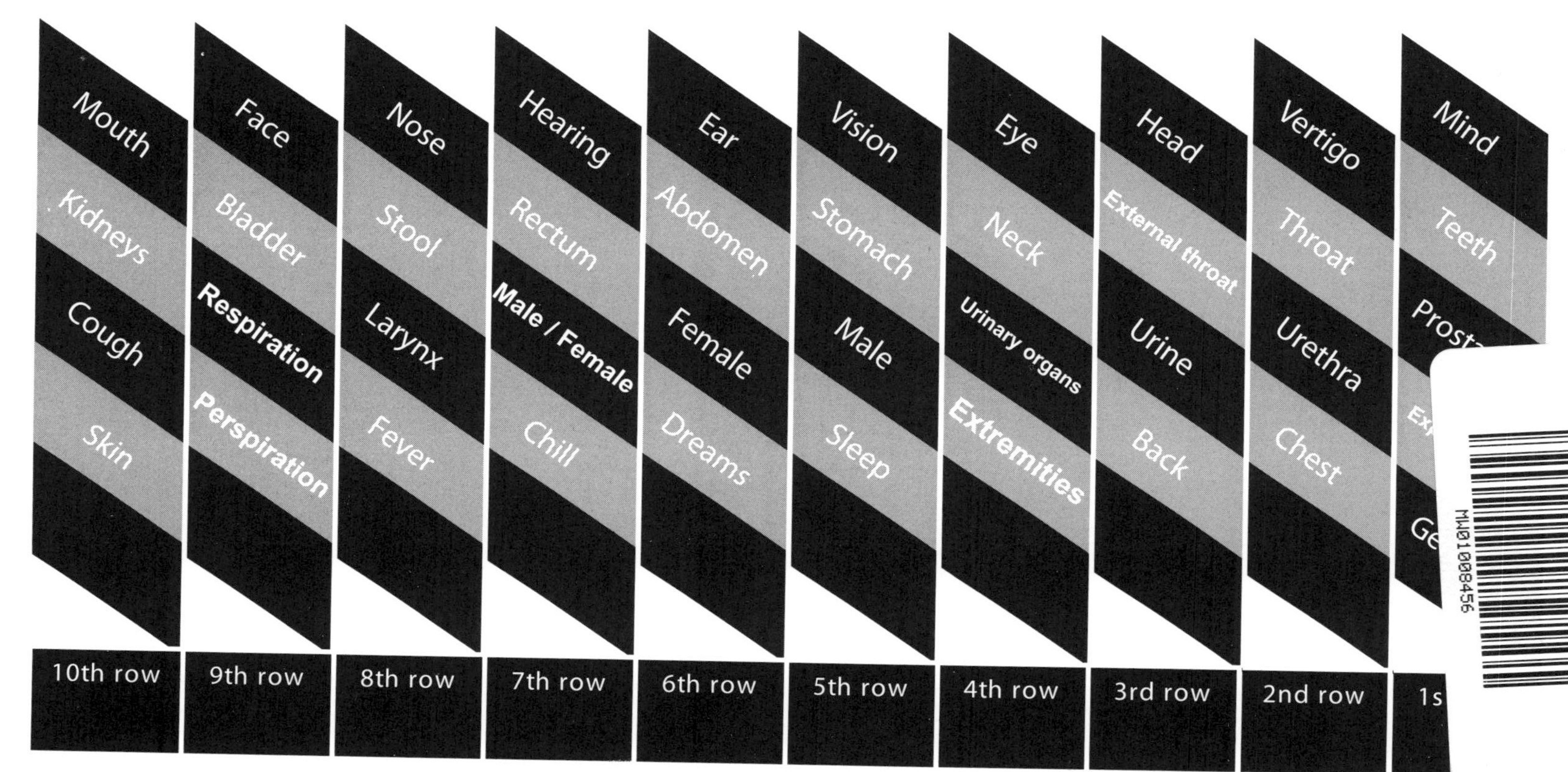
Mind
Teeth
Vertigo
Throat
Urethra
Chest
2nd row
Head
External throat
Urine
Back
3rd row
Eye
Neck
Urinary organs
Extremities
4th row
Vision
Stomach
Male
Sleep
5th row
Ear
Abdomen
Female
Dreams
6th row
Hearing
Rectum
Male / Female
Chill
7th row
Nose
Stool
Larynx
Fever
8th row
Face
Bladder
Respiration
Perspiration
9th row
Mouth
Kidneys
Cough
Skin
10th row

SYNTHESIS

SYNTHESIS

Repertorium Homeopathicum Syntheticum

The Source Repertory

Edited by Dr. Frederik Schroyens
in collaboration with
leading homeopaths throughout the world

With a foreword by Jeremy Sherr

Edition 9.1

B. JAIN PUBLISHERS (P) LTD.

Reprint history for the English edition:

Synthesis 9.x
2004 August
2006 February
2007 January (Indian Edition)
2007 May (9.1 Indian Edition)
2007 October (Essential Synthesis, 1st Edition)
2008 April (Essential Synthesis, Indian Edition)
2008 June (Essential Synthesis, Indian Edition)
2009 January (Indian Edition)
2009 November (Essential Synthesis, Indian Edition)
2012 February (Essential Synthesis, 2nd Ed., Indian Edition)
2012 February (Full Synthesis 9.1, Indian Edition)
2014 February (Full Synthesis 9.1, Indian Edition)
2016 August (Full Synthesis 9.1, Indian Edition)

Published by Kuldeep Jain for
B. JAIN PUBLISHERS (P) LTD.
D-157, Sector 63, Noida - 201 307, UP (INDIA)
Tel.: +91-120-4933333
Email: info@bjain.com • Website: **www.bjain.com**

Printed in India

ISBN: 978-81-319-3922-2

To all the children,
husbands, wives
and lifetime partners
of all those who made homeopathy
grow one step further,
and especially of those who contributed to
this lighthouse of knowledge.

"Things will grow brighter as minds are brought together
and men think harmoniously.
The more we keep together the better,
and the more we think as one the better."
Dr. James T. Kent , Lectures on Homeopathic Philosophy, Ch. 37

Welcome to anyone who wants to join this project
to complete it, improve or criticise it.

FOREWORD BY JEREMY SHERR

Last year I had the privilege of visiting Dr. Frederik Schroyens in his offices in Ghent, Belgium. It was a hive of activity. A constant stream of information poured in - additions, corrections, provings, translations, revisited classics and new manuscripts. Frederik explained the pyramid structure of the organization, how homoeopaths from all over the world gathered information, later passing it on to smaller teams who checked and rechecked it until it arrived at the Ghent office where the final sifting, confirming, corroborating, editing and publishing were performed. I was very impressed. From my own experience of repertorising, I have learnt to appreciate the enormous time and work that goes into each rubric, remedy, cross reference and annotation. It is the work of ants and a labour of love.

But it was not only the industriousness that impressed me. It was the dedication to detail and accuracy that filled me with a renewed confidence in the repertory. The repertory is our daily tool; it is our right arm, the gateway to materia medica and to healing. On this tool the health of our patients depends, and we must be able to rely on it in the way a carpenter relies on his plane, a soldier on his sword, a baker on his oven, a writer on her pen. It must be sharp and accurate, all-encompassing but not over-inflated. I found the Synthesis to be all these things, and the tool felt right in my hand.

Repertorising in the 21st Century provides challenges we have never faced before.
The information highway traverses homoeopathy, gathering ever-increasing amounts of data from a growing number of practitioners, provings and toxicological reports. Computers have trawled the materia medica looking for lost symptoms and confirmations. This valuable information must be catalogued. But these prolific contributions create new difficulties and challenges. Such an incredible amount of new information creates a danger of inflating the rubrics and repertory to unmanageable sizes. If we stretch this sycotic tendency to its extreme, the result will be a large number of giant rubrics, each containing the same remedies and suffering from a loss of individual identity. As regards the sub-rubrics, flooding the repertory with numerous permutations of small rubrics does nothing to stem this tide. In this new era of homoeopathy we must proceed with care.

Another challenge that lies ahead is differentiating the quality of information. From the most reliable symptoms, namely provings confirmed by repeated clinical experience, to the uncertain additions derived from a single clinical experience or a dream proving, the repertory writer must retain, sort, filter and edit information with the utmost caution. It requires extreme discrimination and responsibility.

It is through these turbulent waters that Frederik Schroyens has navigated his ship, and he has done so with remarkable precision. One of his main tools has been structural and technological innovation. In an age where computers have collected vast amounts of data, we must use computers to organize it. In an age where data quality is extremely variable, we need new techniques of differentiation. By restructuring sensations and location he has created a more efficient tool. By including remedies from sub-rubrics into their 'mother rubrics' we have been given the choice of a larger and more accurate remedy base. By utilizing the 'virtual confidence factor' more information has been collected while enabling choice of quality for the user.

Reproducing this versatile format in book form is another challenge. Computers can catagorize data in ways which the printed page cannot. Yet Synthesis 9.1 lives up to its name by retaining many of the qualities of its electronic counterpart.

Kent published his first repertory in 1897, the second edition in 1910. It is good to know that, a century later, homoeopathy is thriving and this work is being continued. I salute Frederik Schroyens and his team for this work and thank them for the gift of Synthesis.

Jeremy Sherr
June 2004

FOREWORD FOR SYNTHESIS 9

Synthesis 9 is the first version that is being released in two steps[1]. Synthesis 9.1 has more or less the same content as Synthesis 9.0. The difference between these two versions is a long awaited, crucial step in the development of the repertory. I have been dreaming about this improvement ever since I became accustomed to my very first Kent's Repertory, which I bought in 1977.

What then is this change?

1. STREAMLINING AND RESTRUCTURING

The change to Synthesis 9.1 addresses a problem well known to deft repertory users: *a lot of information is hidden in the subrubrics of the pain descriptions*. Let's clarify this with an example.
A patient tells you his pain in the eye is definitely better from rubbing the eye. Synthesis 9.0 offers 7 remedies with this modality in the rubric "EYE - PAIN - rubbing - amel.". The meaningful bit of information here is "rubbing amel.". The experienced repertory user knows that the "eye – pain" section contains other symptoms which include this same modality. These are hidden as subrubrics of the pain descriptions, as follows:

"EYE - PAIN - burning - rubbing - amel."
"EYE - PAIN - foreign body; as from a - rubbing amel."
"EYE - PAIN - pressing, pressure, etc. - rubbing - amel."
"EYE - PAIN - sand, as from - rubbing - amel."

These four rubrics all contain remedies whose pain in the eye is improved with rubbing. The relevance is that, if we combine these rubrics, we now look at 13 remedies instead of 7! Considering these additional remedies may increase the likelihood of choosing the correct remedy.

How has this issue been addressed in Synthesis 9.1?
In all the symptoms of the pain sections, the description of pain was always on level 3 ("eye – pain – *burning* - morning"). In Synthesis 9.1 this description has been moved to the last level of the symptom. The above symptoms therefore became:

"EYE - PAIN - rubbing - amel. – burning"
"EYE - PAIN - rubbing - amel. - foreign body; as from a"
"EYE - PAIN - rubbing - amel. - pressing pain"
"EYE - PAIN - rubbing - amel. - sand; as from"

---

[1] Synthesis 9.0 was finalized on November 21, 2003 and released as a software program in English on November 24, 2003 . This version was only translated into German (December 22, 2003) and not printed in any language. Synthesis 9.1 was finalized on June 4, 2004 and released as a software program in English in July 2004. Version 9.1 will be translated into several languages and is the basis for the new printed version. The new veterinary information has been added to Synthesis 9.1 to create Synthesis 9.1V.

As a consequence, these rubrics containing the same modality are now positioned next to each other, on the same page or screen. In Synthesis 9.0 they were pages apart, pages that were seldom turned. This 'hidden' information is now easily visible and usable.

This **restructuring** increases the number of remedy choices for thousands of modalities, sides, times, extensions and localizations. These hidden symptoms and their remedies were hardly ever looked at before. Now it has become very easy to consider this information when necessary.

In addition, the remedies of these symptoms expressing the same side, time, modality, extension or localization have been **copied to the common superrubric**. Reverting to the example above, this means that "EYE - PAIN - rubbing - amel." has 13 remedies in Synthesis 9.1 (in stead of 7 in Synthesis 9.0). For each remedy the source rubric has been indicated[2].

In order to achieve this drastic change, it had to be preceded by another step: a thorough **streamlining** of all symptoms. Here is the explanation why:
The modality "cold air agg." is expressed in several ways at different places in the Repertory. For example, in Synthesis 9.0:

HEAD - PAIN - *cutting* - cold - air agg.
HEAD - PAIN - *tearing* - air - cold; from

If we restructure this information, these rubrics would become:

HEAD - PAIN - cold - air agg. - *cutting*
HEAD - PAIN - air - cold; from - *tearing*

This would result in a cluttered pattern of rubrics with identical meanings, expressed in different ways. Therefore, we have streamlined the modality "cold air agg." throughout the Repertory into "cold - air - agg." before undertaking the restructuring.

In Synthesis 9.1 the above rubrics have become:

HEAD - PAIN - cold - air - agg. - *cutting*
HEAD - PAIN - cold - air - agg. - *tearing*

As a consequence of this streamlining and restructuring process, some familiar rubrics may have undergone some changes.

---

[2] Only visible in the software: if you click on the 'down arrow' following the remedy you see the source rubric (in "Full Synthesis View").

First of all, the symptom level expressing the description of pain has been moved.
There is only one thing to remember in order to find the new symptom location: *move the "description of pain" to the last level of the symptom* and you will find the symptom in Synthesis 9.1. This applies only to pain symptoms that contain a "description of pain" (e.g. burning, cramping, tearing, etc.). Some examples:

Symptom in Synthesis 9.0	*Symptom in Synthesis 9.1*
HEAD - PAIN - stitching - evening	HEAD - PAIN - evening - stitching
HEAD - PAIN - stitching - coughing, when	HEAD - PAIN - coughing, when - stitching
HEAD - PAIN - stitching - Forehead - extending to - Occiput	HEAD - PAIN - Forehead - extending to - Occiput – stitching
HEAD - PAIN - stitching - Temples	HEAD - PAIN - Temples - stitching

Second, the streamlining may have moved a familiar rubric to a different place altogether, even considering the first explanation above. You look for a symptom modified with "air – cold", and in fact in Synthesis 9.1 you will find it under "cold – air"; not under the letter "a"(ir), but under "c"(old).

It may take some time to adjust to the new streamlined modalities and locations. The advantage is that this streamlining is now consistent throughout the repertory. Previously this was not the case. In Synthesis 9.0 and prior versions there were 36 ways to express "cold air agg."[3]!
Now either "cold – air – agg." or the collapsed form[4] "cold air agg." is used– and that's it. This simplifies the search for rubrics in the repertory from now on.

Here are some rules that we have followed while streamlining.

– If a combined modality contains an element indicating **temperature**, then this latter part was put first: "cold air agg"; "cold bathing amel."; "warm food"; "warm bed"; etc. The only important exception to this rule is that we did not touch the existing groups under "weather" and "wind": they remain as they were ("weather – warm – amel."; "wind – cold – agg."; etc.).

---

[3] air - cold/ air - cold - agg./ air - cold air - sensitive to/ air - cold air; sensitive to/ air - cold, from/ air - cold, in/ air - cold; from/ air - cold; in/ air - open – cold/ air; in cold open/ cold – air/ cold - air - agg./ cold - air – from/ cold - air - sensitive to/ cold - air agg./ cold - air, from/ cold - air, in/ cold - air; from cold/ cold - air; from exposure to/ cold - air; in/ cold - air; in cold/ cold - being in the/ cold - open air; in/ cold air/ cold air - agg./ cold air - sensitive to/ cold air agg./ cold air, from/ cold air, in/ cold air, when in/ cold air; exposure to/ cold air; in/ cold open air; in/ cold; to – air/ sensitive - cold – air/ sensitive - cold - air; to

[4] A modality is collapsed when there are no similar modalities next to it. If "cold – air – amel." would be the next symptom, then these modalities would not be collapsed for that symptom.

- As much as possible and where applicable we have reduced modalities to either "**agg.**" or "**amel.**". "Walking – from"; "walking – when"; walking – while"; etc. have all been merged into "walking - agg.". Where doubt existed we kept a difference that will need to be clarified from a study of the Materia Medica. An example: you will find some remedies and subrubrics at "eating agg." and others at "eating while" because this is the way the original rubrics were written. These rubrics have not been merged as it could have induced errors.
- All through Synthesis the difference between "**after xxx agg.**" and "xxx agg." was maintained, even if in some instances this difference appeared to be minimal: is there a difference between "turning head agg." and "turning head agg.; after"? Further study of Materia Medica will answer in each instance.
- The difference between an **aggravation from food** and from *eating* that food has been maintained. The reason being that "eating warm food" indicates that the aggravation takes places while eating – or at least should indicate this. The modality "warm food" normally indicates that the aggravation takes place because of warm food, but not only and not necessarily *while* eating it. The same has been done for aggravation from *drinking* a drink and the aggravation from that drink (e.g. "tea" as opposed to "drinking tea"). In all these instances the original symptom information was carefully preserved.
- At last, some modalities that were depending from **common superrubrics** were split. In Synthesis 9.0 you will find "air – open"; "air – draft of"; etc. These rubrics depend from the common superrubric "air". In Synthesis 9.1 these modalities became "air agg."; "air agg.; in open" and "air agg.; draft of". The reasons for this change are to have a more obvious structure, that is easily perceived and to facilitate translation of these modalities.

These are some of the examples of the rules that we used for streamlining. More information can be found in the Textbook. Although dramatic changes have been applied, great care has been taken to avoid oversimplifying matters and inducing errors thereby.

For the software users there is an additional aid to easily find any restructured and/or streamlined symptom. At the end of Synthesis 9.1 there is an additional **chapter "Old symptoms"**. It contains all symptoms that have undergone a change, but in the "old format". Here you will find the rubric that you are used to, e.g.: "OLD SYMPTOMS - EXTREMITIES - PAIN - stitching - Ankle – standing". Hit enter and you will be at the restructured symptom: "EXTREMITIES - PAIN - Ankles - standing - agg. - stitching pain".

Likewise, software users have additional flexibility to use or not the remedies copied from the subrubrics. The **"Full Synthesis, rmd copied" view** contains all copied remedies. All other views do not contain these additional remedies. These views are a mouse click apart. In the printed version the remedies of the subrubrics have been copied as described. Such remedies are identified by a 'down arrow'.

Still another aid is available: software users get Synthesis 9.0 (without streamlining and restructuring) as well as Synthesis 9.1, they can both be used at the same time.
With all this flexibility and precision, it should be easy to start using Synthesis 9.1. This is important because it is our intention to build on Synthesis 9.1. Streamlining and restructuring is a major milestone[5] in the development of Synthesis. If any change is needed, it is to improve this idea.

Some further improvement is still needed.
First, we did not streamline the Mind chapter. There were too many exceptions to undertake this with an automated process. It will be done manually for the next version of Synthesis. The Dreams chapter was not streamlined because there are no sides, times, extensions, etc.

Second, most of this process was creating and testing the programs and tables for this restructuring and streamlining. Once all was perfectly functional the actual conversion went very quickly[6]. Nevertheless we kept on improving our tables and insights until the end. As a result the first chapter we processed (Head) was restructured and streamlined up to 95 % of the ideal, and the last chapter (Generals) up to 98 %. You may not even notice this as I am referring to relatively small differences.

2. BÖNNINGHAUSEN AND BOGER

This brings me to the second major innovation of Synthesis 9[7]: adding the Repertory information of Bönninghausen and Boger.
Much could be said to explain why this was done. In this foreword I will mention two reasons: today's homeopathic community is increasingly aware of the value of these authors and Kent only partially included their information in his repertory.

---

[5] This was also the title of the lecture when I first presented the ideas of Synthesis 9.1 to a wider audience: The Milestone Lecture. This happened on November 6, 2003 in London during a meeting organized by the Faculty of Homeopathy. At that time this meeting was coincident with my 25 years graduation from that same Faculty (June 1978). It comforted me most of all that each of the skilful repertory users there who spoke to me, told me that they grasped the idea within minutes (among others Roberto Bianchini, Nick Churchill, Phil Edmonds, Peter Fisher, Peter Fraser, Brian Kaplan, Bob Leckridge, Russell Malcolm, Jeremy Sherr and Elaine Walker).
[6] The first time we did a test with *Eye* was October 17, 2003. The final streamlining and restructuring procedure then started with *Head* on April 9, 2004. This chapter still had to be processed 5 times before we could finalize it (May 11). By that time the programs had become so intelligent that we could finalize all other chapters by June 4 – amazing programmers-magicians once again!
[7] Most of the following features apply to Synthesis 9.0 as well as to Synthesis 9.1. From now on, when referring to Synthesis 9, both versions are meant (except where indicated).

The gap between these two repertory worlds is now closing as both types of information, Kent and Bönninghausen/Boger has become available in Synthesis 9. Here is what we did.

A separate repertory was created for each of the **six b-bg repertories**[8]. A team added the symptoms to an Excel file, which was converted into an empty repertory (no remedies). Others then added the remedies to this empty repertory, and while doing so, checked the work of the previous people. Once a separate repertory was complete, it was printed in the same format as the original book, including the remedy abbreviations used in the original book. Again different people checked this print-out against the original book.

When a b-bg repertory had gone through all these steps, remedy abbreviations were converted to comply with the Synthesis standards. For each repertory the original printed version has been used, either German or English.

At last, for b4 and b7, the additions and corrections as written down by Bönninghausen's son have been added with the author abbreviations b4a and b7a[9]. These original **handwritten additions** are preserved in the Library of the Pierre Schmidt Foundation, St. Gallen, Switzerland and graciously given to us by Hans-Jörg Hee for integration into our databases. This work is substantial as it counts for more than 19,000 author references.

As a consequence a highly accurate and complete version of the repertory work of Bönninghausen and Boger is made available for the first time ever. These six repertories, or any single one of them, can be used next to Synthesis 9, and symptoms from different repertories can be added to the same repertorization. But we went one challenging step further.

We decided to **integrate the b-bg repertory information** into Synthesis.
This was a challenging decision as you may be aware that the type of information in both repertories (b-bg repertories and Synthesis) is based on a different concept.

The b-bg repertories offer predominantly generalized information (e.g.: "STOMACH - NOON"), which indicates that stomach symptoms of whatever type tend to occur at noon. The corresponding remedies have been added to the new Synthesis rubric "STOMACH - NOON". They have been kept separate from any other more specific Synthesis rubrics, such as "STOMACH - PAIN - noon".
The same has been done for generalized b-bg symptoms expressing sides, times, modalities or localizations. Most chapters in Synthesis 9 have such symptoms, which only contain generalized remedies as coming from the b-bg repertories. As a result, Synthesis 9 is easily recognized because the first rubric now is "MIND – DAYTIME".

---

[8] Bönninghausen's "Therapeutic Pocket Book (b2)" and both volumes of his "Systematisch-Alfabetisches Repertorium (b4 b7)" and Boger's "Bönninghausen Rerpertory (bg2)" as well as his "Synoptic Key (bg3)" and the "General Analysis (bg11)".

[9] One example: in the rubric "MIND – MORNING": Apis with author b7a.de.

On the other hand and most important: the existing, individualized and *known rubrics, from Synthesis 8 or Kent's repertory, were left as they were.*

Nevertheless, some symptoms could not easily be integrated into the existing 38 Synthesis chapters. These symptoms related to localizations that were larger than the existing chapter. In order to resolve this, we have created **three new chapters**:

- *Neck* (this chapter contains symptoms related to the whole neck - the part joining the head to the body. It should be compared with the chapters "External throat" for the anterior part, and with "Back" (which contains the cervical region) for the posterior part.)
- *Urinary organs* (all urinary organs as a whole)
- *Male and female sex/genitalia* (if gender does not play a role, as this is often not specified in the b-bg repertories)

Synthesis 9, at least in the software version, now contains 42 chapters, because of another additional chapter: a **Personal chapter**. In this chapter you can add symptoms without respect for the structure of the repertory. As a consequence it will not be possible to exchange these additions with others, nor to add symptoms of someone else's "Personal chapter" to your Synthesis. Additions to this chapter are only useful as a temporary solution and the best way to add information to Synthesis remains the correct place within the existing chapters.

Synthesis 9 was ready to receive the information from the b-bg repertories. One more mammoth task was needed: to **link the rubrics** of the b-bg repertories to the correct Synthesis symptoms. This had to be done manually for each single b-bg rubric! A special thanks to the people who took care of this painstaking part of the job: Paul Debruyn (Belgium), Natasha Pelech (Canada), Dr. P. Sivaraman (India), Erik Van Woensel (Netherlands) and Peter Vint (Germany).

After the links were made, the remedies were copied from one b-bg repertory after the other into Synthesis by a computer program. In this way the vast majority of Bönninghausen's and Boger's repertory work was integrated, adding more than 481,000 author references[10] to Synthesis 9. This figure corresponds to b2, b4, b7 and bg2. The smaller bg3 and bg11 are already available as separate repertories and will be integrated into a later version of Synthesis.

There is one further aspect to this integration. In the separate repertories, the degrees were entered as in the original. The definition of **degrees** in the b-bg repertories is quite different from what we are used to in Kent and Synthesis. Looking at the rubrics of any of these repertories immediately shows that there are many more remedies in the third degree. These degrees were converted to the Synthesis standard following the table on the next page:

---

10 As some remedies existed in Synthesis already, only an author reference was added to that remedy, not a new remedy.

b-bg degree	Synthesis degree
1	1
2	1
3	2
4	3

This table corresponds to the way Kent converted b-bg degrees in his repertory for the rubrics he did use[11]. Maintaining the degrees definition of Kent and previous versions of Synthesis guarantees a stable consistency in our repertorization results, where the degree sometimes is a deciding factor.

This integration of b-bg repertories has been **abundantly documented**.
In every separate repertory each symptom contains two types of information:

- Its origin: the page number, and for bg2 even the symptom number on the page (at the bg2 symptom "MIND - Homicidal, murder, etc.": you read "{{BG2-0203-24}}" in the symptom note (user).
- The Synthesis symptom text to which this b-bg symptom is linked (at the same symptom you read "{{Synthesis: MIND - KILL; desire to}}" in the symptom note (Synthesis).

In Synthesis, every addition derived from the b-bg repertories is labeled with an author reference as usual. Clicking on this reference shows the origin of the symptom. In the symptom "MIND - PROSTRATION of mind", as you click on b2.de at the remedy *Acon.*, you see:

> [B2.DE-171 :: Empfindungen und Beschwerden - Äußere und innere Körperteile im Allgemeinen - Nervenschwäche :: acon.2 :: DG1]

This shows, in this order: the source, the page number (B2.DE-171) :: the original symptom text :: the remedy abbreviation with the original degree (acon. 2) :: the degree as used in Synthesis (DG1).

In some instances, several b-bg symptoms are linked to the same Synthesis symptom. This is why some author references in Synthesis will mention more than one link. This is especially the case in bg2, where a lot of information was repeated. Clicking on bg2 at *Agn.* in the same symptom shows:

> [BG2-0208-22 :: MIND - Intellect, impaired, mental exhaustion, weakness of, etc. :: agn.1 :: DG1]
>
> [BG2-0935-11 :: SENSATIONS AND COMPLAINTS IN GENERAL - Weakness, exhaustion, prostration, infirmity - nervous, nervous debility, neurasthenia :: agn.1 :: DG1]

In other words, the source information has been integrated into Synthesis with the greatest care. Together with the Materia Medica notes integrated into Synthesis, we now have about 488,000 notes with source information in Synthesis 9. When printed, this source information alone

---

[11] See the Textbook about this topic.

would amount to 21,480 pages, using courrier font 10. This is why we decided, with some pride, to give this Synthesis the epithet of **The Source Repertory**.

3. OTHER FEATURES

The b-bg repertories were made available as separate repertories for another reason: if anyone wants to use just one of these repertories (with Radar) he can do so. In a similar way **additional separate repertories** are available for the software user[12]. The relevance for Synthesis is that the repertories of **Boericke** and **Phatak** have been integrated into Synthesis 9, following the same procedure as for the b-bg repertories. This amounts to 70,078 and 63,791 additional author references respectively, including source information as explained above.

We will integrate the information of the other separate repertories into a later version of Synthesis[13]. Even if separate repertories are offered, we maintain our vision to *synthesize* all homeopathic information, such as these repertories, into one work.

I have always stressed that copying remedies to superrubrics had to be a thoughtful process. As explained above, this has now been done for the remedies hidden in the subrubrics of the descriptions of pain. This was also done for the whole Mind chapter, but not blindly. Each mind rubric received a label indicating if remedies could be copied to superrubrics or not. An example is that remedies of "MIND – JESTING – aversion" were not copied to its superrubric "MIND – JESTING". If remedies were to be copied, then superrubrics to which the remedies should *not* be copied were indicated if needed. It is only after this careful labeling of each single rubric that the computer took over and **copied the remedies to the appropriate superrubrics of mind**.

Another feature of Synthesis 9.1[14] concerns one further step in the **sorting of symptoms**.
Sorting all symptoms in alphabetical order may appear to be the ultimate solution, yet it is not. There is a homeopathically meaningful relationship between certain symptoms and it makes sense to have these on the same page, rather than scattered because of the alphabet.

Here is the way that Synthesis 9.1 sorts symptoms according to this new perspective.

- The symptoms of *sides* have been kept together so you can easily compare the remedies affecting the left and the right side.
- The symptoms expressing *time* have been kept together so you can easily compare the remedies with an aggravation at certain times of the day or night.

---

12 The known repertories of Boericke, Clarke, Phatak, Roberts and Ward as well as the "Repertory Compilation 1.0" with contains 9 smaller Separate Repertories on specific topics. Finally, three different repertories by Roger Van Zandvoort are now available with Radar 9.

13 Except for the repertories of Roger Van Zandvoort.

14 Not yet applied to Synthesis 9.0.

- The *modalities* and *descriptions* of pain are sorted alphabetically within one alphabet. You do not need to reflect any more whether "pain - rheumatic" would be a modality or a description of pain.
- All *extensions* depend from the rubric "extending to" and are sorted alphabetically.
- All *localizations* are sorted alphabetically[15].

The sorting order of symptoms therefore is:
- sides
- times (in chronological order)
- modalities and descriptions of pain (one alphabet)
- extensions (all subrubrics of "extending to")
- localizations (alphabetical)

In addition, from this Synthesis version onwards, the sorting order on all levels is now the same. You may not have been aware but in Kent's repertory, in Synthesis 8 and previous versions, level 2[16] was the exception to whatever rules were used elsewhere. In most chapters, the sorting order on that level was: sides / times / the rest of the symptoms[17]. In Synthesis 9.1, if you look for a localization at level 2, you will need to look at the end of the chapter, just as for any other level of symptom (where you were doing so already).
This is important if you look for generalized b-bg localization rubrics, such as "ABDOMEN - SOLAR PLEXUS; complaints of". Also some known Kentian rubrics, incoherently sorted, have now been moved applying only this one scheme: "PERSPIRATION - SINGLE parts"; "FEVER - COVERED PARTS"; "CHILL - SIDE not lain on"; etc.

4. NEW CONCEPTS

Concepts are a fabulous tool to more easily find symptoms in Synthesis. Four new concept chapters bring thousands of new concepts and a greater ability to find physical, mental, pediatric and latent psora symptoms.

Up to this point concepts were mostly focused on mind symptoms. The work of Dorin Dragos (Rumania) accomplishes this in a wonderful way for the physical symptoms. It is based on Roger **Morrison's DeskTop Companion**, with his kind permission. Roger initially divided the main complaints of the local chapters in the repertory into several categories. Example: headache related to weather, to cold air, to emotions, etc.

---

[15] In Synthesis 8, all localizations were already sorted alphabetically, except for EXTREMITIES (which remained anatomically sorted). In Synthesis 9.1 we make no exception for EXTREMITIES.

[16] Level 2 is the level of pain, as in "HEAD – PAIN".

[17] To mention one exception most of us were used to: *sides* are in the beginning of the chapter, except in Generals, where it is in the middle of the alphabet. Were you aware of this? Now in Synthesis 9.1 it is in the beginning, as in all other places.

Dorin has taken this work a step further by adding numerous symptoms of Synthesis to all these categories. This allows you to find all the symptoms where cold air affects headaches in one easy step. In this instance, as in many other, there are many more symptoms for this category than the known rubric "head - pain - cold air agg.".
There are about 1,000 new concepts to choose from.

Dorin Dragos also divided the symptoms of the mind into several practical categories. In order to do so, he used the **classification of mental symptoms** of Roget's Thesaurus of English Words and Phrases (new edition prepared by Betty Kirkpatrick MA, Penguin Books Ltd, London, 1999).
One example: "thinking" is divided into three possible disturbances: increased, decreased, and difficult thinking. For each category the repertory offers several precise symptoms, which are now easy to find.
There are about 200 new concepts to choose from.

Roberto Petrucci (Italy), listed more than **2,900 children's symptoms** in meaningful categories. This includes groups such as "dentition", "infectious diseases" and "development". Other concepts come straight out of the practice of Roberto and make many unknown repertory symptoms easily visible: "attitude towards animals", "attitude towards family", "observations during the night", "non-verbal symptoms - observed by the parents", etc.

Hahnemann drew our attention to the symptoms of **Latent Psora** in his "Chronic Disease". Isidre Lara (Spain) has collected these symptoms for each chapter so that they are an easy reference during the consultation.

5. NEW FAMILIES REPERTORY 2.1

Concepts are in fact a repertory working in the background of the Synthesis software version. There is still another source of information, working in the background: the Families repertory[18].
This needs to be addressed because there is a rapidly growing interest among homeopaths to investigate the concordances between remedies bearing relationship to one another. This may be by way of taxonomic classification, chemical composition, source, or other forms of presumed resemblance.
In order to meet that interest, Radar 9 integrates this Families repertory with several new and improved functions for use in case analysis.

In the context of this Synthesis foreword we will focus on the data.
The previous version of the Families repertory has been thoroughly upgraded by about two year's work by Will Taylor (USA).

---

18 The functioning of these concepts and families repertories is most relevant for the software version of Synthesis.

The Families 2.1 repertory now offers a choice of more than 4,000 families.
The Kingdoms (minerals, plants and animals) are divided into 455 families and the Periodic Table contains 175 different families. For plants, they offer the three main classification systems: Cronquist, Dahlgren and Uppsala (Angiosperm Phylogeny Group).
Other families include: Bönninghausen Concordances[19], Bowel Nosode related remedies, Boyd's Groups of remedies, Dorsci's Diathesis and Notions, families according to the five elements, Miasms, Nosodes, related remedies (more than 1,800 categories), families of state of matter and Teste's groups of remedies.
In addition there is a "Preferences"chapter where the user can create their own families.

These figures do not indicate all the effort Will made, with the help of different other specialists[20], to assure that some obsolete homeopathic remedy names were correctly interpreted. Synthesis 9 has the most complete and accurate homeopathic remedy family information so far available!

6. THE NEW INFORMATION

Synthesis 9 comes with even more new information.

- All the information from the Introduction and the Mind sections of all the remedies in **Boericke's Materia Medica** (br1) has been integrated (14,717 additions).

- New clinical information from André **Saine** (Canada) has been added to Synthesis 9 (more than 3,200 additions).

- More than 10,600 additions have been made on the basis of the popular book "Clinical Observation of Children's Remedies" by Farokh **Master** (India).

- The **major new remedies** in Synthesis 9.0 are: Argemone pleicantha (Todd Rowe, USA); Bitis arietans (Craig Wright, South Africa); Brosimum gaudichaude (Mateus Marim, Brazil), Chironex fleckeri - box jellyfish (Alastair Gray, Australia), Bungarus fasciatus (Master, India), Coca cola (Rajan Sankaran, India), Cypraea eglantina (Anne Schadde, Germany), Desoxyribonucleicum acidum - DNA (Phillip Robbins), Dioxinum (Philip Robbins, Australia), Ficus macrophylla (Alastair Gray, Australia), Gardenia jasminoides (Regina Vale, Brazil), Hippocampus kuda - seahorse (Susan Sonz et al., USA), Lapis lazuli (Anne Schadde, Germany), Lavendula angustifolia (Clayton Collyer and Jackie Davis, UK), Melaleuca alternifolia - tea tree (Alastair Gray, Australia), Musca domestica - house

---

[19] Based on the Therapeutic Pocket Book (b2).

[20] Vilma Bharatan (Department of Botany, The Natural History Museum, London, England), Bernhard Bloesy (Germany), Michael Bonnet (England), Mitch Fleisher (USA), Caroline Vandeschoor (Homeoden-Heel, Belgium), Emiel Van Galen (Medicines Evaluations Board, Ministry of Health, Den Haag, Netherlands) and Prof. Walter Verraes (Department of Biology, University of Gent, Belgium)

fly (Susan Sonz and Robert Stewart, USA), Neptunium muriaticum (Didier Lustig and Jacques Ray, France), Ozone (Anne Schadde, Germany), Pertussis vaccine (Prakash Vakil, India), Phascolarctos cinereus - Australian Koala secrettion (Philip Robbins, Australia), Pycnoporus sanguineus - a South-African fungus (Catherine Morris, South Africa), Saccharum album (Salvador Gamarra, Brazil) and Tempestas - storm (Mary English, UK).

- Remedies described in Julian's "Materia Medica of the **Nosodes** (jl2)" have been integrated such as: Colibacillinum, Diphthero-tetano-typho-paratyphoidinum, Diphtherotoxinum, Eberthinum, Enterococcinum, Flavus, Gonotoxinum, Malaria nosode, Malandrinum, Morbillinum, Oscillococcinum, Osteo-arthriticum, Ourlianum, Parathyreoidinum, Pertussinum, Pneumococcinum, Serum anti colibacillinum, Streptococcinum, Toxoplasma gondii, Tuberculinum avis, Tuberculinum denys, Tuberculinum marmoreck, Tuberculinum residuum Koch, Vaccin atténué bilié, Vaccininum, Yersinium, etc.

- The information on **magnets** introduced by Bönninghausen, but kept out of the Repertory by Kent, has been added again - Magnetis polus arcticus, Magnetis polus australis and Magnetis poli ambo.

- There are also remedies whose information has increased substantially. 197 remedies contain more than **50% extra information** as compared to Synthesis 8.1V. Most remedies are expanded on the basis of different author references. The most important ones are: Adrenalinum, Aqua marina, Azadirachta indica, Bacillinum, Cassia sophera, Cina, Diosma lincaris, Gettysburg aqua, Heloderma, Manganum aceticum, Metylenum coeruleum, Natrium salicylicum, Ornithogalum umbellatum, Piper nigrum, Proteus, Rosmarinus officinalis (Bernard Long and P Cayrel), Strophantus sarmentosus (Stephenson), Strychninum phosphoricum, Sulfonalum, Ulmus campestris, Vanadium metallicum, Viola tricolor, and Xanthium spinosum.

While our core team was streamlining and restructuring Synthesis 9.0, some other collaborators continued adding new information. As a result Synthesis 9.1 comes with some additional new information as compared to Synthesis 9.0:

- The major new remedies in Synthesis 9.1 (so not yet existing in Synthesis 9.0) are: **Ancistrodon piscivorus** (Michael Thompson, Ireland); **Bellis perennis spagyricus** (Louise Deacon and Alan Ribot-Smith, England); **Bothrops atrox** (Michael Thompson); **Chlamydia trachomatis** (Richard Boocock et al., England); **Heroinum** (Janet Snowdon, England); **Loxosceles laeta** (Michael Bonnet, England); **Lignum naufragium helvetiae** (Mary English, England); **Oxyuranus scuttellatus** – taipan snake (Paul Masci and Philip Kendall, USA); **Petroleum raffinatum** (Nandita Shah, India); **Spectrum** (Gill Dransfield, England); **Taosca aqua** (Anne Irwin, Ireland); **Thallium** (Jeremy Sherr, England) and **Threskiornis aethiopica** – the holy ibis (Elisabeth Schulz, Germany).

- 161 remedies contain more than **50 % extra information** as compared to Synthesis 9.0. The most important ones are: Aesculus glabra, Bothrops lanceolatus, Calcarea hypophosphorosa, Dulcamara*, Ferrum aceticum, Glycerinum, Guaco, Indolum, Kalium sulphuricum*, Lappa arctium, Latrodectus mactans, Mentholum, Mercurius praecipitatus ruber, Myrtus communis, Naphthalinum, Pilocarpinum, Plumbum aceticum, Polygonum hydropiperoides, Quassia amara, Radium bromatum, Ruta*, Sanguinarinum nitricum, Solidago, Spongia*, Stellaria media, Strophanthus hispidus, Triticum vulgare*, Vanilla aromatica*, Xerophyllum asphodeloides and Zincum valerianicum.
  The remedies with an "*" now also contain extended proving information from Peter Friedrich, Germany.

7. THE PRINTED VERSION

This printed version is very similar to book version 8.1.
Although so much more information has been added, we were able to stick to the **one volume** concept for the repertory part.
Information per page has been condensed to the maximum now, as had been done before for the French Synthesis 8.1.
In addition, we kept the larger paper size of the English Synthesis 8.1 (larger than the French Synthesis 8.1 paper size). As a result the repertory part of this Synthesis 9.1 book counts "only" 2,090 pages[21].
Therefore we could again include the catalogs of remedies and authors in the repertory volume.

The **Full Synthesis View** was printed, with the possibility to differentiate information. The remedies copied to the superrubrics are included in the printed version.
The footers indicate some of these elements:

- A 'down arrow' following a remedy indicates that this remedy is copied from a similar subrubric.
- A black dot following a remedy indicates that this remedy is added either because of a more recent or because of a lesser-known author. These remedies correspond to the difference between the Millennium View (progressive) and the Quantum View (conservative); this is to say that remedies followed by a dot indicate more progressive information. Many thanks to Gregory Pais (USA)[22] who has gone through the author catalogue with the greatest care to differentiate these views.
- The black dot should not be confused with the asterisk, which, as before, follows the remedy if more authors confirm its presence in the rubric.
- The more hypothetical remedies, if not confirmed by other authors, are now in a second alphabetical order, at the end of the rubric and surrounded by square brackets. This is an

---

[21] The repertory part of the English Synthesis 8.1 counted 1,912 pages, the repertory part of the French Synthesis 8.1 counted 2,068 pages (condensed page content, but smaller paper size, and including a dictionary for each chapter).

[22] For several years Gregory has been my ghost writer. If you understand my English, it is with his help – thanks Gregory!

idea which we first implemented in the French Synthesis 8.1 and which was more useful than mixing them into one alphabetical order, as was done in English Synthesis 8.1.
- As a result, remedies without brackets and without a dot are the more classical ones.
- The descriptions and modalities are now contained within one alphabetical order. So the differentiation by symbols at the first modality and then at the first description is not needed any more.

The most important innovation of the printed version 9.1 is that we decided to make the information, normally reserved for the software users, available with the book. It is presented on a CD and compiled into **two additional volumes**.

The former Blueprint is now called the "*Textbook of Repertory Language*". It contains the following elements:
- The rules of Repertory Language Formatting – as before, but updated.
- Explanations about the integration of Bönninghausen, Boger and the separate repertory information.
- Interesting explanations of key symptoms (symptom notes).
- Index of important changes and corrections – as before, but updated.

The second additional volume is called "*Companion to Synthesis*". It contains all the information which may be helpful to find symptoms in Synthesis:
- An alphabetical listing of all concepts, with the main remedies per concept and the related symptoms per concept.
- The chapters of some often used concepts so that related information is in the same place.
- Index of words with page numbers of rubrics in Synthesis – as before, but updated.

More comprehensive information about these additional volumes can be found on the CD itself. In addition, the CD contains a demo version of the Radar 9 software.

8. THE FIGURES

The actual catalogue of **remedies** offers 4,497 standardized remedy names and abbreviations, and Synthesis 9.1 describes 2,373 of them[23].
The actual catalogue of **authors** describes 3,827 bibliographical references and Synthesis 9.1 uses 886 of them[24].

In the author catalogue there is an important change: the **language of the source** is now indicated. This is done by adding two letters behind the author abbreviation, e.g. *b2.de*. This

[23] Synthesis 9.0 describes 2,310 remedies. Synthesis 8.1 described 2,277 remedies and its catalogue offered 4,200 remedy names.

[24] Synthesis 9.0 uses 805 bibliographical references. Synthesis 8.1 used 655 bibliographical references and its catalogue described 3,031 bibliographical references.

indicates that we based ourselves on the German edition to make additions of b2 (Therapeutisches Taschenbuch) and not on the English version.
The letters to abbreviate a language are the ones of ISO 639[25]. If no letter follows, the book used is in English. These letters do not indicate that the original source is in that language: the original book may be written in English or in German.
This improvement allows increased precision. If someone makes additions based on the English translation of Hahnemann's Materia Medica Pura, he should use "h1". If based on the German version: "h1.de". This will permit us to assign a different confidence level to these two "different" authors.

The number of annotated corrections (**xxx**) has increased to 707[26].

Synthesis 9.1 has 1,066,987 **remedy occurrences**[27] and 1,773,453 **author occurrences**[28].

Speaking about quantity we have to remind you that this version of Synthesis now includes an enormous amount of source information as well. This is why the number of megabytes has exploded from 47.3 Mb (version 8.1V) to 205.4 Mb (Synthesis 9.1).

The information in Synthesis 9.1 has not been duplicated, except for a limited copying of remedies as described above. To your skill I therefore entrust what is probably the most complete and accurate repertory ever.

Dr. Frederik Schroyens
Gent, June 4, 2004[29]

---

25 The most often used languages are Dutch: nl; French: fr; German: de; Italian: it; Portuguese: pt and Spanish: es.

26 Synthesis 8.1 had 620 xxx references.

27 Synthesis 8.1 had 760,000 remedy occurrences and Synthesis 9.0 has 926,000.

28 Synthesis 8.1 had 1,074,000 author occurrences and Synthesis 9.0 has 1,491,000.

29 June 4, 2004 was the last day that we worked on the content of Synthesis 9.1, until the very late hours. This foreword was written later, in Elios, Greece, after I gave the "First Seminar Ever With Synthesis 9.1" on Alonissos, Greece. The sunny seafront horizons and the scent of pine trees have been a true inspiration. As for the music, this version of Synthesis has been accompanied by the chanting of Lama Gyourme, I guess because, after all, it's a monk's work.

DAYTIME: ambr b7.de ant-c b7.de aur b4.de bism bg2 bov b4.de *Caust* b4.de merc b4.de nat-m b4.de sulph b4.de

MORNING: acon bg2 agar b4.de* all-c bg2 aloe bg2 alum b4.de* am-c b4.de* am-m b7.de* ambr bg2 anac bg2 ang b7.de* ant-t b7.de* *Apis* b7a.de arn bg2 **Ars** b4a.de* asaf bg2 asar bg2 aur bg2 bar-c bg2 bell bg2 bism bg2 borx b4a.de* bov b4.de* bry b7.de* *Calc* b4.de* canth b7.de* caps b7.de* carb-an b4.de* carb-v b4.de* caust bg2 cham bg2 *Chel* b7a.de chin bg2 cic bg2 clem b4.de* coc-c bg2 cocc b7.de* con b4.de* gels bg2 *Graph* b4.de* guaj b4.de* hep bg2 hyos bg2 ign b7.de* ip b7.de* kali-bi bg2 kali-c b4.de* kali-n bg2 kali-p bg2 kreos b7a.de lach bg2 led b7.de* lyc bg2 mag-c b4.de* mag-m bg2 merc bg2 mez b4.de* nat-c b4.de* nat-s bg2 nit-ac b4.de* *Nux-v* b7.de* petr b4.de* ph-ac b4.de* phos b4.de* phyt bg2 plb b7.de* ran-b bg2 *Ran-s* b7.de* *Rhod* bg2 *Rhus-t* bg2 rumx bg2 ruta bg2 sabin b7.de* samb bg2 sars b4.de* sel bg2 seneg bg2 sep b4.de* sil bg2 squil b7.de* stann bg2 staph bg2 stram b7.de* sul-ac b4.de* sulph bg2 tarax b7.de* tarent bg2 thuj b4.de* verat b7.de* zinc bg2

- **evening**; and: kali-c bg2

FORENOON: am-m b7.de* anac b4.de* ant-c b7a.de ars b4.de* aur b4.de* calc b4.de* cann-xyz bg2 canth b7.de* carb-an b4.de* *Carb-v* b4.de* cic b7.de* lach bg2 lyc b4.de* mag-c b4.de* mag-m bg2 mosch b7.de* nat-c b4.de* nat-m b4.de* ph-ac bg2 phos b4.de* *Ran-b* b7.de* sars b4.de* sep bg2 sil b4.de* sul-ac bg2 sulph bg2 zinc bg2

NOON: ars bg2 bell bg2 kali-bi bg2 tab bg2

AFTERNOON: aloe bg2 alum b4.de* anac b4.de* ang b7.de* ars b4.de* asaf b7a.de* aur b4.de* borx b4a.de* bov b4.de* bry bg2 bufo bg2 calc b4.de* cann-s b7.de* canth b7.de* carb-an b4.de* carb-v b4.de* chin bg2 cina b7.de* cocc b7.de* con b4.de* dulc b4.de* ferr bg2 graph b4.de* hell b7.de* hyos b7.de* ign b7.de* iod b4a.de kali-c b4.de* kali-n b4.de* laur b7.de* lyc bg2 mag-c b4.de* mag-m b4.de* mang b4.de* mur-ac b4.de* *Nat-c* b4.de* nat-m b4.de* nit-ac b4.de* nux-v b7.de* petr bg2 ph-ac b4.de* phos b4.de* plat b4.de* plb b7.de* rhus-t b7.de* ruta b7.de* sabin bg2 sars b4.de* sep b4.de* staph b7.de* teucr b7.de* viol-t b7.de* *Zinc* b4.de*

EVENING: acon b7.de* agar bg2 aloe bg2 alum b4.de* *Am-c* b4.de* am-m b7.de* ambr b7.de* anac b4.de* ant-c b7a.de ant-t b7.de* arn b7.de* ars b4.de* aur b4.de* bar-c bg2 bell b4.de* berb bg2 bism bg2 borx b4a.de* bov bg2 bry b7.de* cact bg2 calad b7a.de* *Calc* b4.de* camph b7a.de carb-an b4a.de* *Carb-v* b4.de* caust b4.de* cham b7.de* chin b7.de* clem bg2 cocc bg2 croc b7.de* cycl b7.de* dig b4a.de* dros b7.de* euphr bg2 ferr bg2 graph bg2 hep b4.de* ign b7.de* ip bg2 kali-c b4.de* lach b7.de* laur b7.de* **Lyc** bg2 m-arct b7.de mag-c b4.de* mag-m b4.de* merc b4.de* merc-c b4a.de mez bg2 mosch b7.de* mur-ac b4.de nat-c b4.de* nat-m b4.de* *Nit-ac* bg2 *Nux-v* b7.de* ph-ac b4.de* phos b4.de* plan bg2 plat b4.de* plb bg2 *Puls* b7.de* ran-b b7.de* ran-s b7.de* rhus-t b7.de* ruta b7.de* sabin bg2 sars bg2 *Sep* b4.de* *Sil* b4a.de* spig b7.de* stann b4.de* stront-c bg2 sul-ac bg2 *Sulph* b4.de* valer b7.de* verat b7.de* viol-t b7.de* *Zinc* b4.de*

- **amel.**: tarent ptk1
- **sunset**; at: puls b7.de*

NIGHT: acon b7.de* alum bg2 am-c b4.de* am-m bg2 ant-c b7.de* arg-n bg2 arn bg2 *Ars* b4.de* aur b4.de* bar-c b4.de* *Bell* b4.de* bry b7.de* **Calc** b4.de* camph b7a.de cann-s b7a.de* canth bg2 carb-an b4.de* *Carb-v* b4.de* caust b4.de* cham b7.de* *Chin* b7.de* cic b7.de* cina bg2 cocc b7.de* coff b7.de* con b4a.de* dig b4a.de* dulc b4.de* ferr b7.de* *Graph* b4.de* hell b7.de* *Hep* bg2 hyos bg2 ign b7.de* iod b4.de* jal bg2 kali-br bg2 kali-c b4a.de* lyc b4.de* m-ambo b7.de m-arct ↓ *Mag-c* b4.de* merc b4.de* nat-c b4.de* nat-m b4a.de* *Nit-ac* b4.de* nux-v b7.de* petr b4a.de* phos b4.de* plb b7.de* puls b7.de* ran-s b7a.de* *Rheum* b7.de* rhus-t b7.de* sabad bg2 sep b4.de* *Sil* b4.de* spong b7.de* squil ↓ sulph bg2 *Verat* b7.de* zinc b4.de*

- **midnight**:
  - **after**: *Ars* bg2 chin b7.de coff b7.de ign b7.de m-arct b7.de *Nux-v* b7.de rhus-t b7.de squil b7.de
  - **before**: puls b7.de*

ABANDONED (See Forsaken)

ABASHED (See Ailments - embarrassment)

ABDOMEN agg.; complaints of: asaf b7.de*

ABILITY; mental (See Mental exertion - desire; Mental power - increased)

ABROAD; desire to go (See Travelling - desire)

ABRUPT (= rough): (↗*Answering - abruptly; Answering - hastily; Answering - snappishly; Brutality; Hurry; Impulsive; Irritability - questioned; Laconic; Rash; Rudeness; Snappish; Speech - abrupt; Taciturn*) (non:absin hr1) *Anac* ↓ ars a* *Aur-m* ↓ bac ↓ **Calc** st* *Carb-v* mrr1 **Caust** mtf cham ptk1* chir-fl ↓ dendr-pol sk4• graph ↓ haliae-lc srj5• hep vh* heroin ↓ *Kali-i* ↓ kola ↓ lac-leo sk4• *Lach* ↓ lil-t mtf lyc vh* lyss ↓ med ptk1* nat-m k* nit-ac vh* **Nux-v** vh* op wbt• pitu-a ↓ plat k2* podo ↓ polys sk4• *Puls* vh* rauw tpw8* sal-fr sle1• sanguis-s hrn2• *Sep* mtf sil gl1.fr• *Staph* mtf sulph vh* *Tarent* k* tub jl2* [rubd-met stj2 tax jsj7]

- **affectionate**; rough yet: (↗*Affectionate*) *Aur-m* vh* lyc mtf33* nat-m gk nux-v gl1.fr• podo fd3.de• **Puls** mtf33*
- **harsh**: *Anac* vh* ars gl1.fr• bac ↓ *Carb-v* mrr1 **Caust** gl1.fr• chir-fl gya2 dendr-pol sk4• graph gl• hep gl1.fr• *Kali-i* kr1* kola stb3• *Lach* gl1.fr* lyss kr1 med st1 *Nat-m* gl1.fr* nit-ac gl• **Nux-v** gl1.fr* pitu-a ft *Sep* st1 *Staph* st1* sulph gl• *Tarent* vh* [heroin sdj2]
  - **children**; in: bac bn

ABSENCES (See Unconsciousness - frequent)

ABSENT FATHER syndrome (See Ailments - neglected - father)

ABSENT MOTHER syndrome (See Ailments - neglected - mother)

ABSENTMINDED: (↗*Absorbed; Abstraction; Concentration - difficult; Dream; as; Fancies - absorbed; Forgetful; Memory - weakness; Mistakes; Staring; Thoughts - wandering; Unobserving [=inattentive]*) *Acon* k* act-sp k* adam srj5• adlu jl aesc k* agar k* *Agath-a* nl2• **Agn** k* aids nl2• *All-c* bg2* *Alum* k* alum-p k2* alum-sil k2 *Am-c* k* am-m k* ambr gl1.fr• *Anac* k* anders bnj1 *Androc* srj1• androg-p bnj1 ang k* *Ant-c* ↓ **Apis** k* aq-mar jl1* arag br1* aran-ix jl arg-met arg-n bg2* *Arn* k* ars k* ars-s-f k2 arum-i a1 arum-t k* asaf j5.de asar k* atro a1 *Aur* k* aur-ar k2 aur-m-n wbt2• aur-s k2* bamb-a stb2.de• bapt bg2 *Bar-c* k* *Bar-m* j *Bell* k* berb j5.de bit-ar wht1• bol-la a1* *Bov* k* bros-gau mrc1 brucel sa3• bry ↓ bufo k1 *Calad* k* calc k* calc-p ptk1 calc-s k* calc-sil k2* **Cann-i** k* cann-s k* cann-xyz bg2* *Canth* bg2* caps carb-ac k* carb-v bg2 carbn-s k* carc tpw2* cardios-h rly4• *Carl* k* cassia-s ccrh1* **Caust** k* *Cench* k2* cent a1 **Cham** k* chel k* chin k* chin-b ↓ chir-fl gya2 chlam-tr bcx2• chlorpr pin1* choc srj3• chord-umb rly4• *Cic* k* clem k* coca bg2 *Cocc* k* coff k* *Colch* k* coleus-a bnj1 coloc k* con cor-r ptk1* cortico tpw7 cot a1 croc k* crot-c sk4• crot-h *Cupr* k* cycl k* cypra-eg sde6.de• cystein-l rly4• daph k* dendr-pol sk4• dirc k* dream-p sdj1• dub c1 dubo-m br1 dulc k* elaps k* falco-pe nl2• ferr-ar k2 fic-m gya1 fl-ac bg2 galeoc-c-h gms1• gels bg2* germ-met stj2*• gink-b sbd1• *Graph* k* grat j5.de guaj ham **Hell** k* helo-s rwt2• hep k* hura k* hydr a1 hydrog srj2*• *Hyos* k* ictod hr1* *Ign* k* ind kr1* irid-met stj2*• jug-c k* kali-bi bg2* *Kali-br* k* *Kali-c* k* kali-n ↓ *Kali-p* kali-s kali-sil k2* ketogl-ac rly4• *Kola* stb3• *Kreos* k* kres mg1.de* *Lac-c* k* lac-h htj1• lac-lup ↓ **Lach** k* lap-la sde8.de• *Laur* ptk1 led k* limest-b es1• lon-c ↓ luf-op rsj5• luna kg1• *Lyc* k* lyss m-ambo b7.de* m-aust b7.de *Mag-c* k* maias-l ↓ manc mang k* med bg2* melal-alt gya4 menis a1 *Merc* k* merc-c h1 **Mez** k* moni ↓ *Morph* ↓ mosch bg2* mur-ac ↓ naja k* nat-ar a1 nat-c k* **Nat-m** k* nat-p neon ↓ nept-m lsd2.fr nit-ac k* **Nux-m** k* *Nux-v* k* *Ol-an* bg2* olib-sac wmh1 *Olnd* k* *Onos* *Op* k* ozone sde2• *Petr* k* *Ph-ac* k* *Phos* k* **Plat** k* *Plb* k* plut-n srj7• podo fd3.de• positr nl2• propr ↓ psil jl* psor st **Puls** k* quas a1 querc-r svu1• ran-b j5.de ran-s a1 rheum ↓ rhod k* *Rhus-t* k* rhus-v k* ruta sabad ↓ sacch-a ↓ sal-ac sf1.de *Sal-fr* sle1• santin a1 saroth jl sars k* *Sel* sf1.de* **Sep** k* *Sil* k* sinus rly4• spig b7.de* spong k* squil ↓ stann k* staph bg2* stict bg2* stram k* sul-ac k* sul-i ↓ *Sulph* k* suprar ↓ *Syph* bg2* tab bg2 taosc iwa1• tarent k* tell bro1* thiop jl thuj k* *Tritic-vg* fd5.de *Tub* ↓ tung-met stj2*• ulm-c ↓ valer j5.de* vanil fd5.de **Verat** k* verb k* viol-o k* viol-t k* zinc k* [alumin stj2 alumin-s stj2 ant-t stj2 astat stj2 aur-m stj2 bar-br stj2 bar-i stj2 bar-met stj2 bism-sn stj2 bro-r rcb1 buteo-j sej6 cadm-met stj2 cadm-s stj2 caes-met stj2 cinnb stj2 hafn-met stj2 iod stj2 lac-mat sst4 lanth-met stj2 lith-i stj2 mang-i stj2 merc-d stj2 merc-i-f stj2 osm-met stj2 plb-m stj2 plb-p stj2 polon-met stj2 rhen-met stj2 tant-met stj2 tax jsj7 thal-met stj2 zinc-i stj2]

- **morning**: bros-gau mrc1 dulc fd4.de guaj k* hydrog srj2• nat-c ph-ac phos suprar rly4•
- **forenoon** | **11**-16 h: kali-n
- **noon**: mosch

- **afternoon**: all-c hr1 ang k* dulc fd4.de
  - **coffee** or wine; after: *All-c* a1*
- **evening**: dulc fd4.de hydrog srj2• [tax jsj7]
- **air**; in open: plat a1*
- **alternating** with:
  - **animated** (See Animation - alternating - absentmindedness; Vivacious - alternating - abstraction)
  - **cheerfulness** (See Cheerful - alternating - absentmindedness)
- **anxiety**; with (See Anxiety - absentmindedness)
- **children**: agar mtf33 bar-c ↓ caust mtf33 hyos mtf33 kali-c mtf33 kali-sil mtf33 mag-c mtf33 phos mtf33 plb mtf33 spong fd4.de
  - **schoolchildren**: bar-c pc
- **conversing**, when: *(↗spoken)* am-c a1* chin-b hr1* chir-fl gya2 chord-umb rly4• *Dulc* fd4.de plut-n srj7• psil jl
- **dreamy** (= daydreaming): *(↗Dream)* *Acon* b7.de* agar ptk1 ambr ptk1 anac ptk1 ang b7.de* *Ant-c* ptk1* arg-n bg2* arn b7.de* bry b7.de* calc-p lmj cann-xyz ptk1 cench c1* cham b7.de* chin bg2* chlam-tr bcx2• clem mtf11 cocc bg2 *Coff* bg2 cycl ggd dream-p sdj1• *Dulc* fd4.de falco-pe nl2• hyos b7.de* *Ign* lmj lac-h sze9• lac-lup hrn2• *Lach* bg2* lon-c mtf11 m-ambo b7.de maias-l hrn2• merc mtf33 moni rfm1• *Morph* br1 **Nat-m** lmj neon srj5• nux-m b7.de* nux-v b7.de* olnd b7a.de* **Op** bg2* ozone sde2* **Phos** bg2* positr nl2• propr sa3• puls b7.de* rheum b7.de* sabad bg2 sep st* sil mtf33 *Spong* fd4.de squil b7.de staph st* stram b7.de* sulph a1* thuj mtf33 *Tritic-vg* fd5.de *Tub* lmj ulm-c jsj8• vanil fd5.de verat ptk1 verb ↓ [hydrog stj2 stann stj2]
  - **amorous**: ant-c bg2 verb bg2
- **driving**; while: galeoc-c-h gms1• sacch-a gmj3
- **epileptic** convulsions | **before**: lach kl
- **inadvertence**: *(↗Heedless)* adam srj5• *Alum* gl1.fr• am-c gl1.fr• cham gl1.fr• dulc fd4.de gink-b sbd1• irid-met srj5• neon srj5• nux-v gl1.fr• ruta fd4.de spong fd4.de staph gl1.fr• vanil fd5.de [tax jsj7]
- **menses**; during: *(↗Menses - during)* calc mur-ac ptk1
- **old** age; in: am-c k1 *Ambr* vh* *Bar-c* vh* *Con* sf1.de *Lyc* sf1.de
- **periodical** | **short** lasting attacks of absentmindedness: bros-gau mrc1 (non:chlorpr c1) fl-ac *Nux-m*
- **reading**; while: *(↗Concentration - difficult - studying; Reading - agg.)* agn (non:ang a1) bar-c pc dulc fd4.de lach *Nux-m* ph-ac sul-i k2
  - **sleep**; going to: (non:ang a1)
- **spoken** to; when: *(↗conversing)* am-c gl1.fr• am-m gl1.fr• ambr gl1.fr• bar-c gl1.fr• dream-p sdj1• nux-v gl1.fr•
- **stands** in one place and never accomplishes what he undertakes: *Dulc* fd4.de *Med* vh* *Nux-m* a1*
- **starting** when spoken to; but (See Starting - spoken)
- **vertigo**; during: hep h2
- **waking**, does not know where he is or what to answer; on: *Nux-m* kr1
- **work**; when at: dulc fd4.de hura a1 spong fd4.de
- **writing**; while: kola stb3• mag-c

ABSORBED: *(↗Absentminded; Abstraction; Brooding; Dream; as; Dwells - past; Execution; Fancies - absorbed; Forgetful; Frown; Introspection; Meditating; Plans - making; Sitting - inclination - meditates; Sitting - inclination - wrapped; Theorizing; Thoughts - thoughtful; Unobserving [=inattentive]; FACE - Expression - vacant; SLEEP - Dreaming - awake)* acon k* aloe alum j5.de am-c gl1.fr• am-m ambr gl1.fr• androc srj1• anh sp1 ant-c k* apis ↓ arge-pl rwt5• arizon-l nl2• *Arn* k* *Aur-m-n* wbt2• aur-s wbt2• bar-c gl1.fr• bell k* bov bros-gau mrc1 bruc j5.de bufo gk calc calc-s ↓ cann-i cann-s b7.de* canth k* *Caps* carb-an ptk1* *Carl* caust cham k* chin k* cic k* clem *Cocc* k* con k* cupr cycl k* dendr-pol sk4• dream-p sdj1• dulc fd4.de elaps euphr j5.de falco-pe nl2• *Ferr* ↓ fic-m gya1 fl-ac ↓ germ-met srj5• grat guaj j ham **HELL** k* hydrog srj2• hyos bg2 ign k* indg j5.de ip irid-met srj5• kali-s fd4.de kiss a1 *Kola* stb3• kreos j lach bg2 lil-t limest-b es1• loxo-recl knl4• mag-m j5.de mang merc **Mez** k* mosch k* mur-ac nat-c k* *Nat-m* nat-p nat-s ↓ nat-sil fd3.de• nit-ac **Nux-m** k* *Nux-v* j5.de* ol-an olib-sac wmh1 *Onos* *Op* petr-ra shn4• phel phos k* plb j5.de* psor ↓ *Puls* k* pyrid rly4• ran-b b7.de* rheum *Rhus-t* b7.de* ribo rly4• ruta fd4.de sabad k* sars sel c1* sep bg2 spig k* spong fd4.de stann staph bg2 stram stront-c j5.de **Sulph** k* thuj j5.de* tritic-vg fd5.de vanil fd5.de verat mrr1 viol-o b7.de* vip j5.de [calc-sil stj2 heroin sdj2 kali-sil stj2 plat stj2]
- **daytime**: elaps
- **morning**: bros-gau mrc1 *Nat-c* k* nux-v k*
- **afternoon**: mang

Absorbed: ...
- **evening**: am-m k* *Sulph*
- **alternating** with | **frivolity** (See Frivolous - alternating - absorption)
- **become** of him; as to what would: *(↗Anxiety - future)* dulc fd4.de nat-m k*
- **business** matters; in: *(↗Talking - business)* apis mrr1 *Ferr* mrr1 nat-s mrr1 *Nux-v* mrr1
- **concentrate** on inner world, wants to (See Introspection)
- **eating** | **after**: aloe
- **family** matters; in: apis mrr1 dulc mrr1
- **future**, about: ruta fd4.de spig h1*
- **horrible** thoughts; in: psor ptk1
- **thoughts**; in (See Absorbed)
- **menses**, during: *(↗Menses - during)* mur-ac k*
- **misfortune**, imagines: *(↗Delusions - misfortune)* calc-s st1
- **sexual** desire; in the fulfillment of his: fl-ac mrr1
- **spoken** to he seems absorbed as if walking in a dream; when (See Absentminded - dreamy)
- **vertigo**; during: hep b4a.de

ABSTRACT THINKING (See Thinking - abstract)

ABSTRACTION OF MIND: *(↗Absentminded; Absorbed; Concentration - difficult; Forgetful; Spaced-out; Unobserving [=inattentive])* acon b2.de* acon-l st1 *Agath-a* nl2• agn b2.de* *Alum* k* am-c b2.de* aml-ns anac b2.de* ang b2.de* *Apis* b7a.de arg-met b7.de arizon-l nl2• *Arn* b2.de* aur b2.de* *Bar-c* b2.de* bell b2.de* berb j5.de bov b2.de* bufo gk *Calad* b2.de calc b2.de camph *Cann-i* k* cann-s b2.de canth b7.de caps j5.de carb-ac k* carc fd2.de• caust k* *Cham* b2.de* chin b2.de choc srj3• cic k* *Cocc* b2.de* colch b2.de* con cortico mg1.de* *Croc* b2.de* cycl k* cystein-l rly4• dream-p sdj1• dulc b2.de elaps *Falco-pe* nl2• gink-b sbd1• *Graph* b2.de* guaj k* *Hell* k* hep b2.de hydrog srj2• *Hyos* ictod j5.de *Ign* b2.de* ignis-alc es2• irid-met srj5• kali-c b2.de* **Kali-p** ↓ kali-s fd4.de *Kreos* lach b2.de* laur led b2.de* limest-b es1• lyc k* *Lyss* k* m-ambo b2.de* m-aust b2.de* mag-c b4.de* mang b2.de* *Merc* b2.de* *Mez* k* mob-ray bcx1• mosch b2.de* nat-c b2.de* *Nat-m* k* nit-ac b2.de **Nux-m** k* nux-v b2.de* *Oena* *Ol-an* j5.de olnd b2.de* *Onos* op k* petr b2.de* ph-ac k* *Phos* k* plat k* plb j5.de psil ↓ **Puls** b2.de* ran-b st1 rhod b2.de* rhus-t b2.de ruta fd4.de sabad sal-fr sle1• sars b4.de* sec sel **Sep** b2.de* sil k* spig b2.de spong b7.de* stann b4.de* stram k* sul-ac b2.de* *Sulph* k* symph fd3.de• thuj b2.de* *Tub* st1 *Verat* b2.de* verb b2.de* vesp viol-o b2.de viol-t b2.de *Visc* [bell-p-sp dcm1 heroin sdj2 tax jsj7]
- **morning**: guaj k*
- **alternating** with | **vivacity** (See Vivacious - alternating - abstraction)
- **driving** the car; when: *Falco-pe* nl2• gink-b sbd1• sal-fr sle1•
  - **missing** the turning: sal-fr sle1•
- **eyes**; with fixed: psil ft1
- **menses**; after: kali-c b4a.de
- **work**; while at: **Kali-p** fd*

ABSURD (See Foolish)

ABUNDANCE: adam srj

ABUSED; being (See Ailments - abused)

ABUSIVE (= abusive language): *(↗Anger - vex others; Censorious; Contemptuous; Cursing; Dictatorial; Disobedience; Impolite; Insolence; Quarrelsome; Rage - insults; Reproaching others; Rudeness; Slander; Speech - offensive; Threatening)* abies-n vh *Acon* j5.de agath-a nl2• alco a1 am-c k* am-m *Anac* k* androc srj1• apis mtf arizon-l nl2• arn a1 ars gl1.fr• atro a1 *Aur* j5.de* aur-m-n wbt2• aur-s wbt2• bar-c b4a.de *Bell* k* borx k* bufo gk *Bung-fa* mtf calc-p ↓ camph bg2 canth j5.de* caps ↓ caust k* cere-s bro1 **Cham** bg2* chin gg* cic gl1.fr• *Con* k* cor-r j5.de* croc bg2* *Crot-c* sk4• cub a1 *Cupr* b7a.de cupr-act kr1 cupr-f ↓ cupr-m ↓ cupr-p ↓ cur vml3• dendr-pol sk4• der a1 dulc k* elae a1 *Ferr* bg2* ferr-f ↓ ferr-lac ↓ ferr-n ↓ ferr-sil ↓ gal-ac a1* granit-m es1• hep k2* hist mg1.de *Hyos* k* ign bg3* ip k* *Kali-i* k2* *Lac-c* bro1 lac-d sk4• lac-leo sk4• lach vh* lil-t bro1 **Lyc** k* *Lyss* k* m-aust j5.de mag-c mg1.de med mtf33 merc j5.de* mosch k* nat-c bg2 *Nat-m* ↓ *Nit-ac* k* **Nux-v** k* oci-sa ↓ oena a1 oxal-a rly4• ozone ↓ pall bg2* pert-vc ↓ *Petr* k* petr-ra shn4• phos mtf33 plat ptk1* plb k* raja-s jl3 ran-b k* rhus-g tmo3• ruta fd4.de sarr a1 *Seneg* k* *Sep* k* sil bg2* spong k* staph bg2* **Stram** k* stront-c sk4• sulph ptk1* syph st1* *Tarent* ptk1* thuj ↓ toxi mtf2• tritic-vg fd5.de *Tub* k* *Verat* k* vinc-ma ↓ viol-t k* [tax jsj7]

- **forenoon**: ran-b k*
- **evening**: am-c k* vinc-ma br1
- **angry**; without being: *(↗Anger)* dulc k*
- **care** what she is saying; does not: agath-a nl2•
- **causeless**: *Stram* bg2
- **children**: am-m ↓ aur-m-n ↓ calc-p ↓ *Cham* mtf33 ferr mtf33 hyos ↓ ip mtf33 lach ↓ *Lil-t* ↓ **Lyc** ↓ mag-c ↓ med mtf33 merc ↓ *Nat-m* ↓ *Nux-v* ↓ phos mtf33 plat mtf33 plb mtf33 sep mtf33 staph mtf33 stram mtf33 tarent ↓ **Tub** ↓ verat mtf33
  - **parents**; children insulting: *(↗family; husband; mother)* am-m vh* aur-m-n wbt2• calc-p mp1• cham vh* hyos vh* lach mtf33 *Lil-t* vh* **Lyc** vh* mag-c mtf33 med mtf33 merc mtf33 *Nat-m* mtf33* *Nux-v* vh* **Plat** vh* tarent vh* **Tub** mp1•
  - **towards** one's children: kali-i k2*
  - **weeping**; with: stram mtf33
- **drunkenness**; during: hep gl1.fr• nux-v gl1.fr• petr gl1.fr•
- **family**; towards one's: *(↗children - parents; husband; mother)* kali-i k2*
- **followed** by | **weakness**: mosch bg2 nat-c bg2
- **friends**; even to his best: *(↗Mocking - friends)* gal-ac a1 oci-sa sk4•
- **husband**: *(↗children - parents; family; mother)* thuj ptk1
  - **insulting**; husband is:
    - **wife** and children: lyss a1 petr-ra shn4•
    - **wife** before children or vice versa: *Anac* vh* ars vh* **Lach** vh* nux-v vh* **Verat** vh*
  - **towards** her husband: dulc fd4.de thuj ckh1
- **insulting**: *(↗Malicious - insulting)* caps ptk1 cham mtf33 dendr-pol ↓ ferr stj2* **Lach** sne mag-c mtf33 med mtf33 merc mtf33 nux-v mtf33 ozone sde2• pert-vc vk9 tarent mtf33 tub jl2* verat mtf33 [cupr stj2 cupr-act stj2 cupr-f stj2 cupr-m stj2 cupr-p stj2 ferr-f stj2 ferr-lac stj2 ferr-n stj2 ferr-sil stj2]
  - **dog**; calls everyone a: dendr-pol sk4•
  - **indignation**; others: ozone sde2•
- **menses** | **before**: cham ptk1*
- **mother**; towards: *(↗children - parents; family; husband)* *Sep* mp1• thuj ptk1*
- **pains**; with the: ars mp1• **Cham** mp1• cor-r k* nux-v mp1•
- **person** in the street; towards a: con ptk1*
- **scolds** until the lips are blue and eyes stare and she falls down fainting: *(↗FACE - Discoloration - bluish - angry)* *Mosch* k*
- **typhoid** fever; during: lyc j5.de

ACAROPHOBIA (See Fear - insects)

ACCEPTANCE: limen-b-c hrn2• *[Spect* dfg1]

ACCIDENT-PRONE: *(↗Awkward - strikes; Heedless)* **Arn** ggd aster ↓ *Caps* lmj *Lyss* lmj maias-l ↓ **Med** lmj nat-m lmj *Plut-n* srj7• *Puls* ggd sep lmj **Staph** lmj sulph lmj
- **car**: aster sze10• maias-l hrn2•

ACHIEVE things, desire to: dream-p sdj1•

ACROPHOBIA (See Fear - high)

ACTION:
- **changing** attitude to action; suddenly (See Inconstancy)
- **delayed** (See Postponing)
- **incomplete** (See Undertaking - many)

ACTIONS with hidden, irrational motives (See Irrational - hidden)

ACTIVITY:
- **after** | **agg.**: ars bg2
- **amel.** (See Occupation - amel.)
- **desires** activity: *(↗Buoyancy; Busy; Delusions - activity; Exertion - physical - amel.; Impulse - occupation - amel.; Industrious; Irritability - idle; Mental exertion - amel.; Occupation - amel.; Overactive; GENERALS - Exertion - desire)* acon gl1.fr• acon-f a1 adam ↓ agar a1* aids nl2• alco ↓ *Aloe* ↓ amn-l sp1 ang ↓ ant-m ↓ *Apis* mrr1 arg-met ↓ arg-n ↓ arg-p ↓ *Ars* vh* aur mtf33 aur-ar k2 *Aur-i* vh* *Aur-m* vh* bad a1 bar-c gl1.fr• bell-p-sp ↓ benz-ac ↓ bry a1* bung-fa mtf cadm-m ↓ cadm-met ↓ cadm-s ↓ calc ↓ calc-sil ↓ cann-i a1 *Cann-s* ↓ canth a1 carb-ac a1 carbn-o a1 carbn-s a1 carc fd2.de• chin mtf33 chinin-s ↓ choc srj3• cic jl3 clem a1 cob-n jl3 coca a1 *Coca-c* sk4• **Coff** vh coff-t a1 cycl ↓ **Dulc** fd* ephe-si hsj1• *Falco-pe* nl2• form a1 fuc a1 galv c1 gels a1 germ-met ↓ gink-b sbd1• gran ↓ ham fd3.de• hura a1

Activity – desires activity: ...
hydrog ↓ *Hyos* a1* iber a1 ignis-alc es2• ina-i mlk9.de ind ↓ **Iod** mtf33 irid-m ↓ irid-met ↓ iris a1 kali-c ↓ *Kola* stb3• lac-ac stj5• lac-del hrn2• lac-h htj1*• lac-leo ↓ lac-lup ↓ **Lach** mtf33* lil-t a1 limest-b ↓ lyc ↓ lycps-v ↓ mag-c mtf33 mag-m mtf33 manc a1 med mtf33 mez a1 *Moly-met* ↓ morph a1 mosch a1 mur-ac a1 naja a1 nat-ar k2 nat-s mtf33 neon ↓ nep mg1.de* nept-m lsd2.fr nicotam rly4• niob-m ↓ nitro-o a1 nux-v br1 oci-sa ↓ olib-sac wmh1 **Op** a1* ozone sde2• pall ↓ petr-ra shn4• phys a1 pip-m a1 plac-s rly4• plb stj2* podo ↓ positr nl2• propr sa3• *Psil* ↓ raph a1 rhodi ↓ rubd-c ↓ ruta ↓ ruth-met ↓ sarr a1 scand-met ↓ *Sep* mtf33* sil a1 *Spect* ↓ spig a1 staph mtf33 stront-met ↓ stry a1 suis-em rly4• *Sulph* vh* sumb a1 symph ↓ syph jl2 tarent mtf33 tax ↓ techn ↓ tell ↓ thea a1 *Ther* ↓ tub mtf33 *Tung-met* bdx1• ulm-c jsj8• **Verat** vh* viol-o ↓ visc sp1 wies a1 xen ↓ zinc ↓ zinc-fcy a1 zing a1 [am-f stj2 bar-br stj2 *Brom* stj2 heroin sdj2 lith-f stj2 zinc-m stj2 zinc-n stj2 zinc-p stj2]
  - **morning**: bung-fa mtf oci-sa sk4•
  - **evening**: chinin-s ↓ lycps-v a1 olib-sac wmh1
    - **21 h** | **walking** in the open air; after: chinin-s a1
  - **night**: olib-sac wmh1
  - **alternating** with:
    - **dullness**: cycl j5.de
    - **indifference**: aloe ptk1 aur ptk1 sarr a1 [bell-p-sp dcm1]
    - **lassitude**: *Aloe* k* *Aur* calc-sil k2 carc mlr1• choc srj3• falco-pe nl2• gink-b sbd1• kola stb3• positr nl2• [heroin sdj2]
    - **prostration**; mental: *Aloe* a1 limest-b es1• [spect dfg1]
    - **weakness**: olib-sac wmh1 ruta gk [tax jsj7]
  - **business**; in: *(↗Business - desire)* brom a1 manc a1
  - **creative** activity: *(↗Art - ability; Concentration - active; Delusions - creative; Ideas - abundant; Innovative; Memory - active; New ideas; Plans - making; Theorizing; Thoughts - profound; Thoughts - thoughtful)* adam srj alco mtf ang vh aur mtf calc mtf *Cann-i* mtf *Cann-s* vh carc mtf *Chin* mtf choc srj3• *Coca* mtf *Coff* a1* coff-t mtf falco-pe nl* germ-met srj gran mtf hydrog srj irid-met mtf* kali-c mtf lac-del hrn2• lac-leo hm lac-lup hm *Lach* mtf lyc mtf *Med* mtf ozone sde• *Phos* mrr1* podo fd3.de• *Psil* mtf sil mtf staph mtf *Sulph* mtf symph fd3.de• tarent mtf *Ther* mtf zinc mtf [ant-m stj arg-met stj arg-n stj arg-p stj cadm-m stj cadm-met stj cadm-s stj heroin sdj2 ind stj iod stj irid-m stj *Moly-met* stj neon stj niob-m stj pall stj rhodi stj rubd-c stj ruth-met stj scand-met stj *Spect* dfg1 stront-met stj techn stj tell stj xen stj]
  - **emotional** activity: (non:germ-met srj5) viol-o a1
  - **mental** activity (See Mental exertion - desire)
  - **perspiration**; during: **Op** a1
  - **physical** exercise; desires (See Exertion - physical - desire)
  - **sleeplessness**; with: bung-fa mtf
  - **weakness**; with physical: mosch bg2
  - **work**; at: benz-ac a1 ham fd3.de•
- **fruitless** (See Busy - fruitlessly)
- **restless**: *(↗Restlessness)* *Coff* vh* dig a1 haliae-lc srj5• ign mtf33* irid-met srj5• lycps-v a1* medul-os-si rly4• nicotam rly4• *Nux-v* j5.de* plac-s rly4• positr nl2• pyrid rly4• verat j5.de* viol-o ptk [heroin sdj2]
- **sleeplessness**; with: dig a1 rhus-t a1 thea a1 zinc a1 [heroin sdj2]
  - **evening** (See SLEEP - Sleeplessness - evening - thoughts)
  - **thoughts** of activity; from (See SLEEP - Sleeplessness - thoughts - activity)

ACUTENESS (See Memory - active)

ADAPTABILITY; loss of: *(↗Schizophrenia - paranoid)* *Anh* mg1.de* psor jl2

ADDICTED; tendency to become: carc mlr1•

ADMIRATION, excessive: *(↗Sentimental; Veneration)* cic gl1.fr•

ADMONITION: *(↗Ailments - reprimands; Sensitive; Sulky)*
- **agg.**: *(↗Ailments - reproaches; Confusion - vexation - after; Delusions - accused; Delusions - confusion; Delusions - criticized; Delusions - despised; Delusions - insulted; Delusions - laughed; Delusions - looked; Delusions - watched; Fear - humiliated; Offended; Sadness - vexation; Sensitive - criticism; Sensitive - reprimands; Weeping - admonition; Weeping - remonstrated; COUGH - Grief;*

- **agg.**: ...
  DREAMS - Theft - accused; EYE - Pupils - dilated - reprimands; GENERALS - Convulsions - unjustly) *Bell* k* calc j5.de carc st* chin mtf coloc ptk* dulc fd4.de germ-met srj* ham fd3.de• *Ign* mtf kali-c bg2* med mtf *Nat-m* ↓ nit-ac j5.de* *Nux-v* gl1.fr• op ptk* pall ptk1* *Phos* ↓ *Plat* k* sal-fr sle1• sep ↓ sil mrr1 stann mtf staph ptk* tarent ptk* *Zinc* ↓
  - **children**; in: carc c1 med c1
  - **kindly**; even: bell b4.de* carc vh* chin b7.de* ign b7.de* *Nat-m* b4a.de nux-v b7.de* *Phos* b4a.de *Plat* b4.de* sep b4a.de *Sil* b4a.de stann bg2 *Zinc* b4a.de

ADULTEROUS: *(↗Deceitful; Love - perversity; Perfidious)* calc vh* canth vh* caust vh* ign oss• lach vh* *Lyc* mrr1 med mtf* phos vh* plat vh* puls vh* *Sabal* rmk1• staph vh* verat vh* [vip bcj1]

ADVENTUROUS: *(↗Courageous; Rash; Travelling - desire)* carc gk6 ignis-alc es2• maias-l hrn2• *Med* mtf *Tub* mtf

AFFABILITY: alco mtf apis a1 dulc fd4.de hypoth jl3 kali-s fd4.de phos mtf podo fd3.de• tub mtf
- **enemy**; to an: alco a1

AFFECTATION: *(↗Eccentricity; Haughty; Vanity)* alum bt* carb-v lmj* carc fb* caust lmj* con lmj* dream-p ↓ graph lmj* *Hyos* vh* *Ign* lmj *Lyc* vh* mez h2* nat-m lmj* *Nux-m* ↓ pall gg petr gl1.fr• plat ptk1* puls lmj ruta ↓ sep lmj sil mtf *Staph* lmj *Stram* k* sulph lmj thuj lmj *Verat* vh*
- **children**; in: alum lmj **Carb-v** lmj *Carc* lmj caust lmj con lmj *Graph* lmj hyos lmj *Ign* lmj *Lyc* lmj mez lmj nat-m lmj *Nux-m* lmj petr lmj **Plat** lmj puls lmj sep lmj *Staph* lmj *Stram* lmj sulph lmj thuj lmj **Verat** lmj
- **gestures** and acts; in: *(↗Speech - affected; Strange - crank)* hyos gl1.fr• mez h2 stram mtf33 verat mtf33*
- **loves** affection (See Sympathy - desire)
- **words**; in: *(↗Speech - affected)* dream-p sdj1• lyc gl1.fr• plat mtf33* ruta fd4.de verat mtf33*

AFFECTED (See Affectation)

AFFECTION: *(↗Consolation; Consolation - amel.)*
- **full** of affection (See Affectionate)
- **rejecting** affection (See Consolation - agg.)
- **returning** affection (See Affectionate - returns)
- **show** affection; unable to (See Reserved)
- **yearning** for affection: *(↗Caressed - wants)* carc mtf olib-sac wmh1 phos mtf

AFFECTIONATE: *(↗Abrupt - affectionate; Anxiety - others; Attached - strongly; Benevolence; Consolation - amel.; Familiarity; Magnetized - desire; Mildness; Sympathetic)* acon k* agar a1 *Agath-a* nl2• aloe sne alum gl1.fr• anac *Ant-c* k* ars j5.de* aur ckh1 *Aur-m-n* wbt2• bar-c gl1.fr• **Bell** ckh1 borx k* bry ckh1* *Calc* ckh1 calc-p mtf33 carb-an carb-v k* carc fb* *Caust* gl1.fr* cham ckh1 chin ckh1 choc srj3• coff colum-p sze2• *Croc* k* dulc fd4.de *Flav* jl2 graph mtf33* **Ham** fd* hura hydr a1 **Hyos** ckh1 *Ign* k* irid-met srj5• *Kali-s* fd4.de kola stb3• lac-ac stj5• lac-del hrn2• lach ckh1* lec oss• lil-t ckh1 limen-b-c hrn2* lyc ckh1* *Murx* ↓ nat-c ckh1 *Nat-m* k* nat-s mrr1 nat-sil fd3.de• nit-ac gl1.fr• *Nux-v* k* *Olib-sac* wmh1 op a1* ox-ac par ph-ac ckh1* *Phos* b4.de* plat k* podo fd3.de• positr nl2• **Puls** k* rhus-t mrr1 seneg sep mrr1* *Sil* st* *Staph* mrr1* stram a1* *Sulph* mrr1* symph fd3.de• thea a1 *Tung-met* bdx1• ulm-c jsj8• valer ckh1 vanil fd5.de verat k* vero-o rly4• [cupr stj2 cupr-act stj2 cupr-f stj2 cupr-m stj2 cupr-p stj2 heroin sdj2 nicc-met stj2 nicc-s stj2 rhodi stj2 tax jsj7]
- **evening**: choc srj3•
- **alternating** with:
  - **anger** (See Anger - alternating - affectionate)
  - **irritability** (See Irritability - alternating - affectionate)
  - **laughing** (See Laughing - alternating - affection)
  - **moroseness** (See Morose - alternating - affectionate)
  - **rage** (See Rage - alternating - affectionate)
  - **sadness**: plat j5.de
- **children**: carb-v mtf33
- **kisses** and caresses children: phos ckh1 *Puls* kr1*
- **returns** affection: *Phos* st1* podo fd3.de• ulm-c jsj8•
- **women**: *Murx* br1

AFRAID (See Anguish; Anxiety; Fear)

AGGRESSION (See Anger; Fight; Irritability; Quarrelsome; Rage; Violent)

AGILITY, mental: *(↗Ideas - abundant; Mental exertion - desire; Mental exertion - wine; Mental power - increased; Quick; GENERALS - Agility)* cocain br1 **Coff** br1* form a1 ham fd3.de• irid-met srj5• lac-f wza1• nux-v br1 **Op** ptk1 ozone sde2• stry br1 tritic-vg fd5.de [heroin sdj2]

AGITATION (See Excitement)

AGONY before death (See Death - agony)

AGORAPHOBIA (See Fear - crowd; Fear - open; Going)

AICHMOPHOBIA (See Fear - pins)

AILMENTS FROM:
- **abstinence**; sexual (See celibacy)
- **abused**; after being: **Acon** ↓ am-m mtf ambr tsm1* anac mrr1* androc ↓ **Arg-n** ↓ **Arn** ↓ ars ↓ aster ↓ aur ↓ aur-m ↓ bapt ↓ bell-p-sp ↓ berb ↓ calc-p mtf cann-i ↓ carc mrr1* caust mrr1 chin ↓ coff mrr1 croc ↓ cupr ↓ cur mrr1 cycl ↓ falco-pe ↓ foll ↓ hura ↓ *Hyos* mtf **Ign** ↓ kreos ↓ *Lac-c* mtf* lac-f ↓ *Lach* ↓ lyc mtf *Lyss* mtf *Med* mtf *Melis* ↓ *Naja* ↓ nat-c ↓ *Nat-f* ↓ **Nat-m** mtf nux-v ↓ **Op** ↓ *Orig* ↓ oxyg ↓ petr-ra shn4• *Plat* ↓ puls ↓ **Sep** ↓ *Staph* mrr1* stram hu3 thuj gy3 toxi ↓ tub ↓ ust ↓ xanth ↓ [lac-mat sst4]
  - **children**: carc mlr1•
  - **indignation**; with: carc mp1*•
  - **physically**: lyss mrr1
  - **marriage**; in: *Anac* mtf **Arg-n** mtf aur mtf carc mtf chin mtf hura mtf hyos mtf *Lach* mtf lyc mtf *Lyss* mtf *Naja* mtf *Nat-m* mtf puls mtf *Sep* mtf stram mtf
  - **sexually**: *(↗Humiliated - sexual; FEMALE - Sexual desire - incest; MALE GENITALIA/SEX - Sexual desire - incest)* **Acon** mp• am-m sfr1 ambr tsm1 anac mp• androc fe* **Arn** mp• ars bse aster ↓ aur-m ptk bapt dkl1 berb lga* calc-p ptk cann-i zr1 **Carc** fd* caust mrr1* croc zl cupr sst• cur vh cycl fe falco-pe nl2• foll vml hyos ptk* **Ign** mp• kreos zl lac-c cza lac-f vml lyc dx1* lyss bse* *Med* mp• *Melis* ptm nat-c zr1 **Nat-m** mp• nux-v mp• **Op** mp• *Orig* mrr1* petr-ra shn4• *Plat* mp* **Sep** mp• **Staph** nh* stram mrr1* thuj svp* toxi fe tub kjm (non:ust hr1) xanth knl• [bell-p-sp dcm1 *Nat-f* stj oxyg stj]
    - **children**; in: acon mp• anac mp• arn mp• *Carc* mp*• ign mp• kreos lrp1• lac-c lrp1• lyc mp• *Med* mp• nat-m mp• nux-v mp• op mp• *Plat* mp• sep mp• staph mp• thuj mp•
    - **rape**: aster sze10• *Carc* mlr1•
  - **violence**; from: *Carc* mlr1•
    - **children**: *Carc* mlr1•
- **accusations** (See reproaches)
- **admonition**; from (See Admonition - agg.)
- **affection**; lack of (See neglected)
- **alcoholism**: *(↗Alcoholism; Beer; GENERALS - Family - alcoholism)* agar c1 **Arn** b7a.de ars b4a.de* asar vh *Bell* k* calc b4a.de* *Calc-ar* ↓ **Cann-s** b7a.de caps ↓ carbn-s ↓ chin b7a.de *Cocc* b7a.de* con hep b4a.de *Hyos* b7a.de lach gl1.fr• *Lyss* nux-v b7.de* op b7a.de* ph-ac gl1.fr• *Phos* hr1 *Stram* k* sulph gl1.fr• zinc sf
  - **abstinence** of alcohol: asar vh *Calc-ar* kr1* caps br1 carbn-s br1
- **ambition**: *(↗Ambition - increased)*
  - **deceived**: aur mtf bell gl1.fr• merc gl1.fr• nat-m gk *Nux-v* kr1* plat gl1.fr• puls gl1.fr• verat mtf* zinc mtf
  - **excessive**: *Asar* mrr
- **anger**: *(↗Mania - vexation; Vexed - intolerance)* **Acon** k* agar aids nl2• *Aloe* vh1 alum k* alum-sil k2* am-c am-m ↓ ambr ↓ anac sf1.de* anan oss• ang vh ant-c bg2 *Ant-t* k* *Apis* k* arg-met k2* arg-n am k* *Ars* k* ars-s-f k2* **Aur** k* aur-ar k2 *Aur-m* aur-m-n c1* aur-s ↓ bamb-a ↓ bar-c bg2 *Bell* k* bros-gau ↓ *Bry* k* cadm-s calc k* calc-ar k2 *Calc-p* k* calc-s calc-sil k2* camph c1 carb-an bg2 carc sst*• caust k* **CHAM** k* chin k* cimic cina bg2 cist *Cocc* k* *Coch* kr1 *Coff* k* colch bro1 **Coloc** k* colum-p ↓ *Cortico* ↓ croc k* crot-c ↓ cupr k* dendr-pol ↓ dulc fd4.de falco-pe ↓ ferr k* ferr-p fum ↓ *Gels* k* *Germ-met* ↓ gink-b ↓ glon ↓ graph k2 grat bro1 haliae-lc ↓ ham fd3.de• hep ↓ hyos k* **Ign** k* ilx-a mtf11 iod bg2 **Ip** k* kali-bi gk kali-br c1* *Kali-p* *Lach* k* lachn ↓ lil-t mrr1 *Lyc* k* lyss ↓ m-ambo b2.de* m-arct b2.de* m-aust b2.de* mag-c k* mag-m k* mag-p ↓ manc merc bg2 mez k* *Moni* ↓ mur-ac ↓ nat-ar k2 nat-c k* *Nat-m* k* nat-p nat-s nux-m k* **NUX-V** k* ol-an bg2* olnd b2.de* **Op** k* petr k* *Ph-ac* k*

- **anger**: ...
Phos k* pin-con ↓ pin-s mtf11 **Plat** k* podo fd3.de• positr nl2• pot-e rly4• *Puls* k* ran-b b2.de* rhus-t k* ruta ↓ sacch a1* samb k* scroph-n c1 sec k* sel k* *Sep* b2.de* sil k* spect ↓ spig gk spong ↓ stann k* **STAPH** b2.de* stram k* stront-c b2.de* sulph k* symph fd3.de• *Tarent* tritic-vg fd5.de tus-p ↓ ulm-c ↓ vanil fd5.de verat k* verat-v bg vesp k2 vinc c1 zinc k* zinc-p k2*
  - **anxiety**; with: (↗*fright; Anxiety*) **Acon** k* alum k* **Ars** k* aur k* *Bell* k* bry k* calc k* carc mlr1• *Cham* k* cocc k* coff k* *Cupr* k* *Gels* bg2 hyos k* **Ign** k* lyc k* nat-c k* nat-m k* **Nux-v** k* *Op* k* petr k* phos k* *Plat* k* *Puls* k* rhus-t k* samb k* sep k* stann k* stram k* sulph k* verat k*
  - **bitterness**; with: **Coloc** b4a.de
  - **fright**; with: (↗*anxiety; mental shock*) **Acon** k* *Aur* *Bell* k* calc k* *Carc* mlr1• cocc k* coff kr1 cupr k* *Gels* bg2 glon bg2 **Ign** k* nat-c k* *Nux-v* k* *Op* k* *Petr* k* *Phos* k* *Plat* k* *Puls* k* samb k* sep k* **Stram** bg2 sulph k* zinc k*
  - **indignation**; with: (↗*reproaches; scorned; Anger - indignation; Hatred; Indignation*) ambr tsm1 ars bg2 *Aur* bros-gau mrc1 bry br1 carc fd2.de*• cham br1 **Coloc** k* germ-met srj ham fd3.de• ip k* lyc m-ambo bg2 merc mur-ac *Nat-m* k* *Nux-v* k* plat k* **STAPH** b2.de*
  - **vehemence**; with: **Acon** b2.de* aur b2.de* bell b2.de* *Bry* b2.de* **Cham** b2.de* *Coff* b2.de* hyos b2.de* lyc b2.de* nat-m b2.de* **Nux-v** b2.de* phos b2.de* *Plat* b4a.de sep b2.de* *Staph* b7a.de sulph b2.de* verat b2.de* zinc b2.de*
  - **vexation**; with: *Bry* b7.de* *Cham* b7.de coff b7.de* nux-v b7a.de
  - **silent** grief; with: (↗*Grief*) *Acon* bg2 alum k* am-m sf1.de* ars k* aur k* aur-ar k2 *Aur-m-n* wbt2• bell k* *Bry* bg2 carc gk6* cham bg2* *Chin* sf1.de *Cocc* k* *Coloc* k* gels bg2 hyos k* **Ign** k* **Lyc** k* nat-c k* **Nat-m** k* nux-v k* *Ph-ac* k* phos k* plat k* puls k* **Staph** k* verat k* zinc bg2
  - **suppressed**: (↗*domination - long; scorned; Emotions - suppressed; Mildness - masking*) acon vh1 agar zr* anac mrr1 aur k* *Aur-m-n* wbt2• aur-s wbt2• bamb-a stb2.de• carc gk6* cham k* **Coloc** b4a.de* colum-p sze2• *Cortico* tpw7 crot-c sk4• cupr sst3• dendr-pol sk4• falco-pe nl2• fum rly1• *Germ-met* srj5• gink-b jl (non:haliae-lc srj5) hep bg2 *Ign* k* ilx-a bh• *Ip* kr1* lachn a1 **Lyc** kr1* lyss sk• mag-m mtf33 *Moni* rfm1• *Nat-m* kr1* pin-con oss2• podo fd3.de• pot-e rly4• ruta fd4.de sep k* spong fd4.de **Staph** k* stront-c sk4• tritic-vg fd5.de ulm-c jsj8• vanil fd5.de [mag-p stj spect dfg1 tus-p stj]
- **anticipation**: (↗*Anticipation; Anxiety - anticipation; Anxiety - anticipation - engagement; Anxiety - future; Anxiety - railroad; Anxiety - time; Clairvoyance; Death - presentiment; Excitement - anticipating; Fear - happen; Hurry - time; Hurry - walking; Time - slowly; Timidity; Timidity - public; RECTUM - Diarrhea - anger; RECTUM - Diarrhea - anticipation*) acon bg* aesc bg aeth st* agn bg *Aloe* sne alum sf1.de am-c bg ambr tsm1 *Anac* c1* androc srj1• ang vh apis bg* **ARG-N** bg2* *Ars* bg2* *Aur-m-n* wbt2* aur-s wbt2• bamb-a stb2.de• *Bar-c* sf1.de bry st* **Calc** bg* camph st* canth j5.de *Carb-v* bg3* **Carc** c1* *Caust* bg* cench k2 chin bg* chinin-s ptk1 chlorpr jl *Cic* st *Cocc* c1* coff st* crot-h a1 cupr mtf cypr vml3• dig sf1.de dys fmm1• *Elaps* sf1.de* epiph c1 fl-ac st* **GELS** bg2* **Graph** sf1.de* hydrog srj2• hyos st* **Ign** bg2* irid-met srj5• kali-br st kali-c bg *Kali-p* kr1 ketogl-ac rly4• *Kola* stb3• *Lac-c* kr1* lach bg levo jl **Lyc** bg3* lyss st* **Med** bg2* merc st* **Mez** st morg fmm1• mosch j5.de mur-ac mtf naja bg* *Nat-c* kr1* nat-m bg2* nux-v st* ox-ac sf1.de ozone sde2• petr st* *Ph-ac* bg2* *Phos* bg* *Plb* bg* **Psor** bg* **Puls** kr1* rhus-t sf1.de sal-fr sle1• sep bg **Sil** bg3* spig bg* staph st still kr1* stram bg stront-c st* sul-ac gk sulph a1* symph fd3.de• thuj st* tritic-vg fd5.de tub bgs* verat bg* [arg-met stj1 calc-n stj1 *Titan* stj zinc stj1]
  - **anxiety**: aur k2* calc st calc-p c1 carc mlr1• cimic hr1* cocc tl1 hyos j5.de ign b7a.de* kali-p k2* lyc a1* nit-ac a1 op mtf33 ph-ac j5.de pic-ac ↓ **Ruta** fd* samb hr1* **Sil** kr1 *Spong* fd4.de staph a*
    - **prolonged**; from: aur sne carc fb pic-ac k2
- **appreciated**; from not being: (↗*Delusions - appreciated*) **Ham** fd*
- **asking** for help: [card-m stj]
- **bad** news: (↗*Dullness - bad; Excitement - bad; Fear - bad; Sadness - bad; Wildness - unpleasant; CHILL - Sad; EAR - Trembling - sad; EXTREMITIES - Trembling - hand - news; GENERALS - Orgasm - disagreeable; PERSPIRATION - News; RECTUM - Diarrhea - bad news; SLEEP - Sleepiness - sad news; STOMACH - Sensitiveness - bad*) acon bro1* aln c1 alum kr1 alumn c1* ambr k2* *Apis* k* *Am* st ars bro1 art-v c1 aster sze10• aur bro1 aur-m st bapt pfa *Bry* bro1 **Calc** k* calc-p k* calc-s tl caust bro1 *Cham* bro1 chin cic ptk1* cinnb cocc bro1 colch bro1* *Coloc* bro1 cupr

- **bad** news: ...
dig c1 dros form k* **GELS** a2* grat bro1 hist mg1.de hyos bro1* *Ign* k* kali-c kali-p k* kola stb3* lac-v al lach k* lyc st lyss k* mag-c sne manc vh *Med* k* mez k2 *Nat-m* k* nat-p nit-ac st *Nux-v* bro1 paeon k* *Pall* k* ph-ac c1* phos podo hr1 puls k* *Ruta* fd4.de sabin k13 sep bro1 *Sil* st spong fd4.de *Staph* bro1 stram *Sulph* k* tarent c1* teucr k13 *Vanil* fd5.de zinc kr1
- **betrayed**; from being: rhus-g tmo3•
- **business** failure: (↗*Business - aversion; Insanity - business*) *Ambr* sf1.de* *Aur* mrr1* calc k2* *Cimic* hr1* coloc k2 *Hyos* hr1 ign hr1 kali-br c1* kali-p sne nat-m sf1.de nux-v sf1.de* ph-ac k2 puls gl1.fr• rhus-t gl1.fr• sep gl1.fr• sulph gl1.fr• verat gl1.fr•
- **cares**, worries: (↗*Cares full; Cares full - Relatives; Prostration - Cares; GENERALS - Weakness - Nursing and; SLEEP - Sleeplessness - Cares; from*) *Ambr* sf1.de arg-n c1 ars c1 *Calc* k2* carc mlr1* *Caust* k2* **Cocc** gk* con sf1.de cypra-eg sde6.de• germ-met srj hippoc-k szs2 ign c1* kali-br c1 kali-p k2* lyc a1 mag-c br1 nat-m sf1.de nit-ac mrr **Nux-v** sf1.de *Ph-ac* *Phos* j5.de* pic-ac k2* sanic c1 *Staph* j5.de* *Vanil* fd5.de
  - **loved** one; over a: (↗*Cares full - relatives*) **Cocc** mrr1 vanil fd5.de
- **caressing**; amorous: caps b7.de
- **celibacy**: (↗*GENERALS - Sexual desire - suppression - agg.*) agn hr* alum mgg* apis dm* calc ptk* *Cann-i* ptk caust mgg* con h2* fl-ac ptk* lyc ptk* **Phos** bg* pic-ac ckh1 plat ptk* sep mrr1*
- **continence** (See celibacy)
- **contradiction**: (↗*Contradiction - intolerant*) anac jl *Aur* b2.de* aur-ar k2 cael jl cham k2 elaps kr1 ham fd3.de• helon bg ign b2.de* **Lyc** bg2 med st nux-v b2.de* olnd b2.de* sil sf1.de spong fd4.de
- **criticized**; from being: agar bg2 gels bg2 ign bg2
- **death** of loved ones: (↗*Death - agony*) **Acon** lmj *Ambr* k* anthraci vh **Ars** lmj aster ↓ *Aur-m-n* ↓ calc lmj calc-sil ↓ caps lmj carc lmj caust lmj gels lmj **Ign** lmj *Kali-br* lmj kali-p ↓ lac-c ↓ **Lach** lmj lyc pcr mur-ac ↓ nat-m gk* nat-s mrr1 nit-ac ↓ nux-m ↓ nux-v lmj **Op** lmj **Ph-ac** lmj plat c1* podo fd3.de• rhod ↓ sal-fr ↓ spig gk **Staph** lmj sulph lmj tritic-vg fd5.de **Vanil** fd* verat lmj
  - **child**; of a: calc k2 caust gl1.fr• *Gels* kr1 **Ign** kr1* *Kali-br* kr1 lach gl1.fr• lyc pcr **Nat-m** c1* nux-v gl1.fr• ph-ac gl1.fr• plat c1 sal-fr sle1• staph gl1.fr• sulph gl1.fr• tritic-vg fd5.de **Vanil** fd*
  - **children**; in: **Acon** lmj ambr lmj **Ars** lmj calc lmj calc-sil lmj caps lmj carc lmj caust lmj gels lmj **Ign** lmj kali-br lmj kali-p lmj **Lach** lmj nat-m lmj nit-ac lmj nux-m lmj nux-v lmj **Op** lmj **Ph-ac** lmj *Plat* lmj **Staph** lmj sulph lmj verat lmj
  - **parents** or friends; of: ambr c1* anthraci vh ars gk aster sze10• aur-m-n wbt2• calc k2 **Caust** mtf33* **IGN** kr1* kali-br ptk lac-c mtf lyc pcr* mur-ac ggd1 nat-m gk* nit-ac kr1* nux-v gl1.fr• plat c1 rhod mtf staph gl1.fr• tritic-vg fd5.de **Vanil** fd* [ph-ac stj1]
    - **mother**; of: *Aur-m-n* wbt2•
- **debauchery**: (↗*GENERALS - Debauch; GENERALS - Debauch - after*) agar k13 anac b4a.de *Anan* vh* ant-c kr1* arg-n c1 calad vh carb-v c1 *Cimic* sne dig c1 *Fl-ac* k2* lach bg* *Nux-v* c1* pic-ac k2* sel c1* sep k2* spig kr1 stram ptk sul-ac bg*
- **deceived**; from being: (↗*friendship; Grief - deception*) **Aur** mtf **IGN** mtf lach mtf **Lyc** mtf merc mtf **Nat-m** mtf *Nux-v* mtf op mtf ph-ac mtf puls mtf sep mtf staph mtf verat mtf
- **disappointment**: (↗*honor; scorned; Indifference - disappointment*) acon bro1 agath-a nl2• all-c vh1 alum c1* ant-c tl1 apis gw* ars bro1 aster sze10• **Aur** bro1* *Aur-m-n* wbt2• *Aur-s* wbt2• bell b4a.de *Bry* bro1 calc-p tl1 caps dg carb-v k13 carc sk• caust bro1 cham dh* cimic ↓ cocc bro1* colch bro1 *Coloc* bro1 dig a *Gels* bro1 grat bro1 hyos bro1 **IGN** br1* kali-c h2 *Lach* k2* *Lyc* st* **Merc** st* **Nat-m** c1* nat-s gk *Nux-v* bro1* *Oci-sa* ↓ *Op* st **Ph-ac** bro1* phos dh plac rzf5• plat k2* *Podo* fd3.de• **Puls** bro1* ruta fd4.de sep bro1* spig gk **STAPH** k1* *Tritic-vg* fd5.de vanil fd5.de verat st [am-c stj1 am-m stj1 am-s stj1]
  - **deception**: cimic sne *Oci-sa* sk4•
  - **new**: **IGN** st
  - **old**: **NAT-M** st
- **discords** between: (↗*Quarrelling - aversion*)
  - **chief** and subordinates: **Ars** ckh1 graph gl1.fr• hep ckh1 lach ckh1* *Lyc* vh* mag-m vh* merc ckh1* nat-m ckh1* nit-ac ckh1* *Nux-v* gl1.fr* sulph gl1.fr•
  - **family**: *Lac-e* hrn2•
  - **friends**; one's: abies-c oss4• ars gl1.fr• aur-m-n wbt2• **Graph** hr1* hep gl1.fr• ign gy lach vh* mag-m vh* merc vh* nat-m vh* nit-ac vh* nux-v vh* sulph vh* tax-br oss1•

- **parents**; one's: abies-c oss4• ars gl1.fr• aur-m-n wbt2• **Graph** hr1* h e p gl1.fr• ign gy lach vh* *Mag-m* vh* med gk merc vh* nat-m vh* nit-ac vh* nux-v vh* sulph vh* tax-br oss1• [*Mag-c* stj1]

- **domination**: *(↗opportunities; Independent)* *Anac* ↓ *Aur-m-n* ↓ brach ↓ calc ↓ carc sst2• coff mrr1 cupr-act mlk erech ↓ eup-per ↓ eup-pur ↓ falco-pe nl2• ferr-i ↓ *Foll* oss• hyos ↓ *Ign* ↓ kali-i ↓ liat ↓ *Lyc* ↓ *Mag-c* ↓ *Mag-m* ↓ manc ↓ med ↓ merc mtf naja ↓ nat-m ↓ nit-ac ↓ **Podo** ↓ ruta ↓ sep ↓ ser-ang ↓ sil ↓ *Staph* mrr1 stram ↓ symph ↓ thuj ↓ tritic-vg fd5.de tub mtf vanad ↓ zinc ↓
  - **children**; in: *Anac* mp1* *Aur-m-n* ↓ *Carc* sk1* cupr-act mlk ferr-i ↓ foll rma2 hyos ↓ kali-i ckh1 *Lyc* szw1* manc ↓ med mp1* naja mtf33 nat-m mp1* nit-ac mtf33 **Podo** fd* ruta fd4.de sep dx1* ser-ang ↓ sil mp1* *Staph* mp1* symph fd3.de• thuj mp1* vanad ↓ zinc ↓ [erech stj]
    - **parental** control; long history of excessive: *Aur-m-n* wbt2• c a r c tpw* hyos sk7• kali-i ↓ manc ↓ naja mtf33 nit-ac ↓ ser-ang vml3• vanad dx* [ferr-i stj1 zinc stj1]
      - **harsh** upbringing: carc sst2• kali-i ckh1 nit-ac mtf33
      - **religious** upbringing: manc vwe2
  - **father**; by: [brach stj eup-per stj eup-pur stj liat stj]
  - **long** time; for a: *(↗anger - suppressed; Emotions - suppressed)* calc mtf carc gk6* falco-pe nl2• foll jsa *Ign* mtf lyc dx1* *Mag-c* mtf *Mag-m* mtf sep dx1 *Staph* mtf stram mtf

- **egotism**: *(↗Dictatorial)* *Calc* k* lac-leo mtf *Lach* vh* *Lyc* k* med vh merc *Pall* k* *Plat* vh* sil *Sulph* k*

- **embarrassment**: *(↗honor; mortification; reproaches; scorned; Confidence - want; Dullness - mortification; Indignation; Speech - embarrassed; Timidity; Timidity - bashful; Weeping - mortification; DREAMS - Embarrassment)* *Ambr* ptk1* *Bar-c* vh* bar-s zr bung-fa mtf carb-v mtf chin mtf coloc crot-c sk4• dig mtf dys bh* ferr mtf gels k2* germ-met mtf hydrog mtf hyos mtf *Ign* k* kali-br al* lac-e mtf lac-h sk4• loxo-recl knl4• melal-alt gya4 *Merc* mtf *Nat-m* hu *Op* k* petr-ra shn4• ph-ac phos mtf plat plut-n srj7• puls mrr1 sep staph k* **Sulph** k* tarent mtf vanil fd5.de [heroin sdj2]
  - **poor** job performance; of: lac-e hrn2•

- **emotionally** suppressed; from being (See Emotions - suppressed)

- **emotions**: *Acon* b2.de* aloe bg2 alum b2.de* am-m b2.de* *Aml-ns* bg2 ant-t b2.de* **Arg-n** bg2 arn b2.de* ars b2.de* asar b2.de* *Aur* b2.de* bar-c b2.de* *Bell* b2.de* *Bry* b2.de* calc b2.de* camph bg2 caps b2.de* carb-an b2.de* *Caust* b2.de* *Cham* b2.de* chin b2.de* cic b2.de* cimic bg2 cist bg2 *Cocc* b2.de* *Coff* b2.de* colch b2.de* **Coloc** b2.de* con b2.de* croc b2.de* cupr b2.de* cycl b2.de* ferr b2.de* *Gels* bg2 graph b2.de* hep b2.de* **Hyos** b2.de* **Ign** b2.de* ip b2.de* kali-c b2.de* kali-n bg2 *Lach* b2.de* laur b2.de* *Lyc* b2.de* m-ambo b2.de* m-arct b2.de m-aust b2.de mag-c b2.de* mag-m b2.de* merc b2.de* mosch bg2 nat-c b2.de* *Nat-m* b2.de* nit-ac b2.de* *Nux-m* b2.de* **Nux-v** b2.de* olnd b2.de* *Op* b2.de* petr b2.de* **Ph-ac** b2.de* *Phos* b2.de* plat b2.de* podo bg2 *Psor* bg2 **Puls** b2.de* ran-b b2.de* rhus-t b2.de* samb b2.de* sars bg2 sec b2.de* sel b2.de* seneg b2.de* sep b2.de* *Sil* b2.de* spong b2.de* stann b2.de* **Staph** b2.de* *Stram* b2.de* stront-c b2.de* sulph b2.de* teucr b2.de* *Verat* b2.de* verb b2.de* z i n c b2.de*
  - **sad**: calc b4a.de caust b4a.de nit-ac b4a.de ph-ac b4a.de

- **excitement**: *(↗Excitement; Irritability - excited)* *Acon* bg2 ambr bg2 arg-n bg2 caust bg2 **Cham** bg2 *Cocc* bg2 coff bg2 *Gels* bg2 **Ign** bg2 **Phos** bg2 sep bg2 *Staph* bg2
  - **depressing**: gels c1 nat-m bg2
  - **emotional**: *(↗Excitement; Irritability - excited)* acet-ac k* *Acon* j5.de* agar c1 anac k2* apis gsd1 *Arg-n* k* *Arn* ars hr1 asaf sf1.de aster *Aur* *Aur-m-n* wbt2• bad a1 bamb-a stb2.de• *Bell* j5.de* bry j5.de* *Calc* calc-ar calc-p **Caps** carb-v ↓ *Carc* mlr1• castm c1 *Caust* cham a1 cimic st cina a1 *Cist* *Cob* *Cocc* k* coch cod c1 **Coff** k* coff-t c1* colch b **Coll** coloc a1* *Con* convo-s sp1 cot br1 crat br1 croc ckh1 cupr st cypr c1 epiph c1 ferr c1* **Gels** k* *Glon* goss st* hyos j5.de ign k* *Kali-br* kali-c j5.de *Kali-p* k* kreos lach j5.de* laur gt lil-t mrr1 lyc *Lyss* mag-c a1 mang c1 med ptk2* merc ↓ mosch a1 nat-c *Nat-m* k* nit-ac nux-m k* *Nux-v* op gt* *Pall* petr br1* **Ph-ac** k* *Phos* phys c1 plat k2* *Psor* **Puls** pyrog ckh1 **Ruta** fd* sacch c1 samb c1 scut c1 *Sep* k1* spig gk *Spong* fd4.de stann c1* **Staph** stram bg sumb a1 symph fd3.de• *Tarent* st* thuj ↓ tritic-vg fd5.de **Tub** st vanil fd5.de *Verat* vesp k2 *Zinc* zinc-val ckh1
    - **children** are ill at certain moments: acon lmj bell lmj calc lmj caps lmj carb-v lmj caust lmj ign lmj *Lach* lmj lyc lmj merc lmj op lmj psor lmj **Puls** lmj *Sep* lmj *Staph* lmj thuj lmj tub lmj verat lmj
    - **slight**: psor ptk1

- **excitement – emotional**: ...
    - **sudden**: caust br1
  - **long** lasting: petr ptk
  - **moral** (See moral)
  - **religious**: stram gt sulph gt verat gt
  - **sexual** (See sexual excitement)
  - **sudden**: coff br1
  - **suppressed**: con c1 cot br1 cupr vh kali-c vh kali-p c1 lach gsd

- **expectations** of parents too high: carc sst2•

- **failure**:
  - **literary**, scientific failure: *(↗rejected; Sadness - failure)* calc gl1.fr• ign gl1.fr• lyc gl1.fr• nux-v gl1.fr• puls gl1.fr• sulph gl1.fr•
  - **social** failures: *(↗position; Fear - social)* pers jl

- **father**; absence of: carc sst2•

- **fear**: *(↗Fear)* **Acon** c1* *Act-sp* vh1 arg-met k2* *Arg-n* c1* ars st1 *Bell* j5.de* c a l c st calc-sil k2 carc c1* *Caust* k2* cocc c1 coff c1 cupr sf1.de **Gels** k2* glon c1* graph c1 *Ign* c1* kali-p sf1.de lac-del hm2• lyc c1 med st1 nat-m st1 *Op* j5.de* p h - a c st1 phos c1 puls sf1.de* sil sf1.de *Spong* fd4.de stram vh* verat j5.de*

- **financial** loss (See money)

- **forced**; from being: *(↗Autism)* [cina stj]

- **fortune**; from reverse of: *(↗Insanity - fortune - losing; Mania - fortune; Sadness - fortune)* ambr sf1.de con sf1.de dig sf1.de lach sf1.de stann sf1.de staph sf1.de **Symph** fd* **Vanil** fd*

- **freedom**; loss of (See domination)

- **friendship**; deceived: *(↗deceived; rejected; Delusions - betrayed; Delusions - friendless; Forsaken)* aur hr1 aur-m-n wbt2• ign gl1.fr• mag-c gl1.fr• mag-m gl1.fr• nux-v gl1.fr• ph-ac gl1.fr• rhus-g tmo3• sil gl1.fr• sulph gl1.fr•

- **fright**: *(↗Fright - menses; Mental shock; Anxiety - Fright - after; Fear - Fright; Fear - Fright - previous; Horrible; Indifference - Fright; Insanity - Fright; Sensitive - Noise; Starting - Fright; Suicidal - Fright; CHEST - Palpitation - Fright; CHILL - Fright; COUGH - Fright agg.; FACE - Expression - Frightened; FEMALE - Metrorrhagia - Fright; GENERALS - Catalepsy - Fright; GENERALS - Faintness - Fright; GENERALS - Trembling - Externally - fright; HEAD - Heat - Fright; PERSPIRATION - Fright; RECTUM - Urging - Fright; VERTIGO - Fright)* **Acon** k* act-sp hr1* agar bg2* anac k* androc srj1• *Apis* k* arg-met k2* *Arg-n* k* arn k* ars k* *Art-v* k* aster gt *Aur* k* a u r - m k* *Bell* k* bry k* *Bufo* st calc k* calc-sil k2* camph gl1.fr• carb-v b2.de* carbn-s carc c1* *Caust* k* cham k* cic b2.de* cimic hr1* cina bg2* cocc b2.de* *Coff* k* coloc bg2* crot-h c1 *Cupr* k* dulc fd4.de **Gels** k* *Glon* k* *Graph* k* ham fd3.de• hep b2.de* *Hyos* k* *Hyper* k* *Ign* k* iod *Kali-br* bg2* kali-c bg2* kali-p sf lac-del hm2• *Lach* k* laur b2.de* **Lyc** k* lyss hr1* mag-c k* *Manc* mrr1 merc k* *Morph* br1* nat-c *Nat-m* k* nit-ac nux-m hr1* *Nux-v* k* **Op** k* *Petr* hr1* **Ph-ac** k* **Phos** k* *Plat* k* **Puls** k* ran-b gt* *Rhus-t* k* sabad k* samb k* sec k* *Sep* k* **Sil** k* spong b2.de* stann b2.de* staph ↓ *Stram* k* sulph b2.de* *Vanil* fd5.de verat k* verb b2.de* vib ptk1 visc c1 zinc k* zinc-p k2*
  - **accident**; from sight of an: **ACON** st *Calc* vh* **OP** st*
  - **anger**; with (See anger - fright)
  - **children**; in: *Carc* mlr1• op mtf33
    - **excitable**; highly: *Carc* mlr1•
    - **nervous** (See excitable)
  - **coition**; during: *Lyc* hr1*
  - **fear** of the fright remaining (See Fear - fright)
  - **fear**; with: *Acon* b7a.de *Op* b7a.de puls b7a.de
  - **long** lasting: carc mlr1•
  - **menses**; during: *(↗fright; Menses - during)* acon lp* bell vh* *Coff* kr1 **Ign** vh* lach vh* nux-v vh* op vh* ph-ac vh* phos vh* staph vh* *Verat* vh*
  - **movies**; after seeing scary: *(↗Horrible)* *Manc* mrr1 vanil fd5.de
  - **old** fright: nat-m hr7 op fb*
  - **ordeal**, of an: **Arg-n** bg2 **Gels** bg2
  - **remembrance** of previous (See old)
  - **severe**: carc mlr1•
  - **shock**, in: hyper bg

- **grief**: (↗love; Cares full; Grief; Insanity - grief; Weeping; CHILL - Grief; COUGH - Grief; GENERALS - Catalepsy - grief; HEAD - Heat - grief; RECTUM - Diarrhea - grief; SLEEP - Sleeplessness - grief; STOMACH - Indigestion - grief) Acet-ac vh1 acon tl1 alum lsa1.de alum-p k2 am-m k* **Ambr** bg2* aml-ns ptk anac ant-c k* anthraci ↓ Apis k* Arn br1* ars k* art-v c1 **Aur** k* aur-ar k2 Aur-m-n wbt2• aur-s k2 bar-s k2 Bell b2.de* Bry st* cadm-s bg2 cael jl calc b2.de* Calc-p k* caps b2.de* carc mlr1*• **Caust** k* cham ry chin lsa1.de clem Cocc k* coff mrr1 colch Coloc k* con k* Crat st crot-h ptk cycl k* cypr kr1 cypra-eg sde6.de• dig sf1.de Dros st* elaps gk Gels k* Graph k* hippoc-k szs2 Hura st* Hyos k* **IGN** k* ip st* Kali-br hr1* kali-c b2.de* kali-p k* **Lach** k* laur k2 lob-c lob-s kr1* lyc k* mag-c c1 naja nat-c b2.de* **NAT-M** k* nat-p mrr1 nat-s mrr1 nit-ac k* nux-m k2 Nux-v k* Op bg2* paull hr1 **Ph-ac** k* **Phos** b2.de* phys c1 pic-ac bg2* Plat k* psor gg Puls k* pyrus a rhus-t b2.de* Samb c1* Sep b4a.de* seq-s bhk1• Sol-o st spig vh **Staph** k* stram b2.de* sulph j* tarent tritic-vg fd5.de tub dx1 Uran-n dx1 **Vanil** fd* verat k* Zinc kr1*
  - **drowsiness**; with (See SLEEP - Sleepiness - grief)
  - **prolonged**: aur-s vh1 carc mlr1* caust br1* cocc k2 kali-p k2 ph-ac k2*
  - **recent**: ign c1
  - **silent** grief: (↗Grief - silent) anthraci mrr1 carc mlr1• **Nat-m** mta1* tub pc
    - **indignation**; with (See Grief - silent - indignation)
  - **undermining** constitution (See Grief - undermining)
- **homesickness**: Aur sne **Caps** k* carc mlk Clem k* eup-pur bro1 hell bro1 Ign bro1 mag-m bro1 op ckh1 **Ph-ac** kr1* senec bro1
- **honor**; wounded: (↗disappointment; embarrassment; mortification; reprimands; reproaches; scorned; Dullness - mortification; Hatred; Haughty; Indignation; Injustice; Timidity; Weeping - mortification) agath-a nl2• aur gk aur-m-n wbt2• Aur-s wbt2• bamb-a stb2.de• carc mlr1*• cham kr1 ign kola stb3• lac-leo sk4• Nat-m vh* nat-s vh nux-v k* pall tl plat ptk2 podo fd3.de• Staph k1* sulph gk verat kr1* [heroin sdj2 tax jsj7]
- **humiliation** (See mortification)
- **hurry**: Acon gl1.fr• aids nl2• Alum vh* am-c gl1.fr• Arn ptk1* benz-ac bg2 Bry vh1* carc mlr1• coff hr1* Nit-ac gl1.fr• nux-v gl1.fr• positr nl2• Puls gl1.fr• rhus-t gl1.fr• sulph gl1.fr• [art-v stj]
- **indignation**: (↗rejected; Haughty) acon j* ambr tsm1 Ant-c bg aur-m-n wbt2• bell bg bry bg carb-v bg carc mlr1• chinin-s a Coloc k* ferr hs ferr-p a gels vh hecla alm• Ign vh* ip k* lac-leo sk4• led sne Nat-m vh* Nux-v k* oci-sa sk4• plat sal-fr sle1• **STAPH** k*
- **injuries**, accidents; mental symptoms from: (↗Confusion - injury - after; Delirium - injuries; Dullness - injuries; Insanity - injuries; Memory - loss - injuries; Prostration - injuries; Sadness - injuries; Sighing - shock; Taciturn - sickness) acon gcj arn gcj camph kr1 carc mlr1• cic hr1* Glon bro1* hyper bro1* mag-c bro1* **Nat-s** k2* rhus-t gcj ruta gcj* stram mrr1 sul-ac hr1 [bell-p-sp dcm1]
- **injustice**; form (See Injustice)
- **insults** (See offended)
- **intolerance**: nux-v a
- **irritability**: cist lpc
- **jealousy**: (↗Jealousy; GENERALS - Catalepsy - jealousy) Apis hr1* Aur-m-n wbt2• ham fd3.de• **Hyos** b2.de* Ign b2.de* Lach b2.de* **Nux-v** b2.de* ph-ac b2.de* Phos vh* **Puls** st* staph bro1 tritic-vg fd5.de
- **job**; having lost his: (↗position) ign pc plat pc staph pc sul-ac mtf
- **joy**: (↗RECTUM - Diarrhea - exciting) Acon ↓ bad bg2 caust bg2 coff bg2 croc bg2 cycl bg2 helon ↓ hir ↓ Manc ↓ nat-c bg2 op bg2 Ped ↓ puls bg2 tarent ↓ trom ↓ verat ↓
  - **excessive**: (↗surprises - pleasant; Ecstasy; Fear - surprises; Weeping - joy from; GENERALS - Catalepsy - joy; HEAD - Pain - joy; HEAD - Pain - laughing; RECTUM - Diarrhea - excitement; SLEEP - Sleeplessness - joy) Acon Bad sf1.de caust k* **Coff** k* croc k* cycl k* helon sf1.de hir mtf Manc st nat-c k* Op k* Ped st Puls k* tarent a trom mtf verat gl1.fr•
  - **sudden**: **Coff** kr1* op c1
- **laughing**; excessive: ars-met c1 Coff kr1
- **love**; disappointed: (↗grief; rejected; Brooding - disappointment; Despair - love; Dwells - disappointments; Dwells - past; Grief - silent - love; Inconsolable; Insanity - love; Laughing - love; Rage - love; Sadness - love; Suicidal - love; Weeping - sad - thoughts; CHEST - Palpitation - unrequited; DREAMS - Disappointments; FEMALE - Menses - suppressed - love; GENERALS - Weakness - love) acon bg2 androc srj ant-c k* asaf vh **Aur** b2.de* Aur-m-n wbt2• Aur-s wbt2• Bell vh* Bufo st* cact bg2* calc ↓ Calc-p k* carc mlr1* Caust k* Cimic k* Coff k* Con bg2*
- **love**; disappointed: ... cypra-eg sde6.de• dig c1 ham fd3.de• Hell k* hippoc-k szs2 **Hyos** k* **IGN** b2.de* iod c1* kali-c k* kali-p bg2 Lach k* **NAT-M** k* Nat-sil fd3.de• nux-m nux-v k* oci-sa sk4• orig mrr1 ozone sde2• petr-ra shn4• **Ph-ac** k* phos bg2* pitu-a ft **Plat** vh3.fr* psor gg rhus-g tmo3• sacch sst1• sal-fr sle1• sep k* seq-s bkh1 **Staph** b2.de* stram he1 sulph st tarent k* til a1 tub lsa1.de vanil fd5.de verat kr1* [am-s stj1 nat-p stj1 spect dfg1]
  - **animals**; for: carc mlr1•
  - **excitement**; with general: Bell st*
  - **lesbian**: calc st* **Plat** st*
  - **unhappy** (See love)
- **magnetized**; being: borx h2* hyper c1 sulph c1
- **masturbation**: (↗GENERALS - Masturbation) aur-ar k2*
- **meditation**: arg-met bg*
- **mental** exertion: (↗Mental exertion - agg.; Mental exertion - aversion) agar h2* Alum-p k2* alum-sil k2* ambr sf1.de Anac kr1* arg-n c1* arn br1* ars sf1.de Ars-i c1* ars-met c1 aven sf1.de bar-act sf1.de bell gl1.fr• calc c1* Calc-p c1* calc-sil k2 caps c1* Carc mrr1 chin sf1.de coca c1 cocc c1* con sf1.de **Cupr** kr1* cupr-act c1 cypr hl Epig sf1.de epiph c1 fl-ac k2 Gels bro1 graph h2* **Ham** fd* hyos j5.de ign k2* iod k2 iris sf1.de kali-br sf1.de Kali-c sf1.de **KALI-I** st Kali-p st* Kali-s fd4.de Lach sf1.de lyc k* mag-p c1 med sf1.de melal-alt gya4 mur-ac tl1 **Nat-c** c1* nat-m nat-p k2 nux-m c1* **NUX-V** k1* Ph-ac c1* phos Pic-ac c1* pip-m sf1.de psor c1 rhus-t sf1.de rib-ac mtf11 ruta fd4.de sabad c1 sabal ptk2 scut c1 sel sf1.de sep sf1.de* Sil bro1* **Spong** fd* **Staph** gl1.fr• **TUB** st vinc c1
  - **prolonged**: agar k13 Arg-n br1
- **mental** shock; from: (↗anger - fright; fright; Anxiety - fright - after; CHEST - Palpitation - fright) acet-ac mtf acon st* Am-c mtf ambr k2* apis c1* Arn br1* both-a mtf both-ax tsm2 camph mtf carc mlr1* cham mtf cic mtf coca c1 coff mtf dulc fd4.de gels k2* hecla mtf hep mtf hyper br1* Ign br1 iod c1 kali-p c1 mag-c k2* merc mtf morg-g fmm1• nat-m br1* nit-ac k2* nux-m k2* nux-v hr1* Op hr1* orni mtf11 pert jl2 ph-ac k2* Pic-ac hr1* plat k2* puls mtf sec mtf sil a1 Spong fd4.de stront-c mtf sulph mtf **Vanil** fd* verat mtf [heroin sdj2 resc rcb1]
- **mentally** suppressed; from being: carc sst2•
- **money**; from losing: (↗Grief - money; Sadness - money - losing) Arn k13* ars hr1* Aur k2* Calc jsa* dulc fd4.de Ign jsa* mez k13 nat-m gl• nux-v jsa puls jsa Rhus-t jsa* Sars hr1 stann gl• Verat jsa*
- **moral** excitement: (↗Injustice) Acon vh* **Bell** vh* ham fd3.de• **Ign** vh* **Ph-ac** vh* Phos vh* Staph vh*
- **mortification**●: (↗embarrassment; honor; reproaches; rudeness; scorned; Dullness - mortification; Hatred; Haughty; Humiliated; Indignation; Insanity - black - fear; Insanity - mortification - from; Weeping - mortification; HEAD - Pain - mortification; RESPIRATION - Difficult - mortification; SLEEP - Sleeplessness - mortification) Acon b2.de* agath-a nl2• all-c vh1 alum j* am-m ptk1 ambr tsm1 anac k2* Apoc vml3• Arg-n ars b2.de* aster sze10• Aur k* Aur-m k* Aur-m-n wbt2• bell k* Bry k* calc hr1* camph j carb-an b2.de* carb-v j Carc fd2.de*• caust ptk1 Cham k* Chin hr1 cocc bg2* **COLOC** b2.de* con gl1.fr• Dulc fd4.de falco-pe nl2• form a1 gels ptk1 graph dp• haliae-lc srj ham fd3.de• **Ign** k* ip b2.de* kali-br sne lac-c zzb Lach j5.de* **Lyc** k* Lyss m-ambo j merc k* Mur-ac hr1* **Nat-m** k* nit-ac bg2 Nux-v b2.de* oci-sa sk4• Op k* **Pall** k* Petr j* **Ph-ac** k* phel bg phos j* plac rzf5• plat k* podo fd3.de• positr nl2• Puls k* ran-b b7a.de* Rhus-g tmo3• rhus-t sacch-a fd2.de• Seneg k* sep k* sil mtf spong fd4.de **STAPH** b2.de* stram k* Sulph k* symph fd3.de• Tritic-vg fd5.de vanil fd5.de verat k* vip fkr4.de zinc bg2* [heroin sdj2 mang stj1]
  - **afternoon** | **15**-16 h: rhus-g tmo3•
  - **anger**; with: **COLOC** st [heroin sdj2 mang stj1]
  - **chagrin** (See mortification)
  - **indignation**; with: **STAPH** st
  - **sexual** (See sexual humiliation)
- **music**: (↗Music - agg.; GENERALS - Music - agg.) Ign vh* kali-s fd4.de phos c1
- **neglected**; being: (↗rejected) am-c ↓ aur ↓ carc ↓ graph ↓ ign ↓ lac-h ↓ lach ↓ lyc ↓ mag-c ↓ mag-m ↓ mag-s ↓ med ↓ Nat-m ↓ Nux-v ↓ pall ↓ plat ↓ puls ↓ sacch sst1• sacch-a ↓ sep ↓ staph ↓ sulph ↓ thuj ↓ verat ↓ [oxyg stj]
  - **father**; by one's: am-c mtf aur mtf lach mtf lyc mtf mag-c mtf mag-s mtf nat-m mtf Nux-v mtf staph mtf sulph mtf verat mtf

- **mother**; by one's: carc mtf graph mtf ign mtf lac-h mtf mag-m mtf med mtf *Nat-m* mtf nux-v mtf pall mtf plat mtf puls mtf sacch-a mtf sep mtf thuj mtf
- **nervous** shock (See mental shock)
- **news**; bad (See bad)
- **noise**: cocc c1
- **nursing** the others (See cares)
- **obliged** to do things against his will; being (See domination)
- **offended**; being: acon tl1 **Anac** sne ang h1 calc h2 *Cham* h1 cocc h1 *Coloc* bro1 dros h1 glon hr1 gran a *Ign* lp lyc bro1 *Merc* hr1 *Nat-m* b4a.de* nit-ac lpc *Op* hr1 *Pall* sne *Seneg* b4a.de *Staph* kr1* stram k13 sulph h2
- **opportunities** to realize his abilities; lack of: (↗*domination*) carc sst2•
- **overwork** (See mental exertion)
- **pecuniary** loss (See money)
- **place**; loss of (See position)
- **position**; loss of: (↗*failure - social; job; reputation; Insanity - black - fear; Insanity - job; Sadness - position*) bry tl1 glon tl1 *Ign* gl1.fr• nux-m tl1 *Nux-v* hr1 op tl1 (non:pers jl) petr tl1 *Plat* gl1.fr• staph gl1.fr•
- **pregnancy** (See Pregnancy)
- **pride** of others: grat c1*
- **prostration** of mind: am-c bg2 arn br1 carb-v bg2 colch bg2 *Kali-p* fd* *Vanil* fd5.de [kali-n stj1]
- **protection** | **parental** protection; excessive: bar-c mtf calc mtf sil mtf
- **punishment**: agar ptk anac mrr1 *Carc* fd2.de*• chin mtf33 cupr sne dam c1 ign bg2* nat-m vh* podo fd3.de• tarent c1
  - **children**: carc mlr1• nat-m mtf33
- **quarrelling**: (↗*Quarrelling - aversion; Quarrelsome*) berb bg2* **Carc** fd* chion bg2* cic bg2* dulc fd4.de germ-met srj glon bg2* ham fd3.de• hydrog srj2• ign gt kali-chl bg2* kali-s fd4.de mag-c mrr1 nat-m mtf33 podo fd3.de• ran-b ↓ spig bg2* symph fd3.de• thuj bg2* tritic-vg fd5.de verat ↓
  - **father**; with one's: (↗*DREAMS - Killing - father; DREAMS - Murdering - father; DREAMS - Quarrels - father*) nat-m mtf ran-b mtf thuj mtf verat mtf
- **rage**, fury: *Apis* hr1* *Arn* kr1 carc mlr1• *Coloc* b4a.de phos b4a.de plat b4a.de seq-s bkh1
- **rejected**; from being: (↗*failure - literary; friendship; indignation; love; neglected; scorned; Fear - rejection; DREAMS - Rejected*) *Aur* mtf *Aur-s* mtf carc mtf33 *Caust* mtf **Lyc** mtf *Nat-m* mrr1 *Pall* mtf sep mtf *Sil* mtf sul-ac mtf *Sulph* mtf thuj mtf **Tritic-vg** fd*
- **remorse**: arn br1* *Aur* jsa *Con* jsa symph fd3.de• tritic-vg fd5.de
- **reprimands**: (↗*honor; Admonition; Sensitive - reprimands*) asar vh *Carc* fd* coloc ptk1 ham fd3.de• *Ign* ptk1 op ptk1 podo fd3.de• spong fd4.de staph ptk1
- **reproaches**: (↗*anger - indignation; embarrassment; honor; mortification; scorned; Admonition - agg.; Anger - reproaches; Anger - reproaches - others; Confusion - vexation - after; Delusions - accused; Delusions - confused; Delusions - confusion; Delusions - criticized; Delusions - insulted; Delusions - looked; Delusions - watched; Despair - criticism; Fear - reproaches; Hatred; Haughty; Indignation; Offended; Sadness - vexation; Sensitive - reprimands; Sulky; Weeping - admonition; Weeping - remonstrated; CHEST - Palpitation - vexation; DREAMS - Vexatious; FACE - Discoloration - pale - vexation; FACE - Discoloration - yellow - vexation; GENERALS - Convulsions - unjustly*) agar bg2* **Ambr** vh *Aur* sne bell vh cadm-s mg calc-sil k2 carc c1* *Cham* h cina k13 coloc k* croc bg2 dulc fd4.de dys ptj• gels bg2* germ-met srj* ham fd3.de• *Ign* k* med mg1.de mosch k13 nat-m dx1 nit-ac j* nux-v ctc• **OP** b2.de* ph-ac k* *Plat* gsh sep gk* *Staph* k* *Stram* kr1 sulph gk tarent c1* [calc-br stj1 heroin sdj2]
- **reputation**; loss of: (↗*position*) ham fd3.de• kali-br ptk1* *Sulph* vh*
- **responsibility**: (↗*Responsibility*) aur ptk aur-m-n ↓ carc sej* mag-m mtf33
  - **early**; too: carc gk6*
  - **unusual**: aur-m-n wbt2•
- **rudeness** of others: (↗*mortification; scorned*) acon tl1 anac dx1* bar-m bra *Calc* carc ot* cocc k* *Colch* k* ham fd3.de• hyos st1 lac-c st1 *Lyc* st1* mag-m vh med dgt mur-ac bra **Nat-m** k* nux-v ph-ac puls vh **Staph** k* symph fd3.de•
- **scolded**; from being (See reproaches)

Ailments from: ...
- **scorned**; being: (↗*anger - indignation; anger - suppressed; disappointment; embarrassment; honor; mortification; rejected; reproaches; rudeness; Hatred; Haughty; Indignation; Sensitive - rudeness*) acon adam srj alum k1 ang vh *Aur* *Aur-m-n* wbt2• bell **Bry** k* carc fd2.de• **Cham** coff *Coloc* falco-pe nl2• ferr ham fd3.de• hyos ip lyc lyss mrr1 **Nat-m** k* **Nux-v** olnd *Par* *Phos* *Plat* podo fd3.de• sep *Staph* stront-c sulph *Tritic-vg* fd5.de verat
- **self**-confidence; from want of: carc sst2•
- **sexual** abstinence (See celibacy)
- **sexual** abused (See abused - sexually)
- **sexual** excesses: (↗*Forgetful - sexual; Hysteria - sexual - excesses; Indifference - masturbation; Insanity - masturbation; Insanity - wantonness; Libertinism; Nymphomania; FEMALE - Sexual desire - insatiable; FEMALE - Sexual desire - violent; GENERALS - Masturbation; GENERALS - Sexual excesses; MALE GENITALIA/SEX - Erections - easy; MALE GENITALIA/SEX - Erections - excessive; MALE GENITALIA/SEX - Erections - frequent; MALE GENITALIA/SEX - Sexual desire - excessive; MALE GENITALIA/SEX - Sexual desire - increased; MALE GENITALIA/SEX - Sexual desire - violent*) agar k* agn hr1* alum *Alum-p* k2* **Apis** bg2 arg-n st arn c1* ars asaf aur aur-ar k2 *Bov* *Calad* k* **Calc** k* calc-p st calc-sil k2* carb-an bg2 *Carb-v* **Chin** k* chinin-ar coca gt cocc *Con* k* dig c1* *Iod* kali-br bg2* *Kali-c* kali-p kali-s kali-sil k2* lil-t k* **Lyc** mag-m *Merc* k* *Nat-c* nat-m nat-p k2* nit-ac **Nux-v** ol-an bg2* onos st petr **Ph-ac** **Phos** plat k2* plb st psor al *Puls* samb c1 sec st sel *Sep* k* *Sil* spig **STAPH** k* sulph symph st thuj upa st zinc zinc-p k2* [vip bcj1]
- **sexual** excitement: con c1 cot br1 falco-pe nl2• kali-br kr1 kali-p c1 *Nat-m* kr1* *Plat* k2* psor vh* staph k2 [vip bcj1]
- **sexual** humiliation: falco-pe nl2•
- **shame**: (↗*Shameful*) agath-a nl2• aur k2* carc fd2.de• falco-pe nl2• *Ign* kr1* nat-m bro1 **Op** hr1* podo fd3.de• *Staph* bro1 sulph gk [heroin sdj2]
- **shock**; mental (See mental shock)
- **striving** for perfection (See mental exertion)
- **suppression** (See anger - suppressed; domination; writing; Desires - suppressing; Destructiveness - emotions; Emotions - suppressed; Somnambulism - emotions)
- **surprises**: (↗*HEAD - Congestion - excitement - during*) alum vh1 chin ↓ coff br1 ferr ↓ gels ptk1 merc bg2 *Op* ↓ verat ↓
  - **pleasant**: (↗*joy - excessive; Fear - surprises; Weeping - joy from; HEAD - Congestion - excitement - after - surprise; HEAD - Pain - joy; RECTUM - Diarrhea - excitement; RECTUM - Diarrhea - exciting; SLEEP - Sleeplessness - joy*) chin h1* **Coff** k* ferr sf1.de *Op* gl1.fr• verat gl1.fr•
  - **unpleasant**: gels ptk1
- **unhappiness**: *Acon* bg2 ambr bg2 *Ars* bg2 carc fb* caust tl1 *Cham* bg2 coff bg2 dig bg2 gard-j ↓ *Ign* bg2 lyc bg2 nat-c bg2 nat-m bg2* nit-ac mtf33 *Nux-v* bg2 phos bg2 *Plat* bg2 sep bg2 sil bg2 spong bg2 stram bg2 sulph bg2 verat bg2*
  - **influence** of other people; due to: carc fb* gard-j vlr2•
- **unusual**; anything: ambr ptk1*
- **vexation** (See anger)
- **violence**: (↗*Violent*) anac mrr1 *Aur* kr1 *Bry* kr1* *Carc* mlr1• caust mrr1 coff kr1 *Stram* mrr1
- **weeping** (See Weeping - agg.)
- **weather**; cloudy (See Weather - cloudy)
- **work**, manual fine (See Manual)
- **writing**: asaf kr1* med kr1* sil h2* stann jl
- **writing** left-handed; suppression of: alum sk• staph gk*

AILUROPHOBIA (See Fear - cats)

AIR castles (See Theorizing)

AIR; in open:
- **agg.**: agar b4.de* arn bg2 ars b4.de* cina b7a.de* con b4.de* hep b4a.de hyos bg2 lach b7.de* lyc bg2 nit-ac b4.de* nux-m b7.de* nux-v b7.de* petr b4.de* ph-ac bg2 phos bg2 plat bg2 rhod b4.de* rhus-t b7.de* sep bg2 sulph b4.de* *Thuj* b4a.de
- **amel.**: agar bg2 am-m b7.de* ant-c bg2 asar srj bar-c b4.de* bar-s k2 bell bg2 bry b7.de* calc b4.de* cann-i k2* carc fd2.de• chir-fl ↓ clem bg2 coc-c bg2 coff b7.de* croc b7.de* dream-p sdj1• dulc bg2 hippoc-k szs2 hydr-ac bg2 laur b7.de* *Lyc* b4a.de mag-c bg2 mag-m b4.de* meny b7.de* merc b4.de* nat-c b4.de* nit-ac bg2 par bg2 plat b4.de* positr nl2• puls b7.de* rhod bg2 rhus-t bg2 *Sulph* b4a.de [spect dfg1]
  - **seaside** air: (↗*Seaside - amel.*) chir-fl gya2

- **desire**: irid-met srj5•

ALCOHOL:

- **agg.**: acon b7.de *Agar* b4a.de *Alum* b4a.de *Am-m* b7.de* anac b4a.de ang b7.de* arg-met b7.de ars b4a.de bell b4.de* *Bov* b4a.de chin b7.de cocc b7a.de con b4.de* laur b7.de *Nux-v* b7.de* *Op* b7a.de *Puls* b7.de rheum b7.de rhod b4a.de samb b7a.de squil b7.de *Stram* b7a.de taosc iwa1• valer b7a.de zinc b4a.de
- **amel.**: olnd bg2

ALCOHOLISM:

(↗Ailments - alcoholism; Delirium tremens; Drinking - more; Drunkenness; Korsakoff - alcoholism; Libertinism; GENERALS - Family - alcoholism; GENERALS - Food and - alcoholic - desire; GENERALS - Intoxication) *Absin* kr1 acon b2.de* adon sf1.de **Agar** b2.de* agav-t jl3 agn mrr1 **Alco** sne alum b2.de* am-m b2.de* anac b2.de* ange mtf11 anis kr1* *Ant-c* b2.de* *Ant-t* bg2* *Apoc* bro1 apom c1* arg-met bg2 arg-n sf1.de arn b2.de* ars k* ars-s-f k2 *Asaf* bg2 *Asar* bg2* *Aur* bg2* aur-m-n wbt2• *Aur-s* wbt2• *Aven* c1* bar-c kr1 *Bell* b2.de* bism bro1 borx b2.de* bov b2.de* *Brucel* sa3• bry bg2* bufo k* cadm-s kr1* *Calc* k* calc-ar c1* camph bg2 cann-i kr1* *Caps* bg2* carb-ac sf1.de carb-an b2.de* *Carb-v* b2.de* *Carbn-s* k2* carc mlr1• card-m kr1* caust k* cham bg2 *Chel* b2.de* chim kr1* **Chin** b2.de* *Chin-su* bro1 chinin-m c1* cic bg2 *Cimic* kr1* coc-c kr1* coca mtf11 *Cocc* b2.de* *Coff* b2.de* con k* croc bg2 **Crot-h** kr1* *Cupr-ar* bro1 dig bg2* *Eup-per* kr1* *Ferr* bg2* fl-ac b4a.de* *Gels* kr1* glon sf1.de *Graph* bg2* *Hell* bg2 hep k* hydr c1* *Hyos* b2.de* ichth br1* *Ign* b2.de* ip bg2 *Kali-bi* bg2* kali-br kr1* kali-c bg2 kali-i bro1 kola bro1* lac-ac sf1.de *Lac-c* kr1 *Lach* k* *Laur* b2.de* *Led* b2.de* lob c1* loxo-recl knl4• lup bro1 *Lyc* b2.de* mag-c k* *Med* ↓ meph kr1* merc k* mez bg2 mosch bg2 *Nat-c* b2.de* *Nat-m* b2.de* nat-n sf1.de nat-s kr1 *Nux-m* b2.de* *Nux-v* k* olib-sac wmh1 op k* passi sf1.de* petr k* ph-ac bg2* *Phos* kr1* pisc mtf11 plat gl1.fr• plb bg2 plut-n srj7• positr nl2• psor bro1 puls k* *Quas* sf1.de *Querc* c1* querc-r c1* querc-r-g-s mtf11 **Ran-b** b2.de* raph c1* *Rhod* b2.de* *Rhus-t* b2.de* rumx sf1.de *Ruta* b2.de* sabad b2.de* samb bg2 sang c1* sars bg2 sec bg2 **Sel** b2.de* *Sep* b2.de* *Sil* b2.de* *Spig* b2.de* spong bg2 staph *Stram* b2.de* stront-c b2.de* *Stroph-h* c1* stry a *Stry-n* bro1* *Sul-ac* b2.de* *Sulph* k* **Syph** c1* tarax bg2 thuj ptk1 tub br* valer bg2 *Vanil* fd5.de *Verat* b2.de* *Zinc* b2.de* [heroin sdj2]

- **acute**: acon ptk1 *Apoc* br1 bell ptk1 *Op* ptk1
- **constipation**; with: *Apom* br1
- **diabetes**; with: med gm1 nux-v mtf
- **drinking** on the sly: *Med* gk *Sulph* k1*
- **excitement**, from alcoholism: *(↗Excitement)* stram sf1.de zinc sf1.de
- **get** up at night to drink; must: ars k2 caps k2 nux-v k2
- **grief**; after: caust mrr1
- **hereditary** (See GENERALS - Family - alcoholism)
- **hypochondriasis**, with: *(↗Hypochondriasis)* **Nux-v** kr1
- **idleness**, from: lach gl1.fr• nux-v gl1.fr• sulph gl1.fr•
- **irritability**, with: *Nux-v* kr1*
- **menses**; before: *(↗Menses - before)* **Sel** k*
- **nausea**; with (See STOMACH - Nausea - drunkards)
- **oblivion** is like; drinking to see what: positr nl2•
- **pregnancy**, during or after: nux-v gl1.fr•
- **remove** the habit of drinking; to: ange bro1 bufo bro1 *Chin-su* bro1 kola br1* *Querc* bro1 *Querc-r-g-s* br1 stroph-h ptk1* stry-n st1 sul-ac bro1 sulph bro1
- **sleeplessness**; with (See SLEEP - Sleeplessness - drunkards)
- **timidity**; from: med mrr merc mrr
- **upper** limbs; with complaints of: **Ars** bg2 lach bg2 *Nux-v* bg2 sulph bg2
- **weakness** of character; from: *(↗Weak character)* ars gl1.fr• petr gl1.fr• puls gl1.fr•
- **withdrawal** from; to support the: ange a1* asar al1* bufo gw calc-ar cda carc mlr1• kola stb3• passi cda phos mtf11 stroph-h cda

ALERT:

agath-a nl2• allox tpw4 anh sp1 arizon-l nl2• ars a* bell mtf calc-p mtf carc mtf choc srj3• coca-c ↓ *Coff* mrr1 eup-a hl* *Ferr-p* mrr1* flor-p rsj3• haliae-lc srj5• hir rsj4• hydr br1 hydrog srj2• ign br1* *Lac-h* htj1• lac-lup hrn2• *Lup* br1 lyc mtf melal-alt gya4 op h1* phos mtf33 sal-fr sle1• stram a* sulph mrr1* thuj mtf tub mtf **Tung-met** bdx1• [bell-p-sp dcm1 temp elm1]

- **morning**: lac-h htj1•
- **evening**: lac-h htj1•
- **alternating** with:
  - **confusion**: coca-c sk4•
  - **exhaustion**: coca-c sk4•
- **movement**; of every: calc-p fb ferr-p fb phos fb
  - **doctor**; of: *(↗Fear - doctors)* calc-p fb ferr-p fb phos fb

Alert: ...

- **waking**; on: lac-h htj1•

ALGOPHOBIA (See Fear - pain)

ALIENATED (See Estranged - family)

ALONE; being:

- **agg.** (See Company - desire - alone)
- **amel.** (See Company - aversion - alone)
- **aversion** of being alone (See Company - desire)
- **desire** to be alone (See Company - aversion)
- **fear** of being alone (See Fear - alone)
- **sensation** of being alone (See Delusions - alone; Forsaken)

ALOOF:

(↗Reserved) brass-n-o srj5• hott-p mtf11

ALTERNATING:

- **mental** symptoms (See Mood - alternating)
- **mental** symptoms with physical symptoms (See Mental symptoms - alternating - physical)

AMATHOPHOBIA (See Fear - dirt)

AMATIVENESS (= amorous; erotic):

(↗Amorous; Lascivious) agn k* ang gl1.fr• *Ant-c* kr1 calc gl1.fr• **Canth** bg3* *Caust* gl1.fr• *Con* hr1* *Hyos* bg3* ign j5.de kali-br st *Lach* bg3* **Lyc** bg3* *Merc* hr1* nat-m gl1.fr• nat-s mrr1 olib-sac wmh1 ph-ac gl1.fr• *Phos* bg3* *Plat* bg* sulph gl1.fr• tritic-vg fd5.de *Ust* hr1* verat bg3* [heroin sdj2]

- **want** of amativeness:
  - **men**; in: con gl1.fr• **Lyc** gl1.fr•
  - **women**; in: caust gl1.fr• lyc gl1.fr• sulph gl1.fr•

AMAXOPHOBIA (See Fear - riding)

AMBITION:

(↗Haughty; Insanity) dulc fd4.de med gk nat-m gk spig j

- **blocked**: nauf-helv-li elm2•
- **increased**: *(↗Ailments - ambition; Contradiction - intolerant)* acon bg2 alum gl1.fr• anac j* apis mgm• arg-met ↓ arg-n ↓ ars j* asar mrr1* aur j* *Aur-m-n* wbt2• aur-s ↓ bar-s mtf berb mtf bov j* calc j* camph j* canth mgm• carb-an j* carc mlr1• *Caust* bg2* cina j* *Cocain* vh/dg* cocc j* coloc j* con gl1.fr• crot-c mgm• crot-h mgm• cupr sht* cur mtf cycl j* dros j* ferr ↓ form mgm• graph mtf33* ignis-alc es2• kali-c gg* kola mtf* lac-e mtf* lac-h mtf lac-leo sk4• *Lach* mgm* lil-t mtf lyc mtf33* med gk mosch mtf nat-ar mrr1 nat-m j* **Nux-v** mrr1* ozone sde2• *Pall* sf1.de* phos j* **Plat** sf1.de* polys sk4• puls bg2 ran-b j* rhus-t mrr1 sars j* sil j* spig j* staph gl1.fr• *Sulph* j* tanac hl* thres-a ↓ ulm-c jsj8• vanad dx **Verat** mtf33* verat-v ↓ vesp mgm• vip mgm•
  - **best**; he will be the: cupr sst3•
  - **competitive**: *(↗Fastidious - prove)* apis mgm* arg-met mtf arg-n mtf aur mtf33 canth mgm• carc mtf crot-c mgm• crot-h mgm• cupr mtf33 ferr mtf form mgm• lach mgm* lyc mtf nux-v mgm* sil mtf sulph mtf thres-a sze7• verat mtf verat-v mtf vesp mgm• vip mgm•
  - **fame**; for: alum gl1.fr• aur-s wbt2• con gl1.fr• graph gl1.fr• lach gl1.fr• nux-v gl1.fr• staph gl1.fr•
  - **means** employed; every possible: lyc gl1.fr• plat gl1.fr• *Verat* mtf33*
  - **money**; to make: *(↗Gambling - passion - make)* ars gl1.fr• calc gl1.fr• carc mlr1• lyc gl1.fr• nux-v gl1.fr• sulph gl1.fr•
  - **social** position: [berb stu1]
- **loss** of: am-m gl1.fr• *Ambr* vh* apoc a1 arag br1 arb-m oss1• arg-n a1* ars gl1.fr• bar-c vh bro-r mtf11 calc-sil k2 caps ptk caust a1* chinin-ar ↓ clem mtf11 dios a1 dream-p sdj1• erig a1 helo-s ↓ kali-c ↓ merc ↓ nat-c ↓ nat-p a1 nux-v ptk1* pall sf petr a1 plac rzf5• polys sk4• rob a1 ros-ca mtf11 sang ↓ *Sep* a1* skat br1 *Sulph* vh* tax-br oss1• tub rb3 ulx-eu mtf11 viol-o mfm
  - **evening**: helo-s rwt2•
  - **cloudy** wet weather; in: sang a
  - **disappointment**; from: *(↗Laziness)* nux-v ptk1*
  - **discouragement**; from: nux-v mtf
  - **money**; to make: chinin-ar gl• kali-c gl• merc gl• nat-c gl•
  - **trifles**; from: polys sk4•
- **not** enough ambition (See Indifference)
- **unfulfilled**: nauf-helv-li elm2•

AMNESIA (See Memory - loss)

AMOROUS: (*↗Amativeness; Ecstasy - amorous; Kissing - everyone; Lascivious; DREAMS - Amorous; FEMALE - Sexual desire - increased)* acon b2.de* agar gl1.fr• *Agn* vh/dg* *Anan* vh* androc srj1• *Ant-c* b2.de* *Apis* bg2* asaf vh aur-m-n wbt2• **Bell** b2.de* bufo bg2 calad b2.de* **Calc** b2.de* camph bg2 cann-i sf1.de *Cann-s* b2.de* canth b2.de* *Carb-v* b2.de* **Caust** vh* **Chin** b2.de* coff b2.de* coloc b2.de* con b2.de* croc b2.de* crot-c sk4• diosm br1 dulc b2.de* fl-ac bg2 galeoc-c-h gms1• **Graph** b2.de* *Hyos* b2.de* *Ign* b2.de* *Iod* bg2* kali-c b2.de* kola stb3• lac-del hrn2• lach sze9• *Lach* b2.de* lil-t bg2* *Lyc* b2.de* m-aust b2.de meny b2.de* *Merc* b2.de* mosch b2.de* murx bg2 nat-c b2.de* *Nat-m* b2.de* *Nit-ac* bg2* nux-m b2.de* **Nux-v** b2.de* olib-sac wmh1 op b2.de* ph-ac vh* phos b2.de* pic-ac bg2 **Plat** b2.de* *Plb* b2.de* plb-act gl1.fr• positr nl2• puls b2.de* rhus-t b2.de* ruta b2.de* *Sabin* b2.de* sanic bg2 sars bg2 sel b2.de* senec ckh1 *Sep* bg2* *Sil* b2.de* squil ckh1 stann bg2 *Staph* b2.de* *Stram* b2.de* sulph b2.de* taosc iwa1• thuj b2.de* tritic-vg fd5.de vanil fd5.de **Verat** b2.de* verb b2.de* zinc b2.de* [heroin sdj2 temp elm1]

- **fits** of amorousness: acon b7a.de* ant-c b7a.de hyos b7a.de op b7a.de* stram b7a.de verat b7a.de
- **impotence**; with: lach ptk1
- **menses** | **before**: ant-c vh stram ptk1*
- **paroxysmal**: diosm br1

AMUSEMENT:

- **aversion** to: (*↗Going; Indifference - pleasure; Playing - aversion; Serious)* androc srj1• *Bar-c* k1* hep ptk1* *Ign* hr1* lil-t k* meny olnd k* *Sulph* k1*
- **desire** for: (*↗Cheerful; Content; Desires - full - cheerful; Excitement - desire; High-spirited; Jesting; Laughing; Laughing - desire; Mirth; Occupation - amel.; Playful; Playing - desire; Pleasure; Smiling; Travelling - desire; DREAMS - Parties)* agam-g mlk9.de *Aur* mtf *Bell* mtf calc mtf calc-p mtf calc-sil mtf cann-i hl* carc mtf cere-b mtf coca hl coca-c sk4• con mtf *Croc* mtf *Crot-c* mtf* ferr mtf *Kali-i* mtf **Kali-s** fd* lac-del hrn2• lac-h mtf lac-lup mtf* *Lach* lil-t mtf lyc mtf marb-w es1• *Med* mtf nat-p mtf nit-ac mtf nux-m mtf *Olib-sac* mtf pall mtf petr-ra shn4• *Phos* mtf pieri-b mlk9.de pip-m k* polys sk4• puls mtf *Sep* mtf spong fd4.de stram mtf stront-c sk4• *Sulph* mtf sumb hl tarent mtf thuj mtf tritic-vg fd5.de *Tub* mrr1* tung-met bdx1* vanil fd5.de verat mtf [heroin sdj2]
  - **night**: med jl2

ANAL FIXATION: (*↗Fastidious; Greed; Obstinate)* *Kali-c* mtf kali-s mtf kali-sil mtf sil mtf sulph mtf thuj mtf

ANALYTICAL THINKING (See Thinking - analytical)

ANARCHIST: (*↗Contradiction - disposition; Fanaticism; Protesting; Rebellious; Revolutionist; Unobserving [=nonconformism])* *Arg-n* vh* *Caust* mtf33* kali-c ptk *Merc* vh* sep cd [astat stj2]

- **revolutionary**: (*↗Revolutionist)* **Merc** vh*

ANDROPHOBIA (See Fear - men; of [=male)

ANEMOPHOBIA (See Fear - air; Fear - wind)

ANGER: (*↗Abusive - angry; Anger - asthmatic; Anger - waking; Anxiety - anger; Anxiety - anger - during; Ardent; Barking - bellowing; Breaking; Delirium - angry; Destructiveness; Fight; Indignation; Insanity - anger; Irritability; Offended; Passionate = choleric]; quarrelsome; rage; tearing - things; tranquillity - anger; wildness; chill - anger; cough - anger; dreams - anger; face - discoloration - bluish - angry; face - discoloration - brown - angry; face - discoloration - pale - anger; face - discoloration - red - anger; face - discoloration - yellow - anger; fever - anger; generals - convulsions - anger; generals - faintness - anger; generals - heat - flushes - anger; perspiration - anger; rectum - diarrhea - anger; vertigo - anger)* abrom-a bnj1 abrom-a-r ↓ abrot sf1.de* acet-ac sf1.de **Acon** k* act-sp adam srj5• aesc *Aeth* j5.de* agam-g ↓ agar k* agath-a nl2• agn k* aids nl2• all-c allox sp1 aloe k* *Alum* bg2* am-c k* *Am-m* j5.de* ambr k* **Anac** k* anan a androc srj1• androg-p bnj1 ang a1 anh ↓ *Ant-c* b7a.de* *Ant-t* j5.de* anthraci ↓ *Apis* k* arg-met arg-n arge-pl rwt5• arizon-l ↓ arn k* **Ars** k* ars-h kr1 *Ars-i* ars-met ↓ art-v ↓ arum-t sf1.de* *Asaf* bg2 asar k* aster k* atp ↓ atro **Aur** k* aur-ar k2 aur-m-n wbt2• aur-s k2* bac ↓ bamb-a stb2.de• bar-act ↓ bar-c k* bar-i k2* bar-m bar-ox-suc ↓ bart ↓ *Bell* k* berb j5.de *Bond* a1 borra-o oss1• *Borx* j5.de *Bov* j5.de* bros-gau mrc1 **Bry** k* bufo k* *Bung-fa* mtf buth-a mg1.de cact cael ↓ *Cain* ↓ calad k* *Calc* k* calc-ar k2* calc-hp ↓ calc-i ↓ *Calc-p* k* calc-s k2* calc-sil k2 camph b7.de* cann-i mrr1 cann-s k* canth k* *Caps* k*

Anger: ...
Carb-an k* *Carb-v* k* *Carbn-s* carc mlr1• *Card-m* kr1 cardios-h rly4• carl carneg-g rwt1• cartl-s rly4• cassia-s cdd7• castm j5.de caul ↓ *Caust* k* cench k2 cer-s ↓ cere-s c1 **CHAM** k* chel *Chin* b7.de* chinin-ar chinin-s ↓ chir-fl gya2 chlor choc ↓ chord-umb rly4• cic sf1.de cimic cimx ↓ *Cina* sf1.de* cinnb k* *Cist* ↓ clem *Cocc* k* coch ↓ *Coff* k* colch bg2 *Coloc* k* colum-p sze2• *Con* k* cop cor-r j5.de cortiso gse *Croc* k* *Crot-c* ↓ crot-h kr1* crot-t **Cupr** b7.de* cupr-act ↓ cur k* cycl k* cyn-d ↓ cyna jl3 cypr cyt-l sp1 daph j5.de *Dendr-pol* sk4• des-ac jl3* dig digin ↓ dioxi rbp6 dirc a1 dream-p ↓ dros k* *Dulc* k* elae a1 elaps eupi *Falco-pe* nl2• ferr k* ferr-ar ferr-f ↓ ferr-i ferr-lac ↓ ferr-m k* ferr-ma j5.de ferr-n ↓ ferr-p ferr-sil ↓ ferul a1 fl-ac k* form a1 fuma-ac rly4• galeoc-c-h gms1• galla-q-r nl2• galv c1 gamb a1 gels *Germ-met* srj5• gink-b jl3 gnaph ↓ gran granit-m es1• *Graph* k* grat j5.de haem j5.de haliae-lc srj5• ham hell k* helo-s bnm14• helon ↓ **HEP** b4a.de* heroin ↓ hipp ↓ hir jl3 hura a1 hydr hydr-ac j5.de* hydrog srj2*• *Hyos* k* ictod ↓ **Ign** k* ignis-alc ↓ ina-i ↓ ind ↓ indg kr1 iod b4a.de* ip b7.de* irid-met srj5• iris a1 kali-ar kali-br kr1* **Kali-c** k* kali-chl j5.de kali-cy a1 kali-fcy ↓ *Kali-i* j5.de* kali-m k2* kali-n k* *Kali-p* **Kali-s** k* kali-sil ↓ ketogl-ac rly4• kola ↓ *Kreos* j5.de* kres mg1.de lac-c sf1.de* *Lac-cp* sk4• lac-d ↓ *Lac-e* hrn2• lac-h sze9• *Lac-leo* hrn2*• lac-lup ↓ *Lach* b7.de* *Lact* j5.de lact-v a1 lap-la sde8.de• laur j5.de* *Led* k* lil-t k2* limen-b-c hrn2* loxo-recl knl4• luf-op ↓ *Luna* kg1• **Lyc** k* lycpr j5.de lyss a1* m-ambo b7.de* m-arct j5.de *M-aust* b7.de* macro a1 *Mag-c* h2* *Mag-m* h2* mag-s k* manc kr1 mang k* marb-w ↓ med jl2 melal-alt gya4 meli kr1 meph **Merc** b4.de* merc-cy a1 merl *Mez* k* *Moni* rfm1• morg-g fmm1• *Mosch* k* *Mur-ac* k* musca-d ↓ myric nat-ar *Nat-c* b4.de* **Nat-m** k* nat-ox rly4• nat-p *Nat-s* nat-sil fd3.de• nauf-helv-li ↓ neon srj5• nept-m ↓ nicc *Nicc-met* sk4• nid ↓ **Nit-ac** k* nit-s-d j5.de nuph kr1 nux-m **NUX-V** k* ol-an sf1.de olib-sac wmh1 olnd k* op k* opun-s ↓ orot-ac rly4• osm osteo-a ↓ oxal-a ↓ ozone sde2• *Pall* par j5.de* ped a1 *Pegan-ha* tpi1• **Petr** k* petr-ra shn4• *Ph-ac* k* phasco-ci ↓ phel j5.de *Phos* k* pin-con ↓ pitu-a ↓ plac rzf5• plac-s rly4• plat k* plb b7.de* plut-n srj7• polys sk4• positr nl2• pot-e rly4• prot jl2* pseuts-m oss1• *Psor* k* ptel a1* puls k* puls-n a1 pycnop-sa ↓ rad-br ↓ ran-b k* rat rheum bg2 *Rhus-g* ↓ *Rhus-t* k* *Ros-d* wla1 ruta k* sabad k* *Sabal* ↓ sabin j5.de* sacch sst1• sacch-a ↓ sal-al blc1• *Sal-fr* sle1• samb bg2* sang sanic ptk sarcol-ac ↓ saroth mg1.de sars h2* scroph-n a1* *Sec* b7.de sel jl3* senec ptk1 seneg k* senn ↓ **Sep** k* sieg mg1.de sil k* sinus rly4• sol-mm j5.de sol-ni ↓ *Spig* b7.de* spong j5.de* squil k* *Stann* k* **Staph** k* stram k* *Stront-c* k* stront-met ↓ suis-em rly4• suis-hep rly4• suis-pan rly4• sul-ac k* **Sulph** k* sumb sf1.de suprar rly4• syc bka1*• symph ↓ syph ptk1* tab ↓ taosc iwa1• tarax ↓ **Tarent** k* tarent-c ↓ tax ↓ tell k* teucr j5.de* thal-xyz ↓ thea j5.de *Thuj* k* thyr ptk1* til ↓ toxi ↓ tril-c ↓ tril-p *Tritic-vg* fd5.de *Tub* ptk1* tub-k ↓ upa a1 v-a-b jl3* valer k* **Vanil** fd* verat k* verb j5.de* vinc j5.de* vip ↓ wye ↓ *Zinc* k* zinc-act ↓ zinc-cy a zinc-p ↓ [am-br stj2 am-caust stj2 am-f stj2 ant-m stj2 ant-met stj2 aur-m stj2 bar-br stj2 bell-p-sp dcm1 brom stj2 buteo-j sej6 cadm-met stj2 fl-pur stj2 lac-mat sst4 lith-f stj2 merc-i-f stj2 osm-met stj2 oxyg stj2 *Spect* dfg1 tung-met stj2]

- **morning**: am-m j5.de ars ↓ bar-ox-suc ↓ *Bell* ↓ bov j5.de bros-gau mrc1 *Calc* h2* canth j carb-an j5.de* castm j *Cham* ↓ chin ↓ heroin ↓ hydrog ↓ *Kali-c* kali-p ↓ lac-cp ↓ lac-lup ↓ lach ↓ *Lyc* ↓ mag-c ckh1 mang h2* nat-s j5.de *Nit-ac* ↓ *Nux-v* oxal-a rly4• *Petr* k* phasco-ci ↓ phos ↓ pitu-a ↓ plut-n ↓ rhus-t ↓ sars ckh1 *Sep* k* staph j5.de stram ↓ sul-ac j *Sulph* vanil ↓
  - **waking**; on: ars bg2* bar-ox-suc rly4• *Bell* bg2 canth j5.de carb-an castm j5.de *Cham* bg2 chin bg2 hydrog srj2• *Kali-c* k* kali-p bg2 lac-cp sk4• lac-lup hrn2• lach bg2 *Lyc* bg2* *Nit-ac* vh* **Nux-v** vh* petr k* phasco-ci rbp2 phos bg1* pitu-a vml2• plut-n srj7• rhus-t bg2 stram bg2 sul-ac j5.de sulph h2* vanil fd5.de [heroin sdj2]
- **forenoon**: *Arg-n* ↓ carb-v dulc fd4.de nat-c j5.de* phos h2* sulph ↓
  - **11** h: *Arg-n* kr1 sulph
- **noon**: am-m j5.de zinc h2*
- **afternoon**: androc srj1• aster ↓ bov j5.de canth j5.de cench k2* dulc fd4.de kali-c j5.de mur-ac ↓ opun-s a1 plac-s rly4• rhus-g ↓
  - **12**-14 h: aster a1
  - **15**-16 h: rhus-g tmo3•
  - **air**; in open: mur-ac a1
- **evening**: *Am-c* k* androc srj1• ant-t j5.de bov j5.de *Bry* *Cain* *Calc* h2* canth j5.de cench ↓ choc srj3• *Croc* k* dulc fd4.de hydrog ↓ *Kali-c* kali-chl k13 kali-m k2 **Lyc** nat-c h2* nat-m j5.de* *Nicc* k* *Op* *Petr* plac-s rly4• sil k* zinc h2*
  - **18** h: cench k2
  - **19**.30 h: hydrog srj2•
  - **20**.30 h: cench k2

  - **amel.**: nat-s j5.de verb j5.de
- **night**: graph h2* lyc j5.de* mag-s j5.de rhus-g ↓ rhus-t j5.de
  - **midnight**:
    - **after** | **1**-2 h: rhus-g tmo3•
- **abdomen**; with complaints in: *Cham* bg2 coloc bg2 staph bg2 sulph bg2
- **absent** persons while thinking of them; at: *(↗Excitement - absent; Irritability - absent; Quarrelsome - absent)* *Aur* kali-c kali-cy a1 lyc sal-fr sle1•
- **abused**; after being: carc mlr1•
  - **children**: carc mlr1•
- **activity**; with great physical: *Plat* kr1
- **agg.** (See Ailments - anger)
- **alternating** with:
  - **affectionate**: croc j5.de* **Dulc** fd*
  - **antics**; playing: op j5.de
  - **cares**: ran-b j5.de
  - **cheerfulness**: *(↗sudden - alternating - cheerfulness)* ant-t j5.de aur cann-s j5.de caps caust j5.de cocc j5.de *Coff* vh* croc k* ign nat-m j5.de op j5.de seneg j5.de spong j5.de stram zinc j5.de
  - **contentment**: caps k*
  - **discontentment**: ant-t j5.de ran-b j5.de
  - **discouragement**: ran-b j5.de zinc j5.de
  - **exhilaration**: ant-t j5.de bov j5.de caps j5.de *Op* hr1* seneg j5.de
  - **exuberance** (See exhilaration)
  - **hysteria**: croc bg ign bg2 lyss kr1 mez bg olnd j5.de vinc j5.de
  - **indifference**: carbn-s a1 cham chin k* nid jl3
  - **jesting**: caps j5.de cocc j5.de ign j5.de
  - **kindness** (See mildness)
  - **lasciviousness** (See Lascivious - alternating - anger)
  - **laughing**: croc j5.de crot-c sk4• *Plat* kr1 stram j5.de
  - **mildness**: cench j5.de* kali-c gl1.fr• lil-t mrr1
  - **mirth** (See Mirth - alternating - anger)
  - **repentance**; quick: *(↗Irritability - remorse; Remorse - quickly)* anan a1 bung-fa mtf cortiso gse croc k* lac-h sk4• lyss kr1* mez olnd h1* spong fd4.de *Sulph* h2* symph fd3.de* tritic-vg fd5.de vinc j5.de
  - **sadness**: ambr k* coff k* lac-h sze9• limen-b-c ↓ sumb sf1.de zinc k* [tax jsj7]
    - **mother** who died eight years ago; over: limen-b-c hrn2•
  - **singing**: croc k*
  - **tenderness** (See affection)
  - **timidity**: ran-b j5.de zinc j5.de
  - **tranquillity**: *Croc* hr1* falco-pe nl2• ina-i mlk9.de kali-c j5.de* positr nl2• [heroin sdj2]
  - **vivacity**: cocc j5.de nat-m j5.de
  - **weeping**: *(↗laughing - alternating - weeping)* bell j5.de cann-s j5.de lac-c sf1.de plat kr1
- **amel.**: positr nl2•
- **answer**; when obliged to: *(↗Answering - aversion; Answering - refusing; Irritability)* *Arn* ars h2* bry dgt1 coloc haliae-lc srj5• nat-m **Nux-v** k* *Ph-ac* puls
- **appeased** easily: phos ctc•
- **approached** by a person; when being: cham vn10.fr
- **aroused**; when: sil k2 zinc k2
- **asthmatic** respiration; with: *(↗respiration; Anger)* *Ars* carc mlr1• **Cham** k* manc rb2 nux-v bro1 pitu-a vml2•
- **attention**; at every little: ant-c br1*
- **authority**; against: lac-d sk4•
- **bad** news; about: calc-p a1
- **beating** friends (See Striking - anger - his)
- **beside** oneself; being: *(↗Irritability - trifles)* **Acon** vh1 anh sp1 carl ↓ cupr-act j5.de dros ↓ *Dulc* fd4.de hyos a1 kali-ar k2 kali-c j5.de lac-leo sk4• lyc h2* melal-alt gya4 merc mtf33 nit-ac sf1.de **Nux-v** kr1* ph-ac sf1.de phos h2* *Puls* j5.de* ruta fd4.de sol-ni j5.de spong fd4.de tarax j5.de vanil fd5.de *Verat* j5.de*
  - **trifles**; with: *(↗Irritability - trifles)* carl rb2 dros mtf33 ruta fd4.de
- **bite**; with desire to (See Biting)
- **breaking** things from (See Breaking)
- **bursting** with anger: galla-q-r nl2•
- **business**; about: chir-fl gya2 ip a1
- **caressing**; from: *(↗Caressed - aversion)* chin cina cd nit-ac dx1
- **cat**:
  - **crying** of a cat; from: galeoc-c-h gms1•
  - **meow**; from cat: galeoc-c-h gms1•
- **catalepsy**; from: art-v kr1
- **causeless**: *Carc* mlr* cassia-s cdd7• chel a1 cyn-d jl3 dioxi rbp6 dulc fd4.de hydrog srj2• *Mez* a1 ped a1 positr nl2• pot-e rly4• rad-br sze8• sal-fr sle1• sel rsj9• vanil fd5.de [tax jsj7]
- **children**; in: *(↗Irritability - children in)* abrot sf* *Acon* kr1 anac ptk ant-t ptk arn hr1 bac bn bell j carb-v hr1 carc cd* **Cham** kr1* *Cina* mrr1* dros wta dulc fd4.de galeoc-c-h gms1• hep c1 ip sf kali-c hr1 *Lyc* hr1 med jl2 merc mtf33 nux-v mtf33 op wbt• *Phos* kr1 prot fmm1• sacch sst1• sanic c1* sep mtf33 sil fl spong fd4.de staph wta* stram dt syph jl tarent mtf33 thuj mtf33 tub wta* tub-k jl
  - **causeless**: carc mlr1•
  - **lifted**; when: stram mtf33
  - **unaccountable** (See causeless)
- **chill**:
  - **during**: bry h1 caps j5.de
  - **from** anger; chill (See CHILL - Anger)
- **coffee**: | **agg.**: calc-p bg1 chlor a1
- **coition** | **after**: *Calc* j5.de* (non:calc-ar a1)
- **cold** and detached: *Falco-pe* nl2•
- **cold**; after taking: adam srj calc h2*
- **colors**:
  - **brown**:
    - **agg.** | **dark** brown: ign vk4 plat vk4
  - **gray** | **agg.**: plat vk4
  - **red** | **agg.**: sep vk4
- **consoled**; when: *(↗Consolation - agg.; Inconsolable)* ars cham dulc fd4.de ferr vh *Hell* kr1 *Nat-m* nux-v k2 sabal bg1* vanil fd5.de
- **contradiction**; from: *(↗refused; Contradiction - intolerant; Haughty; Irritability - contradiction; Violent - contradiction)* aesc k2* aloe am-c *Anac* al4* ars **Aur** k* aur-ar k2* bros-gau mrc1 *Bry* k* cact calc-p cassia-s ccrh1* choc ↓ cocc k* crot-c sk4• dendr-pol sk4• **Dulc** fd* falco-pe nl2• **Ferr** k* ferr-ar k1 granit-m es1• grat ham fd3.de• helon hura k* **Ign** k* ignis-alc es2• lac-h sk4• lac-leo hrn2* **Lyc** k* med hu merc nat-ar k* nat-c nat-sil k2* *Nicc* k* nit-ac gl1.fr• *Nux-v* k* olnd op petr k* petr-ra shn4• pitu-a ft* prot jl2* ros-d wla1 *Ruta* fd4.de **Sep** k* *Sil* k* spong fd4.de stram k* sulph mtf tab brm* tarent k* *Thuj* k* til tritic-vg fd5.de tub mrr1 *Vanil* fd5.de *Verat* mtf33* [ars-met stj2 aur-m stj2 aur-s stj2 ferr-f stj2 ferr-lac stj2 ferr-n stj2 ferr-sil stj2 heroin sdj2 ind stj2 kali-ar stj2 nicc-met stj2 stann stj2 tax jsj7]
  - **plans**; changed: choc oss•
- **controlled**; being: *Plut-n* srj7• positr nl2•
- **conversation**; from: chir-fl gya2 *Dulc* fd4.de puls a1 tarent a1
- **convulsions** | **before** (See GENERALS - Convulsions - anger)
- **cough**:
  - **anger**; from (See COUGH - Anger)
  - **before**: asar k* bell cina
- **cramps**, after: cham sf
- **cursing**, with (See Cursing - desire)
- **delirium**, in (See Delirium - angry)
- **delusions** during menopause; with: **Coloc** kr1 *Nux-v* kr1 *Zinc* kr1
- **despair**; with: *Spong* fd4.de tarent ptk1* *Vanil* fd5.de
- **destroy** things; with tendency to: *(↗Destructiveness)* carc mlr1*
  - **children**; in: carc sst2•
- **diarrhea**, during: *(↗RECTUM - Diarrhea - anger)* gnaph a
- **difficult** respiration; with (See respiration)
- **dinner**; during: kali-c h2*
- **disease**; about his: canth mgm•
- **disorder**; about: *(↗objects)* olib-sac wmh1 *Tritic-vg* fd5.de vanil fd5.de [heroin sdj2]
- **dreams** | **after**: mur-ac h2*
- **drinking** coffee and wine; while: chlor a1
- **driving**, while: dulc fd4.de haliae-lc srj5• ruta fd4.de tritic-vg fd5.de vanil fd5.de

- **easily**: (↗*trifles)* abrom-a-r bnj1 acon mtf adam srj5• aesc kr1 androc srj1• arg-n hr1* arge-pl rwt5• ars cp1* aur mtf aur-ar k2 bar-m k2* bell h1.de* bry gk bufo dw5* calad a1* calc hr1* calc-hp ptk2* calc-s k2* calc-sil k2* *Caps* h1.de* carbn-s mtf **Cham** hr1* chel mtf chinin-ar k2 chir-fl gya2 *Cocc* a1* *Coloc* bg3* con dh6* *Crot-h* kr1 dioxi rbp6 dros bg3* *Dulc* hr1* *Ferr* kr1 ferr-i k2 galla-q-r nl2• *Gels* hr1* granit-m es1• *Graph* a1* *Hell* btw1* hep mtf hydr mtf ign mtf iris kr1 kali-m mtf *Lac-cp* sk4• **Lyc** h2* mang mtf meph kr1 mez mtf musca-d szs1 nat-c mtf nat-m mtf nat-p mtf nauf-helv-li elm2• nept-m lsd2.fr nicc mtf nit-ac mtf **Nux-v** hr1* *Phos* lpc2* *Plat* hr1* *Psor* a1* pycnop-sa mrz1 ran-b hr1* ruta fd4.de sal-fr sle1• sep mtf spong fd4.de squil kr1 staph mtf teucr vh* *Thuj* lpc2* valer kr1 *Zinc* h2* [heroin sdj2]
  - **consolation** amel.: adam srj5•
- **eating** | **after** | **amel.**: (↗*Eating - after - amel.)* am-m j5.de
  - **obliged** to eat; when: ars h2*
- **epileptic** convulsions:
  - **before**: indg kr1
  - **anger**; from (See GENERALS - Convulsions - epileptic - anger)
- **exaggerated** (See beside)
- **face**:
  - **blue**; scolds until face is (See Abusive - scolds; FACE - Discoloration - bluish - angry)
  - **pale**, livid face; with: ars *Carb-v* k* *Con* k1* **NAT-M** st* petr plat **STAPH** st* verat bnt
  - **red**:
    - **face**; with red: (↗*FACE - Discoloration - red - anger)* **BELL** kr1* *Bry* vh* calc vh* **Cham** kr1* hyos vh* **Nux-v** st* puls vh* spig j5.de spong fd4.de staph k1* stram vh*
    - **spots** in face; with red: am-c kr1
    - **tip** of nose; with red: vinc kr1
- **family**; toward one's: pseuts-m oss1•
- **fever**:
  - **anger**; from (See FEVER - Anger)
  - **during**: anan a1 hipp a1
- **fits**; in (See sudden)
- **followed** by:
  - **remorse**: croc bg2
  - **tranquillity**: plut-n srj7•
  - **weakness** (See GENERALS - Weakness - anger)
- **forgetfulness**; during: hydr a1
- **friend**; at one's: plac rzf5•
- **fright**; after: acon kr1*
- **happen**; anger at what he thinks may: sol-mm a1
- **head**; with complaints of: *Agar* b4a.de
- **heartbeat**; with irregular: adam srj5•
- **heat**:
  - **flushes** of heat after anger (See GENERALS - Heat - flushes - anger)
  - **from** anger; heat (See FEVER - Anger)
  - **perspiration**; with (See FEVER - Anger - perspiration)
  - **with**: (↗*FEVER - Anger)* cham h1
- **helpful** | **bystanders**; at: nicc-met sk4•
- **hemorrhage**; from arrest of: *Ign* kr1
- **himself**; with: (↗*Hiding - himself - children)* adam srj5• agar a1 agath-a nl2• aloe br1 anac ptk2 ars kr1 bell kr1* elaps a* germ-met srj gink-b sbd1• ign a1* lac-lup hm2• lyc h2 neon srj5• nux-v gl1.fr• *Rhus-g* tmo3• sep ↓ staph gl1.fr• *Sulph* kr1 vanil fd5.de [heroin sdj2]
  - **alternating** with | **Lumbar** region; pain in: aloe br1
  - **constipated**; when: aloe al1*
  - **others**; and: sep vn10.fr
  - **spoken** to; does not wish to be: elaps hr1*
- **humiliated**; after being: carc mlr1•
- **husband**; towards: *Adam* srj5• aids nl2• dulc fd4.de luna kg1• ruta fd4.de
- **indignation**; from: (↗*Ailments - anger - indignation; Indignation - misdeeds)* lac-leo hm2• syc fmm1•
- **internalized**: plut-n srj7•
- **interruption**; from: (↗*Disturbed; Interruption - agg.; Interruption - intolerance; Spoken - agg.; Spoken - aversion)* androc srj1• cench k2 *Cham* k* cocc *Dulc* fd4.de germ-met srj granit-m es1• graph h2 *Hell* kr1 ignis-alc es2• _kola stb3• lac-cp sk4• lac-h htj1• marb-w es1• *Nux-v* k* petr-ra shn4• positr nl2• spong fd4.de
- **involuntary**: carb-v a1*
- **jaundice** from anger (See SKIN - Discoloration - yellow - anger)
- **jealousy**; with: hyos hr1 lach kr1
- **kicked** or punched; on being: (↗*touched)* stram mtf33
- **kill**; with impulse to: (↗*Kill)* prot jl2 [buteo-j sej6]
- **laughing**; anger with: *Croc* kr1 lach ptk1 *Plat* ↓ rhus-g ↓
  - **alternating** with | **weeping**: (↗*alternating - weeping; Laughing - alternating - weeping)* *Plat* kr1 rhus-g tmo3•
- **laughter**; with burst of (See laughing)
- **legs**; rising from his: sal-fr sle1•
- **leukorrhea** ceases; as soon as: *Hydr* kr1
- **light**:
  - **bright** | **agg.**: colch ptk1*
- **listening** to other people (See talk)
- **love**; from disappointed: hyos *Lach* vh* nat-m st
- **lying** down | **amel.**: lac-cp sk4•
- **menses**:
  - **before**: (↗*Menses - before)* anthraci vh1 atp rly4• kali-fcy zr luna kg1• *Sep* k*
  - **during**: (↗*Menses - during)* acon ↓ am-c j5.de castm j5.de caul sf1.de cimic sf1.de hyos sf1.de kreos sf1.de luna kg1•
    - **anxiety**; with (See Anxiety - menses - during - anger)
    - **beginning** of: acon b7.de*
  - **suppression** of menses from anger (See FEMALE - Menses - suppressed - anger)
- **mental** exertion | **after**: calc-sil k2
- **milk** of mother:
  - **suppression** of milk; anger causes: *Cham* kr1
  - **vomits** from anger of mother; child: coch kr1 valer
- **mistakes**, about his: (↗*Anxiety - conscience; Hiding - himself - children; Remorse; Reproaching oneself)* ars kr1 aur-m-n wbt2• aur-s wbt2• bell kr1 bros-gau mrc1 carc pd* ham fd3.de• ignis-alc es2• neon srj5• *Nit-ac* nux-v gl1.fr• sal-fr sle1• *Staph* *Sulph* k*
- **misunderstood**, when: (↗*Delusions - misunderstood)* *Bufo* k1* haliae-lc srj5• ham fd3.de• laur gt* marb-w es1• nicc-met sk4• *Ruta* fd4.de sal-fr sle1• *Vanil* fd5.de
- **mother**; about the meddling of: plac rzf5•
- **neglected**; from being: pin-con oss2• rad-br sze8•
- **never** angry: staph zr
- **noise**; at: adam srj5• bamb-a stb2.de• calad ↓ falco-pe nl2• hep gl1.fr• ignis-alc es2• ip a1 luf-op vml3• ruta fd4.de stront-c sk4•
  - **sleep**; during: calad a1
- **objects** are not in their proper place; if: (↗*disorder)* nux-v mrr1
- **odors** | **agg.**: colch ptk1 lac-h htj1•
- **pains**: (↗*Irritability - pain; Sensitive - pain)*
  - **about**: (↗*Irritability - pain; Sensitive - pain; Violent - pain)* androc srj1• ars b4a.de* canth j5.de *Cham* hr1* *Coloc* sf1.de* dulc ↓ merc gl• nux-v mrr1 op j5.de* ruta fd4.de staph gl•
    - **Head**; in | **stitching** pain: dulc h1*
  - **agg.**: ant-t bg1* cham k2 tarent-c ccrh1•
- **paralysis** from anger: **Nat-m** kr1 *Nux-v* kr1 staph ↓
  - **one** side; on: staph kr1
- **paralyzed**; feels as if: calc-p kr1 *Cist* kr1
- **past** events; about: (↗*Remorse - indiscretion)* calc carb-an dulc fd4.de *Rhus-g* tmo3• sars kr1 sep spong fd4.de sulph kr1 [spect dfg1]
- **pregnancy**; during: *Nux-m* kr1
- **pushes** the table away: staph lpc*
- **questioned**; when: (↗*Irritability - questioned)* coloc hr1*
- **recovery**; if one spoke of her: *Ars* a1
- **refused**; when things he wants are: (↗*contradiction)* bry al cham al1* cina mta1 kreos mta1* vanil fd5.de
- **reproaches**; from: (↗*Ailments - reproaches)* cadm-met ↓ calc-p ↓ croc ↓ *Ign* ↓

- **others**; from hearing reproaches to: (*↗Ailments - reproaches; Sympathetic)* cadm-met mg1.de calc-p a1 croc a1 *Ign* j5.de*
- **resentment**; from (See indignation)
- **respiration** difficult; with: (*↗asthmatic)* arn ars k* **Cham** k* cupr sst3• dulc fd4.de *Ign* bg2 ran-b bg2* *Rhus-t* staph k* thuj mtf33
  - **children**; in: arn ptk1
- **seizes** the hands of those around him: op a1
- **sensation** as if he were beside himself (See beside)
- **sexual** excitement; after: lil-t mrr1
- **sleep**:
  - **after**: chinin-s a
  - **during**: cinnb ↓ plut-n srj7•
    - **first** sleep: cinnb a
- **spoken** to; when: (*↗Answering - offensive; Hiding - himself - children; Spoken - aversion)* *Cham* kr1 *Elaps* kr1 *Hell* kr1 spong fd4.de tritic-vg fd5.de
- **stabbed** anyone; so angry that he could have: (*↗Kill; desire; Violent)* anac j5.de chin *Dulc* fd4.de **Hep** melal-alt gya4 merc mosch j5.de neon ↓ nux-v stront-c j5.de zinc j5.de zinc-act j
  - **person** who lied to her and amel. while alone: neon srj5•
- **stiffening** out of body, bend backwards; with: (*↗Kicking - children - carried)* cham mtf33
- **stitches** in head; from: dulc a
- **stomach** | **felt** in (See STOMACH - Anger)
- **stool** | **before**: **Calc** j5.de*
- **striking**; with (See Striking - anger)
- **sudden**: (*↗Rage)* acon ↓ aur mtf33 bar-act a1 bar-c ↓ bell mrr1* cann-s ↓ caps ↓ cere-s c2 chir-fl gya2 croc ↓ dendr-pol sk4• dulc fd4.de galla-q-r nl2• germ-met srj granit-m es1• hep vn10.fr* hyos ↓ ign ↓ luna kg1• lyc vn10.fr melal-alt gya4 merc k2 morg-g fmm1• phos wta positr nl2• prot ptj*• puls wta ruta fd4.de sal-fr sle1• seneg ↓ *Staph* c2 stram ↓ stront-c ptk1 stront-met ckh1 *Syc* fmm1• taosc iwa1• tub ptk1*
  - **alternating** with | **cheerfulness**: (*↗alternating - cheerfulness)* acon j5.de *Aur* cann-s j5.de caps croc hyos j5.de ign seneg j5.de stram
  - **causeless**: hep vn10.fr
  - **ceasing** suddenly; and: germ-met srj phos gk2 puls wta*
  - **cowardice**; with: bar-c kr1
- **suffocative** attack; with: *Cham* kr1
- **superficiality**; at: positr nl2•
- **support**; desires: adam srj5•
- **suppressed** (See Ailments - anger - suppressed)
- **sympathy** | **agg.** (See consoled)
- **taciturnity**; with: (*↗Taciturn)* am-m j5.de bros-gau mrc1 hydrog srj2• *Ign* j5.de nat-m j5.de petr j5.de puls j5.de sal-fr sle1• stann j5.de stront-c mg sul-ac j5.de verat mg
- **talk**; when hearing other people: (*↗Answering - offensive; Sensitive - noise - voices)* con gink-b sbd1• mang j5.de plac-s rly4• rhus-t j5.de teucr zinc [bell-p-sp dcm1]
  - **patient**; when listening to a: gink-b sbd1•
- **tear** himself to pieces; could: (*↗Hiding - himself - children; Pulling - hair; Striking - himself; Tearing - himself)* sulph kr1
- **teeth**; with complaints of: *Ars* b4a.de
- **temper** tantrums (See Temper)
- **thinking** of his ailments: (*↗Thinking - complaints - agg.)* *Aur-m* k* vanil fd5.de
- **throat**-pit; with constriction of: (*↗LARYNX - Constriction - throat-pit - anger)* staph kr1
- **throwing** things around: (*↗Throwing things)* androc srj1• camph vh cham vh* *Cina* vh* coff j5.de* *Coloc* kr1* dulc fd4.de hydrog srj2• ignis-alc es2• *Kreos* vh* melal-alt gya4 op wbt• ozone sde2• prot ptj• spong fd4.de **Staph** k1* *Tarent* vh* thea vh *Tub* st* [tax jsj7]
- **tickled** or pinched; on being: stram a
- **time**; wasting | **others** are wasting time: galeoc-c-h gms1•
- **touched**; when: (*↗kicked; Touched - aversion)* *Ant-c* **Cham** vh* cina fr falco-pe nl2• iod lac-e hrn2• lach j **Tarent** k*
- **traffic**; in: lac-e hrn2•
- **trembling**; with (See GENERALS - Trembling - externally - anger)

Anger: ...

- **trifles**; at: (*↗easily; Irritability - trifles; Trifles; Trifles - important)* *Acon* kr1* adam srj5• agam-g mlk9.de anac k2 *Ars* h2* atro a1 aur k2 aur-m-n wbt2• *Bar-c* bg2 bart a1 bell h1* bry st bung-fa mtf cael jl calc-i k2 cann-s h1* *Caps* mhn1 caust a1 cere-s a1 *Cham* c1 *Chel* kr1 chin gl1.fr• chir-fl gya2 *Cocc* hr1* *Con* a1* croc a1 cupr sst3• digin a1 dream-p sdj1• dros kr1* *Dulc* fd4.de elaps fkr8.de ferr mtf33 hell a1 *Hep* al1* ip h1* kali-c a1 kali-s fkr2.de kali-sil k2* kola stb3• kreos a1 *Lac-cp* sk4• luf-op vml3• lyc a1 lyss kr1 mang a1* melal-alt gya4 meph jl *Mez* a1* nat-ar k2 nat-c a1 *Nat-m* a1* nat-p a1* nat-sil fd3.de• *Nit-ac* kr1 *Nux-v* c1* petr a1* petr-ra shn4• ph-ac h2 phos bg1* pitu-a ft *Plat* a1* plut-n srj7• positr nl2• pycnop-sa mrz1 *Rhus-t* a1* *Ruta* fd4.de sabad a1 sacch-a fd2.de• sang mg sanic c1 sarcol-ac jl sel jl seneg a1 sep bg1* sil ↓ spong fd4.de squil h1 *Staph* gl1.fr• sul-ac k2 thuj a1* toxi mtf2• tril-c a1 *Tritic-vg* fd5.de *Vanil* fd5.de verat mg vip fkr4.de wye ah1 zinc a1 zinc-p k2
  - **ovulation**; during: pitu-a vml2•
  - **weakness**; from extreme: sil h2
- **uncontrollable**: *Lac-cp* sk4•
- **understood**; when not (See misunderstood)
- **vex** others; inclined to: (*↗Abusive; Quarrelsome)* **Chin** kr1 dulc fd4.de kali-m ckh1 mez j* spong fd4.de
- **vexations**; about former: *Calc* carb-an carc mlr1• chir-fl gya2 lyc h2 sars kr1 sep sulph kr1
- **violent**: (*↗Rage; Temper; Violent)* **Acon** adam srj5• ambr j5.de **Anac** k* androc srj1• anthraci vh1 *Apis* ars k* **AUR** k* aur-m-n wbt2• aur-s k2* bamb-a stb2.de• bar-c *Bell* k* borx j5.de bros-gau mrc1 *Bry* bufo gk *Bung-fa* mtf cain *Calc* cann-s j5.de *Carb-v* carbn-s *Caust* j5.de* cer-s c cere-s c1 **Cham** k* *Chel* hr1* chin h1* cimx c1 cocc j coff *Croc* j5.de* *Crot-c* sk4• cypr hr1* dendr-pol sk4• des-ac rbp6 dros hr1* *Dulc* fd4.de elaps fkr8.de falco-pe nl2• ferr ferr-p *Graph* grat **Hep** hydrog srj2• *Hyos* k* ictod j5.de ign iod st *Kali-c* j5.de* kali-chl j5.de kali-i kola stb3• *Lac-leo* sk4• lach j5.de led j5.de *Lyc* lyss hr1* *M-aust* j5.de mag-c c1 mag-s j5.de melal-alt gya4 *Meli* hr1* mez j5.de mosch j5.de* *Nat-m* k* nat-s j5.de* neon srj5• **Nit-ac** k* **NUX-V** k* olnd j5.de op wbt• osteo-a knp1• ozone sde2• pall *Petr* petr-ra shn4• ph-ac j5.de phos k* *Plat* j5.de positr nl2• *Prot* fmm1• ros-d wla1 ruta fd4.de seneg j5.de *Sep* k* sil j5.de spong fd4.de *Stann* j5.de* **Staph** k* stram j5.de* stront-c j5.de sulph suprar rly4• taosc iwa1• **TARENT** k* tell hr1* thal-xyz srj8• thuj ↓ tritic-vg fd5.de tub mrr1 vanil fd5.de verat zinc k* zinc-p k2* [heroin sdj2]
  - **evening**: cain kr1
  - **breaking** everything: cimx tl
  - **gestures**; with: sep kr1
  - **offense**; from slightest: *Anac* kr1
  - **things** don't go as he wishes; when: **Dulc** fd* spong fd4.de thuj h1 *Vanil* fd5.de
- **voice**; with complaints of: staph bg2
- **voices** of people (See talk)
- **waiting**; when: dioxi rbp6 rhus-g tmo3•
- **waking**; on: (*↗Anger)* arizon-l nl2• *Ars* ckh1 bar-ox-suc rly4• bell j5.de carb-an j5.de castm j5.de caust j5.de cham j5.de* chinin-s a1 **Lyc** j5.de* lyss kr1 mag-s j5.de petr j5.de plut-n srj7• positr nl2• rhus-t j5.de *Sabal* vh* senn vh* staph vn10.fr suis-pan rly4• sul-ac j5.de tab bg* [heroin sdj2]
- **weeping** from pain; with: merc gl1.fr• op gl1.fr• staph gl1.fr•
- **weeping**; with (See Weeping - anger - during)
- **will**; if things do not go after his: lac-h sk4• thuj h1 *Vanil* fd5.de
- **win**; if he does not: plac rzf5•
- **wine** agg.: chlor a
- **work**:
  - **about**: nat-m a1 spong fd4.de tritic-vg fd5.de
  - **aversion** to: bov j5.de dulc fd4.de m-aust j5.de
  - **cannot**: calc-p a1*
- **worm** complaints; in: *Carb-v* kr1 *Cina* kr1

ANGIOPHOBIA (See Fear - heart - pain)

ANGUISH: (*↗Anxiety; Mania - anguish; Remorse; Shrieking - anguish)* acet-ac k* **ACON** k1* *Adren* vh1 aeth k* ail ↓ aloe alum k* am-c k* am-caust k* am-m h2 ambr k* aml-ns ↓ amp rly4• amyg a1 *Anac* androc srj1*• anh jl3 ant-ar st1 ant-t k* *Apis* aran jl3 aran-ix jl3 arg-met jl *Arg-n* k* *Arn* k* **ARS** al1* **Ars-i** ↓ ars-s-f c1 asaf hr1* asar h1* asc-t ↓ *Aur* k* aur-ar k2 bamb-a stb2.de• **Bell** k* *Bism* k* *Bism-sn* br1 both fne1• bov k* brass-n-o srj5• bry h1* bufo buni-o jl3 buth-a sp1* calad a1 **Calc** k* **Calc-ar** k2* calc-f jl3 calen a1 camph k* **Cann-i** k* cann-xyz ptk1 canth ↓ carb-ac ↓ carb-an ↓ *Carb-v* k*

Anguish: ...
carbn-o a1 *Carc* mlr1• cardios-h rly4• carl↓ **Caust** k* cedr k* cham hr1* chin j5.de* chinin-s↓ chlol↓ chlorpr jl3 cic a1 cimic k2 *Cina*↓ cob-n mg1.de coca kr1 cocc↓ *Coff* k* colch↓ coloc *Croc* hr1 *Crot-c* crot-h k* *Cupr* k* *Cupr-act* kr1 cupr-ar↓ cyt-l jl3 der k* des-ac jl3 **Dig** k* *Dios*↓ dor↓ *Dros*↓ *Elec* c1 eupi↓ falco-pe nl2• foll jl3 galv c1 *Gels* hr1* gins↓ glon↓ **Graph** k* halo jl3 ham↓ hed jl3 hell a1* **Hep** k* hoit jl3 *Hydr* hr1* *Hydr-ac*↓ hydrog srj2• *Hyos* k* ictod↓ ign hr1 *Ip*↓ iris↓ *Jatr-c* kr1 *Kali-ar* kali-bi↓ kali-br↓ kali-c jl3 kali-i k* **KALI-S**↓ kres↓ lac-d↓ lac-h↓ lach bg3* lact hr1* lact-v hr1 *Lat-m* st1 levo jl3 *Lob* hr1* loxo-lae bnm12• **Lyc** vh* *Mag-c* k* mag-m jl3 mag-s mg1.de *Med*↓ meph↓ *Merc* h1 merc-c↓ merc-pr-r↓ *Mez* hr1 mosch hr1* mur-ac k* murx a1* naja nat-ar nat-c *Nat-s*↓ nep mg1.de* nicc↓ nit-ac gl1.fr• *Nux-v* vh* oena a1 onop jl3 op hr1* orni↓ ox-ac a1 perh jl3 ph-ac↓ phel↓ *Phos* k* phyt↓ plan hr1* **Plat** k* *Plb* hr1* pneu jl3 podo↓ psil ft1 *Psor* *Puls* k* ran-b↓ rauw jl3 rhus-t hr1* *Rob*↓ ruta fd4.de samb↓ saroth jl3 *Sars* hr1* sec hr1* sep k* sil↓ spig↓ **Spong**↓ stann jl3 **Staph**↓ *Stram* h1* sul-ac↓ sulfonam jl3 sulph hr1* tab↓ tanac a1 tarent k* thala jl3 thea a1 thiop↓ thuj a1 thuj-l jl3 thyr jl3 thyreotr jl3 tril-c a1 tril-p tritic-vg fd5.de v-a-b srb2.fr* verat k* verat-v↓ vip k* vip-a jl3 xan↓ *Zinc-val* hr1*

- **daytime**: graph mag-c merc murx k* nat-c psor puls stann
  - **5**-17 h: psor
- **morning**: *Alum* calc carbn-o↓ lach↓ meph jl3 nux-v k* puls verat
  - **waking**; on: carbn-o a lach kr1
- **forenoon**: chlorpr↓ nicc ran-b rhus-t
  - **9** h: chlorpr sp1
- **noon**: bell h1*
- **afternoon**: am-c h2* cupr k1* eupi a1 nux-v k13* ph-ac k1* rhus-t k1* staph vh*
  - **siesta**, after: **Staph** vh*
- **evening**: ambr k* ars h2* bell h1* buth-a↓ calc gl1.fr• carb-v k* chlorpr↓ dig c1 foll jl3 hep br1* kres mg1.de* *Mur-ac* k2* *Phos* podo a1 thiop jl3
  - **19** h: buth-a sp1 chlorpr sp1
  - **pressing** in head; during: ars a
  - **sunset**; at: foll jl
- **night**: alum↓ ambr k* arn k* ars gt cob-n mg1.de hep br1 nat-s k* nux-v plan puls gl1.fr•
  - **midnight**:
    - **after**: alum↓ ars gt *Nux-v*↓
      - **4** h: alum *Nux-v* kr1
      - **4**-5 h: alum a1
    - **1** h; before: plan a
  - **paralyzing** anguish, it is impossible to call or move, with heat in head: cob-n mg1.de
  - **perspiration**; during: *Arn* a1
  - **suicidal** thoughts; with: hep br1
  - **waking**; on: *Nat-s* kr1
- **abortion**; in threatening: *Cham* kr1
- **abscess** of sinus maxillaris; from: *Mez* kr1
- **air**; in open | **amel.**: **Cann-i** *Puls* gl1.fr•
- **alone**, when: *Phos* hr1*
- **alternating** with | **death**; presentiment of (See Death - presentiment - alternating - anguish)
- **amenorrhea**; during: *Graph* kr1 *Plat* kr1
- **anger**, from: *Plat* hr1*
- **anxiety**; with (See Anxiety - anguish)
- **bed** | **after** going to bed amel.: cham gt mag-c kr1
- **cardiac**: *Acon* hr1* **Arn** hr1* *Ars* hr1* *Aur* vh* bell hr1* *Carb-v* hr1* *Cham* hr1 *Dig* hr1* **Spong** hr1*
  - **angina** pectoris; during: **Arn** kr1
  - **paroxysms**; during: **Spong** kr1
- **causeless**: mosch kr1
- **children**; in: acon j* aeth j* arg-n mtf33 ars j* bufo j* *Cina* kr1 hyos hr1 loxo-lae bnm12• nux-v j samb j*
  - **sick**; when: aeth br1
- **chill**, during: *Arn* k*
- **choking** during influenza; from: ip kr1
- **cholera**; in: *Arg-n* kr1 ars kr1 hydr-ac kr1 jatr-c kr1 tab kr1
- **clothes** too tight when walking in open air; as if: arg-met a1
- **coldness** of body; with: carb-ac a nux-v a*
- **colic**; with: *Coff* kr1
- **constriction** of chest; with: *Adren* br1*
- **constricted**; as if everything became: *Ars* a1
- **convulsions** of extremities; with: cocc kr1
- **crowded** room: levo jl
- **cough**; during: (↗*Anxiety - cough - during*) dros mtf33
- **delivery**:
  - **after**: thuj kr1
  - **during**: acon kr1 aml-ns kr1 arn kr1 bell kr1 cham kr1 chlol c1 ign kr1 nat-c hr1 puls kr1
- **drinking**; when: *Puls* a
- **driving** from place to place: (↗*Touching; Touching - impelled - everything*) **Acon**↓ **Ars** k* **Ars-i**↓ **Bism**↓ *Rhus-t* hr1*
  - **restlessness**, with: (↗*Restlessness - driving*) **Acon** hr1* **Ars** hr1* **Ars-i** vh* **Bism** hr1*
- **eating**:
  - **after**: *Asaf* hr1* hyos c1 *Sep* hr1*
  - **during**: hyos c1 sep
- **fainting** after anguish: nux-v kr1 verat kr1
- **fever**; during: acon bro1
- **friend**; from losing his: calc fyz ign fyz **Nit-ac** hr1*
- **headache**; during (See pain - head)
- **heat**:
  - **during** heat; anguish: *Arn* *Calc* kr1 *Kali-c* kr1
  - **from** anguish; heat: **KALI-S** st*
- **horrible** things; after hearing: (↗*Excitement - hearing; Horrible; Sensitive - cruelties*) calc gl1.fr• lac-h sze9•
- **joyful** things; by most: *Plat* kr1
- **lamenting**, moaning: tarent k2*
- **light** | **room** full of light: levo jl
- **lying** | **must** lie down: (↗*Anxiety - lying - amel.*) mez k1 ph-ac k1 phel k1
- **mania**; during (See Mania - anguish)
- **meningitis**; during: ars hr1 bufo kr1
  - **red** or purplish streaks on the neck and back; with: bufo hr1
- **menses**:
  - **before**: (↗*Menses - before*) *Graph* *Murx* hr1* stann a
  - **during**: (↗*Menses - during*) *Bell* calc cocc a coff ign merc nit-ac phos *Plat* stann xan
    - **beginning** of menses; at the | **amel.**: *Murx* kr1 stann kr1
- **metrorrhagia**; during: croc kr1
- **motion** amel.: des-ac jl
- **nausea**, with: ail a1* *Ars* h2* **Dig** hr1* lac-d kr1
- **nursing**; after: *Cham* kr1
- **oppression**, with: *Am-caust* vh1 *Ars* h2* *Calc* hr1 *Cann-i* hr1* *Op* hr1* verat hr1*
  - **desire** to sit up or jump out of bed: *Verat* hr1*
- **pain**; from:
  - ○ **Abdomen**; in: *Calc* hr1 cham pfa coff kr1 colch ptk *Coloc* hr1 cupr-ar hr1 *Dios* hr1 ham kr1 lach a1* merc-c a1 merc-pr-r a1 naja a1 nit-ac a* plb a1 sul-ac a1 tab a *Verat* hr1
  - **Hypogastrium**: *Murx* kr1
  - **Head**; in: *Acon* k13 *Aur* kr1 coloc kr1 glon kr1
  - **Sciatic** nerve; in: acon bro1 ars bro1
  - **Stomach**: aeth kr1 cann-i a *Crot-h* hr1 gins a* iris a* kali-bi a kali-br a *Lyc* hr1 med a merc-c a1 merc-pr-r a1 orni c1 ox-ac↓ phyt bg *Rob* hr1 sul-ac a1* verat-v a
    - **Pit** of stomach: *Med* a ox-ac a
  - **Teeth**; in: *Coff* kr1
- **palpitation**, with: **Ars** h2* aur hr1* *Calc* hr1* *Mosch* hr1* **Phos** hr1 plat h2 *Puls* hr1* spig lp *Verat* hr1*
- **peritonitis**; during: **Acon** kr1
- **perspiration** | **cold** perspiration; with | **Forehead**; on: **Verat** kr1
  - **during**: *Ambr* kr1* *Arn* k* chinin-s kr1
    - **night**: ambr kr1 arn a1
- **placenta**; with retained: bell kr1 canth kr1 cimic kr1 *Coff* kr1 *Ip* kr1 *Sec* kr1
- **respiration**, preventing: *Acet-ac* vh1 ars a1 verat hr1

- **rest** amel.; perfect: *Coca* kr1
- **restlessness**; with: *(↗sitting - still)* **Acon** ptk2 *Ars* br1 aur fyz bell kr1 **Bism** hr1
- **room** with light and people agg. (See crowded; light - room)
- **sadness**; in: *Arg-n* kr1 crot-h kr1
- **self**-destruction; leading to: aur fyz
- **shock** from injury, in: *Op* hr1*
- **sinking** sensation; with: carb-an kr1
- **sitting | still**; cannot sit: *(↗restlessness)* graph h2* sil h2*
- **skin** eruptions; with: psor mrr1
- **sleep**:
  - **after** short sleep: **Staph** vh*
  - **during**: dor a
- **sleeplessness**; with: bell a1 crot-h kr1 kali-i kr1 *Thuj* kr1
- **stool**:
  - **before**: acon ictod k* merc k* verat
  - **during**: merc verat k2*
  - **urging**; with ineffectual: *Cham* kr1
- **suicide**; attempts to commit (See Suicidal - anguish)
- **toothache**, with (See pain - teeth)
- **tossing** about, with: *(↗Restlessness - bed - tossing)* **Acon** hr1* *Ars* h2* **Cham** hr1* coff hr1* des-ac jl3 *Hydr-ac* kr1
- **tremulous** anguish, rest agg., motion amel.: *Puls* kr1
- **uremia**, in: *Hydr-ac* kr1
- **vomiting**, with: *Aeth* hr1* *Ant-t* a1 ars h2* asar h1* mez ↓ ox-ac a1
  - **carcinoma** ventriculi; with: mez kr1
- **waking**, on: arn h1* des-ac jl *Dig* hr1* nat-s kr1 nux-v kr1
- **walking** in open air: arg-met arg-n bell k* canth cina plat tab
  - **after**: asc-t a dig a
- **weather**; in stormy: *Phos* kr1
- **weeping**, with: bell a1
- **whooping** cough; during: *Dros* kr1

ANIMAL consciousness: lac-leo hrn2•

ANIMALS:
- **disgust** of: nux-v mtf tub ↓
  - **cats**: tub mp4•
- **agg.**: petr-ra shn4•
- **love** for animals: *(↗Nature - loves; Sympathetic - animals)* aeth vh1* ambr tsm1 bar-c a bufo vh calc a calc-p gk* carc fb* caust a *Crot-c* mtf ign ↓ lac-c ↓ lac-del hrn2• lac-f wza1• lac-leo hrn2• *Lach* mtf limest-b es1• med vh* merc ↓ nat-m gg* nuph a* phos kkb* plat ↓ podo ↓ psor a* puls vh sep gk sulph vh* taosc iwa1• tarent a thuj ↓ *Tub* ↓
  - **cats**: aeth ckh1 calc mtf lac-f wza1• lach dtn1 podo fd3.de• *Sulph* vh* thuj sej4 *Tub* vh*
  - **children**; in: carc fb*
  - **dogs**: aeth ckh1 carc mtf lac-c mtf phos mtf
  - **horses**: carc mtf ign mtf lach mtf plat mtf
  - **pet**; her: med mrr1 nat-m ctc* podo fd3.de•
    - ⁝ **children**; in: med mrr1
  - **talking** to animals: aeth mtf33

ANIMATED (See Vivacious)

ANIMATION:
- **agg.**: *Coff* bg3* **Hyos** bg3* **Lach** st* par st *Sabad* st* **Valer** st*
- **alternating** with | **absentmindedness**: alum a1

ANIMUS POSSESSION: *(↗Mannish - women; Quarrelsome)* hyos mtf ign mtf lil-t mtf plat mtf

ANNOYED (See Irritability)

ANOREXIA MENTALIS (See Anorexia nervosa)

ANOREXIA NERVOSA: *(↗Eating - refuses; Indifference - eating - to/ Insanity - eating - refuses)* arb-m oss1• arg-n fyz* **Ars** vh* asar mrr1 aur mrr1 aur-m-n wbt2• bacls-10 pte1* *Brucel* sa3• caesal-b zzc1• calc gl• cann-i sne carc cd* **Chin** vh* chinin-s ↓ chlorpr pin1• coli jl2 *Cycl* tl1 des-ac rbp6 diph-pert-t mp4• diphtox jl2 enteroc jl2 ferr ↓ gent-l c2 gent-q c2 germ-met srj5• hir rsj4• ign sne* influ jl2* interf sa3• kali-p fyz lac-f wza1* lach gl* lat-h bnm5• lat-m bnm6• levist mtf11 levo jl3* lob-c c2 loxo-lae bnm12•

Anorexia nervosa: ...
loxo-recl bnm10• med mtf11 merc gl• *Nat-m* kl* nat-p sne perh jl3 pert jl2 ph-ac gl1.fr• phos sne plat sne prun-v c2 puls vh* rhus-t a1* sacch sst1• sep sst* sil sne staph gl• sulph vh* syc pte1*• tarent gl1.fr• *Tetox* pin2• thuj sne tub jl2 tub-a jl2 tub-d jl2 tub-m jl2 *V-a-b* ↓ verat vh* [*Vanad* stj1]
- **anorexia**-bulimia (See Bulimia - nervosa)
- **aversion** to all food; with: ferr tl1
- **bulimarexia** (See Bulimia - nervosa)
- **children**: carc mlr1• lat-m bnm6•
- **nausea**; with: chinin-s bg2 *V-a-b* jl2
- **palpitations**; with: coca bro1

ANSWERING:
- **abruptly**: *(↗Abrupt; Disobedience; Impatience; Impolite; Rudeness)* ars ars-h bit-ar wht1• cham k2* *Cic* coff dendr-pol sk4• galeoc-c-h gms1• gels *Hyos* jatr-c lac-leo sk4• mur-ac *Nux-v* vh* *Ph-ac* k* phos plb rhus-t sec sin-n k2* *Stann* *Sulph* k* symph fd3.de• *Tarent* vanil fd5.de [mag-m stj1]
  - **incomplete** but correct, in imbecility: anac kr1
- **aversion** to answer: *(↗refusing; Anger - answer; Irritability - questioned; Taciturn)* acon vh1 *Agar* k* alum alum-p k2 am-c am-m ambr anac *Ant-c* bro1 ant-t bro1 apom a1 arg-met k2 *Arn* k* ars ars-i ars-s-f k2 atro *Aur* st aur-m-n wbt2• bell k* bry k2* bufo gk cact k* calc-s calc-sil k2 carb-an bro1 carbn-h carc gk6* caust cham bro1* chin chinin-s chlol a1 cimic cocc coff *Coloc* k* con cupr dulc fd4.de euphr *Gels* bro1 germ-met srj5• **Glon** k* haliae-lc srj5• hell bg2* **Hyos** k* ign bro1 iod k* irid-met srj5• juni-v a1 kali-ar *Kali-p* lil-t lyss mag-m k* **Manc** k1* merc mosch mur-ac bro1 naja bro1 *Nat-m* k* nat-s bro1 **Nux-v** k1* op oxyt bro1 petr h2 **Ph-ac** k1* *Phos* k1* *Puls* rhus-t k* sabad sal-fr sle1• sars bro1 *Sec* sil bro1* spong *Stann* k* stram *Stry* *Sul-ac* k* *Sulph* k* tab tarent vanil fd5.de verat k* vib [heroin sdj2 merc-i-f stj2]
  - **morning**: mag-m
  - **alternating** with | **loquacity** (See Loquacity - alternating - answer)
  - **sings**, talks, but will not answer questions: *(↗Awkward; Foolish)* agar
- **civil**, cannot be: *(↗Impolite; Rudeness)* **Cham** kr1* lac-leo sk4•
- **confusedly** as though thinking of something else: bar-m *Hell* mosch puls ↓
  - **mania**; in puerperal: puls kr1
- **dictatorial**: *(↗Dictatorial)* *Dulc* fd4.de *Lach* vh* *Lyc* kr1* plat vh *Sulph* vh*
- **difficult**: alum vh1* androc srj1• carbn-o a1 chlol cocc k2 dream-p sdj1• dulc fd4.de hell kr1* iod a1 kola stb3• loxo-lae bnm12• ph-ac k2 *Phos* *Sul-ac* sulph verat
  - **emotions**; from: kola stb3•
- **disconnected**: *(↗Confusion; Thoughts - disconnected - talking)* coff coff-t a1 *Crot-h* kali-br lac-e hrn2• phos stram stry
- **distracted**: *Lyc* kr1 plect a1
- **drowsy**: tong a
- **evasively**: cimic kr1* *Lyc* kr1
- **foolish**: *(↗Childish; Foolish; Frivolous; Speech - foolish)* ars bell
- **gestures**; with: *(↗Gestures - indicates)* carbn-s a1
- **grunting**; by: atro-pur kr1
- **hastily**: *(↗Abrupt; Hurry; Impatience; Impulsive; Quick; Speech - hasty)* ars bell bry bufo gk carc mlr1• cimic cocc cystein-l rly4• dendr-pol sk4• hep lach *Lyc* k* rhus-t k* stry
- **hesitating**: *(↗Speech - hesitating)* graph a1 sec a1
- **imaginary** questions: atro *Hyos* phos ptk1 plb stram tarent
- **imperfect** (See unsatisfactory)
- **inappropriate** (See irrelevantly)
- **incoherently**: *(↗Schizophrenia - paranoid; Speech - incoherent; Thoughts - disconnected - talking)* ail k2 bell cann-i chlol coff-t crot-t j5.de cupr j5.de cycl hyos *Ph-ac* kr1 phos raja-s jl valer vip a
- **incorrectly**: *(↗unsatisfactory; Speech - incoherent)* ail k2 *Bell* carb-v *Cham* cystein-l rly4• dulc fd4.de *Hyos* kali-br sne merc nat-sil fd3.de• nux-m sf1.de *Nux-v* *Op* kr1 ph-ac *Phos* stram kr1 *Verat* kr1 [tax jsj7]
- **indifferent**: atro a
- **irrelevantly**: atro a1 bell carb-v k* cimic *Hyos* k* lac-e hrn2• (non:led k1) (non:lyss k1) *Nux-m* k1* (non:nux-v k1) (non:petr k1) ph-ac k* (non:phos ptk1) (non:sabad k1) (non:sec k1) *Sil* ptk1 (non:stram k1*) sul-ac k* (non:sulph) tarent *Thuj* ↓ valer
  - **delivery**; after: *Thuj* kr1
- **loudly**: iod mtf33

- **monosyllables**; in: (↗*Rudeness; Taciturn)* achy jl acon c1 agar-pa a1 alum vh1 arg-met vh ars-i vh bell gl1.fr• carbn-h carbn-s carc gk6* crot-c ↓ gels hyos ↓ kali-br lach sk4• lac-leo sk4• merc vh* mur-ac h2 **Ph-ac** k1* plb *Puls* k* sep k* sil ↓ spong fd4.de thuj kr1* tritic-vg fd5.de tub st **Verat** vh* zinc ↓
  - **no** to all questions: (↗*Imbecility - negativism)* crot-c hyos kali-br sil vml1.nl tub st* zinc vml1.nl
  - **yes** or no: arg-met vh puls ptk2 sil jsa tub k13* zinc jsa
- **nodding**; by: puls ptk1*
- **offensive**: (↗*Anger - spoken; Anger - talk)* lyss a1
- **one** word; with (See monosyllables)
- **questioned**; does not answer, when: (↗*refusing; Confusion; Loquacity - answers)* alum a apom a camph ptk1 chlol a cocc a *Colch* vh* dulc fd4.de hyos a mosch a op a ozone sde2• tarent k1 thuj hr1 zinc cda
- **questions**; in: (↗*Confusion; Questions) Aur* h2* colch gk
- **rapidly**: carc mlr1• lyss kr1 *Sep* kr1 stry a1 tritic-vg fd5.de
- **reflecting** long: (↗*Reflecting)* alum vh *Anac* arb-m oss1• *Bar-c* gk* **Cocc** k* *Cupr* k* grat **Hell** merc k2 *Nux-m* **Ph-ac** k* **Phos** ●* polys sk4• zinc k2* [tax jsj7]
- **refusing** to answer: (↗*aversion; questioned; Anger - answer; Schizophrenia - paranoid; Secretive; Taciturn) Agar* ambr *Arn* ars *Atro* a1* bac bn bell bry mrr1 bufo gk calc-sil k2 *Camph* caust *Chin* k* chinin-ar *Cimic Hell Hyos* kali-act k13 kali-ar k2 led lyss med vh **Nit-s-d** h nux-m *Nux-v* k* petr ph-ac **Phos** k* sabad sal-fr sle1• sec staph sne *Stram* k* *Sul-ac* k* **Sulph** k* tab a1 tarent *Verat Verat-v* kr1
- **reluctantly** (See aversion)
- **repeats** the question first: (↗*Dullness - understand - questions - repetition)* ambr *Caust* k* hell kr1 kali-br *Med* vh* sulph k* *Zinc* k*
- **signs** with the hands; by making (See gestures)
- **sleep**; during: arn bg *Bapt* bg *Hyos* bg med c1 ph-ac bg
- **sleeps** at once; answers, then (See stupor)
- **slowly**: (↗*Slowness; Speech - slow)* acon sf1.de agar-ph **Alum** vh1* *Anac* arb-m oss1• arn ptk1 ars ars-h kr1 ars-s-f k2 bapt ptk1 *Carb-v* k* carbn-h carbn-s mrr1 choc srj3• chr-met dx *Cocc* k* *Con* cupr k* cupr-act a1 dulc fd4.de **Gels** bg2* **Hell** k1* hyos ptk1 *Kali-br* lyc bg2* med bg2 **Merc** k* nat-sil fd3.de• *Nux-m* op k* ox-ac **Ph-ac** k* **Phos** k* plb rhod bg2* *Rhus-t* k* sep sul-ac *Sulph Thuj* k* zinc k* [heroin sdj2]
- **snappishly**: (↗*Abrupt; Impolite; Rudeness; Snappish) Ant-c* vh* aran-ix mg bac bn* calc-p a1 **Cham** kr1* *Crot-h* hr1 galeoc-c-h gms1• granit-m es• lac-cp sk4• lac-h htj1• lac-leo sk4• lyss ↓ petr-ra shn4• polys sk4• *Sep* mrr1 sin-n a1 *Staph* ptk2* [mag-m stj1]
  - **headache**; during: lyss al
- **spoken** to, yet knows no one; answers when: *Cic*
- **stupor** returns quickly after answering: (↗*Stupor - answers) Ant-t* kr1* **Arn** k* **Bapt** k* brom bg2* chin cda cic k1 **Hyos** k* *Nux-v* kr1 olnd bg2 *Op* bg2* *Ph-ac* bg2* phos bg2 plb *Ter* kr1 visc a1
- **unable** to answer: agar ↓ alum ↓ ars a1 atro ↓ aur-m-n ↓ bar-p ↓ calc ↓ card-m ↓ chinin-ar ↓ crot-c ↓ dendr-pol ↓ gels ↓ *Ign* ↓ *Kali-c* ↓ lon-x a1 lyc ↓ *Mag-c* ↓ *Mag-m* ↓ *Naja* ↓ nat-c ↓ *Nat-m* ↓ nat-p ↓ nux-m ↓ op ↓ ph-ac ↓ *Phos* ↓ plat ↓ plb ↓ *Puls* ↓ sep ↓ sil ↓ **Staph** ↓ stram ↓ symph ↓ tarent ↓
  - **hurt** emotionally; when: (↗*Polite - too; Quarrelling - aversion; Sensitive - quarrels; Sensitive - rudeness; Yielding)* agar mtf alum mtf atro mtf aur-m-n mtf bar-p mtf calc mtf card-m mtf chinin-ar mtf crot-c mtf dendr-pol mtf gels mtf *Ign* mtf *Kali-c* mtf lyc mtf *Mag-c* mtf *Mag-m* mtf *Naja* mtf nat-c mtf *Nat-m* mtf nat-p mtf nux-m mtf op mtf ph-ac mtf *Phos* mtf plat mtf plb mtf *Puls* mtf sep mtf sil mtf **Staph** mtf stram mtf symph mtf tarent mtf
- **unconscious**; as if: arn mrr1 plat a1
- **unintelligibly**: (↗*Speech - unintelligible) Chin* coff-t hell k2 *Hyos* **Ph-ac** kr1 *Phos*
- **unsatisfactory**: (↗*incorrectly) Anac* kr1 atro a1 phos a1*
- **unwillingly** (See aversion)
- **vaguely**: alum mrr1 dig a1
- **violently**: dendr-pol sk4•
- **wandering** (See evasively)
- **whispering** (See Speech - whispering)

ANTAGONISM with herself: (↗*Conflict; Confusion - identity; Confusion - identity - duality; Contradictory - actions; Contradictory - speech; Hiding - himself - children; Irresolution; Thoughts - two; Undertaking - things; Will - contradiction; Will - two) Anac* k* anh mg ant-t kr1 aur k* aur-m-n wbt2• aur-s wbt2• bar-c ptk1* cann-i ptk* cann-s ptk cann-xyz ptk1 *Crot-c* sk4• dendr-pol sk4• irid-met bg2 *Kali-c* k* kali-p fd1.de*

Antagonism with herself: ...
lac-c *Lac-h* sk4• lil-t mrr1 op bg2 paro-i jl sal-fr sle1• *Sep* sf1.de* *Sil* gl• taosc iwa1• verb kr1 [nicc-met stj2 nicc-s stj2]

ANTHROPOPHOBIA (See Fear - people)

ANTICIPATION: (↗*Ailments - anticipation; Anxiety - anticipation; Anxiety - anticipation - engagement; Anxiety - time; Clairvoyance; Excitement - anticipating; Fear - church; Hurry - time; Laziness - difficulties)* acon bg* aeth st1* agam-g mlk9.de alum sf1.de ambr tsm1 anac vh1* androc mtf **Arg-n** k* ars tl1* *Bar-c* sf1.de borx ↓ bry st1* calad ↓ **Calc** st1* calc-p ↓ calc-sil mtf33 camph st1* canth j5.de *Carb-v* sf1.de* **Carc** fd* caust k2* chlorpr jl3 *Cic* st1 cina ↓ *Coca* ↓ *Cocc* st1 coff st1* crot-c ↓ crot-h a1 cupr sst3* *Cypr* ↓ cypra-eg sde6.de• dig sf1.de fl-ac st1 **Gels** k* **Graph** sf1.de* hell h1 hep ↓ hydrog mtf hyos st1* ign sf1.de* ina-i mlk9.de *Kali-br* ↓ *Kali-p* kr1 *Lac-c* kr1* lach ↓ levo jl3 **Lyc** k* lyss st1* mag-c ↓ *Maias-l* ↓ med bg3* merc st1* mez tl1 mosch j5.de nabal ↓ *Nat-c* kr1* nat-m kr1* nat-p ↓ nat-s ↓ nux-v st1* ox-ac sf1.de petr st1* *Ph-ac* k* phos bl7* *Pic-ac* ↓ pin-con ↓ **Plb** sf1.de* prun-cs ↓ **Psor** kr1* **Puls** kr1* rhus-t sf1.de sec al2 sep ↓ **Sil** sf1.de* spig sf1.de staph st1* still kr1* stront-c mtf stroph-h ↓ sulph ↓ *Syph* ↓ thuj tl1* tritic-vg fd5.de *Tub* ↓ vanil fd5.de verat h1* *Zinc* ↓ [lac-mat sst4 tax jsj7]
- **morning**: nabal a1
- **ailments** from (See Ailments - anticipation)
- **dentist**, physician; before going to: (↗*Fear - dentist)* calc st *Gels* st hep mrr1 mag-c mg1.de *Phos* st* *Tub* st
- **examination**; before: (↗*Fear - failure - examinations) Aeth* st anac c1* arg-n bl* carb-v ptk* carc st* cupr st* *Gels* st hydrog srj2• nux-v st* pic-ac st* sil k2* thuj ptk
- **excitement**; with (See Excitement - anticipating)
- **gay** (See Excitement - joy)
- **impending** evil; sensation of: *Maias-l* hrn2• merc ptk
- **relatives**; for his: carc mlr1•
- **stage** fright: (↗*Timidity - public)* acon fry ambr bnt anac bro1 arg-n bro1* ars st1 borx fry calad fry calc-p fry carb-v fry carc mlr1• cina vnk *Coca* bnt coff fry crot-c fry crot-h fry *Cypr* fry *Gels* br1* hyos fry ign bnt *Kali-br* fry kali-p bnt lach dgt lyc dgt* lyss fry *Maias-l* ↓ *Med* dgt *Merc* fry *Nat-m* dgt nat-p fry nat-s fry ox-ac fry petr fry *Ph-ac* dgt *Pic-ac* fry pin-con oss2• plb fry psor fry puls fry sep fry *Sil* mrr1 stroph-h fry sulph fry *Syph* fry thuj fry *Tub* dgt *Zinc* fry [prun-cs rcb1]
  - **singers** and speakers; in: **Gels** kr1
  - **unusual** ordeal; of any: *Maias-l* hrn2•

ANTICS; playing: (↗*Childish; Delirium - absurd; Delusions - absurd; Foolish; Frivolous; Gestures; Gestures - strange; Grimaces; Strange)* androc srj apis a1 astra-m br1 aur-m-n wbt2• *Bell* k* carb-an ↓ *Carb-v* ↓ cic b7.de* croc b7.de* cupr k* dat-m a **Hyos** k* ign b7.de* kali-bi c1 lac-del hrn2• lach b7a.de* lact k* lact-v ↓ lyc ↓ merc k* *Nux-v* hr1 op k* phos k* plb k* sacch ↓ sec hr1 stram k* tub ↓ verat b7.de* [helia stj]
- **alternating** with:
  - **anger** (See Anger - alternating - antics)
  - **sadness**: *Op* kr1
  - **weeping**: carb-an j5.de cupr j5.de
- **children**; in: apis bt *Bell* bt *Carb-v* lmj cic bt croc bt cupr bt* **Hyos** lmj* ign bt kali-bi bt lact bt lyc lmj **Merc** lmj* nux-v lmj op bt* *Phos* lmj plb bt* sacch sst1• stram bt tub lmj verat bt*
- **delirium**; during: bell cupr **Hyos** lact lact-v a1 op phos plb stram
- **drunkenness**; during: bell gl1.fr• stram gl1.fr•

ANTISOCIAL: (↗*Estranged - society)* acon bg aesc bh• alum bg ambr bg anac ptk1* *Aur* bg *Bar-c* bg carb-an bg chin bg cic bg con bg cupr bg granit-m es• *Hyos* bg ilx-a bh• lyc bg *Nat-c* bg pseuts-m oss1• *Puls* bg sacch ↓ sanguis-s hrn2• sel bg stann bg sulph bg *Syph* ptk1* [heroin sdj2]
- **children**; in: sacch sst1•

ANXIETY: (↗*Ailments - Anger - anxiety; Anguish; Brooding; Cares full; Cautious; Delirium - Anxious; Dwells - Past; Fear; Frightened; Laughing - Anxiety - during; Restlessness - Anxious; Starting - Anxious; Timidity - Public - talk; Weeping - Trifles - children; ABDOMEN - Anxiety; BLADDER - Urination - Urging - anxious; CHEST - Anxiety; CHEST - Apprehension; CHEST - Palpitation - Anxiety; CHEST - Palpitation - Anxiety - with; CHILL - Anxiety; DREAMS - Anxious; FACE - Expression - Anxious; FACE - Expression - Haggard; FACE - Heat - Anxiety; GENERALS - Anxiety; GENERALS - Trembling - Externally - anxiety - from; PERSPIRATION - Anxiety; RECTUM - Diarrhea - Anxiety;*

Anxiety: ...
RESPIRATION - Anxious; SLEEP - Sleeplessness - Anxiety; SLEEP - Sleeplessness - Cares; from; STOMACH - Anxiety; TEETH - Pain - Anxiety; VERTIGO - Anxiety) abel↓ abies-c↓ *Abrot* k* acer-circ↓ *Acet-ac* k* achy↓ **Acon** k* acon-c a1 *Acon-f* k* act-sp k* adam srj5• *Adon* vh1 *Adren*↓ *Aeth* k* aether a1 agar k* *Agar-em*↓ agar-ph a1 *Agath-a* nl2• agn k* agre jl3 agri↓ aids nl2• ail k* alco a1 alet↓ *All-c* k* all-s a1* allox sp1 aln↓ aloe k* *Alum* k* alum-p↓ *Alum-sil* k2* alumn k* *Am-c* k* am-caust↓ am-f↓ am-m k* *Ambr* k* *Aml-ns* a1* amor-r↓ amyg a1 *Anac* k* anag↓ anan↓ androc srj1*• ang k* anh mg1.de* ant-ar j5.de* *Ant-c* k* *Ant-t* k* anthraci↓ anthraq↓ antip↓ apis k* apoc↓ aq-mar skp7* aran hr1* aran-sc a1 *Arg-met* k* **Arg-n** k* arge-pl rwt5• arist-cl↓ arizon-l↓ *Arn* k* **ARS** a al b2.de b4.de b4a.de Bg **Bg** br bro Gvt k mrr **Mtf3** ptk tl vh/dg vhx3 *Ars-h* k* **Ars-i** ars-met↓ **Ars-s-f** a1* arum-m hr1* arund a1* asaf k* *Asar* k* asc-t↓ aspar astac a1* aster k* asthm-r↓ atis ckh1 atra-r bnm3• atro a1* *Atro-s* hr1 **Aur** k* aur-ar↓ aur-br↓ aur-i↓ aur-m-n a1 **Aur-s** k* avic mtf11 bac↓ bacls-10 pte1*• *Bamb-a*↓ bapt↓ bar-act a1 *Bar-c* k* bar-i k2* *Bar-m* k* bar-ox-suc↓ **Bar-s**↓ bart↓ **Bell** k* benz-ac k* berb k* beryl↓ beryl-m↓ **Bism** k* bit-ar wht1• blum-o bnj1 bond a1 bor-pur↓ borra-o↓ *Borx* k* both-a rb3 both-ax↓ **Bov** k* brass-n-o srj5• brom a1* bros-gau mrc1 brucel sa3• **Bry** k* bufo k2 bung-fa↓ buni-o jl3 but-ac sp1* buth-a sp1 **Cact** k* cadm-s k* cain calad k* **Calc** k* calc-act a1* **CALC-AR** kr1* calc-br sf1.de *Calc-f* a1* calc-i k2 calc-lac↓ calc-m↓ calc-met↓ **Calc-p** k* **Calc-s** calc-sil↓ calen a1* calth a1 **Camph** k* **Cann-i** k* cann-s k* *Cann-xyz*↓ *Canth* k* caps k* carb-ac↓ *Carb-an* k* **Carb-v** k* *Carbn-o* **Carbn-s** k* carc st* card-b a1 *Cardios-h* rly4• *Carl* k* carneg-g rwt1• cartl-s rly4• *Casc* j5.de cassia-s cdd7* caste↓ *Castm* j5.de caul k2 **Caust** k* cedr a1 *Cench* cent a1 *Cham* k* chap↓ *Chel* k* **Chin** k* *Chinin-ar* k* *Chinin-s* k* chir-fl gya2 chlam-tr↓ chlf a1* (non:chlol a1) *Chlor* a1* choc↓ chr-m↓ chr-met↓ chr-s↓ *Cic* k* cic-m a1 cimic k* *Cimx* k* cina k* cinnb a1 cinnm hr1* cist ptk1 clem k* cob↓ cob-m↓ cob-n sp1 cob-p↓ coc-c k* coca kr1 *Coca-c* sk4• *Cocc* k* coch k* cod hr1* *Coff* k* coff-t a1* colch k* coli jl2* *Coloc* k* **Con** k* conch↓ *Convo-s* sp1* cop↓ corn a1 corn-s a1 cortico sp1 cot a1 croc k* *Crot-c* k* *Crot-h* k* crot-t k* cub k* culx k2* *Cupr* k* *Cupr-act* j5.de* cupr-ar k* cupr-f↓ cupr-m↓ cupr-p↓ cupr-s j5.de* cur cycl k* cyclosp↓ cypr hr1* cypra-eg↓ cystein-l rly4• cyt-l mg1.de daph↓ dendr-pol↓ der a1 des-ac↓ **Dig** k* digin a1 *Dios*↓ dioxi rbp6 diph jl2 diphtox jl2 dirc↓ dor↓ *Dream-p* sdj1• *Dros* k* dulc k* *Dys* fmm1• elaps elat j *Elec* c1* ephe-si hsj1• ergot jl3 eric-vg↓ euon k* eup-per k* *Euph* k* euph-c a1* euph-re dp1.fr euphr↓ falco-pe nl2• *Ferr* k* *Ferr-ar* ferr-c↓ ferr-f↓ *Ferr-i* ferr-lac↓ *Ferr-m* j5.de* ferr-ma a1 ferr-n↓ ferr-p ferr-sil↓ fil hr1* *Fl-ac* k* fl-pur↓ foll↓ *Form* hr1 formal br1 franz a1 frax↓ fum rly4• fuma-ac rly4• gaert↓ gal-ac↓ gal-met↓ gal-s↓ gala↓ galeoc-c-h↓ galla-q-r nl2• galv c1 gamb a1 *Gels* k* ger-i rly4• germ-met srj5• gink-b↓ gins j5.de* glon k* goss a1 gran a1 granit-m↓ *Graph* k* grat k* grin sf1.de *Guaj* b4a.de guare a1* haem a1 haliae-lc srj5• halo mtf11 ham↓ hed sp1* heli-n↓ *Hell* k* hell-f a1 helo-s bnm14*• *Hep* k* hip-ac sp1* hipp↓ hist sp1 hura *Hydr-ac* j5.de* hydrog srj2• hydroph jl3 *Hyos* k* *Hyper* hr1* hypoth jl3 *Ictod* kr1 *Ign* k* ignis-alc↓ indg k* inul a1* **Iod** k* ip k* irid-met srj5• iris↓ ix bnm8• jab a1 *Jal* hr1* *Jatr-c* juni-v↓ kali-act a1 **KALI-AR** k* kali-bi a1 kali-br k* **Kali-c** k* kali-chl k* *Kali-i* k* kali-m k2* kali-met↓ *Kali-n* k* **Kali-p** k* **Kali-s** k* kali-sil br1 *Kalm* a1* ketogl-ac rly4• kiss a1 *Kola*↓ kreos k* kres mg1.de kurch↓ *Lac-ac*↓ lac-c al2* lac-cp↓ lac-del↓ *Lac-e* hrn2• lac-h htj1• lac-leo↓ lac-loxod-a↓ lac-lup hrn2• lac-mat↓ *Lach* k* lact k* lact-v a1 lam↓ lap-la↓ lat-h↓ lat-m k* *Laur* k* lavand-a↓ lec oss• *Led* k* lepi↓ lept↓ levo mtf11 lil-s↓ *Lil-t* k* limen-b-c↓ limest-b es1• lip jl3 lipp a1 *Lith-c* kr1 lith-f↓ lith-i↓ lith-m↓ lith-met↓ lith-p↓ lith-s↓ lob a1* lol a1* loxo-lae bnm12• loxo-recl knl4• luna kg1• **Lyc** k* *Lyss* k* *M-ambo* b7.de* *M-arct* b2.de* m-aust b2.de* mag-br↓ *Mag-c* k* mag-f mg1.de *Mag-m* k* mag-n↓ mag-p↓ *Mag-s* k* maias-l hrn2• malar↓ manc k* mand sp1 mang k* mang-act br1 mang-i↓ mang-m↓ mang-met↓ mang-n↓ mang-p rly4• mang-s↓ mang-sil↓ marb-w↓ med k* medul-os-si rly4• medus a1* mela↓ melal-alt gya4 meli↓ meny k* *Merc* k* *Merc-c* k* merc-i-f↓ merc-i-r↓ merc-n a1 merc-ns a1 merc-s-cy a1 merc-sul a1 merl↓ **Mez** k* mill k* mim-p rsj8• miml-g mtf11 moly-met↓ *Moni*↓ morg fmm1• morg-g pte1• morg-p pte* morph a1 mosch k* mukul bnj1 *Mur-ac* k* murx j5.de* musca-d↓ mygal k* myos-a rly4• myric↓ naja nat-act↓ **Nat-ar** nat-br↓ **Nat-c** k* nat-caust↓ nat-f↓ nat-lac↓ *Nat-m* k* nat-met↓ nat-ox rly4• *Nat-p* k* *Nat-s* a1* nat-sil↓ neon srj5• nicc k* **Nit-ac** k* nit-s-d a1 nitro↓ nitro-o a1 *Nux-m* a1* *Nux-v* k* nyct c1* oci-sa jl* oena a1 ol-an j5.de* ol-j a1 olib-sac wmh1 olnd k* onos↓ *Op* k* *Orig* a1* *Orig-v*↓ orot-ac rly4• oscilloc jl2 osm hr1* *Ox-ac* k* oxal-a rly4• oxyg↓ ozone↓ paeon k* pall st1 pant-ac rly4• par a1 parth↓ passi↓ perh↓ *Petr* k* petr-ra shn4• *Ph-ac* k* phel k* **Phos** k* phys↓ physala-p bnm7• phyt↓ pic-ac↓ pieri-b↓ pilo a1 pin-con↓ pin-s a1 pip-n↓ pitu sp1 pitu-p sp1 plac-s rly4• plan k* *Plat* k* *Plb* k* plumbg↓ plut-n↓ pneu jl2

Anxiety: ...
podo a1* polys↓ pop mtf11 positr nl2• pot-e rly4• propr sa1*• pseuts-m oss1• psil↓ **PSOR** k* ptel a1* **Puls** k* puls-n a1 pyrid rly4• *Pyrog* k* quas↓ querc-r svu1• rad-br c11* ran-a a1 ran-b k* ran-s k* raph k* rat bg3* *Rauw* sp1 reser jl3 rheum k* rhod k* rhus-g tmo3• **Rhus-t** k* ribo rly4• rob↓ rosm a1 *Ruta* k* *Sabad* k* *Sabin* k* sacch a1 sacch-a↓ sal-ac hr1* sal-al blc1• sal-fr sle1• *Samb* k* sang k* sanguis-s↓ sanic↓ *Sarcol-ac*↓ sarr↓ sars k* scroph-n↓ scut mrr1 **Sec** k* sel sf1.de *Seneg* k* *Sep* k* ser-a-c↓ *Sil* k* sin-n a1 sinus rly4• sol c1 sol-ni↓ sol-t-ae↓ **Spect**↓ *Spig* k* spira↓ spirae↓ *Spong* k* squil k* *Stann* k* staph k* still a1 *Stram* k* streptoc rly4• stront-c k* stroph-s jl3 stroph-xyz↓ stry k* suis-em rly4• suis-hep rly4• suis-pan rly4• sul-ac k* sul-i a1* sulo-ac a1* **Sulph** k* sumb k* suprar rly4• symph↓ syph mrr1 *Tab* k* tanac a1 taosc iwa1• tarax hr1* *Tarent* k* tarent-c↓ tax a1 tax-br oss1• tep a1 ter a1 tere-la↓ teucr b7.de thal↓ thala↓ thea a1 *Ther* hr1* thiam rly4• thioc-ac rly4• thiop k2* *Thuj* k* thyreotr jl3 *Til*↓ tong j5.de trach a1 *Tril-p*↓ trios↓ *Tritic-vg* fd5.de tub al2* tub-m al* ulm-c↓ urol-h↓ *Uva*↓ v-a-b jl3* *Vac* jl2 valer k* vanad↓ *Vanil* fd5.de vario jl2 **Verat** k* *Verat-v* hr1* verb a1 verin a1 vero-o rly4*• vesp a1* vichy-g↓ vichy-h↓ viol-o k* viol-t k* vip j5.de* visc sf1.de wies a1 wildb a1 xan yttr-met↓ *Zinc* k* zinc-act a1 zinc-i↓ zinc-m a1 zinc-o↓ zinc-p k2 zinc-s a1 [arg-p stj2 aur-m stj2 bell-p-sp dcm1 heroin sdj2 zinc-n stj2]

- **daytime**: ambr ant-c k* ant-t aur-ar k2 aur-i k2* *Bell* k* bov a1 caust k* cham h1* chinin-ar laur mag-c k* mang merc nat-c k* nit-ac k* phyt plat psor puls k* ruta sul-ac verb hr1 zinc
- **morning**: *Ail* k* *Alum* k* alum-p↓ am-c anac k* arg-n↓ **Ars** k* *Ars-s-f* k2* **Asaf** sne **Asar** sne aster a1 bar-c h2* berb a1 bry h1* calc-s k2* calc-sil↓ canth k* carb-an k* *Carb-v* k* carbn-o↓ *Carbn-s* castm↓ *Caust* k* chel↓ *Chin* k* coca-c sk4• cocc k* con k* dioxi↓ fl-ac↓ ger-i rly4• **Graph** ign ip kali-ar *Lac-e*↓ **Lach** led *Lyc* mag-c mag-m k* mag-s mez nat-m k* nat-ox rly4• nat-s k2* nit-ac k* *Nux-v* oxal-a rly4• **Phos** k* plat plut-n↓ psor↓ puls rhus-t ruta fd4.de sep spect↓ spong↓ squil↓ *Staph* st1 sul-ac *Sulph* tax↓ ulm-c↓ verat k* zinc k* zinc-p k2*
  - **perspiration**; during: *Sep* a1 sulph a1
  - **rising**:
    - **after**: arg-n k* carb-an a1 mag-c rhus-t
      - **amel.**: carb-an castm fl-ac nux-v rhus-t sep
    - **on**: arg-n k* berb a1 carb-an h2* mag-c rhus-t k*
  - **waking**; on: *Alum* alum-p k2 anac arg-n mrr1 **Asaf** sne **Asar** sne calc-s k2 calc-sil k2 carb-an k* *Carb-v* carbn-o a1 *Caust* k* chel *Chin* cocc dioxi rbp6 ger-i rly4• **Graph** k* ign ip kali-ar k2 *Lac-e* hrn2• **Lach** k* *Lyc* mag-c mag-m mag-s nat-m *Nit-ac* k* *Nux-v* *Phos* plat plut-n srj7• psor al2 puls rhus-t sep spong ckh1 squil ulm-c jsj8• [spect dfg1 tax jsj7]
    - **bed**; driving out of: anac j5.de
- **forenoon**: acon alum alumn am-c *Arg-n*↓ bar-c k* berb a1 cact a1 calc k* canth k* caust h2* clem *Lyc* k* *Nat-m* k* paeon k* plat k* ran-b sars k* sulph
  - **11 h**: *Arg-n* k*
- **noon**: aster↓ bar-c k* chinin-s cic h1* mag-c a1 mez
  - **12-15 h**: aster
- **afternoon**: aeth k* am-c k* aq-mar↓ arg-n *Ars* hr1* bell k* berb a1 both-ax tsm2 bov cact calc k* canth a1 carb-an carb-v k* cench k2 *Chel* hr1* *Coc-c*↓ con↓ crot-t cupr franz a1 gamb k* kali-n k* kali-s fd4.de *Lyc*↓ mag-c mag-m k* nat-c nit-ac nux-v petr-ra↓ ph-ac k* phel phos puls k* pyrid rly4• rhus-t ruta **Staph**↓ stront-c tab k* thuj↓ zinc zinc-p k2*
  - **14-16 h**: aq-mar jl* *Coc-c* vh*
    - **amel.**: aq-mar jl
  - **15 h**: pyrid rly4•
  - **15-18 h**: con
  - **16 h**: *Lyc* tab
  - **16-17 h**: thuj
  - **16-18 h**: carb-v k*
  - **17-18 h**: am-c
  - **evening**; until: con kali-n mag-m nat-c h2
  - **sleep**; before: petr-ra shn4•
  - **siesta**; after: **Staph** vh*
- **evening**: acon agar k* *Alum* k* alum-p k2* alum-sil k2* am-c *Ambr* anac k* androc↓ ant-c↓ ant-t k* **Ars** k* **Ars-s-f** k2* bar-c k* *Bar-m* bar-s↓ bell berb a1 *Borx* bov k* bry k* buth-a↓ cact k* calad **Calc** k* calc-act↓ **Calc-ar** k2* **Calc-s** calc-sil↓ camph tl1 carb-an k* **Carb-v** k* *Carbn-s* *Caust* k* *Cench*↓ cham↓

- **evening**: ...
chel k* chin *Chinin-ar* *Cina* cinnb a1 coca kr1 cocc coff colch k* **Dig** digin a1 *Dros* k* *Fl-ac* graph k* *Hep* k* hipp hura kali-ar kali-c kali-chl k13 kali-i kali-m k2 kali-n kali-p kali-s kali-sil k2* lac-c sne lact *Laur* lil-t ↓ *Lyc* m-arct j5.de mag-c mag-m k* mang-p ↓ marb-w ↓ *Merc* k* mez k* mur-ac nat-ar nat-c *Nat-m* nat-p nat-s ↓ nat-sil k2* *Nit-ac* k* nux-m k* *Nux-v* k* ox-ac ↓ ozone ↓ paeon k* petr k* *Phos* k* plat plb hr1 podo a1 propr sa3• psor ↓ *Puls* k* ran-b *Rhus-t* k* ruta sabin **Sep** k* sil spig k* *Stann* k* stront-c **Sulph** k* tab ter ↓ tub k2* verat k*
  - **18** h: chel a1 *Dig*
  - **19** h: am-c a1 buth-a sp1 dros a1 petr a1
    - **19**-20 h: am-c k* dros
  - **20** h: chin c1 dros a1 marb-w es1• mur-ac
  - **23** h; until: *Borx* k*
  - **midnight**; until: tub k2*
  - **amel.**: aloe vh1 alum gk am-c chel k* mag-c med gk sul-ac *Syph* gk verb k* zinc
  - **bed**; in: am-c **Ambr** anac ant-c **Ars** **Ars-s-f** k2 *Bar-c* bar-s k2 berb kr1 *Bry* calad *Calc* calc-act a1 *Calc-ar* k1* *Calc-s* calc-sil k2 carb-an **Carb-v** *Carbn-s* *Caust* *Cench* cham *Cocc* *Graph* hep kali-ar kali-c kali-m k2 kali-n kali-p kali-s kali-sil k2 laur lil-t *Lyc* *Mag-c* *Mag-m* mez mur-ac nat-ar nat-c nat-m nat-s k2 nit-ac *Nux-v* ozone sde2• phos psor al2 *Puls* sabin sep sil stront-c *Sulph* ter verat
    - **amel.**: am-c j *Mag-c* k*
    - **closing** the eyes; on: *Mag-m*
    - **sadness**; with: ozone sde2•
    - **uneasiness** and anguish; must uncover from: *Bar-c* mag-c nat-m *Puls*
  - **exercise**; from violent: ox-ac k*
  - **twilight**, in the: *(↗Darkness - agg.; Light - desire)* ambr androc srj1• *Ars* *Calc* *Carb-v* k* *Caust* dig laur nux-v *Phos* k* podo a1 *Rhus-t* k* sep [mang-p stj2]
- **night**: *(↗Fear - children - night; Fear - night)* abel ↓ *Acon* k* act-sp hr1 agar agre ↓ aids ↓ aln ↓ *Alum* k* alum-p k2* *Alum-sil* k2* *Alumn* k* am-c k* am-m ambr androc ↓ ang hr1* ant-c k* arg-met arg-n arge-pl rwt5• arn k* **Ars** k* *Ars-s-f* k2* *Aster* k* aur-ar k2 aur-br ↓ aur-i k2* bac ↓ *Bar-c* k* bar-s k2* *Bell* k* borx bov k* bry k* cact k* *Calc* k* *Calc-ar* k2* *Calc-s* calc-sil k2* camph k* cann-s canth k* *Carb-an* k* *Carb-v* k* carbn-o ↓ *Carbn-s* carc tpw2* carneg-g ↓ caste ↓ castm *Caust* k* cench k2 *Cham* k* chap ↓ chel ↓ *Chin* k* chinin-ar chinin-s k* *Chlol* ↓ *Chlor* ↓ cina clem k* cob-n mg1.de coc-c ↓ cocc coff colch ↓ con k* convo-s ↓ cupr sst3• cupr-act sf1.de cupr-ar sf1.de cycl k* cyclosp ↓ dig k* *Dros* k* dulc *Ferr* k* ferr-ar ferr-p gels ↓ ger-i rly4• *Graph* k* *Haem* k* (non:ham a1) *Hep* *Hyos* *Ign* k* jatr-c kali-ar kali-bi k* **KALI-BR** ↓ kali-c k* kali-chl k13 kali-m k2 kali-n h2* kali-p kali-s kali-sil k2* kola stb3• kreos j5.de lac-ac lac-c *Lach* k* lact k* laur ↓ lil-t lith-c lyc m-arct j5.de *Mag-c* k* mag-m mang *Merc* k* merc-c k* *Mur-ac* ↓ nat-ar k* nat-c *Nat-m* k* nat-p nat-s ↓ nat-sil k2* *Nit-ac* k* nux-v olib-sac ↓ pant-ac ↓ petr ph-ac ↓ phel j5.de *Phos* k* pitu jl3 plan plat plb k* psor hr1 **Puls** k* quas ↓ ran-b ran-s j5.de rat j5.de *Rhus-t* k* ruta ↓ sabad sabin j5.de *Samb* k* sep k* ser-a-c jl2 sil k* spong squil stram bg2 stront-c suis-em ↓ *Sulph* k* tab k* taosc iwa1• thuj k* tritic-vg fd5.de *Tub* st valer ↓ *Verat* k* zinc k* zinc-p k2
  - **midnight**:
    - **before**: am-c ambr androc ↓ ars bar-c bar-s k2 borx k2 *Bry* *Carb-v* *Carbn-s* caust cina ↓ *Cocc* cyclosp ↓ ferr kr1 gels *Graph* *Hep* kali-c laur *Lyc* *Mag-c* mag-m merc *Mur-ac* nat-c *Nat-m* nat-p nat-s k2 nat-sil k2 nux-v phos *Puls* ruta ↓ sabin sil stront-c *Sulph* tub k2 verat
      - **22** h: androc ↓ cyclosp sa3•
        - **22**-0 h: androc srj1•
      - **23** h; until: borx k2* ruta
      - **waking**, on: borx ↓ caust h2 cina ↓
        - **children**; in: cina hr1
    - **at**: aids nl2• sil ↓
      - **rising** amel.; on: sil k*
    - **after**: acon a1 alum ant-c **Ars** k* calc carb-an ↓ carneg-g ↓ castm *Cench* chin chinin-s j5.de coc-c ↓ colch con ↓ dulc ger-i rly4• graph hep ign ↓ kali-c ↓ lyc m-arct j5.de mang j5.de nat-m ↓ **Nux-v** olib-sac ↓ pant-ac rly4• ph-ac ↓ psor ↓ quas a1 rat j5.de *Rhus-t* sil ↓ **Spong** kr1* squil verat ↓
      - **0**-2 h: carb-an
      - **1** h: ars ↓ hep ↓ mang a1

- **night – midnight – after – 1** h: ...
  - **1**-2 h: ars k2
  - **1**-3 h: ars pkj1 hep
  - **2** h: chin c1* coc-c ↓ graph a1 kali-c a1 nat-m
    - **2**-4 h: coc-c k2
  - **3** h: ant-c ↓ **Ars** k* carneg-g rwt1• ger-i rly4• olib-sac wmh1 rhus-t ↓ sil verat ↓
    - **3**-5 h: ant-c h2*
    - **after**: *Ars* rhus-t verat
  - **4** h: alum
    - **4**-5 h: alum a1
  - **5** h: nat-m a1 psor ↓
    - **5**-17 h: psor
  - **half** waking; on: con h2
  - **waking**; on: calc h2 ign lyc ph-ac
  - **amel.**: quas a1
  - **bed**; in: aln vva1• *Mag-m* mrr1
  - **children**; in: *(↗Fear - children - night; Fear - night)* abel jl acon kr1 agre jl arg-met jl **Ars** kr1 aur-br vh1 bac bn bell fyz **Borx** st* *Calc* sf1.de* carb-v k13 carc mlr1• caste jl cham kr1 chap jl chel dx1 *Chlol* kr1* *Chlor* kr1 *Cina* kr1* convo-s jl cupr sht• hyos mg **KALI-BR** kr1* kali-c fyz *Kali-p* kr1* *Stram* kr1 **TUB** st valer fyz zinc mg
  - **dentition**; during: **Kali-br** dgt1
  - **orgasm** of blood; with: carb-an a1*
  - **waking**; on: *Alum* arg-n *Ars* carb-v carbn-o a1 chel *Cina* a1* con *Dros* graph kali-ar k2 lac-ac lyc nat-c h2 *Nat-m* nit-ac *Phos* plat h2 psor al2 *Puls* rat sep h2 sil suis-em rly4• **Sulph** zinc
- **abdomen**; with complaints of: *(↗ascites)* ars b4a.de cic b7a.de *Coloc* b4a.de cupr b7a.de mosch b7a.de
- **abdomen**; with distension of: *(↗ascites)* mag-m h2 mur-ac ↓
  - **burst**; sensation as if abdomen would: mur-ac h1*
- **abortion**:
  - **after**: *Cimic* kr1 *Op* kr1 *Sabin* kr1
  - **threatening**: *Acon* kr1 arn mtn bell mtn croc mtn kali-c mtn *Sec* mtn
- **absentmindedness**; with: anac h2
- **acids**; after: sulph a
- **activity** amel.: positr nl2•
- **ailments** from (See Ailments - anxiety)
- **air**; in open: acon anac k* ant-c arg-met k* bar-c bell k* cina k* cupr sst3• hep k* ign k* lach k* nux-v bg2 plat k* spig tab
  - **amel.**: alum aml-ns kr1 aq-mar jl* arund k* *Bry* k* calc calc-s **Cann-i** carl coca-c sk4• *Crot-t* kr1 graph j5.de grat **Kali-s** k* laur *Lyc* *Mag-m* k* *Puls* *Rhus-t* spong *Sulph* kr1 *Til* valer verat zinc kr1
- **alone**; when: *(↗Company - desire; Company - desire - alone; Fear - alone; Watched - desires)* alco a1 *Arg-n* mrr1 **Ars** k* cadm-s caust sf1.de cortico jl* cupr sst3• *Dros* falco-pe nl2• fum rly4• gaert ptj• gal-ac a1 hep j5.de *Kali-br* bg2* kali-c sf1.de lec oss• *Mez* k* morg ptj*• morg-p fmm1• musca-d szs1 nit-ac sf1.de **Phos** k* pin-con oss2• pseuts-m oss1• rat *Rhus-t* kr1 sal-fr sle1• sep sf1.de tab tritic-vg fd5.de zinc [heroin sdj2]
  - **evening**: *(↗Fear - alone - evening)* dros a1
  - **night**: cupr sst3•
  - **amel.**: *(↗company)* lavand-a ctl1•
- **alternating** with:
  - **cheerfulness**: agar mtf33 ant-t j5.de* castm j5.de *Ruta* fd4.de spig j5.de spong j staph j5.de
  - **contentment**: arizon-l nl2• dream-p sdj1• zinc j5.de [heroin sdj2]
  - **exhilaration**: spig j5.de spong j5.de
  - **fainting**: vip a
  - **heat**; flushes of: *Calc* hr1* *Dros* hr1* *Plat* hr1*
  - **indifference**: ant-t kr1 nat-m k* [heroin sdj2]
  - **irritability**: chin sp ran-b sp
  - **joy**: spig sp spong sp
  - **mania**: bell j
  - **rage** (See Rage - alternating - anxiety)
  - ○ **Joints**; pain in | **gouty**: asaf k2
- **amenorrhea**; during: *Cycl* kr1

- **anger**: *(↗Anger)*
  - **after**: lyc j verat j*
  - **during**: *(↗Anger)* caps h1 carc mlr1• sep verat h1
- **anguish**; with: *Psor* mrr1
- **anticipation**; from: *(↗Ailments - anticipation; Anticipation)* arg-n mrr1* arge-pl ↓ *Ars* ↓ aur-m-n ↓ bar-ox-suc rly4• bros-gau mrc1 calc-sil stj2* canth j5.de *Carb-v* ↓ carc mlr1• chir-fl gya2 chlam-tr bcx2• choc srj3• galla-q-r nl2• **Gels** ↓ granit-m es1• hydrog srj2• *Lac-e* hrn2• levo jl *Lyc* ↓ *Lyss* ↓ maias-l hrn2• marb-w es1• *Med* ↓ mosch j5.de **Nat-m** ↓ petr-ra ↓ ph-ac ↓ pop mtf11 positr nl2• sal-fr sle1• sel gmj2* *Sil* ↓ streptoc rly4• suis-pan rly4• *Thuj* ↓ ulm-c jsj8• vanil fd5.de [arg-met stj2 ars-met stj2 brom stj2 calc-lac stj2 calc-met stj2 chr-m stj2 chr-met stj2 chr-s stj2 cob stj2 cob-m stj2 cob-p stj2 cupr-act stj2 cupr-m stj2 cupr-p stj2 ferr stj2 ferr-f stj2 ferr-lac stj2 ferr-n stj2 ferr-sil stj2 gal-met stj2 gal-s stj2 germ-met stj2 kali-ar stj2 kali-met stj2 kali-sil stj2 mang-act stj2 mang-i stj2 mang-m stj2 mang-met stj2 mang-p stj2 mang-s stj2 mang-sil stj2 nat-ar stj2 nat-br stj2 tax jsj7 yttr-met stj2 zinc stj2 zinc-i stj2 zinc-m stj2 zinc-n stj2 zinc-p stj2]
  - **morning**: choc srj3•
  - **cope** when time comes; but able to: lyc tl1
  - **engagement**; an: *(↗Ailments - anticipation; Anticipation)* **Arg-n** k* arge-pl rwt5• *Ars* vh* aur-m-n wbt2• *Carb-v* vh* carc tpw* **Gels** k1* granit-m es1• hydrog srj *Lyc* vh* *Lyss* vh* *Med* k1* **Nat-m** vh* petr-ra shn4• ph-ac vh* *Sil* vh* suis-pan rly4• *Thuj* vh*
- **apparition** while awake; anguish from horrible: *(↗dreams)* *Camph* kr1 zinc
- **ascending** stairs; on: **Ars** bg iod bg *Nit-ac* k* onos mg ox-ac a1
- **ascites**; during: *(↗abdomen; abdomen; with distension)* fl-ac kr1
- **asthma**; with: *Arg-n* kr1 ars j* *Dig* kr1 hydr-ac j kreos j m-ambo j plat j
- **attacks** of anxiety (See paroxysms)
- **attempting** things: kali-p fyz
- **away** from home: *(↗Fear - away)* rhus-g tmo3•
- **bad** days are approaching; that: cassia-s ccrh1• tarent-c ckh1
- **bathing** the feet; after: nat-c sep fyz
- **bed**:
  - **driving** out of bed: anac j5.de **Ars** h2* ars-s-f fyz bar-s fyz bry j5.de carb-v h2* carbn-s j caust j5.de *Cham* j5.de chin j5.de chinin-s j5.de germ-met srj *Graph* h2* *Hep* j5.de lyss kr1* melal-alt gya4 nat-m j5.de nit-ac h2* *Puls* kr1 *Rhus-t* h1* sul-ac fyz
  - **in** bed: alco a1 am-c *Ambr* anac ant-c **Ars** *Ars-i* ↓ *Bar-c* k* berb *Bry* calad *Calc* calc-ar k2 *Camph* canth ↓ carb-an *Carb-v* *Caust* *Cench* *Cham* k* chinin-s *Cocc* cupr-act kr1 *Ferr* *Graph* *Hep* *Ign* k1* kali-c kali-n laur *Lyc* lyss kr1 *Mag-c* mag-m nat-ar nat-c nat-m nat-p nat-sil k2 nit-ac nux-v phos plac-s rly4• *Puls* **Rhus-t** sabin sep sil spong ↓ stront-c *Sulph* *Tarent* ↓ ter verat
    - **heat**; from: ars-i k2*
    - **passing** off on sitting up in bed (See sit)
    - **sit** up; must: carb-v j5.de spong kr1*
    - **tossing** about; with: ars kr1 *Ars-i* vh* camph kr1 canth kr1 *Cupr-act* kr1 *Ferr* kr1 *Tarent* vh*
    - **turning** in bed; when: lyc j5.de
- **beer**; after: ferr a1
- **beside** oneself from anxiety; being: *Acon* j5.de ars j calc vh* carc mlr1• cham j* chel vh* chin j convo-s sp1 *Graph* j5.de heli-n mtf11 kali-br mrr1 **Lyc** vh* m-arct j mag-c j5.de mag-s j5.de* maias-l hrn2• merc vh* **Nux-v** j* pop mtf11 *Psor* vh* **Puls** vh* sol-ni a2 spong j *Staph* vh* *Sulph* vh* tritic-vg fd5.de tub vh*
- **breakfast**:
  - **after**: con kali-c
  - **amel.**: nat-s k2
- **breathing**:
  - **amel.**: agar agath-a nl2• *Hell* vh* plut-n srj7• rhus-t
  - **deeply**: acon ger-i rly4• *Spig*
  - **must**: agath-a nl2• caps h1
  - **suffocative**: lac-e hrn2•
- **burning** of stomach and coldness of body; with: **Jatr-c** a1*
- **business**; about: *(↗Avarice; Delusions - poor; Fear - poverty)* acet-ac br1 anac aq-mar rbp6 arn j bar-c bg2 bry bg2* calc bg2 carc mlr1• caust j chel j dros j dulc fd4.de gels bro1 kali-m ckh1 kali-n j lac-h htj1• lac-lup hrn2• mang j melal-alt gya4 nat-c j nat-m j **Nux-v** bg2* op j ph-ac j *Psor* st* puls k* rhus-t j5.de* sep j spig j stann j sulph bg2 thuj j [heroin sdj2 spect dfg1]
- **calmness**; with: chir-fl gya2
- **career**; about (See Fear - social)
- **carried** by someone who is dancing; when (See Dancing - agg. - child)
- **causeless**: arge-pl rwt5• **Bry** k* cassia-s ccrh1• chir-fl gya2 fil mtf11 kali-ar k2* oscilloc jl2 oxal-a rly4• phos k* positr nl2• sabad sf1.de sal-fr sle1• spong fd4.de tab k* tarent k* thal c1 thala jl3 tritic-vg fd5.de
- **chagrin**; after (See mortification)
- **chest**:
  - **felt** in chest; anxiety (See CHEST - Anxiety)
  - **pain** in chest; with: kola stb3• mand sp1
  - **stitching** in chest; from: ruta h1
- **children**: *(↗family)*
  - **about** his: *(↗family; others; Maternal)* acet-ac k* acon mtf *Ars* mtf calc mtf carc mlr1• cupr sst3• dream-p sdj1• falco-pe nl2• lac-del hrn2• ph-ac gl1.fr• phos mtf polys sk4• rhus-t ptk1* sep fyz1 *Sulph* mrr1 symph fd3.de• vanil fd5.de [heroin sdj2]
  - **in**: *Acon* ↓ aeth mtf33 arg-n mtf33 ars mtf33 *Borx* k* calc calc-p k* calc-sil mtf33 carc mlr1* *Cham* ↓ *Cina* kr1 *Gels* graph mtf33 *Kali-c* loxo-lae bnm12• passi bro1 rhus-t j5.de sil mtf33 stram mtf33 tritic-vg fd5.de
    - **infants**: *Acon* kr1 *Cham* kr1
    - **lifted** from the cradle; when: borx k2 calc k1 *Calc-p* k*
    - **rocking**; during: *(↗rocking)* **Borx** j5.de*
- **chill**:
  - **after**: *Ars* j5.de *Chel* k* kali-c *Puls* hr1
  - **before**: ars ars-h k* **Chin**
  - **during**: **Acon** k* am-c bg2 anh sp1 apis b7a.de* arg-n bg2 arn k* **Ars** k* ars-h k* bov bg2 calad b7.de* **Calc** k* **Calc-ar** k2* calen a1* **Camph** k* caps k* carb-v *Cham* bg2 chin k* chinin-ar chinin-s bro1 cimx k* *Cocc* k* coff bg2 con bg2 cycl k* gels hep b4a.de* hura ign k* lam laur k* merc b4a.de* *Mez* hr1* nat-m nux-v k* phos k* plat k* **Puls** k* rheum bg2 *Rhus-t* k* sec k* sep k* sulph bg2 thuj bg2 *Verat* k*
- **church** bells; from hearing: *(↗Music - agg.; Weeping - music - bells)* *Lyss*
- **closing** eyes; on: aeth calc carb-an sf1.de **Carb-v** k* *Caust* cypra-eg sde6.de• *Mag-m* k* *Psor* kr1
- **clothes**:
  - **loosen** clothes and open windows; must: nux-v st* *Puls* st* sulph h2
  - **walking** out of doors; as if clothing too tight when: arg-met kr1
- **coffee**:
  - **after**: bart a1 cham ign nux-v stram k*
  - **amel.**: morph a1
- **coition**:
  - **after**: carb-an b4a.de kali-c k2 *Ph-ac* b4a.de sep k*
    - **amel.**: agar vh1
  - **during**: kreos hr1*
  - **thought** of; from | **women**; anxiety in: *Kreos* k*
- **cold**:
  - **becoming**, from: carb-ac a1* manc k* nux-v a1 psor vh
    - **thought** of becoming cold: marb-w es1•
  - **drinks**:
    - **amel.**: acon *Agar-em* aq-mar ↓ sulph
      - **ice**-cold drinks: aq-mar skp7*•
- **coldness**:
  - **during**: cupr-act j marb-w es1• nit-ac j olib-sac wmh1 thuj ↓
    - **Feet** at night; of: thuj a1
    - **Limbs**: cupr-act j
- **colors** | **black** | **agg.**: *(↗dark - agg.)* nit-ac vk4
  - **dark** colors | **agg.**: *(↗black - agg.)* nit-ac vk4
- **company**; when in: *(↗alone - amel.; Company - aversion)* *Acon* *Ambr* aq-mar jl bell cadm-s des-ac rbp6 dream-p sdj1• lac-h htj1• lyc *Petr* plat spong fd4.de stram k*
  - **amel.**: aq-mar jl* lec oss•
- **compelled** to do something; when: falco-pe nl2•
- **condition**; about her: lac-lup hrn2•

- **conflicts**; about (See Quarrelling - aversion)
- **congestion**:
  - **chest**; anxiety from congestion to: kali-n h2 sep h2
  - **heart**; to: nit-ac h2
- **conscience**; anxiety of: *(↗duty; salvation; Anger - mistakes; Comply; Delusions - crime - committed; Delusions - criminal he; Delusions - neglected - duty; Delusions - performing - pressured; Delusions - reproach; Delusions - right - doing; Delusions - wrong - done; Escape - crime; Fear - punishment; Remorse; Reproaching oneself; Reproaching oneself - animal; Reproaching oneself - morning; Restlessness - conscience; Sadness - criminal; Thoughts - tormenting)* achy jl adam srj5• agath-a nl2• aids nl2• **Alum** k* alum-p k2 alum-sil k2 *Am-c* am-m vh1 *Ambr*↓ **Anac** bg2* androc srj1• arizon-l nl2• arn st **Ars** k* *Ars-s-f* k2 aster vh atro a1 **AUR** k1* aur-ar k2 aur-br vh1 *Aur-m-n* wbt2• aur-s k2 *Bamb-a* stb2.de• *Bell* j bros-gau↓ bry gl1.fr• bung-fa↓ cact calc h2* canth carb-an kr1 *Carb-v* carbn-s *Carc* fd2.de* *Caust* cham j5.de* **Chel** chin gl1.fr• cina k* cob a1* *Cocc* *Coff* b7a.de* *Con* k* croc ptk crot-c sk4• cupr k* cycl k* **Dig** k* dioxi rbp6 dream-p sdj1• falco-pe nl2• *Ferr* ferr-ar ferr-p *Germ-met* srj5• granit-m es1• *Graph* *Hell* vh* hip-ac sp1 *Hyos* k* *Ign* irid-met srj5• *Kali-bi* kr1 kali-br hr1* kalm bg lac-e hrn2• lac-h sk4*• *Lach* j5.de* led↓ limest-b es1• *M-arct* j5.de m-aust b7a.de mag-c mg1.de mag-s *Med* *Merc* k* *Moni* rfm1• myric a1 *Nat-m* neon srj5• nit-ac *Nux-v* olib-sac wmh1 *Orig* sne *Orig-v* sne ozone sde2• petr-ra shn4• *Ph-ac* bg2* phos pieri-b mlk9.de *Plat* kr1* positr nl2• **Psor** *Puls* b7a.de* rheum rhus-g↓ *Rhus-t* ruta k* sabad *Sal-fr* sle1• sanguis-s hrn2• sarr a1 *Sil* k* *Spig* gl1.fr• (non:spira a1) spirae a1* staph vh* *Stram* b7a.de* stront-c **Sulph** k1* symph fd3.de• *Thuj* k* *Tritic-vg* fd5.de vanad dx vanil fd5.de *Verat* k* *Zinc* zinc-o j5.de [*Brom* stj1 calc-br stj1 heroin sdj2 mag-br stj1 tax jsj7]
  - **afternoon**: *Am-c* st carb-v j
  - **absent**: phasco-ci rbp2
  - **anger**; after: bung-fa mtf
  - **dreams**; in: bros-gau mrc1 lach j5.de led j5.de
  - **eating** habits; about her: rhus-g tmo3•
  - **forgetfulness**; with: thuj a1
  - **masturbation**; after: *(↗Sadness - masturbation)* *Ambr* vh1 *Ph-ac* kr1*
  - **no** rest night or day, prevents lying down: *Phos* kr1
  - **observed**, on being: germ-met srj5•
  - **partner's** bad mood; she is to be blamed for her: bamb-a stb2.de•
- **constipation**; with: tarent mrr1*
- **constriction**; from: ars↓ gins↓ guaj↓ nit-ac↓ ozone↓ positr↓ stann↓ [ars-met stj2 kali-ar stj2]
  - **chest**, in: ars a1 gins a1 ozone sde2• positr nl2• stann h2
  - **heart** region, in: nit-ac h2
  - **stomach**; in: guaj h2
- **continence** prolonged; from: *Con*
- **control** over senses is lost; with feeling that: lac-lup hrn2•
- **conversation**; from: *(↗Conversation - agg.)* alum *Ambr* k* androc srj1• plat stram
- **convulsions**:
  - **as** if threatened with an epileptic fit: alum hr1*
  - **before**: cic st*
  - **between** | **epileptic**: cupr kr1 *Lyc* j5.de
- **coryza**; during: *Ars* b4a.de
- **cough**:
  - **after**: *Cina* kr1
  - **before**: ars *Cupr* k* iod *Lac-ac* kr1 (non:lach k1) lact k*
  - **during**: *(↗Anguish - cough)* *Acon* b7.de* adam srj5• *Ars* b4a.de brom kr1 cina b7.de* *Coff* b7.de* cupr b7a.de hep b4a.de* iod b4a.de* *Ip* b7a.de *Kali-c* kr1 meli kr1 *Mez* b4a.de nux-v b7a.de* *Rhus-t* b7.de* spong fd4.de stram bg2* tritic-vg fd5.de
  - **from**: apis↓ arund k* cina↓ kali-s fd4.de merc-c nit-ac spong fd4.de stram tritic-vg fd5.de
    - **burst**; something will: apis tl1
    - **paroxysm**: cina tl1
- **cough**: ...
  - **whooping** cough:
    - **before**: *Cupr* k*
    - **during**: *Mosch* hr1* *Stram* hr1*
- **cramp**:
  - **as** from: lyc h2*
  - **during**:
    - **Rectum**, in: calc h2
    - **Stomach**, in: kali-c h2
- **crowd**; in a: *(↗Fear - crowd)* **Acon** k* **Ambr** k* *Arg-n* vh* *Aur* vh* bell carc hbh* caust ckh1 hydr-ac bro1 *Kali-ar* vh* lyc mag-c mtf33 *Petr* plat k* *Puls* vh* spong fd4.de stram tab vh taosc iwa1• [mang-n stj2]
- **cruelties**; after hearing of: *(↗Excitement - hearing; Horrible)* *Calc* carc mlr1•
- **dancing**; when carried by someone who is (See Dancing - agg. - child)
- **dark**; in: *(↗Darkness - agg.; Fear - dark; Fear - dark; of; Fear - walking - of - dark; Light - desire)* aeth aur-i k2 calc sf1.de *Cann-xyz* bg2 carb-an sf1.de carb-v k2* hypoth jl nat-m ozone sde2• phos k* *Puls* k* rhus-t ruta fd4.de **STRAM** bg2* tritic-vg fd5.de zinc sf1.de [heroin sdj2]
- **delirium**, before: sang hr1
- **delivery**, during: *Cham* b7a.de cupr kr1
- **dentition**; during: kali-br jl
- **despair**; with: ars gm1 dulc fd4.de *Ruta* fd4.de *Vanil* fd5.de
- **diabetes**; in: cod hr1* *Nat-s* hr1*
- **diarrhea**:
  - **before**: haliae-lc srj5•
  - **suppressed**; from: abrot k2
- **dinner**:
  - **after**: ambr k* bell h1* canth k* gins k* hyos k* mag-c a1 mag-m h2* nat-c a1 nat-m k* *Phos* k* psor hr1 sil k* verat k*
    - **amel.**: sulph
  - **during**: mag-m k*
- **discouragement**; with (See Discouraged - anxiety)
- **disguises**; which he vainly: alco a1
- **do** something; compelled to: *(↗Thoughts - compelling)* *Bry* kr1* lac-lup↓
  - **knows** not what: lac-lup hrn2•
- **domestic** (See household)
- **dreams**; on waking from frightful●: *(↗apparition)* abrot a1 *Ars* calc h2 chin cina j dulc fd4.de frax a1 gink-b sbd1• graph hep h2 hydroph rsj6• **Kali-br** hr1* lach-h sze9• lyc h2 mag-c st mag-m a1 mur-ac h2 *Nat-m* nicc op gk ozone sde2• petr h2 ph-ac h2 plac-s rly4• psor al2 puls sil h2 **Spong** kr1* **Staph** vh* tarent a1 tritic-vg fd5.de vanil fd5.de zinc h2 [bell-p-sp dcm1 heroin sdj2]
- **drinking**:
  - **after**: *Cimx* k* *Puls* a1
  - **cold** water amel.: acon a1* aq-mar jl sulph a1
  - **lemonade**; amel.: lac-e hrn2•
- **driving** from place to place: *(↗Restlessness - anxious - driving)* acon j aeth j alum j am-c j ambr j anac j ars k2* asaf j aur sf1.de bell j bov j bry k2* calc j camph j caps j carb-an j carb-v j carneg-g rwt1• caust j chin j chinin-s j coff j coli rly4• con a1 crot-h j dros j graph mtf33 *Iod* k* lact j m-arct j meny j merc k* musca-d szs1 nat-c j nat-m j nit-ac j nux-v j op j ph-ac j phos j plat j puls j rhus-t j ruta j sabad j sep j spig j spong j staph h1 sul-i k2 valer j verat j
- **duty**; as if he had not done his: *(↗conscience; Delusions - neglected - duty)* alum h2 ars a1 maias-l hrn2•
- **eating**:
  - **after**: aloe *Ambr* k* *Arg-n* k* asaf k* bell k* canth k* carb-an k* *Carb-v* k* *Caust* k* cham k* chin k* *Coc-c* k* con k* ferr hr1* ferr-m ferr-ma k* ferr-p hyos k* kali-c k* kali-p kali-sil k2* lach mag-m merc k* *Nat-c* *Nat-m* nat-p nat-sil k2* *Nit-ac* k* **Nux-v** k* ph-ac k* phel *Phos* k* psor ran-b rhus-t b7a.de sep sil sulph b4a.de thuj k* verat viol-t k*
  - **amel.**: *(↗Eating - after - amel.)* aur k* ignis-alc es2• *Iod* k* mez k* plut-n srj7• streptoc rly4• sulph
  - **before**: mez plac-s rly4• ran-b
  - **while**: *Carb-v* k* kali-sil k2 mag-c k* mez ran-b c1 sabad k* *Sep*
    - **warm** food: mag-c k*
- **eczema**; with chronic: asthm-r mtf11

- **emissions** (See pollutions)
- **epilepsy** (See convulsions)
- **epistaxis** amel.: kali-chl j5.de*
- **eructations**:
  - **amel.**: kali-c mag-m k* mez h2*
  - **ending** with: verat h1*
- **eruptions**; after suppressed: mez mrr1
- **everything**; about: carc mlr1• sarr a1*
- **exaggerated** (See beside)
- **excitement**; from: (*↗Excitement)* asaf aur-m kr1 carc mlr1• *Cocc* kr1 irid-met srj5• kali-i a1 mang k2 melal-alt gya4 *Phos Plat* kr1
- **exercise**:
  - **amel.**: chel st iod mrr1 tarent
  - **from**: (*↗Manual)* **Iod** st *Sarcol-ac* jl3
- **exertion** of eyes; from: (*↗Prostration) Sep*
- **expected** of him; when anything is: (*↗Responsibility - aversion) Ars* k* lac-e hrn2•
- **face**:
  - **anxious** expression of (See FACE - Expression - anxious)
  - **heat** of face; with: *Acon* j5.de* arg-n j5.de* bell j5.de* **Carb-v** k1* graph k1 merc j5.de* puls a1*
  - **pale** face; with: aeth sf1.de *Crot-h* kr1* puls j5.de*
  - **perspiration** of face; with: ars j5.de cic j5.de crot-h ↓ mur-ac j5.de nat-c j5.de
    - **cold**: ars j5.de crot-h j5.de* mur-ac j5.de
  - **red** face; with: *Acon* j5.de *Cupr* kr1 *Kali-i* kr1 sep j5.de
- **faintness**:
  - **after** faintness; anxiety: ars-s-f hr1*
  - **from** anxiety; faintness (See GENERALS - Faintness - anxiety)
  - **with** faintness: *Arg-n* kr1 ars j5.de* cic j5.de *Crot-h* st *Dig* kr1 ign j5.de nux-v j5.de *Plb* br* **Spong** kr1*
- **family**; about his: (*↗children; children - about; others; Fear - happen - parents; Love - family)* acet-ac kr1 *Aeth* vh1 ambr tsm1 apis oss• ars j5.de* aur-m-n wbt2• borra-o oss1• calc oss• calc-i oss• calc-sil k2* carc ib* *Cocc* mrr1 crot-c sk4• cupr sst3*• dendr-pol sk4• *Dulc* mrr1 falco-pe nl2• form mgm• hep h2* lac-cp ↓ lac-del hrn2• lac-e ↓ oxal-a rly4• petr hr1* phos j5.de* plat mrr1 podo fd3.de• puls oss• rhus-t j5.de sulph j* taosc iwa1• tax-br oss1• [cupr-act stj2 cupr-f stj2 cupr-p stj2 heroin sdj2 zinc-p stj2]
  - **occupation** amel.: lac-cp sk4•
  - **safety** of family; for: lac-e hrn2•
- **fasting**; when: iod h
- **fear**; with: (*↗Fear)* **Acon** k* aeth j *Alum* alum-p k2 am-c *Am-m* amor-r jl **Anac** *Androc* srj1• ant-c ant-t **Ars** ars-s-f k2 *Aur* aur-ar k2 aur-s k2 *Bar-c* bar-s k2 bell k* berb bov j bry calad *Calc* calc-ar k1 calc-s *Canth* caps j carb-an j *Carb-v* j5.de carbn-s *Carc* mlr1• **Caust** chel *Chin* chinin-ar *Chinin-s* cic cina clem *Cocc Coff* con j5.de crot-h j *Cupr Dig* dros dulc elec j ferr ferr-ar ferr-p gels gt granit-m es1• *Graph* heli-n mtf11 hell *Hep* hydrog srj2• hyos **Ign** ignis-alc es2• iod j *Kali-ar Kali-c* kali-i kali-n *Kali-p* kali-s kali-sil k2 *Kreos* lach limest-b es1• *Lyc* m-arct j5.de *Mag-c* mag-m j manc mang marb-w es1• meny *Merc* mez mosch j5.de murx j5.de nat-ar nat-c *Nat-m* nat-p nicc *Nit-ac* nux-m nux-v onos op gt ph-ac j phel *Phos Plat* plb j **Psor** k* *Puls* rat *Rhus-t* ruta sabin samb sang kr1 **Sec** *Sep* k* sil j5.de *Spig* spong staph *Stront-c* sul-ac j sulph tab thuj til valer j5.de *Verat* vesp kr1 zinc j5.de
  - **menopause**; during: androc srj1•
- **fever**:
  - **as** from: carb-v h2* **Puls** a1
  - **during**: (*↗Fear - fever - during)* **Acon** k* ail k2 *Alum* k* am-c k* **Ambr** k* anac k* *Ant-c* ↓ ant-t bg2 anthraci jl2 apis bg2 arg-met b2.de* arn k* **Ars** k* ars-s-f k2* *Asaf* k* **Bar-c** k* **Bar-s** k2* bell k* berb k* bov k* *Bry* k* *Calc* k* *Calc-ar* k* calc-s canth k* caps bg2 carb-an k* carb-v b2.de* casc k* caust b2.de cham k* chel bg2 chin k* chinin-ar *Chinin-s* chlor hr1 cina b7a.de* cocc b7.de* coff k* colch b2.de* con b2.de* crot-h k* cycl k* dros k* euph b2.de* *Ferr* k* ferr-ar ferr-p fl-ac graph k* grat guare k* hep k* hyos b2.de* hyper k* ign k* **Ip** k* kali-c lach k* laur k* lyc b2.de* *M-arct* b2.de* *Mag-c* k* mag-m k* merc k* merc-c bg2 *Mur-ac* k* nat-ar nat-c k* nat-m k* nat-p nat-s k2* nicc k* nit-ac b2.de* nux-v k* ol-an j5.de op k* par k* *Petr* k* ph-ac k* *Phos* k* plan plat k* plb k* *Puls* k* rheum k* rhod b2.de* *Rhus-t* k* *Ruta* k* sabad j5.de sabin k* *Sec* k* **Sep** k* sil b2.de spig k* *Spong* k* *Squil* j5.de stann k* staph bg2 stram k* sulph k* thuj b2.de* *Tub* k* valer k* verat k* *Viol-t* k* *Zinc* k* zinc-p k2*
    - **intermittent** fever; during: *Ant-c* kr1 *Ant-t* kr1 *Cocc* kr1 **lyc** kr1
    - **puerperal** fever; during: *Plat* kr1
  - **prodrome** of; during: ars chin k* nux-v b7a.de puls b7a.de rhus-t b7a.de
- **fits**:
  - **before**: cic vh* kali-m sne
  - **with** fits: alum ars kr1 bell calc kr1 carc mlr1• caust cocc cupr ferr *Hyos* ign
- **flatus**:
  - **emission** of, amel.: calc calc-act a1
  - **from**: cic br1 coff k* *Lyc* h2 *Nux-v* k*
  - **obstructed** flatus; with: raph vh sulph h2
- **flatulence**; from: cic b7a.de
- **flushes** of heat: (*↗GENERALS - Orgasm)*
  - **during**: (*↗GENERALS - Heat - flushes; GENERALS - Orgasm - anxiety)* ambr androc srj1• arn ars sne calc camph sne cham sne coff sne cop sne croc sne dros graph ign merc h1 nat-c h2 op phos plat puls *Sep* spong sul-i sne
- **followed** by:
  - **apathy** (See indifference)
  - **indifference**: *Acon* kr1 phos h2
- **food**:
  - **about**: lac-h htj1•
  - **warm** food | **agg.**: mag-c mrr1
- **foot**-bath; after a: nat-c
- **free**-floating: (*↗Fear - free-floating)* limen-b-c hrn2•
- **friends** at home; about his: (*↗others; Fear - accidents - friends)* bar-c *Phos* k* phys *Sulph*
- **fright**:
  - **after**: (*↗Ailments - fright; Ailments - mental shock)* acon both-ax tsm2 *Carc* mlr1• *Cupr* kr1 dulc fd4.de gels *Ign* kr1 *Kali-br* sf1.de lyc *Manc* mrr1 merc nat-m op k* rob *Sil* vanil fd5.de *Verat* kr1
  - **remains**; anxiety if the fear of the fright: **Op** hr1*
- **future**, about: (*↗Absorbed - become; Ailments - anticipation; Avarice - anxiety; Delirium - anxious - future; Fear - happen; Forebodings; Grief - future; Lamenting - future; Thoughts - future; Weeping - future)* acon k* adam srj5• aeth j5.de agar k* agri mtf11 allox sp1* *Aloe* sne alum k* alum-p k2* *Anac* k* anan a1 ant-c k* ant-t k* anthraq rly4• arg-n k2* arist-cl jl3 arn k* ars hr1* aster ptk1* aur j5.de* *Aur-m-n* wbt2• *Aur-s* wbt2• bamb-a stb2.de• *Bar-c* k* *Bar-m* bar-s k2* bros-gau mrc1 **BRY** k* bufo k2 buth-a sp1* calad k* **Calc** k* calc-act a1* *Calc-ar* calc-f jl3 calc-s k* carb-an j carb-v j carbn-s carc az1.de*• cassia-s ccrh1• *Caust* k* cham k* chel k* *Chin* k* **Chinin-s** k* chir-fl gya2 choc srj3• **Cic** k* cimic ptk1 clem gt cocc coff j *Con* k* conch fkr1* crot-c sk4• cupr bg2* *Cupr-ar* mgm• cycl k* dendr-pol sk4• *Dig* k* dirc k* *Dros* k* *Dulc* k* *Dys* fmm1• euph k* euphr bg2 falco-pe nl2• ferr-c ferr-i *Ferr-p* fl-ac k* fum rly1*• *Gels* k* gins k* granit-m es1• *Graph* k* grat k* ham fd3.de• hep gl1.fr• hipp k* hura a1 *Iod* k* kali-br a1 kali-c k* kali-m ptk1* *Kali-n* j kali-p kali-s fd4.de kalm ketogl-ac rly4• *Kola* stb3• lac-leo hrn2• *Lach* k* lil-t k* m-arct b7.de* mag-c j* mang k* meny j merc j5.de* miml-g mtf11 *Mur-ac* k* nat-act a1 nat-ar k* *Nat-c* k* *Nat-m* k* nat-p nat-s k2* nat-sil stj2*• *Nit-ac* j5.de *Nux-v* k* *Op* j ozone sde2• parth vml3• petr k* petr-ra shn4• *Ph-ac* k* **Phos** k* plac-s rly4• plat ptk1* podo fd3.de• *Psor* k* *Puls* k* ran-b k* *Rhus-t* k* ruta fd4.de *Sabin* scroph-n a1* *Sep* b4a.de* *Sil* b4a.de* sol-t-ae a1 *Spig* k* **Spong** k* *Stann* k* *Staph* k* stram stront-c sk4• sul-ac j5.de *Sulph* k* symph fd3.de• tab j taosc iwa1• tarent tere-la rly4• thioc-ac rly4• thuj k* *Tritic-vg* fd5.de tub al ulm-c jsj8• vanil fd5.de verat k* vichy-g a1 vichy-h a1 viol-t a1 wies a1 xan [am-caust stj2 am-f stj2 bar-i stj2 beryl stj2 beryl-m stj2 bor-pur stj2 calc-lac stj2 calc-met stj2 calc-sil stj2 cupr-act stj2 cupr-f stj2 cupr-m stj2 cupr-p stj2 ferr-n stj2 fl-pur stj2 heroin sdj2 hydrog stj2 lith-c stj2 lith-f stj2 lith-i stj2 lith-m stj2 lith-met stj2 lith-p stj2 lith-s stj2 mag-n stj2 mang-i stj2 mang-met stj2 mang-n stj2 merc-i-f stj2 moly-met stj2 nat-br stj2 nat-caust stj2 nat-f stj2 nat-lac stj2 nat-met stj2 nitro stj2 oxyg stj2 pall stj2 spect dfg1 tax jsj7 zinc-i stj2 zinc-n stj2 zinc-p stj2]
  - **afternoon** | **16** h: bamb-a stb2.de•
  - **evening**: buth-a ↓ *Caust* hr1

- **evening**: ...
  - ⁝ **19** h: buth-a jl3
- **day**; about the coming: arg-n mrr1 [heroin sdj2]
- **dreams**; on waking from frightful: lac-leo hrn2•
- **sadness**; with: ozone sde2•
- **twilight**: caust ptk2
- **waking**; on: lac-leo hrn2•

- **germs** | **catch** germs from others; will: *(↗health - own; Fear - disease)* limen-b-c hrn2•
- **grief**; as from: *(↗Fear - grief)* am-m br1
- **head**:
  - **congestion** to; with: acon j5.de **AUR** kr1 carb-v j5.de *Cupr* kr1 cycl kr1 *Ign* kr1 musca-d szs1 puls j5.de*
  - **heat** of; with: carb-v j5.de *Cupr* kr1 laur j5.de *Mag-c* j5.de *Phos* j5.de sil h2 sulph h2*
    - ⁝ **cold** feet; and: *Sulph* kr1
  - **perspiration** on forehead; with: ars j5.de carb-v j5.de *Nux-v* j5.de* *Phos* j5.de* sep j5.de
    - ⁝ **cold**: *Nux-v* kr1 *Sep* j5.de*
- **headache**; with: *Acon* k* aeth j5.de* ambr bg2 ant-c bg2 ant-t bg2 *Ars* k* bell bov *Calc* j5.de* carb-an bg2 carb-v j5.de caust k* cic bg2 cimic bg2 *Cycl* a1 fl-ac k* gels psa glon k* kali-n h2* lach bg2 *Lyss* kr1* nat-c bg2 nit-ac h2 plat h2* ran-b bg2 rheum bg2 ruta j5.de* sep bg2* spig bg2 stront-c bg2 tub vanil fd5.de
- **health**; about: *(↗Delusions - sick - being; Delusions - sick - going; Fear - disease; Hypochondriasis; Thoughts - disease)* acet-ac ↓ acon bg2 adam ↓ **AGAR** ↓ agn ckh1 alum bg2 alum-p ↓ alum-sil ↓ am-c bg2 androc ↓ ant-t bg2 *Arg-met* ↓ **Arg-n** ↓ arn bg2 ars bg2 *Ars-h* ↓ *Aur-m* ↓ *Aur-m-n* wbt2• *Aur-s* wbt2• *Bar-c* vh bar-ox-suc rly4• bell ↓ borx bg2 bov ↓ brom ↓ bry b7a.de* bufo ↓ calad bg2 *Calc* b4a.de* calc-ar ↓ calc-f ↓ calc-p ckh1 calc-s ↓ calc-sil ↓ cann-i ↓ canth ↓ carb-an bg2 *Carc* mlr1• *Chinin-ar* ↓ choc ↓ *Cocc* ↓ cop ↓ crot-c sk4• cupr ↓ eric-vg mtf11 galeoc-c-h gms1• glon ↓ grat ↓ hep b4a.de* hyos ↓ ign bg2 **KALI-AR** ↓ *Kali-br* ↓ *Kali-c* b4a.de* kali-m ckh1 kali-n ↓ kali-p ↓ *Kali-sil* ↓ kreos b7a.de* *Lac-c* bg2 lac-e hrn2• lac-h ↓ *Lach* bg2 lat-h thj1 *Lil-t* ↓ lob ↓ **Lyc** ckh1 m-arct ↓ mag-m ↓ malar jl2 *Med* ↓ merc bg2 moni ↓ morg ptj1* morg-p fmm1*• mosch ↓ musca-d szs1 nat-ar ↓ nat-c bg2 nat-m bg2 nat-p ↓ nit-ac b4a.de* nux-m ↓ **Nux-v** bg2 orot-ac rly4• ozone sde2• petr-ra shn4• ph-ac b4a.de* **Phel** ckh1 *Phos* b4a.de* plat bg2 podo ↓ positr nl2• psor bg2 *Puls* bg2 ruta lp sabad bg2 sel ↓ sep b4a.de* sil ↓ stann bg2 staph ↓ streptoc rly4• sulph bg2 *Syph* ↓ tab bg2 thuj bg2 trios ↓ tritic-vg fd5.de *Uva* ↓ [cupr-act stj2 cupr-f stj2 cupr-p stj2 **Spect** dfg1 tax jsj7]
  - **others**; of: agar vh1 *Cocc* br1*
  - **own** health; one's: *(↗germs - catch; Delusions - disease - every; Despair - health; Despair - recovery; Doubtful - recovery; Fear - disease; Fear - health - ruined; Hypochondriasis; Narrating - agg.; Thinking - complaints - agg.; Thoughts - disease; Weeping - telling - sickness)* acet-ac *Acon* k* adam srj5• **AGAR** kr1* agn vh* alum alum-p k2 alum-sil k2 am-c a1* androc srj1• ant-t a1 *Arg-met* k* **Arg-n** k* arn **Ars** k* *Ars-h* kr1* *Aur-m* vh* bar-c mrr1 bell j borx j bov vh brom sf1.de bry bufo a1* *Calad* k1* *Calc* k* calc-ar k1* calc-f mrr1 *Calc-p* vh* calc-s calc-sil k2 cann-i mrr1 canth j carc sk1* *Chinin-ar* kr1 choc srj3• *Cocc* k* cop a1 cupr j galeoc-c-h ↓ glon sf1.de grat hyos j ign **KALI-AR** k* *Kali-br* hr1 *Kali-c* k* kali-n mrr1 kali-p k* *Kali-sil* k2* lac-c k* lac-h sze9• lach *Lil-t* br1 lob j* *Lyc* vh* m-arct j mag-m malar jl2 *Med* mrr1 merc j moni rfm1• mosch mrr1 nat-ar mrr1 nat-c nat-m j nat-p **NIT-AC** k* nux-m nux-v *Ph-ac* k1* **Phel** vh* **Phos** k* plat vh5 podo sf1.de positr nl2• *Psor* k* *Puls* k1* sel sf1.de* *Sep* k* sil staph sulph k* *Syph* mrr1 trios rsj1•
    - ⁝ **menopause**; during her: *Kali-br* kr1 sil
    - ⁝ **pregnant**; wondering if she is: galeoc-c-h gms1•
  - **relatives**; of: *(↗Fear - health - loved)* *Ars* vh* bar-c vh carc mlr1• cocc a1* **Hep** ckh1* merc ckh1* moni rfm1• *Phos* vh* plat mrr1 tritic-vg fd5.de [*Uva* stj]
- **heart** failure; in congestive: **Carb-v** mrr1
- **heart** region; contraction of: nit-ac h2
- **heart**; about his: *(↗Fear - heart)* maias-l hrn2• ol-an ckh1 phos ckh1 samb ckh1 stroph-xyz ckh1
- **heart**; with pressure in: kola stb3•
- **himself**; about: *(↗Hiding - himself - children)* nat-c a1 *Sil* kr1
- **home**; about: nat-p a1
- **hot** air; as if in: **Puls**
- **house**, in: alum ars aster *Bry* carl chel kali-c **Lyc** *Mag-m* plat positr ↓ **Puls** k* rhod ↓ **Rhus-t** spong *Til* valer
  - **amel.**: ign
  - **entering**; on: alum positr nl2• rhod
- **household** matters; about: ars mp1• bar-c mtf carl br1 chir-fl gya2 hyos mtf lac-leo sk4• nux-v mtf ph-ac mtf puls a2 rhus-t mtf sep mtf *Stann* ↓ sulph psj1
  - **morning**: puls a1
  - **pregnancy**; during: bar-c kr1 *Stann* kr1
- **hungry**, when: *Iod* k* *Kali-c*
- **hurry**, with: *(↗Hurry)* *Alum* vh* *Carc* mlr1• kurch bnj1 **Nat-m** hr1* neon srj5• positr nl2•
- **hypochondriacal**: *(↗Delusions - disease - deaf; Delusions - disease - every; Delusions - disease - unrecognized; Delusions - sick - being; Despair - hypochondriasis; Doubtful - recovery; Hypochondriasis)* *Acon* j5.de **Agar** vh* agn vh* *All-s* vh1 alum j5.de am-c anac k* anag vh1 *Arg-n* hr1* *Arn* k* *Ars* k* asaf k* asar bg2 *Aur* sne *Bell* j5.de bry j5.de calad k* *Calc* h2* **Calen** mgm• canth k* *Carc* mlr1• caust j5.de cham k* *Con* j5.de* conch fkr1• cupr j5.de dros k* ferr-p graph j5.de *Grat* hyos j5.de ign j5.de *Iod* j5.de **Kali-ar** vh* *Kali-c* j5.de kali-chl kali-p lach j5.de **Lec** sne lyc j5.de* m-arct j5.de mosch k* nat-c j5.de* **Nat-m** k* **Nit-ac** k* *Nux-v* j5.de* orot-ac rly4• ox-ac sf1.de ph-ac k* **Phos** k* plat j5.de psor st1 *Puls* j5.de *Raph* j5.de *Rhus-t* j5.de *Sep* j5.de squil j5.de staph j5.de* sulph j5.de valer k* [*Spect* dfg1]
  - **read** books; mania to: **Calc** ↓ carc mlr1• *Nux-v* ↓ *Puls* ↓ staph ↓ sulph ↓
    - ⁝ **medical** books: **Calc** gl1.fr• *Nux-v* gl1.fr• *Puls* gl1.fr• staph gl1.fr• sulph gl1.fr•
- **hysterical**: *(↗Hysteria)* *Asaf* hr1* carc mlr1• con h2* **Ther** kr1 tritic-vg fd5.de
- **ice**-cold drinks (See cold - drinks)
- **ill**, as if he would be: *(↗Fear - disease)* maias-l hrn2•
- **inactivity**, with: bov j5.de *Cench* j5.de coff j5.de laur j5.de merc j5.de
- **incarnate** in physical world; to: [lac-mat sst4]
- **ineffectual** desire (See stool - ineffectual)
- **intense** (See beside)
- **journey**; before a: adam srj5• tritic-vg fd5.de
- **joyful** things; from most: *Plat* kr1
- **late**; to be too (See time)
- **laughing** and crying from anxiety ending in profuse perspiration: *Cupr* kr1
- **looking** steadily: *(↗Staring)* *Sep*
- **lying**: androc srj1• ars bar-c ↓ calc-s carb-v k* *Cench* hep kr1 kali-c ↓ *Mag-m* mrr1 nux-v **Phos** ↓ puls *Sil* k* spong stann
  - **amel.**: *(↗Anguish - lying - must)* mang k* mang-act br1
  - **head**; with | **raised** amel.: oci-sa sk4•
  - **side**, on: bar-c kali-c phos k1* puls
    - ⁝ **right** | **flatulence**; from: kali-c
    - ⁝ **left**: bar-c **Phos** k* puls
- **manual** labor:
  - **during**: aloe anac *Graph* **Iod** k*
  - **from**: *(↗Manual)* iod
- **masturbation**, from: cann-i sf1.de staph vh
- **menopause**; during: acon bro1* *Aml-ns* bro1* ars sf1.de cimic sf1.de glon sf1.de *Kali-br* hr1 puls sf1.de sep bro1* *Tril-p* st
- **menses**:
  - **after**: *(↗Menses - after)* *Agar* lac-e hrn2• *Pall* hr1* phos k* sec
    - ⁝ **morning**: lac-e hrn2•
    - ⁝ **sleep**; which prevents: agar
  - **before**: *(↗Menses - before)* acon am-c k* aur-m-n wbt2• calc st1* carb-an k* carb-v carbn-s *Cocc* k* con k* foll oss• *Graph* k* *Ign* kali-bi kola stb3• m-arct mag-m sf1.de manc c1 mang k* merc *Nat-m* k* *Nit-ac* *Nux-v* ph-ac b4a.de puls b7a.de* *Stann* k* *Sulph* k* zinc
  - **during**: *(↗Menses - during)* acon *Bell* k* calc k* calc-sil k2* canth caul sf1.de cimic cina cocc hr1* coff con hyos sf1.de ign inul k* *Kali-c* hr1* kali-i kali-sil k2* kreos sf1.de lac-e ↓ lach ↓ mag-m sf1.de* merc k* merl c1 nat-c a1 *Nat-m* k* nit-ac k* nux-v op ↓ ph-ac ↓ phos k* *Plat* sec **Sil** k* stann staph ↓ sulph k* verat sf1.de verat-v ↓ zinc k* zinc-p k2*
    - ⁝ **morning**: lac-e hrn2•
    - ⁝ **amel.**: stann k* zinc
    - ⁝ **anger**; with: acon gl1.fr• bell gl1.fr• *Ign* gl1.fr• lach gl1.fr• nux-v gl1.fr• op gl1.fr• ph-ac gl1.fr• staph gl1.fr• verat gl1.fr• verat-v gl1.fr•

- **mental** exertion, from: *(↗Mental exertion - agg.)* acon ars aur-m kr1 benz-ac kr1 calc calc-sil k13 camph cham k* cupr *Cupr-act* kr1 iod kali-p mrr1 mang k2 nat-c nat-m j *Nit-ac* nux-v phos pic-ac br1 plan puls rhus-t sec verat
- **metrorrhagia**; during: acon kr1 *Cann-i* kr1 ham kr1 *Sabin* kr1
- **mistakes**; making: carc sst2•
- **moaning**; with: acon lpc alum lpc ant-t lpc ars lpc cham lpc par lpc phos lpc rheum lpc sep h2
- **money** matters, about: *(↗Fear - poverty)* *Agath-a* nl2• aids nl2• aq-mar rbp6 aur fyz bac bn bamb-a stb2.de• *Bry* vh* calc mrr1 calc-f a1* calc-sil k2* chinin-s mrr1 choc srj3• dulc fd4.de fuma-ac rly4• ign fyz kali-p fyz kali-s fd4.de moni rfm1• positr nl2• spong fd4.de [tax jsj7]
- **mortification**; after: lyc
- **motion**:
  - **agg.**: acon aloe berb borx calc-p ckh1 cocc kr1 coff-t ↓ **Dig** kr1* *Gels* ↓ *Hyos* kr1 kali-i k2 *Lach* kr1 mag-c mang k2 nat-c nicc psor ↓ rheum sanic ↓ stann stram kr1
    - **airplane**, of: *(↗Fear - flying - airplane)* **Borx** st*
    - **cable** railway, of: **Borx** st*
    - **downward** motion: *(↗Fear - falling)* **Borx** k* coff-t kr1 *Gels* psor ckh1 sanic sf1.de
    - **elevator**; of: **Borx** st*
    - **upward** motion: borx k2
  - **amel.**: *(↗Occupation - amel.)* acon act-sp k* aq-mar skp7• *Ars* hist sp1 iod k2* kali-i k2 mag-m k2 naja ph-ac *Puls* seneg k* sil k* tarax
- **mountain** climbing; from: coca br1
- **mucus**; from accumulation of | **bronchi**; in: *(↗Fear - suffocation; LARYNX - Mucus - air)* arund kr1*
- **music**, from: *(↗Music - agg.)* bufo k2 dig *Nat-c* k*
- **nausea**; increases with the: *(↗STOMACH - Nausea - anxiety - with)* ant-t a1*
- **nausea**; with (See STOMACH - Nausea - anxiety)
- **nervous**: antip br1
- **new** things; when seeing: cupr sst3* *Lyc* br1
- **news**; as though he would hear unpleasant (See Fear - bad)
- **night** watching, from: *Aur* vh* *Carc* mlr1• caust *Cocc* k2* cupr **Nit-ac** *Nux-v* vh*
- **noise**, from: *(↗Sensitive - noise)* agar alum ars gm1 **Asar** vh* *Aur* bar-c caps *Caust* chel k* kali-p fd1.de• **Lyss** ↓ nat-c petr puls **Sil** k* **Stram** ↓ *Ther* vh* tritic-vg fd5.de
  - **water**; of rushing: **Lyss Stram**
  - ○ **Ear**, in: puls lpc sil h2
- **nursed**; when the child is:
  - **after** being nursed | **newborns**; in: cham mtf33
- **nursing**:
  - **after**: *Cham* hr1* cocc k2
  - **during**: cocc mrr3*
- **oppression**, with: ars a1 chel a1 lob mrr1 maias-l hrn2• **Spong** fd* sulph h2* tritic-vg fd5.de
- **others**, for: *(↗children - about; family; friends; Affectionate; Benevolence; Cares full - others; Despair - others; Mildness; Sympathetic)* abies-c oss4• *Acon* vh* aeth ↓ ambr tsm1 anan oss• androc srj1• arg-n vh* *Ars* k* *Aur-m-n* wbt2• *Aur-s* wbt2• *Bar-c* k* calc oss• calc-f ckh1 calc-p vh3* calc-s a carb-v fyz carc vh* caust j5.de chel vh chinin-s mrr1 **Cocc** k* cupr sht*• *Dulc* k* falco-pe nl2• *Ferr* hr1 fl-ac vh germ-met srj graph ckh1 hep h2* irid-met srj5• *Manc* gk merc j naja a1 nat-c fyz *Nux-v* vh* perh jl3 ph-ac gl1.fr• **Phos** k* sacch ↓ sep ckh1 *Staph* vh* *Sulph* tritic-vg fd5.de vanil fd5.de [calc-m stj1]
  - **loved** persons: aeth gk sacch sht• *Tritic-vg* fd5.de vanil fd5.de
- **overheated**; when: *Ruta* mrr1
- **pains**, from the: *Acon* alet ↓ apoc vh1 *Ars* k* bar-m ↓ bell b4a.de bell-p-sp ↓ bry k2 calc ↓ carb-v k* carc mlr1• **Caust** k* *Cham* b7a.de coff b7a.de *Coloc* h2* cupr ↓ daph ↓ dulc fd4.de gink-b ↓ graph ↓ haem ↓ kali-s ↓ lac-loxod-a hrn2• lap-la ↓ mag-p ↓ manc ↓ mela ↓ mez ↓ *Nat-c* k* nit-ac k2 **Phos** vh* phys ↓ pip-n ↓ plumbg ↓ psil ft1 rhod b4a.de sars hr1 *Sil* ↓ spig ↓ *Spong* fd4.de sulph ↓ vanil fd5.de *Verat* b7a.de
  - **cancer**; of: carc mlr1•
  - ○ **Abdomen**: calc vh *Cham* bro1 cupr h2 dulc fd4.de mag-p bro1 mez h2 spig h1 spong fd4.de
  - **Anus**: alet hr1 mela a1 *Nit-ac* hr1 phos h2 pip-n c1 *Sil* bg
  - **Chest**; in the: gink-b sbd1• *Spong* fd4.de vanil fd5.de
- **pains**, from the: ...
  - **Eyes**: manc a1 phys a1 plumbg a1 spig h1
  - **Heart**; in the: daph a1 gink-b sbd1• haem ↓ kali-s ↓ lap-la sde8.de• spig kr spong fd4.de vanil ↓ [bell-p-sp dcm1]
    - **inspiration**; on deep: spig kr
    - **Region** of: haem a1 kali-s fd4.de spong hr1 vanil fd5.de
  - **Stomach**: bar-m j dulc fd4.de graph h2 nit-ac bro1 sulph h2
- **paralyzed**, as if: am-m hr1* cob-n mg1.de*
- **paroxysms**, in: **Acon** ckh1 *Aloe* kr1* alum ckh1 ars h2* bar-c ckh1 bell ckh1 calc a1* calc-i k1 cann-i ckh1 *Carb-v* hr1* *Carc* mlr1• *Cham* h1* *Cocc* ckh1 cupr h2* *Cupr-act* kr1 ferr ckh1 *Hyos* hr1* ign ckh1 nat-c h2* nat-s ckh1 nit-ac phos j5.de plat ckh1 rhus-g tmo3• sep h2* spong h1* *Sulph* h2* *Tab* ckh1 thuj ckh1 urol-h rwt•
- **periodical**: am k* *Ars Calc-i* k2* camph tl1 *Cham* cocc nat-c k* nat-m *Phos* plat *Sep* k* spong *Sulph* verb ↓
  - **day**; every: nat-c a1 verb kr1
- **perspiration**:
  - **agg.**: (non:aq-mar jl3)
  - **amel.**: agar a1* aq-mar jl* calc h2*
  - **cold**, with: acon kr1 am-c j5.de ars a1 *Crot-h* kr1 euph-c sf1.de *Ferr* kr1 ferr-m j5.de *Nux-v* kr1 *Plb* j5.de* sep j5.de *Tab* kr1 verat kr1
  - **during**: acon bg2 *Alum* b4a.de* ant-c b7.de* am b7.de* **Ars** b4a.de* *Bar-c* bg2 *Bell* bg2 benz-ac bg2* bov bg2 bry b7.de* **Calc** b4.de* canth bg2 carb-v bg2 caust bg2 **Cham** b7.de* **Chin** bg2 cic bg2 *Coff* bg2 croc b7.de* **Ferr** b7a.de* fl-ac bg2 granit-m ↓ graph bg2 hep bg2 ign b7.de* kali-n b4a.de* kreos b7a.de* lyc bg2 m-arct b7.de **Mang** b4a.de* merc bg2* *Merc-c* bg2 mez bg2 mur-ac bg2 **Nat-c** b4a.de* nat-m bg2 nit-ac bg2 *Nux-v* b7.de* **Ph-ac** bg2 phos b4a.de* *Plb* b7.de* *Puls* b7a.de* rheum bg2 *Rhus-t* b7.de* sabad b7.de* *Sel* b7a.de* **Sep** b4a.de* sil bg2 *Spong* b7.de* *Stann* bg2 staph b7.de* stram b7.de* **Sulph** b4a.de* **Thuj** bg2 *Verat* bg2
    - **hands**; with perspiration and trembling of: cic h1 granit-m es1•
- **playing** piano, while: *(↗Fear - piano; Music - agg.)* *Nat-c* k*
- **pneumonia**; in: verat-v mrr1
- **pollutions**; after: carb-an k* petr k* *Phos* kr1
- **pregnancy**, in: *(↗Fear - pregnancy)* acon hr1* *Ant-t* hr1* bar-c hr1* con bg2 ign hr1* kali-br hr1 psor hr1* stann hr1*
- **present**, about: calc-act a1 chel h1* *Con* gl1.fr• *Iod* br1* [merc-i-f stj2]
- **pressure**; from:
  - ○ **Chest**; on: *Acon* kr1 aur h2 bell h1 **Carb-v** kr1 coca kr1 *Dig* kr1 *Ign* vh* *Lach* vh* ph-ac kr1 *Plat* kr1 *Psor* kr1 sabad kr1 **Sulph** *Tab* kr1
  - **Epigastrium**; in: cham j con h2 crot-t a1 guaj h2 lyc bg nux-v hr1 sang a1
  - **Throat**; in: plut-n srj7•
- **pulsation** in the abdomen, with: alum h2* calc vh cann-s a1 lyc h2
- **pursued**, as if: *(↗Delusions - persecuted; Delusions - pursued; Insanity - persecution)* anac a1* cypra-eg sde6.de• dros mtf33 hyos sf1.de* kali-br sf1.de lac-e hrn2• spong fd4.de [zinc stj2 zinc-i stj2 zinc-m stj2 zinc-n stj2 zinc-p stj2]
  - **walking**, when: *(↗GENERALS - Walking - Rapidly - amel.)* *Anac* k*
- **railroad**, but amel. while in train; when about to journey by: *(↗Ailments - anticipation)* arg-n k2 ars
- **reading**: *(↗Reading - agg.)*
  - **preventing**: quas a1
  - **while**: *Mag-m* k* *Sep*
- **reassured**; is easily (See Reassured - easily - anxious)
- **respiration**; anxious (See RESPIRATION - Anxious)
- **respiration**; with impeded: acon b7.de* *Anac* b4a.de ant-t b7.de* am b7.de* ars b4.de* cann-s b7a.de *Cina* b7a.de *Colch* b7a.de croc b7.de* dys fmm1• ger-i rly4• ign b7a.de kali-n b4a.de lach b7a.de **Lob** mrr1 lyc b4.de* *Nit-ac* b4a.de *Nux-v* b7.de* op b7a.de phos b4a.de* *Plat* b4a.de puls b7.de* rhus-t b7.de* ruta b7.de* sabad b7a.de samb b7a.de *Sars* b4a.de spig b7a.de spong fd4.de stann b4.de* staph b7a.de thiam rly4• *Thuj* b4a.de valer b7.de* vanil fd5.de verat b7.de* viol-o b7.de* viol-t b7.de* [bell-p-sp dcm1 heroin sdj2]
  - **hysterical** women; in: acon vh1
- **rest**, during: act-sp kr1* hist sp1 iod k2* seneg a1
- **retarding** the action of the remedy: merc-i-f kr1
- **retching**; with: ars ↓ bar-m a1* bism ↓ cupr ↓ podo ↓
  - **ineffectual** retching: ars bro1 bism bro1 cupr bro1 podo bro1

- **riding**, while: *(↗Riding - carriage - aversion)* acon↓ adam↓ *Arg-n* hr1* ars↓ *Aur Borx* carc↓ falco-pe↓ *Lach* k* lyc↓ nat-m↓ phos↓ psor k* sep stram↓ vanil fd5.de
  - **amel.**: aq-mar skp7•
  - **down** hill: **Borx** k* *Psor*
  - **driving** himself; when: acon gb• arg-n fd* borx gb• falco-pe nl2• lyc gb• nat-m gb• phos fd* stram gb•
  - **fast** in a car: *(↗Fear - driving a)* adam srj5• ars mrr1 carc az1.de* vanil fd5.de
- **rising**:
  - **after**: arg-n carb-an k* chel k* m-ambo h1 mag-c k* nat-m a1 rhus-t
  - **lying**, from: alum c1 verat h1
  - **seat**; from a: berb k* verat
    - **amel.**: carb-an h2 mill
- **rocking**, during: *(↗children - in - rocking)* **Borx** kr1*
- **room**, on entering a: alum h2
- **salvation**, about: *(↗conscience; Delusions - doomed; Delusions - lost - salvation; Despair - religious; Doubtful - salvation; Religious - too)* ant-c br1 aq-mar jl3 **Ars** ars-s-f k2* **Aur** k* aur-ar k2 aur-s k2* *Calc* k* *Calc-ar* k2* calc-s *Camph* cann-i carbn-s chel coloc↓ *Graph* k* hura ign kali-p **Lach** k* **Lil-t** k* *Lyc* k* *Med* merc↓ *Mez* nat-m nux-v gl1.fr* olib-sac wmh1 ph-ac gl1.fr* plat plb k2* podo k2* *Psor Puls Staph* gl1.fr* *Stram* k* **Sulph** k* *Thuj* k* **Verat**
  - **morning**: psor
  - **night**: calc-ar k2*
  - **faith**, about loss of his: coloc gl1.fr• merc gl1.fr• nux-v gl1.fr• staph gl1.fr• sulph gl1.fr•
  - **hell**, of: *Plat* kr1
  - **scrupulous** (= religious scruples): ars gl1.fr• ign gl1.fr• lyc gl1.fr• nux-v gl1.fr• ph-ac↓ puls gl1.fr• staph gl1.fr• **Sulph** gl1.fr•
    - **practices**; as to their religious: ign gl1.fr• *Lyc* gl1.fr• ph-ac gl1.fr• **Staph** gl1.fr• sulph gl1.fr•
- **screaming** (See Shrieking - anxiety)
- **secrets** revealed: lac-e hm2•
- **sedentary** life; from: *Ars* graph
- **sewing**: *Sep* k*
- **sexual** desire; from suppressed: con mrr1* **Staph** vh*
- **shaving**, while: calad k*
- **shivering**; during: *Acon* b7a.de *Ars* b4a.de **Calc** b4a.de caps b7.de ign b7.de puls b7.de
- **shuddering**, with: *(↗GENERALS - Shuddering)* *Ars* vh* bell calc carb-an h2* carb-v k* **Hell** vh* kreos j nat-c olib-sac wmh1 plat puls sulph a1 tab verat
- **sitting**: ant-t j5.de benz-ac carb-an *Caust* dig digin a1 *Graph Iod* vh* kreos j nit-ac ph-ac phos puls rhus-t↓ sil staph h1 tarax
  - **amel.**: *(↗Sitting - inclination)* iod
  - **bent**: rhus-t
    - **forward** amel.: chinin-ar hr1*
  - **up** in bed amel.: spong kr1
- **sleep**:
  - **before**: alum k* ambr berb k* calad k2 lac-h sze9• *Mag-c* nat-c *Rhus-t* st sil *Sulph* gk
    - **evening**: berb k*
  - **during**: acon agar ang arn **Ars** k* aster kr1 *Bell* k* bry j camph castm cham *Cocc* k* con cycl dig dor a1 dulc ferr k* gala br1 *Graph* hep k* ip h1 *Kali-c Kali-i* kr1 kali-n j *Lyc* mag-c j merc *Merc-c* b4a.de* merc-i-r a1 *Nat-c* j5.de *Nat-m Nit-ac* nux-v op petr k* *Phos* phys puls ran-b bg2 rhod a1 rhus-t samb sil a1 *Spong* stann h2 stram verat zinc kr1
  - **going** to, on: acon *Calc* carb-v k2 *Caust* cench haliae-lc srj5• hep *Lach* lil-s a1 *Lyc* merc nat-m *Puls* quas a1 rhus-t
  - **loss** of: *Calc* vh* *Carc* mlr1• *Cocc Nit-ac*
  - **menses** | **after**: *(↗Menses - after)* agar aster **Cocc** *Kali-i Merc-c* zinc
  - **partial** sleep in the morning; during: juni-v k*
  - **preventing** (See SLEEP - Sleeplessness - anxiety)
  - **starting** from, on: am-m kr1 apis gt clem cystein-l rly4• ruta fd4.de samb
- **soup** | **after**: *Mag-c* ol-an
- **speaking**, when: alum *Ambr* (non:aq-mar jl) *Hell* vh* irid-met srj5• ketogl-ac rly4• nat-c k* plat stram
  - **amel.**: aq-mar skp7•
  - **company**, in: *(↗Timidity - public; Timidity - public - talk)* irid-met srj5• plat
- **standing**, while: aloe anac berb k* cina ph-ac sil *Verat*
  - **amel.**: calc phos tarax
- **still**; when keeping: iod k2*
- **stitching** in spine, from: ruta h1
  - **sitting**; while: ruta hr1
- **stomach**; felt in (See STOMACH - Anxiety)
- **stool**:
  - **after**: acon ant-c bg2 ars b4a.de *Borx* k1* *Calc* k* carb-v k* *Caust* k* coloc crot-t k* jatr-c *Kali-c* b4a.de* kali-i lach bg2 laur merc k* nat-c st1 **Nat-s** st1 *Nit-ac* k* nux-v rhus-t
    - **bloody**: kali-c h2*
  - **as** for stool: cham h1* sep h2*
  - **before**: acon k* ambr k* ant-c *Ars* k* bar-c k* berb *Borx Bov* cadm-s k* calc calen a1* canth k* caps k* caust k* cham k* crot-h bg2 crot-t haliae-lc srj5• kali-ar kali-c k* mag-m k* *Merc* k* mez k* rhus-t sabin sul-i bg2 **Verat** k*
  - **during**: acon ant-c b7a.de ars k* ars-s-f k2* calen hr1* camph canth caust k* cham jal hr1* kali-c h2* mag-c merc merc-c k2 mez bg2 plat raph *Rheum* b7a.de sec k* sep stram sulph k* tab *Verat* k*
  - **ineffectual** desire for stool; from: **Ambr** k* **Caust** kr1
  - **straining** at, while: *Caust*
- **stooping**: bell rheum
  - **amel.**: bar-m
- **stormy** weather (See weather - stormy)
- **strangers**, in the presence of: *(↗Stranger - presence - agg.)* *Ambr* vh* bar-c vh *Carb-v* stram k*
- **studying**, while: sel vh*
- **success**; anxiety from doubt about: *(↗Confidence - want; Delusions - fail; Delusions - succeed; Fear - failure; Succeeds; Undertaking - nothing)* aloe a1 *Lac-c* kr1 ruta a1
- **sudden**: ang hr1* bar-c chel a1* *Cocc* k* granit-m es1• hep ictod kr1 lac-lup hm2• lat-m bnm6• nat-m h2* plat k* plut-n srj7• *Puls* ruta kr1 *Tab* k* thuj k* tritic-vg fd5.de
- **suicidal** disposition, with: *(↗Fear - suicide; Suicidal - anxiety)* *Aur* bell j carc mlr1• caust chin j *Dros* hep *Merc* nux-v plat *Puls Rhus-t* staph
- **supper** | **after**: caust h2 mag-c mag-m mrr1 nux-v
- **suppressed**: dioxi rbp6
- **swoon**, after: ars-s-f k2
- **talking** in public; of (See Timidity - public - talk)
- **taste** in mouth; with bitter: plut-n srj7•
- **teeth**; during complaints of: clem b4a.de* coff b7a.de* mag-c bg2 olnd b7.de* *Puls* b7.de*
- **television** agg.: marb-w es1•
- **terrible** (See beside)
- **therapy** from anxiety; wants: ars gb• phos fd*
- **thinking** about it, from: *(↗Thinking - complaints - agg.)* alum ambr bry *Calc* caust con *Nit-ac* petr-ra shn4• staph tab
- **thoughts**, from: alum↓ calc clem↓ cocc↓ dulc fd4.de phos↓ rhus-t↓ sep↓ spong↓
  - **disagreeable**: phos h2* sep h2*
  - **sad**: alum h2 clem h2 cocc c1 rhus-t h1* spong fd4.de
- **thunderstorm** (See Fear - thunderstorm)
- **time** is set, if a: *(↗Ailments - anticipation; Anticipation; Conscientious)* *Alum* vh* aq-mar rbp6 *Arg-n* k* aur-ar mtf aur-m-n wbt2• bros-gau mrc1 carc gk6* coca-c↓ cupr sst3• dulc fd4.de galeoc-c-h gms1• gels kali-n mtf lac-del↓ lac-e hm2• med musca-d szs1 nat-m mrr1* olib-sac wmh1 sacch-a fd2.de* vanad dx
  - **appointment**; about next day's: coca-c sk4•
  - **wake** up on time; anxious to: lac-del hm2•
- **tobacco**, from smoking: petr sep k* symph fd3.de•
- **torturing**: ars-s-f j5.de* chin j5.de graph j5.de phos j5.de
- **touched**; anxiety from being: ant-c sf1.de am sf1.de cina sf1.de hep sf1.de
- **travelling**; before: arg-n mtf aur mtf aur-m mtf borx mtf caust mtf ign mtf lach mtf mag-c mtf sep mtf sil mtf sulph mtf tab mtf

- **trembling**; with (See GENERALS - Trembling - externally - anxiety - from)
- **trifles**, about: *(↗Trifles; Trifles - important)* abies-c oss4• acer-circ oss• acon tl1 **Aloe** sne anac k* ang vh *Ars* k* aur k2 bar-act a1 bar-c k* borx bung-fa mtf calc k* calc-i k2* caust *Chin* k* coca-c sk4• cocc k* colch rsj2• *Con* k* dream-p sdj1• dys fmm1• *Ferr* k* granit-m es1• graph hydrog srj2• *Ign* mtf kali-chl k13 kali-m k2 kali-sil k2* lac-h sk4• laur a1 limest-b es1• mang k2 mur-ac tl1 nat-m mtf nux-v k* plut-n srj7• sacch-a fd2.de• sep mtf *Sil* k* sulph mtf thuj mtf verat mtf
- **tunnel**: *Arg-n*↓ *Lyc*↓ **Stram** vh*
  - **train** is in a tunnel; when the: *Arg-n* vh* *Lyc* vh* **Stram** st
- **unexpressed**: *Adren* vh1
- **untidiness** and chaos; about: falco-pe nl2•
- **urination**:
  - **after**: dig
  - **before**: *Acon* bro1 alum bell b4a.de borx bro1 *Canth* bro1 dig hep b4a.de ph-ac k* sep
  - **during**: acon k* carb-v bg2 *Cham* k* dig bg2 graph bg2 ph-ac bg2
  - **resisted**; when the desire is: sep h2
  - **urging** to; with: *Cham* h1
- **vaccination**; after: *Thuj* kr1*
- **vexation**: | **after**: acon bov j cham bg2 lyc k* phos sep staph verat k* zinc j
- **voice**, on raising the: cann-s k*
- **vomiting**, on: ant-c h2* ant-t bg2 ars bg2* ars-h a1 asar h1* bar-m bg2 bry bg2 cupr bg2 cupr-act j dig bg2 dulc h2* germ-met srj5• gran a1 *Ign* bg2 kali-bi bg2 *Kali-c* bg2 merc bg2 nit-ac bg2* nux-v j* plat bg2 samb hr1 sang bg2 seneg bg2* tab bg2* tarax bg2 tong a1 vip j
  - **before**: sang a1
- **waking**, on: *(↗SLEEP - Waking - anxiety)* acon agar *Agn* st *Alum* alum-sil k2* am-c am-m anac h2* aq-mar↓ arg-met j5.de arg-n *Arn* k* **Ars** k* ars-h hr1* ars-s-f k2* aster bapt bell bism k* borx k* bov a1 bry j5.de bufo *Cact* calc calc-ar k2* calc-s *Caps* st carb-an k* *Carb-v* k* *Carbn-s* carneg-g rwt1• cartl-s rly4• castm j5.de caust k* chel a1 *Chin* k* chinin-ar cina cocc con k* cub dig *Dios* hr1* dream-p sdj1• *Dros* k* elaps fkr8.de ephe-si hsj1• ger-i rly4• glon bg2* *Graph* k* hep ign ip iris kali-ar kali-bi *Kali-c* kali-p kali-s **Lach** k* lepi k* lept lyc k* mag-c nat-ar nat-c nat-m nat-p *Nat-s* hr1* nat-sil k2* nicc j5.de nit-ac *Nux-v* ph-ac *Phel* j5.de *Phos* k* plac-s rly4• plat psor al2 puls ran-s j5.de rat rhus-t *Samb* k* sep sil k* sol-ni a1 sol-t-ae k* *Spong* k* squil *Stram* *Stront-c* j5.de suis-pan rly4• *Sulph* k* suprar rly4• tab j5.de ter a1 thuj tub bg* verat j5.de xan bg zinc zinc-p k2* [heroin sdj2]
  - **agg.**: agar jl (non:aq-mar jl3)
- **walking**:
  - **after**: asc-t a1 dig a1
  - **agg.**: acon aloe alum *Anac* k* ant-c aq-mar jl1 arg-met *Arg-n* bar-c bell cina clem hep ign *Lyc* manc mang nux-v plat spong staph tab
  - **air**, in open: *Anac* arg-met *Arg-n* bell cina k* hep ign **Lyc** nux-v plat spong tab
    - **amel.**: cann-i k2 *Iod* *Kali-i* *Kali-s* **Puls** k* *Rhus-t* *Sep* vh*
  - **amel.**: androc srj1• aq-mar jl* calc-act h1 hist mg1.de* *Puls* vh* *Sep* vh* sil h2* staph h1*
  - **cold** air; in: nux-m a1
  - **rapidly**: *(↗Walking - rapidly - agg.)*
    - **agg.**: nit-ac *Staph* k* tarent bg1*
    - **makes** him walk faster; which: *(↗Hurry - walking; Restlessness - anxious - walking - rapidly; Walking - rapidly - agg.)* arg-met h1 **Arg-n** k* fl-ac bg1* galeoc-c-h gms1• sep bg1*
- **warm** bed; yet limbs cold if uncovered: **Mag-c**
- **warmth**:
  - **from**: gamb **Kali-s** k* *Puls*
  - **amel.**: *Graph* *Phos*
- **weariness**; with: ant-c sf1.de *Aur* j5.de bell j5.de carc mlr1• caust j5.de chin j5.de dros j5.de hep j5.de *Lach* kr1 merc sf1.de *Nux-v* j5.de plat j5.de *Puls* j5.de rhus-t j5.de sil sf1.de spong j5.de staph j5.de
- **weather**:
  - **rain**; about: calc ckh1 *Elaps* ckh1 haliae-lc srj5•

Anxiety – weather: ...

  - **stormy** weather; during: *(↗Fear - thunderstorm; Fear - wind)* falco-pe nl2• gels lp* lac-c mrr1 *Lyc* hr1* nat-c j5.de nat-m j nit-ac h2* *Oscilloc* jl2 phos j* *Rhod* mrr1 tritic-vg fd5.de
- **weeping** amel.: *(↗Weeping - amel.; Weeping - anxiety)* aster kr1 dig graph phos h2* *Tab* k1*
- **wind** on head; direct | **amel.**: aq-mar skp7•
- **wine**; after: coff k2
- **work**:
  - **inclination** to work; anxiety with: calc j5.de* chir-fl gya2
  - **manual** (See manual)
  - **preventing** work; anxiety: mosch a1
  - **unfit** for work; fear of becoming (See Fear - unfit)
- **working**, while: *Graph* j5.de iod bg
- **world**; for the: agath-a nl2• androc srj1•
- **wringing** of hands; with: *Asar* mrr1
- **wrong** things; he has said (See Fear - talking - say)

○ - **Bladder**; with pain in (See BLADDER - Pain - anxiety)

APATHY (See Inactivity; Indifference)

APHASIA: *(↗Forgetful - words; Mistakes - names; Mistakes - speaking; Speech - wandering; GENERALS - Paralysis - one - aphasia)* agar↓ alum↓ am-m kr1* *Anac*↓ *Anac-oc*↓ ant-m kr1* ant-t kr1* apis↓ arag↓ *Arg-n* kr1* arn↓ *Ars* kr1* arum-m kr1* bar-act kr1* *Bar-c* kr1* bell ptk1 bold kr1* *Both* k* *Calc* kr1* calc-p↓ cann-i↓ canth↓ *Caust* bg2* cham bg2* *Chen-a* kr1* chin↓ cimic kr1* *Colch* bg2* con kr1* crot-c↓ crot-h kr1* cupr kr1* dios↓ dulc↓ elaps bg2* falco-pe nl2• galla-q-r nl2• *Glon* k* hydr kr1* hyos kr1* *Ip*↓ *Kali-br* bg2* kali-cy c2* kali-fcy kr1* *Kali-m* kr1* *Kali-p* kr1* lac-c↓ *Lach* bg2* laur kr1* lil-t↓ *Lyc* bg2* *Mag-c* kr1* *Merc* kr1* mez kr1* naja bg2* nat-f kr1* **Nit-ac** kr1* *Nux-m* kr1* *Nux-v* kr1* oci vh oena kr1* olnd kr1* onos bg* op↓ ph-ac↓ *Phos* kr1* plb kr1* podo kr1* positr nl2• *Psor* jl2 puls bg2* rat c2 rhus-t kr1* stram bg2* sulfon kr1* sumb↓ *Syph* kr1* tab kr1* thal-xyz srj8• xero↓ zinc kr1*

- **amnesia**, with: agar bro1 alum bro1 *Anac* bro1 arag bro1 arg-n bro1 arn bro1 calc bro1 calc-p bro1 cann-i bro1* cham bro1 chin bro1 dios bro1 dulc bro1 **Kali-br** a1* lac-c bro1 lil-t bro1 *Lyc* bro1 *Nux-m* bro1 ph-ac bro1 plb br1* sumb bro1 xero bro1
- **apoplexy**: | **after**: *(↗MOUTH - Speech - wanting - apoplexy)* *Ars* kr1* *Bar-c* kr1 both mtf11 crot-c mrr1 *Crot-h* kr1 *Ip* kr1 *Kali-br* kr1 **Nux-v** kr1* *Oena* kr1 *Plb* kr1 **Stram** kr1
- **comprehension** of speech lost, but can speak oneself: elaps br1*
- **exerts** long before uttering a word: **Stram** jsa
- **fear**, after: cupr jsa hyos ptk1
- **fever**; with typhoid-like: apis ptk1 ars ptk1 op ptk1 *Stram* ptk1
- **imbecility**, in: *Anac-oc* kr1
- **paralysis**; with:
  - **one** side: both br1
  - **right** side; of: both fne1• canth ptk1 chen-a ptk1
- **pronounce** any word told, but cannot speak otherwise; can: kali-br br1
- **stomach** pain; from: laur ptk1
- **swallowing** possible; but: *Hep* b4a.de

○ - **Tongue**:
  - **paralysis** of tongue; with: caust mtf33 stram kr1* syph kr1*
  - **protrusion** of tongue; with: syph kr1*
- **Upper** limbs:
  - **numbness** of; with | **right**: mur-ac ptk1
- **Uterus**; with displacement of: nit-ac ptk1

APLOMB (See Confident)

APPEARANCE; PERSONAL (See Personal)

APPRECIATION; longing for (See Delusions - appreciated; Lamenting - appreciated)

APPREHENSIONS (See Anxiety; Fear)

APPROACHED by persons; being: *(↗Estranged - family)*

- **agg.**: *(↗aversion; Fear - approaching - others; Touched - aversion)* *Arn* bg2 *Bry* vh* con bg2 ign bg2 lyc bg2 **Phos** vh* stry bg2

- **aversion** to: *(↗agg.; Escape; Estranged; Fear - approaching - others)* **Ant-c** ptk1 *Arn* ptk1* aur brass-n-o srj5• *Bry* vh* caj canth c1 **Cham** ptk1 cina dg* con ptk1 cupr ptk1* germ-met srj5• granit-m es1• hell helon hipp ign ptk1 *Iod* kali-c ptk1 kola stb3• lil-t *Lyc* k1* ruta fd4.de sanic c1* sil ↓ sulph tarent ptk1 thuj ptk1 [tax jsj7]
  - **children**; in: cina mtf33 cupr sst3* sil mtf33

APPROVAL; desire for (See Delusions - appreciated; Delusions - neglected - he; Longing - good)

AQUAPHOBIA (See Fear - water)

ARACHNOPHOBIA (See Fear - spiders)

ARDENT: *(↗Anger; Elated; Exhilaration; Fanaticism; Impulsive; Irrational; Passionate [=choleric])* alum gl1.fr• apis vh1 ara-maca ↓ aur-m-n wbt2• *Carc* mrr1* caust mrr1* chin mrr1 ignis-alc es2• *Lach* mrr1 loxo-recl knl4• *Med* br1* *Merc* mrr1 nitro-o a *Nux-v* a1* petr-ra shn4• phos ctc* *Plat* mrr1 sanguis-s hrn2• stann gl1.fr• *Stram* mrr1 sulph br* sumb a vero-o rly3• [ant-m stj2 aur-m stj2 cadm-m stj2 chlor stj2 cob-m stj2 cupr-m stj2 lith-m stj2 merc-d stj2 plb-m stj2 rubd-met stj2 sol-ecl cky1 stront-m stj2]

- **desires** to be: ara-maca sej7•

ARGUING: *(↗Quarrelsome)*

- **facility** for: *(↗Quarrelsome)* nux-m c1
- **not** arguing: *(↗Quarrelling - aversion)* **Sil** ↓ staph mtf33
  - **convictions** and keeping them; despite of having firm: **Sil** mrr1

ARGUMENTATIVE (See Quarrelsome)

ARROGANCE (See Haughty)

ART:

- **ability** for: *(↗Activity - desires - creative; Intelligent - artistic; Painting - ability)* ambr gl1.fr• bell ↓ carc mlr* chin gg* euph gl1.fr• falco-pe nl2• med gk nat-c mrr4• nat-s mrr1 nit-ac ↓ phos vh* plb-act gl1.fr• sil mtf staph mtf33 sulph ctc* *Tub* vh*
  - **plastic** arts: bell gl1.fr• falco-pe nl2• nit-ac gl1.fr• sulph gl1.fr•
  - **poetry** (See Verses)
- **inability** for: *(↗Painting - inability)* bell gl1.fr• calc gl1.fr• hyos gl1.fr• lach mtf mag-c mtf33* nux-v ↓ petr gl1.fr• plat gl1.fr• staph gl1.fr• stram mtf33* verat mtf33* zinc mtf33*
  - **plastic** arts: calc gl1.fr• nux-v gl1.fr•

ASCETIC (See Self-control - increased)

ARTISTIC (See Art - ability)

ASCENDING agg.: **Ars** bg2 iod bg2 *Nit-ac* bg2

ASKING:

- **help**; never asking for: [card-m stj]
- **nothing**; for: *(↗Company - aversion; Confidence - want; Desires - nothing; Indifference; Quiet disposition; Reserved; Taciturn; Timidity; Wants - nothing)* alum gl1.fr• ant-c h2* ars a1 *Aur-m* vh* *Bry* k* cocc a1 hell st1 hep a1 hyos gl1.fr• lim a1 (non:linu-c a1) mez a1 mill a1 nicc a1 *Op* k* puls k* rheum k* sep vh *Tritic-vg* fd5.de [card-m stj uva stj]
- **same** thing; constantly the | **time**; the: des-ac rbp6 marb-w es1• tritic-vg fd5.de

ASSERTIVE (See Confident)

ASSURANCE:

- **excess** of assurance (See Confident)
- **want** of assurance (See Confidence - want)

ASTONISHED: cann-i a1 cori-r a1 stram a1

ASTRAPHOBIA (See Fear - lightning; Fear - thunderstorm)

ATHLETICS; ability for: | **increased**: [buteo-j sej6]

ATTACHED: *(↗Clinging; Held - desire)*

- **father**; children are attached to the: cycl dgt
- **strongly** to others: *(↗Affectionate)* carc mrr1 nat-s mrr1

ATTACK others, desire to: *(↗Fight; Striking)* *Dulc* fd4.de **Hyos** vh* lyss a1 nux-v ↓ sep ↓ **Stram** vh* **Tarent** vh*

ATTENDED to; to be: | **desire** (See Watched - desires)

ATTENTION (See Consolation)

ATTENTION DEFICIT HYPERACTIVE DISORDER (See Concentration - difficult; Restlessness)

ATTENTION SEEKING behavior (See Forsaken)

ATTITUDES (See Gestures - strange)

ATTRACTING others: | **insane** people in the street; attracting: rhus-g tmo3•

AUDACITY: *(↗Contradiction - disposition; Courageous; Danger - no; Defiant; High-spirited; Impertinence; Insolence; Meddlesome; Positiveness; Precocity; Presumptuous; Rash; Rudeness; Temerity)* acon agar k* agath-a nl2• androc ↓ ant-t hr1* arizon-l nl2• *Arn* st1 *Aur* ↓ bamb-a stb2.de• bell ↓ calad hr1* *Caps* ↓ carc mrr1 caust ↓ falco-pe nl2• fl-ac ↓ gal-ac ↓ galla-q-r nl2• gels ↓ hep gl1.fr• **Ign** gl1.fr• ignis-alc es2• *Lyss* ↓ m-arct j5.de **Med** ↓ merc k* mur-ac ↓ nat-m ↓ nitro-o a1 op ozone sde2• petr-ra shn4• plat stj2*• pot-e rly4• *Puls* ↓ ribo rly4• sep ↓ sil mtf33 spong ↓ staph mtf33* stram ↓ sulph ↓ tarent ↓ *Tub* ckh1* *Tung-met* bdx1• ulm-c jsj8• verat mtf33 [heroin sdj2 tax jsj7]

- **children**; in: **Agar** lmj androc lmj **Arn** lmj *Aur* lmj bell lmj *Caps* lmj caust lmj fl-ac lmj gal-ac lmj gels lmj *Lyss* lmj **Med** lmj mur-ac lmj nat-m lmj *Puls* lmj sep lmj spong lmj **Staph** lmj stram lmj sulph lmj tarent lmj tub lmj

AUTISM: *(↗Ailments - forced; Development; Indifference - surroundings; Monomania; Reserved; Retardation; Ritualistic; Taciturn; Talking - himself)* agar ↓ bar-c vh1 bufo mtf cact vwe kali-br mrr1 lyc mtf33 olib-sac wmh1 secret mtf *Tub* mrr1*

- **children**; in: agar mtf33 bufo mtf33 lyc mtf33 tub mtf33

AUTOMATIC gestures (See Gestures - automatic)

AUTOMATISM (See Gestures - automatic; Unconsciousness - conduct)

AUTOPHOBIA (See Fear - alone)

AVARICE: *(↗Anxiety - business; Bargaining; Delusions - business - doing; Delusions - fortune; Delusions - money - counting; Delusions - money - sewed; Delusions - money - talks; Delusions - poor; Delusions - ruined - is; Delusions - starve - being; Delusions - starve - family; Delusions - want - he; Delusions - want - they; Delusions - wealth; Desires - full - more; Envy; Fear - poverty; Fear - starving; Greed; Jealousy; Rich - desire; Selfishness; Ungrateful - avarice; GENERALS - Starving)* alum gl1.fr• **ARS** b2.de* bar-c j bry k* calc k* calc-f k* carb-an gl1.fr• carb-v gl1.fr• carc mlr1• caust gl1.fr• cina coloc con gl1.fr• cypra-eg sde6.de• *Dulc* gk gink-b sbd1• granit-m ↓ graph gl1.fr• hep gl1.fr• hyos gl1.fr• lach gl1.fr• *Lyc* k* marb-w es1• med ptk1 meli **Merc** vh* nat-c k* nat-m gl1.fr• nit-ac gl1.fr• nux-v gl1.fr• petr gl1.fr• petr-ra shn4• *Ph-ac* gl1.fr• phos j plat b4a.de* psor gk* **Puls** k* rheum k* *Sep* k* **Sil** mtf33* spong fd4.de stann gl• staph gl1.fr• sulph bg3* tritic-vg fd5.de

- **alternating** with | **squandering** (See Squandering - alternating - avarice)
- **anxiety** about future; avarice from: *(↗Anxiety - future)* *Bry* vh* granit-m es1• *Nux-v* gl1.fr• *Ph-ac* gl1.fr• *Psor* vh* stann gl1.fr•
- **expensive**; everything seems to: lach pc sep pc sil pc spong fd4.de
- **generosity** towards strangers, avarice as regards his family: *(↗Estranged - family; Indifference - loved - strangers)* carb-v gl1.fr• hyos gl1.fr• nat-m gl1.fr• *Nux-v* gl1.fr*
- **squandering** on oneself, but: *(↗Squandering)* calc gl1.fr• hyos gl1.fr• marb-w es1• nux-v gl1.fr• sep gl1.fr•

AVERSION: *(↗Disgust)*

- **affection** for anybody | **pregnancy**; has no affection during: acon kr1 *Sep* vh*
- **approached**; to be (See Approached - aversion)
- **around** him; to those: ars
- **bed**; to (See Bed - aversion)
- **children**, to: *(↗Escape - family; Hatred - children; Indifference - children; towards - mother; Striking - children; striking)* agn cda aster mgm• *Choc* srj *Con* ↓ foll ↓ glon ↓ heroin ↓ irid-met srj5• **Kali-i** ↓ lyc ptk1 medus mgm• *Nux-v* ↓ phos ↓ plat k* positr nl2• raph a1* sep vh verat ↓ xan mgm•
  - **beloved** children become suddenly burdensome for him; his: **Kali-i** kr1

- **get** children; to:
  - **interfere**; feels children will: *Plat* mrr1
  - **world** is so bad; as the: ign vh nat-m vh plat vh staph vh
- **little** girls; to: raph br1
  - **women**; in: raph
- **own**; her: aster vh *Choc* srj3• foll oss• glon k* *Lyc* k* *Nux-v* vh* phos ptk1* plat k* sep vh verat [heroin sdj2]
  - **guilty** feeling; with: aster vh
- **sadness**; from: *(↗Children - flies; Estranged - children)* *Con* kr1

- **colors** (See Colors - aversion)
- **cooking**: des-ac rbp6
- **computers**: dioxi rbp6
- **education**; to: sulph ptk1*
- **embraces** with oppressive sensation in chest: ozone sde2•
- **everything**, to: *(↗Disgust - everything; Indifference - answer)* alumn k* am-m k* ammc a1 ant-c b7a.de* **Apis** b7a.de ars b4.de* *Asar* b7.de* *Aur-m* vh* bamb-a stb2.de• bism h1* *Bov* bg2* calc k* camph b7.de* canth ptk1* caps k* cent a1 *Cocc* b7.de* coloc b4.de* cupr k* ferr a1 grat a1 hep b4a.de hydrog srj2• hyos k* ip k* kola stb3• lach k2* lyc a1 mag-c h2* mag-m a1* merc k* mez k* phos b4.de* plat a1 plb b7.de* plumbg a1 *Puls* k* rheum a1* rhod a1 rhus-t h1* ruta b7.de* sars h2* **Sep** bg2* spong h1* sulph k* thea a1 thuj k* [pop dhh1]
  - **daytime**: *Sep* a
  - **morning**: lyc a plb a
  - **forenoon**: sars h2*
  - **afternoon** | **13** h: grat a1
  - **dinner**; after: bov a
  - **sitting** idle; as soon as: calc kr1
  - **urticaria**; in: bov kr1
- **faces**; to laughing: m-aust c1
- **family**; to members of: *(↗Estranged - family; Unsympathetic - family)* am-c ↓ am-m bg2 aran ccrh1• aur bg2 *Calc* k* calc-s tl cit-ac alw con bg2* *Crot-h* k* *Fl-ac* k* haliae-lc srj5• ham fd3.de• hep bg2* iod ptk1 kali-c st* kali-m ckh1 kali-p bg2* kola stb3• lac-h sze9• lyc bg2* **Merc** bg2* *Nat-c* k* nat-m gl1.fr• nat-ox rly4• phasco-ci rbp2 phos bg2* plat bg2* plb vh* senec ptk1 **Sep** k* spong fd4.de [tax jsj7]
  - **dementia**; in incipient stage of: *Crot-h* kr1
  - **female**: am-c bg2
  - **others**; but talks pleasantly to: *(↗Behavior - children - home; Estranged - family - strangers)* fl-ac ptk1*
- **flowers**; smell of: graph a
- **friends**, to: *(↗Censorious - friends; Company - aversion - friends; Mocking - friends; Unsympathetic - friends)* acon ↓ anac lpc *Aur-m* vh* cedr k* coloc ptk1* *Con* ↓ ferr fl-ac k2* kali-m ccrh1* lac-h sze9• *Led* k* phasco-ci rbp2 pitu-a ft podo fd3.de• [merc-i-f stj2]
  - **pregnancy**, during: acon kr1 *Con* k*
- **fuss**; to: nat-m ptk1*
- **himself** (See Disgust - oneself)
- **husband**, to: *(↗men; to [=male persons] - women; Disgust - body - others - husband; Fear - men; of [=male; Hatred - husband)* adam srj5]● agncda bamb-a stb2.de• chir-fl gya2 choc srj3• *Glon* k* kali-c st1 kali-p *Kola* stb3• *Nat-c* k* nat-m nat-sil fd3.de• pitu-a ft sal-fr sle1• **Sep** k* thuj ptk1* verat k* [spect dfg1]
  - **children**; and: *Glon* kr1 *Verat* kr1
  - **coition**; during: adam srj5•
  - **menses**; before: adam srj
- **interference**, to (See Disturbed; Hindered; Interruption - aversion)
- **marriage**: *(↗Marriage; Marriage - unendurable)* puls k2
- **men**; to [=in general] (See persons - all)
- **men**; to [=male persons]: *(↗Fear - men; of [=male; Hatred - men; of = male; sensitive - noise - voices - male)* am-c↓] calch2 des-ac rbp6 graph bg2 lyc ↓ med ↓ nat-m a1* nat-sil ↓ **Puls** h1* raph ↓ sep ↓ staph ↓ sulph ↓ symph ↓

- **men** to: ...
  - **women**; in: *(↗husband; Delirium - fear; Delirium - fear - men; Fear - men; of [=male; Fear - sex; of; Hatred - men; of = male persons] - women; homosexuality; marriage - unendurable)* am-cj5.de* lyc gl3• med gk nat-m a1* nat-sil fd3.de• puls b7a.de* raph hr1 sep k2* staph bg2* sulph ↓ symph fd3.de•
    - **religious** aversion: *(↗Marriage - unendurable)* lyc k* *Puls* k* sulph k*
- **men**; to (↗old rubric) graph sf1.de stann kr1*
- **mother**, to: *(↗Hatred - mother)* positr nl2• taosc iwa1• thuj ptk1*
- **night**; of: bufo ptk1
- **objects**; to certain: puls hu
- **parents**, to: fl-ac gl1.fr•
- **persons**: *(↗Sensitive - certain)*
  - **agree** with him; to persons who do not (See Hatred - persons - agree)
  - **all**, to: *(↗Contemptuous; Hatred; Misanthropy)* absin a1* cadm-met gm1 calc gl1.fr• chin gl1.fr• cic ↓ ephe-si hsj1• germ-met srj hippoc-k szs2 *Merc* gl1.fr• merc-act gl• nat-m ckh1 *Nux-v* gl1.fr• phos h2 sep ckh1 stann h1* *Staph* gl1.fr• *Sulph* gl1.fr• taosc iwa1•
    - **contempt** for: cic a1
    - **loss** of confidence in: cic a1
    - **pregnancy**; during: sep vh
    - **shuns** the foolishness of: *(↗Humankind - shuns)* cic vml2*
  - **certain**, to: *(↗Prejudiced)* am-c j *Am-m* k* *Aur* b4a.de* aur-m-n wbt2• cadm-met gm1 **Calc** bg2* calc-p gk carc fb* caust gl1.fr• cic ↓ con bg2 crot-h k* fl-ac j* germ-met srj hep bg2* kali-p bg2 limest-b es1• lyc bg2 merc bg2* **Nat-c** k* nat-m mtf33* nat-sil fd3.de• nit-ac gl1.fr• phos bg2 plat bg2 plut-n srj7• sanic ↓ sel sep bg2* *Spong* fd4.de stann taosc iwa1• *Tub* ↓
    - **agree** with him; who don't (See Hatred - persons - agree)
    - **bed**; lying next to him in: sanic mg*
    - **causeless**: *Tub* jl2
    - **sight** of certain persons: cic ptk1
  - **happy** people; seeing (See Sadness - happy)
  - **literary**; to: sulph ptk1*
- **places**; to certain: hep ptk1*
- **plastic**; to: des-ac rbp6
- **raised**; to being: bry br1
- **sex**: *(↗Disgust - sex)*
  - **jokes**; to sexual (See Jesting - aversion - sexual)
  - **opposite** sex; to the (See men; to [=male persons] - women; women - men)
  - **own** sex; to one's own (See women - women)
  - **sexual** intercourse (See FEMALE - Sexual desire - wanting; MALE GENITALIA/SEX - Sexual desire - wanting)
- **shaving**: kola stb3• ozone sde2•
- **strangers** (See Company - aversion - strangers)
- **telephone** calls | **making**: rhus-g tmo3•
- **visits**; to: aloe a1 bell a1 ferr a1
- **waking** up; to: *Dioxi* rbp6
- **water**, to: *Am-c* bg2* kola stb3• *Lyss* vh*
- **wife**, to his: ars k2* *Fl-ac* k2* nat-s k2* plat k2* puls k2* sal-fr sle1• staph k2*
- **women**; to: *(↗men; Hatred - women; Homosexuality)* am-c bapt con vh* *Dios* k* fl-ac ↓ ign a1 *Lach* k* lyc fd1.de• mag-c a1 musca-d ↓ nat-m phos ↓ *Plat* ↓ *Puls* k* raph a1 sep ↓ staph ↓ sulph
  - **mannish**: fl-ac st
  - **men**; in: *(↗women; Delusions - women - evil; Fear - sex; of; Fear - women; Hatred - women - men; Homosexuality; Marriage - unendurable)* am-c j5.de* lyc fd1.de*• musca-d ↓ nat-m a1* phos ↓ *Plat* ↓ puls b7a.de* sep k2* staph bg2* sulph ↓
    - **homosexuality**; with: *(↗Homosexuality)* phos vh *Plat* gl1.fr• puls vh staph vh
    - **old** women: musca-d szs1
    - **religious** aversion: *(↗Hatred - women; Marriage - unendurable)* lyc k* *Puls* k* sulph
  - **women**; in: *Raph* k*

- **work** (See Laziness)

AWAKENING (See Waking)

AWARENESS heightened: *(↗Conflict - higher; SLEEP - Conscious)* *Anh*↓ ara-maca sej7• arizon-l↓ bung-fa mtf chlam-tr↓ *Falco-pe* nl2• *Galeoc-c-h*↓ galla-q-r nl2• haliae-lc↓ hydrog srj2• ina-i↓ irid-met↓ lac-lup↓ limen-b-c hrn2* loxo-recl↓ lyss mrr1 marb-w↓ olib-sac wmh1 podo fd3.de• positr nl2• ruta fd4.de sanguis-s hrn2• **Spong** fd* suis-pan rly4• taosc↓ tritic-vg fd5.de *Tung-met* bdx1• *Vanil* fd5.de [bell-p-sp dcm1 spect dfg1 tax jsj7 temp elm1]
- **animal** awareness: haliae-lc srj5• [spect dfg1]
- **birds**; of the presence of: loxo-recl knl4• marb-w es1• [spect dfg1]
- **body**; of: *(↗Schizophrenia - paranoid)* *Anh* mg1.de* chlam-tr↓ falco-pe↓ *Galeoc-c-h*↓ haliae-lc↓ ina-i mlk9.de irid-met srj5• lac-lup hrn2• marb-w es1• olib-sac wmh1 positr nl2• sanguis-s hrn2• taosc iwa1• tung-met bdx1•
  - **centred** in body; feels: haliae-lc srj5• olib-sac wmh1 positr nl2•
  - **sensuality**; with: falco-pe nl2•
  - **three** dimensional: positr nl2•
  - ○ **Eyes**: marb-w es1•
  - **Heart** beating: galeoc-c-h gms1•
  - **Nose** | **conscious** of having a nose: *Galeoc-c-h* gms1•
  - **Shoulders**; broadness of my: chlam-tr bcx2•
  - **Skin** surface: lac-lup hrn2•
- **colors**; of: loxo-recl knl4• [spect dfg1]
- **sex**; of the own: olib-sac wmh1
- **stillness**; with: falco-pe nl2•
- **thoughts** and feelings; of: arizon-l nl2• tritic-vg fd5.de

AWE (See Veneration)

AWKWARD: *(↗Answering - aversion - sings; Childish; Delusions - walking - cannot - run; Foolish; Gestures; Jesting - aversion; Laughing - constant; Laughing - immoderately; Laughing - serious; Laughing - silly; Laughing - trifles; Loquacity - answers; Mirth - foolish; Runs; Runs - things; Throwing things around - persons; EXTREMITIES - Awkwardness)* abrot bl adam srj5• aeth bg2* *Agar* bg2* aids nl2• alum↓ am-c↓ am-m↓ ambr bg2* *Anac* b4.de* androc srj1• ant-c bl **Apis** b7a.de* arg-n br1 ars-s-r↓ asaf bg2* asar b7.de bar-c ptk2* bit-ar↓ bov b4.de* bry↓ calc bg2* calc-f↓ *Camph* kr1 cann-i a* *Caps* b7.de* *Carb-v*↓ carbn-s a1 caust bl chir-fl↓ cocc b7.de* colch↓ *Con* bg2* cypra-eg sde6.de• cystein-l rly4• dendr-pol sk4• dulc fd4.de falco-pe nl2• fuma-ac rly4• galla-q-r nl2• *Gels* bg2* germ-met srj5• haliae-lc↓ ham fd3.de• hell bg2* hep vn10.fr hydrog srj2• hyos mtf33 *Ign* b7.de* ip b7.de* kali-c bg2 kali-chl c1 kali-p fd1.de• kali-s fd4.de ketogl-ac↓ lac-h htj1*• lac-leo hrn2• lac-loxod-a hrn2• lach bg2* lap-la↓ levo jl lil-t ptk *Lol* j5.de lyc bg2* mag-c↓ med ctc* mosch sf1.de musca-d szs1 *Nat-c* b4.de* *Nat-m* b4.de* nat-s j5.de *Nat-sil* fd3.de* nauf-helv-li elm2• neon srj5• **Nux-v** b7.de* olib-sac wmh1 op↓ oxal-a rly4• *Petr*↓ petr-ra shn4• ph-ac bg2 phos h2* plat↓ plb b7.de* plut-n↓ podo fd3.de• polys↓ positr nl2• puls lpc pycnop-sa↓ rheum bg2* *Ros-d* wla1 ruta fd4.de sabad b7a.de sabin b7a.de* sal-fr sle1• sars j5.de* sel↓ sep↓ sil k1* spong b7.de* stann b4.de* staph pc stram b7.de* suis-pan rly4• sul-ac↓ sulph j5.de* taosc iwa1• tarent↓ thuj a1* *Tritic-vg* fd5.de *Vanil* fd5.de verat b7a.de zinc↓ [heroin sdj2 lac-mat sst4 pop dhh1]
- **forenoon**: anac a1 dulc fd4.de
- **evening**: agar a1
- **anxiety**; with: aeth mtf33
- **accidents** prone (See Accident)
- **bashfulness**; from: *(↗Timidity - bashful)* *Bar-c* vh* calc gl1.fr• *Carb-v* mtf33 nat-c gl1.fr• nat-m gl1.fr• nux-v gl1.fr• sil mtf33* sulph mtf33*
- **breaking** things (See Breaking)
- **children**, in: *Caps* kr1 dulc fd4.de lyc mtf33 med mtf33 plb mtf33 rheum mtf33 thuj mtf33 *Vanil* fd5.de
- **drops** things: *(↗EXTREMITIES - Awkwardness - hands - drops)* aeth bro1* *Agar* bg2* *Ambr* ptk1 anac ptk1 **Apis** bg2* ars-s-r kr1 bar-c ptk1* bit-ar wht1• *Bov* j5.de* bry bg2 calc ptk1 calc-f↓ camph ptk1 **Caps** ptk1 caust ptk1 colch bg2 dulc fd4.de falco-pe nl2• ham fd3.de• hell bg2* ign bro1* ip ptk1 kali-s fd4.de ketogl-ac rly4• *Lach* bro1* lap-la sde8.de• levo jl lil-t ckh1 lol ptk1 mosch bg2* *Nat-m* j5.de* neon srj5• nux-v bg2* plat bg2 plut-n srj7• podo fd3.de• polys sk4• pycnop-sa mrz1 ros-d wla1 ruta fd4.de sal-fr sle1• sel rsj9• stann bg2 staph gl1.fr• tarent bg2* tritic-vg fd5.de *Vanil* fd5.de [heroin sdj2]
  - **menses**, before: *(↗Menses - before)* calc-f dgt

Awkward – drops things: ...
  - **pregnancy**; during: calc ptk1
- **gestures**, in (See Gestures - awkward)
- **haste**, from: *(↗Hurry - awkward)* alum gl1.fr• ambr gl1.fr• apis sf1.de* *Mosch* kr1* nat-m mtf33* sul-ac mrr1 sulph mtf33*
- **pregnancy**, during: **Calc** kr1
- **strikes** against things: *(↗Accident)* adam srj5• caps lpc chir-fl gya2 dulc fd4.de falco-pe nl2• haliae-lc srj5• hydrog srj2• hyos j5.de* ip j5.de* kali-p fd1.de• nat-m gl1.fr• *Nat-sil* fd3.de• neon srj5• nux-v j5.de* op lpc podo fd3.de• positr nl2• pycnop-sa mrz1 ros-d wla1 ruta fd4.de sep gl1.fr• taosc iwa1• tritic-vg fd5.de *Vanil* fd5.de [heroin sdj2]
- **tailoring**, dressmaking, embroidering; in: am-c gl1.fr• am-m gl1.fr• carb-v gl1.fr• con gl1.fr• mag-c gl1.fr• nat-m gl1.fr• nux-v gl1.fr• *Petr* gl1.fr• zinc gl1.fr•
- **working**, while: *Nat-sil* fd3.de• nux-v gl1.fr• puls gl1.fr• spong kr1* sulph kr1*

BACKWARDNESS (See Retardation)

BAD MOOD (See Irritability; Morose)

BAD NEWS (See Ailments - bad)

BAD PARTS; taking everything in (See Offended)

BAD TEMPER (See Anger)

BALANCE in life:
- **absent**; is (See Inconstancy)
- **need** for (See Inconstancy)

BARGAINING: *(↗Avarice; Greed)* bry vh* cypra-eg sde6.de• *Puls* vh* *Sil* vh* sulph vh*

BARKING: *(↗Growling; Howling)* alum↓ anac↓ *Bell* k* *Calc* k* calc-p↓ *Canth* k* cham tl1 **Cupr**↓ hell↓ *Hyos* vh* lyc↓ lyss mrr1 mag-m↓ nat-m↓ nux-m gl1.fr• nux-v↓ phos↓ stram k* sulph↓
- **bellowing**: *(↗Anger; Delirium - bellows)* bell k* *Canth* k* *Cupr* k* *Nux-m* vh* *Stram* a1
  - **convulsions** | **before**: **Cupr** mrr1
- **delirium**, during: *Bell* a1 *Canth* kr1
- **drinking** water agg.: canth br1
- **growling** like a dog: alum k* anac a1 *Bell* k* canth ptk1 hell *Hyos* vh* lyc k* lyss mag-m k* phos bg2*
  - **sleep**, during: lyc h2
- **incessant**: nat-m↓ sulph↓
- **paroxysmal**: canth br1
- **touched**; when | **Larynx**; at: canth br1

BASHFUL (See Timidity - bashful)

BASIC persons (See Simple; Unrefined)

BASPHOBIA (See Fear - walking - of)

BATHING: *(↗Swimming)*
- **aversion** to bathe: *(↗Washing - aversion)* am-c bg2* ant-c bg2 clem bg2 marb-w es1• nat-sil fd3.de• positr nl2• rhus-t bg2 sulph bg2* tritic-vg fd5.de
- **cold** | **amel.**: calc-p bg2 cycl bg2 euphr bg2
- **desire** to bathe: *(↗Washing - desire)* chir-fl gya2 positr nl2• ruta fd4.de spong fd4.de tarent a1 tritic-vg fd5.de zea-i st
- **foot**-bath; after: lyc bg2 nat-c b4.de* nat-m bg2 phos bg2 sep bg2 zinc bg2

BATTLES; talking about (See Talking - battles)

BEATING (See Striking)

BEAUTIFUL things:
- **awareness** of; heightened: chin mtf33 olib-sac wmh1 *Vanil* fd5.de
- **soul**; sensation of beauty of the: olib-sac wmh1
- **yearning** for: aeth ptk1 cur mtf ignis-alc es2• lil-t ptk1* *Olib-sac* wmh1 olnd ms petr-ra shn4• podo fd3.de• positr nl2• sulph ptk1* tritic-vg fd5.de *Vanil* fd5.de

BED:
- **aversion** to, shuns bed: *(↗Escape - jumps; Fear - bed - of)* *Acon* ars bapt calc camph cann-s canth caust *Cedr* k* cench cupr graph ptk1 kali-ar *Lach* k1* lec oss• lyc med mtf33 merc nat-c squil ulm-c jsj8•
- **changing** position: androc bnm2•
- **desire** to go to bed early: lavand-a ctl1•

- **fall** out; as if he would (See Delusions - bed - falling - out)
- **get** out of bed; wants to: *Bapt* kr1 *Bry* kr1 *Camph* kr1 cham ptk1 graph ptk1 **Hyos** kr1 lac-c ptk1 led ptk1 merc ptk1 verat ptk1 zinc kr1
  - **morning**; in the (See SLEEP - Waking - early)
  - **cerebrospinal** meningitis; in: *Verat* kr1
  - **chill**, during: *Hyos* kr1
  - **delivery**; during: cham kr1
- **in** bed:
  - **agg.**: am-c bg2 *Ars* b4.de* caust b4.de* graph b4.de* kali-c b4.de* mag-m b4.de* phos b4.de* rhod b4.de* *Sep* b4.de*
  - **amel.**: hep b4a.de mag-c b4.de*
- **jumps** out of, wants to destroy himself but lacks courage: *(↗Escape - jumps; Fear - suicide; Jumping - bed; Suicidal)* chin sabad ↓ sulph ↓
  - **runs** recklessly about; and: sabad sulph kr1
- **refuses** to go to bed: *Med* hu
- **remain** in bed; desire to: *(↗Desires - full - more; Disturbed; Slowness; GENERALS - Lie - desire)* adam srj5• alum alumn am-c ↓ ant-c h2* *Arg-n* k* arge-pl rwt5• aur-m-n wbt2• bamb-a stb2.de* cact ↓ choc srj3• coca mfj con cupr mtf33 dream-p sdj1• dros dx1 dulc fd4.de falco-pe nl2• hydrog ↓ *Hyos* k* ip ↓ kali-p fd1.de• kali-s ↓ *Kola* stb3• lyc ↓ merc olib-sac wmh1 phasco-ci rbp2 phos ↓ plut-n srj7• podo fd3.de• psor puls h1* rhus-t ↓ rob **Ruta** fd* sal-fr sle1• *Sil* kr1* spong fd4.de symph fd3.de• taosc iwa1• tritic-vg fd5.de ulm-c ↓ *Vanil* fd5.de verat-v
  - **morning** (= late riser): *(↗SLEEP - Waking - late)* ferr-m a1 hydrog srj2• kali-s fd* lyc fd* podo fd3.de• psor gk puls fd* rhus-t gb• *Sep* h2* tritic-vg fd5.de ulm-c jsj8• *Vanil* fd5.de
  - **menses**; during: am-c mtn* cact mtn ip mtn phos mtn
  - **sexual** excitement, from: verat kr1

BEER agg.: *(↗Ailments - alcoholism)* alum b4a.de bell b4.de* chin b7.de* ferr b7.de* ign b7.de* stram b7a.de

BEGGING (= entreating; supplicating): *(↗Begging - sleep; Delirium - crying - help)* ars k* aur bg2 bell bg2 kali-c bg2 lyss mtf plat bg2 plb mtf puls bg2 stann ↓ stram k* [oxyg stj]
- **agg.**: ars bg2 stram bg2
- **help**; for (See Shrieking - help)
- **pray** for him to, and not to leave him alone: lyss kr1
- **sleep**, in: *(↗Begging)* stann k*

BEHAVIOR PROBLEMS: *(↗Insolence; Rudeness)* agar ↓ anac mrr1 bufo ↓ cham ↓ cina ↓ cupr ↓ ferr ↓ hep ↓ hyos ↓ lach ↓ lyc ↓ med ↓ merc ↓ nux-v ↓ p-benzq ↓ plat ↓ psor ↓ rhus-t ↓ staph ↓ **Stram** ↓ sulph ↓ syph ↓ tarent ↓ thuj ↓ *Tub* ↓ verat ↓ zinc ↓
- **children**, in: *(↗Destructiveness - children; Disobedience - children; Insolence - children; Kicking; Liar; Mischievous; Moral; Restlessness - children; Rudeness - children; Spoiled; Striking - children; in; Unfeeling)* agar mtf33 anac mrr1 bufo mtf33 cham mrr1* cina mrr1* cupr mtf33 ferr mtf33 hep mrr1 hyos mrr1* lach mtf33 lyc mtf33 med mrr1* merc mtf33 nux-v mrr1* p-benzq mtf11 plat mtf33 psor mtf33 rhus-t mrr1 staph mtf33 stram mrr1* sulph mrr1* syph mtf33 tarent mrr1* thuj ↓ *Tub* mrr1* verat mrr1* zinc mrr1
  - **fears**; with: **Stram** mrr1
  - **home**, but good at school, with strangers, etc.; at: *(↗Aversion - family - others; Contrary - parents; Estranged - family - strangers)* lyc mtf33 thuj mtf33 tub mtf33
  - **nightmares**; with: **Stram** mrr1

BEING in the present; feeling of: ara-maca sej7• *Haliae-lc* srj5• neon srj5•

BELLOWING (See Barking - bellowing)

BELONEPHOBIA (See Fear - pins)

BEMOANING (See Lamenting)

BENDING forward agg.: caust bg2 coloc bg2 glon bg2 hell bg2

BENEVOLENCE: *(↗Affectionate; Anxiety - others; Generous; Mildness; Sympathetic)* agar j am-m j anac j arg-n mrr1 aur j* bell gl1.fr• calc j **Carc** fd* cic j *Cocc* mtf coff hs1 coff-t a1 grat mtf hydrog srj2• ign gl1.fr• kali-s fd4.de lac-f wza1• *Lac-h* mtf lac-leo hrn2• lac-lup ↓ lach j led j limen-b-c hrn2* mang j naja mtf *Nat-c* mtf nat-m j* nit-ac j nux-v gl1.fr• op a1*

Benevolence: ...
phos j* positr nl2• puls gk sil mtf spong fd4.de stann j sulph j taosc iwa1• trios rsj11• *Tung-met* bdx1• vanil fd5.de [osm-met stj2]
- **children**; towards: lac-leo hm2•
- **fortunate**; to others less: lac-lup hm2•

BENUMBED (See Stupefaction)

BEREAVEMENT (See Ailments - death)

BESIDE ONESELF; being: *(↗Self-control - loss)*
- **general**; in: *(↗Self-control - loss)* **Acon** b7.de* anac bg2 anh sp1 ant-t bg2 apis bg2 arn bg2 *Ars* bg2 bar-c bg2 bell bg2 calc bg2 carb-an bg2 carb-v bg2 carc mlr1• caust bg2 **Cham** b7a.de* chin bg2* **Coff** b7.de* colch b7.de* coloc bg2 con bg2 cupr bg2 dros b7a.de* fum rly1• graph bg2 **Ign** bg2 kali-c j5.de* kali-n bg2 lyc h2* mag-s j5.de merc bg2 nat-c bg2 nit-ac bg2* **Nux-v** b7.de* ph-ac bg2* phos h2* plb bg2 *Puls* b7.de* sec b7a.de* sep bg2 sil bg2 spig bg2 stann bg2 stram b7.de* sulph bg2 tarax j5.de ther bg2 thuj bg *Valer* b7.de* *Verat* b7.de* verb bg2
- **anger**; from (See Anger - beside)
- **anxiety**; from (See Anxiety - beside)
- **chill**; during: *Acon* b7.de *Verat* b7.de
- **menses** | **during**: *Coff* b7a.de
- **pain**; from (See Sensitive - pain - beside)
- **teeth**; from pain in: **Acon** bg2 ars bg2 *Bell* bg2 cham bg2 *Clem* b4a.de **Coff** bg2 **Hyos** bg2 ign bg2 merc b4a.de *Nux-v* bg2 *Sep* b4a.de sulph b4a.de
- **trifles**, from (See Trifles)
- **weather**; from bad (See Weather - cloudy)

BEWILDERED (See Confusion)

BILIOUS disposition (See Irritability)

BITING: *(↗Biting - nails; Delusions - animals; Delusions - dogs - he - growls; Fear - bitten; Idiocy; Idiocy - bite; Rage - biting; Violent; FACE - Chewing; MOUTH - Biting; TEETH - Clenching)* acon *Agar* ↓ *Am-br* ↓ am-m ↓ ambr ↓ amp ↓ ant-t k* anthraci arg-n ↓ arn ↓ **Ars** ↓ art-v ↓ **Arum-t** ↓ aster k* *Aur* b4a.de aur-i ↓ bamb-a ↓ **Bar-c** ↓ **Bell** k* *Brom* ↓ bufo k* *Calc* k* calc-f ↓ calc-p ↓ *Camph* cann-i *Canth* k* carb-v carbn-dox ↓ *Carbn-s* carc ↓ castm ↓ caust ↓ chel sne choc srj3• cic k* cina ckh1 cisplat ↓ croc k* cub *Cupr* k* cupr-act a1* cupr-c a1 cupr-o ↓ cur k* dulc ↓ elaps ↓ falco-pe nl2• gaert ↓ gal-ac zr hell ↓ hura hydr-ac k* hydrog ↓ *Hyos* k* ign bg2 iod ↓ irid-met ↓ kali-s ↓ kola stb3• lac-c ↓ lac-e hrn2• *Lach* k* *Lyc* ↓ lys bg2 **Lyss** k* *Mag-c* ↓ mag-sil ↓ **Med** ↓ melal-alt ↓ merc ↓ moni rfm1• morg ↓ morg-g ↓ nat-c ↓ *Nat-m* ↓ nit-ac ↓ nux-v ↓ oena ↓ op phos k* *Phyt* k* pin-con ↓ plb k* podo bg3* puls ↓ *Sacch* ↓ sanic ↓ sec k* senec ↓ sep ↓ *Sil* ↓ squil b7a.de staph ↓ **Stram** k* *Sulph* gk syc ↓ syph ↓ *Tarent* ↓ tritic-vg ↓ tub ↓ upa ↓ *Verat* k* [ant-c stj2 ant-met stj2 cupr-f stj2 cupr-m stj2 cupr-p stj2 heroin sdj2]
- **evening**: croc a1
- **night**: bell k*
  - **sleep**; during: cic ptk1 phos ptk1
- **about** him; bites: falco-pe nl2• phos a1
- **arms**; bites his own: op a1*
- **around** him; bites those (See people)
- **cheeks** (See MOUTH - Biting - cheek)
- **children**, in: ant-t mtf33 **BELL** st* carb-v hr1* carbn-s a1 cupr mtf33 hyos a1* lach hr1 *Op* wbt• stram a1* sulph hu2 tarent hu2 tub hu2
- **clothes**: plb a1* tarent mtf33
- **coition**; during: [heroin sdj2]
- **convulsions**; during: art-v ptk1 bufo ptk1 caust ptk1 croc j5.de *Cupr* hr1* lyss k* oena ptk1 op a1* *Tarent* hr1*
- **delirium**, during: *(↗Delirium - bite)* **Bell** kr1 *Canth* kr1* cupr a2* hydr-ac a1 lyss kr1 phos a1 **Stram** kr1
- **dentition**; during: cham mtf33 phyt hr1
- **desire** to bite (See Biting)
- **disturbs** him; bites everyone who (See people - disturbs)
- **father** (See people - father)
- **fingers**: *(↗hands)* acon ptk1 *Arum-t* k* carc st1* elaps ↓ hydrog srj2• med ptk1* op k* plb k* stram a1 tarent dgt [am-br stj2]
  - **gently** | **children's** fingers; the tips of: carc fb4*
  - **sleep** | **during**: elaps ptk1
  - **tips** of: carc gk6
- **fist**: acon kl1

- **hands**: *(↗fingers)* acon ptk1 arum-t ptk1 elaps ↓ hura med ptk1 op k* plb ptk1
  - **sleep**; during: elaps ptk1
- **himself**: *(↗Hiding - himself - children; Striking - himself)* acon *Agar* vh1 arum-t k1* cupr mtf33 cur mrr1 elaps kr1 hura lyss k* op plb k* stram h1* tarent k*

○ - **Lips** (See MOUTH - Biting - lips)
- **mania**; in puerperal: camph hr1
- **nails**: *(↗Biting)* *Acon* bg2* *Am-br* c2* am-m st ambr st amp rly4• ant-c ar ant-t vh arg-n ar arn st *Ars* bg2* **Arum-t** bg2* aur-i a bamb-a stb2.de• **Bar-c** st* *Brom* vh* bufo a* calc h2* calc-f kkb calc-p a* *Carb-v* mtf33 carbn-dox knl3• carc st* castm mtf caust kkb cina bg2* cisplat jl croc a cupr a* cupr-o ar dulc fd4.de falco-pe nl2• gaert bh* gal-ac a* hura bg2 *Hyos* st* iod a* irid-met srj5• kali-s fd4.de lac-c sne *Lyc* bg3* lys bg2 *Mag-c* vh* **Med** bg3* melal-alt gya4 moni rfm1• morg ar morg-g pte1*• nat-c mtf *Nat-m* h2* nit-ac bg2 phos bg2* pin-con oss2• plb bg2* puls a* *Sacch* sst• sanic st* senec bg2* sep ggd1 *Sil* st* staph a* *Stram* bg2* *Sulph* bg* syc a* syph a *Tarent* gg* tritic-vg fd5.de tub a upa a* **Verat** vh* [heroin sdj2 mag-sil stj2]
  - **children**; in: ant-c mtf11 bar-c mtf33 brom mtf33 bufo mtf33 calc-p mtf33 *Carb-v* mtf33 carc fd* cina mtf33 cupr mtf33 hyos mtf33 lyc mtf33 mag-c mtf33 med gk* nat-m mtf33 phos mtf33 plb mtf33 puls mtf33 sacch sst1• sanic mtf33 sil mtf33 stram mtf33 sulph mtf33 tarent mtf33 verat mtf33
  - **toenails** | **children**; in: sacch sst1•
- **nipples** | **sucking**; while: cupr sst3•
- **objects**: bell h1* bufo kr1* hyos vh* sil vh* **Stram** vh*
- **paroxysmal** (See suddenly)
- **people**: bell h1* carbn-s ↓ falco-pe ↓ lac-c ↓ nux-v mtf33 op wbt• phos a1 stram a1*
  - **disturbs** him; bites everyone who: *(↗Disturbed)* hyos a1*
  - **family**; her: falco-pe nl2•
  - **father**; his: carbn-s a1
  - **head** off; felt like I was trying to bite her (See Delusions - biting - head)
- **pillow**: lyc ptk1 lyss k* phos k*
- **shoe** and swallows the pieces; his: verat j5.de*
- **spits**, barks and bites (See Barking; Biting; Spitting)
- **spoon**: ars k* *Bell* k* cham bg2* cina bg2* cupr k* hell c1* lys bg2 lyss puls bg2* verat bg2*
- **suddenly**: phos a1
- **teeth** (See TEETH - Biting - teeth)
- **tumbler**; his: **Ars** k* cupr mtf33
  - **drinking**; when: **Ars** k* cupr mtf33
- **worm** affections; in: *Carb-v* kr1 croc a1

BLACK (See Colors - black; Fear - black)

BLACKOUT (See Thoughts - vanishing)

BLAMES himself (See Mood - repulsive; Reproaching oneself)

BLANK (See Absentminded; Staring)

BLASPHEMY: *(↗Cursing)* am-m ↓ *Anac* ↓ calc gl1.fr• canth k2* chin-b ↓ coca-c ↓ lyc ↓ nat-c gl1.fr• nat-m mtf* nit-ac mtf* *Nux-v* ↓ op ↓ petr-ra shn4• phos mtf33 spig gl1.fr• staph gl1.fr•
- **cursing**, and: *(↗Cursing)* am-m gl1.fr• *Anac* gl1.fr* canth hr1* chin-b hr1* coca-c sk4• lyc gl1.fr• nat-c gl1.fr• *Nat-m* hr1* *Nit-ac* gl1.fr* *Nux-v* gl1.fr* op gl1.fr• phos mtf33 spig gl1.fr• staph gl1.fr•

BLINDNESS; pretending: *(↗Delusions - blind; Feigning - sick)* verat

BLISSFUL feeling: *(↗Content; Peace - heavenly)* androc srj1• ara-maca sej7• arge-pl rwt5• chir-fl gya2 coff st colum-p sze2• dioxi rbp6 dulc fd4.de falco-pe nl2• helodr-cal knl2• hippoc-k szs2 neon srj5• *Olib-sac* wmh1 *Op* b7.de* sal-fr sle1• spong fd4.de tritic-vg fd5.de vanil fd5.de [tax jsj7]
- **alone**; when: arge-pl rwt5•

BLOOD; cannot look at: *(↗Fear - blood; Frightened - blood; Suicidal - blood; Thoughts - frightful - seeing; Unconsciousness - blood; GENERALS - Faintness - blood)* *Aloe* vh1 **Alum** k* nux-m ptk1* **Nux-v** ↓ phos gg plat ptk1* ruta fd4.de sacch sht• staph mtf33 [mang-n stj2 mang-p stj2]

Blood; cannot look at: ...
- **knife**; cannot look at (See Knife)
- **wounds**; cannot look at: **Nux-v** st staph st*

BLOWING nose:
- **agg.**: euphr b7.de*
- **amel.**: kali-chl ptk1

BLUNT (See Truth - telling)

BLUNTED (See Dullness; Senses - dull)

BLUSHING: *(↗Excitement - heat - during; Timidity - bashful; FACE - Discoloration - red - excitement; GENERALS - Orgasm - emotions; HEAD - Congestion - anger; HEAD - Congestion - anxiety; HEAD - Congestion - fright; HEAD - Congestion - rage)* *Ambr* a12* aml-ns tsm1* carb-an tsm1 carl tsm1 coca tsm1 ferr tl1* kali-p tsm1 meli tsm1 nux-v tsm1 positr nl2• puls tsm1* ruta fd4.de samb tsm1 stram tsm1 sulph tsm1 [bar-i stj2 merc-i-f stj2]
- **asthmatic** breathlessness; with: aml-ns mtf11

BOASTER (= braggart): *(↗Exhilaration - mania; Haughty; Squandering - boasting)* acon vh1 alco a1 arn gl1.fr• ars gl1.fr• aur-m-n wbt2• aur-s wbt2• bell gl1.fr• calc ↓ hydrog srj2• lach gl1.fr• lil-t gk *Lyc* vh* *Med* vh* merc mtf33* nat-m gl1.fr• nux-v gl1.fr• plat gl1.fr• puls ↓ stram mtf33* **Sulph** mrr1* *Verat* mtf
- **rich**, wishes to be considered as: lach mtf33* lyc gl1.fr• verat gl1.fr•
- **squandering** through ostentation: *(↗Haughty; Squandering; Squandering - boasting)* calc gl1.fr• nux-v gl1.fr• plat gl1.fr• puls gl1.fr•

BOISTEROUS (See Exhilaration)

BOLDNESS (See Courageous)

BORED; being (See Ennui)

BORED with life (See Ennui)

BOREDOM (See Ennui)

BORROWING from everyone: acet-ac ckh1 apis ckh1 bar-c ckh1 calc ckh1* phos gl1.fr• plat gl1.fr• sang ckh1

BOSSY (See Dictatorial)

BOUNDARIES; Lack of (See Doubtful)

BRAGGART (See Boaster)

BRAIN FAG (See Prostration)

BREAKFAST:
- **agg.**: coc-c bg2 lyc bg2
- **amel.**: *Calc* b4a.de carb-ac bg2
- **before**: *Calc* b4.de*

BREAKING things: *(↗Anger; Desires - full - more; Destructiveness; Gestures - hands - breaking; Rage; Sitting - inclination - breaks; Tearing - things; Violent)* androc srj1• *Apis* k* bell k2* calc ↓ carbn-s k2 cypr vml3• dulc fd4.de hura hyos gl1.fr• irid-met ↓ lyss ↓ med ctc* *Nux-v* mrr1* pegan-ha ↓ plut-n srj7• sang a1 sep ↓ sol-t-ae a1 *Staph* gl1.fr* *Stram* k* sulph gl1.fr• tarent fb* *Tub* k* verat gl1.fr• [ant-met stj2]
- **bright** objects: lyss c1
- **desire** to break things: bell gl1.fr• hyos mtf33* irid-met srj5• *Nux-v* mtf33* pegan-ha tpi1• sep sne sol-t-ae a1 staph mtf33* *Stram* k* sulph mtf33* **Tarent** sne *Tub* k* verat gl1.fr•
- **sticks**: calc k13
- **valuables**; other's: *(↗Malicious - hurting)* tub mrr1*

BRIGHT (See Intelligent; Mirth)

BRONTOPHOBIA (See Fear - thunderstorm)

BROODING: *(↗Absorbed; Anxiety; Brooding - troubles - imaginary; Cares full; Delusions - images - dwells; Dwells - past; Grief; Grief - silent; Hatred; Inconsolable; Indignation; Introspection; Meditating; Pessimist; Reflecting; Sadness; Sadness - brooding; Secretive; Sighing; Sulky; Taciturn; Weeping - cannot)* acon h1 agri ↓ alum androc srj1• anh mg1.de* arn aur k* *Aur-m-n* wbt2• aur-s k2* bamb-a stb2.de• bar-c ↓ bar-i k2 bell bit-ar wht1• calc k2 calc-s camph ↓ canth caps carb-an h2* carc vh* caust cham chel k2 clem sf1.de cocc con b4a.de* cupr ↓ cycl k* dulc fd4.de euphr *Gels* goss st1 hell hyos ↓ **Ign** k* ip

Brooding: ...
kali-p kali-s fd4.de kiss↓ *Kola* stb3• lach j5.de* lil-t k2 lyc k2 mez mur-ac k* *Naja* k* nat-m tl1 nat-sil fd3.de• neon srj5• nept-m lsd2.fr nit-ac a1* nux-v olnd op ozone sde2• petr-ra shn4• *Ph-ac* k* plat k2 plb b7.de* *Podo* fd3.de• ran-s a1 *Rheum* j5.de ruta fd4.de sabad b7.de* sabal↓ sacch-a fd2.de• sal-fr sle1• sep h2 spig b7.de* spong fd4.de stram a1* sulph k* symph fd3.de• thuj b4.de* tritic-vg fd5.de ulm-c jsj8• *Vanil* fd5.de **Verat** k*

- **evening**: **Verat** k*
- **alternating** with | **screaming**: verat tl1
- **condition**, over one's: nat-sil fd3.de• *Ph-ac* h2* sabal ckh1 *Spong* fd4.de symph fd3.de• *Vanil* fd5.de
- **corner**; brooding or moping in a: aur bg2 aur-s k2 bar-c bg2 bell bg2 camph bg2 cocc kr1 con k2 cupr bg2 hyos bg2 ph-ac bg2 spong fd4.de **Verat** bg2*
- **disappointment**, over: *(↗Ailments - love; Dwells - disappointments)* **Bell** st petr-ra shn4• *Ph-ac* kr1
- **disease**, over his: cycl↓ lil-t↓ naja↓ ph-ac h2
  - **imaginary** disease; over: cycl ptk1* lil-t ptk1* naja br1*
- **forbidden** things, over: *Plb* hr1*
- **grief**; over: cycl↓ ign ptk1 nat-m tl1 nat-sil fd3.de•
  - **imaginary** grief: cycl ptk1* ign ptk1
- **hidden** cares; tormented by: agri mtf11
- **suicidal** disposition; with: naja ptk1 spong fd4.de
- **symptoms**; over his own: sabal ptk1
- **trifles**; about (See Trifles)
- **troubles**: | **imaginary** troubles; over: *(↗Brooding)* *Ign* kr1 lil-t ptk2 *Naja* c10*
- **unpleasant** things: kiss a1

BROTHERHOOD; sensation of: *(↗Fraternized; Unification; Unification - sensation)* aids nl2• germ-met srj5• kali-s fd4.de neon srj5• phos h2 sal-fr nl2•

BRUSQUE (See Abrupt)

BRUTALITY: *(↗Abrupt; Cruelty; Jealousy - brutal; Malicious; Mischievous; Moral; Rudeness; Unfeeling; Wicked)* absin hr1* alco a1 *Anac* vh* *Aur* vh* nit-ac mtf33 nux-v vh staph mtf33 stram vh sulph↓ tarent vh

- **drunkenness**, during: nux-v gl1.fr• sulph gl1.fr•

BUFFOONERY (See Foolish)

BULIMIA: *(↗Insanity - bulimia; STOMACH - Appetite - ravenous)* abies-c ptk1 abies-n mtf11 adam srj agar b4.de* agath-a nl2• alf br1 all-s c1* anac mgm• ang b7.de* ant-c b7a.de* ant-t mtf33 apoc hs1 *Aq-mar* mgm• ars h2* aur b4a.de* aur-ar mtf aur-i mtf *Bell* b4a.de brass-n-o c1* bry c1* cadm-s vml3• **Calc** b4.de* calen br1 cann-i a1 *Carb-v* b4a.de* carc mlr1• carneg-g rwt1• caust gl1.fr• cham mtf33 **Chin** b7.de* **Cina** b7.de* cocc gk7 coff hs1* coloc hpc2 ephe-si hsj1• euph b4.de* ferr hr1 ferr-s hr1* fl-ac bg2 glon vml4 graph b4a.de* hell b7.de* hep h2 *Hyos* b7a.de ign h1* iod b4.de* ip↓ kali-c h2 kali-m br1 kali-n hpc2 levo jl3 **Lyc** b4.de* mag-c mtf33 **Merc** b4a.de* mosch hpc2 mur-ac b4.de* naja mgm• *Nat-c* b4a.de* nat-m mp1* nat-s mtf33 nux-m b7.de* nux-v hr1* olib-sac wmh1 op a1* petr b4a.de* phos h2* pitu-a vda* plat b4.de* positr nl2• pseuts-m oss1• psor↓ puls b7a.de* raph mgm• sabad hr1* sacch sst1• *Sec* b7.de* **Sep** b4.de* spig h1 spong b7.de* squil b7.de* stann b4.de* staph b7a.de* stram↓ *Sulph* h2* sumb a1 tarent mtf33 thuj mrr1* *V-a-b*↓ **Verat** b7.de* zinc b4a.de* [bell-p-sp dcm1 *Vanad* stj1]

- **night**: psor mtf11
- **alternating** with:
  - **refusal** to eat | **insanity**; with: hyos gl1.fr• ip gl1.fr• stram gl1.fr• verat gl1.fr• [vanad stj2]
- **children**: carc mlr1•
- **nervosa**: anac mgm• aq-mar mgm• iod mgm• lyc mgm• naja mgm• sacch sst• sep mgm• *V-a-b* jl2 [vanad stj1]

BUOYANCY: *(↗Activity - desires; Cheerful)* carc mlr1• eucal kr1 *Fl-ac* kr1* *Nux-v*↓ sarr a1* testis bwa3

- **alternating** with:
  - **despondency** (See sadness)
  - **sadness**: carc mlr1• *Nux-v* kr1

BUSINESS:

- **aversion** to: *(↗Ailments - business; Fear - business; of; Indifference - business; Laziness; Loathing - business; Neglecting - business; Sadness - business)* acon-l st agar am-c anac androc srj1• ange-s oss1• arb-m oss1• arn bg2 ars ars-h asar kr1 aur-m *Brom* k* calc k2 chinin-s cimic *Con* k* cop fl-ac k* gels mrr1 graph hipp kali-ar kali-bi k* kali-br k* kali-c kali-i *Kali-p* br1 kali-s *Kola* stb3• lac-ac *Lach* k* laur lil-t limen-b-c hrn2* lyc h2 mag-s nat-ar k2 nat-c h2* nux-v a1* *Ph-ac* k1* *Phyt* *Puls* k* rhod k2 rhus-t gl1.fr• **Sep** k* stann k2 stram bg2 sulph k* syph k2* tax-br oss1• ther kr1*
- **desire** for: *(↗Activity - desires - business; Industrious)* ars a1 carc mlr1• cere-b a1 con a1 fel a1 *Ferr* mrr1 lach a1 nat-s mrr1 sulph mrr1 tarent a1
- **failure**; ailments from business (See Ailments - business)
- **incapacity** for: *(↗Work - impossible)* acon bg2 agn k* *Alum* bg2 am-c bg2 anac bg2 *Asar* bg2 aur bg2 bell bg2 bry bg2 **Calc** bg2 canth bg2 carb-v bg2 caust h2* chinin-s a1 coff bg2 con bg2 cycl bg2 dros bg2 dulc bg2 falco-pe nl2• gels mrr1 graph bg2 iod bg2 kali-bi k* laur bg2 limen-b-c hrn2* *Lyc* bg2 mag-c bg2 mag-m bg2 meny bg2 meph br1 merc bg2 mez bg2 mit a1 mur-ac bg2 nat-m bg2 nit-ac bg2 nux-v bg2 olnd bg2 *Petr* bg2 *Phos* bg2 plb bg2 puls bg2 *Rhus-t* bg2 ruta bg2 sang↓ sars bg2 sel bg2* sep bg2 *Sil* bg2 spong bg2 squil bg2 stann bg2 staph bg2 sul-i sulph bg2 tab a1 tarax bg2 *Ter* bg2 viol-t bg2 zinc bg2
  - **fever**, during: sang a1
- **neglects** his: *(↗Laziness)* lac-lup hrn2• limen-b-c hrn2* op a1 *Sulph* a1
- **talks** of (See Delirium - business; Talking - business)

BUSINESSMEN: | **worn**-out businessmen; suited to: *(↗GENERALS - Weakness - businessmen)* aur mtf33 **Calc** mrr1 *Coca* kr1 kali-p c1 **Nux-v** kr1* toxo-g jl2

BUSY: *(↗Activity - desires; Delirium - busy; Hurry; Industrious; Insanity - busy; Insanity - crazy; Occupation - amel.; Overactive; Practical; Restlessness - busy; DREAMS - Busy)* absin↓ acon sf1.de aids nl2• allox tpw4 anac sf1.de androc srj1• ant-c↓ *Apis* k* arg-n↓ arn j5.de ars a1 *Aster* mgm• aur j* *Bar-c* bg2* bell j borx↓ *Bry* k* calad calc k* canth↓ caps carc mlr1• cere-b a1 chir-fl gya2 choc srj3• cimic bg2* cina mtf33 cocc con a1 cupr sst3• dig j dioxi rbp6 dulc fd4.de fel a1 ferr-p a1* fic-m gya1 ger-i rly4• helo-s rwt2• hydrog↓ *Hyos* j5.de* ign k* indg br1 *Iod* k2* ip j irid-met srj5• *Kali-br* bg2* kali-i sf1.de kalm bg2* lac-e hrn2• lac-h htj1• lac-leo↓ *Lach* bg2* lavand-a↓ lil-t bg2* m-arct j mag-c j mag-m sf1.de mag-p↓ *Med* jl2 merc sf1.de morg-p pte* mosch bg2* nat-c j nat-ox rly4• *Nux-m* vh* nux-v br1 *Op* sf1.de opun-s a1 (non:opun-v a1) *Oscilloc* jl2 petr-ra shn4• phos sf1.de plac-s rly4• positr nl2• rhus-r slp (non:rhus-t k*) ruta fd4.de sep bg2* stann j staph↓ stram stront-c sf1.de suis-em rly4• sul-ac j *Sulph* k1* *Tarent* bg2* tere-la rly4• ther k2* tritic-vg fd5.de tung-met bdx1• *Valer* bg2* vanil fd5.de *Verat* k* zinc sf1.de* zinc-val sf1.de [bar-i stj2 heroin sdj2 lith-m stj2 mang-i stj2 merc-i-f stj2 niob-met stj2 sel stj2 **Spect** dfg1 zinc-i stj2]

- **evening**: lac-leo hrn2•
- **night**: hydrog srj2•
- **children**: cina mtf33
- **forgets** to urinate, defecate or eat: ant-c ptk2
- **fruitlessly**: *(↗Hurry - aimless; Time - fritters)* absin bro1 *Apis* b7a.de* arg-n bro1* ars bro1 *Bar-c* b4a.de borx bg2* calc h2* canth bro1 cocc b7.de ign b7.de kali-br ptk1* *Lach* b7.de* lavand-a ctl1• *Lil-t* bg1* mag-p ptk1 mosch b7a.de *Sep* b4a.de stann k* sulph bro1* tarent bg* ther k2* **Verat** b7.de*
- **himself**, with: mag-m a1* staph a1*
- **must** keep: **Dulc**↓ iod br1* lil-t br1 tarent br1* ther↓ verat tl1
  - **restlessness**, from: **Dulc** fd* ther k2
  - **sexual** desire; to repress: lil-t bro1
- **tired**; even though: dioxi rbp6
- **weak**; busy and: mosch bg2*

CALCULATING, inability for (See Mathematics - inability - calculating)

CALLED; when being: sulph bg2

CALMNESS (See Tranquillity)

CALUMNIATE; desire to (See Slander)

CAPRICIOUSNESS: *(↗Desires - full; Eccentricity; Impulsive; Inconstancy; Irresolution; Mood - changeable; Persisting; Petulant; Rash; Undertaking - many; CHILL - Changing; FEVER - Changing; GENERALS - Contradictory; GENERALS - Side - alternating; STOMACH - Appetite - capricious)* acon k* act-sp hr1* agar k* *Aloe* sne *Alum* k* alum-sil k2 am-c k* ambr bg2 anac bg2 ang bg2

Capricousness: ...
Ant-c bg2* ant-t↓ apis bg2 arn k* *Ars* k* ars-s-f k2 arum-t↓ asaf k* aur bg2 aur-m bamb-a stb2.de• *Bar-c* k* bar-s k2 *Bell* k* bism ptk1 bov j5.de bran j brom k* **Bry** k* calc k* *Calc-p* bg2 calc-s k* calc-sil k2* cann-i cann-s j5.de canth k* caps k* carb-an carbn-s carc tpw2* cassia-s ccrh1• caste jl3 castm↓ *Caust* j5.de* cench k2 **CHAM** k* *Chin* k* chinin-ar cimic k* **CINA** k* coc-c bg2 coca a1 *Cocc* j5.de* *Coff* k* con bg2 croc k* cycl bg2 *Cypr* hr1* dig dros *Dulc* k* ferr bg2* ferr-act j fl-ac hr1* form bg2 goss vh* graph bg2 grat k* haliae-lc srj5• ham hell bg2 *Hep* k* hera j5.de hyos bg2 *Ign* k* ina-i mlk9.de *Iod* bg2* **Ip** k* kali-ar **Kali-c** k* kali-sil k2* kola stb3• kreos lac-h sk4• lach k* led k* lil-t k2 lyc k* m-arct j5.de m-aust j5.de mag-c hr1* mag-m k* *Mag-p* hr1* marb-w es1• med bgs *Merc* k* *Merc-i-f* a1* mez bg2 moni rfm1• mosch bg2 nat-c bg2* nat-m bg2 nat-n j5.de* nit-ac k* nux-m k* *Nux-v* k* oci-sa sk4• onos bg2 op ozone sde2• par **Petr** bg2 *Ph-ac* gl1.fr• *Phos* k* phys↓ **Plat** j5.de* plb hr1* podo fd3.de• *Puls* k* ran-b↓ raph *Rheum* k* rhod ruta bg2 sacch c1* sarr sars bg2* sec **Sep** j5.de* sil k* sphing a1* spig a1 spong stann bg2 **Staph** k* stram k* *Sul-ac* hr1* *Sulph* k* *Symph* fd3.de• syph mtf33 tarax bg2 tarent br1 thuj k* thymol br1 thyr jl3 tub bgs* valer j5.de* verat bg2* **Verat-v** vh* viol-o bg2 viol-t zinc k* zinc-p k2

- **daytime**: castm j5.de ran-b j5.de
- **morning**: bov st1 *Nit-ac* hr1* staph
- **forenoon**: cann-s j5.de
- **noon**: zinc j5.de
- **afternoon**: cann-s j5.de sars j5.de*
- **evening**: aur j5.de bov j5.de calc-s a1 castm j5.de croc j5.de fl-ac hr1* ign ran-b j5.de zinc j5.de
- **children**; in: carc mlr1•
- **irritability**; with (See rejecting)
- **pain**; with | **Teeth**; in: mag-c mtf33
- **mania**; in: raph a
- **rejecting** the things for which he has been longing; when offered, he is: *(↗Refusing - everything)* ant-t↓ arn bg2* arum-t vh bry j5.de* **Cham** b7a.de* chin tl1 *Cina* b7a.de* *Dulc* j5.de* *Hep* a1* ign j5.de* *Ip* j5.de* kreos bg2* op wbt• phos ptk1 phys ptk1 *Puls* b7.de* **Rheum** j5.de* sec ptk1 **Staph** st*
  - **children**; in: ant-t bro1 bry bro1* cham br1* cina bro1* ip bro1* kreos bro1 rheum bro1* staph br1*

CAPTIVATING others' attention (See Charming)

CARDIOPHOBIA (See Fear - heart - disease)

CAREFREE: *(↗Heedless)* adam srj5• aln vva1• arge-pl rwt5• buteo-j↓ calad bg2 *Cann-i* br1* chir-fl gya2 dream-p sdj1• falco-pe nl2• graph mtf haliae-lc srj5• ham bg2* laur bg2* med vh2 melal-alt gya4 nat-m a1* olib-sac wmh1 op b7a.de* phos bg2* sep rb2 sulph hu2 symph fd3.de• tarax bg2* tritic-vg fd5.de verat b7.de* zinc bg2* [heroin sdj2 temp elm1]

- **desire** to be: [buteo-j sej6]
- **money**; about: adam srj

CAREFULNESS: *(↗Cautious; Censorious; Conscientious; Fastidious; Rest - cannot; Suspicious)* ang b7.de* ara-maca sej7• **Ars** k* aur b4.de* **Bar-c** k* bry b7.de* calc gl1.fr• carc fd2.de• cham bg2 **Chin** b7.de* cocc bg2 cycl bg2 dig bg2 dulc fd4.de ephe-si hsj1• **Graph** b4a.de* hyos bg2 ign bg2 *Iod* k* ip b7.de* kali-s fd4.de *Lach* bg2* *Lyc* bg2* *M-arct* b7.de* *M-aust* b7.de mez b4.de* mur-ac b4.de* nat-c b4.de* **Nux-v** k* podo fd3.de• positr nl2• **Puls** k ●* ran-b rhus-t bg2 *Sep* b4.de* **Sil** b4a.de* spig b7.de* *Stram* bg2 **Sulph** b4a.de* thuj b4a.de* *Verat* bg2* [tax jsj7]

CARELESS (See Heedless)

CARES, full of: *(↗Ailments - Cares; Ailments - Grief; Anxiety; Brooding; Conscientious; Grief; Serious; Weeping - Trifles - children; FACE - Expression - Haggard; SLEEP - Sleeplessness - Cares; from)* acet-ac ptk1 acon↓ *Agath-a* nl2• alum↓ ambr bg2* anac j5.de* apis ptk1 arn j5.de *Ars* j5.de* aur h2* *Aur-m-n* wbt2• *Aur-s* wbt2• *Bar-c* j5.de* blum-o bnj1 brucel sa3• but-ac↓ *Calc* kr1* calc-p bg2* calc-sil k2 cann-i a1 carc mlr1• *Caust* k* chel j5.de *Chin* k* chir-fl gya2 cimic jl3 **Cocc** mtf coff k* colch↓ con sf1.de* cortico tpw7 crot-c↓ dig bg2 dros j5.de* dulc↓ dys↓ erech↓ fic-m↓ gins j5.de granit-m↓ graph j5.de ham fd3.de• hed jl3 hep↓ **Ign** bg2* *Iod* vh* *Kali-br* kr1* kali-c mrr1 kali-n h2* kali-p ptk1 kali-s↓ *Kola* stb3• lac-leo↓ lac-mat↓ lach↓ lil-t↓ limest-b↓ lyc gl1.fr• mag-c ptk1* mag-m mrr1 mag-s↓ mang j5.de* med kr1 merc-i-f↓ mim-p rsj8• moni rfm1• mur-ac h2 *Nat-c* j5.de* *Nat-m* j5.de* nicc↓ nux-v br1* op j5.de ozone↓ petr↓ *Ph-ac* j5.de* phos ptk1 physala-p bnm7• pic-ac sf1.de* plac-s↓ plat↓ podo↓ *Psor* bg2* **Puls** ●*

Cares, full of: ...
rad-br c11 rhus-t↓ sabad↓ sal-ac kr1 sang ptk1 sep h2* sil gl1.fr• *Spig* j5.de stann j5.de* **Staph** bg2* *Sulph* c1* symph↓ term-a bnj1 thuj j5.de tritic-vg fd5.de ulm-c↓ v-a-b jl3* vac kr1* *Vanil* fd5.de verat tl1 zinc↓ [uva stj]

- **day** and night: caust j5.de
- **morning**: alum↓ ham fd3.de• *Puls* h1* staph gl1.fr• symph fd3.de•
  - **bed**, in: alum j5.de
- **evening**: ars↓ dig j5.de graph↓ kali-c j5.de
  - **bed**, in: ars j5.de graph j5.de
- **night**: caust h2 dulc↓ *Psor* kr1
  - **midnight**: dulc j5.de
- **alone**, when: hep j5.de
- **alternating** with:
  - **anger** (See Anger - alternating - cares)
  - **exhilaration** (See Exhilaration - alternating - cares)
  - **irritability** (See Irritability - alternating - cares)
  - **quarreling** (See Quarrelsome - alternating - cares)
- **business**, about his: *(↗Fear - business failure)* acet-ac br1* ambr ptk1 aur mtf33 carc mlr1• caust ptk1 kali-p ptk1 lil-t ptk1 nux-v br1* podo ptk1 psor↓ *Puls* j5.de rhus-t j5.de
  - **successful**; although: psor ptk1
- **causeless**: petr ptk1*
- **company**; with aversion to: *(↗Company - aversion)* con j5.de ham fd3.de• nat-m j5.de
- **daily** cares, affected by: ambr bg2 calc bg2 nat-m bg2 nux-v bg2 plac-s rly4•
- **domestic** affairs, about: bar-c k* *Puls* k* **Sep** ●* ulm-c jsj8•
- **future**; about: carc az1.de• podo fd3.de• symph fd3.de• tritic-vg fd5.de
- **money**; about: aur mtf33 ozone sde2•
- **nature**; for (animals, plants etc.): fic-m gya1 lac-leo hm2•
- **others**, about: *(↗Anxiety - others)* ars bg2 carc sk1• *Caust* gl1.fr• **Cocc** b7.de* crot-c sk4• kali-s stj1* lac-leo hm2• lach gl1.fr• limest-b es1• mag-c sys mag-m sys mag-s lmp puls zr sabad sys staph zr sulph j5.de zinc gl1.fr• [erech stj lac-mat sst4 mang stj1 nicc stj1 uva stj]
- **relatives**, about: *(↗Ailments - cares worries; Ailments - cares worries - loved; Maternal)* acon vh1 ars j5.de* *Caust* gl1.fr• *Cocc* tl1* colch gk dulc mrr1 hep j5.de kali-s fd4.de lach gl1.fr• moni rfm1• phos tl1 plat mrr1 rhus-t j5.de *Spig* gl1.fr• *Sulph* tl1* tritic-vg fd5.de *Vanil* fd5.de zinc gl1.fr•
- **symptoms** disappear during cares: merc-i-f kr1
- **trifles**, about: *(↗Trifles; Trifles - important)* *Ars* k* aur k2 bar-c gk but-ac br1 *Chin* gl1.fr• dys pte1• granit-m es1•
- **waking**, on: alum j5.de ham fd3.de• ulm-c jsj8•
- **walking** in open air: hep j5.de

CARESSED; being:

- **aversion** to: *(↗Anger - caressing; Touched - aversion)* *Ant-c*↓ cham↓ chin mtf *Cina* k* cupr sst3* irid-met srj5• nit-ac h2 positr nl2• sep↓ [heroin sdj2 plat stj2]
  - **children**; in: *Ant-c* jsa* cham vh cupr sst3•
- **wants** to be caressed: *(↗Affection - yearning)* ara-maca sej7• cann-i a1 carc cd* cypra-eg sde6.de• marb-w es1• olib-sac wmh1 *Podo* fd3.de• puls↓ sacch sst1• *Tritic-vg* fd5.de [heroin sdj2 lac-mat sst4]
  - **children**; in: puls br1 sacch sst1•

CARESSING:

- **husband** and child, then pushes them away; caresses: *Anac* hr1* [heroin sdj2]
- **inclination** to caress: carc gk6* falco-pe nl2• irid-met srj5•
- **oneself**: irid-met srj5•

CARING: | **aversion** to care for others: bamb-a stb2.de•

CAROUSAL; as if after a (See Delusions - carousal)

CARPHOLOGIA (See Gestures - hands - picking - bedclothes)

CARRIED:

- **aversion** to be carried: *(↗Fear - carried; Kicking - children - carried)* bell hr1 *Bry* hr1* cham j cina br1 *Coff* c1* cupr sst3•

- **aversion** to be carried: ...
  - **dancing**; when the one who carries is (See Dancing - agg. - child)
- **desire** to be carried: (↗*desire - amel.; Desires - full - more; Irritability - rocking; Morose - children - carried; Quieted - carried; Restlessness - children - carried; Rocking - amel.; Weeping - carried - quiet; GENERALS - Carried - amel.)* acet-ac k* acon k* alumin-sil hr1 ant-c bg2* ant-t k* arn ll1 *Ars* k* aspar hr1* *Bamb-a* stb2.de• bell bg2* benz-ac k* borx bg2* brom k* **Bry** a1 calc-p mrr1 carb-v k* carc cd caust hr1 **CHAM** b2.de* *Chel* bg2* *Cina* k* coff st coloc sf1.de cupr sst3• dros gk dulc fd4.de ign ip bro1* *Kali-c* k* kali-p br3 *Kreos* bg2* *Lyc* k* mag-m h2 med gk* merc bg2* phos gk podo ↓ puls k* rheum mtf33 *Rhus-t* k* sacch sst1• sanic k* stann ↓ staph k* stram ↓ sulph *Tritic-vg* fd5.de vac kr1* vanil fd5.de *Verat* k* [tax jsj7]
  - **amel.**: (↗*desire)* ant-t b7a.de *Cham* b7a.de
    - **not** amel.; but carrying does: cina bwa3*
  - **caressed**; and: acon st cham br1 kreos bg2* *Puls* bg2* sacch sst1•
  - **croup**, in: brom
  - **fast**: acon bg* **Ars** k* bell brom k* rhus-t verat k*
    - **dentition**; during: ars bro1
  - **fondled**; and (See caressed)
  - **laid** down; will not be: benz-ac ptk1* tritic-vg fd5.de
  - **shoulder**; over the: cina bg2* podo bg2* stann bg2* stram gk*
  - **sitting** up: ant-t bg2*
  - **slowly**: *Puls* k*
  - **soothed**; and: ant-c tl1

CARRYING: | **things** from one place to another and back again (See Busy - fruitlessly)

CARS: | **love** for: *Med* mtf merc mtf phos mtf stram mtf *Tub* mtf [bar-f stj1 calc-f stj1 *Fl-ac* stj2 fl-pur stj1 kali-f stj1 nat-f stj1]

CASTING OFF people against her will: (↗*Mood - repulsive)* **Plat** h2*

CASUAL: (↗*Heedless; Indifference; Tranquillity)* polys sk4•

CATALEPSY (See GENERALS - Catalepsy)

CATATONIA: (↗*Schizophrenia - catatonic; Schizophrenia - paranoid)* cic jl3 coli jl2 cortico sp1* diph-t-tpt jl2 kali-br mrr1 puls mrr1 rauw sp1 [verbe-o rcb1]

CATOPTROPHOBIA (See Fear - mirrors)

CATS:
- **fear** of cats (See Fear - cats)
- **loves** cats (See Animals - love - cats)

CAUTIOUS: (↗*Anxiety; Carefulness; Confidence - want; Conscientious; Death - presentiment; Fear - happen; Insecurity; Reserved; Suspicious; Timidity)* acon bg2 am-c j anac j arn j ars bg2* aur j aur-m-n wbt2• bar-c j brom mtf33 cact a1 calc ptk1* carc cd caust chel j chin j cic j coff j *Cupr* bg2* dros j graph k* hyos bg2 *Ign* ptk1 ip k* kali-n j kali-s fd4.de lach j lact j **Lyc** ↓ m-arct mang j nat-c j nat-m j nit-ac j nux-v bg2* oci-sa sk4• op bg2 petr-ra shn4• ph-ac j **Puls** ●* sil ↓ spig j stram bg2* sulph ↓ tax ↓ thuj j verat ptk1
- **anxious**: am-c gl1.fr• bar-c gl1.fr• carc fd2.de• caust **Lyc** ●* **Puls** ●* sil mtf33* sulph gl1.fr• [tax jsj7]

CENSORIOUS: (↗*silent; Abusive; Carefulness; Conscientious; Contradiction - disposition; Contrary; Cynical; Dictatorial; Fastidious; Haughty; Intolerance; Mocking - sarcasm; Mood - repulsive; Prejudiced; Quarrelsome; Reproaching others; Rest - cannot; Slander; Talking - faults)* acon k* adam srj5• agar bg2 alum k* alum-sil k2 am-c k* am-s ↓ androc srj1• apis bro1* aq-pet ↓ *Arn* **Ars** k* ars-s-f k2 aur k* aur-ar k2 aur-m-n wbt2• aur-s k2* *Bar-c* bar-s k2 bell k* ben borra-o oss1• borx k* *Brom* gl1.fr• bros-gau mrc1 calc k* calc-ar k2 calc-p k* calc-sil k2 caps k* carb-v mrr1 carbn-dox knl3• carc mlr1• carl *Caust* k* cench cham k* chin k* chinin-ar chir-fl gya2 cic k* cich mtf11 cocc coli rly4• con sne crot-c sk4• cupr gk cycl dendr-pol sk4• der dulc dys fmm1• fagu mtf11 galeoc-c-h gms1• galla-q-r nl2• ger-i rly4• *Germ-met* srj5• gran granit-m es1• **Graph** bg1* guaj k* haliae-lc srj5• helo ptk1 *Helon* k1* hep mrr1 hydrog srj2*• hyos k* ign k* ignis-alc es2• impa-g mtf11 iod mtf33 *Ip* k* iris k* kali-ar k2 kali-c bg2 kali-cy a1 kali-p fd1.de• kali-s gk ketogl-ac rly4• lac-ac k2* lac-cp sk4• lac-e hrn2• lac-f wza1• lac-h htj1*• lac-lup hrn2• *Lach* k* lil-t k2

Censorious: ...
loxo-recl knl4• lyc k* lyss mrr1 m-arct j5.de mag-c mg1.de *Merc* bg2* mez bg2* morg-g fmm1• morph br1* mosch k* myric naja bg2* nat-m k* **Nat-sil** fd* nicc-met sk4• *Nux-v* k* par k* petr k* petr-ra shn4• *Phos* gl1.fr• pin-s ↓ *Plat* k* plb plut-n srj7• podo fd3.de• polys sk4• positr nl2• pseuts-m oss1• puls bg2 ran-b rhus-r ↓ rhus-t k* ruta fd4.de samb ptk1* sapin a1 sel ptk1* *Sep* k* sil k* sol-t-ae spong fd4.de staph k* **Sulph** k* syc bka1*• **Symph** fd* taosc iwa1• tarent bro1 til tub bgs tus-fr a1 urol-h rwt• *Vanil* fd5.de **Verat** b7.de* verbe-o mtf11 vitis-v mtf11 zinc ptk1* [ars-met stj2 aur-m stj2 heroin sdj2 tax jsj7]
- **afternoon**: dulc podo fd3.de•
- **evening**: rhus-r a1 rhus-t a1 [tax jsj7]
- **blames** others:
  - **family**; blames others in her family: lac-lup hrn2•
  - **wants** to; and make them responsible: lac-lup hrn2•
- **everything**; desire to criticize: guaj ptk1*
- **friends**; with dearest: (↗*Aversion - friends; Mocking - friends; Unsympathetic - friends)* ars-s-f k2 aur-s k2 chinin-ar chir-fl gya2 der *Dulc* fd4.de positr nl2• sep mtf33
- **occupation** amel.: sapin a1
- **oneself**; of: (↗*Reproaching oneself)* aq-pet mtf11 aur ptk1 pin-s mtf11 [heroin sdj2]
- **remarks**; making nasty: [am-s stj1]
- **silent**; disposition to be faultfinding or: (↗*Censorious; Taciturn)* caps fkm1• hydrog srj2• lac-lup ↓ nat-sil fd3.de• *Verat*
  - **husband**; of: lac-lup hrn2•
- **weather**; the: lac-lup hrn2•

CENTERED:
- **not** centered (See Confidence - want)
- **too** much centered (See Confident)

CEREBRAL type (See Emotions - predominated)

CHAGRIN (See Ailments - mortification)

CHANGE:
- **aversion** to: (↗*Conformism; Dogmatic; Fear - new enterprise; Homesickness; Narrow-minded; New ideas - aversion; Obstinate; Pertinacity; Positiveness; Prejudiced; Proper - too; Stability - desire)* acon ↓ agar ↓ *Aloe* sne *Bar-c* ↓ (non:bol-la c1) *Bry* mtf calc-f ↓ caps br1 *Carb-an* ↓ **Carb-v** ↓ coc-c mgm• cupr sst3• dulc ↓ form ↓ germ-met ↓ *Graph* ↓ kali-bi ↓ *Kali-c* mrr1 medus ↓ nicc ↓ polyg-h hr1 puls ↓ skook srj sol-t-ae ↓ **Vip** ↓
  - **children**; in: acon lmj agar lmj *Bar-c* lmj **Bry** lmj **Calc** lmj calc-f lmj *Caps* lmj *Carb-an* lmj **Carb-v** lmj cupr lmj dulc lmj form lmj germ-met lmj *Graph* lmj kali-bi lmj kali-c lmj medus lmj nicc lmj puls lmj sol-t-ae lmj **Vip** lmj
- **desire** for: (↗*Travelling - desire)* aq-mar rbp6 bac jl2 *Bamb-a* stb2.de• *Bry* hr1* carc mlr1• cham k2* **Dulc** fd* hep k2* *Kali-s* fd4.de lac-leo sk4• med mtf33 merc sne pieri-b mlk9.de positr nl2• puls mtf33 ruta fd4.de *Sacch-a* fd2.de• sal-fr sle1• sep a1* *Spong* fd4.de *Tritic-vg* fd5.de tub k2* vanil fd5.de
  - **life**; in: bamb-a stb2.de• *Carc* mrr1 **Dulc** fd* ruta fd4.de sal-fr sle1• spong fd4.de *Tritic-vg* fd5.de **Tub** mrr1 vanil fd5.de

CHANGEABLE (See Mood - changeable)

CHANGING MOOD (See Mood - changeable)

CHAOTIC: (↗*Confusion; Dirty; Disconcerted; Heedless; Idleness; Squandering - order)* agar k* am-c anac androc srj1• *Ars Bell Bov* bry ↓ *Carc* mlr1• chir-fl gya2 dream-p sdj1• euphr falco-pe nl2• germ-met srj5• ip ↓ irid-met srj5• kali-c kali-s fd4.de lac-f wza1• *Lac-lup* ↓ lach a1 mag-m maias-l hrn2• *Merc* mez *Moni* rfm1• nat-c nux-v ↓ olib-sac ↓ *Ph-ac Phos* k* polys sk4• puls ↓ *Rhod* rhus-t ↓ *Seneg* spong fd4.de stram bg* sul-ac mrr1 sulph tl1* syph jl2 thuj tritic-vg fd5.de zinc k* [ant-t stj2 heroin sdj2 lac-mat sst4 pop dhh1 rubd-met stj2 tax jsj7 zinc-m stj2 zinc-n stj2 zinc-p stj2]
- **chill**; during: ars bg2 bell bg2 bry bg2 ip bg2 nux-v bg2 puls bg2 rhus-t bg2
- **orderly** manner; cannot perform anything in: lach a1*
- **planning**, roaming around; unsure, poor: *Lac-lup* hrn2•
- **restlessness**; with: mag-m h2 olib-sac wmh1

CHARACTER, lack of: (↗*Cowardice; Will - weakness)* *Caust* vh* **Lyc** vh* med jl2 *Sil* vh*

CHARLATAN: (↗*Deceitful; Liar)* calc gl1.fr• nat-m gl1.fr• plat gl1.fr• puls gl1.fr• sulph gl1.fr•

CHARMING others: *(↗Mirth; Vivacious; Witty)* marb-w es1• sulph mrr1

CHASING:
- **objects**; imaginary: stram k*
- **persons**; imaginary: cur k*

CHECKING:
- **family** matters: apis mrr1
- **twice** or more; must check: *(↗Forgotten - something; Self-control - loss; Thoughts - compelling)* arg-n dgt ars mrr1 brom mrr carc fd* caust vh* iod mrr1 kali-s fd4.de luna kg1• nat-m ser nat-sil fd3.de• podo fd3.de• spong fd4.de syph vh* tub jl2 [heroin sdj2]
- **verifying** if the doors are locked: syph jl2

CHEERFUL: *(↗Amusement - desire; Buoyancy; Content; Delirium - gay; Exhilaration; Exultant; High-spirited; Hopeful; Jesting; Joy; Laughing; Mirth; Mood - agreeable; Optimistic; Playful; Pleasure; Smiling; Thoughts - persistent - humorous; Vivacious; Witty)* abrot *Acon* k* aesc aeth aether a1 agar k* *Agath-a* nl2• agri mtf11 aids↓ alco j* alf br1 allox tpw4 aloe alum b2.de* alum-p k2 am-c↓ anac anag bro1 anan vh1 androc srj1• ang k* ant-c k* ant-t b2.de* anth a1 apis k* apoc aran↓ *Arg-met* k* arg-n mrr1* arn↓ ars k* ars-s-f k2 arund↓ asaf asar k* asc-t↓ aspar j5.de* aster↓ *Atro* kr1 *Aur* k* aur-i k2 aur-m k* aur-m-n↓ aur-s k2* bad bg2 *Bamb-a* stb2.de• bart a1 *Bell* k* bell-p↓ bism↓ bit-ar wht1• borx bov k* brom bry k* bufo↓ bufo-s jl3 bung-fa mtf cact *Calc*↓ calc-act↓ calc-i k2 calc-p **Cann-i** k* cann-s k* **Cann-xyz** ptk1 canth caps k* carb-ac *Carb-an* k* carb-v k* carbn-dox knl3• carbn-h br1 carbn-o a1 carbn-s carc st1* carl a1 castm j5.de caust k* cench↓ cent a1 ceph a1 chel↓ chin chin-b↓ chinin-s a1 chir-fl gya2 chlol a1 chlor choc↓ **Cic** b2.de* *Cimic*↓ cinch a1 *Cinnb* k2* cist↓ cit-v↓ clem↓ cob k* coc-c↓ coca coca-c sk4• cocc **Coff** k* colch coloc com↓ con k* conch fkr1• corian-s knl6• cot a1 **Croc** k* cupr k* cycl k* cypr bro1* dios j dream-p sdj1• dros dulc fd4.de elae a1 ephe-si hsj1• erig↓ ery-a a1 ery-m a1 eucal k* eug j5.de eupi fago falco-pe↓ ferr k* ferr-ma a1 ferr-p *Fl-ac* k* flor-p rsj3• *Form* bro1 galeoc-c-h gms1• galla-q-r nl2• gamb gast a1 gels germ-met↓ gink-b↓ glon glycyr-g cte1• graph k* *Grat* j5.de* guar kr1 haliae-lc srj5• ham fd3.de• hell↓ *Hep*↓ hippoc-k↓ hir rsj4• hura hydr hydrc kr1 hydrog srj2*• **Hyos** k* *Ign* k* ina-i mlk9.de indg a1 inul a1 iod k* iodof a1 irid-met srj5• jab↓ kali-bi kali-br kali-chl j5.de kali-cy a1 kali-m ckh1 kali-p↓ kali-s stj1* keroso a1 kiss a1 kola stb3• kreos↓ kres mg1.de lac-del hrn2• lac-f wza1• lac-loxod-a↓ lac-lup↓ **Lach** k* lachn↓ lact a1 lact-v a1 lapa↓ laur k* lepi a1 limen-b-c hrn2* limest-b es1• loxo-recl↓ *Lyc* k* lyss jl2 m-arct b7.de* m-aust↓ mag-c↓ mag-m b4.de mag-s manc marb-w es1• mate a1 med↓ melal-alt gya4 meny b2.de* meph↓ merc merc-c b4a.de merc-i-r↓ mez b4.de* mit a1 morph a1 mosch mucs-nas rly4• mur-ac a1 nabal a1 **Nat-c** k* nat-m k* nat-p nat-s nat-sil fd3.de• neon srj5• nept-m lsd2.fr nicc j5.de nicc-met stj2*• nid↓ *Nit-ac* nitro-o a1 *Nux-m* k* *Nux-v* ol-an olib-sac wmh1 *Op* k* orig a1 orot-ac rly4• ox-ac k* ozone sde2• par↓ paull a1 ped a1 peti a1 petr petr-ra shn4• ph-ac k* phasco-ci rbp2 phel↓ *Phos* k* phys pieri-b mlk9.de pip-m k* *Plac* rzf5• *Plat* k* plb k* plut-n srj7• **Podo** fd* polys↓ positr nl2• pot-e rly4• propr sa3• prun a1 psil ft1 psor k* ptel↓ *Puls* b7.de* querc-r svu1• ran-b↓ ran-s↓ rhod rhodi a1 rhodi-o-n c1 rhus-g tmo3• *Rhus-t* mrr1 rhus-v *Ros-d* wla1 ruta sabad k* sacch-a fd2.de• sal-al blc1• sarr *Sars* k* scut sf1.de sec k* sel gmj2 senec↓ seneg k* sep k* sil↓ spig k* spong k* squil k* stann k* staph staphycoc rly4• stram k* *Sul-ac* k* sul-i k2 sulfa↓ *Sulfon*↓ *Sulph* k* sumb↓ suprar rly4• *Symph*↓ tab k* *Tarax* k* *Tarent* k* tell rsj10*• tere-la rly4• teucr thea bro1 ther thres-a sze7• thuj thyr↓ tong j5.de* trios a1* tritic-vg fd5.de *Tub* ulm-c jsj8• upa a1 valer k* vanil fd5.de *Verat* k* verb k* viol-o viol-t b7.de visc jl3 wies a1 *Zinc* k* zing ziz↓ [am-f stj2 ant-met stj2 arg-p stj2 argon stj2 bar-i stj2 *Buteo-j* sej6 cadm-met stj2 cadm-s stj2 calc-s stj1 cob-m stj2 cob-p stj2 cupr-act stj2 cupr-f stj2 cupr-m stj2 cupr-p stj2 ferr-f stj2 ferr-lac stj2 ferr-n stj2 ferr-sil stj2 fl-pur stj2 helium stj2 krypt stj2 lith-f stj2 lith-i stj2 mang stj1 mang-i stj2 mang-m stj2 mang-met stj2 mang-p stj2 mang-s stj2 merc-i-f stj2 oxyg stj2 pall stj2 pop dhh1 rado stj2 sol-ecl cky1 *Spect* dfg1 tax jsj7 temp elm1 tung-met stj2 xen stj2 zinc-i stj2 zinc-m stj2 zinc-n stj2 zinc-p stj2]

- **daytime**: anac ant-t arg-met aur caust k* gink-b↓ mag-m mur-ac nat-s sars
  - **alternating** with | **irritability** | **night** (See Irritability - night - alternating - cheerfulness - daytime)
    - ⁝ **sadness** | **evening**: gink-b sbd1•
- **morning**: aloe↓ androc srj1• borx bov j5.de bung-fa mtf calc-s k* carbn-s caust chin↓ chir-fl gya2 choc srj3• cinnb cit-v a1 clem↓ con k* ery-m↓ *Fl-ac* graph ham fd3.de• hep hura hydr↓ hydrog srj2• kali-p fd1.de• kola stb3• lach (non:mag-m slp) nat-s nept-m lsd2.fr nux-m↓ olib-sac wmh1 *Plat* k* polys sk4• psor ros-d wla1 spig sulph k* tarent↓ tritic-vg fd5.de vanil fd5.de zinc bg2

Cheerful – morning: ...
  - **8** h: hura
  - **air**, in open: plat a1
  - **alternating** with:
    - ⁝ **sadness** | **evening**: calc-s kr1 graph gl1.fr•
  - **flatus**; after: carbn-s k2
  - **rising**, on: hydr
  - **waking**, on: aloe bov j chin k* clem ery-m a1 hydr kali-p fd1.de• nept-m lsd2.fr nux-m tarent
- **forenoon**: aeth k* borx caust k* clem k* com k* graph nat-m nat-s k* phos pip-m a1 plb spong fd4.de zinc
- **noon**:
  - **alternating** with:
    - ⁝ **sadness** | **evening**: zinc hr1*
- **afternoon**: anac k* ang k* *Ant-t* arg-met aster hr1* aur-m calc calc-s k* cann-s lyc mag-c merc-i-f↓ merc-i-r↓ nat-s ol-an↓ ox-ac ped↓ phos plb sars *Staph* thuj k* verb
  - **15** h: ped a1
  - **16**-18 h: merc-i-f a1 merc-i-r a1
  - **17** h: ol-an a1
- **evening**: agar *Aloe* alum am-c k* anac *Ang*↓ ant-c↓ arn↓ asc-t↓ aster k* aur↓ bell k* bism k* borx↓ (non:bufo slp) bufo-s k* calc calc-act a1 calc-s carb-ac k* carb-an↓ carb-v castm chel chin k* chin-b hr1* chinin-s cist k* clem coc-c cupr cycl k* dulc fd4.de ferr k* graph hydrog srj2• **Lach** lachn k* laur lyc↓ lyss k* m-aust↓ mag-c med k* *Merc*↓ merc-i-f merc-i-r k* mez↓ nat-c *Nat-m* nicc-met sk4• *Nit-ac*↓ nux-m k* nux-v gl1.fr• ol-an phel k* phos↓ pip-m plat *Prun*↓ *Puls*↓ ran-b↓ ran-s↓ rhus-t↓ sars *Sep*↓ sil↓ *Spig*↓ spong fd4.de staph↓ sul-ac↓ *Sulph* sumb teucr *Valer* k* verb k* viol-t k* *Zinc* zinc-p k2*
  - **18** h: calc-s a1
  - **21** h: asc-t c1
  - **alternating** with:
    - ⁝ **hypochondriasis** | **daytime**; during: *Sulph* k* viol-t
    - ⁝ **ill** humor (See irritability)
    - ⁝ **irritability** | **daytime** (See Irritability - daytime - alternating - cheerfulness - evening)
    - ⁝ **sadness**:
      - ⁝ **morning**: nux-v gl1.fr•
      - ⁝ **noon**: *Zinc* k*
  - **bed**, in: alum *Ang* j5.de ant-c j5.de arn j5.de aur j5.de borx j5.de carb-an j5.de carb-v j5.de *Lach* j5.de laur j5.de lyc j5.de m-aust j5.de *Merc* j5.de mez j5.de *Nat-m* j5.de *Nit-ac* j5.de *Nux-v* j5.de phos j5.de *Prun* j5.de *Puls* j5.de ran-b j5.de ran-s j5.de rhus-t j5.de *Sep* j5.de sil j5.de *Spig* j5.de staph j5.de sul-ac j5.de *Sulph* j5.de *Zinc* j5.de
- **night**: alum bell k* *Caust* chin croc cupr cypr br1 hyos kreos lyc nicc-met sk4• nitro-o a1 op k* ph-ac sep sil stram sulph verat k*
  - **midnight**:
    - ⁝ **after** | **2** h; until: *Chin*
- **air**, in open: ang j5.de chir-fl gya2 dulc fd4.de kali-s fd4.de merc-i-f k* nux-m j5.de phel vml3• *Plat* plb ruta fd4.de spong fd4.de *Tarent* teucr tritic-vg fd5.de vanil fd5.de
- **alternating** with:
  - **absentmindedness**: alum a1 spong st
  - **anger** (See Anger - alternating - cheerfulness)
  - **anger**; sudden (See Anger - sudden - alternating - cheerfulness)
  - **anxiety** (See Anxiety - alternating - cheerfulness)
  - **confusion**: spong bg2*
  - **dancing** (See Dancing - alternating - cheerfulness)
  - **distraction** (See confusion)
  - **dullness**: jab hr1*
  - **grief**: calc-s hr1* graph j5.de *Op* gl1.fr•

- **ill** humor (See Irritability - alternating - cheerfulness)
- **impatience** (See Impatience - alternating - cheerfulness)
- **indifference** (See Indifference - alternating - cheerfulness)
- **irritability** (See Irritability - alternating - cheerfulness)
- **lachrymose** mood (See weeping)
- **laughter** (See Laughing - alternating - cheerfulness)
- **laziness**: kola stb3• spong k*
- **mania** (See Mania - alternating - cheerfulness)
- **melancholy** (See sadness)
- **moaning**: bell j5.de coff hr1* stram j5.de
- **moroseness** (See Morose - alternating - cheerfulness)
- **pain**: plat
- **palpitation**: spig k*
- **passion**; bursts of (See Anger - sudden - alternating - cheerfulness)
- **physical** symptoms: plat
- **quarreling** (See Quarrelsome - alternating - cheerfulness)
- **quiet** disposition: aur j5.de bell kr1
- **rage** (See Rage - alternating - cheerfulness)
- **sadness**: abrot st1 acon agar k* androc srj1• aran jl3 arg-met jl asar k* *Aur* hr1* aur-m-n wbt2• bell vh* calc calc-s a1* cann-i cann-s j5.de cann-xyz bg2 canth carb-an k* carc mlr1• castm *Caust* k* cench k2* *Chin* k* *Cimic* k* clem k* coc-c k2* coff vh* croc k* cupr hr1* *Dios* ↓ ferr k* fl-ac k* gels graph j5.de hell hippoc-k szs2 hyos vh* ign iod *Kali-chl* k* (non:kali-m a1) lach k2* lapa a1 lyc k* m-arct j5.de med k* mucs-nas rly4• nat-c k* *Nat-m* k* neon ↓ nicc-met sk4• nid jl3 nit-ac *Nux-m* k* *Nux-v* hr1* op j5.de ozone sde2• *Petr* bg2* petr-ra shn4• *Phos* k* *Plat* k* psor k* senec k* sep spig **Spong** fd* staph vh* *Stram* j5.de* sulfa jl3 *Sulfon* br1 *Symph* fd3.de• tarent k* thyr c1 tub br1 *Vanil* fd5.de zinc k* ziz k*
  - ⁝ **looking** down when walking on the street: *Dios* kr1
  - ⁝ **periodical** | **day**; alternate: ferr c1 neon srj5•
- **seriousness**: cann-s j5.de *Chin* ckh1 cycl h1* *Nux-m* hr1 plat spong bg2*
- **shouting** (See Shrieking - alternating - cheerfulness)
- **shrieking** (See Shrieking - alternating - cheerfulness)
- **suicidal** thoughts: loxo-recl knl4•
- **sympathy**; want of: (↗*Consolation - agg.*) merc
- **taciturnity**: asar h1
- **talk**; aversion to (See taciturnity)
- **timidity**: m-arct j5.de
- **vexation** (See Irritability - alternating - cheerfulness)
- **violence** (See Violent - alternating - cheerfulness)
- **weakness**: *Sulfon* br1
- **weariness** of life: borx j5.de
- **weeping**: acon k* alum j5.de arg-met bell k* borx cann-s k* carb-ac carb-an k* chin ptk1 croc bg graph j5.de ign k* iod nux-m tl1 nux-v gl1.fr• phos j5.de plat k* plb podo fd3.de• psor sep spong k* *Stram* j5.de* sumb tritic-vg fd5.de *Vanil* fd5.de
- **work**; aversion to (See laziness)

- **bed**:
  - **in**: *Alum* j *Hep* k*
  - **jumps** out of: **Cic** hr1*
- **causeless**: aur-i k2* falco-pe nl2• sacch-a fd2.de•
- **chill**, during: *Cann-s* k* cann-xyz bg2 *Coff* bg2 croc bg2 *Nat-c* bg2 nux-m k* **Op** bg2 phos k* **Plat** bg2 *Puls* k* rhus-t k* *Sars* bg2 verat k*
- **clapping** ones hands: cic j5.de verat j5.de
- **coition**; after: nat-m k*
- **company**, in: (↗*Company - desire; Excitement - company*) bov k* chir-fl gya2 lac-lup hrn2• pall mrr1
  - **exhausted** afterwards; but: pall br1*
- **constipated**, when: *Calc Psor* k*
- **convulsions**; after: sulph k*
- **dancing**, laughing, singing; with: (↗*Dancing*) *Bell* j5.de* chir-fl gya2 haliae-lc srj5• *Hyos* j5.de kali-s fd4.de *Nat-m* j5.de* nitro-o a1 plat j5.de *Spong* fd4.de *Stram* j5.de tab j5.de vanil fd5.de
- **death**, while thinking of: (↗*Death - desires; Suicidal*) aur k* aur-m-n wbt2•
- **desires** to be cheerful (See Desires - full - cheerful)
- **destructiveness**; with: spong vh*
- **dreams**; after: bamb-a stb2.de• kali-cy a1 mur-ac h2
- **driving**; while: haliae-lc srj5•
- **drunkenness**, during: alum ang h1* *Bell* kr1 cinnb h1* coff k* fl-ac k2 op k* plb k2 spig staph k* tarent k2 teucr j5.de
- **eating**:
  - **after**: carb-v mez ptel ↓
    - ⁝ **followed** by | **depression** an hour later: ptel c1
  - **when**: aids nl2• anac bell carb-ac cist
- **fearful**; but: nat-c ptk1*
- **flatus**, after: carbn-s k2
- **followed** by:
  - **irritability**: clem hyos nat-s ol-an op seneg tarax
  - **melancholy**: gels graph meph jl3 petr plat ziz k*
  - **prostration**: clem spong
  - **sleepiness**: bell k* calc
- **foolish**, and: (↗*Foolish*) acon k* agar anac b4a.de* anan a1 arund kr1 bell k* *Calc* b4.de* carb-an j5.de carb-v k* cic vh dulc fd4.de falco-pe nl2• *Hyos* b7a.de merc k* olib-sac wmh1 par k* seneg k* spong fd4.de **Sulph** kr1
- **headache**, with: *Ther* k2*
- **heart** disease; with: cact ptk1*
- **heat**, during: acon dulc fd4.de mosch j5.de *Op* petr j sabad j5.de sars b4.de thuj h1
- **hysterical**: (↗*Hysteria*) ther k2*
- **intoxicated**, as if: agath-a nl2•
- **itching** eruption; though there is an: gink-b sbd1•
- **lightness**; with sensation of: lac-loxod-a hrn2• limen-b-c hrn2•
- **loquacious**: aeth c1 *Kali-s* fd4.de
- **manual** labor, during: ang h1* tritic-vg fd5.de
- **menses**:
  - **before**: (↗*Menses - before*) acon coca ptk1 fl-ac k* hyos k*
  - **during**: (↗*Menses - during*) *Fl-ac* k* germ-met mtf ozone sde2* pot-e rly4• stram
- **morbidly**: aur-s k2
- **music**, from: chir-fl gya2 *Croc* j5.de nat-sil fd3.de• *Spong* fd4.de symph fd3.de• tarent a1
- **never**: (↗*Laughing - never; Smiling - never*) hep vh* nit-ac vh*
- **pain**:
  - **after**: form ptk1*
  - **during**: spig k*
- **paroxysms**, in: aur-i k2
- **perspiration**, during: apis ars bell clem
- **quarrelsome**, and: *Bell* hr1* podo fd3.de• *Staph* kr1*
- **room**; in the | **amel.**: tarent
- **sadness**:
  - **after**: cench k2 orig c1 spig a1 spong fd4.de
  - **with**: ptel c1 zinc gk*
- **stool** | **after**: *Borx* k* *Calc* vh* nat-c **Nat-s** k* ox-ac
- **supper**; after: bell a1 cist
- **thinking** of death (See death)
- **thoughtless**: alum k2 arn hr1* eug kr1 podo fd3.de•
- **thunders** and lightens; when it: (↗*Weather - Thunderstorm - during; Weather - Thunderstorm - during - amel.; GENERALS - Weather - Thunderstorm - amel.*) bell-p fb1 calc gk *Carc* cd* caust gg **Lyc** ●* **Sep** k ●*
- **tranquillity** (See Tranquillity - cheerful)
- **urination** | **after**: erig a1 eug germ-met srj5• hyos k*
- **waking**, on: bufo bg2 haliae-lc srj5• hydrog srj2• ozone sde2• *Sulph* hr1* tarent k*
- **walking** in the open air and afterwards: alum h2* ang h1* chinin-s a1 cinnb h1* coca a1 dulc fd4.de fl-ac k1 *Kali-s* fd4.de plb k1 spong fd4.de tarent k1 teucr j5.de*
- **weakness**; with: kola stb3•
- **weather** | **cloudy**; in: aur sk1•

O - **Stomach**; with pain in (See Vivacious - stomach)

CHILDBED (See Delivery - after)

CHILDISH behavior: *(↗Answering - foolish; Antics; Awkward; Delusions - child - he; Dementia; Foolish; Frivolous; Gestures - ridiculous; Giggling; Jesting - ridiculous; Laughing - childish; Laughing - silly; Naive; Retardation; Simple; Smiling - foolish; Speech - childish; Speech - foolish; Speech - prattling; FACE - Expression - foolish)* acon k* aeth ptk1 *Agar* bg2* agath-a nl2• alco a1 *Aloe* ptk1 alum ambr ptk1 anac k* ant-c vh *Apis* *Arg-n* k* arizon-l nl2• ars bg2 aur-m-n wbt2• **Bar-c** k* *Bar-m* bell bg2* bufo k* calad *Calc* ctc*• carb-an carb-v k* *Carbn-s* carc mtf33 cham gk chlol **CIC** k* con ptk1 *Croc* k* crot-c cypr vml3• falco-pe nl2• *Hell* ptk1 hyos bg2* *Ign* k* irid-met srj5• kali-br k* kres mg1.de *Lac-ac* stj*• lac-h sze9• lach ptk1 lyc ptk1* *Nat-c* ptk1 *Nux-m* k* nux-v bg2* op bg2* par k* *Ph-ac* ptk1 phos mtf33 pic-ac ptk1 plb ptk1* **Podo** fd* positr nl2• puls k* rhus-t seneg k* sep ptk1* sil ptk1* *Stram* k* sulfa jl3 sulph ptk1* thyr ptk1 *Tritic-vg* fd5.de tub mrr1* vanad dx verat ptk1 viol-o k* [bar-s stj1 heroin sdj2 zinc stj2 zinc-m stj2 zinc-n stj2 zinc-p stj2]

- **body** grows; and only the: bufo ptk1*
- **delivery**; after: apis ptk1*
- **old** people; in: **Bar-c** kr1*

CHILDREN:

- **aversion** to her own (See Aversion - children - own)
- **beget** and to have children; desire to: *(↗Love - children)* lac-h mtf nat-m gl* ox-ac podo fd3.de• puls mtf ruta fd4.de thuj mtf *Tritic-vg* fd5.de
- **covering** their face (See Gestures - hands - covering - face - children)
- **desire** to be with (See Company - desire - children; of)
- **desire** to have more children: plac rzf5• taosc iwa1•
- **dislikes** her own (See Aversion - children - own)
- **flies** from her or his own children: *(↗Aversion - children - sadness; Escape - family; Estranged - family; Forsaking - children)* lyc
- **loves** profoundly her beautiful daughter: *(↗Love - children)* lac-e hrn2•
- **nurture**; desire to: limen-b-c hrn2•
- **striking** one's own children (See Striking - children; striking)
- **watchful** (= who are on the lookout for every gesture): phos st* sulph ↓
  - **everyone** eating; of: sulph mtf33

CHILL; during: bell bg2 *Camph* b7.de *Caps* b7.de cham b7.de cic b7.de dros b7.de hell b7.de kali-c b4.de led b7.de nat-c b4.de nux-m b7.de op b7.de plb b7.de rhus-t b7.de spig b7.de *Stram* b7.de *Verat* b7.de viol-t b7.de

CHOLERIC (See Passionate [=choleric])

CHRISTMAS; sensation of: vult-gr sze5•

CIRCUMSPECTION, lack of (See Indiscretion)

CLAIRAUDIENT: anac br1 cann-i c1 lyss c1

CLAIRVOYANCE: *(↗Ailments - anticipation; Anticipation; Death - presentiment; Deja; Fear - happen; Intuitive; Prophesying; ABDOMEN - Apprehension; BLADDER - Apprehension; CHEST - Apprehension; DREAMS - Clairvoyant; DREAMS - Events - future; DREAMS - Prophetic; DREAMS - Visionary; STOMACH - Apprehension)* *Acon* k* anac k* androc srj1• *Anh* bro1* arn k* ben c1 bry j calc k* cann-i k* carc pd* chir-fl gya2 com ↓ *Crot-c* k* cypra-eg sde6.de• dat-a c1* dulc fd4.de falco-pe nl2• haliae-lc srj5• hydroph jl3 hyos kali-p fd1.de• kola stb3• lac-del hrn2• lac-f wza1• lac-leo sk4• lach k* lap-la sde8.de• *Lyss* k* m-arct j5.de* *Med* k* nabal bro1 nat-p mrr1 nat-sil stj2*• neon srj5• *Nux-m* k* op k* *Phos* k* *Podo* fd3.de• ptel gk pyrus k* ruta fd4.de *Sal-fr* sle1• sil k* spong fd4.de stann k* stram symph fd3.de• taosc iwa1• tarent *Tritic-vg* fd5.de urol-h rwt• valer a1* vanil fd5.de *Verat-v* hr1* [calc-sil stj2 ferr-sil stj2 heroin sdj2 mag-sil stj2 mang stj1 mang-m stj2 mang-met stj2 mang-p stj2 mang-s stj2 spect dfg1]

- **midnight**: cann-i a1
- **dreams**; clairvoyant (See DREAMS - Clairvoyant)
- **sleep**, during: com hr1*

CLARITY of mind: *(↗Ideas - abundant; Mental power - increased)* *Acon* bg2 *Adam* srj arge-pl rwt5• arizon-l nl2• bell ↓ camph bg2 cimic bg2 coca-c sk4• *Coff* ↓ des-ac rbp6 hydr br1 ign b7.de* lac-h sze9• lac-leo hrn2• lac-lup hrn2• lacer c1 lach ↓ lavand-a ctl1• loxo-recl knl4•

Clarity of mind: ...
melal-alt gya4 *Moni* rfm1• myos-a rly4• *Nux-v* b7.de* *Olib-sac* wmh1 *Op* ↓ ozone sde2• ph-ac ↓ phos bg2 positr nl2• rad-br sze8• *Sanguis-s* hrn2• spig ↓ spong fd4.de thuj ↓ tritic-vg fd5.de valer ↓ vanil fd5.de *Vero-o* rly3• viol-o ↓ vult-gr sze5• [bell-p-sp dcm1 buteo-j sej6 heroin sdj2 *Spect* dfg1 tax jsj7]

- **night** | **amel.**: lac-lup hrn2•
- **alcohol**; in spite of: olib-sac wmh1
- **alternating** with | **head**; heaviness of (See HEAD - Heaviness - alternating - clearness)
- **chill**; during: bell bg2 coff bg2 lach bg2 op bg2 ph-ac bg2 phos bg2 spig b7.de*
- **perspiration**; during: *Coff* bg2 lach bg2 *Op* bg2 phos bg2 thuj bg2 valer bg2 viol-o bg2
- **reading** amel.: lac-lup hrn2•
- **yearning** for: olib-sac wmh1 rad-br sze8•

CLAUSTROPHOBIA (See Fear - narrow)

CLEANNESS:

- **aversion** to cleaning itself (See Washing - aversion)
- **desire** for cleaning: vult-gr sze5•
- **mania** for: *(↗Fear - dirt; Washing - desire; GENERALS - Uncleanliness)* alumin-s ↓ ars k2* carc mlr1• chir-fl gya2 ignis-alc es2• *Kali-s* fd4.de lac-f wza1• lyc ↓ nat-m ↓ olib-sac wmh1 rhus-g tmo3• sep ↓ sil gl1.fr• spong fd4.de sulph gl1.fr• syph mtf33 tritic-vg fd5.de *Vanil* fd5.de [heroin sdj2 tax jsj7]
  - **menses**; before: [alumin-s stj2]

CLEARNESS of mind (See Agility; Clarity; Ideas - abundant)

CLEVER (See Intelligent)

CLIMACTERIC PERIOD (See Menopause)

CLIMBING:

- **desire** to: apom sne *Bell* vh* brass-n-o ↓ choc ↓ falco-pe nl2• hyos a1* petr-ra shn4• sep sne stram kr1*
  - **ladder**: brass-n-o srj5•
  - **walls**: choc srj3•

CLINGING: *(↗Attached; Fear - falling - child; Held - desire)*

- **attendant**; to: ant-t ptk2
- **children**; in: *(↗Frightened - wakens - terrified)* ant-t mtf33 bar-c ↓ *Bism* ↓ *Bism-sn* ↓ **Borx** ↓ cina mtf33 cupr mtf33 cupr-act ↓ *Gels* ↓ kali-c ↓ lyc ↓ nat-m ↓ phos ↓ puls ↓ sanic mtf33 sep ↓ sil ↓ **STRAM** ↓ vanil ↓
  - **awakens** terrified, knows no one, screams, clings to those near; child: *(↗Shrieking - waking - on)* **Borx** st* cina a1* **STRAM** k1*
  - **cough**; during: *Ant-t* mtf borx ↓ sanic ↓
    - **downward** motion; at: borx mtf sanic mtf
  - **grasps** the nurse when carried; child: bism bg2 borx k1 cupr hr1 cupr-act hr1 *Gels* bg2*
    - **afraid** of falling; and screams as if: borx br1 gels br1
  - **mother**; child clings to the: *(↗Mother complex; Mother fixation; Oedipus)* *Ant-t* ↓ bar-c mtf33 *Bism* ↓ *Bism-sn* ↓ borx ↓ gels ↓ kali-c ↓ lyc ↓ nat-m sne phos ↓ puls mrr1* sep mtf33 sil ptk1* vanil ↓
    - **hand** of the mother; child will always take the: *(↗Holding - mother's)* *Ant-t* vh1 *Bism* hr1* gels mtf kali-c mtf33 lyc mtf33 phos a* puls a vanil fd5.de [*Bism-sn* stj2]
    - **frightened**; as if: borx mtf33
  - **sick**; when: sep mtf33
- **convulsions** | **before**: *Cic* kr1*
- **grasps** at others: *(↗Gestures - hands - grasping - bystanders)* agar gg ant-t ptk1* ars bg2 *Camph* kr1 lac-cp ↓ op gl1.fr• phos bg2* puls mtf28*
  - **angry**; when: lac-cp sk4•
- **held**; wants to be (See Held - desire)
- **nurse**; to the: bism bg2 gels bg2
- **persons** or furniture; to: *(↗Forsaken)* ant-t vh* *Bar-c* vh* bism sf1.de* borx h2 cina mtf coff gels irid-met srj5• phos h2 puls ctd stram k*
- **restlessness**, with: *Carb-v* kr1*

- **take** the hand of mother, will always (See children - mother - hand)

CLOSED Character (See Reserved)

CLOSING EYES:
- **agg.**: aeth bg2 apis bg2 arg-n bg2 ars bg2 bell b4a.de* bry b7.de* calc b4a.de* carb-an ptk1 *Carb-v* bg2 caust b4a.de* chin b7a.de* euphr bg2 graph bg2 lach bg2 *Led* b7a.de mag-m ptk1 op b7.de puls b7a.de* samb bg2 sep bg2 sil bg2 spong b7.de* stram bg2 sulph bg2 tarent bg2 thuj bg2
- **amel.**: kali-c k* zinc k*

CLOTHES: *(↗Dress)*
- **best** clothes; wearing his (See Haughty - clothes)
- **luxurious** clothing, finery; wants: aeth bg2 lil-t bg2 sulph bg2*

CLOUDINESS, confusion (See Confusion; Stupefaction)

CLOUDS: | **attracted** by: positr nl2•

CLOUDY weather (See Weather - cloudy)

CLUMSY (See Awkward)

CLOWN; playing the (See Antics; Foolish)

COFFEE agg.: arg-n bg2 calc-p bg2 **Cham** bg2 ign bg2 mill bg2 *Nux-v* bg2 plat b4a.de

COITION:
- **after** agg.: bov bg2 *Calc* bg2 dig bg2 mez bg2 nat-m bg2 petr bg2 ph-ac bg2 sel bg2 sep bg2 sil bg2 staph bg2 thuj bg2
- **amel.**: tarent bg2

COLD drinks: | **agg.**: ars b4a.de

COLD hands agg.: graph bg2 puls bg2

COLLECTS many things: *Ars* mrr1 stram mtf sulph mrr1*

COLORS: *(↗Sadness - colors; Sensitive - colors)*
- **attracted** by (See desire)
- **aversion** to: plut-n srj7• spong fd4.de tarent k2*
  - **strong** colors; aversion to: **Tarent** mrr1
- **black**:
  - **amel.**: ign vk4
  - **aversion** to: *(↗Fear - black; Fear - black - everything; Somber - aversion)* ars-i vk4 cocc vk4 *Ign* vk4 ignis-alc es2• med vk4 nat-m vk4 *Nux-v* vk4 *Phos* vk4 podo fd3.de• rob ruta fd4.de *Sep* vk4 stram *Tarent* k* tritic-vg fd5.de vanil fd5.de
  - **desire** for: bung-fa ↓ ign vk4 ignis-alc es2• lac-h sze9• ozone sde2• vanil fd5.de
    - **white**; and: bung-fa shj• *Vanil* fd5.de
- **blue**:
  - **amel.**:
    - **light** blue: ign vk4 mangi vk4
    - **navy** blue: ign vk4
    - **sky** blue: merc vk4
  - **aversion** to: choc srj3• ignis-alc es2• podo fd3.de• sep ↓ tarent a1 vanil fd5.de
    - **dark** blue: sep vk4 vanil fd5.de
  - **desire** for: cocc ↓ *Ign* ↓ *Kali-bi* ↓ lach ↓ neon srj5• *Nux-v* ↓ phos ↓ ruta fd4.de *Sep* ↓ *Sil* ↓ spong fd4.de staph ↓ taosc ↓ tarent a1* tritic-vg fd5.de *Tub* ↓ vanil fd5.de [spect dfg1]
    - **dark** blue: ign vk4 lach vk4 nux-v vk4 ruta fd4.de spong fd4.de staph vk4 vanil fd5.de
    - **light** blue: cocc vk4 *Ign* vk4 *Kali-bi* vk4 *Nux-v* vk4 phos vk4 ruta fd4.de *Sep* vk4 *Sil* vk4 staph vk4 tritic-vg fd5.de *Tub* vk4
      - **men**; in: ign vk4 nux-v vk4 ruta fd4.de sep vk4
    - **turquoise**: nux-v vk4 sep vk4 spong fd4.de taosc iwa1• [spect dfg1]
- **bright**:
  - **agg.**: sil ptk1
  - **amel.**: *Stram* ptk1 *Tarent* ptk1
  - **aversion** to: sil bg2
  - **desire** for: lac-del hrn2•
- **brown** | **aversion** for | **dark** brown: ign vk4 plat vk4

Colors – brown: ...
  - **desire** for:
    - **dark** brown: sil vk4
    - **light** brown: nux-v vk4 sep vk4
    - **wear** it; to: choc srj3• positr nl2•
- **changeable** | **desire** for: puls vk4
- **charmed** by colors (See desire)
- **cream** | **amel.**: phos vk4
- **dark** colors:
  - **aversion** to: ars vk4 ars-i vk4 ign vk4 lach vk4 *Nux-v* vk4 ruta fd4.de *Sep* vk4 vanil fd5.de
  - **desire** for: tarent mtf33
- **desire** for: *Falco-pe* nl2• hippoc-k szs2 lac-h sze9• tritic-vg fd5.de
- **dreams** in colors (See DREAMS - Colored)
- **gold** | **desire** for: [spect dfg1]
- **gray** | **aversion** for: plat vk4
- **green**:
  - **amel.**: ign vk4 kali-i ↓ merc ↓
    - **light** green: kali-i ↓ merc vk4
      - **shirt** and black pants; light green: kali-i vk4
    - **olive** green: ign vk4
  - **aversion** to: choc srj3• lach vk4 mag-c ptk1 *Nux-v* vk4 polys sk4• *Sep* vk4 *Tarent* k1*
    - **dark** green: nux-v vk4
  - **desire** for: dulc fd4.de ign ↓ ignis-alc es2• *Lac-cp* sk4• neon srj5• *Nux-v* vk4 *Sep* ↓ sil vk4 spong fd4.de tarent a1* tritic-vg fd5.de *Tub* ↓
    - **light** green: dulc fd4.de ign vk4 nux-v vk4 *Sep* vk4 sil vk4 *Tub* vk4
    - **men**; in: nux-v vk4
- **light** colors:
  - **amel.**: nit-ac vk4 nux-v vk4 phel vk4 sep vk4 stram mtf33 tarent mtf33
  - **aversion** to: sil mtf33
  - **desire** for: ign vk4 lach vk4 mangi vk4 *Nux-v* vk4 *Sep* vk4 tub vk4 vanil fd5.de
- **nails**, desire to paint: falco-pe nl2•
- **orange**:
  - **aversion** to: *Ign* vk4 lach vk4 nux-v vk4 puls vk4
  - **desire** for: positr nl2• tritic-vg fd5.de
- **paint** nails; desire to (See nails)
- **pink**:
  - **amel.**: calc-p vk4 ign vk4 phos vk4 staph vk4
  - **aversion** to: sep vk4
  - **desire** for: *Ign* vk4 nat-m vk4 nit-ac vk4 *Nux-v* vk4 *Phos* vk4 puls vk4 *Sep* vk4 *Sil* vk4 tritic-vg fd5.de tub vk4 zinc vk4
    - **women**; in: ign vk4 nux-v vk4 sep vk4 tritic-vg fd5.de
- **purple**:
  - **aversion** to: nux-v vk4 sep vk4
  - **desire** for: nat-m mtf33 nux-v vk4 sep vk4 [spect dfg1]
- **red**:
  - **amel.**: ign vk4
    - **deep** red: ign vk4
  - **aversion** to: *Alum* bg2* ars-i vk4 choc ↓ ign vk4 ignis-alc es2• *Nux-v* vk4 polys sk4• *Sep* vk4 *Tarent* k1*
    - **maroon**: choc srj3•
  - **desire** for: aur vk4 dream-p sdj1• ign vk4 ignis-alc es2• lac-h sze9• phos vk4 plut-n srj7• positr nl2• symph fd3.de• taosc iwa1• tarent a1* tritic-vg fd5.de [spect dfg1]
- **violet**:
  - **aversion** to: nux-v vk4 sep vk4
  - **desire** for: nux-v vk4 sep vk4 tritic-vg fd5.de vanil fd5.de
- **white**:
  - **amel.**: ign vk4 nux-v vk4 sep vk4 tub vk4
  - **aversion** to: ign vk4 nux-v vk4
  - **desire** for: *Ars-i* vk4 haliae-lc ↓ ign vk4 ignis-alc es2• kali-bi vk4 kali-p fd1.de• *Lach* vk4 mangi vk4 med vk4 *Nux-v* vk4 *Phos* vk4 polys sk4• *Sep* vk4 *Sil* vk4 *Staph* vk4 sulph vk4 thuj vk4 *Tub* vk4 **Vanil** fd* zinc vk4

- white – **desire** for: ...
  - ⁝ **black**; and (See black - desire - white)
  - ⁝ **hair**; attracted to white: haliae-lc srj
  - ⁝ **men**; in: nux-v vk4 sep vk4 vanil fd5.de
- **yellow**:
  - **aversion** to: *Nux-v* vk4 *Sep* vk4 *Tarent* k1* tritic-vg fd5.de
  - **desire** for: ars-i ↓ (non:brass-n-o srj5) choc ↓ dream-p sdj1• falco-pe nl2• *Ign* ↓ **Podo** fd* ruta fd4.de sep ↓ taosc iwa1• tritic-vg fd5.de vanil fd5.de
    - ⁝ **lemon** yellow: ars-i vk4 *Ign* vk4 sep vk4
      - : **women**; in: ign vk4
    - ⁝ **wear** it; to: choc srj3• podo fd3.de•
  - **everything** looks yellow (See VISION - Colors - yellow - objects)

COMA: (↗*Delirium; Stupor; Unconsciousness; SLEEP - Coma vigil; SLEEP - Comatose)* absin a1 *Acon* bg2* aesc-g a1 aeth bg2* aether a1 agar-cit a1 agar-pa a1 agar-ph a1 agn bg2 agro a1 ail a2 alco a1 alum bg2 am-c bg2* am-caust a2 ambr bg2 amyg a1 anac bg2 ant-t bg2* *Apis* bg2 arg-n a1 **Arn** bg2 ars bg2* asar bg2 atro a2 *Bapt* mrr1 *Bar-c* bg2 *Bell* bg2* ben-n a1 benz-ac a1 benzol br1 both a1 bov bg2 brom bg2 bry a2 bufo a1 cact al4 calc bg2 *Camph* bg2* cann-i a1 cann-s bg2* canth bg2* *Caps* hr1 carb-ac a2 carb-v ↓ *Carbn-h* a1 carbn-o a1 carbn-s a1 caust a1 cench a1 cham bg2 chel bg2 chen-a a2 chin bg2 chir-fl bnm4• chlf a1 chlol ↓ chlor a2 cic bg2* *Cocc* bg2 *Colch* bg2 con bg2* cori-r a1 *Crot-h* a1 **Cupr** bg2* cupr-act a1 cupr-ar ry1 cur pks1 dat-m a1 dig a1 dulc a1 euph-l br1 gels ↓ glon bg2 guaj bg2 *Hell* bg2 hep a1* *Hydr-ac* bg2* **Hyos** bg2* hyosin ↓ *Ign* bg2 iodof a2 ip bg2 jasm mp1• juni-v a1 kali-br a1 *Kali-c* bg2 *Lach* bg2* lat-m bnm6• laur bg2* *Led* ↓ lil-t bg2 lob-p br1 lon-x a1* loxo-lae bnm12• lyc bg2 mag-c bg2 manc mp1• merc bg2* merc-c bg2* merl a1 mez bg2* *Morph* a1 *Mosch* bg2* mur-ac bg2 naja rti2 nat-c bg2 *Nat-m* bg2 nit-ac bg2 **Nux-m** bg2* **Nux-v** bg2* oena a1 olnd bg2* op bg2* oxyg ↓ *Ph-ac* bg2 phos bg2* phyt bg2 plat bg2 plb bg2* *Puls* bg2 pyrog ↓ ran-b bg2 rheum bg2 rhod bg2 *Rhus-t* bg2* ruta bg2 santin a2 *Sec* bg2* sel bg2 sep bg2 sil bg2 sol-ni a1 spig bg2 stann bg2 staph bg2 **Stram** bg2* sul-ac a1 sulph bg2* *Tab* bg2* tanac a2 tarax bg2 tax a1 ter a2* thuj a1 trinit br1 tub al2 valer bg2 verat bg2* verat-v ↓ viol-o bg2 vip bg2* zinc ↓ zinc-s ↓ [heroin sdj2]

- **acidosis**; with respiratory: op mtf
- **alcoholic**: hyos mrr1
- **anoxemic** (See apoplectic)
- **apoplectic**: alco a1 arn mtf bell mtf carbn-h mtf glon mtf hyos mrr1* nux-v mtf op mtf oxyg mtf verat-v mtf
- **asphyxia**; with: ant-t al1 chlor mtf op mtf
- **chills**; with: bell mtf hep al4
- **convulsions**; with: ars a1 bell a2 hydr-ac a1 laur a1 mez a2 op a1 phos hs1 plb a1 stram a1
  - **preceded** by convulsions: ben-n a1 canth a1 juni-v a1 oena a1 plb a1 sec a1
- **deep**: carbn-h a1 op al1
- **delirium**; with: (↗*Delirium - coma vigil)* bapt mtf bell mtf cur mtf hyos mtf lach mtf mur-ac mtf op al1 stram mtf verat mtf zinc mtf
- **diabetes**; in: alum pks1 ars gk2 carb-v gsd1* carbn-o mtf cur mtf* op c8*
- **ear**; with ecchymosis behind ear (= Battle's sign): arn mtf *Led* mtf
- **eyelids**; with falling of: alco a1 cann-i a2
- **face**:
  - **bluish**: agar-ph a1
  - **dark** face; with: ant-t hr1
  - **pale** face; with: ant-t hr1 carb-ac a2 plb a1
  - **purple** face; with: ben-n a1
  - **red** face; with: bell a2 chin ptk1 lon-x mp4• *Mur-ac* op al1
- **fever** | **during**: hyos mrr1 sol-ni a1 tub al2
- **jaw**; with clenched: hydr-ac hr1
- **larynx**; with insensibility of: carb-ac mtf gels mtf hyos mtf lach mtf plb mtf sec mtf stram mtf
- **lips**; with bluish: ant-t hr1
- **liver**; with complaints of: crot-h mtf
- **meningitis**; with:
  - **suppurative**: lyc mtf
  - **tubercular**: tub mtf
- **mouth**; with frothing, foaming from: con a1
- **opisthotonos**; with: camph mtf laur mtf lyc mtf op a1*

Coma: ...

- **persistent** vegetative state (See SLEEP - Coma vigil)
- **pulse**:
  - **frequent** pulse; with: ben-n a1 stram a2
  - **imperceptible**: agar-ph a1 carb-ac a2
  - **irregular** pulse; with: bell a2 ben-n a1
  - **slow** pulse; with: ben-n a1 benz-ac a1 plb mtf
  - **small** pulse; with: bell a2 ben-n a1 stram a2
  - **thready** pulse; with: ant-t btw2 chlol pet1 colch fr1 lach fr1 sec hs1 stram a2
  - **weak** pulse; with: benz-ac a1
- **pupils**:
  - **contracted** pupils; with: agar-ph a1 alco a1 chlf a1 op a2
  - **dilated** pupils; with: bell a2 ben-n a1 carb-ac a2 laur a1 mez a2
  - **insensible**: acon a2 mez a2
  - **unequal** pupils; with: lon-x pfa2
- **renal** failure; with: am-c mtf apis mtf canth mtf merc-c mtf
- **respiration**:
  - **accelerated** respiration; with: (↗*RESPIRATION - Accelerated - coma)* ant-t mtf ars mtf carb-v mtf laur a1 stram a1
  - **arrested** respiration; with: camph mtf cupr mtf cur pks1 hyos mtf lach mtf laur mtf op a2*
  - **difficult** respiration; with: chlor a1 op pew1 stram a2
  - **rattling** respiration; with: agar-ph a1 bell al1
  - **slow** respiration; with: ben-n a1 op a2
  - **stertorous** respiration; with: agar-ph a1 amyg a1 bell htc1 op a2 plb a2
- **septicemia**; with: crot-h hr1 pyrog mtf
- **skin**:
  - **coldness** of skin; with: ben-n a1 benz-ac a1 op a2
  - **heat** of skin; with: bell a2
- **stool**; with involuntary: amyg a1 laur a1
- **stupor**; preceded by: op al1
- **sudden**: ben-n a1
- **throat**; with rattling in: bell a2
- **uremia**; in: *Am-c* bro1 bell bro1 bry bro1 *Carb-ac* bro1 cupr-ar bro1 *Hell* bro1 merc-c bro1 *Morph* bro1 *Op* bro1 verat-v bro1
- **vertigo**; preceded by: aesc-g a1
- **vomiting**; with: dig a1 hyosin a2
- **eyes**:
  - **closed** eyes; with: ben-n a1 laur a1 nux-m al1 plb a1 verat ↓
    - ⁝ **one** eye closed: verat a1
    - ⁝ **opening** eyes when swallowing; only: ter ptk1
  - **glassy** eyes; with: op al1
  - **insensibility** of eyes; with: chlf a1 hell mtf hydr-ac mtf hyos mtf op mtf plb mtf stram mtf zinc mtf zinc-s mtf
  - **open** eyes; with | **half** open: acon a2 lon-x mp4• op al1
  - **sunken** eyes; with: agar-ph a1 chlf a1
  - **swelling** of eyes; with | **one** eye: ter ptk1
- **perspiration**; with: benz-ac ptk1

COMMOTION (See Excitement)

COMMUNICATIVE: (↗*Expansive; Loquacity; Sociability)* acon gl1.fr• alum gl1.fr• ara-maca sej7• arg-n mrr1* bar-c gl1.fr• bov bg2 carc mlr1• chlam-tr bcx2• choc srj3• cimic gk helo-s rwt2• hydrc a1 kali-p fd1.de• kali-s fd4.de lac-del hrn2• *Lach* bg2* *Limen-b-c* hrn2• limest-b es1• marb-w es1• orig sej ozone sde2• **Phos** mrr1* plac rzf5• podo fd3.de• ruta fd4.de spong fd4.de staph mtf33 *Sulph* mrr1* *Tritic-vg* fd5.de ulm-c jsj8• vanil fd5.de [spect dfg1]

- **heart**; desire to be from the: *Limen-b-c* hrn2•

COMPANY: (↗*Sadness - company)*

- **agg.**: (↗*RECTUM - Constipation - presence)* *Acon* ptk1 ambr bg2* anac ptk1 ant-c b7a.de* arg-n bg2 aur bg2* *Bar-c* b4.de* bell bg2* bry bg2 calc bg2 carb-an b4.de* carc fd2.de• *Cham* ptk1 chin bg2 cic bg2* coca br1 con b4.de* cupr bg2 cycl bg2 dig bg2 **Gels** ptk1 graph bg2 hell bg2 hippoc-k szs2 *Ign* bg2* *Lac-leo* hrn2• lavand-a ctl1• led bg2 lyc b4.de* mag-c bg2* mag-m bg2 meny bg2

- **agg.**: ...
nat-c b4.de* nat-m b4.de* nat-sil fd3.de• nux-v bg2* petr b4.de* phos bg2 plb bg2 sal-al blc1• sanguis-s hrn2• *Sep* b4a.de* stann b4.de* stram bg2 sulph b4.de* thuj ptk1 [ferr-f stj2 ferr-n stj2 mang-met stj2]
  - **menses**; during: con ptk1
- **aversion** to: *(↗Anxiety - Company; Asking - Nothing; Cares full - Company; Disturbed; Dullness - Company; Fear - People; Going; Indifference - Company - to; Quiet; wants; Reserved; Restlessness - Company; Retiring - Desire; Secretive; Social - Agg.; Spoken - Aversion; Spoken - Aversion - alone; Suspicious - Solitude; Taciturn; Timidity - Public; HEAD - Pain - Company - agg. - pressing; HEAD - Pain - Company - while)* absin a1* achy jl3 acon k* *Adam* srj5• aesc ↓ agar bg2 agath-a nl2• *Aids* nl2• allox sp1* *Aloe* bg2* **Alum** k* alum-p k2* alum-sil k2* alumin ↓ alumn a1 *Ambr* k* **Anac** k* anan k* *Androc* srj1• ange-s ↓ anh mg1.de ant-c k* ant-t k* *Anth* ↓ aq-mar vml3* arag br1* aran ckh1 arb-m oss1• arg-met ↓ *Arg-n* bg2* arge-pl rwt5• arist-cl jl3 arizon-l nl2• arn k2* ars bg2* *Ars-met* kr1* atro k* *Atro-s* hr1 *Aur* k* aur-i k2* *Aur-m-n* wbt2• *Aur-s* k* bamb-a stb2.de• **Bar-c** k* bar-i k2* bar-m k* bar-s k2* *Bell* k* bov bg2 brom ↓ bros-gau ↓ brucel ↓ *Bry* k* bufo k1* bufo-s k1 *Cact* k* cadm-met mg1.de* caesal-b ↓ caj ↓ calc k* calc-i k2* calc-n ↓ *Calc-p* k* calc-s k* camph ↓ cann-i k* caps br1* **Carb-an** k* *Carb-v* k* carbn-s k1 carc hbh* cardios-h rly4• cartl-s rly4• cassia-s cdd7* caust ↓ cedr k* cench k2* **Cham** k* *Chin* k* chir-fl gya2 choc srj3• chord-umb rly4• **CIC** k1* cimic k* cina ↓ cinnb k* clem k* coca k1* *Coloc* k* *Con* k* convo-s jl cop k* corian-s knl6• cortico tpw7* *Cupr* k* cur k* curc ↓ cycl k* cypra-eg ↓ cystein-l rly4• des-ac rbp6 *Dig* k* dios k* dioxi rbp6 *Dream-p* sdj1• dulc fd4.de *Dys* fmm1• elaps k1 eug k* euph hr1* falco-pe nl2• *Ferr* k* ferr-i k* ferr-p k* ferul a1 fic-m gya1 fl-ac k* fum rly1*• fuma-ac rly4• galla-q-r nl2• **Gels** k* ger-i rly4• germ-met srj5• gink-b sbd1• *Granit-m* es1• graph k* grat k* haliae-lc srj5• halo ↓ ham k* *Hell* k* helo bg2 helo-s rwt2• helon k* *Hep* k* *Hipp* k* hippoc-k szs2 hir skp7• hydr k* hydrog srj2• *Hyos* k* **Ign** k* ignis-alc es2• indg ↓ *Iod* k* irid-met srj5• iris ↓ jug-c k* kali-ar ↓ kali-bi k* kali-br k* kali-c k* kali-i bg2 kali-m ckh1 kali-p k1* kali-s k* ketogl-ac rly4• kola stb3• *Lac-cp* ↓ *Lac-d* k* *Lac-h* htj1*• lac-leo ↓ lac-lup hrn2• *Lach* k* lap-la sde8.de• lavand-a ↓ lec oss• *Led* k* lil-t bg2* limest-b es1• loxo-recl knl4• luna kg1• *Lyc* k* m-aust j5.de mag-c b2.de* mag-m k* mag-s ↓ mang k* marb-w es1• medus ↓ melal-alt gya4 meny k* meph jl merc ↓ merc-i-f ↓ moly-met jl* *Moni* rfm1• *Morg* fmm1• morg-p fmm1• mur-ac ↓ murx j5.de musca-d szs1 nat-br ↓ *Nat-c* k* **NAT-M** b2.de* nat-p k* nat-s k2* **Nat-sil** fd3.de• neon srj5• nept-m lsd2.fr nicc k* nux-m ↓ **Nux-v** k* olib-sac wmh1 op k2* orot-ac rly4• osteo-a knp1• oxal-a rly4• *Oxyt* k* ozone sde2* *Pall* bg2* pana a1 pert-vc vk9 petr k* petr-ra ↓ ph-ac hr1* phasco-ci rbp2 phos k* pic-ac k* pieri-b mlk9.de pin-con oss2• *Plac* rzf5• plac-s rly4• *Plat* k* *Plb* b2.de* plut-n srj7• podo fd3.de• positr nl2• pot-e rly4• prot pte1* pseuts-m oss1• psor k* ptel k* *Puls* k* pycnop-sa mrz1 rad-br sze8• rauw ↓ *Rhus-t* k* ros-d wla1 ruta fd4.de sacch-a fd2.de• sal-al ↓ *Sal-fr* sle1• sanguis-s hrn2• sanic c1 sapin a1 sec k* *Sel* k* **Sep** b2.de* seq-s ↓ sieg mg1.de spong fd4.de *Stann* k* **Staph** bg2* stram b2.de* stront-c sk4• suis-em rly4• suis-hep rly4• sul-ac k* sul-i k2* sulfonam jl3* *Sulph* k* suprar rly4• symph fd3.de• *Syph* bg2* taosc iwa1• *Tarent* k* tax-br oss1• tep k* term-a bnj1 thala jl3 thiop jl *Thuj* k* til k* trinit br1 trios ↓ *Tritic-vg* fd5.de tub ctc• tung-met bdx1• *Urol-h* rwt• ust k* vanil fd5.de verat k* visc ↓ x-ray hr1* [am-br stj2 bell-p-sp dcm1 buteo-j sej6 ferr-sil stj2 helium stj2 heroin sdj2 *Spect* dfg1 tax jsj7]
  - **morning**: alum cortico tpw7 lach br1
  - **forenoon**: alum k*
  - **night** | **spends** night alone to hide his gloominess: indg gt*
  - **age**; people of own: cortico tpw7
  - **alone** amel.; when: adam srj5• agath-a nl2• allox sp1 ambr arge-pl rwt5• *Aur-m-n* wbt2• *Bar-c* bell j bov carb-an carc fd2.de• chir-fl gya2 choc srj3• con convo-s sp1 cortico sp1 cycl ferr ferr-p halo jl ham fd3.de• hell hydrog srj2• iris vh* kali-p fd1.de• kali-s fkr2.de kola stb3• lac-h htj1• lac-lup hrn2• *Lyc* mag-s melal-alt gya4 meny a1 *Nat-c* k* *Nat-m* k* **Nat-sil** fd* ozone sde2• petr ph-ac k2 phasco-ci rbp2 phos plac rzf5• plat j *Plb* k* plut-n srj7• podo fd3.de• rauw sp1 sal-fr sle1• **SEP** k* stann staph stram sulph trios jl visc sp1 [ant-t stj2 buteo-j sej6 moly-met stj2 spect dfg1]

- **aversion** to: ...
  - **alternating** with:
    - **desire** for company (See desire - alternating - aversion)
    - **pleasantry** and sarcasm; bursts of (See Jesting - alternating - company; Mocking - sarcasm - alternating - company)
    - **sarcasm** (See Mocking - sarcasm - alternating - company)
  - **bear** anybody, cannot: *(↗Libertinism)* alumin mtf arg-n mtf elaps fkr8.de ferr mtf *Lac-cp* mtf lac-lup mtf lavand-a ctl1• merc j5.de* nux-v j5.de* sal-al blc1• staph j5.de* *Sulph* j5.de*
  - **children**; in: | **nursed**; when the child is: ant-c mtf33
  - **blanket**; wants to wrap himself in a: plac rzf5•
  - **country** away from people; wants to get into the: *(↗Countryside - desire; Nature - loves; Wilderness - desires)* calc k* calc-p k2 elaps k* merc ptk1 positr nl2• sep ptk1 taosc iwa1•
  - **delivery**; after: *Thuj* kr1 tritic-vg fd5.de
  - **desire** for solitude: achy mtf *Acon* bg2 adam mtf* aesc mrr1 *Aids* nl2• *Allox* mtf *Ambr* b7a.de* ange-s mtf* arg-met vh arn br1 *Aur* b4a.de* bamb-a stb2.de* *Bar-c* b4.de* bell b4.de* bros-gau mrc1 *Bufo* ↓ cadm-met mtf caesal-b bnj1 calc-p bg2 camph b7.de* carb-an b4.de* carc mtf cassia-s mtf chin b7.de* cic b7.de* clem b4.de* con b4.de* cortico mtf cupr b7.de* cur mrr1 curc mtf cycl b7.de* cypra-eg sde6.de• dig bg2 dioxi rbp6 dream-p sdj1• dulc fd4.de eug mtf ferr-p bg2 hep b4a.de* hippoc-k szs2 **Ign** bg2 kali-bi bg2 kali-br bg2 kali-c bg2 kali-s fd4.de kola mtf* lac-h sk4• lac-leo mtf* *Lach* ↓ led b7.de* lyc b4.de* m-aust b7.de* medus mtf melal-alt gya4 meny b7.de* nat-c b4.de* **Nat-m** b4.de* nat-sil fd3.de• nux-v b7.de* olib-sac wmh1 op b7a.de ozone sde2* petr b4.de* petr-ra shn4• *Plat* bg2 *Plut-n* srj7• podo fd3.de• positr nl2• *Puls* b7.de* pycnop-sa mrz1 *Rhus-t* b7.de* ruta fd4.de sal-fr sle1• sanguis-s hrn2• sel gmj2 sep b4a.de* seq-s mtf spong fd4.de stann b4.de* staph ↓ *Stram* bg2 stront-c sk4• sulph b4.de taosc iwa1• term-a bnj1 thuj b4a.de tritic-vg fd5.de tub mtf ust ↓ vanil fd5.de [heroin sdj2 nat-br stj2]
    - **indulge** her fancy; to: *Lach* staph ↓
      - **sexual** fancies: staph br1
    - **masturbation**; to practice: *Bufo* k1* ust k*
    - **reflect**, to: aids nl2•
  - **dullness**; with: gink-b sbd1•
  - **family**; flying from (See Escape - family)
  - **fear** of being alone; yet: *(↗Fear - alone; Fear - people - being)* aids nl2• alum gsh alum-sil k2 ars bg2* brucel sa3• bufo *Clem* k* *Con* k* elaps gels bg hippoc-k szs2 kali-ar k13 kali-br kali-c al lyc k* morg ptj• **Nat-c** k1* *Sep* k* stram bg2* tarent bg1*
  - **friends**, of intimate: *(↗Aversion - friends)* bell cham hr1* coloc k* *Ferr* k* ger-i rly4• gink-b sbd1• granit-m es1• hep c1 *Iod* k* kola stb3• *Nat-c* ruta fd4.de *Sel* spong fd4.de taosc iwa1• [heroin sdj2]
  - **headache**; during: bamb-a stb2.de• lac-cp sk4• melal-alt gya4
  - **heat**, during: con hyos op mtf33 *Puls*
  - **ideally**; if things don't work out: plac rzf5•
  - **lies** with closed eyes (See sight - lies)
  - **loathing** of company: bell gl1.fr• ign gl1.fr• lyc gl1.fr• nux-v gl1.fr• sep gl1.fr• staph gl1.fr• [heroin sdj2]
  - **looked** at; aversion to being (See sight)
  - **meeting** friends, whom he imagines he has offended; to: *(↗Fear - friends - meeting)* ars
  - **men**; the company of: [heroin sdj2]
  - **menses**, during: *(↗Menses - during)* cic ↓ *Con* k* nux-v ↓ plat sapin a1 sep
    - **desires** to be let alone: cic nux-v
  - **mortification**; with: plut-n srj7•
  - **pains**; with the: arn mrr1 lac-h sze9•
  - **perspiration**, during: ars *Bell* lach lyc puls sep
  - **pregnancy**, during: lach *Nat-m* kr1* nux-m sf1.de
  - **quarrelsomeness**; with (See Quarrelsome - company)
  - **sight** of people; avoids the: *(↗Looked - evading)* acon ars gl1.fr• calc st **Cic** *Cupr* k* cur st elaps fkr8.de ferr galla-q-r nl2• *Gels* hydrog srj2• *Iod* k* kola stb3• *Lac-d* st *Led* *Nat-c* nat-m mtf33 positr nl2• psor gg* rhus-t hr1 *Sep* spong fd4.de taosc iwa1• *Thuj*

- **sight** of people; avoids the: ...
  - **lies** with closed eyes, and: kola stb3• sep
  - **shuts** herself up: cur
- **sits** in her room, does nothing: brom hr1*
- **smiling** faces; aversion to: *Ambr*
- **strangers**, aversion to the presence of: *(↗Stranger - presence - agg.)* **Ambr** k* anac vh1 *Bar-c* k* *Bry* bufo calc-p ↓ *Carb-v* caust gk **Cic** cina k2 *Con* *Dys* fmm1• granit-m es1• hep ↓ *Iod* *Lach* hr1 lyc mur-ac ↓ *Nat-c* k2* **NAT-M** gk petr phos mrr1 sacch-a fd2.de• sal-fr sle1• *Sep* spong fd4.de staph gk *Stram* tarent ↓ *Thuj* k* *Vanil* fd5.de [calc-n stj1 merc-i-f stj2]
  - **stool**; during: **Ambr** k* nat-m gk
  - **urination**; during: *(↗Stranger - presence - agg.; BLADDER - Retention - company; BLADDER - Urination - retarded - long - others)* ambr bro1* hep c1* lyc mtf mur-ac bro1* **NAT-M** bg2* tarent ptk1*
- **unpredictable**; thinks people are: ozone sde2•
- **walk** alone, wants to: caj falco-pe nl2•
- **weep**:
  - **has** to; when he: *Anth* vh1 ign gy nat-m br1 vanil fd5.de
  - **weeping** does not amel.: *Cycl* hr1*
  - **with** weeping: podo fd3.de• *Rhus-t* kr1
- **women**; the company of: galla-q-r nl2•

\- **desire** for: *(↗Anxiety - alone; Cheerful - company; Contact; desire; Death - thoughts - alone; Delusions - alone; Delusions - disgraced; Delusions - family; Delusions - forsaken; Delusions - friend - affection; Delusions - friendless; Delusions - help; Delusions - help - calling; Dullness - alone; Estranged - family; Excitement - company; Fear - alone; Fear - death - alone; Fear - happen - alone; Fear - people - being; Fear - solitude; Forsaken; Forsaken - isolation; Inconsolable - alone; Indifference - company - while - amel.; Irritability - alone - when; Laughing - company; Rage - alone; Restlessness - alone; Sadness - alone - when; Social - amel.; Talking - desire; Weeping - alone)* achy ↓ acon gl1.fr• act-sp k* aeth agar ↓ agri mtf11 *Aids* nl2• alco ↓ all-s allox ↓ alum-sil ↓ ambr ↓ androc srj1• ant-c b7a.de* ant-t k* *Apis* aq-mar skp7• **Arg-n** k* **Ars** k* ars-h hr1* asaf k* aur ↓ aur-m k* aur-m-n wbt2• bell k* **Bism** k* bism-o a1 *Bism-sn* br1 bit-ar wht1• bov k* brom k* brucel sa3• bry bufo bung-fa mtf buteo-j ↓ cadm-met ↓ cadm-s *Calc* k* calc-ar k2* calc-n ↓ calc-p calc-sil ↓ *Camph* k* *Cann-s* b7a.de carb-v carc fd2.de*• caust cedr ↓ cench chir-fl ↓ choc srj3• cich mtf11 cimic sne *Clem* coloc *Con* k* cortico ↓ cot a1 crot-c bg2* crot-h cupr ↓ cyna jl cypra-eg sde6.de• dendr-pol ↓ der k* dream-p ↓ dros k* dulc fd4.de dys fmm1• *Elaps* eric-vg mtf11 falco-pe ↓ ferr ↓ *Ferr-ar* ↓ fl-ac bg2 gaert fmm1• **Gal-ac** ↓ galla-q-r nl2• gard-j vlr2• *Gels* germ-met srj5• granit-m es1• haliae-lc ↓ ham fd3.de• hep k* hydrog srj2• **Hyos** k* *Ign* k* irid-met srj5• *Kali-ar* kali-br k* **Kali-c** k* kali-m ckh1 kali-n ↓ *Kali-p* kali-s fd4.de kola stb3• **Lac-c** k* lac-cp ↓ lac-del hrn2• lac-f wza1• lac-h htj1*• lac-leo ↓ lac-lup hrn2• lach b7a.de lec ↓ lepr vk2 *Lil-t* k* limen-b-c ↓ limest-b es1• **Lyc** k* m-aust ↓ mag-m ↓ manc meny ↓ merc k* *Mez* k* *Morg* fmm1• morg-p fmm1• naja bro1* *Nat-c* bg2 nat-m ↓ nat-ox rly4• nat-sil fd3.de• neon srj5• nit-ac sf1.de *Nux-v* oci-sa sk4• oxyg ↓ *Pall* k* petr-ra shn4• ph-ac bg2 **PHOS** b4.de* pieri-b mlk9.de pin-con oss2• plac rzf5• plac-s rly4• plb k* **Podo** fd* polys sk4• pseuts-m ↓ *Puls* k* querc-r svu1• rad-br c11* (non:rad-met) ran-b k* rat rhus-g ↓ *Rhus-t* ↓ ruta fd4.de sal-al blc1• sal-fr sle1• *Sep* k* sil bg2 sinus rly4• skat br1 spong fd4.de stann j5.de *Stram* k* *Stront-c* sk4• *Stry* k* suis-em rly4• suis-hep rly4• sulph gl1.fr• symph fd3.de• syph hr1* tab taosc iwa1• tarent thiop ↓ thymol br1* *Tritic-vg* fd5.de valer ↓ vanad dx vanil fd5.de verat k* verb k* zinc k* zinc-p k2* [bell-p-sp dcm1 heroin sdj2 lith-p stj2 nat-p stj1 tax jsj7 uva stj]

- **evening**: brom k* carc fd2.de• dros dulc fd4.de kali-c kali-s fd4.de plb puls ran-b sal-fr sle1• tab thiop jl
- **night**: *Camph* phos mrr1 puls mrr1 **Stram** k* tab
- **agg.** in company; but: pseuts-m oss1•
- **alone** agg.; when: *(↗Anxiety - alone; Dullness - alone; Fear - alone; Fear - death - alone; Inconsolable - alone; Irritability - alone - when; Rage - alone; Restlessness - alone; Sadness - alone - when; Sadness - company - amel.; Thoughts - persistent - alone; Unconsciousness - alone; Weeping - alone)* aeth bg2 agar bg2 aids nl2• alco sne all-s sne allox sne ambr ant-t bg2 *Apis* bg2 aq-mar sne *Arg-n* sne* **Ars** k* asaf bg2 aur sne bell bg2 bism bg2* bov k* brom bufo bg2 cadm-s k* calc k* calc-sil k2 *Camph* k* caust sne cedr bg2 clem bg2 con k*

Company – desire for – **alone** agg.; when: ...
cortico sne crot-c sk4• cupr sne *Dros* k* elaps k* ferr sne *Ferr-ar* sne *Fl-ac* bg2 **Gal-ac** zr gels bg2 haliae-lc srj5• **Hep** bg2 hydrog srj2• *Hyos* bg2 irid-met srj5• kali-ar sne *Kali-br* sne *Kali-c* k* kali-n sne kali-s fd4.de lac-c k2 lac-cp sk4• lach bg2 lil-t bg2* *Lyc* k* m-aust sne mag-m sne *Merc* bg2 *Mez* k* morg sne nat-c bg2 nat-m bg2 nat-ox rly4• nit-ac sne *Pall* k* ph-ac bg2 **Phos** k* plb bg2 podo fd3.de• ran-b bg2 rat *Rhus-t* sne ruta fd4.de sep bg2 sil k* spong fd4.de stann bg2 *Stram* k* tab taosc iwa1• tarent ↓ tritic-vg fd5.de valer sne vanil fd5.de verat b7a.de* zinc k* zinc-p k2 [*Bism-sn* stj2 cadm-met stj2 calc-n stj1]
  - **fear** of people; yet: *(↗Delusions - enemy - everyone)* ars bg2 bufo bg2 clem bg2 con bg2 tarent bg2
- **alternating** with | **aversion** to company: acon gl1.fr• aids nl2• falco-pe nl2• kali-s fd4.de
- **amel.** in company: *(↗Fear - happen - alone)* aeth bro1 alum-sil ↓ *Arg-n* mrr1 *Bism* bro1 bov ckh1 calc mtf33 carc sst• chir-fl gya2 dream-p sdj1• dros tl1 dulc fd4.de irid-met srj5• kali-c bro1 kali-p fd1.de• kali-s fd4.de lac-h htj1• lec oss• lil-t bro1 *Lyc* bro1* phos mrr1 sal-fr sle1• spong fd4.de *Stram* bro1 [cadm-met stj2 cadm-s stj2 oxyg stj2]
  - **alone** agg.; when: alum-sil k2
- **children**; in: carc mtf33 dros mtf33 phos mtf33 puls mtf33 stram mtf33
  - **rejected**; who are: carc mlr1•
- **children**; of: falco-pe nl2• *Tritic-vg* fd5.de [buteo-j sej6]
- **coryza**; during: merc mtf33
- **deceased** mother: limen-b-c hrn2•
- **family**, of his: aids nl2• [bell-p-sp dcm1]
- **fever**; during: dendr-pol sk4•
- **friend**, of a: aids ↓ dulc fd4.de granit-m es1• kali-p fd1.de• kali-s fd4.de petr-ra shn4• plb *Spong* fd4.de stront-c ↓ *Vanil* fd5.de [buteo-j sej6]
  - **close**: aids nl2•
  - **faithful**: stront-c sk4•
- **go** away from; cannot: *Plac* rzf5•
- **group** together; desire to keep: lac-leo hrn2•
- **happen**; as if something horrible might: *(↗Fear - happen - alone)* *Elaps* kr1
- **headache**, during: meny h1*
- **menses**, during: *(↗Menses - during)* stram
- **mother** | **died** eight years ago; who: limen-b-c hrn2•
- **relax**; of those she can: rhus-g tmo3•
- **spoken** to, but averse to being: achy a1*
- **sudden** desire for certain company: plac rzf5•
- **treats** those who approach him outrageously; yet: *Kali-c* k*
- **undertake** something together; to: plac rzf5•
- **watched** constantly; wants to be: gal-ac a1* lac-del hrn2•

\- **yearning** for: olib-sac wmh1

COMPASSIONATE (See Sympathetic)

COMPELLED to do something; he is (See Thoughts - compelling)

COMPETITIVE (See Ambition - increased - competitive)

COMPLAINING: *(↗Discontented; Grumbling; Indifference - complain; Irritability; Lamenting; Moaning; Morose; Muttering; Nagging; Pessimist; Sadness - complaining; Sulky; Tormenting - others - complaints; Wearisome; Weeping)* abrom-a ckh1 acet-ac k2 acon k* alco a1 aloe bro1 *Alum* k* ambr anac j5.de* *Ant-c* bro1* *Ant-t* ↓ arn *Ars* k* ars-h ↓ asaf j5.de* *Aur* k* bell j5.de* *Bism* k* bism-sn br1* borx bro1 *Bry* k* *Bufo* *Calc* k* **Calc-p** br1* *Canth* k* caps bro1 carc mlr1• caust tl1* **Cham** k* chin k* chinin-ar *Cina* k* cocc k* *Coff* k* colch bro1 coli rly4• *Coloc* con ↓ *Cor-r* cori-r a1 crot-h ptk1* dig k* dulc goss st1 ham fd3.de• hell k* hep vh* hyos j5.de* ign k* indol bro1 *Kali-br* ↓ kali-c bro1* kali-i kali-s fd4.de kiss a1 lac-cp sk4• *Lac-e* hrn2• *Lach* k* loxo-lae bnm12• *Lyc* k* mag-p bro1 marb-w es1• *Merc* bg2* merc-c j5.de* moni rfm1• *Mosch* k* mur-ac tl1* nabal a1 nit-ac bro1* *Nux-v* k* onos mrr1 op k* ozone ↓ petr ph-ac k* phos bg2 plat k* positr nl2• prun ↓ psor bro1 puls k* *Rheum* mrr1 rhus-t bg2 ruta ↓ sal-fr sle1• *Sanic* mrr1 sep sil bg2 spira a1 staph bro1 *Sulph* k* tab bro1 tarent thea a1 tub c1* tus-fr a1 *Verat* bg2* verat-v ptk1 *Zinc* vh* [alum-p stj2 alumin stj2 alumin-s stj2 arg-n stj2 ars-met stj2 aur-m stj2 aur-s stj2 beryl-m stj2 cadm-m stj2 chlor stj2 cob-m stj2 heroin sdj2

Complaining: ...
kali-ar stj2 lith-m stj2 mang-m stj2 merc-d stj2 nat-ar stj2 oxyg stj stann stj2 stront-m stj2 thal-met stj2 zinc-i stj2 zinc-m stj2 zinc-n stj2 zinc-p stj2]

- **day** and night: *Coloc* hr1*
- **morning** | **bed**; in: prun a1
- **night** | **sleep**; in: nux-v j5.de
- **alternating** with | **shrieking** (See Shrieking - alternating - complaining)
- **always**: aloe bg2 nit-ac mtf33
- **childhood**; about: ozone sde2•
- **disease**, of: *Ant-t* hr1* cham h1 **Ham** fd* *Kali-s* fd4.de **Lach** j5.de* *Nux-v* j5.de* ph-ac a1
- **fever**; during: acon bg2 bry bg2 nux-v bg2 verat bg2
- **injury**; of imaginary: (*↗Feigning - sick) Hyos* k*
- **menopause**; during: *Kali-br* kr1
- **never**: (*↗Indifference - complain; Well - says - sick)* agri mtf11 op mtf33 querc-r mtf11
- **offenses**; of long past: (*↗Dwells - past)* calc
- **others**, of: coli rly4• hep dm ruta dm sep hr1*
- **pain**, of: (*↗pitiful - children - ear)* ars-h hr1* *Cham* mrr1 *Hep* mrr1 *Mosch* j5.de* *Nux-v* gl1.fr• prun ↓ verat ↓
  - **waking**; on: prun j5.de verat j5.de
  - ○ **Teeth**; in: nux-v bg2
- **pitiful**: ars h2* puls ↓
  - **children**; in: puls tl1
  - ⁝ **Ear**; with pain in: (*↗pain)* puls tl1
- **pregnancy**, during: *Mosch* hr1*
- **relations** and surroundings, of: *Merc* hr1*
- **sleep**, in: anac ↓ bell k* con j5.de ign k* nux-v j5.de op ↓ rheum hr1 stann ptk1* sulph j5.de
  - **comatose**: anac j5.de op j5.de
- **stomach**; with complaints of: ars bg2 **Nux-v** bg2
- **telling** what is wrong; without: mosch b7a.de
- **threatening**, and: tarent k2*
- **trifles**, of: acon vh1 *Lach* hr1* sal-fr sle1•
- **waking**, on: cina

COMPLAINTS; mental (See Mental symptoms)

COMPLY to the wishes of others; feeling obliged to: (*↗Anxiety - conscience; Delusions - performing - pressured; Servile; Yielding)* mag-m h2 **Tritic-vg** fd*

COMPREHENSION:

- **difficult** (See Dullness)
- **easy**: aesc sf1.de ambr b2.de* anac h2* ang b2.de* anh sp1 aur bg2 bar-c b2.de* bell bro1* borx a1 brom hr1* buth-a mg1.de calc ↓ calc-f mg1.de camph bg2* cann-i sf1.de cann-s b2.de* caust b2.de* **Coff** b2.de* hyos b2.de* ign c1 **Lach** b2.de* lyc b2.de* lyss hr1* meph sf1.de olib-sac wmh1 **Op** b2.de* **Phos** b2.de* *Pip-m* sf1.de *Plat* bg2* puls sf1.de querc-r svu1• rhus-t bg2 sabad b2.de* sal-al blc1• sel bg2 sep b2.de sulph b2.de* tab j5.de thiop jl3 ulm-c jsj8• valer b2.de* *Verat* b2.de* *Viol-o* b2.de* [tax jsj7]
  - **connections** of things; about the: *Olib-sac* wmh1
  - **drunkenness**, during: calc gl1.fr• sulph gl1.fr•
- **heart**; of everything from the: limen-b-c hrn2•
- **not** understand; does:
  - **but** can speak: elaps ptk2
  - **questions** addressed to her (See Dullness - understand - questions)
- **slow**: guaj br1 nat-c br1

COMPULSIONS (See Thoughts - compelling)

COMPULSIVE DISORDERS (See Thoughts - compelling)

COMPUTERS: | **love** for: (*↗Playing - desire - nintendo)* bufo gk7 cann-i mtf kali-br sk2• merc mtf *Sil* mtf *Sul-ac* mtf sulph mtf zinc mtf

COMPULSIVE NEUROSIS (See Checking - twice; Forgotten - something; Gestures; Thoughts - compelling; Washing - desire)

CONCEIT (See Haughty)

CONCEPTUAL THINKING (See Thinking - conceptual)

CONCENTRATION:

- **active**: (*↗Activity - desires - creative; Fancies - vivid; Ideas - abundant; Memory - active; Plans - making; Quick; Theorizing; Thoughts - profound; Thoughts - rapid; Thoughts - thoughtful; Witty; HEAD - Pain - attention)* agath-a nl2• aids nl2• alum bg2* alumin-s ↓ am-c j ambr j anac bg2 androc srj1• *Anh* mg1.de* arg-n j asaf b7.de aur j bell j bros-gau mrc1 calc bg2* calc-f mg1.de* carb-v j caust hr1* chir-fl gya2 choc srj3• coca bg cod a1 coff coff-t st1 coli rly4• con j conch fkr1• cycl j cypra-eg sde6.de• dream-p sdj1• falco-pe nl2• fuma-ac rly4• haliae-lc srj5• ham fd3.de• hell bg2 hydrog srj2• hyos bg2 ign j kali-p fd1.de• kali-s fd4.de kola stb3• lac-h htj1• lac-leo hrn2• lach j lap-la sde8.de• limen-b-c hrn2* loxo-recl knl4• lyc j lyss mrr1 melal-alt gya4 merc j nat-c j nat-m bg2 neon srj5• nit-ac j nux-m j nux-v bg2 *Olib-sac* wmh1 olnd bg2 op b7.de ox-ac k* ozone sde2• petr j petr-ra shn4• ph-ac j *Phos* gl1.fr• positr nl2• pycnop-sa mrz1 rhus-t bg2 sep j sil j spong fd4.de staph bg2 staphycoc rly4• stram j sulph gl1.fr• symph fd3.de• syph bg1* thea thuj j tritic-vg fd5.de vanil fd5.de verat j *Zinc* mrr1 [*Buteo-j* sej6 heroin sdj2]
  - **morning**: androc srj1• ham fd3.de•
  - **evening**: conch fkr1•
  - **alternating** with | **tranquillity**: choc srj3• olib-sac wmh1
  - **menses** | **before**: (*↗Menses - before)* calc bg1* [alumin-s stj2]
- **difficult**: (*↗Absentminded; Abstraction; Confusion - concentrate; Dullness; Dyslexia; Ideas - deficiency; Memory - weakness; Mistakes; Prostration; Slowness; Spaced-out; Thoughts - vanishing; Thoughts - wandering; Unobserving [=inattentive])* abrom-a bnj1 abrot mtf *Acon* k* acon-ac rly4• acon-c a1 acon-l st1 aconin a1 adam srj5• *Aesc* k* *Aeth* k* agar k* *Agath-a* nl2• *Agn* k* *Aids* nl2• ail k* alco a1 alet k* all-c allox tpw3* aln vva1• aloe sf1.de *Alum* k* alum-p k2* alum-sil k2* *Am-c* k* am-m bg2* *Ambr* **Anac** k* anders bnj1 *Androc* srj1• ang k* ange-s jl3 *Anh* mg1.de* ant-c anthraq rly4• *Apis* apoc a1 aq-mar jl3* arag br1* *Aran-ix* mg1.de* aran-sc ckh1 arg-met sf1.de* arg-n bg2 arge-pl rwt5• arizon-l nl2• arn k* ars ars-i k* asaf k* asar k* atp rly4• atro a1 aur bg2 aur-m-n wbt2• aven br1 *Bamb-a* stb2.de• bapt k* **Bar-c** k* bar-i k2* *Bar-m* k* bar-ox-suc rly4• bar-p ↓ bar-s k2* bell k* berb k* beto br1 bit-ar wht1• boerh-d ckh1 *Bov* k* brass-n-o srj5• brom k* bros-gau ↓ bry bufo sf1.de* bung-fa mtf buth-a sp1 cact a1 cadm-met mg1.de* calad bg2* *Calc* bg2* calc-ar k2 *Calc-f* mg1.de* calc-p mtf calc-sil k2* camph cann-i k* cann-s k* *Canth* k* caps j5.de carb-ac k* *Carb-an* **Carb-v** k* carbn-o a1 **Carbn-s** carc mg1.de* *Cardios-h* rly4• cartl-s rly4• cassia-f ↓ cassia-s ckh1 **Caust** k* cench k2* cent cephd-i bnj1 cham k* chel k* chin chinin-s chir-fl gya2 chlam-tr bcx2• chlol k* chlorpr jl3 choc srj3* chord-umb rly4• **Cic** bg2* *Cimic* k* cina mtf cinnb k* clem a1 cloth mtf cob-n sp1 coca bg2 *Cocc* k* cod a1 coff colch k* coleus-a bnj1 coloc k* *Con* conch fkr1• conin a1 *Corn* k* cortico mg1.de* cortiso jl3 croc k* crot-c sk4• crot-h j *Cupr* k* cur a1 cycl cypra-eg sde6.de• cystein-l rly4• dendr-pol sk4• des-ac jl3 diaz sa3• dream-p sdj1• *Dros* k* *Dulc* dys fmm1• elaps ephe-si hsj1• erig mg1.de ery-a esp-g kk1.de* euph-hy a1 euphr eys sp1* fago k* falco-pe nl2• ferr ferr-ar ferr-i ferr-p fic-m gya1 fl-ac k* flor-p rsj3• fum rly1*• galeoc-c-h ↓ galla-q-r nl2• gard-j vlr2• *Gels* k* ger-i ↓ *Germ-met* srj5• gink-b sbd1*• **Glon** k* glyc ↓ goss st1 **Graph** k* grat haliae-lc srj5• halo jl3 ham k* **Hell** k* helo helo-s rwt2• hipp st1 hir mg1.de* hist sp1 hura hydr *Hydr-ac* **Hydrog** srj2*• hydroph mg1.de* *Hyos* k* iber a1 ichth br1 ictod k* ign k* ignis-alc es2• indol ↓ iod k* irid-met br1* iris jal mtf jug-c k* jug-r kali-ar kali-bi ↓ kali-br k* *Kali-c* k* kali-i kali-p kali-s kali-sil k2* kalm ketogl-ac rly4• *Kola* stb3• *Lac-c* k* *Lac-e* hrn2• *Lac-h* htj1• **Lach** k* lact lam lap-la sde8.de• laur *Lavand-a* ctl1• **Lec** k* led k* levo jl3 lil-s a1 *Lil-t* k* limen-b-c hrn2* limest-b es1• lol a1 loxo-recl knl4• luf-op rsj5• *Luna* kg1• **Lyc** k* lycps-v lyss a1* m-ambo ↓ macro a1 mag-c k* mag-m mand mg1.de* mang mang-p ↓ *Med* k* medul-os-si rly4• melal-alt gya4 meli br1 meph jl3 *Merc* k* merc-c merl k* *Mez* k* mim-p ↓ *Moni* rfm1• morph a1 mosch k* mucs-nas rly4• myric a1* myris a1 nad rly4• nalox gmm1.fr narcot a1 **Nat-ar** *Nat-c* k* *Nat-m* k* nat-p nat-sil k2* nauf-helv-li elm2• neon srj5• nicc-met sk4• nicot a1 nicotam rly4• *Nit-ac* k* **Nux-m** k* **NUX-V** bg2* oci-sa jl* ol-an *Olib-sac* wmh1 olnd k* onop jl3 onos c1* op k* orig orot-ac rly4• ox-ac k* ozone sde2• pant-ac rly4• pert-vc vk9 petr k* petr-ra shn4• **Ph-ac** k* **Phos** k* phys k* pic-ac k* *Pieri-b* mlk9.de pin-con oss2• pip-n br1 pitu ↓ pitu-gl br1 *Plat* k* plb ↓ plect plut-n srj7• podo fd3.de• polys sk4• positr nl2• pot-e rly4• propr sa3• pseuts-m oss1• psil ↓ psor st1 ptel k* *Puls* k* pycnop-sa mrz1 pyrid rly4•

- **difficult**: ...
ran-b sf1.de ran-s k* raph rauw sp1* rham-cal br1 rhod rhus-r rhus-t *Rhus-v* rib-ac jl3 ribo rly4• *Ros-d* wla1 *Ruta* fd4.de sabad sacch mtf sacch-a fd2.de* *Sal-fr* sle1• sang k* sanic mrr1* santin a1 saroth mg1.de* sarr k* sars k* scut a1* sec *Sel* k* senec k* seneg **Sep** k* **Sil** k* sin-a a1* sinus rly4• skat br1 spig k* *Spong* k* squil stann k* staph k* stict k* *Stram* k* streptoc rly4• stront-c sk4• suis-em rly4• suis-pan rly4• sul-ac k* sul-i k2 *Sulph* k* sumb a1 suprar rly4• symph fd3.de• syph bg2* *Tab* k* tanac a1 tarax sp1 *Tarent* mtf33 *Tell* rsj10• *Ter* k* thal c1 thal-xyz srj8• ther mtf thioc-ac rly4• *Thuj* k* til toxo-g mtf trios rsj11* *Tritic-vg* fd5.de tub al2* *Tung-met* bdx1• ulm-c ↓ upa a1 *Urol-h* rwt• *Vanil* fd5.de ven-m jl3 verat k* verb k* viol-o xero ↓ *Zinc* k* zinc-p k2* [am-caust stj2 am-f stj2 arg-p stj2 bell-p-sp dcm1 beryl stj2 bism-sn stj2 bor-pur stj2 buteo-j sej6 cadm-s stj2 fl-pur stj2 heroin sdj2 ind stj2 lac-mat sst4 lith-c stj2 lith-f stj2 lith-i stj2 lith-met stj2 mang-i stj2 mang-met stj2 merc-i-f stj2 mur-ac stj2 nat-caust stj2 nitro stj2 oxyg stj2 pop dhh1 rubd-met stj2 sol-ecl cky1 spect dfg1 tax jsj7 thal-met stj2 zinc-i stj2 zirc-met stj2]
  - **morning**: *Anac* arizon-l nl2• canth k* cortico tpw7 gink-b sbd1• kali-p fd1.de• mag-m a1 mang-p rly4• nat-c a1 phos ptel a1 sumb a1 vanil fd5.de
  - **forenoon**: ptel a1 sil a1 symph fd3.de• til a1 vanil fd5.de
  - **afternoon**: aids nl2• ang j5.de cham a1 *Cimic* hr1 dulc fd4.de ery-a a1 h a m fd3.de• kali-s fd4.de myris a1 olib-sac wmh1 sang a1
  - **evening**: am-m j5.de cassia-f ckh1 gink-b sbd1• ham fd3.de• nat-c a1
    - ⋮ **amel.**: lac-h htj1•
  - **abstract** subjects; on: med pc
  - **air**; in open | **amel.**: cinnb a1 conch fkr1• hydrog srj2• nat-ar k2
  - **alcohol** amel.: irid-met srj5•
  - **alternating** with | **uterus**; pain in: gels
  - **attempting** to concentrate; on: androc ↓ arg-n ↓ *Asar* ↓ bell-p-sp ↓ chir-fl ↓ choc ↓ *Gels* ↓ hydrog ↓ kali-c mtf33 mez ↓ nat-m ↓ *Nit-ac* ↓ olnd ↓ ran-b ↓ ros-d ↓ staph ↓ *Tung-met* bdx1•
    - ⋮ **dark** before the eyes; it becomes: (↗*Darkness - agg.*) arg-n
    - ⋮ **vacant** feeling; has a: androc srj1• *Asar* chir-fl gya2 choc srj3• *Gels* hydrog srj2• mez nat-m *Nit-ac* k* olnd ran-b k1 ros-d wla1 staph k1 [bell-p-sp dcm1]
  - **attention**, cannot fix: (↗*Consolation - agg.*) *Aesc* vh* aeth bro1* agar bro1 *Agn* bro1 ail tl1 aloe bro1 alum bro1 *Anac* bro1 apis bro1 arag bro1 arg-n bro1 arge-pl rwt5• arizon-l nl2• atp rly4• bapt bro1 bar-c bro1 bov vh* cann-i bro1 caust bro1 con k2* dream-p sdj1• fago bro1 falco-pe nl2• fic-m gya1 gard-j vlr2• *Gels* bro1 glon bro1 glyc bro1 hell bro1 hipp vh* hyos vh* ichth bro1 ign vh* indol bro1 irid-met bro1* *Kali-p* fd1.de• lac-c bro1* lil-t mrr1 lyc bro1 nat-c bro1 *Nux-m* bro1 *Nux-v* bro1 olib-sac wmh1 op bro1 *Ph-ac* bro1 *Phos* bro1 *Pic-ac* bro1 pitu bro1 positr nl2• sal-fr sle1• sep bro1 *Sil* bro1* **Sin-a** vh* staph bro1 sulph bro1 symph fd3.de• syph bro1 tritic-vg fd5.de *Vanil* fd5.de xero bro1 *Zinc* bro1
  - **aversion** to: calc vh* lyc vh* nux-v vh* ph-ac vh* plb vh* staph vh* tung-met bdx1•
  - **calculating**, while: (↗*Mathematics - inability - calculating*) a e t h mtf33 ail hr1* ger-i rly4• hydrog srj2• kola stb3• lac-h htj1• lyc gl1.fr• *Merc* gl1.fr• **Nux-v** k* *Psor* hr1* ruta fd4.de syph hr1* tung-met bdx1•
  - **children**, in: *Aeth* k* am-c gl1.fr• *Bar-c* k* brom mtf33 calc mtf33 carb-v mtf33 carc st1* graph mtf33* iod mtf33 lach gl1.fr• lyc mtf33 med mtf33 nat-m mtf33 nit-ac mtf33 nux-v mtf33 op wbt• ph-ac gl1.fr• phos mtf33 sacch sst1• sil mtf33 spong fd4.de tarent mtf33 zinc mtf33*
  - **conversation**, during: (↗*Conversation - agg.*) anthraq rly4• bit-ar wht1• *Calc-sil* k2* carc sst2• chir-fl gya2 chord-umb rly4• conch fkr1• cupr sst3• dulc fd4.de falco-pe nl2• fic-m gya1 gink-b sbd1• ignis-alc es2• irid-met srj5• *Kali-s* fd4.de limest-b es1• lyc med br1 mim-p rsj8• moni rfm1• nux-v gl1.fr• pieri-b mlk9.de plut-n srj7• podo fd3.de• psil vml3• ruta fd4.de sanic c1 spong fd4.de symph fd3.de• tarent a1 tritic-vg fd5.de *Vanil* fd5.de [tax jsj7]
  - **crazy** feeling on top of head, wild feeling in head with confusion of ideas: (↗*Delirium*) lil-t
  - **drawing**, when: iod a1*
  - **driving**; while: bamb-a stb2.de• chir-fl gya2 choc srj3• chord-umb rly4• galeoc-c-h gms1• *Germ-met* srj5• hydrog srj2• kali-p fd1.de• melal-alt gya4 positr nl2• sal-fr sle1• suis-pan rly4• tritic-vg fd5.de vanil fd5.de
  - **eating**:
    - ⋮ **agg.**: neon srj5•

Concentration – difficult – eating: ...
  - ⋮ **amel.**: *Calc-f* st*
  - **examinations**; during: (↗*studying*) hydrog srj2•
  - **exhilaration**; from: hist sp1
  - **focus**; inability to: [buteo-j sej6]
  - **food**, when preparing: falco-pe nl2•
  - **headache**, with: cob-n sp1 dulc vh* kali-c vh* [bell-p-sp dcm1]
  - **interrupted**, if: berb k* mez h2* ulm-c jsj8•
  - **masturbation**, from: aven c1
  - **menses**, after: (↗*Menses - after*) *Calc* vh*
  - **noises** in ear; from: kola stb3•
  - **one** subject; on: cann-i c1 helo-s c1 m-ambo al2
  - **piano**; playing: galeoc-c-h gms1•
  - **reading** (See studying)
  - **rubbing** the forehead when trying to concentrate; is: hell mrr1
  - **sleepiness**; with: bit-ar wht1•
  - **spaciness**: [buteo-j sej6]
  - **studying** (= reading): (↗*examinations; Absentminded - reading; Dullness - thinking - long; Studying - difficult; Thoughts - wandering - studying*) acon aesc a1 **Aeth** k1* agar a1* agath-a nl2• *Agn* aids nl2• alco a1 allox tpw3 alum ambr gl1.fr• *Androc* srj1• ang j5.de a n h sp1 apis a1* arag br1 asar aur-m-n wbt2• bamb-a stb2.de• *Bar-c* k* bar-m bell bit-ar wht1• brass-n-o srj5• bros-gau ↓ calc mtf33 calc-f mg1.de calc-sil k2 carb-ac a1 carbn-s carc sst2* cassia-s ccrh1• caust cham chir-fl gya2 chlol a1 choc srj3• *Cimic* a1 coff conch fkr1• conin a1 corn *Dros* k* fago falco-pe nl2• ferr-i k2 ferr-p k2 gard-j vlr2• *Gels* a1 germ-met srj5• ham fd3.de• **Hell** hydrog srj2• hyos a1 iod a1* kali-bi vh* kali-c *Kali-p* st kali-sil k2* ketogl-ac rly4• *Kola* stb3• lach limen-b-c hrn2* l y c a1 merc gl1.fr• mur-ac vh* narcot a1 nat-ar a1 *Nat-c* k1* nat-m mtf33 nat-p st* neon srj5• nicot a1 nicotam rly4• **NUX-V** k1* olnd a1* op wbt• ox-ac ozone sde2• *Pert-vc* vk9 phos mtf33 pic-ac st* pitu-gl skp7• plut-n srj7• puls a1 pycnop-sa mrz1 rham-cal br1 ribo rly4• sacch-a gmj3 sal-fr sle1• scut a1 sin-a a1 skat br1 spig *Staph* mtf33* sul-i k2 sulph sumb a1 syph vh* tab st tanac a1 *Ter* a1 tung-met bdx1• vanil fd5.de xero br1 zinc-p vh* [bar-p stj1 tax jsj7]
    - ⋮ **foreign** language: bros-gau mrc1
  - **talking**, while: (↗*Speech - incoherent*) chir-fl gya2 chord-umb rly4• dream-p sdj1• dulc fd4.de fic-m gya1 gink-b sbd1• kali-p fd1.de• kola stb3• limest-b es1• merc-c *Nat-m* ph-ac br1 podo fd3.de• positr nl2• ruta fd4.de symph fd3.de• tung-met bdx1•
  - **thinking** agg.: aeth mtf33 calad k2 ger-i rly4•
  - **working**, while: bar-ox-suc rly4• galeoc-c-h gms1• hydrog srj2• kali-s fd4.de medul-os-si rly4• melal-alt gya4 plect a1 ros-d wla1 sacch-a gmj3 spong fd4.de symph fd3.de• tritic-vg fd5.de *Vanil* fd5.de
    - ⋮ **work**; must concentrate continuously on his work or 'his hands forget what they are doing'. (See Confusion - muscles)
  - **writing**, while: (↗*Mistakes - writing*) acon arizon-l nl2• dulc fd4.de germ-met srj5• gink-b sbd1• ham fd3.de• hydrog srj2• kola stb3• mag-c k* merc gl1.fr• [tax jsj7]
- **impossible**: allox tpw4 cadm-met tpw6 carc mlr1• hydroph rsj6• pip-n br1 plut-n srj7• scut br1 tritic-vg fd5.de [bell-p-sp dcm1]
- **lack** of: lac-h sze9•
  - **agg.**: *Bell* bg2 *Camph* bg2 cic bg2 gels ptk1 **Hell** bg2*

CONCERNED:
- **details**; over (See Conscientious)
- **general**; in (See Anxiety)
- **personal** appearance; about (See Tidy - appearance)

CONCLUSIONS; difficult to make (See Irresolution)

CONDESCENDING attitude (See Contemptuous)

CONFIDENCE:

- **too** much confidence in himself (See Confident)
- **want** of self-confidence: *(↗Ailments - embarrassment; Anxiety - success; Asking - nothing; Cautious; Cowardice; Cowardice - opinion; Delusions - appreciated; Delusions - business - unfit; Delusions - confidence; Delusions - confusion; Delusions - criticized; Delusions - despised; Delusions - disgraced; Delusions - fail everything; Delusions - forsaken; Delusions - friend - affection; Delusions - insulted; Delusions - laughed; Delusions - looked; Delusions - neglected - he; Delusions - right - doing; Delusions - succeed; Delusions - wife - run; Delusions - wrong - done; Dependent - desire; Discouraged; Fear - business failure; Fear - failure; Fear - opinion; Fear - talking - say; Fear - undertaking; Fear - wrong; Flattered - desire; Forsaken; Helplessness; Impressionable; Insecurity; Irresolution; Lamenting - appreciated; Longing - good; Mocking - others; Mood - repulsive; Postponing; Quiet disposition; Reproaching oneself; Reserved; Responsibility - inability; Succeeds; Suggestible; Timidity; Timidity - bashful; Undertaking - lacks; Undertaking - nothing; Unfortunate; FACE - Discoloration - red - excitement)* abies-c oss4• acer-circ oss• adam srj5• agath-a nl2• agn k* aids nl2• aloe sne alum *Am-br* vh1 am-c gl1.fr• am-caust ↓ am-f ↓ am-m gl1.fr• ambr vh1* amp rly4• **Anac** k* anan ang k* anh mg1.de* anthraq rly4• *Aq-mar* mgm* arb-m oss1• arg-n k* arizon-l nl2• arn oss• ars ptk1* atp rly4• *Aur* aur-i k2 *Aur-m-n* wbt2• aur-s k2 bamb-a stb2.de• bar-act a1* bar-ar sk2• **BAR-C** b4a.de* bar-i oss• bar-s zr bell beryl ↓ bor-pur ↓ *Bry* buth-a sp1 calc *Calc-p* ↓ calc-s ↓ calc-sil k2* calen mgm• canth k* carb-an carb-v k* *Carc* mlr1* caust cerstig-w mtf11 *Chin* k* chir-fl ↓ chlor choc srj3• cob kr1* coca-c sk4• cocain ↓ cocc a1* coli rly4• con pcr* cystein-l rly4• dendr-pol sk4• des-ac rbp6 dioxi rbp6 dream-p sdj1• dros *Dulc* fd4.de dys pte1* falco-pe nl2• ferr-p ↓ fic-m gya1 fl-ac ↓ fl-pur ↓ fuma-ac rly4• galla-q-r nl2• gard-j vlr2• gels germ-met srj5• graph vml1.nl haliae-lc srj5• ham fd3.de• hydrog srj2• hyos ign ina-i mlk9.de iod irid-met srj5• kali-br ckh1 *Kali-c* kali-n kali-p fd1.de* *Kali-s* k1* *Kali-sil* k2* *Kola* stb3• lac-ac ↓ *Lac-c* k* lac-del hrn2• *Lac-e* hrn2• lac-h htj1*• lac-leo sk4• lach k* lar-d mtf11 lavand-a ctl1• limest-b es1• lith-c ↓ lith-f ↓ lith-m ↓ lith-met ↓ *Lyc* k* mag-m ↓ manc vh *Med* vh* melal-alt gya4 merc *Moni* rfm1• morph oss• mur-ac naja kr1* nat-c *Nat-m* k1* nat-sil k2 nit-ac nitro ↓ nitro-o a1 *Nux-v* k* olib-sac wmh1 olnd k* op oxyg ↓ ozone sde2• *Pall* k* pers jl pert-vc vk9 *Petr* vh* *Ph-ac* gg phasco-ci rbp2 phos k* pic-ac ptk1* pieri-b mlk9.de pin-con oss2• plb polys sk4• positr nl2• pseuts-m oss1• psor gsd1* *Puls* k* *Pycnop-sa* mrz1 rad-br sze8• ran-b rhod kgp5• rhus-g tmo3• *Rhus-t* k* ruta sacch sst1• sacch-a fd2.de• sal-fr sle1• santin a1 scler mtf11 sep b4a.de* **Sil** k1* staph j* stram k* stront-c sk4• sul-ac sul-i k2 sulph k* sumb a1 **Symph** fd* syph vh* tab tax-br oss1• thea a1 ther k* thuj mrr1* *Tritic-vg* fd5.de tub ↓ tung-met ↓ ulm-c jsj8• ulm-pra ↓ urol-h rwt• vanad dx *Vanil* fd5.de verat gl1.fr• verb viol-t k* vip fkr4.de visc ckh1 zinc k* [arg-met stj1 bar-p stj1 bell-p-sp dcm1 heroin sdj2 spect dfg1 tax jsj7]
  - **daytime**: lac-h sk4•
  - **evening** | **amel.**: lac-h sk4•
  - **beer**; amel.: thea a1
  - **children**; in: calc-sil mtf33 carc mlr1*• naja mtf33
  - **failure**, feels himself a: *(↗Delusions - right - doing; Delusions - succeed)* aq-mar rbp6 *Bamb-a* stb2.de• carc mlr1• chir-fl gya2 *Dulc* fd4.de germ-met srj5• naja ptk1* phasco-ci rbp2 rhod kgp5• sal-fr sle1• sulph ptk1* ulm-pra mtf11 *Vanil* fd5.de
  - **good**, yet feels: galla-q-r nl2•
  - **inadequacy**; feeling of: ulm-pra mtf11
  - **inferior**; feels: lac-del hrn2•
  - **others** have none, which makes her unhappy; and thinks: *Aur* dulc fd4.de *Ham* fd3.de•
  - **plans**; about realizing her: bamb-a stb2.de• *Dulc* fd4.de ulm-c jsj8• vanil fd5.de
  - **school**; in: *Calc-p* zzl *Carc* zzl ferr-p zzl *Phos* zzl *Puls* zzl *Sil* zzl
  - **seaside** amel.; at the: *(↗Seaside - amel.)* carc bng
  - **self** despising and feelings of inadequacy in the eyes of others, with: arizon-l nl2•
  - **self**-depreciation: *(↗Delusions - body - ugly; Delusions - small - he; Delusions - succeed; Delusions - worthless; Fear - failure; Will - loss)* anac mrr1* anh mtf *Ars* mtf bar-act mtf *Bar-c* vh1 calc hu2 calc-s mtf cob kr1* cocain mtf dulc fd4.de falco-pe mtf gels mtf germ-met mtf haliae-lc mtf hydrog srj2• irid-met srj5• kali-p mtf lac-c br1* lach mtf *Lyc* mtf

Confidence – want of self-confidence – **self**-depreciation: ... merc mtf mur-ac mtf naja bg2* *Nat-c* mtf *Nux-v* mtf *Pall* mtf phos mtf psor mrr1 santin mtf *Sil* mtf21 sulph bg2* thuj mtf tub mtf tung-met mtf ulm-c jsj8• vanil fd5.de
    - **children**; in: naja mtf33
  - **support**; desires: *(↗Despair - supported; Helplessness)* arizon-l nl2• *Bamb-a* stb2.de• kali-p fd1.de• lac-ac stj5• lac-h sze9• mag-m ↓ sacch-a ↓ stront-c mtf [am-caust stj2 am-f stj2 beryl stj2 bor-pur stj2 fl-ac stj2 fl-pur stj2 graph stj2 lith-c stj2 lith-f stj2 lith-m stj2 lith-met stj2 nitro stj2 oxyg stj2]
    - **family** and friends; from: mag-m h2* sacch-a fd2.de•
  - **talking** amel.: falco-pe nl2•

CONFIDENT: *(↗Determination; Firmness; Freedom - doing; Positiveness; Tranquillity - settled)* adam srj5• agam-g mlk9.de *Aids* nl2• *Alum* ↓ ang a1 arizon-l nl2• carc fd2.de• chlam-tr bcx2• choc srj3• corian-s knl6• dream-p sdj1• *Falco-pe* nl2• ferr br1* fic-m gya1 gard-j vlr2• ham fd3.de• *Irid-met* srj5• kali-p fd1.de• kali-s fd4.de *Kola* stb3• lac-e hrn2• lac-h sk4• lyc mtf33 nept-m lsd2.fr nux-v mrr1 olib-sac wmh1 pert-vc vk9 plat zzl plut-n srj7• podo fd3.de• positr nl2• querc-r svu1• *Rhus-g* tmo3• ruta fd4.de sal-fr sle1• senec ckh1 spong fd4.de sulfonam ks2 sulph mrr1 symph fd3.de• tritic-vg fd5.de vanil fd5.de verat zzl [*Buteo-j* sej6 heroin sdj2 *Spect* dfg1 temp elm1]

- **alternating** with:
  - **discouragement**: alum j5.de
  - **timidity**: *Alum* k* falco-pe nl2•
- **aplomb** (See Confident)
- **explore**, feels safe to: aids nl2•
- **naked**, feels safe to be: aids nl2•
- **natural**, feels safe to be: aids nl2•

CONFIDING: *(↗Revealing)* falco-pe nl2• ham fd3.de• hydrc k* kali-s fd4.de kres mg1.de lac-f wza1• mur-ac k* olib-sac wmh1 op a1 spig k*

- **people** confide in him; many: nat-m mrr1

CONFLICT: *(↗Antagonism)*

- **aversion** to (See Quarrelling - aversion)
- **higher** consciousness and worldly existence; between: *(↗Awareness)* hydrog srj2• limen-b-c hrn2* [tax jsj7]
- **religious** ideals; conflict between sexuality and (See Religious - too - sexuality)
- **resolve** a conflict; unable to (See Ailments - anger - suppressed; Emotions - suppressed; Mildness; Will - weakness; Yielding)
- **will**; of the (See Will - contradiction; Will - two)
- **within** oneself (See Antagonism)

CONFORMISM: *(↗Change - aversion; Delusions - trapped; Dogmatic; Obstinate; Proper - too)* coc-c mgm• *Kali-bi* mrr1 **Kali-c** mrr1

CONFOUNDING:

- **objects** and ideas: *(↗Confusion; Disconcerted; Mistakes)* calc cann-s colch hr1* hyos musca-d szs1 nux-v phos ckh1 plat podo fd3.de• sacch-a fd2.de• *Sulph* tritic-vg fd5.de
- **present** with past: anac bg2 cic bg2* croc bg2 staph bg2

CONFUSION of mind: *(↗Answering - disconnected; Answering - questioned; Answering - questions; Chaotic; Confounding - objects; Delirium; Disconcerted; Discontented; Dullness; Forgetful; Forgotten - something; Memory - weakness; Mistakes; Muttering; Orientation - decreased; Prostration; Senses - confused; Speech - confused; Speech - wandering; Strange - everything; Strange - things; Unreal - everything; FACE - Expression - bewildered; FACE - Expression - confused)* abies-c a1 *Abies-n* bro1 absin acet-ac *Acon* k* acon-ac ↓ acon-f a1 acon-s a1 act-sp k* adam srj5• *Aesc* k* aesc-g a1 *Aeth* k* aether a1 *Agar* k* *Agath-a* nl2• agn k* *Aids* nl2• ail k* alco a1 alet br1 alf bro1 all-c k* allox tpw3* aln vva1• aloe k* *Alum* k* alum-sil k2 *Alumn* ↓ *Am-br* sf1.de* am-c k* am-m k* ambr k* aml-ns a1 ammc ↓ amyg a1 amyg-p a1 *Anac* k* anac-oc anan ↓ androc srj1*• ang b2.de* ange-s oss1• anh sp1 ant-c b7.de* *Ant-t* k* anthraci kr1 apis k* *Apoc* k* arag br1* aran k* aran-ix sp1 aran-sc a1 arb-m oss1• arg-met k* *Arg-n* k* arge-pl rwt5• arizon-l nl2• *Arn* k* *Ars* k* ars-i ars-s-f ↓ arum-t ↓ asaf k* *Asar* k* aspar aster a1* astra-e jl3 atha c2 atp rly4• atra-r bnm3• *Atro* a1* *Aur* k* aur-ar ↓ aur-i ↓ aur-m k* *Aur-m-n* wbt2• bac jl2 *Bamb-a* stb2.de• *Bapt* k* *Bar-c* k* bar-i k2* *Bar-m* bar-ox-suc ↓ bar-s ↓ bart a1 **Bell** k* bell-p sp1 benz-ac berb *Bism* k* bism-o a1 bism-sn a1* bit-ar wht1•

Confusion: ...
Borx k* both a1 both-a rb3 *Bov* k* brass-n-o srj5• brom k* bros-gau mrc1 brucel sa3• **Bry** k* *Bufo* k* bung-fa mtf cadm-met tpw6* caj ↓ calad k* **Calc** k* calc-ar br1 calc-i k2 *Calc-p* k* calc-s *Calc-sil* k2 camph b2.de* **Cann-i** k* *Cann-s* k* cann-xyz ↓ *Canth* k* *Caps* k* carb-ac *Carb-an* k* **Carb-v** k* carbn-h a1 carbn-o *Carbn-s* k* carc mg1.de* cardios-h rly4• carl carneg-g ↓ cartl-s rly4• cassia-f ckh1 cassia-s ccrh1* caust k* cedr ↓ cere-b a1 cham k* *Chel Chin* k* chinin-ar chinin-s chir-fl gya2 chlf a1* *Chlol* k* chlor chloram jl3 chlorpr jl3 choc ↓ chol a1 chord-umb rly4• chr-ac a1* cic k* cimic bg cimx cina k* cinnb k* clem k* cob ptm1*• *Coc-c* coca ↓ *Coca-c* ↓ **Cocc** k* cod a1 *Coff* k* coff-t a1 coffin a1 *Colch* bg2* coli jl2* *Coloc* k* com *Con* k* conin a1 convo-s jl3 cop cor-r ↓ cori-r a1 corian-s knl6• corn cortico tpw7* cortiso jl3 cot a1* *Croc* k* *Crot-c Crot-h* k* crot-t cund a1 *Cupr* k* cupr-ar cupr-s a1 cur cycl k* cyn-d ckh1 cypra-eg ↓ cystein-l rly4• daph ↓ dat-a a1 dat-m a1 dendr-pol sk4• des-ac ↓ diaz sa3• dig k* dios diph-t-tpt jl2 dirc a1 dream-p ↓ *Dros* k* *Dulc* k* dys fmm1• eberth jl2 echi k* ephe-si hsj1• erio ↓ ery-a eucal a1 eug euon bro1 euon-a br1 eup-pur euph ↓ euphr k* eupi *Fago* fagu a1 falco-pe nl2• *Ferr* k* ferr-ar ferr-i ↓ ferr-p fic-m gya1 fl-ac k* flor-p rsj3• form bg2* formal ↓ galeoc-c-h ↓ galin jl3 galla-q-r nl2• gard-j vlr2• *Gels* k* gent-c ↓ gent-l germ-met stj2*• gink-b ↓ gins **Glon** k* glyc bro1 gran *Granit-m* ↓ *Graph* k* grat k* grin ↓ guaj ↓ guare a1 haliae-lc srj5• halo jl3 ham a1 *Hell* k* hep k* hipp hura hydr hydr-ac k* **Hydrog** srj2*• *Hyos* k* *Hyper* k* iber a1 ign k* ignis-alc es2• indg indol bro1 iod k* ip k* irid-met br1* iris-foe a1 jab jatr-c jug-c jug-r br1 kali-ar kali-bi k* *Kali-br* k* *Kali-c* k* kali-chl ↓ kali-cy ↓ kali-i k2* kali-n k* kali-p k* kali-s *Kali-sil* ↓ kalm ketogl-ac rly4• *Kola* ↓ *Kreos* k* lac-ac *Lac-c* k* *Lac-e* hrn2• lac-h htj1*• *Lac-lup* hrn2• **Lach** k* lact lact-v a1* lam ↓ lat-m ↓ *Laur* k* lavand-a ctl1• *Lec* k* led k* lil-t limen-b-c ↓ limest-b es1• lina br1 lob k* lob-p br1 lol a1* loxo-recl knl4• luf-op rsj5• *Luna* kg1• *Lyc* k* lyss kr1 m-ambo b7.de* *Mag-c* k* mag-m k* mag-s manc bro1 mand sp1 mang bg2 marb-w ↓ *Med* k* melal-alt gya4 meli menth c1 *Meny* b7.de* meph a1 **Merc** k* merc-c k* merc-i-r ↓ merl ↓ *Mez* k* mill ↓ moly-met jl3* *Moni* rfm1• morph *Mosch* k* mucs-nas rly4• mur-ac bg2* murx musca-d szs1 myric nabal a1 naja narcot a1 nat-ar *Nat-c* k* **Nat-m** k* nat-ox rly4• nat-p nat-s nat-sil fd3.de• neon srj5• nicc nicc-met stj2*• nit-ac k* nit-s-d a1 nitro-o a1 **Nux-m** k* **Nux-v** k* oci-sa jl* oena a1 *Olib-sac* wmh1 *Olnd* b7.de* **Onos** k* **Op** k* opun-s a1 (non:opun-v a1) oreo c1 osm ox-ac ↓ oxal-a ↓ oxeod a1 oxyt ↓ ozone sde2• par k* parathyr jl3 paro-i ↓ ped c1 pert jl2 peti a1 **Petr** k* petr-ra shn4• ph-ac k* phel *Phos* k* phys phyt ↓ *Pic-ac* bro1* pieri-b mlk9.de pip-m a1 pisc bro1 pitu-gl br1 plac rzf5• plac-s rly4• plan plat k* *Plb* k* plb-chr a1 plut-n srj7• **Podo** fd* polys ↓ positr nl2• psil ft1 *Psor* ptel *Puls* k* *Pyrog* k2* pyrus ↓ querc-r svu1• raja-s ↓ ran-b k* ran-s bg2 raph rat ↓ rauw tpw8* rham-cal br1 rheum k* rhod k* rhus-g tmo3• rhus-r ↓ **Rhus-t** k* ruta k* *Sabad* k* sabal br1 sabin k* sacch-a fd2.de• sal-ac *Sal-fr* sle1• samb k* sang sars k* scut br1 *Sec* k* sel bg2* senec a1 *Seneg* k* **Sep** k* ser-a-c jl2 **Sil** k* sinus rly4• *Spig* k* spira a1 spirae a1 spong k* squil k* stann k* *Staph* k* staphycoc ↓ stict c1* *Stram* k* streptoc rly4• stront-c bg2 **Stry** k* suis-em rly4• suis-pan rly4• sul-ac b2.de* sul-i ↓ sulfa sp1* sulfon br1* *Sulph* k* sumb ↓ suprar rly4• symph ↓ syph *Tab* k* tanac a1* taosc ↓ tarax k* tarent ↓ tax a1 tax-br oss1• tell rsj10• ter tere-la ↓ teucr k* thal-xyz srj8• thea ↓ ther thiop jl3 *Thuj* k* thymol sp1* til ↓ tong ↓ trif-p ↓ tril-c a1 tril-p ↓ *Tritic-vg* fd5.de trom tub ptk1* tub-d ↓ tus-fr a1 uran-n ↓ *Urol-h* rwt• ust ↓ vac a1* valer k* **Vanil** fd* *Verat* k* verat-v ↓ verb k* vero-o rly3• vinc ↓ viol-o k* viol-t b7.de* vip visc ↓ xan k* xero bro1 *Zinc* k* **Zinc-p** vh* zinc-val bro1 [alum-p stj2 alumin stj2 alumin-s stj2 am-caust stj2 am-f stj2 arg-p stj2 astat stj2 aur-s stj2 bar-br stj2 bar-met stj2 bell-p-sp dcm1 beryl stj2 bor-pur stj2 buteo-j sej6 cadm-s stj2 caes-met stj2 chr-met stj2 cob-m stj2 cob-p stj2 cupr-act stj2 cupr-f stj2 cupr-m stj2 cupr-p stj2 fl-pur stj2 hafn-met stj2 heroin sdj2 lanth-met stj2 lith-c stj2 lith-f stj2 lith-i stj2 lith-m stj2 lith-met stj2 lith-p stj2 mang-i stj2 mang-p stj2 merc-d stj2 merc-i-f stj2 nicc-s stj2 nitro stj2 osm-met stj2 oxyg stj2 plb-m stj2 plb-p stj2 polon-met stj2 pop dhh1 rhen-met stj2 sol-ecl cky1 tant-met stj2 thal-met stj2 tung-met stj2 zinc-m stj2 zinc-n stj2]

- **daytime**: granit-m es1•
- **morning**: acon *Aesc* ↓ agar aloe alum alum-p k2 alum-sil k2 am-m ambr *Anac* ant-t arg-n arn ars ars-i ars-s-f ↓ arum-t asaf asar astra-e jl3 aur aur-ar k2 aur-i k2 aur-s k2 bamb-a stb2.de• *Bar-c* bar-s k2 bell bism bov bros-gau mrc1 *Bry* bufo *Calc* calc-ar k2* calc-p ↓ *Calc-s* calc-sil ↓ cann-s ↓ canth caps *Carb-an Carb-v* carbn-s caust cham chel *Chin* chinin-ar chinin-s chord-umb rly4• cic cimic ↓ cina ↓ clem cob coc-c ↓ cocc colch k2* coloc con corn kr1 crot-h euphr ferr ↓ ferr-ar ferr-p *Graph* hyos hyper ign iod jug-r kali-ar kali-c kali-n kali-p kali-s kali-sil ↓ **Lach** lact lyc mag-c mag-m mag-s merc merc-i-f ↓ merl ↓ mill moni rfm1• mosch murx *Naja* ↓ *Nat-c* nat-m nat-p k2 nat-s nat-sil k2 nicc nux-v k* olib-sac wmh1 op ox-ac ped ↓ petr ph-ac phos plb ↓ podo psor ↓ puls ↓ ran-b ran-s raph ↓ rheum ↓ *Rhod Rhus-t* ruta sabad ↓ samb sars
- **morning**: ...
seneg sep sil spong fd4.de squil stann staph stram a1 stry sul-ac sul-i k2 **Sulph** sumb *Thuj* til trif-p a1 ust verat zinc zinc-p k2 [tax jsj7]
  - **rising**:
    - **after**: anac arg-n asar aur bell bry calc *Carb-v* cham chel cic cina clem coc-c corn graph ign kali-c lact mag-c mag-m mag-s merc merl nat-m h2 ph-ac phos a1* plb raph rhod rhus-t sabad samb sep sil sulph
      - **amel.**: alum h2 ant-t mag-s phos rhus-t
    - **when**: anac arg-n asar aur bell bry calc *Carb-v* cham chel cic cina clem coc-c corn graph ign kali-c kali-sil k2 lact mag-c mag-m mag-s merc merl ped c1 ph-ac plb raph rhod rhus-t sabad samb sep sil sulph
  - **waking**, on: acon *Aesc* agar alum k2 alum-p k2 alum-sil k2 ambr a1 *Anac* ant-t arg-n ars ars-s-f k2 *Bar-c Bry Calc* k* calc-p calc-s calc-sil k2* cann-s carb-an *Carb-v* carbn-s chinin-ar cimic clem coc-c euphr ferr ferr-ar graph h2 hyper ign **Lach** *Lyc* mag-m h2 mag-s merc merc-i-f *Naja* nat-m petr k2 *Phos* psor puls rheum h rhod ruta *Sil* spong fd4.de sulph *Thuj* k2* til trif-p br1 zinc zinc-p k2
- **forenoon**: phys a1 sep a1 sil a1 sulph a1
- **afternoon**: agar alumn asaf bry calc cann-s a1 carb-v cham chel chin clem coloc crot-t ery-a a1 ferr gard-j vlr2• graph hell hyos kali-bi kali-c kali-cy a1 lac-ac laur nat-m nux-v op petr phel sabin sal-fr sle1• sep sulph verat-v zinc
- **evening**: aloe am-c androc srj1• aran ars ars-i bar-c bar-s k2 bell borx bov calc calc-ar k2* calc-s calc-sil k2 cann-s carb-an *Carb-v* cedr cham chinin-s cinnb a1 coc-c coloc corn cycl dig dios a1 dros dulc euphr ferr ferr-ar ferr-i ferr-p graph hipp hydrog srj2• iod ip kali-ar kali-c kali-n kali-p kali-s kali-sil k2 kalm *Lyc* mag-s mez mill a1* murx nat-ar nat-c nat-m nat-p nat-sil k2 *Nux-m* nux-v olib-sac wmh1 ph-ac phos psor st1 ptel puls rhus-t ruta sars sep sil spig stann sul-ac sul-i k2 sulph thuj urol-h rwt• valer zinc zinc-p k2
  - **amel.**: sars h2
- **night**: acon ↓ am-m ↓ anac ant-t ↓ arg-n ars ↓ aur-m ↓ bar-c ↓ bell ↓ brom ↓ bry ↓ calc calc-s ↓ cedr *Chel* kr1 chin ↓ clem ↓ coc-c ↓ com croc ↓ crot-t dulc ↓ fl-ac *Glon* ↓ grat ↓ hydr-ac ↓ kali-bi ↓ kali-s ↓ lil-t ↓ lyc mag-m ↓ mag-s ↓ mang ↓ meny ↓ merc ↓ merc-i-f ↓ mez ↓ mur-ac nat-c ↓ nat-m ↓ par ↓ phos phyt ↓ plat ↓ psor ptel puls ↓ raph rat ↓ rhus-r ↓ ruta sec sep sil ↓ *Stram* ↓ *Sulph* til
  - **midnight**:
    - **after** | **walking** about; on: *Stram* kr1
  - **lying** down, on: acon am-m ant-t ars aur-m bar-c bell brom bry calc-s clem coc-c croc dulc glon grat a1 hydr-ac kali-s lil-t mag-m mag-s mang meny merc nat-c par phos phyt *Psor* rat rhus-r sulph
  - **waking**, on: *Chel* chin h1 *Glon* k* kali-bi sf1.de merc-i-f mez nat-m k2 phos plat psor puls h1 sil sulph h2
- **abortion**; after: ruta a1
- **air**, in open: agar caust colch con crot-t hyos mag-c h2* nit-ac nux-v rhod spig staphycoc rly4• sulph
  - **amel.**: acon am-m ant-t ars aur-m bar-c bar-s k2 bell bry caj a1 calc-s clem coc-c croc cyn-d ckh1 dulc glon grat a1 hydr-ac kali-s mag-m mag-s mang meny merc nat-c par phos phyt *Psor* rat sal-fr sle1• sulph
- **alcoholic** drinks; after: cocc mrr1
- **alternating** with:
  - **alertness** (See Alert - alternating - confusion)
  - **cheerfulness** (See Cheerful - alternating - confusion)
  - **singing** (See Singing - alternating - confusion)
- **appetite** wanting, with: *Ptel* vml3•
- **arouse** himself, compelled to: (↗*Hiding - himself - children)* **Carb-v** choc srj3• gran hydrog srj2• **Nux-v** *Sulph* k2*
- **ascending** | **agg.**: ptel *Sulph*
- **atrophy**; with: lach bg2
- **bed**, while in: ambr ars ↓ calc cic ↓ merc ↓ phos rhod stram ↓
  - **amel.**: nat-c
  - **jump** out of, makes him: ars j5.de cic j5.de merc j5.de stram j5.de
- **beer**, from: bell calc chin *Coloc* con cor-r crot-t ign
- **bread**; agg.: (↗*GENERALS - Food - bread - agg. - butter)* crot-t
- **breakfast**:
  - **after**: calad coc-c cycl a1
    - **amel.**: bov mag-c
  - **before**: calc fl-ac
- **calculating**, when: (↗*Mathematics - inability; Mistakes - calculating)* nat-m *Nux-v Psor* kr1* *Syph* kr1* vanil fd5.de

- **carousal**; as after a: gran k* mez h2 **Nux-v** k* ph-ac h2
- **carrying** heavy loads, when: agar a1
- **children**; in: aesc ptk1
- **chill**:
  - **between** chill and heat: chel bg2
  - **during**: acon aloe *Calc* bg *Caps Cham* cic coff con dros hell hyos kali-c nat-c nux-m *Phos* h2 plb rhus-t ruta stram suis-pan rly4• verat viol-t
- **closing** eyes, on: atro a1
- **coffee**:
  - **after**: all-c arg-n calc-p mill
  - **amel.**: coca hipp
- **coition**:
  - **after**: bov calc caust mez *Ph-ac* phos rhod sel sep staph vh
  - **amel.**: olib-sac wmh1
- **cold** applications:
  - **head**, to | **amel.**: cycl a1
- **cold** bath | **amel.**: *Arg-n* vh* calc-p euphr *Phos*
- **concentrate** the mind, on attempting to: *(↗Concentration - difficult; Prostration)* ambr k2 androc srj1• asar bell bry calad k2 chir-fl gya2 **Cocc** con croc *Dulc* fd4.de galeoc-c-h gms1• galla-q-r nl2• gels hydrog srj2• lavand-a ctl1• limen-b-c hrn2* mez nat-c vh* nat-m nit-ac olnd k* plut-n srj7• ran-b spong fd4.de staph
- **conversation**: | **agg.**: *(↗Conversation - agg.)* bit-ar wht1• granit-m es1• limen-b-c hrn2* *Sil* tax-br oss1•
- **coryza**; during: staph b7.de*
- **cough** | **before** paroxysm of coughing: cina
- **daily** affairs; about: chir-fl gya2 ham fd3.de• kali-p fd1.de• lyc ptk1* podo fd3.de• symph fd3.de• tritic-vg fd5.de
- **dazed**: *(↗intoxicated)* lac-lup hrn2•
- **describing** complaints properly; not: dulc fd4.de puls ckh1 **Ruta** fd* tritic-vg fd5.de vanil fd5.de
- **dinner**:
  - **after**: arg-n carb-v euphr mag-m nux-v petr h2 phos plan tab thuj zinc h2
  - **during**: mag-m h2
- **disorganized** (See Chaotic; Memory - weakness - objects)
- **dream**, as if in a: *(↗Dream; as; Unconsciousness - dream)* ail sf1.de ambr k2 androc srj1• arn bamb-a stb2.de• bell calc h2 *Cann-i* cann-s carb-an h2 *Carb-v* carneg-g rwt1• cham chin cupr h2 dream-p sdj1• germ-met srj5• grat guaj ign *Lec* k* mez *Nux-m* br1* *Phos* rhus-t sep spig *Spong* fd4.de squil sulph suprar rly4• tax-br oss1• thuj k* **Vanil** fd* zinc
- **drinking** | **after**: bell bry **Cocc** con croc
- **driving**, while: falco-pe nl2•
- **drowsiness**; while resisting: coca a1
- **drugs**; as if under: plac rzf5•
- **eating**:
  - **after**: agar ambr apis aran arg-n bell bufo *Calc* calc-sil k2 *Carb-v* caust coc-c **Cocc** coloc croc cycl euphr ferr ferr-p grat hyos lach led lob *Lyc* mag-m meny *Merc Mez* mill nat-c *Nat-m* nat-p nat-sil k2 nit-ac *Nux-v* olnd op petr *Ph-ac Phos* plan **Puls** sabad sabin *Sep Sil Sulph* tab thuj zinc zinc-p k2
  - **amel.**: agar apis caust fago jug-r lach mez phos
- **ecstatic**: cann-i k2
- **emotions**; about: polys sk4•
- **epileptic** convulsions:
  - **after**: plb k* sil k*
  - **before**: lach gt1* plb gt1* sil gt1*
- **epistaxis**; amel.: carb-an cham
- **eructations**; amel.: bry gent-c sang
- **excitement**; amel.: *(↗Excitement - amel.)* chin a1 cycl a1
- **feelings**; about one's: **Nat-sil** fd*
- **fever**; during: *(↗heat)* ars bg2 *Bell* bg2 bry bg2 chin bg2 ip bg2 nat-c bg2 *Nux-v* bg2 puls bg2 rhus-t bg2
- **fumes**; from inhaling: *(↗smoking - after)* glon mrr1
- **haste**; from: sul-ac mrr1
- **hat** agg.; putting on a: calc-p ferr-i
- **head**:
  - **complaints** of; with: aur bg2 petr bg2
- **head**: ...
  - **pain**; with: agar h2 ammc vh1 bry k2 chinin-s j *Cimic* mrr1 con h2 cycl a1 lac-h htj1• lil-t k2 morph j nat-m h2 petr h2 phos h2 sil h2 tarax h1 xan c1 zinc h2
- **headache**, with: *Cina* a1
- **heat**, during: *(↗fever)* acon bg alum **Ang** bg arg-met *Bapt Bell* bg* bry calc bg camph *Caps* bg carb-v bg carbn-s k2 cham chin coc-c coloc con bg dros dulc k2 formal bro1 *Hyos* ign ip laur merc bg nat-c nat-m bg *Nux-v* bg op phos puls raja-s jl3 rhus-t bg sep sil bg tab a1 thuj valer verat
- **identity**, as to his: *(↗Antagonism; Delusions - body - divided; Delusions - consciousness - belongs; Delusions - divided - two; Delusions - divided - two - cut; Delusions - identity - errors; Delusions - influence; Delusions - person - other; Delusions - place - different; Delusions - robot; Delusions - sees - someone; Delusions - separated - body - mind; Delusions - separated - body - soul; Delusions - someone else - she; Delusions - strangers - control; Delusions - superhuman - control; Delusions - three; Delusions - three persons; Depersonalization; Irresolution; Memory - weakness - names - own; Merging; Schizophrenia - paranoid; Stranger - sensation; Thoughts - persistent - separated - mind; Thoughts - persistent - separated - will; Will - two)* agar ↓ *Agath-a* ↓ aids nl2• **Alum** k* *Alumn* vh* **Anac** ↓ *Anh* mg1.de* ant-c arg-n ↓ aur kr1 aur-m-n wbt2• bapt calc-p ↓ camph gl1.fr• cann-i br1* cann-s cann-xyz ↓ chr-met dx cic k2 cocc ↓ cycl ↓ cypra-eg sde6.de• daph ↓ des-ac ↓ dulc ↓ falco-pe nl2• galeoc-c-h gms1• gard-j vlr2• gels bg haliae-lc srj5• ham fd3.de• hydrog ↓ hyper ↓ irid-met ↓ kali-br lach lil-t ↓ lyc ↓ med moni rfm1• mosch bg musca-d ↓ naja ↓ nat-m ↓ nat-sil fd3.de• neon ↓ nux-m ↓ olib-sac wmh1 op ↓ oxal-a rly4• paro-i ↓ petr petr-ra ↓ phos plb positr nl2• psor ↓ puls ↓ *Pyrog* ↓ pyrus sabin ↓ sal-fr sle1• sec ↓ sep ↓ sil ↓ *Spong* fd4.de stram sulph syph ↓ taosc ↓ ther ↓ thuj k* tril-p ↓ *Tritic-vg* fd5.de valer verat ↓ xan ↓
  - **boundaries**; and personal: *(↗Delusions - dissolving; Depersonalization; Merging)* hydrog nl neon srj5• olib-sac wmh1 positr nl2•
  - **depersonalization** (See Depersonalization)
  - **duality**, sense of: *(↗Antagonism; Delusions - body - cut - two; Delusions - body - divided; Delusions - body - half; Delusions - body - threefold; Delusions - divided - two; Delusions - double - being; Delusions - person - two - personalities; Delusions - place - two; Delusions - separated - body - mind; Delusions - separated - body - soul; Delusions - side - alive; Irresolution; Thoughts - two; Will - two)* agar ptk1 *Agath-a* nl2• alum bg2 **Anac** j5.de* anh jl3 arg-n bg3* **Bapt** bg2* calc-p bg3* cann-i a1* cann-s bg3 cann-xyz bg2* cocc ptk1 cycl bg2* daph ptk1 des-ac jl3 dulc ptk1 *Gels* bg2* ham fd3.de• hyper ptk1 *Lach* bg2* lil-t bg2* lyc bg2 naja st* nat-m bg2 nux-m bg2* op bg2 paro-i jl **Petr** bg2* petr-ra shn4• phos bg2* plb bg2 psor bg2* puls bg2 *Pyrog* bg3* sabin ptk1 *Sal-fr* sle1• sec bg2 sep ptk1 sil bg2* *Stram* bg2* taosc iwa1• ther bg2* thuj bg2* tril-p ptk1 verat ptk1 xan bg3*
  - **head** separated from body; as if (See Delusions - body - divided; Delusions - head - separated)
  - **own**, as if not his: alum bg2 cypra-eg sde6.de• falco-pe nl2• lach bg2 nat-m bg2 syph ptk1 thuj bg2
  - **sexual** identity: *(↗Shameful - sexuality; DREAMS - Sexual identity)* hydrog srj2• irid-met srj5• musca-d szs1
- **influenza**; after: scut tl1
- **injury** to head: | **after**: *(↗Ailments - injuries; Dullness - injuries; Insanity - injuries)* hell mrr1 **Nat-s** k* op mrr1
- **interruption**, from: *(↗Disturbed; Interruption - agg.)* berb colch ↓ *Mez*
  - **logical** thinking impossible: colch a1
- **intoxicated**: *(↗dazed)*
  - **as** after being: *(↗HEAD - Intoxication; HEAD - Intoxication - as)* acon k* agar k* agath-a nl2• am-m k* anac h2 ang k* arg-met k* bell k* *Bry* camph *Carb-v* k* *Chin* k* clem cocc coloc cor-r croc **Dig** dulc h2 *Glon* grin vh kali-c k* kali-n b4a.de* lam laur k* mosch nat-m k* *Nux-v* k* op *Ph-ac* k* psor puls k* rheum k* sabin sal-fr sle1• squil k* valer *Vanil* fd5.de
  - **as** if: abies-c br1 *Acon* agar j5.de agath-a nl2• aids nl2• amyg anan androc srj1• ant-c h2* arg-met h1* arizon-l nl2• asar **Bapt** bell bism h1 bry k2 bufo *Carb-v Carbn-o* **Carbn-s** chinin-s choc srj3• cupr h2 cypra-eg sde6.de• *Dig* erio br1 falco-pe nl2• *Glon* graph grat grin vh* hyos j5.de ign kali-c h2 kali-n lach k2 laur led h1 lyc mag-c h2 mag-m h2

- **as** if: ...
  merl a1 mez j5.de nat-sil fd3.de• *Nux-m* k* nux-v oxyt br1 ph-ac phel ran-b c1 rhus-t sabad sal-fr sle1• *Sil* spong thuj h1 tong *Vanil* fd5.de visc sp1
  ⋮ **waking**; on: **Mag-m** mrr1
- **knows** not where he is: *(↗loses; Mistakes - localities; Recognizing - not - surroundings; Unconsciousness - dream - does)* *Aesc*↓ alum↓ atro a1 bov↓ *Cann-s*↓ cann-xyz↓ **Chin**↓ cic k2 coff↓ coff-t↓ galeoc-c-h gms1• **Glon** k* haliae-lc srj5• limen-b-c hrn2• merc a1 *Mez*↓ neon srj5• **Nux-m** k* *Petr* plat↓ plut-n srj7• positr nl2• puls↓ ran-b sacch-a fd2.de• sel↓ spong fd4.de staph↓ stram mtf33 tax↓ *Vanil* fd5.de viol-t↓
  - **night**: bov a1
  - **objects** around her; and cannot distinguish the: *Aesc* k1* coff-t kr1* limen-b-c mlk9.de *Mez* kr1*
  - **objects** around her; nor recognizes the: limen-b-c hrn2• [tax jsj7]
  - **waking**, on: aesc alum k2 bov bg2 *Cann-s*↓ cann-xyz bg2 **Chin** bg2 coff bg2 merc bg2 plat bg2 puls bg2* sel bg2 staph bg2 vanil fd5.de viol-t bg2
    ⋮ **dream**, from a: *Cann-s* a1
- **laughing**: | **agg.**: ther
- **listening**; while: ignis-alc es2• sacch-a gmj3 tritic-vg fd5.de
- **location** (See knows; loses)
- **loses** his way in well-known streets: *(↗knows; Forgetful - house; Forgetful - streets; Memory - weakness - places; Mistakes - localities; Orientation - decreased; Recognizing - not - streets)* arg-n mtf33 bros-gau mrc1 cann-i mrr1 cic k2* *Coca-c* sk4• cot br1 dulc fd4.de falco-pe nl2• germ-met srj5• **Glon** k* irid-met srj5• kali-s fd4.de *Kola* stb3• *Merc* *Nux-m* k* nux-v gl1.fr• oci-sa sk4• ozone sde2• **Petr** k ●* petr-ra shn4• plb a1 plut-n↓ positr nl2• psil ft1 puls gl1.fr• ran-b *Sal-fr* sle1• spong fd4.de stram mtf33 thuj urol-h rwt•
  - **alone** | **amel.**: plut-n srj7•
- **lost** feeling: *(↗Helplessness)* cot br1 nat-sil fd3.de• olib-sac wmh1 plut-n srj7• [alum-p stj2]
- **lying**; when: brom bry *Carb-v* cham *Grat* lil-t mag-m merc rhus-r sep
  - **amel.**: granit-m es1• nat-m h2 sal-fr sle1•
- **masturbation**, from: *Gels* kr1
- **menses**:
  - **after**: *(↗Menses - after)* graph nat-m
  - **before**: *(↗Menses - before)* aur-m-n wbt2• cimic *Sep*
  - **during**: *(↗Menses - during)* am-c cimic cocc graph h2 lyc phos
  - **suppressed** menses; from: apis b7a.de
- **mental** exertion:
  - **amel.**: carb-v
  - **from**: ang ant-t apis aran *Aur* aur-s k2 bar-ox-suc rly4• borx h2 *Calc* *Calc-p* *Calc-s* k* *Calc-sil* k2 canth *Carb-v* k* carbn-s k2 *Caust* cham *Cocc* k1* euon *Gels* gink-b sbd1• hep iod kali-p fd1.de• *Kali-sil* k2 laur *Lyc* mag-c mag-m mez **Nat-c** *Nat-m* *Nat-p* **Nat-sil** k2* *Nit-ac* *Nux-m* *Nux-v* olib-sac wmh1 olnd ox-ac petr *Ph-ac* *Phos* *Pic-ac* podo fd3.de• *Puls* ran-b scut a1 *Sep* *Sil* k* *Staph* sul-i k2 *Sulph* thuj tritic-vg fd5.de
- **mistakes** (See Mistakes)
- **mixes** subjective and objective: calc bg2 cann-s bg cann-xyz bg2 cypra-eg sde6.de• hyos bg2 nux-v bg2 plat bg2 sulph bg2
- **motion**, from: acon ambr bell borx↓ bry calc-p carb-an↓ cob ign indg kalm k2 lob mosch nat-c nux-v phos *Puls* sulph↓ tab
  - **amel.**: arg-n ferr ferr-p
  - **downward** | **agg.**: borx k2
  - **head**, of the: carb-an h2 sulph h2
- **muscles** refuse to obey the will when attention is turned away: anac ptk1 aster ptk1* gels bg2* *Hell* k* lil-t bg2* phys ptk1* tarent ptk1*
- **nausea**; with: calc-p bg2
- **noise** | **agg.**: *Asar* vh* mag-c h2 *Ther* vh*
- **old** age, in: arg-met vh *Arg-n* vh* *Bar-c* kr1* *Con* sf1.de
- **pain**; during paroxysms of: *Acon* apoc *Cham* *Coff* dulc j5.de verat
- **past** and present: cic k2*
- **periodical**: staph
- **perspiration**, during: acon bg ang bg ars bg **Bell** bg calc bg *Caps* bg *Chin* dros bg graph bg ip bg kali-c bg merc bg nat-c bg *Nat-m* bg *Nux-v* bg op bg ph-ac bg *Phos* bg *Rhus-t* bg sabad bg samb **Sep** bg sil bg *Stram* **Sulph** bg thuj bg *Valer* bg verat bg
- **pollutions**, from: *Sel* sumb a1
- **pregnancy**, during: *Nux-m*
- **provocations**; from small: *Arg-met* vh1
- **reading**, while: agar agn *Alum* ambr ang *Apis* bit-ar wht1• *Calc* canth k2 cocc echi sf1.de ferr-i germ-met srj5• lil-t *Lyc* k* nat-m nux-m *Olnd*↓ *Ph-ac* pip-m a1 podo fd3.de•
  - **understand**, if he attempts to: *Olnd*
- **riding**, while: *(↗Riding - carriage - aversion)* bry sil symph fd3.de•
- **rising** | **after**: *Alum* aur bell bism-sn a1 bov bry kali-c laur merc nat-m nat-s phos rhod
- **rocking**, agg.: borx k2
- **room**, in: ars h2 mag-c h2
- **sadness**; with (See Sadness - confusion)
- **scratching**:
  - **ear**; behind the ear: calc h2
  - **head**; the right side of: sul-ac h2
- **sexual** excesses; as if from: ph-ac h2
- **sexual** identity; about one's (See identity - sexual)
- **sitting**, while: *(↗Sitting - inclination)* am-c asaf asar bar-c bell calc calc-sil k2 carb-an caust cic colch kali-c kali-sil k2 kalm k2 mang merc nat-c nat-m nit-ac op phos phyt puls *Rhus-t* sabad sars sep sil spig sul-ac thuj valer verat
- **situations**, of: anh sp1
- **sleep**:
  - **after**: ambr anac ars bry calc carb-v chel↓ *Con* dulc fd4.de graph hep kali-c↓ lach mill↓ op phos↓ spong fd4.de squil *Sulph* kr1 uran-n sf1.de
    ⋮ **long**: kali-c h2
    ⋮ **siesta**: calc carb-v chel a1 **Con** dulc fd4.de mill hr1 phos
  - **during** | **amel.**: granit-m es1•
  - **loss** of sleep; from | **as** from loss of sleep: zinc a1
- **sleepiness**; with: all-c vh1 ant-t a1 echi bg2* nux-m mrr1 pip-m a1
- **smoking** | **after**: *(↗fumes)* alum bell ferr-i gels petr thuj
- **spirituous** liquors, from: *(↗Libertinism)* *Alum* bell bov *Con* k2* cor-r **Nux-v** petr k2* stront-c vanil fd5.de
- **spoken** to, when: **Alum** vh* *Alumn* vh* lith-c ruta fd4.de *Sep* tax-br oss1• tere-la rly4• thal-xyz srj8•
- **standing**, while: bov bry cic grat lith-c k* mang hr1 plb staph sulph k2 thuj valer verat
  - **amel.**: iris-foe a1
- **stitching** in chest, from: sep h2
- **stool** amel.: *Borx* mag-s *Nat-s*
- **stooping**, when: bov calc caust coloc corn *Glon* kr1 hell nat-m nit-ac phos spig valer vinc
  - **amel.**: verat
- **sun**; in the: *Nat-c* nux-v
- **surroundings**, of: bell-p sp1 coli rly4• kali-p fd1.de• olib-sac wmh1 *Ruta* fd4.de *Spong* fd4.de
- **talking**, while: *(↗Dullness - spoken; Speech - incoherent)* dulc fd4.de glon sf1.de *Kali-s* fd4.de lavand-a ctl1• marb-w es1• *Nat-m* k* nat-sil fd3.de• *Ruta* fd4.de sacch-a fd2.de• sep gl1.fr• *Sil* sf1.de spong fd4.de staph *Thuj*
- **teeth**; with pain in: acon bro1 cham bro1
- **thinking** of it | **agg.**: *(↗Thinking - complaints - agg.)* **Hell** k* olnd ox-ac vh podo fd3.de•
- **time**; as to: *(↗Mistakes - time)* anh↓ arge-pl↓ bapt↓ borx↓ bov bg2 bros-gau mrc1 cann-i mrr1 cann-xyz bg2 caust↓ cic↓ cypra-eg↓ falco-pe↓ galeoc-c-h gms1• *Glon*↓ halo jl hydrog srj2• **Lach** a1* loxo-recl knl4• moni rfm1• **Nat-sil** fd* nux-m bg2 *Ruta* fd4.de *Spong* fd4.de symph fd3.de• tritic-vg fd5.de tub-d jl2 [heroin sdj2]
  - **morning**; as to: arge-pl rwt5•
  - **space**; and: *(↗Mistakes - space - time)* anh bro1 bapt tl1 borx bg2 *Cann-i* bro1* caust bg2 cic bro1 cypra-eg sde6.de• falco-pe nl2• *Glon* bro1 lach bro1 nux-m bg2 **Ruta** fd* tritic-vg fd5.de
- **trifles**; about: carc gk6*
- **unfocused**, fuzzy: *Lac-e* hrn2•
- **urination** amel.: ter
- **vertigo**, with: acon bg2 aesc bg2 agar bg2 am-m bg2 aml-ns vh1 *Anac* bg2 ant-t br1 arg-n bg2 ars bg2* asaf bg2 bell bg2 borx h2* bov bg2 brom bg2 bry bg2 camph bg2 canth bg2 carb-an bg2 *Carb-v* bg2 caust bg2 cham bg2 *Chin* bg2 clem bg2 **Cocc** bg2* coff bg2 coloc bg2 croc bg2 *Cupr-ar* kr1 euph bg2 hell bg2 kali-n bg2 laur bg2 lyc bg2 mag-c bg2 mag-m bg2 merc bg2 nat-c bg2 nux-m bg2 **Nux-v** bg2 *Op* bg2 ph-ac bg2 phos bg2 plac-s rly4• *Puls* bg2 ran-b bg2 rhod bg2

- **vertigo**, with: ...
sabad bg2 sec bg2 seneg bg2 *Sep* bg2 sil h2 spig bg2 spong fd4.de squil bg2 stann h2 staph bg2 *Stram* kr1 sulph bg2* verb bg2 zinc h2
- **vexation**: | **after**: *(↗Admonition - agg.; Ailments - reproaches)* nux-v vanil fd5.de
- **vomiting** amel.: tab a1
- **waking**, on: acon acon-ac rly4• *Aesc* k* agar alum bg2 alum-sil k2 ambr anac ant-t arg-n ars bamb-a ↓ bar-c bell bg2 berb borx a1 bov bg2* bry k* calad calc calc-ar k2 calc-p caps *Carb-v* k* cartl-s rly4• cham chel chin k* clem coc-c cocc con k* euphr gels ptk1* glon *Granit-m* es1• graph k* grat hell sf1.de hep hyper ign *Kali-br* k* kali-c h2 kali-n h2 lac-e hrn2• *Lach* k* lat-m bnm6• lavand-a ctl1• led bg2 *Lyc* k* mag-s merc merc-i-f mez naja nat-c nat-p nat-sil k2 nux-m nux-v bg2 op oxal-a rly4• *Petr* bg2* *Ph-ac* **Phos** k* *Plat* psor *Puls* k* rheum a1* rhod rhus-t ruta sal-fr sle1• samb bg2 *Sep* *Sil* spong bg2* squil stann staph *Stram* suis-em rly4• *Sulph* til trif-p br1 urol-h rwt• *Zinc* k* zinc-p k2
  - **dream**; from a beautiful: bamb-a stb2.de•
- **walking**: acon ↓ agar ang arg-n ars ↓ asar bell borx *Bry* calc camph carb-an carb-v *Carl* ↓ caust ↓ cic coc-c coff coloc con dros ferr *Glon* graph ↓ grat kali-c kali-chl ↓ kali-s ↓ *Lach* **Lyc** ↓ merc-i-f ↓ merc-i-r ↓ mez a1 nat-c nat-m nit-ac *Nux-m* par ↓ *Petr* **Puls** ↓ rhod ↓ rhus-t *Sabad* sal-fr ↓ sep spig ↓ spong *Stram* ↓ sulph tarax thea thuj tub ↓ viol-t
  - **night** | **midnight**, after: *Stram* kr1
  - **after**: nat-m h2
    - **amel.**: caust h2
  - **air**, in open: acon agar ars h2 carb-v caust coff **Glon** kali-chl k* lyc **Nux-m** **Petr** sep spig sulph tub
    - **amel.**: bry *Carl* graph kali-s fd4.de **Lyc** merc-i-f merc-i-r nat-c par **Puls** rhod sal-fr sle1• sulph
  - **amel.**: agar ferr-p sulph tax-br oss1•
- **warm** room, in: acon bell *Iod* kali-s **Lyc** merc-i-f nat-m ph-ac phos **Puls** *Sulph*
- **washing** the face | **amel.**: *Ars* k* calc-p coca cycl euphr ferr ferr-p k2 *Phos* k*
- **weather**:
  - **windy** and stormy weather | **before**: *Rhod* mrr1
- **weeping**: *(↗Weeping)*
  - **amel.**: *(↗Weeping - amel.)* *Sep*
- **will** amel.; strong effort of: glon
- **wine**; after: all-c *Alum* amyg a1 amyg-p a1 bov coloc con kali-chl mill ox-ac petr h2 sal-fr sle1• *Zinc* k*
- **working**, while: kali-s fd4.de merc a1 sacch-a gmj3 spong fd4.de tritic-vg fd5.de
- **wrapping** up head | **amel.**: mag-m
- **writing**, while: *(↗Mistakes - writing)* arg-n bamb-a ↓ brom k* croc ferr-i gent-l germ-met srj5• ham fd3.de• hydrog srj2• laur lil-t nat-c symph fd3.de• tritic-vg fd5.de vanil fd5.de vinc
  - **left**-handed when usually writing right-handed: bamb-a stb2.de•
- **yawning** | **amel.**: bry

CONGESTION of blood agg.: anac bg2 bar-c bg2 bry bg2 calc bg2

CONGESTION of head agg.: acon bg2 carb-v bg2 laur bg2 mag-c bg2 phos bg2 puls bg2 sulph bg2

CONNECTION; sense of (See Unification - sensation)

CONSCIENTIOUS about trifles: *(↗Anxiety - time; Carefulness; Cares full; Cautious; Censorious; Delusions - neglected - duty; Delusions - wrong - done; Dirty; Fastidious; Fear - trifles; Loyal; Moral; Responsibility; Rest - cannot; Sensitive; Trifles; Trifles - important)* ambr tsm1 ang bg2 anh mg1.de apis arge-pl rwt5• **ARS** b4a.de* ars-s-f k2* aur k* aur-ar k2 aur-i k2* bamb-a stb2.de• *Bar-c* k* bry but-ac br1 calc gl1.fr• calc-sil stj2* carbn-s carc lsa1.de* cham k* chin k* chinin-ar chir-fl gya2 cocc bg2 crot-c sk4• cupr sst3* cycl k* *Dig* bg2* dulc fd4.de dys fmm1• ferr ferr-ar ferr-i ferr-p a1* galla-q-r nl2• graph k* ham st1 hep hura c1 hyos k* **Ign** k* ignis-alc es2• iod k* ip bg2 kali-c fd* kali-p fd1.de• **Kali-s** fd* lac-d lac-del hrn2• lac-f c1* lac-h sk4• lach bg2* lap-la sde8.de• loxo-lae bnm12• loxo-recl knl4• **Lyc** k •* *M-arct* b7.de* malus-c mtf11 med st1 merc h1 mez k* *Mur-ac* k* musca-d szs1 nat-ar **Nat-c** k* nat-m vh* nat-sil k2* nit-s-d lsa1.de *Nux-v* k* oci-sa sk4• olib-sac wmh1 ozone sde2• ph-ac gl1.fr• phos mtf pin-con oss2• plat gl1.fr• plb cld* plut-n srj7• podo fd3.de• positr nl2• **Puls** •* rhus-t bg2 ruta fd4.de sacch-a fd2.de• sal-fr sle1• sarr sec **Sep** k •* ser-a-c jl2

Conscientious about trifles: ...
Sil k* spig k* spirae c2* *Spong* fd4.de **Staph** sne* *Stram* k* sul-i k2* **Sulph** k •* tax-br oss1• **Thuj** k* *Tritic-vg* fd5.de tub mtf vanil fd5.de verat k* [arg-met stj2 calc-lac stj2 calc-met stj2 ferr-sil stj2 kali-sil stj2 mag-sil stj2 mang-n stj2 mang-sil stj2 merc-i-f stj2 *Nicc* stj1 sil-met stj2 zinc-i stj2]
- **afternoon** | **16**-20 h: *Lyc*
- **children**; in: carc mlr1• cupr mtf33
- **eating** | **after**: ign
- **occupied** with trifles (See Trifles)
- **religious**: carc mlr1•

CONSCIOUSNESS:
- **alternating** with:
  - **delirium** (See Delirium - alternating - consciousness)
  - **rage** (See Rage - alternating - consciousness)
- **animal**: plut-n srj7•
- **convulsions**; with (See GENERALS - Convulsions - consciousness - with)
- **epileptic** convulsions; with: ign bro1
- **expanded** (See Awareness)
- **higher** consciousness; unification with (See Delusions - consciousness - higher)
- **increased** (See Awareness)
- **loss** of consciousness (See Unconsciousness)
- **paralysis**; with: cur br1 naja br1

CONSERVATIVE (See Conformism; Dogmatic; Obstinate; Proper - too)

CONSOLATION: *(↗Affection; Sympathy - aversion)*
- **agg.**•: *(↗Anger - consoled; Cheerful - alternating - sympathy; Concentration - difficult - attention; Flattered - aversion; Inconsolable; Irritability - consolation - agg.; Rage - consolation; Reproaching oneself; Sadness - consoled; Weeping - consolation - agg.)* acon vh1 *Aloe* sne arg-n ptk1 arn k* *Ars* k* aur bg2* *Aur-m-n* wbt2• *Bell* k* cact k* calc k* *Calc-p* calc-sil k2* *Carc* fb* cham k* chin k* coff bg2 con ↓ cupr sst3• *Dys* fmm1• falco-pe nl2• graph bro1 *Hell* bg2* hydroph rsj6• **Ign** k* kali-c *Kali-p* bg2* kali-s ptk1* kali-sil k2* kalm bg2 *Lil-t* k* lyc melal-alt gya4 merc **NAT-M** b2.de* *Nit-ac* k* nux-v k* *Phos* b4a.de *Plat* k* sabad st1 sabal bg2* sabin bg2 **SEP** b2.de* **Sil** k* staph k* streptoc jl2 sulph bg2* **Syph** bg2* tarent k* thuj visc sp1 *Zinc* b4a.de [ant-c stj2 pall stj2 stann stj2]
  - **sympathy** agg.: ars ptk1 *Bell* ptk1 calc bg2* calc-p bg2 carc mp1• coff bg3 con ptk* hell bg2 **Ign** ptk1* kali-c bg2 kali-s ptk1 merc bg2 *Nat-m* ptk1 *Plat* ptk1 sabal bg3* *Sep* ptk1* *Sil* ptk1
- **amel.**: *(↗Affection; Affectionate; Sympathy; Sympathy - desire)* acer-circ oss• agar mtf33 aids nl2• arg-n vh asaf ptk1* calc-p st* camph ptk1 carc gk6* caust gb• con ckh1 cypra-eg sde6.de• falco-pe nl2• gels ptk1* *Hell* ptk1* kali-s st* melal-alt gya4 musca-d szs1 *Phos* sf1.de* pin-con oss2• prot fmm1• **PULS** bg2* ruta fd4.de sal-fr sle1• sil st* spong fd4.de staph syph st* tritic-vg fd5.de vanil fd5.de [heroin sdj2]
  - **woman**; when consoled by a: sal-fr sle1•
- **kind** words; from: *Carc* mlr1•

CONSTIPATION agg.: aloe bg2 **Nat-m** bg2 nux-v bg2

CONTACT with people; easy to get in (See Company - desire; Forsaken; Sociability; Talking - desire)

CONTACT; desire for: *(↗Company - desire; Forsaken; Talking - desire)*
- **reality** and real people; with: polys sk4•

CONTEMPTUOUS: *(↗Abusive; Aversion - persons - all; Cynical; Delirium - reproachful; Dictatorial; Haughty; Insolence; Laughing - contemptuous; Mocking; Mocking - ridicule; Mocking - sarcasm; Presumptuous; Rudeness; Smiling - sardonic)* agath-a ↓ agn bg aloe bg2 alum k* *Androc* srj1• arn bg2 *Ars* k* aur ↓ bry ptk1 canth cham k* *Chin* k* chir-fl gya2 **Cic** k* cina j5.de com a1 cop ↓ croc j cycl falco-pe nl2• gran j granit-m es1• guaj k* hell j5.de hyos ign k* ignis-alc ↓ *Ip* k* lac-ac lac-c ↓ lac-cp sk4• lac-leo hrn2*• *Lach* k* *Lyc* m-arct j merc j5.de mosch j nat-m nit-ac k* *Nux-v* k* *Pall* bg2 par k* **Plat** k* polys sk4• puls k* rhod kgp5• sacch-a fd2.de• sal-fr sle1• sec sil spong a1 stram b7.de* sulph mrr1 taosc iwa1• thuj ↓ *Verat* bg2*
- **air** or when sun shines into room; in open: plat

- **everything**; of: *Chin* k* cina ip k* **Plat**
- **hard** for subordinates and agreeable to superiors (See Hard)
- **humankind**; of: cic h1* ignis-alc es2•
- **opponents**; of: com a1
- **paroxysms** against her will, in: *Plat*
- **ravenous** hunger and greedy, hasty eating; contemptuous with sudden: *Plat* a1
- **relations**, for: *Plat* sne sec hr1*
- **self**, of: *(↗Hiding - himself - children; Loathing - oneself; Reproaching oneself)* agath-a nl2• agn k* aur bro1* cop falco-pe nl2• lac-c bro1 thuj bro1
  - **alternating** with | **eccentricity** (See Eccentricity - alternating - contemptuousness - self)
- **unfortunate** and beyond redemption; of people who she believes are: ignis-alc es2•
- **values**; of generally accepted: *Chin* bg2

CONTENT: *(↗Amusement - desire; Blissful; Cheerful; Delirium - gay; Delusions - island; Delusions - pleasing; Delusions - right - everything; Jesting; Laughing; Mirth; Peace - heavenly; Playful; Pleasure; Self-satisfied; Smiling)* aids nl2• aloe a1* alum a1 *Androc* srj1• anh br1 aq-mar rbp6 arizon-l nl2• aur b4.de* *Borx* bg2* *Cann-i* br1 *Caps* j5.de* carbn-h a1* carc ↓ carl a1 caust ↓ chir-fl gya2 choc srj3• *Cic* bg2* coca a1 cocc a1 com a1 conch fkr1.de cycl a1 *Des-ac* rbp6 *Dream-p* sdj1• falco-pe ↓ fl-ac a1 galeoc-c-h gms1• gins a1 haliae-lc srj5• hydrog srj2*• kali-s fd4.de ketogl-ac rly4• kola stb3• *Lac-lup* ↓ lat-h ↓ laur j5.de led ↓ limen-b-c hrn2* limest-b es1• mag-s a1 mate a1 meny a1 mez a1 nat-c b4.de* nat-m h2 nat-sil fd3.de• **Neon** stj2*• *Olib-sac* wmh1 *Op* b7.de* orot-ac rly4• phasco-ci rbp2 phos b4.de* plac rzf5• plac-s rly4• plut-n ↓ podo fd3.de• positr nl2• propl ub1• *Rhus-g* tmo3• ruta fd4.de sacch-a fd2.de• sal-fr sle1• sinus rly4• spig a1 spong fd4.de staph j5.de suis-em rly4• tarax b7.de* tritic-vg fd5.de tus-fr ↓ vanil fd5.de *Zinc* b4.de* [helium stj2 heroin sdj2 spect dfg1 tax jsj7]

- **morning**: carc fd2.de• galeoc-c-h gms1• hydrog srj2• neon ↓ [heroin sdj2]
  - **waking**, on: neon srj5•
- **forenoon** | **10**-23 h: tus-fr a1
- **afternoon** | **stool**, after: *Borx* a1*
- **night**: op a1
- **alternating** with:
  - **anger** (See Anger - alternating - contentment)
  - **anxiety** (See Anxiety - alternating - contentment)
  - **sadness**: zinc j5.de
- **forgets** all his ailments and pains: chir-fl gya2 op gl1.fr• [heroin sdj2 tax jsj7]
- **group**; with an uninterrupted flow between self and: aids nl2•
- **himself**, with: *Aids* nl2• carl km• caust a1 chir-fl gya2 cic a1 **Dream-p** sdj1• falco-pe nl2• *Kali-s* fd4.de *Lac-lup* hrn2• lat-h thj1 led a1 mag-s a1 meny a1 olib-sac wmh1 plac ↓ plut-n srj7• tritic-vg fd5.de vanil fd5.de [heroin sdj2]
  - **harmony** with oneself; in: plac rzf5•
  - **world**; and the: olib-sac wmh1
- **life** are ideal; circumstances of: plac rzf5•
- **others**; with: dream-p sdj1•
- **partner**; with an uninterrupted flow between self and: aids nl2•
- **quiet**; and: *(↗Quiet disposition)* neon srj5• op a1 podo fd3.de• spong fd4.de [heroin sdj2]
- **world**; feeling content with the: aids nl2• [heroin sdj2]

CONTENTIOUS (See Quarrelsome)

CONTRADICTION:

- **agg.**: *Asar* bg aur bg2* bry bg2 carc mlr1• cop a1 ferr bg2* helo bg2 ign bg2 lyc bg2 nux-v bg2* olnd bg2 petr bg2 *Sep* bg3 stront-c sk4• [ars stj2 nicc-met stj2 nicc-s stj2]
- **disposition** to contradict: *(↗Anarchist; Audacity; Censorious; Contrary; Corrupt; Defiant; Determination; Dictatorial; Disobedience; Fight; Hypocrisy; Insolence; Irritability; Liar; Obstinate; Perseverance; Pertinacity; Positiveness; Presumptuous; Protesting; Quarrelsome; Reverence - lack; Rudeness; Untruthful)* abrot mtf33 acon c1 alum a1* **Anac** k* androc srj1• ant-c br1* ant-t ptk1* *Apis* kr1 arag br1 *Arg-n* vh* arn k* *Ars* hr1* arum-t ptk1 *Aur* aur-m a1 bar-c gl1.fr• bell mtf33 bry ckh1 bufo ckh1 cael jl3 calc-s mrr1 camph k* *Canth* k* caps b7a.de* **Caust** k* *Cham* ptk1* cina br1* crat ptk1 *Cupr* hr1* cypra-eg sde6.de• dendr-pol sk4• *Dulc* b4a.de* ferr k* ferr-ar k2 grat **Hep** k* hyos ictod k* ign k* iod ptk1

Contradiction – disposition to contradict: ...
kali-p fd1.de• kola mtf* kreos ptk1 lac-c mtf33 **Lach** k* led mrr1 **Lyc** k●* mag-c mg1.de *Merc* k* morph oss• nat-c k* nicc nicc-met sk4• nit-ac k* **Nux-v** k●* *Olnd* k* ozone sde2* petr-ra shn4• *Pulx* br1 rad-br ptk1 ruta k* *Sacch* br1 sanic ptk1 sep bg2* *Sol* mtf staph k2* staphytox jl2 sulfonam jl3 sulph gk* *Symph* fd3.de• syph ptk1 **Thuj** ckh1 tritic-vg fd5.de trom a1* tub mtf33 verat mtf33 vip-a jl3

- **afternoon**: *Canth* k*
- **evening**: nicc a1
  - **amel.**: nicc a1
- **children**; in: *Cina* br1*
- **heart** disease; with: crat br1

- **intolerant** of contradiction: *(↗Ailments - contradiction; Ambition - increased; Anger - contradiction; Excitement - contradiction; Haughty; Intolerance; Kill; desire - contradicts; Moaning - contradicted; Suggestions; Weeping - contradiction)* acon k* alco a1 aloe alum alum-sil k2 am-c *Anac* k1* anan vh1 *Ant-c* bro1* arge-pl rwt5• arn bro1 ars k* asaf bro1 asar bro1 aster k* **Aur** k* aur-ar vh1 aur-m-n wbt2• bell bro1 bros-gau mrc1 *Bry* k* cact calc-p calc-s ptk1 cann-i cann-s c1 canth bro1 *Caps* bro1 carbn-s a1 carc cd* cassia-f ckh1 cassia-s ccrh1• *Caust* mtf *Cham* k2* chin bro1* *Cina* bro1* *Cocc* k* *Colch* bro1 coloc bro1* con k* crot-c sk4• cupr sst3• dendr-pol sk4• *Dulc* fd4.de echi k* *Ferr* k* fl-ac ↓ *Flav* jl2 glon br1* grat hell bro1 helo bg2 *Helon* k* hep bro1 hura hyos bg2 ictod j5.de **Ign** k* ignis-alc es2• ina-i mlk9.de irid-met stj2*• kali-p fd1.de• lac-e ↓ lac-h sk4• lach bro1 lact c1 **LYC** k ●* med st1 merc k* mez bro1 morph bro1 mur-ac bro1 *Nat-c* k1* *Nat-m* bro1* nicc nicc-met sk4• nit-ac bg2* nuph a1* *Nux-m* **Nux-v** k ●* olnd k* op pall bro1 petr k* phos bro1 plan *Plat* bro1* puls bro1 ribo rly4• *Sal-fr* sle1• sars bro1 **SEP** k ●* *Sil* k* spong fd4.de *Staph* bro1* stram sulph kr syph a1* tarent thuj k* thyr bro1* til tub mrr1* ulm-c jsj8• *Verat* gl1.fr• [astat stj2 aur-m stj2 aur-s stj2 bar-br stj2 bar-i stj2 bar-met stj2 bism-sn stj2 cinnb stj2 hafn-met stj2 lanth-met stj2 merc-d stj2 merc-i-f stj2 osm-met stj2 plb stj2 plb-m stj2 plb-p stj2 polon-met stj2 rhen-met stj2 tant-met stj2 tax jsj7 thal-met stj2 tung-met stj2]
  - **forenoon**: nat-c a1
  - **evening** | **amel.**: nicc a1
  - **children**; in: carc sst2* cham mtf33 *Chin* mtf33 ferr mtf33 fl-ac ggd ign mtf33 nux-v mtf33 *Tub* mtf33
  - **restrain** himself to keep from violence; has to: *(↗Violent)* aloe sil
  - **rules**; intolerant of inflexible: lac-e hrn2•
- **unable** to contradict (See Yielding)

CONTRADICTORY:

- **actions** are contradictory to intentions: *(↗Antagonism; Will - contradiction; DREAMS - Contradictory)* arizon-l nl2• phos bg2 puls bg2 ruta bg2 sep bg2 thuj bg2*
- **impulses** (See Antagonism)
- **speech**; intentions are contradictory to: *(↗Antagonism; Will - contradiction; Will - two)* acon vh1 [nicc-s stj2]

CONTRARY: *(↗Censorious; Contradiction - disposition; Defiant; Determination; Dictatorial; Disobedience; Fight; Intolerance; Irritability; Obstinate; Perseverance; Pertinacity; Positiveness; Presumptuous; Quarrelsome)* abrot sf1.de* acon aids nl2• **Alum** k* alum-p k2 alum-sil k2 ambr **Anac** k* anan ant-c k* *Ant-t* ptk1* **Arg-n** k* arizon-l nl2• *Arn Ars* bg3* arum-t sf1.de aur aur-ar k2 *Bar-c* k* bell brom j bry ptk1 calad calc k* calc-caust j calc-s k* calc-sil k2 camph canth j5.de caps carb-an carc ↓ *Caust* k* **Cham** sf1.de* chin sf1.de cina sf1.de *Cocc* con croc k* **Dulc** fd* falco-pe nl2• ferr-act j guaj h2* helo-s rwt2• **HEP** bg2* hydr-ac j ictod j ign k* ip jug-r j* *Kali-c* k* kali-p kali-sil k2* kola stb3• kreos sf1.de **Lach** vh* lact laur k* lavand-a ctl1• led k* lyc k* mag-c mag-m k* **Merc** k* *Merc-c* bg2 morph oss• nicc ↓ *Nit-ac* k* *Nux-v* k* olnd j op wbt• petr phos plat mtf33 plb **Podo** fd* *Puls* k* ruta samb sars sep vh* sil k* spong suis-pan rly4• *Sulph* k* **Tarent** k* *Thuj* k* trom tub ↓ ulm-c jsj8• vanil fd5.de [ant-m stj2 cadm-s stj2]

- **afternoon**: *Canth* a1
- **evening**: nicc a1
- **parents**; with: *(↗Behavior - children - home)* carc mtf33 dulc fd4.de tub vk* vanil fd5.de

CONTROLLING:
- **everything** (See Checking - twice)
- **himself** (See Self-control)

CONVERSATION:
- **agg.**: *(↗Anxiety - conversation; Concentration - difficult - conversation; Confusion - conversation - agg.; Dullness - conversation; Excitement - conversation; Irritability - conversation; Narrating - agg.; Quiet disposition; Reserved; Restlessness - conversation; Sensitive - noise; Spoken - aversion; Taciturn; Talking - agg.; GENERALS - Talking - agg.)* acon alum am-c **Ambr** k* am k2 aur aur-m-n wbt2• borx c1 calc cann-s canth carc tpw2* chin cocc k* coff dios ferr *Fl-ac* granit-m es1• graph helon ptk1* **Ign** k* iod k* kali-c kali-s fd4.de ketogl-ac rly4• lach k2 lap-la rsp1 limest-b es1• mag-m mang mez **Nat-m** k* nat-p *Nux-m* *Nux-v* ph-ac k* plac rzf5• plat k* psil ft1 puls *Rhus-t* ruta fd4.de sal-al blc1• sars *Sep* k* **Sil** k1* spig stann bro1* staph ptk1 sulph thuj tritic-vg fd5.de vanil fd5.de [merc-i-f stj2]
- **amel.**: *(↗Talking - amel.)* aeth ptk1* eup-per bro1* irid-met srj5• kali-p fd1.de• kali-s fd4.de lac-d ptk1* lac-h sk4• oci-sa sk4• **Pall** sne sacch-a fd2.de• sal-al blc1• vanil fd5.de
- **aversion** to: allox tpw3 am-c a1 *Am-m* vh1 *Ambr* hr1* *Ars* h2* ars-s-f k2 asim a1 atro a1 bell a1* bit-ar wht1• caj a1 calc k2* *Carb-an* h2* carc tpw2* *Cham* c1 chel k2* chen-a a1 chin ↓ choc srj3• cortiso tpw7 elaps a1 ferr a1* gels a1* gink-b sbd1• granit-m es1• ham a1 hell a1 kali-p fd1.de• kali-s fd4.de kalm a1 murx a1 myric a1 nat-s a1 ox-ac k2* plb a1* *Ptel* hr1* ruta fd4.de spong fd4.de tarent a1 thea a1 tril-c a1 tritic-vg fd5.de vanil fd5.de ziz a1
  - **superficial** conversation; aversion to: chin oss•
- **desire** for: ars a1 chen-a a1 ham ↓ kali-s fd4.de narcot a1 nicotam rly4• ruta fd4.de spong fd4.de vanil fd5.de
  - **sublime**, to hear: ham a1
- **difficult** to carry on: med jl2
- **easy** to start a conversation with others (See Communicative)
- **remember**; cannot (See Memory - weakness - heard; Memory - weakness - said)

CONVULSIONS; after: ars bg2 camph bg2 cic b7.de* verb bg2

COQUETTISH:
- **not** enough: bell vh* lyc vh* puls vh* staph vh* **Sulph** vh*
- **too** much: *Ambr* ↓ bell vh* calc-f ↓ lac-leo hrn2• lach dtn1 lyc vh* nux-v vh* **Phos** ↓ **Plat** ↓ puls vh* sal-fr sle1• sulph vh* **Verat** ↓ [calc-s stj1 tax jsj7]
  - **children**; in: *Ambr* lmj bell lmj calc-f lmj **Lach** lmj **Phos** lmj **Plat** lmj *Puls* lmj *Sulph* lmj **Verat** lmj

CORRUPT, venal: *(↗Contradiction - disposition; Deceitful; Manipulative)* ars gl1.fr• chin gl1.fr• lyc gl1.fr• petr-ra shn4• puls gl1.fr• sulph gl1.fr• [oxyg stj]

CORYZA; from suppressed: lyc bg2

COSMOPOLITAN (See Travelling)

COUGH:
- **after**: cina b7.de* *Rhus-t* bg2
- **before**: asar bg2 cic bg2 cina b7.de
- **during**: asar b7.de* kali-c bg2 nat-m bg2

COUNTING continually: *(↗Numbers)* *Hyos* hr1* moni rfm1• phys k* sil bg2* sulph sne verat vh*

COUNTRYSIDE:
- **desire** for: *(↗Company - aversion - country; Nature - loves; Wilderness - desires)* androc srj1• calc ckh1 choc srj3• elaps a1 falco-pe nl2• haliae-lc srj5• hydrog srj2• limen-b-c mlk9.de merc ckh1 ruta fd4.de sep ckh1 tritic-vg fd5.de [bell-p-sp dcm1]
  - **go** into the: limen-b-c hrn2•
  - **mountains**: falco-pe nl2• haliae-lc srj5•

COURAGEOUS: *(↗Adventurous; Audacity; Deeds - great; Defiant; Determination; Fearless; High-spirited; Hopeful; Perseverance; Pertinacity; Positiveness; Precocity; Rash)* acon k* agar k* agath-a nl2• alco a1 alum k* ant-t k* *Bell* sne berb *Bov* b2.de* *Calad* b2.de* calc-s tl1 carc mrr1 corian-s knl6• dendr-pol sk4• dros *Dulc* fd4.de falco-pe nl2• ferr-p a1 fic-m gya1 galla-q-r nl2• gins guaj bg2 helo-s rwt2• *Ign* k* ignis-alc es2• lach bg2 loxo-recl knl4• m-arct b2.de* merc k* mez k* nat-c k* *Op* k* pert-vc vk9 phos k* plut-n srj7• *Puls* b2.de* *Rhus-g* tmo3• sal-fr sle1•

Courageous: ...
spong fd4.de squil k* staph ↓ sulph k* tab tarax k* ter st1 tere-la rly4• tritic-vg fd5.de *Tub* ptk1* valer verat k* [heroin sdj2 plat stj2]
- **alternating** with:
  - **discouragement**: merc gl1.fr• op gl1.fr• staph gl1.fr•
  - **fear**: *Alum* j5.de* *Spong* fd4.de

COVERING the head agg.: led bg2 stront-c b4.de*

COVETOUS (See Avarice)

COWARDICE: *(↗Character; Confidence - want; Fear - people; Insecurity; Responsibility - aversion; Timidity)* *Acon* k* agar k* agn k* alco a1 alum alum-sil k2* **Am-c** c1* ambr bg* anac k* ang k* ant-t bg2* arg-n bg2* arizon-l nl2• ars br1 aur k* aur-m-n wbt2* aur-s k2* **Bar-c** k* bar-i k2 bar-m bar-s k2* bell k* *Bry* k* calc k* calc-s k* calc-sil k2* camph canth k* carb-an k* carb-v k* caust k* cham bg2* *Chin* k* chin-b hr1* cocc coloc con k* cupr k* dig dioxi rbp6 dros k* dys ckh1 fic-m gya1 fl-ac gk gard-j vlr2• **Gels** k* germ-met stj2*• graph k* hep gl1.fr• hydr-ac bg2 ign k* iod k* ip k* kali-c k* kali-n k* kali-p kali-sil k2* kreos bg* lach bg* laur led **Lyc** k* marb-w es1• merc mur-ac k* (non:nat-act) nat-m k* nit-ac k* *Nux-m* bg2* nux-v bg2* ol-an bg* olnd bg2 **Op** k* petr ↓ ph-ac phos k* plat k* plb k* positr nl2• *Puls* k* ran-b b7.de* *Rhus-g* tmo3• rhus-t bg2 ruta sabin k* sec sep k* *Sil* k* spig stann k* staph vh* *Stram* bg2* sul-ac k* sul-i k2* sulph k* tab k* ther bg2 thuj k* *Verat* k* verb viol-t k* visc sp1 zinc j
- **alternating** with | **irritability** (See Irritability - alternating - cowardice)
- **anger**; with sudden fit of: bar-c kr1
- **opinion**; without courage to express own: *(↗Confidence - want)* **Bar-c** vh graph mtf33* ign gl1.fr• petr gl1.fr• **Staph** vh
- **sadness**, with: *Sulph* hr1*

CRAFTY (See Deceitful)

CRAWLING:
- **bed**, around in: *Stram* a1*
- **children**; in: camph ↓ med mtf33 sil ↓
  - **howls** and cries; crawls into corners: *(↗Hiding - himself - corner; Playing - aversion - children - sit; Sadness - sits)* camph a1*
  - **nervously**: sil ptk1*
- **floor**; on: absin ptk1 *Acet-ac* a1 bell bg2* cann-i a1 lach k*
- **rolling** on the floor (See Rolling - floor)

CRAZY (See Delusions - insane; Insanity)

CREATIVE (See Activity - desires - creative; Ideas - abundant; Plans - making; Thoughts - thoughtful)

CREATIVITY: | **lost**: dioxi rbp6 lac-h sze9• nauf-helv-li elm2•

CREDULOUS: *(↗Impressionable; Naive)* arg-n vh bar-c dmk1* *Bell* mtf33* *Puls* gl1.fr• staph gl1.fr•

CRETINISM: *(↗Idiocy; GENERALS - Myxedema)* absin bro1 aeth bro1* anac bro1* arn bro1 bac bro1 *Bar-c* bro1* bar-m bro1 bufo bro1* calc-p bg2* carc mtf33 hell bro1 ign bro1 iod bro1 *Lap-a* kr1* lol bro1 nat-c bro1 oxyt bro1 ph-ac bro1 phos mtf33 plb bro1* sil mtf33 sulph bro1* thuj ptk1* *Thyr* br1* tub mtf33 zinc mtf33
- **agile**: calc-p ptk1

CRITICAL (See Censorious)

CROAKING: bell ↓ cina k* cupr k* cupr-act ↓
- **frogs**, as of: cupr a1 cupr-act a1
- **sleep**, in: bell

CROSS (See Contradiction; Contradiction - disposition; Irritability)

CROSSED; being (See Contradiction - intolerant)

CRUELTY: *(↗Brutality; Hardhearted; Indifference - suffering - others; Malicious; Misanthropy; Mischievous; Mocking - ridicule; Moral; Sensitive - want; Unfeeling; Wicked)* abrot k* absin k* alco a1 **ANAC** b4a.de* arizon-l nl2* *Ars* mtf33* *Aur* vh* bell bro1 bry bro1 canth bro1 carc mlr1* chin bg2 chir-fl gya2 chlam-tr ↓ choc srj3• croc k* crot-c sk4• cur cycl b7.de dendr-pol sk4• dream-p sdj1• falco-pe nl2• haliae-lc srj5• *Hell* b7.de **Hep** gl1.fr• *Hyos* b7.de* ignis-alc ↓ *Kali-i* k2* kali-p bg2* kola stb3• *Lach* k2*

Cruelty: ...
Laur b7.de loxo-recl knl4• lyss kr1 marb-w es1• med ptk1* nicc gl1.fr• *Nit-ac* bro1* *Nux-v* k ●* op k* ph-ac b4a.de *Plat* k* plut-n srj7• positr nl2• sabad b7.de* sec b7.de sel gl1.fr• squil j staph bro1* *Stram* b7.de* sulph ckh1 tarent bro1 verat bro1* [heroin sdj2 nicc-met stj2 nicc-s stj2]
- **animals**; to: abrot mtf33 ars mtf33 **Med** mrr1* nit-ac mtf33
- **cats**; toward: ignis-alc es2• [heroin sdj2]
- **family**; to her: chlam-tr bcx2• kali-p k2
- **like** to do something cruel; would: *(↗Cut)* abrot rb2
- **loves** to make people and animals suffer: *Anac* mrr1 **Ars** vh* *Bell* vh* med mrr1
- **seeing** or hearing cruelty; cannot bear: *(↗Horrible)* carc mlr1• mag-m mtf33 **Spong** fd*
  - **children**: carc mlr1•
  - **cinema**; at: carc mlr1•
  - **television**; on: carc sst2•
    - **murder**: carc sst2•
    - **surgery**: carc sst2•

CRYING (See Shrieking; Weeping)

CUDDLE: | **desire** to be cuddled: *(↗Held - desire; Magnetized - desire)* sacch sst1•

CULPABILITY; feelings of (See Anxiety - conscience; Mood - repulsive; Reproaching oneself)

CUNNING: agar bg2 anac bg2 atra-r mtf bell bg2* bufo bg2 cann-i a1 cupr bg2 hyos bg2 lach bg2* mosch k2 nux-v bg2 op bg2* tarent k2* thuj mtf verat bg2*

CURIOUS: *(↗Gossiping; Indiscretion; Learning - desire; Loquacity; Meddlesome; Revealing; Sensitive - want; Spying; Touching - impelled - everything)* acon mtf agar k* ambr k13* *Aran-ix* mtf arg-s mtf aur ptk1* aur-s wbt2• berb mtf bung-fa mtf calc ↓ calc-br mtf cann-i mtf caps mtf carb-v gl* carc mtf* choc srj3* conv mtf dulc fd4.de hyos mtf33* kali-s fd4.de lac-f wza1• lach k* laur ptk1 lyc mtf* med mtf olib-sac wmh1 phos mrr1* positr nl2• puls kl* sep gl1.fr• sulph ptk1* tritic-vg fd5.de verat mrr1* [alum-p stj2 arg-p stj2 cupr-p stj2 hydrog stj2 lith-p stj2 plb-p stj2]
- **children**: hyos mtf33
- **jumping** from one subject to another: *Ambr* k13
- **supernatural** or spiritual matters, about: calc vh
- **training** of the physician; wants to know the: *(↗Impetuous; Indiscretion; Questions; Spying; Touching; Touching - impelled - everything)* phos fd* sulph fd*

CURL UP; desire to: [buteo-j sej6]

CURSING: *(↗Abusive; Blasphemy; Blasphemy - cursing; Despair - rage - cursing; Insolence; Malicious; Rage; Rudeness; Slander)* adam srj5• agath-a nl2• alco a1 aloe am-c **Anac** k* arizon-l nl2• arn kr1 *Ars* k* aur-m-n wbt2• bamb-a ↓ *Bell* bg2* borx k* bov k* bufo gk calc vh* *Camph* hr1 cann-i canth caust vh* cere-s st chin-b kr1 cic ↓ coca-c sk4• cor-r k* cub a1 cupr-s a1 dendr-pol sk4• dream-p ↓ dulc ↓ falco-pe nl2• fum ↓ gal-ac k* hydr bg2* *Hyos* k* ign ↓ ip k* kali-p fd1.de• *Lac-c* k* lac-e ↓ lac-h htj1• lac-loxod-a ↓ *Lil-t* k* *Lyc* k* lyss maias-l ↓ med ↓ melal-alt gya4 merc mtf33 moni rfm1• musca-d szs1 nat-c gl1.fr• *Nat-m* k1* neon srj5• **Nit-ac** k* *Nux-v* k* oena op k* *Opun-s* a1 opun-v ↓ ozone ↓ pall k* pegan-ha ↓ petr k* petr-ra shn4• phos bg2* plb k* puls rhus-t ↓ sanguis-s hrn2• sanic c1* skat br1 spig gl1.fr• spong fd4.de staph gl1.fr• stram k* suprar rly4• tarent bg2* thiam rly4• *Tub* k* valer ↓ vanil fd5.de *Verat* k* [ant-met stj2 ferr stj2 ferr-f stj2 ferr-lac stj2 ferr-n stj2 ferr-sil stj2 pop dhh1]
- **afternoon**: aloe a1 op a1 opun-s a1 (non:opun-v a1)
- **evening**: lil-t a1 nit-ac ↓ opun-s a1 valer a1
  - **home**; when: nit-ac a1 opun-s a1
- **night**: *Verat* h1*
  - **stupid** feeling; and complaints of: verat
- **amel.**: cor-r st
- **children**; in: nit-ac mtf33
- **contradiction**; from: falco-pe nl2• hydr a1 opun-s a1
- **convulsions**, during: ars k* bell he
- **desire** to curse: adam srj5• anac tl1 bamb-a stb2.de• cic sne dream-p sdj1• fum rly1*• ign sne lac-e hrn2• lac-loxod-a hrn2• maias-l hrn2• nat-m tl1 pegan-ha tpi1•
- **discouragement**; with: nit-ac j5.de

Cursing: ...
- **headache**, during: nat-m vh* tarent c1 verat h1
- **involuntary**: opun-s a1
- **mother** and throws food or medicine across room; curses his: *Hydr* hr1*
- **pains**, at: cor-r hr1*
- **rage**:
  - **after**: *Arn* hr1*
  - **in**: anac j5.de* falco-pe nl2• melal-alt gya4 *Nit-ac* j5.de* spong fd4.de verat j5.de*
- **restrain** himself in order not to curse; has to: anac vh dulc fd4.de med vh sanic vh tub vh
- **sleep**, during: rhus-t sst•
- **trifles**; about: ozone sde2•

CUT, mutilate or slit; desire to: *(↗Cruelty - like; Delusions - body - cut; Delusions - body - cut - two; Delusions - divided - two - cut; Impulse - stab - others; Violent)*
- **knife**; with a sharp: crot-c sk4•
- **oneself** (See Mutilating)
- **others**: *(↗Delusions - body - cut; Delusions - body - cut - two; Delusions - divided - two - cut; Impulse - stab - others; Violent)* lyss k* verat k2
- **things**: tarent br1 *Verat* br1*

CYNICAL: *(↗Censorious; Contemptuous; Hatred; Hatred - women; Haughty; Jesting - malicious; Laughing - contemptuous; Laughing - sardonic; Misanthropy; Mocking - sarcasm; Morose; Smiling - sardonic; Suspicious)* galla-q-r nl2• lyc ptk1* nit-ac ptk1* sacch-a fd2.de• sulph mrr1 tarent ptk1* [am-br stj2 am-c stj1 am-caust stj2 am-m stj1 am-p stj1 merc stj2]

CYNOPHOBIA (See Fear - dogs)

DANCING: *(↗Cheerful - dancing; Dancing - agg. - child; Delirium - dancing; Insanity - dancing; DREAMS - Dancing; GENERALS - Dancing)* acon k* aether a1 agar k* agath-a nl2• aids nl2• androc ↓ apis k* atra-r bnm3• *Bell* k* bros-gau mrc1 camph ↓ cann-i k* cann-s ↓ **Carc** k* caust jsa chir-fl gya2 chlol k* *Cic* k* *Cocc* k* con *Croc* k* crot-c sk4• crot-t dendr-pol sk4• fl-ac ↓ grat ham fd3.de• *Hyos* k* ign bg2* irid-met srj5• kali-p ↓ kali-s fd4.de *Kola* stb3• lach fb lat-h ↓ medus mgm• merc k* nat-m k* nat-sil fd3.de• nitro-o a1 nux-m pd olib-sac wmh1 *Orig* mrr1 ozone sde2• *Ph-ac* k* pip-m a1 plat k* positr nl2• rob k* ruta fd4.de sacch-a fd2.de• sal-fr sle1• santin a1 sec ↓ *Sep* bg2* sil bg2* spong fd4.de stann ↓ stict bro1* *Stram* k* sulph ↓ tab **Tarent** k* tela ↓ vanil fd5.de verat gk* [tax jsj7]
- **evening**: nat-m a1
- **ability** for: sulph mtf33
- **agg.**: *(↗GENERALS - Dancing - agg.)*
  - **child** which is carried by someone who is dancing; in a: *(↗Dancing)* *Borx* a1*
- **alternating** with:
  - **cheerfulness**: *Agath-a* nl2• bell bg2*
  - **moaning**: bell h1*
  - **sighing**: bell a1
  - **weeping**: bell j5.de
- **amel.**: *(↗GENERALS - Dancing - amel.)* agath-a nl2• cann-s sf1.de carc fd* caust sf1.de* *Ign* sf1.de* kali-p fd1.de• nat-m sf1.de* nat-sil fd3.de• positr nl2• sal-fr sle1• **Sep** j5.de* sil sf1.de* stann sf1.de* *Tarent* mrr1
- **children**: carc pc* fl-ac pc hyos mtf33 merc mtf33 nat-m mtf33 sep pc spong fd4.de vanil fd5.de
- **desire** to dance; excessive (See Dancing)
- **grotesque**: *(↗Delirium)* agar *Cic* k*
- **impulse** to dance (See Dancing)
- **inability** for: nat-m mtf33 nux-v mtf33
- **jumping**; and: bell a1* cic h1* croc hr1* grat a1 rob a1 sec hr1* stict hl* **Stram** a1 tarent a1* tela hs1*
- **love** to: carc mlr1•
- **naked** in moonlight: irid-met srj5•
- **rhythm**; with marked sense of: carc fb* *Kola* stb3• sep mtf33 [tax jsj7]
- **unconscious**: ph-ac
- **wild**: *(↗Delirium; Wildness)* androc srj1• *Bell* camph k* cann-i a1 carc mlr1• lat-h thj1 tarent k* verat mtf33 [tax jsj7]

DANGER:

- **awareness** of; heightened: olib-sac wmh1
- **as** if in (See Delusions - danger)
- **desire** for: *(↗Runs - dangerous)* lac-lup hrn2•
- **impression** of danger (See Delusions - danger)
- **lack** of reaction to danger: ambr bg2 ars bg2 camph bg2 falco-pe nl2• lyc bg2 positr nl2•
- **no** sense of danger; has: *(↗Audacity; Protected; Tranquillity)* *Agar* mtf falco-pe nl2• hep glh med mtf merc glh **Op** wbt* plat glh stram mtf tub mtf [heroin sdj2]
  - **health**; about the state of his (See Well - says - sick)
- **surrounded** by | **calm**; yet: lac-del hrn2•

DARING (See Courageous)

DARKNESS:

- **agg.**: *(↗Anxiety - dark; Anxiety - evening - twilight; Concentration - difficult - attempting - dark; Delirium - dark; Delusions - images - dark; Delusions - people - behind - walking - dark; Delusions - specters - twilight; Fear - dark; of; Fear - night; Fear - walking - of - dark; Light - desire; Longing - sunshine; Sadness - darkness; Sensitive - light; Weeping - dark; DREAMS - Darkness; EYE - Photomania; GENERALS - Darkness - agg.; GENERALS - Faintness - dark)* acon *Aeth* am-m bg1* ars k* bapt berb *Calc* k* camph cann-s bg *Carb-an* k* *Carb-v* k* *Caust* cupr galeoc-c-h gms1• graph hell bg* *Lyc* nat-m *Phos* k* plat *Puls* k* rhus-t sanic sec bg* sil vh* **Stram** k* stront-c bg1* *Valer* zinc sf1.de
- **aversion** to: *(↗Somber - aversion)* carb-v br1 ignis-alc es2• sanic bg2*
- **desire** for: achy jl3 aeth mtf33 anan a1 arge-pl rwt5• choc srj3• coca br1 irid-met srj5• sanguis-s hrn2• tung-met bdx1•
- **lie** down in the dark and not be talked to, desire to: *Aur* vh* *Aur-m* vh* bry vh tarent k*

DAYDREAMING (See Absentminded - dreamy)

DAZED (See Confusion; Stupefaction)

DEAFNESS; pretended: *(↗Feigning - sick)* verat k*

DEATH:

- **agony** before death: *(↗Ailments - death)* **Acon** bg ant-t ptk1 *Ars* ptk1 aur sne carb-v ptk1 carc mlr1• con sne gels bg lach sne **Lat-m** st oscilloc jl2 plat bg psor sne spig sne syph sne tarent-c ptk1
- **apparent** (See GENERALS - Death)
- **contempt** of: *Op* hr1*
- **conviction** of: *(↗Delusions - die - time)* alum-p k2 ars lp ars-h kr1 bapt kr1* bell kr1 *Canth* kr1 *Coff* kr1 *Cupr-act* kr1 hydr br1* kali-ar k2 nit-ac sne *Phyt* kr1 positr nl2• *Psor* kr1 *Thuj* kr1
  - **after** fever, epistaxis amel.: *Psor* kr1
- **desires**: *(↗Cheerful - death; Desires - full - more; Loathing - life; Pessimist; Suicidal; Weary)* absin ↓ acon bg* adam srj5• agath-a nl2• agn k* agri mtf11 alum a1* alum-sil k2 ambr bg2* anh mg1.de ant-c k2 apis aran k* ars k2 ars-met ars-s-f k2 **Aur** k* aur-ar k2 **Aur-m** k2* *Aur-m-n* wbt2• aur-s *Bell* k* berb bg2* calc k2 caps carb-v carc mlr1• *Caust* bg2* chel *Chin* clem k* cortico mg1.de* cypra-eg sde6.de• der dulc fd4.de euph-c sf1.de *Gad* a1* germ-met srj5• *Glon* kr1 ham fd3.de• hep bg2* hura hydr k* hydrog ↓ ignis-alc ↓ kali-bi kali-br kali-chl ↓ *Kreos* bg2* **Lac-c** k* lac-d k2* lac-h sk4*• *Lach* k* led lil-t lyc *Merc* k* merc-aur sf1.de mez moni rfm1• nat-c k* *Nat-m* nat-s *Nit-ac* k1* nux-v k* op orig hl1 ozone sde2• pegan-ha tpi1• phos k* phyt plat k* plb k* plut-n srj7• positr nl2• psor puls gl1.fr• ran-b k2* rat sf1.de rhus-g tmo3• *Rhus-t* *Rob* kr1 ruta ↓ sec bg2* *Sep* k* *Sil* k* spig ↓ spong k* *Staph* k* stram j5.de* sul-ac **Sulph** k* thuj k* vanil fd5.de verat-v k2* vip zinc gl1.fr• [*Spect* dfg1]
  - **morning** | **waking** on: germ-met srj5• hydrog srj2• nat-c phyt
  - **forenoon**: apis
  - **afternoon**: ruta
  - **evening**: **Aur** ruta
  - **alternating** with:
    - **laughing** (See Laughing - alternating - death)
    - **rage** (See Rage - alternating - death - desire)
  - **anguish**, from: bell gl1.fr•
  - **anxiety**, from: bell h1* caust h2*
  - **chill**, during: kali-chl k* spig
  - **convalescence**, during: *(↗Despair - recovery - convalescence)* absin *Aur* lac-c sep

Death – desires: ...

  - **despair**, from: *Kreos* sf1.de ozone sde2•
  - **dishonored**; instead of being: ignis-alc es2•
  - **headache**; from: ozone sde2•
  - **meditates** on easiest way of self-destruction (See Suicidal - thoughts - meditates)
  - **menses**, during: *(↗Menses - during)* berb k*
  - **pains**, during (See Suicidal - pains)
  - **rage**, during intervals from: bell kr1
  - **walking** in open air, while: bell k*
- **dying**, sensation as if: *(↗Delusions - dying - he)* acon kr1 ant-t vh lyss kr1 ruta fd4.de *Sep* kr1 *Sil* kr1 *Spong* fd4.de *Ther* kr1 vesp kr1
- **presentiment** of: *(↗Ailments - anticipation; Cautious; Clairvoyance; Delusions - die - about; Fear - death; Fear - happen; Prophesying)* **Acon** k* *Agn* k* aloe k1 alum alum-p k2* anac *Anthraci* kr1 **Apis** k* *Arg-n* arn k* *Ars* k* ars-h a1* bapt k* bar-m **Bell** k* *Bry* k* *Cact* hr1* *Calc* k* *Camph* hr1 cann-i canth k* carb-v k2 *Caust* hr1 *Cench* *Chel* k* cimic k* *Coff* hr1 *Cupr* k* dendr-pol sk4• dig a1 ferr sne ferr-br c1 gels c1 *Graph* k* hell a1 *Hep* k* hydr ptk1 kali-ar kali-br a1 kali-c k* kali-n k* lac-d *Lach* k* lap-la sde8.de• lob j5.de *Lyc* k* lyss hr1* *Med* k* **Merc** k* mosch k* nat-m k* *Nit-ac* k* nux-m c1* *Nux-v* k* ox-ac hr1 petr k* *Phos* k* *Phyt* hr1 *Plat* k* podo positr nl2• *Psor* hr1* puls k* *Raph* j5.de* rhus-t k* sep k* staph k* stram k* sul-ac a1 sulph bg2* tab j5.de* thea st *Thuj* hr1 ulm-c jsj8• verat k* vip zinc k* zinc-p k2* [bell-p-sp dcm1 *Spect* dfg1]
  - **alternating** with:
    - **anguish**: raph hr1*
    - **rage** (See Rage - alternating - death - presentiment)
  - **calmly** thinks of death: zinc k* [bell-p-sp dcm1]
  - **predicts** the time: *(↗Delusions - dying; Fear - death - predicts; Prophesying - predicts)* **ACON** k1* *Aloe* kr1 alum st1 *Arg-n* k* cench k2 hell k2* *Lac-d* hr1* thea st
  - **respiration**; with asthmatic: *Ars* bro1 psor bro1*
  - **settling** his affairs; must be: petr hr1*
  - **soon** and that she cannot be helped; believes that she will die: *Agn* k*
  - **sudden** death, of a: *Cench* st1
  - **vomiting**, with: med c1
- **sensation** of: *(↗Delusions - dying - he; Shrieking - dying)* acon hr1* aesc aether a1 *Agn* k* **Am-c** kr anh sp1 apis bg2 *Ars* k* asaf a1 camph cann-i k* cench chinin-s sne cic k* cimic hr1 cypra-eg sde6.de• ferr a1 gels c1 *Graph* k* hydrog srj2• kali-bi k* kali-br k* kali-n **Lat-m** st1* lyss hr1 morph a1 nux-v op *Phos* k* *Plat* k* *Sep* hr1 sil k* *Ther* hr1 v-a-b jl3* verat vesp hr1 *Zinc* gl1.fr•
  - **evening**: aether a1
  - **chill**, during: cann-i k*
  - **lying**, while: cench k2
  - **spasm**, during: nux-v
- **talks** of: mosch k2 spong fd4.de vanil fd5.de
- **thoughts** of: *(↗Suicidal - thoughts)* **Acon** k* *Agar* vh1 agath-a nl2• agn k* aloe bg2* alum ↓ am-c k* *Apis* k* aq-mar rbp6 *Arg-n* vh* arn st1 *Ars* k* ars-h hr1* *Aur* sf1.de* aur-br vh1 *Aur-m* vh* aur-m-n wbt2• aur-s wbt2• camph cann-i k* carb-an k* cartl-s rly4• caust k* *Cham* hr1* chel clem a1 *Coff* b7a.de* *Con* k* cortico sp1* cortiso sp1* *Crot-c* k* *Crot-h* k* cupr k* cypra-eg ↓ dendr-pol sk4• *Dig* bg2* *Ferr* k* ferr-ar galla-q-r nl2• **Graph** k* haliae-lc srj5• hist sp1 hura hydrog srj2• kali-ar kali-c kali-p fd1.de• lac-d k2 lac-h sk4• *Lach* hr1* lat-m sp1* *Lob* bg2* loxo-recl knl4• lyc ↓ merc ↓ mez ↓ *Nat-m* sne nux-v k* olib-sac wmh1 op k* oxal-a rly4• ozone sde2• *Phos* b4a.de* plat bg2* positr nl2• *Psor* k* *Puls* hr1* rauw sp1 rhus-t j5.de rob k* ruta fd4.de sal-fr sle1• *Sep* b4a.de spong j5.de stram k* symph fd3.de• tarent k* tax-br ↓ thuj b4a.de* tritic-vg fd5.de tung-met bdx1• ulm-c jsj8• vanil fd5.de verat k* verat-v sf1.de vinc j5.de* *Zinc* k* [tax jsj7]
  - **morning**: con k* lyc gl1.fr•
  - **afternoon**: tarent k* zinc h2*
  - **evening**: *Zinc* sf1.de
  - **alone**, when: *(↗Company - desire)* *Crot-c* k*
  - **amel.**: zinc mrr1

- **thoughts** of: ...
  - **calmly** thinks of death (See presentiment - calmly)
  - **everything** is dead: mez ptk1
  - **father**; the death of his: positr nl2• tritic-vg fd5.de
  - **fear**, without: apis bg2* *Coff* bg2* cypra-eg sde6.de• merc bg2 tax-br oss1• verat-v bg2*
  - **joy**; give him (See Cheerful - death)
  - **waking**, on: alum b4a.de lyc j5.de

DEBAUCHERY (See Libertinism)

DEBILITY (See Wearisome)

DECEITFUL (= sly): *(↗Adulterous; Charlatan; Corrupt; Delusions - lie; Dishonest; Hypocrisy; Intriguer; Liar; Manipulative; Perfidious; Slander; Unreliable; Untruthful)* agar bg2* anac bg2 androc srj1• arg-met ptk1* arg-n k* *Ars* vh* *Aur-m-n* ↓ aur-s j* *Bell* bg2* bufo k* calc vh* chin mtf chlol k* chlor a1 coca corv-cor bdg• crot-c sk4• cupr bg2* dendr-pol sk4• dig h2 dros k* fl-ac st1 hep mtf hyos bg2* kola stb3• lac-leo sk4• **Lach** bg2* lyc vh* marb-w es1• *Med* mtf merc bg3* morph mtf mosch mtf nat-c a1 *Nat-m* gl1.fr• nit-ac mtf **Nux-v** bg2* *Op* bg2* petr-ra shn4• plat mtf33* plb bg3* puls mtf33* *Sacch-a* fd2.de• sep gl1.fr• sil vh* sulph mtf33* *Tarent* c1* thuj k2* verat bg2* [ant-c stj2]

- **blame**; avoids: dendr-pol sk4•
- **fraudulent**: bell gl1.fr• calc gl1.fr• lach pc lyc pc merc gl1.fr• puls pc sil pc
- **grief** and mortification; causes: *Aur-m-n* wbl2•
- **perjured**: hep gl1.fr• nat-m gl1.fr• nit-ac gl1.fr•

DECEPTION: carc ↓ corian-s knl6• loxo-recl knl4•

- **grief**; causing: carc mlr1•
- **humiliation**; causing: carc mlr1•

DECISIVE: *(↗Positiveness; Practical; Will - strong)* adam srj5• phasco-ci rbp2 polys sk4• positr nl2• sal-fr sle1• vanil fd5.de [tax jsj7]

- **practical** (See Practical)

DECOMPOSITION of shape: *(↗Schizophrenia - paranoid)* anh mg1.de* crot-h ↓ falco-pe ↓ mur-ac ptk1 phos ptk1 pyrog ptk1 sec ptk1

- **rapidly**: crot-h ptk1
- **space**, of: anh mg1.de* falco-pe nl2•

DEEDS:

- **good** deeds; desire to perform: coff-t a1 ignis-alc es2•
- **great** deeds; sensation as if he could do: *(↗Courageous; Delusions - better; Delusions - creative; Delusions - great; Delusions - superhuman; Delusions - superiority; Fancies - exaltation; Haughty; Plans - making - gigantic; Theorizing)* *Cocain* br1* *Hell* k* ignis-alc es2•
- **useful**; desire to be (See Useful)

DEFENSE mechanisms; weak (See Helplessness)

DEFENSELESS (See Helplessness)

DEFENSIVE (See Offended)

DEFIANT: *(↗Audacity; Contradiction - disposition; Contrary; Courageous; Disobedience; Fight; Haughty; Impertinence; Inciting; Insolence; Obstinate; Pertinacity; Positiveness; Presumptuous; Quarrelsome)* acon agath-a nl2• alum sf1.de am-c sf1.de anac k* androc srj1• arizon-l nl2• *Arn* k* *Bar-c* mtf bell sf1.de* bufo gk* canth **Caust** k* chir-fl gya2 *Cina* bg2* **Dulc** fd* guaj *Ign* bg2* irid-met srj5• kreos sf1.de *Lyc* k* merc mtf33 morph oss• nux-v k* ph-ac sf1.de puls mtf ruta fd4.de* sacch sst1• sal-fr sle1• sec sf1.de sep st1* sil sf1.de* spong sulph sf1.de tritic-vg fd5.de tub mtf [mag-br stj1 tax jsj7]

DEFORMATION of all objects (See VISION - Distorted)

DEJA VU: *(↗Clairvoyance; Delusions - experienced - before)* anh mtf crot-c mtf positr nl2• staph mtf sulph gk5

DEJECTION (See Sadness)

DELICATE (See Elegance; Sensitive; GENERALS - Delicate)

DELIRIUM: *(↗Coma; Concentration - difficult - crazy; Confusion; Dancing - grotesque; Dancing - wild; Delusions - home - at; Delusions - home - away; Fear - approaching - others - delirium; Gestures; Insanity; Irritability - sends - doctor; Recognizing - not - house; Recognizing - not - streets; Refusing - medicine - delirium; Runs; Speech - delirious; Unreal - everything)* absin k* acet-ac k* *Acon* k* *Act-sp* k* aegle-f bnj1 aesc *Aeth* k* aether a1 **Agar** k* agar-cps a1 agar-pa a1 agar-ph a1 agar-pr ↓ *Agarin* ↓ agath-a ↓ agn hr1* ail k* alco a1 alum kr1 alumn hr1 am-c k* ambr ↓ amyg a1* anac k* anag hr1* anan k* androc bnm2• anh c1* ant-c k* ant-s-aur ↓ ant-t k* anthraci k* apis k* arg-met k* arg-mur ↓ arg-n arn k* **Ars** k* ars-i ↓ ars-s-f k2 art-v hr1 **Arum-t** k* astac a1* atra-r bnm3• atro a1* atro-s ↓ *Aur* k* aur-ar ↓ aur-m hr1* *Bapt* k* bar-c k* **Bell** k* ben-n ↓ bism k* bol-lu a1 bomb-pr a1* borx br1 bov ↓ brom sf1.de **Bry** k* bufo cact k* calad k* *Calc* k* *Calc-ar* ↓ calc-caust j calc-p ↓ calc-sil ↓ calen hr1* *Camph* k* **Cann-i** k* cann-s k* cann-xyz ptk1 *Canth* k* caps k* carb-ac k* carb-an ↓ carb-v k* *Carbn-s* *Carl* a1 caul hr1* *Caust* ↓ *Cham* k* **Chel** k* chin k* chinin-ar chinin-s k* chlf hr1* chlol k* *Chlor* hr1 chloram jl3 chr-ac hr1* *Cic* k* cic-m a1 cimic k* *Cina* k* clem k* *Cocc* b7a.de* cod ↓ coff k* *Colch* k* coli ↓ coll ↓ coloc k* *Con* k* convo-s sp1* cop k* cor-r cori-r k* croc b2.de* **Crot-c** k* *Crot-h* k* crot-t ↓ *Cupr* k* *Cupr-act* j5.de* cupr-ar a1* cur a1 cyt-l mg1.de dat-f c1* dat-m a1* *Dig* k* (non:diph) dor k* dub a1* dubo-m a1 *Dulc* k* euph bg2 euph-l br1 fagu a1 ferr-p bg2 gal-ac c1* *Gels* k* gins ↓ glon k* granit-m ↓ graph guaj ↓ guar a1 ham hr1* hell k* helo-s bnm14• hep k* hipp k* hippoz hr1* hydr hr1* hydr-ac ↓ hydrog ↓ **Hyos** k* hyosin a1* *Hyosin-hbr* ↓ hyper k* ign k* indg ↓ iod k* iodof c1* *Ip* iris kr1 iris-fl c1* iris-foe a1 ix bnm8• jab a1 jatr-c juni-v a1 kali-ar kali-bi hr1* kali-br k* kali-c k* *Kali-chl* hr1 kali-cy ↓ *Kali-i* hr1* *Kali-m* kr1 kali-n k* kali-p kalm hr1* kou br1 kreos ↓ lac-c hr1* lac-del ↓ lac-lup ↓ lacer a1* **Lach** k* lachn k* lact k* lact-v ↓ lat-h bnm5• lat-k a1 lat-m bnm6• *Laur* hr1 led ↓ lept hr1* lil-t k* lob lob-p ↓ lol a1 loxo-lae bnm12• loxo-recl bnm10• lup a1 **Lyc** k* lyss k* mag-c ↓ malar ↓ manc sf1.de mand kr1* *Meli* k* meny k* *Merc* k* merc-c b4a.de* merc-cy merc-i-r hr1* merc-meth ↓ merc-n a1* merc-ns a1 merc-sul a1 merl k* methyl ↓ mez k* *Mill* hr1* morph a1 mosch b7a.de* mur-ac k* mygal k* naja nat-c ↓ nat-m k* nat-s hr1* nat-sal ↓ nicot a1 **Nit-ac** k* nit-s-d a1* nitro-o a1 *Nux-m* k* *Nux-v* k* *Oena* k* **Op** k* oper br1 ox-ac k* paeon a1 par k* passi ↓ past a1 paull a1 *Petr* k* ph-ac k* *Phos* k* phys ↓ phyt k* pilo ↓ plat k* *Plb* k* podo k* psor k* *Puls* k* pyre-p c1* pyrog k2* raja-s ↓ ran-b k* ran-s k* rheum k* rhod k* **Rhus-t** k* ruta ↓ sabad k* sabin k* sal-ac k* samb k* sang hr1* santin a1 sapin a1 sarr **Sec** k* sel bg2 *Sep* ↓ sil sin-n hr1* sol-mm ↓ sol-ni spig bg2 spig-m ↓ spong b2.de* squil ↓ stigm c1* **Stram** k* stry k* sul-ac k* sul-h a1* sul-i ↓ sulfa jl3 *Sulph* k* syph hr1* tab k* tang a1 tarax k* tarent k* tarent-c sf1.de tax k* *Ter* thal-xyz srj8• thea thuj ↓ thyr ↓ til ↓ trach ↓ trach-v ↓ trinit br1 tub hr1* valer k* vanil fd5.de vario hr1* **Verat** k* **Verat-v** k* verin a1 vesp k* vip k* vip-a jl3 xan hr1* zea-i c1 zinc k* zinc-act sf1.de zinc-p k2* zinc-s a1 [ant-met stj2 arg-p stj2 bar-i stj2 cupr-f stj2 cupr-m stj2 cupr-p stj2 merc-i-f stj2 zinc-m stj2 zinc-n stj2]

- **day** and night: *Op* hr1* *Stram* hr1*
- **morning**: ambr bry k* con dulc hell hep merc nat-c nat-m ↓
  - **sunrise**, at: **Bry** con
  - **waking**, on: ambr dulc hell hep nat-m
- **noon**: bell a1 bry a1 *Lach* ↓
  - **12**-0 h: *Lach* kr1
- **afternoon** | **16**-0 h: *Stram* kr1
- **evening**: ars a1 *Bell* k* bry *Calc-ar* ↓ canth k* colch a1 croc k* cupr hr1* lach lyc mygal ↓ nux-v ↓ phos plb k* *Psor* hr1 sulph
  - **18** h: phos a1
  - **20** h: mygal a1
  - **dark**, in the: *Calc-ar* k* cupr k*
  - **nap**, during: nux-v k*
- **night**: **Acon** k* *Aeth* j5.de aether *Apis* am j5.de **Ars** k* ars-i ars-s-f k2* atro j5.de* aur h2* aur-ar k2 **Bapt** k* bar-c h2* *Bell* k* *Bry* k* *Cact* k* calc k* camph k* cann-i k* *Canth* k* carb-v k* *Carbn-s* carl a1 *Cham* j5.de *Chel* k* chinin-ar chinin-s cod k* coff k* colch k* coloc j5.de con j5.de cor-r *Crot-h* k* dig k* dulc k* gal-ac a1* granit-m es1• graph hep k* hippoz hr1* hydr hr1* jab k* *Kali-ar* *Kali-c* k* kali-chl hr1 kali-m kr1 kali-p **Lach** k* *Lachn* ↓ lyc k* *Lyss* k* malar jl2 meli sne *Merc* k* merc-c k* merc-cy hr1* merc-sul k* *Mur-ac* ↓ nit-ac j5.de nux-v op k* *Plb* k* *Puls* k* rheum rhus-t hr1* sec sep k* sil k* *Stram* k* sul-ac sul-i k2* sulph syph hr1* tub br1 verat k*
  - **midnight**:
    - **before**: *Mur-ac* hr1
    - **after**: apis kr1 *Lachn* ↓

• **midnight – after**: ...
 : **1-2 h**: *Lachn*
• **waking**, on: *Cact* hr1*
- **abandons** her relatives: sec k*
- **abortion**: | **after**: ruta k*
- **absurd** things, does: *(↗Antics; Foolish)* bell h1* sec k*
- **addresses** objects: stram bg2
- **air** amel.; in open: bry k2
- **alcoholic** (See Delirium tremens)
- **alternating** with:
• **colic** (See abdomen)
• **coma** (See unconsciousness)
• **consciousness**: acon a1 bell a1 *Phos* hr1*
• **convulsions**; tetanic: stram
• **excitement**: agar
• **lamenting**: bell k*
• **sadness**: *(↗gay - alternating - sadness)* plb hr1 tub br1
• **sleep**: acet-ac atro hr1 bell a1 bry↓ cocc k* *Coloc* k* *Lach* hr1 phos↓ plb k* vip k*
 ⁝ **comatose** sleep: bry c1 plb
 ⁝ **deep**: acet-ac atro hr1 bell a1 cocc k* *Coloc* k* *Lach* hr1 phos a2 plb k* vip k*
• **sleeplessness**: *Tub* hr1*
• **sopor** (See sleep)
• **stupefaction**: acet-ac st1
• **stupor**: *Atro* kr1 atro-s hr1
• **unconsciousness**: *Atro* hr1* cann-i a1 *Coloc* hr1 *Phos* hr1 plb stram
○ • **Abdomen**; colic in: plb k*
• **Limbs**; pain in: plb ptk1
- **angry**: *(↗Anger)* *Cocc* k* dulc fd4.de zinc mrr1
- **answering**:
• **abruptly**: cimic bro1 *Lach* bro1 stram bro1 verat bro1
• **correctly** when spoken to, but delirium and unconsciousness return at once (See Answering - stupor)
• **slowly**: arn bro1 bapt bro1 diph bro1 *Hell* bro1 *Hyos* bro1 *Ph-ac* bro1 phos bro1 sulph bro1
- **antics**; playing (See Antics - delirium)
- **anxious**: *(↗Anxiety)* *Acon* k* anac apis ptk1 *Ars* sf1.de *Bell* k* *Brom* sf1.de bry tl1 calc bg2 camph k* *Canth* sf1.de *Croc* b7a.de cupr hr1* hep hydrog srj2• *Hyos* k* ign hr1* lac-c hr1* mez gk nux-v k* *Op* k* phos plb puls bg2 sil k* *Stram* k* sulph h2* *Verat* k*
• **business**: bry tl1
• **fever**; during: acon bg2 bell bg2 croc bg2 *Hyos* bg2 nux-v bg2 *Op* bg2 puls bg2 sil bg2 *Stram* bg2
• **future**; about the: *(↗Anxiety - future)* bry tl1 verat tl1
- **apathetic**: *(↗Indifference)* ph-ac verat
- **apoplectic**: hyos mrr1 lach mrr1
- **arms**:
• **extends**: sep bg2 stram bg2
• **throws** about: *(↗Violent)* bell k*
- **aroused**, on being: dat-f a1 hep phos sec k2
• **answer** questions; could be aroused to: *Hyper* kr1
- **attacks** people with knife: *(↗Violent)* hyos k*
- **barking**; with (See Barking - delirium)
- **bed**:
• **attempts** to leave (See Escape - jumps)
• **creeps** about in: *Bell* vh* stram k*
• **escapes**, jumps up suddenly from bed: *(↗Escape - jumps; Jumping - bed)* **Acon** j5.de* *Agar* kr1 alco a1 *Ars* j5.de* atro a1 **Bell** j5.de* *Bry* j5.de* chin *Chinin-s* kr1 cic a1 *Coloc* j5.de *Crot-h* kr1 *Cupr* j5.de* dig j5.de* gal-ac a1* glon *Hyos* a1* iod sf1.de merc-c a1 merc-meth a1 morph a1 **Nit-ac** kr1 nux-v j5.de op j5.de* past a1 phos a1 plb a1 puls sf1.de rhus-t sf1.de sec hr1* sol-mm a1 *Stram* kr1* sul-ac a1 *Verat* j5.de* *Zinc* kr1
- **bellows** like a calf: *(↗Barking - bellowing)* cupr k*
- **bite**, desire to: *(↗Biting - delirium)* anthraci vh **Bell** hr1* *Canth* hr1* cupr kr1* hydr-ac a1* lyss hr1* **Stram** hr1*
- **blames** himself for his folly: *(↗Reproaching oneself)* op k*
- **books**; endeavors to grasp: atro a1
- **business**, talks of: *(↗Industrious; Talking - business)* ars atro a1* bell k* *Bry* k* canth k* cimic dor k* **Hyos** k* mygal op k* phos k* plb k* *Rhus-t* bg2* stram sulph k*
- **busy**: *(↗Busy; Industrious)* arum-t k2* bapt k* bell k* *Bry* k* camph k* chlol hr1 *Hyos* k* kali-cy a1 rhus-t *Stram* k* sulph
- **carotids** pulsating, with: *Bell* hr1*
- **catches** at flocks in air (See Gestures - hands - grasping)
- **changeable**: lach ptk1 stram ptk1
- **changing** subject rapidly: *(↗Loquacity - changing)* **Lach** stram bg
- **cheerful** (See gay)
- **chill**, during: acon bg2 *Aeth* hr1* *Arn* ars k* astac hr1* *Bell* k* bry bg2 calc bg2 caps b7a.de* carb-v bg2 cham k* chin bg2 cina bg2 dulc bg2 *Hyos* bg2 ign bg2 iod bg2 kali-c bg2 lac-del hrn2• **Nat-m** k* nux-v k* **Op** bg2 ph-ac bg2 phos bg2 plat bg2 podo bg2 puls samb bg2 *Sep* stram k* *Sulph* k* *Verat* k*
- **closing** the eyes, on: bapt *Bell* *Bry* calc graph *Lach* k* led pyrog k* stram sne sulph
- **cold** | **catching**; after: *Op* kr1
- **coldness**, with: lact br1 *Verat*
- **collapse**, with: colch sf1.de cupr hr1*
- **coma**; with (See Coma - delirium)
- **coma** vigil; with: *(↗Coma - delirium)* cur bro1 *Hyos* bro1 *Lach* kr1 mur-ac bro1 op bro1 phos bro1
- **comical**: ant-c c1 *Hyos* k* *Stram* verat k*
- **confused**: coli jl2
- **congestion**, with: *Apis* kr1 aur-m hr1* **Bell** kr1* brom sf1.de hyos h1 iod sf1.de
- **constant**: bapt k* bell h1* *Canth* a1 con k* *Lach*
- **convulsions**:
• **after**: absin k* arg-mur vh bell k* kali-c kali-chl gt1* oena c1 sec k*
• **before**: *Kali-m* kr1 op sul-h a1
• **during**: acon hr1* *Aeth* hr1* amyg hr1* ars k* *Bell* hr1* *Camph* hr1* crot-h k* cupr sf1.de *Dig* hr1* dulc h2 hyos br1 *Kali-chl* hr1 *Kali-m* kr1 *Mosch* j5.de op a1* plb a1*
- **crying**, with: *(↗Weeping)* *Acon* kr1 agar sf1.de agar-pr a1 apis sf1.de atro a1 bell *Canth* kr1 *Caust* *Chinin-s* kr1 *Cina* crot-h kr1 *Cupr-act* kr1 dat-m a1 ferr-p sf1.de merc sf1.de phos a1 stram a1
• **help**, for: *(↗Begging; Delusions - help; Delusions - help - calling; Helplessness; Shrieking - help)* Canth stram kr1
- **dancing**; with: *(↗Dancing)* cic br1
- **dark**, in: *(↗Darkness - agg.; Light - desire)* *Calc* *Calc-ar* k* *Carb-v* *Cupr* k* *Stram*
- **death**, talks about: *Acon* hr1*
- **decency**; with loss of (See naked)
- **delusions**, with: absin br1 aeth bg2 agar tl1 anac jl3 *Ars* sf1.de *Bell* bg2* camph tl1 *Cann-i* sf1.de* *Cann-xyz* bg2 cham bg2 cocc↓ croc tl1 dig sf1.de graph bg2 *Hyos* bg2* *Kali-bi* hr1* op bg2* petr sf1.de* plb a1* sep bg2 sil bg2 spong bg2 *Stram* bg2* *Sulph* bg2
• **sees** rolling live things: cocc tl1
- **depletion**; after: *(↗loss; Prostration)* *Chin*
- **devils**, sees: op vh*
- **distension** of abdomen and constipation; with: *Acet-ac* vh*
- **dogs**, talks about: bell h1*
- **dress** and go out, wants to: lachn kr1
- **drunkards** (See Delirium tremens)
- **eating** | **amel.**: anac bell
- **embraces** the stove and wishes to climb upon it as on a tree: *(↗Delusions - stove - mistakes; Embraces - inanimate)* hyos
- **encephalitis**; with: *Acon* kr1 *Cocc* kr1 hell mrr1 *Puls* kr1
- **envy**, with: lyc a1
- **epilepsy**:
• **after**: *Arg-met* plb k*
• **during**: *(↗GENERALS - Convulsions - epileptic - during)* hyos j op k*
- **erotic**: *(↗Lascivious; Lewdness; Naked; Nymphomania; Obscene; Shameless)* camph cann-i k* *Canth* k* *Hyos* bro1* kali-br k* *Lach* *Phos* k* *Plat* vh* *Sec* st1 *Stram* k* *Tarent* vh* verat bro1
- **escapes** in abortion; she: *(↗Escape; Escape - delirium)* *Coloc* kr1
- **exaltation** of strength, with: *Agar* k* *Aur* k* bell mrr1 hyos sec vh* stram k* *Tarent* vh*

- **exhaustion**, with: agar hr1* ail sf1.de am-c sf1.de *Bapt* sf1.de* dor sf1.de hyos sf1.de lyc sf1.de
- **extravagant** language, with: bell a1
- **eyes**; with brilliant: ail ptk1
- **face**:
  - **distorted**; with: *Plb* kr1
  - **livid**: *Bell* kr1
  - **muscles** constantly in play: (*↗grimaces*) *Stram* kr1
  - **pale**: *Hyos* k*
  - **red**: *Ail* sf1.de *Bapt* sf1.de *Bell* k* dor k* *Gels* sf1.de **Hyos** k* op k*
- **fantastic**: alum j ambr j *Bell* k* calc j carbn-s cham con dulc graph hyos lyc j nat-m j nux-m j op plat j rhod j sep sil spong *Stram Sulph*
- **fatigue**, overexertion, study; from: (*↗Prostration*) lach
- **fear**; with: (*↗Aversion - men; to [=male persons] - women; Fear; Fear - men; of [=male; Fear - people)* *Acon* br1] bell↓ *Plat*↓
  - **men**; of: (*↗Aversion - men; to [=male persons] - women; Fear - men; of [=male; Fear - people)* bell *Plat* k*]
- **fever**:
  - **after**: arg-met vh1
  - **during**: (*↗Loquacity - fever*) *Acet-ac* hr1 *Acon* b7.de* act-sp a1* aeth a1* agar hr1* ail a1 anag hr1* anan a1 *Ant-c* b7a.de* ant-t hr1* *Anthraci* kr1 *Apis* b7a.de* *Ars* b4a.de* *Arum-t* hr1* **Bapt** hr1* bar-c a1 **Bell** b4.de* *Bry* b7.de* bufo bg2* **Calc** b4a.de* *Camph* hr1* *Canth* bg2* *Caps* b7a.de* *Carb-v* b4a.de* *Cham* b7.de* chel hr1* *Chin* b7.de* *Chinin-s* kr1 chlol hr1 cimic hr1* *Cina* b7.de* cocc bg2 coff b7.de* colch sf1.de croc bg2 *Crot-h* hr1* cupr bg2 cur a1 dor hr1* *Dulc* b4a.de* granit-m es1• *Hell* bg2* helo-s bnm14• *Hep* b4.de* hydrog srj2• *Hyos* b7.de* ign b7.de* iod b4a.de* juni-v a1 kali-c b4a.de* lac-lup hrn2• *Lach* bg2* meny b7.de* *Merc* hr1 merc-i-r hr1* morph a1 mur-ac sf1.de *Nat-m* b4a.de* *Nit-ac* bg2 nux-v b7.de* op b7.de* *Ox-ac* hr1* petr hr1 *Ph-ac* b4a.de* phos bg2 plat b4a.de* podo bro1* psor hr1* **Puls** b7.de* **Rhus-t** bg2* *Sabad* b7.de* sal-ac sf1.de *Samb* b7.de* sang hr1 *Sec* hr1* *Sin-n* hr1* *Spong* bg2* *Stram* b7.de* sul-ac a1 sulph b4a.de* *Ter* hr1 til a1 vario hr1* verat b7.de* verat-v sf1.de
    - **intermittent** fever: sabad br1
  - **intense** (See FEVER - Intense - delirium)
- **fierce**: (*↗Violent*) agar *Bapt* hr1* bell k* hyos *Stram*
- **fire**, talks of: *Calc* cupr vh
- **foolish**, silly: (*↗nonsense; Foolish*) acon aeth agar st1 bell k* calc-sil k2 *Cic* sf1.de* *Hyos* k* merc k* *Op* k* *Stram* k* sulph bg3*
- **foreign**:
  - **countries**; talks of: cann-i
  - **language**; talks in a: lach ptk1* nit-ac ptk1 *Stram* k*
- **frightful**: (*↗terror*) *Acon* anac *Atro* k* bar-c hr1* **Bell** k* calc k* canth carb-v j caust j chin j cic colch coloc dig hep sf1.de* *Hyos* lyc j merc j mez gk nat-m nit-ac j nux-v *Op* k* phos k* *Plb* k* *Puls* rhod a1 samb j sec sil **Stram** k* sulph j *Verat* zinc zinc-p k2*
- **fruit**; after sour: podo br1
- **furious**: bell vh* *Bry* vh* canth br1 verat vh* verat-v br1
- **gangrene**; during: ran-b tl1
- **gather** objects off the wall, tries to: bell k* hyos
- **gay**, cheerful: (*↗Cheerful; Content*) acon k* agar k* agath-a nl2• ant-t kr1 aur *Bell* k* cact cann-s con croc↓ cupr↓ hyos k* lact lact-v↓ op k* plat↓ spig-m↓ spong↓ *Stram* k* sulph k* verat k*
  - **midnight**; after | **morning**; until: lact-v a1
  - **alternating** with:
    - **crying** (See weeping)
    - **laughing**: stram
    - **melancholy** (See sadness)
    - **sadness**: (*↗alternating - sadness*) agar
    - **singing**: stram
    - **weeping**: plat dh1* spig-m a1* stram k*
    - **whistling**: stram
  - **fever**; during: *Bell* bg2 croc bg2 cupr bg2 *Hyos* bg2 spong bg2 stram bg2 verat bg2
- **gestures**; with funny: (*↗Gestures*) cic br1
- **giggling**: hyosin a1
- **grimaces**, with: (*↗face - muscles; Grimaces*) *Bell* hr1*
- **grinding** teeth; with: **Bell** kr1
- **groping** as if in dark: plb a1
- **headache**:
  - **during**: acon agar k* ail hr1* arg-n bg arn bg ars *Aur* hr1 bell bg* calc bg cham bg cimic hr1* *Colch* k* coloc bg crot-h hr1* crot-t bg glon kalm bg mag-c *Meli* hr1* mosch nat-m bg *Nux-v* hr1* sec k* sep bg stram hr1* syph bro1 tarent verat k*
  - **from** headache, delirium: atro kr1 *Aur* kr1 aur-m kr1 syph br
- **heat** | **agg.**: bry k2 dulc hr1 stram
- **hemorrhage** | **after**: arn k* ars k* bell ptk1 chin chinin-ar k2 ign k* lach k* lyc k* ph-ac k* phos k* sep k* squil k* sulph k* verat k*
- **home**, wants to go: (*↗Delusions - home - away - must*) bell a1 **Bry** br1* *Cupr-act* kr1
- **horses**, talks about: *Stram* a1
- **hot** head, with: *Bell* kr1 bufo kr1
- **hysterical**, almost: (*↗Hysteria*) bell k* *Hyos* hr1* ign tarent verat
- **imperious**: lyc a1
- **injuries** to head; after: (*↗Ailments - injuries*) bell bg2* hyos bg2* op bg2* stram bg2* verat bg2*
- **intermittent**: con k* **Stram** hr1*
- **intoxicated**, as if: *Agar* br1* agath-a nl2• am-c sf1.de carb-an a1 chinin-s kr1 cori-r a1 vip a1
- **irrational** actions and thoughts: stram h1*
- **jealousy**, from: (*↗Jealousy*) **Hyos** hr1* **Lach** vh*
- **jerking**, with: acon a1 hyos↓
  - **angular**: hyos tl1
- **jumping**, with: acon a1 bell a1 lact a1 merc a1
- **laughing**: (*↗Laughing - delirious*) acon *Bell* k* colch con *Hyos* k* hyosin a1 *Ign* lach lact op plb sal-ac a1* sec sep k* *Stram* k* sulph thea verat zinc
- **lips** move as if talking: (*↗FACE - Motion of facial - constant - lips - delirium*) bell k*
- **lochia**, during: verat j5.de
- **look** fixed on one point (= staring): (*↗Staring*) *Acon* kr1 art-v bell j bov camph cann-s j canth cham j *Cic* j cupr dor sf1.de guaj j hell j *Ign* k* kreos j mez j nat-c j ran-b stram
  - **wrinkled** face; with: stram
- **loquacious**: (*↗Loquacity*) agar k* apis↓ aur k* bapt bar-c *Bell* k* bry camph k* cann-i bro1 **Cimic** k* *Crot-h* k* *Cupr* k* dat-m a1 dor a1 gels **Hyos** k* **Lach** k* **Lachn** lyss k* meli a1* merc-cy bro1 naja oena k* *Op* k* oper br1* par petr *Phos* k* *Plat* plb k* podo c1* *Rhus-t* k* **Stram** k* *Sulph* hr1* thea↓ *Verat* k*
  - **fever**; during: bell bg2 cupr bg2 lach bg2 rhus-t bg2 *Stram* bg2 verat bg2
  - **indistinct**: apis bell a1 *Hyos Op* a1*
  - **rhyme**; talking in: thea a1
- **loss** of fluids, from: (*↗depletion*) *Chin Chr-ac Hell Lach* k* *Nat-s Sulph Verat* verat-v
- **maniacal**: (*↗Mania*) acon k* *Aeth* agar ptk1 ail k* ant-c apis kr1 ars k* **Bell** k* bry bg3* *Camph* cann-i *Canth* k* carbn-s chinin-s *Cic* hr1* *Coff* colch con cori-r k* crot-h *Cupr* dig sf1.de glon sf1.de *Hell* **Hyos** k* indg *Kali-bi* hr1* *Lach* sf1.de led lob lyc k* merc merc-c nat-m nit-ac ptk1 nux-m *Oena* k* *Op* k* *Phos*↓ plb rhod *Sec* k* **Stram** k* tarent ter thuj↓ *Verat* k* zinc zinc-act sf1.de
  - **love**, from disappointed: *Phos* hr1*
  - **trifles**; about: thuj ptk1
- **meningitis** cerebrospinalis: (*↗FEVER - Cerebrospinal*) *Apis* kr1* *Chr-ac* hr1* *Hell* hr1* naja kr1 *Nat-s* hr1* *Sulph* hr1* *Verat* hr1* verat-v hr1* zinc mrr1
- **menses**:
  - **before**: (*↗Menses - before*) ars bell cocc tl1 hyos lyc k* verat hr1*
  - **during**: (*↗Menses - during*) acon apis bell cocc k* hyos k* lyc k* nux-m k* puls stram verat k*
    - **menstrual** difficulties, with: (*↗Menses - during*) apis k1
  - **suppressed** menses; from: *Apis* b7a.de
- **mental** exertion, from: *Lach* k*
- **merry** (See gay)
- **mild**: *Apis* kr1 **Bapt** kr1 *Ph-ac* kr1 *Puls* kr1 pyrog jl2 rhus-t bg2* sec j5.de **Stram** kr1 *Valer* kr1 *Vario* kr1 verat j5.de
- **miscarriage** (See abortion)
- **moaning**, with: (*↗Moaning*) bell hr1* *Crot-h* hr1*
- **mouth**, puts stones in: merc k*

- **moving**:
  - **constantly** from place to place; moving: *Oena* kr1
  - **queer**; moving: **Stram** hr1*
  - **rhythmical**: stram tl1
- **murmuring**: *(↗Muttering)* arn k* calad k* *Hyos* k* *Lyc* k* merc ↓ ph-ac *Phos* k* rhus-t *Stram* k* tab k* *Zinc* hr1*
  - **himself**, to: hyos merc a1 tab
  - **slowly**: ph-ac
- **music**; from hearing: plb ptk1
- **muttering**: *(↗Muttering)* *Agar* br1* *Ail* k* *Amyg* hr1* *Ant-t* hr1* *Apis* k* *Arn* k* ars k* arum-t k2* *Bapt* k* *Bell* k* **Bry** k* calad k* calc-sil k2 chel *Cic* hr1* *Colch* k* convo-s jl* *Crot-h* k* dor k* gels k* hell k* *Hep* k* **Hyos** k* *Iris* kr1 kali-br kali-cy a1 *Lach* k* *Lyc* k* *Merc* k* *Mur-ac* k* nat-m k* nux-v k* *Op* k* ph-ac k* **Phos** k* raja-s jl3 *Rhus-t* k* *Sec* k* **Stram** k* *Sulph* hr1* *Tab* *Tarax* k* *Ter* k* *Verat* k* verat-v ptk1
  - **fever**; during: **Apis** bg2 bell bg2 hyos bg2 mur-ac bg2 *Op* bg2 ph-ac bg2 stram bg2 tarax bg2
  - **himself**, to: bell k* hyos k* rhus-t tab k* tarax ptk1
  - **sleep**, in: ant-t k* ars k* bry k* *Gels* hr1* sulph
  - **slowly**: ph-ac
- **naked** in delirium, wants to be: *(↗Lascivious)* *Bell* k* **Hyos** k* merc k* *Phos* phyt *Sec* stram hr1*
- **nausea** and retching; with: cimic kr
- **noisy**: agar bg2 *Bell* k* *Camph* *Hyos* k* **Stram** k* verat bg2
- **nonsense**, with eyes open: *(↗foolish)* anac ars bapt *Canth* cham coll coloc crot-h *Hyos* op *Stram* k* tarent **Verat**
- **not** know anybody; does (See recognizes)
- **pains**:
  - **from**: acon kr1 ars kr1 aur kr1 **Bell** kr1 bry kr1 calc kr1 *Cham* kr1 chin kr1 dulc kr1 **Hyos** hr1* ign kr1 *Iod* kr1 kali-c kr1 nat-m kr1 nux-v kr1 **Op** kr1 *Ph-ac* kr1 plat kr1 samb kr1 **Stram** kr1 sulph kr1 **Verat** hr1*
  - **with** the: *(↗Shrieking - pain)* acon bg2 arg-met bg2* arg-n bg2 bov bg2 dulc k* tarent-c bg2* *Verat* k*
- **paroxysmal**: *Bell* k* con k* *Gels* hyos hr1 naja kr1 phos plb sabad gk
- **periodical**: *Bell* kr1 samb stram ↓
  - **fever**; during: bell tl1 stram tl1
- **persecution** in delirium; delusions of: *(↗Delusions - persecuted - he)* ars gl1.fr• calc gl1.fr• hyos gl1.fr• lach gl1.fr• merc gl1.fr• nat-m gl1.fr• rhus-t gl1.fr• stram gl1.fr• verat gl1.fr•
- **perspiration**:
  - **amel**.: aeth k*
  - **cold** perspiration; with: *Verat* kr1
  - **with**: acon bg2 ars bg2 aur bg2 **Bell** bg2 bry bg2 calc bg2 *Cham* bg2 chin bg2 cina bg2 dulc bg2 gal-ac br1 granit-m es1• *Hyos* bg2 ign bg2 iod bg2 kali-c bg2 nat-m bg2 nux-v bg2 **Op** bg2 *Ph-ac* bg2 plat bg2 samb bg2 **Stram** bg2 sulph bg2 *Verat* bg2
- **picking** at nose or lips, with: *(↗FACE - Picking - lips)* *Arum-t* k* **Bry** camph kr1 *Carb-v* *Chel* chin chlf kr1 croc cupr **Hyos** hyosin a1 kali-p kr1 op past a1 *Ph-ac* phos plb rhus-t sec tab valer verat
- **pupils**, with dilated: acon hr1* *Bell* hr1* *Cimic* hr1*
- **quarrelsome**: bell a1 *Chr-ac* hr1 nit-ac ptk1 verat-v hr1
- **quiet**: **Bry** calc-sil k2 camph kr1 *Carb-v* *Chel* chin chlf kr1 chlor ckh1 croc cupr cupr-act a1 **Hyos** hyosin a1 kali-p kr1 op past a1 *Ph-ac* phos plb rhus-t sec tab valer verat
  - **alternating** with | **restlessness** (See Restlessness - alternating - delirium - quiet)
- **rabid**: bell canth lyss *Stram* k*
- **raging** (= raving): *(↗Rage)* *Acon* k* *Act-sp* *Aeth* aether k* **Agar** k* agar-pa a1 ail kl alco a1 anac k* ant-c ant-s-aur *Ant-t* apis sf1.de arg-met arg-n ars k* ars-s-f k2 atro kr1 **Bell** k* bry k* calc k* *Camph* k* cann-i cann-s a1 cann-xyz bg2 **Canth** k* *Carbn-s* cham ↓ chel chin chinin-s k* cic k* *Cimic* cina k* clem kr1 colch coloc k* cori-r a1 *Cupr* k* cupr-act a1 dat-f a1 dig dulc glon granit-m ↓ graph *Hell* helo-s bnm14• hep **Hyos** k* hyper jatr-c juni-v a1 *Kali-i* kr1 lach bg2* lob lol bg2 **Lyc** *Merc* k* merc-cy k* morph a1 mosch mur-ac a1 nat-m **Nit-ac** nux-m k* nux-v a1 *Oena* k* **Op** k* par phos *Plb* k* *Puls* rheum k* **Sec** k* *Sol-ni* k* **Stram** k* sul-ac sulph *Tab* tarent trach a1 trach-v a1 **Verat** k* verat-v kr1 vip zinc zinc-p k2
- **raging**: ...
  - **fever**; during: acon bg2 bell bg2 *Bry* bg2 granit-m es1• *Hyos* bg2 lyc bg2 op bg2 *Stram* bg2
  - **pains**, from: arg-met k2 cham bg2
- **rambling**: atro k* *Bell* k* chlol a1 *Chlor* hr1* hyos *Nat-m* hr1* plb k* sec hr1* *Sulph* hr1*
- **raving** (See raging)
- **recognizes** no one: *(↗Recognizing - not - anyone)* agar hr1* **Ail** hr1* bell k* calad hyos merc k* nux-v op stram k* tab verat
  - **throws** wine and medicine at nurse: agar kr1
- **refuses** to take the medicine (See Refusing - medicine - delirium)
- **religious**: *(↗Religious - too)* agar bg2* alco a1 aur lach **Verat** k*
- **repeats** the same sentence: *(↗Speech - repeats)* camph k* plb b7a.de
- **reproachful**: *(↗Contemptuous)* hyos lyc k*
- **restless**: *(↗Restlessness)* *Absin* vh1 acon ail k2* ars a1 atro k* *Bapt* hr1 bell a1 bry sf1.de gal-ac br1 **Hyos** hr1* iod sf1.de merc-sul hr1* *Mur-ac* hr1 oper br1 phos a1 plb k* *Stram* a1* sulph sf1.de *Verat* hr1*
- **rocking** to and fro: bell hyos k*
- **rolling** on floor: *(↗Rolling - floor)* calc ptk1 *Op* k*
- **romping** with children: agar k*
- **running**, with: bell a1 con a1 helo-s bnm14•
- **sad**: *(↗Sadness)* acon bg2* bell bg2 puls bg2
- **same** subject all the time; talking about the: petr k*
- **scolding**: chr-ac hr1* hyos merc k* stram k* verat-v hr1*
- **sepsis**, from: anthraci vh *Bapt* sf1.de *Bar-c* kr1 crot-h sf1.de* dor sf1.de *Lach* sf1.de mur-ac sf1.de *Pyrog* sf1.de *Rhus-t* sf1.de sec sf1.de tarent-c sf1.de ter sf1.de *Verat* sf1.de *Verat-v* sf1.de *Vip* sf1.de
- **shrieking**; with: *Agar* br1 crot-h bg2 cupr bg2 helo-s bnm14• merc bg2
- **shy**, hides himself: *(↗Hiding - himself)* **Stram** hr1*
- **silent**: agar k* ant-c ↓ bell ↓ *Hyos* ↓ mur-ac ↓ sec k* verat ↓
  - **fever**; during: ant-c bg2 bell bg2 *Hyos* bg2 mur-ac bg2 verat bg2
- **singing**: *(↗Singing)* *Agar* br1* cic br1* lact a1 stram a1
  - **talking**, but won't answer; and: agar tl1
- **sleep**:
  - **after**: *Lach* hr1* petr sf1.de
    - **amel**.: bell *Cact* calad mrr1
  - **aroused** (See aroused)
  - **during**: acon k* ant-c hr1* **Apis** k* arn b7a.de ars k* aur b4a.de *Bar-c* hr1* **Bell** k* **Bry** b7.de* *Cact* k* *Calc* hr1* *Camph* b7a.de cham cina coloc b4a.de cupr cupr-act a1 dig b4a.de dulc b4a.de *Gels* k* hyper lach k* lat-m bnm6• *Lyc* hr1* merc morph a1 mur-ac *Nit-s-d* hr1* nux-v b7.de* *Op* k* phos b4a.de* puls ↓ rheum k* santin sec ↓ sep b4a.de spong k* stram k* sulph b4a.de verat k*
    - **comatose**: acon j5.de ant-c j5.de arn j5.de bry j5.de camph j5.de coloc j5.de puls j5.de sec j5.de
  - **going** to sleep; on: *Bell* *Bry* cact calc camph caust *Chin* *Gels* k* gins guaj ign merc ph-ac *Phos* rhus-t *Spong* *Sulph*
- **sleepiness**, with: acon ant-c j5.de arn *Bry* k* calc-p camph a1* coloc *Crot-h* hr1* hyos bg2 lach *Op* hr1* **Puls** k* sec j5.de
- **sleeplessness**:
  - **from**: *Lach* hr1*
  - **with**: acon bro1 ail k2* alum j5.de aur j5.de* *Bapt* hr1* *Bell* bg2* bry b7a.de* cact bro1 calc bg2* *Cann-i* bro1 chin bg2* *Cimic* bg2* *Coloc* bg2* cupr-act a1 cyt-l mg1.de* dig bg2* dulc bg2* *Gels* hr1* hyos bg2* ign bg2* iod a1 kali-br bro1 lact br1 led j5.de lyc bg2* merc j5.de *Mur-ac* hr1 nat-c bg2* nux-m c1 nux-v bg2* op j5.de* passi sf1.de petr j5.de ph-ac j5.de* phos bg2* plat bg2* *Plb* hr1* puls bg2* rhus-t bg2* sabad bg2* samb ptk1* sel bg2* *Sil* j5.de spong b7a.de* *Stram* bg2* sulph bg2* *Tub* hr1* verat bg2* vip-a j
- **smallpox**; after: *Bell* bro1 stram bro1 verat-v bro1
- **sopor**, with: aeth bro1 agar bro1 *Ail* bro1 am-c bro1 *Ant-t* bro1 *Apis* bro1 arn bro1 *Bapt* bro1 bell bro1 ben-n bro1 *Camph* bro1 *Carb-ac* bro1 diph bro1 gels bro1 *Hell* bro1 *Hyos* bro1 kali-c hr1* lach bro1 laur bro1 lob-p bro1 mur-ac bro1 nit-s-d bro1 nux-m bro1 *Op* hr1* *Ph-ac* bro1 phos bro1 pilo bro1 *Rhus-t* bro1 stram bro1 ter bro1 thyr bro1 *Verat* hr1* *Zinc* bro1
- **sorrowful**: acon agar a1 bell dulc lyc puls
- **specters**; sees: op vh*

- **staring** at one fixed point (See look)
- **stove** and wishes to climb upon it as on a tree; embraces (See embraces)
- **stupid**: *Stram* a1*
- **terror**, expressive of: *(↗frightful)* bell a1
- **thirst**, with: camph hr1* *Verat* hr1*
- **throwing** from windows: calc k2 sil k2
- **tongue** | **brown** discoloration: *Phos* kr1*
- **trembling**, with: acon ptk1 apis ptk1 ars ptk1 bell ptk1 bry ptk1 calc ptk1 chin ptk1 hyos ptk1 ign ptk1 lact br1 nat-m ptk1 op ptk1 phys ptk1 plat ptk1 *Puls* ptk1 rhus-t ptk1 sabad ptk1 samb ptk1 stram ptk1 sulph ptk1 valer verat ptk1 verat-v ptk1
- **tremens** (See Delirium tremens)
- **twitching** of muscles; with: hyos br1
- **typhoid** fever; during: agar bro1 *Agarin* bro1 ars bro1 bapt bro1 *Bell* bro1 cann-i bro1 *Hyos* bro1 *Hyosin-hbr* bro1 lach bro1 methyl br1* op bro1 ph-ac bro1 phos bro1 rhus-t bro1 *Stram* bro1 ter bro1 valer bro1
- **urinating**:
  - **floor**; tries to urinate on the: *(↗Dirty - urinating and - everywhere - children; Insanity - urinating)* plb
  - **pot**; outside the: *(↗Dirty - urinating and - everywhere - children)* bell
- **vertigo**:
  - **after**: jatr-c hr1*
  - **with**: nux-m b7a.de* sec j
    - **violent**: nux-m c1
- **vexation**, from: bell j **Hyos** hr1* plat j
- **violent**: *(↗Violent; Violent - deeds)* *Acon* aeth ptk2 agar alum kr1 alumn hr1 *Apis* **Ars** k* atro k* aur hr1* **Bell** k* camph k* canth k* chlf hr1* con k* *Cupr* dig a1 **Hyos** k* *Lach* k* *Op* k* phos plb k* puls *Sec* k* **Stram** k* verat verat-v sf1.de zinc k* zinc-p k2*
  - **night**: ars tl1
  - **restrained** and calmed with great difficulty, is: zinc
- **vivid**: bell k* *Stram* k*
- **waking**, on: aur bell k* bry k* cact carb-v chel cina k2 coff colch cur dulc granit-m es1• *Hyos* k* *Lach* k* lob merc nat-c par sep stram zinc sf1.de*
- **wandering** (See Wandering - desire)
- **warm** room agg.: bry k2
- **water**, jumping into: bell k* sec k*
- **wedding**, prepares for: *Hyos* k*
- **well**, declares she is: *(↗Delusions - well; Irritability - sends - doctor; Obstinate - nothing; Well - says - sick)* apis *Arn* k* *Ars* k* op k2
- **wild**: *(↗Violent; Wild feeling)* *Acon* bg2 anac bg2 ars bg2 atro a1* **Bell** k* *Bry* bg2* *Calc* bg2 calen hr1* camph k* cann-xyz bg2 canth k* chlol k* cic bg2 *Cina* bg2 colch k* coloc bg2 cupr k* gal-ac a1 gels hr1* hydr-ac k* *Hyos* k* *Kali-br* hr1* lach k* lol bg2 merc bg2 nat-sal a1 nux-m bg2 *Op* bg2* **Plb** k* rheum bg2 sec bg2 **Stram** k* *Valer* hr1* *Vario* hr1* *Verat* k*
  - **night**: bell hr1 gal-ac a1* plb
  - **sudden**: *Canth* bg2
- **wraps** up in fur during summer: hyos k*
- **wrongs**, of imagined: hyos

DELIRIUM TREMENS: *(↗Alcoholism; Insanity - drunkards; Libertinism; Unconsciousness - delirium tremens)* acon k* aether c1* **Agar** k* agar-pr a1 alco a1 anac bg2* ant-c *Ant-t* hr1* *Arn* k* **Ars** k* ars-s-f k2* asar mrr1 *Atro* a1* aur bg2 aven br1* *Bell* k* *Bism* k* bry c1 bufo k2 *Calc* k* calc-s *Cann-i* k* cann-xyz bg2 *Caps* c1* carb-v carc mlr1• *Cedr* ↓ chir chinin-s j5.de* chlf c1* chlol k* *Chlor* kr1 cimic k* *Coff* k* cori-r a1* *Crot-h* k* cypr hr1* dig k* dor sf1.de ferr-p k* gels *Glon* hr1* *Graph* hr1 grat hell *Hyos* k* *Hyosin-hbr* bro1 ign k* *Kali-bi* ↓ *Kali-br* k* kali-p k* **Lach** k* lact-v br1 led lol c1* lup bro1 lyc lyss jl2 *Merc* k* nat-c **Nat-m** k* **Nux-m** k* **Nux-v** k* Oena k* olden-h gsb1 **Op** k* *Passi* a1* *Past* a1* *Phos* k* plb bg2* puls **Ran-b** k* rhod rhus-t ruta scut c1* sel sep sil spig **Stram** k* **Stry** k* stry-n bro1 sul-ac sulph sumb bro1 teucr bro1 thea c1* thuj bg2 tus-p c1 verat zinc k* zinc-act sf1.de [mag-lac stj2 mag-met stj2]

- **coldness**, with: lact-v br1
- **confusion**; with: lach br1
- **delusions**, with: *Bell* sf1.de calc sf1.de cann-i sf1.de *Cimic* hr1 *Kali-bi* hr1* *Lach* sf1.de *Op* hr1* *Stram* hr1*
  - **night**: stram tl1
  - **elephants**; of: cann-i tl1
- **escape**, attempts to: *Bell* sf1.de stram sf1.de
- **excitement**, with: chlf hr1* *Zinc* hr1*

Delirium tremens: ...

- **face**; with red, bloated: *Bell* kr1* *Crot-h* kr1 *Kali-br* hr1 stram sf1.de
- **loquacity**, with: *(↗Loquacity)* *Lach* hr1* *Ran-b* hr1*
- **maliciousness**; with (See Malicious - delirium)
- **mild** attacks: *Cypr* hr1*
- **old** emaciated persons, in: **Op** hr1*
- **oversensitiveness**, with: **Nux-v** hr1*
- **praying**, with: *(↗Praying)* *Aur* vh* **Stram** hr1*
- **sleeplessness**, with: *Cimic* kr1* *Gels* hyos sf1.de kali-p sf1.de lact-v br1 *Nux-v*
- **small** quantity of alcoholic stimulants, from: **Op** hr1*
- **sopor** with snoring: **Op** hr1*
- **tongue**:
  - **trembling** of tongue; with: stram kr1*
  - **white** discoloration of the tongue; with: **Stram** kr1* zinc kr1*
- **trembling**, with: *Cedr* kr1 *Hyos* kr1 lach br1 lact-v br1 *Stram* kr1

DELIVERY: | **after**: *(↗Sadness - delivery - after)* acon b7.de* *Apis* b7a.de bell b4a.de lil-t k* sec bg2 *Sep* b4a.de stram b7.de*

DELUSIONS (= imaginations): *(↗Mania; Schizophrenia - paranoid; Thoughts - persistent)* abel jl3 abies-c ↓ abrot ↓ absin k* *Acer-circ* ↓ acet-ac kr1 *Acon* k* act-sp ↓ *Adam* ↓ aesc ↓ *Aeth* aether ↓ agar k* *Agath-a* ↓ *Agn* ↓ *Aids* ↓ ail ↓ alco a1 allox ↓ aloe ↓ alum k2* alum-p ↓ alum-sil ↓ alumin ↓ alumin-s ↓ alumn ↓ am-br ↓ am-c ↓ am-caust ↓ am-f ↓ *Am-m* ↓ *Ambr* k* ambro ↓ aml-ns ↓ anac k* anag ↓ anan *Androc* ↓ ang b2.de anh c1* ant-c k* ant-t bg2 anthraq ↓ *Antip* bro1 ap-g ↓ apis apoc ↓ *Aq-mar* ↓ ara-maca ↓ *Aran* ↓ aran-ix sp1 aran-sc ↓ arb-m ↓ arg-met **Arg-n** k* arge-pl ↓ arizon-l ↓ arn k2* *Ars* k* ars-h ↓ ars-i ars-met kr1 ars-s-f k2 art-v kr1 arum-t ↓ asaf ↓ asar jl3 asc-t ↓ astat ↓ *Aster* ↓ astra-m br1 atra-r ↓ atro a1* *Atro-s* ↓ *Aur* k* aur-ar k2 *Aur-m* *Aur-m-n* wbt2• aur-s ↓ bac ↓ bad ↓ *Bamb-a* stb2.de• *Bapt* k* bar-act ↓ bar-br ↓ bar-c k* bar-i k2 *Bar-m* ↓ bar-met ↓ bar-p ↓ bar-s ↓ **Bell** k* bell-p-sp ↓ ben ↓ *Benz-ac* ↓ benzo ↓ benzol br1 berb j5.de beryl ↓ bism bg2 bism-sn ↓ bit-ar ↓ bold ↓ bor-pur ↓ *Borx* ↓ *Bov* ↓ brach ↓ brass-n-o ↓ brom ↓ bros-gau ↓ bry k* bufo ↓ bufo-s ↓ buteo-j ↓ *Cact* ↓ cadm-met ↓ cadm-s ↓ caes-met ↓ cain ↓ caj ↓ *Calad* ↓ *Calc* k* calc-act ↓ calc-ar k2* calc-br ↓ calc-caust ↓ calc-f ↓ calc-i k2 calc-p ↓ calc-s **Calc-sil** ↓ calen ↓ *Camph* camph-br ↓ camph-mbr ↓ **CANN-I** k* *Cann-s* k* *Cann-xyz* ptk1 canth k* caps ↓ carb-ac ↓ carb-an k* carb-v k* carbn-h ↓ carbn-o ↓ *Carbn-s* ↓ *Carc* mlr1• carl a1 carneg-g ↓ casc ↓ cassia-s ↓ *Caul* ↓ caust k* cench cere-b ↓ cham h1* chel kr1 chen-a ↓ chim ↓ chin k* chin-b ↓ chinin-ar chinin-s ↓ chir-fl ↓ chlf a1 chlol br1* chlor kr1 chloram jl3 chlorpr jl3 choc ↓ chord-umb ↓ chr-ac ↓ cic k* cimic k* cimx ↓ cina k* cinnb ↓ cinnm ↓ cist ↓ cit-v ↓ clem ↓ clem-vit ↓ cob ↓ cob-m ↓ cob-n ↓ cob-p ↓ coc-c ↓ coca a1 coca-c ↓ cocain bro1 **Cocc** k* cod ↓ *Coff* k* coff-t ↓ colch k* coli rly4• coll ↓ coloc bg2 con k* conch ↓ conin ↓ convo-s sp1* cop ↓ cor-r ↓ cori-r ↓ corian-s ↓ cortico sp1 cortiso ↓ corv-cor ↓ cot ↓ croc k* *Crot-c* bro1* crot-h k* crot-t ↓ cub ↓ culx ↓ cund ↓ *Cupr* b2.de* cupr-act kr1* cupr-f ↓ cupr-m ↓ cur ↓ *Cycl* ↓ cypra-eg ↓ cystein-l rly4• cyt-l jl3 *Daph* ↓ dat-a ↓ *Dendr-pol* ↓ der ↓ des-ac ↓ dig bg2 digin a1 dios ↓ dioxi ↓ dirc ↓ dor ↓ dream-p ↓ **Dros** ↓ dub ↓ dubo-m ↓ dulc k* *Dys* ↓ eberth jl2 elaps eos ↓ ephe-si ↓ equis-h ↓ erig ↓ eucal ↓ eug ↓ *Euon* ↓ euon-a ↓ *Eup-per* ↓ eup-pur euph ↓ euph-a ↓ euph-l br1 euphr b2.de eupi ↓ falco-pe nl2• *Ferr* ↓ ferr-f ↓ ferr-lac ↓ ferr-n ↓ ferr-p ↓ ferr-sil ↓ fic-m ↓ fl-ac fl-pur ↓ foll ↓ form ↓ fum ↓ gala ↓ galeoc-c-h ↓ *Galla-q-r* ↓ gamb ↓ gard-j ↓ gast ↓ *Gels* ↓ gent-c ↓ ger-i ↓ germ-met ↓ gink-b ↓ *Glon* gnaph ↓ gran granit-m ↓ graph bg2* grat ↓ guaj ↓ guan ↓ hafn-met ↓ *Haliae-lc* ↓ halo ↓ *Ham* ↓ helia ↓ *Hell* k* helo-s ↓ *Hep* b2.de* *Hipp* ↓ hippoc-k szs2 hoit jl3 hom-xyz ↓ hura hydr ↓ hydr-ac kr1 **Hydrog** ↓ **Hyos** k* hyper ↓ iber ↓ **Ign** k* ignis-alc ↓ ilx-a ↓ indg ↓ indol ↓ iod k* iodof ↓ ip ↓ irid-m ↓ *Irid-met* ↓ iris-foe ↓ iris-t ↓ itu ↓ jab ↓ jug-r ↓ junc-e ↓ *Kali-ar* ↓ kali-bi kr1 *Kali-br* k* kali-c b2.de* kali-chl ↓ kali-cy ↓ kali-i ↓ kali-m ↓ kali-n ↓ kali-p *Kali-s* ↓ kali-sil k2 keroso ↓ kola stb3• kreos ↓ kres ↓ lac-ac ↓ lac-c k* lac-cp ↓ *Lac-d* ↓ lac-del hrn2• lac-e hrn2• lac-f ↓ *Lac-h* ↓ lac-leo ↓ *Lac-loxod-a* ↓ *Lac-lup* ↓ lac-mat ↓ **Lach** k* lachn kr1 lact ↓ lact-v ↓ lam ↓ lanth-met ↓ lap-la ↓ lappa ↓ lat-h ↓ lat-k ↓ lat-m bnm6• lath ↓ *Laur* ↓ lavand-a ↓ led k* lepi ↓ levo jl3 *Lil-t* ↓ limen-b-c ↓ limest-b es1• lina ↓ lith-c ↓ lith-f ↓ lith-p ↓ lith-s ↓ lob ↓ *Lol* sf1.de loxo-recl bnm10• luna ↓ *Lyc* k* *Lycpr* ↓ lycps-v ↓ *Lyss* m-ambo ↓ m-arct b2.de m-aust ↓ macro ↓ **Mag-c** ↓ mag-m k* *Mag-p* kr1 mag-s ↓ magn-gl ↓ magn-gr ↓ maias-l hrn2• malar ↓ *Manc* mrr1 mand ↓ mang ↓ mang-m ↓ mang-met ↓ mang-p ↓ mang-s ↓ marb-w ↓ med k* melal-alt ↓ meli ↓ meny j5.de meph ↓ *Merc* k* merc-act ↓ merc-c ↓ merc-d ↓ merc-i-f ↓ merc-i-r ↓ merl ↓ methys ↓ mez bg2 mill ↓ mim-p ↓ *Moni* ↓ morph a1 mosch bg2* mucs-nas ↓ mur-ac k* murx sf1.de musca-d ↓ myos-a ↓ myric ↓ nad ↓ *Naja* ↓ nat-act ↓ *Nat-ar* ↓ nat-c bg2 nat-f ↓ nat-hchls ↓ nat-m bg2 nat-n ↓ nat-ox ↓ nat-p nat-pyru rly4•

Delusions: ...
nat-s ↓ nat-sal bro1 *Nat-sil* ↓ *Neon* ↓ nep ↓ nept-m ↓ nicc ↓ nicc-met ↓ nicot ↓ *Nit-ac* k* nitro ↓ nitro-o ↓ nux-m bg2* *Nux-v* k* oci-sa ↓ *Oena* kr1 ol-j ↓ olib-sac ↓ *Olnd* ↓ onos ↓ *Op* k* orig kr1 (non:orig-v kr1) orot-ac rly4• osm-met ↓ ovi-p ↓ ox-ac a1 oxal-a ↓ oxyg ↓ oxyt ↓ ozone sde2• paeon ↓ **Pall** ↓ pant-ac rly4• par j5.de paraf ↓ paro-i ↓ passi sf1.de past a1 paull ↓ *Pegan-ha* ↓ pen ↓ pert-vc ↓ peti ↓ **Petr** k* petr-ra ↓ **Ph-ac** k* phasco-ci ↓ phel ↓ *Phos* k* *Phys* ↓ phyt ↓ pic-ac ↓ pieri-b ↓ pin-con ↓ pip-m ↓ pip-n ↓ plac ↓ plac-s ↓ plan ↓ *Plat* k* plat-m ↓ plb k* plb-m ↓ *Plut-n* ↓ pneu ↓ *Podo* ↓ polon-met ↓ polys ↓ pop ↓ *Positr* ↓ pot-e ↓ prim-v ↓ *Propr* ↓ prot ↓ prots-m ↓ pseuts-m ↓ psil jl3 *Psor* ptel ↓ *Puls* k* pycnop-sa ↓ pyrog br1* pyrus ↓ querc ↓ rad-br ↓ raja-s ↓ ran-b ↓ ran-s ↓ raph ↓ rat ↓ rauw ↓ rhen-met ↓ rheum bg2 rhod bg2 rhod ↓ rhodi-o-n ↓ *Rhus-g* ↓ rhus-r ↓ *Rhus-t* k* rob ↓ rosm ↓ russ a1 *Ruta* ↓ **Sabad** k* sabal ↓ sabin ↓ sacch ↓ sacch-a ↓ sacch-l ↓ sal-ac a1 sal-al ↓ *Sal-fr* ↓ sal-p ↓ samb k* *Sang* ↓ sanguis-s hrn2* sanic ↓ santin a1 sarr ↓ sars ↓ scop ↓ scroph-n ↓ *Sec* k* sel ↓ senec ↓ seneg b4a.de sep k* seq-s ↓ *Sil* k* sin-n ↓ sinus ↓ sol-ni ↓ sol-t-ae ↓ **Spect** ↓ **Spig** ↓ spira ↓ spong k* squil ↓ *Stach* ↓ stann k* *Staph* k* *Stict* ↓ **STRAM** k* streptoc ↓ stront-c ↓ stront-met ↓ stroph-h ↓ stry ↓ stry-p ↓ suis-em ↓ sul-ac ↓ sul-i ↓ sulfon br1 sulfonam jl3 **Sulph** k* sumb ↓ suprar rly4• *Symph* ↓ *Syph* ↓ tab ↓ tanac ↓ tant-met ↓ taosc ↓ tarax ↓ tarent tax ↓ tax-br ↓ tell ↓ tep ↓ ter ↓ tere-ch jl3 tere-la ↓ tet ↓ thal-met ↓ thal-xyz ↓ thea bro1 ther thiam ↓ thiop ↓ thres-a ↓ thuj k* thyr c1 til ↓ titan ↓ toxi ↓ trif-r ↓ trion bro1 tritic-vg fd5.de *Trom* ↓ tub hr1* tung-met ↓ tus-p ↓ ulm-c ↓ upa ↓ urol-h ↓ v-a-b ↓ *Valer* k* vanil fd5.de vario ↓ ven-m ↓ verat k* verat-v sf1.de verb k* verin a1 vero-o ↓ *Vesp* ↓ vib ↓ vichy-g ↓ vinc ↓ viol-o k* vip ↓ visc c1* vult-gr ↓ wies ↓ x-ray ↓ xan kr1 *Zinc* zinc-i ↓ zinc-m bro1 zinc-n ↓ zinc-o ↓ zinc-p ↓ *Zing* ↓ [arg-p stj2 cupr-p stj2 heroin sdj2 plb-p stj2]

- **day** and night: aeth j5.de ars j5.de kali-c j5.de
- **morning**: ambr ↓ bry j5.de con j5.de* dulc ↓ hell ↓ hep ↓ nat-c ↓
  - **bed**, in: ambr j5.de dulc j5.de hell j5.de hep j5.de nat-c j5.de
- **evening**: alum ↓ ambr ↓ bell ↓ bry j5.de *Calc* ↓ camph ↓ carb-an ↓ *Carb-v* ↓ carc ↓ chin ↓ falco-pe ↓ graph ↓ guaj ↓ ign ↓ lach j5.de lyc j5.de merc ↓ nat-c ↓ nit-ac ↓ nux-v ↓ ph-ac ↓ phos ↓ rhus-t ↓ spong ↓ sulph j5.de
  - **bed**, in: alum j5.de ambr j5.de *Calc* j5.de camph j5.de carb-an j5.de *Carb-v* j5.de carc mlr1• chin j5.de falco-pe nl2• graph j5.de ign j5.de merc j5.de nat-c j5.de nit-ac j5.de nux-v h1* ph-ac j5.de rhus-t j5.de sulph j5.de
  - **going** to sleep; on: bell j5.de bry j calc j5.de camph j chin j guaj j5.de ign j merc j nat-c j ph-ac j phos j5.de spong j sulph j
- **night**: *Acon* j5.de aeth j5.de am j5.de ars j5.de aur j5.de bac jl2 *Bell* h1* *Bry* h1* calc-ar k2 camph j5.de* cann-i a1 canth j5.de* carb-v j5.de carc mlr1• carl a1 cham j5.de chinin-ar coloc j5.de con j5.de dig j5.de *Dulc* j5.de falco-pe nl2• kali-c j5.de lyc j5.de meny j5.de *Merc* nit-ac j5.de nux-v j5.de op j5.de *Plb* j5.de *Puls* j5.de *Rheum* j5.de sec j5.de sep j5.de sol-ni a1 sulph j5.de tub br1 valer br1 vip j5.de zinc j5.de
  - **towards** morning:
    - **alternating** with | **sleep**; confused: ars a1
  - **children**; in: bac jl2
  - **sleeplessness**; with: carc mlr1•
- **above** it all, she is: aids nl2•
- **abroad**, being: verat vh*
- **absurd**, ludicrous: *(↗Antics; Foolish)* agath-a nl2• ambr ↓ arg-met ↓ camph ↓ cann-i caust ↓ cic ↓ cypra-eg ↓ op ↓ taosc iwa1• tarent ↓
  - **figures** are present: *(↗figures - seeing)* ambr arg-met camph cann-i caust cic cypra-eg sde6.de• op tarent
- **abundance** of everything, she has an: adam srj5• sulph h2
- **abused**, being: *(↗insulted)* *Bar-c* bro1* cocain br1* cur vml3• falco-pe nl2• hyos bro1* ign bro1* lyss kr1 pall bro1* petr-ra shn4• *Rhus-g* tmo3• *Staph* bro1* [berb stu1]
  - **mother** is abused; her: [berb stu1]
- **abyss**: alco ↓ calc ↓ carbn-s ↓ galla-q-r ↓ *Kali-c* ↓ ozone sde2• sulph ↓
  - **behind** him: *Kali-c* bg2*
  - **falling** down an abyss; fear of: alco a1 carbn-s c1
    - **others** would fall down an abyss, as they stand close to it: calc mrr sulph mrr
  - **standing** at the edge of an abyss, he is: galla-q-r nl2•
- **accidents**:
  - **fatal**; he will have a: maias-l hrn2•
- **accidents**: ...
  - **sees** accidents: anac j* ars j* bell j canth j hep j maias-l hrn2• nat-c j op j phos ↓
    - **relatives**; of: phos h2
  - **threatened** with an accident; he was: alum ↓ coli rly4• kali-i hr1
    - **fatal** accident: *(↗Fatalistic)* alum rb2
- **accused**, she is: *(↗criticized; thieves - accused; Admonition - agg.; Ailments - reproaches; Suspicious)* laur zinc [heroin sdj2 nicc stj1]
- **act** and yet cannot; must: *(↗do - unable)* pop rb2
- **activity**, with: *(↗Activity - desires)* *Bell Hyos Stram*
- **adolescent**; he was again an: androc srj1•
- **adrift**; being (= feels cut): phasco-ci rbp2
- **affection** of friends, has lost (See friend - affection; Forsaken; Forsaken - isolation; Insecurity; Sadness - friends)
- **afternoon**, it is always: lach stann
- **air**:
  - **cold** air; he were entering: tarent rb2
  - **go** into the air and busy himself; he must: anac rb2
  - **hovering** in the air (See floating - air)
  - **in** the air like a spirit; he were hovering (See floating - air - spirit)
  - **lighter** than air; he was (See body - lighter)
  - **stepped** on air (See step - air)
  - **suspended** in the air: sep rb2
  - **tremulous** motion; the air were in: sabad rb2
- **alarm**, of | **waking**, on: agn rb2
- **alien**, she is: limen-b-c hrn2•
- **alive**; something (See living things)
- **Aladdin** on his carpet: *Agath-a* nl2•
- **alone**, being: *(↗forsaken; Company - desire; Forsaken; Forsaken - isolation)* *Androc* ↓ bamb-a ↓ bit-ar wht1• camph ↓ carc ↓ chir-fl ↓ choc ↓ cycl ↓ cypra-eg ↓ *Dendr-pol* sk4• germ-met ↓ *Ham* ↓ hura ↓ *Kola* ↓ *Lac-h* ↓ lepi ↓ moni ↓ *Nat-sil* ↓ petr-ra ↓ phos ↓ *Phys* ↓ plac ↓ pseuts-m oss1• **Puls** ↓ rhus-t ↓ *Ruta* ↓ sal-al blc1• sep ↓ stram ↓ tax-br ↓ tritic-vg fd5.de vanil fd5.de [astat stj2 aur stj2 aur-m stj2 aur-s stj2 bar-br stj2 bar-i stj2 bar-met stj2 bism-sn stj2 caes-met stj2 cinnb stj2 hafn-met stj2 heroin sdj2 irid-met stj2 lanth-met stj2 merc stj2 merc-d stj2 osm-met stj2 plat stj2 plb stj2 plb-m stj2 plb-p stj2 polon-met stj2 rhen-met stj2 tant-met stj2 thal-met stj2 tung-met stj2]
  - **always** alone; she is: *(↗friendless; Forsaken)* carc fd2.de• chir-fl gya2 *Lac-h* sk4• *Nat-sil* fd3.de• petr-ra shn4• **Puls** k ● stram
  - **belong** to anyone; she did not: carc fd2.de• *Ham* fd3.de• *Nat-sil* fd3.de• puls rb2 *Ruta* fd4.de
  - **castaway**; being a: *(↗Forsaken)* cypra-eg sde6.de• germ-met srj *Phys* kr1
  - **dead** and still; and all about her were: rhus-t rb2
  - **graveyard**; alone in a: *(↗Forsaken)* lepi sep
  - **presence** of friends; in the: plac rzf5•
  - **wilderness**; alone in a: *(↗Forsaken)* stram k*
  - **world**; alone in the: *(↗Forsaken)* *Androc* srj1• bamb-a stb2.de• camph choc srj3• cycl k2* cypra-eg sde6.de• germ-met srj hura irid-met srj5• *Kola* stb3• lac-h sk4• moni rfm1• *Plat* k* pseuts-m sne *Puls* tax-br oss1• [heroin sdj2 phos stj1]
- **ancestors**:
  - **about**: positr nl2•
  - **one** with her ancestors; she is: positr nl2•
- **angels**, seeing: aether a1 cann-i a1 irid-met srj5• olib-sac wmh1 stram k2* [merc stj2 spect dfg1]
- **animals**: *(↗Biting)* absin adam ↓ aeth ail ↓ alum bg2 am-c bg2 am-m bg2 arn bg2 *Ars* k* aur aur-ar k2 aur-s k2 *Bell* k* *Calc* cham choc srj3• chord-umb rly4• *Cimic* k* cina colch con *Croc* ↓ *Crot-h* cycl ↓ dulc ↓ falco-pe ↓ ger-i ↓ germ-met ↓ *Hyos* k* *Kali-br* sne lac-c lac-lup hrn2• lach ↓ lyc bg2 lyss mag-m bg2 maias-l hrn2• med merc bg2 moni ↓ mosch bg2 musca-d ↓ nicc-met sk4• nux-v bg2 olib-sac ↓ **Op** k* phos bg2 *Plb* ↓ puls k* sal-fr sle1• sanguis-s hrn2• santin sec sil bg2 spect ↓ *Stram* k* sul-ac bg2 sulph k* tarent thuj valer verat bg2 zinc bg2 [arg-n stj2]
  - **abdomen**, are in: *Croc* vh* falco-pe nl2• *Thuj* k* [spect dfg1]

- **bed**:
  - **dancing** on the: con k*
  - **on**: ars j5.de* bell sne cimic hr1 colch k* *Plb* k* stram valer
  - **under** it: cham kr1*
- **being** an animal right through: choc srj3• lach rb2
- **black** animals; seeing: bell ↓ sal-fr nl2*• stram ↓
  - **walls** and furniture; seeing black animals on: bell stram vh
- **changing** shape: adam srj5•
- **corners**; coming out of: stram sf1.de
- **creeping**: ail ↓ bell ↓ cycl ↓ dulc ↓ lac-c stram ↓
  - **in** her: cycl a1 dulc fd4.de stram
  - **on** him: ail k2 dulc fd4.de
  - **shirt**; in: bell kr1
- **cup**, moving in a: hyos
- **dark** colored: bell k*
- **devoured** by:
  - **being**: maias-l hrn2• moni rfm1• *Stram* j5.de*
  - **had** been: *Hyos*
- **fierce**, with horns and bushy heads: *Bell* kr1
- **fire**, in the: bell k*
- **frightful**: *Bell* k* cham hr1* *Crot-h* hr1* olib-sac wmh1 *Op* k* *Stram* k* tarent k*
- **grotesque**: absin k*
- **hideous** (See ugly)
- **jumping**:
  - **bed**; on the (See bed - dancing)
  - **her**; jump at: *Merc* k1*
  - **out** of the ground: stram k*
- **large** animal is running over her whole body: cycl a1
- **lying** near her: valer kr1
- **objects**; are: hyos ptk1
- **passing** | **before** her: thuj
- **persons** are animals: *Aeth* ↓ bell vh *Calc* ↓ chord-umb rly4• *Cimic* ↓ hyos *Med* ↓ stram
  - **rats**, mice, insects etc.: *Aeth* bell *Calc* vh* *Cimic* *Med* stram
  - **unclean** animals: bell
- **she** is an animal: choc srj3• ger-i rly4• germ-met ↓ musca-d szs1
  - **wild** animal locked in; a: germ-met srj5•
- **starting** up: stram bg2
- **suckling**: choc srj
- **surrounded** by ugly animals: crot-h kr1* cycl tl1 plb tl1
- **ugly** (= hideous): *Crot-h* a2*

- **annihilation**; about to sink into: calc h2 cann-i carbn-h *Carc* fd2.de• moni rfm1•
- **answers** to any delusion: anh sp1 aster hr1*
- **ants**: hyos ↓ plb ↓ psil ft1
  - **bed** is full of ants: plb
  - **letters** are ants: hyos h1
- **anxious**: *Acon* j5.de *Anac* j5.de calc j5.de carb-v j5.de ign j5.de kali-br ↓ mag-c j5.de med st *Phos* j5.de *Puls* j5.de sep j5.de verat j5.de
  - **pregnancy**; during: kali-br tl1
- **apoplexy**:
  - **he** has an: arg-met k* carb-v h2*
  - **he** will have an (See Fear - apoplexy)
- **apparition**; he would see an: *(↗images; visions)* brom rb2 olib-sac wmh1
- **appreciated**, she is not: *(↗body - ugly; criticized; despised; insulted; neglected - he; persecuted - he; Ailments - appreciated; Confidence - want; Egotism; Flattered - desire; Forsaken; Haughty; Lamenting - appreciated; Longing - good; Respected - desire; Selfishness; Suspicious; Timidity)* acer-circ oss• *Aids* nl2• *Androc* srj1• arg-n gg arge-pl rwt5• aur gg caps kr1* *Carc* fd2.de*• *Ham* fd3.de• limest-b es1• musca-d szs1 *Pall* k* plat polys sk4• positr nl2• puls vh
- **appreciated**, she is not: ... pycnop-sa mrz1 rad-br sze8• seq-s bkh1 spong fd4.de sulph mp1* *Thuj* mrr1 tritic-vg fd5.de urol-h rwt• vanil fd5.de [helia stj heroin sdj2 oxyg stj tax jsj7]
- **approaches** and recedes; everything: cic rb2
- **argument**, making an eloquent: cann-i k*
- **arms**:
  - **belong** to her; arms do not: agar k* bapt st carc gk6* ign ptk1 op ptk1 symph fd3.de•
  - **bound** to her body; arms are: caj c1* cimic
  - **cut** off; arms are: bapt st
  - **four** arms; she has: adam srj5• sulfon vh*
  - **many** arms; she has too: pyrog ptk1
    - **legs**; and: *(↗crowded; legs - many - arms)* pyrog rb2*
  - **no** arms; he has: kola stb3•
  - **reach** the clouds | **sleep**; when going to: pic-ac
  - **separated** from body; are (See separated - body - arms)
  - **stiff**; arms were very: bamb-a stb2.de•
  - **three** arms; she has: petr
  - **wing**; left arm feels like a broken: haliae-lc srj5•
- **army** passed him in the street; a silent | **walking**; while: cann-i a1
- **arousing** (See awakening)
- **arrested**, is about to be: *(↗pursued - police; Fear - arrested; DREAMS - Arrested)* am ars *Bell* k* cupr germ-met srj5• kali-br meli k* plb ruta a1* tab c1* *Zinc* k*
- **asleep** (See sleeping)
- **assaulted**, is going to be: *(↗attacked; injury - about; Fear - injury - being; Suspicious)* abel jl3 androc srj1• maias-l hrn2• podo fd3.de• sacch-a fd2.de• tarent [tax jsj7]
- **assembled** things, swarms, crowds etc.: acon bg2 ambr bg2 anac bg2 ars bg2 bell bg2 bry bg2 cann-s bg cann-xyz bg2 con bg2 graph bg2 hell bg2 lyc bg2 merc bg2 nat-act bg2 op bg2 phos bg2 plb bg2 **Stram** bg2* sulph bg2 tab bg2
- **asylum**:
  - **mental** asylum; sent to: lach k2
  - **she** will be sent to: cench lach k13
- **atmosphere**:
  - **beautiful** (See beautiful - atmosphere)
  - **heavy** and thick; atmosphere in room were: agn rb2
  - **warm** atmosphere:
    - **entering** a warm atmosphere when eating; he was: puls rb2
    - **in** a; he was: puls rb2
- **attacked**; being: *(↗assaulted)* arizon-l nl2• crot-c sk4• granit-m es1• lac-leo sk4• lyss kr1 polys sk4• positr nl2• [bell-p-sp dcm1]
  - **women**, by: positr nl2•
- **auditory** (See hearing)
- **authority** | **work**; in his: rhus-g tmo3•
- **awake** | **night**; he has been awake all: puls rb2
- **awakened**; he is:
  - **fright** or alarm; awakened in: agn rb2 bell rb2
  - **just** been awakened; he has: cic ↓ cycl rb2 irid-met srj5• mang rb2
    - **fever**; from: cic rb2
  - **someone** were trying to awake him: carb-v ↓ cur rb2
    - **dream**; from a: carb-v rb2
- **awakening**; he is: *(↗waking)*
  - **himself**:
    - **dream**; from a: carb-v rb2
    - **sleep**; from a heavy: rheum rb2
  - **never** get awake; she would: ang rb2
- **babies**:
  - **helpless** as a baby in a cradle; she is as: aids nl2•
  - **odious**; baby looks: *Puls* kr1*
  - **two** babies are in bed: petr
- **back**:
  - **loosened**; back is: bamb-a stb2.de•
  - **opens** and wings are forming: choc srj

- packed in streaks of fog; back is: bamb-a stb2.de•
- bad:
  - **temper**; he is in a bad: zinc rb2
  - **triumphs** over good because good is not good enough: dioxi rbp6
- balancing:
  - **bridge**; as if balancing over water when crossing a: ferr rb2
  - **head** (See head - balance)
  - **himself** to and fro; as if balancing: ferr rb2 gard-j vlr2•
- **ball**, he is sitting on a (See RECTUM - Lump)
- **banished**; she is: galla-q-r nl2•
- **barriers**: (*↗curtain)*
  - **oneself**; being not in touch with: polys sk4•
  - **removed** between himself and others; are: aids nl2•
  - **things** around; between oneself and (See separated - world - he)
- **bats**, of: bell j5.de
- **beads** | **she** was one of a long string of beads suspended in space: galla-q-r nl2•
- **bear**:
  - **feet**, he has bear's: positr nl2•
  - **seeing** bears: positr nl2• sal-fr ↓
    - **chains**, sees a black bear in: sal-fr sle1•
  - **walking** behind him; bear: plut-n srj7•
- **beaten**, he is being: bry j5.de elaps sal-fr sle1•
- **beautiful**: *(↗visions - beautiful)* aids ↓ anh sp1 bell k* *Cann-i* k* coca coff ↓ coff-t ↓ dat-a ↓ eug ↓ germ-met ↓ hippoc-k ↓ hydrog ↓ irid-met ↓ lac-del ↓ *Lach* musca-d ↓ neon ↓ olib-sac ↓ olnd ↓ op mp1• petr-ra shn4• plac ↓ positr nl2• psil ↓ *Sulph* k* tab ↓ taosc iwa1•
  - **atmosphere**, in: dat-a a1 plac ↓
    - **himself** in a beautiful atmosphere; he finds: plac rzf5•
  - **kitsch** is beautiful: olib-sac wmh1
  - **landscape**; of: (non:coff k2*) coff-t slp irid-met srj5• *Lach* olib-sac wmh1 petr-ra shn4•
  - **old** ragged woman seemed beautiful: psil ft1
  - **people** look: positr nl2•
  - **rags** seem, even: *Sulph* k*
  - **she** is beautiful and wants to be: stram st
  - **things** look: bell bg2 eug a1* germ-met srj hippoc-k szs2 hydrog srj2• lac-del hrn2• musca-d szs1 neon srj5• olnd bg2 plac rzf5• positr nl2• sulph h2* tab bg2 taosc iwa1•
  - **urination**; all things seem beautiful after: eug
  - **visions** (See visions - beautiful)
  - **youth**, beauty, love and peace: aids nl2•
- **bed**:
  - **bouncing** her bed up and down; someone is: bell canth
  - **bound** to the bed by suction: sars rb2
  - **covered** the whole bed; she: pyrog rb2*
  - **creases**; bed is full of: *Stram* kr1
  - **drawn** from under her: ars ↓ stram k*
    - **alighted** on the floor; and she had: ars rb2
  - **falling**: *(↗SLEEP - Falling - falling)*
    - **on** her: stram rb2
    - **out** of bed: arg-met ↓ arg-n bg2* ars bg2* ars-s-f kr1* crot-c bg2*
      - **head** were falling out of bed: *(↗head - fall - bed)* arg-met rb2*
    - **through** the bed: *(↗SLEEP - Falling - falling)* bell rb2 benzol br1 chinin-s rb2 dulc rb2 lach rb2 rhus-t rb2 sacch rb2 sec rb2
      - **floor**; and: benzol c1*
  - **floating**; is (See floating - bed - is)
  - **forced** him out of the bed; as if something: rhus-t k*
  - **hard**, too (See GENERALS - Hard)
  - **headboard** was swaying: lac-c kr1

- **bed**: ...
  - **large** enough; bed were not (See small)
  - **lumps** in bed: arn ptk1 mag-c ptk1
  - **lying** on his bed; he is not: asar nh hyper ↓ stict nh valer nh
    - **waking**; on | **4** h; at: hyper
  - **motion**, in: clem rb2 lac-c k*
  - **naked** man is wrapped in the bedclothes with her: *Puls* k*
  - **noise**; something under her bed were making a: *(↗someone - under - knocking; Fear - waking - under)* bell h1* calc bg2 canth bg2 colch bg2
    - **knocking**; as if someone were (See someone - under - knocking)
  - **occupied** (See someone - in)
  - **old** ragged woman; is: psil ft
  - **out** of bed; as if forced (See forced)
  - **raised**; is: canth
  - **sinking**:
    - **bed** is sinking: bapt bro1* *Bell* k* *Benz-ac* bro1 bry k* calc-p k* chinin-s k* dulc kali-c k* *Lach* k* lyc ptk1 plb st rhus-t k* sacch sec rb2
      - **closing** the eyes; on: sec rb2
    - **everything** is sinking down in bed: lyc rb2 sacch-a fd2.de•
    - **patient** were sinking down; bed and: lach rb2
    - **she** is sinking:
      - **down** deep in bed: bry rb2 xan rb2
      - **through** the bed: bell rb2 chinin-s rb2 dulc rb2 lach rb2 rhus-t rb2
      - **with** the bed: lach rb2
  - **small**; too: germ-met srj5• sulph rb2*
  - **sold** his bed; someone has: nux-v
  - **someone**:
    - **comes** near his bed; as if someone: carb-v j5.de
    - **gets** into his bed and there is no more room: nux-v
    - **in** the bed; as if someone is: anac ↓ apis ↓ *Bapt* ↓ carb-v ↓ cycl ↓ graph ↓ nux-v ↓ op ↓ petr bro1 *Puls* ↓ rhus-t ↓ ruta ↓ samb xxb1 sec ↓ stram ↓ valer ↓
      - **two** persons lay in the bed; as if | **overlapped** hers by half; and the body of the other: cycl rb2
      - **with** him: anac apis *Bapt* carb-v graph sf1.de nux-v op petr k* *Puls* rhus-t ruta fd4.de sec stram k* valer k*
        - **strange** boy; a: apis rb2
    - **menacing**, is standing at the foot of the bed; someone who is: chlol
    - **over** the bed; someone is: calc
    - **take** away the bedclothes; someone tries to: bell
    - **under** the bed; someone is: *(↗enemy - bed; thieves - house - bed; Fear - waking - under)* am-m ars k* **Bell** k● calc canth colch
      - **knocking**: *(↗noise)* **Bell** j5.de* calc k* canth k* colch bg2
  - **strange** objects, rats, sheep in the bed: cimic kr1
  - **surrounded** by devils; is: op j
  - **swaying**; bed is:
    - **back** and forth: zinc rb2
    - **side** to side; from | **hammock**; like a: tub rb2
  - **swimming** (See floating - bed - swimming)
  - **tipping** over; is: ars tl1
  - **touch** the bed when lying; as if she did not: *(↗Floating - bed - swimming; VERTIGO - Lying - Agg. - touch)* asar rb2 chin rb2 coff rb2 lac-c br1* nat-m rb2 nux-v rb2 op rb2 ph-ac rb2 rhus-t rb2 spig rb2 stict rb2 stram rb2 thuj rb2*
    - **floating**; and body and limbs were: stict rb2
  - **trembling**; is: kola stb3•
  - **turned**:
    - **about**: nux-v rb2 plb rb2 puls rb2 sin-n rb2
    - **circle**; bed turned in a: con rb2 sol-ni rb2
  - **two** persons in bed with her: cycl petr vh
  - **warm** | **hot**; sensation as if bed is: op ptk2*
  - **whirling** around with her: nux-v rb2

- • **yard**; looks for it in | **pregnancy**; during: puls kr1
- bees; sees: puls
- **beetles**, worms etc.: ars bell dulc fd4.de hyos k2 kres mg1.de* nep jl *Stram*
- **behind** him; that someone is (See people - behind)
- **bells**; hears ringing of: *(↗hearing - illusions)* aether↓ ars h2* cann-i k* kres mg1.de* med gg neon↓ petr-ra↓ ph-ac k* thea valer a1 verat gg
  - • **door** bell: *(↗hearing - illusions)* neon srj petr-ra shn4• thea
  - • **funeral**, his: *(↗dead - he - funeral)* aether
  - • **sweet** toned bells; numberless: cann-i k*
- **belong** here; does not (See Estranged - family; Forsaken)
- **belong** to her own family; she does not: *(↗Estranged - family; Forsaken)* lac-lup hrn2• *Plat*
- **bend**; she cannot: positr nl2•
- **beside** oneself; being | **trifles**; with: carl rb2
- **betrayed**; that she is: *(↗deceived; Ailments - friendship)* adam srj5• dros mtf33 falco-pe nl2• hydrog srj2*• lac-h sze9• petr-ra shn4• rad-br sze8• *Rhus-g* tmo3• urol-h rwt• [heroin sdj2 spect dfg1]
- **betrothal** must be broken: fl-ac k* sal-fr sle1•
- **better** than others; he is: *(↗great; Deeds - great; Haughty)* cic ptk1* germ-met srj5• granit-m es• kola stb3• myric plat mp1•
- **bewildered**; he is: xan rb2
- **bewitched**, he is: *(↗charmed)* cann-i loxo-recl knl4• rhus-t mtf
- **bier**, is lying on a: anac k* cann-i
- **bird**:
  - • **being** a bird; he runs about chirping and twittering until he faints, as if: lyss kr1
  - • **high** as a bird, he is: falco-pe nl2•
  - • **picking** feathers from a bird; he is: hyos
  - • **seeing** birds: bell haliae-lc↓ irid-met srj5• kali-c lac-c nicc-met sk4• thres-a sze7•
    - ⁝ **eagles**: haliae-lc srj5•
- **biting** | **head** off; as if he was trying to bite her: galeoc-c-h gms1•
- **bitten**, will be: *Hyos* j5.de stram bg2
- **black**:
  - • **gods**: sanguis-s hrn2•
  - • **objects** and people, sees: *Bell* j5.de falco-pe nl2• op j puls j5.de stram k* tarent gg [plat stj2]
  - • **she** is: sulph h2*
- **blanket**, under a thick: galla-q-r nl2•
- **blessed** state; she is in a: positr nl2•
- **blind**; he is: *(↗Blindness)* bell h1 hyos j mosch stram j verat
- **blood**:
  - • **ceased** to flow | **vertigo**; during: seneg rb2
  - • **circulate** well; blood does not: *Atro* a1*
  - • **pouring** out of mouth: choc srj
  - • **rushed** through like roar of many waters: alumn k2* cann-i k*
- **blown** at; of being: lyss kr1
- **board**; as if lying on a (See BACK - Board)
- **boat**:
  - • **founder**, his boat will: aids nl2•
  - • **owns** a boat; he/ she: limest-b es1•
- **body**: *(↗Schizophrenia - paranoid)*
  - • **above**: ara-maca sej7•
  - • **absent**; is: cocain ptk1 germ-met srj ozone sde2•
  - • **adherent** to a woolen bag; is:
    - ⁝ **night** | **half** awake; while: coc-c
  - • **alive** on one side of the body and buried on the other (See side - alive)
  - • **black**, it is: sulph k*
  - • **brittle**, is: *(↗delicate; thin; emaciation; glass - she; Insanity - touched; Touched - aversion)* des-ac↓ falco-pe nl2• gard-j vlr2• ign bg2 lac-leo sk4• nux-v bg2 sars bg* seq-s bkh1 stram mrr1 *Thuj* k* [tax jsj7]
    - ⁝ **afternoon**: gard-j vlr2•
    - ⁝ **break** in two; will: des-ac rbp6

- **body**: ...
  - • **broad**: lac-lup hrn2•
  - • **brown**; spotted (See spotted)
  - • **continuity** of body would be dissolved: thuj rb2*
  - • **covers**:
    - ⁝ **bed**; covers the whole: pyrog k*
    - ⁝ **earth**; covers the whole: cann-i
  - • **cut** through; he is: *(↗Cut; Cut - others)* *Bell*↓ *Stram* thuj↓ [plat stj2]
    - ⁝ **two**; in: *(↗divided; Confusion - identity - duality; Cut; Cut - others)* *Bell* vh* plat stram vh*
  - • **dashed** to pieces, being: calc a1
  - • **deformed**, some part is: acon vh* **Sabad** a1*
  - • **delicate**, is: *(↗brittle)* *Thuj* k*
  - • **diffused** (See enlarged - body)
  - • **diminished**; is: *(↗small - things - appear; Size - incorrect)* agar carc fd2.de• falco-pe nl2•
    - ⁝ **left** side of body is smaller: *(↗half - right; half - right - bigger)* cinnm k* limest-b es1•
  - • **disintegrating**: *Lach* a1 marb-w es1•
  - • **divided**, is: *(↗cut - two; half; threefold; divided - two; head - separated; place - two; side - alive; Confusion - identity; Confusion - identity - duality)* *Agath-a* nl2• cann-i choc srj3• lil-t a1 olib-sac wmh1 *Petr* ruta fd4.de sil *Stram* j5.de
  - • **dragging** down; is: [spect dfg1]
  - • **dry**, is: positr nl2•
  - • **elongated**: plut-n srj7•
  - • **enlarged**; body is (See enlarged - body)
  - • **expanded** (See enlarged - body)
  - • **fibre** in her right side, feels every: nux-v st1 sep k*
  - • **forehead** was pulled into a peak like a helmet worn in a joust: agath-a nl2•
  - • **greatness** of, as to: *(↗great; tall; tall - he; Haughty)* *Cann-i* *Coca* vh* *Hell* vh* *Plat* staph taosc iwa1•
  - • **half**: *(↗divided; Confusion - identity - duality)*
    - ⁝ **right** half: *(↗diminished - left)*
      - : **bigger** than left half; is: *(↗diminished - left)* adam srj5•
      - : **have** a right half; she does not: galla-q-r nl2•
    - ⁝ **left** half | **belong** to her; does not: sil k*
  - • **headless**; is (See head - no)
  - • **heavy** and thick; body has become: *(↗Heaviness)* nat-c a1 positr nl2•
  - • **hollow**; body is (See hollow - body)
  - • **immaterial**, is: anh sp1 thuj sp1
  - • **immovable**, parts of body are: asar vh
  - • **imperfect** (See ugly)
  - • **inner** structure; sees the completeness of its: positr nl2•
  - • **internal** tissues; she sees the: neon srj5•
  - • **jelly**; made of (See jelly)
  - • **lighter** than air; body is: *(↗floating - air; floating - air - spirit; flying; light [=low - is)* agn↓] asarjl galla-q-r nl2• gels↓ ignis-alc es2• irid-met srj5• lac-loxod-a hrn2• lac-lup hrn2• lach limest-b es1• olib-sac wmh1 *Op* psil ft1 sanguis-s hrn2• thuj k* visc jl xan c1
    - ⁝ **embrace**, after: agn a
    - ⁝ **hysteria**; in: gels ptk1
    - ⁝ **masturbation**; from: gels ptk1
  - • **no** body; he had: psor rb2
  - • **one** with his body; is: positr nl2•
    - ⁝ **world**; and at odds with the: positr nl2•
  - • **out** of the body: *(↗Depersonalization; Merging; DREAMS - Lifted)* agar mtf agath-a↓ alum vh5 *Anh* mtf ara-maca sej7• arge-pl rwt5• bit-ar wht1• *Cann-i* mrr1 carneg-g rwt1• clem-vit rcb4• cypra-eg sde6.de• falco-pe nl2• galeoc-c-h gms1• *Hydrog* srj2• lac-c↓ lac-lup hrn2• nux-m mtf *Op* mtf phos mrr1 *Plut-n* srj7• pyrus↓ [lac-mat sst4]

- **out** of the body: ...
  - **crazy** if she could not get out of her body; she would become: lac-c rb2
  - **enjoy** to provoke out of body experiences: agar vh1
  - **lying** in bed; when: plut-n srj7•
  - **observe** herself, can: agath-a nl2• carneg-g rwt1• cypra-eg sde6.de• pyrus a1*
  - **second** self outside of patient (See double - being - outside)
  - **someone** else saw or spoke outside: alum a1 galeoc-c-h gms1•
- **parts**:
  - **absent**; parts of body are: cot br1 dream-p sdj1• ignis-alc es2• ozone sde2• stram br1
    - **muscle**; only feels a thin: ozone sde2•
  - **separated**; are: bapt br1 daph br1
  - **shrunken** (See diminished - shrunken)
  - **taken** away; parts of body have been: *Bapt* st* daph st*
  - **thick**; are: acon br1
- **pieces**:
  - **coming** in pieces; body is in danger of: thuj a1*
  - **falling** to pieces; body is: gard-j vlr2• *Lac-c* bg2* xan rb2
    - **rage**; after: gard-j vlr2•
  - **relief** to fall to pieces; it would be a great | **kept** herself together; only by great effort she: sacch-l rb2
  - **torn** to pieces: positr nl2•
    - **two** pieces: positr nl2•
  - **were** in several pieces; he:
    - **afternoon**: gard-j vlr2•
    - **adjusted**; and could not get them: phos rb2
- **putrefy**, will: *(↗Fear - putrefy)* *Ars* bell
- **rags**; body torn into: phyt ptk1 plat ckh1
- **scattered** about; body was: *Bapt* hr1* caj ↓ coca-c ↓ daph bro1 *Petr* bro1 phos bro1 pyrog k13 stram bro1
  - **bed**; in the: bapt br1*
  - **tossed** about to get the pieces together; he: *Bapt* k* caj br1 coca-c sk4• daph st petr *Phos* pyrog k2*
- **seize** up and turn to stone; will: positr nl2•
- **separated** (See separated - body - mind)
- **shapeless**, is: galla-q-r nl2•
- **shrunken**, like the dead; body is: *Sabad*
- **sink** down between the thighs; body will: bell
- **spotted** brown, is: bell k*
- **state** of his body, to the erroneous: cypra-eg sde6.de• *Haliae-lc* srj5• lac-lup hrn2• positr nl2• pyrog k2 **Sabad** k* stram k2 thiam rly4•
- **stone**, is: positr nl2•
  - **stony** tomb: positr nl2•
- **sweets**, is made of: merc k*
- **thick**, is: nat-c h2
- **thin**; is: *(↗brittle)* limest-b es• thuj k* [spect dfg1]
- **threads**; body inside is made of: nux-v a1
- **threefold**, has a: *(↗divided; Confusion - identity - duality)* ars petr
- **together**; is stronger and more: aids nl2•
- **ugly**; body looks: *(↗appreciated; wretched; Confidence - want - self-depreciation; Disgust - body; Reproaching oneself; Wretched - body)* *Acer-circ* ↓ bar-c vh bry ptk1 bufo ptk1 *Cham* ptk1 cina ptk1 falco-pe nl2• haliae-lc srj5• lac-h ↓ loxo-recl knl4• melal-alt gya4 *Nux-v* ptk1 positr nl2• pycnop-sa mrz1 *Thuj* mrr1 tub al [calc-s stj1 heroin sdj2]
  - **fat**; too: *Acer-circ* oss• lac-h sze9•
- **vibrating**: vero-o rly3•
- **withering**, is (See withering)
- **wrapped**: cact ptk2

- **bomb** | **exploded**; has just: plut-n srj7•
- **bones** | **fragments** and cannot fit pieces together; in: phos kr1
- **boots**; seeing black: falco-pe nl2•
- **born** into the world; he was newly: cor-r ↓ cori-r a1 ignis-alc ↓ irid-met ↓ lac-h sze9• olib-sac wmh1 plut-n srj7• spect ↓ symph fd3.de•
  - **wonder** at the novelty of his surroundings; and was overwhelmed with: (non:cor-r k1) cori-r k1 ignis-alc es2• irid-met srj5• [spect dfg1]
- **bottle**:
  - **ninety**-four colored bottles; of: plut-n srj7•
  - **soda** water; he is a bottle of: *Arg-n* k* cann-i ↓
    - **running** to and fro: cann-i a1*
- **boundaries** | **soft** and diffuse (See Confusion - identity - boundaries)
- **brain**:
  - **absent** | **clarity** because of this; and has great: ignis-alc es2•
  - **balanced** on a slight point and was likely to be turned over; brain were: camph rb2
  - **confused**; brain were: coca rb2
  - **cracking**; brain is: nux-m st*
  - **dissolving** and she were going crazy; brain were: calc rb2
  - **dry** and compressed, is: cypra-eg sde6.de• sal-fr sle1•
  - **far** from skull; as if too (See space - between)
  - **fog** in brain; there is: galeoc-c-h gms1• rhod b4a.de sulph rb2
  - **glass**; made of: *Dig* hr1
  - **half** of his brain; has only the left: positr nl2•
  - **hard**; brain is: mez h2
  - **intoxicated**; brain is | **blood**; by degraded: crot-h rb2
  - **loose**; brain is (See HEAD - Looseness)
  - **lump** in the left side of his brain, there is a heavy: aids nl2•
  - **moving**; brain is: aids nl2• ars tl1 cycl rb2* sulph tl1
    - **vertigo**; with: cycl bg2
  - **muddled**; brain is (See confused)
  - **rearranging** itself: aids nl2•
  - **round** and round; brain seemed to go: sabad rb2
  - **skull**; brain is smaller than (See HEAD - Smaller - brain)
  - **smoke** on brain: op rb2
  - **soft**: lavand-a ctl1•
  - **softening**: *(↗Fear - brain)* abrot k* *Arg-n* hr1* cann-i k1 crot-h br1
  - **stomach**; has brain in: acon bro1
  - **swashing**; brain is | **walking**; when: spig rb2
  - **swimming**; brain is: sol-ni rb2
  - **tightening**: asaf tl1 sulph tl1 visc c1
  - **turning** around; were: bry rb2 sabad rb2
  - **wavering**; brain were: aids nl2• nux-v ↓ phos rb2 phys ↓ sul-ac rb2
    - **revolving**; and: nux-v rb2
    - **walking**; when: phys rb2
  - **whirled** round and round; brain: cimic tl1 sabad rb2
  - **wobble**; brain seems to: ars rb2 cycl ↓ spira ↓
    - **to** and fro: cycl rb2 spira rb2
- **brandy**; he had taken: puls rb2
- **break**:
  - **she** would break:
    - **down**: arg-met rb2
    - **lay** too long in one position; if she: pyrog rb2
- **breaking** in; someone is (See thieves - house)
- **breathe**:
  - **cannot** breathe: hippoc-k szs2
  - **water**; can breathe under: hippoc-k szs2
- **brittle**; he is (See body - brittle)
- **broad**; things are: lac-lup hrn2•
- **bubbles**:
  - **blood**; sensation as if bubbles in: ara-maca sej7•
  - **seeing** bubbles: *Aids* nl2•
    - **popping** up: *Aids* nl2•

- **seeing** bubbles: ...
  - ⁝ **rising** to the surface: aids nl2•
- **bugs** and cockroaches; of: *(↗cockroaches; insects)* kres mg stram kr1 [alum stj2]
- **bugs**; sees: ars↓ choc↓ *Cocain* br1 sanguis-s↓
  - **bed**; crawling over: ars tl1
  - **page** when writing; crawling down the: choc srj3•
  - **small**, black bugs running across the floor; hundreds of: sanguis-s hrn2•
- **building** stones, appearance of: positr nl2• thuj k*
- **bulls**, of: bell j5.de
- **buried** | **snow**; under: sal-fr sle1•
- **burn**; desire to: lac-lup hrn2•
- **business**:
  - **accomplished**; business could never be: med rb2
  - **doing** business; is: *(↗Avarice; Industrious)* bell *Bry* canth cupr *Phos Rhus-t* sf1.de
  - **occupied** about business: *Bry* bro1 op bro1
  - **ordinary**, they are pursuing: *(↗Industrious)* ars atro bell plb stram
  - **success**; is a: phos h2
  - **unfit** for, he is: *(↗succeed; Confidence - want; Fear - failure; Succeeds; Timidity)* *Croc* sacch-a fd2.de•
- **butterflies**, of: bell k* cann-i k* chir-fl gya2 cupr glon melal-alt gya4 rhus-g tmo3•
- **buzzing**; everything seems to be: bit-ar wht1•
- **caged**: dendr-pol sk4• thres-a sze7•
- **calls**:
  - **absent** persons, for: hyos k*
  - **him**; someone calls (See someone)
  - **someone** calls: anac ant-c k* ars↓ bell bg2* cann-i k* dros dulc↓ hyos gg kali-c k* med pc* plat j* *Plb* k* rhod kr1 rhus-t↓ rosm lgb1 ruta j5.de *Sep* kr1 stram gg sulph kr1* taosc iwa1• thuj k* verat gg
    - ⁝ **absent** mother or sister call his name: anac h2*
    - ⁝ **sleep**; someone calls him during: **Sep** ●*
    - ⁝ **waking**; on: ant-c ars bell bg1* dulc h2 rhod ptk2 rhus-t
- **cancer**, has a: *(↗disease - incurable)* carc mlr1• ruta fd4.de sabad br1 verat k* [spect dfg1]
- **car** stands still, although driving fast: ozone sde2•
- **caressed** on head by someone: *(↗touched - head)* *Med* vh*
- **carousal**; as if after a: *(↗debauch)* mez a1 phys rb2
- **carriages** | **splendid** carriages; seeing: carbn-s a1
- **carried** somewhere and conversed with another person; she was: raph rb2
- **castles** and palaces; sees: plb
- **casualties**; sees (See accidents - sees)
- **catches**:
  - **imaginary** appearance; at: *Hyos* j5.de* **Stram** j5.de*
  - **people**, at: stram j5.de
- **cathedral**; he is in a: cann-i↓ olib-sac wmh1
  - **choirs**; on hearing: cann-i
- **cats**:
  - **he** is a cat: marb-w es1•
    - ⁝ **kitten**; he is a newly born: marb-w es1•
  - **sees**: absin *Aeth* k* arn *Bell Calc* daph hyos mosch gt op vh* positr nl2• puls k* *Stram* k*
    - ⁝ **black**: bell puls
- **caught**; he will be: *(↗Suspicious)* bell germ-met srj5•
- **cellar**: | **shut** in a dark cellar; he is: nat-p rb2
- **centipedes**: atro kr1
- **chair**:
  - **jumps** away like a hare: kola stb3•
  - **repairing** old chairs; he is: cupr cupr-act a1
  - **rising** up; chair is: phos
  - **something** hanging over a chair were a person (See person - something)
  - **standing** in middle of bed; chair were: thuj rb2
- **changeable**: hyos bg2
- **changed**; everything is: *(↗strange - everything; Strange - everything)* aids↓ *Arg-n* k* bar-m carb-an nad rly4• *Nux-m* bg1* *Plat* k* positr nl2• stram kr1
  - **growing** and transforming: aids nl2•
  - **home**; at (See home - changed)
- **changelings** and will leap up and attack her; her children are (See child - not - attack)
- **changing** suddenly: cann-i k* hyos bg psil ft1
- **charmed** and cannot break the spell: *(↗bewitched)* *Lach* kr1*
- **cheated**; being: rhus-g tmo3•
- **cherries**, sees: santin a1
- **child**:
  - **drive** children out of the house; he must: fl-ac
  - **he** is a child: *(↗teenager; Childish)* agath-a nl2• aids nl2• arizon-l nl2• *Cic* k* plut-n↓ symph fd3.de• vanil fd5.de
    - ⁝ **acts** like a child; and: *Cic* k2* plut-n srj7• symph fd3.de•
    - ⁝ **vulnerable**; and: *(↗injury - about)* aids nl2•
  - **not** hers; child is: anac k* falco-pe↓ nit-ac yl
    - ⁝ **attack** her; her children are changelings and will leap up and: falco-pe nl2•
  - **nursing** her child (See nursing)
  - **wish** and need for another child: plac rzf5•
- **childish** fantasies, has: lyc olib-sac wmh1
- **chill**; during: bell bg2 bry bg2 kali-c bg2 op bg2 phos bg2 rhus-t bg2 sulph bg2
- **chin**:
  - **divided** horizontally by a line; sensation as if: gard-j vlr2•
  - **long**; is too: glon
- **choir**; he is in a cathedral on hearing music of a: *(↗hearing - illusions)* cann-i
- **choked**:
  - **forms**; being choked by: phos bg2
  - **he** is about to be: cann-i↓ ozone sde2• phos↓ *Plat*↓
    - ⁝ **night** | **waking**; on: cann-i phos j5.de* *Plat* gl1.fr•
  - **ice**-cold hands, by: canth
- **Christ**, himself to be: *(↗divine; great)* cann-i **Verat** k2* [plb stj2]
- **churchyard**:
  - **dancing** in, he is: cic a1 stram
  - **visits** a: anac arn *Bell* stram k*
- **ciphers**, sees (See VISION - Ciphers)
- **clairvoyant**; she is: pyrus a
- **clear**, everything is too: aids nl2• ambr j5.de dream-p sdj1•
- **climbing** up: hyos bg2
- **clock** strike; he hears the: *(↗hearing - illusions)* ph-ac
- **closing** eyes; on: anh mg* *Calc* h2* led h1* spong h1
- **clothes**:
  - **beautiful**; clothes are: aeth olib-sac wmh1 **Sulph** k ●
  - **fit**; did not: verat-v a
  - **fly** away and become wandering stars; clothes will: | **undressing**; on: cann-i
  - **heavy**; too (See GENERALS - Clothes - heavy)
  - **near** them; cannot get clothes though: caj rb2
  - **rags**; is clad in: *Cann-i*
  - **tight**; too (See GENERALS - Clothes - tight)
  - **uncomfortable**: spong c1
  - **wearing** clothes; not (See naked)
  - **wet**; are (See GENERALS - Clothes - wet)
- **clouds**:
  - **being** a cloud: aids nl2•
  - **black** cloud enveloped her; a heavy: *(↗Sadness - cloud)* *Adam* srj5• arg-n bro1* *Cimic* k* dendr-pol sk4• galla-q-r nl2• irid-met srj5• *Lac-c* bro1 melal-alt gya4 plut-n srj7• puls bro1 sal-fr sle1•
  - **head** were confused by a cloud: crot-t rb2 melal-alt gya4 pert-vc↓
    - ⁝ **sun**; after exposure to: pert-vc vk9
  - **ideas** were floating in clouds: dat-a rb2

- • **reach** the clouds; he seems to: irid-met srj5• pic-ac ↓
  - ⁝ **arms**, face, tongue and forepart of brain seem to reach to the clouds: pic-ac rb2
- • **rocks**; looking over clouds and: mag-m
- • **sees**: aids nl2• hep mag-m rhus-t
  - ⁝ **billowy**: aids nl2•
- • **strange** clouds settle upon patients or dance about the sun: cann-i

- **cobwebs**; seeing: galla-q-r nl2•
- **cockroaches** swarmed about the room: *(↗bugs; insects)* bell kres mg stram kr1
- **collect** senses; unable to: cham rb2 hyos rb2
- **colors** are muted: hippoc-k szs2
- **comfortable** while sitting on something hard; that he is: psil ft1
- **commander**; being a: *(↗general; officer)* cann-i a1 cupr bg2
- **companions**:
  - • **are** half men, half plants: cann-i
  - • **youth**; is with companions of his: aether
- **company**; people are averse to her (See appreciated; outcast)
- **compelled** to do certain things; he is (See Thoughts - compelling)
- **complaints** amel. by a single, very deep breath: *(↗GENERALS - Breathing - deep - amel.)* caps h1
- **confidence** in him; his friends have lost all: *(↗Confidence - want; Foolish; Forsaken; Succeeds; Timidity)* aur hura
- **confused**; as if: *(↗criticized; Ailments - reproaches)* sul-ac ↓ sulph ↓ tub rb2 verat-v rb2
  - • **sleep**; from insufficient: sulph rb2
  - • **smoke** in head caused confusion: sul-ac rb2
- **confusion**; others will observe her: *(↗criticized; Admonition - agg.; Ailments - reproaches; Confidence - want; Fear - observed; Suspicious; Timidity)* *Calc* k* choc srj3• limest-b es1• sal-fr sle1•
- **connected**; being (See Unification - sensation)
- **conscience**; as if he had a bad (See wrong - done; Anxiety - conscience)
- **consciousness**:
  - • **belongs** to another: *(↗identity; Confusion - identity)* *Alum* k*
  - • **higher** consciousness; unification with: hydrog srj2• podo fd3.de•
  - • **lose** consciousness; he would: brom rb2 calc rb2 camph rb2 dig rb2 dios rb2 mag-m rb2 oxyt rb2 plat rb2 taosc iwa1• thea rb2 [spect dfg1]
    - ⁝ **confusion**; after: syph rb2
    - ⁝ **lying** down; on: agar rb2
    - ⁝ **momentarily**; he had lost consciousness: lyss rb2
    - ⁝ **vertigo**; during: nat-n rb2
  - • **outside** of his body; his consciousness were: alum b4a.de*
- **conspiracies**:
  - • **against** her father; the landlord's bills are conspiracies: kali-br k*
  - • **against** him; there are conspiracies: ars k* kali-br hl1* lach k* plb k* puls ptk1 sal-fr sle1•
- **contaminated**: *(↗dirty)*
  - • **being** contaminated; she is: ignis-alc es2•
  - • **everything** one is touching is contaminated: *(↗dirty - he; sick - being - imaginary; Washing - desire - hands)* aids nl2• ars galla-q-r nl2•
- **control**; out of:
  - • **he** is running out of control (See Fear - control)
  - • **organization**; losing control over one's: lac-e hrn2•
- **controlled**: *(↗double - being - controls)*
  - • **higher** power; under the control of (See influence)
  - • **movement** and thought is; every: germ-met srj
- **convent**, she will have to go to a: lac-d olib-sac wmh1
- **conversing**; as if: *Bell* bg2 nat-m bg2 raph ↓ stram bg2
  - • **carried** somewhere; and: raph rb2
- **convulsions**; as if he would go into: pyrus rb2 raph rb2
  - • **after**: absin a

- **corners**: *(↗creeping - corner)*
  - • **faces** were looking out of every corner; horrible (See faces - corner)
  - • **head** fitted into each corner of the room; part of (See head - corner)
  - • **people** coming out of; sees: *Stram* kr1
  - • **project**; corners of the houses: *(↗Fear - narrow)*
    - ⁝ **walking** in the street; so that he fears he will run against them while: *(↗Fear - corners)* *Arg-n* k*
  - • **something** coming out of the corner; sees: *(↗creeping - corner)* *Phos* k* stram fr1*
- **corpses** (See dead - persons)
- **corruption**; surrounded by: musca-d szs1
- **couch** moved; as if: plb rb2
- **council**; holding a: arn bg2 cham bg2
- **counteracted**; he is (See hindered - everyone)
- **country**, then in another; he were now in one: chlol rb2
- **court**; called before | **menopause**; during: zinc kr1
- **coward**:
  - • **he** is a: germ-met srj
  - • **people** leaving him are cowards: cann-i
- **crabs**, of: hyos k*
- **crack** in his soul, or in the universe: haliae-lc srj5•
- **crazy** (See insane)
- **creative** power; has: *(↗great; knowledge; Activity - desires - creative; Deeds - great)* agath-a nl2• cann-i ignis-alc es2• psil ft1
- **creep** into his own body; he would crouch together as much as he could and: cimx rb2
- **creeping** things; full of: phos ↓ stram kr1
  - • **corner**; out of every: *(↗corners; corners - something)* phos rb2
- **crime**:
  - • **about** to commit a: *Kali-bi* kr1 kali-br k* *Lach* vh* thea rb
  - • **committed** a crime; he had: *(↗Anxiety - conscience; Remorse)* agath-a nl2• alum alum-sil vh am-c rb2 anac ars k2* carb-an kr1 carb-v caust ptk1 chel bg1* chinin-s rb2 cina br1* cocc rb2 conch fkr1.de cycl k* dig rb2 hell k2 *Ign* bro1* *Kali-bi* kr1 kali-br k* lac-h sze9• lach k2* med c1 merc a1* nux-v bro1* petr-ra shn4• plb k2 puls rb2 rheum rb2 rhus-t rb2 ruta bro1 sabad staph bro1 *Verat* bro1* zinc br1* zinc-o rb2 [ars-met stj2 germ-met stj2 heroin sdj2 kali-ar stj2 nat-ar stj2 spect dfg1]
  - • **impelled** to commit a: thea rb2
- **criminal**, he is a: *(↗prisoner; pursued; wrong - done; Anxiety - conscience; Reproaching oneself - animal)* agath-a nl2• alum j* am-c j ars j calc-br ↓ carb-v j caust j cina j cob cob-m ↓ cob-p ↓ coff j crot-c sk4• cycl dig ferr j graph j hyos *Ign* k* m-arct j *Merc* nat-c j nux-v j op phos puls j ruta j sabad rb2 sarr sil j stront-c j sulph j thuj k* verat j [alumin stj2 heroin sdj2 zinc stj2]
  - • **executed**, to be: **Op** kr1
  - • **others** know it; and: calc-br mtf cob k* [cob-m stj2 cob-p stj2 heroin sdj2]
- **criminals**, about: alum am-c *Ars* bell k* carb-v caust *Chel* cina *Cocc* coff dig *Ferr* k* graph *Hyos* k* merc k* nat-c nit-ac nux-v puls ruta sil stront-c sulph verat [ferr-f stj2 ferr-lac stj2 ferr-n stj2 ferr-sil stj2 stront-met stj2 zinc-i stj2 zinc-m stj2 zinc-n stj2 zinc-p stj2]
- **crippled** old man; he is a (See man - old - being)
- **criticized**, she is: *(↗accused; appreciated; confused; confusion; despised; insulted; laughed; looked; watched; Admonition - agg.; Ailments - reproaches; Confidence - want; Despair - criticism; Fear - opinion; Fear - reproaches; Flattered - desire; Haughty; Offended; Sadness - slight; Sensitive; Sensitive - criticism; Sensitive - opinion; Suspicious; Timidity)* arizon-l nl2• bar-act a1* *Bar-c* k* calc gg carc sej3* carneg-g rwt1• cocain bro1* *Dys* fmm1• germ-met srj5• ham fd3.de• hydrog srj2*• hyos bro1 ign bro1 lac-ac stj5• lac-leo sk4• *Lac-lup* mtf* lach gg* laur loxo-recl knl4• lyss c1 marb-w es1• nat-m mrr1 pall bro1 pin-con oss2• plb podo fd3.de• positr nl2• prot fmm1• rad-br sze8• rhus-r k* sacch sst1• sal-fr sle1• staph bro1* *Symph* fd3.de• toxi mtf2• vanil fd5.de [heroin sdj2 spect dfg1 titan stj]
  - • **children**; in: sacch sst1•
- **crowded** with arms and legs: *(↗arms - many - legs; legs - many - arms)* *Pyrog* c1* pyrus st
- **crumble**; she is about to: [heroin sdj2]

Mind

- **crushed**:
  - **bedclothes**; crushed by the: pic-ac rb2
  - **everybody** rushing; crushed by: tub rb2
  - **houses**; crushed by the: arg-n bro1*
  - **she** is: positr nl2• sulph nl
- **cry**; he could: apoc↓ caj rb2
  - **nothing** but cry; he could do: apoc rb2
- **cucumbers** on the bed; sees: *Bell*
- **cursing**, with: *Anac* vh/dg* *Nit-ac* vh* verat j5.de
- **curtain**: *(↗barriers)*
  - **heavy** curtain hangs between her and others: *Galla-q-r* nl2•
- **cut** through; he is (See body - cut)
- **cylinder**, being a: cann-i
- **damage** to mind and body; the proving caused irreparable: phasco-ci rbp2
- **dancing**:
  - **he** were dancing: agar rb2 ars-s-f rb puls rb2 [buteo-j sej6]
    - **walking**; he were dancing up and down when: ars-s-f rb2
  - **night**; he had been dancing all: clem rb2 sabin rb2
  - **objects** were dancing on the floor: *Brom* b4a.de
  - **revolving**, twirling and spiralling dancers; of: plut-n srj7•
  - **satyrs** and nodding mandarins: cann-i k*
- **danger**, impression of: *(↗Fear - danger; Fear - happen; Fear - misfortune)* camph rb2 carneg-g rwt1• falco-pe↓ fl-ac k* gard-j vlr2• haliae-lc srj5• kali-br k* lac-del hrn2• lac-lup hrn2• macro rb2 maias-l hrn2• mez gk moni rfm1• olib-sac wmh1 plb↓ rhus-g↓ *Stram* k* toxi mtf2• valer k*
  - **calm**; yet: lac-del hrn2•
  - **family**, from his: kali-br
  - **fear**; but without: falco-pe nl2• fl-ac hr1
  - **life**, to his: maias-l hrn2• plb
  - **risk** he feels relieved; enjoying the exposure to danger and when at: lac-lup hrn2•
  - **world** is dangerous: rhus-g tmo3•
- **dark**: carb-v↓ carneg-g↓ cimic↓ hippoc-k szs2 maias-l hrn2• plut-n↓ **Stram** kr1
  - **balancing** with the light: plut-n srj7•
  - **cloud**; he is enveloped in a dark (See clouds - black)
  - **in** the dark; delusions: carb-v j5.de
  - **objects** and figures; sees dark: carneg-g rwt1• cimic bg2*
- **dead**: [heroin sdj2]
  - **child** was, her: (non:kali-bi kr1) *Kali-br* k* tritic-vg fd5.de [bell-p-sp dcm1]
  - **corpse**:
    - **acquaintance** on sofa and has dread; corpse of absent: ars k*
    - **bier**; on a: anac cann-i
    - **brother** and child, corpse of: calc-sil k2 con plb
    - **husband**, corpse of: calc-sil k2 plb
    - **mutilated** corpse: ant-c arn con mag-m merc nux-v sep
    - **near** him: anac h2
    - **sister**, corpse of: agar
    - **tall** yellow corpse is trying to share the bed with him | **ejected**; and he is promptly: bell
  - **everything** is: *(↗Indifference - dead)* kali-p fd1.de• mez rhus-t↓
    - **alone**; everything is dead and still and she is: *(↗forsaken)* rhus-t rb2
  - **friends** are dead and she must go to a convent; all her: *Lac-d*
  - **he** himself was: agn ptk1 anac anh sp1 apis k* ars ptk1 camph cann-i choc srj3• cypra-eg sde6.de• graph ptk1 *Lach* k* mosch bro1* oena rb2 *Op* bro1* phos k* plat ptk1 raph rb2 sil rb2 stram tanac↓
    - **funeral**; and preparations were being made for her: *(↗bells - funeral)* lach rb2*
    - **half** dead, half alive: tanac ptk2
  - **lover**; is his: positr nl2•
  - **mother** is, his: *Anac* aur-m-n wbt2• lach nat-m h2

- **dead**: ...
  - **persons**, sees: agar alum k* am-c k* *Anac* k* arg-n k* am k* *Ars* k* ars-i aur bg2 bar-c bar-i k2* *Bell* k* brom bry calc k* calc-ar k2* calc-i k2* calc-sil k2* cann-i↓ canth caust cocc k* con k* fl-ac gard-j vlr2• graph k* *Hep* k* hura *Hyos* iod kali-ar k* *Kali-br* *Kali-c* k* kali-p kali-sil k2* *Lach* laur k* *Mag-c* k* mag-m nat-c k* nat-m nat-p nit-ac nux-v k* olib-sac wmh1 op k* paull a1 *Ph-ac* k* *Phos* k* *Plat* k* plb k* rad-br sze8• ran-s sars sil stram bg2 stry k* sul-ac sul-i k2* sulph thuj k* verb zinc k* zinc-p k2* [alum-p stj2 alumin-s stj2 ant-t stj2 ars-met stj2 cupr-m stj2 cupr-p stj2 merc-i-f stj2 nat-ar stj2 zinc-i stj2 zinc-m stj2 zinc-n stj2]
    - **morning**:
      - **waking**; on | **frightened** by images of dead persons: hep
    - **midnight** | **waking**; on: cann-i k*
- **deaf** and dumb: *(↗hearing - illusions)* verat k*
- **death** approaching (See die - time)
- **debate**, of being in: hyos k*
- **debauch**; as after a: *(↗carousal; Reveling; GENERALS - Debauch - sensation)* caj↓ clem a conin a* kreos a lact a lyc a nux-v rb2 op a* ox-ac a
  - **afternoon**: caj a
- **decayed**, tarnished and impure; everything is: positr nl2•
- **deceived**; being: *(↗betrayed; trapped)* bamb-a stb2.de• crot-c sk4• dros ptk1* *Ign* mtf lyss mtf naja mtf *Nat-ar* mtf nicc mtf nicc-met sk4• ozone sde2• ruta ptk1* spong fd4.de *Staph* mtf stront-c mtf
- **decline**; is going into a: *Xan* kr1
- **deer**; seeing | **antlers**, with large: positr nl2•
- **deity**; huge Tibetan: adam srj5•
- **delightful** | **she** is or wants to be delightful: *(↗pleasing)* stram st
- **delirious**:
  - **become** delirious; he would: bry↓ gels rb2
    - **night**: bry
  - **was** delirious; he: cann-i nit-ac rb2 [ars stj2]
- **delirium** tremens; after: *Kali-br* hr1
- **demoniacal**, is (See devil)
- **demons**; of (See devil; monster - chair)
- **depending** on him; everything is: lac-lup hrn2• lil-t bc
- **depressive**: ambr ptk1* *Aur* sf **Kali-br** ptk1* murx j nux-v j plat j
- **deranged**; becoming (See insane - become)
- **deserted** (See forsaken)
- **despised**; is: *(↗appreciated; criticized; disgraced; insulted; laughed; looked; neglected - he; repudiated; worthless; Admonition - agg.; Confidence - want; Fear - opinion; Forsaken; Forsaken - isolation; Lamenting - appreciated; Mocking - others; Suspicious)* **Arg-n** arizon-l nl2• cob mg* ham fd3.de• hura hydrog srj2• lac-c lach ptk2* moni rfm1• *Orig* hr1* (non:orig-v kr1) phasco-ci rbp2 positr nl2• prots-m sne pseuts-m oss1• rhod kgp5• rhus-g tmo3• [cob-m stj2 cob-p stj2 heroin sdj2]
  - **loves** him; by everybody who: phasco-ci rbp2
  - **sexual** desire; with violent: orig hr1
- **destruction** of all near her; impending: *Kali-br* kr1
- **devil**: absin↓ alum↓ ambr↓ anac bg2 ars↓ *Bell* bg2 borx↓ camph↓ cann-i↓ cupr bg2 cupr-act↓ cupr-f↓ cupr-p↓ dulc↓ *Hell*↓ hyos bg2 ignis-alc↓ *Kali-br*↓ kali-c↓ lach↓ *Manc*↓ mand↓ meli↓ nat-c↓ *Op*↓ orig↓ ozone↓ pegan-ha↓ phos↓ *Plat* bg2 *Plb*↓ positr↓ psil↓ *Puls*↓ stram↓ sulph↓ tax↓ [cupr-m stj2 zinc stj2 zinc-i stj2 zinc-m stj2 zinc-n stj2 zinc-p stj2]
  - **after** her; is: *Hyos* vh* *Manc* vh* orig↓ *Zinc* kr1
    - **sexual** desire; with violent: orig hr1
  - **all** persons are devils: meli sne **Plat** k* *Plb* kr1
  - **belongs** to the devil; he: pegan-ha tpi1•
  - **connected** to devil, he is arrogant towards those who strive to purity, light and love: ozone sde2•
  - **he** is a devil: **Anac** k* camph cann-i *Hyos* vh* kali-br pegan-ha tpi1• positr nl2• stram [tax jsj7]
  - **persecuted** by the devil; he is: *(↗pursued - fiends)*
    - **crimes** he had never done; for: zinc rb2
  - **possessed** of a devil: alum gk borx↓ cann-i↓ *Hyos*↓ mand sp1 meli↓ plat↓ positr↓ psil↓ stram↓
    - **everyone** is: meli
    - **he** is: *(↗possessed)* borx k2 cann-i a1 *Hyos* k* plat vh* positr nl2• psil↓ stram c1*
      - **god** and by the devil; alternately by: psil ft1
  - **present**, is: anac cann-i op phos **Plat** [tax jsj7]

- **sees**: *(↗faces - diabolical)* absin fyz ambr *Anac* ars *Bell* cann-i cupr k* dulc *Hell* *Hyos* k* ignis-alc es2• *Kali-br* sne kali-c lach *Manc* vh* nat-c *Op* k1* orig sne *Plat* *Puls* stram sulph *Zinc* [cupr-act stj2 cupr-f stj2 cupr-p stj2]
  - **bed**; sees devils about his: op j5.de
- **sits** in his neck; devil: *Anac* kr1
  - **prompting** to offensive things: anac rb2
- **speaking** in one ear, prompting to murder: *(↗voices - hearing - follow; whispering)*
  - **angel** in the other ear, prompting to acts of benevolence; and an: *(↗voices - hearing - follow)* *Anac* kr1*
- **squeezed** dry in the devil's fist; she is: positr nl2•
- **taken** by the devil; he will be: *(↗Fear - devil of)* bell gl1.fr• manc *Puls* kr1
- **whispers** blasphemous words: *Anac* kr1

- **devoured** by animals (See animals - devoured)
- **die**:
  - **about** to die; one was: *(↗disease - incurable; dying - he; Death - presentiment)* **Acon** agn c1 alum a1 am-c rb2 ant-t rb2 *Arg-n* arn k2 ars k2 asaf rb2 asar rb2 bar-c bar-m k2 bell sf1.de cact kr1 calc gl1.fr• cann-i caps a1* caust rb2 cench k2 *Chel* *Croc* cupr gels rb2 glon rb2 graph rb2 hell h1* iris-t c1 kali-c lac-d *Lach* kr1* lil-t rb2 lyc kr1* lyss rb2 mag-p kr1 magn-gr rb2 med c1* meli sne merc j5.de mur-ac rb2 musca-d ↓ nat-hchls ↓ *Nit-ac* nux-v petr k* phos a1* *Plat* kr1* *Podo* k1* pop ↓ positr nl2• psor rb2 puls rb2 pyrus rb2 raph rb2 rhus-t ruta rb2 sil rb2 stram sulph rb2 tab rb2 thea rb2 *Thuj* v-a-b jl verat rb2 vinc ↓ *Xan* kr1 zinc rb2
    - **alive** again; and: musca-d szs1
    - **delivery**; during: **Acon** mrr1
    - **dissected**; and soon will be: *Cann-i*
    - **exhaustion**; she would die from: lach rb2
    - **fit**, which makes him walk faster; thinks he will have a: *Arg-n*
    - **heart** trouble; in: *(↗heart - disease - going; Fear - death - heart)* *Cact* ↓ pop rb2
      - **rheumatism**; with: *Cact* kr1
    - **help** her off; and wishes someone would: lach rb2
    - **lie** down and die; she must: kali-c rb2
    - **sink** down and die; one would (See sinking - dying)
    - **sleep**; she would die on going to (See Fear - death - sleep - falling - on)
    - **stool**; before: nat-hchls a1*
    - **suddenly**: thea rb2
    - **weakness**; one would die from: asar rb2 lyc rb2 vinc rb2
    - **wrong** from which they die; she gives people something (See wrong - gives)
  - **must**; she: *Mag-p* ↓ nux-v rb2 ruta fd4.de [spect dfg1]
    - **tetanus**, with pain in the right leg; must die of: *Mag-p* kr1
  - **rather** die than live; one would: xan rb2
  - **time** has come to: *(↗Death - conviction)* ars bell k* dendr-pol sk4• lach med c1 sabad thuj
  - **waiting** to die; being old and: plut-n srj7•
- **diminished**: *(↗tall; tall - he; GENERALS - Smaller)*
  - **abdomen** has fallen in (See abdomen - fallen)
  - **all** is: *(↗small - things - appear; Size - incorrect)* cann-i carc fd2.de• cinnm grat hydrog srj irid-met srj5• lac-c sabad sulph
  - **body** is diminished (See body - diminished)
  - **everything** in room is diminished; while she is tall and elevated: *(↗great; Haughty)* plat
  - **objects** are (See small - things - appear)
  - **others** are: granit-m es1•
  - **short**, he is: lac-c
  - **shrunken**, parts are: carc fd2.de• cypra-eg sde6.de• nux-m sf1.de* positr nl2• *Sabad* k*
  - **small**, he is (See small - he)
  - **thin**, he is too: thuj k*
- **dirt**, eating: verat
- **dirty**: *(↗contaminated; Dirty)*
  - **everyone** is: ignis-alc es2•
  - **everything** is: cur ignis-alc es2• musca-d szs1 positr nl2• [heroin sdj2]
  - **he** is: *(↗contaminated - everything; Fastidious; Washing - desire - hands)* aster vh carc fd2.de• hydrog srj2*• *Lac-c* k* limest-b es1• lycps-v k* nat-p fkr6.de neon srj5• olib-sac wmh1 plut-n srj7• positr nl2• rhus-t k* sanguis-s hrn2• *Syph* bg* thuj gk vanil fd5.de
    - **inside** and smells badly: aster vh
  - **sexuality** is dirty: [berb stu1]
    - **delivery**; since: [berb stu1]
    - **menses**; during: [berb stu1]
    - **mother**; since being a: [berb stu1]
    - **pregnancy**; since: [berb stu1]
- **disabled**, she is: cit-v dulc fd4.de
- **disagreeable**; everything seems: valer ptk1
- **disappear**; she will: gard-j ↓ limest-b es1•
  - **left** side: gard-j vlr2•
- **disappearing**; dreams are: dream-p sdj1•
- **discoveries**; makes: nitro-o a
- **disease**:
  - **belong** to her, her disease does not: sal-fr sle1•
  - **deaf**, dumb and has cancer; he is: *(↗hearing - illusions; Anxiety - hypochondriacal)* verat
  - **every** disease; he has: *(↗heart - disease; sick - being; Anxiety - health - own; Anxiety - hypochondriacal; Hypochondriasis)* *Aur-m* stram
  - **imaginary** (See sick - being)
  - **incurable** disease; he has an: *(↗cancer; die - about; health; Despair - health; Despair - recovery; Doubtful - recovery; Fear - disease - incurable; Fear - recover; Thoughts - disease - incurable)* acon sf1.de adam srj5• alum h2* *Arg-n* k* arn k2* cact k* calc sf1.de calc-sil k2 chel *Ign* sf1.de lac-c br1* *Lach* sf1.de *Lil-t* kr1* macro a1 mag-c mg1.de nit-ac sf1.de petr-ra shn4• phos hr1 plb podo k2 positr nl2• *Sabad* *Stann* sf1.de *Syph* cda [spect dfg1]
  - **loathsome**, horrible mass of disease; he were a: lac-c rb2*
  - **throat** disease, which ends fatal; has: **Sabad** kr1
  - **unrecognized** disease; he has an: *(↗Anxiety - hypochondriacal)* raph
  - **yellow** fever; has: camph kr1
- **disgraced**: *(↗despised; repudiated - relatives; Company - desire; Confidence - want; Forsaken; Forsaken - isolation; Succeeds; Timidity)*
  - **family** or friends; he has disgraced his: plat hr1 sarr k*
  - **she** is: caust mtf33 kali-s sk• mag-s sk• nat-s sk• nux-v he plat rob a1 (non:sarr a1) (non:sec a1*) staph sk• sulph k*
- **disintegrating**, the world is: falco-pe nl2•
- **disorder**; objects appear in: glon st op a1
- **dispossessed**; he will be: granit-m es1•
- **dissected**, he will be: cann-i
- **dissolving**, she is: *(↗existence; existence - own; Confusion - identity - boundaries)* aids nl2• ham fd3.de• neon srj5• olib-sac wmh1
- **distances**; of: *(↗enlarged - distances; Distances - inaccurate)* anac ↓ bros-gau ↓ cann-i st* cann-s st* magn-gr rb2 nux-m st*
  - **objects** were too distant: anac rb2 bros-gau mrc1
- **distinguished**; he is: *(↗great; noble; Haughty; Insanity)* marb-w es1• phos h2 stram verat
- **disturbed**; being | **sleep**; during (See sleep - disturbed)
- **divided**: *(↗side - alive)*
  - **four** parts; into: choc srj3•
  - **two** parts; into: *(↗body - divided; Confusion - identity; Confusion - identity - duality)* *Anac* vh* aq-mar rbp6 *Bapt* bell gl1.fr• cann-i cypra-eg sde6.de• des-ac rbp6 fic-m gya1 ham fd3.de• lil-t a1 neon srj5• olib-sac wmh1 ozone sde2• petr positr nl2• puls *Ruta* fd4.de sal-fr sle1• sil stram thuj
    - **cut** in two parts; or: *(↗Confusion - identity; Cut; Cut - others)* bell gl1.fr• plat stram gl1.fr•
    - **left** side did not belong to her; and: sil rb2*
    - **real** him, one is not the: sal-fr sle1•

- **two** parts; into: ...
  - **which** part he has possession on waking; and could not tell of: thuj k*
- **divine**, being: *(↗christ; great; mary; power - disease; superhuman)* cann-i glon sf1.de ignis-alc es2• stram
- **division** between himself and others: *(↗separated - world - he)* arge-pl rwt5• dream-p sdj1• falco-pe nl2• hippoc-k szs2 hydrog srj2• nat-c k2* nat-sil fd3.de• phasco-ci rbp2
- **dizzy** (See vertigo)
- **do**:
  - **dreadful** while trembling; he were going to do something: visc c1*
  - **nothing**; he could do: *(↗worthless)* lyss rb2
  - **unable** to do anything, yet something must be done: *(↗act and)* pop rb2
- **doctors** come; three: sep
- **dogs**:
  - **attack** him: nit-ac ↓ pall ↓ **Stram** k*
    - **gnawing** flesh and bones: nit-ac tl1 pall tl1 stram tl1
  - **barks** at them to be understood; others are dogs, he: *Stram* kr1
  - **biting** his chest: stram k*
  - **black**: arn h1* *Bell* k* positr nl2• puls j5.de
  - **he** is a dog: bell ↓ irid-met ↓ lyss ↓ plut-n srj7•
    - **growls** and barks: *(↗Biting)* bell hr1* irid-met srj5• lyss hr1*
  - **sees**: *Aeth* k* arn k* aur h2* **Bell** k* *Calc* k* calc-ar k2* calc-sil k2* cina k2 limest-b es1• lyc merc mosch gt neon srj5• olib-sac wmh1 puls sil *Stram* k* sulph verat zinc
  - **swarm** about him: bell k* *Calc* hr1* stram
- **doing** enough | **not** done enough; he has (See neglected - duty)
- **dolls**, people appeared like: plb k*
- **dominated**; he is: polys sk4•
- **doomed**, being: *(↗lost - salvation; purgatory; Anxiety - salvation)* acon bro1 ars k2* aur k2* bell gl1.fr• cycl bro1 hell k2* hyos k2* *Ign* hr1* *Kali-br* hr1* *Kali-p* hr1* lach bro1* *Lil-t* hr1* lyc bro1 med hr1* meli bro1 nat-m gl1.fr• op bro1 *Plat* hr1* psor bro1 puls bro1* stram bro1 sulph j5.de* *Verat* bro1 [germ-met stj2 heroin sdj2]
  - **drunkards**, in: *Lach* gl1.fr•
  - **expiate** her sins and those of her family; to: *Lil-t* kr1
  - **soul** cannot be saved: | **cries** and rages: *Ign* kr1
- **door**; someone was coming in at the | **night**: con
- **double**:
  - **being**: *(↗person - two - personalities; standing - beside; Confusion - identity - duality)* alum *Anac* k* anh mg1.de* ara-maca sej7• *Bapt* k* calc-p ptk cann-i k* glon haliae-lc srj5• lach lil-t mosch *Nux-m* op a1 *Petr* k* phos h2 psil ft1 pyrog bg rhus-t fr sec sil h2 *Stram* k* tab ↓ thuj k* valer bro1 [heroin sdj2]
    - **conquer** the other; there were another self and he is not sure which will: op rb2
    - **controls** the other; one self: *(↗controlled)* *Cann-i* br1
    - **fever** would not run alike in both; and: pyrog al2*
    - **lying** on one side:
      - **one** person; she were | **another** person when lying on the other side; she were: pyrog rb2
    - **one** person when lying on the left side; he were | **another** person when lying on the right side; and (See lying - one - another)
    - **outside** of patient; there were a second self: *Bapt* hr1* tab rb2
    - **smaller**, the outer person loosely put on; the inner person being a little | **get** up; the inner person is urging the outer to: anac rb2
    - **watching** his other self playing; his real conscious self seemed to be: nux-m c1
  - **existence**; having a double: ara-maca sej7• cann-i rb2
- **double**: ...
  - **head** and pairs of limbs are (See head - double; limbs - double - pairs)
  - **limb** is; one (See limbs - double)
  - **mouth** is (See mouth - double)
  - **nose** is (See nose - double)
  - **objects** are: *Anh* mg1.de zinc sf1.de* [zinc-i stj2 zinc-m stj2 zinc-n stj2 zinc-p stj2]
  - **sensations** present themselves in a double form: cann-i k*
- **downward**; pulled: hydrog srj
- **dragged** from the lowest abyss of darkness: thea
- **dragons**, of: cann-i a1 op a1
- **drawing**:
  - **circle**; something were drawing her round in a | **head** straight; and she could not hold her: lyss rb2
  - **legs**; he were drawn forth and wafted quickly in the direction of his: tell rb2
  - **right** when walking; something were drawing her to the: sil rb2
- **drawn** | **floor**; he were drawn from the | **difficult** to place foot to the floor: euon-a rb2
  - **organs** seem to be drawn together: *Naja* br1
- **dream**; as if in a (See Dream)
- **dreaming** when awake; he was (See Dream; as)
- **dreams**:
  - **belong** to another; dreams: choc srj3•
  - **stolen**; dreams have been: choc srj3•
- **drinking**:
  - **had** been drinking; he: aran-sc rb2
  - **is** drinking; he: bell
- **driving** a car:
  - **closing** the eyes: ferr a1*
  - **uphill** though road is flat: adam srj5•
- **driving** animals:
  - **peacocks**: hyos k*
  - **sheep**: acon k*
- **drugged**; as if: falco-pe nl2• marb-w es1• melal-alt gya4 olib-sac wmh1 op rb2 plut-n srj7• positr nl2• sal-fr sle1•
  - **someone** drugged him: melal-alt gya4
- **drunk**:
  - **been** drunk; he had:
    - **night**; before: bry rb2
    - **week**; for a: onos rb2
  - **is** drunk; he: acet-ac ↓ acon ↓ agar rb2 alum ↓ ant-c rb2 arg-met ↓ arg-n rb2 asc-t rb2 aur rb2 bell rb2 bufo rb2 calc ↓ chlf rb2 chlol ↓ cot rb2 croc rb2 ferr ↓ graph ↓ kali-br rb2 lat-k ↓ meph rb2 mez rb2 nept-m lsd2.fr nux-m rb2 oena rb2 op rb2 phys rb2 pip-m rb2 querc rb2 sacch-a fd2.de• sal-fr sle1• sil rb2 stram rb2 sul-ac rb2 sulph rb2
    - **all** the time: arg-met rb2
    - **cloudiness**; with: alum rb2
    - **head**:
      - **heavy**; with a: acet-ac rb2
      - **in**: calc rb2
    - **nausea**; with: acon rb2
    - **partially**: chlol rb2
    - **rising**; on: graph rb2 sacch-a fd2.de•
    - **side** were drunk; affected: lat-k rb2
    - **smoke** in brain; from: op rb2
    - **vertigo**; with: ant-c rb2 ferr rb2
- **drunkard** | **coming** toward her and lying down beside her; a huge drunkard were: cic kr1*
- **dull**:
  - **intoxication**; as after an: podo fd3.de• squil rb2
  - **liquor**; from taking: sabad rb2
  - **sleep**; head were dull from loss of: nicc rb2

- **study**; head were dull from too much: nat-n rb2
- **dumb**, he is: verat
- **dying**: *(↗Death - presentiment - predicts)*
  - **friend** is; beloved: bar-c kr1
  - **he** is: *(↗die - about; Death - dying; Death - sensation)* acon rb2* ant-t vh apis br1* cact rb2 cann-i k* chlf rb2 *Lac-lup* hrn2• morph rb2 nux-v op rb2 podo rb2 pot-e rly4• rhus-t stram ther rb2 thyr rb2 vesp rb2 xan rb2 [arg-n stj2]
- **earth**:
  - **exploding**; of seeing earth: plut-n srj7•
  - **shifting** | **feet**; under my: galeoc-c-h gms1•
- **earthquake**; one were in an: fl-ac rb2 fum rly1*•
- **eating**:
  - **cannot** eat: myric ptk1
  - **is** eating; he: limest-b es1•
  - **must** not eat; she: kali-m k2
- **ego**; had lost their: limest-b es1•
- **elephant**; sees an: aids nl2•
  - **enormous**, gentle and passive: aids nl2•
- **elevated**:
  - **air**; elevated in the: *(↗floating - air)* calc ↓ falco-pe nl2• ignis-alc ↓ irid-met srj5• mosch ↓ (non:nit-ac a1) nitro-o k* phos rb2 rhus-t rb2 sil rb2
    - **fall**; and would: mosch rb2
    - **looking** down on a cesspool of ignorance and vulgarity; and: *(↗inferior; Haughty)* ignis-alc es2•
    - **pressed** forward; and: calc rb2
  - **bed** is raised: canth
  - **carried** to an elevation: oena k*
  - **step** over; has to: euph kr1
- **emaciation**; of: *(↗body - brittle; thin - he; DREAMS - Emaciated)* *Anh* mg nat-m bg2 sabad bg2 sulph k* thuj k1 [tax jsj7]
- **emperor**:
  - **is** an: *(↗great; prince; queen)* cann-i
  - **talked** of: carbn-s
- **emptiness**; of: *(↗GENERALS - Emptiness)* am-c ptk aur ↓ *Calad* st cann-i a **Cocc** st *Gels* kr1 germ-met srj *Ign* st irid-met br1 kali-br ↓ *Kali-c* st *Kola* stb3• lac-loxod-a hrn2• *Mur-ac* st oena a *Olnd* st ozone sde1• petr-ra shn4• *Plat* kr1 plut-n srj7• **Puls** st sars st **Sep** st stann st* stry a* *Sulph* st tritic-vg fd5.de *Vanil* fd5.de *Zing* st [bell-p-sp dcm1 heroin sdj2 neon stj2]
  - **around** and under one on standing; emptiness: kali-br rb2
  - **behind** one on turning around; emptiness: kali-c rb2
  - **internal**: aur st
- **encaged** in wires: *(↗wires)* *Cimic* k*
- **enchantment**, of: coff-t a1
- **enclosed**; she is: germ-met srj
- **enemy**: *(↗Suspicious - enemy)*
  - **bed**; enemy is under the: *(↗bed - someone - under; pursued - enemies)* am-m
  - **everyone** is an: *(↗hindered - everyone; pursued - enemies; Company - desire - alone - fear; Forsaken; Forsaken - isolation; Suspicious - enemy)* granit-m es1• *Merc* k* plat k* puls hr1*
  - **injury**; an enemy is constantly lying in wait to inflict an: *(↗pursued - enemies)* alco a1
  - **pursued** by (See pursued - enemies)
  - **rest**; enemy allowed him no: dros rb2
  - **surrounded** by enemies: *(↗pursued - enemies; Suspicious - enemy)* ambr tsm1 *Anac* k* carbn-s *Crot-h* dros h1 lac-del hrn2• marb-w es1• *Merc* moni rfm1• verat gk [thal-met stj2]
- **energy**:
  - **air**; moving around in the: hydrog srj2•
  - **plug** on my energy; as if someone pulled a: galeoc-c-h gms1•
  - **scattered**; his energy is: rhus-g tmo3•
  - **stream** of energy from right to left: galla-q-r nl2•
- **engaged**:
  - **lawsuit**; in a (See lawsuit)
  - **occupation**; he is engaged in some: *(↗Industrious)* acon ars atro bell cann-i cupr hyos lyss plb rhus-t stram verat
    - **ordinary** occupation: *(↗Industrious)* ars atro bell plb stram
- **enlarged**: *(↗large - he; swollen; tall)* acon adam ↓ agar ↓ alum *Anh* ↓ apis a1 *Aran* sf1.de arg-met sf1.de *Arg-n* sf1.de atro ↓ aur ↓ bad ↓ *Bapt* sf1.de bell berb bit-ar ↓ *Bov* sf1.de caj c1 camph ↓ **Cann-i** cann-s ↓ carb-ac ↓ carb-v ↓ caust ↓ cench ↓ cham ↓ chord-umb ↓ cic ↓ cob-n ↓ coc-c coca-c ↓ con sf1.de corian-s ↓ cypra-eg ↓ dream-p ↓ euph falco-pe ↓ ferr a1 gard-j ↓ *Gels* sf1.de glon haliae-lc ↓ hydrog srj2• *Hyos* c1* irid-met srj5• kali-ar sf1.de kali-bi sf1.de kali-br c1 kola stb3• lach sf1.de laur levo ↓ limest-b es1• loxo-recl knl4• mang mang-m ↓ mang-met ↓ mang-p ↓ mang-s ↓ meph ↓ mim-p ↓ nat-c neon ↓ nux-m sf1.de nux-v *Op* ox-ac sf1.de pall ↓ *Par* br1* phos sf1.de pic-ac pip-m sf1.de *Plat* plut-n ↓ positr ↓ puls sf1.de pyrog ↓ rhus-t sf1.de sabad sacch-a ↓ sal-fr ↓ sil ↓ spig sf1.de stann ↓ staph ↓ stram k* sulph ↓ *Trom* ↓ tub ↓ xan ↓ zinc
  - **body** is: acon ↓ adam srj5• alum ↓ anh ↓ aran ↓ arg-n br1* bad ↓ bapt ↓ bell rb2 bit-ar ↓ *Bov* wd* caj rb2 cann-i ↓ carb-v ↓ cench k13 cic rb coca-c sk4• corian-s knl6• dream-p ↓ gard-j vlr2• haliae-lc ↓ hydrog srj2• hyos ↓ irid-met srj5• kali-br ↓ kola stb3• limest-b es1• mang ↓ mim-p jl3 neon ↓ nux-m ↓ op h1 par rb2 pic-ac ↓ plut-n srj7• positr ↓ stram ↓ sulph ↓ xan c1
    - **right** side: cann-i a
    - **alternating** with | **small**; delusions that body is very: sulph rb2
    - **enormously**: cic rb2 neon srj5•
    - **fat**; feeling: bit-ar wht1• corian-s ↓ haliae-lc ↓ positr ↓
      - **pale** and ugly: corian-s knl6• haliae-lc srj5• positr nl2•
    - **parts** of body: *(↗neck - too; Size - incorrect)* acon sf1.de alum anh jl aran sf bad ptk bapt fr bell hr1 bov sf cann-i k2 carb-v k2 dream-p sdj1• hyos kali-br ↓ limest-b es1• mang sf1.de nux-m a1* op pic-ac stram
      - **growing** too long; as if: kali-br c1
  - **chin** is: glon k* sabad k2*
  - **distances** are: *(↗distances; Distances - inaccurate; Size - incorrect)* camph **Cann-i** k* cann-s cob-n mg1.de cypra-eg sde6.de• glon hydrog srj2• nux-m stann [*Arg-n* stj2]
  - **everything** is: *(↗large - everything)* euph bg1
  - **eyelashes** are: cann-i
  - **eyes** are: *(↗eyes - big)* bell levo jl3 op k*
  - **forearm** is: aran jl3
  - **hands** are: dream-p sdj1•
  - **head** is: *(↗head - large; head - large - too; HEAD - Enlarged)* acon k* *Bapt* sf1.de berb sf1.de *Bov* sf1.de caj wd cann-i k* carb-ac a1 falco-pe nl2• *Gels* sf1.de glon sf1.de kali-ar k* limest-b es1• mang sf1.de meph sf nux-m sf1.de *Par* sf1.de pip-m sf1.de *Plat* vh* sil h2 zinc [mang-m stj2 mang-met stj2 mang-p stj2 mang-s stj2]
    - **right** side (See head - diminished - left)
  - **leg** is longer, one: cann-i haliae-lc srj5• sacch-a fd2.de•
  - **letters**: *Anh* st*
  - **nose**: *(↗NOSE - Enlarged - sensation)*
    - **other** people's noses seem enlarged: sal-fr sle1•
  - **objects** are: *(↗longer; Size - incorrect)* agar br1 *Anh* mg1.de atro a1 **Cann-i** k*
    - **diminished** and: *Anh* st*
  - **persons** are: *(↗large - people)* berb ↓ cann-i caust k* cham ↓ chord-umb rly4• falco-pe nl2• *Trom* ↓ tub ↓
    - **twilight**, in: berb bc
    - **vertigo**; during: caust k* cham bg1* *Trom* vh tub bg1*
  - **scrotum** is swollen: sabad k*
  - **tall**; he is very: *(↗tall - he; Haughty)* aur rb hydrog srj2• *Irid-met* srj5• op pall k* plat k* pyrog staph h1 stram
- **enlightened**; is: ignis-alc es2•
- **enrage** him; least provocation would: aids nl2• sumb ↓
  - **mirth**; with: sumb rb2
- **enslaved**; he is: limest-b es1•

- **entering**; someone is (See person - entering)
- **epilepsy**:
    - **has** epilepsy; he: atro
    - **would** have an epileptic fit; he: alum rb2 cina rb2 lyss rb2
- **eternity**:
    - **he** was in: cann-i
    - **lived** an eternity; he has: aether a1
    - **merged** with present: anh sp1
- **ether** in his head; he had taken: cain rb2
- **evil**: absin ↓ cycl ↓ lach ↓ lat-h ↓ meny ↓ *Pegan-ha* ↓ positr nl2• zinc ↓
    - **done** some evil; had: *(↗wrong - done)* cycl rb2 lat-h thj1 zinc rb2
    - **eye** is put on him: *Pegan-ha* tpi1•
    - **happened** to him; feeling as though some evil had: lach a1 meny ptk1
    - **haunted** by evil images: absin vh1
    - **he** is evil and does not care: positr nl2•
    - **sex** is (See Fear - moral)
- **exaggerated**; everything: cann-i tl1
- **exalted**; as if: cann-i tl1 lac-c rb2 plat rb2*
- **excited**; as if: coff kali-i ↓
    - **intoxicated**; and: kali-i rb2
- **execute** him; people want to: nux-m sne *Op* kr1
- **executioner**; visions of an: stram
- **exhausted**; he was: coca rb2 [**Spect** dfg1]
- **existence**: *(↗dissolving)*
    - **begun** his existence; he had just that moment: camph rb2
    - **doubt** if anything had existence: *(↗Nihilistic)* agn
    - **longer**; she cannot exist any: thuj rb2*
    - **own** existence; he doubted his: *(↗dissolving)* cann-i
    - **surroundings** did not exist: agn rb2 nux-m rb2 puls rb2
    - **two** existences; to have: cann-i k2*
    - **without** form in vast space: cann-i a1
- **expanding**:
    - **he** is: coca-c sk4• gard-j vlr2•
    - **passersby** are expanding: *(↗Size - incorrect)* cann-i
- **expectant**; he is: coca rb2
- **expecting** unpleasant news; he is (See news - expecting - unpleasant)
- **experienced** | **before**; thought everything had been: *(↗Deja)* dendr-pol sk4• kali-br oci-sa sk4• pant-ac rly4• *Ruta* fd4.de
- **eyelashes** prolonged: cann-i a1
- **eyelids**; he has two sets of: positr nl2•
- **face**:
    - **air**; feeling them in the: [heroin sdj2]
    - **distorted**: lac-h htj1•
    - **four** faces; she has: adam srj5•
    - **unfamiliar**; her own face looks: choc srj3•
- **faces**, sees: *(↗images)* acon ↓ aeth ↓ *Ambr* k* anac ↓ anh ↓ apis arg-n k* ars k* aur **Bell** k* *Bry* ↓ *Calc* k* calc-sil cann-i k* carb-an carb-v caust k* cham chin ↓ cimic br cocc ↓ crot-c ↓ *Cupr* euphr ↓ germ-met ↓ kali-c hr1* *Lac-c* k* lac-h ↓ lac-loxod-a ↓ laur k* lyc ↓ maias-l ↓ med k* merc k* *Nat-m* ↓ *Nux-v* **Op** k* orot-ac rly4• phos k* pic-ac ↓ plut-n ↓ positr ↓ samb stram ↓ stry *Sulph* *Tarent* k* [heroin sdj2]
    - **ape**-like: plut-n srj7•
    - **closing** eyes, on: aeth anh mg1.de* *Arg-n* k* ars **Bell** *Bry* k* **Calc** k* carb-v caust k* chin euphr k* germ-met srj5• maias-l hrn2• *Op* samb sulph *Tarent*
    - **corner**; looking out of every: phos rb2*
    - **dark**, in the: chin **Lac-c** k*
    - **diabolical** faces crowd upon him: *(↗devil - sees)* *Ambr* carb-an caust tarent
        - ⁝ **get** away of them; cannot: ambr k1
    - **distinguished** people, of: cann-i k*
    - **distorted**: *(↗images - distorted)* ambr h1 arg-n a1 caust h2* cupr ↓ lac-c k2* lac-h htj1*• laur a1
- **faces**, sees – **distorted**: ...
        - ⁝ **lying** down in the daytime; on: ambr arg-n cupr laur
    - **elongated**: stram
    - **every** ones face in a glass except his own: anac c1
    - **father**; of her: plut-n srj7•
    - **grotesque**: phos bg2
    - **hideous** (See ugly)
    - **larger**; grow: acon aur
    - **looking** from behind bed and furniture: med c1
    - **mask**-like: anh mg1.de* op j5.de
    - **noises**; because of slight: kali-c lt
    - **oars** or spades instead of hair; with: positr nl2•
    - **reaching** the clouds | **sleep**; on going to: pic-ac a1
    - **ridiculous**: cann-i k*
    - **scheming**: anh mg1.de*
    - **stooping**, when: *Nat-m* k*
    - **supplicating**: germ-met srj
    - **ugly** (= hideous): *(↗grimaces)* *Ambr* k* *Bell* k* **Calc** k* calc-sil cann-i k* carb-an caust k* cocc sf crot-c sk4• cupr sst3• *Kali-c* hr1* lac-c lac-loxod-a hrn2• lyc j5.de merc k* nux-v **Op** phos bg1 stram sf stry sulph j5.de *Tarent*
        - ⁝ **coming** out at him: lac-loxod-a hrn2•
        - ⁝ **pleasing**; seem: cann-i
    - **waking**, on: ambr vh
    - **warriors** and peacemakers: plut-n srj7•
    - **wherever** he turns his eyes, or looking out from corners: aur med *Phos* k*
- **fail**, everything will: *(↗succeed; wrong - everything; wrong - everything goes; Anxiety - success; Confidence - want; Fear - failure; Sadness - failure; Succeeds; Timidity; Undertaking - nothing)* act-sp k* aq-mar rbp6 *Arg-n* k* *Aur* k* *Aur-m-n* wbt2• bamb-a stb2.de• carc mlr1• chir-fl gya2 cob-n mg conch fkr1• *Kali-s* fd4.de kola stb3• lac-c lpc lac-e hrn2• merc k* nux-v k* psor jl2* sil k* spong fd4.de [tung-met stj2]
    - **his** understanding: arg-n br1
- **failure**; he is a (See Confidence - want - failure)
- **faint**; he would: ang rb2 beryl tpw5 bry rb2 bufo ↓ calc rb2 calen rb2 carb-v ↓ cocc rb2 cupr kr1* dig rb2 kali-c rb2 lappa rb2 levo jl3 mag-c rb2 med rb2 mosch a1 nat-m rb2 sabad rb2 sep rb2 sil rb2 spong rb2 stann rb2* sulph kr1 thea rb2 upa rb2 zing rb2 [cupr-act stj2 cupr-f stj2 cupr-m stj2 cupr-p stj2]
    - **emptiness** of stomach; with: bufo rb2
    - **lying** down; on: sulph rb2
    - **qualmishness**; with: upa rb2
    - **standing**; while: dig rb2
    - **waking** any longer; if he had postponed: carb-v h1*
- **fairies**; searching for: *(↗specters; spirit)* marb-w es1•
- **fall**; something would | **him**; on: kali-s fd4.de tarent rb2
- **falling**:
    - **asleep**; delusions on falling (See sleep - going)
    - **backward**: bry ptk1 calc ↓ chin rb2* dub rb2 kali-n rb2 led ptk1 nux-v ↓ prim-v rb2 rhus-t ptk1 spong rb2 staph rb2 tub ↓
        - ⁝ **bed**; on getting out of: rhus-t rb2
        - ⁝ **rocking** in a chair; going over backward when: tub rb2
        - ⁝ **side**; he would fall backward or to one: calc rb2 nux-v rb2
    - **bed** (See bed - falling)
    - **bodies**: *Borx* bg2
    - **brother** fell overboard in her sight; her: kali-br
    - **clings** and asks to be held: stram kr1
    - **dancing**; he would fall on: puls rb2
    - **elevated** and would fall; he were: mosch rb2
    - **fire** on walking past it; one would fall into a: onos rb2
    - **forward**:
        - ⁝ **backward**; and: rhus-t rb2
        - ⁝ **is** falling forward; she: alum ptk1 alum-sil chel rb2 chlf rb2 cupr ↓ dig ptk1 elaps k* gels rb2 mang ptk1 (non:mosch j*) nat-m rb2*

- **forward** – **is** falling forward; she: ...
  Nux-v ptk1 petr rb2 phos rb2 pic-ac rb2 rhus-t ptk1 ruta rb2 senec rb2 sil rb2 spig rb2 stram k13 tarax rb2 ter ↓ xan rb2
  : **turning** around in head; as if: cupr rb2
  : **walking**; when: ter rb2*
  : **must** fall forward; she: nat-hchls rb2
  : **rising** from a seat; on: vib rb2
  : **stooping**; when: berb rb2 puls rb2
- **he** is: alum-sil ambro rb2 apis rb2 aran rb2 bell rb2* bism rb2 calc rb2 caust rb2 chen-a rb2 chim ↓ clem rb2 coloc rb2 cupr rb2* equis-h rb2 gels rb guaj ↓ ham fd3.de• lappa rb2 lyss rb2 mag-m rb2 mag-p rb2 med rb2 mosch k* puls rb2 rhus-t rb2 sabin rb2 sec ↓ sep rb2 spig rb2 stram k* tub rb2 upa rb2 vib ↓ visc rb2 wies rb2 zinc rb2 [arg-n stj2 ars stj2 ars-met stj2 bism-sn stj2 cupr-act stj2 cupr-f stj2 cupr-m stj2 cupr-p stj2 kali-ar stj2 nat-ar stj2]
  : **asleep**; when: vib rb2*
  : **awakening**; when: guaj rb2* sec rb2
  : **children**; in: gels rb2
  : **deep**: bell rb2
  : **head**; on: chim rb2
  : **suddenly**: clem rb2
  : **unpleasantly**; she would fall not: lappa rb2
- **height**; from a: bell tl1 calen rb2 caps tl1 caust ptk1 gels ptk1 mosch c1* *Thuj* tl1
- **hold** onto something; she would fall if she did not: sabad rb2
- **hole** close by; danger of falling into a: carbn-s c1*
- **is** falling; she or he (See he is)
- **looks**:
  : **down**; falls if he looks:
  : **downstairs**; when going: onos rb2
  : **standing** or when walking; when: spig rb2
  : **up**; falls if he looks: puls rb2
- **open** space; he would fall in: ars rb2 coca-c sk4•
- **over**; he would fall: ars rb2 zinc rb2
- **pieces** to (See body - pieces - falling)
- **seat**; he would fall from a: alumn rb2 stram rb2
- **side**; to one: am-m rb2 aur ↓ calc rb2* camph ↓ cocc ptk1 dirc ↓ eup-pur ↓ itu ↓ merl ↓ nat-m ↓ nux-v ptk1 rheum rb2 ruta ↓ sacch-l ↓ squil ↓ zinc ↓
  : **left**; to: aur rb2 calc rb2 dirc rb2 eup-pur rb2 merl rb2 nat-m rb2
  : **right**; to: camph rb2 itu rb2 ruta ↓ sacch-l rb2 zinc ↓
  : **height**; when at a: zinc rb2
  : **walking**; when: ruta rb2
  : **rising**; he would fall to one side on: squil rb2
- **showers**: plb bg2
- **stands**; he will fall if he: alum-sil k2 oxyt rb2
- **things** will be: hyos stram
- **turns**; if he:
  : **head**; he would fall if he turns his: spig rb2
  : **right** or left; to: der rb2
- **walking**; when:
  : **if** she walks: calc rb2 iod rb2
  : **step**; he would fall at every: dor rb2
- **walls**: *(↗house - crush; walls - crush; walls - surrounded; Fear - narrow)* arg-n k* cann-i carb-v rb2 lyss st1
  : **epileptic** fit; walls seem to fall inward before an: carb-v k* *Lyss* vh*

- **family**, does not belong to her own: *(↗Company - desire; Estranged; Forsaken; Forsaken - isolation)* lil-t ↓ nat-sil fd3.de• plat k*
  - **get** along with her; cannot: lil-t bc
- **fancy**, illusions of: *(↗images; objects; visions; Fancies - absorbed)* *Acon* *Aeth* k* agar k* alum bg2 alum-sil k2 am-c bg *Ambr* k* anac k* ang anh sf1.de* ant-c k* ant-t apis arn k* *Ars* k* ars-i k* *Aur* aur-ar k2 aur-s k2 bar-c bar-i k2* *Bell* k* berb bism bit-ar wht1• bry k* (non:bufo slp) bufo-s slp calc k* calc-ar k2* calc-p calc-sil k2* camph k* **Cann-i** k* cann-s *Cann-xyz* bg2 canth k* carb-an k* carb-v k* carbn-s k2 caust k* cham k* chin chinin-ar chinin-s cic k*

- **fancy**, illusions of: ...
  Cina k* *Cocc* coff colch k* coloc k* con croc k* *Crot-c* cupr k* cycl bg dig dros k* dulc k* euphr k* falco-pe ↓ *Fl-ac* k* graph hell k* hep k* **Hyos** k* **Ign** indg iod k* kali-ar *Kali-br* kali-c k* *Kali-p* kali-sil k2* lac-c **Lach** k* lact j *Laur* b7.de* led k* lyc *Lyss* m-arct ↓ mag-c bg *Mag-m* k* mag-s meny ↓ *Merc* k* musca-d ↓ nat-c k* nat-m bg2 *Nit-ac* *Nux-m* k* nux-v k* olib-sac wmh1 olnd j *Op* k* par petr j *Ph-ac* k* phos k* *Plat* k* plb positr nl2• psil ft1 puls k* rheum k* rhod k* *Rhus-t* k* *Sabad* k* samb k* sec k* sel ↓ sep sil k* spong k* stann *Staph* k* **Stram** k* sul-ac bg sul-i k2* **Sulph** *Tarent* thuj valer k* vanil fd5.de verat k* verb viol-o k* visc zinc zinc-p k2* [zinc-m stj2]
  - **evening** | **bed**; in: calc h2 hell h1
  - **air**; in open | **amel.**: *Plat*
  - **chill**, during: kali-c nit-ac phos sulph
  - **closing** the eyes; on: calc h2 falco-pe nl2• led h1 sep h2
  - **decreased**: cann-xyz bg2 sel bg2
  - **followed** by | **garbage**: musca-d szs1
  - **heat**, during: bell bg2 bry bg2 carb-v k* hyos k* mag-m k* merc k* *Op* bg2 ph-ac bg2 phos rhus-t bg2 samb k* stram k*
  - **sleep**:
    : **during**: *Ant-c* b7a.de *Bell* b4.de* calc b4a.de camph b7.de* *Cham* b7.de* led b7a.de m-arct b7.de meny b7.de* *Merc* b4.de* nat-c b4.de* nux-v b7.de* phos b4a.de puls b7.de* rheum b7.de* *Sep* b4a.de *Sil* b4a.de stram b7.de*
    : **falling** asleep; when: calc h2* puls h1*
  - **waking**; on: meny b7.de*
- **fantasies** are forced upon him; a multitude of: bell br1 berb ↓ cypra-eg sde6.de• *Psor* kr1 verb kr1
  - **dozing**; when: berb kr1
- **far** away; as if everything is (See separated - world - he)
- **far** off; as if: bit-ar wht1• med rb2 sec ↓
  ○ • **Head**; in: sec rb2
- **farewell**; she had bid | **friend**; to a near: rhus-t rb2
- **fasting**; as after (See GENERALS - Weakness - fasting)
- **fatigue**:
  - **banished**; fatigue were forever: cann-s rb2
  - **work** without fatigue; he could: pip-m rb2
- **feather** duvet, the person beside him is a: aids nl2•
- **feet**:
  - **belong** to her; do not: carc sde•
  - **grown** longer; have: kola stb3•
  - **plunked** in the ground and someone had put a strengthening thing around her spine; feet had been: aids nl2•
  - **separated** from body, are (See separated - body - feet)
  - **slip** from under her; feet would: nicc rb2
  - **touch** scarcely the ground: calc-ar ↓ camph ↓ dat-a a1 falco-pe nl2• peti ↓ tep ↓ thuj ↓
    : **walking**; when: calc-ar rb2 camph rb2 peti a1* tep rb2 thuj rb2
- **feminine**; is soft, round and: dream-p sdj1•
- **fence** | **image** of a black painted fence: galla-q-r nl2•
- **fermenting** | **everything** were fermenting: nux-v rb2
- **fever**:
  - **coming** on; fever were: vichy-g rb2
  - **during**: bell a1* calc st
- **fiery**: bell a1
- **fighting**; people are: op stram
- **figures**: *(↗images)*
  - **seeing** figures: *(↗absurd - figures; people - seeing)* acon sf1.de agar sf1.de ambr ↓ anac kr1 anh mg1.de arg-n ↓ ars ↓ atro **Bell** k* bry sf1.de *Calc* camph ↓ carb-v caust ↓ chin c1 cic j5.de cimic sf1.de cina sf1.de coca cocc sf1.de con ↓ cupr cypra-eg sde6.de• graph ↓ hell hep ↓ *Hyos* sf1.de kali-br ↓ kali-c kali-p kali-s fd4.de merc ↓ mosch ↓ nat-c nit-ac nux-m nux-v ↓ *Op* sf1.de ph-ac *Phos* ↓ plat ↓ plb positr ↓ rhus-t sf1.de samb ↓ santin sec sf1.de sil ↓ spong *Stram* j5.de* sulph j5.de tarent tritic-vg fd5.de valer kr1 *Verat* ↓ visc ↓ zinc ↓
    : **closing** eyes; on: chin c1
    : **corners**; coming out of: stram sf1.de

- **seeing** figures: ...
  - **delirium**; seeing frightful figures during (See Fancies - exaltation)
  - **dozing**; when: visc sp1
  - **faceless**: positr nl2•
  - **gigantic**: atro
  - **hurled** bottle at them, and (See throws)
  - **large** black figures were about to spring on him: mosch
  - **marching** in the air:
    - **evening** | **asleep**; while half: nat-c
  - **old** repulsive persons: *Kali-c* kr1
  - **strange** (= grimaces): agar b2.de* ambr b2.de* *Anac*↓ arg-n bg2 ars bg2 *Bell* b2.de* bry b2.de* calc b2.de* camph b7.de caust b2.de* chin b2.de* cic bg2 *Cocc* b2.de* con b2.de* cupr bg2 graph bg2 hep b2.de* *Hyos* b2.de* kali-br bg2 merc b2.de* nux-v bg2 *Op* b2.de* ph-ac b2.de* *Phos* b2.de* plat bg2 rhus-t b2.de* samb b2.de* sec b2.de* sil b2.de* *Stram* b2.de* sulph b2.de* *Verat* b2.de* zinc bg2
    - **accompany** him, one to his right, the other to his left: *Anac* kr1*
  - **sleep**; during: kali-c h2
    - **half** asleep (See dozing)
  - **stone** or clay; made of: positr nl2•
- **throws** bottle at: chlol chlor kr1

- **filthy** (See dirty)
- **fingernails** seem as large as plates | **drowsiness**; during: cann-i
- **fingers**:
  - **cut** off: mosch k*
  - **thousand** fingers | **scratching** the body: musca-d szs1
  - **thumbs**; fingers are (See thumbs)
  - **together**; are grown: kola stb3•
- **fire**: alum↓ am-m↓ anac↓ ars↓ bar-c↓ *Bell*↓ *Calc*↓ calc-ar↓ calc-p↓ clem↓ croc↓ daph↓ *Hep*↓ ignis-alc↓ kali-n↓ kreos↓ lac-h sze9• lach↓ laur↓ lyss↓ mag-m↓ mez↓ nat-m↓ op↓ **Phos**↓ *Puls*↓ rad-br↓ rhod↓ rhus-t↓ spect↓ spig↓ spong↓ stann↓ stram↓ sulph↓ tet↓ verat↓ zinc↓ zinc-m↓ zinc-p↓ [ant-t stj2 heroin sdj2 plat stj2]
  - **night**: lach br1
  - **balls** of fire were rolling over bedclothes: stram rb2
  - **flame** of fire seems passing through him, a: *(↗Fire - set)* **Phos** k*
  - **head** is surrounded by: am-m k*
  - **home**; on a distant: bell
  - **house**, on: bell k* hep k* stram k* [spect dfg1]
  - **neighbor's** house on fire: hep
  - **noise** is a cry of fire and she trembles; every: *(↗hearing - illusions)* bar-c
  - **room** is on: stram k*
  - **visions** of: alum am-m k* anac k* ant-t k* ars *Bell* k* *Calc* k* calc-ar k2* calc-p k* clem croc daph k* *Hep* k* ignis-alc es2• kali-n kreos laur k* lyss k* mag-m mez bg2 nat-m op k2 phos k* plat *Puls* k* rad-br sze8• rhod rhus-t spig spong k* stann k* stram sulph k* tet a1 zinc zinc-p k2* [zinc-m stj2]
    - **evening**: rad-br sze8•
  - **world** is on: *Hep* ignis-alc es2• puls hr1* verat k2* [spect dfg1]
    - **night**; during: puls hr1
- **fishes**, flies, etc.; sees: bell *Stram*
- **fit** and walks faster, she will have a: *Arg-n*
- **flat**; everything is: positr nl2•
- **flatus**; that everybody notices his: zinc-p vh*
- **fleas** creeping over body; sees: gent-c c1
- **flesh** was off bone and edges sticking out: lac-d c1
- **flies**; sees: bell a1 lyc k2* streptoc jl2
- **flight** from objects: *Stram* a
- **floating**: *(↗lifted)* *Acon*↓ agar↓ agath-a↓ *Aids*↓ *Ambr*↓ anag↓ anh↓ ara-maca↓ *Arg-met*↓ arg-n↓ arge-pl↓ arn↓ asar↓ bell↓ brass-n-o↓ bry↓ calc↓ calc-ar↓ camph↓ cann-i↓ canth↓ carc↓ chir-fl↓ chlf↓ cocain↓ con↓ cypra-eg↓ dat-a↓ dub↓ dulc↓ *Euon*↓ euon-a↓ falco-pe↓ fic-m↓ galla-q-r↓ germ-met↓ haliae-lc↓ hippoc-k↓ hura↓ hyos↓ hyper↓ irid-met↓ jug-r↓ kali-br↓ keroso↓ *Lac-c*↓ lac-f↓ *Lac-loxod-a*↓ lac-mat↓ *Lach*↓ lact↓

- **floating**: ...
  lact-v↓ lat-h↓ loxo-recl↓ luna↓ m-aust↓ manc↓ moni↓ mosch↓ mucs-nas↓ musca-d↓ nat-ar↓ nat-m↓ nat-ox↓ *Nux-m*↓ olib-sac↓ *Op*↓ ozone↓ passi↓ pen↓ *Ph-ac*↓ phos↓ phys↓ pieri-b↓ pin-con↓ pip-m↓ plut-n↓ psil↓ rhus-g↓ sep↓ **Spig**↓ *Stach*↓ stict↓ stram↓ stroph-h↓ suis-em↓ suprar↓ *Tarent*↓ tell↓ tep↓ ter bg2 thuj↓ tung-met↓ urol-h↓ valer↓ visc↓ xan↓
  - **above** it all (See Detached; Estranged)
  - **air**, in: *(↗body - lighter; elevated - air; flying; lifted; lifted - air; swimming - air)* *Acon* bg3* agar vh agath-a nl2• *Aids* nl2• *Ambr* vh* anh sp1 ara-maca sej7• *Arg-met* vh* arge-pl rwt5• arn dx1 asar k* bell sf1.de* brass-n-o srj5• bry rb2 calc c1 calc-ar k2 cann-i canth carc fd2.de• chir-fl gya2 chlf a1 cocain rb2 cypra-eg sde6.de• dat-a a1* dub↓ dulc fd4.de *Euon* sf1.de* euon-a c1* falco-pe↓ fic-m gya1 galla-q-r nl2• germ-met srj5• haliae-lc srj5• hippoc-k szs2 hura hyos c1 hyper br1* irid-met srj5• jug-r c1* kali-br *Lac-c* bg3* lac-f wza1• *Lac-loxod-a* hrn2• *Lach* lact c1 lact-v c1* lat-h bro1 loxo-recl knl4• luna kg1• m-aust c1* manc rb2 moni rfm1• mosch rb2 mucs-nas rly4• nat-ar bro1 nat-m bg3* nat-ox rly4• *Nux-m* k* olib-sac wmh1 *Op* bg3* ozone sde2• passi c1* pen c1* *Ph-ac* c1* phos k* phys c1* pieri-b mlk9.de pin-con oss2• pip-m rb2 psil↓ rhus-g bro1* sep b4a.de* **Spig** bg3* *Stach* sf stict bg3* stroph-h c1 suis-em rly4• suprar rly4• *Tarent* c1* tell c1* tep rb2 ter bg1* thuj bg3* tung-met bdx1• urol-h rwt• valer bg3* visc c2* xan c1* [arg-n stj2 lac-mat sst4]
    - **evening**: bell
    - **kite** or a balloon on a string; like a: falco-pe nl2• galla-q-r nl2•
    - **legs** were floating: stict rb2
    - **sitting**; when: xan rb2
    - **spirit**; like a: *(↗body - lighter; light [=low - is)* asar k*] lac-ck2 lach k2* tell rb2
      - **sleep**; on going to: tell rb2
    - **upper** part of body: visc c1*
    - **walking**; while: asar dub bro1 lac-c bro1 spig ptk1
  - **back**; on a man's: musca-d szs1
  - **bed**:
    - **is** floating: con rb2 cypra-eg sde6.de•
    - **resting** on the bed:
      - **arms** and hands are not resting on the bed: plut-n srj7•
      - **he** is not: *Lach* stict
    - **suspended** in bed: bell h1 stram h1
    - **swimming** in bed: *(↗bed - touch)* bell h1* stram h1*
  - **boat**; floating in a: bell rb2
  - **closing** eyes, on: pen a1
  - **driving**, while: dulc fd4.de haliae-lc srj5•
  - **maze**, in a wavy: keroso a1
  - **polystyrene**; he was a piece of: agath-a nl2•
  - **things** are floating | **writing**; things are floating to and fro on: anag rb2
- **floor** (See ground)
- **flowers**; of:
  - **gigantic** flowers; of: cann-i a1
  - **seed** pods which pop open; changing into: aids nl2•
- **fluid** resisting passage; surrounded by ethereal: cann-i
- **fly** to pieces; he could (See Fear - control)
- **flying**: *(↗body - lighter; floating - air)* adam↓ anh sp ars-s-f↓ asar bell sf1.de buteo-j↓ calc-ar br1* camph k* *Cann-i* dendr-pol sk4• dulc↓ euon sf1.de falco-pe nl2• galla-q-r nl2• haliae-lc srj5• irid-met srj5• jug-r rb2 lach lact rb2 lat-h↓ lil-t↓ manc rb2 nitro-o a1 oena olib-sac wmh1 op sal-fr sle1• thiam rly4• thuj↓ tub↓ valer rb2 verat↓ vult-gr↓
  - **abyss**; flying from a rock into a dark | **bed**; on going to: cann-i
  - **Andes**; over the: vult-gr sze5•
  - **church**; in the: olib-sac wmh1
  - **constant**: lat-h bnm5•
  - **could** fly; as if he: adam srj5• camph rb2 cann-i tl1 dulc↓ lil-t rb2 olib-sac wmh1 tub rb2
    - **raised** from the ground; and he were: cann-i rb2 dulc fd4.de
  - **must** fly; as if he: ars-s-f rb2 bell rb2 verat rb2

- • **rushing** towards the stars: falco-pe nl2•
- • **skin**; out of his: thuj bg2
- • **walking**; while: [buteo-j sej6]
- • **would** fly away; as if he: galla-q-r nl2•
- **fog** | **wet** mist hanging over everything: galla-q-r nl2•
- **followed**; he is (See walking - behind)
- **foolish**: *Bell* j5.de hyos j5.de merc j5.de merc-act j nux-v j5.de
- **footsteps**; hearing: (↗*hearing - illusions)* canth k* carb-v k* crot-c *Med*↓ nat-p taosc iwa1•
  - • **behind** him: crot-c *Med* vh*
  - • **next** room, in: nat-p k*
- **forced**; that she is: crot-c sk4•
- **forehead**, she must look out under: ph-ac h2
- **forgetful**; he is: bar-c rb2 ham fd3.de• nat-sil fd3.de• podo fd3.de• [arg-n stj2 bar-i stj2 iod stj2 merc-i-f stj2]
- **forms** | **strange** forms accompanying him (See figures - seeing - strange)
- **forsaken**; is: (↗*alone; dead - everything - alone; friend - affection; friendless; outcast; repudiated - relatives; Company - desire; Confidence - want; Fear - forsaken; Fear - separation - husband; Fear - separation - parents; Flattered - desire; Forsaken; Forsaken - isolation; Longing - good; Timidity)* agath-a nl2• aids nl2• **Arg-n** *Aur* sf1.de *Aur-m-n* wbt2• bamb-a stb2.de• bar-c bit-ar wht1• camph cann-i carb-an carb-v carc fd2.de• chin crot-c sk4• *Cycl* cypra-eg sde6.de• *Dendr-pol* sk4• dream-p sdj1• *Ham*↓ hura hyos *Kali-br* *Kola* stb3• lach↓ lil-t limest-b es1• lyss **Mag-c** gg marb-w es1• nat-c nat-sil fd3.de• ozone sde2• pall phasco-ci rbp2 *Plat* positr nl2• **Puls** k ●* rhus-t↓ sal-al blc1• samb↓ sanic c1 *Stram* thuj mrr1 tritic-vg fd5.de [heroin sdj2]
  - • **morning** | **waking**; on: lach rb2
  - • **care** for her; no one would: *Ham* fd3.de• hura jsl lil-t rb2
  - • **doctor**; by her: samb bat1•
  - • **friend**; she has been forsaken by a near: rhus-t rb2
  - • **god**; by: kali-br mrr1
- **fortunate**; he is: lac-lup hrn2•
- **fortune**, he was going to lose his: (↗*poor; Avarice; Fear - poverty)* psor staph
- **foul**, everything appears: cur k*
- **fowls**, sees: stram k*
- **fragile** (See body - brittle)
- **friend**:
  - • **accident**; his friend had met with an: ars
  - • **affection** of; has lost the: (↗*forsaken; friendless; neglected - he; Company - desire; Confidence - want; Fear - separation - friends; Forsaken; Insecurity; Sadness - friends; Succeeds; Timidity)* agath-a nl2• ars gm1 *Aur* k* aur-m-n wbt2• hura hydrog srj2• hyos k2 rhus-t ckh1 *Thuj* mrr1 [bell-p-sp dcm1]
  - • **fantasy** world of imaginary friends; lives in a: calc ctc•
  - • **lose** a friend; she is about to: (↗*Forsaken)* hura [bell-p-sp dcm1]
  - • **never** seen his friends; he had | **walking**; after: stram kr1
  - • **offended**; has: ars
  - • **surrounded** by friends; being: aids nl2• bell cann-i germ-met srj5• *Hydr-ac*↓ [heroin sdj2]
    - ⁝ **shaking** hands and calling them by name: *Hydr-ac* kr1
  - • **unwanted** by friends: *Lac-h* sk4•
- **friendless**, he is: (↗*alone - always; forsaken; friend - affection; Ailments - friendship; Company - desire; Fear - separation - friends; Forsaken; Forsaken - isolation; Weeping - goes)* aids nl2• (non:alum h1) carc fd2.de• falco-pe nl2• *Ham* fd3.de• lac-h sk4• lach hr1 mag-m k* oci-sa sk4• phasco-ci rbp2 positr nl2• sars *Thuj* mrr1 [alum-p stj2 alumin stj2 alumin-s stj2 bell-p-sp dcm1 tax jsj7]
  - • **morning** | **waking**; on: lach rb2
- **fright**:
  - • **after**: (↗*visions - horrible - fright)* bapt rb2 bell j5.de calc-p rb2 dulc fd4.de merc rb2 plat j5.de
  - • **as** if in a fright: apis↓ bell↓ borx rb2 calc-p rb2 iber rb2 lac-c tl1 lach↓ lyc↓ m-aust↓ mag-p↓ magn-gl↓ nat-ar rb2 paeon rb2 phys↓ psor rb2 sacch-l rb2 samb↓ sars↓ stram rb2 ter rb2 zinc rb2
    - ⁝ **dream**; by a: borx rb2
- **fright** – **as** if in a fright: ...
    - ⁝ **trembling**; and indefinable dread with: iber rb2
    - ⁝ **vision** behind him; by a: lach rb2
    - ⁝ **waking**; on: apis rb2 bell rb2 lyc rb2 m-aust rb2 mag-p rb2 magn-gl rb2 phys rb2 samb rb2 sars rb2
- **frightening** others; that she is: hydrog srj2•
- **frightful** (See images - frightful; visions; Fancies - exaltation)
- **furniture** to be persons; imagines: (↗*inanimate)* nat-p tl1*
  - • **night**: nat-p
    - ⁝ **waking**; on: nat-p k*
- **galaxies** spiralling: adam srj5•
- **gallows** with fear; vision of: *Bell*
- **garbage**:
  - • **beautiful**; is: musca-d szs1
  - • **moving**; is: musca-d szs1
- **gathering** objects from pictures and walls; making efforts at: bell a1
- **gave** way:
  - • **everything** under him gave way: sanic rb2
  - • **ground** under him gave way (See ground - gave)
- **geese**:
  - • **is** a goose; he: con
  - • **sees**: hyos k*
  - • **threw** themselves into water, thinking themselves to be geese: con
- **general**, he is a: (↗*commander; great; officer)* cupr k* [cupr-act stj2 cupr-f stj2 cupr-m stj2 cupr-p stj2]
- **genitals** | **shrunken**, are: positr nl2•
- **gentle** | **everything** is gentle, natural and clean: aids nl2•
- **ghosts** (See specters)
- **giants**, sees: bell k*
- **gifts**; she is showered with: positr nl2•
- **giraffe**, he is a: cann-i k* falco-pe nl2•
- **glass**:
  - • **behind** a glass; as if: plac rzf5•
  - • **bubble**; as if in a: plac rzf5•
  - • **she** is made of: (↗*body - brittle)* falco-pe nl2• thuj k*
  - • **wood**, glass, etc.; being made of: eupi bro1 rhus-t bro1 *Thuj* bro1*
- **gliding** in the air; he is (See floating - air)
- **glittering** | **objects** were glittering and too bright: bell camph rb2 falco-pe nl2•
- **glowworms**, of: (↗*insects - shining)* cann-i a1
- **gnome**; being a: cann-i a1 positr nl2•
  - • **woman**: positr nl2•
- **God**:
  - • **communication** with God; he is in: chord-umb rly4• olib-sac wmh1 psil ft1 stram thres-a sze7• verat k*
  - • **god's** works are ill made and ill done: positr nl2•
  - • **he** is God, then he is the devil: (↗*iris)* **Stram** kr1
  - • **messenger** from God; he is a: (↗*messenger)* verat mrr1
  - • **presence** of God; he is in the: hydrog srj2*•
  - • **sees** God: aether a1
  - • **vengeance**; he is the object of God's: **Kali-br** k*
- **goitre**:
  - • **has** a: indg zinc↓
    - ⁝ **cannot** see over when sitting down; has one which he: zinc
- **goose** (See geese)
- **granddaughter**; bond will be broken with: des-ac rbp6
- **granted**; being taken for: polys sk4•
- **grasshoppers**: (↗*tomato)* choc srj
- **grave**, he is in his: anac jl3 *Gels* kr1 lepi stram

- **great** person, is a: *(↗better; body - greatness; christ; creative; diminished - everything; distinguished; divine; emperor - is; general; humility; inferior; knowledge; messenger; noble; officer; prince; proud; queen; rank; superhuman; superiority; tall - he; visions - grandeur; wealth; Deeds - great; Dictatorial - power; Haughty; Insanity; Plans - making - gigantic; Power - sensation; Respected - desire)* aeth *Agar* alum st1 bell *Cann-i* k* cic sne *Coca* vh* crot-c sk4• cupr cur a glon bg graph kr1 ham ↓ ignis-alc es2• iod sne *Kola* stb3• lac-leo sk4• *Lach* bg l y c bg *Lycpr* gl• lyss marb-w es1• phos *Plat* sal-fr sle1• stram bg sulph *Syph* st taosc iwa1• *Verat* k* verat-v kr1 [buteo-j sej6 heroin sdj2]
  - **reverenced** by all around her; she ought to be: ham a1
- **grid** of white lines, sees: positr nl2•
- **grief**:
  - **anger**; delusion from grief and: bell j5.de *Zinc* kr1
  - **weighed** upon him; a grief: am-m rb2 con rb2
- **grimaces**, sees: *(↗faces - ugly)* ambr j5.de* caust j5.de cocc sf1.de *Op* j5.de* stram sf1.de sulph j5.de*
  - **falling** asleep, on: sulph j5.de
- **groans**:
  - **hears**: *(↗hearing - illusions)* *Crot-c*
  - **with**: bell j5.de *Cham* j5.de
- **grotesque**: cann-i a1 hyos ↓ plb a1 sulph bg2
  - **people** appear: hyos a1
- **ground**:
  - **coming** up to meet him; ground were: *(↗stairs; stairs were)* bell bg2* calc bg2* cann-xyz bg2* pic-ac rb2* sil bg2*
  - **down**; as if ground was a long way: lavand-a ctl1•
  - **elastic**; as if floor were: alum b4a.de calc b4a.de
  - **gave** way beneath his feet: arg-n ptk1 con ptk1 cypra-eg sde6.de• d i g i n rb2 *Kali-br* hr1* sulph ptk1 tep rb2 visc ptk1
  - **moving**; ground were: clem rb2 podo fd3.de•
  - **sinking**; floor is: *(↗sinking - floor)* lepi rb2
  - **slipped** back and forth beneath her; the ground: tep rb2
  - **soft** like wool while walking; floor is: *(↗walking - wool)* xan c1
  - **touch** the ground; she would hardly: aids nl2• ars-met rb2 calc-ar rb2 camph ↓ dat-a rb2 thuj mlk1
    - **lighter**; he were: camph rb2
    - **walking**; when (See feet - touch - walking)
  - **unsteady**; the ground were: tep rb2
  - **wavering**; the ground were: chlf ↓ sulph rb2
    - **closing** the eyes; on: chlf rb2
    - **stood** was wavering; the ground on which he: sulph rb2
- **grow**:
  - **everything** is growing and transforming (See changed - growing)
  - **larger** and longer; he grew: *(↗tall - he)* aids nl2• aur rb2 plat rb2 stram rb2
  - **slowly** and dreamily; growing: aids nl2•
- **growling** as of a bear, hears: *(↗hearing - illusions)* mag-m
- **guilt**; of (See wrong - done)
- **gun**, uses a stick for a: *(↗shoot)* bell j5.de*
- **hair**; of:
  - **falling** out: nit-ac oss•
  - **increased**:
    - **facial** | **body**; and: plut-n srj7•
- **half** does not belong to her (See body - half - left)
- **hall**, illusions of a gigantic: cann-i
- **hammock**; swinging in a | **treetops**; above the: coff-t rb2
- **hand**:
  - **amputated**, she has no hands as if: galla-q-r nl2•
  - **behind** him: stront-c sk4•
  - **belong** to her, does not: carc sde•
  - **bound**: hyos ↓ positr nl2•
    - **chains**; with: hyos kr1
  - **four** hands; she has: adam srj5•
- **hand**: ...
  - **larger**; hands are becoming: choc srj3• falco-pe nl2• limest-b es•
  - **passes** over body: carb-v h2*
  - **separated** from body, is (See separated - body - hand)
  - **smoothing** her; felt a hand: med rb2
    - **head**; smoothing her: med k*
  - **taking** her hand; something | **midnight**: canth k*
  - **visions** of white, outspread hand coming toward face in the darkness: ben
  - **water**; lying in a puddle of (See EXTREMITIES - Water - hand - puddle)
- **hang** himself, wants to: *Ars* h2*
- **hanging**; is:
  - **he** or she were hanging:
    - **downward**; with his head: glon rb2 plut-n srj7•
    - **standing** high; hanging or: phos
    - **three** feet from the ground | **asleep**; on falling: hura
  - **persons** who were hanging; sees: ars k*
- **happen**; something terrible is going to (See Fear - happen - terrible)
- **happened**; something has: calc gl1.fr• med ↓ nux-v gl1.fr• *Staph* gl1.fr• sulph gl1.fr•
  - **dreadful** has happened; something: med rb2
- **happy** in his own house, he will never be: ars
- **hard**; everything is: adam srj lac-e hm2•
  - **sitting** or lying; while (See GENERALS - Hard bed - everything)
- **hardship**; life is: lac-e hm2•
- **harlequin**, he is a: hyos
- **harmony**:
  - **heaven** and earth; between: neon srj5•
  - **order** and clarity of everything: adam srj5•
- **hat** is a pair of trousers which he tries to put on: stram k*
- **hated**; by others: adam srj5• galla-q-r nl2• lach ptk1 sanic mg
- **haywire**; things going: polys sk4•
- **head**:
  - **back** of head is elongated: choc srj3•
  - **balance** his head; he has to | **vertigo**; during: aesc rb2
  - **balloon**, rising up and stretching the neck; head is a hot air: bamb-a stb2.de•
  - **belongs** to another: *Alum* bg2* cann-i st1 cann-xyz bg2 nat-m bg2* ther k* thuj bg2*
  - **circle**; head were going around in a: bry rb2 iber ↓ tub rb2
    - **occiput** were turning around: iber rb2
  - **cold** breeze blows on: petr
  - **compacted**, is: positr nl2•
  - **corner** of the room; part of head fitted into each: cann-i rb2
  - **deceased** acquaintances without bodies; heads of: nux-v k*
  - **diminished**: grat vml2* limest-b ↓
    - **left** side has diminished: limest-b es1•
  - **disease** will break out of head: stram k*
  - **divided**; is: psor al2* ther hr1* xan br1
  - **double**; is: sulfon gl1.fr•
  - **empty**; head were (See HEAD - Empty)
  - **enlarged** (See enlarged - head)
  - **fall**; head would:
    - **backward**: chinin-s rb2 chir-fl gya2
    - **bed**; out of: *(↗bed - falling - out - head)* arg-met rb2*
    - **directions**; in all: cann-s rb2
    - **forward**: agn rb2 calad ↓ cupr rb2 *Hipp* jl2
      - **walking**; on: calad rb2 hipp rb2
    - **off**: nux-m c1
    - **side**; to one: spong rb2
  - **floating**: jug-r br1* nat-hchls ↓ rauw ↓ zinc ↓

- **floating**: ...
  - **off**: *(↗separated)* nat-hchls ↓ rauw sp1
    - **top** of head were floating off: nat-hchls rb2
  - **up** and down | **images** of fancy; head were floating up and down with a similar floating of the: zinc rb2
- **flying** | **round** and round: eup-pur rb2
- **friend's** head stick out of a bottle; sees his: bell
- **headless**; is (See no)
- **heavy**; his own head seemed too: bry cham rb2 lac-lup hrn2• puls rb2
- **hold** his head straight; he could not | **right** side; head would constantly incline to the: ferr rb2
- **inflated**; head were: merl rb2
- **large**: *(↗enlarged - head)*
  - **grimaces**; large heads make:
    - **evening** | **closing** the eyes; on: euphr
  - **too** large; seems: *(↗enlarged - head)* acon allox tpw4 melal-alt gya4 meph sf1.de sil h2
- **lift** it off; can: ther
- **light**; head is: jab rb2 sarr rb2
- **longer**; back of head is (See back)
- **monstrous** head on a distant wall of the room: aur h2 cann-i
- **motion** | **up** and down | **similar** floating of images of fancy; with a: zinc rb2
  - **within** head were in motion; all: verat rb2
- **no** head; there were: *(↗separated)* asar ptk1* aur-ar vml2• calc-i ptk1 cocc rb2 nit-ac ptk1 nux-v j5.de
- **open** and his consciousness is expanding above him; top of head is: falco-pe nl2•
- **opens** and a choir of golden angels ascends from it: aids nl2•
- **pain** in head; having: bamb-a stb2.de•
- **pendulum**; head seems an inverted oscillating: cann-i
- **pillow**, but did not know where the rest of the body was; the head was on the: pyrog rb2
- **pulled** backward: chir-fl gya2
- **pushed**; head were | **forward**: ferr-p rb2
- **reeled** to and fro; head (See swaying - head - back)
- **rolling** about in head; something were: sep rb2
- **separated** from body; head is: *(↗floating - off; no; body - divided)* allox k1* alum st anac vh ant-t st* arg-n bg2 bell bg2 bufo bg2 cann-i rb cocc k1 *Daph* a1* falco-pe nl2• kali-bi bg2 lac-lup hrn2• lyc bg2 m-ambo b7.de mez bg2 nat-c st plut-n srj7• **Psor** b4a.de* ther k1*
- **shaking** the: bell cham
- **strange** head; his head were another: ther rb2
- **stupefied**; head were: podo fd3.de• psor ↓ rheum rb2
  - **left** half of head: psor rb2
- **swaying** | **head** were swaying | **back** and forth: carb-v rb2 zinc rb2
  - **in** head; swaying | **walking**; when: daph rb2
- **swimming**: ars-h rb2
- **swinging**; head were | **forward**; from behind: pall rb2
- **teeming**; head were | **whirling** around it; with live things: sil rb2
- **topsy**-turvy; head were | **walking**: cham rb2
- **transparent** and speckled brown: bell k*
- **two** heads, having: *Bell* b4a.de mosch gt nux-m k* sulfon gl1.fr•
- **undulating** in head: indg rb2 stroph-h ↓
  - **body**; and whole: stroph-h rb2
- **whirling** in head: chel rb2 chinin-s ↓ chlf rb2 coff ↓ ovi-p rb2 sec rb2 viol-o rb2
  - **mill** wheel; like a: chinin-s rb2
  - **thinking**; when: coff rb2

- **headache**; having a (See head - pain)
- **headless** (See head - no)
- **health**, he has ruined his: *(↗disease - incurable; Despair - recovery)* bamb-a stb2.de• chel k*
- **hear**, he cannot: *(↗hearing - illusions)* hyos j5.de mosch verat
- **hearing**: *(↗hearing - illusions; messages; voices - hearing; HEARING - Illusions)*
  - **ear**; not with his own (See HEARING - Illusions - own)
  - **illusions** of: *(↗sounds; bells; bells - door; choir; clock; deaf; disease - deaf; fire - noise; footsteps; groans - hears; growling; hear he; hearing; help; help - calling; music - hearing; noise - hearing; people - noise; shouting; sight; sounds; voices - hearing; voices - own voice seems; voices - own voice sounds; HEARING - Illusions)* absin k1 agar bro1 am-c k1 *Anac* bro1 anh jl *Antip* br1* ars bro1 atro k1 atro-s hr1 bell j5.de* bold mg1.de calc j5.de *Cann-i* k1* canth j5.de* carb-v bg2* carbn-o k1 carbn-s k1* **Cham** bro1* cocain br1* colch j5.de con k1 conin c1 corv-cor bdg• dulc fd4.de elaps bro1 eup-pur k1 hyos k1 iodof a kali-ar k1 lyss c1 mag-m j5.de med k1 merc bro1 naja bro1 nat-p bro1 nux-m c1 ph-ac j5.de puls bro1 rhodi-o-n c1 stram k1* streptoc jl2 thea k1* thres-a sze7• vanil fd5.de [cann-s xyz62]
  - **mania**; in: *Stram* kr1
  - **noise** of colors: cann-i tl1
  - **objects** moving: ph-ac h2
  - **retching**: musca-d szs1
  - **someone** approaches his bed: carb-v kr1
  - **songs**: thres-a sze7•
  - **sounds**: *(↗illusions; HEARING - Illusions - sounds)*
    - **distant**; are (See HEARING - Distant - sounds)
    - **left** side; from (See HEARING - Illusions - sounds - left)
    - **remaining** longer (See HEARING - Illusions - sounds - remained)
  - **talk** seems distant: aran jl bros-gau mrc1 galeoc-c-h gms1•
  - **talk** seems loud: *Lac-e* hrn2•
  - **tone**:
    - **split**; is: anh sp
    - **world**; as from an other: **Carb-an** kr1 galeoc-c-h gms1•
  - **voice** seems changed; his own (See strange - voice)
  - **wrist**-watch; winding up of: ambr a
- **heart**: *(↗CHEST - Ceases - will)*
  - **absent**; is: ozone sde2•
  - **disease**: *(↗disease - every)*
    - **going** to have a heart disease and die; is: *(↗die - about - heart; Fear - death - heart)* arn k2* germ-met srj *Kali-ar* vh lac-c lach st podo k2
    - **having** an: *(↗Fear - heart - disease)* arn k13 calc h2 germ-met srj graph bg2 *Kali-ar* vh* *Lac-c* hr1 lach st *Nat-c* kr1 podo k2
  - **hung** by a thread (See CHEST - Thread)
  - **large**, too (See CHEST - Enlarged - heart)
  - **live** without; he can: *Nux-v* kr1
  - **open**; is: coca-c sk4•
  - **rock**; is like a: rhus-g tmo3•
  - **stitches** will kill him: psor kr1
  - **stone**; is a: positr nl2•
  - **stops** beating when sitting: *(↗CHEST - Ceases)* *Arg-n* hr1* gels vh
  - **thread**; heart hung by a (See CHEST - Thread)
  - **turning** around, is: aur k*
- **heat** from epigastrium; has a furious, radiating: cann-i
- **heaven**, is in: calc-ar rb2 cann-i k* hydrog srj2• neon ↓ op *Verat* hr1*
  - **kissed** by heaven: neon srj5•
  - **talking** with God: *Verat* hr1*
- **heavy**; is: *(↗Heaviness)* alum ptk1 atro kr1 chr-ac kr1 eup-per ↓ eup-pur ↓ hippoc-k szs2 hyper ↓ nat-c *Nit-ac* kr1 ovi-p ↓ *Positr* nl2• sacch-a fd2.de• sarr kr1 thuj k* [heroin sdj2]
  - **bed**; he was too heavy in: hyper rb2 ovi-p ↓

- **heavy**; is: ...
  - ⁝ **break**; and bed would: ovi-p rb2
  - · **fall**; and he will: eup-per hr1* (non:eup-pur kr1)
- **hedgehog**:
  - · **sees** hedgehogs: choc srj3•
  - · **she** is a: choc srj3•
- **held** | **sitting**; he is held up high when: rhus-t rb2
- **hell**:
  - · **chains** of; in: *Orig* hr1* (non:orig-v kr1)
    - ⁝ **sexual** desire; with violent: orig hr1
  - · **confess** his sins at gate of; obliged to: agar
  - · **going** to hell because he had committed a unpardonable crime: *(↗sinned - unpardonable)* med c1
  - · **in**; is: *(↗purgatory)* camph k* cann-i germ-met srj haliae-lc srj5• hydrog srj2• ignis-alc es2• lyss hr1* merc k* *Orig* hr1* (non:orig-v kr1)
  - · **shadows**; of demoniac:
    - ⁝ **midnight**; at | **waking**; on: cann-i
  - · **torments** of hell without being able to explain; suffers the: lyss kr1* *Merc* k1*
- **help**: *(↗hearing - illusions; Company - desire; Delirium - crying - help; Forsaken; Forsaken - isolation; Helplessness; Shrieking - help)*
  - · **calling** for: *(↗hearing - illusions; Company - desire; Delirium - crying - help; Forsaken; Forsaken - isolation; Helplessness; Shrieking - help)* plat
  - · **wanted**; is not: dioxi rbp6
- **hemorrhage**; after: chinin-ar
- **hens** bound with chains: *Hyos* hr1*
- **herbs**, gathering: bell k* cupr k*
- **herself**; she were not (See person - other)
- **high**:
  - · **building**; stepped from a high: dub rb2
  - · **he** were high: camph ↓ plut-n srj7•
    - ⁝ **houses**; higher than the: camph rb2
  - · **steps** were too high: agar bg2 onos bg2 tab rb2
- **himself**; he is not (See person - other)
- **hindered**; he is: *(↗work - hindered; Hindered)* anh sp1 *Chin* ↓ *Lac-e* hrn2• lac-leo ↓ mosch ↓ ruta fd4.de tritic-vg fd5.de
  - · **everyone**; by: *(↗enemy - everyone)* *Chin* gl1.fr• lac-leo sk4• mosch bg2*
- **hippopotamus**; being a: cann-i a1*
- **hole**:
  - · **black** hole with spider's webbing coming from it; seeing a: aids nl2•
  - · **chasm**; a small hole appears like a frightful: agar
  - · **chest**; in his: melal-alt ↓ rhus-g tmo3•
    - ⁝ **black** hole: melal-alt gya4
    - ⁝ **extending** through | **back**; to: rhus-g tmo3•
  - · **digging** a big: maias-l hrn2•
  - · **world** through a hole; views the: androc srj1•
- **hollow**:
  - · **body** is hollow; whole: aur st *Kali-c* hr1* pall a1 [spect dfg1]
  - · **organs**; being hollow in: *Cocc* bro1 galeoc-c-h gms1• oxyt bro1
    - ⁝ **Nose**: galeoc-c-h gms1•
- **home**:
  - · **arrived** home; has: neon srj5•
  - · **at** home, when he is not; thinks he is: *(↗Delirium)* cann-i hyos
  - · **away** from home; he is: *(↗house - own; Delirium)* acon k* *Aster* kr1* bell **BRY** k ●* calc calc-p ↓ cic cimic ↓ *Coff* k* des-ac rbp6 germ-met srj *Hyos* lach k* limest-b es1• meli merc h1 *Nux-v* vh* *Op* k* par j5.de plb bg2* puls st *Rhus-t* valer k* verat vip
    - ⁝ **abortion**, in threatening: *Op* mtn
    - ⁝ **delirium** tremens, in: *Coff* kr1
    - ⁝ **must** get there: *(↗Delirium - home; Home - desires)* **Bry** bro1* calc ptk1 calc-p bro1 cimic bro1 hyos bro1 lach ptk1 *Op* bro1*
  - · **changed**; everything at home has: arg-n k*
- **home**: ...
  - · **every** place in nature or a big strange city could be one' s home: plac rzf5•
  - · **way** home were too long: glon rb2
- **honest**:
  - · **is** honest; she: marb-w es1• olib-sac wmh1
  - · **not** honest; is: stram hr1*
- **horizon** moving towards oneself; of: falco-pe nl2•
- **horrible**: *(↗Horrible; Strange - everything)* lac-c ptk1
  - · **everything** seems: *(↗Horrible; Strange - everything)* **Calc** kr1 cic br1 kali-bi ↓ *Plat* positr nl2•
    - ⁝ **delirium** tremens; in: kali-bi kr1
  - · **person**; everyone can see she is a horrible: positr nl2•
  - · **visions** (See visions - horrible)
- **horses**: *(↗Horrible)* bell ↓ cann-i ↓ falco-pe ↓ m-aust ↓ mag-m ↓ stram ↓ zinc ↓ [ars-met stj2]
  - · **riding** a horse: cann-i k* stram he1
  - · **seeing**: bell m-aust j mag-m zinc
  - · **she** is a reined in wild stallion that desires to be free: falco-pe nl2•
- **hostage**; being taken as: phasco-ci rbp2
- **house**:
  - · **burning** down; her house is: haliae-lc srj5•
  - · **coming** down on her; house is: sabad rb2
  - · **crush** him; houses on each side would approach and: *(↗falling - walls; Fear - narrow)* arg-n
  - · **enlarged**, is: aids nl2•
    - ⁝ **explore** it, and he wants to: aids nl2•
  - · **falling** on her; as if houses were: sabad rb2
  - · **fragile**, is: vesp mgm•
  - · **movable**; house seems: cann-i
  - · **move** as she walks; houses: tep rb2
  - · **own** house; not being in one's: *(↗home - away; Recognizing - not - house)* *Op* hr1* verat a1*
  - · **people**; house is full of: ars cann-i con lach lyc merc nat-m nux-v sil stram
  - · **place**; house is not in the right | **walking** in the street; while: glon
  - · **stage** setting; house looks like a: plut-n srj7•
  - · **surrounded**; house is: lac-e hrn2• stram
  - · **turned** upside down; house were: bufo rb2 eug rb2
- **hovering** in the air; one were (See floating - air)
- **humility** and lowness of others; while he is great: *(↗great; tall; tall - he; Haughty)* germ-met srj ignis-alc es2• plat staph
- **hunted**, he is: *(↗pursued)* plut-n srj7• positr nl2•
  - · **running** scared: positr nl2•
- **hunter**, he is a: cann-i sanguis-s hrn2• verat
- **husband**; he is not her: *(↗Forsaken)* *Anac* k*
- **hydrothorax**; he has a: alco a1* phos a1*
- **hypnotized**, he is: positr nl2•
- **ichthyosaur**; seeing an: cann-i a1
- **ideas**:
  - · **floating**:
    - ⁝ **clouds**; in the: dat-a rb2
    - ⁝ **outside** of brain: *(↗thoughts - outside)* dat-a a1
  - · **gather** ideas from a far; he has to: dat-a rb2
  - · **rush** of ideas prevented him from completing work: stann rb2
- **identity**: *(↗consciousness - belongs; Stranger - sensation)*
  - · **boundaries** and is everywhere; his identity has no (See Confusion - identity - boundaries)
  - · **errors** of personal identity: *(↗person - other; robot; Confusion - identity)* aids nl2• *Alum* k* androc srj anh jl ant-c bapt cann-i st cann-s cic k2 gard-j vlr2• kali-br hl lac-c lach lil-t hl mosch st myric hl naja hl ol-j hl orig hl petr phos plb pyrog k2* (non:pyrus slp) raja-s jl spong fd4.de stram k* thuj k* valer **Verat** mrr1

- **errors** of personal identity: ...
  - **turning** his body from one side to another; when: Pyrog jl2
- **someone** else, she is: Alum vh* cann-i st cann-s gels Lach k1* mosch bg1 phos plb pyrog k2 Valer k1

- **ill** (See sick)
- **ill**-treated by everyone; he is: sumb rb2
- **images**, phantoms; sees: *(↗apparition; faces; fancy; figures; sight; specters; visions)* acon alum j5.de Ambr anac↓ androc↓ anh↓ Apis Arg-n arn j5.de Ars atro↓ bar-c **Bell** berb bit-ar wht1• brom bry↓ calc calc-ar k2 calc-s calc-sil k2 camph cann-i↓ canth carb-an Carb-v carbn-o↓ caust cham chin chinin-ar cic cina↓ coca cocain↓ con↓ croc↓ Crot-h cupr cur↓ cycl↓ cypra-eg↓ dros dulc fl-ac↓ gels↓ graph hell Hep hydrog↓ Hyos ign kali-ar kali-br kali-c kali-p kali-sil k2 lac-c k2 **Lach** lachn hr1* lact j5.de laur↓ led limest-b↓ Lyc mang↓ marb-w↓ Merc mur-ac↓ nat-c Nat-m nat-p nit-ac nux-m j5.de nux-v olib-sac wmh1 olnd j5.de Op oxal-a rly4• ozone↓ petr↓ ph-ac Phos k* plat puls rhod j5.de rhus-t Samb sanguis-s hrn2• sars↓ sec↓ sep sil spect↓ spong Stram sulph tab Tarent thres-a sze7• Thuj toxi↓ valer k2 verat verb j5.de Zinc zinc-p↓ [Cann-s xyz62]
  - **afternoon**: lyc
  - **evening**: calc carb-an a1 lyc nit-ac
    - **bed**; in: nit-ac
  - **night**: acon ambr arg-n arn bell berb calc calc-ar k2 calc-sil k2 Camph canth carb-an carb-v cham chin crot-h cupr cur graph ign Kali-br kali-c kali-sil k2 led lyc Merc nat-m nit-ac nux-v op phos puls Sep sil spong tab Thuj valer zinc zinc-p k2
  - **all** over: bry k2 merc Sil
  - **alone**, when: fl-ac lach
  - **black**: arn ars Bell k* caust cypra-eg sde6.de• hydrog srj2• op plat k* puls k* **Stram** k*
  - **closing** eyes, on: anh mg1.de Arg-n **Bell** k* **Calc** calc-ar k2 Caust cupr↓ graph limest-b es1• nat-m h2 oxal-a rly4• puls samb k* sep Sil k1 sulph Tarent Thuj
    - **bed**; in: Bell vh* Calc vh* cupr samb sulph
  - **dark**, in the: *(↗Darkness - agg.; Light - desire)* Bell Carb-v hell petr puls Stram k*
  - **disappearing** and reappearing: nit-ac h2
  - **distorted**: *(↗faces - distorted)* caust h2 lac-c k13
  - **dozing** during day; sees images while: lachn kr1
  - **dwells** upon: *(↗Brooding)* arn nux-m sil
  - **ever** changing: carbn-o mur-ac↓
    - **past** to present: mur-ac
  - **frightful**: *(↗visions - horrible; Fancies - exaltation - frightful)* Ambr anac androc srj1• anh br1 arg-n arn ars atro bar-c Bell k* bry h1 **Calc** k* calc-s camph Carb-an Carb-v Caust k* chin k* chinin-ar cina k2 coca cocain br1 con k* croc gels graph k* Hep k* hyos ign kali-ar Kali-br kali-c k* kali-p k1 kali-sil k2 Lac-c Lach laur limest-b es1• lyc k* mang marb-w es1• Merc k* mur-ac nat-c nat-p nit-ac nux-v k* Op k* petr k* ph-ac Phos k* puls k* rhod rhus-t k* samb sars k* sec sil k* spect↓ spong Stram k* sulph k* tab tarent toxi↓
    - **evening**: caust gt
    - **night**: calc-s↓ sil ckh1 spect↓
      - **sleep**; while trying to: calc-s sil h2 [spect dfg1]
    - **closing** the eyes; on: toxi mtf2•
  - **increasing** and decreasing; sees images: nit-ac h2
  - **moving** up and down; sees images: zinc h2
  - **pleasant**: bell kr1 cann-i cycl cypra-eg sde6.de• Lach
  - **rising** out of the earth: **Stram** k ●*
  - **running**; sees images: nit-ac h2
  - **side**; at his: **Stram** k ●
  - **sleep**:
    - **before**: carb-an merc nit-ac sep
    - **during**: lyc
      - **hateful** | **afternoon**: lyc a1
    - **going** to; on: arg-n a1 calc-s k2 calc-sil k13 carb-an a1 chin nat-m h2
    - **preventing**: alum ambr k2 arg-n lyc op tab
  - **suppressed** for long; that are: ozone sde2•

- **images**, phantoms; sees: ...
  - **twilight**: berb k2
  - **wall**, on the: lyc samb
- **immortality**, of: anh sp1*
- **impotent**; being: stry-p ptk1
- **imposter**, is an: sal-fr sle1•
- **inanimate** objects are persons: *(↗furniture; person - something)* bell k* calc nat-p stram
- **inconsolable**; being: stram rb2
- **incubus**; being weighed down by an (See Sadness - burden)
- **incurable** (See disease - incurable)
- **indispensable** | **together**; holds everything: des-ac rbp6
- **inferior**; people seem mentally and physically: *(↗elevated - air - looking; great; tall; tall - he; Haughty; Vanity)* granit-m es1• nicc-met↓ plat↓ Psor jl2
  - **entering** the house after a walk; when: plat k*
  - **stupid** and thick; that others are: nicc-met sk4•
- **influence**; one is under a powerful: *(↗possessed; strangers - control; superhuman - control; Confusion - identity)* ambr tsm1 carc mlr1• cere-b dream-p sdj1• foll asm• Hyos vh* irid-met srj5• kali-br sne Lach k* ozone sde2• positr nl2• psil ft1 Sal-fr sle1• Stram kr1 thuj rb2* verat vh
- **inhuman**, animal-like: dendr-pol sk4•
- **injury**:
  - **about** to receive injury; is: *(↗assaulted; child - he - vulnerable; Fear - injury - being)* aq-mar rbp6 ars bell k2 berb↓ cann-i carbn-s con dendr-pol sk4• fum↓ galeoc-c-h gms1• hyos st irid-met srj5• lac-h sze9• lach lyc merc nux-v oci-sa sk4• Op kr1 polys sk4• rad-br sze8• sil stram k* sulph symph fd3.de• [tax jsj7]
    - **friends**; from his: fum rly4• lach k2
    - **woman**; as a: [berb stu1]
  - **being** injured; is: bry cact canth elaps **Hyos**↓ kali-br lach lyss naja kr1* phos plat↓ rhus-g tmo3• rhus-t **Stram** k* sulph k*
    - **head**; at: naja kr1
    - **sleep**, during: plat a1
    - **surroundings**; by his: **Hyos** k1* Lach Naja k1*
  - **fingers** and toes are being cut off; his: mosch
  - **someone**; is about to inflict injury on: limest-b es1•
- **inkstand**:
  - **saw** one on the bed; he: lact
  - **was** an inkstand; he: cann-i k*
- **insane**: *(↗Insanity)*
  - **become** insane; one will: *(↗mind - out; Fear - insanity)* Acon k* act-sp vh1 agar rb2 ail rb2 alum bg2* ambr bg2* antip↓ aq-mar mgm• arg-n br1 ars bg2 asar vh brom rb2* Calc bg2* **Cann-i** k* cann-s st* cann-xyz bg2 cham sne Chel k* chlor bg2* **Cimic** k* coff↓ colch bg2 cupr rb2* cycl rb2 cypra-eg sde6.de• Eup-per kr1 falco-pe nl2• gels rb2 glon rb2 ham bg2 hydrog srj2• hyos rb2 Ign kr1 iod rb2* iris-t rb2 kali-bi rb2 kali-br bg2* kali-p wd lac-c bg2* Lac-e hrn2• lam a1 lil-t k* limen-b-c hrn2* maias-l hrn2• **Manc** k* med k* merc k* nat-m k* nat-s rb2 nat-sil fd3.de• nitro-o a1 nux-v bg2* pall hr1* phys bg2* plat bg2* psor c1* sil rb2 spig↓ streptoc jl2 sulph rb2 Syph br1* tanac tarent bg2* vario wd [am-br stj2 bar-br stj2 bar-i stj2 merc-i-f stj2]
    - **delivery**; during: cimic kr1* coff kr1
    - **hammering** over left eye; with: Ham kr1
    - **head**; from snapping in: antip rb2
    - **headache**, from: spig hr1
    - **hold** himself; if he did not: lil-t rb2
    - **itching**; with: ail kr1
    - **pain**; from: kali-bi rb2
    - **sitting** still and thinking; when: lac-c hr1*
    - **thinking** long about anything; when: ars rb2
    - **unless** she got out of her body: lil-t kr1
  - **crazy** | **he** is (See he)
  - **everyone** is: androc srj1•
  - **he** is insane: Cimic bg2 falco-pe nl2• germ-met srj5• Kali-br kr1 maias-l hrn2• ol-j kr1 orig sne pall rb2 phys bg2* sanic rb2 spong kr1 sulph rb2 Thuj b4a.de [alum stj2 cupr-act stj2 cupr-f stj2 cupr-p stj2 heroin sdj2]
    - **tell** everyone, and must: falco-pe nl2•

- • **people** think her or him being insane: aids nl2• **Calc** germ-met srj hydrog srj2• sal-fr sle1•
- **insects**, sees: *(↗bugs; cockroaches)* *Abel* vh* agar b4a.de agath-a ↓ *Am-m* b7a.de **Ars Bell** k* carc fd2.de• caust k* choc srj3• *Cimic* gk cocc b7.de c o f f b7a.de colch sf dig k* galeoc-c-h gms1• hydrog ↓ hyos irid-met srj5• *Lac-c* k* loxo-recl knl4• merc k* musca-d szs1 nat-sil fd3.de• op sf phos plb puls sanguis-s hm2• *Stram* k* tarent k*
  - • **head**; on back of: hydrog srj2• irid-met srj5•
  - • **neck**; on back of: agath-a nl2•
  - • **shining**: *(↗glowworms)* bell k*
- **insecure**; everything is (See Insecurity)
- **insignificant**; he is (See Confidence - want)
- **insulted**, he is: *(↗abused; appreciated; criticized; despised; laughed; Admonition - agg.; Ailments - reproaches; Confidence - want; Fear - humiliated; Fear - opinion; Haughty; Offended)* adam srj5• alco a1 aur-ar a1* aur-m-n wbt2• bell cham cocc rb2 crot-c ↓ granit-m es1• haliae-lc srj5• ign k* ilx-a mtf11 kali-br lac-c *Lac-e* hm2• lyss k* nat-m mrr1 nux-v k* oci-sa sk4• *Pall* k* puls k* staph ptk1* sulph rb2 tarent [heroin sdj2]
  - • **boarders** in hotel, by: kali-br a1
  - • **looked** down upon: crot-c sk4•
- **insulting**; with: lyc j5.de
- **intelligence** | **joyful** intelligence; he had received: lyss rb2
- **interest** in anything; felt no: dulc fd4.de nux-v rb2
- **intoxicated**:
  - • **been**; he had: iodof rb2 kali-c rb2 rheum rb2 squil rb2
  - • **is**; he: agar rb2 aids nl2• ang rb2 bufo rb2 carb-ac rb2 cench ↓ chinin-s rb2 chlor rb2 cic rb2 cocc rb2 cor-r rb2 cot rb2 croc rb2 cur rb2 falco-pe nl2• ferr rb2 gard-j vlr2• gels rb2 glon rb2 hydr rb2 hyos rb2 jug-r rb2 kali-br rb2 kali-c rb2 kali-i ↓ lact rb2 lil-t rb2 lyc rb2 m-aust rb2 mag-p rb2 med rb2 merl rb2 mez rb2 mill rb2 nicc rb2 nux-m rb2 nux-v rb2 olnd rb2 op rb2 oxyt ↓ petr rb2 ph-ac rb2 phos rb2 pip-m rb2 psor rb2 ptel rb2 puls rb2 ran-b rb2 raph rb2 rat rb2 rhod rb2 rhus-t rb2 sabad rb2 sec rb2 sep rb2 sol-ni rb2 spig rb2 staph rb2 sul-ac rb2 sulph rb2 tab rb2 tarax rb2 thuj rb2* valer rb2 verat rb2 zinc ↓ [spect dfg1]
    - ⁝ **morning**; in: thuj rb2
    - ⁝ **afternoon** | **16** h and in the evening: cench rb2
    - ⁝ **coal** gas; from: zinc rb2
    - ⁝ **debauch**; after a: psor rb2
    - ⁝ **excited**; and: kali-i rb2
    - ⁝ **head** is held erect; if: nux-v rb2
    - ⁝ **move**; when trying to: gels rb2
    - ⁝ **night** reveling; from: nux-v rb2
    - ⁝ **pleasantly**; he were: oxyt rb2
    - ⁝ **room** but not in the open air; in a: croc rb2
    - ⁝ **tobacco** smoking; as after: spig rb2
    - ⁝ **undressing**; while: sec rb2
    - ⁝ **water** when walking; on seeing flowing: ferr rb2
- **invaded**; one's space is being: gard-j vlr2• granit-m es1• positr nl2• [heroin sdj2 spect dfg1]
  - • **mother**; by her: positr nl2•
- **invader**; he is an: lac-lup hm2•
- **invincible**; he is: kola stb3• loxo-recl knl4•
- **invisible**; she is: aq-mar rbp6 loxo-recl knl4• positr nl2•
- **iodine**; illusions of fumes of: iod
- **iris**; being the goddess: *(↗god - he)* irid-met srj5•
- **iron** shield around him, has an: falco-pe nl2•
- **irresistible**; he is: *Kola* stb3•
- **island**; he is happy on a distant: *(↗Content)* phos
- **jarring** her; she were in some vehicle which was moving and (See vehicle - jarring)
- **jealousy**:
  - • **lovers** concealed behind stove; wife has: *(↗wife - faithless)* *Stram* kr1
  - • **with**: *Lach* j5.de* stram kr1
- **jelly**; the body is made of: cypra-eg sde6.de• eupi br1* plac rzf5•
- **jostling** against everyone she meets: acon rb2
- **journey**; he is on a: *(↗travelling)* bell k* brom cann-i cann-xyz bg2 chinin-ar rb2 crot-h hyos k* lach mag-m nat-c op sang sil
- **joy**: | **nothing** could give her any joy: stram rb2
- **juggler**, he is a: bell
- **jumping**:
  - • **high** place; off a: arg-n tl1
  - • **impelled** to jump out of the window: thea rb2
  - • **safely**; she can jump from a height and land: marb-w es1•
  - • **things** jumped upon the ground before her; all sorts of: brom k* ther ptk1 [am-br stj2]
- **keep** herself together only by a great effort; she can: sacch-l rb2
- **kidnapped**: positr nl2•
- **kill** (See murder)
- **knees**; he walks on his (See walking - knees)
- **knives** | **body**; shot into the: [buteo-j sej6]
- **knocking**:
  - • **bed**; under the (See bed - someone - under - knocking)
  - • **door**; someone is knocking at the (See noise - knocking - door)
- **knowing** | **not** knowing where one were (See Recognizing - not - surroundings)
- **knowledge**; he possesses infinite: *(↗creative; great; Haughty)* cann-i psil ft1 verat-v cda [tax jsj7]
- **labor** or thinks she has pain; she pretends to be in: *(↗pregnant)* verat k*
- **landscape**; beautiful (See beautiful - landscape)
- **large**: *(↗longer)*
  - • **everything** looks larger: *(↗enlarged - everything)* acon bro1 a g a r bro1 *Arg-n* bro1 atro bro1 bov bro1 *Cann-i* bro1 eug br1 euph br1 *Gels* bro1 glon bro1 *Hyos* bro1 op bro1 par bro1
  - • **he** himself seems too: *(↗enlarged; tall - he)* alum ptk1 irid-met srj5• plat ↓ pyrog staph h1 stram
    - ⁝ **entering** the house after walking: plat
  - • **parts** of body seem too large: *(↗Size - incorrect)* acon sf1.de alum anh jl aran sf1.de bad ptk bapt fr bell hr1 bov sf1.de cann-i k13 carb-v k13 clem ↓ *Dulc* b4a.de fic-m gya1 *Hyos* kali-br ↓ mang sf mim-p jl nux-m sf1.de op pic-ac stram
    - ⁝ **growing** too long; as if: kali-br c1*
    - ⁝ **hands**: clem a1*
  - • **people** seem too large: *(↗enlarged - persons)*
    - ⁝ **vertigo**; during (See enlarged - persons - vertigo)
  - • **surroundings** seem too large: *(↗Size - incorrect)* ferr
- **lascivious**: ambr h1* bell j5.de calc j5.de sil j5.de *Stram* j5.de verb hr1*
- **laughed** at and mocked at; being: *(↗criticized; despised; insulted; Admonition - agg.; Confidence - want; Fear - laughed; Fear - opinion; Mocking - others; Offended; Suspicious; Suspicious - talking; Timidity - bashful)* adam srj5• *Aq-mar* mgm• arizon-l nl2• **BAR-C** k* des-ac rbp6 germ-met srj5• haliae-lc srj5• ham fd3.de• ign vh* lac-leo sk4• lach vh lyss mrr1 nux-v vh* oci-sa sk4• ph-ac vh* psor gg* rhod kgp5• sep vh* *Symph* fd3.de• [bar-m stj1 bar-p stj1 bar-s stj1 heroin sdj2]
  - • **street**; whenever she goes into the: bar-c rb2
- **laughter**, with: op j5.de sep j5.de *Stram* j5.de *Verat* j5.de
- **lawsuit**; being engaged in a: *(↗Litigious)* *Nit-ac* a1*
- **lazy** | **move**; too lazy to: eucal rb2
- **learn** | **anew** everything she wished to do; she would have to learn: sep rb2
- **legs**:
  - • **belong** to her; her legs don't: *Agar* k1* *Bapt* st* coll ptk1* ign ptk1 k o l a stb3• op st* sumb st symph fd3.de•
  - • **conversing**; legs are: *(↗talking - limbs; talking - part)* bapt k*
    - ⁝ **toe** is conversing with thumb: *Bapt* kr1
  - • **cut** off; legs are: aq-mar rbp6 bapt st bar-c halo jl med lz stram tarent
  - • **four** legs; has: sulfon vh*
  - • **glass**; were made of: *Thuj* b4a.de
  - • **go** from under him; legs would: staph rb2
  - • **guitar**, man's legs are a: sal-fr sle1•
  - • **long**; legs too: cann-i sacch-a fd2.de• [heroin sdj2]
  - • **many** legs; too: pyrog ptk1

- many legs; too: ...
  - arms; and too many: (↗arms - many - legs; crowded) pyrog rb2
- pull out her leg; little gray man wanted to (See pull out)
- shorter; her legs are: haliae-lc srj5• neon stj2*• positr nl2•
- sidewalk; legs were all over the: kali-br rb2
- springy, legs feel: haliae-lc srj5•
- stiff; as if: nux-v ptk
- three legs; has: petr stram sf1.de
- tin case filled with stair rods; leg is: cann-i k*
- lie; all she said is a: (↗Deceitful; Hypocrisy; Liar) lac-c k*
- lied to, that she is being: aids nl2•
- life:
  - burdened by my life: aloe ptk1 des-ac rbp6
  - careering from life to: cann-i a1
  - cut off from life: bamb-a stb2.de•
  - no life in him: dub rb2
  - short, like a house is too big and you have to explore every room; life is too: aids nl2•
  - simple; life is: arizon-l nl2•
  - symbols of life; all past events revolve rapidly on wheels as: cann-i
  - threatened; life is: kali-br
  - unfair to him; that life is (See unfair)
- lifted; she was being: (↗floating; floating - air) hyper↓ mosch↓ ozone sde2• plut-n srj7• stroph-h↓
  - air; high in the: (↗floating - air) hyper rb2
  - couch; from a: stroph-h rb2
  - falling; with fear of: hyper hr1* mosch hs1*
  - sleep; during: stroph-h ptk1
- light [=brightness]:
  - abdomen; in his: rhus-g tmo3•
  - ascending light; of: irid-met srj5•
  - dark; and: plut-n srj7•
  - too much light in room on falling asleep: ambr
  - two points of white light merging into one: neon srj5•
- light [=low weight]:
  - coition; after: agn b7.de*
  - float; he was so light he could: camph rb2 lac-leo hrn2• manc rb2 tep rb2
  - is light; he (= incorporeal): (↗body - lighter; floating - air - spirit; EXTREMITIES - Lightness) agar sf1.de agath-a nl2• ara-maca sej7• Asar sf1.de bit-ar wht1• camph rb2 cann-i sf1.de chin hr1 chir-fl gya2 coca-c sk4• Coff sf1.de Croc sf1.de dendr-pol sk4• dig h2* eup-pur a1 falco-pe nl2• gels rb2 haliae-lc↓ hippoc-k szs2 ignis-alc es2• lac-c sf1.de lac-leo hrn2• lac-lup hrn2• lach rb2 lact sf1.de lact-v br1 manc rb2 mez h2* mim-p skp7• musca-d szs1 neon srj5• op sf1.de ozone sde2• petr-ra shn4• phos h2* pieri-b mlk9.de Plut-n srj7• puls a1 rhus-g tmo3• spig↓ Stict sf1.de stram sf1.de tep rb2 thuj sf1.de* valer br1* zinc sf1.de [zinc-i stj2 zinc-m stj2 zinc-n stj2 zinc-p stj2]
    - internal organs: ara-maca sej7•
    - skeleton: ara-maca sej7•
    - walking; when: haliae-lc srj5• spig rb2* tep rb2 thuj rb2*
- limbs:
  - brain; have own: dioxi rbp6
  - crooked; limbs are: sabad k2
  - double:
    - one limb is double: petr k*
    - pairs of limbs are double: sulfon ckh1*
  - no limbs; she had: stram rb2
  - separated; limbs are: bapt st falco-pe nl2• stram h1*
    - car, when riding in a: falco-pe nl2•
- line:
  - heavy line through his body; there is a: aids nl2•
- line: ...
  - parallel lines or railway; sees: haliae-lc srj5•
- lions: lac-lup hrn2•
- lip is swollen; lower: glon
- liquor | taken liquor; she had: bapt rb2 pip-m rb2 sabad rb2
- live | she could not live: vib rb2
- liver disease; that he will have: podo k2
- living:
  - lack of strength to continue: lac-lup hrn2•
  - not living under ordinary relations: cic
  - three hours distant from his house: Op a
- living things:
  - mouth (See mouth - living)
  - vagina (See vagina - living)
  - walls, floor and chair; on the: cocc ptk1*
- locality is transformed: bar-m a
- locked away within herself: (↗Forsaken - isolation) positr nl2•
- locomotive:
  - he is a locomotive: cann-i
  - run over by a locomotive; to be: phos rb2
- longer; things seems: (↗enlarged - objects; large) berb camph dros kreos nit-ac sacch-a fd2.de• sulph zinc bg2*
- looked down upon; she is: (↗criticized; despised; spied; Admonition - agg.; Ailments - reproaches; Confidence - want; Fear - opinion) ham fd3.de• Lac-c k* lac-lup hrn2• pin-con oss2• vanil fd5.de
- looking: (↗spied)
  - down; he were looking: haliae-lc srj5• phos rb2 **Plat**↓ Plut-n↓
    - high place; from a: **Plat** mrr1 Plut-n srj7•
  - everyone is looking at her: (↗spied; watched; Looked - cannot) meli k* petr-ra shn4• rhus-t sanguis-s hrn2•
  - persons are looking at her (See watched)
  - someone is looking | shoulder; over her (See people - behind - looking)
- loquacity, with: Bell j5.de hyos j5.de lach j5.de op j5.de rhus-t j5.de Stram j5.de Verat j5.de
- lost; she is: aesc↓ arg-n↓ arge-pl rwt5• ars k13 Aur↓ coca-c↓ cot br1* des-ac rbp6 hell↓ hippoc-k szs2 hura↓ ign↓ kali-p fd1.de• Lach↓ orig↓ plb↓ Ruta fd4.de urol-h rwt• [cupr stj2 cupr-act stj2 cupr-f stj2 cupr-p stj2 heroin sdj2]
  - city; in a big: coca-c sk4•
  - everything is lost: ign mg
  - salvation; for: (↗doomed; Anxiety - salvation) aesc↓ arg-n↓ ars k2 Aur hell k2 hura Lach↓ orig↓ plb
    - despised in erotomania; and: orig hr1*
    - predestination, from: Lach gl1.fr•
    - sexual desire; with violent: orig hr1
    - world, to the, beyond hope: arg-n kr1
- love is impossible: dioxi rbp6 hippoc-k szs2
- loved by parents; she is not: (↗Forsaken - beloved) sacch sht•
- low down; everything beneath him seems too: staph h1
- ludicrous: (↗strange - familiar - ludicrous) bell a1 calc j5.de cann-i k* cic↓ hyos j5.de Nux-m plat h2 sulph j5.de
  - antics; plays: Bell j5.de cic j5.de
- luminous (See light [=brightness])
- lying:
  - crosswise: stram k*
  - down; as if she could lie: kali-c rb2 nux-m rb2 sabad rb2
  - someone is lying:
    - near him: cic↓ petr
      - drunken man is coming toward her and lying down beside her; a huge: cic rb2
  - turned around in bed; he is lying: calc h2 calc-act a1
- machine; he is working a: plb
- maelstrom; carried down a psychical: cann-i
- magician, is a: (↗DREAMS - Magic - gifts) bell
- maggots; seeing: musca-d szs1

- **maleness** (See Masculinity - increased)
- **mammae** are too big or too small: bar-c vh
- **man**:
  - **back** of a man in front of her; seeing the: plut-n srj7•
  - **bed** at night; men are on the: merc
  - **black** men; seeing: *Puls* b7a.de
  - **does** all the things he does; a man: *(↗Imitation)* ars
  - **huge** drunk man coming to her (See drunkard - coming)
  - **hung** himself; saw a man who: ars
  - **little** gray man wanted to pull out her leg (See pull out)
  - **muffled** man starts from the wall | **walking** in the streets; when: cann-i
  - **naked** man in bed: *Puls* k*
  - **old** men:
    - **alone** and lost after the death of their wives: sanguis-s hrn2•
    - **being** an old man: gink-b sbd1• hydrog srj2• limest-b es1•
    - **seeing**: laur
      - **beards** and distorted faces; seeing old men with long: laur
  - **perforate** his throat with a gimlet; man in the room intending to: merc-i-f
  - **same** man is walking before and after him; the: euph k*
- **mandarin**; mistook friend for a Chinese: cann-i k*
- **marble** statue; felt he is a: cann-i
- **marriage**: *(↗wedding)*
  - **dissolve** marriage; must: fl-ac k* melal-alt gya4 petr-ra shn4•
  - **going** to be married; is: hyos
  - **is** married; he: ign k*
- **married** (See marriage)
- **martyr**; of being a: carc mlr1•
- **Mary**; Virgin: *(↗divine)*
  - **she** is: cann-i stram he1 verat gk
- **mask**:
  - **is** behind a mask: plut-n srj7•
  - **seeing**: bell kali-c *Op*
    - **laughing** masks:
      - **night** | **bed**; in: *Bell* kr1
- **meaningless**; everything is: bamb-a stb2.de• **Spong** fd* [am-caust stj2 am-f stj2 beryl stj2 bor-pur stj2 fl-ac stj2 fl-pur stj2 lith-c stj2 lith-f stj2 lith-p stj2 lith-s stj2 nat-f stj2 nitro stj2 oxyg stj2]
- **medicine**:
  - **taken**; he had: bit-ar ↓ lina rb2
    - **placebo**: bit-ar wht1•
- **melancholy**: alum k* *Aur* sf1.de **Kali-br** hr1* murx j5.de nux-v j5.de plat j5.de
  - **night**; while half awake at: nux-v
- **melodies**, mostly from the past, come into her mind: *(↗music - hearing)* sulph h2*
- **melting** away, agg. from change of position, amel. when lying: oxal-a rly4• sumb
- **memory** failed; as if: puls rb2
- **mesmerized** by her absent pastor; she is: meli
- **messages**; hears: *(↗hearing)* irid-met srj5•
- **messenger**; she is a: *(↗god - messenger; great)* irid-met srj5•
- **metamorphic**: musca-d szs1
- **mice**:
  - **bed**; mice in his: colch j5.de*
  - **sees**: absin ↓ *Aeth* bg2* ail ↓ bell *Calc* k* *Cimic* k* colch k* cortico jl* galeoc-c-h gms1• hyos k2 lac-c lach bg2* mag-s op k* pot-e rly4• stram bg2*
    - **chair**; running from under a: *Aeth* bro1 *Calc* vh* *Cimic* kr1* lac-c bro1
- **military**; about: arg-met kr1
- **mind**:
  - **out** of his mind; he would go: *(↗insane - become)* ambr c1 calc gsy cot a1* eup-per hr1* ham hr1* *Kali-br* hr1* *Lac-c* al nit-ac c1 ol-j rb2 paraf hs petr c1 visc ah
    - **waking**; on: cot rb2
- **mind**: ...
  - **separated**; mind and body are (See separated - body - mind)
  - **weak**; mind is (See Prostration)
- **mingled**; objects were: camph rb2
- **mirror**:
  - **face**; seeing everybody's face in the mirror except his own: anac ptk1 [alum stj2]
  - **wretched**; she looks (See wretched)
- **miscarries**; as if everything (See wrong - everything)
- **misfortune**: *(↗misfor; poor; Absorbed - misfortune)* brass-n-o ↓ calc-s k2 cupr ↓ *Verat* ↓
  - **approaching**; as if some misfortune were: brass-n-o srj5• cupr gt *Verat* br1
  - **inconsolable** over imagined misfortune: *(↗poor; Lamenting - misfortune; Pities; Unfortunate)* calc-s k13 *Verat*
- **mission**; one has a: ignis-alc es2• *Plat* sne
- **misunderstood**; she is: *(↗Anger - misunderstood)* carc fd2.de• *Dulc* fd4.de germ-met srj5• limest-b es1• olib-sac wmh1 *Propr* sa3• rad-br sze8• ruta fd4.de sal-fr sle1• *Tritic-vg* fd5.de vanil fd5.de
- **money**:
  - **counting** money; he is: *(↗poor; Avarice)* alum bell cycl mag-c zinc
  - **sewed** up in clothing; is: *(↗poor; Avarice)* kali-br
  - **talks** of: *(↗poor; Avarice)* calc canth bg carb-v bg carbn-s kali-br hl ph-ac phos j5.de
- **monster**; of a: *(↗visions - monsters)*
  - **chair**; some horrid monster would come from under his: lac-c rb2
- **mortification** | **after**: *Aur* sf1.de bell j5.de nux-v j5.de *Puls* j5.de
- **mother**:
  - **cold**, harsh, cruel; is: taosc iwa1•
  - **whore**; mother is a: [berb stu1]
- **motion**:
  - **all** parts being in motion: kreos a
    - **rest**; during: kreos a1
  - **bed** and ground; motion of | **waking**; on: clem a1
  - **chair** and table in different directions; motion of | **sitting**; while: chlf a1
  - **everything** were in motion: *(↗move - everything - all)* cycl tl1 sabad rb2
    - **seesaw** motion; making a: cycl rb2
  - **horizon**; of (See horizon)
  - **slow** motion; things happen in: haliae-lc srj5•
  - **up** and down; delusion of a motion: lach st plb st *Spong* st
- **mountain**; he is on the ridge of a: cann-i cycl ↓
  - **descending**: cycl rb
- **mouth**:
  - **cannot** open mouth, lower jaw stiff and painful: lyss kr1
  - **double**; mouth is: choc srj3•
  - **living** things are creeping into his mouth | **night**: merc [heroin sdj2]
  - **offensive** odor from: hyos kr1
- **move**:
  - **everything** is moving:
    - **all** directions; in: *(↗motion - everything)* anac rb2 tab rb2
    - **circle**; in a | **stooping**; on: sol-ni rb2
    - **inside** her: positr nl2•
    - **rapidly** and confusedly around her: sang rb2
    - **side** to side; from: cic j*
    - **slowly**; everything about him is moving: hydr-ac rb2
    - **to** and fro: cic h1 form rb2
  - **he** moves:
    - **not** move; he could: hom-xyz ↓ m-arct h1 (non:m-aust rb2) (non:mag-p rb2)
      - **yet** amel. by motion: hom-xyz rb2

- **he** moves: ...
  - ⁝ **to** and fro; he moves | **sitting** and lying; when: thuj rb2
- **hears** things that are moving high up near him out of sight: ph-ac phos j5.de
- **things** moving; sees: germ-met ↓ phos j5.de podo fd3.de• [lac-mat sst4]
  - ⁝ **stationary** car moves through his field of vision while driving: germ-met srj5•

- **multiple**: pyrog tl1
- **murdered**: *(↗Kill; desire - somebody; Suspicious - plotting; Suspicious - plotting - house)*
  - **being** murdered; he is: absin bro1 germ-met ↓ kali-br bro1 plb bro1 stram ↓ sulph rb2
    - ⁝ **roasted** and eaten; he was murdered: stram k*
    - ⁝ **shot** in the head like a horse or dog: germ-met srj5•
  - **had** murdered someone; he: *(↗stabbed - person)* ars k2* phos h2*
  - **mother** had been murdered; her: nux-v
  - **someone** being murdered; sees: *(↗stabbed - person)* calc
  - **will** be murdered; he: *(↗Fear - murdered)* absin vh1 am-m ars ↓ *Bell Calc* camph a1 cann-i ↓ carc mlr1• cimic sne fic-m ↓ hep vh* hydrog ↓ *Hyos* ign kali-c lac-c sne lact lyc mag-c merc *Op* phos k* plb rb2 positr nl2• *Rhus-t* sacch-l ↓ staph sf1.de *Stram* tab ↓ verat zinc
    - ⁝ **bribed** to murder him; persons are: cann-i k*
    - ⁝ **coming** to murder him; someone is: tab c1*
    - ⁝ **conspire** to murder him; others: ars hydrog srj2• plb tab rb
    - ⁝ **mother** wants to murder her: fic-m gya1 sacch-l c1*
    - ⁝ **serial** killer; by a: positr nl2•
  - **women** are by men: lac-lup hrn2•
- **murderer**; everyone around him is a: **Op** ↓ *Plb* k*
  - **executed**; to be: **Op** kr1
- **murdering**; he is:
  - **family** with a hatchet; she will murder her: jab k* kali-br ptk1
  - **had** murdered someone; he (See murdered - had)
  - **has** to murder someone; he: ars camph ↓ hep rb2 hyos j5.de* lach k2 spong fd4.de
    - ⁝ **street**; when on the: camph rb2
  - **husband** and child; she is about to murder her: kali-br
  - **struck** friends who came to help him: *Stram* kr1
- **mushroom**; he is commanded by a:
  - **confess** his sins; to fall on his knees and to: agar k*
  - **rip** up his bowels; to: agar k*
- **music**:
  - **hearing** music: *(↗hearing - illusions; melodies; Music - agg.)* aether ↓ calc b4a.de cann-i tl1 cann-s ↓ *Lach* ↓ lyc ↓ nat-c b4a.de olib-sac ↓ *Plb* ↓ psil ↓ puls ↓
    - ⁝ **evening** he hears the music he heard in the day; in the: lyc
    - ⁝ **delightful**: lach plb puls
    - ⁝ **delirium**; during: *Plb* kr1
    - ⁝ **sweetest** and most sublime melody: cann-i *Lach* olib-sac wmh1 psil ↓
      - ⁝ **primitive** music; when listening to: psil ft1
    - ⁝ **unearthly**: aether cann-s st
  - **influence** of music; he is under the | **pleasant** and quick music; of: zinc-p rb2
  - **thinks** he hears: anh mg1.de **Cann-i** k* croc dulc fd4.de ign h1 *Lach* lyc merc st nat-c st plb puls sal-ac sarr a1 spong fd4.de *Stram* thuj k*
- **mutilated** bodies; sees: ant-c arn con mag-m maias-l hrn2• marb-w es1• merc *Nux-v* sep
- **mystery**; everything around seems a terrifying: *(↗Mysticism)* aether a1 androc srj1• cann-i
- **mystic** hallucinations: *(↗Mysticism)* aether a1 irid-met srj5•
- **nails** of toes are flying off: pyrog al2*
- **naked**, he is: *(↗Naked)* aids nl2• irid-met srj5• lac-loxod-a hrn2• nad rly4• stram sulph rb2
  - **unprotected** and exposed: aids nl2•
- **names**:
  - **calls** things by wrong names (See Mistakes - speaking - words - wrong - names)
  - **meaning**; names have a peculiar: kola stb3•
- **narrow**; everything seems too: guaj irid-met srj5• plat k*
- **natural**; everything feels: aids nl2•
- **near** | **things** were near him even when not looking at them; felt: valer rb2
- **neck**:
  - **elongated**; is: falco-pe nl2•
  - **too** large; is: *(↗enlarged - body - parts)* kali-c k* positr nl2•
- **needles**; sees: *(↗pins)* merc k* *Sil* k*
- **neglected**:
  - **duty**; he has neglected his: *(↗reproach; wrong - done; Anxiety - conscience; Anxiety - duty; Conscientious; Discontented - himself; Fear - duty - neglect; Remorse; Reproaching oneself; Responsibility - taking; Sensitive - moral)* arizon-l nl2• *Ars* a1 **Aur** k* aur-m-n wbt2• aur-s stj2*• crot-c sk4• cur ptk cycl k* dream-p sdj1• dulc fd4.de falco-pe nl2• hell k2* hyos ign k* kali-br br1 kola stb3• lac-e hrn2• *Lyc* k* melal-alt gya4 myos-a rly4• naja a1 nat-ar k* petr-ra shn4• ptel a1 puls ruta fd4.de staph sne symph fd3.de• ulm-c jsj8• vanil fd5.de [aur-m stj2 heroin sdj2]
    - ⁝ **headache**, during: naja a
    - ⁝ **performed** in perfunctory manner: ptel a
    - ⁝ **reproaches**, deserves (See reproach)
  - **friends**, his: *Aur* k13
  - **he** or she is neglected: *(↗appreciated; despised; friend - affection; Confidence - want; Flattered - desire; Forsaken; Insecurity; Longing - good)* *Arg-n* k* aur-m-n wbt2• carc fd2.de• crot-c sk4• *Ham* fd3.de• kola stb3• lac-f ↓ *Lac-h* sk4• mag-m h2 marb-w es1• naja nat-m ctc* nat-sil fd3.de• nicc-met sk4• oci-sa sk4• **Pall** k* petr-ra shn4• plat mtf positr nl2• puls k2* rad-br sze8• sacch sht• sep ctc• staph sne *Stram* ↓ stront-c sk4• symph fd3.de• tritic-vg fd5.de [buteo-j sej6 heroin sdj2 oxyg stj tax jsj7]
    - ⁝ **children**; in: sacch sst1•
    - ⁝ **husband**; by her: *Stram* hr1*
    - ⁝ **women**; in: lac-f wza1•
- **nerve** were strung to the highest pitch; every: pip-m rb2
- **nesting**; as if she is: lac-h htj1• [tax jsj7]
- **net**; as if in a: cypra-eg sde6.de• nat-m rb2
- **new**; everything is: asar ckh1 *Hell* k* *Irid-met* srj5• stram k* symph fd3.de•
- **news**:
  - **agitated** by unpleasant news: alumn rb2
  - **expecting** news:
    - ⁝ **bad** news: aster rb2
    - ⁝ **joyful** news: lyss rb2 valer rb2
    - ⁝ **unpleasant** news: dros rb2 lyss rb2 mez rb2 spong fd4.de
  - **heard** news; he had:
    - ⁝ **joyful** news: *Lyss* kr1
    - ⁝ **unpleasant** news: lyss rb2
- **newspapers**; he sees: atro
- **night** watching; as after long: op rb2 vib rb2
- **noble**; being: *(↗distinguished; great; Haughty; Insanity)* marb-w es1• phos plat k2*
- **nobody**; being: agn rb2 germ-met srj5• symph fd3.de•
- **noise**:
  - **bed**; under (See bed - noise)
  - **clattering** above the bed | **asleep**; when falling: calc
  - **exaggerated**, loud; seems: lac-e hrn2•
  - **gnashing** their teeth around his bed; hears wild beasts: ars rb2
  - **hearing** noise: *(↗hearing - illusions; Sensitive - noise; HEARING - Illusions)* anh mg1.de bell calc canth bg2 carb-v cham coff k2 colch con crot-c sk4• dulc fd4.de hyos lac-e hrn2• mag-m naja gw olib-sac wmh1 ph-ac bg2 rad-br sze8• spong fd4.de sulph h2 verat j5.de
  - **knocking** | **door**; at the: ant-c h2* *Neon* srj5• petr-ra shn4• ruta fd4.de
  - **making** noise; delusions with: verat j5.de
  - **vehicles**; hears shout of: *Cann-i* k1*

- **not** being connected (See Forsaken - isolation)
- **nothing**:
  - **do** nothing; he could: lyss rb2 *Vanil* fd5.de
  - **exists** (See existence - surroundings)
- **nothingness**, nowhere; going into (See dissolving)
- **numb**; being: alum ptk1* galla-q-r nl2• positr nl2• [gnaph stj]
- **numeral**:
  - **nine** inches long; he appeared:
    - **night**:
      - **waking**; on | **lying** on the other side amel.: sulph
- **nun**; she is a: olib-sac wmh1
- **nursing** her child; she is: atro thiam rly4•
- **nuts**; cracking: hyos a1
- **objects**; about: *(↗fancy)*
  - **altered**; are (See different)
  - **animals**; objects are: hyos ptk2 ruta fd4.de tritic-vg fd5.de
  - **approach**: cic br1 ruta fd4.de
  - **blood**; covered with: stront-c ptk
  - **bright** objects; delusions from: *(↗Shining - agg.)* anh mg1.de canth bg2 irid-met srj5• kola stb3• **Stram**
  - **closing** the eyes; appear on: scroph-n a1
  - **colored**; brilliantly: androc srj1• anh mg1.de bell camph h1 dream-p ↓ psil ft1 spong fd4.de
    - **red**: dream-p sdj1•
  - **crooked**: glon
  - **deformed**: anh sp
  - **different**; appear: *(↗Strange - everything)* cic h1 germ-met srj nat-m k*
  - **far** off; too: anac rb2 sal-fr sle1• stann rb2
  - **flight** away from objects: **Stram** a1*
  - **follow** her; objects leave their place and: coff-t rb2
  - **glittering** (See glittering - objects)
  - **imaginary** objects: *Cupr-act* kr1 lyss kr1 med ptk1 tritic-vg fd5.de
  - **immaterial** objects in the room; about (See imaginary)
  - **large**: hyos tl1 nux-m c1
  - **lean** forward and about to fall; high objects: arn ptk1
  - **motion**, in: *Anh* mg1.de* carb-ac rb cic a1 kali-cy rb2 kali-p fd1.de• mosch rb2 nat-sal rb2 nux-v rb2 phos bg2 sep rb2 thuj rb2
    - **right**; to the: nat-sal rb2
    - **backward** and forward: *(↗recede)* carb-ac rb2 cic h1*
    - **small** objects appear in motion (See small - motion)
    - **up** and down: kali-p fd1.de• phos rb2
  - **near**, when not looking at them: valer a
  - **numerous** objects in room; too: phys
  - **open** air, in: atro
  - **persons**; are: bell ptk1 calc ptk1 nat-p ptk1 stram ptk1
  - **recede**: *(↗motion - backward; recedes)* cic br1
  - **reel**: bell rb2 bry rb2 glon rb2 kali-s fd4.de merc-i-r rb2
  - **run** | **into** each other: iris-foe rb2
  - **seize** objects; tries to: ars a1 atro a1 bell a1 hyos a1 oena a1
  - **shining**: irid-met srj5• plut-n srj7•
  - **strange**; objects were (See strange - objects)
  - **taken** from him; objects around him had been: valer rb2
  - **thick**, sometimes thin; objects were sometimes | **closing** the eyes in slumber; on: camph
  - **tossed** up from below in every direction; objects were: lac-d rb2
  - **turned**:
    - **round** and round: cod ↓ coff-t ↓ cycl rb2 laur rb2 psor rb2 sabad rb2
      - **circle**; in a: coff-t rb2
      - **closing** eyes; objects turned around with him on: cod rb2
    - **upside** down; objects are turned: guan rb2
- **objects**; about – **turned** – **upside** down; objects are turned: ...
  - **unworthy** (See Unworthy)
  - **waver** (See waver - objects)
- **obscene**: *(↗Obscene)* *Phos* ↓ stram k*
  - **action** of which she had not been guilty; accuses herself of an obscene: *Phos*
- **observing** oneself (See seeing - herself)
- **obstacles**:
  - **in** his way: aur a
  - **wants** them to be removed: cham lpc
- **obstructed**, being (See hindered - everyone)
- **occupied** about business (See business - occupied)
- **occurred** | **things** done today occurred a week ago: med rb2
- **ocean** | **middle** of the ocean, not knowing what direction to swim; being in the: galeoc-c-h gms1•
- **odor** (See NOSE - Odors)
- **offended** people; he has: aids nl2• ap-g vml3• **Ars** k1* cere-b ah **Hyos** gl1.fr• nit-ac gl1.fr•
- **officer**, he is an: *(↗commander; general; great)* agar bell cann-i *Cupr* k* cupr-act a1* [cupr-f stj2 cupr-p stj2]
- **old**:
  - **feels** old: adam srj5• haliae-lc srj5• loxo-recl knl4• mag-m mrr1 olib-sac wmh1 plut-n srj7• positr nl2• vanil fd5.de [calc-sil stj2 hydrog stj2 pop dhh1 spect dfg1]
  - **looks** old; he: mag-m mrr1
  - **men** (See man - old)
  - **timeless**, ancient feeling; having a: lac-loxod-a hrn2•
  - **woman** seemed beautiful; old ragged (See beautiful - old)
- **olfactory** (See smell)
- **opiate**: *(↗Morphinism; GENERALS - Narcotics - opium)*
  - **influence** of an opiate; he were under the: *(↗GENERALS - Narcotics)* cann-i rb2 carb-ac ↓
    - **morning**: carb-ac a
- **opposed** by everyone; he is (See hindered - everyone)
- **oppressed**; he were: carb-v rb2 positr nl2•
- **optic** (See seeing - herself; visions)
- **ordeal**; is about to undergo an: positr nl2•
- **ostracized**, she is (See banished)
- **outcast**; she were an: *(↗forsaken)* anac mtf androc srj* atra-r mtf crot-c mtf crot-h mtf germ-met srj5• haliae-lc srj5• hura mtf thuj mrr1*
- **outside** of his body (See body - out)
- **outsider**; being an: phasco-ci rbp2
- **ox**; riding an (See riding - ox)
- **painful**, with sadness: *Kali-br* kr1
- **pains** | **sleep**; he has pain during: alum h2
- **paradise**:
  - **lost**; the fall from grace: plut-n srj7•
  - **seeing**: (non:coff k*) coff-t slp
- **parallel** states:
  - **dyslexia** and clarity: des-ac rbp6
  - **emotions** and clarity or lightness; terrible: des-ac rbp6
- **paralyzed**; he is: agar rb2 cist rb2 con rb2 cycl rb2 falco-pe nl2• hippoc-k szs2 sacch-l rb2 sang rb2 syph c1*
  - **about** to be paralyzed: syph rb2
  - **walk**; after a short: con rb2
- **parasite**; she is a: galla-q-r nl2•
- **parchment**; she is made of: neon srj5•
- **pass** | **not** pass a certain point on walking without falling; he could: arg-n rb2 kali-br ptk1
- **past**:
  - **anxious** thoughts and things are present; past: sanguis-s hrn2• staph h1
  - **generations**; elbowing way through crowd of past: plut-n srj7•
  - **living** in the past: [lac-mat sst4]
  - **long** past events: atro hyos k2 op j5.de

- **patient** | **outside** of patient; as if a second self were (See double - being - outside)
- **peacocks**:
  - **chasing**: hyos
  - **frightening** away: hyos a1
- **pendulum** | **vertigo** were like the vibration of a pendulum: bell rb2
- **penis**:
  - **cut** off penis; sees a: marb-w es1•
  - **two** penises; he had: dendr-pol sk4•
- **people**: *(↗person)*
  - **averse** to her company; people are (See appreciated; outcast)
  - **beautiful** (See beautiful - people)
  - **behind** him; someone is: *(↗person - present; walking - behind; Fear - behind; Looking - backwards; Looking - backwards - followed)* am-br↓ anac k* bar-br↓ bell bg2* brom k* calc casc cench crot-c k* crot-h rb2* dendr-pol sk4• dulc fd4.de ephe-si hsj1• ferr↓ kali-s fd4.de lach led ptk1 mag-m jl *Med* k* naja a ozone sde2• psil ft1 ruta sacch-l bg2* sal-fr sle1• sanic ptk1 sil staph stront-c sk4• thuj mlk1 tub rb2*
    - **ascending** from cellar; when: ozone sde2•
    - **coming** up behind: sal-fr sle1• staph rb2
    - **looking** over her shoulder: *(↗strangers - looking)* brom k* sal-fr↓ [am-br stj2 bar-br stj2]
      - **left** shoulder: sal-fr sle1•
    - **sneaking** up behind her: sanic rb2
    - **walking**, when: calc rb2* ferr↓ kali-s fd4.de sanic↓ *Staph* gl1.fr•
      - **dark**, in the: *(↗Darkness - agg.; Light - desire)* ferr sanic
    - **whispering**: med ptk*
  - **beside** him; people are: anac apis *Ars* atro a1 bell calc camph carb-v cench dulc fd4.de hyos tl1 *Med* mrr1 nux-v petr pyrog tl1 thuj valer
    - **doing** as he does: *(↗Imitation) Ars*
    - **lies** down; another person: petr rb2
    - **strange** person; a: thuj br1*
    - **stranger**; a: anac rb2
    - **walking** beside her: calc rb2
  - **conversing** with absent people: agar aur bell calc k2 cham h1 crot-c dig hyos lach op *Stram* thuj k* *Verat* kr1
  - **distant**; feel: vero-o rly3•
  - **entering** the house at night: con
  - **front** of him; people in: alum ptk1 con bg2*
  - **hear** him; don't: cortico tpw7
  - **noise**; people are making: *(↗hearing - illusions)* puls st
  - **pranks** with him; people carry on all sorts of: hydrog srj2• **Nux-v** kr1
  - **questions** and he must answer; people address him with: **Nux-v** kr1
  - **say** "come": med kr1*
  - **seeing** people: *(↗figures - seeing) Ars* atro bar-c↓ **Bell** k* *Bry Calc* vh* calc-ar↓ calc-sil↓ chin con *Hyos* kali-c kali-s fd4.de kola stb3• lac-loxod-a hrn2• lyc lyss mag-c j5.de* mag-s med merc bg2 nat-m op petr k2 plb *Puls* rheum rhus-t↓ sep spong fd4.de *Stram* sulph thuj k* valer verat
    - **day** and evening | **entering** the room; on: lyc a1
    - **morning** | **waking**; on: sulph h2
    - **closing** eyes; on: ars **Bell** k* bry **Chin** nat-m
    - **disagreeable**; people: calc-ar k2 calc-sil k2 lac-loxod-a hrn2•
    - **looking** at him: *(↗watched; Looked - cannot)* bar-c kr1 med↓ rhus-t
      - **night**: med c1
    - **seize** them; a number of strangers and tries to: stram kr1
  - **threatening** her, and she screams horribly: ars-met kr1
- **performing** | **pressured** by those about him to perform: *(↗Anxiety - conscience; Comply)* mag-m h2*
- **persecuted**: *(↗Anxiety - pursued; Insanity - persecution)*
  - **he** is persecuted: *(↗appreciated; pursued; Delirium - persecution; Forsaken; Suspicious)* abrot tl absin gl• aids nl2• allox jl ambr tsm1 anac bg2* androc srj1• ars bg2* aur bg2 bell bg2* brom bl calc gl1.fr• canth mgm• *Cench* k2* **Chin** k* choc srj *Cocain* br1 con bg2* crot-c sk4• crot-h gl• cupr gl• *Cycl* k* dendr-pol sk4• dream-p sdj1• **Dros** k* falco-pe nl2• hell gl• hydrog srj2• *Hyos* k* *Ign* vh* iodof cda **Kali-br** k* lac-leo sk4• *Lach* bg2* lyc gl• manc mrr med tl meli gl• merc gl1.fr• moni rfm1• nat-c gl• nat-m gl1.fr• nux-v vh* petr-ra shn4• podo fd3.de• positr nl2• puls gl• rhus-t bg2* sal-fr sle1• sil gl• spong kr1 staph bg2* stram stry gl• *Sulph* vh* syph gl• tarent sne thiop↓ thyr ptk1 urol-h rwt• verat gl1.fr• verat-v bg2 *Vesp* mgm• *Zinc* kr1 [spect dfg1]
    - **backward**; and looks: staph gl•
    - **delirium**; during (See Delirium - persecution)
    - **dementia**; during: thiop jl
    - **everyone**; by: *Cycl* kr1
  - **scene** of some mournful event of the past; he is persecuted and tormented by a (See Dwells - past - frightful)
- **person**: *(↗people)*
  - **come** in, look at her, whisper and say "come" (See people - say)
  - **entering** his room; he hears a person: con j5.de*
  - **following** him; is (See walking - behind)
  - **other** person; she is some: *(↗identity - errors; robot; someone else - she; Confusion - identity; Observer - being - oneself; Stranger - sensation)* androc srj1• cann-s k* dream-p sdj1• gels bg2 haliae-lc srj5• ignis-alc es2• lac-c k2 *Lach* k* mosch bg2 olib-sac wmh1 oxal-a rly4• phos plb puls rb2 pyrog↓ valer
    - **existed** in another person; she: pyrog rb2
  - **present**; someone is: *(↗people - behind)* arizon-l nl2• hyos kali-p fd1.de• lyc olib-sac wmh1 thuj k*
  - **room**; another person is in the: anac bg2* brom bg2* cann-i con bg2* hyos rb2 lyc bg2* ruta fd4.de
    - **waking**; on: mag-p ptk1
  - **shroud**; person with coat seemed covered by: psil ft1
  - **something** hanging over the chair is a person sitting there: *(↗inanimate)* calc k*
  - **three** persons; thinks he is (See three)
  - **two** | **personalities** opposing each other in himself; there are two: *(↗double - being; Confusion - identity - duality)*
    - **discussing** their disease; two personalities who are: paro-i jl
    - **persons**; thinks he is two (See double - being)
- **pieces**; he were falling to (See body - pieces - falling)
- **pigeons** flying in room which he tries to catch: *Kali-c* hr1*
- **pins**; about: *(↗needles)* **Nux-m** vh *Sil* k* spig
- **pitch** (See falling)
- **pitied** on account of his misfortune and he wept; he is: *Nat-m* h2*
- **place**:
  - **cannot** pass a certain place; he: *Arg-n* kali-br
  - **different** places at a time; of being in: *(↗Confusion - identity)* cann-i *Lyc* plb raph
  - **no** place in the world; she has: germ-met srj *Plat* kr1
  - **strange** place; he was in a: *(↗Recognizing - not - surroundings)* cic gt* hyos bro1 par↓ plat bro1 podo fd3.de• tub bro1
    - **solitary** place; in a strange and:
      - **night** | **waking**; on: par
  - **two** places at the same time; of being in: *(↗body - divided; Confusion - identity - duality) Cench Lyc* k* *Sil*
  - **wrong** place; he was in the: *(↗Recognizing - not - surroundings)* dioxi rbp6 hyos
- **pleasing** delusions: *(↗delightful - she; Content)* aeth a atro bell↓ cann-i nitro-o a1 op k* phos h2 psil ft1 stram
  - **morning** | **sleep**; after: bell

- **poisoned**:
  - **he**:
    - **about** to be poisoned; he is: *(↗Fear - poisoned - being)* carc mlr1• dulc fd4.de falco-pe nl2• *Hyos* j5.de* *Kali-br* k* lach bro1* meli sne plb **Rhus-t** k* verat-v bro1* [ferr stj2 ferr-f stj2 ferr-lac stj2 ferr-n stj2 ferr-sil stj2 zinc stj2 zinc-i stj2 zinc-m stj2 zinc-n stj2]
    - **has** been: *(↗Fear - poisoned - has)* agar rb ang rb bufo rb caj a1* carb-ac rb chinin-s rb chlor rb cic rb cimic cocc bg2* cor-r rb croc rb culx k2 cur rb cypra-eg sde6.de• euph rb2 ferr rb gels rb glon rb hydr rb hydrog srj2*• *Hyos* iodof rb jug-r rb kali-br rb kali-c rb kali-i rb lac-c bg2* lac-h sze9• *Lach* bg2* lact rb lil-t rb lina rb2 lyc rb m-aust rb mag-p rb marb-w es1• med rb merl rb mez rb mill rb naja ckh1 nicc rb nux-m rb nux-v rb olnd rb op rb petr rb ph-ac rb phos rb pip-m rb plat-m psor rb ptel rb puls rb ran-b rb raph rb rat rb rheum rb rhod rb **Rhus-t** •* sabad rb sec rb sep rb spig rb squil rb staph rb stram he1 sul-ac rb sulph rb tab rb tarax rb thuj rb valer rb vip ckh1 zinc rb [heroin sdj2 *Spect* dfg1 zinc-p stj2]
  - **medicine**; being poisoned by: cimic k2 cypra-eg sde6.de• hyos k2 lach lina rb2 rhus-t fyz
- **poisoning** people, she is: limest-b es1• sulph h2*
- **poked**, is being: *Agath-a* nl2•
- **policeman**:
  - **calls** on him; officers: *Cupr* vh*
  - **coming** into house; he sees a policeman: ars k2 hyos k* kali-br k*
  - **physician** is a policeman: bell
  - **pursued** by the police (See pursued - police)
- **poor**; he is: *(↗fortune; misfor; misfortune - inconsolable; money - counting; money - sewed; money - talks; ruined - is; starve - being; starve - family; want - he; want - they; Anxiety - business; Avarice; Fear - poverty; Fear - starving)* bamb-a stb2.de• bell bry gg calc-f coli rly4• gink-b sbd1• hep mez nux-v psor k2 sal-fr sle1• *Sep* stram valer [heroin sdj2]
- **popping**, bubbles and seed pods: aids nl2•
- **position**; she is not fitted for her: *(↗unfit - work)* stram kr1
- **possessed**; being: *(↗devil - possessed - he; influence; superhuman - control)* alum gk *Anac* k1* bell canth k2 carb-v k2 helo-s rwt2• hydrog srj2• *Hyos* k1* ignis-alc ↓ lach sne **Manc** vh* mand sp1 op sf1.de orot-ac rly4• plat sf1.de* positr nl2• psil ft sal-fr sle1• sil sf1.de stram gl1.fr• *Sulph* sf1.de verat sf1.de
  - **evil** forces; by: ignis-alc es2• manc mrr1
- **power**:
  - **all**-powerful; she is: *(↗strong; superhuman)* adam srj5• cann-i tl1 thuj ckh1 verat gk
  - **diseases**; he had power over all: *(↗divine)* *Stram* kr1
  - **evil** power had control of the whole of him: *(↗superhuman - control)* cann-s ↓ ignis-alc es2•
    - **will** power; except of his: cann-s rb2
  - **hands** of a strong power; he were in the (See influence)
- **powerful** influence (See influence)
- **pregnancy**; during: lyss jl2 puls hr1
- **pregnant**, she is: *(↗labor; Feigning - pregnancy; CHEST - Milk - pregnancy; in)* apis a1 berb c1 carc gk6 *Caul* kr1* cimic gk *Croc* kr1* cycl bro1 galeoc-c-h gms1• galla-q-r nl2• gink-b sbd1• hydrog srj2*• ign lap-la sde8.de• nux-v c1* *Op* bro1 ozone sde2• *Puls* kr1* *Sabad* k* sal-fr sle1• sulph bro1 taosc iwa1• thuj k* *Verat* k* [*Spect* dfg1]
  - **distension** of abdomen from flatus; with: ign c1 ozone sde2• **Sabad** hr1*
  - **menses**, after: *Ign* kr1
  - **mirror**; on looking in a: *Galla-q-r* nl2•
- **present**; someone is (See person - present)
- **pressed** down by a great force: sal-fr sle1•
- **presumptuous**: lyc j5.de
- **primitive** man; is a: *Plut-n* srj7•
- **prince**; he is a: *(↗emperor - is; great; Haughty)* adam ↓ verat
  - **Indian** prince; an: adam srj5•
- **prisoner**; she is a: *(↗criminal he)* dulc fd4.de falco-pe nl2• germ-met stj2*• haliae-lc srj5• *Moni* rfm1• olib-sac wmh1 positr nl2•
- **project**; as if corners (See corners - project)
- **prostitute**, is a: falco-pe nl2• lac-c mtf
- **prostration**; cannot endure such utter: *Chinin-ar* kr1 eup-per rb2
- **protection**, defense; has no: carc sde• dioxi rbp6
- **proud**: *(↗great; Haughty)* lach j5.de plat k* stram verat
- **pull** out her leg; a little gray man wanted to: puls hr1
- **pulled**:
  - **he** was:
    - **backward**: germ-met ↓ merc rb2
      - **and** up by the neck: germ-met srj5•
    - **downward**: agath-a nl2• hydrog srj2•
    - **threads**; and torn into: coca-c sk4• plat rb2
    - **two** directions, in: haliae-lc srj5• positr nl2•
  - **mind** were pulled downwards; as if: hydrog srj2•
- **pump** log; he was a: cann-i a1*
- **pure**; she is: ignis-alc es2• stram st*
- **purgatory**; one is in: *(↗doomed; hell - in)* ignis-alc es2•
- **pursued**; he was: *(↗criminal he; hunted; persecuted - he; Anxiety - pursued; Fear - ghosts; Impulse - run - followed; Insanity - persecution; Looking - backwards - followed)* absin aids nl2• alco ↓ ambr tsm1 *Anac* k* apis ↓ ars aur sf1.de bell k* brom b4a.de* bry carc mlr1• carneg-g ↓ *Chin* ↓ choc srj3• cic ↓ *Cocain* ↓ con sf1.de crot-h ↓ *Cupr* ↓ cupr-act ↓ cupr-f ↓ cupr-m ↓ cupr-p ↓ cycl vh dros vh germ-met ↓ hell ↓ hydrog srj2*• *Hyos* bg2* *Kali-br* k* lach k2* lepi ↓ lyc ↓ manc mrr1 med st meli ↓ merc rb2* moni rfm1• nat-c ↓ nux-v bg2 op bg2 phos ↓ plat tl1 plb positr nl2• *Puls* ↓ rhus-t k* sanguis-s hrn2• sil bg2 spong fd4.de staph stram k* stry ↓ thuj k2* verat bg2 verat-v sf1.de vip ↓ [am-br stj2 bar-br stj2 cob stj2 nicc stj1 spect dfg1 zinc stj1]
  - **animals**; by: nux-v ptk1
  - **devil**, by: [vip bcj1]
  - **enemies**, by: *(↗fiends; enemy - bed; enemy - everyone; enemy - injury; enemy - surrounded)* absin anac k* ars aur *Bell* carneg-g rwt1• *Chin* k* cic *Cocain* bro1 con crot-h cupr k* cycl vh* dros k* hell *Hyos* k* *Kali-br* k* *Lach* k* lepi lyc med tl meli merc nat-c nux-v bro1 plb k* positr nl2• *Puls* rhus-t k* sil stram k* stry zinc [cupr-act stj2 cupr-f stj2 cupr-m stj2 cupr-p stj2]
  - **fiends**, by: *(↗enemies; devil - persecuted)* apis a3 plb k*
  - **friends**; by: plb a1
  - **ghosts**, by: *(↗specters - pursued; Fear - ghosts)* lepi k* plat stram stry mrr1
  - **horrid** thing, by some: anac
  - **hunted** (See hunted)
  - **murderers**; by: alco
  - **past**; mournful events of the (See Dwells - past - frightful)
  - **perspiration**; with cold: hydrog srj2•
  - **police**, by: *(↗arrested)* alco a1 ars k2 bell *Cupr* k* germ-met srj5• *Hyos* *Kali-br* meli k* phos plb zinc k* [cupr-act stj2 cupr-f stj2 cupr-m stj2 cupr-p stj2]
  - **robbers**; by: alco
  - **robbing** a friend; for: *Kali-br* a1*
  - **sadist**, by a: positr nl2•
  - **soldiers**, by: absin bell bry nat-c gl1.fr• plb
- **pushed** backwards; he was: germ-met srj5•
- **queen**, she is a: *(↗emperor - is; great; Haughty)* cann-i olib-sac wmh1
- **quiet** (See patient)
- **rabbits**, sees: stram k*
- **rags** are as fine as silk; old: *(↗Dirty)* **SULPH** k •*
- **railway** train:
  - **ear**; there is a train or car in his: *Stram* kr1
  - **go** off by railway; he was obliged to: atro
  - **in** a railway car; she is: sang rb2
    - **begs** others to hold her; and: *Sang* kr1
    - **jarring** her; which was moving and: sang rb2
  - **she** is a rushing: haliae-lc srj5•
- **rain**:
  - **hearing** the rain: calc gl1.fr• chin gl1.fr• ph-ac gl1.fr• staph gl1.fr• sulph gl1.fr• verat gl1.fr•
  - **it** is raining: naja hr1

- **out** in the rain from having a wet cloth on the head; thought he had been: atro k*
- **tears** of the world; rain is: ignis-alc es2•

- **rainbows**; of: haliae-lc srj5• irid-met srj5•
- **rainstorm**; she is in a: naja hr1
- **raised** up; she were being: cann-i ↓ sil rb2
  - **fly**; and could: cann-i rb2
- **rank**; he is a person of: *(↗great; Haughty)* cupr phos verat
- **rats**, sees: *(↗visions - monsters - strange)* absin a1 *Aeth* k* ail ↓ *Ars* k* bell k* *Calc* k* choc srj *Cimic* k* colch bg2* cortico sp galeoc-c-h gms1• hyos k2* lac-c hr1 lach bg2 med k* op j5.de* stram k* [thal-met stj2]
  - **colors**, of all: absin
  - **large** rats:
    - **night** | **room**; in the: med hr1*
  - **running**:
    - **leg**; up the: ail k1* *Calc* k1*
    - **room**; across the: *Aeth* k* ail k* ars cimic med
- **reading**:
  - **after** her, which makes her read faster; someone is reading: *(↗Imitation)* mag-m k*
  - **wrong**; it seems: lach a
- **real** | **nothing** seems (See unreal - everything)
- **reason**; losing his (See insane)
- **recedes**; everything approaches and: *(↗objects - recede)* cic rb2
- **reel**:
  - **she** was reeling: gamb ↓ spig rb2 tax ↓
    - **rest**; when at: tax rb2
    - **side** to side; from: gamb rb2
- **rejected** by others (See repudiated - others)
- **religious**: *(↗Religious - too)* alum-sil vh *Anac* hr1* *Ars* sf1.de aur sf1.de bell sf1.de croc sf1.de *Hyos* sf1.de ignis-alc ↓ *Kali-br* hr1* lach j5.de* lyc sf1.de med hr1* merc sf1.de nux-v sf1.de olib-sac wmh1 plat sf1.de *Puls* j5.de* *Stram* j5.de* *Sulph* sf1.de tarent sne *Verat* j5.de*
  - **redemption** and devil; about: ignis-alc es2•
- **reproach**; he has neglected his duty and deserves: *(↗neglected - duty; wrong - done; Anxiety - conscience; Forsaken; Remorse; Reproaching oneself)* *Aur* germ-met srj5•
- **reproved** | **expects** to be reproved; he: dig rb2
- **repudiated**; he is: *(↗despised)*
  - **others**; by: pin-con oss2• rad-br sze8•
  - **relatives**; by his: *(↗disgraced; forsaken; Forsaken; Forsaken - isolation)* aq-mar mgm• arg-n falco-pe nl2• hura ulm-c jsj8•
  - **society**; by: hydrog srj2•
- **repulsive** fantastic: *Fl-ac* maias-l hm2•
- **resin** exuding from every pore: cann-s a1
- **respiration**; attention must be centered on: chlor rb2
- **restlessness** with anxiety: olib-sac wmh1
- **reveling**; he had been | **night**; all: rhod rb2
- **reversed**; directions are: camph-br br1 camph-mbr bro1
- **revolving**; he is | **axis**; around his: nux-v rb2
- **rich**; that he is (See wealth)
- **ridiculed**; he is (See laughed; Mocking - others)
- **riding**; as if:
  - **closed** eyes; with: cycl rb2
  - **horse**; riding on a (See horses - riding)
  - **lying** down; when | **closing** the eyes agg.: ferr rb2
  - **ox**; riding on an: bell
- **right**:
  - **doing** nothing right; he is: *(↗succeed; wrong - done; Anxiety - conscience; Confidence - want; Confidence - want - failure; Fear - failure; Remorse; Reproaching oneself; Succeeds; Timidity)* anac arg-n *Aur Carc* fd2.de• germ-met srj5• *Kali-s* fd4.de nat-c plac-s rly4• vanil fd5.de
  - **everything** is right the way it is: *(↗Content)* plac rzf5• positr nl2•
  - **nothing** seems right (See wrong - everything)
- **ringing** | **door**; someone is ringing at the: *Neon* srj5•
- **rising**: bar-c ↓ dig ↓ falco-pe nl2• lach ↓
- **rising**: ...
  - **could** not rise up; he | **stooped**; could not rise up again if he: bry rb2 puls rb2 rhus-t rb2
  - **falling**; then: bar-c bg2* lach bg2*
  - **time** for rising; it were: dig rb2
- **road** is long: ozone sde2•
- **roaming**: lac-lup hm2• rhus-t ↓
  - **fields**; in the: rhus-t
- **robbed**, is going to be: *(↗thieves)* bar-c vh* borx vh* caust vh* maias-l hm2• rhus-g tmo3• sep vh*
- **robot**; one is a: *(↗identity - errors; person - other; Confusion - identity; Stranger - sensation)* *Alum* mrr2* anac mtf *Cann-i* mtf hell ng1 med mrr2 stry sej4
- **rocked**; one were being: bell rb2 calad rb2 nat-m rb2
  - **lying** down and closing the eyes; when: calad rb2 nat-m rb2
- **rocks** in air: mag-m bg2
- **rolling**:
  - **him**; something will roll on: cocc c1
  - **wall**, the floor or anywhere; something alive is rolling on the: cocc c1
- **room**:
  - **close** and hot; is: plan a
  - **desolate**: valer a
  - **falling** to pieces; room were: cann-i rb2
  - **house**; room is a: calc
  - **large**; room is too: tub rb2
  - **own** room; he is not in his: coloc a1
  - **people**; sees:
    - **babies**; full of white and colored: morph a
    - **bedside**; at his: atro con lyc ↓
      - **entering**, on: lyc
    - **passing** in and out, who wanted to take her away; room were full of strange men: bell rb2
  - **round**; went (See turning)
  - **sea**; room is like the foam of a troubled: sec k*
  - **small**; room is too: carb-v bg2 cycl bg2* germ-met srj5• nat-c bg2
  - **smaller**; is: germ-met srj
  - **turning** in a circle; room were: *(↗turn - everything - circle)* calc-caust rb2 cann-s rb2 cod rb2 dub rb2 grat rb2 kali-bi rb2 nux-v rb2
  - **walls** (See walls)
  - **whirling**; room were: nux-v rb2
- **round** | **everything** seems: arizon-l nl2•
- **round** and round:
  - **everything** went | **looking** at water; when: ferr rb2
- **rowdies** would break in if she was alone (= disorderly persons): elaps rb2
- **royal** birth; of (See noble)
- **ruined**:
  - **is** ruined; he: *(↗poor; Avarice; Fear - poverty)* calc vh* **Ign** vh* verat vh* [heroin sdj2]
  - **will** be ruined; he: puls rb2
- **run**:
  - **against** something; she ran: arg-met rb2
  - **away**; she had to run: ars-met rb2
  - **backward**; he were chased and had to run: sep rb2
  - **long** way; he could run a: coca rb2
  - **never** before; she could run as: agar rb2 taosc iwa1•
  - **people** are running over her: [gnaph stj]
  - **up** and down and scream; she would like to run: calc rb2
- **sacrificed**: positr nl2•
  - **acceptance** of being slaughtered like something innocent; final: positr nl2•
- **sadness**, with (See depressive)
- **safe**; she is not: lac-del hm2•

- **satyrs**; vision of dancing: cann-i a1
- **saw** darting up and down; he was a huge: cann-i k*
- **says** something, it seems to him as though somebody else has said it; when he: *(↗talking - someone; talking - someone - he)* alum k1*
- **scalp** too small: stict c1
- **scapegoat**; he is a (See wrong - suffered)
- **scattered** about; he is (See body - scattered)
- **scorpions**; sees: **Op** k*
- **scratching** on linen or similar substance; someone was: asar
- **scream**:
  - **obliging** to scream (See Shrieking - must)
  - **with** screaming: canth j5.de hyos j5.de *Stram* j5.de* verat j5.de
- **scrotum** is swollen; his: **Sabad**
- **sea**:
  - **at** sea; he were: cocc rb2
  - **immersed** in the sea; being: lac-loxod-a hrn2•
  - **on** the sea; he were | **rough** sea; he were tossing on a: lac-ac rb2 sacch-l rb2
- **seasick**; he is: der hippoc-k szs2 magn-gr rb2 nitro-o a1 sanic ↓ spong fd4.de tab rb2
  - **riding** on horseback in the dark; after: sanic rb2
- **seat**:
  - **moving**; seat is | **to** and fro: thuj rb2
  - **tottering**; seat were: chlf rb2
  - **undulating**; seat were | **morning**; when sitting up in bed in the: zinc rb2
- **secure**, even within chaos; feels: falco-pe nl2•
- **seeing**:
  - **cannot** see; he: alum ↓ dream-p sdj1• hyos j5.de phel ↓ stram j5.de
    - **head** that he could not see over; something projected from: phel rb2
    - **transfer** himself into another, and only then he could see; he could: alum rb2
  - **dead** animals with insects eating out eyes: musca-d szs1
  - **eggs**; insect and fish: musca-d szs1
  - **herself**: anh sp1 stram he1
  - **miles** and miles; can see for: lavand-a ctl1•
  - **physicality** of the world; through: bit-ar wht1•
  - **river** of tar: dioxi rbp6
  - **would** see something; he | **turned** around; if he: brom rb2
- **seeking** | **something**; he is seeking: stram rb2
- **sees** something; when he | **someone** else's eyes; seems as though he saw through: *(↗Confusion - identity)* alum k1 gard-j vlr2• spong fd4.de
- **seized**, as if: canth k* *Hyos* hr1* phos bg2
- **self**-control; she would lose all (See Self-control - loss - as)
- **selfish**; others are: polys sk4•
- **sensations**; misrepresents his: bell
- **senses**:
  - **deprived** of his senses: cycl rb2
  - **vanish**:
    - **had** vanished; senses: spira rb2
    - **would** vanish; senses: plat rb2 ran-b rb2
- **sensual** fancies: phos gt tritic-vg fd5.de verb kr1
- **separated**:
  - **body**:
    - **arms** are separated from the body: bapt ptk1* cypra-eg sde6.de• daph ptk1* psor ptk1*
    - **chest** is separated from body: melal-alt gya4
    - **extremities** are separated from the body: *(↗EXTREMITIES - Separated - leg - body)* falco-pe nl2• stram br1
    - **feet** are separated from the body: falco-pe nl2• kola stb3• stram h1
    - **hand** is separated from the body: daph cda dream-p sdj1• falco-pe nl2• germ-met srj* stram h1

- **separated – body**: ...
    - **mind** are separated; body and: *(↗soul; spirit; Confusion - identity; Confusion - identity - duality; Thoughts - persistent - separated - mind)* anac k* arb-m oss1• arge-pl rwt5• bit-ar wht1• cann-i k13 corv-cor bdg• cypra-eg sde6.de• dioxi rbp6 dream-p sdj1• ham fd3.de• lac-lup hrn2• limest-b es1• loxo-recl knl4• melal-alt gya4 mucs-nas rly4• musca-d szs1 ozone sde2• polys sk4• sabad bg2 suis-em rly4• thuj k* [lac-mat sst4 spect dfg1]
    - **soul**; body is separated from: *(↗mind; spirit; Confusion - identity; Confusion - identity - duality; Depersonalization)* *Anac* k* cann-i k* *Hydrog* srj2• nit-ac bro1 plut-n srj7• rhus-g tmo3• thuj k*
    - **spirit** had separated from body: *(↗mind; soul)* anac rb2 loxo-recl knl4• *Plut-n* srj7• [spect dfg1]
  - **floating** in his inner self; he is: irid-met srj5•
  - **group**; he is separated from the: des-ac rbp6 lac-del hrn2• musca-d szs1
  - **himself**; he were separated from: ara-maca sej7• ham fd3.de• sabad ↓ [heroin sdj2]
    - **evening**; in the: sabad rb2
  - **senses** are separated from objects: aeth rb2
  - **thoughts** are separated from him; strange: falco-pe nl2• sabad bg1*
  - **world**; from the:
    - **he** is separated: *(↗division; Forsaken - isolation)* adam srj5• aids nl2• *Anac Androc* srj1• *Anh* mg1.de* arge-pl rwt5• arizon-l nl2• bit-ar wht1• carc sde• choc srj3• coca rb2 dioxi rbp6 dream-p sdj1• falco-pe nl2• galla-q-r nl2• germ-met srj5• haliae-lc srj5• *Ham* fd3.de• hippoc-k szs2 **Hydrog** srj2*• ignis-alc es2• irid-met srj5• lac-del hrn2• lavand-a ctl1• loxo-recl knl4• mang-p rly4• moni rfm1• nat-sil fd3.de• nicc-met ↓ pin-con oss2• plac rzf5• plut-n srj7• polys sk4• positr nl2• sal-fr sle1• sanguis-s hrn2• symph fd3.de• taosc iwa1• thiop jl thuj mrr1 tung-met bdx1• ven-m jl [heroin sdj2 lac-mat sst4 **Spect** dfg1]
      - **detached** from it; being in the present yet: falco-pe nl2•
      - **religious** songs; listening to: nicc-met sk4•
- **serious**, is not taken: [erig stj]
- **serpent** fastening on his neck; a crimson (See snakes - crimson)
- **servants**; he must get rid of: fl-ac
- **seven** seemed significant: *(↗VISION - Ciphers)* irid-met srj5•
- **sewing**, she is: atro
- **sex** | **opposite**; belonging to the opposite: pegan-ha tpi1•
- **shadows**, of: hom-xyz mgm•
- **shapeless**, he is: galla-q-r nl2•
- **sheep**:
  - **driving**: acon h1*
  - **seeing**: *Cimic*
- **shell** and her protection; feels she has lost her: *Aids* nl2•
- **shining** objects; of (See objects - shining)
- **ships**:
  - **seeing** ships on the ocean: limest-b es1•
  - **storm**; they are on board of a ship in a: alco
- **shock**:
  - **electric** | **fell** suddenly from an electric shock; he: clem rb2
- **shoot** with a cane; tries to: *(↗gun)* bell j5.de* merc
- **shopping** with her sister; of: atro
- **should** have done this or that (See Anxiety - conscience)
- **shoulder**; people are looking over his (See people - behind - looking)
- **shouting**; to be: *(↗hearing - illusions)* cann-i
- **shoved** forward; he is:
  - **closing** the eyes: ferr a1*
  - **lying** down; when: ferr a1*

- **shroud**; person with coat seemed covered by (See person - shroud)
- **sick**: *(↗Hypochondriasis)*
  - **being**: *(↗disease - every; Anxiety - health; Anxiety - hypochondriacal; Feigning - sick)* ambr bg2 arg-n k* *Ars* k* asar bg2 bar-c k* bell **Calc** bg2* caust gl1.fr• cham bg2 chel bg2 chlol ↓ cic bg2 *Colch* bg2 graph k* hell k2 *Iod* k* *Kali-c* lac-c k2 laur bg2 led bg2 *Lyc* k* merc lpc mosch bg2* murx naja mrr1 nat-c k* nat-m k* nit-ac nux-m bg2 **Nux-v** bg2 petr k* phos k* podo k* psor **Puls** bg2 *Sabad* k* sel bg2 sep k* spig bg2 spong bg2 *Staph* bg2 stram tarax rb2 *Tarent* k2* valer bg2 verat bg2* [bar-i stj2 calc-sil stj2 merc-i-f stj2 stann stj2]
    - **imaginary** disease, syphilis, to others; he will give his: *(↗contaminated - everything)* chlol hr1
    - **mind** and body; in: merc lpc
    - **work**; and for this reason will not: calc vh* caust vh* nux-v vh* sep gl1.fr•
  - **family** were sick; members of the: hep
  - **friend** is sick and dying; a beloved: bar-c
  - **going** to be sick; he is: *(↗Anxiety - health)* nat-p nicc rb2 podo sacch-a fd2.de•
    - **severe** illness were impending: nicc rb2
  - **someone** else is: gels bg2*
  - **two** sick people were in bed, one of whom got well and the other did not: sec
- **side**:
  - **alive** on one and buried on the other; he is: *(↗body - divided; divided; Confusion - identity - duality)* stram
  - **left** side; she does not own her (See body - half - left - belong)
  - **right** side:
    - **elongated**; right side of body and head is: adam srj5•
    - **have** a right side; she does not (See body - half - right - have)
    - **muscle** and fibre of her right side; she can feel every: sep k1
  - **the** same; left and right side are not: bamb-a stb2.de• positr nl2•
- **sidewalk** | **rising** up before him; sidewalk is: spig rb2
- **sight** and hearing, of: *(↗hearing - illusions; images)* anac jl bell sf1.de carc fd2.de• eup-pur k* kali-br a1*
- **sin**; one has committed a (See sinned)
- **singing**; to be: cann-i
- **sinking**; to be: asar ↓ bapt sf1.de ben ↓ benzo a1 benzol sf1.de *Cimic* c2 gala br1 glon ↓ *Hell* br1 hyos ↓ *Ign* c2 kali-c sf1.de kali-cy br1 lac-e hrn2• lyc h2 lyss rb2 nat-m ↓ phos ↓ plac-s rly4• *Sulph* c2
  - **bridge**; stones were sinking under his feet, when crossing a stone: nat-m rb2
  - **dying**; and: asar rb2
  - **floor**; through the: *(↗ground - sinking)* ben ptk1 hyos ptk1 phos rb2*
  - **quicksand**; in: lac-e hrn2•
  - **warm** room | **working** in a hot room; when: glon rb2
- **sinned**; one has: ars ↓ aur ↓ chel ↓ hell ↓ kali-p ↓ med ↓ neon ↓ plb ↓ podo ↓ psor ↓ puls mrr1 stram ↓ sulph ↓ thuj sne
  - **day** of grace; sinned away his: ars k2 aur k2 kali-p k2 plb k2 podo k2 psor k2 puls k2 stram c1* sulph k2
  - **unpardonable** sin; he had committed the: *(↗hell - going)* aur k2 chel rb2 hell k2 med hr1* neon ↓
    - **forgiven**, and was: neon srj5•
- **sitting**:
  - **high**; he is sitting too: aloe rb2
  - **wet**; sitting in: morph rb2
- **skeletons**, sees: crot-c k* op k* [heroin sdj2]
- **skin** is very thin (See SKIN - Thin - sensation)
- **skull**:
  - **diminished**: chel ptk glon ptk grat ptk
  - **raised** and lowered; being: stict c1
- **sleep**:
  - **deprived** of sleep (= too little sleep): merl rb2 rheum rb2 rhus-t rb2 zinc rb2
- **sleep**: ...
  - **disturbed**; sleep is being: agar rb2
  - **falling** asleep; delusions on: arg-n a bell j5.de bry j5.de *Calc* j5.de camph j5.de carc mlr1• chin j5.de falco-pe nl2• guaj j5.de ign j5.de merc j5.de merc-act j ph-ac j5.de phos j5.de spong j5.de sulph j5.de
  - **going** to sleep; he were: asar rb2 camph ↓ lappa rb2 merc-act j mur-ac rb2 plat rb2
    - **deep** sleep; into a state of: camph rb2
  - **ought** to sleep; he: ant-t rb2
  - **short**; after: op a
- **sleeping**: *(↗sleepy)*
  - **awake**; insists that he was sleeping while: acon alco a1
  - **half** asleep; he were: con rb2 rheum rb2
  - **he** were sleeping: irid-met srj5• rhus-t rb2 ter rb2
  - **just** falling asleep (See sleep - going)
  - **night**; he had slept all: euph rb2 lina rb2
  - **not** been sleeping; he had:
    - **morning** | **waking**; on: trif-r rb2
  - **not** slept enough; he had: ars rb2 bapt rb2 bell rb2 calc rb2 colch rb2 con rb2 dig rb2 eucal rb2 ham ↓ lac-ac rb2 magn-gr rb2 nux-v rb2 phos rb2 ran-b rb2 rhus-t rb2 ruta rb2 sulph rb2 thuj rb2
    - **morning**; in the: bell rb2 ham rb2
  - **sound** sleep; he were in a: visc rb2
  - **stupid** sleep; he were in a: ant-t rb2
- **sleepy**; he is: *(↗sleeping)* merl rb2 nat-m rb2 nux-m rb2
- **sliding** | **impelled** by an invisible agent; he is sliding along the ground: op a1*
- **slow**; bus goes: cortiso sp
- **small**: *(↗GENERALS - Smaller)*
  - **body** is smaller: acon k* agar k* agath-a nl2• alum-sil k2 ambr vh *Bar-c* vh* cact bg2 calc k* carb-v carc fd2.de• croc b2.de* crot-c sk4• falco-pe nl2• gard-j vlr2• glon bg2 graph bg2 grat mrr1 hydrog srj2*• kola stb3• kreos b2.de* loxo-recl knl4• naja bg2 neon srj5• nux-m bg2 nux-v bg2 olib-sac wmh1 plut-n srj7• podo fd3.de• sabad sanguis-s hrn2• sulph bg2 tarent k* zinc bg2 [cob stj2]
    - **alternating** with | **large**; delusions that the body is (See enlarged - body - alternating - small)
    - **epileptic** convulsions; before: carb-v
  - **he** is: *(↗Confidence - want - self-depreciation)* aids nl2• choc srj3• grat hydrog srj2• ozone sde2• sanguis-s hrn2•
  - **motion**; small objects appear in: anh sp1
  - **things**: *(↗tall - he)*
    - **appear** small; things: *(↗body - diminished; diminished - all; tall; Size - incorrect; VISION - Small)* agar bg anh jl1 aur berb ptk1 cact bg carb-v k* cop tl1 cycl ptk1 hyos sf1.de irid-met srj5• merc-c ptk1 nat-c bg1* ozone sde2• phys **Plat** k* puls sf1.de staph vh* stram k* sulph ↓ tab bg thuj sf1.de
      - **he** were very large; and: stram c1*
      - **large**; sometimes very small and sometimes very: sulph rb2
    - **grow** smaller; things: camph carb-v nit-ac *Plat* j5.de* stram j5.de
- **smell**, of: *Agn* bro1 *Anac* c2* aran-ix sp1 ars br1* *Aster* mgm• carc fd2.de• cic k2 cina k2 corv-cor bdg• der vml3• euph-a c2* *Kali-bi* c2 lach vh* lact-v c1* musca-d szs1 *Op* bro1 par bro1 puls c2* *Sang* c2 sulph c2* vanil fd5.de zinc-m bro1
  - **own** body has offensive odor: aster mgm•
- **smoke**; of: *Bry* bg2 fl-ac ↓ petr bg2 ran-b bg2
  - **hot** smoke is coming through all orifices; as if: fl-ac ptk1
- **smoking** | **marijuana**: vero-o rly3•
- **smooth**; being: alum ptk1*
- **smoothed** by a delicate hand; she were: *(↗touched)* med rb2
- **snakes**: *Abel* ↓ ail ↓ anh ↓ arg-n ptk1 bell ↓ bit-ar ↓ calc ↓ crot-c ↓ cund ↓ dendr-pol ↓ gels bg2* *Hyos* ↓ ign ↓ *Lac-c* br1* lach ↓ lachn ↓ olib-sac ↓ op ↓ phys bg2 phyt ↓ rhus-g ↓ stram ↓ tab ↓ tub ↓ viol-o bg2
  - **black**: arg-n bg2
  - **crawling** up the leg; feels a snake: ail st
  - **crimson** serpent fastening on his neck: bell k*
  - **hose** of shower is snake: olib-sac wmh1

• **in** and around her: *Abel* vh* ail k2 anh sp1 arg-n bell k* bit-ar wht1• calc crot-c sk4• cund bg1* dendr-pol sk4• gels bg1* *Hyos* k* ign bg1* *Lac-c* k* lach lachn bg1* op phys bg1 phyt st* rhus-g ↓ stram hr1* tub bg3* viol-o bg1*
⁝ **cobra** | **stomach**; in his: rhus-g tmo3•
• **lying** on a large snake; she were: lac-c rb2
• **seeing**: olib-sac wmh1 tab a2
• **white**: ign bg2
- **snow** blankets; sees black: ozone sde2•
- **snowed** under; being (See buried - snow)
- **soda** water; he is a bottle of (See bottle)
- **sold**:
• **bed**; someone has sold his (See bed - sold)
• **brain** turned solid; as if his: phos b4a.de
• **being**: hyos
- **soldiers**:
• **bed**, on his: lact k*
• **being** a soldier | **night**: chel a1*
• **cutting** him down | **cool** amel.; on getting: bry k*
• **march** | **air**; march about in front of her in the:
⁝ **evening** | **partial** sleep; in: nat-c h2
⁝ **silently** past: cann-i
• **seeing**: bar-c *Bell* bry nat-c h2* op
• **surrounded** by: nat-c vh*
- **someone** (See people/ person)
- **someone** else | **she** were someone else: *(↗person - other; Confusion - identity)*
⁝ **power**; and in the hands of a strong: lach rb2
• **speaking**; someone else were: cann-s rb2
- **something** else:
• **chest**; something else comes from above which is pressing the: sep h2
• **objects** appear as if something else: staph
- **shower** of soot fell on him: cann-i k*
- **sorrow**; everyone he meets has a secret: cann-i
- **soul**:
• **body** was too small for the soul, or separated from the soul (See separated - body - soul)
• **exchanged**; were: olib-sac wmh1
• **something** presses on her: bamb-a stb2.de•
- **sounds**: *(↗hearing - illusions)*
• **color**; are like: anh br1*
• **double**, whistling; are: med hr1
• **listens** to imaginary sounds: hyos
• **muffled**: hippoc-k szs2
• **muted**: hippoc-k szs2
• **remained** longer (See HEARING - Illusions - sounds - remained)
- **space**:
• **between** brain and skull; there is empty space: caust k*
• **carried** into space; he was:
⁝ **lying**; while: cann-i k2 coca germ-met srj *Lach*
⁝ **orbit**; and compelled to describe a vast | **lying**; while: cann-i a1
• **contraction** of: irid-met srj5•
• **decomposition** of space and shape: anh sp cypra-eg sde6.de•
• **expansion** of: *(↗Distances - exaggerated)* cann-i k* cypra-eg sde6.de• falco-pe nl2• nux-m vh* [ferr-f stj2 ferr-lac stj2 ferr-n stj2 ferr-sil stj2]
• **he** is in: germ-met srj
• **large** space in the head; having a: bit-ar wht1•
- **sparkling**, everything is: adam srj5•
- **specters**, ghosts, spirits: *(↗fairies; images; Fear - ghosts)* acon ↓ agar ↓ am-c ↓ ambr ↓ apis ↓ arn ↓ ars bg2* ars-met ↓ atro ↓ *Atro-s* hr1 aur ↓ bell bg2* berb ↓ bov ↓ *Bry* ↓ *Calc* ↓ camph bg2 *Cann-xyz* bg2 carb-an bg2 carb-v bg2 cassia-s ↓ caust bg2 chin ↓ cimic bg2 cocc ↓ *Croc* ↓ *Crot-c* mrr1* crot-h ↓ *Cupr* ↓ *Cupr-act* ↓ cupr-f ↓ dig ↓ dros bg2 dulc bg2 hell bg2 hep ↓ hura ↓ hyos bg2 hyper ↓ ign ↓ kali-br bg2 kali-c bg2 kali-i ↓ kali-sil ↓ lac-mat ↓ lach bg2 led ↓ lepi ↓ lyc ↓ mag-m bg2 merc bg2 nat-c bg2 *Nat-m* ↓ nit-ac ↓ *Nux-v* bg2 *Op* bg2 orot-ac rly4• ph-ac bg2 phos bg2 phys ↓ plat bg2 plut-n ↓ *Psor* ↓ puls ↓ ran-b ↓ rhus-t bg2 ruta bg2 sal-fr ↓ samb ↓ sars ↓ sep bg2 sil bg2 sinus rly4• spect ↓ spig ↓ spong ↓ stram bg2* stry ↓ *Sulph* ↓ tarent ↓ *Thuj* ↓ tritic-vg fd5.de verat bg2 verb ↓ visc ↓ zinc ↓ [alum stj2 alum-p stj2 alumin stj2 alumin-s stj2 am-br stj2 ant-t stj2 arg-n stj2 bar-br stj2 brom stj2 cupr-m stj2 cupr-p stj2]
• **day** and night: *Ars*
• **morning**:
⁝ **waking**; on: dulc zinc
⁝ **enlarge** until it disappears; a specter continues to: dulc
• **evening** | **appear**; a specter will: brom
• **bed**, in: atro a1
• **black** forms when dreaming: arn ars puls
• **chill**, during: nit-ac
• **closing** eyes, on: apis arg-n *Bell* k* *Bry* *Calc* cassia-s ccrh1* chin ign *Lach* led nat-m samb sep spong stram *Sulph* *Thuj*
• **clutches** at: hyos
• **conversing** with; he is: nat-m gl1.fr• plat gl1.fr•
• **death** appears as a gigantic black skeleton: crot-c crot-h tl1
• **fire**, in: bell
• **forced** upon him in multitude; are: plut-n srj7• *Psor* kr1 verb kr1
• **hovering** in the air: aur lach k2*
• **pursued** by, is: *(↗pursued - ghosts)* lepi plat k1 stram stry mrr1
• **seeing**: acon sf1.de agar alum am-c ambr ant-t *Ars* k1* ars-met kr1 atro aur **Bell** bov brom sf1.de *Calc* vh* *Camph* carb-v cocc *Croc* b7a.de *Cupr* k* *Cupr-act* kr1* dig c1 dulc hell hep hura *Hyos* hyper ign *Kali-br* sf1.de kali-c kali-i c1* kali-sil k2 lach lepi lyc merc *Nat-c* *Nat-m* nit-ac *Op* k1* phos sf1.de phys plat psor kr1 puls ran-b sf1.de sal-fr sle1• sars sep sil spig *Stram* *Sulph* tarent thuj verb kr1 visc a1* zinc [cupr-f stj2 lac-mat sst4 spect dfg1]
⁝ **night**: atro a1 merc a1
• **twilight**: *(↗Darkness - agg.; Light - desire)* berb
- **sphere**; he transformed into a cylinder or a: cann-i
- **spiders**, sees: *(↗Fear - spiders)* kola stb3• *Lac-c* k*
- **spied**; being: *(↗looked; looking; looking - everyone; stalked; watched)* aq-mar mgm• lach gl1.fr• med al olib-sac wmh1 positr nl2•
- **spinal** column is a barometer: cann-i
- **spinning**, is: hyos k* stram
- **spirals**, awe at (See Spirals - awe)
- **spirit**, he is a: *(↗fairies)* cann-i ignis-alc es2•
- **spotted** brown (See body - spotted)
- **squanders** money: *(↗Squandering)* falco-pe nl2• *Verat* hr1*
- **square** surrounded by houses a hundred stories high; sees a colossal: cann-i
- **stabbed**:
• **back**; in the: rhus-g tmo3•
• **person** who passed on the street; he had stabbed a: *(↗murdered - had; murdered - someone)* *Bell*
• **somebody** threatened to stab him; as if: op j5.de
• **will** be: | **knife**; on seeing a: rhus-g tmo3•
- **staggering**; as if: carb-ac rb2 olnd ↓
• **weakness**; from: olnd rb2
- **stairs** of stones fitting perfectly together: *(↗ground - coming)* galla-q-r nl2•
- **stairs** were coming up to meet him: *(↗ground - coming)* pic-ac rb2
- **stalked**; he is being: *(↗spied)* lac-e hrn2•
- **standing**:
• **beside** oneself: *(↗double - being)* anh sp1 [heroin sdj2]
• **head**; standing on: ars bg2* asaf bg2 dios ptk1* elaps ptk1* glon bg2* lach bg2* nux-v bg2 ph-ac bg2* phos ptk1 thuj bg2*

- head; standing on: ...
  - ⁝ **bed** were tilted and she were standing on her head; as if: *Ph-ac* vh*
- **must** stand up | **sitting**; when: sep rb2
- **securely**; he were not standing: asar rb2 calc-act rb2

- **standstill** in body; as of a general | **chill**; during: lyc b4a.de
- **stars** in his plate; saw: cann-i
- **starve**:
  - **being** starved: *(↗poor; Avarice; Fear - starving)* lap-la rsp1 naja a1
  - **family** will: *(↗poor; Avarice; Fear - poverty; Fear - starving)* ars calc-sil k2 lap-la rsp1 *Sep* staph
  - **he** must: *(↗Fear - poverty; Fear - starving)* (non:kali-chl c1) kali-m k*
  - **humankind** will starve: lap-la rsp1
- **statue**: cann-i ↓ positr nl2• *Stram* ↓
  - **admired**; poses as a statue to be: *Stram* vh*
  - **Egyptian**; sees: positr nl2•
  - **marble** statue; he was a: cann-i rb2
- **stepping**:
  - **air**; stepping on: dub rb2 dubo-m br1 nat-m rb2
  - **down** when walking; steps on feather: der rb2
  - **easily** as one; she could take ten steps as: puls rb2
  - **person** is stepping hard; a: aloe ptk1
  - **space**; stepped on empty (See air)
- **stimulant**; had taken a: nux-v rb2 sabad rb2
- **stolen** something; she has: lach k2
  - **thinks** it; or somebody: lach k2
- **stone**:
  - **turn** to stone; she will: positr nl2•
  - **turned** to stone; one has | **waking**, on: positr nl2•
- **stool** | **obliged** to go to: spig rb2
- **stove**:
  - **heats** stove in heat of summer: merc j5.de
  - **mistakes** stove for a tree: *(↗Delirium - embraces)* hyos
    - ⁝ **climb** it; and wants to: *Hyos* j5.de*
- **strain** herself; she could easily: sep rb2
- **strange**:
  - **everything** is: *(↗changed; Strange - everything)* aids nl2• anac bg2* *Anh* mg1.de bac bn *Bar-m* camph a1 cann-i a1* cann-s k2* cann-xyz bg2 carb-an *Cic* k* coca-c sk4• cypra-eg sde6.de• glon bg *Graph Hydrog* srj2• lyss ↓ nad rly4• *Nux-m* k* petr bg2* *Plat* k* plb bg2* podo fd3.de• positr nl2• sep kr1 staph stram tub al* valer j [germ-met stj2 heroin sdj2]
    - ⁝ **disagreeable**; and: valer ptk
    - ⁝ **horrible**; and: cic br1* plat rb2
    - ⁝ **pregnancy**; during: lyss ptk
    - ⁝ **room**; in the: tub rb2
    - ⁝ **standing** agg.: glon a
  - **familiar** things seem strange: *(↗Strange - everything)* arg-n atro bar-m bell bov sf1.de calc *Cann-i Cann-s* kr1* carb-an carc gk6* choc srj3• cic *Cocc* bg1* croc dream-p sdj1• glon *Graph* hydrog srj2• hyos irid-met srj5• kali-p bg1* lyss mag-m med merc bg1* mosch *Nux-m* bg1* op petr bg1* phos bg1* *Plat* puls bg1* ran-b bg1* rhus-t staph stram sulph bg1* thuj bg1* tub bg1* valer verat [heroin sdj2]
    - ⁝ **horrible**, are: plat
    - ⁝ **ludicrous**, are: *(↗ludicrous)* cann-i hyos nux-m
  - **houses** seem strange; loses his way in the streets, the (See streets)
  - **land**; as if in a strange: aids nl2• bry cypra-eg sde6.de• par plat verat [heroin sdj2]
  - **notions** seem: *Lyss*
  - **objects** seem: cann-s rb2 carbn-s a1 cic h1 cimic kr1* germ-met srj stram tl1 valer rb2

- **strange**: ...
  - **places** seem strange (See surroundings)
  - **streets**, the houses seem strange; loses his way in the: *Glon* kr1
  - **surroundings** seem strange: aids nl2• cic k* des-ac rbp6 glon ↓ hyos ptk1* op tl1 plat ptk1* rhus-r sal-fr sle1• tub rb2*
    - ⁝ **headache**; after: glon
  - **symptoms** do not belong to him; his (See symptoms)
  - **thing** inside her: ozone sde2•
  - **voice** seemed strange; her own: *(↗Strange - voices)* alum h2* *Cann-i* cic k13 galeoc-c-h gms1•
- **strangers**:
  - **control** of; under: *(↗influence; Confusion - identity)* aster bry galeoc-c-h ↓
    - ⁝ **aliens**: galeoc-c-h gms1•
  - **familiar**; seem: germ-met srj5• [bell-p-sp dcm1]
  - **friends** appears as strangers: *(↗Recognizing - not - friends)* bry neon srj5• stram
  - **knitting**; she sees strangers while: mag-s
  - **looking** over shoulder: *(↗people - behind - looking)* brom k*
    - ⁝ **see** someone on turning; and she should: brom br1
  - **midst** of strangers; he were in the (See surrounded)
  - **room**; seem to be in the: *Bell* ↓ bry j5.de *Tarent Thuj* k*
    - ⁝ **snatch** at her; who: *Bell* kr1
  - **seeing**: anac b4a.de* cann-i mag-s nit-ac gl1.fr• nux-v *Puls* gl1.fr• stram *Thuj* k*
  - **surrounded** by: androc srj1• aster hr1* irid-met srj5• nit-ac vh* *Puls* vh* [heroin sdj2]
  - **wherever** he goes he is a stranger: positr nl2•
- **strangled** (See choked)
- **street** | **rising** when walking; were: sep rb2
- **strength** | **failing** him; all his strength were: coloc rb2
- **strike** | **like** to strike; he would | **anyone** who spoke to him; in the face of: nux-v h1*
  - **struck**; being: ara-maca sej7•
- **strong**; he is: *(↗power - all-powerful; superhuman)* aids nl2• androc srj1• cc⁑ hr1 dendr-pol sk4• hydrog srj2• lac-leo sk4• plac ↓ plat sne
  - **good**; and: plac rzf5•
- **study**; after: hyos j5.de nux-v j5.de
- **stumble**; he would | **legs**; over his own: caj rb2
- **stunned**; he was: laur rb2
- **stupefied** (See intoxicated)
- **stupid**; one is: moni rfm1•
- **succeed**, he does everything wrong; he cannot: *(↗business - unfit; fail; fail everything; right - doing; unfit - world; Anxiety - success; Confidence - want; Confidence - want - failure; Confidence - want - self-depreciation; Fear - failure; Pessimist; Succeeds; Timidity; Undertaking - nothing)* adam srj5• *Anac* k* *Arg-n* k* arn ry *Aur* k1* *Aur-m-n* wbt2• bamb-a stb2.de• bapt k2 *Bar-c* vh* gels ry germ-met srj5• lyc mtf33 melal-alt gya4 naja dm* nat-c nat-m ry ozone sde2• petr-ra shn4• phos ry sal-fr sle1• sulph ptk1* tritic-vg fd5.de vanil fd5.de [brach stj]
- **sucked** up; she is being: galla-q-r nl2•
- **sucking** people dry; she is: galla-q-r nl2•
- **suckling**; she is | **animals** or hairy babies: choc srj3•
- **suffering** | **women** through the ages; conscious of: aster sze10• lac-lup hrn2•
- **suffocated**; she will be: petr-ra shn4• *Stram* kr1
- **suffocating**; as if: arum-t ↓ galla-q-r nl2• ignis-alc es2• irid-met srj5• rad-br sze8• *Tub* mtf vib tl1
  - **chest** is blown up with air: galla-q-r nl2•
  - **sleep**; on going to: arum-t rb2
- **suicide**; impelled to commit: alum ↓ ars j5.de dros ↓ hyos j5.de rhus-t rb2 thea rb2 verat j5.de
  - **drowning**; by: dros rb2
  - **knife**; on seeing a: alum rb2
- **sulfur** vapors; of: x-ray szh

- **sun**:
  - **pushed** her down and she had to rest in the shade in order to walk on: psor rb2
  - **reeling**; sun is: cann-i a1
- **superhuman**; is: *(↗divine; great; power - all-powerful; strong; Deeds - great)* cann-i ignis-alc es2• psil ft
  - **control**; is under superhuman: *(↗influence; possessed; power - evil; Confusion - identity; Insanity)* agar anac k* carc mlr• cypra-eg sde6.de• des-ac rbp6 falco-pe nl2• kali-br sne *Lach* k* *Naja* op bro1* petr-ra shn4• plat bro1* psil ft1 sal-fr sle1• *Thuj* k*
- **superiority**, of: *(↗great; Deeds - great; Haughty)* crot-c sk4• germ-met srj granit-m es• *Kola* stb3• musca-d ↓ *Plat* k* polys sk4• [astat stj2 aur stj2 aur-m stj2 aur-s stj2 bar-br stj2 bar-i stj2 bar-met stj2 bism-sn stj2 caes-met stj2 cinnb stj2 hafn-met stj2 irid-met stj2 lanth-met stj2 merc stj2 merc-d stj2 osm-met stj2 plb stj2 plb-m stj2 plb-p stj2 polon-met stj2 rhen-met stj2 tant-met stj2 thal-met stj2 tung-met stj2]
  - **inferiority** at the same time; and: musca-d szs1
- **support | himself**; he could not support: tab rb2
- **surrounded** by friends (See friend - surrounded)
- **surroundings**:
  - **capacious**; are: ferr
  - **exist**; do not (See existence - surroundings)
- **suspended**:
  - **he** is suspended in the air: hyper ↓ sep rb2
    - ⋮ **bed**; and not lying in: hyper rb2
- **swallow**, cannot: lyss hr1*
- **swaying** to and fro; he is: cic tl1 paraf ↓
  - **sitting**; when: paraf rb2
- **sweets**; is made of: merc ptk
- **swimming**, is: calc-ar ↓ cann-i k* galeoc-c-h gms1• lac-c ↓ lact ↓ manc ↓ ox-ac ↓ rhus-t valer ↓
  - **air**, in the: *(↗floating - air)* calc-ar rb2 lac-c k2* lact rb2 manc rb2 valer rb2
  - **bed**; in (See floating - bed - swimming)
  - **lying** down; when: ox-ac rb2
- **swine**, men are: hyos
- **swinging**; he were: camph ↓ ign rb2 lact ↓ merc rb2 sulph rb2
  - **bed**; in: camph rb2 lact rb2
  - **cradle**; in a: ign rb2
- **swirls**; of: sal-fr sle1•
- **swelling**; he is gradually: cann-i tl1
- **swollen**, is: *(↗enlarged; GENERALS - Swollen)* acon bro1 *Aran* bro1 *Arg-n* bro1* asaf bro1 bapt bro1 *Bov* bro1 *Cann-i* k* carbn-s glon bro1 kali-br ↓ op bro1 plat bro1*
  - **convulsion**; before: kali-br vh
- **sword** hanging over head: am-m k*
- **symptoms** come from outside of himself; his: bamb-a stb2.de•
- **tactile** (See touch)
- **taken** from him; objects around him had been (See objects - taken)
- **talking**:
  - **asleep**; as if: musca-d szs1
  - **behind** him; someone: *Med* vh*
  - **dead** people; with: *(↗Talking - dead)* bell **Calc-sil** k1* canth k* hell *Hyos* k* med k2 nat-m stram
    - ⋮ **sister**; with his: bell hr1* *Hyos* kr1
      - ⋮ **churchyard**; in: bell j5.de*
  - **friends** are talking about her: *(↗people)* lach k2
  - **hears** talking; he: dream-p ↓ elaps a1 galeoc-c-h gms1•
    - ⋮ **head**, inside his: dream-p sdj1•
  - **imaginary** persons; loudly and incoherently to: atro a1 bell a1 chlol kr1*
  - **inanimate** objects with names, but observes no one standing near him; to: stram j5.de*
  - **insane**: nit-ac h2
  - **inside** or outside myself: galeoc-c-h gms1•
- **talking**: ...
  - **irrationally**: nit-ac h2*
  - **limbs** talking to each other: *(↗part; legs - conversing)* bapt ptk1*
  - **part** of body is talking to another part; one: *(↗limbs; legs - conversing)* bapt k2* urol-h rwt•
  - **people** talk about her: *(↗friends; Fear - talking - people)* crot-c sk4• lac-cp sk4•
  - **persons** as though near; talking of | **midnight**; about: sep
  - **rapidly**; all around her are talking: *Sang* kr1
  - **she** is: op ↓ raph
    - ⋮ **herself**; she is talking with: op rb2
  - **someone** is talking: *(↗says)*
    - ⋮ **echo** chamber; in an: galeoc-c-h gms1•
    - ⋮ **he** is speaking; when: *(↗says)* alum a1* cann-s k2* cann-xyz ptk1 galeoc-c-h gms1• nux-m sne [lac-mat sst4]
  - **spirits**, with: bell j5.de nat-m st* nit-ac ptk1 *Plat* st* stram k*
- **tall**: *(↗body - greatness; diminished; enlarged; humility; inferior; small - things - appear)*
  - **he** or she is tall: *(↗body - greatness; diminished; enlarged - tall; great; grow - larger; humility; inferior; large - he; small - things; Haughty)* arizon-l nl2• cob ptm1*• cop crot-c sk4• eos bg1* fic-m gya1 hydrog srj2• iodof a *Irid-met* srj5• limest-b es1• op bg2* pall a1* plat j5.de* plut-n stj2*• staph h1* **Stram** k ●* *Sulph* ckh1 tung-met bdx1• [heroin sdj2]
    - ⋮ **vertigo**; with: eos br1
    - ⋮ **walking**; had grown while: pall
  - **things** grow taller: berb j5.de camph dros kreos nit-ac sulph
    - ⋮ **pulse** is throbbing; as the: berb ↓ camph j5.de
      - ⋮ **diminish**; and: berb j5.de
- **tankard**, chased with dragons; he saw a huge: cann-i a1
- **tartars**; of a band of: cann-i a1
- **taste**, of: cina k2 staph vh*
- **tears**; he would burst into: cot rb2
- **teenager**; she is a: *(↗child - he)* germ-met srj5•
- **terrible**; everything seems: cic ptk1 plat ptk1
- **terrified**; as if (See fright - as)
- **tetanus**, with pain in the right leg; must die of (See die - must - tetanus)
- **thicker** than natural; everything he touched were: coc-c rb2
- **thieves**: *(↗robbed)*
  - **accused** of robbing; he has been: *(↗accused)* kali-br
  - **frightened** on waking and thinks dream is true; dreams of robbers: nat-m ↓ verat
    - ⋮ **search** is made; and will not believe the contrary until: nat-m
  - **house**, in: *(↗Fear - robbers)* ars k* cann-i k* con gl1.fr• *Cupr-act* kr1 dulc fd4.de *Lach* k* merc k* *Nat-m* k* plut-n srj7• sil sol-t-ae
    - ⋮ **bed** is full of thieves; and space under: *(↗bed - someone - under)* *Ars* k*
  - **jump** out of window; therefore wants to: *Lach* kr1
  - **seeing**: alum k* arn bg2 ars k* aur bell carneg-g rwt1• cupr k* cupr-act kr1* kali-c kali-sil k2 lach bg2 mag-c mag-m merc k* nat-c *Nat-m* k* petr phos sanic c1 sil k* sol-t-ae a1 verat zinc k* [ars-met stj2 cupr-f stj2 cupr-m stj2 cupr-p stj2 kali-ar stj2 nat-ar stj2 zinc-i stj2 zinc-m stj2 zinc-n stj2 zinc-p stj2]
    - ⋮ **night**: *Ars*
    - ⋮ **listens** under the bed: ars hr1
- **thin**:
  - **body** is: limest-b es1• moni rfm1• thuj k*
    - ⋮ **enlarged**; but arms and hands are: limest-b es1•
  - **he** is getting: *(↗emaciation; wasting)* limest-b es• sulph
- **think**:
  - **cannot** think; she: *Chel* kr1 crot-t ↓ onos rb2
    - ⋮ **outside** of herself: crot-t rb2
- **thoughts**:
  - **grasp** any thoughts; he could not: phos rb2
  - **neck**; are in right side of the: fic-m gya1

- **outside** of body; thoughts are: *(↗ideas - floating - outside)* sabad bg2*
- **read** thoughts; can: kola stb3•
- **separated** from her (See separated - thoughts)
- **stomach**; come from: acon h1*
- **two** different trains of thought influenced him at the same time: lyss rb2 sal-fr sle1•
- **vanish**:
  - **had** vanished; thoughts: dream-p sdj1• kali-c rb2
  - **would** suddenly vanish; as if thoughts: croc rb2 kali-c rb2

- **three** dimensional; two dimensional objects are: *(↗Confusion - identity)* anh sp
- **three** persons, he is: *(↗Confusion - identity)* anac sf1.de bapt st1 cann-i a1 *Nux-m* k* *Petr* sf1.de psil ft1
- **throat**; someone with ice-cold hands took her by the (See choked - ice-cold)
- **thumbs**, fingers are: **Phos** a1*
- **tigers**: positr nl2• rad-br sze8•
- **time**:
  - **earlier**; time seems (= passes too quickly): *(↗Time - quickly)* *Cocc* bro1* galeoc-c-h gms1• hippoc-k szs2 kali-s fd4.de lac-e hrn2• podo fd3.de• sacch-a fd2.de• sulph taosc iwa1• thea a ther bro1
  - **exaggeration** of time (= passes too slowly): *(↗Time - slowly)* *Alum* bro1 ambr bro1 anh bro1 aq-mar rbp6 *Arg-n* bro1 **Cann-i** k* cann-s cere-b a con sf1.de dirc a fic-m gya1 galeoc-c-h gms1• germ-met srj* hippoc-k szs2 hydrog srj2• kali-p fd1.de• lac-e hrn2• limest-b es1• med bro1 nat-sil fd3.de• nux-m k* nux-v bro1 onos pall rb2 petr-ra shn4• taosc iwa1• thres-a sze7• vanil fd5.de
  - **hum** of time; can hear: galeoc-c-h gms1•
  - **space**, and, lost or confused (See Confusion - time - space; Mistakes - space - time)
  - **timeless** and in the present: falco-pe nl2•
  - **working** against: nat-ar bc
- **tipping** over | **sitting** or walking; when: euon-a rb2
- **tired**:
  - **born** tired; as if: bamb-a stb2.de•
  - **speaks** as if: cann-i rb2 nat-sil fd3.de•
  - **world**; pressure of the: [spect dfg1]
- **titan** in seven-league boots; she is: neon srj5•
- **tobacco**: | **vertigo** were from tobacco: rhod rb2
- **toes**:
  - **cut** off: mosch
  - **longer** (See EXTREMITIES - Longer - toes)
- **together**:
  - **himself** together; could not get: caj rb2
    - **air**; in open | **amel.**: caj a1
- **tomato** was a grasshopper: *(↗grasshoppers)* choc srj3•
- **tongue**:
  - **disintegrating**: positr nl2•
  - **long**; tongue is too: aeth
  - **pulling** out his tongue; someone is: bell
  - **seems** to reach the clouds; tongue | **sleep**; when going to: pic-ac
  - **wood**; tongue is made of: *(↗wood - he; EXTREMITIES - Wooden)* apis ars b4a.de carb-v b4a.de
- **tormented**; he is: *Aq-mar* jl1 *Chin* k* dendr-pol sk4• lyss k*
- **torture**: med ↓ ozone ↓ positr nl2•
  - **rid** her mind of the torture; she must do something to: med rb2
  - **tortured**; he is: ozone sde2•
- **tottered** | **surroundings** or he himself tottered: anac rb2
- **touched**; he is: *(↗smoothed)* anac bro1* bapt ↓ canth bro1* fic-m ↓ irid-met srj5• **Med** ↓ op bro1* par vml3• *Rhus-t* ptk1 stram bro1* *Thuj* ptk1 tritic-vg fd5.de
  - **head**; someone touched her: *(↗caressed)* fic-m gya1 **Med** vh*
  - **sides**; someone touched him on both: bapt rb2
- **touching**:
  - **anything**; she could not touch: pall c1*
  - **everything**; he was touching: bell
    - **rough**; everything is too (See GENERALS - Touch - illusions - rough)
- **town**, he is in deserted: carb-an j5.de
- **toys**:
  - **objects** seemed as attractive as toys: cic
  - **playing** with toys: atro
- **train** (See railway)
- **transferred**:
  - **room**; to another: coloc
  - **world**, to another: cann-i
- **transformed**; he is:
  - **mentally**: aids nl2•
  - **several**, strange transformations; he is subject to: cann-i a1
- **transition**; she is in: neon srj5• [*Spect* dfg1]
- **transparent**:
  - **bell**; he is in a transparent: ozone sde2•
  - **everything** is: *Anh* mg1.de*
  - **he** is: anh mg1.de* bell j5.de cann-i k* falco-pe nl2• urol-h rwt•
  - **head** and nose are: bell k*
  - **people** are: kola stb3•
  - **solid** things: cycl tl1
- **trapped**; he is: *(↗deceived; Conformism; DREAMS - Trap - being)* dendr-pol sk4• falco-pe nl2• haliae-lc srj5• hippoc-k szs2 ign mtf irid-m ↓ lac-e hrn2• lath mrr1 limest-b es1• naja mtf plut-n ↓ positr nl2• sal-fr sle1• stry mrr1 *Tub* mtf [heroin sdj2 spect dfg1]
  - **magnetic** field; in a: irid-m srj5•
  - **walking** in a trap: [heroin sdj2]
  - **underworld**; in the: plut-n srj7•
- **travelling**, of: *(↗journey)* aether ↓ *Bell* gl1.fr• cann-i k* [am-br stj2 bar-br stj2 brom stj2]
  - **worlds**; through: aether k*
- **tread** | **lightly** to avoid injuring or disturbing his companions; he must tread: cupr rb2
- **trees**:
  - **higher**; trees seem: [pop dhh1]
  - **people** in fantastic costume; seem to be:
    - **afternoon** | **riding**; while: bell
- **trembling**:
  - **everything** was trembling:
    - **circle**; and was turning in a: plb rb2
    - **on** him was trembling; everything: sulph
    - **wavering**; and: aml-ns rb2
  - **he** was trembling | **without** trembling; but: carb-v rb2 med rb2 sul-ac rb2 zinc rb2
- **trial**; she is on: positr nl2•
- **tribal** | **belongs** to a tribal people; he/she: aids nl2•
- **tricked**; being: rhus-g tmo3•
- **troubles**:
  - **broods** over imaginary troubles (See Brooding - troubles - imaginary)
  - **great** troubles had just come over him: cycl rb2
  - **impending**; troubles were: am-c rb2 anac ↓
    - **trifle** would lead into great troubles; every: anac rb2
- **truth** | **telling** the truth; she were not: macro rb2
- **tumble** | **he** would tumble: calc rb2
- **turn**:
  - **everything** turned: agn ↓ alum rb2 bell ↓ chel ↓ cycl ↓ laur ↓ lyc rb2 mag-c rb2 nat-m ↓ phos ↓ plb ↓ staph ↓ valer rb2 verat ↓ zinc ↓
    - **circle**; in a: *(↗room - turning)* agn rb2 bell rb2 chel rb2 cycl rb2 laur rb2 nat-m rb2 plb ↓ verat rb2 zinc rb2
      - **trembled**; and: plb rb2
      - **walking**; when: nat-m rb2

- **everything** turned: ...
  - **half**-circle; in: staph rb2
  - **round** and round: laur rb2
  - **sitting** up; on: chel rb2
  - **with** her: phos rb2
- **she**:
  - **had** been turned | **circle**; in a: puls rb2 thuj rb2
  - **was** turning: agar rb2 alum↓ anac↓ ang↓ arg-n↓ aur↓ aur-m↓ bry rb2 carl↓ chel↓ con↓ junc-e↓ merc↓ mosch↓ pieri-b mlk9.de ruta↓ tub↓
    - **backward** and around: ang rb2
    - **circle**; in a: alum rb2 anac rb2 arg-n rb2 aur rb2 aur-m↓ carl rb2 chel rb2 con rb2 junc-e↓ merc rb2 ruta rb2 tub rb2
      - **rest**; during: junc-e rb2
      - **stooping**; when: aur-m rb2
    - **left**; to: anac rb2
    - **rapidly** that he perceived a current of air produced by the motion; so: mosch rb2
  - **would** turn: alum rb2
- **surroundings** were turned | **with** him in a circle: am-c rb2
- **things**:
  - **around** each other; things were turning: sabad rb2
  - **with** her; things were turning: aloe rb2 anac rb2 arn rb2 calc rb2 ferr rb2

- **turtles** in room, sees large: bell
- **two**:
  - **individuals**; she were two (See Confusion - identity - duality)
  - **things** happening at once; two: adam srj5•
  - **wills** (See Will - two)
- **typhoid** fever, he will have: nat-p
- **ugly** (See body - ugly)
- **umbrella** was a knife: androc srj1•
- **understand**:
  - **being** understood; she was not: dendr-pol sk4•
  - **not** understand anything; she could: sep rb2
  - **understands** everything: verat-v cda
- **unearthly**, of something: cann-i a1
- **unfair** to him; that life is: ign sej nux-v sej stry sej
- **unfit**:
  - **loved**; to be: germ-met srj5•
  - **work**; for: *(↗position)* cupr dx1 meph kr1 sacch-a fd2.de•
  - **world**; he is unfit for the: *(↗succeed)* *Aur* kr1* aur-m-n wbt2• aur-s wbt2• plat h2
- **unfortunate**, he is: *(↗Pities; Unfortunate)* bry caust k* *Chin* cub dream-p sdj1• graph k* hura ip lyc petr-ra shn4• sep *Staph* gl1.fr* verat
- **unhampered** by a material body; he is: chin-b rb2
- **unpleasant**: alum a1 am-c bell k* carbn-s a1 hep gl1.fr• op↓ phos
  - **distinct** from surrounding objects: bell k* op a1
- **unreal**: *(↗Unreal - everything)*
  - **everything** seems unreal: *(↗Strange - everything; Unreal - everything)* ail *Alum* k* aml-ns kr1 *Anac* kr1* androc srj1• anh sp1 aran jl aran-ix mg beryl tpw5 bit-ar wht1• cann-i cann-s cann-xyz ptk1 cic sf1.de *Cocc* bg1* con c1 cypra-eg sde6.de• dat-a hl dream-p sdj1• *Dulc* fd4.de germ-met srj gink-b jl halo jl hydrog srj2*• irid-met srj5• lac-c lac-h sze9• lil-t limest-b es1• loxo-recl knl4• *Med* k* nad rly4• nat-sil fd3.de• plut-n srj7• podo fd3.de• psil ft rauw sp1 sacch-a fd2.de• *Spong* fd4.de staph taosc iwa1• tere-la rly4• [cadm-met stj2 cadm-s stj2 heroin sdj2 lac-mat sst4 spect dfg1]
    - **company**; while in: psil ft1
    - **hemorrhage** after delivery; in: cann-s kr1
  - **life** were unreal: med rb2 podo fd3.de• taosc iwa1•
- **unseen** things; delusions of: tarent
- **unsupported**: falco-pe nl2•
- **unveiled**; she is: germ-met srj5•
- **upright**; she has become: neon srj5•
- **urine** | **she** were turning into urine: lac-ac rb2
- **used** and discarded; being: polys sk4•
- **vagina** | **living** things creep into vagina at night: merc
- **valued**, she is: positr nl2•
- **valued**; he is not: polys sk4• rad-br sze8• [bell-p-sp dcm1]
- **vampires**:
  - **bats**; delusions of vampire: plut-n srj7•
  - **energetic**:
    - **he** is an energetic vampire: pegan-ha tpi1•
    - **power** from him; energetic vampires get: pegan-ha tpi1•
    - **surrounded** by energetic vampires; he is: *Pegan-ha* tpi1•
- **vanish**:
  - **everything** will: lyc
  - **senses** vanish; seems as if his: cann-s k2 merc plat c1
- **vegetable**:
  - **existence**, leading a: cann-i
  - **green** vegetables, he is selling: (non:cupr slp*) cupr-act a1* [cupr-f stj2 cupr-m stj2 cupr-p stj2]
- **vehicle** | **jarring** her; she were in some vehicle which was moving and: sang rb2
- **veil** | **mind** and reality; between: bit-ar wht1•
- **vengeance**, divine (See god - vengeance)
- **vermin**: alum↓ am-c↓ *Ars*↓ bov↓ calc↓ kali-c↓ lac-c k2* mur-ac↓ musca-d szs1 *Nux-v*↓ petr-ra↓ phos↓ ran-s↓ sil↓ sulph↓
  - **bed** is covered with; his: ars
  - **seeing** vermin crawl about: alum am-c *Ars* k* bov calc gl1.fr• kali-c lac-c k2* mur-ac *Nux-v* petr-ra shn4• phos ran-s sil sulph vh*
- **vertigo**:
  - **become** dizzy; he would: brom rb2 gard-j↓ mag-m↓ malar rb2
    - **consciousness**; and lose: mag-m rb2
    - **rage**; after: gard-j vlr2•
  - **beginning**:
    - **ears** and pressed to vertex; beginning in front of: sal-p rb2
    - **eye**; from left: lob rb2
    - **stomach**; from: kali-c rb2
  - **having** vertigo: aml-ns rb2 bell rb2 bufo rb2 ferr rb2 gels rb2 jug-r rb2 magn-gr↓ sacch rb2 stram rb2
    - **seasickness**; from: magn-gr rb2
  - **moved** now in one, now in another direction: coff-t rb2
  - **overpowering** vertigo coming over her: con rb2
- **vexation**:
  - **after**: bell j5.de *Plat* j5.de
  - **offenses**; of vexations and: cham chin dros
- **victim**; she is a: lac-lup hm2• [oxyg stj]
- **vindictive**: agar j5.de
- **violence**, about: kali-br k* lac-h sze9•
- **violent**: *Bell* j5.de hyos j5.de positr nl2• sec j5.de stram j5.de [ars stj2]
- **Virgin** Mary; being (See mary - she)
- **visions**, has: *(↗apparition; fancy; images; VISION - Illusions)* absin k* agar bro1 alum alum-sil k2 ambr k* anac jl3 anh bro1* antip br1* apis↓ arg-n arn kr1 *Ars* j5.de* *Atro* bro1 atro-s hr1 aur mrr1 **Bell** k* berb↓ borx br1 brom↓ *Bry*↓ *Calc* k* calc-ar kr1 *Calc-s* calc-sil↓ camph j5.de* cann-s bg cann-xyz bg2 canth carb-an j5.de* carb-v j5.de* carbn-o br1 *Carbn-s* k* carc gb• caust j5.de cench cere-b↓ cham k* *Chin*↓ chlol chlorpr jl3 choc↓ cic cimic k* *Cina* kr1 coca↓ cocain bro1 cocc↓ coff k2 coff-t↓ con convo-s sp1 cortico sp1 *Crot-c* cupr↓ dig c1 dros j5.de* dulc j* germ-met↓ graph haliae-lc↓ hell j5.de* *Hep* k* hippoc-k szs2 *Hyos* k* *Ign*↓ indol↓ kali-br bro1 kali-c j5.de* *Lac-c*↓ lac-del↓ *Lach* k* lact j lat-h↓ led↓ lyc mag-m j* mag-s j5.de merc j5.de* methys jl3 *Morph* bro1 musca-d↓ naja kr1 nat-c j* *Nat-m* nat-sal bro1 nicot↓ nit-ac nux-m *Nux-v* j5.de* olib-sac wmh1 olnd j *Op* k* orot-ac rly4• oxal-a↓ past bro1 petr↓ *Ph-ac* h2* phos bg2* plat k* plb↓ plut-n↓ positr↓ psil jl3 *Psor*↓ *Puls* k* pyrog↓ rad-br↓ rhod rhus-t k* samb↓ sanguis-s hm2• santin bro1 scop↓ sec bg2* sep *Sil* spong *Stram* k* *Sulph* k* tab↓ tarent k2 ther c1 thuj↓ tritic-vg fd5.de valer k* vanil fd5.de verat j* zinc↓
  - **daytime**: bell lac-c lyc nat-m stram
  - **morning** | **bed**, in: hep c1
  - **evening**: brom carb-an carb-v chin *Cina* kr1 cupr ign phos puls
    - **children** wake in; with: **Cina** kr1

- **night**: camph kr1 canth cham dulc fd4.de spong *Stram* kr1 thuj kr1
- **above** and below; simultaneously: choc srj
- **beautiful**: (↗*beautiful)* anh ↓ bell *Cann-i* coca lac-c lach musca-d ↓ olib-sac wmh1 olnd **Op** k* psil ft1
  - **kaleidoscopic** changes; varied: anh br1 musca-d szs1
- **black** objects (See black - objects)
- **closing** the eyes, on: anh mg1.de apis *Arg-n* ars **Bell** k* *Bry* **CALC** k1* camph carb-v fry caust *Chin* cocc cupr germ-met srj graph hell *Ign* lac-del hrn2• *Lach* led lyc nat-m op fry plb *Psor* fry *Puls* pyrog fry samb sec sep spong *Stram* k* *Sulph* tarent thuj
- **clouds** of colors: lach spong fd4.de
- **colorful**: (↗*VISION - Illusions - colorful)* anh br1*
- **coma** vigil; in: *Op* kr1
- **comets**; of: plut-n srj7•
- **creeping** things; of: *Lac-c* kr1
- **delight**; visions of | **night**; filled his brain all: op rb2
- **fantastic**: ambr br1 arn kr1 ars bell br1* *Chlol* kr1 hyos lach nit-ac op psil ft1 stram ptk1 verat ptk1
- **fire** (See fire - visions)
- **goddess**; of a: *Sanguis-s* hrn2•
- **grandeur**, of magnificent: (↗*great; Haughty; Insanity)* cann-i kr1 carbn-s (non:coff slp) coff-t slp olib-sac wmh1
- **hide**; wishes to: bell kr1
- **horrible**: (↗*images - frightful; Fancies - exaltation - frightful)* absin k* ambr k2 atro a1 **Bell** berb ↓ **CALC** k1* calc-sil k2 camph carb-an carb-v *Caust Dulc* fd4.de hell ↓ hep sf1.de ign kr1 indol br1 *Kali-br* k* lac-c *Lach* ↓ lyc merc nat-m ↓ nicot a1 nit-ac ↓ *Nux-v* kr1* op petr ↓ phos positr nl2• *Puls* rad-br sze8• rhod a1 samb scop ↓ sil spong ↓ *Stram* k* sulph tab ↓ tarent tritic-vg fd5.de vanil fd5.de zinc ↓
  - **evening**: calc a1 carb-v a1
  - **night**: camph a1 dulc fd4.de nit-ac a1 phos a1 tab a1 vanil fd5.de
  - **behind** him: *Lach* kr1
  - **beside** him: *Stram* j5.de
  - **dark**, in the: *Bell Carb-v* hell ign lach petr puls scop stram
  - **events**, of past: spong a1
  - **fright**; from: (↗*fright - after)* bell kr1 nat-m kr1 samb kr1
  - **sleep**; before falling to: calc h2 ign a
  - **twilight**; in | **children**; in: berb ptk1
  - **waking**; on: ign a vanil fd5.de zinc
- **light**, not in the dark; sees visions in the: *Lac-c* tl
- **monsters**, of: (↗*monster)* anh br1 *Bell* k* camph cann-i cic cimic ↓ ign ↓ *Kali-br* sne lac-c lat-h thj1 olib-sac wmh1 op j5.de samb *Stram* tarent
  - **going** to sleep and on waking; on: ign
  - **strange** objects and rats: (↗*rats)* cimic
- **persecuted** in visions: hyos rb2
- **power**, of imaginary: cann-i psil ft1
- **rainbows** in the sky (See rainbows)
- **rats**; strange objects and (See monsters - strange)
- **real**; visions are: lach rb2
- **shadows** of light: plut-n srj7•
- **simultaneous** from above and below: choc srj3•
- **sleep**; during: *Nat-m* kr1 *Stram* ↓
  - **restless**: *Stram* kr1
- **strikes** at them and holds up the cross: *Puls* kr1*
- **suns**; of two: haliae-lc srj5•
- **symmetrical**: cann-i a1 cere-b a1
- **telling** him; about what they are: psil ft1
- **wonderful**: anh br1 calc camph cann-i lach oxal-a rly4• psil ft1

- **visual** (See visions)
- **vitality**; vivid consciousness of usually unnoticed operations of: cann-i a1 [spect dfg1]
- **vivid**: *Absin* bro1 acon bro1 aether a1 agar bro1 ambr bro1 ars bl bell k* *Calc Cann-i* bro1 carc mlr1• cham k* dub bro1 gast a1 hyos k* irid-met srj5• kali-c bro1 *Lach* k* lyc op k* phos a1 *Plat* kr1 plb psil ft1 puls rhus-t bro1 scop bro1 spong k* *Stram* k* sulph bro1 *Verat* bro1
- **voices**:
  - **hearing**: (↗*hearing; hearing - illusions)* abrot acon bg2* agar anac k* anh sp1 aster k* bell k* benz-ac calc bg2 calc-sil k2 cann-i *Cann-s* kr1 cann-xyz bg2 canth bg2 carb-v bg2 carbn-s cench **Cham** b7a.de* chir-fl ↓ chlol k* coca k* coff bg2* con bg2 *Crot-c* k* crot-h *Cupr-act* kr1 dros bg2 *Elaps* k* germ-met srj hyos hyper ↓ ign bg2 *Kali-br* k* *Kola* stb3• lac-c lach lyc mag-m bg2 manc k* med k* nat-m nit-ac ptk1 petr ph-ac bg2 *Phos* k* plb plut-n ↓ rhus-t a1 sabal ↓ sol-ni spong fd4.de stram k* *Sulph* ↓ tarent sne thal-xyz srj8• thuj ↓ ulm-c ↓ verat bg2 *Zinc* kr1 [lac-mat sst4]
    - **night**: *Cham* chir-fl gya2 spong fd4.de *Sulph* vh ulm-c jsj8•
    - **abdomen**; voices are in his: thuj k*
    - **absent** persons; of: (↗*distant)* anac h2 cham h1* germ-met srj5•
    - **abusive** and filthy language; voices from within him are speaking in: *Zinc* kr1 [lac-mat sst4]
    - **answers**; and: aster kr1 calc-sil k2
    - **calling** | **him** | **night**: sulph vh*
      - **his** name: anac
    - **cease** when listening intently in bed: abrot
    - **commit** crime; voice commands him to: lach k2
    - **confess** things she never did; she must: lach k2
    - **confused** | **swallowing** or walking in open air agg.: benz-ac petr phos
    - **crime**; a voice commands him to commit a (See commit)
    - **dead** people, of: anac br1* *Bell* calc-sil k2* hyper st* nat-m stram
    - **distant**: (↗*absent)* anac br1* bell cann-s kr1 cham nat-m sabal ptk stram
    - **filthy** language; voices from within him are speaking in abusive and (See abusive)
    - **follow**, that he must: (↗*devil - speaking; devil - speaking - angel; whispering)* anac k2 crot-c lach k2 thuj h1*
    - **kill**; that she must steal and (See commit)
    - **name**; a | **nose**; from behind her: plut-n srj7•
    - **saying** "come" (See people - say)
    - **sleep**, during: cham gt spong fd4.de
    - **steal** and kill; that she must (See commit)
    - **strangers**, of: bell gl1.fr• *Cham* gl1.fr• crot-c tl1
    - **unpleasant** voices about himself: coca ptk1
  - **own** voice seems to be distant; his: (↗*hearing - illusions)* aids nl2•
  - **own** voice sounds strange and seems to reverberate like thunder; his: (↗*hearing - illusions)* cann-i
- **vow**:
  - **breaking** her vow; she is: ign
  - **keep** it, must: verat j5.de
- **waiting**:
  - **had** to wait; he: anh sp1
  - **is** waiting; he: limest-b es1• *Propr* sa3•
- **waking**; on: (↗*awakening)* anthraq rly4• arizon-l nl2• aur j5.de carb-v j5.de colch j5.de* dulc j5.de merc j5.de nat-c j5.de par j5.de ph-ac hr1*
- **walked**:
  - **had** walked; she:
    - **long** distance; a: eup-per rb2 lac-ac rb2
    - **too** far: verat rb2
- **walking**:
  - **air**:
    - **in** air; walks: aur-m rb2 lact rb2
    - **on** air; walks: asar rb2 chin rb2 coff rb2 lac-c br1* merc-i-f rb2 nat-m rb2 nux-v rb2 op rb2 ph-ac rb2 phos rb2 rhus-t rb2 spig rb2 stict rb2 stram rb2 thuj rb2*
  - **backward**; she walks | **forward**; when walking: paull a1 sil rb2
  - **behind** him; someone walks: (↗*people - behind; Fear - behind)* anac jl crot-c lach tl1 mag-m jl med st* musca-d szs1 sanic c1 sil k2 *Staph* h1*
  - **beside** him; someone walks: calc k* petr k2 sil k2 thuj k2
  - **cannot** walk, he: apis ↓ hell ↓ *Ign* k1* pneu jl stram sf1.de
    - **run** or hop, must: (↗*Awkward; Foolish)* apis hell

- **cotton**; he walks on: **Alum** b4a.de* apis bg2 calc b4a.de carb-v bg2 onos rb2* phos bg2 *Sulph* b4a.de zinc bg2
- **effortlessly**: neon srj5•
- **forever**; she could walk: fl-ac rb2
- **he** has been walking | **years**; for: plut-n srj7•
- **knees**, he walks on his: *Bar-c* k* bar-m k* med lz
- **same** one is walking after him, who is walking before him: euph k*
- **slowly**; she walks | **quickly**; when walking: adam srj5• fic-m gya1
- **stones**; on (See EXTREMITIES - Stones - sensation)
- **up** and down rooms | **dreams**; in his: agar rb2
- **velvet**; on: sec ptk1
- **wool** on walking; floor were soft like: *(↗ground - soft)* xan rb2*

- **walls**:
  - **crush** him; walls will: *(↗falling - walls; Fear - narrow)* *Arg-n*
  - **falling**; walls are: *(↗Fear - narrow)* arg-n st* cann-i st* carb-v ↓ falco-pe ↓ lyss st*
    - **inward**: arg-n rb2 carb-v rb2 falco-pe nl2• lyss st
  - **gliding** together; walls seem to be: cann-i [arg-n stj2]
  - **horrible** things on the walls; sees: bell cann-i hyos samb
  - **surrounded** by high walls; being: *(↗falling - walls; Fear - narrow)* cann-i carc fd2.de•
- **want**:
  - **he** will come to: *(↗poor; Avarice; Fear - poverty; Fear - starving)* calc-f chlor rb2 dulc fd4.de sulph tritic-vg fd5.de
  - **they** had come to: *(↗poor; Avarice; Fear - poverty)* cann-i
- **war**: bell ↓ ferr ↓ ferr-f ↓ ferr-lac ↓ ferr-n ↓ ferr-sil ↓ hyos ↓ ignis-alc es2• ran-b ↓ rhus-g ↓ thuj ↓ verb ↓ [plat stj2]
  - **being** at: bell j5.de ferr bg2* hyos bg2 ignis-alc es2• plat bg2 ran-b bg2 thuj bg2* verb bg2 [ferr-f stj2 ferr-lac stj2 ferr-n stj2 ferr-sil stj2]
    - **evil**; with: ignis-alc es2•
  - **inside** her: rhus-g tmo3•
- **warts**, he has: mez
- **washing**, of: bell k* syph bg2
- **wasting** away: *(↗thin - he)* naja gm1
- **watched**, she is being: *(↗criticized; looking - everyone; people - seeing - looking; spied; Admonition - agg.; Ailments - reproaches; Fear - observed; Looked - cannot; Offended)* adam srj5• aids nl2• aq-mar jl3* **Ars** k* *Bar-c Calc* bg1* choc srj3• dream-p sdj1• falco-pe nl2• fum ↓ *Hyos* k* *Kali-br* sne *Kola* stb3• med pc* meli musca-d szs1 nat-pyru rly4• olib-sac wmh1 petr-ra shn4• rhus-t sanguis-s hm2• spong fd4.de [titan stj]
  - **night**: med c1
  - **herself**; by: fum rly1*•
- **water**:
  - **blue** water; of: cann-i
  - **disasters** by: cann-i
  - **flowing** water; sees: *Merc* sal-fr sle1•
  - **foul**: musca-d szs1
  - **green** water, of: sal-fr sle1•
  - **nectar**; water is delicious | **drinking**; when: cann-i
  - **of**: alum bg2 am-m bg2 ant-t bg2* ars bg2 bov bg2 dig bg2 ferr bg2 graph bg2 ign bg2 iod bg2* kali-c bg2 kali-n bg2 mag-c bg2 mag-m bg2 meph bg2 merc h1* nat-c bg2 ran-b bg2 sal-fr sle1• sep bg2 sil bg2
  - **smells**: agath-a nl2•
  - **spoonful** of water seems like a lake; a: *(↗Hydrophobia)* agar
  - **talking** of water; with: *Sal-fr* sle1• sep j5.de
  - **under** water; he is: hippoc-k szs2 irid-met srj5• limest-b es1•
  - **wades** in water; he: ant-t j5.de
- **waver**:
  - **everything** wavers and trembles (See trembling - everything - wavering)
  - **objects** waver: cycl rb2 grat rb2 til rb2
- **waves** going through head (See HEAD - Waving)
- **waves**, of: falco-pe nl2•
- **waving**:
  - **he** was waving lengthwise | **lying**; while: merc rb2
- **wealth**, of: *(↗great; Avarice; Haughty; Insanity - purchases)* adam srj5• agn alco bell k* calc cann-i k* cann-xyz ptk1 kali-br nit-ac bg2 *Nux-v* ↓ phos bro1* *Plat* bro1* *Pyrog* k* *Sulph* k* verat k* [tax jsj7]
  - **purchases**; and make useless: *Nux-v* kr1
- **wedding**, of a: *(↗marriage)* alum bg2* hyos h1* irid-met srj5• mag-m bg2 nat-c bg2 [alum-p stj2 alumin stj2 alumin-s stj2]
- **weep**; he would: aster rb2 cot rb2
- **weeping**; with: acon j5.de dulc j5.de lyc j5.de merc j5.de stram j5.de
- **weight**:
  - **no** weight; has: cann-i k* hyos c1* op
  - **pressing** down from above: irid-met srj5•
- **well**, he is: *(↗Delirium - well; Irritability - sends - doctor; Obstinate - nothing; Well - says - sick)* *Apis* aq-mar skp7• **Arn** k* ars bell j5.de cinnb hyos *Iod* bg2* kreos merc op bg2* podo fd3.de• psil ft1 puls
- **went** around with her; everything: ferr rb2
- **wheelwright**; is a: stram kr1
- **whimsical**: cann-i a1
- **whirled** around:
  - **he** | **coal** screen; and had been placed in a: eup-per hr1*
  - **surroundings**: aloe ↓ alum rb2 bry ↓ op ↓ rhus-t ↓ zinc rb2
    - **standing**; when: bry rb2
    - **with** her: aloe rb2 op rb2 rhus-t rb2
  - **things**:
    - **circle**; in a: verat rb2
    - **opposite** direction; in the | **shuts** the eyes; if he: sabad rb2
- **whirling** | **everything** round him; he is whirling with (See whirled - surroundings - with)
- **whiskey** | **fumes** of whiskey gone to his head: ars-met rb2
- **whispering** to him; someone is: *(↗devil - speaking; voices - hearing - follow)* anac ptk1 chir-fl gya2 med k2* rhodi c1
  - **blasphemy**: anac c1*
- **whistling**, with: bell j5.de stram j5.de
- **white** coating around him; has a: ozone sde2•
- **wicked** deed; she had committed a: cocc rb2
- **wife**:
  - **faithless**; wife is: *(↗jealousy - lovers; Forsaken; Jealousy)* hyos k* stram k*
  - **run** away from him; wife will: *(↗Confidence - want; Forsaken)* staph k*
- **wild**; he would go: lob rb2
- **wilderness**; being in: stram j
- **will** power; as if loss of: *(↗Will - loss; Will - weakness)* carb-v rb2 chinin-s j5.de nit-ac rb2 pop rb2
- **wills**; possessed by two (See Will - two)
- **wind** sighing in chimney sounded like the hum of a vast wheel | **reverberated** like a peal of thunder of a grand organ; and: cann-i
- **window**:
  - **closed**; should be: lyss kr1
  - **thrown** out: [tus-p stj]
- **windsurfing**, as if: falco-pe nl2•
- **wine**; he had taken: sabad rb2
- **wings**:
  - **back** were opening and wings were forming; as if: choc srj3•
  - **carried** on wings when walking: thuj rb2*
  - **has** wings; she: irid-met srj5•
- **wires**; is caught in: *(↗encaged)* cact st1 cimic k*
- **witches**; believes in: sep b4a.de
- **withering**, body is: positr nl2• sabad k2
- **wolves**, of: agath-a nl2• bell k* kola stb3• positr nl2• stram
- **womb** is soft and would give abortion: abies-c c1
- **women**: *(↗Hatred - women)*
  - **bedside**; by: med kr1
  - **dark**-haired | **dripping** black teeth: galeoc-c-h gms1•

- women: ...
  - **evil** and will injure his soul; women are: *(↗Aversion - women - men; Hatred; Homosexuality)* puls
  - **lewd** women; his mother's house is invaded by: kali-br
  - **old**:
    - **ragged** woman seemed beautiful; old (See beautiful - old)
    - **wrinkled** women; and: calc-sil k* cann-i
  - **surrounded** by women, he is too much: galla-q-r nl2•
- **wood**:
  - **brain** is made of wood and he could not think; back of: staph rb2
  - **he** is made of wood: *(↗tongue - wood; EXTREMITIES - Wooden)* kali-n k* petr ptk2
- **words** | **think** of words; she cannot: verat rb2
- **work**:
  - **accomplish** her work; she cannot: bry a1* dulc fd4.de limen-b-c hrn2•
  - **advance** fast enough; does not: gamb a
  - **hard**; is working: bell bg2 bry bg2 canth bg2 phos bg2 rhus-t k* verat k*
  - **harm**; work will do him: *(↗Laziness - work - harm) Arg-n*
  - **hindered** at work; is: *(↗hindered) Chin*
  - **home**; will create a feeling of being: des-ac rbp6
  - **stop**; cannot: des-ac rbp6
  - **too** much work; he has: ozone sde2•
- **world**:
  - **absurd**: taosc iwa1•
  - **cold**: hippoc-k szs2
  - **dark**: hippoc-k szs2
  - **different** world; being in a: cann-i a1 [heroin sdj2 *Spect* dfg1]
    - **parallel** world: [heroin sdj2]
  - **lost** to the world, beyond hope; he is: *Arg-n* kr1
  - **modern**: taosc iwa1•
  - **new** world; he is moving in a: camph rb2
  - **ordered**, that the world is perfectly: aids nl2•
  - **rested** upon him; the world: tab rb2
  - **shabby**; is: germ-met srj
  - **she** has her own little: bell ptk1 camph kr1 cypra-eg ↓
    - **clear**, outside is uncertain; in which things are: cypra-eg sde6.de•
  - **small**; is: [spect dfg1]
  - **stony**: hippoc-k szs2
  - **top** of the world; feeling on: allox tpw4 tell rsj10•
- **worms**: am-c ↓ bov ↓ cann-i ↓ coca-c ↓ *Cocain* br1 kali-c ↓ mur-ac ↓ *Nux-v* ↓ phos ↓ ran-s ↓ sil ↓ [alum stj2 ars stj2 heroin sdj2]
  - **bed**; are in: ars a1
  - **covered** with; he is: cocain
  - **creeping** of: alum bg2 am-c bg2 ars bg2 bov bg2 coca-c sk4• kali-c bg2 mur-ac bg2 *Nux-v* bg2 phos bg2 ran-s bg2 sil bg2
  - **vomitus** is a bunch of: cann-i
- **worthless**; he is: *(↗despised; do - nothing; Confidence - want - self-depreciation; Discontented - himself - good; Honor - sense - no)* adam srj agn vh* anac ptk1 aur k2* falco-pe nl2• lac-c mtf33 lac-h sk4• nat-ar a1 positr nl2• thuj mrr1*
- **wretched**; she looks: *(↗body - ugly)* des-ac ↓ limest-b ↓ **Nat-m** mtf33 sal-fr ↓ [calc-s stj1]
  - **looking** in a mirror; when: *(↗Unfortunate)* des-ac rbp6 limest-b es1• **Nat-m** k •* sal-fr sle1•
- **writing** seemed untidy; her: hydrog srj2•
- **wrong**: [heroin sdj2]
  - **doing** something wrong; he is: *Carc* fd2.de• dulc fd4.de (non:germ-met srj5) hell ptk1* vanil fd5.de

Delusions – wrong: ...
  - **done** wrong; he has: *(↗criminal he; evil - done; neglected - duty; reproach; right - doing; Anxiety - conscience; Confidence - want; Conscientious; Pessimist; Remorse; Reproaching oneself; Sadness - fault; Sadness - wrong; Succeeds; Timidity)* agath-a nl2• aids nl2• alum a1* *Ars* k* *Aur* k* aur-ar k2 *Aur-m-n* wbt2• aur-s wbt2• cina ptk1* cob rb cocc c1* con rb2 crot-c sk4• cycl k* dig digin a1 ferr rb2 germ-met srj* granit-m es1• *Hell* hyos st *Ign* k* lac-h sk4• *Lach* vh* *Lil-t* bc lyc merc k* *Moni* rfm1• myric mg naja k13 nat-ar *Nux-m* rb2* op mtf33 positr nl2• puls ruta rb2* sarr a1 sil sf1.de sulph h2 symph fd3.de• thuj k* verat rb2 [brom stj1 calc-br stj1 heroin sdj2]
    - **others** know it; and (See criminal, he - others)
    - **look** anyone in the face as others knew this; and could not: cob rb2
    - **punished**; and is about to be: op mtf33
  - **everything** goes wrong: *(↗fail)* androc srj bac bn bamb-a stb2.de• calc bg2 coloc bg2 falco-pe nl2• hep bg2 kali-br rb naja bg2* nux-v bg2* phys ptk1 plac-s rly4• [heroin sdj2]
  - **everything** she said was wrong: aids nl2•
  - **gives** people something wrong from which they die; she: sulph h2*
  - **something** were wrong: kali-br rb2 sal-fr ↓ thuj ptk1
    - **waking**; as if something wrong within her on: sal-fr sle1•
  - **suffered** wrong; he has: *(↗Forsaken)* adam srj5• bac bn bar-c mtf33 carc sst* chin dx1 **Hyos** k* lach *Lyss* naja k* petr-ra shn4• positr nl2• sal-fr sle1• ulm-c jsj8• [heroin sdj2 tax jsj7]
    - **children**; in: bar-c mtf33 carc sst2• naja mtf33
- **young**, she is again: agath-a nl2• musca-d szs1

○ - **Abdomen**:
  - **alive** in; something is (See ABDOMEN - Alive)
  - **enlarged**: falco-pe nl2• haliae-lc srj5• symph fd3.de•
  - **fallen** in; abdomen is: **Sabad** k*
- **Eyes**:
  - **big**; of: *(↗enlarged - eyes) Lac-c* kr1* op h1* *Puls* kr1
  - **darting** like an animal: musca-d szs1
  - **falling** out (See EYE - Falling - out)
  - **further** round side of head: haliae-lc srj5•
  - **half**-closed eyes; looking at world through: adam srj5•
  - **hundred** eyes; seeing: musca-d szs1
  - **iris**; looking through her own: neon srj5•
  - **moving** slower than head: bit-ar wht1•
- **Nose**:
  - **double**; nose is: merl k*
  - **longer**; nose seems: agath-a nl2• choc srj3• *Glon* kr1 *Verat* kr1
  - **smaller**; nose is: choc srj3•
  - **someone** else's nose; has: lac-c k*
  - **takes** people by the nose: merc
  - **touched** with a metallic substance: cinnb c1
  - **transparent** nose; has a: bell k*
  - **two** noses, has (See double)
- **Stomach**:
  - **devoured**; his stomach is: **Sabad**
  - **enlarged** (See STOMACH - Distension - sensation; STOMACH - Enlarged - sensation)
  - **hole** in stomach cannot be filled: kola stb3•
  - **own** stomach; is not his: plut-n srj7•
  - **mental** acts were performed in: acon rb2
  - **ulcer** in stomach; has corrosion of an: acet-ac kr1 ign sabad

DEMANDING (See Dictatorial; Manipulative)

DEMENTIA: *(↗Childish; Retardation; Schizophrenia - paranoid)* *Acon* ↓ *Aesc-g* ↓ aeth ptk1 *Agar* bro1 *Agn* ↓ alco a1 alum mrr1* *Ambr* ↓ *Anac* bro1* ant-c h2* anth vh1 apisin bro1 arg-n mrr1* ars ptk1* aur ↓ *Aur-i* ↓ aza ↓ *Bad* ↓ bapt ↓ bar-act ↓ *Bar-c* ↓ bell bro1* bry ↓ bufo bg2 calc bro1 calc-p bro1 cann-i br1* canth ↓ carbn-s a1 carc mrr1* caust ↓ cic mrr1 cimic ↓

Demetia: ...
coca a1 con bro1* croc a1 crot-c mrr1 crot-h c1* dam ↓ *Ferr-i* ↓ gaert ↓ glon mrr1 graph mrr1* hell bro1* hydroph ↓ *Hyos* bro1 ign bro1 iodof ↓ kali-i a1 kali-p ↓ lach gl1.fr• laur ↓ *Lil-t* c1* lyc bg* med ↓ merc bro1 nat-i ↓ nat-m ↓ *Nat-sal* bro1 nit-ac ↓ *Nux-v* ptk1 *Oena* ↓ op bro1* orch c1 *Ph-ac* bro1 *Phos* bro1* *Pic-ac* bro1 plb mrr1* puls mrr1 sec ↓ sep ↓ sil mrr1* sol-crl ↓ *Staph* ↓ stram c1 sulph bro1* sumb bg tarent a1* thiosin ↓ *Verat* bro1 verat-v ↓ vip c1 zinc bg2* [alum-p stj2 alumin stj2 alumin-s stj2 am-caust stj2 am-f stj2 arg-met stj1* arg-p stj2 bar-i stj2 beryl stj2 bor-pur stj2 cob stj2 cupr stj2 cupr-act stj2 cupr-f stj2 cupr-m stj2 cupr-p stj2 fl-ac stj2 fl-pur stj2 iod stj2 lith-c stj2 lith-f stj2 lith-i stj2 lith-m stj2 lith-met stj2 lith-p stj2 mang-i stj2 mang-p stj2 merc-i-f stj2 nitro stj2 oxyg stj2 zinc-i stj2 zinc-m stj2 zinc-n stj2 zinc-p stj2]

- **alternating** with | **excitement**: carbn-s br1
- **cares** about business; from: lil-t ptk1
- **dialysis** dementia: alum mtf bar-c mtf kali-p mtf ph-ac mtf zinc-p mtf
- **epileptics**, of: acon bro1 *Bell* bro1 cimic bro1 cupr bro1 *Cupr-act* bro1 *Ferr-i* kr1 laur bro1 *Oena* bro1 *Sil* bro1 sol-crl bro1 stram bro1 verat-v bro1
- **incipient**: nat-sal br1
- **masturbation**, with: *Agn* bro1 calc-p bro1 canth bro1 caust bro1 dam bro1 nux-v bro1 op bro1 *Ph-ac* bro1 phos bro1 pic-ac bro1 *Staph* bro1
- **paretic**: *Acon* bro1 *Aesc-g* bro1 agar bro1 ars bro1 *Bad* bro1 bell bro1 cann-i bro1 cimic bro1 cupr bro1 hydroph rsj6• hyos bro1 ign bro1 iodof bro1 merc bro1 *Phos* bro1 *Plb* br1* stram bro1 verat-v bro1 zinc bro1
- **sadness**, with: tarent k2*
- **senilis**: *(↗Mental exertion - agg. - impossible - old)* agn sf1.de alum mrr1 *Ambr* mrr1 anac bg2* ant-c bg2* arg-met jl aur bg2 *Aur-i* bro1 aza jl3 bapt bg2 bar-act bro1 *Bar-c* bg2* bell gl1.fr• bry gl1.fr• bufo ↓ calc-p bro1 carc mlr1• *Con* bg2* *Crot-h* kr1* *Cupr* mrr1 gaert fmm1• ign gl1.fr• lach bg2 lil-t c1 *Lyc* ↓ med ↓ nat-i bro1 nat-m gl1.fr• nux-v gl1.fr• op ↓ phos bg2* plb mrr1 puls mrr1 sec bg2* sep gl1.fr• sulph gl1.fr• thiosin br1
  - **premature**: *Ambr* mrr1 bufo br1 *Lyc* br1 med jl2
  - **talking**, with foolish: bar-c gl1.fr• con gl1.fr• op gl1.fr• plb gl1.fr• puls ↓
    - **night**: puls gl1.fr•
- **sexual** excesses; from: lil-t ptk1
- **syphilitics**, of: aur-i bro1 *Kali-i* bro1 merc bro1 nit-ac bro1 sulph bro1
- **weakness**; with: pic-ac br1

DENTITION; during: *Acon* b7.de* *Cham* b7.de* *Coff* b7.de* *Nux-v* b7.de* *Rheum* b7a.de *Rhus-t* b7.de*

DEPENDENT of others: *(↗Forsaken)* adam srj agar mrr1 ars ↓ bar-c sk• bar-s ↓ bism ↓ gels ↓ lac-ac stj5• marb-w es1• nux-v ↓ *Phos* ↓ **Puls** mrr1 sep ↓ sil ctc• stram ↓

- **desire** to be: *(↗Confidence - want; Responsibility - aversion)* adam mtf ars vh* bism mtf gels mtf marb-w es1• nux-v mtf puls mtf sep mtf sil mtf stram mtf [bar-s stj1]
- **physician**; on the: *Phos* mrr1

DEPERSONALIZATION: *(↗Confusion - identity; Confusion - identity - boundaries; Delusions - body - out; Delusions - separated - body - soul; Disruption; Merging)* alum mtf anac mtf *Anh* mg1.de* bapt mtf cann-i mtf falco-pe nl2• hydrog mtf irid-met srj5• nat-sil fd3.de• stram mtf *Thuj* mtf [bell-p-sp dcm1 heroin sdj2]

DEPRAVITY: *(↗Moral)* *Anac* hr1* *Bufo* ptk1 tarent ptk1

DEPRECIATION; feeling: [berb stu1]

DEPRESSION (See Sadness)

DEPRESSIVE MANIA (See Mania - alternating - depression)

DESCENDING agg.: **Borx** bg2 *Gels* bg2

DESERTED (See Forsaken)

DESIRES: *(↗Longing; Yearning)*

- **full** of desires: *(↗Capriciousness)* agav-t jl aids nl2• alco ↓ ambr ↓ ant-c bg2 *Ars* mp1• ars-s-f ↓ bar-s ↓ berb bg2 bry j5.de* calc-sil ↓ carc mlr1• castm bg2 chin ↓ cina j5.de *Coca* ↓ coff bg2 cur ↓ dioxi ↓ dream-p ↓ dulc j5.de* elaps ↓ galeoc-c-h ↓ *Ham* ↓ hippoc-k ↓ ign j5.de ip j5.de kali-c ↓ lach ↓ lap-la ↓ mag-m ↓ *Manc* ↓ *Med* mrr1 musca-d ↓ nat-m ↓ nux-m j op ↓ phasco-ci ↓ phos ↓ phyt ↓ positr ↓ *Puls* j5.de* querc-r ↓ rheum j5.de* rhus-t bg2 sang ↓ santin ↓ sil ↓ spect ↓ *Spig* gl1.fr• sulph ↓ taosc ↓ *Ther* ↓ tritic-vg fd5.de tub mrr1 verat ↓ vero-o ↓ zinc-p ↓ [heroin sdj2]

Desires – full of desires: ...

- **anxious** desires; full of: *Castm* kr1
- **beautiful** things; desire for (See Beautiful - yearning)
- **cavern**; desire to be in a: elaps a1
- **cheerful**; desires to be: *(↗Amusement - desire)* aids nl2• chin a1 *Manc* ↓
  - **ineffectually**: *Manc* kr1
- **death**; for: | **vomiting**; to relieve: phyt ptk1
- **dive**; to: ambr tsm1
- **everything**; desire for: nat-m ↓ phos ↓ santin a1 verat ↓
  - **another** person is using; which: nat-m gb• phos gb• verat gb•
- **exercise**; desire for physical (See Exertion - physical - desire)
- **fast** things; for: dioxi rbp6
- **fell** all non-native trees: phasco-ci rbp2
- **fluffy** things, for: positr nl2•
- **grandeur**; desire for: *Coca* vh* cur a1 *Ham* fd3.de• sulph vh [heroin sdj2]
- **hair** cut bald; having: hippoc-k szs2
- **holidays**; for: musca-d szs1
- **husband**; for: vero-o rly3*•
- **impatiently** desires many things (See Petulant)
- **indefinite**: bry a1 chin a1 ip a1* lach a1* lap-la sde8.de• *Puls* a1 sang a1 sil a1* *Ther* a1
- **inexpressible** desires; full of: aids nl2• dream-p sdj1• *Ip* kr1* kali-c mtf33
- **know** for what; does not (See inexpressible)
- **lake**; to live near: galeoc-c-h gms1•
- **look** behind; to (See Looking - backwards - desire)
- **more** than she needs: *(↗Avarice; Bed - remain; Breaking; Carried - desire; Death - desires; Flattered - desire; Greed; Home - leave; Kill; desire; Light - desire; Mental exertion - desire; Talking - desire; Travelling - desire)* *Ars* h2* ars-s-f k2 bar-s k2 bry j5.de zinc-p k2
- **new**; something: querc-r svu1•
- **numerous**, various things; desire for: *Cina* a1* phos a1*
- **origins**; for: [spect dfg1]
- **paint** nails; to (See Colors - nails)
- **present**, things not: calc-sil k2
- **refuses** when offered; but (See Capriciousness - rejecting)
- **singing** (See Singing)
- **snuggle** up; to: phasco-ci rbp2
  - **sleep**; during: phasco-ci rbp2
- **things** which are opposed, if proposed by others (See Capriciousness)
- **this** and that; for (See Capriciousness)
- **unattainable** things; desire for: bry b7.de* mag-m mtf33 op a1* puls b7.de* rheum b7.de* [heroin sdj2]
- **uncontrollable**: alco a1
- **vexatious** things; desire to say (See Speech - vexatious)
- **watched**; to be (See Watched - desires)
- **wind** takes me away: phasco-ci rbp2
- **woman**, ideal: ant-c a1 nat-m mp1• taosc iwa1•

- **group** together; to keep: lac-leo hm2•
- **nothing**; desires: *(↗Asking - nothing; Indifference; Wants - nothing)* ars a1* cocc a1* *Hell* ckh1 hep a1* lim a1 (non:linu-c a1*) mez a1* mill a1* neon srj5• nicc a1* olib-sac wmh1 op br1 ph-ac mtf phos mtf podo fd3.de• tritic-vg fd5.de
- **pain**: lac-lup hm2•
- **suppressing** his desires: carc sk1• sil mtf33 staph mtf33
- **touch** things (See Touching - impelled - everything)

DESOLATE, room appears: valer a1

DESPAIR: *(↗recovery; religious; Helplessness; Inconsolable; Pessimist; Sadness; Sadness - despair; Sadness - diabetes; Sensitive - colors; Suicidal - despair; Suicidal - thoughts; Weeping - despair)* *Acon* k* act-sp hr1* adam srj5• aesc bg2* agar k* agath-a nl2• agn k* all-c k* all-s ↓ aloe *Alum* k* alum-sil k2* am-c k* am-m b2.de* **Ambr** k* *Anac* b4.de* androc srj1• anh sp1 ant-c bro1* *Ant-t* k* *Apis* b7a.de aq-mar ↓ *Arg-n* k* arizon-l nl2• arn k* **Ars** k* ars-h a1 *Ars-i* ars-s-f k2* aster k* **AUR** k* aur-ar k2 aur-i ↓ *Aur-m-n* wbt2• *Aur-s* ↓ bad k* bamb-a stb2.de• *Bapt* ↓ bar-c b2.de* bell k* ben a1 bit-ar wht1• borx ↓ bov k* brom bros-gau mrc1 bry k* bufo k2 cact br1 cadm-met tpw6* calad ↓ **Calc** k* calc-ar ↓ calc-i k2* calc-s *Calc-sil* k2* calen a1 camph b2.de* *Cann-i* k* canth k* carb-an k* *Carb-v* k* carbn-s *Carc* mlr1• carl a1 carneg-g rwt1• castn-v mtf11 *Caust* k* cham k* chel k* *Chin* k* chinin-ar chinin-s j5.de chir-fl gya2 chlol ↓ chloram ↓ choc srj3• cic bro1 cimic ↓ clem k* *Cocc* k* *Coch* ↓ **Coff** k* colch k* coli jl2 **Coloc** ↓ *Con* k* crat sf1.de crot-c mre1.fr crot-h k* *Crot-t* cupr k* *Cupr-act* kr1 cur cycl ↓ der k* des-ac rbp6 dig k* dioxi rbp6 dol ↓ dream-p sdj1• dros b7.de **Dulc** fd* eup-per k* euph b4a.de falco-pe nl2• ferr sne *Gad* st1 gamb gels bro1 germ-met stj2*• *Graph* k* haliae-lc srj5• ham ↓ **HELL** k* helon k* hep k* hippoc-k szs2 hura hydr-ac hydrog srj2• hyos k* hyper ↓ **Ign** k* iod k* ip b7.de irid-met srj5• kali-ar kali-br k* kali-c tl1 kali-i ptk1 kali-n *Kali-p* k* kali-s fd4.de ketogl-ac rly4• kola stb3• kreos j5.de lac-c ↓ lac-e hrn2• lac-h ↓ lac-loxod-a hrn2• lac-lup ↓ *Lach* k* laur b7.de* *Led* b7.de *Lept* bg2* *Lil-t* k* lith-c k* loxo-recl knl4• **Lyc** k* lyss jl2 m-arct b2.de* mag-c ↓ mag-m ↓ mag-p hr1 med bg2* *Merc* k* *Mez* k* moni rfm1• morph k* musca-d szs1 naja *Nat-ar* *Nat-c* k* **Nat-m** k* nat-s k* nat-sil k2* neon srj5• *Nit-ac* k* nitro-o a1 *Nux-m* ↓ nux-v k* olib-sac wmh1 onos ↓ *Op* b7.de* orig k* orot-ac rly4• ozone sde2• petr k* petr-ra shn4• ph-ac b2.de* phasco-ci rbp2 phos b2.de* pic-ac bro1 pin-con oss2• plat plb k* plut-n srj7• podo positr nl2• pot-e rly4• prun-cf mtf11 pseuts-m ↓ psil ↓ **Psor** k* *Puls* k* ran-b ↓ rhus-g ↓ *Rhus-t* k* ruta b2.de* sacch-a ↓ sal-fr sle1• sec k* sel c1* senec ↓ *Sep* k* sil k* spig b2.de* **Spong** ↓ stann k* *Staph* bro1* *Stram* k* streptoc ↓ sul-ac b2.de* sul-i k2* **Sulph** k* sumb k* syph hr1* tab ptk1* *Tarax* b7a.de *Tarent* ↓ tax ↓ ther k* thuj k* thymol bro1 *Thyr* ↓ til ban1• toxi mtf2• tritic-vg fd5.de tub k* v-a-b jl2 valer k* *Vanil* fd5.de **Verat** k* verb k* viol-t b7.de vip j5.de* vult-gr sze5• wies a1 zinc ↓ [ant-met stj2 buteo-j sej6 heroin sdj2 lar-d rcb1 nat-caust stj2 nat-lac stj2 nat-met stj2 *Spect* dfg1 titan stj2]

- **morning**: ozone ↓ psor vh
  - **waking**: ozone sde2•
- **night**, all: lith-c kr1
- **alternating** with:
  - **euphoria**: ozone sde2•
  - **hatred** (See Hatred - alternating - despair)
  - **hope** (See Hopeful - alternating - despair)
  - **indifference**: ars gm1
  - **irritability** (See Irritability - alternating - despair)
  - **stupor**: chlol gm1
- **anger**; with (See Anger - despair)
- **anxiety**; with (See Anxiety - despair)
- **black** cloud; as if in: [buteo-j sej6]
- **black** hole, looking into a: falco-pe nl2•
- **chill**, during: *Acon* k* ant-t k* **Ars** k* *Aur* k* aur-ar k2 bell bry k* *Calc* k* *Cham* k* chinin-ar cupr graph k* hep k* **Ign** k* merc k* nux-v k* rhus-t k* *Sep* k* *Tarent* hr1* *Verat* k*
- **comforted**; wants to be: ozone sde2•
- **company** | **amel.**: [buteo-j sej6]
- **condition**; of his: streptoc jl2
- **criticism**; from the smallest: *(↗Ailments - reproaches; Delusions - criticized; Sensitive - criticism)* ham fd3.de• *Med* st* spong fd4.de
- **cure**; of his: bry ptk1 psor jl2 streptoc jl2
- **death**:
  - **fear** of; with: bamb-a ↓ **Calc** kr1
    - **separate** him from his children; death will: bamb-a stb2.de•
  - **thoughts** of; with: *(↗Suicidal - thoughts; Suicidal - thoughts - meditates)* dulc fd4.de (non:germ-met srj5) ruta fd4.de spong fd4.de stram
- **delivery**, during: *Coff* kr1
- **destiny**; everything is controlled by: bamb-a stb2.de•
- **eating** | **amel.**: *Kola* stb3•
- **empty** shell, sensation of being a fully functioning: falco-pe nl2•
- **existence**, about miserable: carc mlr1• nat-m hr1 *Ruta* fd4.de *Sep* st1
- **fever**; during: *Carb-v* b4a.de
- **future**, about: *Dulc* fd4.de falco-pe nl2• kali-s fd4.de *Nat-m* hr1* nat-sil fd3.de• orot-ac rly4• plut-n srj7• positr nl2• *Psor* mrr1 ruta fd4.de sal-fr sle1• *Spong* fd4.de *Vanil* fd5.de
  - **planet**; of the: positr nl2•
- **head**; with complaints of: agar bg2
- **health**, of: *(↗recovery; Anxiety - health - own; Delusions - disease - incurable; Hypochondriasis)* adam srj5• *Agn* mrr1 calc k* carc mlr1• *Sep* b4a.de staph [tax jsj7]
- **heart** disease; in: aur ptk1*
- **heat**, during: *Acon* k* ant-t hr1* *Ars* k* bell calc-s *Carb-v* k* cham k* chel chinin-ar con k* graph k* ign k* lyc bg2 *Nux-m* bg2 petr h2* ph-ac bg2 puls k* rhus-t sep k* *Spong* k* stann k* stram sulph k* verat k*
- **hypochondriasis**, in: *(↗Anxiety - hypochondriacal)* *Arg-n* hr1*
- **impotence**; with: *(↗Sadness - impotence)* onos mrr1
- **itching** of the skin, from: carbn-s ckh1 dol vml3• **Psor** k*
  - **suppressed**: psor al1
- **life**, of: arizon-l nl2• *Ars* h2 calc h2* cimic jl3 kali-p fd1.de• lac-h sk4• lac-lup hrn2• mag-m mrr1 *Ruta* fd4.de **Spong** fd* **Vanil** fd* [heroin sdj2]
- **liver** complaints; with: lept ptk1
- **lost**, thinks everything is: aur j5.de falco-pe nl2• ign j5.de
- **love**, from disappointed: *(↗Ailments - love; Sadness - love)* caust gl1.fr• *Hyos* hr1* nat-sil fd3.de• plut-n srj7•
- **masturbation**, in: *Op* hr1*
- **menorrhagia**, in: *Cocc* hr1*
- **menses**:
  - **before**: *(↗Menses - before)* verat
  - **during**: senec vml3•
- **nausea**, with: positr nl2•
- **noises** in ear; from: kola stb3•
- **others**; about: *(↗Anxiety - others)* *Arg-n* ↓ *Aur* k* falco-pe ↓
  - **oneself** and: *Arg-n* kr1 aur kr1
  - **poverty** and ugliness, in: falco-pe nl2•
- **pains**, with the: *(↗Sensitive - pain; Shrieking - pain; Suicidal - pains/ Weeping - pain - with)* **Acon** k •* act-sp hr1* agar vh1 aloe k2 ant-c ↓ *Ars* k* **Aur** aur-ar k2 calc st* carb-v k* *Carc* mlr1• **Cham** k •* chin k* chinin-ar clem h2* *Coch* ↓ **Coff** k •* colch k* *Dulc* fd4.de hyper *Kali-i* sne lac-h sze9• lach lil-t mag-c **Nat-m** gg nux-v psil ft1 rhus-g tmo3• **Ruta** fd* stram vh* syph gk tritic-vg fd5.de vanil fd5.de *Verat* vip bg2*
  - ○ **Abdomen**; in the: ars mtf33
  - **Stomach**, in the: ant-c *Coch* kr1 *Coff*
- **periodical**: *Ars* *Aur* aur-ar k2
- **perspiration**, during: acon bg2 **Ars** k* *Aur* bg2 bry bg2 calc k* *Carb-v* k* *Cham* k* con bg2 *Graph* k* ign bg2 lyc k* nat-m bg2 nux-v bg2 rhus-t bg2 sel bg2 *Sep* k* stann k* verat k*
- **pregnancy**, during: nat-m bg2
- **rage**, bordering on: *Agar* kr1 **Nit-ac** ↓
  - **cursing** and imprecations, with: *(↗Cursing)* **Nit-ac** gl1.fr•
- **recovery**, of: *(↗health; Anxiety - health - own; Delusions - disease - incurable; Delusions - health; Despair; Doubtful - recovery)* *Acon* k* adam srj5• agar hu agath-a nl2• agn c1* all-s a1* **Alum** bg2* am-c j ambr tsm1 ant-t a1* aq-mar rbp6 **Ars** k* ars-s-f vh aur-ar k2 aur-i k2* aur-m-n wbt2• *Aur-s* k2* *Bapt* k* bar-c k* borx j *Bry* k* cact k2* calad j **CALC** k* calc-ar k2 calc-s k* cann-i *Carc* mlr1• caust vh* cham chlol k* cimic jl3 **Coloc** cda1* der sne1* dulc fd4.de germ-met srj5• ham fd3.de• *Hell* hura *Ign* k1* kali-ar k* kali-br kali-c k* kreos lac-c sf1.de lach j5.de* *Lyc* h2* m-arct j mag-c mg1.de med br1* *Merc* vh* nat-c j nat-m j nat-s k* nit-ac k2* *Nux-v* k* ph-ac j* phos j plut-n srj7• pseuts-m oss1• *Psor* al *Al* **AL** **Awy** *Bg* **Bg** br btw *Btw* c cda cp **DGS** fr gm gsd *Gsw* gtk *Gvt* hr hsa hsw k *Lpc* mhn **MP** mrr mta **Nh** nsk *Pfa* ptk *Ptk* samkn shc shs svr5 *Tl* vwe2 puls hr j ran-b mrr1 *Ruta* fd4.de sal-fr sle1• *Sep* *Bg* *Gvt* hr k mrr1 sil *Bg* cd1.es k *Spong* fd4.de sulph j mrr5 **Syph** br cp *Gvt* *K* *Lp* mhn **MP** mta ptk *Ptk* samkn shc st wl1 ther *Thyr* ckh vh vh/dg vhx1 verat *Gvt* hr k2 zinc k* [tax jsj7]
  - **convalescence**, during: *(↗Death - desires - convalescence)* **Alum** st **Ars** st **Calc** st carc mlr1• med jsa *Psor* k* **Syph** st
  - **heat**, during: calc-s k2
- **religious** despair of salvation: *(↗Anxiety - salvation; Despair; Doubtful - salvation; Religious - too; Remorse; Suicidal - despair - religious)* *Arg-n* **Ars** **Aur** aur-ar k2 aur-i k2 aur-s k2 *Calc* calc-ar k2 *Camph* carc mlr1• *Chel* cycl sf1.de hell hura ign kali-br mrr1 *Kali-p* **Lach** *Lil-t* k* *Lyc* med *Mez* nat-m ozone sde2• plat plb podo *Psor* **Puls** k1* *Stram* *Sulph* *Thuj* **Verat** k*
  - **alternating** with | **sexual** excitement: *Lil-t* k* *Plat* ptk1

· **menses**; during suppressed: **Verat**
- **restlessness**; with (See Restlessness - despair)
- **rising**; on | **amel.**: chloram jl
- **sexual** craving, from: aster kr1
- **shrieks** of despair; paroxysmal: lyss kr1
- **skin**; from itching of the (See itching)
- **social** position, of: *(↗Fear - opinion; Fear - social; Flattered - desire; Flattered - desire - gives)* calc gl1.fr• haliae-lc srj5• ham fd3.de• ign gl1.fr• puls gl1.fr• rhus-t gl1.fr• sep gl1.fr• staph gl1.fr• sulph gl1.fr• **Verat** k* [heroin sdj2]
- **stomach**; with complaints of: ant-c bg2
- **stupor**; before: chlol gm1
- **supported**; wants to be: *(↗Confidence - want - support)* *Bamb-a* stb2.de• dulc fd4.de spong fd4.de vanil fd5.de
- **trifles**, over: *(↗Trifles; Trifles - important)* *Graph* k* ham fd3.de•
- **typhus** fever; in | **epistaxis** amel.; after: **Psor** kr1*
- **vomiting**, during: ars-h a1
- **waking**, in intermittent: *Ant-t* kr1
- **work**, over his: anac h2* dulc fd4.de ham fd3.de• kali-s fd4.de nat-sil fd3.de• ruta fd4.de sacch-a fd2.de• spong fd4.de
- **world**; for the: plut-n srj7•

DESPISING (See Contemptuous)

DESPONDENCY (See Sadness)

DESPOTIC (See Dictatorial)

DESTRUCTIVENESS: *(↗Anger; Anger - destroy; Breaking; Rage; Tearing - things; Throwing things; Violent)* agar k* anac ↓ anan k* androc srj1• apis k* aur-m-n wbt2• bac bn *Bell* k* bufo k* calc *Camph* canth k* carbn-s carc gk6* *Chel* sne *Cimx* hr1* *Con* hr1* crot-c ↓ *Cupr* k* cur dulc fd4.de fl-ac ptk1* gal-ac zr hep k2* hura *Hyos* k* *Ign* ↓ iod hr1* kali-p dx1 lach k* laur lil-t bro1 med bra merc mrr1 merc-i-f k* moni rfm1• morph oss• mosch *Nux-v* bg2* oena hr1* op k* ozone sde2• phos k* plat k* plb k* prot ptj• sec bro1 sep sne sol-t-ae k* spong fd4.de staph **STRAM** bg2* stront-c sulph k* *Tarent* k* tritic-vg fd5.de *Tub* k* vanil fd5.de *Verat* k* verat-v bro1 [bar-i stj2 cupr-act stj2 cupr-f stj2 cupr-m stj2 cupr-p stj2 lith-i stj2 mang-i stj2 tung-met stj2 zinc-i stj2]
- **alone**; when: tarent mtf33
- **alternating** with:
  · **fear** of being harmed: crot-c sk4•
  · **mildness**: tub mtf33
- **children**; in: *(↗Behavior - children)* bufo mtf33 carc sst* cupr mtf33 hyos mtf33 iod mtf33 lach mtf33 phos mtf33 stram mtf33 tarent mtf33 *Tub* mrr1*
- **clothes**, of: *(↗Rage - tearing)* *Bell* *Camph* hyos kr1 *Ign* nux-v gl1.fr• plb bg1* *Stram* k* *Sulph* k* **Tarent** k* *Verat* k*
  · **cuts** them up: *Verat*
- **cunning**: *(↗Mischievous)* *Tarent* k*
- **drunkenness**, during: bell gl1.fr• verat gl1.fr•
- **emotions**; destructiveness from suppressed: anac vh bell vh ign vh moni rfm1• nux-v vh tub vh

DETACHED: *(↗Hardhearted)* adam srj5• *Agath-a* nl2• aids nl2• *Androc* srj1• anh sp1 arge-pl rwt5• arizon-l nl2• brass-n-o srj5• cann-i mtf carneg-g rwt1• choc srj3• corv-cor bdg• cypra-eg sde6.de• dioxi rbp6 dulc fd4.de *Falco-pe* nl2• galeoc-c-h gms1• germ-met srj5• *Granit-m* es1• haliae-lc srj5• *Ham* fd3.de• hippoc-k szs2 hydrog srj2• hyos mrr1 irid-met srj5• kali-p fd1.de• lac-del hrn2• *Lac-h* htj1*• *Lac-lup* hrn2• lat-h thj1 loxo-recl knl4• *Luna* kg1• med ↓ nat-sil fd3.de• neon srj5• *Olib-sac* wmh1 *Plut-n* srj7• podo fd3.de• positr nl2• rauw tpw8 rhus-g tmo3• ruta fd4.de *Sal-fr* sle1• sanguis-s hrn2• sel rsj9• *Sep* mrr1 *Spong* fd4.de sulph mrr1 symph fd3.de• syph al2* trios rsj11• tritic-vg fd5.de vanil fd5.de ven-m rsj12• vero-o rly3*• [*Bell-p-sp* dcm1 heroin sdj2 **Spect** dfg1 tax jsj7]
- **coition**, during: adam srj5•
- **daily** activity; from: arizon-l nl2• falco-pe nl2•
- **dreams**; from: [bell-p-sp dcm1]
- **ego**; from: lac-h htj1•
- **headache** and nausea; with: androc srj1•
- **observing**; as if | **outside**; from: plut-n srj7•
- **rational** thoughts: dioxi rbp6
- **sensation** of being: med ptk1 plut-n srj7• syph ptk1
- **waves** of detachment: falco-pe nl2•

DETAIL; exaggerated attention to (See Conscientious)

DETERMINATION: *(↗Confident; Contradiction - disposition; Contrary; Courageous; Disobedience; Firmness; Obstinate; Perseverance; Pertinacity; Positiveness; Will - strong)* *Agar* ↓ aur mtf *Bar-c* ↓ calc ↓ *Calc-p* ↓ *Caust* mtf cupr ↓ des-ac ↓ **Ferr** mtf lach mtf *Lyc* mtf merc mtf nat-c b4.de *Nit-ac* sys* **Nux-v** mtf *Phos* ↓ polys sk4• pyrus ↓ sal-fr sle1• sil mtf sulph mtf vanil fd5.de verat mtf vip ↓ [heroin sdj2]
- **gloomy**: *(↗Sadness)* *Agar* *Bar-c* sf1.de calc *Calc-p* cupr a1 des-ac jl3 *Phos* pyrus a1* vip a1

DEVELOPMENT of children arrested: *(↗Autism; Retardation; GENERALS - Development; GENERALS - Development - arrested)* abrot oss• *Agar* sf1.de* ancis-p tsm2 ant-c vh aur bl bac bn *Bar-c* k2* bov mtf bufo k2* calc sf1.de *Calc-p* sf1.de carc jl2* chap jl *Cic* mrr1 cupr a1* des-ac jl kali-br mrr1 nitro-o fb op wbt• *Phos* sf1.de syph jl2* thuj bl* toxo-g jl2 tub ↓
- **injury** of head; after: *Cic* mrr1
- **mental** development: carc mlr1•
- **reading**: tub vh

DIARRHEA: | **amel.**: cimic ptk1

DICTATORIAL: *(↗Abusive; Ailments - egotism; Answering - dictatorial; Censorious; Contemptuous; Contradiction - disposition; Contrary; Dogmatic; Egotism; Haughty; Heedless; Insanity - dictatorial; Insolence; Intolerance; Manipulative; Obstinate; Pertinacity; Positiveness; Presumptuous; Reproaching others; Rudeness; Selfishness; Suggestions; Suspicious)* allox sp1* *Androc* srj1• apis st aran-ix mtf arizon-l nl2* arn k* ars ctc• aur k1* aur-m-n wbt2• *Aur-s* wbt2• bamb-a stb2.de• borra-o oss1• calc-s mrr1 *Camph* k* carc mtf caust k* cham chel vh* *Chin* vh* chir-fl gya2 cich mtf11 con k* *Cupr* h2* dendr-pol sk4• *Dulc* mrr1* falco-pe nl2• ferr k* *Fl-ac* mrr1 granit-m es1• ignis-alc ↓ kali-c h *Kola* stb3• lac-e hrn2• lac-h sk4• lac-leo hrn2• lach k* lil-t ptk1 **Lyc** k* *Med* vh* *Merc* nux-v lmj* ozone sde2• pall ptk1* phos hr1* *Plat* ptk1* polys sk4• puls lmj ruta ↓ sal-fr sle1• sep lmj *Sil* mtf spong fd4.de stram vwe sul-ac mtf *Sulph* ptk1* tax ↓ thuj mrr1 vanil fd5.de verat b7.de* vitis-v rcb1* [heroin sdj2]
- **power**, love of: *(↗Delusions - great; Haughty; Insanity)* granit-m es1• ignis-alc es2• lyc k*
- **talking** with air of command: arn j5.de cupr j5.de **Dulc** fd* falco-pe nl2• lac-leo hrn2• *Lyc* j5.de* *Phos* kr1* ruta fd4.de spong fd4.de [tax jsj7]

DIFFUSION (See Loquacity)

DIGESTION:
- **during**: iod bg2
- **disturbed** | **agg.**: arg-n ptk1 kali-bi bg2 lyc bg2

DIGNIFIED: *(↗Pompous; Solemn; Walking - slowly; Walking - slowly - dignified)* caj a1 calc mtf nat-c samkn *Nat-m* mrr1 staph al1

DIPLOMATIC: *(↗Polite - too; Quarrelling - aversion)* lyc mtf mag-m vh5

DIPSOMANIA (See Alcoholism)

DINNER agg.: arg-n bg2 carb-v bg2 coloc bg2 euphr bg2

DIRECT (See Truth - telling)

DIRECTION; sense of (See Orientation)

DIRECTIONLESS (See Irresolution)

DIRTY: *(↗Chaotic; Conscientious; Delusions - dirty; Delusions - rags; Indifference - appearance; Indifference - external things; Untidy; Washing - aversion; GENERALS - Bathing - aversion; GENERALS - Uncleanliness)* **Am-c** br1* arizon-l nl2• ars ↓ aur ↓ bry ↓ calc-p ↓ calc-s tl *Caps* c1* carc ↓ chel ptk1 coca wm crot-h vh* dulc fd4.de *Graph* ptk1* *Hyos* ↓ ign ↓ kali-s fd4.de lach ptk1 lyc ↓ lycps-v ptk *Merc* bro1* nat-m gl• nux-v ptk1* petr gl1.fr• petr-ra ↓ phos ptk1* *Plat* vh* pluv ↓ positr nl2• *Psor* bro1* sep ptk1* *Sil* bro1 staph vh* stram ↓ *Sulph* br1* verat bro1*
- **aversion** to dirtiness (See Tidy - dirtiness)
- **defecating** | **indoors**: sep ↓
- **everything**; dirtying: am-c gl1.fr• bry brm* *Nat-m* mtf33* petr-ra shn4•
- **plays**:
  · **dirt**; with: hyos vh
  · **feces**; with: hyos mtf33

- **sensation** of being (See Delusions - dirty - he)
- **sitting** or lying in feces:
  - **unaware** | **children**; in: hyos mtf33
- **skin**, with dirty: am-c k* ars k* lyc k* nux-v k* psor vh sulph vh
- **urinating** and defecating: (↗*Insanity - urinating)*
  - **everywhere**: *Hyos*↓ *Sep*↓ sil↓ staph↓ sulph↓
  - ⋮ **children**: (↗*Delirium - urinating - floor; Delirium - urinating - pot) Hyos* vh* *Sep* mtf33* sil mtf33* staph mrr1 sulph mtf33*
- **urinating** deliberately | **indoors**: aur↓ ign↓ sep↓

DISAGREEABLE (See Irritability)

DISCERNMENT; lack of (= judgment): (↗*Discrimination; Grumbling)* alum gl1.fr• con gl1.fr• hep gl1.fr•

DISCIPLINE: (↗*Proper)*
- **easy** to: nat-m vh
- **want** of: ars ctc• calc ctc• limen-b-c hm2• morph oss• nat-m ctc* syph jl2

DISCOMFORT: (↗*FACE - Expression - distressed)* aeth ptk1 agar a1 ammc a1 ang↓ ant-t↓ arg-met↓ ars a1 asaf a1 asc-t ptk1 aur a1 bar-act↓ bol-s a1 brom↓ bry a1 calad a1* calc↓ calc-p a1 calc-s a1 *Camph* a1 caust↓ cedr ptk1 cimic↓ cina a1 clem a1 colch a1 coloc↓ crot-t↓ cupr bg2* digin a1 dros ptk1 ferr a1 form a1 glon a1 gran a1 graph ptk1 *Grat* a1 guaj ptk1 hell a1 hipp a1 hydr-ac a1 ign↓ iod↓ kali-bi a1 kali-c a1 kali-chl a1 lach a1* led↓ loxo-lae bnm12• lyc a1 mag-c a1 mang↓ mez↓ morph a1 mosch a1 nat-c a1 nat-sil fd3.de• nicc a1 nux-v↓ ol-an↓ olnd↓ op a1 par a1 petr a1 ph-ac↓ phys↓ plect a1 puls-n↓ quas a1 rad-br sze8• ran-b↓ rheum a1* sabad a1 sec a1 seneg↓ sep ptk1 sil↓ spira a1 stann ptk1 *Sulph* a1 thuj a1 valer a1* verat-v ptk1 wye br1 zinc a1
- **morning**: ang a1 ant-t↓ cimic a1 hipp a1 mag-c a1 plect↓
  - **walking**, on: ant-t a1 plect a1
- **forenoon**: agar a1 lyc a1 mag-c a1
- **noon**: mez a1
- **afternoon**: ang a1 mang a1 sil a1
- **evening**: ars a1 brom a1 calc a1 coloc a1 ign a1 led a1 sabad a1 sulph a1
- **night**: nicc a1 petr a1 puls-n a1
- **bathing**, after: phys a1
- **chill**, during: ars a1
- **colors**:
  - **black** | **agg.**: sep vk4
  - **dark** | **agg.**: nux-v vk4 sep vk4
  - **shiny** | **agg.**: nux-v vk4
- **eating**, after: bar-act a1 bry a1 clem a1 crot-t↓ iod↓ ol-an↓ olnd a1 petr↓ ph-ac a1 seneg↓ sil↓ zinc a1
  - **dinner**, after: crot-t a1 iod a1 ol-an a1 zinc a1
  - **supper**, after: petr a1 seneg a1 sil a1
- **heat**, during: ran-b a1
- **pickled** fish, after: calad a1
- **walking**, after: arg-met k* caust k*

DISCONCERTED: (↗*Chaotic; Confounding - objects; Confusion; Mistakes; FACE - Expression - bewildered; FACE - Expression - confused)* brom k* ign k* mim-p rsj8• ozone sde2•

DISCONNECTED FEELING (See Estranged)

DISCONNECTED THINKING (See Thoughts - disconnected)

DISCONTENTED: (↗*Complaining; Confusion; Disgust; Frown; Grumbling; Indifference - answer; Irritability; Lamenting; Moaning; Morose; Muttering; Petulant; Shrieking - pleased; Sulky; Unfriendly; FACE - Expression - discontented; FACE - Expression - sullen)* abrot bg2 acon k* adam↓ adon↓ aesc↓ aeth agar agath-a nl2• agn k* aids nl2• alet all-c *All-s*↓ aloe k* alum k* alum-p k2* alum-sil k2* am-c k* *Am-m* k* ambr↓ ammc j5.de **Anac** k* androc srj1• ang k* *Ant-c* bg2* ant-t bg2* anthraq rly4• apis k* aq-mar↓ aran↓ arg-met↓ arizon-l nl2• arn k* *Ars* k* ars-i ars-s-f k2 asaf j5.de* asar k* *Aur* k* aur-ar k2 aur-br vh1 aur-m *Aur-m-n* wbt2• aur-s k2 *Bamb-a* stb2.de• bar-c k* bell k* berb *Bism* k* *Bism-o* a1 bism-sn br1 *Borx* k* bov k* brom k* *Bry* k* *Buteo-j*↓ calad↓ calc k* calc-ar k2 calc-i k2 **Calc-p** k* calc-s calc-sil k2 camph j cann-s k* canth k* caps k* carb-ac bg2* carb-an carb-v bg2 carbn-s carc st1* castm↓ caul ptk1 caust k* cench k2 *Cham* k* *Chel Chin* k* chinin-ar chir-fl↓ cic k* *Cina* k* cinnb cinnm a1 clem k*

Discontented: ...
cob a1 cocc k* coff k* *Colch* k* coloc k* *Con* bg2* croc↓ crot-t k* *Cupr* k* cycl j* cystein-l rly4• dig j dioxi rbp6 dream-p sdj1• dros j* dulc k* eug j5.de falco-pe↓ ferr ferr-ar ferr-p fl-ac k* fum rly4• galeoc-c-h↓ *Germ-met*↓ goss vh* graph k* grat guaj j* ham hell helo↓ helon↓ **Hep** k* hipp hura hydr-ac j *Hyos* bg2 ign k* indg indol br1* iod k* ip k* jug-r a1 kali-ar kali-br↓ *Kali-c* k* kali-m k2* kali-n kali-p kali-s kali-sil k2 *Kola* stb3• kreos k* lac-e hrn2• lac-h↓ lac-lup↓ lach k* lact j laur k* led k* lepi lil-t k* *Lyc* k* lyss kr1 m-arct j m-aust b7.de* mag-c k* mag-m k* mag-p bro1 mag-s manc mand mg1.de mang k* marb-w↓ med↓ meny k* **Merc** k* merc-c j5.de mez k* moly-met jl3* moni rfm1• mur-ac k* naja↓ nat-ar *Nat-c* b4a.de* **Nat-m** k* nat-p nat-sil fd3.de* neon srj5• *Nit-ac* k* *Nux-v* k* ol-an olib-sac wmh1 *Olnd* j* op opun-s a1 (non:opun-v a1) orig ozone↓ *Pall* k* pana a1 par k* petr k* ph-ac k* phasco-ci↓ phos k* pin-con oss2• *Plat* k* plb k* podo↓ positr nl2• prun psor bro1 *Puls* k* querc-r svu1• ran-b k* rheum bg2* rhod *Rhus-r*↓ *Rhus-t* k* rob ruta k* sabad j sabin j* sacch sst1• sal-fr sle1• samb k* sars k* sel bg2* *Sep* k* sieg↓ *Sil* k* sin-n spong k* *Stann* k* *Staph* k* stram k* stront-c bg2* suis-em rly4• suis-hep rly4• sul-ac j* sul-i k2 **Sulph** k* symph↓ syph vh* tab bg2* *Tarax* b7a.de tarent k* teucr bg2* thea↓ ther *Thuj* k* til tong↓ tritic-vg fd5.de **Tub** al* ulm-c↓ ust↓ vanil fd5.de verat bg2 verb bg2 viol-o↓ viol-t k* vip j zinc bg2* ziz↓ [ant-met stj2 arg-n stj2 arg-p stj2 bar-i stj2 cupr-p stj2 heroin sdj2 lith-i stj2 lith-p stj2 mag-n stj2 mang-i stj2 mang-met stj2 mang-n stj2 merc-i-f stj2 nitro stj2 plb-p stj2 pop dhh1 tax jsj7 thal-met stj2 zinc-i stj2 zinc-m stj2 zinc-n stj2 zinc-p stj2]
- **daytime**: ars k* led
- **morning**: hipp k* *Lyc* sf1.de *Nux-v* sf1.de phasco-ci rbp2 plb k* puls k*
- **afternoon**: *Borx*↓ grat mur-ac k* nat-m op k* zinc
  - **stool** | **before**: *Borx*
- **evening**: calc fl-ac k* hipp k* ign k* jug-r a1 *Puls* ran-b k* *Rhus-r* a1 *Rhus-t* k*
  - **amel.**: aloe puls sf1.de
- **air**, in open: bov fl-ac mur-ac k* spong fd4.de
- **alternating** with:
  - **anger** (See Anger - alternating - discontentment)
  - **quarreling** (See Quarrelsome - alternating - discontentment)
- **always**: cina mtf33 **Hep** gl1.fr• lach gl1.fr• **Merc** gl1.fr• nit-ac mtf33*
- **causeless**: clem ptk1*
- **childish** peevishness in adults: sulph br1
- **children**: brom mtf33 calc-p mtf33 carc vh* dulc fd4.de ip mtf33 merc mtf33 spong fd4.de
- **coition**, after: *Calc* k* sel sf1.de
- **eating**, after: bov fl-ac k*
- **everything**, with: (↗*Disgust; Disgust - everything; Loathing - general; Morose; Offended; Pessimist; Selfishness; Thoughts - disgusting)* acon j adon bg2 aesc bg2 agn bg2 aids nl2• *All-s* vh1 alum k* alum-sil k2* am-c am-m bg2 ambr j* ammc j5.de anac k* ant-c j* ant-t hr1 apis k* aran bg2 arg-met bg2 arg-n bg2 arn k* ars k* aur h2* *Aur-m-n* wbt2• bamb-a stb2.de• bell j5.de* berb a1 bism k* bism-o a1 bov bg2 brom bg2 bry bg2 calc h2* calc-p mtf33 calc-s k2* calc-sil k2* cann-s k* canth j5.de* caps j carb-ac bg2 carb-an h2* carb-v bg2 carc mlr1• caust j* cham k* chel h1* chin bg2 chinin-ar *Cina* hr1* clem bg2 cocc k* coff colch k* *Coloc* j5.de con j* croc j cupr h2* dig bg2 dros k* dulc a1 eug ferr-p k2 graph k* grat ham j5.de hell bg2 helo bg2 helon bg **Hep** k* hipp hura ign k* iod k* ip k* kali-br bg2 kali-c k* kali-p bg2 kali-s k2* *Kola* stb3• kreos k2* lac-lup hrn2• lach gl1.fr• lact j laur j led j lil-t k2* lyc j mag-c k* mag-m j* marb-w es1• med bg2 meny **Merc** bg2* merc-c j5.de mez k* mur-ac k* naja bg2 nat-c k* **Nat-m** k* *Nat-sil* fd3.de* nit-ac nux-v bg2* *Pall* petr ph-ac bg2 phos j* *Plat* gl1.fr• plb j* psor bg2 *Puls* k* ran-b bg2 rheum st sacch sst1• samb sars sel bg2 *Sep* k* sieg mg1.de sil j spong stann k* staph k* suis-hep rly4• sul-ac k2* *Sulph* k* thea ther a1* thuj j tub jl2 ulm-c↓ ust bg2 viol-o bg2 viol-t bg zinc bg2 [*Buteo-j* sej6 pop dhh1]
  - **exertion** | **amel.**: ulm-c jsj8•
- **headache**, during: aids nl2• ign gl1.fr•
- **health**, about: phos h2*
- **himself**, with: (↗*Delusions - neglected - duty; Hiding - himself - children; Remorse; Reproaching oneself)* adam srj agath-a nl2• *Agn* k* aloe k* ambr↓ arn↓ *Ars* k* asaf ptk1* aur aur-br vh1 aur-m-n wbt2• bamb-a stb2.de• bell k* bry calc-p k* *Carc* fd2.de*• caust k* cham k* chir-fl gya2 cinnb k* cinnm a1 cob k* cocc k* colch↓ con ptk1* dioxi rbp6 dream-p sdj1• *Dulc* fd4.de falco-pe nl2• *Germ-met* srj *Hep* k* kali-c *Kali-s* fd4.de lac-h htj1• lyc m-aust j5.de mang meny merc k* mez k* moni rfm1• mur-ac k* *Nit-ac* k* nux-v gl1.fr• olib-sac wmh1 ozone sde2• pana a1 ph-ac k* podo fd3.de• *Puls* k*

- **himself**, with: ...
ruta k* sacch sst1• sal-fr ↓ sep ↓ spong fd4.de staph k2* *Sulph* symph fd3.de• tarent ther tong ↓ vanil fd5.de viol-t k* zinc ↓ ziz a1* [pop dhh1]
  - **alternating** with | **Lumbar** region; pain in: aloe br1
  - **good** for nothing; sensation of being: *(↗Delusions - worthless)* ambr sgp arn hr1 colch hr1 sal-fr sle1• sep a1 tong a1 (non:zinc hr1)
  - **weeping**: carc mlr1•
  - **whatever** he did; about: ruta a1
- **inanimate** objects: caps
- **menses**, during: *(↗Menses - during)* castm tarent k*
- **others**; with: hep ptk1* lac-lup hrn2• podo fd3.de• ruta ptk1*
- **rainy** weather; during (See weather - rainy)
- **reserved** displeasure: *(↗Reserved)* aq-mar rbp6 aur ptk1 dulc fd4.de ign ptk1 ip ptk1* nat-m ptk1 ruta fd4.de *Staph* ptk1* tritic-vg fd5.de
- **stool** | **before**: *Borx* k*
- **surroundings**, with: ang h1* calc-p mtf33 carc mlr1• *Cham* a1 chel a1 galeoc-c-h gms1• meny a1 merc a1 mez a1 par a1 plat a1 podo fd3.de• spong fd4.de
- **weather** | **rainy** weather; during: aloe
- **weeping**:
  - **amel.**: *(↗Weeping - amel.)* *Nit-ac* k* ziz
  - **with**: aeth ckh1 calad ckh1 nit-ac ptk1 ziz a1*
- **wrong**, everything another does is: *Cham* h1*

DISCORDS (See Ailments - discords)

DISCOURAGED: *(↗Confidence - want; Eyes - downcast; Helplessness; Insecurity; Pessimist; Resignation; Sadness; Succeeds; Timidity)* *Acon* adam srj5• agar k* agath-a nl2• agn k* aloe alum alum-p k2* alum-sil k2* am-br sf1.de am-c ↓ ambr k* *Ammc* j5.de* *Anac* k* ang k* ange-s jl3 anh mtf ant-c k* ant-t k* *Apis* aq-mar rbp6 arg-met arg-n mtf11 arizon-l nl2• arn k* *Ars* k* ars-h hr1* ars-i aur k* bamb-a mtf bar-c k* bar-n mtf bell k* brom hr1* bros-gau ↓ bry k* bufo-s caj a1 calad k* *Calc* k* calc-i k2* calc-p mtf calc-sil k2 camph canth k* carb-an k* **Carb-v** k1* carbn-s carc mlr1• *Carl* k* caust k* cench k2* cham *Chin* k* chinin-ar *Chinin-s* *Cocc* k* coff colch k* coloc k* con k* convo-d cop a1 cortico tpw7 cupr dam mtf11 der k* des-ac jl3 dig k* dioxi rbp6 *Dros* k* dulc fd4.de ephe-si hsj1• falco-pe nl2• ferr-p ↓ fum rly4• gent-am mtf11 gran k* graph k* haliae-lc srj5• hell k* hep k* hipp hydr a1* hydr-ac k* hyos hypoth jl3 iber a1 *Ign* k* ina-i mlk9.de iod ip irid-met srj5• iris kali-bi k* kali-c k* kali-chl k13 kali-i sf1.de kali-m bg* kali-n kali-p k* kali-s kali-sil k2* *Kola* stb3• lac-ac k* lac-e mtf lac-leo mtf **Lach** k* laur k* limen-b-c mtf lith-c sf1.de* *Lyc* k* *M-arct* j5.de mag-m k* mand jl3 mang med mtf merc k* merc-c k* moly-met jl3* mur-ac myric ptk1 nat-ar nat-c nat-m k* nat-n mtf nat-p k* nat-s k* nat-sil k2* nit-ac k* *Nux-v* k* olnd op k* pen a1 *Petr* k* ph-ac k* phos k* pic-ac mtf11 plat plb k* podo prot mtf *Psor* k* *Puls* k* pyrus ran-b ran-s ↓ rhus-g tmo3• *Rhus-r* a1 *Rhus-t* k* **Ruta** fd* sabin sacch-a fd2.de* samb ↓ sarcol-ac jl3 sec k* *Sep* k* *Sil* k* spig spong fd4.de *Stann* k* staph ↓ stram sul-ac sul-i k2* *Sulph* k* suprar rly4• tab k* tarent k* ther k* thuj k* tritic-vg fd5.de tub al2* tub-r jl3* ulm-c jsj8• valer vanil fd5.de **Verat** k* verb viol-t k* vip j5.de visc jl3 xan hr1 zinc k* zinc-pic mtf11 [lac-mat sst4 spect dfg1 tax jsj7]
- **daytime** and night: carb-an j5.de
- **morning**: hipp kali-p fd1.de• plat puls j sep sulph
  - **bed**, in: puls j5.de
- **afternoon**: con dulc fd4.de
- **evening**: ant-c j5.de ant-t j5.de calc dulc fd4.de ferr-p k* *Puls* ran-s k* *Rhus-r* a1 *Rhus-t* k* suprar rly4•
  - **eating** amel.: tarent k*
- **night**: carb-an j dulc fd4.de graph j5.de
- **air**, in open: *Ph-ac*
  - **amel.**: coff j5.de

Discouraged: ...
- **alternating** with:
  - **anger** (See Anger - alternating - discouragement)
  - **confidence** (See Confident - alternating - discouragement)
  - **courage** (See Courageous - alternating - discouragement)
  - **exaltation** (See Exhilaration - alternating - discouragement)
  - **exhilaration** (See Exhilaration - alternating - discouragement)
  - **exuberance** (See Exhilaration - alternating - discouragement)
  - **haughtiness** (See Haughty - alternating - discouragement)
  - **hope** (See Hopeful - alternating - discouragement)
  - **irritability** (See Irritability - alternating - discouragement)
  - **quarreling** (See Quarrelsome - alternating - discouragement)
- **anxiety**, with: *Acon* j5.de bar-c j5.de canth j5.de *Cham* j5.de *Graph* j5.de *M-arct* j5.de puls j5.de
- **business**, aversion to: *Calc* vh* puls j5.de
- **children**, in: *Carb-v* mtf33 lyc j5.de sulph mtf33
- **chill**; during: ars b4a.de
- **coition**, after: sep k* staph vh
- **cursing**, with (See Cursing - discouragement)
- **disgust**, with (See Disgust - discouragement)
- **future**, about: *Dros* hr1* dulc fd4.de kali-p fd1.de• kali-s fd4.de merc j5.de podo fd3.de• *Ruta* fd4.de
- **household** matters; about: carl br1
- **impatience**, with (See Impatience - discouragement)
- **irresolution**, with: *(↗Irresolution)* bros-gau mrc1 dulc fd4.de puls j5.de
- **irritability**, with (See Irritability - discouragement)
- **menses** | **before**: *(↗Menses - before)* carl
- **moaning**, with: *(↗Moaning)* cham j5.de nux-v j5.de verat j5.de
- **morose**, and: *(↗Morose)* op j5.de
- **pain**, from: acon bg2 ars bg2 colch j5.de dulc fd4.de hep j5.de* lach j5.de nux-v j5.de tritic-vg fd5.de vip bg2
- **praying**, with: puls j5.de ruta fd4.de
- **quiet**, and: lyc j5.de spong fd4.de
- **rage**, with (See Rage - discouragement)
- **reproaches** himself: *(↗Hiding - himself - children; Reproaching oneself)* dulc fd4.de *M-arct* j5.de*
- **waking**, on: *Graph* *Puls*
- **walking**, while: am-c k* ph-ac k*
- **weeping**, with: bar-c j5.de *Carb-v* j5.de chinin-s j5.de laur j5.de *Lyc* j5.de nux-v j5.de samb bat1• tritic-vg fd5.de
  - **amel.**: *(↗Weeping; Weeping - amel.)* nit-ac

DISCRIMINATION, lack of: *(↗Discernment)* **Alum** vh* con vh* hep vh* nitro-o a1 podo fd3.de•

DISCUSS:
- **desire** to: agav-t jl1 hist vml3• morph oss• olib-sac wmh1 trios jl3
- **political** disputes, inclined to: *(↗Eccentricity - political; Excitement - debate; Politics)* caust h2*
- **symptoms** with everyone, discusses her: *(↗Loquacity - health; Tormenting - others - complaints)* *Arg-n* vh* phos vh pop-cand vh*

DISGUST: *(↗discouragement; Aversion; Discontented; Discontented - everything; Ennui; Loathing - general; Thoughts - disgusting; DREAMS - Disgusted; DREAMS - Disgusting)* agath-a nl2• aloe bg2* *Ambr* ↓ arn j5.de **Ars** k* asar vh aster ↓ aur j5.de *Bar-c* ↓ camph j5.de caps j5.de carc mlr1* caust j5.de cimx coloc con j5.de *Croc* j5.de crot-h ↓ dulc h1 *Falco-pe* nl2• fl-ac ↓ germ-met srj5• gink-b ↓ *Hep* j5.de ign ↓ ignis-alc ↓ iod ↓ ip j5.de *Kali-c* j5.de kali-i j5.de kali-p ↓ kola stb3• **Lac-c** kr1* *Laur* j5.de led j5.de lyc ↓ m-aust ↓ mag-c j5.de mag-m j5.de med gk *Merc* k* mez neon ↓ nux-v j5.de orig ↓ orig-v ↓ petr j5.de phos pitu-a ↓ **Plat** sne plb j5.de positr nl2• ptel gk **Puls** k* pyrog ↓ samb j5.de sars j5.de senec ↓ sep ↓ sil j5.de spirae ↓ spong j5.de *Stram* vh* **Sulph** k* **SYPH** st* tarent kr1 thea j5.de thuj j5.de visc ↓ [berb stu1]
- **animals**; of (See Animals - disgust)
- **body**; of the: *(↗Delusions - body - ugly)*
  - **others**; of the body of:
    - **husband's** odor: *(↗Aversion - husband)* sep mrr1
    - **pregnancy**; during: sep mrr1

- **body**; of the – **others**; of the body of: ...
  - **own** body odor; but loves his: lac-c ptk1 **Sulph** mrr1
  - **own** body; of one's: ambr ↓ falco-pe nl2• positr nl2• pyrog ↓ **Sulph** ↓ *Thuj* mrr1
    - **effluvia**; to nausea from her own (See odor - nausea)
    - **odor**; of the: (*↗Perfume - loves)* ambr tsm1 pyrog ptk1 sulph mtf33
      - **nausea**; to the point of: **Sulph** kr
      - **secretions**: ambr tsm1
- **colors**:
  - **gray**:
    - **agg.**: ign vk4
    - **aversion** to: ign vk4
- **consciousness** of his unnatural state of mind: tarent kr1
- **deceit** of others, at the: falco-pe nl2•
- **dirt**; with: (*↗Fastidious)* **Caps** b7a.de carc mlr1•
- **discouragement**; with: (*↗Disgust; Loathing - life)* caust j5.de falco-pe nl2•
- **everything**, with: (*↗Aversion - everything; Discontented - everything; Loathing - life; Weary)* arn j5.de aur j5.de carc mlr1• caust j5.de con j5.de ignis-alc es2• ip j5.de kali-i j5.de *Laur* j5.de *Led* j5.de mag-c j5.de mag-m j5.de* *Merc* j5.de nux-v j5.de orig hl1 orig-v sne petr j5.de phos j5.de *Plat* sne positr nl2• *Puls* j5.de* samb j5.de sars j5.de spong j5.de *Sulph* vh* **Syph** vh* thea j5.de *Thuj* j5.de
- **exhilaration** of others; at: m-aust j5.de
- **grossness** of physical things; at the: positr nl2•
- **oneself**: (*↗Hiding - himself - children; Reproaching oneself)* *Bar-c* ↓ crot-h bg* falco-pe nl2• fl-ac bg* *Germ-met* srj5• gink-b sbd1• iod bg* kali-p bg* lac-c ptk1* lyc bg* *Merc* ↓ neon srj5• phos bg* pitu-a ft plat bg* positr nl2• senec bg* sep bg* spirae a
  - **live** with himself; has no courage to: *Bar-c* vh* *Merc* kr1
- **laughing** of others; at: *Ambr* j5.de*
- **medicine** bottle, on sight of the: (*↗Refusing - medicine)* visc sp1
- **sex**, kissing etc.: (*↗Aversion - sex)* asar vh aster sze10•
- **society**, with the shortcomings of: positr nl2•
- **stool** | **odor** of his own stool: ambr tsm1
- **woman** | **being** a: [berb stu1]

DISHONEST: (*↗Deceitful; Hypocrisy; Liar; Untruthful)* arg-n mtf33 ars vh* bry vh* calc vh* ferr mtf iod mtf lach vh* mag-c mtf puls vh* sil vh* sulph vh* tarent mrr1 thuj mrr1

DISOBEDIENCE: (*↗Abusive; Answering - abruptly; Contradiction - disposition; Contrary; Defiant; Determination; Impolite; Mischievous; Obstinate; Pertinacity; Positiveness; Quarrelsome; Reverence - lack; Rudeness; Slander)* acon agar ↓ agn k* alum ↓ *Am-c* k* am-m *Arg-n* vh* arn bufo gk cact ↓ calc gl1.fr• calc-p mtf33 canth caps carc sst* **Caust** k* *Chin* k* cina mtf33 colch ↓ coloc ↓ *Dig* k* dulc fd4.de elae a1 fl-ac ↓ guaj hep ↓ *Lach* sne *Lyc* k* mag-m mtf33 **Med** ↓ **Merc** h1* moni rfm1• morph oss• nit-ac nux-v p-benzq ↓ petr h2* petr-ra shn4• phos **Plb** ↓ sacch ↓ *Sang* ↓ sep mtf33 sil gk* spig spong j staph j* stram gk* sulfonam jl3 sulph *Syph* vh* **Tarent** k* *Tub* mrr1* *Verat* mrr1* viol-o b7a.de* *Viol-t* k* vip ↓
- **children**, in: (*↗Behavior - children)* agar lmj agn lmj alum lmj cact lmj calc-p mtf33 **Caps** lmj carc tpw* *Caust* lmj *Chin* hr1* cina mtf33 colch lmj coloc lmj dulc fd4.de fl-ac lmj hep lmj lyc lmj* mag-m mtf33 **Med** lmj merc mtf33 moni rfm1• nit-ac lmj nux-v lmj p-benzq mtf11 phos lmj **Plb** lmj sacch sst1• *Sang* lmj sep mtf33 sil mtf33 spong lmj staph lmj* stram mtf33 sulph lmj syph mtf33 **Tarent** lmj *Tub* lmj* *Verat* lmj* vip lmj
  - **masturbation**; in boys with: sil mtf33

DISORDER, sensitive to: (*↗Fastidious; Rest - cannot)* ham st kali-p fd1.de• olib-sac wmh1 oscilloc jl2 spong fd4.de tritic-vg fd5.de vanil fd5.de [heroin sdj2]

DISORDERLY (See Chaotic; Untidy)

DISORGANIZED (See Chaotic)

DISORIENTED; easily (See Orientation - decreased)

DISPLEASED (See Discontented)

DISPOSING of things: (*↗Tidy)* agath-a nl2• **Ruta** ↓
- **old** things: **Ruta** fd*

DISPUTE:
- **ability** to (See Irritability; Quarrelsome)
- **aversion** to (See Quarrelling - aversion)

DISRUPTION; personal: (*↗Depersonalization)* anh mg1.de* aur hr1* [heroin sdj2]

DISSATISFIED (See Discontented)

DISSOCIATION from environment: anh mg1.de* phos vh *Tung-met* bdx1• verat vh [bor-pur stj2]

DISTANCES:
- **exaggerated**; are: (*↗Delusions - space - expansion; Size - incorrect)* anac k2* bros-gau mrc1 *Cann-i* k* glon kali-s fkr2.de nux-m sf1.de* nux-v ↓ ox-ac sf1.de stram kr1 sulph sf1.de ther sf1.de vero-o rly4•
  - **runs** against things which appear to be distant to him: stram kr1
  - **time** as well; and | **sleepiness**; during: nux-v j5.de
- **great** distances; desires to see: choc srj3• falco-pe nl2•
- **inaccurate** judgement of: (*↗Delusions - distances; Delusions - enlarged - distances; Mistakes - localities; Size - incorrect; HEARING - Distant; HEARING - Distant - sounds; VERTIGO - Objects - far; VISION - Distant; VISION - Nearer)* agar bg2 anac bg2 arg-n bg2 atro hl bros-gau mrc1 *Cann-i* k* cann-xyz bg2 carb-an c1 coca hl cypra-eg sde6.de• dat-m c1 des-ac rbp6 glon bg2 hyos h1 irid-met srj5• lac-h htj1• magn-gr rb nux-m bg2* onos ptk2 op bg2 ozone sde2• petr-ra shn4• podo fd3.de• sal-fr sle1• stann bg2 *Stram* k*
  - **ground**; to the | **walking**; while: cypra-eg sde6.de• ozone sde2•

DISTRACTION (See Abstraction; Concentration - difficult; Confusion)

DISTRUSTFUL (See Suspicious)

DISTURBED; averse to being: (*↗Anger - interruption; Bed - remain; Biting - people - disturbs; Company - aversion; Confusion - interruption; Going; Hindered; Ideas - deficiency - interruption; Interruption - agg.; Interruption - intolerance; Irritability - disturbed; Quarrelsome - disturbed; Quiet; wants; Rest - desire; Sitting - inclination; Taciturn; Thoughts - vanishing - interrupted; Touched - aversion; Weeping - disturbed)* ant-c k2* ant-t k2* bamb-a stb2.de• **Bry** k* cench k2 cham mtf33 chinin-ar kr1 *Cocc* hr1* gels k* gink-b sbd1• hell hr1* iod mtf33 kali-m ckh1 lil-t k2 naja mtf33 nat-ar k2 *Nux-v* vh* plut-n srj7• sec a1 *Sep* vh* sulph mtf33 tub c1* ulm-c jsj8•

DIVERSION amel. (See Occupation - amel.)

DOCILITY (See Yielding)

DOGMATIC: (*↗Change - aversion; Conformism; Dictatorial; Obstinate; Pertinacity; Positiveness; Preaching; Prejudiced; Religious - too)* allox tpw4 bamb-a stb2.de• bry mtf camph bg2* caust bg2* con bg cupr mtf des-ac rbp6 dulc mrr1 ferr bg2 kali-bi mrr1 **Kali-c** mrr1* lach bg2* lyc lpc1* merc bg2* prot jl2 puls mrr1 verat mrr1
- **children**: kali-c mtf33

DOMINATED; easily (See Yielding)

DOMINEERING (See Dictatorial)

DOTAGE (See Dementia)

DOUBLE CHECKING (See Checking)

DOUBTFUL: (*↗Irresolution)* *Acon* ↓ agn ↓ aloe sne alum ptk1* alumn ↓ anh mg1.de* arn ↓ **Ars** ↓ ars-h ↓ aster sze10• **Aur** ↓ bar-c gl1.fr• bell ↓ brucel sa3• bry ↓ *Calc* ptk1 calc-sil ↓ **Carb-v** mtf33* carc ↓ cecr ↓ chel ↓ cic b7.de* croc ↓ cycl ↓ dig ↓ dulc fd4.de falco-pe nl2• *Graph* mtf33* hyos ↓ *Ign* mrr1 ina-i mlk9.de kali-c ↓ kali-p fd1.de• kali-s fd4.de kola ↓ kreos ↓ lac-c ↓ *Lach* gl1.fr• *Lept* ↓ *Lil-t* ↓ *Lyc* ↓ mag-c ↓ merc ptk1 nat-s ↓ nit-ac ↓ nux-v ↓ *Petr* gl1.fr• ph-ac ↓ phos mrr1 psil ft1 psor ↓ **Puls** ↓ ruta ↓ sars ↓ sel ↓ sep gl1.fr• ser-a-c jl2 spong fd4.de *Stann* ↓ staph gl1.fr• stram ↓ sul-i ptk1 *Sulph* ↓ syph ↓ tax ↓ tritic-vg fd5.de *Tung-met* bdx1• vanil fd5.de *Verat* ↓ [alumin stj2 alumin-s stj2 heroin sdj2]
- **himself** (See Confidence - want)
- **recovery**, of: (*↗Anxiety - health - own; Anxiety - hypochondriacal; Delusions - disease - incurable; Despair - recovery; Hypochondriasis; Pessimist)* *Acon* k* agn k* *Alum* h2* alumn a1* arn sf1.de **Ars** j5.de* ars-h hr1* aur st1 bry calc calc-sil k2* carc mlr1• cecr jl3 *Ign* k* kali-c kreos j5.de lac-c sf1.de

- **recovery**, of: ...
lach *Lept* sf1.de lil-t sf1.de *Lyc* sf1.de mag-c dx1* *Merc* gl1.fr• nat-s j5.de nit-ac sf1.de nux-v ph-ac k* phos psor puls ruta fd4.de sars ↓ sep *Stann* sf1.de sulph syph st1 [tax jsj7]
  - **medicine** is useless; thinks: *(↗Refusing - medicine)* alumn j5.de* ars j5.de* [tax jsj7]
  - **menopause**; during: sars kr1
- **salvation**; of: *(↗Anxiety - salvation; Despair - religious; Religious - too)* **Ars Aur** bell calc chel croc cycl bg2 dig hyos **Lach** k* *Lil-t* k* lyc nux-v **Puls** k* sel stram *Sulph* j5.de* *Verat* k*
- **skeptical**: carb-v pc cic bg2 dulc fd4.de graph pc lach pc petr pc [heroin sdj2]
- **welfare**; of souls: kola stb3•

DRAMA: | **desire** for (See Excitement - desire)

DRAWING:
- **inability** for: nux-v mtf33 sulph mtf33
- **talented** for: sulph gl•

DREAD (See Fear)

DREAM; as if in a: *(↗Absentminded; Absentminded - dreamy; Absorbed; Confusion - dream; Fancies - absorbed; Forgetful; Introspection; Meditating; Sitting - inclination - wrapped; Spaced-out; Thoughts - thoughtful; Unconsciousness - dream; Unobserving [=inattentive]; Unreal - everything; FACE - Expression - vacant)* absin k* acon aids nl2• ail k* allox tpw3 alum *Ambr* k* aml-ns *Anac* k* *Androc* srj1* ang anh mtf *Ant-c* ptk2* *Apis* ara-maca sej7* arb-m oss1• arge-pl rwt5• arizon-l nl2• arn k* ars k* atro k* bamb-a stb2.de• *Bell* k* bell-p-sp ↓ bit-ar wht1• buth-a sp1* *Calc* *Cann-i* k* *Cann-s* k* carb-ac carb-an k* *Carb-v* carneg-g rwt1• *Cench* k2 cham chord-umb rly4• *Cic* ↓ cocc h1* *Con* k* cupr k* cypra-eg sde6.de• dioxi rbp6 dream-p sdj1• elaps ↓ falco-pe nl2• ger-i rly4• germ-met srj5• glon k* *Gran* mtf *Hell* hep hydrog srj2• *Hyos* irid-met srj5• kali-p fd1.de• *Kola* stb3• lac-h htj1*• lac-mat ↓ *Lach* lavand-a ctl1• lil-t k* limest-b es1• *Med* k* melal-alt gya4 merc moni rfm1• morph br1 nat-c ↓ *Nat-m* k* nat-sil fd3.de• neon srj5• **Nux-m** k* oena ol-an k* olnd h1* **Op** k* oxal-a rly4• *Ph-ac* *Phos* phys k* pieri-b mlk9.de *Podo* fd3.de• pyrog br1* rad-br sze8• rheum bg2* sal-al blc1• *Sal-fr* sle1• sang rb2 sars rb2 sil squil k* *Staph* ↓ **Stram** k* *Sulph* taosc iwa1• tere-la rly4• thuj k* tritic-vg fd5.de tung-met bdx1• urol-h rwt• valer **Vanil** fd* *Verat* k* *Visc* k* zinc b* zing vh ziz bg2* [heroin sdj2 spect dfg1 tax jsj7]
- **daytime**: ars k* elaps *Kola* stb3• [lac-mat sst4]
- **night**: aids nl2• nat-c k* [bell-p-sp dcm1]
- **beautiful**: absin a1*
- **convulsions**; after: *Cic* mrr1
- **dinner**, after: nux-m c1
- **done**; for what he just has: acon br1
- **escapes** in a world of dreams: anh jl
- **future**, about the: olnd ↓ *Staph* hr1*
  - **poetical** future; about a: olnd
- **happened** during the day; had dreamt everything that: lach rb2
- **pleasant**: sal-fr sle1•

DREAMS; after: puls b7.de*

DREAMINESS (See Absentminded - dreamy)

DRESS: *(↗Clothes; Extravagance; Haughty - clothes; Personal; Strange - crank - dressing)*
- **aversion** to: *Con* kr1 nat-m ↓ *Sulph* ↓
  - **sadness**; in: *Con* kr1 nat-m mtf *Sulph* vh*
- **conservative**: *(↗Narrow-minded)* kali-c mrr1
- **extravagant** (See Extravagance)
- **incorrectly**, dresses: aids nl2•
- **indecently**, dresses: *(↗Elegance - want; Indifference - external things; Lewdness; Naked; Shameless; Tastelessness)* canth mtf cub mtf hell b7.de* hyos b7.de* lyss mtf phos mtf plat mrr1* sal-fr sle1• sec st* stram b7.de* *Tarent* mtf tub mtf verat mtf [heroin sdj2]
- **ridiculously**; wants to dress: *(↗Gestures - ridiculous; Mocking - ridicule)* sil pc sulph pc
- **sensually** (See indecently)
- **striking**, bright and vivid: dendr-pol sk4• lac-f wza1•
- **unable** to: lac-h sze9• merc a1
- **womanly**: [heroin sdj2]

DRINKING:
- **agg.**: bell b4.de* *Cocc* b7.de* con b4.de*
- **amel.**: acon bg2 sulph bg2
- **more** than she should: *(↗Alcoholism)* ars h2* [heroin sdj2]

DRINKING alcohol; complaints after (See Ailments - alcoholism)

DRIVEN (See Ambition)

DRIVING:
- **amel.**: nit-ac bg2*
- **desire** for driving: androc mtf aur-m ↓ falco-pe ↓ galla-q-r ↓ haliae-lc srj5• hydrog ↓ mag-sil ↓ med ↓ nux-v ↓ *Tub* ↓
  - **fast**: aur-m vml3• falco-pe nl2• galla-q-r ↓ haliae-lc srj hydrog srj2• med mtf nux-v zr2 *Tub* mtf [mag-sil stj2]
    - **reckless** and indifferent to consequences: falco-pe nl2• galla-q-r nl2•
- **roundabout** several times; driving round the same: falco-pe nl2•

DROMOMANIA (See Impulse - run)

DROWSY (See Dullness; SLEEP - Sleepiness)

DRUGS: *(↗Medicine)*
- **desire**:
  - **heroine**: phasco-ci rbp2
  - **injection**; by: [vip bcj1]
  - **psychotropic**: *(↗Morphinism)* androc srj1• aur mrr1 lach mrr1 med mtf33 nat-m mrr1 nat-s mrr1 nux-v br1 pegan-ha tpi1• phasco-ci rbp2 positr nl2• [*Hydrog* stj2 lith-s stj2]
    - **puberty**; in: med mtf33
- **taken** drugs; as if one had: ara-maca ↓ bit-ar wht1• rhus-g ↓ [heroin sdj2]
  - **love**-drug; a: ara-maca sej7•
  - **marijuana**: rhus-g tmo3•
- **withdrawal**; as if in: phasco-ci rbp2

DRUNKEN; seems as if (See Stupefaction)

DRUNKENNESS; symptoms during: *(↗Alcoholism; GENERALS - Intoxication)*
- **abusive** (See Abusive - drunkenness)
- **antics**, plays (See Antics - drunkenness)
- **brutality** (See Brutality - drunkenness)
- **cheerful** (See Cheerful - drunkenness)
- **clairvoyant** dreams (See DREAMS - Clairvoyant - drunkenness)
- **coition**, desire for (See FEMALE - Sexual desire - increased - drunkenness; MALE GENITALIA/SEX - Sexual desire - increased - drunkenness)
- **comprehension**; easy (See Comprehension - easy - drunkenness)
- **destructiveness** (See Destructiveness - drunkenness)
- **dullness** (See Dullness - drunkenness)
- **intelligent**, more (See Intelligent - drunkenness)
- **jealousy** (See Jealousy - drunkenness)
- **kill**, desire to (See Kill - drunkenness)
- **loquacity** (See Loquacity - drunkenness)
- **morose** (See Morose - drunkenness)
- **naked**, wants to be (See Naked - drunkenness)
- **quarrelsome** (See Quarrelsome - drunkenness)
- **rage** (See Rage - drunkenness)
- **sadness** (See Sadness - drunkenness)
- **sexual** excitement (See FEMALE - Sexual desire - increased - drunkenness; MALE GENITALIA/SEX - Sexual desire - increased - drunkenness)
- **shrieking** (See Shrieking - drunkenness)
- **sleepiness** (See SLEEP - Sleepiness - drunkenness)
- **sleeplessness** (See SLEEP - Sleeplessness - drunkenness)
- **striking** (See Striking - drunkenness)
- **suicide**; desire for (See Suicidal - drunkenness)
- **talking** foolishly (See Speech - foolish - drunkenness)
- **weeping** or being sentimental (See Sentimental - drunkenness; Weeping - drunkenness)

DRYNESS (See Emotions - dryness)

DUALITY; sense of (See Confusion - identity - duality)

DULLNESS: (↗*Concentration - difficult; Confusion; Ennui; Ideas - deficiency; Indifference; Mental exertion - agg.; Mental exertion - aversion; Mistakes; Prostration; Senses - dull; Slowness; Stupefaction; Thinking - aversion; Torpor; Unconsciousness; Unconsciousness - dream; Unobserving [=inattentive]; FACE - Expression - stupid; FACE - Expression - vacant; GENERALS - Heaviness; GENERALS - Heaviness - externally; GENERALS - Lassitude; GENERALS - Lie - desire; GENERALS - Sluggishness; GENERALS - Weakness; GENERALS - Weariness)* abel↓ abies-c vh1 abies-n k* abrot k* absin kr1 acet-ac *Acon* k* acon-ac rly4• aconin a1 adam srj5• aesc aesc-g bro1 aeth k* aether a1 *Agar* k* *Agath-a* nl2• agn k* *Aids* nl2• *Ail* bg2* alco a1 alf br1 all-c↓ allox tpw3* *Aloe* br1* *Alum* k* alum-p k2 alum-sil k2* am-c k* am-m b2.de* *Ambr* k* *Ammc* j5.de* amor-r jl amyg a1 *Anac* k* anan kr1 androc srj1• anemps br1 ang b2.de* anh mg1.de* ant-c k* *Ant-t* b2.de* antip vh1 *Apis* k* apoc↓ apom a1 aq-mar skp7* aran↓ arb-m oss1• *Arg-met* k* **Arg-n** k* arn k* ars k* ars-i ars-met kr1 arund a1* asaf b2.de* asar k* asc-c kr1 asc-t a1* asim br1 aster atro a1 aur k* aur-m-n wbt2• aur-s k2 bad kr1 bamb-a stb2.de• **Bapt** k* **Bar-c** k* bar-i k2 **Bar-m** k* **Bell** k* bell-p sp1 benz-ac↓ berb k* bism k* bit-ar wht1• bol-la a1 *Borx* b2.de* *Bov* k* brass-n-o srj5• *Brom* b4a.de bros-gau mrc1 **Bry** k* bufo bufo-s↓ cact cadm-met tpw6 cadm-s↓ caj a1 *Calad* b2.de* **Calc** k* calc-act↓ calc-ar calc-caust a1 calc-i k2 **Calc-p** k* **Calc-s** calc-sil k2 camph k* cann-i k* *Cann-s* k* cann-xyz↓ canth k* caps k* carb-ac k* carb-an b2.de* **Carb-v** k* carbn-o *Carbn-s* k* carc tpw2* carl cartl-s rly4• cassia-s ccrh1* castm↓ caul↓ *Caust* k* cedr a1 cench k2 cent a1 cere-b↓ *Cham* k* *Chel* k* chen-a↓ chim a1 *Chin* k* chinin-ar *Chinin-s* chir-fl gya2 *Chlf* a1* chlol a1 chord-umb rly4• chr-ac a1* *Cic* k* cimic cimx cina b7a.de cinnb↓ cit-ac rly4• *Clem* k* coc-c coca bg2* *Cocc* k* coch a1* cod a1 coff b2.de* *Colch* k* coli rly4• coloc b2.de* colum-p sze2• com↓ *Con* k* conin a1 conv br1 *Cop* corn cortico mg1.de* cortiso mg1.de* corv-cor bdg• cot a1 crat br1 croc k* crot-c sk4• *Crot-h* k* crot-t cupr k* cupr-ar cur↓ *Cycl* k* cyn-d ckh1 cypra-eg sde6.de• cyt-l br1 dendr-pol sk4• des-ac jl *Dig* k* dios a1 diosm↓ dioxi rbp6 dirc a1 dros k* dubo-m br1 dulc k* echi epil a1 ery-a kr1 esp-g↓ eucal a1* eug vml3• eup-pur a1 euphr b2.de* fago a1 falco-pe nl2• *Ferr* b2.de* ferr-i kr1* ferr-m a1 ferr-ma j5.de ferr-p bg2 fl-ac bg2 flor-p rsj3• form a1 gad a1 galeoc-c-h gms1• galla-q-r nl2• galv c1 gard-j vlr2• **Gels** k* gent-l a1 ger-i rly4• germ-met stj2*• get a1 gink-b↓ gins *Glon* k* glyc bro1 gran a1 **Graph** k* grat↓ **Guaj** k* guare a1 gymno a1* haem a1* haliae-lc srj5• halo jl ham a1* **Hell** k* helon *Hep* k* hipp hir jl* hist jl hura↓ *Hydr* j5.de* *Hydr-ac* k* hydrog srj2• hydroph jl* **Hyos** k* hyper↓ iber a1* ign k* ind k* indg indol br1* iod k* ip k* irid-met stj2*• iris jug-c a1 juni-c a1 juni-v a1 kali-bi bg2* **Kali-br** k* **Kali-c** k* kali-chl c1 kali-i kali-m k2* kali-n k* kali-p k* *Kali-s* kali-sil↓ kali-sula a1* kalm↓ ketogl-ac rly4• *Kola* stb3• *Kreos* k* lac-c lac-e hrn2• lac-f wza1• lac-h sk4*• lac-loxod-a hrn2• lac-mat↓ **Lach** k* lact lact-v hr1* lap-la rsp1 lat-h↓ lat-m bnm6• **Laur** k* lec br1* led k* lepi lil-t k* lim a1 limen-b-c hrn2* limest-b es1• lina a1 linu-c a1 linu-u a1 lob a1 lol a1 *Luf-op* rsj5• **Lyc** k* lycps-v a1 *Lyss* k* m-ambo b7.de *M-arct* b2.de* m-aust b2.de* macro a1* mag-c b2.de* *Mag-m* k* mag-p br1 mag-s↓ maland st malar jl2 manc a1 mang b2.de* mang-p↓ med k* melal-alt gya4 *Meli* meny b2.de* meph a1 *Merc* k* *Merc-c* k* *Merc-i-r* kr1 merl *Mez* k* mill↓ mim-p rsj8• mit a1 *Moni* jl2* morph a1 mosch k* mucs-nas rly4• mur-ac k* myric naja nat-act a1 **Nat-ar** **Nat-c** k* **Nat-m** k* nat-n br1 *Nat-p* nat-pyru rly4• *Nat-s* k* nat-sil fd3.de• nauf-helv-li↓ neon srj5• nicc nicot c1 nicotam rly4• *Nit-ac* k* nitro-o a1 **Nux-m** k* *Nux-v* k* oci-sa↓ ol-an j5.de olib-sac wmh1 *Olnd* k* **Op** k* ox-ac a1 oxal-a rly4• ozone sde2• par k* paull a1 ped a1 pen a1 penic jl *Pert-vc* vk9 *Petr* k* petr-ra shn4• **Ph-ac** k* **Phos** k* phys **Pic-ac** k* pin-s a1 pip-m k* pitu↓ plan a1 plat k* **Plb** k* plect a1 plut-n srj7• podo bg2 polys sk4• *Positr* nl2• pot-e rly4• psil jl* *Psor* k* ptel k* **Puls** k* puls-n a1 pyrid rly4• rad-br c1* raja-s jl ran-b k* ran-s k* raph a1 rham-cal br1 rheum k* *Rhod* k* rhus-g a1 rhus-r↓ *Rhus-t* k* rhus-v ribo rly4• ros-d wla1 ruta k* sabad k* sabin b2.de* sacch a1 sacch-a↓ sal-ac sal-n a1 sal-p a1 samb b2.de* sang sanguis-s hrn2• santin a1 sapin a1 saroth sp1 sarr a1* *Sars* k* scut mrr1 *Sec* k* *Sel* k* **Seneg** k* **Sep** k* serp a1 **Sil** k* sin-n a1 skat br1 sol-mm c1 *Spig* k* *Spong* k* squil b2.de* stach↓ *Stann* k* **Staph** k* stict bg2* still *Stram* k* streptom-s vk2 stront-c b2.de* stry a1 suis-em rly4• suis-pan rly4• sul-ac k* sul-i k2 sulfa sp1 sulfonam ks2 **Sulph** k* sumb suprar rly4• *Syph* bg2* *Tab* k* tanac br1 tarax k* *Tarent* tart-ac br1 tax-br oss1• *Ter* a1 tere-la rly4• tetox pin2• teucr k* thala jl ther *Thuj* k* thyr vh til toxi mtf2• trif-p a1 trios↓ tritic-vg fd5.de **Tub** k* tub-a jl2 ulm-c jsj8• upa a1 uran-n kr1 urol-h rwt• ust a1 v-a-b jl valer k* vanil fd5.de *Ven-m* rsj12• *Verat* k* verb k* *Verbe-o*↓ vero-o rly4*• viol-o k* viol-t b2.de* vip j5.de* xero br1* **Zinc** k*

Dullness: ...
Zinc-p k2 *Zing* st [ant-met stj2 bell-p-sp dcm1 bism-sn stj2 buteo-j sej6 cob stj2 cob-m stj2 cob-p stj2 ferr-f stj2 ferr-lac stj2 ferr-n stj2 ferr-sil stj2 heroin sdj2 lith-i stj2 mang-i stj2 mang-met stj2 nicc-met stj2 nicc-s stj2 niob-met stj2 osm-met stj2 pop dhh1 *Spect* dfg1 tax jsj7 tell stj2 zinc-i stj2]

- **daytime**: abies-n a1 am-c h2 am-m h2 calc h2 carb-v h2 cinnb a1 con h2 kali-c h2 luf-op↓ lyc h2 mag-c h2 merc a1 nat-ar a1 nat-c h2 nat-m h2 phos h2 sep h2 sulph h2 tell rsj10•
  - **wakeful** | **night**: abies-n br1 luf-op rsj5•
- **morning**: acon b7.de aesc agar k* alum b4.de am-c j5.de am-m b7.de *Ambr* k* ammc↓ **Anac** k* arg-n↓ arn asaf b7.de asar b7.de aur b4.de bamb-a stb2.de• bapt↓ bar-c k* berb k* bism b7.de* bit-ar↓ borx bov b4.de brom a1 bry b7.de* calc b4.de* canth k* caps k* carb-ac↓ carb-an k* carb-v b4.de* carbn-s caust b4.de cere-b a1 cham b7.de chel↓ **Chin** k* cic b7.de clem b4.de coc-c↓ cocc b7.de coli rly4• coloc a1 con b4.de cortico sp1 cycl sf1.de dulc fd4.de ferr↓ form a1 germ-met srj5• *Graph* k* guaj guare a1 ham↓ hyos b7.de hyper a1 ign k* *Iod* b4a.de kali-c k* kali-n k* kali-p kali-sil↓ lach lact j5.de laur mag-c b4.de mag-m b4.de* manc a1 mang-p rly4• melal-alt↓ merc k* mez mit a1 nat-ar nat-c nat-s a1 nux-v b7a.de* oci-sa↓ ox-ac k* petr a1 *Ph-ac* k* phos k* phys plat psor al2 puls puls-n a1 ran-s b7.de rhod k* *Rhus-t* b7.de* ruta b7.de* *Samb* b7.de* sarr a1 scut↓ seneg b4.de sep b4.de* sil k* spong fd4.de squil b7.de* stann b4.de staph k* stram↓ sul-ac k* sulph k* *Sumb* k* suprar rly4• tell a1 *Thuj* k* urol-h rwt• verat b7.de* zinc k*
  - **8 h**: nat-ar a1 phys a1
  - **noon**; until: oci-sa sk4•
  - **bed**, in: brom a1 chel j5.de cocc j5.de
  - **old** people; in: ambr br1
  - **rising**, on: ammc a1 bapt↓ calc h2* *Carb-v* h2* coc-c a1 ham a1* mag-m petr h2 phos scut a1 stram zinc h2
    - **after**: bapt a1
  - **waking**, on: *Aesc* *Alum* mrr1 anac arg-n a1 arn bar-c h2* berb k* bit-ar wht1• bry k2 caps k* carb-ac carb-an carb-v **Chin** k* cic j coli rly4• dulc fd4.de ferr a1 graph mrr1 ham vh* ign kali-c kali-n kali-sil k2* **Mag-m** mrr1 melal-alt gya4 merc plat puls ruta h1 sil stann staph sulph k2 suprar rly4• thuj
- **forenoon**: *Anac* ars bar-c a1 bism canth b7.de carb-an a1 carb-v h2 galeoc-c-h gms1• lach lyc b4.de mag-c mag-m b4.de* mosch b7.de mur-ac myric a1 nat-ar a1 nat-m ph-ac b4.de phys a1 psor k* ran-b b7.de sars k* sep k* sil sul-ac b4.de sulph k* zinc b4.de
  - **11 h**: galeoc-c-h gms1•
- **noon**: ars con esp-g kk1.de* zinc
- **afternoon**: agath-a nl2• all-c k* anac ang arg-n ars h2* asaf b7.de atro k* bry b7.de cadm-s a1 caj k* calc b4.de cann-s carb-v b4.de cham h1* chin b7.de cimic a1 cod a1 con dendr-pol↓ dios k* dulc fd4.de ferr b7.de* graph k* ham k* *Hell* k* hyos k* kali-c b4.de laur k* lil-t m-arct b7.de merc-c b4a.de nat-m *Nux-v* b7.de* petr b4.de pip-m k* plan k* puls k* rhus-r sabin b7.de sel rsj9• *Sep* k* *Sil* *Staph* b7a.de sulph h2* trios↓ zinc b4.de*
  - **16 h**: trios rsj11•
    - **amel.**: dendr-pol sk4•
  - **amel.**: anac j5.de
- **evening**: am-c j anac a1* bar-c b4.de bov b4.de* caj↓ calc-s k* cann-s carb-an b4.de carb-v b4.de* cham b7.de coca coch a1 cod a1 dig dios a1 dulc *Euphr* b7.de* graph b4.de hipp ign ip b7.de irid-met srj5• kali-c k* lach lyc k* mag-m j5.de mez b4.de* mill k* mur-ac j5.de myric a1 naja a1 nat-m k* nat-pyru rly4• nux-v b7.de* ph-ac b4.de phos b4.de* pip-m k* puls b7.de* ran-s j5.de rhus-t k* ruta b7.de* sel b7a.de sep k* *Sil* b4.de spig b7.de stann b4.de* sul-ac b4.de *Sulph* k* valer b7.de
  - **amel.**: agar k2* alum-sil vh1 aur-m-n vml3• (non:bufo slp) bufo-s slp cic puls sil sulph j5.de
  - **going** to bed, after: caj a1
- **night**: aesc↓ bapt k2 com↓ ery-a a1* kali-c j lyc↓ lyss a1 mur-ac↓ phos b4.de plat↓ psor↓ ran-s j rhod b4a.de rhus-t b7.de verat↓
  - **amel.**: *Agar* k2*
  - **bed**, in: mur-ac a1
  - **waking**; on: aesc bapt k2 com a1 ery-a a1 lyc h2 lyss a1 phos plat psor al2 verat
- **air**:
  - **open** air; in: hyos lyc↓ nat-ar k2 plat
    - **after** being in open air: lyc h2

- **open** air; in: ...
  - **amel.**: bell h1* cinnb k* cyn-d ckh1 dulc a1 graph j5.de **Lyc** mag-m meny k* nat-ar k2
- **wet** air | **from**: *(↗Laziness - weather)* *Calc* *Carb-v* *Cimic* vh* *Dulc* vh* merc k2 *Nat-s* vh* puls *Rhus-t* sil sulph h2* verat
- **alone**, when: *(↗Company - desire; Company - desire - alone)* ph-ac
- **alternating** with:
  - **activity**; desire for (See Activity - desires - alternating - dullness)
  - **cheerfulness** (See Cheerful - alternating - dullness)
  - **clearness** of mind (See Ideas - abundant - alternating - dullness)
  - **dim** vision (See vision)
  - **excitement** (See Excitement - alternating - dullness)
  - **ideas**; abundant (See Ideas - abundant - alternating - dullness)
  - **memory**; active (See Memory - active - alternating - dullness)
  - **mental** exertion (See Mental exertion - desire - alternating - dullness)
  - **mirth** and hilarity (See Mirth - alternating - dullness)
  - **singing** (See Singing - alternating - dullness)
  - **vision**; dim: bell h1*
  - **vivacity** (See Vivacious - alternating - dullness)
  - **work**; desire for (See Activity - desires - alternating - dullness)
- **bad** news, from: *(↗Ailments - bad)* calc-p
- **beer**, after: coloc
- **brain**; with complaints of the: diosm br1
- **breakfast**, after: bapt a1 calad hr1 tritic-vg fd5.de
- **cares** for his business, from: ph-ac k2*
- **carousal**; as after a: kreos hr1 phys a1
- **chagrin**; from (See mortification)
- **children**, in: *(↗Laziness - children)* abrot sf1.de aeth mtf33 *Agar* k2* apis ↓ **Arg-n** k* **Bar-c** k* *Bar-m* k2* bufo gk *Calc* k* **Calc-p** k* calc-s mtf33 carb-v mtf33 *Carbn-s* carc fb* caust mtf33 cupr mtf33 dulc fd4.de graph mtf33 iod kali-sil k2 lach j5.de lat-h bnm5• *Lyc* med k2* merc k* nat-s mtf33 op wbt• phos mtf33 sep mtf33 *Sil* **Sulph** k* *Syph* vh* tax-br oss1• *Tub* vh* zinc
  - **puberty**; at | **girls**: apis ptk1
  - **school** children: carb-v mtf33
- **chill**, during: agar hr1* ang bg2 aur j bell k* borx b4a.de* bry k* *Calc* b4.de* *Caps* k* *Cham* chin h1* cic k* cimx con b4a.de* dros b7.de* *Hell* k* ip bg2 *Kali-c* b4.de* *Lach* led k* **Nat-c** b4.de* nat-m bg2 nux-m k* *Nux-v* bg2 op bg2 ph-ac bg2 phos k* plb k* rhus-t k* ruta b7a.de* sep bg2 stann valer bg2 verat bg2
- **closing** eyes, on: zinc
  - **amel.**: kali-c
- **coition**, after: bar-c bg2 bov b4.de* calc b4a.de* *Sep* k*
- **company**, in: *(↗Company - aversion)* plat k2*
- **condition**, could not think of her: chel *Ruta* fd4.de *Spong* fd4.de tritic-vg fd5.de *Vanil* fd5.de
- **conversation**, from: *(↗Conversation - agg.)* sacch-a fd2.de• sil staph
- **copious** flow (See urine)
- **coryza**; as from: aeth bg2 berb bg2 caul bg2 chin bg2 coc-c bg2 colch bg2 coloc bg2 con bg2 euphr bg2 graph bg2 hep bg2 ign bg2 ol-an bg2 sep bg2 staph bg2
- **coryza**, during: anemps br1 ars h2* bamb-a stb2.de• bov b4a.de *Cham* b7.de* chen-a vml3• chin b7.de* dulc b4.de* euphr b7.de* hell b7.de* kola stb3• lach b7a.de lyc b4.de* *Nux-v* b7a.de phos b4.de* rhod b4.de* sabad b7a.de seneg b4a.de
- **cough**, during: hep h2*
- **damp** air (See air - wet)
- **diabetes**, in: *Helon* hr1* *Op* hr1* ph-ac mtf sul-ac hr1*
- **dinner**:
  - **after**: arg-n a1 carb-an mag-c h2 zinc a1
  - **during**: mag-m h2 sulph h2
- **dreams**, after: arn bell caps chin cocc eug vml3• sil
- **drinking**; after: bell b4a.de cocc b7a.de
- **drunken**, as if: agath-a nl2• anan a1 *Bell* hr1* dulc fd4.de *Op* hr1*
- **drunkenness**, during: op gl1.fr• stram gl1.fr•
- **eating**, after: ambr b7a.de bell b4a.de calc-s caust b4a.de chel j5.de cocc b7a.de graph led st meny b7a.de* nat-m b4a.de nux-v b7a.de petr b4a.de* ph-ac b4a.de phos b4a.de* *Rhus-t* tab tritic-vg fd5.de
  - **amel.**: *(↗Eating - after - amel.)* fago a1 *Iod* *Mez* *Nat-c* *Phos* sep sil
- **emissions** (See pollutions)
- **emotions**, from: acon *Dulc* fd4.de op ph-ac staph
- **epilepsy**:
  - **before**: *Caust*
  - **with**: *Verbe-o* br1
- **epistaxis** | **amel.**: psor vml
- **eruptions**; from suppressed: bar-c k2
- **fog**, as if enveloped in a: agath-a nl2• arb-m oss1• kola stb3• olib-sac wmh1 petr st1 tere-la rly4• *Tritic-vg* fd5.de
- **forehead**; with complaints of: acon bg2 aloe bg2 bar-c bg2
- **gassing**, by: *Caust* **Glon**
- **head**:
  - **complaints** of head; with: agar bg2 am-c bg2 aran bg2 ars bg2 asar bg2 *Bapt* bg2 berb bg2 bov bg2 bry bg2 calc bg2 castm bg2 con bg2 cupr bg2 dulc bg2 echi bg2 gels bg2 hell bg2 *Hyos* bg2 led bg2 mur-ac bg2 nat-c bg2 nux-m bg2 ph-ac bg2 phos bg2 puls bg2 sep bg2 sil bg2 squil bg2 sulph bg2
  - **enlarged** with nausea and ill humor (See HEAD - Enlarged - nausea)
- **headache**, with: *(↗HEAD - Pain - stunning)* acon bg agar bg am-c bg aran bg* ars bg asar bg asc-c hr1* *Bapt* bg bar-c b4.de* bell a1 berb bg bov bg* bry bg* calc bg *Calc-p* a1* carb-an b4.de* carb-v bg carc zzl *Caust* b4.de* cham b7.de* chel a1 **Cimic** mrr1 con bg cupr bg dulc b4.de* echi bg ferr b7.de* fl-ac bg2 gels bg2 gink-b sbd1• glon k2 graph b4.de* hell bg* hyos b7.de* kola stb3• led bg *Mag-p* hr1 merc b4.de* merc-i-r bg moni rfm1• mur-ac bg nat-c b4.de* nat-m b4.de* nit-ac b4.de* nux-m bg ozone sde2• pert-vc vk9 petr b4.de* ph-ac b4.de* phos bg puls bg ruta fd4.de sep b4.de* **Sil** b4.de* spig b7.de* squil bg sulph b4.de* zinc h2*
- **heard**, what he has: ruta fd4.de sel k2* tritic-vg fd5.de
- **heat**:
  - **after**: sep a1
  - **during**: *(↗Indifference - fever)* acon bg2 **Ang** b7.de* *Arg-met* b7.de* *Arg-n* k* **Ars** b4.de* *Bapt* hr1* bell b4.de* borx b4a.de* bry b7.de* calc bg2 caps k* carb-v k* *Cham* k* chinin-s con bg2 dros b7.de* *Hyos* hr1* *Ign* k* ip b7.de* *Kali-c* b4.de* merc bg2* *Nat-c* b4.de* nat-m bg2 *Nux-v* b7.de* op bg2 ph-ac bg2 **Phos** b4.de* *Puls* k* rhus-t b7a.de* ruta b7.de* **Sep** b4.de* sil k* sulph hr1* *Valer* b7.de* **Verat** b7.de*
- **impotence**, with: ph-ac k2
- **injuries** of head, after: *(↗Ailments - injuries; Confusion - injury - after)* arn cic hell bg* hyper merc **Nat-s** mrr1 rhus-t
- **interrupted**, when: colch a1
- **intoxicated**; as if: agath-a nl2• rhus-g tmo3•
- **laughing**; with silent: *Bell* b4a.de
- **looking** out the window lasting for hours: mez a1*
- **loss** of fluids, after: *Chin* *Nux-v* sulph
- **lying**, while: bry
  - **amel.**: zinc
- **masturbation**, after: *Gels* hr1* *Nat-p* vh* ph-ac k2* **Staph** hr1*
- **menses**: *(↗Menses - during)*
  - **after**: alum b4a.de nat-m b4.de thuj b4a.de
  - **before**: aur-m-n wbt2•
  - **during**: *(↗Menses - during)* calc k* germ-met srj5• graph ↓ lyc lycps-v
    - **beginning** of: graph b4.de
- **mental** symptoms; during: alum bg2 bov bg2 caust bg2 sil bg2
- **mental** exertion, from: aeth vh1 agar j5.de *Anac* arb-m oss1• asaf j aur *Bar-c* vh* berb j *Calc* k* *Calc-p* cham j cocc ger-i rly4• *Glon* a1 graph hep hura ign lach limen-b-c hrn2* lyc mag-c **Nat-c** nat-m *Nat-sil* k2 nauf-helv-li elm2• *Nux-v* *Olnd* ph-ac k2 pic-ac puls ran-b sabad j sars j sel j5.de* *Sil* *Sulph*
- **mortification**, after: *(↗Ailments - embarrassment; Ailments - honor; Ailments - mortification)* ign lach *Staph*
- **motion**:
  - **agg.**: bry k2* kalm k2

- amel.: rhus-t
- **news** (See bad)
- **occiput**; with complaints of: carb-v bg2 merc-i-r bg2
- **old** people, of: abel vh1 *Abies-n* vh1 **Ambr** k* *Arg-met* vh* *Arg-n* vh* **Bar-c** k* *Con* sf1.de *Lyc* sf1.de **Plb** gk
- **pain**; with: abies-c↓ cham nh ruta fd4.de tritic-vg fd5.de
- ○ • **Stomach**; at: abies-c gb•
- **painful**: dig h2* meny h1* nat-c h2* phos h2*
- **palpitation**, with: kali-c h2*
- **paroxysmal**: sep h2* zinc h2*
- **periodical**: chin
- **perspiration**, during: acon bg2 ang bg2 ars k* **Bell** bg2 *Bry* bg2 calc bg2 caps k* chin k* dros bg2 graph k* hyos ip bg2 kali-c bg2 merc bg2 nat-c bg2 *Nat-m* bg2 *Nux-v* bg2 op bg2 ph-ac bg2 *Phos* bg2 *Puls* b7a.de *Rhus-t* bg2 ruta bg2 sabad k* **Sep** bg2 sil bg2 sulph k* thuj k* *Valer* bg2 verat bg2
- **pollutions**:
  - **after**: caust k* ind a1 nat-p mrr1
  - **with**: **Kali-br** kr1
- **pressing** in hypogastrium, from: calc-act h*
- **pulse**; with slow: dig br1
- **reading**: acon aeth ptk1 agn alum ambr k* bism cann-s k2 *Carb-v* cocc c1 coff colch k2 **Con** dros ferr-i *Glon* hell ptk1 hipp ind iod a1 kali-p fd1.de• kali-sil k2 kola stb3• lac-c *Lach* *Lyc* mez *Nat-c* nat-p nat-sil k2 nux-m *Nux-v* k* olnd **Op** *Ph-ac* **Pic-ac** mrr1 ruta fd4.de sel k2* sil *Sulph* k* vanil↓
  - **hearing** or reading; about what he is: ruta fd4.de sel ptk1 vanil fd5.de
- **respiration**; with impeded: sep b4.de*
- **riding** in a carriage | **amel.**: nit-ac k2
- **rising** from bed: ox-ac ozone sde2•
- **room**, in a: meny
- **says** nothing: arn j5.de dulc fd4.de *Hell* hr1* *Lach* j5.de *Rheum* j5.de spong j5.de
- **sexual** excesses, after: *Cocc* vh* *Sel* sf1.de *Staph* vh*
- **shivering**; during: *Ruta* b7.de*
- **siesta**; after: bar-c kr1 eug vml3• *Graph* lyc h2 *Nat-s* vh* **Staph** vh*
- **skin** over brain; as if from a tense: ang b7.de*
- **sleep**:
  - **after**: bry k2 dendr-pol sk4• dulc fd4.de
  - **sound**; after: alum-sil k2 berb kr1 mez
- **sleepiness**, with: (↗*Stupefaction - sleepiness*) arn j5.de benz-ac a1 bit-ar wht1• cact hr1* calad j5.de cann-s j5.de carb-an j5.de carb-v j5.de caust j5.de chin j5.de clem j5.de coff j5.de colch j5.de croc j5.de crot-h j5.de *Cupr* hr1* dig j5.de ferr j5.de *Gels* j5.de *Hyos* j5.de ketogl-ac rly4• kreos j5.de lact hr1* lyc j5.de mag-s j5.de *Merc* hr1* nat-m j5.de nux-m j5.de *Phos* hr1* plb a1 sep j5.de staph j5.de tax-br oss1• zinc j5.de
- **sleeplessness**, with: agath-a nl2• carc mlr1• dulc j5.de lact j5.de ran-s j5.de
- **smoking**, from: acon petr a1
- **speaking**, while: (↗*Speech - incoherent*) am-c cypra-eg sde6.de• kali-c *Lyc* mez petr-ra shn4•
- **spoken** to, when: (↗*understand - questions; Confusion - talking*) bry k2* dulc fd4.de lob a1
- **standing** | **agg.**: bov bry guaj
- **stiffness** cervical region; with: **Cimic** mrr1
- **stool**, after: apoc vh1 calc bg2 cycl
- **stooping**, on: sulph h2*
- **stramonium**; from: tab hr1*
- **studying**; when: (↗*Studying - difficult*) aeth ptk1 *Agar* bg2 agn bg2 anac bg2 aq-mar skp7• ars bg2 bar-c bg2 calc bg2* calc-p bg2* carb-v mtf33 caust bg2 con bg2 hell ptk1 luf-op rsj5• mag-p bg2 nat-m bg2 nux-v ptk1 olnd bg2 ph-ac bg2 phos bg2
- **thinking**:
  - **long**; unable to think: (↗*Concentration - difficult - studying; Mental exertion - agg. - impossible/ Studying - difficult*) anac arb-m oss1• bamb-a stb2.de• *Bar-c* vh* carbn-s k2 cham cinnb con dendr-pol sk4• ery-a **Gels** k* *Kali-p* fd1.de• *Limen-b-c* hrn2• moni rfm1• oci-sa sk4• **Ph-ac** k* **Phos** k* **Pic-ac** k* rhus-g tmo3• stram [tax jsj7]
  - **slowly** (See Dullness)
- **toothache**, from: clem h2*
- **understand**; does not:
  - **happening**; what is: hell mrr1

Dullness – understand; does not: ...
  - **questions** addressed to her: (↗*spoken*) ambr↓ *Caust*↓ cocc↓ hell↓ kali-br↓ med↓ *Phos*↓ *Sulph*↓ tarent k* thuj hr1 *Zinc*↓
    - ⁝ **repetition**; only after: (↗*Answering - repeats*) ambr *Caust* cocc hell hr1* kali-br med st1 *Phos* k* *Sulph* *Zinc*
  - **words**; the meaning of: plut-n srj7•
- **urine** amel.; copious flow of: *Gels* k* *Ter* kr1
- **vertigo**; during: acon bg2 agar bg2 alum bg2 am-c bg2 ambr bg2 anac bg2 ant-t bg2* arg-n bg2 *Arn* bg2 ars bg2 asaf bg2 asar bg2 aur bg2 bamb-a stb2.de• *Bell* bg2 bry bg2 calc bg2 cann-xyz bg2 caps bg2 caust h2 chin bg2 colch bg2 *Con* bg2 croc bg2 cycl bg2 dig bg2 dulc bg2 graph bg2 hell bg2* hep bg2 *Hyos* bg2 ign bg2 iod bg2 kali-c bg2 *Lach* bg2 laur bg2 led bg2 mag-m bg2 meny bg2 merc bg2* mez bg2 mosch bg2* nat-m bg2 nit-ac bg2 nux-m bg2 nux-v bg2 olnd h1* op bg2* petr bg2 ph-ac bg2 phos bg2* pitu a1 plb bg2 ptel kr1 rhod bg2 rhus-t bg2 sabad bg2* sec bg2 sel bg2 sil bg2 spig bg2 spong bg2 stach bg stann bg2 staph bg2 sulph bg2 ther bg2 verat bg2 verb bg2 *Zinc* bg2
- **vexation**; after: ign lach
- **vomiting** amel.: asar h1*
- **waking**, on: allox tpw3 alum alum-sil k2* am-m j5.de ambr h1 anac arn bar-c bell berb k* bov j5.de calc b4a.de* *Cann-s* j5.de caps k* chel chin chir-fl gya2 clem cocc con cur dig j5.de grat j5.de guare↓ ham vh* ind↓ **Lach** *Med* hr1* nat-c nat-sil k2* nux-m j5.de op **Phos** pic-ac plat psor k* *Puls* j5.de rheum j5.de sel sil sol-mm j5.de stann staph j5.de stram thuj j5.de verat
  - **dream**; from a: guare a1
  - **emissions**; after: ind a1
- **walking**: ham a1 nat-m↓ ph-ac phys rhus-t sulph↓
  - **after** walking rapidly: nat-m h2 sulph h2
  - **air**; in open | **amel.**: borx galeoc-c-h gms1• graph j5.de **Lyc** nat-ar plan
  - **amel.**: kola stb3•
- **warm** room, on entering a: acon *Puls*
- **washing**, amel. from cold: *Calc-p* a1*
- **wet** air (See air - wet)
- **weather**; in cold: merc k2
- **wine**, after: acon all-c mill petr a1 zinc
- **words**, with inability to find right: (↗*Mistakes - speaking - words - wrong*) lil-t kr1 tritic-vg fd5.de [lac-mat sst4]
- **working** amel.: cycl sf1.de
- **writing**, while: acon arg-n k* cann-s chinin-s galeoc-c-h gms1• glon k* kali-sil k2* mag-c nat-pyru rly4• nux-m rhus-t *Sil*

DUPLICITY (See Deceitful)

DUTY: (↗*Responsibility*)
- **aversion** to: aur-ar↓ bell-p↓ brom↓ calc-p hr1 cench↓ cit-l↓ dulc fd4.de falco-pe↓ *Kali-s* fd4.de *Lyc*↓ *Nux-v*↓ petr-ra↓ podo fd3.de• ruta fd4.de **Sep**↓ *Sil*↓ spong fd4.de sul-i↓ *Sulph*↓ tritic-vg fd5.de
  - **domestic** duty: aur-ar mtf bell-p mtf brom↓ cench k2 cit-l kr1 dulc fd4.de falco-pe nl2• *Lyc* mtf *Nux-v* mtf petr-ra shn4• **Sep** mtf *Sil* mtf spong fd4.de sul-i k2 *Sulph* mtf tritic-vg fd5.de
    - ⁝ **children**; in: brom mtf33
- **no** sense of duty: (↗*Indifference - duties; Moral*) alum gl1.fr• ambr gl1.fr• anac gl1.fr• ars gl1.fr• **Calc** a1* carc mlr1• cench k13 cob ptm1• coloc gl1.fr• hep gl1.fr• kali-s fkr2.de lach gl1.fr• *Merc* st* nat-m gl1.fr• olib-sac wmh1 podo fd3.de• ptel a1 sil st* sulph st*
- **performs** in a perfunctory manner: ptel vml3•
- **stimulate** sense of duty; to (See no)
- **too** much sense of duty: (↗*Love - family; Proper - too; Responsibility - taking; Serious*) agar mtf33 androc↓ *Ars* lmj aur mtf33 **Calc** lmj* calc-p lmj calc-sil bt* caps↓ carc tpw* caust lmj choc oss• cupr sst3* ign lmj kali-ar oss• kali-bi oss• **Kali-c** vh* kali-i oss• kali-n oss• *Kali-s* fd4.de kali-sil oss• kali-sula oss• lac-c↓ lac-e hrn2• lyc lmj mag-m mrr1* mang↓ naja↓ nat-m lmj* *Nat-s* mrr1 **Nit-ac** lmj nux-v lmj sacch-a fd2.de• *Sep* lmj *Thuj* lmj* **Tritic-vg** fd* vanil fd5.de vip↓ zinc lmj
  - **children**; in: androc lmj *Ars* lmj **Calc** lmj calc-p lmj calc-sil lmj caps lmj **Carc** lmj caust lmj *Cupr* lmj ign lmj kali-bi lmj kali-c lmj lac-c lmj lyc lmj mang lmj naja lmj nat-m lmj **Nit-ac** lmj **Nux-v** lmj *Sep* lmj *Thuj* lmj vip lmj **Zinc** lmj

DWELLS: (↗*Introspection; Memory - active - past; Sadness - dwelling; Thoughts - disagreeable*)
- **childhood**, on his: *Aids* nl2• *Tritic-vg* fd5.de

- **childhood**, on his: ...
  - **equanimity**; with: aids nl2•
- **disappointments**, on: (*↗Ailments - love; Brooding - disappointment*) *Nat-m* vh* *Ph-ac* kr1
- **grief** from past offenses: calc gl1.fr• rhus-g tmo3• staph gl1.fr•
- **happy** moments; dwells on past: carb-an mrr1 carc az1.de• *Dulc* fd4.de ruta fd4.de *Sacch-a* fd2.de• spong fd4.de tritic-vg fd5.de vanil fd5.de
- **health**; on his own broken: aur-m k2
- **mother** earth, beautiful, strong and benevolent but abused and disregarded; on: positr nl2•
- **mothers** and grandmothers: positr nl2•
- **offenses** come back to him; long forgotten: (*↗recalls - old; Grief - offenses; Speech - vexations*) glon kr1
- **past** disagreeable occurrences, on: (*↗Absorbed; Ailments - love; Anxiety; Brooding; Complaining - offenses; Grief; Grief - past; Hatred; Introspection; Meditating; Pessimist; Remorse - indiscretion; Sadness; Sighing; Thoughts - persistent - unpleasant; Thoughts - tormenting - past; Weeping - past*) aids nl2• am-c k* *Ambr* k* anthraq rly4• arg-n asar jl3 *Aur-m-n* wbt2• aur-s zr* ben-n ↓ *Benz-ac* k* borra-o oss1• bros-gau mrc1 bung-fa mtf calc j* caust gk* *Cham* *Chin* cob-n mg1.de *Cocc* *Con* cop k* cur sne cycl sne dros sne *Dulc* fd4.de elaps gk fic-m gya1 form glon k* goss vh* granit-m es1• graph ↓ haliae-lc srj5• hep k* hydrog srj2• hyos bg2* **Ign** vh* kali-c ↓ *Kali-p* st1 kali-s fkr2.de kiss a1 kola stb3• kreos lac-h sk4• lac-lup hrn2• lil-t k2 luna kg1• **Lyc** ●* meny mez musca-d szs1 **NAT-M** k ●* *Nit-ac* k* op gl1.fr• opun-s a1 *Ph-ac* ↓ phos bg2* pin-con oss2• plac rzf5• *Plat* positr nl2• psor bg* puls gb• *Rhus-g* tmo3• rhus-t ros-d wla1 sal-fr sle1• sanguis-s hrn2• sars kr1 *Sep* k* spong h1 staph gl1.fr• suis-em rly4• *Sulph* k* symph fd* syph st1 thuj bg2* tritic-vg fd5.de ulm-c ↓ vanil fd5.de verat sf1.de visc sp1*
  - **evening** | **bed**; in: aur-m-n wbt2•
  - **night**: ambr k2* ben-n a1 benz-ac k2 caust chin graph kali-c kali-p vh* **Lyc** k* nat-m sf1.de* *Plat* **Rhus-t** k* *Sulph*
    - **midnight**; after: *Nat-m* vh* **Rhus-t**
  - **cannot** cease talking about old vexations: cham h1 dulc fd4.de
  - **disappointments**; on: *Ph-ac* kr1 *Tritic-vg* fd5.de ulm-c jsj8•
  - **forgiveness**, with: positr nl2•
  - **frightful** scene of some mournful event of the past; tormented by a: spong kr1
  - **grieve** therefore; to: nat-m gl1.fr•
- **recalls**:
  - **disagreeable** memories: am-c ptk1* ambr ptk1 aur-m-n wbt2• benz-ac ptk1 calc st* carc mlr1• cham ptk1 hep st* hyos st* **Lyc** ●* **Nat-m** ●* nit-ac st* phos st* psor ptk1 **Sep** ●* sulph st* thuj ptk1
  - **old** grievances: (*↗offenses; Weeping - vexation - old*) glon k* neon srj5• *Rhus-g* tmo3• sars kr1 sulph kr1
- **sexual** matters; on: staph br1
- **thinking** of everything that others have done to displease her: (*↗Excitement - evening - thinking*)
  - **lying** awake thinking of it | **forgotten** about it; in the morning she has: am-c k1
- **unpleasant**, disagreeable things: *Benz-ac* ptk1* cocc ptk1

DYNAMIC (See Activity)

DYSLEXIA: (*↗Concentration - difficult; Heedless - talking; Memory - weakness; Mistakes - reading; Mistakes - speaking - spelling; Mistakes - writing; Writing - inability*) anac mtf *Bar-c* mtf *Calc* mtf *Calc-p* mtf calc-s mtf calc-sil mtf carc gk* *Caust* mtf chin mtf **Germ-met** stj2*• graph mtf hyos mtf ign mtf kali-br mtf *Kali-p* mtf lac-c mtf33 lyc mtf mag-c mtf *Med* mtf merc mtf nux-v mtf *Phos* mtf sal-fr sle1• sil mtf stram mtf sul-ac mtf sulph mtf thuj mtf tub mtf11 zinc mtf

EARLY:
- **riser**; early (See SLEEP - Waking - early)
- **too** early; always (See Anxiety - time)

EARNESTNESS (See Serious)

EARTHY (See Simple; Unrefined)

EASE, feeling of: (*↗Protected; Tranquillity*) coca ↓ falco-pe nl2• gamb a1 hir rsj4• lat-h thj1 nept-m lsd2.fr olib-sac wmh1 ozone sde2• ruta fd4.de thea a1 tritic-vg fd5.de [heroin sdj2]

Ease, feeling of: ...
- **business**, in: coca a1

EATING:
- **after**: tritic-vg fd5.de
  - **evening** | **amel.**: (*↗Sadness - evening - eating*) tarent k2
  - **agg.**: agar bg2 *Aloe* ptk1 alum bg2 am-c bg2* ambr b7.de* anac b4a.de* aq-mar mgm• arg-n bg2 arn b7.de* ars bg2* asaf b7.de* asar b7.de* bar-c bg2 bell b4.de* borx b4a.de bov b4.de* bry b7.de* calc bg2* cann-s bg cann-xyz bg2 canth b7.de* caps b7.de* carb-an b4.de* carb-v b4.de* caust b4a.de* cham b7.de* chel b7.de* *Chin* bg2* cocc b7.de* *Coloc* ptk1 *Con* b4.de* ferr b7.de* graph bg2 hep ptk1 hyos b7.de* ign ptk1 iod b4.de* ip bg2 **Kali-bi** ptk1 kali-c bg2* lach bg2* *Lyc* bg2* mag-m b4.de* meny b7.de* merc b4.de* nat-c b4.de* *Nat-m* bg2* nit-ac bg2* nux-m bg2 **Nux-v** b7.de* petr b4.de* ph-ac b4.de* *Phos* b4.de* plb b7.de* podo ptk1 *Puls* b7.de* rhus-t b7.de* rumx ptk1 sabin b7.de* sars bg2 sel bg2 sep b4.de* sil b4.de* sulph b4.de* teucr b7.de* thuj b4.de* verat ptk1 viol-t b7.de* zinc b4.de*
  - **amel.**: (*↗Anger - eating - after - amel.; Anxiety - eating - amel.; Dullness - eating - amel.; Forgetful - eating - amel.; Irritability - eating - after - amel.; Sadness - eating - after - amel.*) *Anac* ptk1 apis b7a.de bov ptk1 calc-f mg1.de caust b4.de* cham ptk1 chel ptk1 con ptk1 dicha mg1.de fl-ac ptk1 goss st graph ptk1 hep ptk1 **Ign** ptk1 iod bg2* kali-bi ptk1 kalm ptk1 lach ptk1 mez b4.de* **Nat-c** ptk1 nat-m ptk1 petr bg2 phos b4.de* plb ptk1 psor ptk1 rad-br ptk1 rhod ptk1 sep ptk1 spong ptk1 tarent k2* valer ptk1 *Zinc* ptk1
- **before**: calc b4.de*
- **company**; in | **amel.**: aids nl2•
- **desire** to | **hands**; with the: plut-n srj7•
- **feces** (See Feces - swallows)
- **fed**, desire to be: aids nl2•
- **greedily** (See Bulimia)
- **hunger**; without: calad ptk1 olib-sac wmh1
- **more** than she should (See Bulimia)
- **refuses** to eat: (*↗Anorexia nervosa; Indifference - eating - to; Insanity - eating - refuses; Nursed - aversion*) anac ptk1 ant-c ↓ apis hr1 ars astra-m br1 bar-c ptk bell *Borx* kr1* carc mlr1• caul st caust *Chin* mtf33 cocc croc des-ac rbp6 grat hell ptk1 **Hyos** k* *Ign* kali-bi hr1 kali-br gk (non:kali-chl a1*) **Kali-m** k* kali-p lach k2 malar jl2 morg-p pte* op paull kr1 **Ph-ac** k* *Phyt* k* plat puls *Rhus-t* hr1 sep spong fd4.de stann ↓ sulph dx1* **Tarent** k* **Verat** k* **Viol-o** k* zinc-chr ptk1*
  - **alternating** with | **bulimia** (See Bulimia - alternating - refusal - insanity)
  - **asked**; eats only when: ant-c ptk1
  - **children**; in:
    - **birth** trauma; after: (*↗GENERALS - History - birth*) borx mtf33
    - **nurslings** | **vomiting**; after: ant-c mtf33
  - **fear** of becoming ill; for: malar jl2
  - **weakness**; from: bar-c ptk1 stann ptk1
- **spoon**; cannot eat with a: bell a1
- **when**:
  - **agg.**: aur bg2 cann-xyz bg2 carb-v bg2 caust bg2 cocc bg2 coloc bg2 hep bg2 kali-c b4.de* lyc bg2 mag-m b4.de* merc b4.de* mez bg2 nux-v bg2 olnd b7.de* ph-ac b4.de* plat b4.de* ran-b b7.de* sep bg2 sul-ac bg2 sulph bg2
  - **amel.**: aids nl2• anac ptk aur b4.de* bell ↓ caust bg2 galeoc-c-h gms1• **Goss** vh* grat bg2 *Iod* vh* kali-bi bg2 *Phos* vh* *Sep* vh* tarent ↓
    - **little**: bell k2* tarent ptk1

ECCENTRICITY: (*↗Affectation; Capriciousness; Extravagance; Mirth; Queer; Strange*) aesc a1 agar ↓ agn a1 alco a1 am-c j5.de* ambr gl1.fr• ang j5.de *Anh* vh* apis hr1 apoc ↓ ara-maca sej7• arg-n hr1* ars ↓ ars-h hr1* *Asar* j5.de* asc-t hr1* *Bell* a1* *Cann-i* a1* caps ckh1 caust ptk1 coff hr1* coff-t a1 con ptk1* cub hr1* cupr j5.de* cupr-act kr1 cupr-ar a1 cycl hr1* dendr-pol sk4• form a1 glon sf1.de hoit jl3 hyos a1 iodof hr1* kali-c jl3 lac-ac a1 **Lach** hr1* lact j5.de loxo-recl bnm10• lyss a1 **Med** mrr1 muru a1 nitro-o a1 nux-v gl1.fr• *Op* a1* pall sf1.de petr j5.de* plat sf1.de puls ↓ raja-s jl3 sang a1 sel ↓ sep hr1* spig j5.de stram j5.de* sul-ac j5.de* sulph a1 sumb a1* *Tarent* hr1* teucr a1* thea a1 valer j5.de* verat k* verat-v hr1* verb j5.de zinc mtf [tax jsj7]
- **evening**: asc-t hr1* teucr a1*
- **night**: op a1

- **alternating** with:
  - **contemptuousness** | **self**, of: agn j5.de
  - **sadness**: petr j5.de* *Stram* hr1*
  - **timidity**: sul-ac j5.de
- **chorea** with: *Cupr* hr1* *Cupr-act* kr1 sumb hr1*
- **epilepsy**; before: *Cann-i* kr1
- **fancies**, in: agar h2* apoc a1 arg-n hr1* glon sf1.de lact a1 pall sf1.de plat sf1.de *Verat-v* hr1*
- **metrorrhagia**, after: *Sep* hr1*
- **political**: *(↗Discuss - political; Politics)* ars gl1.fr• caust mrr1* lach gl1.fr•
- **religious**: *(↗Religious - too)* puls gl1.fr• stram gl1.fr• sulph h2 verat gl1.fr• [sel stj2]

ECSTASY: *(↗Ailments - joy - excessive; Excitement; Exhilaration; Joy; Loquacity - ecstasy; Sentimental)* **Acon** k* aether a1 *Agar* k* agn k* am-c k* androc srj1• ang k* *Anh* mg1.de* *Ant-c* k* apis bg2 arn k* astra-e jl3 bell k* berb sf1.de bry k* camph cann-i k* *Cann-s* bg *Cann-xyz* bg2 canth bg2 carb-v ↓ carbn-h castm sf1.de cham k* chin ↓ *Cic* cinnb ↓ coca a1 *Cocc* *Coff* k* croc bg2* crot-h cupr k* cupr-am-s a1 cur cypr k* dream-p ↓ ery-a a1 falco-pe nl2• fl-ac a1 galla-q-r nl2• hyos k* ign bg2 iod a1* irid-met srj5• jatr-c k* keroso c1* kres mg1.de* *Lach* k* laur ↓ lyss kr1 m-arct b2.de maias-l hrn2• myos-a rly4• *Neon* srj5• nit-ac ↓ nitro-o a1 nux-m olnd k* *Op* k* ph-ac k* **Phos** k* pic-ac ↓ plat k* plb *Podo* fd3.de* puls bg2 sabad ↓ sal-fr sle1• sel bg2 senec ↓ sil bg2 stann b2.de* staph bg2 stram k* sulph ↓ sumb a1 thea tritic-vg fd5.de tung-met bdx1• valer k* verat b2.de* vero-o rly4•

- **morning** | **waking**; on: crot-h a1 maias-l hrn2•
- **night**: **Ant-c** ↓ cur k* *Cypr* ↓ verat ↓
  - **waking**, on: *Cypr* verat gk
  - **walking** in moonlight: *(↗Moonlight)* **Ant-c** k*
- **alternating** with | **sadness**: senec
- **amorous**: *(↗Amorous)* ant-c h2 dream-p sdj1• op k* phos ↓ pic-ac k* thea a1
  - **sleep**, during: phos k*
- **chill**; during: *Acon* bg2 bell bg2 lach bg2 op bg2 *Phos* bg2 stram bg2
- **heat**, during: chin *Cic* hr1 coff laur puls sabad
- **joy**, as after excessive: lach a1 maias-l hrn2•
- **periodical**: *Cic* hr1*
  - **twice** a day; seems to be dying: *Cic* kr1
- **perspiration**; during: carb-v iod nit-ac sulph
- **rainbow** arches at her feet; as: maias-l hrn2•
- **sublime**: crot-h a1 lach a1
- **walking** in open air; on: *(↗Moonlight)* cinnb a1 falco-pe nl2•

ECSTATIC (See Absorbed; Ecstasy)

EFFEMINATE: calc vh* fl-ac sne lyc vh* *Plat* vh* **Puls** vh* sil vh* [heroin sdj2]

EFFICIENT, organized: *Lac-e* hrn2* [heroin sdj2]

- **clutter**; bothered by: lac-e hrn2•
- **compensation** for mental confusion; must be: lac-e hrn2•

EGOCENTRIC (See Egotism)

EGOISM (See Selfishness)

EGOTISM: *(↗Delusions - appreciated; Dictatorial; Envy; Haughty; Helping - aversion; Loquacity - self-satisfied; Self-indulgent; Selfishness; Talking - others; Talking - pleasure; Vanity)* act-sp kr1 *Agar* ↓ alco a1 *Alum* anac sf1.de anan kr1 androc srj1• anh sp1 aq-mar rbp6 arn gl1.fr• aster sze10• aur sf1.de* aur-m-n wbt2• *Aur-s* wbt2• bufo cda *Calc* cic ↓ cich mtf11 cimic kr1 cur a1 des-ac jl1* dream-p sdj1• eric-vg mtf11 fl-ac mrr1 granit-m es• hydrog srj2*• ignis-alc es2• ina-i mlk9.de *Iod* lac-leo sk4• *Lach* k* lith-f mtf *Lyc* sf1.de* marb-w es1• *Med* k* merc nicc-met sk4• *Nux-v* bg2* *Pall* k* par j5.de phos bn **Plat** k* plb mrr1 positr nl2• ribo rly4• sal-fr sle1• sal-l mtf11 senec bg3* *Sil* staph gl1.fr• stram sf1.de *Sulph* k* taosc iwa1• *Verat* sf1.de* [tax jsj7]

- **children**; in: lach mtf33
- **inferior**; others are (See Delusions - inferior)
- **nymphomania**, in: *Agar* kr1
- **overestimation** of himself: cic ptk*
- **reciting** their exploits: agar a1
- **speaking** always about themselves in company: lach mtf33* par j5.de staph mtf33*

EJACULATION; after: bov bg2 calc bg2 carb-an bg2 sil bg2

ELATED: *(↗Ardent; Exhilaration)* *Agath-a* nl2• aids nl2• caust ↓ chir-fl gya2 chlor hs coca a1* coff ↓ dream-p sdj1• dulc fd4.de ery-a a1 falco-pe nl2• fl-ac br1 haliae-lc srj5• hippoc-k szs2 hydrog srj2• iod a1* iodof a1* kali-p fck kali-s fd4.de merc-i-f sk• musca-d szs1 nux-m hs olib-sac wmh1 op a1* ox-ac hs ozone sde2• plat lsr plut-n srj7• podo fd3.de• *Ros-d* wla1 ruta fd4.de sal-al blc1• senec ↓ sinus rly4• *Sul-ac* ↓ teucr sfa valer a vanil fd5.de *Visc* sp [bell-p-sp dcm1]

- **morning**: cinnb ↓ crot-h ↓ hydrog srj2•
  - **waking**; on: crot-h a1*
  - **walking** in the open air: cinnb a1*
- **night**: hydrog srj2•
- **alternating** with | **sadness**: *(↗Exhilaration - alternating - sadness)* aids nl2• caust zr coff ptk1 hippoc-k szs2 senec a1* valer a1 visc sp [*Sul-ac* stj]

ELEGANCE: *(↗Pretty; Tasteful; GENERALS - Delicate)* chin mtf33 plat mtf33 *Sil* mrr1 verat mtf33

- **want** of elegance: *(↗Dress - indecently; Indifference - appearance; Indifference - external things; Tastelessness)* am-c vh* am-m vh* ars gl1.fr• calc ↓ caps vh* caust gl1.fr• lach gl1.fr• nat-c vh* nat-m vh* nux-v vh* plat ↓ sep gl1.fr• sil vh* sulph vh*
  - **women**; in: calc gl1.fr• nat-m gl1.fr• nux-v gl1.fr• plat gl1.fr• sil gl1.fr•

ELEVATION; mental (See Elated)

ELOQUENT: *(↗Loquacity; Speech - fluent)* cann-i a1 cann-s h1 lachn lp op a1

EMBARRASSED (See Timidity)

EMBARRASSMENT (See Ailments - embarrassment)

EMBITTERED: ambr b7.de* ang j5.de ars j aur-m-n wbt2* coloc b4a.de* ign gl1.fr• ilx-a mtf11 mang bg2* nit-ac bg2* phenob srb2.fr* puls gl1.fr• sal-l mtf11 seq-s bkh1* staphycoc rly4• stry mrr1 *Sulph* j5.de* valer k2* [am-c stj1 am-m stj1 am-s stj1]

- **children**: nit-ac mtf33
- **offenses**, from slight: ang a1

EMBRACES: *(↗Kissing)*

- **anything** in the morning, agg. in open air: plat
- **companions**, his: agar anac ↓ *Phos* hr1* plat k*
  - **hands**; his companions': agar anac
- **desire** to be embraced: rhus-g tmo3•
- **everyone**: *(↗Kissing - everyone)* agar ptk1 caps *Croc* k* hyos sf1.de kres mg1.de mand mg1.de* phos plat kr1* stram *Verat*
  - **alternating** with moroseness: croc
- **himself**: olib-sac wmh1
- **inanimate** objects, even: *(↗Delirium - embraces)* *Verat* hr1*
- **menses**; before: *(↗Menses - before)* *Verat* zinc
- **trees**; wants to embrace: ozone sde2•

EMOTIONAL excitement (See Ardent; Excitement)

EMOTIONS (= type of emotions): *(↗Theorizing)*

- **changeable**; quickly (See Mood - changeable - quickly)
- **dryness**: positr nl2•
- **excited** easily (See Ardent; Excitement)
- **loss** of: dioxi rbp6 lac-lup hrn2• **Nat-sil** fd* phasco-ci rbp2
- **predominated** by the intellect: *(↗Intellectual; Practical; Self-control - increased; Theorizing)* kali-c mtf33 lyc vh* nat-m mrr1 nit-ac ctm plb tl1* *Tritic-vg* fd5.de valer st* *Viol-o* b7a.de* [zinc stj1]
- **respiration**; with complaints of: *Acon* bg2 arg-n bg2 ars bg2 **Cham** bg2 coff bg2 **Ign** bg2 **Nux-v** bg2
- **spontaneous** and natural: limen-b-c hrn2•
- **strong**; too: dioxi rbp6
- **subdued** (See suppressed)
- **sudden**, hastens onset of chill: *Gels* kr1
- **suppressed**: *(↗Ailments - anger - suppressed; Ailments - domination - long)* aeth vh1* arge-pl rwt5• arizon-l nl2• aster sze10• carc sk1* caust h2* coff mrr1 cot br1 cupr sst3• des-ac rbp6 falco-pe nl2• *Glycyr-g* cte1• *Ign* mtf lath mrr1 lyc mtf mag-c mtf *Mag-m* mtf naja mtf nat-ar mrr1 nat-m mtf **Staph** vh* *Tritic-vg* fd5.de [heroin sdj2 mag-lac stj2 mag-met stj2 mag-sil stj2]
- **tenderness**; of (See Affectionate)
- **unclear** about one's feelings: **Dulc** fd*

- **voice**; with complaints of: hyos bg2 puls bg2

EMPTINESS of the mind; sensation of (See Delusions - emptiness)

ENCOPRESIS (See Dirty - urinating and - everywhere)

ENDANGERED; as if (See Delusions - danger)

ENEMY; considers everybody an (See Delusions - enemy - everyone)

ENERGIZED feeling: *Agar*↓ *Arn*↓ *Aur*↓ bit-ar wht1• *Fl-ac*↓ lac-h↓ **Lach**↓ *Lyss*↓ **Med**↓ nux-v↓ stram↓ tarent↓ verat↓ [temp elm1]
- **children**; in: *Agar* lmj *Arn* lmj *Aur* lmj *Fl-ac* lmj lac-h lmj **Lach** lmj *Lyss* lmj **Med** lmj nux-v lmj stram lmj tarent lmj verat lmj

ENNUI (= tedium): *(↗Disgust; Dullness; Ideas - deficiency; Indifference; Indifference - ennui; Loathing - life; Mental exertion - agg.; Mental exertion - aversion; Pessimist; Prostration; Thinking - aversion; Time - fritters; Wearisome; Weary; FACE - Expression - vacant; GENERALS - Lassitude; GENERALS - Lie - desire; GENERALS - Sluggishness; GENERALS - Weariness)* acon-ac rly4• agam-g mlk9.de *Alum* k* alumn ambr j amph a1 androc srj1• *Ant-c* bro1 arb-m oss1• arizon-l nl2• ars k2* aur k* bamb-a stb2.de• bar-c k* berb↓ borx cain calc k2 **Calc-p** mrr1 camph canth j *Caps*↓ carb-an j carc mlr1• cere-s a1 chin k* choc srj3• *Clem*↓ *Con* b4.de* croc j cupr cur cystein-l rly4• des-ac rbp6 dream-p sdj1• elaps ferr galeoc-c-h gms1• germ-met srj5• hippoc-k szs2 hura hydr k* hydrc *Hydrog* srj2• ign ip j irid-met srj5• kali-bi kali-br bro1 kali-i a1 kali-n k* kiss a1 lac-c bro1 lac-d bro1 *Lac-e* hrn2• lac-h htj1*• lach k* laur lavand-a ctl1• led bg2 **Lyc** b4.de* mag-c j* mag-m k* manc **Merc** vh* mez mosch j naja bro1 *Nat-c* k* nat-m j nat-s bro1 nat-sil fd3.de• nit-ac k2* *Nux-v* k* olib-sac wmh1 ozone sde2• paull a1 petr k* phasco-ci rbp2 phos bro1* pieri-b mlk9.de pip-m plat k* *Plb* b7.de* podo bro1* positr nl2• ran-b j rhus-t k* sal-fr sle1• sinus rly4• *Spig* gl1.fr• spira st1 spirae a1 sulph j* tab bro1 taosc iwa1• tarent *Thuj* bro1 tub k2* ven-m jl3 verat bro1 zinc k* [am-f stj2 aur-m stj2 aur-s stj2 heroin sdj2 lith-f stj2]
- **morning**: germ-met srj
- **forenoon**: alum hydrog srj2•
- **afternoon**: plb
- **evening**: mag-m h2
- **entertainment** amel.: *(↗Occupation - amel.)* aur lil-t *Pip-m*
- **homesickness**, with: alum vh* *Caps* st* *Clem* st des-ac rbp6
- **laziness**; with: *Bamb-a* stb2.de•
- **menses**, during: *(↗Menses - during)* berb kr1
- **silent**: nat-sil fd3.de• *Plb* vh*
- **sitting** at writing: lyc a

ENTERTAINMENT (See Excitement; Occupation)

ENTHUSIASM (See Ardent)

ENVIRONMENTAL orientation (See Orientation)

ENVY: *(↗Avarice; Egotism; Envy - hate; Insanity - envy; Jealousy; Sadness - happy; Selfishness; Slander)* *Am-c* gl1.fr• am-m↓ anac bg2 *Apis* bg2 aran-ix mtf arg-n sne **Ars** k1* aur-m-n wbt2• aur-s wbt2• bry calc camph bg2 cench k2 *Chin*↓ cub cur germ-met srj5• hell helon↓ **Hyos** bg2* ign bg2 ilx-a mtf11 kola stb3• *Lach* bg2* lil-t k* lyc k* marb-w es1• nat-c nat-m↓ nit-ac↓ nux-v bg2* *Pall* sne ph-ac↓ *Plat* mtf33* **Puls** k ●* rhus-t↓ sacch sht• sarr sep spig gl1.fr• stann↓ *Staph* k* sulph gl1.fr• tarent mtf thres-a↓ tritic-vg fd5.de zinc a1 [am-p stj1]
- **avidity**, and: *(↗Greed)* *Ars* sf1.de* *Chin* mtf33* lyc sf1.de nit-ac gl1.fr• nux-v gl1.fr• ph-ac gl1.fr• *Puls* j5.de* rhus-t gl1.fr• sep sf1.de stann gl1.fr• staph gl1.fr• sulph gl1.fr•
- **happy**; seeing other people: hell a* helon ptk1 tritic-vg fd5.de
- **hate**, and: *(↗Envy; Hatred)* am-c vh* am-m gl1.fr• calc vh* nat-c vh* nat-m mtf* nit-ac gl1.fr• puls vh*
- **qualities** of others, at: ars st1 calc st1 kola stb3• lach st1* lyc st1 puls st1 sulph st1 thres-a sze7•

EPILEPSY; after (See Convulsions)

EPISTAXIS:
- **agg.**: con bg2
- **amel.**: borx bg2* kali-chl bg2

ERETHISM (See Irritability; Sensitive)

ERGASIAPHOBIA (See Fear - responsibility)

EROTIC (See Amorous)

ERRATIC (See Eccentricity; Mood - changeable)

ERUCTATIONS: | **amel.**: arg-n bg2 bry bg2 sang bg2 sumb bg2

ERUPTIONS; mental symptoms after suppressed: *Ail* a1 anac bg2 ant-c bg2 *Apis* hr1 arn bg2 *Ars* b4a.de* asaf ptk bar-c k13 bell b4a.de* *Calc* kr1 caust bg2* cupr bg2 fl-ac bg2 *Hep* hr1 hyos bg2 ign bg2 lach bg2 *Lyc* bg2* nux-v bg2 ph-ac b4a.de phos bg2 *Psor* hr1* sep bg2 stram k13 *Sulph* b4a.de* verat bg2 *Zinc* bg2*

ESCAPE, attempts to: *(↗Approached - aversion; Delirium - escapes; Fear - escape; Hiding - himself; Home - leave; Insanity - escape; Jumping - bed; Runs)* acon k* adam↓ *Aesc* aeth↓ *Agar* agar-st a1 alco a1 all-s alum↓ am-c↓ ambr tsm1 androc srj1• anh↓ arg-n↓ *Ars* k* ars-met arum-t *Aur*↓ bapt bar-c **BELL** b4.de* *Bry* k* calc-sil↓ camph caust k* cham chel bg2* chin k* chlor choc srj3• cic k* *Cocc* k* coloc k* crot-c sk4• *Crot-h* k* *Cupr* k* cupr-ar↓ dendr-pol sk4• *Dig* k* dulc fd4.de falco-pe↓ gels↓ germ-met srj *Glon* k* haliae-lc srj5• hell hydrog↓ **Hyos** k* ign ignis-alc es2• ina-i mlk9.de iod bg2 irid-met srj5• kali-br bg2* kali-m↓ kola stb3• lac-e↓ lac-h↓ lac-leo sk4• *Lac-lup* hrn2• lach k* lath mrr1 lil-t limest-b es1• loxo-recl knl4• lyc bg2 meli merc k* merc-c k* mez bg2* nat-sil↓ *Nux-v* k* *Oena* olib-sac wmh1 *Op* k* oper br1 ozone sde2• petr-ra shn4• *Ph-ac* b4a.de phasco-ci rbp2 phos k* plat↓ plb k* *Positr* nl2• puls k* ran-b rhus-t k* rib-ac jl3 *Sal-fr* sle1• samb *Sep*↓ sol-ni spong fd4.de *Staph*↓ *Stram* k* sul-ac k* sulph k* *Thuj* b4a.de tub valer bg2 *Verat* k* verat-v↓ zinc k* zinc-p k2
- **night**: merc a1*
- **alternating** with:
  - **stupor**: *Coloc* kr1
  - **unconsciousness**: *Coloc* kr1
- **angles** of; looking for: lac-lup hrn2•
- **anxiety** at night, with: bell kr1 hyos kr1 *Merc* kr1
- **children**; in: cupr mtf33 op mtf33 verat mrr1
- **crime**, for a fear of having committed a: *(↗Anxiety - conscience)* *Merc* k*
- **delirium**; during: *(↗Delirium - escapes)* acon bro1 *Agar* bro1 alco a1 bell a* bry br1* *Coloc*↓ *Cupr* kr1* dig a2 hell bro1 hyos br1* merc a1 oena a1 op bro1 oper bro1 phos a1 rhus-t br1* *Stram* a* sul-ac a verat a*
  - **abortion**; in: *Coloc* kr1
- **delusions**; during: ars kr1 *Hyos* hr1 merc a1 op bg2 puls bg2
- **dreams**; in a world of: anh jl lac-h sze9•
- **family** and children; attempts to escape from her: *(↗Aversion - children; Children - flies; Estranged - children; Estranged - family; Forsaking - children; Indifference - children; towards - mother; Indifference - family; Responsibility - aversion)* adam srj5• am-c pc* choc srj3• falco-pe nl2• lac-e hrn2• lyc k* nat-sil fd3.de• nux-v pc* phasco-ci rbp2 phos pc* positr nl2• *Sep* pc* staph pc* [plat stj2]
- **fever**, during: *Chlor* kr1 *Coloc* j5.de* *Hell* kr1 *Op* kr1 **Rhus-t** hr1
- **house**; wants to get out of the: falco-pe↓ germ-met srj merc↓ *Verat* hr1*
  - **fright**; after: falco-pe nl2• merc kr1
- **jumps** up suddenly from bed: *(↗Bed - aversion; Bed - jumps; Delirium - bed - escapes; Jumping - bed)* *Ars* bg2 bell chin *Crot-h* kr1 glon hyos↓ nux-v **Rhus-t** bg2* *Verat* kr1
  - **change** beds, to: **Ars** hyos
- **mania** puerperalis, in: *(↗Insanity - puerperal)* *Stram* kr1
- **meningitis** cerebrospinalis, in: *Verat* kr1 verat-v mtf
- **pregnancy**; during: *Bar-c* kr1 *Puls* kr1
- **restrained** with difficulty, is: *Stram* kr1 zinc
- **run** away, to: alum k2 bar-c kr1 *Bell* k* bry chel bg1* *Cupr* dig falco-pe nl2• glon hydrog srj2• hyos kola stb3• meli br1 *Merc* kr1 mez tl1* nux-v op ozone sde2• positr nl2• rhus-t sal-fr sle1• *Verat* k*
  - **hide** as she insists that everyone is looking at her; and: meli c1
  - **mania**; in: bell lpc cupr lpc dig lpc nux-v lpc verat lpc
- **shrieking**, with: stram kr1
- **society**, from: cic h1 kali-m ckh1
- **strategy**; concern about: lac-lup hrn2•
- **street**; into: agar-st a1 bell a1 *Hyos* kr1 op a1
  - **gesticulating** and dancing in their shirts: *Bell* kr1

- **surrounded** and captured from men; as if: *Hyos* kr1
- **throw** himself into the river; tries to: *Hell* kr1
- **vigilance** of friends; avoids the: *Chlor* kr1
- **visit** his daughter; wants to: ars
- **waking**; on: *Cupr-act* kr1 cupr-ar kr1 *Staph* ↓
  - **children**: *Staph* kr1
- **window**, from: *(↗Suicidal - throwing - windows)* *Aesc* aeth ptk arg-n ptk *Aur* ptk *Bell* bry calc-sil st1 camph ptk gels ptk glon valer

ESTRANGED: *(↗Approached - aversion; Delusions - family)* aids nl2• am-c ↓ anac ↓ aq-mar ↓ arn ↓ ars ↓ *Aster* ↓ choc ↓ cimic ↓ con ↓ cycl ↓ cypra-eg ↓ dendr-pol ↓ dream-p ↓ dulc ↓ falco-pe ↓ granit-m ↓ hep ↓ hipp ↓ hydrog ↓ irid-met ↓ kali-s ↓ lac-e ↓ lac-h ↓ *Lach* ↓ *Lil-t* ↓ limest-b ↓ lyc ↓ melal-alt ↓ *Nat-c* ↓ *Nat-m* ↓ nat-s ↓ nat-sil ↓ *Nit-ac* ↓ nux-v ↓ phasco-ci ↓ phos ↓ plat ↓ plut-n ↓ positr ↓ psor ↓ *Puls* ↓ rhus-g tmo3• ribo ↓ sanguis-s ↓ *Sep* ↓ spect ↓ spong ↓ staph ↓ *Sulph* ↓ ther ↓ *Tritic-vg* fd5.de *Vanil* ↓ *Verat* ↓ [bell-p-sp dcm1 berb stu1]

- **children**; flies from her own: *(↗Aversion - children - sadness; Escape - family; Forsaking - children; Indifference - children; towards - mother; Neglecting - children; Responsibility - aversion)* falco-pe nl2• lyc
- **convulsions**; during: cimic kr1
- **cut**-off; feels: dendr-pol sk4•
- **family**; from his: *(↗Approached; Avarice - generosity; Aversion - family; Children - flies; Company - desire; Delusions - belong to; Escape - family; Forsaking - children; Indifference - family; Irritability - family; Love - friends; Mocking - relatives)* am-c gl1.fr• anac arn c1 ars choc srj3• con dream-p sdj1• falco-pe nl2• hep hydrog srj2• lac-e hrn2• limest-b es1• lyc ↓ *Nat-c* *Nat-m* nat-s nat-sil fd3.de• *Nit-ac* nux-v gl1.fr• phasco-ci rbp2 phos plat plut-n srj7• positr nl2• psor k2* puls ↓ *Sep* k* staph gl1.fr• *Tritic-vg* fd5.de verat ↓ [bell-p-sp dcm1]
  - **strangers**, but not with his entourage and his family; being kind with: *(↗Aversion - family - others; Behavior - children - home)* lyc mtf33* nux-v gl1.fr• puls gl1.fr• verat gl1.fr•
- **friends** and relatives: *(↗Indifference - loved)* aids nl2• granit-m es1• hydrog srj2• kali-s fd4.de lac-h sk4• nat-c k2 ribo rly4• spong ↓ *Tritic-vg* fd5.de [spect dfg1]
  - **forgetful** of (See Memory - weakness - family)
  - **ignores** his: spong fd4.de
- **husband**; from her: aids nl2• falco-pe nl2• nat-c hr1
- **menopause**; during: *Aster* st cycl st hipp st *Lach* st *Lil-t* st *Puls* st *Sep* st *Sulph* st ther st *Verat* st
- **self**, from: aq-mar rbp6 falco-pe nl2• **Tritic-vg** fd* *Vanil* fd5.de
- **society**, from: *(↗Antisocial)* anac choc srj3• cypra-eg sde6.de• dream-p sdj1• dulc fd4.de falco-pe nl2• limest-b es1• positr nl2• sanguis-s hrn2• *Vanil* fd5.de
- **wife**, from his: ars falco-pe nl2• irid-met srj5• melal-alt gya4 nat-s phasco-ci rbp2 plat staph [bell-p-sp dcm1]

EUPHORIA: *Agar* vh1 *Agath-a* nl2• androc srj1• ange-s jl anh sp1 aran-ix sp1* arge-pl rwt5• asar jl3 aster ↓ chloram jl3 choc srj3• cob-n sp1 cortiso jl3 dulc fd4.de ephe-si hsj1• falco-pe nl2• galla-q-r nl2• germ-met srj5• haliae-lc srj5• hippoc-k szs2 irid-met srj5• kola stb3• kres mg1.de* lac-h sze9• lac-loxod-a hrn2• limest-b es1• mand ↓ mang-p rly4• marb-w es1• meph ↓ myos-a rly4• nat-pyru rly4• nept-m lsd2.fr nid ↓ *Olib-sac* wmh1 onop ↓ ozone sde2• palo jl3 phasco-ci rbp2 podo fd3.de• pyrid rly4• ros-d wla1 sacch-a fd2.de• sinus rly4• suis-hep rly4• suis-pan rly4• suprar rly4• thyr jl3 tritic-vg fd5.de tung-met bdx1• vanil fd5.de [heroin sdj2 spect dfg1]

- **alternating** with:
  - **despair** (See Despair - alternating - euphoria)
  - **indifference** (See Indifference - alternating - euphoria)
  - **quarreling** (See Quarrelsome - alternating - euphoria)
  - **quiet**; desire for: asar jl
  - **sadness**: *(↗Excitement - alternating - sadness; Mania - alternating - depression)* asar jl3 aster jl cortiso jl3 *Dulc* fd4.de hippoc-k szs2 mand jl3 meph jl nid jl onop jl podo fd3.de• [heroin sdj2]
  - **weariness**: lac-loxod-a hrn2•
- **anesthesia** by chloroethylene; with feeling of lightness as after: asar jl
- **dinner**; after: ozone sde2•
- **driving**, while: haliae-lc srj5•

Euphoria – **driving**, while: ...

  - **high** speed; at: haliae-lc srj5•
- **lightness**; feeling of: hippoc-k szs2
- **out**; when going: ozone sde2•

EVADING: | **look** of other persons; the (See Looked - evading)

EXACT (See Censorious/ Conscientious)

EXACTING; too (See Fastidious)

EXAGGERATING: agar ptk1* asaf ↓ bufo ↓ calc ptk1* calc-f ↓ cann-i ckh1 cann-xyz ptk1 cham ↓ flav jl2 iob ↓ lyc mtf33 naja ↓ onos ptk1* plat tl1* plb ↓ positr nl2• stram ptk1* v-a-b ↓ [gent-am rcb1]

- **symptoms**; her: agar dgt1 asaf ptk1* bufo ptk1 calc-f dgt1 cham ptk1* flav jl2 iob mrr1 naja mrr1 plb ptk1* v-a-b jl2

EXALTATION (See Exhilaration)

EXAMINATION FEAR (See Fear - failure - examinations)

EXASPERATED (See Embittered)

EXCITEMENT: *(↗Ailments - excitement; Ailments - excitement - emotional; Alcoholism - excitement; Anxiety - excitement; Ecstasy; Mirth; Restlessness; Sensitive - excitement; Starting; Vivacious; Witty; ABDOMEN - Apprehension; BLADDER - Apprehension; CHEST - Apprehension; COUGH - Nervous; FACE - Discoloration - red - excitement; STOMACH - Apprehension)* abies-n ↓ abrom-a ↓ abrot absin a1* acet-ac acetan vh1 **Acon** k* adam srj5• aeth aether a1 agar k* agar-st a1 *Agath-a* nl2• agav-t jl3 agn k* *Aids* nl2• alf ↓ aloe ↓ alum k* alum-p k2 alum-sil k2 alumn k* am-c k* am-caust ↓ *Am-m* ↓ *Am-pic* ↓ *Am-val* ↓ ambr k* aml-ns vh1 ammc amyg ↓ **Anac** k* anag kr1 anan kr1 *Androc* srj1*• ang k* *Anh* mg1.de* ant-c k* ant-s-aur ↓ ant-t k* anthraci kr1 anthraco ↓ antip vh1 ap-g ↓ *Apis* k* apoc k2 aqui ↓ arg-met bg2* **Arg-n** k* arizon-l nl2• *Arn* k* *Ars* k* *Ars-h* *Ars-i* ars-s-f k2 art-v arum-t k2* *Asaf* k* *Asar* k* aspar ↓ aster atha ↓ atp rly4• atra-r bnm3• atro a1 **Aur** k* aur-ar k2 *Aur-i* k2 *Aur-m* *Aur-m-n* wbt2• **Aur-s** k2 aven ↓ bad sf1.de bamb-a stb2.de• bapt bg2 bar-act ↓ **Bell** k* bell-p jl3 ben-n a1 benz-ac berb ↓ bit-ar wht1• bond ↓ bor-ac ↓ borx bg2* bov ↓ brom k2 *Bruc* j5.de brucel sa3• *Bry* k* bufo k2* bung-fa mtf but-ac ↓ *Cact* ↓ calad *Calc* k* calc-ar calc-br ↓ *Calc-p* *Calc-s* calc-sil k2 *Camph* k* camph-br c1 *Camph-mbr* ↓ *Cann-i* k* *Cann-s* b2.de* cann-xyz ↓ canth k* caps k2 carb-ac a1 carb-an h2 carb-v k* carbn-h ↓ *Carbn-s* *Carc* mlr1• *Carl* carneg-g rwt1• cartl-s rly4• castm bg2* caul k2 **Caust** k* *Cean* ↓ cedr c1* ceph a1 **Cham** k* *Chel* *Chin* k* chinin-ar chinin-s chlf a1 chlol br1 chlor a1 choc srj3• *Cic* k* *Cimic* bg2* cina ptk1 cinnb ↓ cist k2 cit-v a1 clem k* *Cob* k* cob-n sp1* coc-c ↓ coca bro1 coca-c sk4• cocain bro1 cocc k* *Coch* kr1 **Coff** k* coff-t a1 coffin ↓ colch b2.de* **Coll** coloc k* con convo-s sp1* cop ↓ *Corh* ↓ cori-r a1 cortiso ↓ cot ↓ crat br1 croc k* crot-h k* cryp a1 cub *Cupr* k* cupr-act ↓ cupr-ar sf1.de cycl k* cypr c1 cyt-l mg1.de* *Daph* dendr-pol sk4• *Dig* k* digin a1 diosm ↓ dol ↓ dros b2.de* dubo-m a1 dulc fd4.de *Dys* ↓ elaps elec c1 eucal k* eup-a ↓ eup-per falco-pe ↓ *Ferr* k* ferr-ar ferr-i *Ferr-p* fic-m gya1 fl-ac k* foll ↓ form fum ↓ gaert bh* galeoc-c-h gms1• gard-j vlr2• gast ↓ *Gels* k* *Glon* k* glyc ↓ goss ↓ gran granit-m ↓ **Graph** k* guar kr1* guare a1 haliae-lc srj5• ham k2 hedeo ↓ hell k* helo-s bnm14• helon ↓ hep bg2* hipp hippoc-k szs2 hir rsj4• hoit jl3 hura hydr-ac j5.de hydrog ↓ **Hyos** k* hyosin c1* *Hyosin-hbr* ↓ hyper iber a1 *Ign* k* indg br1 indol ↓ *Iod* k* irid-met srj5• jab ↓ jug-r *Kali-ar* kali-bi k* **Kali-br** kali-c k* **Kali-i** kali-m k2 kali-n ↓ *Kali-p* k* *Kali-s* kali-sil k2 kalm ↓ kola stb3• kreos k* kres mg1.de **Lac-c** lac-h sze9• lac-lup hrn2• **Lach** k* lachn lapa a1 lappa a1 lat-m bnm6• lath mrr1 laur k* lavand-a ctl1• *Lec* k* lil-t k* limest-b es1• *Lith-c* k* lob a1 *Lol* sf1.de loxo-lae bnm12• loxo-recl bnm10• *Lup* br1 *Lyc* k* *Lycps-v* lyss k* m-ambo b2.de* m-arct b2.de* m-aust ↓ mag-c c2 *Mag-m* mag-p mrr1 mag-s malar jl2 mand a1 mang k2 mate a1 *Med* ↓ medul-os-si ↓ meny b2.de* meph k* *Merc* k* merc-c k* *Merc-cy* br1* merc-d a1 merc-i-f ↓ merc-p j merl meth-ae-ae a1 *Mez* bg2 mill mim-p rsj8• moni ↓ morg ↓ morph a1* **Mosch** k* mur-ac k* *Murx* ↓ mygal sf1.de myos-a rly4• myric kr1 myrt-c ↓ *Naja* nat-ar *Nat-c* k* **Nat-m** k* nat-p nat-s k2 nat-sil k2 neon srj5• nep mg1.de nicc ↓ nicc-met ↓ nicc-s ↓ **Nit-ac** k* nit-s-d ↓ nitro-o ↓ *Nux-m* ↓ **Nux-v** k* oena a1 ol-j olib-sac wmh1 olnd ↓ **Op** k* ov ↓ ox-ac paeon pall k* palo jl3 par passi mtf11 paull bro1 pegan-ha tpi1• pert ↓ pert-vc ↓ *Petr* k* petr-ra ↓ **Ph-ac** k* phel ↓ phenob ↓ **Phos** k* phys bro1 physala-p bnm7• phyt ↓ pic-ac ↓ pin-s a1 pip-m a1* pisc bro1 plac rzf5• plac-s rly4• plan *Plat* k* plb bg2 plect a1 plut-n ↓ *Podo* positr nl2• prun j5.de *Psor* k* **Puls** k* pyre-p a1 pyrid ↓ pyrog ↓ rad-br ↓ ran-b k2 ran-s ↓ raph rauw sp1 reser jl3 rham-cal ↓ rheum rhod mrr1 rhodi ↓ rhus-t k* rob ↓ rumx k2 ruta b2.de* sabad k* sabal ↓ sabin ↓ sacch-a ↓ sacch-l c2 sal-ac sal-fr sle1• sal-n ↓ samb sang k* santin a1

Excitement: ...
saroth a1* *Sars*↓ scut c1 sec k* sel k* senec kr1* seneg k* *Sep* k* ser-a-c jl2 *Sil* k* sol bg2* sol-ni↓ spartin-s↓ *Spect*↓ *Spig* bg2* *Spong* k* *Stann* k* **Staph** k2* stict↓ *Stram* k* stront-c↓ **Stry** succ↓ *Sul-ac* k* sul-i k2 *Sulph* k* sumb k* symph fd3.de• syph↓ tab tanac↓ *Tarent* k* tela↓ tell temp↓ *Ter* a1* tere-ch jl3 *Teucr* k* *Thal* jl3 thal-xyz srj8• *Thea* k* ther bg2* thiop↓ *Thuj* k* thyr↓ thyreotr jl3 tril-c a1 tril-p trios↓ tritic-vg fd5.de tub *Tub-m*↓ ulm-c↓ uncar-tom mp4• v-a-b jl3* vac jl2 *Valer* k* vanil fd5.de *Verat* k* verat-v sf1.de verb k* vero-o rly3• vib↓ *Viol-o* b2.de* viol-t bg2 vip visc↓ voes a1 wildb↓ wye c2 xan c2 yohim bwa3* zinc b2.de* **Zinc-p** k2 zinc-val↓ ziz [am-f stj2 arg-p stj2 bell-p-sp dcm1 cadm-met stj2 cadm-s stj2 cob-m stj2 cob-p stj2 cupr-f stj2 fl-pur stj2 heroin sdj2 ind stj2 lith-i stj2 lith-met stj2 lith-p stj2 lith-s stj2 mang-i stj2 tax jsj7 thal-met stj2 zinc-i stj2]

- **morning**: aeth ars k* calc canth chin chinin-s choc srj3• con cop k* kalm lach k* *Lyc* k* mang k* nat-c nat-m k* nat-s *Nux-v* olib-sac wmh1 sep k* spong
- **forenoon**: aeth a1 chinin-s a1 elaps a1
- **noon**: bry a1 dulc fd4.de hura a1 sulph a1
- **afternoon**: aloe ang k* aspar a1 cann-i k* dulc fd4.de iod k* lyc k* nux-v hr1 phos a1 thiop jl3 tritic-vg fd5.de ulm-c↓ vanil fd5.de
  - **14** h: ulm-c jsj8•
- **evening**: agar am-c k* am-caust vh1 anac *Ang*↓ ant-c↓ arn↓ atha a1 *Aur*↓ borx↓ *Bruc* j5.de bry↓ *Calc* carb-an↓ carb-v k* caust↓ chel k* chin cocc↓ daph k* dulc fd4.de elaps a1 ferr ferr-p fl-ac k* graph k2* haliae-lc srj5• hyper jug-r↓ kali-c↓ kali-s k2* *Lach* laur↓ lyc k* lycps-v m-aust↓ *Merc*↓ mez k* mim-p rsj8• *Nat-m*↓ *Nit-ac*↓ *Nux-v* k* ox-ac k* phel k* phos positr nl2• *Prun*↓ *Puls* ran-b↓ ran-s↓ rhus-t↓ sabad↓ *Sep*↓ sil↓ spig↓ staph↓ sul-ac↓ *Sulph*↓ sumb k* teucr ther thiop jl3 tritic-vg fd5.de valer viol-t↓ zinc k*
  - **bed**, in: agar j *Ang* j5.de ant-c arn *Aur* borx bry j *Calc* carb-an k1 carb-v caust j chin j cocc j graph j jug-r a1* kali-c j lach laur lyc j5.de m-aust j5.de *Merc* mez *Nat-m* *Nit-ac* **Nux-v** *Phos* *Prun* j5.de *Puls* ran-b ran-s rhus-t sabad j *Sep* sil spig staph sul-ac *Sulph* viol-t j zinc
  - **thinking** of the things others have done to displease her: *(↗Dwells - thinking)* am-c
- **night**: agar j am-c k* ambr k* ammc a1 androc bnm2• ant-s-aur a1 *Apis* arg-n k* *Arn* hr1 ars-s-f hr1* *Aster* k* berb k* borx j bry j calc carb-an h2* carbn-h a1 carbn-s chel a1* chin j chlol hr1* coc-c↓ *Coff* con j cop hr1* cupr-ar sf1.de cypr vml3• dig k* *Ferr* k* fum rly1*• *Graph* k* haliae-lc srj5• hep j hura hyos j kali-br hr1* kali-c j kali-n j *Lach* laur j5.de loxo-lae bnm12• lyc m-arct j mez j5.de mosch j5.de nat-m nit-ac k* *Nux-v* op j ph-ac j plat j plect a1 *Puls* pyrid rly4• saroth mg1.de sep k* sil j spong j *Sulph* k* *Tarent* hr1* thea↓ ther c1 thuj k* zinc
  - **rushing** in ears, with: ther c1
  - **sleep**, during: lyc
  - **waking**, on: berb a1* coc-c k* thea a1 thuj
- **absent** persons, about: *(↗Anger - absent)* aur
- **agg.**: *Acon* bg2* agar sf1.de ambr bro1* aml-ns ptk1 anac sf1.de* arg-met sf1.de arg-n bg2* aur bro1* aur-m-n wbt2• bell ptk1 borx j5.de *Bry* ptk1 calc k2* carc mlr1• *Caust* sf1.de* **Cham** sf1.de* chin bro1 cist k2* cob a1* coch hr1 coff bro1* *Colch* bro1 coll hr1* **Coloc** bro1* con bro1* cupr-act bro1 dys fmm1• ferr sf1.de* *Gels* bro1* hyos bg2* **Ign** bro1* kali-c bg2* kali-p bro1 *Lach* ptk1 lyc bg2 lyss br1* nat-c bg2 nat-m bg2* nit-ac sf1.de nit-s-d bro1 **Nux-v** bro1* *Op* ptk1 *Pall* hr1* pert jl2 petr bro1 **Ph-ac** bro1* **Phos** bg2* phyt ptk1 plat bg2* psor ptk1 **Puls** ptk1 sel bg2 sep bg2* sil br1* spong hr1* stann sf1.de* *Staph* bro1* *Stram* ptk1 tub ptk1 verat ptk1 zinc bg2
- **agreeable**: carc mlr1• pip-m a1
- **ailments** from emotional excitement (See Ailments - excitement)
- **alcohol** amel.: coca-c sk4•
- **alternating** with:
  - **convulsions**: **Stram** k*
  - **delirium** (See Delirium - alternating - excitement)
  - **dementia** (See Dementia - alternating - excitement)
  - **dullness**: alum-p k2 anac moni rfm1• (non:tub lmj)
  - **idiocy**: aeth c1*
  - **indecision**: cortiso jl3
  - **indifference**: alum-p k2 ambr k2 cypr vml3• phenob srb2.fr sabad j5.de
  - **prostration** of mind: kali-c vh*
- **alternating** with: ...
  - **sadness**: *(↗Euphoria - alternating - sadness; Mania - alternating - depression)* ambr h1* aster a1* colch jl3 *Con* cortiso jl3 ferr-p k2 foll jl3 ox-ac k2 petr j phenob jl3 *Plb* kr1 rauw jl3 sul-ac j5.de thyreotr jl3
  - **sleep**; deep: phos a1
  - **sleepiness**: alum hr1 androc↓ *Kali-br* kr1
    - ⁝ **children**; in: androc bnm2•
  - **taciturnity** | **afternoon**: thiop jl
  - **unconsciousness**: *Kali-br* hr1*
  - **weakness**: granit-m es1• [bell-p-sp dcm1]
- **amel.**: *(↗Confusion - excitement; Idleness - agg.)* asaf vh aur aur-m-n wbt2• aur-s wbt2• falco-pe nl2• kali-p bro1 lil-t merc-i-f pall bro1 pert-vc vk9 *Pip-m* k* *Sep* vh*
- **amnesia**; followed by transient: agav-t jl1
- **anticipating** events, when: *(↗Ailments - anticipation; Anticipation)* *Arg-n* arizon-l nl2• *Carc* mlr1• *Dulc* fd4.de *Dys* fmm1• *Gels* haliae-lc srj5• hydrog srj2• med morg fmm1• symph fd3.de• vanil fd5.de
- **bad** news, after: *(↗Ailments - bad)* alumn hr1 *Apis* *Calc* *Calc-p* k* carc mlr1• chin cinnb cupr form **Gels** *Ign* kali-c kali-p lach nat-c nat-m *Phos* k* puls stram *Sulph*
- **bath**, during: gast a1
- **beer**, after: coc-c k* wildb c1
- **beside** oneself: plac rzf5•
- **cardiac** symptoms, with: crat br1
- **champagne**:
  - **as** after champagne: amyg↓ chlol a1 form a1
    - ⁝ **followed** by sudden unconsciousness: amyg kr1
- **children**, in: absin br1* aloe ptk1 ambr c1* carc mlr1• caust mrr1* hyosin c1 lat-m bnm6• loxo-lae bnm12• lyc c1 sep mrr1*
- **chill**:
  - **before**: *Cedr*
  - **during**: **Acon** k* ars k* *Asar* bro1 aur k* aur-ar k2 bell bg2 bry bg2 bufo bg2 calc k* cann-s bg cann-xyz bg2 canth caps k* carb-v k* caust *Cean* hr1* **Cham** k* cimic bro1 cocc bg2 **Coff** k* croc bro1 *Gels* bro1 goss bro1 *Hep* k* ign bg2 lach lyc k* *Nat-m* k* *Nux-v* k* phos k* puls sep bg2 spig k* sulph k* teucr bg2 verat k*
- **coffee**:
  - **after**: fic-m gya1
    - ⁝ **as** after: chin j5.de *Chinin-s* j5.de fic-m gya1 haliae-lc srj5• sulph j5.de valer j5.de
- **coition**, after: *Calc* k*
- **colors**:
  - **black** | **agg.**: sep vk4
- **company**, in: *(↗Cheerful - company; Company - desire)* ambr k2 irid-met srj5• kali-s fd4.de *Lec* k* *Pall* k* sal-fr sle1• *Sep* k*
- **confusion**, as from: choc srj3• nux-m k*
- **contradiction**, from slightest: *(↗Contradiction - intolerant)* *Ferr* kr1* spong fd4.de
- **conversation**, from hearing: *(↗Conversation - agg.)* ambr mrr1 *Lyss*
- **convulsions**:
  - **after**: agar-st a1
  - **with**: *Cic* hr1*
- **convulsive**: canth k* *Lyss*
- **cough** | **during**: cadm-s c1
- **crying**; till (See weeping)
- **dancing**, singing and weeping; with: tarent k2
- **darkness**; in: choc srj3•
- **debate**, during: *(↗Discuss - political)* *Caust* dulc fd4.de *Nit-ac*
- **desire** for: *(↗Amusement - desire)* carb-v mrr1 carc mrr1 cot a1 *Med* mrr1 nat-s mrr1 *Plat* mrr1 puls↓ **Tub** mrr1 [heroin sdj2]
  - **children**; in: puls ptk1
- **easily** excited: abrom-a ckh1 calc-s mtf33 carc mlr1• gard-j vlr2• ign tl1 kali-m ckh1 ther↓
  - **perspiration**; with cold: ther ptk1
- **eating**:
  - **after**: positr nl2•
  - **amel.**: bell k2 dulc fd4.de

- **epilepsy**; before: *Art-v* coff k2 *Indg* kr1
- **excretions**; from suppression of: acon gl1.fr• asaf sf1.de carc mlr1• merc sf1.de
- **exertion**, after: sulph h2
- **face**:
  - **cold** perspiration of; with: iber kr1
  - **heat** of, with: *(↗FACE - Heat - flushes - excitement)* aloe kr1
- **faintness**; with: cocc bg2 coff bg2 kali-c bg2 ph-ac bg2 *Verat* ptk1
- **fever**; during: **Acon** bg2 alum bg2 *Apis* b7a.de* **Bell** b4a.de* bry bg2 **Cham** bg2 cocc b7a.de* *Coff* b7a.de* **Con** b4.de* ign bg2 kali-c bg2 m-arct b7.de mag-c b4a.de* mosch bg2 *Nux-v* bg2 op bg2 *Petr* b4a.de* *Sars* bg2 stram bg2 **Teucr** b7.de* valer bg2
- **feverish**: ant-t k* aspar a1 bry a1 chlf k* chlor colch k* cub k* merc k* merc-c k* phos k* rhod ↓ sec k* seneg k* sep ↓ sul-i k* sulph ↓
  - **evening**: merc-c
  - **night**: sulph
  - **dinner**, after: sep k*
  - **menses**, during: *(↗Menses - during)* rhod k*
- **hairline**, short and bristly; from seeing: choc srj3•
- **headache**:
  - **before**: cann-i br1
  - **with**: crat br1
- ○ **Head**; with perspiration of: bamb-a stb2.de•
- **hearing** horrible things, after: *(↗Anguish - horrible; Anxiety - cruelties; Fear - cruelties; Horrible)* *Calc* carc mlr1• **Chin** k2* cic k2* cocc falco-pe nl2• gels ign *Lach* nat-c nux-v *Teucr* vanil fd5.de *Zinc* k*
- **heat**:
  - **during** heat; excitement: *(↗Blushing)* *Acon* bro1 alum anthraco kr1 *Apis* ars-h kr1 bell k2 cham kr1 chinin-s coff kr1 coff-t kr1 *Ferr* kali-c lach kr1 mag-c mosch op *Petr Rhus-t Sars* stram sulph tarent tela bro1 valer verat
    - **puerperal** heat: *Cham* kr1 coff kr1 *Lach* kr1
  - **from** excitement; heat: **Caps** kr1
  - ○ **Head**; with heat of: meph
- **hemorrhage**, after: *Chin* hr1*
- **hope**, as in joyous: aids nl2• *Aur* h2* choc srj3•
- **hungry**, when: kali-c
- **hurried**, as if: *(↗Hurry)* carb-v carc mlr1• coff **Dulc** fd* plut-n srj7• [fl-ac stj2]
- **hydrocephalus**, in: *Apis* kr1 *Carb-ac* hr1*
- **hysterical**: camph ↓ ign k2
  - **convulsions**; with: *(↗GENERALS - Convulsions - hysterical)* camph br1
  - **coryza**; during: ign b7a.de
- **intellectual**: guar vml3• *V-a-b* jl2
- **joy**, from: caust vh* **Coff** hr1* crot-h a1* plut-n srj7• puls vh* tritic-vg fd5.de
- **lascivious**, with painful nocturnal erections: *(↗Lascivious - erections - painful)* *Merc* kr1
- **leukorrhea**; after suppressed: asaf sf1.de
- **menopause**; during: arg-n sf1.de cimic sf1.de coff sf1.de glon sf1.de ign sf1.de lach sf1.de ov c2 phys kr1 ther sf1.de valer sf1.de zinc sf1.de
- **menses**:
  - **after**: *(↗Menses - after)* ferr k*
  - **before**: *(↗Menses - before)* alum-sil aur-m-n wbt2• croc *Kreos* k* *Lach* hr1* *Lyc* b4.de* mag-c mag-m k* nat-m sf1.de *Nux-v* rob k* sacch-a fd2.de• thuj k*
  - **during**: *(↗Menses - during)* caul sf1.de cimic cop k* ferr k* hyos sf1.de kreos sf1.de *Mag-m* k* *Nat-c* hr1* nat-m sf1.de puls k* rhod rob a1 senec *Tarent* k* verat sf1.de
  - **return** of menses; excitement brings: **Calc** kr1
- **mental** exertion; from: ambr c1 dulc fd4.de ind kali-p med nat-p kr2* tub bg
- **motions**, performed with uncontrollable zeal; quick and brusque: cit-v kr1
- **music**, from: *(↗Music - agg.)* *Aur* vh* carc mlr1• *Graph* vh* *Kreos* pall hr1* sumb k* *Tarent* k*
- **nervous**: *(↗Restlessness; Sensitive - nervous)* abies-n bro1 absin br1* **Acon** k* agar br1* alf br1* *Am-pic* br1 *Am-val* bro1 *Ambr* j5.de* aml-ns bro1 *Anac* bro1 ap-g bro1* apis bro1 aqui bro1 arg-n k* arn br1* *Ars* bro1 asaf bro1* *Asar* j5.de* aster br1 aur bro1* aven bro1 *Bell* bro1* bond a1 bor-ac mtf borx br1*
- **nervous**: ... bov bro1 brom mtf33 bry a1 bufo br1 but-ac bro1 calad k2 calc ↓ calc-br bro1 calc-p mtf33 camph-br c2* *Camph-mbr* bro1 caps ↓ carneg-g rwt1• *Castm* br1* caul ptk1* caust bro1* cedr br1* cham bro1* *Chin* ptk1* choc srj3• *Cimic* bro1* cina bro1 cinnb k* *Coca* bro1 cocain bro1 cocc ptk1* coff k2* coffin a1 colch rsj2• **Con** bro1* *Corh* br1 crat ↓ cupr bro1* cypr bro1 diosm br1 dol br1 *Dulc* fd4.de eup-a bro1 ferr bro1 ferr-p br1 fic-m gya1 gels bro1* glyc bro1 goss bro1* graph mrr1 haliae-lc srj5• hedeo br1* *Hell* ↓ helon bro1 *Hyos* br1* *Hyosin-hbr* bro1 iber br1* **Ign** br1* indol br1* iod j5.de* jab br1* kali-ar br1 *Kali-br* bro1 kali-c bro1 *Kali-p* hr1* lac-c bro1 **Lach** bro1* lat-m bnm6• *Lil-t* bro1* lup br1 mag-c bro1* mag-m ptk1* mag-p bro1* med br1* medul-os-si rly4• merc ptk1* morph bro1 *Mosch* ptk1* *Murx* ↓ mygal br1 myrt-c br1 nat-c k2* nat-m ptk1* nicc bro1 nicc-met br1 nicc-s br1 nit-ac ptk1* nitro-o a1 nux-m bro1* **Nux-v** br1* olib-sac wmh1 op bro1* ov bro1 passi br1 petr ↓ *Ph-ac* ↓ phos k* pic-ac ptk1* plac rzf5• *Podo* ↓ prun ptk1* psor bro1 **Puls** bro1* pyrog ptk1 rad-br ↓ rham-cal br1 rhod mrr1 rhodi br1 rhus-t ↓ sabad br1 sabal ptk1* sabin ↓ sal-n br1 santin bro1 scut ↓ sec bro1 senec br1* **Sep** bro1* sil br1* sol-ni ↓ spartin-s bwa2 spig ↓ staph bro1* stict br1* *Stram* bro1* stry k* succ br1 sul-ac k* *Sulph* ptk1 *Sumb* br1* syph mtf33 tanac br1 tarent k* ter ↓ teucr j5.de* thea k* ther bro1* thyr ptk1* trios br1* tritic-vg fd5.de *Tub* jl2* *Tub-m* jl2 v-a-b jl2 vac br1 valer k* vanil fd5.de *Verat* ptk1 vib ptk1* visc ptk1* wye br1 *Xan* br1* *Zinc* bro1* zinc-p bro1 zinc-val bro1* [temp elm1]
  - **children**; in: absin br1 agar mtf33 ambr br1 arg-n mtf33 borx br1 brom mtf33 calc-p mtf33 cypr br1 ign mtf33 syph mtf33 tub br1*
    - **intestinal** complaints; from: cypr br1
  - **chill**; during: bell bg2 calc bg2 chin bg2 coff bg2 *Con* bg2 nux-v bg2 phos bg2 rhus-t bg2 sep bg2 teucr bg2
  - **coryza**; with: *Acon* bg2 ign bg2 merc bg2 *Nux-v* bg2
  - **dentition**; from: **Acon** bg2* agar bro1 *Bell* bg2* borx bg2 cham bg2* cimic bro1 **Coff** bg2 cypr br1* dol bro1 *Hell* bro1 kali-br bro1 *Podo* bro1 sol-ni bro1 ter bro1 *Zinc* bro1
  - **explosive**: rad-br sze8• stry br1
  - **fever**; during: apis bg2 *Bell* b4a.de* caps bg2 *Cham* bg2 **Cocc** bg2 **Coff** bg2 **Con** bg2 kali-c bg2 *Nux-v* bg2 petr bg2 ph-ac bg2 sep bg2 **Teucr** bg2 valer bg2
  - **music**; from: sabin br1
  - **pain**; during: *Acon* ↓ am-val ↓ ars ↓ *Cham* ↓ *Coff* br1 crat ↓ gels ↓ *Mag-p* ↓ spig ↓
    - **cervical** region; in: crat br1
    - **occiput**; in: crat br1
    - **sciatic** nerve; in: *Acon* bro1 am-val bro1 ars bro1 *Cham* bro1 *Coff* bro1 gels bro1 *Mag-p* bro1 spig bro1
  - **paroxysmal**: mosch br1
  - **perspiration**; during: acon bg2 apis bg2 *Bell* bg2 caps bg2 **Cham** bg2 *Chin* bg2 *Coff* bg2 ferr bg2 kali-c bg2 **Nux-v** bg2 petr bg2 *Ph-ac* bg2 **Sep** bg2 sulph bg2 *Teucr* bg2 valer bg2 verat bg2
  - **rheumatic** complaints; with: *Cimic* br1
  - **women**; in: *Murx* br1 scut ptk1
  - ○ **Extremities**; with heaviness of: *Cimic* br1
  - **Ovaries**; with irritation of: *Cimic* br1
  - **teeth**; after extraction of: staph br1
  - ○ **Uterus**; with cramping pain in: *Cimic* br1
- **pain**, during: aloe k2 arg-met k2 *Aur* carc mlr1• cham k2 lat-m bnm6•
- **palpitation**, with violent: alum kr1* ambr k1 ars k1 *Asaf* k1 *Cact* kr1* calc k1 calc-ar k1* carc fd2.de• *Cocc* kr1* coff k1* *Lil-t* kr1* lith-c k1* *Nit-ac* kr1* ox-ac k1 *Plat* kr1* ruta fd4.de sacch-a fd2.de• stann k1 staph k1 stront-c k1
- **perspiration**, during: *Acon* k* *Bell* k* **Cham** k* *Cocc* k* **Coff** k* *Con* k* *Lyc* k* nux-v k* ph-ac k* *Sep* k* **Teucr** k*
- **pregnancy**, during: *Acon* hr1* ambr hr1* croc sf1.de *Gels* hr1* *Nux-m* hr1*
- **reading**, while: *(↗Reading - agg.)* *Coff* med ph-ac v-a-b ↓
  - **foreign** language, in: v-a-b srb2.fr
- **religious**: *(↗Exhilaration - religious; Religious - too)* agar a1 *Aur* plb hr1 *Verat* hr1* [tax jsj7]
- **sadness**, after: *(↗Sadness)* *Cann-i* sf1.de spig k*
- **sexual** (See Ailments - sexual excitement)
- **sleep**:
  - **before**: nat-m psor

- **preventing** (See SLEEP - Sleeplessness - excitement)
- **speech** stammering with: dys bh*
- **stammers** when talking to strangers: *(↗Stranger - presence - agg.)* dig k* dys fmm1• merc vh
- **stool**; after: *Nit-ac* b4a.de
- **swallows** continually while talking: *Staph* k1*
- **talking**, while: *(↗Speech - incoherent)* am-c k* *Am-m* k* ambr k* ammc a1 caust hr1* dulc fd4.de graph merc k* mosch ptk1* petr-ra shn4• [tax jsj7]
- **tea**, after: sulph
- **tea**; as if under the influence of: hyper a1*
- **teeth**; with complaints of: *Sep* b4a.de
- **tongue | mapped**; with: (non:calad vk1) phys hr1*
- **trembling**, with: aur a1 bruc j5.de **Cocc** hr1* dulc fd4.de lat-m bnm6• nitro-o a1 **Nux-v** hr1* petr j5.de* *Psor* st spig hr1* *Teucr* j5.de ulm-c jsj8• *Valer* j5.de yohim c1*
  - **inward**: petr hr1*
  - ○ **Intestines**: ulm-c jsj8•
  - **Nerves**; of: ulm-c jsj8•
- **trifles**, over: *(↗Frightened - trifles; Trifles; Trifles - important)* *Arg-met* vh1 bar-act a1 carl k* chinin-ar cinnb digin a1 ferr hr1* kali-s fd4.de lac-h sk4• lachn k* med morph st nit-ac phos sacch-a fd2.de• sep a1 spong fd4.de sul-ac k2* sumb st tarent a1 thuj mtf33 *Tritic-vg* fd5.de verat h1 zinc
- **urination**, during: aloe cimic ptk2
- **waking**, on: bell k2 coc-c k* *Merc* ↓ nat-m k* sep thuj
  - **frightened**, as if: *Merc* kr1
- **walking**:
  - **after**: caust k* fl-ac k* nat-m k*
  - **air**; in open: alum j5.de ant-c h2* caust ↓ choc srj3• sulph h2*
    - ⁝ **after**: caust h2
- **water** poured out, from hearing: *(↗Hydrophobia)* **Lyss** k* **Stram**
- **weakness**, with: *Calc* h2* caust gl1.fr• coff gl1.fr• *Con* hr1* *Phos* hr1* puls gl1.fr• tritic-vg fd5.de
- **weather**:
  - **windy** and stormy weather: carc mlr1• *Rhod* ↓ [*Spect* dfg1]
    - ⁝ **before**: *Rhod* mrr1
- **weeping**, till: carc mlr1• *Con* vh* *Lach* vh*
- **wine**:
  - **after**: ambr a1 cann-s a1 coff k2 con k2 iod a1 kali-n ↓
    - ⁝ **one** glass: kali-n c1
  - **as** from: camph hr1* chinin-s j5.de jug-r a1 kali-i lyc k* mosch k* naja valer j5.de
- **women**, in: cedr c1 con c1 ign c1*
- **working**, when: ang j *Dulc* fd4.de mur-ac olnd tritic-vg fd5.de
- **writing**, while: med

EXCLAIMING (See Shrieking)

EXCLUSIVE, too: *(↗Extravagance; Haughty)* calc vh* carc fd2.de• nat-m vh* plat vh* ruta fd4.de spong fd4.de

EXECUTION lost as the result of overpowering visual sensations: *(↗Absorbed; Fancies - absorbed)* anh sp1

EXERCISE; mental symptoms amel. by physical (See Exertion - physical - amel.)

EXERTION:

- **mental** (See Mental exertion)
- **physical**: *(↗GENERALS - Exertion)*
  - **after**: benz-ac bg2 iod bg2 kali-c bg2 sel bg2 spong b7.de* zinc bg2
  - **agg.**: agar bg2 ars bg2 calc bg2 calc-p bg2 caust bg2 cocc bg2 hyper bg2 nat-c b4.de* plb ptk1 senec bg2 sep bg2 sulph bg2 ther bg2 verat bg2
  - **amel.**: *(↗Activity - desires; Industrious; GENERALS - Activity - amel.; GENERALS - Exertion - amel.)* *Agar* mtf aloe sne bar-i mtf calc ptk1 *Calc-p* mtf carc fd2.de* *Iod* k* *Merc* mtf *Nat-sil* fd3.de• positr nl2• querc-r svu1• rad-br sze8• sacch-a fd2.de• spong fd4.de *Sulph* mtf tarent ptk1 vanil fd5.de
  - **aversion**: act-sp vh1 adam skp7• calc-sil k2 ham fd3.de• positr nl2• sacch-a fd2.de• vanil fd5.de
  - **desire**: *(↗Impulse - run)* agam-g mlk9.de *Agar* mtf **Bell** a1 *Calc-p* mtf cann-i a1 coca a1 crot-c a1 dulc fd4.de erech a1 eucal a1* galeoc-c-h gms1•

Exertion – physical – desire: ...
musca-d szs1 *Nat-sil* fd3.de• nicc-met ↓ olib-sac wmh1 orig a1* phos a1* podo fd3.de• polys mtf sacch-a fd2.de• *Sulph* mtf taosc ↓ teucr ↓ tritic-vg fd5.de vanil fd5.de ziz a1 [spect dfg1]
- ⁝ **air**; in open: galeoc-c-h gms1• *Nat-sil* fd3.de• sacch-a fd2.de• taosc iwa1• teucr a1
- ⁝ **but** walking is difficult: nicc-met sk4•

EXHAUSTED (See Prostration)

EXHIBITIONISM (See Naked - exhibitionism)

EXHILARATION: *(↗Ardent; Cheerful; Ecstasy; Elated; Jesting; Loquacity; Loquacity - cheerful; Mirth; Pleasure; Spaced-out; Vivacious; Wildness)* absin c1 acon k* aesc a1 aether a1 *Agar* k* agar-se a1 *Agath-a* nl2• agn k* agra a1 aids nl2• alco a1 alf br1 allox tpw3* alum alum-p k2 am-c k* anac ↓ anag k* androc ↓ ang a1 ant-c arg-met arg-n ↓ arizon-l nl2• arn j ars-h k* asar k* asc-t ↓ *Bell* k* bit-ar wht1• borx ↓ bov a1 calc-f sp1 camph k* **Cann-i** k* canth bro1* caps h1 carb-ac k* carb-an h2 carb-v h2 *Carbn-s* k* *Carc* mrr1* carneg-g rwt1• castm j5.de caust j5.de chel k* chin h1 chinin-ar chinin-s k* chir-fl gya2 *Chlor* ↓ cimic hl *Cinnb* k* clem k* cob k* *Coca* k* cocain bro1 cocc k* cod a1* **Coff** k* colch k* coll a1 cortico sp1 cortiso sp1 *Croc* j5.de* cub hr1* cupr k* cupr-ar a1 cycl hr1 cypra-eg sde6.de• dulc fd4.de ephe-si hsj1• erio a1 eucal hr1* eug j5.de falco-pe nl2• ferr ↓ *Fl-ac* *Form* k* galla-q-r nl2• gels *Graph* haliae-lc srj5• ham ↓ hippoc-k ↓ hydr a1 hydrog srj2• hyos h1* ign gl1.fr• ignis-alc es2• iod k* iodof hr1 *Kali-br* hr1* kali-n a1 *Kola* stb3• lac-ac a1 **Lach** k* laur sf1.de limest-b es1• lyc h2 lyss k* mand sp1 med k* meny c1 merc-cy bro1 mez gl1.fr• muru a1 myric k* nitro-o a1 nux-v bro1 *Olib-sac* wmh1 **Op** k* *Ox-ac* oxal-a rly4• ozone sde2• paull bro1 petr j5.de ph-ac j5.de phel k* phos phys bro1 *Pip-m* k* pisc bro1 plat h2* plut-n srj7• podo fd3.de• puls ↓ rhus-g ↓ ros-d wla1 ruta fd4.de sabad sf1.de sacch-a fd2.de• sang a1 sec k* senec spig h1 spong h1 **Stann** gl1.fr• *Stram* k* sul-ac k* sulfa sp1 sulph a1 sumb k* symph fd3.de• tanac a1 taosc iwa1• **Tarent** k* teucr k* thea k* thioc-ac rly4• thuj trios rsj11• tritic-vg fd5.de *Tung-met* bdx1• ulm-c jsj8• valer k* vanil fd5.de verat j5.de* visc sp1 zinc sf1.de ziz a1*

- **daytime**: cob a1 lyss a1
- **morning**: bov k* cinnb k* dulc fd4.de phys a1 tritic-vg fd5.de
- **afternoon**: arg-n
- **evening**: anac asc-t hr1 carc mlr1• chin cycl dulc fd4.de graph k2* ham fd3.de• med k2* phos sacch-a fd2.de• teucr k*
- **night**: *Med* k* op a1
- **air**, in open: chir-fl gya2 dulc fd4.de phel spong fd4.de tritic-vg fd5.de vanil fd5.de
- **alternating** with:
  - **anger** (See Anger - alternating - exhilaration)
  - **anxiety** (See Anxiety - alternating - exhilaration)
  - **cares**: op j5.de
  - **discouragement**: *Dulc* fd4.de petr j5.de sul-ac j5.de
  - **fear** (See Fear - alternating - exhilaration)
  - **grief**: op mtf33*
  - **moroseness** (See Morose - alternating - exhilaration)
  - **sadness**: *(↗Elated - alternating - sadness)* agn androc srj1• carc mlr1• croc gl1.fr• *Dulc* fd4.de ferr j5.de hippoc-k szs2 ox-ac k2* petr j5.de plat j5.de **Spong** fd* *Stram* hr1*
  - **timidity**: petr j5.de sul-ac j5.de
- **blissful**: chir-fl gya2 falco-pe nl2• *Op* j5.de* symph fd3.de•
- **children**; in: bell mtf **Cann-i** mtf caust mtf **Coff** mtf graph mtf *Hyos* mtf ign mtf iod mtf *Kali-br* mtf **Lach** mtf lyc mtf med mtf nux-v mtf **Op** mtf petr mtf phos mtf *Pip-m* mtf plat mtf **Stann** mtf *Stram* mtf sulph mtf *Tarent* mtf thuj mtf verat mtf zinc mtf
- **coition**, after: borx
- **diarrhea**, during: ox-ac
- **followed** by | **exhaustion**: clem a1
- **going** out; when: rhus-g tmo3•
- **himself**; about: *Kola* stb3•
- **intoxicated**; as if: agath-a ↓ cypra-eg sde6.de•
  - **champagne**; by: agath-a nl2•
- **mania**; in: *(↗Boaster)* *Chlor* kr1
- **perspiration**, during: op
- **politics**, about: *Caust* vh* lach vh*
- **recall** things long forgotten, can: *(↗Memory - active)* *Gels*
- **religious**: *(↗Excitement - religious)* puls pc* stram pc* verat pc

- **sadness**, after: ziz a1*
- **walking** in open air, while: chir-fl gya2 cinnb dulc fd4.de spong fd4.de

EXPANSIVE (= too demonstrative): *(↗Communicative; Loquacity)* *Acon* vh* alum vh bar-c vh *Bov* b4.de* carc mlr1• ham fd3.de• helo-s rwt2• **Kali-s** fd* lac-ac stj5• lac-del hrn2• limen-b-c hrn2* nat-ox rly4• psor jl2 spong fd4.de staph mtf33 *Sulph* mrr1* tritic-vg fd5.de

EXPRESSING oneself:

- **cannot** express oneself: *(↗Memory - weakness - expressing)* ham fd3.de• podo fd3.de• puls ptk1* *Ruta* fd4.de tritic-vg fd5.de *Vanil* fd5.de
- **desire** to express oneself: anh sp1 lac-f wza1• *Med* mrr1 podo fd3.de• [tax jsj7]
  - **mimic**; in: lac-f wza1•
  - **verbally**: lac-f wza1•
- **difficult**: allox tpw3 chlam-tr bcx2• plut-n srj7• thuj bg2 zinc mtf33

EXTRAVAGANCE: *(↗Dress; Eccentricity; Exclusive; Fanaticism; Fear - extravagance; Foppish; Gestures - extravagant; Haughty; Jewelry - desire; Laughing - immoderately; Speech - extravagant; Squandering - money; Vanity)* aids nl2• am-c ang a1 ara-maca sej7• *Bell* k* buteo-j ↓ cann-i a1 *Carb-v* st1* castm j *Caust* chin k* chinin-s j *Con* croc k* guar a1* iod k* lach mtf33 merc h1 musca-d szs1 *Nat-m* st1* nux-m a1 op a1 paull a1 petr k* petr-ra shn4• ph-ac phel plat k* sal-fr sle1• stram taosc iwa1• verat

- **purchases**; in: [buteo-j sej6]
- **work**, and hard: guar vml3•

EXTREMES; goes to (See Eccentricity; Mood - changeable)

EXTROVERTED people (See Communicative; Excitement; Expansive; Loquacity)

EXUBERANCE (See Exhilaration)

EXULTANT: *(↗Cheerful)* agath-a nl2• cann-i a1

EYES:

- **downcast**: *(↗Discouraged; Looked - evading)* stann h2* verat ptk1
  - **walks** with the eyes downcast: *(↗Sadness - looking)* cham kr1 dioxi rbp6 plut-n srj7•
- **evading** the look of other persons (See Looked - evading)

FACE:

- **hot**; with face: op bg2

FACES; making (See Grimaces)

FACETIOUSNESS (See Jesting)

FAILURE: | **literary** or scientific failure (See Ailments - failure - literary)

FAITH: | **maintain**; need to: stront-c sk4•

FAITHLESS (See Religious - want)

FALTERING (See Irresolution)

FAMILIARITY: *(↗Affectionate)* chlf a1 irid-met srj5•

FANATICISM: *(↗Anarchist; Ardent; Extravagance; Impetuous; Intolerance; Obstinate; Obstinate - children; Passionate [=choleric]; Religious - too - fanaticism; Superstitious; Thoughts - persistent; Violent)* aur-ar k2 carc mlr1• caust cupr sst3• lach gb• limest-b es1• nux-v mtf33 puls k2* rob sel **Sulph** k ● *Thuj* k*

- **gives** up; never: cupr sst3•

FANCIES:

- **absorbed** in: *(↗Absentminded; Absorbed; Delusions - fancy; Dream; as; Execution; Forgetful; Plans - making; Theorizing)* anh jl1 arn k* aur-ar k2 bar-i k2 bell br1 cann-i br1 cocc br1 cupr dream-p sdj1• irid-met srj5• kali-p k2 limest-b es1• marb-w es1• ozone sde2• positr nl2• sil stram k*
- **absurd**: *(↗Foolish)* alco a1 carbn-s a1 marb-w es1•
- **anxious**: fl-ac a1 sep ↓
  - **night** | **fever**; during: sep a1
- **childish**: lyc mtf33
- **confused**: *(↗Memory - weakness)* *Ail* hr1* **Bapt** hr1* camph hr1* chin h1* con a1* *Glon* hr1* ham hr1* **Hyos** k* *Lil-t* hr1* phos k* **Stram** k*

Fancies: ...

- **exaltation** of: *(↗Deeds - great; Plans - making; Theorizing)* *Absin* *Acon* k* *Agar* k* agn k* alum k* alum-sil k2* *Am-c* k* *Ambr* k* *Anac* k* anan a1 androc srj1• *Ang* k* anh mtf ant-c k* apoc k* arg-n k* arn k* *Ars* k* *Asaf* aur k* aur-ar k2 aur-m-n wbt2• aur-s k2 bar-c bg2* bar-ox-suc rly4• **Bell** k* borx ↓ *Bry* k* (non:bufo slp) bufo-s a1* calc k* calc-sil k2* camph bg2 **Cann-i** k* cann-s b7a.de* cann-xyz ptk1 *Canth* k* carb-an bg2 carb-v k* *Carbn-s* caust k* cham k* chel *Chin* k* chinin-ar k2 *Cic* bg2 coca cocc bg2 *Coff* k* coff-t a1 coloc ↓ con k* convo-d croc k* *Crot-c* cupr bg2 cycl k* dig k* *Dulc* ↓ elaps euphr bg2 fl-ac k* *Graph* k* hell k* hep bg2 hipp ↓ hydr ↓ hydr-ac ↓ **Hyos** k* ign k* iod bg2 irid-met srj5• kali-ar kali-br ptk1 kali-c k* kali-n ↓ kali-p kali-s fd4.de *Lac-c* ptk1* **Lach** k* lact k* *Laur* b7.de led bg2 lil-t k2* *Lyc* k* *M-arct* ↓ m-aust b7.de mag-m k* meph k* *Merc* k* merc-c bg2 mosch bg2 mur-ac k* naja nat-c ↓ nit-ac k* nitro-o a1 *Nux-m* k* nux-v k* olnd *Op* k* ox-ac *Petr* ph-ac k* *Phos* k* pic-ac sf1.de pip-m k* plan k* *Plat* b4a.de* *Plb* positr nl2• psor k* puls k* pyrog ptk1 rhus-t bg2 sabad k* samb bg2 *Sec* bg2 seneg bg2 sep k* *Sil* k* spong k* stann bg2 staph k* **Stram** k* sul-ac b4.de* *Sulph* k* thuj k* valer k* vanil fd5.de verat bg2* verb k* viol-o k* viol-t ↓ *Zinc* k* zinc-p k2* ziz k* [nicc stj1]
  - **day** and night: ambr j5.de caust j5.de
  - **daytime**: elaps a1
  - **morning**: canth j5.de chin ↓ con k* *Nux-v* j5.de
    - **bed**, in: chin j5.de
  - **afternoon**: anac j5.de ang j5.de lyc
  - **evening**: agar ↓ alum ↓ am-c ambr ↓ anac k* *Bry* ↓ *Calc* ↓ camph ↓ carb-an ↓ *Carb-v* ↓ *Caust* chel k* chin j5.de cocc ↓ cycl graph ↓ hell ↓ ign ↓ *Kali-c* ↓ kali-s fd4.de lyc ↓ merc ↓ naja nat-c ↓ *Nux-v* ↓ ph-ac ↓ *Phos* *Puls* ↓ rhus-t ↓ sabad ↓ *Sil* ↓ staph ↓ sulph k* viol-t ↓
    - **bed**, in: agar j5.de alum j5.de ambr j5.de *Bry* j5.de *Calc* h2* camph j5.de carb-an j5.de *Carb-v* j5.de caust j5.de *Chin* j5.de cocc j5.de graph j5.de hell j5.de ign j5.de *Kali-c* j5.de lyc j5.de merc j5.de nat-c j5.de *Nux-v* j5.de ph-ac j5.de phos j5.de *Puls* j5.de rhus-t j5.de sabad j5.de *Sil* j5.de staph j5.de *Sulph* j5.de viol-t j5.de
    - **twilight**, in: *Caust*
  - **night**: agar j5.de androc srj1• ars k* aur k* *Bar-c* borx j5.de *Bry* j5.de **Calc** canth carb-an carb-v k* caust *Cham* k* *Chin* j5.de* coff k* con j5.de *Graph* h2* hep j5.de hipp k* hydr *Hyos* j5.de ign k* *Kali-c* j5.de kali-n j5.de *Lach* j5.de *M-arct* j5.de *Nit-ac* *Nux-v* j5.de *Op* j5.de petr k* ph-ac j5.de phos plat j5.de plb puls sep sil spong j5.de *Sulph* j5.de *Zinc* j5.de
  - **alone**, when: ars j5.de
  - **business**, of: bell a1
  - **closing** the eyes in bed; on: bell j5.de *Calc* camph j5.de *Graph* h2* led lyc sep *Sulph* j5.de
  - **frightful**: *(↗Delusions - images - frightful; Delusions - visions - horrible)* **Calc** k* *Caust* hydr k* hydr-ac k* *Lac-c* k* merc k* *Op* *Sil* **Stram** k*
  - **going** to bed, after: chin hell ign *Phos*
  - **happened**, thinks they had: *Staph* gl1.fr•
  - **heat**, during: acon bg2 ars b4a.de bell bg2 carb-v b4.de chin k* coff k* *Dulc* b4a.de iod b4.de lach bg2 laur k* nit-ac b4.de* *Op* b7.de* phos bg2 puls k* sabad k* stram bg2 sulph b4.de *Thuj* bg2 valer bg2
  - **sleeplessness**, with: agar j5.de alum ambr k2 anh mg1.de *Arg-n* *Bell* k* borx j5.de bry j5.de calc h2* caust j5.de *Chin* j5.de cocc j5.de coloc j5.de *Graph* j5.de hep j5.de kali-c j5.de kali-n j5.de led j5.de *Lyc* j5.de merc nat-c *Nux-v* j5.de *Op* j5.de* petr j5.de ph-ac phos k* plat j5.de *Puls* j5.de sabad j5.de *Sep* j5.de *Sil* j5.de spong a1 staph j5.de sulph j5.de thuj viol-t j5.de
  - **walking** in open air: ant-c j5.de sulph j5.de
  - **working**, while: ang j5.de mur-ac j5.de olnd j5.de
- **excitement**; after: ign k2
- **fits**; in: acon bg2 viol-o bg2
- **frightful** (See Delusions - images - frightful)
- **lascivious**: *(↗Lascivious; Lewdness; Naked; Nymphomania; Obscene; Shameless; Thoughts - intrude - sexual; Thoughts - tormenting - sexual)* am-c k* *Ambr* k* anac k* androc srj1• arund aur k* bell bufo mtf11 *Calad* hr1* *Calc* k* calc-s a1 camph a1* *Canth* j5.de carb-v k* *Chin* cod hr1* *Con* j5.de* cop a1* crot-c sk4• dig k* *Fl-ac* ↓ *Graph* k* hipp k* ign irid-met srj5• *Kali-br* hr1* *Lach* j5.de lil-t *Lyc* k* lyss hr1* nat-c hr1* *Nat-m* j5.de* *Nuph* a1* nux-v gl1.fr• *Onos* ↓ *Op* k* *Orig* hr1* plat gl1.fr• psor gl1.fr• sang *Sel* j5.de* sep j5.de* *Sil* hr1* sin-n hr1* staph mrr1* stram j5.de tarent k2* thuj k* *Ust* hr1* vanil fd5.de verb k* yuc a1 *Zinc* hr1* [heroin sdj2]

- **lascivious**: ...
  - **forenoon**: hipp a1
  - **evening**: am-c a1 anac a1
  - **night**: aur h2*
  - **dreaming**, even when: ambr h1*
  - **impotence**, with: *(↗Lascivious - impotence; Thoughts - sexual - impotence; MALE GENITALIA/SEX - Sexual desire - increased - weakness)* calad k2 *Chin* kr1 *Fl-ac* vh* *Onos* mrr1 *Op* kr1 *Sel* kr1
  - **lying** down, while: thuj a1
  - **religious** duties; from aversion to: orig hr1
- **laughable** | **before** going to sleep: sulph a1
- **lively** (See vivid)
- **periodically** returning: ars
- **perspiration**, during: *Acon* bg2 carb-v k* iod k* nit-ac k* *Op* bg2 *Phos* bg2 sulph k*
- **pleasant**: *(↗Pleasure)* **Cann-i** k* cimic hl coca cod a1 cycl k* lach olib-sac wmh1 **Op** k* stram k*
- **reading**, on: coff j5.de *Mag-m* ph-ac j5.de
- **repulsive**, when alone: *(↗Mood - repulsive)* fl-ac k* sel k* tarent
- **sleep**:
  - **going** to sleep, on: arg-n bell j5.de bry a1 *Calc* camph j5.de chel a1 chin j5.de coff a1 ign j5.de *Spong* j5.de sulph
  - **preventing**: *Arg-n* k* *Op* hr1* phos *Staph* hr1* viol-t hr1*
- **strange**: lyss ↓ **Stram** h1*
  - **pregnancy**, during: *(↗Thoughts - strange - pregnancy - during)* lyss a1
- **unpleasant**: olib-sac wmh1 op a1 phos ↓ rumx a1
  - **bed**, after going to: phos a1
- **vanishing** rapidly: viol-o b7.de
- **vivid** (= lively): *(↗Concentration - active; Ideas - abundant; Memory - active; Witty)* acon k* alco a1 ambr b7a.de androc srj1• *Ang* b7.de* bell bg2* *Cann-i* kr1 cann-s b7.de* carb-an cham coff k* croc cycl dig k* hell hyos k* ign k2 kali-br **Lach** k* lact *Lyc* meph k* morph a1 naja nat-m nitro-o a1 nux-v bg2 op k* par b7.de phos k* pic-ac bg2 puls k* sabad b7.de **Stram** k* valer b7.de* *Viol-o* b7.de* zinc kr1
  - **evening**: cycl a1 hell a1
  - **midnight**, after: puls
  - **going** to sleep; when: nat-m
  - **heat**, followed by: phos
- **waking**, on: calc ign j5.de kali-n j5.de *Lach* plat j5.de puls sep sil j5.de sulph
- **walking** in open air; when: dulc fd4.de marb-w es1•
- **wild**: cimic hr1 con a1 rhus-v c1 stram hr1

FANTASY (See Delusions)

FAR away from everything (See Detached; Dream; as; Indifference; Time - slowly)

FAREWELL: | **separation** is difficult: *(↗Homesickness)* olib-sac wmh1

FASCINATING others (See Charming)

FASTIDIOUS: *(↗Anal; Carefulness; Censorious; Conscientious; Delusions - dirty - he; Disgust - dirt; Disorder sensitive; Offended; Order - desire; Proper - too; Rest - cannot; Tidy; Trifles; Trifles - important)* **Aloe** sne alum st1 *Anac* vh* androc srj arg-n dx1 **Ars** k* ars-i ser* asar vh aur k* *Aur-m-n* wbt2• *Aur-s* wbt2• bamb-a ↓ bell-p fb bit-ar wht1• bufo ↓ *Carc* c* *Caust* mrr1 chir-fl gya2 choc oss• con st1 cupr sht* dream-p sdj1• falco-pe nl2• galla-q-r nl2• *Graph* bg2* haliae-lc srj5• ignis-alc es2• iod k2* *Kali-ar* gk kali-bi k2* *Kali-c* gg* kali-p fd1.de• **Kali-s** fd* lac-ac hr1* lac-e hrn2• lac-f wza1• lac-h htj1• lob vh* lyc k2 med hbh moni rfm1• morg-g ptj*• musca-d szs1 nat-ar mrr1 *Nat-m* k2* nat-s vh* **Nat-sil** fd* *Nux-v* k* orot-ac rly4• oxal-a rly4• phos fb* pin-con oss2• pip-m vh plat k* plb cld• podo fd3.de• polys sk4• positr nl2• puls pc* pycnop-sa mrz1 ruta fd4.de sep k* sil k* spong fd4.de stann ggd1 sulph mrr1* syc fmm1• thuj vh* vanil fd5.de [heroin sdj2 *Nicc* stj1 sil-met stj2]
- **cleanliness**; for (See Cleanness - mania)
- **disease**; in: carc mlr1• pip-m ckh1
- **eating**; in: bufo a1
- **order**; for (See Order - desire)
- **perfect** way; wants to perform in a: bamb-a stb2.de•

Fastidious: ...
- **personal** appearance; about: *(↗Tidy - appearance)* falco-pe nl2• galla-q-r ↓ positr nl2•
  - **others**, of: galla-q-r nl2•
- **possessions**; about his: ars-i st
- **prove** himself; he has to: *(↗Ambition - increased - competitive)* *Anac* mrr1 cupr sst3*
- **stressed**; only when: lac-f wza1•
- **time**; being on (See Anxiety - time)
- **work**; in his: carc sst2•

FATALISTIC: *(↗Delusions - accidents - threatened - fatal; Fear - accidents - fatal; Indifference - future; Indifference - stoical; DREAMS - Accidents - fatal)* lavand-a ctl1• nit-ac mrr1

FAULTFINDING (See Censorious)

FEAR (= apprehension, dread): *(↗Ailments - fear; Anxiety; Anxiety - fear; Delirium - fear; Frightened; BLADDER - Apprehension)* **Abel** ↓ abies-c ↓ abrot kr1* absin acet-ac achy ↓ achy-a bnj1 **Acon** k* acon-f ↓ act-sp kr1* adam ↓ adon ↓ *Adren* ↓ aesc ↓ aeth aether a1 agar k* agath-a ↓ agav-a ↓ agn k* agre ↓ aids ↓ alco ↓ *All-c* kr1 all-s ↓ aloe k* *Alum* k* alum-p ↓ alum-sil k2 alumin ↓ alumin-s ↓ alumn a1 am-br sf1.de am-c k* *Am-caust* ↓ *Am-f* ↓ am-m b7.de* *Am-p* ↓ ambr b7.de* aml-ns a1 *Ammc* ↓ amyg ↓ anac k* anag ↓ anan ↓ androc srj1• ang k* *Anh* ↓ ant-c k* ant-m ↓ *Ant-met* ↓ ant-s-aur kr1 ant-t k* *Anth* ↓ anthraq ↓ antip ↓ apis b7a.de* aq-mar rbp6 ara-maca ↓ aral a1 aran ↓ aran-sc ↓ arg-met bg2* **Arg-n** k* arg-p ↓ arge-pl ↓ arist-cl sp1 arizon-l nl2• *Arn* b7.de* **Ars** k* ars-h kr1* ars-i *Ars-met* ↓ ars-s-f a1* art-v kr1 arum-m kr1 **Arum-t** ↓ asaf k* *Asar* ↓ aspar kr1 astac kr1 astat ↓ *Aster* ↓ asthm-r ↓ atra-r ↓ atro a1 *Atro-s* hr1 **Aur** k* aur-ar k2 *Aur-br* ↓ aur-i ↓ *Aur-m* ↓ *Aur-m-n* ↓ *Aur-s* ↓ bac jl2 bad ↓ *Bamb-a* ↓ bapt bar-act ↓ bar-br ↓ *Bar-c* k* bar-i ↓ bar-m k* bar-met ↓ bar-s ↓ **Bell** k* bell-p-sp ↓ benz-ac ↓ berb j5.de* *Beryl* ↓ beryl-m ↓ bism bg2 *Bism-sn* ↓ bit-ar ↓ *Bor-pur* ↓ **Borx** k* both-a rb3 both-ax ↓ bov b4.de bran ↓ brom bg2* bros-gau ↓ bruc ↓ *Bry* k* bufo bufo-s ↓ bung-fa ↓ but-ac sp1* *Cact* cadm-m ↓ cadm-met ↓ cadm-s ↓ caes-met ↓ calad k* **Calc** k* calc-act ↓ *Calc-ar* ↓ calc-f sf1.de* calc-i ↓ calc-lac ↓ calc-m ↓ calc-met ↓ calc-n ↓ **Calc-p** k* *Calc-s* calc-sil k2* *Calen* ↓ calli-h ↓ camph k* cann-i k* cann-s cann-xyz bg2 canth b7.de* *Caps* k* carb-ac ↓ carb-an k* *Carb-v* k* **Carbn-s** carc c1* cartl-s ↓ cassia-s ↓ caste ↓ castm caul c1* *Caust* k* cean ↓ cecr ↓ cedr ↓ *Cench* ↓ cent ↓ cham k* chel bg2 chen-a ↓ chin k* chinin-ar **Chinin-s** ↓ chir-fl ↓ chlam-tr ↓ chlol kr1 chlor choc ↓ chord-umb ↓ chr-m ↓ chr-met ↓ chr-s ↓ **Cic** k* cich ↓ cimic k* cina b7.de* cinnb ↓ cist ptk1 cit-ac ↓ clem b4.de* cob ↓ cob-m ↓ cob-n sp1 cob-p ↓ coc-c *Coca* coca-c ↓ *Cocc* k* cocc-s ↓ coff k* *Coff-t* kr1 colch b7.de* coli rly4• coloc k* *Con* k* cop ↓ cor-r ↓ cori-r ↓ corn-a ↓ cortico sp1 corv-cor bdg• croc k* **Crot-c** ↓ *Crot-h* k* *Crot-t* ↓ culx ↓ *Cupr* k* cupr-act a1 cupr-ar bg2 *Cupr-f* ↓ cupr-m ↓ *Cupr-p* ↓ *Cur* ↓ cycl bg2* cypr ↓ cypra-eg ↓ cystein-l rly4• cyt-l sp1 daph dendr-pol ↓ der ↓ des-ac ↓ **Dig** k* digin ↓ dios ↓ diosm ↓ dioxi ↓ dirc ↓ dream-p ↓ dros k* dulc k* dys pte1*• echi elaps elat ↓ elec al2 epiph ↓ eric-vg ↓ *Eup-per* ↓ eup-pur ↓ euph k* euphr a1 fago ↓ fagu ↓ falco-pe nl2• ferr k* ferr-act ↓ ferr-ar ferr-f ↓ ferr-lac ↓ *Ferr-n* ↓ ferr-p ferr-sil ↓ ferr-t ↓ fl-ac bg2 *Fl-pur* ↓ foll ↓ *Form* frax ↓ fum ↓ fuma-ac rly4• gaert fmm1• gal-ac ↓ gal-met ↓ gal-s ↓ galeoc-c-h ↓ galla-q-r ↓ gard-j vlr2• *Gels* k* genist ↓ gent-c *Germ-met* ↓ gink-b ↓ gins j5.de glon glycyr-g ↓ gran ↓ granit-m ↓ **Graph** k* grat bg2 *Grin* ↓ guaj ↓ guar ↓ guare ↓ hafn-met ↓ haliae-lc ↓ ham ↓ hed sp1 heli-n ↓ hell k* helo-s ↓ helon ↓ *Hep* k* hera ↓ heroin ↓ hipp ↓ hippoc-k szs2 hir ↓ hoit jl3 hom-xyz ↓ hura ↓ hydr ↓ hydr-ac hydrc ↓ hydrog ↓ *Hyos* k* hyper hypoth ↓ iber a1* **Ign** k* ignis-alc ↓ ind ↓ *Iod* k* ip k* irid-met ↓ iris ↓ ix ↓ jatr-c a1 **Kali-ar** kali-bi ↓ *Kali-br* k* *Kali-c* k* kali-cy ↓ kali-fcy ↓ kali-i kali-m ↓ kali-met ↓ kali-n k* kali-p k* kali-s kali-sil ↓ kali-tel ↓ kalm ↓ ketogl-ac ↓ *Kola* ↓ kreos kr1 kres mg1.de lac-ac stj5• lac-c mrr1 lac-cp ↓ *Lac-d* ↓ lac-del hrn2• *Lac-e* ↓ lac-f ↓ lac-h ↓ lac-leo ↓ lac-lup ↓ lac-mat ↓ lach k* lact j5.de lanth-met ↓ lap-la ↓ lappa ↓ lat-m sp1 laur b7.de* lavand-a ↓ *Lec* ↓ led bg2 lepi ↓ lept ↓ levo ↓ lil-s ↓ *Lil-t* limest-b ↓ lipp a1 *Lith-c* ↓ *Lith-f* ↓ lith-i ↓ lith-m ↓ *Lith-met* ↓ lith-p ↓ lith-s ↓ lob lol a1 loxo-recl ↓ luf-op ↓ lup ↓ **Lyc** k* lycps-v ↓ lys ↓ **Lyss** k* m-arct b7.de* m-aust b7a.de macro a1 mag-br ↓ mag-c k* mag-f ↓ mag-i ↓ mag-lac ↓ *Mag-m* k* mag-met ↓ *Mag-n* ↓ mag-p ↓ mag-s sp1 mag-sil ↓ maias-l hrn2• malar ↓ manc k* mang b4.de* mang-act br1 mang-i ↓ mang-m ↓ mang-met ↓ *Mang-n* ↓ mang-p ↓ mang-s ↓ mang-sil ↓ marb-w ↓ med bg2* melal-alt ↓ *Meli* meli-a ↓ meli-xyz c2 menis ↓ meny b7.de* *Merc* k* *Merc-act* ↓ merc-br ↓ merc-c bg2* merc-d ↓ *Merc-i-f* ↓ merc-i-r merl ↓ mez k* moly-met ↓ moni ↓ *Morb* ↓ morg fmm1• morg-g pte1*• morg-p ↓ morph ↓

Fear: ...
Mosch k* mur-ac k* murx k* musca-d ↓ mygal br1 nad rly4• *Naja* ↓ *Nat-ar* nat-br ↓ **Nat-c** k* *Nat-caust* ↓ *Nat-f* ↓ *Nat-lac* ↓ *Nat-m* k* nat-met ↓ nat-n ↓ *Nat-p* k* nat-s nat-sil ↓ nicc nicc-met ↓ nicc-s ↓ niob-met ↓ nit-ac k* nit-s-d ↓ *Nitro* ↓ nux-m b7.de *Nux-v* k* *Oci-sa* ↓ oena ↓ ol-j ↓ olib-sac wmh1 olnd ↓ *Onos* *Op* k* orig a1 *Oscilloc* ↓ osm ↓ osm-met ↓ osm-o ↓ ovi-p ↓ ox-ac a1* oxal-a ↓ *Oxyg* ↓ ozone ↓ paeon ↓ *Pall* ↓ parth ↓ paull ↓ perh ↓ pert-vc ↓ *Petr* k* petr-ra shn4• ph-ac b4a.de* phasco-ci ↓ phase ↓ *Phel* ↓ **Phos** k* *Phys* ↓ physala-p bnm7• *Phyt* pic-ac ↓ pieri-b ↓ pin-con ↓ pip-m pip-n br1 pitu ↓ pitu-a ↓ plac ↓ **Plat** k* plb b7.de* plb-m ↓ plb-p ↓ plut-n ↓ pneu ↓ podo sf1.de polon-met ↓ polys sk4• pop ↓ positr nl2• pot-e rly4• prim-v ↓ prot fmm1• prun-cf ↓ **Psor** k* ptel ↓ *Puls* k* pyrog bg2 pyrus ↓ querc-r ↓ rad-br br1* rad-met ↓ ran-b k* ran-s bg2 raph rat ptk1 rauw sp1* rhen-met ↓ rheum k* rhod rhodi ↓ rhus-g ↓ *Rhus-t* k* rhus-v rob ↓ rubd-met ↓ rumx ↓ ruta k* ruth-met ↓ sabad bg2 *Sabal* ↓ sabin b7.de* sacch ↓ sacch-a ↓ sal-fr sle1• samb b7.de* samb-c ↓ sang bg2* sanguis-s hrn2* sanic ↓ sars bg2 scand-met ↓ scol ↓ *Scut* ↓ sec k* *Sel* ↓ seneg bg2 **Sep** k* seq-s ↓ ser-a-c ↓ sieg ↓ sil k* sil-met ↓ *Sin-n* ↓ sinus rly4• sium ↓ sol-ni ↓ sol-t-ae ↓ *Spig* b7.de* spirae ↓ *Spong* k* squil k* *Stann* k* staph k* staphycoc ↓ **Still** ↓ **Stram** k* streptoc ↓ *Stront-c* k* stront-m ↓ stront-met ↓ *Stroph-h* ↓ stroph-s sp1* stry succ ↓ succ-ac ↓ succ-xyz c1* suis-em rly4• suis-pan rly4• *Sul-ac* k* sul-i ↓ *Sulph* k* sumb ↓ suprar rly4• syc bka1*• **Symph** ↓ *Syph* al* *Tab* k* tanac ↓ tant-met ↓ taosc ↓ tarax ↓ tarent tarent-c ↓ tart-ac ↓ tax ↓ tax-br ↓ techn ↓ tell jl3 temp ↓ ter ↓ tere-ch jl3 tere-la ↓ thal-met ↓ thea a1 *Ther* bg2* thres-a ↓ thuj k* til *Titan* ↓ titan-s ↓ tong ↓ toxi ↓ trach ↓ tril-c ↓ tril-p ↓ **Tritic-vg** fd* trom ↓ tub ptk1 *Tub-k* ↓ *Tung-met* ↓ tus-fa ↓ ulm-c ↓ urol-h ↓ v-a-b ↓ *Vac* ↓ valer k* vanad ↓ *Vanil* fd5.de vario ↓ *Verat* k* *Verat-v* ↓ vero-o rly4*• vib ↓ vichy-g ↓ vinc ↓ viol-o ↓ viol-t bg2 visc sp1 vult-gr ↓ wye a1 xan a1 xanth ↓ yttr-met ↓ zinc b4.de* zinc-i ↓ zinc-m a1 *Zinc-n* ↓ **Zinc-p** k2 zinc-val ↓ *Zing* ↓ zirc-met ↓ [buteo-j sej6 miml-g rcb1 spect dfg1]

- **day** and night: ars j5.de
- **daytime**, only: lac-c k* *Lyc* a1 mur-ac k* pip-m a1 sul-ac
- **morning**: alum bg2 alum-sil ↓ anac bg2 arg-n k* arn ↓ ars bg2 carb-an bg2 carb-v bg2 carbn-s caust k* chin bg2 *Graph* k* ign bg2 ip bg2 kali-ar ↓ led k* *Lyc* k* mag-c bg2 mag-m bg2 mag-s mur-ac nicc nit-ac bg2 *Nux-v* k* phos bg2 plat bg2 puls k* rhus-t bg2 sep bg2 sul-ac k* *Verat* bg2
  - **until** evening: sul-ac
  - **bed**, in: lyc j5.de nux-v j5.de
  - **rising**, on: arg-n k*
  - **waking**, on: alum-sil k2* arn k2 kali-ar gk puls
- **forenoon**: am-c nicc a1 paeon a1
- **noon**: aster ↓ zinc a1*
  - **12**-15 h: aster
- **afternoon**: aeth k* am-c ant-t aster ↓ berb k* carb-an k* carb-v castm dig hura ↓ mag-c mag-s nat-c nat-s nicc k* *Nux-v* stram fyz stront-c *Sulph* *Tab* k*
  - **14** h: hura vh
  - **15** h: aster fyz
  - **16** h: berb ↓ tab
    - **sleep**; until going to: berb a
  - **17** h: nux-v
- **evening**: agar ↓ alum k* alum-p k2* *Am-c* am-m ↓ anac k* ant-t k* arg-p ↓ *Ars* aur-ar k2 bar-c k* bar-s k2* berb a1 brom k* calad k* **Calc** k* calc-ar k2* carb-an k* *Carb-v* **Caust** k* coc-c k* *Cupr* cupr-p ↓ dig *Dros* form k* *Graph* ↓ hep hipp k* *Kali-ar* *Kali-c* k* kali-i kali-p lach lith-p ↓ *Lyc* *Mag-c* mag-m k* merc k* nat-ar nat-c k* nat-m nit-ac nux-v k* paeon petr k* *Phos* k* plat plb-p ↓ **Puls** k* ran-b k* *Rhus-t* sep ↓ stront-c tab k* valer k* verat *Zinc* zinc-p k2*
  - **amel.**: mag-c zinc hr1*
  - **bed**, in: agar h2* *Ars* calc *Graph* *Kali-c* mag-c merc nat-ar
    - **amel.**: mag-c k*
  - **twilight**: am-m sf1.de berb k* brom bl *Calc* *Caust* k* kali-i mag-c fyz *Phos* k* **Puls** rhus-t k* sep fyz [alum-p stj2 arg-p stj2 cupr-p stj2 lith-p stj2 plb-p stj2 zinc-p stj2]
  - **walking**, while: *Nux-v* k*
- **night**: (↗*terror - night; Anxiety - night; Anxiety - night - children; Darkness - agg.)* abel vh1 acon bg2 aesc ↓ agar ggd1 am-c arn k* *Ars* k* *Ars-s-f* k2* aur c1 aur-ar k2 *Bell* k* *Borx* st bung-fa mtf *Calc* k* calc-ar k2* *Calc-s* k* calc-sil k2* **Camph** k* cann-i ↓ carb-an *Carb-v* k* *Carbn-s* *Carc* mlr1• caust k* cham *Chin* chinin-ar chlol ggd1 cina mtf33 cob-n ↓ coca-c ↓ cocc k* colch con k* *Crot-c* dros dulc eup-per gard-j vlr2• graph hep ign ip *Kali-ar* *Kali-br* br1* kali-c

- **night**: ...
kali-p br1 kali-s k2* kola stb3• *Lach* lyc k* mag-c maias-l hrn2• manc mang ↓ *Merc* k* *Merc-act* ↓ nat-c *Nat-m* *Nat-p* nit-ac op hr1* paeon bg ph-ac phos k* psor jl2 *Puls* rat j5.de **Rhus-t** k* rob k* samb ↓ sanic c1 scut br1 sil sol-ni br1 spong stann stram k* *Sulph* suprar rly4• syph ↓ tab thea toxi ↓ tritic-vg fd5.de tub jl2* verat br1 zinc zinc-p k2*
  - **midnight**: con manc
    - **after**: **Ars** ↓ ign kali-c ↓ mang a1 rat j5.de
      - **3** h: **Ars** kr1 kali-c
  - **children**; in: *(↗terror - night - children)* borx ckh1 calc-s mtf33 *Carc* mlr1• cina mtf33 kali-br tl1 kali-p ckh1 tub mtf33
  - **flee**; with desire to: merc hr1*
  - **grief**; with: *Merc* kr1
  - **intestinal** spasms; from: *Op* kr1
  - **lie** in bed; cannot: *Rhus-t* br1* syph ptk1
  - **meningitis**; during tubercular: *Tub* kr1
  - **sleep**; on going to: cob-n sp
  - **waking**, after: aesc k2* cann-i a1 carb-v k2* coca-c sk4• con k* lach k2* lyc k2* maias-l hrn2• phos k2* samb k2* spong k2* toxi mtf2•
- **abandoned**; of being (See solitude)
- **abdomen**:
  - **arising** from abdomen: asaf k*
  - **pain** in abdomen; with (See pain - during - abdomen)
- **abortion** from fear; threatening (See FEMALE - Abortion - fear - from)
- **accidents**, of: *(↗approaching - vehicles; crossing; crossing - street; run over; fear of being - going; Injuring)* acon k* adam srj5• alum ↓ androc srj1• ara-maca sej7• arg-n gl* ars mtf bit-ar wht1• calc mrr1 carb-an h2 *Carb-v* *Caust* ↓ choc srj3• coca-c sk4• cupr k* cupr-act stj2* dulc fd4.de falco-pe nl2• *Gins* k* graph fyz* hydrog srj2*• iod hr1* kali-i h* kali-s fd4.de kola stb3• lac-del hrn2• mag-c hr1* mag-s hr1* maias-l hrn2• musca-d szs1 naja hr1* oci-sa sk4• osm mtf perh jl3 petr jl* phos mtf rhus-t kr1* samb-c a1* tarent ccrh1* tarent-c ckh1 tere-la rly4• tritic-vg fd5.de vanil fd5.de [bar-i stj2 calc-m stj1 cupr-f stj2 cupr-m stj2 cupr-p stj2 ferr stj2 ferr-f stj2 ferr-lac stj2 ferr-n stj2 ferr-sil stj2 lith-i stj2 mang-i stj2 mang-m stj2 mang-met stj2 mang-p stj2 mang-s stj2 merc stj2 merc-i-f stj2 mur-ac stj2 nicc-met stj2 nicc-s stj2 pall stj2 tax jsj7 tell stj2 zinc-i stj2]
  - **bed**; all day, relieved after going to: mag-c gt
  - **car**: maias-l hrn2• tritic-vg fd5.de
  - **child**; to: ars fyz
  - **fatal** accident; as if threatened by some: *(↗Fatalistic)* alum rb2 dulc fd4.de maias-l hrn2•
  - **friends**; happening to: *(↗Anxiety - friends)* ars k* *Caust* gk
  - **loved** ones; to: phos h2
  - **others**; to: osm a
- **accomplish** things; cannot: *Dys* fmm1•
- **age**; of one's own: *(↗old)* cortico sp1 ruta fd4.de
- **agoraphobia** (See open)
- **AIDS**; of: ars mrr1 (non:bor-pur mrr1) calc mrr1 carc mlr1• con vml2• iod mrr4• kali-ar mrr4• nit-ac mrr1 phos hu2 sulph mrr1 syph mrr1 [am-f stj2 arg-n stj2 lith-f stj2 mag-sil stj2]
- **air**:
  - **draft** of air; of: caps br1
  - **fresh**; of: caps c1 *Coff* kr1
  - **open**; in: anac k* arg-met bg2 bell bg2 cina bg2 cycl ptk1 *Hep* k* ign bg2 lach bg2 med jl2 nux-v k* plat bg2
    - **amel.**: bry k2 cann-i k2 cypra-eg sde6.de• plat *Valer*
- **air** raids; of: acon bl* arg-n bl* arn fyz ars spd cham fyz gels bl* ign bl* nat-m fyz ph-ac bl
- **airplane**; in (See flying - airplane)
- **aliens**; of: manc mrr1
- **alone**, of being: *(↗neglected; solitude; Anxiety - alone; Company - aversion - fear; Company - desire; Company - desire - alone; Watched - desires)* abel mtf11 acon k* act-sp agath-a nl2• all-s aloe vh1 ant-t k* *Apis* **Arg-n** k* *Arist-cl* sp1 **Ars** k* *Ars-h* ↓ *Ars-s-f* k2 asaf k* aster sze10• aur-ar k2 aur-m-n ↓ bar-c bl bell k* bism k* bov j brom k* bry bufo bung-fa ↓ cadm-s k* calc calc-ar k2 calc-p vh1* *Camph* k* carb-v gk carc sst*• chir-fl gya2 cimic sne

- **alone**, of being: ...
Clem k* Con k* **Crot-c** k* der sne dros dys ptj*• *Elaps* k* falco-pe ↓ gaert fmm1• gal-ac a1* galeoc-c-h ↓ *Gels Hell* ↓ hep **Hyos** k* kali-ar k* kali-br k* **Kali-c** k* *Kali-p Lac-c* k* lil-t bg* limest-b es1• **Lyc** k* lyss k* **Manc** gk med rb menis bg meny ↓ merc mez naja gw* nat-c sf1.de nat-s mtf33 nit-ac sf1.de nux-v oxal-a rly4• **Phos** k* pin-con oss2• pitu-a ft plb k* prot ptj• psor al2* *Puls* k* rad-br c1* ran-b k* rat sal-fr sle1• *Sep* k* sil fl spong fd4.de *Stram* k* syc pte1*• tab k* tarent k* thres-a sze7• toxi mtf2• *Tritic-vg* fd5.de tub hu* valer ptk vanil fd5.de verat zinc c1* [alum-p stj2 am-br stj2 ant-c stj2 ant-m stj2 ant-met stj2 arg-p stj2 *Ars-met* stj2 aur-m stj2 bar-br stj2 beryl-m stj2 *Bism-sn* stj2 cadm-m stj2 chlor stj2 chr-m stj2 cob-m stj2 cupr-m stj2 cupr-p stj2 ferr-lac stj2 kali-met stj2 kali-sil stj2 lith-m stj2 lith-p stj2 mag-p stj1 mang-m stj2 mang-p stj2 merc-d stj2 mur-ac stj2 *Nat-ar* stj2 *Nat-caust* stj2 *Nat-lac* stj2 nat-p stj1 nat-sil stj2 nicc-met stj2 nicc-s stj2 plb-m stj2 plb-p stj2 stront-m stj2 zinc-i stj2 zinc-m stj2 zinc-n stj2 zinc-p stj2]
  - **evening**: *(↗evening; Anxiety - alone - evening)* brom k* dros kali-br ↓ kali-c puls ran-b k* tab
    - **bed**; in: kali-br fyz
  - **night**: abel vh1 arg-n vh* aur-m-n wbt2• bung-fa mtf *Camph* k* carb-v k2 *Caust* k* falco-pe nl2• gaert ptj• *Hell* st1 hep oss• kali-br mrr1 lyc mrr1 *Med* vh* oxal-a rly4• **STRAM** k1* tab a1
  - **aversion** to company, with (See Company - aversion - fear)
  - **away** from partner: galeoc-c-h gms1•
  - **bed**; on going to: caust bg2
  - **darkness**; in the: camph kr1 kali-br ptk1 kali-p fyz med dx puls hu* rad-br c11* *Stram* tl1* valer ptk1
  - **desire** of being alone, but: con hr1* *Dys* fmm1• kali-c fyz lyc fyz
  - **headache**, with: meny st1
  - **lest**:
    - **he** die: *(↗death - alone)* *Arg-n* **Ars** k1* *Ars-h* k1* bell k1 *Kali-c Phos*
    - **injuring** himself (See Injuring - fear)
  - **menses**; during: ars mtn* con hr1* elaps mtn
- **alternating** with:
  - **courage** (See Courageous - alternating - fear)
  - **exhilaration**: coff gl1.fr•
  - **mania**: *Bell* hell fyz
  - **rage** (See Rage - alternating - fear)
  - **sadness**: zinc bg2*
- **amenorrhea** from fear: *Op* kr1
- **angry**; of becoming: lyss jl2
- **animals**, of: *(↗bees; birds; bugs; cats; chickens; cockroaches; creeping things; devoured; dogs; flies; frogs; horses; insects; mice; rats; scorpions; snakes; spiders; wasps; wolves)* abel jl3 *Alum* sne **Bell** ptk1* bufo k* calc vh* carc fd* caust k* **Chin** k* chinin-s mrr1 elaps gk hyos k* nat-m bg phos mtf33 plat mrr1 plb cld• positr nl2• puls gk* ruta ld sil mtf33 *Stram* k* sulph mtf33 syc pte1* tarent mtf33 *Tub* bg3* [arg-n stj2]
  - **night** | **venomous** animals; of: abel jl3
  - **black**: bell hr1
  - **domestic**: **Chin** mrr1
  - **furred**: tub mrr1*
- **anorexia** from fear: carc mlr1• *Ign* kr1
- **anthropophobia** (See people)
- **antidoting** his homeopathic remedies; of: **Cann-i** mrr1 nit-ac mrr1
- **apoplexy**, of: *(↗paralysis)* abel jl3 *Acon* vh1 *Alum* a1* aml-ns vh1 apis k* *Arg-met* k* arg-n arn k* *Aster* k* bell brom bg2* calc gk cann-i a1 carb-v k* cench *Coff* k* colch rb2 elaps k* *Ferr* k* (non:ferr-p k*) ferr-t a1* fl-ac k* glon bg2* kali-ar mrr1 kali-br bg2* kali-cy rb2 lach nat-c k* nux-v gg phos plat vh* prim-v rb2 psor al2 *Puls* h1* sel sf1.de *Sep* h2* staph vh* tarent rb2 ter k* thuj verat k* *Zinc* bg2* [am-br stj2]
  - **morning**: alum a
  - **evening**: *Puls* h1*
  - **night** | **feeling** as if head would burst at night; with: *Aster*
  - **palpitation**, with: arg-met
  - **respiration**; with anxious: thuj fyz
  - **stool**, during: verat k*
  - **waking**, on: arn h1* carb-v h2* glon k*
- **appearing** in public, of: *(↗Timidity - public)* anac ptk1 arg-n ptk1* carb-v tl1* *Dys* fmm1• **Gels** hr1* *Lyc* k2* *Sil* k2* spong fd4.de
- **approaching**; of: *(↗crossing - street; near; run over; fear of being - going)* acet-ac ↓ acon ↓ *Ambr* ↓ anac ↓ anth ↓ **ARN** ↓ ars ↓ bar-c ↓ bar-i ↓ *Bell* ↓ cadm-s ↓ cann-i ↓ caust ↓ *Cham* ↓ chin ↓ *Cina* ↓ coff ↓ con ↓ *Cupr* ↓ *Cupr-act* ↓ cupr-f ↓ cupr-p ↓ falco-pe ↓ graph ↓ hydr-ac ↓ *Hyper* ↓ *Ign* ↓ iod ↓ irid-met ↓ kali-c ↓ lach ↓ *Lyc* ↓ lyss ↓ mag-p ↓ mang-i ↓ meli ↓ merc-i-f ↓ nux-v ↓ op ↓ petr ↓ phos ↓ plb ↓ rhod ↓ sep ↓ spong ↓ *Stram* ↓ stry ↓ tarent ↓ tell ↓ ther ↓ *Thuj* ↓ valer ↓ [ant-c stj2 ant-met stj2 ant-t stj2 cupr-m stj2 lith-i stj2]
  - **others**; of: *(↗Approached - agg.; Approached - aversion; Timidity)* acet-ac acon ↓ *Ambr* anac *Ant-c* vh* ant-t ↓ **ARN** bg2* ars tl1 bar-c bg2* *Bell* cadm-s k* cann-i caust ptk1 *Cham* vh* chin ↓ *Cina* ↓ coff ↓ con *Cupr* k* *Cupr-act* kr1* falco-pe nl2• graph fb *Hyper* sne *Ign* k* iod k* irid-met srj5• kali-c ↓ lach ↓ *Lyc* k* mag-p ↓ meli sne nux-v kr1 op petr ptk1 phos ptk1 plb ptk1 rhod st sep ptk1 spong fd4.de *Stram* stry bg2 tarent ptk1 tell ↓ ther ptk1 *Thuj* k* valer ↓ [bar-i stj2 cupr-f stj2 cupr-p stj2 mang-i stj2 merc-i-f stj2]
    - **children** cannot bear to have anyone come near them: ambr fyz *Ant-c* vh* arn fyz bell fyz *Cina Cupr* k* ign fyz kali-c fyz* lach fyz stram fyz valer fyz
    - **delirium**, in: *(↗Delirium)* cupr ign gk plb gk stram *Thuj*
    - **menstrual** colic; during: ant-t a
    - **starting**; with: *Bell* kr1
    - **touched**, lest he be: *(↗touched; Touched - aversion)* acon ptk1 **ARN** k1* ars fyz chin fyz coff fyz kali-c fyz lach fyz mag-p fyz plb gk rhod st stram fyz tell fyz valer fyz
  - **vehicles**, of: *(↗accidents)* anth hydr-ac k* lyss st phos
- **arrested**; of being: *(↗Delusions - arrested)* ars ptk1 bell fyz meli c1* plb ptk1 ruta vh tab ptk1 zinc ptk1
- **ascending**, of: *Nit-ac* sf1.de*
- **asking** what I want: dioxi rbp6
- **attacked**; fear of being: *(↗injury - being)* bit-ar wht1• carc mlr1• crot-c sk4• falco-pe nl2• lac-h sze9• petr-ra shn4• *Stram* h1 streptoc rly4• suis-pan rly4• tritic-vg fd5.de
  - **partner**; by: falco-pe nl2•
- **authority**; of: *(↗Servile)* aids nl2• lac-h sze9•
- **away** from home; when: *(↗Anxiety - away)* haliae-lc srj5• ign vh* spong fd4.de [moly-met stj2]
- **baby** will die in utero: *(↗pregnancy)* kali-fcy zr phos zr tritic-vg fd5.de vib zr
- **bad** news; of hearing: *(↗Ailments - bad)* acon bg2* ambr bg2* anac bg2 apis vh *Ars* bg2 asaf bg2 aster kr1* aur bg2 bar-c bg2 bell bg2 *Bry* bg2 calad bg2 calc h2* *Calc-p* k* camph bg2 caps bg2 carb-v bg2 caust bg2 cham bg2 chin bg2 chinin-s bg2 cina bg2 cocc bg2 coff bg2 croc bg2 crot-h bg2 cupr bg2 cycl bg2 dig bg2 dirc a1 dros k* gels fyz graph bg2 hep bg2 kali-c fyz lac-leo hrn2• *Lyss* k1* merc bg2 nat-m bg2* nat-p nux-v bg2 petr bg2 phos bg2 *Psor* bg2 sabad bg2 sil bg2 *Verat* bg2
- **bath**; of taking a: adam srj5• ant-c fyz* rhus-t fyz sep fyz* spig fyz sulph tl2*
- **bed**:
  - **child** fears to go to bed alone: caust gt*
  - **of** the: *(↗Bed - aversion)* *Acon* k* alumn ptk1 *Ars* bapt calc st *Camph* k* cann-s k* cann-xyz ptk1 canth carb-v ↓ *Caust* k* cedr k* cench cent cupr hr1* kali-ar kali-c *Lach* k* lyc k* merc nat-c nat-m j5.de squil syph fyz xan ↓ [heroin sdj2]
    - **alone**; when: ars fyz *Camph* kr1 *Caust* hr1* xan bg
    - **dark**; in: carb-v bl caust fr
  - **raised** himself in, when he: ox-ac a1
  - **turn** over in; to: acon ll1*
- **bees**, of: *(↗animals)* *Hep* vh* [nat-caust stj2]
- **behind** him; someone is: *(↗people - behind; Delusions - people - behind; Delusions - walking - behind; Looking - backwards; Looking - backwards - followed)* anac k* brom k* crot-c lach k* med k* merc vh *Phel* vh* sal-fr sle1• staph fyz
- **betrayed**; of being: bell mtf hyos k* ign mtf lach mtf lyss fyz nat-m mtf petr-ra shn4•
- **birds**: *(↗animals)* aesc fyz *Apis* vh1 bufo a* calc-ar bng calc-s vh* gels sys ign vh* kali-c sys lyss ↓ *Nat-m* gk* op gk ph-ac dgt tub ser
  - **chickens** (See chickens)
  - **imaginary** birds; is frightened by: kali-c h2
  - **mouse**; thought that a bird was a: lyss kr1
- **biting** teeth together; of | **fall** out; for fear they would: nit-ac

- **bitten**, of being: *(↗Biting)* abrot asaf choc srj3• falco-pe nl2• *Hyos* k* *Lyss*
- **black**: *(↗Colors - black - aversion)*
  - **everything**: *(↗Colors - black - aversion)* ars fyz rob **Stram** st tarent fyz verat fyz
  - **men**: musca-d szs1
- **blind**; of going: agre jl3 atro fyz *Nux-v* hr1* *Sulph* hr1*
- **blood**; fear when looking at: *(↗Blood)* alum ptk2* plat gk
- **brain**; fear of softening of: *(↗Delusions - brain - softening)* abrot *Arg-n* hr1 *Asaf* k* calc-sil k2 vanad dx
- **breakdown**; of nervous: *(↗control)* kali-p fyz lyc mtf33 nat-m fyz sil fyz
- **breath** away; takes: *Rhus-t* *Spong* fd4.de *Verat*
- **brilliant** objects or cannot endure them; fear of: *(↗mirrors)* anan vh1 cann-i a1 canth ptk1* lach ptk1* lyss ptk1 stram k*
- **bugs**; of: *(↗animals; insects)* *Calc* vh*
- **buildings**:
  - **in** buildings: dys fmm1•
  - **of** buildings: *(↗fall upon)* arg-met ckh1 arg-n hr1 calc sej4 kali-p ckh1 visc ckh1
- **burden**, of becoming a: raph k* [spect dfg1]
- **buried** alive; of being: atro hs tub al *Zinc* hr1* [moly-met stj2]
- **burns**; of: calc-s mtf33
- **bus**; in: dys fmm1•
- **business** failure; of: *(↗business failure; business; of; career; failure; job; poverty; unfit; Cares full - business; Confidence - want; Succeeds; Timidity)* acon fyz arg-n jsa arn vh *Aur* gk* bry fyz calc fyz carb-an vh cimic fyz gels vh iod vh *Kali-c* gk kali-p fyz lac-c vh lyc jsa* moni rfm1• nat-m vh nux-v fyz phos vh *Psor* k* sil jsa sulph vh
- **business**; of: *(↗business failure; Business - aversion)* *Graph* kr1 *Lil-t* kr1 [arg-n stj2]
- **calamity** (See disaster)
- **called** by his name; being: sulph fyz
- **cancer**; of: *(↗death - cancer; Thoughts - disease - incurable)* **Agar** st* arg-n vh* **Ars** st* aster↓ aur-m-n wbt2• bac bn* bamb-a stb2.de• bar-c mtf cadm-met mtf calc st* calc-f vh* calc-p vh* carc gk6* chinin-ar st* clem mtf11 cupr sst3• falco-pe nl2• fl-ac st* ign st* kali-ar st* lac-c fyz* lac-e mtf* lac-h mtf* *Lob* gk luf-op vml3• lyc mrr1 mag-m dgt **Manc** gk med st miml-g mtf11 nat-m fyz* *Nit-ac* st* phos vh* **Plat** hr1 plut-n srj7• *Positr* nl2• **Psor** k1* ruta ld* scol mtf sep fyz* streptoc jl2* sulph mrr1 verat fyz* [am-caust stj2 am-f stj2 beryl stj2 beryl-m stj2 bor-pur stj2 ferr-n stj2 fl-pur stj2 graph stj2 lith-c stj2 lith-f stj2 lith-met stj2 mag-n stj2 mang-n stj2 nat-ar stj2 nitro stj2 oxyg stj2 spect dfg1 stann stj2 tax jsj7 zinc-n stj2]
  - **brain** tumor: bamb-a stb2.de• ruta fd4.de
  - ○ **Mammae**: aster sze10•
- **captured**; of being: phasco-ci rbp2
- **career**; for one's: *(↗business failure; failure)* carc mlr1•
- **carried**, fear of being: *(↗Carried - aversion)* *Borx* bro1 bry bro1 sanic bro1*
- **cars** and vehicles in the street; of: hydr-ac br1
- **catalepsy**; of: art-v fyz
- **cats**; of: *(↗animals; Hatred - cats)* absin fyz aur mtf *Bac* vh* calc mtf calc-ar mtf carc mtf chin vh* elaps gk ign↓ lyc ser med vh3* nat-m↓ plb cld• sil pc* syph dx1* *Tub* bg2* [merc stj2]
- **caught**; of being: crot-c sk4•
- **causeless**: acon tl1* alco *Ars* calc-f sf1.de cann-i carc mlr1• chlol a1 falco-pe nl2• granit-m es1• lac-ac stj5• maias-l hrn2• melal-alt gya4 phos mrr1 plb ptk1* pop mtf11 positr nl2• psor jl2 sabad sf1.de samb k* seq-s bkh1 spong fd4.de* tarent a1* tritic-vg fd5.de zinc mtf33 zinc-val ptk1 [alum stj2 *Am-caust* stj2 *Am-f* stj2 arg-n stj2 *Beryl* stj2 beryl-m stj2 *Bor-pur* stj2 *Cupr-f* stj2 ferr-n stj2 *Fl-ac* stj2 *Fl-pur* stj2 *Graph* stj2 *Lith-c* stj2 *Lith-f* stj2 lith-m stj2 *Lith-met* stj2 lith-p stj2 lith-s stj2 mag-n stj2 mang-n stj2 *Nat-f* stj2 *Nitro* stj2 *Oxyg* stj2 sil stj2 tax jsj7 zinc-n stj2]
- **cemeteries**; of: merc mrr1 nat-m mtf phos mtf staph mtf stram mrr1*
- **censured** of being (See reproaches)
- **change**; of any sudden: limest-b es1•
- **chickens**: *(↗animals)* calc-p dgt chin gk ign sej2*
- **children**, in: **Bar-c** st1 *Borx*↓ calc ptk1* carc fb* caste↓ caust j5.de* dulc fd4.de hyos mtf33 **Kali-br**↓ kali-p↓ *Lyc* st1 sep mrr1 *Staph*↓ **Tub**↓
  - **night**: *(↗Anxiety - night; Anxiety - night - children)* *Borx* st *Calc* st caste jl3 **Kali-br** st kali-p st1 *Staph* sne **Tub** st
- **children**, in: ...
  - **behavior** problems; with (See Behavior - children - fears)
- **chill**, during: *Calc* k* carb-an cycl fyz hura↓ sulph lpc verat fyz
  - **bed**; on going to: hura lpc
- **chlorosis**; during: *Calc* st
- **choking**; of (See suffocation)
- **cholera**; of: arg-n fyz ars gl1.fr• jatr-c kr1 **Lach** k1* **Nit-ac** k* ph-ac kr1 sulph gt verat gl1.fr•
- **chronic**: *(↗continuous; lifelong)* *Acon* ptk1 hyos ptk1 op ptk1 petr ptk1
- **church** or opera, when ready to go: *(↗Anticipation)* **Arg-n** k* bry dys ptj• *Gels* k* plb cld• sanic
- **claustrophobia** (See narrow)
- **climbing** boys should be harmed, that: caust a1
- **closed** places; of (See narrow)
- **closing** eyes, on: aeth k* *Carb-an* *Carb-v* ptk1 *Caust* k* mag-m ptk1*
- **coal** scuttle, of: cann-i
- **cockroaches**; of: *(↗animals)* alum vh1* grat mtf manc gl• petr-ra shn4• phos vh* toxi mtf [vanad stj2]
- **coition**:
  - **during**: *(↗impotence)* sin-n kr1
    - ⁝ **impotence** from fear; with: *Sin-n* kr1
  - **rape**: ozone sde2•
  - **thought** of coition in a women; at: arn vh *Kreos* k* ozone sde2•
- **cold**, of taking: chin↓ nat-c k* nux-v↓ staph↓ sulph k* syph dx1
  - **head**; of the: chin gl• nux-v gl• staph gl•
  - **heat**, during: sulph h2*
- **cold** air; of: med jl2 pyrog jl2
- **coldness**; with: am-c kr1
- **company**, of: cic kr1 cupr ptk1 cupr-act ptk1 dys fmm1• mag-c mtf33 morg-g pte1*• sel hr1* til ptk1
- **complaints**, of imaginary: hydr-ac kali-c ptk1 laur ptk1 sep ptk
- **concussion**; of: arg-met hr1
- **confusion** of mind; that people would observe her (See Delusions - confusion)
- **consumption**, of: *Calc* k* guar vml3• kali-c jl3 lac-c paull k* puls fyz sep k* tarent *Tub* kr1
- **contagion**: *(↗contagion; disease - contagious; infection)* aids nl2• **Ars** lmj* borx b4a.de* bov vh* calc vh* **Carc** lmj* falco-pe nl2• ign lmj lac-c lmj lach vh* *Med* lmj nat-m mrr1 oscilloc jl2 psor lmj ruta fd4.de sil lmj sulph lmj syph lmj* vanil fd5.de [oxyg stj2]
  - **children**; in: **Ars** lmj **Calc** lmj **Carc** lmj ign lmj lac-c lmj lach lmj *Med* lmj psor lmj sil lmj sulph lmj **Syph** lmj
  - **disease**; contagious (See disease - contagious)
- **continuous**: *(↗chronic; everything)* ign k2 lyc mtf33
- **control**; losing: *(↗breakdown; insanity; self-control)* *Aeth* vh1 **Ars** mrr1 cann-i vh* carc vh1* cupr sst3*• galeoc-c-h↓ kali-s fd4.de lac-e hrn2• lyc br1 olib-sac wmh1 thea vh thuj mrr1 *Vanil* fd5.de [cupr-act stj2 cupr-f stj2 cupr-m stj2 cupr-p stj2 heroin sdj2]
  - **ocean**; to the: galeoc-c-h gms1•
- **conversation**, of: *(↗Timidity)* bar-s k2
- **convulsions**:
  - **before**: cic k2*
  - **epileptic**; of: alum arg-n k* bamb-a stb2.de• merc j5.de [cupr stj2 cupr-act stj2 cupr-f stj2 cupr-m stj2 cupr-p stj2]
    - ⁝ **morning**: alum
  - **of** convulsions; fear: bamb-a stb2.de•
  - **with**: **Stram** mrr1
- **corners**; fear to walk past certain: *(↗Delusions - corners - project - walking)* *Arg-n* k* *Kali-br* k*
- **corpses**; fear of: psor sys
- **coughing**; of: ant-t dx1 apis↓ cina mtf33 dros dx1 phos hr1 *Spong*↓
  - **burst**; lest something will: apis k2*
  - **children**; in: cina mtf33 phos↓
    - ⁝ **bronchial** catarrh; with: phos k*
    - ⁝ **keeps** still and does not move or talk; child: cina mtf33
  - **whooping** cough; during: *Spong* kr1

- **crazy**; fear of becoming (See insanity)
- **creeping** out of every corner, of something: med *Phos* k*
- **creeping** things; of: (↗*animals*) chin mtf33
- **criminals**; of: [oxyg stj]
- **crossing**: (↗*accidents*)
  - **bridge** or a place: (↗*walking - of - street*) ang ptk arg-n k2* bar-c gl1.fr• borx vh crot-c wn ferr gl1.fr• puls gl1.fr• sulph ptk ter vh
  - **street**: (↗*accidents; approaching*) *Acon* ll1* bry sne ferr-p fyz gaert ptj• hydr-ac bro1* kali-p fyz oci-sa sk4• plat bro1*
- **crowd**, in a: (↗*Narrow; Open; Anxiety - Crowd; GENERALS - Faintness - Crowded - room; GENERALS - Faintness - Crowded - street; GENERALS - Room - Full - people; HEAD - Pain - Room - crowded*) abel vh1 **Acon** k* aloe am-m ambr vh aran vh *Arg-n* k* arn bg2* ars ars-s-f k2* asaf bg2* asthm-r mtf11 *Aur* k* aur-ar k2 aur-i k2* *Aur-m-n* wbt2• aur-s k2* bamb-a stb2.de• bar-c k* bar-s k2* bell bg2 bufo calc k* carb-an carc vh1* caust cic cocc vh con dios *Dys* ↓ elaps gk ferr k* ferr-act ferr-ar ferr-p k* gard-j vlr2• gels bg3* glon br* graph k* hep k* hippoc-k szs2 hydr-ac k* ignis-alc es2• *Kali-ar* kali-bi kali-c kali-p k* lac-d vh lac-del hrn2• lac-h sze9• led levo jl3 *Lyc* k* lyss mrr1 mag-c mtf33 merc mrr1* morg-g pte1*• morg-p pte1*• nat-ar nat-c *Nat-m* k* nat-s k2* nat-sil fd3.de• nux-m gk *Nux-v* k* petr bg2 petr-ra shn4• phos plat bro1* plb k* pneu mtf11 *Puls* k* rhus-t ruta fd4.de sel k* sep ptk1 ser-a-c jl2 sil gk* spong fd4.de stann k* staph vh sulph tab til visc ptk1 [am-caust stj2 arg-met stj1* astat stj2 aur-m stj2 bar-br stj2 bar-i stj2 bar-met stj2 beryl stj2 beryl-m stj2 bism-sn stj2 bor-pur stj2 caes-met stj2 cinnb stj2 cupr-f stj2 ferr-f stj2 ferr-lac stj2 ferr-n stj2 ferr-sil stj2 hafn-met stj2 irid-met stj2 lanth-met stj2 lith-c stj2 lith-f stj2 lith-i stj2 lith-m stj2 lith-met stj2 lith-p stj2 lith-s stj2 mang-n stj2 merc-d stj2 merc-i-f stj2 nat-f stj2 nitro stj2 osm-met stj2 oxyg stj2 plb-m stj2 plb-p stj2 polon-met stj2 rhen-met stj2 tant-met stj2 thal-met stj2 tung-met stj2 zinc-n stj2 zirc-met stj2]
  - **menopause**; during: *Glon* st
  - **public** place; in a crowded: *Acon* arg-met ckh1 *Arg-n Arn Dys* ckh1 **Gels** hippoc-k szs2 phos sne
  - **street**; in a crowded: (↗*GENERALS - Faintness - crowded - street*) carc fb*
- **cruelties**, from report of: (↗*Excitement - hearing; Horrible*) calc k*
- **cutting** himself when shaving: **Calad** k1*
- **damned**, of being: arg-n fyz lach gt med fyz psor fyz verat k2
- **danger**, of impending: (↗*evil; happen; misfortune; Delusions - danger; DREAMS - Danger*) aether ambr tsm1 arg-n tl1 camph kr1 carb-ac ↓ carc mlr1• caust kr1* choc srj3• *Cic* kr1 cimic *Cocc* kr1 coff ↓ coff-t ↓ crot-c sk4• *Dulc* fd4.de fl-ac rb2 gels tl1 granit-m es1• kali-br hl lac-del hrn2• macro a1 *Maias-l* hrn2• meli c1* nat-m fyz olib-sac wmh1 samb fyz samb-c a sanic cda tarent tl1 *Tritic-vg* fd5.de vanil fd5.de [ant-m stj2 aur-m stj2 beryl-m stj2 cadm-m stj2 chlor stj2 chr-m stj2 cob-m stj2 cupr-m stj2 lith-m stj2 mang-m stj2 merc-d stj2 mur-ac stj2 plb-m stj2 stront-m stj2 zinc-m stj2]
  - **night**: aether a1 carb-ac fyz
  - **going** to sleep, on: (non:coff a1) coff-t a1*
  - **urging** to stool; with: *Caust* kr1
- **dark**; but curiously enough not in the: (↗*walking - of - dark; Anxiety - dark*) lac-c al2*
- **dark**; of: (↗*walking - of - dark; Anxiety - dark; Darkness - agg.; Light - desire*) *Acon* k* aeth st1 am-m ant-c mtf33 arg-n ptk1* ars k2* *Aur-s* wbt2• bapt bell bro1* brom k* calad st1 *Calc* k* calc-act a1 calc-ar a1 calc-p k* calc-s k* *Camph* k* **Cann-i** k* *Cann-s* bg3 *Cann-xyz* bg2* *Carb-an* k* *Carb-v* k* carc fb* cassia-s ccrh1* *Caust* k* chin j chinin-s vh* chir-fl gya2 *Cupr* k* dys ptj*• gaert ptj*• gal-ac zr galeoc-c-h gms1• gard-j vlr2• gels st1 grin st1 hyos bro1* kali-bi st1 kali-br ptk1 kali-c mrr1 kali-s bl lac-c al* lac-e hrn2• lac-h sze9• loxo-recl knl4• *Lyc* k* manc vh* *Med* k* merc mrr1 miml-g mtf11 morg bg morph oss• nat-m vh* nat-p mrr1 nux-m st1 nux-v vh* op bro1 ozone sde2• *Phos* k* pop mtf11 prot ptj• ptel gk *Puls* k* querc-r svu1• rad-br c11* rhus-t k* sanic k* sep bl sil st1* **STRAM** bg2* *Stront-c* k* sulph hu syc ptj*• thres-a sze7• *Tub* ser* *Tub-k* wta valer k* xan bg zinc sf1.de* [alum-p stj2 am-br stj2 arg-p stj2 bar-br stj2 *Buteo-j* sej6 cadm-met stj2 cadm-s stj2 cupr-act stj2 cupr-f stj2 cupr-m stj2 cupr-p stj2 graph stj2 heroin sdj2 lith-p stj2 mang-p stj2 mur-ac stj2 nat-sil stj2 plb-p stj2 zinc-i stj2 zinc-m stj2 zinc-n stj2 zinc-p stj2]
  - **children**; in: bell mtf33 brom mtf33 calc-s mtf33 carb-v mtf33 carc mlr1* caust mtf33 hyos mtf33 lac-c mtf33 med mtf33 nux-v mtf33 puls mtf33 sanic mtf33 sil mtf33 *Stram* mrr1*
  - **closing** eyes; on: carb-an ptk1
  - **trembling** of hands; with: ozone sde2•
- **dawn**, of the return of: kali-i k*
- **death**, of: (↗*Death - presentiment*) **ACON** b7.de* act-sp adam skp7• *Adren* vh1 *Aeth* ↓ *Agn* k* aids nl2• all-s aloe alum k* alum-p k2 am-c k* anac k* anan k* *Ang* ↓ anh mg1.de* ant-c k* ant-t k* *Apis* k* aq-mar rbp6 aran jl3 *Arg-n* k* *Arn* bg2* **ARS** b4.de* ars-h vh *Ars-s-f* k2 asaf k* asar vh aur k* aur-ar k2 aur-m-n wbt2• aur-s k2* bapt bar-c k* bar-s k2 *Bell* k* *Bism* mrr1 *Bry* k* bufo k* *Cact* k* calad **Calc** k* *Calc-ar* k2* calc-s calen mgm• camph k* *Cann-i* k* cann-s bg cann-xyz bg2 canth caps k* carb-an j5.de carb-v k2 carbn-s *Carc* mlr1• cassia-s ↓ *Caust* k* *Cench* ↓ chel k* chin b7a.de* **Cimic** k* *Cocc* k* *Coff* k* con k* cop corv-cor bdg• croc *Crot-c* k* culx k2 *Cupr* k* *Cupr-act* ↓ cur *Cycl* cystein-l rly4• *Dig* k* diosm br1 dros a1 *Elaps* vh* fago a1 ferr k* ferr-ar *Ferr-p* *Fl-ac* k* gard-j vlr2• **Gels** k* germ-met ↓ gink-b ↓ glon k* *Graph* b4.de* haliae-lc srj5• ham ↓ heli-n mtf11 *Hell* k* *Hep* k* hydr bro1 hydr-ac ptk1 hydrog srj2*• hyos ign k* iod j5.de* ip k* iris **Kali-ar** k* kali-bi ↓ kali-br ↓ *Kali-c* k* kali-fcy a1 *Kali-i* k* *Kali-n* k* kali-p kali-s ketogl-ac rly4• **Lac-c** k* lac-h ↓ *Lach* k* lat-m jl3* led *Lil-t* bro1 lob k* *Lyc* k* mag-c ↓ mag-s k* **Manc** gk med k* menis ↓ *Merc* j5.de* miml-g mtf11 *Mosch* k* mygal k* naja bro1 nat-c j5.de* *Nat-m* bg2* nat-p mrr1* **Nit-ac** k* nit-s-d ↓ nux-m k* **Nux-v** k* oci-sa sk4• olnd ↓ *Op* k* ox-ac ozone sde2• petr k* *Ph-ac* phase bro1 **Phos** k* phyt **Plat** k* pneu jl3* podo k* pot-e rly4• *Psor* k* *Puls* k* rad-br sze8• raph rheum k* *Rhus-t* k* rob *Ruta* b7a.de* sabad bro1 *Sec* k* sep k* sium a1 *Spong* k* squil k* stann bro1 staph bro1* still bro1 stram k* sulph k* symph fd3.de• syph bro1* tab k* tarax tarent k* thea ↓ trach a1 tril-p tritic-vg fd5.de tub gb• v-a-b ↓ *Vanil* fd5.de vario a1* *Verat* k* verat-v k* vinc visc sp1 xan c1 zinc k* zinc-p k2* [am-caust stj2 am-f stj2 ant-met stj2 ars-met stj2 astat stj2 aur-m stj2 bar-br stj2 bar-i stj2 bar-met stj2 beryl stj2 beryl-m stj2 *Bism-sn* stj2 bor-pur stj2 brom stj1 caes-met stj2 calc-p stj1 cinnb stj2 cupr-f stj2 ferr-f stj2 ferr-lac stj2 ferr-n stj2 ferr-sil stj2 fl-pur stj2 hafn-met stj2 irid-met stj2 lanth-met stj2 lith-c stj2 lith-f stj2 lith-i stj2 lith-m stj2 lith-met stj2 lith-s stj2 mag-n stj2 mag-p stj1 mag-sil stj2 mang-i stj2 mang-m stj2 mang-met stj2 mang-n stj2 mang-p stj2 mang-s stj2 merc-d stj2 merc-i-f stj2 moly-met stj2 nat-ar stj2 nat-br stj2 nat-caust stj2 nat-f stj2 nat-lac stj2 nat-met stj2 nat-sil stj2 nitro stj2 osm-met stj2 oxyg stj2 plb stj2 plb-m stj2 plb-p stj2 polon-met stj2 rhen-met stj2 sil stj2 spect dfg1 tant-met stj2 thal-met stj2 tung-met stj2 zinc-i stj2 zinc-m stj2 zinc-n stj2]
  - **morning**: con kali-p fd1.de• lyc
  - **afternoon** | **17**.30 h: nux-m a1
  - **evening**: *Calc* nat-m ↓ *Phos*
    - **bed**; in: nat-m h2
  - **night**: act-sp k* am-c h2 *Arn* k2* ars k2 calc-ar k2 chel kali-s k2 *Phos* syph jl2
    - **midnight**:
      - **after**:
        - **1**-2 h: ars k2
        - **1**-3 h: ars st
  - **abortion**; in: *Acon* mtn apis mtn coff kr1 gels mtn kali-c mtn *Sec* mtn stram mtn
  - **alone**, when: (↗*alone - lest - he; Company - desire; Company - desire - alone*) act-sp ↓ *Arg-n Arn* st1 **Ars** ars-h bell camph fyz *Caust* ↓ cupr ↓ *Kali-ar* gk *Kali-c* k2* lac-h sze9• menis bg *Phos* k* tub tl
    - **evening** | **bed**; in: (↗*SLEEP - Sleeplessness - Dark*) act-sp vh *Ars Caust* kr1 cupr sst3• kali-c *Phos*
  - **alternating** with | **laughing** (See Laughing - alternating - fear)
  - **amenorrhea**; in: plat kr1 *Xan* kr1
  - **anger**; from: *Plat* hr1*
  - **angina** pectoris; during: (↗*heart*) acon kr1 *Dig* kr1 lat-m ah1 squil kr1
  - **bed**:
    - **going** to; on: ars hr1* camph fyz caust fyz *Lach* kr1
    - **in**: nat-m h2
  - **cancer**; of: (↗*cancer*) carc mlr1•
  - **cholera** asiatica; during: *Cupr* kr1 *Cupr-act* kr1 **Verat** kr1
  - **convalescence**; during: tarent kr1
  - **convulsions**; during: acon kr1 kali-br kr1
  - **delivery**:
    - **after**: agn c1
    - **during**: **Acon** k* *Coff* k* plat k*
  - **desire** for death; fear with: *Aur* kr1*
  - **diarrhea**; during: ham kr1

- **dream**, from: alum j5.de cench k2
- **dyspnea**; with: *(↗respiratory)* psor kr1
- **epistaxis**; with: *Croc* kr1
- **farewell** messages; prepares: lyc kr1
- **fatal** end of disease; of: ant-t kr1 calc hr1 kali-c hr1 lil-t hr1 *Ph-ac* kr1 *Spong* hr1*
- **fright**; after: plat kr1
- **gastritis**; during: *Cocc* kr1
- **head**; with complaints of: lach bg2
- **heart** symptoms, during: *(↗angina; Delusions - die - about - heart; Delusions - heart - disease - going)* **Acon** kr1* *Ang* kr1 *Arn* kr1* asaf cact k2 carb-v k2 cench k2 **Dig** kr1* germ-met srj5• gink-b sbd1• *Naja* kr1 *Plat* kr1 *Psor* kr1*
  - **dyspepsia**; in: *Ang* hr1*
- **heat**, during: acon bg2* *Ars* bg2 bry k* calc k* cocc k* dig ↓ ip k* mosch k* *Nit-ac* k* *Nux-v* bg2 phos bg2 *Plat* bg2 **Puls** bg2 rhus-t bg2 **Ruta** k* *Verat* bg2
  - **intermittent**: dig kr1
- **hemoptysis**; during: **Acon** kr1
- **hemorrhage**; during uterine: *(↗GENERALS - Hemorrhage - easy - accompanied - death)* acon kr1 *Coff* kr1 nux-m kr1 **Plat** kr1
- **hunger**; from (See starving)
- **hypochondriasis**; with (See Hypochondriasis - fear)
- **impending** death; of: acon tl1* agn gt am-c kr1 arg-n tl1 *Ars* gl1.fr• a s a f kr1 **Bell** gl1.fr• bry gl1.fr• calc tl1 **Cann-i** kr1 caps kr1 carc mlr• caust kr1 cimic gt *Croc* kr1 cupr sst3*• glon gt lach gl1.fr• lat-m bnm6• *Lob* kr1 **Merc** gl1.fr• nit-ac gt nux-v gl1.fr• op st **Phos** kr1 ruta fd4.de sec gt sep gl1.fr• staph gl1.fr• v-a-b jl2*
- **kill** her; that those in the house might: *Cimic* kr1
- **labor**, during (See delivery - during)
- **laughing** alternating with weeping; with: *Plat* kr1
- **loquacity**; with: **ACON** hr1
- **lying** down; on: act-sp vh mosch k2
- **medicine**; therefore useless to take: ars tl1
- **menses**:
  - **after**: acon mtn sec mtn
  - **before**: *(↗Menses - before)* acon kali-bi plat sec sulph xan
  - **during**: *(↗Menses - during)* acon plat *Sec* mtn verat
- **metrorrhagia**; during (See hemorrhage)
- **migraine**; during (See pain - head)
- **moving** about amel.: camph kr1
- **pain**, from: anan a1 ars ↓ cact k2 **Coff** **Kali-i** ↓ naja ↓ olnd ↓
  - **Head**; in: ars kr1
  - **Heart**; around: naja kr1*
  - **Root** of tongue: **Kali-i** hr1*
  - **Teeth**; in: olnd a
- **pale** face; with: *Mosch* kr1
- **paralysis**; during: *Caust* kr1
- **perspiration**, during: *Acon* bg2 ars bg2 bry bg2 kali-n k* *Nit-ac* bg2 nit-s-d lpc nux-v bg2 phos bg2 plat bg2 puls bg2 rhus-t bg2 **Verat** bg2
- **predicts** the time: *(↗soon; Death - presentiment - predicts; Prophesying - predicts)* **Acon** k* apis vh *Arg-n*
- **pregnancy**, during: **Acon**
- **pressure** in hypogastrium, with: ph-ac h2
- **prolapse** of uterus; with: **ACON** hr1
- **reason**; and loss of: *Plat* kr1
- **relatives**; of (See Anxiety - family; Cares, full - relatives)
- **respiratory** complaints; with: *(↗dyspnea; lung)* ars ll1* lob ll1*
- **sadness**; with: *Agn* br1 cupr ptk1* *Plat* kr1 vinc kr1
- **scarlatina**; after: *Hell* kr1
- **sitting** agg.: ph-ac a rhus-t ↓
  - **bent** over: rhus-t a

- **death**, of: ...
  - **sleep**:
    - **die** if he goes to sleep; fear he will: *Aeth* ↓ cassia-s ccrh1• lach kr1* led ↓ nux-m c1* symph fd3.de•
      - **nightmare**; after a: *Aeth* vh* *Lach* kr1 led k*
    - **during**: aeth dx1 ign dx1 pot-e rly4•
    - **falling** asleep:
      - **after**: acon vh1 *Aeth* vh1 cupr sst3• lach rb2
      - **on** falling asleep: lach rb2 led ↓
        - **nightmare**; after a: led fyz
    - **followed** by | **deep** sleep: vario kr1
    - **going** to sleep; on: nux-v bg2
  - **soon**; that one will die: *(↗predicts)* acon br1 *Agn* k* cench k2 plat bc *Sep* gl1.fr•
  - **starvation**; from (See starving)
  - **strength**; with loss of: *Rhus-t* kr1
  - **sudden** death; of: *Arn* *Ars* *Cench* k2 cupr sst3• lat-m ah tab mg thea
  - **suffocation**; from: *Spong* kr1
  - **suicidal** tendency; with (See Suicidal - fear - death)
  - **teeth**; during pain in (See pain - teeth)
  - **uterus**; from pain in: cact kr1 *Con* kr1
  - **vertigo**; during: nat-c a rhus-t b7.de*
  - **vexation**, after: ars
  - **vomiting**: *Ars* k* ars-h vh mag-c h2
  - **waking**, on: alum *Ars* kr1 ars-h vh con j5.de *Ign* ↓ kali-p fd1.de•
    - **afternoon** sleep; from: *Ign* vh*
  - **walking**, while: *Dig*
  - **weary** of life (See Weary - fear)
  - **weeping**; with laughing alternating with (See laughing)
  - **whooping** cough; in: *Anac* kr1
  - **wires** encaging him; saw: *Cimic* kr1
- **delusions**; fear from: *(↗imaginary)* falco-pe nl2• manc mrr1 spong fd4.de **Stram** st *Tritic-vg* fd5.de
- **dentist**; of going to: *(↗Anticipation - dentist)* calc st1 galeoc-c-h gms1• hep mrr1 puls wta* tritic-vg fd5.de tub wta [mang-n stj2]
- **descending**; of (See downward)
- **destination**, of being unable to reach his: galeoc-c-h gms1• lyc k*
- **destruction** of all near her; of impending: *Kali-br* kr1
- **devil**, of being taken by the: *(↗hell; Delusions - devil - taken; Religious - too)* anac sf1.de manc puls fyz
- **devils**, of: *(↗hell)* **Manc** mrr1 zinc j5.de [astat stj2 aur stj2 aur-m stj2 aur-s stj2 bar-br stj2 bar-i stj2 bar-met stj2 bism-sn stj2 caes-met stj2 cinnb stj2 hafn-met stj2 irid-met stj2 lanth-met stj2 merc stj2 merc-d stj2 merc-i-f stj2 osm-met stj2 plat stj2 p l b stj2 plb-m stj2 plb-p stj2 polon-met stj2 rhen-met stj2 tant-met stj2 thal-met stj2 tung-met stj2]
- **devoured** by animals; of being: *(↗animals)* hyos h1 positr nl2• stram
- **diarrhea**:
  - **fear**; with: acon k1 aeth sf1.de* arg-n kr1 coff fyz *Crot-t* kr1 gard-j vlr2• **Gels** kr1 ign kr1 *Kali-p* kr1 **Op** kr1 phos fyz *Puls* kr1 verat fyz
  - **from**: arg-n kr1 dulc fd4.de **Gels** kr1 ign kr1 *Kali-p* kr1 **Op** kr1 *Verat* kr1
  - **suppressed**; with: abrot k13
- **dinner**, after: mag-m k* phel k*
- **diphtheria**; of: bac bn
- **dirt**; of: *(↗Cleanness - mania; Washing - desire)* carc mlr1• oscilloc jl2
- **disaster**; of (= calamity): calc ptk2 calli-h rb2 elat ketogl-ac rly4• lac-c mrr1 lil-t med jl2 psor *Puls* rhus-t rb2 *Scut* br1 tab tub al wye c1 zinc rb2 [bar-i stj2 iod stj2 merc-i-f stj2]
  - **someone** were rapidly approaching a disaster: tab rb2
- **disease**, of impending: *(↗head - something; mammae; respiratory; Anxiety - germs - catch; Anxiety - health; Anxiety - health - own; Anxiety - ill; Thoughts - disease)* acon k* adam skp7• aether agar *Agn* bro1 all-s ↓ *Alum* k* alum-p k2 am-c k* anac bro1 ant-t bg2* *Apis* bro1 *Arg-n* k* *Arn* bg2* ars k* ars-h ↓ *Aur* bro1 *Aur-m-n* wbt2• bamb-a stb2.de• bar-c ↓ bell-p-sp ↓ *Borx* k* bov st1 bry k* bufo k* bung-fa ↓ *Cact* bro1 calad k* *Calc* k* *Calc-ar* k2* calc-sil k2* cann-i bro1 carb-ac k* carb-an k* carc sk1* cecr ↓ chin sne chlor sf1.de chord-umb ↓ cic k* cimic bro1* coca-c ↓ cocc ↓ cupr sst3• cur ↓ *Dig* bro1 diosm br1 dulc fd4.de elaps elat bg eup-pur k* gels bro1 graph bro1* helo-s rwt2•

- **disease**, of impending: ...
hep k* hydr k* ign k* iris kali-ar mrr1* **Kali-c** k* kali-p kali-s fd4.de kali-tel a1 kreos k* *Lac-c* k* lac-e hrn2• lach k* lap-la sde8.de• *Lec* k* *Lil-t* k* lyc h2* m-arct j5.de malar jl2 med bro1 merc k* moni rfm1• naja bro1 nat-ar k* nat-c k* nat-m k* nat-p k* nat-sil fd3.de• *Nit-ac* k* *Nux-v* k* oxal-a rly4• ozone sde2• paull petr-ra ↓ *Ph-ac* k* phase bro1 **Phos** k* *Plat* bg2* pneu jl3* podo k* psor bg2* *Puls* bg2* raph ↓ rhus-t bro1 *Ruta* fd4.de sabad bg2* sacch-a fd2.de• sec bro1* *Sel* sf1.de* *Sep* k* *Spong* hr1* stann bg2* staph bro1* still bro1 stram mrr1 sulph k* *Syph* bro1* tab bg2 tarent thuj k* tril-c a1 tril-p tritic-vg fd5.de ulm-c jsj8• vanil fd5.de verat bro1 [am-caust stj2 am-f stj2 am-p stj1 ant-c stj2 ant-met stj2 arg-met stj1* ars-met stj2 bar-i stj2 beryl stj2 beryl-m stj2 bor-pur stj2 brom stj1 calc-lac stj2 calc-met stj2 cupr-f stj2 *Ferr-n* stj2 fl-ac stj2 fl-pur stj2 iod stj2 lith-c stj2 lith-f stj2 lith-i stj2 lith-m stj2 lith-met stj2 lith-p stj2 lith-s stj2 mag-lac stj2 mag-met stj2 mag-p stj1 mang-i stj2 *Mang-n* stj2 mur-ac stj2 nat-f stj2 *Nitro* stj2 oxyg stj2 sil stj2 tax jsj7 zinc-i stj2 *Zinc-n* stj2]
  - **night**:
    - **bed**; in: ars-h ↓ carb-ac
      - **waking**; while: ars-h kr1
  - **Alzheimer's**: lac-e hrn2•
  - **cancer** (See cancer)
  - **contagious**, epidemic diseases; of: (↗*contagion; infection)* bar-c j borx c1* bov a1* **Calc** c1* chin sne cur dx1 lach vh* med sne* nat-m gg sil ↓ *Sulph* vh5* *Syph* vh* [bell-p-sp dcm1 tax jsj7]
    - **children**; in: sil lmj
  - **deadly** disease:
    - **morning** | **waking**; on: coca-c sk4•
  - **dependent** on others; to be: cupr sst3•
  - **incurable**, of being: (↗*recover; Delusions - disease - incurable; Thoughts - disease - incurable)* acon bg2 all-s a1 alum bg2 ant-t a1 arg-n sf1.de arn bg2 ars a1* bung-fa mtf cact k2* calc bg2 calc-sil k2* carc mlr1• cecr jl3 chord-umb rly4• cimic jl3 cocc h1 ign bg2* lac-c bg2 lach bg2 lil-t bg2* petr-ra shn4• ruta fd4.de stann bg2 syph al*
  - **pain**; during: diosm br1
  - **sadness**; with (See Sadness - fear - with - disease)
  - **trembling** from the idea: ign fyz
  - **unrecognized**: lil-t fyz raph fyz
  - **walking** in the open air agg.: hep
- **disfigured**, of being: hep gl1.fr•
- **disgrace**; of: rob fyz
- **disputes** (See quarrels)
- **disturbed**, of being: agar h2*
- **disturbing** someone; of: (↗*Humility)* lac-h sze9• mosch a1
- **doctors**: (↗*medical; operation; Alert - movement - doctor)* aloe vh1 arg-n fyz *Arn* vh* coff ↓ dys ptj• *Ign* vh* iod k* nat-m vh* nux-v kr1* *Phos* vh* sep vh* staph mrr1 *Stram* kr1* thuj k* tub fyz* verat fyz verat-v k* [bar-i stj2 lith-i stj2 merc-i-f stj2 zinc-i stj2]
  - **surgeon**: coff kr1
- **dogs**, of: (↗*animals)* abies-c oss4• androc srj1• *Bac* c1* **BELL** k1* bufo ptk1* calc vh* calc-p vh1 carc sv* *Caust* k* **Chin** k* choc srj3• cupr sst3• dulc fd4.de gaert dgt *Hyos* k* lac-c mrr1 lac-f wza1• lac-h sze9• lach mtf33 lyss st1 med dx* merc gb• nat-m vh* nat-p pd phos fd* plat bra plb cld• polys sk4• *Puls* vh* sil cda* **Stram** k* sulph gb* syc pte1* symph fd3.de• *Tub* k* tub-k wta verat fyz
  - **big** dogs: stram mtf
  - **black** dogs; of: *Bac* jl2 bell hr1 stram kr1 tub jl2
  - **children**; in: tub jl2
- **door**:
  - **bell** ringing, on hearing (See ringing)
  - **closed**; lest the door should be: (↗*narrow)* lac-d k2* syph jl2 tritic-vg fd5.de
  - **opened**; when the door is: cic h1* con ptk1 lyc ptk1
  - **opening** the door; when there is a difficulty in: cic h1* con bg2* lyc bg2*
- **downward** motion, of: (↗*falling; falling - descending)* **Borx** k1* calc k13 coca st coff-t ↓ cupr st1* gels k* hyper ptk1 lac-c ptk1* lil-t st1 sanic br1* sil ptk1 zinc ptk1 [*Bor-pur* stj2]
  - **hammock**; while asleep of: coff-t kr1
- **drawn** upward (See upward)
- **dreams**; of terrible: (↗*waking - dream)* lac-lup hrn2• **Nux-v** hr1* spong dx1 *Sulph* hr1* [heroin sdj2]
- **drinking**; of: (↗*liquids; water)* ars hr1 bell br1 hyos ↓ jatr-c ↓ malar al plb a1 tarent ↓
  - **nausea**; during: jatr-c a
  - **offered**; what is: hyos fyz
  - **thirst**; with: lach ptk1 tarent a
- **driving** a car; of: (↗*Anxiety - riding - fast)* androc srj1• arg-n mrr1 bit-ar wht1• borx bg2 gins st lac-c mrr1 lac-e ↓ lach bg2 lyss mrr1 [cupr-m stj2]
  - **snow**; in the: lac-e hrn2•
- **driving** him from place to place: (↗*Restlessness - driving; Touching; Touching - impelled - everything)* acon j aeth j alum j am-c j ambr j asaf j bell j bov j camph j caps j carb-an j carb-v j caust j chin j chinin-s j cimic lp coff j crot-h j dros j lact j m-arct j meny *Merc* j nat-c j nat-m j nit-ac j nux-v j op j ph-ac j phos j plat j puls j rhus-t j ruta j sabad j sep j spig j spong j staph j valer j verat j
- **drought**; of: falco-pe nl2•
- **drowned**, of being: (↗*Suicidal - drowning; DREAMS - Drowned)* cann-i k* gard-j vlr2•
- **drunkards**, in: *Kali-p* hr1*
- **duty**:
  - **neglect** his duty; to: (↗*Delusions - neglected - duty)* aur gl1.fr• [heroin sdj2]
  - **unable** to perform her duties; she will become: *Lac-c* kr1 [tax jsj7]
- **earthquakes**; of: lac-c mrr1* phos mrr1
- **eaten**; of being: stram bg2
- **eating**; after: asaf bg2 canth carb-v bg2 caust k* chin fyz hyos bg2 kali-c b4a.de* lach mag-m nit-ac bg2 nux-v bg2 onos fyz petr fyz phel phos b4a.de tab thuj b4a.de* viol-t bg2
  - **amel.**: anac dx1 graph dx1
- **eating**; of: bran a1 caust k* grat k* hera a1 op k* puls k* tarent k* trom fyz [arg-n stj2]
- **eclampsia**; during: *Cocc* kr1
- **electric** energy; like: marb-w es1•
- **electricity**; of: ran-b fyz
- **elevators**; of: arg-n mrr1 borx k2 dys fmm1• staph dtp [alumin-s stj2 bor-pur stj2 ferr-n stj2 mag-n stj2 mang-n stj2 nitro stj2]
- **end** of world crisis: morg fmm1•
- **endure**; cannot: lyss ptk
- **enemies**, of: anac jl3 bell ↓ dros fyz hyos sf1.de sil ↓ [merc stj2 plb stj2]
  - **pursuing**: bell fyz sil fyz
- **epilepsy**; of (See convulsions - epileptic)
- **escape**; with desire to: (↗*Escape)* *Bell* j5.de *Bry* j5.de coloc j5.de cupr j5.de dig j5.de dulc fd4.de merc kr1 positr nl2• puls j5.de spong fd4.de stram j5.de verat j5.de
- **events**:
  - **important** events: *Dys* fmm1•
  - **sudden** events: cocc h1*
- **everything**, constant of: (↗*continuous)* acet-ac a1* acon fyz anac tl1 bell a1 *Calc* hr1* carc mlr1• gard-j vlr2• *Hydr-ac* br1* *Hyos* hr1* kali-br tl1 lac-c tl1 *Lyc* hr1* nat-c hr1* pitu-a ↓ psor jl2 *Puls* hr1* stram ↓ tub kr1
  - **measles** do not come out; and: stram hr1
  - **menses**; before: pitu-a ft
  - **ringing** of door bell, even at (See ringing)
- **evil**; fear of: (↗*danger; happen; misfortune; Religious - too; Thoughts - persistent - evil; Weeping - evil)* acon k* agar *Agn* bro1 alum k* am-c ambr bg2 anac k* ant-c k* *Apis* bro1 *Arg-n* k* arn *Ars* k* ars-i ars-s-f k2 asaf bg2 aster k* aur k* aur-ar k2 aur-i k2 *Aur-m* kr1 aur-s k2 bar-c k* bar-i k2* bar-m bar-s k2 bell h1* bry k* *Cact* bro1 calad k* **Calc** k* calc-act a1 calc-p bg2 calc-s k* camph bg2 cann-i bro1 caps bg2 carb-an *Carb-v* k* carc mlr1• castm *Caust* k* cham bg2* *Chin* k* chinin-ar **Chinin-s** k* *Cimic* bro1 cina k* clem rb2 *Cocc* k* *Coff* k* colch croc bg2 crot-c sk4• crot-h bg2* cupr bg2 cycl k* dig k* dros dulc euph ferr ferr-ar ferr-p gels bro1 graph k* hell hep bg2 hydr bro1 hydr-ac j hyos ign bro1 ignis-alc es2• *Iod* k* *Kali-ar* kali-c k* **Kali-i** k1* kali-m k2* kali-p kalm lac-c bro1 *Lach* *Laur* *Lil-t* k* limest-b es1• lyc gl1.fr• *Lyss* m-arct j5.de mag-c *Mag-s* j5.de *Maias-l* hrn2• **Manc** mrr med bro1 meny merc k* mosch mur-ac naja bro1 nat-ar *Nat-c* *Nat-m* k* nat-s k2 nicc kr1 nit-ac k* nux-v k* *Onos*

- **evil**; fear of: ...
  Pall petr k* phase bro1 *Phos* k* *Plat* bro1 podo bro1 **Psor** k* puls k* rauw sp1 rhus-t k* rumx rb2 ruta sabad bg2* sabin sec k* *Sep* k* sil bg2 spig spong squil *Stann* bro1* *Staph* k1* still bro1 stram kr1 stront-c stry mrr1 sul-ac sulph syph bro1 tarent thuj *Tritic-vg* fd5.de tub ↓ verat k* [ant-met stj2 ant-t stj2 merc-i-f stj2]
  - **morning** | **waking**; on: mag-s sulph lpc
  - **afternoon**: chinin-s
  - **evening**: **Alum** cina ↓ graph sulph
    - **walking** in open air, while: cina
  - **night**: chinin-ar k2
  - **family**; impending on his: podo fd3.de• tub al*
  - **forebodings**; of evil: maias-l hrn2• podo fd3.de• psor gt
  - **overwhelming** her: alum tl1 bar-c kr1 calc tl1
  - **possessed** by evil; they are: **Manc** mrr
  - **sadness** and weeping, with: **Kali-i** kr1
  - **trifles**, from: stram kr1
- **examination**:
  - **before** (See failure - examinations)
  - **medical** examination (See medical)
- **excitement**: *Acon* bro1 hydr-ac bro1 morg-g fmm1• plat bro1
- **exertion** | **of** exertion; fear: (*↗work; Mental exertion - agg.*) calad calc-sil k2 guaj mez ph-ac phos phyt sul-i tab thea
- **exposure** by uncovering; of (See FEVER - Uncovering - aversion)
- **extravagance**, of: (*↗Extravagance*) op k*
- **extreme**: androc srj1• hed sp1 hydrog srj2•
- **faces** looking at him:
  - **hideous** faces: bell mtf camph mtf crot-h mtf hydr-ac mtf hyos mtf phos mtf stram mtf tarent mtf
  - **looking** at him: phos k2
- **failure**, of: (*↗business failure; career; mistakes; new enterprise; undertaking; Anxiety - success; Confidence - want; Confidence - want - self-depreciation; Delusions - business - unfit; Delusions - fail; Delusions - fail everything; Delusions - right - doing; Delusions - succeed; Postponing; Succeeds; Timidity; Undertaking - nothing*)
  Aeth ↓ aids nl2• aloe a1* alumin-s ↓ anac mrr1 ara-maca sej7• arg-n bg2* arn bg2* *Aur* vh1* *Aur-m-n* wbt2• *Aur-s* wbt2• *Bamb-a* stb2.de• carb-v ↓ carc gk6* chin sma cich ↓ cob-n mg1.de crot-h fe cupr sst3*• gels bg2* iod sf1.de* kali-p ↓ kali-s fd4.de *Kola* stb3• *Lac-c* kr1 lach-h ↓ lyc gsd1* med ↓ naja jl* nat-m bg2* nux-v mrr1 olib-sac wmh1 ph-ac ↓ phos bg2* pic-ac ↓ plb cld• podo ↓ *Psor* jl2* rhod kgp5• rhus-g ↓ sacch sst1• sal-fr sle1• sil k2* sulph bg2* tax-br oss1• thuj ↓ *Tritic-vg* fd5.de vanad dx* zirc-met ↓ [alum stj2 am-br stj2 am-caust stj2 am-f stj2 ars stj2 ars-met stj2 bar-br stj2 bar-i stj2 beryl stj2 beryl-m stj2 bor-pur stj2 brom stj2 calc-lac stj2 calc-met stj2 calc-sil stj2 chr-m stj2 chr-met stj2 chr-s stj2 cob stj2 cob-m stj2 cob-p stj2 cupr-act stj2 cupr-f stj2 cupr-m stj2 cupr-p stj2 ferr stj2 ferr-f stj2 ferr-lac stj2 ferr-n stj2 ferr-sil stj2 fl-ac stj2 fl-pur stj2 gal-met stj2 gal-s stj2 germ-met stj2 graph stj2 heroin sdj2 kali-ar stj2 kali-met stj2 kali-sil stj2 lith-c stj2 lith-f stj2 lith-i stj2 lith-m stj2 lith-met stj2 lith-p stj2 lith-s stj2 mag-n stj2 mag-sil stj2 mang-act stj2 mang-i stj2 mang-m stj2 mang-met stj2 mang-n stj2 mang-p stj2 mang-s stj2 mang-sil stj2 merc-i-f stj2 moly-met stj2 mur-ac stj2 nat-ar stj2 nat-br stj2 nat-f stj2 nat-sil stj2 nicc-met stj2 nicc-s stj2 niob-met stj2 nitro stj2 oxyg stj2 scand-met stj2 sel stj2 sil-met stj2 *Titan* stj2 titan-s stj2 zinc stj2 zinc-i stj2 zinc-m stj2 zinc-n stj2 zinc-p stj2]
  - **business** (See business failure)
  - **children**; in: aur mtf33 carc sst2• naja mtf33 psor mtf33 sacch sst1•
  - **confirmation**; needs constant: cupr sst3•
  - **examinations**; in: (*↗Anticipation - examination*) *Aeth* st* aids nl2• anac c1* arg-n st* ars fyz carb-v fyz carc hbh* cupr sst3• *Gels* st* kali-p fyz lac-h sk4• lyc wr* med fyz* ph-ac fyz pic-ac br1* podo fd3.de• rhus-g tmo3• sil k2* thuj fyz* [alumin-s stj2 calc-sil stj2 cob stj2 cob-m stj2 cob-p stj2 ferr-sil stj2 kali-sil stj2 mag-sil stj2 mang-sil stj2 nat-sil stj2 nicc-met stj2 nicc-s stj2 niob-met stj2 sil-met stj2 titan-s stj2 zinc stj1 zirc-met stj2]
  - **plans** to avoid; making: aur-s wbt2•
  - **things** not done in the way he wants, in: [cich stj]
- **fainting**, of: *Acon* vh *Arg-n* ars-s-f hr1* aster k* carb-an cimic zr kola stb3• **Lac-c** k* *Plat* a1 tritic-vg fd5.de [calc-n stj1 lac-mat sst4 mag-n stj2 moly-met stj2]
- **faith**; to lose his religious: (*↗Religious - too*) coloc vh* merc vh* nux-v vh* staph vh* *Sulph* vh*
- **fall** upon him; high walls and building will: (*↗buildings - of; narrow*) *Arg-n* k* *Arn* k* choc srj3• hydr-ac br1*
- **falling**, of: (*↗Downward; Anxiety - Motion - agg. - downward; Unconsciousness - Looking - downward; FACE - Expression - Anxious - downward; GENERALS - Descending - Agg.; GENERALS - Riding - Streetcar; downhill - agg.*) acon k* alum k* alumn arg-n bg2* *Arn* ↓ ars h2* *Borx* k* brom ↓ calc gl1.fr• caust fyz chin bg2* coca ↓ cocc ↓ coff bg2* crot-c sk4• *Cupr* k* cur daph ↓ der ↓ dulc fd4.de *Gels* k* glycyr-g cte1• graph fyz hir ↓ hura ↓ hydr-ac ↓ hyper bg2* ix ↓ kali-c bg2* kali-p fd1.de• kali-s *Lac-c* k* lac-f ↓ *Lil-t* k* lyc ↓ lys bg2 lyss bg1* med k2 nat-m ↓ nat-p ↓ nux-v k* oci-sa sk4• olib-sac wmh1 onos bg2* ovi-p c1 perh ↓ phos fyz plut-n ↓ prim-v br1 prot ptj• psor ↓ *Puls* ↓ ran-b ↓ rhod kgp5• sabin ↓ sanic bg2* sil fr1 *Stram* bg2* suprar rly4• *Symph* fd3.de• tab bg2* tarent ↓ tub vh zinc bg2* [alumin-s stj2 astat stj2 aur stj2 aur-m stj2 aur-s stj2 bar-br stj2 bar-i stj2 bar-met stj2 bism-sn stj2 caes-met stj2 cinnb stj2 cupr-act stj2 cupr-f stj2 cupr-m stj2 cupr-p stj2 gal-met stj2 germ-met stj2 hafn-met stj2 irid-met stj2 lanth-met stj2 merc stj2 merc-d stj2 merc-i-f stj2 moly-met stj2 osm-met stj2 plat stj2 plb stj2 plb-m stj2 plb-p stj2 polon-met stj2 rhen-met stj2 scand-met stj2 sel stj2 tant-met stj2 thal-met stj2 tung-met stj2 zinc-i stj2 zinc-m stj2 zinc-n stj2 zinc-p stj2]
  - **morning**, from vertigo: sabin kr1
  - **afternoon**: nux-v
  - **evening**: lyss
  - **night**: kali-s k13
  - **backward** | **looking** up; when: hir rsj4•
  - **carried**; while: **Gels** kr1
  - **child** holds on to mother: (*↗Clinging*) borx al *Cupr* kr1 *Cupr-act* kr1 **Gels** kr1* sanic al
  - **children**; in: cupr-act kr1
  - **descending** stairs; when: (*↗downward*) borx mrr1 lac-c kr1* lac-f al ovi-p c1
  - **everything** is falling on her: stram kr1 tarent a
  - **fire**; into: onos a2* psor fyz
  - **forwards**: alum ptk1 *Cur* ↓
    - **rising**; on: *Cur* kr1
  - **height** (See high)
  - **houses**; of: hydr-ac ptk
  - **letting** things fall, of: coca plut-n srj7•
  - **rising**; on: ix bnm8•
  - **room** agg.; in: lil-t
  - **sleep**, on going to: coff
  - **stooping**; on: ix bnm8•
  - **turning** head, on: *Arn* brom daph der lyc nat-p *Puls* ran-b
  - **walking**, when: coca cocc fyz hura a1 lyss a1 nat-m *Symph* fd3.de•
  - **water**; into: perh jl
- **family**: falco-pe ↓ *Staph* ↓ [calc-sil stj2 cupr-m stj2 kali-ar stj2 zinc stj2 zinc-i stj2 zinc-m stj2 zinc-n stj2]
  - **bring** up his family; to: falco-pe nl2• *Staph* vh*
  - **matters**, about: calc-sil k2*
- **fasting**, of: kreos k*
- **father**; to become like his: ozone sde2•
- **fever**:
  - **after** fear; fever (See FEVER - Fright)
  - **during** fever: (*↗Anxiety - fever - during*) acon bg2* ambr ptk1 ars bg2* bar-c ptk1 cact bg2 ip ptk1 nux-m bg2 sep ptk1 spong bg2
  - **of** the fever:
    - **chilly**; while: calc st sulph
    - **going** to bed; on: hura
    - **typhus** fever; of: tarent
- **financial** loss; of (See poverty)
- **fire**: cupr sst3* dulc fd4.de hep mrr1 lyss ↓ olib-sac wmh1 onos ↓ pieri-b mlk9.de podo fd3.de• psor al2* stram k2 vanil fd5.de [cupr-act stj2 cupr-f stj2 cupr-m stj2 cupr-p stj2 merc stj2 *Tung-met* stj2]
  - **things** will catch: cupr *Cupr-act* kr1* *Dulc* fd4.de hep mrr lyss fyz onos fyz psor fyz stram k2* vanil fd5.de

- **fit**, of having a: agar alum k* aml-ns kr1 *Arg-n* k* ars-s-f hr1 *Calc* sne cann-i k* carb-an carb-v rb2 grat hr1* helon fyz lach j5.de lyss hr1* med gk merc j5.de nux-m phos puls
  - **fainting**; after: *Ars-s-f* kr1
- **flies**, of: *(↗animals)* abel jl3
- **floating** of single limbs; during sensation of: **Cann-i** mrr1
- **fluids**, of (See water; Hydrophobia)
- **flying**; of: acon ↓ arg-n ↓ ars ↓ calc ↓ calc-n ↓ lup ↓ lyss ↓ nat-m ↓ phos ↓ psor ↓ tritic-vg fd5.de [alum stj2 alumin-s stj2 am-caust stj2 am-f stj2 beryl stj2 beryl-m stj2 bor-pur stj2 cupr-f stj2 ferr-n stj2 fl-ac stj2 fl-pur stj2 graph stj2 lith-c stj2 lith-f stj2 lith-m stj2 lith-met stj2 lith-p stj2 lith-s stj2 mag-n stj2 nat-f stj2 nitro stj2 oxyg stj2 sil stj2]
  - **airplane**; in: *(↗Anxiety - motion - agg. - airplane; GENERALS - Aviator's)* acon vh1* arg-n fd* ars vh calc fd* lup vh lyss mrr1 nat-m vh phos fd* psor ser tritic-vg fd5.de [calc-n stj1 oxyg stj]
- **food**; after (See eating; after)
- **food**; to obtain her (See starving)
- **forebodings**; fear of evil (See evil - forebodings)
- **forsaken**; of being: *(↗neglected; solitude; Delusions - forsaken; Forsaken)*
  - **children**; in: borx mtf33 bufo mtf33 calc mtf33 kali-c mtf33 puls mtf33 sil mtf33
- **free**-floating: *(↗Anxiety - free-floating)* maias-l hm2•
- **friend** has met with accident, that a (See accidents - friends)
- **friends**; of his: androc srj1• ars fyz cedr k* lyc ↓ phos fyz phys fyz sep ↓ sil ↓ sulph fyz [lith-p stj2]
  - **meeting** his friends; of: *(↗Company - aversion - meeting)* lyc fyz sep al1* sil fyz
- **fright**: *(↗Ailments - fright)*
  - **previous** fright; because of a: *(↗Ailments - fright)* *Acon* k2 bell kr1 merc kr1 nat-m kr1 **Op** gt* *Verat* kr1
  - **remains**; anxiety if the fear of the fright remains (See Anxiety - fright - remains)
- **frogs**; of: *(↗animals)* carc sst*
- **full** of fear: *(↗Timidity)* acon gt ars gt aur gt bell gt caps ↓ carb-an gt chin gt cupr gt dys pte1• graph ↓ ign gt kali-c br1 phos gt psor gt* puls gt verat gt [rubd-met stj2]
  - **morning**: graph gt
  - **waking**, on: caps gt
- **future**; of the (See Anxiety - future)
- **gallows**, of the: *Bell* k*
- **germs**; of (See contagion)
- **ghosts**, of: *(↗Delusions - pursued; Delusions - pursued - ghosts; Delusions - specters)* absin fyz *Acon* k* agar vh *Ars* k* ars-s-f k2 aur-s wbt2• bell k* brom k* calc vh* cann-i *Carb-v* k* carc mlr1• *Caust* k* chin chinin-ar clem gl• cocc k* *Crot-c* mrr1* dros k* gal-ac zr gard-j vlr2• *Hyos* bro1* *Kali-br* sf1.de kali-c k* kali-i k2 **Lyc** k* *Manc* k* *Med* bro1* merc mrr1 nat-m fyz* op bro1* **Phos** k* *Plat* k* plut-n srj7• *Puls* k* rad-br bro1 (non:rad-met) ran-b k* rhus-t k* sep k* spong stram k* *Sulph* k* tarent tl1 thres-a sze7• *Valer* b7a.de zinc k* zinc-p k2* [am-br stj2 ant-c stj2 ant-met stj2 bar-br stj2 lac-mat sst4 zinc-i stj2 zinc-m stj2 zinc-n stj2]
  - **evening**: brom k* lyc k* *Puls* k* ran-b k*
  - **night**: *Acon* ars *Carb-v* chin chinin-ar k2 cocc h1* gard-j vlr2• *Lyc* phos vh *Puls* ran-b *Sulph*
  - **conversing** with; thinks he is: *Nat-m* vh* **Plat** vh*
  - **dark**; in the: brom mtf33
  - **sleeplessness**; with: *Carb-v* b4a.de cocc b7a.de
  - **waking**, on: *(↗SLEEP - Waking - fear)* cocc h1* phos vh sulph j5.de
- **glistening** objects (See brilliant)
- **going** out, of: *(↗Open; Going; GENERALS - Faintness - Crowded - street; VERTIGO - Walking - Air; VERTIGO - Walking - Air - agg.)* acon ↓ anth k* ars ↓ bar-c bl dys pte1*• ign ↓ kali-p fyz *Lyss* gk pitu-a ↓ pneu jl3 sep jl3 tarent ccrh1• tarent-c ckh1
  - **alone**: ars bl ign bl pitu-a ft
  - **menses**; before: acon mtn
- **graveyard**; of (See cemeteries)
- **green** stripes; on seeing: thuj ptk1
- **grief**, as from: *(↗Anxiety - grief; Grief; Inconsolable)* am-m kr1 phos k*
- **grieved** about something; as if (See grief)
- **groundless** (See causeless)
- **gun**; thunder of a: borx br1
- **hair**; that she is losing her: nit-ac gy3
- **hallucinations**, of: falco-pe nl2•
- **hanged**, to be: **Plat** vh*
- **happen**, something will: *(↗danger; evil; misfortune; Ailments - anticipation; Anxiety - future; Cautious; Clairvoyance; Death - presentiment; Delusions - danger; Forebodings; Prophesying; ABDOMEN - Apprehension; CHEST - Apprehension; DREAMS - Clairvoyant; DREAMS - Events - future; DREAMS - Prophetic; DREAMS - Visionary; STOMACH - Apprehension)* *Abel* vh1 acet-ac k2* *Acon* br1 aesc ↓ agar ↓ alum k* alum-p k2* am-c rb2 ambr tsm1 aml-ns a1* anac k2 androc srj1• anth a1 apis k2 *Arg-n* bg2* arge-pl rwt5• arn h1* *Ars* k* aur-m-n wbt2• bar-c k2* bufo cact **Calc** calc-s ↓ calen vh* carb-an h2* *Carb-v* carc sne* cartl-s rly4• **Caust** k* chel k2* choc srj3• **Cimic** sne cocc k2* *Coloc* vh* corn-a c1 crot-c [illegible] crot-t k* cupr ↓ cypra-eg sde6.de• dendr-pol sk4• dig k2 *Dulc* fd4.de *Elaps* falco-pe nl2• fl-ac k* fuma-ac rly4• *Gels* glon ↓ graph ham fd3.de• hydroc srj2• ign k2 *Iod* irid-met srj5• *Kali-ar* *Kali-br* kali-c k2 kali-p kali-s fd4.de kalm a1 kola stb3• *Lac-c* hr1* lac-e hm2• lac-h sze9• lappa rb2 *Lil-t* k* limest-b ↓ *Lyc* *Lyss* k1* mag-c k* mag-s ↓ maias-l hm2• *Manc* gk mang marb-w es1• *Med* st* melal-alt gya4 merc k2* mez k2 moni rfm1• mosch a1* nad rly4• nat-ar k* *Nat-m* k* *Nat-p* nicc k* nit-ac ↓ **Nux-v** gl1.fr• *Oci-sa* sk4• *Onos* *Pall* hr1* *Ph-ac* **Phos** k* *Plat* hr1* plb k2* plut-n srj7• podo ↓ **Psor** jl2 pyrus rat a1 rhus-t hr1 *Ruta* fd4.de sacch-a fd2.de• sanic mrr1 scut vh* *Sep* ↓ spong hr1* still br1 stront-c sk4• stry suis-em rly4• sul-i k2* *Sulph* ↓ suprar rly4• **Symph** fd* tab tarent bg* thea *Tritic-vg* fd5.de **Tub** k* urol-h rwt• vanil fd5.de vult-gr ↓ wye a1 xan zinc ↓ *Zing* ↓ [heroin sdj2 mang-i stj2 mang-m stj2 mang-p stj2 mang-s stj2 moly-met stj2 spect dfg1 tax jsj7]
  - **night**: *Arn* st nat-p st
  - **air** amel.; fresh: aml-ns kr1 *Crot-t* kr1 rhus-t kr1 spong kr1 *Sulph* kr1 zinc kr1
  - **alone**, amel. by conversation; when: *(↗Company - desire; Company - desire - amel.; Company - desire - happen)* rat
  - **family**; to his: ambr tsm1 ars kr1* calc fyz calc-s a1 carc mrc* caust fyz* phos fyz psor fyz sep fyz tub a1
  - **himself**; to: ambr tsm1 ars kr1* calc fyz calc-s a1 carc mrc* caust fyz* phos fyz psor fyz sep fyz tub a1
  - **home**; before he got: *Zing* kr1
  - **horrible**; something: *(↗terrible)* ambr tsm1 aml-ns rb2 *Calc* kr1 calen vh carc mlr• cupr sst3• cypra-eg sde6.de• elaps rb2 fl-ac kr1 ign kr1 irid-met srj5• lac-e hm2• lappa rb2 lyss rb2 mang fyz med rb2 onos rb2 pall rb2 psor a pyrus rb2 *Sep* a thea rb2
  - **husband**; that he would never return: ars fyz bar-c fyz caust fyz *Plat* k* sep fyz vanil fd5.de
  - **leaves** the room, when someone: falco-pe nl2•
  - **parents**; child is afraid something bad will happen to his: *(↗health - loved; Anxiety - family)* phos mrr1
  - **pollutions**; after: carb-an a1
  - **sad**: aesc a *Calc* kr1 *Phos* a **Still** a
  - **still**, cannot sit: aml-ns kr1
  - **terrible** is going to happen; something: *(↗horrible)* aml-ns vh1 *Calc* hr1* *Calen* ckh1 carc mlr1• cimic sne elaps kr fl-ac a1* fuma-ac rly4• ign ry1* limest-b es1• *Lyss* k* med br nit-ac oss• onos rb pall kr1* podo fd3.de• ruta fd4.de scut mtf suis-em rly4• vult-gr sze5•
  - **unpleasant**; something: agar rb2 caust rb2 glon rb2 lyss rb2 mag-c rb2 mag-s rb2
  - **uterine** hemorrhage, in: **Plat** kr1
  - **waking**; on: lyss kr1
  - **warmth** of bed amel.: *Caust* mag-c
- **harmed**, that others should be: caust h1*
- **head**:
  - **something** wrong in her head: *(↗disease)* bamb-a stb2.de•
  - **water**; to have the head under: calc gy3 puls gy3 stram gy3*
- **health**: *Agn* ↓ calc ↓ carc ↓ chel ↓ *Cocc* ↓ eric-vg mtf11 hep ↓ merc ↓ miml-g mtf11 morg-p fmm1• staph ↓ succ-ac ↓ [ars stj2 ars-met stj2 cupr stj2 cupr-m stj2 cupr-p stj2 kali-ar stj2 nat-ar stj2]

- loved persons; about health of: *(↗happen - parents; Anxiety - health - relatives)* carc ib* *Cocc* mrr1* hep gl1.fr• merc gl1.fr• succ-ac rly4•
- **ruined**, that she has: *(↗Anxiety - health - own; Hypochondriasis)* *Agn* mrr1 calc st chel staph st

- **heart**: *(↗Anxiety - heart; about)*
  - **arising** from: aur lyc meny merc-c mez
  - **cease** to beat unless constantly on the move; heart will: *(↗disease - stop; CHEST - Ceases)* both-a rb3 both-ax tsm2 *Gels* k* lach ptk1
  - **disease** of the heart: *(↗Delusions - heart - disease - having)* acon cd* aml-ns vh1 *Apis* ↓ arg-n vh* arn k2* ars mrr1* *Aur* k* bapt both-a ↓ cact *Calc* k1* calc-p vh* calc-s k2 cassia-s ↓ caust fyz coca ↓ cupr sht*• daph a1* dig ↓ fum rly1*• **Gels** ↓ germ-met srj hed sp1 hydrog srj2• *Kali-ar* vh* lac-c lac-cp ↓ lach k* *Lil-t* k* lob cd* meny c1 mez cd nat-m vh* nux-m kr1 *Phos* vh* plac rzf5• podo k2 psor fyz rhus-t fyz ruta fd4.de sars vh sin-n kr1 *Spong* tarent fyz tritic-vg ↓ vib ↓ [ars-met stj2 astat stj2 aur-m stj2 aur-s stj2 bar-br stj2 bar-i stj2 bar-met stj2 bism-sn stj2 caes-met stj2 calc-n stj1 cinnb stj2 cupr-act stj2 cupr-f stj2 cupr-m stj2 cupr-p stj2 ferr-n stj2 hafn-met stj2 irid-met stj2 lanth-met stj2 mag-n stj2 mang-n stj2 merc stj2 merc-d stj2 merc-i-f stj2 nat-ar stj2 nitro stj2 osm-met stj2 plat stj2 plb stj2 plb-m stj2 plb-p stj2 polon-met stj2 rhen-met stj2 tant-met stj2 thal-met stj2 tung-met stj2 zinc-n stj2]
    - **night**: arn mrr1
    - **organic** disease; of: *Apis* kr1* *Aur* a1* calc a *Spong* fd4.de
    - **stop**; heart will: *(↗cease; CHEST - Ceases; CHEST - Ceases - would)* both-a rb3 cassia-s ↓ coca vh dig mrr1 **Gels** mrr1 lac-c tl1 lac-cp ↓ lach ptk1 tritic-vg fd5.de vib tl1
      - **fright**; from: lac-cp dmd1.fr
      - **sleep**; during: cassia-s ckh1
  - **pain** about heart; from: daph a1

- **heat**:
  - **during**: acon k* *Ars* k* cact bg2 cham hr1* nux-m k* spong k* sulph ↓
    - **cold**; during a: sulph h2
  - **from**: chen-a kr1 hyos kr1 lyss kr1
- **hell**; of: *(↗devil of; devils)* manc gl•
- **high** places, of: *(↗High places - agg.)* abies-c oss4• aeth dgt* aids nl2• *Arg-n* k* ars gb• aur ptk* *Aur-m-n* wbt2• aur-s zr* bell gb• calc fd* calc-ar mtf calc-f cd* calc-p dgt carb-an mrr1 carb-v gb• *Carc* gk* caust gb• cob-n sp1 coca dm* con gb• crot-c wn* cupr gb• dendr-pol sk4• gels ptk* hep oss• hyos ptk1 hyper br1 kali-p fd1.de• lach fd* lyc fd* manc vh med gk* merc mrr1* morg-g mtf nat-m ctc* petr-ra shn4• phos vh* pin-con oss2• plut-n srj7• psor mtf ptel gk puls k* rhod kgp5• sil st* staph k* stram md* sulph k* thuj fyz zinc vh* [alumin-s stj2 ant-c stj2 ant-m stj2 ant-met stj2 ant-t stj2 arg-met stj1* arg-p stj2 astat stj2 aur-m stj2 bar-br stj2 bar-i stj2 bar-met stj2 bism-sn stj2 brom stj1 cadm-m stj2 cadm-met stj2 cadm-s stj2 caes-met stj2 calc-lac stj2 calc-met stj2 calc-n stj1 calc-sil stj2 chr-s stj2 cinnb stj2 gal-s stj2 hafn-met stj2 ind stj2 iod stj2 irid-met stj2 lanth-met stj2 lith-i stj2 lith-s stj2 mang-i stj2 mang-s stj2 merc-d stj2 merc-i-f stj2 moly-met stj2 nicc-s stj2 niob-met stj2 osm-met stj2 pall stj2 plat stj2 plb stj2 plb-m stj2 plb-p stj2 polon-met stj2 rhen-met stj2 rhodi stj2 rubd-met stj2 ruth-met stj2 sel stj2 stann stj2 stront-m stj2 stront-met stj2 tant-met stj2 techn stj2 tell stj2 thal-met stj2 titan-s stj2 *Tung-met* stj2 yttr-met stj2 zinc-i stj2 zinc-m stj2 zinc-n stj2 zinc-p stj2 zirc-met stj2]
  - **others** on; seeing: *Sulph* mrr1
  - **pushed** by someone behind him; might be: aids nl2•
- **homosexuality**; of: hydr-ac vml3• manc vh musca-d szs1 *Puls* vh *Staph* vh
- **horror** movies; of: calc mtf
- **horses**; of: *(↗animals)* hydr-ac br1* led ↓ nux-v ↓ [mag-i stj]
- **hospital**; going to the: arg-n mrr1* calc sys kali-s fd4.de
- **house**; on entering the (See room)
- **humiliated**, of being: *(↗Admonition - agg.; Delusions - insulted)* *Carc* vh* falco-pe nl2• nat-m mrr1 nux-v mrr1 puls gl1.fr• *Sep* gl1.fr• staph mtf [moly-met stj2]
- **hungry**, when: grat iod k2* [bar-i stj2 lith-i stj2 mang-i stj2 merc-i-f stj2 zinc-i stj2]
- **hurry** followed by fear: *(↗Hurry)* benz-ac
- **hurt**, of being: *(↗injury - being; Sensitive - mental impressions)* *Arn* ptk1 carc mlr1• chin ptk1* hep ptk1 kali-c ptk1 lap-la sde8.de• nat-m mtf33 *Rhus-t* ckh1 ruta ptk1 spig ptk1 symph fd3.de• vanil fd5.de [lact stj]
  - **soldiers**, in children; by: [lact stj]

- **hurt**, of being: ...
  - **emotionally** (= feelings will be hurt by others): carc mlr1• chin ptk
- **husband**; something would happen to (See happen - husband)
- **hydrocephalus**, in: *Zinc* hr1*
- **ill**; becoming (See disease)
- **imaginary**: *(↗delusions)*
  - **animals**, of: **Bell**
  - **things**; of imaginary: acon b7.de* ars bad bg **Bell** k* brom bg2* calc-sil st1 cham b7a.de chin b7a.de dros b7a.de *Hell* b7.de* hydr-ac br1* hyos b7a.de iod k* laur k* lyc **MED** st merc nat-c fyz *Phos* k* rhus-t b7a.de *Sabad* b7a.de sep fyz **Stram** b7.de* verat b7.de* zinc bg2
- **imbecile**, to become: stram
- **impotence**; of: *(↗coition - during)* nat-m fyz onos fyz phos ↓ pitu jl rhod kgp5• stry ↓ tritic-vg fd5.de [am-f stj2 cob stj2 cob-m stj2 cob-p stj2 fl-ac stj2 lith-f stj2]
  - **old** people; in: phos fyz stry fyz
- **impulses**; of his own: alum ptk1* androc srj1• germ-met srj merc k2* osm a sulph mrr1 [alum-p stj2 alumin stj2 alumin-s stj2]
- **inevitable** things: cob ptm1•
- **infection**, of: *(↗contagion; disease - contagious)* aids nl2• *Borx* k* bov a1* bufo calad k* **Calc** k* carc mlr1• falco-pe nl2• galla-q-r nl2• lach positr nl2• psor tl1 sulph mrr1 *Syph* mrr1 [ars stj2 bor-pur stj2]
- **injury**:
  - **being** injured; of: *(↗attacked; hurt; raped; Delusions - assaulted; Delusions - injury - about; Secretive - exposure)* anthraq rly4• arn ptk1* ars k2 calad k* calc-s sej* cann-i carc mtf cartl-s rly4• chin ptk1* choc srj3• *Cimic* mrr1 crot-c sk4• cupr-act kr1 falco-pe nl2• fuma-ac rly4• gels hr1 hep ptk1* hyos k* kali-br mrr1 kali-c ptk1* kola stb3• lyss fyz* mag-c mrr1 oxal-a rly4• phasco-ci rbp2 rhus-g tmo3• ruta dm* sep mtf spig ptk1* staph mrr1 **Stram** k* *Stry* suis-pan rly4• symph fd3.de• valer mtf vanil fd5.de
    - **dark**; in: valer fyz
    - **sewing**; when: sep fyz
  - **others**; of injuring: *(↗Thoughts - accidents - others)* androc srj1• arg-n mrr1 nat-m ↓ osm-o a1
    - **himself**; for fear of being hurt: nat-m mtf33
- **insanity**: *(↗control; Delusions - insane - become; Mania - insane)* acon k1* agar k1 *Alum* k* alum-p k2* alum-sil k2 *Alumn* a1 ambr b7a.de* anac vh* antip br1* aq-mar jl arg-n bg2* ars k1* ars-i k1 bov k1 bry k1 cact k2 **CALC** k* *Calc-ar* k2* calc-i k2 calc-s k1 **Cann-i** k* *Cann-xyz* ptk1 carb-an carbn-s k1 *Carc* mlr1• *Chel* bg2* chlor k* chord-umb rly4• *Cimic* bg2* cupr k1* cypra-eg sde6.de• dendr-pol sk4• *Dig* k1 *Eup-per* kr1 falco-pe nl2• gels k1 *Graph* bg2* guare a1 haliae-lc srj5• *Hell* gk hydrog srj2*• ign k1 iod k1* irid-met stj2*• kali-bi k1 *Kali-br* k1* kali-c gk *Kali-s* hr1* *Kola* ↓ *Lac-c* bg2* *Lac-e* hm2• lac-h sze9• lach k1* lat-m jl* laur k1 levo jl lil-s a1* *Lil-t* bg2* limest-b es1• *Lyss* kr1* mag-c k1 maias-l hm2• malar jl2 **MANC** k1* med br1* *Merc* k* merl k1 mosch k1 mur-ac mtf *Nat-m* bg2* *Nux-v* k1 ol-j kr1 *Phos* k1* phys k1 pin-con oss2• plat kr1* prun-cf mtf11 psor al2* **Puls** k1* rhod k1 sanic c1 sec mrr1 *Sep* k1* spong kr1 *Staph* gl1.fr• *Stram* k* sul-i k2 sulph k1 sumb hr1* syph k1* taosc iwa1• tarent k1 thuj k1 verat bro1 [alumin stj2 alumin-s stj2 astat stj2 aur stj2 aur-m stj2 aur-s stj2 bar-br stj2 bar-i stj2 bar-met stj2 bism-sn stj2 caes-met stj2 cinnb stj2 mang-i stj2 mang-m stj2 mang-met stj2 mang-p stj2 mang-s stj2 merc-d stj2 osm-met stj2 plb stj2 plb-m stj2 plb-p stj2 polon-met stj2 rhen-met stj2 spect dfg1 tant-met stj2 tax jsj7 thal-met stj2 tung-met stj2 zinc-n stj2]
  - **evening** | **bed**; in: falco-pe nl2• nat-m h2
  - **night**: calc a1 manc kr1 *Merc* phys
  - **chorea**; in: sumb kr1
  - **crying**; with: *Puls* kr1
  - **fright**; after: *Ign* kr1 stram kr1
  - **headache**; with: ambr b7a.de cimic ↓
    - **vertex**; in: cimic kr1
  - **menopause**; during: *Cimic* st*
  - **repose**, he must always move; if he wants to: *(↗Kill - rest)* ars k2* iod k2*
  - **restlessness** and heat; with: **Chel** kr1
  - **senses**; of losing one's: alum calc cann-i carb-an chlor *Kola* stb3• stram

- **typhoid**; after: *Manc* kr1
- **vertigo**; with: *Phys* kr1

- **insects**; of: *(↗animals; bugs)* **Abel** jl* ars bng* bufo a* *Calc* vh* calc-ar bng carc vh1* cartl-s rly4• cimic kk lyc kk* *Nat-m* vh* nat-p pd* phos kk* puls dgt* s u l p h hu* [arg-n stj2 ferr-n stj2 mag-n stj2 mang-n stj2 nat-caust stj2 nitro stj2]
- **insensible**; of becoming: lyc bg2 nux-v bg2 sulph bg2
- **intangible** (See causeless)
- **intense** fear (See terror)
- **invalidity**: ign bng
- **jarred**; of being: am mrr1
- **job**, to lose his lucrative: *(↗business failure)* calc jsa* ign jsa* puls jsa* rhus-t jsa* sep gl1.fr• staph gl1.fr• sulph gl1.fr• verat jsa*
- **joints** are weak, that: sep
- **jumps**:
  - **bed** from fear; out of: *(↗Jumping - bed)* *Ars* k* **Bell** kr1 chlol ↓ stann kr1
    - **typhoid** fever; during: chlol gm1
  - **touch**, on: bell
  - **window**, out of the: ars hir rsj4•
- **killed**; of being (See murdered)
- **killing**, of: *(↗Kill; desire)* absin k* alum gk alumn am-m arg-n gk *Ars* k* *Chin* gl1.fr• coff ↓ der k* *Hyos* vh kali-br hr1 manc ↓ med oss• merc k2 *Nux-v* k* *Rhus-t* k* sep ↓ sil ↓ sulph thea k*
  - **child**; her: ars fyz coff fyz manc gl• merc gg *Nux-v* gg rhus-t fyz sep gg sil fyz *Sulph* vh* thea mrr1
  - **herself**, that she may kill (See suicide)
  - **knife**, with a: ars k* der k* *Nux-v* k*
- **knives**; of: *(↗Knife)* alum bg2* ars bg2* chin h1* hyos bg2* lac-c kr1 lys bg2 lyss bg1* merc vh nux-v hr1* *Plat* ckh1 symph fd3.de• [alum-p stj2 alumin stj2 alumin-s stj2 mang-p stj2 oxyg stj2]
- **labor**:
  - **after**: iod k*
  - **during**: acon k* ars coff *Op* hr1* plat
  - **of**: borx c1 cimic ↓ gels ↓ kali-c c1 puls ↓
    - **approaching**: cimic vh gels kr1 puls kr1
- **lasting** fear (See chronic)
- **laughed** at and mocked at; being: *(↗Delusions - laughed)* calc hu2
- **late**; of being (See Anxiety - time)
- **lectophobia** (See bed - of)
- **life**; of embracing: dioxi rbp6 lac-h sze9•
- **lifelong**: *(↗chronic)* am-c gl1.fr• am-m gl1.fr• calc gl1.fr• *Carc* mlr1• lyc gl1.fr• petr gl1.fr• puls gl1.fr• sil gl1.fr• stann gl1.fr• sulph gl1.fr• zinc gl1.fr•
- **lightning**, of: *(↗noise; thunderstorm)* bell bg2 cycl bg2 dig bg2 gard-j vlr2• lach bg2 phos bg2 phys bg2 sil bg2* taosc iwa1•
- **liquids**; of: *(↗drinking; water)*
  - **thirst**; with: agn am-c androc srj1• arn ars st **Arum-t** lp *Bell* cann-i *Canth Caust Cocc Hell Hyos* jatr-c c1 lac-c *Lach Lyc* lyss merc nat-m *Nux-v* rhus-t samb sel *Stram* tarent
- **literary** work (See mental - of - literary)
- **liver**, in affections of: *Mag-m* vh* podo k2
- **looked** at; being (See observed)
- **looking**:
  - **before** her, when: sulph
  - **first** thing he sees; fear looking at the: stram rb2
- **loss**; of suffering a: **Ruta** fd* tritic-vg fd5.de [calc-lac stj2 calc-met stj2 calc-sil stj2]
- **losing** breath; of (See suffocation)
- **liberty**; losing one's: [temp elm1]
- **losing** objects; of: irid-met srj5•
- **losing** his reason; of (See insanity)
- **losing** senses; of (See insanity - senses)
- **losing** one's way home; of: cassia-s ccrh1*
- **lumps** in mammae, of (See mammae)
- **lung** disease; of: *(↗death - respiratory; pneumonia; respiratory)* a n h st *Aral* a1* arg-n fyz podo fd3.de•
- **lying**:
  - **amel.**: mang-act br1
  - **bed**; in: androc srj1• falco-pe nl2• kali-c mosch ↓
- **lying – bed**; in: ...
    - **lest** she die: mosch k2*
- **Lyme** disease: ars mrr1 (non:bor-pur mrr1) calc mrr1 sulph mrr1 syph mrr1
- **mammae**; lumps in: *(↗disease)* bamb-a stb2.de•
- **mania**; in: bell lpc cupr kr1 ign ↓ plat ↓ sec ptk1 stram kr1
  - **fright**; after: ign kr1 plat kr1 stram kr1
- **manual** labor, after: *(↗Manual)* iod k*
- **marriage**; of (See Marriage - unendurable)
- **Martians**; of: manc mrr1
- **medical** examinations; of: *(↗doctors)* ant-t nh* phos fb* puls wta* sanic bj* tub wta*
- **medicine**: all-s ↓ carc ↓ crot-h ↓ falco-pe nl2• hyos ↓ iber ↓ ruta ↓
  - **homeopathic** remedies; of antidoting (See antidoting)
  - **poison**; being: hyos tl1
  - **selecting** remedies, when: crot-h a1
  - **taking** too much medicine; fear of: *(↗Refusing - medicine)* a l l - s k* iber ruta fd4.de
  - **unable** to bear any kind of; of being: all-s kr1* carc mlr1•
- **memory** would fail; that his: [pop dhh1]
- **men**; of [=in general] (See people)
- **men**; of [=male persons]: *(↗Aversion - husband; Aversion - men; to [=male; Aversion - men; to = male persons] - women; delirium - fear; delirium - fear - men; hatred - men; of [=male; sensitive - noise - voices - male; head - pain - voice)* acon bg2] ambr bg2 anac bg2 aur bg2 bar-c bg2 bell bg2 cic bg2* con bg2 *Hyos* bg2 kali-bi bg2 lach cd1 lyc bg2* merc bg2 nat-c bg2* **Puls** bg2* rhus-t bg2 sel bg2 stann bg2* sulph bg2 tritic-vg fd5.de [tung-met stj2]
- **men**; of (↗old rubric) bar-m choc srj3• dream-p sdj1• ign marb-w es• phos *Plat* sep sinus rly4• stram brm sulph
- **menses**:
  - **after**: *(↗Menses - after)* *Pall* hr1* *Phos* hr1* thuj ↓
    - **closing** the eyes: thuj mtn
  - **before**: *(↗Menses - before)* *Acon* borx calc con hr1* hep kali-bi hr1* kali-br mang k* pitu-a ft plat sec sep sulph k* xan
  - **during**: *(↗Menses - during)* acon ant-t ↓ bell vh cina mtn *Coff* hr1* c o n k* **IGN** vh *Lach* vh mag-c manc gl• *Nat-m* k* nux-m vh nux-v fyz oena hr1* op vh *Ph-ac* vh phos plat rhus-t fyz sec sep staph vh sulph mtn verat vh
    - **menstrual** colic, during: *(↗Menses - during)* ant-t
  - **suppressed** menses from fear: acon st act-sp kr1 *Calc* kr1 *Lyc* kr1 *Nux-m* kr1
  - **suppressed** menses; fear from: *Cocc* b7a.de
- **mental** exertion:
  - **after** mental exertion: calc-sil k2
  - **amel.**: falco-pe nl2•
  - **of** mental exertion: aloe ↓ calc-p k2 con sf1.de graph k2 lyc ↓ nat-p k2 *Nux-v* ↓ ph-ac vh pic-ac vh *Sil* ↓ sulph ↓
    - **literary** work: aloe vh lyc fyz *Nux-v* k1* *Sil* sulph
      - **morning**: nux-v a
- **mice**: *(↗animals; rats)* **Calc** mrr1 calc-f mrr1 carc sst2* colch ↓ cupr sst3• mag-m dgt pot-e rly4• puls gk sep fyz [tung-met stj2]
  - **waking**; on: colch j5.de
- **mirrors** in room, of: *(↗brilliant)* bufo camph k* cann-i k* *Canth* carbn-s fyz carc fb *Lyss* puls gsy* *Stram* k*
  - **lest** he should see himself: camph kr1
- **mischief**; he might do: *(↗wrong - commit)*
  - **night** | **waking**; on: canth fyz *Phys*
- **misery**; of (See poverty)

- **misfortune**, of: *(↗danger; evil; happen; Delusions - danger; Unfortunate)* acon k* agar alco a1 alum alum-p k2* alumn a1 am-c k* ambr bg2* aml-ns kr1 *Ammc* vh1 *Anac* k* ant-c arn k* ars bg2* ars-i k2* asaf bg2 astac↓ aster k* atro k* aur bg2 aur-m rb2 bamb-a stb2.de• bar-c j5.de* bell bg2 bros-gau mrc1 bry bg2* bufo k* cact calad k* *Calc* k* calc-f k* calc-i k2* calc-p bg2 calc-s camph bg2 caps bg2 carb-v bg2 carbn-s carc mlr1• castm j5.de *Caust* j5.de* cham bg2 chin bg2 **Chinin-s** k* cic cina bg2 *Clem* k* cocc bg2 coff bg2 colch k* croc bg2 crot-h bg2 crot-t k* cupr k* cycl k* dig k* digin a1 dros k* ferr k* ferr-ar k2 ferr-p fl-ac genist fr1 gins glon k* *Graph* k* *Hell* h1* hep bg2 hura hydr-ac ign hr1* *Iod* k* ip j5.de kali-i k* kali-p rb2 lach laur j5.de lil-t lipp a1 lyss k* mag-c k* mag-s k* mang j5.de **MED** st1 meny *Merc* j5.de* merc-c mez mur-ac h2* naja a1 *Nat-c* bg1* nat-m k* nat-p k* nat-s k* nicc **Nux-v** k* petr bg2 phel k* phos k* **Psor** k* *Puls* rhus-t k* rumx sabad bg2 sabin j5.de sanic rb2 sec a1 sil bg2 spong j5.de* stram sul-i k2* sulph k* tab k* tarent valer verat j5.de* vichy-g a1* vinc wye a1 zinc hr1* [heroin sdj2]
  - **daytime**: phel k*
  - **morning**: am-c mag-s k*
  - **forenoon**: am-c k*
  - **noon** | **15** h; until: astac a
  - **afternoon**: castm hura tab a1
    - ⁝ **14** h: hura
  - **evening**: ferr k* mag-c↓ nat-m k*
    - ⁝ **bed**; in | **amel.**: mag-c
  - **air** amel.; open: calc-s fyz
  - **chilliness**, during: cycl k*
  - **heat**, during: atro k* cycl h1*
  - **hysteria**, weeping amel.: *Aster* kr1
  - **losing** something of great value: sec fyz
  - **play**; in: phel a
  - **twilight**; in: caust ptk1
- **mistakes**; of making: *(↗failure; talking - say)* cob ptm1• coca-c sk4• crot-c sk4• lac-ac stj5• lac-h sze9• vanil fd5.de
- **monomania**; religious: *(↗Religious - too)* lach tl1
- **monsters**; of: lac-c mtf33 med mtf33 tarent tl1
  - **dark**; in the: med mrr1
    - ⁝ **not** in the dark; in light and: lac-c mtf33
- **moral** obliquity: lil-t k* manc mrr1
  - **alternating** with | **sexual** excitement: lil-t k*
- **motion**, of: *Bry* bro1 calad br1* chel a1 cina↓ gels hr1* hyos h1* mag-p bro1 mur-ac h2
  - **cough**; lest it brings on: bry al cina al
- **motoring**; of (See driving a)
- **multiple** sclerosis; of: ars mrr1
- **murdered**, of being: *(↗Delusions - murdered - will; Schizophrenia - paranoid)* absin k* ars fyz* caps fyz *Cimic* k* lac-h sze9• op k* phos k* *Plat* stj2*• plb k* rhus-t bg2 staph bg2 stram k* tab ptk1 [am-f stj2 arg-n stj2 ars-met stj2 aur stj2 aur-m stj2 aur-s stj2 bar-met stj2 caes-met stj2 cinnb stj2 fl-ac stj2 fl-pur stj2 hafn-met stj2 irid-met stj2 kali-ar stj2 lanth-met stj2 lith-f stj2 merc-d stj2 nat-ar stj2 nat-f stj2 osm-met stj2 rhen-met stj2 tant-met stj2 thal-met stj2 tung-met stj2]
- **music**, from: *(↗Music - agg.)* *Acon* bro1 *Ambr* bro1 bar-c fyz bufo bro1 cocc fyz dig *Nat-c* k* nat-s k2* nit-ac fyz nux-v bro1 phos fyz *Sabin* bro1 sulph fyz tarent bro1 thuj bro1*
- **narrow** place, in: *(↗vaults; Crowd; Door - closed; Fall upon; Suffocation; Delusions - Corners - project; Delusions - Falling - walls; Delusions - House - crush; Delusions - Walls - crush; Delusions - Walls - falling; Delusions - Walls - surrounded; COUGH - Cellars; GENERALS - Faintness - Crowded - room; GENERALS - Faintness - Crowded - street; GENERALS - Room - Close; GENERALS - Room - Close - agg.; GENERALS - Room - Full - people; GENERALS - Vaults; HEAD - Pain - Room - crowded; HEAD - Pain - Vaults)* abies-c oss4• absin vh **Acon** k* aids nl2• ambr jsa* ant-c gb*• aran jl aran-sc st **Arg-n** k* ars kk* *Aur-m-n* wbt2• *Bamb-a* stb2.de• bar-c↓ bry kk *Calc* vh* carb-an kk carc pd* caust↓ chinin-ar vh chlam-tr bcx2• cimic ptk1 cocc st coli rly4• dirc jsa dulc↓ dys pte1*• falco-pe nl2• ferr mtf33 ham fd3.de* *Ign* vh* ignis-alc es2• kali-ar vh kali-c kk *Lac-d* k2* lach kk lavand-a ctl1• *Lyc* mrr1* lyss mrr1* manc vh med kk* morg ptj• morg-g pte1* nat-m vh* nat-s mtf33 nat-sil stj2*• nux-m gk nux-v st pert-vc vk9 petr-ra shn4• pin-con oss2• plb kr1* positr nl2• psor vh *Puls* mrr1* ruta ld sep kk sil gk*
- **narrow** place, in: ... stann gb*• staph gl1.fr• staphycoc rly4• **Stram** k* succ br1* succ-xyz↓ suis-pan rly4• sulph st* tab k* til a1 *Tritic-vg* fd5.de valer st* vanil fd5.de vult-gr sze5• [ant-m stj2 ant-met stj2 ant-t stj2 arg-met stj1* arg-p stj2 bar-i stj2 cadm-m stj2 cadm-met stj2 cadm-s stj2 calc-n stj1 calc-sil stj2 *Ferr-n* stj2 ferr-sil stj2 heroin sdj2 ind stj2 iod stj2 kali-n stj1 kali-sil stj2 *Mag-n* stj2 mag-sil stj2 *Mang-n* stj2 mang-sil stj2 merc-i-f stj2 moly-met stj2 nat-n stj1 niob-met stj2 *Nitro* stj2 pall stj2 rhodi stj2 rubd-met stj2 ruth-met stj2 sil-met stj2 stront-m stj2 stront-met stj2 techn stj2 tell stj2 yttr-met stj2 *Zinc-n* stj2 zirc-met stj2]
  - **trains** and closed places; fear of: *(↗rail)* acon vh aids nl2• arg-n fyz bar-c gl• cimic fyz dys pte1*• ferr gl• ham fd3.de• nat-m fyz puls gl• succ bro1 succ-xyz c1* tritic-vg fd5.de vanil fd5.de [calc-n stj1 ferr-n stj2 zinc-n stj2]
  - **vaults**, churches and cellars; fear of: *(↗narrow)* *Ars* sf1.de bry sf1.de* *Calc* sf1.de carb-an sf1.de carc gk6* caust sf1.de dulc sf1.de* dys pte1• nat-s sf1.de* *Puls* sf1.de sep sf1.de stram sf1.de tritic-vg fd5.de
- **nausea**; after: **Ant-t** br1* calc a1 **Nux-v** kr1 tab k* tarax↓
  - **sitting**; while: tarax a
- **near**; of those standing: *(↗approaching)* bell
- **neglected**, of being: *(↗alone; forsaken; solitude)* aur-s wbt2• crot-c sk4• musca-d↓ **Psor** vh* **Puls** k2* thuj mrr1
  - **wife**; by his: musca-d szs1
- **nervous**: *Kali-p* br1 *Scut* br1
- **new** enterprise; of undertaking a (= new situation; of a): *(↗failure; new persons; undertaking; Change - aversion)* aster sze10• *Aur-m-n* wbt2• aur-s wbt2• bar-c mrr1 lyc mtf33 plb cld• *Sil* kr1 stront-c sk4• [cupr stj2 cupr-act stj2 cupr-f stj2 cupr-m stj2 cupr-p stj2]
- **new** persons, of: *(↗new enterprise)* lyc k2* stront-c sk4•
- **new** situations (See new enterprise)
- **noise**, from: *(↗lightning; Sensitive - noise)* acon bro1 aloe alum *Ant-c* k* *Asar* bro1 *Aur* bar-c *Bell* bro1* *Borx* k* calad bro1 calc↓ calc-p brm cann-s canth↓ carc↓ *Caust* *Cham* bro1 chel chin gl1.fr• cic k* *Cocc* k* coff dulc fd4.de ferr bro1 hipp hura hyos↓ ign bro1 kali-c bro1 lac-h↓ limest-b↓ *Lyc* k2* **Lyss**↓ mag-m bro1 med bro1 mosch k* nat-c k* *Nat-s* nit-ac bro1 nux-v k* oxal-a rly4• ozone↓ *Phos* bro1* *Ruta* fd4.de sabad sep↓ sil bro1* **Stram**↓ sulph gl1.fr• tab tanac bro1 tarent bro1 ther bro1* zinc bro1* [arg-n stj2 bor-pur stj2 zinc-i stj2 zinc-m stj2 zinc-n stj2 zinc-p stj2]
  - **night**: aloe↓ bar-c *Caust* *Nat-s* oxal-a rly4•
    - ⁝ **pollution**; after: aloe kr1
  - **door**:
    - ⁝ **at**: *Aur* k* cic *Lyc* k*
    - ⁝ **moving** in the dark: ozone sde2•
  - **gun**; thunder of a (See gun)
  - **menses**; during: carc sde•
  - **rattling**: aloe bg2 calad↓
    - ⁝ **newspaper**; of: calad fyz
  - **rushing** water; of: *(↗Hydrophobia)* bell fyz canth fyz hyos k2 **Lyss** **Stram** k* sulph fyz
  - **slight** noise: aloe↓ aur ptk1
    - ⁝ **pollutions**; after: aloe hr1
  - **street**, in: bar-c k* *Caust* k*
  - **sudden**, of: *Borx* *Cocc* lac-h sze9• limest-b es1• ruta fd4.de
  - **unusual**; of: borx tl1
- **nose** | **cut** off; of having the nose: ars glh
- **observed**; of her condition being: *(↗Delusions - confusion; Delusions - watched; Looked - cannot; Timidity)* ambr tsm1 anthraq rly4• aq-mar mgm• atro k* bamb-a stb2.de• **Calc** k* chel k* choc srj3• falco-pe↓ germ-met srj* limest-b es1• marb-w es1• sal-fr sle1• sanguis-s hm2• taosc iwa1• [am-br stj2 ars stj2 ars-met stj2 bar-br stj2 calc-sil stj2 chr-m stj2 chr-met stj2 chr-s stj2 cob stj2 cob-m stj2 cob-p stj2 cupr-act stj2 cupr-f stj2 cupr-m stj2 cupr-p stj2 ferr stj2 ferr-f stj2 ferr-lac stj2 ferr-n stj2 ferr-sil stj2 gal-met stj2 gal-s stj2 iod stj2 kali-ar stj2 kali-met stj2 kali-sil stj2 mang-act stj2 mang-i stj2 mang-m stj2 mang-met stj2 mang-n stj2 mang-p stj2 mang-s stj2 mang-sil stj2 merc stj2 nat-ar stj2 nat-br stj2 nicc-met stj2 nicc-s stj2 sel stj2 tell stj2 titan-s stj2 zinc stj2 zinc-i stj2 zinc-m stj2 zinc-n stj2 zinc-p stj2]
  - **morning** | **bed**; in: falco-pe nl2•
- **occupation**, of: lyc fyz sel k* sil fyz
- **ocean**: galeoc-c-h gms1•

- **power** of the: galeoc-c-h gms1•
- **offended**, of being: puls k2
- **offending** his associates: tus-fa a
- **old**; of getting: *(↗age)* lach dtn1 lyc dtn1 marb-w es1• sep dtn1
- **open** spaces; fear of: *(↗Crowd; Going; Going; GENERALS - Faintness - Crowded - street; VERTIGO - Walking - Open)* *Acon* bg2* *Anth* vh1 *Arg-n* bg2* *Arn* bg2* ars fyz* bar-c mrr1* *Calc* bg2* carc mlr1• crot-h gl1.fr• ferr gl1.fr• glon bg2 hydr gl1.fr• hydr-ac ll1* hyos fyz kali-bi ll1 *Kali-p* bg2* lac-c fyz levo jl lyc fyz* lyss mrr1 merc mrr1 morg jl nux-v bg2* phos ll1* prot ptj• puls gl1.fr• ser-a-c jl2 stram mrr1 succ-ac rly4• tab hs visc bg2* [alum stj2 am-caust stj2 arg-met stj1 ferr-n stj2 fl-ac stj2 mag-n stj2 moly-met stj2 nat-f stj2 oxyg stj sil stj2 zinc-n stj2]
  - **menopause**; during: *Glon* st
- **operation**, of each: *(↗doctors)* aeth gg calc st1 phos mtf33 [am-caust stj2 am-f stj2 beryl stj2 beryl-m stj2 bor-pur stj2 fl-ac stj2 fl-pur stj2 graph stj2 lith-c stj2 lith-f stj2 lith-met stj2 oxyg stj2]
- **opinion** of others, of: *(↗Confidence - want; Delusions - criticized; Delusions - despised; Delusions - insulted; Delusions - laughed; Delusions - looked; Despair - social; Flattered - desire; Mocking - others; Sensitive - opinion; Timidity - bashful)* **Ambr** vh ars mrr1 aur-m-n wbt2• bar-c dx1 bar-s mtf calc mtf33 *Germ-met* srj5• nux-v vh* ozone sde2* prot ptj* puls vh* thuj mrr1 [heroin sdj2 zinc-p stj2]
- **ordeals**, of: *Arg-n* bg2* arn bg3* ars fyz carb-v fyz *Gels* bg2* kali-br bg3* lys bg2 lyss bg1* *Stroph-h* bg3* thuj fyz
- **osteoporosis**, of: calc gg
- **others** (See people)
- **out** of doors; to go (See going)
- **overpowering** (See terror)
- **overwhelming** fear (See terror)
- **pain**:
  - **during**: acon tl1 bism ↓ carc mlr1• dulc fd4.de merc-br a1 plb ↓ **Ruta** fd* sars ptk1 tritic-vg fd5.de
    - ⁝ **Abdomen**; in: bism mrr1
  - **of** the pain: *(↗pins; suffering)* all-c mtf **Arn** sne aur bl* bry fyz* calc st carc ↓ clem st coff fyz* cor-r fyz* cori-r a1 der a1* eup-per fyz* jil-t fyz* lyc mtf phos fyz* pip-m a1 pip-n fyz* *Ruta* fd4.de *Spong* fd4.de tritic-vg fd5.de vanil fd5.de
    - ⁝ **distracted** from pain; that she will become: all-c gt
    - ⁝ **unbearable**; that the pain will become: all-c ptk1* carc mlr1•
- **palpitation**, with: abel vh1 *Acon* bg2* alum hr1 aur-m hr1* ferr vh* hydrog srj2• *Merc* hr1* nat-m bg2* nit-ac sf1.de* *Op* hr1* *Puls* hr1* spong kr1 tritic-vg fd5.de *Vanil* fd5.de
- **panic** attacks (See sudden)
- **paralysis**, of: *(↗apoplexy)* *Anac* k* arn k* asaf k* bapt c1* bell dulc fd4.de kali-p fyz nux-m c1 syph k*
- **people**; of (= anthropophobia): *(↗Company - aversion; Cowardice; Delirium - fear; Delirium - fear - men; Hatred; Humankind - shuns; Timidity)* acet-ac *Acon* k* aloe k* alum k* alum-p k2 am-m k* ambr k* *Anac* k* *Anh* mg1.de *Arist-cl* mg1.de ars k* ars-i ars-s-f k2 *Aur* k* aur-ar k2 aur-i k2 *Aur-m-n* wbt2• aur-s k2* bar-act a1 *Bar-c* k* bar-i k2* bar-s k2 bell k* bufo-s calc k* calc-i k2 camph k2 carb-an k* *Carb-v* k* carbn-s carc ↓ *Caust* mtf33* cham ↓ chin k* *Cic* b7.de* clem ↓ cocc ptk1 *Con* k* crot-h k* crot-t cupr k* cycl tl1 dig sf1.de dios k* dream-p sdj1• dros tl1 ferr k* ferr-ar ferr-p fl-ac bg2 gard-j vlr2• gels bro1 granit-m es1• graph k* hep k* hydrc a1 **Hyos** k* hypoth vml3• ign k* *Iod* k* *Kali-ar* k* kali-bi k* kali-br *Kali-c* k* kali-i ptk1 kali-p k* kali-s ketogl-ac rly4• lach k* *Led* k* **LYC** k •* *M-aust* b7a.de meli bro1 merc k* musca-d szs1 *Nat-ar* k* **Nat-c** k* *Nat-m* k* nat-s k2 phos k* *Plat* k* *Puls* k* rhus-g a1* **Rhus-t** k* sel k* sep k* sil ptk1 spong fd4.de stann k* staph bg2* sul-i k2 sulph k* tab k* tarent ↓ til vult-gr sze5• [ars-met stj2 astat stj2 aur-m stj2 bar-br stj2 bar-met stj2 bism-sn stj2 caes-met stj2 cinnb stj2 cupr-act stj2 cupr-f stj2 cupr-m stj2 cupr-p stj2 ferr-f stj2 ferr-lac stj2 ferr-sil stj2 hafn-met stj2 irid-met stj2 lanth-met stj2 mag-p stj1 merc-d stj2 merc-i-f stj2 nat-br stj2 nat-caust stj2 nat-lac stj2 nat-met stj2 nat-sil stj2 osm-met stj2 plb stj2 plb-m stj2 plb-p stj2 polon-met stj2 rhen-met stj2 tant-met stj2 thal-met stj2 tung-met stj2]
  - **approaching** him (See approaching - others)
  - **behind** him might hit him; fear that people: *(↗behind)* alum vh*
  - **being** alone; yet fear of: *(↗being; Company - aversion - fear; Company - desire)* ars ptk1 clem ptk1* con j5.de* kali-br ptk1 lyc ptk1* sep ptk1* stram ptk1* tarent ptk1
  - **children**, in: **Bar-c** k* carb-v mtf33 caust mtf33 cham tl1 cupr ↓ *Lyc* k*

- **people**; of – **children**, in: ...
    - ⁝ **fever**, during: cupr st
  - **confidence** in; from loss of: cic a1
  - **contempt** for; with: cic a1
  - **fever**; during: con bg2 hyos bg2 *Puls* bg2
  - **menses**; during: carc sde• con hr1
  - **shuns** the foolishness of: cic
  - **stool**:
    - ⁝ **before**: ambr b7.de*
    - ⁝ **complaints** of stool; with: ambr bg2
- **perspiration**, with: acon bg ars bg2 *Bell* bg2 *Calc* bg carc mlr1• caust bg *Cham* bg kali-i fyz lach bg2 lyc bg2 nux-v bg *Petr* bg *Phos* bg puls bg2 sabad bg samb bg sep bg2 *Spong* bg* sulph bg
  - **cold** perspiration: ars br1
- **physician** (See doctors)
- **piano**, when at: *(↗Anxiety - playing; Music - agg.)* *Kali-br* hr1* *Phos* k*
- **pins**; of (= pointed things): *(↗pain - of)* *Alum* ptk1* *Apis* bg2* ars ptk1 bov ptk1 lac-f bg2* merc ptk1* nat-m st plat ptk1* **Sil** k* **Spig** k* symph fd3.de* [oxyg stj]
- **pitied**, of being: chin gl1.fr• nat-m vh
- **places** (See crowd; narrow)
- **places**; open (See open)
- **pneumonia**: *(↗lung)*
  - **during**: acon mrr1
  - **of** pneumonia; fear: chel k*
- **pointed** things (See pins)
- **poisoned**: *(↗Schizophrenia - paranoid)*
  - **being** poisoned; fear of: *(↗Delusions - poisoned - he - about)* agre jl all-s k* alum ↓ anac bg2* apis k* *Ars* gk* ars-met k* bapt bg2* *Bell* k* bry cimic dros fyz euph h2 falco-pe nl2• glon k* **Hyos** k* ign vh* (non:kali-bi hr1) *Kali-br* k* *Lach* k* lyss fyz maias-l hrn2• meli mrr1* nat-m bg2* oxal-a rly4• ph-ac vh* phos plb k* **Rhus-t** k •* stram he1 *Verat* b7.de* verat-v k* [ant-c stj2 ant-met stj2 kali-ar stj2 mag-sil stj2 nat-ar stj2]
    - ⁝ **night**: ars-met
    - ⁝ **aluminium**; by: alum tl1
  - **has** been: *(↗Delusions - poisoned - he - has)* euph h2* glon k* hyos h1*
  - **mania**, in puerperal: *Verat-v* kr1
- **police**; of (See Delusions - pursued - police)
- **pollutions**, after: aloe carb-an k* petr ptk1
- **position** (See job; social)
- **possessed**; being (See Delusions - possessed)
- **poverty**, of: *(↗business; starving; Anxiety - business; Anxiety - money; Avarice; Delusions - fortune; Delusions - poor; Delusions - ruined - is; Delusions - starve - family; Delusions - starve - he; Delusions - want - he; Delusions - want - they)* agath-a nl2• aids nl2• ambr ars ptk1* bamb-a stb2.de• borx gt **Bry** k* *Calc* k* *Calc-f* k* calc-s tl calc-sil k2* chinin-s mrr chir-fl gya2 chlor cit-ac rly4• coca-c sk4• dream-p sdj1• dulc fd4.de falco-pe nl2• gink-b sbd1• graph gk hydrog srj2• iris gt kali-c st1 kali-s fd4.de lach gt meli merc mrr1* moni rfm1• nit-ac mrr1 nux-v k* phasco-ci rbp2 positr nl2• *Psor* k* puls sec gk *Sep* k* sil gk spong fd4.de staph ptk1 suis-em rly4• sulph k* syph jl2 tritic-vg fd5.de [alumin-s stj2 *Am-f* stj2 ant-c stj2 aur-s stj2 cadm-s stj2 calc-lac stj2 calc-met stj2 chr-s stj2 cinnb stj2 *Cupr-f* stj2 *Fl-ac* stj2 *Fl-pur* stj2 gal-s stj2 *Lith-f* stj2 lith-s stj2 mang-s stj2 *Nat-f* stj2 nicc-s stj2 *Oxyg* stj2 stann stj2 titan-s stj2]
  - **spending** money in order not to be short of it in future; fear of: *Nux-v* gl1.fr• spong fd4.de stann gl1.fr•
- **pregnancy**, during: *(↗baby; Anxiety - pregnancy)* *Acon* hr1* *Ant-t* kr1 bar-c kr1 *Caul* st *Cimic* k* con bg2 ign kr1 kali-br tl1 lyc hr1* lyss k* *Nux-m* hr1* op ↓ psor kr1 stann
  - **abortion** in latter part; of: op fyz
- **pregnant**; of getting: *Sep* fd
- **problems** of my proximate friends; to be mixed with the | **afternoon**: gard-j vlr2•
- **process**, of a: *Nit-ac* gl1.fr•
- **processions**, in: stram j5.de
- **prolapse**; of:
  - ○ **Anus**; of: ign fyz* nit-ac fyz

- **Uterus**; of: *Lil-t* hr1*
- **public** places:
  - **crowded** (See crowd)
  - **empty** (See open)
- **pulsation**; of:
  - **body**; in: carb-v j
  - ○ **Head**; in: aml-ns hs1*
- **punishment**; of: *(↗Anxiety - conscience)* calc sne camph↓ carc mlr1• crot-c↓ moni rfm1• olib-sac wmh1 plb cld* tritic-vg fd5.de
  - **child**: camph kr1
  - **divine**: crot-c sk4•
- **pursued**; of being (See Anxiety - pursued; Delusions - pursued; Insanity - persecution)
- **pursuit**; of (See Anxiety - pursued; Delusions - pursued; Insanity - persecution)
- **putrefy**, body will: *(↗Delusions - body - putrefy)* bell
- **rage**, to fly into a: calc ckh1* chin ckh1* *Nux-v* ckh1* staph ckh1*
- **rail**, of going by: *(↗narrow - trains)* bar-c vh* ferr vh* puls vh*
- **rain**, of: calc vh cor-r fyz dulc fd4.de *Elaps* k* gard-j vlr2• lap-la sde8.de• naja br1*
- **raped**; of being: *(↗injury - being)* arn vh crot-c sk4•
- **rats**: *(↗animals; mice)* absin fyz bell hr1 **Calc** mrr1 calc-ar mtf cimic ptk1* hyos mrr1 olib-sac wmh1 op fyz* phos fyz* sep fyz* [tung-met stj2]
- **recover**, he will not: *(↗disease - incurable; Delusions - disease - incurable)* all-s a1* ant-t a1 carc mlr1• falco-pe nl2• hep gl1.fr• ruta fd4.de sars↓
  - **menopause**; during: sars st
- **recurrent**: arn bg2 ars bg2 carc mlr1• cham bg2 cocc bg2 nat-c bg2 nat-m bg2 phos bg2 plat bg2 sep bg2 spong bg2 sulph bg2
- **red**, anything: *Alum* vh*
- **rejection**; of: *(↗Ailments - rejected)* *Aur* mtf aur-m-n mtf carc mtf *Ign* mtf kali-c mtf lac-c mtf *Mag-c* mtf mag-m mtf *Nat-m* mtf plat mtf *Staph* mtf thuj mtf
- **reflecting** objects (See brilliant; mirrors)
- **reproaches**; of: *(↗Ailments - reproaches; Delusions - criticized)* camph mtf caps k* carc mlk* dig a1 nux-v sne plb mtf
- **reptiles**; of: calc-s sej
- **respiration**; of: bell hr1 osm a1 viol-o↓
  - **painful**: viol-o a
- **respiratory** disease; of a: *(↗disease; lung)* lac-c tl1 lob mrr1
- **responsibility**: *(↗Responsibility - aversion)* arg-n fyz ars tl1* aur ptk carc↓ kali-p fyz lyc vn10.fr sil fyz*
  - **much** responsibility; of too: carc mlr1•
- **restlessness** from fear (See Restlessness - fear)
- **riding** in a carriage, when: *(↗Riding - carriage - aversion)* acon dx1 androc srj arg-n fd* ars sne aur gb• *Borx* k* (non:bry) carc dgt cimic↓ cocc fyz cupr sht*• dulc fd4.de falco-pe nl2• gins st1 *Lach* k* lipp a1 mag-m dgt nat-m dgt olib-sac wmh1 pitu-a ft *Psor* k* (non:sanic) **Sep** k ●* succ ptk2 vanil fd5.de [calc-m stj1]
  - **closed** carriage and being obliged to jump out; in a: cimic br1* succ ptk1
- **ringing** at the door; from: *Lyc* hr1*
- **roasted**, to be: stram j5.de
- **robbers**, of: *(↗Delusions - thieves - house)* agar fyz alum anac k2* aq-mar vml3• *Arg-n* k* arizon-l nl2• **ARS** bg2* aur aur-s k2* bell k* *Con* k* crot-c sk4• cupr↓ dulc fd4.de elaps *Ign* k* kali-p st1 lac-del hrn2• lac-h sze9• *Lach* lyc hu mag-c mag-m k* maias-l hrn2• *Merc* moni rfm1• nat-c **Nat-m** k ●* *Phos* k* plut-n srj7• positr nl2• psor hu puls mrr1 sal-fr sle1• sanic k* sil sol-t-ae stront-c sk4• sulph k* tritic-vg fd5.de verat *Zinc* k* zinc-p k2* [*Oxyg* stj]
  - **night**: ars↓ cupr fyz dulc fd4.de *Ign*↓ lach gl1.fr• nat-m↓ sanic c1 sulph↓
    - **midnight** | **waking**; on: ars fyz *Ign* nat-m h2* sulph
  - **waking**, on: merc j5.de nat-m j5.de sil j5.de
- **room**, on entering: alum k* *Bry*↓ hydr-ac ptk1 lyc k* plat k* til k* *Valer* k*
  - **air** amel.; open: *Bry* kr1
- **ruin**; of financial (See poverty)
- **run** against something; to: arg-met hr1 tarent a1
- **run** over; fear of being: *(↗streets - busy; walking - of - street)*
  - **going** out; on: *(↗accidents; approaching; walking - of - street; Going)* anth hydr-ac lyss op hr1 **Phos** k ●
- **sadness**, with: *(↗Sadness)* am-m bg2 cic bg2 croc bg2 *Crot-h* hr1* *Dig* a1 hep bg2 *Kali-br* hr1* kali-c bg2 **Kali-i** hr1* lyc bg2 *Nat-m* hr1* plat hr1* *Plb* hr1* rhus-t hr1* syph mtf11 tab bg2 vinc hr1*
- **say** something wrong; lest he should (See talking - say)
- **scorpions**; of: *(↗animals)* abel jl3 op gl•
- **sea**; of the: *Morb* vh* [mang-i stj2]
- **see** wounds, to (See wounds)
- **self**-control, of losing: *(↗control)* alum gk* *Arg-n* k* bamb-a stb2.de• cann-i bng crot-c sk4• cupr sht* *Cupr-act* kr1 cypra-eg sde6.de• des-ac rbp6 **Gels** k ●* germ-met srj *Merc* kr1 mur-ac h2 nux-v gg ozone sde2• rhod kgp5* *Staph* k* sulph gg thea gg thuj gk [mag-br stj1 tax jsj7]
- **senses**; with exalted state of (= smell, taste, touch): lyss kr1
- **separation**; of:
  - **children**; from: calc mtf phos mtf puls mtf
  - **friends**; from: *(↗Delusions - friend - affection; Delusions - friendless)* lac-c mtf
  - **husband**; from: *(↗Delusions - forsaken)* ign mtf puls mtf sep mtf staph mtf
  - **parents**; from: *(↗Delusions - forsaken)* lac-ac mtf puls mtf
  - **partner**; from: galeoc-c-h gms1•
- **serious** thoughts, of: *(↗Serious)* crot-h plat
- **sex**; of opposite: *(↗Aversion - men; to [=male persons] - women; Aversion - women - men)* kali-p fyz lac-f mlk6 puls fyz sep fyz staph fyz
- **sexual**:
  - **assault**: musca-d szs1
  - **obliquity** (See moral)
- **shadows**: acon ptk calad↓ *Calc* bg2* caust fr lyc↓ med dx phos gl* staph mtf33 stram↓ xan bg
  - **candlelight**; thrown by: calc hr1
  - **his** own shadow; of: acon ptk calad st* *Calc* kr1* lyc c1* staph c1*
- **sharks**; of: nat-lac mtf nat-m mtf
- **shining** objects (See brilliant; mirrors)
- **shivering** from fear: **Gels** kr1 granit-m es1• hydrog srj2•
- **sighing**, with: ip a1 *Rhus-t* hr1*
- **sin**; of: manc mrr1
- **sitting** amel.: *(↗Sitting - inclination)* iod k*
- **sleep**:
  - **before**: acon arg-n calad k* calc carb-v chir-fl gya2 cob-n sp1 gels lac-h sze9• nat-c *Rhus-t* k* sars [mag-m stj1]
  - **close** the eyes lest he should never wake; fear to: aeth k* ang kr1 hypoth jl plac rzf5• [mang-sil stj2]
  - **go** to sleep; fear to: aeth mrr apis ld bapt kr1 cadm-s br1 calad kr1* calc st calc-sil bc camph k* caust↓ cench k2 cob-n↓ coff he dig k2 grin k2 *Hydr-ac* kr1 kali-s fd4.de *Lach* k* *Led* k1* med gb• merc nat-m *Nux-m* nux-v *Rhus-t* *Sabal* br1* *Syph* bgs thea dx1 [heroin sdj2]
    - **night**: cob-n sp1
    - **dark**; in the: caust fyz
    - **die**; lest he (See death - sleep - die)
    - **dreams**; lest he (See dreams)
    - **pain**; because of increasing: lach tl1
    - **suffocate**; lest he (See suffocation - sleep)
  - **jerking** on falling asleep; from: sabal ptk1
  - **lack** of; of: daph fyz
  - **loss** of sleep; from: cocc ptk1 corv-cor bdg• *Nit-ac* ptk1 tritic-vg fd5.de
  - **never** sleep again, he will: *Ign*
- **sleeplessness**; of: op fyz
- **smallpox**, of: *Vac* kr1* vario br1*
- **snakes**, of: *(↗animals)* *Abel* jl3* arg-n fyz* ars gm1 bell tl1* calc gy* calc-s sej* carc nl* *Elaps* vh* hep vh* ign mrr* **Lac-c** tl1* lac-f wza1• *Lach* vh* lob samkn nat-m hu* puls hu* ruta ld sep vh spig vh* sulph vh* syph vh urol-h rwt• [ferr-n stj2 mag-n stj2 mang-n stj2 nitro stj2]
- **social** position; about his: *(↗Ailments - failure - social; Despair - social)* chel mtf ign mtf *Lyc* mrr1 sep gl1.fr• staph gl1.fr• verat k* [calc-f stj1 mag-f stj1]

- **society** (See company)
- **sold**; of being: bell lpc bry lpc *Hyos* k* lyss fyz rhus-t lpc
- **solitude**, of: *(↗alone; forsaken; neglected; Company - desire)* act-sp vh1 *Ars* a1* ars-s-f k2 berb vh1 cadm-s ptk1 *Carc* fd2.de*• lyc a1 stram tl1 vanil fd5.de
- **sounds**; unusual (See noise - unusual)
- **space**; open (See open)
- **speak**; to (See talking)
- **spiders**, of: *(↗animals; Delusions - spiders)* *Abel* jl* calc bng* carc bcn* cupr sst3• ign bng lac-c tl1* lec oss• mag-m dgt nat-m vh1* phos bng puls gk sep dgt stram fyz tarent gg* [arg-n stj2 ferr-n stj2 mag-n stj2 niob-met stj2 nitro stj2]
  - **children**; in: carc sst2•
- **spirits**; of (See ghosts)
- **spoken** to, when: *Kali-br* k* sep
- **stage** fright (See Anticipation - stage; Timidity - public)
- **starting**, with: *(↗Starting)* bar-c kr1 bell kr1 calc-p kr1 carc mlr1• *Hyos* kr1 kali-br kr1 nit-ac kr1 *Op* kr1 phos kr1 stram j5.de *Verat* kr1
- **starving**, of: *(↗poverty; Avarice; Delusions - poor; Delusions - starve - being; Delusions - starve - family; Delusions - starve - he; Delusions - want - he)* ars ptk1 *Bry* hr1* calc k* grat lpc kali-m sla lap-la rsp1 op a1 *Sep* hr1* staph sne sulph tritic-vg fd5.de
- **stomach**:
  - **arising** from: *(↗STOMACH - Apprehension)* adon sf1.de asaf *Aur* bry *Calc* *Cann-s* canth carc mlr1• *Dig* euph sf1.de euphr bg2 hydrog srj2• *Kali-c* k* *Lyc* **Mez** k1* *Phos* positr nl2• thuj
  - **ulcer** in, of: ign nat-m fyz sabad j5.de
- **stool**:
  - **after**: calc ptk1 caust ptk1* kali-c ptk1* nit-ac ptk1
  - **complaints** of stool; with: ambr bg2 caust bg2
  - **dark** stool and urine, with urging for: ozone sde2•
  - **involuntary** stool; of: aloe ↓ carb-v ↓ nat-m ↓ nat-p ↓ nat-s ↓ olnd ↓ ozone ↓ ph-ac ↓ phos kr1 podo ↓ sep h2 sulph ↓ verat ↓
    - **flatus** or urinating; when passing: *(↗urine - involuntary)* aloe vh carb-v fyz nat-m fyz nat-p fyz nat-s fyz* olnd fyz ph-ac fyz podo fyz sulph fyz verat fyz
    - **green**, gushing, exhausting: verat kr1
    - **hemorrhoids**; with: ozone sde2•
  - **painful** | **children**; in: nux-v mrr1 sulph mtf33
  - **passing**; on account of pain: sulph al
- **stoppage** of circulation; with sensation of | **night**: *Lyc* kr1
- **storm**; of (See wind)
- **strange** places; of: carc mlr1•
- **strange** things; of (See unfamiliar)
- **strangers**, of: *(↗Stranger - presence - agg.)* ambr *Arn* bg2 aur-m-n wbt2• *Bar-c* k* bufo gl* cadm-s bg2 *Carb-v* k* carc sst*• caust k* *Con* hr1 *Cupr* k* dys ptj*• ign bg2 kali-p fyz lach k* lyc k2* plb cld• puls wta rhod kgp5• sil gg* *Spong* fd4.de stram k* stront-c sk4• stry bg2 *Thuj* k* tub wta [alum stj2 am-caust stj2 am-f stj2 arg-n stj2 beryl stj2 beryl-m stj2 bor-pur stj2 cupr-act stj2 cupr-f stj2 cupr-m stj2 cupr-p stj2 ferr-n stj2 fl-ac stj2 fl-pur stj2 graph stj2 lith-c stj2 lith-f stj2 lith-i stj2 lith-m stj2 lith-met stj2 lith-s stj2 mag-n stj2 mang-n stj2 nat-f stj2 nitro stj2 oxyg stj2 zinc-n stj2]
  - **children**; in: bar-c mtf33 cupr mtf33 lach mtf33
  - **menses** | **during**: con ptk2
- **strangled**, to be: **Plat** st1* [*Ant-met* stj2]
- **streets**: *(↗walking - of - street)*
  - **busy** streets; of: *(↗run over; walking - of - street)* *Acon* vh* bar-c fyz carc vh1* caust fyz **Psor** vh* [oxyg stj]
  - **crowd** in streets; of the (See crowd - street)
- **stroke**; of having a (See apoplexy)
- **struck**: *(↗touch)*
  - **approaching** him; of being struck by those: **Arn** kr1 bell a1* ign a1 kali-c a1 lach a1 stram a1 thuj a1*
  - **walking** behind him, by those: alum st
- **subways**; of: *(↗tunnels)* **Acon** vh
- **sudden** (= panic attacks): *(↗terror)* achy mtf *Acon* br1* androc srj5• apis br1 arg-n gsd1 arn ptk1 *Ars* br1 ars-i mp1• atra-r bnm3• bamb-a stb2.de• bar-c ↓ borx ↓ *Cann-i* mrr1 carb-v gsd1 carc mlr1• cypra-eg sde6.de• diosm br1 foll vml3• gard-j vlr2• gels c2* germ-met srj5• glon ptk1* heli-n mtf11 hydrog srj2• hyos tl1 ign ↓ kali-ar mrr1 kali-c bl7 lac-h sze9• levo jl3 med rb3 meli mrr4• meli-a c1 merc mrr1 nit-ac mrr1 op ↓ ozone sde2• ph-ac ↓ plb gk* *Ruta* mrr1 stry sej4 ther mrr1 *Tritic-vg* fd5.de *Vanil* fd5.de [alum stj2 bell-p-sp dcm1 cupr-p stj2 oxyg stj2 sil stj2]
  - **night**: achy ↓ ars gsd1 bar-c ↓ gard-j ↓ [bell-p-sp dcm1]
    - **midnight**:
      - **after** | **0**-2 h: **Ars** mrr1
    - **waking**; on: achy jl3 bar-c vh1 gard-j vlr2•
  - **followed** by:
    - **diabetes** mellitus: op hr
    - **grief**: ign kr1
  - **overheated**; when: *Ruta* mrr1
  - **trembling** and weakness of legs; with: *(↗tremulous)* diosm br1
  - **urination**; before: alum bg2 borx bg2 ph-ac bg2
  - **voice**; with complaints of: hyos bg2
- **suffering**, of: *(↗pain - of)* achy jl3 acon fyz all-c ↓ aur bl bry k* calc k* carc mlr1• cham gk* clem st coff fyz cor-r k* cori-r a1 der k* epiph mgm• eup-per k* fl-ac vh* hep vh* hom-xyz mgm• lach ↓ lil-t k* merc-br a1 parth vml3• phos fyz pip-m k* pip-n fyz sanic mgm• spig k2* stram fyz syph br1 vanil fd5.de
  - **exhaustion** while walking; from: lach fyz syph fyz
  - **unbearable**; will become: all-c ptk
- **suffocation**, of: *(↗narrow; throat; Anxiety - mucus - bronchi)* **Acon** k* acon-f c1 aeth a aether a agar ↓ am-br c1* am-c mg amyg st1 anan a1 apis bg2 arn ↓ *Ars* bg2* aur-m ↓ bapt ↓ *Bell* ↓ *Bry* gl1.fr• cact ↓ carb-an k* carb-v bg2* *Chin* ↓ cupr-act br1 *Dig* bg2* *Dulc* fd4.de falco-pe nl2• *Graph* ↓ *Grin* bg2* ignis-alc es2• ip ↓ *Kali-i* sf1.de lac-d k2 lach bg2* lat-m bg3* *Lob* hr1* *Lyc* ↓ lyss vh* med ↓ melal-alt gya4 merc k* *Merc-i-f* ↓ mosch ↓ nat-sil ↓ nux-v gl1.fr• *Phos* k* *Puls* ↓ (non:rob slp) ruta fd4.de samb hr1* seneg k2 sil ↓ *Spig* hr1* *Spong* k* *Staph* hr1* *Stram* k* *Sulph* bg2* tritic-vg fd5.de vanil fd5.de [ant-c stj2 ant-met stj2 ant-t stj2 *Buteo-j* sej6 nicc stj1 tax jsj7]
  - **evening**: aether a1
  - **night**: *Aeth* vh1 agar k* *Ant-t* st arn k* ars aur-m st cact *Chin* st *Dig* hr1* ip c1 *Lyc* h2* med st *Puls* st ruta fd4.de sil h2* *Spong* hr1* *Sulph* st
  - **asthma**; with: *Phos* kr1
  - **bed**; driving out of: *Dig* kr1
  - **closing** eyes, on: carb-an
  - **dark**; in the: aeth vh
  - **eating** amel.: *Graph* st1
  - **goitre**, in: *Merc-i-f* st
  - **heart** disease, in: *Dig* st1 *Lach* vh* *Spong* st1
  - **lying**, while: ars fyz* carb-an k* dig fyz mosch k* sil fyz
  - **motion**, with dyspnea; on: *Spig* kr1
  - **mucus**; from:
    - **Bronchi**; in (See Anxiety - mucus - bronchi; LARYNX - Mucus - air)
    - **Throat**; in: carb-an h2* nat-sil fd3.de• spong fd4.de tritic-vg fd5.de
  - **rubber** dam is placed in the mouth by dentist; after a: *Stram* prf
  - **sit** up; must: [*Buteo-j* sej6]
  - **sleep**, during: bapt vh*
  - **swallow**; with desire to: *Bell* bg2
  - **walk** about; must: am-br c1
- **suicide**; of: *(↗Anxiety - suicidal; Bed - jumps; Impulse - stab - his; Injuring - fear; Insanity - split; Insanity - suicidal; Kill; desire - herself; Suicidal; Suicidal - anguish; Suicidal - drunkenness; Suicidal - fear; Suicidal - fear - window; Suicidal - fright; Suicidal - sight - cutting; Weary - sight)* *Alum* k* arg-n *Ars* caps tl1 lach fyz med rb* *Merc* k* *Nat-s* *Nux-v* kr1 plat kr1* *Rhus-t* k1* sep tub bgs [astat stj2 aur stj2 aur-m stj2 aur-s stj2 bar-br stj2 bar-i stj2 bar-met stj2 bism-sn stj2 caes-met stj2 cinnb stj2 hafn-met stj2 irid-met stj2 lanth-met stj2 merc-d stj2 merc-i-f stj2 osm-met stj2 plb stj2 plb-m stj2 plb-p stj2 polon-met stj2 rhen-met stj2 tant-met stj2 thal-met stj2 tung-met stj2 zinc-p stj2]
  - **knife**; on seeing a: alum rb2 merc vh

- **supernatural** forces; of (See evil; ghosts; Delusions - pursued - ghosts; Delusions - specters - pursued; Thoughts - persistent - evil)
- **superstitious**: (↗*Superstitious*) rhus-t k*
- **supper**, after: caust k*
- **surgery**: *Aeth* vh1
- **surprises**, from pleasant: (↗*Ailments - joy - excessive; Ailments - surprises - pleasant*) *Coff* k*
- **swimming**; fear of | **deep** water; only in: med hu2 psor sys
- **syphilis**, of: *Hyos* k* merc gl1.fr• **Syph** vh*
- **talking**: (↗*voice of*) arg-met k2 bamb-a ↓ bry ↓ cina ↓ germ-met ↓ *Lil-t* ↓ med ↓ meli ↓ nux-v ↓ pall ↓ puls ↓ rhus-g ↓ sep
  - **cough**; lest it brings on: bry al cina al
  - **crowd**; fear of talking in front of a (See Timidity - public - talk)
  - **kill** her; as if talking loud would: meli k*
  - **people** are talking about him/her: (↗*Delusions - talking - people*) nux-v gl1.fr• pall dx1 puls dmk1*•
  - **say** something wrong; lest he should: (↗*mistakes; Confidence - want; Timidity*) bamb-a stb2.de• germ-met srj *Lil-t* k* med ptk1 rhus-g tmo3•
- **telephone**, of: nat-p vh* visc ptk1*
- **terror**: (↗*sudden*) acon bg2* androc srj1• ars bg2 aur bg2 *Aur-br* ↓ bamb-a stb2.de• bell bg2 calc ↓ carb-v bg2 carc fd2.de*• caust bg2 cham bg2 chin bg2 chlol ↓ cic ↓ *Cina* ↓ cocc bg2* coff bg2 cupr ↓ cypr ↓ dig bg2 falco-pe nl2• gaert ↓ gard-j ↓ **Kali-br** ↓ *Kali-p* ↓ maias-l hm2• morg-g ↓ nux-v bg2 phos bg2 plat bg2 positr nl2• puls bg2 rhus-t bg2 scut ↓ sol-ni ↓ spong ptk1* stram ptk1* sulph bg2 syc ↓ tarent ptk1* toxi mtf2• *Tritic-vg* fd5.de tub ↓ *Vanil* fd5.de verat bg2 zinc ↓
  - **night**: (↗*night; DREAMS - Nightmares*) acon bro1 *Aur-br* bro1 calc bro1* *Carb-v* mtf33 cham bro1 chlol bro1* cic bro1 *Cina* bro1* cupr sst3* cypr bro1 gaert pte1*• gard-j vlr2• *Kali-br* hr1* *Kali-p* br1* morg-g pte1*• scut bro1 sol-ni bro1 *Stram* bro1* syc pte1*• tub bro1 zinc bro1
    - **children**; in: (↗*night - children*) calc mtf33 chlol br1 cina mtf33 cupr mtf33 **Kali-br** hr1
    - **followed** by strabismus | **children**; in: kali-br hr1*
  - **causeless**: maias-l hm2•
  - **sudden** (See sudden)
- **theater**; being in a (See crowd; narrow)
- **things**; of real and unreal: cann-i a1
- **thinking**:
  - **disagreeable** things; when thinking of: phos
  - **sad** things; of: rhus-t
- **thoughts**, of his own: androc srj1• camph
- **throat**; from sensation of swelling of: (↗*suffocation; THROAT - Anxiety*) *Glon* k* nat-m h2*
- **thunder** of a gun (See gun)
- **thunderstorm**, of: (↗*lightning; Anxiety - weather - stormy; Weather - thunderstorm - during*) arizon-l nl2• bell vh beryl-m ↓ *Borx* bg2* *Bry* k* calc vh5* calc-p dp* carc gk6* caust sf1.de *Coloc* vh* con vh* cupr sst3• cycl vh dig vh dulc fd4.de dys dgt* elec j* gard-j vlr2• *Gels* k* glycyr-g cte1• *Graph* vh* hep hyos mta1 ignis-alc es2• lac-c vh* lach k* *Lyc* kr1* merc vh* *Nat-c* k* *Nat-m* k* nat-p mrr4*• *Nit-ac* k* *Oscilloc* jl2 **PHOS** bg2* plut-n srj7• psor bro1 *Rhod* k* rhus-t fyz *Sep* sil bro1 *Staph* vh* stram wta* sulph tritic-vg fd5.de tub lmj [alum-p stj2 *Am-p* stj1 arg-p stj2 *Cupr-p* stj2 ferr-p stj1 lith-p stj2 mang-p stj2 plb-p stj2 zinc-p stj2]
  - **before**: (↗*Weather - thunderstorm - before*) gels hr1* *Nat-c* sf1.de *Phos* nh3* *Psor* vh* *Rhod* vh*
  - **children**; in: calc-p mtf33 carc sst2* lac-c mtf33 lach mtf33 nat-m mtf33 nit-ac mtf33 stram mtf33 [beryl-m stj2]
- **toilet**; in: *Lac-d* st
- **torticollis**; after: *Nux-v* kr1
- **touched**; of being: (↗*approaching - others - touched; struck; Touched - aversion*) *Acon* bro1 *Ant-c* bro1* ant-t bro1* apis bro1 **Arn** k* ars fyz asar jl *Bell* bro1 bruc bro1 calc-sil k2* **Cham** bro1* *Chin* bro1 cina bro1* coff *Colch* bro1 con ptk1 cupr ptk1* *Hep* bro1* ign ptk1 iod bro1* *Kali-c* k1* lac-h sze9• lach k* lyc ptk1 mag-p bro1 nit-ac bro1 nux-m bro1 *Nux-v* kr1* ph-ac kr1 phos bro1 *Plb* bro1 sanic bro1 sep bro1 sieg mg1.de *Spig* bro1 stram bro1 stroph-s ↓ sulph bro1 tarent bro1* tart-ac st *Tell* k1* thuj bro1* valer fyz [bar-i stj2 cupr-act stj2 cupr-f stj2 cupr-m stj2 cupr-p stj2 lith-i stj2 mang-i stj2 merc-i-f stj2 zinc stj2 zinc-i stj2 zinc-m stj2 zinc-n stj2 zinc-p stj2]
  - **chest** wall; on: stroph-s sp1
  - **colic**; in: *Nux-v* kr1
  - **feet**, cries out; on: kali-c kr1
  - **gout**; in: **Arn** kr1*
  - **sore** parts; on: ph-ac kr1 tell ptk1
- **trains**; of: succ br1
- **travelling** by car; of (See Anxiety - riding - fast)
- **travelling**, of: [oxyg stj]
- **tread** lightly or will injure himself, must: (↗*GENERALS - Jar - agg.*) cupr
- **trembling**; with (See tremulous)
- **tremendous** (See terror)
- **tremulous**: (↗*sudden - trembling*) abrot bg2 acon bg2 ambr bg2 ant-c bg2 ars bg2 *Aur* bg2* bell bg2 *Calc* bg2* carb-v j5.de* caust j5.de* *Cham* bg2* cina bg2 coff bg2 croc bg2 cupr bg2 diosm br1 dys pte1• elaps ptk1 **Gels** kr1 granit-m es1• graph bg2 hydrog srj iber hr1* lach bg2 *Mag-c* j5.de* marb-w es1• merc sne mosch bg2 *Nat-c* bg2 nicc j5.de **Op** hr1* oxal-a rly4• ozone sde2• phos bg2 *Plat* j5.de* puls j5.de* ran-b hr1* rat a1 rhus-t bg2 *Ruta* fd4.de sars bg2 sep bg2 ther bg2 tritic-vg fd5.de verat bg2
- **trifles**, of: (↗*Conscientious; Starting - trifles; Trifles; Trifles - important*) acon ptk1 anac fyz *Ars* borx but-ac ↓ calc st1 chin fyz dys ptj• ign k* iod stj2* *Kali-c Lyc Nat-c Nat-m* rhus-t fyz sep ptk1 thuj ptk1 [bar-i stj2 calc-sil stj2 ferr-sil stj2 kali-sil stj2 mag-sil stj2 merc-i-f stj2 nat-sil stj2 sil stj2 sil-met stj2]
  - **head**; during pain in: but-ac br1
- **troubles**; imaginary (See complaints)
- **tuberculosis**; of: calc ptk1* ruta fd4.de syph mrr1 tub ↓
  - **incipient**; in: tub kr1
- **tunnels**; of: (↗*subways*) *Acon* vh* **Arg-n** vh* cimic fyz *Lyc* vh* nat-m fyz **STRAM** st* succ fyz [ferr-n stj2 mag-n stj2 mang-n stj2 nitro stj2 tung-met stj2 zinc-n stj2]
- **twilight**; in: calc bg2 caust ptk1 rhus-t bg2
- **unaccountable**, vague (See causeless)
- **unconsciousness**; of: alum h2* alumn a1 thuj ↓ til a1
  - **sunstroke**; in: thuj kr1
- **undertaking** anything; of: (↗*failure; new enterprise; Confidence - want; Irresolution; Postponing; Responsibility - aversion; Succeeds; Timidity; Undertaking - nothing*) alum gl1.fr• am-c gl1.fr• *Arg-n* k* *Ars* k* **Bar-c** vh* coli rly4• kali-p fyz lach gl1.fr• **Lyc** k* puls gl1.fr• sil bg2* tax-br oss1•
- **unendurable**: lyss ptk1
- **unfamiliar** objects: aur k2 bar-act a1 bar-c vh1 calc-i k2 granit-m es1• hydrog srj2• kali-m k2 kali-sil k2 laur a1 limest-b es1• mang k2 *Psor* k1* zinc-m a1
- **unfit** for work; of becoming: (↗*business failure*) cean kr1 symph fd3.de•
- **unknown**; of the: ars bl aur fyz brom jsj1 calc vh3* carc mtf30 lach cd1 lyc cd1 med rb* morg ptj• sacch sst• stram sk7• tarent gsd1 tub hu2 vanil fd5.de [oxyg stj]
- **unreasoning**: acon tl1 calc tl1
- **upward**, of being drawn: calc-p gk camph k* falco-pe nl2•
- **urinating**, after: sulph hr1*
- **urine**:
  - **involuntary** loss of urine; fear of: (↗*stool - involuntary - flatus; wet*) *Phos* kr1 pitu jl
  - **retention** of urine from fear: *Op* kr1
- **vertigo**; of: bamb-a stb2.de• op fyz sumb k*
- **vexation**; after: *Ars* hr1* cham k* coff kr1 lyc bg2 *Petr* kr1 verat bg2
- **violated**, of being (See raped)
- **violence**, of (See Cowardice; Horrible; Violence - aversion)
- **voice**, of using: (↗*talking*) cann-i k*
- **voices**; of: *Crot-c* mrr1 gard-j vlr2• phos ↓ stram fyz
- **vomiting**; of: acon bro1 lach mrr1
- **waking**, on: (↗*Frightened - waking*) abrot ↓ *Agn* aids nl2• alum alum-p k2 alum-sil k2 am-c ant-t ptk1 arn k2* ars ptk1 aster *Bell* bism k* *Borx* k* bov ↓ *Bry* bg2 bufo *Cact Calc* bg2* *Caps* kr1* carb-an carb-v gm1 *Cham* bg2 chin ↓ cina kr1* cocc con cupr sf1.de dioxi rbp6 frax ↓ graph ↓ hep hyos bg2 ign irid-met srj5• iris kali-br bg2 kali-c bg2 *Lac-c* kr1 lach k* lepi k* lept *Lyc* k* lyss kr1 mag-m ↓ mag-s *Med* kr1 nat-c *Nat-m* nat-p nat-sil k2 nit-ac *Nux-v* ph-ac phos ↓ psor ptk1 *Puls* rat samb ↓ *Sil Spong* k* *Stram* k* *Sulph* suprar rly4• syph ↓ tarent ↓ ter a1 toxi ↓ **Tub** ptk1* xan bg1 zinc k* zinc-p k2

- **aggravation** on waking; of the: syph k2
- **dream**, from a: (↗*dreams*) abrot a1 alum bov chin a1 cina frax a1 graph a1 *Lyc* mag-m a1 ph-ac phos samb bat1• sil tarent a1 toxi mtf2•
- **under** the bed, of something: (↗*Delusions - bed - noise; Delusions - bed - someone - under*) bell

- **walking**: (↗*Walking - slowly; Walking - slowly - dignified*)
  - **of** walking: *Acon*↓ alum↓ ang↓ arg-n↓ beryl↓ beryl-m↓ bor-pur↓ *Carbn-s*↓ carc↓ crot-h↓ fl-pur↓ galeoc-c-h↓ kali-p↓ lith-c↓ lith-f↓ lith-i↓ lith-m↓ lith-met↓ lith-s↓ nat-m nitro↓ oxyg↓ **Psor**↓
    - **canal**; by: ang ptk1
    - **dark**; in the: (↗*dark; dark; of; Anxiety - dark; Darkness - agg.; Light - desire*) *Carbn-s* galeoc-c-h gms1•
    - **street**; across a busy: (↗*crossing - bridge; run over; run over; fear of being - going; streets; streets - busy*) *Acon* carc vh* crot-h bg kali-p fyz **Psor** vh* [alum stj2 arg-n stj2 beryl stj2 beryl-m stj2 bor-pur stj2 fl-pur stj2 lith-c stj2 lith-f stj2 lith-i stj2 lith-m stj2 lith-met stj2 lith-s stj2 nitro stj2 oxyg stj2]
  - **rapidly** (See Anxiety - walking - rapidly - agg.)
  - **when** walking (See Anxiety - walking)
- **want**; of (See poverty)
- **war**: cupr sst3•
- **warm** room:
  - **in**: iod sf1.de
  - **of**: *Puls* st valer
- **washed**; of being: ant-c fyz* sulph k2*
- **wasps**; of: (↗*animals*) hep vh [nat-caust stj2]
- **water**, of: (↗*drinking; liquids; Hydrophobia; GENERALS - Water*) acet-ac k* agar br1 agav-a bro1 alum vh* anag bro1 ant-c bro1* *Bell* k* cann-i k* canth k* carc mlr1• cocc-s bro1 cupr k* fagu a1* gels k* **Hyos** k* iod k* jatr-c a1 *Lach* k* lap-la sde8.de• laur bro1 lycps-v mrr **LYSS** k* med hu merc bg nux-v k* perh jl3 phel a1 *Phos* k* plb k* psor jl2 ruta sabad k* spirae bro1 **Stram** k* sulph k2* tanac bro1 tarent k* verat bro1 xanth bro1 [am-br stj2 ant-m stj2 aur-m stj2 bar-br stj2 bar-i stj2 beryl-m stj2 brom stj1* cadm-m stj2 chlor stj2 chr-m stj2 cob-m stj2 cupr-act stj2 cupr-f stj2 cupr-m stj2 cupr-p stj2 lith-i stj2 lith-m stj2 mang-i stj2 mang-m stj2 merc-d stj2 merc-i-f stj2 moly-met stj2 mur-ac stj2 plb-m stj2 stront-m stj2 zinc-m stj2]
  - **deep**: phos mtf stram mtf
  - **faucets**; of (= tap): (↗*running*) lyss st*
  - **ocean** or lake; of swimming in an (See swimming - deep)
  - **running** water; of: (↗*faucets; VERTIGO - Water - crossing; VERTIGO - Water - looking*) lyss pfa2* stram mtf33
  - **washing** hair: cupr sst3•
- **weary** of life, with: (↗*Weary*) carc mlr1• kali-p hr1* *Lyc* hr1* *Nit-ac* hr1* *Plat* hr1* rhus-t hr1* [alum stj2 am-f stj2 arg-n stj2 beryl stj2 beryl-m stj2 bor-pur stj2 fl-pur stj2 graph stj2 lith-c stj2 lith-f stj2 lith-i stj2 lith-m stj2 lith-met stj2 lith-p stj2 lith-s stj2 mag-n stj2 mang-n stj2 nat-f stj2 nitro stj2 oxyg stj2 zinc-n stj2]
- **weeping** amel.: (↗*Weeping - amel.*) *Aster* hr1* dig **Graph** k* phos a1 tab k*
- **wet** his bed; fear he will (= incontinence in bed): (↗*urine - involuntary*) alum k* cob ptm1•
- **wind**, of: (↗*Anxiety - weather - stormy*) ars *Cham* k* cupr sst3• *Dys* fmm1• gard-j vlr2• glycyr-g cte1• lac-c mrr1 lyc nat-m mrr1 nat-p mrr1 *Oscilloc* jl2 psor jl2 puls *Rhod* br1* **Sil** st1* *Tarent* thuj st* [bar-m stj mang stj]
- **wolves**; of: (↗*animals*) bell hr1
- **women**; of: (↗*Aversion - women - men; Hatred - women; Homosexuality*) *Lyc*↓ puls k* raph a1 sep fyz sil sne staph gg
  - **children**; in: | **boys**: puls mtf33
  - **men**; in: *Lyc* cd1
- **work**; of: (↗*exertion - of; Laziness; Loathing - work*) *Arg-n* k* aur-i k2 cadm-s k* calc calc-f sp calc-sil k2 cham chin k2 coloc h2 *Con* graph h2* hyos ind iod bg2* *Kali-c* kali-p kali-s kali-sil k2 lyc fyz nat-m nat-p k2 *Nux-v* gl1.fr• ozone sde2• petr phos h2 plb gl1.fr• *Puls* ran-b sanic sel k* *Sil Sulph* tab tarax tong tritic-vg fd5.de zinc h2 [bar-i stj2 lith-i stj2 mang-i stj2 merc-i-f stj2]
  - **afternoon**: *Arg-n* a1
  - **daily**, of: calc-f sp1 nux-v k2
  - **headache**, during: gran
  - **literary**; of (See mental - of - literary)
  - **persuaded** to work; cannot be: *Con* kr1

Fear – **work**; of: ...
  - **prolonged**: con fyz nat-m fyz
  - **unfit** for work; fear to become (See unfit)
- **worm** diseases; with: stann hr1
- **worms**; of: aesc fyz ars fyz nat-m fyz* [oxyg stj]
- **wounds**; to see: calc gl1.fr•
- **wrong**, of something: (↗*Confidence - want*) *Kali-br* hr1* *Merc*↓ [bell-p-sp dcm1]
  - **commit** something: (↗*mischief*) *Merc* kr1

FEARLESS: (↗*Courageous; Heedless; Power - sensation*) *Agar* h2* anh vh1 bell br1* calad fyz cocain bro1 coff-t a1 falco-pe nl2• fl-ac↓ galeoc-c-h gms1• gels br1 haliae-lc srj5• ham↓ hell a1 *Ign* a1 lac-del hrn2• loxo-recl knl4• mosch a1 *Op* h1* ozone sde2• sil bro1 tung-met↓ [heroin sdj2 mill stj]
- **danger**; in spite of: falco-pe nl2• fl-ac hr1 tung-met bdx1• [heroin sdj2]
- **hemorrhage**; with: ham bro1
- **menses**; during: fl-ac mtn
- **water**, in the: lac-del hrn2•
- **waves**; plunged through big: lac-del hrn2•

FEASTING (See Reveling)

FECES:
- **licks** up cow-dung, mud, saliva: (↗*Insanity - eating - dirt; Licking*) *Hyos* vh* merc k*
- **passed** on the floor: cupr k* **Hyos** vh* sulph st
- **swallows** his own: (↗*Insanity - eating - dirt*) (non:camph kr1) *Hyos* vh* merc bg2* sulph j verat k* visc bg2
- **urinating** and going to stool everywhere, children (See Dirty - urinating and - everywhere - children)

FEELINGS (= emotions):
- **flitting** by quickly (See Mood - changeable - quickly)
- **lost** (See Emotions - loss)
- **unfamiliar** (See Estranged)

FEET; stamping (See Gestures - feet - stamping)

FEVER:
- **agg.**: bry b7.de* dros b7.de* ip b7.de* laur b7.de* *Nux-v* b7.de* *Valer* b7.de*
- **before** | **agg.**: chin b7.de*

FEIGNING:
- **fainting**: tarent k2
  - **paroxysms**; in: *Tarent* k1
- **pregnancy**: (↗*Delusions - pregnant*) verat
- **sick**; to be: (↗*Blindness; Complaining - injury; Deafness; Delusions - sick - being; Hypochondriasis; Pities - sick*) aethyl ggd aethyl-act↓ arg-n k* bell k* calc bg2 ign mtf33 kali-c bg2 lac-c↓ lach lmj lyc lmj mosch vh* op ptk1* petr-ra shn4• plb k2* *Puls* lmj sabad bg2* sep bg2* sil gl1.fr• syph ggd *Tarent* k* verat k* [sal-l rcb1]
  - **children**; in: aethyl-act lmj arg-n lmj bell lmj ign lmj lac-c lmj lach lmj lyc lmj *Mosch* lmj op lmj plb lmj *Puls* lmj sabad lmj sep lmj sil lmj syph lmj tarent lmj **Verat** lmj
  - **shrieking**; with: ign bg2 verat bg2

FEMININITY: lac-ac stj5•
- **increased** sensation of: sanguis-s hrn2•

FERVENT (See Ardent)

FICKLE (See Capriciousness; Inconstancy; Irresolution)

FIDGETY (See Restlessness; EXTREMITIES - Restlessness)

FIERY temperament (See Ardent)

FIGHT, wants to: (↗*Anger; Attack; Contradiction - disposition; Contrary; Defiant; Quarrelsome; Rage; Violent*) anac mrr1 *Androc* srj1• atro a1 bell bov bung-fa mtf chir-fl gya2 cocc a1 *Crot-c* sk4• *Dendr-pol* sk4• **Dulc** fd* falco-pe nl2• ferr mtf33 granit-m es• hipp hyos lac-ac stj5• lac-d sk4• lac-e hrn2• *Lac-leo* sk4• lach mtf med hu* merc k* *Nux-v* vh* pegan-ha tpi1• phasco-ci rbp2 sec sulo-ac a* symph fd5.de• *Tarent* vh* tritic-vg fd5.de tub al* [heroin sdj2]
- **boxing** | **desire** for: dendr-pol sk4•
- **helpless** people; for: (↗*Injustice*) dendr-pol sk4•

- **space**; for one's: phasco-ci rbp2

FILLS pockets with anything: stram a1*

FINANCES:
- **ability** to manage: ars gl1.fr• lyc gl1.fr• puls gl1.fr•
- **inability** to manage: ars gl1.fr• cypra-eg sde6.de• dulc fd4.de lyc gl1.fr• puls gl1.fr• **Sil** st*

FINERY (See Beautiful)

FINGERS into mouth; putting (See Gestures - fingers - mouth)

FIRE:
- **fear** of (See Fear - fire)
- **near** the fire; desire to be: ignis-alc es2• naja a1*
- **seeing** fire (See Delusions - fire - visions)
- **set** things on fire; wants to: *(↗Delusions - fire - flame)* alco a1 ant-t b7a.de* **BELL** st* carc mrc2 **HEP** bg2* hyos ckh1* phos st staph st stram ckh1*
- **thinks** and talks of: *Calc* hr1* taosc iwa1•
- **throwing** things into: *(↗Throwing things)* hep fyz staph
  - **child**; her own (See Kill; desire - throw - fire)

FIRMNESS: *(↗Confident; Determination; Positiveness; Tough; Will - strong)* aids↓ dulc fd4.de ferr mrr1 ferr-p↓ haliae-lc srj5• ham fd3.de• irid-met srj5• kali-p fd1.de• kali-s fd4.de lach a1 olib-sac wmh1 podo fd3.de• polys↓ positr nl2• ruta fd4.de sacch-a fd2.de• sal-fr sle1• spong fd4.de squil a1 symph fd3.de• *Vanil* fd5.de
- **morning**: ferr-p a1
- **desire** to be tough: polys sk4•
- **drawing** the line (See Determination)
- **obligations**; not to be encumbered by unnecessary: aids nl2•

FISHING:
- **aptitude** for: lyc pc sil pc
- **inaptitude** for: nit-ac pc nux-v pc staph pc
- **likes**: nux-v dgt

FISTS; makes (See Gestures - hands - fists)

FITFUL (See Capriciousness)

FIXED ideas (See Thoughts - persistent)

FIXED notions (See Delusions)

FLASHBACK (See Thoughts - past)

FLAT (See Indifference)

FLATTERED:
- **aversion** to be: *(↗Consolation - agg.)* lil-t a1
- **desire** to be: *(↗Confidence - want; Delusions - appreciated; Delusions - criticized; Delusions - forsaken; Delusions - neglected - he; Desires - full - more; Despair - social; Fear - opinion; Haughty; Lamenting - appreciated; Longing - good; Sensitive - opinion; Vanity)* carb-v gk* carc fb lac-ac stj5• lyc↓ marb-w es1• *Pall* k* puls↓ sulph mrr1 [mang stj1]
  - **gives** everything, when flattered: *(↗Despair - social)* lyc mtf33* puls gl1.fr• sulph mtf33*

FLATTERING: *(↗Pleasing - desire)* **Ambr**↓ arn gl1.fr• carb-v gl1.fr• carc↓ caust↓ fl-ac↓ hyos↓ *Lach*↓ **Lyc** mtf33* med↓ merc↓ nux-v gl1.fr• pall↓ petr gl1.fr• **Phos**↓ plat gl1.fr• puls gl1.fr• sil gl1.fr• staph mtf33* sulph gl1.fr• thuj↓ tub↓ **Verat**↓
- **seducing** behavior in children: *(↗Precocity)* **Ambr** lmj *Carb-v* lmj carc lmj caust lmj fl-ac lmj hyos lmj *Lach* lmj lyc lmj med lmj merc lmj nux-v lmj pall ggd **Phos** lmj plat lmj *Puls* lmj *Sil* lmj *Staph* lmj *Sulph* lmj thuj lmj tub lmj **Verat** lmj

FLATULENCE agg.: camph bg2 *Nux-v* bg2

FLATUS; passing: | **amel.**: all-c bg2 calc bg2 sulph bg2

FLEEING AWAY (See Escape)

FLEXIBILITY; loss of (See Dogmatic)

FLIRTING (See Amorous)

FLOATING sensation (See Delusions - floating - air)

FLOWERS:
- **loves**: *(↗Sensitive - flowers)* nat-m mtf33 phos mtf
- **sensitive** to (See Sensitive - flowers)

FLYING: | **desire** to fly: choc srj3•

FOCUS (See Concentration)

FOGGED (See Confusion; Dullness)

FOOLISH behavior: *(↗Answering - aversion - sings; Answering - foolish; Antics; Awkward; Cheerful - foolish; Childish; Delirium - absurd; Delirium - foolish; Delusions - absurd; Delusions - confidence; Delusions - walking - cannot - run; Fancies - absurd; Frivolous; Gestures - ridiculous; Giggling; Grimaces; Impulse - absurd; Insanity - crazy; Jesting; Jesting - ridiculous; Laughing - immoderately; Laughing - ludicrous; Laughing - silly; Laughing - trifles; Loquacity - answers; Ludicrous; Mirth - foolish; Runs; Serious - absurdities; Smiling - foolish; Speech - foolish; Thoughts - foolish; Thoughts - ridiculous; Throwing things - persons; DREAMS - Absurd; FACE - Expression - foolish)* absin acon k* aeth↓ aether k* agar k* all-c k* alum bg2 **Anac** b4a.de* anan androc srj1• ant-c *Apis* k* arg-n k* arn c1* *Ars* k* aur↓ bamb-a stb2.de• **Bar-c** k2* *Bar-m* *Bell* k* bufo k2* cact↓ calc k* *Camph* bg2* cann-i k* cann-xyz bg2 canth k* carb-an k* carb-v k* *Carl* a1 caust↓ *Chin* k* **Cic** k* cocc bg2 cod a1 con k* cori-r↓ cortico mg1.de* cot a1 croc k* cupr k* der dulc bg2 falco-pe nl2• ferr bg2 ferr-p sne galla-q-r nl2• hell bg2 **Hyos** k* ign k* kali-bi↓ kali-c k* kola stb3• lach k* lact *Lyc* k* *Merc* k* mosch bg2 nat-hchls a1 nux-m k* nux-v k* *Olib-sac* wht1• op k* ozone sde2• par k* ph-ac k* *Phos* k* phys *Plb* k* podo fd3.de• psil↓ pyrus a1 sacch↓ sal-fr sle1• *Sec* k* seneg k* sep bg2 sil↓ spong↓ **Stram** k* **Sulph**↓ tab↓ tanac *Tarent* bg2* tritic-vg fd5.de tub↓ *Verat* k* verb bg2 [cann-s xyz62 cupr-act stj2 cupr-f stj2 cupr-m stj2 cupr-p stj2]
- **morning** | **waking**; on: aur
- **night**: cic k*
- **air**, in open: nux-m
- **alternating** with | **rage**: aeth ptk1
- **children**; in: androc lmj apis lmj bar-c lmj *Bell* lmj carb-v mtf33 chin mtf33 cic lmj croc lmj cupr lmj hyos mrr1* ign lmj kali-bi lmj lach lmj lyc mtf33 **Merc** lmj nux-v lmj op lmj phos mtf33 plb mtf33 psil lmj sacch lmj sil lmj spong lmj stram mtf33 tarent lmj tub lmj verat mtf33
- **epilepsy**:
  - **after**: tab ptk1
  - **before**: caust k*
- **fever**, during: acon j5.de *Cic* b7a.de ferr-p sne
- **grotesque** behavior: agar a1 cact a1 cori-r a1
- **happiness** and pride: *(↗Haughty; Vanity)* **Sulph** k*
- **spasms**, during: sec
- **talking** foolishly (See Speech - foolish)

FOPPISH: *(↗Extravagance; Vanity)* chin mtf33* lach mtf33* nux-v mtf33* petr-ra shn4• phos mtf33* *Plat* mtf33* verat mtf33* [tax jsj7]

FORAGING: | **desire** for: choc srj3•

FORBEARANCE: *(↗Self-control - increased)* positr nl2•

FORCED; being: | **aversion** to (See Contradiction - intolerant; Obstinate)

FORCING HIMSELF to do something: | **has** to force himself to do something (See Discouraged; Prostration)

FOREBODINGS: *(↗Anxiety - future; Fear - happen)* *Acon* b7.de* aesc bg2* agn bg2* am-c bg2 aml-ns vh1 apis bg2 arg-n bg2 ars bg2* bell b4a.de *Calc* b4a.de* carb-v bg2 *Carc* mlr1• *Caust* bg2* chin bg2 cimic bg elaps bg2* *Fl-ac* b4a.de gels bg2 graph gsd1 kali-c bg2* lach bg2* lyc bg2 maias-l hrn2• med bg2 melal-alt gya4 naja bg2 nat-m hr1* phos b4a.de* plat b4a.de plb bg2 *Psor* bg2* sec a1 sep bg2* sil bg2 spig b7.de* still c1* stram bg2 thuj b4a.de verat bg2 [heroin sdj2 tax jsj7]
- **gloomy**: *Still* br1

FOREIGN countries: | **yearning** for (See Travelling - yearning)

FORGER (See Deceitful - fraudulent)

FORGETFUL: *(↗Absentminded; Absorbed; Abstraction; Confusion; Dream; as; Fancies - absorbed; Memory - weakness; Mistakes; Mistakes - speaking; Senses - confused; Speech - confused; FACE - Expression - bewildered; FACE - Expression - confused)* a b r o t k* absin bro1 acet-ac *Acon* k* adam skp7*• *Aeth* k* agar k* agath-a nl2• *Agn* k* *Aids* nl2• ail k2* allox tpw3 *Alum* k* alum-p k2 alum-sil k2 am-c k* **Ambr** k* **Anac** k* anders bnj1 *Androc* srj1• androg-p bnj1 *Anh* bro1* ant-c ↓ a p i s k* aq-mar skp7• aran ckh1 arg-met sf1.de* *Arg-n* k* arge-pl rwt5• *Arn* k* a r s k* ars-s-f k2 arum-t *Aur* k* aur-ar k2 *Aur-m-n* wbt2• aur-s k2* aza bro1* *Bamb-a* stb2.de• bapt ↓ bar-act br1 **Bar-c** k* bar-i k2 bar-s k2 *Bell* k* benz-ac ↓ berb k2 bit-ar wht1• borx j5.de **Both** ↓ bov k* brass-n-o ↓ brom k* bros-gau mrc1 brucel sa3• bry k* bufo-s ↓ bung-fa mtf cact ↓ cain calad k* *Calc* k* *Calc-p* k* calc-s calc-sil k2 camph k* *Cann-i* k* cann-s cann-xyz ↓ *Canth* k* caps k* carb-ac *Carb-an* k* *Carb-v* k* carbn-dox knl3• **Carbn-s** carc gk6* card-m k* *Cardios-h* rly4• carneg-g rwt1• cassia-s ccrh1* *Caust* k* cench br1* cham k* *Chel* k* chen-a ↓ chin chinin-ar chir-fl gya2 chlam-tr bcx2• choc srj3*• chord-umb rly4• *Cic* cimic cinnb k* *Cinnm* kr1 cit-ac rly4• clem cob-n ↓ **Cocc** k* coff **Colch** k* coloc *Con* k* conch ↓ corian-s knl6• *Corn* cortico jl3 cortiso mg1.de cot ↓ *Croc* k* crot-h cupr cycl k* cyn-d ckh1 cypra-eg sde6.de• cystein-l rly4• *Dig* k* dioxi rbp6 dream-p sdj1• dulc fd4.de elaps eug ↓ falco-pe nl2• ferr ferr-ar *Ferr-p* *Fl-ac* k* form *Formal* br1 gad ↓ galeoc-c-h gms1• *Gels* germ-met stj2*• gink-b sbd1*• gins mtf11 *Glon* glyc bro1 *Glycyr-g* cte1• *Graph* k* *Guaj* k* *Guare* ↓ gymno haem ↓ haliae-lc srj5• ham hell k* helo ↓ helo-s ↓ hep hipp hippoc-k szs2 hydr hydr-ac hydrog srj2• h y d r o p h mg1.de* hyos k* ichth br1* ign k* iod k2* ip *Irid-met* srj5• kali-bi *Kali-br* k* kali-c k* kali-i kali-m ckh1 kali-n k* *Kali-p* k* kali-s kali-sil k2* kalm ketogl-ac rly4• kiss ↓ kola stb3• kreos k* *Lac-c* k* lac-e hrn2• lac-leo hrn2• *Lach* k* lat-m bnm6• laur k* lavand-a ↓ lec k* led lil-t lith-i ↓ loxo-recl knl4• luf-op rsj5• luna kg1• **Lyc** k* lyss m-ambo b7.de mag-c *Mag-p* ↓ manc med bro1 melal-alt gya4 meli **Merc** k* mez *Mill* mim-p rsj8• *Moni* rfm1• morph mosch k* **Mur-ac** vh* murx ↓ musca-d szs1 naja k* nat-ar nat-c k* *Nat-m* k* *Nat-p* nat-s k2 nat-sil k2* neon srj5• nept-m lsd2.fr nicotam rly4• nit-ac k* *Nux-m* k* *Nux-v* k* oci-sa sk4• olib-sac wmh1 olnd k* *Onos* ↓ op k* orot-ac rly4• oxal-a rly4• o z o n e sde2• pert-vc ↓ **Petr** k* petr-ra shn4• **Ph-ac** k* **Phos** k* *Phys* ↓ *Pic-ac* k* plan **Plat** k* plb k* plut-n ↓ podo ↓ pop ↓ pop-cand ↓ positr nl2• prot ↓ psil ft1 psor k* ptel puls pyrid rly4• querc-r svu1• ran-b raph rheum rhod k* rhus-g ↓ *Rhus-t* k* rhus-v *Ros-d* wla1 ruta sabin k* sacch-a fd2.de• sal-ac *Sal-fr* sle1• sanic sarr k* sars sec k* *Sel* k* sep k* sil k* sil-met ↓ sinus rly4• spig k* spong fd4.de stann k* staph k* staphycoc ↓ stram k* stront-c k* stry a1 suis-pan rly4• *Sulph* k* suprar rly4• symph fd3.de• syph k2* tab k* taosc iwa1• tarax tarent a1 tarent-c ckh1 tell k* thioc-ac rly4• *Thuj* k* thyr bro1 tritic-vg fd5.de trom *Tub* k* tung-met stj2*• ulm-c jsj8• *Urol-h* rwt• v - a - b ↓ vac jl2 vanil fd5.de verat k* verat-v verb k* viol-o k* visc sp1 *Zinc* k* zinc-i ↓ **Zinc-p** k2* zinc-pic bro1 zing zirc-met ↓ [am-br stj2 am-caust stj2 am-f stj2 ant-t stj2 arg-p stj2 aur-m stj2 bar-br stj2 beryl stj2 bor-pur stj2 chr-met stj2 ferr-sil stj2 fl-pur stj2 heroin sdj2 lith-c stj2 lith-f stj2 lith-met stj2 mag-sil stj2 mang-p stj2 mang-sil stj2 merc-d stj2 nitro stj2 oxyg stj2 stront-met stj2 tax jsj7 zinc-m stj2 zinc-n stj2]

- **morning**: **Anac** k* berb a1* bros-gau mrc1 bufo-s chord-umb rly4• *Kali-br* ↓ kali-p fd1.de• olib-sac wmh1 oxal-a rly4• ph-ac phos sil j5.de stann j5.de stram *Thuj* k*
  - **amel.**: fl-ac k*
  - **waking**, on: berb a1* *Kali-br* oxal-a rly4• stann *Thuj*
- **afternoon**: anac h2* graph kali-s fd4.de laur a1 sep
  - **amel.**: *Anac* k*
- **evening**: bufo-s a1 dulc fd4.de fl-ac *Form* kali-s fd4.de laur lyc naja nat-m rhus-t sep
- **night**: chin sil sulph
- **anxiety** of conscience; with (See Anxiety - conscience - forgetfulness)
- **appetite**; with loss of: anac kr1
- **business**; about: *(↗profession; work)* cystein-l rly4• oxal-a rly4• sel j* [tell stj2]
- **busy**; when: ant-c ptk1*
- **chill**, during: ars bg bell con hyos podo hr1* rhus-t
- **clean** himself thoroughly: rhus-g tmo3•
- **coition**, after: *Sec*
- **connection** of consecutive thoughts, of: op mtf33
  - **apoplexy**; after: *Op* kr1
- **daily** things: ulm-c jsj8•
- **drunkards**, forgetfulness in: *Calc* bg2 lach bg2 merc bg2 **Nux-v** bg2 *Op* bg2 puls bg2 *Sulph* bg2
- **eating**, after: calc-s ferr mag-c nat-m rhus-t *Sulph* kr1
  - **amel.**: *(↗Eating - after - amel.)* sil
- **emotions**, from: *Acon* bg2 op bg2 ph-ac bg2 *Staph* bg2
- **epilepsy**:
  - **before**: *Caust*
  - **happened** before; of what: *(↗Memory - loss - epileptic)* absin st*
- **epistaxis**, after: *Kreos* hr1* rhus-t kr1
- **errands**; for (See purchases)
- **everything**: *(↗immediately)* ant-c ptk1 galeoc-c-h gms1• gymno ptk1 *Ign* ↓ *Lach* ↓ merc ptk1
  - **dreams**; except of: *Ign* kr1
  - **occurred** for six years; that had: *Lach*
- **examinations** agg.: [nat-sil stj2 sil stj2 sil-met stj2]
- **food**; while preparing: falco-pe nl2• vanil fd5.de
- **friends** and relatives, of: *(↗Indifference - family; Indifference - loved; Indifference - relations)* lyss hr1*
- **fright**, after: *Cupr* hr1*
- **going**, forgets where she is: cench vh* chord-umb rly4• *Merc* mtf33* *Ruta* fd4.de staphycoc rly4•
- **headache**; during: apis bell h1* calc k* caps h1* dulc k2 glon ptel a1 sarr hr1 zinc hr1* [tax jsj7]
- **heat**:
  - **after**: *Mag-p* hr1* podo hr1*
  - **during**: *Alum* hr1* *Arn* hr1* cocc hr1* form br1 *Guare* hr1* rhus-t sf1.de
- **house** was; on which side of the street his: *(↗streets; Confusion - loses; Mistakes - localities; Recognizing - not - streets)* **Glon** *Nux-m* nux-v gl1.fr• *Petr*
- **hungry**; when: petr-ra shn4•
- **ideas**: cann-i k2 dream-p ↓
  - **last**, for: dream-p sdj1•
- **immediately**, of everything: *(↗everything)* aids nl2• *Dig* kr1
- **injury**; after: stront-c kr1
- **masturbation**; after: *(↗sexual)* *Dig* kr1 kali-br sf1.de staph c1*
- **menopause**; during: *Lach* kr1* *Phys* kr1*
- **menses**, during: *(↗Menses - during)* raph ulm-c jsj8•
- **mental** exertion, from: anac aur bg2 calc bg2 lach bg2 nat-c bg2 nat-m k* *Nux-v* bg2 puls bg2 sil bg2 *Sulph* bg2
- **motion**, on: laur
- **names** (See Memory - weakness - names)
- **old** people, of: am-c k2* *Ambr* anac sf1.de *Bar-c* coff gl1.fr• *Con* sf1.de *Crot-h* hr1* lach gl1.fr• *Lyc* k* *Ph-ac* rhus-t sf1.de sulph gl1.fr•
- **periodical**: carb-v
- **phoning**; in: chlam-tr bcx2•
- **possessions**; leaves behind: lac-leo hrn2•
- **profession**, forgets her: *(↗business)* tarent k2*
- **purchases**; goes off and leaves the: *(↗Memory - weakness - do)* absin vh agn anac st bamb-a stb2.de• bar-c ckh1 bell caps bl carneg-g rwt1• caust st iod irid-met srj5• kali-s fd4.de *Lac-c* lac-e hrn2• manc bg* med ckh1 nat-m st orot-ac rly4• pyrid rly4• ruta fd4.de sal-fr sle1• tritic-vg fd5.de urol-h rwt• [lith-i stj2 pop dhh1 tax jsj7 zinc-i stj2]
- **remembers** everything before her disease; but: syph ptk
- **sentence**; cannot finish (See Speech - finish)
- **sexual** excesses, after: *(↗masturbation; Ailments - sexual excesses)* calad kali-br sf1.de *Nat-p* *Ph-ac* *Sec* kr1 *Staph* hr1*
- **shaving** or dressing, of: aids nl2• chel k*
- **sleep** he remembers all he had forgotten, during: calad sel
- **stool** | **after**: cycl hr1*
- **streets**, of well-known: *(↗house; Confusion - loses; Mistakes - localities; Recognizing - not - streets)* cann-i mrr1 *Crot-h* hr1* germ-met srj **Glon** k* hydrog srj2• *Nux-m* k* *Petr* k* plb cld• ruta fd4.de urol-h rwt•
- **thinking** of something agg. the forgetfulness, diversion amel.: lil-t k2
- **time** and place; for: merc lpc*
- **tobacco** poisoning, from: *Calad* k2*
- **waking**, on: chin cob-n sp1* kali-br kali-n sf1.de ptel sil stann thuj
- **walking** after eating; while: rhus-t
- **weather** | **stormy**: *Am-c* br1

- **wind** his watch, to: fl-ac k*
- **words** while speaking; of (= word hunting): *(↗Aphasia; Memory - weakness - expressing; Memory - weakness - words; Mistakes - speaking - words; Speech - incoherent)* acet-ac a1 adam srj5• agar k* agath-a nl2• am-br sf1.de am-c a1 anac ptk1 anh sp1 *Arg-n* k* **Arn** k* bapt gk *Bar-c* k1* bar-s k2 bell b4a.de benz-ac **Both** k1* brass-n-o srj5• bros-gau mrc1 cact calc gl1.fr• **Cann-i** cann-xyz bg2* carb-an carb-v k* carbn-s carc fd2.de• *Cham* rb3 chen-a k1 cocc sf1.de colch con↓ conch fkr1• cot a1 crot-h bg2* cypra-eg sde6.de• dulc k* falco-pe nl2• gad a1 germ-met srj5• gink-b sbd1• glon bg2 haem a1 ham helo st helo-s rwt2• hydr ign a1 irid-met srj5• *Kali-br* k* kali-c↓ kali-p kali-s fd4.de kiss a1 *Lach* k* lavand-a ctl1• lil-t *Lyc* k* *Med* k* moni rfm1• morph a1 murx a1 *Nat-m* neon srj5• nux-m b7a.de *Nux-v* *Onos* pert-vc vk9 petr-ra shn4• **Ph-ac** k* phos ptk1 *Plb* sf1.de* plut-n srj7• podo pop-cand c1 positr nl2• prot ptj• ptel hl puls↓ rhod k* *Ruta* fd4.de sil bg2* staph bg2* sulph syph st tab a1 *Thuj* b4a.de* tritic-vg fd5.de ulm-c jsj8• v-a-b jl2* verat [zirc-met stj2]
  - **chill**; during: podo kr1
  - **looks** around for help: *Arg-n* kr1
  - **vertigo**; with: con bg2 kali-c bg2 lyc bg2 nux-v bg2 puls bg2 thuj bg2
- **work**; in matters relating to: *(↗business)* *Cardios-h* rly4•

FORGETTING (See Memory - weakness)

FORGIVING:

- **easy** to forgive (See Benevolence)
- **unable** to forgive (See Hatred)

FORGOTTEN:

- **sleep**; forgotten things come to mind in: *(↗Memory - active; Memory - weakness)* calad k* sel k*
- **something**; feels constantly as if he had forgotten: *(↗Checking - twice; Confusion; Memory - weakness; Thoughts - compelling)* aids nl2• arg-n gk calc st *Caust* k* cham gk *Iod* k* mill a1* musca-d szs1 podo fd3.de• puls vh syph mrr1 tub vh* zinc vh [pop dhh1]

FORMAL (See Affectation)

FORSAKEN feeling: *(↗beloved; Ailments - friendship; Clinging - persons; Company - desire; Confidence - want; Contact; desire; Delusions - alone; Delusions - alone - always; Delusions - alone - castaway; Delusions - alone - graveyard; Delusions - alone - wilderness; Delusions - alone - world; Delusions - appreciated; Delusions - belong to; Delusions - confidence; Delusions - despised; Delusions - disgraced; Delusions - enemy - everyone; Delusions - family; Delusions - forsaken; Delusions - friend - affection; Delusions - friend - lose; Delusions - friendless; Delusions - help; Delusions - help - calling; Delusions - husband; Delusions - neglected - he; Delusions - persecuted - he; Delusions - reproach; Delusions - repudiated - relatives; Delusions - wife - faithless; Delusions - wife - run; Delusions - wrong - suffered; Dependent; Fear - forsaken; Forsaken - isolation; Friendship - maintain; Helplessness; Lamenting - appreciated; Longing - good; Weeping - forsaken; Weeping - goes)* abies-c oss4• agath-a nl2• *Aids* nl2• allox sp1 alum k* *Anac*↓ androc srj1• ange-s oss1• anh sp1 *Ant-t* mtf aq-mar rbp6 aran-ix mtf *Arg-n* k* arist-cl jl *Ars* mtf asar vh **Aur** k* *Aur-m-n* wbt2• *Aur-s* wbt2• bamb-a stb2.de• bar-c k* bar-s mtf *Bism* mtf *Bit-ar*↓ brass-n-o srj5• bros-gau mrc1 bufo mtf bung-fa mtf calc k* *Calc-s* a* camph k* cann-i k* cann-s↓ carb-an k* carb-v k* carc az1.de*• cench mgm• *Cham* mtf (non:chin k*) chin-b hr1* chir-fl gya2 choc srj3• chord-umb rly4• chr-ac mtf *Cina* mtf coca↓ coff bg2 coli rly4• conch fkr1• cortico sp1* *Crot-c* sk4• crot-h mgm• *Cycl* k* cypra-eg↓ cystein-l rly4• dendr-pol mtf* des-ac rbp6 dioxi↓ dros bg2 *Dulc* fd4.de elaps mgm• falco-ch sze4• falco-pe nl2• fl-ac↓ galeoc-c-h a galla-q-r↓ gard-j vlr2• gels mtf germ-met srj5• gink-b sbd1• granit-m es1• haliae-lc srj5• *Ham* fd3.de• hell bg2 helo-s rwt2• helon mgm• hippoc-k szs2 hott-p mtf11 hura hydrog srj2• *Hyos* mtf hyosin wd *Ign* mtf ip bg2 irid-met↓ kali-br k* kali-c k* kali-p fd1.de• kali-s fd4.de keroso a1 *Kola* stb3• lac-ac↓ lac-c mtf lac-d k* lac-del hrn2• *Lac-h* mtf* lac-leo hrn2*• lac-lup↓ *Lach* k* lact lam k* lap-la↓ laur bg2 lavand-a ctl1• lil-t k* limest-b es1• lith-c k* loxo-recl↓ lyc↓ lyss k* m-aust *Mag-c* st1 mag-m k* *Mag-s* mtf mang-p↓ marb-w↓ *Meny* bg2* *Merc* st* moni rfm1• musca-d szs1 naja mgm• *Nat-c* k* *Nat-m* ser* **Nat-sil**↓ neon srj5• nicc-met sk4• oci-sa sk4• op mtf ozone sde2• pall k* par mtf petr-ra shn4• phasco-ci rbp2 *Phos* mtf pin-con oss2• pip-m↓ plac↓ *Plat* k* plb cld• *Plut-n*↓ podo fd3.de• polys↓ positr nl2• pseuts-m oss1• psil↓ **Psor** k* **Puls** k* *Pycnop-sa* mrz1 rad-br sze8• rhus-t k* *Ruta* fd4.de sabin bg2* sacch sst1• sal-al↓ *Sal-fr* sle1• samb bat1• sanic c1 sars bg2 sec bg2* sep bg2* sil↓ spig bg2 spong fd4.de *Stram* k* stront-c sk4• succ-ac rly4• sul-ac mtf sulph mtf *Symph* fd3.de• tab↓ taosc iwa1• *Thuj* mrr1 tritic-vg fd5.de *Tub* mtf valer k* vanil fd5.de verat vip mgm• wye ah [bell-p-sp dcm1 buteo-j sej6 gnaph stj heroin sdj2 impa-g rcb1 mag-met stj2 spect dfg1 tax jsj7]

- **morning**: carb-an k* carb-v carc fd2.de• dulc fd4.de *Lach* k*
- **afternoon**: gard-j vlr2•
- **evening**: androc srj1• bar-c k* dulc fd4.de kola stb3• *Puls*
- **air** amel.; in open: rhus-t
- **beloved** by his parents, wife, friends; feeling of not being: *(↗Delusions - loved; Forsaken; Orphans)* aids nl2• *Ars* mtf33* calc gl1.fr• camph mrr1 lac-h mtf* lyc mtf33* *Mag-c* st* moni rfm1• nat-m gk* phos gk **Puls** mrr1 sep gl1.fr• sil mtf33* sulph gl1.fr• *Thuj* mrr1 *Tritic-vg* fd5.de vanil fd5.de
- **friendless**; feels (See Delusions - friendless)
- **friends** or group; by: lac-leo hrn2•
- **headache**, during: meny bg1*
- **isolation**; sensation of: *(↗Company - desire; Delusions - alone; Delusions - despised; Delusions - disgraced; Delusions - enemy - everyone; Delusions - family; Delusions - forsaken; Delusions - friendless; Delusions - help; Delusions - help - calling; Delusions - locked; Delusions - repudiated - relatives; Delusions - separated - world - he; Forsaken)* abies-c oss4• aids nl2• allox sp *Anac* *Androc* srj1• *Anh* mg1.de* *Arg-n* arist-cl jl3 *Bit-ar* wht1• camph k* cann-i cann-s a1 carc fd2.de• choc srj3• coca coli jl2* cortico mg1.de crot-c sk4• cypra-eg sde6.de• cystein-l rly4• dendr-pol sk4• des-ac rbp6 dioxi rbp6 falco-pe nl2• fl-ac mrr1 galla-q-r nl2• *Germ-met* stj2*• *Ham* fd3.de• hippoc-k szs2 hura *Hydrog* srj2• irid-met srj5• *Kola* stb3• lac-ac stj5• lac-del hrn2• lac-h htj1*• lac-lup hrn2• lap-la sde8.de• loxo-recl knl4• lyss mrr1 mang-p rly4• marb-w es1• merc mrr musca-d szs1 **Nat-sil** fd* op mgm• ozone sde2• phasco-ci rbp2 pip-m mgm• plac rzf5• plat *Plut-n* srj7• polys sk4• *Positr* nl2• psil mgm• psor mrr1 puls dx1 pycnop-sa mrz1 rad-br sze8• **Ruta** fd* sal-al blc1• sal-fr sle1• stram *Symph* fd3.de• tab mgm• taosc iwa1• thuj mrr1 *Vanil* fd5.de vip fkr4.de [buteo-j sej6 heroin sdj2 phos stj1]
  - **terror**; with: falco-pe nl2• stram nl
- **joyless**, feels: *(↗Indifference - joyless)* (non:alum h2) aur a3 [heroin sdj2]
- **old** people; in: aur dx1* psor dx1
- **sighing**; with: lith-c lpc
- **waking**, on: *Arg-n* dulc fd4.de *Lach* k*
- **warmth** of sun; from: gels hr1
- **weeping**; with (See Weeping - forsaken)

FORSAKING:

- **children**; his own: *(↗Children - flies; Escape - family; Estranged - children; Estranged - family; Responsibility - aversion)* chlam-tr bcx2• lyc phasco-ci rbp2 sep a1
- **relations**: phasco-ci rbp2 sec

FRAGILE people (See GENERALS - Delicate)

FRAIL; sensation of being (See Delusions - body - brittle)

FRANTIC, frenzy (See Beside; Mania; Rage)

FRATERNIZED with the whole world: *(↗Brotherhood; Unification; Unification - sensation)* aloe a1

FREE-SPIRITED (See Libertinism)

FREEDOM:

- **doing** what he had to do; remarkable freedom in: *(↗Confident)* ara-maca sej7• banis-c mtf hippoc-k szs2 kola mtf* op a* ozone sde2• [temp elm1]
- **desires** (See Conformism; Libertinism)

FREETHINKER (See Libertinism)

FRENZY (See Beside; Mania; Rage)

FRETFUL (See Anger; Morose)

FRIENDLY (See Affectionate)

FRIENDSHIP: *(↗Unification; Unification - sensation)*

- **end** his; desire to | **anger**; to avoid: *(↗Quarrelling - aversion)* rhus-g tmo3•
- **maintain**; need to: *(↗Forsaken)* stront-c sk4•
- **outpourings** of; sweet: *(↗Love - friends; Unification; Unification - sensation)* alco a1

FRIGHT (See Fear - sudden)

FRIGHT; complaints from (See Ailments - fright)

FRIGHTENED easily: *(↗Anxiety; Fear; Restlessness; Senses - acute; Sensitive - noise - slightest; Starting; Starting - easily; Timidity)* abrot a1 *Acon* k* act-sp vh1 aether a1 aids↓ ail a1 aloe↓ alum alum-sil a1* alumin↓ alumin-s↓ alumn am-c am-caust j5.de* am-m *Ambr*↓ *Anac* st1 ang ant-c ant-t aq-mar skp7• **Arg-n** k* *Arn* k* **Ars** k* *Ars-s-f* k2 aur aur-ar k2 aur-s k2 **Bar-c** k* bar-s k2 **Bell** k1* benz-ac berb bism sf1.de **Borx** k* brom mtf33 *Bry* bufo cact hr1* calad *Calc* calc-p a1* *Calc-sil* k2* calen j5.de* *Camph* a1 cann-i cann-s j5.de* canth *Caps* *Carb-an* k* *Carb-v* k* carbn-s k2 carc mlr1• casc↓ castm↓ *Caust* cham chin↓ *Chlol*↓ chlor a1 cic cimic br1 *Cina*↓ *Cit-ac* j5.de clem cob a1 cocc k* coff con crot-c↓ cub a1 cupr k* cupr-act a1* cur a1 cypr br1 cypra-eg sde6.de• daph a1 dicha↓ *Dig* dulc fd4.de *Erig*↓ *Euphr*↓ eupi↓ gard-j vlr2• glon a1 **Graph** k* guaj hep↓ *Hyos* hyper iber a1 *Ign* k* iod a1* iris a1 juni-v a1 kali-ar kali-br sf1.de *Kali-c* k* kali-i *Kali-p* k* kali-s kali-sil k2* kiss a1 *Lach* lat-h↓ led loxo-lae bnm12• **Lyc** k* m-arct a1 m-aust j5.de *Mag-c* mg1.de* mag-m kr1* mag-n↓ *Med*↓ *Meph*↓ *Merc* mez mit↓ morph a1 mosch mur-ac j5.de **Nat-ar** k* **Nat-c** k* *Nat-m* k* nat-p nat-s k2 *Nat-sil* k2* *Nit-ac* nux-m a1 **Nux-v** k1* ol-an↓ *Op* orig a1 *Petr* k* ph-ac *Phos* k* phys a1 pieri-b mlk9.de plat plb a1 plut-n↓ psor al2* *Puls* rhus-t ruta↓ *Sabad* k* sacch-a fd2.de* *Samb* k* sang↓ sarr *Scut* br1 **Sep** k* *Sil* sol-ni↓ spong *Staph* st1 **Stram** k* stront-c a1 stry a1 sul-ac k* sul-i↓ *Sulph* sumb tab a1 tarent↓ ter↓ thea a1 ther k2* tritic-vg fd5.de **Tub** al* verat k* vult-gr↓ xan a1* zinc j5.de* [alum-p stj2 arg-met stj2 arg-p stj2 ars-met stj2 bar-i stj2 cupr-f stj2 cupr-m stj2 ferr stj2 ferr-f stj2 ferr-lac stj2 ferr-m stj1 ferr-sil stj2 heroin sdj2 lith-p stj2 merc-i-f stj2 nat-br stj2 nat-lac stj2 nat-met stj2 plb-p stj2 stann stj2 zinc-i stj2]

- **noon**: bar-s↓ *Calc-sil*↓ nat-c↓ nit-ac↓ zinc k2*
  - **nap**, after: bar-s k2* *Calc-sil* k2* nat-c a1 nit-ac a1
- **evening**: carb-an h2* iber a1 lach a1 merc k2* ol-an a1 *Sep* a1 sulph sf1.de
- **night**: **Ars**↓ castm a1 cham↓ cimic hr1* con↓ crot-c a1 *Euphr*↓ *Ign* hr1* lat-h↓ *Lyc* a1* merc↓ *Nat-m* k* nat-p↓ ph-ac a1 samb hr1* sang a1 sep a1 *Spong* ter↓ thea a1
  - **midnight**:
    - **before** | **23** h: merc a
  - **noise**: nat-p a
  - **starting** up as if falling from a height into water: ph-ac a
  - **waking**, on: **Ars**↓ cham↓ con↓ *Euphr* a1 lat-h thj1 *Sep* a1 ter sne
    - **3** h: **Ars** cham kr1 con a1
- **alternating** with sadness: zinc j
- **blood**, at sight of: *(↗Blood)* *Alum* stj2*• *Calc* vh* ruta fd4.de [alum-p stj2 alumin stj2 alumin-s stj2 mag-n stj2]
- **chill**, during: verat
- **closing** the eyes: op j5.de
- **cough**; during: *Acon* b7.de* arg-n bg2
- **delusions**, from: **Stram** st1
- **fever**, during: acon bg2 *Bell* bg2 calc bg2 caps bg2 ign bg2 nat-m bg2 nux-v bg2 op bg2 petr bg2 phos bg2 puls bg2 sabad j5.de sep bg2 sulph bg2 **Verat** j5.de*
- **going** to sleep; on: *Aur* *Nit-ac* nux-v phos
- **menses** | **before**: *(↗Menses - before)* *Calc*
- **noise**; at a (See Starting - noise)
- **pains**, from: sulph h2
- **palpitations**, from: iber vml3•
- **perspiration**; during: acon bg2 bell bg2 *Calc* bg2 caust bg2 *Cham* bg2 nux-v bg2 *Petr* bg2 *Phos* bg2 puls bg2 sabad bg2 samb bg2 sep bg2 spong bg2 sulph bg2
- **pollutions**, after: aloe k*
- **pregnancy**; during late: kali-br tl1
- **roused**, when: *Calc* nat-ar kr1
- **shadow**, his own: calad k2*
- **sneezing**, at: *Borx* vult-gr sze5•
- **touch**, from: *(↗Touched - aversion)* *Kali-c* k* ruta a1
- **trifles**, at: *(↗Excitement - trifles; Trifles; Trifles - important)* am-c k* am-m k* ang k* ant-t k* arn k* bar-c borx bufo calc k* calen a1 caust hyper k* kali-ar **Kali-c** k* kali-i k* kali-s k* kiss a1 *Lach* k* *Lyc* k* merc k* mez k* *Nit-ac* k* nux-v k* *Phos* k* psor al2 rhus-t k* sacch-a fd2.de• sep k* sumb k*
  - **menses**, before: *(↗Menses - before)* calc
- **urinating**; before: alum a1

Frightened easily: ...

- **wakens**:
  - **noise**; in a fright from least: nux-v
  - **terrified**, knows no one, screams, clings to those near: *(↗Clinging - child)* *Stram*
- **waking**, on: *(↗Fear - waking)* abrot↓ aids nl2• *Am-m* *Ambr* hr1* ant-c hr1* *Ars* *Bell* bism hr1* borx sf1.de *Cact* k* *Calc* hr1* *Caps* casc↓ *Cham* sf1.de chin↓ *Chlol* hr1* *Cina* *Cocc* h1* con↓ dicha↓ dig sf1.de *Erig*↓ *Euphr* k* eupi k* *Graph* h2* hep *Hyos* sf1.de ign sf1.de kali-br *Kali-c* kr1* *Lach* led k* lyc k* mag-m↓ *Med* hr1* *Meph*↓ mit a1 *Nat-m* hr1* nit-ac k* nux-v k* op sf1.de plut-n srj7• sil sf1.de sol-ni a1 spong *Staph*↓ stram sf1.de sul-i k* sulph h2 tarent↓ tub br1 verat k* zinc k*
  - **dream**, from a: abrot a1 casc kr1 chin a1 con a1 dicha mg1.de *Erig* mg1.de graph a1 *Ign* kr1 **Lyc** kr1 mag-m a1 *Meph* a1* plut-n srj7• *Staph* vh* *Sulph* kr1 tarent a1
- **weeping** amel.: *(↗Weeping - amel.)* phos k* puls vh

FRITTERS away his time (See Time - fritters)

FRIVOLOUS: *(↗Answering - foolish; Antics; Childish; Foolish; Gestures - ridiculous; Grimaces; Jesting - joke; Laughing; Laughing - serious; Laughing - silly; Laughing - trifles; Mirth - foolish; Smiling - foolish; Speech - foolish; Trifles; Trifles - important; FACE - Expression - foolish)* agar gl1.fr• aids nl2• apis hr1* arg-n k13* *Arn* k* bar-c k* bell gl1.fr• calad bg2 con gl1.fr• falco-pe nl2• lach mtf33* **Merc** k* par k* *Puls* bg2* sep j* sil mtf33* spong k* stram hr1* sulph mtf33* [heroin sdj2]

- **alternating** with | **absorption**: arg-n falco-pe nl2•

FROWN, disposed to: *(↗Absorbed; Discontented; Frown; Gestures; Irritability; Mood - repulsive; Morose; Sulky; Unfriendly; FACE - Expression - sullen; FACE - Wrinkled - forehead)* canth sne **Cham** kr1* equis-h a1 hell k* hyos ptk* *Lyc* k ●* mang nat-m sne **Nux-v** k ●* plb vh rheum c1* rumx dx1* sanic c1* sep ckh1* stram k* sulph ptk* verat ckh1* viol-o↓

- **contraction** of skin of forehead; from: lyc tl1 sanic c1
  - **pneumonia**; during: lyc tl1
- **knitting** his brows: viol-o ptk

FRUSTRATED (See Ailments - anger - suppressed; Ailments - moral; Discontented; Impatience; Indignation)

FUR; wraps up in summer in: *(↗Roving - wrapped; GENERALS - Warm - clothing - desire)* hep ptk1 hyos k* kali-ar ptk *Psor* ptk1*

FUROR (See Excitement)

FURY (See Rage)

FUSSY (See Censorious; Conscientious; Fastidious)

FUZZINESS (See Confusion)

GAMBLING:

- **passion** for gambling: ars k* bell k* bros-gau mrc1 calc k* caust k* chin k* dulc fd4.de lyc k* mag-c mtf33 mag-m mtf33 merc k* *Nat-c*↓ nux-v k* plat sne puls↓ spong fd4.de staph mtf33 sulph k* verat k*
  - **make** money; to: *(↗Ambition - increased - money)* bell a1 calc gl1.fr• lyc gl1.fr• mag-m mtf33* *Merc* gl1.fr• *Nat-c* gl1.fr• plat gl1.fr• puls gl1.fr• staph gl1.fr• sulph gl1.fr•

GARDENING: | **love** for: *(↗Nature - loves)* carc mtf elaps mtf *Med* mtf scand-met mtf sulph mtf thuj mtf tub mtf

GAY (See Cheerful; Vivacious)

GENEROUS; too: *(↗Benevolence)* bros-gau mrc1 carb-v↓ cere-b a1 dulc fd4.de hyos↓ kali-s fd4.de nat-m↓ nux-v gl1.fr• olib-sac wmh1 op a1* ruta fd4.de staph mtf33* sulph ctc* taosc iwa1• *Tritic-vg* fd5.de *Vanil* fd5.de [stann stj2]

- **strangers**; for: carb-v mtf33* hyos gl1.fr• nat-m gl1.fr• nux-v gl1.fr• *Vanil* fd5.de

GENTLENESS (See Mildness)

GESTURES, makes: *(↗Antics; Awkward; Delirium; Delirium - gestures; Frown; Grimaces; Ritualistic; EXTREMITIES - Motion - involuntary; GENERALS - Catalepsy; HEAD - Motions in; HEAD - Motions of; HEAD - Motions of - involuntary)* *Acon*↓ aeth↓ aether↓ agar↓ agar-ph↓ alco↓ all-c↓ alum↓ alumn↓ am-c↓ aml-ns↓ anac↓

Gestures, makes: ...
androc↓ anh↓ ant-c↓ **Ant-t**↓ apis↓ apoc↓ aq-pet↓ arg-met↓ arg-n↓ *Arn*↓ ars ars-s-f↓ *Art-v*↓ *Arum-t*↓ asaf↓ *Asar*↓ asc-t a1 atro↓ aur↓ bapt↓ **Bar-c**↓ *Bell* k* bism-met↓ **Borx**↓ bry↓ bufo a1 calad↓ *Calc*↓ calc-ox↓ calc-p↓ camph k* cann-i cann-s↓ *Canth*↓ caps↓ carb-an↓ carb-v↓ carc mlr1• caust↓ cean↓ *Cham*↓ chen-a↓ chin↓ chinin-s a1 choc↓ cic cic-m↓ *Cina*↓ clem↓ coca↓ *Cocc* k* coff↓ *Colch*↓ *Coloc*↓ *Con*↓ conin↓ cor-r↓ cori-m↓ croc↓ crot-c↓ cupr j dat-a↓ dat-m↓ dros↓ dub↓ dubo-m↓ dulc fd4.de elec↓ enterob-v↓ falco-pe↓ fl-ac↓ gamb↓ glon↓ graph↓ hell k2 *Hep*↓ hir↓ hydr-ac↓ hydrog↓ *Hyos* k* hyosin↓ *Ign*↓ **Iod**↓ iodof↓ **Ip**↓ kali-bi↓ *Kali-br*↓ kali-c↓ kali-i↓ kali-n↓ *Kali-p*↓ kres mg1.de* lac-h↓ lach mtf laur↓ lil-t↓ *Lyc*↓ lyss↓ mag-c↓ malar↓ med↓ meph↓ merc j morph↓ mosch k* **Mur-ac**↓ mygal↓ naja↓ nat-c↓ *Nat-m*↓ nat-s↓ nitro-o a1 nux-m k* nux-v oena↓ onos↓ **Op**↓ orot-ac rly4• paeon↓ par↓ ped↓ petr↓ **Ph-ac**↓ phel↓ **Phos**↓ phys↓ pip-m↓ plat plb podo↓ polys↓ *Psor*↓ puls pyrog↓ pyrus↓ raja-s↓ ran-b↓ rheum↓ *Rhus-t*↓ *Rumx*↓ *Sacch*↓ sang↓ sanic↓ sars↓ sec↓ sep k* sil↓ *Sol-ni*↓ spong fd4.de staph↓ *Stram* k* streptoc↓ stry↓ *Sulph*↓ *Syph*↓ tab↓ tanac↓ *Tarent* k* tax↓ ther↓ thuj↓ thyr↓ tritic-vg↓ tub jl2 valer↓ vanil↓ verat verat-v↓ verbe-o↓ wies↓ *Zinc*↓ *Zinc-i*↓ *Zinc-m*↓ *Zinc-n*↓ *Zinc-p*↓

- **evening** | **asleep**; on falling: sil h2*
- **actions**; repeated (See repeating)
- **actor**; like an: hyos a1
- **affectation** in gestures (See Affectation - gestures)
- **angry**: *(↗Rage)* cann-i k* dulc fd4.de *Hep* meph↓ sep k* spong fd4.de
  - **somnambulism**; in: meph kr1
- **animated** (See lively)
- **answering** with gestures (See indicates)
- **automatic**: *(↗repeating; Schizophrenia - paranoid; Unconsciousness - conduct)* anac bg2* anh mg1.de* bell ptk1* calc bg* cann-i a1 falco-pe nl2• hell bg2* hyos bg* lyc ptk1* mag-c ptk1* *Nux-m* bg2* phos bg* polys sk4• sil ptk1* *Stram* ptk1* syph jl2 tab a1 tub mrr1 *Verat* mrr1 zinc bg* [hydrog stj2]
  - **sleep**, during: phos a1
- **awkward** in: *(↗cautious; shy; uncertain)* caps gl1.fr• nat-c gl1.fr• nat-m gl1.fr• (non:nux-m gl1.fr) nux-v gl2.fr*• sil gl1.fr• sulph gl1.fr• syph jl2 **Verat** vh*
- **carphologia** (See hands - picking - bedclothes)
- **cautious**: *(↗awkward; shy; uncertain)* pip-m a1
- **childish**: anac h2* verat vh
- **clawing** (See hands - clawing)
- **coition**; motions as of: caust ptk1 phos ptk1
- **confused**: *Acon* a1 sil a1
- **convulsive**: acon a1 aeth↓ aether a1 alco a1 ant-t a1 apis arg-n↓ ars a1 aur↓ bell k* camph a1 cann-s k* canth a1 caust↓ cocc↓ cori-m a1 cupr↓ hydr-ac a1 hyos mrr1 ign a1 iod a1 kali-bi a1 mag-c↓ malar↓ merc a1 morph a1 nux-v a1 op a1 petr a1 plb puls↓ pyrus a1 rhus-t↓ sec a1 sol-ni a1
  - **drink**, at sight of: bell
  - **sleep**, during: acon bg aeth a1 arg-n bg caust bg cocc bg cupr bg *Hyos* bg mag-c bg malar jl2 puls bg rhus-t bg
  - **thinking** of motion; when: aur a1
- **decided**: fl-ac a1
- **drinking**; as if (See hands - drinking)
- **enthusiastic**: *(↗lively; sublime)* aq-pet mtf11 nitro-o a1 verbe-o mtf11
- **extravagant**: *(↗Extravagance)* bell a1 dulc fd4.de stram a1 *Verat* vh*
- **feet**; involuntary motions of the:
  - **shuffling** about as if dancing: *(↗EXTREMITIES - Walking - shuffling)* nitro-o a1
  - **spinning** around on the foot: cann-s
  - **stamping** the feet: *(↗Kicking)* acon h1 anac st ant-c k* ant-t bg2 bell↓ cann-i a1 cham h1 cina a1* dulc h2* hyos h1* *Ign*↓ kali-c↓ lyc st* nitro-o a1 nux-v st* op st* phos mtf33 plb a1 podo fd3.de• puls c1* sep↓ *Stram* k* streptoc↓ sulph ctc* tarent sne **Verat** bg2*
    - **lying**; while: streptoc mtf11
    - **sleep**; during: bell j *Ign* h1* kali-c h2* sep h2*
      - **children**: *Ign* ●* kali-c mtf33 sep mtf33
    - **talking**; while: nux-v mtf33
  - **walking**; ways of (See EXTREMITIES - Walking)
- **fighting** with hands: mosch j
- **fingers**: *(↗EXTREMITIES - Restlessness - hand)*
  - **mouth**; children put fingers into the: *(↗hands - grasping - mouth - everything; tics; Sucking - into; MOUTH - Fingers)* *Calc* k* calc-ox jl* calc-p bg2* cean bg2* *Cham* k* hell sne hyos hr1 **Ip** k* kali-p kl* lyc a1* med bg* merc bg2* nat-m bg2* nat-s bg2* plb mtf *Sacch* sst1• sil h2* sulph bg2* tarent hr1* ther sne verat nh* zinc gk [tax jsj7]
    - **Night**: sacch sst1•
  - **picking** at fingers: ars bg2 *Art-v* hr1 arum-t bg2* bapt he calc k13* canth hs cina al *Con* bg2* hell k13 hydrog srj hyos bg2* *Kali-br* bg2 kali-n ptk1 *Lach* bg2* mur-ac k13 petr a1 tarent bg2* ther ptk1 thuj bg2*
    - **tips**: arum-t k2 hydrog srj2•
  - **playing** with the fingers: *(↗Timidity)* arum-t ptk1* *Asar* vh* bell calc k* con hr1* crot-c k* *Hyos* k* kali-br kali-n ptk1 lach ptk1* nat-m sne rhus-t h1* tarent st* ther ptk1 zinc-p k2
    - **sleep**, during: rhus-t a1
- **fists** (See hands - fists)
- **foolish** (See ridiculous)
- **frightful**: *Hep* hr1* hyos j5.de
- **furious** (See angry)
- **genitals**; handling (See FEMALE - Masturbation; MALE - Handling)
- **grasping** (See hands - grasping)
- **groping**; as if: cocc↓ croc↓ hyos bg2 op↓ plb↓ stram↓
  - **dark**; in the: cocc k* croc k* hyos k* op k* plb k* stram a1
- **hair** | **face**; pushing one's hair out of one's: choc srj3•
- **hands**; involuntary motions of the: *(↗tics; EXTREMITIES - Motion - hands)* acon↓ agar↓ alco↓ all-c↓ alum↓ alumn a1 am-c↓ aml-ns↓ ant-c↓ **Ant-t**↓ arg-met↓ *Arn*↓ ars ars-s-f k13 art-v↓ *Arum-t*↓ asaf↓ *Asar*↓ atro↓ aur↓ bapt↓ **Bar-c**↓ bell **Borx**↓ bry↓ bufo↓ calad↓ calc bg2 calc-p↓ camph↓ cann-i canth↓ carb-an↓ carb-v↓ carc↓ caust *Cham*↓ chin↓ cic *Cina*↓ coca cocc↓ *Colch*↓ con↓ cor-r↓ cupr↓ dat-a↓ dat-m↓ dros↓ dub↓ dubo-m↓ *Dulc* fd2.de• falco-pe↓ fl-ac a1 glon↓ graph↓ hell k2 *Hep*↓ hir rsj4• hydr-ac↓ *Hyos* k* hyosin↓ ign↓ **Iod**↓ ip↓ kali-bi↓ kali-br kali-i↓ *Kali-p*↓ lac-h↓ lach↓ lil-t↓ *Lyc*↓ lyss↓ merc mosch **Mur-ac**↓ naja↓ nat-c↓ nat-m nux-m k2 nux-v↓ oena↓ **Op**↓ paeon↓ **Ph-ac**↓ *Phos* a1 plat↓ plb↓ *Psor*↓ puls k* raja-s↓ *Rhus-t*↓ *Rumx*↓ sang a1 sanic↓ sars↓ sec↓ sil *Sol-ni*↓ spong↓ staph↓ stram stry↓ sulph tab a1 tarent mtf33 tax↓ ther↓ thuj↓ thyr↓ valer↓ vanil fd5.de verat verat-v↓ *Zinc*↓ zinc-m↓ zinc-p↓
  - **breaking**: *(↗Breaking)*
    - **pins**: **Bell** calc k2
    - **sticks**: *Bell* k2 calc k2
  - **brushing** the face or something away; as if: *(↗picking - bedclothes; strange; GENERALS - Catalepsy)* alum k2 cham st hyos k*
  - **buttons** of his clothes; plays with the: *(↗Playing - desire - buttons)* *Asar* vh* mosch k1 nux-v↓ staph mtf33
    - **talking**; while: nux-v mtf33
  - **clapping**: *Bell* k* cic k* sec↓ *Stram* verat k*
    - **overhead**: bell a1 sec st stram mtf33
  - **clawing**: falco-pe nl2•
  - **clenching**:
    - **fingers** (See EXTREMITIES - Clenching - fingers)
    - **thumbs** (See EXTREMITIES - Clenching - thumbs)
  - **counting** money; as if: calc mtf33* *Hyos* vh* nux-v gl1.fr• staph mtf33*
  - **covering** | **face** with their hands, but looking through their fingers | **children**; in: **Bar-c** st*
    - **mouth** with hands: *(↗Timidity)* am-c ckh1 arg-met ckh1 cor-r ckh1 cupr ckh1 ip st kali-bi st lach st *Rumx* st thuj ckh1
  - **crossing** hands: carb-v ckh1 graph ckh1 mosch
  - **drinking**; as if: bell j5.de*
  - **face**; to the: stry vanil fd5.de
  - **fists**:
    - **doubling** as if in furious anger: calc hr1*
    - **makes** fists | **fright**; after: ign kr1
  - **folding**:
    - **coverings**; folding and unfolding: plb k*
    - **hands**: puls

• **grasping** (= reaching at something, at flocks): acon↓ alco↓ all-c↓ aml-ns vh1 **Ant-t**↓ arn k* ars arum-t kr1* asaf↓ atro a1* *Bell* k* *Borx* calad↓ *Calc*↓ calc-p camph↓ *Cham* chin sf1.de *Cic*↓ cina k* cocc k* colch a1 con a1 dat-m a1 dros↓ dub a1 dubo-m a1 dulc a1 falco-pe↓ glon↓ *Hell*↓ **HYOS** b2.de* hyosin a1 *Iod* a1* lil-t ckh1 *Lyc* lyss↓ merc↓ mosch mur-ac sf1.de naja↓ nux-v↓ oena op k* paeon a1 *Ph-ac* k* phos plat *Psor* puls mtf33 raja-s jl rhus-t k* sil mtf33 *Sol-ni* spong↓ **Stram** k* sulph k* thyr ckh1 *Verat* vh/dg* *Zinc* k1* zinc-m a1 zinc-p k2
  ⁝ **evening** | **going** to sleep; on: sil h2
  ⁝ **night**: atro a1 sol-ni a1
  ⁝ **air**, at: **Hyos** a
  ⁝ **bedclothes**; picks at (See picking - bedclothes)
  ⁝ **blaze** of fire, at: stram a
  ⁝ **bystanders**, at: *(↗Clinging - grasps)* **Ant-t** a1 bell h1* camph kr1 cocc a1 merc j phos stram j
  ⁝ **chewing** and swallowing, on: dulc a1 *Sol-ni*
  ⁝ **fingers**; picks at (See fingers - picking)
  ⁝ **flies**, at: *Stram* kr1
  ⁝ **frightened** manner, in: *Cic* kr1
  ⁝ **genitals** (See FEMALE - Masturbation; MALE - Handling)
  ⁝ **head**: ars↓ glon bg2 *Hell* hr1
    : **stool**; during: ars bg2
  ⁝ **hurriedly**: hyos bg2 merc bg2 stram bg2
  ⁝ **knees**: falco-pe nl2•
  ⁝ **lips** (See FACE - Picking - lips)
  ⁝ **mother**, in sleep; at: **Borx** a1
  ⁝ **mouth**: *(↗mouth)* *Calc*↓ dulc a1 lyc↓ merc↓ *Sulph*↓
    : **everything** in the mouth: *(↗fingers - mouth; MOUTH - Put everything)* *Calc* kr1 lyc mtf33 merc mtf33 *Sulph* h2*
    : **fingers** in the mouth (See fingers - mouth)
  ⁝ **nose**; at: *(↗NOSE - Boring)* *Arum-t*↓ *Cina*↓ stram a1*
    : **lips**; or: *(↗mouth; FACE - Picking - lips)* *Arum-t* kr1 *Cina* kr1
  ⁝ **objects**; at real or imaginary: dat-m c1 hyos a1 *Psor* kr1* *Stram* a
  ⁝ **quickly**: *Stram*
  ⁝ **rest**; during: alco a1
  ⁝ **sides** of the bed; at: nux-v
  ⁝ **sleep**; during: *Bell* b4a.de phos b4a.de
  ⁝ **throat**: acon bg2* all-c bg2* ars bg2 arum-t bg2* asaf ptk1 calad bg2 cina bg2 dros bg2* iod bg2* naja bg2* phos ptk1 spong bg2 stram bg2
  ⁝ **trachea**: cina bg2
  ⁝ **wrong** things; at: lyss hr1*

• **hasty**: *Bell*
• **head**, to the: *Ars*↓ calc-p↓ carc gk phos h2* plb *Stram* verat
  ⁝ **screams**; and: calc-p bj•
  ⁝ **sleep**, during: *Ars* kr1*
• **joining** the hands | **convulsions**; during tetanic: stram
• **kneading** bread; as if: sanic ptk1
• **knitting**, as if: tarent
• **lifting** up hands: ars
• **mother**, in sleep; at: **Borx** a
• **mouth**; to: *(↗grasping - mouth; grasping - nose - lips)* dulc a nux-v ptk2
  ⁝ **right** hand: nux-v ptk1*
• **nuts**; as if opening: hyos h1
• **opening** and shutting: stram ptk2
• **picking**:
  ⁝ **bedclothes**; at the (= carphologia): *(↗brushing)* acon agar bro1 alco mtf ant-c *Arn* k* *Ars* k* ars-s-f k2 art-v kr1 arum-t k2 atro k* *Bell* k* cham k* chin k* *Cina* cocc *Colch* con dat-a mtf dub mtf dulc *Hell* k* hep **Hyos** k* *Iod* k* *Kali-br* *Lyc* k* *Mur-ac* k* *Nat-m* *Op* k* *Ph-ac* k* *Phos* k* *Psor* *Rhus-t* k* sol-ni **Stram** k* sulph k* tarent ptk1* thuj mtf33 valer bg2 verat-v k* *Zinc* k* zinc-m k* zinc-p k2 [tax jsj7]
    : **chill**; during: arn bg2 **Ars** bg2 cham bg2 *Hep* bg2 *Hyos* bg2 **Iod** bg2 *Op* bg2 ph-ac bg2 *Phos* bg2 rhus-t bg2 stram bg2 *Sulph* bg2
    : **fever**; during: arn bg2 ars b4a.de* **Bell** b4a.de* cham bg2 chin bg2 hep b4a.de* *Hyos* bg2 iod b4.de* **Mur-ac** b4a.de* **Op** b7a.de* **Ph-ac** b4a.de* phos b4a.de* rhus-t b7.de* stram bg2 sulph bg2

- **hands**; involuntary motions of the – **picking** – **bedclothes**; at the: ...
    : **perspiration**; during: acon bg2 *Ars* bg2 **Bell** bg2 cham bg2 chin bg2 *Hep* bg2 hyos bg2 iod bg2 **Mur-ac** bg2 *Op* bg2 *Ph-ac* bg2 *Phos* bg2 *Rhus-t* bg2 stram bg2 *Sulph* bg2 thuj bg2
    : **sleep**; during: hyos b7.de* op b7.de* *Rhus-t* b7a.de stram b7.de*
  ⁝ **nose**; in (See NOSE - Picking - nose)
  ⁝ **one** spot; at: arg-met↓ ars ptk1 arum-t ptk1* cham ptk1 cina↓ con ptk1 kali-br ptk1 lach ptk1 ph-ac↓ phos↓ tarent ptk1* thuj ptk1* zinc↓
    : **sore** or bleeding; until it is: arg-met ptk1 arum-t ptk1* cina ptk1 con ptk1 ph-ac ptk1 phos ptk1 zinc ptk1
  ⁝ **Lips**; at (See FACE - Picking - lips)
• **playing** with hands: *(↗Playing - desire)* calc bg2 *Mur-ac* hr1 rhus-t bg2
• **pouring** from hand to hand; as if: bell
• **rage**, in: *Stram* kr1
• **rest**, during: alco a
• **restlessness** of hands (See EXTREMITIES - Restlessness - hand)
• **rubbing**:
  ⁝ **face**; the: alum k2 nux-v ptk1
  ⁝ **together**; rubbing hands: bapt a2* cann-i hyos a1
• **scratching** thighs: sars h2
• **sleep**, during: phos a1
• **spinning** and weaving: hyos k* sars bg2 *Stram* k*
• **squeezes** things: kali-i bg2
• **tapping** one's skull with his fingertips: carc hbh*
• **throwing** about: ars↓ atro bell bry canth carb-an hydr-ac↓ mosch nat-c phos sil stram
  ⁝ **head**; over: ars bell hydr-ac mosch stram
• **typhoid** fever; during: *Iod* kr1 *Lyc* kr1
• **waving** in the air: bry op stram
• **weeping**, with: calc-p hr1
• **wild**: *(↗Wildness)* acon camph kr1
• **winding** a ball; as if: agar k* stram
• **wringing** the hands: *(↗Sadness - wringing)* *Ars* bg2* *Asar* mrr1* aur bufo k2* cic bg2 kali-br k* *Kali-p* lac-h htj1• *Phos* k* plat *Psor* puls *Stram* k* *Sulph* k* *Tarent* k* ther ptk1*
  ⁝ **walks** the floor, and: bufo dm*
• **wrong** things: lyss kr1

- **impatient**: coca a1
- **indicates** his desires by gestures: *(↗Answering - gestures)* *Stram*
- **intoxicated**; as if: **Hyos**
- **involuntary** motions of hands (See hands)
- **knees**; grasping (See hands - grasping - knees)
- **labored**: conin a1
- **light**: chin a1 clem a1 coff a1 phel a1 wies a1
- **lips** move as if talking (See Delirium - lips)
- **lively**: *(↗enthusiastic; sublime)* alco a1 dulc fd4.de *Hyos* kr1 ped a1
- **morose**: *Canth* b7a.de *Cic* b7a.de hyos b7a.de nux-m b7a.de *Stram* b7a.de *Verat* b7a.de
- **mouth** in place of hands; desire to use: choc srj3•
- **nervous**: phys a1 tarent a1 *Verat* vh*
- **one** arm or leg or head: apoc ptk1 bry ptk1 hell ptk1 iodof ptk1 mygal ptk1 pyrog ptk1 zinc ptk1
- **perseverance**, with great: anac a1 arg-n a1 *Bell* a1 cic a1 croc a1 *Cupr* a1 **Hyos** a1 ign a1 kali-p a1 *Lach* a1 merc a1 *Mosch* a1 *Nux-m* a1 nux-v j5.de* op a1 *Sep* a1 stram a1 *Tarent* st1 verat a1
- **picking** (See hands - picking)
- **pulls** hair of bystanders: *(↗Pull - hair)* bell
- **pushing** things away in sleep: cocc a1
- **putting** everything in mouth (See hands - grasping - mouth - everything)
- **repeating** the same actions: *(↗automatic)* chen-a a1* lach bg2 plat bg2 *Syph* jl2 tub mrr1 **Verat** mrr1 *Zinc* stj2* [*Zinc-i* stj2 *Zinc-m* stj2 *Zinc-n* stj2 *Zinc-p* stj2]
  • **cutting** papers: *Verat* mrr1
  • **stacking** things: verat mrr1
  • **tearing** things: *Verat* mrr1

- **verifying** if the doors are locked (See Checking - verifying)
- **ridiculous** or foolish: (↗*Childish; Dress - ridiculously; Foolish; Frivolous; Jesting - ridiculous; Thoughts - ridiculous)* androc srj1• arg-n a1 *Bell* k* cic k* croc *Cupr* k* elec c1 **Hyos** k* ign kali-p *Lach* merc k* *Mosch Nux-m* k* nux-v j5.de* op par vml3• *Sep Stram* k* *Tarent* k2* *Verat* k*
  - **air**; in open: nux-m
  - **chorea**, in: *Cupr* kr1
  - **standing** on the street; while: *Nux-m*
- **shy**: (↗*awkward; cautious; uncertain)* arg-n a1
- **slow**: (↗*Slowness - motion)* chinin-s a1 conin a1 **Phos** a1 plb a1 verat a1
- **spinning**; imitates (See hands - spinning)
- **squirming** (See wriggling)
- **strange** attitudes and positions: (↗*hands - brushing; Antics; Schizophrenia - paranoid; Strange)* agar gl1.fr• agar-ph a1 camph a1* caust st *Cina* ptk1 cocc ptk1 *Coloc* ptk1 gamb ptk1 hyos gl1.fr• lyc a1* merc ptk1 *Nux-m* hr1* nux-v ptk1* op a1* *Plb* kr1* rheum h* sep c1* stram a1* sulph gl1.fr• tanac cda zinc ptk1
  - **gait**, in: nux-v gl1.fr• sep gl1.fr•
  - ○ **Arms**, of: hyos gl1.fr• sep gl1.fr• stram gl1.fr•
  - **Head**, of: agar gl1.fr• sulph gl1.fr•
- **stroke** her hair; desire to: choc srj
- **sublime**: (↗*enthusiastic; lively)* hyos a1 nitro-o a1
- **talking**:
  - **lips** move as if (See Delirium - lips)
  - **while** talking; gesticulating: cic ↓ *Dulc* fd4.de lyc ↓ nux-v gl1.fr• puls ↓ sep gl1.fr• sulph ↓ tritic-vg fd5.de
    - **arms**; with: cic ptk1 dulc fd4.de nux-v pc* sep pc tritic-vg fd5.de
    - **head**; with: cic ptk1 lyc mtf33* puls gl1.fr• sulph mtf33*
- **throwing** about arms: cina gw
- **tics**; nervous: (↗*fingers - mouth; hands; Grimaces; Tourette's; EXTREMITIES - Twitching; EYE - Twitching; EYE - Winking; FACE - Involuntarily; FACE - Tic; FACE - Twitching; GENERALS - Twitching; HEAD - Twitching; MALE AND - Handling; MALE GENITALIA/SEX - Handling; MALE GENITALIA/SEX - Twitching - penis; MOUTH - Fingers; MOUTH - Grasping; NOSE - Picking - nose - constant)* agar mtf11 arg-n bro1* ars ptk1 bism-met ↓ carc jl2* caust mrr1 croc mrr1 cupr mrr1 enterob-v ↓ hyos bro1* ign mrr1 laur bro1* lyc bro1* nux-v mrr1 ran-b ptk1 rhus-t mrr1 sep bro1* staph mrr1 stram mrr1 syph jl2 tanac mtf11 tarent bro1* *Verat* mrr1 zinc bro1*
  - **children**; in: carc sst2•
  - **painful**: bism-met mtf11 enterob-v mtf11
- **tired**; acts as if born: onos ptk1
- **twisting** (See wriggling)
- **uncertain**: (↗*awkward; cautious; shy)* acon a1 bell a1 *Phos* a1 sil a1 verat a1
- **usual** vocation; of his: ars bell plb stram
- **violent**: (↗*Violent)* agar k* *Bell* k* *Camph* k* cic-m a1 dulc fd4.de *Hep Hyos* k* kali-br a1 plb a1 sep ↓ *Stram* verat hr1
  - **angry**; when: sep mtf33
- **waking**; on: stram b7.de*
- **walking** in a peculiar way (See EXTREMITIES - Walking)
- **whimsical**: op a1
- **wild**: (↗*Wildness)* bell gg camph a1
- **wriggling**: valer ptk1*
- **wringing** (See hands - wringing)

GET ONESELF TOGETHER; as if one cannot (See Confusion)

GIFTED (See Talented)

GIFTS to his wife or son; husband making no: (↗*Indifference - family)* **Lach** gl1.fr•

GIGGLING: (↗*Childish; Foolish)* adam srj5• *Agath-a* nl2• aids nl2• androc srj1• arizon-l nl2• bamb-a stb2.de• bufo k2* cann-i choc srj coca-c sk4• coli rly4• cypra-eg sde6.de• dulc fd4.de falco-pe nl2• galla-q-r nl2• germ-met srj5• hyosin a* irid-met srj5• kali-f stj* nat-m vh neon srj5• nept-m lsd2.fr positr nl2• stry a ulm-c jsj8• [calc-s stj heroin sdj2]

GLITTERING objects: *Canth* bg2

GLOOMY (See Sadness - gloomy)

GLUTTONY (See Bulimia)

GODLESS (See Religious - want)

GOING OUT; aversion to: (↗*Amusement - Aversion; Company - Aversion; Disturbed; Fear - Going; Fear - Open; Fear - Run over; fear of being - going; VERTIGO - Walking - Air; VERTIGO - Walking - Air - agg.)* am-c k* anth k* caps ptk2 clem k* *Cycl* k* gink-b sbd1• haliae-lc srj5• hydr k* *Pneu* jl2* **Sep** vh* spong fd4.de

GOOD FOR NOTHING; sensation of being (See Discontented - himself - good)

GOOD-HUMORED (See Cheerful)

GOSSIPING: (↗*Curious; Indiscretion; Lamenting - others; Loquacity; Meddlesome; Revealing; Slander; Spying; Talking - desire)* ars b4a.de* borra-o mtf* calc gl1.fr• caust gl1.fr• *Hyos* k* lach gl1.fr• par sf1.de stram k* verat k* [tax jsj7]

GOURMAND: (↗*Reveling)* all-s br1 berb br1 calc gl1.fr• carb-v vh* chin gl1.fr• ip mtf33* mag-c mtf33* merc mtf33* nat-c gl1.fr• nux-v mtf **Verat** mtf33*

GRACIOUS: | **not** gracious (See Elegance - want)

GRATITUDE: neon srj5• olib-sac wmh1 plut-n srj7• positr nl2• tritic-vg fd5.de vanil fd5.de

GRAVITY (See Serious)

GREED, cupidity: (↗*Anal; Avarice; Bargaining; Desires - full - more; Envy - avidity; Possessiveness; Rich - desire; Selfishness)* ant-t hr1 *Ars* sf1.de* aur-m-n wbt2• aur-s wbt2• calc st1* cham mhn1 *Chin* st1* graph mtf33 *Hyos* kr1 ip st1 *Lyc* kr1* mag-c st1 *Merc* st* nat-c st1 nit-ac gl1.fr• nux-v gl1.fr• ph-ac gl1.fr• phos hr1 *Puls* a1* rhus-t gl1.fr• *Sep* kr1* stann gl1.fr• staph gl1.fr• sulph gl1.fr• thuj cd1 verat st1
- **food**; greed for (See Bulimia)
- **grasping** greedily with both hands anything offered him: *Hyos* kr1

GRIEF: (↗*Ailments - anger - silent; Ailments - grief; Brooding; Cares full; Dwells - past; Fear - grief; Inconsolable; Love - love-sick; Moaning; Sadness; Sighing; Weeping; Weeping - cannot; Weeping - sad - thoughts; RESPIRATION - Sobbing)* acet-ac k* acon k* adam srj5• adren ↓ aeth mtf33 agar k* agn bg2 ail bro1 alum k* am-c k* am-m k* *Ambr* bg2 *Anac* j* ant-c k* **Anthraci** ↓ apis br1 aq-mar rbp6 arge-pl rwt5• *Arn* j* *Ars* k* asaf ↓ asar bg2 **Aur** k* aur-ar k2 aur-m bg *Aur-m-n* ↓ bar-c k* *Bell* bg2 benz-ac bg2 bov bg2 *Bry* bg2 cael jl3 calc k* calc-f mrr1* calc-p bro1* *Cann-xyz* bg2 caps b7.de* carb-an k* carc sk1• card-m bg2 **Caust** k* *Cham* ↓ chel j* chin h1* choc srj3• *Cic* j5.de* *Cimic* bro1 clem bg2 cocc b7.de* coff j5.de* colch ptk1 *Coloc* k* colum-p sze2• con b4a.de* conv ↓ *Croc* bg2 crot-c ↓ cycl k* des-ac rbp6 *Dig* bg2* dream-p ↓ *Dros* j* *Ferr* bg2 *Gels* ↓ gink-b ↓ granit-m ↓ *Graph* k* *Hell* b7.de* hep bg2 hippoc-k szs2 hyos k* *Iber* bro1 **IGN** k* indg ↓ iod bg2 ip ↓ irid-met srj5• kali-bi bg2 kali-br bg2 kali-c b4a.de* kali-fcy ↓ kali-n j kali-p k2 ketogl-ac ↓ *Lac-c* ↓ *Lach* k* lact laur bg2 lil-t ↓ limest-b es1• loxo-recl knl4• *Lyc* k* mag-m bg2 mang j* meny bg2 *Merc* k* mez bg2 mur-ac bg2* naja ptk1 nat-ar mrr1 nat-c b4a.de* **Nat-m** k* nat-p mrr1 nat-s mrr1 nat-sil fd3.de• nit-ac bg2* *Nux-v* k* olnd bg2 *Op* k* orni mtf11 peti ↓ petr bg* *Ph-ac* k* phos b4a.de* phys ↓ pin-con oss2• plat bg2 plut-n ↓ pseuts-m mtf* psor ↓ **Puls** k* ran-s bg2 **Rhus-t** bg2* ruta bg2 sal-ac ↓ samb ptk1 sars bg2 sec bg2 *Sep* k* sil bg2* spig bg2 stann ↓ **Staph** k* stram b7.de* stront-c bg2 stry mrr1 suis-em rly4• sul-ac k* *Sulph* bg2* **Symph** ↓ *Tarent* thuj j* v-a-b jl2 vanil fd5.de verat k* viol-o bg2 viol-t bg2 zinc bg2*
- **day** and night: caust gl1.fr•
- **daytime**: staph
- **morning**: alum j5.de nux-v gl1.fr• phos puls
- **afternoon**: *Tarent* k*
- **evening**: *Graph* j5.de*
  - **amel.**: nux-v gl1.fr• staph gl1.fr•
- **night** | **bed**; in: graph h2 ph-ac h2
- **ailments** (See Ailments - grief)

- **alternating** with:
  - **cheerfulness** (See Cheerful - alternating - grief)
  - **exhilaration** (See Exhilaration - alternating - grief)
  - **vivacity** (See Vivacious - alternating - grief)
- **boisterous** (See turbulent)
- **business** in morning; when thinking of his: *Puls* kr1
- **chronic** (See prolonged)
- **complaining**, with: caust bg*
- **condition**; about his: staph
- **consequences**, about: **Staph** kr1
- **cry**; cannot (See Weeping - cannot)
- **deception**, from: *(↗Ailments - deceived)* **Aur** vh **IGN** st lach gl• **Lyc** vh merc gl• **Nat-m** st *Nux-v* vh op vh ph-ac gl• puls gl• sep vh verat vh
- **delivery**; during: ign kr1
- **delusions** from: *Zinc* hr1*
- **diabetes**; with: aur mtf aur-m-n mtf ign mtf mag-m mtf nat-s mtf ph-ac mtf tarent mtf
- **easily**: conv br1
- **fear** at night, with: *Merc* hr1*
- **financial** loss; from (See money; Sadness - money - losing)
- **fits** of grief: asaf kr1
- **fright**, after: *Ign* kr1
- **future**; for the: *(↗Anxiety - future; Lamenting - future)* gink-b sbd1• mang h2 nat-c **Nat-m** k ● stann h2 *Vanil* fd5.de
- **headache** from (See HEAD - Pain - grief)
- **hunting** for something to grieve oneself: lil-t
- **inconsolable** (See Inconsolable)
- **insults**, over: *Op* kr1
- **jealousy**, with: *Hyos* kr1
- **losing** objects; after: dream-p sdj1• **Ign** kr1
- **loved** ones; long lost: hippoc-k szs2
- **money**; from losing: *(↗Ailments - money)* aur mp1• calc-f mrr1 mez mp1• psor mp1•
- **offenses**; from long past: *(↗Dwells - offenses)* calc h2* *Cham* kr1 *Ign* kr1* *Op* kr1 *Staph* mrr1*
- **paralytic** state of body and mind, from: phys ptk1
- **past** events, about: *(↗Dwells - past; Remorse - indiscretion)* adam srj5• arge-pl rwt5• *Plat* hr1* plut-n srj7• *Vanil* fd5.de
- **prolonged**: aq-mar rbp6 carc mlr• caust mrr1 *Graph* gl1.fr• *Nat-m* bg* **Nat-sil** fd* ph-ac tl1* phos bg *Staph* mrr1
- **punishment**, after: *Ign* kr1
- **sensitive** to: *Cocc* kr1
- **sighing**; with: acet-ac hca ail h **Cimic** kr *Iber* kr ign st nat-m lp op j orni bh• puls hr
- **silent**: *(↗Ailments - grief - silent; Brooding; Sadness - quiet; Taciturn)* adren vh aeth mtf33 *Am-m* vh1 **Anthraci** vh1 apis lsr *Aq-mar* mgm• *Aur* b4a.de* aur-ar k13 *Aur-m* vh* *Aur-m-n* wbt2• bell gb• carc fb* *Coff* hr1* *Coloc*↓ crot-c bdg* *Cycl* k* *Gels* hr1* granit-m es• **Ign** k* indg hr1 ip vh* kali-fcy zr ketogl-ac rly4• loxo-recl knl4• lyc k2* mag-m gb• *Mur-ac* br **Nat-m** k* nat-sil fd3.de• nux-v h1* peti a1 *Ph-ac* ptk1* phos↓ *Puls* k* sal-ac hr1* sep gb• staph mrr1 sulph nh4 **Symph** fd* [merc stj2]
  - **alternating** with | **quarreling** (See Quarrelsome - alternating - silent)
  - **anger**, after: *Ign* kr1
  - **indignation**, with: carc mlr1• *Coloc* hr1* staph vh
  - **love**; from disappointed: *(↗Ailments - love; Inconsolable)* *Aur-m-n* wbt2• **Ign** **Nat-m** k* nat-sil fd3.de• **Ph-ac** k* phos
  - **menses**, before: *Ign* mtn
  - **submissiveness**, with: **Puls** hr1*
- **suppressed** (See silent)
- **trifles**, over: *(↗Trifles; Trifles - important)* ars h2 bar-c k* conv br1
- **turbulent**: nat-m ptk1
- **undemonstrative** (See silent)
- **undermining** the constitution: carc mgg• *Phos* hr1*
- **waking**, on: *(↗Sadness - waking)* alum b4a.de* *Lac-c* hr1* *Lach* hr1* ph-ac j5.de

Grief: ...

- **weeping** (See Sadness - weeping; Weeping - sad - thoughts)

GRIMACES: *(↗Antics; Delirium - grimaces; Foolish; Frivolous; Gestures; Gestures - tics; FACE - Expression - foolish)* absin bg2 agar bg2* agath-a nl2• *All-c* vh ars↓ bell *Camph* sne cann-s↓ carb-ac↓ carc jl2* cina *Cupr* k* dulc fd4.de gels bg2* hell *Hyos* k* ign bg2* meli sne merc↓ nux-m *Olnd* op↓ pall plat k* *Rhus-t*↓ spong fd4.de *Stram* k* tritic-vg fd5.de verat-v zinc mrr1 [ant-met stj2]

- **children**; in: carc sst2•
- **convulsions** | **before**: absin a1
- **hide** the grimaces; trying to: *Cupr* mrr1
- **ill**-mannered faces; makes: *(↗Haughty; Rudeness - children)* hyos a1*
- **sleep**; during: bell hr1 op h1
- **strange** faces; makes: agar sf agath-a nl2• all-c dgt1 ars a1 bell k* cann-s a1 carb-ac a1 carc mlr1• cupr vh dulc fd4.de gels sf hell hyos k* ign sf merc a1 nux-m olnd pall k* plat k* *Rhus-t* vh* *Stram* k* tritic-vg fd5.de verat-v k* zinc vh
- **talking**, while: bell h1

GROANING (See Moaning)

GROPING; as if (See Gestures - groping)

GROUNDED:

- **not** grounded (See Confidence - want)
- **too** much grounded (See Confident)

GROWLING: *(↗Barking)* alum↓ ars bg2 caust↓ hell↓ lyc↓ nat-m↓ nux-v↓ phos↓ puls↓ sep↓

- **dog**; at any male: alum bg2 hell bg2 lyc bg2
- **strangers**; at: caust↓

GRUDGE (See Hatred)

GRUMBLING: *(↗Complaining; Discernment; Discontented; Lamenting; Moaning; Muttering; Tormenting - others - complaints)* alum a1* anac a1 aur ptk1 bell j5.de* con↓ loxo-lae bnm12• morb↓ sang ptk1* thyr ptk1* valer ptk1* [ant-c stj2 ant-met stj2 ant-t stj2 arg-n stj2 tell stj2 zinc stj2 zinc-i stj2 zinc-m stj2 zinc-n stj2 zinc-p stj2]

- **night**: con a1
- **children**; in: morb jl2

GRUNTING: *(↗Moaning; Muttering; Sighing)* bell hell k* ign mag-c↓ puls sep↓

- **angry**, when: mag-c dgt
- **sleep**, during: ign k* sep h2

GUIDANCE; need for: stront-c sk4•

GUILT (See Reproaching oneself)

GUILTY; as if (See Anxiety - conscience; Mood - repulsive; Remorse; Reproaching oneself)

GULLIBLE (See Naive)

HAIR:

- **cut**; having hair:
  - **desires**: choc↓ gink-b↓ hippoc-k↓ positr nl2•
    - **bald**; desires having hair cut: hippoc-k szs2
    - **short** and bristly; desires having hair cut: choc srj3• gink-b sbd1•
  - **refuse**; children: cina st

HALLUCINATIONS (See Delusions)

HANDLE THINGS any more; cannot (See Discouraged; Excitement; Prostration; Sadness)

HANDLED; being: | **aversion**: *(↗Touched - aversion)* abrot bl cina st nat-m bl sep bl

HANDYMAN: nux-v mtf

HAPHEPHOBIA (See Fear - touched)

HAPPY (See Cheerful)

HAPPY; envy when seeing others (See Envy - happy)

HARD for inferiors and kind for superiors: *(↗Indifference - loved - strangers)* lach gl1.fr• lyc ●* plat gl1.fr• verat gl1.fr•

HARDHEARTED: *(↗Cruelty; Detached; Indifference - suffering - others; Malicious; Mischievous; Mocking - ridicule; Moral; Rudeness; Sensitive - want; Unfeeling; Unsympathetic; Wicked)* adam srj5• aids nl2• alco sf1.de* *Anac* b4a.de* arizon-l nl2• ars gl1.fr• aur-ar vh1 bism j5.de* cench k2* chin bg2 con j5.de* croc j5.de* cupr vh* haliae-lc srj hep gl1.fr• hyos j5.de* *Kali-i* k2* kali-p bg2 lac-leo sk4• *Laur* j5.de* lil-t ↓ lyss a1* nat-m mrr1* (non:neon srj5) *Nit-ac* mrr1* nux-v mrr1* *Op* j5.de* par mrr1 plat j5.de* positr nl2• sabad j5.de* *Sep* mrr1 squil j5.de* sulph gl1.fr• verat mrr1 [bism-sn stj2 cadm-met stj2 cadm-s stj2 heroin sdj2]
- **alternating** with | **mildness**: croc j5.de* lil-t mrr1
- **family**, with his: kali-i k2
- **himself**; to: cupr sst3•
- **others**; to: cupr sst3•

HARMONY: | **desire** for: *(↗Quarrelling - aversion; Sensitive - rudeness)* carc zzh kali-p fd1.de• kali-s fd4.de lac-f wza1• mag-c mrr1 mag-m mtf mag-s mtf *Moni* rfm1• nat-c ms nat-m mtf33 olib-sac wmh1 podo fd3.de• *Ruta* fd4.de vanil fd5.de

HARSH (See Unfeeling)

HASTINESS (See Hurry)

HATRED: *(↗Ailments - anger - indignation; Ailments - honor; Ailments - mortification; Ailments - reproaches; Ailments - scorned; Aversion - persons - all; Brooding; Cynical; Delusions - women - evil; Dwells - past; Envy - hate; Fear - people; Hatred - humankind; Indignation; Loathing - general; Malicious; Misanthropy)* acon k* adam srj5• *Agar* k* agath-a nl2• aloe k* am-c am-m b7a.de* am-s ↓ ambr tsm1 **Anac** k* androc srj1• ang ↓ anh ↓ ars ↓ *Aur* k* *Aur-m-n* wbt2• *Aur-s* wbt2• bar-c k* cadm-i gm1 *Calc* k* calc-s ↓ caust mrr1 *Cham* ptk1* **CIC** b7.de* colum-p sze2• crot-c ↓ cupr k* dulc fd4.de falco-pe ↓ fl-ac bg2 gaert fmm1• galla-q-r nl2• germ-met srj5• granit-m es• hep bg2* hydr bg2 ign k* ignis-alc ↓ ilx-a ↓ iod ↓ kali-c st1 kali-i kola stb3• *Lac-c* lac-h sze9• *Lac-leo* ↓ *Lach* k* *Led* k* luna ↓ lyc k* mang k* med ↓ medus ↓ merc ↓ *Moni* rfm1• mygal bg2 nat-c b4.de **NAT-M** b4.de* neon ↓ **Nit-ac** b4a.de* *Nux-v* sf1.de* op bg2 opun-s ↓ pegan-ha ↓ ph-ac gl1.fr• phos k* pitu-a ft* plut-n ↓ polys sk4• positr nl2• pseuts-m sne* puls gl1.fr• *Raph* ↓ *Rhus-g* ↓ rhus-t sal-l mtf11 sep ↓ skat br1 stann k* stram ptk1 streptoc ↓ stront-c ↓ stry mrr1 **Sulph** k* taosc iwa1• tarent a1* tax ↓ tritic-vg fd5.de vip ↓ zinc ↓ [*Am-caust* stj2 am-p stj1 heroin sdj2 plat stj2]
- **night**: opun-s a1
- **absent** persons, better on seeing them; of: fl-ac k*
- **alternating** with | **despair**: ars gm1
- **bitter** feelings for slight offenses; has: *(↗Offended)* ang
- **cats**; of: *(↗Fear - cats)* ignis-alc es2•
- **children**; of: *(↗Aversion - children)* anac vh *Lyc* vh *Nux-v* vh **Plat** vh
- **envy**; with (See Envy - hate)
- **humankind**; of: *(↗Hatred; Humankind - shuns; Misanthropy)* cic h1* galla-q-r nl2• ignis-alc es2• *Led* kr1* positr nl2• [am-c stj1 am-m stj1]
- **husband**; of: *(↗Aversion - husband)* dulc fd4.de *Lac-leo* hrn2• luna kg1• [am-s stj1]
- **jealousy**; from: ilx-a mtf11
- **life** itself, of: *(↗Weary)* positr nl2•
- **men**; of [=in general] (See Hatred)
- **men**; of [=male persons]: *(↗Aversion - men; to [=male]; Fear - men; of [=male])*
  - **women**; in: *(↗aversion - men; to [= male persons] - women)* plut-n srj7• sep ptk2*
- **morbid** ideas; from: sulph kr1
- **mother**; of: *(↗Aversion - mother)* pegan-ha tpi1•
- **persons**:
  - **abusing** him: rhus-g tmo3•
  - **agree** with him; who do not: calc-s k*
  - **close** to him: positr nl2•
  - **enjoying** life, who are: medus bc

Hatred – persons: ...
  - **offended** him; hatred of persons who: *(↗Offended)* agar lpc am-c lpc ambr tsm1 anh br1 *Aur* k* *Aur-m-n* wbt2• *Aur-s* wbt2• calc gl1.fr• cic lpc granit-m es1• iod mtf33 lach lpc* led lpc mang med hu merc gl1.fr• *Nat-m* k* neon srj5• nit-ac k* nux-v mtf33* ph-ac lpc *Rhus-g* tmo3• sep st stann lpc staph gl1.fr• sulph taosc iwa1• [heroin sdj2]
  - **unmoved** by apologies: **Nit-ac** k*
- **relatives**; of close: pegan-ha tpi1•
- **repels** everyone: aloe kr1
- **revengeful**; hatred and: *(↗Plans - making - revengeful)* am-c gl1.fr• ambr tsm1 aur-m-n wbt2• calc ptk1* crot-c sk4• lach k2* med hu **Nat-m** ptk1* neon ↓ *Nit-ac* ptk1* *Nux-v* ptk1* *Ph-ac* gl1.fr• pseuts-m oss1• *Rhus-g* tmo3• streptoc rly4• stront-c sk4• tritic-vg fd5.de vip bcj1* zinc ↓ [stann stj2 tax jsj7]
  - **alone** amel.; while: neon srj5•
  - **alternating** with | **irritability**: zinc bg2
- **unreasonable**: fl-ac bl
- **vengeful** and detached: falco-pe nl2•
- **women**, of: *(↗Aversion - women; Aversion - women - men - religious; Cynical; Delusions - women; Fear - women; Homosexuality)* **Puls** k ● *Raph* a* sep ↓
  - **men**; in: *(↗Aversion - women - men)* sep ptk2*

HAUGHTY: *(↗Affectation; Ailments - honor; Ailments - indignation; Ailments - mortification; Ailments - reproaches; Ailments - scorned; Ambition; Anger - contradiction; Boaster; Boaster - squandering; Censorious; Contemptuous; Contradiction - intolerant; Cynical; Deeds - great; Defiant; Delusions - appreciated; Delusions - better; Delusions - body - greatness; Delusions - criticized; Delusions - diminished - everything; Delusions - distinguished; Delusions - elevated - air - looking; Delusions - enlarged - tall; Delusions - great; Delusions - humility; Delusions - inferior; Delusions - insulted; Delusions - knowledge; Delusions - noble; Delusions - prince; Delusions - proud; Delusions - queen; Delusions - rank; Delusions - superiority; Delusions - tall - he; Delusions - visions - grandeur; Delusions - wealth; Dictatorial; Dictatorial - power; Egotism; Exclusive; Extravagance; Flattered - desire; Foolish - happiness; Grimaces - ill-mannered; Haughty - alternating - discouragement; Impertinence; Indifference - company - while; Insanity - haughty; Insolence; Lamenting - appreciated; Laughing - contemptuous; Longing - good; Loquacity - self-satisfied; Pedant; Pompous; Presumptuous; Reproaching oneself; Reproaching others; Rudeness; Selfishness; Speech - extravagant; Squandering - money; Talking - pleasure; Vanity; Walking - self-sufficient; Walking - slowly; Walking - slowly - dignified)* acon bg2 agar agn ↓ alum k* anac k* arn k* ars ↓ asar vh aur k* aur-m-n wbt2• aur-s zr* bac al bell bg* calc vh* cann-i k* cann-xyz bg2 carb-v mrr1 carc mlr1• *Caust* k* chin k* chir-fl gya2 cic k* cina j5.de coloc k2 con k* cupr k* daph dulc k* elaps gk* ferr k* ferr-ma k* gard-j vlr2• glon ↓ gran j5.de* granit-m es1• *Graph* ↓ grat k2* guaj k* ham k* hell j5.de* hep ↓ hott-p rcb1* *Hyos* k* ign k* ignis-alc es2• *Ip* k* kali-c kali-i bg2 kola stb3• lac-f ↓ lac-leo hrn2*• *Lach* k* lap-la sde8.de• lil-t bg1* **LYC** b2.de* marb-w es1• merc k* myric hl nat-m st* nitro-o a1 nux-v k* *Pall* k* par k* phos k* **PLAT** b2.de* podo fd3.de• positr nl2• *Puls* b7a.de* rhus-g tmo3• rob k* sabad sal-fr sle1• sec sep gk *Sil* vh* squil *Staph* k* *Stram* k* stront-c **Sulph** k* thuj k* tung-met stj2*• vanil fd5.de **Verat** k* *Verat-v* ↓ [ant-c stj2 ant-m stj2 ant-met stj2 ant-t stj2 arg-met stj1* arg-n stj2 arg-p stj2 astat stj2 aur-m stj2 bar-br stj2 bar-i stj2 bar-met stj2 bism-sn stj2 cadm-m stj2 cadm-met stj2 cadm-s stj2 caes-met stj2 cinnb stj2 cupr-act stj2 hafn-met stj2 heroin sdj2 ind stj2 iod stj2 irid-met stj2 lanth-met stj2 lith-i stj2 mang-i stj2 merc-d stj2 merc-i-f stj2 moly-met stj2 niob-met stj2 osm-met stj2 plb stj2 plb-m stj2 plb-p stj2 polon-met stj2 rhen-met stj2 rhodi stj2 rubd-met stj2 ruth-met stj2 stann stj2 stront-m stj2 stront-met stj2 tant-met stj2 techn stj2 tell stj2 thal-met stj2 zinc-i stj2 zirc-met stj2]
- **alternating** with | **discouragement**: *(↗Haughty)* agn
- **clothes**: *(↗Dress)* con ptk1
  - **best** clothes; likes to wear his: *Con* kr1* irid-met srj5• lac-f wza1• tung-met bdx1•
  - **colorful** clothes: lac-f wza1•
  - **tasteful** clothing: lac-f wza1•
- **intelligent**; but: nux-v mtf33
- **look**, self-contented: *(↗Hiding - himself - children)* ferr hr1* ferr-ma j5.de*

- **mania**; in: cupr bg2 glon bg2 *Graph* kr1 hyos bg2 *Lach* bg2* lyc bg2 **Plat** bg2* stram bg2 sulph bg2 *Verat* bg2* *Verat-v* kr1
- **menses**, before: verat mtn
- **pregnancy**, during: *Verat* hr1*
- **races**; to other human: ars j hep j phos j plat j sep j
- **religious** haughtiness: *(↗Religious - too)* *Plat* hr1*
- **stiff** and pretentious: *Lyc* hr1*
- **stupidity** and hatred: bell gl1.fr• calc gl1.fr• lyc gl1.fr• plat gl1.fr• stram gl1.fr• verat gl1.fr•
- **women**: *Grat* mrr1
- **wounded** self-esteem; wishes to be flattered: **Pall** kr1* plat tl1* puls vh verat ptk1

HAZY feeling (See Confusion)

HEAD-BANGING (See Striking - himself - knocking)

HEADSTRONG (See Obstinate)

HEAT:
- **during**: arg-met b7.de bry b7.de camph b7.de *Cham* b7.de chin b7.de *Cina* b7.de coff b7.de dulc b4a.de *Hyos* b7.de *Ign* b7.de laur b7.de meny b7.de mosch b7.de *Op* b7.de phos b4.de *Puls* b7.de *Sabad* b7.de sep b4.de *Valer* b7.de *Verat* b7.de
- **hands** agg.; of: carb-v bg2
- **head** agg.; of: carb-v bg2 laur bg2 mag-c bg2 phos bg2 sulph bg2

HEAVINESS; sensation of: *(↗Delusions - body - heavy; Delusions - heavy; Sadness)* *Agath-a* nl2• cocc br1 cortico↓ cortiso tpw7 galla-q-r nl2• gels↓ hell-o↓ hir rsj4• *Hydroph* rsj6• lac-h sze9• lat-h bnm5• pitu-gl↓ *Plut-n* srj7• sel rsj9• trios rsj11• tritic-vg fd5.de [bell-p-sp dcm1 heroin sdj2]
- **morning**: cortico tpw7 tritic-vg fd5.de
- **afternoon** | **14**-17 h: pitu-gl skp7•
- **night**: hell-o a1
- **alternating** with | **clearness** of mind: agath-a nl2•
- **influenza**; after: gels tl1

HEEDLESS: *(↗Absentminded - inadvertence; Accident; Accident-prone; Carefree; Casual; Chaotic; Dictatorial; Fearless; Impertinence; Impetuous; Improvident; Impulse - reckless; Impulsive; Indifference; Indiscretion; Loquacity - heedless; Meddlesome; Neglecting; Rash; Revealing; Sensitive - want; Unobserving [=inattentive]; Untidy)* abies-c k* agar k* agn ail k* alco a1 aln vva1• *Alum* k* alum-p k2* am-c k* am-m ambr *Anac* apis b7a.de* arn gl1.fr• asaf aur-m k* aur-m-n wbt2• *Bar-c* k* *Bell* k* bov bufo-s a1 calad b7.de* camph gl1.fr• cann-i a1 cann-s canth carl k* *Caust* *Cham* k* cic clem coff *Con* cortico jl3 cot↓ croc cupr cur a1 cypra-eg sde6.de• daph k* euon falco-pe nl2• *Gels* k* guaj ham sf1.de *Hell* k* hep *Hyos* k* ign ind a1* kali-c kali-sil k2* kreos lac-lup hrn2• *Lach* laur sf1.de loxo-recl knl4• *Lyc* lyss hr1 m-ambo b7.de* m-arct j5.de melal-alt gya4 *Merc* k* mez myris↓ nat-c *Nat-m* k* nat-p nit-ac *Nux-m* k* nux-v k1* *Olnd* *Op* k* ped a1 ph-ac k* phasco-ci rbp2 *Phos* k* plat k* podo fd3.de• positr nl2• puls b7.de* rhod rhus-t rib-ac jl3 ruta sabad hr1 sep k* sil spig staph mtf33* stram gl1.fr• sulph gl1.fr• tarax sf1.de thuj valer verat k* zinc zinc-p k2* [heroin sdj2 tax jsj7]
- **morning** | **waking**; on: cot a1
- **all** around; of: cann-i a
- **business**; about: myris a1
- **exhilaration**, from: hell a op a
- **fix** thoughts, cannot: ind kr1
- **mental** derangement, in: op kr1
- **talking** and writing; in: *(↗Dyslexia)* carl a1
- **think**; of what others: lac-lup hrn2•

HELD: *(↗Mania - held)*
- **amel.** being held: *(↗Magnetized - amel.)* ars ptk1 *Bry* ptk1 calc-p bg2 carb-an ptk1 diph ptk1 dros ptk1 eup-per ptk1 *Gels* ptk1 glon ptk1 *Lach* bg2* lil-t ptk1 murx ptk1 nat-s ptk1 nux-m ptk1 nux-v ptk1 rhus-t ptk1 sang ptk1 *Sep* bg2* sil ptk1 stram bg2* sul-ac ptk1 sulph ptk1
- **desire** to be held: *(↗Attached; Clinging; Cuddle - desire; Magnetized - desire; Mania - held)* *Ars* bg2* coff bg2 diph bg dulc fd4.de *Gels* bg2* germ-met srj5• iod bg2 iodof a irid-met srj5• kali-p bg2 kola stb3• lach bg2* *Nux-m* bg2* *Nux-v* bg2* phos bg2 plb bg2 rhus-t bg2 sacch sht• *Sang* bg2* *Sep* bg2* *Stram* bg2* sul-ac bg* sulph bg2* vanil fd5.de

HELPING OTHERS:
- **aversion** to help others: *(↗Egotism; Indifference - welfare; Selfishness)* calc pc plat pc sil pc [tax jsj7]

Helping others: ...
- **desire** to help others (See Benevolence)

HELPLESSNESS; feeling of: *(↗Confidence - want; Confidence - want - support; Confusion - lost; Delirium - crying - help; Delusions - help; Delusions - help - calling; Despair; Discouraged; Forsaken; Impressionable; Inconsolable; Insecurity; Irresolution; Pathetic; Pessimist; Shrieking - help; Succeeds)* agar mtf agath-a nl2• aids nl2• alum gk* am-c↓ ambr mtf anac bg2* anh sp1 ant-t a arg-n vh* ars h2* aur-m-n wbt2• *Bamb-a* stb2.de• *Bar-c* mtf33 bell a1 *Calad* st1 calc-sil mtf33 camph mtf cann-i a1 carc↓ cench↓ **Chel** sne chir-fl gya2 coca-c sk4• crot-c sk4• cypra-eg sde6.de• ferr ms foll mtf *Gels* hr1* germ-met stj2*• haliae-lc srj5• ham fd3.de• hecla alm• hell k* hydrog srj2* ign mtf jasm a1 kali-br k* kali-p fd1.de* *Kola* stb3• lac-c mtf lac-h sze9• lac-leo↓ lith-c hl* **Lyc** bg2* lys mtf *Moni* rfm1• naja mtf nat-m sne nat-sil fd3.de• olib-sac wmh1 ozone sde2• petr ph-ac mrr1 phos k* polys sk4• puls ctc• rad-br sze8• rhus-t c1* *Sacch-a* fd2.de• sal-fr sle1• *Sang*↓ sep lp2* *Sil* mtf staph sne stram k* *Symph* fd3.de• tax k* toxi mtf tritic-vg fd5.de vero-o rly3• [bell-p-sp dcm1 buteo-j sej6 spect dfg1]
- **afternoon**: kali-br k*
- **night**: *Lith-c* kr1
- **cough**, during: cench k2
- **menses**; during: foll mtf
- **emotional** level; on: carc sst2•
- **heart** complaints, with: am-c h2
- **infant**, feels like an: hell kr1
- **mental** exertion, from: gels hr1
- **mental** level; on: carc sst2•
- **nausea**; with: bamb-a stb2.de•
- **overwork**; from: **Kali-p** fd*
- **paralyzed**, from sensation of being: *Sang* cda
- **sensitivity** to: lac-leo hrn2•
- **vomiting**, after: hell a
- **weakness**, in mental exertion; from: *Gels* kr1

HEMATOPHOBIA (See Fear - blood)

HEMOPHOBIA (See Fear - blood)

HEMORRHAGES; after: arn bg2 ars bg2 bell bg2 ign bg2 lach bg2 lyc bg2 ph-ac bg2 phos bg2 sep bg2 squil bg2 sulph bg2 verat bg2

HEMORRHOIDS; after suppressed: anac bg2 ant-c bg2 arn bg2 ars bg2 bell bg2 caust bg2* cupr bg2 fl-ac bg2 hyos bg2 ign bg2 lach bg2 lyc bg2 nux-v bg2 phos bg2 sep bg2 sulph bg2 verat bg2 zinc bg2*

HESITATING (See Irresolution)

HIDING: *(↗Secretive)*
- **desire** to hide (See himself)
- **food**; desire to hide: choc srj3•
- **himself**: *(↗Delirium - shy; Escape; Longing - anonymity; Looked - cannot; Runs; Timidity)* adam↓ ars k* aur k13 *Bar-c*↓ **Bell** k* calc↓ camph chin↓ chlol k* *Chlor* kr1 choc srj3• coca hl crot-c sk4• cupr k* cypra-eg sde6.de• dulc fd4.de elaps mgm• eug j5.de falco-pe nl2• fic-m gya1 galeoc-c-h gms1• *Hell* k* hippoc-k szs2 hyos k* *Ign* hr1* kali-s fkr2.de lac-h sze9• lach limest-b es1• marb-w es1• med↓ meli br1* op mtf33 plut-n srj7• *Puls* k* sal-fr sle1• *Sanguis-s* hrn2• sil↓ spong fd4.de staph j* *Stram* k* sulph↓ tarent k* verat mtf33
  - **children**: *(↗Anger - himself; Anger - mistakes; Anger - spoken; Anger - tear; Antagonism; Anxiety - himself; Biting - himself; Confusion - arouse; Contemptuous - self; Discontented - himself; Discouraged - reproaches; Disgust - oneself; Haughty - look; Irritability - himself; Loathing - oneself; Reproaching oneself)* aur st1* bar-c mtf33 dulc fd4.de meli↓ tarent mtf33 verat mtf33
    - **mother**; behind: bar-c mrr1*
    - **run** away; and: meli ptk
    - **strangers**, from: *Bar-c* c1*
    - **visitors** laugh at them and they hide behind furniture; they think: *Bar-c* k*
  - **corner**; in: *(↗Crawling - children - howls; Playing - aversion - children - sit; Sadness - sits)* camph hr1 elaps a hyos hr1 puls hr1
  - **earth**; desire to hide in the: adam srj5•
  - **fear**, on account of: *Ars* *Bell* k* calc ckh1 cupr k* dulc fd4.de hyos kr1 sil↓ tarent↓
    - **assaulted**; of being: tarent k2*

- **himself**: ...
  - **mania**, in puerperal: *Puls* kr1
  - **old** people, in: op hr1
  - **running** away; and: meli ptk1*
- **things**: bell k* *Staph* hr1* tarent k2*

HIDING HER/HIS WEAKNESS (See Insecurity - hiding)

HIGH pitched: musca-d szs1

HIGH PLACES:
- **agg.**: (*↗Fear - High; Suicidal - Throwing - height; GENERALS - Ascending high - Agg.; VERTIGO - High - Places)* *Arg-n* k* *Aur* k* coca ptk1 gels k* puls k* staph k* *Sulph* k*
- **desire**: irid-met srj5•

HIGH-SPIRITED: (*↗Amusement - desire; Audacity; Cheerful; Courageous; Jesting; Mirth; Smiling - involuntarily - speaking; Temerity; Vivacious)* *Agath-a* nl2• carc mlr1• coca-c sk4• ephe-si hsj1• hydr k* hyos k* op spig spong ulm-c jsj8• verat verb [temp elm1]
- **children**: carc mlr1•

HILARITY (See Mirth)

HINDERED; intolerance of being: (*↗Delusions - hindered; Disturbed)* cina ↓ ferr-p a1 granit-m es1• ignis-alc es2• nauf-helv-li elm2•
- **children**; in: cina mtf33

HISTORY, awareness of: positr nl2•

HOLD (See Held; Holding)

HOLDING: | **head** | **moaning**; and vomiting when: cimic ptk1
- **mother's** hand; child constantly holding: (*↗Clinging - children - mother - hand)* *Bism* c1* kali-c al lil-t al lyc al [*Bism-sn* stj2]

HOME:
- **desires** to go: (*↗Delusions - home - away - must)* acon bg adam srj5• arge-pl rwt5• bell k* **Bry** k* *Calc* k* calc-p k* *Carb-an* a1 cassia-s ccrh1• chlol cic cimic bg clem a1 coff bg cupr *Cupr-act* kr1 eup-per a1 falco-pe nl2• galla-q-r nl2• germ-met srj granit-m es1• ham fd3.de• hell a1 hyos k* kola stb3• lac-cp sk4• *Lach* limest-b es1• lipp a1 loxo-recl knl4• mag-c a1 meli bg merc a1 nit-ac a1 *Op* plan plb a1 *Pneu* jl2 psor k2 puls a1 rhus-t ruta fd4.de sacch a1 senec a1 sil a1 spong fd4.de* stram a1 tritic-vg fd5.de valer bg verat vip [bell-p-sp dcm1 spect dfg1]
  - **go** out; and when there to: *Bry* kr1 *Calc* kr1 **Calc-p** kr1 *Cupr-act* kr1
- **leave** home; desire to: (*↗Desires - full - more; Escape)* adam ↓ elaps al elat fl-ac k2 lac-e hrn2• myos-a rly4• petr-ra shn4• phasco-ci rbp2 phos ↓ sal-fr sle1• spong fd4.de tub mtf33 vanil fd5.de [lac-mat sst4]
  - **night**; at: elat br1
  - **and** lead a clear not muddled life without her family: adam srj5•
  - **retiring**; when: elaps a
- **talks** of home: bell *Bry*

HOMEOPATHY; aversion of: (*↗Refusing - medicine)* caust pc hep pc lyc pc nit-ac pc nux-v pc sep pc

HOMESICKNESS: (*↗Change - aversion; Farewell - separation; Sentimental)* acon bg2* ant-c mtf33 *Aur* k* aur-m-n wbt2• bamb-a stb2.de• bar-c h2 *Bell* k* bit-ar wht1• bros-gau mrc1 *Bry* bg2* *Calc* fry calc-p k* **CAPS** b7.de* **Carb-an** k* carc mlk carl k* *Caust* cent k* chlol a1 chlor a1 cimic bg2* *Clem* k* *Cocc* vh* *Coff* bg2* corian-s knl6• dream-p sdj1• dros elaps elat st1 (non:eup-per a1) eup-pur k* galeoc-c-h gms1• *Galla-q-r* nl2• gard-j vlr2• ger-i rly4• germ-met srj haliae-lc srj5• *Hell* b7.de* hipp k* hyos k* **Ign** k* iris-t c1* kali-m ccrh1* *Kali-p* k* lac-cp sk4• lach k* limest-b es1• lipp a1 mag-c k* *Mag-m* b4.de* manc k* mang-p rly4• meli bg2* **Merc** k* *Nat-m* k* *Nit-ac* k* olib-sac wmh1 op bg2* orot-ac rly4• petr k* **Ph-ac** k* *Phos* st1* plan k* plb bg2* positr nl2• psor mtf33 puls k* puls-n c1* ribo rly4• ruta fd4.de sacch a1* (non:sacch-l k*) senec k* sep *Sil* k* *Staph* k* streptoc rly4• trios rsj11• valer bg2* verat k* vero-o rly4*• vult-gr sze5• *Zinc* fry* [ferr-p stj1 mag-p stj1 nat-p stj1 zinc-p stj]
- **morning**: carb-an k*
- **evening**: hipp k*
- **anguish**, with: [merc stj]
- **children**; in: bros-gau mrc1 sacch sst1•
- **fauces**; with heat: **Caps** pc
- **heat** in throat; with: **Caps** kr1*
- **house**; even in her own: [eup-pur stj]

Homesickness: ...
- **mental** derangement, in: [manc stj]
- **red** cheeks, with: *Caps* k*
- **silent** ill humor, with: mag-m h2 nit-ac *Ph-ac*
- **sleeplessness**, with: (*↗Sentimental)* **Caps** k*
- **weep**; with inclination to: galeoc-c-h gms1• [ph-ac stj]

HOMOPHOBIA (See Fear - homosexuality)

HOMOSEXUALITY (= love with one of the own sex; tribadism): (*↗Aversion - men; to [=male persons] - women; Aversion - women; Aversion - women - men; Aversion - women - men - homosexuality; Delusions - women - evil; Fear - women; Hatred - women; Marriage - unendurable; CHEST - Palpitation - woman)* *Anh* mg1.de* aur-ar vh1 calc gl1.fr• calc-p hydrog srj2• hyos gg hypoth jl *Lach* med ser* nat-m k* orig vh pegan-ha tpi1• phos k* **Plat** k1* plut-n srj7• *Puls* st* sep st* *Sulph* syph c1 thiop jl tub jl2 [merc stj2]

HONEST: (*↗Injustice; Objective; Truth; Truth - telling)* calc-sil mtf33 olib-sac wmh1 *Sep* sne **Staph** sne tritic-vg fd5.de vanil fd5.de [am-br stj calc stj heroin sdj2 nux-v stj spect dfg1 sulph stj]

HONOR:
- **sense** of honor: (*↗Moral)*
  - **no** sense of honor: (*↗Delusions - worthless)* anac gl1.fr• ars gl1.fr• hyos gl1.fr• lach gl1.fr• verat gl1.fr• [psor stj]
  - **strong** sense of honor: aur mtf33
- **wounded**; ailments from (See Ailments - honor)

HOPEFUL: (*↗Cheerful; Courageous; Optimistic)* acon k* aids nl2• alum j ambr j androc srj1• ant-t j ars j (non:aur h2) bov ↓ calc bg2 canth j carb-an j carb-v j carc ↓ caust j chin j cocc j colch j dig j falco-pe nl2• ferr-ma k* graph j hydr k* hydrc a1 hyos j hyper a1 ign j kali-c a1 ketogl-ac rly4• kola stb3• lach j lyc j *Merc* ↓ nat-m h2 nit-ac j olib-sac ↓ *Op* ↓ orot-ac rly4• phasco-ci rbp2 podo fd3.de• puls j raph a1 rhus-t j ruta fd4.de sang hr1* seneg *Staph* ↓ stram j *Sulfon* ↓ sulph bg2* **Tub** k ●* valer j vanil fd5.de verat bg2 [*Spect* dfg1 temp elm1]
- **alternating** with:
  - **despair**: acon j5.de* aids nl2• bov j5.de carc mlr1• falco-pe nl2• kali-c bg1*
  - **discouragement**: alum j5.de kali-c j5.de *Merc* gl1.fr• *Op* mtf33* *Staph* gl1.fr•
  - **sadness**: acon kali-c j5.de* raph k* *Sulfon* br1
  - **timidity**: kali-c j5.de
  - **weakness**: *Sulfon* br1
  - **weeping**: aids nl2• raph a1
- **disease**; in long-lasting: aur ckh1
- **lungs**; with complaints of: aur ptk1
- **recovery**, of: olib-sac wmh1 sang hr1*

HOPELESS (See Despair)

HORRIBLE things, sad stories affect her profoundly: (*↗Ailments - fright; Ailments - fright - movies; Anguish - horrible; Anxiety - cruelties; Cruelty - seeing; Delusions - horrible; Delusions - horrible - everything; Delusions - horses; Excitement - hearing; Fear - cruelties; Sadness - stories; Sensitive - cruelties; Sensitive - crying; Sensitive - sad; Sympathetic; Talking - unpleasant; Weeping - anecdotes)* alum gk ambr tsm1 ars gt1* *Aur* gt1* *Aur-m* gt1* *Aur-m-n* wbt2• aur-s wbt2• benz-ac k2 **CALC** b2.de* carb-v dx1* carc fb* carl km• *Caust* gt1* cench k2 *Chin* k13* **Cic** k* cimic gk* coca vnk cocc coloc ↓ *Con* st* cypra-eg sde6.de• *Falco-pe* nl2• ferr gt1* gels *Hep* gt1* ign k* **Iod** gt1* kali-bi gk *Kali-c* gk kali-p mrr1 lac-h sze9• lac-lup hrn2• *Lach* limest-b es1• *Lyc* gt1* mag-m mtf33 manc vh* marb-w es• med gk moni rfm1• nat-c *Nat-m* lmj *Nit-ac* gt1* *Nux-v* op fry ozone sde2• *Phos* gt1* plat lmj plut-n srj7• positr nl2• prot dx1 *Puls* gt1* *Ruta* fd4.de *Sep* gt1* *Sil* gt1* **Spong** fd* **Staph** h1* *Sulph* gt1* *Teucr* k* *Thuj* lmj *Vanil* fd5.de *Zinc* k* [calc-s stj mag-s stj1 tax jsj7]
- **misfortune** of others: coloc ptk1 ruta fd4.de
- **thoughts** during delivery; her: plat kr1

HORROR (See Anxiety; Fear)

HORROR MOVIES: | **love** for: stram hu3 [cench bdt]

HOUSE (= familiar surroundings):
- **in** the house; being:
  - **agg.**: plat bg2 til bg2
  - **aversion** being kept in the house: falco-pe nl2• lyc a1 phos ↓

HOUSEKEEPING: *(↗Neglecting - household)*
- **aversion** to: aster mgm• helon mgm•
- **unable** to do housekeeping; women: *(↗Neglecting - household)* cit-l kr1 falco-pe nl2• lyc vh* nux-v vh* pitu-a ft sil vh* sulph vh*

HOWLING: *(↗Barking; Lamenting; Shrieking)* *Acet-ac* a1 **Acon** b7.de* *Alum* j5.de arn bg2* ars bg2 *Aur* bg2 bell bg2* brom bg2* bufo br1* calad b7.de* camph b7.de* canth a1 caps b7.de* *Cham* b7.de* *Cic* b7.de* cina b7a.de* coff b7.de* cupr bg2 cupr-act a1 ign b7.de* ip b7.de* lyc j5.de merc j5.de morph a1 nat-m j5.de nux-v b7.de* op b7.de* *Phos* j5.de plat sne stann bg2 *Stram* b7.de* tarent a1 verat b7.de* *Verat-v* j* verb j* viol-t b7.de*
- **night**: stram a1 *Verat* k*
- **anger**; with: arn bg*

HUGGING (See Embraces)

HUMANKIND: *(↗Men)*
- **shuns** the foolishness of humankind: *(↗Aversion - persons - all - shuns; Fear - people; Hatred - humankind; Misanthropy)* **Cic** k*

HUMBLE (See Humility)

HUMILIATED; feeling: *(↗Ailments - mortification)* ara-maca sej7• *Carc* ↓ staph mtf33 [berb stu1 heroin sdj2]
- **anger**; with (See Anger - humiliated)
- **punishment**; from: carc mlr1•
- **rape**; after: *(↗sexual)* carc mlr1•
- **sexual** abuse; after: *(↗rape; Ailments - abused - sexually)* *Carc* mlr1•
  - **shame**; from: carc mlr1•

HUMILITY: *(↗Fear - disturbing; Modesty; Simple; Singing)* bry sys cupr ms kali-s fd4.de podo fd3.de• psor mrr1 ruta fd4.de symph fd3.de• [*Spect* dfg1]

HUMMING (See Talking - humming)

HUMOR (See Mood)

HUMOROUS (See Cheerful; Jesting)

HUNGRY; when: iod bg2

HUNTING: | **desire** to go hunting: nux-v mtf sulph mtf tub mtf

HUNTING for words (See Forgetful - words)

HURRIED; being: *(↗Hurry)*
- **cannot** be hurried: *(↗Slowness)* **Alum** mrr1 [spect dfg1]

HURRY (= hastiness): *(↗Abrupt; Answering - hastily; Anxiety - hurry; Busy; Excitement - hurried; Fear - hurry; Hurried; Impatience; Impetuous; Impulsive; Quick; Rash; Slowness - behindhand; Speech - hasty; Speed - desire; Thoughts - rapid; Time - quickly; Time - slowly; Touching; Touching - impelled - everything)* achy-a bnj1 *Acon* k* adam srj5• agath-a nl2• aids nl2• allox tpw4 aloe alum k* alum-p k2* am-c gl1.fr• ambr k* *Anac* b4a.de anan k* androc srj1• apis k* aq-mar ↓ *Aran-ix* mg1.de* arg-met br1* *Arg-n* k* arge-pl rwt5• arist-cl ↓ *Ars* k* *Ars-i* ars-s-f k2* asar vh atro ↓ aur k* aur-ar k2 aur-i k2 *Aur-m-n* wbt2* aur-s k2* *Bar-c* k* bar-i k2* bar-s k2* *Bell* k* benz-ac berb ↓ bit-ar ↓ bov k* bros-gau mrc1 *Bry* k* cact k* calad k* calc k* *Calc-f* mg1.de* calc-p ptk1 calc-s calc-sil k2* *Camph* k* cann-i cann-s h1* cann-xyz bg2 canth k* caps k* carb-an k* carb-v k* *Carbn-s* carc mlr1* caust hr1* cham bg3* choc ↓ cimic bg2* cina ↓ clem ↓ coca ↓ coca-c sk4• cocc *Coff* k* con k* conch fkr1• cortico ↓ *Crot-c* k* cupr ↓ cur bg2 cystein-l rly4• dendr-pol sk4• dig k* dioxi rbp6 dubo-h hs1 **Dulc** k* elaps fkr8.de ephe-si ↓ esp-g kk1.de* *Falco-pe* nl2• ferr-p ↓ fic-m gya1 *Fl-ac* mrr1 fum rly4• fuma-ac rly4• galeoc-c-h ↓ ger-i rly4• gink-b sbd1• gins ↓ *Glycyr-g* cte1• graph k* grat k* haliae-lc srj5• ham ↓ *Hell* ↓ helo-s rwt2• *Hep* k* hist shj• hydrog srj2*• hyos k* *Ign* k* ignis-alc es2• *Iod* k* ip ptk1 irid-met stj2*• kali-ar *Kali-c* k* kali-p kali-s k* ketogl-ac ↓ *Kola* stb3• kurch bnj1 lac-ac stj5• *Lac-cp* ↓ lac-e hrn2• lac-h ↓ lac-lup hrn2• *Lach* k* laur k* **Lil-t** k* lob-p c1 loxo-recl knl4• lyc lycps-v ptk1 *M-ambo* b7.de* *M-arct* b7.de* m-aust b7.de* mag-m k2 mang ↓ **Med** k* melal-alt ↓ meny k* **Merc** k* merl mez b4.de* moni rfm1• morph k* mosch k* nat-ar nat-c k* **Nat-m** k* nat-ox rly4• nat-p neon srj5• *Nit-ac* ptk1* nux-m b7.de *Nux-v* k* olib-sac wmh1 olnd ↓ onos ↓ op k* orot-ac rly4• ox-ac k* oxal-a rly4• ped ↓ petr mp1• petr-ra ↓ *Ph-ac* k* phos k*

Hurry: ...
pin-con oss2• pip-m ↓ plan ↓ plat bg2* plb bg2* plect ↓ plut-n srj7• podo ↓ polys sk4• positr nl2• prun ↓ psor gg ptel k* *Puls* k* querc-r svu1• ran-b c1 rheum ptk1 rhus-g tmo3• rhus-t j5.de* ribo rly4• sabad ↓ sacch-a fd2.de• sal-al blc1• sal-fr sle1• sep k* **Sil** gl1.fr• staph gl1.fr• *Stram* k* streptoc rly4• suis-hep rly4• **Sul-ac** k* sul-i k2* **Sulph** k* sumb k* symph fd3.de• syph ↓ **Tarent** k* thiam rly4• *Thuj* k* ulm-c ↓ urol-h rwt• valer ptk1 verat k* viol-t k* visc sp1 zinc stj2* zinc-val bro1 [alumin stj2 alumin-s stj2 am-f stj2 arg-p stj2 cinnb stj2 cob stj2 cob-m stj2 cob-p stj2 fl-pur stj2 gal-s stj2 lith-f stj2 lith-i stj2 lith-s stj2 mag-n stj2 mang-i stj2 merc-i-f stj2 moly-met stj2 mur-ac stj2 nicc-s stj2 niob-met stj2 nitro stj2 *Rhodi* stj2 spect dfg1 tax jsj7 titan-s stj2 zinc-i stj2 zinc-m stj2 zinc-n stj2 zinc-p stj2]
- **morning**: med jl2
- **afternoon**: ferr-p a1 hydrog srj2•
- **evening**: ulm-c jsj8•
- **night**: lach
- **agg.** (See Ailments - hurry)
- **ailments** from (See Ailments - hurry)
- **aimless**: *(↗Busy - fruitlessly)* *Lil-t* br1*
- **alternating** with | **tranquillity**: irid-met srj5•
- **always** in a: arg-n tl1 ars-s-f k2 dulc gl1.fr• lil-t tl1 med tl1 nux-v gl1.fr• sil gl1.fr• staph mtf33* sul-ac rb2
- **awkward** from hurry: *(↗Awkward - haste)* alum gl1.fr• ambr gl1.fr• apis sf1.de choc srj3• *Mosch* kr1* nat-m mtf33* sulph gl1.fr•
- **breath**; with short: caust kr1
- **children**; in: med jl2
- **chill**, during: cann-s k*
- **coffee**; as after: fic-m gya1
- **desire** to: *Rhus-g* tmo3•
- **drinking**, on: anac ptk1 *Ars* kr1 *Bell* b4a.de* bry kr1* cina kr1* *Coff* *Hell* kr1 *Hep* k* lyc kr1 merc ↓ *Stram* kr1* *Zinc* kr1*
  - **fever**; during: *Hep* bg2 merc bg2 stram bg2 zinc bg2
  - **unconsciousness**; during: hell ptk1
- **driving**; when: lac-h sk4• sacch-a gmj3
- **duties**; as by imperative: **Lil-t** a1 *Sacch-a* fd2.de•
- **eating**; while: anac br1* androc srj1• arg-n st* *Ars* b4a.de aur b4a.de* *Aur-s* wbt2• bell kr1* berb kr1 bros-gau mrc1 bry bro1 calad k* **Caust** k* clem bg2* coca-c sk4• *Coff* b7.de* conch fkr1• cupr b7.de* ephe-si hsj1• fl-ac mrr1 graph bg2 ham fd3.de• hell bro1 **Hep** k* kali-c st* *Lach* k* lyc h2* nux-m b7.de* olnd b7.de* petr-ra shn4• phos b4a.de pip-m k* **Plat** b4a.de* plect a1 *Rhus-t* vh* sabad b7.de* **Sul-ac** k* sulph h2* *Zinc* b4a.de*
- **everybody**:
  - **moves** too slowly: allox tpw4 ham fd3.de• irid-met srj5• *Lac-cp* sk4• med k2* positr nl2• *Tarent* vh*
  - **must** hurry: arg-n bro1 cann-i bro1 galeoc-c-h gms1• lach k2* med mtf33 nat-p k2* *Nux-m* bro1 nux-v mrr1 sul-ac mrr1 **Tarent** k* [tax jsj7]
- **fatigued**; gets: coca-c sk4•
- **headache**, during | **hot** face; with: ptel hr1
- **itching**; with | **Genitals**; of: tarent mrr1
- **menses**:
  - **before**: [alumin-s stj2 tax jsj7]
  - **during**: ign ptk1
- **mental** exertion; during: ambr aur k* calc mtf33 ign *Kali-c* k* laur op *Sul-ac* *Thuj*
- **movements**, in: acon adam srj5• arg-n ptk1 ars ars-s-f k2 atro a1 aur ↓ *Bell* k* camph k* cann-i k* coca coff k* con k* gins k* *Hyos* k* kali-c ketogl-ac rly4• melal-alt gya4 meny k* merc k* merl k* **Stram** k* **Sul-ac** k* *Sulph* **Tarent** k* *Thuj* k* viol-t k*
  - **fast** enough; cannot do things: aur **Sul-ac**
  - **involuntary** hurry in movements: **Sulph** a1
- **occupation**, in: *(↗work)* acon arist-cl rbp3• aur aur-m-n ↓ bit-ar wht1• calc-f mg* camph carb-v k* caust mrr1 cimic bg1* cortico ↓ dioxi rbp6 **Dulc** fd* hep hr1* hist shj• *Kali-c* kali-p k2* ketogl-ac rly4• kola ↓ **Lil-t** *Med* ↓ moni rfm1• nat-ox ↓ onos vml3• op k* plan ↓ plut-n srj7• positr ↓ ptel mg puls ribo rly4• sep **Sul-ac** k* *Thuj* k* viol-t [tax jsj7]
  - **desire** to do several things at once: aur aur-m-n wbt2• cortico tpw7 kola stb3• **Lil-t** k* *Med* ↓ nat-ox rly4• plan plut-n srj7• positr nl2• [tax jsj7]
  - **finish** any, but cannot: *Med* ckh1 positr nl2•
- **slow** execution; with: alum ptk1 bit-ar wht1•

- **speech** (See Speech - hasty)
- **time**; hurry to arrive at the appointed: *(↗Ailments - anticipation; Anticipation)* aids nl2• aq-mar rbp6 **Arg-n** k* med mtf33 sul-ac dgt ulm-c jsj8•
- **trifles**; about: med ptk1* sul-ac ptk1 sulph ptk1*
- **walking**, while: *(↗Ailments - Anticipation; Anxiety - Walking - rapidly - makes; GENERALS - Walking - Rapidly - amel.)* acon alum ptk1 **Arg-n** k* canth carb-an h2* dendr-pol sk4• fl-ac bg2 hist shj• iod k* mang bg2* mosch prun sep bg2 stram **Sul-ac** k* sul-i k2* *Sulph* k* syph ptk1 **TARENT** k* *Thuj* k*
- **walks** to and fro, cannot be amused by thinking or reading: lil-t hr1*
- **work**, in: *(↗occupation)* aloe ↓ calc-f mg1.de* caust mrr1 cimic a1 op a1 petr-ra shn4• ribo rly4• sacch-a fd2.de• sep gl1.fr• sul-ac k2 sul-i k2 symph fd3.de• *Tarent* mrr1
  - **afternoon**: aloe a1
- **writing**, in: alum j coca a1 falco-pe ↓ ign mtf33* lyc j ped a1 podo fd3.de• ptel k* **Sul-ac** k*
  - **calm**, while feeling: falco-pe nl2•

HURT; easily:

- **mentally** hurt (See Insecurity; Offended; Sensitive - mental; Sensitive - moral)
- **physically** hurt; as if going to be (See Delusions - injury - about)

HURTING oneself (See Injuring)

HURTING other people's feelings (See Malicious - hurting)

HUSBAND; aversion to (See Aversion - husband)

HYDROPHOBIA (= rabies): *(↗Delusions - water - spoonful; Excitement - water; Fear - noise - rushing; Fear - water; Irritability - water; Rage - water; Sensitive - noise - water; Shining - surface; GENERALS - Bathing - aversion; GENERALS - Water - seeing)* acet-ac k* acon a1 aconin a1* agar ld* agav-a c1* anag br1 anan c1* ant-c bg2* anthraci al apis bg2 arg-n k* ars k* *Aspar* hr1* **Bell** k* brom mtf33 calc k* camph bg2 cann-i k* **Canth** k* cedr c1* ceto br1 chlol k* chlor kr1 cocc-s c1* crot-h k* *Cupr* k* *Cur* k* fagu c1* gels bg2 gent-c c1 gua c1* *Hydr-ac* bg2* **Hyos** k* hyper c1* iod k* jatr-c bg2 **Lach** k* laur bg2* lys bg2 **LYSS** c2* merc k* nux-v bg2 phel k* **Phos** k* plb bg2 ran-s k* ruta b2.de* *Sabad* k* scut c1* spirae c1* **Stram** k* stry a1 strych-g c1* sulph bg2* tann-ac c1 tarent bg2 ter k* trach a1 verat k* (non:xan)

- **bright** objects agg.: cocc-s br1
- **contact** renews paroxysm: *Bell* kr1
- **delirium**; with: stram tl1
- **hear** the word "water" without shudder of fear; cannot: *Lyss* kr1
- **prophylaxis** of: *Bell* tl1* canth bro1* hyos bro1* *Lyss* ptk1 stram bro1*
- **screams** or howls in a high voice: *Stram* hr1*
- **thought** of water causes paroxysm: lyss kr1

HYPERACTIVE CHILDREN (See GENERALS - Energy - excess - children)

HYPOCHONDRIASIS: *(↗Alcoholism - hypochondriasis; Anxiety - health; Anxiety - health - own; Anxiety - hypochondriacal; Delusions - disease - every; Delusions - sick; Despair - health; Doubtful - recovery; Fear - health - ruined; Feigning - sick; Lamenting - sickness; Sensitive - complaints; Thinking - complaints - agg.)* abies-n c1* acon bg2 aesc ↓ agn b7.de* alf bro1 aloe bg2* alum bg2* am-c ↓ *Ambr* bg2* *Anac* b4.de* anag kr1* anan kr1 *Ant-t* kr1 arg-met jl *Arg-n* bg2* arn b7.de* **Ars** b4.de* arum-m kr1 *Asaf* b7a.de* **Aur** b4.de* aur-m bro1 aur-s j aven bro1 aza jl3 bamb-a stb2.de• bell b4.de* **Benz-ac** kr1 bism bg2* both fne1• bran j brom bg2* bry bg2 **Cact** kr1* *Calc* b4.de* *Cann-s* b7a.de canth b7.de* *Caps* bg2* card-m ptk1 caust b4a.de* *Cham* b7.de* chin b7a.de* chion br1 *Cimic* c1* coca bro1 *Cocc* b7.de* coff j5.de* **Con** b4.de* croc b7.de* cupr bg2 cur ↓ *Cycl* b7.de* dig b4.de* esp-g jl3 euphr b7.de* ferr bg2* ferr-p k2 gels bg2 gran j5.de *Graph* j5.de* *Grat* kr1* hell b7.de* helon bro1 *Hep* b4.de* hera j5.de hydr-ac bro1 *Hyos* kr1* **Ign** j5.de* *Iod* b4.de* *Ip* kr1 kali-br bro1 kali-c bg2 kali-chl j5.de* *Kali-p* bg2* kreos ↓ *Lach* bg2 lath br1 *Lyc* j5.de* lycps-v c1 lyss ↓ m-arct ↓ mag-c mg1.de **Mag-m** b4.de* malar jl2 merc b4.de* merc-d bg2* **Mez** b4.de* *Mill* kr1* mosch b7.de* naja mrr1 **Nat-c** b4.de* **Nat-m** j5.de* nep mg1.de* **Nit-ac** j5.de* nux-m b7.de* **Nux-v** b7.de* *Ol-an* j5.de* op bg2 *Petr* b4.de* *Ph-ac* b4a.de* *Phos* b4.de* plat b4a.de* plb b7.de* pneu jl2 podo bg2* **Puls** b7.de* rhus-t bg2 sabad bg2* sabin b7.de* *Sel* bg2* seneg b4.de* *Sep* b4a.de* sil ↓

Hypochondriasis: ...
sin-n kr1 *Spong* b7.de* *Stann* b4.de* *Staph* b7.de* stram bg2 sul-ac bg2 *Sulph* b4a.de* sumb bro1 **Syph** vh* tab bg2* tarent bro1 *Ter* kr1* thuj bro1 tub jl2* v-a-b jl3* *Valer* b7.de* verat b7.de* vib-t c1* *Viol-o* b7.de* *Zinc* b4.de* zinc-o c1* zinc-val c1* *Zing* kr1 ziz c1* [mag-n stj2]

- **daytime**:
  - **alternating** with:
    - **cheerfulness** in the evening (See Cheerful - evening - alternating - hypochondriasis - daytime)
    - **irritability** (See Irritability - alternating - hypochondriasis - daytime)
    - **merriness** in the evening (See Cheerful - evening - alternating - hypochondriasis - daytime)
- **morning**: alum j5.de anac kr1 lyc j5.de
- **forenoon**: nux-m j5.de
- **afternoon**: cocc j5.de graph j5.de zinc j5.de
- **evening**: kreos j5.de lyss kr1 nux-v j5.de phos j5.de puls j5.de
- **night**: alum j5.de calc j5.de lach j5.de m-arct j5.de nat-m j5.de
- **abdomen**; with complaints of: calc bg2 cham bg2 **Nux-v** bg2 stann bg2 staph bg2 sulph bg2
- **air**; in open: *Con* j5.de petr j5.de
- **alone**, when: ars j5.de
- **drunkards**, in: *Nux-v* kr1
- **eating**, after: anac b4a.de* chin kr1 *Nat-c* b4a.de* *Nux-v* b7a.de* sulph b4a.de zinc b4a.de*
- **epistaxis** amel.: kali-chl sf1.de
- **eruption**; after suppression of: **Sulph** kr1
- **fear** of death; with: nit-ac mrr1
- **fever**, during: nux-m j5.de
- **gastrointestinal** complaints; with: *Nux-v* br1
- **head**; with complaints of: *Nux-v* bg2 staph bg2
- **hemorrhoids**; with: aesc bro1 grat bro1 *Nux-v* bro1
- **insult**; from: staph kr
- **interest** in his surroundings; takes no: *(↗Indifference - surroundings)* euphr kr1
- **masturbation**, after: *Tarent* kr1
- **menses**:
  - **during**: *(↗Menses - during)* cur kr1
  - **suppression** of: *Con* k*
- **morose**: *(↗Morose - hypochondriasis)* con j5.de graph j5.de grat j5.de m-arct j5.de petr j5.de phos j5.de **Puls** j5.de* sabin j5.de sulph j5.de
- **pollutions**, after: anac bg2 sil bg2 staph bg2
- **sexual**: anac ↓ calc ↓ chin ↓ **Con** ↓ mosch br1* nat-m ↓ nux-v ↓ *Ph-ac* ↓ sep ↓ **Staph** ↓ sulph ↓
  - **abstinence**, from: **Con** kr1 mosch kr1
  - **excesses**, from: anac j calc j chin j **Con** kr1* nat-m j nux-v j *Ph-ac* kr1* sep j **Staph** kr1* sulph j
- **stomach**; with complaints of: calc bg2 *Cocc* bg2 grat bg2 ign bg2 mag-c bg2 *Nat-c* bg2 **Nux-v** bg2 stann bg2
- **stool**; about: aloe vh1
- **suicide**; driving to: alum gl1.fr• aur gl1.fr• calc gl1.fr• caust gl1.fr• chin gl1.fr• con gl1.fr• graph gl1.fr• hep j5.de *Nat-m* gl1.fr• sep gl1.fr• **Staph** gl1.fr• sulph gl1.fr•
- **vertigo**; with: phos bg2
- **waking**, on: *Alum* j5.de lyc j5.de
- **weeping**, with: am-c j5.de calc j5.de kali-c j5.de mez kr1 plat j5.de *Puls* j5.de* stram j5.de viol-o j5.de

HYPOCRISY: *(↗Contradiction - disposition; Deceitful; Delusions - lie; Delusions - lie; all; Dishonest; Liar; Liar - lies; Manipulative; Slander; Untruthful)* bar-c gl1.fr• caust vh* **Lyc** ●* marb-w es1• merc vh* nux-v vh* phos k* *Puls* ●* sep vh* *Sil* vh* *Sulph* vh*

HYSTERIA: *(↗Anxiety - hysterical; Cheerful - hysterical; Delirium - hysterical; Laughing - hysterical; RESPIRATION - Asthmatic - hysterical)* abies-n vh1 abrot k* absin k* *Acet-ac* *Acon* k* aether a1 *Agar* agath-a nl2• agn k* aloe c2* *Alum* bro1 alum-sil k2* am-c k* am-val br1* ambr k* aml-ns c1* *Anac* k* anag c1* androc ↓ ang vh anh br1* ant-c k2* antip vh1 apis k* aqui c1* aran ↓ arg-met k2* *Arg-n* k* arn bg2 *Ars* k* ars-s-f k2* *Art-v* hr1* arund k* **Asaf** k* asar k* asc-c hr1* asc-t hr1* aster k* atra-r bnm3• **Aur** k* aur-ar k2 aur-i k2* aur-m-n wbt2• aur-s k2* bad ↓ bapt c1*

Hysteria: ...
Bar-c bar-i k2* bar-s k2 bell k* benz-ac borx k2 bov↓ brom k* bry k* bufo bg2 *Cact* k* *Caj* hr1* calad k2* *Calc* k* *Calc-s* calc-sil k2* *Camph* k* camph-br c1* camph-mbr bro1 cann-i bro1 cann-s k* *Canth* k* caps↓ carb-an↓ carb-v↓ *Carbn-s* *Carc* mlr1• *Castm* kr1* catar br1 *Caul* k* **Caust** k* cedr k* *Cham* k* chel↓ *Chen-a* chim hr1* chin b7a.de* chinin-s *Chlf* hr1* *Chlol* k* chlor kr1 cic k* *Cimic* k* *Cinnm* hr1* cob bro1 *Coca* kr1 **Cocc** k* *Coff* k* *Coff-t* hr1* **Con** k* conv br1 convo-s sp1 cop k* cor-r k* cot c1* *Croc* k* crot-h hr1* crot-t cupr c1* cycl↓ cypr des-ac↓ *Dig*↓ *Diosm* br1 *Elaps* elec c1* *Eup-a* br1* eup-pur k* euphr↓ *Ferr* k* ferr-ar ferr-i ferr-p **Gels** k* *Graph* k* *Grat* k* haliae-lc srj5• hell k2* heln-ov bta1• helon mrr1 hep↓ hura c1* *Hydr-ac* hr1* *Hyos* k* hyper k2 *Ictod* kr1* **Ign** k* *Indg* j5.de* iod k* ip k* kali-ar kali-br mrr1 *Kali-c* k* kali-i↓ **Kali-p** k* kali-s kali-sil k2* *Lac-ac* hr1* lac-c k2* lac-d↓ **Lach** k* lact lact-v c2 lat-h thj1* *Lil-t* k* lob c1* *Lyc* k* m-arct↓ mag-c k2* **Mag-m** k* *Manc* mrr1 mand a1* (non:mang) mang-act bro1 melis lsr4.de• meny↓ *Merc* k* mez bg2 *Mill* k* moni rfm1• morph k* **Mosch** k* mygal k* narc-ps ah1* nat-ar *Nat-c* k* nat-hchls c1* **Nat-m** k* nat-p nat-s k2* nat-sil k2* **Nit-ac** k* nitro-o c1* **Nux-m** k* **Nux-v** k* ol-an j5.de* op k* orig hr1* *Pall* k* par c1* passi br1 petr↓ *Ph-ac* k* *Phos* k* phys c1* physala-p bnm7• **Plat** k* *Plb* k* polyg-h kr1* polyg-xyz c2 prot jl2* pseuts-m oss1• psoral-p bta1• **Puls** k* pyrus c1* *Raph* k* rheum↓ *Rhus-t* *Ruta* b7a.de* sabad k2 sabin k* sacch c1 sacch-l c1* sal-n br1 samb↓ sang sars↓ scut c1* *Sec* k* *Sel* b7a.de senec k* seneg↓ **Sep** k* **Sil** k* spartin-s bwa2 spig↓ spira c1* spong↓ stann k* staph k* stapl-g bta1• *Stict* k* stram k* stront-c↓ stry-p br1* succ br1 succ-xyz c1* sul-ac bg2 sul-i k2* *Sulph* k* sumb k* tab↓ **Tarent** k* ter↓ thal jl3 *Ther* k* thuj bg2 thyr c1* *Tub* st1 ust **Valer** k* vanad br1 **Verat** k* vib hr1* *Viol-o* k* viol-t↓ visc sp1 xan c1* zinc k* zinc-cy c1* *Zinc-val* br1* *Ziz* c1* [am-f stj2 arg-p stj2 cupr-act stj2 cupr-f stj2 cupr-m stj2 cupr-p stj2 lith-c stj2 lith-f stj2 lith-met stj2 lith-p stj2 merc-i-f stj2 thal-met stj2 zinc-i stj2 zinc-m stj2 zinc-n stj2 zinc-p stj2 zirc-met stj2]

- **evening**: aether a1 androc srj1• kali-s k2*
  - **18 h**: androc srj1•
- **night**: *Senec* hr1*
- **alternating** with | **anger** (See Anger - alternating - hysteria)
- **amenorrhea**, in: *Xan* kr1
- **attacks**, in: absin a1 carbn-s a1
- **changing** symptoms: carc mlr1• **Puls** hr1*
- **children**; in:
  - **girls**: | **love**; from disappointed: ant-c mtf33
- **chlorosis**; with: tarent br1
- **coition**:
  - **agg.**: lac-c ptk1
  - **amel.**: con sf1.de
- **contradiction**: | **agg.**: prot fmm1•
- **deep** scrofulous constitution, psora or syphilis; in: asaf k1
- **delivery**; during: caul mrr1
- **discharges**; after suppression of: **Asaf** k* *Lach* k*
- **enuresis**; with: ign bro1 valer bro1
- **excessive** irritation of genitals; from: orig hr1*
- **fainting**, hysterical: (↗*GENERALS - Faintness - hysterical*) am-c st1* arn kr1* ars *Cham* cimic **Cocc** k* *Dig* kr1* **Ign** k* lac-d *Mosch* k* *Nat-m* *Nux-m* *Nux-v* puls samb stict kr1 *Sumb* kr1 ter
- **fever**; with intermittent: aran bro1 cocc bro1 ign bro1 tarent bro1
- **fright**: | **after**: sabad ptk1
- **globus** hystericus (See THROAT - Lump)
- **grief**, from: bar-s k2* *Gels* hr1* *Ign* hr1*
- **hemorrhage**:
  - **after**: stict ptk1
  - **with**: bad bro1 croc bro1* hyos bro1 ign bro1 kali-i bro1 merc bro1 stict bro1 sulph bro1
- **hypochondriasis**; with: acon b2.de* agn b2.de* alum b2.de* am-c b2.de* ambr b2.de* *Anac* b2.de* arn b2.de* ars b2.de* *Asaf* b2.de* asar b2.de* **Aur** b2.de* bar-c b2.de* *Bell* b2.de* bov b2.de* bry b2.de* calc b2.de* cann-s b2.de* canth b2.de* caps b2.de* carb-an b2.de* carb-v b2.de* *Caust* b2.de* cham b2.de* chel b2.de* chin b2.de* cic b2.de* cocc b2.de* *Coff* b2.de* **Con** b2.de* croc b2.de* cycl b2.de* dig b2.de* euphr b2.de* ferr b2.de* graph b2.de* hell b2.de* hep b2.de* hyos b2.de* *Ign* b2.de* *Iod* b2.de* ip b2.de* kali-c b2.de* lach b2.de* *Lyc* b2.de* m-arct b2.de mag-c b2.de *Mag-m* b2.de* meny b2.de* merc b2.de* mez b2.de* *Mosch* b2.de* **Nat-c** b2.de* *Nat-m* b2.de* nit-ac b2.de* *Nux-m* b2.de* **Nux-v** b2.de* op b2.de* petr bg2 ph-ac b2.de* *Phos* b2.de* **Plat** b2.de* plb b2.de* *Puls* b2.de* rheum b2.de* rhus-t b2.de* ruta b2.de* *Sabin* b2.de* sars b2.de* sel b2.de*
- **hypochondriasis**; with: ... seneg b2.de* *Sep* b2.de* sil b2.de* spig b2.de* spong b2.de* *Stann* b2.de* *Staph* b2.de* stram b2.de* stront-c b2.de* sul-ac b2.de* sulph b2.de* tab bg2 **Valer** b2.de* *Verat* b2.de* viol-o b2.de* viol-t b2.de* zinc b2.de*
- **injure** herself; desire to: (↗*Injuring*) *Hydr-ac* kr1 kali-s fd4.de
- **injury**: | **Coccyx**; of the: hyper k2
- **intestinal** complaints; with: asaf mrr1
- **lascivious**: (↗*Lascivious; Lewdness; Naked; Nymphomania; Obscene; Shameless*) agn hr1* mosch *Plat* k* *Tarent* k*
- **lie** down, must: *Stict* hr1* ther hr1*
- **light** and noise agg.: *Stict* hr1*
- **looked** at; when: (↗*Looked - cannot*) plb ptk1
- **loss** of:
  - **blood**; after: *Stict* kr1*
  - **fluids**; after: *Chin* kr1 *Cinnm* kr1
- **ludicrous**: *Tarent* a1*
- **man**, in a: carc mlr1• croc c1 mosch a1*
- **menopause**; at: cimic sf1.de ign bro1 *Lach* kr1 *Ph-ac* kr1* ther kr1* valer bro1 zinc-val bro1
- **menses**:
  - **after**: (↗*Menses - after*) ferr bro1 *Mag-m*↓ **Nux-m**↓ nux-v↓
    - **copious**: *Mag-m* kr1 (non:nux-v hr1)
    - **scanty**: **Nux-m** kr1
  - **before**: (↗*Menses - before*) caul bro1 *Cimic* kr1* cocc con elaps gels bro1 *Hyos* k* ign b7.de* *Mag-m* bro1 *Mosch* k* nux-m nux-v bro1 *Plat* k* puls bro1 senec bro1 vib bro1
  - **during**: (↗*Menses - during*) cact c1 caul bro1* caust hr1* *Cimic* k* cocc bg* gels bro1 ign bro1* mag-m bro1* mosch sf1.de **Nux-m** hr1* nux-v bro1 plat bro1 puls bro1 raph↓ sec k2 senec bro1 stram hr1* verat hr1* vib bro1
    - **amel.**: *Zinc*
    - **first** day of: raph k*
  - **suppressed** menses; from: hell b7a.de
- **metrorrhagia**; with: caul bro1 cimic bro1 mag-m bro1
- **moaning** agg. and sighing amel.: tarent k1*
- **moon** | **increasing** agg.: *Sulph* kr1
- **move** any part of body; cannot: ter kr1
- **music** amel.: (↗*Music - amel.*) **Tarent** k*
- **orgasm**; at the height of: lac-c ptk1
- **pain**; from: des-ac rbp6
- **plethoric** subjects, in: (↗*GENERALS - Plethora - constitution*) *Acon* hr1* *Gels* hr1*
- **pollutions**, after: anac bg2 sil bg2 staph bg2
- **pregnancy** and delivery; during: *Chlol* c1* **Gels** hr1*
- **puberty**, at: ant-c kr1* *Lach* hr1* *Ther* hr1*
- **respiration**; with complaints of: *Acon* bg2 asaf bg2 aur bg2 *Bell* bg2 caust bg2 cham bg2 *Coff* bg2 con bg2 cupr bg2 **Ign** bg2 ip bg2 lach bg2 **Mosch** bg2 *Nux-m* bg2 **Nux-v** bg2 phos bg2 *Puls* bg2 stann bg2 *Stram* bg2 sulph bg2
- **salivation**; with: merc kr1*
- **sexual**:
  - **excesses**, after: (↗*Ailments - sexual excesses*) agar anac con lach *Ph-ac* k* sep *Staph* vh*
  - **excitement**; from suppression of sexual: *Brom* vh* **Con** kr1*
- **sleep**; with disturbed: carc mlr1•
- **sleeplessness**, with: carc mlr1• croc sf1.de *Kali-br* hr1* mosch hr1* *Senec* hr1* *Stict* hr1*
- **spasms**; with:
  - O **Back**; of: cimic mrr1
  - **Cervical** region; of: cimic mrr1
- **stomach**; with complaints of: calc bg2 *Cocc* bg2 grat bg2 **Ign** bg2 mag-c bg2 nux-v bg2 stann bg2
- **teeth**; with pain in: **Ign** bg2 sep bg2
- **tongue**:
  - **stiffness**: sep kr1*
  - **white** discoloration of the tongue; with: *Lyc* kr1*
- **touch** and pressure; intolerance of: *Tarent* kr1
- **tuberculous** patients; in: viol-o br1
- **uterus**:
  - **complaints** of the; with: cimic tl1 helon mrr1

- **prolapse** of the; with: helon mrr1

IDEAL; sensation as if everything is (See Content)

IDEALISTIC: *(↗Injustice)* aq-pet mtf11 **Caust** mrr1 *Chin* mrr1 *Ign* mtf ignis-alc es2• lyc mtf *Plat* mtf

IDEAS: *(↗Thoughts)*

- **abundant**: *(↗Activity - desires - creative; Agility; Clarity; Concentration - active; Fancies - vivid; Memory - active; Mental exertion - desire; Mental exertion - wine; Mental power - increased; New ideas; Plans - making; Quick; Reason increased; Theorizing; Thoughts - profound; Thoughts - rapid; Thoughts - thoughtful; Witty)* acon *Adam* srj5• aesc aether a1 agar agath-a ↓ aloe ↓ alum alum-p k2 am-c am-f ↓ ambr aml-ns kr1 anac anag kr1 ang anh mg1.de* ant-c kr1 aq-mar rbp6 arg-met kr1* arg-n k* *Ars* ars-s-f kr1 ars-s-r kr1 asaf j5.de asar aster ↓ aur aur-ar k2 aur-s k2 *Bar-c* b4.de *Bell* borx *Bry* bufo gk caj *Calc* k* calc-f jl3 calc-p calc-sil ↓ camph gl1.fr• cann-i cann-s canth carb-ac a1* carb-v a1 carbn-s carc ↓ cartl-s rly4• caust k* cham **Chin** k* chinin-ar *Chinin-s* chlor kr1 choc srj3• cimic *Cinnb* kr1 cob k* coc-c coca cocc j **Coff** k* *Coff-t* kr1* colch coloc con j cypr vml3• cypra-eg sde6.de• der dream-p sdj1• eupi falco-pe nl2• ferr-p k* flor-p jl3 gels germ-met srj5• glon k* graph haliae-lc srj5• ham ↓ hell hep hyos hyper kr1 ign ignis-alc es2• iod sne irid-met srj5• kali-br a1 kali-c kali-n kali-p kr1 kali-s kola stb3• kreos a1 lac-ac a1 **Lach** lat-h thj1 laur led ↓ *Lyc* k* lycps-v ↓ lyss m-arct j med ptk1* melal-alt gya4 menth a1 mentho a1 meph sf1.de merc mez mim-p rsj8• morph mur-ac nat-ar nat-c nat-p nat-sil fd3.de• neon srj5• nit-ac k* *Nux-m* kr1 *Nux-v* *Olib-sac* wmh1 olnd **Op** k1* opun-v a1 ox-ac ↓ ozone sde2• pall bg2 ph-ac **Phos** phys kr1 pic-ac *Pip-m* a1* plat k* *Podo* fd3.de• positr nl2• *Puls* querc-r svu1• rhus-t sabad sacch-a fd2.de• sal-fr sle1• sep sil spig spong staph stram *Stry* *Sulph* k* sumb symph fd3.de• tab ter thea thuj *Thymul* ↓ *Tub* *Tung-met* bdx1• ulm-c ↓ v-a-b jl valer verat k* verb viol-o viol-t zinc k* zing kr1 [arg-p stj2 cob-m stj2 cob-p stj2 heroin sdj2 sol-ecl cky1 *Spect* dfg1]
  - **morning**:
    - **restless** sleep; after: carc fd2.de• ham a1 olib-sac wmh1
    - **rising**; after: *Thymul* sa3•
  - **forenoon**: ham fd3.de• olib-sac wmh1 ox-ac
  - **afternoon** | **13**-14 h: germ-met srj5•
  - **evening**: *(↗Plans - making - evening)* agar ↓ anac arg-n bry ↓ *Calc* ↓ caust ↓ **Chin** k* cocc ↓ *Coff* graph ↓ kali-c ↓ kali-p fd1.de• **Lach** lyc lycps-v kr1 nat-p nat-sil fd3.de• *Nux-v* olib-sac wmh1 phos *Puls* rhus-t ↓ sabad sil *Staph* sulph ↓ *Sumb* symph fd3.de• *Valer* viol-t
    - **bed**, in: agar bry *Calc* caust chin k* cocc graph kali-c *Lyc* **Nux-v** *Puls* rhus-t sil sulph symph fd3.de•
  - **night**: *(↗Plans - making - night)* aloe borx *Calc* calc-sil k2 *Cham* kr1 *Chin* k* chinin-ar *Chinin-s* coca cocc j *Coff* colch graph hep kali-c *Lyc* *Nux-v* olib-sac wmh1 *Op* pic-ac puls sabad sep sil *Staph* sulph tab ulm-c ↓ viol-t
    - **bed**; in: *Chin* mrr1
    - **sleep**; before: ulm-c jsj8•
  - **alternating** with:
    - **deficiency** of ideas (See dullness)
    - **dullness**: agath-a nl2• alum-p k2 cann-i a1 colch rsj2*
    - **lassitude**: choc srj3• olib-sac wmh1
  - **chill**, during: phys k* spig k*
  - **closing** the eyes, on: led spong
  - **communicate** them; and ability to: falco-pe nl2• med jl2
  - **headache**, after: aster hr1*
  - **heat**, during: bell bg2 coff bg2 lach bg2 op bg2* stram k* thuj b4.de*
  - **perspiration**, during: valer viol-o
  - **uncertain** in execution; but: *(↗Irresolution)* med ptk1* [am-f stj2 graph stj2]
  - **urination**, after: cann-i
  - **weakness**; with: mur-ac k2
- **deficiency** of: *(↗Concentration - difficult; Dullness; Ennui; Memory - weakness; Prostration; Slowness; Thinking - aversion; Thoughts - vanishing)* acet-ac k* *Acon* k* *Aeth* br1 agn k* all-s hr1* alum k* alum-p k2 alum-sil k2* *Am-c* k* ambr b7.de* *Anac* k* ang bg2 anh mg1.de apis b7a.de arg-met sf1.de arg-n am bg2* arund a1* asaf asar k* aster jl atro k* aur k* bamb-a stb2.de• bar-c k* bell k* borx b4a.de bov k* brom a1 bry b7.de* caj k* calc k* *Calc-p* k* calc-sil k2 camph k* cann-s k* canth k* caps j *Carb-v* k* carc jl2 *Caust* k* cham k* *Chin* k* chlf a1 cic k* clem k* cocc coff colch ↓ *Con* b4a.de* corn k* cot a1 croc cupr k* cycl k* dig k* dulc fd4.de glon k* graph gl1.fr• guaj k* **Hell** k* hep bg2 *Hyos* k* iber a1 ictod j ign k* iod ip k* *Kali-br* k* kali-p ↓ kreos *Lach* k* laur k* lepi lil-t k* **Lyc** k* *Lycps-v* ↓ m-arct j5.de m-aust b7.de meny k* *Merc* k* merc-c k* *Mez* k* mit a1 mosch j myric a1 nat-c k* *Nat-m* k* nat-p *Nit-ac* k* nitro-o a1 *Nux-m* k* nux-v gl1.fr• olnd k* **Op** k* petr k* **Ph-ac** k* **Phos** k* plat b4.de* *Plb* k* ran-b c1 ran-s b7.de* rheum st rhod bg2 rhus-t k* ruta bg2 sal-p a1 *Sel* b7.de* sep k* ser-a-c jl2 sil k* spig bg2 stann b4.de* **Staph** k* stram b7.de* sulph k* tab a1 *Tarent* k* thuj k* trif-p a1 trom hr1* upa a1 valer k* vanil fd5.de verat k* xan c1 *Zinc* k* [spect dfg1]
  - **daytime**: calc-sil k2*
  - **alternating** with | **clearness** of mind (See abundant - alternating - dullness)
  - **brain** fag, in: kali-p fd1.de• *Ph-ac* hr1*
  - **child**: carc jl2
  - **interruption**, from any: *(↗Disturbed; Thoughts - vanishing - interrupted)* colch k*
  - **menses**, during: *(↗Menses - during)* *Lycps-v* kr1
  - **overexertion**, from: kali-p fd1.de• *Mez* kr1 olnd
  - **vomiting** amel.: asar k*
- **fixed** ideas (See Thoughts - persistent)
- **insane**, ridiculous (See Thoughts - insane)
- **new** (See New ideas)
- **unconnected**: alum bg2 am-c bg2 gels c1 med jl2 nat-c bg2 ph-ac bg2 sacch-a fd2.de• sulph bg2 zinc b4a.de*

IDIOCY: *(↗Biting; Cretinism; Imbecility; Retardation; FACE - Expression - idiotic)* absin k* *Aeth* k* agar k* alum bg2* anac k* anan k* ant-c k* antip vh1 apis gl1.fr• ars bg2* bac c1* *Bar-c* k* *Bar-m* k* bell k* bell-p st1 *Borx* ↓ bufo k* *Calc-p* k* caps carbn-o a1 *Carbn-s* carc gk6* caust ↓ cent k* cham chlol k* cic k* *Hell* k* helo c1 helo-s rwt2• hyos k* kali-br a1 *Lac-c* ↓ lach bg2* lyc bg2* med mtf33 merc k* mez a1 mosch bg2* nux-m k* oena ↓ olnd bg2* op gl1.fr• orig ↓ ph-ac sf1.de *Phos* k* plb k* sanic bg sarr k* sars sec bg2* stram bg2* stry ↓ sulph bg2* tab k* thuj bg2* thyr c1* *Tub* k* verat bg2* [zinc stj2 zinc-m stj2 zinc-n stj2 zinc-p stj2]

- **alternating** with:
  - **excitement** (See Excitement - alternating - idiocy)
  - **furor** (See Excitement - alternating - idiocy)
  - **irritability**: aeth br1
- **bite**; desire to: *(↗Biting)* **Bell** st1 **Stram** st1
- **children**; in: aeth tl1 calc-p mtf33 carc jl2
- **convulsions**; with: oena mrr1
- **cretinism**: carc mlr1•
- **giggling**: stry a1
- **idiotic** actions: ant-c k* caust ↓
  - **epilepsy**; before: caust
- **masturbation**; after: bufo st med st* orig hr1*
- **pulling** feathers out of bed: ant-c h2*
- **shrill** shrieking, with: *Borx* st *Lac-c* st1 *Tub* st1

IDLENESS: *(↗Chaotic; Laziness)* tritic-vg fd5.de vanil fd5.de

- **agg.**: *(↗Excitement - amel.)* tarax b7.de* verat b7.de*
- **sadness**; with (See Sadness - idleness)

ILL feeling (See Delusions - sick - being)

ILL HUMOR (See Irritability; Morose)

IMAGINARY disease (See Delusions - sick - being)

IMAGINATIONS (See Delusions)

IMBECILITY: *(↗Idiocy; Laughing - imbecility; Memory - loss - imbecility; Mischievous - imbecility; Retardation)* acon agar k* agn bg2 alco a1 **Aloe** *Alum* k* alum-p k2 alum-sil k2* *Am-c* **Ambr** k* **Anac** k* anac-oc c1* anil a1* ant-c k* ant-t k* apis arg-met c1* *Arg-n* k* *Ars* k* ars-s-f k2 art-v asar k* *Aur* k* aur-ar k2 aur-s k2* *Bapt* bg2* **Bar-c** k* **Bar-m** bar-s k2* **Bell** k* bov k* brom sf1.de* **Bufo** k* **Bufo-s** calad k2 *Calc* k* calc-p k* calc-s calc-sil k2* camph *Cann-s* k* *Caps* k* carb-an carb-v k* carbn-o a1 **Carbn-s** carc fb* *Caust* k* cham k* *Chel* chin chlol k* chlor a1 *Cocc* k* **Con** k* croc k* *Crot-h* cupr k* cycl k* dig k* *Dios* dulc k* *Fl-ac* *Hell* k* *Hep* ↓ **Hyos** k* *Ign* k* kali-bi a1 *Kali-br* k* kali-c kali-chl k13 kali-m k2 *Kali-p* kali-sil k2* **Lach** k* *Laur* k*

Imbecility: ...
loxo-recl ↓ **Lyc** k* mang j5.de *Med* meli *Merc* k* *Merc-c* k* mez k* mosch k* mur-ac k* nat-ar *Nat-c* k* nat-i sf1.de *Nat-m* k* *Nat-p* nat-sil k2* nit-ac **Nux-m** k* **Nux-v** k* olnd k* **Op** k* *Oxyt* *Par* k* *Petr* k* **Ph-ac** k* *Phos* k* **Pic-ac** k* *Plat* *Plb* k* *Puls* k* ran-b k* rheum k* *Rhus-t* k* ruta k* *Sabad* k* *Sabin* sars k2 sec k* sel k* seneg k* *Sep* k* **Sil** k* sol-ni j5.de *Spig* k* spong k* stann k* *Staph* k* **Stram** k* stry a1 sul-ac k* **Sulph** k* *Syph* k2* tax a1 *Ther* thuj tub mrr1 **Verat** k* verb k* viol-o zinc zinc-p k2* [am-br stj2 bar-br stj2 bar-i stj2 iod stj2 merc-i-f stj2]

- **aphasia**, with: *Anac-oc* kr1
- **epilepsy**; before: *Caust*
- **laughing** for no reason: hyos dmk1*• stram gl1.fr•
- **negativism**: (↗*Answering - monosyllables - no)* hell st1 ign st1 loxo-recl bnm10•
- **old** rags are as fine as silk: **Sulph** k*
- **rage**, stamps the feet: anac st lyc st nux-v st op st verat st
- **sexual** excitement, with: *Bell* st1 *Hep* st1 *Hyos* st1 *Phos* st1 *Staph* st1 *Stram* st1
- **shrieks** when occupying with him: *Hell* st1 *Ign* st1

IMITATION, mimicry: *(↗Delusions - man - does; Delusions - people - beside - doing; Delusions - reading - after)* aur-m-n wbt2• bell bg2 cupr bg2* dulc ↓ haliae-lc srj* hyos bg2 lach ptk1* *Lyc* ↓ nux-m ptk1* spong fd4.de stram bg2* verat bg2 [cupr-act stj2 cupr-f stj2 cupr-m stj2 cupr-p stj2]

- **voices** and motions of animals; of: dulc fd4.de *Stram* kr1
- **writing**; in | **without** knowing signification; imitates writing: *Lyc* hr1*

IMPATIENCE: *(↗Answering - abruptly; Answering - hastily; Hurry; Impetuous; Impulsive; Intolerance; Irritability - questioned; Quick; Rash; Restlessness; Selfishness; Speech - hasty; Time - slowly; Weeping - impatience)* achy-a bnj1 *Acon* k* act-sp *Adam* srj5• aesc mtf11 aeth j5.de agar-ph a1 aids nl2• alco a1 all-s k* allox tpw3* aln vva1• *Aloe* sne alum ptk1 ambr k* amph a1* anac k* *Androc* srj1• ant-c bro1 anthraci ↓ *Apis* k* aral bg2* arb-m oss1• *Arg-n* bro1* arizon-l nl2• arn ckh1 *Ars* k* *Ars-h* *Ars-i* ars-s-f k2* aster k* atp rly4• aur k* aur-ar k2 aur-i k2* aur-m-n k* bamb-a stb2.de• bar-c k* bar-i k2* bar-s k2* bell k* bit-ar wht1• borra-o oss1• bros-gau mrc1 *Bry* bufo k* bung-fa mtf *Calc* k* calc-f mg1.de* calc-i k2* calc-p ptk1 calc-s calc-sil k2* *Carb-ac* hr1* carb-v k* *Carc* mlr1• carneg-g rwt1• **Cham** k* chin k* chinin-ar chir-fl gya2 chlam-tr ↓ choc srj3• cic sne cimic k* *Cina* bg2* coca-c ↓ colch k* *Coloc* k* colum-p sze2• conch fkr1• crot-c sk4• crot-h br1 cub culx k2* digin a1 dioxi rbp6 dream-p sdj1• dros k* *Dulc* k* dys fmm1• ferul a1 fic-m ↓ galeoc-c-h ↓ gard-j vlr2• gels k* ger-i rly4• germ-met srj5• gink-b sbd1• gins j5.de* goss st1 graph k2* haliae-lc srj5• ham ↓ hell k* helo-s rwt2• helodr-cal knl2• *Hep* k* hist mg1.de* hura hydrog srj2• *Hyos* k* **Ign** k* ignis-alc es2• impa-g mtf11 ina-i mlk9.de *Iod* k* **Ip** b7.de* irid-met srj5• kali-ar *Kali-bi* k* *Kali-c* k* kali-p kali-s k* kali-sil k2* ketogl-ac rly4• kola stb3• *Kreos* bg2* lac-cp sk4• lac-e hrn2• lac-h sk4*• *Lac-leo* hrn2*• lac-lup hrn2• *Lach* k* lap-la ↓ lil-t k* luna kg1• *Lyc* k* lycps-v ptk1 lyss k* m-ambo b7.de manc mang lsa1.de *Med* k* meli lsa1.de meny lsa1.de merc k* mez ↓ morg-g pte1*• mosch hr1* murx hr1* musca-d ↓ nat-ar nat-c nat-caust ↓ *Nat-m* k* nat-p nat-pyru rly4• nauf-helv-li elm2• neon srj5• nep mg1.de* nicc k* nicc-met sk4• nid jl3 *Nit-ac* k* nuph hr1* nux-m bg2 **Nux-v** k* *Olib-sac* wmh1 onos op k* osm k* pall k* pant-ac rly4• pert-vc vk9 petr-ra shn4• ph-ac k* *Plan* k* *Plat* k* plut-n srj7• podo fd3.de• polys ↓ positr nl2• pot-e rly4• pseuts-m oss1• *Psor* *Puls* k* *Pulx* br1 pycnop-sa mrz1 rheum k* rhus-g tmo3• *Rhus-t* k* ros-d wla1 *Ruta* fd4.de *Sacch-a* fd2.de• sal-fr sle1• sang k* sanguis-s hrn2• sars sel gmj2 **Sep** k* **Sil** k* sol-a ↓ spig spong stann k* *Staph* k* *Stram* ptk1 suis-em rly4• suis-hep rly4• *Sul-ac* k* sul-i k2* **Sulph** k* tarax sp1* tarent k* tax k* tell rsj10• thal c1* thiam rly4• thiop jl3 thuj k* *Tritic-vg* fd5.de urol-h rwt• vac k* valer ptk1 vanil fd5.de verat ptk1 viol-t vip-a jl3 wies a1 zinc k* zinc-p k2* [alumin-s stj2 arg-met stj1* arg-p stj2 bell-p-sp dcm1 buteo-j sej6 cadm-met stj2 cadm-s stj2 chr-s stj2 cinnb stj2 cob stj2 gal-s stj2 heroin sdj2 lith-s stj2 mag-n stj2 mang-i stj2 merc-i-f stj2 mur-ac stj2 nicc-s stj2 nitro stj2 osm-met stj2 rubd-met stj2 spect dfg1 thal-met stj2 titan-s stj2]

- **daytime**: lyss a1
- **morning**: bamb-a stb2.de• dulc k* fic-m gya1 sulph k* vanil fd5.de
- **forenoon** | **11** h: sulph
- **noon**: dulc fd4.de hura a1
- **afternoon**: nit-ac k* sang k*
- **alternating** with:
  - **cheerfulness**: tell jl3
  - **patience**: lac-lup hrn2•
- **always**: merc gl1.fr• sil gl1.fr•

Impatience: ...

- **anger**, with: aids nl2• vanil fd5.de [heroin sdj2]
- **apoplexy**; before: aster kr1 plan ↓
  - **dull**, stupid feeling in brain; with: plan kr1
- **boredom**; with: lac-e hrn2•
- **children**; about his: anac st* bamb-a stb2.de• chlam-tr bcx2• dulc fd4.de haliae-lc srj5• kali-c h2 musca-d szs1 ruta fd4.de spong fd4.de [heroin sdj2]
- **contradiction**; at slightest: alco a1 lap-la rsp1 nuph kr1
- **convulsions** | **before**: *Mosch* kr1
- **coryza**, with: ham fd3.de• **Nux-v** hr1* tritic-vg fd5.de
- **cure** him at once, doctor should: cham c1
- **delivery**; during: cham kr1
- **dinner**, during: sulph k*
- **discouragement**; with: *Calc* j5.de *Spong* fd4.de
- **driving**; while: haliae-lc srj5• ruta fd4.de spong fd4.de vanil fd5.de
- **eating**, while: merc a
- **head**; with complaints of: plat bg2
- **headache**, during: lyss manc pall k* *Sulph* zinc h2*
- **heat**, with: *Acon* bg2 apis bg2 ars k* bell k* *Cham* bg2* chinin-ar k2 ign bg2 *Ip* k* lyc k* *Merc* bg2 *Nat-m* k* *Nux-v* k* *Puls* k* *Rhus-t* bg2 viol-t bg2*
- **house**, in: aster k* tritic-vg fd5.de
- **intermittent** fever, in: chinin-ar
- **interruption**; from: plut-n srj7•
- **itching**, from: osm k* sars hr1*
- **larynx**, from heat and irritation in: kali-bi kr1
- **menses**:
  - **after**: *Nat-m* mtn
  - **before**: anthraci vh1 [nat-caust stj2]
  - **during**: *Cham* mtn ign ckh1 *Nux-v* mtn
- **others**; with: allox tpw3 galeoc-c-h gms1•
- **pain**, from: **Cham** k ● *Coloc* sne hura murx hr1*
- **people**; with | **unhelpful**: lac-e hrn2•
- **perspiration**, during: *Acon* bg2 apis bg2 aur k* *Cham* bg2 ign bg2 merc bg2 mez rhus-t bg2 sul-ac k* zinc k*
- **playing** of children, by: anac dulc fd4.de
- **reading**, while: nat-c k*
- **room**, in a warm crowded: *Plat* hr1*
- **runs** about, never sits or sleeps at night: *Iod* hr1*
- **rush** about; he must: coca-c sk4•
- **sadness**, in: *Kali-c* kr1
- **sitting**, while: *(↗Sitting - inclination)* *Sep* k*
- **slowly**; everything goes too: androc srj1• *Cham* kr1 **Dulc** fd* ham fd3.de• kali-s fd4.de polys sk4• *Sacch-a* fd2.de• spong fd4.de *Tritic-vg* fd5.de vanil fd5.de
- **spoken** to, when: *Lil-t* vh* *Nux-v* hr1*
- **suicidal** disposition, with: carb-v h2
- **supper**, after: nit-ac k*
- **talk** of others, during: *(↗Petulant)* kali-s fd4.de zinc k*
- **tossing** about: *Acon* hr1*
- **trifles**, about: *(↗Trifles; Trifles - important)* *Carc* fd2.de• kali-p *Med* merc k* nat-m *Sacch-a* fd2.de• sang a1 sol-a a1 *Sul-ac* k* *Sulph* vanil fd5.de [heroin sdj2]
- **urinating**; before: sulph
- **waking**, on: *Lyc* kr1
- **walking**, while: *Cimic* ↓ lyc *Sacch-a* fd2.de•
  - **tires** soon: *Cimic* kr1
- **work**, for: *Ip* kr1
- **working**; when: galeoc-c-h gms1• gink-b sbd1• kali-s fd4.de *Nux-v* sf1.de podo fd3.de• polys sk4• ros-d wla1 ruta fd4.de sep gl1.fr• tritic-vg fd5.de

IMPERIOUS (See Haughty)

IMPERTINENCE: *(↗Audacity; Defiant; Haughty; Heedless; Insolence; Meddlesome; Pert; Precocity; Presumptuous; Rudeness)* acon ckh1 bell j bufo gk canth graph hyos gl1.fr• ign j lach gl1.fr• *Nat-m* gl1.fr• nit-ac nux-v j* pall phos sacch c1 spong a1 staph gl1.fr• *Stram* st *Tub* st verat

IMPETUOUS: *(↗Curious - training; Fanaticism; Heedless; Hurry; Impatience; Impulsive; Indiscretion; Quick; Rash)* acon *Anac* arg-n mrr1* arn he* *Ars* ↓ aur lsr* *Bry* calc lsr* calc-s tl* *Carb-v* caust *Cham* cocain hs croc ferr ↓ ferr-p fic-m ↓ glon ptk* **Hep** *Hyos* hr1 ictod kr1 ignis-alc es2• *Iod* gk* *Kali-c* kali-i kali-p kali-s k2 lach k2 laur led mag-c c1* med br1 morph oss• nat-c *Nat-m* **Nit-ac** **Nux-v** olnd petr-ra shn4• phos rheum **Sep** *Staph* k* stram ↓ stront-c sul-ac lsr* *Sulph* tab ptk* thuj ↓ *Zinc* zinc-p k2

- **daytime**: nit-ac
- **morning**: fic-m gya1 staph
- **afternoon**: caust
- **evening**: ferr-p k*
- **heat**, with: sep
- **perspiration**, with: _Acon Ars Bry_ carb-v ferr _Hep_ hyos nat-m phos stram sulph thuj
- **urination**; before: sulph

IMPOLITE: _(↗Abusive; Answering - abruptly; Answering - civil; Answering - snappishly; Disobedience; Insolence; Reverence - lack; Rudeness; Slander)_ aran-ix jl _Hep_ vh* lac-leo sk4• lyc vh* _Merc_ vh* plat vh*
- **children**: _(↗Rudeness)_ lyc mtf33*

IMPORTANT person; behaving as a (See Pompous)

IMPORTUNATE (See Meddlesome)

IMPRESSIONABLE: _(↗Confidence - want; Credulous; Helplessness; Irresolution; Naive; Sensitive - external; Sensitive - mental exertion; Sensitive - mental impressions; Sensitive - moral; Sensitive - sensual; Sympathetic)_ am-c gl• ambr mtf ant-c kr1 _Ars_ lmj aur gl* aur-m bt* bar-c gl* **Calc** lmj calc-p lmj* _Canth_ hr1 **Carc** st* **Caust** lmj _Chin_ lmj **Cic** lmj **Cocc** c1* coff br1 con bt* croc bg2 cypra-eg sde6.de• dulc fd4.de ferr lmj* **Gels** lmj graph c1 hep lmj* ign lmj* **Iod** st* kali-p fd1.de• lach lmj* lyc lmj* _Nat-c_ lmj _Nat-m_ lmj nit-ac lmj* nitro-o a1 _Nux-v_ br1* phos kr1* plat lmj* positr nl2• **Puls** lmj* rosm ↓ sel gmj2 sep lmj* _Sil_ lmj _Staph_ lmj* sulph lmj* _Symph_ ↓ tarent bg2 teucr lmj* _Thuj_ lmj tritic-vg fd5.de **Tub** st vanil fd5.de _Verat_ gl• viol-o c1 _Zinc_ lmj*
- **children**: _Ars_ lmj aur lmj aur-m lmj **Calc** lmj calc-p lmj carc mlr1* **Caust** lmj _Chin_ lmj **Cic** lmj cocc lmj con lmj ferr lmj **Gels** lmj hep lmj ign lmj iod lmj lach lmj lyc lmj _Nat-c_ lmj _Nat-m_ lmj nit-ac lmj _Nux-v_ lmj **Phos** lmj plat lmj puls mtf33 rosm lgb1 sep lmj _Sil_ lmj _Staph_ lmj sulph lmj teucr lmj _Thuj_ lmj zinc mtf33
- **pleasure**; to: _Coff_ br1
- **unpleasantly** impressed by everything: _Con_ kr1 _Symph_ fd3.de•
- **women** and girls; in: viol-o c1

IMPROVIDENT: _(↗Heedless)_ alum gl1.fr• aur-m-n wbt2• caust gl1.fr• nat-m a1* podo fd3.de•

IMPRUDENCE (See Indiscretion)

IMPUDENT (See Insolence)

IMPULSE; morbid: _(↗Meddlesome)_ acon ↓ adam ↓ agar-st ↓ all-s ↓ alum bg2* anac bg2 androc ↓ arg-n bg* ars bg2* bac ↓ _Bar-p_ ↓ bell ↓ bufo ↓ bung-fa ↓ cact ↓ _Calc_ ↓ cann-i ↓ carc mlr1• caust bg2* cham ↓ chin ↓ coca-c ↓ coff ↓ crot-c sk4• _Dendr-pol_ ↓ dig ↓ ferr ↓ fl-ac ↓ glon ↓ hep bg2* hyos mrr1 iod bg2* kali-i ↓ kali-s fd4.de lac-h ↓ lac-leo ↓ lach bg2* lil-t ↓ lyc bg2 _Lyss_ ↓ mag-c ↓ mang ↓ merc bg2* mez ↓ naja ↓ nicc-met ↓ nux-v ↓ op wbt• opun-s a1 _Orig_ ↓ phos ↓ phys ↓ _Plat_ ↓ podo ↓ positr ↓ psor ↓ sal-fr ↓ sep ↓ staph ptk1* stram mrr1 sulph ↓ syph ↓ tarent mtf33 tax ↓ thea mrr1 _Thlas_ ↓ thuj ↓ **TUB** ↓ valer ↓ verat ↓ [fl-pur stj2]
- **absurd** things; to do: _(↗Foolish)_ alum gk arg-n mtf33
- **argue**; to: bung-fa mtf
- **burn**; to | **matchsticks**: lac-h sk4•
- **busy** amel.; when (See occupation - amel.)
- **cable** cars; to ride: coca-c sk4•
- **climb** out of running train; to: dendr-pol sk4•
- **contradictory**: anac ckh1
- **destroy** himself; to (See Suicidal)
- **fight**; to (See Fight)
- **hurt** others; to: dendr-pol sk4•
- **jump** (See Jumping - impulse)
- **kill**; to (See Kill)
- **move**, to: bac jl
- **occupation** | **amel.**: _(↗Activity - desires; Occupation - amel.)_ icd ptk1*
- **peculiar**: arg-n br1*
- **pinch**, to: coff bg2
- **rash**: bell gl1.fr• _Hyos_ gl1.fr• kali-s fd4.de nux-v st1 staph st1* _Stram_ gl1.fr• verat gl1.fr•
- **reckless** things; impelled to do: _(↗Heedless)_ lyss rb2
- **run**; to (= dromomania): _(↗Exertion - physical - desire; Mania - jumps; Roving - senseless; Runs)_ agar-st ↓ all-s a1* anac ↓ androc srj1• bell a1 bufo bg _Calc_ ↓ cann-i a1 dig h2 glon a1 _Iod_ k* lac-h sk4• lach ↓ mang bg2

Impulse; morbid – **run**; to: ...
mez a1 _Orig_ a1* phys a1 positr nl2• sal-fr sle1• **Stram** mtf33 tarent a1* **TUB** st* [tax jsj7]
  - • **night**: iod h
  - • **convulsive** paroxysms, in: agar-st a
  - • **followed**, thinks he is: _(↗Delusions - pursued)_ anac vn10.fr
  - • **fright**, after: bell kr1
  - • **menses** | **before**: lach ptk1
  - • **up** and down: _Calc_ kr1
- **sexual**: _(↗FEMALE - Sexual desire - violent; MALE GENITALIA/SEX - Sexual desire - violent)_ caust pc chin pc mag-c pc nux-v pc phos pc positr nl2• staph pc verat pc
- **speak** in abusive language; to: bung-fa mtf
- **shriek**; to (See Shrieking - must)
- **stab**; to:
  - • **his** flesh with the knife he holds; to stab: _(↗Fear - suicide; Injuring; Injuring - fear; Kill; desire - knife - sight; Kill; desire - knife - with)_ adam srj5• alum gk ars mrr1 kali-s fd4.de _Lyss_ k* positr nl2•
  - • **others**; to stab: _(↗Cut; Cut - others; Kill; desire)_ adam srj hep mrr1 merc mrr1 plat mrr
- **strange** things; to do: _(↗Strange - things)_ arg-n mtf33 cact ptk1*
- **suffocate**; to | **teacher**; a: lac-h sk4•
- **tease**; to:
  - • **women**: | **sexually**: dendr-pol sk4•
- **touch** to (See Touching)
- **violence**, to do: _(↗Kill; desire)_ alum gk crot-c sk4• _Dendr-pol_ sk4• hep mrr1 _Iod_ br1* lac-leo sk4• merc k2* nux-v mrr1 op wbt• _Plat_ mrr1 podo fd3.de• _Stram_ mrr1 sulph mrr1 thea mrr1
- **walk**; to: acon ptk1 arg-n ptk1 _Ars_ ptk1 _Bar-p_ ckh1 cham bg2 ferr ptk1 fl-ac ptk1* kali-i ptk1 lil-t ptk1 lyc ptk1 mag-c ptk1 merc ptk1* naja ptk1* phos ptk1 sep ptk1* tarent br1* _Thlas_ ptk1 thuj ptk1 valer ptk1
- **wash**; to: psor ckh1 syph ckh1
- **wring** and turn someone's neck around to break it: nicc-met sk4•

IMPULSIVE: _(↗Abrupt; Answering - hastily; Ardent; Capriciousness; Heedless; Hurry; Impatience; Impetuous; Indiscretion; Irrational; Meddlesome; Mood - changeable; Quick; Rash; Speech - hasty; Thoughts - rapid; Time - slowly)_ agath-a nl2• alum k2 **Arg-n** k* _Ars_ k* _Aur_ _Aur-m-n_ wbt2• aur-s wbt2• bung-fa mtf cadm-met gm1 camph carc mlr1• caust a1 cere-b a1 choc srj3• _Cic_ coca-c sk4• croc ptk1 cupr ptk1* dendr-pol sk4• ephe-si ↓ fic-m gya1 gins k* hep k2* **Ign** br1* iod k2* irid-met srj5• lac-e hrn2• lach k2 marb-w es1• med ptk1* merc k* morph oss• nux-v k* pert-vc vk9 petr-ra shn4• phos dt **Podo** fd* **Puls** j5.de* rheum mtf33 rhus-t sacch-a fd2.de• staph symph fd3.de• tarent ptk1* thea tritic-vg ↓ [am-f stj2 cupr-f stj2 fl-ac stj2 lith-c stj2 lith-f stj2 lith-i stj2 lith-met stj2 lith-p stj2 lith-s stj2 rubd-met stj2 temp elm1 tung-met stj2]
- **alternating** with:
  - • **fear** | **control**; losing: dendr-pol sk4•
- **secrets**; must blurt out (See Revealing - impulsively)
- **shopping**; impulsive to go: ephe-si ↓ nux-v zr tritic-vg fd5.de
  - • **someone**; for: ephe-si hsj1•

INACTIVITY: _(↗Laziness)_ adam srj5• allox tpw3 androc bnm2• ara-maca sej7• aran mtf11 bapt a1 _Bar-c_ mrr1 buteo-j ↓ cadm-met tpw6 carbn-dox knl3• _Cardios-h_ rly4• cassia-s ccrh1* _Chel_ br1* chir-fl bnm4• choc srj3• colch rsj2• con tl1 conin-br c1* corian-s knl6• dig br1 _Falco-pe_ nl2• fic-m gya1 gels br1 germ-met srj5• haliae-lc srj5• hydroph rsj6• ign tl1 kali-p br1 lat-h ↓ limest-b es1• loxo-lae bnm12• loxo-recl bnm10• _Luna_ kg1• _Mag-m_ mrr1 mand rsj7• nat-sil fd3.de• nauf-helv-li elm2• op br1 positr nl2• puls mtf33 rad-br c11 ruta fd4.de spong fd4.de succ-ac mtf11 tamrnd vk2 tetox pin2• thal-xyz srj8• trios rsj11• vanil fd5.de vero-o rly3• _Zinc_ br1 [bell-p-sp dcm1 heroin sdj2]
- **morning**: adam skp7• trios rsj11•
- **persistent**: lat-h bnm5•
- **unmotivated**; and: [buteo-j sej6]

INADVERTENCE (See Absentminded)

INATTENTIVE (See Absentminded; Heedless)

INCARNATION; lack of: [lac-mat sst4]

INCENSE (See Anger; Hatred; Rage)

INCEST (See Ailments - abused - sexually)

INCITING others: (↗*Defiant)* cimic coloc hyos k* plb

INCONSOLABLE: (↗*Ailments - love; Anger - consoled; Brooding; Consolation - agg.; Despair; Fear - grief; Grief; Grief - silent - love; Helplessness; Irritability - consolation - agg.; Quieted; Sadness; Sulky; Weeping - cannot; Weeping - consolation - agg.)* A c o n k* ambr k* ant-c bl* arist-cl mg *Ars* k* asar jl3 bell b4a.de *Brom* hr1* calc-p lmj calc-s k13 carc lmj *Caust* gl1.fr• *Cham* k* *Chin* k* cic fyz coff cupr sst3• dig j5.de graph j hep b4a.de **Ign** lmj *Jal* mrr1 kali-br hr1* kali-c lmj kali-p lmj kali-s lmj kali-sil lmj lil-t lmj *Lyc* k* *M-arct* b7.de* mag-s a1 mang h2* merc lmj n a t - c k* *Nat-m* k* nit-ac vh* *Nux-v* k* par c1 pert mp• *Petr* phos *Plat* bg2* *Puls* rhus-t b7.de* *Spong* k* *Stann* gl1.fr• staph lmj stram k* sulph k* syph lmj tab lmj tarent lmj vanil fd5.de *Verat* k*

- **actions**, over all her: sulph h2
- **air** amel.; in open: coff gl1.fr•
- **alone**; agg. when: (↗*Company - desire; Company - desire - alone)* stram
- **anxiety** about his family during a short journey; from: *Petr* kr1
- **children**: brom mtf33 *Cham* mrr1* chin mtf33 nat-m mtf33 vanil fd5.de verat mtf33
  - **infants**: *Cham* mrr1 vanil fd5.de
- **dark**; agg. when: stram
- **dreams**; in his: tab j5.de
- **heat**, with: spong b7.de*
- **misfortune**; over imagined: (↗*Unfortunate)* **Verat**
- **suicide**, even to: (↗*Suicidal)* **Chin** kr1
- **weeping** from consolation; continuous: (↗*Weeping - consolation)* nat-c gl1.fr•

INCONSTANCY: (↗*Capriciousness; Irresolution; Mood - changeable; Persisting; Undertaking - many)* acon h1* acon-l a1 act-sp k* agar k* alum j5.de* am-c j5.de* *Ambr* bg2* anac bg2 ang bg2 anh mg1.de ant-c bg2 apis bg2* arg-met mtf arg-n mtf arn gl1.fr• ars k* asaf k* aur bg2* bar-c bg2 bell h1* bism k* borx k2 calc mtf *Calc-p* bg2 cann-s h1* canth k* carc mlr1• cassia-s ccrh1• cham bg2 chin bg2 cimic k* cina bg2 coc-c bg2 cocc mtf coff k* con bg2 *Croc* bg2 cycl bg2 dros ferr bg2 form bg2 gels mtf *Graph* j5.de* hell bg2 hyos bg2 **Ign** k* iod bg2 **Kali-br** hr1* kali-c bg2* kali-p ↓ l a c - c k* lach k* led k* lith-f mtf lyc bg2* m-arct c1 m-aust j5.de mag-m bg2 *Med* mtf merc ↓ mez bg2 moni rfm1• mosch bg2 nat-c k* nat-m bg2* nicc mtf nit-ac bg2 *Nux-m* bg2 nux-v bg2* olib-sac ↓ olnd h1 onos bg2 op k* opun-s a1 (non:opun-v a1) pall mtf petr bg2* plan plat bg2* *Puls* bg2 ruta bg2 sars bg2 *Sep* bg2 sil sphing k* spig stann bg2* staph bg2 stram bg2* sulph bg2* syph st1 tarax bg2 thuj k* v-a-b c1 valer bg2* verat bg2* viol-o bg2 voes a1 zinc k*

- **thoughts**, of: alum j5.de am-c j5.de hell j5.de kali-p fd1.de• merc j5.de* mez j5.de olib-sac wmh1 thuj j5.de

INDECISION (See Irresolution)

INDEPENDENT: (↗*Ailments - domination; Libertinism; Positiveness)* adam srj5• aeth mrr1 aids nl2• *Bell* vh* calc hu2 cina bg2 cupr sst3* des-ac rbp6 dulc fd4.de hippoc-k szs2 lac-ac stj5• mag-c mtf *Nux-v* vh* orot-ac rly4• plac rzf5• raph mgm• sep mgm*• spong mgm• *Sulph* vh* *Tritic-vg* fd5.de [ruth-met stj2 tax jsj7]

- **lack** of independence: anac b4a.de bar-c b4a.de nat-m b4.de* ulm-c jsj8•

INDIFFERENCE: (↗*Asking - nothing; Casual; Delirium - apathetic; Desires - nothing; Dullness; Ennui; Heedless; Mood - repulsive; Neglecting; Pessimist; Reserved; Sensitive - want; Wants - nothing)* abel ↓ abrom-a ckh1 absin acet-ac a1 *Acon* adam skp7*• aesc ↓ agam-g ↓ *Agar* k* agath-a nl2• *Agn* k* aids nl2• ail k* *All-c* vh1 allox tpw3* aloe bg2* **Alum** b2.de* alum-p k2* alum-sil k2 alumn a1* am-c j5.de* am-m k* ambr ammc ↓ amor-r jl3 **Anac** b2.de* *Anac-oc* kr1 anan a1 *Androc* srj1• *Anh* mg1.de* ant-t k* *Anthraci* ↓ **Apis** k* aq-mar jl3 arag br1* aran ↓ arb-m oss1• *Arg-n* k* arge-pl rwt5• arizon-l nl2• *Arn* k* *Ars* k* ars-h kr1 ars-i ars-s-f k2 a r u m - t kr1 arund ↓ asaf k* asar k* asim br1 aster atro a1 *Aur* ↓ aur-ar ↓ a u r - b r vh1 *Aur-m* ↓ aur-m-n wbt2• aur-s ↓ bac ↓ *Bamb-a* stb2.de• bapt k* *Bar-c* bar-i k2* bar-m bar-s k2 *Bell* k* bell-p ptk1 bell-p-sp ↓ berb k* bism k* bit-ar wht1• borx h2* *Bov* k* brass-n-o srj5• brom k* bros-gau mrc1 brucel ↓ bry br1 bufo k* but-ac sp1 buth-a mg1.de* *Cadm-m* ↓ cadm-met mg1.de* calad kr1* *Calc* k* calc-ar k2* calc-f jl3 calc-i k2 *Calc-p* k* calc-s camph k* cann-i cann-s cann-xyz bg2 canth ↓ caps k* *Carb-an* k* **Carb-v** k* carbn-o a1 *Carbn-s* carc mg1.de* card-m br1 carneg-g rwt1• cartl-s rly4• caust k* cench ↓ *Cham* k* *Chel* k* **Chin** k* *Chinin-ar* *Chinin-s* chion br1 chir-fl ↓ chlf kr1 chloram jl3

Indifference: ... chlorpr jl3 choc ↓ cic k* *Cimic* cina k* cit-l ↓ clem k* cob ↓ coc-c ↓ coca a1 coca-c sk4• cocain ↓ *Cocc* k* cod a1 coff ↓ colch rsj2• coli rly4• coloc j5.de* colum-p sze2• com ↓ **Con** b2.de* conch ↓ conin-br c1* corian-s ↓ corn cortico tpw7 croc k* **Crot-c** *Crot-h* k* cupr k* cupr-s a1* *Cur* ↓ *Cycl* k* cypr cypra-eg sde6.de• cystein-l rly4• cyt-l br1* dendr-pol ↓ des-ac rbp6 dig k* digin ↓ dioxi rbp6 dream-p sdj1• dros b7a.de* *Dulc* kr1* eberth jl2 elaps ephe-si ↓ esp-g kk1.de euphr k* fago ↓ *Falco-pe* nl2• ferr k* ferr-ar ferr-i k* ferr-p fic-m gya1 fl-ac k* fuma-ac rly4• galla-q-r nl2• *Gels* k* germ-met stj2*• gink-b ↓ glon glyc ↓ *Granit-m* es1• *Graph* k* grat ↓ guaj guare kr1 gymno haliae-lc srj5• ham bg2* harp jl3 **Hell** k* helo helo-s rwt2• helodr-cal knl2• hep hipp jl2 hippoc-k szs2 hura hydr ↓ hydr-ac j5.de hydrc a1 hydrog srj2• hydroph ↓ *Hyos* k* *Ign* k* ind jl3* indol ↓ iod k* ip k* *Irid-met* srj5• jatr-c jug-r st1 *Kali-ar* kali-bi k* kali-br k* *Kali-c* k* kali-chl j5.de* kali-i ↓ kali-m k2* kali-n j5.de *Kali-p* kali-s kali-sil k2 ketogl-ac rly4• *Kola* stb3• kres mg1.de* lac-ac stj5• lac-c *Lac-cp* ↓ lac-d kr1* lac-e hrn2• *Lac-h* ↓ *Lac-lup* hrn2• *Lach* k* lap-la sde8.de• laur k* lavand-a ↓ lepi levo jl3 lil-s a1 **Lil-t** k* limest-b es1• linu-c a1 lith-c stj2*• loxo-recl knl4• luf-op mg1.de* *Luna* kg1• *Lyc* k* lyss a1* mag-c a1 mag-m manc mand kr1* marb-w ↓ med ckh1 melal-alt ↓ *Meli* meny k* meph jl3 *Merc* k* m e r c - c b4a.de merc-i-f a1* merl ↓ **Mez** k* moly-met jl3* moni rfm1• morph a1 mur-ac k* myos-a rly4• myric br1 myris ↓ nad rly4• naja narz a1 nat-ar kr1 **Nat-c** k* **Nat-m** k* **Nat-p** k* nat-s k2 nat-sal br1 nat-sil fd3.de* neon srj5• nep mg1.de* nept-m ↓ nid jl3 nig-s mp4• *Nit-ac* k* nit-s-d sf1.de* nitro-o ↓ *Nux-m* k* nux-v k* oci-sa sk4• *Olib-sac* wmh1 olnd k* **Onos** k* **Op** k* osteo-a jl2 oxal-a rly4• ozone sde2• ped c1 pegan-ha tpi1• petr k* petr-ra shn4• **Ph-ac** k* **Phos** k* phys ↓ *Phyt* k* *Pic-ac* k* pitu ↓ pitu-gl skp7• **Plat** k* plb k* plut-n srj7• *Podo* fd3.de• polys sk4• *Positr* nl2• prun pseuts-m ↓ psil jl *Psor* k* ptel bg2* **Puls** k* pycnop-sa mrz1 querc-r svu1• rad-br ptk1 raja-s ↓ ran-b j5.de raph rat ↓ rauw tpw8* rheum k* rhod k* rhus-g a1 rhus-t k* rhus-v ↓ rib-ac ↓ ric a1 rumx r u t a k* sabad k* sabal br1* sabin k* sacch a1 sacch-a ↓ *Sal-fr* sle1• sal-l mtf11 sang bg2* *Sanguis-s* hrn2• sapo br1 saroth sp1 sarr c1 sars *Sec* k* sel k* seneg k* **Sep** k* sieg mg1.de *Sil* k* spig ↓ spong squil k* stann k* **Staph** k* s t r a m k* sul-ac kr1* sul-i k2 sulfa jl3 sulfon br1 sulfonam ks2 *Sulph* k* *Symph* fd3.de• *Syph* br1* *Tab* bg2* tanac ↓ taosc ↓ tarax jl3 tarent k* tax a1* *Tell* bg2* term-c gsb1 teucr ptk1 thal jl3 thal-xyz srj8• thala ↓ ther thiop jl3 *Thuj* k* *Thuj-l* jl3 **Thyr** ptk1* til ban1• tong ↓ toxi ↓ trinit br1 *Tub* bg2* *Tung-met* bdx1• ulm-c ↓ *Urol-h* rwt• **Vanil** fd* ven-m jl3 *Verat* k* verb k* vero-o rly4• *Viol-t* k* vip j5.de* visc sp1* xan zinc k* zinc-p k2 ziz [alumin-s stj2 am-caust stj2 am-f stj2 ant-c stj2 ant-met stj2 bar-br stj2 bism-sn stj2 bor-pur stj2 cadm-s stj2 carp-b rcb1 chr-s stj2 cinnb stj2 fl-pur stj2 gal-s stj2 heroin sdj2 kali-met stj2 lac-mat sst4 lact stj lith-f stj2 lith-i stj2 lith-m stj2 lith-met stj2 lith-p stj2 lith-s stj2 mang-i stj2 mang-m stj2 mang-met stj2 mang-p stj2 mang-s stj2 nat-f stj2 nicc-s stj2 nitro stj2 oxyg stj2 titan-s stj2 zinc-i stj2]

- **daytime**: anac dig digin a1 merc verat xan kr1 zinc-p k2
- **morning**: all-c a1 bamb-a ↓ brucel sa3• com a1 cortico tpw7 dream-p sdj1• ham fd3.de• hep ↓ mag-c a1 mag-m ↓ manc a1 petr ↓ **Ph-ac** a1 phyt ↓ positr ↓ sacch-a fd2.de• sep ↓ staph ↓ tarent ↓
  - **8** h: sep a
  - **15** h; until: tarent a1
  - **waking**; on: all-c kr1 bamb-a stb2.de• hep mag-m manc petr *Ph-ac* phyt positr nl2• staph sf1.de
- **forenoon**: alum sars sep a1 ulm-c jsj8•
- **afternoon**: aids nl2• con ham st1 mag-c a1
  - **17-18** h: con a
- **evening**: aids nl2• aloe dig kali-chl k* phos sacch-a fd2.de• tarent [tax jsj7]
- **act** for herself; no longer wishes to: *Cur* kr1
- **adverse** circumstances; to: conch fkr1• ham fd3.de• ph-ac ptk1 podo fd3.de•
- **agreeable** things; to: (↗*pleasure)* ambr k* anac k* apis k2 cina k* corn merc gl1.fr• op k* rhod k* staph k* stram k* [heroin sdj2]
- **air**, in open: con mur-ac plat
  - **amel**.: nat-ar a1
- **alternating** with:
  - **activity** (See Activity - desires - alternating - indifference)
  - **anger** (See Anger - alternating - indifference)
  - **anxiety** (See Anxiety - alternating - indifference)
  - **cheerfulness**: agn androc srj1• meny j5.de* ozone sde2• tarent k*
  - **despair** (See Despair - alternating - indifference)
  - **euphoria**: ozone sde2•

- • **excitement** (See Excitement - alternating - indifference)
- • **irritability** (See Irritability - alternating - indifference)
- • **jesting** (See Jesting - alternating - indifference)
- • **mental** exertion; desire for (See Mental exertion - desire - alternating - indifference)
- • **restlessness** (See Restlessness - alternating - indifference)
- • **sadness** (See Sadness - alternating - indifference)
- • **sensitiveness** (See Sensitive - alternating - indifference)
- • **timidity** (See Timidity - alternating - indifference)
- • **vexation** (See Irritability - alternating - indifference)
- • **weeping** (See Weeping - alternating - indifference)

- **annoyance**; after least: *Kali-bi* kr1
- **anosognosia**: thala jl3
- **answer**, indifference when questioned, says nothing; aversion to: *(↗Aversion - everything; Discontented; Torpor; Unattractive)* Colch vh*
- **anxiety**, after: *Acon* kr1 phos h2
- **appearance**; to his personal: *(↗Dirty; Elegance - want; Untidy)* arizon-l nl2• aur-s wbt2• calc mrr1 cocain br1 conch fkr1• dream-p sdj1• ephe-si hsj1• kola stb3• lac-h htj1• nat-sil fd3.de• petr-ra shn4• phyt br1 positr nl2• psor jl2 **SULPH** k ●* [lac-mat sst4 oxyg stj tax jsj7]
- **beloved** ones; to (See loved)
- **business** affairs, to: *(↗intellectual; money; Business - aversion)* aesc vh agam-g mlk9.de agar *Arg-n* arn j5.de bamb-a stb2.de• *Calc* vh* con br1 falco-pe nl2• *Fl-ac* gink-b sbd1• ham st1 *Kali-bi* kali-p k2 myric myris k* nat-ar *Ph-ac* phys ckh1 phyt k2* plut-n srj7• podo fd3.de• positr nl2• psil ft1 *Ptel* br *Puls* rhus-t a1* sal-fr sle1• sanguis-s hrn2• *Sep Stram Sulph* symph fd3.de• [heroin sdj2]
- **cares**, to: nit-ac lpc
- **caresses**, to: **Cina** k*
- **children**; in: *(↗Striking - children; in)* phos mtf33
- **children**; towards: | **mother** towards her children; indifference of: *(↗family; Aversion - children; Escape - family; Estranged - children; Neglecting - children; Striking - children; striking)* aur-ar k2 choc srj3• irid-met srj5• kali-i *Lyc* k* nat-c **PHOS** k2* plut-n srj7• sacch-a gmj3 **SEP** k1* [heroin sdj2]
- **chill**, during: apis bg2 arn k* **Chin** bg2 con k* ign k* kali-chl bg2* (non:kali-m a1) lach bg2 **Op** k* **Ph-ac** k* **Phos** k* puls k* sel bg2 **Sep** bg2 sil k* verat k*
- **coition**:
  - • **after**: *Calc* ptk1 sep ↓
    - ⁝ **menses**; before: sep mtn
  - • **during**: lyss a1
- **coma**, after: bufo kr1
- **company**, society:
  - • **to**: *(↗Company - aversion)* irid-met srj5• rhod j5.de rhus-t h1 *Tung-met* bdx1•
  - • **while in**: *(↗Haughty)* androc srj1• **Arg-n** k* bov *Kali-c* k1* kali-m ccrh1• lyc hr1* mez c1 nat-c nat-m *Plat* k* plut-n srj7• rhus-t [tax jsj7]
    - ⁝ **amel.**: *(↗Company - desire)* bov k*
- **complain**; does not: *(↗Complaining; Complaining - never; Well - says - sick)* apis wm coca-c sk4• colch ↓ *Hyos* k* **OP** k1* *Podo* fd3.de• **Stram** k*
  - • **unless** questioned; says nothing of his condition: colch
- **concussion** of brain, after: **Arn** kr1 *Cic* kr1
- **condition**; to his: *(↗suffering)* *Gels* br1* [heroin sdj2]
- **conscience**, to the dictates of: *(↗Moral)* cann-i caust gl1.fr• con gl1.fr• falco-pe nl2• graph gl1.fr• petr gl1.fr•
- **conversation**; from: carc jl sil ptk1
- **danger**, to: falco-pe nl2•
- **dead** to him; everything seems: *(↗Delusions - dead - everything)* hydrog srj2• **Mez** kr1 *Ph-ac* mrr1 **Vanil** fd*
- **dearest** friends; even towards: *(↗loved)* nat-sil mtf33 phos mtf33 [bell-p-sp dcm1]
  - • **alcoholism**; in chronic: *Phos* kr1
- **delirium**; after: cupr kr1 op a1
- **desire**, nor action of the will; has no: *(↗Will - weakness)* hell *Kali-p* fd1.de• podo fd3.de• *Verat* kr1
- **disappointment**; after: *(↗Ailments - disappointment)* aesc vh1
- **done** for her; about anything being: *(↗Ungrateful)* **Lil-t** kr1* til ban1•
- **drinking**, to: chin k2 irid-met srj5•
- **drowsiness**, with (See sleepiness)
- **duties**; to: *(↗Duty - no)* androc ↓ ars gl1.fr• aur-ar ↓ brom ↓ bros-gau ↓ **Calc** kr1* carb-v st cench k2 chir-fl ↓ *Cimic* kr cit-l ↓ cypr vml3• cypra-eg sde6.de• falco-pe nl2• gink-b sbd1• kali-p fd1.de• **Kali-s** fd4.de* lach gl1.fr• merc gl1.fr• nat-m gl1.fr• neon ↓ petr-ra ↓ podo fd3.de• *Ptel* kr1 sal-fr sle1• *Sanguis-s* hrn2• sep ↓ sil gl1.fr• sul-i k2 sulph gl1.fr• ulm-c jsj8• [heroin sdj2]
  - • **domestic**, to: androc srj1• aur-ar k2 brom k2* bros-gau mrc1 chir-fl gya2 *Cimic* kr1 cit-l kr1 neon srj5• petr-ra shn4• sep ste sul-i k2 [heroin sdj2]
- **dying**; to: sapo br1
- **eating**:
  - • **after**: aloe lach ptk1 lyc ptk1 *Ph-ac* ptk1 sacch-a fd2.de• sel ptk1
  - • **to** eating: *(↗Anorexia nervosa; Eating - refuses)* bac bn chin h1* granit-m es1• irid-met srj5• kali-p fd1.de• lac-h htj1• merc mtf33* nat-c gl1.fr• nat-m gl1.fr• *Staph* gl1.fr• [tax jsj7]
- **emaciation** and weakness, with: **Ph-ac** kr1
- **ennui**, with: *(↗Ennui)* alum j5.de carneg-g rwt1• choc srj3• con j5.de *Kali-n* j5.de lach j5.de lyc j5.de *Nat-c* j5.de *Nux-v* j5.de petr j5.de *Plb* j5.de positr nl2• zinc j5.de [heroin sdj2]
- **epilepsy**, in: *Crot-h* kr1 kali-br kr1 *Op* kr1
- **everything**, to: *(↗Neglecting - everything; Unattractive)* acet-ac *Acon* adam srj5• agar k* agn bro1 ail ambr k2 anac androc srj1• *Apis* bro1 arg-n bro1 arn k* *Ars* j5.de* asaf j5.de *Aur* vh* *Aur-m* vh* aur-m-n wbt2• bamb-a stb2.de• bapt bro1* bell berb gt bism j5.de bov bry bro1* buth-a mg1.de **Cadm-met** vh* calc hr1 cann-s canth caps **Carb-v** k* carneg-g rwt1• cham j5.de chin j5.de* choc srj3• cic j5.de *Cimic* bro1* *Cina* con k2* croc cypr cystein-l rly4• cyt-l bro1 dig *Falco-pe* nl2• fl-ac bro1 *Gels* bro1 germ-met srj5• gink-b sbd1• glyc bro1 granit-m es1• *Ham* fd3.de• *Hell* k* hydr hydr-ac bro1 hyos j5.de ign k* indol bro1 irid-met srj5• kali-ar kali-chl j kali-m ckh1 *Kali-p* fd1.de• kali-s fkr2.de kola stb3• *Lac-h* htj1• lach bro1 lepi lil-t bro1 *Lyc* j5.de mag-c mtf33 meny c1 *Merc* k* merl mez k* nat-c j5.de *Nat-m* j5.de* nat-p k2* *Nat-sil* fd3.de• nit-ac k2 *Nit-s-d* kr1* nux-m k* *Nux-v* kr1* *Op* j5.de* ozone sde2• petr-ra shn4• **Ph-ac** k* *Phos* k* phyt bro1 *Pic-ac* k2* pitu ckh1 *Plat* kr1* podo fd3.de• polys sk4• *Positr* nl2• psil jl *Puls* j5.de* pycnop-sa mrz1 *Rheum* j5.de rib-ac jl sal-fr sle1• sec k* sel gt *Sep* k* stann j5.de **Staph** k1* sulph syph k2 thuj bro1 **Thyr** vh* verat j5.de* ziz [heroin sdj2 tax jsj7]
- **excitement**, after: ambr k2 ham fd3.de•
- **exciting** events, to: ferr-p k2 ozone sde2• petr-ra shn4•
- **exertion**:
  - • **after**: nat-m h2
  - • **during**: bamb-a stb2.de•
- **exposure** of her person, to: *(↗naked; Lascivious; Lewdness; Naked; Nymphomania; Obscene; Shameless)* corian-s knl6• *Hyos* k* petr-ra shn4• *Phos Phyt Sec* stram verat
- **external** impressions; to: choc srj3• con a1 *Hell* kr1 lyc a1 nat-sil fd3.de• [heroin sdj2]
- **external** things; to: *(↗Dirty; Dress - indecently; Elegance - want; Tastelessness; Untidy; Washing - aversion)* agn am-c gl1.fr• am-m gl1.fr• anac a1* berb j5.de* bit-ar wht1• bov j5.de* buth-a sp1 calc-p sne canni-i cham k* cic k* coca-c sk4• con a1 euphr j5.de falco-pe nl2• *Hell* kr1* *Kola* stb3• lyc k* merl olib-sac wmh1 op k* ozone sde2• petr-ra shn4• *Ph-ac* hr1* plat j5.de polys sk4• rumx k* stann k* staph k* **SULPH** k ●* tarent thuj j5.de verat k* vip j5.de [heroin sdj2]
- **fame**; to: am-m gl1.fr• ars gl1.fr• sep gl1.fr•
- **family**, to his: *(↗children; towards - mother; husband; parents; relations; Escape - family; Estranged - family; Forgetful - friends; Gifts)* carb-v k2 falco-pe nl2• granit-m es• ham fd3.de• hell a1 hep b4a.de melal-alt gya4 merc mtf33 nat-p k13 nat-sil fd3.de• nit-ac sf1.de petr-ra shn4• **Phos** st* plut-n srj7• podo fd3.de• positr nl2• sacch-a gmj3 sal-fr sle1• sel gmj2 **Sep** b4.de* sil b4a.de staph tl1 sulph tl1 [bell-p-sp dcm1 heroin sdj2]
- **feel** almost nothing, seems to: nit-s-d kr1 petr-ra shn4•
- **feeling**; with desire for: [heroin sdj2]
- **fever**, during: *(↗typhoid; Dullness - heat - during)* ail k2 *Apis* kr1 aran kr1 *Arn* k* **Bapt** hr1 bufo ↓ chin k* *Chinin-s* kr1 **Con** k* ferr-p bn iod bro1 kali-c ↓ *Nit-s-d* kr1* **Op** k* **Ph-ac** k* phos k* *Puls* k* *Sep* k* stram verat viol-t k*
  - • **delivery**; after puerperal: kali-c kr1
  - • **heat** and cold feet; with: bufo kr1
- **fine** feeling, to: op j5.de

- **fright**, after: *(↗Ailments - fright)* plat kr1
- **future**, to: *(↗Fatalistic)* syph kr1
- **gaiety**, after: carbn-s a
- **happiness**, to: *(↗joyless)* ars-i k2
- **head**, with hot: bufo kr1
- **headache**; during: bism hr1
- **himself**, to: lavand-a ctl1• phos bg* sep bg* thuj-l jl ulm-c jsj8• [lac-mat sst4 tax jsj7]
- **household** affairs: *(↗Neglecting - household)* brom k2 cimic ptk1 falco-pe nl2• ham fd3.de• kali-p fd1.de• sacch-a gmj3 [bell-p-sp dcm1 lac-mat sst4]
- **husband**; towards: *(↗family)* falco-pe nl2• luna kg1• melal-alt gya4 podo fd3.de• sacch-a gmj3
- **important**: *(↗Neglecting - important)*
  - **news**, to: ars-h kr1
  - **things**, to: calc fl-ac nat-sil fd3.de• symph fd3.de• [lact stj]
- **increasing** gradually: *Plb* kr1
- **influenza**: | **after**: *Cadm-m* vh*
- **intellectual** occupation; to usual: *(↗business)* androc srj1• neon srj5• tung-met bdx1• [heroin sdj2 tax jsj7]
- **interrogatories**, to: tanac a1
- **irritability**, with: asaf kr1 con↓ tung-met bdx1• ziz kr1
  - **afternoon** | 17-18 h: con kr1
- **irritating**, disagreeable things; to: ambr k* anac k* borx k* cina k* coc-c k* coca-c sk4• coff k* op k* rhod k* [heroin sdj2]
- **jesting**, to: *(↗joyless)* sabad a1
- **joy** of others; to: *(↗pleasure)* acon a1 alum a1 am-c a1 ambr a1 anac↓ *Anthraci*↓ apis k13 aur k13 bamb-a stb2.de• bell j cadm-met gm1 cann-s j carb-v↓ cartl-s rly4• cham a1 cina↓ coloc a1 **Croc** a1 dioxi rbp6 dros a1 falco-pe↓ hell↓ ip j kali-p k2 laur a1 lyc a1 meny j nat-ar k2 *Nat-m* j nat-sil fd3.de• nit-ac j *Op* kr1 podo fd3.de• positr nl2• prun a1 *Puls* j sabin j tab a1
  - **and** suffering: *(↗suffering - others)* ambr j5.de* anac j5.de *Anthraci* vh1 carb-v k2 cina j5.de falco-pe nl2• hell j5.de *Op* j5.de* puls j5.de
- **joyless**: *(↗happiness; jesting; pleasure; Forsaken - joyless)* adam srj5• alum h2* apis k2 aur k2 aur-m-n wbt2• bell j5.de camph b7a.de cann-s j5.de card-m ptk1 cham b7a.de coff b7.de dros b7.de falco-pe nl2• hell b7.de ip b7.de* kali-p fd1.de• laur b7.de* loxo-recl knl4• mag-m b4.de meny j5.de *Nat-m* b4a.de* neon srj5• nit-ac j5.de *Op* j5.de* podo fd3.de• positr nl2• *Puls* j5.de sabin b7.de* sars b4.de *Sep* b4a.de spig b7.de **Vanil** fd* [heroin sdj2]
- **lies** with eyes closed: apis wm arg-n cocc *Sep*
- **life**, to: absin a1 *Ars* a1* bov a1 cham sf1.de dioxi rbp6 fago hl granit-m es• hydroph rsj6• lyc kr1 *Merc* gl1.fr• *Ph-ac*↓ phos sf1.de *Phyt* a1* plut-n srj7• rhus-v hl *Sep* kr1 sulph sf1.de *Tab* sf1.de toxi mtf2• *Xan* kr1 [heroin sdj2 tax jsj7]
  - **affairs** of life: *Ph-ac* kr1
- **loved** ones, to: *(↗dearest; parents; Estranged - friends; Forgetful - friends)* *Acon* aids nl2• *All-c* vh1 allox tpw3* arge-pl rwt5• ars ars-i k2 bell dx1 carb-v k2 carc ib* cina mtf33 dendr-pol sk4• dream-p sdj1• falco-pe nl2• *Fl-ac* k* ham fd3.de• **Hell** k* kali-p k2 kali-s fkr2.de kali-sil k2 ketogl-ac rly4• lavand-a ctl1• lil-t bc melal-alt gya4 merc myric hl nat-p k* nat-sil k2* petr-ra shn4• **Phos** k* plat k* positr nl2• pseuts-m sne* sal-fr sle1• **Sep** k* *Syph* k2* [bell-p-sp dcm1 heroin sdj2]
  - **strangers**; and animated to: *(↗Avarice - generosity; Hard)* *Fl-ac* kr1
- **mania**; in: camph h1
- **masturbation**, after: *(↗Ailments - sexual excesses)* **Staph**
- **matter**; it does not: positr nl2•
- **menopause**; in: *Cycl* kr1
- **menses**:
  - **before**: *(↗Menses - before)* nit-ac k2
  - **during**: germ-met↓ hydrog srj2• rhod mtn sep mtn
    - **beginning**, at: germ-met srj
- **mental** exertion:
  - **after**: nat-m
  - **during**: bamb-a stb2.de•
- **misfortune** to (See adverse)
- **money**; to making: *(↗business)* chin gl1.fr• cob ptm1• kali-c gl1.fr• merc gl1.fr• nat-c gl1.fr• sep gl1.fr•
- **morose**: am-c j5.de bac bn bov j5.de *Con* kr1 lach j5.de *Verat* br1*
- **music**, which he loves; to: *Carb-v* k* caust j5.de ign b7.de* polys sk4•
- **naked**, to remain: *(↗exposure)* **Hyos** st petr-ra shn4•
- **notices** nothing: *Verat* kr1
- **opinion** of others; to: agath-a nl2• androc srj1• falco-pe nl2• lac-cp sk4• petr-ra shn4• symph fd3.de• taosc iwa1• ulm-c jsj8• [tax jsj7]
- **ordinary** matters, to: com a1 kali-p fd1.de• podo fd3.de•
- **others**, toward: *(↗welfare; Selfishness)* all-c dgt1 arge-pl rwt5• arizon-l nl2• caust↓ fl-ac mrr1 granit-m es1• kola stb3• *Lac-cp* sk4• marb-w es1• *Osteo-a* jl2 plat gg podo fd3.de• positr nl2• sabad gg sulph urol-h rwt• [heroin sdj2 tax jsj7]
- **pain**:
  - **to** pain: arund a1* *Chin* hr1 des-ac rbp6 jatr-c kr1 nitro-o a1 op h1* positr nl2• puls gl• sapo br1 [heroin sdj2]
  - ○ **Head**; with pain in: bamb-a stb2.de• plut-n↓
    - **pressing** pain: plut-n srj7•
  - **Stomach** and precordial region; with pain in: kali-bi c1
- **parents**; to: *(↗family; loved)* all-c vh1 cina mtf33 phos j* sep bl* [heroin sdj2]
- **periodical**: ars st chin st
- **personal** appearance (See appearance)
- **persons**; to all: eberth jl2 kali-m ccrh1* mez a plut-n srj7•
- **perspiration**, during: apis bg2 **Ars** k* *Bell* k* **Calc** k* *Chin* bg2 *Lach* k* **Ph-ac** bg2 **Phos** bg2 *Puls* bg2 sel bg2 *Sep* bg2
- **pining** boys; in: aur br1
- **pleasure**, to: *(↗agreeable; joy of; joyless; Amusement - aversion)* alum anac androc srj1• *Arg-n* *Ars* ars-i k2 *Aur-m-n* wbt2• calc-ar k2 cartl-s↓ cench k2 *Cham* chinin-ar k2 *Chinin-s* cocc croc dioxi↓ ferr-p k* germ-met srj graph **Hell** k* hep hura ip kali-ar kali-c kali-m k2 kali-p k2 kali-sil k2* mag-c mg1.de mag-m meph jl mez mur-ac nat-ar nat-c **Nat-m** k* *Nit-ac* k1* **Op** k* petr plut-n↓ positr nl2• prun *Puls* sal-fr sle1• sars *Sep* k* spig stann staph stram **Sulph** k* *Syph* st tab ther [heroin sdj2]
  - **things** usually enjoyed: androc srj1• cartl-s rly4• dioxi rbp6 plut-n srj7•
- **possessions**; to his personal: sulph mtf33
- **puberty**, in: *(↗Loathing - general - puberty; Puberty)* bar-c st lach st ph-ac sf1.de
- **pulse** retarded: ant-t kr1
- **quiet**: *(↗Taciturn)* crot-h kr1
- **reading**, while: mez a1
- **recovery**, about his: ars h2 aur-m-n vh* *Calc*
- **relations**, to: *(↗family; Forgetful - friends)* acon k2 bac bn bell bg2 falco-pe nl2• *Fl-ac* granit-m es• ham fd3.de• **Hell** hep hydrog srj2• hyos bg2 kali-p k2 merc bg2 nat-c nat-p k2 petr-ra shn4• **PHOS** k1* plat positr nl2• **SEP** k1* *Syph* st verat bg2
- **religion**, to his: *(↗Religious - want)* anac coloc med cd sil ptk2
  - **not** caring if he went to heaven or to hell: med rb2
- **reprimands**, to all: *(↗Laughing - reprimands)* ham fd3.de• *Merc* gl1.fr• petr-ra shn4• podo fd3.de• symph fd3.de• tub mrr1* verat mrr1
- **sadness**; with: cic br1 hell↓ *Kali-ar* kr1 *Kali-br* kr1 nat-sil fd3.de• ph-ac tl1 *Plat* kr1
  - **typhoid**; after: hell kr1
- **setback**; to a (See adverse)
- **sex**; to opposite: puls vh* **Sep** vh* thuj k*
- **sleepiness**, with: acon j5.de am-m j5.de ammc j5.de ant-t j5.de ars j5.de carb-an j5.de carb-v j5.de chel j5.de cinnb j5.de com kr1 corn kr1 croc j5.de dig j5.de dulc j5.de grat j5.de ip j5.de irid-met srj5• lap-la sde8.de• laur j5.de lyc j5.de mag-c j5.de mag-m j5.de nat-c j5.de nep vs rat j5.de sapo br1 sars j5.de tong j5.de verb j5.de *Zinc* j5.de
- **sleeplessness**, with: *Nit-s-d* kr1
- **society** (See company)
- **stoical** to what happens: *(↗Fatalistic)* ail kr1* myric hl op ptk1*
- **stool**, after: arn↓ *Cycl* st*
  - **every**: arn ptk1
- **suffering**; to: *(↗condition; Well - says - sick)* anac↓ androc srj1• bac bn chir-fl gya2 con fkr8.de *Hell* *Lac-h* htj1• **Op** plut-n srj7• **Stram** tax↓ tung-met bdx1• [heroin sdj2]
  - **others**; of: *(↗joy of - and; Cruelty; Hardhearted)* anac j *Lac-h* htj1• plut-n srj7• [tax jsj7]
- **superiority**; with feeling of: ozone sde2•
- **surprises**; not affected by: polys sk4•
- **surroundings**, to the: *(↗Autism; Hypochondriasis - interest; Involvement - reduced)* abel jl allox jl androc srj1• arge-pl rwt5• ars-i k2 bac bn bufo bj• calc-s k2 carneg-g rwt1• ham fd3.de• kali-p k2 levo jl merc h1 mez c1

- **surroundings**, to the: ...
  nat-sil k2 phos k2 phyt kr1* pic-ac ptk1 polys sk4• raja-s jl rumx kr1* sel kr1* sul-i k2 thuj-l jl tung-met bdx1•
- **taciturn**: *(↗Taciturn)* allox sp1 bac bn bamb-a stb2.de• calc j5.de* *Hell* kr1 irid-met srj5• kali-p fd1.de• nat-sil fd3.de• *Nit-s-d* kr1 plat j5.de staph j5.de
- **typhoid** fever; in: *(↗fever)* ail k2 *Apis Arn* chin *Chinin-s* kr1 *Colch* kr1 *Nit-s-d* kr1 *Ph-ac* **Rhus-t** hr1 *Verat* kr1
- **unfeeling**; with: plat bg2 sabad bg2 sulph bg2
- **vexation** with distress in stomach; after least: *Kali-bi* kr1
- **walking** in open air, while: *Con*
- **weariness**; with: ozone sde2•
- **weather** | **stormy**: sang ptk1 tub ptk1
- **weeping**, with: *(↗Weeping)* caust j5.de ign j5.de *Plat* kr1
- **welfare** of others, to: *(↗others; Helping - aversion; Selfishness)* a d a m srj5• androc srj1• ars gl1.fr• caust gl1.fr• germ-met srj5• granit-m es1• ham fd3.de• lach gl1.fr• marb-w es1• moni rfm1• nat-m gl1.fr• *Nux-v* gl1.fr• ozone sde2• plat gl1.fr• sacch-a gmj3 sep gl1.fr• **Sulph** k*
- **window**; looking for hours out of the (See Looking - window)
- **women**, to: nat-m a1
- **work**: *(↗Laziness)* agar ↓ allox tpw3 androc ↓ arge-pl rwt5• cadm-met ↓ camph ↓ chir-fl gya2 ign ↓ irid-met ↓ kali-m ckh1 kali-p ↓ lach ↓ lavand-a ctl1• nept-m ↓ plut-n ↓ positr ↓ pycnop-sa ↓ rhod ↓ sacch-a gmj3 squil ↓ staph ↓ tung-met ↓ [bell-p-sp dcm1]
  - **aversion** to work; with: *(↗Laziness)* agar j5.de allox sp1 androc srj1• cadm-met tpw6 camph kr1 ign j5.de irid-met srj5• kali-p fd1.de• lach j5.de nept-m lsd2.fr plut-n srj7• positr nl2• pycnop-sa mrz1 rhod kr1 squil j5.de staph j5.de tung-met bdx1•

INDIGESTION agg.: kali-bi bg2

INDIGNATION: *(↗Ailments - anger - indignation; Ailments - embarrassment; Ailments - honor; Ailments - mortification; Ailments - reproaches; Ailments - scorned; Anger; Brooding; Hatred; Injustice; Violent - reproached)* acon j* adam srj ambr k* androc srj1• arge-pl rwt5• *Ars* k* aster ↓ aur aur-m-n wbt2• bros-gau mrc1 bry gl1.fr• *Calc-p* k* caps carc mlr1• cham gl1.fr• chin k* cocc *Colch* ↓ *Coloc* k* croc falco-pe nl2• ferr-p a1 fic-m gya1 foll oss• gels vh germ-met srj5• granit-m es1• graph h2 hep oss• ign ip st1* irid-met srj5• lac-c zzb lac-cp sk4• lac-e hrn2• lac-leo hrn2*• led sne m-ambo h1 med jl nat-c *Nat-m* sne nitro-o a1 nux-v vh* o e n a a1 op ↓ pip-m ↓ podo fd3.de• positr nl2• psor bgs sabad wf sal-fr sle1• *Spig* gl1.fr• spong fd4.de **Staph** k* stry mrr1 sulph h2 suprar rly4• tere-la rly4• verat gl1.fr• [heroin sdj2 oxyg stj]
- **morning**: ars k*
- **alternating** with:
  - **mildness**: *Ars* a
  - **mirth**: aster sze10• aur caps croc ign k*
- **discomfort**; from general: op
- **dreams**; at unpleasant: calc-p
- **emission**, after: pip-m a
- **hypocrisy**; by society: bros-gau mrc1
- **irritability**, with: coloc h2
- **misdeeds** of others; at the: *(↗Anger - indignation)* *Colch* a1* coloc h2 podo fd3.de• *Staph* bro1*
- **pregnant**, while: nat-m k*
- **rage**, with: falco-pe nl2•
- **slandering**, with: spig gl•

INDISCRETION: *(↗Curious; Curious - training; Gossiping; Heedless; Impetuous; Impulsive; Loquacity; Meddlesome; Rash; Revealing; Sensitive - want; Touching; Touching - impelled - everything)* acon agar alum gl1.fr• arn vh* aur bg aur-s wbt2• *Bar-c* vh* bov vh* bry bufo gk calad calc gl1.fr• camph caps caust gl1.fr• con gl1.fr• croc j5.de cypra-eg sde6.de• germ-met srj graph gl1.fr• hyos k* ign kali-c jl3 lac-f wza1• lach laur k* lyc gl1.fr• meny *Merc* gl1.fr• nat-m k* *Nux-v* k* op vh* phyt c1 plat gl1.fr• **Puls** k ●* sep gl1.fr• spong vh* staph mtf33* *Stram* k* sulph gl1.fr• verat vh*

INDOLENCE (See Laziness; Time - fritters; Undertaking; Undertaking - many)

INDUSTRIOUS (= mania for work): *(↗Activity - desires; Business - desire; Busy; Delirium - business; Delirium - busy; Delusions - business - doing; Delusions - business - ordinary; Delusions - engaged - occupation; Delusions - engaged - occupation - ordinary; Exertion - physical - amel.; Insanity - busy; Irritability - idle; Mental exertion - amel.; Mental exertion - desire; Occupation - amel.; Perseverance; Rest - cannot; Restlessness - busy; Talking - business)* acon j5.de* adam srj5• aeth bro1 agar k* aids nl2• allox sp1 aln vva1• aloe bg2* ang bg2 apis b7a.de* ara-maca sej7• arist-cl sp1 arn k* ars k* **Aur** k* aur-ar k2 aur-m-n wbt2• *Aur-s* zr *Bar-c* k* bell k* brom bg2* bry k* bufo gk calc k* calc-act a1 calc-ar a1 calc-f jl3 calc-p k* calc-sil mtf33 cann-xyz bg2 caps k* carc hbh* caust gl1.fr• cere-b k* chin k* chir-fl gya2 choc srj3• cic b7a.de cimic bg2* cit-v a1 clem k* cob-n sp1 coca ↓ *Cocain* bro1 cocc k* **Coff** bg2* cupr sst3• cycl bg2 des-ac rbp6 dicha a1* dig k* dream-p sdj1• *Eucal* bro1 euph b4a.de* euphr bg2 falco-pe nl2• fic-m gya1 fl-ac bg2* gamb a1 guare a1 haliae-lc srj5• ham fd3.de• helo bg2 *Helo-s* rwt2• *Helon* bro1 hydrog srj2• *Hyos* k* hyper a1 *Ign* k* ina-i mlk9.de indg *Iod* bg2* ip k* irid-met srj5• kali-br bg2 kali-c st kali-p ↓ kola stb3• kreos lac-e hrn2• lac-leo hrn2• lac-lup hrn2• *Lacer* bro1 *Lach* k* laur b7.de* led lil-t bg2 loxo-recl knl4• *Lyc* bg2* *M-ambo* b7.de* m-arct b7.de* mag-c k* mag-m bg2 manc a1 mand sp1 marb-w es1• med gk melal-alt gya4 menth a1 merc gk mez k* mosch k* mur-ac k* murx a1 musca-d szs1 nat-c k* nat-m a1 nat-s k* neon srj5• nux-v bg2* *Op* k* p e d a1* petr-ra shn4• phos k* pic-ac bg2 pip-m k* pisc bro1 plac ↓ plan a1 plb k* *Plut-n* srj7• podo fd3.de• positr nl2• puls bg2 querc-r svu1• rhus-g ↓ rhus-t k* sacch-a fd2.de• sal-fr sle1• sanguis-s hrn2• sars b4.de* seneg j5.de *Sep* k* sil bng *Spig* gl1.fr• stann k* staph bg2* stram bg2 sul-ac k* sulph bg2* **Tarent** k* tere-la rly4• ther j5.de* thuj b4a.de* **Tub** vh* *Valer* bg2 verat k* verb b7a.de* viol-o bg2 zinc b4.de* [bell-p-sp dcm1 ferr-i stj1 heroin sdj2 kali-m stj1]
- **morning**: coca ↓ sacch-a fd2.de•
  - 7-9 h: coca a1
- **afternoon**: sacch-a fd2.de• sars a1
- **evening**: kali-p fd1.de• lac-leo hrn2• *Lach* stann mg
- **night**: coca a1 ham fd3.de• kali-p fd1.de• sacch-a fd2.de•
- **coition**, after: calc-p k*
- **dispatches** things quickly: menth c1
- **efficient**: lac-lup hrn2•
- **fever**; during: op bg2 sars bg2 *Thuj* b4.de* verb bg2
- **finish** his work | **desire** to: carc sst2• cupr sst3• med jl2
- **heat**, during: op sars *Thuj* verb
- **household** affairs; in: plac rzf5• [bell-p-sp dcm1]
- **menses**: *(↗Menses - before)*
  - **before**: *(↗Menses - before)* ars dgt *Bar-c* k* bell k* bry k* *Calc* k* *Calc-p* k* carc sst2* chin k* cocc k* *Hyos* k* *Ign* k* ip k* kreos k* **Lach** k* *Mag-c* k* mag-m dgt mez k* mosch k* mur-ac k* nat-c k* *Phos* k* rhus-t k* **Sep** k* stann k* sul-ac k* **Verat** k*
  - **during**: rhus-g tmo3•
- **pain**; although: *Des-ac* rbp6
- **weary**; although: dicha jl mosch bg2

INEFFICIENT; feeling (See Confidence - want; Delusions - fail, everything; Fear - failure)

INEXORABLE (See Hardhearted)

INFANTILE behavior (See Childish)

INFERIORITY (See Confidence - want)

INFLEXIBLE (See Obstinate)

INHIBITION: *(↗Reserved; Timidity)* **Ambr** vh1 lach mrr1 staph mrr1
- **social** inhibition; lack of (See Indiscretion; Truth)

INHUMANITY (See Cruelty)

INITIATIVE, lack of: *(↗Irresolution; Will - weakness)* agar vh1 anh sp1 aur gl1.fr• calc a1* calc-f jl hydroph rsj6• ign bl iod gl1.fr• lach gl1.fr• l y c gl1.fr• onop jl rhus-t gl1.fr• saroth sp1 sil a1* sulph gl1.fr• *Symph* fd3.de• thala jl [tax jsj7]

INJURIES (See Ailments - injuries)

Mind

INJURING himself: (*↗Fear - accidents; Hysteria - injure; Impulse - stab - his; Loathing - life - injury; Masochism; Mutilating; Suicidal)* agar↓ cimic br1 lac-h sk4• lyss↓ *Nat-s*↓ tarent mtf33 [lac-mat sst4]
- **fear** to be left alone, lest he should injure himself: (*↗Fear - suicide; Impulse - stab - his; Kill; desire - herself; Loathing - life - injury; Suicidal)* alum arg-n ars k* *Cimic* kr1 kola stb3• *Merc* k* *Nat-s* k* sep
- **frenzy** causing him to injure himself: agar k* lyss a1
- **sensation** as if she could easily injure herself: germ-met srj lyss↓ sep
  - • **rage**; out: lyss a
- **shooting** himself from satiety; must use self-control to prevent: *Nat-s* k*

INJUSTICE, cannot support: (*↗Ailments - honor; Ailments - moral; Fight - helpless; Honest; Idealistic; Indignation; Sympathetic)* ambr tsm1* ars mtf aur lmj* aur-m-n wbt2• *Aur-s* wbt2• bell mtf bry mtf bung-fa mtf calc ctc* calc-p lmj* **Carc** fd* **Caust** vh* chel vml* chin lmj coloc mrr* crot-c sk4• cupr sht* dros skp* *Dulc* fd4.de elaps mtf *Falco-pe* nl2• fic-m gya1 *Foll* oss• *Ham* fd3.de• hecla alm* hep oss• *Ign* lmj* ignis-alc es2• *Kali-i* gk *Kola* stb3• lac-e gk* mag-c lmj* mag-m gk* med dx1* merc sht* naja mtf nat-c↓ *Nat-m* lmj* nit-ac lmj nux-v h1* pall↓ petr-ra shn4• ph-ac dgt phos lmj* plat mtf plb cld* *Podo* fd3.de• positr nl2• *Puls* mtf rhus-g tmo3• sep hsa* *Spong* fd4.de **Staph** lmj* sulph gk* symph fd3.de• tub lmj verat bg [am-c stj1 am-m stj1 cupr-act stj2 cupr-f stj2 cupr-m stj2 cupr-p stj2]
- **children**; in: am-c lmj am-m lmj aur lmj *Calc-p* lmj **Caust** lmj chin lmj **Coloc** lmj dros lmj *Ign* lmj *Mag-c* lmj *Mag-m* lmj *Merc* lmj nat-c lmj **Nat-m** lmj nit-ac lmj **Nux-v** lmj pall lmj phos lmj sep lmj **Staph** lmj tub lmj
- **cool** in the face of unjustified anger: falco-pe nl2•

INNOVATIVE: (*↗Activity - desires - creative)* chin mtf sulph mtf tub mtf

INNOCENT (See Childish; Naive)

INQUISITIVE (See Curious; Indiscretion; Spying)

INSANITY (= madness): (*↗Ambition; Delirium; Delusions - distinguished; Delusions - great; Delusions - insane; Delusions - noble; Delusions - superhuman - control; Delusions - visions - grandeur; Dictatorial - power; Insanity - crazy; Mania; Monomania; Rage; Stupefaction; Wild feeling; Wildness; DREAMS - Insane)* absin acon k* aeth k* aether a1 *Agar* k* agn↓ ail alco a1 all-c k* *Alum* alum-p k2* alum-sil k2 *Am-c* k* ambr k2* *Anac* k* anag kr1 anan kr1 anh br1 ant-c k* ant-t *Apis* k* *Arg-met* k* arg-n k* *Arn* k* **Ars** k* ars-i ars-s-f k2 arum-t aster↓ atro sf1.de *Aur* k* aur-ar k2 aur-i k2 aur-s k2* bac c1* bacls-7↓ bar-c *Bar-m* **Bell** k* berb bg2 borx k2 bov brom bry b7a.de bufo buth-a↓ cact calad *Calc* k* calc-ar k2 calc-i k2 *Calc-p*↓ calc-s calc-sil k2 *Camph* cann-i cann-s k* *Cann-xyz*↓ *Canth* k* carb-an carb-v↓ carbn-s carc mlr1• carneg-g↓ *Caust* k* cench k2 cere-b c1* cham↓ *Chel* kr1 *Chin*↓ chinin-s chlol *Chlor*↓ *Cic* k* *Cimic* k* *Cocc* k* coff k* colch coleus-a bnj1 coloc k* *Con* k* cori-r↓ cortiso sp1 *Croc* k* *Crot-c* crot-h k* crot-t↓ *Cupr* k* *Cupr-act*↓ cur *Cycl* dig k* diphtox↓ *Dulc* k* eberth jl2 euph ferr-p↓ fl-ac gaert↓ gels sf1.de germ-met srj5• *Glon* k* *Graph*↓ *Grat*↓ haliae-lc srj5• *Hell* k* helo-s bnm14*• *Hep* k* hipp↓ **Hydr-ac**↓ **Hyos** k* *Hyper*↓ *Ign* k* ind↓ indg iod k* ip↓ kali-ar kali-bi a1 *Kali-br* k* kali-c *Kali-chl* k* kali-i *Kali-m* hr1* kali-ox *Kali-p* kola stb3• kreos↓ lac-c↓ *Lach* k* lat-m bnm6• led k* *Lil-t* lob a1 *Lol* sf1.de **Lyc** k* lyss↓ mag-m↓ *Manc* mand sp1 med k2* melal-alt↓ meli c1* meli-xyz c2 **Merc** k* merc-c mez morg↓ mosch sf1.de murx sf1.de naja nat-c k* nat-i↓ *Nat-m* nat-s nat-sal↓ nit-ac↓ *Nux-m* k* **Nux-v** k* oena olnd k* *Op* k* opun-s a1 (non:opun-v a1) *Orig*↓ *Ox-ac* par k* passi sf1.de penic srb2.fr *Petr*↓ ph-ac *Phos* k* phys phyt↓ *Pic-ac*↓ *Plat* k* plb k* *Psor* *Puls* k* raph rhod *Rhus-t* k* sabad sec k* sel↓ senec↓ seneg sep k* ser-a-c↓ sil sol-ni sf1.de squil k* stach-a↓ stann a1* **Staph**↓ **Stram** k* stry↓ sulfonam↓ *Sulph* k* syph ptk1* **Tarent** k* ter k* ther↓ thuj thyr↓ *Tub* hr1* **Verat** k* verat-v verb↓ vip ptk1 zinc k* zinc-p k2* [alumin stj2 arg-p stj2 astat stj2 aur-m stj2 bar-br stj2 bar-i stj2 bar-met stj2 bism-sn stj2 caes-met stj2 cinnb stj2 cupr-m stj2 cupr-p stj2 hafn-met stj2 irid-met stj2 lanth-met stj2 lith-i stj2 mang-i stj2 merc-d stj2 merc-i-f stj2 osm-met stj2 pall stj2 plb-m stj2 plb-p stj2 polon-met stj2 rhen-met stj2 tant-met stj2 thal-met stj2 tung-met stj2 zinc-i stj2 zinc-m stj2 zinc-n stj2]
- **evening**: ambr st
- **night**: stry a
- **alternating** with:
  - • **fever**; inflammatory: tub c1
  - • **mental** symptoms; other: *Con* sabad k* stram b7a.de

Insanity – alternating with: ...
  - • **metrorrhagia**: crot-c
  - • **physical** symptoms: (*↗Mental symptoms - alternating - physical)* cere-b a1 *Croc* hyos *Lil-t* *Plat* tub k2*
  - • **sadness**: tub br1
  - • **stupor**: apis dm* *Hyos* ptk1 op
- **amenorrhea**, from: (*↗Wicked - amenorrhea)* *Cocc* kr1
- **anger**, from: (*↗Anger)* bell j5.de* *Ign* *Lach* gl1.fr• lyc j5.de melal-alt gya4 op j5.de *Plat* k1* staph gl1.fr•
- **anxiety**, with: *Agar* b4a.de ars j5.de bell j5.de* cupr b7a.de* kali-c j5.de lyc b4a.de nat-c j5.de *Stram* b7a.de* verat j5.de verb↓
  - • **neuralgia**; in facial: verb kr1
- **apoplexy**: | **after**: hell ptk1*
- **appetite**, with loss of: verat lpc
- **black** insanity with despair and weariness of life | **fear** of mortification or loss of position; from: (*↗mortification; mortification - from; Ailments - mortification; Ailments - position)* calc gl1.fr• ign gl1.fr• puls gl1.fr• rhus-t gl1.fr• staph gl1.fr• sulph gl1.fr• verat gl1.fr•
- **blood** circulation; with complaints of: cupr b7a.de
- **break** pins; she will sit and: bell calc
- **brutal**: absin ptk1*
- **bulimia**; with: (*↗Bulimia)* chin gl1.fr• **Verat** gk*
  - • **alternating** with refusal to eat (See Bulimia - alternating - refusal - insanity)
- **burrows** in ground with his mouth, like a pig: stram kr1
- **business** failure; from: (*↗Ailments - business)* *Cimic* kr1* *Lil-t* kr1
- **busy**: (*↗Busy; Industrious)* **Apis** k* bell j5.de hyos k2 *Iod* kr1 kali-br k*
- **capricious**: raph kr1
- **character**; of somber: nat-sal a
- **cheerful**, gay: bell b4a.de* cann-s b7a.de* croc b7.de* cupr b7a.de* *Hyos* b7a.de ign b7.de* mez j5.de stram b7.de* verat j5.de
- **chill**; during: acon bg2 ars bg2 bell bg2 *Cann-xyz* bg2 canth bg2 hyos bg2 lyc bg2 nit-ac bg2 nux-v bg2 op bg2 plat bg2 stram bg2 sulph bg2 verat bg2
- **chilliness**, with: calc crot-h↓ phyt kr1
  - • **coldness** of skin; and: crot-h
- **cold**, after taking: bell j
- **company**; with desire for | **light**; and: **Stram** kr1
- **convulsions**, with: cupr kr1 *Hyos* kr1 oena hl phos kr1 *Stram* kr1 *Verat-v* kr1 *Zinc* kr1
- **cough**; with: bell lpc1 verat lpc1
- **crawls** on the floor (See Crawling - floor)
- **crazy** person; behaves like a: (*↗Busy; Foolish; Insanity)* cann-xyz bg2 croc bg2 germ-met srj hyos bg2 kali-ar lach bg2 nux-m bg2 sec bg2 stram bg2* tarent bg2 verat bg2
- **dancing**, with: (*↗Dancing)* bell j5.de cic j5.de* hyos j5.de* ph-ac j5.de
  - • **stripping** himself; and: *Bell* a1*
- **delivery**; during: (*↗puerperal)* bell lpc kali-p ptk lach ptk phos ptk sec hs1
- **despair**; with: calc gl1.fr• ign gl1.fr• puls gl1.fr• rhus-t gl1.fr• staph gl1.fr• sulph gl1.fr• verat gl1.fr•
- **dictatorial**: (*↗Dictatorial)* **Lyc** j5.de*
- **discharge** of blood, with: merc j
- **dispute**, to: camph lpc
- **distortion** of mouth, with: ph-ac lpc
- **distress**, with: *Stram* kr1
- **domestic** calamity, after: *Lach* kr1
- **dresses** in his best clothes: con
- **drunk**, as if: oena kr1
- **drunkards**, in: (*↗Delirium tremens)* **Ars** k1* ars-s-f k2 aur-ar k2 *Bell* k1* calc cann-i carb-v chin *Coff* crot-h dig hell hep *Hyos* *Lach* merc nat-c **Nux-v** *Op* puls *Stram* sulph
- **eating**:
  - • **dirt**: (*↗Feces - licks; Feces - swallows)* meli sulph j5.de*
  - • **dung**: merc st
  - • **refuses** to eat: (*↗Anorexia nervosa; Eating - refuses)* bell gl1.fr• carc mlr1• verat gl1.fr•
- **emaciation**, with: sulph lpc
- **ensue**; sensation as if it would (See Fear - insanity)
- **envy**, with: (*↗Envy)* **Lyc** gl1.fr•

- **erotic**: *(↗Lascivious; Shameless)* **Apis** k* *Bar-m* k* bell j5.de* bufo ptk1* *Calc-p* a1* camph c1 *Canth* c1* dulc↓ *Grat* vh/dg* *Hyos* k* kali-br kola stb3* lyss *Nux-v* c1 *Orig* k* *Phos* k* *Pic-ac* c1 **Plat** k* *Puls* stann a1 *Stram* j5.de* *Sulph* **Tarent** k* **Verat** k* zinc k*
  - **girl**, in hysterical: *Plat* kr1
  - **jealousy**, with: *Hyos* kr1
  - **menses**:
    - **after**: *(↗Menses - after)* *Kali-br* kr1
    - **before**: dulc ptk1 stann ptk1
- **eructations** amel.: mag-m ptk
- **eruptions**; after suppressed: ant-t cda ars j bell *Caust* k* *Hep* kr1 mez stram *Sulph* k* *Zinc* k*
- **escape**, desire to: *(↗Escape)* ars j5.de* *Bell* j5.de* cupr j5.de dig j5.de nux-v j5.de *Op* gl1.fr• stram gl1.fr• verat j5.de
- **face**:
  - **heat** of; with: verat lpc
  - **pale**; with: camph kr1 cortiso kr1 croc j5.de* merc j5.de **Stram** kr1 verat j5.de
  - **red**; with: aur-i k2 calc j5.de kali-br sne op j5.de stram mrr1 verat j5.de
  - **wild** look; with: cupr lpc
- **fanatics**, of: aur-ar k2
- **foolish**, ridiculous: *Bell* b4a.de* cic j5.de **Hyos** j5.de* merc j5.de nux-m j5.de nux-v j5.de
- **fortune**:
  - **gaining**; after: bell gl1.fr• *Caust* gl1.fr• puls gl1.fr• stram gl1.fr• verat gl1.fr•
  - **losing**, after: *(↗Ailments - fortune)* calc gl1.fr• ign gl1.fr• rhus-t gl1.fr• verat gl1.fr•
- **fright**, from: *(↗Ailments - fright)* **Ars** gl1.fr• **Bell** gl1.fr• *Ign* lach kr1 meli sne merc kr1 plat sabad ptk stram kr1
- **gesticulations**, with: bell a
- **gluttony** (See bulimia)
- **graveyards**; visiting: bell j stram j
- **grief**, from: *(↗Ailments - grief)* **Ars** gl1.fr• **Bell** gl1.fr• *Cocc* kr1 ign sne meli sne *Plat* kr1
- **haughty**: *(↗Haughty)* lach j5.de **Lyc** gl1.fr• phos br1 *Stram* gl1.fr•
- **head** washing in cold water amel.: sabad ptk1
- **headache**; from (See pain; from - head)
- **heart** enlargement; with: aur-i k2
- **heat**; with: ant-c bg2 *Ars* bg2* bell k* cact bg2* calc j canth bg2 *Chin* kr1 **Cic** bg2 dulc bg2 hyos j5.de* *Kali-p* kr1 *Op* bg2 stram k* verat k*
- **hemorrhage**, after: carb-v *Chin* k* *Cupr* k* kreos ph-ac *Sep* k* staph verat
- **hysterical**: ign k2 orig hl
- **immobile** as a statue: *(↗Stupefaction - sits; Unconsciousness - remains - motionless)* cham j5.de fl-ac k2 hyos j5.de* ser-a-c jl2
- **injuries** to the head, from: *(↗Ailments - injuries; Confusion - injury - after)* alco a1 nat-s k*
- **insensibility**; with general: *(↗GENERALS - Painlessness)* **Hydr-ac** gl1.fr• hyos gl1.fr• stram gl1.fr•
- **job**; from fear to lose the: *(↗Ailments - position)* calc gl1.fr• ign gl1.fr• puls gl1.fr• rhus-t gl1.fr• staph gl1.fr• sulph gl1.fr• verat gl1.fr•
- **joy**, from, with headache: croc kr1
- **lamenting**, moaning; only: *(↗Lamenting)* bell j5.de* hyos gl1.fr• stram gl1.fr•
- **lascivious**: *(↗Lascivious)* hyos bg2* *Plat* b4a.de tarent hr1 *Verat* bg2
- **laughing**, with: *(↗Mania - laughing)* camph kr1 *Hyos* mrr1 op j5.de sec j5.de *Stram* j5.de *Tarent* kr1 *Verat* j5.de *Verat-v* kr1
- **loquacious**: *(↗Loquacity)* *Anac* b4a.de bell j5.de bry gl1.fr• buth-a jl *Cimic* sne cupr b7a.de hyos j5.de* **Lach** b7a.de* *Meli* sne par b7.de* *Stram* b7.de*
- **love**; from disappointed: *(↗Ailments - love)* tarent a1
- **malicious** (= malignant): *(↗Malicious)* agar j5.de *Bell* vh* cann-s j5.de *Cupr* k* gaert fmm1• *Hyos* vh* lyc j5.de morg fmm1• **Stram** vh*
  - **old** age; in: morg fmm1•
- **malignant** (See malicious)
- **masturbation**, from: *(↗Ailments - sexual excesses)* anan kr1 bufo k* *Cocc* k* *Hyos* k* op ptk1 orig vh *Plat* vh* *Plb* kr1
- **megalomania**: anac lmp bacls-7 fmm1• cupr b7a.de* glon sf1.de *Graph* kr1 *Hyos* b7.de* *Lach* b7a.de* lyc sf1.de *Phos* kr1 *Plat* b4a.de* *Puls* b7a.de *Stram* b7.de* sulph sf1.de *Syph* st* *Verat* b7.de* *Verat-v* kr1
- **melancholy**: bell gl1.fr• calc gl1.fr• hyos gl1.fr• *Ign* j5.de* *Kali-br* kr1 *Petr* gl1.fr• ph-ac gl1.fr• *Puls* gl1.fr• rhus-t gl1.fr• staph gl1.fr• sulph gl1.fr• verat gl1.fr•
- **menopause**, during: aster cimic jl cycl kr1* hipp kr1* *Lach* *Lil-t* kr1* *Puls* *Sep* *Sulph* kr1* ther *Verat* kr1*
- **menses**:
  - **before**: cimic ptk1 dulc ptk stann ptk
  - **copious**, with: **Ign** vh* sep k*
  - **during**: *(↗Menses - during)* acon b7.de* *Bell* bg2* cham b7.de coff b7.de *Hyos* b7.de lach bg2 puls bg2 stram b7.de* verat b7.de*
  - **profuse**, with (See copious)
  - **suppressed**, with: apis ptk1 ign k* kali-br sne *Puls* k* sec sne
- **mental** exertion; from: *(↗Mental exertion - agg. - impossible - crazy)* hyos ind↓ *Kali-p* k* *Lach* k* **Nux-v** k1* *Phos* k* **Tub** st
  - **headache**; with: ind kr1
- **mild**: croc b7.de* verat b7.de*
- **misfortune** after: calc jsa ign jsa nat-m jsa rhus-t jsa
- **mortification**: *(↗black - fear)*
  - **fear** of; from: calc gl1.fr• ign gl1.fr• puls gl1.fr• rhus-t gl1.fr• staph gl1.fr• sulph gl1.fr• verat gl1.fr•
  - **from**: *(↗black - fear; Ailments - mortification)* bell j5.de *Lach* gl1.fr• **Nux-v** j5.de* plat gl1.fr• *Puls* j5.de **Staph** gl1.fr*
- **neuralgia** | **disappearance** of; with: cimic k* *Nat-m* k*
- **noisy**: chlol kr1 *Chlor* kr1
- **old** people; in: bell pc ign pc nat-m pc nux-v pc sep pc sulph pc
- **orgasm**, at height of: lac-c ptk
- **pain**; from intolerable: *(↗Sensitive - pain)* **Acon** kr1* *Bell*↓ canth↓ *Colch* kr1 croc↓ cupr↓ *Hyper* kr1 **Verat** h1*
  - ○ **Abdomen**, in: canth lpc cupr lpc
  - **Head**; in: *Bell* kr1 croc lpc1 verat lpc1
  - **Larynx**, in: canth lpc1
- **painlessness** (See insensibility)
- **paralysis**, with: ant-c bro1 ars bro1* aur bro1 bell hr1* *Cann-i* bro1 caust bro1 chlol hr1 crot-h ptk2 hyos k13* kali-br c1* kali-i bro1 *Lach* st lol ah merc-c bro1 nat-i bro1 nux-v bro1 op bro1 *Phos* c1* phys bro1 plb bro1 stram bro1 sulph bro1 verat bro1
- **paroxysmal**: *Bell* cic kr1 *Dig* gels kali-i *Nat-m* kr1 nat-s phos stram k2 *Tarent*
- **periodical**: *Con* k* nat-s k* *Plat* k* staph vh *Tarent* k1*
- **persecution** mania: *(↗Anxiety - pursued; Delusions - persecuted; Delusions - pursued; Schizophrenia - paranoid)* **Ars** gl1.fr• calc gl1.fr• caust gl1.fr• lach gl1.fr• sulfonam jl verat gl1.fr•
- **perspiration**:
  - **cold**; with: stram ptk1
  - **fits** of insanity followed by perspiration: cupr
- **position**; from fear to lose his (See job)
- **prayer**:
  - **insists** upon saying his prayer at the tail of his horse: euph
  - **raising** hands and kneeling as in prayer: *Ars* a1
- **pregnancy**, in: *Bell* j5.de* cimic k1 hyos bro1 *Stram* kr1
- **puerperal**: *(↗delivery; Escape - mania; Jumping - wild; Mania - puerperal)* agn bg2* *Aur* k* bar-c *Bell* k* bry gl1.fr• *Camph* k* *Cann-i* sf1.de cann-xyz bg2 canth bg2* *Chlol* hr1* cic bg2* *Cimic* k* crot-h *Cupr* k* *Cupr-act* kr1 ferr-p k2 *Hyos* k* *Kali-bi* kr1 kali-br kali-c kali-p c1 *Lyc* k* merc c1 nat-m bg2 *Nux-v* bg2* *Petr* kr1 phos bg2* *Plat* k* *Puls* k* *Sec* bg2* senec bg2* *Stram* k* *Sulph* kr1 thuj ptk1 thyr al* *Verat* k* verat-v k* zinc k* [cann-s xyz62]
- **pulse**; with frequent: ars j5.de crot-h j5.de cupr j5.de *Cupr-act* kr1
- **purchases**; makes useless: *(↗Delusions - wealth; Squandering)* carneg-g rwt1• con *Nux-v* kr1
- **putting** tongue out (See tongue - putting)
- **quarrelsome**: *(↗Quarrelsome)* hyos ptk1* *Verat* hr1
- **rage**: ars-s-f k2 germ-met srj *Hyos* mrr1 oena hl *Tarent* kr1
- **religious**: *(↗Mania - religious; Religious - too; Religious - too - fanaticism; Religious - too - melancholia)* anac k2 *Ars* b4a.de* aur b4a.de* aur-ar k2 bell sf1.de *Calc* b4a.de camph ptk1 croc sf1.de *Hyos* br1* *Kali-br* kr1* *Lach* j5.de* lil-t k2 lyc b4a.de* meli sne merc sf1.de nat-c k2* nux-v sf1.de *Plat* b4a.de* *Puls* b7a.de* sel b7a.de **Stram** b7a.de* *Sulph* b4a.de* tarent sne *Thuj* b4a.de *Verat* b7.de*
- **reproaches** others: *(↗Reproaching others)* **Lyc** gl1.fr•

- **restlessness**, with: *(↗Restlessness)* *Ars* j5.de* bell gl1.fr• bry gl1.fr• canth j5.de chin gl1.fr• *Hyos* j5.de* meli sne merc j5.de nux-v j5.de* puls gl1.fr• rhus-t vh staph vh stram j5.de* tarent vh verat gl1.fr•
  - **lower** limbs; of: *(↗EXTREMITIES - Restlessness - lower)* **Tarent** k1
- **sadness**; with: *(↗Sadness)* bac al bell gl• calc gl• diphtox jl2 hyos gl• *Ign* j *Kali-br* kr1 nat-sal ↓ petr gl• ph-ac gl• rhus-t gl• sulph gl• verat gl•
  - **paroxysms**; in: nat-sal br1
- **secretive**: *(↗Secretive)* dig b4a.de*
- **sensation** of (See Delusions - insane - he)
- **sexual** excesses, from: anan kr1 *Apis* ptk1 *Lach* gl1.fr• lil-t kr1 *Phos* kr1 staph gl1.fr•
- **shy**: *(↗Timidity)* agar j5.de* *Anac* b4a.de
- **signs**, writes unintelligible (See writes)
- **silent**: *(↗Quiet disposition)* bell b4a.de verat j5.de *Verat-v* kr1
- **sleeplessness**, with: *Bell* st* carc mlr1• *Cocc* kr1 *Hyos* st* meli sne nux-m j5.de op j5.de *Stram* kr1 *Tarent* kr1
- **split** his head in two with an axe; suddenly wants to: *(↗Fear - suicide; Suicidal)* *Naja* a1
- **stamps** the feet: ant-c stram gl1.fr• verat
- **staring** of eyes: *(↗Staring; EYE - Staring)* *Bell* j5.de* *Camph* kr1 crot-t j5.de stram j5.de
- **strength**; with increased: *(↗Rage - chained)* agar k* *Bell* k* canth cori-r hyos k* *Plat* sne *Plb* vh* *Stram* k* **Tarent** k*
- **stupidity**; with: arn b7a.de cic b7a.de hyos b7a.de op b7a.de stram b7a.de verat b7a.de
- **suicidal** disposition, with: *(↗Fear - suicide; Suicidal)* ars j5.de* aur br1 hyos j5.de naja br1* orig hl verat j5.de
- **syphilis**, in: anag kr1 syph ptk1
- **taciturnity**; with: ant-c b7a.de *Aur* b4a.de dig b4a.de hell b7a.de hyos b7a.de *Lyc* b4a.de
- **talking**; with wild: *(↗Speech - wild)* *Hyos* mrr1
- **thoughts**; with persistent: anac bg2 sulph bg2
- **tapping** about the room: hyos j
- **threatened**; when: meli sne
- **threatening** destruction and death: *(↗Threatening; Violent)* **Tarent** k1
- **throwing** stones: bell j
- **timidity**; with (See shy)
- **tongue**:
  - **putting** tongue out, clicking, distortion of face; with: bell j5.de*
  - **white** discoloration of tongue; with: nux-v kr1*
- **touched**, will not be: *(↗Delusions - body - brittle; Touched - aversion)* meli sne *Thuj* k*
- **travel**, with desire to: *(↗Travelling - desire)* bell gl1.fr• bry gl1.fr• chin gl1.fr• hyos gl1.fr• nux-v gl1.fr• puls gl1.fr• stram gl1.fr• tub k2 verat gl1.fr•
- **trembling**: ars lpc
- **urinating** on the floor: *(↗Delirium - urinating - floor; Dirty - urinating)* plb ptk1
- **varicose** veins:
  - **after**: anac ptk1 ant-c ptk1 arn ptk1 ars ptk1 bell ptk1 caust ptk1 hyos ptk1 ign ptk1 lach ptk1 lyc ptk1 nux-v ptk1 phos ptk1 sep ptk1 sulph ptk1 verat ptk1
  - **with**: arn ptk1 ars ptk1 fl-ac ptk1 lach ptk1 lyc ptk1 sulph ptk1 *Zinc* ptk1
- **vertigo**, with: nux-m lpc
- **violent**: agar b4a.de* apis bg2 ars bg2 bell bg2 *Bry* b7a.de *Cann-s* b7a.de *Cupr* b7a.de *Hyos* b7.de* lyc b4a.de merc bg2 *Plb* b7a.de sec bg2 *Stram* b7.de*
- **vomiting**, with: cupr-act lpc
- **wantonness**, with: *(↗Ailments - sexual excesses)* bell j5.de cupr *Hyos* merc j5.de mez j5.de stram verat
- **weariness** of live; with: *(↗Weary)* calc gl1.fr• ign gl1.fr• puls gl1.fr• rhus-t gl1.fr• staph gl1.fr• sulph gl1.fr• verat gl1.fr•
- **wedding**; preparing for: *(↗Marriage - unendurable)* hyos ptk1
- **weeping**, with: *(↗Weeping)* ars k13 merc j5.de *Puls* kr1 stram j5.de
- **women**; in: *Acon* bg* apis ptk1 *Bell* bg* cimic ptk1 *Orig* ptk1 plat bg* *Puls* bg* stram bg* verat bg*
  - **alternating** with stupor: apis ptk1*
  - **reproaching** herself; from: *(↗Reproaching oneself)* hell ptk1
- **writes** unintelligible signs: ars a1
- **eye**:
  - **complaints** of eyes; with: cupr b7a.de

Insanity – **eye**: ...

  - **inflammation** of; during: croc lpc op lpc
- **stomach**; with burning in: oena hr1*
- **throat**; with burning in: oena hr1*

INSECURITY; mental: *(↗Cautious; Confidence - want; Cowardice; Delusions - friend - affection; Delusions - neglected - he; Discouraged; Helplessness; Irresolution; Longing - good; Reproaching oneself; Suggestible; Timidity; Timidity - bashful)* agath-a nl2• aids nl2• alum-sil vh1 *Aml-ns* kr1 anac mrr1 anh sp1 aq-mar rbp6 arizon-l nl2• ars vh atp rly4• bamb-a stb2.de• berb ↓ *Bry* a1 calc-sil mtf33 cann-xyz bg2 caps ckh1 cham bg2 choc srj3• cypra-eg sde6.de• dioxi rbp6 dulc fd4.de dys fmm1• falco-pe nl2• galeoc-c-h ↓ gels mrr1 granit-m es1• hydrog srj2• kali-p fd1.de* kali-s fd4.de lac-del ↓ pin-con oss2• plb ↓ positr nl2• pycnop-sa mrz1 rhod kgp5• ros-d wla1 *Ruta* fd4.de *Sacch-a* fd2.de• sil mrr1* staph tl1 sumb a1 tritic-vg fd5.de tus-p ↓ vanil fd5.de [buteo-j sej6 erech stj helia stj heroin sdj2]
- **afternoon**: hydrog srj2•
- **hiding** it; but is: galeoc-c-h gms1• [helia stj tus-p stj]
- **sensation** of: lac-del hrn2•
- **woman**; as a: [berb stu1]
- **working**; while: ros-d wla1

INSENSIBILITY (See Unconsciousness)

INSIGHTFUL: *(↗Thoughts - past - insightful; Will - loss - insight)* lac-leo hrn2• [tax jsj7]

INSIGNIFICANT; sensation as if one is (See Confidence - want)

INSOLENCE: *(↗Abusive; Audacity; Behavior; Contemptuous; Contradiction - disposition; Cursing; Defiant; Dictatorial; Haughty; Impertinence; Impolite; Laughing - contemptuous; Mocking; Presumptuous; Reverence - lack; Rudeness; Slander; Smiling - sardonic)* acon kl aloe sne *Anac* bg2* arn h1* ars bro1 bar-c bg2 bell bufo bro1* calc gl1.fr• *Canth* k* caust ↓ cham bg2* chin bro1 cic sne cupr bro1 granit-m es1• *Graph* k* hell bg2 *Hyos* k* ign b7.de* *Lac-c* k* lach bg2* lil-t ptk1 **LYC** k • * lyss k* m-arct b7.de* med ptk1 morph oss• nat-m bg2* nit-ac k* nux-m bg2 *Nux-v* k* op bg2 pall k* par ptk1 *Petr* phos k* **Plat** k* *Psor* sacch c1 spong bg2* *Staph* bro1* stram k* sulph ptk1 tarent bro1 *Tub* st **VERAT** bg2*
- **afternoon**: *Canth*
- **acts**; in: stram gl1.fr• verat gl1.fr•
- **children**, in: *(↗Behavior - children)* caust mtf33 graph br1* plat mtf33 sacch c1*
  - **explanation** from parents; always demanding: caust mtf33
- **laughing** at reproof (See Laughing - reprimands)
- **servants** to chiefs, of: lyc gl1.fr• nat-m gl1.fr•

INSTABILITY (See Mood - changeable)

INSULTING (See Abusive - insulting)

INTELLECT predominates emotions (See Emotions - predominated)

INTELLECTUAL: *(↗Emotions - predominated; Learning - desire; Philosophy; Philosophy - ability; Theorizing)* acon mtf anac mtf aur mtf33 bapt mtf bar-s mtf bell mtf cann-i mtf carc mtf33 cocc mtf conv mtf cupr-act mtf germ-met mtf hell mtf hyos mtf ign mtf lach mtf lyc tl2* merc mtf nat-c mtf nat-m mtf nux-v mtf op mtf33 ph-ac mtf phos mtf33 plat mtf puls mtf rhus-t mtf sep mtf33 sil mtf stram mtf **Sulph** mrr1* tritic-vg fd5.de verat mtf33 viol-o mtf
- **children**: *Carc* mlr1• hyos mtf33
- **work**; desire for (See Mental exertion - desire)

INTELLIGENT: *(↗Learning - desire; Studying - easily)* alum ↓ am-c ↓ bell mtf33 bufo ↓ calc mtf33 carc cd* con ↓ gaert bh* glycyr-g cte1• *Graph* ↓ lach mtf33 *Lyc* hr1* nicc-s ↓ *Petr* ↓ phos mrr1 sil mtf33 sulph mtf33 tub ↓ [ant-c stj2 ant-met stj2 irid-met stj2 osm-met stj2 plat stj2]
- **children**: bell mtf33 calc mtf33 lach mtf33 sil mtf33 sulph mtf33
- **artistic**: *(↗Art - ability)* carc mlr1•
- **drunkenness**; more intelligent during: calc gl1.fr• sulph gl1.fr•
- **lazy**; but: alum gl1.fr• am-c gl1.fr• con gl1.fr• *Graph* gl1.fr• *Petr* gl1.fr•
- **narrow** field; in a: bufo gk
- **weakness**; with muscular: lyc hr1* nicc-s br1 sil mtf33 tub mtf33

INTEMPERANCE (See Violent)

INTENSE personality (See Ardent)

INTERFERENCE:
- **aversion** to (See Disturbed; Hindered; Interruption - aversion)
- **self**; by talking of: eric-vg mtf11

INTERRUPTION:
- **agg.**: *(↗intolerance; Anger - interruption; Confusion - interruption; Disturbed; Irritability - disturbed)* cina stj* colch bg2* culx k2 staph bg2 verat bg2 [hydrog stj2]
- **aversion** to: bar-c bl* calc-p bl* cham bl* cina mtf nat-m bl* sanic bl* sil bl* sulph bl* [*Buteo-j* sej6]
  - **children**; in: cina br1* nat-m mtf33
- **intolerance**: *(↗agg.; Anger - interruption; Disturbed)* cham a1 cocc h1* germ-met srj granit-m es1• ignis-alc es2•

INTOLERANCE: *(↗Censorious; Contradiction - intolerant; Contrary; Dictatorial; Fanaticism; Impatience; Quarrelsome)* ars gl1.fr• bar-c gl1.fr• carbn-s br1 caust gl1.fr• cham↓ choc srj3• con gl1.fr• dulc fd4.de ferr-p↓ ferr-p-h c1 galeoc-c-h↓ irid-met srj5• lac-e↓ lac-h htj1• lac-leo sk4• merc h1* nux-v↓ positr nl2• psor st1 streptoc jl2 suprar rly4• taosc iwa1• *Tritic-vg* fd5.de ulm-c jsj8• [heroin sdj2]
- **afternoon**: ferr-p a1
- **ambiguity**: lac-e hrn2•
- **cat**; to: galeoc-c-h gms1•
- **complaints**; intolerance of his: cham↓ nux-v a1
  - **children**; in: cham mtf33
- **contradiction**; of (See Contradiction - intolerant)
- **hindrance**, of (See Hindered)
- **interruption**, of (See Interruption - intolerance)
- **noise**, of (See Sensitive - noise - slightest)
- **others**; of (See Company - aversion - bear)
- **spoken** to; of being (See Spoken - aversion)
- **vexation** of (See Vexed - intolerance)
- **wind**; to (See Weather - wind - intolerance)

INTOXICATION (See Confusion; Stupefaction)

INTRIGUER: *(↗Deceitful)* ars gl1.fr• bell gl1.fr• hyos gl1.fr• lach cd1* verat gl1.fr•

INTROSPECTION: *(↗Absorbed; Brooding; Dream; as; Dwells; Dwells - past; Meditating; Pessimist; Reflecting; Reserved; Serious; Sitting - inclination - wrapped; Talking - himself; Theorizing; Thoughts - thoughtful; FACE - Expression - vacant)* *Acon* b7.de* aids nl2• allox tpw4 aloe↓ alum k* am-m b7.de* ambr b7a.de* *Anh* mg1.de* arg-met jl arge-pl rwt5• arist-cl wm arn b7.de* *Aur* k* *Aur-m-n* wbt2• bamb-a stb2.de• bell k* bism b7.de* bov k* *Camph*↓ cann-i a1 canth b7.de* caps b7.de* carb-an k* carc dx1 carl a1 caust k* cham k* *Chin* k* choc srj3• cic a1 clem k* **Cocc** k* con dx1 cupr dx1 cycl k* dig k* dream-p sdj1• dros b7.de* dulc fd4.de euph k* euphr b7.de* falco-pe nl2• ferr-ma↓ germ-met srj5• gink-b sbd1• glycyr-g cte1• *Granit-m* es1• haliae-lc srj5• hell k* hyos b7.de* **Ign** k* *Indg* hr1* *Ip* k* irid-met srj5• kali-c dx1 kali-s fd4.de ketogl-ac rly4• lac-del hrn2• lac-h sk4• lach mrr1 lil-t k2* luna kg1• lyc bg2* mag-m k* *Mang* b4a.de med al* meny b7.de* *Merc* vh* mez k* morg ptj*• morg-p fmm1• mur-ac k* nat-c dx1 nat-m mrr nat-s dx1* neon srj5• nux-v k* ol-an a1* *Olib-sac* wmh1 olnd bg2 op b7.de* ozone sde2• petr b4a.de *Ph-ac* b4a.de phel a1 phos↓ plb b7.de* plut-n srj7• positr nl2• psor gg **Puls** k* rheum b7.de* ruta fd4.de sabad b7.de* sal-fr sle1• sars k* *Sep* hr1* sil b4a.de spong fd4.de stann k* staph b7.de* stram b7.de* suis-em rly4• *Sulph* k* thuj b4a.de* tritic-vg fd5.de ulm-c jsj8• vanil fd5.de verat b7.de* viol-o a1 viol-t b7.de* [rhodi stj2 **Spect** dfg1 tax jsj7]
- **morning**: nat-c a1
- **forenoon**: phos
- **afternoon**: hell
- **night**: *Camph* a1 spong fd4.de
- **agg.**: lac-h htj1•
- **awareness** of environment; with: olib-sac wmh1
- **eating**, after: aloe a1 ferr-ma a1
- **fright**, after: *Ign* kr1

INTROVERTED people (See Introspection; Reserved)

INTUITIVE: *(↗Clairvoyance; Sensitive)* acon gl• cann-i a lac-leo hrn2• plut-n srj7• sep↓ syph jl2 vanil fd5.de [*Spect* dfg1]

Intuitive: ...
- **weakness** of others, to: *(↗Mocking - sarcasm - weaknesses)* sep mrr

INVOLVEMENT:
- **reduced**: *(↗Indifference - surroundings)*
  - **practical**, logical behavior (See Chaotic)

IRASCIBILITY (See Anger; Quarrelsome)

IRKSOME, everything is (See Ennui; Weary)

IRONY: *(↗Jesting; Mocking; Witty)* anh mg1.de* dulc fd4.de kali-p fd1.de* *Lach*↓ spong fd4.de [lith-m stj2]
- **satire**; desire for: *Lach* a1*

IRRATIONAL: *(↗Ardent; Impulsive; Unreasonable)* arg-n k13* atra-r bnm3• bell a cann-i↓ chir-fl bnm4• lil-t k13 *Nux-v* kr1 op a plb a stram h1
- **alternating** with | **rationalism**: cann-i k13
- **hidden** irrational motives; actions with: arg-n br1*

IRRELIGIOUS (See Religious - want)

IRRESOLUTION (= indecision): *(↗Antagonism; Capriciousness; Confidence - want; Confusion - identity; Confusion - identity - duality; Discouraged - irresolution; Doubtful; Fear - undertaking; Helplessness; Ideas - abundant - uncertain; Impressionable; Inconstancy; Initiative; Insecurity; Longing - good; Mood - changeable; Persisting; Postponing; Sensitive - mental impressions; Thoughts - two; Timidity; Undertaking - lacks; Undertaking - many; Undertaking - things; Will - two)* act-sp k* adam srj5* *Agar* allox tpw3 *Alum* k* alum-p k2* alum-sil k2* alumn am-c *Anac* k* androc srj1• ang k* anh mg1.de* apis *Aran-ix* mg1.de *Arg-n* k* arn *Ars* k* ars-i asaf k* aster sze10• aur k* aur-ar k2 aur-i k2 aur-m-n wbt2• aur-s k2 *Bar-act* a1* **BAR-C** b4.de* bar-i k2 *Bar-m* bism bros-gau mrc1 brucel sa3• bry bufo gl1.fr• bufo-s buth-a sp1* cact *Calc* calc-ar k2 calc-f calc-i k2 calc-p calc-s *Calc-sil* k2* camph cann-i cann-s canth carb-v↓ *Carbn-s* *Carc* fd2.de* carneg-g rwt1• cartl-s rly4• caust k* cench k2 cham k* chel chin k* chinin-s chir-fl gya2 *Chlol* chord-umb rly4• cic c1 cimic jl3 cina clem coca coca-c sk4• *Cocc* k* coch j* coff *Coli* jl2 coll coloc j *Con* cortico sp1* crot-c sk4• crot-h kr1 cub a1 cupr k* *Cur* k* cyn-d ckh1 cypra-eg sde6.de• daph k* des-ac rbp6 dig k* dream-p sdj1• dros dulc ephe-si hsj1• erig↓ falco-pe nl2• ferr ferr-ar ferr-i ferr-m j5.de* ferr-ma ferr-p↓ fic-m gya1 gard-j vlr2• germ-met srj5• gink-b↓ granit-m es1• *Graph* k* grat guare guat sp1* haliae-lc srj5• ham↓ **Hell** k* helon mgm• hydrog srj2• hyos k* **Ign** k* ina-i mlk9.de iod k* *Ip* irid-met srj5• kali-ar kali-br k* kali-c k* kali-m k2 kali-p kali-s k* *Kali-sil* k2* kiss a1 *Kola* stb3• lac-c k2* lac-d lac-h htj1*• *Lac-lup*↓ **Lach** k* laur led lil-t bg* *Lyc* k* lyss m-ambo b7.de* *M-arct* b7.de* m-aust b7.de* mag-m k* malar jl2 mand mg1.de mang *Merc* *Mez* k* *Moni* rfm1• mur-ac k* musca-d szs1 *Naja* k* nat-c *Nat-m* k* nat-sil k2 nit-ac *Nux-m* k* *Nux-v* k* **Onos** k* **Op** k* osteo-a jl2 ozone sde2• pall pert-vc vk9 **Petr** b4.de* petr-ra shn4• *Phos* k* pic-ac plat k* plb propr↓ pseuts-m sne* *Psor* *Puls* k* pycnop-sa mrz1 rauw sp1 rheum rhod kgp5• rhus-r ros-d wla1 ruta k* sacch sst1• sacch-a fd2.de• sal-fr sle1• sanic santin a1 seneg *Sep* k* *Sil* k* sinus rly4• spig *Stann* gl1.fr• staph sne* suis-em rly4• suis-hep rly4• sul-ac k2* *Sulph* k* **Symph** fd* syph jl2 tab taosc iwa1• tarax k* tarent thuj k* vanad dx verat↓ xan mgm• zinc zinc-p k2 [am-caust stj2 am-f stj2 beryl stj2 beryl-m stj2 bism-sn stj2 bor-pur stj2 fl-ac stj2 fl-pur stj2 heroin sdj2 lith-c stj2 lith-f stj2 lith-i stj2 lith-m stj2 lith-met stj2 lith-p stj2 lith-s stj2 nitro stj2 oxyg stj2 pop dhh1 scler rcb1 spect dfg1 tax jsj7 *Titan* stj]
- **morning**: des-ac jl kali-p fd1.de• nat-c h2 pall
- **afternoon**: hyos
- **evening**: calc ferr-p a1 m-arct j5.de nat-sil fd3.de• propr sa3• *Puls*
  - **eating**; after | **amel.**: propr sa3•
- **acts**, in: bar-act sne **Bar-c** carc fd2.de• chin cur br1 ham fd3.de• hydrog srj2• kali-p fd1.de• **Kali-s** fd* *Lac-lup* hrn2• **Lyc** k●* nat-c nat-sil k13* nux-m **Onos** k* ozone sde2• ros-d wla1 *Sacch-a* fd2.de• stann ptk1 **Symph** fd* tarent
- **air**; in open | **amel.**: asaf j5.de
- **alternating** with | **excitement** (See Excitement - alternating - indecision)
- **anxious**: carc fd2.de• *Graph* gl1.fr•
- **changeable**: asaf j5.de aur-m-n wbt2• bism j5.de cann-s j5.de carc mlr1• gink-b sbd1• ign j5.de led j5.de m-aust j5.de nux-v j5.de op j5.de plat j5.de sil j5.de thuj j5.de
- **children**; in: bar-c mtf33 sacch sst1•
- **choosing** things; in: carc az1.de* chir-fl gya2 **Symph** fd*
- **debility**; in nervous: *Cur* kr1* *Kali-p* fd1.de•

- **discouragement**; with (See Discouraged - irresolution)
- **execution** when a decision is made; but prompt: m-arct c1*
- **ideas**, in: cur br1 m-aust j5.de nat-m nat-sil fd3.de• *Sacch-a* fd2.de• sulph k* tarent
- **indolence**; with (See laziness)
- **irritability**, with: chin h1
- **laughing**: coca-c sk4•
- **laziness**; with: *(↗Laziness)* ham fd3.de• nat-sil fd3.de• puls j5.de tarax j5.de
- **life** choices; about big: *Des-ac* rbp6
- **marry**, to: *(↗Marriage - unendurable)* carb-v gl1.fr• dream-p sdj1• ign gl1.fr• lach vh* lyc mtf nat-m gl1.fr• nux-v vh* phos gl1.fr• plat gl1.fr• sil gl1.fr• staph vh* verat gl1.fr•
  - **avarice**; from: lyc kl*
- **projects**, in: ars j5.de asaf j5.de **Bar-c** bufo-s cact cham cortico sp dream-p sdj1• *Nux-m* j5.de *Onos* mrr1 rhus-r
- **shopping**: ozone sde2•
- **sleepiness**, with: hyos j5.de
- **trifles**, about: *(↗Trifles; Trifles - important)* ars kr1* **Bar-c** carc fd2.de• ferr-p a1 graph ptk1* ham fd3.de• irid-met srj5• *Kola* stb3• **Lyc** k •* lyss nat-sil fd3.de• pic-ac mg **Symph** fd* [erig stj titan stj]
  - **strong** in important things; but: [erig stj]
- **waking**, on: lyc a1
- **weakness**, from: helon mgm•

IRRITABILITY: *(↗Anger; Anger - answer; Complaining; Contradiction - disposition; Contrary; Discontented; Frown; Morose; Offended; Petulant; Quarrelsome; Sensitive; Sulky; Unfriendly; Violent; FEVER - Irritative; GENERALS - Irritability - excessive)* abies-c abrom-a ks5* abrot k* absin a1* *Acet-ac* k* **Acon** k* act-sp *Adam* skp7*• adlu jl3 *Aesc* k* *Aeth* *Agar* k* agath-a nl2* agn b7.de* *Aids* nl2* *Ail* alco a1 alf br1 all-s vh1 allox tpw3* aln vva1• *Aloe* k* **Alum** k* alum-p k2* am-c k* am-caust a1* *Am-m* b2.de* am-s ↓ ambr k* ammc a1 amn-l sp1 *Anac* k* anan androc srj1*• ang k* ange-s oss1• anh mg1.de* **Ant-c** k* ant-m ↓ ant-o a1 *Ant-t* k* anthraci ↓ anthraq rly4• **Apis** k* apoc ↓ arag br1 aral vh1 aran jl3 aran-ix mg1.de* arb-m oss1• *Arg-met* k* *Arg-n* k* arge-pl rwt5• arist-cl ↓ arizon-l nl2• *Arn* k* **Ars** b2.de* *Ars-i* ars-s-f k2 *Art-v* arum-t k* *Asaf* k* *Asar* k* asc-t kr1 ascar-l ↓ asim br1 aspar aster atha ↓ atis ckh1 atro a1 **Aur** k* aur-ar k2 aur-i k2 aur-m *Aur-m-n* wbt2* *Aur-s* k2 bac jl2 bacls-10 pte1*• *Bamb-a* stb2.de• bar-act a1 *Bar-c* k* bar-i k2 bar-m bar-s k2 **Bell** k* bell-p mg1.de* ben a1 ben-n a1 benz-ac a1 berb *Bism* k* bism-o a1 bit-ar wht1• bol-la a1* bol-s a1 bomb-chr mlk9.de bond a1 borra-o oss1• *Borx* k* **Bov** k* brach a1* brass-n-o srj5• brom bros-gau mrc1 brucel sa3• **Bry** k* bufo k* bung-fa mtf buth-a mg1.de cact cadm-met bg* cadm-s k* cain ↓ calad calam sa3• **Calc** k* calc-act ↓ calc-ar k2 calc-br c1* calc-f jl* calc-i k2 calc-m ↓ *Calc-p* k* **Calc-s** calc-sil k2* calen j5.de* camph k* cann-i a1 cann-s k* cann-xyz ↓ *Canth* k* *Caps* k* *Carb-ac* k* carb-an k* **Carb-v** k* **Carbn-s** k* carc sp1* card-b ↓ card-m k* *Cardios-h* rly4• *Carl* carneg-g rwt1• cartl-s rly4• cass ↓ cassia-f ckh1 cassia-s ccrh1• caste jl3 castm *Caul* k* **Caust** k* cedr bg2* cench k2 cere-b a1 cere-s a1 **Cham** k* cheir c1 chel k* chim-m ↓ *Chin* k* *Chinin-ar* chinin-s chion a1* chir-fl gya2 chlam-tr ↓ chlol chlor chlorpr pin1* *Choc* srj3• chord-umb rly4• cic k* cimic k* cimx *Cina* k* cinnb *Clem* k* cob ↓ cob-n mg1.de coc-c coca k* coca-c ↓ *Cocc* k* *Coff* k* *Colch* k* coli rly4* *Coloc* k* *Con* k* conch fkr1* conv br1 cop cor-r cori-r a1 corian-s ↓ corn cortico sp1* cortiso mg1.de* crat br1* *Croc* k* *Crot-c* sk4• *Crot-h* k* crot-t k* cub c1 *Cupr* k* cupr-act kr1 cupr-ar a1 cupr-s cur mrr1 *Cycl* k* cyn-d jl3 cyna jl3 cypr mtf11 cystein-l rly4• cyt-l mg1.de* daph k* *Dendr-pol* sk4• der des-ac jl3* *Dig* k* digin a1 dios diosm ↓ dioxi rbp6 dirc a1 dor a1 dream-p sdj1• dros k* *Dulc* k* elae a1 elaps enteroc jl2 ephe-si hsj1• equis-h a1 erig ↓ ery-a ↓ euon euon-a br1 eup-a ↓ eup-per bg2* euphr eupi fago k* falco-ch sze4• falco-pe nl2• fel a1 *Ferr* k* ferr-ar ferr-i ferr-p *Ferr-s* ↓ fic-m gya1 fil ↓ fl-ac k* **Foll** ↓ form a1 fum rly1*• fuma-ac rly4• gaert pte1*• gal-ac a1* galeoc-c-h ↓ galv c1 *Gamb* gard-j vlr2• *Gels* k* ger-i rly4• germ-met srj5• gink-b sbd1• glon a1* glycyr-g cte1• *Gran* *Granit-m* es1• **Graph** k* grat k* guaj k* guat sp1 haliae-lc srj5• ham hell k* helo st helo-s rwt2• helodr-cal knl2• *Helon* k* **Hep** k* hip-ac sp1* hipp hippoc-k szs2 hir mg1.de* hist sp1* hura a1 *Hydr* k* hydr-ac *Hydrog* srj2• hydroph rsj6* *Hyos* b2.de* hyper iber a1* ichth br1 ictod br1 ign k* ignis-alc ↓ ina-i mlk9.de ind ↓ *Indg* **Iod** b2.de* *Ip* k* irid-met srj5• iris ix bnm8• *Jal* ↓ jatr-c jug-r ↓ just br1 kali-ar *Kali-bi* k* *Kali-br* kr1 **Kali-c** k* kali-chl bg2 kali-cy ↓ kali-f a1 kali-fcy ↓ **Kali-i** k* kali-m k2* kali-n k* *Kali-p* k* **Kali-s** k* kali-sil k2 kalm k* ketogl-ac rly4• kiss a1 kola stb3• kreos k* kres mg1.de* kurch bnj1 *Lac-c* k* *Lac-cp* sk4• lac-d lac-del hrn2• lac-e hrn2• lac-h htj1• *Lac-leo* hrn2*• lac-lup hrn2• lac-mat ↓ *Lach* k* lachn lact lact-v ↓

Irritability: ...
lap-la sde8.de• lat-m bnm6• laur k* lavand-a ctl1• *Lec* k* *Led* k* lept a1 **Lil-t** k* limen-b-c ↓ limest-b ↓ linu-c a1 *Linu-u* br1 lipp a1* lith-i ↓ lon-p c1* loxo-recl bnm10*• luf-op mg1.de **Luna** kg1• **Lyc** k* lycpr j5.de *Lycps-v* kr1* lyss k* m-ambo b2.de* m-arct b2.de* m-aust b2.de* macro c1 **Mag-c** k* mag-f mg1.de* mag-m k* mag-p mrr1 *Mag-s* j5.de* maias-l ↓ manc mand mg1.de* *Mang* k* mang-i ↓ mang-m ↓ mang-p rly4• mang-s ↓ marb-w ↓ *Med* k* medul-os-si rly4• melal-alt gya4 meli menis a1 meny bg2 meph *Merc* k* *Merc-c* k* merc-i-f ↓ *Merc-i-r* merc-sul ↓ merl *Mez* k* mill a1 mim-p jl3* *Moni* rfm1• *Morg* fmm1• morg-g pte1*• morg-p pte1*• morph br1 mosch k* *Mur-ac* k* *Murx* myos-a rly4• myric k* nabal a1 nad rly4• naja nat-ar **Nat-c** k* **Nat-m** k* nat-ox rly4• nat-p nat-pyru rly4• *Nat-s* k* nat-sil fd3.de• nauf-helv-li ↓ neon srj5• nep mg1.de* nept-m ↓ nicc k* nicc-met sk4• nid jl3 **Nit-ac** k* nit-s-d j5.de nitro-o a1 nux-m **Nux-v** k* oci a1 oci-sa ↓ oena a1 ol-an olib-sac wmh1 *Olnd* k* onop jl3 onos mrr1 *Op* k* opun-s a1 opun-v ↓ orch mtf orig a1 orot-ac rly4• osm osteo-a jl2* ox-ac a1 oxal-a rly4• ozone sde2• paeon a1 *Pall* k* palo jl3 pant-ac rly4• par k* ped a1* *Pegan-ha* tpi1• pen ↓ pers jl3 pert-vc vk9 **Petr** k* petr-ra shn4• **Ph-ac** k* phasco-ci ↓ phel k* **Phos** k* phys a1 physala-p bnm7• *Phyt* pic-ac pieri-b mlk9.de pin-con oss2• **Pip-m** ↓ plac rzf5• plac-s rly4• plan **Plat** k* plb a1* plect plut-n srj7• podo c1* polyg-h ↓ polyg-pe ↓ polys ↓ positr nl2• pot-e rly4• propr sa3• prot pte1* prun pseuts-m oss1• *Psor* k* ptel k* **Puls** k* puls-n a1 *Pulx* br1 **Pycnop-sa** mrz1 pyrog bg2* quas a1 querc-r svu1• rad-br c11* (non:rad-met) **Ran-b** k* ran-s rat rauw tpw8* rham-cal br1 rheum k* rhod k* *Rhus-g* tmo3• **Rhus-t** k* rhus-v ribo rly4• *Ros-d* wla1 rumx *Ruta* k* *Sabad* k* sabal ptk2 sabin k* sacch a1 sacch-a ↓ sal-ac ↓ sal-al blc1• *Sal-fr* sle1• sal-p a1 *Samb* k* sang k* sanguis-s ↓ sanic k* santin a1 sapin a1 sarcol-ac jl3 saroth mg1.de* *Sars* k* sec a1* sel k* senec k2* seneg k* **Sep** k* **Sil** k* sin-n sinus rly4• skat br1 sol-a ↓ sol-ecl ↓ sol-mm c1* sol-t-ae a1* *Spig* k* spira a1 spong b7.de* squil k* *Stann* k* **Staph** k* staphycoc rly4• stel br1 *Stram* k* stront-c k* **Stry** k* succ-ac rly4* suis-em rly4• suis-hep rly4• suis-pan rly4• **Sul-ac** k* sul-i k2 sulfa sp1 sulfon br1 sulfonam jl3* **Sulph** k* *Sumb* bg2* suprar rly4• syc pte1*• **Symph** ↓ syph ptk1* tab k* tanac br1 tarax k* *Tarent* k* tarent-c ckh1 tell k* tep tere-la rly4• teucr k* thal c1* thal-xyz srj8• thea k* thioc-ac rly4• **Thuj** k* thymol br1 thyr al* til tong ↓ toxi mtfw2• tril-c a1 tril-p trios rsj11* **Tritic-vg** fd* *Tub* k* tub-m jl2 ulm-c ↓ upa a1* (non:uran-met k) uran-n *Urol-h* rwt• ust v-a-b jl2 vac k* valer k* **Vanil** fd* ven-m ↓ *Verat* k* **Verat-v** verb b7.de* vero-o rly4*• vib k* vinc viol-o k* *Viol-t* k* vip a1 vip-a jl3 visc sp1* voes a1 wye a1 x-ray jl* yuc a1* **Zinc** k* zinc-m a1* zing a1 ziz a1* [ant-met stj2 bell-p-sp dcm1 buteo-j sej6 chr-m stj2 heroin sdj2 mag-n stj2 pop dhh1 **Spect** dfg1 tax jsj7 zinc-i stj2 zinc-n stj2 zinc-p stj2]

- **day** and night: cham ptk1 lac-c ptk1 op ptk1 psor ptk1 stram ptk1
- **daytime**: am-c anac k* ant-c k* bism k* bism-o ↓ bros-gau mrc1 calc carb-v caust k* cycl dulc ham fd3.de• ip iris kali-s fd4.de kreos lyc mag-c *Med* hr1* merc *Merc-c* k* nat-c nat-m petr phel phos plat plut-n srj7• puls sars sep stann staph sul-ac sulph verb viol-t zinc
  - **alternating** with | **cheerfulness** | **evening**: bism-o a1 sulph viol-t
    - **mirth**: | **evening**: sulph viol-t
  - **increasing** as the day proceeds: plut-n srj7•
  - **only**: lyc ptk1 med ptk1
- **morning**: agar ↓ am-c k* am-m k* ang a1 ant-c ant-t k* arg-n a1 arizon-l nl2• ars ↓ ars-s-f ↓ aur-m-n wbt2• *Bell* ↓ bov k* brucel sa3• bry k2 bufo ↓ calad k* *Calc* k* calc-act a1 calc-sil k* camph ↓ canth k* carb-an k* carb-v k* *Carbn-s* carc ↓ *Carl* ↓ castm cham k* chin chlol chlor k* cob-n mg1.de coc-c a1 coca ↓ cocc k* coff ↓ con k* cupr ↓ cycl k* cystein-l rly4• dream-p sdj1• dulc fd4.de erig mg1.de gamb ↓ gink-b sbd1• graph k* grat haliae-lc srj5• hep ↓ hipp *Iber* hr1* irid-met ↓ iris ↓ jatr-c ↓ kali-ar kali-c kali-p kali-s kali-sil k2 kalm ketogl-ac rly4• kola stb3• kreos *Lach* lil-t ↓ luf-op ↓ **Lyc** ↓ mag-c mag-m manc ↓ *Mang* *Med* jl2 *Merc-i-r* mez ↓ moni ↓ myric a1 nat-c j5.de *Nat-m* k* nat-p *Nat-s* nicc nit-ac k* nux-v oci-sa ↓ *Petr* ph-ac ↓ phasco-ci ↓ phos k* plat plb ↓ polys sk4• psor k* *Puls* ↓ ran-b c1 rhus-g tmo3• rhus-t ↓ sabad sacch sst1• sal-fr sle1• sang k* sars seneg sep k* sil spect ↓ spong j5.de **Staph** k* stram sul-ac sulph tarax tax ↓ thuj *Til* k* **Tub** ↓ verat zinc zinc-p k2
  - **7 h**: calad sep
  - **rising**, after: arg-n a1 arizon-l nl2• bov a1 bry k2 calc canth k* carc gk6* *Carl* a1 cham h1* coff gamb a1 hep mag-m manc a1 nat-s phos sulph
  - **stool** | **before**: calc a1
  - **waking** on: agar ant-t arg-n ars ars-s-f k2 *Bell* bov bry bufo camph carb-an cham *Chin* ↓ coca con cupr cycl st dulc fd4.de gamb haliae-lc srj5• irid-met srj5• iris jatr-c kali-ar *Kali-c* kali-p kali-s lil-t luf-op rsj5• **Lyc** mag-m k1 *Merc-i-r* mez moni rfm1• nat-m nat-s **Nit-ac** k* **Nux-v** k*

- **waking** on: ... oci-sa sk4• petr ph-ac phasco-ci rbp2 phos h2* plat plb *Puls* rhus-t *Staph* sne sul-ac *Sulph* thuj **Tub** al* [spect dfg1 tax jsj7]
  - **9** h: luf-op rsj5•
  - **children**, in: ant-t tl1 *Chin* st dulc fd4.de tub mtf33
- **forenoon**: aeth agar a1 am-c k* am-m k* ant-c h2* ant-t k* arg-met cadm-met tpw6 carb-an carb-v k* caust cinnb dulc fd4.de grat hipp kalm hr1 lil-t a1 lyc a1 mag-c mag-m *Mang* nat-c j nat-m k* nat-p nicc phos plect a1 ran-b seneg sil verat
- **noon**: am-m aster a1 cinnb a1 dulc fd4.de kali-c mez a1 nat-c j5.de nat-m rumx teucr zinc k*
  - **amel.**: aeth oci-sa sk4•
- **nose**; with complaints of: arn bg2 ars bg2 vinc bg2
- **afternoon**: aeth k* aloe alum anac androc srj1• ant-t *Borx* bov k* brom a1 calc-s a1 cann-i a1 cann-s k* canth j cardios-h rly4• castm chel k* colch *Con* k* cycl k* dulc fd4.de elaps falco-pe nl2• graph hydr-ac ign iod kali-c j lil-t m-arct a1 mag-c mang merc-c k* mez ↓ mur-ac nat-m nit-ac op opun-s a1 (non:opun-v a1) osteo-a ↓ ox-ac ozone ↓ paeon ↓ plb rhus-g tmo3• ruta sal-fr sle1• sang k* sars sil a1 sumb k* symph fd3.de• thuj k* urol-h rwt• zinc [heroin sdj2]
  - **14** h: bov a1 mez a1
  - **16** h: borx osteo-a ↓ ozone sde2• symph fd3.de•
    - **16**-18 h: osteo-a jl2
  - **17** h: paeon a1 sil a1
  - **17**-18 h: *Con*
- **evening**: adam srj5• aesc alf br1 aloe am-c k* am-m k* androc srj1• ant-c ant-t k* bamb-a ↓ bar-c bar-m bar-s k2* bov k* cain *Calc* k* *Calc-s* k* calc-sil k2* canth k* carbn-s carneg-g rwt1• castm k1 cob ↓ coc-c a1 coloc a1 *Con* cycl k* dios dream-p sdj1• dulc fd4.de fago k* hydrog ↓ ign indg jug-r k* *Kali-c* kali-chl k13 kali-m k2 kali-p *Kali-s* kali-sil k2* kalm k* kola stb3• lach j5.de lil-t limest-b es1• *Lyc* k* lyss k* mag-c mag-m mill a1 mur-ac nabal a1 *Nat-c* nat-m k* nat-sil k2* neon srj5• nicc *Osteo-a* jl2 ox-ac oxal-a rly4• pall phos plan podo hr1 positr nl2• psor a1 *Puls* ran-b rhus-g ↓ sabad a1 sacch-a fd2.de• sal-fr sle1• sel rsj9• sil spig **Sulph** sumb trios rsj11* upa ↓ **Zinc** k* **Zinc-p** k2* *Zing* hr1*
  - **18** h: bamb-a stb2.de•
  - **19**.30 h: hydrog srj2•
  - **20**.30 h: cob ptm1•
  - **amel.**: aloe am-c bism calc mag-c nat-m nat-s j nicc sal-fr sle1• verb viol-t zinc
  - **bed**, in: upa a1
  - **sunset**; after: rhus-g tmo3•
- **night**: anac ant-t ckh1 anthraci borx bufo a1 camph k* cham chin k* cinnb ↓ coloc sf1.de graph j hydrog ↓ *Jal* ckh1 lac-c ckh1 lyc nicc a1 nux-v ckh1 petr a1 phos pic-ac a1 psor ckh1 rheum ckh1 **Rhus-t** sabad thea ↓
  - **midnight**:
    - **before** | **22** h | **amel.**: plut-n srj7•
    - **22**-2 h: thea a1
  - **alternating** with:
    - **cheerfulness** | **daytime**: *(↗children in - good)* ant-t ptk1 *Jal* br1* lac-c ptk1 nux-v ptk1 psor ptk1* rheum ptk1*
  - **children**; in: | **babies**; in sick: *(↗children in - sick)* *Psor* kr1
  - **only**, good all day and cross all night (See alternating - cheerfulness - daytime)
  - **retiring**, after: bufo cinnb k* hydrog srj2•
  - **visions**, with frightful: camph kr1
  - **waking**, on: lyc phos ↓ *Psor*
- **abortion**:
  - **in**: *Caul* kr1
  - **threatened**, in: *Cham* kr1
- **absent** persons, with: *(↗Anger - absent)* aur k* fl-ac k* kali-cy k* lyc k*
- **afterpains**; during: *(↗delivery)* *Nux-v* kr1
- **air**, in open: aeth k* am-c arn borx calc *Con* dream-p sdj1• kali-c mur-ac nux-v plat puls rhus-t spong fd4.de
  - **amel.**: adam srj5• anac k* calc coff ign mag-c *Rhus-t* stann staph sne tritic-vg fd5.de
- **alone**:
  - **when**: *(↗Company - desire; Company - desire - alone)* cortico mg1.de dream-p sdj1• phos k*
  - **wishes** to be alone: adam srj5• arge-pl rwt5• bry kr1 choc srj3• gels c1 hydrog srj2• kali-p fd1.de• lac-h htj1• lec oss• podo fd3.de• pycnop-sa mrz1 tritic-vg fd5.de vanil fd5.de
- **alternating** with:
  - **affectionate**: croc j plat sal-fr sle1•
  - **anxiety** (See Anxiety - alternating - irritability)
  - **cares**: ran-b j5.de*
  - **cheerfulness**: *(↗joy)* aids nl2• ant-t k* ars *Aur* aur-ar k2 *Borx* k* bov j carc gk6* caust k* chin cocc croc k* cycl k* kali-c j lyc merc merc-c k* nat-c nat-m k* ozone sde2• plat sanic k* spig spong k* *Stram* j5.de sul-i k2 sulph ↓ tell jl3 viol-t ↓ zinc k*
    - **evening**: sulph viol-t
  - **cowardice**: ran-b bg2* zinc j
  - **despair**: ars gm1
  - **discouragement**: aids nl2• *Kali-p* fd1.de• zinc j5.de
  - **hypochondriasis** | **daytime**; during: sulph viol-t
  - **idiocy** (See Idiocy - alternating - irritability)
  - **indifference**: asaf bell k* carb-an k* cham chin k* chir-fl gya2 colch jl3 kali-p fd1.de• sep ziz kr1
  - **jesting**: cocc j5.de
  - **joy**: *(↗cheerfulness)* acon bg3 *Coff* bg3 croc bg3 cycl kr1* op bg3
  - **laughing**: croc sanic k* stram
  - **merriness** (See cheerfulness)
  - **mirth**: caust k* cocc croc cycl a1 dream-p sdj1• nat-m spong sul-i k2
  - **patience**: arge-pl rwt5• nid jl3
  - **prostration**: conch fkr1•
  - **remorse**: *(↗Remorse - quickly)* mez j5.de
  - **sadness**: ambr k* arist-cl rbp3• asar jl3 gink-b sbd1• lac-h sze9• melal-alt gya4 ptel bg2 puls bg2 zinc k*
  - **singing**: agar k* croc
  - **tenderness** (See affection)
  - **timidity**: *(↗Timidity)* ran-b j5.de zinc j5.de
  - **tolerance** (See patience)
  - **tranquility**: hippoc-k szs2 positr nl2•
  - **weeping**: acon j alum j aur sf1.de bell k* graph j kali-i k* phos j plat j puls mrr1
    - **laughter** at trifles; and: graph
- **anxiety**, with: acon h1 aspar j bros-gau mrc1 carc mlr1• chir-fl gya2 nauf-helv-li elm2• **Nux-v** hr1* phos h2
- **aroused**, when: berb a1 bufo gk choc srj3• hyos a1 nux-m k* op sil k2*
- **breakfast**:
  - **after**: con sacch ↓
    - **amel.**: sacch sst1•
  - **before**: nat-p sacch sst•
  - **until**: sacch sst1•
- **burning** in right lumbar region; from: nit-ac h2
- **business**:
  - **about**: borx j5.de ip nat-m
  - **important**, in an: *Borx* k1
  - **proceed** fast; when does not: lac-e hrn2•
- **cardiac** symptoms, with: crat br1*
- **causeless**: brom mtf33 carc mlr1• dulc fd4.de hir skp7• hydrog srj2• limest-b es1• med jl2 *Psor* jl2 spong fd4.de vanil fd5.de
- **children**, in: *(↗Anger - children)* abrot k* ant-c k* ant-t k* ars k* ascar-l mtf11 aur mtf33 bell mtf33 benz-ac borx *Calc* hr1 calc-br c1 *Calc-p* k* camph a1* carc mlr1• **Cham** k* *Chin* vh* **Cina** k* cupr st1* dros gk dulc sf1.de graph *Iod* ip st1 jal ↓ kali-br c1 kali-p ptk1 kreos mrr1 lac-c ptk1* loxo-recl bnm10• lyc k* **Mag-c** k* med jl2 nux-v mrr1 physala-p bnm7• psor ↓ puls rheum sf1.de* rhus-t mrr1 *Sacch* br1 sanic k* sep *Sil* k* **Staph** hr1* sulph ptk1* syph *Tub* c1* vanil fd5.de verat mtf33 zinc k*
  - **cross** all day, good all night: lyc ptk1* med ptk1

- **good** all day, cross all night: (*↗night - alternating - cheerfulness - daytime)* jal br1* psor mtf33
- **infants**: **CHAM** mrr1
- **pushes** nurse away: lyc sf1.de*
- **shriek** when touched: **Ant-t** kr1
- **sick**, when: (*↗night - children - babies) Lyc* st1* puls gk
- **sleepless** | **day** and night: psor st1*

- **children**, towards: bamb-a stb2.de• calc-m ↓ chlam-tr bcx2• *Choc* ↓ dream-p sdj1• dulc fd4.de haliae-lc ↓ kali-i a1* kola stb3• limest-b es1• luna ↓ polys sk4• positr nl2• pycnop-sa mrz1 ribo rly4• ruta fd4.de **Sep** ↓ spong fd4.de vanil fd5.de [bell-p-sp dcm1]
  - **own**; his: *Choc* srj3• dulc fd4.de haliae-lc srj5• luna kg1• ruta fd4.de **Sep** mrr1 spong fd4.de vanil fd5.de [calc-m stj1]
- **chill**, during: acon alum anac am *Ars* ars-s-f k2* aur aur-ar k2 bell borx bry **Calc** calen camph **Caps** k* carb-v castm *Caust* k* cham chin chinin-ar cimx cocc coff **Con** cycl gels hep k* hyos *Ign* kali-ar kreos **Lyc** m-aust mag-c merc mez nat-c *Nat-m Nit-ac Nux-v Petr* phos plan **Plat** *Puls* **Rheum** *Rhus-t* sabad k* sep sil *Spig* staph *Sulph* teucr thuj verat
- **coffee**, after: calc-p k* symph fd3.de•
- **coition**:
  - **after**: agar aster hr1 bov calad **Calc** calc-s k* calc-sil k2* *Chin* dig graph *Kali-c* kali-p *Kali-sil* k2 mag-m *Nat-c* nat-m nat-sil k2 nit-ac nux-v *Petr* k* ph-ac *Phos Sel* k1* **Sep Sil** k* staph thuj bg1*
  - **amel.**: tarent bg1*
- **cold**; after taking: calc h2
- **colors** | **green**:
  - **agg.**:
    - **dark** green: ign vk4
    - **olive** green: phos vk4 staph vk4
  - **purple**:
    - **agg.** | **dark** purple: ign vk4
- **company**: arge-pl rwt5•
- **concentration**; from difficult: aids nl2• carc vh* sapin a1
- **consolation**: | **agg.**: (*↗Consolation - agg.; Inconsolable) Bell Cact* calc *Calc-p* calc-sil k2* carc mlr1• chin dulc fd4.de hell **Ign** k* kali-c kali-sil k2 lil-t lyc merc **Nat-m** k* *Nit-ac* nux-v *Plat* sabal st **Sep** k* **Sil** k* staph
- **contradiction**; from: (*↗Anger - contradiction)* apis mrr1 arge-pl rwt5• aur ↓ bros-gau ↓ bung-fa mtf helon ↓ **Ign** ↓ kola stb3• nept-m ↓ pert-vc ↓ sel gmj2 thyr ↓ *Vanil* fd5.de [pall stj2 plat stj2]
  - **slightest**; at: aur br1 bros-gau mrc1 helon br1 **Ign** kr1* kola stb3• nept-m lsd2.fr pert-vc vk9 thyr br1
- **conversation**, from: (*↗talking; Conversation - agg.) Ambr* k* dros c1 dulc fd4.de kali-s fd4.de ketogl-ac rly4• lap-la rsp1 plac-s rly4• plect a1 rhus-g tmo3• spong fd4.de tritic-vg fd5.de vanil fd5.de
- **convulsions**:
  - **before**: agar sne art-v *Aster* bufo ↓ ign ↓ *Lach*
    - **epileptic**: (*↗GENERALS - Convulsions - epileptic - vexation) Art-v* kr1 bufo bro1 ign tl1 *Lach* kr1
  - **between**: cic tl1 nux-v tl1 stry tl1
- **cough**, from: *Bry* ↓ *Cina* bg2* *Cupr-act* ↓ irid-met srj5•
  - **whooping** cough, in: *Bry* kr1 *Cupr-act* kr1
- **crying** and weeping: bamb-a stb2.de• cortiso skp7• nux-v gb• plat gb• [iod stj2]
- **delivery**, during: (*↗afterpains)* caul br1 **Cham** kr1* *Hyos* kr1
- **dentition**, during: ars bro1 calc calc-p k* **CHAM** k1* cina kreos k* nux-v bro1* op bro1 **RHEUM** kr1* *Zinc* mtf33
- **diabetes**, in: *Helon* hr1* *Lycps-v* kr1*
- **diarrhea** | **after**: guaj a1 kali-p k2
- **difficulty** with someone; after: dulc fd4.de tarent a1
- **dinner**:
  - **after**: am-c cham h1* coc-c k* crot-t a1 *Hydr* iod a1 mill k* *Nat-c* ol-an a1 teucr k* til k* zinc a1
  - **before**: phos
  - **during**: teucr k*
- **disappointment**; from: carc mlr1•
- **discouragement**; with: *Anac* j5.de ars j5.de bism j5.de carb-an a1 carb-v j5.de dig j5.de lach j5.de mag-c j5.de mur-ac j5.de myric a1 nat-ar a1 nat-m j5.de orig j5.de pall j5.de phys a1 pip-m j5.de psor j5.de sars j5.de sep j5.de sil j5.de sulph j5.de [heroin sdj2]
- **disease**; during the | **acute** disease: ant-t mrr1
- **disturbed**, when: (*↗questioned; Disturbed; Interruption - agg.)* ant-t k2* bros-gau mrc1 calam sa3• choc srj3• *Dulc* fd4.de falco-pe nl2• gard-j vlr2• germ-met srj5• graph j5.de* ix bnm8• limest-b es1• op a1 positr nl2• *Ruta* fd4.de sacch-a fd2.de• sal-fr sle1• *Spong* fd4.de symph fd3.de• *Tritic-vg* fd5.de [heroin sdj2 tax jsj7]
- **drinking** wine and coffee, while: chlor a1
- **driving** a car: bros-gau mrc1 limen-b-c hrn2•
- **easily**: abies-c a1* abrom-a bnj1 aids nl2• ant-t ptk1 arge-pl rwt5• bit-ar wht1• cassia-s ccrh1• *Cham* a1 cinnb hr1 digin a1 dros ptk1 *Dulc* fd4.de glon br haliae-lc srj5• ham a1 kali-c a1 kali-fcy a1 kali-s fd4.de lach a1 merc h1 myric a1 plan a1 plat a1 *Psor* st1 *Pycnop-sa* mrz1 rad-br ptk1 sacch-a fd2.de• sang a1 sarcol-ac a1 staph mtf33 *Tritic-vg* fd5.de vanil fd5.de zinc a1
- **eating**:
  - **after**: aeth am-c am-m j5.de ambr arn k* ars bamb-a stb2.de• bar-act a1 *Borx Bry* k* carb-v k* cham k* chlor k* clem a1 con graph *Hydr* hr1* iod *Kali-c* kali-i merc merc-sul *Nat-c Nat-m Nux-v* olnd a1 ph-ac a1 plat *Puls* teucr k* thuj zinc a1
    - **amel.**: (*↗Eating - after - amel.)* am-c am-m kali-bi *Kola* stb3• nat-s phos sacch sst•
  - **amel.**: ignis-alc es2•
  - **during**: chlor kr1 kali-c b4a.de teucr j5.de
  - **satiety**; to: merc h1
- **eggs** | **agg.**: syc fmm1•
- **emission**; after: coff dig *Lil-t* nat-c *Nux-v* sang st sel k* **Staph** ust
- **epilepsy** | **before** (See convulsions - before - epileptic)
- **events**; about imagined (See imagined)
- **everything** causes: lac-lup hrn2• *Psor* jl2
- **excited**, when: (*↗Ailments - excitement; Ailments - excitement - emotional)* arg-n chin k* syc fmm1•
- **exertion**; from: ham fd3.de• kali-p fd1.de• sacch-a fd2.de• *Sep* sulph [calc-sil stj2]
- **expression**, from unintelligible: ham fd3.de• sol-t-ae a1
- **family**, to her: (*↗husband; loved; mother; Estranged - family)* anthraq rly4• *Carb-v* mrr1 cardios-h rly4• chir-fl gya2 coli rly4• kali-p fd1.de• ketogl-ac rly4• lac-h htj1*• melal-alt gya4 nat-ox rly4• opun-s a1 (non:opun-v a1) podo fd3.de• positr nl2• ribo rly4• sacch-a gmj3 sinus rly4• suis-em rly4• symph fd3.de• thuj k* vanil fd5.de [heroin sdj2 tax jsj7]
- **fever**; during: acon bg2 *Ars* bg2 bell bg2 calc bg2 *Cham* bg2 con bg2 lyc bg2 mosch bg2 **Nat-c** bg2 nux-v bg2 puls bg2 *Rheum* bg2 staph bg2 thuj bg2
- **flatulence**, from: cic br1*
- **flippancy** of others; from: (*↗talk of)* rhus-g tmo3•
- **forgetful**, because: aids nl2• *Anac* sp1 carc mg1.de* ham fd3.de•
- **friend**; to her: hir rsj4•
- **grief**, from: carc mlr1• *Kali-br* hr1* mag-c sf1.de tarent a1
- **headache**, during: *Acet-ac* k* acon aeth *Am-c* k* am-m *Anac* k* ant-c *Ars* k* aur-m-n wbt2• bell bov k* bros-gau mrc1 bry k* calc calc-i k2* calc-p k* calc-sil k2* *Cham* bro1 *Chin* bg* *Chinin-ar* kr1 chinin-s chir-fl gya2 coca con crat br1 cycl dulc graph helon k* hipp hydrog srj2• ign hr1* ind iod k* kali-ar kali-c kali-p *Kreos Lac-c* k* lac-h sk4• lach k* lachn laur luf-op rsj5• lyss mag-m *Mag-p* maias-l hrn2• mang meph merc *Mez* nat-m *Nicc Nux-v* k* ol-an st op pall k* *Phos* plac-s rly4• plat sal-fr sle1• *Sang* hr1* sil spong stann **Syph** k* teucr j5.de thuj vanil fd5.de vip zinc zinc-p k2* [tax jsj7]
- **head**; with complaints of: anac bg2 bell bg2 bov bg2 chin bg2 con bg2 kreos bg2 laur bg2 merc bg2 plat bg2 sil bg2 thuj bg2
- **heart** disease; with: crat br1
- **heat**:
  - **after**: am-c k* *Cina* kr1 hipp
  - **during**: acon k* ail k2 anac *Ant-c* vh aran hr1* *Ars* k* atha j5.de bell bg2 *Bry* calc bg2 carb-v card-b a1 caust *Cham* k* chim-m hr1* chlol gm1 cina vh* con bg2 *Ferr* hep j5.de ip hr1* lach k* lyc bg2 m-arct j5.de mosch k* **Nat-c** k* *Nat-m Nux-v* k* petr ph-ac phos plan *Psor* puls k* ran-b a1 *Rheum* k* spong fd4.de staph k* *Sulph* hr1* thuj bg2 ust hr1* [tax jsj7]
  - **typhoid** fever; in: *Bry* bro1 chel bro1 chlol gm1 hydr bro1 lept bro1 *Merc* bro1 nux-v bro1
- **hemorrhoids**, with: *Apis* kr1 **Nux-v** kr1

- **himself**; with: *(↗Hiding - himself - children; Reproaching oneself)* adam srj5• ars a1 aur a1 *Elaps* a1 sel rsj9• syph jl2 *Tritic-vg* fd5.de vanil fd5.de
- **hungry**; when: iod mtf33 *Kola* stb3• lac-e hrn2•
- **husband**; towards: *(↗family)* adam srj5• aids nl2• bamb-a stb2.de• dulc fd4.de kali-p fd1.de• luna kg1• nat-sil fd3.de• symph fd3.de• ulm-c jsj8• vanil fd5.de
  - **menses**; before: adam srj
- **idle**, while: *(↗Activity - desires; Industrious)* calc nux-v mtf33 stann a1 ulm-c jsj8•
- **illness**; preceding onset of: ix bnm8•
  - **one** day; by about: ix bnm8•
- **imagined** events; about: meph a1
- **impotence**, with: pers jl *Pic-ac* kr1
- **indefinite**: ix bnm8•
- **insincerity** of others, from: positr nl2• tritic-vg fd5.de
- **insults**, from: *(↗reproaches)* canth a1 [ars stj2 iod stj2 kali-ar stj2 merc stj2 nat-ar stj2 zinc-i stj2]
- **itching**, from: anac br1 *Ros-d* wla1
- **labor** pains; during: caul c1*
- **leukorrhea** ceases; as soon as: *Hydr* kr1
- **lies**; when hearing: **Podo** fd*
- **little** things; about (See trifles)
- **liver** trouble, in: *Bry* kr1 *Cham* kr1 **Nux-v** kr1 *Podo* kr1
- **looked** at: *(↗Looked - cannot)* *Ant-c*↓ *Cham*↓ *Cina*↓ gels↓ *Nux-v*↓ sacch-a↓ sanic↓ *Sil*↓ thuj↓ [ant-t stj2 bar-i stj2 iod stj2 lith-i stj2 merc-i-f stj2]
  - **spoken** to or touched: *Ant-c*↓ ant-t↓ *Cham*↓ *Cina*↓ gels↓ *Nux-v*↓ sacch-a↓ sanic↓ *Sil*↓ thuj mlk1
    - **children**; in: *Ant-c* bro1* ant-t bro1 *Cham* bro1 *Cina* bro1 gels bro1 *Nux-v* bro1 sacch-a gmj3 sanic bro1 *Sil* bro1 thuj bro1
- **loved** ones, to: *(↗family; Malicious - loved)* thuj k2 vanil fd5.de [am-s stj1 *Ferr-s* stj1]
- **lying** amel.; on: sulfonam jl
- **masturbation**, after: *Hyos* hr1*
- **medicine**; at thought to take the: *(↗Refusing - medicine)* mim-p jl*
- **menopause**; during: arg-n bro1 *Lach* bro1 *Morg* fmm1• morg-p fmm1• *Psor* st
- **menses**:
  - **after**: *(↗Menses - after)* berb k* bufo carb-ac c1 ferr nat-m
  - **appear**; as if menses would: bamb-a stb2.de•
  - **before**: *(↗Menses - before)* anthraci vh1 arge-pl rwt5• *Aur-m-n* wbt2• *Aur-s* wbt2• bamb-a stb2.de• berb k* bros-gau mrc1 calc carc sst2• carneg-g rwt1• *Caust* *Cham* k* choc srj3• cocc bro1 cycl gk des-ac rbp6 eupi bro1 falco-pe nl2• **Foll** oss• gink-b sbd1• hep hu irid-met srj5• kali-c kali-p fd1.de• kreos k* lac-e hrn2• lac-h htj1• lach mrr1* lil-t bro1* loxo-recl knl4• luna kg1• *Lyc* k* mag-m k* moni rfm1• morg-g pte1• *Nat-m* k* *Nux-v* k* ozone sde2• pic-ac c1 ptel gk *Puls* vh* sacch sst1• sacch-a fd2.de• *Sep* k* suis-pan rly4• sulph ser thyr jl3 [calc-m stj1 heroin sdj2 tax jsj7]
  - **during**: *(↗Menses - during)* acon h1 aeth am-c k* aran asaf bell berb k* bry calc castm caust k* *Cham* k* cimic cina cocc bro1 con crot-c a1 eupi k* ferr germ-met srj5• gink-b sbd1• ind kali-c kali-p kali-s kola stb3• kreos k* lil-t bro1 lyc k* mag-c mag-m k* mag-s nat-c nat-m nat-p *Nux-v* k* petr ph-ac k* plat prot fmm1• puls sars sep k* stram *Sulph* tarent tritic-vg fd5.de zinc k* zinc-p k2* zing
  - **intermission** of; during an: eupi sacch-a fd2.de•
- **mental** exertion; from: bamb-a stb2.de• calc-sil k2 kali-p mrr1 pic-ac k2 *Prot* jl2 sapin a1
- **mother**; to her: *(↗family)* lac-h sk4•
- **mucous** membranes; with chronic complaints of: pen br1
- **music**: *(↗noise)*
  - **during**: *(↗Music - agg.; Sensitive - noise)* anac sf1.de *Calc* sf1.de caust coca-c sk4• *Mang* nat-c sf1.de nat-m k2* nat-s sne nux-v sf1.de pycnop-sa mrz1 sep sf1.de tarent st viol-o sf1.de zinc sf1.de [mang-i stj2 mang-m stj2 mang-p stj2 mang-s stj2 zinc-i stj2 zinc-m stj2 zinc-n stj2 zinc-p stj2]
  - **harsh**, from: sumb a1
  - **piano**, of: anac sf1.de *Sep* h2* zinc sf1.de
  - **violin**, of: viol-o sf1.de
- **nausea**; with: mag-m bg2
- **nervousness**; with: ambr br1 castm br1 *Chin* br1 ery-a↓ eup-a br1 gard-j vlr2• staph br1 syc fmm1•
  - **urination**; with painful: ery-a br1
- **noise**, from: *(↗music; Rage - mischievous - noise; Sensitive - noise; Sensitive - noise - slightest)* acon vh1 allox tpw3* androc srj1• ant-t k* ars *Asar*↓ bell calam sa3• cardios-h rly4• caust cinnb k* cocc k* dulc fd4.de falco-pe nl2• *Ferr* k* gard-j vlr2• helo-s rwt2• iod k* ip irid-met srj5• kali-c kali-p fd1.de• kali-s fd4.de ketogl-ac rly4• *Kola* stb3• lavand-a ctl1• lyc↓ med jl2 nat-c k2 nat-m k2* nat-sil fd3.de• neon srj5• ozone sde2• phos pip-m k* plect k* plut-n srj7• ptel puls-n rhus-g tmo3• ruta fd4.de sanguis-s hrn2• sel rsj9* spong fd4.de stront-c sk4• suis-em rly4• tanac br1* thal-xyz srj8• trios rsj11* tritic-vg fd5.de *V-a-b* jl2 *Vanil* fd5.de ven-m rsj12* [bar-i stj2 ferr-i stj1 ferr-s stj1 merc-i-f stj2 tax jsj7]
  - **city**; of: ozone sde2•
  - **crackling** of newspapers; even from: *Asar* sf1.de *Ferr* lyc k2 nat-c k2
- **objects**; with inanimate: aids nl2• vanil fd5.de
- **odor** | **vinegar**; of: hydrog srj2•
- **ovulation**; during: bung-fa mtf
- **overwork**; from: **Ham** fd*
- **pain**, during: *(↗Anger - pains; Anger - pains - about; Sensitive - pain)* acon tl1 aloe k2 alum↓ apoc vh1 arn mrr1 ars sf1.de canth j5.de *Cham* b7a.de* chin b7a.de *Coff* b7a.de colch gt1* coloc k2 crat↓ crot-t a1 diosm br1 glycyr-g cte1• hep hydrog srj2• ign kreos↓ *Nux-v* b7a.de *Op* brm* *Phos* b4a.de phys c1 pot-e rly4• *Puls* b7a.de rhus-t↓ sal-fr sle1• sep↓ visc↓ [ant-t stj2]
  - **colic**; from: coloc bro1
  - **rheumatic**: cham bro1 coff bro1 rhus-t bro1
  - ○ **Cervical** region; in: crat br1
  - **Chest**; in: visc c1
  - **Face**; in: cham bro1 coff bro1 kreos bro1 nux-v bro1
  - **Occiput**; in: crat br1
  - **Teeth**; in: alum bg2 sep bg2
- **people**; with: allox tpw3* corian-s knl6• gard-j vlr2• rad-br sze8• sel rsj9• tell rsj10• trios rsj11• ven-m rsj12• [bell-p-sp dcm1]
- **perspiration**, during: ang bell bg2 bry k* *Calc* k* calc-p *Cham* k* chin bg2 clem con bg2 hep k* ketogl-ac rly4• mag-c merc k* nat-m nux-v bg2 puls bg2 **Rheum** k* rhus-t bg2 sabad bg2 samb bg2 sep *Sulph* k* thuj k*
- **pollutions**, after: *Aur* bro1 calad bro1 *Calc* bro1 *Chin* bro1 *Cimic* bro1 coff con bro1 dig dios bro1 gels lp kali-br bro1 *Lil-t* nat-c *Nux-v* k* ph-ac bro1 phos bro1 sang st sel k* **Staph** k* ust
- **pregnancy**, during: *Cham* hr1* *Sep* sne
- **prolapsus** uteri, in: *Lil-t* hr1*
- **puberty**, in: *Phos* sf1.de*
- **questioned**, when: *(↗disturbed; spoken; Abrupt; Anger - questioned; Answering - aversion; Impatience)* androc srj1• apis *Arn* k* bry k2 bufo gk bung-fa mtf *Cham* k* chir-fl gya2 coloc k* conv c1 haliae-lc srj5• nat-m k* **Nux-v** k* ozone sde2• petr-ra shn4• *Ph-ac* k* **Pip-m** sne puls rad-br sze8• ruta fd4.de sinus rly4• spong fd4.de ust *Vanil* fd5.de [bell-p-sp dcm1 heroin sdj2 tax jsj7]
- **reading**, while: *(↗Reading - agg.)* med nat-c
- **remorse**; with easy and quick: *(↗Anger - alternating - repentance)* arg-n mrr1 bung-fa mtf dulc fd4.de *Sulph* kr1 vanil fd5.de
- **reproaches**; from: *(↗insults)* bamb-a stb2.de•
- **restlessness**, with: gard-j vlr2• lat-m bnm6• ozone sde2• positr nl2•
- **rocking** fast: *(↗Carried - desire)*
  - **amel.**: *(↗Rocking - amel.)* cina
- **sadness**, with: aids nl2• ant-c j5.de asar h1* aur j5.de bit-ar wht1• bov j5.de dig j5.de gink-b sbd1• kali-br kr1 *Kali-c* hr1* **Kali-i** kr1 kola stb3• lyc j5.de *Nat-m* kr1 nit-ac j5.de plat j5.de polyg-h kr1 polyg-pe vml2• ptel bg1* sal-ac kr1 sep j5.de sul-ac j5.de *Sulph* kr1 tarent-c ckh1 *Vanil* fd5.de ziz a1* [sol-ecl cky1]
- **sends**: *(↗Obstinate - nothing; Refusing - medicine)*
  - **doctor** home, says he is not sick: *(↗Delirium; Delirium - well; Delusions - well; Reproaching others - doctor; Well - says - sick)* *Apis* k1* **Arn** k* **Cham** k*
  - **nurse**:
    - **home**: *Fl-ac*
    - **out** of the room: **Cham**
- **sexual** desire; from loss of: sabal ptk1*
- **sexual** excesses; from: ol-an sf1.de
- **sexual** excitement; from: | **women**; in: *Nux-v* kr1

- **sexual** weakness; with: *Pic-ac* kr1
- **sitting**, while: *(↗Sitting - inclination)* aeth ammc a1 calc mang nat-m k*
- **sleep**; when aroused by noise during: calad *Thuj* kr1
- **sleepiness**, with: ind hr1* lachn lpc
- **sleeplessness**, with: bell hr1* calc j5.de *Coff* sf1.de **Hyos** hr1* *Kali-br* hr1* mosch hr1* *Nat-m* hr1* plat hr1* psor st1 spong fd4.de
  - **children**, in: psor st1
- **spoken** to, when: *(↗questioned; Spoken - aversion)* arge-pl rwt5• ars aur aur-ar k2 bamb-a stb2.de• bry k2 bufo gk carbn-s **Cham** *Dulc* fd4.de elaps gels germ-met srj5• *Graph* hyos *Kali-p* kola stb3• lap-la rsp1 *Lil-t* kr1* mang j nat-m nat-s neon srj5• *Nit-ac* nux-v puls-n a1 rhus-t ruta fd4.de sal-fr sle1• *Sep* sil spong fd4.de staph stram *Sulph* tep tritic-vg fd5.de ust *Vanil* fd5.de verat k* [mang-i stj2 mang-m stj2 mang-p stj2 mang-s stj2]
- **stool**:
  - **after**: graph sf1.de laur bg2 nat-c k* *Nit-ac* k* rheum sf1.de
  - **before**: aloe *Borx* k* *Calc* k* merc sf1.de *Nux-v* bg2*
- **sudden**: brom mtf33 ham fd3.de• limest-b es1• *Podo* fd3.de• puls hr1 ros-d wla1 stront-c ptk1 suis-em rly4•
- **supper**, after: am k* nat-c petr a1 seneg a1
- **suspicious**: *(↗Suspicious)* cham j5.de lyc j5.de merc j5.de
- **taciturn**: *(↗Taciturn)* am-c j5.de ars j5.de coloc j5.de kali-s fd4.de puls j5.de pycnop-sa mrz1 ruta fd4.de sulph j5.de [heroin sdj2]
- **taking** everything in bad part: *(↗Offended)* alum c1 bov caust *Croc* *Dulc* fd4.de granit-m es1• kali-s fd4.de kola stb3• nat-m *Pall* puls *Vanil* fd5.de
- **talk** of others; from: *(↗flippancy)* plut-n ↓ *Rhus-g* tmo3• sacch-a gmj3 sel ↓
  - **loud**: *(↗Sensitive - noise - voices)* plut-n srj7• sel rsj9•
- **talking**: *(↗conversation)*
  - **amel.**: abrom-a ks5
  - **while**: allox tpw3 alum ambr k* cham kali-m ckh1 ketogl-ac rly4• lap-la rsp1 mang nicc ozone sde2• psor sacch-a gmj3 staph sul-ac teucr tong a1 zinc [mang-i stj2 mang-m stj2 mang-p stj2 mang-s stj2]
- **teeth**; with complaints of: rhus-t bg2 sep b4a.de
- **thunderstorm** | **before**: nat-c sf1.de
- **time**; about wasted: nicc-met sk4•
- **touch**, by: *Ant-c* hr1* *Arn* vh* *Cham* vh* lach j5.de phos ↓ tarent ptk1* [ant-m stj2 *Ant-met* stj2 ant-t stj2 iod stj2 lith-i stj2 merc-i-f stj2 zinc-i stj2]
- **travelling**:
  - **bus**; by: ven-m rsj12•
  - **slow**: cortiso tpw7*
- **trifles**, from: *(↗Anger - beside; Anger - beside - trifles; Anger - trifles; Petulant; Trifles; Trifles - important)* acon vh1 ang a1 ant-c j5.de anthraq rly4• arg-met j5.de arge-pl rwt5• *Ars* h2* aspar hr1* *Aur-m-n* wbt2• *Bell* h1* ben c bit-ar wht1• borx a1 brass-n-o srj5• bros-gau mrc1 bry br1 bung-fa mtf *Calc* j5.de* calc-sil k2 cann-xyz bg2 *Caps* a1 carb-v j5.de carc mlr1* cassia-s cdd7• *Caust* j5.de* *Cham* bg2 chel a1 chir-fl gya2 choc srj3• *Cimic* kr1* cina bg2 clem bg2 cob ptm1• *Cocc* j5.de* con a1 cortico tpw7 croc bg2 crot-c sk4• cupr sst3• *Cycl* a1 dendr-pol sk4• digin a1 dream-p sdj1• dros ptk1* *Dulc* fd4.de falco-pe nl2• fl-ac a1 gink-b sbd1• granit-m es1• graph k2 haliae-lc srj5• *Ham* fd3.de• hell bg2* *Hep* bg2* hist mg1.de* hydrog srj2• ign j5.de ip bg2 kali-bi bg2 kali-m k* kali-p fd1.de• *Kali-s* fd4.de ketogl-ac rly4• kola stb3• kreos bg2* *Lac-cp* sk4• lac-leo sk4• lach bg2 lact-v a1 limest-b es1• *Lyc* bg2* lycpr a1 lyss a1 mang h2* marb-w es1• **Med** kr1* meph a1 merc-i-r a1 mez bg2 mim-p rsj8• moni rfm1• nat-c bg2 *Nat-m* bg2* nat-p k2 *Nat-sil* fd3.de• **Nit-ac** bg2* **Nux-v** bg2* oci-sa sk4• opun-s a1 (non:opun-v a1) ozone sde2• petr j5.de petr-ra shn4• *Phos* bg2* *Plat* j5.de* plut-n srj7• *Podo* fd3.de• positr nl2• pot-e rly4• *Ptel* kr1 puls a1 *Pycnop-sa* mrz1 rhus-t h1 ruta fd4.de sacch-a fd2.de• sal-fr sle1• sanic ptk1 saroth jl3 sars a1 sel gmj2 seneg bg2 sep bg2* sil j5.de sol-a a1 spong fd4.de stram bg2 stront-c sk4• suis-pan rly4• sul-ac k2 sulph j5.de **Symph** fd* *Tritic-vg* fd5.de *Tub* ptk1* *Vanil* fd5.de verat h1* [lac-mat sst4 mang-i stj2 mang-m stj2 mang-p stj2 mang-s stj2 pall stj2]
  - **jocose**, though: *Caps* a1
- **violent** | **children**; in: carc mlr1•
- **waking**, on: agar aids nl2• anac ant-t k* arg-n *Ars* k* bamb-a stb2.de• *Bell* k* berb bov brom k* bry k* bufo calad hr1* camph carb-an k* carb-v a1 cass a1 castm caust cham chel k* chin chinin-ar chinin-s *Cina* kr1 clem k* coca cupr *Cycl* k* gamb iris jatr-c *Kali-c* k* kali-p ketogl-ac rly4• *Lach* lil-t **Lyc** k* m-aust mag-m *Merc-i-r* mez nat-m k* nat-s nat-sil k2* neon srj5• *Nit-ac* k* nux-v pall petr *Ph-ac* phos ptk1 plat plb pseuts-m oss1• *Psor* puls rhus-t sanic c1* sep

Irritability – **waking**, on: ...
staph mrr1 suis-em rly4• suis-pan rly4• sul-ac sulph tarent a1 thuj **Tub** al* [zinc stj2]
  - **amel.**: caps
  - **immediately** when opening eyes: tub jl2
  - **whooping** cough; on: *Bry* vh*
- **walking**, when: am-c h2 berb *Borx* clem con sumb a1 thuj
  - **open** air amel.; in: mag-c **Rhus-t** symph fd3.de•
- **warm** room, in: anac calc ign *Puls*
- **water**; on hearing or seeing: *(↗Hydrophobia)* **Lyss** k*
- **weakness**: *(↗weariness)*
  - **from**: mur-ac sf1.de*
  - **with**: *(↗Well - says - sick; GENERALS - Irritability - lack)* bamb-a stb2.de• caul c1 **Chin** hr1* gal-ac c1 *Kali-p* hr1*
- **weariness**: *(↗weakness)*
  - **during**: bit-ar wht1• crot-t a1 hydrog srj2• kali-p fd1.de• ruta gk **Sep** mrr1 tritic-vg fd5.de vanil fd5.de
- **weather**; in rainy or cloudy: aloe am-c dulc fd4.de ruta fd4.de
- **weeping**; with (See crying)
- **working**, when: aids nl2• cadm-met tpw6 galeoc-c-h gms1• ham fd3.de• kali-s fd4.de plan a1 sacch-a fd2.de• symph fd3.de• tong a1 tritic-vg fd5.de [bell-p-sp dcm1]
- **worm** affections; in: abrot gsy* *Carb-v* kr1 **Cina** kr1* fil kr1 nat-p tl1 teucr ↓
  - **followed** by | **squinting**: nat-p tl1
  - **threadworms**: teucr hr1
- **writing** | **while**: med kr1*

ISOLATION; sensation of (See Forsaken - isolation)

JEALOUSY: *(↗Ailments - jealousy; Avarice; Delirium - jealousy; Delusions - wife - faithless; Envy; Jealousy - drunkenness; Love - love-sick; Quarrelsome - jealousy; Sadness - happy; Selfishness; Slander; Suspicious)* *Aml-ns* vh1 anac bg2* anan k* *Apis* k* arg-n sne ars gl1.fr• *Aur-m-n* wbt2• bamb-a stb2.de• bell ↓ bufo gk calad ↓ *Calc* ↓ calc-p k* *Calc-s* k* camph k* carc ↓ caust ↓ *Cench* cham gsy chin ↓ chir-fl ↓ *Cocain* br1 cocc dx1 coff coloc k2 con ↓ crot-c sk4• cystein-l rly4• gal-ac gels cda haliae-lc srj5• ham fd3.de• **HYOS** b7.de* ign k* ilx-a bh* ip kr1* kali-act kr1 kali-ar kr1* kali-c vh* kali-p sne kali-s tl1* *Kola* stb3• lac-c sne lac-leo hrn2• **LACH** b7.de* lil-t bg2* lob ↓ lyc bg2* mag-c ↓ *Med* st1* merc pd* morg-g pte1*• nat-m fd* nat-sil fd3.de• *Nux-m* st* **Nux-v** b7.de* op k* ozone sde2• petr ↓ ph-ac phos ↓ pin-con oss2• plat gl* positr nl2• *Puls* k* raph sabad dgt sacch sht*• sal-fr sle1• sep gl• *Staph* k1* *Stram* k* sulph mrr1* ther sne thuj k2* tritic-vg fd5.de verat mrr1* [am-s stj bar-s stj ferr-s stj heroin sdj2 *Mag-s* stj1 nat-s stj sul-ac stj vip bcj1]
- **accuses**:
  - **husband**:
    - **faithless**; of being: positr nl2•
    - **neglect**; of: ham fd3.de• nat-sil fd3.de• *Stram* hr1*
  - **wife** of being faithless: *Stram* hr1*
- **ailments** (See Ailments - jealousy)
- **animal** or an inanimate object; for: caust vh* hyos vh* lach vh* nux-v vh*
- **appreciate** anything; desires that others shall not: ham fd3.de• *Ip* kr1*
- **attention**; others getting all: ozone sde2•
- **brutal** from jealousy; gentle husband becoming: *(↗Brutality)* calc gl1.fr• lach gl1.fr• nux-v gl1.fr• sulph gl1.fr•
- **children**:
  - **between**: ars vh* calc-s mrr1* carc cd* med gk nat-m vh* nux-v vh* sep vh* sulph mrr1 verat ms
    - **girls**: nux-v mtf33
  - **in**: calc-p mtf33 hyos mtf33 ip mtf33 lach mtf33 lyc mtf33 med mtf33 nux-v mtf33 sacch sst1• staph mtf33 stram mtf33 thuj mtf33
  - **newborn** gets all the attention; when the: *Hyos* hr1 ign hr1
- **crime**, to a: *(↗kill)* hyos gl1.fr• lach mtf33*
- **drunkenness**, during: *(↗Jealousy)* *Hyos* gl1.fr• lach gl1.fr• nux-v gl1.fr• puls gl1.fr• staph gl1.fr•
- **happy**; seeing others (See Envy - happy)
- **images**, with frightful: *Lach* hr1*
- **impotence**, with: calad gl1.fr• nux-v vh*

- **insane**: lach ptk1*
- **insult**, driving to: *Nux-v* hr1*
- **irrational**: cocain ptk1* ham fd3.de•
- **irresistible** as foolish as it is: *Lach*
- **kill**, driving to: (↗*crime; Kill; desire*) **Hyos** kr1 lach tl
- **loquacity**, with: (↗*Loquacity*) lach gl1.fr• mag-c mtf33* petr gl1.fr•
- **love**; from disappointed: hyos *Lach* vh* nat-m st sacch sst1•
- **men**, between: ars vh* lach vh* puls vh* verat vh*
- **menses** | **before**: **Lach** mrr1
- **neglect**, accuses husband of (See accuses - husband - neglect)
- **people** around, of: chir-fl gya2 op a1
- **quarrelling**, reproaches and scolding; with: (↗*Quarrelsome - jealousy*) gal-ac a1 *Lach* kr1 *Nux-v* kr1*
- **rage**, with: **Hyos** hr1* *Lach* vh*
- **revenge**, wants to take: hyos gl•
- **sadness**, with: chir-fl gya2 *Kali-ar* hr1* lob mp1• tritic-vg fd5.de
- **saying** and doing what he would not normally say and do: bell gl1.fr• lach gl1.fr• sulph mtf33*
- **sexual** excitement, with: calc gl1.fr• caust gl1.fr• chin gl1.fr• con gl1.fr• hyos kr1 nux-v gl1.fr• phos gl1.fr•
- **strike** his wife; driving to: (↗*Striking*) *Calc* vh* lach vh* nux-v vh* sulph vh*
- **tearing** the hair: (↗*Pulling - hair*) lach mtf33*
- **value** or appreciate anything, desires that others shall not: *Ip* kr1
- **vindictive**: (↗*Malicious*) hyos gl1.fr• positr nl2•
- **weeping**, with: caust vh* nux-v vh* petr vh*
- **women**:
  - **between**: ars vh* nat-m vh* nux-v vh* sep vh*
  - **in**: *Apis* kr1

JESTING: (↗*Amusement - desire; Cheerful; Content; Exhilaration; Foolish; High-spirited; Irony; Laughing; Loquacity - jesting; Mirth; Mocking; Playful; Pleasure; Teasing; Vivacious; Witty*) aeth k* aether a1 agam-g mlk9.de agar ↓ *Agath-a* nl2• agav-t jl3 alco a1 aloe alum ↓ androc srj1• arg-met ars k* bar-c bell k* bry k* cact ↓ calc cann-i k* *Caps* k* carb-v k* chlol a1 choc srj3• *Cic* *Cocc* k* coff ptk1* con ↓ conch fkr1.de **Croc** k* cupr cur ↓ dulc fd4.de falco-pe ↓ ferr-p k2 galla-q-r nl2• glon k* ham fd3.de• hyos k* **Ign** k* ip k* kali-cy a1 *Kali-i* k* kali-s fd4.de kola stb3• lac-del hrn2• *Lach* k* limest-b es1• lyc marb-w ↓ medul-os-si rly4• meny b7a.de* merc k* merl nat-m k* *Nux-m* nux-v ↓ olib-sac wmh1 op k* oxal-a ↓ peti a1 petr-ra shn4• phos ctc• plac rzf5• plat k* *Podo* fd3.de• positr ↓ psil ft1 psor a1 puls ↓ rad-br ↓ rhus-r *Rhus-t* mrr1 ruta fd4.de sacch-a fd2.de• sars k* sec spong k* *Stann* gl1.fr• staph gl1.fr• *Stram* k* sul-ac k* sumb a1 tab k* tanac ↓ *Tarax* b7a.de *Tarent* k* tere-la rly4• tritic-vg fd5.de vanil fd5.de verat mtf33 [ant-c stj2 ant-met stj2 heroin sdj2 lappa stj pop dhh1 tax jsj7]

- **afternoon** | **15**.30 h: aloe a
- **evening**: aether a
- **alternating** with:
  - **anger** (See Anger - alternating - jesting)
  - **company**; aversion to: rad-br st rhus-r k1
  - **indifference**: meny j5.de
  - **irritability** (See Irritability - alternating - jesting)
  - **seriousness**: cann-i a2 plat j5.de positr nl2•
  - **taciturnity**: plat j5.de
  - **vexation** (See Irritability - alternating - jesting)
  - **weeping**: cur a2 *Ign* j5.de nux-m ll1 peti c1
- **aversion** to: (↗*joke; Awkward; Serious*) *Acon* am-c ang k* apis ars asar ↓ borx bov cann-s b7a.de caps carb-an *Cina* cocc cycl ignis-alc es2• *Merc* k1* nat-m nux-v puls sabin sil k* spig k* staph gl1.fr• sulph thuj k* viol-t b7.de
  - **sexual** jokes: asar mrr1
- **black** humor: galla-q-r nl2•
- **erotic**: bell gl1.fr• *Calc* gl1.fr• galla-q-r nl2• hyos mrr1* nux-v gl1.fr•
- **everything**; makes jest of: dulc fd4.de nux-m c1 sacch-a fd2.de•
- **facetious**; desire to do something: aeth a cact a1 dulc fd4.de
- **fun** of somebody; making (See Jesting)
- **gravity**; jesting after: plat
- **indifference**; jesting after: meny

Jesting: ...

- **joke**; cannot take a: (↗*aversion; Frivolous*) *Acon* kr1* ang kr1 aur-m-n wbt2• caps gl1.fr• cina h1 **Iod** gl1.fr• lyc mtf33* merc mtf33* nat-m h2* nux-v gl1.fr• puls gl1.fr• *Ran-b* a1 *Spig* a1 sulph gl1.fr•
- **licentious**: alco a1
- **malicious**: (↗*Cynical; Malicious; Mocking - sarcasm*) ars k* choc srj3• marb-w es1• oxal-a rly4•
- **practical** joker (See Mocking)
- **problems**, at: falco-pe nl2•
- **puns**, makes: cann-i k* choc srj3• dulc fd4.de ruta fd4.de sacch-a fd2.de•
- **ridiculous** or foolish: (↗*Childish; Foolish; Gestures - ridiculous*) androc srj1• bell *Cic* croc falco-pe nl2• hyos *Stram* tanac tritic-vg fd5.de *Verat*
- **roguish**: puls j5.de
- **sadness**; during: limest-b es1•
- **trifles** with everything: agar alum gl1.fr• con gl1.fr•
- **waking**, on: tarent a1

JEWELRY: | **desire** to wear: (↗*Extravagance; Vanity; DREAMS - Jewelry*) lac-f wza1• oci-sa sk4•

JOKING (See Jesting)

JOURNEYS (See Travelling)

JOVIAL (See Cheerful; Jesting; Sociability)

JOY: (↗*Cheerful; Ecstasy*) abrom-a ckh1 agri mtf11 anac ↓ ars ↓ *Asaf* ↓ bufo ↓ chir-fl gya2 cimic ↓ cupr ↓ dulc fd4.de falco-pe nl2• hippoc-k szs2 kali-s fd4.de lac-lup hrn2• limen-b-c hrn2• maias-l hrn2• nat-sil fd3.de• neon srj5• *Olib-sac* wmh1 plac ↓ ruta fd4.de sacch-a fd2.de• thres-a sze7• tritic-vg fd5.de vanil fd5.de verb ↓ vult-gr sze5• [sulph stj1]

- **ailments** (See Ailments - joy)
- **alternating** with | **irritability** (See Irritability - alternating - joy)
- **death**, when thinking of (See Cheerful - death)
- **diarrhea**; with sudden (See RECTUM - Diarrhea - joy)
- **fits** of joy with bursts of laughter: *Asaf* k1 maias-l hrn2• plac rzf5• verb kr1*
- **followed** by | **sadness**: olib-sac wmh1
- **giving** out presents at Christmas: lac-lup hrn2•
- **grandchildren**; looking at one's: **Nat-sil** fd*
- **happiness**; at other's: limen-b-c hrn2•
- **headache** | **from** joy; headache (See HEAD - Pain - joy)
- **misfortune** of others; at the: (↗*Malicious; Malicious - laughing*) anac gg ars k* cupr cda*
- **nature**, in: falco-pe nl2• *Tritic-vg* fd5.de *Vanil* fd5.de
  - **birds**, in the flight of: falco-pe nl2•
- **rainbow**; seeing a: maias-l hrn2•
- **sleeplessness** from excessive joy (See SLEEP - Sleeplessness - joy)
- **spontaneous** feelings of pleasure: limen-b-c hrn2•
- **trembling**, mirth, playfulness and clear intellect; with: cimic hr1*
- **trembling**; with (See GENERALS - Trembling - externally - joy)
- **waking**; on: bufo bg maias-l hrn2•

JOYLESS (See Indifference - joyless)

JOYOUS (See Cheerful)

JUMPING: absin ↓ acet-ac ↓ *Acon* ↓ aeth ↓ agar k* alco ↓ ambr ↓ ant-t ↓ apis ↓ *Arg-met* kr1 *Arg-n* ↓ *Ars* ↓ asar bg2 atra-r ↓ atro ↓ *Aur* bg2 bell k* bry ↓ calc ↓ calc-f ↓ camph ↓ cann-i a1 **Chin** ↓ chinin-ar ↓ *Chinin-s* ↓ chlol ↓ cic k* **Cina** ↓ *Croc* k* *Cupr* ↓ *Cupr-act* ↓ dubo-m ↓ dulc ↓ gal-ac ↓ *Glon* ↓ grat hell ↓ hydr-ac ↓ hyos lach ↓ lact lyss ↓ *Merc* ↓ merc-c ↓ merc-meth ↓ morg-p ↓ morph ↓ nux-v hr1* **Op** ↓ past ↓ petr ↓ phos ↓ pip-m a1 plb ↓ *Puls* ↓ rumx ↓ sabad ↓ sol-mm ↓ stict bg2 stram k* sul-ac ↓ *Syph* ↓ tarent bg2* tax ↓ verat ↓ **Verat-v** ↓ zinc ↓

- **evening**: *Cina* kr1
- **night**: cic a
- **air**, into: cann-i a
- **alternating** with | **sighing**: bell a1
- **bed**, out of: (↗*Bed - jumps; Delirium - bed - escapes; Escape; Escape - jumps; Fear - jumps - bed; Restlessness - bed - driving*)

- **bed**, out of: ...
absin ptk1 acet-ac↓ *Acon* aeth c1* alco a1 ambr h1 ant-t a1 apis dm *Arg-n* *Ars* atro a1 **Bell** k* bry calc h2 calc-f↓ camph k* **Chin** k* chinin-ar *Chinin-s* chlol cic *Cupr* cupr-act kr1 dubo-m a1 dulc↓ gal-ac k* *Glon* hell fyz **Hyos** k* lach lyss *Merc* merc-c a1 merc-meth a1 morph↓ **Op** k* past a1 phos plb a1 puls rumx sabad sol-mm a1 **Stram** k* sul-ac a1 *Syph* kr1* verat mtf33 **Verat-v** kr1 zinc mtf33 [tax jsj7]
  - **crawls** on floor, and: acet-ac ptk1
  - **delirium**, in: *Chinin-s* kr1
  - **dreaming**: calc-f ptk1 dulc↓
    - **frightful**: dulc h2
    - **waked** him; which: calc-f hr1
    - **when** dreaming: calc-f ptk1
  - **fell** and knees gave out: *Glon* kr1
  - **fever**, during: chinin-ar chlol↓ *Hyos* hr1* morph a1
    - **typhoid** fever: chlol gm1
  - **happy**, childish state, in: **Cic** kr1
  - **mania**, in: (↗*Mania*) *Cupr-act* kr1 *Puls* hr1*
  - **returning** to bed continually; and: bell a1
  - **shrieking**; and (See Shrieking - jumping)
  - **waking**, on: *Stram* kr1
- **children**; in: *Bell*↓ cina mtf33
  - **evening**: **Cina** kr1
  - **chairs**, tables and stove; on: *Bell* kr1
- **convulsively**: hydr-ac a
- **dancing**; and (See Dancing - jumping)
- **dream**; because of a (See bed - dream)
- **frantically**: atra-r bnm3•
- **impulse** to jump: agar ptk1 arg-met↓ *Aur* ptk1 calc-f↓ croc ptk1 lach sne morg-p fmm1• stram ptk1 tarent ptk1*
  - **bridge**; when crossing a (See Suicidal - throwing - river)
  - **dreams**, in: calc-f ptk*
  - **epilepsy**, after: arg-met ptk*
  - **height**; from a (See Suicidal - throwing - height)
  - **pregnancy**, during: **Aur** kr1
  - **river**; into the (See Suicidal - drowning; Suicidal - throwing - river)
  - **window**; from a (See Suicidal - throwing - window)
- **running** recklessly; and: sabad ptk1
- **suddenly**, as from pain: cina ptk1*
- **wall**: petr c1
- **wild** leaps in puerperal mania: (↗*Insanity - puerperal*) *Nux-v* kr1

JUMPING UP:
- **lying** down, after: carb-ac a
- **menses**, during: *Oena* kr1
- **sleep**; during: acon b7.de*

JUMPY nerves (See Excitement)

JUSTICE: | **desire** for (See Injustice)

KICKING: (↗*Behavior - children; Gestures - feet - stamping; Striking; Violent*) atro a1 *Bell* k* borx↓ carb-v k* carc↓ cham h1* cina↓ dendr-pol sk4• dulc fd4.de gal-ac zr hyos h1 *Ign*↓ *Lyc* k* med hu* nat-c↓ nat-m↓ nux-v vh* ozone sde2• phos↓ plut-n srj7• prot jl3* sacch sht• sanic c1* stict↓ *Stram* k* stry k* *Sulph*↓ tarent k* tub↓ vanil fd5.de verat-v k* [ant-c stj2 ant-met stj2 cupr stj2 cupr-act stj2 cupr-f stj2 cupr-m stj2 cupr-p stj2]
- **anger**; during: bell ctc• borx bl nat-m ctc• nux-v ctc• tub ctc• vanil fd5.de
- **children**; in: bell mtf33 borx mtf33 *Cham* mrr1 cina↓ cupr↓ **Lyc**↓ med mtf33 nux-v mtf33 sanic mtf33 tarent mtf33 vanil fd5.de
  - **carried**; child becomes stiff and kicks when: (↗*Anger - stiffening; Carried - aversion*) *Cham* k* cina st* cupr sst3*
  - **cross**, kicks and scolds on waking; child is: **Lyc** k* sanic c1*
- **heels**; with: stict ptk1
- **legs**; with | **convulsions**; during: *Ign* hr1*
- **sleep**, in: **Bell** k* carc zzh cina k* nat-c h2* phos h2* *Sulph* k* tub gk*
- **tantrum**, in (See anger)
- **worm**-complaints; during: *Carb-v* kr1 cina cd

KILL; desire to: (↗*Anger - kill; Anger - stabbed; Desires - full - more; Fear - killing; Impulse - stab - others; Impulse - violence; Jealousy - kill; Kill - drunkenness; Rage - kill; Thoughts - persistent - homicide; Thoughts - persistent - murder; Threatening - kill; Violent*) acon vh1 agar k* aids nl2• alco a1 alum sf1.de anac k* androc srj arg-n vh *Ars* k* *Ars-i* aur-m-n wbt2• *Bell* k* calc k* camph k* caust sne chin k* chlf↓ cimic sne crot-c sk4• cupr k* cur dendr-pol sk4• der↓ (non:germ-met srj5) haliae-lc srj5• **Hep** bg2* **Hyos** k* *Iod* k* jab↓ kali-ar k2 kali-br↓ lac-lup hrn2• *Lach* k* *Lyc* gl1.fr• lys↓ lyss *Med* gk* meli↓ *Merc* k* *Nat-s*↓ nicc-met sk4• nit-ac mrr1 *Nux-v* op k* pegan-ha tpi1• *Petr* petr-ra shn4• *Phos* k* *Plat* k* positr nl2• prot ptj• pseuts-m sne* rauw↓ rhus-g tmo3• rumx↓ sec sil bg2* spong fd4.de *Staph* kr1* *Stram* k* sulfon↓ sulph↓ syph bg2* taosc iwa1• tarent mrr1 thea k* thuj↓ thyr c1 tritic-vg fd5.de x-ray jl* [cinnb stj2 merc-i-f stj2]
- **animals**: haliae-lc srj5• spong fd4.de tritic-vg fd5.de
- **barber** wants to kill his customer: *Ars* *Hep*
- **beer** bottle; a: lac-lup hrn2•
- **beloved** ones: alum gk ars bro1 chin bro1 hep k2 jab ptk kali-br ptk merc bro1 *Nux-v* bro1 *Plat* bro1* thea mrr1
- **car**; by running into people with her: bell ser
- **child**, the own: (↗*throw*) alum gk androc srj1• arg-n vh haliae-lc srj5• merc gl1.fr• nux-v gk *Plat* c1* thea c1*
- **children**; in: | **parents**; to kill the: der vh*
- **contradicts** her; the person that: (↗*Contradiction - intolerant*) dendr-pol sk4• *Merc* k*
- **delirium**, in: chlf c1
- **drunkards**, in: (↗*drunkenness*) *Ars* kr1
- **drunkenness**; during: (↗*drunkards; Kill; desire; Rage - drunkenness*) bell vh* hep vh* **Hyos** vh* nux-v vh plat vh
- **everyone** he sees: aids nl2• hyos vh* taosc iwa1•
- **fear** that she may get a desire to kill (See Fear - killing)
- **herself**; sudden impulse to: (↗*Fear - suicide; Injuring - fear; Suicidal*) alum kr *Ars* mrr1 iod ptk1* meli ptk1* merc k2 *Nat-s* k* *Nux-v* kr1 rauw sp1 rumx gg thea a1 thuj
- **husband**; impulse to kill her beloved: *Merc* *Nux-v* *Plat* k*
  - **menses** agg.; during: (↗*Menses - during*) *Merc* kr1
  - **razor**; therefore implores him to hide his: *Merc* kr1
- **hysterical** sadness, with: *Merc* kr1
- **injure** with a knife; impulse to (See knife - with)
- **knife**:
  - **sight** of a; at the: (↗*Impulse - stab - his; Thoughts - frightful - seeing*) *Alum* ars fyz *Merc* vh* nux-v sne* plat
    - **gun**; or a: *Alum* k*
  - **with** a knife: (↗*Impulse - stab - his*) *Alum* k* ars h2* chin bg2* crot-c sk4• der vml3• *Hep* kr1* *Hyos* bg2* **Lyc** gl1.fr• lys bg2 *Merc* kr1* nicc-met sk4• *Nux-v* kr1* plat *Stram* kr1 thea c1
- **menses**:
  - **before**: (↗*Menses - before*) x-ray jl*
  - **during**: (↗*Menses - during*) *Merc* kr1 x-ray jl*
- **offended** him; those who: rhus-g tmo3•
- **offense**; sudden impulse to kill for a slight: (↗*Offended*) *Hep* *Merc* *Nux-v*
- **poison**, impulse to: ars gl1.fr• lach gl1.fr• nux-v gl1.fr•
- **rest**; during: (↗*Fear - insanity - repose*) iod
- **somebody**; thought he ought to kill: (↗*Delusions - murdered*) camph *Hyos* kr1
- **sudden** impulse to kill: **Alum** vh* arg-n vh *Ars* *Ars-i* crot-c↓ dendr-pol sk4• *Hep* *Hyos* vh* iod k* kali-ar med gk merc k2* nicc-met sk4• *Nux-v* *Plat* k* rauw sp staph vh sulfon vh sulph vh tarent ptk thea k* thuj mlk1
  - **disturb** him; those who: crot-c sk4•
  - **herself** (See herself)
- **threatens** to kill (See Threatening - kill)
- **throw** child; sudden impulse to: (↗*child*)
  - **fire**; into: hep k2 lyss merc↓ *Nux-v* thea
  - **window**; out of the: lyss kr1*
- **walking** in open air and street, while: camph hyos gl1.fr•
- **woman**; irresistible impulse to kill a: *Iod* kr1

KILLED; desire to be: (↗*Suicidal*) *Ars* k* bell k* carc mlr1• coff-t k* lac-h↓ *Phyt* hr1* plat↓ stram k*
- **alone**; rather than left: lac-h sk4•

- **labor**, in: *Coff-t* kr1
- **menses**, during: plat mtn
- **stabbing** heart; by | **midnight**; after: *Ars* a1

KIND people: | **yearning** for: *(↗Sympathy - desire)* olib-sac wmh1 *Vanil* fd5.de

KINDNESS (See Consolation; Mildness)

KISSING: *(↗Embraces)*
- **children** are caressing and kissing: *Puls* hr1*
- **everyone**: *(↗Amorous; Embraces - everyone; Lascivious)* caps *Croc* k* hyos bg2* kres mg1.de mand mg1.de* phos k* plat kr1* stram *Verat* k* [zinc stj2 zinc-i stj2 zinc-m stj2 zinc-n stj2 zinc-p stj2]
- **hands** of his companions: agar k* anac
- **mania** puerperalis, in: *Verat* kr1
- **menses** | **before**: *(↗Menses - before)* *Verat* k* zinc
- **wants** to be kissed: *Stram* kr1*

KLEPTOMANIA: absin k* ars *Art-v* k* **Bell** mtf33* bry calc gl1.fr• carb-v mtf33* carc mlr1* caust cic bro1 *Cur* k* gal-ac zr hyos bro1 kali-br zr kali-c k* lac-h sze9• lach ctc* lyc k* mag-c ↓ mand mgm• nat-c ↓ nat-m mtf33* *Nux-v* k* op tl1* oxyt bro1 phos ↓ plat bro1* **Puls** ●* sep k* sil gl1.fr• staph k* stram k* *Sulph* k* syph bg* tarent k* thuj gy* [nat-f stj2]
- **boy** with epilepsy: *Art-v* kr1
- **dainties**, steals: mag-c mag-m mtf33 nat-c
- **goes** about house searching for something: *Staph* kr1
- **money**, steals: art-v ckh1 **Calc** k ●* cur ckh1 nux-v ckh1 **Puls** ●* tarent ckh1
  - **necessity**; without: art-v ptk1 cur ptk1 nux-v ptk1 tarent ptk1

KNEELING (See Praying)

KNIFE; cannot look at a: *(↗Fear - knives)* **Alum** k* nux-m ckh1 plat bg* staph mtf33

KORSAKOFF's psychosis: | **alcoholism**: *(↗Alcoholism)* agar mtf11 verat mtf11

LACONIC: *(↗Abrupt)* chin h1 merc h1 mur-ac h1*

LAID down; does not want to be (See Carried - desire)

LAMENTING: *(↗Complaining; Discontented; Grumbling; Howling; Insanity - lamenting; Moaning; Muttering; Pessimist; Shrieking; Sighing; Tormenting - others - complaints; Weeping)* *Acet-ac* *Acon* k* act-sp agar ↓ *Alum* k1* alum-p k2 am-c ambr *Anac* k* ant-t ↓ arg-n arn k* *Ars* k* ars-s-f k2 asaf **Aur** k* aur-ar k2 aur-m-n wbt2• aur-s k2 bar-s k2 *Bell* *Bism* *Bism-o* a1 brom k* *Bry* bufo calad *Calc* calc-ar k2 calc-s k2 calc-sil k2* camph *Canth* k* caps caust gl1.fr• *Cham* k* *Chin* k* *Cic* *Cina* k* cocc *Coff* k* *Coloc* *Cor-r* cupr cupr-act a1 cycl dig dulc gard-j ↓ gels ↓ **Ham** fd* hell hyos ign ignis-alc ↓ ip kali-ar kali-br kali-i kali-p kali-s fd4.de *Lach* k* lat-m bnm6• **Lyc** lyss kr1 m-arct ↓ mag-p kr1 merc *Moni* rfm1• morph a1 *Mosch* nat-ar nat-c k2* nat-m nit-ac nux-m **Nux-v** k* *Op* ozone ↓ petr ph-ac phos pin-con oss2• plat plb **Puls** k* ran-b rheum rhus-t rob sal-fr sle1• sec sep sil spong fd4.de stann staph gl1.fr• stram stry *Sulph* k* syph k2 tarent thal jl3 til a1 tub bgs **Verat** k* **Verat-v** viol-t zinc k*
- **morning** | **waking**; on: *Cina* kr1
- **evening**: **Verat** k*
- **night**: sil ↓ spong fd4.de stram h1* verat k*
  - **waking**; on: sil h2
- **alternating** with:
  - **crying** (See Weeping - alternating - lamenting)
  - **delirium** (See Delirium - alternating - lamenting)
  - **laughing** (See Laughing - alternating - lamenting)
- **anxiety** in epigastrium, about: ars h2*
- **anxious**: plb hr1* puls a1
- **appreciated**, because he is not: *(↗Confidence - want; Delusions - appreciated; Delusions - despised; Flattered - desire; Forsaken; Haughty)* calc-s k* *Ham* fd3.de•
- **cold**; from: ozone sde2•
- **convulsions**, during: ars k*
- **cough**; lamenting causes: arn br1
- **cramp** in feet; from: ozone sde2•
- **fever**, during: acon bg bry bg nux-v bg puls j5.de* til a1 verat bg
- **future**, about: *(↗Anxiety - future; Grief - future)* lyc k*

Lamenting: ...
- **heat** of whole body except hands, with: **Puls** a1*
- **hoarse**: brom kr1*
- **involuntary**: *Alum* gl1.fr•
- **loud**, piercing: *Ars* h2*
- **menses**, during: *(↗Menses - during)* ars h2* *Cocc* hr1*
- **misfortune**; over his imaginary: *(↗Delusions - misfortune - inconsolable)* alum-p k2*
- **others**, about: *(↗Gossiping; Sympathetic)* merc
- **pain**, about: *(↗Sensitive - pain)* agar vh1 ars h2* cham gl1.fr• **Coloc** hr1* dulc fd4.de gels sys **Lach** gl1.fr• *Mag-p* hr1* *Mosch* j *Nux-v* h1* *Spong* fd4.de
- **perspiration**, during: *Acon* bg2 bry bg2 ign k* nux-v bg2 verat bg2
- **sadness**, in: kali-s fd4.de *Puls* hr1*
- **sickness**, about his: *(↗Hypochondriasis)* arg-n **Ham** fd* *Kali-s* fd4.de **Lach** gl1.fr• nux-v gl1.fr• ph-ac
- **sleep**; during: alum arn bry j5.de *Cham* *Cina* k* gard-j vlr2• m-arct j5.de op j5.de ph-ac h2* phos stann h2 stram sulph
- **stool** | **before** stool, in children: **Rheum** st
- **trifles**, over: *(↗Trifles; Trifles - important)* acon vh1 *Coff* k* ham fd3.de• moni rfm1•
- **waking**, on: ant-t j5.de cina k* merc j5.de sil j5.de *Stram* j5.de
- **world**; about the sadness and suffering of the: ignis-alc es2•

LANGUAGES:
- **inability** for: lyc gl1.fr• olnd gl1.fr• rhus-t gl1.fr• sulph gl1.fr• syph jl2
- **understanding** (See Comprehension)

LASCIVIOUS: *(↗Amativeness; Amorous; Delirium - erotic; Delirium - naked; Fancies - lascivious; Hysteria - lascivious; Indifference - exposure; Insanity - erotic; Insanity - lascivious; Kissing - everyone; Lewdness; Libertinism; Naked; Nymphomania; Obscene; Obscene - songs; Pleasure - lascivious; Restlessness - lascivious; Shameless; Shameless - exposing; Shameless - exposing - person; Thoughts - intrude - sexual; Thoughts - tormenting - sexual)* *Acon* bg2* agar agath-a nl2• agn ptk1 aloe *Ambr* k* androc srj1• ang b7a.de ant-c b7.de* *Apis* k* aq-mar skp7• arund aster kr1* aur bell bg2* borx bov a1 *Bufo* bg2* *Calad* k* *Calc* k* calc-p sf1.de calc-s calc-sil k2 camph bg2* *Cann-i* sf1.de cann-s b7a.de* *Canth* k* caps ↓ carb-an bg2 *Carb-v* k* carl a1 *Caust* mtf33* cedr c1* cere-s a1 *Chin* k* chir-fl ↓ coc-c cod a1 coff b7.de* coloc bg2 *Con* k* cop croc bg2* des-ac jl3 *Dig* k* dulc bg2 euphr ↓ falco-pe nl2• *Fl-ac* k* *Gamb* mrr1 *Graph* k* hydrog srj2• **Hyos** k* hyper ign k* iod bg2 irid-met srj5• kali-br st kali-c bg2 **Lach** k* **Lil-t** k* lyc k* lyss m-ambo b7.de* m-arct a1 meny b7a.de* merc k* mosch k* *Murx* bg2* nat-c bg2* nat-m k* nat-s mrr1 nit-ac k* nuph a1 nux-m bg2* nux-v b7.de* *Onos* ↓ op k* **Orig** k* ph-ac gl1.fr• **Phos** k* **Pic-ac** k* **Plat** k* plb bg2* plut-n srj7• *Puls* k* raja-s jl3 *Raph* k* rhus-t b7.de* ruta bg2 *Sabin* bg2* sanic bg2 sars bg2* *Sel* k* senec bg* *Sep* k* *Sil* k* sin-n ↓ spig k* squil bg* stann bg2* **Staph** k* staphycoc rly4• *Stram* k* sulph bg2* *Tarent* k* tere-ch jl3 thuj bg2 *Tub* st* ust sf1.de *Verat* k* verb b7.de* zinc k* [heroin sdj2]
- **daytime**: lach a1
- **morning**: coc-c a1 sil ↓
  - **bed**, in: sil a1
- **afternoon**: lyss a1
- **evening**: calc a1 nat-m ↓
  - **bed**, in: nat-m a1
- **alternating** with:
  - **anger**: lil-t mrr1
  - **despair**; religious (See Despair - religious - alternating - sexual)
  - **remorse**: lil-t mrr1
- **coitus**; disappearing after: *M-aust* b7a.de
- **constantly**: orig hr1
- **dreaming**, after: sil j5.de
- **eating**, with feeling of weakness in parts; after: lyss kr1
- **emotions**, with violent: cop kr1
- **erections**:
  - **with**: lyss kr1 op kr1 sin-n kr1
  - **without**: ambr b7.de* calad b7.de* caps b7.de* *Ign* b7.de* meny b7.de* *Sel* b7.de*
  - **painful**: *(↗Excitement - lascivious)* lyss kr1
- **followed** by | **epilepsy**: *Lach* kr1

- **impotence**, with: *(↗Fancies - lascivious - impotence; MALE GENITALIA/SEX - Sexual desire - increased - weakness)* calad b7a.de* *Chin* kr1 *Ign* b7.de* *Lach* b7a.de meny b7.de* *Nux-m* b7a.de *Onos* mrr1 *Op* kr1 *Sel* b7.de* *Stram* b7a.de
- **itching** of genitalia; with: euphr b7a.de staph b7a.de
- **looking** at women on the street: calad ptk1* chir-fl gya2 fl-ac ptk1*
- **menses** | **before**: kali-c b4.de*
- **ogling** at women (See looking)
- **prostate**; with enlarged: dig ptk1*
- **touch**; women become lascivious at every: *(↗FEMALE - Sexual desire - increased - touch)* *Murx* sf1.de* *Plat* mrr1
- **uncovers** genitalia: **Hyos** kr1

LATE:

- **riser**; late (See Bed - remain - morning; SLEEP - Waking - late)
- **too** late; always: acon acon-l a1* agar aids nl2• alco a1 alum am-c ambr anac anan arn ars arund asaf *Aur* bar-c sf1.de* *Bell* calc vh* **Cann-i** cann-s caps carb-v caust cic coff con cor-r a1 cori-r *Croc* crot-h *Cupr* cypr sf1.de cypra-eg sde6.de• elae a1 *Ferr* ferr-ar graph hell *Hyos* **Ign** kali-bi kali-p keroso a1* kreos *Lach* lepi lil-t *Lyc* merl moni rfm1• nat-ar nat-c *Nat-m* nept-m lsd2.fr *Nux-m* nux-v op peti a1 *Phos* plat vh* plb positr nl2• puls k* ran-s rob sabad santin a1 sarr sec *Sep* sil k* spong **Stram** stry sulph sumb tab tarax *Tarent* valer verat verb zinc zinc-s
- **too** late; never (See Anxiety - time)

LAUGHING: *(↗Amusement - desire; Cheerful; Content; Frivolous; Jesting; Smiling)* abrom-a ↓ acon k* acon-f a1 acon-l a1* aether a1 agar k* *Agath-a* nl2• aids ↓ alco a1 aloe alum k* alum-p ↓ alum-sil k2 alumn ↓ am-c k* ambr amyg ↓ anac k* anan k* androc srj1• apis k* ara-maca sej7• arg-met arg-n ↓ arizon-l nl2• arn k* ars k* ars-s-f k2 arund k* asaf k* *Asar* ↓ atro a1* atro-s ↓ *Aur* k* aur-ar k2 *Aur-m-n* ↓ aur-s ↓ bamb-a ↓ bar-c sf1.de* *Bell* k* beryl ↓ *Borx* bov ↓ *Bufo* *Calc* k* calc-sil k2 *Camph* ↓ camph-br ↓ **Cann-i** k* cann-s k* cann-xyz ptk1 canth ↓ caps k* carb-an ↓ carb-v k* carbn-s ↓ carc mlr1* castor-eq caust k* *Cedr* ↓ chir-fl gya2 chlf a1 chlol a1 choc ↓ cic k* cimic ↓ coca ↓ cocc ↓ coff k* *Colch* ↓ coli rly4• con k* conch fkr1.de cor-r a1 cori-r k* *Croc* k* crot-c ↓ crot-h *Cupr* k* cypr hr1* cypra-eg ↓ des-ac ↓ dulc fd4.de elae a1 *Elec* ↓ falco-pe ↓ *Ferr* k* ferr-ar galla-q-r ↓ germ-met ↓ granit-m ↓ graph k* haliae-lc srj5• ham ↓ hell k* hura hydr-ac ↓ hydrog srj2*• *Hyos* k* hyosin a1 hypoth ↓ **Ign** k* irid-met ↓ iris ↓ junc-e ↓ kali-bi k* kali-p k* kali-s tl1* keroso a1* *Kola* stb3• kreos k* lac-del hrn2• lac-h ↓ lac-leo ↓ lac-mat ↓ *Lach* k* lepi lil-t limest-b ↓ loxo-recl knl4• *Lyc* k* lyss jl2 mang ↓ mang-act ↓ mang-p rly4*• marb-w ↓ med ↓ melal-alt ↓ **Merc** k* merc-meth ↓ merl k* mosch br1 naja b nat-ar nat-c nat-hchls ↓ *Nat-m* k* neon ↓ nept-m lsd2.fr nid ↓ *Nit-ac* ↓ nitro-o a1 *Nux-m* k* nux-v k* oci-sa ↓ *Oena* ↓ *Olib-sac* wmh1 op k* oxyg ↓ ozone sde2* par ↓ ped a1 peti a1 petr-ra ↓ ph-ac ↓ *Phos* k* phyt ↓ pieri-b mlk9.de plac rzf5• plac-s rly4• *Plat* k* plb k* plut-n srj7• podo ↓ positr nl2• psor ↓ puls k* ran-b ↓ ran-s rob k* rubd-met ↓ ruta fd4.de sabad k* **Sacch-a** ↓ sal-ac ↓ sal-fr sle1• samb ↓ santin a1 sarr sec k* *Sel* ↓ *Sep* k* sil k* sol-ni ↓ spig-m ↓ spong *Staph* ↓ **Stram** k* stry k* stry-p br1 succ-ac ↓ sul-ac ↓ sulph k* sumb k* symph fd3.de• syph k2 tab k* tarax k* *Tarent* k* tax ↓ thala ↓ ther ↓ thres-a sze7• thuj ↓ thyr ↓ til ban1• tritic-vg fd5.de ulm-c ↓ valer vanil fd5.de verat k* *Verat-v* ↓ verb k* zinc k* zinc-o ↓ zinc-ox ↓ zinc-s k* ziz hr1 [ant-t stj2 cadm-met stj2 cadm-s stj2 cupr-act stj2 cupr-f stj2 cupr-m stj2 cupr-p stj2 heroin sdj2 mang-i stj2 mang-m stj2 mang-met stj2 mang-s stj2 pop dhh1 rhodi stj2 zinc-i stj2 zinc-m stj2 zinc-n stj2 zinc-p stj2]

- **daytime**: peti a1
- **morning**: graph hura lach phos plat k* psor
  - 7-8 h: hura a1
- **forenoon**: graph a1 nux-m k*
- **evening**: aether a1 coli rly4• cupr k* dulc fd4.de nat-m k* sulph j5.de valer zinc
- **night**: alum ambr caust cic k* cupr a1 cypr ↓ kreos lyc op sep sil stram b7a.de* sulph verat
  - **midnight**: kreos a1 sil a1
  - **children**: cypr hr1*
- **actions**, at his own: dulc fd4.de falco-pe nl2• iris spong fd4.de stram
- **agg.**: *(↗GENERALS - Laughing)* carb-v mtf33 carc jl2 ther ptk1
- **ailments** (See Ailments - laughing)
- **air**, in open: *Nux-m* k* *Plat* tritic-vg fd5.de
- **alternating** with:
  - **affection**: croc j5.de

Laughing – alternating with: ...

- **anger** (See Anger - alternating - laughing)
- **anguish** (See fear)
- **cheerfulness**: stram bg1
- **convulsions**: alum bg2
- **death**; desire for: aur j5.de
- **delirium**; gay (See Delirium - gay - alternating - laughing)
- **fear** of death: *Plat* kr1
- **frenzy** (See Rage - alternating - laughing)
- **gaiety** (See cheerfulness)
- **groaning** (See moaning)
- **irritability** (See Irritability - alternating - laughing)
- **lamenting**: ars-s-f k2
- **loathing** of life: *Aur*
- **loquacity**: bell k* carbn-s
- **metrorrhagia**: crot-c
- **moaning**: ars-s-f k2* bell k* crot-c hyos ozone sde2• stram k* verat k*
- **moroseness** (See Morose - alternating - laughing)
- **quarreling** (See Quarrelsome - alternating - laughter)
- **quiet**; desire to be: hyos j5.de nux-m j5.de
- **rage** (See Rage - alternating - laughing)
- **sadness**: androc srj1• canth caust nat-c nid jl3 *Phos* k* **Sacch-a** fd* stram zinc
- **seriousness**: aids nl2• nux-m k* plat sul-ac ptk1
- **shrieking** (See Shrieking - alternating - laughing)
- **singing**: stram a1
- **spasms** (See convulsions)
- **taciturnity**: plat j5.de
- **tenderness** (See affection)
- **vexation**, ill humor (See Irritability - alternating - laughing)
- **violence** (See Violent - alternating - laughing)
- **weeping**: *(↗Anger - laughing - alternating - weeping)* *Acon* k* alum alum-p k2 alumn a1 *Asaf* bg2* *Aur* k* aur-s k2 bell k* borx k* bov ckh1 bufo gk *Calc* camph-br c1* cann-i k2 cann-s cann-xyz bg2 caps k* carbn-s k2 *Coff* k* con *Croc* bg2* graph *Hyos* k* hypoth jl *Ign* k* kali-p k* *Lyc* **Merc** k* **Mosch** bg2* nat-m **Nux-m** k* nux-v *Phos* k* *Plat* k* **Puls** k ●* samb sep spig-m a1 *Stram* k* sulph sumb k* tarent *Valer* bg2* verat ziz k* [lac-mat sst4 rubd-met stj2]
  - **anger**; after: *Plat* hr1
  - **fear** of death; with (See Fear - death - laughing)
- **whining** (See moaning)

- **anger**:
  - **after**: borx mtf33
  - **during** (See Anger - laughing)
- **annoying**: bell k*
- **anxiety**:
  - **after**: *Cupr* hr1* lyc h2*
  - **during**: *(↗Anxiety)* lyc k*
- **asthma**; with: *(↗RESPIRATION - Difficult - laughing)* bov c1*
- **aversion** to: *(↗never; Serious; Smiling - never)* alum ptk1* *Ambr* b7a.de* bar-c bg2 cann-s b7a.de *Led* b7a.de
- **balloons**; on thinking and seeing: hydrog srj2•
- **barking** dog, as a: *Aether* a1
- **bed**, in: agar a1
- **beside** herself; claps hands over head: sec ptk1
  - **abortion**; after: *Sec* kr1*
- **cannot** laugh (See never)
- **causeless**: *(↗easily; Smiling - involuntarily - speaking)* aether a1 *Agath-a* nl2• arn gl1.fr* bar-c bg2* bufo bg2* cann-i a1 carbn-s a1 podo fd3.de• sal-ac a1 sal-fr sle1• stram hr1 syph k2* tab a1 ulm-c jsj8• [tax jsj7]
- **childish**: *(↗Childish)* agath-a nl2• bar-c bg2* bufo k2* croc bg2* falco-pe nl2• neon srj5• vanil fd5.de
- **children**, in: aloe kr1 camph ↓ cypr sf1.de dulc fd4.de spong fd4.de tritic-vg fd5.de

- **insane**: camph kr1
- **chill**, during: agar hr1* calc
- **chilliness**, followed by: hura
- **chorea**; in: caust ptk1
- **company**, in: *(↗Company - desire)* tarent
- **constant**: *(↗Awkward)* **Cann-i** k* cann-s a1 cann-xyz ptk1 *Hyos* hr1* nat-m a1 nept-m lsd2.fr olib-sac wmh1 verat k* *Verat-v* hr1* *Zinc* bg2*
- **contemptuous**: *(↗Contemptuous; Cynical; Haughty; Insolence; Mocking; Mocking - sarcasm; Smiling - never)* alum k*
- **convulsions**:
  - **before**, during or after: aether a1 *Alum* j5.de* alumn a1 *Bell* j5.de* calc j5.de *Camph* hr1* *Caust* k* con j5.de cupr a1 *Ign* j5.de* oena a1 *Plat* hr1* stram stry a1 zinc k*
  - **between**: alum ptk1 plat ptk1
  - **from** laughing: *Coff* hr1* *Cupr* hr1*
- **cyanosis**, with: cann-i sf1.de cann-xyz bg2
- **delirious**: *(↗Delirium - laughing)* apis bg2 bell bg2* cupr bg2 hyos bg2 op bg2 stram k* verat bg2
- **desire** to laugh: *(↗Amusement - desire)* *Agath-a* nl2• choc srj3• galla-q-r nl2• haliae-lc srj5• nitro-o a1 olib-sac wmh1 sal-fr sle1• *Tarent* a1
- **dream**, during: bell a1 *Sulph* ↓
  - **comic** dream, laughing continues after waking; during a: *Sulph* kr1
- **drunk**; as if: nept-m lsd2.fr
- **easily**: *(↗causeless)* agath-a nl2• arg-n mrr1 arn h1 ars a1 arund a1* *Bufo* hr1* *Calc* hr1 carb-v a1 choc srj3• *Coff* hr1 dulc fd4.de ham fd3.de• lac-del hrn2• nat-m a1 nept-m lsd2.fr positr nl2• *Puls* kr1* sacch-a fd2.de• tritic-vg fd5.de
- **eating** | **after**: puls k*
- **epileptic** convulsions:
  - **after**: *Bufo* kr1 caust
  - **before**: *Bufo* kr1 caust
  - **during**: *(↗GENERALS - Convulsions - epileptic - during)* *Bufo* kr1 caust
- **everything** (See ludicrous)
- **exhausted** condition, during: con a1
- **foolish**: *Hyos* ptk1
- **forced**: hyos k* tritic-vg fd5.de
- **giggling** (See Giggling)
- **grief**; from: ign lp
- **grinning**: agath-a nl2• bell st1 podo fd3.de•
- **heartily**, wholeheartedly: olib-sac wmh1
- **hysterical**: *(↗Hysteria)* *Agath-a* nl2• alum-sil k2* *Asar* mrr1 calc hr1 elec al hydrog srj2• kali-p hr1 limest-b es1• nux-m hr1* puls hr1 santin a1 sumb a1 tarent hr1
- **idiotic**: *Atro* hr1* atro-s hr1 merc-meth a1
- **ill** humor, with: stram hr1*
- **imbecility**, in: *(↗Imbecility)* hyos gl1.fr• stram gl1.fr•
- **immoderately**: *(↗Awkward; Extravagance; Foolish)* abrom-a ckh1 aether a1 alco a1 *Am-c* k* anac bro1 aur-m-n wbt2• bar-c gl1.fr• *Bell* hr1* **Cann-i** k* cann-xyz ptk1 carb-v coff gl1.fr• *Croc* j* cupr k* *Ferr* k* granit-m es1• graph *Hyos* bro1 *Ign* bro1* *Kola* stb3• *Mosch* bro1 **Nat-m** k* nitro-o a1 *Nux-m* k* *Nux-v* olib-sac wmh1 *Plat* bro1* plb a1 ran-s sf1.de stram k* *Stry* *Stry-p* bro1 tarent k* verb hr1* zinc zinc-o bro1
- **involuntarily**: *(↗uncontrollable)* agar k* asaf vh aur h2* aur-m-n wbt2• bell k* *Borx* *Cann-i* k* carbn-s choc srj3• con k* croc k* *Elec* j* (non:hyos) **Ign** k* *Kola* stb3• lach gk lyc mang br1* mang-act br1 *Nat-m* *Nit-ac* k1* nitro-o a1 oci-sa sk4• op phos k* plb puls bg2 sep sil gk staph gk *Tarent* zinc hr1* zinc-o c1 zinc-ox c zinc-s c1
  - **pressure** on spine; during: agar ptk1
  - **sadness**; with (See Sadness - laughing - involuntary)
  - **talking**; when: aur ptk1
- **irritation** in stomach and hypochondria, from: con h2
- **joy**, with excessive: *Agath-a* nl2• asaf hr1* stram bg2 verb hr1*
- **joyless**: lyc h2
- **looked** at, when: *(↗Looked - cannot)* lyc k*
- **loudly**: agar bg2* **Bell** k* cann-s croc k* dulc fd4.de hydr-ac *Hyos* k* op k* *Stram* k* [beryl stj2]
- **love**; from disappointed: *(↗Ailments - love)* *Hyos* kr1
- **ludicrous**, everything seems: *(↗Foolish)* agath-a nl2• dulc fd4.de hydrog srj2• hyos k* lyc *Nux-m* k* ruta fd4.de sabad spong fd4.de
- **menopause**; during: ferr vh*
- **menses**:
  - **before**: *(↗Menses - before)* *Hyos* k* *Nux-m* k* phos ptk1
  - **during**: *(↗Menses - during)* ars ptk1 **Nux-m** hr1 plat ↓
    - **convulsive**: plat gt
    - **hysterical**: nux-m gt
- **mistakes** of others; at: *Ars* b4a.de
- **misfortune**, at: apis phos
- **mocking**: *(↗Mocking)* tarent a1
- **nervous**: asar vh cupr sst3• hura a1 mosch ptk1* tarent ptk1*
- **never**: *(↗aversion; Cheerful - never; Serious)* aloe sne am-c gl1.fr• am-m gl1.fr• arg-met vh **Ars** st1* bamb-a stb2.de• hep hr1* positr nl2• [tax jsj7]
- **overwork**, after: *Cupr* hr1*
- **pain**:
  - **nervous** laugh; every paroxysm excites a: hura
  - **own** pain; with their: des-ac rbp6 nux-v bg2
- **paroxysmal**: bell st1* conch fkr1.de stram k* tarent ptk2
- **peculiar** to herself; in a way: thyr ptk1*
- **perspiration**, ending in profuse: *Cupr* hr1*
- **rage**, with: *Stram* j5.de*
- **reprimands**, at: *(↗Indifference - reprimands)* bar-c gk graph k*
- **reproach**, at: graph st*
- **sad**, when: *(↗Sadness - laughing)* lac-leo hrn2• limest-b es1• phos k*
- **sardonic**: *(↗Cynical; Mocking; Mocking - sarcasm; Smiling - sardonic)* amyg a1 **Bell** k* camph bg2* cann-i a1 *Caust* k* *Cedr* hr1 cic h1* *Colch* k* con k* croc a1 *Cupr* hr1 hydr-ac bg2* hydrog srj2• *Hyos* k* ign k* med hr1 nux-m k* *Oena* k* ozone sde2• phyt bg2* plb k* ran-b hr1* ran-s k* *Sec* k* sol-ni *Stram* k* stry k* tarent verat k* zinc k* zinc-o k* zinc-ox j5.de zinc-p k2
  - **epileptic** convulsion; during (See GENERALS - Convulsions - epileptic - during - laughter)
- **serious** matters, over: *(↗Awkward; Frivolous)* *Anac* k* apis arg-n arn h1* *Aur-m-n* wbt2• aur-s wbt2• bufo k2 cann-i cann-xyz ptk1 castor-eq cypra-eg sde6.de• germ-met srj5• hydrog srj2• ign k* lac-h htj1• lil-t lyc k* melal-alt gya4 *Nat-m* k* nux-m petr-ra shn4• phos h2* *Plat* k* sil mtf33 spong fd4.de sulph k* tritic-vg fd5.de
  - **air**, in open: *Plat*
- **sexual** excitement; with: stram ptk1
- **shrieking**: croc bg2* cypr bg2* ozone sde2•
  - **before** (See Shrieking - laughing - after)
- **silly**: *(↗Awkward; Childish; Foolish; Frivolous)* aether agath-a nl2• apis sf1.de bamb-a stb2.de• bell k* bufo k2* cann-i a1 cic cimic mtn croc st1 crot-c k* dulc fd4.de falco-pe nl2• **Hyos** k* irid-met srj5• *Lach* k* lyc merc k* nux-m bg2 ozone sde2• par bg2 podo fd3.de• spong fd4.de stram k* stry symph fd3.de• ulm-c jsj8• zinc-p k2*
  - **children** on all occasion, in: croc st1
- **sleep**:
  - **during**: alum k* bell a1* caust k* coca a1 croc k* cypr hr1* dulc fd4.de *Hyos* k* junc-e a1 kreos k* **Lyc** k* nat-hchls a1 ph-ac k* sep k* *Sil* k* *Stram* k* succ-ac rly4• **Sulph** k ●* [oxyg stj2]
  - **going** to; on: sulph j5.de
- **smiling** (See Smiling)
- **spasmodically**: *(↗GENERALS - Convulsions - epileptic - during)* acon k* aether *Alum* k* alum-p k2 alumn am-c k* anac k* ant-t bg2 apis b7a.de* arn bg2 ars bg2* asaf k* **Aur** k* *Bell* k* bov ↓ *Calc* k* cann-i a1* cann-s b7a.de* carb-an bg2 *Caust* k* cic k* cocc bg2 *Coff* b7a.de colch *Con* k* croc k* cupr k* hyos k* **Ign** k* lyc k* mosch b7a.de* nat-c bg2 nat-m k* nux-m k* oena a1 op phos k* plat k* sec k* sel b7a.de* **Sep** b4a.de sil k* *Stram* k* stry vh* sulph b4a.de* sumb thala jl thres-a sze7• thuj k* *Tritic-vg* fd5.de valer k* verat k* zinc k* zinc-o j5.de zinc-p k2
  - **asthma**; with: bov ptk1
  - **chill**; during: ign b7a.de *Sel* b7a.de
  - **epileptic** convulsion; after: cupr ptk1
- **speaking**, when: aur bell k*
- **speechlessness**, with: stram hr1*
- **stupid** expression, with: apis sf1.de atro a1 *Nux-m* hr1* *Tarent* a1*

- **tears**; with (See weeping - same)
- **tension**; from (See nervous)
- **tittering** (See Giggling)
- **trifles**, at: *(↗Awkward; Foolish; Frivolous; Trifles; Trifles - important)* am-c androc srj1• ars k* arund a1* bufo k2 *Cann-i* k* cann-xyz ptk1 carb-v a1 carc fd2.de• coli rly4• dulc fd4.de graph k* ham fd3.de• hydrog srj2• *Hyos* gl1.fr• limest-b es1• *Lyc* h2* marb-w es1• nept-m lsd2.fr op a1 ped c1 podo fd3.de• *Puls* hr1 ruta fd4.de spong fd4.de *Stram* gl1.fr• tarent a1* zinc k* [heroin sdj2]
- **unbecoming**: croc a1*
- **uncontrollable**: *(↗involuntarily)* atro a1 bell h1 bufo mtf33 cann-i a1* cann-xyz ptk1 caps ptk1 coli rly4• croc mrr1 dulc fd4.de melal-alt gya4 *Mosch* br1* nitro-o a1 oci-sa sk4• *Stry-p* br1
- **vexation**, at: lyc sf1.de
- **violent**: bell a1 dulc fd4.de ran-s bg2* stram a1* tritic-vg fd5.de
- **waking**, on: plac-s rly4• sep j5.de stram bg2
- **weakness**, during: con h2*
- **weeping**:
  - **all** occasions; weeping or laughing on: calc-sil k2* caps ptk1 *Caust* gl1.fr• ign ptk1 **Puls** gl1.fr• sep gl1.fr• *Staph* gl1.fr• sumb ptk1
  - **same** time; weeping and laughing at the: agath-a nl2• aur st camph h1 cann-i k2 cann-s a1 ferr ↓ granit-m es1• ign ptk1 lyc gl1.fr• nat-m br1 nux-m br1 sumb ptk1*
    - ⁝ **asleep**; on falling: lyc ptk1
    - ⁝ **menopause**; during: ferr st
- **wild**: *(↗Wildness)* atro a1 bell a1 calc stram mrr1
- **word** said, at every: **Cann-i** kr1
- **wrong** moment; at the (See serious)
- **wrong** places; at the (See serious)
- **yawning**; after: agar br1*

LAZINESS: *(↗Ambition - loss - disappointment; Business - aversion; Business - neglects; Fear - work; Idleness; Inactivity; Indifference - work; Indifference - work - aversion; Irresolution - laziness; Laziness - postponing; Loathing - work; Mental exertion - agg.; Mental exertion - aversion; Postponing; Quiet disposition; Time - fritters; Undertaking - many)* abrot acon k* acon-l a1 adam skp7*• aesc k* *Agar* k* agar-cit a1 agn b7.de aids nl2• ail alco a1 alet bro1 alf bro1 all-c ↓ aloe k* *Alum* k* alum-p k2 alum-sil k2* alumn ↓ am-c k* am-m k* ambr st1 ammc a1 *Anac* k* androc srj1• ang b7.de anh br1 ant-c k* ant-t k* anth a1 *Apis* k* apoc aq-mar skp7• arag br1* arb-m oss1• arg-met b7.de* *Arg-n* k* arge-pl rwt5• *Arn* k* ars k* ars-h ars-i ars-met kr1 ars-s-f k2 asaf k* *Asar* k* asc-t a1* *Aster* kr1 atis bnj1 atro kr1 *Aur* k* aur-ar k2 aur-i k2 *Aur-m* k* aur-s k2 *Bamb-a* stb2.de• *Bapt* k* bar-act a1 *Bar-c* k* bar-i k2 bar-s k2 bell k* berb j5.de berb-a bro1 bism ↓ bit-ar wht1• blatta-a a1 **Borx** k* bov b4.de* bran a1 brom k* bros-gau mrc1 *Bry* k* bufo bufo-s a1 bung-fa mtf cadm-met mg1.de cadm-s a1* caj a1 *Calc* k* *Calc-ar* k2* *Calc-f* mg1.de calc-i k2 *Calc-p* k* calc-s k2 calc-sil k2 camph k* cann-i ↓ *Cann-s* b7.de* **Canth** b7.de* *Caps* k* *Carb-ac* k* carb-an h2* *Carb-v* k* **Carbn-s** carl a1 cassia-f ckh1 cassia-s cdd7*• *Caust* k* cench k2 cere-b a1 cham k* **Chel** k* **Chin** k* chinin-ar chinin-s chir-fl gya2 choc srj3• cic cinnb *Cit-ac* ↓ cit-l ↓ clem b4.de* cob *Cob-n* mg1.de coc-c *Coca* k* cocc k* coff b7.de* colch k* coloc b4.de con k* *Corn* a1* cortico tpw7 croc k* crot-h k* crot-t culx k2 cupr b7.de* *Cur* ↓ *Cycl* k* cyn-d jl3 dendr-pol sk4• dicha mg1.de* dig k* digin ↓ dios dirc dor ↓ dream-p ↓ dros b7.de* dulc k* elaps a1 erig eug a1 euon a1 euphr k* falco-pe nl2• ferr a1* ferr-i ↓ ferr-p ferul a1 *Form* bg2* franz ↓ gamb *Gels* bg2* gent-ch bnj1 germ-met srj5• get ↓ gink-b sbd1• gins a1 glon a1* gran sf1.de **Graph** k* grat guaj k* haliae-lc srj5• *Ham* kr1* hell b7a.de* hell-o a1* helo st1 helo-s ↓ helon k* *Hep* k* hera a1 hipp ↓ hir skp7• hura hydr a1 hydr-ac a1 hydrog srj2• hyos k* hyper a1 ign k* ind kr1 indg indol bro1 *Iod* k* ip k* jug-r kali-ar *Kali-bi* bg2* kali-br *Kali-c* k* kali-cy a1 kali-m ckh1 kali-n b4.de* *Kali-p* k* kali-s k* *Kali-sil* k2* kiss a1 *Kola* stb3• lac-ac k* *Lac-c* lac-cp sk4• lac-d lac-h sk4*• lac-leo hrn2• lac-lup hrn2• **Lach** k* lact j5.de* lat-m bnm6• laur k* lec bro1* lil-t a1* *Limen-b-c* hrn2• limest-b es1• linu-c a1 *Lyc* k* m-arct b7.de* m-aust b7.de* mag-c k* mag-f mg1.de *Mag-m* k* mag-p bro1 mag-s manc marb-w es1• mate a1 med ↓ melal-alt gya4 meli menis ↓ meny b7.de* *Meph* k* *Merc* b4.de* merc-i-f ↓ merl a1 *Mez* k* mill k* mur-ac b4.de* musca-d szs1 myos-a rly4• nat-ar nat-c k* nat-hchls a1 **Nat-m** k* nat-n sf1.de nat-p nat-s k2 nat-sil k2 neon srj5• nicc-met sk4• nicc-s bro1 nid jl3 **Nit-ac** k* nitro-o a1 nux-m ↓ **Nux-v** k* oci-sa sk4• ol-an j5.de* olnd k* op k* opun-s a1 opun-v ↓ osm osteo-a jl2* ox-ac a1 oxyt br1* ozone sde2• pall kr1 par b7.de* paull a1 pert-vc vk9 petr k* petr-ra shn4• *Ph-ac* k* phasco-ci rbp2 **Phos** b4.de* phys a1* phyt ↓ **Pic-ac** k1* pieri-b mlk9.de pip-m k* pitu-gl skp7• plan a1 plat

Laziness: ...
plb k* plect a1 plut-n srj7• podo fd3.de• polys sk4• positr nl2• prun ↓ *Psor* k* *Puls* k* ran-b b7.de* ran-s k* raph a1 rat ↓ rham-cal bro1 rheum k* rhod b4.de* rhus-g a1 rhus-t k* rob rumx kr1* ruta k* sabad k* *Sabin* k* sacch-a fd2.de* sal-al blc1• sal-fr sle1• sang k* *Sanguis-s* hrn2• sarcol-ac bro1 saroth jl3 sarr a1 sars k* sec k* sel b7.de* senec ↓ seneg a1* **Sep** k* sieg mg1.de *Sil* b4a.de* sol-t-ae ↓ sphing ↓ spig k* spirae a1 **Spong** k* squil k* stann k* *Staph* b7.de* stel br1 stram k* stront-c k* stry-p bro1 sul-i k2 sulfa k2* sulfonam ks2 **Sulph** k* sumb a1 symph fd3.de• syph st1 tab tanac bro1 taosc iwa1• tarax b7.de* tarent tarent-c ckh1 tela ckh1 *Teucr* k* thea j5.de *Ther* k* *Thuj* k* thymol bro1 tong j5.de* tritic-vg fd5.de **Tub** br1* uran-n sf1.de urol-h rwt• valer a1 vanil fd5.de verat gl1.fr• verb k* viol-o ↓ viol-t b7.de* visc sp1 wildb a1 *Zinc* k* zinc-chl ptk1 zinc-chr bg **Zinc-p** k2 zing ziz a1 [bell-p-sp dcm1 osm-met stj2 *Oxyg* stj tax jsj7]

- **daytime**: digin a1 phos a1 plan a1 ran-b a1
- **morning**: all-c k* aloe alum am-c am-m ambr vh* ammc kr1 anac ang h1* ant-t *Bamb-a* ↓ canth carb-an *Carb-v* carbn-s cham ↓ chel chinin-s ↓ choc srj3• clem *Cocc* dig ↓ dream-p ↓ falco-pe nl2• ham vh* helo vh* helo-s rwt2• hep k* hipp indg kali-n k* kali-p fd1.de• lac-c a1 lach j5.de lact j5.de* mag-c med ↓ merc vh* nat-c ↓ *Nat-m* nat-s nux-v op ↓ ox-ac pall phyt plat ran-b ran-s k* rheum h *Rhod* vh* rhus-t rumx sabin sacch-a ↓ sal-fr sle1• seneg vh* spong fd4.de squil sulph symph ckh1 syph vh tarax ther j5.de *Tub* vh* verat vh* verb [tax jsj7]
  - **bed**, in: *Carb-v* kr1
  - **rising**, on: cham a1 dig nat-c nat-m h2 op sacch-a fd2.de• spong fd4.de verb
  - **waking**, on: *Bamb-a* stb2.de• chinin-s dream-p sdj1• med cd sal-fr sle1•
- **forenoon**: *Alum* alumn a1 anac get a1 hipp a1 indg a1 lach a1 mag-c nat-m vanil fd5.de verat hs
- **noon**: aloe chinin-s a1
- **afternoon**: aloe anac a1 *Borx* (non:bufo slp) bufo-s a1* chel erig gels hyos lyc k* mag-c mag-s melal-alt gya4 nat-ar a1 nat-m k* op a1 osteo-a ↓ petr podo fd3.de• sep sil viol-t
  - **14** h: chel
  - **16**-18 h: osteo-a jl2
  - **amel.**: anac j
- **evening**: agar bamb-a stb2.de• calc-p k* cann-s carb-v coca dios dream-p sdj1• erig ferr-i form a1 franz a1 mag-c mag-m mur-ac j nat-m a1 pall plb puls ran-s sphing k* spig a1 sulfonam jl **Sulph** viol-o mfm viol-t
  - **amel.**: aloe bism clem sulph
- **night**:
  - **midnight**:
    - ⁝ **before** | **22** h: sol-t-ae a
- **air**, in open: arn
  - **amel.**: calc graph
- **alternating** with:
  - **activity**; mental (See Mental exertion - desire - alternating - laziness)
  - **cheerfulness** (See Cheerful - alternating - laziness)
  - **desire** to work: cycl a1
- **amenorrhea**, in: cycl kr1
- **amused**, when not: carbn-s a1 *Dulc* fd4.de
- **anger**, after: *Nux-v* kr1
- **bathing** | **hot** amel.: lac-leo hrn2•
- **breakfast**, after: nat-s
- **burning** in the right lumbar region; with: nit-ac h2
- **business**:
  - **quits** his thriving: calc k2
  - **transacting**; when: kali-p fd1.de• nux-v a1 opun-s a1 (non:opun-v a1)
- **children**, in: *(↗Dullness - children)* bar-c lach mag-c mtf33 psor mtf33 sulph mtf33
- **chill**, during: camph crot-h j lach j
- **coition**, after: nat-c j5.de
- **content**, with: spong fd4.de ziz kr1
- **difficulties**, in face of: *(↗postponing; Anticipation; Postponing)* cocc kr1
- **dinner**, after: agar k* ant-c bar-c *Chel* kr1 *Chin* mag-c tong a1 zinc k*
- **disappointment**; after: aesc vh1 nux-v ptk

- **drowsiness**, from (See sleepiness)
- **eating**, after: agar anac b4a.de* ant-c asar k* bar-c k* bov cann-i chel *Chin* k* dig h2* ign sf1.de *Kali-c* sf1.de lach *Lyc* sf1.de mag-c *Nat-m* b4a.de* nux-m sf1.de nux-v ol-an st *Ph-ac* b4a.de* *Phos* k* plat sf1.de plb sel ptk sep b4a.de sulph b4a.de thuj k* zinc
- **emissions** (See pollutions)
- **exhaustion**, in nervous: *Coca* kr1
- **fever**, during: ammc a clem bg2
- **followed** by | **mania** for work: aur-s k2 bit-ar wht1•
- **gonorrhea**, in: tarent kr1
- **head**; with complaints of: dulc bg2 laur bg2 ph-ac bg2
- **headache**, during: dulc a
- **heaviness** of limbs, with: merc-i-f kr1 sanguis-s hm2•
- **housework**; aversion to her usual: arb-m oss1• bamb-a stb2.de• cench k2 *Cit-ac* cit-l kr1 nat-sil fd3.de• sep ptk1 suli k2 symph fd3.de• vanil fd5.de [tax jsj7]
- **intellectual** (See Mental exertion - aversion)
- **intelligent**; although very (See Intelligent - lazy)
- **irritability**; with: bit-ar wht1•
- **loquacity**, with: eug vml3•
- **masturbation**, after: *Dig* kr1 *Gels* kr1
- **menses**:
  - **before**: *Agar* mtn cocc mtn nux-v mtn
  - **during**: agar mtn graph b4a.de nux-v mtn petr-ra shn4• senec mtn
- **movement**; with difficulty of: sep h2
- **nervous** exhaustion, in: *Coca* kr1
- **new** ideas; with aversion for: hep glh kali-c glh lyc glh nit-ac glh sil glh
- **ordinary** matters; as to: ferr-p a
- **physical**: agar bro1 aids nl2• alco a1 alf bro1 *Aloe* bro1 *Anac* bro1 arag bro1 aur-m bro1 bapt bro1 bar-c kr1* calc bro1* *Caps* bro1 carb-ac kr1* caust bro1 cham a1 chel a1 chin a1* choc srj3• cob kr1 coca bro1 con bro1 cycl a1* franz a1 gels bro1* glon bro1 hell bro1 indol bro1 iod a1 *Kali-bi* kr1 *Kali-p* bro1 **Kali-s** fd* lec bro1 *Lil-t* kr1 lyc gl1.fr• mag-p bro1 menis a1 nat-c c1* nat-m sf1.de* nicc-s bro1 nit-ac bro1 nux-v bro1* oxyt bro1 *Ph-ac* bro1 phos bro1 *Pic-ac* bro1 positr nl2• puls bro1* rham-cal bro1 sec a1 sel bro1 sep a1* sil bro1 spong fd4.de stry-p bro1 *Sulph* a1* tanac bro1 thymol bro1 tritic-vg fd5.de vanil fd5.de *Zinc* bro1
- **pollutions**, after: *Dios* kr1 nat-c h2 sep
- **postponing** the work: (↗*difficulties; Laziness; Loathing - work; Mental exertion - agg.; Postponing)* *Cench* k2 dream-p sdj1• *Dulc* fd4.de *Kali-s* fd4.de *Nat-m* gl1.fr• podo fd3.de• *Ruta* fd4.de sal-fr sle1• spong fd4.de vanil fd5.de
- **respiratory** complaints, with: puls j
- **rest**, during: nat-c a
- **routine**; not wanting to depart from the usual: caps vh1
- **sad**, making him: sabin kr1
- **sadness**, from: *Bamb-a* stb2.de• berb j5.de bov j5.de crot-t j5.de dor j dros j5.de kali-s fd4.de laur j5.de mez j5.de prun j5.de *Spong* fd4.de zinc j5.de
- **siesta**, after: anac borx
- **sitting**, while: (↗*Sitting - inclination)* nat-c nit-ac ruta
- **sleep**, after: borx chinin-s dulc fd4.de mez pip-m k* vanil fd5.de
- **sleepiness**, with: acon j5.de am-m j5.de ammc j5.de ant-t j5.de ars j5.de bit-ar wht1• carb-an j5.de carb-v j5.de* chel j5.de* chin a1 cinnb j5.de clem j5.de colch j5.de coloc j5.de croc j5.de dig j5.de dulc j5.de grat j5.de ip j5.de laur j5.de lyc j5.de mag-c j5.de mag-m j5.de nat-c j5.de rat j5.de ruta fd4.de sang kr1 sars j5.de spong fd4.de tong j5.de verb j5.de *Zinc* j5.de
- **started**; but works well after having: spong fd4.de tarax kr1
- **stool**:
  - **after**: colch k* coloc a1
  - **before**: *Borx* k*
- **stretching** of limbs, with: cann-s j
- **sudden**: calc ptk1* [tax jsj7]
- **vaginitis**, in: *Cur* kr1
- **waking**, on: *Aloe* kr1 pip-m a1
- **walking**:
  - **after**: caust h2
  - **while**: arn caust a1 chinin-s coff a1 nit-ac sabin
- **weariness**; with (See Ennui - laziness)
- **weather**; in damp: (↗*Dullness - air - wet - from)* sang

Laziness: ...
- **work**:
  - **aversion** to (See Laziness)
  - **harm**; he thinks the work will do him: (↗*Delusions - work - harm)* *Arg-n* ↓ helo c1 helo-s rwt2• ther hl
    - : **hypochondriasis**; in: *Arg-n* kr1

LEARNING:
- **desire** for: (↗*Curious; Intellectual; Intelligent; Studying - easily)* des-ac rbp6 graph mtf33 lyc mtf33 sulph mtf33
- **studying** (See Studying)
- **talk**; to (See Talking - slow)
- **walk**; to (See GENERALS - Walk - learning)

LECHEROUS (See Lewdness; Obscene)

LETHARGY (See Inactivity)

LETTING GO (See Tranquillity)

LEVITATION (See Delusions - floating - air)

LEWDNESS: (↗*Delirium - erotic; Dress - indecently; Fancies - lascivious; Hysteria - lascivious; Indifference - exposure; Lascivious; Libertinism; Naked; Nymphomania; Obscene; Obscene - songs; Shameless)* agn alco ↓ alum gl1.fr• androc srj1• apis aur ↓ bell bufo ↓ calc gl1.fr• *Camph* *Canth* k* carb-v gl1.fr• *Caust* gl1.fr• chin gl1.fr• chlf ↓ con gl1.fr• *Cub* dig ↓ fl-ac bg* *Hyos* k* *Lach* lil-t a1 lyc gl1.fr• lyss merc gl1.fr• nat-m gl1.fr• nux-m ↓ nux-v op orig gl1.fr• *Phos* *Pic-ac* k* *Plat* k* puls gl1.fr• raja-s ↓ *Raph* a1 rob staph gl1.fr• stram k* sulph mtf33* tarent verat k*
- **fancies** (See Fancies - lascivious)
- **old** men; in: dig ptk1
- **songs**: alco a1 canth k2 *Hyos* op raja-s jl3 *Stram* verat k2
- **talk**; lewd: (↗*Obscene - talk)* aur *Bell* bufo gk camph chlf a1 cub *Hyos* k* *Lil-t* nat-m ↓ nux-m j *Nux-v* phos plat *Stram* k* **Verat** k*
  - **coition**; during: hyos mrr1 nat-m mrr1

LIAR: (↗*Behavior - children; Charlatan; Contradiction - disposition; Deceitful; Delusions - lie; Delusions - lie; all; Dishonest; Hypocrisy; Manipulative; Slander; Untruthful)* agath-a nl2• alco k* androc srj1• arg-met ckh1 arg-n st1* calc sne* calc-p gg carb-v mtf33* caust gl1.fr• coca a1* con gl1.fr• dendr-pol sk4• *Kola* stb3• lyc mtf33* med mtf33 merc mtf33* **MORPH** bro1* nat-m gl1.fr• nux-v c1* olib-sac wmh1 **Op** kr1* plat cda1 puls gl1.fr• sep bng sil mtf33* staph mtf33* sulph mtf33* *Syph* st1* tarent mrr1 thal-xyz ↓ thuj mrr1 *Verat* k*
- **charlatan** and (See Charlatan)
- **lie**; believes all she says is a (See Delusions - lie)
- **lies**, never speaks the truth, does not know what she is saying: (↗*Hypocrisy)* alco st1 arg-n st1 calc ckh1 coca st *Morph* st1 nux-v st **Op** bg2* *Syph* st1* *Verat* bg2*
- **memory** gaps; making up stories to fill: thal-xyz srj8•

LIBERTINISM: (↗*Ailments - sexual excesses; Alcoholism; Company - aversion - bear; Confusion - spirituous; Delirium tremens; Independent; Lascivious; Lewdness; Moral; Nymphomania; Shameless; Travelling - desire; CHILL - Alcohol; COUGH - Debauch; GENERALS - Intoxication; GENERALS - Narcotics - agg.; GENERALS - Reveling; SLEEP - Sleeplessness - wine)* act-sp hr1* agar ptk1 aids nl2• alum gl1.fr• anh mtf ant-c ptk1 arg-n c arn j bar-c j bell gl1.fr• calc gl1.fr• cann-i mtf *Canth* gl1.fr• carb-v c* *Caust* gl1.fr• chin gl1.fr• con gl1.fr• dig c falco-pe nl2• ferr-i mtf fl-ac k13* haliae-lc srj5• hyos gl1.fr• ign mtf lac-f mtf lach ptk1 lyc mrr1* **Med** gg* merc mtf* nat-m gl1.fr• *Nux-v* k* orig gl1.fr• petr-ra shn4• ph-ac gl1.fr• *Phos* gl1.fr• pic-ac k* *Plat* puls gl1.fr• *Raph* a1 sel c* sep k13* spong j *Staph* stram ptk1* sul-ac ptk1 sulph gl1.fr• **Tub** mtf verat gl1.fr•

LICKING up things: (↗*Feces - licks)* merc bg2

LIE on bare floor; wants to: *Camph* hr1*

LIFE:
- **change** in life; desire for (See Change - desire - life)
- **struggle**; has been a long hard: carc fb*
- **weary** of (See Weary)

LIFELESS (See Indifference)

LIFTING agg.: psor bg2

LIGHT:
- **abundance** of; sees an: anh sp1 haliae-lc srj5• irid-met srj5•
- **amel**. (See Darkness - agg.)
- **aversion** to: *(↗EYE - Photophobia)* achy jl3 ambr↓ androc↓ bell↓ bufo↓ **Con**↓ hyos↓ irid-met↓ sanguis-s↓ stram k2* tarent bg2 zinc↓
  - **brilliant** objects: bufo ptk1 irid-met srj5•
  - **shuns**: *(↗Sensitive - light; EYE - Photophobia)* ambr androc srj1• bell k2 **Con** hyos sanguis-s hrn2• stram k2 tarent bg1* zinc
- **desire** for: *(↗Anxiety - dark; Anxiety - evening - twilight; Darkness - agg.; Delirium - dark; Delusions - images - dark; Delusions - people - behind - walking - dark; Delusions - specters - twilight; Desires - full - more; Fear - dark; of; Fear - walking - of - dark; Longing - sunshine; Sadness - darkness; Weeping - dark; DREAMS - Darkness; EYE - Photomania; GENERALS - Faintness - dark)* *Acon* *Am-m* asar jl3 bamb-a stb2.de• **Bell** bism fyz *Calc* cann-i st cann-s bg* carb-an bg1* choc↓ cimic sne **Gels** grin bg1* haliae-lc srj5• ignis-alc es2• irid-met srj5• kali-br sne *Kola* stb3• lac-c nat-m phasco-ci rbp2 phos bg1* plb bg1* rad-br fyz ruta sanic bg1* spong fd4.de **Stram** k* *Stront-c* vh* valer [spect dfg1]
  - **sunlight**; to be in: choc srj3• ruta fd4.de spong fd4.de
- **shuns** (See aversion - shuns)
- **sunlight** | **amel**.: nux-v b7.de plat b4.de* sel b7.de

LISTENED TO; being: | **desire** to (See Delusions - appreciated; Delusions - neglected; Forsaken)

LISTLESS (See Indifference)

LITERARY WORK:
- **aversion** to (See Mental exertion - aversion - literary)
- **desire** for (See Mental exertion - desire - literary)

LITIGIOUS: *(↗Delusions - lawsuit; Quarrelsome)* ars gl1.fr• caust gl1.fr• lach gl1.fr• nit-ac mtf nux-v gl1.fr• plat pd* staph pd*

LIVELY (See Vivacious)

LOATHING:
- **business**; his: *(↗Business - aversion)* ars-h
- **general** loathing: *(↗Discontented - everything; Disgust; Hatred; Misanthropy; Thoughts - disgusting)* acon k* aloe↓ alum alumn↓ ang k* ant-c↓ ant-t k* arg-met jl *Arg-n* k* arn k* asar k* aur↓ bamb-a stb2.de• bell k* benz-ac k* bufo *Calc* k* canth k* carbn-o a1 carc mlr1• cham k* chel k* coli gmj1 cop↓ hep k* hyos k* ip gl1.fr• jatr-c kali-bi k* kali-c k* kali-chl j *Lach*↓ laur *Lyc*↓ mag-m merc k* mez gl1.fr• mosch↓ myric k* nat-c↓ paull a1 phel k* phyt k* pic-ac↓ plat k* *Plb* gl1.fr• plect↓ *Puls* k* raph k* rat k* sapin a1 sec k* sel gmj2 seneg k* sep↓ stram k* sulph↓ sumb k* tab↓ tarent k* thea tong↓
  - **morning**: mag-m phyt k*
    - **waking**, on: phyt
  - **forenoon**: tong a1
  - **noon**: pic-ac a1
  - **evening**: alum alumn a1 *Hep* k* raph k* sulph gl1.fr•
  - **eruption**; before: cop
  - **fear** of death, during: cop a1
  - **old** age, in: aur k2* calc k2*
  - **pain**:
    - **during**: aloe a1
    - **from**: phyt sf1.de
  - **puberty**, in: *(↗Indifference - puberty; Puberty)* ant-c st1
  - **rising**, when: plect a1
  - **smoking**, when: sep a1
  - **vertigo**; with: mosch bg2
  - **stomach**; with complaints of: tab bg2
  - **waking**, on: *Lach* *Lyc* nat-c
- **himself** (See oneself)
- **life**: *(↗Death - desires; Disgust - discouragement; Disgust - everything; Ennui; Pessimist; Suicidal; Weary)* act-sp agn alum alum-p k2 alum-sil k2 am-c am-m *Ambr* k* ang vh **Ant-c** k* ant-t am oss• **Ars** ars-s-f k2 **Aur** k* *Aur-ar* k2* *Aur-m* *Aur-m-n* wbt2• *Aur-s* k1* bell k2* berb bov cadm-met gm1 *Calc* calc-ar k2 calc-s calc-sil k2 carb-an *Carb-v* carc mlr1• caust cere-b↓ **Chin** *Chinin-ar* cic jl3 cop dendr-pol sk4• dros gels gk* grat hep

Loathing – life: ...
hydroph jl3 hyos kali-bi kali-br kali-chl↓ kali-m k2 *Kali-p* kreos **Lac-c** vh/dg* lac-d st1 *Lach* laur led *Lyc* mag-m mrr1 **Merc** mez moni rfm1• nat-ar nat-c **Nat-m** *Nat-s* k* nat-sil k2 *Nit-ac* **Nux-v** k* op *Ph-ac* gl1.fr• **Phos** *Plat* *Plb* k1* pneu jl3 podo *Puls* *Rhus-t* *Rhus-v* ruta sec *Sep* **Sil** k* spig *Spong* **Staph** k* stram sul-ac *Sulph* *Ter* **Thuj** *Valer* k2* zinc *Zinc-p* k2 ziz
  - **morning**: *Lach* **Lyc** nat-c
  - **evening**: **Aur** dros hep kali-chl k* rhus-t spig
  - **alternating** with | **laughing** (See Laughing - alternating - loathing)
  - **anxiety**, with: *Lach* kr1
  - **eating** amel.; on: cic jl
  - **injury**, must restrain herself to prevent doing herself: *(↗Injuring; Injuring - fear)* **Nat-s**
  - **menses** | **before**: *(↗Menses - before)* cere-b
  - **old** people; in: calc k2
  - **perspiration**; during: alum bg2 *Ars* bg2 *Aur* bg2 **Calc** bg2 hep bg2 *Merc* bg2 nux-v bg2 puls bg2 rhus-t bg2 sep bg2 sil bg2 *Spong* bg2 thuj bg2
- **oneself**: *(↗Contemptuous - self; Hiding - himself - children)* agath-a nl2• arizon-l nl2• falco-pe nl2• galla-q-r nl2• germ-met srj5• lac-c bg1* musca-d szs1 positr nl2• spirae a1
- **speaking**: *(↗Taciturn)* anac dios
- **work**: *(↗Fear - work; Laziness; Laziness - postponing; Mental exertion - aversion)* anac br1 arg-n am calc chin gl1.fr• con gl1.fr• croc gl1.fr• ham fd3.de• hyos kali-c lach gl1.fr• lact-v a1 merc gl1.fr• nat-m nit-ac h2 petr *Puls* k● ran-b reser↓ *Sil* stann k2 staph gk sulph tab k1 tarax ther a1 tub br1
  - **evening**: reser jl
  - **alternating** with | **singing** (See Singing - alternating - loathing)

LOCALITY, errors of (See Mistakes - localities)

LOCATION; sense of (See Orientation)

LOGICAL THINKING (See Thinking - logical)

LONELINESS (See Forsaken)

LONGING: *(↗Desires; Yearning)*
- **anonymity**: *(↗Hiding - himself)* sanguis-s hrn2•
- **good** opinion of others; for: *(↗Confidence - want; Delusions - appreciated; Delusions - forsaken; Delusions - neglected - he; Flattered - desire; Forsaken; Haughty; Insecurity; Irresolution; Succeeds; Timidity; Vanity)* acer-circ oss• carc fd2.de• falco-pe nl2• lyc mtf33 *Pall* k* sulph mrr1 *Tritic-vg* fd5.de [heroin sdj2]
- **knows** not what for: croc bg2 dream-p sdj1• kali-c bg2
- **repose** and tranquillity; for: *(↗Rest - desire)* **Kali-s** fd* nux-v sacch-a fd2.de• sulph h2 [*Spect* dfg1]
- **sense** of: agath-a nl2•
- **sun** and salt water; for: chir-fl gya2
- **sunshine**, light and society, for: *(↗Darkness - agg.; Light - desire)* grin kali-s fd4.de stram k*
- **things** which are rejected when offered; for (See Capriciousness - rejecting)
- **yearning** (See Yearning)

LOOKED AT; to be: **Ant-c** bg2 ant-t bg2 **Ars** bg2 calc bg2 hell bg2
- **always** wants to be looked at (See Watched - desires)
- **aware** that her legs are looked at: lac-lup hrn2•
- **cannot** bear to be looked at: *(↗Delusions - looking - everyone; Delusions - people - seeing - looking; Delusions - watched; Fear - observed; Hiding - himself; Hysteria - looked; Irritability - looked; Laughing - looked; Weeping - looked)* ambr bg2 *Ant-c* k* *Ant-t* k* **Ars** *Aur-m-n* wbt2• aur-s wbt2• bamb-a stb2.de• bar-c hu brom mtf33 calc bg2* *Cham* k* *Chin* k* *Cina* k* cupr sst3*• hell a1 *Iod* k* kali-br kr1 kali-c tl1 lyc bg2 mag-c k* med gk merc bg2* *Nat-m* bg* nux-v phasco-ci rbp2 puls ckh1 rhus-t sanguis-s hrn2• sanic mtf33 sil bg2* stram k* sulph k* tarent bg2 thuj mtf33 *Tub* st1* [ant-m stj2 *Ant-met* stj2 bar-i stj2 cupr-act stj2 cupr-f stj2 cupr-m stj2 cupr-p stj2 mang-i stj2]
  - **children**; in: *(↗Shrieking - children - looked)* *Ant-c* b7a.de* ant-t tl1 brom mtf33 calc mtf33 cham tl1* chin mtf33 cina tl1* cupr mtf33 iod mtf33 mag-c mtf33 nat-m mtf33 sanic mtf33 sulph mtf33 thuj mtf33 tub mtf33

- **desires** to be looked at (See Watched - desires)
- **evading** the look of other persons: *(↗Company - aversion - sight; Eyes - downcast)* agar mtf cupr sst3* nat-m↓ plb↓ *Stram* kr1
  - **spoken** to; when: nat-m mtf33 plb a1
- **looking** down when looked at: *(↗Sadness - looking; Timidity)* agar zr

LOOKING:
- **anything** agg.; at: nat-m bg2 psor bg2 sulph↓
  - **front** of him; in: sulph bg2
- **backwards**: *(↗Delusions - people - behind; Fear - behind)*
  - **desire** to look backwards: brom tl1 lach tl1 med tl1 sanic tl1
  - **followed**; as if: *(↗Delusions - people - behind; Delusions - pursued; Fear - behind)* med vh sanic c1* staph gl1.fr•
- **bed**, as if to find something; about: ign ptk1
- **directions**; in all: *Brom*↓ calc ptk2 hyos↓ kali-br ptk2 *Puls*↓ tarent↓
  - **hysteria**; to observe the effect of her actions on others, in: tarent ptk2
  - **puerperal** mania; in: *Puls* kr1
- **down** on the street (See Sadness - looking)
- **mirror** agg.; into the: camph b7a.de nat-m b4a.de
- **observing**: adam srj5•
- **sideways**: stram bg2
- **stars** in the night sky; at the: neon srj5• tritic-vg fd5.de
- **window** agg.; out of the | **hours**; for: androc srj ham fd3.de• mez h2* [tax jsj7]

LOQUACITY: *(↗Communicative; Curious; Delirium - loquacious; Delirium tremens - loquacity; Eloquent; Exhilaration; Expansive; Gossiping; Indiscretion; Insanity - loquacious; Jealousy - loquacity; Revealing; Sensitive - want; Speech - babbling; Speech - fluent; Speech - hasty; Speech - prattling; Talking - desire; Talking - listens)* abrot acon k* adam srj5• aeth aether a1 agar k* agath-a nl2• agav-t jl1* agn aids nl2• alco a1 aln↓ aloe alum a1 am-c↓ ambr k* anac k* anh sf1.de* ant-t apis aran↓ aran-ix mg1.de *Arg-met* k* arg-n mtf33 arn ars k* ars-h ars-i ars-s-f k2 atro a1 *Aur* k* aur-ar k2 aur-s k2 bamb-a stb2.de• banis-c mtf bapt k* bar-c bar-i k2 bar-s k2 *Bell* k* ben-n a1 bit-ar wht1• borx k* bov k* bry↓ bufo sf1.de* bung-fa mtf buth-a sp1 calad k* calc k* calc-act a1 *Camph* *Cann-i* k2* cann-s b7a.de* cann-xyz ptk1 canth k* carbn-s carc st1* *Carl* caust cham mtf chel k* chin↓ chir-fl gya2 choc mtf chord-umb rly4• *Cimic* k* cina h1 coc-c cocain br1* *Cocc* k* coff k* coli rly4• colum-p sze2• con sf1.de *Croc* k* *Crot-c* k* crot-h k* *Cupr* k* cystein-l rly4• dendr-pol sk4• dig↓ dros mtf **Dulc** k* ephe-si hsj1• eug k* eup-pur ferr-m ferr-p k* frax bg gamb gast a1 *Gels* germ-met mtf gink-b jl3 glon k* glycyr-g cte1• graph mtf grat k* guare hep bg2* hydrc hydrog srj2• **Hyos** k* ichth mtf ign k2 *Iod* b4.de* iodof bg2 ip kali-c b4a.de *Kali-i* kali-m ckh1 kali-s fd4.de ketogl-ac rly4• *Kola* stb3• kres mg1.de* lac-e hrn2• lac-h htj1*• lac-loxod-a hrn2• **LACH** b7.de* *Lachn* k* lil-t limest-b es1• lob mtf loxo-recl↓ lyc bg1 lyss m-arct b7.de* mag-c manc a1 marr-vg↓ meli mrr1* meph k* merc-cy a1* merc-i-f *Mosch* b7a.de* *Mur-ac* nabal mtf nat-ar *Nat-c* k* nat-m nat-sil fd3.de* nept-m↓ nicc nicotam rly4• nux-m nux-v k* oci mtf oena olib-sac wmh1 onos *Op* k* ozone sde2* *Par* b7.de* parth c1 past c1* pert-vc vk9 petr ph-ac mtf *Phos* k* phys bg2 physal-al bro1 pieri-b mlk9.de pip-m vml3• plat k2* *Plb* *Podo* k* polys sk4• psor puls mtf pyre-p a1* *Pyrog* k* rad-br gk **Ran-b** sne raph↓ rhus-t ribo rly4• ruta fd4.de sabad mtf sacch sst* sacch-a↓ sal-ac a1 sal-fr sle1• sec *Sel* k* sol-t-ae mtf stann k* staph k* stict **Stram** k* stroph-h mtf sulph tab taosc iwa1• tarax k* tarent k* teucr k* thal-xyz srj8• thea ther k* thres-a sze7• thuj k* thymol sp1* *Tritic-vg* fd5.de trom tub jl2* valer bro1 vanil fd5.de *Verat* k* verat-v bg* viol-o viol-t b7.de* zinc k* zinc-p k2 [eric-vg rcb1 heroin sdj2 tax jsj7]
- **daytime**: arg-met caust h2* dulc fd4.de
- **forenoon**: caust k*
- **afternoon**: *Nux-v* hr1*
- **evening**: adam srj5• aln vwa1• calc calc-act a1 dulc fd4.de **Lach** k* nux-v k* sacch-a fd2.de* sel k* sol-t-ae sulph teucr hr1* tritic-vg fd5.de vanil fd5.de verat-v viol-t a1
- **night**: *Aur* *Lachn*↓ lyss plb puls gl1.fr• sacch-a fd2.de•
  - **1-2 h**: *Lachn*
- **alternating** with:
  - **answer**; aversion to: cimic
  - **detachment**: lac-loxod-a hrn2•

Loquacity – alternating with: ...
  - **laughing** (See Laughing - alternating - loquacity)
  - **maliciousness** (See Malicious - alternating - loquacity)
  - **rage** (See Rage - alternating - loquacity)
  - **sadness**: arg-met jl tritic-vg fd5.de
  - **silence** (See taciturnity)
  - **taciturnity**: bell h1* buth-a mg1.de* cimic hr1* ign a1* nat-m vh sal-fr sle1•
- **answers** no questions, but: *(↗Answering - questioned; Awkward; Foolish)* *Agar*
- **busy**: lach j5.de ther j5.de
- **changing** quickly from one subject to another: *(↗Delirium - changing; Speech - wandering)* agar k* ambr bg* aran↓ arg-met k2 arg-n bg2* bar-c↓ bit-ar wht1• bry ptk1 choc srj3• *Cimic* k* hyos bg* ketogl-ac rly4• **Lach** k* lachn cda loxo-recl knl4• lyc k* marr-vg ckh1 *Meli* sne meph↓ nux-v hr1* onos bg* par k* phos ptk1 podo bg* raph mgm• rhus-t ptk1 sel bg* stram ptk1 teucr bg* tritic-vg fd5.de tub bg2* valer ptk1
  - **important** matters about; on: agar b aran b cimic b lach b meph b par b
  - **headache** | **during**: bar-c ptk1 lach ptk1 stram ptk1
- **cheerful**, exuberant: *(↗Exhilaration)* aeth mtf33 agath-a nl2• chir-fl gya2 croc j5.de grat j5.de iod j5.de kali-i j5.de kali-s fd4.de lach j5.de nat-c j5.de *Par* j5.de *Podo* fd3.de* ruta fd4.de tab j5.de verat j5.de
- **children**; in: bufo mtf33 hyos mtf33 lach mtf33 sacch sst1• stroph-h↓ verat mtf33
  - **precociously** loquacious: *(↗Precocity)* stroph-h ptk1*
- **chill**, during: *Podo* k* teucr zinc bg*
- **coughing** | **after**: dros ptk1*
- **domineering**: ozone sde2•
- **drunk**, as if: *(↗Speech - intoxicated)* meph hr1* *Mosch* sf1.de nept-m lsd2.fr
- **drunkenness**, during: caust gl1.fr• hep gl1.fr• lach gl1.fr• mag-c gl1.fr• petr gl1.fr• sulph gl1.fr•
- **ecstasy**, with: *(↗Ecstasy)* lach j5.de
- **excited**: *(↗Speech - excited)* *Cupr* sf1.de *Lach* gl1.fr• sel a1* teucr ptk1 *Ther* sf1.de
- **exhausted**, until: nat-c bg2
- **fever**; during: *(↗Delirium - fever - during)* ars-h sne ars-i sne *Bapt* gk coff k* *Ferr-p* sne *Gels* kr1 hyos gk *Lach* k* lachn c1 lob bg2 m-arct j5.de ph-ac kr1 *Podo* k* *Pyrog* k2* stram k* sulph bg2 **Teucr** k* *Tub* k* zinc bg*
- **foolish**: *(↗Speech - foolish)* *Ambr* mrr1 dulc fd4.de par j5.de
- **fruit**; after sour: podo br1
- **hasty**: *(↗rapid; Speech - hasty)* acon kr1 hyos j5.de
- **headache**:
  - **before**: cann-i br1
  - **during**: cann-i bro1
- **health**, about his: *(↗Discuss - symptoms)* **Nux-v** st1
- **heat**; during (See fever)
- **heedless**: *(↗Heedless)* *Iod* hr1*
- **hilarity**; with: *Podo* fd3.de• ruta fd4.de ther ptk1*
- **hoarseness**; only kept in check by: *Lach* kr1
- **incoherent** (See changing)
- **insane**: *Apis* kr1 bell j5.de *Hyos* j5.de* lach j5.de *Par* hr1* *Staph* hr1* *Stram* j5.de* verat gk *Verat-v* hr1*
- **jesting**, with: *(↗Jesting)* croc j5.de cystein-l rly4• kali-i j5.de* kali-s fd4.de lach j5.de
- **listen**, would not: dulc fd4.de *Hep* kr1
- **menopause**; during: *Phys* kr1*
- **menses**:
  - **before**: *Apis* b7a.de
  - **during**: *(↗Menses - during)* *Bar-c* k* hyos b7.de *Lach* *Stram* k*
- **mental** exertion, after: lach j5.de
- **nonsense**: *(↗Speech - nonsensical)* agar bg2 arg-met k2 cimic bg2 lach bg2* lyc bg2 meph bg2 par bg2 stram bg2
- **openhearted**: anh sf1.de bov gl1.fr• *Kali-s* fd4.de
- **perspiration**, during: ars k* bell k* *Calad* k* cocc k* cupr ptk1* hyos k* *Lach* bg2* *Sel* k* tarax k*
- **pregnancy**, during: *Bar-c* hr1*
- **question** after another; asks one: ambr k2* aur ptk1*

- **questioning** (See question)
- **rambling** (See changing)
- **rapid**: *(↗hasty)* arg-met k2
- **religious** subjects, about: *(↗Religious - too)* *Verat* a1*
- **rheumatic** pains; with: **Cimic** mrr1
- **selected** expressions, in: lach j5.de
- **self**-satisfied: *(↗Egotism; Haughty; Selfishness)* par j5.de
- **sleep**, during: ambr k* cupr graph mtf33 ign k* op k*
- **sleepiness**; with: *Lach* b7a.de
- **sleeplessness** with loquacity | **midnight**; especially before: Lach kr1
- **speeches**, makes: am-c bg arn k* cham k* chin bg dig bg ign bg2 *Lach* k* lyc bg viol-t bg
- **stupid** and irritable, then: lachn hr1*
- **vivacious**: *(↗Speech - vivacious)* *Hyos* j5.de kali-s fd4.de nat-c j5.de *Par* hr1* *Podo* fd3.de• tritic-vg fd5.de
- **witty**: croc j5.de

LOSING:
- **things** (See Memory - weakness - objects)
- **way**; his (See Confusion - loses)

LOSING ONE'S TEMPER (See Anger - easily; Offended)

LOSS; sense of: *(↗Yearning)* agath-a nl2•

LOVE:
- **anal** coition with a woman: *(↗perversity)* caust gl1.fr• nux-v vh plat gl1.fr•
- **animals** (See Animals - love)
- **appreciation** for fatherly love: | **younger** and older men; between: lac-lup hrn2•
- **children**; for: *(↗Children - beget; Children - loves)* *Ars* mtf *Hep* mtf lac-e↓ lac-h mtf lac-mat mtf *Limen-b-c* hrn2• ox-ac mtf phos mtf plat mtf rad-br sze8• sep mtf taosc iwa1•
  - **danger**; without awareness of imminent: limen-b-c hrn2•
  - **daughter**; for | **limited** in expression of it; but: lac-e hrn2•
  - **responsibilities**; yet naive about: *Limen-b-c* hrn2•
- **coming** towards her and from her; feelings of love: limen-b-c hrn2• ulm-c jsj8• *Vanil* fd5.de
- **disappointed** love:
  - **ailments** (See Ailments - love)
  - **anger**; with (See Anger - love)
  - **grief**; with silent (See Grief - silent - love)
  - **jealousy**; with (See Jealousy - love)
  - **laugh**; with inclination to (See Laughing - love)
  - **rage** from disappointed love (See Rage - love)
  - **sadness** from disappointed love (See Sadness - love)
  - **suicidal** disposition from disappointed love (See Suicidal - love)
  - **talk**; with incoherent (See Speech - incoherent - love)
- **exalted** love: *(↗Unification; Unification - sensation)* adam srj5• aids nl2• ant-c b7.de* cypra-eg↓ hydrog↓ *Hyos* b7a.de limen-b-c hrn2* olib-sac wmh1 plut-n srj7• *Podo* fd3.de• rhus-g tmo3• tritic-vg fd5.de vanil fd5.de
  - **family**; for her: *(↗family)* adam srj5• plut-n srj7• vanil fd5.de
  - **humanity**; for: aids nl2• cypra-eg sde6.de• hydrog srj2• limen-b-c hrn2*
- **family**; for: *(↗exalted - family; parents; Anxiety - family; Duty - too; Responsibility - taking)* acet-ac mtf aeth mtf *Ars* mtf *Aur* mtf *Calc* mtf calc-ar mtf calc-i mtf calc-sil mtf cand mtf carb-an mtf carc mtf *Caust* mtf coff hr1 cupr mtf germ-met mtf *Hep* mtf ign mtf kali-bi gk *Kali-c* mtf lach mtf limen-b-c hrn2• mag-m mtf nat-m mtf nat-s mtf petr mtf phos mtf puls mtf *Rhus-t* mtf *Spig* mtf sulph mtf *Tax-br* mtf zinc mtf
- **friends**; for: *(↗Estranged - family; Friendship - outpourings)* aur-s mtf bar-p mtf calc-p mtf kali-p mtf lac-c mtf mang-p mtf ph-ac mtf phos mtf
- **homosexuality** (See Homosexuality)
- **husband**; for: limen-b-c hrn2•
- **imaginary** love for a person: olib-sac wmh1
- **love**-sick: *(↗Grief; Jealousy)* aids nl2• *Ant-c* k* cypra-eg sde6.de• hydrog srj2• til k*
- **married** man, with: *(↗wrong)* *Nat-m* st

Love: ...
- **nature**; for (See Nature - loves)
- **openness**; and | **friends**; for: lac-lup hrn2•
- **opposite** sex: musca-d szs1
- **overflowing** love (See exalted)
- **parents**; for: *(↗family)* nat-m mtf33
- **pedophilia** (See Pedophilia)
- **people** in the group; for: ara-maca sej7•
- **perversity**; sexual: *(↗anal; Adulterous; Pedophilia; Seduction - desire)* agn ptk1 anac mrr1 *Canth* br1 *Fl-ac* mrr1 gamb mrr1 *Grat* mrr1 hura a1 *Hyos* mrr1 ind c1* kali-n a1 *Lyc* mrr1 manc mrr1 med mrr1 merc mrr1 mosch mrr1 murx mrr1 nux-v c1* orig mrr1 plat c1* polys sk4• sabal ptk1 staph ptk1* stram mrr1 tarent mrr1 tub mrr1 zinc mrr1 [stann stj2]
- **romantic** love; desire for: *(↗Sentimental)* germ-met srj5• musca-d szs1
- **sight**; at first (See Amorous)
- **wrong** person; with the (= out of social context): *(↗married)* aur-m-n wbt2• nat-m k2* olib-sac wmh1
- **yearning** for: olib-sac wmh1 *Vanil* fd5.de

LOW-MINDED (See Cowardice; Mood - repulsive)

LOW-SPIRITED (See Sadness)

LOYAL: *(↗Conscientious; Secretive)* calc-sil mtf33 **Kali-c** mrr1 *Nat-m* mrr1 staph↓
- **relationships**; in: nat-m mtf staph mtf

LUCIDITY; feeling of (See Clarity)

LUDICROUS, things seem: *(↗Foolish)* calc j cann-s falco-pe nl2• hyos j nat-m *Nux-m* plat h2 stram sulph j tarent

LUSTFUL (See Lascivious)

LUXURY, desire for: cur a1*

LYING:
- **agg.**: bry b7.de* canth b7.de* carb-v bg2 cham bg2 croc b7.de* merc b4.de* nux-v b7.de* phos b4.de* puls b7.de* sil bg2 viol-t b7.de*
- **amel.**: *Bell* b4a.de cina b7.de* euphr bg2 nit-ac bg2 teucr bg2 zinc b4.de*
- **bed**; in: calad b7a.de cham b7.de* ign bg2 laur b7.de* mosch b7.de* nux-v b7.de*
- **down**; after lying: ars b4.de* calc b4.de* carb-v b4a.de graph b4.de* hep bg2 ign b7.de mosch b7.de* nux-v b7.de* sep b4a.de sulph b4.de*
- **side**; on left: phos bg2 puls bg2

LYPOTHYMIA (See Prostration - grief)

MADNESS (See Insanity)

MAGIC: | **rainbow** feels like: maias-l hrn2•

MAGNETIC state: | **sensation** of increased personal power (See Power - sensation)

MAGNETIZED: *(↗GENERALS - Magnetism)*
- **amel.**: *(↗Held - amel.; GENERALS - Magnetism)* chin mtf33 cypra-eg sde6.de• graph mtf33 [am-p stj1]
- **desire** to be: *(↗Affectionate; Cuddle - desire; Held - desire)* **Calc** k* calc-sil dx1* cupr mtf33 lac-del hrn2• *Lach* k* limen-b-c hrn2* nat-c **Phos** k* podo fd3.de• polys sk4• **Sil** k* *Spong* fd4.de
- **easily** magnetized: caust gl1.fr• cypra-eg sde6.de• lac-f wza1• lach gl1.fr• phasco-ci rbp2 phos vh sep gl1.fr•
- **seems** as if he is magnetized; to others it: oena k*

MAGNETIZING others: | **desire** for: marb-w es1• podo fd3.de•

MAKING FUN of somebody (See Jesting; Mocking)

MALICIOUS: *(↗Brutality; Cruelty; Cursing; Hardhearted; Hatred; Insanity - malicious; Jealousy - vindictive; Jesting - malicious; Joy - misfortune; Misanthropy; Mischievous; Moral; Plans - making - revengeful; Rage - mischievous; Thoughts - persistent - injury; Unfeeling; Whistling - jolly; Wicked)* abrot k* *Acon* k* adam srj5• agar k* alco a1 aloe am-c k* am-m k* ambr **ANAC** b2.de* androc srj1• arn k* **Ars** k* ars-s-f k2* *Aur* k* aur-ar k2 aur-m-n wbt2• aur-s wbt2• bar-c k* *Bell* k* berb borra-o oss1• *Borx* k* bros-gau mrc1 bry c1 bufo *Calc* calc-s cann-s cann-xyz bg2 canth k* caps k* carb-an k* carc ot* carneg-g rwt1• caust k* *Cham* br1* chin k* choc srj3• cic k* clem coca gl1.fr• cocc k* coloc k* com k* con k* croc k* crot-c sk4• *Cupr* k* cycl j5.de cyna jl3 dendr-pol sk4•

Malicious: ...
falco-pe nl2• fl-ac gl1.fr• germ-met ↓ glon granit-m es1• guaj k* haem a1 *Hep* k* hydr k* *Hyos* k* ign k* ip j5.de irid-met srj5• kali-c j5.de* kali-i k* *Lac-c* lac-cp sk4• lac-h htj1• lac-leo sk4• *Lach* k* lat-m bnm6* *Led* k* levo jl3 *Lil-t* vh* limest-b es1• *Lyc* k* mang k* marb-w es1• med mrr merc k* moni rfm1• mosch k* *Nat-c* k* nat-m k* nat-ox rly4• neon srj5• nicc nicc-met stj2*• *Nit-ac* k* **Nux-v** k* oci-sa sk4• op k* opun-a ↓ opun-s ↓ opun-v ↓ osm ↓ ozone sde2• par k* ped a1 petr k* petr-ra shn4• *Ph-ac* vh* phasco-ci rbp2 phos k* plat k* plut-n srj7• polys sk4• pseuts-m oss1• (non:puls gl1.fr) ran-b j5.de rhus-g ↓ rhus-t mrr1 sacch sst1• sacch-a fd2.de• sarr a1 sec k* sep k2* sol-mm j5.de spong j squil k* stann k* *Staph* mtf33* **Stram** k* stront-c k* sulph syph st1 taosc iwa1• tarent ptk1* thuj bg2 tritic-vg fd5.de **Tub** st1* tus-fr a1 verat k* zinc k* zinc-p k2* [cupr-act stj2 cupr-f stj2 cupr-m stj2 cupr-p stj2 nicc-s stj2 tax jsj7]

- **evening** | **amel.**: hydr a
- **night**: *Calc* gl1.fr• opun-a a opun-s a1 (non:opun-v a1) *Sulph* gl1.fr•
- **alternating** with:
  - **loquacity**: ars-s-f k2
  - **mildness**: tub mtf33
- **anger**, with: anac j5.de bar-c j5.de calc kr1 canth j5.de *Caps* j5.de carb-an j5.de *Chin* j5.de* hep j5.de *Lyc* j5.de *Nat-m* j5.de nicc j5.de petr gl1.fr• taosc iwa1• zinc j5.de [plat stj2]
- **children**; in: sacch sst1•
- **chocolate**, after: sacch sht•
- **convulsions**:
  - **after**: *Cupr* kr1
  - **during**: cham kr1
- **delirium** tremens, in: **Nux-v** kr1
- **delivery**:
  - **after**, puerperal: cham kr1
  - **during**: cham kr1
- **dirty** tricks on others or on their teachers; desire to play: lach ↓ phos mtf33 zinc mtf33
  - **schoolboys**: lach gl1.fr• zinc gl1.fr•
- **dogs**, to: tub vh
- **dreams**, in: lac-h htj1• lach j5.de*
- **good** becomes malicious; man who was: puls pc
- **guilty**; without feeling: ozone sde2•
- **hurting** other people's feelings: *(↗Breaking - valuables; Mocking - sarcasm)* chin br1* lat-m mtf rhus-g tmo3• tarent mtf tub mtf33
- **injure** someone, desire to: androc srj1• levo jl3 osm a1* tritic-vg fd5.de
- **insulting**: *(↗Abusive - insulting)* hyos j5.de merc j5.de
- **laughing**: *(↗Joy - misfortune)* cupr j5.de* marb-w es1•
- **loved** ones, to: *(↗Irritability - loved)* germ-met srj sep k2*
- **murder** someone, as if she could: *Hep* kr1
- **sadness**, in: **Kali-i** hr1*
- **savage**: cupr kr1
- **sweets**; after: sacch sst1•

MALINGERING (See Feigning - sick)

MANIA: *(↗Delirium - maniacal; Delusions; Insanity; Jumping - bed - mania; Rage; Religious - too - mania; Schizophrenia - paranoid; Violent; Wild feeling; Wildness)* absin k* acon k* acon-l a1* aeth aether a1* *Agar* bg2* agn ↓ agre ↓ ail alco a1* aloe ↓ *Alum* alum-p k2* *Anac* k* anag kr1* anan kr1* androc bnm2• anh k1* ant-c ant-t bg2* *Apis* k* *Arg-met* *Arn* k* **Ars** k* ars-met ↓ ars-s-f k2 *Arum-t* astra-m br1 atro c1* *Aur* k* aur-ar k2 aur-i k2 aur-s k2 bapt k1* bar-c k* *Bar-m* k* **Bell** k* *Brom* bry k1* bufo cact *Calad* *Calc* calc-i k2 calc-p ↓ *Camph* *Cann-i* k* *Cann-s* j5.de* cann-xyz ↓ **Canth** k* carbn-s k2 *Carc* mlr1• caust bg2* cedr br1 cham bg2* chel *Chin* k* chinin-s chir-fl ↓ *Chlol* k* cic *Cimic* k* coca *Cocc* k* coff colch k* coli ↓ *Con* k* cori-r c1* cortico k1* croc j5.de* crot-c k* crot-h k* *Cupr* k* cupr-act c1* *Cupr-s* ↓ cur ↓ *Cycl* cyt-l ↓ dat-f c1* dat-m c1* der c1* dig diosm br1 dros bg2* dulc bg* eberth jl2 *Elat* ↓ euph ↓ ferr-p k2* gels bg2* glon k* grat c1* haliae-lc srj5• *Hell* helo-s rwt2• *Hep* heroin ↓ *Hydr-ac* ↓ **Hyos** k* hyosin c1* hyper ↓ *Ign* k* indg *Iod* k* iodof c1* iris-t c1* kali-bi bg2* **Kali-br** k* kali-c bg2* (non:kali-chl a1) kali-i **Kali-m** k* *Kali-p* kres k1* *Lach* k* lact ↓ lat-h ↓ lat-m bnm6• laur k1* led lil-t bg2* lol bg2 **Lyc** k* lyss c1* maias-l hrn2• *Manc* k* mand k1* med bg2* meli mrr1 **Merc** k* merc-c murx bg2* musca-d ↓ nat-m k* nat-p ↓ *Nat-s* ↓ nit-ac bg2* *Nux-m* **Nux-v** k* oena **Op** k* orig k1* oscilloc jl2 ox-ac par c1* passi k1* petr bg2* ph-ac bg* *Phos* k* *Phyt* ↓ pic-ac k1* pisc k1* *Plat* bg2* plb k* positr nl2• *Psor* puls k* *Raph* k* rhod rhus-t j5.de* ruta bg2* sabad k* sal-n ↓

Mania: ...
Sec k* senec c1* seneg bg2* *Sep* k* ser-a-c ↓ sil c1* sol-ni c1* spig-m c1* spong k1* stann ↓ staph c1* **Stram** k* streptoc ↓ sul-h c1* sulfa ↓ *Sulph* k* *Tarent* k* ter thea c1* thyr c1* tub c1* tub-k c1* ust k1* vanad ↓ **Verat** k* verat-v k* vip bg* zinc k* [am-f stj2 arg-n stj2 caes-met stj2 fl-ac stj2 fl-pur stj2 irid-met stj2 lith-c stj2 lith-f stj2 lith-met stj2 lith-p stj2 lith-s stj2 zinc-m stj2 zinc-n stj2 zinc-p stj2]

- **morning**, early: kali-c j
- **evening**: croc j crot-c a1
- **night**: bell j cact ↓ cic h1* kali-i a1 *Staph* ↓ verat j
  - **midnight**, agg.; about: cact ↓ *Staph* kr1
    - **heat**; from burning: cact a
  - **dancing**, laughing and striking; with: cic gl1.fr•
- **abuses** everyone: anac mp1• *Camph* hr1* lach mp1• *Stram* kr1 *Tarent* hr1*
- **action**, must be constantly in: *Iod* kr1
- **acute**: *Canth* br1 carc mlr1• euph br1 *Gels* ↓ passi br1
  - **tongue** | **white** discoloration of the; with: *Gels* kr1*
- **alcoholic** drinks; from (See Delirium tremens)
- **albuminuria**, in: *Phyt* kr1
- **alternating** with:
  - **cheerfulness**: bell k* *Cann-i* cann-s croc
  - **depression**: *(↗Euphoria - alternating - sadness; Excitement - alternating - sadness)* anac mp1* arg-met jl aur mrr1 bell mp1• cann-i mrr1 *Carc* mlr1• coff mp1• coli jl2 *Con* hr1* cyt-l jl3 hyos mp1* ign mtf33 kres jl3 **Lach** mp1* lil-t mrr1 *Med* mp1* *Nat-s* hr1* phos mrr1 pic-ac gm1 psor jl2* sep ↓ ser-a-c jl2 *Staph* hr1* stram h1* sulfa jl3 tub br1* verat mrr1 [heroin sdj2 lith-c stj2 lith-met stj2 vanad stj2]
    - **children**; in: sep mtf33
  - **fear** (See Fear - alternating - mania)
  - **frenzy**: hyos j
  - **loathing**: bell j
  - **metrorrhagia**: *Crot-c* bg2*
  - **mirth**: bell *Cann-i* caust lpc croc
  - **sadness** (See depression)
  - **silence** and refusing to talk: verat br1*
  - **tranquillity**: positr nl2•
- **amenorrhea**, from: *Cocc* kr1
- **anguish**, during: *(↗Anguish)* ars a1 carc mp1*• stram mp1•
- **boisterous** (See Exhilaration - mania)
- **brain** | **congestion** or irritation of brain; from: ferr-p kr1 *Kali-br* kr1 *Meli* kr1 verat-v kr1
- **business**: | **failure**, from (See Insanity - business)
- **capricious** (See Capriciousness - mania)
- **cold** perspiration, with (See perspiration)
- **coldness**, with: lact br1
- **constipation**. during: *Verat* kr1
- **convulsions**:
  - **after**: arg-met bg2 cur kr1
  - **before**: *Lach* kr1 nux-v kr1
  - **clonic**: cupr kr1
  - **epileptic**: dig kr1
  - **mental** excitement; with: zinc kr1
  - **paroxysmal**; every half hour: stram kr1
  - **puerperal**: verat-v kr1
  - **sudden** furious attack, with: *Oena* kr1
  - **with**: oena mrr1 verat-v tl1
- **demonic**: agre jl *Anac* bg2* bell bg2* *Hell* kr1 hyos bg2* op bg2* plat bg2* sil bg2* sulph bg2* verat bg2*
- **destruction**, followed by laughter and apologies; of: tarent kr1
- **domestic** calamity, after: lach kr1
- **drunk**, as if: oena kr1
- **eruptions**; after suppressed: ant-t cda *Caust* kr1 *Hep* kr1 *Zinc*
- **excitement** in gesture or speech: *Hydr-ac* hr1* *Zinc* ↓
  - **from**: *Zinc* kr1
- **fever**, during: *(↗heat - during)* *Ars* ↓ bell k2* calc c1 *Chin* ↓ *Elat* ↓ kali-p kr1 *Phyt* ↓ verat sne1

- **fever**; during: ...
  - **chill**; with:
    - **night**: *Phyt* kr1
    - **suppressed**: *Elat* kr1
  - **delivery**, after, puerperal: *Kali-p* kr1
  - **intermittent** fever; during: *Ars* kr1 *Chin* kr1
- **fortune**; from reverse of: (↗ *Ailments - fortune*) *Anac* j5.de *Bell* j5.de *Hyos* j5.de *Lach* j5.de *Phos* j5.de *Stram* j5.de *Verat* j5.de
- **hands**:
  - **claps**: bell ptk1 *Stram* kr1*
  - **washing** face; while: musca-d szs1
  - **wringing** hands; runs about day and night: *Hell* kr1
- **haughty** (See Haughty - mania)
- ○ - **Head**; with pain in: *Sil* kr1
- **heart**:
  - **affected**, with: cupr kr1
  - **pain** in region of, with: ars-met kr1
- **heat** | **during**: (↗ *fever*) cact bg2*
- **held**, wants to be: (↗ *Held; Held - desire*) **Ars** k*
- **homicidal**: thea c2
- **indecent**: op kr1
- **indifference**; with (See Indifference - mania)
- **insane**, declares she will go: (↗ *Fear - insanity*) cimic lpc streptoc jl2
- **jumps** over chairs and tables: (↗ *Impulse - run*) bell a1*
- **lascivious**: calc-p mp1• *Hyos* br1 *Plat* mp1• *Raph* a1 stann mp1• *Tarent* mp1•
- **laughing** and gaiety; with: (↗ *Insanity - laughing*) *Croc* br1 maias-l hm2•
- **liver** complaints, with: *Merc* kr1
- **lochia**, from suppressed: cimic sf1.de plat sf1.de verat sf1.de
- **masturbation**; after: (↗ *MALE GENITALIA/SEX - Masturbation - mania*) anan kr1 plb ↓
  - **duration**; eight or ten years of: plb kr1
- **menopause**; during: cimic mg verat mg
- **menses**:
  - **before**: (↗ *Menses - before*) cimic bro1* sep
  - **during**: *Bell* kr1 cimic bro1 *Sep* mtn stram mtn
  - **suppressed**, after: aloe j apis pe *Cimic* kr1 *Puls* k1 stram bro1* verat nh
- **mental** exertion, after: camph kr1 *Kali-br* kr1 lach *Merc* kr1
- **monomania** (See Monomania)
- **morphine**, from: (↗ *Morphinism*) nat-p c1
- **neuralgia**, after disappearance of: cimic kr1*
- **noisy**: verat bg2*
- **pain** | **after** | **sciatic** nerve; in: cimic bro1
  - **from**: *Ars* bg2* colch ↓ hyper ↓ *Verat* ↓
    - **evening**: colch kr1
    - **delirium**; with: *Verat* kr1
    - **paroxysms**: hyper kr1
- **paroxysmal**: carc mlr• cic hr1* diosm br1 kali-i ↓ *Nat-m* hr1 nat-s br1 stram k2 *Tarent* k* tub br1
  - **headache**, with: kali-i kr1
  - **wet**, after becoming: *Nat-m* kr1
- **periodical**: arg-n *Nat-s* k* staph hr1 *Tarent* tub br1
- **perspiration**; with cold: camph k2* **Cupr** ↓ stram k2*
  - **ending** in: **Cupr** kr1
- **philosophical**: (↗ *Philosophy - ability*) *Sulph* k13*
- **praying** (See Praying)
- **puerperal**: (↗ *Insanity - puerperal; Praying*) agn bro1 bell c2* *Camph* mp1• *Cann-i* bro1 cimic c2* coli jl2 hyos c2* *Kali-br* hr1 kali-p c2 plat bro1 puls c2 sec bro1 senec c2* *Stram* bro1* verat br1* verat-v c2* zinc bro1*
- **pulse**, with full, hard: *Cupr-act* kr1
- **quiet** and meditation amel.: *Iod* kr1
- **rage**, with: acon k13 agar h2* anac k13 ant-t j5.de arg-met j* ars bg2* *Bell* k* camph hr1* cann-i sf1.de cann-s j5.de cann-xyz bg2 *Canth* j5.de con k13 croc bg2* cupr j5.de* cur hr1 *Dig* hr1 **Hyos** bg2* kali-c k13 lach sf1.de lat-h thj1 lol bg2* **Lyc** k* *Merc* bg2* nux-v hr1* *Op* j5.de* ph-ac bg2 phos bg2* plat k13 plb j5.de* puls k13 *Sec* j5.de* sol-ni j5.de *Stram* a1* *Tarent* mrr1 *Verat* k* verat-v bg2 zinc bg2
- **religious**: (↗ *Insanity - religious*) stram br1

Mania: ...
- **restlessness**; with (See Restlessness - mania)
- **running** about (See Runs - mania)
- **running** away (See Escape - run - mania)
- **sadness**; with: verat br1
- **scratching** themselves: (↗ *Scratching*) bell a1
- **sexual** abuse; after: *Phos* hr1
- **sexual** mania: **Apis** ↓ bar-m br1 camph c2 cann-i ↓ canth br1 chir-fl ↓ *Dulc* ↓ heroin ↓ *Hyos* br1 **Phos** ↓ plat ↓ *Raph* ↓ sal-n br1 stram ↓ *Tarent* ↓ verat ↓
  - **alternating** with | **stupor** (See Stupor - alternating - mania)
  - **increased** sexual desire; from: apis vh1 *Bar-m* kr1
  - **men**; in: apis st chir-fl gya2 **Phos** st *Raph* a1 *Tarent* st
  - **menses**:
    - **before**: cann-i bro1 *Dulc* bro1 plat bro1 stram bro1 verat bro1
    - **during**: cann-i bro1 *Dulc* bro1 plat bro1 stram bro1 verat bro1
  - **women**, in: **Apis** kr1* **Phos** st *Raph* a1 *Tarent* st [heroin sdj2]
- **shrieking** in: (↗ *Shrieking*) *Bell* sf1.de cic jl3 lach bg2* stram
- **singing**, with: (↗ *Singing*) bell j5.de* cann-i lpc cic jl3 *Cocc* h1* croc br1 cupr lpc hyos lpc *Nux-m* hr1* plat kr1 stram lpc *Tarent* hr1* *Verat* j5.de
  - **puerperal** mania; in: *Plat* kr1
- **sleep**:
  - **during**: kali-c ↓ ph-ac j phos k2
    - **dreaming**: kali-c j
- **sleeplessness**, with: lach mrr1 lact br1 meli sne
- **spasmodic** sensation; with: maias-l hm2•
- **spasms**, after (See convulsions - after)
- **spit** and bite at those around him, would: (↗ *Spitting*) *Bell* a1*
- **stamping** feet: verat j
- **strength**; with increased (See Insanity - strength)
- **sudden** beginning: carc mlr1•
- **suicidal**: *Ars* h1* aur ↓ thea c1* verat kr1
  - **sexual** symptoms; with: aur hr1*
- **sunstroke**, after: hyos h1
- **syphilis**, in: anag kr1
- **tearing**: (↗ *Tearing - himself; Tearing - things*)
  - **clothes**: nux-v gl1.fr• *Tarent* kr1 *Verat* j5.de*
  - **hair**, own: bell j5.de canth gl1.fr• stram gl1.fr• tarent a1 verat gl1.fr•
  - **himself** to pieces with nails: canth gl1.fr• stram gl1.fr• verat gl1.fr•
- **tongue** | **white** discoloration of the; with: *Gels* vk1
- **trembling**, with: lact br1
- **typhus**, in: hyos a
- **vertigo**, with: *Cocc* kr1
- **vexation**; after: (↗ *Ailments - anger*) bell j hyos j ign j nux-v j ph-ac j plat kr1 staph j
- **violence**, with deeds of: (↗ *Violent - deeds*) ars j5.de *Bell* j5.de hyos j5.de lach mrr1 *Plat* hr1* sec j5.de stram j5.de* tarent mrr1 verat br1*
  - **bed** with difficulty; can be kept in: lach kr1
- **wandering** (See Wandering - desire - mania)
- **washing** head in cold water amel.: sabad lpc
- **work**; for (See Industrious)
- ○ - **Eyes**:
  - **delusions** of sight, with: *Stram* kr1
  - **immovable**: *Bell* kr1
  - **inflamed**: *Cupr-act* kr1
  - **open**, staring: *Bell* kr1
  - **protrusion** of eyes; with (See EYE - Protrusion - mania)
  - **wild** look, with: *Cupr-s* hr1*

MANIA A POTU (See Delirium tremens)

MANIC-DEPRESSIVE (See Mania - alternating - depression)

MANIPULATIVE: (↗ *Corrupt; Deceitful; Dictatorial; Hypocrisy; Liar; Untruthful*) cot br1 lach ↓ *Puls* vh* sanic mrr1 sil mrr1 staph zr *Sulph* mrr1 tarent mrr1 thuj zr* tub mrr1 [heroin sdj2]
- **children**: lach ↓ puls mtf33 tub mtf33
  - **nurslings**: lach mtf33

MANKIND (See Humankind)

MANNERLY (See Polite)

MANNISH:

- **girls**; mannish looking: carb-v mtf33* cimic mg cortiso mg *Nat-m* mtf33* petr gl1.fr• plat mtf33* staph vh
- **women**: (↗*Animus; GENERALS - Hair - distribution)* fl-ac st *Graph* vh* plut-n srj skook srj sulph mrr1

MANUAL WORK, fine work; mental symptoms from: (↗*Anxiety - exercise - from; Anxiety - manual - from; Fear - manual)* graph k* hep b4a.de iod k*

MARRIAGE: (↗*Aversion - marriage)*

- **obsessed** by idea of marriage; girls are sexually excited and: bell gl1.fr• *Caust* mtf33* plat gl1.fr• verat gl1.fr•
- **thoughts** of, amel.: orig ptk1*
- **unendurable**; idea of marriage seemed: (↗*Aversion - marriage; Aversion - men; to [=male persons] - women; Aversion - men; to [=male persons] - women - religious; Aversion - women - men; Aversion - women - men - religious; Homosexuality; Insanity - wedding; Irresolution - marry)* fl-ac mp1• *Lach* k* **Lyc** mp1* *Med* st **Nux-v** ptk1* pic-ac k* puls k* staph gl1.fr•

MASCULINITY: | **increased** sensation of: chlam-tr bcx2• musca-d szs1 *Plut-n* srj7•

MASOCHISM: (↗*Injuring; Mutilating; Reproaching oneself)* caust cd1 lach ↓ nat-c gg* nat-m gg tub gg

- **sexual**: lach gg

MASTURBATION agg.: sec b7a.de

MATERIALISTIC: (↗*Unrefined)* con mrr1 *Fl-ac* mrr1 plb mrr1 polys sk4• positr nl2• [heroin sdj2]

MATHEMATICS:

- **ability** for: cocc gl1.fr• lach gl1.fr• nux-v gl1.fr• plb cld• sil dgt* [calc-sil stj2 ferr-sil stj2 kali-sil stj2 mag-sil stj2 mang-sil stj2 nat-sil stj2 sil-met stj2]
- **inability** for: (↗*Confusion - calculating)* ail ↓ *Alum* ↓ *Ambr* ↓ anh ↓ arb-m ↓ aur mtf33 bell gl1.fr• calc gl1.fr• *Carb-v* ↓ caust mtf33 con ↓ crot-h ↓ falco-pe nl2• graph ↓ kali-c mtf33* kali-p ↓ lyc mtf33* merc a1 mosch ↓ nat-c ↓ nat-m ↓ *Nux-v* ↓ ph-ac ↓ *Psor* ↓ rhus-t a1 sil ↓ staph mtf33 sulph ↓ *Sumb* ↓ symph ↓ syph st*
  - **algebra**: alum gl1.fr• caust gl1.fr• graph gl1.fr• staph gl1.fr•
  - **astronomy**: aur gl•
  - **calculating**: (↗*Concentration - difficult - calculating; Mistakes - calculating; Slowness - calculating; Studying - difficult - mathematics)* alum gl1.fr• arb-m oss1• bell gl1.fr• calc k2* *Carb-v* mtf33 caust gl1.fr• crot-h sf1.de graph gl1.fr• kali-c gl1.fr• lyc gl1.fr• merc a1 mosch mlk2 nat-c k2 nat-m k2 *Nux-v* vh* ph-ac k2 *Psor* kr1 rhus-t a1 staph k2* syph k2*
    - **aversion** to: sil mtf33 sulph mtf33
  - **geometry**: ail kr1 *Alum* gl1.fr• *Ambr* gl1.fr• calc gl1.fr• caust gl1.fr• con gl1.fr•
  - **horror** of: calc gl1.fr• lyc gl1.fr• nat-m gl1.fr• sil gl1.fr• staph st sulph mtf33*
  - **summing** up is difficult: anh sp1 kali-p fd1.de• *Sumb* a1 symph fd3.de•

MATERNAL INSTINCT; EXAGGERATED: (↗*Anxiety - children - about; Cares full - relatives)* ars mtf bar-c mtf calc mtf carc mtf cocc mtf lac-d mtf lac-mat mtf sep mtf

MATURE, behaves as a much older child (See Precocity)

MEANINGLESSNESS; feeling of (See Delusions - meaningless)

MEDDLESOME: (↗*Audacity; Curious; Gossiping; Heedless; Impertinence; Impulse; Impulsive; Indiscretion; Presumptuous; Rash; Unobserving [=nonconformism])* alum gl1.fr• atro k* aur-s wbt2• con gl1.fr• hyos k* hyosin a* lyc gl1.fr• plb a1*

- **children**: | **disturbing** parents when they are conversing: hyos mtf33
- **hands**; with his: hyos mtf33

MEDICINE: (↗*Drugs)*

- **aversion** to (See Refusing - medicine; Remedies - aversion)
- **desire** to swallow large doses of: cact a1 [tax jsj7]

MEDITATING: (↗*Absorbed; Brooding; Dream; as; Dwells - past; Introspection; Sitting - inclination - meditates; Sitting - inclination - wrapped; Thoughts - thoughtful; FACE - Expression - vacant)* am-m anh mtf ant-c arb-m oss1• aur k* bar-c vh berb kr1 calc-s k13 *Cann-i* mtf cann-s canth **Carb-an** cham j chin choc srj3• cic clem cocc coch ↓ coff gl1.fr• con cycl eug euph kr1 falco-pe nl2• galeoc-c-h gms1• germ-met srj guaj j haliae-lc srj5• ham hell *Hyos* ign ina-i mlk9.de ip irid-met srj5• kali-n kreos j lac-e ↓ lac-leo hrn2• *Lach* led sf1.de limen-b-c ↓ lyc mtf lyss kr1 manc mang j5.de meny kr1 mez mur-ac nat-c ol-an kr1 olib-sac wmh1 op ↓ ozone ↓ petr-ra shn4• phel phos plac rzf5• plan hl plb positr nl2• ran-b rhus-t ruta fd4.de sabad sanguis-s hrn2• senec hl sep spig staph *Sulph* k* suprar rly4• thuj tritic-vg fd5.de vanil fd5.de [heroin sdj2]

- **evening**: coch j senec hl
- **night**: op gl1.fr•
- **as if**: ozone sde2•
- **deeply**: cocc j positr nl2• suprar rly4• **Vanil** fd*
- **desire** for: limen-b-c hrn2•
- **difficult**: lac-e hrn2•
- **menses**, during: senec mtn
- **prostration**, with extreme: plan hl

MEDITATION agg.: arg-met b7.de* olnd b7.de* ran-b b7.de*

MEETING OF SOULS; sensation of a (See Brotherhood; Unification - sensation)

MEGALOMANIA (See Insanity - megalomania)

MELANCHOLY (See Despair; Grief; Sadness)

MEMORY:

- **active**: (↗*Activity - desires - creative; Concentration - active; Exhilaration - recall; Fancies - vivid; Forgotten - sleep; Ideas - abundant; Plans - making; Quick; Thoughts - profound; Thoughts - rapid; Thoughts - thoughtful; Witty)* acon k* acon-f a1 *Agar Agath-a* ↓ ail ↓ *Aloe* alum anac k* ang k* anh sp1* ant-c am ars ars-s-f k2 asaf *Asar* ↓ *Aur* k* aur-ar k2 *Bad* bapt a1 *Bar-c* bg3 **Bell** k* bov brom bros-gau ↓ bufo gk *Calc* bg3 calc-p camph cann-i cann-s caps carb-v carc mlr1• chin k* cimic cob k* coc-c coca cocc **Coff** k* coff-t a1 con bg3 croc k* cub cupr cycl k* dig dulc fd4.de elae ↓ elaps ↓ fl-ac form ↓ *Gels* germ-met ↓ glon grat guaj ↓ ham ↓ hell bg hipp **Hyos** k* iber a1 kali-p kola stb3• lac-ac a1 **Lach** k* limest-b ↓ **Lyc** bg3 lyss k* manc meph *Merc* bg3 **Nat-m** gg nat-p *Nux-m Nux-v* olib-sac wmh1 olnd ↓ **Op** k* ox-ac *Ph-ac* bg3 *Phos* k* phys pip-m k* plat plb plut-n ↓ puls raph rhus-t sanguis-s ↓ senec kr1 seneg k* sil sol-t-ae ↓ spig spong fd4.de staph bg3 *Stry Sul-ac* sulph symph fd3.de• syph ↓ ter ther thres-a ↓ thuj tritic-vg fd5.de valer verat verb viol-o k* zinc zing a1 ziz [tax jsj7]
  - **morning**: fl-ac a1*
  - **afternoon**: anac h2* ang h1*
  - **evening**: agar **Coff** ↓ kali-p fd1.de• **Lach**
    - **midnight**, until: **Coff**
  - **alternating** with:
    - **dullness**: rhus-t
    - **lassitude**: *Aloe*
    - **weakness** of memory: acon gl1.fr• ars-s-f k2 cycl rhus-t b7.de*
  - **dates**; for: plb mtf33
  - **done**; for what one has: bapt lpc cann-i lpc elae lpc fl-ac lpc seneg lpc sol-t-ae lpc
  - **fever**, during: op a1
  - **involuntary** remembrance: croc b7a.de fl-ac bg2 hyos b7.de* nat-m bg2 seneg sfa
  - **music**, for: croc j5.de* lyc lpc*
  - **names**, for proper: *Asar* jl3 germ-met srj ham fd3.de•
  - **narrow** field; in a: bufo gk
  - **numbers**; for: plb cld*
  - **past** events, for: (↗*Dwells)* *Agath-a* nl2• ail ↓ anh sp1 bell a1 bros-gau ↓ dulc fd4.de elaps a1 form a1 *Hyos* j5.de* *Kali-p* ↓ limest-b ↓ plut-n srj7• sanguis-s hrn2• seneg j5.de* syph ↓ thres-a sze7•
    - **happened**; which have not: limest-b es•

- **past** events, for: ...
  - **haunted** by and longing for remembering past events: bros-gau mrc1 *Kali-p* kr1
  - **previous** to his illness: syph br1
  - **remembered** as happened to someone else or as read: ail kr1
- **read**; for what one has: bapt lpc cann-i lpc elae lpc fl-ac lpc seneg lpc sol-t-ae lpc
- **seen**; for what one has: bapt lpc cann-i lpc elae lpc fl-ac lpc seneg lpc* sol-t-ae lpc
- **sexual** desire; from suppressed: lach
- **short**, but: calc gl1.fr• sil gl1.fr• staph gl1.fr• sulph gl1.fr•
- **words**; for: anac j croc j guaj j lyc j olnd j rhus-t j sulph j*

- **confused**: (↗*false)* *Agath-a* nl2• anac a1 anh sp1 arg-n tl1 bell b4a.de chinin-s a1 cupr sf1.de lach ↓ naja a1 op hr1* petr sf1.de podo fd3.de• **Ruta** fd* sel sf1.de sep b4a.de ser-a-c jl2 sinus rly4• spong fd4.de *Stram* hr1* syph jl2 [plb stj2]
  - **epileptic** convulsions; before: lach bro1
- **overexertion** of | **agg.**: m-ambo b7.de*
- **false** memory: (↗*confused)* limest-b es1•
- **loss** of memory: absin br1* acon bro1 *Aeth* bro1 agath-a nl2• *Agn* bro1 ail tl1 *Alum* bro1 am-c ↓ ambr bro1 *Anac* b2.de* anh bro1 aq-mar ↓ *Arg-n* bg2* arn bro1 *Aur* bro1 aza bro1 bamb-a stb2.de• bar-c bg2* bell b2.de* bry b2.de* calad bro1 *Calc* bro1 calc-p bg2* *Camph* b2.de* *Cann-i* bro1 carb-v bro1 carbn-s c2 chen-a ↓ chinin-ar ↓ chlorpr ↓ *Cic* ptk1 cocc bro1 *Coli* jl2 *Con* b2.de* convo-s sp1 cori-r c2 cycl b2.de* des-ac mtf11 *Dig* c2 diph-t-tpt jl2 elec c1 euon-a br1 fago br1 glon ↓ glyc bro1 graph b2.de* hell b2.de* hippoc-k szs2 hyos b2.de* *Hyper* bg2 ichth bro1 kali-br bg2* kali-c b2.de* kali-m ckh1 kali-p br1* kali-x br1 *Lac-c* bro1 lac-e hm2• *Lach* b7a.de* lat-h bnm5• lat-m bnm6• lec bro1 lyc b2.de* mand sp1 med bro1* merc bro1 *Nat-c* bro1 *Nat-m* b2.de* nat-s tl1 nit-ac bro1 nux-m bro1* *Nux-v* bro1 olnd b2.de* onos br1 op b2.de* perh-mal jl3 **Petr** b2.de* petr-ra shn4• ph-ac bro1* phos br1* *Pic-ac* bro1 plb bg2* pneu jl2 podo fd3.de• psor jl2 puls b2.de* rhod bro1* rhus-t b2.de* *Ruta* fd4.de sel b2.de* sep bro1 sil b2.de* spig b2.de* *Spong* fd4.de staph b2.de* *Stram* b2.de* sulfa sp1 sulph b2.de* syph br1* tab bg2 tell bro1 thyr bro1 trif-p br1 vanil fd5.de **Verat** b2.de* visc sp1 *Zinc* bro1 *Zinc-p* bro1 zinc-pic bro1
  - **aphasia**, in: cann-i sf1.de
  - **apoplexy**, after: **Anac** kr1 chen-a vml3• *Plb* kr1
  - **catalepsy**, after: camph a1*
  - **coma**, after: cori-r a1
  - **concussion** of the brain; after: (↗*injuries; injuries - head)* hell fb3 *Hyper* sf1.de
  - **epileptic** fits, after: (↗*Forgetful - epilepsy - happened)* absin kr1* calc kr1 cic sf1.de *Zinc* kr1
  - **fear**, from: anac kr1
  - **hearing**; with loss of: sulfa sp1
  - **imbecility**, in: (↗*Imbecility)* *Anac* kr1
  - **injuries**; after: (↗*concussion; Ailments - injuries)* am-c bg1 **Arn** ↓ chinin-ar st cic ↓ hyper ↓ merc ↓ *Nat-s* ↓ rhus-t ↓
    - **Head**; of: (↗*concussion)* am-c bg2 **Arn** bg2 cic bg2 hyper bg2 merc bg2 *Nat-s* vh* rhus-t bg2
  - **insanity**, in: aur kr1 *Merc* kr1 *Stram* kr1
  - **life**; about his past: nux-m ptk1
  - **mental** exertion, from: aq-mar skp7• bamb-a stb2.de• *Kali-p* fd1.de• *Nat-c* kr1*
  - **periodical**: cic tl1 con tl1 nat-m tl1 nux-m tl1
  - **retrograde**: chen-a vml3•
  - **sudden**: aq-mar skp7• calc bg2 carb-v bg2* chlorpr pin1• nux-v bg2 syph bg2
  - **sunstroke**, after: *Anac* glon *Lach*
  - **transient**: chlorpr pin1* **Spong** fd*
  - **urinary** or intestinal trouble; after: coli jl2
- **short** term memory; poor (See weakness - facts - recent; weakness - happened - just; weakness - heard - just; weakness - read - just)

- **weakness** of memory: (↗*Absentminded; Concentration - difficult; Confusion; Dyslexia; Fancies - confused; Forgetful; Forgotten - sleep; Forgotten - something; Ideas - deficiency; Mistakes; Recognizing - not - relatives; Thoughts - vanishing)* abrot absin a1* acet-ac a1* *Acon* k* acon-c a1 act-sp adam srj5• aesc k* aeth k* agar agath-a nl2• **Agn** k* agre jl *Aids* nl2• ail alco a1 all-s kr1 allox tpw3* aloe ↓ *Alum* k* alum-sil k2* alumn a1 am-c k* am-m **Ambr** k* **Anac** b2.de* *Anac-oc* kr1 anan androc srj1• androg-p bnj1 anh bro1* ant-t bg2 anthraci ↓ *Apis* k* aq-mar ↓ arag ↓ arb-m oss1• *Arg-met* bg2* **Arg-n** k* arge-pl rwt5• arizon-l nl2• *Arn* k* **Ars** k* ars-h kr1 ars-met br1 art-v ptk1 arum-t asaf bg2* asar ↓ asc-t a1* aster jl atis bnj1 *Atro* kr1 atro-s ↓ *Aur* k* aur-ar k2 aur-m a1 *Aur-m-n* ↓ aur-s a1* aza bro1 *Bamb-a* stb2.de• bapt a1 bar-act br1* **Bar-c** k* bar-i k2 bar-s k2 **Bell** k* bell-p-sp ↓ berb bit-ar ↓ bol-la kr1 borx k* *Bov* k* brass-n-o srj5• brom k* bros-gau mrc1 *Bry* k* **Bufo** k* **Bufo-s** cact ↓ cadm-met mg1.de* cael ↓ calad k* *Calc* b2.de* calc-ar k2 *Calc-p* k1* calc-s calc-sil k2 camph k* *Cann-i* k* cann-s cann-xyz ptk1 caps a1 carb-ac *Carb-an* k* *Carb-v* k* carbn-o a1 **Carbn-s** carc mg1.de* card-m *Cardios-h* rly4• carl a1 **Caust** k* cedr ↓ cench k2* cham chel k* *Chin* k* *Chinin-ar* chinin-s ↓ chlam-tr ↓ chlf kr1 *Chlol* chlor k* chlorpr jl* choc ↓ chr-ac ↓ *Cic* cimic cinnb ↓ cit-ac rly4• *Clem* cob-n sp1 *Coca* ↓ **Cocc** k* coff **Colch** k* coli ↓ coloc **Con** k* conch ↓ convo-s jl* cop cor-r ↓ cori-r com k1 cortico jl* cortiso jl* cot a1 croc k* crot-c k* *Crot-h* k* crot-t k* cub culx k2 *Cupr* k* cupr-act kr1 *Cycl* k* cypra-eg ↓ cystein-l rly4• dendr-pol sk4• der a1 diaz ↓ *Dig* k* dios ↓ dirc ↓ dream-p sdj1• dubo-m br1 dulc bg2 dys fmm1• elaps erio a1 *Euon* ↓ euon-a ↓ *Euphr* k* eupi a1 fago br1 *Falco-pe* nl2• ferr *Ferr-p* k1* *Fl-ac* k* *Form* gad ↓ galeoc-c-h ↓ gard-j ↓ *Gels* germ-met srj5• gink-b sbd1• gins a1* **Glon** k* glyc bro1 gran ↓ granit-m es1• *Graph* k* *Guaj* k* guare a1* guat sp1 gymno a1 haem sf1.de haliae-lc ↓ halo ↓ ham a1* **Hell** k* helo k1 helo-s rwt2• *Helon* **Hep** k* hipp hist sp1 *Hydr* k* hydrog srj2• **Hyos** k* hyper *Iber* kr1* ichth bro1 *Ign* k* ignis-alc ↓ iod k2* ip irid-met srj5• iris jug-c a1 juni-v a1 kali-ar kali-bi k* *Kali-br* k* kali-c k* kali-cy a1 kali-i k1* kali-m ↓ kali-n sf1.de **Kali-p** k* kali-s kali-sil k2 kalm kiss ↓ *Kola* ↓ kreos k* *Lac-ac* *Lac-c* k* lac-d lac-e hm2• lac-h ↓ *Lac-lup* ↓ **Lach** k* *Lact* ↓ lap-la ↓ lat-m bnm6• *Laur* k* lavand-a ↓ lec bro1* led k* lil-t k* lim ↓ limest-b es1• linu-c a1 linu-u ↓ lipp a1 lith-c ↓ *Lith-m* ↓ loxo-recl ↓ **Lyc** k* lyss m-arct b2.de* macro a1 mag-c manc mand mg1.de* mang **Med** k* meli k* **Merc** k* *Merc-c* methys jl *Mez* k* mill mit a1 *Moni* rfm1• morph a1 mosch k* *Mur-ac* ↓ murx musca-d szs1 nad rly4• naja *Nat-ar* *Nat-c* k* *Nat-m* k* *Nat-p* nat-sal a1 nat-sil k2 nicotam rly4• nid jl **Nit-ac** k* nitro-o a1 **Nux-m** k* *Nux-v* k* *Oena* a1* okou jl *Olnd* k* onos ptk1 *Op* k* ox-ac k2 ozone sde2• pall ↓ perh ↓ peti a1 *Petr* k* petr-ra shn4• **Ph-ac** k* phenob jl* **Phos** k* phys bg2 *Pic-ac* k* pip-m sf1.de plan **Plat** k* **Plb** k* plut-n ↓ pneu jl podo ↓ polys sk4• pop ↓ positr nl2• prun ↓ psil jl* psor k* ptel *Puls* k* pyrid ↓ ran-s a1 raph a1 rauw jl* rhod k* rhus-g a1 *Rhus-t* k* rob ↓ rosm mtf11 ruta sabad sabin k* sacch-a ↓ sal-al blc1• sal-fr sle1• sanic sapin a1 sarr k* sars ↓ sec k* *Sel* k* seneg **Sep** k* serp a1 *Sil* k* sol-ecl ↓ sol-ni ↓ *Spig* k* spong *Stann* k* *Staph* k* staphycoc rly4• *Stram* k* stront-c k* stry suis-hep rly4• sul-ac k* sulfa jl* *Sulph* k* sumb ↓ symph ↓ *Syph* k* tab a1* taosc iwa1• tarax jl* *Tarent* tax ↓ tela ckh1 tell bg2* tep a1 tetox pin2• thal-xyz srj8• ther ↓ thiop ↓ *Thuj* k* thyr br1* trif-p br1 *Tritic-vg* fd5.de *Tub* k* upa a1 *Urol-h* rwt• v-a-b ↓ valer vanil fd5.de **Verat** k* verat-v verb k* *Viol-o* k* viol-t visc sp1 wildb a1 xero ↓ yuc a1 *Zinc* k* *Zinc-m* a1 *Zinc-p* k2* zinc-pic bro1 zing kr1 zirc-met ↓ [heroin sdj2 mang-met stj2 *Spect* dfg1]
  - **alternating** with | **active** memory (See active - alternating - weakness)
  - **arteriosclerotic** disease; with: plb mrr1
  - **business**, for: agn androc srj1• chel falco-pe nl2• fl-ac hyos kali-c kreos mag-c j phos sabin sel sulph tell tep
  - **children**, in: agar k2* bar-c mtf33 caust mtf33 spong fd4.de
  - **chill**; during: ars bg2 bell bg2 con bg2 hyos bg2 *Rhus-t* b7a.de*
  - **colors**, for: lyc gl1.fr• sil gl1.fr• staph gl1.fr•
  - **congestion** to head; with: chin bg2 *Merc* bg2 *Rhus-t* bg2 *Sulph* bg2
  - **dampness**; from exposure to: calc bg2 **Carb-v** bg2 puls bg2 **Rhus-t** bg2 sil bg2 *Verat* bg2
  - **dates**, for: acon k* *Con* crot-h dulc fd4.de falco-pe nl2• fl-ac haliae-lc srj5• kali-bi kali-br limest-b es1• med k2 merc nad rly4• nat-sil fd3.de• nux-v gl1.fr• petr-ra shn4• podo fd3.de• *Ruta* fd4.de staph gl1.fr• symph fd3.de• syph tritic-vg fd5.de vanil fd5.de [heroin sdj2]
  - **details**, for: cadm-met sp1 falco-pe nl2• nat-sil fd3.de• *Ruta* fd4.de
  - **diabetes**; in: kali-br mtf lyc mtf nux-m mtf nux-v mtf ph-ac mtf
  - **do**; for what was about to: (↗*Forgetful - purchases)* agath-a nl2• agn allox tpw3* bamb-a stb2.de• *Bar-c* k* bell bit-ar wht1• bros-gau mrc1 calc-p calc-s k* cann-s *Carb-ac* k1* carb-an bg2* carbn-s kr1* carc az1.de•

- **do**; for what was about to: ...
Card-m Chel chlam-tr bcx2• choc srj3• cinnb cor-r mrr1 cortico mg1.de* diaz sa3• *Dulc* fd4.de falco-pe nl2• fl-ac germ-met srj5• gran ham fd3.de• hydr hydrog srj2• iod k2 irid-met srj5• jug-c kali-p fd1.de• kali-s k2 kreos *Lac-c* kr1 limest-b es1• manc k* med ptk1 moni rfm1• nat-m h2* nat-sil fd3.de• *Nux-m* k* *Onos* ozone sde2• petr-ra shn4• phos h2 plut-n srj7• podo fd3.de• positr nl2• psil jl *Ruta* fd4.de sacch-a gmj3 sal-fr sle1• spong fd4.de *Sulph* symph fd3.de• [sol-ecl cky1 tax jsj7]
- **done**; for what he just has: absin *Acon* agar aids nl2• allox tpw3* androc srj1• aster *Bar-c* borx bov (non:bufo slp) bufo-s slp calad *Calc-p* camph chel choc srj3• cic ptk1 dream-p sdj1• *Dulc* fd4.de falco-pe nl2• fl-ac granit-m es1• graph *Hyos* irid-met srj5• *Kali-c* gk kali-p fd1.de• kali-s fd4.de lac-c lach laur lavand-a ctl1• limest-b es1• loxo-recl knl4• lyc nat-m ptk1 *Nux-m* k* *Onos* ozone sde2• petr-ra shn4• plut-n srj7• positr nl2• psil ft1 rauw sp1 rhus-t rosm lgb1 *Ruta* fd4.de sabin sanic c1 spong fd4.de symph fd3.de• taosc iwa1• thuj tritic-vg fd5.de vanil fd5.de zinc h2 [plb stj2 tax jsj7]
- **events**; for (See happened)
- **everyday** things, for: agath-a nl2• carc mg1.de* cortico tpw7 dream-p sdj1• dulc fd4.de falco-pe nl2• halo jl irid-met srj5• kali-p fd1.de• nat-sil fd3.de• *Ruta* fd4.de sacch-a gmj3 spong fd4.de symph fd3.de•
- **expressing** oneself, for: (↗*words; Expressing - cannot; Forgetful - words; Thoughts - vanishing - speaking)* acet-ac a1 agar am-c a1 arg-n bamb-a stb2.de• bell k* cann-i sf1.de cann-s k* carb-an h2 carbn-s a1* cimic kr1 *Coca* a1* cocc colch a1* cot a1 crot-h sf1.de dulc k* falco-pe nl2• gad a1 haem a1 hydrog srj2• ign a1 *Kali-br* a1* *Kali-c* k* kali-p sf1.de *Kali-s* fd4.de kiss a1 lac-c lach *Lact* kr1 lap-la rsp1 lil-t a1 *Lyc* morph a1 murx a1* *Nat-m* *Nux-v* k* *Ph-ac* a1* phys a1 **Plb** k* puls k* sep a1 *Spong* fd4.de *Stram* kr1* tab a1 thuj k* vanil fd5.de zinc mtf33
- **faces**; for: syph rb3*
- **facts**, for: (↗*happened)* ail ↓ allox ↓ aza ↓ bell gl1.fr• cael ↓ **Calc** gl1.fr• camph ↓ carb-v ↓ carbn-s ↓ coff ↓ ferr-p c1 graph ↓ hyos ↓ lach ↓ limest-b ↓ lyc ↓ med k2 nat-m ↓ nux-m ↓ nux-v ↓ *Ruta* fd4.de spong fd4.de sulph ↓ symph ↓ tritic-vg fd5.de verat gl1.fr•
  - **past** facts; for: ail k2 bell a1 calc gl1.fr• camph a1 coff ↓ hyos a1 lach a1 limest-b es1• lyc gl1.fr• nux-m k2 sulph a1
    - **old** people, in: coff gl1.fr•
  - **recent** facts, for: allox jl aza jl bell gl1.fr• cael jl calc gl1.fr• carb-v gl1.fr• carbn-s a1 graph k2* hyos gl1.fr• lach ↓ nat-m k2 nux-v gl1.fr• *Ruta* fd4.de sulph gl1.fr• symph fd3.de• tritic-vg fd5.de verat gl1.fr•
    - **old** people, in: lach gl1.fr• sulph gl1.fr•
- **family**; for: limest-b es1• lyss kr1
- **figures** (See numbers)
- **forms**, for: agath-a nl2• ambr gl1.fr• lyc gl1.fr• staph gl1.fr• sulfa jl sulph gl1.fr•
- **friends**; for: limest-b es1• lyss kr1
- **grief**, after: anthraci vh con k2 ign j
- **happened**, for what has: (↗*facts)* absin c1 acet-ac c1* adam ↓ aids nl2• ail k2 allox ↓ androc ↓ anh ↓ borx a1 bufo-s calad k2 carb-ac bg1* *Carb-v* ↓ cic k2 cocc k2 coli ↓ cycl ↓ graph hydr bg1* irid-met ↓ *Lach* limest-b es1• *Med* ↓ *Nat-m* *Nux-m* petr-ra shn4• podo fd3.de• rhus-t *Ruta* fd4.de sacch-a ↓ spong fd4.de sulph syph k2* tritic-vg fd5.de vanil fd5.de [heroin sdj2]
  - **just** happened: absin br1* adam skp7• ail ptk1 allox sp1 androc srj1• anh sp1 carb-ac bg2 *Carb-v* bg2* coli jl2 cycl a1 graph ptk1* hydr bg2 irid-met srj5• *Med* jl2 rhus-t ptk1 *Ruta* fd4.de sacch-a fd2.de• tritic-vg fd5.de
- **head**; with complaints of: caps bg2 carb-v bg2 chin bg2 crot-h bg2 cycl bg2 kreos bg2 mang bg2 mez bg2 nit-ac bg2 rhus-t bg2 sars bg2 sil bg2 stann bg2 sulph bg2
- **headache**, during: bell h1 gels c1 kali-c j mosch j
- **heard**; for what he has: agar ail k2 allox ↓ aq-mar skp7• bros-gau mrc1 calc cann-i carb-ac gk carb-v cypra-eg sde6.de• **Hell** k* hydr gk **Hyos** iber ↓ irid-met srj5• *Kola* stb3• *Lach* lavand-a ctl1• *Med* st mez nat-m *Nux-m* ozone sde2• plat k* podo fd3.de• positr nl2• psor pyrid rly4• sacch-a gmj3 sulph vanil fd5.de
  - **just** heard: allox tpw3* iber jl
- **letters**: (↗*Mistakes - speaking - letters; Mistakes - speaking - sleeplessness; Mistakes - speaking - words - mispronouncing; Mistakes - writing)*
  - **capitals**: med a1
  - **make** several letters; how to: chr-ac kr1
  - **names** of the letters; for the: *Lyc* k*
- **loss** of vital fluids; from: *Chin* bg2 **Nux-v** bg2 *Sulph* bg2
- **mental** exertion; for: (↗*Studying - difficult)* acon aloe asar bar-c kr1* calc ↓ calc-p mtf33 colch ↓ *Con* cycl *Gels* graph-ign k2 laur lyc naja **Nat-c** k* **Nat-m** nux-v ↓ *Ph-ac* *Pic-ac* plat ↓ psil ft1 puls ↓ sel sep *Sil* sol-ni spig spong staph sulph mtf33 ther thuj
  - **child** cannot be taught: *Bar-c* kr1*
  - **fatigue**, from: calc colch gels nat-c nat-m nux-v ph-ac plat puls sep sil
- **music**, for: galeoc-c-h gms1• ign k2 lyc gl1.fr• staph gl1.fr• sulfa jl
  - **piano**; what song he was playing on the: galeoc-c-h gms1•
- **names**: (↗*Mistakes - names)* adam ↓ allox tpw3* alum ↓ anac bg2* bar-act bro1 chinin-s ↓ *Chlor* bg2* cic ↓ cortico tpw7* croc bg2 *Euon* bro1 euon-a ↓ guaj bg2* hep bro1 hist sp1 kali-br ↓ kali-m ↓ lac-h sze9• lim br1 lith-c ↓ lyc bg2* med bg2* merc bg2 nat-sil ↓ olnd bg2 ph-ac ↓ rhus-t bg2 sec ↓ sil mtf33 sulph bro1* syph bro1* valer ↓ xero br1* [bell-p-sp dcm1 *Lith-m* stj2 zirc-met stj2]
  - **friend**; of intimate: adam skp7• med mtf33
  - **members** of family; of the: euon-a br1 ph-ac k2 sec a1
  - **objects**; of: adam skp7• chinin-s ptk1 kali-m ckh1 lith-c ptk1*
  - **own** name; his: (↗*proper; Confusion - identity)* alum cic c1 kali-br *Med* k* nat-sil fd3.de• sulph k* valer
  - **persons**; of (See proper)
- **numbers**: galeoc-c-h gms1• *Med* jl2 petr-ra shn4•
- **objects**; for where he has put: irid-met srj5• *Lac-lup* hrn2• plut-n srj7• tritic-vg fd5.de vanil fd5.de [heroin sdj2]
- **occurrences** of the day, for: acet-ac k2 calad k2 *Carc* gk* cic k2 nat-m nat-sil fd3.de• perh jl *Ph-ac* plb *Rhus-t* spong fd4.de symph fd3.de•
- **orthography**, for: (↗*Mistakes - writing)* con gl1.fr• crot-c gl1.fr• dulc fd4.de hydr gl1.fr• *Lach* gl1.fr• *Lyc* gl1.fr• *Ruta* fd4.de sil gl1.fr• sulph gl1.fr• tab gl1.fr• vanil fd5.de
- **pain**; from: am-c ptk1* anac ptk1 arg-n ptk1* bell ptk1* hep ptk1* laur ptk1* nux-m ptk1* pall ptk1* prun ptk1* puls ptk1*
- **periodical**: carb-v k* chin bg2* cic k2 nat-m k*
- **persons**, for: (↗*Mistakes - persons)* acet-ac agar ail ambr gl1.fr• anac bamb-a stb2.de• bell cedr cham chlor croc *Crot-h* kr1 ham fd3.de• hyos kali-p fd1.de• kali-s fd4.de lyc c1* merc nux-v op ph-ac k2 podo fd3.de• *Ruta* fd4.de staph gl1.fr• stram sulph gl1.fr• syph k2 thuj tritic-vg fd5.de verat [bell-p-sp dcm1]
- **pining** boys; in: aur br1
- **places**, for: (↗*Confusion - loses; Mistakes - localities; Recognizing - not - streets)* allox tpw3* calc gl1.fr• *Crot-h* kr1 dulc fd4.de falco-pe nl2• *Hep* sf1.de kali-p fd1.de• merc nad rly4• nux-m psor *Ruta* fd4.de sil mtf33* **Staph** gl1.fr• sulph gl1.fr• syph k2
- **pollutions**; after: staph bg2
- **proper** names: (↗*names - own)* adam skp7*• allox tpw4* alum gl1.fr• *Anac* k* aur gk *Aur-m-n* wbt2• aur-s wbt2• aza jl bamb-a stb2.de• bell bit-ar wht1• cann-i carl a1 caust gl1.fr• chinin-s chlor k* choc srj3• coli jl2 cortico mg1.de* croc *Crot-h* dulc fd4.de euon br1 ferr-p c1 fl-ac germ-met srj5• glon *Guaj* k* ham fd3.de• hist mg1.de* irid-met srj5• kali-br kali-m ckh1 kali-p c1 kola stb3• lac-e hrn2• lach lim br1 linu-u a1 lith-c *Lyc* *Med* k* merc moni rfm1• musca-d szs1 nat-ar nat-m gl1.fr• nat-sil fd3.de• nux-v gl1.fr• olnd k* ozone sde2• perh jl petr-ra shn4• ph-ac k2 plut-n srj7• positr nl2• ptel puls *Rhus-t* k* sec spig spong fd4.de staph b7a.de* stram *Sulph* k* syph tab gl1.fr• tritic-vg fd5.de urol-h rwt• [pop dhh1 tax jsj7]
- **read**; for what he has: (↗*Thoughts - vanishing - reading)* allox tpw3* ambr anac arn ars-met bell bros-gau mrc1 cann-i carb-ac chlor cocc k2 coff colch corn gard-j vlr2• guaj halo jl ham **Hell** hipp hydr *Hyos* jug-c kali-p fd1.de• lac-c lac-d lac-h htj1• **Lach** lavand-a ↓ *Lyc* *Med* *Merc* nat-c *Nat-m* k* nicotam rly4• *Nux-m* olnd *Onos* *Op* perh jl *Ph-ac* phos psor sacch-a gmj3 sal-fr sle1• **Staph** syph k2* tep tub al* viol-o
  - **just** read: allox tpw3 **Arn** kr1* lavand-a ctl1• *Med* al ph-ac gl1.fr• sal-fr sle1• viol-o kr1

- **recent** events; for (See happened - just)
- **said**; for what he has: adam srj5• aids nl2• ail k2 arg-met sf1.de *Arn* k* *Bar-c* calc a1 calc-sil k2 *Cann-i* carb-an *Carb-v* cench k2 cic k2 colch croc diaz sa3• **Hell** hep **Hyos** kali-n kali-p fd1.de• kali-s fd4.de lach lavand-a ctl1• mag-c j *Med* merc mez k1 *Mur-ac* nat-sil fd3.de• nux-m ozone sde2• plut-n srj7• podo fd3.de• *Psor* k* rhod spong fd4.de stram sulph tep verat [plb stj2]
  - **just** said: calc-sil k2* kali-p fd1.de• nat-sil fd3.de• podo fd3.de•
- **say**; for what he is about to: *(↗Speech - finish; Thoughts - vanishing - speaking)* adam srj5• agath-a nl2• aids nl2• allox tpw4* am-c k* arg-met k2* *Arg-n* *Arn* atro atro-s hr1 **Bar-c** k1* *Cann-i* cann-s carb-an card-m carl a1 colch conch fkr1• cot a1 dulc k2 germ-met srj5• gink-b sbd1• *Granit-m* es1• ham fd3.de• **Hell** k* hydr hyper k* ignis-alc es2• iod k2* kali-p fd1.de• kali-s k2 lil-t *Med* k* merc *Mez* *Nat-m* nat-sil fd3.de• nux-m *Onos* ph-ac k2 plut-n srj7• podo rhod rhus-t bg2* *Ruta* fd4.de sacch-a gmj3 *Staph* gl1.fr• stram *Sulph* taosc iwa1• thuj tritic-vg fd5.de verat [tax jsj7]
- **seen**; for everything what he has: aids nl2• *Anac* kr1
- **sexual** excesses; from: *Agn* bro1 *Anac* bro1 arg-n bro1 aur bro1 chin bro1 nat-m bro1 nux-v bro1 *Ph-ac* bro1 *Staph* bro1
- **streets**; familiar: *(↗Recognizing - not - streets)* cann-i bro1 dulc fd4.de *Glon* bro1 lach bro1 nux-m bro1 *Ruta* fd4.de sal-fr sle1•
- **studying**; young people when (See mental)
- **sudden** and periodical: *Anac* hr1* *Arg-met* vh1 calc bg2 calc-s *Carb-v* k* chin bg1* gels c1 laur st nux-v bg2* syph bg2*
- **sunstroke**; after: *Anac* kr glon kr *Lach* kr
- **thought**, for what he just has: acon agar aids nl2• alum anac bell *Cann-i* *Cocc* colch fl-ac galeoc-c-h gms1• *Hyos* kali-s fd4.de *Med* nat-m nat-sil fd3.de• ozone sde2• ran-s rob *Ruta* fd4.de sacch-a gmj3 staph stram sulph gl1.fr• *Vanil* fd5.de verb
- **time**, for: *(↗Mistakes - time)* bamb-a stb2.de• falco-pe nl2• *Lach* j5.de merc *Ruta* fd4.de *Spong* fd4.de taosc iwa1• *Vanil* fd5.de [tax jsj7]
- **transient**, but perfect consciousness of what he himself said or did: nux-m c1
- **verses**, to learn: nux-v gl1.fr• puls gl1.fr• sulph gl1.fr•
- **vexation** agg.: am-c ptk1
- **words**; for: *(↗expressing; Forgetful - words; Mistakes - speaking - words; Speech - incoherent)* adam mrr1* agar k* agath-a nl2• allox tpw3* alum bg2* *Anac* k* anh mg1.de* arag bro1 *Arg-n* k* *Arn* k* bamb-a stb2.de• **Bar-c** k* bros-gau mrc1 cact calc bg2* calc-p bro1 cann-i k* *Cann-s* j5.de cann-xyz bg2 caps j5.de *Carbn-s* carc fd2.de• cham k* chin bro1 cimic coca bg2 *Cocc* k* coli jl2 con k* crot-h cupr cycl a1 dios bro1 *Dulc* k* falco-pe nl2• gink-b sbd1• ham k* *Hell* helo c1 helo-s rwt2• *Hep* sf1.de hist mg1.de* hydrog srj2• irid-met srj5• *Kali-br* k* *Kali-c* k* *Kali-p* kola stb3• lac-c bro1* *Lach* k* lap-la rsp1 lil-t k* *Lyc* k* lyss med murx j5.de musca-d szs1 *Nat-m* k* nat-sil fd3.de• *Nux-m* bro1 *Nux-v* k* *Op* gl1.fr• ozone sde2• *Ph-ac* k* **Plb** k* podo bg2* psor jl2 **Puls** bg2* rhus-t j5.de sil bg2* staph bg2* sulfa jl *Sulph* k* sumb bro1 symph fd3.de• thiop jl thuj k* tritic-vg fd5.de v-a-b jl2 vanil fd5.de xero bro1 [bell-p-sp dcm1 heroin sdj2 *Spect* dfg1]
- **write**; for what he is about to: *(↗Mistakes - writing; Thoughts - vanishing - writing)* **Cann-i** chr-ac a1 colch *Croc* cypra-eg sde6.de• dirc galeoc-c-h gms1• gink-b sbd1• kali-s fd4.de kola stb3• lach j med st *Nat-m* k* nat-sil fd3.de• *Nux-m* petr-ra shn4• rhod a1 rhus-t
- **written**, for what he has: *(↗Mistakes - writing)* calad cann-i dulc fd4.de gard-j vlr2• nux-m staphycoc rly4•

MEN: *(↗Humankind)*
- **dread** of (See Fear - men; of [=male; Fear - people)

MENDACITY (See Liar)

MENOPAUSE agg.: *(↗FEMALE - Menopause; GENERALS - Menopause)* acon bg2] aml-ns bg2 aqui br1 arg-n bg2 ars bg2 *Cimic* bg2 coff bg2 glon bg2 ign bg2 kali-br bg2 **Lach** bg2 lil-t bg2 puls bg2 sep bg2* tab bg2 ther bg2 valer bg2 verat bg2 zinc bg2

MENSES:
- **about**: ferr bg2
- **absent** agg.: cocc bg2 puls bg2

Menses: ...
- **after**: *(↗Anxiety - menses - after; Anxiety - sleep - menses - after; Concentration - difficult - menses; Confusion - menses - after; Excitement - menses - after; Fear - menses - after; Hysteria - menses - after; Insanity - erotic - menses - after; Irritability - menses - after; Moaning - menses - after; Morose - menses - after; Nymphomania - menses - after; Nymphomania - menses - suppressed; Prostration - menses - after; Remorse - menses; Restlessness - menses - after; Sadness - menses - after; Shrieking - menses - after; Sighing - menses - after; Unconsciousness - menses - after; Weeping - menses - after)* agar bg2 alum bg2 aur bg2 berb bg2 bufo bg2 carb-ac bg2 chin bg2 cupr bg2 ign bg2 nat-m b4.de* phos bg2 *Stram* b7.de* ust bg2
- **before**: *(↗Alcoholism - menses; Anger - menses - before; Anguish - menses - before; Anxiety - menses - before; Awkward - drops - menses; Cheerful - menses - before; Concentration - active - menses - before; Confusion - menses - before; Delirium - menses - before; Despair - menses - before; Discouraged - menses - before; Embraces - menses; Excitement - menses - before; Fear - death - menses - before; Fear - menses - before; Frightened - menses - before; Frightened - trifles - menses; Hysteria - menses - before; Indifference - menses - before; Industrious - menses; Industrious - menses - before; Irritability - menses - before; Kill; desire - menses - before; Kissing - menses - before; Laughing - menses - before; Loathing - life - menses - before; Mania - menses - before; Morose - menses - before; Nymphomania - menses - before; Prostration - menses - before; Restlessness - menses - before; Sadness - menses - before; Sensitive - menses - before; Sensitive - music - menses; Sentimental - menses - before; Shrieking - menses - before; Shrieking - sleep - menses - before; Sighing - menses - before; Speech - delirious - menses; Starting - menses - before; Starting - sleep - from - menses - before; Suicidal - menses - before; Thoughts - vanishing - menses; Unconsciousness - menses - before; Weary - menses - before; Weeping - menses - before)* **Acon** bg2 agar bg2 am-c b4.de* anthraci vh aur bg2 *Aur-m-n* wbt2• bar-c bg2 bell bg2 berb bg2 borx bg2 brom bg2 cact bg2 calc b4.de* carb-an bg2 caust b4.de* *Cham* bg2* cimic bg2 cinnb bg2 cocc bg2 coloc bg2 *Con* b4.de* croc bg2 cupr bg2 cycl bg2 elaps mrr1 ferr bg2* fl-ac bg2 gels bg2 graph bg2* hyos b7.de* ign bg2 kali-bi bg2 kali-c b4.de* *Kreos* bg2* lac-c bg2 lach bg2* lil-t mrr1 luna kg1• **Lyc** b4.de* mag-c bg2 mag-m b4.de* mang b4.de* merc bg2 mosch bg2 murx bg2 **Nat-m** b4.de* nit-ac bg2* nux-m bg2 **Nux-v** bg2 *Phos* bg2 plat bg2 **Puls** bg2* sec bg2 sep b4.de* *Stann* b4.de* stram bg2 sulph bg2 tarent bg2 thuj bg2 verat b7.de* zinc bg2 [heroin sdj2]
  - **amel.**: cimic ptk1
- **during**: *(↗beginning; Absentminded - menses; Absorbed - menses; Ailments - fright - menses; Anger - menses - during; Anguish - menses - during; Anxiety - menses - during; Cheerful - menses - during; Company - aversion - menses; Company - desire - menses; Confusion - menses - during; Death - desires - menses; Delirium - menses - during; Delirium - menses - during - menstrual; Discontented - menses; Dullness - menses; Dullness - menses - during; Ennui - menses; Excitement - feverish - menses; Excitement - menses - during; Fear - death - menses - during; Fear - menses - during; Fear - menses - during - menstrual; Forgetful - menses; Hypochondriasis - menses - during; Hysteria - menses - during; Ideas - deficiency - menses; Insanity - menses - during; Irritability - menses - during; Kill; desire - husband - menses; Kill; desire - menses - during; Lamenting - menses; Laughing - menses - during; Loquacity - menses - during; Moaning - menses - during; Morose - menses - during; Nymphomania - menses - during; Praying - menses; Prostration - menses - during; Quarrelsome - menses - during; Quiet disposition - menses; Rage - menses - during; Reserved - menses; Restlessness - menses - during; Sadness - menses - during; Sensitive - menses - during; Sensitive - noise - menses; Shrieking - menses - during; Sighing - menses - during; Starting - menses - during; Starting - night - menses; Starting - sleep - from - menses - during; Stupefaction - menses; Stupor - menses - during; Suicidal - menses - during; Taciturn - menses; Thoughts - wandering - menses; Unconsciousness - menses - during; Violent - contradiction - menses; Weary - menses - during; Weeping - menses - during)* **Acon** b7.de* agar bg2 aloe bg2 alum bg2 *Am-c* b4.de* ant-t bg2 ars bg2 asar bg2 aur bg2 *Bell* b4.de* berb bg2 borx bg2 brom bg2 bry bg2 cact bg2 calc b4.de* canth bg2 carb-an bg2 caul bg2 *Caust* bg2 *Cham* b7.de* chel bg2 chin bg2 cic bg2 *Cimic* bg2* cinnb bg2 *Cocc* bg2 *Coff* b7.de* coloc bg2 con bg2 croc bg2 cupr bg2 cycl bg2 elaps bg2 ferr ↓ gels bg2 glon bg2 *Graph* b4.de* hell bg2 hydr-ac bg2

- **during**: ...
Hyos b7.de* **Ign** bg2 ip bg2 kali-c bg2 kali-i bg2 *Lac-c* bg2 lach j* lob bg2 *Lyc* b4.de* mag-c bg2 mag-m b4.de* mang bg2 merc bg2 mosch bg2 mur-ac b4.de* nat-c bg2 *Nat-m* b4.de* nit-ac j* *Nux-m* bg2 *Nux-v* bg2 ol-an bg2 petr bg2 phos bg2 plat bg2* plb bg2 puls j* rhod bg2 rhus-t bg2 sars bg2 sec bg2 senec bg2 *Sep* b4.de* *Sil* bg2 stann bg2* **Stram** b7.de* sul-ac bg2 sulph bg2 tab bg2 tarent bg2 thuj bg2 *Verat* b7.de* zinc bg2
  - **beginning** of menses; at: *(↗during)* acon b7.de* brom bg2 cham b7.de* cocc bg2 con bg2 ferr bg2 graph bg2 lyc b4.de* mag-m bg2 *Nat-m* b4.de*
  - **copious** flow amel.: cycl k2
- **suppressed** menses; after: *Ferr* b7.de* nux-m bg2 plat ptk1 puls b7a.de sulph b4a.de

MENTAL DETERIORATION (See Idiocy; Imbecility)

MENTAL EXERTION:

- **agg.**: *(↗Ailments - Mental exertion; Anxiety - Mental; Dullness; Ennui; Fear - Exertion - of; Laziness; Laziness - Postponing; Prostration; Sensitive - Mental exertion; Will - Weakness - mental; VERTIGO - Mental; VERTIGO - Mental - Agg.)* abies-n ↓ abrom-a ks5 abrot k* achy jl3 *Acon* ↓ *Act-sp* vh1 *Agar* k* agn b2.de* *Aloe* k* *Alum* ↓ alum-p k2 alum-sil k2 am-c k* ambr k* aml-ns bro1 ammc ↓ *Anac* k* androc ↓ ang k* anh ↓ apoc ↓ arag ↓ *Aran-ix* mg1.de **Arg-met** k* **Arg-n** k* arn k* ars k* ars-i k* ars-met c1 ars-s-f ↓ asaf j5.de asar k* astra-e ↓ atra-r skp7• **Aur** k* aur-ar k2 *Aur-i* k2 aur-m st1 aur-s k2 aven sf1.de bacls-7 fmm1• bamb-a ↓ *Bapt* ↓ bar-act sf1.de bar-c k2 bell k* berb j5.de bit-ar wht1• borx k* brom ↓ buth-a ↓ cadm-met mg1.de* calad k* **Calc** k* *Calc-ar* k2* calc-caust sf1.de calc-f jl3 calc-i k2 **Calc-p** k* calc-sil k2 camph ↓ *Cann-s* b7a.de *Canth* ↓ caps c1 *Carb-ac* *Carb-v* k* *Caust* cere-s ↓ cham k* chel ↓ *Chin* k* chinin-s ↓ chir-fl gya2 cimic bg2* cina k* cist coca a1* *Cocc* k* coff k* *Colch* k* *Con* k* cop ↓ cortiso mg1.de* crot-h bg2 *Cupr* k* *Cupr-act* c1 cycl ↓ dendr-pol sk4• dig k* dirc ↓ dulc fd4.de echi bg2 *Epig* sf1.de equis-h ↓ fago ↓ *Ferr* ↓ ferr-pic sf1.de fl-ac bg2* form ↓ *Gels* k* germ-met ↓ gins ↓ *Glon* k2* *Graph* b4a.de* grat ↓ gymno ↓ haem ↓ halo jl3 ham ↓ hell k* *Hep* bg2 hipp ↓ hydr ↓ *Hydr-ac* ↓ **Hyos** bg2* hypoth ↓ **Ign** k* ind ↓ iod k* iris bg2* kali-ar k* *Kali-br* kali-c k* **Kali-p** k* kali-s kali-sil k2 kalm ↓ kiss ↓ kreos ↓ **Lach** k* lact ↓ lact-v ↓ laur k* **Lec** k* led b7.de* lil-t k2 limen-b-c ↓ luf-op rsj5• **Lyc** k* lyss ↓ m-ambo b2.de* m-arct b2.de m-aust b2.de* mag-c k* mag-m k* mag-p c1* mand rsj7• mang k* med meli ↓ meny k* meph bg2 merc ↓ mez ↓ moni rfm1• morph ↓ *Naja* bg2* *Nat-ar* **Nat-c** k* **Nat-m** k* nat-p k2* *Nat-s* k* *Nat-sil* k2* nauf-helv-li elm2• *Nit-ac* k* *Nux-m* k* **Nux-v** k* *Olnd* k* *Op* k* par k* *Petr* k* *Ph-ac* k* *Phos* k* **Pic-ac** k* pip-m sf1.de plan plat k* plb k2 *Psor* k* ptel c1 *Puls* k* ran-b k* rauw sp1 rhus-t k2* ruta fd4.de *Sabad* k* sabal ptk2 *Sars* j5.de scut c1 **Sel** k* **Sep** k* sieg ↓ **Sil** k* sol-mm ↓ spig b7.de* spong b7.de* squil c1 stann k* **Staph** k* *Stram* bg2 sul-i k2 sulfonam jl3 *Sulph* k* *Sumb* ↓ tab ↓ tarax k* tarent ↓ tell ↓ *Ter* ↓ thal ↓ *Thuj* ↓ thymol bro1 **Tub** k13* tub-m vs* v-a-b jl vanil fd5.de verat h1* verb bg2 vib ↓ vinc c1 vip visc ↓ zinc k* zinc-p k2
  - **crazy**; seems to drive him (See impossible - crazy)
  - **fatigues**: *(↗GENERALS - Lassitude - Mental; GENERALS - Lassitude - Mental - agg.; GENERALS - Weariness - Mental)* abrot kr1 achy kr1* *Acon* kr1 **Aur** kr1 cocc kr1 coff kr1* **Con** kr1 dulc fd4.de *Graph* kr1 hypoth kr1* *Ign* kr1 *Kali-p* fd1.de* *Kali-s* fd4.de lach kr1* limen-b-c hrn2• lyc kr1* **Nat-c** kr1* *Nux-v* kr1* *Pic-ac* kr1* ruta fd4.de *Sel* kr1 sil kr1* staph kr1* sulph kr1* v-a-b kr1* vanil fd5.de
  - **impossible**: *(↗Dullness - thinking - long; Studying - difficult)* abies-n kr1 abrot kr1 acon j5.de* agar j5.de agn j5.de* *Alum* j5.de* am-c j5.de *Ambr* j5.de* ammc a1 *Anac* j5.de* androc srj1• anh mg1.de* apoc sf1.de arag bro1 *Arg-met* kr1* arn j5.de* ars j5.de* ars-s-f ↓ asar astra-e jl aur j5.de* bamb-a stb2.de• *Bapt* a1* bar-c k2 berb k2* borx j5.de* brom sf1.de buth-a mg1.de cadm-met mg1.de calad k2 *Calc* calc-ar k2 camph gl1.fr• *Canth* kr1 caps j5.de carb-ac sf1.de *Carb-v* j5.de* caust k2* cere-s a1 chel k2 chin k2 chinin-s cocc k2 coff j5.de *Con* sf1.de* cop crot-h j5.de* cycl dig dirc a1 dulc sf1.de equis-h a1 fago ↓ *Ferr* form ↓ *Gels* k* germ-met srj5• gins sf1.de glon graph j5.de* grat sf1.de gymno haem sf1.de ham *Hell* j5.de* hep gl1.fr• hipp a1 hydr j5.de *Hydr-ac* j5.de* hyos ign j5.de* ind ↓ *Kali-br* sf1.de *Kali-p* mrr1 kalm kiss a1 kreos kr1 *Lach* j5.de* lact j5.de lact-v a1 laur j5.de lil-t a1* limen-b-c ↓ lyc lyss kr1 m-arct j5.de mag-c mg1.de mag-m j5.de* mag-p sf1.de mang k2 *Med* meli k1 merc sf1.de* mez j5.de morph naja a1 nat-ar a1 **Nat-c** *Nat-m* j5.de* nat-p k2 nat-s nit-ac j5.de *Nux-v* k1* olnd j5.de* op j5.de *Petr* j5.de* *Ph-ac* h2* *Phos* k* pic-ac k* psor al2 ptel *Rhus-t* k2* sabad sf1.de sars h2* sel j5.de* sep h2* sieg mg1.de *Sil* sf1.de sol-mm j5.de *Spig* a1 spong j5.de stann j5.de *Staph* kr1* *Sumb* tab sf1.de tarent mtf33 tell jl *Ter* sf1.de thal jl *Thuj* kr1* verat j5.de* vib visc jl *Zinc* j5.de*
    - **morning**: agar sf1.de *Ph-ac* kr1
    - **afternoon**: fago a1 hyos a1 sil gl1.fr•
    - **evening**: *Ign* kr1
    - **night**: form a1
    - **air**, in open: nat-ar a1
    - **burning** in right lumbar region; from: nit-ac h2
    - **continuous** active work is: agar k2 arn br1
    - **crazy**; owing to the impotence of his mind seems to drive him: *(↗Insanity - mental)* ind *Kali-p* limen-b-c hrn2• med
    - **eating**, after: ars-s-f k2
    - **exertion**, after: dulc fd4.de nat-m h2
    - **headache**, during: ammc vh1 sep h2
    - **interruption**, by least: berb kr1
    - **old** people; in: *(↗Dementia - senilis)* *Ambr* kr1
    - **sexual** excesses, after: ph-ac sf1.de pic-ac sf1.de *Sel* sf1.de
    - **siesta**, after: graph h2*
  - **puberty**; agg. from mental exertion in: calc-p st kali-p st
- **amel.**: *(↗Activity - desires; Industrious; GENERALS - Activity - amel.)* aesc vh1 bamb-a stb2.de• calc calc-p bg2 croc k* *Ferr* k* gels ptk1 helo ptk1 *Helon* *Nat-c* k* nat-m sf1.de nat-sil fd3.de• rauw sp1 vanil fd5.de *Verat* gl1.fr• zinc sf1.de
- **aversion** to: *(↗Ailments - mental exertion; Dullness; Ennui; Laziness; Loathing - work; Thinking - aversion)* acet-ac **Acon** k1 act-sp vh1 adam skp7• aesc agar k* alf bro1 **Aloe** k* alum k* alum-p k2 alum-sil k2* alumn am-c j am-m h2 anac k* ant-c a1 anth a1 arag bro1 arg-n bg ars j asaf a1 atro *Aur* aur-ar k2 aur-i k2 aur-m k* aur-s k2 **Bapt** k* bar-c k* bar-s k2 bell berb sf1.de *Borx* sf1.de brom bry k2 bufo a1 bufo-s buth-a mg1.de* cadm-s cain calc k* calc-p calc-s calc-sil k2 cann-i *Caps* bro1 *Carb-ac* k* carb-an carb-v carbn-s a1 *Carl* caust bro1* cham **Chel** **Chin** k* *Chinin-ar* chinin-s cic a1 cinnb clem cob k* coca bro1 cocc j *Colch* coloc con k* corn croc a1 crot-h j crot-t a1 cycl k* dam a1 dig a1 dros h1 dulc echi euon j fago *Ferr* ferr-p *Form* sf1.de galeoc-c-h gms1• *Gels* k* germ-met srj5• get ↓ glon bro1 graph k2* grat *Ham* hell bro1 helo-s c1 hep hipp hir rsj4• hura a1 hydr hydrog ↓ hyos hyper ign j ind indol bro1 *Iod* a1* ip irid-met srj5• jug-r a1 *Kali-bi* kali-c h2 *Kali-i* st kali-n kali-p bro1* kali-s kali-sil k2 kalm kola stb3• lac-d lac-h htj1• lac-leo hrn2• *Lach* **Lec** k* *Lil-t* limen-b-c mlk9.de lyc k* mag-c j mag-m mag-p k* mag-s a1 med meph merl mill a1 mur-ac nat-ar nat-c c1* *Nat-m* *Nat-n* br1* nat-p k2 nat-sil fd3.de• nicc-s bro1 *Nit-ac* k* **Nux-v** k* olnd op osm a1 ox-ac sf1.de oxyg a1 oxyt bro1 ozone sde2• pall par petr petr-ra shn4• *Ph-ac* k* **Phos** k* *Phyt* *Pic-ac* k* plan plat k* plb podo fd3.de• polys sk4• ptel *Puls* k* ran-s raph rham-cal bro1 *Rhus-t* rhus-v a1 rumx sacch-a fd2.de• sanic sapin a1 sapo a1 sars a1 scut sec a1 sel bro1 *Sep* k* *Sil* k* sol-ni spig spong j5.de squil stann k2 staph k* stry-p br1* sulfonam j1* *Sulph* tab a1 tanac bro1 teucr thea ther a1 *Thuj* thymol bro1 **Thyr** vh* tub k* tung-met bdx1• upa c1* valer vanil fd5.de verb a1 viol-o viol-t yuc a1 zinc h2* zinc-p k2 [bell-p-sp dcm1]
  - **morning**: hydrog srj2• kali-n h2
  - **forenoon**: fago ↓ get a1
    - **11 h**: fago a1
  - **afternoon**: hyos nat-ar a1
  - **literary** work: calc gl1.fr• ign gl1.fr• ip a1 lyc gl1.fr• *Nux-v* a1 puls gl1.fr• *Rhus-t* a1 sulph gl1.fr•
  - **widows**, in: con k2
- **desire** for: *(↗Agility; Desires - full - more; Ideas - abundant; Industrious; Playing - desire - scrabble)* acon a1 acon-f a1 agam-g mlk9.de aloe ang a1 anth apis ckh1 arn aur k* aur-s k2 bad k* **Bell** a1 *Brom* k* carb-ac k* carbn-o a1 carbn-s a1 carc mlr1• chin chlor a1 choc srj3• cic ↓ clem k* cob k* coca coff a1 cortico ↓ cypra-eg ↓ dig j dream-p sdj1• eaux a1 eucal a1 eug a1 fago ↓ flor-p jl form a1 galeoc-c-h gms1• gels k* graph ↓ ham a1 hydrog ↓ hyos a1 hyper a1 iber a1 irid-met srj5• kali-s k2 lac-h sk4• lac-leo ↓ lach a1* laur led a1 lyc a1 lycps-v ↓ m-arct j manc a1 morph a1 naja k* nat-ar k2 nat-m gl1.fr• nat-p a1 nat-s a1 nept-m lsd2.fr nitro-o a1 nux-v ckh1 op a1 opun-s a1 (non:opun-v a1) ozone sde2• ped a1 penic jl phos a1* *Phys* a1 pip-m sf1.de plb a1 polys sk4• puls ↓ querc-r svu1• raph a1 reser jl rhus-g ↓ rhus-r slp (non:rhus-t slp) ruta fd4.de sarr ↓ seneg sil a1 sin-n ↓ spig a1 spong fd4.de stry a1 sulph sumb a1 **Tarent** k* ther thiop ↓ tub jl2 ulm-c ↓ valer ckh1 **Verat** j* viol-o a1 zing a1
  - **morning**: acon gl1.fr•

- **desire** for: ...
  - **evening**: cic graph k2 hydrog srj2• irid-met srj5• lac-leo hrn2• *Lach* lycps-v a1* nat-p a1 puls rhus-t a1
  - **night**: **Coff**↓ cortico↓ dig a1 fago↓ gels↓ graph↓ ham fd3.de• hydrog srj2• *Lach* a1* lycps-v↓ nitro-o a1 sin-n a1 thiop↓ ulm-c↓
    - **midnight**:
      - **after**:
        - **1** h: gels a1 ulm-c jsj8•
        - **2** h; until: thiop jl
        - **4** h; after: cortico jl
        - **5** h: fago a1 lycps-v a1
      - **until**: **Coff** a1 graph k2
  - **alternating** with:
    - **dullness**: acon gl1.fr• irid-met srj5•
    - **indifference**: sarr a1
    - **indolence** (See laziness)
    - **laziness**: *Aloe* a1 lac-h sk4•
    - **weakness**: *Aloe* a1
  - **fatigue**; during: rhus-g tmo3•
  - **literary** work: sulph a1
  - **routinizing** work: cypra-eg sde6.de•
- ○ **Respiration**; with complaints of: acon bg2 *Bell* bg2 **Cocc** bg2 **Cupr** bg2 *Merc* bg2 *Nux-v* bg2 phos bg2 **Puls** bg2 sep bg2 sulph bg2
- **mouth**; with complaints of: nit-ac bg2
- **wine** for mental exertion; needs: *(↗Agility; Ideas - abundant; Prostration)* hep gl1.fr•

MENTAL OVERSTIMULATION (See Concentration - active; Ideas - abundant; Mental exertion - desire; Mental exertion - wine; Thoughts - rapid; Thoughts - rush)

MENTAL POWER:
- **increased**: *(↗Agility; Clarity; Ideas - abundant)* adam srj5• agath-a nl2• aids nl2• anag a1 ang bg2 anh sp1 ars a1 *Bapt-c* c1 bit-ar wht1• camph a1 cann-i a1 clem a1 cod a1 dig a1 dulc fd4.de eaux a1 ferr a1 gard-j vlr2• ham fd3.de• hyos bg2 hyper st kali-p fd1.de• kali-s fd4.de lac-h sk4• lach bg2* lyss mrr1 nep mg1.de* olib-sac wmh1 op a1* ozone sde2• pip-m a1 polys sk4• positr nl2• querc-r svu1• sal-al blc1• symph fd3.de• thea a1 thuj a1 tritic-vg fd5.de vanil br1 verat a1 visc sp1 [tax jsj7 temp elm1]
  - **alternating** with | **sadness** and weeping: ozone sde2•
  - **followed** by | **weakness**; physical: olib-sac wmh1
  - **sharp** and alert: aids nl2•
- **loss** of: *(↗Prostration)* anac ptk2 arg-met ptk2 carp-b mtf11 olnd ptk2

MENTAL SYMPTOMS: **Abrot**↓ *Acon* b2.de* agar b2.de* agn b2.de* alum b2.de* am-c b2.de* am-m b2.de* ambr b2.de* **Anac** b2.de* ang b2.de* ant-c b2.de* ant-t b2.de* antip c2 *Apis*↓ *Arg-met*↓ arg-n↓ arn b2.de* **Ars** b2.de* asaf b2.de* asar b2.de* astra-e↓ **Aur** b2.de* bapt ptk1 bar-c b2.de* bar-m↓ **Bell** b2.de* bism b2.de* borx b2.de* bov b2.de* bry b2.de* calad b2.de* *Calc* b2.de* camph b2.de* cann-s b2.de* cann-xyz ptk1 canth b2.de* caps b2.de* carb-an b2.de* carb-v b2.de* carc↓ *Caust* b2.de* cere-b↓ *Cham* b2.de* chel b2.de* chin b2.de* cic b2.de* *Cimic*↓ cina b2.de* clem b2.de* *Cocc* b2.de* coff b2.de* colch b2.de* coloc b2.de* *Con* b2.de* croc b2.de* cupr b2.de* cycl b2.de* dig b2.de* *Dios* c2 diosm br1 dros b2.de* dulc b2.de* elat↓ euon-a br1 euph b2.de* euphr b2.de* ferr b2.de* gink-b↓ *Graph* b2.de* guaj b2.de* hell b2.de* hep b2.de* hippoc-k↓ **Hyos** b2.de* hyper c2 **Ign** b2.de* iod b2.de* ip b2.de* kali-c b2.de* kali-n b2.de* kreos b2.de* **Lach** b2.de* laur b2.de* led b2.de* lil-t ptk1 **Lyc** b2.de* m-ambo b2.de m-arct b2.de m-aust b2.de mag-c b2.de* mag-m b2.de* mand↓ mang b2.de* meny b2.de* *Merc* b2.de* mez b2.de* mosch b2.de* mur-ac b2.de* *Murx*↓ **Nat-c** b2.de* *Nat-m* b2.de* *Nat-s*↓ nit-ac b2.de* nux-m b2.de* *Nux-v* b2.de* olnd b2.de* *Op* b2.de* par b2.de* petr b2.de* ph-ac b2.de* **Phos** b2.de* plat b2.de* plb b2.de* **Puls** b2.de* ran-b b2.de* ran-s b2.de* rheum b2.de* rhod b2.de* rhus-g↓ rhus-t b2.de* ruta b2.de* sabad b2.de* sabin b2.de* samb b2.de* sars b2.de* sec b2.de* sel b2.de* seneg b2.de* *Sep* b2.de* *Sil* b2.de* spig b2.de* spong b2.de* squil b2.de* stann b2.de* staph b2.de* **Stram** b2.de* stront-c b2.de* sul-ac b2.de* *Sulph* b2.de* tarax b2.de* teucr b2.de* thuj b2.de* toxo-g jl2 tub↓ valer b2.de* **Vanil**↓ **Verat** b2.de* verb b2.de* viol-o b2.de* viol-t b2.de* zinc b2.de* [bell-p-sp dcm1]
- **daytime** | **amel.**: alum br1
- **afternoon** | **15**-18 h: rhus-g tmo3•

Mental symptoms: ...
- **accompanied** by:
  - ○ **Ear**; noises in: puls bg2
  - **Epigastrium**; pain in: calc bg2 cham bg2 cupr bg2
  - **Eyes**; pain in the: agar bg2
  - **Face**:
    - **heat**: acon bg2 arg-n bg2 bell bg2 carb-v bg2 graph bg2 merc bg2
    - **pale**: puls bg2
    - **perspiration**: ars bg2 cic bg2 mur-ac bg2 nat-c bg2
    - **red**: acon bg2 sep bg2
  - **faintness**: ars bg2 cic bg2 ign bg2 mag-m bg2 nit-ac bg2 op bg2 ran-b bg2
  - ○ **Feet**; cold: graph bg2
  - **physical** symptoms: **Acon** b2.de agar b2.de alum b2.de am-c b2.de am-m b2.de ambr b2.de anac b2.de ant-c b2.de ant-t b2.de *Arg-met* b2.de arn b2.de *Ars* b2.de asaf b2.de aur b2.de bar-c b2.de *Bell* b2.de bov b2.de bry b2.de calad b2.de **Calc** b2.de* camph b2.de canth b2.de carb-an b2.de carb-v b2.de caust b2.de *Cham* b2.de chel b2.de chin b2.de cic b2.de cina b2.de cocc b2.de coff b2.de coloc b2.de con b2.de croc b2.de cupr b2.de dig b2.de dulc b2.de ferr b2.de graph b2.de hell b2.de hep b2.de hyos b2.de ign b2.de iod b2.de ip b2.de kali-c b2.de kali-n b2.de *Lach* b2.de *Laur* b2.de led b2.de lyc b2.de mag-c b2.de mag-m b2.de *Merc* b2.de mez b2.de *Mosch* b2.de nat-c b2.de nat-m b2.de nit-ac b2.de nux-m b2.de **Nux-v** b2.de olnd b2.de op b2.de par b2.de petr b2.de ph-ac b2.de **Phos** b2.de plat b2.de plb b2.de **Puls** b2.de ran-s b2.de rhod b2.de rhus-t b2.de ruta b2.de sabad b2.de sabin b2.de sars b2.de sec b2.de sel b2.de seneg b2.de sep b2.de sil b2.de spig b2.de spong b2.de squil b2.de stann b2.de staph b2.de **Stram** b2.de stront-c b2.de sulph b2.de *Verat* b2.de verb b2.de zinc b2.de
  - ○ **Pupils**; small: cocc bg2
  - **Stomach**; complaints of: agar bg2 alum bg2 am-m bg2 ars bg2 bar-m bg2 calc bg2 cupr bg2 nit-ac bg2 nux-v bg2 phos bg2 puls bg2
  - **weakness**: acon bg2 agn bg2 alum bg2 am-c bg2 ang bg2 ars bg2 aur bg2 borx bg2 calc bg2 carb-an bg2 carb-v bg2 caust bg2 cic bg2 ign bg2 kali-n bg2 mag-c bg2 op bg2 phos bg2 rhus-t bg2 sil bg2 verat bg2
- **acute** mental symptoms: *Coff* ptk1 mand↓ *Op* ptk1 ph-ac tl1 *Ruta*↓ sil↓ **Vanil**↓
  - **weakness**; with physical: mand c1 *Ruta* fd4.de sil ptk1 **Vanil** fd*
- **alternating** with:
  - **insanity** (See Insanity - alternating - mental)
  - **leukorrhea**: murx k*
  - **mental** symptoms; other: *(↗Mood - alternating)* alum mtf aur mtf *Bell* mtf con mtf croc mtf ferr mtf hippoc-k szs2 **Ign** mtf **Mosch** mtf *Plat* mtf sabad b7a.de stram b7a.de* sul-ac mtf valer mtf *Verat* mtf zinc mtf
  - **physical** symptoms: *(↗Insanity - alternating - physical; Sadness - alternating - lungs; GENERALS - Alternating)* **Abrot** vh* agar mrr2* alum st* *Arn* k* astra-e jl aur vh* bell vh* carc gk* cere-b c1 *Cimic* k* con vh* *Croc* bg2* ferr vh* gink-b sbd1• hippoc-k szs2 hyos gb• **Ign** bg3* lach c1 *Lil-t* k* *Murx* ptk1* *Nux-m* ckh1 **Plat** b4a.de* *Rheum* b7a.de stram ckh1 *Sul-ac* ckh1 tub k2* *Valer* ckh1 *Verat* ckh1 zinc ckh1
  - ○ **Heart**; complaints of: lil-t ptk1
  - **Uterus**; complaints of: arn ptk1 lil-t ptk1
- **moon** phases agg.: bell mtf
- **dementia**; during: con bg2
- **followed** by | **physical** symptoms: nat-m bg2
- **injuries** to head; from: *Nat-s* br1
- **leukorrhea**; with: murx bro1
- **limbs**; with trembling of: plat k2
- **malaria**; from suppressed: elat br1
- **menses**; from suppressed: plat br1
- **milk**; with increased flow of: bell bg2 stram bg2
- **nervous**: diosm br1
- **pregnancy**; during: acon bg2 *Bell* bg2 cupr bg2 lach bg2 merc bg2 plat bg2 **Puls** bg2 stram bg2 verat bg2
- **voice**; with complaints of: staph bg2
- **women**; in: *Apis* b7a.de

MENTAL WORK (See Mental exertion)

MENTALLY drained (See Prostration)

MERCURY; complaints after abuse of: *Nit-ac* b4a.de

MERGING OF SELF with one's environment: *(↗Confusion - identity; Confusion - identity - boundaries; Delusions - body - out; Depersonalization; Unification - sensation - universe)* *Anh* mg1.de* cann-i mtf carc mtf hydrog srj2• lac-c mtf lac-mat mtf stram mtf

MERRY (See Cheerful)

MESMERIZED; being (See Magnetized)

MESMERIZING others (See Magnetizing)

METICULOUS (See Conscientious)

MILDNESS: *(↗Affectionate; Anxiety - others; Benevolence; Polite - too; Quarrelling - aversion; Quiet disposition; Sympathetic; Tranquillity; Yielding)* abies-c oss4• *Acon* aids nl2• aln c1 alum hr1* ambr k* amph a1 anac k* ant-c mrr1 anthraci vh1 arb-m oss1• **Arn** k* **Ars** k* *Ars-i* asar k* aur k* *Aur-m-n* wbt2• bell **Borx** k* bov k* *Cact* *Calad* k* *Calc* k* calc-sil k2* calen oss• *Cann-i* caps k* carb-an k* *Carc* gg* carl km• castm j5.de caust k* cedr chel chim-m hr1* chin bg cic k* *Cina* clem k* **Cocc** k* coff mrr1 coli rly4• colum-p sze2• cor-r kkb *Croc* k* *Cupr* k* cycl cypra-eg sde6.de• dream-p sdj1• euph k* euphr k* falco-pe nl2• fuma-ac rly4• ham fd3.de• hell k* hydr j5.de hypoth jl3 *Ign* k* *Indg* k* iod k* kali-c k* kali-cy a1 kali-p lac-ac ↓ lac-c st laur j5.de *Lil-t* limen-b-c hrn2• loxo-lae bnm12• *Lyc* k* *M-arct* b2.de* mag-m b2.de* manc a1 mang k* mosch k* mur-ac k* murx bro1 naja mrr1 nat-ar nat-c k* **Nat-m** k* *Nit-ac* *Nux-v* b7.de* op k* ph-ac k* *Phos* k* plb k* podo fd3.de• positr nl2• propl ub1• **Puls** k* **Rhus-t** k* sal-ac c1 *Sep* k* **Sil** k* *Spong* stann k* staph bg* *Stram* k* *Sulph* k* sumb a1 symph fd3.de• tax-br oss1• *Thuj* k* tub lp* urol-h ↓ vanad dx *Verat* k* viol-o zinc k* [cupr-act stj2 cupr-f stj2 cupr-m stj2 cupr-p stj2 kali-s stj1 mang-met stj2 nicc stj1 sol-ecl cky1 tax jsj7 zirc-met stj2]

- **evening**: croc a1
- **alternating** with:
  - **anger** (See Anger - alternating - mildness)
  - **destructiveness** (See Destructiveness - alternating - mildness)
  - **hardness** (See Hardhearted - alternating - mildness)
  - **maliciousness** (See Malicious - alternating - mildness)
  - **obstinacy** (See Obstinate - alternating - mildness)
  - **violence** (See Violent - alternating - mildness)
- **children**; in: aur mtf33 borx mtf33 carc mtf33 cupr mtf33 lac-ac stj5• lyc mtf33 mag-m mtf33 nat-m mtf33 phos mtf33 puls mtf33 sep mtf33 sil mtf33 staph mtf33 stram mtf33 thuj mtf33
- **complaining**; bears suffering, even outrage without: *(↗Well - says - sick)* *Ign* kr1
- **convulsions**; between: cic tl1
- **epileptic** convulsions; after: *Indg* hr1*
- **masking** violence: *(↗Ailments - anger - suppressed)* stram mtf
- **waking**; on: urol-h rwt•

MIRTH: *(↗Amusement - desire; Charming; Cheerful; Content; Eccentricity; Excitement; Exhilaration; High-spirited; Jesting; Mood - agreeable; Playful; Vivacious; Witty)* acon aeth *Agar* k* aloe alum am-c *Anac* anag anan ang ant-t apis arg-met arn ars ars-i arund asaf asar asc-t aster ↓ *Aur* bar-c *Bell* *Borx* ↓ brom bufo-s ↓ *Calc* calc-s camph **Cann-i** cann-s caps carb-an carb-v *Carbn-s* castm ↓ caust cham chel ↓ chin chin-b ↓ chinin-s chlor cic cimic cit-v ↓ clem cob coc-c cocc **Coff** con *Croc* cupr cycl dendr-pol ↓ dros dulc fd4.de eupi falco-pe nl2• *Ferr* ferr-ar ferr-i ferr-p *Fl-ac* form gamb gels graph haliae-lc ↓ ham fd3.de• hell ↓ **Hyos** k* ign iod ip jab ↓ kali-c kali-p kola stb3• kreos **Lach** lachn laur led limest-b ↓ *Lyc* m-arct ↓ mag-c mag-m ↓ mag-s meny merc merc-c merc-i-f merc-i-r merl mez naja nat-ar **Nat-c** nat-m nat-p *Nat-s* ↓ neon ↓ nept-m lsd2.fr nit-ac *Nux-m* k* *Olib-sac* wmh1 olnd ↓ **Op** k* ox-ac par petr *Ph-ac* phel *Phos* pip-m ↓ *Plat* plb podo fd3.de• psil ft1 psor puls rhus-t ruta fd4.de sabad **Sacch-a** ↓ sal-fr sle1• sars seneg sep sil ↓ spig spong squil stann staph *Stram* sul-ac sulph sumb tab *Tarax* *Tarent* teucr ↓ ther thuj til ban1• tritic-vg fd5.de ulm-c jsj8• valer vanil fd5.de *Verat* verb viol-t ↓ *Zinc* [hydrog stj2 pall stj2 rhodi stj2 tax jsj7]

- **daytime**: ant-t mag-m a1
- **morning**: chin ↓ cit-v a1 con k* *Fl-ac* k* graph k* kola stb3• mag-m k* sulph k*
  - **waking**; on: chin
- **forenoon**: graph nat-m zinc
- **afternoon**: ang k* *Ant-t* arg-met cann-s k* lyc k* merc-i-f k* nept-m lsd2.fr olib-sac wmh1 olnd a1 phos k* *Staph* verb

Mirth: ...

- **evening**: aloe alum am-c k* anac aster k* bell k* bufo-s calc calc-s k* carb-v castm chel *Chin* k* chin-b hr1 coc-c k* croc cupr cycl k* dulc fd4.de falco-pe nl2• ferr k* ham fd3.de• **Lach** k* lachn k* laur mag-c *Nat-m* ph-ac phel k* pip-m k* sars *Sulph* valer k* verb hr1 viol-t k* *Zinc* k*
  - **alternating** with | **irritability** | **daytime** (See Irritability - daytime - alternating - mirth - evening)
    - **sadness** | **morning**: calc-s kr1
  - **bed**; in: alum
- **night**: alum bell k* caust *Chin* k* croc kreos lyc naja ph-ac sep sil stram sulph verat k*
  - **midnight**:
    - **after** | **2** h; until: *Chin*
- **air**; in open: phel plb teucr
- **alternating** with:
  - **anger**: *Op* kr1
  - **dullness**: jab spong h1*
  - **indignation**; bursts of (See Indignation - alternating - mirth)
  - **irritability** (See Irritability - alternating - mirth)
  - **lachrymose** mood (See weeping)
  - **mania** (See Mania - alternating - mirth)
  - **palpitation**: spig k*
  - **sadness**: cann-i caust croc k* ferr hell limest-b es1• nat-c neon srj5• nit-ac petr *Phos* plat sep tarent zinc
  - **seriousness**: cann-s j5.de cycl a1 haliae-lc srj5• plat **Sacch-a** fd* spong st
  - **taciturnity**: asar h1
  - **talk**; aversion to (See taciturnity)
  - **weeping**: arg-met carb-an iod plb k* psor k* sep spong k* sumb
- **chill**; during: nux-m
- **emission**; after an: pip-m
- **foolish**: *(↗Awkward; Foolish; Frivolous)* acon agar anac j5.de arund hr1 bell k* calc carb-an j5.de carb-v k* merc olib-sac wmh1 par *Podo* fd3.de• seneg spong fd4.de **Sulph** hr1
- **heat**; during: acon thuj h1
- **sleep**; during: alum bell caust croc hell j hyos kreos lyc m-arct j ph-ac sil sulph
- **stool**; after: *Borx* *Nat-s*
- **wretched**; simulating hilarity while he feels: apis k13 dendr-pol sk4•

MISANTHROPY: *(↗Aversion - persons - all; Cruelty; Cynical; Hatred; Hatred - humankind; Humankind - shuns; Loathing - general; Malicious; Mischievous; Moral; Wicked)* acon k* adam srj5• ail-c *Am-m* k* *Ambr* *Anac* ant-c arizon-l nl2• ars bg* *Aur* k* bar-c bell *Calc* k* cic k* clem bg2 con cop crot-h cupr cur a1 ferr bg fl-ac bg galla-q-r nl2• germ-met srj5• graph bg grat guaj haliae-lc srj5• hep bg hydrc k* *Hyos* ign bg iod kali-bi kali-c gl1.fr• kola stb3• lach *Led* k* *Lyc* k* mag-m jl3 merc **Nat-c** bg2* nat-m k* nit-ac olib-sac wmh1 pall bro1 *Phos* k* plat k* psor jl2 *Puls* rhus-g a1 rhus-t sel bg sep bg* *Stann* k* staph gl1.fr• stram bg2 sulph k* tab taosc iwa1•

MISCHIEVOUS: *(↗Behavior - children; Brutality; Cruelty; Destructiveness - cunning; Disobedience; Hardhearted; Malicious; Misanthropy; Moral; Rage - mischievous; Wicked)* *Agar* k* aids nl2• aloe **Anac** k* apis ↓ arn k* *Ars* k* aur ↓ aur-m-n wbt2• aur-s wbt2• bar-c k* bufo gk *Calc* k* calc-ar k2* **Cann-i** k* cann-xyz ptk1 *Caps* ↓ caust ↓ **Cham** c1* **Cina** vh* *Cupr* k* dam c1 gal-ac ↓ germ-met srj5• *Hyos* k* *Lach* lyc ↓ medul-os-si rly4• *Merc* k* **Nux-v** k* phos mtf33 plat ↓ puls c1 sacch ↓ sep ↓ spong j5.de **Stann** gl1.fr• *Stram* k* *Tarent* k* *Tub* vh* *Verat* k* [heroin sdj2]

- **children**; in: **Agar** lmj anac lmj apis lmj aur lmj calc lmj *Caps* lmj caust lmj gal-ac lmj hyos lmj lyc lmj merc lmj plat lmj puls lmj sacch lmj sep lmj *Tarent* lmj verat lmj
- **imbecility**, in: *(↗Imbecility)* *Merc* kr1

MISERABLE (See Unfortunate; Wretched)

MISERLY (See Avarice)

MISERY (See Horrible)

MISFORTUNE of others affects one profoundly (See Horrible - misfortune)

MISTAKES; making: *(↗Absentminded; Concentration - difficult; Confounding - objects; Confusion; Disconcerted; Dullness; Forgetful; Memory - weakness; Prostration)* acet-ac↓ acon↓ adam↓ adlu↓ aegle-m↓ aesc↓ *Agar*↓ agath-a↓ aids↓ ail↓ alco↓ all-c↓ allox sp1 alum bg2* alum-sil↓ am-br↓ am-c bg2 am-m↓ aml-ns↓ anac↓ anders↓ androc↓ *Anh*↓ anthraq↓ apeir-s↓ ara-maca↓ arag↓ *Arg-n*↓ arist-cl↓ arizon-l↓ *Arn*↓ atro↓ aur-m-n↓ aza↓ bad↓ bamb-a↓ bapt↓ bar-c↓ *Bell*↓ bell-p-sp↓ benz-ac↓ bit-ar↓ borx↓ *Both*↓ bov bg2 brom↓ bry↓ bufo↓ *Buteo-j*↓ cadm-met↓ cadm-s↓ calc bg2 *Calc-p*↓ calc-s↓ calc-sil↓ camph↓ camph-br↓ *Cann-i*↓ *Cann-s*↓ cann-xyz↓ canth↓ carb-an↓ carbn-o↓ carbn-s↓ carc↓ caust bg2 cench↓ cere-b↓ cere-s↓ cham bg2 *Chen-a*↓ chin bg2 *Chinin-s*↓ chlam-tr bcx2• choc↓ chr-ac↓ *Cic*↓ coca↓ *Coca-c*↓ *Cocc*↓ colch↓ coli rly4• coloc↓ colum-p↓ con↓ conv↓ corian-s↓ cortico sp1 croc↓ crot-h bg2 cupr↓ cycl↓ cypra-eg↓ cystein-l rly4• des-ac↓ *Dios*↓ dirc↓ dream-p↓ dulc bg2 elaps↓ elec↓ erig↓ esp-g↓ falco-pe↓ fic-m↓ *Fl-ac*↓ galeoc-c-h↓ galin↓ galla-q-r↓ gard-j↓ *Germ-met*↓ gink-b↓ **Glon**↓ *Graph* bg2 haem↓ haliae-lc↓ halo↓ ham↓ hell↓ helo↓ helo-s↓ hep bg2 heroin↓ hippoc-k szs2 hura↓ hydr↓ *Hyos*↓ *Hyper*↓ *Ign*↓ irid-met↓ iris-foe↓ kali-bi↓ kali-br bg2 kali-c bg2 *Kali-p*↓ *Kali-s*↓ kali-sil↓ kiss↓ *Kola*↓ lac-ac bg2 *Lac-c*↓ lac-e↓ lac-h↓ lac-loxod-a↓ lac-mat↓ lach bg2 lachn↓ lact↓ lap-la↓ lil-t↓ lob-s↓ loxo-recl↓ luna↓ lyc bg2 lyss↓ m-arct↓ mag-c↓ mang↓ mang-m↓ mang-met↓ mang-p↓ mang-s↓ *Med*↓ melal-alt gya4 meli↓ *Merc*↓ *Moni*↓ morb↓ morph↓ murx↓ musca-d↓ nat-ar↓ nat-c↓ nat-m bg2 **Nat-sil**↓ neon↓ nept-m↓ *Nux-m* bg2 nux-v bg2 oci-sa↓ olib-sac↓ onop↓ onos↓ *Op*↓ opun-s↓ opun-v↓ osm↓ ozone↓ pall↓ par↓ **Petr**↓ petr-ra↓ ph-ac↓ phasco-ci↓ phos↓ pieri-b↓ plac-s↓ plat↓ plb↓ *Plut-n*↓ podo↓ pop↓ positr↓ psil↓ psor↓ ptel↓ puls bg2 pycnop-sa↓ pyrid↓ pyrog↓ ran-b↓ rauw sp1 rhod bg2 rhus-r↓ rhus-t↓ ros-d↓ **Ruta**↓ sacch↓ sacch-a↓ sal-fr↓ sars↓ sec↓ sel rsj9*• sep bg2 sil↓ sinus↓ *Spong*↓ stann↓ staph↓ *Stram*↓ suis-hep rly4• sul-ac↓ sulph bg2 *Sumb*↓ symph↓ syph↓ tab↓ taosc iwa1• thal-xyz↓ ther↓ **Thuj**↓ *Tritic-vg* fd5.de tub↓ tung-met↓ ulm-c↓ valer↓ *Vanil* fd5.de verat↓ *Verat-v*↓ visc sp1 *Xero*↓ yuc↓ [alum-p stj2 alumin stj2 alumin-s stj2 ars stj2 hydrog stj2 tax jsj7 zinc stj2 zinc-m stj2 zinc-n stj2 zinc-p stj2]

- **calculating**, in: *(↗Confusion - calculating; Mathematics - inability - calculating)* ail *Am-c* k* arist-cl rbp3• calc k2 chinin-s chlam-tr bcx2• con *Crot-h* dulc fd4.de fic-m gya1 galin jl kali-p↓ lac-e hm2• lac-h htj1• lach gl1.fr• *Lyc* k* merc moni rfm1• nat-sil fd3.de• neon srj5• *Nux-v* petr-ra shn4• plb mtf33 podo fd3.de• rhus-t *Ruta* fd4.de *Sumb* syph thal-xyz srj8• *Thuj*↓ vanil fd5.de
  - **adding**; in: chinin-s a1 kali-p fd1.de• lac-e hm2• *Ruta* fd4.de *Sumb* a1*
  - **cannot** calculate | **delivery**; after: *Thuj* kr1
- **computer** | **deletes** program: lac-e hm2•
- **differentiating** of objects, in: calc bg2 cann-xyz bg2 dulc fd4.de hyos bg2 nux-v bg2 plat bg2* *Ruta* fd4.de sulph bg2 tritic-vg fd5.de [cann-s xyz62]
- **direction**; in the sense of (See Orientation - decreased)
- **distances**; in judgement of (See Distances - inaccurate)
- **gender**; in: musca-d szs1
- **headache**; during: med pc
- **homework**; in | **children**; in: med jl2
- **left** and right side; about (See side)
- **localization** of parts of body: pyrog jl2
- **localities**, in: *(↗Confusion - knows; Confusion - loses; Distances - inaccurate/ Forgetful - house; Forgetful - streets; Memory - weakness - places/ Recognizing - not - streets; Recognizing - not - surroundings)* aesc aml-ns bg2 anh sp1 arg-n bg2* atro bapt bg2 bell k* bov k* bry k* calc bg2 camph bg2 camph-br c1 cann-i k* cann-xyz bg2 cham cic coca bg2 *Coca-c* sk4• *Cocc* bg2 coloc bg2 croc bg2 dulc fd4.de falco-pe nl2• fl-ac bg2* **Glon** k* graph bg2 hell bg2 hura *Hyos* bg2 irid-met srj5• kali-bi bg2 *Kali-br* kr1 *Kali-p* st kali-s fd4.de lach lil-t bg2 lyc bg2 med bg2 merc k* musca-d szs1 nat-m k* **Nux-m** k* nux-v gl1.fr• *Op* bg2 ozone sde2• par k* **Petr** k* phos k* pieri-b mlk9.de plat bg2* plut-n srj7• positr nl2• psor puls bg2* ran-b bg2 *Ruta* fd4.de sep bg2 sil bg1* spong fd4.de stram k* sulph k* thuj bg2 tub bg2 valer k* verat k*
- **measure**; in estimation of: *(↗Size - incorrect)* kali-s fd4.de nux-v

Mistakes; making: ...

- **names**, in: *(↗Aphasia; Memory - weakness - names)* dios a1 dulc fd4.de galla-q-r nl2• hippoc-k szs2 kali-s fd4.de* musca-d szs1 positr nl2• sacch-a fd2.de• *Stram* a1 symph fd3.de• tritic-vg fd5.de vanil fd5.de [heroin sdj2]
- **objects**; about: musca-d szs1 sinus rly4•
- **perception**, of: *(↗Thoughts - erroneous - perception)* arg-n br1 cupr mtf33 **Dulc** fd* germ-met srj5• morb jl2 nux-m tl1 **Ruta** fd* *Spong* fd4.de *Tritic-vg* fd5.de vanil fd5.de
  - **misunderstands** what she has seen or heard: dulc fd4.de germ-met srj5• spong fd4.de
- **persons**, in: *(↗Memory - weakness - persons)* alco a1 cham a1 dulc fd4.de kali-s fd4.de *Ruta* fd4.de spong fd4.de [bell-p-sp dcm1]
- **reading**, in: *(↗Dyslexia; Reading - unable)* bar-c gg bit-ar↓ calc gg carc gg* cham chin gg conv c1 ham fd3.de• *Hyos* lac-c mtf33 lac-h htj1• lach a1 lact c1 lyc k* melal-alt gya4 merc plb a1* podo fd3.de• sep ptk1 sil *Spong* fd4.de stann suis-hep rly4• tritic-vg fd5.de vanil fd5.de
  - **reversing** letters and words: *Lyc* mrr1
  - **skipping** lines: bit-ar wht1•
  - **words**:
    - **adding** words: lac-c mtf33
    - **omitting** words: lac-c mtf33
- **right** and left side; about (See side)
- **salt** instead of sugar in his tea; puts: cadm-met gm1
- **side**; about left and right: *(↗speaking - words - wrong - side)* adam srj5• agath-a nl2• dulc fd4.de germ-met srj5• hydrog srj2• kali-s fd4.de melal-alt gya4 ozone sde2• plut-n srj7• symph fd3.de• *Vanil* fd5.de
- **size**; in (See Size; Size - incorrect)
- **space**; in: bapt↓ borx↓ bov sf1.de *Cann-i* br1* caust↓ falco-pe↓ hydrog srj2• lac-h↓ melal-alt gya4 nux-m sf1.de petr-ra↓ taosc↓ tritic-vg↓
  - **time**; and in: *(↗time; Confusion - time - space)* bapt tl1 borx bg2 bov sf1.de *Cann-i* br1* caust bg2 falco-pe nl2• hydrog srj2• lac-h htj1• melal-alt gya4 nux-m bg2* petr-ra shn4• taosc iwa1• tritic-vg fd5.de
- **speaking**, in: *(↗Aphasia; Forgetful; Speech - incoherent; Unobserving [=inattentive])* acet-ac adam srj5• aegle-m↓ *Agar* k* agath-a nl2• all-c↓ allox↓ *Alum* k* alum-sil k2* am-br sf1.de *Am-c* k* am-m androc srj1• anthraq rly4• apeir-s mlk9.de arg-n *Arn* aur-m-n wbt2• aza↓ *Bell* b4a.de* bell-p-sp↓ benz-ac↓ bit-ar wht1• *Both*↓ bov k* brom mtf33 bufo cadm-met gm1 *Calc* k* calc-p calc-s calc-sil k2* cann-i↓ cann-s canth carbn-s carc fd2.de• caust k* cere-s a1 *Cham* k* *Chen-a*↓ *Chin* k* chinin-s choc↓ coca *Cocc* con k* corian-s↓ cortico sp1 croc b7.de* crot-h cupr cycl cypra-eg sde6.de• des-ac rbp6 dios dirc dream-p↓ *Dulc* k* esp-g bg* falco-pe↓ fic-m↓ *Fl-ac*↓ galla-q-r↓ gard-j↓ germ-met stj2*• gink-b sbd1• graph k* haem haliae-lc↓ ham helo↓ helo-s↓ hep k* hydrog srj2• hyos hyper ign k* irid-met srj5• iris-foe a1 kali-br k* *Kali-c* k* kali-p kali-s fd4.de kali-sil k2 kiss a1 *Kola* stb3• lac-ac↓ *Lac-c* k* lac-h↓ lac-loxod-a hm2• lach k* lap-la sde8.de• lil-t k* lob-s↓ luna kg1• *Lyc* k* lyss↓ mang k* *Med*↓ melal-alt gya4 meli↓ *Merc* k* *Moni* rfm1• murx musca-d↓ nat-c ptk1 **Nat-m** k* *Nat-sil*↓ neon↓ nept-m↓ nux-m k* nux-v k* oci-sa↓ olib-sac wmh1 onop↓ onos osm ozone↓ petr-ra shn4• ph-ac phos↓ plac-s rly4• plb mtf33 *Plut-n*↓ positr nl2• *Puls* k* pycnop-sa mrz1 rauw↓ rhod b4.de* rhus-r ros-d wla1 *Ruta* fd4.de sacch-a fd2.de• sars↓ sec sel k* sep k* sil k* *Spong* fd4.de staph k2* stram sul-ac sulph symph fd3.de• syph mtf33 taosc↓ tax↓ *Thuj* k* tritic-vg fd5.de ulm-c↓ *Vanil* fd5.de *Verat-v*↓ visc sp1 xero↓ yuc↓ zinc k* [lac-mat sst4 mang-m stj2 mang-met stj2 mang-p stj2 mang-s stj2 tub bcj]
  - **answers** | **wrong** answers; giving: cann-s nat-m k* nat-sil fd3.de• nux-v phos
  - **chill**; during: cham b7.de
  - **exertion** agg.: agar
  - **fast** thoughts; from: *(↗hurry)* hydrog srj2•
  - **hurry**: *(↗fast)* *Ign* gl1.fr•
  - **intend**, what he does not: adam srj5• alum h2* cham h1 dulc fd4.de germ-met srj5• ham fd3.de• kola stb3• *Nat-m* k* plut-n srj7•
  - **letters**: *(↗Memory - weakness - letters)*
    - **reversing**: *(↗words - reversing)* *Lyc* mrr1
  - **mispronounces** words (See words - mispronouncing)
  - **old** people; in: am-c k1
  - **sleeplessness**, after: *(↗Memory - weakness - letters)* agar st
  - **sounds**; transposing: caust k* chin ptk1 germ-met srj5• [tax jsj7]

- **spelling**, in: (*↗Dyslexia)* adam srj5• aegle-m ckh1 agar k2* all-c k* allox tpw4* am-c androc srj1• aza jl calc-sil k2* corian-s knl6• *Cortico* jl* crot-h cypra-eg sde6.de• dream-p sdj1• fic-m gya1 fl-ac germ-met srj5• helo helo-s c1* *Hydrog* srj2• hyper lac-ac lac-h htj1• *Lach* lob-s a1 *Lyc* k* *Med* k* melal-alt gya4 nux-m nux-v oci-sa sk4• petr-ra shn4• plut-n srj7• rauw tpw8* stram sulph k* ulm-c jsj8• xero br1 [tax jsj7]
- **syllables** | **wrong** syllables: caust kali-c gm1 kola stb3• **Lyc** k* nat-sil fd3.de• onop jl sel vanil fd5.de
- **vertigo**; with: am-c bg2 calc bg2 caust bg2 cham bg2 chin bg2 con bg2 graph bg2 hep bg2 kali-c bg2 mang bg2 merc bg2 nat-m bg2 nux-v bg2 sep bg2 sil bg2
- **words**: *(↗Forgetful - words; Memory - weakness - words)* adam ↓ agar ↓ agath-a ↓ all-c ↓ *Alum* ↓ alum-sil ↓ am-br bg2 *Am-c* ↓ apeir-s ↓ *Arg-n* ↓ *Arn* ↓ bell-p-sp ↓ benz-ac ↓ bit-ar ↓ *Both* ↓ bov bg2 bufo ↓ *Calc* ↓ *Calc-p* ↓ calc-s ↓ calc-sil ↓ canni-i ↓ cann-s ↓ canth ↓ carbn-s ↓ *Caust* ↓ cere-s ↓ cham bg2 *Chen-a* ↓ *Chin* bg2 *Chinin-s* ↓ choc ↓ *Cocc* ↓ con ↓ cortico ↓ crot-h ↓ cupr ↓ cycl ↓ cypra-eg ↓ des-ac ↓ *Dios* ↓ dirc ↓ *Dulc* ↓ esp-g ↓ falco-pe ↓ fic-m ↓ *Fl-ac* ↓ galla-q-r ↓ gard-j ↓ germ-met ↓ gink-b ↓ graph ↓ haliae-lc ↓ ham ↓ helo ↓ helo-s ↓ hep ↓ hydrog ↓ *Hyos* ↓ hyper ↓ irid-met ↓ iris-foe ↓ *Kali-br* ↓ kali-c ↓ kali-p ↓ *Kali-s* ↓ kali-sil ↓ kola ↓ *Lac-c* ↓ lac-loxod-a ↓ lac-mat ↓ *Lach* ↓ *Lyc* bg2 lyss ↓ mang bg2 med ↓ melal-alt ↓ meli ↓ merc bg2 moni ↓ musca-d ↓ nat-c ↓ nat-m bg2 *Nat-sil* ↓ neon ↓ nept-m ↓ *Nux-m* bg2 *Nux-v* ↓ onop ↓ onos ↓ osm ↓ ozone ↓ petr-ra ↓ ph-ac ↓ *Plut-n* ↓ positr ↓ puls ↓ pycnop-sa ↓ rhod ↓ *Ruta* ↓ sacch-a ↓ sars ↓ sep ↓ sil bg2 spong ↓ staph ↓ *Stram* ↓ *Sulph* ↓ symph ↓ syph ↓ taosc ↓ tax ↓ *Thuj* ↓ tritic-vg ↓ tub ↓ ulm-c ↓ *Vanil* ↓ *Verat-v* ↓ yuc ↓ zinc ↓
  - **misplacing** words: adam srj5• agath-a nl2• all-c k* alum am-c apeir-s mlk9.de *Arn* bit-ar wht1• bov bufo *Calc* calc-s calc-sil k2 cann-s carbn-s caust cham **Chin** k* choc srj3• cocc con crot-h cycl fl-ac graph hep hyos hyper kali-br kali-c kali-p kali-s kali-sil k2* *Lac-c Lach Lyc* k* med k2 melal-alt gya4 merc moni rfm1• nat-c *Nat-m* nept-m lsd2.fr *Nux-m* k* *Nux-v* osm petr-ra shn4• puls rhod sep sil *Stram Sulph* taosc iwa1• thuj k* tritic-vg fd5.de [tax jsj7]
  - **mispronouncing** words: *(↗Memory - weakness - letters)* adam skp7• *Caust* dulc fd4.de germ-met srj5• *Kali-s* fd4.de lach c1 neon srj5• petr-ra shn4• symph fd3.de• ulm-c jsj8• *Vanil* fd5.de
  - **new** words; makes: moni rfm1•
  - **omitting** words: benz-ac bro1 cere-s bro1 cham h1* gard-j vlr2• helo st helo-s rwt2• *Kali-br* bro1 lac-c bro1 lach bro1 *Lyc* bro1 melal-alt gya4 meli bro1 *Nux-m* bro1 nux-v a1* onos vml3• petr-ra shn4• staph mtf33 *Verat-v* kr1
  - **reversing** words: *(↗reversing; letters - reversing)* agath-a nl2• calc caust *Chin* cycl des-ac rbp6 kali-br kali-s fd4.de *Lyc* mrr1 melal-alt gya4 *Nat-sil* fd3.de• onop jl osm positr nl2• stram sulph vanil fd5.de
  - **wrong** words; using: *(↗Dullness - words)* adam srj5• agar agath-a nl2• *Alum* alum-sil k2 am-br sf1.de *Am-c* k* *Arg-n* a1 *Arn* bit-ar wht1• *Both* bov bufo *Calc Calc-p* cann-i a1 cann-s canth caust cham a1 *Chen-a* **Chin** k* chinin-s a1 *Cocc* con cortico mg1.de* crot-h cupr k* cypra-eg ↓ *Dios* kr1 dirc *Dulc* esp-g bg* falco-pe nl2• fic-m gya1 fl-ac a1 galla-q-r nl2• gard-j vlr2• germ-met srj5• gink-b sbd1• graph haliae-lc srj5• ham fd3.de• hep hydrog ↓ *Hyos* a1 hyper a1 irid-met srj5• iris-foe ↓ *Kali-br* kali-c kali-s fd4.de kali-sil k2 kola stb3• lac-c lac-loxod-a hrn2• **Lyc** k* lyss med k2 musca-d szs1 nat-sil fd3.de• neon ↓ **Nux-m** *Nux-v* kr1* osm kr1 ozone sde2• ph-ac gl1.fr• *Plut-n* srj7• pycnop-sa mrz1 *Ruta* fd4.de sacch-a fd2.de• sars a1 sep sil sf1.de spong fd4.de staph gl1.fr• *Stram* kr1 sulph ↓ syph mtf33 tax ↓ *Thuj* k* tritic-vg fd5.de ulm-c ↓ vanil fd5.de yuc a1 zinc k* [bell-p-sp dcm1 lac-mat sst4 tub bcj]
    - **names**; calls things by wrong: am-c calc cypra-eg sde6.de• *Dios* k* falco-pe nl2• hydrog srj2• lac-c *Ruta* fd4.de sep *Stram* k* sulph tritic-vg fd5.de ulm-c jsj8• [bell-p-sp dcm1 tax jsj7]
    - **opposite**, hot for cold: irid-met srj5• *Kali-br* nux-m ulm-c jsj8•
    - **plums**, when he means pears; says: agath-a nl2• dios falco-pe nl2• **Lyc** k ●* ozone sde2• *Stram* vanil fd5.de
    - **seen** instead of the one desired; name of the object: am-c calc *Lac-c* neon srj5• sep sulph tub
    - **side** or vice versa; putting right for left: *(↗side)* *Chinin-s Dios Fl-ac* hyper iris-foe kali-s fd4.de neon srj5• ulm-c jsj8• vanil fd5.de

- **speaking**, in – **words** – **wrong** words; using: ...
  - **stop** in the middle of a sentence and to change it entirely; obliged to: neon srj5• nux-m c1
- **spelling** (See speaking - spelling)
- **time**, in: *(↗space - time; Confusion - time; Memory - weakness - time; Time - slowly)* acon alum anac *Anh* br1* ara-maca sej7• arist-cl rbp3• arizon-l ↓ atro bad bamb-a stb2.de• borx bov sf1.de camph cann-i k* carc fd2.de• cere-b choc srj3• cic cocc k* colum-p ↓ con croc dirc dulc fd4.de elaps elec c1 falco-pe nl2• fl-ac galeoc-c-h ↓ germ-met srj5• glon haliae-lc ↓ halo jl ham fd3.de• hura hydrog srj2• irid-met srj5• kali-p ↓ kali-s fd4.de* *Kola* stb3• lac-h sk4• lac-loxod-a ↓ *Lach* k* loxo-recl knl4• med k* melal-alt gya4 moni rfm1• **Nat-sil** fd* neon ↓ nept-m lsd2.fr nux-m nux-v k* olib-sac ↓ op ozone sde2• pall petr k* petr-ra shn4• phasco-ci rbp2 plac-s rly4• plb k* podo fd3.de• psor st pycnop-sa mrz1 pyrid rly4• *Ruta* fd4.de sacch-a fd2.de• sal-fr sle1• *Spong* fd4.de stann ↓ staph ↓ sulph symph ↓ ther k* tritic-vg fd5.de **Vanil** fd* [cadm-met stj2 cadm-s stj2 cann-s xyz62]
  - **afternoon**, always imagines it is: *Lach* stann
  - **conception** of time; has lost the: anh sp1 arizon-l nl2• colum-p sze2• galeoc-c-h gms1• haliae-lc srj5• hydrog srj2• kali-p fd1.de• kali-s fd4.de lac-loxod-a hrn2• lach tl1 med tl1 **Nat-sil** fd* neon srj5• olib-sac wmh1 symph fd3.de• **Vanil** fd*
  - **confounds**:
    - **days** of the week: bamb-a stb2.de• kola stb3• pycnop-sa mrz1 *Ruta* fd4.de spong fd4.de vanil fd5.de
    - **future** with past: *Dulc* fd4.de staph mtf33
    - **present** with future: anac k* neon srj5•
    - **present** with past: anac b4a.de* *Cic* k* croc k* med k* nux-m nux-v b7a.de ozone sde2• staph k*
  - **past** events; about: hydrog srj2• med kr neon srj5•
  - **present** merged with eternity: anh sp1
- **traffic** lights; in red and green: ozone sde2•
- **weight**; in estimation of: nux-v positr nl2•
- **work**, in: acet-ac agath-a nl2• aids nl2• all-c androc srj1• bell carc fd2.de• chinin-s dulc fd4.de kali-p fd1.de• kali-s fd4.de kola stb3• meli nat-c nept-m lsd2.fr phos *Ruta* fd4.de sep spong fd4.de tritic-vg fd5.de ulm-c jsj8• vanil fd5.de [pop dhh1]
- **writing**, in: *(↗Concentration - difficult - writing; Confusion - writing; Dyslexia; Memory - weakness - letters; Memory - weakness - orthography; Memory - weakness - write; Memory - weakness - written; Writing - inability)* adam ↓ adlu jl agar k2* agath-a nl2• aids nl2• allox jl* alum k* alum-sil k2* am-br sf1.de *Am-c* k* am-m vh1 anders bnj1 androc srj1• anthraq ↓ arag br1 arizon-l nl2• aza jl bamb-a stb2.de• benz-ac bit-ar wht1• bov k* brom mtf33 calc a1* *Calc-p* k* cann-i *Cann-s* k* cann-xyz ↓ carb-an carbn-o a1 carbn-s caust ↓ cench k2 cere-s a1 *Cham* k* *Chin* k* chinin-s choc srj3*• chr-ac colch con fkr8.de* cortico ↓ croc crot-h k* cypra-eg sde6.de• des-ac ↓ dios dirc a1 *Dulc* sf1.de erig ↓ fl-ac k* galin jl galla-q-r nl2• gard-j ↓ germ-met stj2*• gink-b sbd1• graph k* ham fd3.de• helo st helo-s rwt2• hep k* hippoc-k szs2 hydr hydrog srj2• hyper k* ign k* irid-met srj5• iris-foe *Kali-br* kali-c sf1.de *Kali-p* kali-s kali-sil k2 kola stb3• lac-ac *Lac-c* k* lac-e ↓ lac-loxod-a hrn2• **Lach** k* lachn ↓ lil-t lob-s a1 loxo-recl knl4• **Lyc** k* m-arct b7.de* mag-c k* med k2* melal-alt gya4 meli ↓ morph a1 nat-ar a1 nat-c k* *Nat-m* k* nat-sil ↓ neon srj5• *Nux-m* k* nux-v k* olib-sac wmh1 onos op ↓ opun-s a1 (non:opun-v a1) ozone sde2• petr-ra shn4• phos pieri-b mlk9.de plac-s rly4• plut-n srj7• podo ↓ positr ↓ psil ft1 ptel puls k* pycnop-sa mrz1 rauw sp1 rhod k* rhus-t k* *Ruta* fd4.de sacch a1 sacch-a fd2.de* sal-fr sle1• sars ↓ sel gmj2 sep k* sil *Spong* fd4.de staph k2* stram suis-hep rly4• sulph k* *Sumb* k* syph ↓ tab gl1.fr• taosc ↓ tax ↓ **Thuj** k* tritic-vg fd5.de tung-met bdx1• ulm-c jsj8• vanil fd5.de visc sp1 *Xero* ↓ yuc a1 zinc mrr1* [*Buteo-j* sej6 tub bcj]
  - **adding** letters: gink-b sbd1• *Lyc* a1 podo fd3.de• *Ruta* fd4.de spong fd4.de tritic-vg fd5.de [tax jsj7]
  - **confounding** letters: dulc fd4.de ham fd3.de• lac-loxod-a hrn2• lyc ozone sde2• sacch-a gmj3 spong fd4.de
  - **fast** thoughts; from (See thoughts)
  - **hurry**, from: *(↗thoughts)* hydrog srj2• *Ign* gsd1*
  - **old** people; in: am-c k1 *Crot-h* kr1
  - **omitting**:
    - **letters**: adam ↓ bamb-a stb2.de• benz-ac bro1 bit-ar wht1• cere-s bro1 cham bro1 choc srj3• colch k1 dulc fd4.de erig mg1.de galla-q-r nl2• germ-met srj5• *Hydrog* srj2• *Hyper* kali-br k* kali-s fd4.de *Lac-c* k* lach bro1 **Lyc** k ●* med jl2 melal-alt gya4 meli k* *Nux-m* k* nux-v k* onos

- **omitting – letters**: ...
  op a1 opun-s a1 podo fd3.de• puls *Ruta* fd4.de sacch-a gmj3 spong fd4.de stram *Thuj* k* tritic-vg fd5.de vanil fd5.de zinc k* [tax jsj7]
  - **first** letter: adam srj5• opun-s a1
  - **last**; final: meli vml3•
  - **syllables**: bov *Cham* colch kali-br *Lyc* kr1 nux-v ozone sde2• *Thuj* k*
  - **words**: benz-ac k* *Cann-s* cere-s bro1 *Cham* k* erig mg1.de gard-j vlr2• hyper kali-br k* lac-ac lac-c bro1 lach bro1 lachn *Lyc* k* meli k* nat-sil fd3.de• *Nux-m* bro1 nux-v k* (non:opun-v a1) *Rhod Ruta* fd4.de sacch a1 *Thuj* k* vanil fd5.de [buteo-j sej6]
- **repeating** words: *Calc-p Cann-s* choc srj3• kali-br kali-s fd4.de lac-c sulph syph jl2
- **spelling** errors: [buteo-j sej6]
- **thoughts**; from fast: *(↗hurry)* hydrog srj2• ign h1* onos a2*
- **transposing**:
  - **letters**: adam srj5• allox tpw4 caust *Chin* choc srj3• des-ac rbp6 germ-met srj5• irid-met srj5• kali-s fd4.de lac-e hrn2• *Lyc* melal-alt gya4 opun-s a1 (non:opun-v a1) podo fd3.de• psil ft1 spong fd4.de stram tub ser *Xero* ↓ [tax jsj7]
    - **last** letters of words first; writes: *Xero* br1
  - **words**: agath-a nl2• hydrog srj2• vanil fd5.de
- **vertigo**; with: am-c bg2 bov bg2 cann-xyz bg2 cham bg2 chin bg2 crot-h bg2 graph bg2 hep bg2 *Lach* bg2 nat-c bg2 nat-m bg2 nux-v bg2 puls bg2 rhod bg2 sep bg2
- **wrong**:
  - **letters**, figures: agath-a nl2• am-c a1 bit-ar wht1• dulc fd4.de galin jl galla-q-r nl2• *Germ-met* srj5• hydrog srj2• kali-p fd1.de• *Med* jl2 melal-alt gya4 neon srj5• plut-n srj7• spong fd4.de stram mtf33 taosc iwa1• [*Buteo-j* sej6]
  - **syllables**: *Lyc* br1
  - **words**: allox tpw3 anthraq rly4• bit-ar wht1• bov kr1 *Calc* kr1 calc-p a1 cann-i a1 cench k2 chinin-s a1 choc srj3• cortico tpw7 dirc a1* fl-ac a1 gard-j vlr2• germ-met srj5• ham fd3.de• hydrog srj2• hyper a1 irid-met srj5• kali-s fd4.de *Kola* stb3• lac-c mtf33 loxo-recl knl4• *Lyc* a1* *Nat-m* ↓ neon srj5• nux-m ↓ ozone sde2• positr nl2• *Ruta* fd4.de sacch-a fd2.de• sal-fr sle1• sars a1 sep a1* suis-hep rly4• thuj kr1 tritic-vg fd5.de yuc a1
    - **headache**, during: *Nat-m* ckh1 nux-m kl

MOANING: *(↗Complaining; Delirium - moaning; Discontented; Discouraged - moaning; Grief; Grumbling; Grunting; Lamenting; Muttering; Sighing; Tormenting - others; Tormenting - others - complaints)* abrot br1 **Acon** k* aether a1 agar vh1 *Ail* ↓ aloe ↓ alum k* am-c ambr a1 anac ↓ ang **Ant-c** ↓ ant-t k* *Apis* k* *Arn* ↓ *Ars* k* ars-h ↓ aur nh4 aur-s k2 bamb-a stb2.de• *Bapt* ↓ *Bar-c* k* bar-s k2 **Bell** k* *Borx* a1* *Bry* k* bufo ↓ cadm-s ↓ *Calad Calc* k* *Calc-p* vh* calc-sil k2 *Camph* **Cann-i** cann-s bg cann-xyz bg2* canth caps ↓ *Carb-ac* carb-an b4.de* carb-v carbn-o carbn-s caust *Cham* k* chin chinin-ar chlf kr1 *Cic* k* cimic kr1 *Cina* k* clem ↓ coc-c a1* coca a1 *Cocc* k* coff k* *Colch Coloc* kr1 con ↓ cop ↓ *Crot-c* crot-h *Cupr* k* cupr-act kr1 dig dulc emb-r bnj1 erio ↓ eup-per *Eup-pur* kr1 ferr-s a1 gels graph k* hell k* hep ↓ hipp ↓ hoit jl3 hura a1 hydr kr1 hydr-ac hydrc a1 *Hyos Ign* k* *Ip* k* juni-v a1 *Kali-br* **Kali-c** k* kali-cy a1 *Kali-i* kr1 kali-m k2 kali-p kali-s fd4.de kreos lac-d kr1 lach lachn a1* lat-m sp1 laur lavand-a ↓ led ↓ *Lyc* ↓ m-ambo ↓ mag-c mang k* med gk merc k* merc-c mez kr1 mill bg2* *Mur-ac* k* naja nat-c *Nat-m* ↓ nit-ac *Nux-v* k* oena a1 olib-sac wmh1 op k* ox-ac petr a1 ph-ac ↓ *Phos* k* phys kr1 phyt plat ↓ plb ↓ plect ↓ podo psor *Puls* k* pyrus a1 rheum rhus-t k* rumx-act a1 ruta fd4.de sacch c1* samb xxb1 sang bg sars *Sec* sel kr1 sep b4.de* *Sil* ↓ sol-ni ↓ squil stann ↓ *Stram* k* stry a1 sul-ac sulph tab tanac tarent thres-a ↓ *Thuj* ↓ **Tub** hr1* verat k* **Zinc** k* [alum-p stj2 alumin stj2 alumin-s stj2]

- **daytime**: zinc
- **morning**: *Agar* vh1 *Borx* a1*
- **afternoon**: bell a1 cina
- **evening**: ars k* coca a1
  - **sleep**, during: ars k*
- **night**: *Ars* k* bell a1 cupr k* *Dulc* ↓ hep k* **Kali-c** ↓ phyt hr1* plat hr1* podo hr1* rhus-t hr1 sec sol-ni a1 tarent k* verat hr1 zinc k*
  - **midnight**:
    - **after** | 3 h: **Kali-c**

Moaning – night: ...
  - **tossing** about, with: ars h2* *Dulc* hr1*
- **alternating** with:
  - **cheerfulness** (See Cheerful - alternating - moaning)
  - **dancing** (See Dancing - alternating - moaning)
  - **laughing** (See Laughing - alternating - moaning)
  - **singing** (See Singing - alternating - moaning)
  - **songs**, gambols (See Singing - alternating - moaning)
- **anxious**: **Acon** hr1* alum a1* *Ars* hr1 calad ptk1* plb hr1*
- **breath**; with every: bell ptk1*
- **children**, in: **Ant-c** vh* ant-t k2 borx kr1* *Calc-p* vh* caust a1 **Cham** kr1* *Cina* kr1* emb-r bnj1 lach ptk1* mill ptk1* phyt hr1* *Podo* hr1* psor jl2 puls ↓ sacch c1
  - **carried**, while being: puls h1*
  - **wanted**, piteous because they cannot have what they: **Cham** a1*
- **chill**, during: am chinin-ar cupr *Eup-per Nat-m* samb hr1*
- **constant** moaning and gasping for air: kreos kr1* mang kr1* merc kr1 phyt
- **contradicted**, when: *(↗Contradiction - intolerant)* tarent k*
- **convulsions**, in: cic br1 *Ign* hr1* *Sil* hr1* *Tub* hr1*
- **coryza**; during: bamb-a stb2.de•
- **cough**, during: *(↗Weeping - cough - during)* bell cina *Cupr-act* ↓ podo
  - **whooping** cough, during: *Cupr-act* kr1
- **dentition**, in: **Cham** hr1* phyt hr1* *Podo* hr1*
- **discouragement**; with (See Discouraged - moaning)
- **dreaming**, while: graph j5.de
- **ear** lobes, with hot: *Alum* hr1*
- **fate**, about the: *Kali-br* hr1*
- **fever** (See heat)
- **heat**, during: acon k* *Arn* k* ars bg2 bell k* bry bg2 cham k* chinin-ar cocc bg2 coff k* eup-per k* ign j5.de* ip k* lach *Mur-ac* hr1* nux-v k* podo hr1* **Puls** k* *Rhus-t* bg2 sep bg2 thuj k* verat
- **hemicrania**, with: cop k* dulc fd4.de
- **honor**, from wounded: *Nux-v* hr1*
- **ill** humor, from: cham h1*
- **involuntary**: *Alum* bg2* *Cham* h1* crot-c a1 hell gl1.fr•
- **lifted**, when: sul-ac bg2*
- **loud**: *Mur-ac* br1* stram hr1* stry a1
- **menses**:
  - **after**: *(↗Menses - after)* *Stram* a1*
  - **during**: *(↗Menses - during)* *Ars* k* *Cocc* hr1* *Coff* b7a.de lyc plat
  - **suppressed** menses; from: *Cocc* b7a.de
- **objects**, about: caps h1*
- **offense**, happened long ago; for trifling: *Cham* a1*
- **old** age, in: *Bar-c* k*
- **pain**, from: *Bell* kr1 cham gl1.fr• *Coff* kr1 *Coloc* kr1 crot-c mre1.fr dulc fd4.de *Eup-per* kr1* hura a1 *Hydr* kr1 lachn kr1 lat-m sp1* *Merc* kr1 *Nux-v* gl1.fr• phos h2 sil bg2* thres-a sze7• *Thuj* kr1
- **perspiration**, during: acon bar-c bry camph chin cupr *Merc* phos stram verat
- **pollutions**, after: hipp a1
- **restlessness**, with: **Cham** hr1* petr a1 *Stram* hr1*
- **sleep**, during: *Acon* ↓ *Ail* k* aloe *Alum* k* am-c anac h2* ant-t hr1* apis k1 arn h1* *Ars* k* ars-h hr1* **Aur** k* *Bar-c* b4.de* *Bell* k* **Bry** k* bufo k* cadm-s k* **Calad** k* calc b4a.de* *Carb-an* b4.de* caust j5.de *Cham* k* chin h1* *Cina* hr1 clem k* coc-c a1 (non:cocc k*) coff k* con k* *Crot-c* k* erio a1 eup-per hr1* graph k* *Hell* bg2* hyos k* *Ign* k* *Ip* k* *Kali-br* hr1* kali-p k* kreos c1 lach k* lavand-a ctl1• led hr1* *Lyc* k* m-ambo b7.de* mag-c j merc b4.de* *Mur-ac* k* nat-m *Nit-ac* j5.de* *Nux-v* k* oena a1 *Op* k* ph-ac k* phos j5.de plb a1 plect a1 *Podo* k* *Puls* k* rheum h* ruta fd4.de *Samb* hr1* sep k* sil k* stann k* *Stram* b7.de* *Sulph* k* *Thuj* hr1* verat h1*
  - **chill**; during: cham bg2 lach bg2 nux-v bg2
  - **fever**; during: *Acon* bg2 *Arn* bg2 bar-c bg2 *Bell* bg2 bry bg2 calc bg2 *Cham* bg2 cocc bg2 *Ign* bg2 *Ip* bg2 mur-ac bg2 nux-v bg2 *Puls* bg2 sil bg2 thuj bg2
  - **grinding** of teeth, with: *Kali-br* hr1*

- **sleep**, during: ...
  - **perspiration**; during: acon bg2 arn bg2 bar-c bg2 *Bell* bg2 bry bg2 calad bg2 calc bg2 *Cham* bg2 cocc bg2 *Ign* bg2 ip bg2 *Mur-ac* bg2 nux-v bg2 puls bg2 sil bg2 stram bg2 thuj bg2
  - **rolling** of the head and closing half the lids; with: *Podo* kr1 *Samb* kr1
- **sleepiness**, with: *Cham* hr1*
- **sleeplessness**, with: ant-t bro1 arn bro1 ars h2* aur bro1 *Bapt* bro1 *Bell* bro1 carb-v bro1 *Cham* bro1 cic bro1 crot-h hr1 cupr-act bro1 *Gels* bro1 *Hell* bro1 hyos bro1 kali-br bro1 lach bro1 lyc bro1 *Mur-ac* bro1 nat-m bro1 nit-ac bro1 *Op* bro1 *Podo* bro1 puls bro1 rhus-t bro1 verat bro1
- **stool**; before: puls b7.de*
- **teeth**; with complaints of: coff bg2
- **touch**, on: ant-t a1* chin a1
- **trifle**, about every: bar-c ptk1 caust h2*
- **twice** each time | **babies**; in: ant-t zr
- **waking**, on: am-c j5.de cina j5.de*
- **weakness**, from: (↗*Prostration)* graph k2*
- **weeping**, with: *Hell* hr1*
- **why**, does not know: *Hyos* hr1*

MOCKING: (↗*Contemptuous; Insolence; Irony; Jesting; Laughing - contemptuous; Laughing - mocking; Laughing - sardonic; Mocking - ridicule; Mocking - sarcasm; Rudeness; Teasing; Unfriendly)* acon b7.de* alco ↓ aloe sne alum bg2* am-br ↓ am-caust ↓ androc ↓ anh sp1 arist-cl ↓ ars k* aur-m-n ↓ bry ↓ cann-i ↓ *Carb-v* mtf33 carbn-o ↓ caust ↓ cham mtf33 chin k* choc ↓ cinnb ↓ conv ↓ crot-c ↓ *Dulc* ↓ **Graph** ↓ guaj bg2 hyos b7.de* hyper ↓ ign b7.de* ip k* kali-p fd1.de• lac-ac ↓ *Lach* k* lat-m ↓ loxo-recl knl4• lyc ↓ nit-ac ↓ nux-m ptk1* nux-v b7.de* pall ↓ par k* ped a1 petr ↓ plat k* rad-br ↓ rhus-g ↓ rhus-r ↓ rhus-t ↓ ruta fd4.de sacch-a fd2.de• sacch-l ↓ sal-fr sle1• sec ↓ **Sep** ↓ stann gl1.fr• suis-hep rly4• tarent k* tax ↓ verat b7.de*

- **friends**, at his: (↗*Abusive - friends; Aversion - friends; Censorious - friends; Unsympathetic - friends)* alco a1
- **fun** of somebody; making (See Mocking)
- **jealousy**, with: *Lach* hr1*
- **old** age; aged people with their: *Tarent* hr1*
- **others** are mocking at him; thinks: (↗*Confidence - want; Delusions - despised; Delusions - laughed; Fear - opinion)* ham fd3.de• ign gl1.fr• lyss mrr1 nux-v gl1.fr• petr-ra shn4• ph-ac gl1.fr• sep gl1.fr•
- **relatives**, at his: (↗*Estranged - family)* sec k*
- **ridicule**; passion to: (↗*sarcasm; Contemptuous; Cruelty; Dress - ridiculously; Hardhearted; Mocking)* acon k* conv br1 hyos k* lach k* nux-v k* verat k* [pall stj2]
- **sarcasm**: (↗*ridicule; Censorious; Contemptuous; Cynical; Jesting - malicious; Laughing - contemptuous; Laughing - sardonic; Malicious - hurting; Mocking; Smiling - sardonic; Speech - sharp; Witty)* androc srj anh sp arist-cl rbp3• *Ars* h2* aur-m-n wbt2• bry gl1.fr• cann-i a1 **Carb-v** gl• carbn-o a1 caust gl1.fr• cham dx1* chin mrr1 choc srj3• cinnb a1 crot-c sk4• *Dulc* fd4.de **Graph** gl* hyper dx1 ign gl1.fr• lac-ac hr1* *Lach* j5.de* lat-m ↓ loxo-recl knl4• lyc gsd nit-ac ptk* nux-v gl1.fr• pall sf1.de* par mrr1 petr gl• rad-br st rhus-g tmo3• rhus-r ↓ sacch-a fd2.de• sacch-l sna* sec hr1* sep mrr1* tarent ptk [am-br stj2 am-caust stj2 stann stj2 tax jsj7]
  - **alternating** with | **company**; aversion to: rad-br st rhus-r k1
  - **weaknesses**; with great intuition concerning other people's: (↗*Intuitive - weakness)* androc mtf lat-m mtf **Sep** mrr1
- **satire**, desire for: ars a1* lac-ac kr1 *Lach* lpc2* sec kr1 stann gl•

MODESTY, increased: (↗*Humility; Reproaching oneself)* sacch a1

MONOMANIA: (↗*Autism; Insanity; Pertinacity; Talking - one; Thoughts - persistent)* *Absin* bro1 acon agath-a nl2• **Aloe** sne ambr tsm1 anac a1 anan k* androc mtf aur bg2 bell j bufo mtf33 camph carb-v k* carc mlr* cham j* chin j cic bg2* cocc j con j croc j cupr j dream-p sdj1• dros j galla-q-r nl2• hell hyos j* *Ign* k* ignis-alc es2• iod j lach j limest-b es1• mag-c j* nux-m oxyt bro1 plat j* positr nl2• puls rhus-t j *Sil* k* stram k* sulph k* tarent bro1* thuj k* verat j [nat-sil stj2 plb stj2]

- **children**; in: bufo mtf33
- **grotesque** manner; to appear in a public place in a: (↗*Walking - self-sufficient)* *Anan* k*
- **photographs**, taking: galla-q-r nl2•

MOOD:

- **agreeable**: (↗*Cheerful; Mirth)* abrot acon-ac rly4• aesc hl ant-t asc-t hl chel hl chir-fl gya2 cist hl croc fago hl ign lach lat-h thj1 meny nept-m lsd2.fr olib-sac wmh1 orig hl *Plac* rzf5• plat positr nl2• sacch-a fd2.de• scut hl spong fd4.de sul-ac zing [sol-ecl cky1]
- **alternating**: (↗*Mental symptoms - alternating - mental)* *Acon* k* agar a1 agn k* *Aloe* sne **Alum** k* alum-p k2 ambr h1* anac bg2* *Androc* srj1• ange-s oss1• *Anh* mg1.de* ant-t k* arg-n a1 arn k* ars k* ars-i asaf k* asar k* aur k* aur-i k2* *Aur-s* wbt2• *Bar-c* k* bar-i k2* **Bell** k* bism k* borx **Bov** k* buth-a sp1 calc cann-i br1 cann-s k* caps k* *Carb-an* k* *Carc* mlr1• caust k* *Cench* c10* *Chin* k* cob br1 cob-n sp1 cocc j con k* conch fkr1• cortico sp1 cortiso sp1* *Croc* k* cupr k* cycl k* *Des-ac* rbp6 dig j* *Dros* k* falco-pe nl2• **Ferr** k* ferr-ar ferr-i *Ferr-p* fum rly1• *Graph* k* hippoc-k szs2 hist sp1 hydrog srj2• hyos k* **Ign** k* ina-i mlk9.de **Iod** k* irid-met srj5• *Kali-c* k* kali-p fd1.de• kali-s lac-c k2* lac-leo hrn2• led bg2 lil-t mrr1 limest-b es1• **Lyc** k* m-arct b2.de* mag-c j mand jl3 med k* meny j merc k* merc-i-f a1 mez j* moni rfm1• myos-a rly4• *Naja* k* nat-c k* *Nat-m* k* nid jl3 nit-ac j* *Nux-m* k* olib-sac wmh1 op k* pant-ac rly4• petr j* *Phos* k* pic-ac bg2 pieri-b mlk9.de **Plat** k* plb bg2 podo fd3.de• psor bg2* *Puls* k* ran-b j *Ruta* fd4.de sabad b7.de* sabin bg2 sacch sst1• sacch-a fd2.de• **Sars** k* seneg k* sep k* sil bg2 spig j* spong j* stann k* staph stram b2.de* **Sul-ac** k* *Sulph* k* tarent thiam rly4• thuj bg2 *Tritic-vg* fd5.de *Tub* k* valer k* *Verat* j* verb vero-o rly4*• viol-o bg2 **Zinc** k* [bell-p-sp dcm1 tax jsj7 vanad stj2]
  - **children**; in: ign mtf33 lyc mtf33 naja mtf33 sacch sst1• tub mtf33
  - **fever**; during: alum bg2 ferr bg2 *Ign* bg2 nux-m bg2 plat bg2 zinc bg2
  - **periodical** | **evening**; alternate: ferr bg2
  - **perspiration**; during: alum bg2 *Aur* bg2 croc bg2 *Ferr* bg2 **Ign** bg2 *Plat* bg2 stram bg2 sul-ac bg2 valer bg2 zinc bg2
  - **sudden**: tarent br1
  - **wavelike**: conch fkr1•
- **bad** mood (See Irritability; Morose)
- **changeable**: (↗*Capriciousness; Impulsive; Inconstancy; Irresolution; Persisting; Undertaking - many; CHILL - Changing; FEVER - Changing; GENERALS - Contradictory; GENERALS - Side - alternating; STOMACH - Appetite - capricious)* abrom-a ckh1 *Acon* k* acon-l st adam skp7*• agar k2 agath-a nl2• agn k* alco a1 aloe k* *Alum* k* alum-p k2 alum-sil k2 am-c ↓ ambr k* anac anan a1 androc srj1• ang c1 anh sp1 ant-t k* *Apis* k* arg-met k* *Arg-n* arn k* *Ars* k* ars-h kr1 ars-i asaf k* asar k* astra-e jl *Aur* k* aur-i k2 aur-m *Aur-m-n* wbt2• aur-s k2 bac jl2 bamb-a stb2.de• *Bar-act* sf1.de *Bar-c* *Bell* k* bism k* *Borx* bov k* brucel sa3• bry k* bufo buth-a jl *Calc* calc-s calc-sil k2 camph-mbr bro1 cann-i br1 cann-s k* canth b7.de* caps k* carb-an k* carb-v h2* carbn-o a1 carbn-s k* *Carc* mlr1• carl cassia-s ccrh1• castm bro1 caul ↓ caust k* cerstig-w mtf11 cham ptk1 *Chin* k* chir-fl gya2 choc srj3*• cic ↓ cimic k2* cina ptk1 cob bro1 coc-c sf1.de coca a1 coca-c sk4• *Cocc* k* *Coff* bro1* con cortico jl* *Croc* k* *Cupr* k* cur a2 cycl k* cypra-eg sde6.de• *Des-ac* rbp6 *Dig* dioxi rbp6 dros k* emb-r bnj1 eup-per kr1 falco-pe nl2• *Ferr* k* ferr-ar ferr-i k2 form sf1.de fum rly4• gels k* gink-b sbd1• graph k* guare a1 hyos k* **Ign** k* iod k* ip ptk1 irid-met srj5• *Kali-c* k* kali-p k* kali-s kali-sil k2* *Kola* stb3• lac-c lac-d k2* lac-h htj1• lac-leo hrn2• lac-loxod-a hrn2• lach k* lachn laur ↓ led b7.de* lil-t bro1 limest-b es1• luna kg1• **Lyc** k* m-arct b7.de* m-aust j5.de *Mag-c* k* mang-act bro1 med k2 melal-alt gya4 meny *Merc* k* merc-c b4a.de* mez *Moni* rfm1• morph mosch bro1* mur-ac h2 nat-c k* nat-m k* neon srj5• nid jl nit-ac k* **Nux-m** k* nux-v sf1.de* onop jl op k* ozone sde2• *Petr* ph-ac ↓ phel *Phos* k* pitu-gl skp7• plac-s rly4• plan *Plat* k* plb k2 propr sa3• *Psor* k* **Puls** k* pulx br1 ran-b rat rheum a1 rhod ↓ rhus-g tmo3• *Rhus-t* ↓ sabad k* sal-fr sle1• sang a1 sanic k* sapin a1 **Sars** k* scler mtf11 senec ptk1* seneg k* *Sep* k* ser-a-c jl2 sil k* spig k* spong k* *Stann* k1* *Staph* k1* *Stram* k* streptoc rly4• suis-em rly4• *Sul-ac* k* sul-i k2 sulph k* *Sumb* bro1 suprar rly4• *Symph* fd3.de• *Syph* jl2 tab ↓ taosc iwa1• tarent k* thal-xyz srj8• thiam rly4• thuj k* *Tub* k* *Valer* k* vanil fd5.de verat k* verb viol-o sf1.de yuc a1 **Zinc** k* zinc-p k2* *Zinc-val* bro1 ziz bro1 [ant-c stj2 ant-m stj2 *Ant-met* stj2 arg-p stj2 bar-i stj2 bism-sn stj2 cadm-met stj2 cadm-s stj2 chr-met stj2 chr-s stj2 heroin sdj2 lac-mat sst4 lith-i stj2 mang-i stj2 merc-i-f stj2 rubd-met stj2 spect dfg1 tax jsj7 zinc-i stj2 zinc-m stj2 zinc-n stj2]
  - **evening**: aur croc
  - **night**: carb-v gl1.fr• cic jl
  - **anxiety**; with: propr sa3•
  - **children**; in: chin mtf33 cupr mtf33 emb-r bnj1 ign mtf33 kali-sil mtf33 mag-c mtf33 nit-ac mtf33 plat mtf33 sep mtf33 tub mtf33
  - **delivery**; during: caul mrr1

- **changeable**: ...
  - **dinner**, after: aloe
  - **epistaxis** amel.: borx st
  - **heat**, during: *Nux-m*
  - **menses** | **before**: cham ptk1 luna kg1•
  - **opinions**, in: bell gl1.fr• graph gl1.fr• kali-c gl1.fr• lyc gl1.fr• petr gl1.fr• plat gl1.fr•
  - **perspiration**, during: **Aur** *Bell* bg2 **Bry** bg2 calc bg2 *Chin* bg2 *Croc* ip bg2 laur bg2 nux-v bg2 op bg2 ph-ac bg2 **Puls** bg2 rheum bg2 *Rhus-t* bg2 stram k* **Sul-ac** verat bg2 zinc
  - **quickly**: des-ac rbp6 rhus-g tmo3•
  - **sudden**: asaf ptk1 cassia-s ckh1 croc tl1* rhod ptk1 sep ptk1 tab ptk1 tarent tl1* tub ptk1 *Valer* ptk1
    - **touch**; on: asaf ptk1
  - **supper**, after: am-c gl1.fr• carb-v gl1.fr•
- **contradictory**: puls br1
- **heavy** (See Sadness)
- **holy** mood: olib-sac wmh1
- **insupportable**: calc h2*
- **lachrymose** mood (See Weeping)
- **repulsive**: (↗*Casting; Censorious; Confidence - want; Fancies - repulsive; Frown; Indifference; Morose; Quarrelsome; Unsympathetic; FACE - Expression - cold)* acon aloe↓ alum ambr *Anac* gg ant-c arg-n mtf33 arizon-l nl2• arn ars aur bell camph caps carb-ac a1 carc mlr1• caust con croc *Dulc* fd4.de ferr j gink-b sbd1• *Hep* k* ign ip kali-c lact laur led lyc mag-c mag-m *Merc* *Nat-sil* fd3.de• neon srj5• nit-ac nux-v ozone sde2• par mrr1 petr phos plb *Psor* st1* **Puls** k ● *Ruta* fd4.de samb sars sep gl1.fr• sil spong sulph thuj k* tritic-vg fd5.de upa c1 vanil fd5.de
  - **milk**; after: mag-c mtf33
  - **repels** everyone: aloe kr1* arizon-l nl2•
- **stuck** and tight: lac-lup hrn2•

MOON: | **full** moon agg.: sulph bg2

MOONLIGHT agg.: (↗*Ecstasy - Night - walking; Ecstasy - Walking; Sentimental - Moonlight; EAR - Pain - Full; EYE - Light - Moonlight - amel.; GENERALS - Light - Agg. - moonlight; VISION - Light; from - Moonlight - amel.)* *Ant-c* k* bell cypra-eg sde6.de• meph jl3 thuj

MOPING (See Indifference; Sadness)

MORAL FEELING; want of: (↗*Behavior - children; Brutality; Conscientious; Cruelty; Depravity; Duty - no; Hardhearted; Honor - sense; Indifference - conscience; Libertinism; Malicious; Misanthropy; Mischievous; Religious - want; Sensitive - moral; Slander; Unfeeling)* abrot bro1* acetan bro1 achy jl3 alco a1 am-c a1 *Anac* k* androc srj1* arizon-l nl2• ars a1* aster a1 **Bell** ptk1 bism *Bufo* sf1.de* cass a1 cere-s bro1 chin sf1.de choc srj3• clem a1 *Coca* br1* *Cocain* br1* cocc coloc con convo-d a1 croc cur falco-pe nl2• fl-ac mrr1 flav jl2 granit-m es1• haliae-lc srj5• hep gl1.fr• hura a1 **Hyos** k* *Kali-br* k* kali-n a1 lac-c lac-h sze9• lach↓ *Laur* k* merc↓ *Morph* bro1* nat-m a1* nit-ac sf1.de nux-v bg* op k* ozone sde2• ped a1 petr-ra shn4• ph-ac ptk1 phasco-ci rbp2 pic-ac bro1 *Plat* j5.de* plut-n srj7• polys sk4• psil jl3* sabad *Sep* sf1.de* squil j5.de **Stram** ptk1 stry-p bro1 syph mtf33 *Tarent* bg* tub mrr1 **Verat** sf1.de* [absin stj art-v stj heroin sdj2]
- **criminal**, without remorse; disposition to become a: ars gl1.fr• bell gl1.fr• hep gl1.fr• lach gl1.fr• merc gl1.fr• [heroin sdj2]
- **weeping**; with: bell br1

MOROSE (= gloomy, fretful, ill humor, sullen): (↗*Complaining; Cynical; Discontented; Discontented - everything; Discouraged - morose; Frown; Irritability; Mood - repulsive; Muttering; Pessimist; Petulant; Sulky; Unfriendly; Wearisome; FACE - Expression - sullen)* abies-c a1 abrom-a ckh1 abrot hr1* acet-ac k2* *Acon* b2.de* adam srj5• *Aesc* a1* aeth k* aether a1 *Agar* k* agn b7.de* aids↓ alco a1 alf bro1 aloe k* alum k* alum-sil k2* *Alumn* a1 *Am-c* k* am-m b2.de* ambr a1 ammc a1* **Anac** k* ang b2.de* **Ant-c** b2.de* *Ant-t* b7.de* anth vh1 anthraco a1 apis b7a.de* arag br1 aral vh1 *Aran* k* arg-met b7.de* arg-n mrr1 **Arn** k* *Ars* b2.de* ars-s-r hr1* *Art-v* k* arum-t sf1.de *Asaf* b2.de* *Asar* b2.de* asc-t a1* aspar j5.de* aster hr1* atro a1* *Atro-s* hr1 **Aur** k* **Aur-m**↓ aur-m-n wbt2• aur-s a1* bac al bar-act a1 bar-c b2.de* bart a1 **Bell** k* benz-ac↓ berb j5.de* *Bism* k* *Bism-o* a1 bol-la a1 bond a1 *Borx* b2.de* *Bov* b2.de* bran a1 brom a1* bros-gau mrc1 bruc↓ **Bry** k* bufo bro1* bufo-s a1 cact a1* cadm-s c1

Morose: ...
Calad↓ **Calc** k* calc-act a1 calc-ar↓ calc-br c2* calc-caust↓ *Calc-p* bg2* calc-s k* calc-sil k2* calen a1* camph b7.de* cann-s b2.de* *Canth* k* *Caps* b2.de* carb-ac k* carb-an k* carb-v k* *Carbn-s* *Carc* mlr1• card-b a1 carl a1 cas-s↓ cass↓ castm j5.de* *Caul* hr1* caust k* **Cham** b2.de* chel k* chin b2.de* chin-b↓ chinin-s chlol k* chlor a1 cic b2.de* *Cimic* mrr1 *Cina* k* cinnb k* clem k* cob-n jl3 coc-c a1* coca↓ cocc k* *Coff* b2.de* *Colch* k* **Coloc** k* com a1 *Con* k* conch fkr1• cop k* cor-r j5.de* *Corn* a1* corv-cor bdg• *Croc* bg2* *Crot-h* hr1* *Crot-t* k* cub a1 cupr k* cupr-act a1 cur a1 *Cycl* k* daph a1* des-ac jl dicha jl3 *Dig* k* digin a1 dios hr1* dirc a1 dros b2.de* dulc b2.de* elae a1 elaps a1 elec al eug↓ euon a1 euph-a a1 euphr b7.de* fago↓ fel a1 ferr k* ferr-act↓ ferr-ma a1 ferr-p *Fil*↓ fl-ac bg2* form k* franz a1 galv c1 gamb a1 *Gels* bg2* gent-l j5.de* gnaph c1 *Gran* a1 *Graph* b2.de* *Grat* j5.de* guaj k* haem a1 ham a1 hell a1 helon hr1* *Hep* b2.de* hera a1 heroin↓ hipp a1 hydr a1* hydr-ac a1* hydrog srj2• *Hyos* b2.de* iber bro1* ictod kr1 *Ign* k* ind hr1* *Indg* j5.de* indol bro1 *Iod* b4.de* *Ip* k* irid-met srj5• iris a1 *Jal*↓ jatr-c a1 *Jug-c*↓ jug-r a1* kali-ar k* **Kali-bi** bg2* *Kali-br* hr1* *Kali-c* b2.de* kali-chl j5.de* kali-cy↓ kali-i a1 kali-n b4.de* *Kali-p* k* kalm a1 ketogl-ac rly4• kiss a1 kola stb3• kreos k* lac-c bro1 lac-f al *Lach* b2.de* lachn a1 lact-v a1 *Laur* b2.de* *Led* k* lil-t a1* lina a1 linu-c a1 lipp a1 *Lyc* k* lycpr j5.de lyss k* m-ambo j m-arct b7.de* *M-aust* b2.de* mag-c k* *Mag-m* b2.de* mag-s a1* magn-gr c1 malar al manc mang k* med jl2 meli al menis a1 meny b2.de* meph j5.de* **Merc** k* *Merc-c* b4a.de* *Merc-cy*↓ merc-i-f a1 merc-i-r a1 merc-sul↓ merl k1 *Mez* k* morph a1 mosch b7.de* *Mur-ac* k* myric a1 naja a1 nat-ar a1 *Nat-c* b2.de* *Nat-m* b2.de* nat-n a1 nat-p a1 *Nat-s* j5.de* neon srj5• nicc a1* *Nit-ac* b2.de* nit-s-d j5.de nux-m a1 **Nux-v** k* oena↓ ol-an j5.de* olib-sac↓ *Olnd* b7.de* *Op* b7.de* opun-s a1 (non:opun-v a1) orig hr1* osm a1 ox-ac↓ ozone sde2• paeon a1 *Pall* hr1* palo jl3 par j5.de *Petr* b4.de* *Ph-ac* k* *Phel* j5.de* *Phos* k* pic-ac a1 plac↓ *Plan* k* *Plat* k* *Plb* k* plect a1 plumbg a1 podo c1 *Prun* j5.de* *Psor* bg2* ptel a1 **Puls** k* puls-n a1 pyrog al rad-br bro1 (non:rad-met) ran-b b2.de* ran-s a1 rat j5.de* rauw sp1 rheum k* rhod b4.de* **Rhus-t** b2.de* rhus-v a1 rob a1 ruta k* sabad b2.de* sabal c1 sabin b2.de* sacch a1 sacch-a↓ sacch-l c1 sal-n c1 *Samb* b7.de* sang k* sapin a1 sars k* sel b7a.de* seneg b2.de* *Sep* b2.de* serp a1 **Sil** k* sin-n a1* sol-t-ae a1 spig b7.de* spirae a1 *Spong* b2.de* squil b2.de* stann k* *Staph* b2.de* *Stram* b2.de* *Stront-c* b2.de* *Stry* *Sul-ac* b2.de* sulfon bro1 *Sulph* k* sumb a1 *Syph* bro1* tab j5.de* tarax j5.de* tarent a1* tep a1 terebe↓ tet c1 teucr b2.de* thea j5.de* thuj k* thymol bro1* til a1 tong↓ tril-c a1 *Tritic-vg* fd5.de tub hr1* upa a1 uran-n k* uva a1 vac a1* valer k* vanil fd5.de verat b2.de* verat-v bro1 verb k* vinc j5.de* viol-o a1 viol-t b2.de* vip j5.de visc jl3 voes a1 wies a1 xan bg *Zinc* k* *Zinc-o* j5.de *Zinc-ox* j5.de zinc-p k2* zinc-val↓ [ant-met stj2 bell-p-sp dcm1]
- **daytime**: *Cham* hr1* *Cina* k* ip a1 iris a1 kreos a1 lyc a1* *Med* hr1* merc *Merc-c* a1 nat-m a1 phel a1 phos a1 plat a1 staph a1 sul-ac a1 sulph a1 viol-t a1
- **morning**: agar↓ am-c j5.de* am-m ant-t a1 *Ars* j5.de* asaf j5.de aur-m-n wbt2• bell↓ bov j5.de* bruc j5.de bry j5.de *Calad* a1* calc j5.de* calc-act a1 calc-ar a1 calc-caust a1 canth a1 carb-an↓ castm j5.de* chin a1 chlor a1 coca a1 coff a1 con hep hipp kali-ar↓ kali-c j kalm hr1* kola stb3• kreos j5.de* *Lach* hr1* *Lyc* k2* lyss c1 mag-c h2 mag-m mang med↓ merc-i-r a1* mez j *Nat-m* a1* nat-s nit-ac *Nux-v* j5.de* petr j ph-ac j5.de phos plat h2* plb j puls↓ rhus-t j sars h2* sep j5.de **Staph** a1 sul-ac j5.de sulph tarax j5.de* thuj j vanil fd5.de zinc
  - **bed**, in: *Ars* h2* bell j5.de bry j5.de castm j5.de* kali-c j5.de *Lyc* j5.de mez j5.de nit-ac j5.de nux-v j5.de petr j5.de ph-ac j5.de plat j5.de plb j5.de puls j5.de rhus-t j5.de thuj j5.de
  - **waking**, on: agar a1 bell a1 carb-an a1 coca a1 kali-ar k2 med jl2 merc-i-r gt* nat-m a1 nit-ac a1 sul-ac a1 thuj a1
- **forenoon**: am-c k* am-m k* ant-t a1 canth a1 caust colch con k* des-ac jl3 grat j5.de* hipp a1 kreos↓ *Mag-c* j5.de* *Mang* a1 *Nat-m* a1* nat-p a1 nicc a1 phos k* sars h2* seneg j5.de* sil a1 verat a1
  - **10-22 h**: kreos a1
- **noon**: dulc fd4.de zinc a1*
- **afternoon**: aeth alum anac a1 ant-c a1 borx bov j5.de* brom↓ cann-s canth chel a1 cinnb k* clem↓ colch con j5.de* cycl↓ elaps a1 hell a1 hydr-ac a1 kali-c laur mag-s mang merc-c a1 mur-ac nat-c nat-m a1 nit-ac j5.de olib-sac wmh1 op a1 ox-ac a1 puls ruta a1 sang a1 sars k* zinc
  - **17-18 h**: *Con* kr1
  - **amel.**: mag-c j5.de
  - **siesta**, after: brom a1 clem a1 cycl a1
  - **twilight** (See evening - twilight)
- **evening**: aloe a1 am-c a1 am-m j ant-c j5.de bar-c a1 bov a1 calc a1 calc-s a1 castm a1 chin j con j5.de cycl a1 dios a1 fago a1 form a1 hep sf1.de ign j5.de indg a1 kali-c h2* kali-cy a1 kalm j lyc a1* lyss a1 m-aust j5.de mag-c h2* mag-m h2* mur-ac h2* nat-c a1 nat-m a1 ox-ac a1 pall a1 phos a1* puls j5.de* rhus-t j spig a1 **Sulph** a1* upa↓ zinc

- **and** next forenoon: kalm hr1*
- **amel.**: bism j euph-a a1 puls sf1.de
- **bed**, in: chin j5.de rhus-t j5.de upa a1
- **twilight**, in: am-m sf1.de *Phos* gl1.fr•

- **night**: anac j5.de ant-t bro1 borx j5.de camph a1* cham j5.de chin j5.de chinin-s j *Jal* bro1 lyc j5.de lyss a1 m-arct j5.de nux-v bro1 phos j5.de* *Psor* hr1* rheum bro1 **Rhus-t** j5.de* sabad j5.de
- **air**, in open: *Aeth* j5.de* borx j5.de calc j5.de* *Con* j5.de mur-ac j5.de plat a1 rhus-t a1 stann j5.de
  - **amel.**: anac j asar j5.de calc k* coff j5.de stann k*
- **alternating** with:
  - **affectionate**: plat j5.de
  - **cheerfulness**: acon j5.de ant-t j5.de* ars h2* *Aur* j5.de* borx j5.de bov j5.de calc-p j5.de carb-v j5.de *Chin* j5.de chin-b hr1* croc j5.de cycl j5.de* eug j5.de* form sf1.de kali-c j5.de kali-chl j5.de* mag-m j5.de merc-c j5.de* nat-c j5.de nat-m j5.de* oena j5.de ol-an j5.de plat j5.de
  - **embracing** (See Embraces - everyone - alternating)
  - **exhilaration**: aids nl2• ant-t j5.de*
  - **exuberance** (See exhilaration)
  - **laughing**: borx j5.de croc j5.de
  - **singing**: croc j5.de
  - **tenderness** (See affectionate)
  - **weeping**: bell a1
- **business** does not proceed fast; when: ip a1
- **caressing** agg.: chin gl1.fr•
- **causeless**: aloe a1 bry a1 chel a1 clem a1* cycl a1 *Nat-m* a1 ptel a1 rhod a1
- **children**, in: *Ant-c* j5.de* **Ant-t** kr1* ars j5.de benz-ac hr1 borx j5.de calc k2* calc-p mtf33 *Carc* mlr1• **Cham** hr1* **Cina** k* dulc fd4.de graph j5.de hep c1 *Jug-c* hr1 *Nat-m* ↓ op wbt• *Psor* c1 *Puls* j5.de* rheum st sacch c1* sil j5.de* **Staph** ↓ terebe c1
  - **morning**; early: **Staph** kr1
  - **carried**, desire to be: *(↗Carried - desire)* benz-ac hr1* cham hr1*
  - **cry**, when touched: **Ant-c** kr1
  - **spoken** to, when: *Nat-m* hr1*
- **chill**, during: anac b4a.de* am bg2 ars b4a.de* bry bg2 **Calc** bg2 calen a1* camph j caps b7.de* caust *Cham* b7.de* chin bg2 **Con** b4a.de* hep j5.de* ign bg2* kreos b7a.de* **Lyc** bg2 m-aust j5.de merc bg2 mez j5.de* nat-m a1 nit-ac bg2 petr bg2 phos bg2 plat b4a.de* puls k* *Rheum* bg2 rhus-t bg2 sabad bg2 sil bg2 *Spig* b7.de* *Sulph* bg2 thuj bg2
- **coffee**, after: calc-p a1
- **coition**, after: ang a1 calc bg2 nat-c j5.de *Nat-m* a1* *Sel* b7.de*
- **colors**:
  - **rusty** | **agg.**: sil vk4
- **contradiction**, by: bros-gau mrc1 **Dulc** fd* ign a1 tarent a1 *Verat* a1
- **conversing** amel.: lyss hr1*
- **convulsions** | **before**: zinc kr1* zinc-val sf1.de
- **coryza**; during: hep b4a.de *Nux-v* b7a.de *Puls* b7a.de
- **cough**: *(↗whooping)*
  - **before** fits of: ant-t sf1.de asaf a1 bell a1
  - **during**: bell b4.de* *Cham* b7a.de nux-v b7a.de spong b7.de*
- **dentition**, in: **Cham** hr1*
- **discouragement**; with (See Discouraged - morose)
- **dreams**, by: op a1
- **drunkenness**, during: caust gl1.fr• hydr gl1.fr• lach gl1.fr• nux-v gl1.fr•
- **ear** lobes, with hot: *Alum* hr1*
- **eating**, after: am-c hr1* am b7a.de* *Borx* b4a.de* bov j5.de bry a1 calad hr1* carb-v cham ferr-act sf1.de ferr-ma a1 *Graph* a1* iod j5.de kali-c kalm j merc a1 *Merc-cy* hr1* merc-sul nat-c k* nux-v b7a.de* ol-an j5.de phos puls sil j thuj
- **epistaxis** amel.: kali-chl j5.de*
- **fever**:
  - **after**: am-c a1 card-b a1 hipp a1 sil b4a.de
  - **during**: *Acon* j5.de* *Aran* j5.de* *Ars* b4.de* asar j5.de bell bg borx j5.de calc bg *Cham* bg cic j5.de con bg *Ferr* hr1* ip hr1* kali-n b4a.de lyc j5.de* m-aust j5.de mosch b7.de* **Nat-c** bg nux-v bg petr j5.de puls b7.de* rheum b7.de staph bg *Sulph* hr1* thuj bg
- **fly** on wall, by: sars a1
- **followed** by | **repentance**: bros-gau mrc1 vinc kr1
- **forgetfulness**, from: *Anac* hr1* ham fd3.de•
- **heat** in head, with: aeth hr1*
- **hiccough**; during: *Agn* b7a.de
- **house** agg.; in | **open** air amel.; on walking in: calc h2 mag-c a1 **Rhus-t** a1*
- **hurry**, with: carc mlr1• thuj hr1*
- **hypochondriasis**, in: *(↗Hypochondriasis - morose)* carc mlr1• grat hr1* *Mosch* hr1* **Puls** hr1*
- **interruption**, from: cham j5.de
- **laughing**, followed by loud: stram hr1*
- **menopause**; at: *Psor* st
- **menses**:
  - **after**: *(↗Menses - after)* bufo kr1 ferr k*
  - **before**: *(↗Menses - before)* *Cham* hr1* *Lyc* k* *Nux-v* k* plac rzf5•
  - **during**: *(↗Menses - during)* am-c b4.de* cas-s a1 castm a1 caust b4a.de* *Cham* a1* ferr a1 ind a1 lyc a1 mag-c a1 mur-ac a1 plat a1 tarent a1 zinc b4a.de
    - **beginning** of: cham b7.de
  - **suppressed**, in: cycl hr1*
- **music**: *(↗Music - amel.)*
  - **joyous**; during: *Mang* h1*
  - **sad** | **amel.**: mang h1*
- **nausea**, with: sang hr1
- **oneself**, with: ars a1 aur a1
- **pain**, after: **Cham** a1 crot-t a1 hep j5.de* ign j5.de
- **perspiration**, during: mag-c
- **pollutions**, after: *Dig* kr1 nat-c b4.de* *Nux-v* b7a.de *Thuj* kr1
- **puberty**, in: *(↗Puberty)* *Cina* st ph-ac sf1.de
- **questioned**, when: nat-m a1 spong fd4.de
- **sexual** desire; with violent: orig hr1*
- **shivering**; during: m-aust b7.de
- **sleep**, in: anac j5.de nux-v j5.de rhus-t j5.de
  - **amel.**: caps j5.de
- **sleepiness**, with: calc j5.de calc-act a1 calen j5.de carb-an j5.de hyos j5.de kali-c j5.de ol-an j5.de ph-ac j5.de sabad j5.de sep j5.de
- **stomach**; with complaints of: *Nat-m* b4a.de
- **stool** | **before**: *Borx* b4a.de* calc a1
- **storm**, during (See weather - stormy)
- **taciturn**: *(↗Taciturn)* *Chin* gl1.fr• *Stann* gl1.fr• tong a1 viol-t kr1 [heroin sdj2]
- **talk**; indisposed to (See taciturn)
- **talking** of others, on: zinc hr1*
- **tearful**: dig c1
- **thinking** of his ailments when alone; on: **Aur-m** kr1
- **thunderstorm**, from: am-c st
- **trifles**, about: aspar hr1* *Bell* a1 carb-v a1 **Cham** a1* chel a1 con a1 *Cycl* a1 hep a1 lact-v a1 lyc a1 meph a1 merc-i-r a1 myric a1 *Nux-m* a1 *Ptel* hr1* sacch-a fd2.de• sil hr1*
- **waking**, on: anac j5.de ant-t j5.de* *Ars* j5.de bell j5.de* borx j5.de bry j5.de calc sf1.de cass a1 caust j5.de cham j5.de chel j5.de* *Cina* kr1 clem a1 cycl j5.de* ign j5.de jatr-c a1 kali-c j5.de **Lyc** j5.de* lyss hr1* m-aust j5.de med jl2 mez j5.de* nit-ac j5.de nux-v j5.de* petr j5.de ph-ac j5.de phos j5.de* plat j5.de* plb j5.de rhus-t j5.de sabad j5.de sep sf1.de tarent a1 thuj j5.de*
- **walking** in open air; after: am-c j calc j con j m-aust j puls gl1.fr•
- **weather**:
  - **bad**; from: am-c gl1.fr•
  - **cloudy**; from: aloe st am-c st dulc fd4.de
  - **rainy**; from: am-c st
  - **stormy**: *Am-c* kr1*
- **weeping** amel.: nit-ac j5.de *Plat* j5.de
- **whooping** cough; in: *(↗cough)* *Bry* kr1 cupr-act kr1
- **women**, in: calc gl1.fr• nat-m gl1.fr• nux-v gl1.fr• plat gl1.fr• sil gl1.fr•
- **work**, with inclination to: sars k*
- **worm** affection, in: *Carb-v* kr1 **Cina** kr1 *Fil* kr1

MORPHINISM: *(↗Delusions - opiate; Drugs - desire - psychotropic; Mania - morphine; GENERALS - Medicine - allopathic - addiction; GENERALS - Narcotics; GENERALS - Narcotics - desire)* agar sf1.de *Anh* mtf apom c1* ars sf1.de aur sf1.de *Aur-m-n* sne *Aven* c1* bell sf1.de* calc gl1.fr• cann-i bro1* *Cham* sf1.de* cic sf1.de cimic bro1 coff sf1.de hyos sf1.de ip c1* kali-perm sf1.de *Lach* sf1.de lob bro1* *Macro* bro1 med mtf m e r c gl1.fr• mur-ac sf1.de nat-p c1* nux-v br1* op a1* ox-ac st1 *Passi* br1* phos sf1.de plat sf1.de puls sf1.de sep sf1.de zinc sf1.de [heroin sdj2]

MORTIFICATION; ailments from (See Ailments - disappointment/ Ailments - mortification)

MOTHER COMPLEX: *(↗Clinging - children - mother; Mother fixation; Oedipus)* aur-m mtf calc-lac mtf lac-h mtf mag-lac mtf

MOTHER FIXATION: *(↗Clinging - children - mother; Mother complex; Oedipus)* bar-c mtf *Bism* mtf lac-del mtf lac-h mtf lach ggd1 mag-lac mtf mag-m mtf plut-n mtf positr mtf puls mtf sil mtf

MOTION:
- **agg.**: acon bg2 ambr b7.de* *Bell* b4.de* berb bg2 bry b7.de* calc b4.de* mag-c b4.de* nux-v b7.de* phos b4.de* puls b7.de* rhod bg2
- **amel.**: bry bg2 ferr bg2 mag-c b4.de* nat-c b4.de* puls b7.de*
- **head** agg.; of: samb b7.de*

MOTIONS (See Gestures)

MOTIVATION:
- **lacking** (See Laziness; Will - loss)
- **strong** (See Ambition)

MOUNTAINS: | **desire** for (See Countryside - desire - mountains)

MOVE CONSTANTLY; must (See Restlessness - move - must)

MUDDLED (See Confusion)

MURDER, desire to (See Kill)

MURMURING (See Muttering)

MUSIC:
- **ability** for: staph mtf33 sulph mtf33
- **agg.**: *(↗Ailments - music; Anxiety - church; Anxiety - music; Anxiety - playing; Delusions - music - hearing; Excitement - music; Fear - music; Fear - piano; Irritability - music - during; Restlessness - music; Sadness - music; Sensitive - music; Suicidal - music; Thoughts - persistent - music; Unconsciousness - music; Weeping - music; Weeping - music - bells; GENERALS - Music - agg.)* **Acon** k* *Aloe* kr1 *Ambr* k* *Anac* a1* aur-m-n wbt2• bufo st cact st *Calc* sf1.de* *Carc* st1* caust sf1.de* *Cham* sf1.de* chir-fl gya2 cop ↓ *Croc* sf1.de *Dig* k* **Graph** k* *Ign* k* *Kali-br* hr1 *Kali-c* ↓ kreos b7a.de* *Lyc* k* mang a1 merc st **Nat-c** k2* nat-p st *Nat-s* k* **Nux-v** k* pall sf1.de *Ph-ac* sf1.de *Phos* c1* *Sabin* k* **Sep** sf1.de* sumb a1 symph fd3.de• *Tarent* k* thuj k* *Viol-o* sf1.de zinc sf1.de*
  - **brass** of: zinc glh
  - **organ**: graph mtf33 lyc thuj
  - **piano** playing, from: anac b4a.de* calc b4a.de* cham st cop a1 *Kali-br* hr1 kali-c sf1.de* *Nat-c* b4.de* phos hr1* sep b4.de* zinc b4a.de*
  - **violin** playing: calc b2.de* *Kali-c* b2.de* *Viol-o* b2.de*
- **agreeable**, is (See desire)
- **amel.**: *(↗Hysteria - music; Morose - music; Sadness - music; Sensitive - noise - music)* am-m st ambr tsm1 androc srj1• anh sp1* **Aur** k* *Aur-m* k* *Aur-m-n* wbt2• *Aur-s* wbt2• bufo k2 carc st* carneg-g rwt1• chir-fl gya2 cop st* cupr stj2* dulc fd4.de hydrog srj2• kali-p fd1.de• kali-s fd4.de lac-leo hm2• lach mtf mang k* merc st* nat-m bg2* *Nat-sil* fd3.de• podo fd3.de• positr nl2• *Ruta* fd4.de spong fd4.de stront-c sk4• suis-em rly4• sul-ac bg2* sumb bg2* symph fd3.de• **Tarent** k* *Thuj* bg2* tritic-vg fd5.de tub bg2* [cupr-act stj2 cupr-f stj2 cupr-m stj2 cupr-p stj2 rubd-met stj2]
- **aversion** to: **Acon** bg2* alum gl1.fr• bell ↓ bufo kr1* cadm-met gm1 carc c1* caust a1* cham a1* hep gl1.fr• kali-s fd4.de lac-cp sk4• mang ↓ merc j5.de* n i t - a c gl1.fr• nux-v bg2* sabin bg2* sep mg1.de* symph fd3.de• viol-o a1*
  - **children**; in:
    - ⁝ **nurslings** | **nursed**; when the child is: bell mtf33
  - **joyous** music, but immediately affected by the saddest: mang kr1

Music – aversion to: ...
  - **violin**, of: viol-o a1*
- **carried** by; sensation of being: anh sp1 falco-pe nl2• spong fd4.de
- **cough** agg. (See COUGH - Music - agg.)
- **desire** for: aur ↓ bamb-a stb2.de• bar-ox-suc ↓ bufo gk* bung-fa ↓ cann-i a1* **Carc** fd* chin mtf33 chlf ↓ coca-c ↓ *Dulc* fd4.de ign h1* kali-m ckh1 *Kola* stb3• mang ↓ nat-c ↓ oxal-a ↓ ozone ↓ *Plat* ↓ positr nl2• ruta fd4.de spong fd4.de s t a p h mtf33 suis-em rly4• symph fd3.de• **Tarent** sf1.de* tritic-vg fd5.de ulm-c ↓ vanil fd5.de [mang-met stj2]
  - **children**; in: aur ↓ bufo ↓ carc mtf33 chin mtf33 staph mtf33 tarent ↓
    - ⁝ **nurslings** | **nursed**; when the child is: aur mtf33 bufo mtf33 t a r e n t mtf33
  - **piano**; desire to play the: bar-ox-suc rly4• chlf a1 oxal-a rly4• *Plat* kr1
  - **sad** music: *(↗Sadness - music - amel. - sad)* bung-fa mtf m a n g ptk1 nat-c mrr1 ozone sde2•
  - **shape**, structure and energy; for its: positr nl2•
  - **soft** music: coca-c sk4•
  - **varying**: ulm-c jsj8•
- **drums** produce euphoria: anh sp1
- **earache** from (See EAR - Pain - music - from)
- **faintness** on hearing music (See GENERALS - Faintness - music)
- **headache** from (See HEAD - Pain - music)
- **lessons**; cannot give her music: *Kali-br* kr1
- **palpitation** when listening to (See CHEST - Palpitation - music)
- **piano**; desire to play (See desire - piano)
- **sensitive** to music (See Sensitive - music)
- **sleepiness** from (See SLEEP - Sleepiness - music)
- **trembling** from music:
  - **general**; in (See GENERALS - Trembling - externally - music)
- **weariness**:
  - **from** music (See GENERALS - Weariness - music)
  - **playing** piano, from (See GENERALS - Weariness - playing)

MUTILATING his body: *(↗Injuring; Masochism; Suicidal; Tormenting; Tormenting - himself)* agar bro1 ars k* bac mtf bell bro1 carc mtf chlol btw2 choc knl• cupr mtf cur mrr1* dict knl• dig mtf helium knl• hyos bro1 lach mtf lat-h thj1 lil-t mtf lyc gk lyss knl• manc mrr1 med mrr* plb mtf positr nl2• sec mtf staph mp1• stram bro1 syph bcr tab mtf t a r e n t knl* tub mp1* [am-f stj2 bor-pur stj2 heroin sdj2 lith-c stj2 lith-f stj2 lith-i stj2 lith-met stj2]

MUTISM (See Taciturn; Taciturn - mutism)

MUTTERING: *(↗Complaining; Confusion; Delirium - murmuring; Delirium - muttering; Discontented; Grumbling; Grunting; Lamenting; Moaning; Morose; Stupor - murmuring; Talking - himself; Unconsciousness - muttering; MOUTH - Speech - unintelligible)* aether a1 ail k* alum anac a1 *Anac-oc* ↓ ant-t bro1 *Apis* *Arg-n* ↓ *Arn* ars ars-s-f k2 arum-t bg2 atro a1* atro-s hr1 *Bapt* bg2* bar-act ↓ *Bar-c* ↓ **Bell** k* bry st1 calad calc st1 calc-sil k2 camph ↓ cann-s caust st1* cham chel chlf a1 chlol a1 chlor a1 cic kr1 *Cocc* colch con ↓ conin a1 cortico ↓ *Crot-h* k2* dulc hell bg2 *Hep* **Hyos** k* indg ↓ irid-met srj5• iris kali-br ↓ **Lach** k* *Lyc* k* *Merc* morph a1 **Mur-ac** ↓ nat-m *Nit-s-d* ↓ nux-v k* *Op* k* ph-ac *Phos* plb raph ↓ *Rhus-t* *Sec* sil stann **Stram** k* sul-ac **Sulph** ↓ tab tarax *Verat* vesp a1 vip
- **evening**: bell calc-sil ↓ con a1 *Phos* plb sil ↓
  - **bed**, in: sil
  - **going** to sleep; on: calc-sil k2
- **night**: *Arg-n* kr1 atro a1 sil ↓
  - **waking**, on: atro a1 sil
- **absurd** things: verat mtf33
- **alternating** with | **vivacity** (See Vivacious - alternating - muttering)
- **apoplexy**, in: *Arn* hr1* *Cocc* hr1* *Crot-h* hr1*
- **fever**; during: *Apis* b7a.de bell b4a.de *Mur-ac* b4a.de *Op* b7a.de ph-ac b4a.de
- **himself**; to: hyos b7.de* lach b7a.de op b7a.de stram b7a.de *Tarax* b7a.de

- **old** people; in: *Bar-c* kr1
- **sleep**, in: (↗*Talking - sleep)* alum k* *Apis* b7a.de* ars k* bar-act a1 bar-c j5.de *Bell*↓ camph k* con conin a1 cortico tpw7 *Hyos* k* indg kali-br bg2 lyc bg2 merc k* morph a1 **Mur-ac**↓ *Nit-s-d* hr1* op↓ *Ph-ac*↓ *Phos* b4a.de raph j5.de* *Rhus-t* k* *Sil* b4a.de sul-ac j5.de **Sulph** j5.de*
  - **chill**; during: apis bg2 ph-ac bg2 phos bg2 rhus-t bg2
  - **fever**; during: apis bg2 *Bell* bg2 **Mur-ac** bg2 op bg2 *Ph-ac* bg2 phos bg2 rhus-t bg2 sil bg2
  - **perspiration**; during: apis bg2 bell bg2 *Mur-ac* bg2 op bg2 ph-ac bg2 *Phos* bg2 *Rhus-t* bg2 sil bg2
- **sleeplessness**, with: **Hyos** hr1*
- **unintelligible**: *Anac-oc* hr1* *Ars* a1 bell a1 cann-s a1 *Hell* hr1* hyos a1 *Nux-v* hr1* plb a1

MYSOPHOBIA (See Fear - contagion; Fear - dirt)

MYSTICISM: (↗*Delusions - mystery; Delusions - mystic; Religious - too; Superstitious)* aether mtf agri pfa2 anh sp1* calc mtf33 camph mtf chen-a mtf kali-fcy mtf lach mtf med mtf ser-ang mtf

NAGGING: (↗*Complaining; Tormenting - others)* cann-i vh5 fagu mp4• kali-c sk7• lyc ptk1 nux-v bg3* plat ptk1 [mag-lac stj2]

NAIVE: (↗*Childish; Credulous; Impressionable; Reassured - easily; Simple; Truth)* arg-n mrr1 arizon-l nl2• *Bell* vh* bov vh* chin mtf33 *Cic* gl1.fr* falco-pe nl2• hyos↓ ignis-alc es2• *Phos* mrr1 stram vh* sulph mrr1 vanil fd5.de **Verat**↓

- **intelligent**, but very: bell mtf33 *Chin* gl1.fr• hyos gl1.fr• *Stram* mtf33* *Sulph* mtf33* **Verat** gl1.fr*
- **open**, honest and childlike: falco-pe nl2•

NAKED, wants to be: (↗*Delirium - erotic; Delusions - naked; Dress - indecently; Fancies - lascivious; Hysteria - lascivious; Indifference - exposure; Lascivious; Lewdness; Nymphomania; Obscene; Roving - naked; Shameless; Undressing; MALE GENITALIA/SEX - Handling - public)* aids nl2• ara-maca↓ bamb-a stb2.de• *Bell* k* bufo gk* camph k* cham k* **HYOS** k1* irid-met srj5• mag-c↓ merc k* merc-c k* nat-m mrr1 *Phos* k* phyt puls↓ sabin↓ *Sec* k* spong fd4.de *Stram* k* sulph↓ tarent ptk1* vanil fd5.de *Verat* st1*

- **morning** | **bed**; in: *Hyos* gl1.fr• mag-c a1* phos gl1.fr•
- **bares** her breast in puerperal mania: *Camph* kr1
- **bed**; in: mag-c mtf33
- **constantly**: *Stram* st
- **dancing** naked (See Dancing - naked)
- **delirium**, in (See Delirium - naked)
- **drunkenness**, during: hyos gl1.fr•
- **exhibitionism**: (↗*Shameless - exposing; Shameless - exposing - person; FEMALE - Masturbation - public; MALE GENITALIA/SEX - Handling - public; MALE GENITALIA/SEX - Masturbation - public)* **Hyos** mrr1
- **hyperesthesia** of skin, in: *Hyos* kr1
- **natural**; because it is: aids nl2•
- **riding** a horse: aids nl2•
- **sleep**, in: ara-maca sej7• bamb-a stb2.de• hyos st1* merc gl1.fr• puls gl1.fr• sabin gk sulph mtf33*
- **swimming** in the sea: aids nl2•

NARCISSISM (See Egotism; Haughty; Self-indulgent; Self-satisfied; Selfishness)

NARRATING her symptoms:

- **agg.**: (↗*Anxiety - health - own; Conversation - agg.; Thinking - complaints - agg.; Weeping - telling - sickness)* aur-m-n wbt2• **Calc** k* cic k* ign **Nat-m** vh* *Puls* k* teucr k* [*Graph* stj]
- **difficulty**; with great: dulc fd4.de med pc

NARROW-MINDED: (↗*Change - aversion; Dress - conservative; New ideas - aversion; Prejudiced)* alum bg* am-c bg* bar-c bg* con bg*

Narrow-minded: ...

- **religious** questions; in (See Religious - too - narrow-minded)

NASTY (See Malicious)

NATURE:

- **loves**: (↗*Animals - love; Company - aversion - country; Countryside - desire; Gardening - love; Plants - loves; Seaside - loves; Sensitive - nature; Wilderness - desires)* bit-ar wht1• carc sk1* caust mtf33 coff hr1 dulc fd4.de elaps mtf falco-pe nl2• ignis-alc es2• kali-s fd4.de lac-f wza1• lac-leo hm2• limest-b es1• med mtf33 phos mtf podo fd3.de• rad-br sze8• rhus-g tmo3• ruta fd4.de taosc iwa1• tritic-vg fd5.de vanil fd5.de [buteo-j sej6]
  - **children**; in: carc sst2•
- **yearning** for: olib-sac wmh1

NAUSEA:

- **after**: tab bg2
- **during**: *Ars* bg2 bar-m bg2 *Calc* bg2 crot-t bg2 gran bg2 graph bg2 nux-v bg2 puls bg2

NEAT (See Tidy)

NECROPHOBIA (See Fear - death)

NEGATIVE (See Mood - repulsive)

NEGLECTING: (↗*Heedless; Indifference)*

- **appearance**; his personal (See Indifference - appearance)
- **business**: (↗*Business - aversion)* op a1 opun-s a1 *Sulph* a1
- **children**, her: (↗*Estranged - children; Indifference - children; towards - mother)* aster sze10• aur-ar k2 *Aur-m* vh* mur-ac mtf thuj mtf
- **everything**: (↗*Indifference - everything)* am-c gl1.fr• bar-c gl1.fr• caust gl1.fr• kali-p fd1.de• tell a1*
- **himself** (See Indifference - appearance)
- **household**, the: (↗*Housekeeping; Housekeeping - unable; Indifference - household)* aur-ar k2 sul-i k2 [bell-p-sp dcm1]
- **important** things: (↗*Indifference - important)* alum gl1.fr• con gl1.fr• podo fd3.de•

NERVOUS (See Excitement; Excitement - nervous; Hurry; Petulant; Restlessness)

NERVOUS breakdown (See Irritability; Prostration)

NEURASTHENIA (See Discouraged; Prostration; Sadness; GENERALS - Weakness - nervous)

NEUROSIS (See Anxiety; Sadness; Thoughts - compelling)

NEW (See Delusions - new)

NEW IDEAS: (↗*Activity - desires - creative; Ideas - abundant; Prejudiced - traditional)*

- **aversion** to: (↗*Change - aversion; Narrow-minded; Obstinate; Prejudiced; Prejudiced - traditional; Proper - too)* hep glh kali-c glh lyc glh nit-ac glh sil glh

NEWS (See Delusions - news)

NIBBLE; desire to: *Aeth* bg2* *Ars* mtf bar-c a1* bung-fa mtf calc bg2* **Chin** b7a.de* graph mtf *Ip* b7a.de* kali-p mtf mag-c ptk1* mag-m b4.de* **Nat-c** b4.de* nat-m mtf petr bg2* rhus-t b7a.de* rib-ac mtf

NIGHT WATCHING; from (See Sleep - loss)

NIGHT-TERROR (See Fear - terror - night)

NIHILISTIC ATTITUDE: (↗*Delusions - existence - doubt; Religious - want)* nit-ac mrr1 syph mrr1

NO; cannot say (See Yielding)

NOISE:

- **agg.**: chir-fl gya2
- **amel.**: graph ckh1
- **aversion** to: (↗*Sensitive - noise)* asar ptk1 borx ptk1 con ptk1 ferr a1 kali-c ptk1 kali-m sla* op ptk1 raph a1 zinc a1
- **inclination** to make noise: (↗*Tourette's)* acon ptk1 **Bell** a1* cham ptk1* cic ptk1 merc a1 op a1 verat a1

NOISY persons (See Noise - inclination)

NOSOPHOBIA (See Fear - disease)

NOSTALGIA (See Homesickness; Yearning)

NOTHINGNESS; sensation of (See Delusions - emptiness)

NUMBERS: *(↗Counting)*
- **even** numbers; drawn to: neon srj5•
- **three**; drawn to the number: positr nl2•

NURSED in children; being: | **aversion**: *(↗Eating - refuses)*
- · **moistening** mouth amel.: borx tl1 bry tl1
- **desire**:
- · **daytime** only: apis ptk1
- · **all** the time: calc-p ptk1

NURSING HER CHILD: | **aversion**: bamb-a stb2.de•

NURSING OTHERS (See Cares, full)

NYCTOPHOBIA (See Fear - dark; of; Fear - night)

NYMPHOMANIA: *(↗Ailments - sexual excesses; Delirium - erotic; Fancies - lascivious; Hysteria - lascivious; Indifference - exposure; Lascivious; Lewdness; Libertinism; Naked; Satyriasis; Shameless; Thoughts - intrude - sexual; Thoughts - tormenting - sexual; FEMALE - Sexual desire - increased; FEMALE - Sexual desire - violent; GENERALS - Masturbation; GENERALS - Sexual excesses)* agar k* ambr k* androc srj1• anh jl3 *Ant-c* **Apis** k* asaf b7a.de* aster bro1* *Aur* b4a.de aur-m-n c1 *Bar-c* b4a.de *Bar-m* k* *Bell* k* calad k* calc k* *Calc-p* k* camph k* *Cann-i* k* *Cann-s* k* *Canth* k* carb-v cedr k* *Chin* k* chlor bg2 coca bro1 cocc ↓ *Coff* k* *Croc* bg2* cyna jl3 *Dig* k* dulc k* *Ferul* c1* *Fl-ac* k* gins bro1 graph **Grat** k* **Hyos** k* ign b7.de* *Kali-br* k* kali-c ↓ kali-p c1* **Lach** k* *Lil-t* k* *Lyc* k* manc bro1* med mrr1 *Merc* k* mosch k* *Murx* k* nat-c nat-m k* *Nux-v* k* op **ORIG** k* ozone sde2• ph-ac c1* *Phos* k* pic-ac bro1 **PLAT** k* plb k* positr nl2• psil jl3 *Puls* k* *Raph* k* *Rob* k* *Sabad* k* sabin k* *Sal-n* c1* *Sec* ↓ sil k* *Staph* k* **Stram** k* stry bro1 sul-ac ↓ sulph k* *Tarent* k* valer bro1 *Verat* k* *Zinc* k* zinc-pic c1* [zinc-i stj2 zinc-m stj2 zinc-n stj2 zinc-p stj2]
- **chorea**, with: tarent kr1
- **coition** agg.: *Tarent* hr1*
- **loquacity**, with: *Verat* hr1*
- **menopause**; at: lach sf1.de manc sf1.de murx sf1.de
- **menses**:
- · **after**: *(↗Menses - after)* sul-ac sf1.de
- · **before**: *(↗Menses - before)* calc sf1.de calc-p k* kali-c sf1.de *Phos* k* stram *Verat* k*
- · **during**: *(↗Menses - during)* calc sf1.de *Hyos* kali-br k* kali-c sf1.de *Plat Sec Verat*
- · **suppressed**, after: *(↗Menses - after)* ant-c canth chin cocc hyos *Murx* phos *Plat* sil stram sulph verat zinc
- **metrorrhagia**, during: mosch murx plat sabin c1* sec
- **pregnancy**, during: phos kr1 zinc k*
- **puerperal**: *(↗FEMALE - Sexual desire - increased - delivery; FEMALE - Sexual desire - increased - delivery - after)* bell j5.de *Chin* k* kali-br k* *Plat* k* verat k* zinc kr1*
- **worms**, from: plat lp sabad lp*
- **young** girl, in a: *Orig* hr1*

OBEDIENCE: kali-c mtf33 zinc mtf33
- **too** obedient (See Yielding)

OBJECTIVE, reasonable: *(↗Honest; Reason increased)* alum gl1.fr• bell gl1.fr• falco-pe nl2• galeoc-c-h gms1• hep gl1.fr• lach gl1.fr• merc gl1.fr• nat-m gl1.fr• nit-ac gl1.fr• plat gl1.fr• ruta fd4.de sep ctc• sil gl1.fr• symph fd3.de• *Tritic-vg* fd5.de [tax jsj7]

Objective, reasonable: ...
- **alternating** with | **irrationalism** (See Irrational - alternating - rational)

OBLIGATIONS: | **aversion** to (See Cowardice; Duty - aversion)

OBLIGED to comply to the wishes of others; feels (See Comply)

OBSCENE, lewd: *(↗Delirium - erotic; Delusions - obscene; Fancies - lascivious; Hysteria - lascivious; Indifference - exposure; Lascivious; Lewdness; Naked; Obscene - songs; Shameless)* agn alco ↓ alum gl1.fr• anac bro1 apis aur ↓ bell bufo sf1.de calc gl1.fr• *Camph Canth* k* carb-v gl1.fr• *Caust* gl1.fr• chin gl1.fr• chlf ↓ con gl1.fr• *Cub Hyos* k* *Lach* k* lil-t a1* lyc gl1.fr• lyss merc gl1.fr• murx bro1 nat-m gl1.fr• nux-v *Olib-sac* wmh1 op orig gl1.fr• *Phos* k* *Pic-ac Plat* k1* puls bro1* raja-s ↓ rob staph bro1* stram k* sulph gl1.fr• tarent tub jl2 verat k*
- **man** searching for little girls: *(↗Pedophilia)* caust gl1.fr• phos gl1.fr• plat stj2*• verat gl1.fr•
- **songs**: *(↗Lascivious; Lewdness; Obscene; Singing)* alco a1 canth k2 *Hyos* k* op raja-s jl stram k* verat k2*
- **talk**: *(↗Lewdness - talk; Tourette's)* aur *Bell* bufo sf1.de *Calc* gl1.fr• camph k* chlf a1 cub *Hyos* k* *Lil-t Nux-v* olib-sac wmh1 phos plat *Stram* k* tub jl2 verat

OBSEQUIOUS (See Servile)

OBSERVANT (See Alert)

OBSERVER:
- **being** an: galeoc-c-h ↓ limen-b-c hm2•
- · **oneself**; of: *(↗Delusions - person - other)* galeoc-c-h gms1•
- **detail**; of everything in (See Conscientious)

OBSESSION (See Thoughts - persistent)

OBSTINATE: *(↗Anal fixation; Change - aversion; Conformism; Contradiction - disposition; Contrary; Defiant; Determination; Dictatorial; Disobedience; Dogmatic; Fanaticism; New ideas - aversion; Perseverance; Pertinacity; Positiveness; Quarrelsome; Shrieking - obstinate; Suggestions; Sulky; Thoughts - persistent)* abrot bg2* *Acon* k* act-sp k* *Agar* k* alco a1 aloe k* **Alum** k* alum-p k2* alum-sil k2* alumn am-c k* am-m vh1 ambr tsm1 **Anac** k* androc srj1• *Ant-c* bg2* ant-t k* apis **ARG-N** k1* arizon-l nl2• arn k* *Ars* k* ars-s-f k2* arum-t bg2* aur k* aur-ar k2 aur-m-n wbt2* aur-s k2* bamb-a stb2.de• bar-act a1 bar-c oss• **Bell** k* borra-o oss1• *Bry* k* bufo gk **Calc** k* calc-ar k2 calc-p j *Calc-s* k2* camph k* canth k* *Caps* k* carb-an k* carb-v k* carbn-s a1 carc c1* *Caust* k* **Cham** k* chel k* *Chin* k* chinin-s chir-fl ↓ choc oss• *Cina* k* coca kr1 coloc sf1.de croc *Crot-h* hr1* cupr b7a.de* cycl k* dendr-pol sk4• des-ac rbp6 dig k* dros k* *Dulc* mrr1 emb-r bnj1 euph b4a.de ferr k* ferr-ar ferr-p galv c1 gard-j vlr2• guaj k* hell k2* *Hep* k* hura hydrog srj2*• *Hyos* k* *Ign* k* ignis-alc es2• ip k* kali-ar oss• kali-bi oss• *Kali-c* k* kali-chl k13* kali-i k* kali-m k2 *Kali-p* k* kali-s kali-sil k2* kalm kreos k* lac-e hrn2• lac-f wza1• lach k* *Lyc* k* *Mag-m* k* *Med* hu medul-os-si ↓ menis a1 merc k* mez b4a.de morph oss• mosch k2* mur-ac k* nat-c h2 nat-m gk nat-sil fd3.de• nicc-met sk4• *Nit-ac* k* **Nux-v** k* oscilloc jl2 p-benzq ↓ *Pall* k* pert-vc vk9 petr a1* *Ph-ac* k* phel j5.de phos k* plat mtf33* plb positr nl2• *Prot* jl2* *Psor* k* puls mrr1 rhus-t j* ruta b7a.de* sanic k* sec k* sep gl1.fr• *Sil* k* *Spong* k* *Staph* bro1 stram k* *Sulph* k* *Symph* fd3.de• syph jl2* **Tarent** k* *Thuj* b4a.de* thymol br1 *Tub* mg1.de* verat gl1.fr• viol-o viol-t b7.de* zinc k* zinc-p k2* [ant-m stj2 bell-p-sp dcm1 bism-sn stj2 caes-met stj2 osm-met stj2 oxyg stj2 ruth-met stj2 tax jsj7]
- **forenoon**: chinin-s a1
- **evening**: ign j5.de* mur-ac a1
- **night**: dig a1
- **alternating** with | **mildness**: *Cupr* hr1*
- **amiable**, tries to appear: *Pall* kr1
- **children**: *(↗Fanaticism)* abrot sf1.de am-c j5.de *Ant-c* sf1.de ars sf1.de arum-t sf1.de aur sf1.de* aur-m-n wbt2• bell j5.de calc mtf33 calc-s mtf33 *Caps* ↓ carc fb* *Cham* hr1* *Chin* hr1* *Cina* kr1* cupr mtf33 dros gk ferr mtf33 hyos st1 kali-c mtf33 kreos sf1.de lyc j5.de* mag-m mtf33 med gk nit-ac mtf33 nux-v mtf33 p-benzq mtf11 plat mtf33 *Psor* ↓ sanic c1* sec j5.de sil j5.de* syph st1 tarent mtf33 thuj hr1* **Tub** st1*
- · **annoy** those about them: *Psor* hr1*
- · **chilly**, refractory and clumsy: *Caps*

- **children**: ...
  - **cry** when kindly spoken to; yet: *(↗Spoken - aversion)* sil k*
  - **fat**, inclined to grow: **Calc**
  - **masturbation** in boys; after: aur sf1.de
- **eruption**, during: psor hr1*
- **fever**, during: acon j5.de
- **menorrhagia**, in: *Nux-v* hr1*
- **menses**:
  - **before**: cham ptk1
  - **during** | **beginning** of menses: *Cham* k*
- **nothing** the matter with him, declares there is: *(↗Delirium - well; Delusions - well; Irritability - sends; Well - says - sick)* apis k* Arn k*
- **plans**; in the execution of: chir-fl gya2 dros a1* ignis-alc es2• medul-os-si rly4• *Symph* fd3.de•
- **queerest** objection; against whatever was proposed, he had the: Arg-n k*
- **resists** wishes of others: alum a1 **Dulc** fd* **Nux-v** kr1*
- **simpleton**, as a: des-ac rbp6 lyc gl1.fr• plat gl1.fr• *Tub* st verat gl1.fr•
- **stool**, during: sulph h2*
- **tossing** about impatiently: *Acon* hr1*

OBSTRUCTION of nose agg.: zinc bg2

OBTUNDED (See Dullness)

OCCULTISM (See Mysticism)

OCCUPATION (= diversion):

- **amel.**: *(↗Activity - desires; Amusement - desire; Anxiety - motion - amel.; Busy; Ennui - entertainment; Impulse - occupation - amel.; Industrious; Sadness - occupation; Thinking - complaints - agg.; GENERALS - Activity - amel.)* aesc k2* agar k* alum androc srj1• apis sf1.de ars st aur *Aur-m-n* wbt2• bar-c borra-o oss1• brucel sa3• calc calc-p bro1 calc-sil k2* carc sst2• chin chir-fl gya2 colch gk *Con* k* *Croc* k* *Cupr* k* *Cycl* sf1.de* falco-pe nl2• *Ferr* k* galeoc-c-h gms1• granit-m es1• haliae-lc srj5• ham fd3.de• *Hell* k* *Helon* k* *Ign* k* ignis-alc es2• *Iod* k* irid-met srj5• **Kali-br** k* *Kola* stb3• lac-h htj1• *Lil-t* k* limest-b es1• lyc mag-m dgt* med mtf33 *Merc-i-f* merc-i-r ptk1 mez mur-ac sf1.de *Nat-c* k* nat-sil fd3.de• *Nux-v* k* orig ptk1 ox-ac bro1 pall ptk1 petr-ra shn4• pieri-b mlk9.de *Pip-m* k* pip-n bg2 positr nl2• pseuts-m oss1• puls k2 **Sep** k* sil spig sf1.de spong fd4.de stram suis-em rly4• tarent bro1 thuj tritic-vg fd5.de *Tung-met* bdx1• ulm-c jsj8• vanil fd5.de verat [buteo-j sej6 calc-n stj1 heroin sdj2 pop dhh1]
- **aversion** to (See Business - aversion)
- **changing** constantly: ruta fd4.de *Sanic* st
- **desire** to: carc mlr1• *Dulc* fd4.de naja a1 opun-s a1 ozone sde2• rhus-t a1 ruta fd4.de spong fd4.de sumb a1 ther a1 tritic-vg fd5.de tub mrr1

OCCUPIED with the objects immediately around him: carbn-s a1 carc mlr1•

OCEAN (See Seaside)

ODDS with oneself; at (See Anger - himself; Discontent - himself; Loathing - oneself)

OEDIPUS COMPLEX: *(↗Clinging - children - mother; Mother complex; Mother fixation)* calc mtf calc-m mtf lac-ac mtf lac-c mtf lac-h mtf lach ggd1 mag-lac mtf mag-m mtf nat-lac mtf nat-m mtf plut-n srj7•

OFFENDED, easily (= taking everything in bad part): *(↗Admonition - agg.; Ailments - reproaches; Anger; Delusions - criticized; Delusions - insulted; Delusions - laughed; Delusions - watched; Discontented - everything; Fastidious; Hatred - bitter; Hatred - persons - offended; Irritability; Irritability - taking; Kill; desire - offense; Petulant; Sensitive; Sensitive - complaints; Sulky; Wrong)* *Acon* k* agar aids nl2• *Aloe* sne *Alum* k* anac k* ang k* ant-c ptk1* ant-t ptk1* *Apis* k* arg-n hr arge-pl rwt5• arn **Ars** k* ars-s-f k2 *Aur* k* aur-ar k2 *Aur-m-n* wbt2• aur-s k2 *Bamb-a* stb2.de• *Bar-c* hu *Bell* j5.de* borra-o oss1• borx k* *Bov* k* *Bufo* st* **Calc** k* calc-ar k2 calc-s k* camph k* cann-s k* *Caps* k* carb-an h2* *Carb-v* k* carbn-s **CARC** fd* carneg-g rwt1• **Caust** k* cench k2 cham k* *Chel* chin k* chinin-ar cic bg2 cimic ptk1* *Cina* k* cinnb *Cocc* k* coff a1 *Coloc* k* *Croc* k* cupr sst3* *Cycl* k* dros k* dulc fd4.de *Foll* oss* germ-met srj5• *Granit-m* es1• *Graph* ham fd3.de• hell hr1 hep ptk1* hyos st1 ign al* **Iod** j5.de* irid-met stj2*• kali-n j5.de kola stb3• *Lac-c* sne lac-e hrn2• lac-leo sk4• lac-lup hrn2• *Lach* st1* lap-la sde8.de• lil-t mrr1 limest-b es1• loxo-recl knl4•

Offended, easily: ...
Lyc k* lyss mag-s j5.de* marb-w es1• merc k* mim-p vml3• nat-c j5.de *Nat-m* k* nit-ac a1 **Nux-v** k* *Op* ↓ *Pall* k* pert-vc vk9 *Petr* k* phos k* *Plat* k* podo fd3.de• positr nl2• pseuts-m sne* *Puls* k* ran-b k* sacch-a fd2.de• sanic ptk1* *Sars* k* *Seneg* b4a.de *Sep* k* *Sil* j5.de* *Spig* k* spong fd4.de stann j5.de* **Staph** k* stram sul-ac bg2 *Sulph* k* *Symph* fd3.de• syph al* tarent mtf33 teucr a1 thuj j5.de* **Tritic-vg** fd* **TUB** st1* *Vanil* fd5.de *Verat* k* viol-o bg2* viol-t st *Zinc* zinc-p k2 [astat stj2 heroin sdj2 lanth-met stj2 merc-d stj2 merc-i-f stj2 moly-met stj2 oxyg stj2 plb stj2 tax jsj7]

- **children**; in: acon mtf ant-c mtf ant-t mtf cham mtf cimic mtf **Cina** mtf hep mtf puls mtf sanic mtf tub mtf33
- **offenses**, from past: calc gl1.fr• *Cham* kr1 *Ign* kr1* mim-p vml3• *Op* kr1 *Staph* gl1.fr• [oxyg stj]

OLD, sensation of being: agath-a nl2• med ↓ vanil fd5.de

- **men**; in: med jl2

OLD people agg.: bar-c b4a.de*

OLDER child; behaves as a much (See Precocity)

ONE IDEA: | **attention** is fixed on one idea; all one's (See Monomania; Thoughts - persistent)

OPEN (See Communicative; Sensitive - external; Truth - telling)

OPENING eyes agg.: *Alum* b4a.de

OPHIDIOPHOBIA (See Fear - snakes)

OPINIONATED (See Obstinate)

OPINIONS: | **respected**; expects her opinions to be: *(↗Respected - desire)* ham a1 podo fd3.de•

OPTIMISTIC: *(↗Cheerful; Hopeful)* *Aids* nl2• androc srj1• anh mg1.de anthraq rly4• arizon-l nl2• *Calc* gl1.fr• choc srj3• dream-p sdj1• falco-pe nl2• ferr-m a1 fl-ac st1 galin ↓ hydrc a1 hydrog srj2*• kali-c ↓ kali-s fd4.de lac-e hrn2• loxo-recl knl4• lyc gl1.fr• marb-w es1• mucs-nas rly4• nat-sil fd3.de• nep mg1.de* nux-v gl1.fr• podo fd3.de• puls gl1.fr• rib-ac jl3 sil gl1.fr• *Sulph* gl1.fr• symph fd3.de• *Tub* jl2* visc sp1* [spect dfg1 tax jsj7 tung-met stj2]

- **weakness**; in spite of the: *(↗Well - says - sick)* falco-pe nl2• galin jl kali-c jl

ORDER:

- **desire** for: *(↗Fastidious)* aster sze10• carc mlr1• chir-fl gya2 fic-m gya1 **Kali-s** fd* lac-f wza1• marb-w ↓ sal-fr ↓ *Tritic-vg* fd5.de vanil fd5.de [heroin sdj2 tax jsj7]
  - **everything** into order; desire to put (See Rest - cannot)
  - **life**; in one's: chir-fl gya2 marb-w es1• sal-fr sle1• tritic-vg fd5.de

ORDERLY MANNER; cannot perform anything in (See Chaotic)

ORGANIC MENTAL SYNDROME: nux-m mrr1

ORGANIZED and methodical; desire to be (See Fastidious)

ORIENTATION; sense of:

- **decreased**: *(↗Confusion; Confusion - loses; Recognizing - not - streets)* **Alum** mrr1 aml-ns bg2 arg-n bg2 bapt bg2 bell bg2 bov bg2 *Bry* bg2 buteo-j ↓ calc bg2 camph bg2 camph-br ↓ cann-xyz bg2 coca bg2 *Cocc* bg2 coloc bg2 cortico sp1 croc bg2 des-ac rbp6 fl-ac bg2* galeoc-c-h gms1• **Glon** bg2 graph bg2* hell bg2 *Hyos* bg2 irid-met srj5• kali-bi bg2 kola stb3• lac-h sze9• lac-lup hrn2• lil-t bg2 lyc bg2 med bg2 merc bg2 nat-m bg2 neon srj5• **Nux-m** bg2 *Op* bg2 par bg2 *Petr* bg2 phos bg2 *Plat* bg2 puls bg2 rad-br sze8• ran-b bg2 sep bg2 *Stram* bg2 sulph bg2 thuj bg2 tub bg2 valer bg2 *Verat* bg2 vult-gr sze5• [am-caust stj2 am-f stj2 beryl stj2 bor-pur stj2 fl-pur stj2 lith-c stj2 lith-f stj2 lith-m stj2 lith-met stj2 lith-p stj2 nitro stj2 oxyg stj2]
  - **direction**; sense of | **driving**; while: [buteo-j sej6]
  - **north** seems south and east seems west: camph-br hs1*
- **increased**: adam srj5• anh mg1.de* falco-pe nl2• haliae-lc srj5• irid-met srj5•

ORPHANS: *(↗Forsaken - beloved)* aur mtf crot-c mtf crot-h mtf lac-h mtf lach mtf *Mag-c* k2 mag-m mtf puls mtf

OUTGOING (See Expansive; Sympathetic)

OVERACTIVE: *(↗Activity - desires; Busy)* **Dulc** fd* hyos bg2 *Kola* stb3• med mtf33 op bg2* ruta fd4.de spig bg2 spong bg2 tritic-vg fd5.de vanil fd5.de verat bg2 verb bg2

OVERBEARING (See Haughty)

OVERBURDENED (See Cares, full)

OVERSENSITIVE (See Sensitive)

OVERWEENING (See Haughty)

OVERWHELMED (See Helplessness)

OVERWORKED (See Ailments - mental exertion)

PAIN:
- **during**: *Acon* bg2 agar bg2 aloe bg2 ant-t b7.de* am bg2 *Ars* b4a.de* *Bell* bg2 cact bg2 canth bg2 carb-v b4a.de* caust b4.de* **Cham** b7.de* clem bg2 *Coff* b7a.de* coloc b4a.de con bg2 cupr bg2 dulc b4a.de* hep bg2 hyos bg2 kali-c bg2 *Mag-c* b4a.de mag-m bg2 med bg2 mez bg2 nat-c b4a.de* nit-ac bg2 nux-v b7.de* plat bg2 plb bg2 ruta b7.de* sars b4a.de* sep bg2 sil bg2 stann bg2 stram bg2 **Verat** b7.de* zinc bg2
- **abdomen** agg.; pain in: acon bg2 alum bg2 am-m bg2 ant-t b7.de* *Ars* bg2 aur bg2 bell bg2 borx bg2 bov bg2 bry b7.de* *Carb-v* bg2 cham b7.de* cic bg2 coff bg2 coloc bg2 cupr bg2 hep bg2 ign bg2 lyc bg2 merc bg2 mosch bg2 nux-v bg2 *Phos* bg2 plat bg2 puls bg2 rhus-t bg2 sec bg2 sep bg2 sul-ac bg2 sulph bg2 *Verat* bg2
- **extremities** agg.; pain in: ars bg2 bell bg2
- **eyes** agg.; pain in (See Mental symptoms - accompanied - eyes)
- **head** agg.; pain in: acon bg2 alum bg2 aml-ns bg2 ant-c bg2 arg-n bg2 arn ↓ aur b4a.de bell b4a.de* bov bg2 bry ↓ calc bg2 carb-v bg2 castm bg2 caust bg2 coff ↓ crot-h bg2 cycl ↓ gels bg2 glon bg2 gran bg2 graph bg2 hydr-ac ↓ lach ↓ laur bg2 mag-c bg2 manc bg2 meny bg2 naja bg2 phos bg2 puls bg2 rhod ↓ ruta bg2 sel bg2 sil b4a.de sulph bg2 *Vip* bg2 zinc bg2
  - **right**: arn bg2 coff bg2 gels bg2 hydr-ac bg2 lach bg2
  - **left**: bry bg2 cycl bg2 rhod bg2 sulph bg2
- **heart** agg.; pain in: bar-c bg2 carb-v bg2 cham bg2 nit-ac bg2 rhus-t bg2 spong bg2
- **stomach** agg.; pain in: bar-m bg2 calc bg2 carb-v bg2 cham bg2 ferr bg2 graph bg2 merc bg2
- **teeth**; during pain in: merc-c bg2

PAINTING:
- **ability** for: *(↗Art - ability)* chin mtf33 staph mtf33
- **inability** for: *(↗Art - inability)* sil mtf33

PALPITATION agg.: acon bg2 alum bg2 am-c bg2 ant-t bg2 borx bg2 calc bg2 *Cham* bg2 ferr bg2 glon bg2 ign bg2 mosch bg2 nat-m bg2 nit-ac bg2 nux-v bg2 phos bg2 plat bg2 *Puls* bg2 sil bg2 verat bg2

PANIC (See Fear - sudden)

PARADOXICAL (See Contradictory; GENERALS - Contradictory)

PARALYSIS: | **Facial** nerves, peripheral nerves, 1st and 8th cranial nerves not affected: thal-xyz srj8•

PARANOIA (See Delusions - pursued; Suspicious)

PARTIAL (See Prejudiced)

PASSIONATE [=ardent] (See Ardent)

PASSIONATE [=choleric]: *(↗Anger; Ardent; Fanaticism; Rage)* alco a1 alum gl1.fr• ampe-qu br1 *Anac* bg2* androc srj1• ars a1 aur b4.de* *Aur-m* vh* *Bar-c* bg2 *Bell* bg2 *Bry* bg2* calc gl1.fr• cann-i a1 canth a1 *Carb-v* bg2* carbn-s a1 caust mtf33* coff b7.de* con kr1 croc bg2 hep bg2* hura a1 hyos a1 ign bg2 *Ip* bg2* *Kali-c* kr1* **Kali-i** a1* **Lach** vh* laur a1 led bg2 lyc a1* m-ambo b7.de merc mtf33 **Nat-c** gl1.fr• nat-m b4.de* nat-s bg2* **Nux-v** b7.de* olnd bg2* petr bg2* ph-ac bg2 phos a1 plat gl1.fr• *Psor* kr1* sabad bg2 seneg bg2 *Sep* bg2* stann bg2 stram a1 *Sulph* bg2* sumb a1 tarent a1 *Thuj* kr1 [ferr stj2 ferr-f stj2 ferr-lac stj2 ferr-n stj2 ferr-sil stj2]
- **morning**: nat-s a1
- **alternating** with | **cheerfulness** (See Anger - sudden - alternating - cheerfulness)
- **trifle**, at every: nat-m a1 ph-ac a1 phos a1 sumb a1

PASSIVITY (See Inactivity)

PATHETIC: *(↗Helplessness; Speech - pathetic)* aids nl2• am-m mtf calc-sil mtf lyc mtf mag-m mtf nat-m mtf *Sep* mrr1 stram bg* sulph mtf

PATIENCE: *(↗Tranquillity)* adam srj5• chlam-tr bcx2• choc srj3• dream-p sdj1• dulc fd4.de falco-pe nl2• galeoc-c-h gms1• haliae-lc srj5• ham fd3.de• kali-s fd4.de lac-h sk4• lac-leo hrn2• mag-m b4.de* melal-alt gya4 phos a1 plb mtf positr nl2• spong fd4.de tritic-vg fd5.de [heroin sdj2]
- **alternating** with | **irritability** (See Irritability - alternating - patience)

PAVOR NOCTURNUS (See Anxiety - night - children; Fear - terror - night - children)

PEACE:
- **heavenly** peace; sensation of: *(↗Blissful; Content)* aids nl2• arb-m oss1• arg-met kr1* gard-j vlr2• olib-sac wmh1 rhus-g tmo3• sal-fr sle1• [arg-p stj2 helium stj2 heroin sdj2 hydrog stj2 neon stj2]
- **yearning** for: olib-sac wmh1

PEACEMAKER (See Ailments - discords; Ailments - quarrelling; Quarrelling - aversion; Sensitive - quarrels; Sensitive - rudeness)

PECKING (See Gestures - hands - picking)

PEDANT: *(↗Haughty)* *Carc* fd2.de• kali-p fd1.de• **Nat-sil** fd* plat gl1.fr• puls gl1.fr• ruta fd4.de sil gl1.fr•

PEDOPHILIA: *(↗Love - perversity; Obscene - man)* calc pc plat pc

PEEVISH (See Complaining; Discontented; Irritability; Petulant)

PERCEPTIONS:
- **changed** (See Fancies - exaltation)
- **errors** of (See Mistakes - perception)
- **increased** (See Alert)
- **slowness** of (See Dullness)

PERFECTIONIST (See Conscientious; Fastidious)

PERFIDIOUS: *(↗Adulterous; Deceitful)* *Ars* gl1.fr• **Lach** gl1.fr• lyc gl1.fr• nat-c a1* nit-ac gl1.fr• nux-v gl1.fr• phos gl1.fr• sep gl1.fr• sulph gl1.fr•

PERFUME:
- **aversion** to use perfume: *(↗NOSE - Smell - acute - perfumes)* nux-v mtf phos mtf puls mtf
- **loves** to use perfume: *(↗Disgust - body - own - odor; Vanity)* ambr mtf anh mtf cann-i mtf carc mtf ign mtf med mtf mosch mtf phos mtf *Sulph* mtf tarent mtf tub mtf

PERIODICITY: anac bg2 ars bg2 aur bg2 carb-v bg2 cham bg2 *Chin* bg2 *Con* bg2 *Cupr* bg2 *Ferr* ↓ puls bg2 sulph bg2
- **day** | **other** day; every: *Ferr* b7.de*

PERSPIRATION:
- **amel.**: sulph bg2
- **during**: chin b7.de* hyos b7.de* *Samb* b7.de*
- **forehead** agg.; perspiration of: ars bg2 carb-v bg2 nux-v bg2 phos bg2 sep bg2
- **hands** agg.; perspiration of: cham bg2 merc bg2

PERSEVERANCE: *(↗Contradiction - disposition; Contrary; Courageous; Determination; Industrious; Obstinate; Pertinacity; Positiveness; Thoughts - persistent; Will - strong)* acon bg2 alum bg *Ars* b4a.de aur-s wbt2• bry bg2 caps b7a.de* chir-fl gya2 cupr sst3* dig bg2 dros b7.de* *Dulc* fd4.de *Ferr* mtf guare a1 *Lac-c* bg lach bg lim ↓ linu-c ↓ lyc bg2 nat-c bg2* nit-ac bg2 nux-v b7.de* phos bg2 *Sil* bg spong fd4.de sulph bg2 [senec stj thal-met stj2]
- **duties**, in performing irksome: chir-fl gya2 lim a1 (non:linu-c a1)
- **resistance**, against: [senec stj]

PERSEVERING: | **not** persevere in anything; can (See Undertaking - many)

PERSISTING in nothing: *(↗Capriciousness; Inconstancy; Irresolution; Mood - changeable; Undertaking - many; Will - weakness)* alum bg aur h2 bar-c j bism-o a1 cann-i mrr1 lac-c lach lyc a1 med vh plan *Sil* bg* stann h2 sulph bg* ulm-c jsj8• [tax jsj7]

PERSONAL APPEARANCE: (↗*Dress; Pretty)*
- **coquettish**:
  - **not** coquettish enough (See Coquettish - not)
  - **too** coquettish (See Coquettish - too)
- **indifference** to one's personal appearance (See Indifference - appearance)
- **tidy** in one's personal appearance (See Tidy - appearance)

PERT: (↗*Impertinence; Vivacious)* olib-sac wmh1 pall a1 spong h1*

PERTINACITY: (↗*Change - aversion; Contradiction - disposition; Contrary; Courageous; Defiant; Determination; Dictatorial; Disobedience; Dogmatic; Monomania; Obstinate; Perseverance; Positiveness; Quarrelsome; Thoughts - persistent)* aids nl2• caps dros ignis-alc es2• nat-sil fd3.de• polys sk4• positr nl2• ruta fd4.de sal-fr sle1• spong fd4.de stram symph fd3.de• tritic-vg fd5.de ulm-c jsj8• [tax jsj7]

PERVERSE (See Love - perversity; Moral)

PESSIMIST: (↗*Brooding; Complaining; Death - desires; Delusions - succeed; Delusions - wrong - done; Despair; Discontented - everything; Discouraged; Doubtful - recovery; Dwells - past; Ennui; Helplessness; Indifference; Introspection; Lamenting; Loathing - life; Morose; Serious; Succeeds; Suicidal; Suicidal - thoughts; Undertaking - lacks; Weary; Wrong)* agar-st jl agav-t jl3* *Alum* sne arg-n sne ars gl1.fr• aur k2* aur-m-n wbt2• aur-s wbt2• bar-c gl1.fr• bros-gau mrc1 calc h2* caust gl1.fr• cecr jl3 cic k2 *Cimic* sne falco-pe nl2• galeoc-c-h gms1• halo jl3 hyos gl1.fr• ketogl-ac rly4• lach gl1.fr• lavand-a ctl1• *Nat-m* sne *Nit-ac* mrr1 *Nux-v* gl1.fr• parathyr jl2 pers jl3 plut-n srj7• *Positr* nl2• *Psor* jl2* puls sne *Ruta* fd4.de sacch-a fd2.de• sep gl1.fr• stann jl3* staph sne tub jl2 vip-a jl3 [cadm-m stj2 nat-caust stj2 nat-lac stj2 nat-met stj2 nat-sil stj2]

PETTINESS (See Trifles)

PETULANT: (↗*Capriciousness; Discontented; Impatience - talk; Irritability; Irritability - trifles; Morose; Offended; Sulky; Unfriendly)* acon ptk1 alco a1 am-c ptk1 *Ant-c* ptk1 ant-t ptk1 aur ptk1 bamb-a stb2.de• *Calc* ptk1 calc-p ptk1 calc-s a1 caps ptk1 carb-ac hr1 *Cham* ptk1* cina br1* clem ptk1 cocc ptk1 cop ptk1 corn a1* kali-c ptk1 lyc ptk1 merc-c a1 nat-ar a1 nux-m a1 olnd ptk1 opun-s a1* phos a1* rat ptk1 *Rheum* h2* staph ptk1* sulph ptk1 syph ptk1 tritic-vg fd5.de zinc ptk1

PHILOSOPHY: (↗*Intellectual)*
- **ability** for: (↗*Intellectual; Mania - philosophical; Theorizing)* anac gl1.fr• ars-s-f mtf calc k2 cann-i tl1 chin mtf dream-p sdj1• halo ↓ hep gl1.fr• hydrog srj2• ign mtf kali-bi mtf lach mtf33* *Nat-c* mtf nit-ac gl1.fr• olib-sac wmh1 petr-ra shn4• ruta ↓ *Sulph* j5.de* tritic-vg fd5.de tub mtf vanil ↓ verat mrr1 [cadm-met stj2 ruth-met stj2]
  - **evening** | **21** h; after: halo jl
  - **reveries**; great inclination to philosophical: dream-p sdj1• hydrog srj2• ruta fd4.de sulph h2 tritic-vg fd5.de vanil fd5.de

PHLEGMATIC (See Dullness; Indifference; Slowness)

PHOBIA (See Anxiety; Cares, full; Fear; Timidity - public)

PHOTOMANIA (See Light - desire)

PHYSICAL symptoms:
- **alternating** with:
  - **insanity** (See Insanity - alternating - physical)
  - **mental** symptoms (See Mental symptoms - alternating - physical)

PICKING (See Gestures - hands - picking)

PICTURE TAKEN, aversion to having his/her: *Nat-m* ser

PIETY, nocturnal: (↗*Praying; Religious - too)* stram

PINCHING: | **children**; in: cham mrr1 *Cina* mrr1 hyos hpc2*

PITIES herself: (↗*Delusions - misfortune - inconsolable; Delusions - unfortunate; Unfortunate)* agar k* aids nl2• androc srj1• anthraq rly4• *Aur-m-n* wbt2• aur-s wbt2• bamb-a stb2.de• cadm-i gm1 **Calc** gl1.fr• carc mlr1• chir-fl gya2 cich mtf11 des-ac rbp6 dream-p sdj1• eric-vg mtf11 germ-met srj5• gink-b sbd1• granit-m es1• graph gsd1 hydrog srj2• ign gsd1 lach gsd1 moni rfm1• musca-d szs1 nat-sil fd3.de• nit-ac k* podo fd3.de• puls wl1* sal-l mtf11 *Staph* gl1.fr• suis-hep rly4• sulph wl1 tarent ↓ tere-la rly4• ulm-c jsj8• vanil fd5.de [ant-m stj2 cadm-m stj2 chr-m stj2 plb-m stj2 tax jsj7 zirc-met stj2]
- **pains**; for the: bamb-a stb2.de•
- **sick**; desire to show being: (↗*Feigning - sick)* tarent a1*

PLACIDITY (See Mildness; Tranquillity)

PLAINTIVE (See Complaining)

PLANS:
- **carrying** out his plans; insists on (See Obstinate - plans)
- **making** many plans: (↗*Absorbed; Activity - desires - creative; Concentration - active; Fancies - absorbed; Fancies - exaltation; Ideas - abundant; Memory - active; Programming - everything; Theorizing)* adam srj5• agar ↓ aloe ↓ anac k* ang k* arg-n arizon-l nl2• carc zzh *Chin* k* *Chinin-s* chir-fl gya2 *Coff* k* cortico tpw7 crot-c ↓ cupr ↓ *Ham* fd3.de• hydrog srj2• ignis-alc es2• *Kali-s* fd4.de lach ↓ lec oss• nat-m ↓ nux-v olnd k* op plb ↓ polys sk4• ruta fd4.de sep k* sul-ac mrr1 *Sulph* k* tab bg2 tritic-vg fd5.de ulm-c ↓ vanil fd5.de visc jl3
  - **evening**: (↗*Ideas - abundant - evening)* *Chin* k* *Chinin-s*
  - **night**: (↗*Ideas - abundant - night)* **Chin** k*
    - **bed**; in: *Chin* mrr1
  - **bold** plans: agar a1
  - **day**; for the whole: cupr sst3•
  - **future**; for the: (↗*Talking - future)* ulm-c jsj8•
  - **gigantic** plans: (↗*Deeds - great; Delusions - great)* op k*
  - **realize** them; but don't: cortico tpw7
  - **revengeful** plans: (↗*Hatred - revengeful; Malicious)* agar k* aloe mtf crot-c mtf* lach mtf nat-m mtf *Nux-v* mtf op mtf plb mtf

PLANTS:
- **agg.**: petr-ra shn4•
- **loves**: (↗*Nature - loves)* cupr mgm• limest-b es1• tritic-vg fd5.de vanil fd5.de [uva stj]

PLAYFUL: (↗*Amusement - desire; Cheerful; Content; Jesting; Mirth; Vivacious)* aids nl2• aloe bell a1 bufo gk cimic k* cocc k* croc bg2 dream-p sdj1• elaps falco-pe nl2• ign bg2 lac-del hrn2• lac-leo hrn2• lach k* melal-alt gya4 meny k* naja k* ox-ac k* *Podo* fd3.de• positr nl2• psor mtf33 sal-fr sle1• seneg k* tarent k* vero-o rly3• [heroin sdj2]
- **alternating** with | **sadness**: psor
- **water**; in the: lac-del hrn2•

PLAYING:
- **aversion** to play: (↗*Amusement - aversion)* arum-t ↓ aur-m-n ↓ bar-c b4a.de* bar-m bg2 calc ↓ calc-p ↓ carc ↓ cham ↓ cina bg2 cupr ↓ diphtox ↓ *Hep* ↓ ign ↓ lach ↓ *Lyc* ↓ med ↓ merc ↓ nat-m ↓ phos ↓ puls ↓ **Rheum** bg2 sep ↓ staph ↓ *Sulph* ↓ tab ↓ tub ↓
  - **daytime** | **children**; in: cina mtf33
  - **children**; in: (↗*Serious)* arum-t vh aur-m-n wbt2• *Bar-c* k* bar-m carc mlr1* cham ↓ *Cina* k* cupr mtf33 diphtox jl2 *Hep* k* lach hr1 *Lyc* k* merc gl1.fr• **Rheum** k* staph ↓ *Sulph*
    - **favorite** toys; with their: cham mtf33 rheum mtf33 staph mtf33
    - **pain** in abdomen or physical illness; from: rheum mtf33
    - **sit** in corner; and: (↗*Crawling - children - howls; Hiding - himself - corner; Sadness - sits)* bar-c kr1* bar-m kr1
  - **fluffy** or feathery toys; with: calc mtf carc mtf med mtf puls mtf tub mtf
- **desire** to play: (↗*Amusement - desire; Gestures - hands - playing)* agar ↓ ars ↓ bar-c ↓ bell a1 bufo ↓ calc ↓ calc-p ↓ calc-sil ↓ **Cic** ↓ cimic *Cocc* a1 *Con* kr1 croc bg cupr ↓ cypr ↓ dream-p sdj1• elaps ↓ ign bg lac-leo hrn2• lach limen-b-c hrn2* lyc ↓ *Med* ↓ meny mosch ↓ naja mtf33 nux-v ↓ ox-ac phos ↓ pieri-b mlk9.de positr nl2• puls ↓ sacch-a fd2.de• seneg sil ↓ spong fd4.de stram ↓ sulph ↓ tarent k* tub ↓ vanil fd5.de vero-o rly4• [heroin sdj2]
  - **night**: cypr hr1* *Med* kr1*
    - **children**: cypr br1 med mtf33
  - **buttons** of his clothes, with the: (↗*Gestures - hands - buttons)* mosch
  - **dirty** tricks on others; play (See Malicious - dirty)
  - **dolls**; with: bar-c k2 puls mtf

- **desire** to play: ...
  - **gambling**; for (See Gambling)
  - **games** | **board** games: phos mtf33
  - **grass**, in the: elaps
  - **guns**, soldiers; with: agar mtf bell mtf cupr mtf tub mtf
  - **hide** and seek, at: bell kr1* stram mtf tarent mtf
  - **scrabble**: *(↗Mental exertion - desire)* calc-p mtf calc-sil mtf lyc mtf sil mtf sulph mtf
  - **Lego**; with: calc mtf lyc mtf phos mtf sil mtf
  - **Nintendo**: *(↗Computers - love)* ars mtf bufo mtf calc mtf nux-v mtf sil mtf tarent mtf tub mtf
  - **toys**; with: | **childish** toys: **Cic** kr1*
- **inability** to play: borra-o oss1• cupr sst3• merc gl1.fr• sulph gl1.fr•

PLEASANTRY (See Jesting)

PLEASED:
- **aversion** to be pleased (See Flattered - aversion)
- **desire** to be pleased (See Flattered - desire; Longing - good)

PLEASING:
- **desire** to please others: *(↗Flattering; Quarrelling - aversion; Yielding)* aur-m-n wbt2• bar-c oss• *Carc* fd2.de*• dulc fd4.de falco-pe nl2• germ-met srj5• **Kali-s** fd* pin-con oss2• puls mtf33 rhus-g tmo3• sil-mar oss• spong fd4.de thuj mlk1* vanil fd5.de
  - **make**-up; puts on: falco-pe nl2•
  - **parents**: carc sst2•
    - **father**: carc sst2•

PLEASURE: *(↗Amusement - desire; Cheerful; Content; Exhilaration; Fancies - pleasant; Jesting; Vivacious)* aether a1 anag a1 ang k* ara-maca sej7• bell ↓ cann-i k* carb-ac a1 cod a1 falco-pe nl2• galeoc-c-h gms1• kali-s fd4.de lac-del hrn2• limen-b-c ↓ mate a1 neon srj5• sec ↓ spong fd4.de thea ↓ til k* tritic-vg fd5.de
- **amel.**: kali-p ptk1 pall ptk1
- **morning**: til a1
- **lascivious** ideas, only in: *(↗Lascivious)* bell
- **nothing**; in (See Discontented - everything; Indifference - everything)
- **seeking** (See Amusement - desire; Occupation - amel.)
- **sleeplessness**, during: sec
- **spontaneous** feelings of: limen-b-c hrn2•
- **talking**; in his own (See Talking - pleasure)
- **voluptuous** (See Lascivious)
- **wakefulness** at night; during: galeoc-c-h gms1•
- **waking** from a dream of murder, on: thea

POETRY (See Verses)

POLITE:
- **not** polite (See Insolence; Rudeness)
- **too** polite: *(↗Answering - unable - hurt; Diplomatic; Mildness; Quarrelling - aversion; Yielding)* carc sk1• staph mtf33 *Vanil* fd5.de

POLITICS: *(↗Discuss - political; Eccentricity - political; Revolutionist)*
- **ability** for: choc srj3•
- **aversion** to political engagement: plac rzf5•
- **occupied** with politics; too: *Sulph* b4a.de

POLLUTION agg.: petr-ra shn4•

POMPOUS, important: *(↗Dignified; Haughty; Solemn; Walking - slowly; Walking - slowly - dignified)* alco a1 bell ptk1 calc ptk1* cann-i a1 cupr ptk1 ferr lpc ferr-ma a1 glon bg2 hyos lpc ignis-alc es2• *Lyc* ptk1 phos ptk1 **Plat** bg2* stram bg2 sulph bg2 *Verat* bg2*

PONOPHOBIA (See Fear - pain - of; Fear - work)

POSITIVENESS: *(↗Audacity; Change - aversion; Confident; Contradiction - disposition; Contrary; Courageous; Decisive; Defiant; Determination; Dictatorial; Disobedience; Dogmatic; Firmness; Independent; Obstinate; Perseverance; Pertinacity; Power - sensation; Tough; Will - strong)* adam srj aids nl2• anac androc srj1• arizon-l nl2• ars gl1.fr• aur-s wbt2• bell camph k* carc fd2.de* *Caust* b4.de* chir-fl gya2 choc srj3• dioxi rbp6 **Dulc** fd* ferr k* ham fd3.de• hydrog srj2• hyos

Positiveness: ...
ignis-alc es2• lac-h htj1• *Lach* b7.de* limen-b-c hrn2• m-arct b7.de *Merc* b4.de* nux-v gl1.fr• op ozone sde2• plat **Podo** fd* positr nl2• ruta fd4.de sal-fr sle1• sep gl1.fr• sil spong fd4.de sulph symph fd3.de• tritic-vg fd5.de ulm-c jsj8• vanil fd5.de verat [heroin sdj2 tax jsj7 temp elm1]
- **alternating** with | **sadness** (See Sadness - alternating - positiveness)
- **children**; in: caust mtf33 ferr mtf33
- ○ **Lumbar** region; with pain in dioxi rbp6
- **waking**; on: hydrog srj2• ozone sde2•

POSSESSIVENESS: *(↗Greed)* ars mtf33 cich mtf11 des-ac ↓ eric-vg mtf11
- **same** things; a number of: des-ac rbp6

POSTPONING everything to next day: *(↗Confidence - want; Fear - failure; Fear - undertaking; Irresolution; Laziness; Laziness - difficulties; Laziness - postponing; Responsibility - aversion; Undertaking - lacks)* acon-ac rly4• adam srj5• androc srj1• anh sp1 apis st arg-n mtf ars mtf bamb-a stb2.de• bar-s mtf calc mtf chir-fl gya2 coli rly4• dendr-pol sk4• dream-p sdj1• dulc fd4.de falco-pe nl2• hydrog srj2• irid-met srj5• kali-p fd1.de• *Kali-s* fd4.de lar-d mtf11 lyc mtf *Med* hr1* miml-g mtf11 nat-m mtf33 nauf-helv-li elm2• nux-v k* ozone sde2* petr-ra shn4• plat k* plb mtf *Podo* fd3.de• sal-fr sle1• scler mtf11 sil k* streptoc rly4• sulph mrr1 vanil fd5.de [lac-mat sst4 tax jsj7]

POWER:
- **excited** by power: adam srj
- **love** of power (See Ambition; Dictatorial - power)
- **mental** power (See Mental power)
- **sensation** of: *(↗Delusions - great; Fearless; Positiveness)* androc srj crot-c a ferr a germ-met srj phos hr1 rhus-g tmo3• [*Buteo-j* sej6 heroin sdj2]
- **will**; power of (See Will; Will - strong)

POWERLESS (See Helplessness)

PRACTICAL: *(↗Busy; Decisive; Emotions - predominated)* apis mrr1 polys sk4•

PRAISED; being: | **desire** (See Flattered - desire)

PRAYING: *(↗Delirium tremens - praying; Mania - puerper; Piety; Religious - too)* aids nl2• *Alum* gl1.fr• *Anac* mtf arn *Ars* k* **Aur** k* *Bell* k* carc mtf cer-s ↓ cere-b cere-s a1* euph haliae-lc srj5• hyos hyper hu ignis-alc es2• lyss kr1 manc mtf med mtf mygal mtf nat-s k* nat-sil fd3.de• op opun-s a1 (non:opun-v a1) petr-ra shn4• plat **Puls** k* rhus-t gl1.fr• ruta fd4.de *Sep* gl1.fr* stann mtf **Stram** k* sul-ac sulo-ac a1 sulph k2 vanil fd5.de **Verat** k* [heroin sdj2]
- **morning**: op k* opun-s a1 (non:opun-v a1)
- **night**: cer-s a1* cere-s a1* stram
- **children**; in: nat-s mtf33
- **discouragement**; with (See Discouraged - praying)
- **fervent**: alum gl1.fr• aur mtf **Sep** gl1.fr•
- **kneeling** and: *Ars* nat-s *Stram* verat k*
- **loud** in sadness: *Plat* kr1
- **menses**, during: *(↗Menses - during)* *Stram* hr1*
- **others** to pray for him; begs: lyss kr1
- **piety**, nocturnal: stram
- **quietly**: arn hr1* ars hr1*
- **timidly**: stann hr1*
- **vomiting**; constantly praying even with the: med c1

PREACHING: *(↗Dogmatic)*
- **religious** psychotic preaching: verat vh4*

PREARRANGING (See Programming - everything)

PRECOCITY of children: *(↗Audacity; Courageous; Flattering - seducing; Impertinence; Loquacity - children - precociously)* *Acon* lmj *Asar* ggd *Aur* lmj aur-m-n wbt2• bell hr1* *Calc* k2* calc-f lmj *Calc-p* lmj carc fb* chel lmj cina mrr1* crot-h al fl-ac lmj hyos lmj ign bl1* iod lmj lac-f lmj **Lach** lmj lyc br1* lyss lmj **Med** lmj *Merc* k* nat-m mrr1 nux-v hr1* orig lmj par vml3• petr lmj phos hr1* puls mtf33 sep lmj* sil hr1* staph lmj stroph-h c1 sulph lmj* syph mtf33 tub lp* **Verat** vh*

PREDICTING:
- **death**; time of (See Death - presentiment - predicts)
- **future** events (See Clairvoyance)

PREGNANCY:
- **during** pregnancy: acon bro1 *Apis* b7a.de *Bell* k* cham bro1 chin k* *Cimic* bro1 con k* ign k* lys bg2 lyss nat-m k* *Nux-m* bg2 **Puls** b7.de*
- **false** pregnancy (See Delusions - pregnant)

PREJUDICED: *(↗Aversion - persons - certain; Censorious; Change - aversion; Dogmatic; Narrow-minded; New ideas - aversion)* ars gl1.fr• calc ↓ carb-v ↓ gins mtf11 lach gl1.fr• lyc ↓ plat ↓ plut-n ↓ verat ↓
- **traditional** prejudices: *(↗New ideas; New ideas - aversion; Proper - too)* calc gl1.fr• carb-v gl1.fr• lach gl1.fr• lyc gl1.fr• plat gl1.fr• plut-n srj7• verat gl1.fr•

PREMENSTRUAL tension (See Menses - before)

PREMONITION (See Anticipation; Fear - happen; Forebodings; Prophesying)

PREOCCUPIED (See Absentminded; Absorbed)

PRESENTIMENT (See Anxiety - future; Clairvoyance; Fear - happen)

PRESSURE; external:
- **amel.**: croc b7.de*
- **hand**; of | **amel.**: hydr bg2

PRESUMPTUOUS: *(↗Audacity; Contemptuous; Contradiction - disposition; Contrary; Defiant; Dictatorial; Haughty; Impertinence; Insolence; Meddlesome; Rudeness)* arn gl1.fr• calc gl1.fr• *Lyc* k* plat gl1.fr• staph gl1.fr•

PRETTY: *(↗Elegance; Personal; Tasteful)* aur-m sgw1 plat mrr2

PRIDE (See Haughty)

PRIM (See Affectation)

PROCRASTINATING (See Postponing)

PROFANITY (See Cursing)

PROGRAMMING: | **everything** (= prearranging): *(↗Plans - making)* **Ars** mrr1 kali-s fd4.de nat-m vh tritic-vg fd5.de

PROMISCUOUS (See Adulterous; Love - perversity)

PROPER: *(↗Discipline)*
- **too**: *(↗Change - aversion; Conformism; Duty - too; Fastidious; New ideas - aversion; Prejudiced - traditional; Responsibility - taking; Serious; Truth - telling)* arg-met mtf arg-n mtf arg-p mtf ars-n mtf aur mtf aur-m mtf aur-s mtf bar-c mtf cadm-met mtf calc mtf caps mtf cinnb mtf cob-m mtf cupr-m mtf kali-bi mtf **Kali-c** mrr1* kali-i mtf lyc mtf mag-met mtf merc mtf merc-d mtf merc-i-f mtf merc-i-r mtf *Nat-m* mrr1 neon mtf puls mtf sil mrr1* staph mtf sulph mtf tell mtf thal mtf tub ↓
  - • **children**; in: kali-c mtf33 sil mtf33 tub mtf33

PROPHESYING: *(↗Clairvoyance; Death - presentiment; Fear - happen; DREAMS - Clairvoyant; DREAMS - Visionary)* Acon k* agar k* *Agn* ↓ alum ↓ anh sp1 ant-c bro1 apis b7a.de *Arg-n* ↓ camph chir-fl gya2 con hell ↓ *Lac-d* ↓ **Lach** a1* med a1 nux-m k2* olib-sac wmh1 podo fd3.de• sol-ni vml3• stram k* thea ↓ tritic-vg fd5.de [tax jsj7]
- **disagreeable** events, of: med st1
- **predicts** the time of death: *(↗Death - presentiment - predicts; Fear - death - predicts)* **Acon** k* *Agn* vh* alum st *Arg-n* k* hell k13 *Lac-d* hr1 thea st

PROPORTION disturbed; sense of (See Exaggerating)

PROSTRATION of mind: *(↗Anxiety - Exertion; Concentration - Difficult; Confusion; Confusion - Concentrate; Delirium - Depletion; Delirium - Fatigue; Dullness; Ennui; Ideas - Deficiency; Mental exertion - Agg.; Mental exertion - Wine; Mental power - Loss; Mistakes; Moaning - Weakness; Senses - Dull; Slowness; Stupefaction; Thinking - Aversion; Torpor; Unconsciousness; Unobserving [=inattentive]; EYE - Open lids; FACE - Expression - Haggard; FACE - Expression - Vacant; GENERALS - Collapse; GENERALS - Heaviness - Externally; GENERALS - Lassitude; GENERALS - Lie - Desire; GENERALS - Sluggishness; GENERALS - Weakness; GENERALS - Weakness - Exertion - agg. - slight; GENERALS - Weariness; SLEEP - Sleepiness)* abies-c br1* abrot k* acet-ac bg2 *Acon* b2.de* adam skp7*• adox a1 *Aeth* c1* agar k* agath-a nl2• agn b2.de* aids nl2• ail hr1* alco a1 alet br1 alf br1* allox tpw3 *Alum* k* alum-p k2* alum-sil k2* alumin ↓ alumin-p ↓ alumin-s ↓ alumn br1 am-c b2.de* am-m ↓ ambr k* amyg j *Anac* k* ang b2.de* anh c2* *Ant-c* h2* apis k* aran-sc a1 **Arg-met** k* *Arg-n* k* arn b2.de* ars k* ars-i ars-s-f k2* *Art-v* ↓ arum-i ptk2 asaf bg2* asar b2.de* asc-t a1 aster astra-e ↓ atra-r ↓ **Aur** k* aur-ar k2 aur-i k2* **Aur-s** k2* *Aven* c2* bacls-7 pte1*• bamb-a stb2.de• **Bapt** a1* *Bar-c* k* bar-i k2* bar-m k2* **Bell** b2.de* bell-p ↓ berb k2* bism-o a1 bit-ar wht1• boerh-d bnj1 both-a rb3 bov bg2 *Bry* k* bufo k2 buni-o jl3 buth-a sp1 cadm-met tpw6 caesal-b bnj1 calad k* *Calc* k* calc-ar k2* calc-f sp1 calc-i k2* calc-p k* calc-s calc-sil k2* camph b2.de* cann-i k* *Cann-xyz* bg2 canth b7.de* *Caps* j5.de* **CARB-AC** st1 carb-an k* *Carb-v* k* carbn-dox knl3• *Carbn-s* carc cpd*• carl a1 cassia-s ccrh1• castm bg2* *Caul* ↓ caust h2* cham k* chin b2.de* chinin-ar sf1.de chion c2 chir-fl gya2 choc srj3• chord-umb rly4• cic k* *Cimic* ↓ cinnb k* clem a1 cob bro1 cob-n sp1 coca c1* coca-c sk4• *Cocc* k* *Coff* b2.de* coff-t a1 colch k* coli jl2 coloc j5.de **Con** k* convo-d a1 convo-s sp1* cordyc mp4• corn a1* corn-f ↓ cortico tpw7* cortiso tpw7 crat br1 croc b2.de* cub a1 **Cupr** k* *Cupr-act* kr1* cur bro1 cycl b7.de* cypr c1 dam bro1 dig k* digin a1 diph-t-tpt ↓ dulc bg2 dys bh* eberth jl2 elaps a1 epiph br1 equis-h a1 eucal a1 eup-a c2 ferr k2* ferr-p ↓ **Ferr-pic** fl-ac bg2* gard-j vlr2• *Gels* k* germ-met stj2*• gink-b mtf11 glon a1 glyc bro1 gran a1 granit-m ↓ *Graph* k* grat a1* haliae-lc srj5• ham k2* *Hell* b2.de* hell-o a1* *Helon* bro1 *Hep* k* *Hipp* a1* *Hir* rsj4• *Hydroph* rsj6• **Hyos** b2.de* hyper k* *Ign* b2.de* ignis-alc ↓ ind a1* indg br1 influ mp4• iod k* ip h1* kali-ar c2 kali-br bg2* kali-c bg2* *Kali-hp* bro1 kali-i a1* kali-n b2.de* **Kali-p** k* *Kali-s* fd4.de *Kali-sil* k2* *Kola* stb3• lac-ac stj5• lac-d k2* lac-h sk4• lac-loxod-a hrn2• **Lach** k* lat-h bnm5*• lat-m sp1* lath bro1 laur k* lavand-a ctl1• **Lec** k* *Led* k* lil-t ↓ lim br1 limen-b-c hrn2* *Lob* hr1* lob-p bro1 lol a1 loxo-lae bnm12• loxo-recl bnm10• *Luf-op* rsj5• **Lyc** k* lyss hr1* *M-arct* b2.de m-aust b2.de mag-c a1* mand sp1 mang a1 marb-w es1• med al melal-alt gya4 meli menis a1 meny bg2 merc k* *Merc-c* bg2* methyl c2 mez bg2 morg-p pte* morph a1 mosch b2.de* *Mur-ac* b2.de* naja nat-ar **Nat-c** k* *Nat-m* k* **Nat-p** k* nat-s hr1* nat-sil k2* nicot c1 nid jl3 **Nit-ac** k* *Nit-s-d* ↓ *Nux-m* k* **Nux-v** k* ol-an ptk1 *Olib-sac* wmh1 olnd bg2* onos c2* op k* orch mtf osm ↓ osteo-a ↓ ox-ac a1* pall hr1* par bg2 petr k* petr-ra shn4• **Ph-ac** k* **Phos** k* phys a1* **PIC-AC** bg2* pip-m c2* *Plan* plat k* *Plb* bg2* plut-n srj7• podo positr nl2• prot pte1*• psor a1* ptel a1 *Puls* k* pyrog bg2* querc-r svu1• quinhydr mtf11 rad-br c11* ran-b bg2 ran-s ↓ raph a1 rauw sp1 rhod b4.de* rhus-t k* ruta b7a.de* sabad bg2 sabal c2 sabin b2.de* sacch bro1 sanic c1* sarcol-ac bro1 *Sars* k* *Scut* bro1 sec b2.de* *Sel* k* senec c2 seneg k* **Sep** k* ser-a-c jl2 **Sil** k* sium a1 sol-ecl ↓ sol-ni mtf11 *Spig* k* spong k* squil b7.de* stann k* *Staph* k* **Stram** b2.de* *Stry-p* c2* stry-val bwa3 *Sul-ac* k* sul-i k2* **Sulph** k* sumb hr1* syc pte1*• syph k2* tab a1* tanac a1* tarax bg2 tarent bro1 teucr k* thuj k* thymol ↓ thyr c2 trif-p br1 trios rsj11* *Tritic-vg* fd5.de tub bro1* tub-d ↓ ulm-c ↓ uncar-tom mp4• valer k* *Vanil* fd5.de ven-m ↓ **Verat** b2.de* verat-v a1 verb bg2 verbe-h bro1 verbe-o br1 *Viol-o* b2.de* *Viol-t* ↓ vip c2 visc sp1 xan c1* *Zinc* k* **Zinc-p** k2* *Zinc-pic* bg2* zinc-val c1 [arg-p stj2 bell-p-sp dcm1 cent-u rcb1 cupr-f stj2 cupr-m stj2 cupr-p stj2 irid-met stj2 lac-mat sst4 lith-i stj2 mang-i stj2 mang-p stj2 merc-i-f stj2 nat-caust stj2 osm-met stj2 zinc-i stj2 zinc-m stj2 zinc-n stj2]
- **morning**: arg-met k2 berb j5.de canth j5.de carb-v j5.de graph mtf33 kali-p fd1.de• **Lach** hr1* med jl2 osteo-a jl2 ph-ac j5.de *Phos* h2* ran-s a1 spong fd4.de syph jl2 tritic-vg fd5.de ven-m rsj12• [sol-ecl cky1]
- **noon**: carb-v phos
- **afternoon**: anac j5.de gard-j vlr2• kali-s fd4.de mur-ac ↓ nat-m j5.de olib-sac wmh1 sep j5.de sil j5.de ulm-c jsj8•
  - • **air**; in open: mur-ac a1
- **evening**: am-m j5.de astra-e jl3 atra-r skp7*• bamb-a stb2.de• bufo a1 cham k* ign j5.de kali-s fd4.de merc-c a1 nat-m j5.de* osm a1 pall sne positr nl2• sel rsj9• tritic-vg fd5.de
- **night**: ign a1* kali-c j5.de nux-v a1* ran-s j5.de
- **abortion**, after: *Caul* hr1*

- **ailments** from (See Ailments - prostration)
- **alternating** with:
  - **activity**; desires (See Activity - desires - alternating - prostration)
  - **alertness** (See Alert - alternating - exhaustion)
  - **excitement** (See Excitement - alternating - prostration)
  - **irritability** (See Irritability - alternating - prostration)
- **anxiety**, after: calc k2 **Lec** sne
- **business**, from: nux-v mrr1 podo c1
- **cares**, from: *(↗Ailments - cares; GENERALS - Weakness - nursing and)* *Cocc* mrr1 ph-ac k2* pic-ac k2*
- **children**; in: aeth mtf33 bar-c mtf33 calc-p mtf33 carb-v mtf33 graph mtf33 kali-sil mtf33 zinc ptk1
- **chill**; during: bell bg2 bry bg2 lach bg2 podo bg2
- **coition**, after: *Calc* st1 sep bg2* staph vh
- **conversation**:
  - **after**: *(↗talking - from)* granit-m es1• ruta fd4.de vanil fd5.de
  - **during**: granit-m es1•
- **convulsions**, from: *Staph* hr1*
- **diarrhea** | **suppression** of; prostration of mind from: ph-ac k2
- **dreams**; from: kola stb3•
- **eating**, after: anac a1 ignis-alc es2• lach nat-m a1 nux-m b7a.de ph-ac b4a.de
- **emissions** (See pollutions)
- **epilepsy**, in: *Art-v* hr1*
- **excitement**, after: calc k2
- **eye** strain, from: phos k2
- **fever**:
  - **after**, prolonged: *(↗FEVER - Intense - followed - prostration)* sel k2
  - **during**: ail vh1 *Anac* kr1 *Bapt* kr1 lil-t bg2 *Nit-s-d* kr1 rhod a1 sep bg2 tub-d jl2
- **followed** by:
  - **restlessness**: pyrog jl2
  - **weakness**; physical: ph-ac br1
- **grief**; from: diph-t-tpt jl2 **Ign** kr1* *Influ* jl2 kali-br ptk1 **Lec** sne nux-m ptk1 *Ph-ac* mrr1 phys ptk1
- **head** | **pain** in; during: arg-n bro1 med pc nux-v bro1 pic-ac mrr1 sil bro1
- **heart** failure, with: crat br1
- **influenza**:
  - **after**: cypr c1* lyc tl1
  - **during**: bapt tl1
- **injuries**, from: *(↗Ailments - injuries)* *Acet-ac* vh* camph vh* hyper vh* *Sul-ac* vh* verat vh*
- **menses**:
  - **after**: *(↗Menses - after)* **Alum** k* [alumin stj2 alumin-p stj2 alumin-s stj2]
  - **before**: *(↗Menses - before)* *Cinnb* hr1*
  - **during**: *(↗Menses - during)* aids nl2•
- **mental** exertion, slight: granit-m es1• *Kali-p* fd1.de• *Kali-s* fd4.de phos k2
- **motion** amel.: kali-i k2
- **nursing**, after: *Nit-ac* hr1* *Zinc* hr1*
- **old** age, in: **Bar-c** hr1* sel br1
- **pain**; from: bamb-a stb2.de• *Ruta* fd4.de tritic-vg fd5.de
- **pneumonia**; after: ferr-p tl1
- **pollutions**, after: bell-p c1 calc st carb-an *Cypr* kr1 *Gels* kr1 ph-ac bro1 *Phos* kr1 *Sel* *Viol-t* kr1
- **prostatic** complaints; in: thuj ptk1
- **reading**, from: *(↗Reading - agg.)* aur kali-p fd1.de• *Pic-ac* mrr1 *Sil*
- **respiration**; with impeded: ars bg2
- **room**, in closed: tanac br1*
- **sexual** excesses; after: agar bro1 *Agn* bro1 *Anac* bro1 calad k2* *Chin* bro1 coca bro1 dam bro1 gels bro1 *Graph* bro1 lec bro1 lyc bro1 nat-m bro1 nux-v bro1 onos bro1* *Ph-ac* bro1 *Phos* bro1 *Pic-ac* bro1 plat bro1 sabal bro1* sel k2* sep bro1 staph bro1* thymol bro1 zinc-pic bro1

Prostration of mind: ...

- **sexual** prostration (See FEMALE - Sexual desire - diminished; MALE GENITALIA/SEX - Sexual desire - diminished)
- **sleep**, from loss of: pic-ac k2*
- **sleepiness**, with: corn hr1 corn-f kr1
- **sleeplessness**, with: ambr bro1 ars bro1 aur bro1 *Aven* sf1.de *Carc* mlr1• castm sf1.de caust sf1.de *Cimic* bro1 coff bro1* **Cupr** hr1* lach sf1.de nux-v bro1 ph-ac sf1.de zinc-p bro1
- **study**; prolonged: graph ptk1 *Kali-p* fd1.de• ph-ac k2 *Pic-ac* mrr1 zinc mtf33
- **talking** | **from**: *(↗conversation - after)* alum tl1 calc h2 *Calc-p* kali-p fd1.de• **Nat-m** kr1
- **thoughts** | **doing** anything; of | **agg.**: bacls-7 fmm1•
  - **work**; of | **agg.**: bacls-7 fmm1•
- **tobacco**; from: calad k2*
- **trembling**, with: arg-n sf1.de cann-i hr1* con sf1.de stann sf1.de
- **trifles**, from: *(↗Trifles; Trifles - important)* am-c br1 *Phos*
- **vexation**, from: *Staph* sf1.de
- **waking**, on: op a1 osteo-a jl2 *Syph* hr1*
- **wine** agg.: con k2
- **women**: | **housewives**: bamb-a stb2.de•
- **working** too hard: carc sst2•
- **writing**, after: granit-m es1• kali-p fd1.de• pic-ac a1 *Sil*

PROTECTED feeling: *(↗Danger - no; Ease; Tranquillity)* *Caps* ckh1 olib-sac wmh1 ozone sde2• rhus-g tmo3• vanil fd5.de

PROTECTING: | **desire** to protect: nicc-met sk4•

PROTESTING: *(↗Anarchist; Contradiction - disposition; Quarrelsome)* ars jsa *Caust* jsa* lach jsa merc jsa sep jsa *Symph* fd3.de• tritic-vg fd5.de

PROUD (See Haughty)

PROVING ONESELF; need for (See Fastidious - prove)

PROVOKING others (See Inciting)

PRYING (See Curious)

PSYCHOSIS (See Delusions; Insanity; Mania; Mental symptoms)

PUBERTY; in: *(↗Indifference - puberty; Loathing - general - puberty/ Morose - puberty)* acon st ant-c bg2 ant-s-r st ant-t st apis dm *Ars* st aur sf bar-c st *Bell* st *Calc* st caul ↓ caust st *Cham* st *Cimic* ↓ cina lsr *Graph* st *Hell* bg2* helon sf *Kali-p* st lach st manc bg2 nat-m bg2 ph-ac sf *Phos* st *Puls* st rhus-t st *Staph* st *Sulph* st *Teucr* st

- **girls**; in: caul bro1 *Cimic* bro1

PUBLIC places agg.: hippoc-k szs2

PULLING:

- **collar** | **desire** to pull one's: ant-c bg2* lach bg2*
- **hair**: *(↗Anger - tear; Gestures - pulls; Jealousy - tearing; Striking - himself)* *Ars* ↓ bar-c ↓ *Bell* k* canth gb• *Cupr* ↓ dig ptk2 dulc ↓ germ-met ↓ lach gb• *Lil-t* med ↓ merc ↓ mez ↓ stram gb• tarent tub gb• verat gb• xanth ↓ [ant-c stj2 ant-met stj2]
  - **desire** to pull: *(↗HEAD - Hair - pulls)*
    - **her** own hair: *(↗HEAD - Hair - pulls)* *Ars* ptk1 *Bell* ptk1* *Cupr* ptk1* dig ptk1 germ-met srj5• lach mtf33 lil-t hr1* med ptk1 tarent ptk1* tub hr1* xanth ptk1
      - **pain**; from: tub mtf33
    - **someone's** hair: ars bg2* bar-c mrr **Bell** k* cupr bg2* dulc fd4.de lach *Lil-t* k* med bg2* merc mrr mez bg2* tarent k* tub bg2* xanth bg2
  - **presses** her head; and: tarent a1*
- **nose** | **one's** nose in the street: merc k*
- **teeth** | **one's**: bell

PULSATION in body agg.; during: m-ambo b7.de pyrog bg2

PUNCTILIOUS (See Conscientious)

PUNISHMENT agg. (See Ailments - punishment)

PURITY:

- **desire** for: positr nl2•
- **heart**; sensation of purity of: olib-sac wmh1

PURPOSEFUL: **Dulc** fd*

PYROMANIA (See Fire - set)

PYROPHOBIA (See Fear - fire)

QUAKING: vesp a1*

QUALMISH (See Remorse)

QUARRELLING:

- **aversion** to: (↗*Ailments - discords; Ailments - quarrelling; Answering - unable - hurt; Arguing - not; Diplomatic; Friendship - end - anger; Harmony - desire; Mildness; Pleasing - desire; Polite - too; Sensitive - quarrels; Sensitive - rudeness)* atro a1 aur-m-n wbt2• card-m vh dulc fd4.de *Kali-s* fd4.de lyc vh* mag-c vh* mag-m vh* nat-m mtf33 nit-ac gk ruta fd4.de staph mrr1* symph fd3.de• tritic-vg fd5.de vanil fd5.de [mag-br stj1 nicc stj1 spect dfg1 uva stj]
- **desire** to (See Quarrelsome)

QUARRELSOME: (↗*Abusive; Ailments - quarrelling; Anger; Anger - vex others; Animus; Arguing; Arguing - facility; Censorious; Contradiction - disposition; Contrary; Defiant; Disobedience; Fight; Insanity - quarrelsome; Intolerance; Irritability; Litigious; Mood - repulsive; Obstinate; Pertinacity; Protesting; Reproaching others; Rudeness; Snappish; Speech - offensive; Violent; Weeping - opposition; Weeping - remonstrated)* acon k* acon-c adam srj5• agar k* agath-a nl2• agav-t jl1 alco a1 allox tpw3* aloe bg2 alum k* am-c k* ambr k* *Anac* k* anan k* androc srj1• ang bg2 anh sf1.de ant-c ↓ ant-t k* apis b7a.de* arizon-l nl2• *Arn* k* *Ars* k* ars-s-f k2* *Asaf* bg2 asar k* aster k* atro a1* **Aur** k* aur-ar k2 aur-s k2* bamb-a stb2.de* bar-c k* *Bell* k* borra-o oss1• borx *Bov* k* *Brom* k* *Bry* k* bufo gk bung-fa mtf cael jl3 calc k* calc-s k* *Camph* k* cann-s j canth k* caps carb-an j carb-v j carc az1.de• caste jl3 *Caust* k* cench *Cham* k* chel k* chin k* chir-fl gya2 choc srj3• chord-umb rly4• *Chr-ac* hr1 cocc j coff bg2 colch bg2 *Con* k* conch fkr1• cop a1 cor-r k* *Croc* k* crot-h k* culx k2* *Cupr* k* cycl j cyn-d jl3 dendr-pol sk4• dig k* dream-p sdj1• *Dulc* k* elae a1 elaps ferr k* ferr-act j ferr-ar fl-ac germ-met srj5• gran j5.de granit-m ↓ graph j grat j5.de haliae-lc srj5• hell j helo-s rwt2• *Hep* b4a.de* hipp hir mg1.de *Hist* mg1.de* hydrog srj2• **HYOS** b7.de* ictod j5.de **Ign** k* ina-i mlk9.de iod j* ip k* kali-ar k* kali-bi bg2 *Kali-c* k* *Kali-chl* j5.de* kali-i k* kali-m ↓ kali-p k2* kola stb3• *Lac-cp* sk4• lac-e hrn2• lac-h sk4• *Lac-leo* sk4• lac-loxod-a hrn2• lac-lup hrn2• *Lach* k* led j lepi k* *Lyc* k* lyss k* m-ambo b7.de m-aust b7.de* mag-c mg1.de* mag-s sp1 mang j marb-w es1• meph jl3 *Merc* k* merl k* mez k* moni rfm1• morph oss• *Mosch* k* mur-ac j nat-ar *Nat-c* *Nat-m* k* nat-s *Nat-sil* fd3.de• neon srj5• nicc k* nicc-met stj2*• *Nit-ac* k* *Nit-s-d* j5.de **Nux-v** k* olib-sac ↓ olnd op bg2* ozone sde2• p-benzq ↓ pall k* **Petr** k* petr-ra shn4• *Ph-ac* k* *Phos* k* *Plat* k* plb positr nl2• pot-e rly4• prot fmm1• *Psor* k* puls gl1.fr• *Ran-b* k* raph ↓ rat k* reser jl3 rheum *Rhus-t* bg2* rib-ac jl3 ruta k* sabad j sacch a1* seneg k* *Sep* k* *Sil* j5.de* sinus rly4• sol-t-ae vml3• spong k* stann k* *Staph* k* *Stram* k* stront-c sul-ac k* sulfonam jl3* **Sulph** k* **Symph** fd* **TARENT** k1* tax ↓ thea *Thuj* k* thyr ↓ til k* trios rsj11• tritic-vg fd5.de tub al* upa c1 *Verat* k* *Verat-v* k* vinc ↓ viol-o bg2 viol-t k* zinc k* [am-br stj2 bar-br stj2 bar-i stj2 cupr-act stj2 cupr-f stj2 cupr-m stj2 cupr-p stj2 ferr-f stj2 ferr-lac stj2 ferr-n stj2 ferr-sil stj2 heroin sdj2 lith-i stj2 mang-i stj2 merc-i-f stj2 nicc-s stj2 zinc-i stj2]

- **morning**: *Lyc* sf1.de petr k* psor k* ran-b spong fd4.de staph sf1.de
- **forenoon**: ran-b a1
- **noon** | **12**-14 h: aster
- **afternoon**: alum k* dulc lyss ↓
  - **16** h: lyss
- **evening**: am-c j5.de ant-c nat-m neon srj5• nicc k* op a1 psor k* sil k* til a1
- **night**: olib-sac wmh1 verat
- **absent** persons; disputes with: (↗*Anger - absent)* lyc k*
- **alcoholism**; in: p-benzq mtf11
- **alternating** with:
  - **cares**: ran-b k*
  - **cheerfulness**: croc k* *Lach* gl1.fr• spong k* *Staph* j5.de*
  - **discontentment**: ran-b k*
  - **discouragement**: ran-b j5.de
  - **euphoria**: thyr jl
  - **gaiety** (See cheerfulness)
  - **laughter**: croc k* *Lach* gl1.fr• spong *Staph* sf1.de*
  - **remorse**: vinc hr1
  - **repentance** (See remorse)
  - **sadness**: *Con* kr1 sulfonam jl

Quarrelsome – alternating with: ...

  - **silent** grief: *Con*
  - **singing**: croc k*
  - **taciturnity**: *Con* k*
  - **timidity**: ran-b j5.de
- **anger**, without: bell k* bry a1 caust h2* *Dulc* staph h1* stram j5.de*
- **answers**; without waiting for: *Ambr* vh* *Graph* vh*
- **causeless**: granit-m es1• stram j5.de*
- **children**; in: brom mtf33 cham mtf33 ferr mtf33 mag-c mtf33 phos mtf33 sacch sst1• stram mtf33
  - **sweets**; after: sacch sst1•
- **company**; with aversion to: bamb-a stb2.de•
- **delivery**, during: **Cham** kr1
- **disturbed**, if: (↗*Disturbed)* **Nux-v** hr1*
- **drunkenness**; during: (↗*intoxicated)* *Petr*
- **face**:
  - **heat** of; with: mosch j5.de
  - **pale**; with: mosch j5.de
- **family**, with her: (↗*Talking - family)* agath-a nl2• dendr-pol sk4• *Dulc* mrr1 *Ign* mrr1 kali-c ptk1* kali-m ckh1 kali-p k2* lac-h sk4• lac-lup ↓ petr-ra shn4• spong fd4.de thyr jl3
  - **husband**; to: lac-lup hrn2•
- **herself**; with (See Mood - repulsive; Reproaching oneself)
- **intoxicated**; when: (↗*drunkenness)* *Petr*
- **jealousy**; from: (↗*Jealousy; Jealousy - quarrelling)* *Calc-s* vh* *Cench* *Hyos* j5.de* *Lach* nux-v
- **menses**:
  - **beginning** of; at: *Cham* kr1
  - **during**: (↗*Menses - during)* am-c
- **pains**:
  - **before**: cor-r j5.de
  - **during**: cor-r hr1 nux-v h1*
- **pugnacious**: bell j5.de nat-c j5.de nicc j5.de
- **recriminations** about trifles: (↗*trifles)* cop a1
- **sleep**, in: alum gl1.fr• ars *Bell* k* caust gl1.fr• cupr hep gl1.fr• merc gl1.fr• raph j5.de rheum k*
- **staring** of eyes, heat of face, bluish lips and dry mouth; with: mosch j5.de
- **trifles**; about: (↗*recriminations)* bamb-a stb2.de• *Dulc* fd4.de [tax jsj7]
- **waking**, on: lyc k*

QUEER: (↗*Eccentricity; Strange; Strange - crank)* agar ↓ **Bell** k1* calc k1* **Hyos** k1* **Lach** k1* nux-v ↓ puls k1* *Sep* ↓ sil ↓ *Stram* k1* *Sulph* ↓ verat k1*

- **acts**, ideas, opinions: calc jsa sulph jsa *Verat* jsa
- **dressing**, in: sil k1* *Sulph* k1*
- **gait**, in: nux-v jsa *Sep* jsa
- **gestures**; in:
  - ○ **Arms**; of: hyos jsa sep jsa *Stram* jsa
  - **Head**; of: agar jsa *Sulph* jsa

QUESTIONS, speaks continually in: (↗*Answering - questions; Curious - training)* ambr k2* *Aur* k*

- **answer**; without waiting for an: aur br1

QUICK to act: (↗*Agility; Answering - hastily; Concentration - active; Hurry; Ideas - abundant; Impatience; Impetuous; Impulsive; Memory - active; Rash; Speech - hasty; Thoughts - rapid; Vivacious; Witty)* androc srj1• bell sne bros-gau mrc1 choc srj3• coca-c sk4• *Coff* k* *Dulc* fd4.de hep sne ign br1* ignis-alc es2• lac-loxod-a hrn2• *Lach* k* nux-v br1 op a1 oxal-a rly4• spong fd4.de tritic-vg fd5.de ulm-c jsj8• [am-f stj2 fl-ac stj2 lith-f stj2 tax jsj7 tung-met stj2]

QUIET disposition: (↗*Asking - nothing; Confidence - want; Content - quiet; Conversation - agg.; Insanity - silent; Laziness; Mildness; Reserved; Taciturn; Timidity; Touched - aversion; Tranquillity)* abies-c agar bg2 agath-a nl2• aloe *Alum* k* am-c j5.de anac ↓ ant-c mrr1 ars a1 asar k* aur j5.de* aur-m-n wbt2• *Bell* k* bism j5.de* bism-o a1 brom j bruc j5.de *Bry* ↓ bufo k2 *Calc* bg2 cann-i a1 caps k* carb-an b4a.de *Caust* j5.de* cham j5.de* chin bg2 choc srj3• *Cic* k* clem k* coca a1 cocc k* coloc bg2 con ↓ cupr-s a1 cycl bg2 cystein-l rly4• dios a1 dros a1 dulc fd4.de

Quiet disposition: ...
eryth a1 euph k* euphr b7a.de* falco-pe nl2• fic-m gya1 fic-r br1 fuma-ac rly4• *Gels* k* ham fd3.de• *Hell* b7a.de* helodr-cal knl2• hydrog srj2• *Hyos* k* *Ign* k* ip j5.de* kali-m ckh1 lac-h htj1• lac-leo hrn2• lac-loxod-a hrn2• lac-lup hrn2• *Lach* k* lap-la rsp1 lyc k* mag-c bg2 mag-m mtf33 manc br1 mang k* meny a1 mur-ac k* nat-m h2* neon srj5• nit-ac bg2 nux-v k* op b7.de* petr k* petr-ra shn4• **Ph-ac** k* plac-s rly4• plat k* *Plb* k* podo fd3.de• positr nl2• psil ft1 puls k* rheum j5.de* rhus-g tmo3• rhus-t b7.de* ribo rly4• ruta fd4.de sabad j5.de* sabin bg2 sal-fr sle1• sars k* sep sil k* spong bg2* stann k* staph mrr1* thuj bg2* tub c1 ulm-c jsj8• valer kr1 vanil fd5.de *Verat* bg2 viol-t k* zinc k* [arg-met stj2 sel stj2]

- **evening**: choc srj3• dulc fd4.de
- **air**; in open | **amel.**: stann
- **alternating** with:
  - **cheerfulness** (See Cheerful - alternating - quiet)
  - **gaiety** (See Cheerful - alternating - quiet)
  - **laughing** (See Laughing - alternating - quiet)
  - **rage** (See Rage - alternating - quiet)
  - **singing** (See Singing - alternating - quiet)
- **calm**, and: *(↗Tranquillity)* lac-lup hrn2•
- **cannot** be quieted (See Quieted)
- **clasped**, with hands: puls j5.de
- **delivery**, after: *Thuj* kr1
- **discouragement**; with (See Discouraged - quiet)
- **heat**, during: *Bry* *Gels*
- **hypochondriasis**, in: puls j5.de valer kr1
- **light** is intolerable, bright: con j5.de
- **menses**, during: *(↗Menses - during)* am-c j5.de mur-ac j5.de
- **noise**, intolerable to: con j5.de
- **sleep**, after: anac j5.de

QUIET; wants to be: *(↗Company - aversion; Disturbed; Rest - desire; Retiring - desire; Silence - soliciting; Spoken - aversion; Touched - aversion)* agn k2· *Aids* nl2• arge-pl rwt5• arn ↓ ars a1 *Bamb-a* stb2.de• bell borx ↓ brass-n-o srj5• **BRY** ●* cadm-met ckh1 cadm-s st calc-p k2 cann-i chin a1 chir-fl gya2 choc srj3• coca colch ckh1 coli gmj1 con ↓ conch fkr1• crat br1 cupr-s cypra-eg sde6.de• dios dream-p sdj1• *Dulc* fd4.de eryt-j a1 euph **GELS** k ●* gink-b sbd1• *Ham* ↓ hir skp7• irid-met srj5• *Kali-c* ↓ kali-s fd4.de kola stb3• lac-h ↓ lach br1 lap-la rsp1 limen-b-c hrn2• marb-w es1• melal-alt ↓ mur-ac h1* nat-m ↓ nux-v j* ozone sde2• petr-ra ↓ ph-ac ↓ phasco-ci rbp2 phos ↓ pin-con oss2• podo fd3.de• positr nl2• ptel hl rad-br ↓ rhus-g tmo3• ruta fd4.de sabin ↓ sacch-a fd2.de• sal-ac sal-fr sle1• sapin ↓ spong fd4.de sulph ↓ tritic-vg fd5.de vanil fd5.de

- **afternoon**: sapin a1
- **alternating** with:
  - **euphoria** (See Euphoria - alternating - quiet)
  - **laughing** (See Laughing - alternating - quiet)
  - **rage** (See Rage - alternating - quiet)
- **apyrexia**; during: nat-m bro1
- **chill**, during: ars **Bry** *Kali-c*
- **grief**; from (See Grief - silent)
- **headache**; during: bamb-a stb2.de• melal-alt gya4 tritic-vg fd5.de
- **repose** and tranquillity; desires: *(↗Tranquillity)* arn ↓ bell gl1.fr• borx ↓ calc-p ↓ chir-fl gya2 con h2* crat br1 *Ham* fd3.de• kola stb3• lac-h sze9• nux-v k* petr-ra shn4• ph-ac ↓ rad-br sze8• sabin ↓ sacch-a fd2.de• spong fd4.de sulph gl1.fr•
  - **amel.**: crat br1
  - **walking** in open air; on: arn borx calc-p ph-ac j5.de sabin

QUIETED, cannot be: *(↗Inconsolable)* *Ars* ↓ **Cham** ↓ **Cina** k*

- **carried**; only by being: *(↗Carried - desire; Restlessness - children - carried)* *Ars* h2 **Cham**
  - **rapidly**: ars hr1*

RACING mind (See Concentration - active; Thoughts - control; Thoughts - rapid; Thoughts - rush)

RAGE (= fury): *(↗Anger; Anger - sudden; Anger - violent; Breaking; Cursing; Delirium - raging; Destructiveness; Fight; Gestures - angry; Insanity; Mania; Passionate [=choleric]; Restlessness - rage; Violent; Violent - deeds; Wicked; Wildness; FACE - Discoloration - yellow - rage; FACE - Expression - fierce)* *Acon* k* acon-c a1 acon-l a1 *Aeth* **Agar** k* agn kr1 alco a1 aloe ↓ alumn *Anac* k* androc srj1• ant-t k* *Apis* b7a.de* arg-met k2* arg-n k* *Arn* k* *Ars* k* ars-s-f k2 *Atro* kr1* aur bg2 bar-c k* **Bell** k* borra-o oss1• *Borx* sne bry k* bufo calc *Camph* cann-i k* cann-s k* cann-xyz ↓ **Canth** k* carb-v h2 *Carbn-s* cardios-h rly4• *Caust* b4a.de* cere-s ↓ cham k* chel k* chin chin-b ↓ chinin-s chlor ↓ choc ↓ cic k* cimic k* *Cimx* ↓ cina cocc j5.de* *Colch* k* coloc con bg2 cori-r croc k* crot-c sk4• crot-h k* *Cupr* k* cyn-d jl3 dig k* dros k* dulc elec j eupi a1 falco-pe nl2• fl-ac galla-q-r nl2• gels bg2 germ-met srj5• glon k* graph grat ↓ haliae-lc srj5• *Hell* k* hep **Hyos** k* hyper ign bg2* iod bg2 irid-met srj5• jatr-c kali-bi bg2 kali-br mrr1 kali-c k* **Lac-c** lac-cp sk4• lac-e hrn2• lac-leo hrn2*• *Lach* k* lat-h ↓ *Lil-t* bg2* lob *Lol* bg2* loxo-recl knl4• **Lyc** k* lyss ↓ m-ambo c1 manc bg2 med bg2 melal-alt gya4 meli a1* *Merc* k* merc-cy j5.de* merc-meth ↓ **Mosch** murx bg2 nat-c ↓ *Nat-m* k* neon srj5• *Nit-ac* k* nux-m nux-v bg2* oena olib-sac wmh1 olnd ↓ **Op** k* oper br1 opun-s ↓ opun-v ↓ oxal-a rly4• ozone sde2• par petr j5.de* petr-ra ↓ ph-ac sf1.de *Phos* k* plat bg2* plb k* plut-n srj7• positr nl2• psor al2 *Puls* k* raja-s jl3 raph a1 rhus-t bg2 ruta k* sabad k* sal-fr sle1• sang ↓ *Sec* k* seneg k* sep j5.de* *Sol-ni* staph c1* **Stram** k* streptoc rly4• stry k2* sul-ac sulo-ac a1* *Sulph* k* *Tab* taosc iwa1• tarent k* thal-xyz srj8• *Thuj* b4a.de thyr br1 *Trios* rsj11• tub jl2 **Verat** k* vip k* xanth ↓ zinc k* [heroin sdj2 spect dfg1]

- **day** and night: hyos j5.de
- **morning** | **bed**; in: kali-c j5.de
- **evening**: acon anac ars **Bell** croc j5.de* *Hyos* *Lach* merc nit-ac op a1 phos plat puls thyr jl3 trios jl3 zinc
- **night**: acon *Apis* kr1 ars *Bar-c* kr1 *Bell* con *Hyos* lyc merc nat-c nat-m nit-ac plb puls *Verat*
- **ailments** (See Ailments - rage)
- **alone**, while: *(↗Company - desire; Company - desire - alone)* bufo
- **alternating** with:
  - **affectionate** disposition: croc
  - **anxiety**: bell j5.de
  - **cheerfulness**: acon j5.de bell j5.de cann-s h1* croc j5.de hyos j5.de seneg j5.de
  - **consciousness**; return of: acon stram h1*
  - **convulsions**: **Stram** k*
  - **death**:
    - **desire** for: bell j5.de*
    - **presentiment** of: stram hr1*
  - **fear**: bell j5.de
  - **foolish** behavior (See Foolish - alternating - rage)
  - **laughing**: acon j5.de stram k*
  - **loquacity**: stram j5.de
  - **quiet**; desire to be: hyos h1*
  - **religious** excitement: agar
  - **remorse**: lil-t mrr1
  - **repose** (See quiet)
  - **sleep**: ars kr1
  - **unconsciousness**: aloe kr1
  - **weeping**: acon j5.de cann-s h1*
- **amorous** rage:
  - **morning** | **rising**; on: agn a1
- **aroused**, when: phos
- **biting**, with: *(↗Biting)* bell j5.de* *Camph* kr1 canth sf1.de croc j5.de cupr j5.de* falco-pe nl2• sec j5.de *Stram* j5.de *Verat* j5.de
- **blame** others, desire to: camph mrr
- **chained**, had to be: *(↗Insanity - strength)* ars j5.de* *Bell* vh* *Hyos* vh* sec j5.de **Stram** vh* **Tarent** vh*
- **children**; in: tub jl2
- **chill**, during: cann-s j5.de *Cimx* kr1*
- **cold** applications to head amel.: sabad
- **consolation**, from: *(↗Consolation - agg.)* *Nat-m* kr1
- **constant**: *Agar* *Verat* kr1

- **contradiction**, from: grat j *Ign* c1 *Lac-c* kr1 lyc j nux-v j olnd kr1 opun-s a1 *Thuj* a1
- **controlled**: plut-n srj7•
- **convulsions**; rage with: ars *Bell* *Canth* kr1 *Hyos* kr1 plb hr1 *Stram*
- **cursing**, with: alco a1 anac sf1.de falco-pe nl2• lac-c al *Nit-ac* j5.de* ozone sde2• tub mtf33 verat j5.de* [heroin sdj2]
- **delivery**, during: *Bell* kr1
- **delusion** puts him into rage: cann-xyz bg2 *Stram* kr1
- **discouragement**; with: colch j5.de nit-ac j5.de
- **drink** or to touch larynx; when trying to: canth merc-meth a1
- **drinking**, while: bell h1 *Stram*
- **drunkenness**, during: *(↗Kill; desire - drunkenness)* agar a1 taosc iwa1•
- **eating**:
  - **during**: chlor kr1
  - **after**: chlor kr1
- **epilepsy**:
  - **after** epilepsy; rage: *Arg-met* op bro1
  - **with** epilepsy; rage: bell cupr hyos nux-v op plb
- **fever**; during: *Bell* b4.de* lyc bg2 stram bg2 **Verat** b7.de*
- **foaming** mouth, with: *Camph* j5.de*
- **followed** by | **repentance**: *(↗Remorse - anger; Remorse - quickly)* anac mtf croc sf1.de lyss kr1 med mtf
- **hallucinations**, from (See delusion)
- **headache**, with: agar a1 *Ars* **Bell** cimic kr1 croc glon k2 *Lyc* nat-m puls **Stram** *Verat*
- **heat** on body, with: *Verat* j5.de*
- **insults**, after: *(↗Abusive)* lat-h thj1 sang stram taosc iwa1•
- **kill** people, tries to: *(↗Kill)* hep **Hyos** sec *Stram* tarent mrr1
- **know** his relatives, does not: *(↗Recognizing - not - relatives)* *Bell*
- **laughing**, with: *Stram* j5.de*
- **love**; from disappointed: *(↗Ailments - love)* *Hyos* kr1
- **malicious**: *Bell* j5.de cann-s j5.de choc srj3• cocc j5.de cupr j5.de* lyc j5.de mosch j5.de neon srj5• petr j5.de* sec j5.de taosc iwa1•
- **medicine**, from forcible administration of: *Bell* a1
- **menses**:
  - **beginning** of; at: acon a1*
  - **during**: *(↗Menses - during)* acon k* bell hyos k* meli mrr1
- **mischievous**: *(↗Malicious; Mischievous)* agar bell j cann-s j cocc j cupr j lyc j mosch j petr j sec j zinc ↓
  - **noise**; from the slightest: *(↗Irritability - noise; Sensitive - noise; Sensitive - noise - slightest)* zinc mtf33
- **pain**, from: acon sf1.de arg-met k2 *Ars* bg2* cham sf1.de glon k2
- **paroxysms**, in: acon kr1 camph kr1 canth kr1* cere-s a1 chin-b hr1* **Cocc** hr1 croc sf1.de *Cupr* kr1 hyos c1 lac-c br1 mosch c1* *Nit-ac* hr1 oena sf1.de opun-s a1 (non:opun-v a1) *Puls* kr1 *Stram* kr1 taosc iwa1• *Verat* kr1*
- **passing** quickly: germ-met srj5•
- **perspiration**; during: acon bg2 *Ars* bg2 bell bg2 *Canth* bg2 caust bg2 hyos bg2 nit-ac bg2 nux-v bg2 *Op* bg2 sabad bg2 *Stram* bg2 verat bg2
- **pulls** hair of bystanders: ars ckh1 *Bell* k* *Cupr* ckh1 med ckh1 tarent ckh1 tub ckh1 xanth ckh1
- **reading** and writing, by: med kr1
- **sexual** desire; from suppressed: lil-t mrr1
- **shining** objects, from: *(↗Shining - agg.)* bell canth hyos *Stram*
- **shrieking**, with (See Shrieking - rage)
- **sleep**:
  - **followed** by continuous deep: sec kr1
  - **in**: phos j5.de
- **spitting**, with: *(↗Spitting)* bell j5.de *Camph* kr1 cann-s j5.de
- **stand**, unable to: *Stram* kr1
- **staring** looks, with: *(↗Staring)* bell
- **strength** increased: *Agar* **Bell** hyos j5.de*
- **striking**, with (See Striking - rage)
- **suffering**, from: aloe kl
- **suicidal** disposition, with: *(↗Suicidal)* ant-t j5.de* sec sf1.de stram j5.de
- **taken** up, child on being: *Stram* kr1
- **tearing** clothes: *(↗Destructiveness - clothes; Tearing - things)* *Camph* kr1
- **tossing** about in bed, making unintelligible signs: stram kr1
- **touch**, renewed by: *(↗Touched - aversion)* *Bell* lach sf1.de *Op* *Stram*

Rage: ...

- **trifles**, at: bar-c sf1.de cann-s a1 *Chel* sne dros h1 thyr br1
- **violent**: *(↗Violent; Violent - deeds)* agar anac sf1.de bar-c j5.de **Bell** k* canth j5.de cocc j5.de croc j5.de cupr j5.de **Hyos** lyc j5.de lyss mrr1 petr-ra shn4• **Stram** k* tarent mrr1 thal-xyz srj8• *Verat* st
- **water**, at sight of: *(↗Hydrophobia)* *Bell* *Canth* cupr hyos lach merc j5.de *Stram*
- **weeping**, with: cann-i sf1.de cann-s j5.de cann-xyz bg2 irid-met srj5•
- **worm** affections; in: *Carb-v* kr1*
- **writing**; from: med mtf33

RAIN (See Weather - rain)

RASH: *(↗Abrupt; Adventurous; Audacity; Capriciousness; Courageous; Heedless; Hurry; Impatience; Impetuous; Impulsive; Indiscretion; Meddlesome; Quick; Sensitive - want; Speech - hasty; Thoughts - rapid)* aids nl2• arizon-l nl2• *Aur* k* caps cic ptk1* dendr-pol sk4• galla-q-r nl2• meny petr-ra ↓ **Puls** k ● tub ptk1* [temp elm1]

- **driving**, when: aids nl2• petr-ra shn4•

READING:

- **agg.**: *(↗Absentminded - reading; Anxiety - reading; Excitement - reading; Irritability - reading; Prostration - reading; Restlessness - reading; Restlessness - reading - while; Sensitive - reading)* ang k* asaf hr1* *Calc* k* carb-ac hr1* cocc k* colch a1 croc ckh1 fl-ac a1 kali-c ckh1 lyc bg2 mag-m k* mang ckh1 med k* nat-c mrr1 nat-sil k2 olnd k* ph-ac k* sil ckh1 stann k* tarax k*
- **aversion** to read: *Acon* alum gl1.fr• bar-c brom k* carb-ac *Carl* clem coca con gl1.fr• corn cycl hydr kali-bi kali-p fd1.de• lac-ac *Lach* gl1.fr• lil-t nat-ar *Nat-c* vh* nat-m sne nat-sil fd3.de• *Nux-v* ox-ac phys pic-ac gg puls gl1.fr• pyrus *Sil* sulph b4a.de
  - **walking** in open air amel.: ox-ac
- **desires**: adam srj5• aur-s zr *Calc* ↓ carc fb* cocc ptk1 kali-s fd4.de kola stb3• lec oss• *Nux-v* ↓ positr nl2• *Puls* ↓ ruta fd4.de sep mtf33 staph mtf33 stram ↓ sulph mtf33 [lac-mat sst4 *Spect* dfg1]
  - **encyclopaedia**: sulph mtf
  - **children**; in: carc pd*
  - **extravagant** stories: stram pc
  - **medical** books; to read: *Calc* gl1.fr• carc mlr1• *Nux-v* gl1.fr• *Puls* gl1.fr• staph gl1.fr• sulph mtf*
  - **mystery** and detective stories: sulph mtf
  - **passion** to read: carc gk6
  - **read** to; to be: anth a1 chin k* clem k*
- **difficult**; is: *Agn* a1* carc mlr1• *Coca* kr1 *Cocc* h1* hura a1 kali-p fd1.de• nat-sil fd3.de•
- **subject**, must change the: dros kr1
- **unable** to read: *(↗Mistakes - reading)* aeth hr1* agar ↓ alum st bar-c ↓ bell a1 cann-i a1 *Carc* ↓ cycl a1 ham a1 lat-m bnm6• lyc h2* mag-c st* merc a1 narcot a1 nat-m hr1* ptel hl saroth sp1 sep hr1*
  - **children**, in: agar mtf33 alum st* bar-c mtf33 *Carc* mlr1• mag-c st*
  - **written**, what he has: lyc a1*
- **understand**, does not: *Ambr* kr1 *Carc* mlr1• *Colch* kr1 com a1* com-f kr1 vanil fd5.de

REALITY:

- **flight** from reality: *(↗Renunciation - world)* anh k* lac-f wza1•
- **not** real; everything seems (See Unreal - everything)

REASON increased, power of: *(↗Ideas - abundant; Objective)* bry *Calc* carb-v *Cham* coff-t a1 *Lyc* merc mur-ac nit-ac nux-v olib-sac wmh1 phos puls rhus-t sep spig staph *Sulph*

REASONABLE (See Objective)

REASSURED:

- **desires** to be (See Consolation - amel.; Longing - good)
- **difficult** to be reassured (See Censorious; Suspicious)
- **easily**: *(↗Naive)* arg-n ↓ *Phos* mrr1
  - **anxious**; when: arg-n vh [phos stj1]

REBELLIOUS: *(↗Anarchist; Revolutionist)* adam srj5• *Carc* mrr1 **Caust** mrr1

REBELS against poultice: borx h2 bry h1* *Calc* h2* carb-v h2* *Cham* h1* lyc h2 merc h1* mur-ac h2* nit-ac h2* nux-v h1* phos h2* puls h1* rhus-t h1* sep h2* spig h1* staph h1* *Sulph* h2*

RECKLESS (See Rash; Temerity)

RECOGNITION; desire for (See Delusions - appreciated)

RECOGNIZING: | **everything**:

- **move**; but cannot | **catalepsy**; in: cocc sang

- **not** recognize; does:
  - **anyone**: *(↗Delirium - recognizes)* aesc k2 *Glon* kr1 *Hyos* kr1 *Ruta* fd4.de *Verat* kr1
  - **children**; her own: acet-ac ptk1
  - **face**; his own: choc srj3•
  - **friends**: *(↗Delusions - strangers - friends)* kali-br kr1 neon srj5• [cupr stj2 cupr-act stj2 cupr-f stj2 cupr-m stj2 cupr-p stj2]
  - **house**; his own: *(↗surroundings; Delirium; Delusions - house - own)* cic k2 meli merc psor
  - **mother**; her: atra-r bnm3•
  - **relatives**; his: *(↗Memory - weakness; Rage - know)* acet-ac k* aesc↓ agar *All-c* vh1 *Anac* **Bell** k* calad calc-sil k2 cic cupr k* *Glon* **Hyos** k* kali-bi kali-br bg2 *Lach* lyc k2 meli *Merc* nux-m k2 oena *Op* k* phos plb sil h2 *Stram* k* sul-ac tab valer *Verat* k* zinc
    - **waking** on: aesc k2 *Kali-br* hr1* stram mrr1 zinc mrr1
  - **speaking**; the one to whom he is: stram kr1
  - **streets**; well known: *(↗surroundings; Confusion - loses; Delirium; Forgetful - house; Forgetful - streets; Memory - weakness - places; Memory - weakness - streets; Mistakes - localities; Orientation - decreased)* arg-n sf1.de cann-i k* **Glon** k* lach **Nux-m** olib-sac wmh1 **Petr** k* plat sf1.de *Ruta* fd4.de sal-fr sle1•
  - **surroundings**: *(↗house; streets; Confusion - knows; Delusions - place - strange/ Delusions - place - wrong/ Mistakes - localities; Stupefaction - knows/ Unconsciousness - dream - does)* aesc↓ cann-s rb2 dulc fd4.de glon rb2 *Kali-p* kr1* kali-s fd4.de merl rb2 podo fd3.de• *Ruta* fd4.de spong fd4.de tritic-vg fd5.de vib↓
    - **waking**; on: aesc k* vib↓
      - **what** to do on waking; she could not tell where she was or: vib rb2

RECRIMINATING (See Quarrelsome)

RECTIFYING: | **desire** to rectify: *(↗Truth - telling)* **Podo** fd*

REFINED (See Elegance; Sensitive; GENERALS - Delicate)

REFLECTING: *(↗Answering - reflecting; Brooding; Introspection)* *Ambr*↓ aur a1 bar-c j bar-ox-suc rly4• berb hr1* *Carb-an* hr1* chin j chord-umb rly4• *Cocc*↓ cycl a1 dulc fd4.de eug a1* euph hr1* graph j *Hyos* h1* ketogl-ac rly4• lac-h sze9• lac-loxod-a hrn2• lyss hr1* m-arct j meny hr1* mur-ac j nux-v j ol-an hr1* olib-sac wmh1 *Phos* hr1* plac-s rly4• *Plat*↓ positr nl2• ruta fd4.de sal-fr sle1• sil j sulph j thuj j tritic-vg fd5.de *Vanil* fd5.de [tax jsj7]

- **inability** to reflect: acon bg2* *Ambr*↓ aur kr1 lyc bg2 mez bg2 nat-c bg2 nux-m bg2
  - **old** people; in: *Ambr* kr1
  - **studying**, from: *Nat-c* kr1
- **sadness**, in: *Cocc* h1* *Plat* hr1*

REFUSING:

- **cannot** refuse (See Yielding)
- **eat**; to (See Eating - refuses)
- **everything** offered to him: *(↗Capriciousness - rejecting)* oena a1 past a1
- **help**: cina mtf33 des-ac rbp6 tritic-vg fd5.de
- **medicine**; to take the: *(↗treatment; Disgust - medicine; Doubtful - recovery - medicine; Fear - medicine - taking; Homeopathy; Irritability - medicine; Irritability - sends; Remedies - aversion; Suspicious - medicine; Well - says - sick)* agar-pr↓ *Am* st* calad ptk1 cimic k2* *Hyos* k* *Kali-p* kr1 **Lach** st* mim-p skp7*• ruta fd4.de *Stram* kr1* tritic-vg fd5.de *Verat-v* kr1 visc sp1
  - **delirium**; during: *(↗Delirium)* agar-pr a1 hyos vh

Refusing: ...

- **things** asked for (See Capriciousness - rejecting)
- **treatment**; every: *(↗medicine; Well - says - sick)* ars↓ bell gl1.fr• caust gl1.fr• kali-br sne lach gl1.fr• nux-v↓ plat gl1.fr•
  - **sick**; in spite of being very: ars gl1.fr• caust gl1.fr• nux-v gl1.fr•

REGRESSION (See Childish)

REJECTING everything offered to him (See Capriciousness - rejecting; Refusing - everything)

REJUVENATED; feeling of being: olib-sac wmh1

RELAXED (See Tranquillity)

RELIGIOUS AFFECTIONS: *Ars* ptk1 *Aur* ptk1 hyos ptk1 *Lach* ptk1 lil-t ptk1 *Lyc* ptk1 puls ptk1 *Stram* ptk1 *Sulph* ptk1 **Verat** ptk1 zinc ptk1

- **too** occupied with religion: *(↗Anxiety - salvation; Delirium - religious; Delusions - religious; Despair - religious; Dogmatic; Doubtful - salvation; Eccentricity - religious; Excitement - religious; Fear - devil of; Fear - evil; Fear - faith; Fear - monomania; Haughty - religious; Insanity - religious; Loquacity - religious; Mysticism; Piety; Praying; Remorse; Superstitious; GENERALS - Catalepsy - religious)* achy jl *Alum* bg2* alum-sil k2 am-c k* anac k2 aq-mar skp7* *Arg-n* k* *Ars* k* ars-s-f k2 aster sze10• *Aur* k* aur-ar↓ *Aur-m*↓ bar-c *Bell* k* *Calc* camph *Carb-v* k* carbn-s *Carc* mlr1• caust k* *Cham* k* *Chel* cina k* coff k* con k* croc k* crot-c sk4• cycl k* dig k* ferr k* ferr-ar *Graph* k* hura hydrog srj2*• **Hyos** k* hyper a1 *Ign* k* ignis-alc↓ kali-br k* *Kali-p* lac-f wza1• **Lach** k* **Lil-t** k* **Lyc** k* *Med* *Meli* merc k* *Mez* nat-c k2 nat-m nux-v k* oci-sa sk4• *Olib-sac*↓ orig gy *Orig-v* sne petr-ra shn4• ph-ac gl1.fr• *Plat* k* plb↓ plut-n↓ polys sk4• *Psor* k* *Puls* k* raja-s↓ rat mrr1 *Rhus-t* k1* rob ruta k* sabad k* sel k* **Sep** k1* sil k* stann staph vh* **STRAM** bg2* **Sulph** k* tarax a1 thuj **Verat** k* **Zinc** k* [heroin sdj2]
  - **alternating** with:
    - **rage** (See Rage - alternating - religious)
    - **sexual** excitement: lil-t k* *Plat* plut-n srj7•
  - **bible** all day; wants to read the: *Calc* st stram st
  - **children**; in: *Ars* k* *Calc* k* carc mlr1• *Lach* k* plat mtf33 sep mtf33 *Stram* st* *Sulph* k*
  - **fanaticism**: *(↗Fanaticism; Insanity - religious)* aur-ar k2 ignis-alc k2 petr-ra shn4• plb c1 puls k2* rob sel stram c1 sulph thuj k* verat mrr1
  - **haughtiness**; religious (See Haughty - religious)
  - **horror** of the opposite sex (See Aversion - men; to [=male persons] - women - religious; Aversion - women - men - religious)
  - **mania**: *(↗Mania)* *Anac* ptk1* plb c1 sulph c1 verat tl1*
  - **melancholia**: *(↗Insanity - religious)* ars b4.de* *Aur* b4a.de* *Aur-m* bro1 bell j carc mlr1• con gl1.fr• croc j5.de* *Kali-br* hr1* *Kali-p* hr1* *Lach* j5.de* lil-t k2* *Lyc* b4a.de* *Meli* hr1* mez k2* *Plat* hr1* plb bro1 psor c1* puls j5.de* sel j5.de sil k2* *Stram* j5.de* *Sulph* b4a.de* *Verat* j5.de* [heroin sdj2]
    - **remorse**; from: aur gl1.fr• con gl1.fr•
  - **metaphysical** concerns: **Calc** mrr1*
  - **narrow**-minded in religious questions: hyos gl1.fr• puls gl1.fr• *Stram* gl1.fr•
  - **penance**, desires to do: *Plat* kr1
  - **praying** (See Praying)
  - **preaching** (See Preaching - religious)
  - **preoccupations**; religious (See too)
  - **puberty**; in: *Ars* st *Calc* st *Lach* st* *Sulph* st
  - **sex**; religious aversion to the opposite (See Aversion - men; to [=male persons] - women - religious; Aversion - women - men - religious)
  - **sexuality**; conflict between religious ideals and: *Lil-t* mrr1
  - **songs**: olib-sac wmh1 raja-s jl3
  - **speculations**; dwells on: *Olib-sac* wmh1 **Sulph** h2*
    - **asking** questions; he is:
      - **drugs**; did Jesus take: olib-sac wmh1
      - **who** made God?: sulph k2
      - **yearning** eyes; did Jesus have: olib-sac wmh1

- **too** occupied with religion: ...
  - • **taciturnity**, haughtiness, voluptuousness and cruelty; religious affections with: *Plat* kr1
  - • **talking** on religious subjects: *Hyos* kr1
  - • **thoughts**; religious: olib-sac wmh1
  - • **tortured** by religious ideas; at night: camph kr1 lil-t k2 plut-n srj7•
- **want** of religious feeling: (*↗Indifference - religion; Moral; Nihilistic) Anac* k* aster sze10• calc gl1.fr• coloc k* croc k* kali-br ptk1* **Lach** mtf33* laur ptk1* *Lyc* gl1.fr• merc gl1.fr• petr-ra shn4• plat gl1.fr• sil gl1.fr• *Sulph* gl1.fr• ulm-c jsj8•

RELOCATING: (*↗Travelling)*
- **desire** to relocate: hydrog srj2•

REMEDIES, homeopathic: | **aversion** to: (*↗Refusing - medicine)* carc mlr1• caust gl1.fr• hep gl1.fr• lyc gl1.fr• nit-ac gl1.fr• nux-v gl1.fr• sep gl1.fr•

REMEMBERING:
- **bad** memory (See Memory - weakness)
- **not** happened; events which have (See Memory - false)
- **sleep** what he had forgotten; during (See Forgetful - sleep; Forgotten - sleep)
- **strong** memory; too (See Memory - active)

REMORSE: (*↗Anger - mistakes; Anguish; Anxiety - conscience; Delusions - crime - committed; Delusions - neglected - duty; Delusions - reproach; Delusions - right - doing; Delusions - wrong - done; Despair - religious; Discontented - himself; Religious - too; Reproaching oneself; Thoughts - tormenting)* achy jl3 adam ↓ agath-a nl2• agn k2 alum k* alum-sil k2* am-c k* anac bg* anan a1 androc srj1• arg-n ↓ **Ars** k* ars-s-f k* **Aur** k* aur-ar k2 *Aur-m-n* wbt2• *Bell* k* bros-gau ↓ cact bg2 *Calc* st1 calc-p bg2* carb-an bg2 carb-v k* carc tpw2* caust k* cham k* *Chel* k* chin-b hr1* chir-fl gya2 cina k* **Cocc** k* **Coff** k* con k* croc hr1 *Cupr* k* cur sne *Cycl* k* *Dig* k* dulc fd4.de ferr k* ferr-ar fic-m ↓ graph k* *Hell* mrr1 helodr-cal ↓ hep **Hyos** k* *Ign* k* irid-met srj5• kali-br bg2* kali-n ↓ kalm bg lac-e hrn2• lac-h sk4• *Lach* k* lil-t mrr1 lyss al *Med* k* *Merc* moni rfm1• nat-c k* nat-m k* nat-s ptk1* nit-ac k* nux-v k* olnd ↓ *Ph-ac* bg2* phos bg2 plat psor st1 *Puls* k* rheum bg2 ruta k* sabad k* sanguis-s hrn2• sec bg2 sel k* *Sep* mrr1 *Sil* k* spirae a1 spong fd4.de staph vh* **Stram** k* stront-c k* **Sulph** k* symph fd3.de• tritic-vg fd5.de **Verat** k* vinc a1 *Zinc* k* [heroin sdj2]
- **afternoon**: am-c carb-v
- **evening**: *Puls*
- **night**: puls
- **ailments** from (See Ailments - remorse)
- **alternating** with:
  - • **irritability** (See Irritability - alternating - remorse)
  - • **lasciviousness** (See Lascivious - alternating - remorse)
  - • **quarreling** (See Quarrelsome - alternating - remorse)
  - • **rage** (See Rage - alternating - remorse)
- **anger**; after: (*↗Rage - followed - repentance; Sadness - anger - after)* kali-n mrr4•
- **dream**; after a sexual: helodr-cal knl2•
- **excessive**: merc bg2
- **indiscretion**; over past: (*↗Anger - past; Dwells - past; Grief - past)* sanguis-s hrn2• spirae a1
- **menses**, after: (*↗Menses - after)* Ign hr1*
- **quickly**, repents: (*↗Anger - alternating - repentance; Irritability - alternating - remorse; Rage - followed - repentance)* adam srj5• arg-n mrr1 bros-gau mrc1 croc k* fic-m gya1 iyss mrr1 olnd k* spong fd4.de sulph gl1.fr• symph fd3.de• tritic-vg fd5.de
  - • **alternating** with | **anger** (See Anger - alternating - repentance)
- **trifles**, about: (*↗Trifles; Trifles - important) Sil* k* symph fd3.de•
- **waking**, on: fic-m gya1 puls
- **want** of: polys sk4•

RENUNCIATION: (*↗Resignation)*
- **world**; of the external: (*↗Reality - flight)* anh sp1*

REPEATING: lach ptk1* lyc ptk1* stann ptk1* zinc bro1*

Repeating: ...
- **actions**; the same (See Gestures - repeating; Ritualistic)
- **question** first; when answering, repeating the (See Answering - repeats)
- **rhymes** (See Verses - repeating)
- **sentence** when speaking; the same (See Delirium - repeats; Speech - repeats)
- **words** when writing; the same (See Mistakes - writing - repeating)

REPENTING:
- **not** repenting (See Hatred)
- **quickly** (See Remorse - quickly)

REPOSE (See Quiet disposition; Quiet; wants)

REPROACHED; ailments from being (See Ailments - reproaches)

REPROACHING oneself●: (*↗Anger - mistakes; Anxiety - conscience; Censorious - oneself; Confidence - want; Consolation - agg.; Contemptuous - self; Delirium - blames; Delusions - body - ugly; Delusions - neglected - duty; Delusions - reproach; Delusions - right - doing; Delusions - wrong - done; Discontented - himself; Discouraged - reproaches; Disgust - oneself; Haughty; Hiding - himself - children; Insanity - women - reproaching; Insecurity; Irritability - himself; Masochism; Modesty; Remorse; Self-denial; Shameful; Striking - himself; Tearing - himself) Acon* agath-a nl2• agri mp4• alum ptk1* anac bg2* arn ptk1* *Ars* k* *Aur* k* aur-ar k2* *Aur-m-n* wbt2• aur-s wbt2• bros-gau mrc1 calc-p k* calc-sil ↓ *Carc* fd2.de* chel ptk1 clem bg2 cob k* cob-act mtf coca-c sk4• *Cocc* ptk1 coli rly4• con bg2* cortiso gse croc bg2* cupr bg2* cur mrr1 cycl k* dendr-pol ↓ *Dig* k* falco-pe nl2• fic-m gya1 fum rly4• ger-i rly4• germ-met mtf* gink-b jl3 haliae-lc srj5• hell k* hura hydrog ↓ *Hyos* k* *Ign* k* irid-met srj5• kali-br ptk1* kali-c ptk1 kalm ptk1 lac-c br1* lach bg2* limest-b es1• loxo-recl knl4• lyc *M-arct* j5.de* med st* merc k* moni rfm1• mucs-nas rly4• naja mtf28 nat-ar *Nat-m* neon srj5• **Nux-v** bg olib-sac wmh1 olnd bg2 *Op* k* oxal-a rly4• ph-ac k* pin-con oss2• pin-s mtf11 pseuts-m oss1• psor ptk1 *Puls* rhod ↓ sal-fr sle1• *Sarr* sep gk sil bg2* staph tl1* stram sf1.de* sulph sf1.de* symph fd3.de• *Thuj* k* toxi mtf verat sf1.de* [*Buteo-j* sej6 heroin sdj2 nat-br stj2]
- **morning**: (*↗Anxiety - conscience)* hydrog srj2•
- **mother**; about one's: rhod mrr2
- **others** are reproached; when: calc-p ng1
- **passion**; about one's own: med mtf thuj mtf
- **sexual** fantasies; from indulging to: staph mtf
- **animal** or inhuman behavior; about: (*↗Anxiety - conscience; Delusions - criminal he)* dendr-pol sk4•
- **sexual** thoughts; about: dendr-pol sk4•
- **stands** up for himself; then: falco-pe nl2•
- **sterility**; with: ign mtf puls mtf
- **trifles**; from: calc-sil mtf sil mtf [nat-br stj2]

REPROACHING others●: (*↗Abusive; Censorious; Dictatorial; Haughty; Insanity - reproaches; Quarrelsome) Acon* k* aln vva1• alum ambr tsm1 arizon-l nl2• **Ars** k* aur aur-ar k2 aur-m-n wbt2• aur-s wbt2• bell j borx h2 *Calc* vh* calc-p camph mrr caps k* carc gk6* caust j cham **Chin** k* cic *Dulc* fd4.de fic-m gya1 gran k* granit-m es1• *Hyos* k* ign ignis-alc es2• irid-met srj5• kali-p fd1.de• kali-s fkr2.de lac-leo sk4• **Lach** k* *Lyc* k* marb-w es1• **Merc** k* mez k* mosch j musca-d szs1 nat-ar *Nat-m* neon srj5• nit-ac mrr1 *Nux-v* k* par petr j* *Ph-ac* ↓ podo fd3.de• pseuts-m oss1• rhus-t sep k* spong fd4.de *Staph* k* suis-em rly4• sulph gl1.fr• tere-la rly4• tritic-vg fd5.de tub bgs *Vanil* fd5.de **Verat** k1* [heroin sdj2 tax jsj7]
- **morning**: *Ph-ac* gl1.fr•
- **afternoon** | **16** h: borx
- **delirium** reproachful: hyos jsa lyc jsa
- **doctor**; the: (*↗Irritability - sends - doctor)* nit-ac mrr1
- **imaginary** insult, for (See Delusions - insulted)
- **pains**, during: nux-v h1*

REPULSIVE MOOD (See Mood - repulsive)

REPUTATION; ailments from loss of (See Ailments - reputation)

RESENTMENT (See Hatred; Hatred - persons - offended; Malicious)

RESERVED: (↗*Aloof; Asking - nothing; Autism; Cautious; Company - aversion; Confidence - want; Conversation - agg.; Discontented - reserved; Indifference; Inhibition; Introspection; Quiet disposition; Secretive; Spoken - aversion; Taciturn; Timidity; Timidity - bashful)* acon j aeth k* agar j aids nl2• alco a1 *Aloe* sne alum alum-p k2* alum-sil vh1 am-c j* am-m j* ambr j anac j ant-t j apis vh1 aq-mar rbp6 arg-n k* arn gl1.fr• ars k* asar vh* aur k* aur-ar k2 *Aur-m-n* wbt2• aur-s wbt2• bell bism k* borx j bry mrr1 cact sf1.de *Calc* k* cann-i mrr1 canth j caps carb-an carc fb* caust cham chin k* cic j cina j clem cocc j coloc k* con j* cupr j* cycl des-ac rbp6 dig j dioxi rbp6 dros k* dulc vh* elaps gk euph euphr fl-ac k2* *Gels* mrr1 graph j grat guaj j *Hell* k* hep j hydrog srj2*• *Hyos* k* *Ign* k* indg ip irid-met srj5• kalm j lac-h ↓ lach led j lob mrr1 luna kg1• lyc k* mag-c mag-m j *Mang* k* med vh* meny bg2* merc j* mez j moni rfm1• *Mur-ac* nat-c j **Nat-m** k* nat-p mrr1 nat-s vh* nit-ac k* nux-m j nux-v olnd k* op ozone sde2• petr ph-ac **Phos** k* *Plat* k* plb k* *Puls* k* rheum ruta fd4.de sabad sabin sal-fr sle1• sars j sec gk sep j* sil k2* spig j spong squil j *Stann* k* *Staph* sf1.de* stram ↓ stront-c j sul-ac j sulph j thuj j* tritic-vg fd5.de tub gk ulm-c jsj8• vanil fd5.de verat viol-t j [am-br stj2 am-p stj1 am-s stj1 arg-met stj1 bism-sn stj2 calc-f stj1 chr-met stj1 heroin sdj2 nicc stj1 tax jsj7]

- **morning**: cocc hep petr
  - **bed**, in: cocc
- **afternoon**: anac mang
- **evening**: am-m
- **air**, in open: plat a1 stram
- **children**: aur mtf33
- **displeasure**; reserved (See Discontented - reserved)
- **eating**:
  - **after**: plb
  - **while**: lac-h htj1•
- **menses**, during: (↗*Menses - during)* am-c mur-ac
- **sleep**, after: anac
- **walking**:
  - **after**: arn calc
  - **air**; while in open: borx ph-ac sabin

RESIGNATION: (↗*Discouraged; Renunciation; Yielding)* agar bg2* agath-a nl2• agn bg2* *Aloe* vh1 *Alum* hr1* anh sp1 aq-mar rbp6 bry gl1.fr• carc sk1• chin-b hr1* cob ptm1• colum-p sze2• dulc fd4.de falco-pe nl2• hydrog srj2• *Kali-p* fd1.de• lyc hr1* nat-m gl1.fr• *Nat-sil* fd3.de• nit-ac gl1.fr• *Ph-ac* bg2* pic-ac bg2* positr nl2• ros-ca mtf11 *Ruta* fd4.de *Sacch-a* fd2.de• spong fd4.de sulph bg2* symph fd3.de• *Tab* bg2* til ban1• ulm-c jsj8• ulx-eu mtf11 [heroin sdj2]

- **senselessness**; feeling of: **Spong** fd*

RESOLUTE (See Confident; Courageous; Determination; Firmness)

RESPECTED: | **desire** to be: (↗*Delusions - appreciated; Delusions - great; Opinions - respected)* ham br1* lyc mtf33 polys sk4• spong fd4.de *Tritic-vg* fd5.de

RESPECTING: (↗*Reverence)*

- **law**; child is very respectful of the (See Duty - too)
- **rules** too much; the (See Duty - too)

RESPIRATION:

- **complaints** of respiration agg.: acon bg2 am-c bg2 ambr bg2 anac bg2 ars bg2 borx bg2 calc bg2 carb-v bg2 cocc bg2 hep bg2 iod bg2 lyc bg2 nit-ac bg2 nux-v bg2 rhus-t bg2 sil bg2 spig bg2 verat bg2
- **painful** respiration agg.: viol-o bg2

RESPONSIBILITY: (↗*Ailments - responsibility; Conscientious; Duty)*

- **agg.**: lavand-a ctl1•

Responsability: ...

- **aversion** to: (↗*Anxiety - expected; Cowardice; Dependent - desire; Escape - family; Estranged - children; Fear - responsibility; Fear - undertaking; Forsaking - children; Postponing)* agar md* aster sze10• bamb-a stb2.de• gels mrr1 *Lac-ac* stj*• lac-h htj1• lavand-a ctl1• limen-b-c hrn2* lyc vn10.fr* marb-w es1• *Med* st1* phos bn tritic-vg fd5.de [tax jsj7]
- **early**; taking responsibility too: carc fb*
- **give** up her responsibility; wanting to: limen-b-c hrn2•
- **inability** to take: (↗*Confidence - want)* fl-ac br1* olib-sac wmh1 [lac-mat sst4]
- **oneself**; for: olib-sac wmh1
- **strong** (See taking)
- **taking** responsibility too seriously: (↗*Delusions - neglected - duty; Duty - too; Love - family; Proper - too; Serious; BACK)* ara-maca sej7• ars mrr1 aster sze10• aur k13* aur-ar mtf bamb-a mtf calc mrr1* calc-i oss• calc-sil mtf33 carc fb* cocc k2* cupr sst3* cycl lgr* ign sys* kali-c vh* lac-e hrn2• lavand-a ctl1• *Lil-t* bc* lyc lgr* mag-m mrr1* nat-ar bc* nat-m ctc1* *Nat-s* mrr1* puls lgr* stront-c vml2•
  - **children**; in: carc fb*

RESPONSIVE: carc fb* dulc ↓

- **interest**; but without: carc az1.de• dulc fd4.de

REST:

- **agg.**: calc b4.de* *Nat-c* b4a.de *Ph-ac* b4a.de *Sep* bg2
- **cannot** rest when things are not in the proper place: (↗*Carefulness; Censorious; Conscientious; Disorder sensitive; Fastidious; Industrious; Thoughts - persistent; Trifles; Trifles - important)* anac k* *Ars* k* carc fd2.de* chir-fl gya2 fic-m gya1 *Kali-s* fd4.de lac-e hrn2• moni rfm1• musca-d szs1 pycnop-sa mrz1 sep dx1* sulph k13* ulm-c jsj8• [heroin sdj2]
- **desire** for: (↗*Disturbed; Longing - repose; Quiet; wants)* *Aesc* sf1.de alum sf1.de *Anac* sf1.de arn sf1.de bell hr1* brass-n-o srj5• brom sf1.de* *Bry* sf1.de* carc fd2.de• clem a1 coca a1 *Colch* hr1* dulc fd4.de eug cda haem a1 ham fd3.de• kali-bi a1 kali-p fd1.de• kali-s fd4.de kola stb3• lach sf1.de lyc sf1.de mez ↓ morph a1 nat-sil fd3.de• nicc-s br1 nux-v sf1.de olib-sac wmh1 op sf1.de *Ph-ac* sf1.de podo fd3.de• *Ruta* fd4.de sabad sf1.de sacch-a fd2.de• spong fd4.de *Stann* sf1.de *Symph* fd3.de• tritic-vg fd5.de vanil fd5.de vesp hr1* [spect dfg1]
  - **afternoon**: dulc fd4.de mez a1

RESTLESSNESS: (↗*feverish; Activity - restless; Delirium - restless; Excitement; Excitement - nervous; Frightened; Impatience; Insanity - restlessness; Senses - acute; Starting - uneasiness; Touching - impelled - everything; Wandering - desire; Weeping - nervous - all; EXTREMITIES - Restlessness; GENERALS - Restlessness; GENERALS - Shuddering)* abies-c abies-n abrom-a ckh1 abrom-a-r ↓ abrot absin c1* **Acon** k* acon-ac rly4• acon-c acon-f ↓ acon-l ↓ act-sp adam ↓ adel ↓ adon sf1.de aeth k* aether ↓ agam-g mlk9.de *Agar* k* agar-ph a1 agar-st a1 *Agath-a* nl2• agn bg *Aids* nl2• ail k* alco a1 all-c all-s kr1* allox tpw3 aln vva1• aloe k* alum k* alum-sil ↓ alumn k* am-br vh1 am-c k* am-caust ↓ am-m ↓ ambr k* aml-ns ammc amn-l sp1 **Anac** anan k* androc srj1• ang j5.de* ange-s jl3 *Anh* mg1.de* anil ↓ ant-ar sf1.de* ant-c k* ant-o ↓ ant-s-aur *Ant-t* k* anth ↓ anthraci anthraco a1 ap-g vh *Apis* k* apoc apom a1 aq-mar a1* aqui ↓ ara-maca sej7• arag k* aran jl3 *Aran-ix* mg1.de* aran-sc ↓ *Arg-met* **Arg-n** k* arge-pl ↓ arist-cl sp1 arn k* **Ars** k* *Ars-h* **Ars-i** k* *Ars-s-f* ↓ *Art-v* arum-i a1 arum-t *Asaf* k* asar asc-t aspar ↓ aster atis ckh1 atp rly4• atra-r skp7*• atro *Aur* k* aur-ar k2 aur-i k2 *Aur-m* *Aur-m-n* wbt2• aur-s k2 avic mtf11 bac ↓ bad *Bamb-a* stb2.de• **Bapt** k* bar-c k* bar-i k2* **Bell** k* bell-p mg1.de* ben-n ↓ berb k2 bism k* bism-o ↓ *Bol-la* a1 bol-s a1 borx k* both a1 *Bov* k* brach ↓ brass-n-o srj5• *Brom* ↓ bros-gau mrc1 brucel ↓ bry k* bufo br1* but-ac br1 buth-a sp1 cact cadm-met sp1* cadm-s k* cain ↓ calad **Calc** k* *Calc-ar* k2* calc-br c1 calc-caust ↓ *Calc-f* mg1.de calc-i k2 **Calc-p** k* *Calc-s* calc-sil k2 *Calen* a1* calo calth a1 **Camph** k* cann-i k* *Cann-s* cann-xyz ↓ canth k* caps k* carb-ac ↓ carb-an k* *Carb-v* k* carbn ↓ carbn-o a1 *Carbn-s* carc cd* card-m ↓ *Cardios-h* rly4• carl c1 cartl-s rly4• casc a1 cassia-f ckh1 cassia-s ccrh1• castm castn-v ↓ caul *Caust* k* cedr *Cench* k2* ceph a1 cere-b a1 cerv a1 *Cham* k* *Chel* k* chen-a ↓ chim *Chin* k* chinin-ar chinin-s chir-fl gya2 chlf a1 chlol a1 chlor *Chloram* ↓ choc ↓ chr-ac a1 cic bg2* **Cimic** k* *Cina* k* cinch ↓ cinnb cist **Cit-v** clem cob k* cob-n sp1 coc-c coca *Coca-c* sk4• *Cocc* coch c1 cod a1* *Coff* k* coff-t coffin a1 *Colch* coll **Coloc** k* colocin a1 colum-p sze2• com con convo-s sp1* *Cop* cor-r *Corh* br1 corn corn-a br1 *Cortico* tpw7 cot ↓ crat ↓ croc k* *Crot-c* k* crot-h j5.de crot-t cub culx k* cuph ↓ **Cupr** k* cupr-act j5.de* **Cupr-ar** cupr-s cur cycl cyclosp ↓

Restlessness: ...
cyn-d ckh1 cypr sf1.de cypra-eg ↓ cyt-l a1* daph ↓ des-ac jl3 desm-g bnj1 *Dig* k* digin ↓ digox ↓ dios dioxi rbp6 dirc dor *Dream-p* sdj1• dros k* dub a1 dubo-m a1 *Dulc* k* dys pte1*• eaux a1 eberth jl2 elaps *Elec* c1* equis-h ↓ erig ery-a eug eup-a br1 eup-per bg2* euph ↓ euph-a ↓ euph-l a1 euphr eupi fago ↓ falco-ch sze4• falco-pe nl2• **Ferr** k* **Ferr-ar** *Ferr-i* ferr-m ferr-p k* ferul ↓ fic-m gya1 fic-r mg1.de fl-ac k* flor-p rsj3• form sf1.de franz ↓ frax st1 fum rly1• gaert fmm1• gal-ac a1* galeoc-c-h gms1• galla-q-r nl2• galv c1 gamb ↓ gast a1 gels k* gent-c gent-l ↓ ger-i rly4• germ-met stj2*• get ↓ gink-b ↓ gins glon bg* gnaph ↓ goss a1 granit-m ↓ *Graph* k* guaj guar k* guare ↓ haem haliae-lc srj5• hall ↓ halo ↓ ham **Hell** b7.de* hell-v ↓ helo-s bnm14*• helon hep j5.de hipp *Hippoz* ↓ **HIST** sp1* hura ↓ hydr ↓ hydr-ac hydrog srj2*• **Hyos** k* hyosin a1 hyper iber jl3 *Ign* k* ina-i mlk9.de ind k* indg ↓ *Iod* k* *Ip* k* irid-met srj5• iris iris-foe ↓ ix ↓ jab jac-c ↓ jac-g ↓ jal c1* jatr-c jug-c ↓ jug-r ↓ kali-ar k* kali-bi a1 *Kali-br* k* *Kali-c* k* kali-chl kali-cy a1 kali-i kali-m k2 *Kali-n* k* *Kali-p* k* kali-perm a1 *Kali-s* kali-sil k2 kali-sulo a1 kalm kiss ↓ kola stb3• kreos k* kres mg1.de lac-ac *Lac-c* k* *Lac-cp* sk4• *Lac-d* k2* *Lac-e* hrn2• lac-h sk4*• lac-leo ↓ lac-lup ↓ *Lach* k* lachn lact lact-v hr1* lam a1 lat-h bnm5• lat-m sp1* laur k* lavand-a ↓ *Lec* k* *Led* k* lepi lev ah1 levo jl3 lil-s ↓ *Lil-t* k* limest-b es1• lip jl3 lipp a1 lob lob-p c1 *Lol* a1* loxo-lae bnm12• loxo-recl bnm10• luf-op rsj5• **Lyc** k* lycps-v ↓ lyss m-ambo b7.de *M-arct* ↓ m-aust b7a.de* macro a1* mag-c k* mag-m k* *Mag-p* ↓ mag-s maias-l ↓ malar jl2 manc mand a1* *Mang* k* marb-w es1• *Med* k* medul-os-si rly4• melal-alt gya4 meli ↓ menis a1 menth-pu a1 meny k* meph **Merc** k* *Merc-c* k* merc-cy a1 merc-d merc-i-r merc-meth a1 merc-sul a1 merl meth-ae-ae a1 *Mez* k* mill mim-p rsj8• miml-g mtf11 *Moni* rfm1• morg-g pte1*• morph k* *Mosch* k* mur-ac k* musca-d szs1 mygal a1* myric naja *Nat-ar* *Nat-c* k* nat-f sp1* *Nat-m* k* nat-p nat-s nat-sil fd3.de• neon ↓ nep jl3 nicc nicc-s ↓ nicot a1 *Nit-ac* k* nit-m-ac a1 nitro-o a1 nuph a1 nux-m *Nux-v* k* nyct c1* nymph ↓ oena ol-an sf1.de ol-j ↓ *Olib-sac* wmh1 olnd onop jl3 onos *Op* k* opun-s ↓ opun-v ↓ orig a1 osm ost ↓ osteo-a jl2 ox-ac oxal-a rly4• ozone sde2• paeon ↓ par ↓ passi ↓ past a1 paull a1 ped ↓ perh jl3 pert jl2 pert-vc vk9 petr k* petr-ra shn4• *Ph-ac* k* phasco-ci rbp2 phos k* phys physala-p bnm7• phyt k* pic-ac ↓ pieri-b mlk9.de pin-con oss2• pip-m ↓ plac ↓ plac-s rly4• plan *Plat* k* **Plb** k* plb-chr a1 plut-n srj7• podo k2* polyp-p ↓ positr nl2• pot-e rly4• prot fmm1• prun pseuts-m oss1• *Psor* k* ptel **Puls** k* puls-n a1 pyre-p a1 *Pyrog* k2* pyrus st querc-r svu1• rad-br bro1* (non:rad-met) ran-a a1 ran-b k* *Ran-s* ↓ raph ↓ rat rauw sp1* rham-cal br1 rheum k* rhod rhus-g a1 rhus-l xyz67 **Rhus-t** k* *Rhus-v* *Rumx* *Ruta* k* sabad k* sabin sacch sst1• sacch-a fd2.de• sacch-l c1 sal-ac c1 sal-fr sle1• *Sal-n* ↓ *Samb* k* samb-c a1 sang ↓ sanic k* santin a1 sapin ↓ saroth mg1.de* sarr sars ↓ scam ↓ scut **Sec** k* sel rsj9• senec c1 seneg b4.de* senn sf1.de **Sep** k* serp ↓ **Sil** k* sol-mm j5.de* sol-ni sol-t a1 sol-t-ae ↓ spect ↓ spig k* spira ↓ spirae ↓ spong j5.de* squil ↓ *Stann* k* **Staph** k* *Stict* sf1.de **Stram** k* stront-c b4.de* stry a1* suis-em rly4• suis-hep rly4• *Sul-ac* b4.de* sul-i k2 sulfa sp1 **Sulph** k* sumb k* syc pte1*• *Symph* ↓ syph jl2* *Tab* tarax **Tarent** k* tax k* *Tell* tep ↓ ter ↓ *Teucr* ↓ thal jl3 thal-xyz srj8• thea br1 ther br1* thioc-ac rly4• thiop jl3 *Thuj* k* thymol sp1* thyr k* tong a1 tril-c ↓ tril-p ↓ trios br1* *Tritic-vg* fd5.de trom tub bg* tub-a jl2 *Tub-m* jl2 tung-met bdx1• ulm-c ↓ upa a1 uran-n sf1.de urol-h rwt• urt-u bro1 ust k* v-a-b jl2 vac a1* *Valer* k* vanil fd5.de vario jl2 verat k* verat-v bro1 verb ↓ vero-o rly4*• vesp ↓ vib sf1.de* vinc viol-o viol-t b7.de* vip vip-a jl3 visc sp1 voes a1 vult-gr ↓ wies a1 wildb ↓ wye a1 xan c1 yuc a1 **Zinc** k* zinc-act a1 zinc-o j5.de zinc-ox ↓ zinc-p k2* zinc-val bro1 zing [agri rcb1 alum-p stj2 am-f stj2 arg-p stj2 bism-sn stj2 bor-pur stj2 *Buteo-j* sej6 cob-m stj2 cob-p stj2 cupr-p stj2 ferr-f stj2 ferr-lac stj2 ferr-n stj2 ferr-sil stj2 fl-pur stj2 heroin sdj2 lith-c stj2 lith-met stj2 lith-p stj2 lith-s stj2 mag-n stj2 mang-i stj2 merc-i-f stj2 moly-met stj2 nat-caust stj2 niob-met stj2 nitro stj2 osm-met stj2 plb-m stj2 plb-p stj2 pop dhh1 *Rhodi* stj2 sol-ecl cky1 temp elm1 thal-met stj2 tus-p stj vanad stj2 *Zinc-i* stj2 *Zinc-m* stj2 *Zinc-n* stj2]

- **day** and night: canth j5.de chel k2* iod k2* sulph j5.de
- **daytime**: ambr k* aran vh1 bov a1 calc hr1 kali-br nat-c k* nat-m k* pip-m a1 plan k* positr nl2• *Rhus-t* k* staph k* sulph [spect dfg1]
- **morning**: ail k* bamb-a ↓ bell h1* cina ↓ cortico tpw7 dulc k* fago k* gamb k* *Gels* k* guaj ↓ hyos hyper k* iod iris-foe kali-br k* kola ↓ *Lyc* k* meph jl3 mygal ↓ myric k* nat-m k* nit-ac ↓ ph-ac k* phys k* puls ↓ ruta fd4.de sulph k* thuj k* ulm-c ↓ upa a1 zinc zinc-p k2*
  - **bed**, in: guaj h2* ph-ac k*
  - **rising**, after: puls h1*
  - **waking**, on: bamb-a stb2.de* cina dulc k* hyper k* kola stb3• lyc h2* mygal sf1.de nit-ac h2* ruta fd4.de ulm-c jsj8•
- **forenoon**: acon a1 am-m anac calad k* cimic k* fago k* lyss k* nat-c phos sil thuj k*
- **noon**: bell k* cinnb a1 dulc fd4.de lyss k* sulph a1
- **afternoon**: anac ang j5.de apis aur k* borx ptk1 calc-s k* *Carb-v* k* caul k* *Chinin-ar* k1* chinin-s ↓ cimic k* coloc k* dios k* dulc fd4.de fago k* hyos ix bnm8• jug-c k* lyc ↓ merc merc-sul a1 naja nicc k* ruta sapin a1 spong fd4.de staph k* stront-c ↓ tab thuj upa a1 vanil fd5.de vero-o rly4*•
  - **15** h: caul a1 nicc a1
  - **16** h: dios a1 stront-c sk4•
  - **16**-18 h: carb-v lyc
  - **17** h: chinin-s a1 thuj a1
  - **lying**, when: aur a1
  - **twilight** (See evening - twilight)
- **evening**: acon k* aether a1 agar k* *Alum* *Am-c* k* *Ars* k* ars-s-f k2* *Bapt* a1 bov k* *Calc* k* calc-s k* *Carb-v* k* caul **Caust** cham ↓ chinin-s *Chloram* ↓ clem k* dios k* dulc fd4.de equis-h fago k* ferr guare a1 hep k* jab k* kali-ar k* *Kali-br* a1* *Kola* ↓ **Kreos** ↓ lac-h htj1• lach laur lavand-a ↓ lyc k* lycps-v mag-c mag-m k* meph k* *Merc* k* mur-ac k* *Nat-c* k* nat-p nicc nit-ac j5.de nux-v k* olib-sac wmh1 ph-ac k* phos phys positr nl2• *Rumx* ruta sabin scut k* sep sulph k* thuj k* verat j5.de zinc zinc-p k2* zing a1
  - **18**-6 h: **Kreos**
  - **19** h: am-c a1
  - **20** h: calc **Merc**
  - **bed**:
    - **before** going to bed: lavand-a ctl1•
    - **in**: am-c j5.de cham h1* *Chloram* jl3 hep a1 *Kola* stb3• lyc k* **Mag-m** k* nux-v k* phos sabin sep thuj
  - **twilight**; at: caust sf1.de
- **night**: *(↗anxious - night)* abies-c k* abies-n k* abrot k* acon k* acon-c k* adel a1 alum alum-sil k2* am-caust k* am-m k* ambr j5.de* ammc a1 anac k* androc srj1*• ang k* *Anh* mg1.de anil a1 ant-o a1 ant-t k* anth a1* anthraci *Apis* apoc k* *Arg-met* *Arg-n* k* arge-pl rwt5• **Ars** k* *Ars-i* k* *Ars-s-f* k2* arum-t a1 asaf k* asc-t k* aster k* atro k* aur k* aur-ar k2 aur-s a1* bac c1 bad k* *Bamb-a* stb2.de* *Bapt* k* bar-c a1 *Bell* k* bism k* *Bol-la* a1 *Borx* h2* bov k* brach a1 bry k* cact k* cain *Calc* k* calc-ar k2* calc-caust calc-p a1 calc-s a1 calc-sil k2* calen a1* calo a1 camph k* canth k* carb-ac k* carb-an k* *Carb-v* k* carbn a1 carbn-s a1 card-m k* castm castn-v k* *Caul* k* **Caust** k* cedr k* cench k2 *Cham* k* chel a1 chin k* chinin-ar chr-ac k* cic k* cimic k* cina cinch a1 cinnb k* *Cist* k* *Cit-v* k* clem k* coc-c k* coca coff a1 colch sf1.de coloc k* colocin a1 com k* cop a1 cor-r k* corn k* cot ↓ crot-t k* *Cupr* k* cupr-s k* *Cycl* k* cyclosp ↓ cyn-d ↓ cypr sf1.de dig k* digin k* digox a1 dios k* dirc k* dor a1 dulc erig k* euph-a a1 euphr k* eupi k* fago k* *Ferr* k* ferr-ar ferr-i k* ferr-p ferul a1 fic-m gya1 fl-ac k* form k* franz a1 gal-ac a1* gels k* gent-l a1 get a1 glon k* gnaph k* *Graph* k* *Guaj* hall a1 hell hell-v a1 hep a1 hura hydr k* **Hyos** k* hyper k* iber a1 *Ign* k* ind k* indg k* iod k* *Iris* jac-c k* jac-g jal br1 jatr-c jug-c k* **Kali-ar** k* kali-bi a1 *Kali-br* k* kali-c kali-i sf1.de kali-n h2* kali-sil k2* kiss a1 kola ↓ **Kreos** k* *Lac-c* k* lach k* led lil-s a1 **Lyc** k* lycps-v a1 lyss k* mag-c k* *Mag-m* k* mang k* *Med* *Menis* a1 menth-pu a1 **Merc** k* *Merc-c* k* merc-cy k* merc-i-r ↓ merc-meth a1 merc-sul a1 morph k* mosch k* *Mur-ac* k* mygal a1 myric k* *Nat-ar* nat-c k* nat-m k* nat-p nat-s k* nat-sil k2* nicc k* nicot a1 nit-ac k* nux-m k* nux-v k* nymph a1 ol-j br1 olib-sac ↓ op k* opun-s a1 (non:opun-v a1) osm k* ost a1 ox-ac k* par ped a1 petr k* ph-ac k* *Phos* k* phys k* phyt k* pic-ac ↓ pip-m a1 plan k* plat ↓ plb k* *Podo* k* polyp-p a1 positr nl2• psor k2* ptel k* **Puls** puls-n a1 *Ran-b* k* *Ran-s* rauw sp1 rheum al* **Rhus-t** k* rhus-v k* rumx ruta sabad a1* sang k* sanic c1 sapin a1 sars j5.de senec k* senn sf1.de *Sep* k* sil k* sol-t-ae a1 spig j5.de spira a1 spirae a1 spong k* stann j5.de staph h1 stram k* stront-c br1 stry k* sul-ac k* sul-i k* **Sulph** k* syph k2 tab k* tarax k* tarent bg *Teucr* k* thea thuj k* trom ↓ tub tl* uran-n a1* ust k* *Valer* k* verat k* verat-v k* verb k* vesp k* vip k* visc sp1 wildb ↓ yuc a1 zinc k* zinc-p k2* zing ↓ [spect dfg1]
  - **midnight**:
    - **before**: alum k* carbn-s k2 cot k* cyclosp ↓ euphr h2* *Ferr* mag-m mur-ac a1 nat-m h2* phys ↓ pic-ac a1 plat a1 sars k* senec k*
      - **22** h: cyclosp sa3• phys a1
    - **at**: cyn-d ckh1 graph ↓ nat-m k* phyt ↓ plat ↓
      - **waking**; on: graph a1 phyt a1 plat
    - **after**: **Ars** k* bapt a1 bry a1 calc-ar ↓ *Chinin-ar* ↓ cimic ↓ clem ↓ coc-c ↓ com ↓ *Dios* k* fago ↓ ferr ↓ get ↓ graph ↓ iod ↓ kola ↓ *Kreos* ↓ lil-s ↓ lyc mag-m ↓ mang ↓ merc a1 merc-i-r k* myric ↓ nat-ar ↓ nat-m ↓ nicc ↓ *Nit-ac* olib-sac ↓ phos ↓ polyp-p ↓ **Rhus-t** a1 rhus-v k* sil k* stann ↓ sulph k* tarent ↓ trom ↓ tub ↓ wildb ↓ zinc k* zing ↓

- **midnight – after**: ...
  - **1** h: get iod↓ mang h2 nat-ar phos stann h2
    - **1**.30-4.30 h: iod a1
  - **2** h: *Bapt*↓ com ferr graph iod a1 lil-s a1 mag-m myric zing
    - **after**: *Bapt* a1
  - **3** h: ars↓ bapt hr1 calc-ar *Chinin-ar* cimic coc-c fago↓ kola stb3• *Kreos* lil-s a1 nat-ar nat-m nicc↓ olib-sac wmh1 polyp-p a1 tub↓
    - **3-4** h: fago a1*
    - **after**: ars h2 tub jl2
    - **everything** feels sore, must move about: nicc
  - **4** h: clem kreos nit-ac↓ trom wildb a1
    - **until**: nit-ac h2
  - **5** h: tarent
- **closing** eyes agg.; on: **Mag-m** h2* sep a1*
- **heart**; from uneasiness about: phys a1
- **hiccough**; with: *Stram* st1
- **waking**; on: caust h2 lyc h2

- **action**; in his (See busy)
- **agg.**: ars bg2
- **air**; in open | **amel.**: aran-ix jl **Arg-n** hr1 *Aur-m* dream-p sdj1• graph lac-cp sk4• lach laur lyc *Staph* gl1.fr• tritic-vg fd5.de valer
- **alone**, when: *(↗Company - desire; Company - desire - alone)* all-s k* cortico tpw7 gaert fmm1• mez k* *Phos* k*
  - **amel.**: lac-h htj1•
- **alternating** with:
  - **delirium** | **quiet**: *Chlor* hr1*
  - **indifference**: ant-t kr1 fic-m gya1 nat-m k*
  - **sadness**: apis bg2
  - **sleepiness**: ars k* chir-fl gya2
    - **fever**; during: *Ars*
  - **stupor**: *Acon* kr1 **Ars** kr1 op mrr1 thyr br1
  - **unconsciousness**: *Acon* hr1* **Ars** a1
    - **fever**; during: **Ars** k*
  - **weakness**: ars mrr1 brucel sa3•
- **anger**; restlessness from: *Cham* sf1.de **Coloc** kr1 falco-pe nl2• positr nl2• vanil fd5.de
- **angina** pectoris, in: *Aur-m* hr1*
- **anxious**: *(↗Anxiety)* **ACON** k1* adon sf1.de* *Aeth* k* aids nl2• alum alum-sil k2 *Am-c* b4.de* ambr anac k* androc↓ ang b7.de* ant-ar sf1.de ant-t b7.de* aq-mar jl3* arg-n arge-pl rwt5• arn j5.de* **Ars** k* *Ars-i* asaf aspar atro sf1.de *Aur* aur-ar k2 aur-m-n wbt2• *Bell* k* bism k* bov k* *Bry* k* *Calc* k* calc-i k2 calc-p calc-sil k2* camph k* canth k* caps carb-an *Carb-v* k* *Carc* mlr1• cassia-s ccrh1• *Castm* j5.de *Caust* *Cham* k* chel chin k* chinin-ar chinin-s cimic k* clem coff coloc kr1 con a1 croc crot-h *Cupr* k* dig c1 *Dream-p* sdj1• dros dulc fd4.de *Ferr* frax st1 granit-m es1• *Graph* k* haliae-lc srj5• halo jl3 *Hell* *Hep* k* hist sp1 ign tl1 iod k* *Jal* kr1 **Kali-ar** k* **Kali-br** hr1 **Kali-c** k* kali-i kali-n j5.de lac-cp sk4• lac-e hrn2• lach sf1.de lact lact-v a1 laur b7.de* lil-t↓ lol sf1.de **Lyc** gl1.fr• *M-arct* j5.de m-aust j5.de mag-m mang h2* med bg2 meny *Merc* k* mez k2* mur-ac tl1 **Nat-ar** **Nat-c** k* *Nat-m* k* nat-p nat-sil k2 neon srj5• *Nit-ac* nux-m bg2 nux-v k* op ph-ac *Phos* k* plac-s rly4• plat k* plb k* positr nl2• pot-e rly4• prun↓ psor kr1* *Puls* k* pyrog sf1.de rhod b4.de* *Rhus-t* k* ruta *Sabad* sal-fr sle1• sanic sec b7.de* seneg b4.de* sep *Sil* spig k* spong stann b4.de* staph k* stry a1 suis-hep rly4• sul-ac↓ sul-i k2* *Sulph* *Tab* tarax j5.de **Tarent** k* *Thuj* h1* valer k* *Verat* k* vip sf1.de wies a1 zinc zinc-p k2* [heroin sdj2 spect dfg1]
  - **afternoon** | **16**-23 h: lac-cp sk4•
  - **night**: *(↗night)* *Psor* mrr1
  - **activity** amel.: positr nl2•
  - **disorganization** agg.: lac-e hrn2•
  - **driving** from place to place: *(↗Anxiety - driving)* *Ars* ptk1 *Tab* st1
  - **epilepsy**, during intervals of: *Arg-n*
  - **fresh** air amel.: lac-e hrn2•
  - **noise** agg.: lac-e hrn2•
  - **rage**; ending in: canth br1
  - **rest** at any occupation; has no: positr nl2•
  - **smash** things; with impulse to: positr nl2•

- **anxious**: ...
  - **walking**; compelling:
    - **constant**: prun ptk1
    - **rapidly**: *(↗Walking - amel.; Anxiety - Walking - rapidly - makes; GENERALS - Walking - Rapidly - amel.)* androc srj1• *Arg-n* k* **Ars** k* cimic mg lil-t sul-ac **Tarent** k*
- **apyrexia**; during: ars bro1 gels bro1
- **asthma**; with: ars mrr1 tarent mtf33
- **atrophy**; with: caust bg2
- **back**, during tired aching in: calc-f k*
- **bed**: *(↗sleep)*
  - **driving** out of: *(↗Jumping - bed; Suicidal - thoughts - drive)* androc bnm2• arg-met sf1.de **Ars** *Ars-i* aur-ar vh1 *Bell* k* **Bism** k* bry k* carb-an *Carb-v* caust cench k2* *Cham* k* chin chinin-ar chinin-s clem a1 con dulc a1 **Ferr** ferr-ar ferr-p *Graph* *Hep* hyos *Kola* stb3• *Lyc* *Mag-c* k* mag-m merc nat-c nat-m nat-sil k2* nicc nit-ac nux-v phos h2* ptel gk puls rhod k2* **Rhus-t** sep sil tarent hr1 ther
  - **go** from one bed to another; wants to: *Arg-met* vh1 **Ars** k* *Bell* k* *Calc* cham cina *Ferr* *Hyos* merc mez *Plb* *Rhus-t* sep stram *Tarent* k2* verat
  - **heat** of, from: op
  - **in**: *(↗Rolling - bed)* amn-l sp1 apoc a1 arist-cl sp1 arn mrr1 *Bapt* a1 bell a1 caust h2* choc srj3• clem a1 dios a1 dulc fd4.de fago a1 halo jl hura a1 iod a1 nit-ac a1 phos a1 **Puls** a1 rauw sp1 tab a1 tax a1 tell a1
  - **tossing** about in: *(↗Anguish - tossing; SLEEP - Light - tossing)* **Acon** k* adel a1 agar-ph a1 agn b7.de* alco a1 alum k* alumn k* am-c b4.de* anac bg2 ant-t k* ap-g vh apis k* *Arg-n* k* arist-cl rbp3• arn sf1.de* **Ars** k* ars-s-f k2* *Arum-t* asaf atro a1 *Bamb-a* stb2.de• bapt k* bar-c bg2 *Bell* k* ben-n a1 borx k* *Bry* k* bufo bg2 *Calc* k* calc-ar k2* calc-p a1 calo a1 *Camph* k* *Cann-s* b7.de* canth k* carb-an k* *Carb-v* bg2 carbn a1 carbn-o k* *Carl* a1 *Castm* *Caust* k* cench k2 ceph a1 *Cham* k* chel a1 chen-a a1 *Chin* b7.de* chinin-s a1 chlf a1 cic k* cimic bg2 *Cina* k* cinnb a1 cist *Cit-v* a1 clem k* cob a1 coca a1 cocc *Coff* b7.de* coloc b4.de* colocin a1 con h2* cop a1 cor-r corn a1 crot-t k* **Cupr** k* cur k* dig b4.de* dulc k* eup-per gt euph b4.de euphr a1 **Ferr** k* ferr-ar ferr-m ferr-p *Gels* bg2* goss st graph b4.de* guaj k* hell k* hep b4.de* hydr-ac a1 hyos b7.de* iber a1 ign k* ip b7.de* jug-r a1 *Kali-ar* kali-bi bg2 kali-c bg2 kali-n h2* *Kola* stb3• kreos k* lac-lup↓ *Lach* k* lachn c1 laur b7.de* led k* *Lyc* k* m-ambo b7.de* m-arct b7.de m-aust b7.de mag-c b4.de* mag-m k* manc a1 mang b4.de* meny b7.de* *Merc* k* merc-c b4a.de* mosch b7.de* *Mur-ac* k* myric a1 nat-ar a1* nat-c k* nat-m k* nit-ac b4.de* *Nux-v* bg2* op k* osm a1 ozone sde2• par k* petr b4.de* ph-ac bg2 phos k* plan a1 plat h2* podo c1 *Puls* k* pyrog al2* ran-b bg2 *Ran-s* k* rheum k* **Rhus-t** k* ruta b7.de sabad a1 sabin b7.de sang a1 sars bg2 seneg b4.de* senn *Sep* k* serp a1 sil bg2* sol-t a1 *Spig* b7.de* spong bg2 squil k* stann bg2 *Staph* k* *Stram* k* stront-c bg2 *Stry* sul-ac bg2* *Sulph* k* tab bg2* tarax h1* **Tarent** k* tep a1 ter a1 teucr b7.de* thea a1 thuj k* tril-c a1 (non:tril-p a1*) tub al ust a1 valer k* vanil fd5.de *Vario* st* verat k* verb b7.de· zinc bg2*
    - **amel.**: cham bg2* cocc bg2*
    - **cough**; during: *Acon* b7.de* arn b7.de*
    - **sleep**; during: lac-lup hrn2• ozone sde2•
- **busy**: *(↗Busy; Industrious)* acon j5.de *Aur* b4a.de* *Bar-c* b4a.de bell j5.de* *Brom* b4a.de bry j5.de caps h1* chir-fl gya2 choc srj3• cocc h1 dig j5.de dros gk **Dulc** fd* ger-i rly4• hyos j5.de *Ign* h1* ip j5.de *Kali-s* fd4.de *Lach* j5.de* m-arct j5.de *Mosch* j5.de nat-c j5.de nux-v gl1.fr• stann j5.de sul-ac j5.de ther sf1.de tritic-vg fd5.de tung-met bdx1• vanil fd5.de verat h1* [tax jsj7]
- **cardiac** symptoms, with: crat br1 ruta fd4.de
- **chaotic** behavior; with (See Chaotic - restlessness)
- **chest**:
  - **congestion** in chest; from: sep
  - **constriction** of chest; with: kola stb3•
  - **heat** rising up into the mouth from chest; from: nux-v
- **children**, in: *(↗Behavior - children; GENERALS - Energy - excess - children)* absin st1 **Acon** hr1 aeth mtf33 agar vh1* am-c a2 ambr al* anac vh ant-t k* anth vh1 ars j5.de ars-i vh* atra-r bnm3• aur-m-n wbt2• bac jl2 bar-c gk4 bell hr1 borx bry h1* bufo gk *Calc* hr1 calc-br c1 calc-p mtf33 calc-s mtf33 carc gk6* caust mtf33 *Cham* k* chin mtf33 cina st* coca↓ coff hr1 coff-t hr1 cupr sst3• cypr br1 goss st hyos mrr hyosin c1 iod mtf33 ip st1* *Jal* k* kali-c j5.de kali-p↓ *Kreos*↓ lat-m bnm6• lyc mrr med mrr* **Merc** vh* *Moni* rfm1• morph oss• nux-v mrr* op wbt• phos mtf33 psor mtf33 rheum k* **RHUS-T** k1* sacch↓

- **children**, in: ...
sanic mrr1* senec c1 staph↓ stram mrr1* sul-ac hr1 sulph al* tarent mrr1* tritic-vg fd5.de *Tub* vh* tub-a ih tub-m vn* verat mrr* viol-o c1
  - **night**: coca hr1 jal br1* kali-c h2* *Psor*↓ rheum mrr1* staph h1
    - ⁝ **morning** fresh and lively; but in the: *Psor* st*
  - **babies**, in: kali-p c1 tritic-vg fd5.de
  - **carried** about amel.; being: (↗*Carried - desire; Quieted - carried; Weeping - carried - quiet)* ant-t k* ars *Cham* k* cina kali-c
  - **dentition**, during: acon hr1 coca hr1 cypr br1 *Kreos* hr1 **Rheum** st
    - ⁝ **night**: coca br1
  - **eruption**; with (See eruptions - with - children)
  - **roving** (= wandering): (↗*Wandering - desire - restlessly)* bell gl1.fr• bry gl1.fr• nux-v mtf33*
  - **sweets**; after: sacch sst1•
  - **wandering** (See roving)
- **chill**:
  - **beginning** of; at: *Lach* phos
  - **during**: acon k* aeth a1 am-c bg2 anac k* apis bg2 *Arn* bg2 **Ars** k* asaf k* bell k* borx bov bg2 *Calc* b4.de* cann-s caps k* carb-v k* **Cham** j5.de* chin bg2 coff bg2 eup-per k* ip bg2 kali-ar kreos k* lach b7a.de* lam j5.de *Lyc* bg2 merc bg2 mez k* nat-c k* nat-m k* **Nux-v** bg2 petr k* *Ph-ac* bg2 phos bg2 plan plat k* puls bg2 rhus-t k* ruta bg2 sabad bg2 **Sep** bg2 *Sil* b4.de* spig k* tub gk *Verat* bg2
- **chorea**; in: cimic tl1
- **closing** eyes at night agg.: **Mag-m** k* sep k*
- **clutching** hands amel.: med br1*
- **coffee**; as from: ozone sde2• [buteo-j sej6]
- **coition**:
  - **after**: **Calc** cop k* dig mez bg1* petr *Sep* k* staph bg1*
  - **during**: upa a1
- **colors**:
  - **black** | **agg.**: sep vk4
- **company**, in: (↗*Company - aversion)* androc srj1• *Carb-v* mez vh* staph vh*
  - **amel.**: fum rly1•
- **conscience**, of: (↗*Anxiety - conscience)* *Chel* hr1* merc j5.de *Moni* rfm1• *Puls* st1 zinc-o j5.de zinc-ox j5.de [heroin sdj2 zinc dmk1]
- **conversation**, from: (↗*Conversation - agg.)* *Ambr* borx↓ vanil fd5.de
  - **animated**: borx h2
- **convulsions**:
  - **after**: cupr bro1 oena k* plb a1
    - ⁝ **epileptic**: cupr bro1
  - **before**: anan a1 **Arg-n** k* bufo k* caust sf1.de hyos a1* plb gk
- **convulsive**: guar a1 sol-ni br1
- **coryza**; during: *Ars* b4a.de samb b7a.de
- **coughing**, with: acon b7.de* coff b7.de* nux-v b7a.de samb b7.de* sulph h2*
- **dancing**: | **amel.**: positr nl2•
- **dark** room; in a: ulm-c jsj8•
- **delivery**, during: *Acon* kr1 *Camph* kr1 *Cham* b7a.de chlf kr1
- **despair**; with: ars br1* *Ruta* fd4.de
- **diabetic**: helon bro1
- **diarrhea**:
  - **before**: haliae-lc srj5•
  - **during**: cuph ah1 pyrog tl1
- **dinner**:
  - **after**: am-m k* nat-c k* ruta thuj k*
    - ⁝ **amel.**: thuj
- **disguise**, vainly seeks to: alco a1
- **do** something; compelled to: lac-h htj1•
- **dreams**, provoked by: graph gt
- **drink**, at the sight of: bell k*
- **drinking** agg.: *Crot-c*
- **drives** him from place to place: *Ars* vh* bell vh *Calc-p* tl1* *Cedr* vh* cupr mtf33 lac-cp sk4• *Lach* vh* *Lyss* vh* med mtf33 olib-sac wmh1 plut-n srj7• sanic tl1 spong fd4.de tub tl1
- **driving** about: (↗*Anguish - driving - restlessness; Fear - driving him)* acon j5.de *Am-c* j5.de arag br1 *Ars* k2* aur j5.de *Bell* h1* bism j5.de* *Calc-p* k2* canth j5.de carb-v j5.de *Cedr* st cench k2 cimic jl crot-h j5.de *Cupr* sf1.de dream-p sdj1• dros j5.de **Dulc** fd* graph j5.de ham fd3.de• *Hist* mg1.de* hyos j5.de* ign bg2 iod j5.de* kali-i k2* *Kali-s* fd4.de kres mg1.de *Lach* j5.de* lyss hr1* meny j5.de merc j5.de* nat-c j5.de nux-v j5.de plat j5.de prun j5.de puls j5.de sanic c1 sep j5.de sol-mm j5.de spig j5.de stann j5.de staph j5.de *Tab* j5.de* tarax j5.de tarent k2* *Tritic-vg* fd5.de valer↓ vanil fd5.de verat j5.de
  - **air**, in open: lach j5.de nux-v kr1 valer j5.de
- **eating**: am-m↓ bar-c↓ borx carb-an↓ chin↓ cinnb↓ lach↓ nat-c↓ nux-m↓ nux-v↓ petr ph-ac↓ phos↓ rhod↓ rhus-t↓ sulph↓ thuj↓ verat↓
  - **after**: am-m k* bar-c carb-an b4a.de chin cinnb lach nat-c a1 nux-m nux-v petr k* ph-ac phos k* rhod rhus-t sulph thuj a1 verat
- **eructation**, from insufficient: calc ckh1 kali-c h2
- **eruptions**:
  - **with**: **Psor** ckh1
    - ⁝ **children**; in: **Psor** vh*
- **excitable**: dioxi rbp6 loxo-lae bnm12•
- **exertion**, after: cimic st1 *Merc* ptk1*
- **exhaustion**; with (See weakness - during)
- **fear**; from: acon bg2 am-br sf1.de aml-ns kr1 ars bg2* aur bg2 calc tl1 carb-v mtf33 cimic tl1 *Ign* kr1 iod bg2 merc bg2 tarent tl1
- **feverish**: (↗*heat - during; Restlessness)* acon bro1 aeth↓ ail↓ am-c↓ anac a1 apis↓ ars↓ *Bell*↓ camph↓ cham bro1 cimic jl3 cob-n sp1 cupr↓ *Cupr-act*↓ *Hyos*↓ iod bro1 melal-alt gya4 phos a1 pyrog tl1 ran-b a1 rhus-t↓ ruta a1 *Stram*↓ sulph↓ vac jl2 zinc↓
  - **scarlet** fever: aeth bro1 ail bro1 am-c bro1 apis bro1 ars bro1 *Bell* bro1 camph bro1 cupr bro1 *Cupr-act* bro1 *Hyos* bro1 rhus-t bro1* *Stram* bro1 sulph bro1 zinc bro1
- **followed** by:
  - **faintness**: calc
  - **sadness**: vult-gr sze5•
- **headache**, during: aeth hr1 anac k* aran-sc vh1 arg-n k* *Ars* k* *Bell* bry cadm-s calad k* canth cham chin coloc hr1* crat br1 cycl↓ daph k* dulc st gent-c hell bro1 ign k* kali-i *Lach* lil-s a1 *Lyc* lyss hr1* menis br1 morph naja nux-m pyrog bro1 ran-b ruta sil spig bro1 sulph h2* syph *Tab* st vip
  - **forehead**, at night from pain in: cycl
  - **occiput** and neck; pain in: crat br1
- **heat**:
  - **after**: ph-ac puls sep
  - **before**: lach b7a.de phos b4a.de
  - **during**: (↗*feverish)* *Acon* k* acon-l a1 ail k2 am-c k* anac h2 androc srj1• ant-t k* *Apis* bg2* *Arn* k* **Ars** k* ars-s-f k2 atro bapt *Bar-c* k* *Bell* k* *Bov* b4.de* bry b7.de* cadm-s k2 calad b7a.de calc k* calc-ar k2 caps *Carb-v* *Cham* k* chin chinin-ar *Chinin-s* cina clem a1 cob-n sp1 coff b7.de* colocin a1 con k* corh br1 cub *Eup-a* br1 *Eup-per* sf1.de* *Ferr* *Ferr-ar* ferr-p *Gels* graph k2 hyper ign b7.de* *Ip* k* kali-ar kali-c b4.de kali-i k2 kola↓ *Lach* k* lachn *Lyc* k* *M-arct* b7.de* mag-c k* mag-m k* merc b4a.de* merc-c k* mez k2 mosch k* *Mur-ac* k* nux-v bg2 *Op* b7.de* *Ph-ac* b4a.de* phos h2* plan **Puls** k* pyrog mrr1 ran-b a1 rheum k* **Rhus-t** k* rhus-v ruta b7.de* sabad bg2 sabin k* sec sep k* sil b4.de* spong k* stann bg2 staph k* stram k* *Sulph* k* syph dgt thuj k* valer k* verat b7.de*
    - ⁝ **flushes** of heat: kola stb3•
  - **sensation** of | **during**: mag-c cp plut-n srj7•
- **hemorrhages**; after: tril-p c1
- **hormonal** dysfunction; during: aqui mtf11
- **hunger**, with: kali-c hr1* nat-m a1 podo hr1
- **hypochondriacal**: ars j5.de *Asaf* k2* graph a1 valer j5.de
- **hysterical**: *Asaf* k2*
- **idle**; when: bamb-a stb2.de• dulc fd4.de spong fd4.de tritic-vg fd5.de
- **indecision** to do something; with (See irresolution)
- **internal**●: *Acon* k* agar k* aids nl2• ang h1* **Ars** k* atro k* aur-m-n wbt2• bamb-a stb2.de• carb-an k* carl k* chel k* choc srj3• cypra-eg sde6.de• dros dulc fd4.de eupi k* gink-b sbd1• gins k* ina-i mlk9.de *Kola* stb3• lact j5.de lact-v c1 lob k* lyc k* mag-c k* mag-m k* mag-s k* mang h2* melal-alt gya4 meph k* moni rfm1• morph a1 nat-c h2* nat-m k* nat-sil fd3.de• nit-ac h2* olib-sac wmh1 op k* ozone sde2• par k* ph-ac k* phos k* plb k* ran-b k* rheum **Rhus-t** k* sep k* **Sil** k* spong fd4.de stram h1* sulph h2* *Tritic-vg* fd5.de vanil fd5.de viol-t j5.de
  - **morning** | **waking**; on: bamb-a stb2.de• sep k*

- **forenoon** | **walking**; on: acon a1
- **evening** | **bed**; in: bamb-a stb2.de• eupi k*
- **night**, on waking, with headache: agar↓ par k*
  - ⁝ **in** dream: agar h2
- **beat** about herself with hands and feet, as if would: lyc

- **irresolution** to act; with: bamb-a stb2.de•
- **itching**, after: coloc h2 mang mez psor
- **lascivious** thoughts, during: *(↗sexual; Lascivious)* graph a1
- **light**:
  - **sun**; of the | **agg.**: cadm-s k* [cadm-met stj2]
- **lying**, while: alum h2 aur aur-ar k2 borx hr1 calc-p↓ cit-v lat-m↓ lyc↓ mag-m merc h1 nux-v rhus-t vh
  - **amel.**: atis ckh1 mang k2 vanil fd5.de
  - **back** agg. and on side amel.; on: calc-p
  - **cannot** lie down: lat-m bnm6•
- **lower** limbs; with complaints of: ars bg2 cham bg2 coff bg2 ferr bg2 kali-c bg2 merc bg2
- **mania**; in: *(↗Wandering - desire - mania)* ars a cann-i br1 maias-l hm2• meli sne
- **meditation**; during: *Lac-e* hm2•
- **menopause**; at: *Kali-br* kr1 sep mtf11
- **menses**:
  - **after**: *(↗Menses - after)* carb-ac bg2 ferr bg2 mag-c k* nux-v bg2
  - **before**●: *(↗Menses - before)* *Acon* k* amn-l sp1 ang bg2* arist-cl sp1 caul bro1 caust sf1.de *Cham* bro1 *Cimic* bro1 coloc con k* gels bg2 ign bro1 kali-c k* *Kreos* k* *Lach* bro1 lyc k* m-aust mag-c mag-m bro1 *Mag-p* bro1 mang k* nit-ac bro1 nux-m bg2 *Nux-v* k* puls k* *Sal-n* bro1 senec bro1 sep bro1 stann ptk2 **Sulph** k* tril-p bro1 vib bro1 xan c1*
  - **during**: *(↗Menses - during)* abrom-a-r bnj1 *Acon* k* agar↓ am-c ant-t k* apis k* *Ars* k* ars-s-f k2* bell k* borx k* *Calc* k* calc-ar k2* caul bro1 *Cham* k* *Cimic* bro1 cocc k* *Coff* k* croc k* *Cycl* gels k* hyos k* ign k* ip k* kali-ar kali-c k* kali-p kali-s kreos bro1 *Lach* bro1 lil-t bg2 mag-m k* *Mag-p* bro1 merc k* nat-c k* nit-ac k* nux-m bg2 *Nux-v* k* op petr-ra shn4• phos k* plat k* *Puls* k* *Rhus-t* k* *Sal-n* bro1 sec k* senec bg2* *Sep* k* *Stram* k* sulph k* tarent thuj k* tril-p bro1 uran-n bg2 vib k* xan bro1
    - ⁝ **beginning** of; at: agar bg2
  - **suppressed**, during: ars cimic *Ferr* hr1 kali-c nicc nux-v rhus-t sep zinc
- **mental** exertion: *(↗reading)*
  - **amel.**: *Nat-c*
  - **during**: *(↗study)* ambr j borx fago graph k2 ind *Kali-p* k* nat-c h2*
- **metrorrhagia**, during: *Acon Apis* cham hyos stram
- **moon** | **full** moon; during: adam srj5• nat-m brm
- **motion**:
  - **agg.**: berb dgt1 bry k2
  - **amel.**: *(↗move - must)* arn tl1 ferr tl1 granit-m es1• lyc c1 macro c1 positr nl2• puls h1* rhus-t tl1 sanic c1 vanil fd5.de
- **move**:
  - **must** constantly: *(↗motion - amel.)* acon mrr1 aml-ns vh1 ap-g vh1 *Apis* st* *Ars* st* aur h2* bac jl2 *Bell* h1* bism-o a1 canth a1* caust kl cench k2 cimic sf1.de **Dulc** fd* hipp st *Hippoz* vh* hyos h1* ign j5.de *Iod* st* *Kali-br* br1* kali-s fd4.de *Kola* stb3• *Kreos* st* lac-cp sk4• lac-leo sk4• *Led* vh* manc st med jl2 mez pf pip-m br1 plac↓ plut-n srj7• **Rhus-t** br1* sanic c1 sul-i k2 tarent br1* tril-c a1 tril-p c1 trom st *Tub* mrr1 vanil fd5.de verat mrr1
    - ⁝ **amel.**; does not: *Kola* stb3•
    - ⁝ **goes** from one room to the other: ars mrr1 med jl2 plac rzf5•
    - ⁝ **walking** agg; but: tarent br1
  - **weak** to; but too: *Bapt* kr1
- **music**, from: *(↗Music - agg.)* nat-c sabin br1 tarent k*
- **nausea**:
  - **from**: cina a1 phos a1
  - **with**: ign bg2 lac-d st1 vanil fd5.de
- **noise**; from: gaert fmm1•
- **pacing** back and forwards: **Ars** mrr1 plan k* *Tritic-vg* fd5.de vanil fd5.de
- **pain**, from: **Acon** st* androc srj1• arn mrr1 ars h2 bell h1 berb dgt1 bry k2 caust h2 cham b7a.de* chr-ac a1 *Cina*↓ *Coff* b7a.de coloc a1* dios a1 eup-per k2 irid-met srj5• kali-br↓ kali-c bg1* lac-h↓ lyc h2* *M-arct* b7a.de mag-c k2 merc k2 musca-d szs1 plb a1 puls zr rad-br br1 rhod k2 *Ruta* fd4.de sil h2 spig↓ tub gk vib↓ *Zinc*↓ [tax jsj7]
  - ○ **Abdomen**; in: lac-h sze9•
  - **Face**; in: spig bro1
  - **Ovaries**: kali-br bro1 vib bro1 *Zinc* bro1
  - **Sciatic** nerve; in: acon bro1 ars bro1 spig bro1
  - **Stomach**; in: *Cina* hr1
- **painful**: acon-f a1
- **palpitations**; during: *Kola* stb3•
- **paroxysms**:
  - **after**: oena a1
  - **during**: plb k*
- **periodical**: anac↓ *Ars* k*
  - **third** day; every: anac
- **perspiration**:
  - **amel.**: *Sulph* k*
  - **during**: *Acon* bg2 *Am-c* bg2 anac bg2 ant-t bg2 *Arn* bg2 **Ars** bg2 *Bar-c* bg2 **Bell** bg2 *Bov* bg2 **Bry** k* **Calc** bg2 cann-xyz bg2 carb-v bg2 *Cham* bg2 chin bg2 coff bg2 ferr bg2 graph *Hyos* bg2 *Ign* bg2 *Ip* bg2 lachn **Lyc** bg2 *Mag-c* bg2 mag-m bg2 **Merc** bg2 merc-c bg2 *Mosch* bg2 *Mur-ac* bg2 nit-ac bg2 *Nux-v* bg2 op bg2 **Ph-ac** bg2 phos bg2 plat bg2 puls bg2 rheum bg2 **Rhus-t** b7.de* *Ruta* bg2 *Sabad* bg2 *Samb* k* **Sep** bg2 sil bg2 spong bg2 stann bg2 staph bg2 stram bg2 sulph bg2 thuj bg2 valer bg2 *Verat* bg2
- **pneumonia**; during: pyrog tl1 rhus-t tl1
- **pregnancy**, during: acon ambr hr1* cimic tl1 *Colch* hr1* *Nux-m* hr1* nux-v verat
  - **last** month; during: colch ptk1
- **pressing** in liver, from: ruta h1
- **pulse**, from intermittent: digox a1
- **rage**, ending in a: *(↗Rage)* canth
- **reading**: *(↗mental; Reading - agg.)*
  - **amel.**: plut-n srj7•
  - **while**: *(↗Reading - agg.)* dros *Nat-c* ph-ac c1 sumb k* [tax jsj7]
- **rising**, on: atro caust↓ fago germ-met srj5• positr↓ ptel
  - **seat**; from a: caust positr nl2•
- **room**, in: *Iod Kali-s* **Lyc** k* psor al2
- **sadness**:
  - **with**: aur-ar vh1 calc h2* petr-ra shn4• *Plat* hr1* thyr↓ *Vanil* fd5.de
    - ⁝ **alternating** with | **stupor**: thyr br1
- **sanguine** people; in: ozone sde2•
- **septicemia**; with: *Pyrog* br1
- **sexual** excitement, in: *(↗lascivious)* ant-c j canth ptk1 kali-br ptk1 kali-p c1 raph ptk1 staph sf1.de
- **shivering**; during: *Ars* b4a.de asaf b7a.de caps b7.de sabad b7.de
- **sitting**, while: alum ap-g vh ars gb• borx hr1 cact carc gk* *Caust* dirc a1 dulc fd4.de *Ferr* k* germ-met srj5• **Graph**↓ hydrog srj2• ind hr1 *Iod* kali-s fd4.de lac-h htj1• lipp a1 **Lyc** k* mag-c mag-m hr1 mag-p hr1 merc h1* nat-m phos gk* plan plut-n srj7• positr nl2• rhus-t fd* ruta fd4.de sacch↓ *Sep Sil* staph h1 sulph *Symph* fd3.de• syph gb• tung-met bdx1• vanil fd5.de
  - **children**; in: sacch sst1•
  - **work**, while at: ars h2 **Graph** k*
- **sleep**: *(↗bed)*
  - **before**: *Acon* kr1 dulc fd4.de phos thuj
  - **loss** of sleep; from: lac-d ptk1
  - **starting** from; on: apis gt
- **sleepiness**, with: ars j5.de bufo kr1 coloc j5.de *Con* hr1* crot-h j5.de *Hep* hr1* lact hr1* *Merc* hr1* *Petr* hr1* rhus-t j5.de *Sep* hr1* *Stram* hr1*
- **sleeplessness**, from: carc mlr1• coca-c sk4• *Lac-d* hr1* stict kr1* vanil fd5.de
- **smoking**, after: calad k*
- **spine**, affections in: ip k2
- **stool**:
  - **after**: caust bg cench k2 con bg graph bg2 kali-c bg nit-ac bg2 rheum bg2
  - **during**: apis b7a.de *Ars* b4a.de bell cench k2 **Cham** b7a.de *Coloc* b4a.de

- **stomach**; with complaints of: cham b7a.de* m-ambo b7a.de mang b4a.de*
- **storm** (See thunderstorm)
- **strangers** | **presence** of strangers agg.: *(↗Stranger - presence)* dys fmm1• sep bg1*
- **street**; crossing the: gaert fmm1•
- **stretching** backward amel.: *(↗GENERALS - Stretching; GENERALS - Stretching out)* arist-cl rbp3• borx
- **study**, when attempting to: *(↗mental - during; Studying - difficult)* fago ind mim-p rsj8• [tax jsj7]
- **suffocation** threatened: gels c1
- **talking**, after: ambr borx nat-m c1
- **thunderstorm**:
  - **before**: *(↗Weather - thunderstorm - before)* *Gels* hr1* *Psor* k*
  - **during**: *(↗Weather - thunderstorm - during)* adam srj5• gels nat-c k* *Nat-m* *Phos* k* psor k*
- **tossing** about in bed (See bed - tossing)
- **tremulous**: arn k* aur j5.de dulc fd4.de euph h2 *Plat* k* tritic-vg fd5.de valer j5.de
- **typhus** fever; with: agar bro1 *Bell* bro1 *Hyos* bro1 lach bro1 op bro1 ph-ac bro1 phos bro1 *Stram* bro1
- **urinary** complaints; during | **women**; in: meny ptk1
- **urination**:
  - **before**: cain a1 *Coloc* b4a.de ph-ac k*
  - **during**: hipp jl2
- **waiting**, during (See Impatience)
- **waking**, on: am-c am-m hr1* ambr k* ant-s-aur a1 ant-t a1 bell canth k* carb-an b4.de* cedr chin k* chlol a1 chr-ac a1* cina dulc ger-i rly4• graph b4.de* guaj b4.de* hyper m-ambo b7a.de mag-m b4.de* merc b4.de* mur-ac b4.de* *Nat-m* b4.de* oxal-a rly4• ph-ac phos k* plac-s rly4• ruta fd4.de sep k* *Sil* k* squil k* stann tarax k* thea a1 vult-gr sze5• zinc b4.de* [heroin sdj2]
- **walking**, while: acon a1 ambr caust merc paeon ran-b thuj
  - **air**; in open | **amel.**: *(↗Wandering - amel.)* aur-m graph **Lyc** k* ph-ac gl1.fr• **Puls** k* tritic-vg fd5.de
  - **amel.**: *(↗anxious - walking - rapidly)* cench k2 culx k2 cycl hr1 dios nat-m nicc zinc-p k2
- **warm**:
  - **bed**: *Ars-i* *Ferr* *Iod* *Kali-s* *Lach* nat-m *Puls*
  - **room**: psor a1
- **weakness**: *(↗GENERALS - Weakness - restlessness)*
  - **during**: *(↗GENERALS - Weakness - restlessness)* ars tl1 *Bapt* hr1 chinin-ar st mand c1 nicc-s br1 sal-fr sle1•
- **weeping**:
  - **amel.**: hell bg2
  - **while**: rhod ptk1
- **women**, in: castm c1 cedr c1 dulc fd4.de helon c1 kali-br c1 scam c1 sec c1 senec c1 ter c1 xan c1
- **work**; during intervals of (See idle)
- **working**, while: cit-v k* cortico mg1.de *Dulc* fd4.de **Graph** k* kali-s fd4.de kola stb3• nat-sil fd3.de• passi↓ sacch-a fd2.de• spong fd4.de voes a1
  - **tedious**: passi c1
- **worries**; from: carc mlr1•
- **abdomen**; with complaints of: ant-t b7a.de bell b4a.de *Cham* b7a.de *Coloc* b4a.de mosch b7a.de
- **abdomen**; with pain in: aq-mar skp7• choc srj3• coloc bro1 germ-met srj5•
- **head**; with complaints of: *Lyc* bg2 nux-m bg2 par b7a.de ran-b bg2 ruta b7a.de*
- **teeth**:
  - **complaints** of teeth; with: *Acon* b7a.de coff b7a.de* mag-c b4a.de* mang b4a.de* merc b4a.de sep b4a.de spig b7a.de*
  - **pain** in teeth; with: *Mag-c* h2 mang h2 mez h2

RETARDATION; mental: *(↗Autism; Childish; Dementia; Development; Idiocy; Imbecility)* ambr mrr1 ars-i mrr1 aur↓ bar-m mrr1 *Bufo* br1* carc gk6* cic mrr1 des-ac mtf11 iod↓ kali-br mrr1 lyc↓ merc mtf33 pert jl2 phos mtf33 plb↓ sil↓ sulph↓ syph jl2 *Tub* mrr1 zinc mtf33
- **children**: aur mtf33 bufo br1* *Carc* mlr1* iod mtf33 lyc mtf33 merc mtf33 phos mtf33 plb mtf33 sil mtf33 sulph mtf33 tub br1 zinc mtf33
- **injuries**: | **head**; of the: *Cic* mrr1

RETICENT (See Taciturn)

RETIREMENT; desire for: guar vml3• lap-la sde8.de• peti a1* polyp-p a1

RETIRING (= withdrawing):
- **desire**: *(↗Company - aversion; Quiet; wants)* paull a1

REVEALING secrets: *(↗Confiding; Curious; Gossiping; Heedless; Indiscretion; Loquacity; Sensitive - want; Spying)* agar k* alco a1 am-c↓ *Ammc* vh1 *Ars*↓ hyos k* lac-e hrn2• sal-fr sle1•
- **impulsively**: lac-e hrn2•
  - **own**; her: lac-e hrn2•
- **sleep**, in: *(↗Talking - sleep - reveals)* am-c *Ars* k*

REVELING: *(↗Delusions - debauch; Gourmand; GENERALS - Reveling)* agar bg2* ambr bg2* ang bg2* ant-c bg2* ip gl1.fr• kali-c gl1.fr• lach bg2* *Nat-c* gl1.fr• *Nux-v* bg2* petr-ra shn4• sel bg2* sulph bg2*
- **night** reveling; from: *Nux-v* b7.de*

REVENGEFUL (See Hatred - revengeful; Malicious)

REVERENCE for those around him: *(↗Respecting; Veneration)* cocc gl1.fr• coloc ms ham *Hyos* kr1 lac-h↓ nat-m mtf33* nux-v gl1.fr• olib-sac wmh1 plat gl1.fr• podo fd3.de• puls gl1.fr• sil gl1.fr• sulph gl1.fr•
- **lack** of: *(↗Contradiction - disposition; Disobedience; Impolite; Insolence; Rudeness)* anac coloc nux-m gl1.fr• verat gl1.fr•
- **teacher**; towards his: lac-h sk4•

REVERIES (See Absorbed)

REVOLUTIONIST: *(↗Anarchist; Anarchist - revolutionary; Politics; Rebellious)* caust gk2* merc gvt2* [cinnb stj2 merc-i-f stj2]

RHEUMATISM agg.: cimic ptk1

RHYMES; talks in (See Verses)

RICH; to be: | **desire**: *(↗Avarice; Greed; Selfishness)* marb-w es1•

RIDICULED; feels (See Ailments - scorned; Delusions - laughed)

RIDICULOUS actions (See Gestures - ridiculous; Mocking - ridicule)

RIDING:
- **agg.**: lach bg2 psor bg2 sep bg2
- **carriage**; in a:
  - **agg.**: borx b4a.de* lach b7.de* psor bg2 sil b4.de*
  - **aversion** to: *(↗Anxiety - Riding; Confusion - Riding; Fear - Riding; GENERALS - Riding - Streetcar; on - agg.; GENERALS - Riding - Streetcar; on - aversion)* psor k*
  - **wants** to: cupr sst3• psor bg2*
- **horseback**; on | **amel.**: *Lac-e* hrn2•
- **wagon**; in | **amel.**: bry bg2

RIGHT; always claims to be (See Positiveness)

RIGHTEOUS (See Proper - too)

RIGID (See Contradiction - intolerant; Dogmatic; Obstinate)

RISING:
- **after** | **amel.**: m-arct b7.de rhus-t b7.de*
- **agg.**: aur bg2 bism bg2 bry bg2
- **amel.**: sulph bg2
- **bed**; from:
  - **after** rising from bed: bov b4.de* hep b4a.de mag-c b4.de* mag-m b4.de* nit-ac b4.de* rhus-t b7.de* thuj b4a.de
    - **amel.**: nux-v b7.de*
  - **when** rising from bed: asar b7.de* aur b4.de* bell b4.de* berb bg2 bry b7.de* *Calc* b4a.de cham b7.de* cic b7.de* cina b7.de* clem b4.de* *Graph* b4.de* hep bg2 mag-c b4.de* mag-m b4.de* merc b4.de* ph-ac b4.de* phos b4.de* rhod b4.de* rhus-t b7.de* samb b7.de* sep b4.de* sil b4.de* stram b7.de* verb bg2
- **lying**; from: verat b7.de*
- **sitting**; from: asar b7.de* laur b7.de*

- **stooping**; when rising from: chin b7.de* laur b7.de* nat-m b4.de* nux-v b7.de* *Op* b7a.de ox-ac bg2

RITUALISTIC BEHAVIOR: (↗*Autism; Gestures; Superstitious; Thoughts - compelling)* ars mrr1 bell-p mgm• caust gy3 iod gy3* lyss mrr1 rat gy3 rhus-t gy3* ther gy3 tub gy3* [cupr stj2]

ROCKING:
- **agg.**: ars sf1.de *Borx* b4a.de* carb-v sf1.de* *Cocc* sf1.de thuj mtf33
- **amel.**: (↗*Carried - desire; Irritability - rocking - amel.; SLEEP - Sleeplessness - children - rocked)* acon k* calc sf1.de carb-an bg2* cham k* cina k* hyos ↓ kali-c bg2* phos gk puls k* pyrog bg2* rhus-t k* sacch bg2* sec sf1.de
  - **fast**: cina mtf33
  - **to** and fro: hyos mtf33
- **aversion** for being rocked: carb-v mtf33
- **desire** for being rocked: acon bg2 carb-an bg2 carc st1 **CHAM** bg2* cina bg2* kali-c bg2 puls bg2 pyrog bg2 rhus-t bg2 sanic c1* [heroin sdj2]

ROCKS: | **desire** to feel and crawl behind: androc srj1•

ROLLING:
- **bed**; in: (↗*Restlessness - bed - in)* stram mtf33
- **dirt**; in his own: camph ptk1
- **floor**; on the: (↗*Delirium - rolling)* acet-ac ars h2* *Calc* k* cic ptk1 lat-m ↓ **Op** k* paeon ptk1 prot jl3* *Sulph* kr1* tarent ptk1*
  - **pain**; from: ars ↓ lat-m bnm6•
    - **abdomen**; in the: ars mtf33
- **side** to side: am-c ptk1 ars ptk1 lach ptk1 lat-m ↓ tarent ptk1
  - **amel.**: tarent tl1
  - **children**; in: lat-m bnm6•

ROMANTIC (See Sentimental)

ROOM; in a:
- **agg.**: am-m b7.de* ars b4.de* bry b7.de* calc b4.de* croc b7.de* ign b7.de* *Lyc* b4a.de mag-m b4.de* meny b7.de* merc b4.de* *Nat-c* b4a.de ph-ac b4.de* phos b4.de* pic-ac bg2 plat b4.de* puls b7.de* rhus-t b7.de* spong bg2
- **amel.**: aeth bg2 ant-c b7.de* ign b7.de* ph-ac b4.de*

ROUGH (See Abrupt)

ROVING: (↗*Runs; Wandering)* arag ↓ bell ↓ bry ↓ canth ↓ chin ↓ coff ↓ hyos ↓ lyss ptk1* meli sne nux-v ptk1* puls ↓ sabad ↓ stram ↓ verat ↓ [alum stj2 alum-p stj2 alumin stj2 alumin-s stj2]
- **aimless**: arag br1 verat br1*
- **insane** (See senseless)
- **naked**, about: (↗*Naked)* hyos k*
- **senseless**: (↗*Impulse - run; Runs)* bell bry gl1.fr• canth chin gl1.fr• coff hyos meli sne *Nux-v* puls gl1.fr• sabad stram verat
- **wrapped** in fur in the summer: (↗*Fur)* hyos

RUBBING (See Gestures - hands - rubbing; GENERALS - Rubbing)

RUDENESS: (↗*Abrupt; Abusive; Answering - abruptly; Answering - civil; Answering - monosyllables; Answering - snappishly; Audacity; Behavior; Brutality; Contemptuous; Contradiction - disposition; Cursing; Dictatorial; Disobedience; Hardhearted; Haughty; Impertinence; Impolite; Impolite - children; Insolence; Mocking; Presumptuous; Quarrelsome; Reverence - lack; Slander; Speech - offensive; Timidity)* ambr *Anac* bg2* androc srj1• ant-c ↓ aran-ix jl3 arn k* aur aur-s a1 bar-c bg2* bell k* bros-gau mrc1 bufo gk canth k* carc ot* *Cham* bg2* *Chin* ↓ cic sne cina ↓ crot-c sk4• dendr-pol sk4• dulc ↓ eug ferr a1 gal-ac k* granit-m es1• graph k* haliae-lc srj5• hell k* *Hyos* k* ign bg2* *Lac-c* lac-cp sk4• lach bg2* led mrr1 loxo-recl knl4• **Lyc** k* lyss k* med ptk2 nat-m bg2* nicc-met sk4• nit-ac nux-m k* *Nux-v* k* op k* oxal-a rly4• pall par petr-ra shn4• phasco-ci rbp2 phos k* plat mrr1* polys sk4• psor mtf33 rauw tpw8* rheum ↓ sieg mg1.de spong bg2 staph ↓ *Stram* k* stront-c sk4• **Verat** k* [heroin sdj2]
- **ailments** (See Ailments - rudeness)
- **children**; of naughty: (↗*Behavior - children; Grimaces - ill-mannered)* ant-c bg2* bell mtf33 *Carc* mlr1* cham bg2* *Chin* kr1* cina bg2* dulc bg2* rheum bg2* spong fd4.de staph bg2*
- **employees** to the chiefs, of: lyc gl1.fr• nat-m gl1.fr•
- **fever**, during: lyc j5.de
- **women**, in: *Cham* sf1.de

RULES:
- **aversion** to be submitted to the rules (See Contradiction - disposition; Contradiction - intolerant)
- **respecting** the rules too much (See Duty - too)

RUNNING:
- **desire** for: iod ptk1 lac-lup ↓ orig ptk1 verat ptk1
  - **down** the hill: lac-lup hrn2•
  - **everywhere** at a lope: lac-lup hrn2•

RUNNING AWAY (See Escape - run)

RUNS about: (↗*Awkward; Delirium; Escape; Foolish; Hiding - himself; Impulse - run; Roving; Roving - senseless)* acon bg2 agar aids ↓ ars *Bell* k* bomb-chr ↓ bufo k* *Calc* cann-i ↓ canth k* carc cd *Chin* k* clem ↓ *Coff* ↓ con *Cupr* k* cupr-ar dros gk glon haliae-lc srj5• hell **Hyos** k* iod k* lach ↓ meli sne morph ↓ nux-v bg2 orig bg2* *Plat* ↓ plb positr nl2• *Puls* ↓ ruta fd4.de spig-m a1 **Stram** k* *Sulph* tarent k* tritic-vg fd5.de **Verat** k* *Zinc* ↓
- **night**: verat gk
- **dangerous** places, in most: (↗*Danger - desire)* agar a1
- **fright**, as if in: *Zinc* kr1*
- **impulse** to run; morbid (See Impulse - run)
- **lightness** and rapidity, with great: clem a1
- **mania**; in: (↗*naked - mania)* bell lpc con lpc hell lpc stram lpc sulph lpc verat lpc
- **menses** | **before**: lach ptk1
- **naked** | **mania**; in: (↗*mania)* bell lpc hyos lpc
- **paroxysms**, agg. evening; runs in: **Verat** a1
- **people** when walking; runs against: cann-i a1
- **punish** himself; running about to: aids nl2•
- **room**, in: *Coff* kr1 hyos a1 morph a1 *Plat* kr1 tritic-vg fd5.de verat mtf33
- **shirt**, in: bell kr1
- **sleep**; during: (↗*Somnambulism)* positr nl2•
- **streets**; in | **night**: *Puls* kr1
- **things**; runs against: (↗*Awkward)* bell a1 bomb-chr mlk9.de
- **unsteady**: *Coff* kr1

SAD STORIES affect her profoundly (See Horrible)

SADNESS: (↗*Brooding; Delirium - sad; Despair; Determination - gloomy; Discouraged; Dwells - past; Excitement - sadness; Fear - sadness; Grief; Heaviness; Inconsolable; Insanity - sadness; Serious; Sighing; Suicidal - sadness; Weeping; Weeping - sad - thoughts; CHILL - Sad)* *Abies-n* k* abrom-a ckh1 abrot k* acal acet-ac achy jl3 **Acon** k* acon-f a1 act-sp adam skp7*• adlu jl3 adon sf1.de *Aesc* k* aeth j5.de* aether a1 agar k* *Agath-a* nl2• agav-t jl3 *Agn* k* aids nl2• ail alco a1 alf br1* all-c all-s a1* allox tpw4* aln ↓ aloe *Alum* k* alum-p ↓ alum-sil k2 alumn am-br sf1.de *Am-c* k* *Am-m* k* *Ambr* k* *Aml-ns* kr1 ammc amp ↓ amph a1 amyg ↓ *Anac* k* anag vh1 anan androc srj1*• androg-p bnj1 ang h1* ange-s oss1• anh sp1* *Ant-c* k* ant-o c1 *Ant-t* bg2* anthraci mrr1 anthraco a1 anthraq rly4• aphis br1 apis k* apoc k* aq-mar skp7* aqui ↓ ara-maca sej7• *Arag* br1 aran aran-ix mg1.de* arb-m oss1• *Arg-met* k* *Arg-n* k* arge-pl rwt5• *Arist-cl* mg1.de* *Arn* k* **Ars** k* **Ars-i** ars-met kr1* ars-s-f ↓ ars-s-r kr1 art-v ↓ arum-d a1* arum-m kr1 arum-t *Asaf* k* asar k* asc-t kr1 astac kr1 aster k* astra-e jl3 atis bnj1 atra-r bnm3• atro a1* *Atro-s* hr1 **Aur** k* aur-ar ↓ aur-br ↓ aur-i k2 **Aur-m** k* *Aur-m-n* ↓ *Aur-s* k2* aza jl3 bac jl2 bacls-10 pte1*• *Bamb-a* stb2.de• bapt k* bar-act a1 *Bar-c* k* bar-i k2* *Bar-m* bar-ox-suc rly4• *Bell* k* benz-ac k* berb bism ↓ bit-ar wht1• boerh-d bnj1* bol-la borra-o oss1• borx a1 both-a rb3 both-ax tsm2 bov k* bran j brass-c rcb1* brass-n-o srj5• *Brom* k* bros-gau mrc1 bruc ↓ *Brucel* sa3• *Bry* k* *Bufo* k* bufo-s a1 bung-fa mtf buni-o jl3 but-ac bro1 buteo-j ↓ buth-a sp1 cac c1 *Cact* k* cadm-met mg1.de* caesal-b bnj1 caj a1 calad **Calc** k* calc-act a1 **Calc-ar** k* *Calc-f* k* **Calc-i** k2 calc-m ↓ *Calc-p* **Calc-s** calc-sil k2 *Camph* k* camph-br c1* cann-i k* *Cann-s* k* cann-xyz ↓ *Canth* k* *Caps* k* carb-ac a1* **Carb-an** k* *Carb-v* k* carbn-o a1 **Carbn-s** carc jl2* card-m k* *Cardios-h* rly4• carl carneg-g rwt1• cartl-s rly4• cass a1 cassia-s ccrh1• castm k* castn-v mtf11 **Caust** k* cecr jl3 cedr a1 cench k2 cere-b ↓ cerv ↓ **Cham** k* *Chel* k* chen-a ↓ chim a1 **Chin** k* chin-b kr1 *Chinin-ar* *Chinin-s* k* chir-fl ↓ *Chlol* kr1 chlor a1 chloram jl3 chlorpr jl3 choc srj3• chord-umb rly4• chr-ac kr1 *Cic* k* **Cimic** k* *Cina* b2.de* cinnb k* *Clem* k* cob k* cob-n mg1.de* coc-c bg2* coca k* coca-c ↓ *Cocc* k* coch cod ↓ *Coff* k* *Colch* k* coli jl2 *Coloc* k* colocin ↓ colum-p sze2• *Con* k* conch j convo-d a1 convo-s sp1* cop kr1 corian-s knl6• *Corn* cortico tpw7* cortiso jl3 corv-cor bdg• cot a1 crat ↓ *Croc* k* **Crot-c** *Crot-h* k* crot-t cund a1* *Cupr* k* *Cupr-act* j5.de* cupr-ar a1 *Cur* *Cycl* k* cypr c1* cypra-eg ↓ cystein-l rly4• cyt-l mg1.de* *Daph* j5.de*

Sadness: ...
dendr-pol sk4• der a1 des-ac rbp6 *Dig* k* *Dios* kr1 *Dioxi* rbp6 diphtox jl2 dirc c1* dream-p ↓ *Dros* k* *Dulc* dys pte1*• echi k* elae a1 elaps k* elat c1 ergot jl3 erig a1 ery-a kr1 esp-g jl3* eug euon bro1 euon-a br1 eup-per eup-pur euph k* euphr k* fago a1* fagu a1 falco-pe nl2• **Ferr** k* *Ferr-ar* ferr-br ↓ **Ferr-i** ferr-m kr1 *Ferr-p* ferul a1 fic-m ↓ fic-r br1* fl-ac k* flav jl3* flor-p rsj3* foll ↓ form a1 frax st1 fuli br1 fum rly1*• gad a1 gaert pte1*• galla-q-r ↓ gamb k* gard-j ↓ gaul ↓ **Gels** k* ger-i rly4• germ-met stj2*• gink-b sbd1• glon glycyr-g cte1• goss st1 gran j5.de* granit-m ↓ **Graph** k* *Grat* guaj k* **Guar** ↓ guat sp1* haem haliae-lc srj5• halo k* ham k* **Hell** k* helo bg2 helo-s c1* helodr-cal knl2• *Helon* k* *Hep* k* hera j5.de* **Hipp** k* hippoc-k szs2 hir mg1.de* hist mg1.de* *Hura* *Hydr* k* hydr-ac j5.de* hydrc hydrog srj2*• hydroph rsj6* **Hyos** b2.de* hyper k* hypoth jl3 iber a1* ichth br1 **Ign** k* ina-i ↓ ind k* *Indg* k* indol bro1 influ jl2 ing ↓ **Iod** k* *Ip* k* irid-met srj5• iris jac-c a1 jug-c kr1 kali-act a1 *Kali-ar* k* kali-bi k* **Kali-br** k* *Kali-c* k* kali-chl k* kali-fcy a1* *Kali-i* k* *Kali-m* k2* kali-n k* **Kali-p** k* kali-s k* kali-sil ↓ kalm ketogl-ac rly4• *Kola* stb3* kreos k* kres mg1.de **Lac-c** k* lac-cp sk4• *Lac-d* k* lac-e hrn2• lac-h sk4• lac-leo hrn2• lac-loxod-a hrn2• **Lach** k* lachn lact lact-v a1 lam lap-la sde8.de• lapa a1 lat-m sp1* lath c1* *Laur* k* lavand-a ctl1• *Lec* k* led h1* lepi a1 **Lept** k* lil-s a1 **Lil-t** k* lim br1 limen-b-c hrn2* *Limest-b* es1• lipp a1 lith-c bg2* lob k* lob-e c1 lob-p br1 *Lob-s* kr1* lol br1 loxo-lae bnm12• loxo-recl bnm10*• luf-op mg1.de* luna kg1• lup j5.de **Lyc** k* lycps-v lyss a1* m-arct b2.de* m-aust b7.de* macro a1* mag-c k* mag-f mg1.de mag-m k* mag-p sf1.de mag-s k* magn-gr ↓ maias-l ↓ *Manc* k* *Mand* mg1.de* *Mang* k* marb-w ↓ med k* medul-os-si rly4• melal-alt gya4 meli c1 meli-xyz c2 menis a1 meny k* meph jl3 **Merc** k* *Merc-aur* bg2* *Merc-c* k* *Merc-i-f* a1* *Merc-i-r* merc-sul ↓ merl methys jl3 **Mez** k* *Mill* kr1* mim-p rsj8• mit a1 moly-met jl3* morg fmm1• morg-g pte1*• morg-p pte1*• morph k2* mosch mucs-nas rly4• *Mur-ac* k* **Murx** k* musca-d szs1 *Mygal* k* myric k* nabal a1 *Naja* k* **Nat-ar** k* nat-br a1 **Nat-c** k* nat-chl br1 nat-f jl3* nat-hchls a1 **Nat-m** k* nat-n sf1.de nat-ox rly4• *Nat-p* k* **Nat-s** k* nat-sal c1 **Nat-sil** fd* neon stj2*• nep mg1.de* nept-m ↓ nicc nicc-met stj2*• **Nit-ac** k* nitro-o ↓ nux-m k* *Nux-v* k* oena a1 *Ol-an* *Olib-sac* wmh1 olnd k* onop jl3 **Op** b7.de* orig a1 orni br1* orot-ac rly4• osteo-a jl2* ox-ac k2 oxal-a rly4• oxyt k* ozone sde2• palo jl3 pant-ac ↓ parat jl3 *Parathyr* jl2 paull a1 ped c1 *Pegan-ha* tpi1• pen a1 penic jl3 perh jl3 peti a1 *Petr* k* petr-ra shn4• *Ph-ac* k* phasco-ci rbp2 phel phenob jl3* *Phos* k* phys ↓ *Phyt* k* pic-ac k* picro a1 pieri-b mlk9.de pin-con oss2• pin-s a1 pip-n br1 plac ↓ plac-s rly4• plan **Plat** k* plat-m mtf11 *Plb* k* plb-act bro1 plb-xyz c2 plect a1 plumbg a1 plut-n srj7• pneu jl3* podo k* polyg-h kr1 polyp-p a1 polys ↓ positr nl2• pot-e rly4• *Propr* sa3• prot pte1* prun pseuts-m oss1• psil jl3 **Psor** k* ptel **Puls** k* puls-n a1 *Pycnop-sa* mrz1 pyrus a1 querc-r c1 rad-br c11* (non:rad-met) ran-b b7.de* ran-s k* raph k* rauw tpw8* reser jl3 rham-f a1 rheum k* rhod rhus-g tmo3• *Rhus-r* ↓ **Rhus-t** k* *Rhus-v* k* rib-ac jl3 ribo ↓ rob rumx *Ruta* k* sabad k* sabal ↓ *Sabin* b7.de* sacch a1* sal-ac kr1* sal-al blc1• *Sal-fr* sle1• sal-l ↓ samb xxb1 sang sanic k* santin a1 sapin a1 *Sapo* ↓ sarcol-ac bro1 saroth mg1.de* sarr sars k* scop ↓ scroph-n ↓ scut c1 sec k* *Sel* b7.de* senec k* senec-j c1 seneg k* **Sep** k* ser-a-c jl2 sieg mg1.de *Sil* k* sin-n ↓ *Skat* br1 sol-br dsa1• sol-crl bro1 sol-o a1 sol-t-ae a1 spartin ↓ *Spig* k* spira a1 *Spong* k* squil b7.de* **Stann** k* stann-i sf1.de *Staph* k* *Still* k* *Stram* k* streptoc jl2 stront-c k* **Stry** k1* suis-em rly4• *Sul-ac* k* *Sul-i* k2 sulfa sp1 sulfon br1 sulfonam jl3* **Sulph** k* sumb a1 suprar rly4• syc pte1*• **Symph** fd* *Syph* bg3* *Tab* k* taosc iwa1• tarax ptk1* *Tarent* k2* tarent-c ckh1 tax-br oss1• tell k* *Ter* k2* tere-ch jl3 tere-la rly4• teucr ↓ thal c1* thea a1 ther k2* thiam rly4• thioc-ac rly4• thiop jl3 thres-a sze7• **Thuj** k* thuj-l ↓ thymol sp1* thyr ↓ thyreotr jl3 til tong j5.de* toxi ↓ toxo-g ↓ tril-c a1 tril-p trinit br1 trios rsj11* **Tritic-vg** fd* *Tub* bg2* tub-d jl2 tub-r jl3* ulm-c jsj8• ulx-eu mtf11 upa a1 (non:uran-met vh*) *Uran-n* k2* urol-h ↓ ust k* v-a-b jl3* vac jl2 valer k* vanad br1 **Vanil** fd* ven-m jl3 **Verat** k* *Verat-v* k* verb vesp a1* vib vichy-g ↓ *Vinc* j5.de* viol-o b2.de* viol-t k* *Vip* j5.de vip-a jl3 *Visc* k* wildb a1 wye k2* x-ray jl* xan k* yuc a1* **Zinc** k* **Zinc-p** k2* zinc-val ↓ zing ziz k* [alumin-sil stj2 am-caust stj2 am-f stj2 ant-m stj2 ant-met stj2 arg-p stj2 bar-br stj2 bell-p-sp dcm1 beryl stj2 bism-sn stj2 bor-pur stj2 cadm-m stj2 cadm-s stj2 chr-m stj2 chr-met stj1* chr-s stj2 cob-m stj2 cob-p stj2 cupr-f stj2 cupr-m stj2 cupr-p stj2 ferr-f stj2 ferr-lac stj2 ferr-n stj2 ferr-sil stj2 fl-pur stj2 gal-s stj2 helium stj2 heroin sdj2 kali-met stj2 lac-mat sst4 lith-f stj2 lith-i stj2 lith-m stj2 lith-met stj2 lith-p stj2 lith-s stj2 mag-n stj2 mang-i stj2 mang-m stj2 mang-met stj2 mang-n stj2 mang-p stj2 mang-s stj2 merc-d stj2 nat-caust stj2 nat-lac stj2 nat-met stj2 nicc-s stj2 niob-met stj2 nitro stj2 oxyg stj2 pall stj2 plb-m stj2 plb-p stj2 pop dhh1 rubd-met stj2 *Spect* dfg1 tax jsj7 thal-met stj2 titan-s stj2 tung-met stj2 ulm-pra rcb1 zinc-i stj2 zinc-m stj2 zinc-n stj2]

- **day** and night: *Caust* kali-p k2 lil-t ↓ sulph j5.de
  - • **diarrhea** in the morning; with: lil-t

- **day** and night: ...
  - • **weeping**; with: *Caust*
- **daytime**: agn k* aln vva1• ant-c k* bov a1 cact a1 calc-s a1 calc-sil k2* cench k2* cerv a1 dros kali-p k2 lyss hr1* nat-m paull a1 phel stann staph a1 sul-ac sulph k* symph fd3.de• zinc
- **morning**: agar aloe *Alum* k* alum-p ↓ alumn am-c k* ammc ↓ amph a1 anac k* ant-c apis arag br1* arg-met arg-n ars ↓ *Aur* aur-m-n ↓ aur-s k2* bamb-a ↓ bar-c bar-m bit-ar ↓ bruc j5.de calad calc k* calc-s k2 calc-sil k2* cann-i cann-s a1 canth *Carb-an* k* castm caust k* coc-c br1 colocin a1 con k* cop k* cortico tpw7 cycl a1 cystein-l rly4• dulc k* falco-pe ↓ gard-j ↓ granit-m ↓ graph haliae-lc ↓ ham fd3.de• hep hipp ↓ hura hydrog srj2• hyper k* ign ↓ kali-c kali-p kali-s kali-sil k2* *Kola* ↓ kreos lac-leo ↓ **Lach** k* lil-s a1 loxo-recl ↓ *Lyc* k* mag-m mag-p mag-s manc k* mur-ac myric a1 naja *Nat-s* neon srj5• nicc *Nit-ac* nux-m ↓ *Nux-v* ol-an k* op oxal-a rly4• ozone sde2• *Petr* k* ph-ac ↓ phel ↓ *Phos* k* *Plat* k* plb ptel ↓ *Puls* k* rhus-t k* sarr sars sel rsj9• sep k* sil spong fd4.de sul-ac k* sulph symph ↓ tarax tarent ↓ thuj ↓ vanil fd5.de verat ↓ vichy-g a1 xan ↓ zinc k* zinc-p k2*
  - • **alternating** with | **cheerful** | **evening** (See Cheerful - evening - alternating - sadness - morning)
    - ⁝ **mirth**: | **evening** (See Mirth - evening - alternating - sadness - morning)
  - • **amel.**: carb-an k* graph
  - • **bed**; in: dulc a1 spong fd4.de
  - • **rising**; after: ammc vml3•
    - ⁝ **amel.**: sep
  - • **waking**:
    - ⁝ **after**: anac k* ant-c k* cop k* gard-j vlr2• hipp k* nit-ac nux-m k* phel k* ptel k* thuj k* vanil fd5.de
    - ⁝ **on**: **Alum** alum-p k2* ars k* aur-m-n wbt2• bamb-a stb2.de• bar-c bit-ar wht1• bruc j calc-s k2 carb-an k* cop k* falco-pe ↓ granit-m es1• graph mrr1 haliae-lc srj5• ign k* kali-c kali-p *Kola* stb3• lac-leo sk4• **Lach** k* loxo-recl knl4• *Lyc* k* nit-ac ozone sde2• petr j ph-ac phos plat h2* *Sep* symph fd3.de• tarax tarent k* verat xan
      - ⁝ **followed** by | **activity**; manic: falco-pe nl2•
- **forenoon**: alum alumn ↓ am-c ant-c k* apis (non:arg-met slp) arg-n a1* *Cann-s* k* graph j5.de nux-m k* phel j5.de rhus-r a1 sars h2* sel jl3 spong fd4.de thuj
  - • **9-12 h**: alumn k*
  - • **amel.**: graph raph sars
- **noon**: canth caust k* dulc fd4.de phys a1 sarr k* *Zinc*
  - • **alternating** with | **cheerfulness** in the evening (See Cheerful - evening - alternating - sadness - noon)
  - • **amel.**: rhus-g tmo3•
- **afternoon**: aeth k* alum alum-p k2* amyg a1 ant-t k* bamb-a stb2.de• both-ax tsm2 calc-s k* carb-an k* carl k* castm *Chinin-s* cimic k* coc-c k* *Cocc* k* con cop k* dig dulc fd4.de echi gard-j vlr2• *Graph* k* grat k* hydr-ac k* ign iod h* lac-h sze9• mag-c mang k* mur-ac myric k* nicc k* ol-an op orot-ac rly4• *Phos* k* plat puls-n rhus-r k* ruta sulph tarent a1 thuj k* *Zinc* k* zinc-p k2*
  - • **16 h**: bamb-a stb2.de•
  - • **amel.**: agar *Cann-s* rhus-r a1
- **evening**: aeth agar alum am-c k* am-m ↓ amyg a1 androc srj1• *Ant-c* k* ant-t k* arag br1* *Ars* ars-s-f k2* **Aur** aur-ar k2 **Aur-s** k2* bamb-a stb2.de• bar-c k* bov bros-gau ↓ *Calc* k* calc-ar k2 *Calc-s* k* carb-an k* *Carb-v* *Carbn-s* carneg-g rwt1• castm caust coca ↓ colocin a1 con cop a1 cycl k* dig k* dulc fd4.de ferr k* ferr-ar ferr-p fl-ac gink-b sbd1• *Graph* ham ↓ *Hep* k* hyper k* ign k* ina-i mlk9.de kali-ar kali-bi k* kali-c k* kali-chl j5.de* kali-p kali-s kreos k* lact *Lyc* k* lyss a1* m-arct j5.de mag-c mag-s j5.de *Med* vh* murx nabal a1 naja nat-ar nat-c nat-m nat-p k* nept-m lsd2.fr **Nit-ac** k* nux-v j5.de ozone sde2• *Phos* k* *Plat* k* polys sk4• **Puls** k* ran-b sf1.de ran-s k* *Rhus-r* a1 rhus-t *Ruta* sacch ↓ sel rsj9* senec k* seneg k* *Sep* k* *Sil* hr1 spig stram k* stront-c ↓ *Sulph* k* suprar rly4• symph fd3.de• tarent ↓ ther thuj ↓ *Verat* zinc k* zinc-p k2*
  - • **18 h**: coca a1 dig a1
  - • **21 h**: phos a1 sacch a1

- **alternating** with:
    - **cheerfulness**:
        - **daytime** (See Cheerful - daytime - alternating - sadness - evening)
        - **morning** (See Cheerful - morning - alternating - sadness - evening)
        - **noon** (See Cheerful - noon - alternating - sadness - evening)
- **amel.**: aln vva1• aloe am-c bism k* calc cann-s carb-v coca halo jl ham k* kali-c jl mag-c nicc sulph viol-t *Zinc*
- **bed**, in: *Ars Calc* gl1.fr• *Graph* ham fd3.de• kali-c j5.de ozone sde2• puls j *Stram* k* stront-c j5.de *Sulph* thuj a1
- **eating** amel.; when: *(↗Eating - after - evening - amel.)* tarent a1
- **twilight**, in: am-m sf1.de *Ars* bros-gau mrc1 ign *Phos* k* rhus-t

- **night**: alum k* am-c ammc a1 arn *Ars Aur* vh* *Aur-m-n* wbt2• bell j5.de calc k* camph carb-an k* *Caust* k* dream-p sdj1• dulc *Graph* kali-c ↓ kali-p lach k* lil-t m-arct j manc ↓ nat-c *Nat-m* k* ph-ac ↓ *Phos* plat *Propr* ↓ puls-n a1 *Rhus-t* k* stram ↓ sulph ↓
    - **midnight**: plat
        - **before** | **22**-23 h: *Propr* sa3•
        - **after**: manc ph-ac h2* phos h2 rhus-t
    - **amel.**: am-c tarent
    - **bed**, in: *Ars* graph kali-c lil-t *Nat-m* propr sa3• rhus-t j5.de stram sulph
- **acne**, with: aur-br vh1
- **acute**: carc mlr1•
- **air**, in open: aeth con k* cupr hep *Kali-c* mur-ac neon srj5• petr k* *Ph-ac* sabin sep sul-ac sulph
    - **amel.**: arg-n arist-cl jl3 cann-i k2 carl a1 coff j5.de hippoc-k szs2 irid-met srj5• laur j nat-m k2 **Plat** k* **Puls** k* rhus-t tarent
- **alcoholics**; in (See drunkards)
- **alone**:
    - **spends** night alone to hide his gloominess: ind gt
    - **when**: *(↗Company - desire; Company - desire - alone)* aeth all-s k* allox sp1 **ARS** k1* aur *Aur-m-n* wbt2• bov *Calc* carc fd2.de• chir-fl gya2 con dream-p sdj1• *Dros* ferr *Ferr-ar* hep j irid-met srj5• kali-ar kali-c kali-n lyc m-aust j5.de mag-m j5.de *Mez Nat-m* nat-sil fd3.de• phos *Ruta* fd4.de sal-fr sle1• sil spong fd4.de *Stram* trios rsj11• tritic-vg fd5.de valer zinc [buteo-j sej6]
        - **amel.**: allox jl* carc fd2.de• hydroph rsj6• nat-m mp1• rauw tpw8
- **alternating** with:
    - **affection** (See Affectionate - alternating - sadness)
    - **anger** (See Anger - alternating - sadness)
    - **antics**; playing (See Antics - alternating - sadness)
    - **buoyancy** (See Buoyancy - alternating - sadness; Vivacious - alternating - sadness)
    - **cheerfulness** (See Cheerful - alternating - sadness)
    - **contentment** (See Content - alternating - sadness)
    - **delirium** (See Delirium - alternating - sadness)
    - **delirium** gay, cheerfulness (See Delirium - gay - alternating - sadness)
    - **diarrhea**: gamb mrr1
    - **eccentricity** (See Eccentricity - alternating - sadness)
    - **ecstasy** (See Ecstasy - alternating - sadness)
    - **elatedness** (See Elated - alternating - sadness)
    - **energy**; physical: *Aur* carc mlr1• hir jl [bell-p-sp dcm1]
    - **euphoria** (See Euphoria - alternating - sadness)
    - **excitement** (See Excitement - alternating - sadness)
    - **exhilaration** (See Exhilaration - alternating - sadness)
    - **exuberance** (See Exhilaration - alternating - sadness)
    - **fear** (See Fear - alternating - sadness)
    - **hilarity** (See Mirth - alternating - sadness)
    - **hope** (See Hopeful - alternating - sadness)
    - **indifference**: bamb-a stb2.de• sep ptk1

- **alternating** with: ...
    - **insanity** (See Insanity - alternating - sadness)
    - **irritability** (See Irritability - alternating - sadness)
    - **laughing** (See Laughing - alternating - sadness)
    - **loquacity** (See Loquacity - alternating - sadness)
    - **lungs**; inflammation of the: *(↗physical; Mental symptoms - alternating - physical)* gink-b sbd1•
    - **mania** (See Mania - alternating - depression)
    - **mirth** (See Mirth - alternating - sadness)
    - **physical** ailments: *(↗lungs)* cimic tl1
    - **playfulness** (See Playful - alternating - sadness)
    - **pleuropneumonia**: gink-b sbd1•
    - **positiveness**: ozone sde2•
    - **quarreling** (See Quarrelsome - alternating - sadness)
    - **restlessness** (See Restlessness - alternating - sadness)
    - **sexual** desire: lil-t
    - **tenderness** (See Affectionate - alternating - sadness)
    - **timidity**: zinc j5.de
    - **tranquillity** (See Tranquillity - alternating - sadness)
    - **vehemence** (See Violent - alternating - sadness)
    - **violence** (See Violent - alternating - sadness)
    - **vivacity** (See Vivacious - alternating - sadness)
- **amenorrhea**, in: *Anac* kr1 aur kr1 *Caust* kr1 *Cycl* kr1 *Cypr* kr1 ign mp1• *Kali-p* kr1 nat-m mp1•
- **anger**:
    - **after**: *(↗Remorse - anger)* aln vva1• apis ars bell fic-m gya1 hydrog srj2• nux-v petr h2* phos plat puls sep **Staph** mp1*
    - **from**: aur j5.de calc-p j5.de* carc mp1*• ign j5.de lyc j5.de nit-ac j5.de *Puls* j5.de* spig j5.de *Staph* mp1•
- **annoyance** (See vexation)
- **anxious**: *Acon* j5.de asaf j5.de* asar j5.de calc j5.de cann-i br1 carb-an j5.de carb-v j5.de carc mlr1• caust j5.de cic j5.de cop a1 *Croc* j5.de crot-t j5.de cupr j5.de dig j5.de dros j5.de graph j5.de* hep j5.de iod j5.de *Kali-br* hr1* laur j5.de lyc j5.de lyss hr1* *M-arct* j5.de merc j5.de neon srj5• nit-ac j5.de **Plat** j5.de* podo fd3.de• propr sa3• rhus-t j5.de ruta kr1 sep j5.de spig j5.de spong j5.de stann j5.de tab j5.de thuj-l jl3
- **apyrexia**; during: nat-m bro1
- **bad** news, after: *(↗Ailments - bad)* calc-p dulc fd4.de puls k* pycnop-sa mrz1 spong fd4.de
- **bed**, will not leave: aran hr1* *Spong* fd4.de
- **bitter**: calc-s a1 propr sa3•
- **breakfast**; after: con h2 nat-s k2 tritic-vg fd5.de
- **brooding**; with: *(↗Brooding)* *Aur* ckh1 dulc fd4.de naja dm ruta fd4.de spong fd4.de
- **burden**; as from a: cere-b a1*
- **burning** in right lumbar region; from: nit-ac h2
- **business**, when thinking of: *(↗Business - aversion)* *Aur* mp1• kali-s fd4.de mez k2 *Puls* k* spong fd4.de syph st1
- **cancer**; with: ars wl1 carc mp1*• con he1* graph j8* iod gm1
- **canine** hunger, with: ign mtf *Nat-m* hr1*
- **causeless**: aids nl2• androc srj1• bamb-a stb2.de• brass-c mtf11 *Bry* a1 cact a1 calc h2* *Calc-sil* k2* carc mp1*• cardios-h rly4• caust hr1 cench k2* gink-b sbd1• hydroph rsj6• kali-s fd4.de lap-la sde8.de• marb-w es1• *Mur-ac* h2 nat-m ptk1* nept-m lsd2.fr oxal-a rly4• pant-ac rly4• ped a1 phos k* positr nl2• psor jl2 rhus-t k2* *Ruta* fd4.de sars ptk1 sep h2 spong fd4.de staph h1* sulph h2* tarent k* vanil fd5.de
- **cheerfulness**, after: carbn-s a1 *Kali-s* fd4.de **Spong** fd*
- **children**, in: abrot st1 *Ars* k* aur gk* aur-m-n wbt2• *Calc* k* carc fb* caust k* dulc fd4.de *Lach* k* lyc h2* mag-c mtf33 **Nat-m** mp1* rhus-t sep mtf33 sulph k* vanil fd5.de
- **chill**:
    - **before**: *Ant-c*
    - **during**: **Acon** k* alum bg2 am-c anac bg2 anthraco kr1 *Apis* k* **Ars** k* bar-c bg2 bry bg2 calc k* camph h1* cann-s cann-xyz bg2 **Caps** bg2 carbn-s cham k* **Chin** k* chinin-ar cocc k* **Con** k* cupr **Cycl** k* **Graph** k* hell bg2 hep k* **Ign** k* kali-chl j5.de* (non:kali-m a1) lach k* *Lyc* k* merc k*

- **during**: ...
merc-sul hr1* nat-c bg2 **Nat-m** k* *Nit-ac* k* nux-v k* ol-an j5.de petr bg2 p h o s k* *Plat* k* **Puls** k* **Rhus-t** k* sacch a1 sel k* sep k* sil bg2 spig k* *Staph* k* sulph bg2 verat k*
- **chronic** sadness: **Nat-sil** fd*
- **chronic** diseases; in: nat-m br1
- **cloud**; as of a black: (↗*Delusions - clouds - black)* brass-c mtf11
- **coition**, after: *Agar* sf1.de calc cedr hr1* con ham fd3.de• kali-c mrr1 *Nat-m* k* ph-ac mg sel sf1.de* *Sep* k* *Staph* k* sulph ptk1* [heroin sdj2]
- **cold**, from becoming: cimic k2* *Phos* teucr
- **colors**: (↗*Colors)*
  - **purple** | **agg.** | **light** purple: nat-m vk4
    - **aversion** to | **light** purple: nat-m vk4
  - **white**:
    - **agg.**: aur vk4 ign vk4
    - **aversion** to: aur vk4 ign vk4
    - **desire** for white but agg. sadness: lach vk4
- **company**: (↗*Company)*
  - **agg.**: agar lpc euph euphr ptk1 *Lyc* kr1 nat-m mp1• spong fd4.de
  - **amel.**: (↗*Company - desire - alone)* bov k* hippoc-k szs2 irid-met srj5• lec oss• rhus-g tmo3•
  - **aversion** to company, desire for solitude: adam srj5• aids nl2• alum j5.de aur j5.de bamb-a stb2.de• *Con* j5.de* cupr j5.de cycl br1 gink-b sbd1• *Helon* j5.de* *Led* j5.de* melal-alt gya4 murx j5.de nat-c j5.de n a t - m j5.de* pycnop-sa mrz1 rhus-t j5.de sep dx1* vanil fd5.de
  - **desire** for company: bit-ar wht1• stram j5.de*
- **complaining** amel.: (↗*Complaining)* tab
- **confidence**; with lack of: olnd ptk1
- **confusion**; with: toxi mtf2•
- **conscious** of unnatural state of mind; because: maias-l hrn2•
- **consolation**: | **agg.** (See Consolation - agg.)
- **consoled**; cannot be: (↗*Consolation - agg.)* ars kr1* aur mp1• nat-m ctc*• nux-v ctc• olib-sac wmh1
- **constipation**; with: olnd br1
- **continence**, from: bell **Con** k* hyos stram
- **conversation**:
  - **amel.**: dulc fd4.de irid-met srj5• *Lac-d* kr1* rhus-g tmo3•
  - **during**: lac-d c1 vanil fd5.de
- **coughing**:
  - **after**: (↗*Weeping - cough - after)* iod sep
  - **during**: *Caust* kr1 *Petr* kr1
- **criminal**, as if being the greatest: (↗*Anxiety - conscience)* cycl lpc sabad a1
- **darkness**, in: (↗*Darkness - agg.; Light - desire)* am-m sf1.de ars sf1.de calc calc-sil k2 camph *Phos* plat rhus-t stram
- **death** of mother: limen-b-c hrn2•
- **death**, with fear of (See Fear - death - sadness)
- **delivery**:
  - **after**: (↗*puerperal; Delivery - after)* anac ptk1 thuj ptk1
  - **during**: cimic *Ign* k* lach nat-m k* puls k* rhus-t sulph *Verat* zinc
- **dementia**; with (See Dementia - sadness)
- **despair**; with: (↗*Despair)* *Agn* kr1 **Hell** kr1 *Plat* kr1 *Sars* kr1 *Tritic-vg* fd5.de
- **diabetes**; during: (↗*Despair)* *Helon* kr1* *Nat-s* kr1 *Op* kr1
- **diarrhea**:
  - **during**: *Apis* kr1 *Cocc* kr1 crot-h j5.de ferr a1 *Gamb* kr1 *Lyc* kr1 *Merc* kr1
  - **suppressed**; from: gamb mrr1
- **digestion**, during: (↗*eating)* iod h
- **dinner**, after: *Ars* canth a1 *Nat-c* hr1* *Nux-v* k* til k* zinc a1
- **disappointment**, from: bros-gau mrc1 dig a1 dulc fd4.de ign vn10.fr* *Tritic-vg* fd5.de *Vanil* fd5.de
- **disease**, about: (↗*health)* alum a1 carc mp1*• cecr jl3 lac-d ↓ phos ↓ sin-n hr1* *Sulph* hr1* syph hr1*
  - **die** in twenty-four hours; he is sure he is going to: lac-d kr1
  - **incurable** | **heart**: phos kr1
- **diverted** from thoughts of himself; desire to be: *Aur* kr1 camph kr1 spong fd4.de
- **domestic** affairs, over: sep ptk1*
- **doomed** down; as if: lac-cp sk4•
- **dream**, from: agath-a nl2• *Kola* stb3• ozone sde2• phos j5.de* plat j5.de
- **drowsiness**, with (See sleepiness)
- **drunkards**, in: (↗*drunkenness)* alco a1 aur mp1• carc mp1*• cimic st1 lach mp1• nat-m st1 nux-v hr1* puls gl1.fr• staph gl1.fr•
- **drunkenness**, during: (↗*drunkards)* cimic st nat-m st nux-v gl1.fr• puls gl1.fr• staph gl1.fr•
- **dwelling** constantly on her condition: (↗*Dwells)* carc mp1• nat-m mp1• *Spong* fd4.de *Sulph* kr1 tritic-vg fd5.de *Vanil* fd5.de
- **eating**: (↗*digestion)*
  - **after**: alum *Anac* k* ant-c c1 *Arg-n* k* arn b7a.de *Ars* k* asaf k* bar-c canth caust cham *Chin* k* *Cinnb* con galla-q-r nl2• graph ptk1 hyos iod kali-s fd4.de mosch *Nat-c* k* **Nux-v** k* ol-an podo ptel a1 *Puls* til tritic-vg fd5.de zinc k*
    - **amel.**: (↗*Eating - after - amel.)* am-c am-m clem kali-bi mag-m spong fd4.de tarent k*
  - **before**: mag-m
  - **hasty** eating from sadness: sulph j5.de
  - **while**: sep
- **embitterment**; from: sal-l mtf11
- **emission**; from (See pollutions)
- **endogenous**: toxo-g mtf11
- **enjoys** it; and: ign ptk1 nat-m ptk1
- **environment**; about: loxo-recl knl4•
- **epilepsy**:
  - **before** attack of: art-v ↓ zinc sf1.de zinc-val bg
    - **day** and night: art-v kr1
  - **with**: *Indg* br1
- **epistaxis**, after: puls
- **errors** of diet, from: **Nat-c**
- **eruptions**:
  - **history** of; from: mez tl1
  - **suppressed** eruptions; with: mez *Psor* kr1 **Sulph** kr1*
- **excitement**: | **after**: ambr k2 cimic k2 con k2* eug br1
- **exertion**, after: agar *Ars* calc *Coca* kr1 dulc fd4.de hypoth jl kali-c ↓
  - **air**; in open: kali-c h2
  - **amel.**: ferr nat-sil fd3.de•
- **exhilaration**, after: *Dulc* fd4.de myric hr1* plat gl1.fr• ruta fd4.de tritic-vg fd5.de ziz a1*
- **exogenous**: ign mtf11 vac mtf11
- **extreme**: (↗*overwhelming)* hippoc-k szs2 kali-br tl1 orni tl1 ptel tl1 sel mp1• [bell-p-sp dcm1]
- **eyes**:
  - **closed** eyes: *Arg-n* ptk1 kola stb3•
  - **desire** to close the eyes: plac rzf5•
- **failure** to accomplish; from: (↗*Ailments - failure - literary; Delusions - fail everything)* *Dys* fmm1•
- **fault**, as if in: (↗*Delusions - wrong - done)* tarent a1
- **fear**:
  - **from**: cimic k2 nux-m gk sec ptk1* stram gk
  - **with** | **disease**; of: lil-t tl1
- **fever**; during: acon bg2 ant-c ↓ apis bg2 bell bg2 *Brucel* sa3• bufo bg2 cham bg2 chin bg2 *Con* b4.de* ign bg2 lyc bg2 nat-c bg2 op bg2 petr bg2 *Puls* bg2 sep bg2 stann bg2 sulph bg2
  - **intermittent** fever; during: ant-c mtf33
- **flatulence**; with: scop ptk1
- **flowers**; from smell of: (↗*NOSE - Smell - acute - flowers)* hyos k*
- **flushes** of heat, during (See heat - flushes - during)
- **followed** by:
  - **joyfulness**: orig a1*
  - **marriage**; thoughts of: orig a1*
- **fortune**; from reverse of: (↗*Ailments - fortune)* anac j5.de *Calc* j5.de caust j5.de cic j5.de con j5.de *Ign* j5.de *Lach* j5.de nat-c j5.de nat-m j5.de *Ph-ac* j5.de phos j5.de *Puls* j5.de *Rhus-t* j5.de *Sep* j5.de *Staph* j5.de *Sulph* j5.de *Vanil* fd5.de
- **friends**, as if having lost affection of: (↗*Delusions - friend - affection)* *Aur* kr1 *Ham* fd3.de• *Puls* mp1• thuj mrr1 [bell-p-sp dcm1]
- **future**, about the (See Anxiety - future)
- **girls**; in: | **puberty**; before: (↗*puberty)* *Ars* k* calc-p *Hell* k* ign mp1• *Lach* k* nat-m mp1• *Puls* mp1• sep mp1•

- **gloomy**: agn b7.de* alf br1 am-c b4.de* am-m b7.de* ambr b7.de* ang b7.de* apis b7a.de arg-met b7.de* arn b7.de* ars b4.de* asaf b7.de* asar b7.de* aur mp1• bapt bg2 bar-c b4.de* bov b4.de* **Bry** b7.de* calad b7.de* cann-s b7.de* caps b7.de* carb-an b4.de* carb-v b4.de *Caust* b4.de* chel b7.de* chin b7.de* cina b7.de* clem b4.de* cocc bg2 coff b7.de* colch b7.de* coloc b4.de* *Con* b4.de* croc b7.de* cupr bg2* dig b4.de* ferr b7.de* graph b4.de* ham bg2 hippoc-k szs2 hyos b7.de* *Ign* b7.de* iod b4.de* kali-bi bg2 kali-c b4.de* kali-n b4.de* *Kreos* b7a.de *Laur* b7.de* lyc b4.de* mag-c b4.de* mang b4.de* meny b7.de* **Merc** b4.de* mez b4.de* mosch b7.de* mur-ac bg2 *Myric* br1 *Nat-c* b4a.de nat-m b4a.de* nit-ac b4.de* nux-m b7.de* **Nux-v** b7.de* *Op* b7.de* *Petr* b4.de* petr-ra shn4• ph-ac b4.de* phos b4.de* plat b4.de* plb b7.de* puls b7.de* *Rheum* b7.de* rhod b4.de* rhus-t b7.de* rhus-v br1 ruta b7.de* sabad b7.de* sep b4.de* **Sil** b4.de* *Spig* b7.de* stann b4.de* stram b7.de* sul-ac b4.de* sulph b4.de* thuj b4.de* valer b7.de* verat b7.de* viol-o b7.de* *Zinc* b4a.de
  - **evening**: alf br1
- **grief**, after: am-m hr1* *Aur* hr1* aur-m kr1 *Aur-m-n* wbt2• aur-s wbt2• carc mlr1• caust mrr1 cypra-eg sde6.de• *Ign* hr1* limen-b-c hrn2* *Nat-m* hr1* nat-s mrr1 nux-m ptk1 *Ph-ac* hr1* staph mp1•
- **happy**, on seeing others: *(↗Envy; Jealousy)* cic a1* hell b7.de* helon k*
- **hardships** of life; about: coca-c sk4•
- **harsh** word, from a: med kr1 nat-m mp1•
- **headache**:
  - **during**: agar h2* *Agn* hr1* aloe bro1* *Arg-n* bro1 ars j5.de aur hr1* caust hr1* cimic cod hr1* con h2* crot-h k* cycl hr1 *Dulc* hr1* **Guar** hr1* *Ign* bro1 ind bro1 indol mp1• iris kr1* kali-c hr1* lac-cp sk4• lac-d bro1* *Lachn* hr1* lil-t hr1* merl hr1* naja k* nat-c hr1* nat-m k2* ol-an st1 op bg phos pic-ac bro1* *Plb* hr1* ptel hr1* *Puls* bro1 sarr hr1* *Sars* bro1 sel c1 *Sep* hr1* sil bg stann hr1* *Ter* hr1* ther thymol sp1 zinc bro1* [tax jsj7]
  - **after**: cic a1
- **head**; with complaints of: con bg2 crot-h bg2 op bg2 *Sel* bg2 sil bg2
- **health**, about the: *(↗disease)* acon hr1* ars mp1• carc mp1• *Sep* a1* staph hr1*
- **heart**; from:
  - **affections**: aur mp1• cact br1 crat gm1 lyc h2*
  - **pain**: both-ax tsm2
- **heat**:
  - **after**: lob-e c1
  - **during**: **Acon** k* aesc ail k2 *Ant-c* kr1 apis aran kr1 arg-n **Ars** k* ars-s-f k2 *Bell* k* *Bol-la* kr1 bry k* *Calc* calc-ar k2 calc-sil k2 carbn-s chin chinin-ar coca cocc k* *Con* *Dig* *Elat* kr1 *Eup-per* *Gels* kr1 graph k* hipp ign k* *Ip* kr1 kali-ar lyc k* nat-ar *Nat-c* k* **Nat-m** k* nat-p nat-s *Nux-m* op *Petr* k* ph-ac k* *Phos* k* plat k* psil ft1 puls k* *Rhus-t* k* *Samb* kr1 sep k* *Sil* k* *Spong* stann staph k* stram sulph k* tarent vip
  - **flushes** of: | **during**: nat-c h2
- **heaviness**:
  - ○ **Body**; with heaviness of: *Cedr* kr1 dream-p sdj1• graph j5.de positr nl2•
  - **Feet**, in: graph j5.de
  - **Legs**, in: calc h2* con mp1•
- **hemorrhoids** suppressed, after: caps hr1*
- **hiccough**; with: ruta kr
- **horrid**: syph ptk1
- **house**:
  - **in**: dream-p sdj1• *Plat* a1* **Rhus-t** a1*
  - **driving** out of: laur j5.de
  - **entering**, on: plat a1 tarent a1
- **humiliation**; after: *Carc* mlr1•
- **hypertension**; with: aur br1
- **idleness**, while: calc h2
- **impotence**, with: *(↗Despair - impotence)* *Agn* br1* *Aur* hr1* *Calad* hr1* *Gels* hr1* **Kali-br** hr1* *Spong* hr1*
- **injuries**: *(↗Ailments - injuries)*
  - **from**: arn mp1• *Hyper* hr1*
  - **head**, of the: arn carc mp1*• *Cic* con hell mp1• hyper mp1• *Nat-s* k* puls rhus-t sul-ac hr1 sulph
- **insult**; as if from: *Cocc* [tax jsj7]
- **irritability**; with (See Irritability - sadness)
- **isolation**; from sensation of: **Ruta** fd*
- **itching**, from: **Psor**
- **itching**, from: ...
  - **suppressed**: psor al1
- **jealousy** with sadness (See Jealousy - sadness)
- **labor**, during (See delivery - during)
- **lassitude**; with: hippoc-k szs2
- **laughing**: *(↗Laughing - sad)*
  - **after**: plat k*
  - **involuntary**; with: kali-s tl1 *Phos* kr1 puls tl1
- **leukorrhea** amel.: *Murx* kr1
- **light** | **soft** or colored; from: nat-s k2*
- **loathing** of food; with: plat b4a.de
- **looking** down when walking on the street: *(↗Eyes - downcast - walks; Looked - looking)* dios hr1 stann ckh1 verat ckh1
  - **alternating** with | **cheerfulness** (See Cheerful - alternating - sadness - looking)
- **loquacity**, after: aran-ix jl3 tritic-vg fd5.de
- **loss**:
  - **financial** loss; after (See money - losing)
  - **irreparable**; as from: polys sk4•
  - **place**; after loss of (See position)
- **love**; from disappointed: *(↗Ailments - love; Despair - love; Sulky; Weeping - cannot; FEMALE - Menses - suppressed - love)* *Aur* kr1 **Aur-m** vh* *Aur-m-n* wbt2• aur-s wbt2• bell gl1.fr• carc mp1*• dig ptk1* *Hyos* kr1 **Ign** kr1* **Nat-m** kr1* nat-sil fd3.de• *Ph-ac* vh* taosc iwa1•
- **lying** | **amel.**: arg-met vh mang k2 tarent-c ckh1
- **mania**; with (See Mania - sadness)
- **marriage** amel.; thinking of: orig pfa1*
- **masturbation**, from: *(↗Anxiety - conscience - masturbation)* agar **Ars** sne *Aur* hr1* calad cocc *Con* k* *Gels* k* ham *Nat-m* k* nat-p nux-v **Ph-ac** k* *Plat* k* sars sil *Staph* k* sulph *Tarent* hr1
- **menopause**, during: anac jl aq-mar rbp6 *Arg-met* vh* arg-n kr1* arist-cl jl *Aur* kr1* *Aur-m* st buth-a jl *Cimic* bro1* *Con* sf1.de helon c1 hydroph jl ign bro1* *Kali-br* kr1* lac-e hrn2• *Lach* bro1* lil-t sf1.de mag-c gk magn-gr st manc br1* murx c1 *Nat-c* ry nat-m sf1.de penic jl *Psor* a1* puls sf1.de **Sep** st* **Sulph** st *Tab* kr1* thyr bwa valer btw* *Verat* kr1* zinc sf1.de zinc-val bro1*
- **menses**:
  - **after**: *(↗Menses - after)* alum chin *Ferr* k* hell hr1* lac-e hrn2• sapin a1 sil ust
  - **before**: *(↗Menses - before)* acon hr1* am-c k* amp rly4• aur kr1* *Aur-m-n* wbt2• *Aur-s* wbt2• bamb-a stb2.de• bell berb k* brom k* *Calc* carc sst2• carl a1 *Caust* k* *Cimic* bro1 cocc bro1 *Con* cycl des-ac rbp6 dream-p sdj1• ferr k* ferr-p foll oss• ger-i rly4• gink-b sbd1• hell k* helon bro1 *Ign* bro1 iris vh* lac-c lac-d **Lach** mrr1* *Lyc* k* manc k* mim-p rsj8*• *Murx* k* musca-d szs1 nat-c bro1 **Nat-m** k* neon srj5• *Nit-ac* k* phos k* plat bro1 psor st1 ptel gk **Puls** k* rhus-g tmo3• sabal c1 sacch sst1• *Sep* k* **Stann** k* stram tub bgs *Verat* vesp k* vip-a jl3 xan [calc-m stj1 nat-caust stj2]
  - **delayed**, from: **Kali-p** hr1* *Lyc* hr1*
  - **during**: *(↗Menses - during)* am-c k* aqui mtf11 aur k* berb k* brom k* cact calc *Caust* k* chin b7a.de cimic k* cocc bro1 cop k* cur k* *Cycl* st ferr k* graph hell bro1 helon bro1 ign k* *Lac-c* hr1* lac-d lac-h htj1• lyc bro1* macro st mag-m k* merc k* mur-ac k* murx j5.de nat-c k* *Nat-m* k* nat-sil k2* nit-ac k* *Petr* k* phos bro1 pic-ac plac rzf5• plat k* plb *Puls* k* sabin mtf sel ↓ senec *Sep* k* sil k* stann bro1* *Tab* k* thuj ven-m ↓ vesp bro1 zinc
    - **amel.**: arist-cl jl3 *Cycl* k* *Lach* macro a1 *Stann* *Zinc*
    - **beginning** of: nat-m b4.de*
    - **first** day: ven-m rsj12•
    - **menarche**: hell
    - **second** day: sel rsj9•
  - **suppressed**: ars aur aur-ar k2 calc chen-a hr1 cimic *Con* k* croc cycl k* helon br1 nat-m nux-m nux-v ph-ac phos puls k* *Rhus-t* hr1* sep sil staph sulph
- **mental** exertion, after: *Ars* hr1* asar jl3 *Kali-p* hr1* *Nat-m* hr1
- **mercury**, after abuse of: **Aur** **Aur-m** *Hep* *Nit-ac* staph
- **milk**; after disappearance of: agn sf1.de
- **misfortune**; as if from: *(↗Unfortunate)* **Aur** mp1• *Calc* chinin-s cycl ph-ac phel phos puls rhus-t staph sulph
- **missing** mother who died eight years ago: limen-b-c hrn2•

- **money**:
  - **losing**; after: *(↗Ailments - money)* arn ptk1 ars kr1 aur ptk1 mez ptk1* psor ptk1*
  - **problems** with money; about: podo fd3.de•
- **mortification**, after: *(↗vexation)* **Carc** fd* *Ign* hr1* *Puls* kr1 spong fd4.de *Staph* mp1•
- **motion** | **from**: cimic k2 scroph-n a1
- **music**: *(↗Music - agg.; Music - amel.)*
  - **agg.**: *Acon* k* *Ambr* br1 aur-m-n wbt2• cham *Dig* k* *Graph* ign sne kali-p fd1.de• *Kreos* lyc k* *Nat-c* k* nat-m k2 nat-p k* *Nat-s* k* nux-v olib-sac wmh1 phos *Sabin* k* sep tarent k* thuj k* [mang-i stj2 mang-m stj2 mang-p stj2 mang-s stj2]
    - **distant**: lyc ptk1*
    - **lively** music: nat-s kr*
  - **amel.** | **sad** music amel.: *(↗Music - desire - sad)* mang k*
  - **menses**; during: *(↗Sensitive - music - menses)* nat-c mp1• sabin mp1•
- **noise**, from: *(↗Sensitive - noise)* ant-c nat-c k2* phos propr sa3•
- **obesity**; with: gink-b sbd1•
- **occupation** amel.: *(↗Occupation - amel.)* bamb-a stb2.de• tritic-vg fd5.de vanil fd5.de
- **old** age; in: *Aur* a1 esp-g a1*
- **overwhelming**: *(↗extreme)* dendr-pol sk4•
- **pain**, from: both-ax tsm2 carb-v↓ dulc fd4.de germ-met srj5• kali-p br1 nit-ac↓ ribo rly4• *Ruta* fd4.de *Sars* j5.de* staph sne tritic-vg fd5.de
  - **slightest**; from: carb-v h2
  - **stomach**; in: nit-ac bro1
- **palpitations**, with: coca bro1* spartin bwa3
- **past** events; about: aids nl2• luna kg1• psil ft1
- **periodical**: *Ars* asar jl3 *Aur* k* *Aur-m-n* wbt2• *Aur-s* wbt2• brucel sa3• *Con* k* cop k* kali-ar hr1* plat j5.de puls sf1.de sel sf1.de sulph hr1* toxo-g jl2
  - **day** | **alternate**:
    - **alternating** with | **cheerfulness** (See Cheerful - alternating - sadness - periodical - day)
    - **third** day; every: kali-ar kr1
  - **week** | **two** weeks; every: *Con*
- **perspiration**:
  - **after**: lob-e c1
  - **during**: *Acon* k* *Apis* k* ars k* ars-s-f k2 *Aur* aur-ar k2 aur-s k2 bell k* *Brucel* sa3• *Bry* k* *Calc* k* calc-ar k2 calc-s carbn-s *Chin* k* chinin-ar **Con** k* graph k* hep bg2 ign k* lyc *Nat-m* k* nit-ac k* nux-v k* *Ph-ac* bg2 puls k* *Rhus-t* k* sabin bg2 sel *Sep* k* spig k* *Sulph* k* thuj k*
- **pining** boys; in: aur br1
- **pollutions**, from: agar kr1 *Agn* mp1• aur k* *Calad* kr1 *Con* kr1 *Cypr* kr1 dig k* dios k* dys mp1• *Ery-a* kr1 ferr-br sf1.de ham k* **Kali-br** kr1 med kr1 nat-c h2* *Nat-m* kr1 nat-p k* **Nux-v** k* ph-ac k* *Puls* k* sang k* sars kr1 *Sep* kr1 sulph kr1 ust k* zinc ptk
- **position**; after loss of: *(↗Ailments - position)* *Nux-v* kr1
- **pregnancy**, in: aur mp1• bell j chin sf1.de cimic helon mp1• lach k* *Nat-m* k* nux-m sf1.de *Plat* hr1* *Puls* mp1• sanic c1 *Sep* mp1•
- **present**; about the: *Iod* br1
- **pressure** about chest, from: asaf a1 graph k* sanic c1
- **puberty**, in: *(↗girls - puberty)* ant-c bro1* *Ars* st1 aur sf1.de *Calc* st1 caust st1 *Graph* sf1.de* *Hell* hr1* helon sf1.de ign mp1• *Lach* st1 manc br1* *Nat-m* bg2* puls mp1• rhus-t st1 **Sep** mp1• sulph st1
- **puerperal**: *(↗delivery - after)* agn bro1* *Anac* hr1* arg-n dx1* aur bro1* *Aur-m* mp1• bell bro1 *Cimic* bro1* *Con* mp1• foll asm• ign kr1* *Kali-br* mp1• *Lach* mp1• *Lil-t* mp1• manc dx1* nat-m bro1* plat bro1* *Psor* mp1• *Puls* bro1* **Sep** mp1• **Sulph** mp1• thuj dx1* *Tub* mp1• *Verat* sf1.de *Verat-v* bro1 zinc dx1*
- **quarrel** with husband, after: *Anac* hr1* tritic-vg fd5.de
- **quiet**: *(↗Grief - silent)* ars gl1.fr• *Hell* hr1* ign k* kali-s fd4.de nux-v k* ph-ac gl1.fr• plb br1 puls gl1.fr• ziz a1*
- **religious** (See Religious - too - melancholia)
- **respiration**:
  - **asthmatic**; with: nat-s mrr1
  - **impeded**; with: ant-c k* lach laur *Lyc* hr1* sep tab
- **rudeness**; from: [buteo-j sej6]
- **seaside**; at the: *(↗GENERALS - Seaside - Agg.)* nat-m nl positr nl2•
- **sexual** desire | **suppressed** sexual desire; sadness after: con vh*
- **sexual** excesses; from: agar sf1.de con sf1.de
- **sexual** excitement: *(↗Weeping - sexual)*
  - **after**: tarent mp1•
  - **psychopathy**, with: ind mp1•
  - **suppressed**: **Con** mp1*
  - **with** sexual excitement: agar mp1• agn bro1 aur bro1 bell j5.de *Cimic* bro1 con bro1 ind mp1• *Lil-t* bro1 manc br1* nux-v bro1 pic-ac bro1 plat bro1 sep bro1* spong mp1•
- **shock**, from: nitro-o a1
- **sighing**, with: androc srj1• cimic gk **Ign** kr1* lach gl1.fr• nux-v gl1.fr•
  - **amel.**: *Dig* kr1 lach kr1*
- **sits** in corner and does not want to have anything to do with the world: *(↗Crawling - children - howls; Hiding - himself - corner; Playing - aversion - children - sit)* bros-gau mrc1 hipp kr1*
- **sleep** and never to wake, would like to: ars-met kr1
- **sleepiness**, with: calc bg2 calc-p hr1* caust kr1 coca mp1• *Corn* hr1* eup-per hr1* eup-pur kr1 hippoc-k szs2 mag-p sf1.de murx j5.de plb j rhus-t j5.de *Sapo* br1 *Sil* kr1 vanil fd5.de
- **sleeplessness**:
  - **from** sadness; sleeplessness (See SLEEP - Sleeplessness - sadness)
  - **with**: ars hr1* **Aur** mp1• carb-an j5.de **Carc** fd* *Cimic* hr1* gels sf1.de ign hr1* kali-c j rhus-t j sulph j *Thuj* hr1*
- **slight**, from an undeserved: *(↗Delusions - criticized)* *Arg-n* k* *Ham* fd3.de• *Tritic-vg* fd5.de
- **society** (See company)
- **stomach** complaints; with: anac bro1 arg-n bro1 chin bro1 cycl bro1 gaul bro1 hydr bro1 ing br1 lyc bro1 nat-c bro1 nit-ac bro1 *Nux-v* bro1 puls bro1 sep bro1 tab bro1
- **stool** | **after** | **amel.**: nat-m st nux-v st
  - **during**: *Apis* b7a.de
- **stories**, from sad: *(↗Horrible)* calc mp1• **Cic** k*
- **stretching** out on the sofa; on: hep h2
- **stupor**; with (See Stupor - sadness)
- **sudden**: aur mp1• carc mp1• nat-m mp1• tritic-vg fd5.de tub-d jl2
- **suicidal** disposition, with: *(↗Suicidal; Suicidal - sadness)* alum gl1.fr• anac mrr1 *Ars* mrr1 **Aur** hr1* **Aur-m** vh* *Aur-m-n* wbt2• calc gl1.fr• carc jl2* caust gl1.fr• chin gl1.fr• cimic hr1* con gl1.fr• gamb mrr1 graph tl1* *Hep* j5.de* hydrog srj2• ign gl1.fr• med hr1* *Merc-aur* sf1.de morph a1 naja sf1.de *Nat-m* gl1.fr• *Nat-s* sf1.de* op a1 orni tl1 *Psor* a1* ran-b hr1* rhus-v br1 rumx kr1 sep mrr1* *Spig* hr1* **Staph** gl1.fr• sulph gl1.fr• symph fd3.de• zinc mrr1
- **summer**: gels lp
- **sunshine**, in: gels lp *Merc* vh* nat-sil fd3.de• *Stram* k*
  - **amel.**: aur mp1• plat
- **superfluous**, feeling: *Naja* sf1.de
- **supper**, after: nux-v k*
  - **amel.**: am-c k* clem tarent
- **sweets**; after: sacch sst1•
- **sympathy** agg.: carc mlr1• con ptk1
- **taciturn**: *(↗Taciturn; Taciturn - sadness)* **Arg-n** kr1 *Ars* j5.de* bar-c j5.de *Cact* sf1.de gink-b sbd1• ign gl1.fr• mag-c kr1* mur-ac br1 nit-ac j5.de ph-ac gl1.fr• *Puls* kr1* pycnop-sa mrz1 spong fd4.de stann kr1 tarent-c ckh1 verat sf1.de
- **talking**: cimic↓ tarent-c ckh1
  - **constant**: cimic tl1
  - **indisposed** to (See taciturn)
- **taste** | **bitter** taste in mouth; with a: iris a1
- **telling** it to somebody amel.; after: alum-sil k2 falco-pe nl2• petr-ra shn4•
- **tension**; from: dys fmm1•
- **thinking**:
  - **death**; of: dendr-pol sk4• des-ac rbp6
  - **father**; about: *(↗Weeping - anecdotes; Weeping - sympathy)* rhus-g tmo3•
  - **mother**; about: lac-h htj1•
  - **position**; of his: hell gl1.fr•
  - **suicide**; of: aur tl1 ph-ac tl1
- **thunderstorm** amel.: sep k*
- **timidity**; with: plb gk

- **tobacco**, after abuse of: plan br1
- **tongue** | **white** discoloration of the tongue after sadness; with: *Gels* kr1*
- **trifles**, about: *(↗Trifles; Trifles - important)* agar k* bar-act a1 bar-c cocc *Dig* k* *Graph* k* mez saroth jl3 vanil fd5.de
- **typhus** fever; after: *Anac* kr1 *Hell* kr1*
- **unoccupied**, when: nat-sil fd3.de• tarax a1
- **urination**:
  - **amel.**: eug k* hyos
  - **followed** by frequent urination; sadness: mand sp1
- **vertigo**; with: phos bg2 positr nl2•
- **vexation**, after: *(↗mortification; Admonition - agg.; Ailments - reproaches)* calc-p kr1 kali-bi *Plat* kr1 *Puls* kr1
- **vigor**; in spite of: olib-sac wmh1
- **vision**; with dim: cassia-s ccrh1• *Petr* br1
- **vomiting**; with: nux-v bro1
- **waking**: *(↗Grief - waking)*
  - **after** | **amel.**: ozone sde2•
  - **when**: *Alum* k* bell bufo k* calc-p carb-an j5.de cob-n jl3 coc-c ptk1 falco-pe nl2• ign j5.de kali-c *Kali-p* *Lach* k* lepi lyc k* nit-ac op oxal-a rly4• ozone sde2• *Ph-ac* k* plat plb positr nl2• raph rhus-g tmo3• *Sep* j5.de stront-c j5.de tarent thyr jl3 urol-h rwt• x-ray sp1 [heroin sdj2]
- **walking**:
  - **air**, in open: ant-c calc coff *Con* k1* *Cupr* hep kali-c nux-v petr *Ph-ac* rhus-t j5.de *Sep* sulph tab
    - **amel.**: cann-i k2 nat-sil fd3.de• plat *Puls* *Rhus-t* spong fd4.de
  - **amel.**: cop k* hist jl3 nat-sil fd3.de•
  - **during** and after: acon con tab ther thuj
  - **only** while walking: ph-ac ptk1
    - **longer** he walks the worse he gets; the: *Ph-ac*
  - **stand** still or sit down, must: cupr
- **warm** room, in: calc lach k2 *Plat* **Puls** k* rhus-t tarent
- **weakness**; with: calc-p bro1* ign bro1* ph-ac bro1*
- **weather**:
  - **clear**: *Stram* st
  - **cloudy**: am-c *Aur* mp1• plat mp1• sep mp1* [calc-m stj1]
  - **foggy**: sep mtf33
  - **sultry**: sep
  - **wet**: dulc fd4.de *Elaps* kr1 nat-sil fd3.de• rhus-t st spong fd4.de tub bgs
- **weeping**:
  - **agg.**: sep mp1• *Stann* mp1•
  - **amel.**: *(↗Weeping - amel.)* dig k* gink-b sbd1• med k* phos k* puls mp1• tab j*
  - **cannot** weep (See Weeping - cannot)
  - **desire** to weep: *Fum* rly1• hydroph rsj6•
  - **uncontrollable**: kali-br tl1
  - **with**: apis tl1 cycl br1 lac-cp sk4• lil-t tl1 ozone sde2• tritic-vg fd5.de vanil fd5.de
- **wine** amel.: thuj a1
- **work**-shy persons; in: berb j5.de bov j5.de crot-t j5.de dros j5.de gink-b sbd1• laur j5.de mez j5.de prun j5.de zinc j5.de
- **work**; no sadness when there is (See occupation)
- **wringing** the hands: *(↗Gestures - hands - wringing)* ars hr1* *Asar* vh* puls j sulph j5.de syph mp1•
- **wrong** way, as if having done everything in: *(↗Delusions - wrong - done)* bros-gau mrc1 *Naja* a1*

SALVATION: | **yearning** for: olib-sac wmh1

SANGUINEOUS (See Cheerful; Confident; Optimistic)

SARCASM (See Mocking - sarcasm)

SATYRIASIS: *(↗Nymphomania; Shameless; MALE GENITALIA/SEX - Sexual desire - excessive; MALE GENITALIA/SEX - Sexual desire - violent)* adam skp7• agn bg2 ambr bro1 anac jl3 androc srj1• apis bro1* aur-ar vh1 bar-m c1* calc-p bro1* camph bg2* cann-i a1* **Canth** j5.de* con bg2* cyna jl3 ferul bro1 *Fl-ac* hr1* *Gels* hr1 gins bro1 grat hr1* hyos bg2* *Kali-br* hr1* lil-t bro1 *Lyss* hr1* manc bro1 med mrr1 merc bg2* *Murx* bro1

Satyriasis: ...
nat-m bg2* nux-v bg2* orig bro1 pen a1 *Phos* bg2* *Pic-ac* hr1* *Plat* bg2* psor a1 rob bro1 sal-n c1* saroth jl3 *Stram* bg2* sulph bg2* tarent bro1 thymol jl3 tub jl2 ust sf1.de *Verat* bg2* vesp mgm• zinc-pic c1*

SCAPEGOAT (See Delusions - wrong - suffered)

SCARED (See Anguish; Fear)

SCARLET FEVER agg.: *Apis* b7a.de

SCATTERED (See Concentration - difficult; Confusion; Frivolous; Heedless)

SKEPTICISM (See Doubtful - skeptical)

SCHIZOPHRENIA: *Anac* hu* anh mg1.de* aur kr1 *Bell* ↓ carc pd* chlorpr ↓ cic ↓ coli jl2 convo-s ↓ cortico ↓ *Diph-t-tpt* ↓ germ-met srj5• haliae-lc srj5• halo jl3 hyos mrr1 kali-br mrr1 kres jl3 levo jl3 manc mrr1 med ↓ mosch ↓ *Nux-v* ↓ phos mrr1 psil jl3 rauw ↓ reser ↓ ser-a-c ↓ stram mrr1 sulfa jl3 thala ↓ thiop jl3 thuj-l ↓ ven-m jl3 verat mrr1 [lith-p stj2 lith-s stj2]
- **acute**: halo mtf11
- **beginning**: ser-a-c jl2
- **catatonic**: *(↗Catatonia)* chlorpr jl3 cic jl3 coli jl2 convo-s jl3 cortico sp1* halo jl3 rauw sp1 reser jl3 thala jl3 thiop jl3
- **children**; in: hyos mtf33
- **hebephrenia**: anh jl3 chlorpr jl3 *Diph-t-tpt* jl2 halo jl3 kres jl3 reser jl3 thala jl3 thiop jl3 thuj-l jl3
- **paranoid**: *(↗Adaptability; Answering - incoherently; Answering - refusing; Awareness - body; Catatonia; Confusion - identity; Decomposition; Delusions; Delusions - body; Dementia; Fear - murdered; Fear - poisoned; Gestures - automatic; Gestures - strange; Insanity - persecution; Mania; Speech - incoherent; Strange; Stupor; Withdrawal; VISION - Distorted)* *Bell* bg carc mlr1• *Hyos* bg med st1 *Nux-v* bg rauw sp1
- **tongue**:
  - **yellow** discoloration of the | **greenish** yellow: mosch vk1

SCHOOL: | **aversion** to: bac jl2 calc bg2 calc-p bg2* nat-m bg2*

SCOFFING (See Contemptuous)

SCOLDING (See Abusive)

SCORNED (See Ailments - scorned)

SCORNING (See Contemptuous)

SCOWL, inclination to: equis-h a1

SCRATCHING with hands: *(↗Mania - scratching; Striking - boy)* arn ptk1 arum-t ↓ bell a1* calc ↓ *Canth* sne cham ↓ cina mrr1 cupr ↓ falco-pe nl2• hyos a1* marb-w es1• psor ↓ stram k* tarent k* tritic-vg fd5.de [ant-c stj2 ant-met stj2 heroin sdj2]
- **ears**; behind | **agg.**: calc b4a.de
- **coition**; during: [heroin sdj2]
- **face** | **parents**; of his: *(↗Striking - boy)* cupr sst3•
- **head**; on waking child scratches: calc a1
- **himself**: arum-t ptk1 psor ptk1*
- **rage**; during: marb-w es1•
- **walls**; lime off the: arn bg2* canth bg2* cham mtf33 stram hr1*
  - **pain**; from: arn h1* canth k*

SCREAMING (See Shrieking)

SCRUPULOUS (See Conscientious)

SCRUTINY (See Watched)

SEA (See Seaside)

SEARCHING:
- **floor**, on: ign k* plb k* stram k*
- **pins**; for (= pointed things): sil br1*
- **thieves**, at night for: ars dulc fd4.de nat-m ↓
  - **after** having dreamt of them: nat-m

SEASIDE:
- **amel.**: *(↗Air; in open - Amel. - seaside; Confidence - Want - seaside; GENERALS - Seaside - Amel.)* chir-fl gya2 falco-pe nl2• limest-b es1•
- **live** near an ocean; desire to: galeoc-c-h gms1•

- **loves**: *(↗Nature - Loves; GENERALS - Seaside - Desire)* carc sst2• falco-pe nl2• limest-b es1• sal-fr sle1• [heroin sdj2]

SEASONS:

- **autumn**: *(↗GENERALS - Seasons - autumn)*
  - **agg.**: kali-fcy a1 *Stram* b7a.de*

SECRETIVE: *(↗Answering - refusing; Brooding; Company - aversion; Hiding; Insanity - secretive; Loyal; Reserved; Suspicious; Taciturn)* agar bg2 anac bg2 aur bg2* *Bar-c* st* bell bg2 bov bg2 bufo bg2 carc fb caust vh* chlam-tr bcx2• chr-met dx cupr bg2 dig k* galeoc-c-h ↓ galla-q-r nl2• germ-met mtf hyos bg2 *Ign* k* kali-c cd1 lach bg2 *Lyc* st* marb-w es1• naja mtf33 nat-m ptk1* nit-ac bg2 nux-v bg2 op bg2 petr-ra shn4• phasco-ci rbp2 phos bg2 plb bg2* plut-n srj7• *Podo* fd3.de• *Sal-fr* sle1• *Sanguis-s* hrn2• *Sep* st* spong fd4.de staph mtf syph st1 *Thuj* mrr1* tritic-vg fd5.de verat bg2 zinc a1* [heroin sdj2]

- **exposure**; fear of: *(↗Fear - injury - being)* galeoc-c-h gms1•

SECRETS:

- **divulging** secrets (See Revealing)
- **hiding** secrets (See Secretive)

SECURE feeling (See Protected)

SEDUCTION: | **desire** for: *(↗Love - perversity)* olib-sac wmh1

SELF-ABSORBED (See Egotism)

SELF-ABUSE (See Reproaching oneself)

SELF-ACCUSATION (See Mood - repulsive; Reproaching oneself)

SELF-ASSERTION, want of (See Selflessness; Yielding)

SELF-ASSURED (See Confident)

SELF-BLAME (See Reproaching oneself)

SELF-CENTERED (See Egotism)

SELF-CONSCIOUS (See Timidity; Timidity - bashful)

SELF-CONTAINED (See Reserved; Self-control - increased)

SELF-CONTROL:

- **alternating** with | **loss** of self-control: nicc-met sk4•
- **increased**: *(↗Emotions - predominated; Forbearance; Self-denial; Soberness)* ars mtf aur mtf calc mtf33 carc mtf chir-fl gya2 foll mtf haliae-lc srj5• kali-c zr* lyc mtf mosch a1 nat-c a1 nat-m mrr1 nat-s k2* petr-ra shn4• sal-al blc1• sep mtf sil mtf33 stram mtf [nat-br stj2]
  - **children**; in: kali-c mtf33 nat-s mtf33 sil mtf33
- **loss** of self-control: *(↗Beside; Beside - general; Checking - twice)* agar mtf anac ptk1 androc srj1• anh sp1 arg-met ptk1* arg-n ptk1* caust k2* cham mtf33 crot-c sk4• lac-del hrn2• lac-h htj1*• lac-lup hrn2• *Lach* kr1 olnd ptk1 op br1 ozone sde2• petr-ra shn4• sil kr1 staph ptk1* sulph hr1 tarent bg* tub mtf [tax jsj7]
  - **as** if going to lose self-control: gels rb2 lact rb2 olib-sac wmh1
  - **diet**; about: lac-del hrn2•
- **shooting** himself; to prevent (See Injuring - shooting)
- **want** of self-control (See loss)

SELF-DECEPTION: act-sp hr1*

SELF-DENIAL: *(↗Reproaching oneself; Self-control - increased)* agar zr podo fd3.de• staph zr

SELF-DEPRECIATION (See Confidence - want - self-depreciation)

SELF-DESTRUCTIVE: aur br1 haliae-lc srj5• [heroin sdj2]

SELF-DISCIPLINE (See Self-control)

SELF-DISTRUST (See Confidence - want)

SELF-ESTEEM:

- **high** (See Egotism)
- **low** (See Confidence - want)

SELF-INDULGENT: *(↗Egotism; Selfishness)* marb-w es1• plb mrr1 positr nl2• [bell-p-sp dcm1]

SELF-PITY (See Pities)

SELF-RIGHTEOUS (See Injustice)

SELF-SATISFIED: *(↗Content)* carl c1 fl-ac gt olib-sac wmh1 phasco-ci rbp2 podo fd3.de• positr nl2• sacch-a fd2.de•

SELF-TORTURE (See Tormenting - himself)

SELFISHNESS: *(↗Avarice; Delusions - appreciated; Dictatorial; Discontented - everything; Egotism; Envy; Greed; Haughty; Helping - aversion; Impatience; Indifference - others; Indifference - welfare; Jealousy; Loquacity - self-satisfied; Rich - desire; Self-indulgent; Talking - others; Talking - pleasure; Thoughts - himself - cannot; Vanity)* agar k* anac sne androc srj1• anh sp aq-mar rbp6 arizon-l nl2• ars br1* asaf aur-m-n wbt2• bar-s mtf bell gl1.fr• *Calc* tl1* calc-f fl caust gl• cench k2 chin gg* choc srj3• cic ptk crot-t cypra-eg sde6.de• granit-m es1• hydrog srj2• ign ignis-alc es2• *Kola* stb3• lac-h sk4• lach k2* *Lyc* sf1.de* marb-w es1• *Med* k* merc gl1.fr• mosch nat-m ctc• nit-ac mrr1 *Nux-v* sf1.de* ozone sde2• *Pall* c2* petr-ra shn4• phasco-ci rbp2 phos ctc• **Plat** sf1.de* plb mrr1 positr nl2• *Puls* k* pyrus sacch mtf sal-fr sle1• senec ptk1 sep mtf33 sil tl1* staph sne stront-c sk4• *Sulph* k* tarent ptk1 thuj a1 tub bgs* ulm-c jsj8• valer *Verat* vh* [aq-pur stj2 heroin sdj2 *Oxyg* stj tax jsj7]

SELFLESSNESS: *(↗Servile)* anh sp1* aq-mar rbp3 *Carc* fd2.de• iod gl1.fr• *Nat-c* mrr1 podo fd3.de• puls gl1.fr• rhus-t gl1.fr• ruta fd4.de

SENILITY (See Dementia - senilis)

SENSES:

- **acute**: *(↗Frightened; Restlessness; Sensitive; Starting; GENERALS - Sensitiveness - internally; GENERALS - Touch - agg.; HEARING - Acute; MOUTH - Taste - acute; NOSE - Smell - acute; VISION - Acute)* acon bg2* agar mrr1 aids nl2• alco a1 anac k* arg-n arizon-l nl2• *Arn* k* **Ars** k* asaf j5.de* asar bg2* atro bro1 *Aur* bg2* bar-c k* **Bell** k* borx bro1 both-a rb3 cann-i k* caps k* caust gl1.fr• cham b7.de* *Chin* k* choc srj3• cimic ptk1 clem k* **Coff** k* *Colch* bro1 con bg2 *Cupr* b7a.de falco-pe nl2• ferr bro1 galla-q-r nl2• graph c1 helo-s bnm14• hippoc-k szs2 hydr-ac k* hydrog srj2*• hyos b7.de *Ign* k* irid-met srj5• lac-h htj1• lach bg2 *Lyss* k* marb-w es1• melal-alt gya4 morph bro1 mur-ac st1 nad rly4• nitro-o a1 **Nux-v** k* **Op** k* oxal-a rly4• **Phos** k* plb bg2 positr nl2• sil bro1 *Stry* a1* suis-pan rly4• sulph bro1 symph fd3.de• tarent bro1 thea tritic-vg fd5.de *Tung-met* bdx1• valer b7.de* verat bg2 zinc bro1* [heroin sdj2 spect dfg1 tax jsj7 temp elm1]
  - **sensuality**, with: falco-pe nl2•
- **blunted** (See dull)
- **confused**: *(↗Confusion; Forgetful)* acon bg2 aesc bg2 agar bg2 agn bg2 all-c bg2 aloe bg2 *Am-c* bg2 *Ambr* bg2 aml-ns bg2 anh c2 apis bg2 arg-met bg2 arg-n k* *Arn* bg2 ars bg2 *Asar* bg2 aur bg2 bell k* *Bism* bg2 brom bg2 *Bry* bg2 calc bg2 calc-p bg2 camph bg2 cann-xyz bg2 *Caps* bg2 carb-an bg2 caust bg2 chin bg2 chir-fl gya2 coc-c bg2 coff bg2 colch bg2 coloc bg2 con bg2 crot-h bg2 cycl bg2 *Dig* bg2 galeoc-c-h gms1• gels bg2 glon k* gran bg2 graph bg2 grat bg2 hydr-ac bg2 kali-bi bg2 kali-br bg2 kali-c bg2 kali-n bg2 lach bg2 led bg2 lil-t k* lyc bg2 mang k* mosch bg2 nit-ac bg2 nux-m bg2 **Nux-v** bg2 op bg2 phel bg2 rheum bg2 rhod bg2 sang bg2 sec bg2 *Spig* bg2 stram bg2 **Sulph** bg2 valer bg2 verb bg2 viol-t bg2 zinc bg2
- **dull** (= blunted): *(↗Dullness; Prostration; Sensitive - want; Stupefaction)* acon agar k* agath-a nl2• agn ail bro1* alco a1 all-c bg2 alum k* alum-p k2 alum-sil k2 am-c ambr k* anac k* ant-t k* arg-n a1 *Arn* ars ars-i asaf bg2 asar aur k* bapt bro1* *Bell* k* bov k* bry calc k* calc-i k2 calc-s k2 calc-sil k2 *Camph* canth caps k* carb-v k* caust k* cedr *Cham* bg2* chel *Chin* j5.de *Chinin-s* j5.de* *Cic* k* con *Cycl* k* dig k* dros j5.de dulc elec j galla-q-r nl2• gels bro1* graph gl1.fr• **Hell** k* helo-s bnm14• hep gl1.fr• hippoc-k szs2 *Hydr-ac* j5.de* *Hyos* k* ign indg iod irid-met srj5• iris a1 *Kali-br* a1* kali-c *Kali-p* *Lach* k1* lact laur k* led *Lyc* k* m-arct j5.de m-aust j5.de mag-c mag-m j5.de mag-s a1 mang mang-p rly4• melal-alt gya4 meny merc k* mez morph a1 mosch narc-ps a1 nat-c k* *Nat-m* k* nit-ac k* **Nux-m** k* *Nux-v* k1* oci-sa sk4• ol-an k* olnd k* **Op** k* paeon a1 pert jl2 petr k* *Ph-ac* k* *Phos* k* *Plb* bg2* puls ptk1* pyrog ptk1 ran-b ran-s rhod rhus-t k* sabad k* *Sec* k* sel sil k* spong j5.de stann staph stram k* streptoc jl2 sul-i k2 *Sulph* k* tab k* ther verat k* vip a1 zinc zinc-p k2
  - **organs** of hearing, taste and vision unimpaired; yet: **Hell** h1*
- **heightened**: galeoc-c-h gms1•
- **perverted**: arg-n ptk1 bell br1 op ptk1*
- **vanishing** of: *Acon* ↓ agar bg2 alum bg2* ambr ↓ anac k* ang ↓ ant-t k* ars k* asar aur ↓ bar-c ↓ bell k* borx k* bov k* brom bg2 **Bry** k* bufo *Calc* k* *Camph* k* cann-s cann-xyz bg2* canth caps ↓ carb-an k* carbn-o caust ↓ cham

- **vanishing** of: ...
Chel k* chin↓ chlor bg2 cic k* cocc↓ coff con↓ croc crot-h cupr k* cycl c1 dig bg2 gels bg2 glon graph k* hep hyos k* ip↓ kali-c k* kali-sil k2* kreos k* *Lach* k* laur k* lyc bg2 *Mag-c* bg2* *Mang*↓ melal-alt gya4 merc k* mez k* *Mosch* b7.de* nat-m bg2 nat-sil fd3.de• nit-ac k* **Nux-m** bg2* *Nux-v* k* ol-an j5.de op↓ *Petr*↓ ph-ac gl1.fr• phos↓ phys bg2 *Plat* bg2* *Plb* j5.de prun↓ psor bg2 *Puls* ran-b k* rhod k* rhus-t j5.de sec j5.de seneg↓ spong↓ stann k* staph stram k* sulph bg2 tab bg2 valer↓ verat b7a.de*
 • **head**; with complaints of: *Acon* bg2 ambr bg2 aur bg2 cocc bg2 laur bg2 mag-c bg2 *Mang* bg2 mosch bg2 *Petr* bg2 prun bg2 puls bg2 rhus-t bg2
 • **pain**; from: agar bg2 anac bg2 plat bg2 plb ptk1* stann bg2 valer bg2 verat bg2
 • **vertigo**; with: anac bg2 ang bg2 asar bg2 bar-c bg2 borx bg2 bov bg2 bry bg2 calc bg2 canth bg2 caps bg2 carb-an bg2 caust bg2 cham bg2 chin bg2 coff bg2 con bg2 cupr bg2 hep bg2 ip bg2 kali-c bg2 kreos bg2 lach bg2 laur bg2 mag-c bg2 merc bg2 mosch bg2 nat-m bg2 nit-ac bg2 nux-m bg2 *Nux-v* bg2 op bg2 phos bg2 plat bg2 puls bg2 ran-b bg2 rhod bg2 seneg bg2 spong bg2 staph bg2 sulph bg2 tab bg2

SENSITIVE: *(↗Admonition; Conscientious; Delusions - criticized; Intuitive; Irritability; Offended; Senses - acute; Starting; GENERALS - Delicate; GENERALS - Sensitiveness)* abrot↓ absin↓ achy↓ *Acon* k* acon-ac rly4• adam↓ *Aesc* aeth agar↓ *Agath-a* nl2• *Aids* nl2• alco a1 all-s kr1 allox↓ aloe a1 alum k* alum-p↓ alum-sil↓ am-c k* am-m↓ am-val bro1 *Ambr* bg2* **Anac** b4.de* androc↓ ang k* anh sp1 ant-c k* ant-met↓ ant-o a1 ant-s-aur↓ ant-t↓ anthraq rly4• apis k* aq-mar jl3* aqui bro1 aran-ix sp1 arb-m oss1• arg-met k2 **Arg-n** k* arg-p↓ arge-pl↓ arizon-l nl2• *Arn* k* *Ars* k* ars-i ars-s-f k2 asaf k* *Asar* k* aster↓ atro a1* *Aur* k* aur-ar k2 aur-i↓ *Aur-m-n* wbt2• aur-s k2 bac↓ bad↓ bamb-a stb2.de• bapt↓ *Bar-c* bar-i↓ bar-m↓ bar-ox-suc↓ **Bell** k* berb↓ beryl↓ *Bor-pur*↓ **Borx** k* *Bov* k* bros-gau mrc1 bry k* bufo k2 bung-fa mtf *Buteo-j*↓ buth-a sp1 cact↓ cadm-met sp1* cadm-s↓ calad bro1 *Calc* k* calc-ar k2 calc-br↓ calc-f sp1 calc-lac↓ *Calc-m*↓ calc-n↓ calc-p k* *Calc-s* k* calc-sil bro1* calen j5.de camph k* cann-i bro1* cann-s k* *Canth* k* caps k2* carb-an k* *Carb-v* k* carbn-o a1 *Carbn-s* k* carc mg1.de* card-b↓ card-m↓ carl↓ cartl-s rly4• castm **Caust** bg2* cere-s a1 *Cham* k* chel↓ chen-a↓ **Chin** k* chin-b↓ **Chinin-ar** chinin-m bro1 **Chinin-s** k* chir-fl↓ chlam-tr↓ chlol↓ choc srj3• chrysan bro1 cic k* cimic bro1* *Cina* k* cinnb↓ clem cloth↓ coc-c sf1.de* coca-c↓ *Cocc* k* **Coff** k* colch k* coloc con k* convo-s sp1 cop a1 cortiso↓ croc ptk1 *Crot-h* cupr k* cupr-p↓ cyn-d↓ cypra-eg↓ daph dendr-pol sk4• des-ac jl3 dig digin a1 dioxi rbp6 dol↓ dream-p sdj1• dros k* dulc fd4.de dys fmm1• eup-per↓ euph-pi↓ falco-pe↓ *Ferr* k* ferr-ar ferr-f↓ ferr-lac↓ ferr-m↓ ferr-n↓ ferr-p k* ferr-sil↓ fic-m gya1 *Fl-ac* foll↓ fum↓ fuma-ac rly4• gaert fmm1• galla-q-r nl2• gard-j vlr2• **Gels** k* ger-i↓ *Germ-met*↓ gink-b↓ glon bro1 gran graph bg2 haem j5.de haliae-lc srj5• ham k2 hell j5.de helo-s↓ hep k* hippoc-k szs2 hist sp1* hura↓ hydrog srj2*• *Hyos* k* hyper c1* hypoth jl3 **Ign** k* ina-i↓ *Iod* k* ip bg2 irid-met↓ just bro1 *Kali-ar* kali-bi a1 kali-br bro1 *Kali-c* k* kali-i k2* kali-n k* *Kali-p* k* *Kali-s* *Kali-sil*↓ ketogl-ac rly4• kola stb3• kreos lac-ac↓ *Lac-c* k* lac-cp sk4• lac-del↓ lac-e↓ lac-leo hrn2• lac-lup↓ *Lach* k* *Lachn*↓ lat-h↓ *Lat-m* sp1 laur k* lept↓ lil-t k2 limen-b-c hrn2* limest-b es1• lith-met↓ lith-p↓ loxo-recl↓ luna kg1• **Lyc** k* **Lyss** k* m-ambo↓ *M-arct* j5.de m-aust↓ mag-c bg2* *Mag-m* mag-p bro1* mag-s a1 manc↓ mand sp1 mang sf1.de* marb-w↓ mate mg1.de *Med* k* medul-os-si↓ meny sf1.de meph *Merc* k* merc-c a1 *Merc-i-f*↓ mez k* mim-p↓ moly-met↓ moni↓ morph a1* mosch c1* mur-ac h2* murx bg2* musca-d↓ mygal sf1.de myos-a↓ nabal↓ nad↓ naja mtf28 *Nat-ar* *Nat-c* k* **Nat-m** k* *Nat-p* k* nat-pyru rly4• *Nat-s* k* nat-sil fd3.de• nept-m↓ nicc-met↓ **Nit-ac** k* nuph↓ *Nux-m* bro1 **Nux-v** k* *Olib-sac*↓ olnd c1 onop jl3 *Op* bg2* orot-ac rly4• ov↓ ox-ac↓ oxal-a rly4• ozone sde2• paeon ptk1 pall↓ palo↓ pant-ac rly4• par↓ parathyr↓ paull a1 pert-vc vk9 petr k2 petr-ra↓ ph-ac phel↓ phenob jl3* **Phos** k* phos-h c1* phys↓ *Phyt*↓ pieri-b↓ pin-con↓ *Pip-m* br1 plac↓ plan↓ *Plat* k* **Plb** k* plut-n↓ podo↓ positr nl2• prot fmm1• pseuts-m oss1• psil ft1 psor k* ptel↓ **Puls** k* *Pycnop-sa* mrz1 pyrog sf1.de raja-s↓ **Ran-b** k* raph↓ rhen-met↓ rheum↓ rhod mrr1 rhus-g tmo3• rhus-t a1 ribo rly4• ros-d wla1 ruta fd4.de sabad k* *Sabal*↓ *Sabin* sacch↓ sacch-a↓ samb k* *Sang* bg2* sanguis-s↓ sanic sars k* scut↓ sec↓ sel↓ *Seneg* k* *Sep* k* seq-s↓ **Sil** k* sil-met↓ sinus rly4• spig k* spong fd4.de squil↓ stann k* **Staph** b7.de* stram a1* streptoc↓ stront-c↓ stront-met↓ stry a1* succ-ac↓ suis-em rly4• suis-hep rly4• sul-ac↓ sul-i ptk1 sulfonam↓ **Sulph** k* sumb↓ syc pte1*• symph↓ syph↓ tab tanac↓ taosc iwa1• tarax↓ tarent bro1* tax↓ tela↓ tell sf1.de* temp↓ ter ptk1 tere-la rly4• *Teucr* k* thala sf1.de thea a1 **Ther** k*

Sensitive: ...
thiam↓ thuj trios↓ tritic-vg fd5.de tub c1* tub-k↓ tub-m vn* tung-met↓ upa a1* uva↓ v-a-b jl2 **Valer** k* *Vanil* fd5.de vario↓ *Verat* bg2* vesp↓ viol-o b7a.de viol-t k* vip ptk1 visc sp1 voes a1 xan↓ yuc↓ *Zinc* k* zinc-c a1 zinc-cy a1 **Zinc-p**↓ *Zinc-val*↓ [ant-m stj2 aur-m stj2 bar-br stj2 beryl-m stj2 brom stj2 cadm-m stj2 chlor stj2 chr-m stj2 cupr-m stj2 heroin sdj2 lith-m stj2 mang-i stj2 mang-m stj2 mang-met stj2 mang-p stj2 mang-s stj2 merc-d stj2 plb-m stj2 *Spect* dfg1 stront-m stj2 thal-met stj2]
- **daytime**: cadm-met tpw6 carb-v
- **morning**: calc graph hyos a1 iod↓ nat-s k* *Thuj*
 • **evening**; until | **digestion**; during: iod a
- **forenoon**: nat-c a1
- **noon**: zinc j5.de
- **afternoon**: ph-ac j5.de plat j5.de sulph j5.de
- **evening**: *Calc* dulc fd4.de merc j5.de nat-m j5.de ph-ac j5.de plat j5.de ran-b a1
- **night**: kali-c j5.de*
- **abortion**; in threatening: bell mtn nux-v mtn
- **agreeable** impressions; to: arn lpc
- **alternating** with | **indifference**: bell j5.de
- **arts**; to the: carc mlr1*
- **beautiful**, nice things; to: med mtf33
- **causeless**: tub jl2
- **certain** persons, to: *(↗Aversion - persons)* am-m aur calc carc mlr• crot-h cypra-eg sde6.de• falco-pe nl2• **Nat-c** k* sel stann
- **children**●: *Acon* k* agar dx1 ant-c j5.de ant-s-aur ant-t k* *Aur-m-n* wbt2• aur-s wbt2• *Bell* borx j5.de calc calc-sil dx1* *Carc* mrr1* caust dx1* *Cham* chin dx1 cocc↓ coloc dx1 croc dx1 gaert fmm1• *Gels* hr1 *Ign* k13 kali-c dx1* *Kali-p* lyc dx1 med dx1 nat-m dx1 nux-v dx1 *Phos* k* plat dx1 *Puls* k* rheum mtf33 sep mrr1 sil ser spong fd4.de stann dx1 *Staph* k* taosc iwa1• tarent dx1 *Teucr* tub jl2
 • **girls**: cocc br1*
- **chill**, during: **Acon** bg2 aur bg2 bry k* *Caps* k* **Cham** bg2 chin k* **Coff** bg2 colch k* con bg2 hep k* nat-c k* *Nux-v* bg2 petr k* phos k* sel bg2 *Sep* bg2 verat k*
- **chorea**, in: *Cupr* kr1 hyos tl1 mygal kr1
- **coffee**, after: ang sk• **Cham** nux-v k13
- **colors**, to: *(↗Colors; Despair)* choc srj3• dream-p sdj1• falco-pe nl2• hippoc-k szs2 kali-c j5.de plut-n srj7• taosc iwa1• *Tarent* mrr1 tritic-vg fd5.de tung-met bdx1•
- **complaints**; to the most trifling: *(↗Hypochondriasis; Offended)* nux-v
- **confusion**; to: ars br1 aur br1
- **criticism**; to: *(↗opinion; reprimands; reproaches; Admonition - agg.; Delusions - criticized; Despair - criticism)* alum-sil vh1 am-c vh1 ang vh1 arb-m oss1• arge-pl rwt5• ars-s-f vh1 aur vh3* aur-m samkn aur-s samkn bar-c sk• calc bl7* **Carc** vh* chlam-tr bcx2• cupr-m↓ kola stb3• merc vml2• nat-m mrr1 positr nl2• sacch vml3• sep gk5 staph c1* sulph sk7• *Vanil* fd5.de [arg-p stj2 beryl stj2 cadm-m stj2 cadm-s stj2 calc-br stj1 calc-f stj1 calc-lac stj2 calc-m stj1 calc-n stj1 calc-p stj1 calc-s stj1 calc-sil stj2 cupr stj2 cupr-p stj2 ferr stj2 heroin sdj2 lith-met stj2 merc-i-f stj2 plb-m stj2 rhen-met stj2 sil-met stj2 stront-met stj2]
 • **family**; from the: [calc-sil stj2]
 • **menses**; before: [cupr-m stj2]
- **cruelties**, when hearing of: *(↗Anguish - horrible; Horrible)* **Calc** k* *Carc* mlr1• *Caust* vh* dulc fd4.de hep vh* lac-leo hrn2• *Phos* vh* plut-n srj7• positr nl2• *Spong* fd4.de
- **crying** of children, to: *(↗noise; Horrible)* caust phos positr nl2•
- **delirium** tremens, in: **Nux-v** kr1
- **disorder**, to (See Fastidious)
- **drugs**; from: acon c1 ars c1 cham c1 coff c1 lyc c1 nux-v c1 puls c1 sep c1 sil c1 sulph c1
- **eating**:
 • **after**: cann-s j5.de **Nux-v** hr1* teucr j5.de
 • **during**: calc b4a.de hep b4a.de teucr j5.de
- **electricity**; to: marb-w es1•
- **emotions**; to: caust bl1 lac-leo hrn2• thuj br1* *Vanil* fd5.de
- **energies**, to all: gard-j vlr2• positr nl2•
- **everything**; to: canth hr1 gard-j vlr2• kali-p fd1.de• lat-h thj1 mag-p k2 merc mtf33
- **excitement**: *(↗Excitement)* ars bl aur br1 mag-p k2

- **external** impressions, to all: *(↗Impressionable)* anac lpc arg-met k2 am ars hr1* aur lpc bac bn bell k2 *Canth* hr1 caps k2* carc sde*• castm kr1 cham k2* chin mrr1 choc srj3* clem k* *Cocc* coff lpc* *Colch* k* cypra-eg sde6.de• dys fmm1• gaert ptj*• gard-j vlr2• hep k2* hydrog srj2• *Iod* k* irid-met srj5• just br1 kali-p mrr1 *Kali-s* fd4.de kola stb3• lac-c st1 lach k2* limest-b es1• lyc ↓ lyss mrr1 mag-m mtf33 nat-m br1 *Nit-ac* *Nux-v* k* olib-sac wmh1 ph-ac **Phos** k* plat ↓ positr nl2• ptel vml3• sanic c1 sil br1 *Staph* k* stry a1 suis-em rly4• *Tritic-vg* fd5.de [spect dfg1]
  - **delivery**; during: *Cocc* kr1 nux-v kr1
  - **menses**:
    - **before**: nux-v mtn
    - **during**: lyc mtn phos mtn plat mtn
- **fever**; during: acon bg2 bell bg2 carb-v bg2 cham bg2 *Coff* b7a.de* lyc bg2 nat-m bg2 nit-ac bg2 **Nux-v** bg2 **Puls** bg2 sep bg2 teucr bg2 valer bg2
- **flowers**; to: *(↗Flowers - loves)* med mtf33
- **head**; during pain in: ars bro1 *Bell* bro1 *Cham* bro1 chin bro1 coff bro1 *Ign* bro1 *Nux-v* bro1 *Sil* bro1 spig bro1 tela gw*
- **heat**, during: acon bg bell carb-v cham bg coff bg lyc nat-m nit-ac **Nux-v** bg **Puls** teucr valer
- **injustice**, to (See Injustice)
- **insults**, to (See reprimands; reproaches; rudeness; Delusions - insulted)
- **internal** impressions, to all: positr nl2•
- **jar**; to: *(↗touch)* bry bg2 nit-ac br1
- **jesting**; to (See Offended)
- **laughed** at, to being: calc bl
- **light**, to: *(↗Darkness - Agg.; Light - Aversion - shuns; EYE - Photophobia; GENERALS - Light - Agg.; HEAD - Pain - Light; from - agg.)* *Acon* androc srj1• ant-c ↓ aqui br1 arge-pl rwt5• arizon-l nl2• *Ars* aur sf1.de bad h **BELL** k1* borx ↓ bros-gau mrc1 buth-a sp1 *Colch* con j5.de hippoc-k szs2 irid-met srj5• *Kali-p* lac-c k* lyss mrr1 mim-p rsj8• nicc-met sk4• **Nux-v** k* olib-sac wmh1 **Phos** k* positr nl2• sang sf1.de spong fd4.de stram k2 streptoc jl2 thiam rly4• tub bgs tung-met bdx1• vanil fd5.de
  - **bright** light: colch b7.de*
  - **colored** glass; shining through (= as in church): ant-c vh
  - **menses** | **during**: borx mtn ign mtn nux-v mtn
- **lochia**, with profuse: coff kr1
- **magnetic** contact, to: nabal a
- **measles**, in: *Coff* hr1
- **menopause**; during: absin bro1 arg-n bro1 cimic bro1 coff bro1 dig bro1 *Ign* bro1 kali-br bro1 *Lach* hr1* ov bro1 *Ther* bro1 valer bro1 *Zinc-val* bro1
- **menses**:
  - **after**: cimic bro1
  - **before**: *(↗Menses - before)* nit-ac *Nux-v* *Sep*
  - **during**: *(↗Menses - during)* am-c j5.de borx mtn ign mtn lyc hr1* *Nux-v* hr1* phos hr1* plat hr1*
- **mental** exertion; after: *(↗Impressionable; Mental exertion - agg.)* *Kali-p* fd1.de• *Lach* kr1
- **mental** impressions; to: *(↗Fear - hurt; Impressionable; Irresolution)* asar vh dulc fd4.de gaert ptj• nat-m mtf33 nux-v kr1 phos plat kr1 **Spong** fd* *Tritic-vg* fd5.de *Vanil* fd5.de zinc
- **moral** impressions, to: *(↗Delusions - neglected - duty; Impressionable; Moral)* all-s k* aster a1 chin gl1.fr• coff tt dig dulc fd4.de hep tt hydrog srj2• ign k* nuph a1* nux-v gl1.fr• plb a1 positr nl2• psor *Puls* gl1.fr• sacch-a fd2.de• staph gl1.fr• upa a1
- **motion** in the room: lach k2
- **music**, to●: *(↗Music - agg.; GENERALS - Music - agg.)* *Acon* k* aloe bg2* *Ambr* k* anac bg2* androc srj1• arg-met vh am bg2 aur btw *Aur-m-n* wbt2• bry b7a.de* bufo cact *Calc* bg2* carb-an k* carc fb* caust k* *Cham* k* choc srj3• coca-c sk4• coff k* cop bg1* *Croc* bg2* cupr bg2* dig k* falco-pe nl2• *Graph* k* hippoc-k szs2 *Ign* b7.de* ip gsd kali-c bg2 kali-p fd1.de• kali-s fd4.de *Kola* stb3• *Kreos* k* *Lyc* k* lyss ↓ merc k* **Nat-c** k* *Nat-m* k* nat-p *Nat-s* k* **Nux-v** k* pall bg2* *Ph-ac* k* phos k* phys bg2 positr ↓ psil ft1 puls b7a.de* raja-s ↓ ruta fd4.de *Sabal* ptk *Sabin* k* **Sep** k* stann k* staph bg2 suis-em rly4• sulph bg2* *Tab* st1 taosc iwa1• *Tarent* k* thuj k* tub lp* tub-k c1 vanil fd5.de viol-o k* zinc k* zinc-p k2*
  - **amel.** (See Music - amel.)
  - **bird's** song: choc srj3•
  - **children**; in: carc mlr1•
- **music**, to: ...
  - **church** music; to (See sacred)
  - **classical** music: bufo mtf33
  - **continues** to hear music heard before: lyc c1
  - **drums**: carc sde•
  - **stitches** in ear and head from every note: ph-ac c1
  - **happy** music: choc srj3•
  - **menses**; before: *(↗Menses - before; Sadness - music - menses)* carc sst•
  - **opera** music; to: positr nl2• vanil fd5.de
  - **piano**, to: anac sf1.de nat-c j5.de sep j5.de* zinc sf1.de
  - **religious** music; to (See sacred)
  - **sacred** music; to: aur mrr lyss kr1 raja-s mtf *Thuj* st*
  - **violin**, to: positr nl2• viol-o b7.de*
  - **vocal**: nux-v lpc
- **nature** and natural objects, to: *(↗Nature - loves)* falco-pe nl2• lac-leo hm2• med mtf33 positr nl2• *Vanil* fd5.de [heroin sdj2]
- **nervous**: *(↗Excitement - nervous)* **Ambr** br1 cupr bro1 dol br1 sil br1 ther br1
- **noise**, to: *(↗Crying; Noise; Ailments - Fright; Anxiety - Noise; Conversation - Agg.; Delusions - Noise - hearing; Fear - Noise; Irritability - Music - during; Irritability - Noise; Noise - Aversion; Rage - Mischievous - noise; Sadness - Noise; Starting - Noise; Weeping - Noise; CHEST - Palpitation - Noise; CHEST - Palpitation - Noise - strange; FACE - Pain - Noise; GENERALS - Noises - Amel.; HEARING - Acute - Noise; VERTIGO - Noise)* achy jl3 **Acon** k* adam srj5• agar ↓ agath-a nl2• allox sp1 aloe alum k* alum-p k2* alum-sil k2* am-c k* am-m b2.de ambr k* anac b2.de* androc srj1• ang b2.de* anh mg1.de* ant-c k* ant-met ↓ ant-t k* apis k* aqui br1 aran-ix sp1* *Arg-n* arge-pl rwt5• *Arn* k* *Ars* k* *Ars-i* asaf b2.de* **Asar** k* *Aur* k* aur-ar k2 aur-i k2 aur-m k2* aur-m-n wbt2• bad vml3• bamb-a stb2.de• bapt *Bar-c* k* bar-i k2* **Bell** k* **Borx** k* brom ↓ *Bry* k* bufo bung-fa mtf buth-a sp1 cact k* cadm-met gm1 *Calad* b2.de* *Calc* k* calc-f sp1 calc-sil k2* camph k* cann-i a1 cann-s k* canth b2.de* caps k* carb-an k* *Carb-v* k* *Carbn-s* carc gk6* card-b a1* (non:card-m k*) cartl-s rly4• *Caust* k* *Cham* k* chel k* chen-a ↓ **Chin** k* chin-b hr1* chinin-ar k2 chlol hr1* cic k* cimic k* cina b2.de* cinnb k* *Cocc* k* **Coff** k* colch k* **Con** k* convo-s sp1* cop a1 cortiso gse crot-h hr1* cupr b2.de* cyn-d jl3 cypra-eg sde6.de• dig b2.de* dream-p sdj1• dros ↓ dulc fd4.de falco-pe nl2• *Ferr* k* *Ferr-ar* *Ferr-p* *Fl-ac* k* foll jl3* gaert fmm1• gard-j ↓ gels ger-i rly4• **Graph** b2.de* haliae-lc srj5• *Hell* k* helo-s rwt2• hep b2.de* hippoc-k szs2 hura hyos k* *Ign* k* ina-i mlk9.de *Iod* b2.de* *Ip* k* irid-met srj5• kali-ar **Kali-c** k* kali-i *Kali-p* kali-s kali-sil k2* ketogl-ac rly4• *Kola* stb3• lac-ac hr1* *Lac-c* k* lac-cp sk4• lac-del hm2• lac-e hm2• lac-lup hm2• *Lach* k* *Lachn* hr1* *Lat-m* sp1* laur b2.de* lept ↓ lil-t ↓ limest-b ↓ loxo-recl knl4• *Lyc* k* *Lyss* k* m-ambo b2.de* m-arct b2.de m-aust b2.de mag-c b2.de* *Mag-m* k* mag-p k2 manc *Mand* mg1.de* mang k* *Med* medul-os-si rly4• *Merc* k* moni rfm1• mosch *Mur-ac* b2.de* musca-d szs1 myos-a rly4• nad rly4• nat-ar *Nat-c* k* *Nat-m* k* nat-p *Nat-s* k* nat-sil k2* nicc-met sk4• **Nit-ac** k* *Nux-m* b2.de* **Nux-v** k* *Olib-sac* wmh1 olnd b2.de* **Op** k* ox-ac ozone ↓ palo jl3 parathyr jl2 petr k* petr-ra shn4• ph-ac k* phel sf1.de *Phos* k* pieri-b mlk9.de pin-con oss2• plac rzf5• plan a1 *Plat* k* plb b7a.de plut-n srj7• podo fd3.de• positr nl2• ptel k* *Puls* k* raph a1 rhus-t *Ruta* fd4.de sabad k* sabin b2.de* sang bg* sars b2.de* sec hr1* sel b2.de* seneg b2.de* **Sep** k* **Sil** k* *Spig* k* spong fd4.de squil b2.de* stann staph b2.de* stram ↓ streptoc ↓ stront-c sk4• stry a1 suis-em rly4• suis-hep rly4• sul-ac ↓ sulfonam jl3* sulph b2.de* sumb ↓ symph ↓ syph bg1* tab bg2 tanac taosc iwa1• tarax ↓ **Tarent** ↓ *Teucr* ↓ **Ther** k* thuj b2.de* trios ↓ tritic-vg fd5.de **Tub** st1 tung-met bdx1• uva ↓ v-a-b jl3* valer b2.de* *Vanil* fd5.de verat b2.de* viol-o b2.de* visc sp1* xan ↓ yuc a1 **Zinc** k* **Zinc-p** k2* [*Bor-pur* stj2 *Buteo-j* sej6 ferr-f stj2 ferr-lac stj2 ferr-n stj2 ferr-sil stj2 heroin sdj2 spect dfg1 tax jsj7 temp elm1]
  - **morning**: *Fl-ac* a1* ruta fd4.de spong fd4.de vanil fd5.de
  - **evening**: *Calc*
  - **agg.**; noise (See Noise - agg.)
  - **alone** | **amel.**: trios rsj11•
  - **aphthae**; with: borx mrr1
  - **aversion** to (See Noise - aversion)
  - **birds**; of: bamb-a stb2.de•
  - **car** passing on the street: chen-a c1 dulc fd4.de nit-ac k2* spong fd4.de
  - **chill**, during: am bg2 bell **Caps** k* gels *Hyos* nat-c nux-v

• **city**; of: ozone sde2•

• **clocks**, ringing of bells; striking of: ant-c h7a.de* **ASAR** st **Coff** k2* dros st **THER** st verat mtf33

• **crackling** of paper, to: *(↗Starting - crackling)* *Asar* sf1.de ferr hr1* lyc k2* nat-c k2* nat-s ptk tarax h1 ther nh* zinc k2

• **fever**; during: acon bg2 bell bg2 calc bg2 *Caps* b7a.de* **Con** b4a.de* ip bg2 lyc bg2 nux-v bg2

• **hammer**, of: manc lpc

• **heat**, during: acon bg2 bell bg2 calc bg2 *Caps* bg2 con bg2* ip bg2 lyc bg2 nux-v bg2

• **herpes**; with: borx mrr1

• **labor**, during: bell borx *Chin* cimic k* *Coff*

• **loud** noise: ant-c stj2* **Asar** mrr1 *Vanil* fd5.de [ant-met stj2]

• **menses**, during: *(↗Menses - during)* borx mtn ign b7a.de* kali-p k* nux-v mtn

• **music** amel.: *(↗Music - amel.)* anh sp1* **Aur** *Aur-m* jsa bufo k2* carc st* cop st* mang st merc st* nat-m st* sul-ac st* sumb st* **Tarent** k* thuj st* tub st*

• **others** eat apples, hawk or blow their noses; cannot bear to hear: lyss a1* [bor-pur stj2]

• **painful** parts; in (See Noise - agg.)

• **painful** sensitiveness to: am-c hr1* arn hr1* *Coff* hr1* *Con* hr1* *Nux-v* k2* *Sang* hr1* seneg hr1* *Sil* hr1* *Spig* hr1* **Ther** vh*

• **penetrating** noises (See shrill)

• **perspiration**; during: arn bg2 **Caps** bg2 **Cham** bg2 chin bg2 *Coff* bg2 lyc bg2 nat-c bg2 **Nux-v** bg2 sabad bg2 zinc bg2

• **reports** (See sudden - reports)

• **ringing** of telephone: ozone sde2•

• **sawing** wood, to: manc lpc

• **scratching** on linen, silk or strings, to: *Asar* kr1* ferr tl1 tarax tl1 ther tl1

• **shooting**; of: borx b2.de*

• **shrill** sounds, to: *Asar* bg* bar-c bg* *Calc* k* chin bg* cocc bg* con bg* ferr bg* iod bg* lept bg* lil-t bg* lyc bg* manc bg* mur-ac bg* nat-sil fd3.de• *Nit-ac* k* podo fd3.de• ruta fd4.de sabin bg* symph fd3.de• *Ther* bg* tritic-vg fd5.de

• **sleep**, on going to: *Calad* a1* *Calc* lac-del hrn2• ozone sde2• ther mrr1

• **slightest** noise; to the: *(↗Frightened; Irritability - noise; Rage - mischievous - noise)* acon aloe alum-sil k2 am-c a1 ant-c arg-n ars kr1 **ASAR** k1* bad ptk2 bar-c *Bell* a1* *Borx* bufo k2* calad ptk1 chin gsy* cimic br cinnb *Cocc* h1* **COFF** k1* *Ferr* k* gard-j vlr2• ign a1 iod ckh1 irid-met srj5• kali-s fd4.de lach k2 lil-t ckh1 *Lyc* mur-ac ckh1 nat-c k2 nat-s nux-m cda **Nux-v** k* olib-sac wmh1 **Op** k* ozone sde2• petr dx1 *Phos* ptel a1 ruta fd4.de *Sabin* *Sep* st* **Sil** k* streptoc jl2 **THER** k1* tub gb• uva vh* xan c1

⁝ **but** not to loud noise: borx ptk1

• **sneezing**, of: borx a

• **stepping**, of: bamb-a stb2.de• bell lpc **Coff** *Nit-ac* k* **Nux-v** sang *Sil* k* *Teucr* k*

• **sudden**: *Borx* br1* calad ptk1 cocc ptk1 kali-p fd1.de• limest-b es1• nat-c ptk1 nat-m ptk1 podo fd3.de•

⁝ **reports**: borx br1

• **talking**, of: agar kr1 am-c a1* cact kr1 *Cocc* kr1 *Coff* kr1 *Con* kr1 *Ign* kr1 petr hr1* ptel vml3• **Zinc** kr1*

• **vertigo**; with: *(↗VERTIGO - Noise)* ther mrr1

• **voices**, to: *(↗Anger - talk; Irritability - talk of - loud)* agar kr1 am-c a1 *Ars* k* aur aur-ar k2 bar-c hr1 bell ↓ cact kr1 carc sde• chin fry *Cocc* *Coff* kr1 colch fry *Con* ferr fry ferr-ar k2 hyos fry ign kr1 kali-ar *Kali-c* lyss dx1 *Mag-m* mur-ac kr1* nat-c fry *Nat-s* fry *Nit-ac* **Nux-v** ph-ac h2* rhus-t fry ruta fd4.de sel gmj2 sep fry *Sil* stram fry *Teucr* vanil fd5.de verat bg2* **Zinc** k*

⁝ **male**, to: *(↗Aversion - men; to [=male; Fear - men; of = male)* bar-c *Nit-ac*

⁝ own voice: *(↗hearing - acute - voices - her - loud)* bellptk]

• walking; of (See stepping)

• water splashing, to: *(↗hydrophobia)* bromptk1* **Lyss** k* **Nit-ac** k* stram k*

- **odors**, to: *(↗GENERALS - Faintness - Smell; HEAD - Pain - Odors - strong odors; NOSE - Smell - Acute)* ambr tsm1 aran-ix sp1* arge-pl rwt5• ars ptk1 aur ptk1 bell ptk1 calc-f sp1 *Caust* gl1.fr• cham gl1.fr• coff k2* *Colch* b7.de* eup-per ptk1 gink-b sbd1• graph ptk1 hippoc-k szs2 ign ptk1 lac-cp sk4• lach k2 lyc br1* lyss c1* mand mg1.de* merc gl1.fr• *Merc-i-f* ptk1 nat-sil fd3.de• *Nux-v* b7.de* op ptk1 par vml3• phos k2* positr nl2• sabad ptk1 sang ptk1 sanguis-s hm2• sel gmj2 **Sep** ptk1 stann ptk1* staph k2 succ-ac rly4• sul-ac mrr1 sulph k2* taosc iwa1• ther ptk1 tritic-vg fd5.de tung-met bdx1• vanil fd5.de vario ptk1 [lith-p stj2 moly-met stj2 temp elm1]

  • **delivery**, labor, during: nux-v kr1

- **opinion** of others; to the: *(↗criticism; Delusions - criticized; Fear - opinion; Flattered - desire; Timidity - bashful)* ars mrr1 aur mtf33 bov zr *Calc* stj* *Calc-sil* mtf cloth mtf *Dulc* fd4.de gard-j vlr2• *Germ-met* mtf* *Ham* fd3.de• *Kali-sil* mtf nat-m mrr1 nat-sil fd3.de• pall mtf pin-con oss2• **Sil** mtf *Spong* fd4.de stann ptk1 *Staph* br1* thuj mtf vanil fd5.de [arg-met stj1 calc-br stj1 calc-f stj1 *Calc-m* stj1 calc-n stj1 calc-p stj1 *Calc-s* stj1 ferr stj ferr-m stj1 heroin sdj2]

- **pain**, to: *(↗Anger - pains; Anger - pains - about; Despair - pains; Insanity - pain; from; Irritability - pain; Lamenting - pain; Shrieking - pain; Weeping - pains - with; GENERALS - Faintness - pain; GENERALS - Pain - ailments; GENERALS - Pain - intolerable; GENERALS - Sensitiveness - pain)* **ACON** bg2* apis mgm• *Arn* br1* *Ars* bg2* asaf bg2* *Aur* st1* *Bell* sf1.de calc ↓ canth mgm• **CHAM** bg2* chin mtf33 cimic br **COFF** j5.de* colch k2* cupr sf1.de daph j5.de ferr stj2* ferr-p k2 graph k2 **HEP** k2* hyos ↓ *Hyper* vh* ign gt1* *Kali-c* br1 limen-b-c ↓ lyc k2* mag-c mtf33 mag-p ↓ mag-s jl3 mang bg2* mosch mtf nat-m ↓ nat-s k2 nit-ac h2* *Nux-v* bg2* op gl1.fr• *Phyt* vh* *Pip-m* vh* psor st1* sacch sst1• sars h2 scut c1 stann k2 stram sf1.de ther k2 thuj ↓ verat ↓ vesp mgm• [ferr-f stj2 ferr-lac stj2 ferr-n stj2 ferr-sil stj2]

  • **beside** oneself from pain; being: **Acon** tl1* aur k2* calc ptk1 **Cham** tl1* *Coff* ptk1 colch tl1 hep hr1* hyos ptk1 lyc ptk1 mag-p tl1 nat-m ptk1 nit-ac sf1.de* *Nux-v* ptk1 stram ptk1 thuj a1 verat ptk1

  • **children**; in: sacch sst1•

  • **emotional** | **others**; of: limen-b-c hrn2•

  • **noise** agg. pains (See Noise - agg.)

- **people's** inner nature's; to: lac-leo hrn2•

- **people**; to presence of other: carc mlr1• cham bl gard-j vlr2• *Hep* k13 hippoc-k szs2 thuj bl

- **perspiration**, during: *Acon* bg2 aur bg2 bar-c k* bell k* *Cham* bg2 chin k* **Coff** bg2 con bg2 nux-v bg2 sel bg2 *Sep* bg2

- **pregnancy**; during: acon bro1 asar bro1 cimic bro1 *Ther* bro1

- **prolapse** of uterus, in: *Am* kr1

- **psychic** environment; to: dioxi rbp6

- **puberty**, in: *Acon* st1 ant-s-aur st1 ant-t st1 aur st *Bell* st1 calc st1 *Cham* st1 *Kali-p* st1 *Phos* st1 *Puls* st1 *Staph* st1 *Teucr* st1

- **quarrels**; to: *(↗Answering - unable - hurt; Quarrelling - aversion)* ant-c vld carl km• ign hr1 kali-s fd4.de lach hr1 lyc ↓ nat-m mtf33 staph gk

- **reading**, to: *(↗Reading - agg.)* crot-h lach mag-m merc

- **reprimands**, to: *(↗criticism; Admonition - agg.; Ailments - reprimands; Ailments - reproaches; STOMACH - Disordered - reprimands)* aids nl2• arge-pl rwt5• ars ctc• aur-m-n wbt2• aur-s wbt2• *Bamb-a* stb2.de• calc ctc• calc-sil k2* caps c1 *Carc* fb* cina dm *Dulc* fd4.de foll asm*• ham fd3.de• *Ign* c1 kola stb3• lac-leo sk4• lyc mtf marb-w es• *Med* st1 moni rfm1• nat-m ctc* nat-s fb nux-v ctc* oxal-a rly4• ozone sde2• podo fd3.de• puls ctc* ribo rly4• ruta fd4.de sacch sht• spong fd4.de staph mtf33

  • **children**; in: carc fb* med ckh1 nat-s ckh1 sacch sst1• staph mtf33

- **reproaches**: *(↗criticism)* arge-pl rwt5• calc-sil k2 ham fd3.de• kola stb3• lac-leo sk4• sacch-a fd2.de• staph mtf33

- **rhythm**; to: carc mlr1* sep ckh1

- **rudeness**, to: *(↗Ailments - scorned; Answering - unable - hurt; Harmony - desire; Quarrelling - aversion)* aur-m-n wbt2• bar-m vh* *Calc* carc c* cocc *Colch* ham fd3.de• mag-m vh* **Med** mur-ac vh* nat-m k* nat-sil fd3.de• nux-v ozone sde2* ph-ac puls mrr* *Spong* fd4.de stann mrr* **Staph** k*

- **sad** stories, to: *(↗Horrible)* anthraq rly4• bar-ox-suc rly4• cic *Ruta* fd4.de vanil fd5.de

- **said** about her; to what is being (See opinion)

- **sensual** impressions, to: *(↗Impressionable)* *Am-c* k* ars k* ars-i *Aur* k* bar-c k* *Bell* b4a.de berb a calc k* carc tpw2* castm kr1 *Chin* clem bg2 *Coff* mg colch gsy *Con* b4a.de croc bg2 dig k* *Graph* k* hep k* hippoc-k szs2 iod k* irid-met srj5• *Kola* stb3• *Lyc* k* mag-c k* mag-m b4a.de mur-ac b4a.de *Nat-c* k* *Nit-ac* k* nux-v petr st ph-ac b4a.de *Phos* k* positr nl2• sacch-a fd2.de•

- **sensual** impressions, to: ...
  sanguis-s hrn2• seneg b4a.de *Sep* k* sil k* sulph b4a.de taosc iwa1• tarent bg2 thuj valer mg *Vanil* fd5.de *Zinc* k* [heroin sdj2]
  - **children**; in: carc mlr1•
- **shivering**; during: caps b7.de
- **singing**, to: lyss a1* nux-v spong fd4.de
  - **joins** in on hearing anyone sing; involuntary (See Singing - involuntarily - hearing)
- **sound** of passing vehicles; to the (See noise - car)
- **steel** points directed toward her: apis nat-m st **SIL** k1* **SPIG** k1*
- **surroundings**: borx k2 dream-p sdj1• lac-leo hrn2• lach tl1 lyss tl1 nat-p k2 nux-v k2 op tl1 phos mtf33 sabad k2 [tax jsj7]
- **taste** (See MOUTH - Taste - acute)
- **teeth**, during filling of: phys a
- **thinking** of things sensitive to agg.: *Asar* br1
- **time**; passage of: *(↗Time)* fum rly1•
- **touch**, to: *(↗jar; Touched - aversion)* abrot bl *Acon* sf1.de ant-t ↓ arn cda ars k13 *Bell* a caps bl caust k2 chin sf1.de* chinin-ar k13 chir-fl bnm4• cina k2 coff k2* foll jl3* gard-j vlr2• haliae-lc srj5• hep vn10.fr irid-met srj5• kali-c hr1* lac-c mrr1 *Lach* k2* mag-c k2* meny sf1.de mez mrr1 nat-s mtf33 nept-m lsd2.fr nit-ac br1 nux-v ↓ op gl1.fr• phos k2* plb hr1 ruta wm sanic mtf33 sil a1 spig cda staph k2 tarent sk* tell jl3
  - **children**; in: acon tl1 ant-t tl1 chin mtf33 kali-c mtf33 nat-s mtf33 sanic mtf33
- **urticaria**, in: *Bov* kr1
- **walking** of others in the room; to: lach k2
- **want** of sensitiveness: *(↗Cruelty; Curious; Hardhearted; Heedless; Indifference; Indiscretion; Loquacity; Rash; Revealing; Senses - dull; Spying; Unfeeling; Unobserving [=nonconformism])* *Aids* nl2• ant-c st arizon-l nl2• *Arn* ↓ ars ↓ bell k* calc ↓ cann-i a1 chin con cupr cupr-act a1 cycl daph diphtox jl2 euphr *Hydr-ac* gl1.fr• hyos gl1.fr• *Lyc* gl1.fr• **Op** ↓ ozone sde2• *Ph-ac* phos positr nl2• puls ↓ ran-b rheum rhod sabin sel ↓ *Sep* mrr1 staph stram tritic-vg fd5.de tub mrr1 verat mrr1 [heroin sdj2]
  - **chill**; during: *Arn* bg2 ars bg2 calc bg2 chin bg2 *Con* bg2 **Op** bg2 **Ph-ac** bg2 **Phos** bg2 puls bg2 sel bg2 *Sep* bg2 stram bg2 verat bg2
- **weakness**; to other people's (See Abusive; Mocking - sarcasm - weaknesses)
- **wind**; to: *(↗GENERALS - Wind)* *Cham* lpc sulph lpc
- **women**: euph-pi c1 glon c1 ign a*

SENSORIUM (See Senses)

SENSUAL: *(↗FACE - Sensual - lips; FEMALE - Sexual desire - increased; MALE GENITALIA/SEX - Sexual desire - increased; STOMACH - Appetite - ravenous)* bufo mrr haliae-lc srj5• marb-w es1• rhus-g tmo3• taosc iwa1•
- **delights** in his own body: taosc iwa1•

SENSUOUS (See Sensitive - sensual)

SENTIMENTAL: *(↗Admiration; Ecstasy; Homesickness; Homesickness - sleeplessness; Love - romantic; Weeping - drunkenness)* acon *Agn* bro1 alco j* am-c bro1 am-m bro1 ambr sf1.de **ANT-C** bg2* ars k* *Aur* bro1 *Aur-m-n* wbt2• aur-s wbt2• berb a1 bit-ar wht1• cact bro1 calc k* *Calc-p* k* canth k* carb-an bro1 carc fb* castm caust vh* chin chinin-ar cimic bro1 *Cocc* k* *Coff* k* con k* crot-h j5.de* *Cupr* *Cycl* bro1 dendr-pol sk4• dig hr1* dream-p sdj1• *Graph* bro1 hydr-ac iber bro1 **Ign** k* *Indg* bro1 kali-p bro1 kola stb3• kreos j5.de* lac-del hrn2• lac-lup hrn2• lach k* laur j5.de lil-t bro1 loxo-recl knl4• lyc k* manc mur-ac bro1 naja bro1 nat-c bro1* *Nat-m* bro1* nat-s bro1* *Nat-sil* fd3.de• nit-ac j5.de* *Nux-v* k* olib-sac wmh1 petr-ra shn4• ph-ac bro1 *Phos* k* pieri-b mlk9.de plat k* plb vh* podo fd3.de• *Psor* k* *Puls* bg2* rhus-t bro1 ribo rly4• sabad sabin sf1.de sec bro1 *Sel* bro1 *Sep* bro1 *Stann* bro1* *Staph* k* *Sulph* k* thuj bro1 tritic-vg fd5.de **Tub** mrr1 vanil fd5.de zinc bro1* [heroin sdj2 *Ind* stj2 zinc-i stj2 zinc-m stj2 zinc-n stj2 zinc-p stj2]
- **Christmas**; at: lac-lup hrn2•
- **diarrhea**, during: *Ant-c* k*
- **drunkenness**; during: *Caust* gl1.fr• *Lach* k2*
- **ecstasy**, with: dream-p sdj1•
- **girls**: cocc br1*
- **menses** | **before**: *(↗Menses - before)* *Ant-c* k*
- **moonlight**, in: *(↗Moonlight)* **Ant-c** k* petr-ra shn4• vanil fd5.de
- **music**; with: lac-del hrn2•

Sentimental: ...
- **rainbow** colors; gazing at: petr-ra shn4•
- **stars**; gazing at: petr-ra shn4•
- **twilight**: ant-c ptk1*
- **young** persons; in: ant-c c1 ign c1

SERENE (See Tranquillity)

SERIOUS (= earnest): *(↗Amusement - aversion; Cares full; Duty - too; Fear - serious; Introspection; Jesting - aversion; Laughing - aversion; Laughing - never; Pessimist; Playing - aversion - children; Proper - too; Responsibility - taking; Sadness; Smiling - never; Soberness; Solemn)* aeth aids nl2• allox tpw4 *Alum* k* alum-p k2 *Am-c* k* *Am-m* b2.de* ambr k* anac k* ang k* ant-c k* arg-met k* **Ars** b2.de* ars-s-f k2 asar vh aur k* *Aur-m-n* wbt2• aur-s wbt2• bamb-a stb2.de• *Bar-c* k* bart a1 bell k* borra-o oss1• borx k* bov b2.de* bros-gau mrc1 bry j cact a1 calc k* calc-sil mtf33 cann-s k* caust k* *Cham* k* chel j *Chin* b7.de* chord-umb rly4• cic j *Cina* k* **Cocc** k* coff k* *Con* k* cupr hr1* cycl k* dros j **Euph** b2.de* euphr ferr k* ferr-ar graph j grat haliae-lc srj5• ham fd3.de• hydrog srj2*• ign k* ignis-alc es2• iod k* ip j irid-met srj5• lac-lup hrn2• lach sf1.de **Led** k* lob mrr1 *Lyc* k* lyss a1 m-arct j mang j *Merc* k* mez mrr1 mur-ac naja k* *Nat-c* k* *Nat-m* mrr1 nat-p *Nat-s* mrr1 *Nux-m* k* nux-v j olnd k* op orig a1 ph-ac k* *Plat* k* plb k* positr nl2• puls k* rhus-g tmo3• rhus-t k* senec a1 seneg k* sep b2.de* sil mrr1 spig k* *Staph* b2.de* **Sul-ac** k* sulph k* symph fd3.de• **Thuj** k* til ulm-c jsj8• valer a1 verat k* [arg-p stj2 bar-i stj2 cadm-met stj2 cadm-s stj2 ind stj2 lith-i stj2 mang-i stj2 mang-m stj2 mang-met stj2 mang-p stj2 mang-s stj2 merc-i-f stj2 tax jsj7 tung-met stj2]
- **noon** | **amel.**: aeth a1
- **evening**: seneg thuj a1
- **absurdities**, over: *(↗Foolish)* anac bg2
- **alternating** with:
  - **cheerfulness** (See Cheerful - alternating - seriousness)
  - **jesting** (See Jesting - alternating - seriousness)
  - **laughing** (See Laughing - alternating - seriousness)
  - **mirth** (See Mirth - alternating - seriousness)
- **children**: aur mtf33 aur-m-n wbt2• ferr mtf33 sep mtf33
- **ludicrous** things, when seeing: anac

SERVANTS; desire to have: marb-w es1•

SERVILE (= obsequious, submissive): *(↗Comply; Fear - authority; Selflessness; Undignified; Yielding)* agar dgt2 cham h1 gard-j vlr2• *Gels* vh* lyc c1* m-arct c1 **Puls** c1* sil gl1.fr• staph mtf33 streptoc jl2 sulph gl1.fr• [bar-s stj1]

SEXUAL DESIRE (See FEMALE - Sexual desire; MALE - Sexual)

SEXUAL EXCESSES (See Ailments - mortification; Ailments - sexual excesses; Love - perversity)

SEXUAL-MINDED (See FEMALE - Sexual desire - increased; MALE GENITALIA/SEX - Sexual desire - increased)

SHAMEFUL: *(↗Ailments - shame; Reproaching oneself)* fum ↓ hyos mrr1 *Ign* b7.de plut-n srj7• tritic-vg fd5.de tub ↓ [heroin sdj2]
- **children**; in: tub
- **femininity**; about: fum rly1•
- **sexuality**; about: *(↗Confusion - identity - sexual)* fum rly1•

SHAMELESS: *(↗Delirium - erotic; Dress - indecently; Fancies - lascivious; Hysteria - lascivious; Indifference - exposure; Insanity - erotic; Lascivious; Lewdness; Libertinism; Naked; Nymphomania; Obscene; Satyriasis)* aids nl2• alco a1 *Anac* bg2* androc srj1• bell k* *Bufo* bg2* bung-fa ↓ calc camph bg2 cann-xyz bg2 canth k* cub cupr hell k* **Hyos** k* lyc gl1.fr• merc-c k* mosch murx bg2 nat-m nux-m k* *Nux-v* k* *Op* k* **Phos** k* phyt k* *Plat* bg2* positr nl2• sabin bg2 **Sec** staph **Stram** k* *Tarent* *Tub* st* **Verat** k* [cadm-met stj2 cadm-s stj2]
- **bed**, in: *Nat-m* k*
- **children**, in: bufo mtf33 op mtf33 phos mtf33 stram mtf33 *Tub* st*
- **delivery**, during: verat
- **exposing**: *(↗Lascivious; Naked - exhibitionism)*
  - **person**; the: *(↗Lascivious; Naked - exhibitionism)* **Hyos** k* *Phos* k* phyt k* *Sec* k* stram bg2 *Tarent* k* verat st
  - **breasts**; the: bung-fa mtf

- **masturbation**; during: bufo bg2

SHAVING agg.: calad bg2*

SHINING objects:
- **agg.**: *(↗Delusions - objects - bright; Rage - shining; GENERALS - Shining)* **Bell** bufo k* camph cann-i *Canth* glon sf1.de *Hyos* irid-met srj5• lach **Lyss** phos *Stram*
- **aversion** to: bufo lp* irid-met srj5•
- **surface** of water agg.: *(↗Hydrophobia)* irid-met srj5• **Lyss** **Stram** vh*

SHIT, feels like (See Discontented - himself - good)

SHIVERING; during: caps b7.de ruta b7.de

SHORTCOMINGS: | **society** of (See Disgust - society)

SHORT TEMPERED (See Irritability)

SHOUTING (See Shrieking)

SHRIEKING: *(↗Howling; Lamenting; Mania - shrieking; Shrieking - rage; Weeping)* absin a1 acon k* aeth bg2 agar k* agav-t jl3 ail alco a1 allox tpw4 aloe ↓ alum am-c ↓ ambr vh *Aml-ns* ↓ amyg kr1 *Anac* k* androc srj1*• ant-c k* *Ant-t* bg2* **Apis** k* *Apoc* ↓ arg-met k* arn k* ars k* *Art-v* ↓ arum-m a1 arum-t k* atra-r ↓ atro k* *Aur* k* aur-ar k2 *Aur-m* k* bac ↓ bad bg2 bamb-a ↓ *Bell* k* benz-ac ↓ bism-sn ↓ bomb-chr ↓ *Borx* k* bov ↓ bry k* bufo gk cact a1* calad k* *Calc* k* calc-hp sf1.de *Calc-p* k* calc-s ↓ calc-sil ↓ **Camph** k* cann-i a1 *Canth* k* *Caps* ↓ carb-ac k* carb-an k* carb-v k* carbn-o carbn-s carc mlr1• cartl-s rly4• caste ↓ castm j5.de *Caust* k* *Cedr* k* cench k2* *Cham* k* chel ↓ *Chin* k* chinin-s ↓ chlam-tr ↓ chlol a1* (non:chlor a1) chol ↓ **Cic** k* cimic ↓ *Cina* k* cinnm ↓ cocc k* coff k* *Coloc* ↓ con ↓ corv-cor bdg• croc crot-c k* crot-h bg2 **Cupr** k* *Cupr-act* j5.de* cupr-ar k* cycl ↓ cypr ↓ dendr-pol sk4• *Dig* ↓ diph-pert-t mp4• dor ↓ dulc k* elaps k* equis-a sf1.de erig ↓ eup-per a1 eup-pur a1* euph ↓ ferr-p bg2* *Fl-ac* ↓ fuma-ac rly4• *Gels* germ-met ↓ *Glon* k* gran ↓ graph ↓ *Guaj* ↓ haliae-lc srj5• ham ↓ *Hell* k* *Hep* ↓ hydr bg hydr-ac bg2* hydroph ↓ *Hyos* k* hyper bg2* *Ign* k* inul ↓ *Iodof* bg2 *Ip* k* irid-met ↓ *Jal* j5.de* *Jatr-c* ↓ kali-ar k* kali-bi k* *Kali-br* bg2* **Kali-c** k* kali-chl ↓ *Kali-i* ↓ kali-n ↓ kali-p k* kali-s ketogl-ac rly4• kreos sf1.de lac-ac ↓ lac-c bg2* *Lac-cp* ↓ *Lac-e* hrn2• lac-mat ↓ lach b7.de* lat-m k* laur k* lepi a1 levo ↓ lil-t bg2* limest-b ↓ lith-c ↓ **Lyc** k* lyss hr1 mag-c k* *Mag-m* ↓ mag-p ptk1 melal-alt ↓ meny ↓ merc k* merc-c ↓ merc-meth a1 meth-ae-ae a1 *Moni* rfm1• morg-g ↓ mosch bg2 naja ↓ *Nat-c* ↓ nat-m ↓ nit-ac nitro-o a1 nux-m bg2 nux-v k* *Oena* ↓ olnd k* op b7.de* **Pareir** ↓ pert jl2 *Phos* k* **Plat** k* plb k* plb-chr c1* plut-n ↓ podo sf1.de positr nl2• prot ↓ psor al puls k* rad-br sze8• ran-s *Rheum* k* *Rhus-t* ↓ rib-ac ↓ rubd-met ↓ ruta fd4.de samb k* sanic c1 sars sf1.de sec b7.de* seneg k* *Senn* st sep k* sil k* sol-ni spig ↓ spong fd4.de stann ↓ staph ↓ **Stram** k* streptoc rly4• stront-c ↓ *Stry* suis-pan rly4• sul-ac a1 *Sulph* k* syph ptk1 tanac k* tarent k* ter ↓ thal jl3 thuj bg2* toxi ↓ tritic-vg ↓ *Tub* k* urol-h ↓ vac a1 valer a1 vanil fd5.de **Verat** k* verat-v ptk1 viol-t b7.de* vip bg2* *Zinc* k* [ant-met stj2 arg-n stj2 arg-p stj2 ars-met stj2 bar-br stj2 bar-i stj2 brom stj2 cadm-m stj2 cadm-met stj2 cadm-s stj2 cupr-f stj2 cupr-m stj2 cupr-p stj2 ferr stj2 ferr-f stj2 ind stj2 iod stj2 lith-i stj2 mang-i stj2 merc-i-f stj2 moly-met stj2 niob-met stj2 osm-met stj2 rhodi stj2 ruth-met stj2 sel stj2 stront-m stj2 stront-met stj2 techn stj2 tell stj2 thal-met stj2 yttr-met stj2 zinc-i stj2 zinc-m stj2 zinc-n stj2 zinc-p stj2 zirc-met stj2]
- **agg.** other complaints: ant-t b7a.de *Arn* b7.de* cham b7a.de *Verat* b7a.de
- **day** and night: stram k2*
- **evening**: sanic ↓ verat a1
  - **21 h** | **21-0 h**: sanic c1
- **night**: ant-t a1 bell a1 calc h2* carc fb* cypr sf1.de hyos a1 jal sf1.de kreos hr1* lac-ac ↓ mag-c a1 sanic c1* stram a1 [lith-c stj2]
  - **midnight**: lac-ac a1
- **abdomen**; with complaints of: cupr bg2 hyos bg2 ip bg2 viol-t bg2
- **aid**; for (See help)
- **alternating** with:
  - **cheerfulness**: chin bg2*
  - **complaining**: bufo a1
  - **indifference**: sulph hr1
  - **laughing**: kali-p k2* mosch st1 stram hr1 tarent bg [rubd-met stj2]
  - **unconsciousness**: *Apis* kr1 bell k* *Rheum* kr1 tub hr1 *Zinc* vh*
- **anger**, in: arn bg castm j5.de cham j5.de* crot-c sk4• *Dulc* fd4.de fuma-ac rly4• ham fd3.de• *Iod* hr1 irid-met srj5• *Lac-cp* sk4• *Lac-e* hrn2• limest-b es1• melal-alt gya4 nux-v ptk1 plut-n srj7• positr nl2• prot fmm1• puls j5.de ruta fd4.de spong fd4.de tritic-vg fd5.de vanil fd5.de zinc bg*

Shrieking: ...
- **anguish**, from: *(↗Anguish)* lat-m jl3
- **anxiety**, from: calc j5.de chinin-s j5.de cocc h1* *Hyos* j5.de *Lyc* j5.de mosch j plat j ran-s j5.de stann j
- **approaches** bed, when anyone: *Ign* hr1*
- **brain** cry (= cri encéphalique): *Aml-ns* kr1 **Apis** k* arn k* ars *Art-v* hr1* bell k* calc-hp sf1.de canth a1 *Carb-ac* *Cham* hr1* cic coff a1 crot-c a1 cupr *Cupr-act* kr1 cupr-ar a1 dig k* dulc k* *Glon* k* *Hell* k* *Hyos* k* ign hr1* *Kali-br* bg2* *Kali-i* k* *Lyc* k* *Merc* bg2* merc-c phos plb a1 *Rhus-t* k* sol-ni stram sulph k* *Zinc* k*
- **cannot**; wants to scream, but: am-m ptk1 *Stram* hr1*
- **cephalic** (See brain)
- **cheerful** mood; causeless shrieking during: *Chin* h1*
- **child**; like a: cupr b7.de*
- **children**, in: acon bg2 aeth hr1* ail k2* anac k* ant-c ↓ ant-t ↓ *Apis* k* *Arn* ↓ bell k* benz-ac **Borx** k* brom ↓ calc k* *Calc-p* k* camph gl1.fr• carc mlr1• caste jl3 *Cham* k* *Chlol* ↓ *Cina* cinnm ↓ coff k* cupr k* cypr ↓ dor dulc *Glon* hr1* *Hell* hyos ↓ *Ign* k* inul ↓ ip k* *Jal* k* kali-br kali-c ↓ *Kali-p* hr1* *Kreos* k* **Lac-c** k* lyc mag-c mg1.de mag-m ↓ *Moni* rfm1• *Nux-v* hr1* op wbt• phos mtf33 prot fmm1• psor al2 puls bg2 *Rheum* k* sanic c1* *Senn* sil st1 spong fd4.de staph ↓ stram k* **Sulph** ↓ syph c1* ter ↓ thuj ↓ **TUB** st1 *Valer* br1 vanil fd5.de verat mtf33 zinc ↓
  - **day** and night: calc st1
  - **evening**: **Cina** kr1 cinnm hr1* zinc sf1.de
  - **night**: ant-t a1 calc h2* carc mlr1* *Cham* hr1* *Chlol* gl1.fr• cypr br1 jal c1* *Kali-p* hr1* *Lac-c* hr1* nux-v a1 psor hr1* rheum st sanic mtf33 ter sne
  - **causeless**: verat mtf33
  - **colic** with: *Cham* hr1* *Nux-v* hr1*
  - **consolation**: | **agg.**: ant-c tl1 bell kr1 cham tl1
  - **fearfully**: kali-br tl1
  - **fist** in mouth; with: ip h1* vanil fd5.de
  - **looked** at; when: *(↗Looked - cannot - children)* brom mtf33
  - **moved**; when: zinc ptk1*
  - **nursed**, when being: borx st*
  - **sleep**, during: ant-c mtf33 ant-t a1 **Apis** kr1 *Arn* hr1* bell hr1* borx h2* calc ↓ *Calc-p* hr1* carc mlr1* caste jl3 cina mtf33 hell al hyos mtf33 *Ign* hr1* inul hr1* jal j **Kali-br** hr1 lac-c mtf33 *Lyc* hr1* mag-c mtf33 mag-m mtf33 *Psor* st1* **Puls** hr1* rheum j senn j sil j **Sulph** hr1* *Tub* hr1* verat mtf33 zinc mtf33
    - **dreams**; from disturbing: borx mrr1 calc tl1 carc mlr1•
    - **sobbing**; and: hyos ptk1*
  - **spoken** to, when: sil k2*
  - **stool**:
    - **before**: borx ptk1 kreos ptk1
    - **during**: aeth sne *Cham* b7a.de *Kreos* k* **Rheum** kr1 valer ptk1
    - **urging** to; during: **Rheum** st
  - **touched**, when: *(↗Touched - aversion)* ant-t k* cina j mag-c mtf33
  - **waking**, on: borx hr1* cina hr1 ign ↓ **Kali-br** hr1* kali-c hr1 lyc hr1 sanic c1* staph mtf33 sulph hr1 thuj mtf33 zinc ↓
    - **diarrhea**; during: sulph mtf33
    - **trembling**; with: ign ptk1* zinc mtf33
  - **weeping**; and: cham gl1.fr• lac-c ↓ nux-v gl1.fr• psor ↓ rheum ↓
    - **always**: lac-c ptk1 psor ptk1 rheum ptk1
- **chorea**, in: chlol hr1* cina hr1 *Cupr-act* kr1 *Ign* hr1* *Stram* hr1* *Zinc* hr1*
- **convulsions**:
  - **after**: plb k* sil k*
  - **before**: *Aml-ns* *Apis* k* art-v *Bell* k* *Bufo* calc camph canth cedr **Cic** k* *Cina* k* crot-c **Cupr** k* *Hell* bro1 hydr-ac bg2* hyos *Ip* *Kali-br* *Lach* laur *Lyc* nit-ac nux-v *Oena* *Op* k* phos plb sil *Stram* stry *Sulph* verat-v k* *Zinc* k*
  - **between**: bell h1* kali-bi gt1*
  - **during**: acon j5.de *Aml-ns* kr1 ant-t j5.de *Apis* kr1* *Art-v* hr1* bell j5.de* calc h2* *Camph* hr1* canth j5.de *Caust* j5.de* cedr kr1 *Cic* j5.de* *Cina* j5.de* *Crot-h* j5.de* *Cupr* hr1* *Hell* bro1 hyos j5.de* ign hr1 ip j5.de* kali-bi gt1* lach j5.de* *Lyc* h2* *Merc* j5.de* nit-ac kr1 *Nux-v* j5.de* oena sf1.de **Op** j5.de* stann kr1 *Stram* hr1* sulph h2* verat-v kr1 vip j5.de *Zinc* hr1*
  - **epileptic**: *(↗GENERALS - Convulsions - epileptic - during)* *Bufo* kr1 calc h2 cedr kr1 **Cic** h1* crot-h kr1 *Cupr* kr1* hydr-ac sf1.de

- • **epileptic**: ... **Hyos** kr1* ign kr1 *Ip* kr1 *Kali-bi* hr1* *Lach* kr1 *Lyc* b4a.de* nit-ac kr1 *Nux-v* kr1 *Oena* hr1* op kr1 *Sil* hr1* stann kr1 stram kr1* sulph h2* verat-v kr1
- • **puerperal**: ars kr1 *Hyos Iod* kali-c *Lach* hr1* plat puls stram
- **cough**:
- • **after**: cina bg2
- • **agg.**: arn bg2* bell bg2* **Bry** ptk1* caps bg2 chin b7a.de* cina bg2* *Hep* bg2* kali-c mrr1 op b7.de* samb b7.de* sep b4a.de* verat b7a.de
- **cramps**, during: *Cupr* sf1.de *Jatr-c* ↓ *Lyc* ↓ *Mag-p* ↓ plb ↓
- ○ • **Abdomen**; in: cupr k* *Jatr-c* kr1 *Lyc* kr1 *Mag-p* kr1* plb sf1.de
- **delusions**:
- • **from**: ars hr1* kali-c j5.de plat j5.de puls j5.de stram j5.de
- • **with**: canth j5.de hyos j5.de *Stram* j5.de* verat j5.de
- **dentition**, during: *(↗TEETH - Dentition - difficult)* *Apis* kr1 calc-p mrr1 cham mrr1 *Kreos* hr1* *Rheum* kr1 ter hr1*
- **drinking**:
- • **water**: canth br1
- • **while**: nux-v k*
- **drunkenness**, during: caust hyos ign stram
- **dying**; thinks she will be: *(↗Death - sensation)* lat-m gm1 naja ↓
- • **breath**; and looses her: naja gm1
- **face**; with complaints of: acon bg2
- **fever**, during: acon bg2 *Bell* b4a.de* bry bg2 *Caps* b7a.de* cham bg2 coff bg2 cupr bg2 ip bg2 *Lyc* j5.de* op bg2 plat bg2 puls bg2 **Stram** bg2* verat bg2
- ○ - **Genitals**; with grasping of *(↗Tearing - himself - genitals; MALE GENITALIA/SEX - Handling - tearing)* acon ptk1*
- **help**; for: *(↗Delirium - crying - help; Delusions - help; Delusions - help - calling; Helplessness)* *Camph* kr1* hep ↓ *Ign* kr1* kali-c h2 *Laur* kr1 levo jl plat k* plb a rhus-t ↓ stram sk7•
- • **jumping** up from bed: hep j5.de rhus-t j5.de
- • **sleep**; in: hep j5.de kali-c j5.de rhus-t j5.de
- **hiccough**; with: cic ptk1
- **high** pitched: diph-pert-t mp4•
- **hoarse**: bell kr1 stram kr1
- **holds** on to something; shrieking unless she: **SEP** k ●*
- **hydrocephalus**, in: **Apis** kr1 *Cina* kr1 *Dig* hr1* kali-i hr1* *Lyc* hr1* merc hr1* *Zinc* hr1*
- **imaginary** appearances, about: *Kali-c* hr1*
- **inconsolable**: diph-pert-t mp4•
- **interrupting** unconsciousness; shrieking (See alternating - unconsciousness)
- **involuntarily**: hydr-ac ptk1*
- **jumping** out of bed; and: chlol gm1
- **laughing**: | **after**: tarent a1*
- **locomotive**, like a: nux-m st1
- **loudly**: anac ↓ hydr-ac ptk1 plb gk
- • **someone**; as if calling: anac tl1*
- **lower** limbs; with complaints of: coff bg2 lach bg2
- **mania** (See Mania - shrieking)
- **meningitis**; during: apis mrr1
- **menses**:
- • **after**: *(↗Menses - after)* aur bg1*
- • **before**: *(↗Menses - before)* germ-met srj5• *Sep* **Tub** ckh1
- • **during**: *(↗Menses - during)* *Cocc* hr1* *Coff* b7a.de *Coloc* hr1* cupr
- • **suppressed** menses; from: cupr b7a.de
- **must** shriek; feels as though she: adam srj5• *Anac* k* androc srj1• apis ars kr1 aur *Calc* k* calc-p chel ↓ cic cina *Elaps* k* haliae-lc srj5• hell irid-met srj5• kali-c j5.de *Lil-t* k* limest-b es1• merc mrr1 nux-v plat j5.de *Sep* k* sil stann stram j5.de [tax jsj7]
- • **causeless**: chel ptk1
- **nausea**; with: ars bg2
- **obstinate**: *(↗Obstinate)* *Cham* sf1.de sanic c1*
- **pain**, with the: *(↗Delirium - pains - with; Despair - pains; Sensitive - pain; Weeping - pains - with)* **ACON** bg2* alum ↓ apis ptk1* *Apoc* vh1 *Ars* k* atra-r bnm3• atro a1 aur hr1 bamb-a stb2.de• **Bell** k* borx ↓ bov a1 bry k2* **Cact** k* calc-p k2 *Canth* a1 caps h1* **CHAM** bg2* chin ↓ cic bg2* cimic ↓ coff k1* *Coloc* k* cupr ptk1 gels bg2* hep ↓ hyos ↓ kali-c ↓ kali-chl ↓ kali-n h2* lach ↓
- **pain**, with the: ... lat-m br1* mag-c h2* mag-m h2* mag-p bg* nit-ac gk op **Plat** k* plb bg2* podo bg2* puls k* *Sep* hr1* spig ↓ thal dx zinc k2*
- • **inspiration**; on: kali-c mrr1
- ○ • **Abdomen**: hyos bro1 kali-chl a1* lat-m bnm6•
- • **Bladder**: borx mrr1
- • **Ear**: bell mrr1 cham mrr1 hep mrr1 lach mrr1
- • **Feet**: spig h1*
- • **lumbar** region: alum h2 chin h1
- • **labor**-like: cimic bg2
- **paroxysmal**: canth br1 **Cupr** b7a.de *Ign* b7.de* *Lyc* hr1* *Op* b7a.de
- **perspiration**; during: arn bg2 **Bell** bg2 calc bg2 *Camph* bg2 *Cham* bg2 **Cupr** bg2 lyc bg2 **Op** bg2 phos bg2 plat bg2 rheum bg2 stram bg2
- **piercing**: apis br1
- **pleased**; hard to be: *(↗Discontented)* ip ptk1*
- **rage**; during: *(↗Shrieking)* *Anac* kr1 *Bell* kr1* canth j5.de cupr sf1.de hyos j5.de lach sf1.de plb kr1 sec j5.de sol-ni j5.de stram j5.de* *Verat* j5.de*
- **respiration**; with difficult: tarent mtf33
- **restlessness**; with | **night**: jal bg2
- **runs** shrieking through house: bufo kr1 calc rb2
- **sleep**, during: *Agar* bg2* alum h2* am-c k* anac k* ant-c bro1* *Ant-t* b7.de* *Apis* k* *Arg-met* arn k* *Aur* k* bac c1 *Bell* k* bomb-chr mlk9.de **Borx** k* *Bry* k* bufo bg2 calc k* *Calc-hp* bg2* *Calc-p* k* calc-sil k2* camph a1 cann-i a1 *Caps* k* carb-ac carb-an h2* carb-v ↓ carc fb* cartl-s rly4• *Castm* j5.de caust k* *Cham* k* chel chin b7.de* chlam-tr ↓ chlol hr1* *Cic* bro1* *Cina* k* cocc k* croc b7.de* *Cupr-act* bro1 cycl a1* cypr bro1 dig bro1 dor a1* dulc euph k* *Fl-ac* k* gran j5.de* graph h2* *Guaj* *Hell* k* *Hep* k* hydroph rsj6• *Hyos* b7.de* *Ign* bg2* inul hr1* iodof bro1 ip *Kali-br* k1* kali-c h2* kreos *Lac-c* hr1* **Lyc** k* *Mag-c* k* *Mag-m* k* merc hr1 morg-g pte1*• *Nat-c* h2* nat-m k* nit-ac nux-m bro1 op k* phos k* plat j5.de psor bro1* **Puls** k* *Rheum* b7.de* rhus-t ↓ ruta b7a.de sep k* *Sil* k* spong bro1 stram k* stront-c k* stry a1 suis-pan rly4• sul-ac j5.de *Sulph* k* thuj k* toxi ↓ **Tub** hr1* urol-h rwt• *Verat* hr1* **Zinc** k* zinc-p k2* [bism-sn stj2 lac-mat sst4]
- • **dreams**; from disturbing: borx mrr1 chlam-tr bcx2• toxi mtf2•
- • **eyes**; with trembling and fixed: ant-t ptk1*
- • **jumping** out of bed and shrieking for aid: hep j5.de rhus-t j5.de
- • **menses** | **before**: *(↗Menses - before)* carb-v sep sul-ac **Tub** vh* *Zinc*
- **someone**; as if calling: aloe ptk1* *Anac* hr1*
- **stomach**; with complaints of: cham bg2 cupr bg2
- **stool**:
- • **before**: borx h2 kreos ckh1 rheum b7.de* rhus-t b7.de*
- • **during**: canth a1 carb-v h2* **Cham** bg2 *Ip* bg2 kreos bg* **Rheum** bg2 *Sulph* bg2 valer ckh1
- • **curdled** stool; with: valer ptk1
- **stupor** in: hyos ckh1
- **sudden**: apis br1* *Bell* bro1 borx bro1 bry bro1 calc bro1 cham bro1 chin h1* *Cic* bro1 *Cina* bro1 cypr bro1 gels bro1 *Hell* bro1 iodof bro1 kali-br bro1 *Kali-c* hr1* limest-b es1• plb ptk1* stram a1* tub bro1 vanil fd5.de verat bro1 *Zinc* bro1
- **thunderstorm**, during: *(↗Weather - thunderstorm - during)* gels
- **touched**, when: *(↗Touched - aversion)* *Acon* hr1* ant-c sf1.de* ant-t a1* **Arn** k2 canth ↓ hyos ckh1 *Iod* hr1 kali-c ptk1 *Merc* hr1* ruta ptk1 stram ptk1* stry a1
- • **plaintively** shrieking in stupor: hyos ptk1
- • **larynx**; at: canth br1
- **trembling**; with: bell bg2
- **trifles**, at: *(↗Trifles; Trifles - important)* **Kali-c** k* rib-ac jl3
- **unconscious**; until: bufo k2
- **unconsciousness** interrupted by shrieking (See alternating - unconsciousness)
- **urinary** organs; with complaints of: coff bg2
- **urination**:
- • **before**●: *(↗Weeping - urination - before; BLADDER - Urination - dysuria - painful - cry)* acon ptk1* **Borx** k* erig vml3• lach **Lyc** k* nux-v plb b sanic al* *Sars* k* thuj c1
- ⁝ **dentition**, during (See BLADDER - Urination - dysuria - dentition)
- • **during**: borx bg2 **Canth** bg2 erig ptk2* lyc bg2 **Pareir** bg2 sars bg2

- **waking**:
  - **on**: *(↗Clinging - child - awakens)* alum h2* apis k* arn j5.de ars h2* bell a1 *Bry* bg2* **Calc** mtf33 calc-s mtf33 *Caps* st* *Cham* k* chlol a1 chol a1 *Cina* k* con cupr-act c1 gels guaj *Hydr-ac* hr1* *Hyos* k* ign k* *Kali-br* bg2* *Kali-p* hr1* kali-s lach bjj1 *Lyc* k* *Mag-c* j5.de meny h1* phos j5.de rheum c2 ruta b7.de* samb xxb1 sanic c1 sep k* sil j5.de stram k* sulph k* thuj cd1 **Zinc** k*
  - **without** (See sleep)
- **head**; with complaints of: anac bg2 bov bg2 *Coloc* bg2 mag-m bg2 *Sep* bg2 sil bg2 stann bg2 stram bg2

SHY (See Timidity)

SICK feeling (See Delusions - sick - being)

SIESTA; after: calc bg2 carb-v bg2 caust bg2

SIGHING: *(↗Brooding; Dwells - past; Grief; Grunting; Lamenting; Moaning; Sadness; Weeping - sobbing; Weeping - whimpering; RESPIRATION - Sighing; RESPIRATION - Sobbing; RESPIRATION - Whistling)* acet-ac c1 **Acon** k* act-sp aether a1 agar k* agath-a nl2• ail k* alco a1 alum k* am-c k* aml-ns a1 anac androc srj1• ang ant-c c1* apoc bg* aq-mar rbp6 arg-n k* arge-pl rwt5• *Arn* ↓ ars sf1.de atro aur ↓ *Aur-m-n* wbt2• aur-s wbt2• bar-c ↓ **Bell** k* ben-n a1 bor-ac c1 **Bry** b7a.de* *Bufo* ↓ **Calc-p** k* **Camph** k* cann-xyz ↓ carb-ac carb-v ↓ carc mlr1• cedr kr1 *Cench* k1* cere-b a1 *Cham* k* chin k* chinin-s a1 chir-fl ↓ cic ↓ **Cimic** k* clem a1 cob a1* *Cocc* b7.de* *Coff* ↓ colch *Corn* kr1 cortico ↓ croc bg2 cupr cur der a1 dig k* dioxi rbp6 dream-p sdj1• elae a1 elec j* eup-per k2 *Eup-pur* hr1 ferr-m hr1 galv j gast a1 gels a1 germ-met srj5• *Glon* kr1 goss a1 gran a1 graph haliae-lc srj5• *Hell* b7.de* hura *Hydr-ac* ↓ hydrog srj2• hyos bg2 iber kr1* **Ign** k* **Ip** k* irid-met srj5• kali-cy a1 kali-p kali-s fd4.de *Lac-e* hrn2• *Lach* k* lact a1 lil-t kr1 loxo-recl knl4• *Lyc* bg2* lycps-v ↓ lyss a1* *M-arct* j macro a1 mag-c ↓ malar jl2 merc-c a1 mill mit a1 morph a1 mosch a1 mur-ac naja mtf33 nat-c k* nat-m vh* *Nat-p* c1* nit-ac nux-m a1 **Nux-v** bg2* olib-sac wmh1 **Op** k* oxal-a rly4• phos ↓ phys a1* plat k* plb k* podo c1 positr nl2• puls raja-s jl3 ran-s k* *Rhus-t* k* sacch-l c1* *Sars* ↓ *Sec* k* sel a1* *Sep* b4a.de* sil a1 spong bg2 stann sf1.de *Stram* k* sulph tab tax c1 teucr bg2 ther k* thuj ↓ til a1 trad a1 vanil fd5.de verat hr1 verat-v a1 vip a1 xan ↓ zinc hr1 zirc-met ↓ [helia stj7 heroin sdj2]
  - **forenoon**: germ-met srj5• ign ↓
    - **9**.30 h: ign a1
  - **afternoon**: ant-c a1
  - **evening**: chin a1 lycps-v ↓
    - **19** h: lycps-v a1
  - **night**: bry h1* ign ↓
    - **midnight**:
      - **after** | **2** h: ign a1
  - **abdomen**; with complaints in: ign bg2
  - **alternating** with:
    - **dancing** (See Dancing - alternating - sighing)
    - **jumping** (See Jumping - alternating - sighing)
  - **amel.**: *Lach* b7a.de
  - **causeless**: nux-v sf1.de* spong fd4.de
  - **children**; in: chir-fl bnm4• cupr mtf33 puls mtf33
  - **dinner**, after: arg-n a1
  - **epileptic** convulsions:
    - **after**: ign gk
    - **before**: *Bufo* kr1 cic sf1.de *Plb* kr1
  - **heat**, during: acon *Arn* ars bell k* bry carb-v kr1 *Cham* clem a1 cocc *Coff* *Ign* k* ip nux-v puls rhus-t *Sars* bg2 sep stram bg2 *Teucr* bg2 thuj verat bg2
  - ○ **Head**, of: clem a1
  - **honor**, from wounded: *Nux-v* hr1*
  - **hysteria**, in: *Hydr-ac* hr1* **Ign** hr1* *Plat* hr1*
  - **involuntary**: *Calc-p* a1* *Ferr-m* hr1* hell br1* **Ign** al*
  - **leukorrhea**; with: phys ptk1
  - **loud**: ign mrr1
  - **menopause**; during: xan vh*
  - **menses**:
    - **after**: *(↗Menses - after)* nat-p a1 stram
    - **before**: *(↗Menses - before)* *Ign* k* lyc k* nat-p a1
    - **during**: *(↗Menses - during)* ars cimic cocc graph ign nat-p a1 plat

Sighing – menses – during: ...
      - **amel.**: nat-p a1
    - **suppressed** menses; from: *Cocc* b7a.de
  - **old** people: ign mrr1
  - **pain**; from | **Stomach**: cupr bg2
  - **perspiration**, during: acon k* ars k* bar-c bg2 **Bry** k* *Cham* k* chin k* *Cocc* k* cupr k* *Ign* k* *Ip* k* nux-v k* phos k* *Rhus-t* k* *Sep* k* stram k* thuj verat k*
  - **prostration**; from mental and emotional: olib-sac wmh1
  - **respiration**; with complaints of: cocc bg2
  - **sadness**; with (See Sadness - sighing)
  - **shock** from injuries, in: *(↗Ailments - injuries)* *Lach* hr1*
  - **sleep**, in: anac h2* ars j5.de atro a1 aur h2* bell j5.de* camph b7.de* cann-xyz bg2 cortico tpw7 glon bg2 *Kali-p* hr1* *M-arct* j mag-c j5.de op b7.de* puls b7.de* stram b7a.de *Sulph* bg2* [zirc-met stj2]
    - **comatose**: ars j5.de
  - **throat**, with grasping at: **Stram** hr1*
  - **waking**, on: puls j5.de
  - **weeping**; continues long after: *Ign* kr1

SILENCE: | **soliciting** silence: *(↗Quiet; wants)* mosch a1

SILENT (See Grief - silent; Quiet disposition; Sadness - taciturn; Taciturn; Talking - loud)

SILENT GRIEF (See Grief - silent)

SIMPLE persons: *(↗Childish; Humility; Naive; Unrefined)* **Graph** mrr1

SINGING: *(↗Delirium - singing; Humility; Mania - singing; Obscene - songs; Weeping - singing; Whistling)* acon k* agar k* agath-a nl2• aids nl2• alco a1 aln vva1• anan a1* apis k* arg-met ↓ arizon-l nl2• arum-t ↓ aur j *Bell* k* cann-i k* cann-s k* cann-xyz bg2 caps k* carb-v ↓ *Carbn-s* caust mtf33 chin gl1.fr• chlf k* choc ↓ *Cic* k* coca-c sk4• *Cocc* k* cot a1 *Croc* k* cupr k* cupr-act a1 der k* dros ↓ ery-m ↓ eup-pur hr1 ferr-p ptk1 gels germ-met ↓ haliae-lc ↓ ham fd3.de• hep ↓ hipp hydr k* *Hyos* k* *Hyper* hr1 ina-i mlk9.de kali-br a1 kali-c k* kali-p ↓ kali-s fd4.de *Kola* stb3• lac-h ↓ lac-leo ↓ *Lach* k* lachn k* lact limest-b ↓ lob-c a1 lob-s lyc k* lyss k* *M-arct* j5.de mag-c k* manc marb-w es1• merc-i-f k* merl mez k* nat-c k* nat-m k* nat-ox rly4• nat-sil fd3.de• neon ↓ nept-m lsd2.fr nicc-met ↓ nit-ac nux-m k* *Nux-v* ↓ *Oci-sa* sk4• olib-sac wmh1 op k* ozone sde2• peti a1 petr-ra shn4• ph-ac phos k* pieri-b mlk9.de plac ↓ *Plat* k* plb a1* positr nl2• psil ft1 ruta fd4.de sacch-a fd2.de• sal-al blc1• sang ptk1 santin c1 sars sep *Spong* k* stann ↓ staph ↓ *Stram* k* sul-ac sulo-ac a1 sulph gl1.fr• symph fd3.de• tab k* tarent k* *Teucr* k* ther k* thres-a sze7• *Verat* k* verb ↓ [hydrog stj2 sel stj2]
  - **morning**: ery-m ↓ hydrog srj2• kali-p fd1.de• lac-leo ↓ nept-m lsd2.fr oci-sa sk4•
    - **waking**; on: ery-m a1 lac-leo sk4• nept-m lsd2.fr
  - **evening**: bell h1* nat-m a1 oci-sa sk4•
  - **night**: bell j5.de croc j5.de *M-arct* j5.de nicc-met ↓ ph-ac j5.de verat h1*
    - **midnight**: nicc-met sk4•
  - **agg.** complaints: arg-met ptk1* arum-t ptk1* carb-v ptk1 dros ptk1* ferr-p ptk1 hep ptk1 *Nux-v* b7.de* **Phos** ptk1 sang ptk1 sel ptk1* stann ptk1 verb ptk1
  - **alternating** with:
    - **anger** (See Anger - alternating - singing)
    - **confusion**: spong k*
    - **delirium** (See Delirium - gay - alternating - singing)
    - **distraction** (See confusion)
    - **dullness**: spong j5.de
    - **groaning** (See moaning)
    - **hatred** (See loathing)
    - **irritability** (See Irritability - alternating - singing)
    - **laughing** (See Laughing - alternating - singing)
    - **loathing** of work: spong
    - **moaning**: *Bell* k*
    - **moroseness** (See Morose - alternating - singing)
    - **quarreling** (See Quarrelsome - alternating - singing)
    - **quiet** disposition: aur j5.de bell kr1
    - **talking**: *Gels* hr1*

- **alternating** with: ...
  - **vexation** (See Irritability - alternating - singing)
  - **weeping**: *Acon* k* bell k* der k* stram k*
    - ⁝ **and** laughing: stram a1
- **amel.** complaints: positr nl2•
- **exhausted**; until: tarent mtf33
- **boisterous**: alco a1
- **children's** songs: lac-h sze9• plac rzf5•
- **dancing** and weeping; with: tarent k1
- **fever**, during: bell *Op* hr1* *Sars* bg stram k* teucr bg verat
- **headache**, with: ther k2*
- **hilarious** (= joyously): agar bg2 *Agath-a* nl2• aids nl2• choc srj3• haliae-lc srj5• ham fd3.de• hydrog srj2• kali-p fd1.de• *Nat-m* kr1 nat-sil fd3.de• neon srj5• olib-sac wmh1 op bg2 sacch-a fd2.de• verat gk*
  - **night**: verat k*
- **hoarse**, until very: carb-v gl1.fr• caust gl1.fr• lach gl1.fr• *Tarent* a1*
  - **exhausted**; and: *Tarent* a1*
- **inability** for: sil mtf33
- **involuntarily**: *Croc* k* lyc k* lyss k* spong bg2 tarent bg2* teucr k*
  - **hearing** a single note sung; on: *Croc* kr1*
- **joyously** (See hilarious)
- **Latin** paternoster: *Stram* hr1*
- **menses** | **during**: stram ptk1
- **monotonous**: *Op* hr1*
- **obscene** songs (See Obscene - songs)
- **octave** too high or low; one: germ-met srj5•
- **perspiration**; during: *Bell* bg2 croc bg2 kali-c bg2 spong bg2 *Stram* bg2 verat bg2
- **romantic** songs: *Oci-sa* sk4•
- **sadness**, after: merc-i-f kr1
- **shrieking** and weeping, followed by: *Hyper* kr1*
- **sleep**, in: bell k* *Croc* k* hyper a1 lach bg2 *M-arct* b7.de* ph-ac k* stram bg2 sulph bg2*
- **supper**, after: *Nat-c* gl1.fr•
- **trilling**: acon j5.de *Bell* j5.de cocc h1* lyc j5.de* mag-c j5.de nat-c j5.de* nux-v j5.de* phos j5.de staph j5.de* stram hr1 ther j5.de verat h1*
- **waking**, on: limest-b es1• *Sulph* hr1*

SITTING: (↗*GENERALS - Catalepsy)*

- **agg.**: am-c bg2 arg-met b7.de* asaf bg2 asar b7.de* bar-c b4.de* bell b4.de* calc b4.de* canth b7.de* carb-an bg2 caust bg2 cic b7.de* colch bg2 graph b4a.de* kali-c b4.de* mang b4.de* merc b4.de* nat-c b4.de* nit-ac bg2 phos b4.de* puls b7.de* rhus-t b7.de* sep b4.de* sil b4.de* thuj b4.de*
- **amel.**: bry bg2 croc b7.de* iod b4.de*
- **aversion** to sit: iod k* lach k*
- **inclination** to sit: (↗*Anxiety - sitting - amel.; Confusion - sitting; Disturbed; Fear - sitting; Impatience - sitting; Irritability - sitting; Laziness - sitting; Unconsciousness - sitting; GENERALS - Sitting - agg.; GENERALS - Sitting - amel.; GENERALS - Sitting - impulse)* acon *Agar* aloe sne alum alum-p k2 alum-sil ↓ am-c *Am-m* *Ambr* ↓ *Anac* androc srj1• ant-c ant-t arg-met arg-n *Arn* k* *Ars* k* *Ars-i* asar *Aur* aur-s k2 bar-act sf1.de bar-c k* bar-i k2 bar-m k* *Bell* k* borx brom k* bry calc *Calc-p* a1 calc-s ↓ calc-sil ↓ camph *Cann-s* canth caps ptk1 *Carb-v* k* *Carbn-s* caust cench ↓ *Cham* k* *Chel* k* **Chin** k* chinin-ar choc ↓ cimic k2 *Cocc* k* cod a1 colch coloc ↓ **Con** k* croc cupr cycl dream-p ↓ dulc elaps ↓ *Euphr* falco-pe ↓ *Ferr* fl-ac ↓ *Gels* ↓ glon ↓ **Graph** k* **Guaj** k* haliae-lc ↓ ham ↓ hell *Hep* **Hipp** hydrog srj2• *Hyos* ign *Iod* ip irid-met srj5• jac-c a1 kali-ar kali-br ↓ kali-c kali-m ↓ kali-p kali-s fd4.de kali-sil k2 lac-c k* lac-lup hrn2• lach lact j laur lil-t k2* lyc m-aust j mag-c mag-m mag-p ↓ merc k* mez mur-ac nat-ar a1* nat-c *Nat-m* k* nat-p nat-sil ↓ *Nit-ac* **Nux-v** k* ol-an c1 olnd op ozone ↓ petr *Ph-ac* **Phos** k* *Pic-ac* plat plb positr nl2• **Puls** k* ran-b *Ran-s* rheum rhod rhus-g ↓ rhus-t ruta sabin j sal-fr sle1• sanguis-s hrn2• *Sec* *Sep* sil *Spong* **Squil** k* *Stann* k* staph j *Stram* ↓ *Stront-c* sul-ac ↓ sul-i k2 *Sulph* *Tarax* *Teucr* thala ↓ tritic-vg fd5.de vanil fd5.de *Verat* verb viol-t *Zinc* zinc-p ↓ [bell-p-sp dcm1 buteo-j sej6]
  - **bed**; in | **lies** down; and suddenly: *Hyos* ptk1
  - **breaks** pins; and: (↗*Breaking)* **Bell** k* calc k2*
  - **elbows** on knees, bent double; with: coloc ms
  - **erect**: cham bg2 hyos bg2 lyc a1 puls bg2 stram bg2*
  - **head** on hands and elbows on knees; with: glon iod k*

Sitting – inclination to sit: ...
  - **lie** down; sitting in bed and will not: (↗*GENERALS - Lie - will)* kali-br ptk1*
  - **looking** at the ground: stram ptk1
  - **meadow**; in open: rhus-g tmo3•
  - **meditates**, and: (↗*Absorbed; Meditating)* calc ↓ calc-s k* haliae-lc srj5• ham fd3.de• irid-met srj5• kali-s fd4.de lach a1 lil-t ↓ nat-sil fd3.de• positr nl2• ruta fd4.de
    - ⁝ **misfortunes**; over imaginary: calc-s ptk1 lil-t ptk1
    - ⁝ **trifles**; about: calc ptk1
  - **muse**; and: ham st irid-met srj5•
  - **observe** world go by; and: lac-lup hrn2•
  - **place**; on same:
    - ⁝ **headache**; for three or four days during: con
    - ⁝ **looks** into space and does not answer when spoken to: calc-sil mtf33
  - **silent** (See still)
  - **stare**; and: (↗*Staring)* puls mtf33 sanguis-s hrn2•
  - **stiff**, quite: (↗*Taciturn - sits)* *Cham* k* *Hyos* k* kali-c mrr1 kali-m ptk1 nat-p ↓ puls k* *Sep* k* *Stram* k*
    - ⁝ **delirium**, in: sep a1
    - ⁝ **long** time; for a: nat-p ptk1
  - **still**: alum h2 alum-p k2 alum-sil k2 arn aur aur-s k2 bar-c k2 bar-i k2 bar-m k2 brom k* calc k2 calc-sil k2 carbn-s k2 cham k* chinin-ar choc srj3• cimic k2 *Cocc* k* con h2* dulc fd4.de elaps falco-pe nl2• fl-ac k2* *Gels* k* haliae-lc srj5• ham a1 hell k* *Hep* k* **Hipp** hyos k2 ign mtf33 irid-met srj5• kali-ar k2 kali-m k2 kali-sil k2 lyc k2 mag-p ptk1 nat-ar k2 nat-p k2 nat-sil fd3.de• *Nux-v* kr1 ol-an c1 *Pic-ac* k2* *Plat* k* positr nl2• **Puls** k* sal-fr sle1• *Sep* k* spong fd4.de stram thala jl vanil fd5.de **Verat** k1* zinc-p k2
    - ⁝ **corner**; in a: hep ptk1
  - **weeping**: (↗*Weeping)* *Ambr* k* calc-sil k2 cycl c1 puls j sep mtf33 sul-ac hr1 verat a1
  - **wrapped** in deep, sad thoughts and notices nothing; as if: (↗*Absorbed; Dream; as; Introspection; Meditating)* *Ambr* st arn ptk1 aur cench k2 cham h1 cimic k2 *Cocc* k* dream-p sdj1• dulc fd4.de elaps hep ↓ *Hipp* ign mtf33 *Kali-s* fd4.de ozone sde2• plat ptk1 *Puls* k* sal-fr sle1• *Spong* fd4.de *Stram* kr1 *Verat* k*
    - ⁝ **vertigo**; during: hep h1*

SIZE:

- **frame** seems lessened, of: phys
- **incorrect** judgement of: (↗*Delusions - body - diminished; Delusions - diminished - all; Delusions - enlarged - body - parts; Delusions - enlarged - distances; Delusions - enlarged - objects; Delusions - expanding - passersby; Delusions - large - parts; Delusions - large - surroundings; Delusions - small - things - appear; Distances - exaggerated; Distances - inaccurate; Mistakes - measure; VERTIGO - Objects - far; VISION - Large - objects; VISION - Small)* agar k* cann-i mrr1 chinin-s a1 stram

SKEPTICAL (See Doubtful - skeptical)

SLANDER, disposition to: (↗*Abusive; Censorious; Cursing; Deceitful; Disobedience; Envy; Gossiping; Hypocrisy; Impolite; Insolence; Jealousy; Liar; Moral; Rudeness; Untruthful)* am-c anac *Ars* k* bell borx caust vh* cor-r j5.de germ-met srj5• guaj j helon gl1.fr• hyos k* ip lach vh* lyc merc j5.de* nat-c ↓ nat-m ↓ nit-ac *Nux-v* par sf1.de petr phos ↓ sep spig gl1.fr• stram **Verat** k*

- **denounce**: ars gl1.fr• lach gl1.fr• nat-c gl1.fr• nat-m gl1.fr•
- **hypocritical**, and: phos gl1.fr• sep gl1.fr•
- **sneak**: ars gl1.fr• lach gl1.fr• nat-c gl1.fr•

SLEEP:

- **after**: *Acon* b7a.de ambr b7.de* anac b4.de* arn b7a.de ars b4.de* bar-c b4a.de bell b4.de* berb bg2 *Bry* b7.de* calc b4.de* *Camph* b7a.de caps bg2 carb-v b4.de* cham b7.de* chin bg2 con b4.de* euphr bg2 gels bg2 graph b4.de* hep b4a.de* hydr-ac bg2 *Lyc* b4a.de m-arct b7.de op b7.de* petr bg2 puls b7.de* *Rheum* b7a.de sabad b7.de* sang bg2 squil b7.de* stann b4.de* *Staph* b7a.de sulph bg2 tab bg2 *Zinc* bg2
- **before** falling asleep: calad b7.de* rhus-t b7.de*

- **during**: acon b7.de* *Apis* bg2 *Arn* b7.de* bell bg2 *Borx* bg2 *Bry* b7.de* camph b7.de* *Cham* b7.de* chin bg2 cocc bg2 croc bg2 hell b7.de* ign b7.de* ip b7.de* led b7.de* *Lyc* bg2 m-arct b7.de meny b7.de* merc-i-r bg2 nux-v b7.de* op b7.de* ph-ac bg2 *Puls* b7.de* rheum b7.de* rhus-t bg2 *Spong* b7.de* stram b7.de* verat b7.de* **Zinc** bg2
  - **half** asleep; while | **amel.**: sel b7a.de
- **falling** asleep; when: bry b7a.de carb-an b4a.de spong b7a.de
- **loss** of sleep: ambr b7a.de* bry b7a.de* chin b7.de* colch b7.de* ferr bg2 kali-c bg2 *Nit-ac* bg2 *Nux-v* b7.de* op bg2 ph-ac bg2 phos bg2 puls b7a.de* rhod bg2 ruta b7a.de* sel b7.de* sulph bg2 zinc bg2

SLEEPINESS agg.: aloe bg2 ars bg2 bov bg2 euphr bg2 gels bg2 lach b7.de* led bg2 rhus-t bg2

SLEEPLESSNESS agg.: acon bg2 agar bg2 arn bg2 *Ars* bg2 bar-c bg2 *Bell* bg2 bry bg2 carb-an bg2 carb-v bg2 caust bg2 *Cham* bg2 chin bg2 cocc bg2 *Coff* bg2 con bg2 cupr bg2 ferr bg2 graph bg2 *Hep* bg2 *Hyos* bg2 kali-bi bg2 kali-c bg2 laur bg2 mag-c bg2 *Merc* bg2 nat-c bg2 nat-m bg2 nit-ac bg2 ran-b bg2 ran-s bg2 sabin bg2 sep bg2 sil bg2 sulph bg2 thuj bg2 verat bg2

SLOVENLY (See Absentminded; Dirty; Forgetful; Heedless; Untidy)

SLOWNESS•: (↗*Answering - slowly; Bed - remain; Concentration - difficult; Dullness; Hurried - cannot; Ideas - deficiency; Prostration; Speech - slow; Talking - slow; GENERALS - Sluggishness)* acon↓ adam↓ aeth h1* *Aids* nl2• all-c br1 aloe br1 am-m c1 ambr br1* ammc *Anac* k* androc srj1• aq-mar jl3* arb-m oss1• ars k* **Asar** k* *Bamb-a* stb2.de* **Bar-c** ptk1* bell bell-p jl3 bros-gau mrc1 brucel↓ **Bry** bg2* bufo mrr1 cact k* *Calc* k* *Carb-v* k* carc mtf33 *Cardios-h* rly4• cartl-s rly4• caust chel k2* *Chin* k* chinin-s↓ choc srj3• chord-umb rly4• clem c1 *Cocc* bg2* colch b **Con** k* conin a1 cortico sp1* cortiso sp1* crot-h↓ cupr k* cypra-eg sde6.de• diaz↓ diphtox↓ dream-p sdj1• dulc c1 echi ptk1 ergot jl3 falco-pe↓ ferr-ma j5.de* flor-p rsj3* galeoc-c-h↓ galla-q-r nl2• gels sf1.de germ-met stj2*• gink-b sbd1• *Graph* k* halo jl3 **Hell** k* hep c1 hist sp1* hydrog srj2* hyos gl1.fr• ign ip k* irid-met srj5• kali-bi bg2* *Kali-br* bg2* kali-m ptk1 kali-p fd1.de* *Kola* stb3• kreos c1 lach gl1.fr• laur bg2 **Lec** sne lil-t a1 lyc bg2 lycps-v ptk1 m-arct meph jl3 merc c1* nat-chl br1 nat-m j5.de* nux-m nux-v gl1.fr• olib-sac↓ olnd ptk1 onop jl3 onos ptk1 op k* ox-ac ozone sde2• perh jl3 petr-ra shn4• *Ph-ac* bg2* **Phos** k* *Plb* bg2* plut-n srj7* podo fd3.de• positr nl2• **Puls** k •* rhus-t *Ros-d* wla1 ruta sacch-a fd2.de* sal-fr sle1• sanguis-s↓ scler↓ **Sep** k •* spong fd4.de suis-pan rly4• **Sulph** ptk1* syph jl2 tax-br oss1• tell rsj10• thal-xyz srj8• thuj k* trinit br1 tritic-vg fd5.de urol-h rwt• vanil fd5.de verat zinc k2* [alum stj2 am-caust stj2 am-f stj2 art-v stj beryl stj2 bor-pur stj2 fl-ac stj2 fl-pur stj2 heroin sdj2 lith-c stj2 lith-f stj2 lith-i stj2 lith-m stj2 lith-met stj2 lith-p stj2 nitro stj2 oxyg stj2 pop dhh1 sil stj2 tax jsj7 zinc-m stj2 zinc-n stj2 zinc-p stj2]

- **morning**: bamb-a↓ brucel sa3• diaz sa3• dulc fd4.de sanguis-s↓
  - **waking**; on: bamb-a stb2.de• sanguis-s hrn2•
- **behindhand**; always: (↗*Hurry)* *Cact* olib-sac wmh1
- **calculating**; when: (↗*Mathematics - inability - calculating)* calc falco-pe nl2• syph al
- **children**; in: carc mlr1•
- **driving**; while: galeoc-c-h gms1•
- **eating**, while: acon st1 spong fd4.de
- **everybody** else moves too fast: galla-q-r nl2•
- **indifference**: clem mtf11
- **irresolution**; from: scler mtf11
- **motion**, in: (↗*Gestures - slow)* *Anac* k* *Calc* cartl-s rly4• chinin-s a1 choc srj3• chord-umb rly4• cocc ptk1* *Con* conin a1 crot-h k2* diphtox jl2 hydrog srj2• irid-met srj5• ozone sde2• **Phos** k* plb a1 podo fd3.de• positr nl2• ros-d wla1 sep spong fd4.de verat a1
- **old** people, of: cact st calc st **Con** st *Hell* st *Phos* st zinc st
- **pain** in face; with: bamb-a stb2.de•
- **prosopalgia**; during (See pain)
- **purpose**, of: adam srj5• graph k* kali-p fd1.de• ros-d wla1 sanguis-s hrn2•
- **thinking**; in (See Dullness)
- **thought** and action; delay between: plut-n srj7•
- **thought**; of (See Dullness)
- **work**, in: aids nl2• cact k* dulc fd4.de hydrog srj2• kali-p fd1.de• kola stb3• m-arct petr-ra shn4• podo fd3.de• positr nl2• ros-d wla1 sacch-a fd2.de• spong fd4.de tritic-vg fd5.de

SLOWNESS; sensation of: | **bus**; sensation of slowness of: cortiso sp1

SLUGGISHNESS (See Dullness)

SLY (See Deceitful)

SMALLER, things appear (See Delusions - small - things - appear)

SMILING: (↗*Amusement - desire; Cheerful; Content; Laughing)* alco a1 anan a1* ars a1 atro a1* atro-s hr1 aur↓ bell h1* cadm-s↓ carc sk1• chlol a1 croc↓ falco-pe↓ ferr-ma↓ galv↓ **Hyos** hr1* lyc h2 lyss↓ *Merc*↓ op a1 ozone sde2* ph-ac↓ ruta fd4.de sumb a1* tritic-vg fd5.de *Verat* hr1* [sol-ecl cky1]

- **foolish**: (↗*Childish; Foolish; Frivolous)* bell k* falco-pe nl2• hyos lyss k* *Merc* k2* verat k*
- **force** people to smile, wants to: galla-q-r nl2•
- **involuntarily**: aur k* bell k* lyc
  - **speaking**; when: (↗*High-spirited; Laughing - causeless; Vivacious)* aur
- **never**: (↗*Cheerful - never; Laughing - aversion; Laughing - contemptuous; Serious)* alum k* ambr ptk1 **Ars** vh* **Aur** st bell mtf33 lyc mtf33 verat k2*
  - **children**; in: | **girls**; young: verat mtf33
- **sardonic**: (↗*Contemptuous; Cynical; Insolence; Laughing - sardonic; Mocking - sarcasm)* bell k*
- **sleep**, in: cadm-s k* croc j5.de ferr-ma c1 galv c1 hyos j5.de ph-ac h2*

SMOKING agg.: (↗*GENERALS - Tobacco - agg.)* alum b4.de* bell b4.de* petr b4.de* spig bg2

SNAPPISH: (↗*Abrupt; Answering - snappishly; Quarrelsome)* all-c↓ aran-ix mg1.de bung-fa↓ calc-p a1 **Cham** kr1* granit-m es1• **Lil-t** ptk1* **Luna** kg1• phos *Staph* ptk1*

- **children**; in: | **Ear**; from pain in: all-c tl1 cham tl1
- **ovulation**; during: bung-fa mtf

SNARLING like a dog (See Barking - growling)

SNEERING at everyone (See Contemptuous)

SNEEZING:

- **agg.**: borx b4a.de
- **amel.**: lyc bg2

SNUB one who differed from himself; desire to: hydr a1

SOBBING (See Sighing; Weeping - sobbing)

SOBERNESS: (↗*Self-control - increased; Serious)* dulc fd4.de ery-a a1 ferr a1 hyper a1 kali-p fd1.de* nat-sil fd3.de• [osm-met stj2]

SOCIABILITY: (↗*Communicative)* agar h2* aids nl2• alco a1 caps ckh1 carc sk1• kali-s fd4.de lac-h sze9• lac-lup hrn2• lach bg2* limen-b-c hrn2• nat-c bg2* nat-p vh olib-sac wmh1 **Podo** fd* sacch-a fd2.de• stann bg2* stront-c mrr1 sulph mrr1 tritic-vg fd5.de vanil fd5.de

- **alternating** with | **seriousness**: aids nl2•

SOCIAL MEETING:

- **agg.**: (↗*Company - aversion)* coca ptk1* mag-c mtf33 pall ptk1*
- **amel.**: (↗*Company - desire)* ambr↓ bov ptk1*
  - **girls**; young modern: ambr ptk1*

SOCIETY (See Company)

SOLEMN: (↗*Dignified; Pompous; Serious; Walking - slowly; Walking - slowly - dignified)* dulc fd4.de *Hyos* bg2* plat gl1.fr• podo fd3.de•

SOLITUDE:

- **aversion** to (See Company - desire)
- **desire** for (See Company - aversion)
- **sensation** of solitude (See Forsaken)

SOMBER; everything that is: | **aversion** to: (↗*Colors - black - aversion; Darkness - aversion)* ars tl1 rob k* stram *Tarent* verat tl1

SOMNAMBULISM: (↗*Runs - sleep)* **Acon** k* aeth dgt1 agar alum k* alum-sil k2* *Anac* ant-c arg-met jl* *Art-v* k* aur-br c1* aur-m-n wbt2• bell k* **Bry** k* calc h2* camph bg2 *Cann-i* bro1* caste jl3 cham gl1.fr• cic croc crot-h bg2* cur a1* **Cycl** k* des-ac jl3 *Dict* bg2* dros mtf33 hell k2* hipp jl2 hyos ign k* *Kali-br* k* kali-c k* *Kali-p* k* kali-s kalm k* *Kola* stb3• lach luna c2 lyc k* lyss c1* m-ambo b7.de* m-arct b7a.de* mag-m↓ meph k* mosch **Nat-m** k*

Somnambulism: ...
nit-ac gb• *Nux-m* b7a.de **OP** b7.de* paeon bro1 petr k* **Phos** k* plat psor al2 rheum k* rumx bg2* sep k* *Sil* k* spig **Spong** k* stann k* *Stram* k* *Sulph* k* *Tarent* hr1* teucr k* tub jl2* verat **Zinc** k* [alumin-p stj2 am-br stj2 arg-n stj2 arg-p stj2 bar-br stj2 brom stj1* calc-br stj1 cupr-p stj2 mag-br stj1 nat-br stj2 plb-p stj2 titan stj2 titan-s stj2 zinc-i stj2 zinc-m stj2 zinc-n stj2 zinc-p stj2]
- **angry** gestures; with (See Gestures - angry)
- **children**; in: kali-br ptk1
- **climbing** the roofs, the railings of bridge or balcony: lyc gl1.fr• phos gl1.fr• sulph gl1.fr•
- **emotions**; after suppressed: *Zinc* k*
- **eruptions**; after disappearance of old: *Zinc* kr1
- **honor**; from wounded: ign ptk1
- **mental** exertion; doing: phos gl1.fr• sep gl1.fr•
- **moon**:
  - **full** moon: *Sil* kr1*
  - **new** moon: *Sil* kr1*
- **strike** sleepers from vengeance; to: **Nat-m** gl1.fr• nit-ac gl1.fr•
- **work**; to make daily: art-v br1* bry gl1.fr• kali-p vml3• mag-m dgt nat-m gl1.fr• sil sf1.de sulph gl1.fr•

SOPOR (See SLEEP - Deep)

SORROWFUL (See Grief; Sadness)

SPACE:
- **desire** for: irid-met srj5•
  - **one's** own space (See Company - aversion - bear)

SPACED-OUT feeling: *(↗Abstraction; Concentration - difficult; Dream; as; Exhilaration; Stupefaction; Thoughts - wandering)* agar vh *Agath-a* nl2• arizon-l nl2• aur-br vh1 **Bit-ar** wht1• brass-n-o srj5• cann-i vh* corv-cor bdg• dioxi rbp6 falco-pe nl2• fic-m gya1 foli oss• *Granit-m* es1• haliae-lc srj5• hippoc-k szs2 *Hydrog* srj2• lac-del hrn2• lac-h htj1• lac-loxod-a hrn2• limen-b-c hrn2• luna kg1• maias-l hrn2• melal-alt gya4 myos-a rly4• *Neon* stj2*• *Nux-m* mrr1 *Olib-sac* wmh1 orot-ac rly4• phos mrr1 plut-n srj7• *Sal-fr* sle1• sanguis-s hrn2• sinus rly4• thioc-ac rly4• vanil fd5.de [heroin sdj2]
- **anxiety**; with: bit-ar wht1•
- **desire** to have: limen-b-c hrn2•
- **fog** between self and other; sensation as if: lac-del hrn2•

SPEECH: *(↗MOUTH - Speech)*
- **abrupt**: *(↗offensive; Abrupt)* ars a1 bell a1 carc fd2.de• cham h1* germ-met srj5• lyss hr1 mur-ac h2* nat-sil fd3.de• plb a1 podo fd3.de• ruta fd4.de sacch-a fd2.de• sanguis-s hrn2• sul-ac a1 symph fd3.de• **Tarent** a1* tub jl2
- **accent** unusual for him; with an: *(↗foreign)*
  - **American** accent: limest-b es1•
- **affected**: *(↗Affectation - gestures; Affectation - words)* acon bg2 am-c bg2 anac bg2 arg-n ptk1 **Bell** bg2* bov bg2 bry bg2 calc bg2 cann-xyz bg2 carb-an bg2 carb-v bg2 **Caust** bg2* chin bg2 cic bg2 coll ptk1 con bg2 crot-c ptk1 crot-h bg2 cupr bg2 dulc bg2 *Euphr* bg2 *Gels* ptk1 *Glon* ptk1 hep bg2 hyos bg2* kali-br ptk1 kali-i ptk1 kali-p bg2 lac-h htj1• *Lach* bg2* laur bg2 lyc bg2* *Merc* bg2* merc-c ptk1 mez bg2 nat-c ptk1 nat-m bg2* nux-m ptk1 *Nux-v* bg2* olnd bg2 *Op* bg2 ph-ac bg2 phos ptk1 plb bg2 ruta bg2* sec bg2 sil bg2 stann bg2* **Stram** bg2* *Sulph* bg2 thuj bg2 verat bg2
  - **head**; with complaints of: *Lach* bg2 nux-m bg2
- **angry**: castm ↓ zinc hr1*
  - **sleep**, in: castm kr1
- **anxious**, in sleep: alum a1 graph a1 nux-v a1 *Sulph* a1
- **articulate**; cannot (See inarticulate)
- **awkward**: (non:nat-c hr1) *Nat-m* hr1 positr nl2• sacch-a fd2.de•
- **babbling**: *(↗Loquacity)* con sf1.de cortico sp1* dulc sf1.de gels sf1.de *Hyos* k* lach k2* lyc bg1* neon srj5• plb pyrog jl2 ruta fd4.de sel k2* *Stram* kr1*
- **benevolent**: tus-fr a1
- **bombast** (= worthless): crot-h gl1.fr• *Lach* gl1.fr• nux-v gl1.fr• *Olib-sac* wmh1 staph gl1.fr•
- **chattering** (See hasty)
- **childish**: *(↗Childish)* acon k* *Arg-n* k* arizon-l nl2• bar-c k2* lyc st1
- **confused**: *(↗Confusion; Forgetful)* alco a1 atro a1 bell k* ben-n a1 bry calc k* *Cann-s* k* carl a1 *Caust* k* *Cham* h1* choc srj3• *Crot-c* crot-h k* gard-j ↓ *Gels* *Hyos* k* *Lach* lyc k* med mosch k* *Nat-m* k* nux-m k* *Nux-v* c1 olib-sac wmh1 *Op* hr1* sacch-a fd2.de• sec sep gl1.fr• stram k* thuj

Speech – confused: ...
  - **morning** | **waking**; on: atro a1*
  - **night**: calc ↓ cham k* gard-j ↓
    - **sleep**, in: *(↗Talking - sleep)* calc a1 gard-j vlr2•
- **convincing**: op a1 sacch-a fd2.de• ulm-c jsj8•
- **delirious**: *(↗Delirium)* *Bell* a1 **Bry** ↓ camph a1 canth a1 cham ↓ *Cic* kr1 coff ↓ *Cupr-act* a1* dig ↓ hep ↓ *Hyos* a1* lyc ↓ op a1* past a1 phos ↓ plb a1 *Rheum* kr1 sil ↓ *Sulph* ↓ tab a1 til ↓ vip a1
  - **night**: dig a1 rheum a1 sil a1
  - **business**, of: **Bry** a1
  - **chill**, during: cham a1 hep ↓
    - **aroused**; on being: hep a1
  - **eyes**; with wide open: op br1*
  - **fever**, during: coff a1 til a1
  - **menses**; before: *(↗Menses - before)* lyc a1
  - **sleep**:
    - **midnight**; before: rheum a1 *Sulph* a1
    - **going** to sleep; on: phos a1
    - **in**: **Bell** a1
  - **waking**, on: bry a1
- **disconnected**: coff bg2 crot-h bg2 hyos bg2 merc-c bg2 phos bg2 stram bg2 stry bg2
- **distorted**: cupr-act a1* cupr-s a1*
- **embarrassed**: *(↗Ailments - embarrassment)* aeth c1* atro k* carbn-s merc k* morph a1 nat-m c1* pall k* tab c1*
- **enthusiastic**: aq-pet mtf11 cann-i a1 podo fd3.de• verbe-o mtf11
- **excited**: *(↗Loquacity - excited)* morph a1 nat-c a1
- **extravagant**: *(↗Extravagance; Haughty)* aether k* agar dgt1 bell a1 *Cann-i* k* lach k2* *Nux-m* k* plb k* ruta fd4.de stram k*
- **facile** (See fluent)
- **fast** (See hasty)
- **faster** than ever before, especially during fever (See hasty - fever)
- **fine**: hyos k*
- **finish** sentence; cannot: *(↗Memory - weakness - say)* ars bg2 **Cann-i** kr1* cimic jl colch mg haliae-lc srj5• ham fd3.de• irid-met srj5• lach k2 med bg2* onos vml3• plut-n srj7• pop-cand c1 symph fd3.de• thuj kr1
  - **jumping** from thought to thought in the middle of a sentence: irid-met srj5•
- **firmer**, surer in afternoon than in forenoon: anac h2*
- **fluent**: *(↗Eloquent; Loquacity)* cupr-act a1 hyos bg2 kali-c cd1 lach bg2 ped a1 sacch-a fd2.de• sil bg2* thea a1
- **foolish**: *(↗Answering - foolish; Childish; Foolish; Frivolous; Loquacity - foolish)* aur *Bell* k* bry gl1.fr• bufo k2 calc k2* calc-sil k2* caust k2* *Chin* hr1* chir-fl gya2 **Hyos** *Lach* k* merl *Nux-m* par petr ↓ phos k* podo fd3.de• sal-fr sle1• spong fd4.de *Stram* k* tab k*
  - **drunkenness**; during: petr gl1.fr•
- **forcible**: pall a1
- **foreign** tongue, in a: *(↗accent)* camph hr1* lach k* nit-ac ptk1 *Stram* k*
  - **sensation** as if talking in a foreign tongue: olib-sac wmh1
- **future**, about (See Talking - future)
- **hasty**: *(↗Answering - hastily; Hurry; Impatience; Impulsive; Loquacity; Loquacity - hasty; Quick; Rash)* acon k* aids nl2• alco a1 ambr anac bro1 androc srj1• anh mg1.de* arn k* ars k* atro a1* aur bro1 aur-s wbt2• *Bell* k* bit-ar wht1• bry k* bufo gk calc-hp ptk1* *Camph* k* cann-i cann-s k* cann-xyz bg2 caust gl1.fr• chlol cimic k* cina cocc k* *Coff* b7a.de croc b7a.de cyn-d ckh1 fl-ac mrr1 haliae-lc srj5• **Hep** k* **Hyos** k* *Ign* k* irid-met srj5• kali-c st1 kali-p k2* **Lach** k* lil-t bro1 lyc lyss k* **Merc** k* morph a1 *Mosch* k* nux-m mrr1 nux-v k* op bg2 *Ph-ac* k* *Plat* sne plb k* positr nl2• pycnop-sa mrz1 pyrog ↓ sal-al blc1• sal-fr sle1• *Sep* k* stann bg2 *Stram* k* stry bg2 *Thuj* k* verat k*
  - **fever**; during: pyrog k2
  - **loud**; and: mosch b7a.de
  - **monosyllabic**; and: haliae-lc srj5•
  - **stool**; during: *Ars* b4a.de
- **heavy**: aran-sc a1 positr nl2• sacch-a fd2.de•

- **hesitating**: *(↗Answering - hesitating)* absin k* amyg a1 arg-n a1* carbn-s choc srj3• cortico tpw7* kali-br k* lat-m sp1* merc k* morph k* nat-m mrr1 *Nux-m* k* ph-ac *Puls* gl1.fr• vip k* [heroin sdj2]
- **hurried** (See hasty)
- **inarticulate**: *(↗incoherent; MOUTH - Speech - difficult - inarticulate)* *Aesc-g* bro1 agar bro1 anac br1* anh bro1 atro bro1 bar-c bro1 bell bro1 *Both* br1* *Bov* bro1 bufo bro1 cann-i bro1 *Cann-s* bro1 *Caust* bro1* cere-s bro1 cic bro1 cot ↓ *Cupr* bro1 gels bro1 hep ↓ hyos bro1 *Ign* bro1 kali-br bro1 kali-cy bro1 kali-s fd4.de lach br1* laur bro1 linu-u a4 merc bro1 mygal bro1 naja br1* nat-m bro1 nauf-helv-li elm2• nux-m bro1 olnd br1* *Op* bro1 *Phos* bro1 spong fd4.de *Stram* bro1 sulfon bro1 thuj bro1 tritic-vg fd5.de vip bro1
  - **tumbling** over each other; words roll out: hep ptk1
  - **waking**; on: cot br1
- **incoherent**: *(↗inarticulate; Answering - incoherently; Answering - incorrectly; Concentration - difficult - talking; Confusion - talking; Dullness - speaking; Excitement - talking; Forgetful - words; Memory - weakness - words; Mistakes - speaking; Schizophrenia - paranoid; Thoughts - disconnected - talking; Thoughts - vanishing - speaking)* absin aether *Agar* k* alco a1 alum ↓ amyg *Anac* androc bnm2• anh sp1 *Apis* kr1 *Arg-n* k* arn ↓ ars k* ars-s-f k2 *Atro* a1* aur ↓ *Bapt* *Bell* k* **Bry** buth-a sp1 cact calad k* calc ↓ *Camph* k* **Cann-i** k* *Cann-s* bg* *Cann-xyz* bg2 carbn-s cham chel chlol cimic jl3 coca a1 coloc ↓ *Crot-h* k* crot-t ↓ cub cupr k* *Cupr-act* ↓ cycl desm-g bnj1 dubo-m br1 dulc falco-pe nl2• gard-j ↓ *Gels* glon ↓ haliae-lc srj5• hep hydr-ac **Hyos** k* ign ↓ ip ↓ kali-bi k* kali-br k* kali-c kali-p kalm ↓ **Lach** k* merc k* merc-c bg2 merc-meth a1 *Morph* nat-m ↓ *Nux-m* k* op k* par k* past a1 *Ph-ac* **Phos** k* plb k* raja-s jl3* **Rhus-t** sal-ac a1 sep ↓ spig bg2 spig-m a1 **Stram** k* sulfon br1 *Sulph* tanac thal-xyz srj8• verat ↓ vip k* visc k* zinc zinc-p k2
  - **evening**: bell h1*
  - **night**: bell h1* gels kali-bi k* plb a1*
  - **dozing**, after: op k*
  - **epileptic** attack, after: ars a1 plb a1
  - **fever**; during: alum bg2 ars bg2 *Bry* bg2 calc bg2 ip bg2 kali-c bg2 nat-m bg2 phos bg2 *Rhus-t* bg2 verat bg2
  - **head**; with complaints of: arg-n bg2 arn bg2 ars bg2 aur bg2 bell bg2 calc bg2 cham bg2 coloc bg2 crot-t bg2 glon bg2 kalm bg2 nat-m bg2 sep bg2 verat bg2
  - **love**; from disappointed: hyos *Lach* vh* nat-m st
  - **perspiration**, ending with: *Cupr-act* kr1
  - **sleep**: *(↗Talking - sleep)*
    - **during**: cub gard-j vlr2• *Gels* kali-bi phos *Stram* kr1
    - **going** to sleep; on: kali-bi a1
  - **waking**, on: cact k* ign k* op k*
- **inconsiderate**: alco a1 calad a1 mez a1 sacch-a fd2.de•
- **interesting**: thea a1
- **intoxicated**, as if: *(↗Loquacity - drunk as)* amyg androc srj1• carb-an *Gels* **Hyos** lach k13 lyc meph nat-m *Nux-v* vip
- **irrelevant**: atro a1 hyos bg2 nux-m bg2
- **jerks**, by: *Agar* bg2* bov bg2* caust ptk1* mygal bg2* stram vh
- **lost** (See Aphasia)
- **loud**: arn k* ars atro k* aur *Bell* k* bung-fa mtf cann-i a1 cham hr1* dream-p sdj1• *Hyos* k* **Lach** gl1.fr• limest-b es1• nux-m k* *Op* hr1 sil bg2 spong ↓ stram *Sulph* ↓ tritic-vg fd5.de tub mrr1*
  - **each** word louder: hyos ptk1*
  - **sleep**, in: *(↗Talking - sleep)* *Arn* kr1 **Bell** kr1* *Sil* kr1 spong kr1 *Sulph* kr1
- **low**, soft voice: bell sf1.de *Carb-an* sf1.de hydrog srj2• hyos br1 mang-act br1 nux-v sf1.de ruta fd4.de *Sec* sf1.de spong fd4.de staph sf1.de tab sf1.de *Viol-o* b7a.de*
- **merry**: aether a1 agar k* mur-ac k* podo fd3.de• spong fd4.de
  - **sleep**, in: *(↗Talking - sleep)* mur-ac k*
- **monosyllabic**: ars k* haliae-lc srj5• meli merc k* *Nux-v* k* *Ph-ac* *Sul-ac* symph fd3.de• *Thuj* k*
- **monotonous**: anh sp1 irid-met srj5• mang br1 mang-act bro1 mang-o br1*
- **muttering** (See Muttering)
- **nasal** (See LARYNX - Voice - nasal)
- **nonsensical**: *(↗unintelligible; Loquacity - nonsense)* acon aether *Anac* k* androc srj1• arg-met k2 atro aur *Bell* bufo sf1.de* calc-sil k2 camph *Cann-i* canth chlf chlol cina h1 dulc h1 **Hyos** kali-bi a1 kali-br kali-c ↓ merc nat-c nux-m olib-sac wmh1 plb *Stann* kr1 *Stram* *Sulph* k2* tub *Verat* kr1
  - **starting** up while asleep; on: kali-c
- **obscene** (See Obscene - talk)
- **offensive**: *(↗abrupt; Abusive; Quarrelsome; Rudeness)* lyss a1
- **passionate**: olib-sac wmh1
- **pathetic**: *(↗Pathetic)* *Aur* b4a.de lyss hr1*
- **phrases**, in high-sounding: *Nux-v* kr1 sacch-a fd2.de•
- **plaintive**: crot-h ptk1
- **prattling**: *(↗Childish; Loquacity)* acon a1* aids nl2• aloe alum ↓ *Anac* k* *Ars* ↓ atro a1 aur ↓ *Bar-c* ↓ bell a1* **Bry** k* calad k* calc ↓ cupr k2* cyna jl3 **Hyos** k* ign k2* lach gl1.fr• lyc ↓ nux-v k* op par br1* plb sil ↓ *Stram* k* tarax k*
  - **morning**: **Bry** a1
  - **lies** naked in bed and prattles: **Hyos**
  - **sleep**, in: *(↗Talking - sleep)* alum b4.de* anac b4.de* *Ars* b4.de* aur b4.de* *Bar-c* b4.de* calc b4.de* lyc b4.de* *Nux-v* sil b4.de*
- **random** at night, at: plb
- **rapid** (See hasty)
- **rapturous**: aether a1
- **repeats**: *(↗Delirium - repeats)*
  - **everything** said to him | **children**; in: zinc al1*
  - **same** thing; the: arg-n bg2 cann-xyz bg2 cocain bg2 coff-t a1 germ-met srj5• kres mg1.de* lach bg2* limest-b es1• lyc bg2 petr bg2 stram bg2
- **respectful**: agar a1
- **senseless** (See nonsensical)
- **serious**: *Stram* br1
- **sharp**: *(↗Mocking - sarcasm)* carc fd2.de• cham hr1* hyper a1* *Nat-sil* fd3.de• podo fd3.de• ruta fd4.de
- **short**: cham bg2 cupr-n a1
- **shrill** voice; in a: cann-i sf1.de cupr sf1.de stram kr1*
- **silent** (See Talking - loud)
- **slow**: *(↗Answering - slowly; Slowness)* aeth k* agar-ph a1 ant-c k* *Arg-n* ars k* atro k* bell k* caj a1 calen a1 cann-i a1 carb-an k* *Caust* gl1.fr• chinin-s chlf a1 cocc k* cupr bg2 cypra-eg sde6.de• germ-met srj5• haliae-lc srj5• **Hell** k* irid-met srj5• *Kali-br* k* kali-p bg2 ketogl-ac rly4• **Lach** k* lyc bg2 merc k* mez bg2* morph k* nat-c nat-m gl1.fr• nux-m k* *Op* k* ozone sde2• petr *Ph-ac* k* *Phos* k* phys k* *Plb* k* positr nl2• rhus-t k* sacch-a fd2.de• *Sec* k* *Sep* k* spong fd4.de syph k* *Thuj* k* zinc bg2* [heroin sdj2]
- **soft** voice; in a low (See low)
- **strange**: aether camph a1* cham k* gal-ac
- **swallowing** his words (See MOUTH - Speech - swallowing)
- **terse** (= to the point): op a1
- **threatening**: tarent a1
- **unintelligible**: *(↗nonsensical; Answering - unintelligibly)* acon k* amyg a1 arn ↓ ars k* atro ↓ **Bell** k* bufo sf1.de calen a1 castm ↓ cham ↓ euph k* *Fl-ac* hr1 **Hyos** k* lyc k* *Merc* k* mur-ac ↓ naja nux-m ↓ nux-v k* op ↓ *Ph-ac* k* plb a1 *Sec* k* sil k* **Stram** k* sul-ac a1 tab k* *Verat-v* hr1* zinc ↓
  - **evening** | **after** lying down: zinc a1
  - **night** | **midnight**; before: nux-v a1
  - **convulsions**; before epileptic: bufo sf1.de*
  - **sleep**, in: *(↗Talking - sleep)* arn atro castm cham mur-ac
  - **vertigo**; with: bell bg2 nux-m bg2 op bg2
- **unsuitable**: nux-v a1
- **vexations**, about old: *(↗Dwells - offenses)* cham a1
- **vexatious** things; desire to say: mez a1
- **violent**: bell a1 *Nat-c* gl1.fr• podo fd3.de• stram k2*
- **vivacious**: *(↗Loquacity - vivacious)* cann-i a1 **Hyos** kr1 olib-sac wmh1 *Sulph* kr1 ulm-c jsj8•
- **voice**:
  - **low** voice; in a (See low)
  - **shrill** voice; in a (See shrill)
- **wandering**: *(↗Aphasia; Confusion; Loquacity - changing; Thoughts - wandering)* acon aeth agar hr1* *Ambr* k2* *Anac* arn *Ars* ars-s-f k2* *Atro* a1* aur aur-ar k2 **Bell** k* *Bry* k* calc *Camph* cann-s br1 canth

- **wandering**: ...
cham chin chinin-ar cic cina coloc cupr dig↓ dulc haliae-lc srj5• **Hyos** k* ign kali-c *Kali-p* hr1* **Lach** k* **Lyc** merc moni rfm1• **Nux-m** nux-v k* onos vml3• *Op* k* *Par* j5.de* *Phos Plat* plb k* *Puls* pycnop-sa mrz1 rheum k* *Rhus-t* k* sabin sec sep↓ spong **Stram** k* *Sulph* verat
  - **afternoon** and especially evening: *Nux-v* hr1*
  - **night**: ars aur bell bry coloc dig op rheum sep sulph
- **whispering**: *(↗LARYNX - Voice - whispering)* ol-an ptk1 pyrog↓ sil↓
  - **answering** to the mother instead of to the prescriber directly: *(↗Timidity - children)* sil mrr1
  - **herself**; to: pyrog ptk1
  - **sleep**; during: pyrog ptk1
- **wild**: *(↗Insanity - talking)* ars hr1* atro a1 camph a1* hyper↓ lyc a1 plb a1 spig-m a1 stram a1 *Verat-v* hr1*
  - **sleep**, in: *(↗Talking - sleep)* hyper a1
- **worthless** (See bombast)

SPEED: | **desire** for: *(↗Hurry)* dendr-pol sk4• falco-pe nl2• [heroin sdj2]

SPINELESS: *(↗Will - weakness)* am-c gl1.fr• bar-c dmk1*• calc gl1.fr• rhod kgp5• sil mtf33

SPIRALS: | **awe** at: falco-pe nl2•

SPIRITUALITY: hippoc-k szs2 positr nl2•
- **lack** of: anac bg2 coloc bg2

SPITEFUL (See Malicious)

SPITTING: *(↗Mania - spit; Rage - spitting)* aeth a1 ant-t bg* apoc vh1 arn b7a.de ars↓ bac jl2 *Bapt*↓ bar-act a1 bar-c bg* *Bell* b4a.de* bufo mtf33 cadm-s bg2 *Calc* bg2* camph ptk1 cann-i↓ *Cann-s* j5.de cann-xyz bg2 caps↓ carbn-s a1 *Coc-c* a1 cupr j5.de* cupr-act↓ der↓ dulc a1 epiph bg ferr↓ gels↓ glon a1 graph bg2 grat bg2 hydr-ac bg2 hyos↓ ind vml3• laur bg2 lyc gl1.fr• lyss bg* mag-m h2 merc mtf33* merc-c bg2 *Nat-m* bg2 nit-ac bg2 *Nux-v* gl1.fr• phel↓ phos↓ plb mtf33 rhus-t bg2* sabad bg2 sang bg2 sec b7a.de* sep↓ stram bg2* *Sulph* mtf33* *Tab* bg* *Verat* kr1 *Verat-v* kr1 zinc-chr bg*
- **morning**: der a1
- **afternoon**: gels a1
- **anger**, from: *Calc* kr1
- **bile**; of: sang ptk1
- **complaints**; with other: tab ptk1
- **constantly** (See Spitting)
- **directions**, in all: lyss kr1
- **eating**, after: der a1
- **faces** of people, in: *(↗Violent)* ars **Bell** k* bufo gk *Calc* k* cann-i cann-s j5.de* *Cupr* k* cupr-act a1 hyos k* merc phos k* plb *Stram* k* *Verat* k*
- **fever**; during: bell bg2 caps b7a.de*
- **floor** and licks it up, on the: merc k*
- **foamy**: *(↗MOUTH - Saliva - soapy)* phel bg2
- **food**; of: ferr ptk1
- **headache**, in: ind vml3•
- **liquids** put in mouth: *Bapt* hr1
- **nausea**; with: bar-act bg2 grat a1
- **spasmodic**: **Lyss** k*

SPOILED children: *(↗Behavior - children)* am-c gl1.fr• bar-c gl1.fr• lyc gl1.fr• mosch c1 op gl1.fr• par vml3• sulph mtf33*

SPOKEN TO; being:
- **agg.**: *(↗Anger - interruption)* cham bg2* plat bg2
- **aversion**: *(↗Anger - interruption; Anger - spoken; Company - aversion; Conversation - agg.; Irritability - spoken; Obstinate - children - cry; Quiet; wants; Reserved; Starting - spoken; Taciturn; Weeping - spoken)* agar aloe sne am-c anh mg1.de ant-c bg2* ant-t apoc vh arn *Ars* k* *Ars-i* ars-s-f k2 aur aur-ar k2 aur-s k2 bar-s k2 bry k2 caj calc-sil k2 camph *Carbn-s* **Cham** k* con cur bg2 cyn-d jl dream-p sdj1• dulc fd4.de elaps k* fago *Gels* k* granit-m es1• *Graph* ham hell helon *Hipp* hippoc-k szs2 hist mg1.de *Hyos* k* ign **IOD** k1* kali-p kalm k* lil-t lyc k2 mag-c↓ mag-m k* myric *Nat-m* k* *Nat-s* k* nit-ac gl1.fr• nux-v op bg2 petr-ra shn4• *Ph-ac* bg2* plan plat plb bg2 podo fd3.de• puls bg2* puls-n rhus-t k* ruta fd4.de sep bg2 sil k* sin-n bg2 spong fd4.de staph stram *Sulph* *Tarent* tep teucr tritic-vg fd5.de vanil fd5.de verat zinc
  - **morning**: ars mag-c↓ nat-s

Spoken to; being – **aversion** – **morning**: ...
  - ⁝ **waking**; on: mag-c mrr1
  - **alone**; wants to be let: *(↗Company - aversion)* ant-t st aur caj dream-p sdj1• dulc fd4.de granit-m es1• hell helon hipp hippoc-k szs2 *Iod* kali-p fd1.de• lil-t podo fd3.de• *Spong* fd4.de stram a1 *Sulph Tritic-vg* fd5.de
  - **chill**; during: *Hyos*
- **desire** (See Communicative)

SPOONERISMS (See Mistakes - speaking - sounds)

SPYING everything: *(↗Curious; Curious - training; Gossiping; Revealing; Sensitive - want)* agar ant-c gl1.fr• aur bg calc gl1.fr• carb-v gl1.fr• hyos gl1.fr• lach laur bg lyc gl1.fr• neon↓ positr↓ puls kl* sep gl1.fr• sulph gl1.fr• verat gl1.fr•
- **peeping** through the keyhole: neon srj5• positr nl2•

SQUANDERING: *(↗Avarice - squandering; Boaster - squandering; Delusions - squanders; Insanity - purchases)* agar gl1.fr• alum k* *Bell* gl1.fr• bros-gau mrc1 buteo-j↓ calc gl1.fr• caust gl1.fr• con gl1.fr• dulc fd4.de falco-pe nl2• hep gl1.fr• iod sne kola stb3• *Lach* sne lyc mtf **Merc** mtf33* nat-m sne *Nux-v* gl1.fr• petr-ra↓ plat↓ positr nl2• puls↓ sal-fr sle1• sil↓ spong fd4.de stram mtf33* sulph gl1.fr• *Syph* st1 taosc iwa1• tritic-vg fd5.de verat gl1.fr• [kali-f stj1]
- **alternating** with | **avarice**: calc gl1.fr• lach mtf33* merc gl1.fr• sulph gl1.fr•
- **boasting**, from: *(↗Boaster; Boaster - squandering)* calc gl1.fr• nux-v gl1.fr• plat gl1.fr• puls gl1.fr•
- **money**: *(↗Extravagance; Haughty)* agar gl1.fr• alum gl1.fr• *Bell* gl1.fr• calc gl1.fr• caust gl1.fr• con gl1.fr• dulc fd4.de hep gl1.fr• **Merc** gl1.fr• *Nux-v* gl1.fr• petr-ra shn4• spong fd4.de stram gl1.fr• sulph gl1.fr• *Syph* st taosc iwa1• verat k* [buteo-j sej6]
- **order**, from want of: *(↗Chaotic)* lyc gl1.fr• plat gl1.fr• sil gl1.fr•

STABBING (See Impulse - stab)

STABILITY: | **desire** for stability: *(↗Change - aversion)* **Symph** fd*

STAGE FRIGHT (See Anticipation - stage)

STAMMERING (See MOUTH - Speech - stammering)

STANDING:
- **agg.**: bry b7.de* cic b7.de* plb bg2 staph b7.de* thuj b4.de* valer b7.de* verat bg2
- **amel.**: phos b4.de*

STARING, thoughtless: *(↗Absentminded; Anxiety - looking; Delirium - look; Insanity - staring; Rage - staring; Sitting - inclination - stare; EYE - Staring)* androc srj1• bell ckh1 bit-ar wht1• bov ptk1 brom hr1* bros-gau mrc1 carbn-s kr1* cench k2 choc srj3• cic bg2 dream-p sdj1• *Dulc* fd4.de fic-m gya1 guaj br1 haliae-lc srj5• **Hell** hr1* *Hydr-ac* hr1* hyos bg2* ign hr1* irid-met srj5• kali-bi hr1 kali-s fd4.de lac-e hrn2• lat-m bnm6• marb-w es1• meli sne *Merc-c* hr1* nat-sil fd3.de• op ckh1 podo fd3.de• positr nl2• *Puls* hr1* ran-b hr1* *Ruta* fd4.de sal-fr sle1• sanguis-s hrn2• spong fd4.de stram k2* ulm-c jsj8• [heroin sdj2]
- **morning**: *Guaj* hr1* spong fd4.de

STARTING (= startled): *(↗Excitement; Fear - starting; Frightened; Senses - acute; Sensitive)* abrot↓ absin↓ *Acon* k* act-sp br1 aesc↓ aeth↓ *Agar* c1* agath-a nl2• agn b2.de* alco↓ aloe bg2 alum k* alum-p↓ alum-sil↓ am-c b2.de* am-m b2.de* ambr k* aml-ns↓ ammc↓ anac b2.de* ang k* ant-c k* ant-o↓ ant-t k* anthraq↓ apis bro1 arg-met bg2* arg-n↓ arge-pl↓ arizon-l nl2• *Arn* k* **Ars** k* *Ars-h Ars-i Ars-s-f* k2 arum-t↓ *Asaf*↓ *Asar* bro1 *Atro* a1* *Aur*↓ aur-m auran↓ bamb-a↓ bapt↓ bar-act↓ *Bar-c* k* bar-m **Bell** k* benz-ac berb k* bism k* bond↓ *Borx* k* bov↓ brom k* **Bry** k* *Bufo* k* *Cact*↓ cadm-met↓ calad k* *Calc* k* calc-ar k2 calc-i↓ calc-p↓ calc-s calc-sil k2 calen↓ camph k* cann-i↓ cann-s canth b2.de* **Caps** k* carb-ac *Carb-an* k* *Carb-v* k* *Carbn-s* carc mlr1• card-b slp (non:card-m k*) *Carl*↓ carneg-g↓ castm↓ *Caust* k* cham k* chel k* chin b2.de* chinin-ar chinin-s↓ *Cic* cimic bro1 *Cina* b2.de* *Cinnb*↓ cit-v↓ clem↓ coc-c↓ *Cocc* k* coff b2.de* coff-t↓ colch b2.de* *Con* k* convo-d↓ cor-r↓ croc b2.de* *Crot-c*↓ crot-h↓ cub↓ cupr k* *Cur* cycl↓ cypr bro1 daph↓ *Dig*↓ dros b2.de* dulc b2.de* *Elat*↓ euph b2.de* *Euphr*↓ *Ferr*↓ ferr-i *Ferr-ma*↓ *Ferr-p*↓ ferul↓ gels br1 gins↓ glon bg2 glycyr-g↓ granit-m↓ graph k* *Grin*↓ guaj b2.de* ham↓ *Hell*↓ helon↓ hep k* heroin↓ hipp bg2 hura k* hydr-ac a1 hydroph↓ **Hyos** k* hyosin↓ hyper k* *Ign* k* ignis-alc es2• indg↓ inul iod bg2 ip b2.de* iris↓ jac-c↓ *Kali-ar* kali-bi bg2 *Kali-br* k* **Kali-c** b2.de* kali-cy↓

Starting: ...
Kali-i k* kali-n b2.de* **Kali-p** k1* *Kali-s* kali-sil k2 kiss ↓ *Kola* ↓ kreos b2.de* **Lac-c** lac-h ↓ lach k* lat-m ↓ laur b2.de* led k* lil-t limest-b ↓ lob-c ↓ lup ↓ *Lyc* k* lyss kr1 *M-ambo* ↓ *M-arct* ↓ *M-aust* ↓ macro ↓ mag-c k* mag-m b2.de* mag-p ↓ *Mag-s* ↓ *Med* *Menis* ↓ merc k* *Merc-c* ↓ merc-meth ↓ mez b2.de* *Morph* ↓ mosch j5.de* mur-ac k* murx ↓ myris ↓ naja ↓ napht ↓ **Nat-ar** *Nat-c* k* **Nat-m** k* *Nat-p* k* **Nat-s** ↓ *Nat-sil* ↓ nicc ↓ *Nit-ac* k* *Nux-m* k* *Nux-v* k* ol-an ↓ *Olnd* ↓ *Op* k* ox-ac ↓ oxal-a rly4• ozone ↓ paeon ↓ pall ↓ ped ↓ peti ↓ *Petr* k* petr-ra ↓ ph-ac b2.de* *Phos* k* *Phys* bg2* pip-n br1 plat k* plb b2.de* podo ↓ positr nl2• psor k* ptel puls b2.de* *Rat* ↓ rheum ↓ rhod ↓ rhus-t k* *Ruta* ↓ sabad k* sabal ↓ sabin ↓ sacch ↓ sacch-a ↓ samb k* sang ↓ sanic ↓ sars b2.de* *Scut* bro1 *Sec* ↓ sel b2.de* seneg b2.de* *Sep* k* *Sil* k* sol-a ↓ sol-ni sol-t-ae ↓ spig ↓ spong k* stann b2.de* staph b2.de* staphycoc ↓ **Stram** k* **Stront-c** k* stry suis-em rly4• sul-ac k* sul-i ↓ *Sulph* k* sumb a1 symph ↓ tab k* tarax ↓ *Tarent* bro1 teucr b2.de* thal-xyz ↓ thea ↓ *Ther* k* thuj b2.de* tub br* verat k* xan ↓ zinc k* zinc-m ↓ zinc-p ↓

- **daytime**: nux-v a1
- **morning** | **sleep**; starting from: chinin-s clem hura a1 phos a1 sabad spong
- **noon**: chel j5.de hep j5.de mag-c j5.de nat-c j5.de nit-ac j5.de nux-v j5.de sep j5.de *Sil* j5.de *Sulph* j5.de zinc h2
  - **sleep**, in: mag-c h2 nat-c h2* nit-ac h2* sep h2* sil h2* *Sulph* h2*
- **afternoon**: lyss kr1 nicc a1 pall kr1 sulph a1
- **evening**: *Agar* ↓ am-m ↓ ambr ↓ anac ↓ arizon-l nl2• arn ↓ **Ars** ↓ ars-s-f ↓ bar-c ↓ *Bell* ↓ bry ↓ calc ↓ cina ↓ dulc ↓ hell ↓ kali-bi ↓ kali-i ↓ lach ↓ merc-c ↓ nat-c ↓ ped a1 petr ↓ plat a1 *Puls* a1 sacch-a fd2.de• sars ↓ *Sel* ↓ stront-c ↓ *Sulph* ↓
  - **jerking** or twitching, ceasing on falling asleep: *Agar* hell
  - **sleep**; during: calc kali-i petr h2*
  - **sleep**; on going to: *(↗sleep - going)* am-m ambr anac h2 arn **Ars** ars-s-f a1 bar-c *Bell* bry cina mtf33 dulc kali-bi lach merc-c nat-c plat j5.de sars *Sel* stront-c *Sulph*
- **night**: alum am-c ant-t ↓ asaf k2 bism ↓ carb-v castm ↓ euph indg kali-i ↓ lat-m ↓ lyc mag-c mag-m h2 merc-c morph nat-s nit-ac h2 pall a1 sars a1 sil spong staph stram stront-c ↓ sulph *Teucr* ↓ zinc ↓
  - **midnight** in sleep:
    - **about**: lat-m bnm6• mag-c j5.de*
    - **after**: am-c a1 castm a1 *Teucr* a1
    - **before**: alum a1 ant-t j5.de bism j5.de kali-i j5.de mag-m j5.de* stront-c j5.de
  - **menses**, during: *(↗Menses - during)* zinc
- **anxious**: *(↗Anxiety)* aloe apis *Borx* ↓ cupr sf1.de hep j5.de laur ↓ lyc samb j5.de stront-c j5.de *Sulph*
  - **downward** motion, from: *Borx* k* laur ↓
    - **falling**; as if afraid of: borx br1 laur ptk1
- **bed**, in: anac ↓ bry ↓ cic euph ↓ hura merc-meth a1 tab
  - **awake**; while lying: anac bry euph
- **called** by name, when: sulph
- **coition**, after: sep h2
- **consciousness**; on recovering: *Nux-m* k* phys
- **convulsive**: apis hr1 ars calc-p hyos stry
- **crackling** of paper, from: *(↗Sensitive - noise - crackling)* calad k2
- **dentition**, during: calc-p mp• cham sf1.de
- **door**:
  - **opened**; when a door is: hura a1 mosch a1 phos a1
  - **slammed**; when a door is: calad k2 ox-ac a1
- **dreams**, in: acon ↓ am-m ↓ ant-c a1 aur ↓ bar-c ↓ bov ↓ calc ↓ caps ↓ carb-v ↓ colch ↓ cor-r ↓ croc ↓ dig ↓ *Ferr-ma* ↓ indg ↓ kali-i ↓ *Kali-n* ↓ led ↓ m-arct ↓ m-aust ↓ *Mag-c* ↓ *Mag-s* ↓ mez ↓ murx ↓ nat-c ↓ nat-s ↓ nicc ↓ nit-ac ↓ peti ↓ petr a1 *Puls* a1 sars ↓ *Sil* ↓ staph ↓ sulph a1 teucr ↓
  - **from** a dream: acon j5.de am-m j5.de ant-c a1 aur j5.de bar-c j5.de bov j5.de calc h2 caps j5.de carb-v h2* colch j5.de cor-r j5.de* croc j5.de dig j5.de *Ferr-ma* j5.de indg j5.de kali-i j5.de *Kali-n* j5.de led j5.de m-arct j5.de m-aust j5.de *Mag-c* j5.de *Mag-s* j5.de mez j5.de murx j5.de nat-c a1 nat-s j5.de nicc j5.de nit-ac j5.de peti a1 petr j5.de puls j5.de sars j5.de *Sil* j5.de staph j5.de sulph j5.de teucr j5.de
- **driving**; when: granit-m es1•
- **easily**: *(↗Frightened)* *Acon* b7.de* act-sp vh1 aloe sne alum b4.de am-c am-m k* anac b4.de* ang b7.de* ant-c b7.de* ant-t k* *Apis* b7a.de *Arn* b7.de* ars b4.de ars-s-f k2 *Aur* b4.de* bar-c k* bar-m k2 *Bell* b4.de* bism sf1.de **Borx** k* *Bry* b7.de *Bufo* calc k* calc-ar k2 calc-s calc-sil k2 *Camph* cann-s b7.de* caps b7.de* carb-an b4a.de* carb-v k* *Caust* bg2* *Cham* b7.de* cic k* cina bg2 *Cocc* k* con b4.de* *Croc* b7.de* cupr b7.de* *Ferr* b7a.de* granit-m es1• *Graph* b4.de* helon hep b4.de hura hyos b7.de hyper *Ign* b7.de* *Ip* b7.de **KALI-C** b4.de* kali-i **Kali-p** k* kali-s kali-sil k2 kola stb3• lac-c bg2 lach b7.de* *Led* b7.de* limest-b es1• lyc b4.de* *M-ambo* b7.de* m-arct b7.de *M-aust* b7.de mag-c br1 med ptk1* merc k* mez k* mosch b7a.de mur-ac b4.de nat-ar k2 **Nat-c** k* **Nat-m** k* **Nat-p** *Nit-ac* nux-m **Nux-v** k* *Olnd* b7.de* **Op** k* petr b4.de* ph-ac b4.de **Phos** k* phys plat b4.de* *Psor* st* *Puls* b7.de rhus-t b7.de* sabad b7.de* sacch-a fd2.de• samb b7.de* seneg b4.de* *Sep* k* **Sil** k* spong k* stann b4.de *Stram* b7.de* stront-c b4a.de* sul-ac b4a.de *Sulph* k* sumb tab *Ther* verat k* xan c1 zinc k* zinc-p k2 [heroin sdj2]
- **eating**, after: hep h2
- **electric**:
  - **as if**: *(↗GENERALS - Shock - electric-like)* agar cann-s euph kiss a1
  - **shocks** through the body:
    - **awake**; while wide: *(↗GENERALS - Shock - electric-like)* euph a1 mag-m nat-p
    - **sleep**; during: *Arg-met* *Ars* *Nat-m* *Nux-m*
    - **wakening** her: **Arg-met** k* *Ars* *Nat-m* nux-m
- **excitement**: borx k2
- **fall**, on hearing anything: alum a1
- **falling**, as if: bell bism caps h1 mez ph-ac h2*
- **feet**, as if coming from the: lyc
- **frequently**: **IGN** st*
- **fright**; from and as from: *(↗Ailments - fright)* *Acon* alum k2 *Am-c* ambr c1 anac apis arn ars gt atro a1 bamb-a stb2.de• *Bar-c* **Bell** **Borx** k* bry bufo *Cact* calc-p calen kr1 *Carb-v* carbn-s a1 *Caust* chin *Cic* coff coff-t a1 *Con* dig euphr **Hyos** hyper jac-c a1 *Kali-br* **Kali-c** k* **Kali-p** k* kali-s k1 kali-sil k2 *Kreos* lac-h sk4• *Lyc* macro a1 mag-c k* mag-s a1 *Merc* merc-c mosch k* mur-ac a1 napht a1 nat-ar **Nat-c** **Nat-m** nat-p **Nat-s** nat-sil k2 **Nit-ac** nux-v brm op *Phos* k* plb psor ruta a1 sabad sars *Sep* k* *Sil* *Spong* stann staph **Stram** k* stront-c *Sulph* verat k*
  - **children**; in: nat-c ptk1 sulph ptk1
  - **sleep**; during (See SLEEP - Waking - fright)
- **hawking** of others, at: **Borx** k*
- **heat**, during: caps cham sf1.de ferr-p sf1.de ign nat-m op
- **itching** and biting, from: mag-c h2
- **lying**, while: calc-p ↓ lyc mag-c ↓ nit-ac ↓
  - **back**; on: calc-p mag-c nit-ac h2
  - **side**; on the right: mag-c h2
- **menses**:
  - **before**: *(↗Menses - before)* calc k*
  - **during**: *(↗Menses - during)* *Borx* k1 ign sf1.de *Zinc* k1
- **noise**, from: *(↗Sensitive - noise)* acon st act-sp vh1 agath-a nl2• aloe k* alum ang h1* ant-c k* apis arge-pl rwt5• ars asar jl aur bar-act a1* (non:bar-c slp) **Borx** k* bufo cadm-met gm1 calad *Calc* camph cann-s carb-v carc fb* card-b a1 *Caust* chel *Cic* *Cocc* *Con* crot-c sk4• cub granit-m es1• ham fd3.de• hipp hura kali-ar **KALI-C** k1* *Kali-i* *Kali-p* k* kali-sil k2 *Lach* *Lyc* lyss mag-c *Med* k* *Merc* mosch *Nat-ar* **Nat-c** **Nat-m** **Nat-p** **Nat-s** *Nat-sil* k2* nit-ac k* **Nux-v** k* *Op* ox-ac petr-ra shn4• **Phos** vh* pip-n br1 positr nl2• *Psor* jl2 ptel rhus-t sabad sabin sacch-a fd2.de• **Sil** k* spong *Sul-ac* gk sulph tab tarax _echo thal-xyz ↓ ther sf1.de xan bg
  - **violently**: thal-xyz srj8•
- **pain**:
  - **agg.**: arg-n ptk1 lyc ptk1
  - **from**: arg-n ptk2 ars bg2 bry bg2 coc-c bg2 gels bg2 ign bg2 kali-cy a1 lyc bg2 mag-p bg2 merc bg2 nicc a1 sulph h2 sumb a1 xan bg
- **palpitation**, from: dig a1
- **paroxysmal**: ars kali-i a1 rhus-t
- **perspiration**, during: caust cham sabad samb spong
- **prick** of a needle, at the: calc
- **recovering** (See consciousness)
- **shivering**; during: sabad b7.de

- **sleep**:
  - **before**: alum
  - **during**: acon k* aeth br1* agn k* *Alum* k* *Am-c* b4.de* am-m j5.de ambr h1* aml-ns kr1 anac b4.de* ang b7.de* ant-c k* ant-o a1 *Ant-t* b7.de* *Apis* k* *Arg-met* arn k* *Ars* k* *Ars-h* ars-i ars-s-f kr1* arum-t *Asaf* kr1 atro *Aur* k* aur-m k2 auran kr1 bar-c b4.de* *Bell* k* benz-ac kr1 bism k* *Borx* b4a.de* bov j5.de brom bry k* bufo kr1 calad k* *Calc* k* calc-ar k1 calc-i k2 calc-p calc-sil k2 camph k* cann-i kr1 canth caps b7.de* *Carb-ac* kr1 carb-an b4.de* *Carb-v* b4.de* carbn-s carc gk *Carl* a1 castm k* *Caust* k* *Cham* k* chel b7.de* *Chin* b7.de* *Cic* hr1* *Cina* b7.de* *Cocc* b7.de* *Coff* b7a.de* *Colch* k* cor-r kr1 croc b7.de* *Crot-c* crot-h *Cupr* cur cycl *Dig* j5.de* *Dros* b7.de* dulc st* *Elat* kr1 euph b4a.de euphr st ferr-i kr1 ferr-ma j5.de *Ferr-p* kr1 *Gels* bg2* glycyr-g cte1• graph k* *Grin* bg2 guaj *Hell* kr1 *Hep* b4.de* hura **Hyos** k* hyper *Ign* b7.de* indg j5.de inul a1* iod *Ip* k* iris kali-ar kali-bi k* *Kali-br* **Kali-c** k* kali-i *Kali-n* b4a.de* kali-p *Kali-s* *Kreos* k* lac-h sk4• *Lach* b7.de* laur k* led b7a.de* lob-c a1 lyc k* *M-arct* j5.de m-aust j5.de mag-c k* mag-m k* mag-s j5.de* med st* *Merc* k* merc-c k* mez k* *Morph* mosch j5.de myris a1 nat-c k* *Nat-m* k* nat-p *Nat-s* j5.de* nat-sil fd3.de* nicc j5.de *Nit-ac* b4.de* *Nux-m* *Nux-v* k* *Op* k* ox-ac pall c1 petr k* ph-ac k* *Phos* k* plat b4.de* plb b7.de* *Puls* k* *Rat* rheum k* rhod a1 *Rhus-t* b7.de* ruta b7a.de* sabad kr1 sacch a1 *Samb* b7.de* sars k* *Sec* j5.de sel b7a.de seneg k* sep k* sil k* sol-t-ae a1 spig spong k* stann k* staph b7.de* stram k* stront-c b4.de* sul-ac b4.de* sul-i k2 *Sulph* k* symph fd3.de• *Tab* *Tarent* kr1* teucr b7.de* thuj k* *Verat* b7.de* *Zinc* k* zinc-p k2
  - **from**: abrot *Acon* aesc k2 *Agn* alco a1 *Alum* *Am-c* am-m h2 ammc vml3• anac sf1.de ang ↓ *Ant-c* ant-o c1 ant-t *Apis* arg-n k2 arge-pl rwt5• arn ↓ *Ars* asar ↓ aur aur-m bamb-a stb2.de• *Bar-c* **Bell** benz-ac *Bism* **Borx** bry *Cact* *Calad* *Calc* sf1.de calc-p k2 caps carb-v carbn-s carc tpw2* castm **Caust** *Cham* sf1.de chel *Chin* chinin-s cic hr1 cimic *Cina* *Cinnb* cit-v a1 clem *Cocc* *Coff* con convo-d a1 cor-r cycl *Dig* dros *Euphr* k* ferr-i ferr-p sf1.de ferul a1 gins graph guaj hell ↓ *Hep* hydroph mg1.de **Hyos** hyosin a1 ign ip ↓ jac-c a1 kali-bi sf1.de *Kali-br* a1* *Kali-c* a1* kali-i *Kola* ↓ kreos a1 laur a1 led lup lyc mag-c mag-m *Med* *Menis* *Merc* *Merc-c* mez h2 mur-ac murx naja k2 nat-ar *Nat-c* nat-sil k2 *Nit-ac* *Nux-v* ol-an j5.de op sf1.de ozone ↓ petr a1 *Ph-ac* *Phos* plat h2* plb positr nl2• psor sf1.de *Puls* *Rat* rhus-t ↓ ruta sabad sabal ptk2 *Samb* sang sanic c1 *Sars* scut sec ↓ *Sep* *Sil* sol-a a1 **Spong** k* staph a1 *Stram* suis-em rly4• sul-ac *Sulph* *Tarent* thea thuj h1 xan ↓ zinc [cann-s xyz62]
    - **chill**; during: ars bg2 *Lyc* bg2 nux-v bg2 puls bg2
    - **forenoon**: rhus-t a1
    - **comatose** sleep, from: *Ant-t* st hell st sec j5.de
    - **cough**; from: cina b7a.de kali-br bg2
    - **fever**; during: **Acon** b7a.de* *Apis* bg2 arn bg2 *Bell* bg2 bry bg2 **Cham** b7.de* chin bg2 ip bg2 **Lyc** b4.de* phos bg2 **Puls** b7.de* samb bg2 sep bg2 sil bg2 sulph bg2
    - **forgotten** something; as if he had: ozone sde2•
    - **menses**:
      - **before**: *(↗Menses - before)* sep kl
      - **during**: *(↗Menses - during)* *Zinc*
    - **noise**; at a: ang j asar mta borx bg calad hr *Kola* stb3• nux-v mta puls kr sulph h tarent mta
    - **pain** in heart; from: xan c1
    - **suffocative** breathing, from: ammc vml3•
    - **touch**, from slightest: *Ruta*
  - **going** to sleep; on: *(↗evening - sleep; on)* aeth kl *Agar* k* *Alum* alum-p k2 alum-sil k2 am-c j5.de am-m ambr arn **Ars** k* ars-h kr1 ars-s-f a1* arum-t kr1 atro a1 bapt kr1 bar-c **Bell** bism j5.de bond a1 *Calc* kr1 *Carb-an* carb-v *Caust* chin chinin-ar *Cina* k* *Coff* cor-r daph *Dros* j5.de *Dulc* ferr-ma j5.de ham fd3.de• **Hep** ign ip kali-ar kali-bi *Kali-c* kali-s kali-sil k2 kreos *Lach* led h1 **Lyc** mag-c mag-m h2* merc *Merc-c* *Nat-ar* *Nat-c* *Nat-m* nat-p *Nat-s* *Nit-ac* *Nux-v* op ox-ac c1 paeon petr j5.de *Phos* *Phys* kr1* plb podo fd3.de• rat j5.de rhus-t h1* sars *Sel* sep *Sil* stront-c stry **Sulph** k* *Tab* tub verat h1 **Zinc** vh*
    - **feet**; as if the starting begins in: lyc h2
    - **violent** starting: cina mtf33
  - **preventing** (See SLEEP - Sleeplessness - starting)
- **sleepiness** with: ang j5.de ant-t j5.de *Cham* kr1 chel j5.de kali-i j5.de mag-c j5.de merc j5.de plat j5.de *Puls* kr1 sars j5.de seneg j5.de sil ↓ *Tarent* kr1 verat j5.de*

Starting – sleepiness with: ...

  - **afternoon**: sil h2
- **sneezing** of others, at: **Borx** k*
- **spoken** to, when: *(↗Spoken - aversion)* aur-m k2* carb-ac k* ignis-alc es2• phos vh ptel a1* **Sulph** k ●*
- **tossing** of arms, from: merc
- **touched**, when: *(↗Touched - aversion)* bamb-a stb2.de• *Bell* *Cocc* coff st* **Kali-c** k* *Kali-p* kali-sil k2* lac-h sk4• m-aust h1 mag-c k* ruta *Sil* stram c1 stry st*
- **tremulous**: bar-c cham
- **trifles**, at: *(↗Fear - trifles; Trifles; Trifles - important)* *Arn* *Borx* k* calc cham *Cocc* hura *Lyc* *Nat-c* *Nat-m* nux-m *Nux-v* *Petr* *Psor* k1* sabad *Sil* *Spong* sul-ac *Sulph* k* ther ptk1 zinc zinc-m a1
- **twitching**: con
- **uneasiness**, from: *(↗Restlessness)* mur-ac
- **unexpected** news: borx k2
- **urinate**, on beginning to: alum b4a.de*
- **violent**: stront-c ptk1
- **waking**, on: anac anthraq rly4• arizon-l nl2• aur-m ↓ *Bell* brom ↓ *Bry* h1* carneg-g rwt1• chinin-ar k2 coff br1 *Kali-c* *Lach* lat-m bnm6• led lyc nit-ac *Op* ↓ oxal-a rly4• pall staphycoc rly4• sul-i
  - **suffocated**, as if: *(↗RESPIRATION - Difficult - Sleep - during; RESPIRATION - Difficult - Sleep - during - agg.)* aur-m brom mtf33 *Lach* k* *Op*

STARTLED; easily (See Frightened; Starting - easily)

STATING her symptoms with great difficulty (See Narrating - difficulty)

STEALING (See Kleptomania)

STEREOTYPIC BEHAVIOR (See Gestures - repeating)

STEREOTYPIC MOVEMENTS (See Gestures - repeating)

STILLNESS (See Tranquillity)

STIMULANTS (See GENERALS - Food and - stimulants)

STOMACH; after disordered: chin b7.de*

STOOL:
- **after**: aloe ↓ borx ↓ bov ↓ calc ↓ carb-v bg2 caust bg2 chir-fl gya2 cimic ↓ ictod ↓ kali-c bg2 nat-m bg2 nat-s ↓ nit-ac bg2
  - **amel.**: aloe bg2 borx b4a.de* bov ptk1 calc bg2 cimic ptk1 ictod bg2 nat-s bg2*
- **before**: acon bg2 ambr bg2 *Bar-c* b4a.de borx bg2 cadm-s bg2 calc b4.de* canth bg2 caps bg2 caust bg2 cham b7.de* crot-t bg2 kali-c bg2 *Merc* bg2 mez bg2 rheum bg2 verat b7.de*
- **during**: ars bg2 sulph bg2 verat bg2
- **urging** for stool agg.; ineffectual: ambr bg2 *Caust* bg2 *Cham* bg2

STOOPING agg.: bov b4.de* calc b4.de* caust b4.de* coloc bg2 glon bg2 hell bg2 nat-m b4.de* nit-ac b4.de* phos b4a.de *Sulph* b4a.de valer b7.de*

STORIES; agg. by exciting (See Horrible)

STRANGE: *(↗Antics; Eccentricity; Gestures - strange; Queer; Schizophrenia - paranoid)*
- **crank**: *(↗Affectation - gestures; Queer)* bell gl1.fr• calc gl1.fr• carb-v ↓ chin mtf33* hell hr1 hyos gl1.fr• ip mtf33* *Lach* gl1.fr• loxo-recl bnm10• nat-m gl1.fr• puls gl1.fr• sil ↓ stram gl1.fr• sulph ↓ verat gl1.fr•
  - **dressing**, in: *(↗Dress)* carb-v mtf33 hell gl1.fr• sil gl1.fr• sulph gl1.fr•
  - **opinions** and acts, in: calc gl1.fr• sulph gl1.fr• verat mtf33*
- **everything** seems●: *(↗Confusion; Delusions - changed; Delusions - horrible; Delusions - horrible - everything; Delusions - objects - different; Delusions - strange - everything; Delusions - strange - familiar; Delusions - unreal - everything; Unreal - everything)* anac k2* *Bar-m* cann-i sf1.de *Cann-s* kr1* *Cic* b7.de* croc b7.de glon bg1* *Graph* *Hyos* b7.de kali-p *Med* ptk1 nux-m sf1.de *Op* b7.de petr sf1.de plat k* plb sf1.de podo fd3.de• *Ruta* fd4.de sep hr1* spong fd4.de *Stram* b7.de* *Tritic-vg* fd5.de tub k* valer b7a.de* verat b7.de [heroin sdj2]
  - **standing** agg.: glon a1
- **sensations**: arg-n mtf33 nux-m br1

- **things**; impulse to do strange: *(↗Confusion; Impulse - strange)* arg-n k2* cact k* iod ptk lac-leo hrn2• sep ptk1
- **voices** seem: *(↗Delusions - strange - voice)* **Cann-s** cic k2

STRANGER:

- **presence** of strangers: *(↗Restlessness - strangers - presence; Timidity - strangers)*
  - **agg.●**: *(↗Anxiety - strangers; Company - aversion - strangers; Company - aversion - strangers - urination; Excitement - stammers; Fear - strangers; COUGH - Strangers; COUGH - Strangers - presence; PERSPIRATION - Strangers)* *Ambr* k* *Ars*↓ aur-m-n wbt2• *Bar-c* k* *Bry* bufo k* carb-v ptk1 caust bg2* cic mtf cina k2 con iod stj2* **Lyc** k ●* med ser nat-m bg2* petr k* phos bg2* **Sep** k ●* **Spong** fd* staph gk *Stram* k* tarent bg2* *Thuj* k* [calc-n stj1]
    - **children**; in: bar-c mtf33 bufo mtf33 phos mtf33 sep mtf33 stram mtf33 thuj mtf33
    - **coughs** at sight of strangers; child: ambr k1 *Ars* k1 bar-c k1 phos k1
    - **menses**; during: con ptk1
  - **amel.**: thuj ptk1
- **sensation** as if one were a: *(↗Confusion - identity; Delusions - identity; Delusions - person - other; Delusions - robot)* germ-met srj5• nat-m bg1* neon srj5• sal-fr sle1• valer k*

STRENGTH; increased mental (See Mental power - increased)

STRESSED (See Ailments - cares; Ailments - excitement - emotional; Excitement; Hurry; Restlessness; Tension)

STRETCHING: | **agg.**: hep b4a.de

STRIKING: *(↗Attack; Jealousy - strike; Kicking; Violent)* acon↓ alum st1 anac mrr1 anan a1 androc srj1• ant-t↓ apis↓ *Arg-met* k* arg-mur↓ ars↓ atro a1 bac↓ **Bell** k* bov bry↓ bufo↓ bung-fa mtf camph k* cann-i↓ *Canth* k* carb-v k* carbn-s↓ carneg-g rwt1• *Cham* ptk1 chel a1* chen-a↓ **Cina** bg2* con sf1.de* *Croc* b7a.de crot-c sk4• cub *Cupr* k* *Cur* vh* der k* dulc fd4.de elaps gal-ac zr germ-met↓ *Glon* k* glycyr-g cte1• hell k* hep c1 heroin↓ hydr **Hyos** k* *Ign* k* *Kali-c* k* kreos bg2* lac-c sne lac-e hrn2• lac-h sk4• lil-t k* *Lyc* k* *Lyss* k* mag-c↓ marb-w↓ med mtf33 merc sne **Mill**↓ moni rfm1• morph oss• mosch k* *Nat-c* k* nicc-met sk4• **Nux-v** k* op↓ ox-ac↓ ozone↓ phos k* plat k* *Plb* k* polys sk4• *Prot*↓ rhus-t↓ sanic↓ scut↓ sep↓ sieg mg1.de spong fd4.de staph k* *Stram* k* streptoc↓ stront-c k* stry k* sulph↓ suprar rly4• syph al* *Tarent* k* thal-xyz srj8• *Tub* vh* *Verat* k* *Verat-v*↓ [cupr-act stj2 cupr-f stj2 cupr-m stj2 cupr-p stj2]

- **anger**, from: *(↗rage)* anan a1 arg-met sk7• bufo a1 *Bung-fa* mtf cina↓ marb-w es1• *Nat-c* gl1.fr• plat↓ *Prot* fmm1• spong fd4.de stront-c ptk1 tarent↓ tub mrr1
  - **children**; in: cina bwa3
  - **his** friends: plat st* tarent k2*
- **boy** clawing his father's face: *(↗Scratching; Scratching - face - parents)* **Stram** hr1*
- **bystanders**, at: **Bell** a1 carbn-s a1 chen-a a1 hell hr1 *Hyos* a1 lyc h2* stram a1
- **children**; in: *(↗Behavior - children; Indifference - children; in)* **Cham** k* chel a1 **Cina** k* cupr sst3• *Cur* vh* ign mtf33 kali-c mtf33 lac-e hrn2• lyc c1 med mtf33 moni rfm1• nux-v mtf33 op wbt• plb mtf33 prot fmm1• spong fd4.de syph mtf33 tarent mtf33 tub mrr1
  - **reprehended**; when: tub k*
- **children**; striking one's own: *(↗Aversion - children; Indifference - children; towards - mother; Violent; Violent - children - towards)* chel k* ox-ac ptk1
- **convulsions**, after: arg-mur vh cupr hr1* *Glon*↓
  - **puerperal**, after: *Glon* kr1
- **desire**:
  - **push** things; to: coff-t a1
  - **strike**; to: alum st *Anan* vh1 androc srj1• bell k* bufo carbn-s chir-fl gya2 choc srj3• der a1* *Dulc* fd4.de elaps hydr **HYOS** lac-cp sk4• lac-leo sk4• lil-t marb-w es1• nat-c nicc-met sk4• **Nux-v** st pegan-ha tpi1• podo fd3.de• *Rhus-g* tmo3• *Staph* suprar rly4• vanil fd5.de
    - **evening** | **amel.**: hydr a1
    - **betrayed** him; those who: rhus-g tmo3•
- **drunkenness**, during: hep gl1.fr• hyos gl1.fr• nux-v gl1.fr• verat gl1.fr•

Striking: ...

- **fists**, with: anac mrr1 syph al* tub hr1
- **himself**: *(↗Anger - tear; Biting - himself; Pulling - hair; Reproaching oneself; Tearing - himself; Tormenting - himself; Violent)* acon↓ apis↓ ars bac↓ bell k* camph k* cann-i a1 con↓ cur k* germ-met srj5• glon↓ hyos↓ mag-c↓ med↓ **Mill**↓ op↓ ozone↓ *Phos*↓ plat h2* plb↓ rhus-t↓ scut↓ sep sne spong↓ stram gb• sulph↓ syph↓ *Tarent* k* **Tub**↓ *Verat-v* [heroin sdj2]
  - **abdomen**, his: bell
  - **chest**, his: camph plb mtf33 verat-v
  - **face**, his: bell
  - **head**:
    - **hands**, her body and others; strikes her head with her: *Tarent* k1*
    - **his**: *(↗HEAD - Striking - head)* acon ptk1 apis ptk1 ars k* bac mhn1 glon sne hyos bg2* mill ptk1 stram k* syph ptk1 tarent tub ptk1*
  - **knocking** his head against wall and things: *(↗HEAD - Knocking head; HEAD - Motions of)* acon ckh1 apis ars bac mhn1 **Bell** k1* con hyos k* mag-c k* med gb• **Mill** k1* op wbt• ozone sde2• *Phos* gk rhus-t scut ckh1 spong fd4.de sulph gk syph c1* tarent vh* **Tub** k1* [heroin sdj2]
  - **pain**; during: plb bg2
- **imaginary** objects; about him at: *Bell* canth cina mtf33 cupr k* *Hyos* *Kali-c* lyc mosch nat-c nux-v op phos plat *Stram* k* stront-c verat mtf33
  - **dreaming**; while: phos j5.de
- **perspiration**; during: bung-fa mtf
- **quarreling**; when: bung-fa mtf
- **observed**; when not: tarent mtf33
- **rage**; with: *(↗anger)* *Arg-met* hr1 **Bell** hr1 *Carb-v* hr1 cupr sf1.de dulc fd4.de lyc sf1.de marb-w es1• stram hr1* streptoc rly4•
- **touched**; when: *(↗Touched - aversion)* ant-t ptk1 cham mtf33 sanic ptk1 tarent ptk1
- **sleep**; during: camph b7a.de
- **wall**, the: bry a1 canth k* con bg2* nux-v↓ spong fd4.de *Stram* a1 syph al
- **worm** affections, in: *Carb-v* hr1*

STRUGGLE: | **everything** is: lac-e hrn2•

STRUGGLING: lac-lup hrn2•

STUBBORN (See Obstinate)

STUDYING:

- **agg.**: ars-i ptk1* mag-p ptk1*
- **aversion** for (See Mental exertion - aversion)
- **difficult**: *(↗Concentration - difficult - studying; Dullness - studying; Dullness - thinking - long; Memory - weakness - mental; Mental exertion - agg. - impossible; Restlessness - study; Thoughts - wandering - studying)* aesc mtf11 *Agar* mtf33 agn sf1.de* aids nl2* allox tpw3* *Anac* sf1.de* *Ars* sf1.de* *Bar-c* sf1.de* bit-ar wht1• calc sf1.de* calc-p sf1.de* carb-v ptk1* carc jl2* caste jl caust sf1.de* con sf1.de* diphtox jl2 fago br1 falco-pe nl2• flor-p rsj3• kali-sil mtf33 mim-p rsj8• nat-m sf1.de* okou jl olnd sf1.de* ph-ac sf1.de* *Phos* sf1.de* podo fd3.de• positr nl2• rib-ac jl sep mtf33 syph↓ *Vanil* fd5.de [mang-met stj2 plb stj2]
  - **grammar**: syph jl2
  - **mathematics**: *(↗Mathematics - inability - calculating)* syph jl2
- **easily**: *(↗Intelligent; Learning - desire)* camph ptk1* coff ptk1* lach ptk1* phos ptk1* plat ptk1* sal-fr sle1•

STUNNED (See Stupefaction)

STUPEFACTION (= as if intoxicated): *(↗Dullness; Insanity; Prostration; Senses - dull; Spaced-out; Stupor; Torpor; Unconsciousness; Unconsciousness - dream; Unobserving [=inattentive]; FACE - Expression - intoxicated; FACE - Expression - stupid; FACE - Expression - vacant; GENERALS - Weakness - intoxicated; HEAD - Intoxication; HEAD - Intoxication - as)* abies-c↓ absin k* acet-ac k* acon k* act-sp hr1* adon sf1.de aesc k* aesc-g a1 aeth aether a1 agar k* *Agath-a* nl2* *Agn* b7.de* aids nl2• *Ail* bg2* allox tpw4 aloe sf1.de *Alum* k* alum-p k2* alumn↓ *Am-c* b4.de* am-m b7.de* ambr bg2* aml-ns a1* amyg anac b4.de* anan androc srj1• ang b7.de* *Anh* sf1.de* ant-c b7.de* ant-t k*

Stupefaction: ...
Apis k* apoc k2 arb-m oss1• arg-met b2.de* *Arg-n* j5.de* *Arn* b2.de* *Ars* k* ars-i ars-s-f k2* arum-t hr1* asaf k* asar k* asc-c hr1* aur b4.de* aur-m j bamb-a stb2.de• **Bapt** k* bar-c b2.de* **Bell** k* bism k* *Bit-ar* wht1• borx b4a.de* both fne1• *Bov* k* bruc j5.de **Bry** k* bufo sf1.de cact hr1* caj ↓ calad b7.de* *Calc* k* calc-ar k2* calc-caust ↓ calc-p bg2* calc-s calc-sil k2* *Camph* k* *Cann-i* a1* cann-s b2.de* canth b7a.de* caps b2.de* carb-ac a1 carb-an k* *Carb-v* b4.de* carbn-h k* carbn-o a1 carbn-s k* caust k* cench k2* cent a1 cham k* chel k* chin k* chinin-ar chinin-s chlf hr1 chlol a1 chlor k* chr-ac hr1* *Cic* k* cina k* cit-v hr1* clem k* cob *Coc-c* k* coca-c sk4• **Cocc** k* coch hr1* *Coff* b2.de* colch a1* coli rly4• coloc k* *Con* k* cor-r ↓ cori-r corn a1 cortico sp1 croc k* *Crot-h* k* crot-t j5.de cryp a1 *Cupr* k* cupr-act a1 cupr-ar hr1* cur bg2 cycl k* cypra-eg sde6.de• cyt-l a1 dig b4.de* digin a1 diosm br1 *Dulc* k* echi sf1.de ephe-si hsj1• eug br1 eup-pur hr1 euph bg2 euphr b7.de* fagu ↓ ferr k* ferr-ar ferr-i ferr-p fic-m ↓ fl-ac ptk1* gard-j ↓ *Gels* k* gent-l j5.de gins sf1.de glon bg2* gran k* graph k* haem sf1.de *Ham* hr1* **Hell** k* helon *Hep* b4a.de* hipp a1 hippoc-k szs2 *Hydr* hr1* hydr-ac a1 **Hyos** k* *Hyper* hr1 ign b7.de* ind hr1* iod k* ip k* jatr-c just sf1.de kali-bi bg2* kali-br k* **Kali-c** b2.de* kali-chl j5.de* kali-cy a1 kali-i bg2* kali-m ↓ kali-n k* kali-p kali-s fd4.de *Kola* stb3• kreos k* lac-c bg lac-h htj1• lac-lup hrn2• lach k* lachn ↓ lact j5.de* lact-v a1* laur k* led b2.de* lil-t k* lob sf1.de lol a1 lon-c a1 lon-x a1 lup a1* *Lyc* k* *Lycps-v* ↓ lyss hr1* *M-arct* b7.de* m-aust j5.de mag-c b4.de* mag-m k* mang ↓ med bg2* melal-alt gya4 *Meli* hr1* meph bg2* *Merc* b2.de* *Merc-c* merl a1* mez b2.de* mill a1* moni rfm1• morph a1 mosch b2.de* mur-ac b2.de* musca-d szs1 myos-a rly4• myric hr1 myris kr1 narcin a1 nat-c k* *Nat-hchls* nat-m k* nat-p nat-s nat-sil fd3.de• nicc nicot a1 *Nit-ac* b4.de* nitro-o a1 *Nux-m* k* **Nux-v** k* *Oena* ↓ ol-an j5.de* olib-sac wmh1 olnd k* **Op** k* ox-ac a1 ozone sde2• par j5.de *Petr* k* petr-ra shn4• **Ph-ac** k* phasco-ci rbp2 phel j5.de **Phos** k* phys phyt ↓ pic-ac sf1.de plan plat k* *Plb* k* plut-n srj7• podo hr1* positr nl2• psor k* *Ptel* hr1* *Puls* k* pyre-p a1 pyrid rly4• ran-b b7.de* ran-s ↓ raph k* rat j5.de rauw tpw8 rham-cal br1 *Rheum* k* rhod k* **Rhus-t** k* rhus-v k* ribo rly4• ruta b7.de* *Sabad* b2.de* sabin b7.de* sal-ac hr1* sal-fr sle1• samb b7.de* sang j* sars k* scut mrr1 *Sec* k* sel k* seneg k* sep k* ser-a-c ↓ sil k* sol-ni a1 spig k* spong b7.de* squil k* *Stann* k* staph k* **Stram** k* stry a1 sul-ac b4.de* sul-i k2* sulfa sp1 *Sulph* k* *Symph* fd3.de• tab k* tarax b2.de* tarent a1 *Ter* k* teucr b7.de* *Thuj* k* tritic-vg fd5.de tub rb2 uran-n sf1.de valer k* *Vanil* fd5.de **Verat** k* verat-v sf1.de verb k* vib ↓ viol-o b7.de viol-t b7.de* vip *Visc* *Zinc* k* zinc-p k2* [bell-p-sp dcm1]

- **daytime**: nit-ac a1 zinc hr1
- **morning**: acet-ac agar k* am-c ↓ bar-c *Bov* ↓ bry ↓ cham ↓ chel ↓ chin cob graph kali-p fd1.de• lyc a1 nat-c bg1* olib-sac wmh1 phos a1 positr ↓ rhod ↓ rhus-t hr1* sabad ↓ sars sep ↓ spong fd4.de squil *Thuj* k* tritic-vg ↓
  - **amel.**: *Agar* sf1.de
  - **rising**, after: *Bov* a1 bry k2 kali-p fd1.de• rhod sabad sep h2 *Thuj* tritic-vg fd5.de
  - **waking**, on: am-c sf1.de cham chel nat-c k* phos positr nl2•
- **forenoon**: ars ↓ sulph ↓ vanil fd5.de
  - **11** h: sulph a1
  - **11**-18 h: ars
- **noon**: podo fd3.de• zinc a1
- **afternoon**: caj a1 calc k* dulc fd4.de ham fd3.de• lyc lyss hr1 mang a1 olib-sac wmh1 phys *Puls* hr1* tritic-vg fd5.de *Zinc* a1
- **evening**: bov dulc graph a1 lyc h2* lyss hr1 merl a1 podo fd3.de• *Sulph* k* tritic-vg fd5.de vanil fd5.de zinc
- **night**: arg-n a1 bar-c a1 calc k* chel a1 fagu a1 lyss hr1* psor ↓
  - **waking**; must rise on: psor
- **air**, in open: cina *Nux-v*
  - **amel.**: agar a1 bell merc mosch a1 vanil fd5.de
- **alternating** with:
  - **convulsions**: *Aur*
  - **delirium** (See Delirium - alternating - stupefaction)
  - **violence** (See Violent - alternating - stupefaction)
- **anxiety**, with: anac hr1* gard-j vlr2•
- **beer**; from: kali-chl a1
- **brain**; with complaints of the: diosm br1
- **chill**, during: acon bg2 *Arn* bg2 *Ars* b4a.de* bell bg2 *Borx* k* *Bry* bg2 calc bg2 *Camph* b7.de* *Caps* bg2 *Cham* bg2 cic bg2 cocc bg2 con k* hell k* *Hyos* bg2 *Ip* bg2 kali-c bg2 laur bg2 mur-ac bg2 *Nat-m* b4.de* *Nux-m* nux-v bg2 **Op** b7.de* *Ph-ac* bg2
- **chill**, during: ...
Phos bg2 **Puls** b7a.de* *Rhus-t* bg2 **Ruta** bg2 sep bg2 stram k* valer bg2 verat b7.de* viol-t b7.de*
- **conversation**, after animated: borx h2*
- **convulsions**:
  - **after**: plb hr1
  - **between**: *Aur Bufo Cic Hell Hyos* lach *Oena* **Op** *Plb Sec* tarent
- **coryza**; during: hell b7.de*
- **cough**; during: ant-t b7.de*
- **debauchery**; as after: olib-sac wmh1 psor st
- **diarrhea**; with: dulc fd4.de gels a1*
- **dinner**, after: bufo kr1 coloc k* nat-m nux-v plan
- **disease**; about one's: **Ruta** fd*
- **eating**:
  - **after**: bell b4a.de cocc b7a.de hyos b7a.de petr b4a.de zinc b4a.de
    - **agg.**: *Cocc* hyos h1 morph
  - **while**: am-c b4a.de
- **emissions** (See pollutions)
- **epistaxis**, after: zinc
- **eruptions**; from suppressed: **Cupr**
- **fever**:
  - **after**: ars b4a.de
  - **before**: ars b4a.de bell b4a.de ph-ac b4a.de sulph b4a.de
  - **during**: *Apis* bg2 *Arn* b7.de* ars b4.de* *Bell* b4a.de* calc bg2 *Camph* bg2 *Cham* bg2 cocc b7.de* dulc b4a.de **Gels** bg2 *Hell* b7.de* **Hyos** b7.de* *Laur* b7.de* *Mur-ac* b4a.de nat-m b4.de* **Nux-v** bg2 **Op** b7.de* *Ph-ac* b4.de* phos bg2 **Puls** bg2 *Rhus-t* bg2 sep b4.de* stram b7.de* *Verat* bg2
- **head**, from congestion of the: bell a1
  - **with** congestion of the: agath-a nl2• *Kali-c* kr1
- **headache**:
  - **before**: plat h2*
  - **during**: *(↗HEAD - Pain - stunning)* cina a coc-c a1 dulc fd4.de hell mrr1 nat-sil fd3.de• plat h2 ruta fd4.de sabin c1 ser-a-c jl2 tritic-vg fd5.de vanil fd5.de
- **heat**; during: alum bg2 *Apis* k* arg-met bg2 arn bg2* ars bg2 *Bell* bg2 calad k2 calc bg2 *Camph* k* carb-v bg2 *Cham* b7.de* chinin-ar k2 **Cocc** bg2 gels bg2* **Hyos** b7.de* lach bg2 lachn c1 *Laur* b7.de* led bg2 nat-m bg2* **Nux-v** b7a.de* **Op** b7.de* *Ph-ac* bg2 phos bg2 **Puls** b7.de* *Rhus-t* bg2 *Sep* k* stram k* tritic-vg fd5.de *Verat* bg2
- **injury** to head, after: arn bg2* cic bg2* con bg2* hell bg2* puls bg2* rhus-t bg2*
- **knows** not where he is: *(↗Recognizing - not - surroundings; Unconsciousness - dream - does)* merc petr-ra shn4• ran-b thuj vib hr1
- **loquacious**: kali-i sf1.de meph sf1.de
- **menorrhagia**, during: *Cycl* hr1
- **menses**, during: *(↗Menses - during)* *Lycps-v* kr1 *Nux-m* k* zinc k2
- **mental** exertion; after: aeth vh1 ham fd3.de• *Kali-p* fd1.de• mag-c a1 **Nat-c** hr1 petr raph a1
- **motion**:
  - **amel.**: rhus-t hr1 vanil fd5.de
  - **from**: *Staph* thuj
- **paroxysms**, in: zinc h2
- **perspiration**, during: *Arn* bg2 ars bg2 bell bg2 bry bg2 calc bg2 cham bg2 **Hyos** b7.de* laur bg2 nux-v bg2 **Op** bg2 **Ph-ac** bg2 *Phos* bg2 *Rhus-t* bg2 stram k* verat bg2
- **pollutions**, after: caust lact c1 *Sul-ac* vh*
- **reading**, on: lyc k*
- **remains** fixed in one spot: nux-m
- **restlessness**, with: *Bapt* sf1.de kali-i sf1.de rhus-t sf1.de
- **rising**:
  - **after**: ozone sde2•
    - **amel.**: phos
  - **on**: sil
- **rouses** with difficulty: hell lyc **Op** sel sul-ac
- **scarlatina**, from: zinc k2
- **shivering**; during: caps b7.de
- **sits** motionless like a statue: *(↗Insanity - immobile; Unconsciousness - remains - motionless)* cham h1* hyos k* stram k*

- **sitting** at table, while: carb-an a1
- **sleepiness**, with: *(↗Dullness - sleepiness)* agath-a nl2• bapt sf1.de bell j5.de cocc j5.de *Con* kr1 euph j5.de lach j5.de lyc a1 m-arct j5.de **Nux-m** hr1* nux-v j5.de *Plb* hr1* ter sf1.de
- **smoke** in brain; as if from: arg-met b7a.de* op b7.de* sul-ac bg2
- **smoking**, from: acon a1
- **standing**; while: mang hr1
- **stool**; after: carb-an b4.de* nat-m bg2
- **stooping**, on: calc gl1.fr• nicc valer
- **sun**, agg. in: nat-c hr1 *Nux-v* ruta fd4.de
- **suppressed** eruptions (See eruptions)
- **urine** amel.; copious: gels hr1
- **vertigo**:
  - **after**: bufo a1
  - **during**: abies-c vml3• acon aeth agar k* arn *Aur* k* bar-c bell k* *Borx* b4a.de bov k* *Calc* k* cham b7.de* chel b7a.de clem croc sf1.de dulc fic-m gya1 *Gels* gran a1 graph hell hydr hydr-ac ip b7.de* kali-p fd1.de• kreos laur k* merc hr1 mill mosch k* mur-ac *Nat-m* b4a.de nux-m b7a.de op k* phos k* phyt plut-n srj7• psor *Puls* b7a.de ran-b sf1.de ran-s b7a.de *Rhus-t* b7a.de sabad hr1 sabin k* samb bat1• sec *Sep* b4a.de* ser-a-c jl2 sil spong fd4.de stann staph k* sulph tritic-vg fd5.de verat b7.de* zinc ptk1 zinc-p k2
- **vision**; with clear: agath-a nl2•
- **vomiting**; after | **children**; in: aeth c1* dulc fd4.de
- **waking**, on: agar a1 am-c sf1.de bov b4.de cann-s b7.de chel *Chin* b7.de* coff b7.de hyos ptk2 ind hr1* kali-p fd1.de• lac-h htj1• merc b4.de moni rfm1• nat-c *Op* hr1* phos plat b4.de* *Psor* hr1* puls b7.de sel b7.de* spong fd4.de staph b7.de tarent a1 vib hr1 viol-t b7.de
- **walking**, when: alumn **Ars** aur↓ calc gl1.fr• carb-an h2* cina↓ ip kali-p fd1.de• sulph↓
  - **air**, in open: ars aur c1 cina kali-p fd1.de• sulph a1
- **warm**:
  - **feet** get warm amel.; when: *Lach*
  - **room**; in: merl a1 phos
- **weather**, hot: gels hr1
- **wine**, after: ant-c c1 calc-caust a1 cor-r k* kali-m hr1 kali-n c1 petr a1 rhod hr1 sulph a1
- **writing**, while: arg-n k*

STUPIDITY (See Dullness)

STUPOR: *(↗Coma; Schizophrenia - paranoid; Stupefaction; Unconsciousness)* absin a1* acet-ac a1 acetan vh1 achy↓ acon a1* aesc a1* **Aeth** a1* aether a1 agar a1 agar-pa a1 *Agar-ph* a1 agar-se a1 agar-st a1 agav-t a1* **Ail** a1* alet a1* *Alum* a1 *Am-c*↓ *Aml-ns* a1* amyg a1* *Anac* j5.de* androg-p bnj1 ang a1 ant-c a1 *Ant-t* a1* *Apis* a1* apoc a1* aq-mar a1* *Arg-n* a1* *Arn* a1* ars a1* ars-h a1* ars-met↓ *Art-v*↓ astac a1* atro↓ bapt a1* *Bar-c* a1* **Bell** j5.de* ben-n a1 bism a1* boerh-d bnj1 *Bry* a1* bufo a1* cact a1* calad a1 *Calc* a1 *Camph* j5.de* cann-i a1 *Canth*↓ caps j5.de* carb-ac br1 carb-an a1* *Carb-v* j5.de* carbn-o a1 *Carbn-s* br1 *Cham* j5.de* **Chel**↓ chin a1* *Chinin-s*↓ *Cic* a1* clem a1 cocc a1* cod↓ coloc a1 **Con** j5.de* cori-r a1 corn a1* croc a1 crot-c a1 crot-h a1* cupr j5.de* *Cupr-act*↓ cyt-l a1* dat-s a1 *Dig* a1* diph↓ dor a1 dubo-m a1 euph a1 euph-l br1 euphr j5.de* ferr a1 ferr-p a1 *Gels* a1* glon a1 *Graph* a1* grat j5.de* *Ham* a1* *Hell* a1* *Helon* a1* *Hep* j5.de* hydr-ac a1* *Hyos* a1* *Ign* a1 iod a1 *Iris*↓ juni-v a1 kali-br a1 kali-c a1 *Kali-i* a1* *Kali-n* j5.de* kreos a1 lach j5.de* lat-m bnm6• **Led** a1* loxo-lae bnm12• lup a1 lyc a1* *Mag-c*↓ malar jl2 *Meli* a1* merc a1 *Merc-c* a1* merc-ns a1 merc-pr-r a1 morph a1 *Mur-ac* a1* myric a1 nat-br↓ nat-f a1* **Nat-m** a1* nit-ac a1 *Nit-s-d* a1* **Nux-m** a1* **Nux-v** a1* oena a1 *Op* a1* *Orig*↓ osteo-a jl2 ox-ac br1 petr a1* **Ph-ac** a1* **Phos** j5.de* phyt a1 plat j5.de* *Plb* a1* *Puls* j5.de* pyrus a1 ran-b a1 *Rheum*↓ rhus-t↓ sal-ac a1* *Samb*↓ sang a1* sars a1 scroph-n a1 *Sec* j5.de* *Seneg* j5.de* sol-ni↓ sol-t a1 spig j5.de* *Stann* a1* *Stram* a1* stry a1 sul-ac a1 *Sulph* a1* tab a1 tanac a1 tarent a1 tax a1 ter a1 tere-ch a1* valer a1 verat j5.de* verat-v a1* vip a1 visc c1 *Zinc* a1* [heroin sdj2]

- **daytime**: euph j5.de phos j5.de
- **morning**: ars-met a1* *Chinin-s* kr1 *Mag-c* j5.de
- **forenoon** | **10** h: stry a1
- **noon** and afternoon: euph j5.de
- **evening**: acon a1 *Ars* a1* oena a1 stry↓
  - **20** h: stry a1
- **night** | **amel.**: ferr a1

Stupor: ...

- **alcoholic** (See drunk)
- **alternating** with:
  - **convulsions**: agar a1
  - **delirium** (See Delirium - alternating - stupor)
  - **despair** (See Despair - alternating - stupor)
  - **escape**, desire to (See Escape - alternating - stupor)
  - **insanity** (See Insanity - alternating - stupor)
  - **mania**; sexual: apis br1
  - **restlessness** (See Restlessness - alternating - stupor)
  - **restlessness** with sadness (See Restlessness - sadness - with - alternating - stupor)
  - **violence** (See Violent - alternating - stupor)
  - **vomiting**: verat-v bg2 vip bg2
- **answers** questions properly, but stupor immediately returns: *(↗Answering - stupor)* *Hyos* kr1
- **apoplectic**: *Crot-h* kr1 *Hyos* kr1* *Lach* kr1 **Op** kr1* *Plb* kr1 sol-ni a1* *Stram* kr1
- **cold** surface, with: *Canth* kr1
- **concussion** of brain, from: **Arn** kr1*
- **convulsions**, after: *Ars*↓ *Art-v* *Bell* cori-r a1 *Glon* oena mrr1 op tl1 *Plb*↓
  - **epileptic**: *Ars* kr1 oena mrr1 *Plb* kr1
- **delirium**, after: atro a1 **Chel** kr1
- **despair**; after (See Despair - stupor)
- **diarrhea**:
  - **after**: ars a1
  - **during**: zinc c2
- **diphtheria**, in: ail kr1* diph bro1 *Nat-m* kr1 *Sul-ac* kr1
- **drunk**; as if: gels a1 *Glon* kr1 hyos a1* *Kali-br* kr1 *Stram* kr1
- **fever**, during: ail kr1* *Apis* kr1 **Arn** kr1* *Ars* kr1 **Bapt** kr1* calad kr1* *Camph* kr1 cic kr1 *Clem* kr1 crot-h kr1 dor kr1 *Gels* kr1 hyos mrr1 *Iris* kr1 kali-br a1* *Lyc* kr1 *Nat-m* kr1 *Nit-s-d* kr1* **Ph-ac** kr1 *Samb* kr1 sol-ni a1* *Ter* kr1
- **hearing**; with stupor: op gk
- **hydrocephalus**, in: **Apis** *Apoc* a1* *Clem* *Hell* *Hyos* *Lyc* *Nat-m*
- **jaundice**, in: **Chel** kr1
- **jaw** dropping; with: *Lyc* kr1 **Op** kr1 *Sulph* kr1
- **meningitis**, in: *Ant-t* kr1 *Apis* kr1 apoc kr1* *Hell* kr1 *Merc* kr1 *Sulph* kr1 *Verat* kr1 zinc mrr1
- **menses**:
  - **during**: *(↗Menses - during)* nux-m a1
  - **suppressed** from fright; in menses: *Op* kr1
- **murmuring**, muttering: *(↗Muttering)* *Cocc* kr1 dor kr1 *Phos* kr1 rhus-t j5.de*
- **old** age, in: *Bar-c* kr1
- **pain**, after: phyt a1
- **pneumonia**, in: *Chel* kr1 *Phos* kr1
- **restlessness**, with: ter kr1
- **sadness**; with: bapt br1 verat br1
- **scarlatina**, in: *Ail* kr1* *Am-c* kr1 *Apis* kr1 cupr br1 *Cupr-act* kr1 *Gels* kr1 *Lyc* kr1 *Mur-ac* kr1 *Sulph* kr1 ter tl1
- **screaming**; interrupted by: *Apis* kr1* bell a1* *Rheum* kr1 *Zinc* vh*
- **sexual** excitement, with: *Hyos* vh* *Orig* kr1 *Stram* kr1
- **speak**, inability to: bufo kr1 *Phos* kr1
- **starting**; with sudden: apis br1
- **starts** up in a wild manner, but could not keep the eyes open: *Stram* kr1
- **sudden**: canth k2
- **twitching** of limbs, with: *Bell* kr1 *Canth* kr1 *Cupr* kr1 **Hyos** kr1* **Stram** kr1
- **ulcers**; with: bapt bro1
- **uremia**, in: ter kr1
- **vomiting**:
  - **after**: ars a1
  - **during**: ail kr1 ars-h kr1 dor kr1 hep k*
- **wakes** often, but only for a short time: achy jl *Ars* kr1
- **waking**, on: cod a1 nat-br a1
- **warm** room agg.: apis mrr1

SUBMISSIVE (See Servile)

SUCCEEDS, never: (↗*Anxiety - success; Confidence - want; Delusions - business - unfit; Delusions - confidence; Delusions - disgraced; Delusions - fail everything; Delusions - friend - affection; Delusions - right - doing; Delusions - succeed; Delusions - wrong - done; Discouraged; Fear - business failure; Fear - failure; Fear - undertaking; Helplessness; Longing - good; Pessimist; Timidity; Undertaking - nothing)* am-c k* asar k* aur k* canth kali-p fd1.de• lac-h sk4• merc h1* mur-ac nat-c nat-s k* nux-v olib-sac wmh1 podo fd3.de• polys sk4• sal-fr sle1• [heroin sdj2 tax jsj7]

SUCKING: | **fingers** | **own** fingers; sucking one's (See Gestures - fingers - mouth)
- **into** the mouth; sucking objects: (↗*Gestures - fingers - mouth)* chin ↓ sacch sst1•
  - **adults**; in: chin brm

SUGGESTIBLE: (↗*Confidence - want; Insecurity)* *Arg-n* mrr1 *Phos* mrr1

SUGGESTIONS; will not accept: (↗*Contradiction - intolerant; Dictatorial; Obstinate)* helon k* *Podo* fd3.de• ruta fd4.de

SUICIDAL disposition: (↗*Bed - jumps; Cheerful - death; Death - desires; Fear - suicide; Inconsolable - suicide; Injuring; Injuring - fear; Insanity - split; Insanity - suicidal; Kill; desire - herself; Killed; Loathing - life; Mutilating; Pessimist; Rage - suicidal; Sadness - suicidal; Weary; Weary - sight)* acon ↓ adam ↓ *Aeth* ↓ agn ↓ alco a1 *Alum* b4a.de* alum-p k2* alum-sil k2 am-c k* ambr k* *Anac* k* anan anh mg1.de* *Ant-c* k* *Ant-t* k* aq-mar skp7• arg-met ↓ arg-n arn oss• *Ars* k* asaf **AUR** k* aur-ar k2 **Aur-m** k* aur-m-n c1* aur-s k2 bar-ox-suc rly4• *Bell* bg2* berb j bov j buni-o jl3 but-ac ↓ *Calc* calc-p sne calc-sil k2 camph h1 *Caps* k* carb-v k* *Carbn-s* ↓ carc mg1.de* cartl-s rly4• cassia-s ccrh1* caust chel bg2* *Chin* k* chinin-ar chr-met ↓ cic *Cimic* k* clem con ↓ corv-cor bdg• crot-c ↓ crot-h cupr sst3• cur cypra-eg sde6.de• der k* *Dol* ↓ dros k* dulc fd4.de falco-pe nl2• fuli bro1 gamb ↓ gels glon bg2 graph stj2*• grat haliae-lc srj5• hell k* *Hep* k* hipp hippoc-k szs2 hydr-ac j5.de *Hyos* k* *Ign* bro1 iod k* *Iodof* sf1.de iris ↓ kali-ar *Kali-br* k* kali-chl j kola ↓ kreos *Lac-d* lac-e ↓ lac-h ↓ *Lach* k* laur j led j lil-t k* lith-s ↓ loxo-recl ↓ lyc bg2* *Lyss* ↓ manc ↓ marb-w ↓ med k* meli k* *Merc* k* *Merc-aur* bg2* mez k* morg fmm1• morg-p fmm1• morph musca-d ↓ naja k* nat-c j *Nat-m* ptk1* **Nat-s** k* nat-sil ↓ nit-ac k* *Nux-v* k* oci-sa ↓ op gl1.fr• orig orni tl1 ozone sde2• parth vml3• ped ↓ petr-ra shn4• phos k* plat k* *Plb* k* plut-n srj7• positr nl2• prot ↓ pseuts-m oss1• **Psor** bg2* *Puls* k* ran-b ↓ rat ↓ rauw sp1 reser jl3 rhus-t k* rumx ruta j sarr sec k* *Sep* k* sil k* *Spig* k* spong j staph gl1.fr• *Stram* k* sul-ac j sulph k* symph ↓ syph rb2 tab k* tarent k* ter thal c1 thea thuj k* thuj-l jl3 tritic-vg fd5.de tub ptk1* ust bro1 valer ↓ verat k* *Zinc* k* zinc-p k2 ziz br1* [alumin stj2 alumin-s stj2 am-caust stj2 am-f stj2 bar-i stj2 beryl stj2 bism-sn stj2 bor-pur stj2 cinnb stj2 cupr-f stj2 cupr-p stj2 fl-ac stj2 fl-pur stj2 hydrog stj2 lith-c stj2 lith-f stj2 lith-i stj2 lith-m stj2 lith-met stj2 mang-i stj2 merc-d stj2 nat-f stj2 nitro stj2 oxyg stj2 plb-m stj2 plb-p stj2 sel stj2 spect dfg1 stann stj2 thal-met stj2 zinc-i stj2]
- **morning**: lyc nat-c
- **evening**: aur k* chin dros dulc fd4.de hep kali-chl k* rhus-t ruta fd4.de spig
  - **twilight**, in: rhus-t
- **night**: ant-c *Ars* chin nux-v phos bg1*
  - **midnight**, after: *Ars* nux-v
  - **bed**, in: ant-c
- **anger** driving to suicide: carb-v j5.de dulc fd4.de [spect dfg1]
- **anguish**; during: (↗*Fear - suicide)* carc mlr1• hep hr1*
- **anxiety**, from: (↗*Anxiety - suicidal)* aur h2 nux-v h1 puls h1
- **axe**, with an: naja k*
- **blood**; at the sight of: (↗*Blood)* alum br1* ars ↓ nat-s ↓ petr-ra shn4• thuj ↓
  - **abhors** the idea; though she: *Alum*
  - **knife**; blood on a: (↗*Thoughts - frightful - seeing)* alum a1* ars tl1 nat-s tl1 thuj tl1
- **brooding**; when (See Brooding - suicidal)
- **car**; throwing himself under a: alum sf1.de ars sf1.de* *Aur* sf1.de* kali-br bg2* lach ptk1* ozone sde2•
- **courage**, but lacks: (↗*fear - death; talks)* alum arg-n ll1 **Chin** k* nit-ac **Nux-v** k* ozone sde2• phos plat rhus-t k* *Sulph* kr1 tab

Suicidal disposition: ...
- **dagger**; with a (See knife)
- **delusions**, from: ars j5.de hyos j5.de verat j5.de
- **despair**, from: (↗*Despair)* ambr sf1.de ant-c kr1 carb-v sf1.de* hyos sf1.de positr nl2• *Ruta* fd4.de *Sep* ↓ *Spong* fd4.de *Tritic-vg* fd5.de verat ↓
  - **miserable** existence; about his: ruta fd4.de *Sep* kr1
  - **religious**: (↗*Despair - religious)* verat kr1
- **drowning**, by: (↗*Fear - drowned)* ant-c k* *Arg-n* k2* *Aur* bg2* aur-m-n wbt2* *Bell* k* *Dros* k* *Hell* k* hep sf1.de *Hyos* k* ign k* *Lach* k* nux-v gl1.fr• ped st1 *Puls* k* *Rhus-t* k* sec k* *Sil* k* spong fd4.de staph gtk1* sulph k* *Ust* gk verat
  - **love**, from disappointed: *Hyos* hr1*
- **drunkenness**, during: (↗*Fear - suicide)* ars gl1.fr• bell gl1.fr• nux-v gl1.fr•
- **eruptions**; from: plut-n srj7•
- **fear**: (↗*Fear - suicide)*
  - **death**; with fear of: (↗*courage)* alum kr1 *Chin* sf1.de* **Nit-ac** vh3* **Nux-v** lpc2* *Plat* kr1* rhus-t hr1* *Staph* gtk1* tab a1
  - **window** or a knife; with fear of an open: (↗*Fear - suicide)* arg-n camph chin *Merc*
- **fire**, to set oneself on: *Ars* st hep k2
- **fright**, after: (↗*Ailments - fright; Fear - suicide)* *Ars* h2*
- **gassing**, by: ars gl1.fr• nux-v gl1.fr• spong fd4.de
- **grief**; from: (↗*love)* *Nat-s* mrr1
- **hanging**, by: **Ars** b4a.de* aur k2 aur-ar gm1 aur-m-n wbt2* *Bell* bg2* carb-v gl1.fr• hell k2 nat-s k* nat-sil fd3.de• ter k*
- **heat**, during: ars k* bell k* nux-v k* puls k* rhus-t k* stram k*
- **homesickness**, from: caps bg2*
- **hypochondriasis**, by: alum gl1.fr• aur gl1.fr• calc gl1.fr• caust gl1.fr• chin gl1.fr• con gl1.fr• graph gl1.fr• hep j5.de *Nat-m* gl1.fr• sep gl1.fr• **Staph** gtk1* sulph gl1.fr•
- **injury** to head or brain; from: *Nat-s* mrr1
- **intermittent** fever, during: *Ars* chin lach *Spong* stram valer
- **itching** of skin; from: *Dol* mrr1
- **knife**:
  - **sight** of a knife; at the: alum bg2* petr-ra shn4•
    - **abhors** the idea; though she: *Alum* k*
  - **with** a knife: alum k* *Ars* k* aur sne bell k* *Calc* hyos gl1.fr• *Merc* k* nat-sil fd3.de• nux-v ptk1 plb vh3* positr nl2• stram
- **lacks** courage (See courage)
- **love**; from disappointed: (↗*grief; Ailments - love)* *Aur* kr1 bell ptk1* caust ptk1* *Hyos* kr1 plut-n srj7• staph ptk1*
- **menses**:
  - **before**: (↗*Menses - before)* iris vh* *Lach* sne
  - **during**: (↗*Menses - during)* cimic gk *Merc* k* sil
- **music**, from: (↗*Music - agg.)* nat-c k2* symph fd3.de•
- **pains**, from: (↗*Despair - pains)* **Aur** k* aur-m-n wbt2• bell carc mlr1• hep mrr1 lach *Nux-v* k* plut-n srj7• rat hr1* *Ruta* fd4.de sep thuj dp• tritic-vg fd5.de
- **perspiration**, during: alum **Ars** **Aur** aur-ar k2 **Calc** *Hep* **Merc** sil **Spong** k* *Thuj*
- **poison**, by: ars ptk1* *Bell* ptk1* ign kr1 lil-t oci-sa ↓ op a1 puls ptk1*
  - **cyanide**: oci-sa sk4•
- **pregnancy**, during: aur kr1
- **razor**; with a: acon gl1.fr• alum st falco-pe ↓ *Stram* hr1*
  - **opening** a vein, by: falco-pe nl2•
- **run** over, to be (See car)
- **sadness**, from: (↗*Sadness; Sadness - suicidal)* alum gl1.fr• **Aur** hr1* **Aur-m** vh* *Aur-m-n* wbt2• *Aur-s* wbt2• calc gl1.fr• caust gl1.fr• chin gl1.fr• cimic kr1 con gl1.fr• graph gl1.fr• *Hep* j5.de* hydrog srj2• ign gl1.fr• med hr1* *Merc-aur* sf1.de morph a1 naja sf1.de *Nat-m* gl1.fr• *Nat-s* sf1.de* nat-sil fd3.de• op a1 *Psor* a1* ran-b hr1* rumx kr1 *Ruta* fd4.de sep gl1.fr• *Spig* hr1* *Spong* fd4.de **Staph** gl1.fr• sulph gl1.fr•
- **sexual** desire; with violent: orig hr1*
- **shooting**, by: alum sf1.de anac k* *Ant-c* k* aur calc gl1.fr• carb-v k* chin gl1.fr• hep med nat-m gl1.fr• nat-s k* nux-v op gl1.fr• puls sep gl1.fr• **Staph** gtk1* sulph gl1.fr•
- **sight** of; at the:
  - **blood** (See blood)
  - **cutting** instruments: (↗*Fear - suicide)* alum *Merc* positr nl2•

- **sight** of; at the: ...
  - **knife** (See knife - sight)
- **stabbing**, by: ars a2* bell vh1* *Calc* kr1 nux-v gl1.fr•
  - **heart**, his: ars a1
- **starving**, by: merc bg2*
- **stomach**; with complaints of: ant-c bg2
- **talks** always of suicide, but does not commit: *(↗courage)* **NUX-V** st1
- **thinking** about suicide amel.: **Aur** hu*
- **thoughts**: *(↗Death - thoughts; Despair; Despair - death - thoughts; Pessimist)* acon vh1 adam srj5• agn k2 alum alum-p k2 alum-sil k2 *Anac* gk *Ant-c* *Arg-n* k* **Aur** k* *Aur-m-n* wbt2• **Aur-s** k2 but-ac br1 *Caps* k2* carc mlr1• cartl-s rly4• clem a1 dros dulc fd4.de falco-pe nl2• fuli br1 gamb mrr1 haliae-lc srj5• hell mrr1 *Hep* hydrog srj2• *Ign* iris vh* kali-ar k2 kali-br kola stb3• lac-d k2 lac-e hrn2• lac-h sze9• lach k2 lil-t loxo-recl knl4• manc mrr1 marb-w es1• med br1 *Merc* musca-d szs1 naja jl nat-m mrr1 **Nat-s** k* nat-sil fd3.de• nit-ac mrr1 prot jl3* **Psor** k* *Puls* *Rhus-t* k* *Ruta* fd4.de spong fd4.de thuj k* *Thuj-l* jl3 tritic-vg fd5.de zinc mrr1 zinc-p k2 [chr-met stj1* lith-s stj2 *Spect* dfg1]
  - **drive** him out of bed: *(↗Restlessness - bed - driving)* *Ant-c*
  - **meditates** on easiest way of committing suicide: *(↗Despair - death - thoughts)* **Lac-d** vh*
  - **mental** power; from despair about loss of: hell mrr1
  - **offensive** odor of body or discharges; with: psor mrr1
  - **persistent** (See Thoughts - persistent - suicide)
  - **restrains** himself because of his duties to his family: **Nat-s** br1*
  - **wish** for it; without: prot jl2
- **throwing**:
  - **height**; himself from a: *(↗High places - agg.)* acon vh1 anac *Arg-n* k* ars **AUR** k* aur-m-n wbt2• **Bell** bg2* camph crot-h gels k* glon bg2* hydrog srj2• hyos gl1.fr• ign st* iod bg2* iodof sf1.de lach bg2* *Lyss* vh* marb-w es1• *Nux-v* k* orig sec vh* sil vh* staph *Stram* k* sulph ptk1
  - **river**; himself into the: arg-n k* sec sil
  - **windows**, from: *(↗Escape - window)* *Aeth* k* arg-met ptk1 arg-n bg2* *Ars* k* **Aur** k* aur-ar k2 bell k* calc wm calc-sil k2 camph k* *Carbn-s* chin crot-c gels k* *Glon* k* *Iod* bg2* *Iodof* sf1.de lach bg2 nux-v bg2* *Sulph* kr1 thea thuj k* verat
    - ⋮ **delivery**; during: aur kr1 *Thuj* ↓
      - : **after**, puerperal: *Thuj* kr1
    - ⋮ **fear**; from: ars k1
    - ⋮ **headache**, in: *Glon* kr1
    - ⋮ **pain**; from: *Aur* k1*
    - ⋮ **parturition**; during (See delivery)
- **waking**, on: lyc nat-c
- **walking** in open air, while: bell
- **weeping** amel.: *(↗Weeping - amel.)* merc ptk1* phos k*

SULKY: *(↗Admonition; Ailments - reproaches; Brooding; Complaining; Discontented; Frown; Inconsolable; Irritability; Morose; Obstinate; Offended; Petulant; Sadness - love; Unfriendly; FACE - Expression - sullen)* *Agar* am-c vh1* anac k2* **Ant-c** k* arn bg2* ars aur bov calc canth carb-an carbn-s carl carneg-g rwt1• *Caust* chel cina ckh1 cinnb ↓ *Con* dulc fuma-ac rly4• hura kali-bi a1 kali-br *Kali-c* kali-n kola stb3• lac-cp sk4• lyc ckh1* mag-c k* mag-m k* mang menis a1 **Merc** h1* mur-ac *Nux-v* k* op petr ph-ac *Plat* k* sars spong hr1* stann staph h1 stront-c sul-ac sulph tub hr1* zinc k*

- **morning**: kola stb3•
- **afternoon**: cinnb a1

SULLEN (See Morose)

SUMMING UP is difficult (See Mathematics - inability - summing)

SUN; exposure to the: nat-c b4.de* nat-n bg2 nux-v bg2 sel bg2

SUNSTROKE agg.: glon bg2 hyos bg2

SUPERSTITIOUS: *(↗Fanaticism; Fear - superstitious; Mysticism; Religious - too; Ritualistic)* agar mrr2 arg-n mrr2* aster sze10• bell bg2 carc mlr1• *Con* k* granit-m es1• haliae-lc srj5• kali-ar gk lach dtn1 lap-a dgt **Lycps-v** vh* manc mrr med vh* op bg2 rat mrr1* rhus-t a1* stram bg2 syph mtf33* tritic-vg fd5.de tub vml zinc k*

SUPPER; after: caust bg2

SUPPORT; desires (See Confidence - want - support)

SUPPRESSED (See Emotions - suppressed)

SUPPRESSION or disappearance:

- **eruptions**; mental symptoms from suppressed (See Eruptions)
- **hemorrhoids**; mental symptoms from suppressed (See Hemorrhoids)

SURPRISES; unaffected by (See Indifference - surprises)

SUSCEPTIBLE: am-c gl1.fr• bar-c gl1.fr• calc gl1.fr• cypra-eg sde6.de• kali-p fd1.de• symph fd3.de• vanil fd5.de [bar-p stj1]

SUSPENSE (See Ailments - fear; Ailments - fright; Horrible)

SUSPICIOUS: *(↗Carefulness; Cautious; Cynical; Delusions - accused; Delusions - appreciated; Delusions - assaulted; Delusions - caught; Delusions - confusion; Delusions - criticized; Delusions - despised; Delusions - laughed; Delusions - persecuted - he; Dictatorial; Irritability - suspicious; Jealousy; Secretive; FACE - Expression - suspicious)* **Acon** k* adam ↓ *Aids* nl2• ambr k* **Anac** k* anan k* androc srj1• ang anh br1* ant-c k* apis bg2* arge-pl rwt5• *Arn* **Ars** k* ars-s-f k2 *Aur* k* aur-br vh1 *Aur-m-n* wbt2• aur-s k2* bapt bar-act j* **Bar-c** k* *Bar-m* *Bar-s* k2* *Bell* k* *Borx* **Bry** k* bufo gl1.fr• *Cact* cadm-met mg1.de calc b2.de* *Calc-p* calc-s k* **Cann-i** k* cann-xyz bg2* canth k* caps k2* carb-v bg2 carbn-s carc gk6* carneg-g rwt1• **Caust** k* **Cench** k* cham k* chin chinin-ar **Cic** k* *Cimic* k* coca k* *Cocc* con k* cortiso gse crot-c sk4• *Crot-h* k* crot-t ↓ *Cupr* k* dendr-pol sk4• **Dig** k* *Dros* k* *Dulc* gk elaps mrr1 falco-pe ↓ galla-q-r nl2• granit-m es1• graph ham fd3.de• *Hell* k* hydrog srj2• *Hyos* k* ign bg2* ip **Kali-ar** kali-bi bg2* kali-br k* *Kali-p* k* lac-cp sk4• lac-leo hrn2• *Lac-lup* hrn2• **Lach** k* **LYC** b2.de* *Lycps-v* kr1 m-arct b2.de* macro a1 marb-w es1• *Med* vh* meli k* meny k* *Merc* k* mez moni rfm1• *Morph* sf1.de mur-ac *Nat-ar* *Nat-c* k* nat-p nat-s k2* nat-sil fd3.de• nicc-met sk4• *Nit-ac* k* *Nux-v* k* olib-sac wmh1 *Op* k* ph-ac b4a.de* phasco-ci rbp2 *Phos* k* plat sf1.de plb k* plut-n ↓ polys sk4• positr nl2• pseuts-m oss1• psor gk **Puls** k* **Rhus-t** k* ruta k* sacch-a fd2.de• sal-fr sle1• sanic sarr **Sec** k* sel k* *Sep* k* sil *Spig* gl1.fr• *Stann* k* *Staph* k* still sf1.de **Stram** k* streptoc ↓ suis-hep rly4• *Sul-ac* k* sul-i k* **Sulph** k* syph st1 thuj k* thyr ptk1 tritic-vg fd5.de urol-h rwt• vanil fd5.de verat bro1* *Verat-v* k* viol-t k* [heroin sdj2 pall stj2 thal-met stj2]

- **daytime**: *Merc* k*
- **afternoon**: cench ↓ *Lach* k* nux-v
  - **15**-20 h: cench
- **evening**: bar-m cench *Lach*
- **enemy**; considering everybody his: *(↗Delusions - enemy; Delusions - enemy - everyone; Delusions - enemy - surrounded)* *Merc* vh* *Puls* kr1
- **fear** of company: *(↗Timidity - bashful; Timidity - company)* ambr j5.de bar-c j5.de falco-pe nl2• *Nat-c* j5.de
- **foolish** suspicion: adam skp7• apis ptk1
- **friends**, his best: androc srj1• crot-c sk4• dros mtf33 ruta a1 sacch-a fd2.de•
- **hiding** things from him; people are: galla-q-r nl2•
- **insulting**: merc j5.de
- **looking** on all sides: kali-br ptk1
- **medicine**, will not take: *(↗Refusing - medicine)* *Cimic* kr1 tritic-vg fd5.de
- **men**; of: plut-n srj7• polys sk4•
- **menopause**; during: *Cimic* st
- **mistrustful** (See Suspicious)
- **plotting** against his life; people are: *(↗Delusions - murdered)* aids nl2• ars ↓ galla-q-r nl2•
  - **house**; people about the: *(↗Delusions - murdered)* ars a1
- **solitude**, desire for: *(↗Company - aversion)* cic j5.de crot-t j5.de
- **strangers**; toward: cupr sst3•

- **talking** about her, people are: *(↗Delusions - laughed)* aids nl2• aur-m-n wbt2• *Bar-c* k* hyos ptk1 ign ptk1 pall ptk1 stann ptk1 staph ptk1 streptoc rly4• *Tritic-vg* fd5.de
- **walking**, while: *Anac* k*

SWEARING (See Cursing)

SWEETNESS (See Mildness)

SWIMMING: *(↗Bathing)*

- **desires**: ambr tsm1 lac-del hrn2•
  - **night** diving: lac-del hrn2•

SWOONING FITS (See GENERALS - Faintness - sudden)

SYMPATHETIC: *(↗Affectionate; Anger - reproaches - others; Anxiety - others; Benevolence; Horrible; Impressionable; Injustice; Lamenting - others; Mildness; Weeping - sympathy)* acon vh adam srj5• aeth ↓ *Aids* nl2• alco a1 am-c bg2* ambr gg aml-ns vh1 androc srj1• arg-n gk* aur fb *Aur-m-n* wbt2• aur-s wbt2• bar-c gk bell gl1.fr• bit-ar wht1• calc fb *Calc-p* vh* cann-i a1 **Carc** c cd ckh fb fd fd2.de gk6 hbh3.fr *Jl* mg1.de mlr mrr **Mtf3** sk sp *Sst* st vh carl k* *Caust* k* chir-fl gya2 *Cic* cocc bg2* coff mrr1 croc crot-c mgm• cupr sst3• cycl mrr1 cypra-eg sde6.de• dendr-pol sk4• dulc gk1 *Falco-pe* nl2• fic-m ↓ *Foll* oss• germ-met srj5• graph bg2* haliae-lc srj5• ham fd3.de• hell fb hydrog srj2• *Ign* k* iod k* irid-met srj5• kali-p ↓ *Kali-s* fd4.de kola stb3• lac-leo sk4• lac-lup hrn2• lach bg2* limen-b-c hrn2* lyc k* *Lyss* ↓ manc med gk *Moni* rfm1• *Nat-c* k* *Nat-m* k* nat-p mrr1* *Nat-sil* fd* *Nit-ac* k* nuph k* *Nux-v* k* oci-sa sk4• olib-sac wmh1 petr-ra shn4• **Phos** k* plut-n srj7• *Podo* fd3.de• positr nl2• puls k* querc-r svu1• ruta fd4.de sabad lsa1.de sacch-a fd2.de• sal-fr sle1• sep fb* **Spong** fd* staph lmj suis-em rly4• sumb lsa1.de symph fd3.de• tarent bg2* tarent-c sf1.de tritic-vg fd5.de ulm-c jsj8• vanil fd5.de [am-p stj1 bar-p stj1 calc-sil stj2 ferr-p stj1 ferr-sil stj2 tax jsj7]

- **animals**; towards: *(↗Animals - love)* aeth c1* carc fb* dulc fd4.de falco-pe nl2• fic-m gya1 ham fd3.de• kali-p fd1.de• kali-s fd4.de med gk nat-m ser *Nat-sil* fd3.de• nuph c1 podo fd3.de• positr nl2• ruta fd4.de spong fd4.de symph fd3.de• tarent oss• tritic-vg fd5.de vanil fd5.de
  - **suffering**: nuph a
- **black** persons; for: dendr-pol sk4•
- **children**:
  - **in**: nit-ac mtf33
  - **towards**: falco-pe nl2• positr nl2•
- **daughter**; with: lac-lup hrn2•
- **Mafia** leader; towards: crot-c sk4•
- **not** sympathetic (See Unsympathetic)
- **same** pain his brother complained of; felt the: *Lyss* kr1

SYMPATHY from others: *(↗Consolation - amel.)*

- **agg**. (See Consolation - agg. - sympathy)
- **amel**. (See Consolation - amel.)
- **aversion** to: *(↗Consolation)* *Am* kr1 coff ptk1 positr nl2• sabal br1 syph ptk1 vanil fd5.de
- **desire** for: *(↗Consolation - amel.; Kind people - yearning)* androc srj1• calen mgm• caust mtf cypra-eg sde6.de• *Ham* fd3.de• *Kali-s* fd4.de nat-m mtf nat-sil fd3.de• ozone sde2• **PHOS** bg2* puls bg2* rhus-g tmo3• ruta fd4.de sep mtf *Spong* fd4.de vanil fd5.de

SYPHILIS agg.: asaf ptk1 *Aur* ptk1 hep ptk1 lach ptk1 merc ptk1 nit-ac ptk1 phyt ptk1

TACITURN: *(↗Abrupt; Anger - taciturnity; Answering - aversion; Answering - monosyllables; Answering - refusing; Asking - nothing; Autism; Brooding; Censorious - silent; Company - aversion; Conversation - agg.; Disturbed; Grief - silent; Indifference - quiet; Indifference - taciturn; Irritability - taciturn; Loathing - speaking; Morose - taciturn; Quiet disposition; Reserved; Sadness - taciturn; Secretive; Spoken - aversion; Talking - loud; Touched - aversion; MOUTH - Speech - wanting)* abrot k* *Acon* adam skp7*• aeth k* aether a1 *Agar* k* agra ↓ aids ↓ alco a1 aloe alum k* alum-p k2 alum-sil k* am-c k* am-m k* ambr k* amyg a1 anac k* androc srj1• androg-p bnj1 anh sf1.de* *Ant-c* k* ant-m a1 ant-t bro1 apis a1 apoc kr1 *Arg-met* k* arg-mur a1 *Arg-n* k* arge-pl rwt5• arizon-l nl2• **Arn** k* *Ars* k* ars-s-f k2 ars-s-r kr1 arum-m kr1 *Arund* kr1 astac a1 aster atro **Aur** k* aur-ar k2 *Aur-m-n* wbt2• aur-s k2 bamb-a stb2.de• bapt *Bar-c* k* bar-m *Bell* k* berb k* bism k* bism-o a1 bit-ar ↓ borx *Both* a1 bov bran a1 brass-n-o srj5• brom k*

Taciturn: ...
bros-gau mrc1 bry k* bufo bufo-s a1 bung-fa ↓ buth-a sp1 *Cact* k* *Calc* k* calc-p calc-s calc-sil k2* camph cann-i cann-s canth *Caps* k* carb-ac **Carb-an** k* *Carb-v* k* carbn-o a1 carbn-s k* carc mg1.de* carl cassia-s cdd7* castm **Caust** k* *Cham* k* chel *Chin* k* chinin-ar chinin-s a1 chir-fl gya2 chlam-tr bcx2• chlf a1 chlol bg2 cic k* *Cimic* k* cina *Clem* k* **Cocc** k* cod a1 coff k* *Coff-t* ↓ colch *Coloc* k* con k* conch fkr1• cortico jl cortiso sp1 corv-cor bdg• crot-c crot-h a1 crot-t cupr k* cupr-act a1 *Cycl* k* cypra-eg sde6.de• dendr-pol sk4• dig k* dios kr1 dirc dream-p sdj1• dros h1 dulc a1 elaps ↓ ephe-si hsj1• ery-m a1 **Euph** bg2* euphr k* fago falco-pe nl2• *Ferr* k* ferr-ar ferr-m a1 ferr-ma ↓ ferr-p fl-ac k2 *Gels* k* gent-c a1 germ-met srj5• gink-b sbd1• **Glon** k* granit-m es1• graph grat k* guaj k* haliae-lc srj5• ham a1 **Hell** k* helon *Hep* k* hera a1 *Hipp* hippoc-k szs2 hist mg1.de hydr hydr-ac kr1 hydrog srj2• *Hyos* k* **Ign** k* iod *Ip* k* irid-met srj5• jab a1 jatr-c jug-r k* kali-ar kali-bi kali-br a1 kali-c kali-cy a1 kali-m k2 kali-n a1* kali-p k* (non:kali-s slp) kali-sil k2* kola stb3• lac-ac kr1 lac-d lac-h sk4*• lac-leo hrn2• lac-lup hrn2• lach k* lap-la rsp1* laur a1 lavand-a ctl1• lec oss• **Led** k* lil-t linu-u a1 lol a1 loxo-recl knl4• **Lyc** k* *Lycps-v* kr1 lyss jl2 m-arct b7.de* m-aust b7.de* mag-c k* *Mag-m* k* mag-s manc *Mang* k* meny k* *Merc* b4.de* merc-c a1 merc-d a1 mez k* moly-met jl* mosch bg2 *Mur-ac* k* murx myric naja br1* nat-act a1 nat-ar nat-c k* *Nat-m* k* nat-p *Nat-s* k* nat-sil k2* nicc nicc-met sk4• *Nit-ac* k* nux-m **Nux-v** k* oena a1 oeno a1 ol-an olib-sac wmh1 olnd a1 onos **Op** k* orig a1 ox-ac k* oxal-a rly4• oxyt k* ozone sde2• passi a1 pert-vc vk9 petr petr-ra shn4• **Ph-ac** k* **Phos** k* phys a1 *Pic-ac* a1* pieri-b mlk9.de pip-m k* plac rzf5• **Plat** k* *Plb* b7.de* plumbg a1 *Plut-n* srj7• podo fd3.de• positr nl2• psil ft1 ptel **Puls** k* querc-r c1 rad-br sze8• rheum k* *Rhus-t* ruta fd4.de sabad sabin k* sacch a1 *Sal-fr* sle1• sanic bro1 sars k* sec bg2 *Senec* ↓ sep k* ser-a-c jl2 sil k* sol-t a1 spig k* *Spong* k* squil k* *Stann* k* **Staph** k* *Stram* k* stront-c k* stry a1 *Sul-ac* k* **Sulph** k* *Symph* fd3.de• tab k* tarax k* *Tarent* k* tart-ac a1 tax-br oss1• tep a1 thea j5.de* *Thuj* k* tong j5.de tril-p c1 tritic-vg fd5.de tub hr1* ust vanil fd5.de **Verat** k* verat-v a1* vesp a1 viol-o k* *Viol-t* k* vip a1 visc a1 **Zinc** k* zinc-p k2* [bell-p-sp dcm1 heroin sdj2 spect dfg1 tax jsj7 zinc-m stj2 zinc-n stj2]

- **morning**: arg-met vh1 cocc hep kali-p fd1.de• mag-c ↓ mag-m nat-s nit-ac oss• sabin tarax thuj ↓ tritic-vg fd5.de
  - **waking**, on: cocc mag-c mrr1 nit-ac vh thuj
  - **walking**, while: sabin thuj
- **forenoon**: aeth hipp nat-m
- **afternoon**: fago grat hell mag-s nat-ar nat-m sep
  - **alternating** with | **excitement** (See Excitement - alternating - taciturnity - afternoon)
- **evening**: am-m kali-c h2 *Ph-ac* *Plat* symph fd3.de• **Zinc**
  - **amel**.: bism h1 clem
- **air**, in open: ph-ac sf1.de plat
- **alternating** with:
  - **cheerfulness** (See Cheerful - alternating - taciturnity)
  - **jesting** (See Jesting - alternating - taciturnity)
  - **laughing** (See Laughing - alternating - taciturnity)
  - **loquacity** (See Loquacity - alternating - taciturnity)
  - **mirth** (See Mirth - alternating - taciturnity)
  - **quarreling** (See Quarrelsome - alternating - taciturnity)
  - **violence** (See Violent - alternating - taciturnity)
- **children**; in: agra bro1* aur mtf33
- **company**, in: arg-met k1 hydrog srj2• spong fd4.de symph fd3.de• tritic-vg fd5.de
- **cough**; during: verat b7a.de
- **die**, as if he would: *Mur-ac* kr1
- **eating**, after: aloe arg-n ferr-ma mez plb
- **fright**, after: *Ign* kr1
- **head**; with complaints of: ant-c bg2 con bg2 thuj bg2
- **headache**, during: *Anac* kr1 bros-gau mrc1 bung-fa mtf *Coff-t* kr1 con hydrog srj2• nat-ar ox-ac kr1
- **heat**, during: am bg2 ars j5.de *Bell* b4a.de* borx j5.de cham k* *Gels* kr1 ign bg2 lach j5.de lyc k* *Mur-ac* b4a.de* *Nux-m* kr1 nux-v k* *Op* b7a.de* *Ph-ac* b4a.de* phos bg2 *Puls* k* *Tarent* kr1 verat bg2
- **herself**; about: plut-n srj7•
- **loud**; indisposed to talk (See Talking - loud)
- **menses**, during: *(↗Menses - during)* *Am-c* castm elaps mur-ac *Senec*
- **mortification**, after: *Ign* kr1 plut-n srj7• vanil fd5.de [tax jsj7]

- **mutism**: agra br1 hell mtf11 lyc↓ verat mtf11
  - • **children**; in: agra ptk1 lyc ptk1
- **obstinacy**, from: cham gl1.fr• nat-m mtf33
- **overwork**; from: **Kali-p** fd*
- **perspiration**, during: arn bg2 ars kr1 *Bell* bg2 bry bg2* calc bg2* chin bg2* *Ign* bg2 merc bg2* *Mur-ac* bg2* *Op* bg2* **Ph-ac** bg2 **Phos** bg2 *Verat* bg2
- **pregnancy**, during: *Verat* kr1
- **sadness**, in: *(↗Sadness - taciturn)* **Arg-n** kr1 *Ars* j5.de* bar-c j5.de bit-ar wht1• *Cact* sf1.de clem h2 gink-b sbd1• ign gl1.fr• mag-c kr1* nit-ac j5.de ph-ac gl1.fr• *Puls* kr1* *Spong* fd4.de stann kr1 verat sf1.de
- **sexual** excesses, after: **Staph** kr1
- **sickness** or injuries, about: *(↗Ailments - injuries)* **Bapt** kr1
- **sits**, does not move: *(↗Sitting - inclination - stiff)* *Hep* kr1 spong fd4.de stram kr1
- **sufferings**; indisposed to talk about his: alum-sil vh1 ign bg2
- **superficial** matters; aversion to talk about: aids nl2• lyc sej4 plut-n srj7• positr nl2• sal-fr nl2• [heroin sdj2]
- **waking**, on: anac j5.de cocc j5.de
- **walking** in open air, after: arn h1

TAKING everything in bad part (See Offended)

TALENTED:
- **children**: chin mtf33 sulph mtf33
- **very**: carc cd

TALKATIVE (See Loquacity)

TALKING:
- **absent** persons, with: chlol ptk1* dig↓ hyos ptk1 *Stram* a1
  - • **night**: dig a1
- **agg.**: *(↗Conversation - agg.; GENERALS - Talking - agg.)* alum j5.de* am-c j5.de* am-m b7a.de *Ambr* k* anac kl arg-met k2 arn borx b4a.de* calc j5.de chir-fl gya2 cocc dros b7a.de ferr ign bg2 kali-c b4.de* mag-c nat-m bg2 nux-v b7.de* ph-ac b4.de* plat bg2 ptel c1 *Spig* b7.de* stann j5.de* staph b7.de* *Sulph* k* zinc bg2 [zinc-m stj2 zinc-p stj2]
- **alone**; talks to himself when (See himself - alone)
- **alternating** with | **singing** (See Singing - alternating - talking)
- **amel**. the complaints: *(↗Conversation - amel.)* calc-p ms carc↓ chir-fl gya2 dulc fd4.de melal-alt gya4 nat-m↓ pieri-b mlk9.de ruta fd4.de *Tritic-vg* fd5.de
  - • **prolonged**: carc fd2.de• nat-m h2 *Tritic-vg* fd5.de
- **animals**; to (See Animals - love - talking)
- **anxious** to talk in public (See Timidity - public - talk)
- **as** if talking; lips move (See Delirium - lips)
- **aversion** to talk (See Taciturn)
- **battles**, about: *(↗war; DREAMS - Battles)* bell hyos taosc iwa1•
- **business**, of: *(↗Absorbed - business; Delirium - business; Industrious)* ars bell **Bry** k* canth k* cimic dor k* *Hyos* k* mygal op phos plb k* stram sulph k*
- **cares**; talks of nothing but about her: cocc zr uva↓
  - • **amel.**: [uva stj]
- **clich s**; in: germ-met srj5• sal-fr sle1•
- **colors**; about: ozone sde2•
- **complaints**; of her: *(↗disease)* arg-n bg2* asaf ptk1* des-ac rbp6 falco-pe nl2• *Mag-p* bg2* *Nux-v* bg2* olib-sac wmh1 pop-cand br1 *Sep* b4a.de zinc ptk1* [tax jsj7]
- **condition**; anxious about his: *Arg-n*↓ **Nux-v** kr1 sabad↓
  - • **wakes** wife and child | **hypochondriasis**; in: *Arg-n* kr1 sabad sys
- **dead** people, with: *(↗Delusions - talking - dead)* bell **Calc-sil** k* canth hell *Hyos* k* nat-m stram
- **desire** to talk to someone: *(↗pleasure; Company - desire; Contact; desire; Desires - full - more; Gossiping; Loquacity)* *Arg-met* k* *Arg-n* k* caust cystein-l rly4• dulc fd4.de frax ptk1* ip↓ kali-s fd4.de kola stb3• lil-t limest-b es1• nat-sil fd3.de• nux-m kr1 oci-sa sk4• petr phasco-ci rbp2 *Phos* vh* pieri-b mlk9.de podo↓ rhus-g tmo3• *Ruta* fd4.de *Spong* fd4.de stict c1* taosc iwa1• tarax kr1 *Tritic-vg* fd5.de vanil fd5.de [calc-p stj1 spect dfg1 tax jsj7]
  - • **forenoon**: caust ruta fd4.de
  - • **chill**; during: podo ptk1
  - • **conflicts**; in order to solve: calc-p ms nat-sil fd3.de•
  - • **occurrences** of previous day; about: ip mtf33

Talking: ...
- **disease**; only about one's: *(↗complaints)* med ptk2
- **eyes** closed, with: nat-m pcr
- **disinclined** to talking (See Taciturn)
- **emotions**; expresses: lac-lup hrn2•
- **family** controversies; about: *(↗Quarrelsome - family)* dulc mrr1
- **faults** of others; about the: *(↗Censorious)* verat ptk1
- **foolishly** (See Speech - foolish)
- **future**; about: *(↗Plans - making - future)* hyos k* ruta fd4.de
- **himself**, to: *(↗Autism; Introspection; Muttering)* aesc mrr1 *Aeth* vh1 *Ant-t* k* apis *Aur* k* aur-m-n wbt2• bell calc k2* chlol k* crot-h bg2 dulc fd4.de haliae-lc srj5• hydrog srj2• *Hyos* k* ign k2 *Kali-bi* k* lach gl1.fr• m-ambo b7.de* m-arct b7.de* mag-p k* merc mosch k* mur-ac nux-m nux-v gl1.fr• oena olib-sac wmh1 op par vml3• ph-ac plb k* podo fd3.de• pyrog k* ran-b rhus-t *Staph* mrr1 stram k* sul-ac mrr1 tab tarax k* thiam rly4• urol-h rwt• vip
  - • **alone**; only when: *Lach* st* *Nux-v* st* par vml3• **Stram** st*
  - • **gesticulates**; and: mosch ptk1*
  - • **loudly**: nux-m ptk1
- **humming**: lyc gl1.fr• nux-v gl1.fr• staph gl1.fr•
- **imaginary** persons; with (See absent)
- **inability** to talk in public (See Timidity - public - talk)
- **incessant**: pyrog jl2
- **indisposed** to talk (See Taciturn)
- **learning** to talk; late (See slow)
- **listens**; talks and does not care whether anyone: *(↗Loquacity)* *Stict* kr1
- **loud**; indisposed to talk: *(↗Taciturn)* nux-m ckh1 sil
- **murder**, fire and rats; of nothing but: *Calc* calc-sil k2
- **nonsense** (See Speech - nonsensical)
- **one** subject; of nothing but: *(↗Monomania)* *Arg-n* cann-i limest-b es1• lyc med ptk1* petr stram
- **others** agg.; talk of: *(↗Egotism; Selfishness; Violent - Talk; GENERALS - Weakness - Talk of)* acon bg2* agar alum am-c k* ambr bg2* androc srj1• ant-t k2 **Ars** k* aur bros-gau mrc1 *Cact* k* cadm-s k2 carb-an bg2* chin k* *Cocc* k* colch k* *Con* k* elaps ferr ferr-ar *Hell* *Helon* kr1 hydrog srj2• **Hyos** k* *Kali-c* kali-p fd1.de• kalm ketogl-ac rly4• lach k2 limest-b es1• lys bg2 lyss bg1* mag-m k* mang k* mez bg2* nat-ar *Nat-c* k* nat-m bg2* *Nat-s* *Nit-ac* **Nux-v** k* orot-ac rly4• petr bg2* *Ph-ac* bg2* *Phos* b4a.de plac rzf5• rhus-t k* *Sep* k* sil k* *Stram* k* teucr vanil fd5.de verat k* *Zinc* k*
- **pleasure** in his own talk: *(↗desire; Egotism; Haughty; Selfishness)* nat-m k* par k* stram k*
- **public**; timid to talk in (See Timidity - public - talk)
- **recovery** agg.; of: ars bg2
- **same** subject; of the (See one)
- **sex**; about: [heroin sdj2]
- **sleep**, in: *(↗Muttering - sleep in; Speech - confused - night - sleep; Speech - incoherent - sleep; Speech - loud - sleep; Speech - merry - sleep; Speech - prattling - sleep; Speech - unintelligible - sleep; Speech - wild - sleep; DREAMS - Talking)* acon k* agra sne *Ail* hr1* alum k* alum-p k2* alum-sil k2* am-c k* ambr k* anac hr1 ant-t k* apis k* arg-n k* arizon-l nl2• *Arn* k* ars k* atro vh aur j5.de *Bar-act* st bar-c k* bar-m bar-s k2* **Bell** k* both-ax tsm2 brach a1* bry k* bufo k* *Cact* k* *Calc* b4.de* camph k* *Cann-i* k* *Carb-an* k* carb-v k* carbn-s carc mlr1* cassia-s ccrh1• caste jl castm caust k* *Cham* k* *Cina* bro1* cinnb k* coff k* com con cortico tpw7* cupr cur a1 dig bg2* diph ptk1 dulc fd4.de elaps gk fuma-ac rly4• *Gels* hr1* graph k* *Hell* bro1 *Hyos* k* hyper k* ign k* indg jab a1 jac-c a1 kali-ar kali-bi k* **Kali-c** k* kali-chl k13 kali-m k2 kali-p kali-s kali-sil k2* kalm k* kola stb3• *Lac-c* hr1* **Lach** b7a.de* *Led* hr1* limest-b es1• lyc k* m-ambo b7.de m-aust b7.de* mag-c k* *Mag-m* k* malar jl2 med↓ merc k* *Mur-ac* k* nat-c b4.de* *Nat-m* k* nit-ac k* nux-m↓ *Nux-v* k* *Op* k* ph-ac k* phos k* plb k* plect a1 podo bg2 psor al2* *Puls* k* pyrog ptk1 raph k* rheum j5.de *Rhus-t* k* sabin k* sapin a1 sel k* *Sep* k* *Sil* k* spig b7.de* spong b7.de* *Stann* k* *Stram* b7a.de* stry a1 *Sulph* k* tarent a1 thuj k* tub hr1* verat sne zinc k* zinc-p k2* zinc-s k2 ziz a1* [bor-pur stj2 heroin sdj2]
  - • **angry** exclamations, with: castm kr1
  - • **answer** questions: med hr1
  - • **anxious**: alum graph h2* *Mag-m* kr1
  - • **business**, of: com k* rhus-t k* sulph k*

- **sleep**; in: ...
  - **calculating**: sel a1
  - **children**, in: *Ambr* hr1* dulc fd4.de kali-c mtf33 kali-sil mtf33 mag-c mtf33 psor st*
  - **chill**; during: ars bg2 calc bg2 *Cham* bg2 nux-v bg2 puls bg2 sulph bg2
  - **comatose** sleep; in: nux-v j5.de op j5.de raph j5.de
  - **confess** themselves aloud; they: bell gl1.fr• **Hyos** gl1.fr• stram gl1.fr•
  - **excited**: alum castm graph nux-v sulph
  - **gentle** voice, all night in a: *Camph* h1*
  - **loud**: *Arn* h1* ars a1 *Bell* hr1* carb-an h2* jac-c a1 *Kali-c* a1 mag-c a1 mur-ac a1 nux-m ptk1 rhus-t a1 *Sep* hr1* *Sil* a1* spong hr1* *Sulph* h2*
  - **obstacles** to be removed; about: cham h1
  - **old** men; in: bar-c ptk1
  - **raving**: bry bg2 rheum bg2*
  - **reveals** secrets: *(↗Revealing - sleep)* am-c *Ars* k1*
  - **supplicates** timidly: stann kr1
  - **thought** when awake, what he: am-c k*
  - **war**, of (See war - sleep)
- **slow** learning to talk: *(↗Slowness; GENERALS - Development)* agar k* **Agra** sne aloe sne bar-c k* *Bell* gl1.fr• borx k2* calc bg2* calc-p k* caust bg2* mag-c mtf33 med c1* **Nat-m** k* nux-m op wbt• ph-ac k2 phos st* sanic k* sil bg2* sulph bg2* thuj mtf33 tub fry* [plb stj2]
- **spirits**; with (See Delusions - talking - spirits)
- **sufferings**; constantly of his (See complaints)
- **troubles**; of her (See complaints)
- **unpleasant** things agg.; of: *(↗Horrible)* *Calc* k* cic b2.de* ign k* nit-ac bg2 *Teucr* k*
- **war**, of: *(↗battles)* agar bell crot-c sk4• dulc fd4.de hyos
  - **sleep**, in: hyos h1*
- **weary** when talking (See GENERALS - Weariness - talking)

TAPHEPHOBIA (See Fear - buried)

TASK-ORIENTED (See Activity)

TASTE agg.; bitter: am-m bg2 bell bg2

TASTEFUL: *(↗Elegance; Pretty)* carc sk1• dulc fd4.de kali-s fd4.de vanil fd5.de

TASTELESSNESS in dressing: *(↗Dress - indecently; Elegance - want; Indifference - external things)* *Calc* gl1.fr• caust gl1.fr• hell h1 hyos h1 lac-h sze9• lyc gl1.fr• *Nat-m* gl1.fr• nux-v mtf33* sec gl1.fr• staph mtf33* stram h1 *Sulph* gl1.fr*

TEARFUL mood (See Weeping)

TEARING:
- **himself** (= herself): *(↗Anger - tear; Mania - tearing; Reproaching oneself; Striking - himself; Tormenting - himself)* ars bell k* cann-xyz ptk1 carc ↓ cupr mtf33 cur kali-p ptk1 plb k* sec k* **Stram** k* tarent ptk1 verat ptk1
  - **genitals**, her: *(↗Shrieking - genitals; MALE GENITALIA/SEX - Handling - tearing)* sec
  - **hair**, her (See Pulling - hair)
  - **skin** around nails: carc hbh*
- **things** in general: *(↗Anger; Breaking; Destructiveness; Mania - tearing; Rage - tearing; Violent)* agar bro1* ars-i ↓ **Bell** k* *Camph* cann-xyz ptk1 canth *Cimx* bro1* cupr k* cur ↓ gink-b jl3 hyos k* ign iod k* *Kali-p* k* merc *Nux-v* k2* *Oena* kr1 op phos sec ptk1 **STRAM** bg2* sulph k* *Tarent* k2* vanil fd5.de *Verat* k*
  - **clothes**: *Bell* ↓ camph ptk1 cur mrr1 hyos tl1 *Kali-p* ↓ nux-v pc tarent k2* verat k2*
    - **nightdress** and bedclothes: *Bell* kr1 *Kali-p* kr1
  - **garments**; his (See clothes)
  - **pillow** with teeth: phos **Stram** k*
  - **restlessness**; from: ars-i mrr1

TEASING: *(↗Jesting; Mocking)* all-c vh1 aran-ix jl3 arn gl1.fr• caust gl1.fr• cic sne cupr ↓ cupr-act ↓ cupr-f ↓ cupr-m ↓ cupr-p ↓ graph gt* mag-p dgt nux-v gl1.fr• petr-ra shn4• ruta fd4.de [lappa stj stann stj2 tax jsj7]
- **animals**: [cupr stj2 cupr-act stj2 cupr-f stj2 cupr-m stj2 cupr-p stj2]
- **children**; in: graph br1

TEDIUM (See Ennui; Forsaken)

TEETH: | **pulled** out; wants a tooth have: bell bg2

TELLING the symptoms (See Narrating)

TEMERITY: *(↗Audacity; High-spirited)* agar gl1.fr• *Arn* st1 aur-m-n ↓ aur-s ↓ med ↓ op gl1.fr• plat ↓ rhus-g tmo3• spong fd4.de staph gl1.fr• [tell stj2]
- **kick**; temerity to get a: aur-m-n wbt2• aur-s wbt2• med fd* plat mrr

TEMPER TANTRUMS: *(↗Anger - violent)* acon mtf aur mrr2* *Bell* h1* borx mtf33 calc vh1* calc-p sej3 carc mtf28 cere-b mtf **Cham** bl1* che! hr1 cina mtf33 cocc mtf *Cupr* mtf33 hep bc3 *Hyos* mrr3* ign gy3 ip mtf33 lach c10 lyss mtf mag-c nsk1 med hu2 *Nat-m* cd1* nux-v dw1* olnd mtf *Phos* mtf33 plut-n srj7• *Prot* mtf11 puls bkh1* rheum mtf33 sanic mtf33 sil cd1* staph gy3* *Stram* mtf stront-c mtf *Sulph* mtf28 *Tarent* mtf33 thuj mtf33 thyr bnu3 **Tub** mtf33 [tell stj2]

TEMPLES; with pressing in: ant-c bg2 gran bg2

TENDERNESS (See Affectionate)

TENSION, mental: *Acon* br1 aids nl2• ara-maca sej7• *Ars* mrr1 bacls-7 pte1*• *Bamb-a* stb2.de• carc fb *Cocc* mrr1 cortico tpw7 cupr sst3* dulc fd4.de dys pte1*• ham fd3.de• hir rsj4• mim-p rsj8• moni rfm1• morg-g pte1*• morg-p pte1*• mosch br1* olib-sac wmh1 ozone sde2• pin-con oss2• positr nl2• prot pte1* syc pte1*• trios ↓ tritic-vg fd5.de [heroin sdj2 nat-caust stj2]
- **evening**: trios rsj11•
- **children**; in: cupr sst3•

TERRIFIED after dreams (See Fear - waking - dream)

TERROR (See Fear - terror)

TESTAMENT, refuses to make a: *Calc* gl1.fr• hep gl1.fr• nat-m gl1.fr•

THANATOPHOBIA (See Fear - death)

THANKING others (See Gratitude)

THEORIZING: *(↗Absorbed; Activity - desires - creative; Concentration - active; Deeds - great; Emotions; Emotions - predominated; Fancies - absorbed; Fancies - exaltation; Ideas - abundant; Intellectual; Introspection; Philosophy - ability; Plans - making; Thoughts - thoughtful)* androc srj1• ang apis k2 arg-n k* arizon-l nl2• ars *Aur* aur-m-n wbt2• aur-s wbt2• bar-s zr* **Cann-i** k* *Cann-s* ckh1 *Cann-xyz* ptk1 *Chin* k* cocc bro1 *Coff* k* helo-s rwt2• hydrog srj2• kali-c mtf lac-e hrn2• lac-loxod-a hrn2• *Lach* k1* limen-b-c mlk9.de lyc nat-c a1 nitro-o a1 *Olib-sac* wmh1 op a1 positr nl2• puls k* sel k2* *Sep* sil spong fd4.de **Sulph** k* thuj mtf tritic-vg fd5.de vanad dx vanil fd5.de *Verat* gl1.fr•
- **evening**: *Chin* k*
- **night**: chin k2* coff k2*
- **philosophic**; mind dwells on: limen-b-c hrn2•
- **proving** substance; about the: lac-e hrn2•

THINKING: *(↗Thoughts)*
- **abstract** thinking:
  - **images**; abstract concepts become like: anh sp1
  - **inability** for: anh sp1
- **agg.**: ign bg2 par ptk1 [bell-p-sp dcm1]
- **analytical** thinking:
  - **ability** for: anh sp1 ham fd3.de• positr nl2• thuj a1 [zinc stj2 zinc-m stj2 zinc-p stj2]
  - **aversion** to: falco-pe nl2•
- **aversion** to: *(↗Dullness; Ennui; Ideas - deficiency; Mental exertion - aversion; Prostration)* act-sp hr1* agar agn b7.de* *Ail* hr1* aloe bg2 *Alum* b4a.de ambr ↓ *Anac* bg3 *Apis* b7a.de am b7.de* asar b7.de* *Aster* hr1* bamb-a stb2.de* **Bapt** k* berb sf1.de bry k* caps k* carb-ac a1 *Carb-v* k* casc k* **Chin** k* coca a1 con bg corn k* dros b7.de* echi k* ferr k* ferr-p *Gels* gins a1 graph b4.de* ham fd3.de* hyos k* iod b4a.de ip b7.de* kali-bi bg2 kali-n b4.de* kola stb3• lac-ac laur b7.de* **Lec** k* limen-b-c hrn2* *Lyc* k* med mtf mez b4.de* nat-ar nat-c bg nat-m nauf-helv-li elm2• nit-ac b4.de* **Nux-m** bg *Nux-v* b7.de* olib-sac wmh1 olnd bg *Op* bg ozone sde2• par b7a.de petr b4.de* **Ph-ac** k* **Phos** k* phyt bg2 pic-ac bg plan plb mtf ptel rhod b4.de* rhus-t b7.de* rumx ruta mrr1 sabad b7.de* *Sars* b4a.de sel b7.de* sep b4.de* *Sil* bg2* spong b7.de* **Squil** k* *Staph* b7.de* stram k* thea a1 *Vanil* ↓ verat wies a1 zinc bg

- **aversion** to: ...
  - **morning**: ambr br1 kali-n
  - **afternoon**: arn ↓ lyc k*
    - ⁝ **walking** in open air; after: arn
  - **evening**: lyc
  - **television**; only desires to watch: kola stb3• *Vanil* fd5.de
- **conceptual**:
  - **inability** | **environment**; about: anh sp1
- **complaints**:
  - **agg.**; thinking of his complaints●: *(↗Anger - thinking; Anxiety - health - own; Anxiety - thinking; Confusion - thinking - agg.; Hypochondriasis; Narrating - agg.; Occupation - amel.; Weeping - telling - sickness; MALE GENITALIA/SEX - Erections - wanting - thinking)* agar (non:alum bg2*) alum-p k2 alumn kr1* am-c ambr k* arg-met k* *Arg-n* bg2* arn k* ars k* asar b7.de aur k* aur-ar k2 aur-m bad bg2 *Bapt* *Bar-c* k* bar-m sf1.de borx c1 bry k* calad b7a.de calc k* *Calc-p* k* carc mlr1• *Caust* k* cham h1* chinin-ar cimic gk cina b7.de cocc b7.de* coff b7.de *Colch* bg2* con k* dros k* *Gels* k* graph ham c1 *Hell* k* helo bg2 *Helon* k* hura hydr bg2 ign b7.de iod bg2* ip sf1.de lac-c bg2* *Lach* k* laur bg2 limen-b-c hm2* lycps-v ptk1 m-ambo b7.de* m-arct b7.de mag-s **Med** k1* menth-pu c1 meny b7.de merc kr1 mosch nat-m nat-s ptk1 *Nit-ac* k* *Nux-m* bg2* *Nux-v* k* olnd k* **Ox-ac** k* *Oxyt* k* par bg* phos pieri-b mlk9.de *Pip-m* k* pip-n bg2 plan bg2 plb k* plut-n srj7• *Ran-b* k* *Sabad* k* sabal ptk1 sars sec gk sep sin-n c1 spig k* *Spong* k* stann bg2 staph k* sumb c1* thuj thyr ptk1 tub ptk1 zinc bg2
  - **amel.**: **Camph** b2.de* cic k* cocc kr1 *Hell* k* mag-c pall prun k*
  - **constantly** to his ailments: *Ham* st*
- **desire** for: limen-b-c hm2•
- **difficulty** of thinking (See Dullness)
- **disagreeable** things agg.; of (See Thoughts - disagreeable)
- **disappear**; ability for thinking will: limen-b-c hm2•
- **extremes**; in: lac-f wza1•
- **fast** (See Thoughts - rapid)
- **faster** than ever before | **fever**; during: *(↗Thoughts - rapid - fever)* pyrog k2
- **fluids** (See Thoughts - liquids)
- **inability** to think (See Concentration - difficult; Dullness; Prostration; Thoughts - vanishing)
- **logical** thinking:
  - **inability** for: falco-pe nl2• sal-fr sle1•
    - ⁝ **interruption**; from (See Confusion - interruption - logical)
- **long** (See Dullness - thinking - long)
- **mechanical** thinking | **ability** for: sulph mrr1
- **mundane**; is: limen-b-c hm2•

THIRST agg.: cupr bg2

THOUGHTS: *(↗Ideas; Thinking)*
- **accidents**; of: dendr-pol sk4• osm-o ↓
  - **others**; accidents to: *(↗Fear - injury - others)* osm-o a1
- **adulterous** (See sexual - adulterous)
- **albatrosses** circumnavigating globe: neon srj5•
- **amorous** | **troublesome**: osteo-a knp1•
- **arrested** (See stagnation)
- **automatic**: chlorpr jl3
- **beauty**; about her own: marb-w es1•
- **birth**; about: olib-sac wmh1
- **blockades**; to break: olib-sac wmh1
- **business**; of:
  - **evening** | **bed**; in: bell j5.de cocc j5.de sulph j5.de
- **charm**; about her own: marb-w es1•
- **circles**, move in: cann-i a1 choc srj3• dulc fd4.de falco-pe nl2• fic-m gya1
- **clearness** of (See Agility; Clarity; Ideas - abundant)
- **commitment**; about a: [temp elm1]
- **communication**; about human: olib-sac wmh1
- **community**; about relieving: *Olib-sac* wmh1
- **compelling**: *(↗persistent; Anxiety - do something; Checking - twice; Forgotten - something; Ritualistic)* *Anac* mp• anh hu* ant-c gk arg-n mrr1* *Ars* mrr1* aur mp• bell-p mgm• brom mrr calc mrr* carb-v ↓ carc mp* *Caust* mrr1* con mrr* cupr br1* cupr-act mtf foll asm* **Hyos** mp• *Ign* mp•

Thoughts – compelling: ...
Iod mp* kali-c mrr* lac-c mtf33 *Lach* ptk1 lyss mrr1* manc mrr1* **Med** mp• merc mrr1* nat-m mp* *Nat-s* mp• nit-ac ptk1 *Nux-v* mp* passi ↓ phos ↓ pin-s bh• *Plat* mp• psor mp• puls mp* *Rat* mrr1* rhus-t pcr* sil mp* *Staph* mp• sulph mp* *Syph* mrr1* thuj pcr tub jl2* verat mp*
  - **children**; in: arg-n mtf33 ars mtf33 carb-v mtf33 passi br1 phos mtf33 puls mtf33
- **control** of thoughts lost: *(↗instability)* arg-met ↓ ars ↓ *Coff* mrr1 kali-s fd4.de lycps-v a1 morph ↓ nat-m ↓ nux-m ↓ oena a1 puls a1 sulph a1
  - **afternoon** | **14** h: nux-m a1
  - **evening**: nat-m a1
  - **chilliness**, during: ars a1
  - **sitting** and reflecting, while: arg-met a1
  - **undressing**, while: morph a1
- **corpses**: hydrog srj2• olib-sac wmh1
- **creation**; of second day of: neon srj5•
- **crude**: camph a1
- **dead** bodies; about (See corpses)
- **death** of (See Death - thoughts)
- **deep** (See profound)
- **disagreeable**: *(↗Dwells)* alum bg2 *Ambr* k* bar-c k* ben-n ↓ benz-ac bg2* calc k* carc mlr1• *Chin* h1* *Cocc* h1* *Hep* bg2* kiss a1 lyc k* meny a1 mez h2* *Nat-m* bg2* nit-ac k* petr ↓ phos ↓ psor bg2* rhus-t a1 sec sep a1 sulph k* symph fd3.de• thuj bg2 urol-h rwt• verat bg2
  - **agg.**: phos bg2
  - **night**: ben-n a1 chin a1 lyc ↓ petr a1 **Rhus-t** ↓
    - ⁝ **midnight**, after: **Rhus-t** a1
    - ⁝ **waking**; on: lyc gl1.fr•
- **disconnected**: alum a1* ambr sf1.de arg-n a1 *Bell* a1 ben-n a1 berb j5.de cann-i a1* caps bg2 carbn-o a1 carbn-s a1 chin bg2 choc ↓ colch hr1* *Cupr-act* a1 dig a1 dream-p sdj1• gels hr1* *Hell* vh* hydrog srj2• hyos a1 irid-met ↓ kali-i a1 lac-h htj1• lact-v a1 lam hr1* laur bg2 lavand-a ctl1• lyc a1 melal-alt gya4 merc-c ↓ *Nat-c* j5.de* *Nux-v* hr1* ph-ac j5.de pin-con oss2• *Rhus-v* a1* sieg mg1.de sulfa jl3 sulph j5.de* *Syph* hr1* trom hr1* ven-m jl3 verat j5.de* viol-o a1* *Zinc* j5.de* [bell-p-sp dcm1]
  - **read**, cannot: choc srj3• lac-h htj1• *Nat-c* hr1* **Nux-v** hr1*
  - **talking**, when: *(↗Answering - disconnected; Answering - incoherently/ Speech - incoherent)* irid-met srj5• merc-c a1
- **disease**, of: *(↗Anxiety - health; Anxiety - health - own; Fear - disease)* alum *Ars* k2* carc mlr1• chel lepi k* lept merc ↓ murx nat-m nat-p ph-ac phos ruta ↓ sang hr1 sep sulph
  - **incurable**, of some: *(↗Delusions - disease - incurable; Fear - cancer; Fear - disease - incurable)* *Ars* hr1 merc a1 ruta fd4.de
- **disgusting** thoughts with nausea: *(↗Discontented - everything; Disgust; Loathing - general; DREAMS - Disgusted; DREAMS - Disgusting)* carc mlr1• falco-pe nl2• sang k*
- **disordered**: lac-lup hm2•
- **distracted**: lac-lup hm2•
- **do**; about things to: cortico tpw7
- **drugs** and addictions; about: *Olib-sac* wmh1
- **erroneous**: agath-a nl2• lac-lup ↓ sabad ptk1* valer ptk1* verat st1*
  - **perception**; of: *(↗Mistakes - perception)* lac-lup hm2•
- **fast** (See rapid)
- **father**; of her: plut-n srj7•
- **flow**; of (See rush)
- **flying**, of: haliae-lc srj5•
- **foolish** thoughts in the night: *(↗Foolish)* chin k2
- **frightful**: *Alum* ↓ calc *Caust* k* hydr ↓ *Iod* hr1* kiss ↓ lac-c lyss olib-sac wmh1 phos k* phys k* *Plat* hr1* *Rhus-t* thea *Visc* k*
  - **evening**: *Caust* k* lac-c ↓
    - ⁝ **bed**; in: lac-c
  - **night**: alum hr1 hydr a1 kiss ↓ phos a1 phys ↓ *Visc* ↓
    - ⁝ **waking**; on: kiss a1 phys a1 *Visc* k*
  - **seeing** blood or a knife, on: *(↗Blood; Kill; desire - knife - sight; Suicidal - blood - knife)* *Alum* k*
- **funeral**; about: olib-sac wmh1

- **future**, of the: *(↗Anxiety - future)* chin-b hr1* chir-fl gya2 cycl k* dulc fd4.de iod limen-b-c hm2• nat-ox rly4• nat-sil fd3.de• podo fd3.de• senec k* sep k* spig
- **god**; about | **confidence** in God; about: olib-sac wmh1
- **grace**; of her own: marb-w es1•
- **himself**; about:
  - **cannot** think of anyone besides: *(↗Selfishness)* crot-t st1 [tax jsj7]
  - **diverted** from thoughts of himself; desire to be: camph kr1 [tax jsj7]
  - **hears** only his inner thoughts and feelings: arizon-l nl2•
- **hurry** (See rapid)
- **imprisonment**; of others: [temp elm1]
- **incarceration**: [temp elm1]
- **inconstancy** (See Inconstancy - thoughts)
- **insane**: *Lyss*
- **instability** (= unsettled): *(↗control; vanishing)* *Acon* b7.de* ang b7.de* berb bg2 cann-s b7.de cham b7.de *Coff* b7a.de *Lach* b7a.de lyc bg2 *M-aust* b7.de* maias-l hm2• nux-m bg2 nux-v b7.de* op b7.de* puls b7.de* staph bg2 valer b7.de* *Viol-o* b7.de*
- **intrude** and crowd around each other: acon k* aloe ↓ androc srj1• ars arund ↓ bry h1* camph hr1* *Cann-i* k* canth k* cinnb k2* con ↓ *Dulc* fd4.de *Fl-ac* hr1* germ-met srj5• *Graph* ↓ helo-s rwt2• **Kali-s** fd* kola stb3• lach k* maias-l hm2• melal-alt gya4 *Merc* hr1* mur-ac orig ↓ ph-ac phos h2* pic-ac ↓ *Plat* ↓ ruta fd4.de sel ↓ spong ↓ *Staph* ↓ suis-hep rly4• *Sulph* *Tritic-vg* fd5.de tub k2 *Vanil* ↓ verb hr1* [heroin sdj2]
  - **night**: bry h1* tub k2*
  - **closing** eyes, on: spong kr1
  - **reading**, while: **Ph-ac** ●*
  - **sexual**: *(↗sexual; tormenting - sexual; Fancies - lascivious; Lascivious; Nymphomania)* aloe arund st1 con *Graph* k* orig st1* *Phos* pic-ac *Plat* sel k2* *Staph* tritic-vg fd5.de *Vanil* fd5.de
  - **too** weak to keep them off or to hold on to one thought: *Ars* k1
  - **work**, while at: *(↗rush - working)* mur-ac *Sulph* tritic-vg fd5.de
  - **writing**, while: *Lach* hr1*
- **life**; about the meaning of: olib-sac wmh1 *Vanil* fd5.de
- **limits**; to respect: olib-sac wmh1 *Tritic-vg* fd5.de
- **liquids** agg; of: lyss ptk1
- **listen** to; hard to: lac-lup hm2•
- **logical**: lac-lup hm2•
- **lovers**; about:
  - **literature**; in: olib-sac wmh1
  - **past**; of the: [temp elm1]
- **many** (See Ideas - abundant)
- **marriage**; of: hyos mtf orig a1*
  - **masturbation**; in: hyos mtf
- **misery**; about: olib-sac wmh1
- **monotony** of: anh mg1.de* chlol a1 olib-sac wmh1 polys sk4•
- **negative**: fum rly1•
- **Noah's** ark; of: neon srj5•
- **numbers**; of:
  - **number** two: neon srj5•
  - **odd** and even: neon srj5•
- **one** thought excludes all other: limen-b-c hm2•
- **other** people; knows thoughts of (See Clairvoyance)
- **playful**: dioxi rbp6
- **past**, of the: agath-a ↓ androc ↓ atro a1 bros-gau mrc1 cann-i a1 chord-umb rly4• dulc fd4.de granit-m es1• haliae-lc srj5• irid-met srj5• meny a1 nat-m a1 olib-sac wmh1 plut-n srj7• ruta fd4.de sanguis-s hm2• senec ↓ sol-t-ae ↓ spong fd4.de *Symph* fd3.de• *Tritic-vg* fd5.de ulm-c jsj8• vanil fd5.de [nat-caust stj2 nat-lac stj2 nat-met stj2 nat-sil stj2 temp elm1]
  - **evening**: senec a1
  - **drug** experiences; of past: agath-a nl2• androc srj1• olib-sac wmh1
  - **happy** moments (See Dwells - happy)
  - **insightful**: *(↗Insightful)* plut-n srj7•
  - **journeys**: olib-sac wmh1 sol-t-ae a1 spong fd4.de
- **persistent**: *(↗compelling; persistent; Delusions; Fanaticism; Monomania; Obstinate; Perseverance; Pertinacity; Rest - cannot)* acon k* aeth agar bg2 aids nl2• **Aloe** sne alum k* am-c k* *Ambr* k* anac k* androc ↓ ang kr1 anh ↓ ant-c bg2 ap-g a1 apis pc* aq-mar skp7• arb-m ↓ *Arg-n* k* arn bg2 *Ars* k* ars-i asar ↓ asim ↓ **Aur** bg2 *Aur-m-n* wbt2• bamb-a ↓ *Bell* bg2* benz-ac ckh1 brucel sa3• bry b7.de* *Calc* k* calc-s **Cann-i** *Cann-s* b7.de* canth k* caps k2 *Carb-v* k* carbn-s carc mlr1• caust cham k* chel *Chin* k* chinin-ar choc ↓ *Cic* bg2 coca bg2 cocc b7.de* *Coff* bg2 coli jl2* *Con* bg2* croc bg2 crot-c ↓ cupr b7.de* cycl bg2 des-ac rbp6 dros bg2 *Euphr* b7.de* galeoc-c-h ↓ glon bg2 glycyr-g cte1• *Graph* k* hell k* hydrog srj2• hyos k* *Ign* k* *Iod* k* kali-ar kali-c kali-i *Kola* stb3• lac-c ↓ lach bg2* lam laur k* loxo-lae bnm12• lys bg2 lyss bg1* mag-c bg2 *Manc* gk* med ptk1* melal-alt gya4 meli merc k* mez mur-ac myris ↓ **Nat-m** k* nit-ac k* nux-m k* *Nux-v* k* olnd op k* orot-ac rly4• oscilloc jl2 osm oxal-a ↓ parathyr jl2 petr k* *Ph-ac* k* phos k* phys plat k* *Prot* jl2* *Psor* k* *Puls* k* *Rhus-t* k* ruta fd4.de *Sabad* b7.de* sal-fr ↓ sec sep ser-a-c jl2 *Sil* j5.de* spect ↓ spong bg2 stann k* *Staph* k1* *Stram* k* streptoc jl2 stry ↓ suis-em rly4• sul-ac bg2 sul-i k2 *Sulph* k* suprar rly4• syph jl2 tab tarent thea *Thuj* k* tritic-vg fd5.de tub valer bg2 vanil fd5.de *Verat* bg2 verb k* viol-o k* visc jl3 zinc bg2 [bar-i stj2 beryl-m stj2 bor-pur stj2 lith-c stj2 lith-i stj2 lith-met stj2 mag-sil stj2 mang-i stj2 merc-i-f stj2 nat-f stj2 zinc-i stj2]
  - **evening**: caust graph ign kali-c *Nat-m*
  - **night**: ambr tsm1 ant-c k* calc graph kali-ar kali-c petr h2* plat ↓ **Puls** k* suprar rly4• tub [spect dfg1]
    - **midnight**:
      - **before**: graph a1
      - **at**: plat a1
  - **alone**: *(↗rush - alone; Company - desire - alone)* ars kali-c zinc
  - **desires**, of: bry gl1.fr• ign gl1.fr• puls gl1.fr•
  - **dreams**; ideas of thoughts which first appeared in his: carc gk6 *Psor*
  - **evil**, of: *(↗Fear - evil)* androc srj1• crot-c sk4• *Lach* k* manc mrr1 stry mrr1
  - **garment** made the previous day, about a: aeth k*
  - **hedgehogs**; of: choc srj3•
  - **homicide**: *(↗Kill; desire)* calc crot-c sk4• iod op phos stram
  - **humorous**: *(↗Cheerful)* nux-m
  - **injury**; of: *(↗Malicious)* anac ↓ crot-c sk4• manc ↓ sal-fr ↓
    - **himself**; of injuring: manc mrr1
    - **others**; of injuring: anac mrr1 sal-fr sle1•
  - **lying**, while: caust graph kali-c lac-c
  - **murder**, fire and rats; of nothing but: *(↗Kill; desire)* *Calc*
  - **music**; of: *(↗Music - agg.)*
    - **night**: **Puls** st1
    - **evening**: ign
    - **song**: melal-alt gya4 myris ↓
      - **16** h; since: myris a1
  - **occurrences** of the day at night; of the: asim a1
  - **offended** him, of persons who had: glon a1 sal-fr sle1•
  - **one** thought excludes all others: androc srj1•
  - **pins**; about: *Sil* br1*
  - **recur** to his mind; expressions and words heard: lam a1 *Sulph*
  - **separated**:
    - **mind** and body are: *(↗Confusion - identity; Delusions - separated - body - mind)* *Anac* k* arb-m oss1• sabad st thuj k*
    - **will**; thoughts separated from: *(↗Confusion - identity)* anh sp1
  - **sexual** desires; about: galeoc-c-h gms1•
  - **suicide**; of: manc mrr1
  - **unpleasant** subjects, haunted by: *(↗tormenting - past; Dwells - past)* *Ambr* asar jl3 *Aur-m-n* wbt2• caust *Cocc* h1* coli rly4• graph kali-c **Nat-m** petr h2* rhus-t staph gk
  - **vertigo**; of his: *(↗VERTIGO - Thinking)* bamb-a stb2.de•
  - **waking** on: acon bry ign k* oxal-a rly4• plat *Psor* sil
  - **walking** in open air amel.: graph
  - **youth**, beauty and love; of: aids nl2•

- **profound**: *(↗Activity - desires - creative; Concentration - active; Ideas - abundant; Memory - active)* acon b7.de* androc srj1• bamb-a stb2.de• bell k* calc-ar a1 cocc b7a.de* cycl grat k* kres mg1.de* lac-h sze9• mur-ac k* nat-sil fd3.de• olib-sac wmh1 plut-n srj7• podo ↓ ruta fd4.de *Sep* b4.de* spig ↓ *Spong* fd4.de staph b7.de* tritic-vg fd5.de ulm-c jsj8• *Vanil* fd5.de
  - **future**, about his: cycl podo fd3.de• spig vanil fd5.de
- **quick** (See rapid)
- **rapid** (= quick): *(↗rush; Concentration - active; Hurry; Ideas - abundant; Impulsive; Memory - active; Quick; Rash; Vivacious; Witty)* acon adam srj5• aesc alco a1 anac bro1 androc srj1• ang anh mg1.de anthraq rly4• *Ap-g* vh1 bell bro1 caj cann-i k* carb-ac a1 caust cham ↓ chin bro1 choc srj3• cimic bro1 cob k* *Coff* k* conch fkr1• cupr mtf33 cystein-l rly4• fuma-ac rly4• helo-s rwt2• *Hyos* ign k* kalm ketogl-ac rly4• lac-c bro1 lac-lup hrn2• *Lach* k* lavand-a ctl1• limen-b-c hrn2* maias-l hrn2• **Med** vh* morph a1 musca-d szs1 nat-ox rly4• nitro-o a1 onos *Op* k* *Ox-ac* k* ped a1 phos bg2 *Phys* bro1 pic-ac bg2 pin-con oss2• positr nl2• pyrog ↓ sabad k* streptoc rly4• suis-pan rly4• valer k* verat k* viol-o k* *Zinc* mrr1 [ant-t stj2 heroin sdj2]
  - **morning**: helo-s rwt2•
    - **waking**; on: helo-s rwt2•
  - **fever**, during: *(↗Thinking - faster - fever)* cham kr1 pyrog k2
  - **speaking**; too rapid for (See Mistakes - speaking - fast)
  - **writing**; too rapid for (See Mistakes - writing - thoughts)
- **religious** (See Religious - too - thoughts)
- **repetition**, of: aids nl2• ger-i rly4• germ-met srj5• mag-m k2* melal-alt gya4 stram
- **ridiculous**: *(↗Foolish; Gestures - ridiculous)* cann-i *Dubo-m* br1 hydrog srj2• kali-p **Lach** *Stram*
- **rush** (= flow): *(↗rapid)* acon sf1.de agar h2* agath-a ↓ alco a1 aloe ↓ *Alum* j5.de ambr b7a.de* *Anac* j5.de androc srj1• *Ang* b7.de* ant-c ↓ ap-g vh1 arizon-l nl2• *Arn* ↓ *Ars* j5.de* ars-s-f a1 bar-c b4a.de **Bell** bg2* borx j5.de* *Bry* b7.de* caj a1 calad b7.de* *Calc* j5.de* camph gl1.fr• cann-i a1* cann-s b7a.de* canth b7.de* carc ↓ caust b4a.de* cham ↓ *Chin* b7.de* chinin-ar ↓ cimic jl3 coca a1 coca-c ↓ cocc b7.de* **Coff** b7.de* coff-t a1 colch ↓ coli rly4• coloc j5.de con j5.de croc b7.de* cycl k2* der a1 dream-p sdj1• dros mtf33 eupi a1 falco-pe ↓ fl-ac bg2 germ-met srj5• *Glon* a1* *Graph* j5.de hell ↓ hep b4a.de* hura vml3• hydrog ↓ hyos j5.de *Ign* b7.de* *Kali-c* j5.de kali-m j kali-n j5.de kali-p fd1.de• *Lac-c* bg2* lac-h sk4• lac-lup hrn2• **Lach** b7.de* led ↓ lyc j5.de* *M-arct* j5.de maias-l hrn2• meph sf1.de merc a1* morph a1 mur-ac b4a.de nat-m b4a.de* nat-sil ↓ nitro-o a1 nux-m bg2 *Nux-v* b7.de* olib-sac wmh1 *Olnd* b7.de* *Op* b7.de* orig a1 *Ph-ac* j5.de* **Phos** j5.de* pic-ac ↓ pieri-b mlk9.de plat j5.de plut-n ↓ ptel ↓ *Puls* b7.de* rheum ↓ *Rhus-t* b7.de* *Sabad* b7.de* sacch-a ↓ seneg a1 sep j5.de* *Sil* j5.de* sol-t-ae ↓ spig b7.de* spong j5.de staph b7.de* *Stram* b7a.de *Sulph* j5.de* tab a1 ter a1 teucr b7.de* thea a1 **Valer** b7.de* verat b7.de* verb b7.de* viol-o b7.de* viol-t b7.de* zinc j5.de* [heroin sdj2]
  - **day** and night: ambr j5.de caust j5.de
  - **morning**: canth j5.de* chin ↓ con j5.de nux-v j5.de
    - **bed**; in: chin j5.de
    - **rising**; after: nux-v a1
  - **afternoon**: anac j5.de ang j5.de* sol-t-ae ↓
    - **17** h: sol-t-ae a1
  - **evening**: agar ↓ anac j5.de *Bry* ↓ *Calc* ↓ caust ↓ chin j5.de cocc ↓ *Graph* ↓ *Kali-c* ↓ lyc ↓ nux-v gl1.fr• phos j5.de *Puls* hr1* rhus-t ↓ sabad ↓ sacch-a fd2.de• *Sil* ↓ staph ↓ *Sulph* ↓ viol-o ↓ viol-t ↓
    - **bed**; in: agar j5.de *Bry* j5.de *Calc* j5.de caust j5.de *Chin* j5.de cocc j5.de *Graph* j5.de *Kali-c* j5.de lyc j5.de *Nux-v* j5.de *Puls* j5.de rhus-t j5.de sabad j5.de sacch-a fd2.de• *Sil* j5.de staph j5.de *Sulph* j5.de viol-o j viol-t j5.de
  - **night**: acon b7.de* agar j5.de aloe a1 *Ambr* b7a.de androc srj1• ant-c b7a.de *Arn* b7.de* borx j5.de *Bry* b7.de* *Calc* j5.de* *Camph* b7a.de cham b7.de* *Chin* b7a.de* chinin-ar k2 coca a1 coff k2* colch a1 con j5.de falco-pe nl2• *Graph* j5.de hell b7.de* hep j5.de* hyos j5.de *Kali-c* j5.de kali-n j5.de *Lach* j5.de led b7.de* *M-arct* j5.de nat-m sf1.de nat-sil fd3.de• *Nux-v* j5.de *Op* b7.de* ph-ac j5.de pic-ac a1 plat j5.de ptel vml3• *Puls* b7.de* rheum b7.de* sep j5.de* *Sil* j5.de* spong b7.de* *Stram* b7a.de *Sulph* j5.de tab a1 zinc j5.de
    - **midnight**:
      - **after** | **5** h: ptel vml3•
  - **air** amel.; open: coff j5.de
- **rush**: ...
  - **alone**, when: *(↗persistent - alone)* ars j5.de
  - **annoying**: *Nux-m* b7a.de
  - **business** accomplished; about: | **evening**: plut-n srj7• sulph a1
  - **delirium**; during: hydrog srj2•
  - **drunkenness**, as in: valer j5.de
  - **partial** sleep, in: agath-a nl2• hyos a1
  - **reading**, while: coff j5.de olnd gl1.fr• ph-ac j5.de
  - **sad**: hura vml3•
  - **sleeplessness** from: *(↗SLEEP - Sleeplessness - thoughts - activity)* agar h2* borx j5.de bry j5.de calc j5.de carc mlr1• caust j5.de *Chin* h1* coca-c sk4• cocc h1* coloc j5.de *Graph* j5.de hep j5.de kali-c j5.de kali-n j5.de *Lyc* j5.de nat-sil fd3.de• *Nux-v* j5.de *Op* j5.de plat j5.de *Puls* j5.de sabad j5.de* *Sep* j5.de *Sil* j5.de staph j5.de sulph j5.de viol-t j5.de
  - **waking**, on: borx j5.de chin j5.de *M-arct* j5.de **Nux-v** bg2 ph-ac j5.de plat j5.de sil j5.de
  - **walking** in open air, on: ant-c j5.de sulph j5.de
  - **working**, during: *(↗intrude - work)* ang j5.de mur-ac j5.de olnd j5.de
- **sad** things agg.; of: rhus-t bg2
- **sexual**: *(↗intrude - sexual; tormenting - sexual)* agath-a nl2• ambr j5.de androc srj1• aq-mar vml3• arund a1* aster hr1* bamb-a stb2.de• bell j5.de* calad ↓ calc h2* carc fd2.de• cer-s a1 chin ↓ chir-fl gya2 *Con* j5.de* cyna jl dig ↓ dulc fd4.de *Fl-ac* mrr1 ger-i rly4• graph h2* *Hyper* hr1* irid-met srj5• *Kali-br* hr1* kali-p fd1.de• kali-s fd4.de kola stb3• lil-t br1 loxo-recl knl4• manc mrr1 marb-w ↓ med ↓ nat-c j5.de nat-sil fd3.de• neon srj5• *Nux-v* vh* olib-sac wmh1 onos mrr1 orig st* ozone sde2• phos ptk1 pic-ac mrr1 plat sf1.de* positr nl2• ruta fd4.de sal-n br1 *Sel* j5.de* sep j5.de sil j5.de spong fd4.de *Staph* ptk1* *Stram* j5.de streptoc rly4• sulph sf1.de symph fd3.de• taosc ↓ tarent-c ↓ tritic-vg fd5.de *Ust* hr1* vanil fd5.de [heroin sdj2 temp elm1]
  - **day** and night: chin j5.de dig j5.de taosc iwa1• tarent-c ckh1
  - **adulterous**: marb-w es1•
  - **impotence**, with: *(↗Fancies - lascivious - impotence; MALE GENITALIA/SEX - Sexual desire - increased - weakness)* calad mrr1 *Onos* mrr1 *Sel* br1*
  - **masturbation**, with: dulc fd4.de orig mrr1 ust sf1.de
  - **tormenting**: ozone sde2•
  - **woman** he sees; sexual thoughts at every: med mrr
- **slow** (See Dullness)
- **speculative**: limen-b-c hrn2•
- **stagnation** of: arb-m oss1• *Cann-s* j5.de* chin h1* hyos a1 iod j5.de lyc h2* m-arct j5.de nat-sil fd3.de• ph-ac j5.de rhus-g ↓ rumx ↓ seneg a1* sulph j5.de thuj j5.de
  - **evening**: rumx a1
  - **examination**; during: rhus-g tmo3•
- **strange**: arg-n ptk1* calc gl1.fr• canth hr1* lac-h sk4• *Lyss* a1* opun-s a1 *Pyrog* jl2 raph a1 spong fd4.de *Stram* hr1* sulph gl1.fr• verat gl1.fr•
  - **pregnancy** | **during**: *(↗Fancies - strange - pregnancy)* *Lyss* kr1* *Stram* kr1
- **suicidal** (See Suicidal - thoughts)
- **thoughtful**: *(↗Absorbed; Activity - desires - creative; Concentration - active; Dream; as; Ideas - abundant; Introspection; Meditating; Memory - active; Theorizing)* acon alco a1 aloe a1 alum a1 am-m arn k* bamb-a stb2.de• bar-c bart a1 bell k* borx a1 brom calc cann-s canth k* *Carb-an* k* cham k* chin chord-umb rly4• cic k* clem k* *Cocc* cycl k* dendr-pol sk4• euph k* euphr k* grat k* guaj j ham fd3.de• hell ↓ *Hep* gl1.fr• hyos k* *Ign* ip k* irid-met srj5• kali-n a1 *Kola* stb3• kreos j *Lach* k* lyc mag-m k* manc k* mang k* mez k* nat-c nat-m mrr1 nit-ac nux-v k* olib-sac wmh1 op ↓ *Phos* k* plan a1 plb k* positr nl2• *Puls* k* ran-b rhus-t ruta fd4.de sabad sal-fr sle1• senec ↓ *Sep* spig spong fd4.de *Staph* stront-c *Sulph* k1* thea thuj k* til k* vanil fd5.de viol-o k* [tax jsj7]
  - **afternoon**: hell a1 mang a1
  - **evening**: senec a1
  - **all** night: op a1
  - **eating**, after: aloe a1
  - **errors** of others; about the: cic a1
  - **weather**; in cold wet: aloe a1

- **tormenting**: *(↗Anxiety - conscience; Remorse; Tormenting)* acon kr1 alum am-c am-m↓ ambr tsm1 ant-c aq-mar↓ arg-n *Ars* ars-i k2 astra-e jl3 calc-s k2 canth↓ caps k2 carbn-s k2 *Caust* con *Dulc*↓ graph j5.de guat jl3 kali-ar k2 kali-c↓ lac-ac lac-c *Lach* *Lyc* manc mrr1 mez **Nat-m** *Nit-ac* nitro-o a1 phos *Rhus-t* sep spong↓ *Staph*↓ sul-i k2 *Sulph* thea tub k2
  - **evening**: *Caust* graph kali-c
  - **night**: ambr tsm1 ant-c arg-n k2* kali-ar k2 kali-c *Nit-ac* tub k2*
  - **dark**; tormented by delusions and fears in the: manc mrr1
  - **past** disagreeable events, about: *(↗persistent - unpleasant; Dwells - past)* am-c h2* am-m h2 *Dulc* fd4.de spong h1*
  - **sexual**: *(↗intrude - sexual; sexual; Fancies - lascivious; Lascivious; Nymphomania)* aq-mar jl3* canth k2 con graph k* *Staph* k*
- **two** trains of thought: *(↗Antagonism; Confusion - identity - duality; Irresolution; Will - contradiction; Will - two)* anac k* bit-ar wht1• *Cann-i* br1 crot-c sk4• haliae-lc srj5• lyss k* paro-i jl3 *Sil* gl1.fr•
- **unpleasant** (See Dwells - unpleasant)
- **unsettled** (See instability)
- **vacancy** of: aids nl2• brass-n-o srj5• calc↓ chlol a1 falco-pe nl2• galla-q-r nl2• *Gels* a1* guaj br1 haliae-lc srj5• hell br1* hydrog srj2• kali-p fd1.de• kali-s fd4.de ketogl-ac rly4• limen-b-c hrn2• lyc j5.de oena a1 phos h2 sal-al blc1• [heroin sdj2]
  - **menses**; during: calc b4.de
- **vagueness** of: agath-a nl2• bros-gau mrc1 chir-fl gya2 choc srj3• dulc fd4.de fic-m gya1 iod a1 melal-alt gya4 nitro-o a1 rhus-g tmo3• sulph a1 [heroin sdj2]
  - **laugh**; causing him to: rhus-g tmo3•
- **vanishing** of: *(↗instability; Concentration - difficult; Ideas - deficiency; Memory - weakness)* abies-n a1 abrot a1 acon b7.de* acon-f a1 aeth a1* aether a1 agn b7.de aids nl2• *Alum* b4.de* am-br bg am-c b4.de* *Ambr* b7.de* **Anac** k* androc srj1• ang b7.de anh mg1.de* ant-t j5.de apis k* apoc arb-m oss1• arg-n a1 arizon-l nl2• *Arn* b7.de* ars b4.de* ars-s-f kr1* arum-t a1 **Asar** k* *Aur* b4.de* bapt k* *Bar-c* b4.de bell k* berb j5.de bit-ar wht1• borx k* bov b4.de brom a1 *Bry* k* **Calc** k* calc-act bg2 calc-p a1 calc-s *Camph* *Cann-i* *Cann-s* k* canth k* carb-an carb-v bg2 carbn-h a1 caust b4.de* *Cham* k* *Chel* k2* chin b7.de* chlorpr pin1• cic k* cinnb a1 cit-ac rly4• clem b4.de* cocc a1 cod a1 coff k* colch b7a.de coloc a1 **Con** a1 conin a1 corn↓ cortico↓ cot a1 croc b7.de* **Cupr** k* cupr-s a1 cycl b7a.de* dig b4a.de* dirc a1 dream-p sdj1• elaps a1 euon gad a1 galla-q-r nl2• *Gels* k* glon a1 guaj k* gymno a1 hell k* hep k* hydr-ac a1 hydrog↓ hyos b7.de* iber a1 ign b7.de* iod ip b7.de* irid-met srj5• kali-bi k* kali-br bg2 *Kali-c* k* kali-cy a1 kali-p kalm a1 kiss a1 kola stb3• kreos k* lac-c lac-h htj1• **Lach** k* laur k* led a1 lepi a1 lil-t a1 limen-b-c mlk9.de lob bg2 lol a1 *Lyc* k* lycpr a1* (non:lycps-v a1) lyss a1 macro a1 *Manc* k* med melal-alt gya4 *Merc* k* *Mez* k* morph a1 mosch a1 nat-ar a1 **Nat-c** b4a.de* *Nat-m* k* **Nit-ac** k* **Nux-m** k* nux-v k* oena a1 ol-an k* olib-sac wmh1 olnd b7.de op k* orig↓ petr a1 ph-ac k* **Phos** a1 pic-ac↓ pin-s a1 plan plb a1 plut-n↓ positr nl2• *Psor* ptel a1 *Puls* k* **Ran-b** k* ran-s b7.de* rhod k* rhodi a1 **Rhus-t** k* rob kr1 ruta b7.de* saroth mg1.de* sec b7a.de* sel b7a.de* sep b4.de* sil b4a.de* sol-ni a1 spig b7.de* spong b7.de* stann h2* **Staph** k* stram a1* sulph sumb a1 syph hr1 *Tab* bg2* tep a1 ther↓ **Thuj** b4.de* trom a1 valer b7.de verat ptk1* verat-v a1 viol-o k* viol-t bg2 yuc a1 zinc zinc-p k2
  - **morning**: anac a1 *Ph-ac* spong fd4.de
  - **bending** head forward: cortico tpw7
  - **business**; while attending: *(↗work)* limen-b-c hrn2•
  - **chill**, during: bell k* bry k* lach k* rhus-t k*
  - **closing** eyes, on: ther hr1*
  - **company**, in: ambr k2*
  - **exertion**, on: nit-ac a1
  - **headache**, during: apis a1 asar↓ bell k* calc a1 glon a1
    - ⁝ **Forehead**; pressing, drawing pain in: asar br1
  - **interrupted**, when: *(↗Disturbed; Ideas - deficiency - interruption)* berb k* mez h2 *Staph* h1*
  - **menses**; before: *(↗Menses - before)* *Nux-m* kr1
  - **mental** exertion; from: *Asar* canth caust cham euon a1 *Gels* hep mez nat-m *Nit-ac* olnd ran-b staph
  - **overlifting**, after: *Psor*
  - **periodically**: chin bg1*

Thoughts – vanishing of: ...

  - **reading**, on: *(↗Memory - weakness - read)* *Anac* bro1 asar bro1 bry k* camph bro1 *Cann-i* k* corn a1 hyos a1 *Lach* k* lyc bro1 merc a1 **Nux-m** k* *Op* a1 **Ph-ac** k ● pic-ac bro1 staph bro1
  - **rising** quickly: cortico tpw7
  - **sexual** excitement; during: orig vh
  - **speaking**, while: *(↗Memory - weakness - expressing; Memory - weakness - say; Speech - incoherent)* aids nl2• *Anac* bro1 asar bro1 camph bro1 *Cann-i* k* hydrog srj2• *Lach* k* lyc bro1 med k2 *Mez* **Nux-m** k1* pic-ac bro1 plut-n srj7• ruta fd4.de staph k* *Thuj* viol-o kr1
  - **spoken** to, when: sep
  - **standing**, while: rhus-t
  - **stooping**: cortico tpw7
  - **sudden**: *Manc* br1
  - **vertigo**; with: ran-b bg2
  - **work**, at: *(↗business)* *Asar* sf1.de dream-p sdj1• hep a1 melal-alt gya4 plut-n srj7•
  - **writing**, while: *(↗Memory - weakness - write)* *Anac* bro1 asar bro1 camph bro1 *Cann-i* k* croc a1 hydrog srj2• *Lach* k* lyc bro1 **Nux-m** k1* pic-ac bro1 rhus-t k* staph bro1
- **veins** were dark and exploding at the ends: coca-c sk4•
- **violent**: lac-h htj1* urol-h rwt•
- **wandering**: *(↗Absentminded; Concentration - difficult; Spaced-out; Speech - wandering)* *Acon* k* alco a1 alet vh1 all-s k* *Aloe* am-c k* ambr sf1.de anac ang k* anth k* apoc k* *Arn* k* ars-i k2* atro k* bamb-a stb2.de• *Bapt* k* bell k* bit-ar wht1• calc↓ cann-i k* cann-s k* canth k2 carbn-s a1 caust k* chinin-s j5.de chlol k* choc↓ cic k* colch k* coloc k* corn k* crot-h k* cupr dig dulc h1* ery-a a1 ferr k* fic-m↓ germ-met srj5• glon k* *Graph* k* haliae-lc srj5• ham↓ hyos c1* ign k* iod k* iris↓ kali-br k* kali-p fd1.de• **Kali-s** fd* kola stb3• lac-e hrn2• lac-lup hrn2• lach lavand-a ctl1• **Lec** sne lyc k* lycps-v a1 manc k* melal-alt gya4 merc k* merc-c mit↓ naja k* nat-c k* nat-m k* nat-ox rly4• nat-p nicot a1 nit-ac k* nux-m mrr1 olnd k* op k* opun-s a1 (non:opun-v a1) ozone sde2• peti a1 ph-ac k* phos ptk1* phys k* pic-ac k* plb k* plect k* *Puls* k* rauw sp1 ruta fd4.de sanic sol-mm a1 sol-t-ae↓ staph sul-i a1 symph fd3.de• tab k* thuj ptk1* valer viol-o k* yuc a1 *Zinc* zinc-m↓ zinc-p k2* [tax jsj7]
  - **morning**: mit a1
  - **afternoon**: ang a1 atro a1 symph fd3.de•
  - **evening**: caust a1
  - **night**: bell zinc-m a1
  - **eyes** are closed, as soon as: bapt hr1
  - **listening**, while: bit-ar wht1• fic-m gya1 sol-t-ae a1
  - **menses**, during: *(↗Menses - during)* calc k*
  - **studying**, while: *(↗Concentration - difficult - studying; Studying - difficult)* bamb-a stb2.de• choc srj3• ham k* phys k*
  - **talking**, while: fic-m gya1 merc-c sanic c1
  - **work**, at: kali-p fd1.de• sol-t-ae a1 symph fd3.de•
  - **writing**, while: iris **Nux-m** k1*
- **wild**: phos k2
- **worms**; about: coca-c sk4•

○ - **Stomach**; as if thoughts came from acon bg2*

THREATENED; feels (See Delusions - attacked)

THREATENING: *(↗Abusive; Insanity - threatening)* agar h2* choc srj3• crot-c sk4• dendr-pol sk4• galeoc-c-h↓ *Hep* k* hyos↓ lac-cp sk4• lac-leo sk4• *Lach* sne meli↓ plat rbr *Stram* k* **Tarent** k* *Tub* st1* valer a1
- **destroy**; to: tarent kr1*
- **destruction**; words of: galeoc-c-h gms1•
- **kill**; to: *(↗Kill; desire)* *Hep* k* hyos mrr1 meli c1* stram hr1 *Tarent* k*
  - **approach**, those who: meli c1
  - **wife** and children: *Hep* kr1

THROWING things around: *(↗Anger - throwing; Destructiveness; Fire - throwing)* acon k2* agar ptk1 androc srj1• ars bell a1 bry camph k* caust ptk1 cham k* *Cina* k* coff coloc k* dulc k* *Galeoc-c-h*↓ ham fd3.de• *Hydr* hr1 ign↓ ignis-alc↓ kali-s fd4.de *Kreos* k* lil-t↓

Throwing things around: ...
lyss a1 neon ↓ prot jl3* spong fd4.de **Staph** k* stram hr1* sulph a1 symph ↓ tarent k* thea thuj ptk1* tub al* [ant-c stj2]

- **morning**: dulc **Staph**
- **bugs** by handfuls: ars ptk1*
- **cats**: ignis-alc es2•
- **persons**; at: *(↗Awkward; Foolish)* agar bell k* ign pcr lil-t k2 lyss a1 (non:neon srj5) **STAPH** ↓ symph fd3.de• **Tub** ●*
  - **offend**; who: **STAPH** k1*
- **window**; out of: *Galeoc-c-h* gms1• stram mtf33
  - **cat**: galeoc-c-h gms1•

THROWING things away (See Disposing)

THUNDERSTORM (See Weather - thunderstorm)

TICKLISHNESS (See Touched - aversion - ticklishness)

TICS (See Gestures - tics)

TIDY: *(↗Disposing; Fastidious)* bar-c mrr1 carc fb* cupr sst3• ham fd3.de• ignis-alc ↓ ina-i mlk9.de kali-p fd1.de• kali-s fd4.de *Nat-sil* fd3.de• polys ↓ ruta fd4.de sacch-a fd2.de• spong fd4.de sulph ↓ symph fd3.de• *Tritic-vg* fd5.de vanil fd5.de

- **appearance**; in one's personal: *(↗Fastidious - personal)* bar-c mrr1 polys sk4•
- **dirtiness**; aversion to: ignis-alc es2• *Vanil* fd5.de

TIME: *(↗Sensitive - time)*

- **always** on time (See Anxiety - time)
- **asking** the time; constantly (See Asking - same - time)
- **conception** of time; lost (See Mistakes - time - conception)
- **desire** to arrive at the appointed (See Anxiety - time)
- **enough** time; sensation of always having (See Late - too late; always)
- **fritters** away his time: *(↗Busy - fruitlessly; Ennui; Laziness; Undertaking - many)* bamb-a stb2.de• borx h2* cocc k* crot-t j5.de lach j5.de *Nat-c* j5.de* nat-m j5.de nux-v k* petr-ra shn4• rhus-g ↓ sal-fr sle1• stann j5.de* staph gl1.fr• *Sulph* j5.de* tab gl1.fr• [tax jsj7]
  - **going** to his work; by: rhus-g tmo3•
- **hears** time: galeoc-c-h gms1•
- **long** everything would take, obsessed by how: falco-pe nl2•
- **mistakes** in (See Mistakes - time)
- **quickly**, appears shorter; passes too: *(↗Delusions - time - earlier; Hurry)* aids nl2• *Anh* mg1.de* ara-maca sej7• atro bamb-a stb2.de• choc srj3• coca **Cocc** k* cypra-eg sde6.de• elaps galeoc-c-h gms1• galla-q-r nl2• hippoc-k szs2 hydrog srj2• ina-i mlk9.de irid-met srj5• kali-s fd4.de ketogl-ac rly4• *Kola* stb3• lac-loxod-a hrn2• lach b7a.de med ↓ moni rfm1• nat-sil fd3.de• neon srj5• olib-sac wmh1 op polys sk4• positr nl2• psil jl* ruta fd4.de sacch-a fd2.de• sel gmj2 sieg mg1.de sulph *Ther* k* thuj k* tritic-vg fd5.de ulm-c jsj8• visc sp1 [pop dhh1 spect dfg1 tax jsj7]
  - **today** occurred a week ago; as if things done: med ptk2*
- **slowly**, appears longer; passes too: *(↗Ailments - anticipation; Delusions - time - exaggeration; Hurry; Impatience; Impulsive; Mistakes - time)* adam srj5• aids nl2• aloe *Alum* k* *Ambr* bg2* amp rly4• androc srj1• *Anh* mg1.de* arg-met br1* *Arg-n* k* arge-pl rwt5• arizon-l nl2• bar-c bit-ar wht1• bros-gau mrc1 camph **Cann-i** k* **Cann-s** k* cann-xyz ptk1 *Cench* cere-b a1 con corian-s knl6• dirc k* **Dream-p** sdj1• falco-pe nl2• fic-m gya1 galeoc-c-h gms1• galla-q-r nl2• ger-i rly4• germ-met srj5• **Glon** k* haliae-lc srj5• hep gl1.fr• hippoc-k szs2 irid-met srj5• kali-p fd1.de• kola stb3• lach k* limest-b es1• **Lyc** k* mag-m k* *Med* k* *Merc* k* nat-c nat-sil fd3.de• nicc-met sk4• nitro-o a1 *Nux-m* k* *Nux-v* k* onos ozone sde2• pall k* petr petr-ra shn4• *Pieri-b* mlk9.de plb k* plut-n srj7• positr nl2• rhus-g tmo3• ribo rly4• sanguis-s hrn2• sinus rly4• streptoc rly4• symph fd3.de• tritic-vg fd5.de tung-met bdx1• ulm-c jsj8• vanil fd5.de [heroin sdj2 tax jsj7]
  - **night**: nux-v a1
  - **ages**, a few seconds seem: cann-i k* haliae-lc srj5• petr-ra shn4•
  - **believe** the clock; does not: galeoc-c-h gms1•
- **timelessness**; sensation of: lac-loxod-a hrn2• [spect dfg1 tax jsj7]

TIMIDITY: *(↗bashful; Ailments - anticipation; Ailments - embarrassment; Ailments - honor; Asking - nothing; Cautious; Confidence - want; Cowardice; Delusions - appreciated; Delusions - business - unfit; Delusions - confidence; Delusions - confusion; Delusions - criticized; Delusions - disgraced; Delusions - fail everything; Delusions - forsaken; Delusions - friend - affection; Delusions - right - doing; Delusions - succeed; Delusions - wrong - done; Discouraged; Fear - approaching - others; Fear - business failure; Fear - conversation; Fear - failure; Fear - full; Fear - observed; Fear - people; Fear - talking - say; Fear - undertaking; Frightened; Gestures - fingers - playing; Gestures - hands - covering - mouth; Hiding - himself; Inhibition; Insanity - shy; Insecurity; Irresolution; Irritability - alternating - timidity; Longing - good; Looked - looking; Quiet disposition; Reserved; Rudeness; Succeeds; Timidity - fright; Undertaking - nothing; FACE - Discoloration - red - excitement)* abies-c oss4• *Acon* k* adam srj5• aeth ↓ agar vh1 *Aids* nl2• aloe k* *Alum* k* alum-p k2* alum-sil k2* alumin-sil ↓ *Alumn* a1 *Am-br* vh1 (non:am-c k*) am-caust a1* *Am-m* ambr k* *Ammc* vh1 anac k* ang k* anh sp1 ant-t k* anthraq ↓ *Aq-mar* ↓ arb-m oss1• arg-n bg2* arn k* *Ars* ars-i ars-s-f k2* asar vh *Aur* k* aur-ar k2 aur-i k2* *Aur-m-n* wbt2• aur-s k2* bac jl2 bamb-a ↓ bapt ↓ **BAR-C** k* bar-i k2* bar-m k2* *Bar-p* ↓ bar-s ↓ bell k* boerh-d bnj1 *Borx* k* **Bry** k* bufo ↓ **Calc** k* calc-ar k2* calc-br ↓ calc-m ↓ calc-p ↓ (non:calc-s k*) calc-sil k2* camph ↓ cann-i ↓ canth k* carb-an k* *Carb-v* k* *Carbn-s* carc tpw* carl a1 *Caust* k* cench ↓ *Chin* k* chinin-ar cic bg2 *Coca* k* cocc k* coff k* *Coli* jl2 *Con* k* cortico mg1.de* croc *Crot-h* k* *Cupr* k* cypra-eg sde6.de• cystein-l rly4• daph k* dat-m a1* dys pte1*• elaps mgm• elec c1* falco-pe nl2• ferr bg2 ferr-p a1 galeoc-c-h ↓ galla-q-r nl2• gard-j vlr2• **Gels** k* germ-met srj5• *Graph* k* haliae-lc ↓ hep gk hydr-ac j hydrog srj2• hyos k* *Ign* k* iod k* ip *Kali-ar* kali-bi a1 kali-br k* **Kali-c** k* kali-i ↓ kali-n k* *Kali-p* k1* *Kali-s* k* *Kali-sil* k2* ketogl-ac rly4• *Lac-c* sne lac-e hrn2• lac-h sze9• lac-leo sk4• lach c1* lachn ↓ laur lil-t **Lyc** k* *M-arct* b7.de* m-aust b7.de* mag-c k* manc mang ↓ *Med* fd* meli c1 meli-xyz c2 *Merc* k* mez ↓ *Moni* rfm1• morg ↓ mosch a1 mur-ac k* naja jl* *Nat-ar* **Nat-c** k* *Nat-m* k* nat-p nat-s c1 nit-ac k* *Nux-v* olib-sac ↓ olnd ↓ op k* opun-s ↓ opun-v ↓ **Petr** k* petr-ra ↓ *Ph-ac* ↓ **Phos** k* pin-con oss2• pip-m a1 plac ↓ plat **Plb** k* **PULS** b7.de* ran-b k* rhod kgp5• rhus-g tmo3• *Rhus-t* k* ribo rly4• ruta j5.de sabad br1 sacch sst1• sec sel bg2 **Sep** k* **SIL** b4a.de* spig *Spong* squil ↓ stann bg2* staph k* *Stram* k* sul-ac sul-i k2* **Sulph** k* syc pte1*• symph fd3.de• tab k* tarent mtf33 tax ↓ tax-br oss1• thuj oss• *Tritic-vg* fd5.de tub kr* vanil fd5.de verat verb b7a.de* zinc k* zinc-p k2* [alumin stj2 alumin-s stj2 am-f stj2 arg-met stj1* arg-p stj2 bar-f stj1 beryl stj2 beryl-m stj2 bor-pur stj2 fl-ac stj2 fl-pur stj2 lith-c stj2 lith-f stj2 lith-i stj2 lith-m stj2 lith-met stj2 lith-p stj2 lith-s stj2 mang-i stj2 mang-m stj2 mang-met stj2 mang-p stj2 mang-s stj2 merc-i-f stj2 nicc-met stj2 nicc-s stj2 nitro stj2 osm-met stj2 oxyg stj2]

- **daytime**: carb-an nat-m pip-m a1 verb
- **forenoon** | **9** h: carl a1
- **afternoon**: carb-an con ferr-p a1 ran-b
- **evening**: acon ↓ ant-t c1 ars ↓ bapt ↓ camph ↓ cann-i ↓ *Caust* ↓ cench ↓ kali-c ↓ lach ↓ lyc ↓ nat-c a1 ran-b j squil ↓
  - **bed**:
    - **going** to bed; about: acon ars bapt camph cann-i *Caust* cench lach lyc nat-c squil
    - **in**: kali-c
- **night**: *Caust* *Kali-c* **Rhus-t**
- **alcohol** amel.: *(↗GENERALS - Food and - alcoholic - amel.)* nat-m mrr1
- **alone**, when: sil k2*
- **alternating** with:
  - **anger** (See Anger - alternating - timidity)
  - **assurance** (See Confident - alternating - timidity)
  - **cheerfulness** (See Cheerful - alternating - timidity)
  - **confidence** (See Confident - alternating - timidity)
  - **eccentricity** (See Eccentricity - alternating - timidity)
  - **exaltation** (See Exhilaration - alternating - timidity)
  - **hope** (See Hopeful - alternating - timidity)
  - **indifference**: stram j5.de

- **alternating** with: ...
  - **irritability** (See Irritability - alternating - timidity)
  - **quarreling** (See Quarrelsome - alternating - timidity)
  - **sadness** (See Sadness - alternating - timidity)
  - **vexation** (See Irritability - alternating - timidity)
- **appearing** in public; about (See public)
- **bashful**: *(↗Ailments - embarrassment; Awkward - bashfulness; Blushing; Confidence - want; Delusions - laughed; Fear - opinion; Insecurity; Reserved; Sensitive - opinion; Suspicious - fear; Timidity; FACE - Discoloration - red - excitement; GENERALS - Orgasm - emotions)* aids nl2• aloe alumin-sil mtf *Ambr* k* anac k* *Aq-mar* mgm* arg-n k* ars-s-f k2* aur k* *Bar-c* k* *Bar-p* mtf bar-s k2* bell boerh-d bnj1 bufo mtf33 *Calc* k* calc-br mtf calc-m mtf calc-s k2* calc-sil k2* *Carb-an* k* carb-v k* carc mlr1* caust bro1 *Chin* k* **Coca** k* cocc ptk1* coff con k* cortico mg1.de* *Cupr* k* elaps mgm• ferr sf1.de *Germ-met* mtf graph bro1* haliae-lc mtf hyos k* *Ign* k* iod k* kali-bi kali-br k* kali-i ptk1 *Kali-p* k1* lil-t bro1 lyc sf1.de* manc k* mang meli c1* merc k* mez *Nat-c* k* nat-m ptk1* nat-p k2* nit-ac nux-v k* olib-sac wmh1 olnd gl1.fr• op gl1.fr• *Petr* ph-ac k* phos k* **Puls** k* *Rhus-t* ptk1 sep mtf sil bro1* *Staph* c1* *Stram* k* *Sul-ac* j5.de *Sulph* k* tab tarent hr1* thuj mtf tub mtf zinc k*
  - **awkward**, and (See bashful)
- **business**; in transacting: op a1 opun-s a1 (non:opun-v a1)
- **children**; in: *(↗Speech - whispering - answering)* ars ↓ ars-i ↓ bar-c mtf33 borx mtf33 bufo gk2 calc-p ↓ calc-s mtf33 carb-v mtf33 carc tpw* chin mtf33 cupr mtf33 graph mtf33 iod mtf33 kali-c mtf33 kali-sil mtf33 moni rfm1• naja mtf33 nat-m mtf33 phos mtf33 puls mtf33 sacch sst1• sep mtf33 sil mrr1* staph mtf33 sulph mtf33 tarent mtf33 tub al2* zinc mtf33
  - **children**; towards other: ars mtf ars-i mtf calc-p mtf carc mtf phos mtf sil mtf
- **company**, in: *(↗Suspicious - fear)* *Ambr* b7a.de* carb-v j5.de* chin gl1.fr• cortico sp1* falco-pe nl2• hep gk morg fmm1• ph-ac gl1.fr• phos gk staph gl1.fr•
- **fright**, after: *(↗Timidity)* *Acon* a1
- **public**; about appearing in: *(↗Ailments - anticipation; Anticipation - stage; Anxiety - speaking - company; Company - aversion; Fear - appearing)* aeth st* **Ambr** st anac c1* anthraq rly4• arg-n a1* aur-m-n wbt2• bamb-a stb2.de• bar-s zr* *Carb-v* k* chin gl* cocc fyz* cortico tpw7* cupr mtf dys dp• **GELS** k •* graph gk kali-p fyz* lach mtf lachn ↓ *Lyc* a1* *Med* vh* petr mtf petr-ra shn4• *Ph-ac* a1 phos gk plac rzf5• **Plb** k1* **Sil** k* staph a1* symph fd3.de• tax ↓ thuj zr* *Tritic-vg* fd5.de [*Arg-met* stj1]
  - **talk** in public; to: *(↗Anxiety; Anxiety - speaking - company)* *Carb-v* k* cupr st* lach gl1.fr• lachn br1 *Lyc* st* med mrr petr phos gk plac rzf5• *Sil* st* tritic-vg fd5.de [tax jsj7]
    - **capable** to; but: lyc h2
    - **inapt** to talk: petr gl•
- **sleeplessness**, during: graph j5.de
- **strangers**; in presence of: *(↗Stranger - presence)* bar-c mtf33 dys fmm1•
- **talking**; when | **sexual** desire; about her: galeoc-c-h gms1•
- **twilight**; in the: phos gl1.fr•
- **whispering** | **answering** the prescriber directly; to the mother instead of (See Speech - whispering - answering)

TIPSY; as if (See Stupefaction)

TOBACCO: | **amel.**: chir-fl gya2

TOLERANT (See Mildness; Patience)

TORMENTED by fears (See Anxiety - beside)

TORMENTING: *(↗Mutilating; Thoughts - tormenting)*
- **himself**: *(↗Mutilating; Striking - himself; Tearing - himself)* *Acon* ptk1 *Ars* ptk1* bell ptk1 *Lil-t* ptk1 nat-m a1 plb ptk1* tarent ptk1* tub ptk1 [heroin sdj2]
- **others**: *(↗Moaning; Nagging)* *Agar* ↓ alumn kr1 **Calc** kr1 lach a1* oci-sa sk4• *Psor* ↓ **Zinc** ↓
  - **day** and night: **Calc** kr1*
  - **complaints**; everyone with his: *(↗Complaining; Discuss - symptoms; Grumbling; Lamenting; Moaning)* *Agar* vh* *Psor* st* **Zinc** k*

TORPOR: *(↗Dullness; Indifference - answer; Prostration; Stupefaction; Unconsciousness)* aether a1 agar a1* ail a1 all-c vh1 ammc kr1 androc srj1*• apis arum-m a1 berb k* berb-a ↓ cann-i a1 carc jl2* cedr a1 *Cic* k* coca-c sk4• crot-c a1 *Crot-h* cupr kr1 dream-p sdj1• esch br1 fagu a1 gad a1 *Gels* *Hyos* kr1 *Iod* kr1 kali-bi a1 kali-br ketogl-ac rly4• lac-loxod-a hrn2• lepi a1 lob a1 lol a1 *Lyc* *Mag-m* kr1* manc a1 *Merc-c* kr1 naja a1 **Nat-m** nauf-helv-li elm2• **Nux-m** **Op** k* orot-ac rly4• oxal-a rly4• phys a1 plat ↓ *Plb* polyg-h kr1 *Puls* kr1 rheum a1 sang k* sec a1 ser-a-c jl2 staph a1 *Stram* k* toxo-g jl2 vip a1 [tax jsj7]
- **pain**; during | **sciatic** nerve; in: plat bro1

○ - **Liver**; from disturbances of berb-a br1

TORTURING (See Tormenting)

TOUCHED: *(↗GENERALS - Touch)*
- **aversion** to be: *(↗Anger - Touched; Approached - Agg.; Caressed - Aversion; Delusions - Body - brittle; Disturbed; Fear - Approaching - others - touched; Fear - Touched; Frightened - Touch; Handled - Aversion; Insanity - Touched; Quiet disposition; Quiet; wants; Rage - Touch; Sensitive - Touch; Shrieking - Children - touched; Shrieking - Touched; Starting - Touched; Striking - Touched; Taciturn; Weeping - Touched; CHILL - Touch - Agg.; GENERALS - Touch - Agg.)* *Acon* k* adam srj5• *Agar* *Aloe* sne **Ant-c** k* *Ant-t* *Apis* vh1 **Arn** k1* ars asaf jsa asar jl *Bell* *Bry* bufo gk calc calc-p mtf33 camph canth b7.de* carc mlr1• caust ↓ **Cham** k* *Chin* k* *Cina* k* cocc *Coff* k1 colch k* con ptk1 cupr k* cypra-eg sde6.de• emb-r bnj1 *Foll* oss• gels sf1.de granit-m es1• graph mtf33 hell k2 *Hep* jsa hydrog srj2• ign ptk1 ignis-alc es2• iod **Kali-c** k* *Kali-i* lac-e hrn2• lac-f wza1• *Lach* k* (non:lachn a1) lyc ptk1 m-aust b7.de mag-c k* *Med* k* meli sne merc mez moni rfm1• *Nat-m* sne nit-ac ↓ nux-m a1 nux-v k* ozone sde2• phasco-ci rbp2 **Phos** ↓ plb ran-b tl1* sanic k* sep ↓ *Sil* solin ↓ stram sulph ↓ suprar rly4• symph fd3.de• tab ↓ **Tarent** k* ther tl1 *Thuj* k* tub a1* verat k* zinc mtf33 [bar-i stj2 cupr-act stj2 cupr-f stj2 cupr-m stj2 cupr-p stj2 heroin sdj2 mang-i stj2]
  - **caressed**, aversion to being (See Caressed - aversion)
  - **carried**; and yet desire to be: *Cina* mrr1
  - **children**; in: *Ant-c* b7a.de* ant-t tl1 calc-p mtf33 cham tl1* chin mtf33 cina b7a.de* cupr sst3• graph mtf33 kali-c mtf33 mag-c mtf33 med mtf33 sanic mtf33 tarent mtf33 thuj mtf33 verat mtf33 zinc mtf33
  - **cough**; during: acon b7a.de
  - **nurse**; by the: lyc bg2
  - **sexually**: *(↗FEMALE - Sexual desire - wanting)* sep mrr1
  - **ticklishness**: ant-c st calc-p st* caust st graph st* **Kali-c** st1* lach st nat-m st nit-ac st **Phos** st* sep st sil st solin c1* sulph st zinc a1
- **desire** to be (See Magnetized - desire)

TOUCHING: *(↗Anguish - driving; Curious - training; Fear - driving him; Hurry; Indiscretion)*
- **impelled** to touch:
  - **everything**: *(↗Anguish - driving; Curious; Curious - training; Fear - driving him; Hurry; Indiscretion; Restlessness)* all-c ↓ anac ↓ ars ↓ bar-c gk bell h1* bism ↓ canth ↓ carc st* cina mtf33 graph ↓ hyos a1* ign ↓ ip ↓ lac-del hrn2• lyc ↓ lycps-eu ↓ lycps-v k* mag-c ↓ *Merc* mtf33* nat-ox rly4• rheum ↓ sacch sst1* sulph bro1* *Thuj* bro1* tub ↓ verat ↓
    - **children**, in: all-c lmj anac lmj ars ggd1 bell lmj bism lmj canth lmj carc gk6* *Cina* st* graph lmj hyos mtf33 ign lmj ip lmj lyc lmj lycps-eu lmj mag-c lmj merc mtf33 rheum lmj sacch lmj sulph mtf33 thuj mtf33 tub lmj verat mtf
    - **real** until she has touched them; does not know if objects are: sulph kr1
  - **people**: falco-pe nl2• lac-del hrn2•
- **unable** to touch anything: sulph ptk1

TOUCHY (See Offended)

TOUGH: *(↗Firmness; Positiveness; Will - strong)* caust mtf ferr mtf lach mtf lyc mtf merc mtf

TOURETTE'S syndrome (= Gilles de la Tourette): *(↗Gestures - tics; Noise - inclination; Obscene - talk; EXTREMITIES - Twitching; FACE - Tic; FACE - Twitching; GENERALS - Chorea)* *Agar* mtf *Hyos* mtf *Mygal* mtf *Op* mtf *Stram* hu3 stry mtf tarent mtf

TRANCE: *(↗Unconsciousness - trance)* aml-ns hl1 camph bg2 camph-br br1 choc srj3• cypra-eg sde6.de• dulc fd4.de keroso a1 **Lach** hr1* nitro-o a1 op bg2 *Podo* fd3.de• *Stram* ↓ taosc iwa1• ter a1
- **alternating** with | **spasms**: *Stram* kr1
- **convulsions** | **after**: *Stram* hr1*
- **periodical** | **summer**; every: *Stram* kr1
- **plays** on piano with closed eyes, writes letters in an acquired language: *Camph* kr1

TRANQUILLITY (= calmness; serenity): *(↗Casual; Danger - no; Ease; Mildness; Patience; Protected; Quiet disposition; Quiet disposition - calm; Quiet; wants - repose)* absin a1 *Adam* srj5• aesc k* aeth ↓ aether a1 *Agath-a* nl2• *Aids* nl2• alco a1 aloe k* *Alum* kr1* androc srj1• apis bg2* aq-mar rbp6 ara-maca sej7• arb-m oss1• arg-met k* arge-pl rwt5• arizon-l nl2• arn k* *Ars* k* asc-c a1 asc-t a1 aspar a1* aur k* aur-ar k2 bamb-a stb2.de• bell k* borx h2 brass-n-o srj5• bros-gau mrc1 cann-s ↓ caps k* carc fd2.de• carneg-g rwt1• caust k* cere-b a1 *Cham* k* *Chel* k* *Chin* k* chin-b ↓ chinin-s chir-fl gya2 chlam-tr bcx2• chlf k* chlor k* *Choc* srj3• chol a1 *Cic* k* cist a1 clem k* cob ptm1• coca coca-c sk4• cocc k* cod a1 *Coff* k* coli rly4• colum-p sze2• conch fkr1• conin a1 croc k* cycl k* dioxi rbp6 **Dream-p** sdj1• dros k* ephe-si hsj1• eucal a1 euph k* *Falco-pe* nl2• ferr k* ferr-ar k* fic-m gya1 fl-ac k* fum rly1*• fuma-ac rly4• galeoc-c-h gms1• galla-q-r nl2• ger-i rly4• germ-met srj5• gins k* gran k* graph ↓ *Haliae-lc* srj5• ham hr1* *Hell* ptk1 helo-s bnm14• hippoc-k szs2 hydr-ac k* *Hydrog* srj2• *Hyos* k* ign k* ina-i mlk9.de ip k* *Irid-met* srj5• kali-br k* kali-p fd1.de• kola stb3• lac-del hrn2• lac-e hrn2• *Lac-h* htj1*• lac-leo ↓ lac-loxod-a hrn2• lac-lup hrn2• lach k* lap-la rsp1* lat-h thj1 laur k* lavand-a ctl1• led k* lil-t k* lim a1 limen-b-c hrn2* loxo-recl knl4• lyc k* lyss a1 m-arct b7.de mag-s k* maias-l hrn2• manc k* mang-p rly4• medul-os-si rly4• melal-alt gya4 meny k* merl k* mez k* *Moni* rfm1• morph ↓ mosch k* mur-ac k* nad rly4• naja narcot a1 nat-c k* nat-m k* nat-p k* nat-sil fd3.de• *Neon* stj2*• nept-m lsd2.fr nicc-met sk4• nicotam rly4• nit-ac ↓ *Olib-sac* wmh1 onop jl3 **Op** b7.de* orot-ac rly4• oxal-a rly4• ozone sde2• paro-i jl3 pert-vc vk9 petr k* petr-ra shn4• **Ph-ac** k* phasco-ci rbp2 phos k* *Plat* k* plb k* *Plut-n* srj7• podo fd3.de• *Positr* nl2• psil jl3* puls ptk1 pycnop-sa mrz1 querc-r svu1• rauw sp1 rhus-g tmo3• rhus-t b7.de ribo rly4• sacch-a fd2.de• sal-al blc1• *Sal-fr* sle1• sel gmj2 seneg k* **Sep** ptk1 sil k* sinus rly4• spig k* stann k* staph k* suis-em rly4• sul-ac h2* sulph ptk1 symph fd3.de• tarax k* tarent ↓ tell k* ter ckh1 thyr jl3 *Tung-met* bdx1• tus-fr a1 ulm-c jsj8• verat k* viol-t k* zinc k* zinc-act a1 [arg-p stj2 bell-p-sp dcm1 helium stj2 heroin sdj2 **Spect** dfg1 tax jsj7]
- **morning** | **waking**; on: androc srj1• chel k* chir-fl gya2 lac-leo hrn2• manc neon srj5• ulm-c jsj8•
- **forenoon**: aeth hr1*
- **accidents**; after:
  - **car** robbed and no transportation: lac-lup hrn2•
  - **computer** toppled off desk; when: lac-lup hrn2•
  - **daughter** cut herself on glass; when: lac-lup hrn2•
- **alternating** with:
  - **anger** (See Anger - alternating - tranquillity)
  - **concentration**; active (See Concentration - active - alternating - tranquillity)
  - **hurry** (See Hurry - alternating - tranquillity)
  - **sadness**: aids nl2• cann-s j chin-b hr1* croc j graph j m-arct j nit-ac j petr j plat j sep j zinc j
  - **violence** (See Violent - alternating - tranquillity)
- **anger**, after: *(↗Anger)* falco-pe nl2• ip k* sal-fr sle1•
- **cheerful**: conch fkr1•
- **conflict**; during: helo-s bnm14• lac-loxod-a hrn2•
- **eating**, after: haliae-lc srj5•
- **followed** by | **irritability**: nicc-met sk4•
- **hemoptysis**, hemorrhages, in: *Ham* kr1*
- **incomprehensible**: choc srj3• falco-pe nl2• ham fd3.de• ina-i mlk9.de morph nat-sil fd3.de• psil ft1
- **letting** go (See Tranquillity)
- **music** calms him: tarent mrr1
- **obscenities**; with regard to: olib-sac wmh1
- **pettiness**; not caught up in: lac-del hrn2•
- **problems**; not bothered by little: lac-del hrn2•
- **rain**; from heavy: [heroin sdj2]
- **reading**, while: haliae-lc srj5•

Tranquillity: ...
- **reconciled** to fate: aloe a1* cham h1* *Falco-pe* nl2• olib-sac wmh1 *Podo* fd3.de• stann h1
- **seriousness**, with: aids nl2•
- **settled**, centred and grounded: *(↗Confident)* aids nl2• positr nl2•
- **stool**, after: borx
- **tingling** of head; with: neon srj5•
- **tiredness**; with: melal-alt gya4
- **warmth**; with inner: galla-q-r nl2•

TRAPPED feeling (See Delusions - trapped)

TRAUMA; mental (See Ailments - mental shock)

TRAVELLING: *(↗Relocating)*
- **amel.**: *(↗desire)* carc gy ign vh*
- **desire** for: *(↗amel.; Adventurous; Amusement - desire; Change - desire; Desires - full - more; Insanity - travel; Libertinism; Wandering - desire)* am-c gl1.fr• am-m gl1.fr• ambr tsm1 anan k* aur aur-m-n wbt2• bac jl2 **Bar-act** sne bar-c gl1.fr• bell a1* bry lmj* calc k2* **Calc-p** k* *Carc* st* caust gl1.fr• chel ↓ choc srj3• cimic k* colum-p sze2• cur dulc fd4.de elaps falco-pe nl2• goss st *Hipp* hydrog srj2*• *Ign* gk* *Iod* k* kali-s fd4.de *Kola* stb3• lac-c sne lac-e hrn2• lach k* lec oss• lyss ptk1 mag-c mtf33* med gb• *Merc* k* merc-i-f sk• petr-ra shn4• plat gk *Podo* fd3.de• positr nl2• ruta fd4.de sacch-a fd2.de• sanic k* sep gk* spong fd4.de thea gl1.fr• **Tub** k* [buteo-j sej6 kali-p stj1 lith-i stj2 lith-p stj2 mag-p stj1 *Phos* stj1]
  - **morning** | **waking**: chel lpc
  - **almost** uncontrollable desire to travel far away: *Merc* kr1
  - **far** away: merc ptk1
  - **one** place to another (See Wandering - desire)
  - **sudden**: positr nl2•
- **yearning** for: olib-sac wmh1
  - **foreign** countries: olib-sac wmh1

TREMBLING:
- **agg.**; when: ant-t bg2 ars bg2 calc b4a.de* cupr bg2 plat bg2 puls bg2 sars bg2
- **hands** agg.; trembling of: am-c bg2 cic bg2 plat bg2 puls bg2

TRIBADISM (See Homosexuality)

TRICKY (See Deceitful)

TRIFLES: *(↗Anger - trifles; Anxiety - trifles; Cares full - trifles; Conscientious; Despair - trifles; Excitement - trifles; Fastidious; Fear - trifles; Frightened - trifles; Frivolous; Grief - trifles; Impatience - trifles; Irresolution - trifles; Irritability - trifles; Lamenting - trifles; Laughing - trifles; Prostration - trifles; Remorse - trifles; Rest - cannot; Sadness - trifles; Shrieking - trifles; Starting - trifles; Unconsciousness - trifles; Violent - trifles; Weeping - trifles; Wildness - trifles)*
- **agg.**: *Ars* ptk1 **Cham** ptk1 cina ptk1 coff ptk1 dros ptk1 hep ptk1 *Ign* ptk1 nit-ac ptk1 **Nux-v** ptk1 petr-ra shn4• phos bg2 sep bg2 **Sil** ptk1 thuj ptk1
- **important**; seem: *(↗Anger - trifles; Anxiety - trifles; Cares full - trifles; Conscientious; Despair - trifles; Excitement - trifles; Fastidious; Fear - trifles; Frightened - trifles; Frivolous; Grief - trifles; Impatience - trifles; Irresolution - trifles; Irritability - trifles; Lamenting - trifles; Laughing - trifles; Prostration - trifles; Remorse - trifles; Rest - cannot; Sadness - trifles; Shrieking - trifles; Starting - trifles; Unconsciousness - trifles; Violent - trifles; Weeping - trifles; Wildness - trifles)* adam srj5• androc srj1• ars bg2* bar-c gk calc k2* caust ptk1 cham mtf33 cocc bg2 con ptk1* ferr k* *Graph* bg2* *Hep* ptk1 ign ptk1 ip **Kali-s** fd* kres mg1.de lac-del hrn2• lac-e hrn2• lac-lup hrn2• lil-t bg2 mill ↓ nat-m ptk1 **Nat-sil** fd* nit-ac bg2 nux-v bg2* petr bg2 petr-ra shn4• podo fd3.de• positr nl2• sil ptk1* thuj bg2* ulm-c jsj8• [chr-met stj1]
  - **evening**: lac-lup hrn2•
  - **details**, losing themselves in: [mill stj]

TRUTH: *(↗Honest; Naive)*
- **desire** for truthfullness: **Podo** fd*
- **sensitive** to people's truthfulness: lac-leo hrn2•

- **telling** the plain truth: (↗*Honest; Proper - too; Rectifying - desire)* alum gl1.fr• ara-maca sej7• bov gl1.fr• choc srj3• falco-pe nl2• hyos gl1.fr• ina-i mlk9.de lac-e hrn2• olib-sac wmh1 ozone sde2• podo fd3.de• positr nl2• tritic-vg fd5.de *Vanil* fd5.de verat gl1.fr• [heroin sdj2]

TURNING:
- **agg.**: am-c bg2
- **head** agg.: rhus-t b7.de*

TWILIGHT agg.: ars b4a.de* berb bg2 brom mtf33 bros-gau mrc1 *Calc* b4.de* camph b7a.de caust bg2 limest-b es1• *Phos* bg2 plat sf1.de *Puls* b7.de* rhus-t b7.de* valer sf1.de

UNATTRACTIVE, things seem: (↗*Indifference - answer; Indifference - everything)* chin k* ignis-alc es2• vanil fd5.de
- **he** is; thinks (See Delusions - body - ugly)

UNCONCERNED about troubles (See Indifference; Tranquillity)

UNCONSCIOUSNESS: (↗*Coma; Dullness; Prostration; Stupefaction; Stupor; Torpor; GENERALS - Faintness)* absin k* acet-ac k* achy↓ **Acon** k* act-sp a1* adel a1 aesc aesc-g a1* aeth k* aether agar k* agar-cit a1 agar-pa a1 agar-ph a1 agar-pr a1 agar-se a1* agar-st a1 agav-t jl3 agn b2.de* agro a1 aids↓ *Ail* k* alco a1 alet hr1* aloe↓ *Alum* k* alum-p k2 am-c k* am-caust a1 am-m k* ambr k* *Aml-ns* a1* amor-r↓ amyg k* *Anac* k* anan a1 ancis-p tsm2 androc bnm2• anh↓ anil a1 ant-c k* ant-m bg* ant-t k* anthraci *Apis* k* apoc apom a1 aq-mar jl3 arg-met a1* *Arg-n* k* *Arn* k* *Ars* k* ars-h k* ars-met↓ art-v sf1.de *Arum-t* k* *Asaf*↓ asar k* astac hr1* *Aster* k* atro a1* *Atro-s* hr1 aur↓ *Bapt* k* **Bar-c** k* *Bar-m* bar-s k2 *Bell* k* ben-n a1 benz-ac a1* berb↓ bism k* borx↓ both a1 both-ax tsm2 bov k* brom bg2 brucel sa3• *Bry* k* bufo bung-fa tsm2 *Cact* k* cadm-s k* *Calad* k* calc k* calc-ar↓ calc-chln a1 calc-m a1 calc-s hr1* calc-sil k2* *Calen* hr1 *Camph* k* **Cann-i** k* cann-s k* *Cann-xyz*↓ *Canth* k* caps j5.de* carb-ac k* carb-an a1* *Carb-v* k* *Carbn-h* *Carbn-o* k* *Carbn-s* carl a1 cass a1 castm↓ *Caust* k* *Cedr* a1* cench a1 *Cham* k* *Chel* k* chen-a a1 chim-m↓ *Chin* k* chinin-s chir-fl↓ chlf a1 *Chlol* k* *Chlor* a1* *Cic* k* cic-m a1 cimic k* *Cina* k* cit-l a1* *Clem*↓ coca↓ **Cocc** k* cod↓ *Coff* k* coff-t hr1* *Colch* k* coloc hr1 *Con* k* cor-r cori-r k* corn hr1 cortico tpw7* cot↓ croc k* *Crot-c* k* *Crot-h* k* *Cupr* k* *Cupr-act* a1* cupr-ar↓ cupr-s a1* cur a1 *Cycl* k* cyt-l a1* dat-m a1 dat-s a1 dendr-pol tsm2 der a1 *Dig* k* digin↓ dirc a1 dor a1 dub a1 dubo-m a1 dulc k* elaps elec a1* eup-per↓ euph euphr j5.de ferr k* ferr-ar ferr-m a1* fil hr1* fl-ac k* form a1 formal br1 frag k* gaul a1 *Gels* k* germ-met↓ *Glon* k* graph k* grat j5.de guaj k* ham k* **Hell** k* helo-s bnm14• *Helon* kr1 *Hep* k* hipp jl2 home a1 **Hydr-ac** k* **Hyos** k* *Hyper*↓ **Ign** k* iod a1 ip k* *Iris*↓ jasm a1 jatr-c a1 jatr-u a1 juni-v a1 kali-bi *Kali-br* k* *Kali-c* k* kali-chl a1* kali-chls a1 kali-cy a1* kali-i k* kali-m k2 kali-n k* kali-s a1 kali-sula a1* keroso a1* kola stb3• kreos k* *Lac-d* lac-e hrn2• lac-h↓ **Lach** k* lact k* *Laur* k* *Led* lepi a1 lil-t bg2* lon-x a1 loxo-lae bnm12• lup a1 *Lyc* k* lyss a1* m-ambo b2.de* m-arct b2.de* mag-c b4.de* mag-m k* manc k* med↓ meli a1* menth a1 merc k* *Merc-c* k* merc-cy↓ merc-n a1 merc-ns a1 merc-pr-r a1 merl a1 meth-ae-ae a1 mez k* mill↓ morph a1 **Mosch** k* *Mur-ac* k* *Murx*↓ myric a1 naja napht a1 nat-br↓ nat-c k* nat-f sp1* nat-hchls a1 *Nat-m* k* nat-p *Nat-s*↓ nat-sal a1* nit-ac k* *Nit-s-d* a1* nitro-o a1 **Nux-m** k* *Nux-v* k* *Oena* k* oeno a1 ol-an k* olnd k* **Op** k* *Orig*↓ ox-ac k* oxyurn-sc mcp1• paeon↓ *Par* hr1* past a1 *Petr* k* **Ph-ac** k* *Phos* k* phyt bg2 *Plat* k* *Plb* k* plut-n↓ podo↓ psor↓ **Puls** k* pyrus a1 ran-b k* ran-s↓ rheum k* rhod k* rhus-r↓ *Rhus-t* k* rumx-act a1 russ a1 ruta k* sabad k* sabin k* sal-ac a1* salam↓ samb↓ sang a1* santin a1 sapin a1 sars k* scroph-n a1 *Sec* k* sel k* *Senec*↓ *Seneg* j5.de sep k* *Sil* k* sin-a↓ *Sol-ni* sol-t a1 sphing a1 spig k* *Spong*↓ squil stann k* staph k* *Stram* k* stry a1 sul-ac k* sul-h a1 *Sulph* k* sumb↓ tab k* tanac k* taosc iwa1• tarax k* *Tarent* a1* tax k* *Ter* k* tere-ch jl3 thal-xyz srj8• thea↓ *Ther*↓ *Thuj* b4a.de til↓ tub br1 uran-n kr1 valer k* *Verat* k* verat-v k* verb verin a1 vesp k* viol-o k* vip k* vip-a jl3 visc k* wies a1 xero bro1 *Zinc* k* zinc-cy↓ zinc-p k2* *Zing* hr1* [heroin sdj2 xen stj2]
- **daytime**: *Euph* j5.de phos j5.de
- **morning**: agar ars-met a1* *Bell* a1 bov k* **Bry** carb-an chel *Chinin-s* kr1 glon lyc *Mag-c* j5.de nat-c nat-m **Nux-v** k* ph-ac k* phos k* psor stry sulph taosc iwa1•
  - • **alone**, when: *Ph-ac* k*
  - • **rising**, on: **Bry**
  - • **waking**, on: chel nat-c
- **forenoon** | **10** h: stry a1
- **noon**: euph↓ glon a1 zinc

Unconsciousness – noon: ...
  - • **and** afternoon: euph j5.de
- **afternoon**: glon a1 nux-m↓ ol-an↓ zinc zing hr1
  - • **13** h: ol-an a1
  - • **14** h: nux-m a1
- **evening**: acon k* ant-t hr1 ars k* bry a1 calc k* caust k* coloc glon a1 lyc k* mag-c↓ mag-m↓ merl nux-m oena a1 ol-an puls k* sin-a hr1 stry k* thea a1 zinc
  - • **20** h: stry a1
  - • **lying** down, when: mag-c mag-m
- **night**: arg-n bar-c h2* bell k* cann-i k* canth↓ chel con↓ cot↓ digin↓ hep↓ mag-c↓ nat-m k* phos↓
  - • **amel.**: ferr a1
  - • **waking**, on: canth con cot a1 digin a1 hep mag-c phos
- **air**, in open: ferr c1 mosch nux-v k*
  - • **amel.**: tarax
- **alcoholic**: gels a1 *Glon* hr1* hyos a1* *Kali-br* hr1* lach mrr1 *Stram* hr1*
- **alone**, when: (↗*Company - desire - alone)* agar bg bry hell bg **Ign** *Lach* ph-ac k* **Sep** bg stram
- **alternating** with:
  - • **convulsions**: agar k* aur k*
  - • **delirium** (See Delirium - alternating - unconsciousness)
  - • **escape**; desire to (See Escape - alternating - unconsciousness)
  - • **excitement** (See Excitement - alternating - unconsciousness)
  - • **rage** (See Rage - alternating - unconsciousness)
  - • **restlessness** (See Restlessness - alternating - unconsciousness)
  - • **shrieking** (See Shrieking - alternating - unconsciousness)
  - • **violence**; dangerous (See Violent - alternating - unconsciousness)
- **answering** correctly when spoken to: arn al1 cic ckh1
  - • **return** at once; but delirium and unconsciousness (See Answering - stupor)
- **apoplexy**, in: *Acon* hr1* agar a1 *Bar-c* hr1* chel h1 *Crot-h* hr1* cupr hr1* cupr-act kr1 *Hyos* hr1* *Lach* hr1* *Laur* hr1* *Oena* hr1* **Op** h1* *Phos* hr1* *Plb* hr1* *Puls* hr1* sol-ni a1 *Stram* hr1*
- **asphyxia**, with: **Ant-t** hr1*
- **awareness** of surroundings, with: cocc k2
- **biting** tongue; after (See MOUTH - Biting - tongue - followed - unconsciousness)
- **blood**, sight of: (↗*Blood; GENERALS - Faintness - blood)* nux-m k*
- **brain** diseases, in: cupr-ar↓ kali-m k2
  - • **edema** of brain: cupr-ar br1
- **burning**, in: *Calen* kr1
- **candlelight**; from: cann-i
- **cheyne**-Stokes respiration; with: *Op* mrr1
- **chill**:
  - • **before**: *Ars Lach*
  - • **during**: acon bg arn bg *Ars* k* *Bell* camph k* caps cham bg cic k* cocc bg *Con Hep* k* *Hyos* bg kali-c mur-ac bg **Nat-m** nux-v op k* *Ph-ac* bg *Phos* bg puls rhus-t bg sep bg *Spong* hr1* stram k* valer verat bg
- **closing** eyes; on: ant-t ptk1 cann-xyz ptk1
- **coition**, after: *Agar* k* asaf *Dig* k*
- **cold**:
  - • **surface**, with cold: *Canth* kr1
  - • **taking** a cold; after: *Sil* k*
  - • **water**:
    - ⁝ **dashed** in face amel.: glon a1
    - ⁝ **poured** over head amel.: tab k*
- **concussion** of brain, from: **Arn** hr1* *Hyper* vh* *Nat-s* tl1*
- **conduct**, automatic: (↗*mental; riding; Gestures - automatic; GENERALS - Catalepsy)* aids nl2• anac sf1.de anh mg1.de* bufo k2* calc-sil camph cann-i caust cench k2 cic con croc hr1* cur elaps hell k2* hyos

- **conduct**, automatic: ...
  lac-h htj1• lach laur lsa1.de lyc *Nat-m* *Nux-m* k* oena *Phos* plut-n srj7• ruta a1 sec lsa1.de *Sil* *Vesp* k* *Visc* k*
- **convulsions**:
  - **after**: *Ars* ↓ *Art-v* hr1* atro hr1* *Bell* kr1 **Bufo** k* calc ↓ canth k* carb-ac k* chir-fl bnm4• *Cic* k* cori-r a1 *Glon* kr1 *Kali-bi* ↓ *Oena* k* **Op** st plb a1* sec stann ptk1
    - **epileptic**: *Ars* hr1* **Bufo** calc tl1 *Kali-bi* hr1* **Op** k* plb k*
  - **with** (See GENERALS - Convulsions - consciousness - without)
- **cough**:
  - **between** attacks of: *Ant-t* k* cadm-s
  - **during**: *(↗GENERALS - Fall; tendency - cough)* cadm-s a1* *Cina* b7.de* cor-r bg2 *Ip* b7.de* kali-c bg2 rhus-t bg2
  - **from** cough: cadm-s c1 cupr nh8* kali-c h2
- **cries**, with howling: camph a1*
- **crowded** room, in a: ambr ars bar-c con ign *Lyc* nat-c nat-m *Nux-m* *Phos* **Puls** sulph
- **delirium** tremens, in: *(↗Delirium tremens)* **Nux-v** k*
- **delirium**:
  - **after**: atro bry *Chel* kr1 phos
  - **during**: absin br1
- **delivery**, during: *Chinin-s* kr1 *Cimic* k* *Coff* k* *Gels* kr1 *Lach* kr1 **Nux-v** k* *Puls* k* **Sec** k1*
- **diarrhea**, after: ars
  - **vomiting**; and: ars k*
- **dinner**, after: castm til
- **diphtheria**, in: ail k2* *Merc* hr1 *Nat-m* hr1* *Sul-ac* hr1*
- **dream**, as in a: *(↗Confusion - dream; Dream; as; Dullness; Stupefaction)* aesc ↓ alum ↓ ambr anac atro ↓ bov ↓ cann-i *Cann-s* ↓ carb-an cic ↓ con cortico ↓ *Glon* ↓ merc ↓ **Nux-m** *Petr* ↓ phos plat ↓ puls ↓ ran-b ↓ rheum stram valer *Verat*
  - **does** not know where he is: *(↗Confusion - knows; Recognizing - not - surroundings; Stupefaction - knows)* aesc ↓ alum ↓ atro a1 bov ↓ *Cann-s* ↓ cic k2 cortico sp1 *Glon* merc *Nux-m* *Petr* plat sf1.de puls ↓ ran-b
    - **night**: bov a1
    - **waking**, on: aesc alum k2 *Cann-s* ↓ puls a1*
      - **dream**; from a frightful: *Cann-s* h1*
- **driving**, while: germ-met srj5•
- **drunkards**; of: *Phos* kr1
- **eating**, after: caust *Mag-m* *Nux-v* *Ph-ac*
- **emotion**, after: *Acon* am-c camph *Caust* *Cham* **Coff** k* **Ign** k* **Lach** k* mosch sf1.de nux-m *Op* *Ph-ac* verat
- **epilepsy**, after (See convulsions - after - epileptic)
- **erect**, if he remained: chin k*
- **eruptions**:
  - **slow** to appear; when eruption is: **Zinc**
  - **suppression** of eruptions; after: *Zinc* k1*
- **excitement**, after: amyg kr1 chlf kr1 nux-m
- **exertion**, after: *Ars* calc calc-ar *Caust* cocc hyper *Senec* *Ther* *Verat*
- **eyes**:
  - **cannot** open: gels *Sulph* hr1
  - **fixed**; with: aeth k* ars k* bov camph k* canth *Caust* k* cupr k* ign gk stram k*
  - **open**, with: *Cic* kr1
  - **pressure** in eyes and obstruction of sight: seneg
- **face**, with red: *Canth* hr1* *Glon* hr1* *Mur-ac* hr1*
- **fever**, during: *Acon* k* aeth *Agar* hr1* ail k2* anan a1 **Apis** k* **Arn** k* *Ars* k* *Bapt* k* *Bell* k* borx k* bry k* *Cact* *Calad* hr1* calc k* *Camph* bg2* *Cann-s* bg *Cann-xyz* bg2 *Caps* hr1* cham bg2 *Chlor* hr1* cic hr1* *Clem* hr1* *Cocc* bg2 *Colch* k* *Crot-h* hr1* dor hr1* *Dulc* k* eup-per *Gels* hr1* *Hell* bg2 *Hyos* k* *Ip* hr1* *Iris* kr1 kali-br a1 *Kali-c* b4a.de *Lach* k* laur k* *Lyc* hr1* manc hr1* meli hr1* **Mur-ac** k* **Nat-m** k* *Nit-s-d* hr1* *Nux-m* hr1* nux-v k* **Op** k* *Ph-ac* b4.de* *Phos* k* psor bg2 *Puls* k* rhus-t bg2 samb kr1 **Sep** b4a.de* sol-ni *Stram* bg2* sulph k* *Ter* hr1* *Verat* bg2* *Zinc* hr1 zing hr1*
- **frequent** spells of unconsciousness (= absences; petit mal): *(↗incomplete; periodical; remains; standing; sudden; talking; transient; GENERALS - Convulsions - epileptic; GENERALS - Convulsions - epileptiform; VERTIGO - Epileptic)* **Ars** k* *Art-v* br1* *Bapt* bell bro1* bufo mrr1 calc ggd1 caust bro1* cic tl1* cur hr1 *Hyos* k* ign k* kali-br a1* merc-cy *Nat-m* nat-s gk nux-m k2* oena mrr1 *Phos* k* sil tl1 visc br1* zinc ggd1 zinc-cy c2*
  - **absentminded** for long periods: cic mrr1
  - **injuries** to head; after: nat-s ptk1
- **head**:
  - **bending** forward, on: cortico sp1
  - **complaints** of; before: cann-xyz bg2
  - **moving**; on: calc carb-an nat-m rhus-t
  - **turning**, on: *Rhus-t* a1*
- **headache**; with (See HEAD - Pain - unconsciousness)
- **hydrocephalus**, in: **Apis** kr1 apoc a1* art-v hr1 *Clem* hr1* *Grat* hr1 *Hell* hr1* *Hyos* hr1* *Lyc* hr1* *Nat-m* hr1*
- **incomplete**: *(↗frequent)* ars carb-ac chlor crot-h cupr cupr-ar glon a1 ign c1 morph nat-c a1 nitro-o a1 op a1 sec sol-t a1 stram sul-ac
- **interrupted** by screaming (See Shrieking - alternating - unconsciousness)
- **jaundice**, in: **Chel** hr1*
- **jaw** dropping: *Lyc* hr1* **Op** hr1* *Sulph* hr1*
- **kneeling** in church, while: **Sep**
- **lies** as if dead: arn *Carb-v* kr1*
- **looking**:
  - **downward**, on: *(↗Fear - falling)* salam
  - **upwards**: lach
- **lying**, while: *Aeth* ↓ *Canth* ↓ *Carb-v* colch mag-c *Mag-m*
  - **arms**; screaming and tossing with outstretched: *Canth*
  - **stretched** out: *Aeth* kr1
- **meningitis**, in: *Ant-t* hr1* *Apis* kr1 apoc k2* *Gels* kr1 *Glon* hr1 *Hell* hr1* *Hydr-ac* hr1 kali-m k2 *Merc* hr1* *Rhus-t* hr1* *Sulph* hr1* *Verat* hr1* zinc mrr1
- **menses**:
  - **after**: *(↗Menses - after)* chin cupr hr1* *Lach* *Lyc*
  - **before**: *(↗Menses - before)* *Murx* *Nux-m* k*
  - **during**: *(↗Menses - during)* apis cham b7.de chin b7a.de cocc *Ign* **Lach** k* *Mosch* *Nux-m* nux-v plb puls *Sars* sep sulph verat zinc-p k2*
  - **suppression** of: acon cham chin con lyc **Nat-m** **Nux-m** k* nux-v *Op* hr1 verat
    - **fright**; from: *Op* kr1
- **mental** insensibility: *(↗conduct)* con cycl hell *Hyos* laur *Nux-m* oena op ph-ac phos podo fd3.de• sabad sec stram
- **motion**, on least: **Ars** *Verat*
- **music**, from: *(↗Music - agg.)* cann-i k* sumb
  - **piano**; listening to: cann-i a1
- **muttering**: *(↗Muttering)* ars h2 cocc kr1 dor kr1 *Phos* kr1 rhus-t j5.de
- **noise** arouses; every: zinc k2
- **odors**, from: **Nux-v** k* *Phos* k*
- **old** age, in: *Bar-c* hr1*
- **pain**, from: *Hep* k* *Nux-m* k* phyt k* *Valer* k*
- **periodical**: *(↗frequent)* alum-p k2* *Bar-s* k2* *Cic* k* fl-ac lyc vesp k2
- **perspiration**:
  - **cold** perspiration; with: sulph sf1.de
  - **during**: arn bg2 *Ars* bg2 bell bg2 benz-ac k2 calc ↓ camph bg2 cocc bg2 hell bg2 hyos bg2 mur-ac bg2 nat-m bg2 op bg2 *Ph-ac* bg2 rhus-t bg2 samb k* sep bg2 *Stram* bg2*
    - **hot** perspiration: calc ptk1 sep ptk1
- **piano**; listening to (See music - piano)
- **pneumonia**, in: *Chel* hr1* *Phos* hr1*
- **pregnancy**, during: *Absin* *Arg-n* *Arn* *Ars* *Asaf* *Bry* cann-i a1 *Glon* hr1* *Lach* *Nux-m* k* *Nux-v* k* *Sec* k* *Stram*
- **prolonged**: *Cic* ptk1 *Gels* ptk1 hydr-ac ptk1 laur ptk1
- **raising** arms above head, on: *Lac-d* lach
- **reading**, from: asaf k* cycl hell k2 tarax k*
- **remains** fixed in one spot: *(↗frequent)* hyos ↓ nux-m stram ↓
  - **motionless** like a statue: *(↗Insanity - immobile; Stupefaction - sits)* hyos stram

- **restlessness**, with: ter$_{hr1*}$
- **returns** after he has answered (See Answering - stupor)
- **riding**, while: *(↗conduct)* berb grat *Sep* sil
- **rising** up, on: *Arn* **Bry** *Carb-v* *Croc*$_{hr1*}$ *Op*$_{hr1*}$ *Verat*
- **rubbing** soles of feet amel.: chel$_{k*}$
- **scarlatina**, in: *Ail*$_{hr1*}$ *Am-c*$_{hr1*}$ *Ant-t*$_{hr1}$ *Apis*$_{kr1}$ *Chlor*$_{hr1}$ crot-h$_{hr1}$ *Cupr-act*$_{kr1}$ *Dulc*$_{hr1}$ *Gels*$_{hr1*}$ *Lyc*$_{hr1*}$ *Mur-ac*$_{hr1*}$ *Sulph*$_{hr1*}$ **Ter**$_{hr1}$ zinc$_{hr1}$
- **screaming**, interrupted by (See Shrieking - alternating - unconsciousness)
- **semi**-consciousness: ail$_{br1}$ amor-r$_{jl}$ *Carb-v*$_{kr1}$ chinin-s$_{kr1}$ chir-fl$_{bnm4}$• coca$_{kr1}$ cocc$_{kr1*}$ ign$_{kr1}$ kali-br$_{kr1}$ *Laur*$_{kr1}$ *Stram*$_{kr1}$ tarax$_{kr1}$ *Verat*$_{kr1}$ verat-v$_{kr1}$ zinc$_{kr1}$
- **sensation** of: cupr$_{ptk1}$ mag-c$_{bg1}$ podo$_{fd3.de}$• symph$_{fd3.de}$•
- **sexual** excitement, with: *Orig*$_{kr1}$ *Stram*$_{kr1}$
- **shock** from injury, in: *Arn*$_{hr1*}$ chlf$_{hr1*}$
- **shrieking**:
  - **interrupted** by shrieking; unconsciousness (See Shrieking - alternating - unconsciousness)
  - **with**: *Tub*$_{hr1*}$
- **sighing**, with: ail$_{br1}$ glon$_{a1}$
- **sitting**, while: *(↗Sitting - inclination)* aesc$_{a1}$ asaf$_{k*}$ bell carb-ac$_{k*}$ carb-an *Caust*$_{k*}$ *Colch*↓ mosch nat-m sil stram↓ tarax
  - **upright**: *Colch*$_{hr1*}$ stram$_{hr1*}$
- **snoring**, involuntary urination and stool; with: amyg$_{kr1}$ *Op*$_{kr1}$
- **somnolence**, without snoring, eyes being closed; with: ph-ac
- **standing**, while: *(↗frequent)* ant-t aur bov chin$_{h1*}$ lyc$_{k*}$ nux-m rhus-r sars
  - **having** dress fitted: nux-m
- **starts** up in a wild manner, but could not keep the eyes open: *Stram*$_{kr1}$
- **stomach**; with complaints of: bell$_{b4a.de}$
- **stool**:
  - **after**: calc cocc nat-m$_{bg2}$ *Phos Ter Verat*$_{bg2*}$
  - **before**: *Ars* dig
  - **during**: aloe ox-ac *Sulph*
- **stooping**, when: calc$_{k*}$ cortico$_{sp1}$ hell sulph$_{h2}$
- **sudden**: *(↗frequent)* absin bufo$_{k2}$ cann-i *Canth*$_{k*}$ carbn-h carbn-o *Cocc*$_{k*}$ glon$_{c1*}$ helo-s$_{bnm14}$• *Hydr-ac*$_{hr1*}$ *Ign*$_{hr1}$ kali-c$_{k*}$ *Laur*$_{hr1*}$ nux-m$_{mrr1}$ oena$_{hr1*}$ plb$_{k*}$ psor$_{al2}$ tub$_{hr1}$
- **sunstroke**, in: *Bell*$_{kr1}$ cact$_{kr1}$ camph$_{kr1}$ **Glon**$_{kr1}$ lach$_{kr1}$ *Nat-c*$_{vh*}$ **Op**$_{kr1*}$
- **swallow**; with inability to: aml-ns$_{ptk1}$
- **talking**, while: *(↗frequent)* lyc$_{k*}$ sin-a$_{hr1}$ tub$_{hr1}$
- **trance**, as in a: *(↗Trance)* **Lach**$_{k*}$ *Laur*$_{k*}$ tab taosc$_{iwa1}$•
- **transient**: *(↗frequent)* arn$_{mrr1}$ asaf$_{k*}$ bov bufo calad calc cann-i canth carb-an chel chim-m$_{hr1*}$ dig$_{c1}$ hep **Ign** kali-c$_{h2*}$ lyss med *Mosch Nat-m* ol-an **Puls** rhod↓ rhus-r sec sil zinc
  - **morning**:
    - **rising**; on | **drowsiness** in head: rhod
  - **afternoon** | **warm** room; in: **Puls**
- **trifles**, at: *(↗Trifles; Trifles - important)* *Sep*
- **turning** in a circle, during: calc$_{a1}$
- **twitching** of limbs, with: *Agar*$_{vh*}$ *Bell*$_{hr1*}$ *Canth*$_{hr1*}$ *Cupr*$_{hr1*}$ **Hyos**$_{hr1*}$ **Stram**$_{hr1*}$
- **unable** to mediate between loved ones; when: lac-e$_{hrn2}$•
- **uremic** coma: canth$_{kr1}$ *Op*$_{kr1}$ *Tab*$_{sf1.de}$ ter$_{kr1}$
- **urine** | **suppression** of; with: dig$_{ptk1}$ plb$_{k2*}$
- **vertigo**, during: *(↗GENERALS - Faintness - vertigo; VERTIGO - Unconsciousness)* acon$_{k*}$ aeth agar ail alet$_{bro1}$ arg-n arn *Ars*$_{k*}$ bell berb$_{bro1}$ borx bov$_{k*}$ *Bry*$_{bro1}$ camph$_{bro1}$ canth$_{k*}$ carb-an carb-v$_{h2*}$ chel chinin-s chlor$_{hr1}$ cocc con$_{h2*}$ crot-h$_{hr1*}$ ferr glon$_{bro1}$ grat iod jatr-c *Kali-br*$_{hr1*}$ *Kali-c*$_{hr1*}$ kreos lach laur$_{k*}$ lyc$_{k*}$ mag-c manc$_{hr1*}$ merc mez$_{k*}$ mill mosch$_{k*}$ nat-c$_{h2*}$ nat-m nux-m nux-v$_{k*}$ op phos$_{bro1}$ psor$_{al2}$ ran-s$_{k*}$ sabad$_{bro1}$ sars$_{h2*}$ sec$_{k*}$ sep$_{k*}$ sil stann$_{h2*}$ stram tab$_{k*}$ zinc
- **vomiting**:
  - **amel.**: acon$_{k*}$ tab tanac$_{k*}$
  - **with**: ail$_{hr1*}$ ars-h$_{hr1*}$ calen$_{hr1}$ cupr$_{bg2}$ dor$_{hr1*}$
- **wakes** often, but only for a short time: achy$_{jl3}$ *Ars*$_{h2*}$
- **waking**:
  - **after**: con$_{k*}$ kali-br$_{k*}$ sel$_{k*}$ stram$_{k*}$

Unconsciousness – waking: ...

  - **on**: aesc$_{k*}$ aster$_{k*}$ chel chin$_{k*}$ cod$_{a1}$ mag-c mez$_{k*}$ nat-br$_{a1}$ nat-c phos
- **walking**, while: calc$_{k*}$ canth↓ carb-an caust↓ grat hep↓ sulph↓ vesp$_{k2}$
  - **air**; in open: canth caust hep sulph
- **warm** room, in: *Acon Lach Lyc* paeon$_{a1}$ **Puls** tab
- **wine**; after: kali-chl$_{a1}$

UNDERSTANDING (See Comprehension)

UNDERSTOOD; being:

- **desire** for:
  - **family**; by: [buteo-j$_{sej6}$]
  - **friend**; by: [buteo-j$_{sej6}$]

UNDERTAKING:

- **anything** with anybody; does not want to undertake: absin$_{br1}$
- **lacks** willpower to undertake anything: *(↗Confidence - want; Irresolution; Pessimist; Postponing; Will - weakness)* androc$_{srj1}$• *Brucel*$_{sa3}$• haliae-lc$_{srj5}$• ign$_{k2}$ phos *Pic-ac* sal-fr$_{sle1}$• sulph$_{mrr1}$
- **many** things, persevering in nothing: *(↗Capriciousness; Inconstancy; Irresolution; Laziness; Mood - changeable; Persisting; Time - fritters; Will - weakness)* *Acon* alum$_{ptk1*}$ androc$_{srj1}$• anh$_{sp1}$ ant-c$_{br1}$ apis$_{c1}$ arg-n$_{sne}$ asaf$_{ptk1*}$ bism$_{h1*}$ borx$_{h2}$ canth$_{c1*}$ cortico$_{jl*}$ **Dulc**$_{fd*}$ graph$_{gl1.fr}$• grat$_{ptk1*}$ haliae-lc$_{srj5}$• ign$_{gl1.fr}$• *Kola*$_{stb3}$• *Lac-c*$_{k*}$ *Lach*$_{k*}$ **Lil-t**$_{a1}$ lyc$_{a1}$ *Med*$_{vh*}$ nat-sil$_{fd3.de}$• nauf-helv-li$_{elm2}$• *Nux-m*$_{kr1*}$ nux-v$_{ptk1*}$ petr$_{gl1.fr}$• pin-s$_{a1}$ plan ruta$_{fd4.de}$ sanic$_{c1*}$ *Sil*$_{ptk1*}$ spong$_{fd4.de}$ stann$_{gl1.fr}$• sul-ac$_{bng}$ sulph$_{ptk1*}$ tritic-vg$_{fd5.de}$ vanil$_{fd5.de}$ verat$_{h1*}$
- **new** things; cannot undertake: lyc$_{br1}$
- **nothing**, lest he fail: *(↗Anxiety - success; Confidence - want; Delusions - fail everything; Delusions - succeed; Fear - failure; Fear - undertaking; Succeeds; Timidity)* *Arg-n*$_{k*}$ nux-v$_{a1}$ sil$_{k*}$
- **others**; desire to undertake something together with (See Company - desire - undertake)
- **tasks** with enthusiasm (See Activity)
- **things** opposed to his intentions: *(↗Antagonism; Irresolution; Will - contradiction)* agar$_{mtf}$ phos$_{h2}$ sep$_{k*}$

UNDIGNIFIED: *(↗Servile)* alco$_{a1}$

UNDRESSING: *(↗Naked)*

- **aversion** to undress: marb-w$_{es1}$•
- **coldest** weather; in | **children**; in: sanic$_{tl1}$ sulph$_{tl1}$
- **weeping**; and: thyr$_{ptk1*}$

UNEASINESS (See Discomfort; Frightened; Restlessness)

UNFEELING: *(↗Behavior - children; Brutality; Cruelty; Hardhearted; Malicious; Moral; Sensitive - want; Unsympathetic; Wicked)* adam$_{srj5}$• aids$_{nl2}$• alco$_{sf1.de}$ aloe$_{sne}$ **Anac**$_{k*}$ androc$_{srj1}$• anh$_{sp1}$ arizon-l$_{nl2}$• ars$_{gl1.fr}$• aur-ar$_{vh1}$ bism$_{j5.de}$ cench$_{k2}$ choc$_{srj3}$• con$_{j5.de}$ croc$_{j5.de}$ crot-c$_{sk4}$• dendr-pol$_{sk4}$• dream-p$_{sdj1}$• falco-pe$_{nl2}$• galla-q-r$_{nl2}$• granit-m$_{es1}$• ham$_{fd3.de}$• hep$_{mtf*}$ hyos$_{j5.de*}$ ignis-alc$_{es2}$• kali-i↓ lac-h$_{htj1}$• *Lach*$_{kr1*}$ *Laur*$_{j5.de}$ lyss$_{mtf}$ marb-w$_{es1}$• med$_{mtf}$ nat-m$_{bg2*}$ nat-sil$_{fd3.de}$• nicc-met$_{sk4}$• **Nux-v**$_{mtf}$ op$_{j5.de}$ ozone$_{sde2}$• petr-ra$_{shn4}$• plat$_{j5.de*}$ plut-n$_{srj7}$• positr$_{nl2}$• rhus-c$_{uba}$ *Rhus-g*$_{tmo3}$• sabad$_{j5.de*}$ *Sal-fr*$_{sle1}$• *Sep*$_{mrr1}$ squil$_{j5.de*}$ *Sulph*$_{j5.de*}$ sumb$_{a1}$ tub$_{mrr1}$ verat$_{mrr1}$ [heroin$_{sdj2}$ lac-mat$_{sst4}$ tax$_{jsj7}$]

- **family**, with his: *(↗Unsympathetic - family)* arizon-l$_{nl2}$• falco-pe$_{nl2}$• kali-i$_{k2}$ [heroin$_{sdj2}$]

UNFORGIVING (See Dwells - past; Hatred; Hatred - persons - offended)

UNFORTUNATE, feels: *(↗Confidence - want; Delusions - misfortune - inconsolable; Delusions - unfortunate; Delusions - wretched - looking; Fear - misfortune; Inconsolable - misfortune; Pities; Sadness - misfortune; Weeping - pitied; Wretched)* agar$_{a1}$ bry carb-v$_{mtf33*}$ carc$_{fb*}$ caust$_{a1}$ *Chel*$_{j5.de}$ *Chin*$_{k*}$ cub fl-ac$_{ptk1}$ *Graph*$_{b4a.de*}$ hell$_{j5.de}$ hura iod$_{ptk1}$ ip kali-c$_{j5.de}$ kreos$_{ptk1}$ lavand-a$_{ctl1}$• *Lyc*$_{k*}$ merc$_{a1}$ nat-m$_{a1}$ **Nat-sil**$_{fd*}$ plut-n$_{srj7}$• rhus-t$_{j5.de}$ sabad$_{ptk1}$ sars$_{h2*}$ sep$_{k*}$ stann$_{ptk1}$ *Staph*$_{gl1.fr}$• sulph$_{j5.de*}$ *Tab*$_{j5.de*}$ *Tritic-vg*$_{fd5.de}$ **Vanil**$_{fd*}$ verat zinc$_{ptk1}$ [heroin$_{sdj2}$]

UNFRIENDLY humor: *(↗Discontented; Frown; Irritability; Mocking; Morose; Petulant; Sulky)* aloe sne am-c k* anac ckh1 mag-m k* plat k* *Psor* st rauw sp1 *Sacch-a* fd2.de• vanil fd5.de

UNGRACIOUS (See Elegance - want)

UNGRATEFUL: *(↗Indifference - done)* ars gl1.fr• bry ↓ calc gl1.fr• caust gl1.fr• chin gk lach gl1.fr• lyc gl1.fr• nat-m gl1.fr• nux-v gl1.fr• **Plat** mtf33* puls ↓ sil ↓ staph gl1.fr• *Sulph* k2* tarent br1*
- **avarice**, from: *(↗Avarice)* bry gl1.fr• puls gl1.fr• sil gl1.fr• sulph gl1.fr•

UNHAPPINESS (See Ailments - unhappiness)

UNIFICATION: *(↗Brotherhood; Fraternized; Friendship; Friendship - outpourings; Love - exalted)*
- **desire** for: galla-q-r nl2• lac-ac stj5•
- **higher** consciousness; with (See Delusions - consciousness - higher)
- **sensation** of unification: *(↗Brotherhood; Fraternized; Friendship; Friendship - outpourings; Love - exalted)* agam-g mlk9.de aids ↓ arge-pl ↓ haliae-lc ↓ irid-met ↓ lac-leo ↓ olib-sac wmh1 ozone ↓ positr ↓ sanguis-s hrn2• spect ↓ thres-a ↓
  - **animals**; with: lac-leo hrn2•
  - **crystals**; with: positr nl2•
  - **earth**; with the: positr nl2•
  - **everything**; with: arge-pl rwt5• irid-met srj5• ozone sde2•
  - **family**; with his: aids nl2•
  - **fellow** man; with his (See Brotherhood)
  - **partner**; with his: aids nl2•
  - **universe**; with the: *(↗Merging)* aids nl2• haliae-lc srj5• olib-sac wmh1 thres-a sze7• [spect dfg1]

UNLOVABLE; sensation as if one is (See Forsaken)

UNOBSERVING [=inattentive]: *(↗Absentminded; Absorbed; Abstraction; Concentration - difficult; Dream; as; Dullness; Heedless; Mistakes - speaking; Prostration; Stupefaction)* *Acon* bg2 agar mtf33 agn bg2 alum k* am-c bg2* am-m bg2 ambr gl1.fr• anac bg2 ang bg2 arg-n bg2 *Arn* bg2 asaf vh1 asar k* aur bg2 bapt bg2 bar-c k* bell j5.de* bov bg2 bros-gau mrc1 bufo gk calad bg2 calc bg2 cann-s bg2 canth bg2 carb-v bg2 *Caust* k* cham h1* chel bg2 cic bg2 coca bg2 *Cocc* bg2 coff j5.de* colch bg2 croc bg2 cypra-eg sde6.de• fl-ac bg2 gels bg2 graph bg2 grat j5.de *Hell* bg2 hyos bg2 ictod kr1 ign bg2 ind hr1* kali-br bg2 kali-c k* kali-p ↓ lach bg2 led bg2 lyc bg2 m-ambo h1* mag-c j5.de* med bg2 merc k* mez bg2 mosch bg2 nat-c k* nat-m bg2 nux-m bg2 *Nux-v* bg2 olnd bg2* op bg2 ozone sde2• petr k* petr-ra shn4• ph-ac k* phos bg2 plat k* podo ↓ puls h1* rhod j5.de sars bg2 *Sep* k* *Sil* bg2 spig j5.de* spong bg2 stann bg2 *Staph* bg2 stict bg2 stram bg2 sul-ac bg2 sulph k* syph bg2 tab bg2 thuj k* tritic-vg fd5.de vanil fd5.de verat bg2 verb bg2 [heroin sdj2]
- **children**: bar-c mtf33
- **spoken** to, when: am-c gl1.fr• am-m gl1.fr• ambr gl1.fr• bar-c gl1.fr• kali-p fd1.de• podo fd3.de•

UNOBSERVING [=nonconformism]: *(↗Anarchist; Meddlesome; Sensitive - want)* alum asar bar-c *Caust* k* kali-c k* lyc cd1 merc nat-c petr ph-ac plat *Sep* k* sulph thuj k*

UNPRACTICAL (See Awkward)

UNREAL:
- **cannot** tell what is unreal and what is real: limest-b es1•
- **conversation** seems: bit-ar wht1•
- **everything** seems: *(↗Confusion; Delirium; Delusions - unreal; Delusions - unreal - everything; Dream; as; Strange - everything)* ail *Alum* anac k2 anh sp1 aran jl3 arb-m oss1• arizon-l nl2• bit-ar wht1• cann-i cann-s cocc st coli jl2 dulc fd4.de falco-pe nl2• galla-q-r nl2• germ-met srj5• gink-b jl3 irid-met srj5• lac-c lac-h sze9• lil-t k* *Med* nat-sil fd3.de• pin-con oss2• plut-n srj7• podo fd3.de• rauw tpw8* *Ruta* fd4.de sal-fr sle1• *Spong* fd4.de staph tung-met bdx1• *Vanil* fd5.de [heroin sdj2]

UNREASONABLE: *(↗Irrational)* am-c br1 ars-s-f k2 kali-i a1 lil-t k2*

UNREFINED: *(↗Materialistic; Simple)* con mrr1 **Graph** mrr1

UNRELIABLE: *(↗Deceitful)* anh sp1 bell ↓ calc ↓ con ↓ lyc ↓ merc ↓ op ↓ sil ↓ sulph ↓

Unreliable: ...
- **promises**, in his: bell gl1.fr• calc gl1.fr• con gl1.fr• lyc gl1.fr• merc gl1.fr• op gl1.fr• sil gl1.fr• sulph gl1.fr•

UNSCRUPULOUS (See Unsympathetic)

UNSOCIABLE (See Antisocial)

UNSYMPATHETIC: *(↗Hardhearted; Mood - repulsive; Unfeeling)* adam srj5• am-c h2 anac bg2 androc srj1• arg-met ↓ ars gl1.fr• calc h2 carb-an h2 carb-v h2 cham bg2 chin bg2 chir-fl gya2 con h2 **Dig** k1* falco-pe nl2• granit-m es1• ham fd3.de• ignis-alc es2• lac-h htj1• lac-leo hrn2*• marb-w es1• nat-m bg2 nat-sil fd3.de• nit-ac bg2 op bg2 ozone sde2• pant-ac rly4• plat bg2* plut-n srj7• puls gl1.fr• sep bg2 staph h1 sumb a1 [pall stj2 tax jsj7]
- **alternating** with | **cheerfulness** (See Cheerful - alternating - sympathy)
- **family**; even toward closest: *(↗Aversion - family; Unfeeling - family)* plut-n srj7•
- **friends**; towards: *(↗Aversion - friends; Censorious - friends; Mocking - friends)* arg-met ptk1* chir-fl gya2 lac-leo hrn2• plut-n srj7•

UNTIDY: *(↗Dirty; Heedless; Indifference - appearance; Indifference - external things)* adam srj5• anac sne arb-m oss1• aur-ar k2 bit-ar wht1• calc mrr1 carc mlr1*• falco-pe nl2• kali-s fd4.de* *Lac-h* htj1• olib-sac wmh1 plut-n srj7• positr nl2• *Psor* mtf33 ruta fd4.de spong fd4.de stram bg *Sulph* bg2* tritic-vg fd5.de [lac-mat sst4 tax jsj7]
- **perform**; except when he has to: carc gk6*
- **working** on; except for what he is (See perform)

UNTRUTHFUL: *(↗Contradiction - disposition; Deceitful; Dishonest; Hypocrisy; Liar; Manipulative; Slander)* alco arg-met vh *Arg-n* st* *Morph* st* **Op** k1* thuj mrr1 *Verat* k*

UNWORTHY, objects seem: *Chin* k* ignis-alc es2•

UPHEAVAL (See Excitement)

UPTIGHT *[= being strict]* (See Dogmatic)

UPTIGHT *[= nervousness]* (See Restlessness)

URINATION:
- **after**: ter bg2
- **during**: cham b7.de*

USEFUL; desire to be: arn ms aur-s zr **Carc** fd* *Cere-b* a1* positr nl2•

USURER: lyc gl1.fr• puls gl1.fr• sulph gl1.fr•

VACILLATION (See Mood - changeable)

VAGABOND: | **tendency** to become a: [oxyg stj]

VANITY: *(↗Affectation; Delusions - inferior; Egotism; Extravagance; Flattered - desire; Foolish - happiness; Foppish; Haughty; Jewelry - desire; Longing - good; Perfume - loves; Selfishness)* ars bng aur-s wbt2• *Bell* gl1.fr• carc cd fic-m gya1 lyc gl1.fr*• marb-w es1• *Merc* gl1.fr• nux-v mtf33* **Pall** sne plat mtf33* *Puls* mtf33* staph sne sulph gl1.fr• taosc iwa1• verat mtf33

VEHEMENT (See Violent)

VENERATION: *(↗Admiration; Reverence)* anac j ars j aur j bell j (non:coff k*) coff-t a1* croc j dulc fd4.de hyos j lach j lyc j *Podo* fd3.de• puls j spong fd4.de stram j sulph j vanil fd5.de verat j

VERIFYING everything (See Checking)

VERSES: agar bro1 ant-c bro1 lach bro1 stram bro1
- **making**: *(↗Writing - desire; DREAMS - Verses)* *Agar* k* am-c gl1.fr• *Ant-c* k* cann-i k* carb-v gl1.fr• chin mrr1* coff gl1.fr• dream-p sdj1• lach gl1.fr• lyc ckh1* nat-c ptk1* nat-m a1* staph mrr1* stram k* thea thres-a sze7• [nat-p stj1]
  - **sleep**; on going to: nat-m h2*
- **repeating** | **childhood**; from: coca-c sk4•

VERTIGO; during: aloe bg2 bar-m bg2 carb-v bg2 seneg bg2 sil bg2 verat bg2

VEXATION (See Anger; Irritability)

VEXED; being: | **intolerance** of: *(↗Ailments - anger)* ferr-p a1

VINDICTIVE (See Malicious)

VIOLENCE: **Chel** sne meli sne ozone sde2•
- **aversion** to: asar vh calc mtf carc mtf gard-j vlr2• hep mrr1 *Mag-c* mrr1* mag-m stj1* plat mrr1 staph zr* stram mrr1 [alumin-s stj2 mag-f stj1 mag-p stj1 mag-s stj1]

VIOLENT: *(↗Ailments - violence; Anger - stabbed; Anger - violent; Biting; Breaking; Contradiction - intolerant - restrain; Cut; Cut - others; Delirium - arms - throws; Delirium - attacks; Delirium - fierce; Delirium - violent; Delirium - wild; Destructiveness; Fanaticism; Fight; Gestures - violent; Insanity - threatening; Irritability; Kicking; Kill; desire; Mania; Quarrelsome; Rage; Rage - violent; Spitting - faces; Striking; Striking - children; striking; Striking - himself; Tearing - things; Wildness)* abrot k* absin kr1 acon k* aesc agar bg2 agav-t jl alco a1 alum kr1 am-c am-m b7a.de ambr *Anac* k* *Androc* srj1• ang *Ant-t* kr1* apis arn k* ars k* **Aur** k* aur-ar k2 aur-s k2 bar-c k* **Bell** k* borx k* *Bry* k* cadm-met ↓ calc k* calc-p camph canth carb-an ↓ *Carb-v* k* *Carbn-s* carneg-g rwt1• caste jl caust k* *Cham* k* chin bg2 **Cic** k* cocc j5.de* coff bg2* coloc k* colum-p ↓ con bg2* corn croc k* crot-c sk4• cupr k* cyna jl dros k* dulc k* ferr k* gamb ↓ graph k* grat j5.de haliae-lc srj5• helo-s bnm14• **Hep** b4.de* **Hyos** k* ictod j5.de ign bg2 *Iod* bg2* iodof ↓ kali-ar ↓ kali-bi bg2* kali-c k* *Kali-i* j5.de* *Kali-p* kola stb3• *Lach* b7.de* *Led* k* lil-t k2* *Lyc* k* m-ambo b7.de *M-arct* j *M-aust* b7.de* mag-s j5.de mang med mrr1 merc k* merl mez k* mill ↓ moni rfm1• morph oss• mosch k* nat-c k* *Nat-m* k* nat-s j5.de nicc ↓ nit-ac k* nitro-o a1 **Nux-v** k* *Oena* ↓ olnd k* op ↓ *Petr* k* petr-ra shn4• ph-ac h2* *Phos* k* plat k* plb bg2 plut-n srj7• polys sk4• prot jl2 psor ↓ ran-b k* rheum br1 ruta fd4.de sabad sacch a1 seneg k* *Sep* k* sil st spong fd4.de stann k* staph gl1.fr• **Stram** k* stront-c k* *Sulph* k* syph jl2 *Tarent* k* teucr gl1.fr• thuj b4a.de *Tub* mrr1 vanil fd5.de *Verat* k* verat-v bg2 vesp mgm• *Visc* k* zinc b4a.de* [heroin sdj2 hydrog stj2 tell stj2]
- **morning**: calc carb-an a1 carb-v gamb graph iod k2 nat-s j5.de petr psor
- **forenoon**: carb-v k*
- **evening**: caust ↓ *Hep* ↓ mill k* *Nat-m* ↓
  - **siesta**, after: caust
  - **supper**, after: mill
  - **trifles**, at: *Hep* k1* *Nat-m*
- **activity**, with bodily: *Plat* hr1*
- **alternating** with:
  - **cheerfulness**: aur croc stram
  - **laughing**: aur j croc k* stram k*
  - **mildness**: croc gl1.fr•
  - **sadness**: ambr k* cadm-met gm1
  - **stupefaction**: absin
  - **stupor**: absin st
  - **taciturnity**: aur-ar k2
  - **tranquillity**: aur-ar k2
  - **unconsciousness**: absin k*
- **chases** family out of house: *Verat* hr1*
- **children**:
  - **in**: tub jl2
  - **towards**: *(↗Striking - children; striking)* colum-p sze2•
- **contradiction**; from: *(↗Anger - contradiction)* aur br1 **Dulc** fd* *Oena* ↓ *Sil* hr1* tub mrr1
  - **menses**; during: *(↗Menses - during)* *Oena* hr1*
- **deeds** of violence; rage leading to: *(↗Delirium - violent; Mania - violence; Rage; Rage - violent)* agar sf1.de* anac ars gl1.fr• *Aur* vh* bar-c *Bell* k* bry gl1.fr• calc gl1.fr• canth j chin cic st cocc con croc j5.de crot-c sk4• cupr j5.de **Hep** k1* hyos k* *Ign* k* *Iod* k2* iodof sf1.de kali-ar k2 kola stb3• lach lil-t sf1.de lyc mosch nat-c nicc j5.de nit-ac sf1.de *Nux-v* k* phos gl1.fr• plat k* **Stram** k* stront-c j5.de tarent k* *Verat* sf1.de zinc
- **easily**: ferr mtf33 plut-n srj7•
- **exhaustion**; until: **Nat-c** gl1.fr•
- **fever**; during: *Cham* b7a.de* coff bg2 nux-v bg2
- **friends**, to his: kali-ar k2*
- **pain**, from: *(↗Anger - pains - about)* ant-t st **Aur Cham Hep** lyc st
- **perspiration**; during: *Acon* bg2 *Ars* bg2 *Bry* bg2 carb-v bg2 **Cham** bg2 *Coff* bg2 ferr bg2 *Hep* bg2 hyos bg2 nat-m bg2 **Nux-v** bg2 phos bg2 stram bg2 sulph bg2 thuj bg2

Violent: ...
- **reproached**, when hearing another: *(↗Indignation)* calc-p a1
- **sick**, when: bell c1
- **sleep** | **before**: op a1
- **stool**; before: calc j5.de
- **talk** of others, from: *(↗Talking - others)* con gl1.fr• dulc fd4.de mang j5.de
- **touch**, from: lach j5.de
- **trifles**, at: *(↗Trifles; Trifles - important)* androc srj1• caust gl1.fr• *Dulc* fd4.de *Hep* sf1.de* *Nat-c* gl1.fr• *Nat-m* k* *Ruta* fd4.de spong fd4.de

VISION agg.; dim: arg-n bg2 cycl bg2 dig bg2 staph bg2

VISIONS (See Delusions - visions)

VITAL (See Vivacious)

VIVACIOUS: *(↗Charming; Cheerful; Excitement; Exhilaration; High-spirited; Jesting; Mirth; Pert; Playful; Pleasure; Quick; Smiling - involuntarily - speaking; Thoughts - rapid; SLEEP - Sleeplessness - vivacity)* acon bg2 agar b4.de* agn b7.de aloe alum k* am-c b4.de anac bg2 anag a1 *Androc* srj1• ang k* anh mg1.de ant-c b7.de *Apis* mrr1 arg-met ars b4.de* ars-s-f a1 *Aur* b4.de* bart a1 bell bg2 borx bg2 bov bg2 brom a1* bufo-s a1 cact calc-s ↓ cann-s k* **Cann-xyz** bg2 carb-an b4a.de* carb-v bg2 carbn-s a1 *Carc* mlr1• caust ↓ chin k* chlol a1 cimic bg2 cit-v ↓ clem a1 cob k* coc-c ↓ coca-c sk4• cocc cod a1 **Coff** k* con a1 **Croc** b7.de* crot-h k* cupr k* cycl k* dig a1 ery-m a1 eucal kr1 ferr bg2* *Fl-ac* kr1 galv c1 gast a1 gels k* glon k* graph bg2 grat a1 guar a1 ham fd3.de• hep gl1.fr• hipp hydrc a1 *Hyos* k* *Ign* b7.de* indg a1 iod h* ip a1 irid-met srj5• kali-c a1 kali-p bg2 kali-s fd4.de kerose a1 keroso a1 **Lach** k* lact a1 laur bg2 loxo-recl knl4• luf-op a1 lyc bg2* m-aust b7.de mag-m bg2* mag-s a1 merl a1 mez a1 morph a1 mosch ↓ *Murx* ↓ nat-c k* nat-m bg2 nit-ac gl1.fr• nux-m bg2 *Nux-v* k* *Op* b7.de* orig a1 ox-ac ↓ par k* paull a1 peti a1 petr k* *Ph-ac* k* phel a1 *Phos* b4.de* plat bg2 plb bg2 plut-n srj7• podo fd3.de• psor a1 ruta fd4.de sabad k* sarr a1* *Sars* ↓ seneg bg2* sep gl1.fr• spig b7.de* *Spong* b7.de* squil bg2 *Stram* b7.de* sul-ac k* sulph mtf33 sumb a1 *Tarent* bg2* testis bwa3 *Teucr* bg2 thea a1 thuj a1 tritic-vg fd5.de upa a1 **Valer** k* vanil fd5.de *Verat* k* verb b7.de viol-o b7.de* viol-t bg2 zinc b4.de*
- **morning**: cit-v a1 con a1 fl-ac a1 graph a1 mag-m a1 sulph a1
- **afternoon**: ang a1 calc-s a1 cann-s a1 lyc a1 ox-ac a1
- **evening**: am-c a1 androc srj1• bufo-s a1 chin a1 coc-c a1 ferr a1 lach a1
- **alternating** with:
  - **absentmindedness**: alum b4a.de*
  - **abstraction** of mind: alum h2
  - **anger** (See Anger - alternating - vivacity)
  - **despondency** (See sadness)
  - **dullness**: crot-h j5.de
  - **grief**: tarent k*
  - **muttering**: ars-s-f k2
  - **sadness**: caust a1 *Nux-v* kr1 psor a1 sep a1 tarent a1
  - **sorrow** (See grief)
- **depression**, followed by: gels c1 spong fd4.de
- **intoxication**, as from: cann-s a1
- **fever**; during: acon bg2 coff bg2 mosch b7.de nat-c bg2 op b7.de* plat bg2 *Sars* bg2
- **perspiration**; during: apis bg2 ars bg2 bell bg2 *Coff* bg2 croc bg2 **Op** b7.de* *Sars* bg2
- **rising**, after: gels a1
- **women**: *Murx* br1

○ - **Stomach**; with pain in: lyc bg2

VOMITING:
- **after** vomiting | **amel.**: asar b7.de* tab bg2
- **agg.**: am b7.de* asar b7.de* bar-m bg2 crot-t bg2 gran bg2
- **amel.**: am bg asar bg*
- **before**: sang bg2
- **desire** to vomit out all her insides: adam srj5•

VULNERABLE (See Delusions - injury - about; Insecurity; Sensitive)

WAILING (See Lamenting)

WAKING:

- **when**: acon b7.de* *Alum* b4a.de* am-c bg2 ant-t b7.de* arg-met b7.de* ars b4.de* asaf b7.de* bar-c b4.de* bell bg2 bism bg2 borx bg2 *Calc* b4a.de* caps b7.de* carb-an bg2 **Carb-v** b4.de* caust b4.de* *Chel* b7a.de *Chin* b7.de* cina b7.de* clem bg2 con b4.de* graph bg2 hyos bg2 *Ign* b7.de* ip b7.de* kali-c bg2 *Lach* bg2* **Lyc** bg2* m-arct b7.de merc b4.de* nit-ac b4.de* **Nux-m** bg2 *Nux-v* b7.de* petr b4.de* ph-ac b4.de* phos b4.de* plat bg2 plb b7.de* puls b7.de* rhod b4.de* rhus-t b7.de* samb b7a.de* sep bg2 squil b7.de* stann b4.de* stram bg2* **Sulph** bg2 thuj b4.de *Zinc* bg2*
- **after**: arn b7.de* aur b4.de* calc b4a.de* caps b7.de* chin b7.de* con b4.de* ign b7.de* **Lach** ptk1 *Lyc* b4.de* nux-v b7.de* op bg2 plat b4a.de puls b7.de* rheum b7.de* sel b7.de* *Stram* b7.de* thuj b4.de* zinc ptk1

WALKING:

- **while** | **agg.**: agar b4.de* ang bg2 ars b4.de* asar b7.de* bell b4.de* bry b7.de* calc bg2 camph b7.de* carb-an b4.de* carb-v b4.de* cic b7.de* coff bg2 con b4.de* ferr b7.de* hep b4a.de kali-c bg2 m-arct b7.de mag-c b4.de* nat-m bg2 nit-ac bg2 nux-v b7.de* rhus-t b7.de* sep bg2 spong b7.de* tarax bg2 thuj b4.de* viol-t b7.de*
- **agg.**: borx bg2 calc bg2 kali-br bg2 nat-m bg2
- **air**; in the open:
  - **after** | **agg.**: agar bg2 arn b7.de* carb-v b4.de* caust bg2 hep bg2 lyc bg2 m-aust b7.de nat-m b4.de* nux-v b7.de* spong b7.de* sulph b4.de*
  - **agg.**: *Ammc* vh1 anac b4.de* ant-c b7.de* calc b4a.de cina b7.de* coff b7.de* con b4.de* glon ptk1 hep b4.de* ign b7.de* ip b7.de* led b7.de* *M-arct* b7a.de mur-ac b4.de* nux-m b7.de* par b7.de* petr ptk1 ph-ac b4.de phos bg2 plat b4.de* sabin b7.de* spig b7.de* sulph b4.de* tarax b7.de* thuj b4.de*
  - **amel.**: asar b7.de* borx b4a.de cann-i k2 carc fd2.de• dream-p sdj1• falco-pe nl2• galeoc-c-h gms1• graph b4.de* ham fd3.de• hippoc-k szs2 ign b7.de* *Mag-c* mg1.de *Nat-sil* fd3.de• par b7.de* positr nl2• puls b7.de* rhus-t b7.de* stann b4.de* sulph bg2 teucr b7.de*
- **amel.**: androc srj1• *Asar* bg2 rhod bg2 sulph bg2
- **aversion** to: (↗*slowly; slowly - dignified)* cham a1 fago a1 kali-bi a1 nit-ac a1 zinc hr1*
- **bed**; child is walking in: rheum j5.de
- **circle**, walks in a: (↗*GENERALS - Walking - circle)* bell a1 *Stram* a1* *Thuj* hr1*
- **desire** for: calc-s ↓ cassia-s ↓ dream-p sdj1• galeoc-c-h ↓ mag-c mtf33 naja mtf33
  - **air**; in open: (↗*GENERALS - Walking - desire - air)* cassia-s ccrh1• galeoc-c-h gms1•
  - **gone**; but as soon as she sets out for a walk the desire is: calc-s kr1
- **fast** (See rapidly)
- **fear**; from | **perspiration** amel.; until: camph kr1
- **hither** and thither, walks: asaf hr1* kali-p fd1.de• merc h1
- **more** than is good for her: (↗*GENERALS - Walking - Rapidly - amel.)* ars h2
- **Neolithic** man; like a: plut-n srj7•
- **rapidly**:
  - **agg.**: (↗*Anxiety - walking - rapidly; Anxiety - walking - rapidly - makes)* ang b7.de* arg-n nit-ac bg2 sep mtf33 tarent bg2
  - **amel.**: *Galeoc-c-h* gms1• hist mg1.de*
- **self**-sufficient impression of importance; walks along with a: (↗*slowly; slowly - dignified; Haughty; Monomania - grotesque)* ferr-ma a1 ulm-c jsj8•
- **slowly**: (↗*aversion; self-sufficient; Dignified; Fear - walking; Haughty; Pompous; Solemn)* gels bro1 ph-ac bro1 phos bro1
  - **dignified**; and: (↗*aversion; self-sufficient; Dignified; Fear - walking; Haughty; Pompous; Solemn)* caj

WANDERING: (↗*Roving)*

- **amel.**: (↗*Restlessness - walking - air - amel.)* hist mg1.de plut-n srj7•
- **desire** to wander: (↗*Restlessness; Travelling - desire)* arag br1* bapt br1* bell ↓ *Bry* bro1 *Calc* ↓ *Calc-p* k* camph ↓ canth ↓ carc mlr1• cench k2 choc srj3• cimic dros gk* elat bro1 falco-pe nl2• hist ↓ hyos sne *Kali-br* kr1 lach bro1 lyss ckh1 meli vml3• merc nit-ac tl1 nux-v ↓ sanguis-s ↓ sanic ptk1* *Stram* ↓ **Tub** br1* *Valer* ↓ verat k*
  - **night**: *Calc* kr1 *Elat* kr1* sanguis-s hrn2• verat gk
  - **convulsions**; with: camph br1
  - **house**; desires to wander about the: *Valer* kr1
  - **mania**; in: (↗*Restlessness - mania)* verat h1
  - **pregnancy**, during: *Verat* kr1
  - **restlessly**, wanders about: (↗*Restlessness - children - roving)* bell bg2 canth bg2 hist vml3• hyos bg2 nux-v bg2* *Stram* bg2* verat bg2

WANTS:

- **nothing**: (↗*Asking - nothing; Desires - nothing; Indifference)* op st* verat mtf33
- **something** but he does not know what (See Capriciousness)

WARM:

- **agg.**: cact bg2
- **bed** agg.: *Iod* bg2
- **room** agg.: acon b7.de* nat-c b4a.de ph-ac b4.de* *Plb* b7a.de *Puls* b7a.de

WASHING:

- **amel.**: *Cann-s* b7a.de
- **aversion** to wash: (↗*Bathing - aversion; Dirty; Indifference - external things)* *Am-c* sf1.de* *Ant-c* sf1.de arizon-l nl2• borx sf1.de calc sf1.de canth sf1.de *Clem* sf1.de kali-n sf1.de kali-p fd1.de• marb-w es1• mez sf1.de nat-sil fd3.de• nit-ac sf1.de podo fd3.de• positr nl2• psor k2* *Rhus-t* sf1.de sep sf1.de spig sf1.de stront-c sf1.de *Sulph* k2* tritic-vg fd5.de
  - **children**, in: ant-c mtf33 **Sulph** kr1* tritic-vg fd5.de
- **desire** to wash: (↗*Bathing - desire; Cleanness - mania; Fear - dirt)* allox ↓ ars ↓ carc ↓ coca ↓ cur ↓ kali-s ↓ *Lac-c* ↓ *Med* ↓ meph ↓ merc ↓ nat-m ↓ *Nat-sil* ↓ *Oscilloc* ↓ petr-ra ↓ phyt ↓ plat ↓ psor ptk1 puls ↓ sanguis-s hrn2• sep ↓ *Sil* ↓ *Sulph* ↓ syph ptk1 tarent lpc* thuj ↓ tub jl2
  - **bathing**; mania for (See Bathing - desire)
  - **cleanness**; mania for (See Cleanness - mania)
  - **cold** water; in: meph lpc phyt lpc
  - **face**; always washing her: puls mtf33
  - **hands**; always washing her: (↗*Delusions - contaminated - everything; Delusions - dirty - he; GENERALS - Bathing - amel.; GENERALS - Uncleanliness)* allox tpw4 ars bg* carc mlr1• coca st* cur vh kali-s fd4.de *Lac-c* st* *Med* st* merc gk* nat-m bg* *Nat-sil* fd3.de• *Oscilloc* jl2 petr-ra shn4• plat k13* psor k13* sanguis-s hrn2• sep vh* sil k13* *Sulph* k13* *Syph* k* thuj vh* tub jl2
  - **monomania**: *Sil Sulph*
- **face** | **amel.**: ars ptk1 phos ptk1
- **feet**; after washing: nat-c ptk1

WASTING his time (See Time - fritters)

WATCHED; to be:

- **agg.**: **Ant-c** ptk1 ant-t ptk1 *Ars* ptk1 cham ptk1 *Cina* ptk1 lac-h htj1• *Nat-m* ptk1 puls ptk1
- **aversion** to be watched: lac-h htj1•
- **desires** to be watched: (↗*Anxiety - alone; Fear - alone)* gal-ac a1 ham fd3.de• marb-w es1• plac rzf5• sanguis-s hrn2•
  - **by** men, in a woman: sanguis-s hrn2•

WATCHFULNESS (See Alert)

WATER:

- **agg.** (See Hydrophobia)
- **looking** at water agg.: alum b4a.de canth b7.de* ferr ↓ hyos b7.de* stram b7.de*
  - **running** water; at: ferr b7.de*
- **loves**: bar-c mtf calc mtf calc-caust mtf calc-p mtf calc-s mtf carc mtf falco-pe mtf haliae-lc mtf heroin ↓ lac-del mtf lac-leo mtf lac-loxod-a mtf limest-b es1• phasco-ci ↓ phos mtf puls mtf sil mtf sulph mtf tarent mtf tub mtf
  - **live** closer to water; wants to: phasco-ci rbp2
  - **play** in water; desire to: [heroin sdj2]

WEAK CHARACTER: (↗*Alcoholism - weakness; Will - weakness)* aids nl2* *Caust* vh* **Lyc** vh* med jl2 *Sil* br1* syph jl2 *Tub* jl2

- **children**: med jl2

WEAKNESS (See Prostration)

WEARISOME: *(↗Complaining; Ennui; Morose)* acon k* aeth k* allox tpw3 alum k* am-c ↓ am-m anac k* ant-c k* arg-n k* arn k* ars k* asar k* bell k* bism k* both-ax tsm2 bov k* bry k* cadm-met tpw6 calc k* *Calc-s* k* cann-s k* caps k* carb-an k* carb-v ↓ carc fb* caust k* cham k* chel tl1 chin k* clem k* cocc colch k* coloc k* con k* cupr k* cur c2 cycl k* cypr c2 dig k* *Euon* graph k* *Grat* k* guaj hep k* hir rsj4• ign k* indg ip *Kali-c* kali-n h2* kreos lach led lyc mag-c ↓ *Mang* med jl2 melal-alt gya4 merc mez mur-ac nat-c nat-m nat-s nit-ac nux-v olnd paull a1 petr petr-ra shn4• *Ph-ac* phos plat puls ran-b rat rauw tpw8 rheum rhus-t sabin samb sars scut ↓ sep spong squil *Staph* *Stront-c* stry a1 *Sul-ac* sulph teucr thuj vario jl2 verb viol-t *Zinc* ziz kr1 [tax jsj7]
- **morning**: am-c k* med jl2
- **evening**: bov a1 cadm-met tpw6 mag-c puls *Zinc*
- **air**, in open: aeth sabin
- **cares**; from: chin tl1 scut tl1
- **causeless**: am mp1• *Ars* mp1• carb-v mp1• lach mp1• merc mp1• sul-ac mp1•
- **exercise**; violent | **amel.**: rauw tpw8
- **exertion**; after slightest: petr-ra shn4•
- **influenza**; after: lyc tl1

WEARY OF LIFE: *(↗Death - desires; Disgust - everything; Ennui; Fear - weary; Hatred - life; Insanity - weariness; Loathing - life; Pessimist; Suicidal)* act-sp ↓ agn k* aloe bg2* alum bg2 am-c k* ambr k* ant-c k* ant-t bg2* apis aran-ix mg1.de* **Ars** k* **Aur** k* aur-ar k2 *Aur-m* kr1 *Aur-m-n* wbt2• *Bell* k* berb bov k* bros-gau mrc1 buth-a mg1.de calc k* calc-ar k2 calc-sil k2 carb-v k* carc mlr1• caust k* *Chin* k* chinin-ar con gl1.fr• cypra-eg sde6.de• dioxi rbp6 dros j5.de* dulc fd4.de euph-c sf1.de grat hep k* hipp hydrog ↓ hyos k* kali-bi bg2* *Kali-br* kr1 kali-chl j5.de* *Kali-p* kola stb3• kreos k* *Lac-d* kr1 lac-f wza1• lac-h sk4*• lach k* laur k* led k* lyc k* manc *Merc* b4.de* mez k* mur-ac naja ↓ nat-c k* *Nat-m* k* *Nat-s* j5.de* nep mg1.de* *Nit-ac* k* *Nux-v* k* op bg2 *Ph-ac* gl1.fr• **Phos** k* phyt k* pic-ac bg2* *Pitu* ckh1 plat k* plb k* plut-n srj7• pneu jl2 psor bg2* *Puls* k* *Rhus-t* k* rhus-v rib-ac jl3 ruta k* sec bg2 sep k* *Sil* k* spig bg2* spong k* staph k* stram k* sul-ac k* sulph k* *Symph* fd3.de• *Ter* kr1 thuj k* tritic-vg fd5.de tub tl* tub-r jl3 valer k* *Vanil* fd5.de verat zinc kr1 ziz kr1 [ulx-eu rcb1]
- **morning**: hydrog srj2• *Lach* kr1 lyc ↓ nat-c j5.de phyt ↓
  - **bed**, in: lyc
  - **waking**, on: lyc j5.de nat-c phyt
- **forenoon**: apis
- **afternoon**: mur-ac ruta
- **evening**: **Aur** dros dulc fd4.de hep kali-chl k* rhus-t ruta spig
- **night**: ant-c nux-v
- **air**, in open: bell j5.de mur-ac
- **alternating** with | **cheerfulness** (See Cheerful - alternating - weariness)
- **company**, in: *Lyc* kr1
- **despair** about trifles, with: act-sp kr1
- **drunkards**, in: *Ars* kr1
- **fear** of death, but: *Kali-p* kr1 *Nit-ac* kr1* *Plat* bg2* *Rhus-t* kr1 *Spong* fd4.de
- **future**, from solicitude about: *Lach* kr1
- **heat**, during: **Ars** bg2 bell chin lach k* nux-v bg2 puls bg2 rhus-t bg2 sep bg2 *Spong* b7.de* stram thuj bg2 valer k*
- **humiliation**; after (See mortification)
- **menses**:
  - **before**: *(↗Menses - before)* berb kr1
  - **during**: *(↗Menses - during)* berb
- **mortification**, after: carc mlr1• *Puls* kr1
- **music** | **agg.**: *Tub* jl2
- **old** age, in: *Ars* vh* aur k2 calc k2
- **pains**, from the: ars bg2 phyt bg2* **Ruta** fd*
- **perspiration**, during: alum *Ars* bg *Aur* **Calc** hep *Merc* nux-v bg puls bg rhus-t bg sep bg sil *Spong* bg thuj bg
- **sight** of blood or a knife, at: *(↗Fear - suicide; Suicidal)* alum j5.de
- **syphilis**, in: *Lyc* kr1
- **unfit** for life: carc mlr1• plat bg2 sep ptk1
- **unworthy** of the gift of life: carc mlr1• naja bg2 *Nat-s* ptk1 plat ptk1
- **waking**, on: lyc j5.de nat-c j5.de

Weary of life: ...
- **walking** in open air: bell

WEATHER:
- **cloudy**:
  - **agg.**: aloe bg2* alum bg2 *Am-c* b4a.de* nat-c bg2 *Phos* bg2* plat k13 sang bg2 [spect dfg1]
  - **loves**: sep mtf33
- **rain** | **trickling** of the rain amel.: lach dgt
- **stormy** weather:
  - **agg.**: nat-c bg2 nat-m bg2 nit-ac bg2 phos bg2
  - **loves**: carc mlr1*•
    - ⋮ **watching**: carc jl2*
- **sultry** agg.: sep bg2
- **thunderstorm**:
  - **before**: *(↗Fear - thunderstorm - before; Restlessness - thunderstorm - before)* bry elec al2 hyper *Nat-c* sf1.de nat-m sf1.de petr sf1.de *Phos* br1 **Rhod** k* zinc kr1*
  - **during**: *(↗Cheerful - thunders; Fear - thunderstorm; Restlessness - thunderstorm - during; Shrieking - thunderstorm)* borx bg2 bry caust elec al2 lach nat-c k* nat-m k* nit-ac k* petr *Phos* k* *Rhod* k* sep *Sil*
    - ⋮ **amel.**: *(↗Cheerful - thunders)* carc sk1• lyc c1 sep st
  - **loves**: carc fb* sep vh*
    - ⋮ **watching**: carc mlr1•
- **wet** | **during**: *Am-c* b4a.de
- **wind** | **intolerance** to: caust lpc *Cham* lpc lach lpc ozone sde2• sel ptk

WEEPING: *(↗Ailments - grief; Complaining; Confusion - weeping; Delirium - crying; Discouraged - weeping - amel.; Grief; Indifference - weeping; Insanity - weeping; Lamenting; Sadness; Shrieking; Sitting - inclination - weeping; Weeping - anxiety; RESPIRATION - Sobbing)* absin ↓ acet-ac a1 **Acon** k* adam srj5• *Aeth* a1* aether a1 agam-g mlk9.de agar ↓ *Agath-a* nl2• *Aids* nl2• ail all-c ↓ all-s ↓ allox tpw4* alum k* alum-p ↓ alum-sil ↓ alumn ↓ am-c k* *Am-m* k* *Ambr* k* amyg *Anac* ↓ anan androc srj1• ang anh sp1 *Ant-c* k* *Ant-t* k* *Anth* ↓ anthraci ↓ anthraq rly4• antip ↓ **Apis** k* apoc kr1* aq-mar rbp6 arb-m oss1• arg-met k* *Arg-n* arge-pl rwt5• *Arist-cl* mg1.de* arizon-l nl2• arn k* **Ars** b4.de* ars-i ars-s-f ↓ arum-m arund ↓ asaf ↓ asar k* astac ↓ aster atro ↓ *Aur* k* aur-ar k2 aur-i k2 aur-m *Aur-m-n* wbt2• aur-s k2 *Bad* ↓ *Bamb-a* stb2.de• bapt st bar-c k* bar-i k2 bar-ox-suc rly4• bar-s k2 *Bell* k* ben berb bor-pur ↓ **Borx** k* both-ax ↓ bov ↓ brass-n-o srj5• brom bg2 bros-gau mrc1 brucel sa3• **Bry** k* bufo bung-fa ↓ buth-a jl* *Cact* k* *Cain* ↓ calad ↓ **Calc** k* calc-act ↓ *Calc-ar* k2 calc-f ↓ *Calc-i* k2 *Calc-p* **Calc-s** calc-sil k2 *Camph* k* cann-i cann-s k* cann-xyz ↓ *Canth* k* caps k* carb-an k* *Carb-v* k* carbn-h ↓ carbn-o ↓ **Carbn-s** *Carc* mlr1• card-m *Cardios-h* rly4• carl cartl-s rly4• cass a1 cassia-s ckh1 caste ↓ castm catar ↓ **Caust** k* cedr cench k2 **Cham** k* chap ↓ *Chel* k* chen-a chin k* chin-b ↓ chinin-ar *Chinin-s* chir-fl ↓ chlf kr1 choc ↓ **Cic** k* cich ↓ *Cimic* k* *Cina* k* cinnm kr1 cit-ac ↓ cit-v a1 clem coca ↓ coca-c ↓ *Cocc* k* **Coff** k* colch k* *Coloc* k* *Con* k* convo-s jl* cop cortiso sp1 **Croc** k* crot-c a1 *Crot-h* k* *Cupr* k* cupr-act a1 cur *Cycl* k* cygn-ol ↓ cypr ↓ cypra-eg ↓ cystein-l ↓ dendr-pol sk4• der *Dig* k* diosm ↓ dioxi ↓ dream-p ↓ dros dulc k* dys fmm1• elec c1 eric-vg ↓ erig ↓ eup-per a1 eup-pur euph ↓ euphr ↓ falco-pe ↓ *Ferr* ferr-ar ferr-i ferr-p ferul a1 fl-ac ↓ foll ↓ fum ↓ galeoc-c-h ↓ galv ↓ gard-j ↓ gels gent-c ger-i rly4• germ-met srj5• gink-b sbd1• gins j5.de* glon glycyr-g cte1• goss st granit-m ↓ **Graph** k* guaj ↓ haem j5.de* haliae-lc ↓ ham ↓ *Hell* k* helo-s rwt2• helon ↓ *Hep* k* hipp ↓ hippoc-k szs2 hir jl* hist sp1 hura *Hydr* kr1 hydr-ac ↓ hydrog srj2• hydroph jl hyos k* hyosin-hbr ↓ hyper ↓ hypoth ↓ iber a1 **Ign** k* ind kr1 *Indg* ↓ *Iod* k* *Ip* b7.de* irid-met srj5• ix ↓ *Jal* j jug-r st kali-ar *Kali-bi* **Kali-br** k* **Kali-c** k* kali-chl j5.de kali-cy ↓ kali-fcy kr1 kali-i kali-m ckh1 kali-n kali-ox a1 *Kali-p* k* kali-s k* kali-sil k2 ketogl-ac rly4• kiss a1 kola stb3• kreos b7a.de* lac-ac ↓ **Lac-c** k* lac-cp sk4• lac-d k2* lac-h sk4• lac-leo hrn2• lac-loxod-a ↓ lac-lup ↓ **Lach** k* lachn lact lam j5.de lap-la ↓ lat-m jl* laur k* lavand-a ↓ led levo jl *Lil-t* k* limest-b ↓ linu-u a1 lith-c k* lob lob-s kr1 loxo-recl knl4• luna kg1• lup ↓ **Lyc** k* lyss m-ambo ↓ *M-arct* b7.de* m-aust b7.de* *Mag-c* ↓ *Mag-m* k* *Mag-p* k1* mag-s *Mang* k* mang-act ↓ *Med* k* *Meli* meny k* **Merc** b4.de* merc-act ↓ merc-c ↓ *Merc-i-r* k1 merc-meth ↓ merl methys jl mez k* mim-p rsj8*• moni rfm1• morg-g pte1*• morg-p pte1*• morph c1 **Mosch** k* mucs-nas rly4• *Mur-ac* ↓ *Murx* ↓ musca-d szs1 naja k* nat-ar k* nat-c k* **Nat-m** k* nat-ox rly4• *Nat-p* *Nat-s* k* nat-sil k2 neon srj5• nicc

Weeping: ...
nicc-met sk4• nid jl *Nit-ac* k* nitro-o a1 *Nux-m* k* *Nux-v* k* oci-sa↓ oena↓ olib-sac↓ olnd↓ *Op* b7.de* orot-ac rly4• osm↓ oxyurn-sc mcp1• ozone sde2• **Pall** k* paull↓ peti a1 *Petr* k* petr-ra shn4• *Ph-ac* k* phel k1 *Phos* k* phys↓ *Phyt*↓ pin-con oss2• pitu-a↓ plac-s rly4• plan↓ **Plat** k* plb plect↓ plut-n srj7• podo fd3.de• polys↓ positr nl2• pot-e rly4• prot pte1*• prun↓ pseuts-m oss1• psil jl psor k* **Puls** k* puls-n↓ pycnop-sa mrz1 pyrid↓ pyrog↓ pyrus a1 querc-r↓ rad-br↓ raja-s jl *Ran-b* k* *Ran-s*↓ raph↓ rheum k* *Rhod*↓ rhodi br1 rhus-g tmo3• **Rhus-t** k* rib-ac jl ribo rly4• rob↓ ruta k* sabad↓ sabin k* sacch-a↓ *Sal-fr* sle1• samb bg2 sanic c1 sarr↓ sars sec sel b7a.de* senec bg2* *Seneg* j senn hr1 **Sep** k* sil k* sol-ni spig k* spira a1 **Spong** k* squil **Stann** k* *Staph* k* staphycoc↓ *Stram* k* streptoc jl2 *Stry* suis-em rly4• suis-hep rly4• *Sul-ac* k* sul-i↓ **Sulph** k* sumb↓ syc pte1*• symph↓ syph kr1* tab *Tarent* tarent-c ckh1 tax↓ tep a1 tere-la rly4• *Teucr*↓ thal jl thala↓ thea a1 ther↓ thiam↓ thuj k* thuj-l jl thyreotr jl til toxi↓ trinit br1 tritic-vg fd5.de tub al* ust k* vac a1* **Vanil** fd* ven-m↓ **Verat** k* *Verat-v*↓ vinc j5.de* **Viol-o** b7.de* viol-t k* vip↓ visc sp1 wies a1 wildb↓ zinc k* zinc-p k2 ziz a1 [ant-m stj2 bell-p-sp dcm1 heroin sdj2 rubd-met stj2 *Spect* dfg1]

- **day** and night: apis k2 med gk
- **daytime**: alum bry caust k1* lac-ac k13 lac-c k1 lyc mez stram b7a.de*
- **morning**: alum k2 alum-p k2 alumn am-c bell borx canth carb-an k* dulc kreos lac-leo hrn2• peti a1 phos k* plat k* podo fd3.de• prun puls k* rhus-t k* sars sil k* spong stram sulph k* tarent k* vanil fd5.de
  - **waking**, on: alum k2 alum-p k2 lac-leo hrn2• podo fd3.de• puls a1 vanil fd5.de
- **forenoon**: canth a1 hura a1 sars j5.de* **Sulph**↓
  - **11** h: **Sulph**
- **afternoon**: bell a1 carb-v castm cop k* dig galeoc-c-h↓ lac-h↓ **Lyc**↓ nicc-met sk4• phos k* puls↓ *Sil* tab j5.de tarent k*
  - **14** h: lac-h sk4•
  - **16** h: puls
  - **16**-20 h: **Lyc**
  - **17** h: galeoc-c-h gms1• lac-h sk4•
- **evening**: acon k* alum am-c am-m *Calc* carb-an k* clem coca galeoc-c-h gms1• *Graph* k* hura a1 hyper k* kali-c kali-chl j5.de kali-i kali-sil k2* lact j5.de lyc j5.de lyss hr1* m-arct j5.de mez k* nat-m ozone sde2• *Plat* k* positr nl2• *Ran-b* k* rhus-g↓ *Rhus-t* sil *Stram* k* sul-i k2* sulph *Verat*
  - **amel.**: am-c castm zinc h2
  - **sunset**; after: rhus-g tmo3•
- **night**: alum k* alum-p k2* am-c anac ant-t j5.de arn k* ars ars-s-f k2* aur aur-s k2* bamb-a stb2.de• bar-c k* bar-s k2* bell k* *Borx* bry calad j5.de calc calc-ar k2* calc-sil k2* camph j5.de caps j5.de carb-an k* *Castm* j5.de caust cham k* chel k* *Chin* chinin-s *Cina* *Cocc* j5.de con k* croc j5.de cupr↓ dendr-pol sk4• euph j5.de graph j5.de guaj j5.de hep j5.de hipp hyos ign indg ip kali-ar kali-c kali-i kali-sil k2* kola stb3• lac-c k* *Lach* lup j5.de lyc k* m-arct j5.de mag-c k* mag-m j5.de merc merc-act j5.de *Nat-c* j5.de *Nat-m* k* nat-sil fd3.de• nicc j5.de nit-ac *Nux-v* op k* ph-ac phos k* phys ckh1 *Phyt* plat j5.de polys sk4• *Psor* k* *Puls* rheum rhus-t ruta j5.de *Sep* j5.de sil k* spong stann *Stram* sul-ac j5.de sulph tab tarent k* thuj k* verat *Zinc* j5.de
  - **midnight**:
    - **before**: alum a1 ars j5.de merc j5.de nux-v j5.de
    - **at**: m-arct j5.de mag-c j5.de
    - **after**: ars j5.de bry j5.de
  - **sleep**, in: alum k* carb-an k* caust cham k* chel a1 con k* ign lach lyc k* nat-m j5.de nit-ac *Nux-v* phos a1 thuj k*
  - **waking**, on: chinin-s cupr sst3* sil k*
    - **consoled**; but won't be: cupr sst3•
  - **weeps** all night, laughs all day: stram
- **abandoned**; as if she had been: *(↗forsaken)* lam a1
- **abdomen**; during complaints in: carb-v bg2
- **admonition**, from: *(↗humiliation; mortification; offense - from; remonstrated; reproaches; Admonition - agg.; Ailments - reproaches)* aids nl2• aur-m-n wbt2• bell *Calc* carc fb* chin ign *Kali-c* *Lyc* med gk nat-m nit-ac plat k* puls gk sal-fr sle1• staph
- **agg.**: ant-t k* *Arn* k* *Bell* k* borx k* canth k* cham k* *Croc* k* *Cupr* k* *Cycl* kr1 hep k* ign sne lach k* m-arct b2.de* *Nat-m* bro1 nit-ac k* puls bro1 *Sep* bro1 stann b2.de* *Teucr* k* *Verat* k*
- **air**, in open: carb-v hura
  - **amel.**: coff *Nat-s* *Plat* k* **Puls**
- **alone**, when: *(↗Company - desire; Company - desire - alone)* *Aur-m-n* wbt2• *Con* k* dream-p sdj1• ign vh lith-c ptk1* lyc hr1 *Nat-m* k* oci-sa sk4• ozone sde2• positr nl2• spong fd4.de tritic-vg fd5.de vanil fd5.de
  - **amel.**: allox tpw4* anth vh *Aq-mar* mgm• *Cycl* hr1
- **aloud** (See sobbing)
- **alternating** with:
  - **anger** (See Anger - alternating - weeping)
  - **anger** and laughing (See Anger - laughing - alternating - weeping)
  - **antics**; playing (See Antics - alternating - weeping)
  - **cheerfulness** (See Cheerful - alternating - weeping)
  - **dancing** (See Dancing - alternating - weeping)
  - **delirium**; gay (See Delirium - gay - alternating - weeping)
  - **hopefulness** (See Hopeful - alternating - weeping)
  - **ill** humor (See Irritability - alternating - weeping)
  - **indifference**: (non:phos k*)
  - **irritability** (See Irritability - alternating - weeping)
  - **jesting** (See Jesting - alternating - weeping)
  - **lamenting**: bufo coff ptk1
  - **laughing** (See Laughing - alternating - weeping)
  - **laughing** and anger (See Anger - laughing - alternating - weeping)
  - **laughing** with fear of death (See Fear - death - laughing)
  - **mirth** (See Mirth - alternating - weeping)
  - **moroseness** (See Morose - alternating - weeping)
  - **rage** (See Rage - alternating - weeping)
  - **singing** (See Singing - alternating - weeping)
  - **vexation** (See Irritability - alternating - weeping)
- **amel.**: *(↗Anxiety - weeping; Confusion - weeping - amel.; Discontented - weeping - amel.; Discouraged - weeping - amel.; Fear - weeping; Frightened - weeping; Sadness - weeping - amel.; Suicidal - weeping)* *Anac* k* androc srj1• *Anth* vh1 astac c1 *Aster* a1 aur-m-n wbt2• cimic ptk1 colch cycl k* cypra-eg sde6.de• *Dig* k* dream-p sdj1• gels vh germ-met srj5• gink-b sbd1• granit-m es1• *Graph* k* ign k* kali-bi gk lac-leo hrn2• lach j5.de* *Lyc* k* mag-m gb• *Med* k* merc nit-ac k* phos k* *Plat* k* *Puls* bg2* sal-fr sle1• sep k* tab k* tritic-vg fd5.de vanil fd5.de [bor-pur stj2 heroin sdj2 spect dfg1]
- **anecdotes**, from: *(↗Horrible; Sadness - thinking - father)* *Lach*
- **anger**:
  - **after**: ambr j5.de arn aur-m-n wbt2• bell bung-fa mtf caust j5.de cham sf1.de *Cocc* j5.de *Coff* j5.de* irid-met srj5• lac-c sf1.de lil-t sf1.de luna kg1• m-aust j5.de *Mosch* kr1 nat-m vh nit-ac gk *Nux-v* k* *Plat* k* puls j5.de sabin j5.de sal-fr sle1• spong j5.de staph j5.de
  - **during**: ant-t bg* ars bg* *Cham* bg2* *Coff* j lac-c bg2 lil-t bg2 moni rfm1• nat-m ckh1 nit-ac gk sacch-a fd2.de• sulph bg* zinc bg*
- **answering** a question, at: **Puls** hr1*
- **anxiety**, after: *(↗Anxiety - weeping; Weeping)* acon aids nl2• am-c j5.de* am-m asaf j asar j5.de bell j5.de calc j5.de camph j5.de* canth j5.de carb-an j carb-v castm j5.de dig j5.de **Graph** j5.de* ign j5.de *Kali-c* h2* **Kali-i** j5.de* lyc h2* nat-m j5.de *Phos* h2* puls j5.de *Spong* j5.de* sul-ac j5.de sulph j5.de zinc j5.de
- **anxious**: am-c hr1* caust h2* coff a1 **Graph** hr1* **Kali-i** hr1* kali-m ckh1 nat-m a1
- **as** if she had been weeping all night; on waking feels: haliae-lc srj5•
- **avoid**; desire to: *Ign* mrr1
- **babies**, thinking of: aids nl2•
- **bathing**, before: sulph k2
- **bells**, sound of (See music - bells)
- **bitter**: hep h2* nat-m ptk1* ruta fd4.de
- **cannot** weep, though sad: *(↗Brooding; Grief; Inconsolable; Sadness - love)* adam srj5• aeth vh* am-m c1* apis a1* arizon-l nl2• *Aur-m-n* wbt2• carc a1* crot-c a1* cypra-eg sde6.de• fic-m gya1 *Gels* k* germ-met srj5• granit-m es1• haliae-lc srj5• **Ign** a1* kali-fcy zr lac-h sze9• lap-la sde8.de• limest-b es1• marb-w es1• **NAT-M** k* nat-sil fd3.de• *Nux-v* k*

- **cannot** weep, though sad: ...
op a1 positr nl2• puls a1 sacch-a fd2.de• *Sep* vh* staph zr tere-la rly4• *Vanil* fd5.de
- **caressing**, from: chin ign
- **carried**, when: chel *Cina* ↓ sil ↓
  - **piteously** if taken hold or carried; child cries: *Cina* k* sil st
  - **quiet** only when carried; child is: *(↗Carried - desire; Restlessness - children - carried)* **Cham** cina
- **catching** of breath; with audible (See sobbing)
- **causeless**: acon k2* anthraci ↓ **Apis** k* *Arn* ars k* bell k* bung-fa mtf cact st* camph carc zzl* *Cardios-h* ↓ caust ↓ chin a1 *Cina* cocc a1 cortiso tpw7* cupr sst3• dys ckh1 *Graph* k* hura kali-ar kali-bi gk kali-br kali-c kreos k* lac-h sk4• *Lyc* k* meli al musca-d szs1 *Nat-m* k* nit-ac k* nux-v gl1.fr• olib-sac wmh1 ozone sde2• petr-ra shn4• phos h2* pot-e rly4• psor al2 **Puls** k* pyrog st1 rhus-t bg2* **Sep** ●* staph k* streptoc jl2 stry a1 **Sulph** k* syph k2* tarent k* thiam rly4• *Tritic-vg* fd5.de tub bgs vanil fd5.de viol-o k* *Zinc*
  - **day** and night: apis ptk1
  - **old** people; in: caust gl1.fr•
  - **without** knowing why: anthraci vh cact st *Camph* hr1 *Cardios-h* rly4• kali-bi gk kali-c pyrog st **Rhus-t** k* sep k* tub al* vanil fd5.de viol-o j
- **child**, like a: ars hr1* calad ↓ *Cupr-act* kr1
  - **illness** with senseless prattling; about: calad kr1
- **children**, in: *(↗trifles - children)* acon c1 aeth ↓ *Ant-t* a1 ars j5.de* arund ↓ aur mtf33 *Bell* j5.de* *Borx* j5.de* calc gg camph j5.de carc fb* caste jl3 caust j5.de* **Cham** j5.de* chap gg chin j5.de cina j5.de *Coff* j5.de dulc fd4.de *Graph* j5.de* *Hyos* j5.de hyosin-hbr j *Ign* j5.de ip gg* *Jal* j5.de *Kali-c* j5.de kreos ↓ *Lac-c* ↓ *Lyc* j5.de med gk nat-m al nit-ac j5.de *Phyt* ↓ *Psor* ↓ *Puls* j5.de **Rheum** j5.de* *Rhod* gg *Seneg* j5.de senn ↓ sep mtf33 sil j5.de* spong fd4.de stann h2 stram ↓ syph gg* thuj gg* tritic-vg fd5.de vanil fd5.de
  - **night**: arund a1* *Borx* kr1 kali-c j kreos ptk2 *Lac-c* hr1* *Lyc* gg *Psor* hr1* *Rheum* j* sil gg stram gg thuj gg
    - **toss** all night: *Psor* vh* *Rheum* vh*
  - **babies**: ars gg bell j5.de borx j5.de calc j5.de camph gg carc gg* caust gg *Cham* j5.de chap gg chin gg coff j5.de *Hyos* gg *Ign* gg ip j5.de jal j5.de *Kali-c* gg *Lyc* gg nit-ac gg psor jl2 *Puls* gg *Rhod* j5.de *Seneg* gg senn j5.de sil gg syph c1 tritic-vg fd5.de vanil fd5.de
    - **birth**:
      - **from** birth on: carc gk6* syph ckh1*
      - **immediately** after: syph a1
  - **difficult** dentition, from: *Phyt* hr1*
  - **nursing**; when: aeth tl1 borx ckh1* lac-c hr1
  - **sick**; when: aeth br1
  - **will** is not done: *(↗contradiction; opposition; refused)* **Cina** kr1 dulc fd4.de spong fd4.de tritic-vg fd5.de vanil fd5.de
- **chill** | **during**: acon k* ars k* *Aur* k* aur-ar k2 **Bell** k* **Calc** k* cann-s cann-xyz bg2 *Carb-v* k* **Cham** k* con k* hep k* ign k* kali-c k* **Lyc** k* m-arct b7.de merc k* nat-m k* *Petr* k* plat k* **Puls** k* sel k* sil k* stram sulph k* verat k* **Viol-o** k*
- **chorea**; in: caust ptk1
- **consolation**: *(↗Inconsolable - weeping)*
  - **agg.**: *(↗Consolation - agg.; Inconsolable)* *Aur-m-n* wbt2• bell cact calc *Calc-p* chin hell ign kali-c lil-t lyc merc nat-c gl1.fr• **Nat-m** k* nit-ac nux-v *Plat* **Sep** **Sil** staph sulph *Tarent* k* thuj
  - **amel.**: cypra-eg sde6.de• kola stb3• lavand-a ctl1• ozone sde2• *Puls* bg2*
  - **comforted**; no desire to be: carb-an pe cupr mtf33 cycl pe helon pe ign pe nat-m pe plat pe stann pe sulph pe thuj pe verat pe
  - **from** consolation: *Tarent* k1*
- **continuously**: ip mtf33 syph ↓ thuj ↓
  - **children**; in: | **newborns**: syph ptk1 thuj ptk1
- **contradiction**, from: *(↗children - will; opposition; refused; Contradiction - intolerant)* carc fd2.de• ign *Nux-v* k* stram tarent k*
- **convulsions**:
  - **after**: caust cina j5.de
  - **during**: absin k* acon j5.de *Alum* j5.de* ant-t j5.de *Bell* j5.de **Camph** hr1* *Canth* j5.de *Caust* j5.de cham cic j5.de cina j5.de cocc j5.de **CUPR** j5.de* hyos j5.de *Ign* j5.de *Indg* ↓ ip k* lach j5.de *Lyc* j5.de *Mag-p* k2* *Merc* j5.de* mosch j5.de *Nux-v* j5.de* op j5.de plb sil j5.de sulph j5.de vip j5.de
- **convulsions – during**: ...
    - **epileptic**: *(↗GENERALS - Convulsions - epileptic - during)* absin a1 **Cupr** hr1* *Indg* hr1* *Lach* hr1*
  - **from**: bell hr1*
- **convulsive** (See spasmodic)
- **coryza**, during: **Puls** b7.de* *Spig* b7.de*
- **cough**:
  - **after**: *(↗Sadness - coughing - after)* arn bell caps cina k* hep k* op
  - **before**: ant-t *Arn* k* **Bell** borx **Bry** **HEP** k ● phos h2*
    - **whooping** cough: arn br1
  - **during**: *(↗Moaning - cough; COUGH - Painful)* ant-t k* arn k* ars *Bad* kr1 *Bell* k* brom bg2 bry ↓ *Cain* *Caps* ↓ *Caust* ↓ cham chin *Cina* k* dros bg2 **Hep** k* ip lyc k* osm ph-ac samb k* sep sil spig spong k* sulph k* tritic-vg fd5.de verat k*
    - **whooping** cough: *Ant-t* kr1 *Arn* kr1* bry bro1 *Caps* bro1 *Caust* kr1 samb bro1
- **dark**; in: *(↗Darkness - agg.; Light - desire)* stram
- **death**; from thought of others' grief at her own: limest-b es1•
- **delirium**:
  - **after**: nat-s
  - **during**: acon k2 stram k*
- **delivery**, during: *Coff* kr1
- **delusions**, after: dulc
- **desire** to weep: ail ↓ am-m hr1* *Ambr* ↓ aster hr1* *Cact* hr1* *Camph* ↓ carc ↓ cassia-s ccrh1• chin-b hr1* *Ferr* ↓ fum rly4• haliae-lc srj5• ham fd3.de• hydrog srj2• *Ip* ↓ kali-c ↓ *Lyc* ↓ merc ↓ merc-c ↓ *Murx* ↓ nat-sil fd3.de• neon ↓ op ↓ plut-n srj7• podo fd3.de• *Puls* ↓ ruta fd4.de samb ↓ *Stram* ↓ symph fd3.de• *Thuj* ↓ [spect dfg1]
  - **all** the time: ail k1* *Ambr* sf1.de *Camph* hr1* carc cd *Ferr* hr1* *Ip* hr1* kali-c hr1* *Lyc* hr1* merc hr1* merc-c hr1* *Murx* hr1* neon srj5• op hr1* *Puls* hr1* samb hr1* *Stram* hr1* *Thuj* hr1*
  - **eyes** are dry; but: *Camph* kr1 nat-sil fd3.de•
- **despair**, from: *(↗Despair)* adam srj5• aids nl2• arg-n ptk1* chel bg2* *Cupr-act* kr1 germ-met srj5• hell bg2* lac-loxod-a hrn2• nat-sil fd3.de• sal-fr sle1• sil bg2 *Spong* fd4.de staphycoc rly4• tritic-vg fd5.de *Vanil* fd5.de [tax jsj7]
- **difficult**: carc mlr1* **Ign** zf
- **dinner**, after: mag-m h2*
- **disappointments**, about: dig a1 *Dulc* fd4.de podo fd3.de•
- **discontented**; when (See Discontented - weeping - with)
- **discouragement**; with (See Discouraged - weeping)
- **disturbed** at work, when: *(↗Disturbed)* *Puls*
- **dreaming**, while: *(↗DREAMS - Weeping)* calc-f ptk1 nat-m a1 plan ptk1 positr nl2• pyrid rly4• spong ptk1 stram ptk1 tarent ptk1 toxi mtf2•
- **drinking**, after: cartl-s rly4• *Caust* gl1.fr• nux-v gl1.fr• petr gl1.fr•
- **drunkenness**; during: *(↗Sentimental)* *Caust* gl1.fr• *Lach* k2*
- **easily**: adam srj5• alum gl1.fr• anan a1 arg-met kr1 arg-n mrr1 arge-pl rwt5• aster kr1 aur-m-n wbt2• *Bell* kr1 brucel sa3• bufo mtf33 *Calc* kr1 carc mlr1• **Caust** kr1* chin gl1.fr• cich mtf11 coff gl1.fr• dioxi rbp6 eric-vg mtf11 *Ferr* hr1 germ-met srj5• gink-b sbd1• *Kali-br* kr1 lyc gl1.fr• med jl moni rfm1• naja a1* *Nat-m* kr1* neon srj5• oci-sa sk4• olib-sac wmh1 *Op* gl1.fr• **Puls** kr1* querc-r c1 rad-br sze8• rhus-g tmo3• rhus-t kr1 sacch-a fd2.de• sal-fr sle1• *Sep* gg staph gl1.fr• toxi mtf2• trinit br1 [bell-p-sp dcm1 heroin sdj2 tax jsj7]
- **eating**:
  - **after**: arg-n arn k* iod mag-m puls
  - **while**: bell ↓ carb-an k* lac-ac ↓ staph ↓
    - **children**, in: bell kr1 lac-ac stj5• staph kr1
- **emissions** (See pollutions)
- **emotions**:
  - **lack** of; about: ozone sde2•
  - **slight**; after: aster k* aur zzb calc zzb **Cupr** st fum rly4• kreos k* *Lach* sf1.de lyc k2* naja k* *Plb* vh* [heroin sdj2]
- **everything**, about: apis a1 carc mlr1• psor a1
- **evil** impended, as if: *(↗Fear - evil)* kali-i a1
- **excitement**, from: antip vh1 ign k2
- **exhausting**: both-ax tsm2
- **face**:
  - **complaints**; with: *Plat* bg2
  - **heat** of face; with: bamb-a stb2.de•

- • **redness** of face; with: bamb-a stb2.de•
- **fear**; from: kali-c bg2 phos bg2 spong bg2
- **forsaken** feeling; from: *(↗abandoned; Forsaken)* *Bamb-a* stb2.de• falco-pe nl2• sal-fr sle1•
  - • **night**: bamb-a stb2.de•
- **fright**; with prolonged: carc mlr1•
- **future**, about the: *(↗Anxiety - future)* lyc k* staphycoc rly4•
- **goes** off alone and weeps as if she had no friends: *(↗Delusions - friendless; Forsaken)* bar-c
- **hallucinations** (See delusions)
- **head**; with complaints of: *Coloc* bg2 ferr bg2 kreos bg2 phos bg2 *Plat* bg2 ran-b bg2 sep bg2
- **headache**, with●: antip vh ars a1 bry kr1 chel a1 *Coff* coloc ferr bg *Kali-c* kreos lac-cp sk4• lac-d al lachn ↓ lyss peti a1 **Phos** k ● plat *Puls* kr1 ran-b **Sep** k ● tritic-vg fd5.de vanil fd5.de zinc kr1
  - • **paroxysmal**: lachn kr1
- **health**; about: | **progressive** disease; with: aeth ptk1 calad ptk1
- **heat**, during: **Acon** k* *Anac* kr1 *Ant-c* kr1 apis **Bell** k* bry calc k* *Caps* cham k* coff k* cupr graph k* ign k* ip *Lyc* k* peti a1 *Petr* k* plat k* **Puls** k* *Spig* k* **Spong** k* *Stram* sulph k* til vac kr1 verat
- **hiccough**; from: bell st1
- **hold** on to something; she would scream if she could not (See nervous - held)
- **hopeless** (See despair)
- **humiliation**; after: *(↗admonition; mortification; offense - from; remonstrated; reproaches; vexation)* carc mlr1•
- **hurt**; seeing others: *(↗sympathy)* carc mlr1•
- **hysterical**: ars hr1* *Asar* mrr1 aur-ar k2 cact hr1* carc mlr1• *Coff* hr1* dulc fd4.de *Kali-p* hr1* *Nat-m* hr1* sumb a1 *Tarent* hr1* *Verat-v* hr1*
- **idiotic**: merc-meth a1
- **illness**, during: calad k* *Cham* b7a.de *Coff* b7a.de *Puls* b7a.de
- **immoderately**: ferr ptk1*
- **impatience**, from: *(↗Impatience)* dulc bg2*
- **impulsive** (See suddenly)
- **incessant**: cupr sst3•
- **intense** (See violent)
- **interrupted**, when: *Puls* k*
- **involuntary**: *Alum* k* alum-p k2* ars ↓ aster vh *Aur* aur-m-n wbt2• *Bell* calc-sil k2 camph gl1.fr• cann-i k* carc mlr1• *Caust* cench k2 cina coff con hr1 croc ptk1 **Cupr** k* cystein-l rly4• **Ign** k* kali-br hr1* kiss a1 kreos a1 lach lil-t tl1 lyc tl1 mang br1* mang-act br1 *Merc* k* morph a1 mosch **Nat-m** k* nat-p k2 olnd ↓ op hr1 peti a1 phos **Plat** k* plb polys sk4• **Puls** k* **Rhus-t** k* sarr a1 **Sep** k* stann stram k* vanil fd5.de verat k* *Vinc* ↓ viol-o
  - • **conversation**, during: carc fd2.de• **Cupr** st
  - • **vinegar** amel.: stram
  - • **weakness**, from: ars st1 olnd st1 *Vinc* st1
- **irritability**; with (See Irritability - crying)
- **irritable**: bamb-a stb2.de• calc a1 carbn-s a1 ip h1 mosch a1 puls h1 sep a1 vanil fd5.de
- **joy**, from: *(↗Ailments - joy - excessive; Ailments - surprises - pleasant)* aids nl2• *Coff* k* falco-pe nl2• kola stb3• lach k* lyc k2* neon srj5• *Plat* puls hr1
- **joyful** or sad things, at: **Puls** hr1*
- **laughing** at same time; weeping and (See Laughing - weeping - same)
- **looked** at; when: *(↗Looked - cannot)* ant-c st brom mtf33 kiss st *Nat-m* k* puls pe *Tarent* kr1
- **loudly** (See sobbing)
- **lying**, while: euphr
- **meeting** people, when: *Aur* lyc ↓
  - • **friend**: lyc ptk
- **menopause**; at: **Sulph** st*
- **menses**:
  - • **after**: *(↗Menses - after)* alum con lyc phos stram
  - • **before**●: *(↗Menses - before)* *Cact* choc srj3• con k* cycl gk foll oss• ger-i rly4• gink-b sbd1• irid-met srj5• loxo-recl knl4• *Lyc* k* neon srj5• nux-v mrr1 petr-ra shn4• *Phos* k* *Puls* sep k* stann mrr1 *Zinc*
  - • **during**: *(↗Menses - during)* *Ars* k* *Aur* b4a.de cact calc caust cit-ac rly4• *Cocc* *Coff* con cycl dream-p sdj1• graph hyos *Ign* ind k* lach
- **menses – during**: ... lyc k* *Nat-m* *Petr* phos *Phyt* *Plat* k* *Puls* k* sec sep *Stram* thuj k* ven-m ↓ verat zinc k* zinc-p k2
  - ⁝ **but** weeping does no good to her: cycl
  - ⁝ **beginning** of: lyc b4.de
  - ⁝ **first** day: ven-m rsj12•
  - • **suppression** of, in: *Chen-a* hr1* *Cycl* hr1*
- **mistakes**; about his: coca-c sk4•
- **moral** feeling; with want of (See Moral - weeping)
- **mortification**, after: *(↗admonition; humiliation; offense - from; remonstrated; reproaches; vexation; Ailments - embarrassment; Ailments - honor; Ailments - mortification)* cocc h1* coff k2* coloc pall sf1.de puls vanil fd5.de
- **movies**; seeing sad: bung-fa mtf
- **music**, from: *(↗Music - agg.)* acon bg2* all-c ↓ *Ambr* bg2* ant-c ↓ aur-m-n wbt2• carc fb* cop ↓ croc bg dig **Graph** k* ham fd3.de• ign sf1.de kali-n kali-s fd4.de *Kola* stb3• *Kreos* k* lac-lup ↓ *Nat-c* k* nat-m st1 nat-s k* *Nux-v* k* olib-sac wmh1 positr nl2• sabin bro1* spong fd4.de tarent bro1 *Thuj* k*
  - • **bells**, of: *(↗Anxiety - church; Music - agg.)* ant-c k* cop st1
  - • **church** music: *(↗organ)* lac-lup hrn2•
  - • **organ**, on hearing: *(↗church)* **Graph** st1*
  - • **piano**, of: all-c ptk1 cop k* *Nat-c* *Nat-s* ptk1
- **nausea**; with: mag-m bg2
- **need**, about an imagined: chin
- **neglect**, from the slightest: coff k2 *Dulc* fd4.de
- **nervous**:
  - • **all** day: *(↗Restlessness)* bry caust lac-c lyc stram
  - • **held** on to something; feels so nervous she would scream unless she: **Sep** k ●
  - • **worse**; feels like crying all the time, but it makes her: stann
- **never** weeping: carc zzl
- **nightmare**, after: *(↗DREAMS - Nightmares)* gard-j vlr2• guaj k*
- **noise**, at: *(↗Sensitive - noise)* aeth ars a1 ign kreos *Lach*
- **nursing** a child; while: (non:lac-c hr1*) **Puls** k*
- **obstinate**: cham sf1.de
- **offense**:
  - • **former** offense; about: caust gl1.fr• ign gl1.fr• lach gl1.fr• staph gl1.fr•
  - • **from**: *(↗admonition; humiliation; mortification; remonstrated; reproaches; vexation)* lac-lup hrn2• *Stram* hr1*
  - • **imaginary**, at least: cham h1
- **old** people for nothing (See causeless - old)
- **opposition**, at least: *(↗children - will; contradiction; refused; Quarrelsome)* nux-v tritic-vg fd5.de
- **pains**:
  - • **after**: glon ptk1
  - • **intermission** of; during: glon
  - • **with** the: *(↗Despair - pains; Sensitive - pain; Shrieking - pain)* acon sf1.de adam srj5• *Apoc* vh1 ars h2* asaf j5.de bamb-a stb2.de• bell a1 bung-fa mtf *Cact* a1 canth j5.de carb-v h2* carc mlr1• catar ↓ cham j5.de* cina j5.de *Coff* k* diosm br1 dulc fd4.de *Glon* hr1* kali-c j5.de kali-cy gm1 *Lach* j5.de* lat-m ↓ lyc h2* *Merc* j5.de* merc-c j5.de mez mosch j5.de *Nux-v* j5.de* op gl1.fr• ozone sde2• *Plat* k* puls *Ruta* fd4.de sep ↓ *Spong* fd4.de *Staph* gl1.fr• stram j5.de ther ↓ tritic-vg fd5.de vanil fd5.de verat j5.de
    - ⁝ **abdomen**; in: catar br1 lat-m bnm6•
    - ⁝ **ear**; in: *Cham* mrr1 puls mrr1
    - ⁝ **teeth**; in: sep h2 ther hr1*
- **palpitation**, during: phos k* *Plat* hr1*
- **paralysis**; during: caust ptk1*
- **paroxysmal** (See suddenly)
- **past** events, thinking of: *(↗Dwells - past)* kola stb3• lyc h2* *Nat-m* k* plut-n srj7• vanil fd5.de [tax jsj7]
- **periodical** every four weeks: *Con* kr1
- **perspiration**, during: acon k* arn aur k* **Bell** k* bry k* *Calc* k* calc-s *Camph* *Cham* k* chin k* **Cupr** k* graph k* **Lyc** k* nux-v k* **Op** k* *Petr* k* phos plat bg2 *Puls* k* rheum k* rhus-t k* sep k* *Spong* k* *Stram* sulph k* verat k*
- **piano** (See music - piano)
- **piteous**: agar vh1 cham h1* **Cina** hr1* lat-m bnm6• puls ↓ stram a1

- children; in: puls tl1
- **pitied**, if he believes he is: *(↗Unfortunate)* **Nat-m** k● tere-la rly4•
- **poetry**, at soothing: lach k* olib-sac wmh1
- **pollutions**, after: hipp *Ust* kr1
- **pregnancy**, during: apis ign lach j5.de *Mag-c* k* nat-m puls sanic c1 stann
- **questioned**; when: cimic ptk1 crot-h ckh1 lach ckh1
- **reading**, while: *Crot-h* k* lac-h htj1• lac-lup hrn2• lach k* ribo rly4•
- **refused**, when anything: *(↗children - will; contradiction; opposition)* bell cham k* *Dulc* fd4.de ign spong fd4.de tarent a1* *Tritic-vg* fd5.de vanil fd5.de viol-o st1
- **remonstrated**, when: *(↗admonition; humiliation; mortification; offense - from; reproaches; vexation; Admonition - agg.; Ailments - reproaches; Quarrelsome)* bell *Calc* k1* calc-p mtf carc fb* ign *Kali-c* nit-ac plat puls mtf spong fd4.de staph
- **remorse**; with: arg-n mrr1
- **reprimanded**, when: sil mrr1
- **reproaches**, from: *(↗admonition; humiliation; mortification; offense - from; remonstrated; vexation)* calc st1 carc gk* moni rfm1• nit-ac j *Plat* bg2*
- **respiration**:
  - **complaints** of; with: *Cupr* bg2 ran-b bg2 rhus-t bg2 samb bg2
  - **difficult**: *Cupr* b7.de* *Led* b7a.de *Ran-s* b7a.de rhus-t b7.de* samb b7.de* tarent mtf33
- **rising**, after: am-c k*
- **room**, in: *Plat* spong fd4.de
- **sad**:
  - **news**, at: carb-v a1 dulc fd4.de ph-ac st1 *Vanil* fd5.de
  - **though** sad, cannot weep (See cannot)
  - **thoughts**, at: *(↗Ailments - love; Grief; Sadness)* alum carb-v k* cartl-s rly4• chir-fl gya2 cina dulc fd4.de kali-c nat-sil fd3.de• phel plat ruta fd4.de *Spong* fd4.de stram k* *Tritic-vg* fd5.de *Vanil* fd5.de [tax jsj7]
- **sea**, by the: falco-pe nl2•
- **sexual** excitement; with: *(↗Sadness - sexual excitement)* *Aster* hr1* stram ptk1*
- **shivering**; during: acon b7.de
- **shock** of a fall; from: both-ax tsm2
- **sickness**; when telling of (See telling - sickness)
- **silently**: cycl ptk1* dulc fd4.de ign ptk1 sep↓
  - **children**; in: sep mtf33
- **singing**, when: *(↗Singing)* hura
- **sits** weeping (See Sitting - inclination - weeping)
- **sleep** | **could** not sleep; because she: lac-leo hrn2•
- **sleep**, in: *(↗sobbing - sleep)* all-s k* *Alum* k* alum-p k2* alum-sil k2* anac j5.de ang bg2 ant-t apis ckh1 *Am* j5.de* ars k* ars-s-f k2* *Aur* aur-ar k2 bar-c bell *Borx* b4a.de* bry j5.de bufo calad j5.de calc k* calc-act a1 calc-sil k2* camph caps j5.de carb-an k* *Carb-v* hr1* carbn-s *Castm* j5.de *Caust* k* **Cham** k* chin chinin-s cina k* *Cocc* j5.de *Con* k* croc b7.de* cur k* euph j5.de fl-ac k* glon k* graph k* hell ckh1 hep b4a.de* *Hyos* k* ign ind j ip kali-ar *Kali-c* k* kali-i kali-sil k2* ketogl-ac rly4• kreos k* *Lach* k* lyc k* m-arct j5.de mag-c k* mag-m k* *Merc* k* *Mur-ac* j5.de *Nat-c* j5.de *Nat-m* k* nicc k* *Nit-ac* k* *Nux-v* k* *Op* *Ph-ac* h2* phos k* *Plat* j5.de psor zs1.fr *Puls* k* rheum k* rhus-t k* rob k* sabin b7.de* *Samb* sarr *Sep* j5.de *Sil* k* *Spong* stann k* stram b7a.de* sul-ac j5.de sulph k* tab k* tarent k* thuj k* verat j5.de wildb a1 *Zinc* j5.de*
  - **child** good during the day, screaming and restless at night: *Jal* k* psor tl1*
  - **moved**; when: zinc mtf33
  - **sensation** as if she had been weeping all night | **waking**; on: haliae-lc srj5•
- **sleepiness**, with: cham hr1* kola stb3• tritic-vg fd5.de vanil fd5.de
- **sobbing**; weeping with: *(↗Sighing; RESPIRATION - Sobbing)* acon j5.de* agar vh1 alum atro a1 aur↓ camph↓ carb-an j5.de carbn-h a1 cham cic *Cocc* hr1* coff k* con j5.de cupr ptk1* dulc fd4.de galv j* hell j *Hep* hr1* hyos k* *Ign* hr1* ip↓ kali-c jl kali-i↓ lach gb• lob hr1* **Lyc** k* lyss hr1* mag-c↓ *Mag-p* hr1* merc j5.de nat-c nat-m nit-ac↓ nux-v k* *Op* mtf33* phos k* plat k* plb a1 plect k* puls rhus-t↓ sabin sal-fr sle1• *Sep* j5.de* staph k* *Stram* a1* sulph vanil fd5.de
  - **sleep**; in: *(↗sleep in)* aur gt* camph bg2 hyos ptk1 ip bg2 kali-i ptk1 mag-c j5.de nat-m bg2* nit-ac bg2 op bg2 puls bg2 rhus-t a1
    - **waking**; without: hyos ptk1
- **spasmodic**: alum b4a.de* aur b4a.de* bell b4a.de* bov↓ carbn-o a1 **Caust** b4a.de* cina b7a.de* cupr b7a.de* cypra-eg sde6.de• ign b7a.de* lach b7a.de* mag-p k* mosch b7a.de* nat-m gl1.fr• ozone sde2• *Phos* h2* plb b7a.de* **Sep** b4a.de stram b7a.de* stry a1 thala jl3 *Thuj* b4a.de
  - **asthma**; with: bov ptk1
  - **shuddering**; with: ozone sde2•
- **spasms**, after: alum ptk1 *Caust* k*
- **speaking**, when: kali-c a1 *Med* hr1* puls a1* sep a1
- **speeches**, when making: cupr st1 cypr vml3•
- **spells** of weeping (See suddenly)
- **spoken** to; when: *(↗Spoken - aversion)* cimic k2* falco-pe↓ ign *Iod*↓ *Med* k* *Nat-m* k* *Plat* k* sil spong fd4.de **Staph** k1* thuj tritic-vg fd5.de *Tub* hr1*
  - **kindly**: falco-pe nl2• *Iod*↓ *Sil*↓ thuj mtf33
    - **children**; in: *Iod* st* *Sil* st thuj mtf33
- **stool**:
  - **before**: borx bg2 phos puls rhus-t k*
  - **during**: *Aeth* k* *Borx* k* carb-v bg2 *Cham* k* cina phos rhus-t sil sulph
- **suddenly**: arg-n mrr1 elec al2 **Kali-br** hr1* *Lac-c* hr1* lap-la sde8.de• phos sep ptk1* stry tritic-vg fd5.de vanil fd5.de
- **supper**, after: am h1*
- **sympathy** with others, from: *(↗hurt; Sadness - thinking - father; Sympathetic)* bar-c gk carc mp1• carl caust k* dulc fd4.de falco-pe nl2• irid-met srj5• lyc gk nat-sil fd3.de• nit-ac gk podo fd3.de• puls gk ruta fd4.de sacch-a fd2.de• sep gk *Spong* fd4.de tritic-vg fd5.de *Vanil* fd5.de
- **symptoms**; when describing (See telling - sickness)
- **taking** cold, after: *Op* kr1
- **teeth**; with complaints of: *Coff* b7a.de kreos b7a.de
- **telling**:
  - **sexual** life; telling about: sep gb•
  - **sickness**; when telling of her●: *(↗Anxiety - health - own; Narrating - agg.; Thinking - complaints - agg.)* adam srj5• agar dgt1 aster mgm• bamb-a stb2.de• bry st* carc st* dulc fd4.de gink-b sbd1• ign fd* *Kali-c* k* **Med** k* nat-m kr* nit-ac gk **Puls** k* **Sep** k* sil gg* staph mrr1* tub gk [*Graph* stj]
- **thanked**, when: ham fd3.de• **Lyc** k*
- **toothache** (See pains - with - teeth)
- **touched**, when: *(↗Touched - aversion)* ant-c k* ant-t k* **Cham** vh* cina sil h2* stram j5.de
  - **children**; in: ant-c b7a.de ant-t b7a.de cina b7a.de
- **trifles**, at: *(↗Trifles; Trifles - important)* agath-a nl2• alum gl1.fr• ant-c arg-met aster hr1 aur mtf aur-m-n wbt2• bamb-a stb2.de• bell h1* ben c1 bufo bung-fa mtf calc k* carc cd **Caust** k* chin gl1.fr• cina cocc k* coff gl1.fr• con graph a1 hypoth jl3 ign gl1.fr• *Kali-br* hr1 kali-p hr1* kola mtf* lyc a1* *Moni* rfm1• nat-m k* nit-ac↓ nux-v gl1.fr• oena br1 *Op* gl1.fr• oxyum-sc mcp1• petr pitu-a vml2* plat gl1.fr• puls k* puls-n a1 rhus-t hr1 sep mtf sil spong fd4.de staph mtf* stram suis-hep rly4• sulph h2 thal mtf tritic-vg fd5.de tub↓ vanil fd5.de ven-m jl3 verat hr1 visc sp1
  - **children** at the least worry●: *(↗children; Anxiety; Cares full)* *Caust* k2* lyc nat-m ptk1 nit-ac k* tub st1
  - **laughing** or weeping on every occasion: *Caust* gl1.fr• **Puls** tl1* sep gl1.fr• *Staph* gl1.fr•
- **undressing**; and (See Undressing - weeping)
- **ungratefulness**, at: *Lyc* gl1.fr•
- **urination**:
  - **before**: *(↗Shrieking - urination - before; BLADDER - Urination - dysuria - painful - cry)* *Borx* **Lyc** k● *Sanic* al* *Sars*
    - **children**: borx b4a.de sanic c1*
  - **during**: erig nat-m a1 *Sars*
- **vertigo**; with: phos bg2
- **vexation**; from: *(↗humiliation; mortification; offense - from; remonstrated; reproaches)* aids nl2• ambr vh arn vh bell j* calad caust vh cham cocc vh coff vh hydrog srj2• ign lac-c vh lach↓ lil-t vh lyc↓ m-aust j mosch vh nat-m↓ nux-v petr plat vh puls vh sabin j* spong j* staph vh sulph tarent vanil fd5.de *Zinc*
  - **old** vexation; from: *(↗Dwells - recalls - old)* caust gl1.fr• cham j ign gl1.fr• lach gl1.fr• lyc j nat-m j staph gl1.fr•
- **violent**: bell h1* borx h2 carl a1 caust h2* cupr mtf33 cygn-ol srj6• hydr-ac k* *Ip* al ix bnm8• nat-m gb• phos h2 sil h2 stram k*

- **waking**, on: alum alum-p k2 am-c am-m ant-t j5.de arn j5.de bell k* borx j5.de bufo k* carb-an k* chinin-s *Cic* c1* cina coff j guaj j5.de hyos k* ign k* kali-i lac-h htj1• lach k* lyc *Mag-c* j5.de merc k* neon srj5• nicc k* nux-v k* op k* paull a1 phos k* plan k* puls k* raph k* ruta j5.de sabad j5.de sabin j5.de sep j5.de sil *Stram* j5.de sulph
- **walking** in open air, when: bell calc coff *Sep*
  - **amel.**: *Puls Rhus-t*
- **washed** in cold water, when: ant-c st1
- **weakness**; from: bamb-a stb2.de• ix bnm8•
- **weather**:
  - **cloudy**: sep mtf33
  - **foggy**: sep mtf33
- **whimpering**: *(↗Sighing)* acon b7a.de* *Alum* bg2 am-c ↓ ambr bg2 anac ↓ ant-t bg2* *Apis* br1* *Arn* b7.de* *Ars* h2* *Aur* k* bar-c ptk1 **Bell** b4.de* *Borx* bg2 *Bry* b7.de* calc k2* calc-p mrr1 *Camph* b7.de* canth b7.de* caps bg2 carb-an bg2* **Caust** j5.de* **Cham** k* *Chin* b7.de* *Cic* b7.de* **Cina** b7.de* cocc b7.de* colch b7a.de* *Cupr* b7.de* hyos k* ign k* *Ip* b7.de* *Kreos* hr1* lac-lup hrn2• lach ↓ lachn ↓ lyc b4.de* m-ambo b7.de mag-c ↓ **Merc** k* nat-m ↓ nit-ac k* **Nux-v** k* op b7.de* ph-ac ↓ phos j5.de* plb bg2 podo ptk1 puls b7.de* *Rheum* b7.de* rhus-t b7.de* sec b7.de* senec ptk1 sil ↓ squil b7.de* stann ↓ **Stram** b7a.de* sulph h2* tub ckh1* *Verat* k* zinc j5.de*
  - **night**: am-c j anac j arn j ars h2* aur j caust j chin j ip j lach j lyc j mag-c j merc j nat-m j nit-ac j nux-v j op j ph-ac j phos h2* rheum j sulph j verat j
  - **aches**; everything: *(↗pain)* lac-lup hrn2•
  - **anger**, with: zinc h2*
  - **fever**; during: bell bg2 cham bg2 *Puls* b7.de* rheum bg2
  - **head**; with complaints of: bell bg2
  - **menses**; after: stram b7.de*
  - **pain**; during: *(↗aches)* lachn
  - **perspiration**; during: acon bg2 bell bg2 bry bg2 camph bg2 *Cham* bg2 *Merc* bg2 rheum bg2
  - **sickness**; before attacks of: ant-t ptk1
  - **sleep**, during: alum b4.de* anac b4.de* *Arn* b7.de* **Ars** b4.de* *Aur* b4.de* *Bar-c* b4.de* borx mtf33 **Bry** b7.de* calc b4.de* calc-p mrr1 *Caust* h2* **Cham** b7.de* *Chin* b7.de* cina b7a.de *Hyos* b7.de* *Ign* b7.de* **Ip** b7.de* lach j5.de lyc b4.de* m-ambo b7.de* mag-c j *Merc* b4.de* nat-m b4.de* *Nit-ac* h2* *Nux-v* b7.de* *Op* b7.de* ph-ac b4.de* phos j5.de podo ptk1* rheum b7.de* sil k* stann b4.de* sulph b4a.de* verat b7.de*
    - **comatose**: anac j5.de op j5.de
    - **toothache**, with: mag-c h2
  - **trifles**; from: tub ptk1

WELL:
- **doing** well; is:
  - **but** says he is very sick (See Despair - recovery - convalescence)
  - **then** agg. (See GENERALS - Well - unusually)
- **says** he is well | **sick**; when very: *(↗Complaining - never; Delirium - well; Delusions - well; Indifference - complain; Indifference - suffering; Irritability - sends - doctor; Irritability - weakness - with; Mildness - complaining; Obstinate - nothing; Optimistic - weakness; Refusing - medicine; Refusing - treatment)* androc srj1• *Apis* k* **ARN** bg2* ars k* atro a1 bell j5.de cann-xyz ptk1 cham dp• cinnb *Coff* b2.de* colch k* hyos iod st* kreos merc **Op** b2.de* plb b2.de* podo fd3.de• **Puls** k ● (non:pyrar k) pyrog zzl stram b2.de* valer b2.de* [cann-s xyz62]

WELL-BEHAVED (See Proper - too)

WELL-BEING: | **sensation** of (See Cheerful)

WHIMPERING (See Weeping - whimpering)

WHIMSICAL (See Capriciousness)

WHINING (See Moaning; Weeping - whimpering)

WHISTLING: *(↗Singing)* agar a1* bell k* calc gl1.fr• cann-i k* cann-s k* caps carb-an k* carbn-s a1* *Croc* k* haliae-lc ↓ *Lach* k* lachn k* lyc k* merc-i-f k* *Plat* k* staph sne *Stram* k* sulph mtf33* tritic-vg fd5.de

Whistling: ...
- **alternating** with | **delirium** (See Delirium - gay - alternating - whistling)
- **fever**, during: caps k*
- **involuntary**: carb-an k* lyc k*
- **jolly**: *(↗Malicious)* carb-an h2* haliae-lc srj5• tritic-vg fd5.de

WICKED disposition: *(↗Brutality; Cruelty; Hardhearted; Malicious; Misanthropy; Mischievous; Rage; Unfeeling)* anac b4a.de* **Ars** jsa bell jsa calc jsa cocc k* cub a1 cupr b7a.de cur k* **Lach** jsa nat-c b4a.de **Nat-m** jsa nux-v b7a.de* sarr a1
- **amenorrhea**; after: *(↗Insanity - amenorrhea)* cocc kr1

WILD feeling in head: *(↗Delirium - wild; Insanity; Mania; HEAD - Wild; VERTIGO - Turning; as - head; whirling)* ambr bg* bapt k* *Cimic* bg* *Hell* mrr1 lil-t k* *Med* k* positr nl2• rhod a1
- **pain** in head; with: bapt a1
- **sexual** desire; from suppression of: lil-t mrr1 med mrr1

WILDERNESS: | **desires**: *(↗Company - aversion - country; Countryside - desire; Nature - loves)* falco-pe nl2• irid-met srj5•

WILDNESS: *(↗Anger; Dancing - wild; Exhilaration; Gestures - hands - wild; Gestures - wild; Insanity; Laughing - wild; Mania; Rage; Violent)* acon k* acon-l a1 agar-st ↓ aids nl2• ant-t k* apoc kkv1 aur k2* bapt k* bell k* calc-p k* camph canth k* carc mlr1• chinin-ar k2 chlf a1 chlol a1 (non:chlor) choc srj3• *Colch* ↓ cot ↓ croc k* cupr k* fagu a1 hyos ign ↓ lil-t bg2 *Lob-s* hr1* lyss a1* m-aust j5.de med k* meli sne mosch k* nat-s k2* op k* petr k* ph-ac k* phos k* *Stram* k* tab bg2 tarent a1* *Verat* k*
- **evening**: ant-t a1 croc k*
- **night** | **waking**; on: cot a1
- **bright** light, strong odors, touch, from: *Colch* k1*
- **children**, in: petr j5.de stram mtf33 verat mtf33
- **convulsions**; before: agar-st a1
- **headache**, during: bapt k*
- **misdeeds** of others, from (See Indignation - misdeeds)
- **sound**; from any: verat mtf33
- **trifles**, at: *(↗Trifles; Trifles - important)* ign k*
- **unpleasant** news, from: *(↗Ailments - bad)* calc-p
- **vexation**, from: ph-ac k*

WILL:
- **contradiction** of: *(↗two; Antagonism; Contradictory - actions; Contradictory - speech; Thoughts - two; Undertaking - things)* acon k* alum bg2 am-c bg2 **Anac** k* ant-t hr1* *Aq-mar* mgm• caps k* chin bg2 crot-c sk4• des-ac rbp6 *Kola* stb3• *Lac-h* sk4• lyc bg2 naja nux-m bg2 rhus-t bg2 sal-fr sle1• sep k* [heroin sdj2]
  - **work** and rest; about: lac-h sk4•
- **control** over his will, does not know what to do; has no: | **head**; with dullness in the: apis a1
- **deficient** (See Irresolution)
- **lack** of will power (See loss)
- **loss** of will power: *(↗Confidence - want - self-depreciation; Delusions - will power)* abrot bro1 acetan bro1 am-c gl1.fr• am-m gl1.fr• *Anac* b4a.de* ang vh *Anh* mg1.de* *Arg-n* ↓ bar-c gl1.fr• *Bar-s* k2 *Calc* j5.de* calc-act a1 calc-sil k2* camph a1 cere-s bro1 chinin-s j5.de clem a1 coca kr1* *Cocain* bro1 *Con* kr1 cortico jl croc j5.de des-ac jl falco-pe nl2• galv c1 grat k2 *Hell* kr1 hypoth jl kali-br bro1 lavand-a ctl1• lyc gl1.fr• malar jl2 *Merc* a1* *Morph* bro1 naja jl nat-br a1 nat-c j5.de *Nat-m* kr1* nat-sil fd3.de• nid jl op j5.de* petr j5.de* phos kr1 *Pic-ac* kr1* *Ptel* kr1 sacch-a gmj3 ser-a-c jl2 sil gl1.fr• stry-p bro1 sulph gl1.fr• **Symph** fd* *Tarent* bro1 thuj-l jl
  - **apoplexy**, after: *Anac* kr1
  - **insight**, self-awareness; with increased: *(↗Insightful)* anh sp1
  - **melancholia**, from: *Arg-n* kr1
  - **walking**, while: chinin-s j5.de*
- **strong** will power: *(↗Decisive; Determination; Firmness; Perseverance; Positiveness; Tough)* aq-pet mtf11 ars mtf aur mtf *Caust* mtf cich mtf11 fagu mtf11 falco-pe ↓ *Ferr* mtf lac-f wza1• lach mtf lyc mtf merc mtf **Nux-v** mtf *Op* mtf phys ↓ sanguis-s hm2• *Sulph* mtf verbe-o mtf11 vitis-v mtf11
  - **amel.**: falco-pe nl2• phys ptk2

- **two** wills; sensation as if he had: *(↗contradiction; Antagonism; Confusion - identity; Confusion - identity - duality; Contradictory - speech; Irresolution; Thoughts - two)* **Anac** k* anh mg1.de cann-i br1 crot-c sk4• *Lach* k* naja polys sk4• sal-fr sle1• taosc iwa1• [heroin sdj2]
  - **commanding** what the other forbids; one: anac rb2
- **weakness** of: *(↗Character; Delusions - will power; Indifference - desire; Initiative; Persisting; Spineless; Undertaking - lacks; Undertaking - many; Weak character; Yielding)* agar vh1 *Alum* bg2* alum-sil k2 am-c gl1.fr• am-m gl1.fr• ambr sf1.de *Anac* bg2* ang vh1 *Anh* mg1.de* ant-c bg2* *Ars* bg2* asaf j5.de* aster sze10• aur-m-n wbt2• *Bar-act* sf1.de **Bar-c** bg2* bism sf1.de bros-gau mrc1 bry bg2 buth-a mg1.de **Calc** bg2* calc-act sf1.de cann-s sf1.de carc jl2* caust gl1.fr• cent-u mtf11 chin bg2 cimic k2 cocc bg2 coff bg2* coloc bg2 *Con* gl1.fr• *Croc* j5.de* *Dioxi* rbp6 dulc bg2 graph sf1.de* grat k2 *Haem* sf1.de hell bg2 ign bg2* ip bg2 irid-met srj5• kali-c bg2 kali-sil k2* *Lach* j5.de* lath mrr1 laur bg2 *Lyc* bg2* malar jl2 merc br1* *Mez* bg2* *Moni* rfm1• nat-c bg2* nat-m bg2* nat-sil fd3.de• nux-v sf1.de op bg2* *Petr* bg2* *Pic-ac* bg2* podo fd3.de• puls bg2 rheum bg2 sil gl1.fr• staph sf1.de sulph gl1.fr• ulm-c jsj8• [tax jsj7]
  - **mental** exertion; from: *(↗Mental exertion - agg.)* *Pic-ac* sf1.de
  - **smoking**; for giving up: dioxi rbp6

WILLFUL (See Obstinate)

WILY (See Deceitful)

WIMPY (See Weak character)

WINDOW; looking for hours out of the (See Looking - window)

WINE agg.: *Agar* b4a.de alum bg2 bell b4.de* bov b4.de* carb-v b4a.de con b4.de* petr b4.de* stront-c b4.de* zinc b4a.de

WIPING eyes: | **amel.**: alum b4a.de

WITHDRAWAL from reality: *(↗Schizophrenia - paranoid)* anh sp1 arb-m oss1• haliae-lc srj5• irid-met srj5• *Plut-n* srj7• rhus-g tmo3• [merc stj2 nicc-met stj2 nicc-s stj2]

WITTY: *(↗Charming; Cheerful; Concentration - active; Excitement; Fancies - vivid; Ideas - abundant; Irony; Jesting; Memory - active; Mirth; Mocking - sarcasm; Quick; Thoughts - rapid)* aeth a1 alco a1 aran-ix mg1.de cann-i a1* caps k* chlol a1 cocc k* *Coff* croc k* dulc fd4.de hydr br1 *Lach* k* olib-sac wmh1 *Op* k* opun-s a1 spong k* sulph ↓ sumb k* thea k* vanil fd5.de verat sne
- **women**; in: sulph mrr1

WOMEN; mannish (See Mannish - women)

WOODS: | **desire** to be in the woods: sanguis-s hm2•

WORD hunting (See Forgetful - words; Memory - weakness - words)

WORK:
- **aversion** to work (See Laziness)
- **desire** to work (See Industrious)
- **impossible**: *(↗Business - incapacity)* arb-m oss1• carc mlr1• gels mrr1 lat-m bnm6• syph jl2

WORK; MENTAL (See Mental exertion)

WORRY (See Anxiety; Cares)

WORTHLESS feeling (See Delusions - worthless)

WRATH (See Hatred - revengeful)

WRETCHED: *(↗Unfortunate)* adam srj5• germ-met srj5• haliae-lc srj5• lat-m bnm6• lavand-a ctl1• neon srj5• **Ruta** fd* *Spong* fd4.de *Tab* br1* *Tritic-vg* fd5.de
- **body**; unhappy with her: *(↗Delusions - body - ugly)* adam srj5•
- **menses**; during: adam srj5•

WRITING:
- **agg.**: asaf hr1* atra-r skp7• caust ckh1 cycl ckh1 kali-c ckh1 laur bg2 mag-p ckh1 med hr1* nat-c bg2 nux-m b7.de* rhus-t b7.de* stann jl sul-ac ckh1 [arg-n stj2]
- **aversion** to: dulc fd4.de hydr k* irid-met srj5• nat-sil fd3.de• ruta fd4.de spong fd4.de squil k* symph fd3.de• thea [tax jsj7]

Writing: ...
- **desire** for: *(↗Verses - making)* chin k* irid-met srj5• kali-p fd1.de• lipp a1 oxal-a rly4• sphing k* spig
- **difficulty** in expressing ideas in: arag br1 cact calc sf1.de cann-s sf1.de carb-an cimic sf1.de dulc fd4.de kali-c sf1.de lach sf1.de lyc sf1.de *Nat-m* sf1.de ruta fd4.de sep a1* sil sf1.de *Symph* fd3.de• tritic-vg fd5.de vanil fd5.de zinc sf1.de
- **fatigues**: kali-p fd1.de• *Sil* hr1*
- **inability** for: *(↗Dyslexia; Mistakes - writing)* ars kr1* atra-r skp7• caust gl1.fr• colch ↓ ign lyc **Nux-v** kr1 podo fd3.de• sil gl1.fr• stram mtf33
  - **connectedly**: colch
  - **learning** to write in children: caust gl1.fr• sil mtf33*
  - **rapidly** as she wishes, anxious behavior, makes mistakes; inability to write as: ign kr1
- **indistinctly**, writes: adam srj5• dulc fd4.de germ-met srj5• kali-br a1 kali-p fd1.de• merc a1 podo fd3.de• positr nl2• ruta fd4.de sacch-a fd2.de• spong fd4.de stram a1 tritic-vg fd5.de [heroin sdj2]
- **left**-handed; ailments from suppression of writing (See Ailments - writing)
- **meanness** to her friends: *Lac-c* kr1*
- **talent** for easier: irid-met srj5• op a1*

WRONG, everything seems: *(↗Offended; Pessimist)* androc srj1• bros-gau mrc1 carc mlr1• cimic mrr1 coloc eug hep *Naja* neon srj5• nux-v sal-fr sle1•

XENOPHOBIA (See Fear - strangers)

YAWNING:
- **agg.**: agar bg2 med bg2
- **amel.**: bry ptk1

YEARNING: *(↗Desires; Longing; Loss)* agath-a ↓ olib-sac wmh1
- **things** lost; for: agath-a nl2•

YIELDING disposition: *(↗Answering - unable - hurt; Comply; Mildness; Pleasing - desire; Polite - too; Resignation; Servile; Will - weakness)* ambr mtf apis gt arb-m oss1• *Aur* b4a.de aur-m-n wbt2• bamb-a stb2.de• bar-c mtf33 bar-m ↓ calc-sil k2* cann-s a1* **Carb-v** lmj *Carc* cd* caust ↓ cic ↓ cocc b7.de* coff mrr1 *Cori-r* j *Croc* b7a.de* crot-h ↓ cupr b7a.de cypra-eg sde6.de• dream-p sdj1• dulc fd4.de fl-ac ↓ *Foll* oss• ham fd3.de• ign k2* kali-c ↓ kiss a1 **Lac-c** ↓ *Lac-d* ↓ lap-la sde8.de• lath mrr1 lil-t gt *Lyc* b4.de* *M-arct* b7.de* mag-m ↓ nat-c ↓ nat-m gt nux-m gt *Nux-v* gl1.fr• olib-sac wmh1 ozone sde2• petr gl1.fr• ph-ac c1 phos lmj* pin-con oss2• plac rzf5• podo fd3.de• **Puls** b7.de* querc-r svu1• sal-fr sle1• sep b4a.de* *Sil* b4.de* spong fd4.de staph lmj* symph fd3.de• **Thuj** lmj *Tritic-vg* fd5.de ulm-c jsj8• vanad dx* **Zinc** ↓ [alum-p stj2 alumin-s stj2 arg-met stj2 arg-p stj2 bar-p stj1 erech stj tax jsj7 uva stj]
- **children**; in: bar-c lmj bar-m lmj calc-sil lmj **Carb-v** lmj *Carc* lmj caust lmj cic lmj cocc lmj croc lmj crot-h lmj **Cupr** lmj fl-ac lmj ign lmj kali-c lmj **Lac-c** lmj *Lac-d* lmj lyc lmj mag-m lmj nat-c lmj nat-m lmj nux-v lmj petr lmj ph-ac lmj phos lmj **Puls** lmj **Sep** lmj sil lmj staph lmj **Thuj** lmj **Zinc** lmj

ZEALOUS (See Ardent; Fanaticism)

ZOOPHOBIA (See Fear - animals)

VERTIGO: (↗*HEAD - Lightness)* abies-c k* abies-n k* abrom-a bnj1 abrom-a-r bnj1 absin k* acet-ac k* **Acon** k* acon-c a1 acon-f a1 acon-l a1 aconin a1 act-sp k* adam skp7• adox a1* adren br1* *Aesc* k* aesc-g a1* *Aeth* k* aethyl-n a1* **Agar** k* agar-cpn a1 agar-em a1* agar-pa a1 agar-pr a1 agar-st a1 agn k* agro a1 aids nl2• **Ail** k* alco a1 alet k* all-c k* all-s a1* allox sp1 *Aloe* k* alst a1 *Alum* k* alumn k* *Am-c* k* am-m k* *Ambr* k* aml-ns amph a1 anac k* anan k* anders bnj1 androc bnm2• androg-p bnj1 ang b2.de* anh sp1* anil a1* anis *Ant-c* k* ant-t k* antip br1 **Apis** k* apoc k* apom a1* aq-mar rbp6 aran-ix sp1 **Arg-met** k* *Arg-n* k* arge-pl rwt5• arist-cl sp1 arizon-l nl2• *Arn* k* *Ars* k* *Ars-h* k* ars-i k* arum-m hr1 arum-t k* arund k* asaf k* asar k* asc-c k* asc-t k* aspar k* *Aster* k* atha a1* atra-r bnm3• atro a1 *Aur* k* aur-i k2 *Aur-m* k* aur-s a1 bad k* *Bamb-a* stb2.de• **Bapt** k* *Bar-c* k* bar-m k* bar-s k2 **Bell** k* bell-p a1* benz-ac k* benzo c2 benzol br1 *Berb* k* bism k* bism-sn a1 bit-ar wht1• boerh-d zzc1• bond a1 borx k* both k* both-a rb3 botul br1 bov k* brach k* brass-n-o srj5• brom k* brucel sa3• **Bry** k* bufo buth-a sp1 *Cact* k* cadm-met tpw6* cadm-s br1 cain caj c2 calad k* **Calc** k* calc-act c2 calc-ar calc-f k* *Calc-p* k* **Calc-s** calo a1 *Camph* k* **Cann-i** k* *Cann-s* k* *Canth* k* caps k* carb-ac k* *Carb-an* k* *Carb-v* k* carbn-dox knl3• carbn-h carbn-o k* **Carbn-s** carc tpw2* cardios-h rly4• carl k* cartl-s rly4• cass a1 castor-eq caul k* *Caust* k* *Cedr* k* cench k2 cent a1 cephd-i zzc1• cere-b a1 cerv a1 *Cham* k* **Chel** k* chen-a k* chim k* *Chin* k* chinin-ar **Chinin-s** k* chir-fl gya2 chlam-tr bcx2• chlf k* chlol k* chlor k* chr-ac a1 *Cic* k* cic-m a1 *Cimic* k* cina k* cinch a1 cinnb k* cist k* cit-v a1 clem k* cob k* cob-n sp1 coc-c k* coca k* **Cocc** k* cocc-s a1 *Coff* k* *Coff-t* c2 coffin a1 colch k* coli jl2* *Coloc* k* colocin a1 com k* **Con** k* conin a1* conin-br a1 convo-d c2 convo-s sp1 *Cop* k* cor-r a1 cori-r a1 corian-s knl6• corn k* cortico sp1 cortiso sp1 cot a1 crat br1 croc k* *Crot-c* crot-h k* crot-t k* culx c2 cund a1 *Cupr* k* cupr-ar k* **Cycl** k* cystein-l rly4• cyt-l a1* daph k* dat-a a1* dat-f a1 der a1 des-ac rbp6 **Dig** k* digin a1* digox a1 dios k* dirc k* dor a1 dream-p sdj1• dros k* dub c2* dubo-h a1* **Dulc** k* echi *Elaps* equis-h erech a1 ery-a a1* eryth a1 eucal a1* euon k* euon-a c2 eup-per k* eup-pur k* euph k* euph-ip a1 euphr k* eupi k* fago k* fagu c2 *Ferr* k* *Ferr-ar* ferr-i k* ferr-ma k* *Ferr-p* k* ferul a1 fl-ac k* form k* formal br1* fuma-ac rly4• galla-q-r nl2• gamb k* gard-j vlr2• gast a1 **Gels** k* gent-c a1 gent-ch bnj1 gent-l a1 ger-i rly4• gins a1* *Glon* k* glycyr-g cte1• gnaph a1 goss k* gran k* granit-m es1• *Graph* k* grat k* *Guare* k* guat sp1 ham k* hed sp1 hell k* helo-s bnm14*• helon k* *Hep* k* hipp a1 hippoc-k szs2 hist sp1 hura hydr-ac k* hydrang br1 *Hydrc* k* *Hydrog* srj2• hydroph rsj6• hygroph-s bnj1 *Hyos* k* hyosin a1 hyper k* iber a1 ign k* ina-i mlk9.de ind a1 indg k* interf sa3• *Iod* k* ip k* iris k* ix bnm8• jab k* jatr-c jug-c k* jug-r k* kali-ar *Kali-bi* k* *Kali-br* k* *Kali-c* k* kali-cy a1 *Kali-i* k* *Kali-n* k* kali-ox a1 kali-p *Kali-s* k* *Kalm* k* ketogl-ac rly4• kou br1 kreos k* lac-ac a1* lac-c k* lac-d lac-del hrn2• lac-h sk4• *Lach* k* lachn k* lact k* lap-la sde8.de• lat-h bnm5• lat-m bnm6• laur k* *Led* k* lepi a1 lept k* lil-t k* lipp a1 lith-br c2 *Lith-m* bro1 lob k* lob-p c2 lob-s a1 lol bg2* lup a1* **Lyc** k* lycps-v lyss k* m-ambo b2.de* m-arct b2.de* m-aust b2.de* mag-c k* mag-m k* mag-s k* magn-gr c2 maland vh malar jl2 *Manc* k* *Mand* sp1 mang k* mang-m a1 mang-p rly4• med k* meli a1 meny k* *Merc* k* *Merc-c* k* merc-cy a1 merc-i-f k* merc-i-r k* merc-n a1* merl a1* *Mez* k* mill k* mim-h a1 mom-b a1 morg fmm1• morg-p fmm1• morph a1* morph-m j2 morph-s hr1 *Mosch* k* mucs-nas rly4• *Mur-ac* k* murx k* musca-d szs1 *Mygal* k* myric a1* nad rly4• naja narcot a1 narcot-m j2 *Nat-ar* nat-bic wd1 nat-br a1 *Nat-c* k* *Nat-hchls* **Nat-m** k* nat-ox rly4• *Nat-p* k* nat-pyru rly4• *Nat-s* k* nat-sal br1* nicc k* nicot bro1 *Nit-ac* k* nit-m-ac a1 nit-s-d a1 nitro-o a1 *Nux-m* k* **Nux-v** k* oci-sa sp1 oena a1* oeno a1 ol-j a1 *Olib-sac* wmh1 olnd k* **Onos** k* **Op** k* oreo br1 orot-ac rly4• ox-ac k* oxal-a rly4• oxeod a1 oxyt c2 ozone sde2• paeon a1* pall a1 pana a1 par k* parathyr jl2 past a1 paull a1 pen a1 **Petr** k* petr-ra shn4• *Ph-ac* k* phal a1* phasco-ci rbp2 phel k* **Phos** k* phys a1* *Phyt* k* pic-ac k* pieri-b mlk9.de pimp a1 pin-con oss2• pin-s a1* pip-m a1 pitu-gl br1* plac-s rly4• plan k* *Plat* k* plb k* plumbg a1 plut-n srj7• pneu jl2 *Podo* k* polys sk4• positr nl2• pot-e rly4• prim-v c2 prot jl2* prun a1 psil ft1 *Psor* k* ptel k* **Puls** k* pycnop-sa mrz1 querc bro1 querc-r c1* querc-r-g-s br1 rad-br bro1 *Ran-b* k* ran-s k* raph k* *Rauw* sp1 rham-f a1 rheum k* *Rhod* k* rhodi br1 **Rhus-t** k* *Rhus-v* k* ric a1 rob a1 rosm a1 rumx ruta k* sabad k* *Sabin* k* sal-ac a1* sal-fr sle1• sal-p a1* salin a1 samb k* **Sang** k* sangin-t c1 sanic sapin a1 sars k* scol a1* scut a1* **Sec** k* sel k* senec k* *Seneg* k* *Sep* k* **Sil** k* sin-a a1 sin-n a1 sinus rly4• sol-a c2 sol-ni c2 sol-t a1 solin a1 *Spig* k* spig-m a1 spira a1 spirae a1 *Spong* k* squil k* stach a1* *Stann* k* staph k* still a1 *Stram* k* strept-ent jl2 streptoc rly4• streptom-s vk2 *Stront-c* k* *Stry* k* suis-em rly4• suis-pan rly4• sul-ac k* sul-h a1* sulfa sp1 sulo-ac a1 **Sulph** k* sumb k* suprar rly4• *Syph* k2* **Tab** k* tanac a1 tang a1 taosc iwa1• tarax k* tarent k* tart-ac a1 tax a1* tax-br oss1• tell k* tep a1* *Ter* k* term-c mtf11 teucr k* *Ther* k* thioc-ac rly4• *Thuj* k* thymol sp1 til a1 titan a1 trach a1 trad a1* trinit br1 trios rsj11• trom a1* tub al*

Vertigo: ...
tung-met bdx1• tus-p a1 upa a1 (non: uran-met k) uran-n *Urt-u* k* ust k* v-a-b jl2 *Valer* k* vanad br1 vario hr1* *Verat* k* *Verat-v* k* verb b2.de* verin a1 vero-o rly4*• *Vesp* k* vesp-xyz c2 vib vichy-g a1 vinc a1 viol-o b2.de* viol-t b7.de* vip a1 visc a1* voes a1* wies a1* wye a1* x-ray sp1 *Zinc* k* zinc-i bg3* zinc-m a1 zinc-p k2 zinc-s a1 zing k* ziz a1 [alumin-s stj2 argon stj2 bell-p-sp dcm1 buteo-j sej6 helia stj7 helium stj2 heroin sdj2 krypt stj2 lac-mat sst4 rado stj2 **Spect** dfg1]

RIGHT side: bapt bg2 crot-t bg2 nat-m bg2

MORNING (= 6-9 h): acon k* *Agar* k* aids nl2• ail k* *Alum* k* alum-p k2* alum-sil k2* *Am-c* k* am-m k* ambr k2* *Arg-n* k* bar-c b4.de* bell k* bism k* *Boerh-d* zzc1• borx b4a.de *Bov* k* *Bry* k* bufo calad k* *Calc* k* calc-i k2* calc-s **Carb-an** k* carb-v b4.de* *Carbn-s Castor-eq* caust k* cer-s a1 cham k* *Chel* k* *Chin* chinin-s *Cinnb* coc-c k* con b4.de* cycl hr1 dig dios k* *Dulc* eup-per eup-pur euphr b7.de* falco-pe nl2• form k* *Gels* k* glon *Graph* k* helo-s rwt2• *Hep* k* hydrog srj2• hyper k* iod k* kali-bi k* *Kali-c* k* kali-n k* kali-p kali-s kali-sil k2* kola stb3• kreos k* **Lach** k* lact **Lyc** k* lyss *Mag-c* k* *Mag-m* k* mag-s k* malar jl2 manc k* merl a1 musca-d szs1 myric a1 myris a1 *Nat-m* k* *Nat-p* nicc *Nit-ac* k* *Nux-v* k* olnd ox-ac k* *Petr* k* *Ph-ac* k* *Phos* k* pip-m a1 plac-s rly4• positr nl2• psor k* *Puls* k* ran-b k* rhus-g tmo3• rhus-t ruta k* sabad b7.de* sabin k* sacch-a fd2.de• sal-ac sne samb b7.de* sang k* sars k* sel k* seneg sep k* *Sil* k* sinus rly4• sol-ni spong fd4.de squil k* stram b7.de* stront-c k* *Sulph* k* tell k* tritic-vg fd5.de tub al* ven-m rsj12• verat k* verat-v k* *Zinc* k* [spect dfg1]

- **night**; until: abrom-a ks5
- **bed** agg.; in: alum borx k* *Calc Carb-v* k* chel con k* form gels graph k* lach k* lyc nat-m k* *Nux-v* bg2 ol-an ph-ac k* phos pip-m k* *Puls* bg2 sep k* sil *Zinc* zinc-p k2*
- **lie** down, compelled to: *Nit-ac* **Puls** tell a1
- **rising**:
  - **after** | **agg.**: am-c bar-c k* calc k* calc-sil k2* chel k* hep k* kali-p fd1.de• lach **Lyc** k* mag-c k* mag-m mur-ac h2* nat-m k* *Nit-ac* **Phos** k* sabad k* sacch-a fd2.de• sil k* stram sulph k* symph fd3.de• **Tell** tritic-vg fd5.de
  - **agg.**: acon *Aids* nl2• *Alum* bro1 am-c *Ambr* aml-ns asar k* atro k* **Bell** k* bov k* **Bry** k* calc k* calc-i k2* calc-sil k2* carb-an h2* carbn-s caul k* *Caust* k* cham k* cimic cob-n sp1 *Con* k* *Dulc* k* fl-ac k* *Gamb* k* glon k* gran k* graph guaj hell k* iod jac-c bro1 kali-bi k* lac-ac a1 lac-h sk4• lach k* lact a1 **Lyc** k* mag-c k* *Mag-m* mag-s manc **Nat-m** k* nat-s nicc k* *Nit-ac* k* nux-v bg2* op bro1 ph-ac k* **Phos** k* pimp a1 pitu-gl skp7• podo bro1* **Puls** k* pycnop-sa mrz1 **Rhus-t** k* ruta sabad samb k* sep k* sil k* sol-ni *Spig* spong fd4.de squil k* sul-i k2* sulph k* thuj k* tril-p tritic-vg fd5.de verat verat-v k* [*Spect* dfg1]
  - **amel.**: caust k* dulc fd4.de rhus-t k*
- **waking**; on: acon allox tpw3 atro brom bry calc caps *Carb-v* caust bg *Chin Dulc* euphr fago falco-pe nl2• fl-ac *Graph* hell hyper (non:iris slp) iris-fl slp *Kali-bi* kola stb3• lac-e hrn2• **Lach** k* lap-la sde8.de• lyc tl1 merc-i-f myris *Nat-m* nit-ac tl1 petr tl1 ph-ac bg positr nl2• pycnop-sa mrz1 rhod bg rhus-t spong fd4.de stann sulph k2 tarent til tritic-vg fd5.de zinc h2

FORENOON (= 9-12 h): acon k* agar ambr k* atro k* bry k* calc k* camph carb-an b4.de* carb-v k* *Caust* k* cham k* chinin-s dulc b4.de* eup-pur fl-ac k* guaj bg2 kali-c b4.de* *Lach* k* lact k* *Lyc* k* lycps-v mag-m b4.de* *Nat-m* k* nept-m lsd2.fr petr-ra shn4• *Phos* k* podo fd3.de• propl ub1• ruta fd4.de sabad b7.de* samb sars k* spong fd4.de stann staph b7.de* sul-ac b4.de* *Sulph* k* tritic-vg fd5.de viol-t k* *Zinc* k* zinc-p k2*

- **11** h: bamb-a stb2.de• ther c1

NOON (= 12-13 h): aeth k* arn *Calc-p* k* *Caust* k* chin k* dendr-pol sk4• dulc k* ham k* kali-c h2* kalm lyc k* mag-m mag-s manc k* merc k* nat-s nux-v petr-ra shn4• *Phos* k* ruta fd4.de sil h2* stram k* stront-c k* sulph zinc k* zinc-p k2*

AFTERNOON (= 13-18 h): *Aesc* k* agar k* aids nl2• alum k* alum-p k2* *Ambr* k* anac b4a.de* apis b7a.de benz-ac k* *Bry* k* carb-an b4.de* carbn-s cench k2* chel k* chin crot-t k* cupr k* cycl k* dios k* eupi k* ferr k* ferr-p glon k* hep b4a.de hura kali-c k* kali-p kali-sil k2* kola stb3• lyc k* merc k* nat-m k* nicc nux-v k* petr-ra shn4• ph-ac phos k* puls k* rhus-t k* sabad k* sang a1 sars k* *Sep* k* sil k* sinus rly4• spong fd4.de staph stront-c k* sul-ac k* sulph k* *Thuj* k* tritic-vg fd5.de vanil fd5.de zinc b4a.de

- **16** h: bamb-a stb2.de•

Vertigo

EVENING (= 18-22 h): aids nl2• alum k* alum-p k2* alum-sil k2* alumn k* *Am-c* k* *Apis* k* arn k* **Ars** k* ars-s-f k2* asaf k* asar b7.de* atra-r skp7*• borx k* bry b7.de* *Calc* k* calc-ar c1* calc-s calc-sil k2* carb-an k* carb-v k* *Carbn-s* caust k* cham k* chel k* chin chinin-ar chir-fl gya2 coloc k* *Cycl* k* dios k* dulc fd4.de eug k* fuma-ac rly4• *Graph* k* *Hep* k* hydr k* indg c1 ip b7.de* iris *Kali-ar* kali-bi k* *Kali-c* k* *Kali-p* kali-s kali-sil k2* *Lach* k* laur k* lyc k* lycps-v m-ambo b7.de* mag-c k* mag-m bg2 meph k* merc k* merc-c b4a.de mosch b7.de* nat-m k* nat-s k* nicc k* *Nit-ac* k* nux-m k* *Nux-v* k* ozone sde2• petr k* *Ph-ac* k* *Phos* k* phys k* phyt pic-ac k* plat k* podo fd3.de• positr nl2• **Puls** k* raph k* *Rhod* k* rhus-t k* rhus-v k* ruta mrr1* sabad sel k* sep k* *Sil* k* spong k* staph k* stront-c k* *Sulph* k* sumb a1 tarent k* thuj k* til k* tritic-vg fd5.de zinc k* [sol-ecl cky1 spect dfg1]

- **19.30 h**: atra-r skp7*•
- **amel.**: indg c1
- **bed** agg.; in: aids nl2• brom k* lach *Mag-c* nit-ac k* nux-m *Nux-v* *Petr* k* *Phos* k* rhus-t sep k* staph k* sulph tritic-vg fd5.de
- **church**; in: ozone sde2•

NIGHT (= 22-6 h): *Am-c* k* bamb-a stb2.de• bar-c bell calc k* carb-an bg2 caust k* chin k* clem k* con b4.de* croc k* cycl dig k* fago k* ham k* hyper kali-p fd1.de• lac-ac c1 lac-c lach lyc b4.de* merc-c b4a.de nat-c k* nit-ac b4.de* nux-v petr b4.de* phos k* phys k* pic-ac positr nl2• rhod k* rhus-t h1* ruta fd4.de sang sarr sars bg2 sep h2* sil k* *Spong* k* stram stront-c b4.de* sulph k* tarent k* ther k* *Thuj* k* tritic-vg fd5.de vanil fd5.de zinc k* zinc-p k2*

- **midnight**:
  - **after** | **1** h: *Mur-ac* hr1
- **bed** | **going** to bed | **amel.**: aur-m carb-an
  - **in** bed | **agg.**: am-c *Arg-met* bar-c *Caust* ind
- **waking** him or her from sleep●: **Nux-v** sil a1
- **waking**; on: *Chin* k* dig k* lac-c lyc k* phos k* sabad k* sil *Spong* stront-c sulph k* thuj k* vanil fd5.de zinc bg1*

ACCOMPANIED BY:

- **anemia** (See GENERALS - Anemia - accompanied - vertigo)
- **anemia** and asthenic fever (See GENERALS - Anemia - accompanied - fever and)
- **atrophy** (See GENERALS - Atrophy - accompanied - vertigo)
- **collapse** (See GENERALS - Collapse - accompanied - vertigo)
- **collapse** and nausea (See GENERALS - Collapse - accompanied - vertigo - nausea)
- **coryza**: chin b7.de* *Gels* bg2 nux-v b7.de* verb bg2
- **cough** (See Cough)
- **deafness** (See HEARING - Lost - accompanied - vertigo)
- **diarrhea**: apis b7a.de *Cham* b7.de* ferr-s hr1 grat bg2 phos bg2 stram b7.de*
- **epistaxis**: acon b7.de* *Ant-c* b7.de* bell bg1* borx bg1 bov bg2 brom hr1 bry j5.de* carb-an bg2* lach b7a.de* lap-la sde8.de• sec k2 sulph b4.de* vip ptk1
- **eructations**: *Acon* b7a.de *Ant-c* b7a.de bell bg2 bism bg2 calc bg2 kali-c bg2 mag-c bg2 nit-ac bg2 nux-m bg2 nux-v b7.de* op bg2 petr h2* phos bg2 *Puls* b7a.de sang bg2 sars bg2 tab bg2
  - **sour**: sars b4a.de
- **hair** being pulled; sensation as if: mur-ac bg2
- **heat**; flushes of: mag-m bg2
- **hemiopia** (See VISION - Hemiopia - accompanied - vertigo)
- **hemorrhage** (See GENERALS - Hemorrhage - accompanied - vertigo)
- **menses**; complaints of: caust ptk1 cycl ptk1
- **nausea** (See Nausea - with)
- **opisthotonos**: cic bro1
- **paralysis** (See GENERALS - Paralysis - accompanied - vertigo)
- **perspiration**: alum bg2 apis bg2 **Ars** b4a.de* bell b4a.de* bov bg2 *Bry* b7a.de* **Calc** bg2 chin bg2 ign b7.de* **Ip** b7a.de* laur bg2 merc-c b4a.de* nux-v bg2 ph-ac bg2 **Phos** bg2 **Rhus-t** b7.de* *Sel* b7a.de* sep bg2 sulph bg2 tab ptk1 *Thuj* b4a.de* *Verat* b7.de*
  - **cold** (See PERSPIRATION - Cold - vertigo)
- **pulse**:
  - **slow** (See Pulse - slow)
  - **spasmodic**: bism hr1

Accompanied by: ...

- **respiration**:
  - **asthmatic** (See RESPIRATION - Asthmatic - accompanied - vertigo)
  - **complaints** of (See RESPIRATION - Complaints - accompanied - vertigo)
  - **difficult** (See RESPIRATION - Difficult - accompanied - vertigo)
- **restlessness**: querc-r svu1• verat bg2
- **salivation**: calc kr1* gran br1 mag-c bg2 phos bg2
- **shivering**: chel b7.de* graph bg2 rhus-t bg2
- **sleeplessness**: ther mrr1*
- **sneezing** agg.: nux-v b7.de*
- **staggering**: *(↗EXTREMITIES - Incoordination - lower; EXTREMITIES - Tottering)* acon k* agar k* *Ail* k* alum bg2 am-c anan ant-t bg *Arg-n* k* atro *Aur* aur-s c1 bamb-a stb2.de• bry *Calc* k* *Camph* caps carb-ac *Carb-an* *Carb-v* k* caust bg2 *Cham* chen-a c1 *Chin* *Cic* coloc *Con* crot-h bro1 cupr-ar dulc a1 *Ferr* k* ferr-ar ferr-p fl-ac form bg2 **Gels** k* glon k2 helo-s rwt2• hydr-ac ign ip kali-br kali-c kali-n c1 kali-s kola stb3• kreos lac-h sk4• lil-t lol bg2 lyc lyss med merc mur-ac nicc *Nux-m* k* **Nux-v** k* olnd op bg ozone sde2• paeon petr petr-ra shn4• ph-ac h2* phasco-ci rbp2 **Phos** k* *Phyt* plat bg2 psor al rhus-t bg2* samb xxb1 sang a1 sars sec *Sep* k* sil h2* *Stram* k* sulph tarax thal-xyz srj8• thuj til vesp kr1*
- **stool**; painful: cob-n sp1
- **taste**; bitter: croc b7.de*
- **thirst**: nit-ac bg2 ox-ac ptk1 stram b7.de* uran-n bg2
- **vision**:
  - **blurred**: agav-t jl1 fuma-ac rly4• kali-s fd4.de melal-alt gya4 positr nl2• psil ft1 ruta fd4.de
  - **complaints** of vision (See VISION - Complaints - accompanied - vertigo)
  - **dim** vision: *(↗VISION - Dim - vertigo - during)* *Acon* act-sp agar k* agav-t jl1 alum h2* amyg *Anac* ant-t apis k* arg-met arg-n k* ars asaf *Bell* k* bism hr1 **Calc** k ● *Camph* canth k* carb-an k* carb-v h2* cassia-s ccrh1• cham chen-a hr1 chin bg2 cic k* cimic k* cina bg2 coff bg2 con k2 *Cupr* k* **Cycl** k* dulc k* euon k* **Ferr** k* *Ferr-ar* ferr-p **GELS** k ●* gink-b sbd1• gins *Glon* k* gran k* graph gymno hell hep hyos *Kali-bi* kalm lac-del hrn2• lach k* lact laur k* lil-t bg2 *Merc* mosch mur-ac vh nat-m h2* *Nit-ac* **NUX-V** k ●* olib-sac wmh1 olnd ozone sde2• par phel bg2 **Phos** k ●* *Phyt* k* plat h2* plb bg2 psil ft1 puls k* raph rhus-t h1* sabad k* *Sabin* k* seneg spong fd4.de *Stram* k* *Stront-c* stroph-h ptk1 *Sulph* tep ter k* ther k2 til valer bro1 vanil fd5.de verat bg2 vinc bro1 zinc
  - **flickering** (See VISION - Flickering - vertigo)
  - **loss** of vision: **Acon** b7.de* agar bg2 alum b4a.de* anac k* ant-t b7.de* apis k* arg-met b7.de* arg-n k* arn b7a.de* ars b4a.de* asaf k* aur b4a.de *Bell* k* *Calc* b4a.de* canth b7.de* carb-an b4.de* *Cham* b7.de* chen-a k* chin c1 cic b7.de* cina b7.de* coff b7a.de* croc b7.de* crot-t dulc b4.de* **Ferr** b7.de* *Gels* hep k* *Hyos* b7.de* ign bg2 kali-n b4.de* *Laur* b7a.de merc k* mez b4.de* morph mosch b7.de* nat-m b4.de* nit-ac b4.de* **Nux-v** k* olnd b7.de* op b7.de* par b7a.de phos b4.de* *Puls* b7.de* rhus-t sabad b7.de* sabin b7.de* sang bg2 scol ah1 sec b7.de* squil b7.de* stram b7.de* sulph b4.de* ter thea thuj b4a.de zinc b4.de*
    - **morning**: scol ah1
    - **hearing**; and loss of: mosch bg2
- **vomiting**: *Acon* b7a.de* ail k* *Ant-c* b7a.de apis b7a.de *Ars* k* bell b4a.de* bry bg2* calad bg2 calc k* calc-p bg2 *Camph* bg2 *Canth* *Chel* k* cimic cocc bg2* con b4a.de crot-h crot-t cycl a1 euon bro1 eup-per bg2* *Glon* gran k* *Graph* k* *Hell* k* hydr-ac bg2 hyos b7.de* ign bro1 ip bg2 kali-bi k* kali-c *Lach* k* lyc b4a.de mag-c k* *Merc* mosch k* *Nat-s* *Nat-sal* sne *Nux-v* k* oena *Petr* k* phos bg2 pilo bro1 *Podo* bro1 *Puls* k* sabad **Sal-ac** sne *Sang* sars sel sep sil h2 streptoc jl2 stront-c bro1 sulph bg2 tab bg2* tell ther k* thuj b4a.de **Verat** k* *Verat-v* k* vip
  - **spasmodic**: caul c1
- **weakness** (See GENERALS - Weakness - vertigo)
- **worms**; complaints of: cina bro1 spig bro1

O - **Abdomen**; complaints in (See ABDOMEN - Complaints - accompanied - vertigo)
- **Back**; pain in: rad-br c11
- **Bones**; pain in: calc-p bg2

- **Brain**:
  - **anemia** of (See HEAD - Anemia - brain - accompanied - vertigo)
  - **complaints** of the (See HEAD - Brain; complaints of - accompanied - vertigo)
  - **congestion** of (See HEAD - Congestion - brain - accompanied - vertigo)
  - **edema** of (See HEAD - Edema - brain - accompanied - vertigo)
  - **inflammation** of (See HEAD - Inflammation - brain - accompanied - vertigo)
  - **movements** in brain; sensation of (See MIND - Delusions - brain - moving - vertigo)
- **Chest** | **pain** in: sars bg2 spig b7.de*
- **Ear**:
  - **complaints** of: arg-n bg2 camph bg2 caust bg2 *Chinin-s* bg2 cic bg2 cocc bg2 dig bg2 glon bg2 nux-v b7.de* onos bg2 *Phos* bg2 puls b7.de* sang bg2 sil bg2
  - **noises** in: (↗*Ménière's*) acon-c a1 alco a1 alum k* alum-p k2 arg-met *Arg-n* k* arn bg2 ars bar-m br1 bell k* benz-ac bg2 bism hr1 calc k* *Camph* k* cann-i a1 carb-v k* *Caust* chen-a bro1* *Chin* bg2 **Chinin-s** k* *Cic* k* *Cocc* k* coff-t hr1 colch com crot-h k* crot-t k* *Dig* k* euph bg2 *Gels* bro1 gink-b sbd1• *Glon* k* gran k* hell k* iris ptk1 kali-br hr1 kali-c kali-n c1 kali-p kali-sil k2 kalm k* kreos bg2 laur mag-c merc-cy a1 myric k* nat-ar nat-c k* nat-m k* nat-p nat-s k* nux-v k* op k* petr k* ph-ac k* **Phos** k* pic-ac k* psor k* ptel a1* puls k* sal-ac k* *Sang* k* seneg k* sep k* *Sil* k* stann *Stry* bro1 tab bg2 tep a1 ther bg2 valer bro1 zinc zinc-p k2
- **Epigastrium**; pain in: kali-bi bg2
  - **burning** pain: ang bg2
- **Extremities**; weakness of: arg-n bg2 con bg2 gels bg2
- **Eye**:
  - **closing** of eyes; involuntary: acon b7.de* ant-t b7.de* *Arg-met* b7a.de sabin b7.de
  - **complaints** of: acon b7.de* ant-t b7.de* sabin b7.de*
  - **fullness** over eyes (See HEAD - Fullness - forehead - eyes - above - vertigo)
  - **glassy**: ph-ac ptk1
  - **heaviness**: aids nl2• pitu-gl skp7•
  - **pain** in the: cimic hr1 ther k2
  - **sensitive**: graph bg2
  - **swelling** (See EYE - Swelling - accompanied - vertigo)
- **Face**:
  - **heat** of face: ant-c bg2 cham bg2 dulc bg2 petr bg2 ruta b7.de* sabad bg2
  - **pale**: crot-h bg2 crot-t bg2 *Dub* bro1 *Dubo-m* br1 lach bg2 led bg2 mag-c bg2 petr b4a.de* *Puls* b7.de* sel b7a.de* *Tab* bro1
  - **red**: *Aur* b4a.de iod bg2 nux-v bg2 stram b7.de*
- **Female** genitalia; complaints of (See FEMALE - Complaints - accompanied - vertigo)
- **Gastrointestinal**:
  - **complaints**: aloe bro1 *Bry* bro1 chin bro1 *Cocc* bro1 ip bro1 kali-c bro1 *Nux-v* bro1 *Puls* bro1 rham-cal bro1 *Tab* bro1
  - **irritation**: cupr bg2
- **Head**:
  - **flushes** of heat extending to top of head: lavand-a ctl1•
  - **fullness** in occiput (See HEAD - Fullness - occiput - accompanied - vertigo)
  - **heat** of head: aeth bro1 puls b7.de* sabin c1 spong b7.de
  - **heaviness** in head: aids nl2• ant-c br1 *Caust* b4a.de guat sp1 hir rsj4• lac-h sk4• *Mag-m* b4a.de rhod b4a.de [heroin sdj2]
  - **pain** in head: (↗*Ménière's*) acet-ac *Acon* k* adox mp4• aeth k* agar agro bro1 ail k* alumn am-m vh1 aml-ns bg2 anac ant-t k* anthraci antip vh1 **Apis** k* aq-mar skp7• arg-met b7.de* *Arg-n* k* *Arn* k* *Ars* k* ars-s-f k2* asaf k* asc-c c1 *Aur* k* aur-ar k2 aur-m k2* aur-s k2* bamb-a stb2.de• *Bar-c* k* **Bell** k* bism a1 *Bov* k* brom k* bros-gau mrc1 bry k* **Calc** k*

Accompanied by – **Head** – **pain** in head: ...
calc-ar bg* calc-f sp1 calc-i k2* *Calc-p* calc-s bg2 calc-sil k2* *Camph* bg2 canth b7.de* carb-an bg carb-v k* carbn-s carc zzh card-m bg2 *Caust* cham bg *Chel* k* chin bg2* chinin-s bro1 *Chlf* hr1 cimic cit-v br1 cob-n sp1 coca *Cocc* k* *Coff* k* coll tl1 **Con** k* croc bg2* crot-h k* *Cupr* k* cycl k* dig bg2 dulc h1* eug k* eup-per k2* *Eup-pur* bro1 ferr k* ferr-ar ferr-p fl-ac k* form k* *Gels* k* *Glon* k* graph b4.de* grat k* guat sp1 hell b7.de* *Hep* k* hipp jl2 hydrog srj2• hyos bg2 *Ign* b7.de* *Indg* hr1* iod bg2* iris tl1 kali-ar *Kali-bi* k* *Kali-br* k* *Kali-c* kali-chl bg2 kali-m bg kali-n b4a.de* kali-p kali-s kali-sil k2* *Kalm* k* kola stb3• lac-c bg2* lac-h htj1• lac-loxod-a hrn2• *Lach* k* lap-la sde8.de• lat-m bnm6• laur k* lept bro1 lil-t ptk1 lob lob-p bro1 lyc bg mag-c k* mag-m k* mag-s sp1 meli sne *Merc* k* merc-c b4a.de mosch b7a.de* mur-ac bg2* nat-c k* *Nat-m* k* *Nat-s* nit-ac b4.de* *Nux-m* **Nux-v** k* onos ptk1 ox-ac ozone sde2• parathyr jl2 petr c1 *Phos* k* pic-ac k* plat bg2 *Plb* k* plut-n srj7• podo bg2* propl ub1• psil ft1 *Psor* ptel c1 *Puls* k* ran-b bg2 rhus-g tmo3• rhus-t h1* ruta fd4.de sabal c1 *Sang* sec k* sep k* **Sil** k* *Spig* k* stram b7.de* stront-c b4.de* sulph k* symph fd3.de• *Tab* k* ther mrr1 tritic-vg fd5.de tub al* ven-m rsj12• verat bg2 *Verat-v* verb b7.de* xan k* *Zinc* k* zinc-p k2*
  - ⋮ **jerking** (See HEAD - Pain - jerking - accompanied - vertigo)
  - ⋮ **twinging** pain (See HEAD - Pain - twinging - accompanied - vertigo)
  - ⋮ **Forehead**: bism hr1 mand rsj7• *Ser-a-c* jl2 *Ven-m* rsj12•
    - : **pressure** | **amel.**: ven-m rsj12•
  - ⋮ **Occiput** (See HEAD - Pain - occiput - accompanied - vertigo)
  - **swelling**; sensation of: cob ptk1
  - **weakness**: caust b4a.de zinc b4a.de
- **Heart**; complaints of (See CHEST - Heart; complaints - accompanied - vertigo)
- **Kidneys**:
  - **inflammation** of (See KIDNEYS - Inflammation - accompanied - vertigo)
  - **pain** in: alum b4a.de
- **Meninges**; inflammation of (See HEAD - Inflammation - meninges - accompanied - vertigo)
- **Mouth**:
  - **dryness** of: plut-n srj7•
  - **spasms** of: mosch bg2
- **Nape** of neck | **pain** in: alum b4a.de
- **Nose**:
  - **discharge** from: calc-p bg2
  - **pressing** pain | **Root** of nose: bapt bro1
- **Occiput**; heaviness in (See HEAD - Heaviness - occiput - accompanied - vertigo)
- **Pelvic** organs; complaints of (See ABDOMEN - Complaints - pelvic - accompanied - vertigo)
- **Pupils**; dilated: crot-h bg2 gels bg2 verat-v bg2
- **Sinuses**; inflammation of: *Sil* mrr1
- **Stomach**:
  - **complaints** of: *Acon* bg2 ambr bg2 **Ant-c** bg2 arn bg2 *Bell* bg2 bry bg2 cham bg2 cocc bg2 eup-per bg2 form bg2 grat bg2 hell bg2 hydr-ac bg2 kali-c bg2 lob bg2 merc bg2 **Nux-v** bg2 petr bg2 **Puls** bg2 rhus-t bg2 ther bg2 verat-v bg2
  - **emptiness**: ozone sde2•
  - **gagging**: cyt-l sp1
  - **pain** in stomach: ambr b7a.de bry bro1 carb-v bro1 chin bro1 cycl bro1 *Grat* bro1 ign bro1 moni rfm1• *Nux-v* bro1 positr nl2• puls bro1 rhus-t bro1
    - ⋮ **pressing**: bism hr1 calc b4a.de
  - **weakness** in stomach | **lie** down; must: ambr c1*
- **Tongue**; white: sabad kr1*
- **Uterus**; complaints of (See FEMALE - Uterus - accompanied - vertigo)

AIR AGG.; DRAFT OF: calc-p mrr1

AIR; IN OPEN:
- **agg.**: acon act-sp aeth *Agar* k* *Alum* b4a.de ambr k* anac anag ang b7.de* arg-n hr1 *Am* b7a.de* ars k* aur aur-s c1* bamb-a stb2.de• bry calc k* calc-act bro1 canth k* *Caust* k* cocc crot-t cycl bg2* dros k* euph euphr bg2 gins *Glon* k* grat k* hydr-ac c1 hyos b7a.de indg c1 ip bg2 kali-ar kali-c k* *Kreos* k* lach k* laur k* manc merc b4.de* merc-c *Mur-ac* k* nicc nux-m bg2 nux-v bg2* ol-an k* olnd b7.de* *Phel* phos tl1 podo psor *Ran-b* k* ruta k* sabad k2 sars senec *Sep* k* sil k* spig b7.de* sulph k* tarax k*
- **amel.**: *Aeth* agar *Am-m* k* aur-m bell k* calc-s *Camph* carbn-s carl *Caust* k* clem conin c1 croc k* genist graph k* *Grat* k* hell hydr-ac hyos kali-bi k* kali-c k* kali-p *Kali-s* lil-t *Mag-m* k* mag-p bg2 mag-s manc merc k* mosch k* mur-ac k* *Nat-c* k* nicc oena ph-ac *Phel* phos k* plb k* *Puls* rhod b4.de* rhus-t b7.de* *Sanic* sil b4a.de* sol-ni staph k* *Sul-ac* k* sulfa sp1 *Sulph* **Tab** k* [sol-ecl cky1]
- **going** into; when: ran-b b7.de*

ALCOHOLIC drinks, from: caust **Coloc** kola stb3• **Nat-m** **NUX-V** k ● ruta fd4.de tritic-vg fd5.de verat
- **sensation** as if from: alum bg2 caust b4.de* *Coloc* bg2 *Nat-m* bg2 *Nux-v* bg2

ALCOHOLICS; in (See Drunkards)

ALTERNATING WITH:
- **colic**: coloc bro1 mag-c bro1 spig bro1 verat
- **sleepiness** (See SLEEP - Sleepiness - alternating - vertigo)
- O - **Kidneys**; pain in (See KIDNEYS - Pain - alternating - vertigo)
- **Teeth**; pain in: cocc-s kr1 merc

ANGER; after: *(↗MIND - Anger)* acon calc k* ol-an bg2

ANXIETY, during: *(↗MIND - Anxiety)* acon aloe k* alum k* arn asar bamb-a stb2.de• bell k* borx h2 *Cact* calc b4a.de caps bg2 *Caust* k* coff k* cypra-eg sde6.de• *Dig* k* ign k* kola stb3• *Lach* b7a.de lyc bg2 merc k* nux-m k* nux-v *Op* k* rhod k* rhus-t k* sel b7a.de *Sulph* k* vanil fd5.de zinc bg2

ARTERIOSCLEROTIC: thiosin br1

ASCENDING; sensation of: aids nl2• am-m *Asaf* asar borx hep laur lyc *Merc* nat-c nux-v olnd bg2 *Phos* k* *Plat* ran-b *Spig* sul-ac valer *Verat* [tax jsj7]

ASCENDING; when: bar-c bg2 borx calc mrr1 dirc k* sulph
- **descending**; and: phys ptk1
- **eminence**; an: borx k* **Calc** k* con gsy1 dig dirc a2 nat-m bg2 phos *Sulph* k*
- **lift**; with a: borx bnt ferr bnt gels bnt
- **stairs**: aloe k* ant-c k* apoc k* ars-h k* borx k* cain k* **Calc** k* carb-ac k* coca con bg2 dig b4.de* duboin ll1* ferr bg2 glon k* *Kali-bi* merc k* par k* phys bg3 pic-ac plat c1 positr nl2• sal-fr sle1• sulph k* tritic-vg fd5.de

AUDITORY (See Ménière's)

AURAL (See Ménière's)

BACK, comes up the●: *Sil* k*

BAD NEWS: | **from**: calc k2*

BALANCING; sensation of: calad ferr k* hist sp1 lact lap-la rsp1 merc suis-pan rly4• thuj k* ulm-c jsj8• zinc

BATHING:
- **after**: nat-m bg2 phys k* samb sol-a a1 sumb k*
- **during**: nat-pyru rly4•

BED:
- **bouncing** up and down in; sensation as if: bar-c c1 bell
- **going** to bed | **when**: nat-m sabad stram
- **in** bed | **agg.**: *Ars* b4a.de borx b4a.de carb-v b4.de* caust b4a.de chel bg2 mag-c b4a.de* nit-ac b4.de* nux-m bg2 *Nux-v* bg2 petr b4.de* ph-ac b4.de* phos b4.de* rhod bg2 sulph b4.de* thuj b4a.de
- **motion**; as if bed were in: arge-pl rwt5• bell bg2 lac-c bg2* lac-h sk4•
- **turning**; seems to be: kola stb3•

BEER; after: ferr a1 kali-n merc k* sulph k* symph fd3.de•

BEGINNING in nape of neck, or occiput: fl-ac b4a.de gels bg2* iber bro1 petr bg2* senec bg2 sil b4a.de*

BENDING head; on: hed sp1
- **backward**: clem c1 glon k* linu-c a1 ruta fd4.de seneg k* stram ptk1
  - **amel.**: ol-an bg2*

Bending head; on: ...
- **forward**: androc srj5• *Anth* vh1 bamb-a stb2.de• bell htc1 clem coca a2 ham a1 hist sp1 lac-h htj1• mag-m merc pic-ac ptel c1 rhus-g tmo3• *Sulph* symph fd3.de• tub c
  - **afternoon** | **17** h: bamb-a stb2.de•
  - **amel.**: hell a1 ol-an bg1

BLOWING THE NOSE AGG.: cod bg3* culx k* iod bg sep k*

BRAIN; deep in: chinin-s bg2 ran-b bg2

BREAD agg.: manc k* sec k*

BREAKFAST:
- **after** | **agg.**: bufo coc-c gels k* lyc k* phos scut a1* sel k* tarent k*
- **amel.**: *Alum* k* calc cinnb k* cocc bg2
- **before** | **agg.**: alum *Calc*
- **during**: con k* *Sil* k*
- **walking** rapidly; after: coloc

BREATHING:
- **deep**:
  - **agg.**: anac ptk1* arge-pl rwt5• *Cact* k* dulc fd4.de
  - **amel.**: acon podo fd3.de• tritic-vg fd5.de
  - **hindering** deep breathing: (non:cur bg1*) dulc fd4.de tritic-vg fd5.de vanil fd5.de

CAR; driving a: lavand-a ctl1•

CARRIED; on being: gels bg2

CARRYING; on: both-a rb3
- **burden** on head: tarent ptk1*

CAUSELESS: glycyr-g cte1•

CERVICAL: bamb-a stb2.de•

CHAGRIN; from (See Mortification)

CHILDREN; in: androc bnm2•

CHILL:
- **after**: colch k* sec k*
- **before**: *Ars* *Bry* corn-f br1 nat-m
- **during**: alum k* ant-t apis b7a.de* ars bg2* bell bg2 bry bg2 bufo bg2 **Calc** k* caps k* chel bg2 *Chin* k* cocc k* *Con* b4a.de* *Ferr* ferr-p gels psa *Glon* ip bg2 kali-bi lac-del hm2• laur k* led b7a.de* lyss med rb2 merc bg2 nat-m nux-m bg2 **Nux-v** k* op ptk ph-ac bg2 phos k* plb k* puls k* *Rhus-t* k* sep bg2 sulph k* verat k* viol-t k*

CHILLINESS; during: apom vh1 caps bg2 gels mag-c bg2 merc-c nept-m lsd2.fr rhus-t k*

CHRONIC: arn br1 **Bell** mrr1 cann-i ptk2 con j5.de nat-m *Nux-v* op j5.de parathyr jl2 **Phos** *Sec*
- **headache**; with one-sided: *Nat-m*

CHURCH; in: ars b4a.de

CLOSED eyes, cannot walk with: *(↗EXTREMITIES - Walking - impossible - eyes)* *Alum* st arg-n st ars st *Stram* st thuj st

CLOSING THE EYES:
- **agg.**●: *Alum* k* alum-p k2 alum-sil k2 *Alumn* k* aml-ns k* *Ant-t* k* *Apis* k* *Arg-n* k* **Arn** k* *Ars* k* bapt bg2 bell b4a.de* bit-ar wht1• calad k* cham **Chel** k* cycl ferr k* ferr-p gels bg2* grat k* *Hep* k* kali-p br kola stb3• **Lach** k* mag-p br1* mag-s merc bg2* mosch bg2 nat-m bg2* pen petr k* *Ph-ac* k* phos k* *Pip-m* plac-s rly4• psor al2 pycnop-sa mrz1 rhus-t sabad **Sep** k* *Sil* k* spong fd4.de *Stram* k* *Tab* bro1 **Ther** k* *Thuj* k* tritic-vg fd5.de verat-v bg2 vib zinc
  - **nausea**; with: *Lach* *Ther*
  - **opening** eyes; or: alum ptk1
  - **sitting**; while: thuj
- **amel.**●: acon bg2* aloe bro1 alum k* alumn br asar br coli rly4• **Con** k ●* dig ferr **Gels** k ● ger br1 graph lol br1* petr-ra shn4• phel *Pip-m* puls bg2* sang bg2* sel sep bg2* sulph tab k* verat-v k*
  - **lying**; while: *Lac-d*

COFFEE:
- **after**●: arg-n **Cham** k ●* cocc k* ephe-si hsj1• fic-m gya1 mosch k* **NAT-M** k ●* *Nux-v* k* phos k* podo fd3.de• symph fd3.de• tritic-vg fd5.de

- **amel.**: cann-i k*

COITION; after: bov b4.de* ph-ac k* sep k*

COLD:
- **applications** | **amel.**: nat-m k*
- **drinks**:
  - **after**:
    - **agg.**: colch bg2*
    - **amel.**: petr-ra shn4•
- **hands** | **with**: merc bg
- **room** | **amel.**: puls k2
- **water**:
  - **agg.** | **overheated**; when: *Ars Kali-c*

COLIC; alternating with (See Alternating - colic)

COLORED glass; from light shining through: art-v k*

CONCUSSION of brain, from: acon k* aloe vh1 *Arn* cic ll1

CONGESTION; from: *(↗HEAD - Congestion - brain - accompanied - vertigo)* **Acon** j5.de* aloe vh1 am-c bg2 aml-ns bg2 apis bg2 apoc bg2 *Arn* j5.de* **Bell** j5.de* bism bg2 borx bg2 cact k2 chin bg2 con bg2 cupr bg2 dig bg2* ferr bg2 ferr-p tl1 *Gels* j5.de* glon bg2* hell bg2* *Iod* bg2* kreos bg2 lac-ac bg2 *Lach* bg2 *Merc* bg2* nit-ac bg2 **Nux-v** j5.de* *Op* j5.de* phos bg2 *Puls* bg2 rhus-t bg2 sang bg2 sec bg2 sil bg2 *Sulph* bg2 uran-n bg2 verat-v j5.de* verb bg2

CONSCIOUSNESS; with loss of (See MIND - Unconsciousness - vertigo)

CONSTIPATION; during: aloe *Ambr* b7a.de bry k2* calc-f bg *Calc-p* k* chin k* crot-h k* indol bro1 nat-s nux-v b7a.de* sulph

CONTINUOUS: borx k* cyt-l ptk2 glycyr-g cte1• helo-s bnm14• kali-sil k2* nux-v bg2 olnd k* phos k* psor k* sec bg2 sil k* verat bg2

CONVERSATION: | **animated**, from: borx h2

CONVULSIONS; BEFORE EPILEPTIC: *(↗GENERALS - Convulsions - epileptic - aura - vertigo)* ars *Calc-ar Caust* **Hyos** indg bg *Lach Plb* sil bg *Sulph Tarent* gsy1 visc bg

CORYZA: | **after** coryza amel.: aloe

COTTON WOOL; sensation of: kola stb3• olib-sac wmh1

COUGH agg.; during: acon k* anac ptk1* ant-t k* ars bg2* calc k* *Coff* k* cupr *Kali-bi* k* kali-c b4a.de led *Mosch* k* naja k* nat-m vh nux-v k* psor bg2 sec b7a.de ther c1 thuj bg2*

CROSSING: | **running** water (See Water - crossing)

CROSSING A BRIDGE agg.: ang arg-n gl1.fr• bar-c k* brom k* *Ferr* k* lyss bro1* puls gl1.fr• *Sulph* k*
- **high** bridge; a: puls staph *Sulph*
- **narrow** bridge; a: bar-c k* ferr k* sulph k*
- **running** water (See Water - crossing)

CROWD, in: cupr sst3• nux-v *Phos* b4a.de

DANCING: dros bnt

DARKNESS:
- **agg.**: agar bg2 alum bg2* *Arg-n* bg2* kali-i ptk1 pic-ac bg2* stram bg2*
- **room** agg.; entering a dark●: agar arg-met bg *Arg-n* kali-i ptk2 *Stram* zinc bg
- **walking** in the darkness agg.: alum ptk1 apis ptk1 arg-n ptk1 gels ptk1 iodof ptk1 stram bro1* zinc ptk1

DESCENDING; as if: lac-loxod-a hrn2• [tax jsj7]
- **mountain**; a: cycl a1*

DESCENDING, on: aloe sne **BORX** k ●* coff con k* **Ferr** k* gels k* kali-p fd1.de• mag-m merl plat ptk1 sanic k* stann tarent ptk1 tritic-vg fd5.de vib ptk1
- **car**; in: bamb-a stb2.de•
- **stairs**: **BORX** k ●* bov bg2 carb-ac k* chr-ac cimic gk **Con** k ●* ferr b7.de* gins kali-p fd1.de• meph bro1 merc k* merl phys k* *Plat* k* positr nl2• *Sanic* bro1 stann bg2 tarent vib ptk2
  - **spiral** stair: sil ptk1

DIARRHEA: phos bg2

Diarrhea: ...
- **before** | **and** after: **Lyc** vh tritic-vg fd5.de

DILATED pupils, with: *Bell* hell teucr

DIM VISION; from (See Accompanied - vision - dim)

DINNER:
- **after** | **agg.**: acon k* aloe bell bufo coloc k* *Cycl* hr1 ery-a k* ferr k* *Hep* mag-s k* *Nat-s* **Nux-v** k* petr k* phos k* *Puls Rhus-t* h1* sel k* *Sulph* thuj k* tub al* vanil fd5.de *Zinc* k* zinc-p k2*
- **agg.**:
  - **rising** from; on: phos phys
  - **walking** agg.; after: *Cocc*
- **amel.**: *Arg-n* dulc sabad
- **during** | **agg.**: arn k* calc-p k* chel *Hep* k* *Mag-c Mag-m* k* mag-s nat-p fkr6.de olnd k* sil tritic-vg fd5.de

DIPLOPIA, with●: arg-n mp1• bell mp1• gels k* glon mp1• nux-v mp1• olnd k* phys bg2 vinc mp1•
- **looking** down; when: olnd

DIRT and garbage: | **sight** of; at: olib-sac wmh1

DISCHARGE:
- **nose**; from | **amel.**: aloe bg2

DOWNWARD motion; from (See Descending, on)

DRINKING:
- **agg.**: crot-t ptk1* *Lyc* k* mang k* *Sep* k*
- **amel.**: oxal-a rly4•
- **water** | **amel.**: op k* paeon bg

DRIVING: calc bg cocc bg dig bg hep bg lyc bg myos-a rly4• petr bg sil bg
- **curves**; on: galeoc-c-h gms1•

DRUNKARDS; in: asar gm1

EATING:
- **after**:
  - **agg.**: acon bg2 aloe *Alum* ambr k* aran bell k* bry k* bufo *Cham* k* chel chin coc-c k* *Cocc* k* cor-r k* cycl gels graph h2* **Grat** k* *Kali-bi Kali-c* k* kali-i kali-p kali-s *Lach* k* lyc mag-s merc k* nat-m k* *Nat-s* k* **Nux-v** k* *Petr* k* ph-ac k* *Phos* k* plb podo fd3.de• **Puls** k* *Rhus-t* k* sabad bg2 sanic sars vh scut sec bg2 sel sep k* sil h2* *Sulph* k* *Tarent* tub c1 zinc k*
  - **amel.**: alum k* anthraq rly4• arg-n cinnb cocc k* dulc k* kali-c bg kola stb3• lac-ac stj5• nux-v ptk1 ruta fd4.de sabad k* spong fd4.de tritic-vg fd5.de
- **before** | **agg.**: dulc b4.de* kali-c b4.de*
- **while** | **agg.**: am-c k* arn k* calc chel cocc bro1 con k* dios k* form k* **Grat** k* hep k* m-ambo b7a.de mag-c k* mag-m k* merc k* nat-c k* *Nux-v* k* olnd k* *Phos* k* puls bro1 sel sil k*

ELEVATED, as if: aloe k* calc k* camph b7a.de cann-i k* (non:cinnb a1) fic-m gya1 hyper k* mosch k* petr-ra shn4• phos k* rhus-t k* sil k* [tax jsj7]
- **evening**: phos k*
- **eating**; after: aloe k*

EMISSIONS agg.; after: bov k* calc caust k* nat-c nat-s ptk1 ran-b c sars k* sep h2*

EMOTIONAL excitement (See Excitement)

EMOTIONS agg.: sil b4a.de

ENTERING house: acon ars carb-ac clem sne lycps-v sne merc nux-v sne pall *Phos* plat *Puls* ran-b sil tab tarent sne
- **walking** agg.; after: arg-met plat tab

EPILEPSY:
- **after** (See GENERALS - Convulsions - epileptic - after - vertigo)
- **during** (See GENERALS - Convulsions - epileptic - during - vertigo)

EPILEPTIC: *(↗GENERALS - Convulsions - epileptic - during - vertigo; MIND - Unconsciousness - frequent)* *Apis* arg-n bro1 art-v k* bell j5.de bufo calc bro1* *Calc-ar* calc-s *Caust* crot-h k* *Cupr* bro1 *Cur* ign k* kalm bro1 *Nat-m Nux-m Nux-v* k* oena hr1 plb k* *Sil* k* sulph j5.de thuj k* *Visc* k*

EPISTAXIS: | **amel.**: brom bg2* carb-an ptk2 card-m bg2*

ERECTIONS during: ran-b c tarent k*

ERUCTATIONS:
- **after**: hep k* nux-v k*
- **during**: cycl a1 gymno k* hep bg2 nat-c bg2 nat-m nux-v k* psor al *Puls* sars

ERUPTIONS:
- **preceding**: cop k*
- **suppressed**: bell bry calc carb-v cham hep ip lach phos rhus-t *Sulph* k*

EXCITEMENT; emotional: acon bg2 calc bg2* op bg2 puls bg2*

EXERTION:
- **agg.**: ars k* berb bism both-ax tsm2 *Cact* k* calc-p k2* chin cop k* cycl dulc fd4.de kali-c kali-s fd4.de kalm k2* merc-c b4a.de mill ptk2 nat-c nit-ac petr-ra shn4• pieri-b mlk9.de ruta fd4.de sol-ni tritic-vg fd5.de vanil fd5.de
  - **air**; in open: (non:coff hs1) (non:nat-c hr1)
  - **violent** exertion: mill ptk1
- **amel.**: mill c1 phos k*
  - **air**; in open: coff hs1 *Nat-c* hr1
- **arms** agg.; of the: berb sep

EXERTION OF THE EYES agg.: all-s *Cur Graph* jab br1 *Mag-p* **NAT-M** k ● onos bg2* **PHOS** k ●* ruta mp1• *Sil* tarent mp1•

EXPIRATION:
- **mouth**; forceful expiration through the | **amel.**: *Phos* b4a.de

EYEBROWS; in: gels bg2

EYES; in: arg-n bg2 bell bg2 lil-t bg2

FAINT-LIKE (See GENERALS - Faintness - vertigo)

FALL, tendency to: *(↗EXTREMITIES - Fall liability; GENERALS - Fall; tendency)* *Acon* k* aeth a1 agar k* alum am-c k* *Ambr* b7a.de anac b4.de* ang apis arg-n bg2 arn k* *Ars* k* asar b7.de* bamb-a stb2.de• bar-c *Bell* k* berb k* both-ax tsm2 bov k* bros-gau mrc1 bufo k2 *Calc* k* calc-ar k1* calc-s camph b7.de* *Cann-i* bg *Cann-s* b7.de* canth b7.de* caps b7.de* carb-ac k* *Carb-an* k* *Carb-v* k* carbn-s caust k* cham b7.de* chin k* *Cic* k* *Cocc* k* coloc k* *Con* k* croc b7.de* crot-h k* *Cupr* k* dig h2* dros euph k* euphr k* *Ferr* k* ferr-ar gels k* *Glon* k* gran bg2 graph k* ham k* hell hep b4.de* hydr-ac bg2* *Hyos* ign b7.de* ip b7.de* kali-bi bg2 *Kali-br* hr1 kali-c k* kali-p kali-s k* kreos k* lac-h sk4• lach lact lat-m bnm6• laur k* led *Lyc* k* m-ambo b7.de mag-c *Mag-m* k* mag-s *Med* hr1 merc k* mez musca-d szs1 nat-c k* nat-hchls nat-m k* *Nat-n* nat-p k* nit-ac k* nux-m k* *Nux-v* b7.de* oena hr1 olnd b7.de* op b7.de* ozone sde2• petr-ra shn4• ph-ac k* *Phel* k* phos b4.de* phyt plb podo fd3.de• psil ft1 *Psor Puls* k* *Ran-b* k* rheum rhod k* *Rhus-t* k* ruta sabad k* *Sabin* k* *Sal-ac* sne sang a1 sarr hr1 sars k* *Sec* b7.de* sel b7a.de sep b4.de* *Sil* k* spig k* *Spong* k* squil stann b4.de* staph b7.de* *Stram* k* stront-c b4.de* *Sulph* k* symph fd3.de• tab tarent *Ter* k* tritic-vg fd5.de upa a1 *Zinc* k* zinc-p k2*
- **right**, to●: *Acon* k* arn b7a.de ars k* ars-s-f k2* *Bell* b4a.de both-a rb3 both-ax tsm2 *Calc* k* camph k* carb-an k* *Caust* k* eup-pur k* euph k* ferr fl-ac bg2 helo bg2* helo-s rwt2• kali-n k* lac-d c1* lycps-v k* lyss mill k* nat-s k* phel bg2 psil ft1* rhus-t k* ruta k* *Sil* k* til ban1• *Zinc* k*
  - **sitting** agg.: stram
- **left**, to●: anac k* *Aur* k* *Bell* k* *Borx* k* both-a rb3 both-ax tsm2 *Calc* calc-act bg2 *Caust* k* cic k* coloc bg2 *Con* bro1 cupr bg2 dirc k* dros k* *Eup-per* k* eup-pur k* euph k* flor-p rsj3• iod bg2* *Iris-foe* kola stb3• *Lach* k* lycps-v merl k* mez k* musca-d szs1 nat-c k* **Nat-m** k* nux-m k* nux-v b7a.de phel bg2 plut-n srj7• positr nl2• sal-ac k* sil h2* spig k* spong b7.de* stram k* *Sulph* k* vib k* vip *Zinc* k*
  - **morning**: zinc
  - **looking** upward: *Caust* k*
  - **sitting** agg.: anac k* spong fd4.de
  - **walking** in open air agg.: aur dros euph a1
- **morning**: ph-ac tl1 tritic-vg fd5.de
  - **waking**; on: *Graph* phos
- **forenoon** | **10h**: visc c1
- **backward**●: absin bg2* agar k* anan k* bell k* bov k* brom k* bros-gau mrc1 *Bry* k* *Calc* k* calc-sil k2* camph b7.de* *Carb-an* k* cassia-s ccrh1• *Caust* k* *Chin* k* chinin-s bg2* chir-fl bnm4• dios k* dub bg2* helo helo-s rwt2• *Kali-c* k* kali-n k* kali-s kali-sil k2* kreos bg2 led k* merc mill k* nat-m bg2 *Nux-v* k* oena k*

Fall, tendency to – **backward**: ...
Ph-ac k* phel k* podo fd3.de• *Rhod* bg2* **Rhus-t** k* sal-fr sle1• sars k* *Sil* k* spig b7.de* *Spong* k* stram k* stront-c bg2* sulph k* til ban1• visc bg2* [sol-ecl cky1]
  - **stooping** agg.: caust
  - **walking** agg.: stram
- **chair**, from: calc-caust c1 podo fd3.de•
- **darkness** agg.: *Stram*
- **direction** turned, in: alum-sil k2
- **fever**; during: *(↗EXTREMITIES - Fall liability - fever)* sep k*
- **forward**●: agar k* agath-a nl2• *Alum* k* alum-p k2* alum-sil k2* arn k* bell b4a.de bov k* bros-gau mrc1 *Bry* bro1 calc bg2 *Calc-p Camph* k* carbn-s carc fd2.de• card-m k* cassia-s ccrh1• *Caust* k* chel k* *Cic* k* con bg2 cupr k* *Elaps* k* *Ferr* k* ferr-p *Graph* k* guar bro1 hell k* hyos iod k* kali-n k* kali-p kali-s k2* *Lach* lat-h bnm5• led k* lyc k* lycps-v mag-c k* mag-m k* mag-p br1* mag-s k* mang k* **Nat-m** k* *Nux-v* k* petr k* *Ph-ac* k* phel k* phos k* *Podo* k* psil ft1 puls k* *Ran-b* k* **Rhus-t** k* ruta b7.de* *Sabin* k* sars k* sec senec *Sil* k* sol-t-ae a1 spig k* stram bg2* stry *Sulph* k* syph bg1* tarax k* tritic-vg fd5.de urt-u bro1 vib bro1 vip
  - **backward**; and: syph bg2 thuj bg2
- **high**:
  - **objects** leaned forward and would fall on him; as if high: arn sabad
  - **walls** fall on him; as if high: *(↗Walls)* arg-n sabad
- **looking** downward agg.: **Spig** k*
- **motion** agg.: sec
- **rising** | **bed**; from | **agg.**: **Rhus-t**
  - **sitting**; from | **agg.**: stram h1
- **sideways**: acon am-m k* amph a1 arg-n k* ars k* *Benz-ac* k* both-ax tsm2 bov k* **Calc** k* calc-act bg2 cann-s k* *Caust* k* *Cic* b7a.de **Cocc** k* *Con* k* cupr sst3• dros k* euph k* euphr b7.de* ip bg2 led k* mez k* **Nux-v** k* olnd b7a.de ph-ac b4a.de phel k* puls k* rheum k* *Sal-ac* sne sil k* squil k* staph k* sulph k* tarax bg2 tritic-vg fd5.de ulm-c jsj8• valer k* zinc k*
  - **walking** agg.: sul-ac
- **sleep** agg.; after: ferr
- **stooping** agg.: cic hr1 merl k*

FALLING; AS IF:
- **height**; from a: *Caust* k* dor hr1 *Gels* k* merl hr1 mosch k*
- **rising**; as if falling and (See height)

FASTING agg.: lac-ac stj5•

FEAR agg.: ther bg2

FEET rose; sensation as if: nat-m bg2 petr bg2 ph-ac h2 spig bg2 stict k13
- **as** if earth was slipping away under his: psil vml3•
- **as** if feet higher than head: spig ptk1*
- **head**; as if he stood on his: glon bg2 ph-ac bg2
  - **morning**, in bed | **closing** the eyes agg.: ph-ac h1

FEVER:
- **before**: arn b7a.de *Ars* b4a.de bell b4a.de bry b7a.de chin b7a.de nux-v b7a.de phos b4a.de puls b7a.de rhus-t b7a.de sulph b4a.de verat b7a.de
- **during**: *(↗FEVER - Vertigo)*
  - **agg.**: *(↗Heat - during; FEVER - Vertigo)* alum b4.de *Apis* b7a.de **Ars** b4.de* *Bry* b7.de* *Calc* b4a.de carb-v ptk1 chin b7.de* cocc ptk1 *Ip* b7a.de kali-c ptk1 laur b7.de *Nux-v* b7.de* phos b4.de puls ptk1 sep b4.de sulph b4.de *Verat* b7.de*
    - **stages**; all: eucal ptk1

FLATULENCE, with obstructed: calc h2*

FLOATING, as if: *(↗Walking - gliding - feet)* abel htj1• acon mp1• agath-a nl2• aids nl2• anthraq rly4• arg-n mp1• asar k* bell k* bit-ar wht1• bry rb2 calad ptk1 calc bg* *Calc-ar* k* calc-s bg1 camph cann-i bg* cann-xyz bg2 chir-fl gya2 cocain rb2 cocc coff mp1• euon bg2* fic-m gya1 ham bg2 hippoc-k szs2 hyos mp1• *Hyper* lac-ac stj5• *Lac-c* k* lac-del hrn2• lac-h htj1• *Lach* k* lact maias-l hrn2• *Manc* mang-p rly4• *Merc* ptk1 *Mez* mosch nat-m mp1• *Nux-m Op* ox-ac ptk1 pen rb2 petr ptk1 ph-ac mp1• phos phys mp1• pycnop-sa mrz1 rhus-t h1 *Sep* k* spig mp1• stict bg2* stram suis-em rly4• *Sulph* bg* tell bg1 thuj ptk1* *Valer* k* xan c1* zinc-i mp1• [tax jsj7]
- **air**; in the: mosch b7a.de

- **body** feels: maias-l hm2•
- **head** feels: stict bg2
- **lying** agg.: lac-c mrr1 ph-ac k2
- **sitting** agg.: xan c1
- **temples** feel: all-c bg2 coloc bg2 cycl bg2

FOLLOWED by:
- **epistaxis**: carb-an h2*
- **perspiration**: helo-s bnm14•
- **retching**: cassia-s ccrh1•

FOREHEAD; in: arn bg2* ars bg2 camph bg2 coca bg2 croc bg2* crot-t bg2 cypra-eg sde6.de• eucal bg2 euon bg2* gels bg2* glon bg2 hyos bg2 indg bg2 kali-bi bg2 nux-m bg2 *Phos* bg2* ran-b bg2 rheum bg2 rhus-t bg2 *Sulph* bg2* thlas bg2
- **right**: culx bg2

FORGETFULNESS; with: | **words** while speaking; of (See MIND - Forgetful - words - vertigo)

FRIGHT; after: *(↗MIND - Ailments - fright)* *Acon* k* aloe vh1 bamb-a stb2.de• crot-h k* *Op* k* ther bg

FRUIT; after: merc-c b4a.de

FULLNESS and aching in vertex: **Cimic** k*

GARGLING, while: carb-v k* *Caust*

GETTING out of a car: aids nl2•

GIDDINESS (See Vertigo)

GRASPS the nurse when carried; child: borx *Gels*

HAIR agg.; binding: sul-i ptk1

HEADACHE:
- **after**: apoc vh1 kali-bi a1 merc bg1* merc-sul c1 merl bg2* phos bg2*
  - **morning**: bov hr1* merc bg
- **before**: *Aran* hr1* *Aren* st calc bg* kali-bi bg phos bg plat hr1* plb ptk1 ran-b bg sep bg til bg*
  - **morning**: bov hr1*
- **during** (See Accompanied - head - pain)

HEAT:
- **before**: chin h1* sep h2*
- **during**: *(↗Fever - during - agg.)* acon k* *Alum* bg2 ang bg2 apis bg2 arg-met k* arn bg2 *Ars* b4.de* bamb-a stb2.de• bell b4.de* bry k* cadm-s k2 *Calc* bg2 *Carb-an* *Carb-v* k* chel bg2 chin k* *Cocc* k* corn-f br1 croc k* hell bg2 ign k* *Ip* b7a.de* *Kali-c* laur k* led k* **Lyc** b4.de* mag-m k* merc k* mosch k* nat-c bg2 nat-m bg2 nux-v k* oxal-a rly4• petr-ra shn4• ph-ac bg2 phos k* *Puls* k* rhus-t bg2 ruta fd4.de sep k* stram k* *Sulph* bg2 verat k*
- **from**: con k* ph-ac a1 ptel k* spong fd4.de
- **intermittent**, during: corn-f br1
- **room**; from (See Warm - room - agg.)
- **sensation** of heat; with:
  - **chest** and about heart; in: lachn
  - **chest** to throat; from: merc
  - **head**; in: kola stb3•
- **sun**; of the | **agg.**: *Agar* castn-v gels glon nat-c *Prot* jl2

HEATED; becoming: | **after**: merc-c b4a.de

HEMORRHOIDS:
- **after**: *Calc* hr1 chin k2 lach j5.de lyc j5.de **Nux-v** hr1 phos j5.de puls j5.de sulph j5.de
- **suppressed**: nux-v a

HIGH:
- **ceiling**; room with high: cupr-act bro1 cupr-ar ptk1
- **places**: *(↗MIND - High places - agg.)* *Arg-n* k* aur **Calc** k* calc-p dgt chinin-s dgt dendr-pol sk4• gels kali-c dgt manc vh *Nat-m* ph-ac vh* phos puls sil vh spig bnt staph **Sulph** vanil fd5.de *Zinc* k*

HOLD to something; must: kreos bg2 lach bg2 sabad bg2 verat bg2

HOLE; as if stepping into a (See Sinking - stepping)

HOUSE:
- **entering**; on (See Entering)
- **in**: agar am-m arg-met bell k* *Croc* crot-t k* cypra-eg sde6.de• kali-bi a1 *Lyc* *Mag-m* merc k* mur-ac k* nat-c par phos *Puls* sil stann staph sul-ac k*
  - **amel.**: *Agar* k* caust k* *Cycl* k* grat kreos k* merc sulph

HUNGRY, when: calam sa3• dulc glycyr-g cte1• *Kali-c* petr-ra shn4• sul-i ptk1

HYPOCHONDRIASIS; with (See MIND - Hypochondriasis - vertigo)

HYSTERICAL (See Nervous)

INJURIES of head; after: arn bg2* cic k* *Nat-s* k* op ptk1 rhus-t gk ruta bg2*

INSPIRATION:
- **deep**:
  - **agg.**: *Cact* k*
  - **amel.**: petr-ra shn4•

INTOXICATED; AS IF: abies-c a1* acet-ac *Acon* k* act-sp k* agar k* aids nl2• ail *Alum* k* alum-sil k2* am-c k* amyg hr1 *Anac* k* anan k* aq-mar rbp6 *Arg-met* k* *Arg-n* k* ars h2* asar k* *Aur* k* bamb-a stb2.de• bapt bg2* *Bell* k* benz-ac hr1 berb bov bg *Bry* k* caj *Camph* k* cann-i caps b7a.de* *Carb-ac* k* carb-v bg2 carbn-s cassia-s ccrh1• caust k* cench k2* *Cham* k* chel k* *Chin* k* chinin-s *Cic* clem k* **Cocc** k* *Coloc* gsd *Con* k* cor-r k* cori-r cot c1 croc k* crot-h cupr-ar hr1 cur k* cypra-eg sde6.de• dig falco-pe nl2• *Ferr* k* ferr-p *Gels* k* *Glon* k* *Graph* k* grat k* ham k* *Hydr* k* hydr-ac c1 *Hyos* k* *Kali-br* kali-c k* kali-i c1 kali-sil k2* kola stb3• kreos lac-h htj1• lach k* lact k* laur k* *Led* k* *Lil-t* lyc k* *M-arct* b7.de* m-aust b7.de mag-c h2* *Med* k* merc merl k* *Mez* mill hr1 mosch k* nat-m k* *Nux-m* k* **Nux-v** k* oena k* olib-sac wmh1 *Olnd* b7.de *Op* k* oxyt bro1 petr k* petr-ra shn4• *Ph-ac* k* phel k* phos k* phyt bg2 pieri-b mlk9.de plut-n srj7• psor hr1 **Puls** k* rhod *Rhus-t* k* sabad sal-fr sle1• sang a1 sarr a1 sars k* *Sec* k* sel k* sep k* *Sil* k* *Spig* k* *Spong* k* stram k* *Tab* k* tarax k* tep k* ter hr1 *Thuj* til k* valer
- **morning**: falco-pe nl2•
  - **waking**; on: falco-pe nl2•
- **evening** | **amel.**: bamb-a stb2.de•
- **driving** a car; after: bamb-a stb2.de•
- **waking**; on: falco-pe nl2•

JERK; sensation of a: m-ambo b7.de

KNEADING bread or making similar motions: sanic k*

KNEELING agg.: bros-gau mrc1 mag-c k* **SEP** k •* stram ther k2*

LEANING:
- **against** something | **agg.**: cycl k* *Dig* tub c
- **cheek** against hand; left: verb
- **head**: verb k*
- **must** lean: kreos bg lach bg sabad bg verat bg
  - **left**; to: lac-del hrn2•

LIFTING a weight: ant-t **PULS** k •*

LIGHT:
- **bright** light; in: agar a1*
- **colored**: art-v bg2*
- **gaslight**, from: *Caust* k*
- **room** with many lights; from being in a: nux-v
- **sunlight**; in: *Agar* b4a.de* aloe vh1 bell bg1 glon ptk1 kali-p ptk1* nat-c bro1*
  - **and** heat: acon k* *Agar* k* bell bg2 brom k* *Glon* k* kali-p bg3 *Nat-c* k* nux-v k*

LIGHT-HEADED (See Vertigo)

LIGHTNING, from: crot-h k*

LIVER disease; with: bry bro1 card-m bro1 chel bro1 *Merc* hr1 mur-ac k2* *Nux-v* hr1 *Podo* hr1

LOATHING of food; with: mosch b7a.de

LOATHING; with general (See MIND - Loathing - general - vertigo)

LOOKING:

- **right**, to: lec
- **back**; when looking: calc b4.de chel bg2 con b4.de* kali-c b4.de
- **concentrated**, focused: alum ptk1 caust b4.de* con bg2 manc bg2 olnd bg2* onos bg2 sabad bg2 sars b4.de* *Sil* bg2 tarent bg2
- **downward**: alum bg2 alumn k* ars ars-s-f k2* bamb-a stb2.de• bell bg2 *Borx* bro1 calad calc k* camph carb-v bg2 cham cina con cypra-eg sde6.de• ferr k* ferr-ar ferr-p graph *Kalm* k* lac-loxod-a hm2• mag-m mang bg2 mang-m k* merc nat-c nit-ac nux-v olnd k* ox-ac petr **Phos** k* podo fd3.de• psor al2* puls rhod rhus-t sal-ac sne salam sep k* **Spig** k* staph **Sulph** k* symph fd3.de• thuj tritic-vg fd5.de vanil fd5.de [pop dhh1]
  - **as** if: phos
- **either** way, right or left: calc bg2 *Con* k* kali-c bg2 lec olnd k* op k* sabad sil bg2 *Spig* k* sulph k* sumb k* thuj k*
- **light**; in colored (See Light - colored)
- **mirror**, into a (See Mirror)
- **movies**; at: cadm-met gm1
- **moving** object, at: *Agar* anac *Cocc* tl1* **Con** k ●* crot-c sk4• *Cur* graph *Jab* laur mosch nat-m olnd prot xyz60 sep *Sulph* thuj b4a.de
- **one** object; at: lach ptk1
- **plain**; at a large: cupr bg2 sep k*
- **revolving** objects, at: aids nl2• **Lyc** k ●*
- **sideways**: thuj b4a.de*
- **steadily**: all-s k* am-c ars *Caust* k* colch con bro1 *Cur Kali-c Lach* k* manc k* **NAT-M** k ●* olnd k* **Phos** k ● sars *Sil* **Spig** k* sulph tarent k*
  - **amel.**: *Dig* k* sabad k*
- **straight** ahead | **amel.**: olnd k*
- **turned**; with the eyes: **Spig**
- **upward**: aeth hr1* *Calc* k* calc-sil k2* carb-v *Caust* k* chinin-ar k* coloc bg2 crot-t k* *Cupr* k* cypra-eg sde6.de• dig digin a1 *Gran* bro1 *Graph* k* hist sp1 iod kali-p k* kali-s kalm bg2 *Lach* mur-ac nat-hchls *Nux-v* k* *Petr* k* **Phos** k* plat k* plb k* psor al2* **Puls** k* sal-ac sne *Sang* k* **Sel** b7a.de sep k* *Sil* k* *Spig* b7a.de stram syph c1* *Tab* k* *Thuj* k*
  - **high** buildings; at: *Arg-n*
  - **light**; at a: chinin-m c1 cupr plb thuj zinc
  - **walking** in open air agg.: *Arg-n* ox-ac *Sep* k*
- **water**; at running (See Water - looking)
- **window**, out of a: camph *Carb-v* k* **NAT-M** k ● ox-ac k*

LOSS of fluids: calc j5.de *Chin* hep j5.de **Phos** k* puls j5.de *Sep* sulph j5.de verat c1

LYING:

- **agg.**: abrom-a ks5 aids nl2• ail bg2* alumn am-c *Apis* k* arge-pl rwt5• ars k* aur bar-c bar-i k2* brom calad k* calc k* calc-sil k2* carb-an bg2 *Carb-v Caust* k* *Cham* k* coca **Con** k* *Crot-c* cycl k* dig ferr b7.de* graph bg2 ham k* hell bg2 iod k* kali-bi bg2* kali-m bg2* lac-c bg1 lac-d *Lach* k* lact m-ambo b7a.de mag-c merc k* merc-c b4a.de merl k* mosch bg nat-c k* nat-s *Nit-ac* k* nux-v k* orot-ac rly4• ox-ac k* petr k* petr-ra shn4• ph-ac k2* phel k* phos k* pic-ac k* plac-s rly4• podo fd3.de• polyg-h bg1 *Puls* k* rhod k* *Rhus-t* k* ruta fd4.de sang k* sep k* sil k* spig spong fd4.de staph k* streptoc jl2 stry k* sul-i k2* sulph k* *Sumb* k* *Thuj* k* tritic-vg fd5.de [heroin sdj2]
  - **feet** were going up; as if: *Ph-ac* stict
  - **opening** the eyes; and: lac-d c1
  - **sinking** down through or with the bed; as if: acetan vh bell benz-ac **Bry** *Calc-p* chinin-s dulc kali-c *Lach Lyc* mosch nat-c rhus-r c rhus-t sacch
  - **touch** the bed; as he did not: (↗*MIND - Delusions - bed - touch)* **Lac-c**
- **amel.**: acon k* alum alum-p k2 alum-sil k2 alumn apis bro1 *Arn* k* atha bro1 aur bro1 aur-m *Bell* b4a.de *Bry* bg2* *Carb-an* k* carb-v bg2 cassia-s cdd7*• cham b7.de* *Chin* k* chinin-s bg2 cic *Cina* k* cocc k* crot-h cupr k* grat ham kalm lac-cp vml2• lach *Lyc* bg2 marb-w es1• med c1* nat-m k* nat-sal sne nit-ac k* olnd op k* ozone sde2• petr k* petr-ra shn4• phel k* phos k* positr nl2• pot-e rly4• psil ft1 puls bg2* rhus-t k* ruta fd4.de sil k* *Spig* b7.de* stann sul-ac k* tell thuj k* tritic-vg fd5.de verat-v bg2
- **back**; on:
  - **agg.**: *Alumn* k* anan *Merc* k* merc-sul k* *Mur-ac* k* nux-v k* *Puls Sil* sulph k*

Lying – back, on: ...

  - **amel.**: lac-h sk4• stram vesp br1*
    - ⁝ **cool** room; in a: castn-v
- **bed**; in | **agg.**: m-ambo b7.de mosch b7.de* *Nux-v* b7.de* rhus-t b7a.de staph b7.de*
- **face**; on the:
  - **agg.**: phos
  - **amel.**: *Coca*
- **head** high; with the | **amel.**: nat-m *Petr* phos bg
- **head** low; with the | **agg.**: nat-m bg2 petr b4.de* phos b4.de*
- **must** lie down: *Ambr* ant-t *Aran* asaf k* *Aur* k* aur-s k2 bry bg2 cassia-s ccrh1• caust h2 chel **Cocc** k* crot-h cupr *Graph* k* helo-s bnm14• *Kali-c* kali-p kali-s kali-sil k2 kalm kreos laur merc mosch k* nat-c k* nat-m nat-s ptk1 *Nit-ac* k* op k* petr-ra shn4• **Phos** k* phys bg2 **Puls** k* sabin sec *Sil* spig bg2* *Sul-ac* tritic-vg fd5.de zinc
- **side**; on:
  - **agg.**: lac-h sk4• stram
  - **amel.**: merc k*
  - **left** | **agg.**: alum bg2 alumn *Iod* k* lac-d bg2* naja oss• onos bg2* **Phos** k●* *Sil* k* zinc bg3 zinc-i ptk1
  - **right**:
    - ⁝ **agg.**: eup-per bg2* **Gels** ●* hell bg1 *Mur-ac* k* *Phos* vh* **Rhus-t** ●* tub xxb
    - ⁝ **amel.**: alum bg2 *Alumn* k* lach bg2 tritic-vg fd5.de

LYING DOWN: | **after** | **agg.**: cham bg2 cina bg2 ferr bg2 graph bg2 *Lach* b7a.de m-ambo b7.de mosch b7.de* nit-ac bg2 nux-v b7.de* puls bg2 *Rhus-t* b7.de*

- **agg.**●: adon bro1 apis bro1 **Bell** k ● brom calad bro1 caust h2 *Con* bro1 ferr kalm lac-d k2 lach bro1 nat-m bro1 nit-ac **Nux-v** k ●* olnd ox-ac petr-ra shn4• rhod bro1 **Rhus-t** k ●* ruta fd4.de sabad sang sil bro1 staph bro1 *Ther* bro1 thuj bro1 tritic-vg fd5.de

MÉNIÈRE'S DISEASE: *(↗Accompanied - ear - noises; Accompanied - head - pain)* aml-ns htc1 apom htc1 arg-n mtf11 arn bro1* aur ptk1 bar-m bro1 bell mrr1 benz-ac ptk1 bry bro1* carbn-s bro1* caust bro1* chen-a br1* chin bwa1* *Chinin-s* bro1* *Chinin-sal* bro1 cic htc1 cocc mrr1 con bro1 crot-h hr1* eucal ptk1 ferr-p bro1 gels bro1 hydrobr-ac bro1 kali-i bro1 kali-m ptk1 kalm htc1 kreos c1 morg-p pte1• nat-sal br1* onos bro1 petr bro1 phos mrr1 pilo c1* prot jl2 pyrus bro1 rad-br ptk1 rhod tl1 sal-ac br1* *Sil* bro1* sulfa mtf11 syph jl2 tab bro1* ther bro1* thyr ptk1 tub jl2

- **accompanied** by | **migraine**: cocc mtf11
- **seasickness**; as if: tab ptk1

MENOPAUSE:

- **after**: con vh
- **during**: con vh *Crot-h* vh *Glon* bro1* lach bro1 *Sang* hr1* tril-p bro1 *Ust* bro1*

MENSES:

- **absent**; with: gels c1
- **after** | **agg.**: agar k* all-s vh ant-t k* con k* *Lach* bg2 nat-m puls k* ust k*
- **before** | **agg.**: acon k* agn k* all-s vh am-c bg2 borx k* bov k* bry calc k* *Calc-p Caul* k* chel k* cimic bg2 cocc bg2 *Con* k* *Cycl* b7a.de* graph b4a.de* *Lach* k* lyc bg2 nat-m bg2 nux-m k* nux-v bro1 phos k* *Puls* k* sep bg2 stann bg2 sul-i ptk1 *Sulph* bg2 tarent bg2 thuj bg2 *Verat* k* *Zinc* zinc-p k2
- **during**:
  - **agg.**: *Acon* k* aesc bg2 aloe bg2 alum bg2 am-c k* aml-ns bg2 ant-t apis bg2 arg-n arn bg2 ars bg2 *Bell* bg2 borx k* bov brom k* cact k* *Calc* k* calc-p k* carb-v k* carbn-s caul k* *Caust* k* cham bg2 chin b7a.de cic bg2 cocc bg2 *Con* k* *Croc* k* crot-t bg2 cub *Cycl* k* elaps k* ferr k* *Ferr-p Gels* k* glon bg2 graph k* hep bg2 hyos bg2 *Iod* k* ip bg2 *Kali-bi* k* kali-c bg2 kreos tl1 *Lach* k* lil-t bg2 lyc k* mag-c bg2 mag-m bg2 mang bg2 merc bg2 mosch k* nat-m bg2 nit-ac bg2 nux-v k* ozone sde2• petr bg2 *Ph-ac* k* *Phos* k* plat k* **Puls** k* rhus-t bg2 sang bg2 sars bg2 *Sec* sep bg2 sil bg2 spong fd4.de stann bg2 stram bg2 sul-i k2* *Sulph* k* tarent bg2 tell bg2 thuj k* tril-p (non:uran-met k) uran-n k* ust verat b7.de* zinc bg2
    - ⁝ **profuse** menses: *Calc* ptk1 ust ptk1
    - ⁝ **stooping** agg.: calc k* caust k*
    - ⁝ **stooping** and rising again; when: *Calc* k*
    - ⁝ **walking** agg.: phos k*
  - **amel.**: all-s k* *Caust* a1 lach
  - **beginning** of menses | **agg.**: iod b4.de* phos b4.de*

- **suppressed** menses; from: *Acon* aloe vh1 bry calc cimic con **Cycl** k* gels lach nux-v phos plat **Puls** k* sabin k* sep sil sulph verat zinc

MENTAL EXERTION: *(↗MIND - Mental exertion - agg.)*

- **agg.**: *(↗MIND - Mental exertion - agg.)* *Agar* k* agn am-c k* anac bg2 arg-met k* *Arg-n* k* arn k* bar-c *Borx* k* calc calc-p k2 calc-sil k2 cham k* cocc bg2 coff k* cupr k* gran k* grat k* ham fd3.de• kalm merc bg2 merc-i-f **Nat-c** k* **Nat-m** k* nat-p k* nat-sil fd3.de• nux-m bg2 **Nux-v** k* *Ph-ac* k* phos bg2 pic-ac k* *Puls* k* sep k* sil k* *Staph*
- **amel.**: phos k*

MERCURY; from abuse of: *Dulc* b4a.de

MIRROR, after looking into: aids nl2• kali-c k*

MORTIFICATION; from: calc k2

MOTION:

- **agg.**: *Agar* ail k* aloe k* *Am-c* am-m k* arge-pl rwt5• arn k* *Aur* k* aur-m bar-c k* *Bell* bism b7.de* bism-sn a1 brom bg2 **Bry** k* *Calc-p* carb-ac carb-an bg2 *Carb-v* k* cassia-s ccrh1• *Chin* k* cob-n sp1 *Cocc* k* *Coff* *Con* k* crot-c sk4• crot-h k* crot-t cupr k* cycl hr1 cystein-l rly4• dig bg2 dulc fd4.de euphr b7.de* ferr bg2* ferr-i fl-ac gels *Glon* k* *Graph* grat k* hed sp1 *Hep* hist sp1 hydr-ac kali-bi bg2 kali-br bg2 kali-c b4a.de kali-s fd4.de *Kalm* k* laur k* lol bg2 lycps-v *Mag-c* k* mag-p br1 *Med* k* nat-ar nat-c nat-m k* nat-ox rly4• nux-v k* oreo c1* oxeod a1 paeon k* phel k* *Phos* k* phys phyt bg2 pic-ac bg2 pitu-gl skp7• *Puls* k* ruta fd4.de sabad k* sang *Sanguis-s* hm2• sec k* sel k* sep bg2 *Sil* k* sin-n sol-ni spong staph sumb tab k* tell k* ther k* tritic-vg fd5.de tub rb2 vanil fd5.de visc sp1 zinc bg2 [bell-p-sp dcm1]
  - **sudden** motion: *Calc* bg2 *Con* bg2 cypra-eg sde6.de• dulc fd4.de ferr gels k* granit-m es1• kali-bi bg2 kali-c bg2 lact orot-ac rly4• phos bg2 ptel k* ruta fd4.de sang bg2 sumb k* tub rb2 vanil fd5.de
  - **vomiting** and nausea: pitu-gl skp7• sel *Ther*
- **amel.**: chinin-ar c1 coff k* cycl k* kali-p fd1.de• mag-m k* phos bg1 ptel c1 rhod k* tritic-vg fd5.de
- **arms**; of | **agg.**: bar-c k* berb dulc fd4.de sep k*
- **bed** in motion; as if (See Bed - motion)
- **continued** motion | **amel.**: bry bg2
- **eyelids**; of | **agg.**: alum chinin-s vh mosch k*
- **eyes**; of:
  - **agg.**: bell chel cocc *Con* cypra-eg sde6.de• *Mur-ac* k* petr plat k* puls spig
  - **sideways** agg.: visc sp1
- **floor**; as from motion of the: gink-b sbd1• sulph bg2*
  - **waves**; floor is moving in: bamb-a stb2.de•
    - **afternoon** | **17** h: bamb-a stb2.de•
    - **fright**; with: bamb-a stb2.de•
- **head**; of:
  - **agg.**: acon k* *Agar* k* aloe am-c k* *Arn* k* atro aur *Bar-c* k* *Bell* k* **Bry** k* *Calc* k* calc-ar carb-an *Carb-v* k* caust chin bg2 clem cob-n sp1 cocc coloc bg2 **Con** k* cupr cypra-eg sde6.de• dig ptk1 echi ferr-p bg2 *Glon* grat bg2 hed sp1 *Hep* hydrog srj2• *Ign* ip kali-bi k* kali-br ptk1 kali-c k* *Lac-d* k* lil-t ptk1 meph mosch k* nat-m k* paeon *Phos* pitu-gl skp7• *Ptel* rhus-t ruta fd4.de samb k* sang k* sel sep spig k* staph bg2 symph fd3.de• tell ther thuj tritic-vg fd5.de verat b7.de*
    - **rapid** motion: adon br1 am-c atro bar-c *Bry* **Calc** calc-s *Carb-v* *Coloc* *Gels* helo helo-s rwt2• ign gk *Kali-c* kreos lac-ac merc sang k* spig *Staph* sulph verat xan c1
  - **amel.** | **rapid** motion: agar
  - **backward** | **agg.**: con bg2
  - **sideways**: con bg2
- **objects** were moving; as if: *Sep* b4a.de
- **slight** motion | **agg.**: asar mrr1 bry mrr1 kali-s fd4.de kalm k2
- **slightest** motion agg.: bell bg2* brucel sa3• carb-v bg2* gels bg2* morph bg2* mosch bg2* ther bg2* thuj ptk1 zinc bg2*
- **violent** motion:
  - **agg.**: bism bg2 phos bg2
  - **amel.**: phos bg2

NARROW places agg.: arg-n bg2

NAUSEA:

- **after**: calc k* cimic gran lyss *Zinc*

Nausea: ...

- **with**: abrom-a ks5 **Acon** k* agar ail k* *Alum* k* alum-p k2 alum-sil k2 *Alumn* *Am-c* k* aml-ns k* amyg ang bg2 *Ant-c* k* ant-t k* apis k* aran-ix sp1 arg-met b7.de* arg-n k* arge-pl rwt5• arist-cl sp1 *Arn* k* ars k* ars-s-f k2 bamb-a stb2.de• *Bapt* *Bar-c* k* *Bell* k* borx brom *Bry* k* cain calad k* *Calc* k* *Calc-p* k* *Calc-s* calc-sil k2 *Camph* k* *Carb-an* k* *Carb-v* cassia-s ccrh1• *Caust* *Cham* k* *Chel* chin k* chinin-ar **Chinin-s** k* cimic *Cinnb* coca **Cocc** k* coff b7.de* colch tl1 coli rly4• coloc *Con* conch fkr1• convo-s sp1 crot-c sk4• crot-h k* crot-t k* *Cycl* cyt-l sp1 ergot mtf11 euon bro1 eup-per k2 falco-pe nl2• **Ferr** k* *Ferr-ar* ferr-p fl-ac k* form bg2 gels *Glon* gran bg2* *Graph* k* gymno *Ham* k* *Hell* k* *Hep* k* hist mtf11 hydrog srj2• hyos b7.de* *Ind* indg br1 irid-met srj5• kali-ar *Kali-bi* k* *Kali-br* k* kali-c k* kali-p kali-s kali-sil k2 *Kalm* kola stb3• *Lac-c* k* lac-h htj1* *Lach* k* lappa ptk1 lepr mtf11 *Lob* k* *Lyc* k* *Lyss* mag-c k* melal-alt gya4 *Merc* k* *Mosch* k* *Mur-ac* k* myric *Nat-m* k* nat-ox rly4• *Nat-s* nat-sil fd3.de• nept-m lsd2.fr nicc nicotam rly4• *Nit-ac* k* *Nux-m* *Nux-v* k* olib-sac wmh1 ozone sde2• penic mtf11 **Petr** k* *Phos* k* phyt bg2 pic-ac pilo bro1 plat h2 *Podo* bro1 positr nl2• pot-e rly4• psor al2* ptel bg2* *Puls* k* pycnop-sa mrz1 *Rhus-t* rumx ruta fd4.de sabad k* **Sal-ac** sne *Sang* k* sanic sars k* sel k* senec *Sep* *Sil* k* *Spig* k* spong k* squil k* *Staph* stram streptoc jl2 stront-c k* sulfa sp1 *Sulph* k* *Tab* k* tarent tell *Ter* tere-la rly4• *Ther* k* thuj b4a.de tritic-vg fd5.de tub al* vanil fd5.de *Verat* *Verat-v* k* vip xan c1 *Zinc* zinc-p k2 [bell-p-sp dcm1 heroin sdj2 tax jsj7]
  - **morning**: *Calc* nat-sil fd3.de• nicotam rly4• nit-ac h2 sabad squil stront-c tritic-vg fd5.de
    - **8** h: pitu-gl skp7•
    - **14** h; until: pitu-gl skp7•
  - **evening**: zinc h2
  - **accompanied** by | **Liver** abscess (See ABDOMEN - Abscess - liver - accompanied - vertigo)
  - **closing** the eyes agg.: falco-pe nl2• *Lach* *Ther*
  - **intoxicated**; as if: cupr bg2
  - **looking** long at one object: *(↗STOMACH - Nausea - looking - moving)* sars
  - **lying**:
    - **agg.**: ars puls k2
    - **amel.**: convo-s sp1
    - **back** or on right side agg.; on: *Mur-ac*
    - **head** low; with the | **agg.**: *Petr*
  - **middle** of chest: bry phos
  - **motion** agg.: nicotam rly4• positr nl2• sel [pop dhh1]
  - **periodical**: **Nat-m**
  - **raising** head agg.: *Merc*
  - **reading** in a car; while: bamb-a stb2.de•
  - **rising** in bed, on: bry **COCC** k ● *Verat-v*
  - **stooping**:
    - **agg.**: mill a1*
    - **amel.**: *Petr*
  - **waking**; on: *Spong*

NERVOUS affections, with: ambr c1* arg-n bro1 arn bg2 *Asaf* bro1 bell bg2 both-a rb3 caj c1 cham bg2 chin bg2 cic j5.de cina bg2 cocc j5.de* con j5.de cycl hr1 ferr mtf11 gels c1* hep bg2 ign c1* kali-p c1 lup br1 lyc j5.de mosch bg2 nux-v bg2* phos j5.de* *Puls* bg2 rhus-t bg2* ther c1* valer bro1 zinc-p c1

NOISE; from: *(↗MIND - Sensitive - noise; MIND - Sensitive - noise - vertigo)* asar k* carc fd2.de• nux-v bro1 *Ther* k*

OBJECTS:

- **approach** and then recede; seem to: *(↗VISION - Approach)* cic
- **far** off; seem to be too: *(↗MIND - Distances - inaccurate; MIND - Size - incorrect)* anac k* gels hr1 **PULS** k ● stann k* stram
- **inverted**: bufo gels hr1
- **large**: caust
- **move**: bamb-a stb2.de• brass-n-o srj5• *Cocc* gink-b sbd1• hydr-ac kali-cy mosch sep thuj
  - **right**; to the: *Lac-d* nat-s sal-ac
  - **left** and downward; to the: tab
  - **seat** on which he sat; the: zinc

- **move**: ...
  - **side** to side, seem to: cic hr1
- **reel**: anac *Bell* *Bry* glon nat-p fkr6.de
- **run** into each other: iris-fl
- **stand** still; seem to: dulc h2
- **turn** in a circle; seem to: *Agar* agn aids nl2• *Alum* alum-p k2 am-c anac arn bar-c bar-m bar-s k2 bell k2 bov *Bry* cadm-s k* **Chel** *Cic* k* coca cocc colch con k* **Cycl** eupi kr1 hell kali-c kali-n h2 kali-p kali-s kali-sil k2 laur lil-t k2 *Lyc* mag-c merc merc-i-r morph mosch *Mur-ac* **Nat-m** nat-p nat-s *Nux-v* olnd op ph-ac *Psor* k* rhus-t sabad k* sel sep sil sol-ni sul-ac **Verat** hr1 zinc h2
  - **air** agg.; in open: *Mur-ac* hr1
  - **looking** at running water; on: *(↗Water - looking)* ferr
  - **room** whirls●: alum h2 cadm-s br1* **Calc** k ● calc-caust c1 cann-s **Caust** k ● cod dub grat kali-bi lac-cp sk4• merc h1 **NUX-V** k ● **Phos** k ● positr nl2• ruta fd4.de sil h2 spong fd4.de tab
  - **walking** agg.: arn br1
- **vibrate**: *Carb-v*

OCCIPITAL●: ang k* bamb-a stb2.de• bell gsy1 bry bg2* cann-xyz bg2 carb-v k* chin k* con bg* crot-h bg2 crot-t bg1 cypra-eg sde6.de• fl-ac **Gels** k* gins bg2* glon k* iber bg2* led bg2* med k* onos bg2* petr k* pic-ac bg2* ran-b k* senec **Sil** k* sphing k* spig k* sulph bg2* tab bg2* thuj bg2* verat bg* *Zinc* k*
- **turning**; when: bamb-a stb2.de•
- **writing** agg.: sphing kk3.fr

ODORS:
- **agg.**: *Phos* b4a.de
- **flowers** agg.; of: *Hyos* k* **Nux-v** k* **Phos** k*

OIL, fumes of: sabal c1

OLD PEOPLE; in●: alum bg2* *Ambr* k* arn bg2* *Ars-i* bro1 aur bg2* *Bar-c* k* bar-m bro1 bell c1 bell-p br* bry ptk1 calc-p k* con bg2* *Cupr* k* dig bro1 fl-ac bg2* galph dx1 glon bg gran bg2* *Iod* bro1 op bro1* phos bg2* **Rhus-t** k ●* sec bg2 *Sin-n* k* stroph-h br1 sulph bro1

OPENING eyes (See Closing - agg.)

PAIN:
- **after**: cimic bg2*
- **before** pain; vertigo agg.: ran-b bg2*
- **during**: *Cycl* b7a.de phos bg2 sil bg2 stann bg2

PAINFUL: phos k* sil a1 tab k* tarent k*

PALPITATION, during (See CHEST - Palpitation - vertigo)

PARALYSIS, before: olnd ptk1

PAROXYSMAL: agar k* aloe ant-t k* *Arg-met* asar vh bell h1* borx h2 calc k* camph h1* caul k* con a1 cupr k* cur bg2 cypra-eg sde6.de• glon bg2 graph h2* kali-bi k* kali-s fd4.de morph k* *Nat-m* k* *Nux-v* k* phos h2* plat k* ptel k* sep h2* sil tab k* thuj bg2 til k* verb h* [tax jsj7]

PERIODICAL: agar ang k* *Arg-met* k* *Camph* k* *Cocc* k* cycl k* gels bg1 *Ign* k* *Kali-c* k* **Nat-m** k* **Phos** k* *Tab* ust
- **every** two weeks: cocc
- **short** time; for: atra-r skp7*•

PERSPIRATION: ign b7.de* *Ip* b7a.de lap-la rsp1 rhus-t b7.de* ruta fd4.de ther k2 verat b7.de*
- **amel.**: nat-s ptk1

PLUMS; after: *Merc-c* b4a.de

PREGNANCY agg.; during: alet bg2* ars bell br1* cocc bro1 *Gels* k* lac-d bg* **Nat-m** k* nux-v bro1 phos

PRESSURE:
- **amel.**: convo-s sp1
- **cheek** agg.; pressure on left: verb b7.de*
- **head**; on | **amel.**: stict bg2

PUBERTY: stroph-h

PULSE: | **slow**: dig mrr1 ther c1*

PUSHED forward, as if: calc h2* euon ptk1 ferr b7.de* ferr-p ckh1
- **closing** the eyes agg.: ferr a1*

RAISING: *(↗HEAD - Hold - up)*
- **arms** | **agg.**: ars bg2 bar-c b4.de* both-ax tsm2 sep bg2 sil bg2

Raising: ...
- **hands** above head | **agg.**: onos ptk1
- **head**: *(↗HEAD - Hold - Up)*
  - **agg.**: *(↗HEAD - Hold - up)* acon k* aeth ant-t k* *Arn* k* bar-c **Bry** k* cact *Calc* k* carb-an *Carb-v* *Chin* *Chinin-s* sne clem cocc bg2 coloc croc hell jatr-c lac-d bg laur mag-s merc merc-c k* morph bg2 *Nux-v* olnd bg2 op *Phos* phyt bg2 pic-ac rhus-t bg2 sal-ac sne sel spig vh stann stram symph fd3.de• verat-v bg2
    - **waking**; from bed on: spig vh

REACHING with the hands up, on: ars bg1 bar-c both-a rb3 cupr bg1 lac-d *Lach* k* sep bg1 sil bg1 sulph

READING:
- **after**: kali-c k* ph-ac k*
- **agg.**: all-s ptk1 aloe vh1 *Am-c* k* ang k* arg-met k* arn k* calc-act bg2 cupr k* *Cur* gran k* *Graph* k* grat k* ham k* hera c1 kali-c bg2 melal-alt gya4 merc-i-f k* merl nat-m bro1 (non:neon srj5) par k* ph-ac bg2 phos bg2 phys k* sars bg2 spong fd4.de stann symph fd3.de•
  - **straightening** spine amel.: neon srj
  - **walking** | **amel.**: am-c k*
- **aloud** | **agg.**: manc k* par k* stann bg2
- **long** time; for a: arn

REELING: acon k* *Agar* k* ail bg2 *Alum* k* anac arg-n bg2* *Ars* k* bamb-a stb2.de• bapt bg2 bar-c bg2 *Bell* k* borx bg2 bruc j5.de bry k* calc h2* camph k* cann-s b7.de* *Caps* k* carb-an b4.de* *Caust* k* cham b7.de* chel a1 chin b7.de* *Cic* k* cimic cocc j5.de con b4.de* croc k* cupr k* dulc b4.de* euph b4.de* euphr bg ferr k* form bg2 gels bg2* *Glon* graph h2* hell b7.de* hydr-ac k* hyos b7.de* ign ptk1 kali-bi bg2 kali-c bg2 kali-i k* kali-m bg kali-n h2* kali-s fd4.de kola stb3• kreos bg2 lach k* led b7.de* lol bg2* *Lyc* k* mag-c k* mag-m k* merc b4.de* mez b4.de* nat-c k* nat-m k* nit-ac bg2 *Nux-m* k* *Nux-v* k* ol-an olnd b7.de* op b7.de* paeon petr-ra shn4• ph-ac k* phasco-ci rbp2 phos bg2* plat j5.de* prun j5.de psor rb2 puls k* rhod b4.de* rhus-t b7.de* ruta j5.de sabad b7.de* sanic sars b4.de* *Sec* k* sel b7a.de seneg k* sep b4.de* sil b4.de* spig b7.de* spong k* *Stram* k* stront-c b4.de* sulph k* sumb a1 symph fd3.de• *Tab* tarax ter teucr b7.de* thuj k* verat k* verat-v ptk1 verb j5.de viol-t k*
- **amel.**: carb-an ptk1*
- **chill**; during: alum bg2 bell bg2 *Caps* b7.de* cic bg2 cocc bg2 nux-v bg2 op bg2 puls b7a.de* rhus-t b7a.de* stram bg2
- **coition**; after: bov ptk1
- **eating**; while: olnd b7a.de
- **fever**; during: alum bg2 *Bell* bg2 bry bg2 caps bg2 mag-m bg2 nux-v bg2 *Op* bg2 ph-ac bg2 stram bg2 sulph bg2 verat bg2
- **standing** agg.: con a1 plat j5.de stram j5.de
- **walking** agg.: agar j5.de alum j5.de am-c j5.de *Ars* hr1 bell j5.de bruc j5.de carb-an j5.de caust j5.de cocc j5.de dros j5.de mag-m j5.de nat-m j5.de petr j5.de ph-ac j5.de* prun j5.de psor al rhod j5.de rhus-t j5.de ruta j5.de sabad j5.de stram j5.de *Sulph* hr1 teucr j5.de verat j5.de verb j5.de

REFLECTING:
- **agg.**: agar k* ang bg2 arg-met k2 arg-n (non:coff k*) coff-t slp gran *Ph-ac* *Puls* k* sil
  - **walking** in open air agg.: agar sil
- **amel.**: phos
  - **thinking** of something else amel.: agar pip-m sep

RELAXATION, after: calc lach

REST:
- **agg.**: acon bell *Calc* k* cycl k* *Lach* manc *Nat-c* k* puls k* rhus-t k* sil k*
- **amel.**: arn br* cann-i k* coca colch br* *Con* cycl br* eupi k* hist sp1 nat-m k* nux-m nux-v k* spig br*

RESTING, supporting head:
- **agg.**: verb b7.de*
- **table**; on | **amel.**: sabad k* verat-v ptk1

RIDING:
- **agg.**: ant-t cocc bg2 crot-c sk4• dig grat hep bg2 kali-c bg2 kola stb3• petr bg2 sil bg2
- **boat**; in a: *(↗STOMACH - Nausea - Seasickness)*
  - **agg.**: *(↗STOMACH - Nausea - seasickness)* apom bro1 **Cocc** bro1* con tl1 petr k2* staph bro1 tab bro1 ther bg2*

- **carriage**; as from riding in a: (↗STOMACH - Nausea - Riding - carriage - agg.) cycl ferr grat hep
- **carriage**; in a:
  - **after** | **moving**; feels as if car is still: ther mrr1
  - **agg.**: (↗STOMACH - Nausea - riding - carriage) acon asar bg calc k* cocc bg2* cypra-eg sde6.de• dig bg2 Hep k* kali-i bg kola stb3• lac-d bro1 lyc k* olib-sac wmh1 petr bg2* prot ptj• sanic pc sel k* Sil k* ther vh*
    - ⁝ **descending** (See Descending, on - car)
  - **amel.**: glon nit-ac ptk1 puls k2 sil
- **horse**; a:
  - **agg.**: cop rhus-t
  - **amel.**: tarent
- **train**; in a: kali-i ptk1

RISING:

- **after** | **agg.**: apoc bar-c Bell bry calc cocc dig eug k* Form gnaph graph kali-s fd4.de Lyc k* lyss k* Mag-c ph-ac Phos sabad stann symph fd3.de•
- **agg.**: absin k* **Acon** k* acon-c k* adon bro1 aeth Aids nl2• Ail k* ambr bg aml-ns anthraq rly4• apoc k* arge-pl rwt5• arizon-l nl2• Arn ars k* arund k* atro k* bamb-a stb2.de• Bar-c k* Bell k* berb k* bov k* **Bry** k* Calc k* Cann-i k* Carb-an k* carbn-o carc fd2.de• Caust k* cedr k* Cham bg chel k* Chin chinin-s chir-fl gya2 Cic cina cocc k* colch k* con k* croc bg cupr Dig k* falco-pe nl2• **Ferr** k* ferr-ar Ferr-p form genist k* Glon k* graph mrr1 grat k* Guaj Ham k* hell k* hep k* hyos ind kali-bi k* kali-c k* kali-chl c1 kali-m k2 kali-p kali-s kali-sil k2 lac-ac k* Lac-d Lach laur lyc a1 lyss k* malar jl2 manc k* meny k* merc morph k* **Nat-m** k* nat-s k* Nat-sal bro1 nit-ac bg nux-v k* oci-sa sp1 olnd k* op k* Petr k* **Phos** k* phyt bg pic-ac k* plat pot-e rly4• ptel k* Puls **Rhus-t** k* ruta fd4.de sabad bg sabin k* sacch-a fd2.de• sang bg seneg sep bg sil k* spig k2 squil bg streptoc jl2* sul-ac sulph k* symph fd3.de• syph xxb **Tab** k* thal-xyz srj8• thuj k* tritic-vg fd5.de trom k* urol-h rwt• vanil fd5.de vario al2 Verat-v k* vib k* vip visc sp1 zinc [bell-p-sp dcm1 ferr-i stj1 ferr-m stj1 ferr-s stj1 heroin sdj2]
- **amel.**: aeth a1 ars Aur caust hell k* mosch k* nat-m phos Rhus-t
- **bed**; from:
  - **after** | **agg.**: aur b4a.de bar-c b4.de* calc b4.de* cham bg2 hep b4a.de lyc b4.de* mag-c b4.de* nat-m bg2 ph-ac b4.de* phos b4a.de* rhus-t bg2 sabad b7.de* sep bg2 sil b4a.de stram b7.de*
  - **agg.**: acon b7a.de* adon ptk1 Agar aids nl2• ail bg2 Arn ars h2 arund c1 asar bg2 bar-c Bell k* bov b4.de* Bry k* Cact calc b4.de* carb-an b4.de* carb-v bg2 caust k* Cham k* **Chel** k* Chin chinin-s cic Cimic Cina b7.de* cinnb **Cocc** k* con k* croc b7a.de cupr dig bg2 dulc k* **Ferr** k* Ferr-p Fl-ac Glon graph grat bg2 hydrog srj2• ind iod kali-bi k* kali-p fd1.de• kali-s ketogl-ac rly4• lach laur bg2 lyc k* mag-m k* mag-s merc bg2 Merc-c merc-i-f ptk1 **Nat-m** k* nat-s nicc Nit-ac k* **Nux-v** k* olnd k* Op ozone sde2• Petr k* Ph-ac k* **Phos** k* **Phyt** k* Pic-ac puls k* Rhus-t k* ruta k* sabad bg2 sabin k* sang hr1 sel b7a.de* Sep k* Sil k* squil b7.de* Stram sul-ac sul-i k2 Sulph k* symph fd3.de• verat-v k* vib ptk1 [ferr-i stj1 ferr-m stj1 ferr-s stj1]
  - **amel.**: hell bg2
- **falling** and rising; as if (See Falling - height)
- **kneeling**; from: carc fd2.de• cere-b
- **lying**; from | **agg.**: cassia-s ccrh1• vanil fd5.de
- **sitting** bent; from:
  - **after**: merc
    - ⁝ **long** time; for a: cham (non:laur a1) ph-ac ven-m rsj12•
- **sitting**; from:
  - **after**: apoc bry chir-fl gya2 cocc dig kali-p fd1.de• nat-sil fd3.de• phos tritic-vg fd5.de
    - ⁝ **long** lasting vertigo: laur a1
  - **agg.**: Acon k* aesc aeth all-s asar k* both-a rb3 both-ax tsm2 bov k* **Bry** k* Calc Calc-p cann-s b7.de* Carb-an k* cham coca cocc tl1 Con k* Dig dulc fd4.de **Ferr** k* gink-b sbd1• grat hell hir rsj4• hydrog srj2• ind iod irid-met srj5• kali-bi kali-c kali-s kalm laur k* Lyc lyss merc k* merc-i-f nat-s bg2 nicc nit-ac k* **Nux-v** ox-ac ozone sde2• Petr k* petr-ra shn4• ph-ac **Phos** k* pic-ac plut-n srj7• ptel **Puls** k* **Rhus-t** k* ruta fd4.de sabad k* Sang sel sep sil b4a.de spig k* staph k* stram b7.de* sul-i k2 Sulph k* sumb symph fd3.de• thuj k* verat verat-v
- **stooping**; from:
  - **after**:
    - ⁝ **agg.**: laur tritic-vg fd5.de zinc

Rising – **stooping**; from – **after**: ...

- ⁝ **amel.**: ars b4.de* aur k* caust b4.de* Hell k* mosch b7a.de phos b4.de* puls bg2
- **agg.**: acon k* ambr bg2 Anac k* apoc Arn k* ars k* bar-c k* **Bell** k* berb bov k* Bry k* Calc calc-sil k2 Carb-an k* carc vh* Cham b7.de* chel bg2 chin b7a.de* cic k* cocc b7.de* Colch b7a.de coloc b4a.de con k* croc b7.de* dig bg2 **Ferr** k* Glon bg2 Graph ham hell kali-s fd4.de laur k* lyss meny k* merc k* nat-m k* nicc Nit-ac k* nux-v k* olnd bg2 Op b7.de* petr bg1* phos k* phyt bg2 pic-ac plat b4.de* Puls k* rhus-t bg2 sabad bg2* Sang k* sanic sel b7a.de seneg b4.de* sep k* sil k* squil b7.de* sul-ac b4a.de sulph k* symph fd3.de• tab bg2 thuj b4a.de* tritic-vg fd5.de tub c1* vanil fd5.de Verat-v bg2 zinc k*
  - ⁝ **quickly** from stooping; rising: Ferr sang
- **supine** position; from: croc merc-c olnd petr puls sel sil

ROCKING:

- **amel.**: sec k*
- **as** if: arge-pl rwt5• bell k* calad k* chir-fl gya2 ferr bg2 Ign b7a.de lap-la rsp1 merc b4.de* plb b7.de* thuj b4.de* zinc b4a.de*
- **from**: borx Coff k* coff-t hr1

ROOM:

- **entering** a room; on: phos bg2 tab bg2
- **in** a room: agar b4.de* am-m b7a.de bell b4.de* croc b7.de* lyc b4a.de* mag-m b4a.de merc b4.de* mur-ac b4.de* nat-c b4.de* phos b4.de* puls b7.de* rhod b4.de* sil b4a.de* staph b7.de* stram b7.de* sul-ac b4.de* tab bg2
  - **amel.**: agar b4.de* caust b4.de* kreos bg2 merc b4.de* sulph b4.de*
- **stuffy** room agg.: gard-j vlr2•
- **turns** in a circle (See Objects - turn - room)

ROTARY (See Turning; as - everything)

RUBBING the eyes amel.: alum

RUNNING; from: luf-op rsj5•

SADNESS; with (See MIND - Sadness - vertigo)

SCRATCHING skin agg.: calc bg2*

SENSES; with vanishing of (See MIND - Senses - vanishing - vertigo)

SEPARATED: | **body**; as if separated from his: cocc mrr1

SEWING, while: graph k* lac-d lact mag-c phel k* sul-ac k*

SHAKING THE HEAD agg.; on: acon k* bry bg2 calc bg* con bg* corn genist glon hep k* kali-c bg* lyc bg2 morph bg* nat-ar bg* sep k* spig k* [tax jsj7]

- **involuntary**: lyc h2*
- **quickly**: sep k*

SHAVING; after: Carb-an k*

SINCIPUT: merl a1

SINKING, as if: bell bg2 bry bg2* cupr bg2 cycl bg2 dulc a1 hyos bg2 kali-br bg2 lach k* Lyc k* merc bg2 nat-m k* ph-ac k* phos bg2 sars bg2

- **stepping**; when: bamb-a stb2.de•

SITTING:

- **agg.**: abrom-a ks5 aeth aloe alum k* alum-p k2 alum-sil k2 am-c k* anac Apis k* arg-met ars k* bell bit-ar wht1• bros-gau mrc1 bry h1 calc k* calc-sil k2 Camph cann-s b7.de* carb-ac Carb-an k* Carb-v k* Carbn-s Caust k* Cham k* chel bg2 chin cic k* coca Cocc k* colch coloc cop crot-h crot-t Cupr dig eug euon fl-ac Glon grat hell k* ind kali-bi Kali-c k* kali-s kali-sil k2 lach k* lycps-v m-aust b7.de mag-p bg2 mang k* melal-alt gya4 meph k* Merc k* merc-cy nat-c nat-m b4.de* nat-p nit-ac k* oci-sa sp1 par k* Petr k* ph-ac k* phel **Phos** k* phyt k2 pic-ac Plat k* positr nl2• pot-e rly4• **Puls** k* ran-s rhod k* Rhus-t k* ruta k* sabad k* sabin k* sanic sars k* Sel b7a.de Sep k* Sil k* Spig k* Spong k* stann k* staph k* stram k* sul-ac k* Sulph k* tab tell thal-xyz srj8• Thuj k* Viol-o k* Zinc k* zinc-p k2
- **amel.**: Acon k* alum tl1 ars h2* aur k* bry Cycl k* form kali-n b4.de* lac-d ptk1 lach lol bg2 ph-ac b4.de* psil ft1* puls k* Sil tritic-vg fd5.de
- **eating**; before: kali-c
- **erect**:
  - **agg.**: Cham k* Hydr petr bg2
  - **amel.**: convo-s sp1
  - **high**; as if too: aloe Phos

- **erect**: ...
  - **impossible**: cyt-l sp1
- **riding** a bicycle; after: hir rsj4•
- **walking**; after: caust h2 colch lach
- **writing**; while: kali-bi merc

SITTING UP IN BED:
- **agg.**: acon c aids nl2• ars *Bry* caust **CHEL** k ● chinin-s **COCC** k ● croc *Cupr* euph eupi ind kali-br merc nat-m nit-ac op petr-ra shn4• **Phos** k ● *Phyt* positr nl2• *Puls* sep *Sil* thuj *Zinc*
- **amel.**: ars bg2 hell k* lac-c bg2 *Lac-d* phos k* puls h1

SLEEP:
- **after**, agg.: ambr ant-t apis k* arn bg2 ars atro *Calc Carb-v* k* *Chin* cimic *Dulc* euphr b7.de *Graph* k* hep hyper bg2 *Kali-c* kali-i **Lach** k* *Lact* laur bg2 *Med* merc nat-m **Nux-v** op k* petr-ra shn4• *Sep Spong* stann k* stict stram stront-c tarent *Ther* thuj zinc
- **amel.**: bell ferr grat pall
- **before**: arg-n bg2 nat-m bg2
- **during**: aeth k* caust ptk1 cimic bg2 crot-h k* kali-n c1 *Lyc Sang* **Sep** *Sil* k* ther k*
- **falling** asleep | **when**: arg-n bg2 nat-m bg2 stann bg2 tell bg2 ther bg2
- **going** to sleep:
  - **on** | **agg.**: arg-n hep h2 lach k2 nat-m stann bg1 tell k* *Ther*
- **half** asleep agg.; when: arg-met petr-ra shn4• *Sil*
- **loss** of; from: **Cocc** k* **Nux-v** k* tritic-vg fd5.de
- **siesta**:
  - **after** | **agg.**: hep bg2

SLEEPINESS; with: adam skp7• aeth k* alum bg2* aml-ns kr1 androc bnm2• ang bg2* ant-t bg2* arg-met k* arg-n bg2* bell bg2* *Con* kr1 crot-h j5.de* crot-t k* *Gels* bg2* *Glon* kr1 *Kali-br* kr1 *Kali-n* kr1 laur k* myric kr1 *Nit-ac* k* nux-m k* phos j5.de* puls k* rhod bg2* sarr *Sil* k* *Stram* b7.de* zinc ptk1

SMOKING agg.: (↗*Tobacco)* alum asc-t borx bov bg2 brom k* calad bnt clem con a3* dulc fd4.de *Gels* k* kali-s fd4.de led a1 **Nat-m** k* nux-v ptk1 op petr h2 sil k* *Tab* k* thuj a1 zinc k*

SNEEZING, from: apis b7a.de* bar-c k* benz-ac k* dios bg2 nux-v k* *Petr* b4a.de *Seneg* k*

SPACINESS; with: lac-del hrn2•

SPASMS; with muscular: calc bg2 cic br1* hyos bg2

SPEAKING; mistakes in (See MIND - Mistakes - speaking - vertigo)

SPEECH: (↗*Talking - agg.)*
- **irrational** speech; with (See MIND - Speech - unintelligible - vertigo)

SPIN; world seems to (See Turning; as - everything)

SPINE; ascending from: sil bg2

SPRING; spells of vertigo in: apis

STAGGERING; with (See Accompanied - staggering)

STANDING:
- **agg.**: abrom-a ks5 *Acon* aeth aloe alum mrr1 am-c ang bg2 apis arg-met arge-pl rwt5• *Arn* atp rly4• aur k* aur-s k2 bamb-a stb2.de• bar-c bar-s k2 *Boerh-d* zzc1• borx *Bov* k* bros-gau mrc1 *Bry* k* *Calc* k* *Cann-s* k* cassia-s ccrh1• *Caust* k* cham *Cocc* coff cop crot-t cycl k* cypra-eg sde6.de• cystein-l rly4• euph euphr fl-ac fuma-ac rly4• gels k* glon graph bg2 kali-bi k* kali-br kali-c k* kali-n k* kali-p kali-s lac-h htj1*• *Lach* laur led k* lyc mag-c k* mang k* marb-w es1• *Merc* k* merc-sul merl nat-m bg2 nux-m *Olnd* k* petr k* *Ph-ac* k* *Phos* k* phyt pic-ac k2 plat k* podo c1 pot-e rly4• *Puls* rheum k* *Rhus-t* k* sabad bg2 *Sabin* k* sars k* sec sel sil sol-ni *Spig* k* stram k* *Sulph* k* symph fd3.de• ter tritic-vg fd5.de valer k* zinc k* zinc-p k2 [bell-p-sp dcm1 heroin sdj2]
- **air** agg.; in open: euph *Podo*
- **amel.**: nux-v k* ph-ac k* phos b4.de*
- **eyes** closed agg.; with: arg-n bro1 lath br1* zinc mtf33
- **feet** together agg.; with: bit-ar wht1•
- **height** agg.; on a: *Zinc*
- **room** agg.; in a: cupr stram
- **walking** agg.; after: bry h1 *Calc* cypra-eg sde6.de•

STARS before eyes; white: alum k* ant-t ptk1

STOMACH:
- **pain** in stomach; with: cic br1*
- **proceeding** from: arge-pl rwt5• *Kali-c* k* tritic-vg fd5.de
- **weakness** in stomach, compelled to lie down; with: ambr k13*

STOOL:
- **after**:
  - **agg.**: alum bg2 apoc k* carb-an k* carb-v bg2 *Caust* k* cupr gran k* lach k* mag-m bg2 *Nat-m* k* petr k* phos k* zinc k*
  - **amel.**: *Cupr* k* lach bg2 ox-ac bg2 phos bg3* zinc bg3*
- **before**: alum k* calc-p bg2* carb-v bg2* caust bg2* chel bg2* cocc bg2* colch bg2* cupr b7a.de* glon bg2* lach k* mag-m h2* mang bg2* nat-c bg1 nat-m bg2 oena phos bg2* ptel bg2* *Zinc* bg2*
- **during** | **agg.**: *Caust* k* cham k* cob k* *Cocc* colch kali-c bg2 ptel k* stram k* tab bg2 zinc k*
- **painful** stool; with (See Accompanied - stool)

STOOPING:
- **agg.**: acon k* act-sp ail aloe vh1 *Alum* k* alum-p k2 *Anac* k* apis b7a.de aran aran-sc *Arg-n Ars* b4a.de *Aur* k* aur-m aur-s k2 bamb-a stb2.de• bapt *Bar-c* k* bar-i k2 **Bell** k* berb k* bit-ar wht1• *Bry* k* *Cact Calc* k* *Calc-p* calc-s calc-sil k2 *Camph* cann-i *Carb-v* k* carbn-s *Caust* k* *Cham* k* *Chel* b7a.de chin k* chinin-s cic k* cimic cinnb coff k* con corn dig ferr c1 *Glon* k* *Graph* k* *Guare Ham Hell* k* helon *Ign* ind inul br1 *Iod* k* *Kali-bi* k* *Kali-br* hr1 *Kali-c* kali-chl c1 kali-m k2 kali-n kali-p kali-s kali-sil k2 *Kalm* k* kreos b7a.de lac-ac lac-h htj1• *Lach* k* led k* *Lyc* k* *Mag-m* b4a.de mang-m med meny k* meph k* *Merc* k* *Merc-c* k* merl mill mosch k* myric nat-m k* nat-s nicc *Nit-ac* k* **Nux-v** k* ol-an op k* oreo c1* oxeod a1 *Petr* k* ph-ac k* *Phos* k* pic-ac k* plb k* podo fd3.de• propl ub1• ptel **Puls** k* *Rhus-t* k* santin sep k* *Sil* k* sol-ni *Staph* k* suis-em rly4• sul-i k2 sulfa sp1 **Sulph** k* sumb syph rb2* ther k* thuj k* tub dx1* valer k* verat
  - **menses**; during (See Menses - during - agg. - stooping agg.)
  - **supper** agg.; after: sep
- **amel.**: am b7.de* carb-an k* petr h2*
- **long** time; after stooping for a: cham spong fd4.de

STRETCHING agg.: apoc k*

STUPEFACTION:
- **barrier** between his organs of sense and external objects; as if there was a: aeth
- **during** vertigo (See MIND - Stupefaction - vertigo - during)

STUPOR agg.: phos bg2

SUDDEN: absin br1 aeth k* agar k* apoc k* *Arg-met* k* ars bg2* aster both-a rb3 both-ax tsm2 *Bov* k* bry k* calc-ar camph carbn-s chen-a c1* chinin-ar cimic tl1 coloc k* ephe-si hsj1• helo-s bnm14• iris kali-bi k* lach bg2 med al meph k* mosch k* mur-ac a1 myos-a rly4• nat-ox rly4• ozone sde2• petr a1 podo fd3.de• *Sal-ac* sne sec k* senec sep k* stann k* stram sulph tarent k* thuj k* tub rb2* verb k* visc bg2

SUMMER; spells of vertigo in: phos *Psor* k*

SUN agg.; facing the: agar ptk glon ptk kali-p ptk nat-c ptk *Prot* jl2

SUPPORTING head amel.: sabad k*

SUPPRESSION of complaints; after: bell bg2 bry bg2 calc bg2 carb-v bg2 cham bg2 hep bg2 ip bg2 lach bg2 phos bg2 rhus-t bg2 **Sulph** bg2

SUSPENSION of the senses: ant-t *Camph Nat-m Nux-m* psil ft1 *Stram* verat
- **as** if there were a barrier between his organs of sense and external objects: aeth k*

SWAYING:
- **right**, to: **Acon** ars berb k* calc carb-an k* caust dios k* euph ferr grat k* helo c1 helo-s c1* kali-n lac-d lycps-v lyss mill nat-s rhus-t ruta sars k* sil *Zinc*
  - **circle**; in a: berb *Caust*
- **left**, to: anac arg-n *Aur* bell *Borx* calc cic dirc dros *Eup-per* eup-pur euph iris-foe lach k2 lycps-v merl k* mez myris k* nat-c nux-m k* positr nl2• sol-ni spig *Sulph Zinc*
  - **morning** | **waking**; on: myris k*
  - **evening**: nux-m k*
  - **lying** agg.: merl k* ox-ac k*
  - **sitting** agg.: anac merl k*

- **left**, to: ...
  - **standing** agg.: merl k*
  - **walking** in open air agg.: aur borx h2 nux-m k* sol-ni sulph
- **to** and fro: *Acon* b7.de* ant-t b7.de* bry b7a.de cham b7.de* hyos b7.de* ign b7.de* ip b7.de* *Kali-c* bg2 m-ambo b7.de *M-arct* b7.de m-aust b7.de* mosch b7.de* *Nux-v* b7.de* olnd b7.de* op b7.de* *Petr* b4a.de puls b7.de* stram b7.de* tarax b7.de* thuj bg2
  - **dancing**; sensation as if he were: puls b7.de*
  - **objects** were swaying; sensation as if: laur b7a.de m-ambo b7a.de mosch b7a.de olnd b7.de*
  - **riding** in a carriage; sensation as if: cycl b7.de* ferr b7.de* grat bg2 hep bg2
  - ○ **Brain**; in: acon b7.de* bry b7.de* cic b7.de* cina b7.de* cycl b7.de* m-arct b7.de nux-v b7.de*

SWIMMING, as if (See Floating)

SWINGING, like: calad coff-t hr1 ferr *Merc* *Sulph* thuj tritic-vg fd5.de zinc
- **hither** and thither: petr h2
- **lying** down; while: ox-ac ptk1
- **waking**; on: phos ptk1

SYNCOPE, with (See GENERALS - Faintness - vertigo)

SYPHILITIC: **Aur** k*

TALKING: | **after** | **excitedly**: borx cham lyc nat-c par stront-c c1 thuj
- **agg.**: *(↗Speech)* alum bg* borx k* cham k* cocc melal-alt gya4 par k* petr-ra shn4• sol-ni
  - **long** time; for a: thuj

TALL; with sensation of being (See MIND - Delusions - tall - he - vertigo)

TEA:
- **agg.**: **Nat-m** k* **Sep** k*
- **amel.**: glon k* kali-bi bg2

TEMPLES, in: coloc bg1

THINKING about it, on: *(↗MIND - Thoughts - persistent - vertigo)* ph-ac bg2 pip-m plb bg2*
- **amel.**: cic bg2

THOUGHTS; with vanishing of (See MIND - Thoughts - vanishing - vertigo)

TINNITUS; after: chin ptk1

TOBACCO agg.: *(↗Smoking)* borx bg2 con a2* rhod bg2 sil bg2 zinc h2*
- **snuff**: sil bg2

TOUCH agg.: cupr k*

TREMBLING: am-c arg-n bg2 ars bell *Camph* k* carb-ac hr1 carb-v k* chin bg2 crot-h k* *Dig* k* *Dulc* k* gels bg2* *Glon* k* gran bg2 lach b7a.de nat-m op bg2 pitu-a vml2• psil vml3• puls spong fd4.de stann bg2 zinc bg2*
- ○ **Hands** and feet: bell b4a.de sep b4a.de
- **Internal**: cupr ptk1

TURNED about; as if bed: cadm-s k2 **Con** k* nux-v k* plb k* *Puls* k* sol-ni
- **whirled**, renewed by thinking about it; and: plb

TURNED, as if house turned upside down: bufo kr

TURNING; as if:
- **couch** is turning; as if: con bg2
- **everything** were turning in a circle; as if: acon k* agn b7.de* aids nl2• aloe *Alum* k* am-c k* anac k* apis b7a.de *Arg-met* b7.de* *Arg-n* k* *Arn* k* asaf k* *Aur* k* bapt bg2 bar-m *Bell* k* berb *Bism* k* bov b4.de* **Bry** k* calad k* *Calc* k* camph k* cann-s b7.de carb-an b4.de* carb-v b4.de* caust b4.de* chel k* *Chin* bg2 *Chinin-s* k* *Cic* k* cocc k* **Con** k* croc b7.de* cupr k* **Cycl** k* dros b7.de* dulc fd4.de euon eup-per eup-pur euph k* ferr k* graph b4.de* grat hell k* hep k* hydr-ac kali-bi k* kali-c b4.de* kali-i bg2 kali-n b4.de* kola stb3• kreos k* lac-cp sk4• lact laur k* *Lyc* k* m-arct b7.de mag-c b4.de* mag-m bg2 merc b4.de* mosch k* *Mur-ac* k* nat-c k* nat-m k* *Nux-v* k* olnd k* op k* par k* ph-ac b4.de* *Phos* k* pieri-b mlk9.de plat b4.de* plb a1 **Puls** k* ran-b k* ran-s b7.de* rhod k*

Turning; as if – **everything** were turning in a circle; as if: ... rhus-t k* ruta k* sabad k* sep b4.de* sil b4.de* spig k* spong b7.de* squil b7.de* stann b4.de* staph k* sul-ac b4.de* sulph k2 tab ter k* thuj b4.de* til tritic-vg fd5.de ust a1 valer k* vanil fd5.de verat k* viol-o k* zinc b4.de*
- **he** turns in a circle: arn ptk1 bamb-a stb2.de• bell k* berb k* bry ptk1 *Calc* k* carbn-o vh caust k* *Con* ptk1 cycl ptk1 cypra-eg sde6.de• helo c1 helo-s c1* nux-v ptk1 phos ptk1 plut-n srj7• *Puls* ptk1 rhus-t ptk1
  - **right**, to: berb *Caust* lac-del hrn2• spong fd4.de
  - **left**, to: bell
- **head** is turning round; sensation as if: bism a1 nux-m c1
- **head**; whirling in: *(↗HEAD - Wild; MIND - Wild feeling)* acon h1 ant-t a1 apis a1 arg-met b7.de* bell h1 bov a1 bry vh1 calc h2 cann-i a1 cann-s a1 carb-v h2* chinin-s a1* con h2 croc a1 eug a1 glon yl1 hell mrr1 kreos a1 lach bg2 m-arct h1 merc h1* merl a1 mur-ac h2* nat-c h2* nux-v b7.de* petr b4.de* phos h2 puls bg2 rob a1 sabad bg2 sep b4.de* sil b4.de* spong h1 sulph bg2 tarax bg2 thuj a1 voes a1 wies a1
  - **menses**; during: **Caust** a1* wies a1*
  - ○ **Brain** | **Front** half of: *Bism* h1
  - **Forehead**; in: euon a1 merc h1* mosch h1 nicc a1 olnd h1* staph h1* tarax b7.de*
  - **Temples**: sulph b4.de*
  - **Vertex**: sabad b7.de*
- **inside** the body was turning around; as if something | **revolving** objects; when looking at: lyc k*
- **objects** seem to turn in a circle (See Objects - turn)
- **room** is turning (See Objects - turn - room)

TURNING IN BED agg.●: **Bell** k* both-a rb3 both-ax tsm2 **Bry** xxb *Cact* k* carb-v k* cean tl1 **Con** k* *Graph* k* ind kalm *Lac-d* k* mang bg2* meph **Phos** k ●* **Rhus-t** k ● **Sulph** k ●* symph fd3.de• syph xxb
- **left**; to: borx k* calc bg calc-p k* coloc bg2* con bg2* gran bg2*
- **right**; to: lach bg3*

TURNING; when: *Agar* am-c amph a1 bit-ar wht1• calc *Con* k* galeoc-c-h gms1• genist glon hydr bg* ind ip *Kali-c* merc nat-m olnd ptk1 ozone sde2• phos *Rhus-t* k* ruta fd4.de tell ther
- **amel.**: staph ptk1
- **around**: agar b4.de* calc b4.de* carb-v b4a.de ip b7.de* kali-c b4.de* merc b4.de* nat-m b4.de* phos b4.de* sang bg2 ther bg2
- **eyes**; when turning: con bro1 plat bg2 spig b7.de*
- **followed** by | **Head**; pain in: rhus-t ptk1
- **head**; or moving the: acon k* *Agar* aloe alum-sil k2 am-c *Arn* atro aur aur-m-n wbt2• bamb-a stb2.de• *Bell* k* bit-ar wht1• **Bry** k* *Calc* k* calc-ar carb-an k* *Carb-v* k* caust clem cocc coloc b4.de* **Con** k* cupr echi k* *Glon* *Graph* hep k* *Ign* ip *Kali-bi* k* *Kali-c* k* kali-p kalm *Lac-d* vh* lec mentho bro1 meph *Morph* bro1 mosch nat-ar bro1 nat-c nat-m orot-ac rly4• paeon *Phos* plut-n srj7• ptel rhus-t samb sang k* sel sep spig k* spong fd4.de staph b7.de* tell ther thres-a sze7• thuj k* tritic-vg fd5.de urol-h rwt• verat b7.de* zinc bg1
  - **left**, to: coloc a1* con a1* tritic-vg fd5.de
  - **quickly**: adon ptk1 aloe alum-sil k2 am-c atro bar-c *Bry* **CALC** k ●* *Carb-v* *Coloc* k* **CON** k ● **Gels** k ● helon a1 *Kali-c* kreos lac-ac merc k* nat-sil fd3.de• **Phos** k ●* *Sang* spig *Staph* sulph *Verat*
    - **amel.**: agar k*
- **heels**; quickly on | **amel.**: staph ptk1
- **right**; to the: cean tl1 lach ptk1 plut-n srj7•
  - **amel.**: alumn ptk1
- **side**; on:
  - **right** | **amel.** (See Lying - side - right - amel.)
- **suddenly**: lavand-a ctl1•
- **upper** part of body from right to left; when turning: eupi c1

UNCONSCIOUSNESS; followed by: *(↗GENERALS - Faintness - vertigo; MIND - Unconsciousness - vertigo)* sil bg2*

URINATION:
- **copious** amel.: gels
- **during**: acon k*
- **urging**, when: dig bg2 *Hyper* k* ruta fd4.de

VERTEX, from: berb bg2* calc k* chel bg2* kreos bg2* lyc bg1 lys bg2 lyss ptk1 med bg2* merc-i-f bg2* phos bg2* scop ptk1 scroph-n bg2* senec bg2
- **left**: brass-n-o srj5•

- **standing** agg.: scroph-n br1

VEXATION; after: calc k* ign nux-v

VIOLENT: diosm br1 meph ptk1

VISION; with obscuration of (See Accompanied - vision - dim)

VOMITING:
- **after** | **amel.**: eup-per ptk1 nat-s ptk1 op k* tab bro1
- **agg.**: arn b7.de* ars bg2
- **before**: nat-s k* phos h2*
- **bile** | **amel.**: eup-per bg2
- **sour** | **amel.**: bapt bg2 kali-bi bg2
- **with** (See Accompanied - vomiting)

WAKING; on: allox sp1 apis bg2 arge-pl rwt5• arn bg2 ars bg2 bell bg2 calc b4.de* carb-an b4.de* carb-v b4.de* caust b4.de* chin b7.de* dig bg2 euphr b7.de* graph b4.de* hyper bg2 *Lach* bg2 laur bg2 **Lyc** bg2 merc b4.de nux-v bg2 op bg2 phos b4a.de* sep bg2 stann bg2 stront-c b4.de* thuj bg2

WALKING:
- **after** | **agg.**: acon arg-met bry calad k* *Calc* k* caust k* colch laur k* lyss k* phos plut-n srj7• rhus-t b7.de* sep a1
- **agg.**: acon k* aesc bg agar k* agn aids nl2• aloe alum k* alum-p k2 alum-sil k2 am-m anac k* ant-t k* *Apis Arg-n* arizon-l nl2• *Arn* k* *Ars* k* ars-i asar k* aster k* atro k* aur hr1 aur-m bamb-a stb2.de• bar-c k* bar-i k2 bar-m bar-s k2 *Bell* k* berb k* bism bit-ar wht1• borx *Bry* k* buth-a sp1 calad *Calc* k* calc-ar k2* calc-i k2 calc-p k* calc-s camph k* cann-i k* cann-s k* carb-an k* *Carb-v* k* carbn-s caust k* cham b7.de* *Chin* k* chinin-ar chir-fl gya2 *Cic* k* coca cocc coff colch *Con* k* cop k* cycl cypra-eg sde6.de• daph dig k* digin a1 dirc k* *Dulc* k* euph h2* *Ferr* k* *Ferr-i* fl-ac *Gels* k* graph *Hell* k* hura hyos k* hyper ign iod ip k* kali-ar kali-bi k* kali-br kali-c k* kali-m k2 kali-n kali-p kali-s kali-sil k2 kola stb3• lac-c lach bro1 laur k* led k* lil-t k* lol bg2 lycps-v *M-aust* b7.de mag-m mag-p bro1 merc k* merl k* mill *Mur-ac* k* nat-ar *Nat-c* k* **Nat-m** k* nat-p *Nat-s* nat-sil fd3.de• *Nit-ac* k* *Nux-m* k* **Nux-v** k* op k* *Oreo* bro1 ox-ac ozone sde2• paeon *Petr* k* *Ph-ac* k* *Phel* k* **Phos** k* phys k* *Phyt* pic-ac k* plut-n srj7• podo fd3.de• pot-e rly4• *Psor* ptel k* **Puls** k* ran-b k* *Rhus-t* k* ruta *Sanguis-s* hm2• sars k* *Sec* sel *Sep* k* *Sil* k* *Spig* k* spong fd4.de stann staph *Stram* k* streptoc rly4• sul-ac sul-i k2 *Sulph* k* sumb tab k* tarax k* tarent k* tell *Ther* bro1 thuj k* tritic-vg fd5.de valer vanil fd5.de verat k* viol-t k* *Zinc* k* zinc-p k2 [spect dfg1]
- **air**; in open: *(↗MIND - Fear - going; MIND - Going)*
  - **after** | **agg.**: anac b4a.de* ham fd3.de• lach b7.de* merc b4.de* phos b4.de*
  - **agg.**: *(↗MIND - Fear - going; MIND - Going)* acon *Agar* k* *Alum* b4a.de *Ambr* k* ang k* arn k* *Ars* k* ars-s-f k2 *Aur* k* aur-ar k2 aur-m aur-s k2 borx b4a.de bry *Calc* k* calc-act c1 calc-ar *Calc-p* calc-sil k2 canth k* carbn-s *Chin* chinin-ar clem coff crot-t *Cycl* bg2* *Dros* k* euph k* gels graph k* hyos b7a.de ip k* kali-ar *Kali-c* kali-p kali-sil k2 kreos k* *Lach* k* laur k* *Led* k* *Lyc* *M-arct* b7.de* merc k* *Mur-ac* k* nicc *Nux-m* k* *Nux-v* k* olnd k* phel *Phos* k* phys psor a12 **Puls** k* rhod rhus-t ruta k* sars senec *Sep* k* sil spig k* stann k* staph hr1 stram streptoc rly4• stry **Sulph** k* symph fd3.de• tab tarax k* tell thea thuj k* til
    - **elevation**; on an: **Sulph**
  - **amel.**: am-m bro1 anac bg2 bell bg2 calc bg2 *Carb-ac* crot-h kali-c k* mag-c mag-m k* mag-p br1* *Nat-c* par k* phos bg2 *Puls* k* rhod *Rhus-t* bro1 sul-ac k2 tab bro1
    - **rapidly**: carb-ac bg2
- **amel.**: abrom-a ks5 *Acon* k* am-c k* apis b7a.de bry k* cadm-met tpw6 calc h2* kali-bi bg2* lil-t mag-c k* podo fd3.de• sabad b7.de* sil k* spira a1 *Staph* k* sulph k* *Zinc* k*
- **circle**; in a | **amel.**: staph bg2
- **continued**:
  - **after** | **agg.**: merl k* nat-m
- **declivity** agg.; near a: sulph
- **eating** agg.; after: *Nux-v*
- **gliding** in the air; with sensation of | **feet** did not touch the ground; as if: *(↗Floating)* agar asar k* aur-m rb2 calc mp1• **Calc-ar** k* *Camph* *Chin* k* coff k* cop dub mp1• hura **Lac-c** k* manc rb2 merc-i-f rb2 nat-m k* nux-m nux-v rb2 op phos k* **Rhus-t** k● sep *Spig* stram *Thuj* valer xan rb2

Walking: ...
- **narrow** path agg.; along a: bar-c
- **open** space agg.; across an: *(↗MIND - Fear - open)* *Ars* chir-fl gya2 psor al2
- **rapidly** | **agg.**: asar vh *Ferr* grat *Puls* sulph vanil fd5.de
- **room** agg.; in a: iris mag-m k* manc k* merc k* nat-c k* nit-ac k* paeon k* tritic-vg fd5.de
- **sideways** agg.: kali-c
- **slowly**:
  - **agg.** | **exertion** does not agg.; violent: mill
- **water** agg.; near: ang k* ferr b7.de* sulph bg2

WALKING ON A SPONGE; as if: helo-s rwt2•

WALLS of house seem to be falling in on her: *(↗Fall tendency - high - walls)* arg-n k* sabad k*

WARM:
- **amel.**: mang-m bro1 sil bro1 stront-c bro1
- **bathing** | **agg.**: neon srj5• sumb bg2
- **bed** | **amel.**: cocc
- **room**:
  - **agg.**: acon k* brom bry k2* cortiso tpw7* *Croc* gard-j vlr2• *Grat* k* kali-s lact lil-t *Lyc* k* *Merc* k* **Nat-c** paeon ph-ac phos k* pieri-b mlk9.de *Ptel* *Puls* *Sanic* sars k* spong fd4.de tab
  - **entering** a warm room; when: arg-met ars bro1 *Iod* bro1 *Phos* k* pieri-b mlk9.de plat k* sep a1 tab k*
- **soup** | **amel.**: kali-bi k*
- **washing** agg.: sumb

WARMTH:
- **agg.** (See Heat - during)
- **rose** from chest to throat; sensation as if (See Heat - sensation - chest to)

WASHING:
- **amel.**: asar b7.de*
- **feet** | **agg.**: merc k*

WATCHING the sick; from (See Sleep - loss)

WATER:
- **crossing** running water: *(↗MIND - Fear - water - running)* *Ang* k* *Arg-met* k* *Bell* k* *Brom* k* crot-c sk4• *Ferr* k* *Hyos* k* lyss ptk1 nat-m bg2 stram *Sulph* k*
- **looking** at running water: *(↗Objects - turn - looking; MIND - Fear - water - running)* ang bg2 arg-met bg2* brom bg2* ferr b7.de* lyc bg2 sulph b4a.de* *Verat* bro1*

WAVELIKE sensations: bamb-a stb2.de• (non:ferr bg) grat c1 meli a2 (non:pot-e rly4) senec a2

○ - **Forehead**:
  - **left**:
    - **extending** to | **right**: bamb-a stb2.de•
- **Heels** | **extending** to occiput: bamb-a stb2.de•

WAVES; in: arge-pl rwt5• chinin-s bg2 chir-fl gya2 ferr bg2 helo-s bnm14• pot-e rly4•

WEAKNESS:
- **agg.**: ambr bg2 bar-act bg2 chin bg2 colch bg2 cur bg2 ran-b bg2 sel bg2 sul-ac bg2 verat bg2
- **with** (See GENERALS - Weakness - vertigo)

WEATHER:
- **cold** agg.: lap-la rsp1 ran-b k2 *Sang*
- **stormy**:
  - **agg.**: falco-pe nl2•
  - **before**: gels bg2 puls bg2
- **warm** | **agg.**: glon bg2 nat-c bg2 [sol-ecl cky1]
- **wet** | **agg.**: brom k* sars k*
- **windy**: *Calc-p* k*

WEEPING; with (See MIND - Weeping - vertigo)

WHITE floor; seeing an expanse of: [bell-p-sp dcm1]

WILL amel.; exertion of: pip-m k*

WINDOW; near a: nat-m $_{bg2*}$

WINE:

- **agg.**: *Alum* am-c $_{bg2}$ bell borx $_{b4a.de}$ bov $_{k*}$ cocc *Con* $_{k*}$ *Nat-c* $_{k*}$ nat-m *Nux-v* ox-ac $_{bg2}$ petr $_{k*}$ sumb $_{k*}$ *Zinc* $_{k*}$ [ferr $_{stj1}$ ferr-i $_{stj1}$ ferr-m $_{stj1}$ ferr-p $_{stj1}$ ferr-s $_{stj1}$]
- **amel.**: arg-n coca gels phos

WIPING THE EYES: | **amel.**: *Alum* $_{k*}$

WRITING:

- **agg.**: arg-met crot-h $_{bg2}$ cypra-eg $_{sde6.de•}$ form *Graph* $_{k*}$ *Kali-bi* $_{k*}$ kali-c $_{k*}$ melal-alt $_{gya4}$ merc $_{k*}$ ph-ac $_{k*}$ ptel rhod $_{k*}$ *Sep* $_{k*}$ sphing $_{a1}$ stram thuj $_{k*}$
- **mistakes** in writing; with (See MIND - Mistakes - writing - vertigo)

YAWNING agg.: agar $_{b4a.de*}$ apoc $_{k*}$ sal-ac $_{sne}$

EXTENDING TO: | **Body**; whole: lac-c $_{bg2}$

Vertigo

DAY AND NIGHT: borx bg2 camph bg2 kreos bg2 led bg2 *Rhus-t* b7a.de* sul-ac bg2 viol-t b7a.de*

DAYTIME: ant-c b7.de*

MORNING: *Agar* b4.de* alum b4.de* am-c b4.de* *Am-m* b7.de* ambr b7a.de anac b4.de* ang b7.de* ant-t b7.de* apis b7a.de arg-met b7.de* arn b7.de* ars b4.de* asaf b7.de* asar b7.de* aur b4.de* bar-c b4.de* bell b4.de* borx b4a.de bov b4.de* *Bry* b7.de* *Calc* b4.de* camph b7.de* *Canth* b7.de* carb-an b4.de* carb-v b4.de* caust b4.de* cham b7.de* *Chin* b7.de* cic b7.de* *Cina* b7.de* clem b4.de* cocc b7.de* coff b7.de* coloc b4.de* con b4.de* *Croc* b7.de* cupr b7.de* dulc b4.de* euphr b7.de* ferr b7.de* *Graph* b4.de* grat bg2 guaj b4.de* hell b7.de* *Hep* b4.de* ign b7.de* iod bg2 ip b7.de* kali-c b4.de* *Kali-i* bg2 kali-n b4.de* *Kreos* b7a.de lach b7.de* laur b7a.de *Lyc* b4.de* *M-ambo* b7.de* *M-arct* b7.de *Mag-c* b4.de* mag-m b4.de* mang b4.de* merc b4.de* mez b4.de* mur-ac b4.de* nat-c b4.de* *Nat-m* b4.de* nat-s bg2 nit-ac b4.de* nux-m b7.de* **Nux-v** b7.de* ox-ac bg2 *Petr* b4.de* ph-ac b4.de* *Phos* b4.de* *Puls* b7.de* ran-b b7.de* rheum b7.de* rhod b4.de* rhus-t b7.de* ruta b7.de* samb b7.de* sang bg2 sars b4.de* sel bg2 seneg b4.de* *Sep* b4.de* sil b4.de* spig b7.de* squil b7.de* stann b4.de* **Staph** b7.de* sul-ac b4.de* sulph b4.de* thuj b4.de* verat b7.de* zinc b4.de*

- **amel.**: kreos bg2
- **bed** agg.; in: bar-c bg2 bell bg2 *Bry* bg2 calc bg2 chin bg2 con bg2 dulc bg2 graph bg2 hep bg2 ign bg2 ip bg2 kali-c bg2 lyc bg2 mag-c bg2 **Nat-m** bg2 nit-ac bg2 **Nux-v** bg2 phos bg2 puls bg2 sulph bg2 thuj bg2
- **rising** agg.: *Bry* bg2 cimic bg2 cycl bg2 *Sulph* bg2

○ - **External** head: alum b4.de* ang b7.de* bov bg2 bry b7.de* cham b7.de* croc bg2 dros b7.de *Graph* b4.de* guaj b4a.de hep b4.de* mez b4.de* nux-v b7.de* seneg b4.de* squil b7.de* staph b7.de* sulph b4.de*

FORENOON: alum b4.de* am-c b4.de* am-m b7.de* ant-c b7.de* apis b7a.de aur b4.de* bar-c b4.de* borx b4a.de bov b4.de* bry b7.de* calc b4.de* *Cann-s* b7.de* canth b7.de* carb-an b4.de* chel b7.de* chin b7.de* cocc b7.de* con b4.de* dig bg2 euph b4.de* fl-ac bg2 graph b4.de* **Hep** b4a.de ign b7a.de kali-c b4.de* kali-n b4.de* lyc b4.de* m-arct b7.de *Mag-c* b4.de* mag-m b4.de* mang b4.de* mur-ac b4.de nat-c b4.de* nat-m b4.de* *Nux-m* b7a.de nux-v b7.de* ph-ac b4.de* *Phos* b4.de* plb b7.de* ran-b b7.de* rhus-t bg2 *Sabad* b7.de* sars b4.de* seneg b4.de* sep b4.de* *Sil* b4.de* **Spig** b7a.de sul-ac b4.de* sulph b4a.de* zinc b4.de*

○ - **External** head: alum b4.de* apis b7a.de phos b4.de* valer b7.de*

NOON: ars bg2 bov bg2 carb-v bg2 cic bg2 con bg2 graph bg2 ign bg2 kali-bi bg2 kali-n bg2 mag-c bg2 mang bg2 mur-ac bg2 nat-c bg2 nat-m bg2 puls bg2 rhus-t bg2 sil bg2 spong bg2 sulph bg2 zinc bg2

AFTERNOON: agar b4.de* aloe bg2 alum b4.de* am-c b4.de* am-m b7.de* ambr b7.de* anac b4.de* ant-t b7.de* *Arn* b7.de* ars b4.de* asar b7.de* aur b4.de* bar-c b4.de* *Bell* b4.de* borx b4a.de bov b4.de* *Bry* b7.de* calad b7.de* calc b4.de* *Canth* b7.de* carb-an b4.de* carb-v b4.de* caust b4.de* chel b7.de* chin b7.de* cic b7.de* *Cocc* b7.de* coff b7.de* *Coloc* b4a.de con b4.de* dig b4.de* dros b7.de* dulc b4.de* euphr b7.de* ferr b7.de* graph b4.de* hell b7.de* ign b7.de* iod b4.de* kali-bi bg2 kali-c b4.de* kali-n b4.de* kreos bg2 lach b7a.de *Laur* b7.de* **Lyc** b4.de* m-arct b7.de mag-c b4.de* mag-m b4.de* mang b4.de* merc-c b4a.de mez b4.de* mur-ac b4.de* nat-c b4.de* nat-m b4.de* nit-ac b4.de* nux-m b7.de* *Nux-v* b7.de* petr b4.de* ph-ac b4.de* phos b4.de* plat b4.de* plb b7.de* puls b7.de* ran-b b7.de* *Rhus-t* b7.de* ruta b7.de* sabin b7.de* sars b4.de* sel b7.de* seneg b4.de* sep b4.de* sil b4.de* spong b7.de* stront-c b4.de* sul-ac b4.de* sulph b4.de* valer b7.de* zinc b4.de*

○ - **External** head: alum b4.de* apis b7a.de calc b4.de* chel b7.de* hyos b7.de* laur b7.de* mag-c b4.de* mag-m b4.de* phos b4.de* rhus-t b7.de* sel b7a.de sep b4.de* zinc b4.de*

EVENING: acon b7.de* agar b4.de* alum b4.de* am-c b4.de* ambr b7.de* anac b4.de* *Ang* b7.de* *Ant-t* b7.de* *Apis* b7a.de arg-met b7.de* *Arn* b7a.de aur b4.de* bar-c b4.de* **Bell** b4.de* *Borx* b4a.de bov b4.de* *Bry* b7.de* *Calc* b4.de* camph b7.de* canth b7.de* carb-an b4.de* carb-v b4.de* caust b4.de* chel b7.de* **Chin** b7.de* cic b7.de* cina b7.de* clem b4.de* *Cocc* b7.de* coloc b4a.de* croc b7.de* cycl b7.de* dig b4.de* dulc b4.de* *Euphr* b7.de* ferr b7.de* graph b4.de* hell b7.de* hep b4a.de* *Ign* b7a.de kali-bi bg2 kali-c b4.de* kali-n b4.de* lach b7.de* laur b7.de* led b7.de* lyc b4.de* m-arct b7.de m-aust b7.de mag-c b4.de* mag-m b4.de* meny b7.de* merc b4.de* *Mez* b4.de* mosch b7.de* mur-ac b4.de* nat-c b4.de* nat-m b4.de* nit-ac b4.de* nux-v b7.de* par b7.de* petr b4.de* ph-ac b4.de* phos b4.de* plat b4.de* plb b7.de* **Puls** b7.de* *Ran-b* b7.de* rhod b4.de* *Rhus-t* b7.de* ruta b7.de* sabad b7.de* sabin b7.de* sars b4.de* seneg b4.de* sep b4.de* *Sil* b4.de* **Spig** b7.de* stann b4.de*

Evening: ... *Staph* b7.de* stront-c b4.de* sul-ac b4.de* *Sulph* b4.de* teucr b7.de* thuj b4.de* *Valer* b7.de* zinc b4.de*

- **21-1 h**: crot-h bg2
- **amel.**: lach bg2 nat-m bg2
- **bed**:
  - **in bed**:
    - **agg.**: camph bg2 carb-an bg2 carb-v bg2 dulc bg2 laur bg2 lyc bg2 mag-c bg2 mag-m bg2 nux-v bg2 ph-ac bg2 phos bg2 plat bg2 rhus-t bg2 sabad bg2 sep bg2
    - **amel.**: anac bg2 mag-c bg2 phos bg2 rhus-t bg2
- **twilight**; in the | **agg.**: aloe bg2 ang b7.de* onos bg2 puls b7.de*

○ - **External** head: agn b7.de* alum b4.de* *Calc* b4.de* caust b4.de* graph b4.de* mag-c bg2 merc b4.de* *Merc-c* b4a.de *Mez* bg2 nux-v b7.de* phos b4.de* puls b7.de* ran-b b7.de* rhod b4.de* sep b4a.de* **Sil** b4.de* staph b7.de* *Stront-c* b4a.de sulph b4.de* thuj b4.de* zinc b4.de*

NIGHT: alum bg2 ambr b7.de* anac b4.de* ang b4.de* ant-t b7.de* arn b7.de* ars b4.de* *Aur* b4a.de *Bell* b4.de* bov b4.de* *Calc* b4a.de camph b7a.de canth b7.de* carb-an b4.de* carb-v b4a.de caust b4.de* **Cham** b7.de* **Chin** b7.de* chinin-s bg2 cic b7.de* croc bg2 dig b4.de* graph bg2 guaj b4.de **Hep** b4.de* kali-bi bg2 kali-c b4.de* kali-i bg2 kali-n b4.de* *Lach* bg2 laur b7.de* **Lyc** b4.de* m-arct b7a.de m-aust b7.de mag-c b4.de* **Merc** b4a.de* *Merc-c* b4a.de mez b4.de nat-c b4.de* *Nit-ac* b4.de* nux-v b7.de* op b7.de* par b7.de* ph-ac b4a.de phos b4.de* plat b4.de* **Puls** b7.de* rhus-t b7.de* sep b4.de* **Sil** b4.de* spig b7.de* stront-c b4.de* **Sulph** b4.de* thuj b4.de* verat b7.de* zinc b4.de*

- **midnight**:
  - **after**: ars b4.de* carb-an b4.de* cham bg2 hep b4.de* ign bg2 kali-c b4.de* ph-ac b4a.de rhus-t b7.de* sep b4.de* **Sil** b4.de* spig b7.de*
  - **at**: arn bg2 ars bg2 cham bg2 hep bg2 kali-c bg2 plat bg2 puls bg2 sep bg2
  - **before**: am-m b7.de* anac b4.de* caust b4.de* *Chin* b7.de* dulc b4.de* lach b7.de* puls b7.de* rhus-t b7.de* sep b4.de*
- **air** agg.; night: plat bg2
- **amel.**: mag-c bg2

○ • **Vertex**: mag-c ptk1

○ - **External** head: bry b7.de* carb-an b4a.de chin b7.de* coloc b4a.de hep b4.de* kali-bi bg2 laur bg2 led b7.de* *Lyc* b4.de* merc-c b4a.de olnd b7.de* par b7.de* rhus-t b7.de* sel b7a.de staph b7.de* sulph bg2 thuj b4.de*

- **Vertex**: laur ptk1

ABSCESS: *Calc* k* *Hep* lyc *Merc* k* *Sil*

○ - **Brain**: arn bro1 bell bro1 crot-h bro1 iod bro1 lach bro1 merc-pr-r mtf11 op bro1 staphycoc jl2 vip bro1

ADHESION:

○ - **Forehead**; of skin of (See FACE - Adhesion)

- **Scalp** to skull; of: arn b7.de* par b7.de*

AIR (= wind):

- **agg.** | **External** head: borx bg2 *Cham* b7a.de lyc bg2 med bg2 naja bg2 *Nux-v* b7.de* sanic bg2
- **filled** with air; as if head: (*↗STOMACH - Distension - sensation - followed - head)* aur b4a.de germ-met srj5• lyss c1
- **sensation** of a current of air:
  - **blowing** on head: petr ptk1
  - **passing** through head: agath-a nl2• am-m bg2* anan k* androc srj1• *Aur* k* benz-ac k* borx bg2 chlam-tr bcx2• choc srj3• colch k* *Cor-r* k* meny mill nat-m k* nit-ac bg2* nux-m bg2* petr puls k* sabin k* sanic k* verat bg1* zinc bg2*
    - **cold** wind: verat bg2
    - **rocking**; on: **Cor-r**
    - **extending** to | **Abdomen**: aloe

○ • **Above** the eyes: borx

- • **Vertex**: *Carb-an*
- **strong** wind agg.: aur b4.de* *Con* b4a.de

AIR AGG.; DRAFT OF: (*↗Cold; Cold - air - agg.)* *Acon* k* arg-n bg2 *Ars* **Bell** k* benz-ac borx k* cadm-s *Calc* k* *Calc-ar* *Calc-p* calc-s tl1 *Caps* cham b7.de* **Chin** k* coloc k* gels *Hep* k* kali-ar *Kali-c* kali-n kali-s lac-c *Mag-m* ptk1 *Merc* mez bg2 naja bg2* nat-s bg2 *Nux-m* *Nux-v* k* phos k* *Psor* ptk1 *Sanic* *Sel* k* **Sil** k* stront-c *Sulph* valer k* verb k*

○ - **External** head: acon b7a.de borx bg2 chin b7a.de naja bg2

Head

AIR; IN OPEN:
- **agg.**: alum b4.de* ang b7.de* arg-n bg2 bell b4.de* bov b4.de* bry b7.de* *Calc* b4.de* *Caps* b7a.de caust b4.de* *Cham* b7.de* chel b7.de* chin b7.de* cina b7a.de *Cocc* b7.de* *Coff* b7.de* con b4.de* ferr b7.de* grat bg2 hep b4a.de* ign b7.de* iod b4.de* ip b7.de* kali-bi bg2 kali-c b4.de* kali-n bg2 laur b7.de* lil-t bg2 lyc b4.de* mag-m bg2 mang b4.de* meny b7.de* mez b4.de* **Nux-v** b7.de* petr b4.de* phos b4.de* rhus-t b7.de* *Spig* b7.de* staph b7.de* sulph b4.de* zinc b4.de*

○ • **External** head: *Calc* b4.de* *Graph* b4.de* guaj b4.de* lyc b4.de*
- **amel.**: acon b7.de* alum b4.de* am-c b4.de* ang b7.de* ant-c b7.de* apis bg2 arg-n bg2 ars b4.de* asar b7.de* aur b4.de* *Borx* b4a.de bov b4.de* bry bg2 camph b7.de* carb-an b4.de* caust b4.de* cimic bg2 coff b7.de* coloc b4.de* *Croc* b7.de* dulc b4.de* glon bg2 *Hell* b7.de* hep b4a.de hydr bg2 hyos b7.de* kali-bi bg2 kali-c b4.de* kali-n b4.de* *Laur* b7.de* *Lyc* b4.de* m-aust b7.de mag-m b4.de* mag-p bg2 mang b4.de* mosch b7.de* nat-c b4.de* nat-m b4.de* olnd b7.de* phos b4.de* phyt bg2 podo bg2 *Puls* b7.de* rhod b4.de* sars b4.de* seneg b4.de* sep b4.de* *Stann* b4a.de sul-ac b4.de* sulph b4.de* tab bg2 tarax b7.de* thuj b4.de* viol-t b7.de* zinc b4.de*

○ • **External** head: hep b4a.de laur b7.de* mag-m bg2
- **going** into; when: laur bg2 mang bg2

ALCOHOLIC drinks:
- **agg.**: acon bg2 *Ant-c* b7.de* *Ant-t* bg2 ars bg2 bell bg2 bry bg2 *Calc* b4a.de* carb-an bg2 **Carb-v** bg2 chin bg2 coff bg2 ip bg2 nit-ac bg2 nux-m b7.de* **Nux-v** b7.de* op bg2 par bg2 ph-ac bg2 phos bg2 *Puls* b7.de* *Ran-b* b7.de* *Rhod* b4a.de rhus-t b7.de* ruta b7.de* sabad b7.de* sabin bg2 *Sel* b7a.de sil bg2 *Sulph* bg2 tarax bg2 *Verat* b7.de* zinc b4a.de
- **amel.**: naja bg2

ALIVE in head; sensation of something: alum-sil k4 ant-t asar k* croc k* crot-c k* crot-t hyper *Nat-m* b4a.de *Petr* k* *Sil* k* sulph k* tarax b7.de* tritic-vg fd5.de
- **night**: hyper
  - **bed** agg.; in: hyper
- **anthill**; as if brain was an: agar
- **crawling**; as of a worm: | **Forehead**; in: alum
- **everything** in head were alive, as if: petr
- **leave** through toes; travels down the body and: alum-sil k4
- **pressing**, crawling pain, spreading out from centre, as of something alive: tarax k*
- **walking** agg.: sil

○ - **Temples**: sang tl1
  - **accompanied** by | **pulsations**; irrepressible: sang tl1

ALOPECIA (See Hair - baldness; Hair - falling; SKIN - Hair - falling)

ANEMIA:
- **agg.**: ars bg2 calc bg2 calc-p bg2 chin bg2 cycl bg2 ferr bg2 kali-c bg2 lac-d bg2 nat-m bg2 ph-ac bg2 senec bg2

○ - **Brain**; of: *(↗Anoxia)* *Alum* k* ambr *Ars* bro1 bar-m br1 borx tl1 *Calc* *Calc-p* k* *Calc-s* camph bro1 *Chin* k* chinin-s con k* *Dulc* **Ferr** k* ferr-p bro1 fl-ac *Hell* kali-br hr1 *Kali-c* k* kali-p hr1* kali-sil k2 *Lyc* *Mag-c* *Mag-p* hr1 malar jl2 mosch mur-ac nat-c *Nat-m* *Nit-ac* *Nux-v* k* petr **Ph-ac** **Phos** k* sang sec bro1 *Sel* *Sep* *Sil* *Stry* sulph tab c2* verat bro1 *Zinc* k*
  - **accompanied** by | **vertigo**: arn bro1 bar-m hr1* calc bro1 *Chin* bro1 chinin-s bro1 con bro1 dig bro1 ferr bro1 *Ferr-c* bro1 hydr-ac bro1 nat-m bro1 sil bro1

ANGER: | **agg.**: mez ptk1

ANOXIA; cerebral: *(↗Anemia - brain; Apoplexy)* op mtf zinc-s mtf

ANXIETY:
- **agg.**: acon bg2 calc bg2 caust bg2 cimic bg2 glon bg2 ran-b b7a.de rheum b7a.de spig bg2

○ - **Head**; in: ant-c a1 apis b7a.de caust bg2 cic b7.de* laur bg2* mag-c hr1 nat-c h2* nat-m h2* phos hr1 psor hr1 sars h2* thuj hr1

APOPLEXY: *(↗Anoxia; Cerebral hemorrhage; Cerebrovascular; GENERALS - Apoplexy)* acon ptk1* ant-c ptk1 ant-t ptk1 arn br1* ars ptk1* aur ptk1 **Bar-c** ptk1* *Bell* ptk1 calc ptk1 chen-a bwa3 **Cocc** ptk1 coff ptk1 **Crot-h** vh ferr ptk1 gels ptk1* *Glon* ptk1 **Hydr-ac** ptk1 hyos ptk1 *Ip* ptk1* kali-br mrr1 kali-m ptk1 lach ptk1* lyc ptk1 nux-m tt1* **Nux-v** ptk1* op k2* ph-ac ptk1 phos tt1* plb mrr1 puls ptk1 rhus-t ptk1 samb ptk1 sep ptk1 sil hr1 staph mrr1 stram ptk1* thuj ptk1 verat ptk1 verat-v a2*

Apoplexy: ...
- **accompanied** by | **diabetes** (See GENERALS - Diabetes mellitus - accompanied - apoplexy)

○ - **Subarachnoid**: gels ptk1

ASCENDING:
- **agg.**: bell ptk1 bry ptk1 calc ptk1 ign b7.de* meny b7.de* nux-v b7.de* rhus-t b7.de* sil ptk1 spig ptk1
- **stairs** | **after** | **agg.**: *M-arct* b7.de*
  - **agg.**: alum b4.de* ant-c b7.de* arn b7.de* bell b4.de* crot-h bg2 cupr bg2 ign b7.de* *Lach* b7a.de lyc b4.de* meny b7.de* mosch b7.de* nat-s bg2 nux-v b7.de* par b7.de* ph-ac b4a.de* rhus-t b7.de* spong b7.de* staph b7.de* sulph b4a.de*
    - **External** head: hell b7.de*

ASLEEP, sensation as if: *(↗Numbness)* alum k* apis k* calad carb-an con k* cupr merc k* mur-ac k* nat-m nit-ac k* op k* sep k*
- **debauch**, after a: *Op* k*
- **eating**; after: con k*
- **lying** agg.: merc k*

○ - **Forehead**:
  - **in**: mur-ac k*
  - **left** half of: calad
- **Sides** | **left**: calad

ATROPHY: caust bg2 lach bg2 stram bg2 sulph bg2

○ - **Brain**; of: *Aur* bro1 *Bar-c* bro1 fl-ac bro1 iod bro1 *Phos* bro1 *Plb* bro1 zinc bro1

BALANCING:
- **difficult** to keep the head erect: glon
- **motion** agg.: crot-h fl-ac lyc rhus-t
- **pendulum**-like: cann-i
- **sensation** in: aesc k* bell k* *Glon* k* lap-la rsp1 lyc k* suis-pan rly4•

○ - **Brain**, to and fro: *(↗Looseness)* aphis rb2 chen-a vml3• chin c1* lyc rti2 sul-ac c1 sulph c1

BALDNESS (See Hair - baldness)

BALL; sensation of a: *(↗Foreign - brain - right; Lump)* ant-t bg2 arn bg2 bufo bg2 chel bg2 ign bg2 plat b4.de* *Sep* b4a.de
- **fastened** in brain: staph k*
- **hot** ball: carb-ac bg2 kali-c bg2
- **lying** on right side agg.: anan
- **rising** up: acon k* ant-t a arn a bufo a chel a cimic ign a lach plat plb k* sep staph
- **rolled** into a ball; as if: ant-t bg2 **Arn** bg2 chel bg2 chin bg2 cocc bg2 staph bg2
- **rolling** in brain: *(↗Rolling in - lead)* anan k* ars bg2* bufo chin b eug bg2 hura k* lach bg2* lys bg2 lyss phos bg2* phys bg2 plat bg2 sep bg2
- **striking** in head | **talking** agg.: sars ptk1

○ - **Forehead**: ant-t bg3* carb-ac bg2* caust bg2* kali-c bg2* lac-d k* ozone sde2• *Staph* k*
  - **headache**; during: ozone sde2•
- **Occiput**; in: staph mrr1
- **Skull**; beating against | **walk**; on beginning to: plat
- **Temple** | **heavy** ball in temple; sensation of a: cob-n sp1
- **Vertex** | **heavy** ball in vertex; sensation of a: cob-n sp1

BAND (See Constriction; Constriction - band)

BATHING:
- **agg.**: **Ant-c** b7.de* bry bg2 calc bg2 canth bg2* nit-ac b4a.de phos bg2 puls bg2 *Rhus-t* b7.de*
- **cold** bathing agg.: *Ant-c* bg2 ars bg2 bry bg2 cycl bg2 glon bg2 lac-c bg2 podo bg2 zinc bg2
- **face** bathing:
  - **cold** bathing face | **amel.**: agar bg2 asar bg2 phos bg2
- **feet** bathing:
  - **amel.**: asc-t ptk1
  - **cold** bathing feet | **amel.**: nat-s bg2

BED AGG.; IN: kali-c bg2

○ - **External** head: ran-b b7.de* staph b7.de*

BEEF agg.; roasted: staph bg2

BEER agg.: *Bell* bg2 ferr b7.de* **Rhus-t** b7.de* verat b7.de*

BENDING:
- **backward**:
  - **amel.** | **Occiput**: cocc ptk1 murx ptk1
- **forward**:
  - **agg.** | **sitting**; when: con bg2
- **head**:
  - **amel.**: seneg ptk1 thuj ptk1
  - **backward**: (↗*BACK - Spasmodic - Cervical*)
    - **agg.**: anac b4.de* aur b4.de* bell b4.de* cupr b7.de* dig b4.de* *Lyc* b4a.de* mang b4a.de* spig bg2 stann b4.de* valer b7.de*
      - **sleep**; during: *Hell* b7a.de *Hep* b4a.de rheum b7.de
    - **amel.**: apis b7a.de* bar-c b4a.de *Bell* b4.de* cann-xyz bg2 cham bg2 cimic bg2 glon bg2 hep bg2 hyper bg2 m-aust b7.de mang bg2 ph-ac bg2 rhus-t b7.de* sil bg2 thuj b4.de* verat b7.de*
    - **must** bend head backward: (↗*Drawn - backward; BACK - Spasmodic - cervical*) ant-t ptk1 arn k* *Cham* k* kali-n k* nat-c ptk1 stram ptk1
      - **walking** agg.: (↗*Falling - backward - walking; Motions of - throwing - backward*) *Arn*
  - **forward**:
    - **must** bend head: tarent k2
      - **floor**; to | **amel.**: sang bg2
      - **walking** agg.: sulph k*
  - **side**; to:
    - **agg.**: chin b7.de*
    - **amel.**: meny b7.de* puls b7.de*

BINDING: | **amel.**: apis ptk1 *Arg-n* ptk1 glon ptk1 hep b4a.de lac-d ptk1 mag-m ptk1 pic-ac ptk1 *Puls* ptk1 pyrog ptk1 sil b4a.de*

BLOOD VESSELS: | **Veins** of temples distended (See FACE - Veins - temples)

BLOWING THE NOSE:
- **agg.**: ambr b7.de* chel b7.de* lyc b4a.de mur-ac bg2 nit-ac bg2 sulph b4.de*
- **amel.**: chel ptk1

BOARD; sensation as if a: (↗*Foreign - brain - right*) nat-m sne

○ - **Front** of head; in●: (↗*Foreign - brain - right*) acon k* aesc k* bapt ptk1 calc k* *Carb-an* k* cocc k* coloc bg2 cupr bg2 *Dulc* k* eug k* guaj bg2 helon k* irid-met srj5• kreos k* **Lyc** k ●* nux-m ptk1 olnd k* op k* plat k* plb **Rhus-t** k ●* sel a1 **Sulph** k ●* tarent-c ptk1 zinc zing k*
  - **forenoon** | **11** h: zing k*
- **Through** head, from temple to temple: plut-n srj7•
- **Vertex**: tab bg2

BODY hot: | **Forehead**; in: kali-c h2*

BOILING sensation: (↗*Bubbling; Motions in; Shaking sensation; Shaking the head; Waving*) **Acon** *Agath-a* nl2• alum alum-sil k2 bufo ck cann-i caust chin coff dig graph grat hell kali-c kali-s kali-sil k2 laur lyc mag-m k* mang med merc sars sil sulph
- **water** in head; as if boiling: acon k* bar-c bg2 indg mag-m bg2 rob

○ - **Forehead**: agath-a nl2•
- **Side** lain on: mag-m k*
- **Vertex** | **left**: lach

BORES head in pillow: (↗*Pain - pillow*) **Apis** k* *Arn* arum-t c1* **Bell** k* *Bry* camph k* cic ptk1 *Cimic* ptk1 crot-t cupr ptk1* dig *Hell* k* helo c1 helo-s c1* hyper k* lach bg2* *Med* k* op ptk1 podo a* psor al sang bg2* *Stram* k* sulph syph ptk1 tarent **Tub** k* verat bg2* verat-v hr1* zinc bg2*
- **children**; in: | **newborns**: cham mtf33
- **delirium**; during: bell mtf33
- **intestinal** disturbances, in: cina bl
- **sleep** agg.; during: apis sf1.de arn st bell b4a.de* cupr mtf33 hell sf1.de hep st hyper k* lach sf1.de spong st verat sf1.de zinc sf1.de

BORING with fingers in nose: | **amel.**: tarent bg2*

BRAIN DAMAGE: (↗*Concussion; Injuries*) diph-pert-t mp4•

BRANDY: | **agg.**: *Ign* b7a.de **Nux-v** b7.de* *Puls* b7.de* ruta b7.de* verat b7.de*

BREAD agg.: zinc bg2

BREAKFAST:
- **after**:
  - **agg.**: bufo bg2 cham b7.de* hyper bg2 iris bg2 lyc b4a.de* nit-ac bg2 *Nux-m* b7.de* nux-v b7.de* par b7.de* plb b7.de* sul-ac bg2
  - **amel.**: am-m b7.de* bov bg2 canth b7.de* con bg2 croc b7.de*

BREATHING: | **deep**:
  - **agg.**: anac bg2* borx b4a.de cact bg2* crot-h bg2 mang bg2 rat bg2*
    - **Vertex**: anac ptk1
- **holding** breath | **agg.**: agar bg2 glon bg2

BRITTLE sensation: nat-m h2*

BUBBLING sensation in: (↗*Boiling; Gurgling; Motions in*) acon k* asaf k* bar-c bg2* bell benz-ac hr1 berb bry k* caust bg2 chinin-s c1 crot-t bg2 dig bg2 glon bg2 grat bg2 hell bg2 hydr-ac bg2 hyos bg2 indg k* kali-c k* kreos k* lach bg2 lyc bg2 mag-m bg2 merc bg2 nux-v k* par k* plb bg2 *Puls* k* rob k* *Spig* k* stroph-h c1 *Sulph* k* tere-la rly4•
- **night**: par k* puls k*
- **leaning** back while sitting | **amel.**: spig k*
- **walking** agg.: nux-v k* spig k*

○ - **Forehead**; as if a bubble was bursting in *Form* k*
- **Occiput**, in: indg k* junc-e a1* sumb

BULGING out of head; sensation as if something was: | **Forehead**: phel a1

CANCER:

○ - **Brain**; of: (↗*Tumors - brain; Tumors - swellings; GENERALS - Tumors - encephaloma*) **Bar-c** mk1• **Bar-i** mk1• *Plb* mk1• **Plb-i** mk1• sil mtf
- **Skull**; of: cadm-met gm1 hippoz gm1
  - **sarcoma**: cadm-met gm1

CARIES: arg-met asaf **Aur** k* caps *Fl-ac* k* *Hep* hippoz mez tl1 *Nat-m* **Nit-ac** k* *Ph-ac* **Phos** **Sil** *Staph*
- **mastoid** process; of (See EAR - Caries - mastoid)

CARRYING things agg.: nat-c bg2

CEPHALHEMATOMA: (↗*Injuries - children - delivery*) *Calc-f* k* *Merc* k* *Rhus-t* b7a.de *Sil* k*

CEREBELLAR diseases: helo bro1 helo-s rwt2• sulfon bro1

CEREBRAL complaints (See Brain; complaints)

CEREBRAL HEMORRHAGE: (↗*Apoplexy; Cerebrovascular; Thrombosis; GENERALS - Paralysis - one - apoplexy*) **Acon** k* ail vh1 **Anac** hr1 anthraci vh1 apis pkj1 arg-n mrr1 *Arn* k* *Ars* hr1 *Aster* hr1 *Aur* k* *Bar-c* k* **Bell** k* **Both** mp1• **Bry** hr1* **Calc** k* *Camph* k* carb-v *Chin* k* cina bl **Cocc** k* *Coff* (non:colch ib) con k* crat pkj1 *Crot-h* k* *Cupr* k* cur a1 dig a1 *Ferr* k* ferr-p a form hr1 **Gels** k* **Glon** hr1 hell a* helon mp1• hydr-ac a1 *Hyos* k* iod hr1 **Ip** k* kali-c pkj1 **Lach** k* laur k* lol a1 *Lyc* merc k* mill hr1* morph a1 *Nat-m* nit-ac *Nux-m* k* *Nux-v* k* oena hr1 **Op** k* ox-ac a1 parathyr jl2 *Phos* k* pitu-gl br1 plb k* *Puls* k* sang hr1 sec a1 sep k2 *Sin-n* hr1 stram k* tab a1* verat a1 *Verat-v* hr1 [kali-m stj1]
- **symmetrical**: anthraci vh

CEREBROVASCULAR ACCIDENT: (↗*Apoplexy; Cerebral hemorrhage; Thrombosis*) alum vh1* aml-ns vh1 hell gvt2 kali-br pks1 lyss bnu3

CHEWING agg.: am-c bg2 am-m b7a.de* ambr bg2 kali-c bg2 olnd b7.de* phos b4.de* ptel bg2 *Sulph* b4.de* thuj bg2 verb bg2

○ - **External** head: thuj b4.de*
- **Temples**: zinc ptk1

CHILDREN; complaints of: *Acon* bg2 *Bell* bg2 calc-p bg2 caps bg2 cham bg2 coff bg2 ign bg2 ip bg2
- **girls**; young: *Acon* bg2 bell bg2 *Puls* bg2

CHILL; during: *Acon* b7.de alum b4.de* am-c b4.de* arn b7.de *Ars* b4.de *Bry* b7.de* calc b4.de caps b7.de carb-v b4.de *Cham* b7.de chin b7.de cina b7.de *Con* b4.de* dros b7.de *Hell* b7.de *Hyos* bg2 ign b7.de kali-c b4.de kali-n b4.de lyc b4.de m-aust b7.de *Mang* b4a.de mez b4.de nat-c b4.de *Nat-m* b4.de* *Petr* b4.de* phos b4.de *Puls* b7.de* *Rhus-t* b7.de sep b4.de sil b4.de spong b7.de sulph b4.de *Tarax* b7.de* viol-t b7.de

Head

CHILLINESS: | **Scalp**: *Agn* b7.de* ambr b7a.de bar-c b4.de calc b4.de carb-v b4.de dulc b4.de kali-c b4.de merc b4a.de *Merc-c* b4a.de nux-v b7.de ph-ac b4.de spig b7.de stann b4a.de staph b7.de *Thuj* b4a.de verat b7.de

CHIRPING: bry b7.de*

CHURCH agg.; air in (See Vaults)

CLOSING THE EYES:
- **agg.**: all-c ptk1 bry b7.de* chin ptk1 cocc bg2 nux-v b7.de* sabin bg2 sil ptk1 *Ther* bg2*
- **amel.**: *Apis* b7a.de bell bg2 *Calc* b4a.de con b4a.de hell b7.de* ip b7.de* *Sep* b4a.de spig b7.de*
  - **partly**; closing the eyes: aloe ptk1

CLUCKING in: sulph
O - **Temples**; in: bry h1

CLUSTER headache (See Pain - cluster)

COFFEE:
- **agg.**: arg-n bg2 calc bg2 caust bg2 *Cham* b7.de* cocc bg2 hep bg2 **Ign** b7.de* kali-n b4.de* lach bg2 lyc bg2 *Merc* bg2 **Nux-v** b7.de* puls bg2
- **hot** coffee agg.: arum-t ptk1

COITION agg.: bcv ptk1 calc bg2 ham ptk1 ph-ac ptk1 sil bg2*

COLD: *(↗Air agg.)*
- **agg.**: ant-c ptk1 bar-c ptk1 bell tl1 grat bg2
O · **External** head: acon bg2 borx b4a.de* naja bg2
- **air**:
  - **agg.**: *(↗Air agg.)* acon a1 ant-c *Ars* k* *Aur* b4.de* *Bar-c* *Bell* k* benz-ac k* borx bov b4.de* brom k* calc b4.de* *Caps* b7a.de *Carb-an* k* *Carb-v* k* card-m **Chin** cocc b7.de* coff b7.de* dulc st eup-per ferr b7.de* ferr-p *Graph* grat k* **Hep** hyos ign b7.de* kali-ar kali-bi bg2* *Kali-c* k* kali-p *Lach* *Lyc* k* mag-c h2* *Mag-m* *Merc* *Mez* k* moni rfm1• *Nat-m* k* nux-m **Nux-v** k* *Phos* k* plat bg2 *Psor* k* puls gk *Rhod* b4a.de *Rhus-t* k* ruta b7.de* sanic *Sep* k* **Sil** k* squil *Stront-c* symph fd3.de• thuj zinc
    - **morning**: carb-v
    - **evening**: ant-c
    - **night**: *Phos*
    - **walking** in cold air: **Carb-v**
    - **External** head: nux-v bg2
      - **chill**; during: acon bg2
    - **Occiput**: sanic ptk1*
  - **amel.**: arg-n bg2 phos b4.de* seneg b4.de*
  - **entering** cold air agg.: *Ran-b* b7a.de verb b7a.de
  - **inspiration** agg.: cimic ptk
- **amel.**: seneg bg2
O · **External** head: mag-m bg2
  - **Vertex**: naja ptk1
- **applications** | **amel.**: aloe ptk1 *Ars* b4a.de* bry ptk1 cycl ptk1 *Glon* ptk1 phos ptk1 *Sil* b4a.de sulph ptk1
- **bathing**:
  - **amel.** | **Occiput**: calc-p ptk1
- **drinks**:
  - **agg.**: *Acon* bg2 ars bg2 *Bell* bg2 dig b4a.de* nat-c bg2 puls bg2
    - **icy** cold agg.: con ptk1 dig ptk1
- **food** | **agg.**: puls bg2
- **washing**:
  - **agg.**: *Bell* b4a.de *Sep* b4a.de
  - **feet** | **amel.**: nat-s ptk1
- **water**:
  - **agg.**: ant-c ptk1 *Nux-v* b7a.de sulph bg2
  - **amel.**: *Aloe* bg2 ant-t b7.de* *Apis* bg2 *Ars* b4.de* asar b7.de* bry b7.de* calc bg2 calc-p bg2 cham b7.de* cimic bg2 cycl bg2 euphr bg2 glon bg2 kali-bi bg2 nat-c bg2 *Nat-m* bg2 nit-ac bg2 psor b4a.de zinc b4.de*

COLD; BECOMING: | **after** | **head**: verb b7a.de
- **agg.**: arn b7.de* *Aur* bg2 bell b4a.de* carb-an bg2 *Hyos* b7a.de rhus-t b7.de* sep bg2 sil bg2 *Stront-c* bg2
  - **feet**: sil bg2
  - **hand**: calc bg2

Cold; becoming – **agg.**: ...
O · **External** head: graph bg2

COLD; TAKING A:
- **after**: **Acon** b7.de* ant-c b7a.de* *Bell* b4.de* bry b7.de* calc b4.de* caust b4.de* *Cham* b7.de* chin bg2 *Coff* b7a.de coloc bg2 *Dulc* b4.de* glon bg2 graph bg2 hep b4a.de hyos b7a.de *Lach* bg2 m-ambo b7.de nit-ac b4.de* **Nux-v** b7.de* petr b4.de* phos b4.de* *Puls* b7.de* rhus-t b7.de* samb b7.de* sep b4.de* sil bg2 verat b7.de*
O · **External** head: led b7a.de *Nux-v* b7a.de
- **tendency**: *Bar-c* b4a.de bell b4a.de borx b4a.de calc b4a.de *Carb-v* b4a.de *Kali-c* b4.de* led b7a.de lyc b4a.de *Nat-m* b4.de* nit-ac b4a.de phos b4a.de *Sil* b4a.de

COLDNESS, chilliness, etc.: abrot k* acon k* **Agar** k* agn k* aloe bg2 alum k* alum-p k2 alumn am-c ambr k* anan ant-c apis *Arn* k* *Ars* k* ars-i asaf asar k* *Aur* bar-c k* bar-i k2 bar-s k2 **Bell** k* benz-ac borx **Calc** k* calc-ar k2 calc-i k2 calc-p k* calc-s calc-sil k2* *Cann-s* cann-xyz bg2* caps carb-an *Carb-v* k* carbn-s caust bg2 chel k* chin bg2 chinin-ar chlam-tr bcx2• chlor choc srj3• cimic cist coca cocc *Colch* *Con* k* *Croc* k* cupr k* dios dulc k* eup-per falco-pe nl2• ferr k* ferr-ar ferr-i ferr-p gels gins glon k* *Graph* grat ham helo bro1 helo-s rwt2• hura hyper bg3* ign bg2 ind iod irid-met srj5• iris c1 kali-ar *Kali-c* k* kali-fcy c kali-p kali-s kali-sil k2 kreos k* *Lach* k* lachn lact *Laur* k* *Led* bg *Lyc* k* mag-m mag-s mang k* *Meny* *Merc* k* **Merc-c** k* merc-i-r morph mosch k* naja *Nat-m* k* *Nit-ac* nux-v k* olnd par mrr1 petr bg ph-ac k* phel *Phos* k* phyt k* *Plat* bg2* plut-n srj7• positr nl2• propr sa3• psor k2 puls b7a.de* raph rhod bg **Rhus-t** k* rhus-v rumx *Ruta* k* sabad sabin bg2 *Sanic* *Sep* k* *Sil* k* spig bg2 spong bg2* **Stann** k* staph k* **Stront-c** k* stry sul-i k2 *Sulph* k* sumb *Tarent* k* thea thuj bg2 til tritic-vg fd5.de valer k* *Verat* k* *Verat-v* bg3* verb vip zing
- **morning**: cedr dios lact positr nl2• sumb *Tarent*
- **afternoon**: ars h2 *Arum-t* gamb gels ol-an valer
- **evening**: alum ars-i dulc hyper kreos merc stry *Sulph* zinc
- **night**: cimic dulc fd4.de lyc mang *Phos* *Sep* stront-c
- **accompanied** by | **Back**; coldness of: *Rhus-t* b7a.de
- **air**; in open:
  - **agg.**: *Ars* phos spong fd4.de
  - **amel.**: *Laur* sep
- **alternating** with | **heat** of head (See Heat - alternating - coldness)
- **begins** in head: *Bar-c* nat-m stann
  - **spreads** from the: mosch valer
- **breakfast** agg.; after: arn
- **burning**; after: sulph
- **cold**:
  - **air**:
    - **agg.**: calc k2 dulc fd4.de grat k2
    - **as** from: acon arg-n cimic k2 *Laur* nat-m petr **Verat** a1
    - **came** from head, as if cold air: falco-pe nl2•
    - **passing** over brain; as if cold air: anan cimic hr1* meny *Petr* *Sanic*
  - **cloth** around the brain; as if: glon k* *Sanic* k*
  - **pain** passing up median lines to vertex and passing down to ear: lac-f c1
- **congestion** of, with: *(↗Congestion - chill)* glon
- **covered**:
  - **amel.**: *Aur* grat kali-i mag-m k2 nat-m sanic
  - **even** when: mang
- **followed** by | **heat**: verat a1
- **hand**; as if touched by an icy cold: helo-s rwt2• hyper c1*
- **hat**; from pressure of a: valer
- **headache**; during: *Ars* ars-s-f k2 calc bro1 calc-act bro1 dulc fd4.de irid-met srj5• phel a* sep bro1 sulph verat bro1
- **heat**; with: androc srj1• chin puls verat h1
- **heated**; from becoming: **Carb-v** k*
- **icy**: *Agar* *Ars* bar-c **Calc** calc-p ind laur nux-v phos *Sep* valer verat k2 vip c
  - **alternating** with | **congestion** of head (See Congestion - alternating - ice-cold)
O · **Scalp**: calc ptk1
- **internally**: acon bg2 agar bg2 arn k* bell k* **Calc** k* chel bg2 cimic bg2 cist bg2 con bg2 cupr bg2 dulc bg2 mosch bg2 petr bg2 phos bg2 puls bg2 sep bg2 staph h1 verat bg2

- **lying** | **amel**.: calc
- **menses**; during: ant-t calc mag-s sep sulph *Verat*
- **motion** agg.: chel sep
- **pain**; with: all-c$_{tl1}$ *Gels* irid-met$_{srj5•}$ *Phos*$_{k*}$
- **painful** parts: *Kali-i*
- **perspiration**; with: merc-c phos$_{b4a.de}$
  - **body**, of: phos$_{h2}$
- **riding**; after: lyc
- **scratching** agg.; after: *Agar*
- **sitting** agg.: mez
- **spot**, as of a cold: agar$_{vh*}$ choc$_{srj3•}$ sulph
- **stool**:
  - **after** | **agg**.: plat
  - **before**: carb-an
  - **during** | **agg**.: staph$_{h1}$
- **stooping** agg.: alum sep
- **walking** | **amel**.: gins
- **warm** room agg.: *Laur*$_{k*}$ merc-i-r tarent
- **water**, as from cold: *Cann-s* carb-an$_{h2}$ croc cupr glon sabad *Tarent*
- **wind** as of a: arg-n$_{bg2}$ petr$_{bg2}$ verat$_{bg1}$

○ • **Occiput**: chel$_{bg2}$ cimic$_{bg2}$
- **wrap** the head; must: calc$_{k2}$ spong$_{fd4.de}$

▽ - **extending** to:

○ • **Brain**; base of: helo-s$_{rwt2•}$
  - **Downward**: castor-eq$_{bg2}$ helo-s$_{rwt2•}$

○ - **Across** head: sil$_{bg2}$
- **Brain**: mosch$_{ptk1}$ phos$_{ptk1}$
- **Forehead**: acon$_{k*}$ *Agar* anac$_{k*}$ arn$_{k*}$ *Ars* ars-s-f$_{hr1}$ bar-c$_{h2*}$ bell$_{k*}$ calc$_{k*}$ calc-p$_{k2}$ calc-s$_{k2}$ *Camph*$_{k*}$ carbn-s cedr cham chin$_{k*}$ chinin-ar cimic$_{k*}$ cina$_{bg2}$ cinnb cist coff$_{k*}$ colch$_{k*}$ dros$_{sne}$ dulc$_{fd4.de}$ gels$_{k*}$ glon *Graph Hep* hydr-ac hyper$_{k*}$ irid-met$_{srj5•}$ *Lachn*$_{k*}$ *Laur*$_{k*}$ lyc$_{k*}$ mag-m$_{k*}$ merc$_{k*}$ mez$_{k*}$ mosch nat-m$_{k2}$ oena ph-ac$_{k*}$ phel plb$_{hr1}$ puls$_{k*}$ ran-s rhus-t$_{hr1*}$ staph$_{k*}$ sul-ac$_{k*}$ sulph tarent verat$_{k*}$ *Zinc*$_{k*}$ zinc-p$_{k2}$
  - **one**-sided: spig$_{h1}$
  - **morning**: cedr
  - **afternoon**: nat-ar
  - **evening**: hyper sulph zinc
  - **night**: lyc
  - **accompanied** by:
    - **Occiput**; heat in: zinc$_{vh*}$
    - **Teeth**; pain in (See TEETH - Pain - accompanied - forehead - cold)
  - **air** | **draft** of; as from a: *Laur* staph$_{h1}$ zinc$_{h2}$
  - **alternating** with | **heat** of forehead (See Heat - forehead - alternating - coldness)
  - **cold** air agg. | **painfully**; penetrates: zinc
  - **externally**: cinnb cist gels laur sulph
  - **headache**; during: ars-s-f$_{k2}$
  - **heat**:
    - **during**: bell$_{bg2}$ chin$_{k*}$ cina$_{b7.de*}$ puls zinc$_{h2}$
    - **external** heat, with: agar$_{k*}$
  - **ice**, as from: agar glon lachn$_{c1}$ laur
  - **menses**; during: sulph
  - **perspiration**; during: carb-v$_{bg2}$ cina$_{bg2}$ lyc$_{b4a.de}$ *Verat*$_{bg2}$
  - **spots**; as of a cold finger in small: *Arn*$_{k*}$
  - **vertigo**; with: lachn$_{c1}$
  - **warm**:
    - **becomes** warm if lightly covered: lyc$_{c}$ sil$_{a1}$
    - **room** | **agg**.: cist *Laur*

○ • **Base** of brain hot: zinc$_{kr1}$
- **Occiput**: acon$_{k*}$ agar$_{k*}$ aloe$_{k*}$ alum$_{k*}$ alum-p$_{k2}$ alum-sil$_{k2}$ anac$_{bg2}$ berb$_{k*}$ *Calc*$_{k*}$ **Calc-p**$_{k*}$ calc-sil$_{k2}$ cann-i cann-xyz$_{bg2}$ castor-eq$_{bg2}$ **Chel**$_{k*}$ chinin-s coc-c$_{k*}$ *Dulc*$_{k*}$ echi ferul$_{bro1}$ gels$_{k*}$ gins helo$_{a*}$ helo-s$_{rwt2•}$ *Ign*$_{b7a.de}$ *Kali-n*$_{k*}$ laur$_{b7.de*}$ mosch$_{bg2}$ nux-m ph-ac$_{b4a.de}$ *Phos*$_{k*}$ plat$_{k*}$ podo rhod$_{bg2}$ sep$_{b4a.de*}$ sil symph$_{fd3.de•}$ tarent thea verat
  - **right** side: *Form*$_{k*}$ lach$_{bg2*}$

Coldness, chilliness, etc – **Occiput**: ...
  - **left** side: cocc$_{h1}$
  - **evening**: alum *Dulc*
  - **accompanied** by | **Head**; pain in (See Pain - accompanied - occiput)
  - **air**; like cold: acon
  - **frozen**, as if: gels nux-v *Sep*
  - **rising** from neck like cold air: **Chel** sep
  - **weather** agg.; cold wet: *Dulc*

▽ • **extending** to:
    - **Feet**: helo-s$_{br1*}$
      - **waves**; in cold: helo-s$_{br1*}$
- **Scalp**: agar$_{b4.de*}$ *Agn*$_{bg2}$ alum$_{b4.de*}$ am-c$_{b4.de*}$ ambr$_{bg2}$ *Apis*$_{b7a.de*}$ asar$_{b7.de*}$ *Bar-c*$_{b4.de*}$ **Calc**$_{b4.de*}$ cann-s$_{b7.de*}$ *Carb-v*$_{bg2}$ chel$_{b7a.de*}$ cimic$_{bg2}$ cist$_{bg2}$ cupr$_{bg2}$ dios$_{bg2}$ dulc$_{bg2}$ glon$_{bg2}$ graph$_{b4a.de*}$ kali-c$_{bg2}$ lach$_{b7.de*}$ laur$_{b7a.de*}$ *Led*$_{bg2}$ lyc$_{bg2}$ mag-m$_{b4.de*}$ mang$_{b4.de*}$ merc$_{bg2}$ *Merc-c*$_{bg2}$ nat-m$_{bg2}$ nux-v$_{bg2}$ petr$_{bg2}$ ph-ac$_{b4.de*}$ phos$_{b4.de*}$ rhod$_{b4.de*}$ **Rhus-t**$_{bg2}$ *Ruta*$_{bg2}$ sabad$_{b7.de*}$ *Sep*$_{b4a.de*}$ spig$_{bg2}$ stann$_{bg2}$ staph$_{bg2}$ **Sulph**$_{b4a.de*}$ **Verat**$_{b7.de*}$
  - **hat**; has to wear a: psor$_{tl1}$
- **Sides**: *Asar* bar-c *Calc* cann-s *Con* croc kali-bi lach lob phos tarent tritic-vg$_{fd5.de}$ verat
  - **one** side: *Calc* con$_{k*}$ lach ruta$_{h1}$
  - **right**: am-m$_{h2}$ bar-c$_{k*}$ *Calc*$_{k*}$ verat
    - **evening**: alum *Dulc*
    - **feels** burning hot; but: bar-c *Calc*
  - **left**: croc$_{b7.de*}$ lach phos$_{k*}$ tritic-vg$_{fd5.de}$
  - **spots**, in: croc
    - **Above** the ear: asar
  - **warmth** | **amel**.: lach
- **Temples**: bell *Berb*$_{k*}$ gamb merc-c ol-an ph-ac plat rhod tarent
  - **right**: berb tarent
  - **left**: gamb$_{a1*}$
- **Vertex**: acon$_{b7.de*}$ agar$_{k*}$ am-c arn *Arum-t* aur$_{bg2}$ aur-m *Bry* calc$_{k*}$ **Calc-p**$_{k*}$ calc-s calc-sil$_{k2}$ *Chin*$_{bg2}$ cimic$_{bg2}$ cist$_{bg2}$ dulc$_{fd4.de}$ elec$_{wd}$ falco-pe$_{nl2•}$ ferr-p grat$_{k*}$ kali-c$_{k*}$ kali-i kali-s kali-sil$_{k2}$ *Laur*$_{k*}$ mang$_{k*}$ myric naja$_{ptk1}$ *Nat-m*$_{k*}$ plat psor *Sep*$_{k*}$ *Sil*$_{k*}$ spong$_{b7a.de}$ sul-i$_{k2}$ sulph$_{k*}$ tarent$_{k*}$ tritic-vg$_{fd5.de}$ valer$_{k*}$ **Verat**$_{k*}$
  - **afternoon**: *Arum-t*
  - **covered**, even when: mang
  - **covering**; as if upper part was without: arum-t
  - **icy** coldness: agar arn *Calc*$_{ptk1}$ *Laur* nat-m$_{gk}$ sep$_{a}$ valer *Verat*$_{k*}$
    - **when** covered: valer
  - **menses**; during: *Sep* sulph *Verat*
  - **motion** agg.: sep
  - **spots**, in: mang *Sulph*
    - **small**: mang
  - **stooping** agg.: sep
  - **warm** room agg.: *Laur*
  - **water**, as from cold: tarent

▽ • **extending** to | **Sacrum**: acon

COMMOTION in head; sensation of a painless: caust$_{k*}$

COMPANY:
- **agg**.: ant-c$_{bg2}$ lyc$_{ptk1}$ mag-c$_{b4a.de*}$ *Plat*$_{ptk1}$ *Plb*$_{ptk1}$ staph$_{ptk1}$
- **large** company agg.: mag-c$_{bg2}$ plat$_{bg2}$

COMPLAINTS of head: **Bell**$_{ptk1}$ *Bry*$_{ptk1}$ calc$_{ptk1}$ *Carb-v*$_{ptk1}$ chin$_{ptk1}$ gels$_{ptk1}$ *Glon*$_{ptk1}$ helodr-cal$_{knl2•}$ *Lach*$_{ptk1}$ lachn$_{br1}$ *Lyc*$_{ptk1}$ *Nat-m*$_{ptk1}$ nat-sal$_{br1}$ *Nux-v*$_{ptk1}$ par$_{ptk1}$ *Phos*$_{ptk1}$ *Prun*$_{br1}$ *Puls*$_{ptk1}$ sabal$_{br1}$ sang$_{ptk1}$ sep$_{ptk1}$ *Sil*$_{ptk1}$ sol-ni$_{br1}$ spig$_{ptk1}$ sulph$_{ptk1}$ tub$_{ptk1}$ [bell-p-sp$_{dcm1}$]
- **morning**: *Am-m*$_{br1*}$
- **abdomen**; as if coming from: graph$_{bg2}$ plb$_{bg2}$ rheum$_{bg2}$

- **accompanied** by:
  - **anger** (See MIND - Anger - head)
  - **appetite**:
    - **ravenous**: chinin-s bg2
    - **wanting**: acon bg2 ant-c bg2 lach bg2 nat-m bg2 sel bg2 seneg bg2 stann bg2 stram bg2
  - **confusion** (See MIND - Confusion - head - complaints)
  - **deafness** (See HEARING - Lost - accompanied - head; HEARING - Lost - accompanied - head - complaints)
  - **despair** (See MIND - Despair - head)
  - **diarrhea** | **schoolgirls**; in: calc-p ptk1
  - **fear** of death (See MIND - Fear - death - head)
  - **gout** (See EXTREMITIES - Pain - joints - gouty - accompanied - head)
  - **heat** of body; general: bov bg2 chin bg2 hep bg2 kreos bg2 sang bg2 sulph bg2
  - **hemiopia** (See VISION - Hemiopia - accompanied - head)
  - **humor**; bad (See MIND - Irritability - head; with)
  - **incoordination**: *Acon* bg2 *Bell* bg2
  - **indolence** (See MIND - Laziness - head; with)
  - **lachrymation**: *(↗EYE - Lachrymation - headache)* asar bg2 bov bg2 carb-an bg2 carb-v bg2 *Ign* bg2 merc bg2 plat bg2 stram bg2
    - **one** side: puls bg2
  - **nausea**: acon b7.de* aloe bg2 alum b4.de* am-c b4.de* *Ant-c* b7.de* *Apis* b4a.de* arg-met b7.de* ars b4.de* *Asar* b7a.de *Borx* b4a.de bry b7a.de calc b4.de* camph b7.de* caps b7.de* *Carb-v* b4a.de *Caust* b4.de* chin b7a.de cic b7.de* **Cocc** b7.de* *Coloc* b4a.de con b4a.de* croc b7.de* dros b7.de* dulc b4.de* graph b4.de* hep b4a.de *Ign* b7.de* *Ip* b7.de* kali-c b4.de* *Lach* b7a.de *Mag-c* b4.de* mosch b7.de* nat-m b4.de* nit-ac b4.de* *Nux-v* b7.de* petr b4.de* phos b4.de* puls b7a.de *Ran-b* b7.de* ruta b7.de* *Sars* b4a.de *Sep* b4.de* *Sil* b4.de* stann b4.de* *Sulph* b4.de* tarax b7.de* verat b7.de*
  - **palpitation**: acon bg2 alum bg2 ant-t bg2 *Bell* b4a.de *Bov* b4a.de bufo bg2 clem bg2 glon bg2 hep bg2 lach bg2 lycps-v bg2 tarent bg2
  - **photophobia**: kali-c bg2 puls bg2 sep bg2
  - **prickling**: aur bg2 chin bg2 ph-ac bg2 viol-o bg2
  - **respiration**; difficult: carb-v bg2 coloc bg2 kali-n bg2 nit-ac bg2 ran-b bg2 sep bg2
  - **restlessness** (See MIND - Restlessness - head; with)
  - **sadness** (See MIND - Sadness - head; with)
  - **shrieking** (See MIND - Shrieking - head)
  - **sleepiness**: *Ant-t* b7a.de ars bg2 calc bg2 cham b7.de* grat bg2 ign b7.de* kali-n bg2 kreos b7a.de* lach bg2 laur b7.de* mur-ac bg2 nux-m bg2 puls bg2 *Ran-b* b7a.de stann b4.de* stront-c bg2 sul-ac bg2 zinc bg2
  - **sour** taste: arg-n bg2 *Nux-v* bg2
  - **syphilis**: apis bg2 asaf bg2 aur bg2 iod bg2 kali-i bg2 merc bg2 mez bg2 nit-ac bg2 sars bg2 still bg2 sulph bg2 syph bg2
  - **talking**; aversion of (See MIND - Taciturn - head; with)
  - **thirst**: agar bg2 arn bg2 chinin-s bg2 cupr bg2 *Lach* bg2 *Mag-m* bg2 mang bg2 nat-c bg2 nat-m bg2 plat bg2 rhus-t bg2 stram bg2 thuj bg2 verat bg2
  - **torticollis**: rhus-r bg2
  - **tottering** gait: agar bg2 camph bg2 graph bg2 kali-c bg2 kali-n bg2 lol bg2 mosch bg2 ph-ac bg2 puls bg2 rhus-t bg2 sep bg2 sil bg2 spig bg2 sulph bg2 tab bg2
  - **trembling**: bar-c b4a.de borx bg2 *Calc* bg2 carb-v bg2 lyc bg2 petr bg2 sep bg2
  - **urination**; frequent: acon bg2* chinin-s bg2 gels bg2* glon ptk1 *Ign* bg2* iris bg2 lac-d bg2* lyc bg2 mosch bg2* ol-an bg2* phys ptk1 sang bg2 sel bg2* sil bg2* verat bg2 vib ptk1
  - **vexation** (See MIND - Irritability - head; with)
  - **vision**:
    - **dim**: am-c bg2 bov bg2 bry bg2 carb-an bg2 croc bg2 crot-h bg2 ferr bg2 mag-m bg2 mur-ac bg2 nat-c bg2 nit-ac bg2 phos bg2 **Puls** bg2 sars bg2 sep bg2
  - **vision**: ...
    - **weak**: nat-c bg2 nux-v bg2 ol-an bg2
  - **weakness** | **Muscles**; of: onos br1
  - **weeping** (See MIND - Weeping - head; with)
  - ○ **Abdomen**; pain in: cina bg2 cupr bg2 hep bg2 kali-n bg2 led bg2 nit-ac bg2 phos bg2 stram bg2 verat bg2 zinc bg2
  - **Back**; pain in: ail bg2 benz-ac bg2 calc-p bg2 fl-ac bg2 graph bg2 merc bg2 mosch bg2 ol-an bg2 op bg2 sabad bg2 sabin bg2 verat bg2
  - **Cheeks**:
    - **red** discoloration of: alum bg2 bov bg2 cann-xyz bg2 ign bg2 zinc bg2
      - **one** side: **Cham** bg2
  - **Chest**; pain in: *Lach* bg2
  - **Ear**:
    - **complaints** of: ferr-p ptk1 merc ptk1 puls ptk1 sang ptk1
    - **noises** in: acon bg2 anac bg2 ars bg2 borx bg2 chin bg2 dulc bg2 lach bg2 op bg2 plat bg2 *Puls* bg2 rhus-t bg2 sang bg2 staph bg2 thuj bg2
    - **pain**: *(↗EAR - Pain - headache)* canth bg2 lyc bg2 meph bg2 merc bg2 mosch bg2 mur-ac bg2 *Puls* bg2 rhus-t bg2 sulph bg2
  - **Extremities**:
    - **heaviness**: carb-v bg2 sil bg2
    - **pain**: acon bg2 carb-v bg2 lach bg2 sang bg2
    - **paralysis**; sensation of: ars bg2 iod bg2
  - **Eyes**:
    - **pain**: acon bg2 bell bg2 bov bg2 **Gels** bg2 ign bg2 lyc bg2 phos bg2
      - **Orbits**: acon bg2 anac bg2 asaf bg2 aur bg2 carb-an bg2 cinnb bg2 cupr bg2 daph bg2 dig bg2 ign bg2 kali-bi bg2 lach bg2 laur bg2 mang bg2 spig bg2 stront-c bg2 zinc bg2
    - **red**: arg-met bg2
  - **Face**:
    - **discoloration**:
      - **pale**: *Acon* bg2 alum bg2 ambr bg2 chinin-s bg2 hell bg2 mag-c bg2 *Verat* bg2
      - **red**: **Acon** bg2 canth bg2 coff bg2 *Ign* bg2 lach bg2 mag-c bg2 mag-m bg2 nat-c bg2 **Nux-v** bg2 **Op** bg2 phos bg2 *Plat* bg2 plb bg2 sil bg2 stram bg2 sulph bg2 tarax bg2 thuj bg2 zinc bg2
    - **heat**: **Acon** bg2 agar bg2 ang bg2 arn bg2 asaf bg2 *Bell* bg2 bry bg2 calc bg2 canth bg2 *Chinin-s* bg2 coff bg2 glon bg2 grat bg2 kreos bg2 laur bg2 mag-c bg2 meny bg2 nat-m bg2 nux-v bg2 op bg2 phos bg2 plat bg2 ran-b bg2 sabad bg2 sil bg2 spong bg2 stront-c bg2 sulph bg2 tarax bg2
    - **pain**: acon bg2 bry bg2 hep bg2 kreos bg2 lach bg2 *Nux-v* bg2 rhus-t bg2 sil bg2 spig bg2 thuj bg2
    - **perspiration**: mag-c bg2 plat bg2 thuj bg2
    - **shivering**: rhod bg2
  - **Feet**:
    - **cold**: camph bg2 sulph bg2
    - **complaints** of: mag-m ptk1
    - **weak**: carb-an bg2
  - **Female** genitalia; complaints of: borx bg2
  - **Fingers**:
    - **cold**: hell bg2
    - **pale**: verat bg2
  - **Forehead**; wrinkled: ars bg2 grat bg2 rheum bg2 *Sulph* bg2 viol-o bg2
  - **Genitalia**; complaints of male and female: cimic bg2 plat bg2 sep bg2
  - **Gums**; pain in: merc bg2 nat-m bg2
  - **Hand** | **coldness**: ambr bg2 benz-ac bg2 borx bg2 camph bg2 merc bg2 ran-b bg2
  - **Heart**:
    - **complaints** (See CHEST - Heart; complaints - accompanied - head - complaints)
    - **pain** (See chest)
  - **Jaw**; lower:
    - **pain** in: ang bg2 bar-c bg2 canth bg2 plat bg2 ran-b bg2 sulph bg2
    - **swelling**: acon bg2 carb-an bg2 nit-ac bg2 par bg2

- **Kidneys**; complaints of: ars bg2 bapt bg2 cann-xyz bg2 canth bg2 dig bg2 kali-ar bg2 merc bg2 phos bg2 plb bg2
- **Leg**:
  - **heaviness**: nit-ac bg2
  - **pain**: calc bg2
- **Liver**; complaints of: bry bg2 card-m bg2 chel bg2 chion bg2 eup-per bg2 iris bg2 mag-m bg2 nux-v bg2 podo bg2 sep bg2 sulph bg2 yuc bg2
- **Nape** of neck:
  - **pain**: bry bg2 caust bg2 cimic bg2 con bg2 graph bg2 lach bg2 phyt bg2 ran-b bg2
  - **stiffness**: ant-c bg2 bar-c bg2 calc bg2 gels bg2 graph bg2 kali-n bg2 lach bg2 mag-c bg2 ph-ac bg2 sep bg2 verat bg2
  - **Glands** in nape of neck; swollen: bar-c bg2 mur-ac bg2
- **Nose**; pain in: *Agar* bg2 ferr bg2 glon bg2 hep bg2 *Lach* bg2 *Lyc* bg2 merc bg2 mez bg2 *Nux-v* bg2 phos bg2
- **Pupils**; dilated: arg-n bg2 *Bell* bg2 calc bg2 dig bg2 verat-v bg2
- **Root** of tongue; heavily white coated: *Glon* kr1*
- **Spleen**; pain in: borx bg2
- **Teeth**:
  - **chattering**: carb-v bg2
  - **grinding**: crot-h bg2 stram bg2
  - **pain** in: borx bg2 calc bg2 carb-v bg2 caust bg2 dig bg2 euphr bg2 ign bg2 kreos bg2 *Lach* bg2 laur bg2 *Lyc* bg2 mag-c bg2 merc bg2 mez bg2 mosch bg2 nat-m bg2 petr bg2 prun bg2 *Puls* bg2 *Rhus-t* bg2 sabad bg2 sars bg2 sep bg2 stram bg2 sulph bg2 zinc bg2
- **Tongue**:
  - **mucus** on: calc bg2
  - **white** discoloration of the tongue | **heavily** coated: *Glon* kr1*
- **Urinary** organs; complaints of (See URINARY - Complaints - accompanied - head)
- **Uterus**; complaints of: cimic bg2* gels bg2 helo bg2 helon ptk1 ign bg2 lach bg2 plat bg2* puls bg2* sep bg2* zinc bg2
- **Vertex**; heat of: calc bg2 carb-an bg2

- **alternating** with:
  - **sleepiness**: ars bg2
  - ○ **Abdomen**; complaints of: aloe bg2* bry ptk1 calc ptk1 cina bg2* podo ptk1 thuj ptk1
  - **Back**; complaints of: ign ptk1 meli ptk1
  - **Chest**; complaints of (See CHEST - Complaints - alternating - head)
  - **Extremities**; complaints of: sulph bg2
  - **Heart**; complaints of (See CHEST - Heart; complaints - alternating - head)
  - **Lumbar** region; pain in: aloe ptk1
  - **Pelvis**; complaints of: gels ptk1
  - **Stomach**; complaints of: ars bg2* bism bg2* ox-ac bg2* plb bg2* verat bg2*
  - **Uterus**; complaints of: gels bg2
- **chronic**: arg-n ptk1 ars ptk1 calc ptk1 nat-c ptk1 nat-m ptk1 psor ptk1 sep ptk1 *Sil* ptk1 zinc ptk1
- **dullness**; with (See MIND - Dullness - head - complaints)
- **flatulence**; as if from: (↗*Pain - flatulence; as*) carb-v bg2 chinin-s bg2 mag-c bg2 nit-ac bg2 sulph bg2
- **increasing** | **gradually**:
  - **decreasing**:
    - **gradually**: nat-m bg2 plat bg2 sang bg2 spig bg2 stann bg2 stront-c bg2
    - **suddenly**: arg-met bg2 sul-ac bg2
  - **suddenly**:
    - **decreasing** | **suddenly**: kali-bi bg2
- **injuries**; after: carc mlr1•
- **memory**; with weakness of (See MIND - Memory - weakness - head; with)
- **paroxysmal**: acon bg2 agar bg2 am bg2 dig bg2 lyc bg2 mur-ac bg2 plat bg2 sil bg2 spig bg2 spong bg2 stann bg2 stront-c bg2 thuj bg2 valer bg2 verat bg2
- **raving**; with (See MIND - Speech - incoherent - head)
- **senses**; with loss of (See MIND - Senses - vanishing - head)
- **speech**; with affected (See MIND - Speech - affected - head)
- **stomach**; as if coming from: alum bg2 carb-v bg2 con bg2 mag-m bg2
- **unconsciousness**; after (See MIND - Unconsciousness - head - complaints)
- **whining**; with (See MIND - Weeping - whimpering - head)
- ▽ **extending** to:
  - ○ **Back**: calc bg2 sep bg2 sil bg2
  - **Backward**: anac bg2 arn ptk1 bapt bg2 *Bell* bg2* **Bism** ptk1 *Bry* bg2* camph bg2 caust bg2 cedr bg2 chel bg2 cimic bg2* coc-c bg2 con bg2 crot-c bg2 form bg2 *Glon* ptk1 iris bg2 kali-bi bg2* lac-d ptk1 lach bg2* lyc ptk1 lycps-v bg2 mag-c bg2 med ptk1 mur-ac ptk1 naja bg2 nat-m bg2* *Nit-ac* ptk1 onos bg2 par ptk1 phos bg2 phyt bg2 pic-ac bg2 prun bg2* ruta ptk1 sabad bg2 sel bg2 sep bg2* stront-c bg2 syph ptk1 thuj bg2* tub ptk1 valer bg2 verat-v ptk1 verb ptk1 zinc bg2*
  - **Body**; over: bry bg2
  - **Bones**: kali-chl bg2 lyc bg2 puls bg2 sulph bg2
  - **Brain**: agar bg2 am-c bg2 bar-c bg2 bov bg2 camph bg2 croc bg2 glon bg2 hell bg2 lach bg2 laur bg2 ox-ac bg2 petr bg2 plan bg2 ran-s bg2 stann bg2
    - **Base**: sep bg2
  - **Cervical** region: bry ptk1 cimic ptk1 cocc ptk1 kali-c ptk1 lach ptk1 nux-m ptk1 nux-v ptk1
  - **Downward**: *Agar* ptk1 aloe bg2 ambr bg2 ant-t bg2* arg-met bg2 asar bg2 bism ptk1 calc ptk1 calc-p ptk1 cham ptk1 chel bg2 *Chin* ptk1 cimic bg2 cina bg2 con bg2 cupr bg2 dulc ptk1 glon bg2 guaj ptk1 hell bg2 hyper bg2* ign bg2* **Ip** ptk1 kali-bi bg2 *Lach* ptk1 *Led* ptk1 mang ptk1 *Med* ptk1 meny bg2* *Mez* ptk1 mur-ac bg2 nit-ac bg2 nux-v bg2* ph-ac bg2 *Phos* ptk1 phys bg2 pic-ac ptk1 plat bg2* **Puls** ptk1 rhus-t bg2* sep ptk1 spig bg2 spong bg2 *Staph* ptk1 stront-c ptk1 sulph bg2 verat bg2 **Verb** ptk1 *Zinc* ptk1
  - **Ears**: cocc bg2 lach bg2 lil-t bg2 lyc bg2 mag-m bg2 thuj bg2
  - **Elbows**: kali-n bg2
  - **Epigastrium**: thuj bg2
  - **Eyes**; through or into: acon bg2 agar bg2 arg-n bg2 asaf bg2 bapt bg2 bry bg2 carb-v bg2* *Chin* ptk1 cimic ptk1 colch bg2 crot-h bg2 dios bg2 gels bg2 ign ptk1 kali-c bg2 kali-n bg2 *Lach* bg2* lith-c ptk1 mang ptk1 nat-c bg2* nat-m bg2 nit-ac bg2* nux-v bg2 op bg2 ph-ac bg2* phos bg2* pic-ac bg2 *Puls* bg2* sil bg2* **Spig** ptk1 sulph bg2* sumb bg2 valer ptk1 zinc bg2*
    - **right**: sang bg2
    - **left**: spig bg2
  - **Face**: bry bg2 hyper bg2 kalm bg2 lach bg2 merc-i-f bg2 phos bg2
  - **Forehead**: agar bg2 canth bg2 gels bg2 iod bg2 lac-c bg2 par bg2 sang bg2 sars bg2 sil bg2 sulph bg2
  - **Forward**: acon ptk1 alum ptk1 arg-n ptk1 *Bell* ptk1 canth ptk1 *Carb-v* ptk1 *Chin* ptk1 cimic ptk1 *Con* ptk1 gels bg2* hydr-ac bg2 laur ptk1 lyc ptk1 mag-p bg2 mang bg2 mur-ac ptk1 ph-ac ptk1 *Rhus-t* ptk1 sabad ptk1 spig bg2 valer bg2 verb ptk1
  - **Hand** | **right**: phos bg2
  - **Heart**: thuj bg2
  - **Jaw**: lach ptk1 phos ptk1 stront-c ptk1
  - **Lids**: chel bg2 phos bg2 spig bg2
  - **Nose**: acon bg2 *Agar* bg2 aloe bg2 am-m bg2 bapt bg2 bism bg2 calc bg2 chel bg2 cimic bg2* colch bg2 coloc bg2 dig bg2 fago bg2 glon bg2 ign bg2 kali-c bg2 kali-n bg2 *Lach* bg2* lachn bg2 lyc bg2 mez bg2* nat-c bg2 ph-ac bg2 phos bg2 plan bg2 plat bg2 ptel bg2 sep bg2 sulph bg2 thuj bg2
    - **Bones**: mez bg2
    - **Dorsum** (= Bridge): colch bg2 dulc bg2
    - **Root**: *Agar* bg2 ant-t bg2 kali-c bg2 lach bg2 lyc bg2 nux-v bg2 phos bg2 zinc bg2
    - **Tip**: bism bg2 brom bg2 kali-n bg2 nat-c bg2
    - **Wings**: carb-v bg2 onos bg2 sep bg2

- **Occiput**: aloe bg2 bell bg2 bry bg2 cann-xyz bg2 cham bg2 chel bg2 chlor bg2 cimic bg2 cina bg2 cinnb bg2 cocc bg2 equis-h bg2 form bg2 hell bg2 ip bg2 kali-bi bg2 lil-t bg2 naja bg2 nat-m bg2 nit-ac bg2 nux-v bg2 phos bg2 phys bg2 phyt bg2 pic-ac bg2 prun bg2 senec bg2 sep bg2 sil bg2 sulph bg2 thuj bg2
  - ⁝ **over** head: anac bg2 cimic bg2 colch bg2 sel bg2 thuj bg2
- **Outward**: acon ptk1 arn ptk1 *Asaf* ptk1 **Bell** ptk1 bism ptk1 *Bry* ptk1 canth ptk1 cham ptk1 chin ptk1 con ptk1 dulc ptk1 ign ptk1 lach ptk1 lyc ptk1 *Mez* ptk1 nat-c ptk1 rhus-t ptk1 sep ptk1 sil ptk1 spig ptk1 sulph ptk1 valer ptk1
- **Parietal** bone: chel bg2 indg bg2
- **Scapula**: hep bg2 lil-t bg2
  - ⁝ **right**: chel bg2
- **Shoulder**: bry bg2 gels bg2 glon bg2 graph bg2 hydr bg2 kalm bg2 lach bg2 mez bg2
- **Sides**: hyper bg2 nit-ac bg2 pall bg2
- **Spine**: cocc bg2 mosch bg2 nux-v bg2 syph bg2
- **Teeth**: ars bg2 carb-v bg2 chin bg2 cupr bg2 ferr bg2 gels bg2 kalm bg2 laur bg2 mag-c bg2 mez bg2 nat-m bg2 psor bg2 rhus-t bg2 sars bg2 staph bg2 thuj bg2 verb bg2 zinc bg2
- **Temples**: arg-met bg2 glon bg2 hell bg2 sars bg2 spig bg2
- **Throat**: anac bg2 chin bg2 croc bg2 graph bg2 hep bg2 kali-n bg2 lach bg2 laur bg2 merc bg2 psor bg2 sars bg2 tarent bg2
- **Tongue**: apis bg2
  - ⁝ **Root**: ip bg2
- **Upward**: bell bg2 bry bg2 calc bg2 cimic bg2 gels bg2 glon bg2 lil-t bg2 meph bg2 onos bg2 ph-ac bg2 phos bg2 rhus-t bg2 sil bg2 staph bg2 verat-v bg2
- **Vertex**: cimic bg2 ferr bg2 kreos bg2 lach bg2 laur bg2 lyc bg2 mag-m bg2 phos bg2 sep bg2 sil bg2 thuj bg2 xanth bg2

○ - **Bones** (See Bones)

- **Brain** (See Brain; complaints)
- **External** head: acon b2.de* agar b2.de* agn b2.de* *Alum* b2.de* am-c b2.de* ambr b2.de* ang b2.de* apis ptk1 arg-met b2.de* **Arn** b2.de* ars b2.de* asar b2.de* aur b2.de* **Bar-c** b2.de* **Bell** b2.de* bism b2.de* borx b2.de* bov b2.de* bry b2.de* **Calc** b2.de* **Calc-p** ptk1 cann-s b2.de* canth b2.de* caps b2.de* carb-an b2.de* carb-v b2.de* *Caust* b2.de* cham b2.de* chel b2.de* *Chin* b2.de* cina b2.de* clem b2.de* cocc b2.de* coloc b2.de* cycl b2.de* dig b2.de* dros b2.de* ferr b2.de* *Graph* b2.de* *Guaj* b2.de* hell b2.de* hep b2.de* hyos b2.de* ign b2.de* iod b2.de* ip b2.de* kali-bi bg2 kali-c b2.de* kali-n b2.de* kreos b2.de* lach b2.de* laur b2.de* led b2.de* **Lyc** b2.de* m-arct b2.de mag-m b2.de* mang b2.de* meny b2.de* *Merc* b2.de* *Mez* b2.de* mosch b2.de* mur-ac b2.de* nat-c b2.de* nat-m b2.de* nit-ac b2.de* nux-m b2.de* **Nux-v** b2.de* olnd b2.de* op b2.de* *Par* b2.de* petr b2.de* ph-ac b2.de* *Phos* b2.de* plat b2.de* puls b2.de* ran-b b2.de* ran-s b2.de* rhod b2.de* **Rhus-t** b2.de* **Ruta** b2.de* sabad b2.de* sars b2.de* sel b2.de* *Sep* b2.de* sil b2.de* *Spig* b2.de* spong b2.de* stann b2.de* **Staph** b2.de* sul-ac b2.de* *Sulph* b2.de* tarax b2.de* *Thuj* b2.de* *Verat* b2.de* viol-o b2.de* *Viol-t* ptk1 *Zinc* b2.de*
  - **right** side: *Agar* b4a.de* *Agn* b7a.de* *Alum* b4a.de* am-c bg2* *Am-m* b7a.de* *Ambr* b7a.de* *Anac* b4a.de* ang b7a.de* *Aur* b4a.de* *Bell* b4a.de* borx bg2* brom bg2 *Bry* b7a.de* **Calc** b4a.de* **Canth** b7a.de* caps b7a.de* carb-an bg2* carb-v bg2* caust bg2* *Chel* b7a.de* chin b7a.de* clem bg2* coloc bg2* **Con** b4a.de* dig bg2* *Dros* b7a.de* graph bg2* *Guaj* b4a.de* hep bg2* *Iod* b4a.de* *Kali-c* b4a.de* *Kali-n* b4a.de* *Kreos* b7a.de* laur b7a.de* *Led* b7a.de* lyc b4a.de* mag-m bg2* *Mang* b4a.de* *Meny* b7a.de* merc bg2* **Mez** b4a.de* mur-ac bg2* *Nat-c* b4a.de* nat-m bg2* *Nit-ac* b4a.de* petr bg2* ph-ac bg2* phos bg2* plat bg2* psor bg2 *Puls* b7a.de* ran-b b7a.de* *Ran-s* b7a.de* rhod bg2* *Rhus-t* b7a.de* *Sabad* b7a.de* *Sars* b4a.de* *Sep* b4a.de* *Sil* b4a.de* spig b7a.de* *Spong* b7a.de* stann bg2* *Staph* b7a.de* stront-c bg2* thuj bg2* *Verat* b7a.de* viol-t b7a.de* *Zinc* b4a.de*
  - **left** side: *Acon* b7a.de* agar bg2* alum bg2* *Am-c* b4a.de* anac bg2* *Ang* b7a.de* *Ant-c* b7a.de* *Ant-t* b7a.de* arg-met b7a.de* *Ars* b4a.de* *Asar* b7a.de* aur bg2* *Bar-c* b4a.de* bell bg2* *Borx* b4a.de* calc bg2* caps b7a.de* *Carb-an* b4a.de* *Carb-v* b4a.de* *Caust* b4a.de* *Cham* b7a.de* chel b7a.de* *Chin* b7a.de* **Clem** b4a.de* *Cocc* b7a.de* *Coloc* b4a.de* *Dig* b4a.de* *Dulc* b4a.de* euph b4a.de *Euphr* bg2* *Graph* b4a.de* *Hep* b4a.de* iod bg2* kali-c bg2* kali-n bg2* laur b7a.de* *Lyc* b4a.de* *Mag-c* b4a.de* mag-m bg2* mang bg2* meny b7a.de* *Merc* b4a.de* mill b7a.de* *Mur-ac* b4a.de* nat-c bg2* *Nat-m* b4a.de* nit-ac bg2* *Olnd* b7a.de*

- **External** head – **left** side: ...
  Petr b4a.de* *Ph-ac* b4a.de* *Phos* b4a.de* *Plat* b4a.de* *Rhod* b4a.de* rhus-t b7a.de* **Ruta** b7a.de* *Seneg* b4a.de* *Sep* bg2* *Sil* b4a.de* *Spig* b7a.de* staph b7a.de* stront-c bg2* *Sulph* b4a.de* *Tarax* b7a.de* **Thuj** b4a.de* *Verb* b7a.de* viol-t b7a.de* zinc bg2*
- **Forehead** | **Bones**: *Coch* br1
- **Internal** head: acon b2.de* agar b2.de* agn b2.de* alum b2.de* *Am-c* b2.de* am-m b2.de* ambr b2.de* *Anac* b2.de* ang b2.de* *Ant-c* b2.de* ant-t b2.de* arg-met b2.de* arn b2.de* *Ars* b2.de* asaf b2.de* asar b2.de* aur b2.de* bar-c b2.de* *Bell* b2.de* *Bism* b2.de* borx b2.de* bov b2.de* *Bry* b2.de* *Calc* b2.de* camph b2.de* cann-s b2.de* canth b2.de* caps b2.de* *Carb-an* b2.de* *Carb-v* b2.de* caust b2.de* cham b2.de* chel b2.de* *Chin* b2.de* cic b2.de* *Cimic* bg2 cina b2.de* clem b2.de* *Cocc* b2.de* coff b2.de* colch b2.de* coloc b2.de* con b2.de* croc b2.de* cupr b2.de* cycl b2.de* dig b2.de* *Dros* b2.de* dulc b2.de* euph b2.de* euphr b2.de* ferr b2.de* *Gels* bg2 **Glon** bg2 graph b2.de* guaj b2.de* hell b2.de* *Hep* b2.de* *Hyos* b2.de* **Ign** b2.de* iod b2.de* ip b2.de* *Iris* bg2 *Kali-c* b2.de* kali-n b2.de* *Kreos* b2.de* lach b2.de* *Laur* b2.de* led b2.de* *Lyc* b2.de* m-ambo b2.de m-arct b2.de m-aust b2.de *Mag-m* b2.de* mang b2.de* meli bg2 meny b2.de* **Merc** b2.de* *Mez* b2.de* mosch b2.de* mur-ac b2.de* *Nat-c* b2.de* **Nat-m** b2.de* *Nit-ac* b2.de* *Nux-m* b2.de* **Nux-v** b2.de* olnd b2.de* **Op** b2.de* par b2.de* **Petr** b2.de* *Ph-ac* b2.de* **Phos** b2.de* *Plat* b2.de* plb b2.de* podo bg2 *Puls* b2.de* ran-b b2.de* ran-s b2.de* rheum b2.de* rhod b2.de* rhus-t b2.de* ruta b2.de* **Sabad** b2.de* **Sabin** b2.de* samb b2.de* sars b2.de* sec b2.de* sel b2.de* seneg b2.de* *Sep* b2.de* **Sil** b2.de* *Spig* b2.de* spong b2.de* squil b2.de* *Stann* b2.de* staph b2.de* stram b2.de* stront-c b2.de* sul-ac b2.de* *Sulph* b2.de* tarax b2.de* teucr b2.de* *Thuj* b2.de* valer b2.de* *Verat* b2.de* **Verb** b2.de* viol-o b2.de* viol-t b2.de* *Zinc* b2.de*
  - **right** side: acon b7a.de* *Agar* b4a.de* *Agn* b7a.de* *Alum* b4a.de* am-c fse1.de *Am-m* b7a.de* ambr b7a.de* anac fse1.de ang b7a.de* ant-c b7a.de* ant-t b7a.de* apis b7a.de arg-met b7a.de* *Arn* b7a.de* ars b4a.de* *Asaf* b7a.de* asar b7a.de* aur fse1.de bar-c fse1.de **Bell** b4a.de* *Bism* b7a.de* *Borx* b4a.de* bov fse1.de *Bry* b7a.de* *Calad* b7a.de* **Calc** b4a.de* camph b7a.de* *Cann-s* b7a.de* *Canth* b7a.de* *Caps* b7a.de* carb-an fse1.de **Carb-v** b4a.de* *Caust* b4a.de* *Cham* b7a.de* *Chel* b7a.de* chin b7a.de* cic b7a.de* *Cina* b7a.de* clem fse1.de cocc b7a.de* coff b7a.de* *Colch* b7a.de* coloc fse1.de con fse1.de croc b7a.de* cupr b7a.de* cycl b7a.de* dig fse1.de *Dros* b7a.de* *Dulc* b4a.de* euph fse1.de euphr b7a.de* ferr b7a.de* *Graph* b4a.de* guaj fse1.de *Hell* b7a.de* *Hep* b4a.de* *Hyos* b7a.de* **Ign** b7a.de* iod fse1.de kali-c fse1.de kali-n fse1.de kreos b7a.de* *Lach* b7a.de* laur b7a.de* led b7a.de* *Lyc* b4a.de* m-arct b7a.de* m-aust b7a.de* *Mag-c* b4a.de* mang fse1.de meny b7a.de* merc fse1.de mez fse1.de mill b7a.de *Mosch* b7a.de* mur-ac fse1.de nat-c b4a.de* *Nat-m* b4a.de* nit-ac fse1.de *Nux-m* b7a.de* *Nux-v* b7a.de* *Olnd* b7a.de* op b7a.de* par b7a.de* petr fse1.de *Ph-ac* b4a.de* *Phos* b4a.de* *Plat* b4a.de* *Plb* b7a.de* *Puls* b7a.de* *Ran-b* b7a.de* *Ran-s* b7a.de* *Rheum* b7a.de* *Rhod* b4a.de* *Rhus-t* b7a.de* *Ruta* b7a.de* **Sabad** b7a.de* *Sabin* b7a.de* samb b7a.de* sars fse1.de sec b7a.de* sel b7a.de* seneg fse1.de *Sep* b4a.de* **Sil** b4a.de* *Spig* b7a.de* spong b7a.de* *Squil* b7a.de* stann fse1.de *Staph* b7a.de* *Stram* b7a.de* *Stront-c* b4a.de* *Sul-ac* b4a.de* *Sulph* b4a.de* tarax b7a.de* *Teucr* b7a.de* *Thuj* b4a.de* *Valer* b7a.de* verat b7a.de* *Verb* b7a.de* viol-o b7a.de* viol-t b7a.de* *Zinc* b4a.de*
  - **left** side: *Acon* b7a.de* agar fse1.de agn b7a.de* alum fse1.de *Am-c* b4a.de* *Am-m* b7a.de* *Ambr* b7a.de* *Anac* b4a.de* ang b7a.de* *Ant-c* b7a.de* ant-t b7a.de* *Apis* b7a.de *Arg-met* b7a.de* *Arn* b7a.de* *Ars* b4a.de* *Asaf* b7a.de* *Asar* b7a.de* aur b4a.de* bar-c fse1.de bell fse1.de bism b7a.de* borx fse1.de *Bov* b4a.de* *Brom* b4a.de *Bry* b7a.de* calad b7a.de* *Calc* b4a.de* camph b7a.de* cann-s b7a.de* canth b7a.de* *Caps* b7a.de* *Carb-an* fse1.de carb-v fse1.de *Caust* b4a.de* *Cham* b7a.de* chel b7a.de* *Chin* b7a.de* *Cic* b7a.de* cina b7a.de* *Clem* b4a.de* cocc b7a.de* coff b7a.de* *Colch* b7a.de* *Coloc* b4a.de* con fse1.de *Croc* b7a.de* *Cupr* b7a.de* *Cycl* b7a.de* *Dig* b4a.de* dros b7a.de* *Dulc* b4a.de* *Euph* b4a.de* euphr b7a.de* ferr b7a.de* *Graph* b4a.de* *Guaj* b4a.de* hell b7a.de* hep fse1.de hyos b7a.de* ign b7a.de* *Iod* b4a.de* *Ip* b7a.de* *Kali-c* b4a.de* *Kali-n* b4a.de* *Kreos* b7a.de* *Lach* b7a.de* *Laur* b7a.de* led b7a.de* *Lyc* b4a.de* *M-arct* b7a.de* *M-aust* b7a.de* *Mag-c* b4a.de* *Mang* b4a.de* *Meny* fse1.de *Merc* b4a.de* *Mez* b4a.de* mosch fse1.de *Mur-ac* b4a.de* nat-c fse1.de nat-m fse1.de *Nit-ac* b4a.de* *Nux-m* fse1.de *Nux-v* b7a.de* *Olnd* b7a.de* op b7a.de* *Par* b7a.de* *Petr* b4a.de* *Ph-ac* b4a.de* *Phos* b4a.de* *Plat* b4a.de* plb b7a.de* psor b4a.de *Puls* b7a.de* ran-b b7a.de* ran-s b7a.de* rheum b7a.de* *Rhod* b4a.de* *Rhus-t* b7a.de* ruta b7a.de* sabad b7a.de* *Sabin* b7a.de* *Samb* b7a.de* *Sars* b4a.de* sec b7a.de* *Sel* b7a.de* seneg fse1.de **Sep** b4a.de* sil fse1.de *Spig* b7a.de* *Spong* b7a.de*

- **left** side: ...
squil b7a.de* *Stann* b4a.de* *Staph* b7a.de* stram b7a.de* stront-c fse1.de *Sul-ac* b4a.de* *Sulph* b4a.de* *Tarax* b7a.de* teucr fse1.de thuj fse1.de valer b7a.de* *Verat* b7a.de* verb b7a.de* *Viol-o* b7a.de* viol-t b7a.de* *Zinc* b4a.de*
- **Meninges**: eberth jl2 morb jl2 ourl jl2
  - **accompanied** by | **measles**: tub-a jl2*
  - **fever**; during: prot jl2
  - **followed** by | **stiffness**: toxo-g jl2
  - **influenza**; after: yers jl2
- **Sides** (See Sides)

COMPRESSION: *(↗Constriction; Pain - pressing pain)*
- **amel.**: apis bg2 arg-n bg2 carb-an bg2 cina bg2 mag-m bg2 nat-m bg2 nux-v bg2 puls bg2 sulph bg2

CONCENTRATION: | **agg.**: nux-v b7.de* sabad b7.de*

CONCUSSION of brain: *(↗Brain damage; Injuries)* *Acon* bro1 **Arn** k* bell k* bry ptk1 carc fb3 **Cic** k* con ptk1 cyt-l sp1 fil sne glon bg2* ham bro1 *Hell* k* hep k* *Hyos* k* **Hyper** k* kali-i bro1 kali-p k* led k* mang c2 merc k* nat-s k* op a* ph-ac k* rhus-t k* sep k* sil c2 sul-ac k* sulph ptk1 zinc k*
- **accompanied** by:
  - **hiccough**: hyos ptk1* lyss hr1
  - **nausea**: *Arn* b7a.de
  - **spasms**: cic tl1
  - ○ **Tongue**; biting of: *Cic* kr1*
- **ailments** after: glon bg2
- **knocking** against anything; when foot was: bar-c ptk1
- **sensation** of | **misstep**; from: led hr1*

CONFUSION in head: fic-m gya1 melal-alt gya4 [bell-p-sp dcm1]
- ○ **Forehead**: all-c bg2 alum bg2 apis bg2 arg-met bg2 arg-n bg2 bar-act bg2 bell bg2 brom bg2 bry bg2 camph bg2 cann-xyz bg2 chin bg2 clem bg2 coff bg2 colch bg2 coloc bg2 croc bg2 crot-t bg2 cycl bg2 graph bg2 hyos bg2 kali-bi bg2 kali-n bg2 laur bg2 lob bg2 lyc bg2 manc bg2 mez bg2 nux-m bg2 op bg2 ph-ac bg2 phos bg2 plat bg2 rat bg2 rheum bg2 rhod bg2 ruta bg2 sabin bg2 sep bg2 squil bg2 staph bg2 sul-ac bg2 *Sulph* bg2 thuj bg2 valer bg2 vinc bg2 zinc bg2
  - **right**: acon bg2 ol-an bg2 op bg2
  - **left**: hyos bg2
- **Occiput**: **Ambr** bg2* arg-n bg2 asar bg2 carb-an bg2 croc bg2 crot-t bg2 fl-ac bg2 gels bg2 lob bg2 manc bg2 mez bg2 nat-c bg2 op bg2 phel bg2 plb bg2 sec bg2 spig bg2 squil bg2 zinc bg2
  - **right**: fl-ac bg2
  - **left**: sep bg2
  - **accompanied** by | **Nape**; peculiar sensation in muscles of: kali-chl a1*
- **Sides**: anac bg2 arn bg2 asar bg2 coloc bg2 laur bg2 sul-ac bg2
  - **right**: crot-t bg2 fl-ac bg2 lob bg2 op bg2 spig bg2 sul-ac bg2
  - **left**: arg-n bg2 con bg2 rhus-t bg2 sulph bg2
- **Temples**: bar-act bg2 coloc bg2 crot-t bg2 lith-c bg2
  - **right**: coff bg2 kali-bi bg2 op bg2
  - **left**: asar bg2 cycl bg2
- **Vertex**: all-c bg2 aml-ns bg2 calc bg2 chel bg2 coc-c bg2 colch bg2 eup-per bg2 kali-bi bg2 lob bg2 merc bg2 phos bg2 sulph bg2
- **Whole** head; in (See MIND - Confusion)

CONGESTION: *(↗Fullness)* acet-ac *Acon* k* aesc aeth agar k* agath-a nl2• all-c k2 aloe k* alum k* alum-sil k2 alumn am-c am-m k* *Ambr* k* aml-ns k* *Anac* k* *Ant-c* k* **Apis** k* arg-met *Arg-n* k* **Arn** k* ars k2* ars-h ars-i ars-s-f k2 asaf k* asar a aster *Aur* k* aur-ar k2 aur-m k2 aur-s bapt k2 bar-c k* bar-i k2 **Bell** k* bit-ar wht1• *Borx* k* bov k* brom k* **Bry** k* *Bufo* k* **Cact** calad k2 **Calc** k* calc-i k2 *Calc-p* *Calc-s* *Camph* k* cann-i *Cann-s* k* *Canth* k* carb-ac *Carb-an* k* **Carb-v** k* **Carbn-s** card-m k2 caust k* *Cedr* cench k2 *Cham* k* chel k* *Chin* k* chinin-ar chlam-tr bcx2• chlol hr chlor choc srj3• cic k* *Cimic* *Cinnb* k* clem coc-c *Cocc* k* *Coff* k* colch coloc k* *Con* k* cop cor-r corn cortico sp1 *Croc* k* crot-h k* crot-t **Cupr** cur *Cycl* k* dig k* dream-p sdj1• *Dulc* k* elaps eug eup-per fago a **Ferr** k* ferr-ar ferr-i *Ferr-p* k* *Fl-ac* form gamb gard-j vlr2• **Gels** k* germ-met srj5• **Glon** k* gran *Graph* k* *Grat* guaj b4a.de* ham bg2 **Hell** k* hura hydr hydr-ac hydrog srj2• *Hyos* k* ign k* indg *Iod* k* ip k2 irid-met srj5• jatr-c kali-ar *Kali-bi* k* *Kali-br* k* *Kali-c* k* kali-chl

Congestion: ...
Kali-i k* kali-n k* kali-p kali-s kali-sil a kalm kreos lac-ac *Lac-d* k2* **Lach** k* lact lat-m bnm6• *Laur* k* lavand-a ctl1• lil-t k* limest-b es1• **Lyc** k* lyss m-arct b7.de *M-aust* b7.de *Mag-c* k* mag-m mag-p k2 *Mag-s* mand mtf11 *Mang* k* mang-act br1 **Meli** k* *Merc* k* merc-c k* merc-i-f mez b4a.de* *Mill* mosch k* naja nat-ar *Nat-c* k* *Nat-m* k* nat-p *Nat-s* *Nit-ac* k* nux-m k* *Nux-v* k* ol-an *Op* k* ox-ac k2 paeon *Par* petr k* *Ph-ac* k* phel **Phos** k* *Pic-ac* plat *Plb* k* podo k2 positr nl2• psil ft1 *Psor* k* *Puls* k* pyrog k2* *Ran-b* k* rauw sp1 rhus-g tmo3• *Rhus-t* k* sabin k* sal-ac sal-fr sle1• **Sang** k* sec seneg k* *Sep* k* *Sil* k* *Spong* k* staph k* *Stram* k* *Stront-c* bg2 *Stry* succ-ac rly4• suis-pan rly4• *Sul-ac* k* **Sulph** k* syph hr1 *Tab* k* tarax k* tarent tell thea thuj k* urt-u usn br valer k* *Verat* k* *Verat-v* k* viol-o k* viol-t bg2 wye vh *Zinc* k* zinc-p k2 zing ziz [bell-p-sp dcm1 calc-n stj1 heroin sdj2 *Spect* dfg1]
- **morning**: calc cham k* chinin-s des-ac rbp6 glon k* lac-ac lach *Lyc* mag-c mag-s naja raph tell k*
  - **rising** agg.: eug lyc
  - **waking**; on: bry k2 *Calc* des-ac rbp6 *Lyc* *Ph-ac* positr nl2• sal-fr sle1•
- **forenoon**: mag-c mag-s
  - **11** h: cact k2
- **noon**: cham naja
  - **evening**; gradually decreasing toward the | **pain**, would press head against wall, and fears going mad; with terrible: stram
- **afternoon**: am-c k* cham chinin-s digin a1 fago a1 graph k* lach k* mang a1 nat-m paeon pimp a1 ran-b sal-fr sle1• sil
  - **17** h until midnight: glon
- **evening**: bar-i k2 calc calc-s k2 caust chinin-s croc fl-ac graph k2 hyos indg mag-m mill nat-c nat-p nux-v phos positr nl2• puls rhus-t sulph h2* trom k*
- **night**: am-c k* anac *Aster* bar-i k2 berb *Calc* k* *Calc-s* calc-sil k2 carb-v cycl kali-c k* kali-sil k2 mill **Psor** puls sil *Sulph* k*
  - **midnight**:
    - ⁝ **before** | **23** h: cact k2
  - **stream** from chest to head like a gust of wind, with epistaxis; a: *Mill*
- **accompanied** by:
  - **palpitations** (See CHEST - Palpitation - accompanied - head - congestion)
  - **vomiting** (See STOMACH - Vomiting - accompanied - head - congestion)
  - ○ **External** throat; pulsation of blood vessels of: lac-ac a1*
  - **Eyes**; hemorrhage from (See EYE - Bleeding - accompanied - head)
- **acute**: *Lycpr* br1
- **air**; in open:
  - **agg.**: lil-t nat-c ran-b *Sulph* [bell-p-sp dcm1]
  - **amel.**: **Apis** *Ars* bry k2 calc-s k2 camph caust *Coc-c* ferr-i k2 grat hell mag-m mosch nat-c h2*
- **alcoholic** liquors agg.: *Calc* k* calc-s *Glon* k* *Lach* k* verat-v hr1 *Zinc*
- **alternating** with:
  - **ice**-cold sensation: *Calc*
  - **palpitation** (See CHEST - Palpitation - alternating - head)
  - ○ **Chest**; congestion of: *Glon* k*
  - **Heart**; congestion to: *Glon* k*
- **anger**; after: *(↗MIND - Blushing)* arn hr1 *Bry* *Cham* k* glon a staph
- **anxiety**; with: *(↗MIND - Blushing)* *Acon* k* *Aur* k* carb-v j5.de *Cupr* hr1 cycl k* *Ign* hr1 musca-d szs1 puls hr1
- **bed**:
  - **in** bed:
    - ⁝ **agg.**: anac kali-c kali-s k2 lyc mill *Sulph*
    - ⁝ **amel.**: nat-c h2*
- **beginning** in:
  - ○ **Abdomen**: crot-t
  - **Back**: *Phos*
  - **Chest**: *Glon* lyss mill sulph
- **bending**:
  - **head** | **backward** | **agg.**: bell
    - ⁝ **forward** | **agg.**: lac-c

- **blowing** the nose agg.: nit-ac
- **bowel** complaints, with: aloe k2
- **chest**, during shocks in: tab k*
- **chill**; during: *(↗Coldness - congestion)* acon bg2 am bg2 ars bg2* bell bg2 bry bg2 calc bg2 cham bg2 **Chin** b7.de* dig bg2 ferr b7.de* hyos bg2 ip bg2 kali-n bg2 lyc bg2 merc bg2 nux-v bg2 phos bg2 puls bg2 rhus-t bg2 sabad bg2 *Sep* bg2 stram bg2 sulph bg2 verat bg2
- **coffee** agg.: am-c bart a1 *Cact* mill k* *Rumx*
- **coition**; after: carb-v bg1
- **cold** applications | **amel.**: ars k2 bry k2
- **coldness** | **Extremities**: verat k2
- **constipation**; during: aster crot-h k* *Nux-v* k*
- **convulsions**:
  - **before**: anan vh calc-ar kr1 **Glon** k* op a sulph a
    - **epileptic**: calc-ar k*
  - **during**: apis tl1 **Bell** canth crot-h **Gels**
- **cough** agg.; during: acon ambr k* anac k* bell calc calc-s calc-sil k2 carb-v caust cham chin dulc ferr hyos iod kali-c kali-p kali-s kali-sil k2 lach laur lyc mag-c mag-m merc mosch nit-ac nux-v phos rhus-t samb seneg sep sil spong stram sul-i k2 sulph
- **dinner**; after: cycl k* nux-m k* psor k*
- **discharges**; from suppressed: cimic **Verat-v** vh
- **eating**:
  - **after** | **agg.**: borx b4a.de* calc k* cinnb k* cop cycl glon guar vml3• nux-m petr k* sil c1 sulph
  - **agg.** | **high** living, from: verat-v k*
  - **before** | **agg.**: (non:uran-met k) uran-n
- **entering** a room: ol-an
- **epistaxis**:
  - **amel.**: psor al1
  - **appearing**; sensation as if epistaxis was: ign lac-ac
  - **with**: *(↗NOSE - Epistaxis - accompanied - face - congestion)* acon b7a.de* alum bg2 anan vh ant-c k* bell k* bry cact mrr1 carb-v k* cham bg2 chin bg2 con bg2 croc k* graph bg2* lach lil-t meli k* nux-v k* pic-ac k* *Psor* k* rhus-t bg2
- **excitement**:
  - **after**: glon br1
    - **surprise**; after a pleasant: *(↗MIND - Ailments - surprises - pleasant)* **Coff**
  - **during**: *(↗MIND - Ailments - surprises)* asaf ferr k2 morg fmm1• *Phos*
- **exertion** agg.: sulph k*
- **fever**; during: acon bg2 ars b4a.de bell b4a.de* bry bg2 carb-v bg2 cham bg2 chin b7.de* *Ferr* b7.de* ign bg2 lach bg2 lyc bg2 nux-v bg2* op bg2 phos b4a.de rhus-t b7a.de* sep b4a.de* sil bg2 squil bg2 stram bg2 sulph b4a.de* verat bg2
- **fright** or grief, from: *(↗MIND - Blushing)* *Ph-ac* k*
- **headache**; before: lyc h2*
- **heart**:
  - **blood** rushed from heart to head; as if: bell tl1 ferr-p tl1 fuma-ac rly4• ger-i rly4• glon tl1 nux-m suis-pan rly4• ven-m rsj12•
  - **throb** of heart; at every: cimic *Glon*
- **heat** of face, with: acon ars k2 asaf canth cham k* chinin-s coff con hr1 cop ferr *Ferr-p* hell kalm mang morg fmm1• phos rhus-t sil *Sulph* k* valer
  - **flushed**: morg fmm1•
- **lifting**; after: nat-c
- **lochia**; from suppressed: acon bell bry cimic
- **lying**:
  - **agg.**: cycl lac-c lyss mang naja
  - **amel.**: nat-c sal-fr sle1•
  - **back**; on | **agg.**: *Sulph*
  - **temple**; on | **agg.**: mur-ac
- **memory**; weakness of (See MIND - Memory - weakness - congestion)
- **menses**:
  - **after** | **agg.**: chin ign k* *Nat-m* sulph thuj
  - **amel.**: apis vh1
- **menses**: ...
  - **before** | **agg.**: *Acon* **Apis** k* aster bro1 *Bell* k* bry k* calc b4a.de cimic bro1 cocc bro1 croc bro1 crot-h kr cupr *Cycl* bro1 des-ac rbp6 ferr-m bro1 ferr-p bro1 gels k* *Glon* k* graph bro1 hep hyper iod *Kali-c* kali-p bro1 kreos bro1 lac-c bro1 lach bro1 lyc manc k* *Meli* *Merc* k* nat-c bro1 *Nat-m* bro1 *Nux-v* bro1 puls bro1 *Sang* bro1 *Sep* bro1 *Sulph* bro1 tril-p *Ust* bro1 verat-v bro1 xan bro1
  - **during** | **agg.**: acon **Apis** aster bro1 *Bell* k* *Bry* k* cact *Calc* k* calc-i k2 calc-p calc-s caust cham k* *Chin* k* cimic bro1 cinnb cocc bro1 con croc bro1 *Cycl* bro1 elaps ferr-m bro1 *Ferr-p* k* gels k* *Glon* k* graph bro1 iod kali-p bro1 kreos bro1 lac-c bro1 lach bro1 mag-c mag-m k* manc k* merc morg fmm1• mosch nat-c bro1 nat-m k* *Nux-m* *Nux-v* k* *Phos* puls bro1 sang k* *Sep* bro1 sul-i k2 **Sulph** k* *Ust* bro1 verat verat-v k* xan bro1
  - **suppressed** menses; from: *Acon* k* *Apis* k* arn **Bell** k* *Bry* k* *Calc* k* calc-s carb-an bg2 cham k* *Chin* **Cimic** k* coc-c *Cocc* con bg2 cycl bg2 dulc bg2 **Ferr** k* **Gels** k* **Glon** k* *Graph* k* ham bg2 ip bg2 kali-c bg2 **Lach** k* lyc bg2 merc k* mosch bg2 op phos bg2 psor bro1 puls bg2 sep bg2* sil bg2 stram sulph k* verat bg2 **Verat-v** k*
- **mental** exertion agg.: agar *Aur* aur-ar k2 **Cact** *Calc* k* cham crot-h kr nux-v *Phos* k* psor
- **motion** agg.: glon grat kali-chl mang nux-v petr sulph
  - **rapid** motion: *Petr*
- **music** agg.: *Ambr* k*
- **painful**: arist-cl sp1 bell-p sp1 calc-f sp1 mag-s sp1 sil h2* visc sp1
  - **air**; in open | **amel.**: arist-cl sp1
  - **fever**; during: acon bg2 apis bg2 ars bg2 bell bg2 *Chin* bg2 *Ferr* bg2 **Hyos** bg2 nat-m bg2 nux-v bg2 phos bg2 puls bg2 *Rhus-t* bg2 sep bg2 **Sulph** bg2 thuj bg2
- **pains** suddenly cease; when: cimic **Verat-v** vh
- **pale** face, with: *Ferr* k* *Glon* k*
- **periodical**: *Cycl* k* ferr morg fmm1•
- **perspiration**:
  - **during**: ant-t bg2 bry bg2 caust bg2 con bg2 nux-v bg2 op bg2 thuj k*
  - **fails** in ague; where perspiration: **Cact**
- **pregnancy** agg.; during: glon bro1* lyss c1
- **rage**; during: *(↗MIND - Blushing)* acon **Bell** hyos lach nux-v *Op* phos *Stram* verat
- **raising** head agg.: lyc
- **redness** of face, with: acon aur a **Bell** cact mrr1 canth coff cop cor-r *Glon* *Graph* meli merc-c phos sil sol-ni
- **riding** agg.: grat k* sulph k*
- **ringing** in ears, with: sang hr1
- **rising**:
  - **agg.**: eug lyc lyss c1 mag-s nat-c sil sulph
  - **amel.**: aur mill
- **sensation** of: guaj b4a.de
- **shaking** the head agg.; on: nit-ac nux-v
- **sitting** agg.: lac-ac mag-c mang nat-c *Phos* thuj
- **sitting** up in bed | **must** sit up: aloe
- **sleep** | **after** | **amel.**: grat
  - **during**: carb-v k2 glon k* sil
- **smoking** agg.: *Bell* *Mag-c* k*
- **spoken** to harshly; when: ign
- **standing**, from: kali-c mang k*
- **stepping** heavily, from: bar-c
- **stool**:
  - **after** | **agg.**: lach k* sulph k*
  - **before**: aloe coloc bg2 **Op** b7.de*
  - **during** | **agg.**: aloe *Bry* k* *Nux-v* k* rhus-t b7.de* *Sulph* k*
- **stooping** agg.: acon am-c aur *Bell* *Calc-p* canth *Cor-r* elaps lach lyc mill myric nat-c nit-ac *Puls* rhus-t seneg sep *Sulph* tell *Verat*
- **streamed** from below upwards or within outwards; as if blood: *Aml-ns* vh1 ox-ac
- **sun**; from exposure to: *Acon* *Bell* *Cact* *Gels* *Glon* sumb a1 verat-v
- **suppressed**; from: **Verat-v** vh
- **talking** agg.: coff k* sulph k*
- **thunderstorm** agg.: morg fmm1•

- **travelling**:
  - **bus**; by: morg fmm1•
  - **train**; by: morg fmm1•
- **uremic** poison, from: am-c apis *Bell* con *Cupr Gels Glon* merc-c *Stram* tab ter verat-v
- **vertigo**; during: **Acon** bg2 *Am* bg2 **Bell** bg2 chin bg2 con bg2 *Lach* bg2 merc bg2 mim-p rsj8• **Nux-v** bg2 *Op* bg2 *Puls* bg2 rhus-t bg2 sabin c1 sil bg2 *Sulph* bg2
- **vomiting** (See STOMACH - Vomiting - head)
- **waking**; on: am-c bell *Calc* k* carb-v sil h2*
- **walking**:
  - **agg.**: caust lach mang ran-b
  - **air**; in open:
    - **agg.**: *Am-c* vh1 caust ran-b
      - **rapidly**: *Phos*
    - **amel.**: cham
- **warm** room agg.: **Apis** bry k2 calc-s *Carb-v Coc-c* ferr-i k2 graph k2 *Kali-s* **Puls Sulph**
- **waves**; in:
  - **accompanied** by | **apoplexy**: glon ptk1
- **wet** agg.; getting the feet: dulc
- **wine** agg.: sil
- **writing** agg.: cann-s

▽ - **extending** to head from ... (See beginning)

○ - **Brain**: absin c2* *Acon* bro1 act-sp bro1 aethyl-n a1 agar bro1 ail tl1 am-br vh1 ambr bro1 *Aml-ns* bro1 arn br1* art-v ptk2 aster bro1 aur h2* *Bell* bg2* *Bry* bro1 *Cact* c2* calc-ar bro1 calc-br c2 carb-v bro1 cham bro1 chin bg2* *Chinin-s* bro1 cimic tl1 cinnb bro1 coff bro1 croc c2* cupr bro1 cupr-act bro1 ferr-p bro1 ferr-py c1* gels bro1 *Glon* c2* hyos bro1 ign bro1 iod bro1 lach bro1 lyc bro1 lycpr bro1 *Meli* bro1 nat-s bro1 *Nux-v* bro1 *Op* bro1 petr bg2 phos bg2 prim-v br1 psor al sabad bg2 sang bro1 sep bro1 sil bro1 spong h1 stram bro1 *Sulph* c2* tub al verat bg2 *Verat-v* br1*
  - **accompanied** by:
    - **convulsions** (See GENERALS - Convulsions - violent - accompanied - brain)
    - **nausea**: verat-v br1
    - **pain**; neuralgic: prim-v br1
    - **vertigo**: *(↗VERTIGO - Congestion)* acon btw1* arn bro1 *Bell* bro1 carb-ac btw2 carbn-o a1 chin bro1 *Cupr* bro1 *Glon* bro1 hydr-ac bro1 *Iod* bro1 nux-v a1* op bro1 pop-cand a2 stram bro1 *Sulph* bro1 verat-v btw2
    - **vomiting**: verat-v br1
  - **bathing** in hot water: apis tl1
  - **cold** agg.; after becoming: glon br1
  - **continued** fever; in: chlol gm1 crot-h gm1 hell gm1 op gm1 zinc gm1
  - **overheated**; after being: glon br1
  - **passive**: aesc bro1 *Chin* bro1 chlol bro1 dig bro1 *Ferr-py* bro1 *Gels* bro1 hell bro1 *Op* bro1 phos bro1
- **Forehead**: aloe k* bad k* *Bapt-c* c1 bell k* cent a1 cimic *Cinnb* k* cortico tpw7* dirc a1 ferr-i k2 *Fl-ac* k* glon k* irid-met srj5• lac-ac k* limest-b es1• mag-s mand rsj7• nat-c k* petr-ra shn4• positr nl2• ran-b k* *Sil* spong k* stann tell a1 tere-la rly4• thres-a sze7• viol-o b7.de* viol-t
  - **waking**; on: tell c1
- **Occiput**: acon bg2 aloe k* apis bg2 bell b4a.de* borx k* calc k2 *Chel* k* coff bg2 *Dulc Gels* k* *Glon* k* ign bg2 lyc bg2 mez bg2 mosch bg2 naja k2 nux-v bg2 ol-an k* petr b4a.de* phel a1 pip-m k* sabad bg2 sal-fr sle1• sep bg2 sil bg2 staph k* *Sulph* k* thuj k* *Verat-v* k*
  - **stooping** agg.; after: lyc h2*
  - **waking**; on: tell c1
- **Sides**: dig a1
  - **left**: androc srj1• dig a1
- **Temples**: ars bg2 chel k* glon k* sil tell a1 thuj bg2 zing
  - **right**: sil b4.de*
- **Vertex**: absin k* cann-i *Cham* bg2 **Cinnb** k* eup-per bg2 irid-met srj5• nat-c h2* phos k* ran-b k* sil *Sulph* bg2 urt-u bg2

CONSTIPATION agg.: alet bg2 **Bry** bg2* chin bg2 coff bg2 colch ptk1 con bg2 crot-h bg2 ign bg2 kali-bi bg2 lach bg2 mag-c bg2 merc bg2 nat-m bg2 **Nux-v** bg2* *Op* bg2* puls bg2 sep bg2 verat bg2

CONSTRICTION: *(↗Compression; Pain - drawing; Pain - pressing pain - constricting; Tension)* *Acon* k* aesc *Aeth* agar agath-a nl2• agn allox tpw3* aloe alum alum-p k2 alum-sil k2 am-br k* am-c ambr b7.de* amn-l sp1 *Anac* k* androc srj1• ang k* *Ant-t* k* antip bro1* **Apis** arg-met *Arg-n Arn* k* ars k* *Asaf* k* *Asar* k* *Aur* b4a.de bac jl2 bamb-a stb2.de• bapt bar-c k* bar-m bell berb bism bg bov *Bry* k* bufo cact k2* cadm-s c1 calc k* calc-s *Camph* k* cann-i cann-s k* carb-ac k* carb-an k* **Carb-v** k* *Carbn-s* carc tpw2* card-m k* cardios-h rly4• cartl-s rly4• **Caust** k* cham k* *Chel* k* chin k* chinin-ar *Chinin-s* chir-fl gya2 cic cimic cina cinnb k2 clem k* cob-n sp1 coc-c coca bg3* *Cocc* k* coff k* colch k* coloc *Con* k* croc *Crot-c* crot-h k* *Cycl* cystein-l rly4• daph dig k* dios dioxi rbp6 dulc eug eup-per bro1 ferr ferr-ar ferr-p fl-ac galeoc-c-h gms1• gamb **Gels** k* gent-c glon k* *Graph* k* *Grat* guan bro1 guare *Hell* helo-s rwt2• helon hep k* hist sp1 hydrc hydrog srj2• hydroph rsj6• hyos k* hyper ign indg iod bg2* *Ip* k* iris kali-ar kali-bi *Kali-br* k* kali-c kali-i kali-m k2 kali-n k* kali-p kali-s kali-sil k2 ketogl-ac rly4• kola stb3• kreos k* lac-ac lac-c lac-e hrn2• lac-h sk4• *Lac-lup* hrn2• lach k* lap-la rsp1 laur lept bro1 lob *Lyc* k* *Lyss* m-aust b7.de mag-c k* mag-m mag-s manc mang k* marb-w es1• med k* *Meny* k* *Merc* k* merc-i-f merl k* *Mosch* k* mur-ac k* nat-c k* *Nat-m* k* nat-p nat-s **Nit-ac** k* nux-m k* *Nux-v* k* olnd k* op k* osm bro1 ox-ac ptk1 pant-ac rly4• *Par* k* *Petr* k* ph-ac k* phel *Phos* k* phys pip-m *Plat* k* plb polys sk4• positr nl2• prun psor k* puls k* pyrid rly4• ran-b ran-s b7.de* rauw sp1 rheum b7a.de rhod k* rhus-t ruta sabad k* sabin sal-fr sle1• samb k* sang hr1 sars ptk1 sel sep *Sil* k* *Spig* k* spong squil bg stann k* staph *Stront-c* k* suis-pan rly4• sul-ac k* **Sulph** k* suprar rly4• tab tarax k* tarent k* teucr b7a.de ther thuj thymol sp1 tritic-vg fd5.de tub bro1 valer k* verat k* verat-v hr1 verb k* viol-o vip xan c1 *Zinc* k* zinc-p k2 [heroin sdj2 spect dfg1]

- **morning**: agar bry carb-ac a1 cham chlor a1 con k* gamb graph kali-bi nat-m k* nux-m sulph sumb k* tarax
  - **amel.**: glon
  - **rising** agg.; after: lyc ped a1
- **afternoon**: agath-a nl2• graph k* mag-c naja nit-ac phos
- **evening**: anac asaf bamb-a stb2.de• camph h1* hyper k* kali-bi merc mur-ac murx phos polys sk4• *Rhus-t* sep stront-c sulph tab tarent valer
  - **amel.**: anac h2*
  - **bed** agg.; in: asaf merc ol-an
- **night**: merc k* mez nux-v
- **accompanied** by:
  - **epistaxis**: cact mrr1
  - **nausea**: nit-ac tl1
- **air**; in open:
  - **agg.**: mang merc nat-m valer
  - **amel.**: berb k* coloc kali-i lach lyc sal-fr sle1•
- **armor**, as if in: agath-a nl2• apis *Arg-n* cann-i **Carb-v** choc srj3• clem coc-c cocc k* *Crot-c Graph* nat-m plut-n srj7•
- **band** or hoop●: *(↗Pain - pressing pain - band)* *Abel* vh1 *Acon* k* aeth k* agath-a nl2• aids nl2• all-c allox tpw4 *Am-br* k* aml-ns bg2* amp rly4• anac k* ant-t k* arg-met *Arg-n* asaf k* aur b4a.de bac c1* bapt k* bell k* brom k* cact bg2* camph cann-s **Carb-ac** k* carb-an *Carb-v* k* carbn-s card-m cardios-h rly4• caust *Chel* k* choc srj3• cinnb rb2 clem k* coca bg2* *Cocc* k* colch bg2 con b4a.de crot-h cupr-s a1* *Cycl* k* cypra-eg sde6.de• cystein-l rly4• dios k* falco-pe nl2• ferr bg2* fic-m gya1 franc rb2 galla-q-r nl2• **Gels** k* glon k* *Graph* k* guaj hell a1 helo c1 helo-s rwt2• *Hep* hippoc-k szs2 hydrog srj2• hyos k* indg k* *Iod* k* ip iris juni-v rb2 kali-c kali-s ketogl-ac rly4• lac-h htj1• laur k* lil-t bg2* med *Merc* k* mill a1 nat-m k* nept-m lsd2.fr **Nit-ac** k* olib-sac wmh1 op osm k* petr phos a1 phys k* pieri-b mlk9.de plat k* plut-n srj7• positr nl2• rhus-t bg2* rhus-v k* sabin sang sars k* *Spig* k* spira a1* spirae a1 stann k* suis-pan rly4• sul-ac **Sulph** k* suprar rly4• symph fd3.de• tab rb2* tarent a1 *Ter* teucr k* ther k* thiam rly4• thuj bg2* tritic-vg fd5.de tub hr* vario rb2* verat xan c1* ziz [bell-p-sp dcm1 heroin sdj2]
  - **amel.**: pic-ac tl1
  - **cold** agg.: helo-s rwt2•
  - **dinner**; after: kali-c k*
  - **eating**; after: kali-c b4a.de
  - **hot**: acon k* chlol hr1* chlor bg2 coc-c k* gels bg2
  - **iron**: acon rb2 bac jl2 fuc rb2 juni-v rb2 tab rb2 tub rb2
  - **rubber**: suprar rly4•

○ · **Behind** the head: psor jl2
  - **Eyes**; passing behind: hydrog srj2•

- **Forehead**: aeth bg2 ant-t b7.de* apis bg2 carb-ac bg2 coca bg2 helo bg2 lac-c bg2 lil-t bg2 med bg2 nat-c bg2 sulph bg2
- **bending** backward | **amel**.: thuj
- **breakfast** | **amel**.: bov k*
- **candlelight**; from: cann-i
- **chill**; during: bell bg2 chin bg2 *Con* bg2 ign bg2 lach bg2 *Nit-ac* bg2 nux-v bg2 *Puls* bg2 sulph bg2 tarent
- **closing** the eyes | **amel**.: *Chel* k* sulph
- **cord**; as if constricted by a (See string)
- **cough** agg.; during: ferr iris petr k*
- **dinner**; after: bar-c kali-c h2* kali-n h2* lyc h2*
- **drinking** agg.: merc
- **eating**; after: clem a1 con dios kali-c lyc nat-m sep k*
- **emotions**; after: nat-m h2*
- **entering** a room: bov
  - **amel**.: hep valer verb
- **hat** | **tight** hat; as from a●: agath-a nl2• agn ptk1 arg-n ptk1 *Berb* ptk1 bry ptk1 cact ptk1 glon ptk1 ign ptk1 lach ptk1 *Meny* ptk1 merc ptk1 onos ptk1 ph-ac ptk1 phys plat ptk1 *Puls* ptk1 *Staph* ptk1
- **hat**; from pressure of a: **Carb-v**
- **heat** of the sun | **amel**.: stront-c
- **heated**; when: **Carb-v**
- **laughing** agg.: iris
- **lean** forward on a table, must: con h2*
- **looking**:
  - **sideways**: dig
  - **steadily** agg.: par *Puls* k*
- **lying**:
  - **amel**.: nat-m
  - **back**; on | **agg**.: mez
- **menses** | **before** | **agg**.: hep k* nat-c sil k*
  - **during** | **agg**.: gels helon iod lac-h htj1• lyc merc plat sulph xan c1
- **mental** exertion agg.: iris par *Sulph*
- **motion**:
  - **agg**.: asar *Bry* carb-v foen hipp iris-foe mez par valer
  - **air**; in open | **amel**.: acon sal-fr sle1•
  - **amel**.: op sulph valer
- **net**, as if in a: apis nat-m
- **paroxysmal**: crot-c
- **periodical**: phos
- **pressure** | **amel**.: aeth k* anac lach meny sal-fr sle1• thuj
- **reading** agg.: agn k* kiss a1
- **rising** | **amel**.: dig laur k* merc k*
- **sitting**:
  - **agg**.: fl-ac
  - **amel**.: asar k* nat-m
  - **bent** forward | **agg**.: asaf
- **sleeping** agg.: graph merc
  - **side**; on the affected: caust
- **smoking** | **amel**.: carb-ac ptk1
- **sneezing** agg.: kali-chl
- **standing** agg.: mag-c
- **stool** agg.; during: coloc
- **stooping** agg.: berb k* coloc cupr-s a1 dig med k* thuj
- **string**; as if constricted by a●: anac asaf k* bell chin cycl **Gels** graph hell iod kalm a1 lach lam a1 merc k* merc-i-r mosch nat-c *Nat-m* nit-ac plat psor sal-fr sle1• **Sulph** k* tub vh

○ • **Nape** to ears; from: anac
  - **Temple** to temple; from: sal-fr sle1•
- **supper** agg.; after: carb-v h2
- **swallowing** agg.: mag-c
- **talking** agg.: nat-m
- **tea**:
  - **green** | **amel**.: carb-ac ptk1
- **thread** were stretched from nape to eyes, as if●: lach k*
- **uncovering** head | **amel**.: *Carb-v*
- **vomiting** | **amel**.: stann
- **waking**; on: anac *Ant-t* bry graph naja nux-v suis-pan rly4• tarent ven-m rsj12•
- **walking**:
  - **agg**.: ang *Asar* *Chin* hipp thea
  - **air**; in open | **amel**.: ox-ac
- **warm** room agg.: acon *Bry* cann-i k* *Carb-v* plat
- **warmth** | **amel**.: stront-c
- **washing** agg.; after: *Ant-t*
- **weather** agg.; wet: sulph
- **wire** cage; as if wrapped in a (See Threads)
- **writing** agg.: gent-l *Lyc*

▽ - **extending** to:

○ • **Eyes** and nose: kali-n c1 nit-ac
  - **Nape**: mosch k2 [heroin sdj2]

○ - **Brain**: caust b4.de* rheum b7.de*
  - **cloth** around the brain; sensation of a tight: asaf b7.de* hell b7.de* mosch b7a.de
  - **compressed**; as if whole brain was: asaf k1* bry ptk1 carc mlr1• lac-c ptk1 nat-m ptk1 nit-ac ptk1 petr h2* sal-fr sle1• sulph ptk1 visc c1
- **Cerebellum**: camph tl1
- **Forehead**: *(↗Contraction - forehead; FACE - Tension - forehead)* *Acon* k* *Aesc* k* aeth k* agath-a nl2• agn k* ail aloe alum k* alum-p k2 alum-sil k2 *Ambr* *Anac* k* *Ant-t* k* apis arg-n k* arizon-l nl2• arn k* ars k* ars-s-f k2 asaf k* asar hr1 asc-c a1* bapt k* *Bar-c* k* bar-s k2 bell k* bell-p c1 berb k* bism k* bond a1 brach hr1 brass a1 bry k* *Cact* ptk1 calc k* *Calc-p* k* calc-s calc-sil k2 camph k* cann-i hr1 cann-s k* *Carb-ac* k* carb-an k* carb-v h2 carbn-s card-m caul hr1 caust k* *Cham* k* chel k* chin k* clem k* cocc coff colch k* coloc k* croc b7.de* crot-t k* *Cycl* k* *Dig* k* dros k* dulc k* elat k* equis-h a1* euph b4.de* fl-ac fum rly1*• galeoc-c-h gms1• gels k* glon k* *Graph* *Grat* k* haem ham k* hell k* helon k* hep k* hura br1 hydr-ac a1 hydrog srj2• hyos k* hyper a1 ign ip iris kali-ar kali-c k* kali-chl a1 kali-n k* kali-p kali-s kali-sil k2 lac-ac lac-c lac-h sk4• lac-lup hm2• lach b7a.de laur k* lepi m-arct b7.de mag-m k* manc k* mang med k* meny k* **Merc** k* mosch k* *Naja* *Nat-c* *Nat-m* k* nat-p *Nit-ac* k* nux-m nux-v k* olnd osm par k* *Phos* k* phys k* phyt k* *Plat* k* plb positr nl2• psor *Puls* k* rheum k* *Rhod* k* rhus-t k* ruta sabad k* sabin k* sal-fr sle1• sars bg2* sep k* *Sil* k* spig k* stann staph *Sul-ac* k* sul-i k* *Sulph* k* sumb a1 symph fd3.de• tarax k* teucr b7.de* ther valer k* ven-m rsj12• verat k* verat-v a1 verb k* viol-o a1 viol-t a1* zinc k* zinc-p k2 ziz a1 [heroin sdj2]
  - **right**: dulc b4.de* nat-c b4.de* *Nux-m* b7a.de
  - **left**: bell b4.de* colch b7.de* croc b7.de* olib-sac wmh1 rhod b4.de*
  - **morning**: naja
    - ⁝ **rising** agg.: sumb k*
  - **alcohol** amel.: granit-m es1•
  - **alternating** with | **expansion** of forehead: bism h1* tarax k*
  - **band**; as from a: aeth agath-a nl2• ant-t apis a bar-c bit-ar wht1• cact bg3 **Carb-ac** *Carb-v* cedr *Chel* chlol bg1* *Coca* fuc c1 gels bg3 granit-m es1• *Graph* helon indg iod iris kali-p fd1.de• lac-c a lil-t manc med k* **Merc** *Merc-c* merc-i-r mill nat-c a phos positr nl2• rauw tpw8 sang sul-i sulph bg3 tarent [bell-p-sp dcm1]
    - ⁝ **noon**: *Chel*
    - ⁝ **air**; in open | **amel**.: rauw tpw8
    - ⁝ **closing** the eyes | **amel**.: *Chel*
    - ⁝ **cold** applications | **amel**.: rauw tpw8
    - ⁝ **coryza**; during: med hr1*
    - ⁝ **exertion** agg.: sang hr1
    - ⁝ **laughing** agg.: iod
    - ⁝ **extending** to | **Neck**: [bell-p-sp dcm1]
  - **bending** forward agg.: med hr1
  - **coryza**; during: sul-ac k2
  - **cough** agg.; during: iris mosch verb
  - **eating**; after: bar-c k* clem a1 rhus-t h1
  - **hand** on part amel.: con h2
  - **intermittent**: arn hyos plat k*
  - **lying** down | **amel**.: granit-m es1•
  - **narrow**, as if too: bar-c a1 gels k*
  - **opening** the eyes agg.: equis-h a1

- **stooping** | **amel.**: con h2
- **string**; as if constricted by a: merc-i-r k* nat-c
- ○ **Above**: chir-fl gya2 con h2 sumb
- **Across**: arn asc-c a1 bar-c cann-i equis-h a1 granit-m es1• ham a1 iris laur lepi naja op par phys sabin sep valer a1 verat
- **Eyes**:
  - **Over** the eyes: aeth anag apis ars asaf bell borx bry *Card-m* chel colch dulc euphr *Glon* iod ip h1 kali-p fd1.de• meny h1 merl nux-m plat h2 polys sk4• positr nl2• *Puls* sang sil sul-i
    - **right**: nat-c h2
    - **left**: arizon-l nl2• borx
    - **hot**: chlol bg1
    - **looking** intently agg.: *Puls*
    - **touch** | **amel.**: meny h1
- **Eyes**; between the: agath-a nl2•
- **Nose**; over root of (See Pain - pressing pain)
- **Orbits**; margin of:
  - **extending** to:
    - **Temples**: cann-s
      - **pressure** | **amel.**: aeth *Anac*

- **Nerves**: graph h2
- **Occiput**: agar k* agath-a nl2• alum k* anac k* arg-n bg2* *Arn* b7a.de *Asaf* bar-c k* bar-s k2 berb k* calc k* calc-s camph bg2* cann-s k* carb-v h2* **Carbn-s** k* carl a1 cartl-s rly4• cassia-s ccrh1• *Chel* k* chin k* *Cimic* coc-c bg2* coca bg2 coca-c sk4• colch bg coloc k* dulc k* euph k* gels bg2 glon k* **Graph** k* grat bg2 guare a1 hell hir rsj4• hydrc a1 hyos k* ip k* kali-chl hr1 kali-i k* kali-s fd4.de lach k* lact k* laur k* lob k* lob-e c1 lyc k* mag-c k* manc k* mang bg2* merc *Mez* k* mosch k* mur-ac k* murx k* nat-c k* nat-m h2* par k* phel a1 pic-ac bg2* pimp a1 plat bg2 psor k* ran-g a1 ruta stann k* staph k* *Sulph* k* sumb k* tab bg2* ther bg2* thuj k* thymol sp1 tong a1 verat k* viol-o k* ziz k*
  - **forenoon**: agar k* alum h2
  - **evening**: kali-s fd4.de mur-ac k* murx k* sumb
  - **night**:
    - **lying** | **back**; on | **agg.**: mez
    - **side**; on | **agg.**: staph
  - **alternating** with | **Face**; tension of: *Viol-o* k*
  - **band**; as from a: anac bg1 arg-n bg1 carbn-s k2 coc-c bg1* con a1 graph ptk1 pic-ac bg1 prim-v c1 psor bg1 sars bl7 tab bg1 thiam rly4•
  - **bending** head agg.: viol-o c
  - **closing** the eyes | **amel.**: cassia-s ccrh1•
  - **cold** water; washing head in | **amel.**: cassia-s ccrh1•
  - **cough** agg.; during: mag-c mosch
  - **heat**: cassia-s ccrh1•
  - **lying** down | **amel.**: cassia-s ccrh1•
  - **mental** exertion agg.: cassia-s ccrh1•
  - **motion** agg.: cassia-s ccrh1•
  - **standing** agg.: mag-c k*
  - **string**; as if constricted by a | **Around** skin of occiput: psor rb2
  - **swallowing** agg.: mag-c k*
  - **waking**; on: anac k* graph k*
  - **wrinkling** forehead, compels: viol-o c
  - **writing** agg.: lyc k*
  - ▽ **extending** to:
    - **Finger** joints: plect
    - **Forehead**: cassia-s ccrh1• *Lach* b7a.de mur-ac h2
    - **Nape** of neck; into: graph h2 nat-c
    - **Upward**, downward and toward ears: **Glon**
  - ○ **Ear** to ear: ox-ac vml3• thuj bg2*
- **Scalp**: adon ptk1 aloe ptk1 asar ptk1 caust ptk1 chin ptk1 merc ptk1 par mrr1 plat ptk1 rauw tpw8* sel ptk1 thioc-ac rly4• viol-o ptk1
- **Sides**: acon a1 aeth a1 ant-t k* apis asaf k* bar-c calc k* caust k* chinin-s clem coloc com a1 dig k* dioxi rbp6 fl-ac k* mur-ac h2 pall a1 pic-ac bg2* ruta h1 spig h1 *Stront-c* k* ther bg2* thymol sp1
  - **right**: bar-c b4.de* calc b4.de* clem b4.de* dig b4.de*

Constriction – Sides: ...

  - **left**: ant-t b7.de* apis b7a.de* *Asaf* b7.de* bar-c b4.de* caust b4.de* coloc b4.de*
  - ▽ **extending** to:
    - **Orbits** and teeth; into: crot-h
    - **Teeth**; upper left:
      - **stitch**-like in spots | **stooping** and rising amel.; on: dig
- **Temples**: absin a1 acon k* agn bg ail k* alum k* ambr k* *Anac* ant-t k* arn k* ars k* bar-c k* bell bg berb k* bov k* bros-gau mrc1 bufo bg2 calc k* *Cann-s* k* *Carb-an* k* carb-v h2* caust k* cinnb k* clem k* coloc k* dig bg elaps elat k* glon k* hell k* hist sp1 hyper k* ip h1 lac-h sk4• lith-c lyc k* mag-m mang h2 merl k* mur-ac k* naja nat-m k* ol-an k* pall k* ph-ac h2* phys a1 *Plat* k* plb k* positr nl2• *Puls* k* rheum sabin c1 *Squil* k* sumb a1 tab thiam rly4• thuj thymol sp1 verat k* verb k* zinc k*
  - **right**: alum b4.de* caust b4.de* mur-ac b4.de* plat b4.de*
  - **left**: equis-h a1
  - **morning**: sulph k*
  - **band** from temple to temple, like a: carb-ac k* kali-p fd1.de• thiam rly4•
  - **cough** agg.; during: lach mag-c merc mosch verb
  - **lying** down | **amel.**: thymol sp1
  - **opening** the mouth agg.: ang h1
  - **pressure** | **amel.**: alum h2
  - **warm**:
    - **applications** | **amel.**: thymol sp1
  - **women**; in: thymol sp1
- **Vertex**: agath-a nl2• anac bg ant-t k* apis k* cact k* calc k* carb-an h2* *Caust* b4a.de chel k* chin bg con fl-ac bg gent-c k* grat bg ign bg ip bg2* kali-bi bg* kali-i k* kali-n h2* laur bg lob bg2* lyc mang a1 meny k* mosch k* naja nat-m nux-m bg2* phel a1 phos phys a1 plat h2 positr nl2• rheum sep h2* spig bg stann h2* staph h1* stront-c k* tong a1 valer bg* verat k* verb k* [bell-p-sp dcm1]
  - **morning**: kali-n h2 staph h1*
  - **afternoon**: kali-n a1
    - **and** night: kali-n h2
  - **evening**: phos h2 positr nl2•
  - **exertion** of the eyes agg.: gent-c k*
  - **menses**; during: lyc nat-m phos
  - **mental** exertion agg.: gent-c k*
  - ▽ **extending** to | **Jaw**: stront-c

CONTRACTION: acon b7.de* agn b7.de* ang b7.de* *Ant-t* b7a.de arn b7a.de asaf b7.de* asar b7.de* bism b7.de* bov b4.de* *Brom* b4a.de camph b7.de* carb-v b4.de* *Caust* b4a.de chel b7.de* *Con* b4a.de *Glon* bg2 *Graph* b4a.de hep b4a.de hyos b7a.de laur b7.de* merc b4.de* nat-c b4.de* nat-m b4.de* petr b4.de* plat b4.de* sep b4a.de squil b7.de* staph b7.de* tarax b7a.de valer b7.de*

- **sensation** of: carb-v bg2 chin bg2
- ○ **Brain**: laur ptk1 *Staph* sne
  - **alternating** with | **relaxation**: bism h1* calc k* glon bg2 ign bg2 lac-c k* med bg2 nux-v bg2 psor bg2 stront-c bg2
- **Forehead**: (↗ *Constriction - forehead*) acon b7.de* alum b4.de* anac b4.de* arn rb2 bapt bro1 bell h1* bell-p c1* *Bism* b7.de* camph b7.de* cann-i c1 cann-s b7.de* caul hr1* caust b4.de* chin b7.de* coff b7a.de *Cycl* dig b4.de* dulc b4.de* gels c1* graph b4.de* grat bro1 *Hell* bro1 lyc k* m-aust b7.de mang b4.de* merc b4.de* *Nux-m* b7a.de par b7.de* phos bro1 plat b4.de* plb b7.de* prim-v bro1 puls b7.de* sabad b7.de* *Sanic* sep b4.de* sumb a1 tarax b7.de* verat-v a1
  - **left**: bov b4.de* valer b7.de*
  - **coryza**; during: sabad b7.de*
- **Glabella**: camph tl1
- **Occiput**: *Acon* b7a.de camph b7.de* chin b7.de* colch bg2 *Graph* b4.de* hura bg2 manc bg2 mang bg2 merc b4.de* nat-m bg2 stann b4.de* thuj b4a.de
- **Scalp**; sensation of contraction of: adon vh1 aeth k* arg-n rb2 arn bg2* bapt bg2* bar-c a1 bell b4.de* bry b7a.de cact k2 *Carb-v* k* chin b7.de* coc-c a1* crot-c bg2* cupr b7a.de gels bg2* graph b4a.de* guare a1 helo bg2 helon bg1 iris bg2* kali-bi bg2* kiss a1 lyc k* lyss k* merc k* nat-m b4a.de* olib-sac wmh1 olnd b7.de* par k* ped a1 plat k* psor al2 ran-s k* rhus-t k* sanic k* sel b7a.de* spig k* stann k* thuj b4a.de* zinc bg2* [heroin sdj2]

Head

- **Sides** | **right**: squil b7.de*
- **Temples**: agn b7.de* anac b4.de* ars bg2 bell b4.de* carb-an b4.de* dig b4.de* ph-ac b4.de* plat b4.de* puls b7.de* squil b7.de* *Verb* b7a.de
  - **right**: croc b7.de*
- **Vertex**: anac b4.de* chin bg2 con b4.de* fl-ac bg2 grat bg2 ign b7.de* kali-bi bg2 laur b7.de* nat-m bg2 nux-m b7.de* phos bg2 *Sel* b7a.de sep bg2 spig b7.de* stann bg2 staph b7.de* valer b7.de*

CONVERSATION: | **amel.**: dulc ptk1 eup-per ptk1 lac-d ptk1

CONVULSIONS:
- **right** side: mygal
- **after**: caust ptk1 *Cupr* b7a.de* kali-br ptk1

CORYZA:
- **agg.**: *Chin* b7a.de *Cina* b7a.de *Sabad* b7a.de
- **amel.**: kali-bi bg2 *Lach* bg2
- **suppressed** coryza; from: acon b7a.de chin b7a.de *Puls* b7a.de

COTTON WOOL; sensation of: | **Vertex**; below the: olib-sac wmh1

COUGH: | **after** | **agg.**: ip b7.de* *Lyc* bg2 *Stann* bg2
- **during**:
  - **agg.**: *Acon* b7.de* alum b4.de* am-c b4.de* *Ambr* bg2 anac bg2 ant-t b7.de* apis b7a.de* arg-n bg2 *Arn* b7.de* ars b4.de* aur b4.de* *Bell* b4.de* brom bg2 **Bry** b7.de* *Calc* b4.de* **Caps** b7.de* carb-an bg2 *Carb-v* b4.de* *Caust* bg2 chel b7.de* *Chin* b7.de* con b4.de* ferr b7a.de* hep b4.de* hyos b7.de* ign bg2 ip b7.de* iris ptk1 kali-bi bg2 kali-c b4a.de* kali-n bg2 kreos bg2 lac-d ptk1 lach bg2 *Led* b7.de* lyc b4.de* m-arct b7.de mang b4.de* med bg2 *Merc* bg2 mez b4.de* **Nat-m** b4.de* nit-ac b4.de* **Nux-v** b7.de* petr b4.de* ph-ac b4.de* *Phos* b4.de* phyt bg2 psor bg2* ptel bg2 *Puls* b7a.de* pyrog bg2 rhus-t b7.de* rumx bg2 ruta b7.de* *Sabad* b7.de* sars b4.de* sep b4.de* spig b7.de* *Squil* b7a.de* stict bg2 sul-ac b4.de* **Sulph** b4.de* verat bg2 viol-o ptk1 zinc bg2
    - **External** head: ant-t b7.de*
    - **Occiput**: ferr ptk1 puls ptk1
    - **Temples**: lyc ptk1
    - **Vertex**: anac ptk1
  - **amel.**: chel ptk1

COVERING head agg.: | **External** head: led bg2

COVERS head (See Coldness - covered - even)

CRACKLING sensation in: acon k* agar bg1* ars k* bry b7a.de calc k* carb-v k* carl a1 cean bg1 cham k* con dig k* dulc fd4.de glon k* kalm k* *Merc* hr1 nux-m bg* par b7a.de puls k* ruta fd4.de sacch-a fd2.de• sep k* spig k* symph fd3.de• zinc bg
- **evening**: acon carl a1
- **blowing** the nose agg.; after: hep k*
- **broke**; as if something: sep
- **chains**; as if from: nux-m c1
- **motion** agg.: acon
- **shivering**; with: kalm k*
- **sitting**:
  - **agg.**: carb-v coff
  - **amel.**: acon
- **sleep** | **siesta**; during: dig k*
- **turning** the head, when: dulc fd4.de sep k*
- **wind** agg.; cold: androc srj1•

○ - **Brain**: calc bg2 coff bg2 puls bg2*
- **Forehead**: acon k* ruta fd4.de spig k* symph fd3.de•
- **Occiput**: agar a1 androc srj1• *Calc* k* carb-v k* *Sep*
- **Sides**: acon k* androc srj1• (non:arn slp) ars h2* calc k* cham k* coff k* *Hep* k*
  - **left**: cham bg2
- **Temples**: acon bg2
- **Vertex**: *Coff* k* con k* kali-bi bg2*

CRADLE CAP (See Eruptions - milk)

CRAWLING, creeping sensation (See Formication)

CROSSING the limbs agg.: bell bg2

CROWN: | **two** crowns (See Hair - crowns)

CUTTING of hair (See Hair - cutting)

DANCING agg.: *Arg-n* bg2*

DANDRUFF (= pityriasis of the scalp): agar bg2 all-s k* aloe vh1 alum k* *Am-m* k* anac bg2 *Ars* k* ars-br vh aur bg2 bad k* *Bar-c* bro1 bran bro1 bros-gau mrc1 *Bry* k* bufo ck *Calc* k* *Calc-s* **Canth** k* **Carbn-s** carc mlr1• cean mtf11 cic bg2 coch br1* crot-h a1 *Dulc* k* fl-ac a* germ-met srj5• granit-m es1• **Graph** k* grat mtf11 hep bro1 hera bro1 hydrog srj2• iod bro1 jab mtf11 *Kali-br* hr1 kali-c k* kali-chl k* kali-m k2 kali-p *Kali-s* k* lac-c *Lach* bg2 led bg2 *Lyc* k* mag-c k* maland al2 *Med* k* merc bg2 *Mez* k* **Nat-m** k* *Olnd* k* para petr bg2* **Phos** k* positr nl2• propr sa3• *Psor* k* quill mtf11 *Rhus-t* bg2 rosm mtf11 ruta fd4.de sanic k* *Sep* k* sil bro1 stann bg2 *Staph* k* sul-i bro1 **Sulph** k* *Thuj* k* tritic-vg fd5.de tub gk vanil fd5.de [nicc stj1]
- **horny**: kola stb3•
- **itching**: med ptk1* positr nl2• propr sa3• ruta fd4.de
- **scaly**: sanic al1*
- **white**●: alum h2* ars ptk1 choc srj3• *Kali-chl* k* kali-m k2* kali-s fd4.de kola stb3• *Mez* k* **Nat-m** k* *Phos* k* **Thuj** k* tritic-vg fd5.de ulm-c jsj8•
- **yellow**●: calc ptk1 **Kali-s** k*

○ - **Occiput**: nat-m bg2 sep bg2

DARKNESS:
- **amel.**: *Brom* b4a.de nat-s ptk1 sep b4a.de*
- **working** in the darkness agg.: cedr ptk1

DESCENDING agg.: *Bell* ptk1 ferr bg2* rhus-t ptk1

DIARRHEA:
- **after** | **agg.**: ambr b7.de* apis b7a.de *Bell* bg2 *Calc-p* bg2 *Hell* bg2 lol bg2
- **agg.**: *Aeth* bg2 agar bg2 bell bg2 con bg2 glon bg2 graph bg2 iris ptk1 kali-n bg2 stram bg2
- **amel.**: apis bg2 podo ptk1

DIGGING in whole head; painless: caust k*

DILATED (See Expanded)

DINNER; after: am-c bg2 calc-p bg2 calc-s bg2 carb-an bg2 kali-bi bg2 nat-m bg2 sulph bg2

DISAGREEABLE sensation in head: cina bg2

DISCHARGE:
- **nose**; from | **amel.**: all-c ptk1 *Bell* bg2 hydr bg2 kali-bi bg2* lach bg2* *Nux-v* bg2 puls bg2 zinc ptk1

DISORDERED STOMACH: | **agg.**: *Ant-c* bg2 arg-n bg2 arn bg2 *Bry* b7.de* *Carb-v* b4.de* chel bg2 chin b7.de* cocc bg2 coff bg2 cycl bg2 euph b4.de* ferr-p bg2 *Ip* b7.de* iris bg2 kali-c b4a.de* lyc b4a.de* mag-c bg2 *Nat-c* b4.de* nux-m b7a.de* **Nux-v** b7.de* op bg2 **Puls** b7.de* rhus-t b7.de* sang bg2 sulph bg2 verat bg2

DISTENSION:
- **sensation** of distension by air: par b7.de ran-b b7.de

○ - **Blood** vessels (See FACE - Veins)
- **Veins**: aloe bg2 am-m gsy1 ars bg2 bell h1* calc bg2 camph bg2 chin bg2 cub bg2 cupr bg2 **Ferr** bg2 glon bg2 sil bg2 *Spig* bg2 staph bg2 sulph bg2 tab bg2 **Thuj** bg2

○ • **Forehead** (See FACE - Veins - forehead)

DISTORTION: cupr bg2

DOZING: | **amel.**: anac bg2 ang bg2 hell b7.de*

DRAFT OF AIR (See Air agg.)

DRAGGING OUT sensation: acon b7.de

DRAGGING sensation in: agar bg2* ant-t calc k* canth k* crot-h gels k* laur k* merl k* nat-m rhus-t k*
- **sitting** and leaning against high pillow amel.: gels k*

▽ - **extending** to | **Shoulders**: gels k*

○ - **Brain**: petr b4.de

DRAWN: *(↗BACK - Opisthotonos)*
- **backward**: *(↗Bending - head - backward - must; Falling - backward; BACK - Opisthotonos)* acet-ac *Acon* k* alum b4a.de* ang bg2 *Ant-t* *Apis* arn bg2 art-v ptk2 asar b7.de* *Bell* k* camph k* cann-i *Carb-ac* carb-v bg2* cedr *Cham* k* *Chin* k* **Cic** k* *Cimic* k* *Cina* k* cocc bg2 colch b7a.de* coloc bg2 *Cupr* k* cur dig b4.de* dros gk *Eup-per* *Gels* *Glon* *Hell* *Hep* k*

- **backward**: ...
hyper bg2 *Ign* k* ip k* kreos k* lach bg2* led bg2 *Lyc Mag-c* k* *Med* k* merc bg2* mur-ac k* nat-c k* *Nat-m Nat-s* bg2* nit-ac k* *Nux-v* k* olnd b7a.de *Op* k* *Phel* phos b4a.de* plb a1 rheum b7.de* rhod bg2 samb k* sil bg2* spig b7.de* *Spong* b7.de* *Stram* k* stry syph a tab bg2 tarent bg2 **Tax** br verat-v k* viol-t k* zinc k*
  - **accompanied** by | **Head**; pain in: bell bro1 cocc bro1 *Goss* bro1
  - **convulsions**, in: **Cic** k* cina k2 *Ign* mosch *Nux-v* k* *Op* tab k* verat-v a
  - **headache** in occiput and vertex, with: arg-n ptk2 spig h1*
  - **menses**; during: zinc k*
  - **sleep** agg.; during: alum cupr mtf33 *Hep*
- **downward**: sulph h2*
- **forward**: acon bg2 agn b7.de apis b7a.de bar-m bell bg2 bry bg2 calc bg2 cic b7.de* cimic sne cupr b7a.de* hydr-ac k* *Ign* b7.de* kali-c bg2 lyc bg2 m-arct b7.de merc k* mur-ac nux-m bg2 nux-v bg2 op bg2 par k* phyt bg2 plb k* puls bg2 ran-b bg2 sang k* sars bg2 sil bg2 staph b7.de* stram bg2 sulph b4.de* verat b7.de* viol-o b7.de*
  - **convulsions**; during: cina gk
- **sideways**: abrot dgt1 apis b7a.de ars asar b7.de* *Bar-c* bell k* calc camph k* caul k* *Caust* k* cham h1 chel chin b7.de* cic k* cina k* cist colch cupr k* dulc eup-pur ferr b7.de* gels hura hyos b7.de* kali-ar lac-c *Lach* k* *Lachn* **Lyc** k* med bg2 merc k* *Nux-v* k* plb k* puls k* *Rhus-t* sabad sil k* spong b7a.de* stram k* sulph tarax b7.de* tax k* tub c1
  - **convulsions**; before epileptic: bufo *Caust* **Lyc**
  - **first** left then right: *Stram*
  - **first** right then left: ang *Nux-m*
  - **left**; to: gels hr1
  - **parotid** gland or glands of external throat; from swelling of: cist hr1*
  - **right**, to: *Caust Ferr* lachn hr1 **Lyc** *Nux-m*
  - **spasmodically**: *Camph* b7.de* *Cupr* b7a.de stram b7.de
  - **upon** shoulders: *Agar* k* hydr-ac k*
- **together** | **sensation** as if: acon bg2 agn bg2 bism bg2 bov bg2 carb-v bg2 chel bg2 chin bg2 con bg2 croc bg2 dig bg2 grat bg2 kali-n bg2 laur bg2 lyc bg2 mang bg2 nat-c bg2 nat-m bg2 nux-m bg2 par bg2 petr bg2 plat bg2 plb bg2 puls bg2 staph bg2 sulph bg2 tarax bg2 thuj bg2 valer bg2
- **upward** | **sensation** as if: hyper bg2 stront-c bg2

DREAMS agg.: *Chin* bg2 puls bg2
- **voluptuous**: borx bg2

DRINKING:
- **agg.**: acon b7.de* *Cocc* b7.de*
- **amel.**: alumn ptk1

DROPSY: *(↗GENERALS - Dropsy - internal)* apoc k2 ars k2

DRUNKARDS; complaints in: *Bar-c* bg2 *Lach* bg2 puls bg2

DRYNESS: bung-fa mtf
- **flaking** | **scalp**: musca-d szs1
- **sensation** of: camph b7.de

○ - **External** head: cann-xyz bg2
  - **only**: rhus-t bg2
- **Vertex**: ars ptk1 frax ptk1

DULLNESS (See MIND - Dullness)

EATING:
- **after**:
  - **agg.**: agar b4.de* alum b4.de* *Am-c* b4a.de* ambr b7.de* anac bg2 *Ant-c* b7.de* ant-t bg2 *Arn* b7.de* *Ars* b4a.de* bar-c bg2 bell bg2 bov b4.de* **Bry** b7.de* *Calc* b4.de* cann-xyz bg2 canth b7.de* caps b7.de* carb-an b4.de* *Carb-v* b4.de* caust bg2 cham b7.de* chel b7.de* *Chin* b7.de* chinin-s bg2 chlor bg2 cina b7.de* *Cocc* b7.de* coff b7.de* con b4.de* crot-t bg2 ferr b7.de* *Graph* b4.de* grat bg2 hyos b7.de* *Ign* b7.de* kali-bi bg2 kali-c b4.de* kali-n bg2 lach bg2 laur b7.de* *Lyc* b4.de* mag-c b4.de* mag-m b4.de* meny b7.de* mur-ac b4.de* nat-c b4.de* nat-m b4.de* nat-s bg2 nit-ac b4.de* *Nux-m* b7.de* **Nux-v** b7.de* petr b4.de* ph-ac b4.de* *Phos* b4.de* plat b4.de* podo bg2 prun bg2 puls b7.de* ran-b b7.de* *Rhus-t* b7.de* ruta b7.de* sel bg2 seneg b4.de* sep b4.de* **Sil** b4.de* staph b7.de* sulph b4.de* valer b7.de* verat b7.de* zinc b4.de*
    - **External** head: hyos b7.de* ran-b b7.de* rhus-t b7.de*

Eating – after: ...
  - **amel.**: aloe bg2 anac bg2 arg-n bg2 bov b4.de* calc-p bg2 carb-an b4.de* caust b4.de* chel b7.de* chin b7.de* cist bg2 con bg2 iod bg2 kali-bi bg2 lach bg2 laur b7.de* *Lyc* bg2 *Mag-c* b4.de* onos bg2 *Phos* b4.de* psor bg2 ptel bg2 rhus-t b7.de* rumx bg2 sabad b7.de* sep bg2 spig b7.de* thuj bg2
- **before** | **agg.**: cann-s b7.de* carb-an b4.de* nux-v b7.de* ran-b b7.de* *Sabad* b7.de* *Sil* b4.de*
- **overeating** agg.; after: acon bg2 ant-c bg2 am bg2 *Bry* bg2 carb-v bg2 ip bg2 *Nux-v* bg2 *Puls* bg2
- **while**:
  - **agg.**: am-c b4a.de bov b4.de* *Cocc* b7.de* con b4.de* dulc b4.de* graph b4.de* kali-c b4.de* kali-n b4.de* lyc b4.de* mag-m bg2 nat-m b4.de* nat-s bg2 nux-v b7.de* ph-ac b4.de* puls b7.de* ran-b b7.de* rhus-t b7.de* sabin b7.de* sars b4.de* sec bg2 verb b7.de* zinc b4a.de*
    - **External** head: merc b4.de* nux-v b7.de* sil b4.de*
  - **amel.**: anac b4a.de chel b7.de* cist ptk1 elaps bg2* lith-c bg2* lyc ptk1 mag-c ptk1 phos ptk1 phyt bg2* psor ptk1 rhod ptk1 sang bg2* sil ptk1 thuj b4a.de*

EBULLITIONS night: borx h2

ECCHYMOSES: **Bar-c** b4a.de
- **sensation** as if from: arn b7.de* ferr b7.de*

EDEMA:

○ - **Brain**; of: cupr-ar br1 hell br1 nat-s mtf33
  - **accompanied** by:
    - **vertigo**: cupr-ar br1
    - **Head**; pain in: cupr-ar br1
  - **threatening** | **dentition**; during: *Apis* bro1 hell bro1 tub bro1 *Zinc* bro1
  - **unconsciousness**; with (See MIND - Unconsciousness - brain - edema)
- **Glabella**; of: kali-c
- **Scalp**; of: *Apis* k* *Ars* k*
  - **children**; in: | **nurslings**: nit-ac mtf33

EJACULATION agg.: bov bg2 calc bg2 ham ptk1 sil bg2

ELONGATED sensation: choc srj3• *Hyper* k* lachn k*

○ - **Forehead** | **shelf**; as if forehead protrudes like a: choc srj3• syph jl2

EMOTIONS agg.: *Acon* b7.de* *Bell* b4a.de *Bry* b7.de* cham bg2 *Chin* b7.de* cocc b7.de* *Coff* b7.de* *Coloc* b4a.de cycl b7.de* ign bg2 kreos b7a.de* nat-m b4.de* nux-v b7.de* *Op* b7.de* rhus-t b7.de* *Staph* b7.de*
- **sad** emotions: calc b4a.de caust b4a.de *Cocc* b7.de* ign b7.de* nit-ac b4a.de *Rhus-t* b7.de* staph b7.de*

○ - **External** head: ph-ac bg2

EMPTY, hollow sensation: *(↗Vacant)* abrom-a bnj1 acon bg2* adax wd1 agath-a nl2• alum alum-p k2 alum-sil k2 am-c anac ant-c k* *Arg-met* k* arge-pl rwt5• arn *Ars* asaf aster bamb-a stb2.de• bar-c bar-s k2 bell berb k* bov bros-gau mrc1 cact cadm-met tpw6 calc k* camph caps k* *Carb-v* k* carbn-s caust k* chin c1 chinin-s k* choc srj3• cimic gk *Cina* k* clem clerod-i bnj1 *Cocc* k* *Coli* jl2 conin-br c2 *Cor-r* k* *Cupr* k* cupr-act bro1 cycl dulc euphr ferr ferr-ar ferr-p galla-q-r nl2• glon gran k* *Graph* k* hipp k* hyos ign k* jab lac-h sk4• lyc *Manc* k* mang k* moni rfm1• myric naja k* nat-ar nat-c k* nat-m k* nat-p nat-sil fd3.de• nux-m bg2* nux-v k* ox-ac *Phel* vh **Phos** k* pic-ac plan plut-n srj7• polyp-p bg1 positr nl2• *Puls* k* rhus-t h1 *Sec* k* *Seneg* k* sep k* spig k* stann bg2* staph k* stram k* suis-pan rly4• *Sulph* symph fd3.de• tetox pin2• thres-a sze7• til ban1• visc sp1 zinc bro1 zing [lac-mat sst4]
- **morning**: anac bov chinin-s euphr sulph verat
  - **7-15 h**: adam skp7•
- **afternoon**: nux-m
- **evening**: bamb-a stb2.de•
- **night** agg. lying on occiput; amel. by pressure of hand: sep
- **air** agg.; in open: cocc sulph
- **bathing**: kola stb3•
- **eating**; after: cocc graph meny
- **headache**; during: calc h2 cocc mrr1 **Graph** mrr1 moni rfm1• plat mrr1
- **hemorrhage**; after: blum-o bnj1
- **intoxicated**; as if: acon agar ambr spig
- **jarring**; when: adam skp7•
- **menses**; during: ferr-p k2*

- **pressure** of hand | **amel.**: mang sep
- **riding** amel.: euphr
- **rising** from squatting: adam skp7•
  - **morning** | **8**-11 h: adam skp7•
- **sitting**:
  - **agg.**: bros-gau mrc1 spig
  - **still** | **amel.**: adam skp7•
- **sleep**; after restless: hipp
- **standing** | **amel.**: adam skp7•
- **stooping** agg.: ign br1
- **talking** agg.: lyc spig *Sulph*
- **turning** head to sides; when: adam skp7•
- **walking** agg.: adam skp7• manc ptk1
- **warm** bed | **amel.**: cocc
- **warm** in bed; becoming | **amel.**: cocc

▽ - **extending** to | **Upward**: plut-n srj7•

O - **Cranial** cavity (See Empty)
- **Forehead**: act-sp bg2* alum **Caust** k* cedr bg2* chel bg2* clem bg2* croc hell bg2* kola stb3• spig k* sul-ac sulph k*
  - **between** forehead and brain; as if: caust k*
- **Occiput**: hell bg2 mang k* nat-c k* sep k* *Staph* k* *Sulph* k*

O • **Brain** in front seems too large; while: hell
- **Sides** | **left**: stann b4.de*
- **Temples**: cycl k*
- **Vertex**: positr nl2• thuj b4a.de*

ENCEPHALITIS (See Inflammation - brain)

ENERGY: | **trapped** inside; sensation as if: hippoc-k szs2

ENLARGED sensation: *(↗Expanded: Large; Swollen feeling; MIND - Delusions - enlarged - head)* acetan c2* acon bg2* **Agar** k* aids nl2• ant-c apis k* apoc aran rb2 **Arg-n** k* **Arn** k* ars k* ars-met k* *Aur* b4a.de bad a bapt k* **Bell** k* *Berb* k* bism b7.de* **Bov** k* bry bro1 cact caj k* *Caps* k* chel tl1 chinin-s sne choc srj3• *Cimic* k* cina b7.de* cob cocc bro1 coll com con bg2 *Cor-r* k* cypra-eg sde6.de• daph k* *Dulc* k* *Echi* ferr k2 *Gels* k* gent-l gins **Glon** k* *Guaj* b4a.de hell *Hyper* indg jug-c bro1* just bro1 kali-ar kali-bi bg2 kali-i lac-ac *Lac-d* lach lachn k* lact laur k* limest-b es1• lith-c k* lyc bg* *Mang* k* meli bro1* mentho bro1 meph k* merc k* merc-c *Nat-c* k* *Nat-m* **Nux-m** k* **Nux-v** k* oxyt bro1 *Par* k* phel pip-m c2* plan bg2 *Plat* k* ptel c1 **Ran-b** k* ran-s k* rhus-t k* *Sil Spig* k* spong b7.de* stry c sulph syph rb2 tarax k* ther k* til tritic-vg fd5.de tub k2 usn bro1 verat *Verat-v* bro1 zing
- **afternoon** | **16** h: *Mang*
- **bandaging**: | **amel.**: *Arg-n*
- **cough** agg.; during: caps
- **elongated**: hyper plut-n srj7•
- **fever**; with intermittent: *Cimic*
- **headache**; during: *Arg-n* hr1 gels **Par** mrr1
- **lying**:
  - **amel.**: dulc
  - **head** high; with the | **amel.**: caps
- **menses**; during: arg-n bad a *Glon*
- **metrorrhagia**; with: bad c1*
- **nausea**; with ill humor and: meph kr1
- **pain**; during: cupr ptk1
- **pregnancy** agg.; during: **Arg-n** k*
- **pulling** on boots agg.: coll
- **rising** from lying: rhus-r
- **stool** agg.; during: caps k2 cob k*
- **weather**; in cold wet: dulc
- **widened**, sensation as if: aloe

O - **Brain** feels large: acon bg2 apis bg2 arg-n bell bg2 berb chin cimic k* clem echi form k* *Glon* k* hell kali-bi bg2 kreos sne meph bg2 nat-m bg2 ozone sde2•
  - **hanging** over eyes; as if: ozone sde2•
- **Occiput**: bry bg2* coc-c bg2 cocc ptk1 dulc k* med k*
- **Vertex** | **upward**; vertex seems extended: lachn k*

EPISTAXIS:
- **agg.**: alum bg2 aml-ns bg2 ant-c bg2 borx bg2 bry bg2 *Dulc* b4a.de ferr bg2 phos bg2 sep bg2
- **amel.**: bell bg2 brom bg2 bry bg2* bufo bg2* cham bg2 chin bg2 con bg2 dig bg2 ferr-p bg2* ham bg2 hyos bg2 kali-bi bg2 *Meli* bg2* petr bg2 phos bg2 pic-ac ptk1 psor bg2* raph bg2 rhus-t bg2 sil bg2 tarent bg2

ERUCTATIONS:
- **agg.**: apis b7a.de calc b4a.de* carb-v bg2 iod bg2 lach bg2 lyc bg2 nat-c bg2 op bg2 sil bg2
- **amel.**: *Bry* bg2 cann-xyz bg2 cham bg2 cimic bg2 graph bg2 ign bg2 lach b7a.de* sang bg2

ERUPTIONS: *Agar* alum b4a.de* anac b4.de* ant-c b7a.de apis b7a.de arg-met b7a.de* arg-n bg2 **Ars** k* ars-i arund aur b4.de* aur-ar k2 bad bg2 *Bar-c* k* *Bar-m* bar-s k2 *Bov* k* bros-gau mrc1 cadm-s **Calc** k* calc-ar a *Calc-s* calc-sil k2 *Carb-an* k* *Carb-v* k* **Carbn-s** *Caust* k* chel bg2 cic k* *Clem* k* con b4.de* *Croc* bg2 crot-h kr crot-t k* cupr cycl k* dulc fuma-ac rly4• gaert pte1*• ger-i rly4• **Graph** k* hell b7a.de* *Hep* k* *Ip* hr1 *Jug-c* k* kali-ar *Kali-bi* kali-br kali-c k* kali-n h2* kali-p *Kali-s* kreos b7a.de* lac-h sk4• lappa br1 *Led* bg2 *Lyc* k* *Mag-c* k* med c1 **Merc** k* **Mez** k* morg-p pte1• mur-ac bg2 naja *Nat-m* k* nat-p *Nit-ac* k* **Olnd** k* par bg2 *Petr* k* ph-ac bg2 *Phos* k* phyt k* plan k* *Psor* k* puls b7a.de querc-r-g-s mtf11 **Rhus-t** k* *Rhus-v* k* *Ruta* k* sabin b7a.de sang bg2 sars bg2 sel bg2* seneg b4a.de **Sep** k* sil k* spig b7.de* spong bg2 **Staph** k* suis-hep rly4• **Sul-ac** k* sul-i k2 **Sulph** k* tell *Thuj* b4a.de ust bg2 vanil fd5.de verat-v bg2 vinc bg2 viol-t bg2 zinc zinc-p k2
- **bleeding** | **scratching**; after: alum *Ars Bov Calc* cupr-ar *Dulc* kola stb3• lach *Lyc Merc Nat-ar* k* petr k* *Psor* staph **Sulph**
- **blotches**: *Apis* arg-n k* sep k*
  - **moist**: arg-n a1 *Psor*
- **boils**: anac k* *Ant-t* bro1 *Arn* k* *Ars* k* aur bro1* bar-c k* bell k* bung-fa mtf *Calc* k* *Calc-m* bro1 calc-s bro1 crot-h kr dulc bro1 *Hep* k* jug-r bro1 kali-bi k* *Kali-c* k* **Kali-i** k* led k* mag-m k* mez k* mur-ac k* nit-ac k* petr-ra shn4• *Psor* k* rhus-t k* sanic mtf11 scroph-n bro1 *Sil* bro1 *Sulph* k* wies a1
  - **slowly** maturing: sanic mtf11

O • **Forehead** (See FACE - Eruptions - boils - forehead)
  - **Occiput**: *Kali-bi* k* *Lyc Nat-c* k*
- **burning**: alum bg2 *Ambr* bg2 anac bg2 *Arg-met* bg2 arg-n bg2 *Ars* k* bar-c st *Bry* bg2 calc bg2 calc-p bg2 *Chin* bg2 cic k* *Dros* bg2 *Graph* k* **Hep** bg2 iod bg2 kali-bi k* mag-c bg2 mang bg2 **Merc** bg2 **Mez** bg2 mur-ac bg2 nat-c bg2 nat-m bg2 nat-sil fd3.de• *Nit-ac* nux-v bg2 ol-an bg olnd bg2 par bg2 petr k* ph-ac bg2 phos h2* puls bg2 ran-b bg2 rhus-t bg2 ruta bg2 sang bg2 *Sars* k* *Sil* kr1 spig bg2 staph bg2 stront-c bg2 sul-ac bg2 **Sulph** k* tarax h1* thuj bg2 *Zinc* bg2
  - **scratching**; after: granit-m es1•
- **carbuncles**: *Anthraci Ars* k* crot-h kr *Hep* k* *Lach* k* *Sil* k* *Sulph* k*
- **chalky**: calc bg2 mez bg2 sars bg2 sel bg2 staph bg2
- **copper**-colored: *Carb-an* k* lyc k* mag-c a ozone sde2• sulph k*
- **cracks**: *Graph Petr* k* *Viol-o* lp viol-t a
- **crusts**, scabs: acet-ac k* aethi-a mtf11 agar alum k* *Ambr* b7a.de anan k* ant-c k* *Ant-t* **Ars** k* *Ars-i* ars-s-f k2 arum-t astac k* *Aur* aur-ar k2 bad bg2 *Bar-c* k* bar-m bar-s k2 *Bov* b4.de* brom k* *Bry* b7.de* *Calc* k* calc-i k2 *Calc-s* k* calc-sil k2 *Canth* bg2 *Caps* carb-ac *Carb-an* b4a.de carb-v carbn-s st *Caust* k* *Chel* k* chin *Cic* k* **Clem** k* *Con* b4a.de **Crot-t** k* dig b4a.de **Dulc** k* *Eup-per* *Ferr* b7.de* ferr-ma a1 *Fl-ac* **Graph** k* hell k* *Hep* k* *Hydr* k* iod k* *Iris Kali-ar* kali-bi kali-c k* kali-chl kali-p *Kali-s Kreos* lach bg2 led b7a.de lith-c *Lyc* k* mag-c b4.de* mag-p bg2 med c1 **Merc** k* *Merc-i-f* **Mez** k* mur-ac **Nat-m** k* nat-p *Nat-s Nit-ac* k* ol-j *Olnd* k* par b7.de* *Petr* k* phos k* *Phyt* k* **Psor** k* *Rhus-t* k* ruta k* sabin b7a.de *Sars* k* sel c1 *Sep* k* *Sil* k* spong mtf11 *Staph* k* sul-ac **Sulph** k* *Thuj* b4a.de* trif-p bro1 ust vanil fd5.de *Vinc Viol-t*
  - **accompanied** by | **Glands**; swelling of: agar b4a.de *Bry* b7a.de calc b4a.de caust b4a.de *Dulc* b4a.de lyc b4a.de mez b4a.de
  - **bloody**: *Calc* ruta fd4.de
  - **brown**: **Dulc**
  - **burning**: ars b4a.de
  - **cracked**: **Mez** hr1*
  - **crusta** lactea (See milk)
  - **destroying** hair: *(↗destroying)* *Dulc* b4a.de
  - **dry**: *Bar-c* b4a.de *Calc* b4a.de mez b4a.de *Sulph* b4a.de trif-p br1
  - **greenish**: *Kali-bi* petr k* sulph
  - **malignant**: *Brom Phos*
  - **moist**: *Alum* b4a.de *Anan* ars b4a.de *Bar-c Calc* carb-v b4a.de *Clem* b4a.de *Graph* k* hep b4a.de* *Lyc* b4a.de med c1 merc b4a.de *Nit-ac* b4a.de *Olnd* b7a.de ph-ac b4a.de **Psor** k* *Rhus-t* b7a.de ruta *Sep* b4a.de **Sil** b4a.de staph k* sul-ac b4a.de *Sulph* b4a.de
  - **painful**: mez gk
    - **sore** to touch: graph mtf33

- **serpiginous**: *Psor Sars*
- **thick**: calc bg2 cic mrr1 mez a1*
- **ulcerated**: ars k* *Mez* k* **Psor**
- **vermin**, with: carb-ac lyc *Mez* k* staph vinc
- **white**: alum *Ars* b4a.de calc k* *Mez* k* **Nat-m** k* tell *Thuj*
  - **thick**: calc mtf33
    - **chalk**; hair like deposits of: calc mtf33
    - **white** pus beneath; with: **Mez** k*
- **yellow**: calc *Calc-s* k* cic mrr1 dulc k* *Kali-bi* k* **Kali-s** med c1 *Merc* k* mez gk nat-p *Petr* k* *Psor* k* ruta fd4.de sep k2 *Spong* k* *Staph* k* sulph *Viol-t* st
  - **oozing**: med c1 petr hr1

○ • **Occiput**: am-c b4a.de *Ars* b4a.de *Calc* b4a.de **Caust** k* *Clem* k* cycl b7a.de euph b4a.de *Hep* b4a.de iod b4a.de *Lyc* k* mez b4a.de *Nat-m* k* *Olnd* b7a.de *Petr* b4a.de ruta b7a.de* sep b4a.de *Sil* k* staph b7a.de* *Sulph* b4a.de *Thuj* b4a.de

- **Vertex**: *Graph* b4a.de nit-ac b4a.de par b7a.de sep b4a.de squil b7a.de zinc b4a.de

- **desquamating**: *Alum* b4a.de* *Calc* k* caust b4a.de clem b4a.de graph bg2 iod b4a.de kali-c bg2 lach k* *Lyc* b4a.de mag-c b4.de* merc k* merc-c mez k* nat-m **Olnd** k* phos k* phyt bg2 rhus-t b7.de* sil b4a.de staph k* *Thuj* b4a.de wies a1
  - **itching**: *Alum* bg2 mag-c bg2 *Staph* bg2
- **destroying** hair: (↗*crusts - destroying; moist - eats)* ars bg2 bell bg2 dulc ptk2 lyc bg2* med c1 merc bg2* mez bg2* rhus-t bg2* sabad bg2
- **dirty**: brom hr1 *Psor* k* sulph syph al* thuj
- **dry**: alum bg2 arg-met bg2 ars k* aur bg2 **Bar-c** b4a.de* *Calc* k* *Carb-an* bg2 chel bg2 *Cic* bg2 clem bg2 *Fl-ac* **Graph** bg2 hell bg2 hep bg2* kali-ar kreos bg2 lach bg2 **Lyc** bg2 mag-c bg2* merc k* *Mez* k* mur-ac bg2 nit-ac bg2 *Olnd* bg2* par bg2 petr bg2 ph-ac bg2 *Phos* bg2 **Psor** k* **Rhus-t** bg2 ruta bg2 sars bg2 seneg bg2 sep k* *Sil* k* *Staph* bg2 sul-ac bg2 **Sulph** k* syc bka1• verat bg2 *Vinc* bg2 *Viol-t* bg2 *Zinc* bg2
  - **offensive**: merc k* psor al2 *Sep* k* *Sulph* k*
- **eczema**: *Agar* alum bg2 *Ant-t* **Ars** k* ars-i k2 ars-s-f k2 *Arum-t* astac bro1 *Aur* bac jl2 bad bg2 *Bar-c Bar-m* brom k* **Calc** k* calc-ar k2 calc-p k2 calc-s calc-sil k2 carb-an bg2 carb-v bl **Carbn-s** *Caust Cic* k* clem bro1 *Cocc* k* *Dulc Fl-ac* **Graph** k* **Hep** k* hydr bro1 iris kali-ar *Kali-bi* k* kali-m k2 *Kali-s* kali-sil k2 *Kreos Lappa* bro1 **Lyc** k* mag-m bg2 melit c1* merc bg2* *Mez* k* nat-c a nat-m nat-p nat-s k2 *Olnd* bro1 **Petr** k* *Phyt* k* **Psor** k* *Rhus-t* k* *Sars* sel c1* sep k2 *Sil* k* staph k* sul-i k2 **Sulph** k* tell bro1 tub al* ust *Vinc* viol-o lp* *Viol-t*
  - **itching**: graph mtf11
  - **weeping**: bac jl2

○ • **Forehead** (See FACE - Eruptions - eczema - forehead)

- **Margin** of hair: kali-sil k2 nat-sil fd3.de•
  - **Ear** to ear posteriorly; from: hydr a kali-sil k2 mez a morg-p a *Nat-m* nit-ac olnd a petr **Sulph**
- **Occiput**: *Caust* st *Lyc Petr Sil* st *Staph* sulph tell br1
- **Scalp**: arist-cl sp1 astac bro1 berb-a bro1 *Calc* bro1 cic bro1 clem bro1 fl-ac bro1 hep bro1 kali-m bro1 lyc bro1 mez bro1 nat-m bro1 *Olnd* bro1 petr bro1 psor bro1 *Sel* bro1 sep bro1 staph bro1 sulph bro1 tub bro1 *Vinc* bro1 viol-o bro1
  - **itching**: cic mtf11 graph mtf11

- **excoriating**: alum bg2 *Ambr* bg2 anac bg2 *Arg-met* bg2 arg-n bg2 ars bg2 *Bry* bg2 *Calc* k* calc-p bg2 *Chin* bg2 *Dros* bg2 *Graph* bg2* *Hep* bg2* iod bg2 kali-bi bg2 mag-c bg2 mang bg2 med c1 **Merc** k* **Mez** bg2 mur-ac bg2 nat-c bg2 *Nat-m* k* *Nit-ac* nux-v bg2 par bg2 **Petr** k* *Ph-ac* k* phos bg2 *Psor* puls bg2 ran-b bg2 rhus-t bg2* ruta bg2 sang bg2 *Sep* spig bg2 staph bg2 stront-c bg2 sul-ac bg2 **Sulph** thuj bg2 *Viol-t Zinc* bg2
- **favus**: aethi-m bro1 *Ars* bg2* ars-i bro1 bar-c bg2 brom bg2 calc bg2* calc-i bro1 *Calc-m* bro1 calc-s bro1 dulc bg2* ferr-i bro1 graph bro1 hep bg2* jug-r bro1 kali-c bg2 kali-s bro1 lyc bg2 merc bg2 mez bg2 nit-ac bro1 phos bg2 sep bg2* *Sil* bro1 *Sulph* bg2* viol-t bg2*
- **hair** | **eats** the hair (See destroying)
- **hard**: ant-c carb-an nat-m suis-hep rly4•
- **herpes**: agar k* *Anan* k* bad k* bar-c *Caps* k* chrysar bro1 cupr kali-c *Lyc* k* mag-c st med k2 nat-m bro1 *Nit-ac* mrr1 olnd bro1 petr st *Psor* k* ran-b k* rhus-t k* *Thuj* k*
  - **circinatus**: (↗*ringworm)* bac vh **Calc** k* **Dulc** k* med k2 *Phyt* k* *Sep* k* tell k* tub k*
- **herpes**: ...

○ • **Occiput**: *Arg-n* k* *Petr* k*

- **impetigo**: ars a bac jl2 bar-c k* calc-p k* *Caust* k* con k* hep k* *Iris* **Merc** k* *Petr* k* phos k* rhus-t k* *Rhus-v* sil k* sulph k* *Viol-t* k*

○ • **Margin** of the hair: *Nat-m*

- **itching**: am-m h2 arg-n bg2 ars k* *Bar-c* bros-gau mrc1 *Carbn-s Cic* crot-t bg2 ferr-m fl-ac granit-m es1• *Graph Hep* hipp kola stb3• lap-la sde8.de• led *Lyc* mag-c **Merc** k* *Mez* k* nat-c h2 nat-m nat-sil fd3.de• *Nit-ac Olnd* k* phos h2 *Phyt Psor* k* rhus-t k* sars bg2 *Sep Sil* k* staph k* sul-i k2 **Sulph** k* zinc
  - **morning**: *Hep* mag-c a1
  - **night**: *Mag-m* k* merc-i-f k* psor k2 rhus-t vinc
  - **menses**; before: *Mag-m* k*
  - **moist**, when: *Psor* tub a
  - **warm**:
    - **evening** agg.: *Lyc Sulph* st
    - **room** | **agg.**: *Clem Mag-m* k*
  - **weather**; rainy: *Mag-c*
- **miliary** before menses: sapin a1* (non:sep a1)
- **milk** crust: *Alum* bg2 ambr b2.de* ant-c b2.de* ant-t vh ars b2.de* astac bro1 aur bg2 **Bar-c** b2.de* bell b2.de* brom bg2 bry b2.de* calc b2.de* calc-i bro1 calc-s bro1* *Carb-an* b2.de* carb-v b2.de* cham b2.de* chel bg2 *Cic* b2.de* clem bg2* con bg2 *Dulc* b2.de* euph bg3 graph b2.de* hell bg2 **Hep** b2.de* kali-c bg2* kali-m bro1 kreos bg2 lappa bro1 *Led* b2.de* *Lyc* b2.de* mag-c bg2* melit c1* merc b2.de* merc-pr-r bro1 *Mez* b2.de* mur-ac bg2 nat-m b2.de* nat-p hr1 *Nit-ac* bg2 ol-j bg3* olnd bg2* par bg2 *Petr* bg2* ph-ac bg2 phos b2.de* psor bg2* rhus-t b2.de* *Ruta* bg2 **Sars** b2.de* scroph-n bro1 seneg bg2 *Sep* b2.de* sil b2.de* *Staph* b2.de* sul-ac bg2 sulph b2.de* *Trif-p* br1* tub bg2* ust bg3* vac jl2 verat bg2 vinc bg2* *Viol-t* b2.de* *Zinc* bg2
  - **children**; in: ars mtf33 *Carb-v* mtf33 graph mtf33 kali-c mtf33 kali-chl c1 lyc mtf33 mag-c mtf33 merc mtf33 merc-i-f c1 nat-m mtf33 phos mtf33 psor mtf33 sil mtf33 staph mtf33 sulph mtf33
    - **newborns**: calc tl1 olnd mrr1 tub xxb
      - **adenitis**; with: am-c st astac ptk bar-c pfa
  - **crusts**; with thick: *Mez* b4a.de
  - **eroding**: staph bg3*
  - **foul**: calc ptk1 staph bg3* sulph ptk1

○ • **Face**; beginning in: *Sars* b4a.de

- **moist**: alum k* *Anan* k* *Ars* k* bad bg2 **Bar-c** k* *Bar-m* bar-s k2 *Calc* k* *Calc-s* bro1 **Carbn-s** *Cham* k* *Cic* k* clem b4a.de* **Graph** k* *Hell* bg2* **Hep** k* *Hydr* k* kali-ar *Kali-bi* kali-s kali-sil kreos bg2 *Lyc* k* *Merc* k* *Mez* k* *Nat-m* nat-s k2 *Nit-ac* k* *Olnd* b7a.de* *Petr* k* *Phyt* plut-n srj7• **Psor** k* *Rhus-t* k* ruta bg2 *Sars* k* sel a sep b4a.de* *Sil* k* *Staph* k* **Sulph** k* tab a *Thuj* k* tub lp* ust vinc k* *Viol-t* k*
  - **eats** the hair; that: (↗*destroying)* ars *Kali-bi Merc* st mez k2 *Nat-m* psor k2 *Rhus-t* staph sne
  - **glutinous** moisture: **Graph** kali-s k2 *Nat-m Sulph*
  - **oozing**: med c
  - **yellow**: *Clem Iris* **Kali-s** *Petr* hr1 *Psor* staph *Viol-t*

○ • **Forehead**, before menses (See FACE - Eruptions - moist - forehead - menses)

- **Margin** of hair: *Clem* bro1 *Galeoc-c-h* gms1• hydr bro1 nat-m bro1 *Olnd* bro1 sulph bro1
  - **left**: galeoc-c-h gms1•
  - **pustular**: galeoc-c-h gms1•
- **Occiput**: *Clem* k* olnd k* *Petr* **Sil** k* *Staph* k* *Thuj*

- **mousy** odor: staph bg2*
- **nodes**: arg-n bg2 asaf *Caust* k* *Chin* k* *Coloc* vh con *Hep* k* *Kali-i* k* mag-c k* nat-c h2* nat-s k* nit-ac *Phyt* k* rhus-t k* **Sil** k* still hr1 thuj k*

○ • **Occiput**: *Mag-m* k*

- **offensive**: bar-m brom calc graph *Hep* k* lyc k* merc k* mez nit-ac *Phyt* psor k* *Rhus-t* k* sep sil staph k* sulph k* tub a vinc k*
- **oranges** agg. (See GENERALS - Food - oranges - agg.)
- **painful**: alum bg ambr bg anac bg arg-met h1* arg-n bg ars bg bar-c h2* *Bry* bg calc bg calc-p bg cann-s k* carbn-s k2 *Chin* bg clem bg *Dros* bg ferr-ma k* **Graph** k* **Hep** k* *Iod* bg kali-bi bg kali-c lyc h2* mag-c mag-m a1 mang bg merc **Mez** bg mur-ac bg nat-c bg nat-m bg nit-ac k2 nux-v bg par petr bg ph-ac bg phos bg puls bg ran-b bg rhus-t bg* ruta bg2 sang bg sul-ac k2 sulph syc bka1• vanil fd5.de
  - **splinter**-like pains: nit-ac k2

- **papules**: staph a1
- **pimples**: act-sp k* agar k* alum am-m b7.de* *Ambr* k* anac k* arg-met b7a.de* **Ars** k* aur k* aur-ar k2 bar-c k* bar-m bar-s k2 bell b4.de* berb hr1 *Bov* k* calc calc-s k* cann-s a1 cann-xyz bg2 carb-v b4a.de carbn-s cench k2 clem bg2 *Con* crot-c k* cund k* cycl k* dulc fd4.de fuma-ac rly4• gal-ac a1 **Hep** k* kali-bi k* kali-c k* kali-p *Kali-s* kreos bg2 lachn hr1 !appa br1 **Led** m-ambo b7.de merc-i-r k* mez k* *Mur-ac* k* nat-c k* *Nat-m* nux-v k* olnd k* petr k* *Phos* k* pin-con oss2• puls hr1 rhus-t b7.de* sec *Sep* hr1 *Sil* k* spig k* staph h1* **Sulph** k* symph fd3.de• tarax b7.de* tarent k* tritic-vg fd5.de vanil fd5 de *Zinc* k*
  - **inflamed** | **Scalp**; hairy: sulph tl1
  - ○ **Forehead** (See FACE - Eruptions - pimples - forehead)
  - **Margin** of hair in front: ambr a1 dulc fd4.de gink-b sbd1• nat-sil fd3.de• nit-ac k* symph fd3.de•
  - **Occiput**: am-m berb hr1 bufo-s clem cob hr1 cycl hydrog srj2• kali-bi kali-n lac-ac hr1 lyc mag-m a1 merc muru a1 nat-sil fd3.de• positr nl2• **Sulph** [bell-p-sp dcm1]
  - **Scalp** like smallpox, having shot-like feeling under them; came all over: am-c k1
- **plica** polonica (See Hair - plica)
- **psoriasis**: *Ars-i* vh **Calc** bg2 cic bg2 *Graph* bg2* led bg2 lyc bg2* merc bg2 **Mez** mrr1 olnd bg2* **Sep** bg2 staph mrr1 **Sulph** bg2
  - ○ **Occiput**: staph mrr1
- **pustules**: ammc k* *Ars* k* ars-s-f k2 arund k* bov *Calc* k* calc-sil k2 cic bro1* clem bg2* crot-h kr gast a1 graph bro1 *Hep* k* *Iris* k* jug-c bro1* kali-br k* kali-n bg2 *Merc* k* merc-i-r k* mez bro1 morg-p pte1*• mur-ac *Psor* k* puls k* rhus-t sep k* *Sil* k* **Sulph** k* vac hr1
  - **burning**: *Cic* mrr1
  - **chronic**: ars mtf33
  - **confluent**: *Cic* mrr1
  - ○ **Forehead** (See FACE - Eruptions - pustules - forehead)
  - **Occiput**: ammc puls **Sil** k*
    - **painful**: sil tl1
    - **ulcers**; join to form: sil tl1
    - **variola**-like: sil tl1
  - **Temples**: mur-ac a1
- **rash**, itching forehead (See FACE - Eruptions - rash - itching - forehead)
- **red** | **spots**; in: tell bro1
- **ringworm**: (*↗herpes - circinatus*) agar bro1 ars bro1 ars-i bro1 *Bac* bro1 bapt c2 bar-m c2* *Brom* bro1 calc bro1 caps hr1 caust tl1 chrysar bro1* *Dulc* ll1* *Graph* bro1 hep bro1 iris tl1 jug-r bro1 *Kali-c* bro1 kali-s bro1 lappa bro1 *Lyc* bro1 med bro1 mez c2* nat-c mrr1 olnd bro1 petr bro1 phos bro1 phys tl1 psor c2* querc-r-g-s mtf11 *Sep* bro1 sil bro1 sulo-ac bro1 sulph bro1 *Tell* bro1 tub bro1* ust bro1 vinc bro1* viol-t bro1
- **scales**: agar bg2 alum k* anac bg2 aq-pet a1 *Ars* k* ars-s-f k2 arund k* aur bg2 bell k* *Bry* bg2 *Calc* k* canth hr1 carbn-s *Cic* k* dulc bg2 *Fl-ac* k* granit-m es1• **Graph** k* *Kali-bi* k* *Kali-c* bg2 kali-n k* *Kali-s* k* *Kreos* k* *Lach* bg2 lap-la rsp1 led bg2 *Lyc* k* mag-c bl merc k* mez k* naja nat-m k* **Olnd** k* petr bg2 phos k* phyt k* plut-n srj7• psor mrr1 puls sne *Rhus-t* bg2 *Sep* k* *Sil* k* *Staph* k* sulph k* syc bka1• *Thuj* k*
  - **bald** spots on: phos k2
  - **bleeding** after scratching: lyc k*
  - **dry**: ars k* *Calc Fl-ac* kali-s bro1 mez k* *Nat-m* bro1 *Ph-ac* phos bro1 phyt bro1 psor bro1 sanic bro1 *Sil* staph syc pte1• thlas bro1 trif-p br1
  - **fine**: clem k* par k*
  - **fish** scales, like: mez
  - **large**: **Olnd** mrr1 ozone sde2•
  - **milk** crust (See milk)
  - **offensive**: *Nit-ac* k*
  - **patches**: graph k* kali-n k* lyc phos k* plut-n srj7• *Sil*
  - **washing** | **amel.**: bros-gau mrc1 **Graph** k*
  - **white**: alum k* calc k* kali-m a *Mez* k* **Nat-m** k* tell k* *Thuj* k* tub dp• wies a1
  - **winter** agg.: bros-gau mrc1 *Sil* k*
- **scratching**; after | **lumps**: granit-m es1•
- **scurfy**: alum ars ars-i arund hr1 bad bg *Bar-c* k* *Bov* bg *Bry* bg *Calc* k* *Canth* bg caust bg *Chel* bg com con corn a1 crot-t bg dulc bg *Ferr* bg **Graph** k* *Hell* hr1 hep iod kali-c h2* lach bg lap-la sde8.de• *Lyc* bg mag-c bg mag-p bg

Eruptions – scurfy: ...
Merc k* *Mez* bg* naja a1 nat-m k* nit-ac bg **Olnd** par bg *Petr* bg *Phos* bg phyt bg *Psor* k* **Rhus-t** bg samb xxb1 sep h2* sil h2* *Staph* k* *Sulph* bg *Viol-t* k*
  - **black**: *Calc-p* k*
  - **dry**: *Bar-c* k* *Calc* hr1
  - **moist**: alum k* *Anan Bar-c* k* *Calc* k* *Graph* k* nit-ac h2*
  - **purulent**: rhus-t hr1
  - **spots**: kali-n c1
  - **white**: nat-m k*
- **sensitive**, extremely: dulc fd4.de **Hep** *Nit-ac* **Staph**
- **serpiginous**: *Ars* bg2 *Calc* k* cic bg2 *Clem* k* con bg2 dulc bg2 graph bg2 lyc bg2 merc bg2 nat-m bg2 ph-ac bg2 *Psor* k* ran-b bg2 rhus-t bg2 *Sars* k* sep bg2 **Sulph** bg2
- **smarting** (See burning)
- **sore**: alum bg2 *Ambr* bg2 anac bg2 *Arg-met* bg2 arg-n bg2 ars bg2 *Bry* bg2 calc bg2 calc-p bg2 *Chin* bg2 *Dros* bg2 galeoc-c-h gms1• graph bg2 *Hep* k* iod bg2 kali-bi bg2 mag-c bg2 mang bg2 **Merc** bg2 **Mez** bg2 mur-ac bg2 nat-c bg2 nat-m k* nux-v bg2 par bg2 petr bg2 ph-ac bg2 phos bg2 puls bg2 ran-b bg2 rhus-t bg2 ruta bg2 sang bg2 spig bg2 staph bg2 stront-c bg2 sul-ac bg2 thuj bg2 *Zinc* bg2
  - **touch** agg.: *Galeoc-c-h* gms1• phos h2*
- **spots**: ars kali-c mang k2 mosch phos k2 syc bka1• vanil fd5.de zinc
- **stings** of insects, like: sarr a1
- **suppurating**: ars *Bar-m* k* *Calc-s* cic k* clem dulc fd4.de graph hep lyc k* *Mez* k* *Psor* k* *Rhus-t* k* *Sep* staph **Sulph** vanil fd5.de vinc
- **tetters**: *Alum* b4.de* graph b4.de* mag-m b4.de* *Petr* b4.de* *Rhus-t* b7.de*
- **tubercles** on scalp: anac ant-c k* bar-c **Calc** carb-an kali-c kali-i k2 *Lyc* nat-m ph-ac phos *Phyt Psor* sil syph k2*
  - **itching**: phos h2*
- **urticaria**: *Agar* k* *Apis* b7a.de rhus-t hr1 urt-u hr1
- **vesicles**: *Ars* k* bov k* clem k* (non:crot-h st) crot-t k* kali-bi k* merc k2 olnd k* ozone sde2• petr k2 psor k* rhus-t k2 sep k* *Sulph* k* tell k* tep k*
  - **purulent**: calc b4a.de kali-c b4a.de *Sil* b4a.de sulph b4a.de
  - ○ **Margins** of hair: nat-m k2 nat-sil fd3.de•
- ○ **Forehead** (See FACE - Eruptions - forehead)
- **Margin** of hair: bros-gau mrc1 calc cypra-eg sde6.de• gink-b sbd1• hydr br kali-n h2 kali-sil lap-la sde8.de• mez bg morg-p pte1• *Nat-m* k* nat-sil fd3.de• nit-ac k* olnd c ozone sde2• petr k* podo fd3.de• rhus-t al sep **Sulph** k* tell k* vanil fd5.de [spect dfg1]
- **Occiput**: am-c b4a.de am-m b4a.de* arg-n ars b4a.de bar-c b4a.de bufo *Calc* b4a.de carb-v b4a.de **Caust** k* chel b7a.de *Clem* k* cycl k* euph b4a.de *Graph* k* *Hep* b4a.de iod b4a.de kali-bi kali-n kali-sil k2 kola stb3• lac-h sk4• *Lyc* k* merc k* merc-i-r bg2 mez b4a.de nat-c nat-m k* nat-sil fd3.de• olnd k* *Petr* k* *Psor* puls k* ruta b7a.de* sep b4a.de **Sil** k* *Staph* k* **Sulph** k* *Thuj* b4a.de vanil fd5.de
- **Scalp**: **Ars** ptk1 bar-c ptk1 *Calc* ptk1 *Graph* ptk1 **Hep** ptk1 *Lyc* ptk1 merc ptk1 mez tl1* **Olnd** ptk1 *Petr* ptk1 **Rhus-t** ptk1 *Sulph* ptk1 viol-t ptk1
- **Sides**: ars b4a.de bar-c b4a.de carb-an b4a.de caust b4a.de coloc b4a.de dros b7a.de kali-c b4a.de ruta b7a.de *Staph* b7a.de
- **Temples** (See FACE - Eruptions - temples)
- **Vertex**: agar b4a.de ars b4a.de bry b7a.de carb-v b4a.de caust b4a.de graph b4a.de* mez b4a.de* nit-ac b4a.de ruta fd4.de sep b4a.de zinc b4a.de

ERYSIPELAS: ant-t *Anthraci* **Apis** apoc k* *Ars* k* ars-s-f k2 bell bg2* *Calc* b4a.de canth mrr1 carbn-s *Chel* k* *Chin* k* crot-t a1 cupr k* dor k* *Euph* k* **Graph** k* kali-i a1 *Lach* k* passi a *Ph-ac* k* *Phyt* k* puls bg2* *Pyrog* a *Rhus-t* k* rhus-v a1* *Ruta* sol-t-ae a1 sulph ter k* verat-v k*

- ▽ **extending** to | **Face**: *Apis*
- ○ **Forehead** (See FACE - Erysipelas - forehead)
- **Occiput**: *Ph-ac* k* rhus-t
- **Sides**:
  - **left**: samb
    - **extending** to | **right**: *Rhus-t*

EXCITEMENT agg.: phos bg2

EXERTION; physical:

- **agg.**: acon bg2 am-c bg2 ambr bg2 anac bg2 ars bg2 calc b4a.de calc-act bg2 calc-p bg2 cocc bg2 glon bg2 mur-ac bg2 nat-c bg2 nat-m bg2 nit-ac bg2 nux-v bg2 rhus-t b7.de* sil b4a.de* spig bg2 spong b7.de* staph bg2 syph bg2 valer bg2
  - ○ **External** head: *Rheum* b7a.de
  - **Occiput**: onos ptk1

EXOSTOSIS: anan bro1* **Arg-met** **Aur** k* aur-m k2* *Calc* **Calc-f** k* carbn-s k2 cupr bro1 *Fl-ac* k* hecla bro1 *Kali-i* k* **Merc** k* merc-p bro1 *Mez* nit-ac k2 **Phos** *Phyt* sars bg2 sep sne sil bro1 still bro1 syph k2*
- **painful**: *Aur* carbn-s k2 *Kali-i* **Merc** syph k2*
- **sensitive**: syph jl2

EXPANDED sensation: *(↗Enlarged; Large; Swollen feeling)* *Acon* bg2 apis b7a.de* *Arg-n* k* arge-pl rwt5• arn b7.de* bapt bg2 bell berb bg2* bism b7.de* bov bg2* cann-i caps b7.de* carb-ac cimic bg2 cina b7.de* dulc euph gels bg2 glon bg2 kola stb3• lac-d k2 laur b7.de* lyc bg2 mang bg2 nux-m k* par bg2* positr nl2• pot-e rly4• ran-b b7.de* ran-s b7.de* sol-ni spig b7.de* stront-c tarax b7.de*
- **inflated**, feels: aids nl2• kali-i olib-sac wmh1 positr nl2•
- **pregnancy** agg.; during: **Arg-n** hr1
- **ring**-like: merc k*
- **shaking** the head agg.; on: carb-ac
- **sleepiness**; with: *Nux-m* br1
- **stool** agg.; during: cob

▽ - **extending** to | **Upward**: plut-n srj7•

○ - **Brain**: bell b4.de
  - · **stooping** agg.: spig h1
- **Forehead**: irid-met srj5• *Nux-m*
  - · **alternating** with:
    - ⁝ **constricion** of forehead (See Constriction - forehead - alternating - expansion)
    - ⁝ **pressing** pain in forehead (See Pain - forehead - pressing pain - alternating - expansion)
    - ⁝ **relaxation** of the forehead: glon k2 *Lac-c*
- **Vertex** | **cone** going upwards; like a: sanguis-s hrn2•

EXPANSION (See Expanded; Swollen feeling)

EXPECTORATION: | **amel.**: lyc bg2

EYES:
- **exertion** of eyes agg.: arg-n bg2 arn bg2 calc-act bg2 cimic bg2 cina bg2 crot-t bg2 gels bg2* hep bg2 lach bg2 nat-m bg2* nicc bg2 onos bg2* par bg2 ph-ac bg2* phys bg2 pic-ac bg2 rhod bg2 ruta bg2* spig bg2 [bell-p-sp dcm1]
- **swelling** of eyes agg.: hyos bg2
- **turning** the eyes: dig bg2 rhus-t bg2 sep bg2

FAINTING; after: | **agg.**: calc bg2 graph bg2 lach bg2 lyc bg2 mosch b7.de* nat-m bg2 nux-v bg2 puls bg2 sil bg2 *Stram* bg2 verat bg2

FALL; from a: | **agg.**: *Arn* b7.de* *Cic* b7a.de *Hyos* b7a.de rhus-t b7.de*

FALLING: *(↗Heaviness - falls)*
- **all** directions; sensation as if head was falling in: cann-s rb2 con rb2
- **backward**: *(↗Drawn - backward)* aeth *Agar* ant-t bov camph cham chin choc srj3• cic k* *Colch* *Dig* k* dios glon *Ign* kali-c kali-m k2 laur *Led* mur-ac oena *Op* *Phel* rhod rb2 samb *Spig* k* tarent
  - · **sitting** agg.: chin *Dig* oena op
  - · **vertigo**; during: led h1 ph-ac h2 *Spig*
  - · **walking** agg.: *(↗Bending - head - backward - must - walking; Motions of - throwing - backward)* *Chin* *Dig* phel
- **forward**: agn bar-c h2* calc calc-sil k2 cham clem *Cupr* elaps gels glon hipp k* hydr-ac k* hyos *Ign* kali-c kali-p laur lyc *Merc* *Nat-m* nux-m *Op* par phos phys pic-ac plat plb *Puls* ran-b sars sec *Sil* staph sulph verat
  - · **and** to left: calc-act h1
  - · **looking** at anything; sinking of head forward when: *Cic*
  - · **rising** agg.: hipp k*
  - · **sensation** of: acon bg2 alum bg2 am-c bg2 bar-c bg2 carb-an bg2 cham bg2 coff bg2 dig b4a.de* grat bg2 kali-c bg2 kreos bg2 laur bg2 nux-v bg2 *Rhus-t* bg2 sabad bg2 sul-ac bg2 thuj bg2
    - ⁝ **Occiput**: bov bg2 cann-xyz bg2 rhod bg2
  - · **sitting** agg.: *Nux-m* oena staph
  - · **stooping** agg.: cic a1 cist *Puls*
  - · **tendency**: emetin mp4•
  - · **vertigo**; during: calc-act h1 *Camph* b7a.de *Cupr* b7a.de* ph-ac h2* podo br1 sars h2*
  - · **walking** agg.: carbn-s hipp k* mez k*
  - · **wrinkling** of forehead and open air amel.: phos

Falling: ...
- **hither** and thither: bar-c bell *Cupr* *Nux-m* phel
- **pieces**; sensation as if head would fall into: xan c1
  - · **stooping** agg.: con bg1 glon
- **sideways** of head: am-c k* aml-ns rb2 ang arn ars cann-s *Cina* dios eup-per ferr fl-ac helo-s rwt2• hyos kali-bi kali-i *Mygal* nux-m op prun stram sulph tarax
  - · **child** leans head, all the time: cina k*
  - · **left** side, to: eup-per rb2 nux-m sil h2*
    - ⁝ **breakfast**; during: sil rb2
  - · **right** side, to: am-c ferr helo-s rwt2• lac-d c1
  - · **vertigo**; with: sil h2* spong h1*
  - · **waking**; on: sulph
  - · **walking** agg.: dios ferr
- **walking** in open air agg.: sul-ac

○ - **Brain**:
  - · **down**; as if brain falls: laur ptk1
  - · **forward**; as if brain was falling: *(↗Looseness)* *Alum* am-c ant-t bar-c bell k2 berb bry carb-an cham coff *Dig* grat hipp kali-c kreos laur mag-s nux-v *Rhus-t* sabad sul-ac
    - ⁝ **and** came up again; a pain as if brain fell forward: sul-ac
    - ⁝ **raising** head | **amel.**: alum
    - ⁝ **stooping** agg.: alum ant-t bar-c *Carb-an* chel coff dig kali-c laur mag-s nat-m *Nat-s* *Nux-v* rhus-t
  - · **out**; sensation as if the brain were falling: *Acon* bg2 bar-c bg2 bell b4a.de* *Bry* b7a.de* chel bg2 hell bg2 hep bg2 kreos b7a.de mez bg2 mosch b7a.de nux-v bg2 puls b7a.de* rhus-t bg2 sep bg2 spig b7.de* staph b7.de*
  - · **side** to side: *(↗Looseness)* nicc sul-ac
  - · **stooping** | **agg.** | **side** to which he stoops: am-c
    - ⁝ **Temple**; as if brain fell to left: nat-s
- **Forehead**; as if everything would fall out of: *Acon* all-c bar-c bell brom bry canth carb-an caust cham chel colch coloc hell hep kali-c kreos mag-m mag-s mez nux-v phos pitu-a vml2• plat puls rat rhod sabad sep spig spong stann staph stront-c tab *Thuj* verb
  - · **coughing**; while: hep
  - · **moving** the eyes; on: puls
  - · **stool** agg.; during: rat
  - · **stooping** agg.: bar-c hell mag-s nat-c h2 spig h1 staph h1

FALSE STEP; at a: | **agg.**: bry b7.de *Led* b7.de* puls b7.de spig b7.de

FASTING agg.: ars ptk1 cact bg2* caust bg2 cist bg2* lach ptk1 lyc bg2* psor bg2 sabad bg2 sang ptk1 *Sil* bg2* sulph ptk1

FAT FOOD agg.: cycl b7.de* *Puls* b7.de*

FATTY degeneration: | **Brain**: pic-ac tl1 plb tl1

FEVER: | **before** | **agg.**: bry b7.de **Chin** b7.de *Cina* b7a.de puls b7.de rhus-t b7.de spong b7.de
- **during** | **agg.**: ant-t b7.de bry b7.de *Chin* b7.de dros b7.de hell b7.de ip b7.de *Nux-v* b7.de spig b7.de *Verat* b7.de

FISSURES: kali-i ptk1 mag-c bg2 *Ruta* b7.de*

FLATTENED, sensation:
- **pressed** flat; as if: spong fd4.de verat

○ - **Forehead**: cor-r k* verat ptk1
- **Occiput**: mag-c k2

FLATUS: | **discharge** of | **amel.**: aeth bg2* cic b7.de* kali-c bg2 m-ambo b7.de m-arct b7.de mag-c bg2 merc-c bg2 sang ptk1
- **movements** of flatus in abdomen | **amel.**: m-ambo b7.de*

FLUCTUATION (See Waving)

FLUID; sensation of (See Water)

FLUIDS agg.; loss of vital: *Calc* bg2 **Chin** bg2 *Nux-v* bg2 sulph bg2 verat bg2

○ - **External** head: *Chin* b7a.de

FONTANELLES:
- **closed** when born: sanic c1

- **open**: ant-c vh *Apis* k* apoc k2* bar-c bnt *Bry* kr1 **Calc** k* **Calc-p** k* *Ip* k* *Merc* k* ph-ac bg2* *Phos* bg2* *Puls* a* *Sep* k* **Sil** k* *Sulph* k* *Syph* k* zinc bro1
  - **abdomen**; with distended: sil ptk1*
  - **close** and reopen: calc-p c1*
  - **sunken**: *Apis* k* calc k* carb-ac bg2
    - **Occipital**: *(↗Sinking - occipital)* calc-p ptk1* mag-c ptk1
- **pulsating** strongly: gels ptk1

FOREIGN body; sensation of a:

○ - **Brain**: con tl1 iod tl1 m-ambo b7.de
  - **right** side: *(↗Ball; Board; Board - front; Lump; Marble)* arg-n bg1 ars bg1 cina bg1 con merc bg1 phos h2* phys bg1
  - **motion** | **amel.**: iod tl1
- **Forehead** | **skin** of; under: plut-n srj7•

FORMICATION: *Acon* k* aesc k* *Agar* aids nl2• alum k* alum-sil k2 am-c k* am-m k* *Ant-c* k* apis bg2* *Arg-met* b7.de* **Arg-n** k* arn b7a.de* ars k* arund atis bnj1 bar-c k* bar-s k2 brom a1 *Calc* k* *Calc-p* k* calc-s cann-s k* carb-v castor-eq caust h2* chel k* chcc srj3• cic bg2* coc-c k* cocc bg2* colch k* cupr k* *Cycl* dulc fago k* *Ferr* k* hipp a1 hist sp1 hydrog srj2• hyos k* ign gk irid-met srj5• kali-bi k* lach k* laur k* *M-aust* b7.de mez k* nat-c nat-s nit-ac k* nux-v k* petr bro1 ph-ac bg2* phos bg2* *Pic-ac* k* *Plat* bg3* psor puls k* ran-b k* ran-r br* rauw sp1 rheum bg2 rhod *Rhus-t* k* sabad bg2 sec gk sep sil spig *Sulph* k* tarax bg2 thuj k* viol-o bg2 zinc bg2
- **right**: germ-met srj5•
- **morning**: arg-n k* thuj k*
- **evening**: bar-c k* calc k*
  - **bed** agg.; in: ran-b ran-r br
- **scratching** until parts bleed: alum k*
- **spots**; in small: hist sp1
- **walking**:
  - **agg.**: *Coc-c*
  - **air** agg.; in open: lyc rhus-t
- **warmth**:
  - **amel.** | **heat** amel.: *Acon* k*

○ - **Brain**: hyper ptk1 ign gk puls h1*
- **Forehead**: alum ptk1 ambr vh apis k* arn k* arund benz-ac k* carc fd2.de• chel k* chin h1* cic k* cocc b7.de* *Colch* k* glon kali-c k* lach b7a.de laur k* m-aust b7.de* manc nux-v ph-ac k* phos h2* plat bg2 puls b7.de* ran-r br rheum bg2 rhus-t k* rhus-v sabad b7.de* sulph bg2 tarax k* viol-o b7.de* *Zinc* k*

○ • **Above** the: kali-c
- **Occiput**: ars bamb-a stb2.de• brom carb-v h2* crot-t bg* lil-t bg2 rhus-t b7.de* *Sep* k* thuj vario bg2
  - **afternoon**: rhus-t h1
- **Scalp**: acon b7.de* agar bg2 alum b4a.de* am-c b4.de* arg-met b7.de* arg-n bg2 *Arn* b7.de* ars b4.de* bar-c bg2 brom bg2 calc bg2 calc-p bg2 camph bg2 cann-s b7.de* carb-v b4.de* caust b4.de* *Chel* b7.de* chin bg2 *Colch* b7a.de* ferr b7.de* kali-bi bg2 kali-c b4.de* lach bg2 laur b7a.de* led b7.de* mez b4.de* nit-ac bg2 nux-v b7.de* plat bg2 ran-b b7.de* rhod b4.de* rhus-t b7.de* sabad b7.de* *Sel* bg2 sil bg2 spig b7.de* staph b7.de* thuj b4.de* trios rsj11• verat b7.de* [tax jsj7]
  - **asleep**; on falling: rauw sp1
  - **pressure** agg.: rauw sp1
- **Sides**: m-aust b7.de
  - **right**: nit-ac h2*
  - **left**: spig h1*
- **Temples**: aesc k* alum k* arund bg1* colch bg2 *Cupr* bg2 guar bg* guare bg1 hyos bg2 *M-aust* b7.de plat k* rheum b7.de sec gk sulph k*
- **Vertex**: agar bg2 aids nl2• arn h1* *Aur* b4a.de calc bg2 calc-p cann-i cann-s bg cann-xyz bg2 caust h2* colch b7.de* crot-t bg2 *Cupr* k* hyos b7.de* hyper bg2 lac-f c1 lil-t m-aust b7.de *Nat-s* nux-v bg2 olib-sac wmh1 positr nl2• rhus-t bg2

FRACTURES:
- **skull**; of: arn tl1 *Calen* st1
  - **slow** repair of broken skull: *(↗GENERALS - Injuries - bones - slow)* calc-p tl1 symph tl1

FRIGHT; after: | **agg.**: *Acon* b7.de* calc b4a.de* chinin-ar ptk1 cic b7.de* cimic ptk1 cupr b7.de* glon ptk1 hyos b7.de* *Ign* b7.de* **Op** b7.de* plat bg2 puls b7.de* samb b7.de*

FROZEN, as if: indg br1

Frozen, as if: ...

○ - **Brain**: ind ptk1 indg br1*

FULLNESS: *(↗Congestion)* abrot **Acon** k* *Aesc* aethyl-n a1 agar ail k* all-c k* allox tpw4 am-c k* *Am-m* k* aml-ns bro1* ang **Apis** k* *Arg-n* k* arn k* arum-t asaf *Aster* aur k* aur-ar k2 aur-s k2 bapt k* *Bell* k* berb *Borx* k* bov k* *Bry* k* **Cact** k* *Calc* k* *Calc-p* calc-s calc-sil k2 cann-i canth caps k* carb-ac carb-an *Carb-v* k* carbn-s *Card-m* *Carl* castm cench k2 cham chin k* *Chinin-ar* k* chinin-s chr-ac cic a1 cimic k* *Cinnb* k* cit-ac rly4• clem cob coc-c cocc coff k* *Con* k* corn crot-h k* crot-t cupr cupr-ar cycl daph k* *Dig* k* *Dios* dulc echi elaps *Ferr* ferr-ar ferr-p fl-ac form fuma-ac rly4• *Gels* k* *Gent-c* gent-l gins **Glon** k* glyc bro1 gnaph k* granit-m es1• graph k* grat k* guaj k* gymno *Ham* k* *Hell* k* hell-o a1* helo helo-s rwt2• hippoc-k szs2 hydr *Hyos* hyper ign k* ip k2 irid-met srj5• iris jac-g jug-c kali-ar kali-bi bg2* kali-c k* kali-i kali-p kali-s kali-sil k2 kalm kreos k* lac-ac *Lac-d* **Lach** lact laur k* lil-t k* lol bg2 lyc mand sp1 meli bg2* mentho bro1 meph k* *Merc* k* merc-i-r mill naja nat-ar nat-c k* nat-m k* nat-p nat-pyru rly4• nat-s k2 *Nicc* nicotam rly4• *Nit-ac* k* *Nux-m* nux-v k* onos op osm oxyt ptk2 *Paeon* *Petr* k* phel *Phos* k* phys phyt pic-ac plan pop br1 *Psor* puls pycnop-sa mrz1 *Ran-b* *Ran-s* k* raph *Rhus-t* k* rumx sabad k2 sabal br1 samb *Sang* *Sel* k* senec sep sil k* sol-ni spig bg2 *Spong* k* stram streptoc rly4• *Stry* k* suis-hep rly4• *Sul-ac* k* **Sulph** k* suprar rly4• syph al* tab tanac tell *Ter* thuj til tung-met bdx1• urol-h rwt• urt-u ust valer k* verat-v k* visc sp1 x-ray sp1 *Xan* *Xanth* ziz [heroin sdj2]
- **morning**: am-m arg-n arn borx cann-i k* carl chinin-s chr-ac cinnb cob *Con* cop dulc hydr indg *Lach* luf-op rsj5• mag-m nat-p nicc petr k* pic-ac rhus-t sul-ac tell urol-h rwt• verat-v a1
  - **waking**; on: arg-n con k* glon kalm lil-t sulph k2 til
- **forenoon** | **10**-22 h: lac-ac
- **noon** until 14 h: pic-ac
- **afternoon**: arg-n coca ferr gels guare jac-c a1 lac-ac lact lith-c mill nat-p osm phys sang stry *Sulph*
  - **night**; until: sil
  - **waking**; on: carb-v k*
- **evening**: arg-n cimic ferr guare ham naja nat-m nat-p thuj
- **night**: arg-n *Aster* chr-ac
- **accompanied** by:
  - **catarrh**: anemps br1
  - **pain** (See Pain - accompanied - fullness)

○ • **Extremities**; coldness of: visc sp1
- **air**; in open | **amel.**: bry k2 carl cinnb grat jac-g
- **ascending**, on: borx
- **bending** head backward agg.: osm
- **breakfast** agg.; after: con hydr
- **burst**, as if would: *(↗Pain - bursting)* am-c aster bell tl1 bry k2 cann-i cimic tl1 daph k* **Glon** ip lil-t merc nit-ac rauw sp1 sarr br1 visc sp1
- **coition**; after: phos
- **cotton**; as by: hippoc-k szs2
- **coughing**, with: kali-p k2
- **descending**, on: **Borx**
- **dinner**; after: gins k*
- **eating**:
  - **after**:
    - **agg.**: borx h2 con gins hydr *Hyos*
    - **amel.**: onos
  - **before** | **agg.**: (non:uran-met k) uran-n
  - **while** | **agg.**: con
- **epistaxis** | **amel.**: tarent ptk2
- **heat**; during: **Glon** lach
- **intermittent**: asaf k*
- **leaning** head to left: chinin-s
- **lying** agg.: naja sep a1
- **menses**:
  - **appearance** of; at: *Glon*
  - **before** | **agg.**: brom
  - **during** | **agg.**: *Apis* arg-n *Bell* *Calc* eupi gent-c *Glon* granit-m es1• puls *Xan* *Xanth*
- **mental** exertion agg.: aur-ar k2 **Cact** cinnb helon k* ind meph *Nat-p* phos *Psor*
  - **amel.**; when mind is employed: helon
- **motion** agg.: calc-p

- **pressure** of hat:
  - **agg.**: calc-p
  - **amel.**: agar arg-n bry$_{k2}$ cop hydr
- **raising** head, on: sulph
- **reading** agg.: cop *Ferr*$_{hr1}$ helon$_{k*}$ indg
- **riding** in a carriage agg.: asaf$_{k2}$
- **rising** agg.: am-m cinnb glon sil$_{k*}$
- **sewing** agg.: petr$_{k*}$
- **shaking** the head agg.; on: car carl glon
- **sitting** agg.: borx glon
- **sitting** up in bed agg.: calc-p
- **sleep**:
  - **after** | **agg.**: hep$_{h2*}$ sulph
  - **amel.**: onos
  - **siesta**:
    - ⁝ **after** | **agg.**: mill
- **sneezing** agg.: hydr
- **stool**:
  - **after** amel.: corn
  - **straining** at | **agg.**: ham
- **stooping** agg.: acon lac-ac merl nicc petr$_{k*}$ pic-ac rhus-t spong
- **talking**; after: sulph
- **urination**; copious | **amel.**: fl-ac$_{a}$ gels
- **vertigo**; during: am-m borx bry chr-ac con crot-t cycl$_{k*}$ gymno$_{k*}$ helon$_{k*}$ lac-ac lact merc nat-m nat-p podo pycnop-sa$_{mrz1}$ sang$_{a1}$ sol-ni til urt-u
- **waking**; on: agar asaf$_{k*}$ carb-v$_{k*}$ guare tung-met$_{bdx1•}$
- **walking** in open air | **amel.**: *Apis* *Borx* hydr *Lyc* **Puls**
- **warm**:
  - **air** agg.: bry$_{k2}$
  - **room** | **agg.**: *Apis* bry$_{k2}$ hydr lact
- **water**; as by: hippoc-k$_{szs2}$
- **wine** agg.: ail
- **writing** agg.: chinin-s

○ - **Forehead**: acon$_{k*}$ aesc agar *Am-c*$_{k*}$ am-m$_{k*}$ ang *Apis* apoc arg-n bapt *Bell*$_{k*}$ berb$_{k*}$ borx *Bry*$_{k*}$ cain calc$_{k*}$ calc-s cann-i carb-an **Carbn-s**$_{k*}$ choc$_{srj3•}$ chr-ac cic$_{a1}$ cimic **Cinnb**$_{k*}$ clem coca con cop euph eupi *Ferr*$_{bg2}$ ferr-p$_{bg2}$ fuma-ac$_{rly4•}$ gels germ-met$_{srj5•}$ *Glon*$_{k*}$ gymno *Ham* hell *Helon*$_{k*}$ hydr hyos ind indg kreos$_{bg2}$ lac-ac lac-cp$_{sk4•}$ laur$_{k*}$ lil-t limest-b$_{es1•}$ mag-s meph naja *Nat-ar* nat-p nicc ox-ac$_{k*}$ pall *Phos* phys phyt pic-ac$_{mrr1}$ pip-m pitu-gl$_{br1}$ podo$_{k*}$ psor ran-s$_{k*}$ rhus-t$_{k*}$ rumx sang$_{k*}$ sep staph stict$_{k*}$ sul-ac *Sulph* thea til
  - **morning**: arg-n borx carl fago glon nat-p til
    - ⁝ **walking** agg.: glon til
  - **forenoon**: rhus-t sul-ac
  - **afternoon**: phys sang
  - **evening**: *Bry* naja nat-m sumb
  - **brain** were packed in front; as if: equis-h$_{a1}$
  - **closing** the eyes | **amel.**: *Bry*
  - **coition**; after: phos$_{k*}$
  - **concentrate**; on attempting to: (↗*mental)* pic-ac$_{mrr1}$
  - **eating** | **amel.**: psor
  - **mental** exertion agg.: (↗*concentrate)* nat-p$_{k2}$
  - **reading** agg.: indg
  - **stool** | **amel.**: fago
  - **stooping** agg.: acon
  - **waking**, while: dig
  - **washing** | **amel.**: psor

○ · **Eyes**:
  - ⁝ **Above**: hydr lil-t nat-p ox-ac
    - ⁝ **pulling** hair amel.: lac-cp$_{sk4•}$
    - ⁝ **vertigo**; with: podo$_{k*}$
  - **Nose**; over | **evening**: naja
- **Occiput**: *Acon* agar$_{k*}$ all-c apis$_{k*}$ arg-n$_{bg2}$ bapt caj cann-i cham$_{k*}$ cinnb coca coff$_{bg2}$ con$_{k*}$ gels$_{bg2*}$ glon$_{k*}$ helon$_{k*}$ kreos$_{k*}$ merc-c$_{b4a.de}$ onos$_{bg2*}$ osm$_{k*}$ puls sulph$_{k*}$ sumb tarent$_{bg2}$ ther thuj$_{k*}$ zinc-s$_{bg2*}$
  - **evening**, in: sumb

Fullness – Occiput – evening: ...
  - ⁝ **walking** in open air agg.: thuj
  - **accompanied** by | **vertigo**: bamb-a$_{stb2.de•}$
  - **cough** agg.; during: all-c
  - **lying** on face amel.: *Coca*

○ · **Ears**, behind: glon$_{bg2*}$
- **Sides**: arg-n asaf cimic cycl fl-ac fuma-ac$_{rly4•}$ glon
  - **right**: galla-q-r$_{nl2•}$
- **Temples**: agar apis bell cic cinnb cob *Echi* glon gnaph jac-c$_{k*}$ jac-g lil-t lith-c nat-m$_{h2*}$ plan rumx sep sumb
  - **right** | **left** and then to nape where it disappears; then to: jac-g
- **Veins** of head: stict$_{c1}$
- **Vertex**: aesc *Am-c* apis calc-p chinin-s chr-ac cimic$_{k*}$ **Cinnb**$_{k*}$ eup-pur fuma-ac$_{rly4•}$ **Glon** gymno ham$_{k*}$ helon$_{k*}$ hyper kali-bi lac-ac meph nat-pyru$_{rly4•}$ osm pic-ac psor suis-hep$_{rly4•}$
  - **evening**: cimic
  - **eating**; after: *Cinnb*
  - **reading** agg.: hell
  - **sitting** up in bed agg.: calc-p
  - **stooping** agg.: pic-ac

FUMES; sensation as from: am-c$_{bg2}$ nit-ac$_{bg2}$ zinc$_{bg2}$

FUNGUS: *Apis*$_{k*}$ bac$_{a}$ calc-i$_{a}$ *Calc-p*$_{k*}$ *Phos*$_{k*}$

FUZZINESS (See Confusion)

GOOSE FLESH:

○ - **Scalp** | **sensation** of goose flesh: (↗*Hair - bristling - sensation)* act-sp$_{vh1}$ vanil$_{fd5.de}$

GRIEF agg.: ign$_{bg2}$ nat-m$_{bg2}$ ph-ac$_{bg2}$ staph$_{bg2}$

○ - **External** head: ign$_{b7a.de}$ *Staph*$_{b7a.de}$

GURGLING: (↗*Bubbling; Motions in)* asaf bry sep

○ - **Temples**: bry

HANDS:
- **holds** head with: glon$_{k*}$ hyos$_{k*}$
  - **apoplexy**; during: glon$_{ptk1}$
  - **cough** agg.; during: **BRY**$_{k\ •*}$ caps$_{bro1}$ nat-m$_{bro1}$ nat-s$_{bro1}$ nicc$_{k*}$ **NUX-V**$_{k\ •*}$ sulph$_{k*}$
  - **vertigo**; during: sabad$_{dgt}$
- **leans** on: iod$_{k*}$
- **rubs** with (See Rubbing - head)

HARD:
- **head** is very; as if: gink-b$_{sbd1•}$
- **pillow** feels hard: coca$_{bg2}$

○ - **Scalp**: ferr-p$_{bg2*}$

HAT:
- **agg.**: alum$_{b4a.de}$ calc-p$_{pd}$ carb-an$_{b4a.de}$ carb-v$_{b4a.de*}$ crot-c$_{pd}$ glon$_{bro1}$ hep$_{b4a.de}$ mez$_{pd}$ nit-ac$_{b4a.de*}$ sil$_{pd}$
- **aversion** to•: (↗*Warm; Warm - coverings; Warm - coverings - agg.)* aur$_{sne}$ calc-p$_{a}$ carb-an carb-v$_{a}$ crot-t$_{a}$ *Iod*$_{k*}$ *Led*$_{k*}$ **Lyc**$_{k\ •*}$ mez$_{a}$ nit-ac$_{a}$ sil$_{a}$ tritic-vg$_{fd5.de}$
- **sensation** of a hat: berb$_{ptk1}$ calc$_{c1}$ calc-s$_{c1}$ cystein-l$_{rly4•}$ eup-per$_{ptk1}$ phys$_{ptk1}$ pyrog$_{ptk1}$
- **sensitive** to a hat (See Sensitiveness - hat)
- **wear** a; must (See Cold - air - agg.)

HAT; from pressure of a: agar$_{bg2}$ calc-p$_{bg2}$ carb-v$_{bg2*}$ crot-t$_{bg2}$ glon$_{bg2}$ lach$_{bg2}$ laur$_{b7.de*}$ led$_{bg2}$ lil-t$_{bg2}$ nit-ac$_{bg2*}$ sil$_{bg2}$ valer$_{b7.de*}$

○ - **External** head: nit-ac$_{bg2}$

HEADACHE (See Pain)

HEADLESS, sensation of being: asar$_{k*}$ aur-ar$_{k2*}$ calc-i cann-i$_{vml2•}$ nit-ac ther$_{vml2•}$

HEAT: abies-n$_{k*}$ acet-ac **Acon**$_{k*}$ acon-c$_{a1}$ aesc aeth$_{k*}$ agar$_{k*}$ ail$_{k2}$ *All-c*$_{k*}$ allox$_{sp1}$ *Aloe* *Alum*$_{k*}$ alum-sil$_{k2}$ *Alumn* am-c$_{k*}$ am-m$_{k*}$ *Ambr*$_{k*}$ aml-ns$_{br1}$ anac$_{k*}$ anan$_{vh1}$ ang$_{k*}$ anh$_{sp1}$ ant-c$_{k*}$ *Ant-t*$_{k*}$ **Apis**$_{k*}$ apoc-a$_{vh}$ apom$_{a1}$ arg-met$_{h1}$ arg-n$_{k*}$ arge-pl$_{rwt5•}$ arist-m$_{a1}$ arn$_{k*}$ **Ars**$_{k*}$ ars-i

Heat: ...
ars-s-f k2 arum-t k2 asaf k* asar aster k* atro a1 *Aur* k* aur-ar k2 aur-i k2 *Aur-m* aur-s k2 bad bamb-a stb2.de• bapt bar-c k* bar-i k2 bar-s k2 bart a1 **Bell** k* benz-ac k* berb k* bism k* bism-sn a1 bit-ar wht1• **Borx** k* brom k* *Bry* k* **Cact** k* cadm-s br1 calad k* **Calc** k* calc-ar calc-i k2 *Calc-p* k* *Calc-s* calc-sil k2 calo a1 camph k* cann-i cann-s k* canth k* caps bg2 carb-ac carb-an k* *Carb-v* k* carbn a1 *Carbn-s* carl a1 casc a1 caust k* cham k* *Chel* k* chin k* chinin-ar chinin-s chlor a1 choc srj3• cic bg2* cic-m a1 cimic k* *Cina* cinch a1 cinnb clem k* cob-n sp1 *Cocc* k* cod a1 coff k* colch k* coli rly4• *Coloc* k* colum-p sze2• *Con* k* conch fkr1• corn cortico sp1 croc k* *Crot-t* cupr k* *Cur* *Cycl* k* cypra-eg sde6.de• cystein-l rly4• daph k* dig k* digin a1 dios dor a1 dros k* dulc k* ephe-si hsj1• euph k* euphr k* eupi fago a1 *Ferr* k* *Ferr-ar* ferr-i ferr-p *Fl-ac* flor-p rsj3• *Form* k* *Frax* bg *Gamb* k* *Gels* k* gent-l a1 gins k* **Glon** k* gran **Graph** k* grat k* gymno haem k* ham fd3.de• *Hell* k* helo helo-s rwt2• helon k* hep bg2 hipp a1 hir rsj4• hura hydr k* hydr-ac k* hyos k* hyper iber a1 *Ign* k* ina-i mlk9.de ind indg k* iod k* *Ip* k* iris jatr-c kali-ar kali-bi k* *Kali-br* k* kali-c k* *Kali-chl* kali-cy a1 kali-i k* kali-n k* kali-p kali-s kali-sil k2 kalm kiss a1 kola stb3• kurch bnj1 lac-ac a1 *Lac-d* **Lach** k* lachn lact k* lap-la rsp1 *Laur* k* led k* lepi a1 lil-s a1 lil-t a1* lup a1 lyc k* lyss m-arct b7.de m-aust b7.de *Mag-c* k* *Mag-m* k* mag-s k* manc mand sp1 *Mang* k* medul-os-si rly4• meli bg meny k* meph a1 merc k* merc-c k* *Merc-i-r* bg* merl k* *Mez* k* mill k2 morph k* *Mosch* k* mur-ac bg2* mygal bg myric a1 nad rly4• naja nat-ar *Nat-c* k* *Nat-m* k* nat-p nat-s k2 nicc k* *Nit-ac* k* nit-s-d a1 *Nux-m* k* *Nux-v* k* oena a1 ol-an k* olib-sac wmh1 olnd bg* *Op* k* orig a1 osm a1 paeon k* par bg ped a1 petr k* petr-ra shn4• ph-ac k* phel k* **Phos** k* phys *Phyt* k* pic-ac k* pieri-b mlk9.de pimp a1 plat k* *Plb* k* plect a1 *Podo* propl ub1• propr sa3• psil ft1 psor ptel a1* puls k* ran-a a1 ran-b k* ran-s k* rat k* rheum k* rhod bg2* rhus-t k* ruta k* sabad k* sabin k* sal-fr sle1• samb h1* sang k2 sapin a1 sarr sars k* sec k* sel bg senec *Sep* k* serp a1 *Sil* k* sol-t-ae a1 spig k* spirae a1 spong k* squil k* *Stann* k* staph k* *Stram* k* *Stront-c* k* suis-em rly4• sul-i k2 *Sulph* k* symph fd3.de• tab k* tarent k* tax tell ther thres-a sze7• thuj k* til k* tong a1 trif-p a1 trios rsj11• tritic-vg fd5.de tub al* upa a1 valer vanil fd5.de *Verat* k* verb vinc k* viol-o k* viol-t bg vip a1 *Xan* *Xanth* zinc k* zinc-p k2 zing a1 ziz a1 [bell-p-sp dcm1]

- **midnight**: aur-m lyc sil h2
  - **after**: nit-ac h2
- **morning**: alum k* alum-p k2 am-m ang h1* ant-c ant-t *Bry* k* calc k* calc-s carb-an k* carb-v h2* chin k* clem cycl k* dios k* euphr k* hipp k* hyper k* indg kali-n *Kalm* k* lyc *Merc-i-r* *Mez* k* nat-ar *Nat-c* **Nux-v** k* petr k* phos k* *Podo* ruta fd4.de sarr a1 sep k* *Sulph* k* til k* tong a1 zinc zing k*
  - **bed** agg.; in: staph h1*
  - **rising**:
    - **agg.**: agar am-m bar-c calc corn cycl dulc
    - **amel.**: sulph
  - **waking**; on: berb calc dulc a1 lyc med al nat-m k* sil stann **Sulph**
- **forenoon**: alum a1 bry k* ham fd3.de• lyc k*
- **noon**: ant-c k* bell k* jatr-c mag-m h2* nat-m h2*
- **afternoon**: anac k* arg-n k* *Arum-t* k* bad berb k* bry k* cann-s k* *Carb-an* k* carbn-s chinin-s coli rly4• dios k* fago k* graph *Hyper* k* ip k* kali-n h2* lyc k* mag-c k* mag-m k* mag-s k* mang k* nat-ar nat-c h2* nat-m nicc k* ol-an k* phos k* phys k* pimp a1 *Puls* k* ruta fd4.de santin sep spong stront-c sulph k* tritic-vg fd5.de vanil fd5.de
  - **16 h**: anac c1 *Mang*
- **evening**: *Acon* k* alum k* alum-p k2 am-m atha a1 bar-c h2* borx calc k* calc-s calc-sil k2 canth carb-v h2* chel k* coc-c cycl k* digin a1 dulc fd4.de gast a1 grat k* indg k* ip h1* jug-r a1 kali-c k* kali-p k2 laur lil-t lob lyc k* mag-c k* mag-m k* merc-i-r nat-c k* nat-p nux-v k* ol-an k* ph-ac k* phys puls ran-b *Rhus-t* k* ruta fd4.de *Sep* k* *Sil* k* sulph k* sumb a1 thuj k* tritic-vg fd5.de tub al* vanil fd5.de zinc k* zinc-p k2
  - **lying** agg.: ars h2
- **night**: aloe sne am-m k* ambr h1* ang *Arg-n* k* arn gsy1 camph cann-s k* carb-an h2* com a1 lyc k* meph k* nat-c k* nat-m h2* nit-ac h2* rhus-r ruta *Sil* k* staph til
  - **bed** agg.; in: aloe sne carb-an k* cortico tpw7* lyc k* nat-m k* **Sulph** k*
  - **waking**; on: arn gsy1 til k*
- **accompanied** by:
  - **breath** deep; desire to: kola stb3•

- **accompanied** by: ...
  - **death** apparent (See GENERALS - Death - accompanied - head)
  - **emaciation** (See GENERALS - Emaciation - accompanied - head - heat)
  - **heaviness** of head: calc a1* hir rsj4• med al2
  - **stool**; complaints of: bell bg2
  - ○ **Face**:
    - **heat** of: aeth arg-n berb bit-ar wht1• bry calc-p cann-s canth clem corn gels psa glon hura iris jatr-c kali-c kali-i kali-n mag-s c1 nat-m op phos sabad sep stront-c sulph tril-p c1 xan c1
    - **redness** of face: aeth arn br1 aster bry cact cann-s coff k2 kali-i mag-c mag-m mag-s merl nat-c phel plb stront-c sulph tarent zinc
      - **coldness** of body; and: arn br1
  - **Hands**; heat of: canth lach laur mag-c ol-an phel phos
  - **Head**; pain in: chinin-s mrr1 mand sp1 nat-m h2 ptel hr1 ruta fd4.de sep h2 tritic-vg fd5.de
  - **Limbs**; coldness of: acon ptk1 *Arn* ptk1 **Bell** ptk1 bry ptk1 calc ptk1 carb-v ptk1 *Chin* ptk1 ferr ptk1 gels ptk1 lach ptk1 mur-ac ptk1 *Sulph* ptk1
  - **Palms**; heat of: borx tarent
  - **Stomach**:
    - **complaints** of (See STOMACH - Complaints - accompanied - head - heat)
    - **pain** in (See STOMACH - Pain - accompanied - head - heat)
  - **Teeth**; pain in (See TEETH - Pain - accompanied - head - heat)
- **agreeable**: camph cann-s k* nicc thuj
- **air** | **surrounded** by hot air; as if: aster k* fl-ac ptk1 plan ptk1 puls ptk1 verat ptk1
- **air**; in open:
  - **agg.**: verat
  - **amel.**: **Apis** *Ars* clem con ferr-i k2 grat kali-i kali-s laur mag-m mang mosch nat-c phel **Phos** sulph
- **alternating** with:
  - **chilliness**: asaf k* phos h2* sep k*
  - **coldness** of head: bell calc gels hr1 kali-n h2 merc *Phos* verat k*
  - **diarrhea**: *Bell*
  - ○ **Back**; rigor in: spong
  - **Hands**; coldness of (See EXTREMITIES - Coldness - hands - alternating with - heat - head; of)
  - **Lower** limbs; coldness in (See EXTREMITIES - Coldness - lower - alternating)
- **anxiety**; with: canth k* carb-v j5.de coff k* *Cupr* hr1 laur j5.de *Mag-c* j5.de phos h2* sil h2* stront-c sulph h2* thuj a1
- **back**, with coldness of: thuj
- **bed**:
  - **in** bed:
    - **agg.**: ang k* arg-n carb-an k* carb-v h2* cycl k* lyc k* nat-c *Nux-v* k* staph k*
    - **amel.**: kali-c k* nat-c h2*
- **beer**; after: chel k* graph gk rhus-t a1 sulph k* vanil fd5.de
- **bending** head | **amel.**: fago a
- **breakfast** agg.; after: laur k*
- **breathing** deep agg.: borx h2
- **burning**: *Acon* bg3* ail *Apis* k* aster aur-s *Bell* bg3* borx bg3* bry k* cact ptk1 calc ptk1 camph *Frax* bg3* *Graph* bg3* hell kali-c h2* lach bg3* merc bg3* *Merc-i-r* bg3* mur-ac h2* nat-c bg3* oena ptk1 olib-sac wmh1 par mrr1 *Phos* k* *Pic-ac* bg* plan sil **Sulph** bg3* verat
  - **right**: bar-c hr1
  - **fire**; like: olib-sac wmh1 psor jl2
  - **warmth**:
    - **amel.** | **heat** amel.: ars k2
- **children**; in: | **nursing** infants; in: *Borx* h2*
- **chill**:
  - **after**: berb caust dros h1* mez h2* phos h2*

- **before**: stram
- **during**: acon k* alum androc srj1• *Apis* **Arn** k* *Ars* k* asar k* aur bg2 *Bell* k* berb borx b4a.de* *Bry* k* calc b4a.de* cann-s b7a.de* canth bg2 **Caust** bg cedr chin k* cina cocc hr1* coff bg dulc bg eup-per ferr bg* gels graph bg hell b7.de* *Ip* b7.de* lach b7a.de* lachn **Mang** b4a.de* merc bg2 *Nat-c* b4a.de* nat-s nux-v k* **Op** ph-ac bg2 phos bg2 *Puls* b7a.de rhod k* rhus-t b7a.de* sabad b7.de* sep bg2 staph bg stram tritic-vg fd5.de verat k*

- **chilliness**:
  - **before**: zinc h2*
  - **during**: androc srj1• ant-c asaf asar h1* *Borx* **Bry** *Cocc* k* colch k* dig h2* hell mag-m mang a1 *Merc*
- **coffee**: | **stopping**; from: cact k2
- **cold**:
  - **applications** | **amel.**: aloe k2 chinin-s mrr1
  - **bathing** | **amel.**: ars k2 euphr ind mez nat-m sep
  - **touch**, though heat; cold to: allox sp1 carb-v k2 hydr
    - **right** side: bar-c hr1
  - **washing**:
    - **hands** | **amel.**: rhus-v
  - **water** | **amel.**: *Apis* ars k2 *Con*
- **coldness**:
  - ○ **Abdomen**; with coldness of: camph h1
  - **Body**; with coldness of: *Acon* agar allox tpw4 **Arn** k* *Ars* asaf bell a *Bufo* *Cact* calc chin chinin-s clem gels glon a hell hipp hyos ip h1 *Lachn* mag-s mang h2 melal-alt gya4 mez h2 nux-v phyt c1 plb ran-b rhus-t a1 staph sne stram sulph verat verat-v a
  - **Extremities**; with coldness of: aloe a *Arn* k* aur aur-m k2 **Bell** k* brom a bry bg2* bufo *Cact* cadm-s calc bg2* camph k* cann-i cann-s chel chin bg2* cic k2 cocc br1 colch bg2* com dulc ptk2 *Ferr* k* gels psa glon jug-r k* kali-br bg2* lach bg2* led lyc k2 naja k2 op bg2* phyt bg2* plb k2 stram sulph bg2* [tax jsj7]
  - **Face**; with coldness of: melal-alt gya4 thuj
  - **Feet**; with coldness of: alum am-c k* anac apis kr1 *Arn* ars bar-c bar-s k2 *Bell* *Cact* *Calc* carb-an h2 cina k2 con *Ferr* k* ferr-ar *Ferr-p* sne *Gels* hell h1 *Ip* kali-ar k2 *Kali-br* hr1 laur mur-ac h2 *Nat-c* nit-ac h2 petr a1* *Ph-ac* h2* ptel hr1 sal-fr sle1• sep k* squil sul-ac k2 *Sulph* k* thuj zinc bg2*
    - **icy** coldness: cob-n sp1
  - **Fingers**; with coldness of: ferr mtf11 hell
  - **Forehead**; with coldness of: nat-ar k2
  - **Hands**; with coldness of: arg-n a1 ars a asaf asar aur-i k2 bar-c bell k* calo hell iod *Ip* *Kali-br* hr1 lact lyc *Nat-c* nat-m bg2* petr h2 ph-ac ran-b c1 sep sulph bl sumb
- **constipation**; during: verat h1*
- **contradiction**, from: cop k* lap-la rsp1
- **convulsions**; before epileptic: calc-ar kr1 *Caust*
- **coryza**; during: am-m b7a.de anac b4a.de* **Arum-t** k* *Bell* b4a.de calc k* graph h2* hell b7.de* jatr-c lach lyc b4.de* mag-m nux-v b7.de* phos b4.de*
- **cough** agg.; during: am-c k* ant-t k* arn *Ars* k* carb-v ip k* *Sulph* k*
- **descending** to toes: *Calc-p*
- **diarrhea**; during: *Apis* k* *Arn* **Bell** *Borx* k* *Bry* hell kali-br ox-ac rhus-t vanil fd5.de
- **dinner** | **after** | **agg.**: alum k* bell h1* berb caust k* cycl k* graph k* mag-m k* phel k* tub al*
  - **during** | **agg.**: grat k* nat-c k* nux-v k* sars
- **during**:
  - **agg.**: *Acon* b7.de am-c b4.de ant-t b7.de arg-met b7.de ars b4a.de bell b4.de calc b4a.de camph b7.de caps b7.de chin b7.de cina b7.de dros b7.de ign b7.de kali-c b4.de lyc b4.de *Nat-m* b4.de* **Nux-v** b7.de *Puls* b7.de rhus-t b7.de ruta b7.de **Sabad** b7.de sep b4.de spig b7.de staph b7.de valer b7.de
    - **External** head: sars bg2
- **eating** | **after**:
  - **agg.**: alum k* alum-p k2 anac c1 bell k* berb k* canth carb-v k* caust clem k* cycl graph *Hyos* *Kali-c* laur *Lyc* k* mag-m nux-v k2 *Petr* k* phel phos ruta fd4.de spong fd4.de ulm-c jsj8•
    - **hot** food: mag-c ruta fd4.de spong fd4.de
  - **soup** | **agg.**: phos
- **epistaxis** | **amel.**: bufo coff k2 *Psor*
- **exertion** agg.: berb con ham fd3.de•
- **fever**:
  - **before**: bell b4a.de sep b4a.de sil b4a.de sulph b4a.de
  - **during** | **agg.**: hell b7.de rhod b4a.de
- **flushes** of: aesc aeth alum-p k2 alum-sil k2 alumn am-m ant-t arn ars arum-t k2 aur aur-i k2 aur-s k2 bar-c h2 bism hr1 cact k2 cadm-s k2 calc-ar k2 calc-p calc-s calc-sil k2 cann-s k2 carb-v k2 carc fd2.de• cench k2 cic clem a1 cocc colch corn dig *Ferr* *Ferr-ar* ferr-p flor-p rsj3• ger-i rly4• *Glon* k* *Granit-m* es1• *Graph* grat k2 hell hep hipp jl2 *Kali-c* kali-p k* kali-s lach k2 lact laur led mag-c mag-m h2 mag-s mang h2 mosch k2 nat-m k* nat-p nat-s k2 oena oxal-a rly4• phos psor k2 ptel rhus-t k2 ribo rly4• sal-fr sle1• sang a1 *Sep* sil h2* *Sulph* tab tarent k2 tub c ulm-c jsj8• verat k2 xan zinc h2 ziz
  - **convulsions**; before epileptic: calc-ar kr1
  - **epistaxis**; with: carb-v k2
  - **headache**; before: lac-f c1
  - **menopause**; during: glon mrr1 sulph k2*
  - **perspiration**; after: nat-p k2
  - ▽ **extending** to:
    - **Stomach**: (↗*GENERALS - Heat - flushes - extending - downward)* *Sang* k*
    - **Top** of head:
      - **accompanied** by | **vertigo** (See VERTIGO - Accompanied - head - flushes)
- **fright**; after: (↗*MIND - Ailments - fright)* *Ph-ac*
- **grief**; from: (↗*MIND - Ailments - grief)* *Ph-ac*
- **headache**:
  - **after**: nat-c h2* ozone sde2•
  - **before**: lac-f c1
  - **during** (See accompanied - head)
- **heart**:
  - **oppression** of heart; during: glon
  - **palpitation** of; with: coloc iod tritic-vg fd5.de
- **heat**; with (See accompanied)
- **hot**:
  - **body**:
    - **fell** forwards; as if a: kali-c
    - **Forehead**; as if in: kali-c h2
  - **iron** around head; as if from a hot: *Acon*
  - **vapor** rising up; sensation as if hot: bufo br1*
  - **water**: all-c indg
    - **thrown** on scalp and penetrating to brain; as from hot water: peti
- **laughing** agg.: ther
- **lying** down:
  - **agg.**: arn ars k* jug-r
  - **amel.**: kali-c nat-c *Phos* rhus-t
- **menopause**; during: *Sulph* vh
- **menses**:
  - **after** | **agg.**: ferr k* ferr-i iod k*
  - **before** | **agg.**: alum b4a.de apis bell *Calc* *Con* *Crot-h* *Ign* *Iod* k* ip *Lyc* k* petr *Thuj*
  - **during** | **agg.**: *Apis* *Arn* *Bell* k* **Calc** k* calc-i k2 carb-an caust cham k* chin b7a.de *Ferr-p* *Ign* ip *Kali-i* lach lyc k* mag-c mag-m k* mag-s nat-m nat-s nux-m petr sulph k*
- **mental** exertion:
  - **agg.**: anac aur aur-ar k2 berb **Cact** calc br1* *Con* *Sil*
  - **amel.**: cham ptk1
- **motion** agg.: calc h2*
- **music** agg.: **Ambr**
- **pain** in abdomen; from: grat
- **painful**: sep h2*
- **pale** face, with: ambr puls thuj vh
- **partial**, with cold other part: kali-c bg2*
- **periodical**: calad
- **pressure**:
  - **amel.**: arg-n carb-ac a1 hydr k* nux-v k*

• **hand**; of | **amel.**: nux-v
- **raising** head agg.: calc h2*
- **reading** agg.: nat-s k*
- **redness** of face; with (See accompanied - face - redness)
- **riding** agg.: lyc k*
- **rising**:
 • **agg.**: bar-c calc mag-s
 • **amel.**: carb-an kali-c sulph
 • **stooping**; from | **agg.**: carc fd2.de• grat nat-c
- **rising** up: aeth borx a1 calad k* canth k* cycl gamb ign b7a.de kali-c *Lil-t* lyc bg2 *Mang* nat-s olib-sac wmh1 plb k* rheum k* rhus-t k*
 • **abdomen**, from: alum cann-s k2 indg kali-c mag-m nat-s plb
 • **back**, from: phos
 • **chest**, from: acon glon *Lil-t* lyss mill *Phos* sulph
- **room**; when entering a: am-m h2* mag-m h2*
- **scratch**; must: mez h2*
- **sensation** of: am-m b7.de chel b7.de graph b4.de hell b7.de ip b7.de laur b7.de lyc b4.de mag-c b4.de mag-m b4.de mang b4.de phos b4.de plb b7.de propr sa3• *Rhod* b4a.de sabad b7a.de *Stront-c* b4.de* thuj b4a.de valer b7.de zinc b4.de
- **sewing**, while: petr k*
- **shivering**; during: acon b7.de ant-c b7.de arn b7.de *Caust* b4a.de *Coff* b7a.de ip b7.de rhus-t b7.de
- **sitting** agg.: canth k* merc k* nat-c k* ph-ac spong
- **sleep**:
 • **amel.**: laur
 • **before**: alum coc-c sulph
 • **during**: aloe sne bell k2
 • **siesta**:
  ⁝ **after** | **agg.**: clem cycl k* rhus-t
- **sleepiness**; with: kreos stann stront-c
- **sneezing** | **amel.**: lil-t
- **speaking**, by: ph-ac k* phos k*
- **spot**, in small: carb-v k* con ptk1 mez
- **standing**:
 • **agg.**: alum canth
 • **amel.**: phos k*
- **stool**:
 • **after** | **agg.**: bell lyc k* nat-c
 • **during** | **agg.**: hyos bg2
 • **urging** to | **during**: clem mag-m ox-ac
- **stooping** agg.: kali-c petr k* valer
- **storm**; on approach of a: nat-c
- **stove**; of | **agg.**: bar-c h2* *Glon Phos* puls b7a.de spig b7a.de
- **thinking** of it agg.: hell
- **toothache**, with one-sided: am-c h2 sil h2
- **touched**; cannot bear to have it: *Cina* h1
- **transient**: agar arn cann-i mag-m sulph tab valer
- **urination** agg.; during: *Sep*
- **vapor**, as from warm: bufo br1* ol-an k*

○ • **Brain**: ant-t ptk1 arg-met bg2 bufo bg2 nux-m bg2 op bg2 sars ptk1 sul-ac bg2 sulph ptk1
- **vertigo**:
 • **after**: aeth ptk1
 • **during** (See VERTIGO - Accompanied - head - heat)
- **waking**:
 • **before**: hyper
 • **on**: arn br1 calc chel k* lyc nat-m phos k* sil spirae a1 stann **Sulph** tarent k* til
- **walking**:
 • **agg.**: borx glon indg mez nit-ac *Phos* sep stront-c
 • **air**; in open:
  ⁝ **agg.**: plb k2
  ⁝ **amel.**: *Phos Sulph*
- **warm** room agg.: **Apis** *Ars Calc-s Carb-v* caust *Coc-c* ferr-i k2 grat k2 indg *Kali-s* lyss mag-m nat-c nicc *Phos* **Puls** ran-s **Sulph**
- **wine**:
 • **agg.**: gink-b sbd1• lyc nux-v petr k*
 • **as** from: rhus-r sabad
- **writing** agg.: aran borx kali-c k* ran-b

▽ - **extending** to | **Toes**: *Calc-p* vh

○ - **Brain**: am-c bg2 bell bg2 cann-xyz bg2 hydr-ac bg2 hyos bg2 kali-c h2* nux-v bg2 phos bg2 plut-n srj7•
 • **boiling** heat: acon bg3* bell ptk1 canth ptk1 glon ptk1 med ptk1 *Phos* ptk1 verat ptk1
 • **swallowing** agg.: form ptk1
- **External** head: **Acon** b7.de* aloe bg2 alum bg2 am-c b4a.de* am-m bg2 ambr bg2 aml-ns bg2 ang b7.de* ant-c bg2 ant-t b7.de* apis bg2 arg-met b7.de* *Arn* b7.de* ars bg2 asaf bg2 *Asar* b7.de* *Aur* bg2 bar-c b4.de* **Bell** b4.de* **Bism** b7.de* *Borx* b4a.de* *Bry* b7.de* *Calc* b4.de* camph b7.de* cann-s b7.de* canth bg2 carb-an b4.de* carb-v b4.de* *Caust* bg2 cham bg2 chel bg2 chin bg2 chinin-s bg2 *Cina* b7.de* coff bg2 coloc b4a.de* con bg2 *Croc* b7.de* cupr bg2 daph bg2 dig b4.de *Dros* bg2 dulc bg2 *Euph* bg2 ferr bg2 glon bg2 graph b4.de* grat bg2 hell bg2 hep bg2 *Ip* bg2 kali-c bg2 kali-i bg2 *Lach* bg2 laur b7.de* led bg2 lyc bg2 m-arct b7.de mag-c bg2 mag-m bg2 *Mang* b4.de* meli bg2 *Meny* bg2 *Merc* bg2 *Mez* b4.de* mosch b7a.de* mur-ac b4.de* mygal bg2 *Nat-c* bg2 nat-m bg2 nit-ac b4.de* nux-v b7.de* olnd bg2 **Op** bg2 par b7.de* petr bg2 **Ph-ac** bg2 *Phos* b4.de* phyt bg2 plat b4.de plb bg2 *Rhus-t* bg2 ruta bg2 **Sabad** bg2 sel bg2 *Sep* b4.de* **Sil** b4.de* spig bg2 spong b7.de* stann bg2 staph b7.de* *Stram* bg2 stront-c bg2 **Sulph** bg2 tab bg2 valer bg2 verat b7.de* viol-t bg2 zinc b4.de*
 • **chill**; during: *Acon* bg2 ant-c bg2 **Arn** bg2 ars bg2 asar bg2 *Bell* bg2 borx bg2 bry bg2 *Calc* bg2 cann-xyz bg2 canth bg2 **Caust** bg2 chin bg2 coff bg2 dulc bg2 ferr bg2 gels bg2 graph bg2 hell bg2 **Ip** bg2 mang bg2 nat-c bg2 nux-v bg2 *Rhus-t* bg2 staph bg2 **Stram** bg2 verat bg2
- **Forehead**: *Acon* k* aeth k* allox tpw4 *Alum* k* alum-p k2 am-m k* androc srj1• ang k* ant-c bg2 ant-t k* **Apis** k* *Arn* b7a.de *Ars* k* ars-s-f k2 arum-d a1 arund a1 asaf k* asar k* aur-m k2 bad bapt k* bart a1 **Bell** k* brom k* calc k* calc-s calc-sil k2 camph k* canth k* carb-an k* *Carb-v* k* carbn-s carc fd2.de• cassia-s ccrh1• caust k* cham b7a.de* chel chin k* chinin-ar choc srj3• cic a1 cimic k* cinnb k* clem k* coc-c cocc k* colch k* coloc conch fkr1* croc crot-h cupr k* cupr-ar j cycl k* digin a1 dor a1 dulc fd4.de elat hr1 euph k* euphr k* eupi k* ferr-i k2 ferul a1 fl-ac k* form a1 gels gins k* *Glon* k* gran k* graph k* grat gymno hell k* hep k* hydr k* hyos k* ind k* indg k* ip bg2 jatr-c kali-ar kali-bi k* kali-c k* kali-i ptk1 kali-n k* kali-p *Kali-s* kali-sil k2 kreos k* lac-f c *Lach* k* lact k* laur k* led k* lob-s a1 lyc k* mag-m k* mag-s manc k* merc merc-c k* *Mez* k* nat-ar *Nat-c* k* nat-m nat-p nicc nit-s-d a1 *Nux-m* **Nux-v** k* ol-an k* op k* oxal-a rly4• petr k* petr-ra shn4• ph-ac k* phel k* *Phos* k* phys pic-ac k* ptel a1* *Puls* k* pycnop-sa mrz1 ran-b k* rat k* rhus-r *Rhus-t* bg2 ruta fd4.de *Sabad* k* sapin a1 sedi a1 senec k* sep k* sil k* sin-n a1* spong k* *Stann* k* staph k* *Stram* k* *Sulph* k* sumb a1 tarax tarent k* tax tell k* thuj k* til k* tub-a jl2 vanil fd5.de vario hr1* verat k* viol-o k* zinc zinc-p k2 [bell-p-sp dcm1]
 • **right**: mosch bg2
  ⁝ **sensation** of: *Carb-v* b4a.de
 • **left**: mag-m bg2 rhus-t bg2
  ⁝ **sensation** of: mag-m b4.de
 • **morning**: am-m k* ant-c k* ant-t k* cycl k* indg k* kali-n h2* ruta fd4.de vac jl
 • **forenoon**: calc k* carb-an k* nat-c k* thuj k*
 • **noon**: zinc k*
 • **afternoon**: chinin-s ip k* nicc k* ruta fd4.de sep k* spong k*
 • **evening**: atp rly4• canth k* gran hell a1 ip h1* lyc k* mag-m k* nat-c k* ran-b k* ruta fd4.de sep h2*
  ⁝ **writing** agg.: *Ran-b*
 • **night**: ang h1* ph-ac k* staph k* til k*
 • **alternately** in either protuberance: lact
 • **alternating** with | **coldness** of forehead: spig h1* staph h1*
 • **chill**:
  ⁝ **after**: caust h2*
  ⁝ **during**: acon bg2 ars h2* cham bg2 lyc bg2
 • **chilliness**; during: acon tl1 asaf k* asar h1* sep k*
 • **cold**:
  ⁝ **air** | **amel.**: alum **Apis** *Phos*
  ⁝ **bathing** | **amel.**: cassia-s ccrh1•
  ⁝ **touch**; but cold to: mag-m h2

- **coldness** of:
  - **Extremities**: chin h1
  - **Hands** and feet: camph h1
- **dinner**; after: alum k* caust h2* *Cor-r* hr1
- **headache**; during: ruta fd4.de sil h2 vanil fd5.de
- **recurrent**: granit-m es1•
- **sensation** of: carb-an b4.de chin b7.de hep b4a.de kali-c b4.de lach b7a.de laur b7.de mag-m b4.de nat-c b4.de
- **sun**: cassia-s ccrh1•
- **walking** agg.: digin a1 mez k*
- **warm**: ketogl-ac rly4•
  - **flowing**; sensation of warm:
    - **Eyes**:
      - **Above** | **left**: nit-ac ptk1
  - **water** trickled down inside; as if warm: glon
  - **wind**; as from warm: staph h1
- **warmth** in middle of forehead, then coldness as from draft of air; feeling of: laur
- **writing** agg.: kali-c k* ran-b a1

○ • **Side** of: ph-ac h2*

- **Occiput**: *Acon* bg2 aesc k* agar bg2 apis bg2 arn bg1 aur bg2 aur-m-n k* bapt bg2 bell brom k* camph k* cann-i k* cann-s k* cann-xyz bg2 carb-v bg2 chlf a1 cic k* cina bg2 cinnb k* coc-c k* *Con* k* dig k* fl-ac glon k* indg k* jatr-c k* kalm k* lob manc k* med merc-i-f k* *Nat-m* nat-s k* nit-s-d a1 nux-m petr-ra shn4• ph-ac phel bg2 *Phos* bg2 pic-ac bg2 puls rhus-r rhus-t bg2 sep bg2 *Sulph* k* sumb tarent k* thuj k* tritic-vg fd5.de vanil fd5.de verat verat-v *Zinc* k*
  - **right** | **sensation** of: zinc b4.de
  - **morning**: sulph k*
  - **evening**: sumb
  - **accompanied** by | **Forehead**; coldness of (See Coldness - forehead - accompanied - occiput)
  - **diarrhea**; during: bell *Zinc*
  - **excitement** agg.: *Con*
  - **flushes** of: aesc lach sumb
  - **walking** in open air | **amel.**: sulph k*
  - **warm** room agg.: coc-c a1 sulph k*
- **Scalp**: anh sp1 *Bell* bg2 camph bg2 cann-s b7.de samb b7.de*
  - **sensation** of: verat b7.de*
- **Sides**: am-m k* calc k* caust k* cinnb k* cycl k* kali-bi k* petr k* phel pic-ac k* tarent k* til k*
  - **one**: kali-c k2
  - **right**: kali-c b4.de* plut-n srj7•
    - **evening**: am-m k*
  - **left**: calc b4.de* thuj b4.de*
  - **flushes**; in: kali-bi
- **Temples**: berb k* bond a1 euph k* glon k* hura ign k* lyc med vh *Merc* bg merl k* nat-n a1 ol-an k* phel k* podo k* upa a1
  - **left**: *Merc* bg2
  - **cold** cheeks, with: berb
- **Vertex**: *Acon* k* agar bg2 ap-g vml3• arn bg2 ars bg2 *Aur Benz-ac* k* *Calc* k* calc-s camph k* carb-an carbn-s caust bg2 cham chel k* *Cimic* bg2 coc-c k* *Con* corn k* *Crot-c Daph* k* *Eup-per* k* eupi k* *Ferr-p* frax ptk1 *Glon* k* **Graph** k* grat helo helo-s rwt2• helon k* hep k* *Hyper* k* *Kali-i* a1 lac-f c **Lach** k* laur k* lepi mag-s k* *Med* melal-alt gya4 *Merc-i-r* k* *Mez Mur-ac* nat-c k* nat-m k* nat-p *Nat-s* k* *Nux-m* k* *Ph-ac Phos* k* *Pic-ac* bg2 plut-n srj7• podo k* ptel bg2* rhus-r sabad bg2 sol-t-ae vml3• **Sulph** k* tarent k* thea tub wd*
  - **morning**: podo k*
  - **night** | 23 h: **Merc-i-r**
  - **accompanied** by | **Head**; complaints of (See Complaints - accompanied - vertex)
  - **chilling** heat: caust h2
  - **cold** applications | **amel.**: sulph k2
  - **descending** agg.: sol-t-ae vml3•
  - **grief**; from: *Calc* k* *Ph-ac Phos* k*

Heat – Vertex: ...

- **hand** were applied, when: lac-v rb2
- **menopause**; during: carb-an vh cimic vh croc vh **Lach** *Sulph* vh
  - **prolapsus**, with: *Lach* vh sep vh
- **menses**; during: ferr-p k2 *Nat-s Sulph*
- **pressure** | **amel.**: eup-per
- **red** hot iron; as if: crot-c tl1
- **sensation** of: hep b4a.de nat-c b4.de nux-m b7.de phos b4.de tarax ptk1
- **spots**, in: *Arn* k* *Graph Mez*
- **thinking**, while: *Nat-s*
- **warm** applications | **amel.**: *Kali-bi Kali-i*

▽ • **extending** to:
  - **left** side of head and face: lac-f c
  - **Downward**: sol-t-ae bg2

HEATED; when becoming: | **agg.**: **Acon** b7.de* am-c b4.de* aml-ns bg2 ant-c ptk1 *Bell* b4a.de* *Bry* b7.de* calc b4a.de* caps b7.de* *Carb-v* b4.de* *Glon* bg2* ign b7.de* ip b7.de* lyc bg2* nit-ac ptk1 sel bg2 sil b4a.de* *Staph* b7a.de thuj bg2 verat-v bg2* zinc ptk1

HEAVINESS: *(↗Pain - pressing pain)* abrom-a ks5* acet-ac achy-a bnj1 *Acon* k* adam srj5• aesc aeth *Agar* k* agn k* aids nl2• ail all-c allox tpw4• aloe k* *Alum* k* alum-p k2 alum-sil k2 am-be mtf11 am-c k* *Am-m* k* ambr aml-ns tl1 amp rly4• anac k* anan anders bnj1 androc srj1• anemps br1 ang ant-t k* **Apis** k* apoc aq-mar skp7*• aran bg2 *Arg-n* k* arizon-l nl2• *Arn* k* *Ars* k* ars-i arum-t asaf k* asar asc-t (non:aur k*) aur-ar k2 aur-i k2 aur-m slp aur-m-n bamb-a stb2.de• bapt k* bar-c bar-i k2 bar-m k* *Bell* k* berb k* bism k* bit-ar wht1• borx k* bov k* brom k* bros-gau mrc1 *Bry* k* bufo buth-a sp1 *Cact* k* *Calc* k* calc-ar calc-i k2 calc-p bg2 *Calc-s Camph* k* *Cann-i* cann-s b7.de* *Canth Carb-ac Carb-an* k* **Carb-v** k* **Carbn-s** *Card-m* cardios-h rly4• cartl-s rly4• cassia-s ccrh1• castm k* caust k* cedr *Cham* k* *Chel* k* **Chin** k* chinin-ar *Chinin-s* chlam-tr bcx2• cic k* cimic k* cinnb *Clem* k* coc-c coca cocc k* coff k* *Colch* k* coli rly4• coloc *Con* k* cop *Corn* cortiso skp7• croc k* *Crot-c* k* *Crot-h Crot-t Cupr* k* cycl cypra-eg sde6.de• desm-g bnj1 *Dig* k* dios *Dros* k* *Dulc* k* echi bg2 *Elaps* eup-per mrr1 euphr k* eupi ferr k* ferr-ar ferr-i ferr-p fl-ac form fuma-ac rly4• galeoc-c-h gms1• galla-q-r nl2• *Gamb* gard-j vlr2• **Gels** k* gent-ch bnj1 ger-i rly4• germ-met srj5• gins k* *Glon* k* glyc bro1 gran k* graph k* grat k* guare guat sp1 gymno haem *Hell* k* hell-o a1* hep k* hipp k* hippoc-k szs2 hir rsj4*• hist sp1 hura hydr k* hydr-ac *Hydrog* srj2• hydroph rsj6• *Hyos* k* hyper k* *Ign* k* indg iod *Ip* k* irid-met vml3• iris k* jatr-c kali-ar *Kali-bi* k* kali-br a1 kali-c k* *Kali-i* kali-m k2 *Kali-n* k* *Kali-p* kali-s ketogl-ac rly4• *Kola* stb3• kreos lac-ac slp (non:lac-c k*) lac-h sk4• **Lach** k* lachn *Lact Laur* k* lavand-a ctl1• led lil-t k* limen-b-c hrn2* limest-b es1• lob lob-e c1 lol ptk1 luf-op rsj5• luna kg1• *Lyc* k* m-aust b7.de *Mag-c* k* *Mag-m* k* *Mag-s* k* manc mand sp1 *Mang* k* mang-act br1 marb-w es1• med melal-alt gya4 meli bro1 *Meny* k* meph *Merc* k* merc-c k* merc-i-f merc-i-r *Merl* mez k* mim-p rsj8• morph mosch k* **Mur-ac** k* muru a1 murx myos-a rly4• naja *Nat-ar Nat-c* k* **Nat-m** k* *Nat-p* nat-s *Nicc* nicc-met sk4• nicotam rly4• **Nit-ac** k* nux-m k* **Nux-v** k* oci-sa sk4• ol-an olib-sac wmh1 *Olnd* k* onos k* *Op* k* oreo br1* osm ozone sde2• paeon par k* parth vml3• **Petr** k* petr-ra shn4• *Ph-ac* k* phasco-ci rbp2 *Phel* k* *Phos* k* phys phyt k* **Pic-ac** k* pieri-b mlk9.de pin-con oss2• pip-m pitu-gl skp7• plan plat k* *Plb* k* *Plut-n* srj7• polys sk4• positr nl2• pot-e rly4• prot jl2 prun ptel *Puls* k* pycnop-sa mrz1 rad-br sze8• ran-b k* ran-s k* rat *Rheum* k* rhod b4a.de *Rhus-t* k* ribo rly4• ruta k* *Sabad* k* *Sabin* k* sal-fr sle1• sang *Sars* k* *Sec* k* sel b7a.de* *Seneg* k* *Sep* k* *Sil* k* sol-ni sphing kk3.fr spig b7.de* *Spong* b7.de* squil k* *Stann* k* *Staph* k* stram k* streptoc rly4• *Stront-c* k* suis-em rly4• suis-hep rly4• suis-pan rly4• *Sul-ac* k* sul-i k2 **Sulph** k* suprar rly4• *Tab* k* *Tarax* k* *Tarent* k* tell ter term-a bnj1 thea ther k* thiam rly4• *Thuj* k* til tritic-vg fd5.de tub c* tub-r jl2 tung-met bdx1• ust k* v-a-b jl2 valer vanil fd5.de verat k* verat-v verb k* viol-o k* *Viol-t* k* vip *Zinc* k* zinc-p k2 zing [heroin sdj2 lac-mat sst4 spect dfg1 tax jsj7]

- **morning**: acon k* agar k* alum k* alum-p k2 am-m k* ars k* art-v hr1 arum-d hr1 arum-t k* berb bov k* bry calc k* calc-sil k2 calen hr1 *Carb-an* k* castm chel chin chinin-ar cimic clem k* coca com k* con k* corn croc k* dirc a1 eupi k* gamb hell hydr hyper k* indg k* kali-c kali-i k* kali-n k* kali-p kali-s kalm *Lach* k* lyc k* mag-m k* mang k* mez nat-m k* nat-s k* nicc k* nicc-met sk4• **Nux-v** k* op k* ox-ac paeon pall *Petr* k* petr-ra shn4• phos k* phys k* phyt pic-ac plb ruta sabin sars k* sep k* sil k* sin-a a1 sol-t-ae a1* spig sul-ac k* sulph tarent k* tell hr1* tritic-vg fd5.de vanil fd5.de verat verat-v a1 zinc k* zinc-p k2
  - **evening**; until: adam skp7•
  - **rising** | **after** | **amel.**: kali-i mag-s *Nat-m* nicc

- • **rising**: ...
  - ⁝ **agg.**: am-m k* anac k* ang ars k* aur aur-ar k2 bell k* caj a1 clem k* coc-c k* coff k* hell k* hipp k* hura kali-bi kali-i kali-p kali-s fd4.de mag-c k* mag-m mur-ac h2* nat-m k* nicc phos rhod sep k* stront-c sulph tong a1 verat a1
- • **waking**; on: allox tpw3 ant-t bar-c k* bell bry calc k* calc-p cann-i k* cham k* chin k* croc crot-c sk4• crot-t k* euphr k* ferr k* fl-ac k* ignis-alc es2• ip h1* lach lil-t lyc mag-s mang h2* nat-m k* nicc k* nicc-met sk4• nit-ac petr-ra shn4• phos rhus-t sol-ni squil k* *Tarent* tong a1 (non:uran-met k) uran-n verat k*
- **forenoon**: ars a1 indg a1 lipp a1 mag-m a1 mang a1 petr-ra shn4• sabin a1 sil a1 verat a1
  - • **10**-11 h: sphing kk3.fr
  - • **night**; until: sil h2
- **afternoon**: all-c alum k* am-c androg-p bnj1 *Arg-n* k* bry k* bufo cham k* chel k* chinin-s crot-c sk4• ferr gamb gels k* hyper k* indg k* jug-r kali-i kali-n h2* lact mag-c k* mag-m mang k* murx nat-c h2* nicc k* nit-ac h2 olib-sac wmh1 pall petr-ra shn4• puls k* sil k* tritic-vg fd5.de
  - • **13**-14 h: sulfonam ks2
  - • **15** h: petr-ra shn4•
  - • **16** h: *Mang*
    - ⁝ **16**-17 h: allox sp1
  - • **amel.**: lac-h sk4•
- **evening**: alum-sil k2 ambr k* apoc k* arg-n ars bar-c k* bar-s k2 bov k* bufo cedr k* chinin-s coloc digin a1 ferr fl-ac k* hydr-ac k* kali-i k* kali-n h2* kalm laur lith-c lyc k* mang a1 petr-ra shn4• phos k* plan k* rumx sep k* sin-a a1 *Stann* k* sulph k* tarent k* thiam rly4• tritic-vg fd5.de vanil fd5.de zinc zinc-p k2
  - • **18** h: choc srj3•
- **night**: arg-n k* carb-an k* kali-i kali-n h2* lil-t mez nicc-met sk4• nit-ac k* sil k* tarent til k* tritic-vg fd5.de
  - • **waking**; on: chel cic k* mez h2* nat-c k* til k*
- **accompanied** by:
  - • **fever** (See FEVER - Heat - head)
  - • **heat** of head (See Heat - accompanied - heaviness)
  - • **nausea**: ozone sde2•
  - • **sleeplessness**: *Boerh-d* zzc1•
  - • **vertigo** (See VERTIGO - Accompanied - head - heaviness)
  - ○ • **Eyes**; heaviness of: bit-ar wht1•
  - • **Hair** being pulled; sensation of the: allox sp1*
- **air**; in open:
  - • **agg.**: laur lil-t
  - • **amel.**: ant-t **Apis** aq-mar vml3• **Ars** carc tpw2* caust clem ferr-i gamb hell hydr lac-h htj1• mang mim-p rsj8• mosch nicc phos *Puls* tab tub-r jl zinc
- **alternating** with:
  - • **clearness** of mind: lacer c1 murx
  - ○ • **Leg**; pain in (See EXTREMITIES - Pain - leg - alternating - head)
- **ascending**, on: lac-h sk4• meny k* rhus-v
- **back** and limbs:
  - • **pain** in; with: apoc
    - ⁝ **and** drowsiness: gamb
- **balancing** sensation, as if falling: lap-la rsp1
- **bandaged**; as if tightly (= enveloped): allox sp1
- **beer**; after: chel k*
- **bending**:
  - • **head** | **backward** | **amel.**: *Cocc* ph-ac
    - ⁝ **forward** | **agg.**: nat-m ph-ac k* pitu-gl skp7•
- **blood**, as if too full of: *Glon* ign k* lil-t k*
- **breakfast** agg.; after: carbn-s
- **chill**:
  - • **after**: dros k*
  - • **during**: dros h1* kali-n h2* sulph k*
- **closing** the eyes | **amel.**: androc srj1• pitu-gl skp7•
- **coffee**; strong: | **amel.**: corn
- **cold**:
  - • **air** agg.: carb-an
- **cold**: ...
  - • **amel.**: chinin-s
- **cold**; after taking a: dulc
- **congestion**, as from: dig h2*
- **cough** agg.; during: euphr tax
- **daily**: nat-m sil
- **darkness**:
  - • **agg.**: sil
  - • **amel.**: brom
- **descending**, on: meny k*
- **dinner** | **after** | **agg.**: am-c k* euphr a1 gins a1 kali-i a1 mag-s a1 nat-c h2* nux-v a1 tab a1
  - • **amel.**: carb-an
- **drinking**, as if had been: acon agar bell h1* cocc dulc kali-n lach laur sabin
- **dull**: apoc k* caj k* calc fl-ac k* glon k* kali-s fd4.de nat-s k* petr-ra shn4• phys k* rumx verb k*
- **eating** | **after** | **agg.**: am-c k* bry k* carb-an hr1 castm cedr euphr k* gins k* graph k* grat guar hr1* (non:jug-r k*) kali-i k* mag-c mag-s k* nat-c k* *Nat-m* k* nux-v op *Phos* sin-a a1 tab k*
  - • **while** | **agg.**: aeth op
- **epistaxis** | **amel.**: dig
- **exertion** agg.: calc
- **exertion** of eyes, on: mur-ac k*
- **exhaustion**; with: kali-p k2
- **falls**: *(↗Falling)*
  - • **backward**, head falls: ant-t borx camph chin kali-c laur mur-ac op phel
  - • **down**, as if brain would fall: alum bell berb hipp
  - • **forward**:
    - ⁝ **brain** would fall; as if: carb-an laur rhus-t sul-ac
    - ⁝ **head** would fall; as if: agn alum bar-c berb chel cub sne hipp kali-c h2 melal-alt gya4 nat-m op par phos plb rhus-t sul-ac sulph tab viol-t zinc [bell-p-sp dcm1]
    - ⁝ **side**, to: arn h1
  - • **side**; as if head would fall to one: anan vh1 bry fl-ac phel
- **fever**; before: calc b4a.de nat-m b4a.de sil b4a.de
- **hands**, must lift head with: eup-per gk
- **headache**; from: kali-s fd4.de lyc h2* vanil fd5.de
- **heat**:
  - • **after**: tarent k*
  - • **during**: ars b4a.de calc b4.de* caust b4.de* dig h2* sep k* thuj k*
  - • **from**: com hell
  - • **sun**; of the | **agg.**: abrom-a ks5 brom hipp jl2 nat-c pitu-gl skp7•
- **holding** head erect, on: dros k* tarax k*
- **lead**; like: carb-v bg2 cimic hr1 sep bg2 sil bg2
  - • **liquid** lead: irid-met vml3•
- **lean** on something, desires to: *Bamb-a* stb2.de• *Bell* gymno k* *Kola* stb3• staph h1*
- **lift**; difficult to: eup-per mrr1 *Gels* k*
- **light**; from | **candlelight** | **agg.**: bov
  - • **strong** light | **agg.**: cact
- **looking**:
  - • **sideways**, while: agn
  - • **steadily**:
    - ⁝ **agg.**: mur-ac
    - ⁝ **amel.**: sabad
- **lying**:
  - • **agg.**: am-c bov *Glon* mag-c merc nicc nicc-met sk4• nux-m puls sep *Sulph* *Tarax*
    - ⁝ **low**; as if head had been too: *Phos*
  - • **amel.**: manc *Nat-m* olnd rhus-t tell
  - • **back**; on | **agg.**: cact mez
  - • **bed**; in | **agg.**: am-c
  - • **head** high; with the | **amel.**: sulph

- **side**; on:
  - **agg.**: meny
  - **amel.**: cact
  - **right** | **agg.**: anan
- **menses**:
  - **after** | **agg.**: all-s$_{k*}$ nat-m$_{k*}$
  - **before** | **agg.**: cimic crot-h$_{k*}$ ign
  - **colic**; menstrual: ant-t
  - **during** | **agg.**: calc$_{k*}$ calc-i$_{k2}$ carb-an ferr-p *Ign* *Kali-c* *Mag-c*$_{k*}$ mag-m$_{k*}$ *Mag-s*$_{k*}$ nat-m nux-v$_{k*}$ zinc$_{k*}$
- **mental** exertion agg.: *Calc* crot-h ferr-i lyc$_{k*}$ **Nat-c** nat-m **Ph-ac**$_{k*}$ **Phos**$_{k*}$ pitu-gl$_{skp7}$• sulfonam$_{ks2}$
- **motion**:
  - **agg.**: abrom-a$_{ks5}$ acon$_{k*}$ arg-n aur-s$_{k2}$ bism bov *Calc* canth colch fl-ac lyc phys$_{k*}$ plat *Sars*$_{k*}$ *Stann*$_{k*}$ *Sulph*$_{k*}$ thuj
  - **amel.**: caj$_{a1}$ com$_{hr1}$ mag-c$_{k*}$ mosch stann$_{k*}$
  - **eyes**; of | **agg.**: bry chin nux-v *Rhus-t*
  - **head**; of | **agg.**: calc indg sars spig
- **noise** agg.: abrom-a$_{ks5}$
- **oil** application | **amel.**: petr-ra$_{shn4}$•
- **old** people; in: bar-m$_{br1}$
- **painful**: cic$_{h1}$* dream-p$_{sdj1}$• gran hell nicc olnd sabad verb
- **paroxysmal**: nat-m$_{h2}$*
- **perspiration**:
  - **amel.**: nat-m$_{h2}$*
  - **during**: *Ars*$_{k*}$ caust eup-per$_{k*}$
- **pressed** forward:
  - **brain**:
    - **compressed**; feels: hyper
    - **forward**; as if brain were pressed: bry canth laur thuj
    - **weight** on brain; like a: chel nux-v pall$_{c1}$ sil
  - **head**; like a weight on: cocc petr-ra$_{shn4}$• phel pycnop-sa$_{mrz1}$
- **pressing** | **Occiput**: ant-t$_{bg2}$ crot-h$_{bg2}$
- **pressure** | **amel.**: agav-t$_{jl1}$ ail$_{k*}$ aq-mar$_{skp7}$*• **Cact** camph cop mur-ac nat-m petr-ra$_{shn4}$• pitu-gl$_{skp7}$• sabin
- **quiet**; keeping | **amel.**: cassia-s$_{ccrh1}$•
- **rage**; after: gard-j$_{vlr2}$•
- **raising** | **eyebrows** | **amel.**: petr-ra$_{shn4}$•
  - **head**:
    - **agg.**: calc dros ign op spong sulph
    - **amel.**: bry
- **reading** agg.: bry *Calc*$_{k*}$ crot-t pimp$_{a1}$ sin-a$_{a1}$
- **rest** | **amel.**: pitu-gl$_{skp7}$•
- **riding** agg.: phyt
- **rising**:
  - **agg.**: am-m ang aur aur-s$_{k2}$ bapt calc hura iod olnd sulph tarax viol-t
  - **amel.**: calc con laur nicc
  - **stooping**; from | **agg.**: grat mag-s sulph viol-t
- **room** agg.; stuffy: gard-j$_{vlr2}$•
- **sewing**, while: petr$_{k*}$
- **shaking** the head; on | **amel.**: gels$_{k*}$
- **sitting**:
  - **agg.**: aeth alum ang ars bism$_{h1}$ caust chin cic manc merc olnd squil *Sulph*
  - **amel.**: sulph$_{k*}$
  - **bent** forward | **agg.**: *Con*
  - **erect** | **agg.**: alum$_{k*}$ con
- **sleep**:
  - **amel.**: laur pitu-gl$_{skp7}$•
  - **loss** of sleep; from | **as** from loss of sleep: zinc$_{h2}$*
  - **siesta**:
    - **after**:
      - **agg.**: bov bry$_{k*}$ mag-c$_{k*}$ petr-ra$_{shn4}$• rhus-t
      - **amel.**: crot-c$_{sk4}$•
- **smoking** agg.: aids$_{nl2}$• ferr-i$_{k*}$ gels$_{k*}$
- **sneezing** agg.: seneg$_{k*}$
- **standing** agg.: alum ars$_{k*}$ bov$_{k*}$ calc$_{h2}$* caust$_{k*}$ kali-c lob-e$_{c1}$ mag-c manc nicc plb
- **stool** agg.; after: apoc$_{k*}$
- **stooping**:
  - **after** | **agg.**: calc$_{h2}$*
  - **agg.**: acon alum alum-p$_{k2}$ bell$_{h1}$ *Berb* bov bry camph *Carb-an* colch con fl-ac grat hell hyos ign$_{br1}$ indg kali-bi kali-i laur nat-m nicc nit-ac *Nux-v* petr *Ph-ac* phos plat **Puls** rhus-t senn spong sul-ac *Sulph* tab urin$_{c1}$
  - **amel.**: dros ign tarax$_{k*}$ viol-t$_{k*}$
- **supporting** head (See lean)
- **swallowing** agg.: kali-c
- **talking** agg.: abrom-a$_{ks5}$ *Ambr*$_{k*}$ cact cassia-s$_{ccrh1}$• ign$_{hr1}$ nat-m$_{k*}$ sulph$_{k*}$ wies$_{a1}$
- **tea**; from drinking: pitu-gl$_{skp7}$•
- **thinking** of it agg.: *Hell*
- **urination**; copious | **amel.**: fl-ac **Gels**
- **vertigo**; with (See VERTIGO - Accompanied - head - heaviness)
- **vexation**; after: mag-c
- **waking**; on: allox$_{tpw3}$* bar-c bell bry calc$_{k*}$ calc-p cann-i cassia-s$_{ccrh1}$• cham chel$_{k*}$ chin cic con$_{k*}$ crot-t euphr ferr fl-ac hir$_{skp7}$• ign$_{k*}$ lach lil-t mag-s nat-c nat-m$_{k*}$ nicc nit-ac rhus-t sal-fr$_{sle1}$• sep sol-ni sol-t-ae$_{a1}$ spong$_{fd4.de}$ squil sulph$_{k*}$ tarent til verat
- **walking**:
  - **agg.**: hell hipp kali-bi laur puls rheum rhus-t spong sulph thea
  - **air**; in open | **after** | **amel.**: bov bufo-s$_{a1}$
    - **amel.**: aq-mar$_{skp7}$• hydr
  - **amel.**: kali-bi mag-c$_{k*}$
- **warm** | **applications** | **amel.**: aq-mar$_{skp7}$•
  - **room**:
    - **agg.**: **Apis** **Ars** chinin-s ferr-i gard-j$_{vlr2}$• hydr laur merc paeon *Phos* pieri-b$_{mlk9.de}$ rhus-t
    - **closed**: abrom-a$_{ks5}$
- **warmth**:
  - **amel.** | **heat** amel.: aq-mar$_{skp7}$*•
- **washing** | **amel.**: mag-c$_{k*}$ phos
- **wine** agg.: rhus-t$_{h1}$*
- **wrinkling** forehead amel.: phos
- **writing** agg.: *Calc*$_{k*}$ ferr-i gent-l$_{k*}$ lyc$_{k*}$

○ - **Brain**: acon$_{bg2}$ bry$_{bg2}$ form$_{ptk1}$ hyper$_{ptk1}$ mag-c$_{ptk1}$ sang$_{a1}$ sil$_{bg2}$ thuj$_{bg2}$

- **Forehead**: *Acon*$_{k*}$ *Aesc*$_{k*}$ aeth$_{k*}$ agar$_{k*}$ ail all-c$_{k*}$ all-s$_{a1}$* allox$_{tpw3}$ *Aloe*$_{bg2}$* *Am-c*$_{k*}$ *Am-m*$_{k*}$ amph$_{a1}$ amyg$_{hr1}$ ang$_{k*}$ *Ant-c*$_{k*}$ ant-t$_{k*}$ apis$_{k*}$ apoc$_{k*}$ arg-met arg-n$_{k*}$ arn$_{k*}$ ars$_{k*}$ *Ars-i*$_{bg2}$* *Ars-s-r*$_{hr1}$ arum-t asaf$_{k*}$ asar$_{k*}$ aspar$_{k*}$ aur-m-n$_{a1}$ *Bapt*$_{k*}$ bar-c$_{k*}$ bar-m bar-s$_{k2}$ *Bell*$_{k*}$ berb *Bism*$_{k*}$ *Bov*$_{k*}$ brom$_{k*}$ **Bry**$_{k*}$ bufo *Calc*$_{k*}$ calc-s calc-sil$_{k2}$ camph$_{k*}$ cann-i$_{k*}$ cann-s$_{bg}$ cann-xyz$_{bg2}$ canth$_{k*}$ *Carb-an*$_{k*}$ carb-v$_{k*}$ carc$_{gk6}$* cassia-s$_{ccrh1}$• cere-b$_{a1}$ *Cham*$_{k*}$ chel$_{k*}$ chinin-s choc$_{srj3}$• *Cic*$_{k*}$ cinnb cist$_{k*}$ clem$_{k*}$ coli$_{rly4}$• *Coloc*$_{k*}$ com$_{a1}$ con$_{k*}$ conv crot-c$_{bg2}$* crot-h crot-t$_{k*}$ dig$_{a1}$ dioxi$_{rbp6}$ dulc$_{k*}$ elaps ferr$_{k*}$ ferr-ar ferr-i ferr-p fl-ac gamb$_{k*}$ *Gels*$_{k*}$ gins$_{k*}$ glon$_{k*}$ gran$_{k*}$ grat$_{k*}$ haem ham$_{k*}$ hell$_{k*}$ hep$_{k*}$ hipp hura hydr$_{k*}$ hydrog$_{srj2}$• hyos$_{k*}$ *Ign*$_{b7a.de}$ indg$_{k*}$ ip$_{k*}$ jac-c$_{k*}$ jac-g jatr-c kali-bi$_{k*}$ kali-c$_{k*}$ *Kali-i*$_{k*}$ kali-m$_{k2}$ kali-n$_{k*}$ kali-p kali-s kali-sil$_{k2}$ ketogl-ac$_{rly4}$• kreos$_{k*}$ lac-c *Lac-d*$_{hr1}$ lac-f$_{c1}$ lach$_{k*}$ lap-la$_{rsp1}$ laur$_{k*}$ led$_{k*}$ lil-t lith-c lyc *Mag-c*$_{k*}$ *Mag-m*$_{k*}$ mag-s mang$_{k*}$ merc$_{k*}$ merc-i-r mur-ac$_{k*}$ musa$_{c1}$ naja nat-ar nat-c *Nat-m*$_{k*}$ nat-p nat-sil$_{fd3.de}$• nicc$_{k*}$ nit-ac nit-s-d$_{hr1}$ nux-m *Nux-v*$_{k*}$ olnd$_{k*}$ op$_{k*}$ *Ox-ac*$_{k*}$ pall pana$_{a1}$ paull$_{a1}$ petr-ra$_{shn4}$• phos$_{k*}$ phyt pic-ac$_{mrr1}$ plb$_{k*}$ prun-p$_{a1}$ psil$_{ft1}$ *Puls* pycnop-sa$_{mrz1}$ rhod$_{k*}$ *Rhus-t*$_{k*}$ ruta$_{k*}$ sabin$_{k*}$ sars$_{k*}$ sep$_{k*}$ **Sil**$_{k*}$ sin-a$_{a1}$ sol-ni spira$_{a1}$ *Stann*$_{k*}$ staph$_{k*}$ staphycoc$_{rly4}$• stict$_{br1}$ stront-c$_{k*}$ suis-em$_{rly4}$• sulfonam$_{ks2}$ *Sulph*$_{k*}$ sumb$_{a1}$ tarent tax tell thea tritic-vg$_{fd5.de}$ verat$_{k*}$ zinc$_{k*}$ zinc-p$_{k2}$ [heroin$_{sdj2}$]
  - **right**: sal-al$_{blc1}$•
    - **blowing** the nose | **amel.**: sal-al$_{blc1}$•
  - **left**: nat-m$_{bg2}$ plut-n$_{srj7}$•
  - **morning**: am-m$_{hr1}$ ars-s-f$_{k2}$ arum-t$_{k*}$ chin$_{k*}$ indg$_{a1}$ kali-sil$_{k2}$ lac-leo$_{sk4}$• nat-m$_{k*}$ nicc$_{k*}$ ox-ac$_{k*}$ pall$_{k*}$ ruta$_{fd4.de}$ sin-a$_{a1}$ sulph$_{k*}$ verat
    - **amel.**: cassia-s$_{ccrh1}$•
    - **rising** agg.; after: ang$_{h1}$*

· **morning**: ...
⁝ **waking**; on: bell h1* calc nat-m k* plut-n srj7•
· **forenoon**: carb-an k* gamb k* *Mang* nicc k* sarr sars h2*
· **noon**: petr-ra shn4• sulph k*
· **afternoon**: am-c k* chel k* chinin-s dioxi rbp6 kali-i k* mag-m h2* mang nicc k* pall k* sil k*
⁝ **14** h: hir skp7•
⁝ **16** h: *Mang*
· **evening**: alum-sil k2 ars-s-f k2 cassia-s ccrh1• coloc k* germ-met srj5• lith-c mag-m k* nat-m k* nat-sil fd3.de• sulph k* tritic-vg fd5.de
⁝ **menses**; during: zinc k*
· **air**; in open | **amel.**: carc a* mang
· **all** would come out, as if: acon k* kreos mag-s
· **brain** were packed in front; as if: equis-h a1
· **concentrate**; on attempting to: pic-ac mrr1
· **dinner**; after: sars h2*
· **eating**; after: aeth k* am-c k* mag-c k*
· **exertion** agg.: cassia-s ccrh1•
· **heat** of the sun agg.: *Brom* k* nat-c
· **lying** down | **amel.**: cassia-s ccrh1•
· **menses**:
⁝ **after** | **agg.**: *All-s* vh1
⁝ **beginning** of menses; at the | **amel.**: *All-s* vh1
⁝ **during** | **agg.**: zinc k*
· **mental** exertion agg.: calc
· **motion** agg.: *Bism* chlol hr1 fl-ac
· **pressure** | **amel.**: cassia-s ccrh1• mur-ac h2*
· **reading** agg.: calc h2*
· **sleep**; as from loss of: nat-m bg2* tell bg2*
· **standing** agg.: hir skp7• mag-c k*
· **stone** lay there, as if: bell h1* ruta
· **stooping** agg.: acon *Carb-an* cassia-s ccrh1• petr-ra shn4• psil ft1* rhus-t tell
· **waking**; on: bell petr-ra shn4• sulph k* tung-met bdx1•
· **walking** agg.: camph k* con sulph k*
· **weight**:
⁝ **falling** forward; as if a heavy weight were: nux-v b7.de* rhus-t bg2
⁝ **pressed** forward in head, must hold head upright; as if a weight: *Acon Rhus-t*
⁝ **sank** down in it: nux-v
· **wine** | **amel.**: dioxi rbp6
· **writing** agg.: *Calc*

○ · **Eyes**:
⁝ **Above**: aml-ns bg2 cist bg2 crot-c bg2 fl-ac bg2 gard-j vlr2• gels bg2 glon bg2 kali-bi bg2 *Nat-m* bg2 petr-ra shn4• polys sk4• sep bg2 sil bg2 tell bg2 tritic-vg fd5.de [tax jsj7]
⁝ **looking** upward | **impossible**: (↗*Pain - forehead - eyes - above - pressure so - pressing)* carb-an a1*
· **Frontal** sinuses: puls pycnop-sa mrz1
· **Upper** part: bell bg2 camph bg2 con bg2 fl-ac bg2 kali-c bg2 kreos bg2 psor bg2

- **Occiput**: *Aesc* k* aeth k* *Agar* k* alumn k* ant-t k* apis k* aur k* aur-m-n k* aur-s k2 bapt bar-c k* bar-m bar-s k2 *Bell* k* *Bism* k* bov k* brom bg2* bros-gau mrc1 *Bry* k* cact k* cain caj k* *Calc* k* *Calc-ar* k* calc-s *Cann-i* k* cann-s k* *Canth* k* *Carb-an* k* **Carb-v** k* *Carl* k* cassia-s ccrh1• cham k* **Chel** k* chin k* chlf a1 chlol a1 cic bg2* cimic gk clem colch k* *Con* k* cop k* *Crot-h* k* *Dulc* k* *Eup-per* *Ferr* k* ferr-p gels k* germ-met srj5• gins k* graph hell k* hipp jl2 hydr bg2 ign indg k* kali-c k* kali-i k* kali-m k2* kali-n k* kali-p k* kali-s kreos k* lac-ac k* *Lach* k* lact k* laur k* *Lyc* k* mag-m k* mang k* *Meph* k* merc-i-r bg2* *Mez* k* *Mur-ac* k* myric k* **Nat-m** k* nat-s k* nicc k* nit-ac nit-s-d a1* nux-v onos bg2* *Op* k* paeon k* pert-vc vk9 **Petr** k* ph-ac k* phos k* pic-ac k* *Plb* k* plut-n srj7• podo bg2 prun psil ft1 psor ptel k* ruta sabin k* sec k* sel k* sep k* sil k2 spig k* spong k* stann k* *Sulph* k* sumb symph fd3.de• tab bg2 tarax k* thuj k* til k* tril-p v-a-b jl2 verat b7.de* zinc k* zinc-p k2

- **Occiput**: ...
· **morning**: cham k* **Lach** sep k* sulph k*
⁝ **menses**; during: mag-m k*
· **forenoon**: indg k*
· **afternoon**: ferr k* lact k* spong h1* upa a1
· **evening**: *All-c* hr1 bov k* kali-i k*
⁝ **18** h: aq-mar skp7•
⁝ **bed** agg.; in: dulc a1
· **night**: chel k* mez k*
⁝ **lying** on back agg.: mez k*
⁝ **raised** from pillow; as if it could not be: *Chel*
· **accompanied** by | **vertigo**: guat sp1
· **bending** head forward agg.: colch con ph-ac
· **chill**; during: cann-i
· **cold** water; washing head in | **amel.**: cassia-s ccrh1*•
· **drawn** backwards; as if: *Alet* vh1 syph xxb
· **draws** eyes together: **Nat-m**
· **exertion** agg.: cassia-s ccrh1•
⁝ **eyes**; on exertion of: *Mur-ac* hr1
· **heat**: acon bg2 *Bell* bg2 cassia-s ccrh1• hell bg2 sep bg2
⁝ **sun**; of the | **agg.**: *Brom* k*
· **lead**, as if full of: kali-c kali-m k2 *Lach* k* mur-ac op k* *Petr* k* spong
· **lying** | **back**; on | **agg.**: bry cact
⁝ **side**; on | **amel.**: cact
· **lying** down | **after** | **agg.**: *Tarax*
⁝ **amel.**: cassia-s ccrh1*•
· **motion**:
⁝ **agg.**: bar-c *Bism* h1* chlol a1 colch k* lyc k* thuj k*
⁝ **amel.**: aq-mar skp7•
· **pressure** | **amel.**: cassia-s ccrh1*•
· **raise**:
⁝ **difficult** to: *Chel Lach* op sep
⁝ **pain** in occiput like a weight, must raise head with hands: *Eup-per* k* op
· **rising** agg.: aur k* tarax h1*
· **sink** backward; as if head would: bros-gau mrc1 ign kali-c kali-m k2 mur-ac op
· **sitting** bent forward agg.: *Con* k*
· **sleep**, as from loss of: nat-m bg1 tell bg1
· **step**, a jolt as if a weight were on occiput; at every: bell
· **stooping** | **amel.**: tarax h1*
· **swallowing** agg.: kali-c k*
· **waking**; on: bry k* cham hell k* **Lach** k*
· **walking**:
⁝ **agg.**: spong
⁝ **air** agg.; in open: staph h1

▽ · **extending** to:
⁝ **Arms**; down: nit-ac
⁝ **Downward**: nit-ac sep sulph
⁝ **Ear** to ear: ferr
⁝ **Forehead**: petr mrr1
⁝ **Nape**, into: sulph
⁝ **Shoulders**, to: bry
⁝ **Vertex**: petr mrr1

- **Sides**: aeth agar bg2 am-c amph a1 arg-n bov *Cact* cedr k* coff bg2 con bg2 elaps eug grat hydr k* kali-c kali-i k* kalm lyc mag-m sabad sabin sin-n bg2 stann sul-ac tarent
· **right**: aeth bg2 am-c k* arg-n bg2 bov k* cact bg2 elaps bg2 hydr a1 kalm bg2 nux-v bg2 phos bg1 plut-n srj7• sabad b7.de* sars h2*
· **left**: ham bg2 hydr bg2 kali-c bg2 lyc bg2 mur-ac b4.de* sabin bg2 stann b4.de* sul-ac b4.de* sulfonam ks2 tarent bg2 [tax jsj7]

- **Skull**: tub-r jl2

- **Temples**: agar k* bell k* bism k* bov k* bros-gau mrc1 cact carb-an k* cimic k* cinnb k* clem k* cortiso tpw7 ferr k* glon kali-bi bg2 kali-i k* led k* nit-ac nit-s-d a1* petr-ra shn4• phyt k* pip-m a1 polys sk4• rhus-t k* ribo rly4• sabad k* sars k* sep k* stann k* sul-h a1 tell k* zinc bg2* zinc-s bg1
  - **right**: dendr-pol sk4• rhus-t bg2
  - **left**: *Phos* bg2 psor jl2
  - **weight** hung at both sides; as if a: agar rhus-t
- **Vertex**: *(↗Pain - vertex - pressing)* acon bg2 aloe bg2 alum b4.de* apis bg2 bry bg2 *Cact* bg2 camph bg2 cann-xyz bg2 canth bg2 chel bg2 con bg2 dig bg2 kali-n bg2 lach bg2 laur b7.de* m-aust b7.de mag-c bg2 mosch bg2 murx bg2 ph-ac bg2 phel bg2 pic-ac bg2 rhus-t b7.de* squil b7.de* stann bg2 sulph bg2 thuj b4a.de*

HEAVING up and down sensation: bell con lyc

HEMORRHAGE:
- **after** hemorrhages agg.: cocc bg2
- ○ **Brain** (See Cerebral hemorrhage)
- **Meninges**: pert jl2

HEMORRHOIDS agg.: lach bg2 *Nux-v* bg2

HICCOUGH agg.: bry bg2

HOLD:
- **backward**: borx k2
- **hands**; holds head with (See Hands - holds)
- **headache**; during: petr h2
- **steady**; unable to hold: arn a1* squil k*
- **up** head; unable to hold: *(↗Lean on; BACK - Weakness - cervical; VERTIGO - Raising; VERTIGO - Raising - head; VERTIGO - Raising - Head - agg.)* abrot br1* *Aeth* k* ant-t apis ptk1 arn a1* atro bapt bar-m k2 bell ptk1 *Calc-p* k* carb-v k2 cham k* cocc ptk1 con croc (non:cupr k*) cupr-s slp dig ptk1 **Gels** k* glon hipp hyos ptk1 kali-br hr1 lil-t lon-x br1 lyc mag-c vh* *Mang* mez nat-m tl1 nux-m nux-v olnd *Op* k* petr petr-ra shn4• phel *Puls* rhus-t sabad sanic tl1* *Sil* sulph mtf33 tab *Verat* k* zinc
  - **leaning** sideways all the time: cina mtf33
  - **weakness**; from: abrot bro1* aeth bro1* calc-p bro1 cocc bro1 nat-m bro1 sulph mtf33 verat bro1*

HOLDING head erect:
- **agg.**: bar-c bg2
- **amel.**: plat b4a.de

HOLLOW (See Empty)

HORRIPILATION (See Hair - bristling)

HOT body; sensation of (See Heat - hot - body)

HUNGER agg.: caust b4a.de sil b4a.de

HYDROCEPHALOID: phos b4a.de *Zinc* b4a.de

HYDROCEPHALUS: abrot bg2 acon k* am-c **Apis** k* apoc k* arg-n bg2* *Arn* b7.de* *Ars* k* ars-i bg2 art-v c2 atro-s mtf11 *Aur* aur-ar k2 aur-s k2 *Bac* c2* bar-c bg2* bell k* *Bism* hr1 *Bry* k* cadm-s **Calc** k* calc-i k2 *Calc-p* k* calc-sil k2* canth bg2* carb-ac k* caust bg2 *Chin* bro1 chinin-s bg2* cina b7.de* coloc bg2 *Con* k* crot-h bg2 cupr bg2 cupr-act c2* cypr br1* cyt-l a* *Dig* k* *Ferr* k* ferr-i galv c2 gels bro1 grat c2 *Hell* k* *Hyos* k* ign b7.de* indg *Iod* k* iodof c2* *Ip* b7.de* kali-br bro1 *Kali-i* k* kali-p lach k* **Lyc** k •* mag-m *Merc* k* *Nat-m* nux-v b7.de* oeno bro1 *Op* k* ph-ac *Phos* k* plat podo bro1 *Puls* rhus-t b7.de* samb k* sep b4a.de **Sil** k* sol-ni c2* spig b7.de* squil b7.de* *Stram* k* *Sulph* k* thuj bg2 toxo-g jl2 tub k* verat bg2* verat-v mtf11 viol-t b7.de* zinc k* zinc-br c2* *Zinc-m* c2*
- **accompanied** by:
  - **blindness**: apoc ptk1
  - **convulsions** (See GENERALS - Convulsions - hydrocephalus)
  - **weakness**; general: sil bg2
  - ○ **Neck**; emaciated: calc-p bg2
- **acute**: apoc br1* cupr mtf11 cyt-l a hell mtf11 merc mtf33 op mtf
  - **measles**; after: merc mtf33
- **beginning** stage: toxo-g jl2
- **cholera**; after | **children**; in: zinc mtf33
- **chronic**: art-v mtf calc-i mtf11 calc-p mtf hed mtf11 kali-i mtf op mtf zinc mtf

Hydrocephalus: ...
- **diarrhea** agg.; after:
  - **children**; in: zinc ptk1*
  - **long**, exhausting diarrhea: cypr br1
- **edematous**: hell br1
- **lies** with head low: apis merc sulph zinc
- **meningitis**; after: apis mtf sol-ni mtf sulph mtf tub mtf
- **perspiration**; with: merc
- **prenatal** therapy for the pregnant mother (See GENERALS - History - hydrocephalic)
- **scarlatina**; after: apis a* merc mtf33

HYPERESTHESIA:
- ○ **Cerebral**:
  - **children**; in young | **overstimulation** of the brain; from: cypr br1

HYPOCHONDRIACS; complaints of (See MIND - Hypochondriasis - head)

INDIGESTION agg.: ant-c bg2 arg-n bg2 bry bg2 calc bg2 carb-v bg2 card-m bg2 chel bg2 cocc bg2 coff bg2 cycl bg2 eup-per bg2 ip bg2 iris bg2 lob bg2 mag-m bg2 merc bg2 myric bg2 nat-m bg2 nat-s bg2 *Nux-v* bg2 *Puls* bg2 sang bg2 sulph bg2 tab bg2

INFLAMMATION:
- ○ **Arteries** of temples: ictod mtf11
- **Brain** (= encephalitis): *Acon* k* aeth bro1 *Ant-t* b7a.de apis k* apoc bro1 arn b7a.de* ars bro1 arum-t c2 bapt bg2* **Bell** k* *Bry* k* cadm-s k* calc bg2* calc-br bro1 calc-p bro1 *Camph* k* cann-s b7a.de* canth k* carb-ac bro1 *Carb-v* b4a.de cham k* chin bro1 chinin-s bro1 chr-o c2* cic bro1 cimic bro1 cina k* *Con* crot-h k* *Cupr* k* cupr-act bro1 cyt-l br1 dig bro1 eberth jl2 echi br1 gels bg2* glon k* *Hell* k* hydr-ac bro1 *Hyos* k* hyper bro1 ign mrr1 influ jl2* iod bg2* iodof bro1 *Kali-br* hr1 kali-i bg2* kreos bro1 lach k* leptos-ih jl2 *Merc* k* merc-c bg2* merc-d bro1 mosch bro1 nux-v k* *Op* k* oreo br1 ourl jl2 ox-ac bro1 par parathyr jl2 *Phos* k* phys k* plb k* puls k* pyrog jl2* rhus-t k* *Sil* bro1 sol-ni bro1 stram k* sulph k* thal-xyz srj8• toxo-g jl2 *Tub* bro1 verat-v k* vip bro1 zinc bg2*
  - **accompanied** by:
    - **fever**; intense: acon mtf11
    - **sleep**; deep: borx
    - **vertigo**: bell btw2
    - **vomiting**: influ mp4•
  - **benign**: raja-s mtf11
  - **children**; in: parathyr jl2 toxo-g jl2
  - **ear** discharge; from suppressed: stram st
  - **eruptions**; after suppressed: cic br1
  - **injuries**; after: acon bro1 *Arn* bro1 bell bro1 *Hyper* bro1 nat-s bro1 sil bro1
  - **sopor**; with (See accompanied - sleep)
  - **tubercular**: *Apis* bro1 *Bac* bro1 bell bro1 bry bro1 calc bro1 *Calc-p* bro1 cocc bro1 *Cupr-cy* bro1 dig bro1 glon bro1 *Hell* bro1 hyos bro1 iod bro1 *Iodof* bro1 kali-i bro1 op bro1 stram bro1 *Sulph* bro1 tub bro1 *Verat-v* bro1 zinc bro1 zinc-o bro1
  - **vaccination**; after: acon mtf11
  - ○ **Base** of brain: *Cupr-cy* bro1 dig bro1 hell bro1 iod bro1 sec bro1 tub bro1 *Verat-v* bro1*
    - **ear** discharge; from suppressed: stram mtf33
  - **Cerebrospinal**: *Agar* bro1 ail bro1 *Apis* bro1 arg-n bro1 atro bro1 *Bell* bro1 bry bro1 *Cic* bro1 *Cimic* bro1 cocc bro1 *Crot-h* bro1 *Cupr-act* bro1 cyt-l bro1 echi bro1 *Gels* bro1 glon bro1 *Hell* bro1 helo-s rwt2• hyos bro1 ip bro1 kali-i bro1 nat-s bro1 op bro1 oreo bro1 phys bro1 sil bro1 stram bro1 sulph bro1 verat-v bro1 zinc bro1 *Zinc-cy* bro1
  - **Medulla** oblongata: chinin-s br1
    - **accompanied** by | **vision**; loss of: chinin-s br1
- **Mastoid** (See EAR - Caries - mastoid)
- **Meninges** (= meningitis): *(↗FEVER - Cerebrospinal)* acon k* aesc-g c2 agar c2 am-c tl1 *Apis* k* arg-n k* *Arn* k* ars hs1* bapt mtf11 **Bell** k* *Bry* k* bufo c2 cadm-s bg* *Calc* *Calc-p* canth k* carb-ac c2 cham b7a.de cic c1* *Cimic* c2 *Cina* k* *Cocc* cor-r hr1 *Cupr* k* diph jl2 dulc btw1 echi br1 *Gels* k* *Glon* k* **Hell** k* helo-s c1 *Hipp* *Hippoz* *Hyos* k* hyper c2 ign mtf11 influ jl2* iodof c2 ip k2 *Kali-br* *Lach* lachn st1 lat-m bnm6• leptos-ih jl2 lyc bg mag-p c2 med c1 meningoc jl2 *Merc* k* merc-d c2* *Nat-m* nat-s k2* *Op* k* oreo br1 *Ox-ac* c2

- **Meninges**: ...
parathyr jl2 *Phos* k* phys kr1 *Plb* pyrog jl2 *Rhus-t* sec btw1* *Sil* k* sol-ni c2* staphycoc jl2 **Stram** k* *Sulph* k* syc bka1*• toxo-g jl2 tub br1* tub-a jl2 verat hr1* verat-v c2* **Zinc** k* zinc-cy c2
  - **abacterial**: coxs mtf11
  - **accompanied** by:
    - **cold** feeling: am-c tl1
    - **hemorrhage**: canth mtf11
    - **hiccough**: *Arn* st1
    - **influenza**: tub-a jl2
    - **pulse**; slow: am-c tl1 cupr-cy hsa1
    - **sharp** stinging pain: apis tl1
    - **strabismus**: tub ptk1*
    - **urine**; pale, clear: bell ptk1 hyos ptk1 lach ptk1 phos ptk1
    - **vertigo**: arn fyz7
    - **vomiting**: leptos-ih jl2
    - **Bladder** irritation: canth br1
    - **Face**; redness of: apis mrr1
    - **Head**; pain in: leptos-ih jl2
    - **Jaw**; chewing motion of (See FACE - Chewing - accompanied - meningitis)
    - **Tongue**:
      - **paralysis** of tongue: *Hydr-ac* kr1*
      - **protruding**: *Apis* kr1* *Hydr-ac* kr1*
      - **swelling**: *Lyc* kr1*
      - **white** discoloration of the tongue | **yellowish** white: *Gels* kr1*
  - **acute**: zinc-s mtf11
  - **children**; in young: toxo-g jl2
  - **injuries**; after mechanical: arn tl1
  - **serous**: apis mtf11
  - **spinal** meningitis (See BACK - Inflammation - membranes)
  - **suppurative** | **coma**; with (See MIND - Coma - meningitis - suppurative)
  - **traumatic**: hyper tl1
  - **tubercular**: apis hr1* bac br1* *Calc* k* *Iod* k* iodof br1* *Lyc* k* *Merc* k* nat-m *Sil* k* *Sulph* k* *Tub* k* *Zinc* k*
    - **coma**; with (See MIND - Coma - meningitis - tubercular)
  - **warm** application agg.: apis tl1
  - ○ **Ear** discharge; from suppressed: merc pf stram tl1*
  - **Ear**; from inflammation of the (See EAR - Inflammation - media - followed - meningitis)
- **Periosteum** (= periostitis): *Aur* *Aur-m* calc-p bg *Daph* bg **Fl-ac** *Kali-i* led *Mang* *Merc* *Merc-c* **Mez** morg-p fmm1• *Nit-ac* **Ph-ac** *Phos* puls *Rhod* *Rhus-t* *Ruta* sars bg *Sil* *Staph*
- **Scalp** and skull; between: sil k2
- **Sinuses**; frontal: hippoz jl2 med jl2

INJURIES of the head; after: (*↗Brain damage; Concussion; Pain - brain - injuries)* am-pic c1 anac bg2 apis bg2 **Arn** k* bell bg2 *Calc* bg2* calen bg1* carc fb* cedr gk1 chin vh* *Cic* k* *Cocc* bg2* con bg2* fic-m gya1 *Fil* sne glon bg2* *Hell* vh* hep bg2* *Hyos* bg2* hyper k* *Kali-p* vh* lach bg2* *Led* vh *Lob* vh* mang vh meli bg2 meny gk1 merc bg2 *Nat-m* k* **Nat-s** k* *Op* bg2* petr bg2 ph-ac bg2 puls bg2* *Rhus-t* bg2* *Sil* bg2* stram bg2* sul-ac bg2* sulph bg2 symph ptk1* *Teucr* c1* vanil fd5.de verat bg2 zinc vh*
- **children**; in: | **delivery**; from: (*↗Cephalhematoma)* carc sst• nat-s mtf33
- ○ **Scalp**: calen bg1*

INSPIRATION agg.: anac b4.de* cimic bg2

INTOXICATION: (*↗MIND - Confusion - intoxicated - as after; MIND - Stupefaction)* lac-c ptk1 lach ptk1 naja ptk1 *Nat-m* nit-ac **Nux-v** olib-sac wmh1 *Op* bg par ph-ac *Pip-m* mrr1 plut-n srj7• psor al ptel *Puls* rhod *Rhus-t* samb spig sul-ac tarax valer vip ptk1 [tax jsj7]
- **agg.**: bry b7.de* cocc b7.de* kreos b7a.de laur b7.de* *Nux-v* b7.de* *Puls* b7.de* stram b7.de*

Intoxication: ...
- **as** from: (*↗MIND - Confusion - intoxicated - as after; MIND - Stupefaction)* *Absin* bro1 acon bro1 aesc *Agar* *Agath-a* nl2• *Ail* bro1 aloe bro1 am-c anac bro1 *Apis* bro1 aran bro1 am bro1 ars asc-t c1 *Bapt* bro1 bell bro1 berb bry k* cann-i bro1 carb-an *Carb-v* k* carbn-s mrr1 caust chel chin bro1 choc srj3• cocc b7.de* croc crot-t cycl dioxi rbp6 euphr eupi gels bg2* *Glon* k* graph k* *Hell* bro1 hydr-ac iod kali-bi bg2 kali-n kreos k* lac-h htj1• laur k* mag-m mentho bro1 mez naja ptk1 nat-c bro1 *Nat-m* nit-ac nux-m bro1 **Nux-v** k* olib-sac wmh1 *Op* b7.de* par ph-ac k* *Phos* bro1 *Pip-m* mrr1 plut-n srj7• psor al ptel *Puls* k* *Querc* bro1 rhod *Rhus-t* k* samb k* sep bro1 spig k* sul-ac *Sulph* bro1 tanac bro1 tarax k* valer k* xero bro1 zinc bro1 [tax jsj7]
  - ○ **Ears** and eyes; between: dioxi rbp6

IRONING agg.: *Bry* ptk1 phos ptk1 sep ptk1

IRRITATION: lap-la rsp1
- ○ **Brain**: absin br1 agar br1
  - **dentition**; during: sol-ni br1
- **Meninges**: phys br1 syc bka1•
  - **accompanied** by | **Muscles**; stiffness of: phys br1

ITCHING of scalp: abrot k* acon k* *Agar* k* agn k* *Alum* k* alum-p k2 alum-sil k2 alumn bro1 *Am-c* k* *Am-m* k* ammc a1 anac k* anag anan *Ant-c* k* *Apis* k* aq-pet a1 arg-met b7.de* *Arg-n* k* arge-pl rwt5• arn b7.de* ars k* ars-i ars-s-f k2 arund k* asar b7.de* aur k* aur-ar k2 aur-i k2 aur-s bad k* bamb-a stb2.de• **Bar-c** k* bar-s k2 bell b4.de* benz-ac k* berb k* bond a1 borx b4a.de *Bov* k* bry k* **Calc** k* calc-i k2 calc-p bg2 **Calc-s** k* calc-sil k2 calen a1 canth tl1 caps k* *Carb-ac* k* *Carb-an* k* *Carb-v* k* **Carbn-s** carneg-g rwt1• *Caust* k* cench k2 cham bg2 chel b7.de* chin b7.de* choc srj3• *Clem* k* cob k* cob-n sp1 cod a1 coff k* coloc k* colum-p sze2• com k* con k* conch fkr1* corn k* *Crot-h* k* crot-t bg2 cupr-ar k* *Cycl* k* cystein-l rly4• daph k* dig k* dioxi rbp6 *Dros* k* elaps eup-pur k* fago k* ferr k* ferr-ar ferr-i ferr-p fic-m gya1 *Fl-ac* k* flor-p rsj3• *Form* k* gels a1* germ-met srj5• granit-m es1• **Graph** k* grat bg2* ham fd3.de• *Hep* k* hera bro1 hura hydrog srj2• hydroph rsj6• ignis-alc es2• ind k* iod k* ip tl1 irid-met srj5• jug-c k* jug-r k* *Kali-ar* kali-bi k* kali-c k* kali-chl k* kali-i kali-n h2* kali-p *Kali-s* kola stb3• lac-h htj1• lach k* *Laur* k* led b7.de* **Lyc** k* m-arct b7.de mag-c k* mag-m k* manc k* mand rsj7• *Med* melal-alt gya4 menis bro1 meph k* *Merc* k* merc-c k* merc-d a1 *Merc-i-f* k* merc-sul k* **Mez** k* mosch b7.de* mur-ac b4.de* **Nat-m** k* nat-s k2 nicotam rly4• nit-ac k* nux-v k* ol-an a1 olib-sac wmh1 *Olnd* k* paeon k* par k* ped a1 pen a1 *Petr* k* petr-ra shn4• ph-ac k* *Phos* k* pic-ac bg2 pin-con oss2• plan a1 plut-n srj7• podo fd3.de• positr nl2• psor bl puls b7.de* ran-s k* rat k* rhod k* rhus-t k* *Ros-d* wla1 *Ruta* k* *Sabad* k* sarr *Sars* k* sel k* seneg b4.de* *Sep* k* *Sil* k* spig b7.de* spira a1 *Spong* k* *Staph* k* streptoc rly4• stront-c b4.de* stry k* suis-hep rly4• *Sui-ac* k* sul-i k2 **Sulph** k* symph fd3.de• tab k* taosc iwa1• tarax *Tarent* k* *Tell* k* ther a1 thuj k* til k* *Trios* rsj11• tritic-vg fd5.de trom vml3• vanil fd5.de verat k* vichy-g a1 vinc k* wies a1 yuc a1 zinc k* zinc-p k2 zing a1 [spect dfg1]
- **daytime**: hydr k* **Olnd** k*
- **morning**: *Agar* bov k* hipp a1 *Kali-c* kali-p kali-s lyc k* lyss k* mag-c k* meph k* ol-an k* plan k* podo fd3.de• ruta fd4.de seneg k* staph k* *Sulph* k* symph fd3.de• tritic-vg fd5.de vanil fd5.de zinc zing k*
  - **waking**; on: sal-fr sle1•
- **forenoon**: kali-s fd4.de mag-c k* podo fd3.de• sabad vanil fd5.de
  - **11** h: ven-m rsj12•
- **afternoon**: aq-pet a1 fago a1 sep k* tritic-vg fd5.de
  - **14** h: chel
- **evening**: agn aq-pet a1 arg-n calc calc-p k* *Carb-v* chinin-s corian-s knl6• *Cycl* kali-p fd1.de• mag-c k* mez h2* ph-ac h2* podo fd3.de• rhod *Sel* k* sep bg1 staph *Sulph* ther k* tritic-vg fd5.de vanil fd5.de
- **night**: agar k* ars k* aur-s k* *Calc* k* cob k* cupr-ar k* hyper k* kali-p *Mez* nuph a1 **Olnd** k* podo fd3.de• ruta fd4.de taosc iwa1• *Trios* rsj11• vanil fd5.de
  - **midnight**:
    - **after** | **3** - 5 h: kali-p
- **accompanied** by | **pricking**: cycl tl1
- **air**; in open | **amel.**: trios rsj11•
- **biting**: agar agn arg-n a1 *Mez* puls k* rhus-t k* staph k* thuj verat h1* vinc wies a1
- **bleeds**; must scratch until it: alum bov carb-an mur-ac *Sabad*
- **burning**: ars berb *Calc* k* calc-s k2 caps dros *Hep* kali-c k* kola stb3• *Mez* *Ruta* sabad *Sil* spirae a1 vinc

- **cold** agg.; becoming: ars sulph k2
- **cold** applications | **amel.**: trios rsj11•
- **corrosive**: ars h2* caps h1* con h2* ruta h1 sep h2* staph h1*
- **crawling**: *Arg-n* lach led h1* sil k*
- **eating**; after: trios rsj11•
- **eruptions**: clem bro1 *Olnd* bro1 sil bro1 staph bro1 *Sulph* bro1
  - • **without**: ars-i k2 ros-d wla1
- **headache**; after: sep h2*
- **intense** (See violent)
- **internal**: *Carb-v* b4a.de dig b4.de* sabad b7.de* sep bg2 tarax b7.de*
- **lice**; as from: bov bg2 caps bg2 laur bg2 led ptk1 merc bg2 mez bg2 *Olnd* bg2 rhod bg2 ruta bg2 sabad bg2 staph bg2 sulph bg2
- **lying** agg.: mez
- **pain**:
  - • **after**: sep bg1
  - • **during**: sabad bg1
- **painful**: ars
  - • **scratching**; after: petr hr1
- **perspiring**: *Ars* b4a.de nat-sil fd3.de• sabad
- **rubbing**:
  - • **agg.**: staph h1
  - • **amel.**: *Dros* nat-m vanil fd5.de
- **scratching**:
  - • **after** | **not** amel.: bov calc carb-an mur-ac h2* ros-d wla1 ruta fd4.de sars h2*
  - • **agg.**: *Calc Lyc* **Phos** *Sil*
  - • **amel.**: agar k* agn a1 bar-c k* caps k* caust cench k2 mag-c k* mez k* nat-m k* ol-an k* *Olnd* k* ph-ac k* ran-s k* ruta h1 sabad sars k* spong fd4.de thuj vanil fd5.de
  - • **changes** place after scratching: *Cycl Mez* sars staph
  - • **must** scratch: granit-m es1• nat-sil fd3.de• positr nl2• ruta fd4.de tritic-vg fd5.de vanil fd5.de
- **sleep**; on going to: agn
- **sore**: zinc h2*
  - • **scratching** agg.; after: petr h2* sil h2*
- **spots**: nat-sil fd3.de• sil zinc h2*
- **stinging**: caust h2* mez h2* sars h2*
- **stooping** agg.: mang a1
- **sudden**: ph-ac k*
- **undressing** agg.: ars
- **violent**: am-c a1 anac a1 crot-h a1 hera a1 merc-sul a1 nuph a1 rhod a1 sabad a1
- **waking**; on: calc bg2
- **walking** in open air agg.: calc k* *Rhus-t* a1
- **wandering**: bar-c k* mag-c k* mosch k*
- **warm**:
  - • **applications** | **agg.**: trios rsj11•
  - • **bed** | **agg.**: bov *Calc Carb-v* lyc *Mez* psor a *Sil* staph *Sulph*
  - • **exercise**; when warm from: **Lyc** sabad
  - • **head** becomes; when: *Bov* mez sabad *Sanic* staph
- **weather**:
  - • **rainy**: *Mag-c*
  - • **wet** | **agg.**: *Mag-c* k*
- ▽ - **extending** to:
  - ○ • **Abdomen**: trios rsj11•
  - • **Chest**: trios rsj11•
  - • **Shoulders**: trios rsj11•
- ○ - **Bones**: kali-n b4.de*
- **Brain**: ferr bg2 laur b7.de* phos b4.de*
- **Forehead**: agar k* agn b7.de* alum k* alum-p k2 am-m k* ambr k* anac k* androc srj1• ars k* arund a1 aur-m k* bell k* berb k* bov k* canth k* caps k* carb-an k* carb-v k* caust k* cham k* chel k* choc srj3• clem k* con k* croc b7.de* fl-ac k* form a1 gamb k* gels a1 gran k* hura hyper k* jug-r a1 kali-bi kali-p fd1.de• lach k* laur k* led k* lyc k* mag-c k* mag-m b4.de* maias-l hm2• merc k* nat-m k* nux-v b7.de* ol-an k* olib-sac wmh1 olnd k* pall ped a1 petr k* phos k* pneu jl2 podo fd3.de• positr nl2• *Rhus-t* k* rhus-v a1 ruta fd4.de samb k*

Itching – Forehead: ...
sars k* sil k* spig k* spong fd4.de squil k* *Sulph* k* tab k* trios rsj11• tus-p a1 vanil fd5.de verat k* vichy-g a1
  - • **evening**: podo fd3.de• *Sulph* k* zinc k*
  - • **air**; in open | **amel.**: gamb
  - • **burning**: *Kali-bi* spong fd4.de
  - • **corrosive**: con h2* ph-ac h2*
  - • **dinner**; during: hep k* mag-c k* sulph k*
  - • **menses**; itching eruption before: sars
  - • **rubbing** | **amel.**: ol-an k* samb k* tab k*
  - • **scratching** | **amel.**: bov mag-c squil vanil fd5.de
- **Occiput**: *Am-c* k* arge-pl rwt5• ars h2* borx h2* calc k* calc-sil k2 *Chel* k* cinnb k* fago k* flor-p rsj3• iodof a1 kali-c k* kiss a1 lap-la sde8.de• melal-alt gya4 mez k* nat-sil fd3.de• paull a1 sars k* *Sep* **Sil** k* spong fd4.de *Staph* k* **Sulph** k* tell k* thuj k* tritic-vg fd5.de vanil fd5.de
  - • **morning**: *Sulph* k* tritic-vg fd5.de vanil fd5.de
  - • **evening**: sep k* *Staph* stront-c tritic-vg fd5.de
  - • **night**: taosc iwa1•
  - • **scratching**:
    - ⁝ **agg.**: *Staph* k*
    - ⁝ **amel.**: chel k* menth-pu a1 ruta spong fd4.de
  - • **warm** room agg.: fago k* sulph
  - ○ • **Ears** | **Behind**: graph bg1 olnd bg1 rhus-t bg1 sabad bg1 sep bg1 staph bg1 sulph bg1
- **Sides**: pall c1 positr nl2• symph fd3.de• vanil fd5.de
  - • **one** side: dig c1
  - • **right**: mang h2* sars h2*
  - • **left**: sil h2* spig h1* tritic-vg fd5.de
- **Temples**: kali-p k2 trios rsj11• vanil fd5.de
  - • **right**: graph h2 lavand-a ctl1•
- **Vertex**: cystein-l rly4• graph bg2* grat a1 hyper a1 ind a1 manc a1 mez a1 mur-ac a1 olib-sac wmh1 pimp a1 sabad a1 sep h2* tell a1 tritic-vg fd5.de vanil fd5.de verat ptk1 zinc a1 [tax jsj7]
  - • **headache**; during: verat ptk1

JAR agg.: *Acon* b7.de* *Arn* b7.de* *Bell* b4.de* *Bry* b7.de *Chin* b7a.de cic b7.de* glon bg2 *Hep* b4a.de mag-m bg2 manc bg2 *Nit-ac* bg2 nux-v b7.de* ph-ac b4.de* phos bg2 phyt bg2 ruta b7.de* sang bg2 sep bg2 sil bg2 ther ptk1

JARS; old: glon tl1

JERKING of the head: *Agar* k* alum k* am-m b7.de ang b7.de ant-t bro1 ars bro1 *Bell* bro1* *Bry* b7.de* bufo bro1 cann-i bro1 canth b7.de caust k* cham b7.de* *Cic* k* cina *Hell* b7.de *Hyos* k* ign kali-ar vh lam bro1 mygal k* nat-c a1 *Nat-m* nicotam rly4• *Nux-m* k* *Nux-v* b7a.de olib-sac wmh1 op b7.de* phos b4.de plb k2 puls b7.de* rhus-t b7.de *Sep* k* spig b7.de *Stram* k* stry k* sumb tarent k2 verat-v k* zinc bro1
- **daytime**: *Sep*
- **accompanied** by:
  - • **sexual** excitement: verat-v ptk1
  - ○ • **Head**; pain in: stram mrr1
- **backward**: alum atro bov *Cic* cina hyper ign bg1 kali-c h2* merc nux-v sep k* stry verat-v hr1
  - • **and** forwards: ars nux-m sep k* stry
- **behind** forward, from: kali-c *Nux-m* ph-ac sep h2* spong *Stram* stry
- **chill**; during: calc bg2 caust bg2 merc bg2 puls bg2
- **forward**: *Sep* b4a.de
  - • **knees** upward during cough; and: bell h1 ther
- **here** and there: chel stram k* stront-c
- **involuntary**, back and forward: *(↗Motions of - backward; Motions of - involuntary)* sep mtf33
  - • **sitting** agg.: sep
- **lying** on back agg.: *Cic Hyper* k*
  - • **off** the pillow; the head jerks clear: **Stram**
- **right**, to: mygal ptk2 *Nat-s*
- **side** to another; from one: ign a kali-ar vh kali-c nat-s nux-m plb samb
- **sitting** agg.: sep

- **sleep** | **during**:
  - **agg.**: *Arn*
  - **head** jerks backwards: *Hyper*
  - **falling** asleep | **when**: puls h1
- **talking** agg.: *Cic*
- **violent**: *Stram* mrr1
- **walking** quickly or ascending stairs, on: **Bell**

JOY; from excessive: | **agg.**: **Coff** b7.de* cycl b7.de* *Puls* b7.de*

KNEELING: | **amel.**: sang bg2*

KNOCKING head against things: *(↗Pulsating; MIND - Striking - himself - knocking)* apis ars **Bell** k* con hyos kali-p fd1.de• mag-c **Mill** k* nat-sil fd3.de• rhus-t scut a staph sne symph fd3.de• syph a **Tub** st* zinc a
- **bed**; against the●: *Apis* ars a con hyos mill prot a* rhus-t scut a stann a tarent a tub a zinc a
- **wall** in sleep: *(↗Striking - wall)* mag-c

KNOCKING in head: *(↗Pulsating)* am-c k* ang
- **ball** striking skull, like a: plat
- ○ **Brain** against skull, as of●: ars chin k* daph glon hydr-ac laur mez nat-m nux-m rheum stann sul-ac sulph
  - **motion** agg.: nux-m *Rhus-t*
- **Occiput**: thuj bg2

LARGE SIZE: *(↗Enlarged; Expanded; Swollen feeling)* apis bg2 bapt ptk1 bar-c bg2* bell k2* (non:caj a1) **Calc** k ●* *Calc-p* k* coloc bg2 (non:cor-r hr1) graph bl7 hell bg2 hyper ptk1 iod hr1 kali-i bg3* lith-c ptk1 lyc sne* mang ptk1 med jl2* merc k* nux-v ptk1 op bg2 ran-b ptk1 *Sil* k* sulph bg2* *Syph* jl2 tub hr1
- **accompanied** by:
  - ○ **Abdomen**; large: calc ptk1
  - **Body**; emaciation of: sil ptk1
  - **Jaws**; small: kali-i ptk1

LAUGHING agg.: bell bg2 nat-m bg2* phos b4.de* zinc b4.de* zing bg2

LAYING hands on the part: | **amel.**: *Apis* b7a.de *Bell* b4a.de meny b7.de* olnd b7.de* par b7.de* rhus-t b7.de* sabad b7.de *Sil* b4a.de spig b7.de

LAYING head sideways agg.: meny bg2

LEAD poisoning; complaints after: sulph b4a.de*

LEAN on something, desire to: *(↗Hold - up)* *Bell* k* carb-v h2* ferr ptk1 gymno kali-c ptk1 *Merc* ptk1 nux-v ptk1 sabad ptk1 spig ptk1 tritic-vg fd5.de

LEANING:
- **head**:
  - **against** something:
    - **agg.**: cann-s b7.de* nux-v bg2
    - **amel.**: bell b4.de* cann-s b7a.de kali-bi bg2 kali-c b4a.de merc b4.de* nat-m b4a.de puls b7a.de rhod b4.de* sabad b7.de* sabin b7.de* seneg b4.de* spig b7.de* sulph b4a.de
  - **side**; to one | **agg.**: cina ptk1 meny b7.de*
  - **table** amel.; on: ign ptk1 sabad ptk1

LEMONADE agg.: sel b7.de*

LICE: *(↗HEAD; MALE GENITALIA/SEX - Crab; SKIN - Lousiness)* am-c apis ars k* bac k* bell-p k* *Carb-ac* k* cocc c1 graph k* lach k* *Lyc* k* m-ambo b7.de *Merc* k* nit-ac olnd k* *Psor* k* sabad b7.de* saroth sp1 **Staph** b7.de* sulph k* tub vinc

LIFTING things agg.: arn bg2 bry bg2 *Calc* bg2 mur-ac bg2 nat-c bg2 nit-ac b4a.de ph-ac bg2 **Rhus-t** bg2 *Sil* bg2

LIFTING up; sensation of: allox tpw3
- ○ **Bones**: bell rb2
- **Brain**: acon b7.de* m-ambo b7.de thuj a1*
- **External** head: hydr bg2
- **Skull**: cann-i cimic c1 glon k2 *Lac-d* k* puls rb2 syph jl2
- **Vertex**: dios hr1* eup-pur a1* lac-ac a1* lac-d hr1* passi c1* til ban1•

LIGHT; from:
- **agg.**: acon bg2 agar bg2 *Apis* b7a.de ars bg2 *Asar* b7a.de **Bell** b4a.de* *Bry* b7a.de cact bg2 chel bg2 croc b7.de* euphr b7a.de glon bg2 *Nat-m* bg2 nux-v b7a.de* phos bg2 sep bg2 sil bg2
- **candlelight** | **agg.**: croc bg2 manc bg2 nat-c bg2
- **daylight** | **agg.**: sang bg2 sep b4a.de* sil bg2
- **fire**; of the: *Bry* b7a.de
- **sunlight**:
  - **agg.**: ant-c b7.de* brom bg2 *Bry* b7a.de camph b7.de* *Euphr* b7a.de ign b7.de* *Lach* b7a.de nux-v b7.de* *Sel* b7.de* *Valer* b7a.de
  - **amel.**: stram b7.de*

LIGHTNESS; sensation of: *(↗VERTIGO - Vertigo)* abies-c bro1 atp rly4• beryl tpw5 chir-fl gya2 coff bg fic-m gya1 helo-s bnm14• hippoc-k szs2 hyos bro1 *Jug-c* bro1 maias-l hrn2• manc bro1 myos-a rly4• nat-ar bro1 nat-hchls bro1 olib-sac wmh1 orot-ac rly4• ozone sde2• plut-n srj7• ribo rly4• stram b7.de* streptoc rly4• [neroin sdj2 tax jsj7]
- **air**; as from lack of: ozone sde2•
- **contents** had greatly diminished in weight; as if the whole: chir-fl gya2 mom-b c1
- **float** off; as if it would: plut-n srj7• stict bg2
- **lying** down | **amel.**: helo-s bnm14•
- **nausea**; after: lyss c1
- **vertigo**; during: op ptk1
- ○ **External** head: coff b7.de*
- **Forehead**: melal-alt gya4
- **Occiput**, in: sec

LIQUID; sensation of (See Water)

LOOKING:
- **concentrated**, focused:
  - **agg.**: cina bg2 mur-ac b4.de* par b7.de* puls b7.de* sabad b7.de* spong b7.de*
    - **External** head: cic b7a.de
    - **Occiput**: mur-ac ptk1
  - **amel.**: agn b7.de* sabad bg2
- **down** | **agg.**: dios bg2 phyt bg2
- **sideways**:
  - **agg.**: acon bg2 dig bg2 merc-c bg2 sil bg2
  - **amel.**: olnd bg2
- **upward** | **amel.**: thuj b4a.de*

LOOSENESS of brain, sensation of: *(↗Balancing - Brain; Falling - Brain - forward; Falling - Brain - side; Motions in; Shaking sensation; Shaking the head)* acon k* aloe bg2 am-c k* ambr ptk1* *Ars* k* asar bg2 *Bar-c* k* bar-m bar-s k2 bell k* bry b7a.de* calc-sil k2 carb-ac rb2 *Carb-an* k* caust k* **Chin** k* chinin-ar k2 cic k* cocc k* coff b7.de* con k* croc k* crot-h bg2 cycl rb2 dig k* elaps fl-ac bg2 genist germ-met srj5• glon k* graph k* guaj k* *Hep* *Hyos* k* hyper ptk1 *Kali-c* k* kali-m k2* kali-n k* kali-s kalm lac-f bg1 lach lact lact-v hr1 laur k* lavand-a ctl1• *Lyc* k* lyss c1 mag-c bg2 mag-s mang b4a.de mez bg2 mosch b7a.de mur-ac k* nad rly4• naja bg2 *Nat-m* k* nat-s k* nicc *Nux-m* k* nux-v k* parth rb2 phos bg2* phys plat b4.de* rheum b7.de* rhod b4a.de **Rhus-t** k* rob rumx bg2* sal-fr sle1• sep k* sil b4a.de sol-ni k* **Spig** k* stann k* staph k* sul-ac k* sulph b4.de* tab bg2 tell thlas rb2 tub bg* verat k* visc sp1 xan
- **morning**: cic guaj
  - **waking**; on: cic
- **ascending** stairs agg.: lyc
- **carrying** a weight, while: mur-ac
- **cough** agg.; during: acon bry carb-an sep sul-ac
- **diagonally** across top, when turning: kalm
- **fall**:
  - ○ **Side** on which he leans; feels as if brain falls to: am-c ambr ptk1* nat-s k2 phys ptk1 sul-ac k2
  - **Side** to side; and would fall from: bar-c k2* sul-ac rb2
- **motion** agg.: am-c ars k* carb-an *Caust* croc mag-s parth vml3• tell
- **rising** from stooping agg.: phos
- **rolling** from side to side: tub rb2
- **shaking** the head agg.; on: ars bar-c con glon nat-m *Nux-m* **Rhus-t** k* stann sul-ac xan
- **sitting** quietly amel.: sul-ac ptk1

- **stepping** agg.: ars k2 bar-c guaj led lyc **Rhus-t** sep **Spig** stann sul-ac
- **stool** agg.; straining at: spig
- **stooping** agg.: bry dig a kali-c laur nat-s k*
- **striking** the sides of the skull; as if: chin mrr1
- **thinking** of pain intensely amel.: cic c1
- **turning** head agg.: kali-c kalm **Spig**
- **waking**; on: cic
- **walking**:
  - **agg.**: acon bar-c carb-an cic c1* cob croc cycl ptk1 guaj led lyc mag-s nux-m nux-v *Rhus-t* sep **Spig** staph sul-ac verat
  - **air** agg.; in open: caust sul-ac
- **weather**; in hot: *Nux-v*

○ - **Forehead**: alum b4.de* bell a* bry b7a.de* caust b4.de* chel k* con k* dig b4a.de glon bg2 laur k* merc bg2 naja al nat-m rhus-t a* spig a *Sul-ac* k* sulph a
- **Occiput**: pic-ac bg2 staph k* thuj bg2
- **Scalp**: *Nat-m* bg2 sang bg2* sep bg2 sulph bg2
- **Temples**: sul-ac
  - **stooping** feels as if brain fell toward left; when: nat-s
- **Vertex**: carb-an bg2 elaps bg2 kalm bg2 rhod bg2 thuj bg2

LUMP; sensation as from a: *(↗Ball; Foreign - brain - right)* ant-t k* aran bg arg-n bg2 arn k* ars bg2 bamb-a stb2.de• caust bg2 cham chel k* cina bg2 *Con* k* cypra-eg sde6.de• fl-ac bg2 merc bg2 phos bg2 phys bg2 pieri-b mlk9.de rhod bg2 *Staph* k* [bell-p-sp dcm1]

○ - **Brain**: *Con* b4a.de
  - **right**: con ptk1
- **Forehead**: bamb-a stb2.de• carb-ac bg2 caust bg2 cham cob-n sp1 kali-bi ptk1 kreos ptk1 pip-m staph k*
  - **falling** forward in forehead on motion: cham rb2

○ - **Eyes**; above | **pressing** on eyes: bamb-a stb2.de•
- **Occiput**: arg-met bg2 con bg2
- **Vertex**:
  - **cold** agg.: *Verat* ptk1
    - **ice**: verat tl1

LUPUS: calc lyc

LYING:
- **after** | **agg.**: calad b7.de* caps b7.de* sel b7.de*
- **agg.**: agar b4.de* am-c b4.de* ambr b7.de* anac b4.de* aur b4.de* bar-c b4.de* **Bell** b4.de* bov b4.de* bry b7.de* calc b4.de* calc-p bg2 camph b7a.de* carb-v b4.de* *Caust* b4a.de *Cham* b7.de* chin bg2 clem b4.de* cocc bg2 coloc b4.de* dulc b4.de* euphr b7.de* glon bg2 hep b4.de* kali-bi bg2 kali-c b4.de* led bg2 lyc b4.de* m-aust b7.de mag-c b4.de* mag-m b4.de* mang b4.de* merc b4.de* merc-i-r bg2 mez b4.de* mur-ac bg2 nit-ac b4.de* nux-m bg2 nux-v b7.de* petr b4.de* ph-ac b4.de* phos bg2 plat b4.de* *Puls* b7.de* ran-b b7.de* rhod b4.de* *Rhus-t* b7.de* sep b4.de* spig b7.de* spong b7.de* stann b4.de* stront-c b4.de* sulph bg2 ther ptk1 *Thuj* b4a.de zinc bg2

○ - **Occiput**: bry ptk1 cact ptk1 carb-v ptk1 **Cocc** ptk1 kali-p ptk1 nux-v ptk1 **Petr** ptk1 phos ptk1 *Sep* ptk1 spig ptk1
  - **Vertex**: manc ptk1
- **amel.**: alum b4.de* ambr b7.de* anac b4.de* arn b7.de* asar b7.de* bell b4.de* *Bry* b7.de* cact bg2 calc b4.de* canth b7.de* *Carb-v* b4a.de chin b7.de* chlor bg2 *Coloc* b4a.de **Con** b4.de* cupr b7.de* dig b4.de* dulc b4.de* eup-per bg2 ferr bg2 ham bg2 hell b7a.de* ign b7.de* kali-c b4.de* lach b7a.de* *Lyc* b4.de* mag-c b4.de* mag-m bg2 mag-p bg2 *Merc* b4a.de mur-ac bg2 nat-c b4.de* **Nat-m** b4.de* nit-ac b4.de* **Nux-v** b7.de* olnd b7.de* petr b4.de* ph-ac b4.de* phos b4.de* psor bg2 puls bg2 rhus-t bg2 sabad b7.de* sang bg2* *Sel* bg2* sep b4.de* sil bg2 spig b7.de* sulph b4.de* thuj b4a.de zinc b4.de*
- **arms** over head amel.; with: *Brom* b4a.de
- **back**; on:
  - **agg.**: agar bg2 bry b7.de* cocc bg2 coloc b4a.de* *Cycl* b7a.de gels bg2 *Nux-v* b7.de* sep bg2 spig b7.de* verat b7a.de*
  - **amel.**: *Bry* b7.de* *Ign* b7.de* nux-v b7.de* par b7.de* puls b7.de* verat b7.de*
- **bed**; in | **agg.**: bry b7a.de *Cham* b7.de* cycl b7.de* ferr b7.de* hell b7.de* laur b7.de* m-arct b7.de mosch b7.de* *Nux-v* b7.de* *Puls* b7.de* ran-b b7.de* rheum b7a.de **Rhus-t** b7.de* ruta b7a.de *Squil* b7a.de staph b7a.de
- **dark** room; in a | **agg.**: onos ptk1
- **hard**; as if on something: *Manc* ph-ac k*

Lying: ...
- **head** high; with the | **amel.**: ars bg2 caps b7.de* gels bg2 nat-m bg2 puls b7.de* spig b7.de* spong bg2
- **head** low; with the:
  - **agg.**: aml-ns bg2 *Bell* bg2 m-aust b7.de puls ptk1 sang ptk1 spig b7.de* stront-c b4.de*
  - **amel.**: arn b7.de* *Bry* ptk1 phys ptk1 spong b7.de* tab bg2 verat-v ptk1
- **head**; on:
  - **agg.** | **External** head: aur b4a.de *Nit-ac* b4a.de rhus-t b7.de* thuj b4.de*
- **low**; as if from lying too: phos
- **occiput**; on:
  - **agg.**: bry ptk1 bufo bg2* cact bg2* carb-v bg2 cocc bg2* eup-per bg2 glon ptk1 graph bg2 kali-p ptk1 nat-m bg2 onos ptk1 petr bg2* phos ptk1 pic-ac bg2 sep bg2* spig ptk1 verat bg2
    - **External** head: nat-m bg2
  - **amel.**: kali-p ptk1 ph-ac ptk1
- **side**; on:
  - **side** lain on: calad bg2 calc bg2 carb-v bg2 *Graph* b4a.de mag-c b4a.de* mag-m bg2 ph-ac b4a.de* sep bg2 stann bg2 thuj b4a.de
  - **side** not lain on: calad b7.de graph bg2
  - **agg.**: *Calad* b7a.de *Ign* b7.de* nux-v b7.de*
  - **painful** side:
    - **agg.**: *Nux-v* b7.de* *Spong* b7.de* zinc bg2
    - **amel.**: arn b7.de* chel bg2 graph bg2 *Ign* b7.de* nux-v b7.de* *Puls* b7.de*
  - **painless** side:
    - **agg.**: bry b7.de* calad b7a.de chel bg2 *Cycl* b7a.de *Ign* b7.de* nux-v b7.de* puls b7.de*
    - **amel.**: ign b7.de* m-aust b7.de *Nux-v* b7.de*
  - **right**:
    - **agg.**: brom bg2 lil-t bg2 *Mag-m* bg2 nux-v bg2 phos bg2* staph bg2
    - **amel.**: brom b4a.de*
- **uncomfortable** position; as if in an: agar bg2 cimx clem lyc k* ph-ac bg2

LYING DOWN:
- **after**:
  - **agg.**: arg-met b7.de* camph b7.de* canth b7.de* *Ign* b7.de* lyc b4a.de m-aust b7.de mag-m b4a.de nux-v b7.de* podo bg2 **Puls** b7.de* *Rhus-t* b7.de* sabad b7.de* *Sep* b4a.de teucr b7.de* zinc b4a.de
  - **amel.**: *Am-m* b7.de* ferr bg2 glon bg2 kali-bi bg2 nit-ac b4a.de **Nux-v** b7.de* olnd b7.de* rhus-t b7.de* spig b7.de*

MARBLE, brain feels as if changed to: *(↗Foreign - brain - right)* cann-i k* cann-xyz ptk1

MEMORY:
- **exertion** of | **agg.**: m-ambo b7.de

MENINGITIS (See Inflammation - meninges)

MENOPAUSE; during: aml-ns bg2 cact bg2 chin bg2 cimic bg2 ferr bg2 glon bg2 ign bg2 lach bg2 ph-ac bg2 sang bg2 sep bg2 spig bg2 stront-c bg2 sulph bg2

MENSES:
- **absent** agg.: cimic bg2 dulc bg2 glon bg2 lach bg2 zinc bg2
- **after**:
  - **agg.**: agar bg2 alum bg2 asar bg2 *Berb* bg2 calc bg2 calc-p bg2 carb-ac bg2 carb-an bg2 chin bg2 chinin-s bg2 ferr bg2 glon bg2* kali-bi bg2 kali-br bg2 kali-p ptk1 lach bg2 lil-t ptk1 lith-c bg2 *Lyc* bg2 mag-c bg2 med bg2 **Nat-m** b4.de* nat-p bg2 plat bg2 puls bg2 *Sep* bg2 thuj bg2 verat-v bg2
    - **copious**: glon ptk1
- **agg.** | **Vertex**: ferr-p ptk1
- **before**:
  - **agg.**: acon bg2 alum bg2 am-c bg2 apis bg2 ars bg2 asar bg2 bell bg2 borx bg2 bov bg2 brom bg2 bry bg2 bufo bg2 cact bg2 *Calc* bg2 calc-p bg2 cann-xyz bg2 carb-an b4a.de* *Carb-v* b4.de* caust bg2 chin bg2 cimic bg2 cinnb bg2 cupr b7.de* *Cycl* bg2 ferr b7.de* ferr-p bg2 gels bg2 glon bg2* *Graph* bg2 ham bg2 hep bg2 hydr bg2 hyper bg2 ign bg2 iod bg2 ip bg2 kali-br bg2 kali-i bg2 kali-p ptk1 *Kreos* bg2 lac-c bg2 laur bg2 lil-t bg2* lyc bg2 mag-c bg2 mag-p bg2 merc bg2 merc-c bg2 nat-c bg2 **Nat-m** b4.de*

Head

- **before** – **agg.**: ...
  nit-ac bg2 nux-m b7.de* ol-an bg2 petr bg2 plat bg2 sang bg2 sars bg2 sep bg2 sil b4.de* stann bg2 *Sulph* b4.de* thuj bg2 verat b7.de* verat-v bg2
  ⁝ **Scalp**: *Sulph* bg2
  ⁝ **Temples**: cham bg2 **Lach** bg2
- **during**:
  - **agg.**: acon bg2 agar bg2 agn bg2 aloe bg2 alum bg2 am-c b4.de* am-m b7.de* aml-ns bg2 apis bg2 arg-n bg2 arn bg2 ars bg2 aur bg2 **Bell** bg2 berb bg2 borx bg2 bov bg2 brom bg2 *Bry* b7.de* bufo bg2 cact bg2 **Calc** b4.de* calc-p bg2 cann-xyz bg2 carb-ac bg2 carb-an b4.de* carb-v b4.de* castm bg2 caul bg2 caust bg2 cham bg2 chel bg2 chin bg2 cic bg2 *Cimic* bg2 cinnb bg2 coc-c bg2 cocc bg2 con bg2 croc b7a.de* crot-t bg2 cupr bg2 cycl bg2 dulc bg2 elaps bg2 ferr bg2 ferr-p bg2 *Gels* bg2 *Glon* bg2* *Graph* b4.de* hydr bg2 hyos b7.de* hyper bg2 ign bg2 iod bg2 kali-bi bg2 kali-c b4.de* kali-i bg2 kali-n bg2 kali-p bg2* *Kreos* bg2 lac-c bg2 lac-d ptk1 **Lach** bg2 laur b7.de* *Lyc* b4.de* *Mag-c* b4.de* mag-m b4.de* mang bg2 med bg2 meli bg2 merc bg2 merc-c bg2 mosch bg2 murx bg2 nat-c b4.de* **Nat-m** b4.de* nat-s bg2 nit-ac bg2 nux-m bg2 **Nux-v** b7.de* ol-an bg2 *Phos* b4.de* plat bg2 **Puls** bg2 rat bg2 rhod b4.de* sabin bg2 **Sang** bg2 sars bg2 *Sep* b4.de* sil bg2 spig b7a.de* stann bg2 **Sulph** bg2 ter bg2 ust bg2 *Verat* b7.de* verat-v bg2 vib bg2 zinc bg2
    ⁝ **Temples**: lyc ptk1
  - **amel.**: verat bg2
  - **beginning** of menses:
    ⁝ **agg.**: brom bg2 bufo bg2 ferr-p bg2 graph bg2 *Hyos* b7.de* kali-p bg2 plat bg2 puls bg2 rhod bg2
    ⁝ **amel.**: alum bg2 bell bg2 kali-p bg2 lil-t bg2
- **suppressed** menses; from: *Apis* b7a.de lith-c ptk1 naja ptk1 psor ptk1

MENTAL EXERTION:
- **agg.**: agn b7.de am-c b4.de ambr b7.de anac b4.de* apis b7a.de arg-met b7.de arg-n bg2 arn b7.de ars-i ptk1 asar b7.de* aur b4a.de* *Bell* b4a.de borx b4a.de *Calc* b4.de* calc-p bg2 cham b7.de *Chin* b7.de* cimic ptk1 cina b7.de* cocc b7.de *Coff* b7.de* colch b7.de* cupr bg2 **Dig** b4.de* glon bg2* graph bg2 hell b7.de ign b7.de* *Iris* ptk1 *Kali-br* ptk1 kali-p ptk1 **Lach** bg2 lyc b4.de* *M-aust* b7.de* mag-c b4.de* mag-p bg2 nat-c b4.de* nat-m b4.de* nat-p ptk1 nicc bg2 **Nux-v** b7.de* olnd b7.de *Par* b7.de* petr b4.de* ph-ac b4a.de* phos b4.de* pic-ac bg2* puls b7.de* sabad b7.de* sel b7.de sep b4.de* *Sil* b4.de* **Sulph** b4a.de* zinc bg2*

  ○ • **Occiput**: visc bg2
- **amel.**: calc b4a.de

MERCURY agg.; abuse of: puls b7a.de
○ - **External** head: *Carb-v* b4a.de *Hep* b4a.de

MICROCEPHALY: syph mtf tub mtf

MIGRAINE (See Pain)

MILK:
- **agg.**: brom b4a.de* bry bg2 lac-d ptk1 verat bg2
- **amel.**: bry bg2* verat bg2*

MOISTURE: | **itching**: sars bg2

MOTION:
- **agg.**: alum ptk1 *Bell* ptk1 camph ptk1 cic ptk1 cina ptk1 *Cupr* ptk1 hyos ptk1 ign ptk1 sep ptk1 spong ptk1 stram ptk1 verat-v ptk1
- **arms**; of | **agg.**: caust bg2 ferr bg2 nat-s bg2 rhus-t b7.de* spong b7.de*
- **body**; of:
  - **after** | **agg.**: dros b7.de* puls b7.de*
  - **agg.**: acon b7.de* *Agn* b7.de* am-c b4a.de ambr b7.de* anac b4.de* ant-t b7.de* apis b7a.de **Arn** b7.de* aur b4.de* *Bell* b4.de* bism b7.de* bov b4.de* *Brom* b4a.de **Bry** b7.de* calc b4a.de* camph b7.de* canth b7.de* **Caps** b7a.de carb-an b4.de* carb-v b4.de* caust b4.de* **Chin** b7.de* coloc b4.de* croc b7a.de cupr b7.de* *Dulc* b4.de* eup-per bg2 ferr-p bg2 hep b4.de* ign b7.de* iod b4.de* kali-bi bg2 *Kali-c* b4a.de kali-n b4.de* *Kreos* b7a.de lach b7a.de laur b7.de* led b7.de* lyc b4.de* mag-c b4.de* mag-m b4.de* mang b4.de* merc b4.de* *Mez* b4.de* mosch b7.de* nat-c b4.de* *Nat-m* b4.de* *Nux-m* b7a.de **Nux-v** b7.de* petr b4.de* ph-ac b4.de* phos b4.de* pic-ac bg2 plat b4.de* rheum b7.de* rhod b4.de* sabad b7.de* samb b7.de* sang bg2 sars b4.de* sep b4.de* sil b4.de* *Spig* b7.de* spong b7.de* stann b4.de* **Staph** b7.de* sul-ac bg2 *Sulph* b4.de* thuj b4.de* verat b7.de*

Motion – **body**; of – **agg.**: ...
  ⁝ **External** head: bry b7.de* calc b4.de* cupr b7a.de dig b4.de* hell b7.de* hyos b7.de* m-ambo b7.de nux-v b7.de* sars b4a.de spig b7.de* spong b7.de*
  - **amel.**: alum b4.de* am-m b7.de* calc b4.de* caps b7.de* cham b7.de* cina b7.de* coloc b4.de* cycl b7.de* dros b7.de* hyos bg2 kali-c b4.de* *Lach* b7a.de lyc b4.de* mag-c b4.de* mag-m bg2 *Meny* b7.de* mosch b7.de* mur-ac bg2 nat-c b4.de* petr b4.de* phos b4.de* *Puls* b7.de* rhod b4.de* *Rhus-t* b7.de* ruta b7.de* seneg b4.de* spong b7a.de sulph b4.de* valer b7.de* verb b7.de*
- **eyelids**; of | **agg.**: coloc b4a.de*
- **eyes**; of:
  - **agg.**: acon b7.de* agn b7.de* apis bg2 arn b7.de* bell b4.de* *Bry* b7.de* calc bg2 *Caps* b7.de* *Chin* b7.de* chinin-s bg2 coloc b4.de* con b4.de* cupr b7a.de* dig b4.de* dros b7.de* gels bg2 hep b4.de* lyc bg2 *M-arct* b7.de* mur-ac b4.de* nat-m ptk1 *Nux-v* b7.de* op b7a.de* pic-ac bg2 ptel bg2 *Puls* b7.de* rhus-t b7.de* sep b4.de* *Sil* b4a.de *Spig* b7.de* staph bg2 sulph b4.de* thuj b4a.de *Valer* b7.de* verat bg2 viol-o bg2
    ⁝ **affected** side; toward: con bg2
- **face** agg.; of muscles of: spig b7.de*
- **head**; of:
  - **agg.**: acon b7.de* am-c b4.de* arn b7.de* bar-c b4.de* bell b4.de* *Bry* b7a.de calc bg2 cann-s b7.de* canth b7.de* *Caps* b7.de* **Chin** b7.de* *Cimic* bg2 cocc b7.de* colch bg2 *Con* bg2 cupr b7.de* euph b4.de* graph b4a.de* ip b7.de* kali-c b4.de* lach bg2 lyc b4a.de merc bg2 mez b4.de* mosch b7.de* nat-c b4a.de *Nat-m* b4a.de ph-ac b4a.de plat b4.de* *Puls* b7a.de rhod b4.de* *Rhus-t* bg2 samb b7.de* sars bg2 sep b4.de* *Spig* b7.de staph b7.de* sulph b4.de* thuj b4a.de verat b7.de* viol-o b7.de*
    ⁝ **sudden**: *Spig* bg2
  - **amel.**: agar bg2 chin b7a.de cina b7.de* sulph bg2
- **limbs**; of | **amel.**: *Ars* b4a.de *Bell* b4a.de
- **upper** body; of | **amel.**: *Bell* b4a.de

MOTIONS in head: *(↗Boiling; Bubbling; Gurgling; Looseness; Shaking sensation; Shaking the head; Surging; Swashing; Waving; MIND - Gestures)* *Acon* k* adam skp7• agar k2 aloe alum am-c k* anan k* ang k* ant-t k* arg-n a1 *Ars* k* bamb-a stb2.de• *Bar-c* bar-m bar-s k2 **Bell** k* *Bry* k* calc k* camph bg3 carb-an carbn-s caust **Chin** k* chinin-ar cic cina bg3 cob cocc con croc k* *Crot-c* crot-h *Cupr* bg3 cycl k* dig k* elaps eug **Glon** graph guaj k* *Hep* *Hyos* ign bg3 indg *Kali-c* k* kali-m k2 kali-n kali-p kali-s kali-sil k2 kalm lach lact *Laur* k* *Lyc* mag-s mez mosch k* mur-ac nat-m nat-s nicc *Nux-m* k* *Nux-v* phel phos plat rheum k* *Rhus-t* **Sep** k* *Sil* k* sol-ni spig k* spong bg3 stann staph stram bg3 stront-c k* sul-ac *Sulph* k* tab tell verat xan xanth
- **morning**: cic grat guaj hyos indg lact nat-s spig tab
  - **rising** agg.: bamb-a stb2.de• bar-c
  - **waking**; on: cic
- **afternoon**: graph mag-m mez nat-m sulph
  - **amel.**: bar-c
- **evening**: eug mag-m nat-m plat stront-c sulph
- **night**: anan hyper puls
  - **waking**; on: par
- **air**; in open:
  - **agg.**: laur
  - **amel.**: indg mag-m
- **ascending** into head; as if something was: acon ptk1 **Bell** ptk1 bry ptk1 *Calc* ptk1 canth ptk1 chel ptk1 chin ptk1 cimic ptk1 gamb ptk1 gels bg2* *Glon* ptk1 iod bg2 kalm ptk1 mang ptk1 *Meny* ptk1 merc ptk1 nat-m ptk1 phos ptk1 **Sang** ptk1 sep ptk1 **Sil** ptk1 **Spig** ptk1
  - **right**: aloe ptk1 *Bell* ptk1 gels ptk1 ign ptk1 meny ptk1 nat-m ptk1 nux-v ptk1 phos ptk1 **Sang** ptk1
  - **left**: arg-n ptk1 chel ptk1 cimic ptk1 colch ptk1 lac-c ptk1 lil-t ptk1 par ptk1 petr ptk1 sabin ptk1 sil ptk1 **Spig** ptk1
- **ascending** stairs, while: bell crot-h lyc nat-m par
- **bending**:
  - **head**:
    ⁝ **agg.**: asar dig hyos ptk1
    ⁝ **amel.**: spig
- **carrying** a weight: lyc

- **constant**: tarent k2
- **cough** agg.; during: acon *Bry* carb-an lact mag-s sep sul-ac
- **drawing** load, while: mur-ac
- **drinking** agg.: acon bry
- **eating**:
  - **after**:
    - **agg**.: alum mag-s
    - **amel**.: aloe
- **leaning** agg.: *Cycl* k*
- **lying** on right side agg.: anan
- **menses**; during: mag-m
- **motion**:
  - **agg**.: acon *Ars* bry calc carb-an *Caust* cic cob croc led lyc mag-c mag-s mang nat-m nux-m nux-v sal-fr sle1• spig staph *Sulph* tab tell
  - **amel**.: lach petr staph
- **motion** of the head; from: am-c *Ars* bar-c calc chinin-ar k* cocc con croc glon kali-c kali-s lach lact mang mez nat-m *Nux-m Rhus-t* sep sol-ni spig squil stann sul-ac *Sulph* thuj xan
- **moved** from back of neck up to head; as if something: glon
- **nodding** the head, on: *Agar* ptk1 aur-s k2 chin ptk1 hyos ptk1 hyper ptk1 ign ptk1 nat-m ptk1 sep ptk1 stram ptk1 *Sulph* verat-v ptk1
- **pressure** | **amel**.: bell
- **rising** up, when: cham indg lyc phos
  - **amel**.: alum laur mill
- **room** agg.: indg mag-m
- **shaking** the head agg.; on: sep h2
- **sitting**:
  - **agg**.: grat sil
  - **amel**.: spig
- **standing** agg.: cycl h1 mang
- **step**, making a: bar-c guaj led lyc **Rhus-t** sep *Sil Spig* thuj
- **stool** agg.; during: spig
  - **jerking** in head: phos bg2
- **stooping** agg.: alum am-c ant-t berb bry carb-an coff dig hydr-ac kali-c laur mag-s mill nat-s nux-v rheum rhus-t
- **stumbling**, from: bar-c led sep sil thuj
- **talking** agg.: acon cocc zinc
- **thinking** about it amel.: cic
- **turning** head agg.: cham *Glon* kali-c kalm spig
  - **suddenly**: nat-ar
- **twisting** in head: kali-c ptk1 mur-ac ptk1 til ptk1
- **waking**; on: cic par phos
- **walking**:
  - **agg**.: acon bar-c bell carb-an cic cob cocc crot-h guaj hyos indg led lyc mag-c mag-s nuph nux-m nux-v rhod *Rhus-t* sep *Sil Spig* staph *Sulph* verat verb viol-t
  - **air** agg.; in open: aloe caust plat *Rhus-t* sul-ac
- **warm** room agg.: lact
- **worm** (See Formication)

▽ - **extending** to | **Eye**: bamb-a stb2.de•

○ - **Brain** | **parts** were changing places; as if: mag-p br1*

- **Forehead** | **morning**: bamb-a stb2.de•

MOTIONS of head: *(↗MIND - Gestures; MIND - Striking - himself - knocking)* agar b2.de* agn b2.de* aloe *Alum* b2.de* am-m b2.de* ang b2.de* ant-t b2.de* arg-met b2.de* arn bg2 ars asar b2.de* aur k* aur-m bell k* benz-ac bry k* bufo *Calc-p Camph* b2.de* cann-i canth b2.de* caust k* cham b2.de* chin b2.de* *Cic* k* *Cina* b2.de* cocc b2.de* colch b2.de* crot-h **Cupr** b2.de* dig b2.de* ferr b2.de* hell b2.de* hep b2.de* *Hyos* b2.de* *Ign* b2.de* kali-c b2.de* kreos b2.de* lach b2.de* *Lyc* b2.de* m-arct b2.de merc b2.de* mez nat-m b2.de* nux-m k* nux-v b2.de* olnd b2.de* op b2.de* par b2.de* phos b2.de* puls b2.de* rheum b2.de* rhus-t b2.de* sec k* sep k* spig b2.de* *Spong* b2.de* staph b2.de* stram k* tarax b2.de* tarent verat b2.de* viol-o b2.de* viol-t b2.de* zinc vh

- **backward** and forward: *(↗Jerking - involuntary)* agar ars bg2 aur caust mtf33 *Cham Cina* lam lyc *Nux-m Ph-ac* sep *Verat-v*
  - **headache**, with: *Lam* br1
- **constant**: *Agar* bro1 ant-t bro1 ars k* arum-t vh *Bell* bro1 cann-i bro1 cham bro1 cocc *Hyos* bro1 lam bro1 mygal bro1 nux-m bro1 op k* *Stram* bro1 stry bro1 verat-v bro1 zinc bro1

Motions of head – **constant**: ...

  - **to** left side: cocc bg2*
- **convulsive**: **Agar** k* ant-c bg2 ars bg2 bell bg2 *Calc Camph* k* *Caust* k* cham bg2 chin bg2 cic bg2 *Cocc* k* *Cupr* k* hell bg2 *Ign* bg2 **Ip** bg2 kali-c bg2 lach bg2 laur bg2 lyc bg2* *Nux-m* k* *Nux-v* bg2 op bg2 *Sep* bg2 sil bg2 spig bg2 s t r a m k* tarent
  - **hiccough**, after: bell h1
  - **right** side; to: *Stram* bg2
  - **talking** and swallowing are impossible; so that: nux-m k*
- **difficult**: colch galla-q-r nl2• hipp kali-i kola stb3• stann
- **forward**: cic bg1* cupr bg2 merc nat-m nux-m bg2* sars bg2 sep stry
- **hither** and thither: agar bg2 ars *Colch* b7a.de cupr b7a.de hyos b7a.de* kali-i bg2 lyc bg2 nit-ac h2 *Nux-m* b7a.de op phos bg2 *Stram* k*
- **impossible**: sphing k* tarent zinc
- **involuntary**: *(↗Jerking - involuntary; MIND - Gestures)* agar alum k* apoc bro1 aur b4a.de bell b4a.de bry bro1 cann-i c1* caust hell k* kali-c b4a.de lyc k* merc nat-m *Sep* b4a.de zinc k*

- **jerking** (See Jerking; Shocks)
- **nodding** of: *(↗wagging)* aur-m aur-s k* bell bg2 calc caust k* cham ign b7a.de* kali-bi lyc k* *Mosch Nat-m* k* ph-ac k* *Sep* bg2* stram bg2* verat bg2 *Verat-v*
  - **agg**.: sulph b4a.de
  - **amel**.: *Chin* bg2
  - **children**; in: nat-m mtf33
  - **speaking**, while: aur-s zr
  - **writing**, while: *Caust* k* ph-ac
  - **yes** or no: *Puls* vh
- **pains**, moves head to relieve: agar dgt1 chin *Kali-i* sec
- **pendulum**-like: cann-i sec
- **recurrent**: cic bg2 kali-c bg2 sep bg2
- **rising** from the pillow, spasmodic: bell stram k*
- **rolling** head: *(↗turning)* *Agar* k* *Apis* k* apoc k2 *Arn* ars **BELL** k •* *Bry* cadm-s a caust k* *Cic Cina* k* clem colch cor-r *Crot-t Cupr* k* cypr a dig ferr-p bg2 gal-ac zr gels k2 *Hell* k* *Hyos* k* ign lp kali-br kali-i lac-c bg2 *Lyc* k* *Med* k* *Merc* k* naja *Nux-m* k* oena *Op* k* ph-ac phos k* *Podo* k* pyrog k* sec *Sil* spong **Stram** k •* **Sulph** k • **Tarent** k •* **TUB** k •* verat verat-v k* zinc k*
  - **day** and night, with moaning•: *Hell Lyc* k*
  - **accompanied** by | **Teeth**; grinding of: zinc ptk1
  - **amel**.: cina bg2
  - **bending** forward agg.: hyos ptk1
  - **brain** affections; in: agar mtf33
  - **business**; from cares of: podo ptk1
  - **concussion** of brain; from: hyos ptk1
  - **fever**; during: agar mtf33
  - **headache** | **during**: gels k2 med hr1 zinc vh
  - **meningitis**; during: hell mrr1 zinc mrr1
  - **paroxysms**; in: merc
  - **side** to side; from | **amel**.: *Agar* ptk1 kali-i ptk1 med ptk1 ph-ac ptk1
  - **sitting**; while: *Nux-m*
  - **sleep**:
    - **during**: apis bro1 *Bell* bro1 hell bro1 *Podo* bro1 tub ih zinc bro1
    - **going** to sleep; on: tub mtf33
  - **weak** to move body; when too•: *Ars*
- **rubbing**:
  - **against** something; rubs head: tarent k*
  - **pillow**; rubs head on: cina mtf33
    - **head**; from pain in: *(↗Pain - rubbing - amel.)* med c1
- **shaking** the head: aloe bg2 ant-t bg2 ars bg2 aur b4a.de* bell b4.de* bry bg2 cann-xyz bg2 carb-v bg2 cham bg2 cocc bg2 kali-n bg2 *Lyc* bg2 mez bg2 tab bg2 *Zinc* b4a.de
  - **amel**.: chin bg2 cina bg2 gels bg2 hyos bg2 lach bg2 phos bg2
  - **involuntary**:
    - **dizzy**; which makes him: **Lyc**
    - **nausea** and closing eyes; with: bry bg1
  - **to** and fro: hyos mtf33

- **shaking** the head: ...
  - • **wild** sensation inside; to dispel the: hell mrr1
- **sideways**: apis a* ars mrr1 arum-t bro1 aur bell k* caust clem cupr mtf33 hell k* lyc *Med* naja gm1 nat-s nux-m podo a* pyrog tl1 tarent teucr a zinc a*
  - • **left**; to: lach bg2
  - • **right**; to: sabad bg2
  - • **rocks** head from side to side to relieve pain: cina a kali-i *Med* tarent
- **swaying**: acon bg2*
  - • **to** and fro: *Hyos* b7a.de
    - ⁝ **sensation** as if: pall ptk1
    - ⁝ **Brain**: *Acon* b7.de* *Chin* b7.de* *Lyc* bg2 *Rhus-t* b7.de*
- **throwing** head:
  - • **about**: *Bell* caust merc phos *Tarent*
  - • **backward**: *(↗Bending - head - backward - must - walking; Falling - backward - walking)* acet-ac *Agar* bro1 art-v bro1 *Bell* bro1 camph camph-mbr bro1 *Cic* bro1 cina cur bro1 *Glon* hell hydr-ac bro1 iodof bro1 kali-n lob med bg1* merc morph bro1 mygal nat-s bro1 op wbt• phyt sec bro1 *Stram* k* sulph bro1 tab tanac *Verat-v* bro1
    - ⁝ **accompanied** by:
      - ⁚ **cough**: samb
      - ⁚ **sneezing**: lyss ptk1
    - ⁝ **headache**; during | **children**; in: ign mtf33
  - • **convulsions**:
    - ⁝ **during** | **epileptic**: lach gt1 stram tl1
  - • **forward**: aethyl-n a1
- **tosses**: *Acon* apoc k2 *Cocc* *Cupr* ign naja a ph-ac *Tarent*
- **turning**: *(↗rolling)*
  - • **backward**, of: laur
  - • **side**, to: op
    - ⁝ **left**: lyc tarent
    - ⁝ **right**: plb
    - ⁝ **wrong** side, when spoken to: *Atro*
- **wagging**: *(↗nodding)* arn bg2 bell k* calc-p bg2 caust bg2 cham k* chin bg2 cupr bg2 hyos b7a.de* nux-m bg2 olib-sac wmh1 op b7.de* rhod bg2 spong bg2 viol-o bg2
  - • **asleep**; before falling: olib-sac wmh1
- **wavering**: kali-c h2
- **writing**; while: caust ptk1

○ - **Scalp**: caust h2 nat-c h2 nat-m h2 sep h2 sulph h2
  - • **forwards** and backwards; drawn: nat-m b4.de* sep b4a.de

MOVE up and down sensation: zinc h2
- **head** seems, to: sep h2

MUCUS; sensation of tenacious: | **Occiput**; in: bamb-a stb2.de•

MUSIC agg.: acon b7.de* ambr b7.de* *Coff* b7a.de* nux-v b7.de* ph-ac bg2* phos b4a.de* sumb bg2 viol-o b7.de*

NARCOTICS: | **agg.**: acet-ac ptk1 coff ptk1

NARROW sensation: gels bg2

NECROSIS: | **Mastoid** | **Temples**: calc-f bro1 caps bro1
- **Skull**; of the: aur bro1 fl-ac bro1 phos a1

NODDING (See Motions of - nodding)

NODULES in scalp: ant-c b7.de ant-t bg2 *Ars* b4.de* aur b4.de* *Calc* b4a.de caust ptk1 daph ptk1 graph ptk1 hell b7a.de *Hep* b4.de* kali-bi bg2 *Kali-i* vh led b7.de* m-arct b7.de mag-m b4.de* nat-m b4.de* nux-v b7.de* petr b4a.de phos b4.de* puls b7a.de ran-b bg2 ran-s b7.de ruta b7.de* sep b4a.de sil b4.de* thuj b4.de*
- **headache**; during: kali-i c1 phos c1 sil c1*
- **painful**: anac bg2 caust bg2 hep ptk1 kali-bi bg2 kali-c bg2 kali-i ptk1 ph-ac bg2 puls bg2 ruta bg2 sil bg2

NOISE agg.: *Acon* b7a.de anac b4a.de* *Ang* b7.de* *Apis* b7a.de arn b7.de* bar-c bg2 *Bell* b4a.de* *Bry* b7a.de cact bg2 calad b7.de* calc bg2 cham bg2 chin b7.de* *Coff* b7a.de* *Colch* b7.de* con b4.de* *Dig* b4a.de hyos bg2 ign b7.de* iod b4.de* m-arct b7.de merc b4.de* mur-ac bg2 nat-c b4.de* nit-ac b4.de* *Nux-v* b7.de* ph-ac b4.de* *Sep* b4a.de sil b4.de* *Spig* b7.de* stann b4.de* ther bg2 tub bg2 zinc b4.de*

Noise agg.: ...

○ - **External** head: hydr bg2

NOISES in head: acon bg2 aethyl-n a1 ars b4a.de* **Aur** bg2* bar-c b4.de* *Calc* b4.de* calc-f ptk1 camph bg2 cann-s bg cann-xyz bg2 carb-v b4a.de* *Carbn-s* c2 **Caust** b4.de* chin bg* *Chinin-s* bg2* cop ptk1 cypra-eg sde6.de• *Dig* b4a.de* dulc fd4.de gard-j vlr2• germ-met srj5• glon bg2 *Graph* b4.de* *Ham* c2 *Hydr* c2 iod ptk1 *Kali-c* b4.de* kalm ptk1 kreos bg2* *Lach* bg2 lap-la rsp1 lyc b4.de* mag-c bg2 mang b4a.de *Merc* c2 mur-ac b4.de* *Nat-sal* c2 nit-ac b4.de* nux-v bg2 ph-ac b4.de* *Phel* bg* phos b4.de* *Plat* bg2* plut-n srj7• ptel bg2 **Puls** bg2* ruta fd4.de sars b4a.de* sep b4.de* sil bg2* stann bg2 **Staph** bg2* **Sulph** b4.de* tril-p bg2 tritic-vg fd5.de verb bg2 *Zinc* bg2*
- **accompanied** by:
  - • **hearing**; lost (See HEARING - Lost - accompanied - head)
  - ○ • **Eustachian** tube; inflammation of (See EAR - Inflammation - eustachian - accompanied - head)
- **bubbles** rushing to the surface; like: germ-met srj5•
- **buzzing**: caust h2 coff mrr1 gard-j vlr2• ven-m rsj12•
  - • **accompanied** by | **Forehead**; pain in (See Pain - forehead - accompanied - buzzing)
  - • **menses** | **after** | **agg.**: kreos b7a.de
    - ⁝ **during** | **agg.**: *Kreos* b7a.de
  - ○ • **Occiput**: coff mrr1
- **chronic**: *Kali-i* vh
- **clanging**: lyc bg2 phel bg2*
- **cracking**: acon bg2 aloe c1 ars bg2 calc bg2 carb-v bg2 cham b7.de* coff b7.de* con bg2 dig bg2 glon bg2 kalm bg2* nux-m bg2 puls b7a.de* sep b4.de* spig b7a.de zinc bg2
  - ○ • **Occiput**: carb-v b4a.de
  - • **Sides**: ars b4.de*
    - ⁝ **right**: hep bg2
  - • **Vertex**: coff bg2 con b4.de*
- **crackling** (See Crackling)
- **crashing**: aloe ptk1 dig ptk1 glon bg2* phos ptk1 puls bg2 zinc ptk1
  - • **falling** asleep; when: dig ptk1 zinc ptk1
- **deafness**; with: carbn-s vh graph vh
- **flapping** and fluttering: kali-c bg2 lac-ac bg2 sars bg2 spong bg2
- **headache**; during: bell j5.de calc j5.de
- **humming**: acon bg2 aml-ns bg2 bar-c b4.de* calc b4.de* carb-an bg2 carb-v b4a.de* caust b4.de* chinin-s vh cocc b7.de* coff b7.de* *Dig* vh dulc fd4.de ferr bg2 graph b4.de* hydrog srj2• kali-bi bg2 kali-i vh kali-p fd1.de• kali-s fd4.de kreos b7a.de* lach bg2* lyc bg2 m-arct b7.de mag-c h2 mang h2 mur-ac bg2 *Nat-s* vh nit-ac bg2 nux-v b7.de* ph-ac b4.de* phos b4.de* *Plat* b4.de* puls b7.de* rhus-t b7.de* sars b4.de* *Sep* b4a.de squil b7.de* stann b4.de* staph b7.de* sulph b4.de* thuj b4.de* tritic-vg fd5.de verat b7.de* viol-t b7.de* zinc b4a.de*
  - • **cough** agg.; during: hep h2
  - • **stool** agg.; during: zinc h2
  - • **undulating** humming in head: calc h2
  - • **walking** agg.: verb h
  - ○ • **Occiput**: graph bg2 sulph bg2
- **rattling**: phos bg2
- **reverberating**: sec bg2 stann bg2 zinc bg2
- **roaring**: alum k* am-c k* aur k* bov k* calc b4a.de cann-s b7.de* caust b4a.de* chinin-s vh *Dig* vh ferr k* graph b4.de* ina-i mlk9.de *Kali-c* b4.de* kali-i vh *Kreos* b7a.de lach b7a.de lyc b4.de* m-ambo b7.de* mag-m k* *Nat-s* vh nit-ac k* nux-v b7.de* petr k* ph-ac b4.de* phos b4.de* plat k* puls b7.de* rhus-t b7a.de ruta fd4.de sars b4a.de sulph k* tritic-vg fd5.de zinc k*
  - • **coryza**; during: sep h2
  - • **perspiration**; during: caust b4a.de
  - • **pollutions**; after: carb-v bg2
- **rushing** sensation: acon vh1
- **seminal** emission; after: carb-v ptk1
- **singing** locusts: bry h1
- **sleep**; on falling: anthraq rly4• rad-br sze8• zinc ptk1
- **talking** agg.: sars ptk1

○ - **Occiput**: calc k* carb-v k* carbn-s bg2 phos k*
- **Sides**: ars b4.de*
- **Vertex**: con b4.de* nat-m bg2

NUMBNESS; sensation of: *(↗Asleep)* acon all-c aloe alum k* alum-p k2 am-c ambr anac k* ang bg ant-t apis ars arund asaf k* asar aur aur-m aur-m-n bapt k* bell berb bg* borx *Bry* bufo bro1 calc calc-ar bro1 calc-p carb-ac carb-an carb-v caust bg cham tl1 chel cob-n sp1 cocc bro1 coff colch coloc con k* cyt-l sp1 daph bg dendr-pol sk4• dig dios *Fl-ac* gels bg glon **Graph** k* ham hell bg helo c1 helo-s c1* hura jatr-c kali-br bg1* kali-fcy c *Lach* lil-t lyc lyss c1 mag-m meny meph merc merc-i-f *Merl* mez mur-ac nat-m **Nit-ac** k* nux-v ol-an olnd k* op orot-ac rly4• ost c2 ozone sde2• par bro1 *Petr* k* petr-ra shn4• phos phys pin-con oss2• *Plat* k* sacch-a fd2.de• sep sil stict bg stram sulph h2 tetox pin2• thuj visc c1 zinc bg1*

- **morning**: carb-v petr hr1
  - **soreness** then numbness extending to body: ambr
  - **waking**; on: cob-n sp1
- **noon** | **amel.**: cob-n sp1
- **evening** | **amel.**: cob-n sp1
- **air**; in open | **amel.**: mang h2
- **cap**, like a: calc k2
- **convulsions**, before: bufo a
- **dinner**; after: carb-v
- **heated**; becoming: petr hr1
- **lying** agg.: merc sulph h2
- **menses**; during: plat
- **mental** exertion agg.: mag-c bg1* staph bg1
- **painful** (See Pain - accompanied - numbness)
- **resting** head on arm: nat-m h2
- **siesta**; after: lyss a*
- **stool** agg.; during: chel dgt
- **walking** in open air | **amel.**: mang *Plat*
- **wooden** sensation | **Occiput**: hell bg2

○ - **Brain**: apis k* bufo k* calc ptk1 *Con* k* cupr bg2 graph ptk1 hell bg2* helo-s bnm14• kali-br k* mag-c nat-ar bg1* nat-m bg2 orot-ac rly4• *Plat* k* staph bg2* thuj a1 v-a-b jl2

- **External** head: acon bg2* aloe bg2 alum bro1 ambr b7a.de ang b7.de* asar bg2 berb bg2 calc b4.de* calc-p bg2 carb-an bg2 castor-eq bg2 caust b4a.de* chel bg2 coloc bg2 con bg2 daph bg2 ferr-br bro1 gels bg2 glon bg2 *Graph* bro1 hell bg2 kali-br bg2 lach bg2 mag-m b4.de* mez b4.de* mur-ac bg2 petr b4.de* phos bg2 plat b4.de* sil bg2 stict bg2
- **Forehead**: ars-met sne bapt k* bar-c brom k* coll dig *Fl-ac* ham k* kola stb3• *Mag-m* k* mang h2 merc mosch bg2 *Mur-ac* k* nat-ar *Phos* **Plat** k* pyrid rly4• sil k* *Staph* sne valer k* [heroin sdj2]
  - **right**: fl-ac bg2
  - **left**: psor jl2
    - **half** of the left forehead: psor jl2
  - **morning** | **waking** and while lying, exercise amel. and wrapping head warmly amel.; on: mag-m
  - **evening**: nat-ar
    - **blow**; as from a: plat
    - **board** lay there, as if a: acon
    - **warm** room agg.: plat
    - **extending** to | **Nose**; bone of: *Plat* [heroin sdj2]
- **Occiput**: acon bg2 *Agar* ammc ars bg2* bry k* cadm-met tpw6 *Calc-p* carb-v caust k* coff bg2 fl-ac k* gels k* hell bg2 irid-met bg2* kali-br bg2* kali-c *Lach* mang h2 merc-i-f k* merl nat-c k* phys bg2 plat raph staph ptk1 tell k*
  - **tightly** bound; as if too: *Carb-v Plat*

▽ • **extending** to | **Spine**; down the: phys ptk1

○ • **Protuberance**; occipital: con bg2

- **Sides**: acon bg2 alum bg2 androc srj1• *Apis* bg2 *Aur* bapt bg2 bell b4.de* bufo bg2 *Calc* k* carb-an b4a.de* *Chel* cina k* coff b7.de* *Con* k* dios bg2 glon bg2 *Graph* b4.de* hura *Kali-br* bg2 kali-n bg2 *Lach* lyc bg2 lyss merc bg2 mez bg2 nat-m bg2 nit-ac bg2 ol-an olnd b7.de* petr b4.de* phos b4.de* plat b4.de* staph bg2 stram bg2 tarax thuj k* zinc bg2
  - **one** side: con bg2 mez bg2*
  - **right**: calc b4.de* *Chel* k* cina b7.de*
    - **followed** by | **left**: anac
  - **left**: lach bg2 lyss ol-an k* par ptk2 stram thuj b4.de* xan c1
- **Temples**: ang h1* aur myric k* phos phys k* **Plat** k* zing k*
- **Vertex**: carbn-s cupr bg2* glon ptk1 graph bg2* *Mez* k* pall k* phos k* *Plat* k* thuj b4a.de* [heroin sdj2]

Numbness; sensation of – **Vertex**: ...

- **preceded** by feeling as if scalp and brain were contracted | **motion** and open air amel.: plat

NURSING agg.: *Chin* b7a.de

OBSTRUCTION of nose agg.: croc bg2 kali-bi bg2 *Lach* bg2 nat-c bg2

ODORS:

- **clothes**; of: | **agg.**: carb-an bg2
- **coffee** agg.; of: lach bg2
- **strong** odors agg.: acon b7a.de* *Anac* b4a.de* arg-n bg2 cact bg2 colch b7.de* *Ign* b7a.de* nux-v b7.de* *Sel* b7.de* sulph b4a.de*

OEDEMA (See Edema)

OILY forehead (See FACE - Greasy - forehead)

OPEN fontanelles (See Fontanelles - open)

OPENING:

- **sensation** as if opened and letting in cold air: *Cimic* k* hippoc-k szs2 neon srj5• plut-n srj7•

○ • **Vertex**: cimic ptk1 cypra-eg sde6.de•

- **shutting**; and (See Pain - opening and)

OPENING THE EYES:

- **agg.**: bell b4.de* **Bry** b7.de* *Chin* b7a.de* coff b7.de* *Coloc* b4a.de *Ign* b7.de* m-ambo b7.de mag-c bg2 *Nux-v* b7.de* rhus-t bg2 *Sep* b4a.de spig b7.de* sulph bg2
- **amel.**: cham bg2

OPENING THE MOUTH agg.: spig b7.de*

○ - **External** head: ang b7.de*

OVERLIFTING agg.: arn b7a.de* *Calc* b4.de* ph-ac b4.de* **Rhus-t** b7.de*

○ - **External** head: ambr b7.de* arn b7.de* *Calc* b4.de* *Rhus-t* b7.de*

PAIN (= headache in general; cephalgia): abies-c oss4• abies-n hr1 abrom-a ks5* abrot absin k* acet-ac acon k* acon-ac rly4• acon-c c2 acon-l ↓ *Aconin* ↓ act-sp adam ↓ adox a1* adren ↓ aesc k* aeth k* aethyl-n a1 agar *Agath-a* nl2• agn bg aids ↓ ail k* alco ↓ alf ↓ all-c all-s c2 allox ↓ aloe k* *Alum* k* alum-p ↓ alum-sil ↓ *Alumn* am-be ↓ *Am-br* ↓ *Am-c* k* am-m am-pic c1* ambr aml-ns c2 ammc amn-l sp1 amp rly4• amph c2 amyg c2 anac k* anag c2* anan ↓ ancis-p tsm2 *Androc* srj1*• androg-p bnj1 ang k* *Ango* c1 anh c2* anil br1 *Ant-c* k* ant-t k* anth c2 **Anthraci Anthraco** anthraq rly4• antip c2* ap-g k* aphis c2 **Apis** apoc apom ↓ aq-mar ↓ aqui ↓ aran c2* aran-sc c2 **Arg-met** k* *Arg-n* k* arge-pl rwt5• arizon-l nl2• *Arn* k* **Ars** k* ars-i ars-met c2 ars-s-f ↓ arum-i c2 arum-t k* asaf k* asar k* asc-c c2 asc-t c2 aster c2 astra-m c2 atha c2 atp ↓ atro ↓ atro-s mtf11 *Aur* k* aur-ar c2* aur-i ↓ aur-m ↓ aur-m-n c2 aur-s k2 aza ↓ *Bac* ↓ bad *Bamb-a* stb2.de• *Bapt* bapt-c c1* bar-act ↓ bar-c bar-i k2 bar-m bar-s ↓ **Bell** k* bell-p c2 ben c2 benz-ac benzol ↓ berb k* berb-a c2 beryl ↓ bism k* bism-sn a1 boerh-d ↓ bol-la c2 bond ↓ bor-ac c2 *Borx* k* both fne1• bov k* brom bros-gau mrc1 bruc c2 *Brucel* sa3• brucin c2 **Bry** k* bufo bung-fa tsm2 but-ac ↓ buth-a sp1 *Cact* k* cadm-met tpw6* cadm-s ↓ caesal-b zzc1• caj c2 calad **Calc** k* calc-act c2 calc-ar c2* calc-f ↓ calc-hp c2 calc-i c2* calc-p k* **Calc-s** calc-sil k2 calen ↓ calth br1 camph k* cann-i k* cann-s k* *Cann-xyz* ↓ canth k* caps bg* *Carb-ac* ↓ carb-an k* *Carb-v* k* carbn-o c2 carbn-s carc gk6* card-b c2 *Card-m* ↓ *Cardios-h* rly4• carl ↓ carneg-g rwt1• cartl-s ↓ cassia-s ↓ castm caul *Caust* k* **Cedr** vh* cench c2* *Cham* k* chel k* chen-a c2 chim-m c2 **Chin** k* chinin-ar chinin-m c2 **Chinin-s** k* chion c2* chir-fl ↓ chlam-tr bcx2• *Chlol* ↓ choc ↓ chord-umb rly4• cic bg* cich c2 *Cimic* k* cimx ↓ cina k* cinch c2 *Cinnb* cinnm c2 cit-v c2 clem k* cob k* cob-n ↓ coc-c coca *Coca-c* sk4• cocain ↓ **Cocc** k* coch c2 *Coff* k* colch k* coli rly4• *Coll* ↓ *Coloc* k* colocin c2 colum-p sze2• com con k* conv convo-d c2 cop ↓ *Cor-r* ↓ corn cortico sp1 cortiso ↓ corv-cor bdg• cot ↓ croc k* **Crot-c** k* *Crot-h* k* *Crot-t* cub ↓ cund k* *Cupr* k* cupr-ar cupr-n a1 cupr-s ↓ cupre-au c2 cur k* cycl k* cystein-l rly4• *Cyt-l* br1* dam mtf11 daph datin hs1 dendr-pol tsm2* der ↓ des-ac ↓ desm-g bnj1 *Dig* k* *Dios* k* diosm br1 dioxi ↓ diph-t-tpt jl2 dirc c2 dol ↓ dor ↓ dream-p ↓ *Dros* k* dubo-m br1 *Dulc* k* dys ↓ *Echi* ↓ elae c2 elaps k* elat elec c1* emblc bnj1 ephe c2 ephe-si ↓ epil a1* *Epiph* c2* equis-h a1 erio ↓ ery-m ↓ esin c2 eucal ↓ eug euon c2 euon-a br1 eup-a br1 eup-per eup-pur c2 euph k* euph-hy c2 euphr eupi k* eys sp1 fago c2 fagu c2 falco-pe nl2• fel c2 *Ferr* ferr-ar st ferr-br c2 *Ferr-i* ferr-m c2 ferr-ma ↓ *Ferr-p* ferr-py c1* ferr-s c2 ferr-t c2 ferul ↓ fic-m gya1 fl-ac k* flav jl2 flor-p rsj3• form c2 franc c2 fuc ↓ fuma-ac rly4• gala ↓ galeoc-c-h gms1• galla-q-r ↓ gamb gard-j vlr2• **Gels** k* genist c2 gent-c k* gent-ch bnj1 gent-l c2 ger-i rly4• *Germ-met* ↓ gink-b sbd1•

Pain: ...
gins k* **Glon** k* glyc ↓ gran granit-m ↓ *Graph* k* grat k* gua br1 guaj k* guan ↓ guar c2 guat ↓ gymno k* haem c2 haliae-lc srj5• ham helia ↓ *Hell* k* hell-o a1* helo ↓ helo-s c1* helon ↓ *Hep* k* hera c2 hip-ac ↓ hipp k* hippoc-k szs2 hir ↓ hist ↓ hist-m mtf11 hom-xyz c2* hura hura-c a1 hydr hydr-ac hydro-v ↓ *Hydrog* srj2• hydroph ↓ *Hyos* k* hyper k* iber ↓ ichth ↓ ictod *Ign* k* ignis-alc ↓ ina-i ↓ ind k* indg k* indol ↓ influ jl2* interf sa3• *Iod* k* iodof c2 ip k* irid-met srj5• **Iris** k* iris-fl c2 iris-foe c2 iris-t c2 jab ↓ jac-g ↓ jal jatr-c joan ↓ jug-c c2 jug-r k* junc-e c2 *Kali-ar Kali-bi* k* *Kali-br* ↓ *Kali-c* k* kali-chl kali-cy c2 **Kali-i** k* kali-m ↓ *Kali-n* k* *Kali-p Kali-s* kali-sil ↓ *Kalm* k* ketogl-ac rly4• kiss ↓ *Kola* stb3• *Kreos* k* kurch bnj1 lac-ac lac-c c2* *Lac-cp* sk4• *Lac-d* k* lac-del ↓ lac-e ↓ lac-f c2* *Lac-h* sk4• lac-loxod-a hrn2• lac-v c2 **Lach** k* lachn k* lact lam c2* lap-la ↓ lapa c2 lat-m sp1* laur k* *Lec Led* k* lepi ↓ *Lept* c2 leptos-ih jl2 lil-s ↓ lil-t k* limen-b-c ↓ limest-b ↓ linu-c ↓ lith-c c2* lob lob-c c2 lob-d c2 lobin a1 lol br1* loxo-lae bnm12• loxo-recl bnm10• **Luna** c2* lup ↓ *Lyc* k* lycpr c2 lycps-v c2 lys ↓ lyss k* m-ambo b7.de m-arct b7.de m-aust b7.de macro c2 mag-c k* *Mag-m* k* **Mag-p** k* mag-s maias-l ↓ malar jl2 *Manc* k* mand sp1 mang k* mang-p rly4• *Med* k* medul-os-si rly4• melal-alt gya4 *Meli* k* meli-xyz c2 meningoc mtf11 menis c2* menth c2 menth-pu c2 mentho ↓ meny bg* meph **Merc** k* merc-c k* merc-i-f merc-i-r ↓ merc-n c1 merl *Mez* k* mill miss ↓ moni ↓ *Morg* ↓ morg-p ↓ morph k* mosch k* mucs-nas rly4• mur-ac muru a1 murx musa ↓ myos-a rly4• myric ↓ naja k* *Nat-ar Nat-c* k* nat-hchls c2 **Nat-m** k* nat-ox rly4• nat-p nat-pyru ↓ *Nat-s* k* nat-sil ↓ nept-m ↓ nicc k* nicc-met br1 nicc-s c2 nicotam rly4• **Nit-ac** k* nit-s-d ↓ nitro-o ↓ nuph c2 *Nux-m* k* **Nux-v** k* nyct c1 *Oci-sa* sk4• oena ol-an br1 ol-j k* olib-sac wmh1 olnd bg* onon c2 onos c2* op k2 oreo mtf11 orot-ac rly4• oscilloc jl2 osm k* ox-ac k* oxal-a rly4• ozone sde2• paeon c2 pall k* *Par* k* paraf ↓ *Parathyr* ↓ parth c2 passi mtf11 paull mtf11 ped ↓ pen c2 pert-vc ↓ peti ↓ *Petr* k* petr-ra shn4• *Ph-ac* k* phase ↓ phase-xyz c2 phel k* phenac c2 **Phos** k* phys k* physala-p bnm7• phyt k* pic-ac k* pieri-b ↓ pimp c2 pin-s ↓ pip-m c2 pip-n c2 pitu-gl skp7• pitu-p sp1 plac rzf5• plac-s rly4• plan plat k* plat-m ↓ plat-m-n c1 *Plb* k* plb-xyz c2 *Plut-n* ↓ pneu mtf11 *Podo* k* polys sk4• positr nl2• pot-e rly4• prim-v br1 propl ub1• propr ↓ prun k* prun-p c2 pseuts-m oss1• psil ft1 **Psor** k* ptel k* **Puls** k* *Pycnop-sa* ↓ pyrog c2* querc-r svu1• rad-br ↓ ran-b k* ran-g c2 ran-s raph k* *Rat* ↓ rauw ↓ rham-cal br1 rheum k* rhod k* rhodi ↓ rhodi-o-n c2 rhus-g c2 rhus-r ↓ *Rhus-t* k* rhus-v ribo rly4• rob ptk1* *Ros-d* ↓ rosm ↓ rumx ruta mrr1* sabad k* sabal c2 *Sabin* bg sacch-a ↓ sacch-l c2 sal-ac ↓ salol c1* samb bg sang k* sangin-n c2* sanguis-s ↓ sanic c2 sapin c2 sarr ↓ sars bg* scarl jl2 scol a1* scut ↓ sec sel k* senec ↓ senec-j c2 seneg k* senn ↓ **Sep** k* serp ↓ **Sil** k* sin-a c2 sin-n ↓ sinus rly4• sol c1* sol-ni k* sol-t-ae c2 sphing ↓ *Spig* k* spirae ↓ spiros-af oss• spong k* squil bg stach c2 stann k* *Staph* k* staphycoc rly4• *Stel* ↓ stict c2 stram k* streptoc mtf11 stront-c c2* stront-n c2 stroph-s ↓ stry stry-xyz c2 suis-em rly4• suis-hep rly4• suis-pan rly4• sul-ac k* *Sul-i* ↓ sulfa sp1 **Sulph** k* sumb ↓ suprar rly4• syc ↓ symph ↓ syph c2* tab k* tanac k* taosc ↓ tarax k* tarent k* tax k* tela ↓ tell tep ↓ *Ter* tere-la rly4• tet ↓ teucr bg thea *Ther* k* thiam rly4• thioc-ac rly4• thres-a sze7• *Thuj* k* thymol sp1 thyr br1 til k* tong ↓ toxo-g ↓ trif-p ↓ tril-p trinit br1 trios c2 tritic-vg fd5.de trom tub c2* tub-d ↓ tub-m jl2 tub-r jl2 *Tung-met* stj2*• tus-p c2 upa c2 urol-h ↓ urt-u usn a2* ust v-a-b jl2 vac mtf11 valer k* vanil fd5.de vario c2 verat k* verat-n c2 *Verat-v* ↓ **Verb** bg vero-o rly4• vib c2 vinc ↓ viol-o viol-t vip visc c1* vult-gr sze5• wies ↓ wye c2 x-ray ↓ xan k* xanth yuc c2 *Zinc* k* zinc-p c2* zinc-pic c2 zinc-s k* zinc-val ↓ zing ziz [am-f stj2 *Ant-met* stj2 bell-p-sp dcm1 *Buteo-j* sej6 heroin sdj2 lac-mat sst4 lith-f stj2 rhen-met stj2 *Spect* dfg1 tant-met stj2]

- **daytime**: agar am-c aur bry calc cann-s caust chel chinin-s cina cist cob cob-n sp1 coca crot-t eup-per ferr fl-ac ger-i rly4• granit-m ↓ ham jac-c k* jac-g kali-c lac-c k2 lyc lyss k* merc-i-f a1 merc-i-r k* *Nat-m* k* nicc petr k* petr-ra shn4• phos k* phys a1 rumx scut a1 sep k* stann k* staph *Sulph* ↓ tritic-vg sna6 ven-m rsj12• zinc h2*
  - **bursting** pain: *Sulph*
  - **pressing** pain: granit-m es1•
- **morning**: acon aesc bro1 **Agar** k* agath-a nl2• aids nl2• alet all-s *Alum* k* alum-sil k2 alumn am-c k* am-m k* ambr k* *Anac* ang ant-t arg-met arg-n arge-pl rwt5• arist-cl sp1 *Arn* k* ars k* ars-i arum-t ↓ asaf asar aspar br1* *Aur* aur-ar k2 aur-i k2 *Bar-c* bar-m *Bell* benz-ac k* berb borx *Bov* bros-gau mrc1 *Bry* k* *Cact Cadm-met* sp1 cadm-s *Calc* calc-f sp1 calc-i k2 *Calc-p* k* calc-s calc-sil k2 camph k* cann-s canth *Carb-an* k* *Carb-v Carbn-s* carc fd2.de• castor-eq caust cedr ↓ cham *Chel* chin chinin-ar chinin-s chlam-tr bcx2• chlorpr pin1• cic cimic ↓ cina k* clem cob k* cob-n sp1 coc-c k* coca coff colch ↓ *Coloc Con* k* croc crot-c sk4• *Crot-t* cund cupr cycl k* dig ↓ dios k* dros ↓ dulc *Eup-per* euphr fago ↓ falco-pe nl2• ferr ferr-ar ferr-i ferr-p *Fl-ac* form gamb ↓ gink-b sbd1• glon k* *Graph* grat guaj gymno ↓ ham ↓ hell

- **morning**: ...
helo-s rwt2• *Hep* k* hipp k* hippoc-k szs2 hir skp7• hyper ↓ *Ign* k* ina-i mlk9.de ind k* indg ↓ iod ip iris jatr-c *Jug-c* k* jug-r kali-bi k* *Kali-c* kali-i kali-m k2 *Kali-n* k* kali-p *Kali-s* kali-sil k2 kalm kola stb3• kreos lac-c lac-d bro1* *Lach* lachn k* lact lact-v ↓ led k* lil-t k* lith-c lyc ↓ lyss ↓ mag-c k* mag-m mag-s ↓ manc k* *Mang* k* merc merc-i-f k* merc-sul *Mez* mim-p rsj8• morg-p pte1*• mur-ac *Murx* k* myric bro1 naja k2 nat-ar nat-c *Nat-m* k* nat-ox rly4• nat-p k* nat-s ↓ nicc k* *Nit-ac* nux-m **Nux-v** k* oci-sa sk4• ol-an op k2 paeon pall pant-ac rly4• *Petr* k* petr-ra shn4• *Ph-ac* k* *Phos* k* phys ↓ phyt pic-ac k2 pip-m ↓ plan ↓ plb ↓ *Podo* k* positr ↓ prot pte1* *Psor* ptel puls pyrid rly4• ran-b ran-s ↓ rheum *Rhod Rhus-t* rumx ruta sabad sacch-a fd2.de• sal-fr sle1• samb sang k* sars scut sel rsj9• *Seneg Sep* k* *Sil Spig* k* spong h1* *Squil Stann* k* *Staph* stel bro1 stram stront-c stry suis-em rly4• sul-ac *Sulph* k* suprar ↓ symph ↓ tab *Tarent* ↓ *Thuj* k* til ↓ tong ↓ tritic-vg sna6 urol-h rwt• vanil fd5.de verat zinc k*

- **3 h** | **stitching** pain (See night - midnight - after - 3 h - stitching)
- **3 to 4 h** | **pressing** pain (See night - midnight - after - 3-4 - pressing)
- **6 h**: brucel ↓
  - **evening**; until: crot-t
  - **dull** pain: brucel sa3•
- **7 h**: pitu-gl ↓
  - **22 h**; until: tetox pin2•
  - **dull** pain: pitu-gl skp7•
- **7.30 h**:
  - **7.30-8 h**: hir ↓
    - **dull** pain: hir skp7•
- **8 h**: bov
- **9-11 h**: oci-sa sk4•
- **10 h**; until: *Arn* lachn k* mag-c k* *Nat-m* vh
- **15 h**; until: aur
- **17 h**; until: mang
- **19 h**; until: aur h2
- **22 h**; until: phys
- **accompanied** by:
  - **hypertension** (See GENERALS - Hypertension - accompanied - head - morning)
  - **scotoma**: aspar br1*
- **amel.**: bov carc fd2.de• caust k* epil a1 fic-m gya1 kreos nat-m k* oci-sa ↓ polys sk4• verat
  - **pressing** pain: oci-sa sk4•
- **apyrexia**; during: nat-m bro1
- **bed** agg.; in: *Agar* alum alum-p k2 am-c anac ant-t arg-n ↓ aur aur-s k2 bar-c bar-s k2 *Bell* berb bov *Bry* calc calc-p carb-an k* carb-v h2* *Carbn-s Cham* chin chinin-s cic coc-c coff con dig dulc ferr ferr-p *Graph* hell *Hep* k* ign ip jug-c *Kali-c* kali-i *Kali-p* kali-s kreos *Lac-d Lach* lact laur k* lyc mag-c mag-m mag-s mang merc merc-i-f a1 mez murx k* nat-m *Nit-ac* **Nux-v** k* petr *Phos Psor* ptel ran-b rheum *Rhod* k* rhus-t ruta squil staph sul-ac sulph thuj verat zinc zinc-p k2
  - **motion** agg.; beginning of: **Bry**
  - **nausea**; with: calc cob *Eup-per* graph nat-m nux-v sep k* sil sulph
  - **tearing** pain: arg-n
- **begins** in morning, increases until noon and ceases toward evening: kali-bi ↓
  - **shooting** pain: kali-bi
- **boring** pain: arg-n k* camph cham dios hep hyper lyss nicc nux-v ruta fd4.de
- **breakfast** | **delayed**; if it is: calc
- **burning**: arn canth glon mur-ac h2 *Nux-v* k* phos phys
- **burrowing**: agar hep k*
- **bursting** pain: am-m dios k* ham k* kola stb3• lac-c lach phos k*
- **ceases** toward evening: abrom-a ks5 agath-a nl2• anis c1 *Bry* calc *Kali-bi* kali-p a kalm *Nat-m* k* nicc a pic-ac k2 plat sang spig sulph
- **comes** and goes with the sun: cact gels mg glon mg kali-bi *Kalm* lac-d k* *Nat-m Sang Spig* k* stann mg staph mg sulph tab

- **cutting** pain: coloc mag-c stry a1
- **drawing** pain: agar k* agath-a nl2• ang k* dros dulc fd4.de hell kali-bi mag-c mez petr rhod sulph tritic-vg fd5.de vanil fd5.de zinc
- **dull** pain: agar k* calc-sil k2 chin h1 dulc fd4.de ham fd3.de• hep h2 ind kali-c h2 lach lact-v hr1 nit-ac h2 petr-ra shn4• ruta fd4.de symph fd3.de• tritic-vg fd5.de vanil fd5.de
- **hammering** pain: colch rsj2• **Nat-m**
- **increasing**:
  - **noon**, or a little later; until | **decreases** gradually; then: fic-m gya1 nat-sil fd3.de• phos sulph
- **increasing** during day: bry a cact calc k2 ozone sde2• petr-ra shn4• pic-ac k2 sang k2 ther c1
- **increasing** till evening; gradually: bry↓ sang↓ sep↓
  - **bursting** pain: bry sang sep
- **lancinating**: mag-c k*
- **menses**; during: kola stb3•
- **opening** the eyes; on first: *Bry*↓
  - **bursting** pain: *Bry*
- **pressing** pain: *Acon* agar alumn ambr arg-n k* asaf benz-ac borx bov *Bry* cann-s caust k* cedr *Cham* chin cimic coloc *Con* k* croc cycl dig h2* fago a1 gamb glon *Graph* ina-i mlk9.de kali-bi kali-n kola stb3• **Lach** lyc k* mez myric nat-c nat-m nat-s nicc k* *Nux-v* paeon *Petr* ph-ac k* phos pip-m podo br1 positr nl2• psor puls rhus-t ruta fd4.de *Sil* spong fd4.de sulph suprar rly4• thuj tong a1 tritic-vg fd5.de vanil fd5.de
- **rising**:
  - **after**:
    - **agg.**: bar-act↓ bar-c↓ calc↓ carc↓ coloc↓ junc-e↓ *Mag-c*↓ olib-sac↓ ozone↓ plb↓ ruta↓ sep↓ squil↓ stront-c↓ tritic-vg↓
      - **burrowing**: bar-act junc-e squil k*
      - **dull** pain: olib-sac wmh1 sep h2 squil h1 tritic-vg fd5.de
      - **lancinating**: coloc mag-c k*
      - **pressing** pain: calc h2* ozone sde2• ruta h1
      - **shooting** pain: mag-c
      - **stitching** pain: bar-c carc fd2.de• *Mag-c* plb stront-c
      - **stunning** pain: calc h2
    - **early** rising; after: mag-c↓
      - **cramping**: mag-c
  - **agg.**: *Agar* am-c am-m apis *Arg-n* k* arist-cl sp1 ars↓ asc-t k* aur-m bar-c bar-i k2 bar-m **Bry** k* camph k* chel chinin-s cimic bg1* cinnb↓ cob cod a1 colch k* crot-t **Cycl** k* dig dulc fago glon k* graph↓ ham k* hep hydr ind k* indg a1 iod ip jug-c *Kali-p* kalm kola stb3• lac-d *Lach* lyc k* mag-c k* mag-m menth c1 merc k* merc-i-f a1 mur-ac nat-m↓ nicc nux-v k* ox-ac↓ ped a1 petr phos *Psor* ptel puls rhus-t k* rumx ruta sabin↓ sang tl1 *Sep* k* spong↓ squil staph stram↓ stront-c sul-i k2 **Sulph** tarent vanil fd5.de [tax jsj7]
    - **drawing** pain: nat-m
    - **nail**; as from a: ptel
    - **pressing** pain: cinnb graph **Lach** lyc mag-c ox-ac psor sabin spong fd4.de squil **Sulph**
    - **sore**: ars
    - **tearing** pain: ip staph stram stront-c
  - **amel.**: *Alum* ars aur↓ cham coc-c crot-h *Graph* *Hep* ign jug-c **Kali-i** k* merc-i-r k* murx k* nat-m *Nit-ac* **Nux-v** ph-ac phos plut-n srj7• ran-g c **Rhod** k* vanil fd5.de
    - **sore**: aur h2
  - **before**: *Nat-hchls*↓ ptel↓
    - **shooting** pain: *Nat-hchls* ptel a1
- **shooting** pain: arum-t k* caust ptel k*
- **sore**: aur bov caust cob con gymno hep hyper ind merc mez nicc **Nux-v** petr plan sul-ac
- **stitching** pain: agar alum am-m arg-met bry k* canth carc fd2.de• cham cic h1 con glon k* grat hep indg lyc mag-c k* mag-s mang nicc petr plb k* ruta fd4.de sars sil stront-c thuj k* til tong a1 vanil fd5.de verat
- **stunning** pain: agar arn k* **Nat-m** **Nux-v** k* psor hr1 rhus-t *Tarent* zinc k*

- **morning**: ...
  - **sun**; increasing and decreasing with the: acon aml-ns vh1 gels a **Glon** k* *Kalm* k* nat-c a* *Nat-m* k* *Phos* *Sang* k* sel ptk *Spig* k* *Stann* stram stront-c mg tab bro1
  - **sunrise**; beginning at: lat-m↓
    - **dull** pain: lat-m bnm6•
  - **tearing** pain: alum arg-n borx bov cic h1 *Coloc* con hyper indg mez nicc nux-v phos ran-s rhod sars sil staph verat
  - **until**:
    - **noon**: ars conv k* ip mag-c h2* *Nat-m* nicc phos k* sep k* *Tab*
      - **tearing** pain: ip
    - **evening**: ant-c↓ zinc↓
      - **tearing** pain: ant-c zinc h2
  - **waking | after**:
    - **agg.**: apis↓ arg-met↓ arum-t↓ aur↓ mez↓
      - **boring** pain: apis arg-met arum-t aur k* mez
    - **on**: agar agath-a nl2• aids nl2• ail allox↓ *Alum* alum-p k2 *Alumn* ambr↓ amp rly4• anac c1 anthraq rly4• *Arg-n* arist-cl rbp3• *Arn* ars k* ars-s-f k2 asc-c hr1 *Aur-m-n* wbt2• bar-ox-suc rly4• bell↓ benz-ac k* bov **Bry** bufo cadm-met tpw6* cadm-s c1 calc calc-f sp1 calc-p calc-s calc-sil k2 cann-i carb-an carbn-dox knl3• carbn-s carc fd2.de• cartl-s rly4• caust cham *Chel* chin chin-b c1 chinin-ar chord-umb rly4• cic k* cimic bg1 cob cob-n sp1 coc-c coff k* colch con *Croc* crot-h crot-t cupr-ar cyclosp sa3• cystein-l rly4• dig dulc↓ elaps erig *Eup-per* euphr fago falco-pe nl2• ferr↓ form fuma-ac rly4• gels↓ **Graph** haliae-lc srj5• ham k2 hell *Hep* hipp hippoc-k szs2 hydr↓ hydrog srj2• ign ind k* jug-c *Kali-bi* *Kali-c* k* *Kali-i* vh kali-m k2 kali-n kali-p kali-s *Kalm* kola stb3• kreos *Lac-c* k* lac-cp sk4• **Lach** k* lap-la sde8.de• lil-t lob luna kg1• *Lyc* mag-c melal-alt gya4 merc-i-f k* mez↓ morph mucs-nas rly4• mur-ac murx k* myric *Naja* **Nat-m** nat-ox rly4• nat-s k2 nept-m↓ nicc **Nit-ac** **Nux-v** ol-an op oxal-a rly4• ozone sde2• peti petr↓ petr-ra shn4• *Ph-ac* phasco-ci rbp2 *Phos* k* phys k* pip-m pitu-gl↓ plac-s rly4• plan k* plat plut-n srj7• positr↓ pot-e rly4• pseuts-m oss1• *Psor* puls rhus-r rhus-t h1* rumx sal-fr↓ sang k2 *Sep* k* squil stann staph succ-ac rly4• suis-pan rly4• sul-ac *Sulph* suprar↓ symph↓ **Tarent** thioc-ac rly4• *Thuj* k* *Thyr* vh trios rsj11• urol-h rwt• vanil↓ ven-m rsj12• verat↓ zinc↓ [bell-p-sp dcm1 heroin sdj2 spect dfg1 uva stj]
      - **10 h**; until: *Arn* lachn c mag-c a *Nat-m* a
      - **burning**: chin coc-c
      - **bursting** pain: aids nl2• cham *Con* k* ham k2 hydr nux-v oxal-a rly4•
      - **drawing** pain: agath-a nl2•
      - **dull** pain: allox tpw3 ars h2 cadm-met tpw6 cob-n sp1 dulc fd4.de melal-alt gya4 pitu-gl skp7• sal-fr sle1• symph fd3.de• vanil fd5.de ven-m rsj12•
      - **hunger**; with: ptel c1
      - **opening** the eyes; on first: bov bro1 *Bry* k* graph bro1 ign kalm *Nat-m* bro1 *Nux-v* k* onos bro1 positr nl2• stry bro1 tab bro1
      - **preceded** by dreams (See SLEEP - Dreaming - followed - head)
      - **pressing** pain: agar alumn anac arg-n bell h1* chord-umb rly4• cob-n sp1 coc-c *Con* ferr gels *Graph* hep kola stb3• mez **Nat-m** nept-m lsd2.fr ol-an ph-ac positr nl2• suprar rly4• ven-m rsj12• zinc
      - **rising** amel.: am-c↓
        - **drawing** pain: am-c
      - **shooting** pain: caust
      - **sore**: ambr anac h2 con *Cupr-ar* *Ign* *Plan* tarent
      - **stitching** pain: caust h2 petr
      - **stunning** pain | **alcoholic** drinks; as from: chin h1 kali-n **Nat-m** *Tarent*
      - **tearing** pain: graph *Phos* puls staph verat
      - **torn**; as if: con h2
- **forenoon**: aeth aids nl2• alum alumn ant-c arg-n a1 *Aur* *Bar-c* bar-i k2 bar-s k2 benz-ac↓ bry k* *Calc* k* canth carbn-s k* caust chel chinin-s cimic k* cinnb k* clem cob k* coc-c k* cocc *Con* cop cupr-ar k* dulc fd4.de fago↓ ferr-ma a1 gamb k* genist k* gink-b sbd1• ham k* hippoc-k szs2 hydr k* ind k* indg k* iod *Ip*↓ jab jac-g *Kali-c* kali-n↓ kali-s kalm lach k* lachn k* lact merc-i-f k* *Nat-c* *Nat-m* nat-sil fd3.de• nicc phel k* phyt k* polyg-h ptel k* puls↓ ran-b rhod rhodi k* rhus-t k* rumx ruta fd4.de sabad k2 *Sars* *Sep* k* sol-ni

- **forenoon**: ...
spong$_{fd4.de}$ sul-ac sul-i$_{k2}$ sulph$_{k*}$ tritic-vg$_{fd5.de}$ trom$_{k*}$ ulm-c$_{jsj8}$• vanil$_{fd5.de}$ ven-m$_{rsj12}$•
  - **9** h: carbn-s$_{k2}$ ozone↓
    - **9-11** h: oci-sa$_{sk4}$•
    - **9-12** h: cedr$_{vh}$ *Meli* psil$_{ft1}$
    - **9-13** h: cedr$_{vh}$ crot-h$_{bg1}$ mur-ac propl$_{ub1}$•
    - **9-16** h: caust cedr$_{vh}$
    - **pressing** pain: ozone$_{sde2}$•
  - **10** h: apis *Aran*$_{vh}$ ars **Borx** cimic *Gels*$_{k*}$ **Nat-m**$_{k*}$ nicc$_{gg}$ petr-ra$_{shn4}$• *Sil*$_{vh}$ thuj
    - **4** h next day; until: petr-ra$_{shn4}$•
    - **10-11** h: nicc$_{c1}$
    - **10-14** h: alum
    - **10-15** h: lac-cp$_{sk4}$• **Nat-m**$_{k*}$
    - **10-16** h: *Stann*
    - **10-18** h: apis psil$_{ft1}$
  - **11** h: aloe$_{hr}$ arum-t$_{vh}$ *Bell*$_{mrr1}$ cann-i$_{a1}$ ip nat-sil$_{fd3.de}$• petr-ra$_{shn4}$• sanguis-s$_{hrn2}$• sol-ni spig sulph$_{k*}$
    - **11-14.30** h: polys$_{sk4}$•
    - **11-15** h: bell$_{vh}$ sal-fr$_{sle1}$•
    - **11-20** h: petr-ra$_{shn4}$•
  - **drawing** pain: kali-c spong$_{fd4.de}$ vanil$_{fd5.de}$
  - **increasing** | **night**; until: sil$_{h2*}$
  - **pressing** pain: benz-ac$_{a1}$ carbn-s$_{k2}$ dulc$_{fd4.de}$ fago$_{a1}$ puls$_{a1}$ ruta$_{fd4.de}$ vanil$_{fd5.de}$
  - **sore**: sep
  - **stitching** pain: canth$_{a1}$ con$_{a1}$ gink-b$_{sbd1}$• tritic-vg$_{fd5.de}$ vanil$_{fd5.de}$
  - **tearing** pain: alum ant-c *Ip* kali-n$_{h2}$
- **noon**: aeth agar alum alum-p$_{k2}$ ant-c arg-met arg-n arizon-l$_{nl2}$• asar bamb-a↓ bell bov calc-ar calc-p$_{k*}$ cann-i carb-v *Cedr* cham$_{k*}$ chel$_{k*}$ chinin-s$_{k*}$ cic cob$_{k*}$ con↓ crot-t$_{a1}$ dulc$_{fd4.de}$ elaps↓ graph gymno$_{k*}$ hippoc-k$_{szs2}$ ign indg$_{k*}$ jab$_{k*}$ kali-bi$_{k*}$ kali-n kalm$_{k*}$ lyc$_{k*}$ lycps-v lyss$_{k*}$ mag-c maias-l$_{hrn2}$• manc↓ mang merc$_{k*}$ mur-ac *Naja* nat-c *Nat-m*$_{k*}$ oci-sa↓ phos$_{k*}$ propr$_{sa3}$• puls rhus-t ruta↓ sang$_{bro1}$ sep↓ sil↓ sol-t-ae$_{a1}$ spira$_{a1}$ spong *Sulph* tab$_{bro1}$ tritic-vg$_{fd5.de}$ vanil$_{fd5.de}$ zinc zing$_{k*}$
  - **evening**; until: sil
  - **midnight**; until: *Caul Sulph*
  - **amel.**: **Bry**↓
    - **drawing** pain: **Bry**$_{k*}$
  - **burning**: *Sulph*
  - **bursting** pain: bamb-a$_{stb2.de}$•
  - **drawing** pain: phos$_{h2*}$
  - **pressing** pain: agar bamb-a$_{stb2.de}$• cedr kali-n$_{h2*}$ manc oci-sa$_{sk4}$• ruta$_{fd4.de}$ sil *Sulph* tritic-vg$_{fd5.de}$ zinc
  - **shooting** pain: calc-p propr$_{sa3}$• sep
  - **sleep** agg.; after: calad↓
    - **pressing** pain: calad
  - **stitching** pain: con elaps
  - **tearing** pain: cham graph zinc
  - **toward**, amel.: bry↓ nat-m↓ ozone↓
    - **pressing** pain: bry nat-m ozone$_{sde2}$•
  - **until** goes to sleep: mur-ac↓
    - **stitching** pain: mur-ac
- **afternoon**: *Acon* aeth *Agar* agath-a$_{nl2}$• allox$_{sp1}$ aloe↓ *Alum*$_{k*}$ alum-p$_{k2}$ alum-sil$_{k2}$ *Am-c*$_{k*}$ am-m ambr anac anan$_{hr1*}$ anders$_{bnj1}$ ang↓ ant-t aq-pet$_{a1}$ arge-pl$_{rwt5}$• arn ars ars-i ars-s-f$_{k2}$ asaf$_{hr1}$ asar aur aur-ar$_{k2}$ aur-s$_{k2}$ *Bad*$_{k*}$ bamb-a↓ bapt↓ bar-c bar-i$_{k2}$ bar-m bar-s$_{k2}$ **Bell**$_{k*}$ berb bov brucel$_{sa3}$• bry bufo cadm-met$_{sp1}$ calad calc calc-ar calc-f calc-p$_{k*}$ calc-s calc-sil$_{k2}$ cann-i↓ canth carb-an *Carb-v* carbn-s cartl-s$_{rly4}$• castm↓ caust cham↓ chel$_{k*}$ chin$_{k*}$ chinin-ar chinin-s cic cimic$_{k*}$ cob coca cocc colch coloc con$_{k*}$ cortiso$_{skp7}$• *Cupr*$_{k*}$ cycl$_{k*}$ dig digin$_{a1}$ dios dros dulc$_{fd4.de}$ ephe-si$_{hsj1}$• epil$_{a1}$ equis-h eup-pur$_{bro1}$ euphr eys$_{sp1}$ fago$_{k*}$ ferr$_{k*}$ ferr-ar ferr-i ferr-p flor-p↓ form$_{k*}$ gamb gels genist$_{k*}$ gink-b$_{sbd1}$• gins↓ glon$_{k*}$ *Graph* grat$_{k*}$ guaj↓ ham$_{k*}$ hell$_{k*}$ hippoc-k$_{szs2}$ hir↓ iber ign ind$_{k*}$ indg$_{k*}$ indol$_{bro1}$ iod$_{k*}$ iris kali-ar *Kali-bi*$_{hr1}$ kali-c kali-i↓ kali-m$_{k2}$ *Kali-n*$_{k*}$ kali-p kali-s

- **afternoon**: ...
kali-sil$_{k2}$ kalm kreos *Lac-c*$_{k*}$ lach lact$_{k*}$ lat-m$_{sp1}$ laur$_{k*}$ lob$_{bro1}$ *Lyc*$_{k*}$ lycps-v lyss$_{k*}$ mag-c$_{k*}$ mag-m mag-s$_{k*}$ maias-l$_{hrn2}$• *Mang* marb-w↓ meli$_{a1*}$ merc-i-f$_{a1}$ merc-i-r$_{k*}$ *Mez Mur-ac* naja↓ nat-ar *Nat-c* nat-m nat-ox↓ nat-p$_{k*}$ nept-m$_{lsd2.fr}$ nicc↓ *Nit-ac* nux-m$_{k*}$ nux-v oci-sa↓ ol-an↓ olib-sac↓ op pall$_{k*}$ pant-ac$_{rly4}$• petr petr-ra↓ *Ph-ac* phel↓ phos$_{k*}$ phyt pic-ac$_{k*}$ plan↓ *Plat* plb polyg-h positr$_{nl2}$• *Propl*$_{ub1}$• psor$_{al}$ ptel$_{k*}$ puls$_{k*}$ ran-b$_{k*}$ rhus-r ruta sabin sal-fr$_{sle1}$• sang$_{hr1}$ sarr$_{hr1}$ *Sars* sec **Sel**$_{k*}$ senec↓ seneg sep$_{k*}$ *Sil* spong stram$_{k*}$ *Stront-c* suis-hep↓ suis-pan$_{rly4}$• sul-ac sul-i$_{k2}$ *Sulph*$_{k*}$ suprar↓ tab$_{k*}$ tarent↓ tell$_{k*}$ tritic-vg$_{fd5.de}$ urol-h$_{rwt}$• v-a-b$_{jl2}$ valer vanil$_{fd5.de}$ *Verat*$_{k*}$ verat-v↓ *Zinc* zinc-p$_{k2}$ zing↓
  - **13** h: ail ars$_{vh}$ coca ham$_{fd3.de}$• lyc mag-c pall$_{hr1}$ phys pic-ac plut-n$_{srj7}$• ptel
    - **13-15** h: ars$_{k2}$ chinin-s ham$_{fd3.de}$• plan
    - **13-17** h: lac-ac mag-c
    - **13-18** h: carc$_{a*}$
    - **13-20** h: abrom-a$_{ks5}$
    - **13-22** h: mag-c plat positr$_{nl2}$• sil spig
    - **twitching**: mag-c
  - **14** h: alum↓ *Ars Chel* gink-b$_{sbd1}$• grat iod$_{h}$ laur lyss maias-l$_{hrn2}$• phys ptel [tax$_{jsj7}$]
    - **14-7** h: *Bad*$_{k*}$
    - **14-15** h: bell$_{vh}$ cadm-met$_{sp1}$ lat-m$_{sp1}$
    - **14-19** h: bad$_{a1*}$
    - **evening**; until late in the: bad chel petr-ra$_{shn4}$•
    - **pressing** pain: alum
  - **15** h: apis **Bell**$_{k*}$ cartl-s$_{rly4}$• fago *Fl-ac* gink-b$_{sbd1}$• guaj hura iber iod$_{a}$ lycps-v lyss naja$_{a}$ nat-ar plut-n$_{srj7}$• sep sil thuj verat-v
    - **15-16** h: brom clem
    - **15-17** h: ephe-si$_{hsj1}$•
    - **15-18** h: rhus-g$_{tmo3}$•
    - **15-21** h: arn lyss nat-ar tarent
    - **15-22** h: calc↓
      - **tearing** pain: calc
  - **16** h: arg-mur arg-n ars-s-f$_{k2}$ asaf↓ bar-c$_{h2}$ caust chinin-s dios dioxi$_{rbp6}$ hell$_{a}$ helon laur↓ lyc$_{a}$ meli nat-m phys pic-ac psil$_{ft1}$ sabad$_{a}$ staphycoc$_{rly4}$• stry suis-pan$_{rly4}$• *Sulph* syph$_{k2}$ verat-v
    - **16-3** h: **Bell**
    - **16-17** h: pitu-gl$_{skp7}$•
    - **16-19** h: allox$_{tpw4*}$ eys$_{sp1}$ hell$_{nh}$
    - **16-20** h: caust hell **Lyc**$_{k*}$
    - **shooting** pain: ars-s-f$_{k2}$
    - **stitching** pain: ars-s-f$_{k2}$ asaf laur
  - **17** h: ars-s-f$_{k2}$ bufo dendr-pol↓ equis-h falco-pe$_{nl2}$• galeoc-c-h$_{gms1}$• helon iod$_{h}$ lac-d$_{a}$ nat-m paeon pic-ac ptel *Puls* sulph
    - **17-18** h: chinin-s lil-t sep
    - **17-21** h: plat
    - **17-22** h: *Puls*
    - **burning**: dendr-pol$_{sk4}$•
  - **until** evening: lyc↓
    - **tearing** pain: lyc
  - **night**; until: carc$_{zzh}$
  - **midnight**; until: crot-c$_{sk4}$•
  - **amel.**: gels$_{ptk}$ ip kola$_{stb3}$• ol-an
  - **boring** pain: aloe mag-s nicc sang$_{k*}$ sep
  - **burning**: canth fago$_{k*}$
  - **burrowing**: ant-t$_{k*}$
  - **bursting** pain: flor-p$_{rsj3}$•
  - **crushed**; as if: marb-w$_{es1}$•
  - **cutting** pain: dulc$_{fd4.de}$ nat-p ptel sang$_{a1}$ suis-hep$_{rly4}$•
  - **drawing** pain: agar ant-t$_{k*}$ dulc gins spong$_{fd4.de}$ tritic-vg$_{fd5.de}$ vanil$_{fd5.de}$ verat-v zing
  - **dull** pain: agath-a$_{nl2}$• bapt dulc$_{fd4.de}$ ham$_{fd3.de}$• hir$_{skp7}$• nat-ox$_{rly4}$• petr-ra$_{shn4}$• ruta$_{fd4.de}$ spong$_{fd4.de}$ suis-hep$_{rly4}$• vanil$_{fd5.de}$
  - **increasing** until midnight | **ceasing** at dawn: syph$_{k2}$
  - **jerking** pain: mag-c$_{h2}$

- **lasting** all night: ars k2 colch cupr petr-ra shn4• syph a verat
  - **until** next evening: cist kali-n
- **pressing** pain: alum ang cann-i carb-an h2* carb-v cham k* coloc dulc fd4.de fago a1 graph hell kali-c kali-n h2* lyc mag-c naja nat-c nit-ac oci-sa sk4• olib-sac wmh1 op ph-ac k* phos ruta fd4.de senec sep k* spong fd4.de stram tritic-vg fd5.de vanil fd5.de
- **shooting** pain: *Ferr* k* plan k* spong fd4.de sulph suprar rly4• tarent
- **sleep**:
  - **after**:
    - **agg.**: calc-p vh
    - **amel.**: adam skp7•
- **sore**: alum bufo nicc phos sang
- **stitching** pain: aeth k* alum k* bov canth cham grat indg *Lyc* mag-c nat-c nicc ol-an phel puls ruta fd4.de sars sep sil h2 stront-c tritic-vg fd5.de vanil fd5.de
- **stunning** pain: cham hell spong fd4.de
- **tearing** pain: aeth bamb-a stb2.de• calc castm caust chel graph grat guaj kali-i kreos laur *Lyc* mag-c mag-s nat-c nicc ol-an sil sulph zinc

- **evening**: acon acon-ac rly4• agar agath-a nl2• ail ↓ **All-c** k* aloe ↓ alum k* alum-p k2 alum-sil k2 am-c *Ambr Anac* ang k* ant-c k* ant-t k* apis ara-maca sej7• arg-met arg-n ↓ arge-pl ↓ ars ars-s-f k2 arum-t ↓ asaf k* aur k* aur-ar k2 aur-s k2 bad bamb-a ↓ bar-c k* bar-m bar-s k2 **Bell** k* borx bov brom k* bry k* calc calc-p ↓ *Calc-s* calc-sil k2 camph canth caps carb-ac ↓ *Carb-an Carb-v* k* *Carbn-s* castm ↓ *Caust* k* cedr cham k* chel k* chin chinin-s cic cimic k* cina k1 cist a1* clem k1* cob a1* coc-c a1* cocc hr1* colch a1* coloc k* croc crot-c sk4• crot-h ↓ crot-t cupr cupr-ar k* cycl k* *Dig* dios k* dream-p sdj1• *Dulc* echi elaps elat k* epil a1 eug k* eup-pur bro1 euphr ferr k* ferr-ar ferr-p fic-m gya1 fl-ac ↓ flor-p rsj3• form glon graph k* grat ↓ ham ↓ hell hep hipp k* hippoc-k szs2 hir rsj4• hydr k* hydr-ac ↓ hyper ign j5.de* ind k* indg k* indol bro1 iris k* jug-c jug-r k* kali-ar *Kali-bi* k* *Kali-c* kali-chl k* kali-i k* kali-m k2 *Kali-n* kali-p k* **Kali-s** k* kali-sil k2 kalm k* lac-ac lac-leo hm2• lach k* lachn k* laur led lepi k* lept lil-t linu-c ↓ lob *Lyc* lycpr c1 lycps-v lyss *Mag-c* k* *Mag-m* mag-p mag-s mang meny meph k* *Merc* k* merc-i-f k* merc-i-r k* **Mez** k* mosch *Mur-ac* murx k* *Nat-ar Nat-c Nat-m* k* nat-ox rly4• nat-p nat-s ↓ nept-m lsd2.fr nicc ↓ *Nit-ac* nux-v ol-an ↓ olib-sac wmh1 olnd ↓ osteo-a knp1• pall ↓ par k* perh-mal jj3 petr k* petr-ra shn4• *Ph-ac Phos* k* phys k* pitu-gl skp7• plan k* *Plat* plb polys sk4• psor ptel a1 **Puls** k* ran-b rat rhod k* rhus-t k* rumx k2 ruta sabad sabin sacch-a ↓ sang sars sel k* *Seneg Sep* k* *Sil* k* spig spira a1 spong fd4.de *Stann* k* staph k* stram k* *Stront-c* suis-pan rly4• *Sul-ac* **Sulph** k* tab ↓ tarent k2 tell k* ter teucr ther thlas bro1 thuj k* til k* tritic-vg fd5.de urol-h rwt• v-a-b jl2 valer vanil fd5.de ven-m rsj12• *Zinc* k* zinc-p k2
  - **18 h**: aeth ↓ cob gels irid-met srj5• lac-leo hm2• nat-s paeon ptel puls rhus-t sacch-a fd2.de• sep
    - **18-4 h**: guaj k2 lac-leo hm2•
    - **18-20 h**: mim-p rsj8•
    - **cramping**: aeth hr1
  - **19 h**: bad *Cedr* chinin-s cocc elaps lyc mag-c nat-m rhod rhus-t sep *Sulph* verat-v
    - **19-22 h**: tetox pin2•
  - **20 h**: gymno lac-ac merc-i-r nicotam rly4• phys sol-ni stry sulph usn a2
    - **20-21 h**: helon indg
  - **21 h**: agath-a nl2• cham k2 coca dios eupi gels lyss osm pic-ac ptel suis-pan rly4•
    - **21-1 h**: crot-h bg1
  - **until** midnight: laur ↓
    - **tearing** pain: laur
  - **amel.**: am-c h2* anis c1 aur-m-n c1 *Bry* calc k2 calc-f coloc ↓ ham k* kali-bi lac-h ↓ lach mang nat-ar *Nat-m* nux-v ↓ phys pic-ac ran-b ↓ sang sol-t-ae a1 spig spirae a1 ter
    - **boring** pain: nux-v
    - **drawing** pain: coloc
    - **dull** pain: lac-h sk4•
    - **pressing** pain: ran-b
  - **bed**:
    - **in** bed:
      - **agg.**: arg-met arg-n ars carb-v cycl dulc fd4.de hipp laur lyc mag-s ↓ *Merc* ↓ nat-c ↓ nat-m phos plan ↓ *Puls* sep sil ↓ suis-pan rly4• **Sulph** thuj ↓ vanil fd5.de zinc k*

- **evening – bed – in** bed **– agg.**: ...
  - **boring** pain: mag-s
  - **burning**: carb-v k* *Merc* nat-c
  - **pressing** pain: carb-v h2*
  - **sore**: plan
  - **stitching** pain: carb-v
  - **tearing** pain: laur sil thuj
  - **amel.**: mag-c **Nux-v** sulph
- **boring** pain: aloe anac h2 arg-n coloc hipp mag-c mag-m nat-s plan puls ruta fd4.de sep zinc
- **burning**: am-c k* carb-ac jug-r merc-i-r nat-c h2 phys k*
- **bursting** pain: caps clem k* ham k* rat
- **cramping**: alum dulc fd4.de
- **cutting** pain: arge-pl rwt5• *Bell* k* dig kali-i
- **drawing** pain: all-c aloe ang k* bov castm crot-h dulc graph hipp k* kali-n kalm ol-an phos ran-b stront-c sul-ac h2* valer k* vanil fd5.de zinc
- **dull** pain: agath-a nl2• carbn-s dulc fd4.de ham fd3.de• ind pall petr-ra shn4• rhus-t h1 ruta fd4.de spong fd4.de vanil fd5.de
- **grinding** pain: anac k*
- **increasing** through the night: puls k2
- **lancinating**: *Bell* kali-i k*
- **lasting** all night: alum calc-sil k2 sulph k2
  - **and** following day: kali-n h2
- **lying** agg.: clem ↓
  - **hammering** pain: clem
- **lying** down agg.; after: stann ↓
  - **pressing** pain: stann
- **pinching** pain: alum k*
- **pressing** pain: acon k* agar alum alum-p k2 ambr *Anac* ang c1 arg-n ars k* bamb-a stb2.de• castm cham chel coc-c colch coloc dig dios dulc k* ferr k* fl-ac k* hell hydr-ac k* hyper k* kali-bi kali-n h2* kalm *Lyss* mag-m mag-s mang h2* nat-c h2 nat-m nat-s nept-m lsd2.fr ol-an phos plat h2* rhod *Rhus-t* ruta h1 sacch-a fd2.de• sep spong fd4.de staph **Sulph** tab tarent thuj tritic-vg fd5.de valer vanil fd5.de *Zinc*
- **shooting** pain: arum-t a1 bell k* dream-p sdj1• tarent
- **sore**: acon bov *Calc* castm chel *Euphr* graph mag-c nit-ac phos *Puls Zinc*
- **stitching** pain: ambr bar-c bell h1 bov calc k* canth carb-an carb-v k* caust chel dig dulc graph hyper indg kali-i linu-c a1 lyc k* mag-c k* mang mur-ac nat-c nat-m nit-ac petr phos k* plat puls rat k* sel sep *Sil* staph k* stram stront-c sulph thuj k* tritic-vg fd5.de valer vanil fd5.de
- **stunning** pain: *Puls*
- **sunset**, after: nat-s ↓
  - **pressing** pain: nat-s
- **tearing** pain: ail alum alum-sil k2 am-c ambr calc-p cocc coloc grat hyper kali-n lachn *Lyc* mag-c mag-m merc nat-c h2 nicc olnd petr *Puls* sars sil *Spig* staph sul-ac sulph
- **toward** evening:
  - **amel.**: kali-bi ↓
    - **shooting** pain: kali-bi k*
- **twilight**; in the: ang k* caj puls
- **walking** agg.: dulc ↓ ther c1
  - **pressing** pain: dulc

- **night**: acon k2 act-sp agar ↓ *Alum* alum-p k2 alum-sil k2 alumn am-c am-m ambr k* anac ang ant-c k2 *Ant-t* ap-g vh1* arg-n k* arge-pl rwt5• am *Ars* k* ars-h ↓ ars-s-f k2 arum-t asaf ↓ aster *Aur* k* aur-m ↓ *Bamb-a* stb2.de• *Bell* benz-ac k2 berb borx bov k* brucel ↓ bufo cact k* *Calc Calc-p* k* *Calc-s* camph canth *Carb-an* k* carb-v k* carbn-s *Caust Cedr* k* cham chel k* *Chin Chinin-ar* chinin-s cic clem k* cob ↓ coca ↓ *Cocc* colch con k* *Crot-c* cupr-ar cycl k* cyclosp sa3• dig dulc elaps epil a1* eug k* glon k* graph grat guaj k* ham helo-s ↓ *Hep* k* hippoc-k szs2 hir skp7• hydr-ac hyos ign ind k* kali-bi k2 *Kali-c Kali-i* kali-n *Kali-p Kali-s* kali-sil k2 kreos lac-ac lac-c lac-lup hm2• lach lact *Laur* led lob loxo-recl knl4• **Lyc** *Mag-c* mag-m mang ↓ **Merc** k* *Merc-c* merc-d bro1 merc-i-r ↓ *Mez* mill nat-ar nat-c nat-m nat-p **Nit-ac** nux-m nux-v op k* par petr-ra shn4• ph-ac *Phos* k* *Phyt* pitu-gl skp7• plat *Pneu* jl2 polys sk4• positr nl2• pot-e rly4• psor al ptel bro1 puls k* raph rhus-r rhus-t rumx k2

- **night**: ...
  ruta fd4.de sars sep k* *Sil* k* sol-ni spig spong fd4.de stram stront-c stry bro1 *Sulph* k* **Syph** k* tarent k* *Thuj* k* til ban1• tritic-vg fd5.de urol-h rwt• vanil fd5.de verat k* zinc k* zinc-p k2 [tax jsj7]
  - **midnight**:
    - **before**: am-m anac caust chin dulc *Lach* puls rhus-t sep
      - **22** h: carbn-s dios ham laur mag-p myric phys
      - **23** h: **Cact** castm dios indg merc-i-r pip-m stram valer
        - **amel.**: adam skp7•
      - **boring** pain: dulc k*
    - **about**: agar all-s arn ars elaps hep *Kali-c* mag-s myric plat puls sep staphycoc rly4• sulph k2
      - **morning**; until: hep
    - **after**: agar ambr a1 *Ars* bamb-a stb2.de• bufo carb-an cham ferr k* hep hippoc-k szs2 ign kali-ar kali-c kali-sil k2 lac-c mrr1 nat-s ph-ac psor rhus-t sep *Sil* spig *Thuj*
      - **1** h: ars vh chin hr1 elaps a1 lavand-a ctl1• (non:pall hr1) uran-n c
        - **1-6** h: cassia-s ↓
          pulsating pain: cassia-s ccrh1•
        - **1-10** h: chin (non:elaps a1)
        - **1-11** h: chin hr1 elaps k*
        - **1-12** h: chin hr1
      - **2** h: ars h2 cimic sulph
        - **pressing** pain: ars
      - **3** h: adam ↓ *Agar* bov *Chin* vh *Chinin-s* k* ferr ↓ nat-m thuj urol-h rwt•
        - **nail**; as from a: adam skp7•
        - **stitching** pain: ferr
      - **3-4** h: thuj ↓
        - **pressing** pain: thuj
      - **4** h: alumn vh1 bamb-a stb2.de• chel con h2 raph stram
        - **waking**; on: sang a1 xan c1
      - **5** h: calc dios kali-bi **Kali-i** luf-op rsj5• mur-ac h2 stann
        - **burning**: kali-i mrr1
        - **stitching** pain: kali-i mrr1
    - **and morning**: ind bg1
  - **accompanied** by | **salivation**: *Verat* kr1*
  - **amel.**: bad c1 bufo chlam-tr bcx2• glon a1 ham k* hir ↓ mag-c ozone sde2• sol-t-ae spira
    - **pressing** pain: hir skp7•
  - **bed**:
    - **driving** out of bed: *Thuj*
    - **in** bed | **agg.**: aloe *Alum* alumn androc srj1• chin j5.de cyclosp sa3• fago hipp hyper merc-i-f ruta fd4.de *Sulph* *Thuj* vanil fd5.de
  - **boring** pain: am-c k* arg-n carb-v clem dulc k* lyc phos k2 ruta fd4.de sep h2 sulph
  - **burning**: arn lyc *Merc* *Sil*
  - **burrowing**: agar
  - **bursting** pain: aster a1 cact carb-an cedr *Hep*
  - **cutting** pain: dig
  - **drawing** pain: agar h2* *Kali-c* nat-m phos rhus-t sep h2*
  - **dull** pain: brucel sa3• nat-c h2
  - **gnawing** pain: merc-i-r k*
  - **lancinating**: am-c a1 tarent k*
  - **lighting** the gas amel.: *Lac-c* sil
  - **pressing** pain: ambr h1* guaj helo-s rwt2• hep lyc mang h2* nit-ac h2* nux-v petr-ra shn4• *Sil* sulph vanil fd5.de
  - **pulsating** pain: asaf tl1 bamb-a stb2.de• ruta fd4.de tritic-vg fd5.de
  - **shooting** pain: tarent k*
  - **sleep**:
    - **amel.**: agar pic-ac k2 sang hr1
      - **preventing**: kali-n h2 sulph h2
  - **sore**: cob coca phos ruta fd4.de
  - **stepping** hard agg.: lyc ↓
    - **gnawing** pain: lyc

- **night**: ...
  - **stitching** pain: am-c arum-t dig hep *Lyc* mag-c h2* nat-m sep sil h2 spig *Sulph*
  - **stunning** pain: arg-n ars-h hr1 kali-n h2 verat hr1
  - **tearing** pain: agar h2 aur-m k2 *Caust* cham hep laur *Lyc* mag-c merc phos k2 *Sil* sulph h2 thuj
  - **waking** him or her from sleep: *Hep* ↓
    - **bursting** pain: *Hep*
  - **waking**; on: *Agar* alumn ambr k* ant-t arg-n ↓ aster bufo canth chlam-tr bcx2• cinnb coloc ferr gels k* gins k* glon hep ↓ hir rsj4• hyper k* kola stb3• lac-ac mag-c mang merc-i-f k* mez nat-ar nat-c ↓ nit-ac h2* nux-v h1* ph-ac plat ↓ pseuts-m oss1• *Psor* rumx
    - **pressing** pain: canth mang h2* nat-c h2* plat h2* *Psor*
    - **stitching** pain: hep k*
    - **tearing** pain: arg-n
- **weekend**; on the (See periodical - week - every)
- **accompanied** by:
  - **anemia** (See GENERALS - Anemia - accompanied - head)
  - **appetite**; ravenous: *(↗STOMACH - Appetite - Increased - headache - during)* phos k2* spong fd4.de
  - **asthenopia**: nicc-met br1
  - **asthma**: lach mtf11
  - **breath**; offensive: calc-act bro1 card-m bro1 euon bro1 gymno bro1 *Puls* bro1
  - **chill**; shaking: bamb-a stb2.de• *Lac-d* mrr1
  - **chilliness**: sang a1
  - **coldness** of the body; icy: cadm-s gm1 lachn c1 verat mrr1
    - **Vertex** (See Coldness - vertex - icy)
  - **company**; aversion to (See MIND - Company - aversion - headache)
  - **constipation**: alet a *Aloe* k* alum k* am-c gsy1 arg-n sne aur bc bell vh **Bry** k* *Calc-p* chin a coff *Coll* k* con crot-h dioxi rbp6 dys fmm1• euon bro1 fl-ac a* gels bro1 graph a *Hydr* bro1 ign iris c1* kali-bi a *Lac-d* k* lach mag-c merc *Nat-m* *Nat-s* nicc a* nicc-met br1 nit-ac bro1 *Nux-v* k* op k* petr *Plb* k* *Podo* *Puls* rat bro1 rhus-t a1 sep bro1 verat k* zinc
  - **deafness** (See HEARING - Lost - accompanied - head - pain)
  - **diarrhea** (See diarrhea - during)
  - **drawn** backward; head being (See Drawn - backward - accompanied - head)
  - **dreams**: menis br1
  - **drinks**; aversion to (See GENERALS - Food and - drinks - aversion - accompanied - head)
  - **empty**, hollow sensation (See Empty - headache)
  - **eructations**: *(↗eructations - amel.)* *Calc* b4a.de* chel mrr1 cimic ptk1 mag-m ptk1
  - **fever**: acon bro1 agar bro1 anders zzc1• apis bro1 ars bro1 astac bro1 *Bell* bro1 bism hr1 cedr bro1 chin bro1 eup-per bro1 ferr-p bro1 ip tl1 nat-m bro1* nux-v bro1 ozone sde2• polyp-p br1* streptoc jl2 wye bro1 [bell-p-sp dcm1]
  - **food**; aversion of (See GENERALS - Food - food - aversion - accompanied - head)
  - **fullness** in head: mand sp1
  - **heat**:
    - **flushes** of (See GENERALS - Heat - flushes - headache)
    - **in** head (See Heat - accompanied - head)
  - **hemorrhoids** (See Hemorrhoids)
  - **herpes**: iris mrr1
  - **hiccough**: aeth st1
  - **indifference** (See MIND - Indifference - headache)
  - **indigestion**: *(↗gastric)* ant-c tl1 chel mrr1 chinin-s mrr1 kali-bi tl1 nat-s mrr1 nicc-met br1 tarent tl1 tub jl2

- **irritability** (See MIND - Irritability - headache)
- **jerking** of head (See Jerking - accompanied - head)
- **lachrymation**: mez ptk1
  - **scalding**: puls br1*
- **leukorrhea** (See FEMALE - Leukorrhea - accompanied - head - pain)
- **malaria** (See GENERALS - Malaria - accompanied - head)
- **myoma**; uterine: til gm1
- **nausea**: *(↗gastric; sides - one - accompanied - nausea)* acon k* acon-ac rly4• aesc aeth hr1 aids nl2• ail aloe bg2* *Alum* k* alum-p k2 alum-sil k2 alumn *Am-c* k* ambr h1 androc srj1• **Ant-c** k* ant-t k* apis arg-met k* arg-n k* arge-pl rwt5• arn k* *Ars* k* ars-s-f k2 asar k* asc-c c1 asc-t br1 aur k* aur-ar k2 aur-s k2 bamb-a stb2.de• *Bell* b4a.de* benz-ac bism hr1 *Borx* bros-gau mrc1 *Bry* k* bung-fa mtf cadm-met sp1 cadm-s c1 calc k* calc-lp br1 *Calc-p* calc-s calc-sil k2 camph k* cann-s *Caps* k* *Carb-ac* *Carb-v* k* *Carbn-s* **Caust** k* *Cedr* cham b7a.de* chel k* chin k* chinin-ar chinin-s k* *Chion* br1 chlf c2 cic k* cimic cina bg2 cit-v br1 clem a1 cob cob-n sp1 **Cocc** k* *Coloc* k* **Con** k* cor-r croc k* crot-h *Cupr* cycl dig bg2 dioxi rbp6 dros k* *Dulc* k* ephe-si hsj1• epiph bg3* *Eug* eup-per k* eup-pur ferr k* fl-ac form k* gels k* ger br1 gink-b sbd1• *Glon* k* *Graph* k* grat guaj b4a.de* guar br1 ham fd3.de• hep hipp hir rsj4• hydrog srj2• hyos b7a.de ign k* ignis-alc es2• ind indol bro1 **Ip** k* **Iris** k* kali-ar *Kali-bi* k* *Kali-c* k* kali-cy br1 kali-p *Kali-s* kali-sil k2 kalm *Kola* stb3• kreos k* *Lac-c* k* *Lac-d* k* lac-h htj1*• *Lach* lap-la rsp1 *Lept* lith-c *Lob* k* lob-p bro1 luna kg1• lyc k* mag-c k* mang-p rly4• med c1 meli mrr1* *Merc* k* mez k* mill moni rfm1• morg-p fmm1• *Mosch* k* naja bg2* nat-ar nat-c *Nat-m* k* nat-p k* nat-s nat-sil fd3.de• nicc-met br1 *Nit-ac* k* *Nux-m* *Nux-v* k* olnd b7.de* onos bg2 *Op* ozone sde2• paull bro1 petr k* petr-ra shn4• *Phos* k* phyt plat plut-n srj7• podo fd3.de• positr nl2• pot-e rly4• prun bg2 ptel c1 *Puls* k* ran-b k* rhus-t k* ruta k* sabin b7a.de sal-al blc1• samb bat1• **Sang** k* sarcol-ac sp1 sarr br1 *Sars* k* seneg *Sep* k* sil k* spig spong fd4.de *Stann* k* stict c1* stram stront-c k* suis-em rly4• *Sulph* k* syc fmm1• symph fd3.de• *Tab* k* taosc iwa1• tarax k* tep ter *Thea* br1 ther k* thuj h1 tritic-vg fd5.de vanil fd5.de ven-m rsj12• verat k* vip bg2 visc sp1 xan c1 zinc k* zinc-p k2 zing [bell-p-sp dcm1 heroin sdj2 spect dfg1 tax jsj7]
  - **end** of the headache; at the: ign bg2
  - **menses**:
    - **after** | **agg.**: syc bka1•
    - **before** | **agg.**: syc bka1•
    - **during** | **agg.**: syc bka1•
- **nausea** and gray tongue: *Kali-c* kr1*
- **nausea** and white tongue: *Lept* kr1*
- **nephrosis** (See KIDNEYS - Nephrosis - accompanied - head)
- **numbness**: bell bg2 calc-f sp1 chel bro1 cocc mrr1 **Graph** bg2* indol bro1 mang h2 phos bg2 plat bg2*
  - **Body**; of whole: cedr ptk1
- **pains**; other: psil ft1
- **palpitations** (See CHEST - Palpitation - accompanied - head)
- **photophobia** (See EYE - Photophobia - headache)
- **psoriasis**: iris mrr1
- **quiet**; wants to be (See MIND - Quiet; wants - headache)
- **respiration**; complaints of (See RESPIRATION - Complaints - accompanied - head)
- **retching** (See STOMACH - Retching - accompanied - head)
- **salivation**: am-c k* cinnb hr1* *Dulc* hr1 epiph bg1* fagu bro1 hipp k* ign k* irid-met bg1 iris c1* kali-bi bg1 lyss hr1 mang bg1 **Merc** k* *Nat-s* k* op bg1 phos h2* sep bg1 vanil fd5.de verat k*
- **sexual** desire: *Pic-ac* kr1* ruta fd4.de sep
- **sleepiness**: galeoc-c-h gms1• sanguis-s hrn2• vanil fd5.de ven-m rsj12•
- **sneezing**; frequent: abrom-a bnj1 cadm-met tpw6 dulc fd4.de lac-cp sk4•
- **sweets**; desire for (See GENERALS - Food and - sweets - desire - headache)
- **taste** in mouth | **bitter**: calc-p ptk1 nat-s mrr1
- **typhoid** fever: acetan bro1 *Bell* bro1 *Bry* bro1 gels bro1 hyos bro1 nux-v bro1 rhus-t bro1
- **urination**:
  - **frequent** (See BLADDER - Urination - frequent - headache)
  - **scanty**: *(↗Brain; complaints of - accompanied - urine)* benz-ac k2
- **vertigo** (See VERTIGO - Accompanied - head - pain)
- **vision**:
  - **blurred** (See VISION - Blurred - headache - during)
  - **colors** before the eyes (See VISION - Colors - accompanied - head)
  - **flickering** (See VISION - Flickering - headache - during)
  - **loss** of (See VISION - Loss - headache - during)
- **vomiting**: *(↗gastric)* *Aeth* agn alum alum-sil k2 anan androc srj1• ant-c k2 ant-t k* *Apis* apom bro1 *Arg-n* k* arn *Ars* k* ars-s-f k2 asar k* bar-m *Bell* *Bry* k* *Cact* cadm-met gm1 cadm-s *Calc* calc-act bro1 calc-s calc-sil k2 *Caps* carbn-s caust k* cham bro1 *Chel* ptk1 chin k* chinin-ar chinin-s bg2 *Chlf* cic bg2 cimic cimx cit-v br1 cocc k* *Coff* coloc con corn *Crot-h* crot-t *Cupr* dioxi rbp6 dulc eug eup-per k2 ferr ferr-ar ferr-p *Form* gaert pte1*• *Gels* glon k* *Graph* *Grat* **Ip** k* *Iris* k* jatr-c kali-ar kali-bi k* kali-c kali-chl kali-p kali-s kali-sil k2 kola stb3• kreos k* *Lac-c* k* *Lac-d* k* lac-h htj1• *Lach* *Lob* k* med **Meli** k* merc bg2 mez k* mosch *Naja* *Nat-m* k* nat-p *Nat-s* *Nux-m* *Nux-v* k* op ozone sde2• petr bro1 *Phos* plat *Plb* **Puls** k* ran-b bg2 rhus-r rob bro1 **Sang** k* sarcol-ac sp1 sarr sars *Sep* k* *Sil* k* spig *Stann* stict c1 *Stram* sulph symph fd3.de• tab k* tarax bg2 *Ther* thuj h1 tub c1* vanil fd5.de verat bg3* verat-v vip xan zinc zinc-p k2 zinc-s bro1
  - **bile** (See STOMACH - Vomiting; type - bile - headache)
- **weakness** (See GENERALS - Weakness - headache - during)
- ○ **Abdomen**:
  - **complaints** (See ABDOMEN - Complaints - accompanied - head)
  - **distension**: mand sp1
  - **flatulence** (See ABDOMEN - Flatulence - headache)
  - **pain** in: cina bro1 coloc bro1 con gt1 hydrog srj2• lept gt1 nept-m lsd2.fr verat bro1
- **Arms**; white discoloration of the: mand mg*
- **Arteries**; tension in (See GENERALS - Tension - arteries - accompanied - head)
- **Back**:
  - **coldness**: berb bro1 dulc fd4.de lac-d c1
  - **pain** in: ail benz-ac cina cob cob-n sp1 daph fl-ac graph hir rsj4• hydr menis merc myric ol-an op sabad sabin *Sil* thymol sp1 verat ziz
    - **Cervical** region (See neck - pain)
    - **Lumbar** region: apoc cob lac-c rad-br bro1 sil
- **Carotids**; pulsation of (See EXTERNAL - Pulsation - carotids; EXTERNAL - Pulsation - carotids - headache)
- **Cervical** region:
  - **cracking** (See BACK - Cracking - cervical - accompanied - head)
  - **pain** in (See neck - pain)
  - **weakness**: fago ptk1
- **Ear**:
  - **discharges** from ears (See EAR - Discharges - accompanied - head)
  - **heat** in left ear (See EAR - Heat - left - accompanied - head)
  - **noises** in (See EAR - Noises - headache)
  - **pulsation** in the ear: bamb-a stb2.de•
  - **stitches** in the left ear: borx h1* neon srj5•
- **Extremities**: bamb-a ↓

- **Extremities**: ...
  - **cold**: carbn-s hr1* dulc fd4.de mand sp1
  - **sore** pain in: bamb-a stb2.de•
- **Eye**: *(↗occiput - accompanied - eye)* petr-ra shn4•
  - **blinking**: lac-cp sk4•
  - **complaints**: aloe bg2 anac bg2 apis b7a.de arg-met b7.de* **Bar-c** bg2 *Bell* bg2 bov bg2 brucel sa3• **Bry** bg2 calc-act bg2 carb-v bg2 chel bg2 cimic bg2 *Cina* b7.de* **Cocc** b7.de* croc b7.de* glon bg2 ign b7.de* kali-bi bg2 kali-n b4.de* kreos bg2 **Lach** bg2 lyc bg2 mag-c bg2 mag-m bg2 merc bg2 mur-ac bg2 nat-c b4a.de* *Nat-m* b4.de* *Nux-v* b7.de* phos bg2 plat bg2 prun bg2 **Puls** b7.de* rhus-t b7.de* *Sabad* b7a.de samb b7.de* seneg bg2 **Sep** bg2 **Sil** bg2 *Spong* b7a.de staph bg2 stram bg2 sulph bg2 *Verat* b7.de* zinc bg2
  - **contraction** of eyelids: sulph h2
  - **discoloration** red (See EYE - Discoloration - red - headache - during)
  - **enlarged** sensation of eyes: arg-n bro1
  - **flickering** before eyes (See VISION - Flickering - headache - during)
  - **heaviness** (See EYE - Heaviness - accompanied - head)
  - **inflammation** of eyes: bad ptk1
  - **pain**: *(↗occiput - accompanied - eye)* *Agar* aloe bro1 *Apis* bamb-a stb2.de• **Bell** cedr bro1 cimic k2* con cor-r br1 *Eup-per* bro1 *Gels* bro1 haliae-lc srj5• hom-xyz bro1 iris tl1 kola stb3• luf-op rsj5• mentho bro1 myrt-c bro1 nat-m bro1 nit-ac h2 olib-sac wmh1 ozone sde2• petr-ra shn4• phel bro1 sanguis-s hrn2• *Scut* bro1 seneg sep sil bro1 *Spig* bro1 stict symph fd3.de• ther tl1 vanil fd5.de zinc h2
    - **burning** (See EYE - Pain - headache - during - burning)
    - **sand**; as from (See EYE - Pain - sand - accompanied - head)
- **Face**:
  - **complaints** of: *Kali-n* b4a.de
  - **neuralgia** (See FACE - Pain - neuralgic - accompanied - headache)
  - **pale**: acon k* aeth k* *Alum* am-c h2* ambr aml-ns ptk1 anac k* *Ars* k* aur-m-n wbt2• bism hr1 *Calc* bro1 canth *Carb-v* chin bro1 *Chinin-s* *Echi* *Hell* hydr k* ign k* ip k* kali-bi tl1 lac-d c1* *Lach* k* lob bro1 mag-c meli bro1* nat-m bro1 *Phos* k* sang sne *Sep* k* sil bro1 spig k* *Stram* tab bro1 valer *Verat* k* *Zinc*
  - **red** (See FACE - Discoloration - red - headache)
- **Gallbladder**; complaints of: chin mrr1 nat-s mrr1
- **Gastrointestinal** complaints (See ABDOMEN - Gastrointestinal - accompanied - head)
- **Hair**; falling of: ant-c a* hep ptk1 nit-ac a* sep a* sil bg2* syph a thuj bg2*
- **Heart**; pain in: crot-h ptk1
  - **lying** on the left side; when: crot-h br1 kalm c1
- **Kidneys**; inflammation of (See KIDNEYS - Inflammation - accompanied - head)
- **Lips**; numbness and tingling of: nat-m bro1
- **Liver**; complaints of: *Chel* bro1* chin mrr1 jug-c bro1 *Lept* bro1 nux-v bro1 ptel bro1
- **Lower** limbs; complaints of: agar bg2 camph bg2 graph bg2 kali-c bg2 kali-n bg2 lol bg2 mosch bg2 ph-ac bg2 puls bg2 rhus-t bg2 sep bg2 sil bg2 spig bg2 sulph bg2 tab bg2
- **Mouth**; complaints of: epiph bg2 kali-bi bg2 phos bg2
- **Neck**:
  - **pain** in: *(↗BACK - Stiffness - cervical - headache)* acon ail *Alum* anac arg-n arn asar *Bamb-a* stb2.de• bar-c *Bell* borx bry bufo bung-fa mtf *Calc-p* cann-i cann-s canth *Carb-v* *Carbn-s* caust chel chin clem con elaps euph fago fic-m gya1 gal-ac **Gels** *Glon* graph *Hell* hura hydr-ac hyos irid-met srj5• jac-g kali-c kali-i *Kalm* kola stb3• lach laur lil-t lyc lyss mag-c mag-s manc merc merc-i-f mosch myric *Nat-m* nat-s k2

- **accompanied** by – **Neck** – **pain** in: ...
  ozone sde2• peti *Pic-ac* plb psor ptel ran-b rhus-r sars serp spong stry sulph tep ziz
  - **Nape** of neck: *(↗BACK - Stiffness - cervical - headache)* aeth alum am-c ambr anac asar bar-c *Bell* berb borx bry *Calc* *Calc-p* calc-sil k2 cann-s carb-an carb-v caust chel cimic c1* cinnb clem **Cocc** k* con corn crot-t **Gels** *Glon* graph *Hell* hydr-ac hyos iod ip kali-c kali-n *Kalm* lac-c lil-t lyc mag-c manc merc mez mosch mur-ac nat-c *Nat-m* nat-s k2 nept-m lsd2.fr op paeon par **Ph-ac** *Phyt* **Pic-ac** plb plect *Puls* ran-b rhus-t k* sabin sang k2* sars sil spong *Stry* sulph tarax tarent tritic-vg fd5.de verat
    - **opening** and closing; as if alternately: cocc tl1
  - **stiffness** in | **Nape** of neck: *(↗BACK - Stiffness - cervical - headache)* **Cimic** mrr1 nept-m lsd2.fr *Rhus-t* mrr1
  - **weakness**: sep mtf11
- **Nose**: oci-sa sk4• ozone sde2• ros-d wla1
  - **catarrh** (See NOSE - Catarrh - accompanied - head - pain)
  - **dry**: dulc br1*
  - **numbness** and tingling of nose: nat-m bro1
  - **obstruction** of: bamb-a stb2.de• calc chir-fl gya2 lach ozone sde2• phos sang *Stict* mrr1 thuj
  - **watery** discharge (See NOSE - Discharge - watery - accompanied - head)
  - **Root** of nose; pain at (See NOSE - Pain - root - headache)
- **Occiput**; coldness in: berb bro1
- **Scalp**; sore pain in: aesc bro1 *Chin* bro1 coloc bro1 sil bro1
- **Spleen**; pain in: borx h2* cean c1 slag pfa2
- **Stomach**:
  - **acidity** in stomach: plat-m a1* rob br1
  - **complaints**: bov bg2 calc-p bg2
  - **distension** of stomach: hydrog srj2• kali-bi tl1 lyc tl1
  - **emptiness** in stomach: cocc dig k2 *Ign* bro1 kali-p bro1 kola stb3• *Nat-m* nit-ac h2 ozone sde2• *Phos* ptel *Sang* **Sep** k*
  - **flatulence** of stomach (See STOMACH - Flatulence of - accompanied - head)
  - **pain** in stomach: bism hr1* cob-n sp1 kola ↓
    - **pressing** pain: kola stb3•
- **Teeth**:
  - **pain** in (See TEETH - Pain - accompanied - head - pain)
  - **stitching**, stinging pain in (See TEETH - Pain - stitching - accompanied - head)
- **Temples** | **Veins**; distention of (See FACE - Veins - temples - accompanied - head)
- **Throat**; pain in: petr-ra shn4•
- **Tongue**:
  - **clean** tongue: *Nat-m* kr1*
  - **gray** discoloration of the tongue: kali-m kr1*
  - **gray** tongue and nausea (See nausea and gray)
  - **numbness** and tingling of tongue: nat-m bro1
  - **stiffness**: *Lach* kr1*
  - **white** discoloration of the tongue: calc-act bro1 card-m bro1* euon bro1 gymno bro1 **Mag-m** kr1* puls bro1*
    - **bluish** white: *Gymno* br1*
  - **white** tongue and nausea (See nausea and white)
- **Uterus**; complaints of (See FEMALE - Uterus - accompanied - head)

- **aching**: acon bro1* *Aesc* bro1 agar ptk1 alf bro1 all-c bro1 aloe bro1* am-c ptk1 ant-c bro1 *Arg-n* bro1 ars bro1* aza bro1 bapt bro1 bell bro1* bism ptk1 bry ptk1 but-ac bro1 cact ptk1 calc ptk1 caps bro1 carb-ac bro1* *Carb-v* bro1* card-m bro1 *Chel* ptk1 chin bro1* *Cimic* bro1 cocc bro1 corv-cor bdg• euon bro1 *Gels* bro1* glon ptk1 *Hell* bro1 *Hydr* bro1 ichth bro1 *Ign* bro1 indol bro1 iris bro1 kali-bi bro1 *Lept* bro1 lil-t bro1 mentho bro1 meny ptk1 myric bro1 naja bro1 nat-ar bro1 **Nat-m** ptk1 *Nux-v* bro1* *Nyct* bro1 onos bro1 oreo bro1 *Petr* ptk1 ph-ac ptk1 *Phel* bro1 phos ptk1 pic-ac bro1 *Plb* bro1 *Puls* ptk1 rauw sp1 rhus-t ptk1 scut bro1

- **aching**: ...
  sep ptk1 sil bro1* *Stann* bro1 *Stel* bro1 *Sulph* ptk1 thuj ptk1 thymol sp1 vero-o rly3• x-ray sp1 zinc ptk1 [bell-p-sp dcm1]
  - **accompanied** by | **Teeth**; pain in: borx bg2 euph bg2 kali-n bg2 lach bg2 puls bg2 thuj bg2 verat bg2
  - **Brain**: *Acon* aloe alum alum-p k2 am-c anac ant-c c1 arg-met arg-n *Ars* k* ars-s-f k2 asaf asar aur bar-c bell bov calc calc-sil k2 camph canth carb-v carc mrr1* caust cham *Chin* chinin-ar k2 *Chinin-s* cina coc-c *Coloc* con corn croc daph dream-p sdj1• dros *Dulc* glon graph guaj k2 hydrog srj2• hyos ign kali-n lach laur lyc mag-c mang *Med* merc *Mosch* mur-ac nat-m *Nit-ac* nux-v olnd petr *Ph-ac* phos phys prun *Psor* ran-b rhod ruta sabad sars sil *Spig* stann *Staph* stram tl1 sul-ac sulph syph hr1 ther thuj tub bg1* zinc [spect dfg1]
- **acids**, from: *Ant-c* hr1 bell morph *Sel*
- **after**:
  - **agg.**: plat bg2
    - ⁝ **External** head: plat bg2 sep bg2
- **agg.** | **External** head: nit-ac bg2 rhus-t bg2 sabad bg2 sil bg2 thuj bg2
- **air**; draft of:
  - **agg.**: *Acon* *Ars* k* aur-s wbt2• *Bell* k* benz-ac cadm-s k* *Calc* calc-sil k2 caps carb-v k2 caust *Chin* k* coloc dulc fd4.de eup-pur bro1 ferr-p bro1 gels *Hep* hir ↓ ichth bro1 ign bro1 iris bro1 kali-ar *Kali-c* kali-n c1 kali-p kali-s kali-sil k2 kola stb3• lac-c lac-h sk4• mag-c ↓ *Merc* nux-m *Nux-v* k* phos psor jl2* rhod bro1 *Rhus-t* k* *Sanic* *Sel* **Sil** k* stront-c *Sulph* til ↓ valer verb
    - ⁝ **drawing** pain: til valer
    - ⁝ **dull** pain: hir skp7•
    - ⁝ **neuralgic**: mag-c mrr1
  - **amel.**: petr-ra shn4•
- **air**; in open:
  - **agg.**: agar ↓ alum ang *Arg-n* ars j5.de* bar-c bar-i k2 bar-m *Bell* bell-p sp1 both-ax tsm2 bov k* bran bro1 bry cadm-s *Calc* calc-ar calc-p *Carb-an* card-m ↓ *Caust* cedr cham *Chel* **Chin** k* cimic cina k* *Cocc* k* coff k* colch *Con* *Cycl* k* dulc fd4.de eup-per euphr ferr glon k* grat *Hep* hipp ign iod ip iris tl1 *Kali-c* kali-m k2 kalm lach laur *Lil-t* lyc mag-m br1* *Mang* meny **Merc** *Mez* mur-ac nat-m *Nux-v* k* ol-an ↓ petr phos phyt a1 plect ↓ psor mrr1 ran-b rat ↓ rhus-t sep bro1 sil hr1 spig k* spong fd4.de staph sulph tritic-vg fd5.de ulm-c jsj8• valer zinc [tax jsj7]
    - ⁝ **burrowing**: agar rat
    - ⁝ **bursting** pain: **Bell** glon mag-m br1
    - ⁝ **cutting** pain: nat-m
    - ⁝ **drawing** pain: *Con* k* grat k* kalm mang k* plect
    - ⁝ **nail**; as from a: coff
    - ⁝ **pressing** pain: agar caust chel *Chin* ferr glon hep laur meny h1 *Merc* nux-v rhus-t valer hr1
    - ⁝ **sore**: calc card-m k2 eup-per
    - ⁝ **stitching** pain: *Mang* sil
    - ⁝ **tearing** pain: calc mang ol-an
  - **amel.**: abrom-a ↓ acon k* act-sp bro1 *All-c* k* aloe *Alum* k* alum-p k2 am-c ambr androc srj1• ang *Ant-c* ap-g k* *Apis* *Aran* k* arg-met c1 arg-n arist-cl sp1 arn *Ars* ars-i asar aur aur-s k2 bamb-a stb2.de• bar-c bar-i k2 bar-s k2 bell berb k* beryl sp1 bov bufo k2 calc calc-s camph cann-i cann-s *Carb-ac* carb-an h2* *Carb-v* carbn-s caust chlol br1 *Cimic* k* cinnb ↓ clem cob k* coc-c *Coca* bro1 *Coff* k* coloc com con cor-r a1 cortiso ↓ cot a1* croc dream-p sdj1• dulc ephe-si hsj1• erig vml3• fago *Ferr* k* ferr-ar ferr-i flor-p rsj3• *Glon* k* granit-m ↓ graph k2 grat ham k* hed sp1 *Hell* hippoc-k szs2 hir ↓ hist sp1* hydr hydr-ac hydroph ↓ hyos indol bro1 iod *Ip* ↓ jatr-c joan bro1 *Kali-bi* kali-c *Kali-i* kali-n *Kali-p* *Kali-s* kola stb3• lac-c lach lap-la sde8.de• laur *Led* lil-t k2 limest-b es1• lith-c **Lyc** lyss *Mag-m* mag-s maias-l hm2• malar jl2 **Mang** mang-c kr2 meli vml3• meny merc-i-f mez mosch myric ↓ naja ↓ nat-ar nat-c *Nat-m* nat-p nat-s k2 *Nicc* nux-v vh olnd op ozone sde2• petr petr-ra shn4• ph-ac phasco-ci rbp2 phel **Phos** k* pic-ac plat **Puls** k* rad-met bro1 ran-b rauw sp1 rhod ruta fd4.de sabin ↓ sal-fr sle1• sang sars sel **Seneg** **Sep** k* sin-a a1 sin-n k* sol-ni spong stann sul-ac sul-i k4 sulph *Tab* k* tarent thuj k* trios ↓ tub xxb tung-met bdx1• vanil fd5.de viol-t visc sp1 xan c1 **Zinc** k* zinc-p k2 [helia stj7 tax jsj7]
    - ⁝ **burning**: *Apis* ars k2 mang myric **Phos**
    - ⁝ **bursting** pain: ars k2 beryl tpw5 kali-bi
    - ⁝ **cutting** pain: am-c

- **air**; in open – **amel.**: ...
    - ⁝ **drawing** pain: asar k* hell k* olnd
    - ⁝ **dull** pain: abrom-a ks5 bamb-a stb2.de• granit-m es1• hir skp7• hydroph rsj6•
    - ⁝ **lancinating**: am-c
    - ⁝ **pressing** pain: alum *Arg-met* bov cinnb coloc *Hell* hydr-ac jatr-c lach lyc mag-m mang *Phos* ruta fd4.de sabin seneg trios rsj11• vanil fd5.de
      - ⁝ **vise**; as if in a: caust
    - ⁝ **pulsating** pain: dream-p sdj1•
    - ⁝ **shooting** pain: naja
    - ⁝ **sore**: ang k* *Ip* k*
    - ⁝ **stitching** pain: am-c cortiso skp7• grat a1 nicc ruta fd4.de sars *Sep* tab
    - ⁝ **tearing** pain: alum ant-c h2 *Arg-met* aur carbn-s mag-s sulph

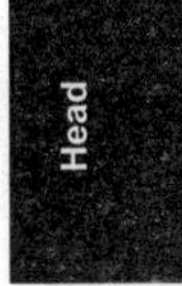

- **alcoholic** drinks:
  - **after**: ruta ↓
    - ⁝ **nail**; as from a: ruta
  - **agg.**: ozone ↓
    - ⁝ **dull** pain: ozone sde2•
- **alcoholics** (See spirituous)
- **alternating** with:
  - **asthma** (See RESPIRATION - Asthmatic - alternating - head)
  - **cough**: lach k* psor
  - **diarrhea**: *Aloe* bro1 mag-p k2 *Podo* k* sec
  - **dreams**; many: ars bg2*
    - ⁝ **sleepiness**; and: ars bg1*
  - **eruptions**: psor a
  - **faintness**: rhodi c1
  - **frightful** dreams: chin k*
  - **heat**; flushes of: lyss hr1*
  - **hemorrhages**: aloe vh
  - **hemorrhoids**: abrot aloe k*
  - **indigestion**: nat-c mrr1
  - **nausea**: androc srj1• squil
  - **oppression** of chest: glon k*
  - **physical** symptoms: ars k2
  - **prolapsus** ani: *Arn*
  - **red** sand in urine: *Lyc*
  - **respiration**; complaints of: *Coloc* b4a.de
  - **rheumatism**: ars k2
  - **sadness**: aur vh
  - **scotoma**: pitu-a ft
  - **sleep** | **deep**: plb a1
  - **sleepiness** | **dreams**; and many (See dreams - sleepiness)
  - **vision**:
    - ⁝ **confusion** of: kali-bi kr1
    - ⁝ **loss** of: *Kali-bi*
  - ○ **Abdomen**:
    - ⁝ **complaints**; uterine and abdominal: aloe k* cina bg1 hippoc-k szs2
    - ⁝ **pain** in: aesc androc srj1• *Ars* bism mrr1 bry bg1 calc-p bg2 cina k* *Gels* hydrog srj2• *Iris* plb k* rhus-r thuj bg1
  - **Back**; pain in: (↗*cervical; lumbar)* acon ptk1 aloe k* alum ptk1 brom k* ign bg2* meli k* sep ptk1
  - **Bladder**; complaints of: alumn a
  - **Bladder**; inflammation of: *Alumn* vh1
  - **Cervical** region; pain in: (↗*back)* hyos
  - **Chest**:
    - ⁝ **oppression** (See CHEST - Oppression - alternating - head)
    - ⁝ **pain** in: lachn
  - **Feet**; perspiration of: merc k2
  - **Fingers**:
    - ⁝ **coldness** in the: *Cupr*

- **Fingers**: ...
  - **Joints** of fingers; tearing pain in: kali-n h2
- **Hypochondria**; stitches in: aesc
- **Joints**:
  - **gouty** pain in: eup-per pd sulph bg1*
  - **pain** in: eup-per k2 *Lyc* sulph
- **Limbs**; pain in: sulph bg1
- **Liver** disturbances: podo k2
- **Lumbar** region; pain in: *(↗back)* aesc mrr1 aloe k* brom lycps-v meli
  - **aching**: aloe brom k*
- **Lumbosacral** region: meli
- **Neck**; pain in nape of: hyos j5.de
- **Ovaries**; pain in (See FEMALE - Pain - ovaries - alternating with - headache)
- **Pelvis**; pain in: *Gels*
- **Shoulder**; pain in: cot c1
- **Stomach**; pain in: *Ant-c* vh1 ars k* bism chel↓ kali-bi gk ox-ac bg1 plb bg1 verat bg1
  - **pressing** pain: chel
- **Teeth**; pain in: kali-p *Lycps-v* psor
- **Throat**; pain in: alumn kr1* lac-c kr1
- **Tonsils**; inflammation of (See THROAT - Inflammation - tonsils - alternating with - head)

- **anger**; after: *(↗vexation)* acon arg-n aur bc aur-m-n wbt2• *Bry* castm *Cham* chin a cocc a* coff coloc dulc ferr-p k2 gink-b sbd1• haliae-lc srj5• ign ip sne kali-c kola stb3• *Lyc* mag-c k* mez k* *Nat-m* *Nux-v* k* oxal-a rly4• *Petr* *Phos* *Plat* ran-b rhus-t sep *Staph* k* verat a
  - **dull** pain: gink-b sbd1•
  - **suppressed** anger; from (See MIND - Ailments - anger - suppressed)
- **animal** fluids (See loss)
- **anticipation**; from: *Aur-m-n* wbt2•
- **apyrexia**; during: puls br1
- **arthritic** (See rheumatic)
- **ascending**:
  - **agg.**: ant-c bro1 bell bro1 but-ac bro1 calc bro1* conv br1* *Meny* bro1
  - **elevator**; with an: calc-f sp1
  - **stairs**:
    - **agg.**: alum alum-p k2 ant-c arn ars↓ aster **Bell Bry** cadm-s **Calc** calc-sil k2 *Carb-v* carbn-s cimic conv br1 crot-h *Cupr* ferr ferr-p *Gels* *Glon* hydr ign *Kalm* lac-c *Lach* lob *Lyc* meny meph *Mosch* nat-ar *Nux-v* par *Ph-ac* *Phos* *Psor* ptel *Rhus-t* sang *Sep* **Sil Spong** staph *Sulph* *Tab* thuj zinc zinc-p k2
      - **jerking** pain: **Bell** *Ign*
      - **pressing** pain: ars lyc **Meny** *Ph-ac*
    - **amel.**: allox tpw3
- **attention**; from too eager: *(↗mental - agg.; MIND - Concentration - active)* anac *Ign* k* nux-v sabad
- **awake**, when trying to keep: phys k*
- **ball** were beating against the skull on beginning to walk; as if a: plat
- **band**; as from a (See pressing pain - band; Constriction - band)
- **bandaging** (See binding)
- **bathing**: *(↗washing)* ant-c bro1
  - **after**: **Ant-c** k* *Bell* bry a *Calc* canth caust chord-umb rly4• kreos nat-ox rly4• *Nit-ac* phos a pot-e rly4• psor tl1 puls *Rhus-t* sep sil spong fd4.de tub a
    - **amel.**: bufo k2 pot-e rly4• psor jl2
  - **amel.**: lac-ac
  - **feet** | **amel.**: asc-t c1 nat-s a1
  - **sea**; in the: *Ars* *Rhus-t* sep
- **beat** head to pieces; sensation as if he could: nit-ac k*
- **beating** (See pulsating)
- **bed**:
  - **going** to bed | **when**: alum ap-g vh1 ars *Lyc* mag-m *Merc* puls sabad sep sulph vanil fd5.de zinc
  - **in** bed:
    - **agg.**: agar↓ brucel↓ hell↓ hipp↓ kalm↓ nat-c↓ nat-s↓ ol-an↓ pip-m↓ plat↓ ran-b↓ rhus-t↓ sulph↓ thuj↓
      - **drawing** pain: agar hell hipp k*
      - **dull** pain: brucel sa3•
      - **pressing** pain: kalm nat-s ol-an pip-m ran-b rhus-t sulph
      - **stitching** pain: nat-c plat thuj
    - **amel.**: *Alum* k* aur-m↓ brucel sa3• caust↓ colch mag-c menth c1 rhus-t sep k* ulm-c jsj8•
      - **tearing** pain: aur-m caust
  - **must** leave the: coloc rhus-t h1* ruta fd4.de sep h2* *Thuj*
- **beer**:
  - **agg.**: all-c bell calc calc-caust caust chim-m c1 *Coc-c* coloc ferr kali-chl merc *Rhus-t* k* verat
  - **amel.**: chim-m c1 pieri-b mlk9.de
- **beer** and bread agg.: crot-t k*
- **bending**:
  - **agg.**:
    - **head**:
      - **back** agg.: anac↓
        - **tearing** pain: anac
      - **forward**:
        - **amel.**: ign↓
          - **tearing** pain: ign
  - **backward**:
    - **agg.**: aur↓ mang↓
      - **boring** pain: aur k* mang k*
      - **pressing** pain: mang
    - **amel.**: *Bell*↓ ph-ac↓ thuj↓
      - **pressing** pain: *Bell* ph-ac thuj
  - **head**:
    - **backward**:
      - **agg.**: anac aur *Bell* k* bry carb-ac *Carb-v* caust chin cic *Clem* cob colch cupr cycl dig dros elaps glon k* hist vml3• ign kali-c kali-s lyc mang osm *Puls* sep spig spong stann valer viol-o
        - **shooting** pain: anac
        - **walks** with head bent backwards: *Arn* *Ars*
      - **amel.**: apis arg-n bell k* bros-gau mrc1 *Cact* *Cham* cocc gels gink-b sbd1• *Glon* *Hep* hydrog srj2• lec murx bro1 ph-ac rhus-t thuj verat
        - **burrowing**: hep k*
    - **forward**: cupr↓
      - **agg.**: *(↗stooping - agg.)* alum-sil k2 androc srj1• arist-cl sp1 bell k2* calc-f sp1 carb-an chlam-tr bcx2• cimic *Cob* k* ferr-p↓ gink-b sbd1• kali-p fd1.de• mand sp1 myos-a rly4• nat-m↓ ph-ac↓ pieri-b mlk9.de pneu jl2 rat *Rhus-t* viol-o visc sp1 [heroin sdj2]
        - **pressing** pain: bell ferr-p nat-m ph-ac
      - **amel.**: abrom-a↓ bamb-a↓ cimic bro1 hyos bro1 ign bro1 ozone↓ sanic tl1
        - **dull** pain: abrom-a ks5 ozone sde2•
        - **pressing** pain: bamb-a stb2.de•
      - **tearing** pain | **burning** pain: cupr
    - **painful** side agg.; to: mez tab
    - **side**; to:
      - **agg.**: chin kali-s meny spong
      - **amel.**: meny *Puls* sep stram
- **bilious**: *(↗STOMACH - Vomiting; type - bile - headache)* am-pic ll1* anac bro1 *Arg-n* bro1 bapt bro1 *Bry* bro1 cham bro1 chel bro1 chion bg3* cycl bro1 eup-per bro1 *Ip* bro1 *Iris* bro1 lob bro1 merc bro1 nat-s bl6* *Nux-v* bro1 podo bro1 *Puls* bro1 rob bro1 *Sang* bro1 stry bro1 tarax bro1 yuc br1*
- **binding**:
  - **hair** up; the | **agg.**: acon alum alum-p k2 alum-sil k2 am-c ambr *Arg-n* arn ars aur aur-ar k2 aur-s k2 bar-c bar-i k2 bar-m **Bell** bry calc calc-i k2

- **hair** up; the – **agg.**: ...
  calc-sil k2 canth carb-an *Carb-v* carbn-s carl chel *Chin* chinin-ar *Cina* cinnb coloc ferr k2 *Glon Hep* indg iod kali-c kali-m k2 *Kali-n* kali-p kreos lach laur lyc mag-c mag-m *Mez* mosch mur-ac nat-c nat-p *Nit-ac Nux-v* petr ph-ac *Phos* psor *Puls* rhus-t sep *Sil* stann sul-i k2 *Sulph* zinc zinc-p k2
- **head**:
  - **agg.**: calc cham lach rhus-t thuj
  - **amel.**: agar a alum-sil k2 apis *Arg-met* **Arg-n** k* arn aur-s k2 bell k* bry *Calc* calc-i k2 carb-ac ephe-si hsj1• glon k2 *Hep* ign a iod bg1 lac-d lach k2 *Mag-m* k* mag-p tl1 merc bg1* mim-p skp7*• nit-ac a nux-v pic-ac pitu-gl skp7• psor **Puls** pyrog a1 rhod sep vh **Sil** spig stront-c a sul-i k2
- **head** up:
  - **amel.**: *Arg-n* ↓ carb-ac ↓ hep ↓ lac-d ↓ mag-m ↓ sil ↓
    - **burrowing**: hep
    - **bursting** pain: lac-d mag-m sil
    - **cutting** pain: carb-ac
    - **pressing** pain: *Arg-n* hep c1
    - **tearing** pain: sil
- **bites** of dogs: lyss c1
- **biting** pain: arg-met bar-c carb-v cham grat k* kali-bi kali-i lyc k* mez k* oci-sa sp1 phel k* ran-s rhod k* sec k*
- **bladder**, with complaints of: senec vml3•
- **blinding**: asar aster *Bell* k* *Caust* k* **Cycl** dys pte1• ferr-p *Gels* k* **Iris** kali-bi tl1 lac-d *Lil-t Nat-m Petr Phos Psor Sil Stram Sulph* thuj tl1 zinc h2*
- **blindness**, followed by violent headache | **sight** returning when headache agg.: *Kali-bi* k*
- **blow**; pain as from a: acon bg1 aeth agn bg2 alum ant-t k* apis bg1 arn k* ars bg1 bell bg1 bov calc bg1 cann-xyz bg2 caust chel k* chord-umb rly4• croc bg1 crot-h bg2 dig bg1 fic-m gya1 galla-q-r nl2• glon bg1 hell k* ign bg1 indg ip bg2 kalm bg1 led k* lyc bg1 m-ambo b7.de mang med mur-ac bg1 naja bg1 nat-m k* nux-m bg1 nux-v k* olnd k* par bg2 ph-ac k* phos bg1 plat k* ran-b rhod bg2 ruta k* sabad k* sol-ni spig k* stann bg1 *Stram* b7a.de streptoc rly4• sul-ac k* tab bg2 tarent bg1 valer k* zinc
- **blowing** the nose agg.: alum h2 ambr aster **Aur** *Bell* calc *Chel* dulc fd4.de euphr h2 ferr **Hep** kali-c ↓ mur-ac nit-ac **Puls** sep ↓ **Sulph**
  - **cutting** pain: sep
  - **pressing** pain: chel dulc fd4.de
  - **shooting** pain: kali-c
  - **stitching** pain: mur-ac k*
- **blows**, from (See injuries)
- **blunt** instrument; as from a: hyos b7.de rheum b7.de
- **body** cold: **Arn** ↓
  - **burning**: **Arn**
- **boring** pain (= digging, screwing): act-sp agar k* am-c k* am-m anac ang k* ant-c k* ant-t k* *Arg-n* k* ars k* asaf k2* aur k* aur-s k2 bar-c bar-m *Bell* k* bism k* borx bov bry cadm-s calc k* camph cann-s canth k* carb-an k* carbn-s **Caust** k* cham chin chinin-ar chinin-s cimic clem k* *Cocc* k* colch *Coloc* k* dros dulc k* fic-m gya1 gink-b sbd1• graph hell *Hep* k* hipp hippoc-k szs2 hydrog srj2• hyper *Ign* k* indg ip kali-c k* kali-i kali-m k2 kali-p *Kali-s* kola stb3• lach k* laur k* led lyc k* mag-c k* mag-m mag-s sp1 mang merc k* merc-c b4a.de *Mez* mosch mur-ac nat-c b4a.de nat-m k* *Nat-s* k* nit-ac nux-v ol-an olnd k* op paeon petr k* ph-ac phel phos pieri-b mlk9.de *Plat* k* puls k* ran-s rhod rhus-t ruta sabad sabin k* samb seneg k* *Sep* k* sil k* sphing kk3.fr *Spig* k* squil stann k* staph k* stram k* sulph *Tab* k* thuj k* tritic-vg fd5.de valer vanil fd5.de zinc k*
  - **needles**; as from: arg-n bg2 cadm-s bg2 calc bg2 caust bg2 cham bg2 chinin-s bg2 clem bg2 cocc bg2 *Coloc* bg2 merc bg2 phos bg2 rhus-t b7.de* sep bg2
- **brain** diseases, from: nat-m k2
  - **edema** of brain (See Edema - brain - accompanied - head)
- **brandy** amel.: sel c1
- **bread** agg.: manc zing
- **bread** agg.: ...
  - **and** beer agg. (See beer and)
- **breakfast**:
  - **after**:
    - **agg.**: agar bad kr1* *Bry* ↓ bufo *Carbn-s* cham chel ↓ hydr k* hyper indg k* *Iris Lyc* merc ↓ *Naja* nat-m nit-ac nux-m *Nux-v* par ph-ac phos plb sars ↓ sphing ↓ sul-ac
      - **boring** pain: sphing kk3.fr
      - **pressing** pain: chel hydr sars
      - **sore**: merc
      - **stitching** pain: *Bry*
  - **amel.**: am-m ap-g arum-t k* bov caj canth k* carb-ac k* cimic cinnb con croc eup-per k* fl-ac ind k* narcot a1 nat-p k* petr psor jl2 ptel vml3• symph fd3.de• vanil ↓
    - **pressing** pain: bov *Psor* vanil fd5.de
  - **before** | **agg.**: calc cimic ind k* rumx
  - **delayed**: calc
  - **during**: sul-ac ↓
    - **tearing** pain: sul-ac
  - **missing**; when: calc vh
- **breathing**:

  - **cold** air through nose (See cold - air - inspiration)
  - **deep** | **agg.**: anac k* cact bg1 crot-h bg1 mang bg1 rat
  - **holding** breath:
    - **agg.**: agar
      - **drawing** pain: agar
- **bruised** (See sore)
- **burning**: **Acon** k* agar k* ail k* alum alum-sil k2 alumn bro1 am-c k* anan ant-t k* *Apis* k* arg-met k* *Arg-n Arn* k* *Ars* k* ars-s-f k2 arum-t k* *Aster* bro1 atro a1 aur aur-ar k2 aur-m aur-s *Bar-c* bar-m bell k* berb bism k* bov *Bry* k* *Calc* k* calc-ar *Calc-p* k* calc-sil k2 *Canth* k* carb-ac carb-an *Carb-v* k* carbn-s *Caust* chel chin cocc k* coff coloc k* colum-p sze2• crot-c crot-t k* cupr k* cystein-l rly4• dig k* *Dros* dulc k* *Eug* k* eup-per k2 ferul a1 *Form Glon* k* graph *Hell* k* helon k* ip k* *Kali-ar Kali-bi* k* kali-c k* kali-i mrr1 kali-p kali-s *Kreos Lach* bro1 lachn k* lact lil-t k* lith-c mag-m h2 manc k* mang med **Merc** k* *Merc-c* merl **Mez** k* mur-ac nat-c h2 nat-m nat-s k* nit-ac k* nux-v k* olib-sac wmh1 ox-ac bro1 oxal-a rly4• par k* *Petr* petr-ra shn4• ph-ac k* phel k* **Phos** k* phys k* plat k* plb pot-e rly4• psor k* rhod k* rhus-t k* rob ruta h1 sabad sang sarr bg1 sars bg2 sec k* sep k* *Sil* k* spig spong fd4.de stann staph k* stront-c k* sul-ac sulph k* tab k* tarax k* tarent k* tax k* tong bro1 tub c verat k* verat-v k* viol-o bro1 zinc bro1 zinc-s k*
  - **accompanied** by | **apoplexy**: glon ptk1
  - **alternating** with | **pain**: brom k*
  - **contracting**: bism k*
  - **fire**; as if brain were on: *Canth* hydr-ac k* *Phos* psor jl2
  - **hot** iron around head; as from | **hot** water in it; or as from: acon coc-c
  - **pressing** pain: mang k*
  - **sparks**, like: nit-ac
  - **tearing** pain: merc
- **burning**, body is cold, and one cannot get warm; head is:
  - **whining** from pain: lachn ↓
    - **plug**; as from a | **split** wide open by a wedge; head was: lachn
- **burnt**; as if: positr nl2•
- **burrowing**: agar k* anac b4a.de* ant-t k* arg-n bg2 aur b4.de* bar-act bar-c bg2 bell bg2 bism b7a.de* bov bg2 bry b7.de* calc h2* caust b4a.de* cham k* chin bg2 clem k* coc-c k* cocc b7.de* colch k* coloc b4a.de* dulc bg2 eupi k* *Hep* k* ign b7.de* kali-m bg2 kola stb3• m-ambo b7.de m-aust b7.de *Mag-m* k* mang bg2 merc bg2 mez bg2 nux-v b7.de* ph-ac bg2 phos k* plat bg2 rat k* sabin b7.de* samb k* sep b4.de* *Spig* k* squil k* til k* *Valer* b7.de* zinc b4.de*
- **bursting** pain: (↗ *tearing - asunder; torn; Fullness - burst)* acon bro1* aesc k* aids nl2• all-c k2 allox sp1 alum alum-p k2 alum-sil k2 am-c k* *Am-m* k* aml-ns bg2 anac b4a.de anil a1 ant-c k* apis k* arg-n k* arn ptk1 ars ars-met asaf k* asar k* aster k* atro bg2 bamb-a stb2.de• bapt bar-c k* bar-s k2 **Bell** k* berb k* beryl tpw5* boerh-d zzc1• bov k* brom k* **Bry** k* cact k* calad k* **Calc** k* calc-f sp1 calc-sil k2 cann-s *Cann-xyz* bg2 canth k2 *Caps* k* carb-an k* carb-v k2

- **bursting** pain: ...
cassia-s ccrh1• *Caust* k* cham k* chel k* **Chin** k* chinin-ar cimic k* clem k* cob k* coc-c cocain bro1 cocc k2* coff k* colch k2 **Con** k* crot-h tl1 cupr cycl sne *Daph* bg2* dendr-pol sk4• dig k* dios k* dol eup-per bg2* euph k* *Euphr* k* fago a1 *Ferr* k* ferr-ar ferr-p flor-p rsj3• form bro1 *Gels* bg2* **Glon** k* *Graph* k* gymno ham k* helo c1 helo-s c1* *Hep* k* hydr k* hyper bg2 ign k* iod bg2 *Ip* k* irid-met srj5• kali-ar kali-bi k* kali-c k* kali-n k* kali-p kali-s kalm k* kola stb3• kreos lac-ac k* lac-c bg2* lac-h htj1• **Lach** k* lachn *Lyc* k* lycpr bro1 **Lyss** k* m-arct b7.de mag-m k* meli bro1* meny bg2 **Merc** k* mez k* mill moni rfm1• mosch naja nat-ar nat-c k* **Nat-m** k* nat-p nat-s k* nicc k* *Nit-ac* k* *Nux-m* k* nux-v b7.de* *Olnd* k* op k* oxal-a rly4• ozone sde2• *Petr* k* petr-ra shn4• ph-ac k* **Phos** k* phys phyt bg2 pic-ac k* pitu-gl skp7• podo k2 prun psor ptel k* *Puls* k* ran-b bg1 *Rat* k* rauw tpw8 rhus-t k* sabad *Sang* k* **Sep** k* *Sil* k* sol-ni *Spig* k* *Spong* k* stann staph b7a.de* streptoc jl2 stront-c k* stry bro1 sul-ac k* *Sulph* k* syph k2* thuj k* usn bg2* vanil fd5.de verat k* verat-v hr1* x-ray sp1 zinc k* [bell-p-sp dcm1]
  - • **accompanied** by:
    - : **sleeplessness**: ozone sde2•
    - : **Ear** | **noises** in ear; hissing: bamb-a stb2.de•
  - • **fly** to pieces; as if it would: arg-n asaf bar-c bry hr1 carb-an caust graph hep irid-met srj5•
  - • **lifted**; as if top of head were being: **Cann-i**
  - • **split** open with a wedge; as if: lachn k*
- **caffeine**; gripping like too much: musca-d ↓
  - • **dull** pain: musca-d szs1
- **candy**, after: ant-c k* chord-umb rly4•
- **cap**; as from a (See pressing pain - cap)
- **cardiac** symptoms; with (See heart)
- **carriage** (See riding - carriage - agg.)
- **catarrh**; from suppressed: *Acon* ↓
  - • **cramping**: *(↗coryza - suppressed)* *Acon*
- **catarrhal**: *(↗forehead - eminence - catarrhal)* acon aesc *All-c* k* *Alum* am-m ambr k* ant-c k2 *Ars* k* *Ars-i* *Aur* bell k* *Bry* k* *Calc* **Calc-s** camph k* *Carb-v* carbn-s caul cench k2 cham chin k* chinin-ar *Chlor* cic k* cimic cina k* dros gk **Dulc** eup-per bro1 **Euphr** k* *Ferr* *Ferr-ar* ferr-p *Gels* k* **Graph** k* gymno hell k* **Hep** *Hydr* k* ign k* *Iod* *Kali-ar* *Kali-bi* k* *Kali-c* **Kali-i** *Kali-s* kalm kola stb3• *Lach* k* laur k* *Lyc* k* *Mang* menth bro1 mentho br1 **Merc** k* merc-i-f mez nat-ar *Nat-m* **Nux-v** k* *Phos* pin-con oss2• pseuts-m oss1• psor k2 *Puls* k* ran-b rumx sabad k* samb k* sang k* senec vml3• sil spig mrr1 staph k* *Stict* k* still k* *Sulph* k* teucr thuj bl tub al*
- **changes** in weather (See weather - change)
- **chewing** agg.: alum-sil k2 am-c bg1 am-m h2* ambr bg1 ind kali-c olnd phos ptel bg1 sulph thuj bg1* verb bg1*
  - • **drawing** pain: sulph
- **chill**:
  - • **after**: acon alum ant-c bg2* (non:ant-t k*) arn berb borx bov caust cedr *Cimx* k* cob dros dulc mrr1 mang **Nat-m** oci-sa sp1 phos h2*
  - • **before**: aesc *Ars* bell *Bry* calc carb-v cedr chin corn-f elat *Eup-per* *Eup-pur* ferr c1 ip kali-n lach nat-c *Nat-m* plan puls rhus-t sang k2 spong symph c1 syph c1 *Thuj*
  - • **during**: acon k* agar alum b4.de* am-c k* anac k* ang k* ant-t k* *Apis* b7a.de* *Aran* *Arg-n* k* arn k* *Ars* k* ars-s-f k2 bapt **Bell** k* bol-la bro1 borx k* *Bry* k* bufo bg2 **Cact** k* *Calc* k* camph caps k* carb-an carb-v k* *Carbn-s* **Castm** k* cham k* *Chin* k* chinin-ar chinin-s k* cimic cina k* coca coff k* coloc con k* conv br1* cor-r k* crot-h *Cupr* daph dros k* dulc elat *Eup-per* k* *Eup-pur* k* euphr bg2 eupi k* ferr k* ferr-ar ferr-p gels k* *Graph* k* hell k* hep k* hipp k* hyper ↓ ign k* ip k* kali-ar kali-bi ↓ kali-c k* kali-n b4.de* *Kali-s* kreos k* lach k* lact led k* lyc k* m-aust b7.de mag-c mang k* merc bg2 mez k* nat-c b4.de* **Nat-m** k* nit-ac b4a.de* **Nux-v** k* *Petr* k* phos k* podo k* puls k* rhod k* rhus-t k* ruta k* sang k* seneg k* **Sep** k* sil b4.de* spig k* *Spong* k* stann bg2 stram *Sulph* k* tarax k* tarent ↓ thuj k* vanil ↓ verat k* viol-t b7.de*
    - : **bursting** pain: alum bg2 *Bry* bg2 spig bg2
    - : **coldness** all over; with: camph ↓ stann ↓
      - : **pressing** pain: camph stann
    - : **congestion**; as from: chin bro1 chinin-s bro1
    - : **dull** pain: petr h2
    - : **pressing** pain: sep tarent vanil fd5.de

- **chill – during**: ...
    - : **stitching** pain: ars bg2 *Bry* bg2 graph bg2 kali-bi bg2 kreos bg2 mang bg2 *Puls* bg2 sep bg2
    - : **tearing** pain: eup-per k2 eupi hyper kali-n h2
  - • **from**: eup-per ↓
    - : **bursting** pain: eup-per k2
  - • **with**: anac ↓
    - : **tearing** pain: anac h2
- **chilliness**:
  - • **during**: eupi ↓ *Glon* ↓ *Sang* ↓ sil ↓
    - : **boring** pain: *Sang* k*
    - : **drawing** pain: eupi *Glon*
    - : **stitching** pain: eupi k* sil h2
  - • **with**: ant-t ↓ arg-n br1* camph bro1 conv bro1 eup-per ↓ ign kr1 kali-c ↓ *Kola* stb3• lac-ac kr1 lact-v bro1 mag-p br1 mang-m bro1 mosch ptk1 *Puls* bro1 ruta fd4.de *Sang* bro1 *Sil* k* vanil fd5.de
    - : **burning**: ant-t k* eup-per k2 kali-c k* sil k*
    - : **stunning** pain: *Puls*
- **choreic** persons, in: *Agar* k*
- **chronic**: aloe bg2 alum bg2 *Alum-sil* vh1 am-c k* arg-n bg2* *Ars* k* asaf bg2 aur b4a.de* calc b4a.de* calc-p bg2 carb-an b4a.de carb-v b4a.de *Caust* k* chinin-s bro1 cocc bro1 con cycl bg2 elaps a kali-ar k2 kali-c bg2 kalm bg2 lac-d k2* lach bg2* lyc b4a.de* lyss br1* mag-c b4a.de mag-m b4a.de meningoc a merc b4a.de nat-m bg2* parathyr jl2 petr b4a.de ph-ac tl1 phos b4a.de* plb bro1 psor bg2* ruta fd4.de sars bg2 sep b4a.de* *Sil* k* *Sulph* k* ter st thuj bg2* tub lp* zinc b4a.de*
  - • **lasting** four days: limen-b-c ↓
    - : **dull** pain: limen-b-c hrn2•
  - • **lasting** seven days: *Caust* h2*
  - • **old** people, of: bar-c bro1 calc-p bro1 iod k* phos bro1
  - • **sedentary** habits; from: anac bro1 *Arg-n* bro1 bry bro1 *Nux-v* bro1
- **church**, while in: zinc ↓
  - • **drawing** pain: zinc
- **clamped** together; as if: am-c bg2 ant-t bg2 berb bg2 tritic-vg fd5.de
- **clawing** pain: *Sep* b4a.de
- **cleaving** (See cutting pain)
- **clenching** teeth amel.: sulph ↓
  - • **shooting** pain: sulph
- **closed** the eyes; as if something: *Cocc* sulph
- **closing** the eyes:
  - • **agg.**: **All-c** k* aloe alumn ant-t apis ars bry a *Chin* clem a1 cocc a ferr ferr-p grat hep ip lac-c lac-d c1 lach nux-v op ph-ac sabad ↓ sabin sep a *Sil* *Ther* thuj
    - : **bursting** pain: *Chin*
    - : **drawing** pain: sabad
  - • **amel.**: abrom-a ↓ *Acon* adam skp7• agar allox tpw3* aloe k* ant-t bro1 anth vh *Bell* k* bros-gau mrc1 *Bry* *Calc* *Chel* k* *Chin* ↓ cocc-s bro1 coff con hell hyos *Ign* k* iod ip kola stb3• lac-h ↓ mim-p skp7*• nat-m *Nux-v* k* oreo bro1 oxeod a1 ozone sde2• pitu-gl ↓ plan plat rhus-t *Sep* **Sil** *Spig* staph sne *Sulph* til a1 zinc
    - : **boring** pain: sep
    - : **bursting** pain: pitu-gl skp7•
    - : **cutting** pain: til k*
    - : **drawing** pain: *Con* a1 til k*
    - : **dull** pain: abrom-a ks5 lac-h sk4•
    - : **pressing** pain: chel
    - : **pulsating** pain: pitu-gl skp7•
    - : **sore**: *Chin* plan sil
  - • **must** close the eyes: *Agar* aloe ap-g vml3• arn bamb-a stb2.de• *Bell* caesal-b bnj1 calc *Carb-v* chinin-s cor-r c euph hydrog srj2• ign gk lac-cp sk4• mez nat-m ozone sde2• podo c1 *Sil*
- **clothing** about the neck agg.: arg-n *Bell* crot-c *Glon* k* *Lach* sep
- **clucking**: sulph h2
- **cluster** headache: *(↗periodical)* cedr vml3•

- **coffee**:
  - **agg.**: acet-ac act-sp br1* am-c arg-n arn arum-t k* *Bell Bry* calc a calc-p k* caust *Cham Cocc* form glon *Guar* hep *Ign* k* kali-n lach lyc merc ill nat-s *Nux-v* k* pall paull bro1 pin-con oss2• podo fd3.de• *Puls* sulph j5.de *Tub* jl2 [helia stj7]
    - **boring** pain: nux-v
    - **pressing** pain: arum-t nat-s
  - **amel.**: act-sp a* anag hr1* cann-i k* chin coloc k* dioxi rbp6 fago a gink-b sbd1• glon k* hyos oxal-a rly4• ruta fd4.de spong fd4.de til vanil fd5.de
    - **dull** pain: gink-b sbd1•
- **coition**: agar arg-n arn *Bov* calad **Calc** *Calc-p* vh calc-sil k2 chin dig graph **Kali-c** kali-sil k2 *Lyc Nat-c* nat-m *Petr Phos* puls **Sep Sil** staph vanil fd5.de [heroin sdj2]
  - **amel.**: olib-sac wmh1
  - **desire** for; with: sep j5.de*
- **cold**:
  - **agg.**: puls ↓ *Rhus-t* ↓
    - **stunning** pain: puls *Rhus-t*
  - **air**:
    - **agg.**: *(↗wind - cold - agg.)* alum-sil k2 am-c **Ars** k* ars-s-f k2 **Aur** aur-ar k2 **Bell** bov *Bry Calc* calc-sil k2 *Camph* carb-an *Carb-v* k* **Caust** **Chin** *Chinin-ar* chlam-tr ↓ *Cocc Coff* **Dulc** ferr ferr-ar grat *Hep* ign ind ↓ *Iris Kali-ar Kali-bi* **Kali-c** kali-chl kali-i ↓ kali-m k2 kali-p kali-sil k2 *Lac-c Lach* led tl1 *Lyc* mag-m st *Mang* nat-m *Nit-ac* **Nux-m Nux-v** petr-ra shn4• *Phos* k* plat *Psor Puls* ran-b k2 **Rhod Rhus-t** ruta sacch-a ↓ sec k2 *Sep* **Sil** k* *Spig* ↓ spong fd4.de stram ↓ *Sulph* thuj ↓ *Verat*
      - **cutting** pain: chlam-tr bcx2• kali-i *Spig* spong fd4.de
      - **drawing** pain: *Caust*
      - **lancinating**: kali-i *Spig*
      - **pressing** pain: ferr sacch-a fd2.de• *Sil*
      - **shooting** pain: iris
      - **sore**: *Chin* ind thuj
      - **tearing** pain: bov caust grat ign rhus-t stram
    - **amel.**: abrom-a ↓ aloe alum-sil k2 arg-n ars aur-i k2 bufo caust cimic croc dros erig vml3• euphr ferr-p *Glon* iod k* kali-s kola stb3• lap-la sde8.de• led mrr1 *Lyc* lyss nat-p fkr6.de **Phos** k* *Puls Seneg* sin-n thuj ↓ trios ↓
      - **boring** pain: phos thuj
      - **burrowing**: phos h2
      - **dull** pain: abrom-a ks5 trios rsj11•
    - **inspiration** through nose: cimic tl1 cor-r br1
  - **amel.**: *Puls* ↓
    - **stunning** pain: *Puls*
  - **anything** cold in mouth; from | **agg.**: chin kr1*
  - **applications**:
    - **agg.**: cystein-l rly4• sacch-a fd2.de• vanil fd5.de zinc-p k2
    - **amel.**: *Acon All-c* bro1 **Aloe** k* alum a alum-sil k4 alumn k* *Am-c Ant-c* ant-t apis bg1 arg-n k2 arist-cl sp1 *Ars* k* asar aur a aur-i k2 aur-m bamb-a stb2.de• *Bell* k* bism k* boerh-d ↓ *Bry* bufo cadm-met sp1 cadm-s a *Calc* calc-f sp1 *Calc-p* caust cedr cham chel vh chinin-s cimic a cinnb coff mrr1 cycl k* cystein-l rly4• ephe-si hsj1• *Euph* euphr ferr ferr-ar ferr-p k* fic-m gya1 *Glon* hist sp1* ictod bro1 ind iod kali-bi kali-s a kalm kola stb3• kreos sne lac-c *Lac-d* k* *Lach* lap-la sde8.de• lappa bg1 *Led* lil-t k2 lyc bro1 mand sp1 meny merc-c merl mosch myric *Nat-m* k* nit-ac a petr-ra shn4• *Phos* k* pic-ac k2 pitu-gl skp7• plan *Psor Puls* k* ran-s sp1 ruta fd4.de seneg *Spig* k* spong fd4.de *Stram* suis-hep ↓ sul-i k2 *Sulph Tab* bro1 til ↓ tritic-vg fd5.de vanil fd5.de visc sp1 xan c1 *Zinc* [bell-p-sp dcm1]
      - **burning**: ars k2*
      - **bursting** pain: ars k2 boerh-d zzc1•
      - **cutting** pain: suis-hep rly4• til
      - **drawing** pain: til k*
      - **lancinating**: *Ars*
      - **pressing** pain: *Phos*
      - **sore**: euph

- **cold**: ...
  - **bathing**:
    - **agg.**: **Ant-c** k* ars a *Bell* bry a *Caps* cycl a form ↓ glon a lac-c a *Nit-ac* phos *Rhus-t* sars sep zinc a
      - **burning**: form
    - **amel.**: hed sp1
  - **drinks**:
    - **agg.**: bry k2 con dig k* kali-c hr1 sulph k2
      - **overheated**; when: bry k2
    - **amel.**: alum bc *Alumn* bism (non:kali-c hr1) petr-ra shn4•
      - **boring** pain: bism hr1
  - **hands**:
    - **amel.**: euphr ↓
      - **stitching** pain: euphr
  - **room**:
    - **agg.**: nat-c k2
    - **amel.**: all-c vh1
  - **washing** | **amel.**: acon aloe ant-t *Ars* asar aur-m *Bry* calc calc-p caust cham cinnb cycl dulc fd4.de euph *Glon* graph c1 ind iod kalm lac-c lach kr1 led k2 myric nat-s *Phos* plan psor spig c1* til c1 tritic-vg fd5.de zinc
  - **water**:
    - **agg.**: sulph ↓
      - **tearing** pain: sulph
    - **amel.**: euphr ↓
      - **pressing** pain: euphr
  - ○ **Feet**: *Bar-c* cham kali-c phos *Puls* **Sil**
    - **amel.**: **Sulph** vh
  - **Head** getting cold; on: *Aur* **Bell** *Calc* carb-an bg1 *Carb-v* k* hep hyos kali-c kali-sil *Led* nat-m *Nux-v* psil ft1* puls **Sep Sil**
- **cold**; after taking a: *Acon* alum k2 ant-c k* arn *Bell* k* benz-ac k2 *Bry Calc* k* calc-sil k2 *Carb-v* carbn-s caust *Cham* chin cimic k2 coff k* coloc con dulc ferr k2 glon hr1 graph k* hep hyos *Kali-bi Kali-c Kali-p* kali-s lach lyc k2 merc nat-m *Nit-ac* nit-m-ac k* *Nux-v* petr k* *Phos* psor al* *Puls* k* rhus-t *Ros-d* wla1 samb sep *Sil Sulph* vanil fd5.de verat
- **cold** agg.; becoming: acon aeth a1 agar ant-c k* *Ars* aur-m-n wbt2• **Bell** **Bry** cadm-s *Calc* calc-s k2 calc-sil k2 carb-an *Carb-v* **Cham** *Chin* chinin-ar cist k2 clem colch *Con* **Dulc** ferr k2 graph k2 grat *Hep* kali-sil k2 lach *Lyc* **Mag-p** k* *Merc Mez* mosch *Nat-m Nit-ac* **Nux-v** petr **Phos** psil ft1 *Puls* ran-b k2 *Rhus-t* **Sil** *Spig Stram Stront-c* sul-ac *Sulph Verat* verb
- **colors**:
  - **red** | **agg.**: thuj vk4
- **combing** hair:
  - **agg.**: alum ↓ alum-sil k2 ars asar ↓ bell k2 *Bry* carb-v carbn-s a chin chinin-ar cina dys pte1*• hell *Hep* ↓ ign kreos lac-c mang ↓ merc-i-f a1 *Mez* nat-m a nat-s ptk* nat-sil fd3.de• nit-ac k2 par ptk2 phos a *Rhus-t* ↓ sars ↓ sel sep *Sil* ↓ *Sulph* ↓
    - **sore**: alum alum-sil k2 *Ars* k* asar carbn-s *Chin Hep* lac-c mang nat-s nit-ac k2 *Rhus-t* sars *Sil Sulph* st
  - **amel.**: form k* glon a2 plut-n srj7• tarent a vanil fd5.de
  - **backward** agg.: kola stb3• puls rhus-t
- **come** off; as if top of head would: alum anth c1* bapt cact cann-s cham cimic k* cinnb bg1 cob k* cupr-s k* helo bg1 helo-s rwt2• iris bg1 kali-bi bg1 lith-c merc passi c1* sang k* sin-n bg1 syph bg1 ther xan hl9*
- **company**:
  - **agg.**: lyc ↓ mag-c ↓
    - **pressing** pain: *(↗MIND - Company - aversion)* lyc mag-c
  - **aversion** to company; with (See MIND - Company - aversion - head)
  - **while** in company or in a crowd: *(↗MIND - Company - aversion)* ketogl-ac rly4• kola stb3• mag-c plat *Plb* staph
- **compressed**; as if: acon bg2 aeth bg2 alum b4.de* am-m b7.de* anac bg2 ant-t bg2 apis b7a.de arg-met b7.de* *Arn* bg2 asaf b7.de* asar b7a.de* bell bg2 bov b4a.de* **Bry** b7.de* cact bg2 calc b4.de* camph b7.de* cann-s b7a.de* carb-v b4.de* caust b4.de* chin bg2 cic b7.de* cina b7.de* cocc b7.de* coloc bg2 con bg2 daph bg2 dulc bg2 euph bg2 graph b4.de* grat bg2 hell b7.de* **Ign** bg2 kali-bi bg2 kali-n bg2 lyc bg2 lycps-v bg2 m-arct b7.de mag-m bg2 meny b7.de*

- **compressed**; as if: ...
merc b4.de* mosch b7.de* nat-m b4.de* nicc bg2 *Nit-ac* b4.de* nux-m b7.de* olnd bg2 petr b4.de* ph-ac b4.de* phos bg2 **Plat** b4a.de* prun bg2 **Puls** bg2 ran-s bg2 rhod b4a.de* rhus-t b7.de* sabad b7a.de* sabin bg2 sars bg2 sep bg2 sil b4.de* spig b7a.de spong b7a.de* stann b4.de* staph b7.de* stront-c bg2 sul-ac bg2 sulph b4.de* tab bg2 ther bg2 thuj b4.de* verb bg2
- **computer**; working with: ephe-si hsj1•
- **concussion**; from: arn *Bell* calc-s cocc ferr-p hep kali-br ptk1 lac-c merc nat-s ↓ phos
  - **neuralgic**: arn tl1 nat-s tl1
- **confusion**; with: agar h2 androc srj1• *Aur* bry k2 calc k2 glon luf-op rsj5• nat-ar nat-c a1 petr stram tarax h1
  - **lose** senses or go mad, as if would●: *Acon* agar chin stram tarent verat
  - **unable** to collect one's senses●: carb-v chin crot-h cycl kreos *Mang* mez nit-ac phos h2 rhus-t sars sil stann sulph
- **congestion**; as from: *Acon* bro1 aloe mrr1 aml-ns bro1 aq-mar rbp6 arg-n bro1* *Bell* bro1 *Bry* bro1 cact bro1* chinin-s bro1 chir-fl gya2 cic hr1 dulc br1 *Ferr-p* bro1 *Gels* bro1 *Glon* bro1 glyc bro1 guaj h2 joan bro1 lach bro1 led mrr1 meli br1* *Morg* fmm1• morg-p pte1*• nat-m bro1 nicotam rly4• nit-ac h2 nux-v bro1 op bro1 phase bro1 puls mrr1 *Sang* bro1 sil bro1 sol-ni bro1 stront-c c2 sulph bro1 syc fmm1• tritic-vg fd5.de usn c2* *Verat-v* bro1 [bell-p-sp dcm1]
  - **passive** congestion: *Chinin-s* bro1 ferr-p bro1 *Ferr-py* bro1 gels bro1 op bro1 sil bro1
- **constant**, continued: acon-ac rly4• arg-met arg-n a1 bros-gau mrc1 cadm-met gm1 cann-s carb-v *Chinin-s* *Cimic* conch fkr1• crot-c sk4• cupr cycl ptk1 dulc dys pte1*• falco-pe nl2• **Ferr** k* *Gels* gink-b sbd1• *Glon* hep hipp jl2 hydr hyos h1* indg *Kola* stb3• lac-d ptk1 lept lob med vh nat-m nat-s tl1 *Parathyr* jl2 petr-ra shn4• ph-ac h2* phos rhod rhus-r rhus-t a1 ruta fd4.de sep still sulph k2 syc fmm1• ter k* thiam rly4•
  - **children**; in: syc fmm1•
  - **fixed**, lasts for weeks, months, even years, with rare intermission: lat-m bnm6• ter
  - **one** week; for: prot jl2
  - **six** weeks; for: lat-h bnm5•
  - **three** to four days; for: pneu jl2
  - **two** or three days: croc **Ferr** k* mag-m vh* ozone sde2• pot-e rly4• ruta fd4.de sulph k2
- **constipated**; while (See accompanied - constipation)
- **constipation**; during: jatr-c ↓
  - **pressing** pain: jatr-c
- **constricting** (See Constriction)
- **contracted**; as if | **skin** of head were contracted; as if: carb-v rb2
- **contracting**: bism h1 chin h1 cycl a1 dig h2 dulc fd4.de hep h2 kali-p fd1.de• lyc h2 mang h2 nat-c h2 nicotam rly4• nit-ac h2 petr h2 podo fd3.de• ruta fd4.de sacch-a fd2.de• sep h2 suis-pan rly4• tritic-vg fd5.de
- **contraction** of muscles of face, at: spig ↓
  - **bursting** pain: spig h1
- **contradiction**, after: *Aur* *Bry* *Coff* lyc mag-c nat-m petr phos rhus-t sep j5.de
- **controversy**, from: bry k2
- **conversation** amel.: dulc br1* *Eup-per* a1 lac-d hr1 olib-sac wmh1
  - **sore**: eup-per
- **convulsions** | **after** | **epileptic**: bufo hr* calc kr1 *Caust* cina cupr k* *Kali-br* hr1 sulph sne
  - **before** | **epileptic**: atro vh1 calc-ar a cina h1* syph a*
- **cooling** of head agg.: carb-an ↓
  - **boring** pain: carb-an k*
- **copper**, abuse of: hep
- **cord**; as if bound with a (See Constriction - string)
- **corrosive**: alum b4a.de* plat h2 staph h1
- **coryza**:
  - **amel.**: arist-cl wm*
    - **fluent** coryza: bell a dulc vh lach a stict ptk2
  - **during**: **Acon** k* *Aesc* *Agar* k* **All-c** k* alum h2* am-m ↓ ambr b7.de* anan ant-c *Apis* bg2 *Arg-n* k* arn *Ars* k* ars-i *Aur* bad bamb-a stb2.de• **Bell** k* bov k* brom k2 bros-gau mrc1 **Bry** k* *Calc* k* calc-i k2 calc-sil k2 camph bro1 carb-v k* caust k* cham k* *Chin* k* *Chinin-ar* **Chlor** k* cic k*

- **coryza – during**: ...
cimic k* cina k* coc-c a coff coloc con cor-r k* croc *Cycl* b7a.de dios dioxi rbp6 dulc k* eup-per bro1 euphr k* *Ferr* ferr-ar ferr-i ferr-p *Gels* k* graph k* hed sp1 hell k* hep k* hydr a hyos ign k* *Iod* jac-c jac-g kali-ar *Kali-bi* k* kali-br bg2 *Kali-c* k* *Kali-i* k* kali-p kali-s kali-sil k2 kalm kola stb3• *Lach* k* laur b7.de* **Lyc** k* mag-m med a **Merc** k* *Merc-i-r* naja nat-ar k* nat-c nit-ac k* **Nux-v** k* petr petr-ra shn4• *Phos* k* phyt propl ub1• psil ft1 psor *Puls* k* rhod k* rhus-t ros-d wla1 rumx sabad k* samb *Sang* k* senec seneg *Sep* k* *Sil* *Spig* k* stann h2* staph b7.de* stict bg2* *Sulph* k* *Thuj* k* tritic-vg fd5.de tub c1* verat k* [calc-m stj1]
    - **dry** coryza: croc melal-alt gya4 rumx *Sep* tritic-vg fd5.de
    - **piercing** pain: bros-gau mrc1
    - **stitching** pain: am-m b7a.de coc-c kali-c lach b7a.de lyc h2* sabad b7.de*
    - **stunning** pain: sabad k2
  - **suppressed** coryza; from: *(↗catarrh; from - cramping)* *Acon* k* alum a am-c ant-c a apis bc arist-cl a ars k* bell k* bry *Calc* carb-v k* cham k* chin k* cina k* croc ↓ **Dulc** vh kali-bi k* kali-c lach k* lyc k* *Nux-v* k* puls k* senec vml3• sep sil *Sulph* bg2
    - **stitching** pain: croc
- **coryza**; as from: *Aesc* vh1 ham fd3.de• melal-alt gya4 mur-ac h2 nit-ac h2* phos h2* sulph h2*
  - **beginning** coryza; as from: sep h2* sil h2*
- **cough**:
  - **after**: lyc ↓
    - **pulsating** pain: lyc ptk1
  - **during**:
    - **agg.**: *(↗jar agg.)* acon k* aesc bc aeth k* allox tpw4* alum k* alum-p ↓ alum-sil k2* alumn ↓ am-c ambr k* *Anac* k* anag vh1 ang ant-t apis k* *Arn* k* ars ars-s-f k2 asc-t bro1 asim aur aur-ar k2 aur-s k2 bad bamb-a stb2.de• bar-c bar-s k2 **Bell** k* **Berb** ↓ beryl sp1 brom **Bry** k* cact cadm-met tpw6 *Calc* k* *Calc-s* **Caps** k* *Carb-v* k* card-m vml3• caust *Chel* *Chin* k* chinin-ar chion choc srj3• cimic ↓ cimx *Cina* coc-c *Coloc* **Con** k* cortico tpw7 *Cupr* dios erig vml3• eup-per k* ferr k* ferr-ar ferr-i ferr-p form bro1 ham hep k* hydr hyos ign *Ip* irid-met ↓ *Iris* k* *Kali-ar* kali-bi *Kali-c* k* kali-n k* kali-p kali-s kreos ↓ lac-ac **Lac-d** *Lach* k* led k* limest-b es1• *Lob* *Lyc* k* mag-s mang med *Merc* k* mez moni rfm1• mur-ac naja **Nat-m** k* nat-sil fd3.de• *Nicc* *Nit-ac* *Nux-v* k* oena ol-an ol-j olib-sac wmh1 ozone sde2• *Petr* k* *Ph-ac* k* **Phos** k* phyt bg1 pitu-gl skp7• pneu jl2 **Psor** ptel c1 *Puls* k* rauw ↓ rhus-t rumx ruta *Sabad* k* samb xxb1 *Sang* sars k* seneg *Sep* k* sil *Spig* k* *Spong* **Squil** k* *Stann* staph stict sul-ac **Sulph** k* tarent tax thuj ↓ tril-p tritic-vg fd5.de tub gk verat k* verb ↓ zinc zinc-p ↓ ziz
      - **blow**; pain as from a: *Ars* b4.de* *Ip* b7.de* lyc b4.de* mang b4.de* *Nat-m* b4.de* *Phos* b4a.de rhus-t b7.de* sul-ac b4.de*
      - **boring** pain: aur k* bell bry *Nux-v*
      - **bursting** pain: apis b7a.de **Bell** k* **Berb** beryl tpw5 **Bry** k* cact calc k* **Caps** k* *Chin* coc-c dios k* hep k* hydr k* irid-met srj5• kali-bi lac-ac *Lach* merc k* **Nat-m** k* nux-v k* ol-j ozone sde2• *Ph-ac* k* *Phos* k* ptel c1 puls k* rumx sep k* sil spig *Spong* staph **Sulph** k*
      - **contracting**: petr b4.de*
      - **cutting** pain: asim bell ziz
      - **drawing** pain: iris
      - **grinding** pain: aur k*
      - **pressing** pain: acon alum b4.de* alumn ambr anac k* *Arn* brom **Bry** k* chel k* coc-c con k* hep kreos k* nat-m b4a.de nit-ac k* petr phos k* rauw tpw8* ruta k* sars k* sep spig verb
      - **shooting** pain: arn bry k* calc k* carb-v k* con k* ferr c1 limest-b es1• mang k*
      - **sore**: sulph b4.de*
      - **stitching** pain: alum k* alum-p k2 anac k* ant-t arn k* *Ars* k* ars-s-f k2 *Bry* k* calc k* calc-s caps k2 *Carb-v* k* caust chel k* cimic cina coloc con k* hep k* hyos k* kali-ar *Kali-c* mez k* nit-ac ph-ac phos ruta k* sabad k* stann sul-ac sulph k* thuj k* verb zinc k* zinc-p k2
      - **stunning** pain: aeth k* kali-n k*
      - **tearing** pain: alum k* arn calc k* cupr mur-ac puls sep k* verat
      - **ulcerative** pain: hep b4a.de
    - **amel.**: arg-mur
  - **suppressed** cough; from: achy-a bnj1

- **covered**, pressing with distress, while: *Led* ↓
  - **pressing** pain: *Led* k*
- **covering** the head (See wrapping up head - agg.)
- **cramping**: *Acon* k* aeth bg2 alum alum-p k2 am-m *Ambr* anac ang k* ant-c c1 *Ant-t* arn b7a.de ars asaf calc k* carb-v k* cina colch *Coloc* croc dig bg2 dulc fd4.de eug gels *Ign* k* kali-c kola stb3• mag-m mez moni rfm1• mosch b7.de* nat-c b4a.de nit-ac nux-v k* olnd petr k* *Ph-ac* *Plat* k* pneu jl2 psor ran-s rheum sars b4a.de sec bg2 sep squil stann k* teucr thuj k* tritic-vg fd5.de verat bg2 verb zinc
- **cramps**; during: hell ↓
  - **shooting** pain: hell
- **crazy** feeling runs up back: lil-t ↓
  - **tearing** pain: lil-t
- **crossing** limbs agg.: bell bg1
- **crushed**; as if (= as if shattered; beaten to pieces): acon aesc k2 aeth k* alum k* alumn k2 aml-ns bg2 anan **Arg-met** k* ars aur k* bar-c bell bov bry ptk1 cact k2 calc camph caul hr1 caust cham *Chin* k* *Cocc* coff *Con* dios bg2* euph glon k2 graph hell hyos **Ign** k* iod *Ip* k* kali-c kali-i k2 *Lach* lyss mang merc mez k2 mur-ac nat-m nat-s k* nit-ac ptk1 nux-v k* ph-ac **Phos** k* puls rhus-t **Ruta** k* *Sep* k* *Sil* stann stront-c sul-ac syph k2* tarent bg2 verat verb bg2*
- **cutting** hair, after●: **Bell** k* bry bro1 glon led nat-pyru mtf11 psor a puls sabad *Sep*
- **cutting** pain: (↗*lancinating)* acon aesc agar k* ail allox tpw3* alum k* alum-sil k2 am-c ambr k* *Apis* k* arg-met k* *Arg-n* arge-pl rwt5• *Arn* k* *Ars* *Aster* bro1 *Aur* k* bell k* bism k* borx bg2 bry k2 cadm-s k* **Calc** k* calc-sil k2 camph k* cann-i bro1 cann-s canth k* caps k* carb-ac *Carb-an* carb-v k* carbn-s caust k* cham tl1 chel chin k* cic bro1 cina cinnb coc-c bg2 cocc k* coli rly4• con k* cortico sp1 croc cupr dig dros k* dulc fd4.de ferr k* ger-i rly4• glon k* graph hell hep hura hydrog srj2• ip **Iris** *Kali-bi* k* kali-c k2 kali-chl *Kali-i* kali-m k2 kreos *Lach* k* lyc k* mag-c manc merc mosch k* mur-ac nat-m k* nit-ac k* nux-m bg2 *Nux-v* bg2 ox-ac bg2 par petr pic-ac bg2 positr nl2• psor puls k* rad-br sze8• rhod bro1 sang k* sanguis-s hrn2• sars h2 sep k* *Sil* spig spong fd4.de squil stann bg2 staph k* suis-hep rly4• suprar rly4• symph fd3.de• tab bro1 tarent til tub k2* verat k* visc c1 zinc-val bro1
  - **brain** were cut to pieces, on stooping, as if: nicc
  - **hot**: hydrog srj2•
  - **knife**; as with a: alum k* *Arg-n* *Arn* *Bell* k* bry k2 calc canth k2 cocc *Con* kali-bi lach mag-c mag-s nat-m ozone sde2•
    - **followed** by | **coldness**; sensation of: arn
  - **split** by a wedge, body icy cold, thirsty; as if: lachn
- **damp** houses; from living in: *Ars* bry bro1 calc *Carb-v* *Dulc* nat-s phys puls rhod *Rhus-t* *Sil* *Verat*
- **dancing**: *Arg-n* k* irid-met srj5•
- **darkness**:
  - **agg.**: aloe ang a carb-an *Carb-v* cedr bro1 lac-c onos puls a *Sil* staph sne
    - **pressing** pain: sil
  - **amel.**: acon arn *Bell* k* brom bry k2 calc k2 chin hipp *Lac-d* mag-p mez nat-s ptk2 petr-ra shn4• *Sang* k* sep *Sil* k* *Stram* sulph k2 zinc
- **days**; lasting several: tab ↓
  - **intermittent** pains: tab bro1
- **debauch**; after: (↗*intoxication - after)* lup br1
- **decreasing** suddenly:
  - **one** hour; after: pitu-gl ↓
    - **pulsating** pain: pitu-gl skp7•
- **deep**-seated: all-c ↓ dulc ↓ grat ↓ kali-p ↓ lach ↓ ruta ↓ tab ↓ verb ↓
  - **stitching** pain: all-c k* dulc a1 grat a1 kali-p fd1.de• lach k* ruta fd4.de tab k* verb c1
- **delirium**; with: agar a bell a chinin-s sil stram syph a verat a
- **dentition**; during: *Acon* bell calc-p *Cham* *Cocc* coff hep hyos ign merc nit-ac nux-v rhus-t sil
- **descending**, on: **Bell** *Ferr* meny merc merc-i-f k* *Rhus-t*
  - **pressing** pain: meny k*
  - **stitching** pain: merc-i-f
- **desk**-work; from prolonged: ruta ↓
  - **dull** pain: ruta fd4.de
- **diagonally**: cycl bg2 gels bg2 iris bg2 lac-ac bg2 phos bg2 sars bg2 zing bg2
- **dialysis**; from: chin mtf ferr-py mtf ferr-r mtf nat-m mtf phase mtf sang mtf
- **diarrhea**:
  - **after** | **agg.**: ambr vh bell a calc-p a hell a lil-t a
  - **amel.**: agar alum apis lachn
  - **during**: (↗*RECTUM - Diarrhea - headache - during)* aeth agar aloe k* ambr apis bamb-a stb2.de• bell a calc-p c1* cham bro1 con glon graph ind jatr-c kali-n podo bro1 *Prot* jl2 stram verat k* zinc vh*
    - **schoolgirls**; in: calc-p tl1
  - **suppressed**; from: podo a
- **diet**; after the slightest error in: calc-ar kr1 guar vml3•
- **digging** (See boring)
- **dinner**:
  - **after**:
    - **agg.**: agar ↓ alum h2* alumn vh1 am-c k* ant-t ↓ ars k2 bar-c ↓ bell k* calc ↓ *Calc-p* *Calc-s* carb-an bg1* carbn-s castm chin ↓ chinin-s cimic con dios k* genist a1 gent-c k* gins k* glon k* grat ↓ hyper k* jug-r k* kali-bi kali-c h2* kali-n k* lob-s k* mag-c ↓ mag-m k* merc-i-f k* mur-ac ↓ nat-c ↓ *Nat-m* nat-p k* nux-v k* ol-an ↓ phel k* phos k* phyt *Puls* ↓ raph k* ruta ↓ seneg ↓ stram *Sulph* tab ↓ thuj ↓ valer k* zinc
      - **boring** pain: zinc
      - **burning**: *Alum* grat
      - **burrowing**: agar kali-c
      - **bursting** pain: kali-bi
      - **drawing** pain: bell k* nat-c k* phos
      - **dull** pain: mag-m h2 nat-c h2
      - **pressing** pain: agar h2 alum h2 alumn calc carb-an k* chin h1 ol-an ruta seneg tab thuj *Zinc*
      - **sore**: mag-m
      - **stitching** pain: ant-t bar-c mag-c mur-ac h2 phos *Puls* k* *Zinc* k*
      - **tearing** pain: carb-an mag-c ol-an zinc
    - **amel.**: arg-n arum-t bapt hr1 genist hir ↓ phos ptel zing
      - **dull** pain: hir skp7•
  - **amel.**: rumx ↓
    - **sore**: rumx
  - **before**: ind k* indg nux-v k*
  - **delayed**; if it is: cact cist lyc
  - **during**:
    - **agg.**: am-c ↓ kali-c ↓ pall c1 zinc ↓
      - **boring** pain: am-c
      - **drawing** pain: kali-c h2*
      - **pressing** pain: pall
      - **stitching** pain: zinc k*
      - **tearing** pain: zinc
- **disappearing** suddenly after one hour: pitu-gl ↓
  - **bursting** pain: pitu-gl skp7•
- **discharges**:
  - **amel.** (See GENERALS - Discharges)
  - **suppressed**: merc k2
- **dispute**, after: bry k2 staph k2
- **drawing** pain: (↗*Constriction)* *Acon* k* aeth k* *Agar* k* agath-a nl2• agn b7.de* ail all-c k2 alum k* alum-sil k2 am-c k* ambr k* ammc a1 ang k* ant-t k* apis k* aran k* arg-met arg-n k* *Ars* k* asar k* aur k* aur-ar k2 aur-m k* aur-m-n a1 aur-s k2 bapt bar-c k* bell k* berb k* *Bism* k* borx k* bov k* *Bry* k* cadm-s bg2 *Calc* k* *Calc-p* k* camph k* canth k* caps k* carb-an k* *Carb-v* k* *Carbn-s* caul bro1 *Caust* k* *Cham* k* **Chin** k* cimic k* cimx k* cina k* coff k* coloc k* *Con* k* croc k* cupr k* cycl k* dulc k* eug k* eupi k* ferr k* ferr-ar *Gels* k* gink-b sbd1• *Glon* k* gran *Graph* k* guaj k* hell k* hipp k* hydr ip k* kali-c k* *Kali-i* k* kali-p kali-s kali-sil k2 kalm *Kreos* k* lach k* lil-t lup a1 lyc k* *Mag-c* k* mang k* meny k* **Merc** k* merc-c mez k* *Mosch* k* mucs-nas rly4• nat-ar nat-c k* *Nat-m* k* nat-p nit-ac k* **Nux-v** k* ol-an k* olib-sac wmh1 petr k* *Phos* k* *Plat* k* *Plb* k* *Puls* k* ran-s k* rheum k* *Rhod* k* *Rhus-t* k* rhus-v a1 ruta k* sabad k* sabin k* sars h2* seneg k* *Sep* k* *Sil* k* spong fd4.de squil k* stann k* *Staph* k* stront-c k* stry suis-pan rly4• *Sul-ac* k* **Sulph** k* thuj k* til k* tong a1 tritic-vg fd5.de valer k* vanil fd5.de verat k* zinc k* zing k*
  - **accompanied** by | **nausea**: croc
  - **forward**: carb-v nat-m
  - **paroxysmal**: carb-v h2* thuj
  - **pendulum** of a clock; like the: *M-arct* b7.de*

Head

- **periosteum**; as if in: *Merc Merc-c*
- **pulsating** pain: ars
- **round** the head: bov carb-v spong fd4.de
- **stripes**; as if in: arg-n
- **thread**; as from a: mosch bg2
- **tightening** pain: asaf bar-c cann-i carb-v *Caust* clem coloc dig *Graph* gymno hep kali-chl lyc mag-c mag-m mang meny *Mosch* nat-c nat-m nit-ac nux-v olnd op par petr rhod sabad samb stram sulph ther verb
- **to** and fro: ambr k1

\- **dreams**, after unpleasant: chin a cob k* puls a sulph h2*
\- **drinking**:
- **after**:
  - **agg.** | **rapidly**: nat-m
  - **cold** water:
    - **heated**; when: bry ↓
      - **pulsating** pain: bry st
  - **milk**: brom lac-d phys
- **agg.**: acon k* bry *Cimx* k* *Cocc* crot-c crot-t kali-bi k2 lyc merc sep sulph k2 vanil fd5.de
  - **pressing** pain: cocc merc
- **amel.**: lavand-a ctl1•
- **cold** water | **agg.**:
  - **heated**; when: **Bry** ↓
    - **bursting** pain: **Bry** xxb
  - **amel.**: kali-c ↓ petr-ra ↓
    - **dull** pain: petr-ra shn4•
    - **jerking** pain: kali-c
- **water**:
  - **amel.**: lavand-a ↓
    - **pulsating** pain: lavand-a ctl1•

\- **drinks** | **aversion** to, with: **Ferr** a
\- **driving** agg.: granit-m ↓
- **lifting** off; head feels as if it is: granit-m es1•

\- **drugs**, after abuse of: dream-p sdj1• nux-v k*
\- **drunk**; as if (See intoxicated)
\- **drunkards**; in: agar tl1 bar-c hr1 cimic sne led mp1• nux-v tl1 puls mp1• sel c1
\- **dull** pain: abrom-a ks5 acon bg* acon-c a1 adam skp7• *Aesc* k* aeth a1 *Agar* k* *Agath-a* nl2• ail k* alco a1 *All-c* k* allox sp1 aloe ptk1 alum k* alum-p k2 alum-sil k2 am-be mtf11 am-c ptk1 *Anac* k* androc srj1• ant-c k* *Apis* k* apoc a1 apom a1* aq-mar skp7* aran-sc vh1 arg-met *Arg-n* k* arge-pl rwt5• ars bg* arum-t k* asaf a1* asar b7.de* asc-t a1 atro a1 bad a1 *Bapt* k* bar-c bar-s k2 bell bg* bism k* bcnd a1 bov k* *Brucel* sa3• bry b7.de* but-ac br1 cact ptk1 cadm-met sp1 caj a1 calc k* calc-p k2 calc-sil k2 camph cann-i k* canth k* caps a1 carb-ac a1* carb-an carb-v k* *Carbn-s* *Card-m* a1 *Cardios-h* rly4• cartl-s rly4• caul a1 caust k* cench k2 cham k* chel k* *Chin* k* chir-fl gya2 chord-umb rly4• cic a1 *Cimic* k* cimx a1 cina k* cinnb a1* *Clem* k* cob-n sp1 *Cocc* k* coch a1* coff coli rly4• *Coll* k* coloc a1 colum-p sze2• con b4.de* conv br1 cot a1 croc k* crot-h k* crot-t cub a1 cupr cystein-l rly4• dendr-pol sk4• dig a1 *Dios* k* dioxi rbp6 dirc a1 dor a1 dream-p sdj1• *Dulc* k* *Echi* ephe-si hsj1• ery-m a1 eucal a1 eup-pur eupi a1 eys sp1 falco-pe nl2• ferr k* ferr-s hr1 fic-m gya1 fl-ac bg2* form a1* fuma-ac rly4• gala br1 gels bg2* gent-l a1 ger-i rly4• gink-b sbd1• glon k* granit-m es1• *Graph* haem a1 ham hell k* hep k* hip-ac sp1 hippoc-k szs2 hir skp7• hydro-v a1 hydroph rsj6• hyos k* *Hyper* k* iber hr1 ign k* *Ind* indg hr1 kali-c a1 kali-i a1 kali-n a1* kali-s fd4.de *Kalm* k* ketogl-ac rly4• kola stb3• kreos a1* lac-ac a1 lac-del hm2• *Lac-h* sk4• *Lach* k* lachn k* lact k* lat-m bnm6• laur k* ied k* lepi a1 **Lil-t** a1* limen-b-c hm2* linu-c a1 lob hr1 *Lyc* k* lyss a1 mag-m k* mag-s a1 mang k* mang-p rly4• melal-alt gya4 meny k* meph *Merc* k* merc-c a1 merc-i-f a1* mez b4a.de* morph a1 mosch k* musa c1 myric a1 *Nat-c* k* nat-m k* nat-p a1* nat-pyru rly4• nat-s k* nat-sil fd3.de• nicc a1 nicotam rly4• *Nit-ac* k* nitro-o a1 nux-m a1 **Nux-v** k* nyct ah1* olnd a1 *Op* k* orot-ac rly4• osm a1 oxal-a rly4• ozone sde2• paeon a1 pall a1* par a1* ped a1 pert-vc vk9 petr k* petr-ra shn4• *Ph-ac* k* phel a1* phos b4.de* phyt a1* pic-ac a1 pin-s a1 pitu-gl skp7• plac-s rly4• plan a1 plat k* *Podo* k* positr nl2• psor a1 ptel a1* **Puls** k* *Pycnop-sa* mrz1 ran-s k* rat a1 rauw sp1 rheum k* rhod k* rhodi br1 rhus-g tmo3• *Rhus-t* k* rhus-v a1 ribo rly4• rob a1* ros-d wla1 rosm a1* rumx hr1 ruta fd4.de sabad k* sal-ac a1 salol c1 *Sang* k* sars k* sec k* sel a1 *Seneg* k* sep k* sil k* sin-a a1* spig k* spirae a1 spong k* squil k* stann a1

\- **dull** pain: ...
staph a1 stram hr1 *Stry* suis-em rly4• suis-hep rly4• suis-pan rly4• sul-ac k* sulph k* sumb a1 suprar rly4• symph fd3.de• tab a1 tarax a1 tarent zzc1• tax a1 tell a1 ter k* teucr k* thiam rly4• thuj k* thymol sp1 til a1 trif-p a1 *Trios* rsj11• tritic-vg fd5.de tus-p a1 urol-h rwt• urt-u k* ust a1 valer a1 vanil fd5.de verat k* verb k* vero-o rly4• viol-o k* viol-t k* vip a1 visc sp1 wies a1 x-ray sp1 xan a1 zinc a1* zing hr1 [bell-p-sp dcm1]
- **alcohol**; as from: ozone sde2•
- **hat**; as from pressure of: cadm-met sp1

\- **eating**:
- **after**:
  - **agg.**: agar **Alum** alum-p k2 alumn ↓ am-c k* ambr anac tl1 ant-c ant-t ↓ arn k* ars k* ars-s-f k2 bamb-a stb2.de• bar-c bar-m bar-s k2 bell bov *Bry* k* bufo cact k2 *Calc* k* *Calc-p* k* *Calc-s* calc-sil k2 canth caps carb-an k* *Carb-v* k* carbn-s castm caust *Cham* k* chel chin k* chin-b kr1 chinin-ar chinin-s choc srj3• cina cinnb clem ↓ *Cocc* *Coff* *Con* k* cop a1 crot-h ↓ crot-t dios euon fago a1 ferr ferr-ar ferr-p gels glon *Graph* k* grat hir ↓ hydr ↓ hydr-ac dp• *Hyos* k* ign ind kali-ar kali-c k* kali-m k2 kali-n kali-s kali-sil k2 lach *Lith-c* lob *Lyc* k* mag-c mag-m meny k* merc merc-i-f mill ↓ mur-ac *Nat-ar* **Nat-c** **Nat-m** k* nat-p nat-s nit-ac k* nux-m k* **Nux-v** k* ol-an ↓ paeon *Petr* *Ph-ac* phel *Phos* k* pip-m ↓ plat prot jl2 prun psor al2 **Puls** ran-b *Rhus-t* k* rumx ruta sars seneg sep k* *Sil* k* staph strept-ent jl2 **Sulph** k* tab ↓ thuj ↓ valer vanil fd5.de verat *Zinc* zinc-p k2
    - **boring** pain: nux-v
    - **bursting** pain: *Graph* nat-s nux-v
    - **drawing** pain: ant-t bell chin crot-h mill nat-c phos
    - **pressing** pain: alumn calc carb-an carb-v clem *Cocc* con graph hir rsj4• hydr hyos kali-c lyc nat-m nat-s ol-an pip-m ran-b ruta sep tab thuj *Zinc*
    - **stitching** pain: alum ant-t bar-c lyc mag-c *Nux-v* a1 phel phos sep k* sulph *Zinc*
    - **stunning** pain: *Cina* hr1 **Nux-v** k*
    - **tearing** pain: carb-an cina a1 mag-c *Nux-v* ol-an phel rhus-t h1 sep zinc
  - **amel.**: *Adam* skp7• allox sp1 aloe *Anac* ap-g vh1 aq-mar skp7• *Arg-n* k* arizon-l nl2• ars-i arum-t bov a bung-fa mtf cadm-s a caj calc-p a carb-ac carb-an card-m caust k* chel chin cist coca con dioxi rbp6 dulc fd4.de ferr a fl-ac a gels genist k* ign sne ind k* iod *Kali-bi* kali-p kali-s fd4.de kola stb3• lachn laur lyc k* mag-c mand a mez nat-c k2 onos a petr phos phys c1 phyt plut-n srj7• psor k* ptel a rhus-t rumx a sabad sal-fr sle1• scut **Sep** k* spig sulph ↓ symph fd3.de• tell k* *Thuj* vanil fd5.de
    - **drawing** pain: con k* sulph
    - **not** amel. when hungry; but: allox tpw4*
- **agg.**: inul ↓ sulph ↓ verb ↓
  - **shooting** pain: inul br1 sulph verb c1
- **amel.**: ind ↓ psor ↓ vanil ↓
  - **dull** pain: ind
  - **pressing** pain: psor vanil fd5.de
- **before** | **agg.**: am-m cann-s carb-an kali-sil k2 nux-v phos k2 ran-b sabad *Sil*
- **impossible**: kali-n h2*
- **nothing**, in spite of ravenous appetite: sulph tl1
- **overeating** agg.; after: coff **Nux-m** k* nux-v a **Puls** sang a tub k2
  - **just** a little bit: nux-m c1*
- **while**:
  - **agg.**: alum-sil k2 am-c k* arn bro1 *Ars* bro1 atro bro1 *Bry* bro1 cact bro1 chel *Cocc* k* coff bro1 con dulc gels k* *Graph* k* ign bro1 ind jug-r a1 kali-c b4a.de lach bro1 *Lyc* bro1 mag-m manc morph a1 nat-m nit-ac nux-v k* *Ph-ac* puls ran-b k* rhus-t sabin scut c1 sec sul-ac tab vanil fd5.de verb zinc
    - **drawing** pain: dulc
    - **pressing** pain: graph h2
    - **tearing** pain: con sul-ac zinc
  - **amel.**: aeth a1 allox tpw3 alum k* *Anac* k* ap-g k* bov cadm-s a carl bro1 chel k* *Chin* choc srj3• coca k* elaps bg1 hydrog srj2• ign k* iod kali-p c1* *Lach* *Lith-c* k* *Lyc* phel phos phyt a psor k* sang bg1 sep sil sin-n spong fd4.de sulph zinc

- **emotions**:
  - **negative**: dioxi rbp6
  - **suppressed**: acetan bro1 ant-c tl1 arg-n bro1 caps tl1 cham bro1 cimic bro1* coff bro1 *Epiph* bro1 *Gels* bro1 *Ign* bro1 mez bro1 ph-ac bro1 *Pic-ac* bro1 plat bro1 rhus-t bro1 sil bro1
- **entering** the house amel.: mang↓ plect↓
  - **drawing** pain: mang plect
- **epistaxis**:
  - **after**: aml-ns bro1 ant-c bro1 *Borx* psor tl1
    - **amel.**: alum bc ant-c bell a bell-p a brom bg1 bry bg1* bufo k* carb-an cham chin bg1 dig ferr-p k* ham k* hyos kali-bi mag-s k* *Meli* k* mill petr *Psor* k* raph bg1 **Rhus-t** hr1* sil a1 tab tarent bg1* tub a
  - **before**: *Carb-an*↓
    - **pressing** pain: *Carb-an*
- **erect** position agg.: *Mur-ac*↓
  - **pressing** pain: *Mur-ac* hr1
- **eructations** | **amel.**: *(↗accompanied - eructations)* arg-n a bry carb-v k2* cham a cimic a cinnb gent-c k* graph a hep bg1 ign bg1 lach ruta fd4.de sang k* tritic-vg fd5.de
- **eruptions**; suppressed: *Ant-c* k* bry k* kali-ar k2 lyc k* **Mez** k* nux-m k* **Psor** k* *Sulph* k*
  - **facial** eruptions: dulc mrr1
- **excitement**:
  - **after**: chinin-s↓
    - **pressing** pain: chinin-s
  - **depressing** or sad news, after: cocc ign nux-v op staph
  - **emotional**; after: *Acon* anac a arg-met *Arg-n Arn Aur Aur-m-n* wbt2• aur-s wbt2• *Bell* benz-ac bry *Cact* calc kr cann-i bro1 carc gk6* cham chin *Chinin-ar* chinin-s *Cocc Coff* con cycl ery-a ferr k2 *Ferr-p Gels* ham fd3.de• ign kali-p *Kola* stb3• kreos *Lach* lil-t vh* *Lyc Lyss* **Nat-m** nat-sil fd3.de• **Nux-v** *Op* ozone sde2• pall bro1 par petr **Ph-ac** *Phos Pic-ac* podo c1 **Puls** k* rhus-t scut **Staph** k* sulph thuj bl tub vanil fd5.de *Verat*
- **exertion**:
  - **agg.**●: acet-ac aloe bro1 ambr h1* anac k* *Arg-n* bro1 arn ars-s-f k2 bac jl2 bamb-a↓ **Bell**↓ berb bros-gau↓ bry k2 *Cact* **Calc** k* calc-f sp1 *Calc-p* carc a* cassia-s↓ chinin-ar c1 coc-c k2 cocc bro1 dulc fd4.de **Epiph** br1* erig vml3• gels bro1 gins glon *Hell*↓ kali-p lact lyc k2 med a* merc mez moni rfm1• naja a nat-c k* **Nat-m** k* *Nux-v* bro1 petr-ra shn4• ph-ac bro1 phos bro1 pic-ac k2* puls mrr1 rhus-r ruta fd4.de sang a* sep bro1 sil k* sol-t-ae vml3• spong til↓ tub bro1 ulm-c jsj8• *Valer* zing
    - **cutting** pain: ambr k* bros-gau mrc1 til
    - **lancinating**: ambr k*
    - **piercing** pain: bros-gau mrc1
    - **pressing** pain: bamb-a stb2.de• **Bell** calc-p k2 dulc fd4.de *Hell Nat-c*
    - **shooting** pain: cassia-s ccrh1• nat-c
    - **slight** exertion: ozone↓
      - **pulsating** pain: ozone sde2•
    - **stitching** pain: ambr h1 nat-c k*
    - **tearing** pain: *Anac*
  - **amel.**: adam skp7• agar apis mag-m merc-i-f mur-ac hr1 naja k2 pitu-gl↓ *Rhod* rhus-g *Sep* tritic-vg fd5.de
    - **bursting** pain: pitu-gl skp7•
    - **pulsating** pain: pitu-gl skp7•
    - **tearing** pain: *Mur-ac* hr1
- **exertion** of the eyes:
  - **agg.**: acetan bro1 *Agar* arg-n *Aur Aur-m-n* wbt2• aur-s k2 bar-m k2 bell *Borx Cact Calc* calc-sil k2 *Carb-v Caust Cimic* k* *Cina Epiph* bro1 gels k* gent-c↓ *Ham* helon↓ jab **Kali-c** kali-p kali-s kali-sil k2 kola stb3• **Lyc** mag-p mim-p skp7• mur-ac *Nat-c* **Nat-m** k* *Nat-p* neon srj5• *Onos* k* par petr-ra shn4• **Ph-ac** k* *Phos* phys pic-ac k2 **Rhod** *Rhus-t* **Ruta** k* sep **Sil** *Spong* staph sulph tritic-vg fd5.de *Tub* k* valer vanil fd5.de zinc
    - **pressing** pain: gent-c helon
  - **amel.**: petr-ra shn4•
- **expectoration** of blood | **amel.**: meli mtf11
- **extreme** (See violent)
- **faintness**; after: mosch
- **falling**; after: arn hyper k* rhus-t
- **false** step; at a: anac bar-c bry cob hep led puls **Sil** sol-ni spig k* thuj vib
- **false** step; at a: ...
  - **tearing** pain: **Spig**
- **fanning** agg.: hir↓
  - **pressing** pain: hir skp9*
- **fasting** agg.●: *Adam* skp7• ars bro1 ars-i cact bro1 calc a carneg-g rwt1• caust k* *Cist* crot-h c1 elaps fl-ac a ind iod k* *Kali-c* kali-p a kali-s kali-sil k2 kola stb3• lach bro1 **Lyc** k ●* mand a nicc-met sk4• nux-v petr-ra shn4• **Phos** ●* psor k2* ptel k* ran-b sabad a *Sang* k* sep mrr1 *Sil* k* spig sul-i k2 **Sulph** k ● thuj (non:uran-met k) uran-n
  - **hunger** is not appeased at once; if●: cact cist elaps **Lyc** k ● *Sang Sulph*
- **fat** food agg.: *Ant-c* hr1 *Carb-v* colch cycl ip nat-c nat-m *Puls* sang sep thuj
- **fever**:
  - **after**: *Ars* b4a.de carb-v b4a.de chinin-ar↓ cic b7a.de coff b7a.de hep b4a.de lach b7a.de plb b7a.de puls b7a.de rhus-t b7a.de
    - **sore**: chinin-ar k2
  - **after** intermittent | **amel.**: leucas-a mtf11
  - **during**:
    - **agg.**: aesc↓ bell↓ dendr-pol↓ nat-m↓ rhod↓ ruta↓ sep↓
      - **bursting** pain: aesc k* bell dendr-pol sk4•
      - **hammering** pain: nat-m bro1
      - **pressing** pain: rhod a1 ruta h1 sep
  - **with** (See accompanied - fever)
- **flatulence**; as from: *(↗Complaints - flatulence)* asc-t a calc-act a calc-p a cann-i a carb-v chinin-s mag-c nit-ac sulph xan a
- **flatulence**; with: asc-t br1 cann-i c1* xan br1
- **flatus**; passing | **amel.**: aeth k* aloe sne carb-v tl1 cic k* kali-i a mag-c a merc-c a sang k2*
- **fluids**; from loss of animal (See loss)
- **flying** pains (See wandering)
- **followed** by:
  - **soreness**: sang a1
  - **sour** things; desire for (See GENERALS - Food and - sour food - desire - headache)
  - **vertigo**: *Nux-v* hr1
  - **vision**; dim: *Nux-v* hr1
  - ○ **Abdomen**; pain in: gels psa
  - **Cheeks**; swelling of: carb-an b4a.de lyc b4a.de
  - **Chest**; complaints of: plat bg2
  - **Heart** | **complaints** of: merc-i-r ptk1
- **foot** steps (See stepping - agg.)
- **foreign** body; as from a: *Con* fl-ac rhod
- **fright**:
  - **after**: **Acon** *Arg-n* calc *Chinin-ar* cic a *Coff Cupr* hipp k* hyos **Ign** *Nux-v Op* ph-ac *Plat* **Puls** samb sil j5.de
  - **least** fright:
    - **agg.**: cic↓
      - **stitching** pain: cic
- **frowning** (See wrinkling)
- **frozen**; head and brain as if: *Indg* vh
- **gastric**: *(↗accompanied - indigestion; accompanied - nausea; accompanied - vomiting)* acet-ac acon aesc ail alum am-c am-pic bro1 *Anac* k* **Ant-c** k* apis *Arg-n* k* *Arn* ars asar atro bapt bro1 bell berb bism k* bor-ac a1 **Bry** k* *Calc Calc-p* calc-s caps k* *Carb-v* k* cas-s br1 caul *Caust* k* cham k* chel bro1 chin h1* *Chion* bro1 cic cina cocc *Coff Coll Corn-f* mtf cycl hr1* *Eup-per* k* euph h2* ferr-i k2 form gamb gels glon hipp a1 *Hydr* k* ign k* indg **Ip** k* **Iris** k* kali-ar kali-bi k* kali-c k* kali-p kali-s kola stb3• lach k* lept k* lob bro1 *Lyc* merc bro1 naja nat-m bro1* nat-s mrr1 nux-m bro1 **Nux-v** k* op par *Phos* phyt plat podo bro1 psor tl1 ptel c2 **Puls** k* rhus-t h1 rob k* **Sang** k* *Sep Sil* stict stry bro1 **Sulph** *Tab* tarax c2* tarent tub k2 verat [ang stj4]
- **gnawing** pain: calc k* canth k* *Coloc* hep kali-m k2 lac-e hm2• led lyc nat-m k* nat-s k2 paeon k* par k* phos k* ran-s k* verat b zinc k*
  - **pulsating** pain: par
- **gouty**: asar bg2 *Bry* bg2 chin bg2 coloc bg2 guaj a2* *Ign* bg2 ip bg2 mosch bg2 **Nux-v** bg2 *Rhus-t* bg2 *Sep* bg2

- **gradually** (See increasing - gradually)
- **grasping** pain: *(↗griping)* arg-n ars k* chin h1* con hell mag-m nat-s k* op bg2 stram bg2 zinc bg2
- **grief**; from: *Aur* hr1* *Calc* hr1* caust ll1 **Ign** k* lach cd1 nat-m k* nat-s k4 op k* *Ph-ac* k* *Phos* hr1* pic-ac al1* *Puls* k* **Staph** k*
- **grinding** pain: agar k* anac k* aur k* clem hr1 myric k*
- **griping** pain: *(↗grasping)* alum h2* chord-umb rly4• con mag-m k* mag-s mez a1 sep
- **grumbling** pain: bamb-a stb2.de• hep k* indg k* sul-ac k*
- **hacking** pain: am-c k* ars k* aur k* kali-n k* lyc k* ph-ac k* *Staph* b7a.de
- **hair** must hang down: bry↓
  - **sore**: bry k2
- **hammering** pain: *Am-c* k* *Ars* k* aur k* aur-ar k2 bamb-a stb2.de• **Bell** cadm-s k* calc k* calc-sil k2 carb-v bg2 carc sst• chel *Chin* k* chinin-ar *Chinin-s* k* cic k* cimic clem k* *Cocc* *Coff* k* colch rsj2• *Cur* dros k* dulc fd4.de **Ferr** k* **Ferr-ar** ferr-p gels k2 gink-b sbd1• **Glon** k* *Hep* k* ign bg2 indg k* iris kali-bi kali-i kola stb3• kreos bg2 lac-h htj1• *Lach* k* m-ambo b7.de mag-s manc k* mez k* **Nat-m** k* nat-ox rly4• nicc nit-ac k* op bg2 ph-ac k* phos b4.de* *Psor* k* puls rheum k* rhod bg2 rhus-t k* ruta fd4.de sang bg2 sars bg2 sep bg2 **Sil** k* *Spong* bg2 stann bg2 suis-pan rly4• **Sulph** k* *Tarent* k* verb h* visc sp1
  - **followed** by | **vomiting**: cadm-s gm1
- **hang** down, letting feet: *Puls*
- **hard** body in head; as from a (See plug)
- **hat**; from pressure of a: agar k* alum k* ang b2.de arg-met k* *Calc-p* k* carb-an k* **Carb-v** k* caust *Crot-t* k* ferr-i k* *Glon* k* hep k* hydr-ac a kali-n k* *Lach* k* laur k* led k* lil-t bg1 lyc k* mez k* nat-m bro1 nat-sil fd3.de• **Nit-ac** k* phys↓ sep *Sil* k* staph stront-c b2.de sulph k* *Valer* k*
  - **drawing** pain: carb-v
  - **pressing** pain: *Calc-p* *Carb-v* *Led* vh nat-sil fd3.de• **Nit-ac** phys sep h2 sulph h2
  - **sore**: carb-v **Nit-ac** *Sil*
- **hawking**, agg.: conv br1*
- **hay** fever, with: sabad↓
  - **pressing** pain: sabad
- **headache**, after intense: lycpr↓
  - **sore**: lycpr c1
- **heart** complaints; with: ars-i k2 lach k2 lycps-v bro1 symph fd3.de•
- **heat**:
  - **after**: *Ars* calc *Carb-v* **Eup-per** k* **Nat-m** sil h2*
  - **and** cold agg.: grat↓
    - **boring** pain: grat
  - **before**: ars b4a.de bry k* *Carb-v* b4a.de chin k* kali-n b4a.de nat-c b4a.de nat-m b4a.de puls k* rhus-t k* sep b4a.de sil h2* spong k*
  - **during**: acon k* aesc agar k* aloe mrr1 am-c k* *Ang* k* ant-t k* **Apis** k* arg-met b7.de* **Arn** k* *Ars* k* asaf bamb-a stb2.de• *Bapt* hr1* bar-c b4a.de **Bell** k* berb borx k* bry k* cact cadm-s k2 calc k* calc-sil k2 camph k* caps k* carb-v k* carbn-s caust sne cham bg2 **Chin** k* chinin-ar chinin-s k* cina k* clem a1 *Cocc* coloc k* con b4.de* corn-f *Crot-h* cupr dros k* dulc k* elat **Eup-per** k* ferr-p a* gels↓ graph k* hell b7a.de* *Hep* k* hipp hir↓ hydroph↓ hyos k* *Ign* k* ip b7.de* kali-ar kali-bi kali-c k* kali-n b4.de *Lach* k* led b7a.de* lob lyc k* mang b4a.de* meny b7.de* merc-i-r c1 mez b4.de* mosch b7.de* nat-c b4.de* **Nat-m** k* *Nux-v* k* *Op* k* petr b4.de* petr-ra shn4• phos b4.de* plan *Podo* *Psor* *Puls* k* rhod b4.de* *Rhus-t* k* ruta k* *Sabad* k* sang a1 sep k* **Sil** k* spig k* staph b7.de* stram bg2 sulph k* syph al ther c1 *Thuj* k* trios↓ valer k* verat k* verat-v hr1
    - **dull** pain: agar h2 dulc fd4.de hir skp7• hydroph rsj6• trios rsj11•
    - **stitching** pain: asaf dulc fd4.de gels *Nux-v* puls k*
    - **tearing** pain: puls
  - **face**; with heat of the: puls↓
    - **boring** pain: puls
  - **stove**; of:
    - **agg.**: bar-c↓
      - **stitching** pain: bar-c
  - **sun**; of the:
    - **agg.**: abrom-a↓ hir↓ tarent↓
      - **dull** pain: abrom-a ks5 hir skp7• tarent zzc1•
    - **amel.**: stront-c↓
      - **drawing** pain: stront-c
- **heated** in bed; from becoming: *Lyc* nux-m
- **heated**; when: am-c↓ carb-v↓ trios↓
  - **drawing** pain: carb-v
  - **pressing** pain: am-c k* trios rsj11•
- **hemorrhage**:
  - **after**: carb-v bro1 chin bro1* ferr bro1 ferr-py bro1 ph-ac bro1 plat k2 sil bro1
    - **amel.**: **Meli** mrr1*
    - **Uterus**; from: *Glon* k*
  - **during**: kali-c↓ visc↓
    - **dull** pain: kali-c h2 visc c1
- **hiccough**:
  - **after**: con↓
    - **dull** pain: con a1
  - **during**: *Bry*↓
    - **pressing** pain: *Bry*
- **high** altitudes; at: *Coca* k*
- **holding** head:
  - **must** hold head: carb-an bro1 glon bg1* petr bro1 sul-ac bro1
    - **headache**; during: caps k2
- **holding** head down | **must** hold head and eyes down: apis
- **holding** head erect | **agg.**: bar-c
- **hoop**; as if with a (See Constriction - band)
- **hot**:
  - **anything** hot in mouth: chin kr1
  - **soup** | **amel.**: kali-bi
- **hot** things, from: *Arum-t*↓
  - **pressing** pain: *Arum-t* k*
- **house** agg; inside: ferr-i k2
- **humiliation**; from: carc mlr1•
- **humming** pain: hep h2 kali-s fd4.de squil h1 staph h1 sulph h2 vanil fd5.de
- **hunger**:
  - **from** (See eating - before - agg.; fasting)
- **hurry**: con k13 ign k2
- **hysterical** headache: agar bro1 aqui bro1 *Arg-n* arn **Asaf** *Aur* aur-ar k2 bell bry cann-s caps k* cham cimic k* *Cocc* *Coff* k* euon bro1 gels hell *Helon* hr1 hep k* hyos *Ign* k* iris kali-bi kali-c bro1 *Lach* lact mag-c mag-m k* *Mosch* nat-m bro1 nit-ac *Nux-m* nux-v k* ph-ac phos *Plat* k* puls bro1 rhus-t ruta scut *Sep* stict stram *Tarent* thuj bro1 *Valer* verat
- **ice** cream agg.: *Ars* caust sne chlam-tr bcx2• dig a* elaps gk ger-i rly4• **Puls**
- **increasing**:
  - **gradually**●: acon brucel sa3• bry carb-v caust con hippoc-k szs2 lact lob petr-ra shn4• psil ft1* ruta fd4.de sars sep a vanil fd5.de
    - **evening**; towards: adam skp7• vanil fd5.de
    - **night** | **22** h: propr sa3•
    - **ceasing** | **suddenly**●: arg-met k* arg-n mrr1 carb-v bg2* caust k* *Ign* *Sul-ac* k*
    - **decreasing**:
      - **bed**; when going to: propr sa3•
      - **gradually**●: arn ars bar-c bufo crot-h glon k* hippoc-k szs2 ip c1 jab kali-bi bg2* luna kg1• mez nat-m k* op pic-ac *Plat* k* psor sabin sang bg2* sars sep bg2* spig k* **Stann** k* staph k* stront-c k* sul-ac mrr1 sulph syph bg2* verb
        - **bursting** pain: mez stront-c
        - **pressing** pain: *Stann*
      - **suddenly**●: arg-met a *Arg-n* **Bell** coca ferr bg1 gink-b sbd1• merc-c *Spig* *Sulph*
  - **suddenly**: *(↗sudden - blow; sudden - stitching)* agar k* *Arg-n* ars-h a1 aster *Bell* berb both-ax tsm2 camph k* cimic croc ferr *Gels* hydroph rsj6• kali-p fd1.de• merc-i-f a1 mez k* morph k* phys k* pneu jl2 podo c1 *Sabin* symph fd3.de• *Tab* k* tell lp* thiam rly4• tub-d jl2 valer *Verat-v* a1
    - **decreasing**:
      - **gradually**: asaf calc fl-ac puls ran-s sabin
      - **suddenly**: arg-n bg2 asaf aster *Bell* k* *Cedr* ferr bg2 fl-ac *Ign* kali-bi mag-p mang-p rly4• med c1* merc-c olib-sac wmh1 ozone sde2• sabal c1 spig bg2 spong bg2 *Sulph* k*

- **suddenly – decreasing – suddenly**: ...
  - . **Forehead**: bell ↓
    - **stunning** pain: bell $_{bg2}$
  - . **Occiput**: bry ↓
    - **stunning** pain: bry $_{bg2}$
  - ⁝ **urination** agg.; during: tab
- **increasing** and decreasing: bar-c ↓
  - **shooting** pain: bar-c
- **influenza**:
  - **after**: sul-ac ↓
    - ⁝ **neuralgic**: *(↗GENERALS - Convalescence - influenza)* sul-ac $_{mrr1}$
  - **during**: camph $_{bro1}$ influ $_{jl2*}$ lob-p $_{c2*}$ naja ↓
    - ⁝ **bursting** pain: naja
- **injuries**; after mechanical: *Arn* $_{k*}$ *Bell* calc *Calc-s* calen $_{hr1}$ carc $_{gk6*}$ *Chel* $_{pd}$ *Cic* con dulc *Glon* $_{vh*}$ *Hep* *Hyper* $_{k*}$ kali-br $_{hr1}$ lach merc *Nat-m* $_{k*}$ **Nat-s** $_{k*}$ nit-ac petr *Ph-ac* $_{sne}$ *Phos* puls *Rhus-t* *Staph* sul-ac sulph
  - **delivery**; during: carc $_{gk6}$
- **inspiration**:
  - **agg.**: *Anac* brom carb-v glon $_{sne}$ kali-c $_{sne}$ rat
    - ⁝ **cold** air through nose (See cold - air - inspiration)
  - **deep** | **agg.**: *Cact*
- **intermittent** pains: agar $_{k*}$ alum-sil $_{k2}$ alumn $_{k*}$ anac arg-met *Ars* cann-i caul chlam-tr $_{bcx2}$• cina coloc $_{k2}$ cupr falco-pe $_{nl2}$• ferr fic-m $_{gya1}$ *Gels* hippoc-k $_{szs2}$ ign $_{k*}$ iod $_{k*}$ iris kalm $_{k*}$ loxo-recl $_{knl4}$• m-ambo $_{b7a.de}$ maias-l $_{hm2}$• mill $_{k*}$ nit-ac $_{k*}$ plan $_{k*}$ plat psor $_{k*}$ sang $_{k*}$ sep $_{k*}$ stann ter $_{k*}$ tet $_{a1}$ trif-p $_{a1}$ tub-d $_{jl2}$ valer $_{k*}$ verat
- **intoxicated**; as if: ambr $_{c1}$ pip-m $_{mrr1}$ podo $_{fd3.de}$•
- **intoxication** | **after**: *(↗debauch)* *Ant-c* bell *Bry* *Carb-v* cocc coff dioxi $_{rbp6}$ glon laur **Nux-v** $_{k*}$ *Puls* spong stram sulph tarax
- **iron**, from abuse of: puls *Zinc*
- **ironing**, from: **Bry** $_{k*}$ sep $_{k*}$
- **irritability**; with (See MIND - Irritability - headache)
- **itching** pain: chin $_{h1}$ sep $_{h2}$ sil $_{h2}$
- **jar** agg.: *(↗Cough - during - agg.; Laughing; Motion; Riding; Stepping - agg.; Walking; Sensitiveness - Jar; Sensitiveness - Stepping)* allox $_{tpw3*}$ aloe $_{a*}$ am-c am-m arn ars $_{k2}$ bar-c bar-s $_{k2}$ **Bell** $_{k*}$ beryl $_{sp1}$ **Bry** $_{k*}$ cadm-met $_{sp1}$ *Calc* calc-p $_{k2}$ calc-s calc-sil $_{k2}$ *Carb-v* *Carbn-s* chel *Chin* $_{k*}$ chinin-ar chion $_{br1}$ cina cob cocc con crot-h $_{k*}$ dioxi $_{rbp6}$ ferr $_{a}$ *Ferr-p* $_{k*}$ *Gels* **Glon** $_{k*}$ grat hell ↓ *Hep* ign $_{k2}$ ind *Kali-c* kali-p *Kali-s* kali-sil $_{k2}$ lac-c lac-d lac-h $_{htj1}$• lach $_{k*}$ **Led** *Lyc* $_{k*}$ *Mag-m* mang med $_{br1}$ meny $_{a*}$ merc mim-p $_{skp7}$• nat-ar *Nat-m* **Nit-ac** *Nux-v* onos op $_{k2}$ petr *Ph-ac* *Phos* phyt *Psor* pycnop-sa $_{mrz1}$ *Rhus-t* $_{k*}$ sabad sang $_{k*}$ *Sep* **Sil** $_{k*}$ *Spig* $_{k*}$ stram $_{k2*}$ *Sulph* *Ther* $_{k*}$ *Thuj* til $_{ban1}$• tritic-vg $_{fd5.de}$ vanil $_{fd5.de}$ vib
  - **bursting** pain: bell beryl $_{tpw5}$ carb-v $_{k2}$ *Chin* sabad $_{k2}$ sil
  - **come** off; as if top of head would: cob merc
  - **cutting** pain: bell $_{k2}$
  - **shooting** pain: bell $_{k2}$
  - **sore**: bar-c **Bell** calc calc-sil $_{k2}$ hell lac-d $_{k2}$ *Led* nit-ac nux-v phyt sil
  - **walking** on tips of toes amel.: *(↗EXTREMITIES - Walking - toes - must)* crot-h $_{br1*}$
- **jar**; as from a: petr-ra $_{shn4}$• sep $_{h2*}$
- **jaundice**; with: sep $_{k2*}$
- **jerking** pain: acon $_{k*}$ aeth agar $_{k*}$ alumn $_{a1}$ am-c am-m $_{bg2}$ ambr $_{k*}$ anac $_{k*}$ ant-t $_{k*}$ apis *Arn* $_{k*}$ asaf $_{k*}$ bar-c $_{k*}$ bar-s $_{k2}$ **Bell** $_{k*}$ bism $_{k*}$ borx $_{k*}$ *Bry* $_{k*}$ calc $_{k*}$ calc-sil $_{k2}$ cann-i cann-s $_{a1}$ canth $_{k*}$ *Carb-ac* carb-an $_{k*}$ carb-v $_{k*}$ *Carbn-s* caust $_{k*}$ cham $_{bg2}$ chel $_{a1}$ *Chin* $_{k*}$ colch $_{b7.de*}$ crot-t $_{k*}$ cycl $_{k*}$ dig $_{b4.de*}$ dulc $_{k*}$ eupi $_{k*}$ glon $_{k*}$ graph $_{k*}$ hell $_{bg2}$ *Ign* $_{k*}$ indg kali-c $_{k*}$ kali-m $_{k2}$ kali-p *Kali-s* kreos $_{k*}$ lach $_{k*}$ laur $_{a1}$ lyc $_{k*}$ m-ambo $_{b7.de}$ mag-c $_{k*}$ mag-m $_{k*}$ meny $_{k*}$ merc $_{k*}$ mill morph $_{a1}$ *Mur-ac* $_{k*}$ nat-c $_{k*}$ *Nat-m* $_{k*}$ nat-s $_{bg2}$ nit-ac $_{k*}$ nux-v $_{k*}$ paeon *Petr* $_{k*}$ ph-ac $_{k*}$ phos $_{k*}$ plb $_{k*}$ prun $_{k*}$ *Puls* $_{k*}$ ran-s $_{bg2}$ rat sabad $_{k*}$ samb $_{k*}$ seneg $_{bg2}$ *Sep* $_{k*}$ sil $_{k*}$ *Spig* $_{k*}$ spong $_{k*}$ squil $_{k*}$ *Stann* $_{k*}$ stram $_{a1}$ stront-c $_{b4.de*}$ **Sul-ac** $_{b4a.de}$ **Sulph** $_{k*}$ teucr thuj $_{k*}$ valer $_{b7.de*}$
  - **accompanied** by | **vertigo**: ozone $_{sde2}$•
  - **behind** forward: ph-ac
  - **wandering** pain: chel stront-c
- **joy**, from excessive: *(↗MIND - Ailments - joy - excessive; MIND - Ailments - surprises - pleasant)* *Coff* croc $_{a*}$ cycl op puls scut
- **knitting**, while: mag-s ↓
- **knitting**, while: ...
  - **tearing** pain: mag-s
- **knocked** in the head; as if: mosch
- **lacerating** (See tearing)
- **lain** with head too low; as if: glon $_{tl1}$ phos $_{h2*}$
- **lancinating**: *(↗cutting pain)* acon acon-ac $_{rly4}$• aesc alum am-c ambr anan arn *Ars* aur-s $_{k2}$ *Bell* cadm-s calc canth $_{k2}$ chord-umb $_{rly4}$• con $_{k2}$ *Cupr* cystein-l $_{rly4}$• dros ger-i $_{rly4}$• gins graph hep hippoc-k $_{szs2}$ hura ip kali-i $_{k*}$ mag-c manc nat-ox $_{rly4}$• oxal-a $_{rly4}$• plac-s $_{rly4}$• podo $_{c1}$ rhodi $_{ptk2}$ ribo $_{rly4}$• sang sphing $_{k*}$ squil suis-em $_{rly4}$• tarent thiam $_{rly4}$•
- **lasting** (See constant)
- **laughing** agg.: *(↗jar agg.; MIND - Ailments - joy - excessive)* allox $_{tpw4*}$ ars ars-met $_{c1}$ bell $_{a}$ chion cocc croc $_{hr1}$ cupr-s ↓ ip iris mang *Nat-m* phos propr $_{sa3}$• ther tong $_{hr1}$ zinc zing
  - **come** off; as if top of head would: cupr-s $_{hr1}$
- **leaning**:
  - **against** something:
    - ⁝ **agg.**: ang bell cann-i $_{a}$ cycl meny $_{a}$ nat-m nux-v $_{a}$
    - ⁝ **amel.**: anac aral aran arn **Bell** brom cann-s con dros gels gymno $_{k*}$ kali-bi *Lycpr* $_{c1}$ meny merc nux-v $_{k*}$ rhod sabad sabin sang seneg spig sulph
  - **head**:
    - ⁝ **hands** amel.; on: dros ↓
      - : **tearing** pain: dros
    - ⁝ **right** side; to:
      - : **amel.**: stram ↓
        - . **sore**: stram
    - ⁝ **table** amel.; on: sulph ↓
      - : **tearing** pain: sulph
- **lemon** amel.: mag-m $_{vh}$
- **lemonade** agg.: *Sel* $_{k*}$
- **lifting** agg.: ambr *Arn* bar-c *Bry* *Calc* $_{k*}$ cocc *Graph* *Lyc* *Nat-c* nux-v *Ph-ac* **Rhus-t** *Sil* sulph valer
- **lifting** off; head feels as if it is: granit-m $_{es1}$•
- **light**; from:
  - **agg.**: *(↗MIND - Sensitive - light)* acon act-sp ↓ agar aloe anac $_{sne}$ anan ant-c $_{k2}$ *Ant-t* ap-g $_{vml3}$• arg-n arizon-l $_{nl2}$• arn *Ars* ars-s-f $_{k2}$ **Bell** $_{k*}$ beryl ↓ *Bov* $_{k*}$ brucel $_{sa3}$• *Bry* bufo cact **Calc** calc-f $_{sp1}$ calc-sil $_{k2}$ cann-i ↓ carb-ac ↓ caul $_{c1}$ *Chin* *Cocc* *Coff* dulc $_{fd4.de}$ euphr ferr $_{bro1}$ *Ferr-p* *Gels* glon $_{k2}$ graph $_{k2}$ hydrog $_{srj2}$• *Ign* $_{k*}$ irid-met $_{srj5}$• kali-bi $_{k*}$ kali-c $_{bro1}$ kali-p kali-sil $_{k2}$ kola $_{stb3}$• lac-c *Lac-d* $_{k*}$ *Lyc* lyss $_{bro1*}$ mag-p $_{k2}$ med $_{k2}$ mim-p $_{skp7}$• *Moni* $_{rfm1}$• nat-ar *Nat-c* *Nat-m* $_{k*}$ nat-p nat-s $_{k2}$ nux-v $_{k*}$ oreo $_{bro1}$ petr-ra $_{shn4}$• *Ph-ac* $_{k*}$ phel $_{bro1}$ *Phos* pin-con $_{oss2}$• plut-n $_{srj7}$• podo sacch-a ↓ sal-fr $_{sle1}$• *Sang* $_{k*}$ sanic scut $_{bro1}$ *Sep* *Sil* $_{k*}$ sol-ni spig $_{bro1}$ spong $_{fd4.de}$ stict *Stram* *Sulph* syph $_{a*}$ tab *Tarent* $_{k*}$ ther $_{k2}$ valer $_{a}$ ziz
    - ⁝ **boring** pain: nux-v
    - ⁝ **burning**: *Glon*
    - ⁝ **bursting** pain: beryl $_{tpw5}$
    - ⁝ **cutting** pain: bell $_{k2}$ carb-ac
    - ⁝ **jerking** pain: carb-ac
    - ⁝ **pressing** pain: act-sp $_{vh1}$ cann-i ph-ac $_{k2}$ sacch-a $_{fd2.de}$•
    - ⁝ **shooting** pain: bell $_{k2}$
  - **amel.**: lac-c sil
  - **artificial** light:
    - ⁝ **agg.**: bufo croc *Glon* manc $_{k*}$ mang nat-c pant-ac $_{rly4}$• pitu-gl ↓ *Sang* **Sep** *Sil* *Stram* zinc
      - : **bursting** pain: pitu-gl $_{skp7}$•
      - : **pulsating** pain: pitu-gl $_{skp7}$•
  - **daylight** | **agg.**: act-sp $_{vh1}$ *Calc* *Hep* nat-m **Phos** sang $_{a}$ sep $_{h2*}$ **Sil**
  - **gaslight** | **agg.**: bell **Glon** *Nat-c* $_{k*}$ nat-s
- **lightning**-like: sang $_{bg2}$ sil $_{bg2}$
- **line**; in a: apis $_{bg2*}$ hydrog $_{srj2}$• syph $_{bg2*}$ tell $_{bg2*}$
- **listening** to reading and talking: *Mag-m*
- **liver** complaints: jug-c $_{br1*}$
- **looking**:
  - **crosswise** | **amel.**: olnd $_{hr1*}$

Head

- **downward**:
  - **from**: alum kalm nat-m olnd phyt k* pic-ac k2 spig sulph [pop dhh1]
  - **out** of window causes vertigo, anxiety, headache and sweat: ox-ac
- **fixedly** at anything:
  - **amel.**: *Agn* k* sabad sars
  - **from**: anac *Aur* cadm-s calc caust cina gent-c glon helon *Ign* lac-c lith-c mur-ac *Nat-m* nux-v olnd **Onos** par pic-ac k2 *Puls Ruta* sabad sars *Spig Spong* sulph tarent
- **moving** objects; at: con k2
- **sideways**:
  - **amel.**: olnd k*
  - **from**: acon dig merc bg1 sil
- **steadily**:
  - **agg.**: helon ↓ *Puls* ↓
    - **pressing** pain: helon k* *Puls*
- **upward**:
  - **amel.**: thuj
  - **from**: acon aeth k* arn arum-t bapt bell *Calc* calc-s caps caust coca colch cupr glon gran graph *Ign Lac-c* lach plat plb ptel bg1 **Puls** sep sil stram *Sulph Thuj*

- **loquacity**; with (See MIND - Loquacity - headache - during)
- **loss** of fluids: *(↗sexual excesses)* ars *Calc Carb-v* k* *Chin* k* cina cocc con ferr bro1 ferr-py bro1 kali-c lach meli sne merc *Nat-m Nux-v Ph-ac* k* phos *Puls Sep Sil* k* *Staph Sulph* verat
- **lying**:
- **abdomen**; on | **amel.**: bell mrr1
- **agg.**: agar alum-p k2 alum-sil k2 *Am-c* ambr anac ant-t ars ars-met bro1 asaf asc-t c1 *Aur* aur-ar k2 aur-s k2 bar-c bar-m bar-s k2 *Bell* k* bov k* cadm-s calam sa3• calc calc-sil k2 camph canth ↓ **Carb-v** k* cham chel chin bro1* cimic clem coc-c k2 *Coloc* k* *Con* crot-h ↓ cupr dios *Dulc* eup-per bro1 euph euphr eupi *Gels* k* *Glon* k* hep ign kali-ar kali-c kola stb3• lac-c lac-leo hrn2• lach k* led lith-c *Lyc* k* mag-c mag-m k* mang *Meny Merc* mez mur-ac nat-c ↓ nat-p nat-s nit-ac nux-m ↓ nux-v onos *Op* ox-ac petr *Ph-ac Phos* phys *Plat* puls ran-b k* rhod *Rhus-t* k* ruta fd4.de sang a1* sanic sep spig spong k2 stann staph stram k2* stront-c sulph **Tarax** ↓ ther k* thuj tritic-vg ↓ vanil fd5.de visc sp1 zinc zinc-p k2
  - **pressing** pain: glon lach *Lyc* merc nat-s nux-v ruta fd4.de **Tarax** tritic-vg fd5.de vanil fd5.de
  - **sore**: aur crot-h euphr nux-m
  - **stitching** pain: canth nat-c puls sep vanil fd5.de
  - **tearing** pain: mag-c thuj zinc h2
- **amel.**: agath-a nl2• *Alum* alum-p k4 alum-sil k4 am-m ambr anac k* ant-c k2 arn asar asc-t c1 *Bell* benz-ac k* beryl sp1 bros-gau ↓ *Bry* k* bufo *Cact Calc* calc-p calc-s camph canth chel *Chin* k* chinin-s *Chion* chlam-tr bcx2• cit-ac ↓ coc-c k* cocc k* colch con dig *Dulc* epiph vh ferr k* ferr-i ferr-p fic-m gya1 fl-ac gels k* glon mtf11 granit-m ↓ ham *Hell* hipp hir ↓ ign k* junc-e ↓ kali-bi *Kali-c* kali-s *Lac-d* k* lach k* *Lyc Mag-c* mag-m bro1 mag-p bg1 meli vml3• merc mosch mur-ac nat-c *Nat-m* nat-ox rly4• nat-s k2 *Nit-ac Nux-v* k* olnd ozone ↓ petr petr-ra shn4• *Ph-ac* k* *Phos* propl ub1• sabad sang k* sel bg1* sep a1* *Sil* k* spig k* spong sulfonam ks2 sulph k* tab tax-br oss1• ther bro1 tritic-vg fd5.de vanil fd5.de visc sp1 zinc zinc-p k2 ziz [heroin sdj2]
  - **burrowing**: junc-e *Spig* k*
  - **cutting** pain: ambr bros-gau mrc1
  - **dull** pain: asc-t c1 granit-m es1•
  - **jerking** pain: chin
  - **lancinating**: ambr cit-ac rly4•
  - **pressing** pain: bell hir skp7• **Lach** nit-ac spig spong fd4.de tritic-vg fd5.de
  - **pulsating** pain: ozone sde2•
  - **sore**: granit-m es1•
  - **stitching** pain: ambr h1 calc dulc nat-m nit-ac *Sep* spig k2 tritic-vg fd5.de vanil fd5.de
  - **tearing** pain: *Calc Calc-p Calc-s Chin Lyc* spig h1

- **lying**: ...
- **back**; on:
  - **agg.**: agar bg1 ail bry cact cinnb *Cocc* coloc cycl a gels bg1 ign lac-c nux-v petr phos plect *Sep* spig vanil fd5.de verat j5.de
    - **burning**: agar
  - **amel.**: bry canth ↓ castn-v ign kali-p nux-v par petr puls spong vanil fd5.de verat
    - **burning**: canth
    - **tearing** pain: ign
- **bed**; in:
  - **agg.**: *Merc* ↓
    - **burning**: *Merc*
- **dark** room; in a:
  - **agg.**: onos
  - **amel.**: acon ars k2 *Aur-m-n* wbt2• bamb-a stb2.de• **Bell** brom *Bry* calc gk chel k2 glon mrr1 *Lac-d* k* lac-h htj1• nat-m mrr1 nat-s a plut-n srj7• podo *Sang* sep **Sil** k*
- **hanging** over side of bed; with head | **amel.**: androc srj1• zinc
- **head** high; with the:
  - **amel.**: androc srj1• arg-met **Ars** bell sne bry calc sne caps k2 carb-v *Con Gels* glon k2* nat-m *Phos* **Puls** *Spig* spong a stront-c
    - **bursting** pain: caps hr1
    - **drawing** pain: gels
    - **pressing** pain: *Spig*
- **head** low; with the:
  - **agg.**: *Rhus-t* ↓
    - **shooting** pain: *Rhus-t*
  - **amel.**: absin arn cadm-s gels lp *Hell* ign laur bg1 *Meli* sne mosch *Nux-v* phys *Spong* thuj vanil fd5.de **Verat-v** sne
- **head**; on:
  - **amel.**: ign ↓
    - **nail**; as from a: ign k2
- **head** straight; with the | **amel.**: adam skp7•
- **must** lie down: alum alum-p k2 am-c anac bell *Bry Calc* calc-i k2 calc-p calc-s calc-sil k2 chin colch ↓ *Con* croc crot-h euphr **Ferr** ferr-act ferr-i ferr-p k2 gels graph iod kali-bi kali-c kali-p kali-s kali-sil k2 lach lyc mag-m melal-alt gya4 mosch nat-c *Nat-m* nat-p nit-ac *Nux-v* olnd op petr ph-ac phos polys sk4• psor puls *Rhus-t* sang sars *Sel Sep* sil stann stict sulph zinc zinc-p k2
  - **tearing** pain: colch *Con Nat-m*
- **occiput**; on | **agg.**: cocc bro1 coloc bro1 nat-m h2*
- **painful** part; on:
  - **agg.**: **Nit-ac** ↓ nux-m ↓ plan ↓ rhus-t ↓ spig ↓
    - **sore**: **Nit-ac** nux-m plan rhus-t k2 spig
- **quietly**:
  - **amel.**: bung-fa mtf
  - **amel.**, towards morning: merc ↓
    - **tearing** pain: merc
- **side**; on:
  - **affected** side:
    - **amel.**: arn ↓ chel ↓ sep ↓
      - **stitching** pain: arn chel sep
  - **agg.**: bar-c ↓ bell calad carb-v k2 graph ign *Kreos* nux-v psor puls h1 stann
    - **pressing** pain: bar-c calad
  - **amel.**: cact *Cocc* ign meny merc sep
  - **left**:
    - **agg.**: cinnb cycl nux-v
    - **amel.**: nux-v petr-ra shn4• symph fd3.de•
  - **painful** side:
    - **agg.**: *Ars* calad calc carb-v chel chin cycl a graph irid-met srj5• *Kali-bi* mag-c *Nux-v* petr ph-ac puls rhus-t sep bro1 *Spong* stann staph zinc a
      - **head**; with:
        - **high**: *Bell* bro1 gels bro1
        - **low**: absin bro1 aeth bro1

- **side**; on – **painful** side: ...
  - **amel.**: anac androc srj1• arn beryl sp1 bry calc gk calc-ar bro1 chel a coff a graph a hipp k* ign k* nux-v plan puls sep thuj a [tax jsj7]
  - **painless** side:
    - **amel.**: ign a mag-c *Nux-v*
      - **stitching** pain: mag-c
  - **right**:
    - **agg.**: alum brom carb-v lil-t bg1 mang merc nux-v petr-ra shn4• phos sang a staph
    - **amel.**: brom cinnb nux-v
- **lying** down:
  - **agg.**: cimic↓ kali-bi↓ *Rhus-t*↓
    - **shooting** pain: cimic kali-bi *Rhus-t*
  - **amel.**: asar↓ beryl↓ bros-gau↓ carb-v↓ cassia-s↓ *Ferr*↓ kali-bi↓ *Lach*↓ mag-m↓ sang↓
    - **bursting** pain: beryl tpw5 carb-v k2 *Ferr* kali-bi *Lach* mag-m sang
    - **drawing** pain: asar
    - **piercing** pain: bros-gau mrc1
    - **shooting** pain: cassia-s ccrh1•
- **lying** on hard stones; as if: plat h2
- **maddening** pain: *Acon* k* ambr antip vh apis ptk1 arg-n bg2 arn bg2 *Ars* k* aur bg2* bamb-a stb2.de• **Bell** k* bry cact cadm-met gm1 *Calc* k* carl a1 *Cham* bg2* *Chin* chinin-s a coloc bg2* crot-t bg2 cupr bg3* cycl a fic-m gya1 **Gels** k* glon bg2 ign ind iod bg2 *Ip* irid-met vml3• kalm bg2 *Kola* stb3* *Lyss* mag-c med a* meli bg3* meny a *Nat-m* k* *Nit-ac* olib-sac wmh1 psor puls ruta fd4.de *Sep* bg2* *Stram* k* syph k2 *Tarent* tritic-vg fd5.de vanil fd5.de verat bg2 zinc-val a
  - **accompanied** by | **afterpains** (See FEMALE - Pain - afterpains - accompanied - head)
- **masticating** (See chewing)
- **masturbation**; after: *Calc* carb-v *Chin* *Con* lyc merc nat-m nux-v phos puls *Sep* spig *Staph* k* sulph
- **measles**; after: bell *Carb-v* dulc hell hyos *Puls* rhus-t *Sulph*
- **meat** agg.: caust pin-con oss2• *Puls* staph
- **menopause**; during: *Aml-ns* bro1 cact bro1 *Carb-v* *Chin* bro1 *Cimic* bro1 croc k* *Cycl* hr1* cypr br1* ferr bro1 glon k* ign bro1 **Lach** k* puls mrr1 *Sang* k* *Sep* k* stront-c bro1 sulph bro1 *Ther* ust
  - **burning**: *Lach*
  - **violent**: ther
- **menses**:
  - **after**:
    - **agg.**: agar all-c vh all-s vh aloe vh1 arg-n a arist-cl sp1 asar berb↓ *Bry* *Calc* calc-p carb-ac k* carb-an *Chin* croc bro1 dream-p sdj1• eupi *Ferr* k* ferr-p glon kali-br lac-d k2 *Lach* k* lil-t bro1 *Lith-c* lyc k* mag-c a med c1 merl a1 mosch naja nat-c sne *Nat-m* k* *Nat-p* ol-an plat psor jl2 *Puls* k* *Sep* k* syc pte1*• thuj ust↓ verat-v hr1 zinc a
      - **morning**, on awaking, after sudden cessation of: *Lith-c* k*
      - **cessation**; on: bry *Carb-v* glon k* lach k2 naja nit-ac **Puls** k*
      - **cutting** pain: *Nat-m*
      - **fly** off; as if top would: ust
      - **pressing** pain: ust
      - **shooting** pain: berb
      - **stitching** pain: berb *Lyc* k* *Nat-m* ol-an plat
      - **tearing** pain: berb
  - **amenorrhea**: gels c1
  - **appearance** of, amel.: cycl↓
    - **stitching** pain: cycl k*
  - **before**:
    - **agg.**: abies-c oss4• *Acon* agn all-s vh aloe vh1 alum k* alum-p k2 alum-sil k2 *Am-c* apis b7a.de arg-n ars *Asar* aster bro1 aur-m-n wbt2• *Bamb-a* stb2.de• *Bell* k* bit-ar↓ *Borx* *Bov* *Brom* *Bry* k* bufo *Calc* k* calc-i k2 calc-p calc-s calc-sil k2 carb-an k* *Carb-v* k* caust cham↓ chion br1 *Cimic* k* *Cinnb* cocc bro1 croc bro1 crot-h↓ cupr k* *Cycl* b7a.de* des-ac rbp6 ephe-si hsj1• ferr k* ferr-ar ferr-i ferr-m bro1 ferr-p bro1 foll oss• *Gels* k* glon k* graph k* ham↓ hep k* hydrog srj2• hyper iod kali-br hr1 *Kali-c* b4a.de kali-p k* **Kreos** k* *Lac-c* k* lac-d k* *Lach* k* laur lil-t *Lyc* manc *Meli* merc moni rfm1• musca-d szs1 nat-ar *Nat-c* k* *Nat-m* k* nat-p k2 nit-ac *Nux-m* k* nux-v k* ol-an oxal-a rly4• petr ph-ac b4a.de phos k* *Plat* prot pte1* *Puls* k* *Sang* bro1 sep k* sil k* stann sul-i k2 *Sulph* k* syc pte1*• thuj k* tritic-vg fd5.de tub a *Ust* bro1 vanil fd5.de *Verat* k* verat-v hr1* vib *Xan* k* *Xanth* zinc zinc-p k2
      - **bursting** pain: brom calc cham ham nat-m
      - **dull** pain: bit-ar wht1• crot-h vml3•
      - **pressing** pain: bamb-a stb2.de• bell carb-an cimic hep *Nat-m* nux-v petr sep sil
      - **shooting** pain: calc-p ferr k* nat-m ol-an
      - **stitching** pain: calc-p *Ferr*
      - **tearing** pain: ars cinnb glon laur
  - **during**:
    - **agg.**: abies-c oss4• acon aeth bro1 agar aloe alum k* alum-p k2 alum-sil k2 am-c k* am-m k* aml-ns vh1 androc srj1• ant-c apis *Arg-n* arn↓ ars ars-s-f k2 asar aster bro1 aven br1* *Bamb-a* stb2.de• **Bell** k* berb borx k* *Bov* brom k* *Bry* k* bufo cact k* *Calc* k* calc-p calc-s calc-sil k2 cann-i bro1 cann-s bro1 canth carb-an k* *Carb-v* k* castm *Caust* cench↓ cham chin k* chinin-ar chion a* cic cimic k* *Cocc* k* coff coloc con k* croc a* cub cupr cur cycl k* dig a dulc eupi k* ferr k* ferr-ar ferr-m bro1 *Ferr-p* k* *Gels* k* gent-c k* **Glon** k* glyc bro1 **Graph** k* guar vml3• ham fd3.de• hep *Hyos* k* hyper k* *Ign* iod↓ kali-ar kali-bi *Kali-c* k* kali-n kali-p k* kali-s kali-sil k2 kalm kola stb3• **Kreos** k* lac-c bro1 *Lac-d* k* *Lach* k* *Laur* k* lil-t bro1 **Lyc** k* *Mag-c* k* mag-m k* mag-s mang↓ med merc↓ *Murx* nat-ar *Nat-c* k* **Nat-m** k* nat-p nat-s c1* nept-m↓ *Nit-ac* *Nux-m* *Nux-v* k* pall c1 *Phos* k* *Plat* *Plat-m* bro1 pneu jl2* positr nl2• *Puls* k* rat rhod k* *Sang* k* sel rsj9• **Sep** k* sil k* spig j5.de stann sul-i k2 *Sulph* k* syc pte1• teucr-s gm1 ther c1 til gm1 ust c2* *Verat* k* verat-v bro1 vib bro1 xan k* xanth zinc zinc-p k2
      - **boring** pain: calc mag-c sep
      - **burning**: nat-m
      - **bursting** pain: berb k* *Bry* calc *Glon* kreos lyc nat-m k* nat-s sang sep
      - **drawing** pain: berb k* mag-c sang
      - **dull** pain: cench k2 ferr-p hr1* kali-p c1* lyc h2 nept-m lsd2.fr
      - **jerking** pain: eupi
      - **nail**; as from a: arn *Ign* *Nux-v*
      - **painful** menses: morg fmm1•
      - **pressing** pain: acon bamb-a stb2.de• bell berb *Bry* castm *Cimic* cycl eupi k* *Gels* *Graph* iod **Kreos** lyc merc *Nat-m* nat-s nux-m nux-v plat *Sep* sil stann *Sulph*
        - **outward**: kreos b7a.de
      - **shooting** pain: apis
      - **sore**: *Gels* st mag-c nux-v zinc-p k2
      - **stitching** pain: acon berb k* calc k* lyc k* mang rat
      - **tearing** pain: am-m h2 calc castm lyc h2 mag-c *Nat-c* (non:rat slp) verat slp
    - **amel.**: all-c k* aloe vh1 bell k* cycl a1* glyc bro1 joan bro1 lach a* lil-t a *Meli* bro1* puls k2 *Verat* *Zinc* k*
    - **beginning** of menses:
      - **agg.**: ant-t berb brom bros-gau mrc1 *Bry* b7a.de carb-an cyclosp sa3• graph hyos k* iod irid-met srj5• *Kali-c* lach laur *Nat-m* nicotam rly4• nit-ac plat plut-n srj7• rhod sal-fr sle1• *Sep* b4a.de
      - **amel.**: all-s k* alum kali-p *Lach* *Meli* k* verat zinc
  - **instead** of: nux-m↓
    - **bursting** pain: nux-m
  - **suppressed** menses; from: acon aeth hr1 alum anag br anagy br apis mtn bell mtn *Bry* *Carbn-s* cocc mtn **Cycl** hr1 gels mtn glon k2 ign mtn ip mtn lac-d mtn lith-c ptk lyc mtn naja ptk nux-v mtn op mtn phos mtn plat mtn psor ptk* **Puls** sang hr1 sep h2* sil mtn sulph mtn tub gk verat-v hr1 vib hs
- **mental** exertion:
  - **after**: anac↓ *Aur*↓ **Chin**↓ daph↓ lyc↓ *Phos*↓ pimp↓ pip-m↓ prun↓
    - **sore**: anac *Aur* **Chin** daph *Phos* prun
    - **stitching** pain: lyc pimp pip-m
  - **agg.**: (↗*attention; school children; students)* acetan bro1 acon agar k* agn allox tpw4* aloe bro1 alum-sil↓ am-c ambr *Anac* k* apis aran arg-met k* *Arg-n* k* arn ars-i asaf asar aster st **Aur** aur-ar k2 aur-br bro1 bac jl2 bell benz-ac beryl↓ borx st *Bry* cact st cadm-s cain **Calc** calc-ar

- **agg.**: ...
  Calc-p k* calc-s calc-sil k2 *Carb-ac* carb-an *Carb-v* carbn-s *Cham* st *Chin* chinin-ar chion bro1 cimic k* cina cinnb *Cist* cob st coc-c *Cocc* k* coff k* *Colch* coloc *Con* crot-h cupr bg1 daph *Dig* dulc fd4.de elaps *Epiph* bro1 fago ferr k2 *Ferr-pic* st* *Gels* k* gink-b sbd1• gins **Glon** k* graph hell helon st hipp hydr st hyper st *Ign* k* *Iris* kali-ar kali-c st kali-n st *Kali-p* k* kali-s fd4.de kali-sil k2 kalm kola stb3• *Lac-c* *Lach* lact lob st **Lyc** *Lyss* *Mag-c* *Mag-m* mag-p br1* manc st meli st merc mez st morph naja *Nat-ar* **Nat-c** k* **Nat-m** **Nat-p** *Nat-s* nicc bro1 *Nit-ac* *Nux-m* **Nux-v** k* ol-an olnd op ox-ac ozone sde2• *Par* *Petr* **Ph-ac** k* phase bro1 *Phos* k* **Pic-ac** k* pimp st *Pip-m* vh pip-n st plat plb st plut-n srj7• prun st *Psor* ptel **Puls** ran-b st rhus-t st rhus-v st rob st *Sabad* k* scut bro1 sel *Sep* k* **Sil** k* *Spig* *Staph* stram sulfonam ks2 *Sulph* ter ther tub al* v-a-b jl2 vanil fd5.de visc sp1 zinc k* zinc-p k2
  - **attention** is concentrated; while: helon ↓
    - **pressing** pain: helon
  - **boring** pain: nux-v
  - **burning**: *Sil*
  - **bursting** pain: arg-n k* beryl tpw5 fago a1 ptel
  - **drawing** pain: borx calc cina coff k* gins nat-m sulph
  - **dull** pain: alum-sil k2
  - **pressing** pain: anac *Arg-n* arn asar *Cact* *Calc* calc-s *Carb-an* cham *Cocc* coff colch dig helon ign kali-c *Lyc* *Mag-c* mez **Nat-c** nat-s *Nux-v* ol-an par *Ph-ac* **Pic-ac** *Sep* sil *Sulph* ter vanil fd5.de
  - **stunning** pain: *Cina* hr1
  - **tearing** pain: *Anac* ran-b
- **amel.**: am-c ars calc-act calc-ar kr1 calc-p gink-b ↓ ham helon k* ign merc-i-f nat-m nit-ac par phos phys k* pic-ac bro1 pip-m psor sabad symph ↓
  - **burning**: helon
  - **dull** pain: gink-b sbd1• symph fd3.de•
  - **reading** or writing: ign ↓
    - **bursting** pain: ign
  - **tearing** pain: calc-act

- **mercury**; after abuse of: arg-n *Asaf* *Aur* carb-v chin clem fl-ac **Hep** *Iod* *Kali-i* led mez **Nit-ac** podo puls *Sars* staph still k* sulph
- **metallic** substances, from abuse of: sulph
- **metrorrhagia**:
  - **amel.** (See menses - during - amel.)
  - **during**: bry b7a.de
- **milk** agg.: brom bro1
  - **sour**: nat-p k2
- **mist** before eyes followed by fleeting pains:
  - ○ **Occipital** protuberances, extending down neck and shoulders; at:
    - **lying** in a dark, quiet place and sleeping amel. | **wandering** pains (See lying - dark - amel.; noise - agg.; occiput - protuberance - extending - neck; occiput - protuberance - extending - shoulders; sleep - after - amel.; VISION - Foggy - followed - occipital)
- **mist** before the eyes: agath-a ↓
- **mortification**; from: *(↗MIND - Ailments - mortification)* bry k2 cham k2 coloc hr1 lyc op
- **motion**: *(↗jar; Stepping - agg.; Walking)*
  - **agg.**: abrom-a ↓ acon k* agn aloe alum-sil k2 am-c am-m ambr *Anac* k* anan *Ant-c* ant-t ap-g vml3• aphis a1* *Apis* k* arg-met *Arg-n* arge-pl rwt5• arn ars k2 ars-i asc-t c1 *Aur* aur-ar k2 aur-s k2 bac jl2 bapt **Bell** k* benz-ac berb beryl sp1 bism bov brucel sa3• **Bry** k* bufo but-ac bro1 cact cadm-met sp1 calc *Calc-p* k* calc-s calc-sil k2 camph cann-s canth *Caps* k* **Carb-v** *Carbn-s* card-m vml3• cartl-s ↓ caust cham chel chen-a vml3• *Chin* k* chinin-ar ↓ chinin-s chion chir-fl ↓ chlor choc srj3• cic *Cimic* k* cinnb cit-ac ↓ cob *Cocc* k* *Coff* colch coloc *Con* croc *Crot-h* *Crot-t* cupr cupr-ar ↓ cycl k* dulc *Elaps* sne eup-per k2 eupi fago *Ferr* ↓ *Ferr-p* fl-ac *Gels* k* gent-c *Glon* k* glyc bro1 granit-m ↓ graph grat ham fd3.de• hell *Hep* hipp hir ↓ hist sp1* hydrog srj2• hyper ↓ ign k* iod iris bro1* kali-ar kali-bi kali-c kali-n kali-s kali-sil k2 kalm *Kreos* lac-c lac-d *Lach* k* laur **Led** lith-c bro1 lob *Lyc* lyss *Mag-c* mag-m k* *Mag-p* mand sp1 *Mang* med k2 *Meli* mentho bro1 meny bro1 merc **Mez** mim-p vml3• *Mosch* naja nat-ar nat-c *Nat-m* k* nat-p nat-s ↓ nicc **Nit-ac** *Nux-m* *Nux-v* k* olnd

- **motion** – **agg.**: ...
  op k2 oreo bro1 oxal-a rly4• ozone sde2• petr petr-ra shn4• *Ph-ac* k* *Phos* phys pic-ac pieri-b mlk9.de plat podo *Psor* ptel k* puls bro1 pycnop-sa mrz1 rat rheum rhod rhus-t a1* rumx ruta fd4.de sabad samb *Sang* k* sanic *Sars* *Sep* k* *Sil* k* sol-ni *Spig* k* spong squil *Stann* k* *Staph* stram k2* stroph-s ↓ sul-i k2 sulph suprar rly4• symph ↓ tab ↓ *Tell* ↓ thea *Ther* k* thuj til ban1• tritic-vg fd5.de tub bg3* vanil fd5.de verat verat-v zing [bell-p-sp dcm1 heroin sdj2]
  - **boring** pain: hep *Sep*
  - **burning**: *Apis* arn
  - **burrowing**: *Spig* k*
  - **bursting** pain: beryl tpw5 caps k* carb-v k2 *Chin* *Coff* colch k2 eup-per k2 *Ferr* kali-bi *Lach* lyss k* mag-m rhus-t k* sep sil sol-ni spig
  - **cutting** pain: bell k2 bry k2 chin phys a1 til k*
  - **drawing** pain: arg-n k* bism k* tab til k*
  - **dull** pain: abrom-a ks5 asc-t c1 dulc fd4.de hir skp7•
  - **jerking** pain: *Chin*
  - **lancinating**: cit-ac rly4•
  - **lifting** off; head feels as if it is: granit-m es1•
  - **pressing** pain: acon agn *Arg-n* **Bell** bism **Bry** *Calc* carb-v cartl-s rly4• chir-fl gya2 cocc colch k2 cupr dulc ferr-p glon *Hell* hyper lach mang h2 mez nat-s ph-ac phos pic-ac rhod *Spig* sulph thuj
  - **pulsating** pain | **violent** pulsating: stroph-s sp1*
  - **rapid** motion: cor-r ephe-si hsj1• ferr k2 hydrog srj2• iod mez h2* nat-c nat-m *Petr* ruta fd4.de xan c1
  - **rest** agg.; and: **Calc** ↓
    - **stunning** pain: **Calc**
  - **shooting** pain: bell k2
  - **sore**: calc-sil k2 caps carbn-s *Chin* st **Cimic** colch k2 cupr-ar glon granit-m es1• iod mang merc nat-ar *Nux-v* st rumx *Tell*
  - **stitching** pain: agn ant-t calc caps cham chin h1 hep h2 hyper kali-c kali-n mag-p nat-m ozone sde2• rat ruta fd4.de *Sep* sil spig k2 spong symph fd3.de• tritic-vg fd5.de vanil fd5.de
  - **stunning** pain: rheum h
  - **sudden** motion: petr ↓ ruta ↓
    - **stitching** pain: petr ruta fd4.de
  - **talking**, even of: dulc ↓
    - **boring** pain: dulc
  - **tearing** pain: *Agn* *Aur* calc canth *Carb-v* carbn-s *Chin* chinin-ar *Cocc* coff colch k2 *Coloc* lith-c phos rat sars h2 sil **Spig** staph tub bg verat
- **air**; in open:
  - **amel.**: acon ↓ ruta ↓
    - **pressing** pain: acon ruta fd4.de
- **amel.**: *Agar* am-m androc srj1• ant-t arg-met *Ars* asaf asar aur ↓ bell ↓ benz-ac k* calc *Caps* cedr cham cic cina coc-c k2 coff coloc com con dros ephe-si hsj1• euph eupi ↓ fago a1 ferr guaj helon ↓ hipp hyos ign indg iod *Iris* kali-i kali-n kali-p kali-s ↓ *Lac-h* sk4• lach k2 lil-t k2 *Lyc* k* mag-c mag-m mang meny merc-i-f mosch *Mur-ac* nat-c *Nux-m* op petr petr-ra shn4• *Ph-ac* ↓ phos pip-m ↓ plut-n srj7• *Pneu* jl2 psor *Puls* *Rhod* k* **Rhus-t** k* ruta samb scut c1 seneg sep a1 spong fd4.de stann staph sul-i k2 sulph k* tarax tub k2* *Valer* vanil ↓ verb
  - **boring** pain: calc
  - **burning**: helon k*
  - **cutting** pain: *(↗rest - agg. - cutting)* kali-i
  - **drawing** pain: arg-met bell eupi *Rhod* *Rhus-t*
  - **jerking** pain: stann
  - **lancinating**: kali-i k*
  - **pressing** pain: *Agar* *Ferr* op pip-m ruta fd4.de sulph *Valer* vanil fd5.de
  - **rapid** motion: lac-h sk4•
    - **dull** pain: lac-h sk4•
  - **slow** motion: puls k2
  - **sore**: aur mur-ac *Ph-ac* *Puls* tub k2
  - **stitching** pain: caps k* kali-s fd4.de lac-h sk4• sulph

- **amel.**: ...
  - **stunning** pain: *Meny Puls* **Rhus-t**
  - **tearing** pain: caps h1 mur-ac *Rhod Rhus-t* sulph
- **arms**; of:
  - **agg.**: bar-c berb bry k2 caust coc-c lept nat-s ptel rhus-t spong
    - **cutting** pain: caust
    - **pressing** pain: rhus-t
    - **stitching** pain: nat-s
- **beginning** of:
  - **agg.**: bry k2 iris *Sep* ther
  - **amel.**: valer
- **continued** motion:
  - **amel.**: calc-act ↓
    - **stitching** pain: calc-act
- **eyelids**; of:
  - **agg.**: **Bell** *Bry Chin Coff* coloc *Ign Nux-v* petr-ra shn4• rhus-t
  - **upper** eyelids: *Coloc* ↓
    - **burrowing**: coloc h2
    - **tearing** pain: *Coloc*
- **eyes**; of:
  - **agg.**: acon agn am-c arn bad bapt bar-c bar-m bar-s k2 **Bell** k* **Bry** k* *Caps* chel *Chin* chinin-s cimic bro1* cinnb *Colch Coloc* k* con crot-t cupr k* dig dros gels k* hell *Hep* hyper ↓ ichth bro1 ign k* ind jug-r kali-c kali-sil k2 mag-s *Mur-ac* k* *Nat-m* **Nux-v** k* *Op* phasco-ci ↓ *Phys* bro1 pic-ac bg1 plat plut-n srj7• ptel c1 puls k* rhus-t k* sang *Sep Sil Spig* k* sulph valer
    - **bursting** pain: chin ptel *Puls*
    - **cutting** pain: dros
    - **pressing** pain: *Bell Chel* hep mag-s c1 phasco-ci rbp2 *Puls*
    - **stitching** pain: caps hyper kali-c
    - **tearing** pain: bell k2 dros *Mur-ac*
    - **torn**; as if: *Rhus-t*
- **face** agg.; of muscles of: apis spig k*
  - **pressing** pain: *Spig*
- **gentle** motion | **amel.**: chin bro1 glon bro1 helon bro1 iris bro1 kali-p bro1 *Puls* bro1
- **head**; of:
  - **agg.**: acon alum alum-p k2 alum-sil k2 *Am-c Arn Ars* ars-s-f k2 *Asar* bac jl2 bar-c bar-s k2 **Bell** berb *Bry* cact ↓ *Calc* calc-i k2 calc-s calc-sil k2 camph cann-s canth *Caps Carb-v Carbn-s* caust *Chin* cic *Cimic* clem coc-c cocc colch coloc ↓ con cor-r corn cupr dros euph **Ferr** *Ferr-ar* ferr-i ferr-p fl-ac **Gels** genist gent-c *Glon* graph *Hell* hep hyper ↓ ind iod ip kali-ar kali-c kali-s kali-sil k2 lac-c lach lact lyc mag-c mang **Mez** *Mosch* nat-ar nat-c *Nat-m* nat-p nat-s ↓ *Nux-m* k* *Nux-v* oxal-a ↓ ph-ac plat puls rhod samb sang sars sec sep *Sil* sol-ni *Spig* k* spong staph sulph symph fd3.de• ther tritic-vg fd5.de tub tl vanil ↓ verat vib viol-o
    - **drawing** pain: cact staph
    - **pressing** pain: coloc h2 *Glon* nat-s oxal-a rly4• staph h1 tritic-vg fd5.de
    - **stitching** pain: caps hyper kali-c nat-m tritic-vg fd5.de vanil fd5.de
    - **stunning** pain: staph h1
    - **sudden**: xan c1
  - **amel.**: *Agar Chin* cina con gels kali-p mag-p ↓ plan sulph h2
    - **shooting** pain: *(↗rest - agg. - shooting)* mag-p sulph
  - **turning** eyes; or: *Cimic* ↓
    - **opening** and shutting; as if: *Cimic* k*
  - **walking**; while:
    - **agg.**: ars ↓
      - **pressing** pain: ars
- **jaw**; of lower:
  - **agg.**: kali-c ↓
    - **stitching** pain: kali-c
- **must** move:
  - **head** and close the eyes; must move: agar ↓
    - **dull** pain: agar
  - **pain**; from: chin ph-ac
- **to** and fro agg.: sep bg2

- **motion**: ...
  - **upward** and downward motion | **amel.**: *Chin*
  - **violent** motion:
    - **agg.**: calc cocc dros *Iris* mez
    - **amel.**: ind vml3• indg bro1 rhus-t bro1 *Sep* k* vanil fd5.de
    - **continued**:
      - **amel.**: sep ↓
        - **bursting** pain: sep
- **music** agg.: acon k* ambr k* cact k* **Coff** k* kali-s fkr2.de lac-h sk4• nux-v k* *Ph-ac* k* *Phos* k* podo k* viol-o k*
- **nail**; as from a: *(↗plug)* acon tl1 adam skp7• *Agar* am-br mtf11 arn *Asaf* k* carb-v caust **Coff** k* der vml3• dulc euon k* *Graph* ham fd3.de• hell *Hep* k* hist sp1 *Ign* k* kali-i k2 kola stb3• lach nat-m *Nux-v* k* oci-sa sp1 olnd ozone sde2• ptel *Puls* ruta sang *Sep* staph tarent tl1 thea **Thuj** k* [bell-p-sp dcm1]
  - **accompanied** by | **coryza**: form ptk1
  - **out** of the skull; as if spikes or sharp nails were trying to come: adam skp7•
- **narcotics**, after abuse of: acet-ac kr1* bell cham coff k* dig graph hyos lach lyc nux-v op puls sep valer
- **nausea**; with (See accompanied - nausea)
- **nervous**: acet-ac k* acon k* **Agar** k* agn ail am-c bro1 am-val bro1 anac k* anh bro1 apis *Arg-met* **Arg-n** k* arn *Ars* **Asaf** k* *Asar* asc-c c1 asc-t aspar bro1 atro aur k* aur-ar k2 aur-m-n wbt2• aven bro1 bell k* benz-ac hr1 bry k* *Cact* calad *Calc* k* *Calc-act* bro1 camph *Cann-i* bro1 cann-s carb-ac bro1 catar br1 caul caust cedr k* *Cham* k* **Chin** k* chinin-ar chion br1* chlor cic cimic k* cina cit-v bro1 coca cocc k* **Coff** k* coloc croc crot-c bro1 crot-t *Cycl* bro1 daph a1 epiph br1* ery-a hr1 form **Gels** k* glon graph guar bro1* hydr k* **Ign** k* indg bro1 iod bg* *Ip* k* iris k* kali-bi bro1 kali-br hr1 kali-c bg2* *Kali-p* k* kreos hr1 *Lac-d* bro1 *Lach* bro1 lact mag-m bg2 mag-p bg2 meli br1* *Menis* bro1 mosch bg2 **Nat-m** k* nicc c2* nicc-met br1 nux-m bg2 **Nux-v** k* *Onos* bro1 op paull bro1 *Petr Ph-ac* k* **Phos** k* pic-ac k2 *Plat* k* plat-m bro1 **Puls** k* rhus-r rhus-t sang k* sapin bro1 scut k* sel bg2 *Sep* k* sil k* spig k* stann bg2* stict *Stram* sulph k* tab bro1 tarent ter thea bro1 *Ther* k* **Thuj** k* tub tl1 ust *Valer Verat* k* verat-v k* verb bro1 xan bro1 **Zinc** k* zinc-p k2 *Zinc-s* bro1 *Zinc-val* bro1 ziz bro1
  - **exhaustion**: acetan bro1 agar bro1 *Anac* bro1 *Arg-n* bro1 *Ars* bro1 aur-br bro1 *Chin* bro1 chion bro1 cimic bro1 coff bro1 *Epiph* bro1 *Gels* bro1 ign bro1 ind bro1 *Kali-p* bro1 lac-d bro1 lob bro1 mag-p bro1 *Nat-c* bro1 nicc bro1 *Nux-v* bro1 ph-ac bro1 phase bro1 *Pic-ac* bro1 sabad bro1 sang bro1 scut bro1 sil bg1* sulph bro1 zinc bro1
  - **hysterical** or scrofulous people: asaf bg3*
- **neuralgic**: *Aconin* bro1 aesc bro1 all-c bro1 am-br br1 am-pic br1 *Arg-met* mrr1 arg-n bro1 *Ars* bro1 *Bell* bro1 bism bro1 cact bg2 *Cedr* bro1 chel bro1 chin mrr1 *Chinin-s* bro1 cimic bg2* *Coloc* br1* der bro1 des-ac rbp6 dulc br1* form bg2 *Gels* bro1 guaj bg2 *Mag-p* bro1 meli bro1 mentho bro1 mez mrr1 oreo br1* pall bro1 phos bro1 prun mrr1 rhod mrr1 rhodi br1 rob mrr1 spig bg2* stann mrr1 sul-ac mrr1 syph hr1 tarent bro1 tub-m jl2 vanil fd5.de zinc-val bro1
  - **accompanied** by | **menses**; suppressed: *Gels* bro1
  - **alternating** with | **leukorrhea**: stann mrr1
  - **wandering** pain: rhodi br1
- **night** watching (See sleep - loss - night)
- **nodding** the head, on: ap-g vml3• lam bro1 sep bro1 *Sulph*
- **noise**:
  - **agg.**: abrom-a ↓ acon k* agar agath-a nl2• alum-sil k2* anac anan k* ang arg-n arn *Ars* k* ars-i bapt k* bar-c bar-i k2 bar-m **Bell** k* borx *Bry* bufo bung-fa mtf *Cact* calad **Calc** calc-f sp1 calc-i k2 *Calc-s* calc-sil k2 cann-s caps carb-ac ↓ carb-an carb-v caust *Chin Chinin-ar* chlam-tr bcx2• cic cimic gk *Cocc Coff* k* colch *Con* k* dream-p sdj1• *Ferr-p* k* gels glon k2 graph hell k* hyos ign k* iod kali-ar kali-bi kali-p kali-s kali-sil k2 *Kola* stb3• *Lac-c Lac-d* k* *Lach* lachn br1* lyc *Lyss* mag-m manc merc merc-i-f k* moni rfm1• mur-ac **Nat-ar** *Nat-c* nat-m k2* nat-p neon srj5• nept-m lsd2.fr **Nit-ac** k* *Nux-v* k* op k2 ozone ↓ petr-ra shn4• *Ph-ac* k* phasco-ci rbp2 phel bro1* *Phos* **Pip-m** sne pitu-gl ↓ plect a1 plut-n srj7• podo ptel k* sang k* sanic scut bro1 sep j5.de* *Sil* k* *Sol-ni Spig* k* *Stann* stict syc ↓ tab k* tarent bro1 **Ther** tril-p c1 tritic-vg fd5.de verat-v a1 yuc zinc k* zinc-p k2 [helia stj7 tax jsj7]
    - **beating** time; clock: anh bro1
    - **boring** pain: nux-v
    - **burrowing**: *Spig* k*
    - **bursting** pain: pitu-gl skp7•

- **agg.**: ...
  - **cutting** pain: carb-ac
  - **distant** talking, of: mur-ac k*
  - **dull** pain: abrom-a ks5
  - **falling** water, of: **Lyss** nit-ac
  - **footsteps**: bell bry **Coff** k* gels lachn vml3• **Nux-v** k* sang j5.de *Sil* k13 ther kr1
  - **hammer** on anvil, of: manc k*
  - **jerking** pain: carb-ac
  - **opening** and shutting; as if: cann-s k2
  - **pressing** pain: *Nit-ac* ph-ac spig
  - **pulsating** pain: ozone sde2• pitu-gl skp7• syc bka1•
  - **rattling** of vehicles: **Nit-ac** *Ther*
  - **sharp** sounds: cop br1 neon srj5•
  - **stitching** pain: spig k2
  - **tearing** pain: coff **Spig**
  - **voices** especially: bar-c cact k2 lyss
  - **wagons**: nit-ac k2
- **amel.**: syc ↓
  - **pulsating** pain: syc fmm1•

- **numbness**; with (See accompanied - numbness)
- **nursing** infant, after: bell bry *Calc* cham chin dulc phos *Puls Sep* sil staph
- **occupation** amel.: calc-sil k2 cham k2 hydrog srj2• pert-vc vk9
- **odors**:
  - **alcohol**, of: sol-t-ae
  - **coffee** agg.; of: lach *Tub* jl2
  - **dirty** clothes, of: carb-an
  - **eggs**: **Sulph** vh
  - **strong** | **and** agreeable: arg-n
  - **strong** odors agg.: *(↗MIND - Sensitive - odors)* acon anac arg-n *Aur* aur-s k2 *Bell* cham chin *Coff* k* *Colch* ephe-si hsj1• gink-b sbd1• graph *Ign* k* kali-p fd1.de• *Lyc* nux-v ozone sde2• *Phos* scut bro1 sel k* *Sil Sulph* k* vanil fd5.de
    - **stitching** pain: sel
- **old** people, of: am-c ambr bar-m br1 cypr br1 gels lp iod lach lp nat-c lp sep lp sulph lp
- **open**; as if: *Carb-an Cimic* k* guan nat-p k2 sil
- **opening** | **eyes** (See light; from; morning - waking - on - opening; motion - eyes - agg.)
- **opening** and shutting; as if: *Cact* ptk1 calc bg3* **Cann-i** k* *Cann-s Cann-xyz* bg2* carbn-s bg2 *Cimic* k* *Cocc* k* cupr ptk1 glon bg3* lac-c bro1* lil-t bg2* lyc k* *Puls* b7a.de sep ptk1 spong ptk1 sulph bg3* tarent ptk1 vib bg2*
- **opening** the eyes | **agg.**:
  - **sleep**; after: rhus-t ↓
    - **pressing** pain: rhus-t
  - **amel.**: *Chin* ↓
    - **bursting** pain: *Chin*
- **opening** the mouth agg.: fago spig k*
  - **boring** pain: spig
  - **burrowing**: *Spig* k*
  - **tearing** pain: spig
- **opium**, from abuse of: acet-ac cham
- **otalgia**, with: ran-s ↓
  - **gnawing** pain: ran-s
- **ovarian**: bell bro1 *Cimic* bro1 *Gels* bro1 helon bro1 ign bro1 joan bro1 lil-t bro1 plat bro1 *Puls* bro1 *Sep* bro1 zinc bro1
- **overeating**; after (See eating - overeating)
- **overheated**, after being: *Kali-c* ↓
  - **tearing** pain: *Kali-c*
- **overheating** (See warm; becoming - agg.)
- **pains**; with other (See accompanied)
- **paralyzed**; as if: ars bg2 calc bg2 carb-v bg2 cina b7.de* lach bg2 sil bg2
- **paroxysmal**: *(↗sides - paroxysmal; waves)* acon agar ambr ant-t arn *Ars* asaf k* aster sze10• **Bell** bufo buth-a sp1 calc calc-sil k2 cann-i tl1 carb-v *Cedr Cham* chin chinin-ar cocc colch *Coloc* crot-t cupr dig ferr ferr-ar ferr-p fic-m gya1 guaj k2 ign *Kali-ar* kali-c kali-m k2 kali-n kali-p kali-sil k2 *Kalm* **Lach**
- **paroxysmal**: ...
  lyc *Mag-p* melal-alt gya4 mosch mur-ac murx nat-ar nat-c nat-p nicc nit-ac nux-m petr ph-ac plat psil ft1 psor ran-b ribo rly4• ruta fd4.de **Sang** k* sars sep *Sil Spig* spong squil stann *Stram* stront-c thuj tub kr1 valer *Verat* viol-t zinc zinc-p k2 [tax jsj7]
- **part** lain on: ph-ac ↓
  - **pressing** pain: ph-ac h2*
- **pecking**: carb-an k* mosch k* nux-v k* rhus-t k* ruta k*
- **penetrating**: cann-xyz bg2 chlam-tr bcx2• hell bg2 *lp* bg2
- **periodical**: *(↗cluster)* acon bro1 act-sp *Aeth* aloe **Alum** alum-p k2 alum-sil k2 am-pic bro1 ambr ammc *Anac Apis* aran arg-n bro1 arn *Ars* k* *Ars-i* ars-s-f k2 asaf aur-ar k2 *Aur-m-n* wbt2• bell k* benz-ac *Cact* k* *Calc* calc-s *Carb-v* card-m k2 **Cedr** k* cham chel k2* **Chin** k* *Chinin-ar* **Chinin-s** *Chion* br1 **Coloc** cupr eup-per k* *Ferr* k* *Ferr-ar* fic-m gya1 gels psa* *Ign* k* *Kali-ar* kali-bi kali-cy bro1 kali-sil k2 *Kreos* lac-d k* *Lach* laur lob *Lyc* mag-m bro1 meli sne* mur-ac *Nat-ar* nat-c **Nat-m** nat-p nat-s nicc k* nicc-br bwa3 nicc-met br1 nicc-s br1* **Nit-ac** *Nux-v Phos* plat podo k2 prun psor k2* *Puls Rhus-t* sacch c2 **Sang** k* *Sel* **Sep** k* **Sil** k* *Spig* k* spong fd4.de *Stram Sulph* syc fmm1• syph c1 tab k* tela bro1 teucr-s gm1 *Tub* k* zinc zinc-p k2 zinc-val bro1
  - **day**:
    - **and** night: borx caust kreos led rhus-t sul-ac viol-t
    - **alternate**: alum alum-p k2 ambr *Anh* bro1 ars cact *Cedr* chin k* cimic eup-per merc-c nat-m nux-v *Phos* psor sang sulph k*
    - **third** or fourth; every: aur eup-per bg3 muru a1 nat-m k2 sang bg3*
    - **every**: *Ars* aur-m-n wbt2• *Bell* calc calc-sil k2 cedr chin mrr1 coloc con eup-per form hep lach lyc mag-c mag-m mang merc-i-r mur-ac *Nat-m Nux-m Nux-v* petr phos sabad seneg sep *Sil* spig stann sulph zinc zinc-p k2
      - **16** h:
        - **coldness** and trembling; with: asaf ↓
          - **stitching** pain: asaf
      - **hour**; at the same: aran vh ars cact br1 cedr vh cimic gels **Kali-bi** mur-ac spig
      - **bursting** pain: *Sulph*
      - **continues** two or three days: croc
      - **earlier** each day: form
    - **third**; every: eup-per bro1 sang hr1
    - **eight** days; every: iris bg3*
    - **ten** days; every: *Lach*
  - **day** at noon; every:
    - **pressure** agg.:
      - **open** air amel.: *Arg-met* ↓
        - **tearing** pain: *Arg-met*
  - **morning**:
    - **7** h: *Ars*
    - **alternate** morning on waking: *Chin* eup-per
    - **every**: *Chin* hep naja k2
    - **awaking** with vertigo and nausea, also in the evening | **pressure**, eating, or open air amel.: kali-bi
  - **forenoon** | **9**-13 h: *Cedr* vh mur-ac
  - **noon** until 22 h: form
  - **afternoon**:
    - **14** h until bed time: sep
    - **16**-3 h: bell
    - **increasing** until midnight, every third attack alternately more or less violent: *Lob*
  - **hour**:
    - **certain**; at: nat-c
    - **same**; at the | **morning**: kali-bi
  - **week**:
    - **every**●: ars k* calc bg3* calc-ar k* calc-sil k2 chin mrr1 epiph bg3* eup-per bg3* gels *Iris* k* *Lac-d* k* lyc meli sne* morg-p pte1• nux-m *Phos* phyt psor sabad bg1* sacch br1 *Sang* k* sep hr1 *Sil* k* spong fd4.de *Sulph* k* syc bka1*• *Tub* k*
      - **Sunday**; on: stann mtf11 sulph mtf11
    - **two** weeks; every: *Ars* ars-s-f k2 calc *Chel* chin chinin-ar ferr bro1* ign nicc phyt psor puls sang *Sulph* k* *Tub* k* [ferr-n stj2 ferr-sil stj2]
      - **lasting** two or three days: **Ferr** k*

- **week**: ...
  - **three** weeks; every: aur bg3 ferr bro1
  - **three** to four weeks; every: cycl hr1
  - **four** weeks; every: meli vml3•
  - **six** weeks; every: **Mag-m** k*
    - **bursting** pain: **Mag-m**
  - **lasting** for days: syc bka1•
- **month** | **two** months; every: ars mrr1
- **children**; in: syc fmm1•
- **pressing** pain: card-m k2
- **stitching** pain: calc mur-ac
- **stunning** pain: *Ars*
- **tearing** pain: anac mur-ac

- **perspiration**:
  - **after** | **agg.**: calc *Chin* merc nux-v k2 puls *Sep* staph sulph
  - **amel.**: aran c1 ars k2 bov bry k2 carbn-s chinin-ar clem graph mag-m *Nat-m* k* nat-s nux-v psor spong *Sulph* k* tarent k* thuj
    - **pressing** pain: thuj
  - **during**: acon b7a.de am-c bg2 ang bg2 *Ant-c* b7.de* ant-t bg2 arn k* ars k* bell h1* **Bry** b7.de* *Calc* bg2 carb-v bg2 caust b4.de* **Cham** b7.de* chin bg2 con bg2 dros bg2 eup-per ferr b7.de* glon bg2 graph bg2 hell bg2 hep bg2 ip bg2 kali-c bg2 kali-n bg2 led bg2 lyc bg2 mang bg2 merc bg2 mez bg2 nat-c bg2 nat-m k* **Nux-v** b7a.de* petr bg2 phos bg2 rhod bg2 rhus-t k* ruta bg2 sel bg2 **Sep** bg2 sil bg2 spig bg2 sulph bg2 thuj *Verat* bg2
    - **stitching** pain: lyc b4a.de
  - **preceded** by headache: asc-c c1 ferr lyc h2* nat-m bg2
  - **profuse**: maias-l hrn2•
  - **suppressed** perspiration; from: *Ars* asc-c c1* *Bell* bry k* *Calc* **Carb-v** *Cham Chin* lyc merc k* *Nux-v* phos *Puls* rhus-t sep *Sulph*
  - **with**: ant-c k* apis arg-met arn *Ars* k* bamb-a stb2.de• *Bry* canth carb-v h2 caust chinin-s dulc fd4.de glon k* graph hyos kali-n lac-loxod-a hrn2• lachn lob bro1 lyc mag-s maias-l hrn2• *Merc* nat-s op ox-ac ozone sde2• phys a1 plat puls ruta fd4.de sil k2 *Sulph* vh tab bro1 tarent visc sp1

- **picking** pain: lach bg2
- **piercing** pain: *Agar* bro1 anan bro1 aqui bro1 calc-f sp1 *Coff* bro1 *Hep* bro1 hist sp1 *Ign* bro1 m-ambo bro1 *Nux-v* bro1 oci-sa sp1 paraf bro1 pneu jl2 rad-br sze8• ruta bro1 sil bro1 *Thuj* bro1 zinc-val bro1
- **pillow**; boring head into: *(↗Bores)*
  - **amel.**: oci-sa sk4• tub jl2
- **pinching** pain: alum k* arn br1 bar-c k* caust k* colch k* kali-c h2 lyc k* mez k* nux-v k* *Petr* k* phos k* sep b4.de* sil k* teucr k* verb [heroin sdj2]
- **plug**; as from a: *(↗nail)* agar bg2 *Anac* k* arg-met k* arn bg2 asaf k* bell bg2 bov k* carb-v bg2 caust cocc k* *Coff* bg2 con k* dulc k* hell bg2 hep k* *Ign* bg2 jac-g kreos k* lyc bg2 mez bg2 nat-m bg2 nicc bg2 nux-m bg2 *Nux-v* bg2 olnd k* plat k* prun k* ran-s k* rhod k* rhus-t k* ruta sil bg2 staph bg2 *Sul-ac* k* thuj bg2
  - **thrust** suddenly in by increasingly severe blows; as if a plug were: sul-ac
- **pollutions**; after: *(↗sexual excesses)* alum bov *Calc* caust cob con ham kali-c lach lyc nat-c *Nux-v* sel sep staph viol-o k*
- **position**; as from wrong: agar h crot-h tl1 dulc h lyc h2* merc h nux-v h staph sne
- **preceded** by drawing in right arm: petr↓
  - **drawing** pain: petr h2*
- **pregnancy** agg.; during: acon bg2 *Bell* k* bry k* calc k* caps caust *Cham* chlam-tr bcx2• cocc k* ferr k2 gels kr1* hyos lac-d k2 lach mrr1 mag-c bg2 nux-m **Nux-v** bg2 plat k* *Puls* k* rhus-t *Sep* k* sulph k* *Verat* bg2
- **press** head upon the floor; desire to: sang↓
  - **pressing** pain: sang
- **press** with hands, must: bamb-a↓ carb-an↓ *Glon*↓ *Mag-m*↓
  - **bursting** pain: bamb-a stb2.de• carb-an *Glon Mag-m*
- **pressing** back of head | **amel.**: sang hr1*
- **pressing** pain: *(↗Compression; Heaviness)* *Acon* k* *Aesc* k* *Aeth* *Agar* k* agath-a nl2• agn all-c allox sp1 aloe k* alum k* alum-p k2 alum-sil k2 *Alumn Am-br Am-c* k* *Am-m* k* ambr k* *Anac* k* androc srj1• ang k* ant-c bg2 *Ant-t* k* apis k* aran arg-met k* *Arg-n* arge-pl rwt5• arizon-l nl2• *Arn* k* ars ars-i

- **pressing** pain: ...
arum-t *Asaf* k* *Asar* k* aster atp rly4• aur k* aur-ar k2 aur-i k2 aur-s k2 bac jl2 *Bamb-a* stb2.de• *Bapt* k* bar-c k* bar-i k2 bar-m bar-s k2 **Bell** k* benz-ac benzol br1 berb *Bism* k* borx bov k* brom *Bry* k* buth-a sp1 cact k2* cadm-s calad k* *Calc* k* calc-i k2 calc-p *Calc-s Camph* k* cann-i cann-s k* canth k* *Caps* k* carb-ac k* *Carb-an* k* **Carb-v** k* **Carbn-s** cartl-s rly4• *Caust* k* cham k* chel k* **Chin** k* chinin-ar *Chinin-s* chion bro1 chir-fl gya2 chlam-tr bcx2• *Chlol* chord-umb rly4• *Cic* k* cimic k* cina k* cinnb clem k* cob-n sp1 coc-c *Cocc* k* *Coff* k* colch b7a.de* coli rly4• *Coloc* k* colum-p sze2• *Con* k* cor-r croc crot-c crot-h crot-t bg2 cub cupr k* *Cycl* k* cyt-l sp1 daph *Dig* k* dios bg2 dioxi rbp6 *Dros* k* dulc k* dys fmm1• echi bg2 epiph bro1 eug *Euon Eup-per* bro1 *Euph* k* euphr k* eupi ferr k* ferr-ar ferr-i ferr-p fl-ac k* fuma-ac rly4• gamb gels k* ger-i rly4• *Germ-met* srj5• gink-b sbd1• **Glon** k* *Graph* k* grat guaj k* ham fd3.de• *Hell* k* helon *Hep* k* hipp hippoc-k szs2 hir skp7• hist vml3• hydr-ac k* *Hyos* k* hyper *Ign* k* ina-i mlk9.de indg iod k* *Ip* k* iris kali-ar kali-bi k* *Kali-c* k* *Kali-i* kali-m k2 *Kali-n* k* kali-p *Kali-s* kali-sil k2 kalm ketogl-ac rly4• *Kola* stb3• *Kreos* k* **Lac-c Lach** k* lact lam lap-la sde8.de• laur k* led k* *Lil-t* limest-b es1• lob *Lyc* k* *Lycps-v Lyss M-arct* b7.de* *Mag-c* k* *Mag-m* mag-s mang k* medul-os-si rly4• (non:meli bro1*) menis slp *Meny* k* **Merc** k* merc-c merc-i-f merc-i-r merl *Mez* k* moni rfm1• morg fmm1• mosch k* mucs-nas rly4• *Mur-ac* myric nat-ar nat-c k* **Nat-m** k* nat-p nat-pyru rly4• nat-s nat-sil fd3.de• nept-m lsd2.fr nicc nicotam rly4• **Nit-ac** k* *Nux-m* **Nux-v** k* ol-an olib-sac wmh1 *Olnd* k* onos bro1 *Op* k* oreo bro1 osm oxal-a rly4• ozone sde2• par k* *Petr* k* petr-ra shn4• *Ph-ac* k* *Phos* k* phyt bg2 pic-ac bg2 pip-m plac rzf5• plac-s rly4• *Plat* k* *Plb* k* plut-n srj7• podo bro1 *Positr* nl2• pot-e rly4• propl ub1• prun **Psor** ptel bg2 **Puls** k* pycnop-sa mrz1 pyrog k2* *Ran-b* k* *Ran-s* k* rauw sp1 rheum k* *Rhod* k* *Rhus-t* k* rhus-v ribo rly4• ros-d wla1 *Ruta* k* *Sabad* k* sabin k* *Samb* k* sang bro1 sars *Sel* rsj9• *Seneg* k* *Sep* k* serp *Sil* k* *Spig* k* *Spong* k* squil k* *Stann* k* *Staph* k* stict bro1 *Stront-c* k* suis-em rly4• suis-pan rly4• sul-ac k* **Sulph** k* suprar rly4• symph fd3.de• tab k* tanac *Tarax* k* *Tarent* ter teucr b7a.de ther *Thuj* k* *Trios* rsj11• tritic-vg fd5.de valer k* vanil fd5.de verat k* verat-v mtf11 verb k* viol-t k* visc sp1 x-ray sp1 xan zinc k* zing
  - **accompanied** by:
    - **Ear**; noises in: thymu br1
    - **Limbs**; pain in: bamb-a stb2.de•
    - **Neck**; pain in nape of: bamb-a stb2.de•
  - **armor**; as if in: *(↗cap)* agath-a nl2• apis *Arg-n* asaf *Berb* cann-i *Carb-v* clem *Cocc Crot-c Cycl Graph* hell *Ip Lil-t* **Nit-ac** peti pyrog *Spig* stry sulph zinc
  - **asunder**: acon k* aesc agath-a nl2• aloe ant-c *Arg-n* k* arn k* ars *Asaf* bro1 asar b7a.de aur bro1 bar-c k* *Bell* k* bov *Bry* k* calc b4.de* calc-p caps k* *Carb-an* k* chel k* **Chin** k* *Cimic* bro1 cocc k* con k* cor-r br1* daph dulc bg2 erio bro1 euph k* fago a1* gels hell hyper k* ign k* irid-met srj5• kali-bi kali-i kali-n k* lach lil-t *Lyc* k* m-arct b7.de* *Menis* bro1 *Merc* k* *Mez* k* nat-m k* nux-m k* *Nux-v* k* par k* ph-ac b4.de* phyt a1 *Prun* k* *Ptel* bro1 puls ran-b k* ran-s bg2 rhus-t k* ruta fd4.de sabad k* sabin k* samb k* *Sep* k* *Sil* k* spig k* *Stann* k* *Staph* k* stront-c k* tarax k* *Thuj* k* tritic-vg fd5.de valer b7.de* viol-t b7.de* zinc k*
  - **band**; as from a: *(↗Constriction - band)* agath-a nl2• bamb-a stb2.de• *Carb-ac* clem cocc coli rly4• cycl tl1 fic-m gya1 franc br1 *Gels* germ-met srj5• glon helo c1 helo-s c1* iod ip *Kola* stb3• med jl2 *Merc* *Mosch* nept-m lsd2.fr *Nit-ac* k* op osm ozone sde2• positr nl2• psil ft1* *Spig* *Stann* **Sulph** tarent bg tub k2* vanil fd5.de
    - **iron** band; as if pressed by an: bac jl2 fuc br1 tarent bg tub br1*
  - **boards**; as if compressed by two: ip
  - **burning**: aloe alum lact mang nux-m sep sul-ac tarax
  - **cap**; as from a: *(↗armor; Skullcap)* acon bg2 agath-a nl2• androc srj1• apis k* *Arg-n* asaf berb k* cann-xyz bg2 *Carb-v* k* carbn-s bg2 clem bg2 coc-c k* *Cocc* crot-c k* *Cycl* k* gels bg2 gink-b sbd1• *Graph* k* hell k* helo bg2 helo-s rwt2• ip kali-s bg2 *Kola* stb3• lach ptk1 *Lil-t* k* lys bg2 mag-p bg2* ozone sde2• peti phys bg2 plut-n srj7• pyrog stry k* sulph suprar rly4• zinc [heroin sdj2]
    - **tight**: berb ptk1
  - **changeable**: bell gins *Ign* k*
  - **congestion**; as from: agath-a nl2• apis chin k* dig h2* meri nux-m rhus-v
  - **constricting** pain: *(↗Constriction)* *Cocc* dulc fd4.de graph *Kola* stb3• olib-sac wmh1 positr nl2• symph fd3.de• tritic-vg fd5.de
  - **cramping**: ars colch ph-ac *Plat* ran-s zinc

- **deep**-seated: agar k* *Arg-n* asc-t c1 *Bell* caust k* cic con gins indg k* lach nat-m nat-s k*
- **digging** pain: bry clem
- **downward**: agar agath-a nl2• ambr ant-t asar cic k* *Cina* cocc con corv-cor bdg• *Cupr* graph bg1 hura laur k* mang meny k* merc k* merc-i-f mur-ac nit-ac k* nux-v *Ph-ac* *Phos* plat rhus-t k* senn sil spig spong *Sulph* vanil fd5.de verat
- **drawing** pain: agar ang ant-c ant-t arg-met ars asaf aur carb-v caust coff hell hep ign iod kali-c mosch nat-c nit-ac nit-s-d a1 olnd ran-b ran-s *Rhod* rhus-t sabad sars spig stann k* staph tarax thuj
- **dull** pain: agath-a nl2• aloe k* alumn bro1 *Anac* bro1 apis *Cact* bro1 canth k* carb-v bro1 cimic k* con k* eup-per bro1 ferr k* hydr-ac k* hyper bro1 *Lach* bro1 lith-c meny bro1 *Naja* bro1 *Nux-v* bro1 op k* petr bro1 *Ph-ac* bro1 *Phel* bro1 phys k* puls bro1 *Sep* bro1 *Sulph* bro1 ther bro1
- **flat**; as if pressing: verat bg2
- **forward**: asar *Bry* nit-ac sil sulph
- **gnawing** pain: *Ran-s*
- **hat**; as from a tight: agath-a nl2• cadm-met tpw6 calc-s k2 germ-met srj5• *Kola* stb3• mang-p rly4• merc k2 sulph
- **intense** (See violent)
- **intermittent**: ph-ac h2 sulph h2
- **inward**: agath-a nl2• allox tpw3* *Alum* amp rly4• *Anac* k* ant-t bg2 arn bg2 asaf bg2 asar k* bapt bg2 bov cact k2 calc carb-v bg2 cham k* *Cocc* coff k* *Dulc* k* falco-pe nl2• graph *Hell* k* ign k* ignis-alc es2• kola stb3• *M-ambo* b7.de* m-arct b7.de mag-c bg2 mag-m bg2 mang bg2 merc mur-ac bg2 nit-ac k* nux-m bg2 nux-v bg2 olnd k* petr ph-ac *Plat* k* plb bg2 *Ran-s* k* sabad k* sep sil spig k* squil bg2 stann k* staph k* sul-ac bg2 *Thuj* b4a.de zing k*
  - **fingertips**; as from: epiph bg2
  - **sharp** corners, as if by: cham k*
- **jerking** pain: dig h2
- **knots**, as from: phos h2
- **outward**: *Acon* k* agar agath-a nl2• all-s vh1 alum-sil k2 *Am-c* anac k* arg-n *Arn* k* ars k* **Asaf** k* asar bamb-a stb2.de• bar-m k2 bar-s k2 *Bell* k* berb *Bry* k* cact k2 calc h2 calc-sil k2 camph k* carb-ac *Carb-an* chel k* cimic k* cob coloc con *Cor-r* k* dros k* dulc k* euph fago a1 ferr k* ferr-ar ferr-p fl-ac k* glon *Hell* hep k* hyper ign k* indg ip a1 kali-ar kali-c k* kali-p k2 kali-sil k2 kiss a1 kola stb3• *Kreos* k* **Lach** laur k* lil-t k* lyc *Menis* a1 meny k* *Merc* k* **Nat-m** nat-s k2 nux-m k* *Nux-v* bg2 *Olnd* ozone sde2• par k* *Ph-ac* k* *Phos* b4a.de* phys phyt pic-ac k* *Prun* psor ptel k* puls bg2* ran-s rhod k* rhus-t b7a.de ruta fd4.de sabad k* sabin samb k* sang bg2 sapin a1 *Sep* k* *Sil* k* spig k* spong stann staph k* sulph k* tarax k* thuj tritic-vg fd5.de vanil fd5.de verb b7a.de *Viol-t* b7a.de zinc k*
  - **contents** would be forced out; as if: lil-t
  - **sharp** instrument; as from a: prun
- **paralyzed**; as if: nat-c h2
- **paroxysmal**: agar carb-v k* cham k* ign **Lach** ter
- **plug**; as from a: anac br1
- **pulsating** pain: arn h1* *Bry* k* *Chin* helo-s rwt2• **Puls** *Ruta* verat h1
- **rhythmical**: ruta k*
- **upward**: fl-ac guaj meph k* ph-ac *Plut-n* srj7• spig
- **violent**: granit-m es1• ruta fd4.de
- **vise**; as if in a: act-sp bro1 aeth k* agar *Alum* am-c am-m ant-t *Arg-n* k* aster atro *Bar-c* bar-s k2 bism bro1 bov bry *Cact* k* cadm-s carb-v caust cham bro1 chel chin cina clem coca-c sk4• *Cocc* daph euph gink-b sbd1• *Glon* graph grat hell lyc k* mag-c mag-s menis bro1 *Meny* bro1 **Merc** k* mucs-nas rly4• *Nat-m* nat-ox rly4• nat-s k2 nicc **Nit-ac** k* olnd op petr ph-ac bro1 **Plat** k* plut-n srj7• pneu jl2 *Puls* k* ran-b ran-s rat rhus-t sabad sars spig stann sul-ac sulph *Tarent* *Verb* bro1 viol-t bro1 [bell-p-sp dcm1]
- **wandering** pain: graph *Ign* symph fd3.de•
- **weight**; as from a: agar agath-a nl2• alum alumn ambr bg2 aq-mar skp7• arn bg2 ars k* aur bg2 bell k* *Bism* *Bry* bg2* bufo bg2 cact calen vml3• cann-s cann-xyz bg2 *Carb-an* b4a.de carb-v k* chel bg2 *Cina* coli rly4• con bg2 cupr dig bg2 hura bg2 ign bg2 kali-n bg2 laur k* led k* lyc bg2 m-arct b7.de mag-p bg2 med bg2* **Meny** k* merc-i-r *Mosch* k* *Nit-ac* k* *Nux-v* k* petr-ra shn4• ph-ac k* phys bg2 plat k* plb bg2 *Rhus-t* k* ruta bg2 sars k* sil k* *Spig* k* squil k* sulph k* *Thuj* k* verat

- **pressing** pain – **weight**; as from a: ...

- **pressure**:
- **abdomen** causes headache; on: **Ars** vh
- **agg.**: *Agar* alum-p ↓ alum-sil k2 am-c k* ant-c *Arg-met* arg-n ↓ *Bar-c* bar-m bar-s k2 bell k* bism bov bry tl1 calc calc-p k2 camph castm chin cic tl1 *Cina* cinnb cortiso sp1 *Cupr* dios bro1 glon k* hep bro1 *Kali-c* kali-m k2 kali-p kali-s lach k* lact lyc *Mag-c* mag-m mand sp1 mang k2 merc-i-f mez mur-ac nat-ar k* nat-c nit-ac mrr1 pall tl1 ph-ac *Prun* ptel bro1 sabin sars sil hr1* sulph teucr tub xxb tung-met bdx1• valer verb
  - **boring** pain: bell
  - **drawing** pain: agar h2* cina
  - **dull** pain: alum-sil k2
  - **pressing** pain: alum-p k2
  - **shooting** pain: verb c1
  - **sore**: arg-met h1 arg-n h1
  - **tearing** pain: agar h2 *Arg-met* bism *Sil*
- **amel.**: abrom-a ↓ acon bg1 acon-ac rly4• aeth hr1 agar agav-t jl1 aloe bg1 alum alum-p k2 *Alumn* **Am-c** *Anac* ant-c *Apis* .* aran *Arg-met* *Arg-n* k* arizon-l nl2• ars sne asaf ↓ **Bell** k* boerh-d ↓ **Bry** k* bung-fa mtf cact cadm-met sp1 caesal-b zzc1• calad ↓ *Calc* calc-f sp1 calc-s camph carb-ac carb-an k* carb-v cassia-s ↓ chel *Chin* k* chion chir-fl ↓ choc srj3• cimic *Cinnb* clem *Coloc* k* con cupr-s ↓ cystein-l rly4• dios ↓ dirc c1 dros dulc fd4.de **Ferr** *Ferr-i* ferr-p fic-m gya1 fum rly1*• galeoc-c-h gms1• gels br1* *Glon* k* guaj hell hep hir ↓ hist sp1* hydr *Ign* bro1 ind indg bro1 iod ↓ ip *Kali-bi* kali-n kalm lac-c bro1 *Lac-d* k* lac-h sk4• **Lach** k* laur lil-t *Lyc* mag-c **Mag-m** k* **Mag-p** k* mand sp1 meny k* merc merc-i-f mez mur-ac nat-c **Nat-m** nat-p *Nat-s* nat-sil fd3.de• nicc nux-m bg1* *Nux-v* k* oci-sa sk4• olnd op ↓ osteo-a knp1• par k* petr-ra shn4• phos *Pic-ac* pitu-gl skp7• plut-n srj7• podo psil ↓ **Puls** k* pycnop-sa mrz1 *Pyrog* ran-s rauw sp1 rhus-t ruta fd4.de sabad sabin samb xxb1 *Sang* k* *Sep* k* *Sil* k* *Spig* k* **Stann** staph suis-em rly4• sul-ac *Sulph* tarent thuj k* trios ↓ tritic-vg ↓ vanil ↓ verat k* visc sp1 *Zinc* zinc-p k2 [bell-p-sp dcm1 tax jsj7]
  - **boring**: hell ip sep
  - **bursting**: boerh-d zzc1•
  - **drawing**: chin
  - **dull** pain: abrom-a ks5 *Apis* cimic cystein-l rly4• hir skp7• lac-h sk4• tarent zzc1• trios rsj11•
  - **grinding**: anac k* dios br1
  - **nail**, as from a: oci-sa sp1
  - **neuralgic**: mag-c mrr1
  - **pressing**: alum alumn *Arg-n* asaf *Cact* chin k* chir-fl gya2 dios dulc fd4.de *Hell* hir skp7• lach *Meny* k* merc nat-m k* nat-s *Nux-v* op *Puls* pyrog sang stann suis-em rly4• thuj tritic-vg fd5.de
  - **pulsating** (See Pulsating - pressure - amel.)
  - **shooting**: bell cassia-s ccrh1• cupr-s lac-h sk4• mag-p
  - **stitching**: aeth calad guaj mur-ac psil ft1 ruta fd4.de sil sulph vanil fd5.de
  - **stunning**, stupefying: iod podo
  - **tearing**: alum h2 *Calc* camph h1 carb-an mag-c mag-m mag-p nat-c sulph
- **cannot** bear pressure though it does not agg.: seneg
- **cold** hand amel.; of: *Calc* carb-ac c1
- **eyes**; on | **amel.**: bamb-a stb2.de• dulc fd4.de vanil fd5.de
- **hand**; of:
  - **amel.**: apis ↓
    - **burning**: apis
- **hard** | **amel.**: *Alumn* vh1 anac arg-n *Bell* bry k2 carb-an **Chin** k* chinin-s mrr1 coloc mrr1 ephe-si hsj1• falco-pe nl2• glon k2 ind bg1 *Mag-m* **Mag-p** mand sp1 meny nux-m petr-ra shn4• *Sang* *Zinc* [tax jsj7]
- **head** against something hard amel.; pressing: (non:sang hr1)
- **head** to floor agg.: sang bg1
- **neck** agg.; on back of: sec
- **not** amel. | **desires** pressure; but: positr nl2•
- **pillow**; on: cupr-ar ↓ **Nit-ac** ↓ *Sil* ↓
  - **sore**: cupr-ar **Nit-ac** *Sil* dx1

- • **slight** | **amel.**: mand sp1
- **pulled** backward; as if: syph ptk1
- **pulled**; sensation as if hair were: acet-ac rb2 *Acon* k* *Aeth* *Alum* k* ambr *Arg-n* k* arn k* ars a1* (non:aur slp) bar-c k* bry b2.de* canth k* carb-an carb-v bg2 caust b2.de* **Chin** k* eupi a1* ferr indg k* iod *Kali-c* k* kali-n k* kali-p rb2 kreos b2.de* lachn vml3• *Laur* k* lept bg2* lyc k* mag-c k* mag-m k* mur-ac k* petr ph-ac k* *Phos* k* psor *Rhus-t* k* sel k* sil sol-ni rb2 stann k* stry rb2 *Sulph* k* vib rb2
  - • **accompanied** by | **vertigo** (See VERTIGO - Accompanied - hair)
  - • **out**: (↗*Hair - pulled*) arn a1 ars bell caps rb2 prun rb2 *Sulph*
- **pulled**; sensation as if scalp were: lyc b4a.de nat-m b4a.de sep b4.de*
- **pulled** upward; as if: camph b7a.de
- **pulling** hair | **amel.**: lac-cp sk4•
- **pulling**; like: acon-l a1 arge-pl rwt5• canth k* galla-q-r nl2• *Lach* petr
  - • **outward**: acon bg2
- **pulsating** pain: (↗*Pulsating*) *Acon* k* acon-ac rly4• act-sp bro1 adren vh1 aeth agath-a nl2• aids nl2• allox sp1 alum k* alum-p k2 alum-sil k2 *Am-c* am-m aml-ns bro1 anac ang anh vh1 ap-g br1 *Apis* arg-n k2* *Ars* k* ars-s-f k2 *Asar* aur-ar k2 aur-m k* bamb-a stb2.de• **Bell** k* beryl sp1 *Borx* bov bg2 bry k* bufo buth-a sp1 cact bro1* *Calc* k* *Calc-p* k* *Calc-s* k* calc-sil k2 camph k* cann-i k2* canth k* caps k* carb-an **Carb-v** **Carbn-s** carc sp1* *Cardios-h* rly4• carneg-g rwt1• caust *Cham* k* *Chel* **Chin** k* chinin-ar k* **Chinin-s** k* chord-umb rly4• cimic bro1 cinch a1 clem cob cocc colch tl1 cortico tpw7* cortiso sp1 croc bro1 crot-h tl1 cupr cupr-s cystein-l rly4• cyt-l sp1 dendr-pol sk4• dream-p sdj1• dulc fd4.de eug k* *Eup-per* k* *Euphr* falco-pe nl2• **Ferr** k* *Ferr-ar* *Ferr-i* ferr-m ferr-ma k* ferr-p k* fic-m gya1 galeoc-c-h gms1• *Gels* k* germ-met srj5• **Glon** k* glyc bro1 guar vml3• guat sp1 ham k* *Hep* hippoc-k szs2 hist sp1 hydr k* hydrog srj2• hyos hyper k* *Ign* k* ind a1* indg k* *Ip* irid-met srj5• iris bro1* jab ptk1 kali-ar kali-bi k* *Kali-c* kali-i kali-p kali-s kali-sil k2 kola stb3• lac-d k2* *Lach* k* lat-m sp1 laur k2* *Led* k* lil-s a1 luna kg1• **Lyc** k* *Lyss* mag-m a1 mag-p k2* manc k* mang h2* mang-p rly4• melal-alt gya4 meli k* merc-i-f a1 mez *Morph* nat-ar nat-c h2* **Nat-m** k* nat-p k* nat-pyru rly4• nat-s k* nicc nit-ac nux-m k* *Nux-v* k* oci-sa sp1 *Op* paull bro1 petr petr-ra shn4• ph-ac k* *Phos* k* pic-ac tl1 pitu-gl skp7• plat positr nl2• pot-e rly4• propr sa3• pseuts-m oss1• **Psor** k* ptel k* **Puls** k* pyrog ptk1* rhod *Rhus-t* k* *Ruta* *Sang* k* sanguis-s hm2• sars h2* sec k* *Sel* rsj9• *Sep* k* *Sil* k* sol-ni *Spig* bro1 spirae a1 spong fd4.de staph ptk1 *Stram* stroph-s sp1 stry suis-pan rly4• **Sulph** k* suprar rly4• syc pte1*• symph fd3.de• taosc iwa1• tarent k* tell rsj10• thiam rly4• thuj h1* tong bro1 *Trios* rsj11• tritic-vg fd5.de upa urol-h rwt• vanil fd5.de verat k* verat-v bro1* visc c1 xan k* xanth zinc h2* [bell-p-sp dcm1 spect dfg1]
  - • **deep** inside: carc tpw2*
    - ⁝ **knocking** against the bone; as if: allox sp1
  - • **waves**; in: nat-m bg2
- **quinine**; after: corn-f br1
- **radiating** in all directions (See extending - all)
- **rain**:
  - • **agg.**: phyt bg1
  - • **amel.**: cham k*
- **raising**:
  - • **arms** to head agg.: sulph
  - • **eyes**:
    - ⁝ **agg.**: *Bry* ↓ *Ign* ↓
      - : **jerking** pain: *Ign*
      - : **pressing** pain: *Bry*
  - • **head**:
    - ⁝ **agg.**: ang ars bar-c bov cact calc caps chinin-s cinnb coca dros ign k* lach linu-c a1 *Nux-m* ox-ac k2 seneg spong squil sulph tarax *Thuj* verat viol-t
    - ⁝ **amel.**: ang carb-v ign kali-c mag-c nat-m rhus-t spig sulfon bro1
      - : **stitching** pain: kali-c
- **raw**; as if: bry bg2 mez bg2 nat-c bg2 prun bg2 staph bg2
- **reading**:
  - • **agg.**: agath-a nl2• agn k* apis aran hr1 arg-met arn asaf aur bell sne borx bov k* bry *Calc* k* calc-f sp1 calc-s carb-v carbn-s caust cham chel chinin-s cimic k* cina cinnb clem coca cocc coff crot-t ery-a ferr-i k* glon k* hell ↓ helon k* hydrog srj2• ign k* kali-p fd1.de• kola stb3• lac-f c1 lac-h sk4• lach lyc lyss k* med c1 merc mez morph a1 **Nat-m** k* nat-s k*

- **reading** – **agg.**: ...
nux-v olnd op par ph-ac *Phys* hr1 pic-ac k2* *Plat* polyp-p a1 ptel k* ruta sabad *Sep* sil sulph *Tub* k*
    - ⁝ **pressing** pain: agn **Bell** *Cocc* hell helon k* *Lyc* k*
    - ⁝ **sore**: aur
    - ⁝ **stitching** pain: carb-v caust lyc
    - ⁝ **stunning** pain: **Calc** caust
  - • **amel.**: ham ign
- **rectangular**; as if: melal-alt gya4
- **recurrent**: granit-m ↓ olib-sac ↓
  - • **pressing** pain: granit-m es1• olib-sac wmh1
- **red** face, vomiting and diarrhea; with: **Bell** ↓
  - • **violent**: **Bell**
- **relaxing** from mental exertion; on: iris gk
- **respiration**; during deep: rat ↓
  - • **stitching** pain: rat k*
  - • **tearing** pain: rat
- **rest**:
  - • **agg.**: caps ↓ cic ↓
    - ⁝ **cutting** pain: (↗*motion - amel. - cutting*) caps
    - ⁝ **shooting** pain: (↗*motion - head - amel. - shooting*) caps tl1 cic tl1
  - • **amel.**: pitu-gl ↓ syc ↓ til ↓
    - ⁝ **cutting** pain: til
    - ⁝ **pulsating** pain: pitu-gl skp7• syc bka1*•
- **resting** head:
  - • **amel.**: kali-bi ↓ pitu-gl ↓
    - ⁝ **bursting** pain: kali-bi pitu-gl skp7•
  - • **amel.**; quietly on a cushion: alum k*
- **resting** head on arm:
  - • **agg.**: nat-m
  - • **amel.**: dros seneg spong fd4.de staph
- **resting** head on hand agg.: bell chin
- **resting** head on table amel.: ang ↓
  - • **boring** pain: ang k*
- **rheumatic**: acon act-sp bro1 am-m arn a1 *Ars* *Asar* asc-t *Aur* aur-ar k2 *Bell* k* benz-ac k* berb **Bry** k* cact calc bro1 *Calc-p* *Caps* *Carbn-s* caul k* *Caust* k* cham chin k* *Cimic* colch k2* **Coloc** k* cycl der bro1 **Dulc** *Eug* eup-per k2 graph *Guaj* k* hep bro1 ign ip bro1 kali-ar kali-bi kali-s k* *Kalm* k* lac-d k2 *Lach* led lyc k* mag-m mag-p k2 mang **Merc** k* *Nat-m* *Nit-ac* nux-v k* petr *Phos* k* *Phyt* k* plat podo prot fmm1• *Puls* k* *Ran-b* k* rhod k2 **Rhus-r** **Rhus-t** k* *Sang* **Sep** k* *Sil* k* spig stict stram sulph k* thuj k2 *Verat* wies a1
  - • **warmth** | **amel.**: ars k2
  - ○ • **External** head: bar-c b4.de* staph b7.de*
- **riding**: (↗*jar agg.*)
  - • **boat**; in a | **agg.**: (↗*STOMACH - Nausea - seasickness*) Cocc colch ferr *Tab*
  - • **carriage**; in a:
    - ⁝ **after**: nat-m *Nit-ac* plat ruta fd4.de **Sil**
    - ⁝ **agg.**: alum-sil k2 ars ars-s-f k2 asaf chin **Cocc** colch con k2 ferr ferr-act ferr-ar k* ferr-p *Graph* *Hep* *Ign* iod *Kali-c* kali-p lach *Lyc* meph naja *Nit-ac* ↓ *Nux-m* phos phyt raph **Sep** *Sil* spong ↓ sulph thuj vanil fd5.de [heroin sdj2]
      - : **noise** and jarring of, agg.: **Nit-ac**
      - : **pressing** pain: cocc *Nit-ac* spong fd4.de vanil fd5.de
    - ⁝ **amel.**: brom graph kali-n merc *Nit-ac* *Sanic*
  - • **cold** wind; in: *Ars-i* bry calc k2 *Calc-i* k* *Carb-v* glon *Kali-c* k* *Kali-i* lyc **Rhus-t** *Sanic*
  - • **horse**; a: | **amel.**: calc
  - • **streetcar**; on a:
    - ⁝ **agg.**: arg-n **Cocc** k* coloc glon ↓ graph bro1 hydrog srj2• kali-c k* lac-h sk4• *Med* k* *Nit-ac* bro1 petr bro1 sulph suprar rly4•
      - : **sore**: glon
    - ⁝ **amel.**: *Nit-ac*

- **rising**:
  - **after**:
    - **agg.**: arn glon laur menth c1 nat-m ox-ac phos pycnop-sa mrz1 stram tarent tritic-vg fd5.de
    - **amel.**: laur↓ ran-b↓ stann↓
      - **pressing** pain: laur ran-b stann
  - **agg.**: agar↓ am-m↓ apis↓ asaf↓ bell↓ bry↓ calc↓ cinnb↓ coloc↓ fic-m gya1 glon↓ hep↓ kalm↓ mag-s↓ mang↓ mim-p↓ nat-m↓ nit-ac↓ ozone↓ phys↓ *Spig*↓ vanil↓
    - **boring** pain: mang k*
    - **cutting** pain: mim-p rsj8•
    - **drawing** pain: bry k* coloc nat-m
    - **pressing** pain: apis asaf bell cinnb glon k* hep c1 mag-s nit-ac *Spig*
    - **shooting** pain: phys
    - **stitching** pain: agar calc ozone sde2• vanil fd5.de
    - **tearing** pain: am-m bell k2 kalm
  - **amel.**: ars↓ asaf cinnb k2 hep ign kali-i kali-p bro1 merc nat-c nat-s nit-ac k* ol-an↓ puls↓ rhus-r ruta fd4.de [heroin sdj2]
    - **dull** pain: ars h2
    - **stitching** pain: ol-an puls
  - **lying**; from:
    - **agg.**: aesc am-m anac ang apis arn ars asar aur-ar k2 aur-m bapt **Bell** bov bry k* *Calc* calc-s calc-sil k2 camph caps carb-an cham chel cinnb clem coca cocc bro1 colch rsj2• coloc con cor-r *Dulc* ephe-si hsj1• fago glon graph hep iod ip kali-n mur-ac nat-c *Nat-p* nux-v olnd **Ph-ac** *Phos* plut-n srj7• propr sa3• puls rhod ruta sep **Sil** squil staph sulph ust vanil fd5.de verat j5.de
      - **stitching** pain: calc h2
    - **amel.**: aloe am-c ambr ars aur **Bell** calad carb-an carb-v cham chin cic cupr ferr gels hep ign *Kali-c* kali-n laur lith-c mag-c nat-m nit-ac nux-v ph-ac **Phos** phys plb puls ran-b rhod rhus-t sabin spig vanil fd5.de verat [heroin sdj2]
  - **sitting**; from:
    - **agg.**: aesc apis *Bell* chin cob ferr grat lam laur lyc mang mur-ac ox-ac puls sil spong verat
      - **stitching** pain: mur-ac
    - **amel.**: arg-met phys spig spong
  - **standing** position, amel.; to: *Alum* ang aur bar-c bry calc canth carb-v chin con dig *Kali-c* laur mag-c nat-c olnd puls rhus-t spig stann teucr
  - **stooping**; from:
    - **agg.**: acon asar calc↓ colch cor-r daph hep *Kali-c* laur lyc mag-m mag-s mang mur-ac nux-v sul-ac viol-t
      - **pressing** pain: lyc
      - **stitching** pain: calc hep mur-ac h2
      - **tearing** pain: mang
    - **amel.**: calc-act con ign indg
  - **upright**:
    - **agg.**: acon agn ang arn ars asar bell bov bry caps caust cham cic dros hell hep ign *Kali-c* lac-d laur lyc mag-m *Mang* *Mur-ac* spong sul-ac tarax verat viol-t
    - **amel.**: ant-t cic mag-c rhus-t sabin
- **rolling** head from side to side amel.: *Agar* cina h1* kali-i med ph-ac
- **room**:
  - **agg.**: am-m↓ bar-c↓ bov↓ coc-c↓ con↓ hyos h1 laur↓ **Lyc**↓ mag-c↓ malar jl2 *Nat-m*↓ *Nat-s*↓ nicc↓ *Phos*↓ **Puls**↓ sel↓ sep↓ sulph↓
    - **pains** coming on in room are amel. out doors and vice versa: mang ran-b
    - **pressing** pain: am-m k* coc-c laur **Lyc** mag-c k* *Nat-m* *Nat-s* *Phos* **Puls** sulph h2
    - **stitching** pain: am-m bar-c bov con nat-m nicc sel sep
  - **amel.**: *Chin*↓ *Hep*↓ mang↓ merc↓ ol-an↓ valer↓
    - **pressing** pain: *Chin* *Hep* merc valer
    - **stitching** pain: mang
    - **tearing** pain: ol-an
  - **closed** room agg.: malar jl2
- **room**: ...
  - **crowded** room agg.: (↗*MIND - Fear - crowd; MIND - Fear - Narrow)* *Lyc* mag-c **Plat** plb rhus-g tmo3•
    - **pressing** pain: mag-c k*
  - **entering** a room; when: bov↓ mag-m↓ tritic-vg fd5.de
    - **cold** air; from: colch con nat-ar k2 puls
    - **open** air; from: aeth a1 *Caust*↓
      - **burning**: *Caust*
    - **pressing** pain: bov
    - **tearing** pain: mag-m
- **room**; as if in a closed: *Agn* bg2
- **room** with open windows amel.: malar jl2
- **rubbing**:
  - **agg.**: alum calc-p caust dios nit-ac staph↓
    - **biting** pain: staph k*
  - **amel.**: (↗*Motions of - rubbing - pillow - head)* ars bamb-a stb2.de• calc↓ canth carb-ac chinin-ar chir-fl gya2 form ham hyos sne indg k* lap-la sde8.de• laur melal-alt gya4 nat-sil fd3.de• ol-an op petr-ra shn4• ph-ac↓ phos phys ruta fd4.de symph fd3.de• tarent hr1* thuj↓ vanil fd5.de
    - **boring** pain: ol-an
    - **burning**: phos k*
    - **bursting** pain: **Phos** k*
    - **pressing** pain: op ph-ac phos
    - **sore**: ars thuj
    - **stitching** pain: canth phos vanil fd5.de
    - **tearing** pain: calc laur phos
  - **forehead**:
    - **amel.**: thuj↓
      - **cramping**: thuj k*
- **running**:
  - **agg.**: *Bry* *Ign* nat-c *Nat-m* k* *Nux-v* **Puls** tarent k*
  - **amel.**: hipp↓
    - **pressing** pain: hipp
- **sadness**; with (See MIND - Sadness - headache)
- **salt**; from: sel mrr1
- **scarlatina**; after: am-c bell *Bry* carb-v cham dulc hell hep lach *Merc* rhus-t
- **school** children: (↗*mental - agg.)* acon bac jl2 bar-c mrr1 bell *Calc* **CALC-P** k ●* *Lac-c* k* lac-d hr1 **Nat-m** k ●* **PH-AC** k ●* phos gk pic-ac k2 psor mtf33 *Puls* k* sabad k2 sang hr1 sulph gk tub al* zinc br1* zinc-m c1
  - **girls**: aur-m-n wbt2• *Calc-p* bro1 kali-p bro1 nat-m bro1* *Ph-ac* bro1 *Pic-ac* bro1 psor bro1 tub bro1 zinc bro1
- **school** headache (See students)
- **scraped**; as if: positr nl2•
- **scratching**:
  - **after**: cob↓ kali-n↓ lach↓ merc↓ ol-an↓ par↓ petr↓
    - **burning**: cob kali-n lach merc ol-an k* par k*
    - **sore**: petr a1
  - **agg.**: kali-i↓
    - **sore**: kali-i k2
  - **amel.**: grat↓ mang plat↓
    - **biting** pain: grat k*
    - **stitching** pain: plat
- **screwed** together; as if: ozone sde2•
- **screwing**; sensation of: alum bg2 bar-c bg2 bell bg2 bov bg2 caust bg2 chel bg2 kali-c bg2 kali-i ptk1 mag-c bg2 onos ptk1 petr bg2 *Plat* bg2 sabad b7.de* sars bg2 stann bg2 sulph bg2 verb bg2 zinc bg2
- **sea**; at the | **amel.**: sul-ac mrr1
- **searing** (See burning; forehead - burning)
- **seething** (See Boiling)
- **sewing**: cina h1* lac-c
- **sexual** desire: apis bro1 chin bro1 nux-v bro1 onos bro1 *Ph-ac* bro1 plat-m bro1 *Sil* bro1
  - **after**: plat k2
  - **suppression** of: camph tl1 *Con* *Puls*
- **sexual** excesses; after: (↗*loss; pollutions)* **Agar** arn *Bov* **Calc** carb-v *Chin* con *Kali-c* kali-sil k2 lach merc *Nat-c* nat-m nat-p *Nux-v* onos br1 ph-ac phos pip-m *Puls* **Sep** **Sil** spig *Staph* *Sulph* *Thuj*

- **shaking** the head; on:
  - **agg.**: acon k* *Arn* ars ars-s-f k2 bac c1 bar-c bar-s k2 **Bell** borx *Bry* calad *Calc* calc-s carb-an *Carb-v* *Carbn-s* carc fd2.de• *Caust* k* chin *Colch* coloc con *Cor-r* corn a1 *Ferr* k* ferr-ar ferr-i a1 ferr-p **Glon** k* *Hep* k* kali-n kali-s lact *Led* lyc k* mang merc *Mosch* *Nat-m* *Nit-ac* *Nux-m* **Nux-v** petr *Ph-ac* *Phos* *Rhus-t* ruta sang *Sep* k* sil sol-ni *Spig* k* squil stann k* staph stram sul-ac sulph tub tl
    - **pressing** pain: **Bell** **Bry** *Chin* coloc h2 ferr-p **Glon**
    - **shattering** pain: mang a1
    - **sore**: *Bell* *Glon* mang nit-ac
  - **amel.**: cina gels hyos phos bg1
- **sharp**: arizon-l nl2• arn br1 chlam-tr bcx2• dendr-pol sk4• fic-m gya1 germ-met srj5• kali-s fd4.de positr nl2• visc c1
- **shattered** (See sore)
- **shattering** pain: irid-met srj5• kali-c h2
  - **glass**; like: choc srj3•
- **shifts** to side lain on, motion amel.; while lying the pain: *Ph-ac* ↓
  - **scraped**; as if: *Ph-ac*
- **shivering**; with: acon b7.de borx b4a.de ferr b7.de kali-c b4.de led b7.de mag-s c1 merc b4.de *Mez* b4a.de phos b4.de puls b7.de rhus-t b7.de
- **shooting** pain: acet-ac *Acon* k* aesc bro1 aeth agar *Alum* alum-sil k2 am-c ambr ant-t apis k* arg-met arn bro1* ars bro1 aur bg2 bar-c bar-s k2 *Bell* k* berb bry k* calc k* calc-i k2 calc-sil k2 caps k* carb-v cassia-s ccrh1• caust *Cedr* bro1 cham k* *Chin* bro1 cimic k* colch coloc bg2* *Con* corn cystein-l rly4• dream-p sdj1• dulc *Eup-per* *Ferr* gels glon bg2 gran *Hell* hep hura hyos ign k* indg iod ip *Iris* bro1 *Kali-bi* k* **Kali-c** k* kali-m k2 kali-n kalm bg2 lac-c bro1 lach k* lact laur *Mag-c* mag-m mag-p k* manc mang merl k* mur-ac naja nat-c *Nat-m* *Nit-ac* nux-v petr phos k2 plan prun bg2* ptel puls k* rhus-r *Rhus-t* sabin c1 sang bro1 *Sep* k* sil k* spig bg2* spong fd4.de staph stront-c bg2 sul-ac bg2 sul-i k2 sulph k* suprar rly4• *Ter* teucr thuj tritic-vg fd5.de tub ptk1 valer vinc bro1
  - **forward**; from behind: nat-m
  - **outward**: alum cinnb nat-c rhus-t sulph
  - **pulsating** pain: aeth **Bell** ferr lac-h sk4• nux-v
  - **upward**: guaj sep sil
- **shopping**, from: bry gk epiph br1 *Sep* k*
- **short** lasting: pneu jl2
- **shriek**; must●: anac *Antip* vh1 *Ars* bov cact camph h1* *Coloc* cupr kali-c lyss k* mag-m petr sang hr1 *Sep* sil stann stram tarent
  - **shooting** pain: sep
- **sick** headache (See accompanied - nausea)
- **singing** agg.: alum ptel k*
  - **shooting** pain: alum ptel k*
- **sitting**:
  - **agg.**: abrom-a ks5 adam ↓ *Agar* alum alum-p k2 alum-sil k2 am-m ang aral arg-met ↓ arn ars asaf asar bell k2 benz-ac ↓ bism borx brucel ↓ bry bufo *Calc* canth carb-an *Caust* cham *Chin* k* cic cina ↓ coff con cycl dros euph ferr ferr-ar ferr-p fl-ac ↓ gent-c grat guaj indg lac-d lac-h sk4• lach led lith-c ↓ lyc mag-c meny merc merc-i-r k* mez *Mosch* mur-ac nat-ar *Nat-c* nicc ↓ nit-ac ↓ *Phos* plat puls ran-b rat rhod rhus-t k* ruta sabad seneg sil k* *Spig* ↓ spong squil *Staph* *Sul-ac* sulph tarax tritic-vg fd5.de vanil fd5.de verat zing
    - **boring** pain: agar k* tritic-vg fd5.de
    - **burning**: canth phos
    - **bursting** pain: phos k*
    - **drawing** pain: arg-met chin meny *Mur-ac* squil
    - **dull** pain: adam skp7• brucel sa3•
    - **pressing** pain: agar alum benz-ac *Bry* fl-ac **Lach** ruta fd4.de vanil fd5.de
    - **stitching** pain: caust chin indg mag-c nit-ac phos rat squil *Tarax*
    - **stunning** pain: caust cina
    - **tearing** pain: indg lith-c mag-c mez nicc phos *Spig*
  - **amel.**: alum-sil k2 ant-t arn ars asar *Bell* calad k* calc *Carb-v* ↓ cic k* cocc coff *Con* dulc fd4.de ferr a1 gels k* glon *Guaj* hipp ign kali-ar kali-c k* kola stb3• *Kreos* lam lith-c mag-c mag-m mang merc nat-m nux-v phos pic-ac ↓ rhus-t sep sulph vanil fd5.de verat
    - **pressing** pain: asar **Bell** calad pic-ac
    - **tearing** pain: *Carb-v* mag-m
- **sitting**: ...
  - **bent** forward:
    - **agg.**: rat ↓
      - **bursting** pain: rat k*
  - **erect**:
    - **agg.**: ign ↓ mang ↓ mur-ac ↓
      - **pressing** pain: mang mur-ac hr1
      - **tearing** pain: ign mur-ac
    - **amel.**: ant-t *Cic* *Gels* kali-c merc phos spong k2
      - **burning**: merc
  - **still** | **amel.**: bung-fa mtf
- **sitting** up in bed:
  - **agg.**: cham ↓ *Lyc* ↓ mang h2* mur-ac ↓
    - **shooting** pain: *Lyc*
    - **tearing** pain: cham h1 *Lyc* mur-ac
  - **amel.**: acon ↓ **Bell** ↓ canth ↓
    - **pressing** pain: **Bell** canth
    - **shooting** pain: acon
  - **half** sitting position | **amel.**: bell bro1
- **sleep**:
  - **after**:
    - **agg.**: (↗*waked)* aesc aeth *Agar* ail alum k* alum-p k2 alum-sil k2 ambr k* *Anac* k* *Ant-t* arg-n arn ars k* ars-s-f k2 *Aur* aur-ar k2 aur-s k2 bad bar-c bar-s k2 *Bell* k* *Bov* *Bry* cadm-s calad *Calc* k* calc-s calc-sil k2 canth b7.de* carb-an *Carb-v* k* **Carbn-s** caust k* cham chin chinin-ar ↓ chinin-s chion cic k* cimic cina cinnb k* clem coc-c k2 *Cocc* coff *Con* k* croc crot-c c1* crot-h dig dros erig eup-per euphr gels *Graph* ham hell hep ign k* ip kali-ar *Kali-bi* *Kali-c* kali-n kali-p kali-s kali-sil k2 **Lach** k* lact luna kg1• *Lyc* k* *Mag-c* mag-m meny merc mill morph k* mur-ac b4.de* *Naja* nat-ar nat-c **Nat-m** nat-p nat-s k* nit-ac k* nux-m *Nux-v* k* op k* ox-ac pall par peti petr ph-ac *Phos* k* plb psor ptel puls k* raph rheum k* rhus-r rhus-t rumx ruta sabad sang tl1 scut c1 sel sep k* *Sil* k* squil staph k* stram sul-ac *Sulph* k* *Tarent* *Thuj* tritic-vg fd5.de tung-met bdx1• vanil fd5.de zinc b4.de*
      - **pinching** pain: rheum
      - **restless** sleep: crot-c k* petr-ra shn4• stram k*
      - **sore**: chinin-ar k2
    - **amel.**: aeth a1 anac al aq-mar skp7• bad c1 bell k* camph k* chel chin-b c1 colch ferr *Gels* ger-i rly4• gink-b sbd1• *Glon* k* graph ham k* hyos kali-n kola stb3• lac-c lap-la sde8.de• laur k* macro a1 nat-m k2 *Pall* petr-ra shn4• **Phos** k* pic-ac plut-n srj7• podo puls *Sang* k* sanguis-s hrn2• *Sep* spong fd4.de thuj h1* vanil fd5.de
      - **good** sleep; by a: epiph c1 **Phos** k● **Sep** k●
  - **agg.**: *Arg-n* ↓ *Bry* ↓ calad ↓ cocc ↓ **Lach** ↓ merc ↓ nat-m ↓ rhus-t ↓ tarent ↓ thuj ↓ *Verat* ↓
    - **pressing** pain: *Arg-n* *Bry* calad cocc **Lach** merc nat-m rhus-t tarent thuj *Verat*
  - **amel.**: galeoc-c-h ↓ *Sang* ↓ sep ↓ stram ↓ thuj ↓
    - **boring** pain: sep
    - **bursting** pain: *Sang* sep
    - **cutting** pain: stram
    - **pressing** pain: galeoc-c-h gms1• thuj
  - **during**: agn androc srj1• ars camph cham k* *Chinin-s* mrr1 colch dendr-pol sk4• dig ferr k* graph hyos led k* mag-c k* petr psor bg1 ptel bg1 ther ptk1 thuj
    - **morning** | **second** sleep, agg.: ham
    - **amel.**: acon bad chlam-tr bcx2• cocc-s bro1 galeoc-c-h gms1• gels bro1 glon hell hydrog srj2• ign kola stb3• nat-m bro1 pall *Sang* bro1 scut bro1 sep sil k*
    - **cutting** pain: dig
  - **going** to:
    - **before**: agar nux-m
    - **on** | **amel.**: anac ang nit-ac
  - **loss** of; from: cimic bro1 cocc bro1* dendr-pol sk4• gink-b sbd1*• *Nux-v* bro1 petr-ra shn4•
    - **dull** pain: gink-b sbd1•

- **loss** of; from: ...
  - **from** late hours: ant-c arg-met *Carb-v* carc mlr1• *Cocc* coff colch dream-p sdj1• *Laur* *Nux-v* rhus-t sulph
  - **night** watching; from: ambr bry carb-v **Cocc** colch *Nux-v* *Puls* sulph
- **preventing**: chinin-ar k2 sulph k2
- **roused** from; on being: *Arn* *Cocc* phos
- **side**; sleeping on the affected:
  - **left**: caust↓
    - **pressing** pain: caust
- **siesta**: | **after**:
  - **agg.**●: bamb-a stb2.de• bov calad calc-p vh calc-s carb-v chel h1 coff glon k2 ign merc-i-f merc-i-r k* nux-m plac rzf5• rhus-t sep sulph k* tritic-vg fd5.de
    - **pressing** pain: calad
  - **amel.**: kali-n pall petr-ra shn4•
- **waked** from sleep by headache: *(↗after - agg.)* ars bg1 hir rsj4• *Kali-br* hr1 pseuts-m oss1• vanil fd5.de

- **sleep**; as from loss of: mag-m bg2 nux-v bg2
- **sleepiness**; with: luf-op↓
  - **dull** pain: luf-op rsj5•
- **smarting**: *(↗sore)* bapt camph canth chin euphr glon ham kola stb3• rhus-t k* sabin k* [helia stj7]
- **smoking**:
  - **agg.**: acet-ac acon alum ant-c bro1 *Ant-t* aran vh1 *Bell* brom calad k* calc k* carb-ac bro1 caust clem k* coc-c cocc ferr k* ferr-i *Gels* k* glon k* hep bro1 *Ign* k* *Lob* k* mag-c k* mand sp1 **Nat-ar** k* nat-m nux-v k* op par k* petr plan positr nl2• *Puls* sil spig k* thuj k* visc sp1 zinc
    - **pressing** pain: *Calad* mag-c k*
    - **stunning** pain: ant-c
  - **amel.**: am-c k* *Aran* k* calc-p k* *Carb-ac* k* glon a1 *Hyper* c1 naja
- **sneezing**:
  - **after**: apis↓ cina↓
    - **pressing** pain: apis cina
  - **agg.**: abrom-a bnj1 am-m apis arn astac a1* bar-c bar-s k2 *Bell* benz-ac *Bry* *Carb-v* cina k* grat hydr *Kali-c* kali-p kali-s *Nat-m* k* *Nit-ac* nux-v **Phos** sabad *Spig* **Sulph**
    - **bursting** pain: nat-m sabad k2
    - **shooting** pain: am-m cina
    - **sore**: arn bell bry grat
  - **amel.**: calc lil-t lyc bg1 mag-m bg1* mur-ac symph fd3.de•
    - **burning**: lil-t
    - **drawing** pain: mag-m h2
    - **frequent**: lil-t↓
      - **drawing** pain: lil-t
- **snow** | **reflection** of snow (= snow headache): *(↗GENERALS - Snow ailments)* glon c1
- **sore**: *(↗smarting; torn)* abrot acon k* aesc aeth ptk1 agar k* aloe alum k* alum-p k2 alum-sil k2 alumn am-c am-m k* ambr k2 anac k* ang bg2 *Apis* *Arg-met* k* *Arn* k* *Ars* k* *Ars-i* st ars-s-f k2 *Aur* k* aur-ar k2 aur-m k2 bad *Bapt* k* bar-c k* bar-i k2 bar-m bar-s k2 **Bell** k* bell-p bro1 benz-ac borx *Bov* k* bry k* cact k2 *Calc* k* calc-i k2 *Calc-p* calc-sil k2 camph k* cann-i *Canth* k* *Caps* *Carb-ac* carb-an b4a.de* *Carb-v* *Carbn-s* cassia-s ccrh1• caust k* cench k2 cham k* chel **Chin** k* chinin-ar *Chinin-s* cimic k* cina k2 *Cinnb* k* cob coff k* colch k2 con k* cop corn *Cupr* k* cupr-ar daph dulc fd4.de euon bro1 *Eup-per* k* eup-pur *Euph* euphr k* *Ferr* k* *Ferr-ar* ferr-p k* fl-ac **Gels** k* *Glon* granit-m es1• *Graph* k* guar bro1 gymno ham *Hell* k* **Hep** k* hipp *Ign* k* ind iod k* **Ip** k* *Iris* ptk1 kali-bi kali-c k2 kali-i k2 kali-m k2 kali-n k* kali-p kali-sil k2 kola stb3• *Kreos* lac-ac lac-c *Lac-d* *Lach* lachn lact laur bg2 led *Lyc* k* lyss *M-ambo* b7.de* *M-arct* b7.de* mag-c k* *Mag-m* manc mang med melal-alt gya4 mentho bro1 **Merc** k* **Mez** mosch k* mur-ac k* naja nat-ar nat-c k* nat-m *Nat-s* nicc **Nit-ac** k* *Nux-m* **Nux-v** k* olnd op k* *Par* *Petr* ph-ac k* phel bro1 *Phos* k* *Phyt* k* pic-ac plan plat k* positr nl2• prun *Puls* k* raph rat rhod k* *Rhus-t* k* *Ruta* sabad sabin b7a.de sang sars sec *Sep* k* **Sil** k* sol-ni sol-t-ae *Spig* stann k* *Staph* k* stict bg2 stram k* stront-c bg2 suis-em rly4• *Sul-ac* k* *Sul-i* *Sulph* k* *Syph* tab bro1 *Tarent* k* tela bg1 tell bg2 tep ter thiam rly4• *Thuj* k* tub k2 *Verat* k* vero-o rly4• zinc k* zinc-p k2 zing [bell-p-sp dcm1]
  - **paroxysmal**: *Verat*

- **sore**: ...
  - **waves**; in: granit-m es1•
- **spasmodic** pain (See paroxysmal)
- **speaking** (See talking)
- **spinal** disease; from: agar bro1 alum hr1*
- **spine** amel.; pain in: kali-p ptk1
- **spinning**, from: carb-an k*
- **spirituous** liquors:
  - **amel.**: androc srj1• arg-n bufo castm gels bro1 hell k* *Ign* *Kreos* naja phos k* sel c1 sep k* spong fd4.de
  - **from**: acet-ac **Agar** k* alum alum-p k2 alum-sil k2 *Ant-c* k* *Ars* ars-s-f k2 asaf *Bell* bry bufo *Calc* calc-f sp1 calc-s calc-sil k2 cann-i carb-v *Chel* *Chin* chlor k* cimic cocc mrr1 *Coff* coloc con dulc fd4.de *Gels* glon mrr1 guar vml3• hell hydr *Ign* k* ip **Lach** *Led* lob k* luna kg1• *Lyc* mand sp1 merc *Nat-m* nit-ac *Nux-m* **Nux-v** k* *Op* paull bro1 *Phos* ptel gk *Puls* **Ran-b** k* *Rhod* k* *Rhus-t* *Ruta* k* sabad *Sel* *Sil* *Spig* spong *Stram* *Sulph* vanil fd5.de *Verat* *Zinc* k*
- **splitting** (See bursting)
- **sprained**; as if: carb-an h2 vanil fd5.de
- **squeezed**; as if: *Acon* b7a.de* ambr b7.de* aml-ns bg2 ang b7.de* aq-mar rbp6 asaf bg2 camph b7.de* colch b7.de* *Coloc* bg2 dios bg2 **Ign** b7.de* laur b7.de* *Nux-v* b7.de* ph-ac bg2 plat bg2 ran-s b7a.de rheum b7.de* squil b7a.de stram b7.de* teucr b7a.de verb b7a.de
- **stabbing** (See cutting pain)
- **standing**:
  - **agg.**: agar alum alum-sil k2 arg-met arn ars calc calc-s canth chin k* cortico↓ dig guaj ip iris tl1 kali-ar kali-c kali-s lith-c↓ *Mag-c* mang *Nat-m* nit-ac↓ plb↓ **Puls** ran-b k* rheum rhus-t **Spig**↓ spong staph *Sulph* tarax tax-br oss1• vanil fd5.de verat zinc
    - **burning**: canth
    - **cutting** pain: agar calc
    - **drawing** pain: agar mag-c
    - **pressing** pain: alum staph h1*
    - **pulsating** pain: cortico sp1
    - **stitching** pain: mag-c nit-ac plb vanil fd5.de
    - **stunning** pain: staph h1
    - **tearing** pain: lith-c ran-b **Spig**
  - **amel.**: calc calc-sil k2 camph dulc fd4.de kali-s fd4.de ran-b tarax
    - **drawing** pain: *Tarax*
  - **impossible**: gels k2
  - **still**:
    - **amel.**: mang↓ *Tarax*↓
      - **stitching** pain: mang
      - **tearing** pain: *Tarax*
- **stepping**:
  - **agg.**: *(↗jar agg.; motion; walking)* aloe↓ alum↓ alumn↓ *Am-c* vh1 ambr↓ *Bell* mrr1 **Bry**↓ coc-c↓ **Coff** dulc fd4.de *Glon*↓ hell↓ lyc↓ **Nux-v** sep↓ *Sil*
    - **burning**: bell k2
    - **cutting** pain: alum ambr
    - **lancinating**: ambr
    - **pressing** pain: **Bell** *Bry* coc-c *Glon* hell lyc
    - **stitching** pain: aloe alum h2 alumn ambr h1 **Bry** k* sep
    - **tearing** pain: bell k2
  - **every** step; at: sep↓
    - **shooting** pain: sep
  - **hard** | **agg.**: aloe alum alum-p k2 alum-sil k2 am-c ambr *Ant-c* bar-c **Bell** **Bry** *Calc* calc-p calc-sil k2 *Carbn-s* *Caust* chel *Chin* coc-c cocc coloc **Con** dros **Glon** hell hydr ign kali-c kali-p kali-s kali-sil k2 *Lach* *Led* *Lyc* *Mag-m* meny mez nat-ar *Nat-m* **Nit-ac** nuph *Nux-v* ph-ac *Phos* *Phyt* *Psor* **Rhus-t** *Sep* **Sil** *Spig* spong sulph thuj
- **sticking** (See stitching)
- **stimulants** (See spirituous)
- **stitching** pain: *Acon* k* aesc bro1 aeth k* *Agar* k* agn k* aids nl2• aloe *Alum* k* alum-sil k2 *Am-c* k* am-m k* ambr k* ammc k* anac k* anan ant-c b7a.de* ant-t k* apis arg-met k* arg-n *Arn* k* ars k* *Ars-i* ars-s-f k2 asaf k* *Aur* k* aur-ar k2 aur-i k2 aur-s k2 bamb-a stb2.de• bapt k* *Bar-c* k* bar-i k2 *Bar-m* bar-s k2 *Bell* k* *Berb* k* *Borx* k* *Bov* k* *Bry* k* cadm-s c1 *Calc* k* calc-f sp1

- **stitching** pain: ...
calc-i k2 *Calc-s* camph k* cann-i k* cann-s k* canth k* *Caps* k* carb-ac carb-an k* carb-v k* carbn-s carneg-g rwt1• castm *Caust* k* cham k* *Chel* k* **Chin** k* chinin-ar *Cic* k* cimic bg2 cina k* cob-n sp1 coc-c k* cocc coloc bg2 *Con* k* cop croc crot-t cupr cycl k* cyt-l sp1 daph dig k* dirc k* dulc k* elaps eug k* *Euon* k* euph b4a.de *Euphr* k* eupi k* falco-pe nl2• ferr k* ferr-ar ferr-i ferr-p fic-m gya1 galla-q-r nl2• gels glon k* grat guaj k* hell *Hep* k* hipp hydr-ac *Hyos* k* *Ign* k* indg iod k* *Ip* k* kali-ar kali-bi k* **Kali-c** k* *Kali-i* k* kali-m k2 *Kali-n* k* **Kali-p** k* **Kali-s** k* kali-sil k2 kalm bg2 ketogl-ac rly4• kola stb3• lach k* lachn k* lact lam *Laur* k* lepi a1 lob lol a1 luna kg1• *Lyc* k* *Mag-c* k* *Mag-m* mag-p k* *Mag-s* k* manc k* *Mang* k* *Merc* k* merc-c k* merc-i-f k* merl k* mez mill miss mfm moni rfm1• mosch *Mur-ac* k* nat-ar *Nat-c* k* *Nat-m* k* *Nat-p* nat-s nicc k* *Nit-ac* k* nit-s-d a1 nux-m *Nux-v* k* ol-an op k* ozone sde2• *Par* k* *Petr* k* *Ph-ac* k* *Phos* k* pieri-b mlk9.de plan plat k* plb k* prun bg2 **Puls** k* raph rat rhod k* *Rhus-t* k* *Ros-d* wla1 ruta h1 sabad k* *Sabin* k* *Sars* k* sel k* seneg k* *Sep* k* serp k* *Sil* k* *Spig* k* spong *Squil* k* stann k* staph k* *Stront-c* k* stry *Sul-ac* k* **Sulph** k* symph fd3.de• tab tarax k* tarent k* teucr k* *Thuj* k* til k* trios rsj11• tritic-vg fd5.de *Valer* k* vanil fd5.de verat k* verb k* viol-t k* x-ray sp1 zinc k* zinc-p k2
  - **backward**: *Bry*
  - **boring** pain: am-c ruta h1
  - **burning**: arg-met h1 ph-ac k* phos h2 rhod k*
  - **drawing** pain: kreos k* *Mang* sil squil
  - **dull** pain: kali-c h2 mag-m k* sep k* sil k*
  - **hot**: meny bg2 staph bg2
  - **intermittent**: ph-ac h2
  - **inward**: *Calc* b4a.de *Canth* b7a.de cina b7a.de petr b4a.de sabin b7a.de squil b7a.de staph b7a.de
  - **jerking** pain: calc h2 *Nat-m* nux-v puls thuj h1
  - **outward**: alum b4a.de* arn b7a.de asaf b7a.de *Bell* b4a.de *Bry* b7a.de calc b4a.de cham b7a.de *Con* b4a.de dulc b4a.de *Lyc* b4a.de ph-ac b4a.de puls b7a.de *Rhus-t* b7a.de sil *Staph* b7a.de sulph b4a.de valer b7a.de
  - **point**; as from a sharp: dios bg2
  - **pulsating** pain: calc ferr kali-n h2 lac-h sk4• *Spig*
  - **tearing** pain: berb k* coloc k* hyos h1 kali-bi k* merc k* mur-ac nat-m phos k*
  - **upward**: thuj

- **stomach** | **distension** of stomach; with (See accompanied - stomach - distension)
- **stool**:
  - **after**:
    - **agg.**: agar bg2 aloe bg2* am-c ambr k* apoc bell bufo carb-an *Carbn-s* caust chel *Chin* b7a.de cupr fago ↓ glon bg2 ign lach linu-c a1 lyc k* nat-c ox-ac petr phos podo k* rat ↓ sabad k* sep k* sil k* spig k* ther zinc
      - **bursting** pain: rat k*
      - **pressing** pain: fago a1 *Lyc* k* sil spig
    - **amel.**: aeth k* agar k* aloe k* apis k* asaf borx corn cupr k* glon bg2* lachn ox-ac k* ptel k* sang bro1 sec bg2 thuj k* tung-met bdx1• verat-v k* *Zinc* bg1
  - **agg.**: alet bg1 aloe bro1 con bg2 ign bro1 nux-v bg2 ox-ac bro1 ptel bg1 rhus-t bg2 verat bg2
  - **before**: agar bg2 aloe k* merc k* nux-v b7a.de ox-ac k* *Puls* verat b7a.de
    - **pressing** pain: merc
  - **during**:
    - **agg.**: acon b7a.de bell bg2 *Calc* b4a.de calc-p bg2 coca bg2 coloc bg2 con bg2 dios bg2 glon bg2 gran ↓ ham bg2 *Lyc* b4.de* merc b4.de* nat-m bg2 nit-ac bg2 *Nux-v* bg2 ox-ac bg2 petr bg2 phos b4a.de* rat bg2 rhus-t b7.de* spig b7a.de* sulph b4a.de*
      - **pressing** pain: coloc gran merc
  - **straining** at:
    - **agg.**: alet bg1 bamb-a stb2.de• bell *Bry* calc-p cob coloc *Con* glon ham hell ign *Ind* iod *Lyc* k* mang bg3 nat-m *Nux-v* ox-ac oxal-a rly4• phos psor *Puls* rat k* *Sil* spig *Sulph* thuj vib
      - **bursting** pain: ind k* rat ptk2
      - **come** off; as if top of head would: ind

- **stooping**:
  - **after**:
    - **agg.**: aloe ↓ calc ↓ rhus-t ↓
      - **stitching** pain: aloe calc rhus-t
  - **agg.**: (↗*bending - head - forward - agg.)* acet-ac acon k* aesc k* agar tl1 aloe *Alum* alum-p k2 alum-sil k2 am-m ang ant-t anth vh *Apis* arg-mur k* arn ars-met bro1 ars-s-f k2 asar bapt *Bar-c* k* bar-m bar-s k2 **Bell** k* berb borx bov k* **Bry** k* *Calc* k* calc-i k2 calc-p k* calc-s calc-sil k2 camph canth caps k* carb-ac k* carb-an ↓ carb-v caul c1 caust cham *Chel* chin chinin-s chion br1 cic cinch a1 cit-ac ↓ cob k* *Cocc Coff* colch *Coloc* k* com con *Cor-r* a1* corn cupr cupr-s ↓ cycl *Dig* k* dros *Dulc* ephe-si hsj1• erig vml3• euphr ↓ *Ferr* ferr-i k* ferr-ma k* ferr-p fl-ac ↓ form gels *Glon* k* ham k* *Hell Helon* k* *Hep* hydr hydr-ac hydrog srj2• hyos *Ign* k* indg ↓ ip ↓ irid-met ↓ kali-bi *Kali-c* kali-m k2 *Kali-n* k* kali-p *Kali-s* kali-sil k2 kola stb3• kreos lach k* laur *Led* lyc k* lyss mag-m manc mand sp1 **Mang** med meny **Merc** merc-c ↓ merc-i-r merl ↓ mill k* moni rfm1• mur-ac nat-ar nat-c *Nat-m* nat-p nat-s nicc *Nit-ac Nux-m Nux-v* k* ozone sde2• par ped ↓ *Petr Phos* k* phys phyt pic-ac k* plat plect k* plut-n ↓ ptel **Puls** k* pycnop-sa mrz1 rheum rhus-r *Rhus-t* rhus-v bro1 rumx ↓ ruta ↓ samb *Sang Seneg* senn **Sep** k* *Sil* k* sol-ni **Spig** k* spong *Stann* staph k* stry sul-ac sul-i ↓ **Sulph** k* teucr *Thuj* tritic-vg sna6 **Valer** *Verat* vib zing
    - **boring** pain: hep merc *Sep*
    - **burning**: *Apis* mang h2* mur-ac h2
    - **bursting** pain: *Ham* k* hep k* hydr k* irid-met srj5• kali-bi lyss k* nat-m k* ptel sep staph hr1 stry k*
    - **come** off; as if top of head would: cupr-s hr1
    - **cutting** pain: arn caust chin dros ferr-p glon a1 nicc k*
    - **jerking** pain: petr h2
    - **lancinating**: arn k* cit-ac rly4• ped a1
    - **pinching** pain: alum k*
    - **pressing** pain: *Bell Bry Calc* canth carb-v cham chel coloc fl-ac hep lyc mag-m merc merc-c merl k* par petr phos plut-n srj7• *Puls* sil *Spig* stann thuj tritic-vg fd5.de zing
    - **shooting** pain: bell hep c1 indg kreos k* nit-ac k* sul-i sulph tritic-vg fd5.de
    - **sore**: bapt *Coloc* hell lyc nicc rumx ruta fd4.de
    - **stitching** pain: alum am-m berb bry calc k* caps cycl k* euphr a1 ferr-p glon *Hep* k* kali-c kali-m k2 mag-m mur-ac nicc *Par* puls staph sulph thuj
    - **stunning** pain: *Hell* hr1 rheum h
    - **tearing** pain: arn asar bov canth carb-an *Coloc* ip rhus-t sil
    - **twitching**: arn k*
  - **amel.**: ang bar-c carb-ac c1 caust *Cina* k* con dig elaps fago *Hyos* ign k* indg laur mang meny bro1 mez nux-v phos k* tarax tritic-vg fd5.de verat verb viol-t
    - **pressing** pain: caust mang tritic-vg fd5.de
    - **rising** or on bending head backwards; returning on: mang ↓
      - **boring** pain: mang
  - **low** down: *Ign* ↓
    - **drawing** pain: *Ign* k*
  - **must** stoop: cann-i ↓ ign ↓
    - **pressing** pain: cann-i ign
- **storm**; before: *Sil* ↓
  - **cutting** pain: *Sil*
- **stove**; from heat of (See warm - stove - agg.)
- **straining** of the eyes (See exertion of - agg.)
- **stretching** agg.: agar ↓
  - **drawing** pain: agar
- **string**; as if by a (See Constriction - string)
- **students**: (↗*mental - agg.)* bac jl2 bar-c mrr1 calc-p c2 diphtox jl2 kali-p k2 mag-p c2 nat-c c2 nat-m c2 ph-ac c2 pic-ac c2 sabal c2 *Tub* jl2 v-a-b jl2*
- **study** and exertion, after ague; from: gels ↓
  - **cramping**: gels
- **stunning** pain: (↗*MIND - Dullness - headache; MIND - Stupefaction - headache - during)* acon k* aeth k* agar k* *Agn* b7a.de alum alum-p k2 alum-sil k2 am-c k* anac k* ant-c k* ant-t k* arg-met *Arg-n* k* *Arn* k* *Ars* k* ars-i asaf k* asar k* aur k* bapt k* bar-c k* bar-i k2 bar-m bar-s k2 *Bell* k*

- **stunning** pain: ... bov$_{k*}$ bry$_{k*}$ *Bufo* **Calc**$_{k*}$ calc-ar$_{k*}$ calc-sil$_{k2}$ *Carb-an*$_{k*}$ **Carb-v**$_{k*}$ caust$_{k*}$ chin$_{k*}$ chinin-s cic$_{k*}$ cimx$_{k*}$ cina$_{k*}$ cinnb cocc$_{ptk1}$ con$_{k*}$ crot-t cupr$_{k*}$ cycl$_{k*}$ dros$_{k*}$ *Dulc*$_{k*}$ fl-ac$_{k*}$ gels$_{bg2*}$ glon$_{k*}$ gran **Graph**$_{k*}$ *Hell*$_{k*}$ hydr-ac$_{hr1}$ *Hyos*$_{k*}$ iod *Iris* kali-bi kali-c kali-m$_{k2}$ *Kali-n*$_{k*}$ kali-p kali-s kali-sil$_{k2}$ *Kola*$_{stb3}$• lac-c *Lach* *Laur*$_{k*}$ *Led*$_{k*}$ *Lyc*$_{k*}$ m-ambo$_{b7.de}$ *Mag-c* mang meny$_{k*}$ *Mez*$_{k*}$ mosch$_{k*}$ *Mur-ac*$_{k*}$ *Naja* *Nat-ar* *Nat-c*$_{k*}$ *Nat-m*$_{k*}$ nat-p nit-ac *Nux-m*$_{k*}$ **Nux-v**$_{k*}$ *Olnd*$_{k*}$ op$_{k*}$ petr ph-ac$_{k*}$ *Phos*$_{k*}$ **Psor**$_{k*}$ ptel$_{bg2*}$ *Puls*$_{k*}$ rheum$_{k*}$ rhod$_{k*}$ *Rhus-t*$_{k*}$ ruta$_{k*}$ sabad$_{k*}$ sabin$_{k*}$ samb$_{k*}$ senec$_{bro1}$ sep$_{k*}$ **Sil**$_{k*}$ spig$_{ptk1}$ spong$_{fd4.de}$ *Stann*$_{k*}$ *Staph*$_{k*}$ sulph$_{k*}$ syph$_{bro1}$ tarax *Tarent* thuj valer$_{k*}$ vanil$_{fd5.de}$ verat$_{a1*}$ verb$_{k*}$ *Zinc*$_{k*}$ zinc-p$_{k2}$
  - **compressed**; as if: *Mosch*$_{k*}$
  - **drawing** pain: asar
  - **pressing** pain: *Ant-t* arg-met arn ars *Asar* calc cic cina *Crot-t* cupr *Dros* dulc *Euon*$_{k*}$ hell *Hyos* *Mez* *Ruta* *Sabad* *Stann* sulph verb
  - **stinging**: verb
  - **throbbing**: nat-m sabin
  - **tightening** pain: asaf olnd
- **sudden**: gins↓ glon↓ ran-b↓
  - **blow**; pain as from a: *(↗increasing - suddenly)* gins$_{bg2}$ ran-b$_{bg2}$
  - **stitching** pain: *(↗increasing - suddenly)* glon$_{bg2}$
- **summer**: aloe$_{sne}$ *Ant-c* bar-c bar-s$_{k2}$ **Bell** *Bry* **Carb-v** **Glon** graph lyc *Meli*$_{sne}$ **Nat-c** *Nat-m* *Nat-s* **Puls** sulph thuj
- **sun**:
  - **agg.**: pitu-gl↓
    - **bursting** pain: pitu-gl$_{skp7}$•
    - **pulsating** pain: pitu-gl$_{skp7}$•
    - **shadow** amel.: brom↓
      - **pressing** pain: brom
  - **exposure** to sun; from: abies-c$_{oss4}$• *Acon* act-sp aegle-f$_{bnj1}$ *Agar* aloe alum$_{dgt}$ androc$_{srj1}$• **Ant-c** *Arum-t* aur-m-n$_{wbt2}$• *Bar-c* bar-s$_{k2}$ **Bell**$_{k*}$ brom bruc **Bry** cact$_{c2*}$ cadm-s *Calc*$_{k*}$ calc-f$_{sp1}$ calc-ox$_{gm1}$ calc-s *Camph* cann-i$_{k*}$ *Carb-v* castn-v *Chin* chinin-s cina$_{k2}$ *Cocc* cortiso$_{sp1*}$ dulc$_{fd4.de}$ euphr ferr-p$_{bro1}$ *Gels*$_{k*}$ genist **Glon**$_{k*}$ glycyr-g$_{cte1}$• hipp$_{k*}$ hist$_{sp1*}$ hyos ign kali-bi$_{c2*}$ kalm$_{c2*}$ **Lach**$_{k*}$ manc mand$_{sp1}$ nat-ar **Nat-c**$_{k*}$ *Nat-m*$_{k*}$ nit-ac↓ *Nux-v*$_{k*}$ petr-ra$_{shn4}$• phos$_{tl1}$ plb$_{gk}$ **Puls**$_{k*}$ sang$_{bro1*}$ *Sel*$_{k*}$ spig$_{bro1*}$ stann$_{tl1}$ *Stram*$_{k*}$ sul-i$_{k2}$ *Sulph* syph *Ther*$_{k*}$ valer verat-v$_{bg1}$ zinc zinc-p$_{k2}$ [heroin$_{sdj2}$]
    - **amel.**: graph stront-c
    - **sore**: manc nit-ac
    - **stitching** pain: bar-c$_{k*}$ sel
    - **stunning** pain: nux-v$_{k*}$
  - **walking** in the sun | **agg.**: stram$_{tl1}$
- **sun**; comes and goes with the (See morning - comes)
- **sun**; increasing and decreasing with the (See morning - sun; increasing)
- **supper** | **after**:
  - **agg.**: carb-v↓ ran-b↓
    - **pressing** pain: carb-v ran-b
  - **amel.**: am-c colch lachn
- **supporting** head on hands amel.: dros↓ hydr↓
  - **cutting** pain: dros hydr
- **suppressed** cough; after (See cough - suppressed)
- **suppressed** discharges (See discharges - suppressed)
- **suppressed** eruptions (See eruptions)
- **suppurating**; as if: *Acon*$_{bg2}$ ars$_{bg2}$ borx$_{bg2}$ bov$_{bg2}$ bufo$_{bg2}$ carb-v$_{bg2}$ caust$_{bg2}$ mang$_{bg2}$ *Nux-v*$_{bg2}$ petr$_{bg2}$ rhod$_{bg2}$ sep$_{bg2}$
- **surging**: lach$_{k2}$ tritic-vg$_{fd5.de}$
- **swallowing** agg.: elaps$_{sne}$ gels kali-c mag-c mag-s↓
  - **drawing** pain: mag-c
  - **stitching** pain: mag-s$_{sp1}$
- **sweets**; from (See candy)
- **sycotic**: thuj$_{tl1}$
- **synchronous** with pulse: bell$_{b4a.de*}$ hell↓ *Ign*$_{b7a.de}$
  - **pressing** pain: hell$_{h1}$
- **syphilitic**: ars$_{bro1}$ ars-i$_{k2}$ asaf *Aur*$_{k*}$ aur-ar$_{c2*}$ aur-m$_{k2}$ fl-ac hep kali-bi$_{k2}$ *Kali-i*$_{k*}$ led *Merc*$_{k*}$ mez *Nit-ac* phyt sars$_{bro1}$ still$_{c2*}$ sul-ac$_{k2}$ *Syph*$_{k*}$ **Thuj**$_{k*}$
- **talk** of others agg.: acon$_{j5.de}$ aran ars$_{j5.de}$ bar-c bell$_{j5.de}$ ign mag-m merc ph-ac$_{k2}$ sep$_{j5.de}$ spig$_{j5.de}$ syph$_{xxb}$
- **talking**:
  - **after**: agar↓ nat-m↓
    - **loudly**: sulph↓
      - **stitching** pain: sulph
    - **stitching** pain: agar nat-m
  - **agg.**: abrom-a↓ *Acon*$_{k*}$ agar alum$_{vh1}$ *Aran* arg-n *Aur* aur-s$_{k2}$ bamb-a↓ *Bell* bry cact$_{k*}$ *Calc* calc-i$_{k2}$ *Calc-s* canth chin$_{k*}$ cic *Cocc* coff$_{k*}$ con dendr-pol↓ dros dulc euphr fl-ac *Gels* glon ham$_{fd3.de}$• hyos *Ign*$_{k*}$ iod jug-c$_{vml3}$• jug-r kola$_{stb3}$• *Lac-c* lac-d led *Mag-m* mang$_{hr1}$ meli merc *Mez*$_{k*}$ **Nat-m** nux-v par pert-vc$_{vk9}$ ph-ac phos psor puls rhus-t sang sars *Sil* spig$_{k*}$ spong sul-i$_{k2}$ **Sulph** syph$_{xxb}$ ther$_{k2*}$ thuj↓ vanil$_{fd5.de}$ zinc zinc-p$_{k2}$
    - **burning**: sil
    - **bursting** pain: bamb-a$_{stb2.de}$•
    - **distant**: mur-ac$_{k*}$
    - **dull** pain: abrom-a$_{ks5}$ dendr-pol$_{sk4}$•
    - **pressing** pain: ph-ac$_{k2}$ vanil$_{fd5.de}$
    - **shooting** pain: nat-m thuj
    - **sore**: aur *Chin* spig
    - **tearing** pain: cocc sars
  - **amel.**: adam$_{skp7}$• allox$_{tpw3*}$ dulc eup-per$_{k*}$ ham hydrog$_{srj2}$• lac-d sil
  - **loudly** agg.: ign↓ psor$_{al}$ spig$_{c1}$
    - **burrowing**: spig$_{k*}$
    - **bursting** pain: ign *Spig*$_{h1}$
    - **pressing** pain: spig
- **tapping** on spine: bell$_{j5.de}$ cina sep$_{j5.de}$ spig$_{j5.de}$ syph$_{dgt}$
- **tea**:
  - **amel.**: adam$_{skp7}$• carb-ac$_{bro1}$ cimic cot$_{c1}$ ferr-p kali-bi
  - **from**: chin guar$_{vml3}$• lach nux-v$_{bro1}$ paull$_{bro1}$ sel$_{k*}$ sep *Thuj*$_{k*}$ verat
  - **green** | **amel.**: carb-ac$_{hr1*}$
  - **strong** | **amel.**: *Carb-ac* glon
- **tearing** pain: *(↗torn)* acon$_{k2}$ aesc aeth agar$_{k*}$ *Agn* ail all-c$_{k2}$ aloe$_{dgt}$ alum$_{k*}$ alum-sil$_{k2}$ am-c$_{k*}$ *Am-m*$_{k*}$ ambr$_{k*}$ *Anac*$_{k*}$ ant-c$_{k*}$ ant-t$_{b7a.de}$ *Arg-met*$_{k*}$ **Arn**$_{b7.de*}$ *Ars*$_{k*}$ ars-i asaf$_{k2}$ asar$_{k*}$ **Aur**$_{k*}$ aur-ar$_{k2}$ aur-i$_{k2}$ aur-m aur-s$_{k2}$ bamb-a$_{stb2.de}$• *Bell*$_{k*}$ *Berb* borx bov$_{k*}$ *Bry*$_{k*}$ calad *Calc*$_{k*}$ calc-p *Calc-s* camph$_{k*}$ cann-s *Canth*$_{k*}$ caps$_{k*}$ carb-an$_{k*}$ *Carb-v*$_{k*}$ castm caust$_{k*}$ *Cham*$_{k*}$ *Chel* *Chin*$_{k*}$ chinin-ar cic$_{b7.de*}$ cimic$_{bg2}$ cina$_{k*}$ cinnb *Cocc*$_{k*}$ coff$_{k*}$ colch$_{k*}$ *Coloc*$_{k*}$ *Con*$_{k*}$ croc$_{k*}$ crot-t cupr *Cycl* dig$_{k*}$ dros eup-per$_{k2}$ eupi ferr ferr-ar ferr-i ferr-p graph *Guaj*$_{k*}$ hell hyos$_{k*}$ hyper *Ign*$_{k*}$ indg iod *Ip*$_{k*}$ kali-ar kali-bi$_{k*}$ *Kali-c*$_{k*}$ kali-m$_{k2}$ kali-n$_{k*}$ kali-p *Kali-s* kali-sil$_{k2}$ *Kalm* kola$_{stb3}$• *Kreos*$_{k*}$ lach$_{k*}$ laur$_{k*}$ led$_{k*}$ lil-t **Lyc**$_{k*}$ m-ambo$_{b7.de*}$ *Mag-c*$_{k*}$ *Mag-m* mag-p mag-s$_{k*}$ manc *Mang* **Merc**$_{k*}$ *Merc-c*$_{k*}$ mez mill *Mur-ac*$_{k*}$ nat-ar nat-c$_{k*}$ **Nat-m**$_{k*}$ nat-p nat-s nicc nit-ac$_{bg2}$ *Nux-v*$_{k*}$ *Ol-an* petr *Ph-ac*$_{k*}$ phel$_{bg2}$ phos$_{k*}$ plat plb$_{k*}$ psor *Puls*$_{k*}$ ran-b$_{k*}$ rat rheum$_{k*}$ rhod$_{k*}$ *Rhus-t*$_{k*}$ ruta samb$_{k*}$ sang$_{k2}$ sars$_{k*}$ sel$_{k*}$ *Sep*$_{k*}$ *Sil*$_{k*}$ **Spig**$_{k*}$ squil$_{k*}$ *Stann*$_{k*}$ *Staph* stram stront-c$_{k*}$ sul-ac$_{k*}$ **Sulph**$_{k*}$ tarax$_{k*}$ ter teucr$_{k*}$ thuj$_{k*}$ til valer$_{k2}$ viol-t vip zinc$_{k*}$ zinc-p$_{k2}$
  - **aching**, tearing, jerking: phos
  - **asunder**: *(↗bursting)* agar am-m coff *Mur-ac* nat-s op *Puls* staph sul-ac *Verat*
  - **bruised**; as if: bov merc
  - **cutting** pain: bell
  - **digging** pain: coloc spig
  - **drawing** pain: am-c calad canth caps cina guaj *Kali-c* lach *Mang* nux-v ol-an rhus-t sil
    - **boring** pain: carb-an
  - **intermittent**: *Coloc* ferr hyos$_{h1}$ nicc rheum *Stann* sulph$_{h2}$
  - **jerking** pain: agar arn *Chin* kali-c mag-c mur-ac paeon puls rat teucr thuj
  - **maddening** pain: mag-c
  - **outward**: lach$_{bg2}$
  - **paralyzed**; as if: nat-c$_{h2}$
  - **paroxysmal**: carb-v$_{h2}$ caust *Coloc* nicc
  - **pressing** pain: aur$_{h2}$ camph chel plut-n$_{srj7}$• samb$_{xxb1}$ sars$_{h2}$ squil

- • **pulsating** pain: ars carb-an *Cocc* mag-m nat-c rhus-t sil spong zinc
- • **saw**; as if with a: *Sulph*
- • **shooting** pain: arg-met berb caust chel chin cic hyos hyper mang h2 phos sil sulph vip zinc
- • **stinging**: caps cocc hyper *Ign* mag-m *Nat-m* nicc ph-ac puls sulph h2 zinc h2
- • **to** and fro: ambr a1*
- • **twitching**: *Chin* kali-c sil
- • **upward**: am-c plut-n srj7•
- • **wandering** pain: ambr ant-c berb colch con nat-s rhus-t sel
- • **waves**; in: caust
- **teeth**:
  - **biting** teeth together: am-c bro1
    - ⁝ **amel.**: crot-c sk4•
- **temperature** | **change** of: carb-v a1* ran-b c1* verb a1*
- **thinking** of it agg.: cham ↓ cocc ↓ dig ↓ *Helon* ↓
  - **pressing** pain: cham cocc dig *Helon* k*
- **thinking** of the pain:
  - **agg.**: ant-c aq-mar skp7• arn bg2* calc-p camph hr1 cham k* chin k* cimic gk con euph h2* ferr-p k* glycyr-g cte1• *Hell* k* helon k* hydr ign nat-s neon srj5• ol-an ox-ac k* pert-vc vk9 pieri-b mlk9.de pip-m k* sabad k* sin-n k* spig vml staph k*
    - ⁝ **cold** applications | **amel.**: aq-mar skp7•
    - ⁝ **pressure** | **amel.**: aq-mar skp7•
    - ⁝ **sleep** | **amel.**: aq-mar skp9*
  - **amel.**: agar k* camph k* *Cic* k* helon bro1 *Ox-ac* bro1 pall prun
    - ⁝ **cutting** pain: cic
- **thread**; like a thick, long: all-c a1*
- **throbbing** (See pulsating)
- **thunderstorm**:
  - **after**: trios rsj11•
  - **amel.**: cob-n sp1
  - **before**●: bry carc fb* dulc fd4.de lach meli sne* *Nat-c* nat-sil fd3.de• **Phos** *Rhod Sep Sil*
  - **during**: carc fb* *Nat-p* k* **Rhod** ↓ sep j5.de
    - ⁝ **drawing** pain: *Rhod*
    - ⁝ **tearing** pain: **Rhod**
- **tightening** (See drawing - tightening)
- **toothache**; with: ail hr1 *Hecla* hr1 *Ign* hr1 *Kali-c* hr1 lac-d hr1 **Lach** hr1 lyss hr1 plan hr1 ros-d wla1 *Sang* hr1 sil hr1 verat hr1 [tax jsj7]
- **torn**; as if: *(↗bursting; sore; tearing)* agar k* alum k* am-m ang arg-met ars aur bell bov camph **Carb-an** caust cham *Chin Coff* k* con k* euphr ferr k* graph hell hep *Hyper* ign k* iod ip kali-n lach mag-c merc mosch *Mur-ac Nicc* nit-ac *Nux-v* k* op k* ph-ac phos plat puls k* *Rhus-t* k* sep k* stann *Staph* k* stront-c sul-ac b4a.de sulph thuj verat k* zinc k*
- **touch**:
  - **agg.**: *Acon Agar* agn all-c alum ambr ↓ ap-g ↓ *Arg-met* ars ↓ bar-c *Bell* k* borx bov bry calc calc-sil k2 camph carb-an carb-v casc castm chel *Chin* k* chinin-ar cina k2 cinnb coloc j5.de con cupr daph dulc ↓ ferr c1 ferr-p bro1 *Gels* grat hep h2* hydrog srj2• *Ign* ip kali-bi *Kali-c* kali-m k2 kali-n kali-p kali-sil k2 *Kalm* lach ↓ lact laur led lyc lyss k* mag-m h2* mag-s mang k2 *Merc* k* merc-i-f a1 **Mez** k* mur-ac nat-m nit-ac nux-m *Nux-v* bg3* ox-ac ↓ par *Ph-ac* phos rhod *Rhus-t* h1* ruta fd4.de sabin sang a1 *Sars* k* sep *Sil* spig k* staph k* *Sul-ac* sulph j5.de tarent k* thlam ↓ vanil fd5.de
    - ⁝ **burning**: ip k* nat-m k*
    - ⁝ **drawing** pain: con **Staph**
    - ⁝ **sore**: ambr k2 ap-g vh1 ars h2 bry k2 dulc fd4.de lach k2 nit-ac h2 ox-ac k2 ph-ac h2 phos h2 sil tl1 sul-ac h2 thiam rly4•
    - ⁝ **stitching** pain: hep ip spig staph
    - ⁝ **tearing** pain: arg-met chel cina a1 ip staph
  - **amel.**: ars asaf bell bry *Calc* coloc con cycl kali-n *Mang* meny *Mur-ac Phos* sars thuj viol-t
    - ⁝ **stitching** pain: ars *Coloc* cycl hr1
    - ⁝ **tearing** pain: mur-ac
  - **hair** agg.; touching the: agar carb-v dulc fd4.de
  - **scalp** agg.; of: lachn c1 melal-alt gya4 ruta fd4.de
- **touch**: ...
  - **vertex** agg.; touching: sabin
- **travelling**: allox tpw4* cortiso sp1
- **trembling**, with (See GENERALS - Trembling - externally - headache)
- **turning**:
  - **agg.**:
    - ⁝ **suddenly**: sil ↓
      - **jerking** pain: sil k*
  - **bed**; in:
    - ⁝ **agg.**: carb-v ↓ chin k2 crot-h meph
      - **bursting** pain: carb-v k2
  - **body** | **agg.**: carb-v k2 cham glon graph lyc merc-i-f nat-c nat-m plan *Sil* vanil fd5.de
  - **eyes**:
    - ⁝ **agg.**: cupr ↓ hep ↓ mur-ac ↓
      - **sore**: cupr hep mur-ac
    - ⁝ **painful** side agg.; to the: con ↓
      - **pressing** pain: con
    - ⁝ **sideways**: *Sil* ↓
      - **pressing** pain: *Sil*
    - ⁝ **upward**: arum-t ↓
      - **shooting** pain: arum-t
  - **head**:
    - ⁝ **after**: lyss ↓
      - **bursting** pain: lyss
    - ⁝ **agg.**: agav-t jl1 ars canth chinin-s clem cocc coloc cupr ↓ erig vml3• *Ery-a* a1 gels genist glon graph hyos ign kali-n lyc k* nat-c nat-m ph-ac phos k* phys pic-ac k* rhod sil spong vanil fd5.de
      - **cutting** pain: cupr
      - **lancinating**: cupr
      - **suddenly**: erig vml3• genist ign irid-met srj5• nat-c
      - **tearing** pain: canth coloc
- **twanging**, as from breaking a piano string: lyc k*
- **twinging**: bell ptk1 *Bry* ptk1 chin ptk1 *Puls* ptk1 sulph ptk1
  - **accompanied** by | **vertigo**: rhus-t ptk1
- **twitching**: arn k* **Bell** k* bry k* carb-v k* chin k* ign k* kali-c k* lyc k* sil k* **Sulph** k*
- **ulcerative** pain: acon k* **Am-c** k* ant-t ars bg2 borx k* *Bov* k* bry bg1 bufo carb-v k* castm caust k* *Chin* bg2 cimic bg2 daph bg2 *Hep* k* kali-bi bg2 kali-c k* kreos lach bg2 lyc bg2 mag-c k* mang k* merc mez bg2 nat-m bg2* nux-v k* olnd bg2 par bg2 petr phos bg2 prun bg2 puls rhod k* rhus-t bg2 sabad bg2 sep k* spig b7a.de stann stront-c k* *Sul-ac* sulph k* *Zinc* bg2
- **unconsciousness**, with: acon aeth agar ambr arg-n arn aur bell *Bov* k* cann-i carb-v castm cocc *Crot-h* cycl ferr glon hep iod kali-c laur mag-c mang *Mosch* **Nat-m** nux-m *Nux-v Petr* k* phos prun puls rhus-t sabin *Sil* stann stram tarax *Verat* verat-v hr1
  - **and** after: bov k*
  - **motion** agg.: calc carb-an rhus-t
- **uncovering**:
  - **body**:
    - ⁝ **agg.**: benz-ac nux-v k2
    - ⁝ **amel.**: cor-r
  - **head**:
    - ⁝ **agg.**: *(↗Uncovering; Uncovering - head - agg.)* bell tl1
    - ⁝ **amel.**: glon bro1 lyc bro1
- **undulating** (See waves)
- **uremic**: am-be mtf11 arn bro1 bapt bro1 cann-i br1* carb-ac bro1 cupr-ar bro1 *Glon* bro1 hyper bro1 phos k2 *Sang* bro1 zinc-pic bro1
- **urination**:
  - **after**:
    - ⁝ **agg.**: caust podo fd3.de•
    - ⁝ **amel.**: agar bg3 fl-ac k* gels mrr1 kali-p fd1.de•
  - **before**, if the call be not attended to: fl-ac k* sep
  - **during**: acon coloc nux-v bg1 *Tab* k* verat hr1
  - **inability** to: con k2*

- **profuse**:
  - **amel.**: *Acon* k* agar bg1 ferr-p **Gels** k* *Ign* k* *Kalm* lac-d al *Meli* *Ph-ac* bro1 sang k* *Sil* k* ter verat k*
- **vaccination**; from: thuj bro1*
- **vaults**, cellars, etc.: *(↗MIND - Fear - narrow)* **Ars** bry carb-an **Puls** *Sep* *Stram*
- **veal**, from eating: kali-n k*
- **vertical**: hydrog ↓
  - **line**; in a: hydrog srj2•
- **vertigo**:
  - **after**: *Calc* kali-bi bg1 phos bg1 plat h2* plb bg2* ran-b bg1 sep h2* til bg1
    - **tearing** pain: plat h2
  - **during** (See VERTIGO - Accompanied - head - pain) *Nat-m* ↓
    - **jerking** pain: *Nat-m* b4a.de
  - **with**: nat-m ↓
    - **lancinating**: nat-m
- **vexation**; after: *(↗anger)* acon *Bry* calc-f sp1 castm *Cham* cocc *Coff* ign ip lyc *Mag-c* **Mez** *Nat-m* nux-v k* *Petr* phos plat k2 ran-b rhus-t **Staph** verat
  - **cramping**: mag-c
  - **cutting** pain: *Mag-c*
  - **shooting** pain: mag-c k*
  - **sore**: **Mez**
  - **stitching** pain: mag-c
- **vinegar**:
  - **agg.**: bell sne teucr k*
  - **applying**, amel.: meli k* op k*
- **violent**: acon k* aesc k2 aeth agar bro1 ail tl1 am-c h2* am-m aml-ns bro1 *Anac* bro1 ant-c h2* *Apis* *Arg-n* k* *Ars* k* ars-s-f k2 asc-c c1 **Aur** bro1* aur-m k2 *Bac* jl2 bamb-a stb2.de• bapt k2 *Bar-c* bar-s k2 **Bell** k* **Bry** k* **Cact** cadm-met gm1 calc-sil k2 cann-s cann-xyz bg2 canth k* carb-v k2 **Carbn-s** caust tl1 chel tl1 *Chin* bro1 cic bg2* *Cimic* bro1 cimx k* cina cinnb coc-c *Cocc* *Coff* colch coloc colum-p sze2• croc k* *Crot-h* k* cupr k* *Cycl* a1 eup-per k2 euphr ferr-ar k2 *Gels* **Glon** k* grat k* *Hell* k* hipp jl2 *Hyos* k* iod h* *Ip* k* kali-ar kali-bi *Kali-br* kali-c *Kali-i* k* kali-p kali-s kali-sil k2 *Kola* stb3• lac-c k2 *Lac-d* **Lach** lat-m bnm6• laur k* led k* **Lil-t** lob-d c1 loxo-recl bnm10• *Lyc* k* lyss mag-c k* mag-p k2 mag-s c1 manc **Meli** k* meph a1 *Merc* *Mez* k* mill k2 *Morph* mosch k* mur-ac bg2 *Nat-m* nat-s k2 nit-ac k2 *Op* k* oreo bro1 *Parathyr* jl2 ph-ac tl1 *Phos* plat k2 plat-m bro1 plb k* psor k2* *Rhus-t* ruta fd4.de *Sang* k* scut bro1 *Sep* **Sil** k* *Sol-ni* spig k2* stann k2 *Staph* h1* *Stram* k* stront-c sk4• stry bro1 sul-ac k2 *Sulph* syph k2 tarax k* ther k* thuj toxo-g jl2 tub k2* vac jl2 valer k2 verat k2 zinc bg2 zinc-val bro1
- **vise**; as if in a: *Anac* bro1 antip bro1 arg-n bro1 *Berb* bro1 *Cact* bro1 cann-i bro1 *Carb-ac* bro1 cimic bro1 coca bro1 *Eup-per* bro1 franc bro1 gels bro1 hyper bro1 mag-p bro1 nit-ac bro1 plac-s rly4• *Plat* bro1 stann bro1 sulph bro1 tub bro1
- **vision**; from complaints of: *Mag-p* k*
- **vivacious** talking, from: **Sulph** ↓
  - **hammering** pain: **Sulph**
- **voice** affects brain; male: *(↗MIND - Fear - men; of [=male)* bar-c
- **vomiting**: acon-ac rly4● agath-anl2• aml-ns vh1 androc srj1• ars k* asar asc-c c1 bamb-a stb2.de• bar-m carc zzh con eug eup-per k2 ferr-p k* gels k2 glon k* **Iris** lach lyc mez nux-v phyt k* pyrog c1 **Sang** tl1 sec sep vanil fd5.de verat [lac-mat sst4]
  - **after**: cham cocc cycl a1 eug ↓ ferr gard-j vlr2• lachn c1 nat-c nat-s ↓ nux-v thuj ↓
    - **burning**: eug k* nat-s k*
    - **tearing** pain: thuj
  - **amel.**: ant-c vh1 arg-n asar k* bry j5.de calc carc zzh chel k2 *Cycl* k* gels glon kali-bi lac-ac stj5• lac-d lach manc k* op k* raph rhus-t hr1 *Sang* k* sep sil stann k* sul-ac k* tab tub c1* vanil fd5.de [heroin sdj2]
    - **pressing** pain: stann
- **waking**:
  - **on**: agar ↓ agath-a ↓ arg-n ↓ canth ↓ cham ↓ chin ↓ choc ↓ cina ↓ cinch ↓ cit-ac ↓ con ↓ galla-q-r ↓ graph ↓ ham ↓ hep ↓ hydr ↓ ind ↓ *Lach* ↓ nux-v ↓ ozone ↓ petr ↓ phos ↓ plan ↓ tarent ↓ thuj ↓ verat ↓
    - **blow**; pain as from a: galla-q-r nl2•
    - **boring** pain: cham

- **waking – on**: ...
    - **bursting** pain: cham k* chin choc srj3• cinch a1 con ham k* hydr *Lach* nux-v
    - **drawing** pain: agar k* agath-a nl2•
    - **lancinating**: tarent
    - **pressing** pain | **outward**: cina a1
    - **pulsating** pain: cit-ac rly4• ozone sde2•
    - **sleep**:
      - **amel.**: sep ↓
        - **boring** pain: sep
    - **sore**: ind plan tarent
    - **stitching** pain: canth k* hep petr thuj
    - **tearing** pain: arg-n graph phos thuj verat
- **walking**: *(↗jar agg.; motion; stepping - agg.)*
  - **about**:
    - **amel.**: canth ↓ hep ↓
      - **stitching** pain: canth hep
  - **after**:
    - **agg.**: bry ↓ hep ↓ nat-c k2 tarax ↓ tell ↓ tritic-vg sna6
      - **stitching** pain: bry hep h2 tarax tell
  - **agg.**: acon act-sp aesc tl1 aeth hr1 agar tl1 allox tpw3* aloe *Alum* alum-p k2 alum-sil k2 am-c k2 anac ang ant-t arn ars ars-i asar aster *Atro* ↓ bar-c bar-i k2 bar-m bar-s k2 **Bell** k* **Bry** bufo ↓ cadm-s calc calc-i k2 calc-p k2 calc-s calc-sil k2 *Caps* k* carb-an *Carb-v* *Carbn-s* cassia-s ↓ castm ↓ caust chel ↓ *Chin* chinin-ar chion cic cina tl1 clem cob *Cocc* coloc con corn crot-t ↓ dig dros ferr ferr-i ferr-p **Glon** gran guaj hell hipp k* hir ↓ hura hyos ign iod kali-bi k2 *Kali-c* *Kali-n* kali-p kali-sil k2 kola stb3• *Lach* k* laur *Led* **Lyc** mag-c mang meny merc merc-i-f mur-ac nat-ar nat-c nat-m k2 nat-p *Nat-s* *Nit-ac* nux-v olnd par *Petr* *Ph-ac* *Phos* phys ↓ phyt plat plb ↓ pneu jl2 podo c1 ptel *Puls* ran-b k* raph rheum rhod *Rhus-t* sabad k* sang k2 *Sars* sel rsj9• *Sep* *Sil* sol-t-ae vml3• spig spong staph stram ↓ stront-c sulph tab tarax tarent tax-br oss1• thea *Ther* thuj ↓ tril-p c1 tritic-vg fd5.de ust vanil fd5.de verat verb viol-t zinc zinc-p k2
    - **boring** pain: bufo coloc k*
    - **burning**: rhus-t
    - **bursting** pain: caps k* carb-an h2 kali-bi sabad k2 stront-c
    - **cutting** pain: calc
    - **drawing** pain: chel coloc k* tritic-vg fd5.de
    - **dull** pain: hir skp7•
    - **jerking** pain: **Bell** *Chin* petr h2
    - **pinching** pain: sil k*
    - **pressing** pain: alum arn ars h2 *Asar* *Bell* *Bry* calc caust *Chin* clem cocc kali-c **Lach** lyc nat-m vanil fd5.de
    - **shooting** pain: bell cassia-s ccrh1• phys
    - **sore**: **Caps** hyos nit-ac nux-v ph-ac phos raph stram
    - **stitching** pain: alum *Atro* a1 bry k* calc carb-an crot-t merc nit-ac plb sep staph k* sulph thuj k*
    - **tearing** pain: castm *Chin* con sars **Spig** tarax
    - **twitching**: **Bell** k*
  - **air**; in open:
    - **after**:
      - **agg.**: *Am-c* bar-c h2 bell *Bov* calc caust chel chin coca coff con h2 ferr *Hep* kali-bi kali-s fd4.de mez mur-ac nicc nit-ac h2 nux-v pall petr plut-n srj7• puls ran-b ran-s rhus-t *Sabad* sep ↓ spig spong **Sulph** zinc
        - **pressing** pain: **Bell** sep zinc
    - **agg.**: acon agar ↓ alum am-c ant-c *Arn* ars-s-f k2 atro bar-s k2 *Bell* borx bov bry *Calc* caust *Chin* chinin-s *Cina* coff *Con* dream-p sdj1• dulc euphr ferr glon ↓ grat hell *Hep* ign kali-ar k2 kali-c kali-m k2 lam laur lil-t *Lyc* mang merc *Mur-ac* nat-c h2 nat-m nicc nit-ac h2 nux-m *Nux-v* par petr plat puls ran-b *Rhus-t* sabad *Sars* sel sep spig *Spong* staph stront-c sul-ac *Sulph* tarax thuj tritic-vg fd5.de vanil fd5.de zinc
      - **burrowing**: agar k*
      - **jerking** pain: *Chin* *Spig*
      - **nail**; as from a: *Thuj*
      - **pressing** pain: agar **Bell** chin con dulc ferr glon hell lil-t staph thuj vanil fd5.de
      - **sore**: *Chin* coff

- **air**; in open – **agg.**: ...
    - **stitching** pain: sul-ac$_{h2}$
    - **tearing** pain: lyc$_{h2}$
  - **amel.**: aeth *Agar* am-c ambr ang **Ant-c** ant-t↓ **Apis** aral aran **Ars** asar bar-c borx$_{k}$* canth carb-an caust chinin-s cimic cina coff coloc cor-r *Croc* crot-t dulc$_{fd4.de}$ eup-pur fago genist glon hep↓ hera$_{c1}$ hippoc-k$_{szs2}$ *Hyos* *Iris* **Kali-s**$_{k}$* *Lach* lap-la$_{sde8.de}$• laur lil-t$_{k2}$* lith-c **Lyc** mag-c *Mag-m* mang merc-i-f mosch *Nat-m* olnd phel **Phos** *Plat* **Puls** ran-b **Rhod** *Rhus-t* sal-fr$_{sle1}$• sang sars *Seneg* *Sep* sol-ni **Sulph** *Thuj* vanil$_{fd5.de}$ viol-t visc$_{sp1}$*
    - **bursting** pain: *Sang*
    - **lancinating**: hep
    - **sore**: *Puls*
    - **tearing** pain: ant-t coloc *Thuj*
- **amel.**: am-c ant-c aran$_{k}$* asar borx calc canth caps carb-ac cham chin chinin-m$_{c1}$ coca coloc *Cycl* dros fago gels glon$_{k}$* *Guaj* ham hep↓ *Hyos* kali-s↓ lac-h$_{sk4}$• **Lyc** mag-c mang *Mur-ac* nad$_{rly4}$• nat-c nat-m$_{k}$* **Phos** puls ran-b **Rhod** **Rhus-t** seneg sep sin-n spig staph sulph symph$_{fd3.de}$• syph$_{xxb}$ *Tarax* *Thuj* vanil$_{fd5.de}$
  - **burning**: canth *Cycl*$_{hr1}$
  - **cutting** pain: *Caps* hep
  - **neuralgic**: mag-c$_{mrr1}$
  - **shooting** pain: *Caps*$_{hr1}$
  - **stitching** pain: *Caps*$_{hr1}$ hep$_{h2}$ kali-s$_{fd4.de}$ vanil$_{fd5.de}$
- **cold** air; in | **agg.**: caps
- **head** erect amel.; with: *Nux-m*
- **must** walk or stand: chin
- **rapidly**:
  - **agg.**: **Bell** **Bry** *Calc* chel ferr-i *Iod* mang nat-c psor$_{al}$ **Puls** tab
    - **lancinating**: *Calc*
- **slowly**:
  - **agg.**: hipp
  - **amel.**: agar coc-c eup-per ferr kali-p$_{k2}$ lyc mur-ac$_{k2}$ **Puls** sep visc
- **tips** of toes; must walk on: crot-h$_{ptk2}$
- **wind**; in the:
  - **agg.**: chin kali-s$_{fd4.de}$ mur-ac nux-v
    - **sore**: chin$_{h1}$

- **wandering** pains: alum-sil$_{k2}$ alumn am-c arg-n$_{bg1}$ berb$_{k2}$ buth-a$_{sp1}$ calc carb-v$_{bg1}$ chin colch dulc$_{fd4.de}$ fic-m$_{gya1}$ glon$_{bg2}$ ign$_{bg2}$ kali-bi$_{k}$* kali-c$_{k2}$ led$_{k}$* luna$_{kg1}$• lyc$_{k}$* mag-p mang$_{bg1}$ med$_{k2}$ *Meli*$_{sne}$ nat-s$_{k}$* ozone$_{sde2}$• phos$_{bg1}$ plan podo *Puls*$_{k}$* ruta$_{fd4.de}$ sabal$_{ptk2}$ *Sang* *Spig* spong$_{fd4.de}$ sulph$_{bg1}$ symph$_{fd3.de}$• tarent$_{k2}$ thuj$_{bg2}$ tritic-vg$_{fd5.de}$ vanil$_{fd5.de}$ [tax$_{jsj7}$]
- **warm**:
  - **applications**:
    - **agg.**: beryl↓ chel$_{k2}$ hir↓ phos$_{k2}$*
      - **bursting** pain: beryl$_{tpw5}$
      - **dull** pain: hir$_{skp7}$•
    - **amel.**: ap-g$_{vml3}$• kali-ar$_{k2}$ mag-p$_{k2}$* symph$_{fd3.de}$• syph$_{k2}$ vanil$_{fd5.de}$
      - **hot** applications: *Arg-n* ars arum-t$_{a}$ *Aur* *Bry* chin cinnb colch coloc fic-m$_{gya1}$ *Gels* glon iris kali-bi$_{a}$ *Kali-c* kali-i kali-p$_{a}$ lach mag-m **Mag-p** nux-m pot-e$_{rly4}$• rhod$_{k2}$ sep$_{k2}$ **Sil** sulph$_{k2}$ symph$_{fd3.de}$•
  - **bathing** | **amel.**: lac-h$_{sk4}$• neon$_{srj5}$•
  - **bed**:
    - **agg.**: arg-n↓ **Bell** *Calc*↓ *Carb-v* **Lyc**$_{k}$* merc↓ *Mez* puls↓ *Staph*$_{hr1}$ sulph↓ thuj↓
      - **boring** pain: arg-n puls
      - **sore**: *Calc* *Carb-v*
      - **stitching** pain: thuj
      - **tearing** pain: lyc merc sulph thuj
    - **amel.**: aur-m↓ caust↓
      - **drawing** pain: caust
      - **tearing** pain: aur-m caust
  - **clothing**: | **agg.**: arum-t$_{c1}$
  - **drinks**:
    - **agg.**: *Arum-t* kali-ar$_{k2}$ **Phos** **Puls** *Sulph* ter$_{a}$ ther$_{k2}$
    - **amel.**: stront-c$_{sk4}$• sulph$_{k2}$ ther$_{k2}$

- **warm**: ...
  - **food**:
    - **agg.**: *Arum-t* mag-c$_{mrr1}$ mez *Phos* *Puls* *Sulph*
      - **hot** food: sulph$_{j5.de}$
  - **hand**; warm | **amel.**: cinnb iris
  - **room**:
    - **agg.**: abrom-a$_{ks5}$ acon aeth **All-c**$_{k}$* allox$_{tpw4}$ aloe *Alum* alum-p$_{k2}$ am-m ant-c **Apis** *Arg-n*$_{hr1}$ *Arn* *Ars* ars-i ars-s-f$_{k2}$ *Arum-t* asaf aur-s$_{k2}$ bar-c bar-i$_{k2}$ bar-s$_{k2}$ *Bell* *Bov* bry bufo calc calc-i$_{k2}$ calc-s$_{k2}$ cann-i carb-an$_{a1}$ **Carb-v** *Carbn-s* *Caust* cham *Chel* *Cimic* cob coc-c coca coff colch com *Croc* euph ferr-i ham hip-ac↓ hydr$_{k}$* hyos *Iod* ip kali-i *Kali-n* **Kali-s**$_{k}$* lact$_{k}$* laur *Led* lil-t$_{k}$* *Lyc* *Lyss* mag-c mag-m *Mang* meli$_{vml3}$• merc-i-f$_{a1}$ mez$_{k}$* *Mosch* *Nat-ar* nat-c *Nat-m* nat-p nicc olib-sac$_{wmh1}$ ph-ac **Phos**$_{k}$* pic-ac$_{k2}$ **Plat** plb ptel$_{c1}$ **Puls** ran-b$_{k2}$ ran-s rhod sal-fr$_{sle1}$• sang sanic$_{c1}$ sec$_{a1}$ sel **Seneg** sep sin-a$_{a1}$ sin-n$_{k}$* sol-ni *Spong*$_{k}$* *Stram* sul-i$_{k2}$ *Sulph* tab thuj$_{k2}$ til$_{k}$* *Verat* verb *Zinc* zinc-p$_{k2}$
      - **burning**: apis **Phos**
      - **dull** pain: hip-ac$_{sp1}$
      - **pressing** pain: acon **Apis** cann-i *Coc-c* **Puls**
      - **sore**: *Coff* *Puls*
      - **stunning** pain: nat-c nat-m *Phos* *Puls*
    - **amel.**: *Am-c* *Aur* bell bov bry *Carb-v*↓ cham chel **Chin** cocc *Coff* dulc$_{fd4.de}$ eup-per ferr graph$_{k2}$ hep kali-c *Lac-c* lycpr$_{c1}$ mag-c **Mang** *Merc* nux-m *Nux-v* rhus-t *Sil* spig staph sul-ac **Sulph** syph$_{c1}$ thuj valer zing
      - **sore**: eup-per
      - **tearing** pain: *Carb-v*
    - **closed**: abrom-a↓
      - **dull** pain: abrom-a$_{ks5}$
    - **entering** a warm room; when | **cold** air; from: caust chel laur mez nat-m *Nicc* *Ran-b* ran-s rhus-t sabad sec$_{a1}$ spong
  - **stove**:
    - **agg.**: **Ant-c** *Apis* *Arn* *Arum-t* *Bar-c* bry bufo$_{k2}$ cimic com euph **Glon** lac-d lyc$_{bg1}$ *Manc* merc nux-v *Phos* *Puls* rhus-t *Sanic* *Zinc*
      - **shooting** pain: bar-c$_{a1}$
      - **stitching** pain: bar-c$_{h2}$
  - **tea**:
    - **amel.**: glon↓
      - **pressing** pain: glon
  - **washing** the hands agg.: phos$_{k2}$
  - **wraps** | **agg.**: arum-t$_{k2}$ sul-i$_{k2}$
- **warm**; becoming:
  - **agg.**: *Acon* *Aloe* am-c **Ant-c** *Apis* arg-n arn ars$_{k2}$ *Arum-t* aster$_{a}$ bar-c bar-s$_{k2}$ **Bell**$_{k}$* brom$_{k2}$ *Bry* calc calc-s calc-sil$_{k2}$ camph caps **Carb-v**$_{k}$* *Carbn-s* chel$_{k2}$ con dig dros form **Glon** grat ign *Ip* *Kali-c* kali-p *Kali-s* kali-sil$_{k2}$ *Kalm* kola$_{stb3}$• **Lyc** nat-ar nat-c$_{vh}$* *Nat-m* nux-m op petr↓ petr-ra$_{shn4}$• phos ptel sel$_{c1}$ *Sep* *Sil*$_{k}$* staph *Stram* sul-i$_{k2}$ *Sulph* *Thuj*$_{k}$* zinc zinc-p$_{k2}$
    - **sore**: petr
    - **walking**, agg. head, but amel. pain of limbs: lyc
  - **amel.**: mosch$_{k2}$
- **warmth**:
  - **agg.**: *All-c*$_{bro1}$ allox$_{sp1}$ aloe$_{bro1}$ bell-p$_{sp1}$ beryl$_{sp1}$ bry$_{bro1}$ calc-f$_{sp1}$ cortiso$_{sp1}$ dulc$_{fd4.de}$ euphr$_{bro1}$ glon$_{bro1}$* hyper$_{bro1}$ kali-i↓ lach$_{mrr1}$ *Led*$_{bro1}$ nicc$_{bro1}$ nux-v$_{k2}$ phos$_{bro1}$* puls$_{bro1}$* sel$_{mrr1}$ sep$_{bro1}$ spong$_{fd4.de}$ thuj$_{k2}$ visc$_{sp1}$
    - **burning**: kali-i$_{mrr1}$
    - **heat** agg.: kali-i↓
      - **cutting** pain: kali-i
      - **lancinating**: kali-i
    - **stitching** pain: kali-i$_{mrr1}$
  - **amel.**: am-c$_{bro1}$ *Ars*↓ chin$_{bro1}$ chlam-tr$_{bcx2}$• coloc$_{bro1}$ ichth$_{bro1}$ mag-c↓ mag-p$_{bro1}$* *Nux-m*↓ nux-v$_{bro1}$ *Phos*$_{bro1}$ rhus-t$_{bro1}$ sil$_{bro1}$* stront-c↓ vanil$_{fd5.de}$
    - **burning**: *Ars*$_{mrr1}$
    - **drawing** pain: stront-c

- **amel.**: ...
  - **heat** amel.: *Arg-n* ars *Aur* aur-ar k2 *Bell* bell-p sp1 *Bry* caps *Caust Chin* cinnb cocc colch *Coloc Gels* hyos *Ign* iris kali-bi k2 *Kali-c* kali-i kali-sil k2 lach *Mag-m* **Mag-p** *Nit-ac Nux-m Nux-v* pot-e rly4• *Psor* rhod *Rhus-t* **Sil** spong fd4.de stann staph *Stram* stront-c sulph sumb syc ↓ symph fd3.de•
    - **cutting** pain: *Lach*
    - **pulsating** pain: syc bka1*•
    - **stitching** pain: kali-c
    - **tearing** pain: mag-p *Rhod Rhus-t* staph stram
  - **neuralgic**: mag-c mrr1
  - **sore**: *Nux-m*

- **washing**: (↗*bathing)*
  - **after**:
    - **amel.**: ferr ↓ phos ↓ *Psor* ↓
      - **pressing** pain: ferr phos *Psor*
  - **face**:
    - **agg.**: cop ↓
      - **stitching** pain: cop
    - **amel.**: petr-ra shn4•
      - **but** agg. after washing: spig ↓
        - **stitching** pain: spig
  - **feet** | **amel.**: nat-s
  - **hands** | **agg.**: rhus-r
  - **head**:
    - **after** | **agg.**: *Am-c Ant-c* bar-c bell k* bry *Calc* calc-s canth carb-v cham glon ham fd3.de• lyc merc nit-ac *Nux-m* olib-sac wmh1 phos puls *Rhus-t* ruta fd4.de *Sep* spig stront-c *Sulph*
- **water**; running:
  - **hearing**: *Lyss* k*
  - **sight** of: lyss bro1*
- **waves**; in: (↗*paroxysmal)* agath-a nl2• ant-t k* asaf k* bamb-a stb2.de• bell chin k* cocc k* cystein-l rly4• ferr fic-m gya1 lach k2 ozone sde2• plat **Sep** spig k* spong fd4.de symph fd3.de• viol-t k* zinc [bell-p-sp dcm1]
- **weather**:
  - **change** of weather: am-c k2 *Ars* benz-ac k2 *Bry Calc Calc-p* k* *Carb-v* k* cimic k2 dulc bro1 guaj bro1 lach mang k2 meli sne* merc ↓ mez moni rfm1• nat-c k2 nat-sil fd3.de• *Nux-m Ph-ac Phos Phyt* bro1 *Psor* k* *Ran-b* k* *Rhod* k* **Rhus-t** k* *Sil* spig bro1 vanil fd5.de verb vip
    - **burning**: merc k2
    - **stitching** pain: merc k2 vip k*
  - **cloudy** weather: | **agg.**: bry *Calc Cham Chin Dulc Mang* merc *Nux-m* **Rhus-t** *Sep* sulph
  - **cold**:
    - **agg.**: acon *Agar Am-c Ars Aur* aur-ar k2 bamb-a ↓ *Bell* **Bry** *Calc* calc-p k2 calc-s *Camph Caps* carb-v *Caust* cocc *Colch* con **Dulc** *Hell* **Hep** hyos ign kali-bi k2 kali-c *Kali-i* lyc *Merc Mosch* nat-m *Nux-m* **Nux-v** *Ph-ac* phos psil ft1 rhod k* **Rhus-t** *Sabad* sep *Spig Stront-c Sulph* trios ↓ verat
      - **dull** pain: trios rsj11•
      - **pressing** pain: bamb-a stb2.de•
    - **dry** | **agg.**: acon *Asar* bry *Caust* **Hep** *Nux-v* sabad *Spong*
    - **wet**:
      - **agg.**: *Am-c* ars brom **Bry Calc** calc-sil k2 carb-an *Carb-v* cimic colch **Dulc** k* **Glon** k* *Lach Lyc Mang* med k2 **Merc** *Mez* mosch nat-c nat-sil fd3.de• **Nux-m Nux-v** phyt **Rhod Rhus-t Sil** *Spig* stront-c **Sulph** thuj k2 tub *Verat* zing
        - **tearing** pain: **Calc** *Rhod Rhus-t*
      - **amel.**: caust ↓
        - **tearing** pain: caust
  - **snowy** | **agg.**: rhod c1
  - **stormy**:
    - **agg.**: asar *Aur* aur-ar k2 aur-s k2 bry cham chin lach meli sne mur-ac nat-c k2 nat-p mrr1 *Nux-m* nux-v phos puls *Rhod* k* *Rhus-t* k* *Spig*
    - **before**: carc jl2
  - **warm**:
    - **amel.**: calc
- **weather – warm**: ...
  - **begins** with the warm weather: dream-p sdj1• dulc fd4.de glon **Nat-c** nat-s
  - **wet** | **agg.**: glon bg1
  - **wet**:
    - **agg.**: **Calc** ↓ calc-f sp1 carb-an ↓ *Nat-s* ↓ oxal-a rly4• phyt ↓ ran-b mrr1 rhod tl1 rhus-t mrr1 sulph ↓ *Tub* jl2
      - **bursting** pain: carb-an
      - **drawing** pain: *Rhod Rhus-t*
      - **pressing** pain: sulph
      - **sore**: **Calc** *Nat-s* phyt
    - **amel.**: caust ↓ ozone sde2•
      - **drawing** pain: caust
  - **windy**: bamb-a ↓
    - **pressing** pain: bamb-a stb2.de•
- **wedge** like (See plug)
- **weeping**; from: aur-m-n wbt2• vanil fd5.de
  - **suppressed**: cypra-eg sde6.de• *Uva* vh
- **weight** on the shoulders, from carrying: mag-s
- **well** especially before the attack; feels: aids nl2•
- **wet** agg.; getting: adam skp7• ars *Bell* bry **Calc** *Colch Dulc* hep kali-c *Led* lyc meli sne *Nat-m* nux-m phos *Puls* **Rhus-t** *Sep*
  - **feet**: gels meli vml3• phos *Puls Rhus-t* sang hr1 sep *Sil*
  - **head**: bar-c *Bell* led phos puls rhus-t k2 sep
  - **perspiration**; during: acon calc *Colch* dulc *Rhus-t* sep
- **wind**:
  - **cold**:
    - **agg.**●: (↗*cold - air - agg.)* *Acon* anag c1 androc srj1• *Aur Bry* calc-p k2 **Hep** *Ign Lac-c* lyc ↓ *Mez Mur-ac* nat-sil fd3.de• **Nux-v** *Psor* **Rhus-t** *Sanic Sep* symph fd3.de•
      - **cutting** pain: lyc h2
    - **amel.**: mur-ac hr1
  - **exposure** to; from: acon bry cham chin dulc fd4.de ham kali-s fd4.de mur-ac nat-s bg1 nux-m k2 nux-v *Phos* pot-e rly4• *Sanic Sep* spong fd4.de
- **wine**:
  - **agg.**: ant-c arn *Ars* bell cact *Calc* calc-sil k2 *Carb-an Carb-v* coff con **Gels** k* glon k* ign kali-chl kali-m k2 lach *Led* lyc nat-ar *Nat-c* nat-m nux-m *Nux-v* k* *Ox-ac* k* petr *Ran-b Rhod* k* rhus-t sabad sang k2 *Sel* k* *Sil* stront-c sulph j5.de symph fd3.de• ter verat **Zinc** k* zinc-p k2
    - **sour** wine: *Ant-c* ars ferr sulph
  - **amel.**: *Arg-n* k* calc coca
- **winking**: *All-c* k*
- **winter** headaches: aloe bro1 *Aur-m-n Bism* k* carb-v bro1 meli vml3• nux-v bro1 sabad bro1 *Sil* **Sulph** k*
  - **alternating** with | **diarrhea** in summer: podo al1*
- **women**; in: calc-sil k2 epiph br1
- **wood** lying across occiput; as if a piece of: psor lp
- **work**:
  - **amel.**: merc-i-f
  - **from**: anac bufo pic-ac tl1
  - **while** doing some disagreeable: chin
- **worm** complaints: *Calc* chin *Cina* graph nux-v plat sabad *Sil* spig *Sulph*
- **worm** creeping; as from a: alum b4a.de*
- **wrapping** up head:
  - **agg.**: *Acon Apis Arum-t Borx* bry *Calc* calc-i k2 *Carb-v* cham *Cob* ferr *Ferr-i* ferr-p gels *Glon* ign **Iod** lach *Led* **Lyc** merc nit-ac op **Phos** pic-ac k2 plat **Puls** sec seneg sep *Spig* staph sul-i k2 *Sulph* thuj *Verat*
  - **amel.**: agar k* apis k* arg-met *Arg-n* k* *Ars Aur Bell* k* benz-ac *Bry Colch Con* cor-r bg1 *Cupr Gels* glon bro1* **Hep** hera c1 hyos ign bro1 kali-ar kali-c k* kali-i kali-m k2 kali-p kali-sil k2 lac-d bro1 *Lach* mag-c *Mag-m* k* *Mag-p* meny mez mur-ac nat-m *Nit-ac Nux-m* **Nux-v** ph-ac *Phos* pic-ac k* *Psor* k* puls bro1 **Rhod Rhus-t** *Sanic Sep* **Sil** k* *Squil Stront-c* k* syph bg1 *Thuj* tub bg1
    - **bursting** pain: *Mag-m*
    - **pressing** pain: kali-c
    - **tearing** pain: *Phos* rhod *Rhus-t* sil
  - **desire** to wrap up head: gink-b sbd1•

- **wrapping** up warmly:
  - **amel.**: aur↓ **Sil**↓
    - ⁝ **burning**: aur **Sil**
- **wrenching**: ozone sde2•
- **wrinkling** forehead:
  - **agg.**: ars mang nat-m k* petr-ra shn4•
  - **amel.**: calc-caust caust phos k* sulph
- **writing**:
  - **agg.**: aran arg-n ars asaf *Aur* borx bung-fa mtf *Calc* calc-sil k2 carb-an caust cimic hr1 clem dros *Ferr* ferr-i gent-l glon ign *Kali-c* kali-p lyc *Lyss* manc meph nat-c↓ **Nat-m** phos ran-b raph bg1 rhus-r *Rhus-t* *Sil* vanil fd5.de
    - ⁝ **boring** pain: dros
    - ⁝ **pressing** pain: borx carb-an ferr-i gent-l k* ign kali-c nat-c vanil fd5.de
    - ⁝ **sore**: aur
    - ⁝ **tearing** pain: ran-b
  - **amel.**: hydrog srj2•
- **yawning**:
  - **agg.**: agar bar-c chin cycl kali-c bro1 mag-c nux-v ozone sde2• phyt propr sa3• staph bro1
    - ⁝ **shooting** pain: bar-c
  - **amel.**: mur-ac nat-m staph
  - **ends** with yawning: ign h1 mur-ac↓ staph h1
    - ⁝ **tearing** pain: mur-ac staph

▽ - **extending** to:
  - **right** side: anac asaf castm eupi hell
  - **left** side: camph cann-s ruta fd4.de *Spig* staph
  - **all** directions: bry bg2 ferr bg2 ip bg2 kalm bg2 lach bg2
    - ⁝ **radiating** from one small spot to (See spot; in - extending - all)
  - ○ **Around** the head: calc-s
  - **Back**: aloe anac bell k* bry bg2 calc k* caust dig graph b4a.de kali-n lyc mag-c mosch nat-m k* nit-ac k* petr phos k* phyt bg2 podo c1 prun *Puls* k* rhod rhus-t ruta fd4.de samb sep sil spig spong stann k* stront-c sul-ac thuj k*
    - ⁝ **Lower** part: gels bg2 med bg2 nat-s bg2 nux-m bg2 nux-v bg2 podo bg2 sep bg2 sulph bg2
  - **Base** of brain: ambr cina laur mang phos senn xan c1
  - **Cervical** region: aids nl2• aml-ns bg2 amp rly4• anac bar-c bell bro1 berb *Bry* k* bung-fa mtf calc-sil k2 chel k* chin cimic k* cocc bg2* des-ac rbp6 dulc bro1 fic-m gya1 gels k2* gink-b sbd1• *Goss* bro1 guaj *Hell* bro1 jac-g kali-bi bg2 kali-c kali-n kalm bg2* ketogl-ac rly4• kola stb3• lac-loxod-a hrn2• *Lach* k* lil-t bg2* lyc k* mand sp1 merc mosch nat-m k* nat-s bro1 nicc-s bro1 nux-m k* *Nux-v* bg2* onos bg2* *Oreo* bro1 *Ph-ac* bro1 phel bg2* *Pic-ac* bro1 pot-e rly4• sabin scut bro1 sep b4a.de *Sil* bro1 spong fd4.de tarent bg2 vanil fd5.de verat-v bro1 viol-o bg2 viol-t bg1 ziz bg1
    - ⁝ **Shoulders**; and: lach bg2
  - **Cheek**: calc b4a.de hep *Hyper* indg rhus-t
  - **Cheeks**: calc↓
    - ⁝ **burrowing**: calc h2
  - **Chest**: cham bg2 con hyper nat-m k* ruta fd4.de
    - ⁝ **left**: con bg2
  - **Chest** or neck: *Nat-m*↓
    - ⁝ **stitching** pain: *Nat-m*
  - **Chin**: hyper bg2* tritic-vg fd5.de
  - **Ear**: nux-v↓ sulph↓
    - ⁝ **tearing** pain: nux-v sulph h2
  - **Ears**: agar cadm-met↓ calc-ar kr1 choc srj3• cist k2 hippoc-k szs2 kola stb3• lach lyc b4a.de mag-m b4a.de merc nit-ac b4a.de nux-v puls rhus-t sep b4a.de tritic-vg fd5.de vanil fd5.de
    - ⁝ **right**: ars-s-f k2
    - ⁝ **boring** pain: sep h2
    - ⁝ **drawing** pain: mag-m h2 sep h2
    - ⁝ **maddening** pain: cadm-met gm1
    - ⁝ **stitching** pain: rhus-t tritic-vg fd5.de
  - **Elbows**: kali-n bg1

- **extending** to: ...
  - **Epigastrium**: thuj bg1
  - **Eyes**: *Arg-n* asaf *Bar-c* b4a.de brom cadm-met↓ *Calc* k* carb-v b4a.de* caust *Chin* bg3 cimic k* croc *Crot-h* dulc fd4.de falco-pe nl2• fic-m gya1 hippoc-k szs2 ign *Kali-c* k* kali-s *Lach* led lith-c bg3 lyc b4a.de *Lyss* mag-m mang bg3 merc nat-c bg3 nat-m k* nat-ox rly4• nicc **Nit-ac** k* ph-ac bg3 **Phos** b4a.de* prun↓ **Puls** rhus-t ruta↓ *Seneg* sep b4a.de *Sil* b4a.de* *Spig* **Sulph** k* symph fd3.de• tritic-vg fd5.de vanil fd5.de *Zinc* b4a.de*
    - ⁝ **left**: dulc fd4.de ger-i rly4• ign hr1 nicc↓ olib-sac wmh1
      - ⁝ **tearing** pain | **paroxysmal**: nicc
    - ⁝ **burrowing**: calc h2
    - ⁝ **drawing** pain: **Nit-ac**
    - ⁝ **maddening** pain: cadm-met gm1
    - ⁝ **neuralgic**: prun mrr1
    - ⁝ **pressing** pain: ruta fd4.de sil h2 tritic-vg fd5.de vanil fd5.de
    - ⁝ **stitching** pain: *Calc* *Kali-c* *Lach* *Spig* **Sulph** vanil fd5.de
    - ⁝ **Out** of: sep↓ sil↓
      - ⁝ **stitching** pain: sep h2 sil h2
      - ⁝ **tearing** pain: sil h2*
  - **Face**: am-m anac ant-t aran arg-met *Bry* calc b4a.de falco-pe nl2• graph k* guaj indg ip mrr1 kola stb3• lyc mag-m nat-m phos puls rhus-t ruta fd4.de sars seneg sil spig squil↓ *Staph*↓ tarent thuj vanil fd5.de
    - ⁝ **drawing** pain: ant-t aran graph mag-m h2 seneg
    - ⁝ **stitching** pain: rhus-t sars
    - ⁝ **tearing** pain: am-m anac bry guaj lyc sil squil *Staph* thuj
  - **Fingers** | **Tips**: camph
  - **Forehead**: aloe arg-n bg2 bar-c **Bell** borx *Bry* carb-v chin cocc bg2 cupr dios ferr fic-m gya1 gran hippoc-k szs2 kali-bi bg2 kali-c kali-s kreos bg2 lach bg2 lact olnd ph-ac prun spig bg2 stann staph sulph til vanil fd5.de viol-t
    - ⁝ **Eyes**; above: hippoc-k szs2
  - **Forehead**; left: ph-ac↓
    - ⁝ **pressing** pain: ph-ac h2
  - **Frontal** eminence: guaj↓
    - ⁝ **stitching** pain: guaj
  - **Heart**: thuj bg1
  - **Here** and there: am-c↓ ambr↓ asar↓ bapt↓ calc↓ hydr-ac↓ ip↓ mag-c↓ mag-s↓ mosch↓ nicc↓ nux-v↓ plb↓ rat↓ stront-c↓ sul-ac↓
    - ⁝ **drawing** pain: ambr ip mosch nux-v
    - ⁝ **shooting** pain: am-c bapt calc hydr-ac mag-c mag-s nicc plb rat sul-ac
      - ⁝ **flying**: asar calc stront-c
  - **Jaws**: amp rly4• *Arg-n* k* bell k* bry bg2 calc-p k* cham bg2 *Chin* bg2 con bg2 gels bg2 kali-c bg2 kali-chl kreos bg2 mez nad rly4• nat-m bg2 *Ph-ac* phos bg2* *Plat* bg2 podo fd3.de• rhus-t bg2 spig stront-c bg2 vanil fd5.de
    - ⁝ **Lower** jaws: arg-met bg2 bar-c bg2 bell bg2 brom bg2 cham bg2 nat-m bg2
    - ⁝ **Upper** jaws: acon bg2 kali-bi bg2 phos bg2
  - **Limbs**, through: acet-ac
  - **Malar** bone: bell↓ cina↓ indg↓ rhus-t↓
    - ⁝ **cramping**: bell
    - ⁝ **pressing** pain: cina a1
    - ⁝ **stitching** pain: indg rhus-t
  - **Malar** bones: brom bg2 kali-chl bg2 mosch bg2 sang bg2
    - ⁝ **Upper**: nux-v h1 tritic-vg fd5.de
  - **Mouth**: ip mrr1
  - **Nape** of neck: *Bar-c* b4a.de calc b4a.de ferr b7a.de graph b4a.de kali-c↓ lyc b4a.de *Mosch* b7a.de puls b7a.de *Sabin* b7a.de sep b4a.de
    - ⁝ **pressing** pain: kali-c h2 lyc h2
  - **Neck** (See cervical) anac↓ *Chin*↓ graph↓ *Kalm*↓ *Merc*↓
    - ⁝ **drawing** pain: graph
    - ⁝ **tearing** pain: anac *Chin* *Kalm* *Merc*
  - **Nose**: agar ant-t ars bism k* borx calc b4a.de* cimic bg1 colch *Glon* guaj **Lach** lachn bg1 lyc k* lyss nat-c nux-v parth gm1 ph-ac bg1 phos rhus-t b7a.de vanil fd5.de zinc b4a.de
    - ⁝ **boring** pain: phos

- **Nose**: ...
  - **burrowing**: calc h2 *Phos*
  - **drawing** pain: ant-t
  - **tearing** pain: lyc nat-c nux-v
  - **Root** of nose: agar *Bism* hydrog srj2• kali-c kali-n *Lach* *Lyc*↓ nux-v h1 rhus-t↓ vanil fd5.de
    - **pulsating** pain: hydrog srj2•
    - **stitching** pain: *Kali-c* *Lyc* rhus-t
  - **Tip**: dig c1
- **Occiput**: *Ars*↓ bell calc calc-sil k2 carb-v cench k2 chel glon helon *Lyc*↓ mag-c↓ nat-c op phos bg1 pieri-b mlk9.de pip-m **Prun** puls rheum↓ *Sep* **Thuj** til vanil fd5.de
  - **right** side: phos **Prun**
  - **left** side: calc-act
  - **drawing** pain: *Ars* glon vanil fd5.de
  - **stitching** pain: carb-v *Lyc* mag-c puls vanil fd5.de
  - **tearing** pain: rheum h
- **Out**; from within: bell↓ dulc↓ puls↓ sep↓ zinc↓
  - **boring** pain: bell b4.de* dulc k* puls k* sep zinc
- **Outward**: acon bg2 asaf bg2 **Bell** bg2 *Bry* bg2 carb-v bg2 *Chin* bg2 con bg2 dulc bg2 kola stb3• kreos bg2 lach bg2 laur bg2 mag-m bg2 nat-m bg2 nux-m bg2 ph-ac bg2 phos bg2 prun bg2 rhod bg2 rhus-t bg2 sabad bg2 samb bg2 sang bg2 *Sep* bg2 *Sil* bg2 spig bg2 spong bg2 stann bg2 staph bg2 sulph bg2
  - **Eyes**; to: usn bg2
- **Scapula**: puls
  - **right**: chel bg1
- **Scapulae**: puls↓
  - **tearing** pain: puls
- **Shoulder**: arge-pl rwt5• glon graph mand sp1 podo c1 spig cp vanil fd5.de
- **Shoulders**, between: glon↓
  - **burning**: glon k2
- **Spine**: kali-n↓ *Mosch*↓ thuj↓ vanil↓
  - **drawing** pain: kali-n *Mosch* thuj vanil fd5.de
- **Spine**; down the: bell bro1 cimic lp* *Cocc* k* dirc c1 dulc bro1 *Gels* bro1 *Goss* bro1 *Hell* bro1 nat-m bro1 nat-s bro1 nicc-s bro1 nux-v bg1 *Oreo* bro1 *Ph-ac* bro1 *Pic-ac* bro1 scut bro1 *Sil* bro1 *Syph* bg1 verat-v bro1
- **Teeth**: calc b4a.de **Chin** crot-h cupr bg1 cystein-l rly4• ferr br1* graph ign ip c1* kalm kola stb3• kreos lach lyc k* lycps-v lyss mag-c bg1 mag-m b4a.de merc mez petr b4a.de psor bg1 puls rhus-t h1* ruta fd4.de sep k* sil staph
  - **boring** pain: sep h2
  - **burrowing**: calc h2
  - **drawing** pain: mag-m h2 sep h2
  - **neuralgic**: kreos mrr1
  - **pulling**; like: staph k*
  - **tearing** pain: chin lyc *Merc* *Staph*
  - **Roots** of: ip hr1 kreos mrr1
- **Teeth**, ears and neck: *Merc*↓
  - **stitching** pain: *Merc*
- **Teeth**; downward into: *Kalm*↓ melal-alt↓ sep↓
  - **shooting** pain: *Kalm* melal-alt gya4 sep
- **Temple**; right: carb-v↓
  - **tearing** pain: carb-v
- **Temples**: asar carb-v↓ fum rly4• sep↓ vanil fd5.de
  - **boring** pain: sep h2
  - **drawing** pain: asar sep h2
  - **stitching** pain: carb-v h2
- **Throat**: anac merc psor bg1 tarent
  - **tearing** pain: anac merc
- **Tongue**: *Ip*
  - **Root** of: ip mrr1
- **Upper** limbs: mand sp1
- **Vertex**: agath-a nl2• glon par sep spig staph vanil fd5.de
  - **shooting** pain: sep

- **extending** to: ...
  - **Whole** head; over:
    - **bed**:
      - **going** to bed:
        - **after**:
          - **returning** daily, after a walk on entering a room: sabad↓
            - **boring** pain | **twisting**, screwing pain from right side of head to both temples: sabad k*
  - **Zygoma**: *Hyper* kali-chl bg1

○ - **Around**: calc-p↓ calc-s↓
  - **tearing** pain: calc-p calc-s
- **Arteries**: caust↓
  - **pulsating** pain: caust h2
- **Back** of head and neck, on: cann-i↓
  - **blow**; pain as from a: cann-i
- **Bones**: acon bg2 agn b7.de* *Ant-c* k* *Arg-met* k* asaf k2 **Aur** k* bar-c k* *Bell* bry *Calc* k* canth k* carb-v k* caust cham k* **Chin** cina bg2 clem h2* coc-c↓ cocc cupr k* eup-per bro1 graph guaj **Hep** hydrog srj2• ign ip k* kali-bi bg2* kalm k2 lach bg2 led↓ *Lyc* mang **Merc** k* *Merc-c* b4a.de merc-i-r c1 *Mez* k* nat-c **Nit-ac** k* nux-v k* ozone sde2• *Ph-ac* k* *Phos* k* phyt k2 *Plat*↓ podo fd3.de• ptel hr1* puls rhod k* rhus-t *Ruta* k* sabad sabin k* samb k* **Sep** *Sil* sphing↓ spig staph k* sulph syph hr1* thres-a sze7• thuj↓ tub k2 vanil fd5.de verat viol-t k* zinc
  - **night**: *Aur* br1 *Syph* mrr1
  - **aching**: tub dp•
  - **boring** pain: led bg2 sphing kk3.fr spig kk3.fr vanil fd5.de
  - **drawing** pain: *Merc* bg2 thuj bg2
  - **hacking** pain: calc bg2
  - **plug**; as from a: *Plat* b4a.de
  - **scraped**; as if: mez k2
  - **tearing** pain: coc-c bg2 kali-bi bg2 *Spig* bg2
- **Brain**: *Acon*↓ *Aesc*↓ aeth↓ agar↓ agath-a↓ *Agn*↓ **Alum**↓ alum-sil↓ am-br↓ am-c↓ anac↓ ang↓ ant-t↓ arg-met↓ arg-n↓ *Arn*↓ ars↓ asaf↓ asar↓ aster↓ aur↓ bapt↓ bar-c↓ *Bell*↓ *Bell-p*↓ bov↓ bros-gau↓ **Bry**↓ calc↓ calc-p↓ camph↓ *Cann-i*↓ *Canth*↓ carb-ac↓ *Carb-v*↓ carbn-o↓ carl↓ cham↓ **Chin**↓ cimic↓ cina↓ coc-c↓ *Cocc*↓ coff↓ colch↓ coloc↓ colocin↓ con↓ *Crot-c*↓ *Cupr*↓ cycl↓ dulc↓ euphr↓ eupi↓ flor-p↓ **Gels**↓ gink-b↓ *Glon*↓ gran↓ graph↓ *Guaj*↓ hell↓ helo↓ helo-s↓ hep↓ hydr↓ hydr-ac↓ hyper↓ *Ign*↓ ind↓ indg↓ iod↓ *Ip*↓ kali-c↓ kali-n↓ kola↓ **Lac-c**↓ *Lach*↓ laur↓ led↓ lil-t↓ lyc↓ mag-c↓ mag-s↓ manc↓ mang↓ med↓ meny↓ *Merc*↓ mez↓ mill↓ morph↓ *Mosch*↓ mur-ac↓ **Nat-m**↓ **Nit-ac**↓ *Nux-v*↓ oci-sa↓ *Olnd*↓ op↓ ox-ac↓ par↓ petr↓ *Ph-ac*↓ phel↓ **Phos**↓ phys↓ phyt↓ plac-s↓ plan↓ plat↓ plb↓ prun↓ *Psor*↓ *Puls*↓ rhod↓ *Rhus-t*↓ rhus-v↓ rumx↓ ruta↓ sabad↓ sabin↓ sars↓ scut↓ sep↓ *Sil*↓ sol-ni↓ *Spig*↓ spong↓ stann↓ *Staph*↓ stront-c↓ sul-ac↓ tarent↓ tell↓ ther↓ thuj↓ tritic-vg↓ *Verat*↓
  - **left**: hydrog srj2•
  - **morning**: kali-bi lach ruta spig tub c1
    - **rising** | **after** | **agg.**: ruta staph
      - **agg.**: staph↓
        - **motion** agg., rest and warmth amel., passes off with yawning | **torn**; as if (See rest - amel. - torn; warmth - amel. - torn; yawning - amel. - torn)
        - **torn**; as if: staph k*
  - **forenoon**: fl-ac indg ran-b
  - **afternoon**: bar-c hell iris lact mag-s merc-i-f phos↓ (non:uran-met k) uran-n
    - **sore**: phos h2
  - **evening**: agn all-c dulc a1 nat-m par phos ran-b zinc
  - **boring** pain: agar bg2 dulc bg2 mur-ac bg2 olnd bg2 stann bg2
  - **burning**: *Acon* alum-sil k2 arn k* bell k* *Canth* carb-ac dulc fd4.de *Glon* helo c1 helo-s c1* hydr-ac k* med k2 ox-ac k2 ph-ac h2* **Phos** k* *Verat*
  - **bursting** pain | **burst** out; as if it would: *Aesc* vh1 alum arg-n cimic con flor-p rsj3• *Glon* k* psor al *Sil* kr1 sol-ni verat
  - **cramping**: bell k2

- **crushed**; as if: rhus-t ptk1
- **dentition**; during: cypr hr1
- **eating** | **after** | **agg.**: canth ign ran-b
  - **amel.**: lach bg1
- **exertion**:
  - **agg.**: merc
  - **amel.**:
    - **slight** exertion: mur-ac↓
      - **torn**; as if: mur-ac
- **eyes**; painful sensation of light penetrating brain on closing the: kali-c fr2*
- **injuries** of head; from: (*↗Injuries*) nat-s mtf33
- **intestinal** pain; with: cypr hr1
- **lying** agg.: ther
- **maddening** pain: plan
- **motion**:
  - **agg.**: bry↓ chin↓ iod h staph↓
    - **sore**: chin hr1
    - **stitching** pain: bry tl1
    - **torn**; as if: staph k*
  - **eyelids**; of | **upper** eyelids: *Coloc*
  - **eyes**; of: mur-ac↓ *Rhus-t*↓
    - **agg.**: mur-ac↓
      - **pressing** pain: mur-ac h2
    - **torn**; as if: mur-ac *Rhus-t* hr1
  - **sitting** up in bed agg., moderate exercise amel.; or | **torn**; as if (See exertion - amel. - slight - torn; sitting up - torn)
- **nail**; as from a: hep tl1 thuj tl1
- **pressing** pain: aster mtf11 oci-sa sk4•
  - **against** the skull; as if pressing: calc-p tl1 glon tl1 kola stb3• mez rhod rhus-v
  - **bound** up; as if: acon aeth agath-a nl2• am-br ant-t k* arg-met asar aur h2 **Bry** k* calc camph *Carb-v* k* cham cimic *Cocc* k* colch *Crot-c* k* cupr cycl gels graph guaj hell h1 hyper indg **Lac-c** k* *Lach* k* laur led k2 mag-s manc meny *Merc* k* morph *Mosch* k* mur-ac h2 **Nat-m** k* **Nit-ac** k* *Olnd* k* op k* par petr *Ph-ac* k* plac-s rly4• plat prun *Psor* k* puls rhus-t sars sil *Spig* k* *Staph* k*
    - **cloth**, by a: cycl
  - **forward**: *Acon* asar bell *Bry* ip kali-c
    - **out** of eyes●: nat-m h2
  - **helmet**; as if by an iron: bros-gau mrc1 *Crot-c*
  - **inward**: asar coff k2 cupr glon spong fd4.de ther rb2
  - **membranes** were too tight; as if: *Acon* carb-v op par psor
  - **on** the brain: agath-a nl2• ars *Cann-i* glon ign manc meny ph-ac h2 phos h2 ruta sep spong fd4.de
  - **outward**: aesc k2 agar *Bell Bry* dulc fd4.de glon guaj hep hydr indg laur lil-t mur-ac h2 *Nat-m* phys psor tl1 stann tritic-vg fd5.de
  - **sharp** corners; as if against: sabad
  - **skull** were too small; as if: gink-b sbd1• *Glon* morph psor jl2 scut
  - **thread**; as from a: asaf b7.de* mosch b7a.de
  - **together**: chin vml
- **reading** agg.: arg-met↓
  - **pressing** pain: arg-met h1
- **rest**:
  - **amel.**: staph↓
    - **torn**; as if: staph k*
- **rising** from stooping agg.: laur
- **shaking** the head agg.; on: *Caust Spig*
- **sitting** erect agg.: hell↓
  - **burning**: hell k*
- **sitting** up in bed agg.: mur-ac↓
  - **torn**; as if: mur-ac

\- **Brain**: ...

- **sore**: anac ang c1 arg-met bro1 *Arn* k* aur bapt a1* bar-c bell bro1 *Bell-p* bro1 bov bro1 **Chin** k* coff *Cupr* dulc fd4.de eupi bro1 **Gels** k* glon hell *Ign* ind iod *Ip* led bro1 mang k2 merc mur-ac k* *Nat-m Nux-v* k* petr bro1 *Ph-ac* phos phys phyt k* plan rhus-t bro1 rumx stann tell verat bro1
  - **accompanied** by | **nausea**: ip tl1
  - **paroxysmal**: *Verat*
- **standing** agg.: arg-met↓
  - **pressing** pain: arg-met h1
- **stitching** pain: *Agn* k* **Alum** k* am-c k* bar-c k* bell *Bry* k* calc k* carl a1 cham k* cina coc-c a1 colch k* colocin a1 cycl k* dulc k* euphr k* gran k* *Guaj* k* hyper kali-c k* kali-n h2* laur k* lyc k* mag-c mill k* nat-m k* petr k* plb k* *Puls* k* sabin k* sil k* thuj k*
  - **needles**; as from: tarent ptk1
  - **needles**; pricking sensation as from thousand: asaf tl1 kola stb3• tarent rb2
  - **upward**: sil h2
- **stooping** agg.: cycl↓
  - **stitching** pain: cycl h1
- **tearing** pain: agar bg2 carbn-o bg2 cham bg2 coloc bg2 kola stb3• phel bg2 puls bg2 sil bg2 spong bg2 stront-c bg2
- **thinking** agg.: daph
- **torn**; as if: coff ptk1 *Rhus-t* hr1 staph ptk1 sul-ac bg2
  - **clasped** by a hand and were being torn and twisted; as if: mur-ac
- **touch**:
  - **agg.**: all-c arg-met bry chin cinnb grat kali-bi lact laur mag-s merc merc-i-f mez mur-ac nat-m par sabin sars staph sulph viol-t
  - **amel.**: sars
- **waking**; on: *Chin* dream-p sdj1• mang phys
- **walking** agg.: gran
- **wandering** pain: am-c chin
- **warmth**:
  - **amel.**: staph↓
    - **torn**; as if: staph k*
- **yawning**:
  - **amel.**: staph↓
    - **torn**; as if: staph k*

▽ • **extending** to | **Forehead**; out through: hydrog srj2• viol-t

○ • **Base** of brain: aesc↓ hyos↓ kola↓ op mrr1
  - **dull** pain: hyos h1
  - **lancinating**: aesc
  - **smarting**: kola stb3•
- **Cerebellum**: sep↓
  - **pulsating** pain: sep br1
- **Middle** of brain: mur-ac↓ phos↓ zinc↓
  - **pressing** pain: mur-ac h2 phos h2 zinc h2
- **Side** lain on: ph-ac↓
  - **pressing** pain: ph-ac h2
- **Spot**; in a: m-ambo↓ zinc↓
  - **pressing** pain: m-ambo al2 zinc h2

\- **Cerebral** | **pressing** pain (See brain - pressing)

\- **Deep** in: *Bac* jl2 carc sp1 hipp jl2 tub bg*

\- **External** head: agn↓ am↓ clem↓ ip↓ lach↓ *Lyc*↓ par↓ phos↓ *Ruta*↓ sars↓ viol-t↓

- **blow**; pain as from a: agn b7.de* arn b7.de* ip b7.de* lach b7.de* par b7.de* phos bg2 *Ruta* b7.de* viol-t b7.de*
- **cutting** pain: clem b4a.de* sars b4a.de*
- **perspiration**; during: **Ars** bg2 **Calc** bg2 graph bg2 hep bg2 **Merc** bg2 mez bg2 nat-m bg2 phos bg2 *Rhus-t* bg2 *Sabad* bg2 *Sep* bg2 sil bg2 staph bg2 thuj bg2
- **scraped**; as if: *Lyc* b4.de* par b7.de*

\- **Eyebrows**: carb-an↓ stront-c↓

- **aching**: stront-c ptk1
- **pressing** down; as if: carb-an k*

- **Eyes**: bell↓ cocc↓ ham↓ rhus-t↓ sep↓
  - **complaints**; with eye: euphr k2
  - **fall** out; as if they would: sep h2
  - **forced** out; as if eyes would be: bell mrr1 cocc tl1 ham ptk1 rhus-t h1
- **Forehead**: abrom-a ks5 acet-ac k* **Acon** k* act-sp↓ adam skp7• *Aesc* k* *Aeth* *Agar* k* agath-a nl2• *Agn*↓ *Ail* k* alf bro1 *All-c* k* allox tpw3* aln↓ *Aloe* k* *Alum* alum-p↓ alum-sil k2 alumn k* **Am-c** k* **Am-m** ambr b7.de* aml-ns↓ ammc k* anac k* anan↓ androc srj1• ang *Ant-c* k* *Ant-t* k* anth a1 antip bro1 ap-g vml3• *Apis* apoc *Aq-mar* skp7• aran k* *Arg-met* *Arg-n* k* arge-pl rwt5• **Arn** k* **Ars** k* ars-i ars-s-f k2 arum-t k* arund *Asaf* k* *Asar* asc-t a1 asim a1 aster atp↓ *Atro*↓ *Aur* k* aur-ar k2 aur-i↓ aur-m k2 aur-m-n a1 aur-s↓ bacls-10 pte1• bad↓ *Bamb-a* stb2.de• *Bapt* k* bar-c k* bar-i k2 bar-m bar-s k2 **Bell** k* benz-ac↓ benzol br1 berb k* beryl tpw5 **Bism** k* bism-sn a1 bit-ar wht1• borx k* bov k* brach a1 brass a1 brom k* bros-gau mrc1 *Brucel* sa3• **Bry** k* bufo bung-fa mtf buth-a↓ cact k* cadm-met tpw6* caj k* calad *Calc* k* calc-i↓ *Calc-p* *Calc-s* calc-sil k2 *Camph* k* cann-i↓ cann-s k* canth k* **Caps** k* *Carb-ac* k* carb-an k* *Carb-v* k* *Carbn-s* carc sp1* card-b↓ card-m *Cardios-h* rly4• carl↓ carneg-g rwt1• cartl-s rly4• cassia-s↓ castm↓ caul k* *Caust* *Cedr* k* cench k2 cent a1 cere-b↓ *Cham* k* *Chel* k* chen-a↓ chim chim-m↓ *Chin* k* chinin-ar *Chinin-s* k* chion br1* chir-fl gya2 chlam-tr↓ chlol choc↓ chord-umb rly4• *Cic* k* cimic k* cimx↓ cina k* cinch a1 *Cinnb* cist cit-ac↓ clem k* cob k* cob-n sp1 coc-c k* coca **Cocc** coff↓ colch coli jl2* *Coll* *Coloc* con k* conch fkr1• conv↓ convo-s sp1 cop↓ cor-r br1 corian-s knl6• corn cortico sp1 cortiso sp1 croc k* *Crot-c* crot-h crot-t k* *Cupr* cupr-ar k* *Cur* *Cycl* cypra-eg sde6.de• cystein-l rly4• cyt-l↓ dendr-pol↓ der a1 *Dig* k* digin a1 *Dios* k* diosm br1 dioxi rbp6 dirc a1 dream-p↓ **Dros** k* *Dulc* k* dys pte1• echi *Elaps* elat k* ephe-si hsj1• erig a1 erio a1 eucal a1 eug↓ euon a1 eup-per a1* euph k* *Euphr* k* eupi a1 eys sp1 fago a1 falco-pe nl2• *Ferr* k* *Ferr-ar* ferr-i *Ferr-p* k* fic-m gya1 fl-ac k* flav jl2 flor-p↓ form k* fuc↓ fuma-ac rly4• galeoc-c-h gms1• gard-j vlr2• gast a1 *Gels* k* gent-c↓ gent-l a1 ger-i rly4• germ-met↓ gink-b sbd1• gins k* *Glon* k* goss↓ gran k* *Granit-m*↓ *Graph* grat k* guaj k* guat↓ gymno haliae-lc srj5• *Ham* k* hed sp1 helio↓ hell k* helon k* **Hep** hera a1 hipp k* hir rsj4*• hist sp1 hom-xyz br1 hura *Hydr* k* hydr-ac k* *Hydrog* srj2• *Hydroph*↓ **Hyos** k* iber a1 **Ign** k* ignis-alc↓ ina-i↓ ind indg a1 indol bro1 inul↓ iod k* *Ip* irid-met srj5• *Iris* k* jab a1 jac-c↓ jac-g↓ jatr-c↓ jug-c k* jug-r a1 kali-ar kali-bi k* kali-br↓ *Kali-c* kali-chl k* kali-cy a1 *Kali-i* kali-m k2 kali-n k* kali-p **Kali-s** kali-sil↓ *Kalm* k* ketogl-ac rly4• kola stb3• *Kreos* k* lac-ac k* **Lac-c** *Lac-d* k* lac-del↓ lac-e hm2• *Lac-h* sk4• lac-leo hm2• lac-lup hm2• *Lach* k* lachn k* lact lact-v↓ lap-la↓ lat-m bnm6• **Laur** k* lavand-a↓ lec led k* lepi a1 *Lept* k* lil-s a1 lil-t k* limest-b↓ linu-c a1 lith-c lob-c a1 lol↓ loxo-recl knl4• luf-op rsj5• luna kg1• *Lyc* k* lycps-v lyss k* m-arct↓ m-aust↓ *Mag-c* *Mag-m* mag-s k* malar jl2 manc k* mand sp1 mang mang-p↓ marb-w↓ *Med* k* medul-os-si rly4• melal-alt gya4 *Meli* k* menis bro1 *Meny* **Merc** merc-c merc-d a1 *Merc-i-f* k* merc-i-r merl k* mez k* mill↓ mim-p↓ mit a1 moni rfm1• morg-p pte1• morph a1 mosch k* mucs-nas rly4• *Mur-ac* k* musa c1 musca-d↓ *Mygal* myric a1 *Naja* narc-ps c1* narcot↓ **Nat-ar** **Nat-c** k* **Nat-m** k* nat-ox rly4• nat-p k* nat-pyru rly4• nat-s k* nat-sil↓ neon srj5• nept-m↓ nicc↓ nicotam rly4• *Nit-ac* k* nit-s-d a1 *Nux-m* k* **Nux-v** k* oci-sa sk4• *Ol-an*↓ ol-j k* olib-sac wmh1 *Olnd* op k* osm *Ost* a1 *Ox-ac* k* oxal-a rly4• oxeod↓ ozone sde2• paeon↓ pall↓ papin a1 *Par* k* ped a1 pen a1 pert-vc vk9 *Petr* k* petr-ra shn4• ph-ac phasco-ci rbp2 phase-vg a1 phel k* **Phos** k* phys k* *Phyt* k* pic-ac k* pieri-b mlk9.de pin-con oss2• pip-m k* pitu-gl skp7• plac-s rly4• plan k* *Plat* *Plb* plect a1 plut-n srj7• podo polyp-p a1 positr nl2• pot-e rly4• propl ub1• *Propr* sa3• prot pte1* prun bro1 prun-p↓ psil ft1 *Psor* k* ptel k* **Puls** k* pulx br1 pycnop-sa mrz1 quas a1 rad-br sze8• *Ran-b* k* ran-s↓ raph k* rat↓ rham-f a1 rheum rhod k* rhodi a1* rhus-g a1 *Rhus-t* k* *Rhus-v* ribo rly4• rob bro1 *Rumx* ruta *Sabad* a1* *Sabin* kr1 sacch-a↓ sal-al↓ samb k* *Sang* k* sanguis-s hm2• sapin a1 sarcol-ac sp1 sarr a1 *Sars* k* *Scut* bro1 sec *Sel* k* senec↓ seneg k* *Sep* k* serp a1 **Sil** k* sin-a a1 sin-n a1 sinus rly4• skat br1 *Sol-ni* **Spig** k* spira a1 spirae a1 *Spong* squil↓ **Stann** *Staph* k* stel bro1 stict k* still a1 stram k* streptoc rly4• stront-c stry succ-ac rly4• suis-em rly4• suis-hep rly4• suis-pan rly4• sul-ac k* sul-i a1* **Sulph** k* sumb a1 suprar rly4• syc pte1• symph fd3.de• *Syph* tab k* tarax k* *Tarent* k* tela zzc1• tell k* tep a1 ter↓ tere-la rly4• tetox pin2• teucr k* thea *Ther* k* thiam rly4• thres-a sze7• *Thuj* k* til k* tong↓ trif-p a1 tril-p *Trios* rsj11• tritic-vg sna6 trom k* tub al *Tub-a* jl2 *Tung-met* bdx1• tus-p a1 upa a1 (non:uran-met k) uran-n urol-h↓ ust k* vac a1 *Valer* k* vanil fd5.de *Ven-m* rsj12• verat verat-v k* verb k* vib k* vichy-g a1 vinc↓ *Viol-o* bro1 viol-t k* vip↓ visc sp1 x-ray sp1 xan k* xanth yuc a1 zinc k* zinc-p↓ zing k* ziz↓ [bell-p-sp dcm1 *Buteo-j* sej6 helia stj7 heroin sdj2 *Spect* dfg1 tax jsj7]
  - **alternating** sides: aloe bg1 apis a1 falco-pe nl2• gins bg1 *Iris* k* **Lac-c** k* lil-t lob bg1 stann bg1 zinc bg1

- **Forehead**: ...
  - **right**: acet-ac k* *Acon* k* agar k* agn↓ aids nl2• aloe alum↓ am-c↓ am-m↓ anac ant-t k* ap-g vh1 apis arg-n arn *Ars* k* ars-s-f k2 arum-t k* asaf bar-c bar-i k2 bar-s k2 *Bell* k* berb bism↓ bit-ar wht1• bov brom bry↓ bufo calc↓ camph↓ cann-i↓ canth caps↓ *Carb-ac* k* *Carb-v*↓ carc sp1 castm caust↓ *Chel* k* chin k* chinin-ar chord-umb rly4• cimx k* cina↓ cinch a1 cinnb coc-c k* cocc colch k* coloc↓ cop br1 cortiso sp1 crot-h cupr-ar k* cycl cystein-l rly4• dig k* dios k* dros dulc fd4.de euphr falco-pe nl2• ferr ferr-ar ferr-i ferr-p fic-m gya1 fl-ac k* flor-p rsj3• germ-met↓ glon k* grat guaj↓ ham fd3.de• hell *Hep* k* hydrog srj2• hyos↓ *Ign* k* indg iod *Iris* kali-bi kali-c↓ kali-n↓ kali-s fd4.de kalm kola stb3• kreos lach lap-la sde8.de• *Laur* k* led↓ loxo-recl knl4• *Lyc* sne lyss m-arct↓ m-aust↓ mag-c↓ mag-m↓ mag-p↓ mand rsj7• *Mang*↓ meny merc *Merc-c*↓ merc-i-f k* *Mez* k* mosch k* nat-c↓ nat-m k* nat-s k* nicc nit-ac↓ *Nux-m*↓ nux-v↓ ol-an olib-sac wmh1 olnd↓ op k* osm par↓ ph-ac↓ phase-vg a1 phel phos *Phyt* pic-ac k* plac-s rly4• plat↓ plb↓ plut-n srj7• podo fd3.de• *Propr* sa3• **Prun** k* psor *Ran-b* k* ran-s↓ rat rhod k* rhodi a1 rhus-r rhus-t↓ rumx ruta sabad k* sabin sang k* sars seneg sep sil k* sinus rly4• spig spong squil stann staph staphycoc rly4• stram k* stront-c↓ suis-pan rly4• sul-ac sulph suprar rly4• symph fd3.de• tarent tax↓ tell rsj10• teucr thuj tritic-vg fd5.de urt-u k* valer k* vanil fd5.de ven-m rsj12• verb viol-t↓ zinc [ang stj4]
    - **morning** | **waking**; on: colch k* phyt
    - **forenoon**: dig k* fl-ac k*
    - **afternoon**: agar k* petr-ra shn4• stram k* tritic-vg fd5.de
    - **evening**: ant-t k* apis ferr-i k2 germ-met srj5• merc-i-r k* nat-m sang k*
    - **night**: merc-i-f a1 sulph k*
    - **boring** pain: am-c b4.de* ant-t b7.de* *Bell* b4a.de caust b4a.de colch bg2 nat-m bg2 nat-s bg2 ruta b7.de* sabin b7.de* sang bg2 zinc b4.de*
      - **inward**: cocc b7.de* kali-c b4.de*
      - **outward**: bell b4.de* bism b7.de* *Dulc* b4.de*
    - **burning**: *Carb-v* b4a.de coloc *Mang* k* *Nux-m* b7a.de sang bg2 **Spig**
    - **burrowing**: am-c b4.de* anac b4.de* ign b7.de* phos b4.de*
    - **compressed**; as if: anac bg2 cocc bg2
    - **drawing** pain: calc b4.de* caps k* dros bg2 ign bg2 kreos b7a.de meny k* nit-ac k* ran-s bg2 rat ruta k* sabin k* spong fd4.de stann k* staph b7.de* sulph bg2
    - **dull** pain: ars-s-f k2 chord-umb rly4• ham fd3.de• ign b7.de* *Merc-c* b4a.de olib-sac wmh1 plac-s rly4• suis-pan rly4• tritic-vg fd5.de [tax jsj7]
    - **hammering** pain: am-m b7.de*
    - **jerking** pain: cann-i c1
    - **nail**; as from a: sabin b7.de* sang bg2
    - **plug**; as from a: anac b4.de*
    - **pressing** pain: anac b4.de* arn b7.de* asaf b7.de* bell b4.de* *Carb-v* b4a.de caust b4.de* chel b7.de* chin b7.de* germ-met srj5• guaj b4.de* hell b7.de* ign b7.de* kali-c b4.de* kali-n b4.de* kreos b7a.de m-arct b7.de meny b7.de* merc b4.de* merc-c b4a.de mez b4.de* mosch b7.de* nux-v b7.de* par b7.de* ph-ac b4.de* plat b4.de* prun mrr1 rhus-t b7.de* ruta b7.de* sabad b7.de* sabin b7.de* sars b4.de* seneg b4a.de spong b7.de* *Staph* b7.de* stront-c b4.de* sul-ac b4.de* *Teucr* b7.de* thuj b4.de* valer b7.de* *Verb* b7.de* viol-t b7.de* zinc b4.de*
      - **asunder**: sabin b7.de*
      - **inward**: olnd b7.de* staph b7.de*
      - **outward**: anac b4.de* asaf b7.de* bry b7.de* cina b7.de* hell b7.de* ph-ac b4.de* rhod b4a.de spig b7.de* spong b7.de*
    - **pulsating** pain: chord-umb rly4• suis-pan rly4•
    - **shooting** pain: **Bell** kali-bi bg2 **Prun** sil bg2 **Spig** k*
    - **stitching** pain: agn b7.de* alum b4.de* anac b4.de* ars-s-f br1 bar-c b4.de* bell b4.de* bov bg2 canth b7.de* carb-v b4.de* cina b7.de* cocc b7.de* dros b7.de* euphr b7.de* guaj b4.de* hell b7.de* hyos b7.de* kali-n bg2 laur b7.de* led b7.de* lyc b4.de* mag-c b4.de* mag-m b4.de* mag-p bg2 mang b4.de* merc b4.de* mez b4.de* nat-c b4.de nux-m b7a.de* ph-ac b4a.de* phos b4.de* plb b7.de* ruta b7.de* sabin b7.de* sars b4.de* *Sep* b4a.de sil b4.de* spig b7.de* squil b7.de* sul-ac b4.de* sulph b4.de tarent bg2 verb b7.de* zinc b4.de*
    - **stunning** pain: cycl bg2
    - **tearing** pain: agn b7.de* bell b4.de* calc b4a.de camph b7.de* caps b7.de* cina b7.de* kali-n b4.de* m-aust b7.de mang b4.de*

- **right** – **tearing** pain: ...
  nat-c b4.de* seneg b4a.de sep b4.de* stann b4.de* sul-ac b4.de* thuj b4.de* zinc b4.de*
  - **warm** room agg.: cortiso sp1*
  - **writing** agg.: phase-vg a1
  - **extending** to:
    - **left**: acet-ac k* aesc aeth cycl ign iris kali-p fd1.de• nat-m **Sabad** sanic
      - **cutting** pain: *Aesc*
    - **Cheek**: dulc fd4.de lachn sang a1
    - **Ear**: dios a1 hydrog srj2• sang a1
    - **Eye**; right: gink-b sbd1•
    - **Neck**: aids nl2•
    - **Nose**: aids nl2•
    - **Occiput**, through head: **Prun** k* symph fd3.de•
    - **Teeth**: aids nl2•
    - **Temple**: bit-ar wht1•
- **left**: acet-ac k* acon aeth agar k* agn↓ aloe↓ alum↓ alumn↓ am-m↓ ambr↓ amp rly4• anac↓ ant-c ant-t k* apis arg-met *Arg-n* arn k* ars↓ asaf *Asar* k* aur aur-i k2 aur-m aur-m-n↓ bar-c↓ bell k* bism↓ bov brass-n-o srj5• *Brom*↓ bry k* cact k* *Calc*↓ camph cann-s↓ canth↓ caps↓ carb-an k* caust cedr↓ cere-b a1 chel k* chin chinin-s chir-fl↓ chord-umb rly4• cic k* cimic↓ cina clem coca cocc colch coloc k* con↓ croc↓ cund cupr cycl↓ cystein-l rly4• dulc euon k* euph falco-pe nl2• ferr↓ fl-ac k* flor-p rsj3• germ-met srj5• glon gran k* grat haem k* ham hed sp1 hell↓ hipp hyos ign↓ iod ip irid-met srj5• kali-bi kali-c↓ kali-i↓ kali-n kali-p fd1.de• kalm kreos *Lac-c* lac-cp sk4• lac-h htj1• lach↓ laur lil-t lith-c luf-op rsj5• lyc k* lyss k* m-arct↓ m-aust↓ mag-c mag-m mand rsj7• mang↓ meny merc k* merc-c↓ *Merl*↓ mez mim-p↓ mur-ac naja mrr1 nat-c k* nat-m nat-s nit-ac↓ nuph a1 *Nux-m*↓ nux-v↓ ol-an olib-sac wmh1 olnd↓ op par petr-ra shn4• ph-ac phel *Phos*↓ phys k* pip-m k* plac-s rly4• plan k* plat plb↓ *Propr* sa3• prun psil ft1 psor ptel ran-b↓ rauw↓ rhod k* rhodi a1 rhus-t k* ribo rly4• sabad↓ sabin sanguis-s hrn2• sars sel seneg sep k* sil spig spong squil↓ stann staph stront-c↓ suis-pan rly4• sul-ac k* sulph k* tab tarax teucr↓ **Thuj** k* tritic-vg fd5.de ulm-c jsj8• valer vanil fd5.de ven-m rsj12• verb viol-o↓ viol-t↓ zinc k*
  - **morning**: mand rsj7•
    - **7** h: sal-al blc1•
  - **forenoon**: dulc fd4.de gink-b sbd1•
  - **afternoon** | **16** h: sal-al blc1•
  - **boring** pain: *Arg-n* bg2 ars bg2 *Calc* b4.de* cimic bg2 kali-c bg2 lyc bg2 merc b4.de* nat-m bg2 ol-an bg2
    - **inward**: kali-c b4.de* mang b4.de*
    - **outward**: bism b7.de* bov b4.de* sep b4.de* spong b7.de* staph b7.de*
  - **burning**: bell b4.de* chir-fl gya2 cupr b7.de* merc k* spig k*
  - **burrowing**: agar k* chin b7.de* kali-c b4.de* phel a1 plat b4.de* spig b7.de*
  - **compressed**; as if: cocc b7.de* valer b7.de*
  - **cutting** pain: aur-m-n a1 caust h2 ferr bg2* iod bg2* kali-p fd1.de• nat-m bg2* sel bg2 sep bg2* stann bg2* staph h1
  - **drawing** pain: aloe bg2 asaf k* bar-c k* calc b4.de* cina k* clem k* colch k* *Coloc* k* cycl k* dulc k* nat-m bg2 *Rhod* k* staph b7.de* thuj k* verb k* viol-o k* viol-t a1
  - **dull** pain: cocc b7.de* dulc b4.de* mim-p rsj8• olib-sac wmh1 rauw sp1 sars b4.de*
  - **hammering** pain: ham bg2 mez b4.de* verb b7.de*
  - **jerking** pain: alum alumn k* anac b4.de* caps stann b4.de* sul-ac b4.de*
  - **nail**; as from a: hell b7.de* thuj k*
  - **plug**; as from a: con b4a.de sul-ac b4.de*
  - **pressing** pain: agn b7.de* ambr b7.de* ant-t b7.de* arg-met b7.de* asaf b7.de* aur b4.de* camph b7.de* cann-s b7.de* caust b4.de* chel b7.de* cic b7.de* cina b7.de* coloc b4.de* dulc b4.de* euph b4.de* ign b7.de* iod b4.de* kali-n b4.de* lac-h htj1• lach b7.de* m-arct b7.de mag-c b4.de* merc-c b4a.de mur-ac b4.de* nat-c b4.de* nat-m b4.de* *Nux-m* b7.de* nux-v b7.de* ph-ac b4.de* plat b4.de* ran-b b7.de* rhod b4.de* sabad b7.de* sabin b7.de* sars b4.de* seneg b4.de* spong b7.de* squil b7.de* stront-c b4.de* sulph b4.de* teucr b7.de* thuj b4.de*
    - **asunder**: acon bg2 camph b7.de* staph b7.de*

- **left** – **pressing** pain: ...
  - **inward**: anac bg2 croc b7.de* spig b7.de* verb b7.de*
  - **outward**: camph b7.de* dulc b4.de* germ-met srj5• *Nux-m* bg2 olnd b7.de* rhus-t b7.de* sep bg2 spig b7.de* staph b7.de*
  - **shooting** pain: bry bg2 cedr bg2 kali-bi bg2 mang bg2 *Merl* nat-m bg2 **Sep** k*
  - **sore**: sul-ac b4.de*
  - **stitching** pain: alum b4.de* am-m b7.de* ant-t b7.de* arg-n bg2 arn b7.de* asaf b7.de* bar-c b4.de* *Brom* b4a.de bry b7.de* calc b4.de* canth b7.de* caust b4.de* chel b7.de* chin b7.de* cocc b7.de* cupr b7.de* euph b4.de* hell b7.de* kali-i bg2 kali-n b4.de* laur b7.de* m-arct b7.de m-aust b7.de mang b4.de* meny b7.de* merc b4.de* merc-c b4a.de mez b4.de* nat-c b4.de* nit-ac b4.de* ph-ac b4.de* *Phos* b4.de* plb b7.de* ptel bg2 sabad b7.de* sabin b7.de* sars b4.de* *Sel* b7.de* sep b4.de* spig b7.de* spong b7.de* stann b4.de* staph b7.de* stront-c b4.de* sul-ac b4.de* sulph bg2 tarax b7.de* verb b7.de*
  - **tearing** pain: agn b7.de* alum b4.de* ambr b7.de* arg-met b7.de* aur b4.de* bell b4.de* camph b7.de* *Caust* b4a.de chel b7.de* cina b7.de* colch b7.de* euph b4.de* kali-c b4.de* mag-m b4.de* mang b4.de* merc b4.de* mez b4.de* nat-c b4.de* sabad b7.de* sep b4.de* spig b7.de* stann b4.de* sul-ac b4.de* zinc b4.de*
  - **extending** to:
    - **right** side: agar chin haem *Iris* lycps-v phos bg1 rhus-r squil
    - **Brain**; deep into: ptel↓
      - **shooting** pain: ptel hl9*
    - **Occiput**: cere-b a1 nat-c
- **midnight**:
  - **morning**; till: hep↓
    - **sore**: hep
- **day** and night: *Lyc*↓
  - **burning**: *Lyc*
- **daytime**: aesc a1 *Calc* cassia-s↓ caust chel chlam-tr↓ con cund dulc fd4.de kali-c kali-sil k2 lach lil-t lyc mag-c mand rsj7• merc-i-f a1 nat-ar k2 nat-m k* nuph op↓ petr phos pic-ac a1 pip-m a1 plut-n↓ ptel ran-b *Seneg* a1 sep sil sol-t-ae k* spig↓ **Stict**↓ sulph a1 tarent ven-m rsj12• zinc
  - **dull** pain: cassia-s ccrh1•
  - **pressing** pain: chlam-tr bcx2• mag-c op k* *Phos* k* plut-n srj7• sil k* **Stict** k*
  - **sore**: sil
  - **stitching** pain: sep h2* spig a1 sulph k*
- **morning**: abrom-a↓ agar k* agath-a nl2• alum alumn am-c↓ am-m ambr↓ ant-t↓ arg-n↓ arn aster k* aur-m bamb-a↓ bapt bar-c↓ bell borx↓ bov brom k* *Brucel* sa3• bry *Calc* *Calc-s* calc-sil k2 canth carbn-s caust↓ chel chinin-s chlam-tr↓ cimic cinnb k2 cob↓ coca colch rsj2• *Coloc*↓ con↓ conch↓ crot-h crot-t cycl dios k* dirc a1 dulc fd4.de equis-h euphr ferr form k* graph↓ grat↓ ham a1 hell↓ hep↓ hydr iris↓ jac-c↓ *Kali-bi* kali-c *Kali-s* kali-sil k2 kola stb3• kreos k* *Lac-c* lac-h↓ lac-leo sk4• **Lach** lact k* lil-t lyc k* lyss mag-c mag-s mand rsj7• med melal-alt↓ merl mez morph a1 mur-ac↓ murx naja nat-ar nat-c *Nat-m*↓ *Nat-s*↓ nicc nit-ac nux-m k* *Nux-v* ol-an ox-ac k* paeon k* peti a1 petr↓ phos phys↓ pic-ac↓ propl ub1• psor pyrid rly4• ran-b↓ raph k* rein↓ (non:rhod slp) rhodi a1* rhus-r rhus-t a1 ruta fd4.de *Sabin*↓ sacch-a gmj3 sars↓ scut seneg sep sil sin-n a1 spong fd4.de squil↓ stram k* stry k* **Sulph** k* symph fd3.de• tarent *Ther*↓ thuj til↓ tritic-vg fd5.de ust k* vanil fd5.de ven-m rsj12• viol-t↓ zinc k* zinc-p k2 zing a1
  - **6** h: sulph xan c1
  - **7-17** h: nat-c↓
    - **bursting** pain: nat-c h2
  - **9-13** h: mur-ac↓
    - **sore**: mur-ac
  - **noon**; until: abrom-a ks5
    - **pressing** pain: abrom-a ks5
    - **pulsating** pain: abrom-a ks5
  - **night**; until: abrom-a ks5
    - **pressing** pain: abrom-a ks5
    - **pulsating** pain: abrom-a ks5
  - **amel.**: mag-s ox-ac petr

Head

- **morning**: ...
  - **bed** agg.; in: anac k* dulc k* graph k* inul k* mez nux-v polyp-p a1 ran-b rhod
  - **boring** pain: arg-n a1 *Bell* calc dios k* ruta fd4.de sulph
  - **burning**: mur-ac h2 nux-v phos k* phys k*
  - **burrowing**: bar-c dulc a1 squil k*
  - **bursting** pain: sulph k*
  - **cutting** pain: coloc viol-t
  - **drawing** pain: agar k* agath-a nl2• am-c mez k* nat-m k* *Nux-v* rein a1 vanil fd5.de
  - **dull** pain: bamb-a stb2.de• lac-h sk4• melal-alt gya4 vanil fd5.de
  - **lancinating**: jac-c a1 viol-t
  - **pressing** pain: abrom-a ks5 agar am-m k* ambr ant-t borx brom calc caust k* chlam-tr bcx2• conch fkr1• dulc fd4.de kola stb3• lyc k* mez k* nat-c *Nat-m* k* *Nat-s* nit-ac h2 *Nux-v* pic-ac *Psor* ran-b ruta fd4.de *Sabin Sil* spong fd4.de **Sulph** *Ther* tritic-vg fd5.de vanil fd5.de zinc
  - **pulsating** pain: abrom-a ks5
  - **rising**:
    - **after**:
      - **agg.**: am-m ↓ calc-act ↓ coloc ↓ con ↓ graph ↓ nat-c ↓ psor ↓ sil ↓ spig ↓ sulph ↓
        - **pressing** pain: am-m a1 calc-act graph k* nat-c psor k* sil h2 spig sulph
        - **stitching** pain: coloc h2 con h2
    - **agg.**: am-m asar bar-c bry carb-an cob coloc ↓ con dulc ferr ham iber kali-bi kali-n kalm lac-d *Lach* lil-t lyc mag-c nat-c nat-m podo fd3.de• psor raph sep sil spong fd4.de squil ↓ vanil fd5.de
      - **burrowing**: bar-c squil k*
      - **lancinating**: coloc
    - **amel.**: anac h2 graph hep **Nux-v** phos ran-b rhod *Sulph*
      - **burning**: nux-v
      - **pressing** pain: *Ran-b*
  - **shooting** pain: iris
  - **sitting** agg.: mez ↓
    - **tearing** pain: mez
  - **sore**: cob hep sil
  - **stitching** pain: arg-n k* bamb-a stb2.de• con k* dulc fd4.de grat k* hell h1 kali-c lyc k* petr k* sars h2 sil k* til a1 tritic-vg fd5.de
  - **tearing** pain: *Coloc* graph mez
  - **waking**; on: acon k* adam skp7• agar agath-a nl2• aids nl2• allox ↓ alum alum-p k2 alumn am-c ↓ anac ant-t arg-met arg-n arn bell berb *Bry* k* cadm-met ↓ calc k* calc-s calc-sil k2 carb-ac carb-an k* carbn-s chinin-s cina cinnb k* coc-c coff colch k* coloc *Crot-h* dig erig euphr fago ferr ferr-p fl-ac k* gels glon k* graph hep hydr hydrog srj2• ign ind *Kali-bi* k* kalm kreos lac-ac lac-c lact lyc lyss mag-c mag-m mez ↓ mim-p rsj8• mit c1 morph myric k* naja nat-ar *Nat-m* ↓ **Nux-v** ol-an ox-ac k* ozone sde2• petr petr-ra shn4• ph-ac phos raph rhus-t rumx ruta sang sol-ni *Spig* ↓ staph *Sulph* k* symph fd3.de• tell k* ther thuj zinc ↓
    - **blow**; pain as from a: sol-ni
    - **boring** pain: *Bell Bry*
    - **bursting** pain: allox sp1
    - **drawing** pain: agar agath-a nl2• am-c *Nux-v* thuj
    - **dull** pain: allox tpw3 cadm-met tpw6*
    - **pressing** pain: agar alumn a1 anac k* ant-t arg-n k* gels k* mag-c mag-m h2 mez k* *Nat-m* ol-an k* *Ph-ac* k* *Spig Sulph* k* zinc k*
    - **sore**: hep sol-ni
    - **stitching** pain: arn petr k*
    - **stunning** pain: ph-ac h2
    - **tearing** pain: graph
- **forenoon**: allox ↓ alum ↓ arn ars-i k* bamb-a stb2.de• brom k* bry k* calc-s carbn-s k2 chin clem k* coc-c k* cocc colch rsj2• coloc con dig k* dulc fd4.de euphr fl-ac k* gamb gels k* gink-b sbd1• graph ↓ guaj a1 hydroph ↓ ign k* kali-c lach luf-op rsj5• lyc k* mag-c mag-m ↓ mag-s mang ↓ meli merc-i-r myric k* nat-ar nat-c ↓ nat-m ↓ nat-s ↓ nicc ↓ peti petr k* plect a1 podo fd3.de• propl ub1• rhus-t k* ruta fd4.de sacch-a ↓ sars sel seneg sep sol-ni spong fd4.de *Sulph* k* symph fd3.de• tell ↓ thuj ↓ tritic-vg fd5.de ust k* vanil fd5.de *Ven-m* rsj12• zinc k*
  - **9** h: ven-m rsj12•
- **forenoon**: ...
  - **10** h: carbn-s ↓ *Gels* med jl2 **Nat-m** psil ft1 thuj ↓
    - **bursting** pain: *Gels*
    - **drawing** pain: carbn-s k2 thuj
    - **pressing** pain: nat-m
  - **10**-15 h: *Nat-m* vh *Tub* vh
    - **stitching** pain: tub c1
  - **11** h: cassia-s ↓ sanguis-s hrn2•
    - **dull** pain: cassia-s ccrh1•
  - **noon**; until: pitu-gl skp7• ven-m rsj12•
  - **evening**; until: sep ↓
    - **boring** pain: sep h2
  - **amel.**: ind lact
  - **bursting** pain: allox tpw3
  - **drawing** pain: *Kali-c* mag-c k* sulph k* thuj k* vanil fd5.de
  - **dull** pain: hydroph rsj6• *Ven-m* rsj12•
  - **menses**; during: sulph ↓
    - **pressing** pain: sulph k*
  - **pressing** pain: cocc mag-c mag-m h2* nat-c k* nat-m k* nat-s k* nicc k* plect a1 ruta fd4.de sacch-a fd2.de• sars k* sulph k* tell rsj10• tritic-vg fd5.de vanil fd5.de zinc h2
  - **sore**: mag-s
  - **stitching** pain: gink-b sbd1• mang k* sars k*
  - **tearing** pain: alum sars
  - **torn**; as if: graph
- **noon**: chel k* chord-umb rly4• con ↓ dirc k* fago k* gent-l ↓ graph ↓ ign k* mur-ac ↓ petr ↓ puls-n ruta fd4.de spong fd4.de **Sulph** k* vanil fd5.de verat k* zinc k* zing ↓
  - **19** h; until: lac-cp sk4•
  - **drawing** pain: petr k* zing k*
  - **pressing** pain: gent-l k* ruta fd4.de *Sulph* k* vanil fd5.de zinc k*
  - **shooting** pain: con
  - **stitching** pain: con k* mur-ac k* zinc kl
  - **tearing** pain: graph zinc
- **afternoon**: aeth ↓ ail k* *Aloe* alum alum-p k2 ambr anac arg-n bad bamb-a ↓ bapt a1 bism ↓ borx bov bry bufo calc-s k* cann-i carb-v ↓ carneg-g rwt1• castm caust chel ↓ chin chinin-s cic cimic cinch a1 coca colch com a1 con cortiso tpw7* cycl dios k* dioxi rbp6 dirc k* dulc fd4.de fago k* form k* gels glon k* graph grat ↓ hell ↓ hipp k* hir skp7• ign ind iris-foe jab *Kali-c* kali-cy kali-n kali-s kali-sil k2 kreos lac-c lact laur lil-t lyc k* lyss mag-c mag-s k* mang melal-alt ↓ merc-i-r k* mosch a1 mur-ac myric k* naja nat-ar nat-c ↓ nat-m nit-ac olib-sac wmh1 op peti ph-ac phos k* pip-m k* plect a1 psil ft1 puls k* ran-b rhus-r ruta fd4.de sacch-a ↓ sang senec sep ↓ serp sil sol-t-ae spong fd4.de stront-c sulph k* tab tarent tritic-vg fd5.de valer vanil fd5.de *Ven-m* rsj12•
  - **13** h: fl-ac ↓ ven-m ↓
    - **amel.**: propr sa3•
    - **pressing** pain: fl-ac ven-m rsj12•
  - **14** h: alum ↓ hir skp7• laur ↓ sep ↓ ven-m rsj12• verat ↓
    - **drawing** pain: verat
    - **stitching** pain: alum
    - **tearing** pain: laur sep
  - **14**-3 h: ant-t ↓
    - **tearing** pain: ant-t
  - **14**-16 h: mag-s ↓
    - **tearing** pain: mag-s
  - **15** h: hura lyc lycps-v sep verat-v
    - **15**-16 h: abrom-a ↓
      - **night**; until: abrom-a ks5
        - **pressing** pain: abrom-a ks5
        - **pulsating** pain: abrom-a ks5
      - **pressing** pain: abrom-a ks5
    - **15**-19 h: tarent
    - **15**-20 h: arn
  - **15**.30 h: ven-m rsj12•
  - **16** h: arg-mur chinin-s phys pic-ac sel ↓ *Sulph* ven-m ↓
    - **dull** pain: ven-m rsj12•
    - **pressing** pain: ven-m rsj12•

- **afternoon** – **16** h: ...
  - **vise**; as if in a: sel rsj9•
  - **17** h: falco-pe nl2• ozone sde2• paeon stram ven-m rsj12•
  - **amel**.: hir skp7• lac-h ↓
    - **dull** pain: lac-h sk4•
  - **boring** pain: bism
  - **dull** pain: vanil fd5.de *Ven-m* rsj12•
  - **lancinating**: sol-t-ae k*
  - **pressing** pain: *Aloe* bamb-a stb2.de• carb-v chin h1 hell a1 *Kali-c* melal-alt gya4 nit-ac h2 ran-b ruta fd4.de sacch-a fd2.de• senec k* spong fd4.de sulph tritic-vg fd5.de vanil fd5.de
  - **riding** in a carriage agg.: lyc
  - **siesta**: | **amel**.: ozone sde2•
  - **stitching** pain: aeth k* alum k* grat k* mag-c k* mur-ac nat-c k* vanil fd5.de
  - **tearing** pain: alum chel graph laur lyc h2 sep sulph
  - **waking**; on: sulph k*
  - **walking** agg.: *Kali-c* k*
- **evening**: acon k* agar k* agn ↓ alum alum-p k2 alum-sil ↓ alumn anac ang k* ant-t k* aran arg-met arg-n k* ars ars-i arum-t bad k* bamb-a stb2.de• bapt k* bar-c bar-i k2 bar-s k2 bism borx bov brach a1 brom bry k* cact k* calc ↓ calc-s camph castm caust chel k* chin k* chinin-s cimic cina cinnb cocc coff ↓ coloc ↓ crot-h *Cycl* k* dig k* digin ↓ dios dulc erig fago k* ferr ferr-ar ferr-i ferr-p fl-ac k* graph ham hell k* hipp k* hir rsj4• hura iber ignis-alc ↓ ind indg iod *Iris* iris-foe jug-r kali-c kali-i kali-n *Kali-s* kali-sil k2 *Kalm* lac-ac lac-e hrn2• lac-leo hrn2• lach k* lepi lil-t luf-op ↓ lyc lycpr lyss mag-c mag-m mag-s mang ↓ merc merc-i-f k* merc-i-r k* mim-p rsj8• myric k* narc-ps a1 nat-c hr1 nat-m *Nat-s* ↓ nit-ac nit-s-d a1 nuph ol-an osm paeon k* ped peti ph-ac phos k* phys k* pic-ac k* plat plb plect a1 podo k* psor *Puls* ran-b ran-s rat rhus-r rumx ruta fd4.de sars sel seneg sep k* sil sin-n k* spong fd4.de staph sul-ac sul-i k2 *Sulph* k* tab tell rsj10• tetox pin2• thuj k* tritic-vg fd5.de (non:uran-met k) uran-n usn ↓ ust k* valer vanil fd5.de ven-m rsj12• yuc a1 zinc
  - **18** h: brom ↓ mag-c ↓
    - **stitching** pain: mag-c
    - **tearing** pain: brom
  - **19** h: chinin-s nat-m *Sulph* verat
  - **19**-20 h: sep
  - **19**-21 h: cocc
  - **20** h: lac-e hrn2• lac-leo hrn2• petr-ra shn4• sol-ni
  - **20**-23 h: *Sil* ↓
    - **stitching** pain: *Sil*
  - **21** h: aq-mar skp7•
  - **amel**.: chin clem k* coca kali-bi naja op phys a1
  - **bed** agg.; in: fl-ac k* mag-s nat-c ↓ sep k*
    - **burning**: nat-c k*
    - **stitching** pain: nat-c k*
  - **boring** pain: calc nat-s ruta fd4.de
  - **burning**: nat-c k*
  - **bursting** pain: rat a1 ruta usn a2
  - **drawing** pain: ang h1* bar-c h2* graph k* kali-c h2* kali-n k*
  - **dull** pain: luf-op rsj5• mim-p rsj8• vanil fd5.de
  - **jerking** pain: alumn k*
  - **pressing** pain: *Acon* k* alum anac k* ang h1 castm coff coloc k* dig k* dulc ignis-alc es2• kali-c k* kalm k* mag-m k* mang h2 nat-c hr1 nat-m k* *Nat-s* *Ph-ac* h2 phos h2* **Puls** ran-b sep h2 *Sulph* k* tab k* thuj k* valer vanil fd5.de *Zinc* k*
  - **shooting** pain: arum-t a1 mag-m
  - **singing**; after: rumx
  - **sitting** agg.: staph ↓
    - **tearing** pain: staph
  - **sore**: ph-ac h2
  - **stitching** pain: alum k* bov k* dig digin a1 dulc fd4.de mag-c h2 mag-m h2* mang k* nat-c k* nat-m k* sel a1 sil k* sulph k* tritic-vg fd5.de vanil fd5.de
  - **tearing** pain: agn alum alum-sil k2 coloc hell lyc mag-m *Merc* *Puls* sars sil staph
- **night**: *Acon* ambr ↓ anac arg-n ars camph carb-v ↓ caust cham ↓ chinin-s cinnb k* croc crot-c a1 crot-h k* cycl fago k* ham k* hep hir skp7• hura kali-c kali-sil k2 lac-ac lachn lyc mag-s melal-alt ↓ merc merc-i-f a1 merc-i-r k* naja nat-m ↓ olib-sac wmh1 pip-m k* plb ↓ ptel puls h1* puls-n raph ruta fd4.de sang k* sil sin-n k* spig spong fd4.de sulph ↓ tarent k* *Thuj* til vanil fd5.de
  - **midnight**: hep k* *Kali-c* ↓ mag-s k* petr k*
    - **before**:
      - **22**.30-1.30 h: ven-m ↓
        - **pressing** pain: ven-m rsj12•
    - **after**: **Lac-c**
      - **1** h:
        - **waking**; on: psor ↓
          - **blow**; pain as from a: psor
      - **2** h; after: cimic
      - **3** h; after: lyc h2
    - **until** morning: hep
    - **coughing**; when: hep ↓
      - **stitching** pain: hep
    - **drawing** pain: *Kali-c* k*
    - **waking** him or her from sleep: vac ↓
      - **bursting** pain: vac jl2*
    - **waking** up: vac ↓
      - **lightning**-like: vac jl2
  - **amel**.: clem phys
  - **bed** agg.; in: sulph ↓
    - **shooting** pain: sulph k*
  - **boring** pain: carb-v k* ruta fd4.de sulph
  - **burning**: lyc k* *Merc*
  - **bursting** pain: *Crot-c*
  - **drawing** pain: nat-m k*
  - **jerking** pain: sil
  - **pressing** pain: melal-alt gya4 vanil fd5.de
  - **stitching** pain: cham h1 nat-m k* spig k* vanil fd5.de
  - **tearing** pain: ambr h1 caust hep lyc *Merc* plb thuj
  - **waking**; on: canth ↓ cinnb k* merc-i-f k* puls-n *Sil* ↓
    - **pressing** pain: canth k* *Sil*
- **accompanied** by:
  - **buzzing**: ven-m rsj12•
  - **hunger**: psor jl2
  - **nausea**: choc srj3• tritic-vg fd5.de vanil fd5.de *Ven-m* rsj12•
  - **sadness**: luf-op rsj5•
  - **vertigo** (See VERTIGO - Accompanied - head - pain - forehead)
  - **Cervical** region:
    - **pain**: ozone ↓
      - **cramping**: ozone sde2•
  - **Eyes**:
    - **coldness**: germ-met srj5•
    - **heaviness** of eyelids: sep
  - **Heart** | **complaints** of the (See CHEST - Heart; complaints - accompanied - head - pain - forehead)
- **aching**: agath-a nl2• merc-i-f ptk1
  - **alternating** with | **jerking** pain in forehead (See jerking - alternating - dull)
- **acupressure** amel.: galeoc-c-h gms1•
- **air**; draft of | **amel**.: ferr-i k2
- **air**; in open:
  - **agg**.: agar k* *Bell* calc caust ↓ chel k* euphr *Glon* ↓ hera a1 kali-bi kalm lac-c lach lachn laur ↓ lil-t *Mang* *Nux-v* ran-b ↓ rhus-t ↓ rumx sil staph valer ↓
    - **boring** pain: calc
    - **cutting** pain: kali-bi
    - **pressing** pain: *Bell* calc caust k* *Glon* k* laur k* mang h2 ran-b k2 rhus-t k* valer
    - **shooting** pain: mang
    - **stitching** pain: *Mang* k* sil k*

- **air**; in open – **agg**.: ...
  - **tearing** pain: lachn c1 mang
  - **amel**.: abrom-a ks5 acon alum ang *Apis* aq-mar rbp6 arg-met aur aur-m berb brom ↓ cact k* calc camph carb-ac cassia-s ↓ cimic k* colch coloc cor-r k* crot-t dulc fd4.de euphr *Ferr Ferr-i Ferr-p* flor-p rsj3• ham k* hell hydr bg1 hydr-ac jac-c jac-g jug-r k* kali-bi lach *Mag-m* mag-s merc *Nat-c* ↓ nuph k* *Phos* k* pic-ac puls bg1 ran-s sp1 *Sabin* ↓ sanic sars sel ↓ seneg sep sin-n a1 stann ↓ sul-ac h2* sulph tab tarax trios ↓ viol-t
    - **burning**: alum **Phos** stann
    - **bursting** pain: cassia-s ccrh1•
    - **pressing** pain: *Alum* **Apis** brom *Ferr* h1* ferr-i *Nat-c Phos Sabin* seneg sep tarax h1
    - **pulsating** pain: trios rsj11•
    - **stitching** pain: sars k* *Sep* k* tab k*
    - **stunning** pain: tarax h1
    - **tearing** pain: alum aur mag-s
    - **vise**; as if in a: sel rsj9•
- **alternating** with:
  - **Chest**; crampy pain in: lachn ↓
    - **followed** by | **tearing** within nose and shoulders: lachn k*
  - **Joints**:
    - **gouty** pain in: eup-per k2 sulph
    - **pain** in: sulph
  - **Lumbar** region; pain in: brom
  - **Occiput**; pain in: acon agn ars bg1 lac-ac c1 mosch ptel bg1 sulph
  - **Side** to side; pain from (See alternating sides)
  - **Vertex**; pain in: cot a1*
  - **Wrist**; drawing pain in: sulph k*
- **anger**; after: petr
- **ascending** stairs agg.: alum ang ↓ *Ant-c* arn **Bell** ↓ cimic dulc fd4.de ign meny par bg1 sulph
  - **pressing** pain: ang h1 arn **Bell** dulc fd4.de meny
- **bandaging**:
  - **amel**.: cassia-s ↓ lac-d ↓
    - **bursting** pain: cassia-s ccrh1• lac-d
    - **dull** pain: cassia-s ccrh1•
    - **pulsating** pain: cassia-s ccrh1•
- **bed** agg.; in: ran-b ↓
  - **pressing** pain: ran-b k*
- **bending**:
  - **backward**:
    - **agg**.: chin ↓ stann ↓
      - **pressing** pain: chin stann
    - **amel**.: *Bell* ↓ *Ign* ↓
      - **pressing** pain: *Bell Ign*
  - **head**:
    - **backward**:
      - **agg**.: chin stann
        - **extending** to | **Temples**; both: chin h1
      - **amel**.: bell sanic thuj verat
    - **downward**:
      - **agg**.: bamb-a ↓ *Coloc* ↓ nat-m ↓
        - **pressing** pain: bamb-a stb2.de• *Coloc* nat-m
    - **forward**:
      - **agg**.: cassia-s ↓ tarent
        - **bursting** pain: cassia-s ccrh1•
      - **amel**.: tril-p c1
- **binding** head up | **amel**.: lac-d
- **biting** pain: spig h1
- **blow**; pain as from a: chel bg2 nat-m bg2 phos bg2
- **blowing** the nose agg.: alum sep ↓
  - **cutting** pain: sep k*
- **boil**; like a: hep c1
- **boring** pain: agar k* am-c bg2 am-m k* anac ang bg2 ant-c k* ant-t apis arg-met k* *Arg-n* k* *Ars* k* aur k* aur-m-n aur-s k2 bar-c bar-s k2 *Bell* k* *Bism* k* bov k* brom k* bry calad k* calc k* carb-v k* carbn-s chel k* chin chinin-s cimic k* colch k* *Coloc* k* cycl dios k* dros k* *Dulc* k* hell k* hep k* hydr-ac k* ign k* ip k* iris kali-c kali-p k2 kali-sil k2 laur k* led k* lyss br1 mag-m mang k* *Merc* mez k* mosch k* *Nat-m Nat-s* k* nicc k* nit-s-d a1 ol-an phel phos *Plat* k* propl ub1• psor puls ruta sabad sabin *Sang* k* sep k* *Sil* k* *Spig* k* *Spong* squil staph sul-ac sulph zinc
  - **intermittent**: arg-met
  - **inward**: bell k* calc k* cocc kali-c
  - **outward**: ant-c k* bell bism k* bov dros k* *Dulc* ip k* sep spig spong *Staph*
- **breaking** sensation after dinner: nat-s ↓
  - **sore**: nat-s
- **burning**: acon k* agath-a nl2• *Alum* k* alum-p k2 am-c k* ant-t k* *Arn* b7a.de *Ars* k* aur k* aur-ar k2 aur-m bell k* bism k* brom a1 bry k* carb-ac k* carb-an k* carb-v k* carc fd2.de• *Caust* k* cham k* chel k* *Chin* coc-c bg2 *Coloc* k* con bg2 conv crot-t cupr dendr-pol sk4• *Dig* b4a.de dulc k* eup-per k* glon k* grat k* helon hr1 *Hep* b4a.de hyos k* ip k* kali-bi bg2 kali-c **Kali-i** k* kali-m k2 kali-p lach b7a.de lil-t k* *Lyc* k* lyss mag-m k* mang k* meny k* merc k* merc-i-r k* mez k* mur-ac k* *Nat-c* k* nat-m k* nat-s bg2 nept-m lsd2.fr nux-m k* *Nux-v* k* ox-ac **Phos** k* phys k* podo pot-e rly4• psor k* rhus-t k* rhus-v k* sabad k* sec k* sep h2 *Spig* k* spong fd4.de stann k* staph k* stront-c k* sul-ac k* sulph bg2 tarent k* teucr k* ther vac jl2 viol-o bg2 xan c1 zinc zinc-p k2
- **burnt**; as if: positr nl2•
- **burrowing**: agar k* anac b4.de* ant-t b7.de* arg-n bg2 bar-c k* bism b7.de* *Bry* b7.de* caust b4a.de cham k* coc-c k* dulc k* eupi k* ign b7.de* kali-c mag-m k* merc b4.de* mez h2 plat k* sabad b7.de* sang a1 sep b4.de* spig k* squil b7.de* sulph bg2 thuj bg2
- **bursting** pain: allox tpw3 *Am-c* k* ant-c k* apis b7a.de* *Ars* bamb-a stb2.de• bar-c k* bar-s k2 *Bell* k* *Bry* b7a.de calad k* *Calc* k* caps k* cassia-s ccrh1• chinin-s crot-c dulc k* *Ferr* k* flor-p rsj3• *Gels Glon Graph* k* hell k* hydr k* indg k* iod bg2 ip bg2 kali-bi bg2 *Kali-c* k* kali-n kali-p kali-sil k2 lac-c lac-d lyc *Mag-m* **Merc** k* mez bg2* moni rfm1• nat-ar *Nat-c* k* **Nat-m** k* nat-s nicc a1 *Nux-v* k* *Olnd* k* petr-ra shn4• prun mrr1 **Puls** k* pycnop-sa mrz1 rat k* ruta sabin c1 *Sang* sep sil k* sol-ni k* spig k* spong k* staph k* stry sulph k* thuj k* ust k* *Vac* jl2 vip bg2 **Zinc** k* [bell-p-sp dcm1]
  - **paroxysmal**: kali-c
  - **small**; as if too: bamb-a stb2.de•
- **business** men: *Arg-met*
- **children**; in: lat-m bnm6•
- **chill**:
  - **after**: mang
  - **before**: oci-sa sp1
  - **during**: arn ↓ *Ars* ↓ cham ↓ coli jl2 eup-pur **Nat-m** petr ↓ ran-b ↓ sep ↓
    - **drawing** pain: petr h2*
    - **dull** pain: cham h1
    - **pressing** pain: *Ars* cham h1 ran-b k2 sep k*
    - **stitching** pain: arn
  - **with**: mang ↓
    - **stitching** pain: mang h2
- **chilliness**; during: sang ↓
  - **boring** pain: sang k*
- **closed**, eyes forcibly: *Cocc*
- **closing** the eyes:
  - **amel**.: *Agar* aloe k* atro a1 **Bell** *Bry* calc *Chel* ↓ nat-m sin-n a1
    - **pressing** pain: *Chel Nat-m*
      - **band**; as from a: *Chel*
  - **must** close the eyes: **Bell** ↓ calc ↓ carb-v ↓ *Nat-m* ↓ nux-v ↓ plat ↓
    - **pressing** pain: **Bell** calc carb-v h2 *Nat-m* nux-v plat
- **coffee** agg.: kali-n ↓
  - **tearing** pain: kali-n

- **cold**:
  - **air**:
    - **agg**.: aran zzc1• *Bell* calc carb-an caust chlam-tr↓ dulc fd4.de ferr *Iris* kali-bi *Nux-v* rhus-t sacch-a↓ sep sil ther k2 zing
      - **pressing** pain: chlam-tr bcx2• *Nux-v* sacch-a fd2.de•
    - **amel**.: lyc **Phos** pip-m
    - **breathing** | **through** nose: cor-r br1
  - **applications**:
    - **amel**.: *Ant-t*↓ *Apis*↓ *Ars*↓ calc↓ cassia-s↓ chel colch↓ *Cycl* dulc fd4.de merl *Phos* **Sulph** tritic-vg fd5.de vanil fd5.de
      - **boring** pain: colch
      - **dull** pain: cassia-s ccrh1•
      - **pressing** pain: *Ant-t Apis Ars* calc dulc fd4.de **Phos**
      - **stitching** pain: cassia-s ccrh1•
  - **drinks** | **agg**.: dig bg1
  - **foot**-bath:
    - **amel**.: nat-s↓
      - **grasping** pain: nat-s k*
  - **forehead**; with: cimic *Cinnb*
  - **hands**:
    - **amel**.: carb-ac k* ozone sde2• *Phos*↓
      - **burning**: carb-ac *Phos*
- **company**:
  - **agg**.: *Plb*
    - **pressing** pain: *Plb*
  - **amel**.: cortico sp1
- **compressed**; as if: acon b7a.de alum b4.de* anac b4.de* bry b7.de* cann-s b7.de* cina b7.de* cocc b7.de* fl-ac bg2 hyos b7.de* lyc b4.de* mosch b7.de* olnd b7.de* plat b4.de* spig b7.de* staph b7.de* sul-ac b4.de* thuj b4.de* verb bg2
- **constant**: conch fkr1• med jl2
- **contracted**; as if | **skin** on middle of forehead were contracted; as if: gels rb2
- **contracting**: bism a1 nicotam rly4• ozone sde2• suis-pan rly4• tritic-vg fd5.de
- **coryza**; during: all-c tl1 *Ars* bg2 *Lyc* bg2
- **cough**:
  - **during**:
    - **agg**.: acon alum↓ anac ant-t *Apis* arn *Asc-t* k* asim **Bell** brom k* **Bry** *Calc* chel k* coc-c k2 coca con↓ cortico tpw7* ferr ferr-i ferr-p form ham↓ hep hyos iod irid-met srj5• iris kali-bi kali-s↓ kreos lyc mez moni rfm1• mosch **Nat-m** nit-ac↓ *Ol-j Phos* plut-n srj7• rumx ruta sars↓ seneg sep spong staph stict sul-ac↓ sulph verb ziz a1
      - **bursting** pain: *Nat-m* ol-j staph stict
      - **cutting** pain: hyos ziz k*
      - **jerking** pain: sul-ac h2
      - **pressing** pain: acon alum arn bell brom bry chel con hep kali-s fd4.de kreos nit-ac phos ruta sars sep spong verb
      - **stitching** pain: anac k* arn k* ham fd3.de• hep k* hyos k* mez sulph k*
    - **amel**.: arg-mur k*
- **cramping**: aeth k* asaf tl1 bell k* calc h2 croc k* ign k* nat-c b4a.de* nat-s bg2 *Plat* k* stront-c b4.de*
- **crowded** room | **pressing** pain (See room - crowded - pressing)
- **cutting** pain: acon aesc agar k* am-c apoc a1 *Arg-n Bell* k* bism calc k* camph carb-ac *Caust Chel* chlam-tr bcx2• cinnb coc-c k* coloc con *Cupr* cycl dios k* dros erio a1 ferr ger-i rly4• glon a1 jug-r kali-bi *Lach* lyc lyss mag-c k* mang nat-m k* phos a1 podo k* sabin sel rsj9• senec a1 seneg sep k* stann staph h1* stram a1 tarent ter trios rsj11• **Valer**
  - **knife**; as with a: *Lach* mang nat-m sabin ter
  - **pulsating** pain: acon
- **descending**:
  - **agg**.: *Bell Ferr* k*
  - **stairs**:
    - **agg**.: *Ferr*↓ meny↓
      - **pressing** pain: *Ferr* meny
- **dinner**; after: *Alum*↓ am-c ant-t↓ aq-mar skp7• calc↓ calc-s chinin-s cimic con grat↓ kali-bi↓ mag-c↓ phos↓ phyt plat↓ sars↓ seneg↓ sulph thuj *Zinc*↓
  - **burning**: *Alum* k* grat k*
  - **drawing** pain: phos k*
  - **pressing** pain: *Alum* k* calc k* con h2 kali-bi plat sars seneg *Zinc* k*
  - **stitching** pain: ant-t k*
  - **tearing** pain: mag-c zinc h2
- **diversion**: *Pip-m* kl
- **drawing** pain: acon k* **Agar** k* agath-a nl2• all-c k* am-c anac k* ang k* ant-c k* ant-t k* *Arg-n* k* *Ars* k* ars-s-f k2 asaf k* asar k* aur b4.de* aur-m aur-m-n k* bad k* bar-c k* bar-s k2 *Bell* k* benz-ac borx k* bry k* calc k* calc-sil k2 cann-i cann-s k* canth k* *Caps* k* carb-ac bg2 carb-an carb-v k* carbn-s castm caust k* chel k* chin k* cic k* *Cimic* cimx a1* cina k* clem k* cocc k* coff b7.de* colch k* *Coloc* k* con k* *Croc* k* cycl k* dulc k* euon a1 eupi k* ferr k* gink-b sbd1• gins k* *Graph* k* *Guaj* k* ham fd3.de• hell k* hipp k* hura br1 *Ign* **Kali-c** k* kali-chl a1 kali-n k* kali-p kali-sil k2 lact k* laur k* led k* lil-t k* *Lyc* k* *Mag-c* k* *Mang* k* meny k* **Merc** k* mez k* mosch *Nat-ar Nat-c Nat-m* k* nat-s k* nit-ac nit-s-d a1 **Nux-v** k* petr k* phos k* *Plat* k* psor k* *Puls* k* ran-b k* rat k* rheum k* *Rhod* k* ruta k* sabad k* sabin k* sel k* seneg k* *Sep* k* sil k* spong fd4.de squil k* *Stann* k* staph k* *Stront-c* k* *Sulph* k* tarax k* ter thiam rly4• thuj k* valer k* vanil fd5.de verb viol-o k* viol-t a1 *Zinc* k* zinc-p k2 zing k*
  - **alternating** with | **Wrist**; pain in: sulph
  - **intermittent**: agar h2* thuj k*
  - **paroxysmal**: zinc h2*
  - **upward**: nit-ac h2
  - **wandering** pain: chel
  - **worm** creeping through; as from a: sulph
- **drinking** | **after**:
  - **cold** water:
    - **agg**.: dig↓
      - **shooting** pain: dig br1
  - **cold** water | **agg**.: dig c1
- **dull** pain: *Aesc Agar* k* agath-a nl2• aloe gsy1 ant-c k* ant-t k* *Apis* b7a.de arn asar k* asc-t c1 bamb-a stb2.de• bapt bros-gau mrc1 cadm-met tpw6 calc k* camph k* cann-i **Carb-ac** carb-v b4.de* cartl-s rly4• cassia-s ccrh1• *Chel* chion br1 chord-umb rly4• cimic k* *Cinnb* cocc k* coff k* coli rly4• *Coll* coloc k* cop br1 **Cupr** cupr-ar *Dulc* k* euph k* *Euphr* falco-pe nl2• ferr b7a.de fic-m gya1 fl-ac form fuma-ac rly4• ger-i rly4• *Glon* k* granit-m es1• graph h2 haliae-lc srj5• ham fd3.de• hell k* hydr *Hydroph* rsj6• hyos ign k* ignis-alc es2• ind iris kali-s fd4.de ketogl-ac rly4• lac-del hrn2• lac-h sk4• laur k* lept limest-b es1• loxo-recl knl4• merc-c b4a.de mim-p rsj8• musa a1 mygal nat-c h2 nat-m k* nicotam rly4• olib-sac wmh1 oxeod a1 ozone sde2• petr-ra shn4• ph-ac k* phos k* plac-s rly4• *Plat* k* plb k* plut-n srj7• podo fd3.de• pot-e rly4• psil ft1 puls k* rheum k* rumx hr1 ruta fd4.de sabad k* sal-al blc1• sars *Sep* spong fd4.de stict br1 succ-ac rly4• suis-em rly4• suis-hep rly4• suis-pan rly4• suprar rly4• tritic-vg fd5.de tung-met bdx1• urol-h rwt• vanil fd5.de *Ven-m* rsj12• verat k* zinc k* [bell-p-sp dcm1]
  - **accompanied** by:
    - **Cervical** region:
      - **pain**: ozone↓
        - **burning**: ozone sde2•
- **eating**:
  - **after**:
    - **agg**.: alum↓ *Am-c*↓ bism↓ carl↓ clem↓ *Cocc*↓ con↓ *Graph*↓ nat-m↓ nat-s↓ nit-ac↓ *Nux-v*↓ sep↓ sulph↓
      - **boring** pain: bism
      - **burning**: *Nux-v*
      - **bursting** pain: am-c *Graph* k* nit-ac h2
      - **pressing** pain: *Am-c* carl k* clem k* *Cocc* con k* graph k* (non:lyc kl) nat-m h2 nat-s
      - **stitching** pain: alum (non:lyc kl) sulph
      - **tearing** pain: sep sulph
    - **amel**.: chel↓
      - **tearing** pain: chel h1

- **eating**: ...
  - **agg.**: alum am-c aran bov brom *Bry* calc-s calen *Carb-v* k* cham chel *Chin* chinin-s clem *Cocc* colch con graph hydr inul jug-r vml3• kali-bi kali-br *Kali-c* kali-n kali-s lyc mag-c *Nat-m* k* nat-s op pert-vc vk9 *Phos* phyt plat sars sulph tab valer zinc
  - **amel.**: anac↓ calc-sil k2 carb-an chel *Cist* dulc↓ genist kali-p↓ kali-s fd4.de phyt k* psor k* **Sep** *Thuj* tritic-vg fd5.de vanil fd5.de
    - **grinding** pain: anac
    - **pressing** pain: chel h1 dulc fd4.de kali-p psor tritic-vg fd5.de vanil fd5.de
    - **shooting** pain: **Sep**
  - **while**:
    - **agg.**: kali-p↓ lyc↓
      - **boring** pain: kali-p k2
      - **pressing** pain: lyc h2
      - **stitching** pain: lyc h2
- **epistaxis** | **amel.**: bufo br1
- **excitement** agg.: dys fmm1• par↓
  - **pressing** pain: par
- **exertion** | **after**:
    - **agg.**: nat-c↓
      - **bursting** pain: nat-c
      - **pressing** pain: nat-c
  - **agg.**: cassia-s↓ *Zinc*↓ *Zing*↓
    - **bursting** pain: cassia-s ccrh1•
    - **drawing** pain: *Zinc* k* *Zing* k*
    - **slight** exertion: *Epiph* vh *Sang* ven-m rsj12•
- **exertion** of the eyes agg.: *Plat*
- ○ **Externally**: ang↓ ars-s-f↓ dig↓ hell↓ hep↓ staph↓ *Tarax*↓
  - **stitching** pain: ang k* ars-s-f a1 dig k* hell k* hep k* staph h1 *Tarax* k*
- **fever**; during: ars↓ cassia-s ccrh1• glon↓ thuj↓
  - **pressing** pain: ars h2 glon k* thuj k*
- **fire**, near a: nux-v
- **foot** steps: **Nux-v Sil**
- **formicating** pain: puls h1
- **gnawing** pain: con dros h1 merc-i-r k* nat-s ran-s b7.de* ruta h1 sulph k* zinc k*
- **grasping** pain: arg-n bg2 bar-c bg2 con b4.de* nat-s bg2*
- **grinding** pain: agar k* anac k*
- **griping** pain: ven-m rsj12•
- **hammering** pain: am-m cham h1* cic k* *Dros* b7a.de **Ferr** kali-i kreos **Lyc** mez nicc olnd rheum h suis-pan rly4• verb
- **hat**; from pressure of a: calc-p k2 carb-v↓ ferr-i k2 glon a1 hep k*
  - **pressing** pain: carb-v
- **heat**: cassia-s↓ tela zzc1• trios↓
  - **before** and after: rhus-t hr1
  - **during**: apis *Ars*↓ corn a1 ferr-i sep k* sulph k*
    - **tearing** pain: *Ars*
  - **pulsating** pain: cassia-s ccrh1• trios rsj11•
- **hiccough** agg.: *Bry*↓
  - **pressing** pain: *Bry* k*
- **house** agg.; in: *Apis*↓ cact↓
  - **pressing** pain: *Apis* cact
- **ice** cream agg.: dig↓
  - **shooting** pain: dig br1
- **increasing** gradually: erech vanil fd5.de
- **intermittent**: agar h2* ant-c stann
- **jar** agg.: acon↓ *Bell*↓ *Bry*↓ germ-met↓ glon↓ petr-ra shn4• podo fd3.de• spig k2 *Sulph*↓
  - **pressing** pain: acon *Bell* *Bry* germ-met srj5• glon *Spig* *Sulph*
- **jerking** pain: apis arn k* borx cann-i carbn-s k2 caust cham k* *Chin* dulc b4.de* lyc k* mag-c b4.de* mang h2 op *Prun* k* *Sep* k* *Sil* k* *Stann* k* *Sul-ac* sulph *Thuj* k*
  - **alternating** with | **dull** aching in forehead: stann
  - **backward**: cann-i c1 *Prun*
- **jerking** pain: ...
  - **outward**: lyc
- **junction** with hairy scalp: stroph-h c1
- **lancinating**: *Am-c* *Bell* *Calc* chord-umb rly4• coloc *Cupr* *Dros* ferr ger-i rly4• gins k* jug-r k* ketogl-ac rly4• lyc nat-ox rly4• ped a1 ribo rly4• sang k2 sel c1 tarent k* thiam rly4•
- **laughing**:
  - **agg.**: iris *Nat-m* zing a1
    - **pressing** pain | **band**; as from a: iris
- **leaning** forward sewing: *Borx*
- **light**; from:
  - **agg.**: act-sp↓ arizon-l↓ bov↓ bros-gau mrc1 cact↓ sacch-a↓
    - **pressing** pain: act-sp vh1 arizon-l nl2• cact sacch-a fd2.de•
    - **stitching** pain: bov
  - **amel.**: bros-gau↓
    - **dull** pain: bros-gau mrc1
- **looking**:
  - **intently**:
    - **agg.**: puls↓ spong↓
      - **pressing** pain: puls spong
  - **steadily**: glon k*
  - **upward** | **agg.**: puls bg1
- **lying**:
  - **agg.**: alum arg-met bov bry camph cassia-s↓ cham h1* chim-m cinnb coc-c k2 coloc fl-ac *Gels* lachn mag-s k* merc k* nat-m↓ nat-s ran-b vanil fd5.de
    - **bursting** pain: *Gels*
    - **drawing** pain: nat-m k*
    - **pressing** pain: vanil fd5.de
    - **stitching** pain: cassia-s ccrh1• cham h1
  - **amel.**: abrom-a ks5 anac bamb-a↓ *Bell* calc calc-sil k2 cassia-s cdd7• chlam-tr↓ con cupr glon ham k* kali-bi kali-p↓ *Lac-d* *Lyc*↓ meli nat-m↓ nat-p nat-s↓ pip-m k* pycnop-sa mrz1 rhus-t sep spig tab *Thuj* tritic-vg fd5.de
    - **bursting** pain: cassia-s ccrh1•
    - **pressing** pain: bamb-a stb2.de• *Bell* chlam-tr bcx2• nat-m nat-s tritic-vg fd5.de
    - **stitching** pain: calc cassia-s ccrh1• *Lyc* *Sep*
    - **tearing** pain: kali-p *Lyc* spig k2
  - **back**; on:
    - **agg.**: cinnb *Coloc* dulc↓
      - **pressing** pain: *Coloc* dulc fd4.de
    - **amel.**: dig nux-v spong
      - **pressing** pain: *Nux-v* *Spong*
  - **face**; on the | **amel.**: bry sys
  - **head** low; with the | **amel.**: *Spong*
  - **side**; on:
    - **amel.**: nat-m
    - **left** | **agg.**: *Cinnb*
    - **right** | **amel.**: cinnb
- **lying** down:
  - **agg.**: camph↓
    - **cutting** pain: camph h1
  - **amel.**: mim-p↓
    - **pulsating** pain: mim-p rsj8•
- **menses**:
  - **after**:
    - **agg.**: ferr plat↓
      - **pressing** pain: *Ferr*
      - **stitching** pain: plat
    - **amel.** when flow begins: kali-p↓
      - **tearing** pain: kali-p
  - **before**:
    - **agg.**: acon bell brom *Calc* cimic cinnb ign↓ kali-p lac-c sil tritic-vg fd5.de
      - **pressing** pain: ign *Sil*

- **menses – before – agg.**: ...
    - **tearing** pain: *Cinnb* kali-p
- **close** of; at: crot-h
- **during**:
    - **agg.**: aesc alum am-c am-m apis bamb-a stb2.de• bell brom k* *Bry* cact cain carb-an castm cench k2 cinnb cycl euph *Gels* graph helon iod kali-bi lac-c ↓ lac-d lyc mag-c merc nat-c nat-m nat-p nux-v phos k* plat rat sang k* sep sil sulph
        - **bursting** pain: lyc nat-m
        - **cutting** pain: apis
        - **drawing** pain: mag-c k*
        - **pressing** pain: bamb-a stb2.de• castm lac-c lyc nux-v *Sep* k* *Sil Sulph*
            - **band**; as from a: bamb-a stb2.de•
        - **shooting** pain: *Rat*
        - **stitching** pain: phos
        - **tearing** pain: castm *Cinnb*
    - **first** day of menses agg.: bamb-a ↓
        - **pressing** pain: bamb-a stb2.de•
- **mental** exertion agg.: abrom-a ks5 agar ↓ anac *Arg-met* arg-n arn asar borx bov *Calc* calc-sil k2 coc-c k2 cocc ↓ coff cop dig fago hydr *Iris* kalm lact k* lyss *Mag-c* ↓ manc meli mez *Nat-c Nat-m* **Nat-p** nat-s *Nux-v* ol-an ox-ac k* ozone sde2• petr *Ph-ac Pic-ac* pip-m plb psor puls rhus-r rob sabad ↓ sep *Sil* k* sulph ↓ symph fd3.de• ter vanil fd5.de ven-m rsj12•
    - **drawing** pain: agar h2* asar h1 calc sulph
    - **pressing** pain: abrom-a ks5 anac arn asar k* borx cocc *Dig* fago a1 *Mag-c* k* mez *Nat-c Nat-s* k* petr ph-ac h2 *Psor* sabad *Sil* vanil fd5.de
    - **pulsating** pain: abrom-a ks5
    - **sore**: ph-ac *Sil*
    - **tearing** pain: anac
- **motion**:
    - **agg.**: acon agn ang ant-t arn ↓ *Ars* ars-s-f ↓ atro aur aur-m aur-s k2 bamb-a ↓ **Bell** bism bov **Bry** *Calc* calc-sil k2 canth carb-v ↓ cassia-s ↓ *Chel* cimic cinnb cocc ↓ cop br1 cortiso ↓ cupr cupr-ar cycl dig dulc fago ferr-i **Glon** graph hep ↓ ign iod kali-bi *Kali-c* kali-s fd4.de *Lac-d Lach* lyc mag-c mag-m ↓ meli meny mim-p ↓ mosch nat-c nat-p nat-s ↓ *Nux-v* olib-sac wmh1 par ↓ ph-ac phys rhod rob rumx sabad sacch-a gmj3 *Sang* sep *Sil* sol-ni *Spig* spong ↓ staph sul-i k2 **Sulph** tab *Ther* til ban1• tritic-vg fd5.de vanil fd5.de
        - **boring** pain: dulc sep
        - **bursting** pain: cassia-s ccrh1• nat-c h2
        - **cutting** pain: acon arn lach
        - **dull** pain: mim-p rsj8•
        - **pressing** pain: ant-t bamb-a stb2.de• **Bell** *Bism Bry* carb-v cocc cupr dulc graph h2 kali-c nat-s par ph-ac sep *Spig* spong h1 staph sulph *Ther*
        - **pulsating** pain: cortiso sp1*
        - **rapid** motion: dros iris ↓ nat-m
            - **shooting** pain: iris
        - **shooting** pain: ars-s-f k2 *Lach*
        - **sore**: cupr-ar hep
        - **stitching** pain: ars-s-f k2 *Bov* cassia-s ccrh1• cycl a1 *Kali-c* lyc h2 mag-c h2 *Sep* spong k* staph h1 tritic-vg fd5.de vanil fd5.de
        - **stunning** pain: ph-ac h2
        - **tearing** pain: agn aur mag-m h2 sil h2 spig k2
    - **amel.**: *Agar* bism ↓ *Cic* ↓ germ-met ↓ hydr *Iris Mag-m* hr1 olib-sac ↓ petr pip-m psor ↓ *Puls Rhod* valer ↓ vanil fd5.de
        - **boring** pain: bism
        - **pressing** pain: *Cic* germ-met srj5• psor valer vanil fd5.de
        - **stitching** pain: olib-sac wmh1
    - **arms**; of:
        - **violent**:
            - **agg.**: caust ↓ rhus-t ↓
                - **cutting** pain: caust h2
                - **pressing** pain: rhus-t h1
    - **eyelids**; of:
        - **agg.**: *Bry* coloc
            - **pressing** pain: coloc h2
- **motion**: ...
    - **eyes**; of:
        - **agg.**: *Bad* bapt bell bry chel chinin-s cimic dros dulc ↓ gels *Hep* ign jug-r kali-c lac-c k2 mur-ac ph-ac ↓ *Pic-ac* puls rhus-t sil spig valer
            - **lancinating**: *Dros*
            - **pressing** pain: *Chel* dulc ph-ac *Puls*
            - **sore**: hep
            - **stitching** pain: *Dros*
    - **hands**; of | **agg.**: coc-c
    - **head**; of:
        - **agg.**: lyss ↓ plat ↓ staph ↓
            - **pressing** pain: lyss plat staph h1
            - **stunning** pain: staph h1
        - **must** move head to and fro: *Agar*
- **nail**; as from a: acon a1 anac k2 caust hell *Ign* lyc nicc bg2 sabin **Thuj**
- **nasal** discharge | **amel.**: hydr bg1 kali-bi bg1 *Lach* bg1 nux-v bg1 puls bg1
- **noise** agg.: abrom-a ks5 acon agar allox tpw3 *Bell* cact cassia-s ↓ *Chinin-s* cit-v colch con *Iod* lac-c lac-d plect a1 *Sil Spig* ther k2
    - **bursting** pain: allox sp1
    - **pressing** pain: abrom-a ks5 **Bell** cact
    - **pulsating** pain: abrom-a ks5
    - **stitching** pain: cassia-s ccrh1•
    - **tearing** pain: spig k2
- **noise** as if hammering before the ears; with: spig ↓
    - **lancinating**: spig c1
- **numbness** of brain; with: hydrog srj2•
- **occupation** amel.: calc-sil k2
- **odors** agg.; strong: sel
- **opening** and shutting; as if: bell bg2
- **opening** the eyes: *Ars* ↓ ph-ac ↓
    - **agg.**: ars ↓ positr ↓ *Sil* ↓
        - **drawing** pain: ars
        - **sore**: positr nl2• *Sil*
    - **hindering** opening eyes: bell ↓
        - **pressing** pain: bell h1
    - **pressing** pain: *Ars* ph-ac
- **paroxysmal**: aesc ant-t ars berb petr-ra shn4• *Psor* **Sep** *Spig*
- **pecking**: carb-an k* nat-m h2 nicc a1
- **periodical**: *Cham* ↓ lac-d laur mag-m merc-c nat-s nux-v plb ↓ *Sil* sulph teucr *Tub*
    - **day** | **alternate** day: merc-c
    - **morning** | **alternate** morning lasting all day: *Calc* carbn-s k2
    - **week**:
        - **every**: dys fmm1•
        - **two** weeks; every: dys fmm1•
        - **four** weeks; every: dys fmm1•
    - **tearing** pain: *Cham* plb
- **periodical**, with constipation: nux-v ↓
    - **ulcerative** pain: nux-v k*
- **pinching** pain: acon k* anac k* calc k* eug k* mez k* nit-ac k* nux-m k* petr pot-e rly4• psor k* rheum staph k* til a1 verat k*
- **plug**; as from a: acon bg2 anac asaf k* caust k* hell bg2 jac-c bg2 jac-g kali-i bg2 kreos bg2 lyc bg2 mez bg2 mosch bg2* nat-s bg2 ptel bg2 puls bg2 rhus-t bg2* sul-ac k*
- **pregnancy** agg.; during: carb-ac mrr1
- **pressing** pain: abrom-a ks5 **Acon** k* *Aesc* k* *Aeth* k* *Agar* k* agath-a nl2• agn k* allox sp1 aln vva1• **Aloe** k* alum k* alum-p k2 alum-sil k2 alumn k* *Am-c* k* am-m k* ambr k* ammc k* *Anac* k* ang k* ant-c *Ant-t* k* **Apis** k* *Arg-met* k* *Arg-n* k* *Arn* k* *Ars* k* *Ars-i* ars-s-f k2 **Asaf** k* asar k* aster atp rly4• atro a1 *Aur* k* aur-ar k2 aur-i k2 aur-m-n wbt2• aur-s k2 *Bamb-a* stb2.de• bapt k* *Bar-c* k* bar-i k2 bar-m bar-s k2 **Bell** k* *Berb* k* *Bism* k* *Bism-sn* a1 borx k* bov k* brach a1 *Brom* k* **Bry** k* buth-a sp1 cact calad k* *Calc* k* calc-i k2 calc-sil k2 camph k* cann-i k* cann-s k* canth k* caps k* carb-an carb-v k* carbn-s card-b a1 carl a1 castm *Caust* k* *Cedr* *Cham* k* *Chel* k* chen-a vml3• chim-m

- **pressing** pain: ...
  Chin k* chinin-ar chlam-tr bcx2• choc srj3• chord-umb rly4• cic k* cimic k* cina k* *Cinnb* cit-ac rly4• clem k* cob-n sp1 *Coc-c* *Cocc* k* coff k* colch *Coloc* k* con k* conch fkr1• cop k* *Cor-r* k* croc k* crot-t cupr k* *Cycl* k* cyt-l sp1 *Dig* k* digin a1 dream-p sdj1• *Dros* k* dulc k* elaps ephe-si hsj1• *Euph* k* euphr k* eupi k* fago a1 *Ferr* k* *Ferr-ar* *Ferr-i* k* *Ferr-p* fl-ac fuma-ac rly4• galeoc-c-h gms1• gast a1 gels k* gent-c gent-l k* germ-met srj5• gins k* *Glon* k* gran k* *Granit-m* es1• graph k* grat k* guaj k* ham helio a1 hell k* hura hydr-ac k* *Hyos* k* *Ign* k* ina-i mlk9.de indg k* inul a1* *Iod* k* ip k* iris jac-c a1 jatr-c kali-ar kali-bi k* kali-br a1 *Kali-c* k* kali-cy a1 kali-i k* kali-m k2 *Kali-n* k* *Kali-p* kali-s fd4.de kali-sil k2 *Kalm* ketogl-ac rly4• kola stb3• *Kreos* k* lac-c lac-h htj1• **Lach** k* lachn k* lact k* lact-v hr1 lap-la sde8.de• laur k* led k* lepi k* lept lil-t k* limest-b es1• linu-c a1 *Lyc* k* lycps-v lyss m-arct b7.de *Mag-c* k* *Mag-m* k* manc k* mang k* mang-p rly4• marb-w es1• melal-alt gya4 meny k* *Merc* k* merc-c b4a.de *Mez* k* moni rfm1• mosch k* *Mur-ac* k* musca-d szs1 naja narcot a1 *Nat-ar* *Nat-c* k* *Nat-m* k* *Nat-p* nat-pyru rly4• *Nat-s* k* nat-sil fd3.de• *Nit-ac* k* nit-s-d a1 nux-m k* **Nux-v** k* *Ol-an* k* olib-sac wmh1 *Olnd* k* *Op* k* osm *Ox-ac* k* paeon a1 pall a1 *Par* k* petr k* petr-ra shn4• *Ph-ac* k* phel a1 **Phos** k* **Phyt** k* pieri-b mlk9.de pip-m k* *Plat* k* plb k* plect k* *Plut-n* srj7• positr nl2• pot-e rly4• prun k* prun-p a1 *Psor* k* ptel *Puls* k* *Ran-b* k* raph k* rheum k* *Rhod* k* rhus-t k* ruta k* sabad k* *Sabin* sacch-a fd2.de• samb k* *Sang* k* *Sars* k* sel rsj9* *Seneg* k* *Sep* k* *Sil* k* *Sol-ni* *Spig* k* *Spong* k* squil k* *Stann* k* *Staph* k* *Stict* k* stram stront-c k* suis-pan rly4• sul-ac k* sul-i k2 **Sulph** k* symph fd3.de• tarax k* tarent k* teucr k* thea *Ther* thres-a sze7• thuj k* til k* tong a1 tritic-vg fd5.de tung-met bdx1• ust *Valer* k* vanil fd5.de verat k* verb k* vinc k* viol-t k* x-ray sp1 *Zinc* k* [heroin sdj2]
  - **alternating** with:
    - **expansion**: tarax k*
    - **stitching**: agar a1 **Valer** k*
  - **asunder**: *Ant-c* b7a.de apis b7a.de bar-c b4.de* *Bell* b4.de* *Bry* b7.de* caps b7.de* chel b7.de* hell b7.de* kali-n b4.de* lyc bg2 mez b4.de* phos b4.de* ran-b b7.de* rhus-t b7.de* *Sabin* b7a.de *Spig* b7.de* stann b4.de* verb b7.de*
  - **backward**: dios spong tab
  - **ball**; as from a: bell con mag-s **Staph**
  - **band**; as from a: *Aeth* agath-a nl2• *Ant-t* aur-s wbt2• bamb-a stb2.de• *Carb-ac* k* carb-v hr1 cedr **Chel** coca con helon indg iod iris kali-p *Lac-c* lil-t med jl2 *Merc* mill ozone sde2• ran-s sp1 **Sulph** tarent vanil fd5.de
    - **iron** band; as from an: fuc br1
  - **cramping**: **Plat**
  - **downward**: agath-a nl2• *Aloe* am-m k* ambr ant-t *Asar* bell bry chinin-s cina cocc *Glon* merc mur-ac *Par* ph-ac **Phos** rhus-t sabin
  - **dull** point; as from a: caust
  - **finger**; as from a: ol-an stront-c
  - **forward**: hydr laur mag-s nux-m rhus-t
  - **hat**; as from a tight: agath-a nl2• *Alum*
  - **intermittent**: arn hyos plat
  - **inward**: aeth a1 agar k* agath-a nl2• aloe alum k* ambr bg2 anac ant-c k* asar b7.de* bapt bell k* brom calc k* cina bg2 cocc croc crot-t bg2 cupr bg2 ferr graph hell k* hep hydr bg2 *Kali-c* k* lach bg2 laur k* mosch k* nat-m bg2 nat-s sne nux-m bg2 *Nux-v* k* olnd *Phos* bg2 *Plat* k* ran-s rhod k* rhus-t k* sep h2 spig **Stann** k* staph sulph k* verb zinc
  - **narrow**; as if too: gels k*
  - **outward**: **Acon** k* agath-a nl2• all-c aloe alum k* alum-p k2 *Am-c* k* anac ang k* ant-c b7.de* arg-n *Arn* k* **Asaf** k* *Bar-c* k* bar-m bar-s k2 *Bell* k* benz-ac *Berb* brom *Bry* k* calc k* calc-sil k2 *Camph* cann-i cann-s k* canth k* *Caps* k* carb-v castm caust k* chel k* *Chin* k* cic cimx k* cina colch *Coloc* k* con k* *Cor-r* k* cupr k* *Dros* k* dulc eupi *Ferr* k* germ-met srj5• graph k* grat bg2 hell hep k* *Ign* b7a.de ip k* *Kali-c* k* kali-m k2 *Kali-p* kali-sil k2 *Kreos* k* **Lach** lact *Laur* b7a.de *Lil-t* lyc lyss m-aust b7.de mag-m k* mag-s mang k* med meny k* merc k* mez k* mur-ac k* nat-c k* nat-m k* nat-p nit-ac bg2 *Nux-m* k* nux-v k* *Olnd* k* op k* ph-ac k* *Phos* k* plat k* prun k* *Psor* ptel *Puls* k* ran-b k* rat rhod k* rhus-t k* ruta fd4.de sabad k* senec *Sep* k* *Sil* k* **Spig** k* *Spong* k* *Stann* k* staph k* *Stront-c* k* sul-ac k* *Sulph* k* tarax k* teucr k* thea thuj k* *Verb* k* viol-t k* zinc-p k2
- **pressing** pain – **outward**: ...
  - **brain** would come out, as though: acon all-c am-c ang arn **Bell** k* brom *Bry* canth caps k2* carb-v caust chel colch coloc *Kali-c* kreos **Lach** k* mag-m mag-s mang med mez nat-c nux-v *Phos* plat puls rat rhod sabad sep *Sil* spig spong stann staph stront-c sul-ac thuj verb
  - **eyes** would jump out; as if: kali-n h2
  - **tumor**; as from a: prun mrr1
  - **paroxysmal**: mur-ac h2 plat sep verat zinc h2
  - **upward**: glon nit-ac h2 valer
  - **wedge**-like (See plug)
  - **weight** or stone; as from a: acon k* am-m k* ant-t b7.de* asar b7.de* aur bell k* berb bg2 cham con h2* dig k* *Glon* k* gran bg2 kali-c mag-s bg2 *Nat-m* k* nux-v bg2 *Par* rhus-t k* sep k* sil b4.de* spig k* **Staph** sne tarax thuj b4.de
    - **sinking** weight; like a: thuj h1
- **pressing** teeth together | **amel.**: aq-mar skp7*•
- **pressure**:
  - **agg.**: agath-a nl2• calc camph cortiso skp7• *Cupr* ↓ dios hydrog srj2• mag-m maias-l hrn2• mur-ac ph-ac spig ↓ teucr
    - **boring** pain: calc
    - **cutting** pain: calc *Cupr* dios a1
    - **lancinating**: *Cupr*
    - **pressing** pain: spig k2
    - **stitching** pain: mur-ac k*
  - **amel.**: abrom-a ks5 ail am-c am-m anac apis aq-mar skp7*• aral aran zzc1• *Arg-n* ↓ **Bell** **Bry** cact k* *Calc* calc-sil k2 carb-ac k* cassia-s ↓ castm *Chel* *Chin* chlam-tr ↓ cimic k* clem colch croc dulc fd4.de *Ferr* galeoc-c-h gms1• gels germ-met ↓ *Glon* ham hell hydr ip kali-i kali-p ↓ kalm *Lac-d* lil-t mang meny merc k* merl mur-ac nat-c **Nat-m** nat-s *Nux-v* olnd op phys k* plut-n ↓ **Puls** sabad k* spig spong fd4.de stann sul-ac sulph tarent tela zzc1•
    - **boring** pain: anac h2 colch
    - **bursting** pain: cassia-s ccrh1•
    - **drawing** pain: mang
    - **pressing** pain: am-c *Arg-n* calc chin chlam-tr bcx2• germ-met srj5• kali-p fd1.de• mur-ac h2 *Nat-m* *Nat-s* plut-n srj7• *Spig* stann
    - **stitching** pain: cassia-s ccrh1•
  - **hard**:
    - **amel.**: cassia-s ↓
      - **dull** pain: cassia-s ccrh1•
  - **slight**:
    - **amel.**: cassia-s ↓
      - **pulsating** pain: cassia-s ccrh1•
  - **temple**; on:
    - **amel.**: calc ↓
      - **pressing** pain: calc h2
- **pulling**; like: plb
  - **visor**; as if pulled down like a: agath-a nl2•
- **pulsating** pain: abrom-a ks5 aeth a1 agath-a nl2• alum *Am-c* *Am-m* *Ars* asar bamb-a stb2.de• **Bell** k* *Bry* k* *Calc* calc-sil k2 cann-i *Caps* carb-v carc tpw2* cassia-s ccrh1• *Caust* k* chlam-tr bcx2• chord-umb rly4• cic cimic k* cinch a1 cocc coloc k* cortiso tpw7* cupr-ar *Dig* k* dulc h2* falco-pe nl2• **Ferr** galeoc-c-h gms1• **Glon** guat sp1 gymno br1 hir rsj4• hist sp1 hydrog srj2• *Ign* k* *Iris* jab a1 kali-c h2* kali-i kali-s fd4.de *Kalm* kreos **Lac-c** **Lac-d** laur k* lavand-a ctl1• **Lyc** k* lyss mag-c k* mand rsj7• meli merc-i-f mez mim-p rsj8• naja nat-c hr1 *Nat-m* k* nat-ox rly4• nicc nux-m olnd ost a1 petr phos h2* plat bg2 positr nl2• pot-e rly4• propr sa3• **Puls** k* ruta sanguis-s hrn2• sec k* sep **Sil** sol-ni spong *Stram* suis-pan rly4• ther trios rsj11• tritic-vg fd5.de ven-m rsj12• verat a1 verb zinc k* [spect dfg1]
- **raising** | **eyes**:
  - **agg.**: arn ↓ puls ↓
    - **drawing** pain: puls
    - **stitching** pain: arn
  - **head**:
    - **agg.**: bar-act ↓
      - **pressing** pain: bar-act

- **raising – head**: ...
  - **amel.**: kali-c ↓
    - **stitching** pain: kali-c
- **reading** agg.: arn bamb-a ↓ borx bov bry$_{k*}$ *Calc* carbn-s ↓ caust chinin-s cocc coff ery-a$_{a1}$ ferr-i kali-p$_{fd1.de•}$ lac-e$_{hrn2•}$ led ↓ lob-s lyc$_{k*}$ lyss *Nat-m* ↓ op phys pip-m rob *Ruta* ↓ tarax
  - **boring** pain: led
  - **candlelight**; by: *Spig*
  - **drawing** pain: borx$_{h2}$
  - **pressing** pain: arn bamb-a$_{stb2.de•}$ borx$_{h2}$ *Calc* carbn-s cocc$_{k*}$ kali-p$_{fd1.de•}$ *Nat-m*
  - **stitching** pain: lyc$_{k*}$ *Ruta*$_{k*}$
- **reflecting** agg.: lyc ↓
  - **stitching** pain: lyc$_{k*}$
- **rest**:
  - **agg.**: cic ↓
    - **stunning** pain: cic$_{hr1}$
  - **amel.**: bros-gau ↓ cassia-s ↓
    - **dull** pain: bros-gau$_{mrc1}$
    - **stitching** pain: cassia-s$_{ccrh1•}$
- **riding**:
  - **agg.**: **Cocc** ↓ vanil ↓
    - **pressing** pain: **Cocc** vanil$_{fd5.de}$
  - **carriage**; in a:
    - **agg.**: acon *Cocc* glon *Lyc* nux-m vanil$_{fd5.de}$
    - **amel.**: kali-n
      - **tearing** pain: kali-n
  - **cold** wind; in: ars-i calc-i *Cocc* glon lyc
- **rising**:
  - **after**:
    - **agg.**: agar ↓ bar-c$_{bg1}$ cob$_{k*}$ cocc$_{bg1}$ coloc ↓ dulc$_{k*}$ ery-a$_{a1}$ glon iber$_{k*}$ ign$_{bg1}$ kalm$_{k*}$ mur-ac$_{k*}$ phys$_{k*}$ *Sang*$_{k*}$ verat
      - **drawing** pain: coloc$_{k*}$
      - **stitching** pain: agar$_{k*}$
    - **amel.**; one hour after rising: adam$_{skp7•}$
  - **agg.**: adam$_{skp7•}$ asaf ↓ *Bell* ↓ kalm ↓ lyc ↓ mag-s ↓ *Spig* ↓ *Stram* ↓
    - **pressing** pain: asaf$_{k*}$ *Bell* mag-s$_{k*}$ *Spig*$_{k*}$ *Stram*
    - **tearing** pain: kalm lyc
  - **amel.**: chinin-s *Cinnb*$_{k*}$ spong sulph
    - **pressing** pain: spong$_{h1}$
  - **bed**; from | **agg.**: abrom-a$_{ks5}$
  - **lying**; from | **agg.**: ars$_{h2}$
  - **stooping**; from | **agg.**: asar *Bell* mag-s
- **room**:
  - **agg.**: abrom-a$_{ks5}$ acon brom ↓ bry cact caust coca colch con jug-r lach nat-c ↓ plat ran-b rhod rhus-t sep
    - **pressing** pain: abrom-a$_{ks5}$ *Acon* brom nat-c
    - **stitching** pain: con$_{k*}$ (non:mang$_{kl}$)
  - **amel.**: bell mang
    - **stitching** pain: mang$_{h2}$
  - **closed** room agg.: abrom-a ↓
    - **pulsating** pain: abrom-a$_{ks5}$
  - **crowded** room agg.: *Mag-c* ↓ *Plat* ↓
    - **pressing** pain: *Mag-c*$_{k*}$ *Plat*
  - **entering** a room; when: *Caust* ↓
    - **burning**: *Caust*$_{k*}$
  - **stuffy** room agg.: luf-op$_{rsj5•}$
- **rubbing**:
  - **amel.**: ars ham nicc$_{c1}$ ol-an op *Phos* phys symph$_{fd3.de•}$
    - **sore**: ars$_{h2}$
- **running** upstairs: ven-m ↓
  - **pulsating** pain: ven-m$_{rsj12•}$
- **sauna**; after: bamb-a$_{stb2.de•}$
- **scratching** agg.; after: granit-m ↓ laur ↓
  - **burning**: granit-m$_{es1•}$ laur$_{k*}$
- **screwed** together; as if: chel$_{bg2}$ grat$_{bg2}$ puls$_{bg2}$ sulph$_{bg2}$
- **sewing**; from: iris lac-c
- **shaking** the head; on:
  - **agg.**: *Calc-s* *Carbn-s* coc-c con *Glon*$_{k*}$ merc-c$_{k*}$ pycnop-sa$_{mrz1}$ sep
    - **pressing** pain: sep
  - **amel.**: hyos ↓
    - **pressing** pain: hyos$_{bg1}$
- **shooting** pain: *Acon*$_{k*}$ aesc agar$_{k*}$ ant-t apis$_{k*}$ arn ars-s-f$_{k2}$ arum-t$_{bg2*}$ *Bell*$_{k*}$ berb cedr$_{bg2}$ chin cic$_{h1}$ cimic$_{bg2}$ cinnb$_{k*}$ *Coloc* **Con** cycl dig dios$_{a1}$ dulc euph ferr$_{k*}$ fl-ac$_{k*}$ *Iris* kali-bi *Kali-c* kali-n kali-sil$_{k2}$ kreos$_{k*}$ lob-c$_{a1}$ mag-c mag-m mang merc merc-i-f$_{k*}$ merl$_{k*}$ mosch naja$_{k*}$ nat-c nat-m$_{bg2}$ pic-ac$_{bg2}$ plb$_{k*}$ propr$_{sa3•}$ **Prun** puls rhod rhus-t$_{k*}$ rumx$_{k*}$ sabad senec$_{k*}$ *Sep* sil **Spig**$_{k*}$ still$_{a1}$ stram$_{k*}$ sulph$_{k*}$ tarent$_{k*}$ til tung-met$_{bdx1•}$
  - **diagonally**: chel
  - **flying**: asar jatr-c sep
  - **intermittent**: mag-c
  - **inward**: canth coloc gels lach
  - **outward**: bell$_{a1}$ berb$_{a1}$ con lyc senec$_{k*}$
  - **rhythmical**: kali-n
- **sitting**:
  - **agg.**: aeth agar *Alum* am-m ↓ aur-m-n bism calc$_{kl}$ (non:calc-act$_{kl}$) castm caust *Chin* con glon ham *Iris* *Lac-d* lach merc mez phos ruta seneg spig spong staph tarax tell ↓ ter vanil$_{fd5.de}$ verat
    - **burning**: *Alum* phos$_{a1}$
    - **drawing** pain: *Aur-m-n*$_{k*}$
    - **pressing** pain: agar alum *Bism*$_{a1}$ *Spong* tell$_{rsj10•}$ vanil$_{fd5.de}$
    - **stitching** pain: chin$_{k*}$
    - **tearing** pain: aeth$_{a1}$ am-m merc **Spig** staph
  - **amel.**: acon ars *Bell* ven-m$_{rsj12•}$
    - **pressing** pain: *Bell*
  - **dark** room; in a | **amel.**: ven-m$_{rsj12•}$
- **sleep**:
  - **after**:
    - **agg.**: ant-c ant-t calc cassia-s ↓ cham cinnb coc-c$_{k2}$ con erig euphr fago hell lyc myric nat-ar ozone$_{sde2•}$ petr-ra$_{shn4•}$ sol-ni stram thuj
      - **stitching** pain: cassia-s$_{ccrh1•}$
    - **amel.**: ars-s-f$_{k2}$ dulc$_{fd4.de}$ kali-bi lac-cp$_{sk4•}$ **Phos** *Sep*
  - **amel.**: thuj ↓
    - **sore**: thuj
  - **going** to sleep; on:
    - **agg.**: alum ↓ ven-m ↓
      - **pulsating** pain: ven-m$_{rsj12•}$
      - **stitching** pain: alum$_{k*}$
- **sleepiness**; with: ars-i ↓ carbn-s ↓ vanil ↓
  - **pressing** pain: ars-i$_{k2}$ carbn-s$_{k2}$ vanil$_{fd5.de}$
- **smarting**: bapt canth carb-an gels graph$_{k*}$ hydr lach
- **smoking** agg.: calad caust coloc ↓ ferr-i *Mag-c* ↓
  - **pressing** pain: calad$_{k*}$ coloc *Mag-c*$_{k*}$
- **sneezing**:
  - **after**: apis ↓
    - **pressing** pain: apis
  - **agg.**: apis arn$_{k*}$ echi *Nat-m*$_{k*}$ sabad
- **sore**: acon am-m$_{bg2}$ ang$_{k*}$ ant-t$_{k*}$ apis *Arn* ars$_{k*}$ ars-s-f$_{k2}$ asaf$_{bg2}$ bapt bufo canth carb-an$_{k*}$ cob coff$_{k*}$ *Coloc* cupr-ar dros$_{h1}$ *Euph* gels$_{k*}$ germ-met$_{srj5•}$ glon$_{k*}$ granit-m$_{es1•}$ graph$_{bg2}$ *Hep*$_{k*}$ hipp hydr ignis-alc$_{es2•}$ indg iod$_{k*}$ lach lil-t lyc mag-s merc merc-i-f mez$_{bg2}$ mur-ac nat-ar nat-c nat-m$_{k*}$ nux-v$_{bg2}$ *Par* ph-ac plan plat$_{k*}$ podo prun **Puls**$_{k*}$ ran-b$_{k*}$ *Rumx*$_{k*}$ sang sarr **Sil** sol-ni spig spong stann$_{k*}$ stram$_{bg2}$ sul-ac sulph tell teucr thuj$_{k*}$ zinc ziz
  - **surface** of brain, as if on: ph-ac
  - **violent** blow, as after: arn chel sol-ni sul-ac
- **sour** food agg.: aq-mar$_{skp7*•}$
- **squeezed**; as if: *Acon*$_{b7.de*}$ ambr$_{b7a.de}$ anac$_{b4.de*}$ ars$_{b4.de*}$ asaf$_{b7a.de}$ colch$_{b7.de*}$ *Ign*$_{b7.de*}$ mez$_{b4.de*}$ plat$_{b4.de*}$ rheum$_{b7.de*}$
- **standing**:
  - **agg.**: agar *Alum*$_{k*}$ ars calc-act canth chin ham$_{k*}$ hir$_{skp7•}$ kali-c mag-c merc phel **Puls** ran-b rheum sang spig spong staph tab tarax

- **standing – agg.**: ...
  - : **burning**: alum
  - : **cutting** pain: agar$_{k*}$
  - : **drawing** pain: agar$_{k*}$ tarax$_{h1*}$
  - : **pressing** pain: **Alum** sang staph
  - : **stitching** pain: alum
  - : **stunning** pain: staph$_{h1}$
  - : **tearing** pain: merc **Spig**
  - : **amel.**: calc iris teucr
  - : **still**:
    - : **amel.**: mang ↓
      - . **stitching** pain: mang$_{k*}$
- **stepping** agg.: alum **Bell** ph-ac *Sep* *Sil* spig$_{k2}$
- **stitching** pain: acon$_{k*}$ aesc$_{k*}$ aeth$_{a1}$ agar *Agn* all-c$_{a1}$ *Alum*$_{k*}$ alum-sil$_{k2}$ am-c$_{k*}$ am-m$_{k*}$ aml-ns anac$_{k*}$ anan ang$_{h1}$ ant-t$_{k*}$ apis$_{k*}$ arg-n$_{k*}$ *Arn*$_{k*}$ *Ars*$_{b4a.de}$ *Asaf*$_{k*}$ *Atro*$_{a1}$ aur$_{k*}$ aur-s$_{k2}$ bar-c bar-m bar-s$_{k2}$ **Bell**$_{k*}$ *Berb*$_{k*}$ borx$_{b4a.de}$ *Bov*$_{k*}$ *Brom*$_{b4a.de}$ bry$_{k*}$ *Calc*$_{k*}$ *Calc-s* calc-sil$_{k2}$ camph$_{k*}$ canth$_{k*}$ caps$_{k*}$ carb-v carneg-g$_{rwt1}$• cassia-s$_{ccrh1}$• caust$_{k*}$ cham$_{k*}$ chel$_{k*}$ *Chin*$_{k*}$ cic$_{k*}$ cina$_{k*}$ cob-n$_{sp1}$ coc-c cocc$_{k*}$ coff$_{a1}$ *Coloc*$_{k*}$ *Con*$_{k*}$ crot-t$_{a1}$ cupr cycl$_{k*}$ dig$_{k*}$ digin$_{a1}$ dros *Dulc*$_{k*}$ *Elaps* euph$_{k*}$ euphr eupi$_{a1}$ ferr$_{k*}$ ferr-p gels$_{k*}$ gins$_{k*}$ goss$_{a1}$ gran$_{k*}$ grat$_{k*}$ guaj ham$_{fd3.de}$• hell$_{k*}$ *Hep*$_{k*}$ hydr-ac$_{a1}$ hyos$_{k*}$ ign$_{k*}$ ip$_{k*}$ *Kali-c*$_{k*}$ kali-m$_{k2}$ *Kali-n*$_{k*}$ kali-p kali-sil$_{k2}$ ketogl-ac$_{rly4}$• kola$_{stb3}$• kreos$_{bg2}$ *Lach* lact$_{k*}$ laur$_{k*}$ led *Lil-t*$_{k*}$ lol$_{a1}$ *Lyc*$_{k*}$ m-aust$_{b7.de}$ mag-c$_{k*}$ *Mag-m*$_{k*}$ *Mang*$_{k*}$ meny$_{k*}$ *Merc*$_{k*}$ *Merc-c*$_{k*}$ merc-i-r$_{a1}$ *Mez*$_{k*}$ mosch$_{k*}$ *Mur-ac*$_{k*}$ nat-c$_{k*}$ nat-m$_{k*}$ nat-p *Nit-ac*$_{k*}$ nux-m$_{b7a.de}$ nux-v$_{k*}$ ol-an$_{a1}$ olib-sac$_{wmh1}$ op$_{k*}$ *Petr*$_{k*}$ ph-ac$_{k*}$ phos$_{k*}$ phys$_{a1}$ plan$_{k*}$ *Plat*$_{k*}$ plb$_{k*}$ podo *Puls*$_{k*}$ rat rhod$_{k*}$ rhus-t$_{k*}$ *Ruta*$_{k*}$ sabad$_{k*}$ sabin$_{k*}$ sang$_{a1}$ *Sars*$_{k*}$ sel$_{k*}$ senec$_{k*}$ *Sep*$_{k*}$ *Sil*$_{k*}$ *Spig*$_{k*}$ spong$_{k*}$ squil$_{k*}$ *Stann*$_{k*}$ *Staph*$_{k*}$ stram$_{k*}$ *Stront-c*$_{k*}$ *Sul-ac*$_{k*}$ *Sulph*$_{k*}$ symph$_{fd3.de}$• tab$_{a1}$ tarax$_{k*}$ tarent$_{a1}$ tax$_{a1}$ ter thuj$_{b4.de*}$ til$_{k*}$ tritic-vg$_{fd5.de}$ valer$_{k*}$ vanil$_{fd5.de}$ verat$_{k*}$ verb$_{k*}$ viol-t$_{k*}$ *Zinc*$_{k*}$ zinc-p$_{k2}$
  - : **alternating** with | **pressing** pain in forehead (See pressing pain - alternating - stitching)
  - : **burning**: cupr$_{h2}$ meny$_{h1}$ phos$_{h2}$ staph$_{h1}$ thuj$_{k*}$
  - : **drawing** pain: aur$_{h2}$ chel$_{h1}$ mang$_{h2}$ ruta$_{h1}$ squil$_{h1}$
  - : **inward**: spig$_{mrr1}$
  - : **itching**: ang$_{h1}$
  - : **jerking** pain: cycl$_{a1}$ lyc$_{h2}$ mang$_{h2}$
  - : **outward**: colch con$_{h2}$ lyc$_{h2}$ sep sulph
  - : **pressing** pain: mang$_{h2}$ nat-m$_{h2}$
  - : **pulsating** pain: sars$_{h2}$ spig$_{a1}$
  - : **rhythmical**: kali-n$_{h2}$
  - : **tearing** pain: cham$_{h1}$
  - : **transversal**: chel$_{h1}$ spong$_{h1}$
  - : **twitching**: mag-m$_{h2}$ mang$_{h2}$ mez$_{h2}$ spong$_{h1}$
- **stool**:
  - : **after**:
    - : **agg.**: bufo chel$_{k*}$ podo$_{k*}$ sep$_{k*}$ spig ↓
      - . **jerking** pain: spig$_{h1}$
      - . **pressing** pain: sep$_{h2}$ spig$_{k*}$
  - : **amel.**: moni ↓ sarcol-ac$_{sp1*}$
    - : **pressing** pain: moni$_{rfm1}$•
  - : **during**:
    - : **agg.**: apis *Bry* ↓ coloc ↓ kali-p ↓ *Nux-v* ↓ rat ↓ *Sil* *Spig* ↓ verb$_{c1}$
      - . **burning**: kali-p
      - . **pressing** pain: *Bry* coloc$_{k*}$ *Nux-v* rat *Spig*
  - : **straining** at | **agg.**: spig$_{k2}$
- **stooping**:
  - : **after**:
    - : **agg.**: hyos ↓
      - . **pressing** pain: hyos$_{h1}$
  - : **agg.**: acon am-c am-m ang arg-mur$_{k*}$ arg-n arn ars-s-f ↓ asar atro aur-m bar-c **Bell** berb$_{k*}$ borx bov brom **Bry**$_{k*}$ *Calc* calc-act ↓ *Calc-s* camph canth caps ↓ carb-an carb-v carbn-s ↓ caust chel cob$_{k*}$ coff *Coloc*$_{k*}$ cortiso$_{skp7}$• cupr cycl dros$_{k*}$ dulc elaps fago fl-ac *Gels* gran$_{k*}$ guaj haem *Hep* hyos ign$_{k*}$ ind ip junc-e kali-bi$_{k*}$ *Kali-c* ↓ kali-i kali-n kali-s$_{fd4.de}$ kreos lact laur$_{k*}$ lyc lyss mag-m manc$_{k*}$ **Mang** **Merc** merc-c mur-ac murx myric nat-c ↓ *Nat-m* *Nux-v* *Par* ↓ phos pic-ac$_{k*}$ plat plut-n$_{srj7}$• ptel **Puls** pycnop-sa$_{mrz1}$ rat *Rhus-v*$_{k*}$ sanic sep ↓ *Sil* sol-ni **Spig** spong ↓ stann staph **Sulph**$_{k*}$ tarent teucr tritic-vg$_{fd5.de}$ **Valer** verat zing
    - : **boring** pain: calc
    - : **burning**: mur-ac$_{h2}$
    - : **cutting** pain: caust
    - : **drawing** pain: borx$_{h2}$ dulc$_{h1*}$ mang
    - : **jerking** pain: sil$_{k*}$
    - : **pressing** pain: acon arg-n$_{k*}$ *Bell* borx **Bry**$_{k*}$ calc canth$_{k*}$ caps$_{k2}$ carb-v$_{k*}$ carbn-s caust chel *Coloc* cupr fl-ac$_{k*}$ kali-n kreos lyss mag-m$_{k*}$ merc$_{k*}$ nat-c *Par*$_{k*}$ plat sep sil *Spig* spong$_{h1}$ stann$_{k*}$ staph tritic-vg$_{fd5.de}$
    - : **shooting** pain: ars-s-f$_{k2}$ kreos$_{k*}$
    - : **sore**: lyc$_{h2}$
    - : **stitching** pain: ars-s-f$_{k2}$ berb$_{k*}$ bry$_{k*}$ cycl$_{hr1}$ *Dros* *Kali-c* mag-m$_{k*}$ mur-ac$_{k*}$ rat staph$_{k*}$ sulph
    - : **stunning** pain: calc-act$_{h1}$
    - : **tearing** pain: asar bov dros$_{h1}$ ip mag-m$_{h2}$ *Stann* staph *Sulph*
  - : **amel.**: bar-c bell caust con verb$_{k*}$
    - : **pressing** pain: bar-c bell$_{h1}$ caust$_{k*}$ con verb
- **straining** the eyes: dulc$_{fd4.de}$ lac-c$_{k2}$ ruta$_{fd4.de}$ vanil$_{fd5.de}$
- **stunning** pain: acon$_{b7a.de}$ agar$_{k*}$ anac$_{k*}$ *Ant-c*$_{k*}$ ant-t$_{b7a.de}$ arg-met$_{k*}$ arn$_{k*}$ *Ars*$_{k*}$ asaf asar$_{k*}$ bapt *Bell*$_{k*}$ bov$_{b4.de*}$ **Calc**$_{k*}$ cann-s$_{k*}$ carb-an$_{k*}$ caust$_{h2*}$ cere-b$_{a1}$ cic$_{k*}$ cina$_{k*}$ con$_{h2}$ cycl dros$_{k*}$ dulc$_{hr1}$ *Euph*$_{k*}$ fl-ac$_{k*}$ gran hep$_{b4a.de}$ *Hyos*$_{k*}$ ign$_{b7.de*}$ *Kali-n*$_{k*}$ laur$_{k*}$ led$_{k*}$ *Mag-c*$_{k*}$ mang$_{k*}$ meny$_{k*}$ mosch$_{b7a.de*}$ *Mur-ac*$_{k*}$ *Nat-c*$_{k*}$ nat-p olnd$_{k*}$ par$_{k*}$ *Ph-ac*$_{k*}$ phos$_{k*}$ plat$_{k*}$ *Rhus-t*$_{b7a.de}$ ruta$_{k*}$ sabad$_{k*}$ sep$_{k*}$ *Stann*$_{k*}$ *Staph*$_{k*}$ syph$_{k2}$ tarax$_{k*}$ thuj$_{k*}$ valer *Verb*$_{k*}$ *Zinc*$_{k*}$
  - : **alternating** with | **Vertex**; stupefying pain in: cot$_{a1*}$
- **sudden**: melal-alt ↓ ther ↓
  - : **pressing** pain: melal-alt$_{gya4}$ ther
- **sunlight**: bov ↓ cortiso$_{skp7}$• ign$_{k*}$ psil$_{ft1*}$
  - : **stitching** pain: bov
- **supper** | **after**:
  - : **agg.**: nat-m ↓ ran-b ↓
    - . **pressing** pain: nat-m$_{h2}$ ran-b$_{k*}$
  - : **during**: zinc ↓
    - : **tearing** pain: zinc$_{h2}$
- **sweats** from anxiety:
  - : **walking** in open air agg.: ant-c ↓
    - : **stunning** pain: ant-c$_{k*}$
- **talking**:
  - : **after**: sil ↓ ther ↓ thuj ↓ vanil ↓
    - : **pressing** pain: sil ther thuj vanil$_{fd5.de}$
  - : **agg.**: cassia-s ↓ cocc iod mang ↓ nat-m *Sil* spig$_{k2}$ vanil$_{fd5.de}$ [tax$_{jsj7}$]
    - : **stitching** pain: cassia-s$_{ccrh1}$•
    - : **tearing** pain: mang$_{a1}$
  - : **loudly** agg.: sulph ↓
    - : **stitching** pain: sulph$_{k*}$
- **tearing** pain: act-sp aeth agar$_{k*}$ *Agn*$_{k*}$ alum$_{k*}$ alum-p$_{k2}$ am-c$_{k*}$ am-m$_{k*}$ ambr$_{k*}$ *Anac*$_{k*}$ ant-c ant-t arg-met arg-n ars$_{k*}$ arum-t asaf asar$_{k*}$ *Aur*$_{k*}$ aur-ar$_{k2}$ aur-m-n aur-s$_{k2}$ *Bell*$_{k*}$ *Berb* bism$_{k*}$ bov$_{k*}$ brom *Bry*$_{k*}$ cact calc$_{k*}$ calc-p calc-sil$_{k2}$ camph$_{k*}$ canth$_{k*}$ *Caps*$_{k*}$ carb-an *Carb-v*$_{k*}$ *Carbn-s* castm caust$_{k*}$ *Cham*$_{k*}$ chel$_{k*}$ chin$_{k*}$ cic$_{a1}$ cina *Cinnb* coc-c cocc$_{k*}$ colch *Coloc* *Con* cupr$_{k*}$ cycl dros$_{k*}$ euphr gran *Graph*$_{k*}$ grat *Guaj*$_{k*}$ hell *Hep*$_{k*}$ hyos$_{k*}$ *Ign*$_{k*}$ indg ip$_{k*}$ kali-ar kali-bi$_{k*}$ *Kali-c*$_{k*}$ kali-m$_{k2}$ kali-n kali-p kali-sil$_{k2}$ kalm kreos *Lach* lachn laur$_{k*}$ led **Lyc**$_{k*}$ mag-c$_{k*}$ mag-m$_{k*}$ mag-s *Mang* **Merc**$_{k*}$ merc-i-r merl *Mez*$_{k*}$ mur-ac$_{k*}$ nat-ar nat-c$_{k*}$ nat-m$_{k*}$ nat-s nit-ac nux-v$_{k*}$ op$_{k*}$ phel phos$_{k*}$ *Plb*$_{k*}$ puls$_{k*}$ rat rhod$_{k*}$ *Ruta*$_{b7a.de}$ sabad samb$_{k*}$ *Sars*$_{k*}$ *Sep*$_{k*}$ **Sil**$_{k*}$ **Spig**$_{k*}$ *Stann*$_{k*}$ staph$_{k*}$ stront-c$_{k*}$ sul-ac *Sulph*$_{k*}$ thuj$_{k*}$ til zinc$_{k*}$ zinc-p$_{k2}$
  - : **alternating** with | **Arms**; pain in: sil
  - : **flying** pain: rat seneg
  - : **intermittent**: agar$_{h2}$
  - : **paroxysmal**: cham$_{h1}$ mur-ac$_{h2}$ *Stann* zinc$_{h2}$

- **tearing** pain: ...
  - **pulsating** pain: mag-c
  - **radiating**: lyc
- **thinking**:
  - **agg.**: abrom-a ks5
    - **pulsating** pain: abrom-a ks5
  - **from** | **pressing** pain (See mental - pressing)
- **thinking** of the pain agg.: chlam-tr ↓
  - **pressing** pain: chlam-tr bcx2• (non:nat-s hr1)
- **thoughts**; with vanishing of:
  - **pressing** pain | **drawing** pain (See MIND - Thoughts - vanishing - headache - forehead)
- **torn**; as if: am-m k* asar k* coff k* graph k* hep mez k* nux-v k* *Puls* thuj h1
- **touch**:
  - **agg.**: alum h2* am-m chin cocc-s kr1 cupr graph ↓ ip *Kali-c* lepi lyc k* mur-ac k* nat-m k* sil spong h1*
    - **burning**: ip k* nat-m k*
    - **smarting**: graph
    - **sore**: nat-m h2
    - **stitching** pain: ip k*
    - **tearing** pain: ip
    - **ulcerative** pain: graph h2
  - **amel.**: bell calc-act chin cycl mur-ac viol-t
    - **drawing** pain: cycl h1*
    - **pressing** pain: cycl h1 mur-ac h2
- **turning**:
  - **eyes**:
    - **sideways**: dig ↓
      - **drawing** pain: dig
    - **upward**: *Lac-c*
  - **head**:
    - **agg.**: canth chinin-s coc-c gels glon k* kali-s fd4.de *Nat-c* a1 *Nat-m* ph-ac k* phos rhod k* spig k2 vanil fd5.de
      - **suddenly**: ign **Nat-c** ph-ac
    - **right** agg.; to: aeth vanil fd5.de
- **twitching**: borx h2
- **ulcerative** pain: graph h2 hep k* kreos b7a.de mur-ac k* nux-v k*
- **uncovering** body amel.: cor-r ↓
  - **pressing** pain: cor-r k*
- **vexation**; after: coli jl2
- **violent**: mand rsj7•
- **vise**; as if in a: sel rsj9• [bell-p-sp dcm1]
- **waking** | **after** | **soon** after waking: psor jl2
  - **on**: adam srj5• agar ↓ aids nl2• anac ↓ ant-t ↓ arg-n ↓ beryl tpw5 cadm-met tpw6 carneg-g rwt1• cartl-s ↓ chlam-tr ↓ choc srj3• chord-umb ↓ cina ↓ gels ↓ hep ↓ melal-alt gya4 mez ↓ *Nat-m* ↓ *Nux-v* ↓ ol-an ↓ *Ph-ac* ↓ propr sa3• puls ↓ rhus-t ↓ suis-pan ↓ sulph ↓ thuj ↓ trios rsj11• zinc ↓
    - **burning**: *Nux-v*
    - **pressing** pain: agar anac ant-t arg-n cartl-s rly4• chlam-tr bcx2• chord-umb rly4• cina gels mez *Nat-m* k* ol-an *Ph-ac* rhus-t k* suis-pan rly4• sulph thuj k* zinc
    - **sore**: hep thuj
    - **tearing** pain: puls h1 thuj
- **walking**:
  - **agg.**: acon anac arg-n ↓ *Arn* ars **Bell** **Bry** *Calc* calc-s calc-sil k2 cassia-s ↓ caust ↓ chin clem coca cocc coloc crot-t ↓ digin a1 dros h1* euphr gran ind k* kali-bi k* *Kali-c* kali-n lac-d lept mag-c mang ↓ merc ↓ naja nat-m ↓ ped a1 peti k* ph-ac phys k* podo fd3.de• *Puls* rat rhus-t ↓ rhus-v sabad sars sep ↓ *Sil* *Spig* ↓ spong sulph ust k* viol-t
    - **boring** pain: arg-n coloc k*
    - **burning**: rhus-t
    - **cutting** pain: calc k*
    - **drawing** pain: arg-n k* mang h2* rat
- **walking – agg.**: ...
    - **pressing** pain: anac arg-n *Arn* *Bry* calc caust *Chin* clem h2 cocc *Kali-c* nat-m *Spig*
    - **shooting** pain: kali-bi kali-n
    - **stitching** pain: cassia-s ccrh1• crot-t kali-n h2 mang merc sep spong h1 sulph
  - **air**; in open:
    - **after**:
      - **agg.**: calc ↓
        - **boring** pain: calc
    - **agg.**: acon am-c ↓ ant-c arg-n asim **Bell** calc carb-ac *Caust* *Chin* *Cina* coca *Cocc* ↓ coff dulc ↓ hell hyos kali-cy lyss merc nat-m plat sars spong sul-ac ↓ tarax *Thuj*
      - **boring** pain: sul-ac
      - **pressing** pain: am-c arg-n **Bell** calc caust *Chin* *Cocc* dulc plat
      - **stitching** pain: merc sars h2 spong h1
    - **amel.**: borx calc ↓ camph cassia-s ↓ chel cor-r crot-h ham hydr hyos *Iris* *Lyc* mag-m phys *Plat* *Sang* ↓ scut sep sulph thuj
      - **pressing** pain: borx calc cor-r *Sang* *Sep*
      - **stitching** pain: cassia-s ccrh1• *Sep*
  - **amel.**: calc-act chin coca dros *Iris* puls ran-b rhod sang staph
  - **rapidly**:
    - **agg.**: caust ↓
      - **pressing** pain: caust
- **wandering** pain: aesc
- **warm**:
  - **applications**:
    - **amel.**: *Ars* cinnb germ-met ↓ kali-c mag-m mag-p *Sil* sulph *Thuj* x-ray ↓
      - **bursting** pain: x-ray sp1
      - **pressing** pain: germ-met srj5•
      - **stitching** pain: kali-c
  - **room**:
    - **agg.**: acon **Apis** bov carb-ac caust cortiso tpw7* ferr-i lac-ac lil-t merc mez *Phos* plat **Puls** ran-b *Sanic* sel *Seneg* sin-n verb
      - **pressing** pain: acon **Apis** ferr-i *Plat* ran-b
      - **tearing** pain: caust
    - **amel.**: am-c ↓ lac-c sil sulph
      - **pressing** pain: am-c
  - **stove** agg.: *Apis* ↓ *Arn* ↓
    - **pressing** pain: *Apis* *Arn*
- **warmth**: calc ferr-i k2
  - **agg.**:
    - **heat** agg.: cassia-s ↓
      - **dull** pain: cassia-s ccrh1•
  - **amel.**:
    - **heat** amel.: calc-sil k2 cassia-s ↓ cinnb mag-m **Sil** stann *Sulph*
      - **stitching** pain: cassia-s ccrh1•
- **waves** of pain: agath-a nl2• kali-s fd4.de **Sep**
  - **pins** and needles; like: agath-a nl2•
- **weather** agg.; cold wet: *Calc* coli jl2 *Dulc* *Rhus-t* *Spig*
- **wet** feet, from: *Spig*
- **wind** agg.; cold: aur *Carb-v* ham fd3.de• lac-c nux-v rhus-t
- **wine** agg.: ran-b k* rhod k*
  - **drawing** pain: rhod k*
- **wrinkling** forehead:
  - **agg.**: nat-m k*
  - **amel.**: phos
- **writing** agg.: aran borx calc calc-sil k2 dros ery-a a1 ferr-i gent-l kali-c lyc k* nat-c ↓ op ran-b sanic sil vanil fd5.de zinc
  - **boring** pain: dros k*
  - **drawing** pain: borx h2
  - **pressing** pain: borx kali-c k* lyc nat-c a1 vanil fd5.de

▽ - **extending** to:
  - **Backward**: agar anac bg1 anan a1* arn bry con bg1 *Crot-c* cupr cystein-l rly4• eup-per form bg1 kali-bi kola stb3• *Lach* lil-t mur-ac h2

Head

- **extending** to – **Backward**: ...
  onos *Phyt* pic-ac bg1 plac-s rly4• **Prun** ran-s ribo rly4• sabad bg1 scroph-n br1 sel bg1 spong stront-c bg1 tab ther **Thuj** valer bg1
  - **Whole** head; over: aids nl2• anac k* **Bry** mrr1 cimic bg1 colch bg1 lach mur-ac petr-ra shn4• sel k* thuj bg1 valer
  - **Brain**; into: agar bg1 croc bg1 glon bg1 hell bg1 laur bg1 pip-m bg1 plan bg1 ran-s bg1 stann bg1
    - **Base** of: sep bg1
  - **Cervical** muscles, then to right arm: bry ↓
    - **tearing** pain: bry
  - **Cheeks**: brom lachn mosch puls sang
    - **And** malar bones: kali-chl bg1 kali-s fd4.de sang hr1 sulph bg1
  - **Chest**: cham bg1
    - **stitching** pain: cham h1
    - **tearing** pain: cham
  - **Ear**: all-c ↓ mang ↓ ozone ↓ rhus-t ↓ squil ↓
    - **bursting** pain: ozone sde2•
    - **drawing** pain: mang h2
    - **stitching** pain: all-c k2 mang h2 rhus-t squil
  - **Ears**: aur-m cystein-l rly4• glon osm ribo rly4• squil ter
  - **Eye**: *Ant-t* ↓ mang ↓ ruta ↓ tritic-vg ↓
    - **stitching** pain: *Ant-t* mang ruta fd4.de tritic-vg fd5.de
  - **Eye** teeth: kalm
  - **Eyes**: acon bg1* agar k* all-c bro1 *Aloe* bro1 ant-t apis arg-n ↓ ars-met bro1 asaf bg1 asar *Bad* k* bapt bg1 bell ↓ borx ↓ bry bg1* calc-p cann-i caps bro1 carb-v bg1 carbn-s ↓ carc fb* caust ↓ cedr bro1 cere-b bro1 cham chel *Cimic* bro1 clem a1 cor-r br1 *Crot-h* epiph bg1 gink-b sbd1• gins glon grat hep k* hydrog srj2• ign k* kali-bi *Kali-c* kali-i bro1 kali-n ↓ kali-p bg1 lac-ac lac-c lach k* laur ↓ lil-t mag-m bro1 mentho bro1 moni ↓ mur-ac nat-c bg1 nat-m ↓ nit-ac nux-m onos bro1 op bg1 ozone sde2• *Phos* *Plat* bro1 prun bro1 psil ft1 *Ptel* bro1 puls ruta fd4.de sabin sacch-a ↓ samb xxb1 seneg *Spig* k* *Stict* bro1 thuj tritic-vg fd5.de vanil fd5.de zinc bg1
    - **burning**: *Spig*
    - **bursting** pain: moni rfm1•
    - **cramping**: nat-c h2
    - **drawing** pain: agar borx a1 cann-i gink-b sbd1• glon hep *Kali-c* lil-t
    - **pressing** pain: asar bell carb-v carbn-s caust h2 *Chel* ign kali-bi kali-c kali-n laur mur-ac h2 nux-m op *Phos* sacch-a fd2.de• samb h1 tritic-vg fd5.de vanil fd5.de
    - **tearing** pain: arg-n a1 *Kali-c* mur-ac nat-c nat-m samb h1* spig
    - **Above**: ketogl-ac rly4• pot-e rly4• tritic-vg fd5.de [bell-p-sp dcm1]
    - **Lids**: chel bg1 phos bg1 spig bg1
    - **Over**: melal-alt ↓
      - **pressing** pain: melal-alt gya4
  - **Face**: acon bro1 *Agar* bro1 all-c bro1 *Aloe* bro1 ambr ↓ ars-met bro1 bad bro1 brom bry bg1* caps bro1 cedr bro1 cere-b bro1 chin *Cimic* bro1 hep bro1 ign bro1 kali-i bro1 kali-s fd4.de *Lach* bro1 lachn mag-m bro1 mentho bro1 meny merc merc-i-f bg1 mosch onos bro1 *Plat* bro1 plut-n srj7• prun bro1 *Ptel* bro1 puls ruta fd4.de sang sep *Spig* bro1 *Stict* bro1 tab vanil fd5.de
    - **tearing** pain: ambr h1
    - **Bones** of: kali-s fd4.de lyss bg1 puls bg1 sulph bg1
    - **Teeth**; down into face and: lyc ↓
      - **tearing** pain: lyc
  - **Head**; over (See backward - whole)
  - **Jaw**:
    - **Lower**: bell bg1 brom bg1 nat-m rhus-t ↓
      - **cramping**: bell h1
      - **drawing** pain: nat-m rhus-t h1
      - **stitching** pain: brom
    - **Upper**: acon bg1 kali-bi bg1 kali-s fkr2.de phos bg1 vanil fd5.de
  - **Lids**: chel bg1 phos bg1 spig bg1
    - **Upper**: chel bg1 phos bg1 spig bg1
  - **Malar** bones: ozone ↓
    - **dull** pain: ozone sde2•
  - **Molars**, upper: *Kalm*
  - **Mouth**: eupi ↓

- **extending** to – **Mouth**: ...
  - **burrowing**: eupi k*
  - **Nape**: anan ↓
    - **stitching** pain: anan
  - **Neck**: bamb-a ↓ berb ↓ borx ↓ *Bry* bro1 chel cystein-l rly4• euon bro1 flor-p ↓ gels bro1 kali-n kalm kola stb3• lac-d bro1 lil-t lyc menis bro1 mosch nux-v bro1 onos *Oreo* bro1 prun bro1 sacch-a ↓ sep bro1 spong ↓ tub bro1 viol-t
    - **bursting** pain: flor-p rsj3•
    - **drawing** pain: borx kali-n *Mosch* viol-t
    - **pressing** pain: bamb-a stb2.de• borx h2 chel sacch-a fd2.de• spong h1
    - **tearing** pain: berb j5.de
  - **Nose**: acon bg1 *Agar* aloe bg1 am-m bg1 bapt bg1 bism ↓ *Calc* calc-p chlam-tr ↓ cina coloc ↓ croc dig bg1* dios dulc fago bg1 ferr a1 glon guaj ↓ *Ign* bg1 kali-bi *Kali-c* kali-n ↓ ketogl-ac ↓ kola ↓ **Lach** lyc ↓ mang mez bg1 mosch nat-c nux-v op ozone ↓ ph-ac phos plan bg1 plect bg1 psor sep thuj bg1 vanil fd5.de
    - **boring** pain: bism mang
    - **bursting** pain: *Dulc*
    - **cramping**: nat-c h2
    - **drawing** pain: **Agar** dulc h1 glon guaj *Kali-c* nux-v
    - **dull** pain: ozone sde2•
    - **pressing** pain: (↗*nose - pressing)* agar aloe am-m *Calc* chlam-tr bcx2• kali-c kali-n c1 lyc mez ph-ac *Phos* vanil fd5.de
    - **shooting** pain: ketogl-ac rly4•
    - **stitching** pain: coloc kola stb3• psor vanil fd5.de
    - **tearing** pain: lyc nat-c
    - **Bones**: mez bg1
    - **Into**: dig ↓
      - **shooting** pain: dig br1
    - **Root**: acon k* *Agar* bro1 all-c bro1 aloe k* ars-met bro1 bad bro1 bamb-a stb2.de• bapt benzol br1 bov ↓ *Bry* bro1 caps bro1 cedr bro1 cere-b bro1 *Cimic* bro1 cina bg1* colch bg1 dulc bg1 glon hep bro1 ign bro1 *Kali-c* kali-i k* *Lach* k* mag-m bro1 mentho bro1 nux-v onos bro1 op ↓ ozone sde2• phos *Plat* bro1 prun bro1 ptel k* *Puls* *Spig* bro1 *Stict* bro1 vanil fd5.de [helia stj7]
      - **pinching** pain: op k*
      - **pressing** pain: ozone sde2•
      - **tearing** pain: bov *Kali-c*
    - **Sides**: carb-v bg1 onos bg1 sep bg1
    - **Tip**: bism bg1 brom bg1 dig ↓ kali-n bg1 nat-c bg1
      - **shooting** pain: dig c1
    - **Wing**: sep ↓
      - **tearing** pain: sep h2
  - **Occiput**: adam skp7• aids nl2• anac ↓ ars ars-s-f ↓ bapt a1 **Bell** bism bov ↓ *Bry* k* calc camph *Cann-s* canth carb-ac *Cedr* ↓ cench k2 *Cham* chel chinin-s chlol **Cimic** cina bg1 cinnb bg1 coc-c cocc bg1 colch con cupr cystein-l rly4• dios diosm br1 dros ↓ euon bro1 eup-per ferr-i ↓ *Form* gels bro1 graph ↓ *Kali-bi* kali-n kali-p kalm kola stb3• kreos *Lac-d* k* *Lil-t* lyc ↓ lycps-v mag-c ↓ menis bro1 merc-i-r mucs-nas rly4• naja nat-c nat-m *Nux-v* k* *Oreo* bro1 par petr ↓ phos phys pic-ac plat **Prun** k* psil ft1 ruta fd4.de sabad sabin sacch-a ↓ *Sep* k* spong ↓ sulph symph fd3.de• ther **Thuj** tritic-vg fd5.de tub bro1 vanil fd5.de zing
    - **and**:
      - **back** again: cop br1
      - **Head**; over (See backward - whole)
      - **Shoulder**: samb bat1•
    - **cutting** pain: *Bell* bism ferr-i k2
    - **drawing** pain: dros h1 graph mag-c h2 *Sep* vanil fd5.de
    - **followed** by | **pain** in whole head: **Bry** mrr1
    - **lancinating**: *Bell*
    - **pressing** pain: anac bry *Cann-s* chel coc-c lyc par sacch-a fd2.de• spong h1 thuj h1 tritic-vg fd5.de vanil fd5.de
    - **shooting** pain: ars-s-f k2 **Bell** cinnb nat-c **Prun Sep**
    - **stitching** pain: ars-s-f k2 *Bell* *Cedr* *Cham* nat-c a1 nat-m h2 petr h2 phos tritic-vg fd5.de vanil fd5.de
    - **stripe**; in a: choc srj3•
    - **tearing** pain: bov kali-n

· **extending** to: ...
: **Orbits**: chel dulc $_{fd4.de}$ gins kali-s $_{fd4.de}$ xan $_{c1}$
: **Outward**: bar-c olnd
: **Parietal** bone: chel ind $_{bg1}$ pert-vc $_{vk9}$
: **Pharynx**: ulm-c ↓
: **burning**: ulm-c $_{jsj8•}$
: **Pituitary** gland: ulm-c ↓
: **burning**: ulm-c $_{jsj8•}$
: **Shoulder**: *Kalm*
: **Sides**: indg ↓ nat-ox $_{rly4•}$ vanil ↓
: **pressing** pain: indg vanil $_{fd5.de}$
: **Sinuses**: ozone ↓
: **dull** pain: ozone $_{sde2•}$
: **Skull**: ozone $_{sde2•}$
: **Spine**; down: *Bry* $_{bro1}$ euon $_{bro1}$ gels $_{bro1}$ lac-d $_{bro1}$ menis $_{bro1}$ nux-v $_{bro1}$ *Oreo* $_{bro1}$ pic-ac $_{k2}$ prun $_{bro1}$ sep $_{bro1}$ tub $_{bro1}$
: **Teeth**: ars $_{bg1}$ rhus-t ↓
: **drawing** pain: rhus-t $_{h1}$
: **Temple**: caust ↓ gran ↓ mang ↓ mur-ac ↓ ruta ↓
: **stitching** pain: mur-ac $_{h2}$ ruta $_{h1}$
: **tearing** pain: caust gran mang $_{a1}$
: **Temples**: arn atp ↓ borx canth *Carbn-s* ↓ chel ↓ choc ↓ cimic dios dulc $_{fd4.de}$ gran ↓ hell hydr ign kali-p $_{k*}$ petr-ra $_{shn4•}$ phys plac-s $_{rly4•}$ psil $_{ft1}$ ruta ↓ sep ↓ stroph-h $_{c1}$ thuj tritic-vg $_{fd5.de}$ vanil $_{fd5.de}$ vero-o $_{rly4•}$ [spect $_{dfg1}$]
: **bending** backward agg.: chin ↓
. **pressing** pain: chin
: **pressing** pain: atp $_{rly4•}$ *Carbn-s* chel choc $_{srj3•}$ gran sep $_{h2}$ vanil $_{fd5.de}$
: **shooting** pain: ruta $_{tl1}$
: **Vertex**: agath-a $_{nl2•}$ alum ↓ calc ↓ caust ↓ chion $_{bg1}$ cic ↓ cimic cystein-l $_{rly4•}$ ferr $_{bg1}$ glon hell ip kreos lac-lup $_{hrn2•}$ laur $_{bg1}$ lyc $_{bg1}$ meny ↓ merc phos $_{bg1}$ puls ↓ ruta sep sil spong $_{fd4.de}$ valer vanil $_{fd5.de}$ xan $_{bg1*}$
: **cramping**: calc $_{h2}$
: **drawing** pain: sep $_{h2}$
: **pressing** pain: glon kreos lyc puls vanil $_{fd5.de}$
: **stitching** pain: caust $_{h2}$ meny $_{h1}$ sep $_{h2}$
: **tearing** pain: alum cic $_{a1}$ merc sil
: **Whole** head (See backward - whole)

○ · **Above**: acon $_{k*}$ *Aloe* ↓ arg-n ↓ calc-p $_{k*}$ chin ↓ coloc ↓ con ↓ dig ↓ dulc ↓ *Iod* ↓ kalm $_{k*}$ lyc $_{h2*}$ merc-i-f $_{k*}$ mez ↓ naja nat-m ↓ ol-an ↓ *Olnd* $_{k*}$ *Par* ↓ psor $_{k*}$ ruta ↓ sal-fr $_{sle1•}$ sep $_{k*}$ *Sil* ↓ sulph ↓ thuj $_{k*}$ zinc ↓
: **morning**:
: **bed** agg.; in: mez ↓
. **stitching** pain: mez $_{h2}$
: **mental** exertion; from: psor
: **pressing** pain: *Aloe* arg-n chin $_{h1}$ coloc con $_{h2}$ dig dulc *Iod* nat-m *Olnd Par* sep $_{h2}$ *Sil*
: **stitching** pain: aloe chin $_{h1}$ mez $_{h2}$ nat-m $_{k*}$ ol-an $_{k*}$ ruta sulph $_{k*}$
: **burning**: chin $_{h1}$
: **dull** pain: mez $_{h2}$
: **tearing** pain: iod $_{h}$ lyc $_{h2}$ zinc $_{h2}$

· **Across**: bry ↓ kalm ↓ lachn ↓
: **tearing** pain: bry kalm lachn

· **Behind** eyes: phos ↓ tritic-vg ↓
: **left**: olib-sac ↓
: **stitching** pain: olib-sac $_{wmh1}$
: **stitching** pain: phos $_{h2}$ tritic-vg $_{fd5.de}$

· **Eminence**; frontal: acon $_{k*}$ agar $_{k*}$ agath-a $_{nl2•}$ agn ↓ aloe ↓ alum ↓ am-c ambr $_{k*}$ anac ↓ arg-met arg-mur ↓ *Arg-n* $_{k*}$ arn ↓ *Asaf* ↓ bacls-10 $_{fmm1•}$ bar-c bar-s ↓ bell $_{k*}$ berb $_{k*}$ bov ↓ brom ↓ calc ↓ calc-sil ↓ canth ↓ *Caust* $_{k*}$ cench ↓ cham ↓ chel ↓ chin ↓ cimx ↓ *Cina* clem $_{k*}$ cocc colch $_{k*}$ cot $_{a1}$ croc $_{k*}$ cupr ↓ dros ↓ dulc $_{k*}$ dys $_{fmm1•}$ euon ↓ *Ferr* ferr-p ↓ gins ↓ gran $_{k*}$ grat $_{k*}$ guaj ↓ hell $_{k*}$ hep $_{bg3}$ hyos $_{k*}$ irid-met $_{srj5•}$ kali-bi $_{k*}$ kali-c *Lach* $_{k*}$ lact ↓ laur $_{k*}$ led $_{bg3}$ lyc ↓ lycps-v mag-m ↓ *Mand* $_{rsj7•}$ mang ↓ melal-alt $_{gya4}$ meny ↓ merc-c $_{k*}$ mez $_{k*}$ mill ↓ morg-p $_{fmm1•}$ mur-ac ↓ myris $_{a1}$ naja nat-c nit-ac $_{k*}$ nux-m $_{k*}$ ol-an ↓

· **Eminence**, frontal: ...
olnd ↓ onos op $_{k*}$ osm ↓ par ↓ ph-ac $_{bg3}$ pip-m $_{k*}$ plan $_{k*}$ plat ↓ plb ↓ polyg-h prot $_{fmm1•}$ prun ↓ puls-n raph ↓ ruta ↓ sabad ↓ *Sabin* ↓ sars ↓ *Sep* ↓ sil ↓ sin-a $_{k*}$ **Spig** ↓ spirae $_{a1}$ spong squil $_{k*}$ stann $_{k*}$ staph ↓ sul-ac ↓ sulph $_{bg3}$ sumb ↓ syc $_{fmm1•}$ teucr ↓ *Thuj* $_{k*}$ verat $_{k*}$ verb $_{k*}$ xan $_{k*}$ zinc $_{k*}$
: **one** side to the other side; from: syph $_{jl2}$
: **deep**-seated: syph $_{jl2}$
: **right**: acon $_{k*}$ am-c ambr ↓ *Arg-met* arg-n ↓ bell ↓ bov ↓ *Caust* cocc colch $_{k*}$ hell $_{k*}$ kali-br kali-p ↓ merc-c $_{k*}$ mez $_{k*}$ nat-c ↓ ph-ac ↓ pip-m ↓ *Sabin* ↓ sep ↓ sin-a $_{k*}$ **Spig** ↓ spong ↓ squil ↓ xan $_{k*}$ zinc $_{k*}$
: **left**; then in: acet-ac ↓
. **dull** pain: acet-ac
: **boring** pain: bell colch
: **pressing** pain: arg-n $_{k2}$ *Caust Hell* $_{h1}$ mez $_{h2}$ ph-ac $_{h2*}$ *Sabin* spong zinc $_{h2}$
: **stitching** pain: bell bov kali-p nat-c $_{a1}$ pip-m squil
: **tearing** pain: ambr *Arg-met* sep $_{h2}$ **Spig**
: **left**: adam $_{skp7•}$ agar $_{k*}$ agn ↓ ambr $_{k*}$ *Arg-n* arn ↓ asaf $_{k2}$ aur-m $_{k*}$ cench ↓ *Cina* croc ↓ dulc $_{k*}$ gran $_{k*}$ kali-c ↓ *Lach Lycps-v* mang ↓ mez ↓ nat-c *Nux-m* ↓ ol-an ↓ onos puls-n sars ↓ squil $_{k*}$ staph ↓ **Thuj** $_{k*}$ zinc $_{h2*}$
: **blow**; pain as from a: squil $_{h1}$
: **boring** pain: **Arg-n** $_{k*}$ ol-an $_{k*}$ thuj
: **dull** pain: cench $_{k2}$
: **grinding** pain: agar $_{k*}$
: **lancinating**: thuj $_{k*}$
: **nail**; as from a: asaf $_{k2}$ **Thuj**
: **plug**; as from a: asaf $_{k2}$
: **pressing** pain: agar $_{k*}$ agn $_{a1}$ ambr $_{k*}$ dulc $_{a1}$ gran $_{k*}$ *Nux-m* squil $_{h1}$ staph thuj $_{h1}$
: **shooting** pain: asaf $_{k2}$
: **stitching** pain: *Arg-n* arn asaf croc mang nat-c sars
: **tearing** pain: asaf $_{k2}$ kali-c mang mez $_{h2}$ nat-c $_{h2}$ *Zinc*
: **extending** to | **Teeth**: cench $_{k2}$
: **Under**: **Spig** ↓
. **tearing** pain: **Spig**
. **extending** to:
Eyes: **Spig** ↓
tearing pain: **Spig**
: **morning**: agar $_{k*}$ agath-a $_{nl2•}$ brucel $_{sa3•}$ *Ferr* ↓
: 3.30 h (See night - midnight - after - 3.30)
: **pressing** pain: *Ferr* $_{k*}$
: **rising** agg., after: *Ferr* ↓
. **pressing** pain: *Ferr* $_{k*}$
: **waking**; on: agar $_{k*}$ lac-h $_{sk4•}$
: **forenoon** | **10**h: thuj
: **afternoon**: arg-n ↓ mag-s $_{k*}$ nat-m $_{k*}$
: **14** h: laur ↓ lyc ↓
. **stitching** pain: laur
. **tearing** pain: lyc
: **15** h: bry ↓
. **pressing** pain: bry
: **16** h: ferr nit-ac ↓
. **stitching** pain: nit-ac
: **stitching** pain: arg-n
: **evening**: alum ↓ dulc $_{a1}$ fl-ac $_{k*}$ lyc ↓ lycps-v nit-ac ↓ plect ↓ sars ↓ sin-a $_{k*}$
: **18** h: lyc ↓
. **stitching** pain: lyc
: **19** h: sars ↓ thuj
. **stitching** pain: sars
: **20** h: thuj
: **21** h: kali-br $_{a1}$
: **pressing** pain: dulc $_{k*}$ plect $_{a1}$
: **stitching** pain: alum lyc nit-ac $_{h2}$ sars
: **tearing** pain: alum
: **night**: anac ↓ calc ↓ *Caust* ↓ ph-ac ↓ spong ↓ zinc ↓

- **Eminence**; frontal – **night**: ...
  - **midnight**: sulph ↓
    - **after** | 3.30 h: thuj
    - **pressing** pain: sulph$_{k*}$
  - **pressing** pain: anac calc *Caust* ph-ac spong zinc
  - **air** agg.; draft of: verb$_{k*}$
  - **air**; in open:
    - **agg.**: ran-b ↓ verb ↓
      - **pressing** pain: ran-b
      - **tearing** pain: verb
    - **amel.**: *Ferr*$_{k*}$ pip-m ↓
      - **pressing** pain: *Ferr*
      - **stitching** pain: pip-m
  - **alternating** with | **Cervical** region; pain in: thuj$_{k*}$
  - **blow**; pain as from a: sul-ac$_{h2}$
  - **boring** pain: am-c arg-met *Bell* led mang ol-an$_{k*}$ *Plan*$_{k*}$ sabad thuj
  - **bursting** pain: bar-c$_{bg2}$
  - **catarrhal**: *(↗catarrhal)* kali-bi
  - **closing** the eyes:
    - **must** close the eyes: calc ↓
      - **pressing** pain: calc
  - **descending** stairs agg.: *Ferr*
    - **pressing** pain: *Ferr*
  - **dinner** | **after**:
    - **agg.**: kali-bi$_{k*}$ zinc$_{h2*}$
      - **pressing** pain: zinc
      - **tearing** pain: *Zinc*
    - **during**:
      - **agg.**: am-c ↓
        - **stitching** pain: am-c
  - **dull** pain: cench$_{k2}$
  - **gnawing** pain: bell$_{k*}$
  - **lancinating**: thuj$_{k*}$
  - **looking** steadily agg.: spong
  - **motion**:
    - **agg.**: staph ↓
      - **stitching** pain: staph$_{h1}$
    - **amel.**: pip-m ↓
      - **stitching** pain: pip-m
  - **noise** agg.: agar ↓
    - **stitching** pain: agar
  - **pressing** pain: agar$_{k*}$ agath-a$_{nl2•}$ agn$_{a1}$ ambr$_{k*}$ anac$_{k*}$ arg-met$_{h1}$ *Arg-n* asaf$_{k*}$ bar-c bell$_{k*}$ brom$_{k*}$ calc *Caust* cham$_{k*}$ chin$_{k*}$ cimx$_{k*}$ clem$_{a1}$ croc$_{k*}$ cupr dulc *Ferr*$_{k*}$ ferr-p gins$_{k*}$ gran$_{k*}$ guaj$_{k*}$ nit-ac$_{h2}$ olnd$_{k*}$ op$_{k*}$ osm$_{k*}$ par$_{k*}$ ph-ac$_{k*}$ plat$_{h2}$ raph$_{k*}$ sabad$_{k*}$ *Sabin* sars$_{k*}$ *Spig*$_{k*}$ spong stann$_{k*}$ sumb$_{k*}$ teucr$_{a1}$ thuj$_{k*}$ verb$_{k*}$ zinc
    - **outward**: anac ph-ac prun spig spong staph$_{h1}$
  - **pressure**:
    - **amel.**: *Ferr*$_{k*}$ lycps-v op ↓
      - **pressing** pain: *Ferr*$_{k*}$ op$_{k*}$
  - **pulsating** pain: agath-a$_{nl2•}$ *Arg-n* nit-ac$_{h2*}$
  - **rest** agg.: thuj$_{k*}$
  - **rubbing**:
    - **amel.**: op ↓
      - **pressing** pain: op$_{k*}$
  - **shaking** the head agg.; on: sul-ac$_{k*}$
  - **sitting** agg.: hell$_{k*}$ spong ↓
    - **pressing** pain: spong
  - **sore**: arn dros$_{h1}$ lach plan plat$_{h2}$ sul-ac$_{h2}$
  - **standing** agg.: canth ↓
    - **stitching** pain: canth
  - **stitching** pain: agar aloe am-c arg-n$_{k*}$ arn *Asaf* bar-c bar-s$_{k2}$ bell$_{h1}$ bov calc canth cham chel chin cocc croc euon grat guaj lact laur led$_{h1}$ lyc mag-m meny mez mur-ac nat-c nit-ac plb raph ruta sabad sars **Spig** stann staph$_{h1}$ sul-ac *Thuj* verb
    - **outward**: bar-c$_{h2}$ bell$_{h1}$ verb

- **Eminence**, frontal – **stitching** pain: ...
    - **pulsating** pain: *Spig*
    - **tearing** pain: chel$_{h1}$ mez$_{h2}$
  - **stooping** agg.: bar-c ↓ dulc lact ↓
    - **stitching** pain: bar-c lact
  - **studying** agg.: cham ↓
    - **pressing** pain: cham$_{k*}$
  - **talking** agg.: mang ↓
    - **tearing** pain: mang
  - **tearing** pain: agn alum ambr arg-met arg-mur asaf$_{k2}$ bell bov calc calc-sil$_{k2}$ chel$_{h1}$ chin cina cocc hell kali-c lyc mang mill nat-c sabad *Sep* sil **Spig** *Thuj* verb *Zinc*
  - **touch**:
    - **agg.**: *Chin* ↓
      - **pressing** pain: *Chin*$_{k*}$
    - **amel.**: thuj ↓
      - **boring** pain: thuj
  - **waking**; on: thuj$_{k*}$
    - **stitching** pain: thuj
  - **walking** in open air agg.: dulc ↓ hell ↓ thuj
    - **pressing** pain: dulc hell$_{h1}$
  - **warm** | **bed** | **agg.**: arg-n
    - **room**:
      - **agg.**: spong$_{k*}$
      - **entering** a warm room; when: spong ↓ verb ↓
        - **pressing** pain: spong verb$_{k*}$
  - **washing**, when: bar-c ↓
    - **stitching** pain: bar-c
  - **extending** to:
    - **Brain**, into: sul-ac ↓
      - **stitching** pain: sul-ac
    - **Ear**: bov ↓ nat-c ↓ zinc ↓
      - **tearing** pain: bov nat-c zinc
    - **Ear**, into: nat-c ↓
      - **stitching** pain: nat-c
    - **Ears**: bov nat-c zinc
    - **Eye**: thuj ↓
      - **right**: calc ↓
        - **pressing** pain: calc
      - **pressing** pain: thuj
    - **Eyes**: calc-act thuj
    - **Jaw**: bell
    - **Nose**: cina croc dulc op squil
      - **stitching** pain: squil
    - **Occiput**: aq-mar$_{skp7•}$ coc-c nat-c spig ↓
      - **pressing** pain: spig$_{h1}$
      - **tearing** pain: spig$_{h1}$
    - **Orbit**: zinc ↓
      - **tearing** pain: zinc$_{h2}$
    - **Outward**: verb
    - **Side** | **right**: cench$_{k2}$
    - **Supraorbital** foramen: aur-m melal-alt$_{gya4}$
    - **Temple**: arg-met ↓ mang ↓ thuj
      - **tearing** pain: arg-met mang
    - **Vertex**: agath-a$_{nl2•}$ *Ferr*
      - **pressing** pain: *Ferr*
  - **Above**: zinc ↓
    - **boring** pain: zinc$_{h2}$
    - **stitching** pain: zinc$_{h2}$
  - **Supraorbital** nerve, in: *Bapt* ↓
    - **stitching** pain: *Bapt*$_{hr1}$
- **Eyebrows**; above: nept-m$_{lsd2.fr}$ [bell-p-sp$_{dcm1}$]
  - **right**: aq-mar$_{skp7•}$ tell$_{rsj10•}$ tritic-vg$_{fd5.de}$
  - **left**: mim-p$_{rsj8*•}$ trios$_{rsj11•}$
- **Eyes**:
  - **right**: bros-gau ↓ buth-a ↓

- **Eyes – right**: ...
  - **piercing** pain: bros-gau mrc1
  - **pressing** pain: buth-a sp1
  - **morning**: allox ↓
    - **pressing** pain: allox sp1
  - **Above**: acon k* aconin bro1 adam skp7• aesc aeth agar agath-a nl2• agn ↓ ail all-c allox ↓ aln ↓ aloe k* alum alum-p k2 alumn ↓ am-c ambr ammc vml3• *Anac* ↓ ang ant-c *Apis* arg-met *Arg-n* arizon-l ↓ *Arn* k* *Ars* k* ars-i ars-s-f ↓ arum-t ↓ asaf k* aspar aster ↓ aur ↓ aur-m aur-m-n ↓ bacls-10 fmm1• bamb-a ↓ bapt bar-act ↓ bar-c bar-i k2 bar-s k2 *Bell* berb *Bism* ↓ borx bov brom bros-gau ↓ *Bry* buth-a ↓ cadm-met tpw6 cadm-s *Calc* calc-caust ↓ calc-i k2 *Calc-p* calc-s calc-sil k2 cann-i cann-xyz ↓ canth caps *Carb-ac* bro1* carb-an carb-v carbn-s ↓ carc sp1 card-b ↓ *Card-m* ↓ cassia-s ↓ caust **Cedr** k* celt ↓ cench ↓ cent ↓ cere-b bro1 *Chel* chim-m *Chin* chinin-ar ↓ *Chinin-s* k* *Chion* br1 chir-fl ↓ chlam-tr ↓ chlol choc ↓ chord-umb rly4• cic b7a.de* cimic k* cina cinnb k* cist cob-n sp1 coc-c ↓ coca coca-c sk4• cocc ↓ colch k* coloc bro1 con cop cortiso sp1* *Croc* k* crot-c ↓ crot-h cupr cupr-ar ↓ dig dios dream-p sdj1• dros dulc fd4.de dys fmm1• echi elaps ephe-si hsj1• euon ↓ euph ↓ eupi ↓ eys sp1 falco-pe ↓ ferr ferr-ar ferr-i ferr-p fl-ac *Gels* *Glon* k* gran ↓ graph ↓ grat ↓ gymno haem ↓ haliae-lc srj5• ham hell *Hep* hipp hist sp1 hura hydr hydrc hydrog srj2• hyos hyper ign k* ind indg ↓ indol bro1 iod ip *Iris* k* jug-r kali-ar *Kali-bi* k* **Kali-c** kali-i k2 kali-n kali-p *Kali-s* kali-sil k2 kalm kola ↓ kreos ↓ lac-ac **Lac-c** *Lac-d* lac-h ↓ **Lach** lachn ↓ lact lap-la rsp1 laur lavand-a ctl1• led ↓ lil-t lith-c (non:lob slp) lob-s slp loxo-recl knl4• luna kg1• *Lyc* k* lyss mag-c mag-m ↓ mag-p mag-s ↓ manc ↓ mang med meli bro1 mentho bro1 meny ↓ *Meph* merc merc-c ↓ merc-i-r merc-sul ↓ merl mez mim-p skp7*• morph ↓ mosch mur-ac ↓ musca-d ↓ naja nat-ar nat-c *Nat-m* nat-ox rly4• *Nat-p* nat-s ↓ nept-m ↓ nit-ac nit-s-d ↓ nux-m k* **Nux-v** k* oci-sa sk4• ol-an olib-sac ↓ onos op osm ox-ac ozone ↓ paeon ↓ **Par** ↓ *Petr* petr-ra shn4• ph-ac phasco-ci ↓ phel bro1 *Phos* *Phys* *Phyt* pic-ac pimp ↓ pip-m ↓ plan plat plb plect ↓ plut-n srj7• podo ↓ polys ↓ *Positr* nl2• pot-e rly4• *Prun* ↓ psil ft1 *Psor* ptel **Puls** k* pycnop-sa mrz1 ran-b k* raph rheum rhodi ↓ rhus-r rhus-t k* ribo rly4• *Ros-d* ↓ ruta fd4.de sabad sabin ↓ sal-fr sle1• *Sang* *Sanic* santin ↓ sarcol-ac sp1 scut ↓ sec a1 *Sel* k* senec ↓ *Seneg* *Sep* **Sil** *Sol-ni* sol-t-ae ↓ **Spig** spong *Stann* staph staphycoc ↓ streptoc rly4• stront-c ↓ suis-pan rly4• sul-i sulph suprar rly4• syph k2 tab tarent tax tell ter teucr ther thuj tritic-vg fd5.de urt-u *Valer* vanil fd5.de verat verb ↓ viol-o bro1 viol-t *Zinc* zinc-p k2 zing
    - **one** side: ozone ↓
      - **dull** pain: ozone sde2•
    - **alternating** sides: irid-met srj5• *Iris* **Lac-c** *Lil-t* sal-fr sle1•
    - **right**: acon aesc agar agn ↓ allox ↓ am-br mtf11 am-m anac ant-c ↓ aran vh arg-n arizon-l nl2• ars arund bro1 aur ↓ aur-m bamb-a stb2.de• bapt *Bell* k* bism k* *Bor-ac* *Bov* ↓ bros-gau ↓ bry cact bg1 **Carb-ac** carb-an carb-v bg1 carc mg1.de* card-m vml3• caust ↓ **Chel** k* *Chin* chord-umb rly4• cinnb cist coc-c coca cocc cocc-s kr1 colch rsj2• com con ↓ cortiso skp7• *Cur* ↓ cycl daph dig dream-p sdj1• dros dulc euon ferr fic-m gya1 fl-ac *Gels* gink-b sbd1• gins glon graph ham helo-s rwt2• hep bg1 hip-ac ↓ hydrog srj2• hyos *Ign* irid-met srj5• iris k* kali-bi bro1 kali-n kali-p fd1.de• kalm mtf11 lac-c lac-d al lach *Lyc* lyss ↓ mag-c br1 *Mag-p* mang meli bro1 merc-i-f mez mur-ac nat-ar ↓ nat-c a1 *Nat-m* nept-m lsd2.fr *Nux-m* *Ol-an* olib-sac ↓ op oxal-a rly4• ozone sde2• phys phyt plat bro1 plut-n srj7• propl ub1• prun bg1 psil ft1 rad-br c11 **Ran-b** rhus-t rumx ruta fd4.de sabad bg1 samb bat1• **Sang** k* sel rsj9• sil bro1 *Spig* spong fd4.de staph stict c1 streptoc rly4• stront-c suis-pan rly4• sulph bg1 suprar rly4• tab tarent thuj ↓ tritic-vg fd5.de tung-met ↓ urt-u ↓ viol-t xan zinc ↓ ziz [heroin sdj2]
      - **morning**: dros ↓
        - **gnawing** pain: dros k*
      - **16** h: sol-ni ↓
        - **shooting** pain: sol-ni
      - **boring** pain: colch k* dulc a1 ol-an bg2 ruta fd4.de sulph k*
      - **cutting** pain: bism bros-gau mrc1 *Chel* nat-ar
      - **drawing** pain: aur carb-v h2* dros a1 dulc gink-b sbd1• ign k* lyss staph h1*
      - **dull** pain: allox tpw3 hip-ac sp1 streptoc rly4• suis-pan rly4• suprar rly4•

- **Eyes – Above – right**: ...
  - **followed** by | **left**: aesc bg1 calc *Lac-c* lyc bg1 *Nat-m* ptel sep sin-n
  - **mental** exertion agg.: phase-vg a1
  - **neuralgic**: *Chel* tl1* sang tl1 thuj tl1
  - **pressing** pain: am-m h2 ant-c bamb-a stb2.de• caust *Chel* con h2 dulc *Ign* kali-p fd1.de• nat-m h2 olib-sac wmh1 plat h2 rhus-t h1 *Sang* sil h2 spig spong h1 staph h1 suis-pan rly4• thuj h1 urt-u zinc h2
    - **upward** and inward: bism
  - **shooting** pain: bry dream-p sdj1• nat-ar **Prun** tung-met bdx1•
  - **stitching** pain: anac h2 bamb-a stb2.de• *Bov* carb-v h2 cortiso skp7• *Cur* cycl a1* *Lyc* *Mag-p* mang nat-ar k2 nux-m bg1 ruta fd4.de tarent
  - **tearing** pain: agn anac bism h1 **Carb-ac** mag-p mang
  - **extending** to:
    - **left**: mez ↓
      - **shooting** pain: mez bg1
    - **Eye**: gink-b sbd1•
    - **Occiput**: *Bism* ↓ **Prun** ↓ sol-ni ↓ tub hr1*
      - **cutting** pain: *Bism* h1 tub al
      - **shooting** pain: **Prun** sol-ni
    - **Side** of head:
      - **right** side: hip-ac ↓
        - **dull** pain: hip-ac sp1
- **left**: acon acon-ac rly4• act-sp bro1 *Aesc* aeth agar ↓ aids ↓ am-c ↓ ambr ant-t arg-met ↓ arg-n bro1 arn *Ars* arum-t asaf atra-r skp7*• bacls-10 fmm1• bamb-a ↓ bar-c berb both-ax tsm2 bov ↓ brass-n-o srj5• brom **Bry** k* caj calc-p camph cann-i carb-v bro1 caul c1 caust ↓ cedr k* *Chel* chin bg1 chinin-s st chlam-tr bcx2• chord-umb rly4• cimic ↓ cocc bro1 *Colch* k* cupr cupr-ar ↓ dream-p sdj1• dulc fd4.de echi elaps gk ephe-si hsj1• euon bro1 euph ferr ferr-i k2 fic-m gya1 germ-met srj5• glon ham hell helo helo-s rwt2• hydr hydrog srj2• ign *Iod* ↓ *Ip* irid-met srj5• iris *Kali-bi* *Kali-c* **Kali-i** ↓ kali-s fd4.de kalm kola stb3• lac-c lac-f k2 *Lach* laur ↓ led bg1 lil-t lob lyc ↓ lyss mag-c mag-s mang-p rly4• mentho bro1 meny merc ↓ merc-c merc-i-r mim-p vml3• mosch mur-ac naja nat-ar ↓ nat-m gk nat-p nit-ac nux-m ↓ *Nux-v* k* onos oreo bro1 ox-ac oxyt bro1 ozone sde2• petr-ra shn4• *Ph-ac* *Phos* pip-m plut-n srj7• positr nl2• psil ft1 psor ptel puls rhus-r ribo rly4• ruta fd4.de sal-fr sle1• sanguis-s hrn2• sapo bro1 sel br1* senec bro1 *Sep* k* **Spig** k* spong fd4.de stann stram suis-pan rly4• sul-ac sulph bg1 tell k* ter ther k2* *Thuj* mrr1 trios rsj11• tritic-vg fd5.de (non:uran-met k) uran-n verat verat-v verb visc ↓ xan bro1 zinc ↓ zing ↓ [heroin sdj2 tax jsj7]
  - **15** h: pip-m ↓
    - **shooting** pain: pip-m
  - **morning**: hydrog srj2•
    - **waking**; on: germ-met srj5•
  - **air**; in open | **amel.**: ozone sde2•
  - **bending** agg.: hydrog srj2•
  - **boring** pain: *Arg-n* k* ars bg2 cimic k* cupr-ar k* kali-c h2 lyc k* nux-m spig
  - **coition**; after: cedr
  - **cutting** pain: aids nl2•
  - **drawing** pain: caul a1 chel mag-c h2* nat-m k* spig thuj k* verat-v a1 zing a1
  - **dull** pain: acon-ac rly4• sal-fr sle1• suis-pan rly4•
  - **lancinating**: chord-umb rly4• ribo rly4• sel c1
  - **lying** on left side | **amel.**: *Bry* ozone sde2•
  - **menses**; day before: xan c1
  - **periodical**: mur-ac ptk1 sep
  - **pressing** pain: *Acon* arg-met h1 bamb-a stb2.de• bry k* camph h1 cupr kola stb3• mur-ac h2 nux-m c1 *Nux-v* phos h2 plut-n srj7• *Sep* sulph h2 *Ther* *Thuj* h1 verb h
    - **followed** by:
      - **dull**, pressive pain in occipital protuberances: bry a1
        - **eating** agg.; quick: bry a1
        - **motion** agg.: bry a1
        - **pulsation** in head; it seemed a distinct: *Bry*
        - **extending** to the whole body: bry a1
  - **shooting** pain: *Acon* agar **Cedr** nat-ar pip-m *Sep* sulph

Head

- **Eyes – Above – left**: ...
  - **stitching** pain: aids nl2• am-c a1 bov a1 caust h2 chel a1 **Kali-i** kola stb3• *Lac-f* mag-c h2 ph-ac h2 psil ft1 ptel ruta fd4.de **Sel** *Sep* thuj h1 visc c1 zinc h2
  - **tearing** pain: aeth arg-met h1 *Iod* laur merc *Merc-c* stann h2 verb h zinc h2
  - **then** right: kali-bi *Lac-c* *Lach* nit-m-ac nux-m bg1 *Psor* sil bg1 sulph bg1 zing
  - **walk** in the sun: sel k2
  - **extending** to:
    - **right**: squil ↓ thuj ↓
      - **shooting** pain: squil bg1
      - **stitching** pain: thuj h1
    - **Eye**: mur-ac hr1
      - **right**: thuj ↓
        - **pressing** pain: thuj h1
    - **Forehead**; increasing and decreasing gradually over whole: *Stann*
    - **Head**: mur-ac hr1
    - **Neck**; nape of: kola stb3•
    - **Nose**: mur-ac hr1
    - **Occiput**: sel rsj9• **Sep** ↓
      - **body**; finally over whole: *Bry*
      - **shooting** pain: **Sep**
    - **Skull**: kola stb3•
    - **Vertex**: ferr-i phyt ↓ spong fd4.de
      - **shooting** pain: phyt
- **daytime**: phos pic-ac sep ↓ sulph
  - **pressing** pain: sep
- **morning**: agar agath-a nl2• alum alumn *Arg-n* bry k2 *Chin* chinin-s coc-c dios dros dulc fd4.de *Kali-bi* kali-n ↓ kola ↓ *Lac-c* lac-h ↓ *Lach* lyc ↓ mag-c ↓ *Mez* nat-ar nept-m lsd2.fr nit-ac ↓ nux-m **Nux-v** petr phys positr nl2• ruta fd4.de sep ↓ sol-ni spong fd4.de *Stann* sulph h2 tritic-vg fd5.de vanil fd5.de
  - **6**-12 h: *Glon*
  - **8** h: hydr
  - **16** h; until: *Mez*
  - **bed** agg.; in: coc-c *Nux-v* ruta fd4.de sol-ni spig
  - **boring** pain: sulph
  - **pressing** pain: alumn kali-n kola stb3• lac-h sk4• lach mag-c h2 petr positr nl2• sulph
  - **stitching** pain: alum k* nit-ac h2 sep k*
  - **tearing** pain: *Chin* lyc h2
  - **waking**; on: agar ↓ alumn ↓ bell h1 hydrog srj2• phos h2 [tax jsj7]
    - **pressing** pain: alumn
    - **shooting** pain: agar
- **forenoon**: allox ↓ chin dulc fd4.de flor-p ↓ glon *Mez* positr nl2• rhus-t ruta fd4.de sulph thuj vanil fd5.de
  - **9** h: lyss petr pip-m
  - **9**-15 h: *Caust*
  - **10** h: cimic ↓ crot-c petr stram tell
    - **boring** pain: cimic
  - **10**-16 h: *Stann*
  - **11** h: mag-p merc-i-r myric *Spig* ↓ verat
    - **boring** pain: *Spig*
  - **dull** pain: flor-p rsj3•
  - **pressing** pain: allox tpw3
  - **walking** agg.: thuj
- **noon**: form ham
- **afternoon**: *Acon* ↓ alum-sil k2 cann-i ↓ carb-v cinnb com dream-p sdj1• kali-bi *Lac-c* lyss ph-ac ↓ puls ruta fd4.de sang sep ↓ sulph tritic-vg fd5.de
  - **13** h: chinin-s dios petr-ra shn4• phys
  - **15** h: hura pip-m
    - **stitching** pain: pip-m
  - **16** h: com
  - **boring** pain: sang k*
  - **burning**: sulph k*
  - **motion** agg.: cinnb

- **Eyes – Above – afternoon**: ...
  - **pressing** pain: *Acon* cann-i carb-v h2 ph-ac h2 sulph h2
  - **shooting** pain: sulph
  - **tearing** pain: sang sep h2
- **evening**: agn ↓ alum-sil k2 ars camph ↓ chel ferr hep ↓ hir rsj4• inul ↓ iod kali-bi ↓ kalm lyss nat-m pip-m ↓ plan *Puls* ran-b ruta fd4.de *Sep* stry tritic-vg fd5.de vanil ↓
  - **18** h: colch dios lil-t
  - **20** h: chinin-s
  - **21** h: lyss petr-ra shn4•
  - **bed** agg.; in: mag-s ↓
    - **boring** pain: mag-s k*
  - **burning**: chel k*
  - **pressing** pain: camph h1 iod h
  - **reading** agg.: *Chel* lyss
  - **stitching** pain: hep k* inul k* kali-bi k* pip-m vanil fd5.de
  - **tearing** pain: agn
- **night**: ars cassia-s ↓ *Chel* *Glon* hyper *Kali-bi* *Lyc* ↓ lyss *Mez* vanil fd5.de
  - **midnight**:
    - **after**: ambr kl
      - **4** h: spig
  - **amel.**: lavand-a ctl1•
  - **burning**: **Ars**
  - **stitching** pain: cassia-s ccrh1• lyc h2 vanil fd5.de
  - **tearing** pain: *Lyc*
- **air**; in open:
  - **agg.**: calc chel colch con c1 conin c1 ham staph ↓
    - **pressing** pain: staph h1
  - **amel.**: aur ↓ aur-m ↓ echi kali-bi merc ↓ phos pip-m rad-br c11 *Sep*
    - **tearing** pain: aur aur-m merc
- **bed**; when going to: atra-r skp7*• ferr
- **blowing** the nose agg.: mag-c ↓
  - **drawing** pain: mag-c h2*
  - **stitching** pain: mag-c h2
- **boring** pain: agar arg-n k* *Ars* asaf k* aster aur-m-n k* **Bell** calc-caust cimic k* colch k* cupr-ar k* dulc k* ephe-si hsj1• ip k* kola stb3• laur k* led k* lyc k* mag-s k* ol-an k* ruta fd4.de sep spig sulph
- **breakfast** agg.; after: hyper *Lyc*
- **burning**: acon k* agar k* **Ars** cent a1 chel k* coloc k* dig dros meny k* merc mur-ac h2 nux-m plut-n srj7• rhus-t k* sil k* sulph k*
- **burrowing**: dulc kali-c plat k*
- **bursting** pain: crot-c kali-bi mag-m nit-ac h2 psil ft1
- **catarrh**; from: cist ↓
  - **pressing** pain: cist tl1
- **closing** the eyes:
  - **amel.**: ip ↓
    - **boring** pain: ip h1
    - **pressing** pain: ip h1
  - **must** close the eyes: *Bell* irid-met srj5• mim-p skp7• nux-v ↓ petr-ra shn4• pot-e rly4•
    - **pressing** pain: nux-v
- **coition**; after: castm cedr
- **cold**:
  - **air** agg.: kali-bi plut-n srj7• sep ↓
    - **boring** pain: sep
  - **applications** | **amel.**: agn cedr chel germ-met srj5• kali-bi lac-d *Lach* *Spig*
- **contraction** of brow: *Arn* k*
- **coryza**; as from: sulph h2
- **cough**:
  - **after**: *Ol-j* seneg k2 *Spig*
  - **during**:
    - **agg.**: hyos ↓
      - **stitching** pain: hyos k*
- **cutting** pain: bry k2 card-b a1 *Hydr* hydrog srj2• kali-i k2 plect a1 sel rsj9• senec a1

- **Eyes – Above**: ...
  - **darkness** agg.: onos
  - **dinner** | **after**:
    - **agg.**: phos ↓
      - **pressing** pain: phos h2
    - **agg.**: am-c ↓ borx ↓
      - **stitching** pain: am-c h2 (non:am-m h2*) borx
  - **drawing** pain: *Agar* k* agath-a nl2• asaf k* aur-m-n a1 bry k* calc *Cann-i* k* cann-xyz bg2 carb-an k* *Chel* colch k* con k* graph k2 *Ign* k* lyss nat-m nit-ac k* *Puls* seneg sil h2* spig stann h2* sulph k* thuj k* zinc k* zing bg2*
    - **projecting**; sensation as if eyes were:
      - **thread** were tightly drawn through eyeball; sensation as if | **brain** with weak vision; and backward into middle of: **Par**
    - **upward**: staph h1*
  - **dull** pain: apis *Arg-n* hr1 ars-s-f k2 cann-i cench k2 chir-fl gya2 falco-pe nl2• ham fd3.de• nat-ar plut-n srj7• podo fd3.de• polys sk4• sal-fr sle1• *Sep* staphycoc rly4• suis-pan rly4• urt-u zinc
  - **eating** | **after**:
    - **agg.**: am-c ↓ bry colch nit-ac sulph h2
      - **stitching** pain: am-c k*
    - **amel.**: chin
  - **heat** of stove agg.: *Arn*
  - **lancinating**: bros-gau mrc1
  - **light**; from: chel chinin-s irid-met srj5• mez nat-m nux-v pic-ac spig
    - **agg.**: sep ↓
      - **pressing** pain: sep h2
  - **looking**:
    - **bright** objects, at: sol-ni
    - **down**: *Nat-m*
    - **intently** at anything: calc k2 puls
  - **lying** down:
    - **after**:
      - **agg.**: chim-m *Ran-b Sang* tell
      - **amel.**: cupr kali-bi tritic-vg fd5.de
    - **amel.**: cassia-s ↓
      - **stitching** pain: cassia-s ccrh1•
  - **menses**:
    - **after** | **agg.**: mag-m
    - **before**:
      - **agg.**: bell graph hir rsj4• hyper nat-p sil tritic-vg fd5.de xan
        - **pressing** pain: sil h2
    - **during**:
      - **agg.**: cench k2 cimic graph lac-c ↓ *Lach Lyc* nat-p phos bg1 sang
        - **pressing** pain: lac-c
      - **amel.**: kali-bi
  - **mental** exertion agg.: calc ↓ ph-ac **Pic-ac** *Puls* sep *Spig*
    - **drawing** pain: calc
  - **motion**:
    - **agg.**: agn ↓ *Bry* cassia-s ↓ cinnb cupr mag-m mim-p skp7• *Nux-v* onos petr-ra shn4• plb *Sang Sep* ↓ sol-ni *Spig* ther k* tritic-vg fd5.de vanil fd5.de
      - **pressing** pain: **Bry** *Sep*
      - **stitching** pain: cassia-s ccrh1•
      - **tearing** pain: agn
    - **amel.**: dios *Puls*
  - **narrow** line, in a: bry
  - **neuralgic**: (↗*EYE - Pain - supraorbital - neuralgic)* arg-n bg2 asaf bg2 bry bg2 cedr bg2 chel bg2 chinin-s bg2 cimic bg2 gels bg2 glon bg2 kali-bi bg2 mag-p bg2 meli bg2 merc bg2 nux-v bg2 ran-b bg2 rhodi br1 ruta bg2 spig bg2 stann bg2 thuj bg2
  - **noise** agg.: chinin-s
  - **numbness**, followed by: *Mez*
  - **opening** the eyes agg.: euph ↓ phys br1 sil ↓
    - **pressing** pain: sil
    - **tearing** pain: euph h2

- **Eyes – Above**: ...
  - **periodical**: *Chinin-s Tub*
  - **pinching** pain: ars h2
  - **pressing** pain: *Acon* aeth agar agath-a nl2• allox tpw3* aln vva1• **Aloe** alum alum-p k2 alumn am-c *Anac* ang ant-c apis arg-met h1 arg-n arizon-l nl2• arn ars ars-i asaf aster bar-c bar-i k2 bar-s k2 *Bell Bism* borx bov brom **Bry** buth-a sp1 calc h2* *Calc-p* cann-i carb-an *Carb-v* carbn-s *Card-m* caust *Chel* chin chinin-ar chlam-tr bcx2• choc srj3• cist con *Crot-h* dig h2 dros h1 dulc euon euph eupi fl-ac *Glon* graph k2 grat gymno haem hep *Ign* indg iod *Kali-ar Kali-c* kali-n kali-p kali-s fd4.de kali-sil k2 kalm kola stb3• kreos lac-h sk4• lach lavand-a ctl1• lil-t lith-c lyc lyss mag-c merc merc-c merc-i-r merc-sul c1 merl mez h2 morph **Nat-m** *Nat-p* nat-s nept-m lsd2.fr nit-ac *Nux-m Nux-v* olib-sac wmh1 op ozone sde2• paeon petr ph-ac h2 phasco-ci rbp2 *Phos* phyt pic-ac plan plect *Positr* nl2• **Puls** rheum h *Rhus-t Ros-d* wla1 ruta sabad santin seneg sep *Sil* sol-t-ae spig h1 spong h1 stann h2 staph streptoc rly4• stront-c suis-pan rly4• sul-i k2 *Sulph* tab teucr ther thuj tritic-vg fd5.de urt-u *Valer* vanil fd5.de zinc zinc-p k2 zing
    - **forced** out; as if eyes would be: bell k2 caps k2 cocc gymno ign lachn med hr1 nat-m phos sabin sang k2 seneg sep sil tarent
    - **inward**: bamb-a stb2.de•
    - **outward**: ang h1 bell h1 ip h1 kali-c h2 lyc h2 phos h2 sec
    - **pressing** down upon the eyes: agath-a nl2• arg-met h1 bell h1 hell h1 *Hep Phos* plat h2 rhus-t h1 sabin spig h1 zinc h2
    - **stunning**: plat h2
    - **wavelike**: plat h2
  - **pressure**:
    - **agg.**: cortiso ↓
      - **stitching** pain: cortiso skp7•
    - **amel.**: *Anac* ↓ apis ↓ cassia-s ↓ chinin-s germ-met srj5• ip ↓ irid-met srj5• kali-p ↓ petr-ra shn4• spong fd4.de tritic-vg fd5.de
      - **boring** pain: ip h1
      - **pressing** pain: apis ip h1
      - **shooting** pain: kali-p
      - **stitching** pain: cassia-s ccrh1•
      - **tearing** pain: *Anac*
    - **eye**; on:
      - **agg.**: arg-met ↓ lyc ↓
        - **tearing** pain: arg-met h1 lyc h2
      - **amel.**: sang hr1
  - **pressure** so severe, when rising, could only half open eyes, could not look up: stram ↓
    - **pressing** pain: (↗*Heaviness - forehead - eyes - above - looking - impossible)* stram
  - **pulsating** pain: agath-a nl2• *Bry* caust chel dig h2 dream-p sdj1• *Glon* st gymno br1 ham *Kali-bi Lach Lyss* st mag-m mim-p skp7• musca-d szs1 nat-c h2 nat-m *Pic-ac* plat ptel **Puls** ruta fd4.de sep *Spig* ther
  - **raising** eyebrow agg.: nat-m ↓
    - **pressing** pain: nat-m h2
  - **reading** agg.: calc chel ph-ac
  - **rubbing**:
    - **amel.**: kali-p ↓
      - **shooting** pain: kali-p
  - **sewing**, while: **Lac-c**
  - **shooting** pain: *Acon* agar am-c ant-c berb bov bry caust **Cedr** *Kali-bi* kali-p lyss nat-ar nat-m nit-ac ph-ac *Prun Sep* sulph zinc
    - **outward**: bar-act bell con ferr glon gran lyc ph-ac puls senec sep sulph verb
    - **upward**: ph-ac scut
  - **sitting** agg.: ter
  - **sleep**:
    - **amel.**: kali-bi petr-ra shn4•
    - **before**: atra-r skp7*•
  - **sneezing** agg.: echi
  - **sore**: cann-i choc srj3• gels *Kali-c* plan plat h2 positr nl2• *Sil*
  - **spectacles**, from wearing: sil hr1
  - **standing** | **amel.**: *Ran-b*

· **Eyes** – **Above**: ...
: **stitching** pain: agar k* aloe alum k* alum-p k2 am-c k* anac ang h1 arum-t bell h1 berb k* borx h2 *Bov* k* bry k* calc h2 caps k* cassia-s ccrh1• *Cedr* celt a1 **Chel** k* cob-n sp1 coc-c k* cocc k* colch k* *Ferr* k* ferr-p kali-c k* **Kali-i** k* kali-p lach k* *Lyc* k* mag-p mag-s k* manc mang mez k* nat-m k* nit-s-d a1 ol-an paeon k* petr h2* ph-ac *Phos* pimp a1 pip-m rhus-t ruta fd4.de sel *Sep* k* sil h2 *Spig* sulph h2 tarent tritic-vg fd5.de valer k* vanil fd5.de
: **stooping** agg.: caps ↓ dros *Ign* ip ↓ kali-bi lyss merc-c ↓ nat-m petr *Puls* sin-n sol-ni *Spig* spong ↓ teucr ↓
. **pressing** pain: caps k2 merc-c spong h1 teucr
. **stitching** pain: ip h1
: **stunning** pain: ars h2 euon k* stann h2
: **sudden**: *Mez*
: **supper**; during: chlor
: **talking** agg.: petr-ra shn4•
: **tearing** pain: agar agn *Ars* aur aur-m calc chel *Chin* ferr-i graph k2 iod kali-ar kali-c kali-i lach laur lyc mag-p mang merc mez phos sang sep sil
. **intermitting**: *Ars*
: **thunderstorm**; in: sep ↓
. **boring** pain: sep
: **waking**; on: allox ↓ bry *Lac-c* nat-ar sol-ni *Spig* tung-met bdx1• ven-m rsj12•
. **dull** pain: allox sp1
: **walking**:
. **about**:
amel.: *Ars* ↓
tearing pain: *Ars*
. **after**:
agg.: con ↓
pressing pain: con h2
. **agg.**: agar aur-m-n ↓ cassia-s ↓ chin petr-ra shn4• plat ↓ puls scroph-n c1 thuj
boring pain: aur-m-n k*
burrowing: plat
stitching pain: cassia-s ccrh1•
. **air**; in open:
agg.: *Sep* ↓
pressing: *Sep* k*
amel.: borx chel hydr nux-v *Phos* ↓ *Sep*
stitching pain: *Phos* sep k*
. **amel.**: ars ↓ dros h1 *Ran-b*
boring pain: ars
: **warm** | **applications**:
amel.: *Arg-met* **Ars** *Aur-m* calc k2 *Mag-p* sang *Thuj*
tearing pain: calc k2
. **room**:
agg.: cortiso tpw7 mez *Puls*
amel.: lac-c k2
: **warmth** agg.: chel mez
: **weather** agg.; cold wet: *Sil Spig*
: **wind**; cold, dry: **Acon** lac-c k2
: **extending** to:
. **Brain**: *Cina* ↓ med ↓
. **pressing** pain | **forced** out; as if eyes would be: med hr1
stitching pain: *Cina* h1*
. **Ear**: aur-m glon lac-ac c1 lac-c lac-d c1 osm
. **Eyes**: con lac-ac c1 lac-d c1 lil-t
. **Eyes**, into: con ↓
pressing pain: con
. **Face**: *Mag-p*
. **Head**: alum k2 gymno
. **Head**; whole: cassia-s ↓
stitching pain: cassia-s ccrh1•
. **Neck**: med ↓
pressing pain | **forced** out; as if eyes would be: med hr1
. **Nose**: all-c bov *Calc* chel bg1 coloc bg1 kola ↓ **Lach** mez bg1 phos bg1 phys ran-b sep bg1

· **Eyes** – **Above** – **extending** to – **Nose**: ...
pressing pain: bov kola stb3•
tearing pain: calc k2
Root of: **Lach**
. **Occiput**: bell bg1 bism bry bg1* cham bg1 chel chlor bg1 cimic dios kali-c bg1 kali-p kalm kreos *Lach* lil-t bg1 lyc naja nat-c bg1 nat-m bg1 phos bg1 pic-ac bg1 rad-br c11 sep sulph bg1 syph k2 ther bg1 thuj bg1 tritic-vg fd5.de tub ↓ zing
shooting pain: tub bg*
. **Outward**: nat-c sec sulph bg1
. **Temples**: *Arn* borx dios hell nat-ar nept-m lsd2.fr phys sang a1
. **Vertex**: arg-n ars-s-f ↓ ferr-i ↓ gymno melal-alt ↓ phos phys podo ↓ rad-br c11
dull pain: ars-s-f k2 melal-alt gya4 podo fd3.de•
stitching pain: ferr-i k2
: **Margin** of orbits: anac ↓ hyos ↓ phasco-ci ↓ spig ↓
. **pressing** pain: anac h2 hyos h1 phasco-ci rbp2 spig h1
. **sore**: spig h1
. **extending** to:
Temples: cann-s ↓ chin ↓
pressing pain: cann-s chin h1
: **Muscles**: bell ↓
. **pressing** pain: bell h1
: **Root** of nose along left orbital arch to external angle of eye; from:
. **dim** sight; with:
beginning in morning, agg. till noon and ceases toward evening: kali-bi ↓
shooting pain | **violent** shooting pains: kali-bi k*
: **Sides** of: aur ↓ caust ↓ clem ↓ coloc ↓ fl-ac ↓ merc ↓ ph-ac ↓ **Spig** ↓
. **burning**: aur k* caust k* clem h2* coloc k* fl-ac k* merc ph-ac **Spig**
: **Upper** lid; down: chel ↓
. **pressing** pain | **pressing** down upon the eyes: chel h1
: **Around**: arizon-l nl2• cortiso tpw7 lat-m sp1
: **afternoon**: cortiso tpw7
: **pressure** agg.: cortiso tpw7
: **warm** room agg.: cortiso tpw7
: **Behind**: acon agath-a nl2• aids nl2• allox tpw3 androc srj1• anthraq rly4• apoc bg1 arge-pl rwt5• arizon-l nl2• asc-t bad bamb-a stb2.de• bar-ox-suc rly4• *Bell* berb bism bit-ar ↓ bry bg1 cadm-met ↓ calc k2 (non:cann-i k*) cann-s kl carc tpw2* caul c1 caust ↓ chel chord-umb rly4• cimic k* cob colch rsj2• coli rly4• cop cor-r br1 corian-s knl6• cystein-l rly4• daph dig dream-p sdj1• fago fic-m gya1 *Fl-ac* fum rly1*• fuma-ac rly4• gels glon granit-m ↓ ham ↓ hep bg1 hydrog srj2• ictod kali-n lach led limen-b-c ↓ lith-c bg1 luna kg1• medul-os-si rly4• merc-c mim-p rsj8• nat-pyru rly4• neon srj5• nept-m lsd2.fr olib-sac wmh1 pall pant-ac rly4• phos h2 phys bg1 plac-s rly4• *Podo* positr nl2• pot-e rly4• puls bg1 rhus-t ribo rly4• ruta fd4.de sacch-l bg1 sal-fr ↓ *Sel* seneg sep squil ↓ streptoc rly4• suis-em rly4• suis-hep rly4• suis-pan rly4• sulph bg1 suprar rly4• symph fd3.de• *Ther* k* thiam rly4• tritic-vg fd5.de ziz [bell-p-sp dcm1 heroin sdj2]
: **right**: amp rly4• ozone sde2• ven-m rsj12• [*Buteo-j* sej6]
. **pulsating** pain: ozone sde2•
: **left**: amp rly4• brass-n-o srj5• lac-lup hrn2• nat-pyru rly4• *Sel* rsj9• staphycoc rly4• suis-pan rly4• tere-la rly4•
. **pressing** pain: brass-n-o srj5•
: **daytime** | **increasing** during the day: allox sp1
: **accompagnied** by:
. **Head**; heaviness of: bit-ar ↓
pulsating pain: bit-ar wht1•
. **Neck**; aching in: bit-ar ↓
pulsating pain: bit-ar wht1•
: **dull** pain: cadm-met sp1 granit-m es1• sal-fr sle1•
: **pinching** pain: pot-e rly4•
: **pressing** pain: bar-ox-suc rly4• caust h2 granit-m es1• ham fd3.de• limen-b-c mlk9.de olib-sac wmh1 rhus-t h1 ruta fd4.de streptoc rly4• ther c1*

- **Eyes – Behind**: ...
    - **pulsating** pain: anthraq rly4• bit-ar wht1• hydrog srj2•
    - **reading** agg.: calc k2
    - **tearing** pain: bism h1 squil h1
    - **waking**; on: allox tpw3
    - **extending** to:
      - **Vertex**: olib-sac ↓
        - **pressing** pain: olib-sac wmh1
  - **Between**: *(↗EYE - Pain - between the)* acon ↓ agath-a nl2• arund mrr asc-c c1 caust ↓ chord-umb rly4• **Cupr** k* des-ac rbp6 ger-i rly4• helo-s ↓ *Hep* ictod kali-s fd4.de lach lyc nat-pyru rly4• phos h2 pot-e rly4• ruta fd4.de streptoc rly4• vanil fd5.de
    - **night**:
      - **midnight**:
        - **after**:
          - **5** h: helo-s ↓
            - **pinching** pain: helo-s rwt2•
    - **bursting** pain: acon bg2
    - **pinching** pain: helo-s rwt2•
    - **pressing** pain: caust h2 nat-pyru rly4•
      - **outward**: acon bg2
    - **extending** to | **Upper** jaw: *Fl-ac*
  - **Over** the eyes: mand ↓
    - **dull** pain (See above - dull)
    - **pressing** pain (See above - pressing)
    - **violent**: mand rsj7•
- **Frontal** sinuses: *(↗FACE - Pain - sinuses - frontal)* allox ↓ kali-i br1 mag-m ↓ syc bka1• symph ↓
  - **coryza**; from chronic: *Ars Kali-bi* kali-c mrr1 *Sang* **Sil** k* *Thuj*
  - **mental** exertion; after: cob-n ↓
    - **stitching** pain: cob-n sp1
  - **pressing** pain: allox tpw3 mag-m h2 symph fd3.de•
- **Interior** parts: cann-i ↓
  - **jerking** pain | **backward**: cann-i c1
- **Lower** part: dios ↓ laur ↓ merc ↓ merc-i-r ↓ senec ↓ sep ↓
  - **right**: bism ↓
    - **cutting** pain: bism bg2
  - **boring** pain: laur bg2
  - **cutting** pain: dios bg2 merc bg2 merc-i-r bg2 senec bg2 sep bg2
- **Margin** of hair: spong fd4.de stroph-h c1 [bell-p-sp dcm1]
- **Meninges**: hyos h1* lob c2
- **Middle** of: agar k* agath-a nl2• ail k* *Ars* atro k* aur ↓ bov ↓ calc carb-ac bg1 *Carb-an* carneg-g rwt1• caust ↓ chel ↓ colch k* crot-c k* *Cupr* dulc ↓ fl-ac k* gels ↓ gink-b sbd1• glon ↓ indg ↓ *Kali-bi* kali-c bg1 **Kali-i** kali-p fd1.de• kola stb3• laur ↓ *Lyc* k* **Merc** mez k* *Nat-ar* mrr1 petr ↓ ph-ac bg1 phos ↓ phys k* pic-ac k* psor k* *Puls* rat k* sabad k* sacch-a fd2.de• sang sanguis-s hrn2• sars ↓ sel k* **Sil** k* spong fd4.de stann ↓ *Staph* stront-c ↓ sul-ac ↓ symph fd3.de• valer ↓ verb [bell-p-sp dcm1]
  - **morning**: bov ↓
    - **tearing** pain: bov
  - **noon**: gels ↓
    - **stitching** pain: gels
  - **afternoon**: gels ↓ mag-c ↓
    - **stitching** pain: gels
    - **tearing** pain: mag-c
  - **evening**: bov ↓ dulc ↓ mag-m ↓
    - **stitching** pain: bov dulc fd4.de mag-m h2
  - **dinner**; after: chel ↓
    - **tearing** pain: chel
  - **eating**; after: nit-ac ↓
    - **stitching** pain: nit-ac h2
  - **foot**-bath | **amel**.: nat-s k*
  - **hammering** pain: **Lyc**
  - **hat**; from pressure of a: sel
  - **menses**; before: *Calc*
  - **motion** agg.: sep ↓
- **Middle** of – **motion** agg.: ...
    - **stitching** pain: sep h2
  - **reading** agg.: *Nat-ar* mrr1
  - **stitching** pain: aur chel dulc fd4.de gels indg sars stann valer
    - **outward**: kali-c ph-ac h2 phos
    - **pulsating** pain: petr h2
  - **stool** agg.; straining at: rat
  - **stooping** agg.: gels ↓ rat ↓
    - **stitching** pain: gels rat
  - **tearing** pain: bov caust h2 glon laur stront-c sul-ac
  - **walking**:
    - **agg**.: sil k*
    - **air**; in open:
      - **agg**.: laur ↓ tarax
        - **stitching** pain: laur
      - **amel**.: sep ↓
        - **stitching** pain: sep h2
  - **extending** to:
    - **left** side: sul-ac ↓
      - **tearing** pain: sul-ac h2
    - **Eye** | **right**: ozone sde2•
    - **Neck**; nape of: kola stb3•
- **Nose**; above: *Acon* aesc ↓ aeth ↓ agar agath-a nl2• *All-s* ↓ am-m ambr ↓ ammc vh1 ant-t arn *Ars Ars-i* asar ↓ asc-c c1 aster bamb-a ↓ *Bapt* bar-c *Bell* berb ↓ *Bism* borx bov ↓ brom *Calc* calc-act ↓ calc-p camph cann-s ↓ canth *Caps* **Carb-ac** ↓ carb-an ↓ *Carb-v* ↓ caust ↓ cench k2 chel chin ↓ chion br1 *Cimic* ↓ cist k2 coc-c coloc conch ↓ **Cupr** dig dulc euphr ↓ falco-pe ↓ ferr gink-b sbd1• *Glon* guaj ham helon ↓ *Hep* hydr ↓ *Ign* iod ↓ kali-bi *Kali-c* kali-chl **Kali-i** kali-n ↓ kiss ↓ kola stb3• kreos lac-h sk4• *Lach* led ↓ lyc ↓ manc ↓ mang ↓ meny ↓ merc *Merc-i-f* mez tl1 mosch nat-ar k2 nat-c k2 nat-m ↓ nit-ac ↓ nux-v petr-ra shn4• ph-ac ↓ phos ↓ phyt ↓ plat *Prun* psor ↓ puls ran-b ↓ raph rheum ↓ rhus-t ↓ *Rhus-v* ruta fd4.de sacch-a fd2.de• sars ↓ sep ↓ sil ↓ spong ↓ **Staph** stict *Sulph* ↓ tarax ↓ til ↓ ulm-c ↓ verb ↓ viol-t xan zinc ↓ zing ↓
  - **left** half: dulc fd4.de mur-ac
    - **extending** to | **Occiput**; base of: oxeod a1
  - **morning**: sil ↓
    - **pressing** pain: sil k*
  - **evening**: ferr
  - **night**: rhus-v
  - **boring** pain: agath-a nl2• bism coloc k* **Hep** mang nat-m *Sulph* k*
  - **changeable**: ulm-c jsj8•
  - **cold**:
    - **amel**.: euphr ↓
      - **pressing** pain: euphr k*
  - **coryza**; during: bamb-a ↓
    - **pressing** pain: bamb-a stb2.de•
  - **cramping**: arn bell ign br1 spong
    - **lose** his senses; as if he would: *Acon* ign
  - **cutting** pain: agath-a nl2• led k*
  - **drawing** pain: acon agar agath-a nl2• asar *Carb-v* caust *Hep* kiss a1 meny h1* merc nat-m phyt a1 rheum spong zing k*
  - **dull** pain: xan c1
  - **gnawing** pain: calc-act merc ph-ac h2* phos raph
  - **menses**; during: arn hep *Ign* kali-bi *Lach*
  - **mental** exertion agg.: nat-m ↓
    - **drawing** pain: nat-m
  - **pressing** pain: *(↗extending - nose - pressing)* *Acon* aesc aeth *All-s* vh1 am-m k* ambr k* ant-t k* arn asar bamb-a stb2.de• *Bapt* bar-c *Bell Bism* k* bov k* brom camph cann-s *Caps* a1* **Carb-ac** carb-v chel h1 chin k* *Cimic Cist Coloc* conch fkr1• *Dulc* hr1 euphr k* falco-pe nl2• glon ham helon k* hep hydr k* *Ign* iod k* kali-n k* manc meny h1* merc mez mosch ph-ac k* raph k* ruta h1 sil k* spong *Stict* tarax til k* verb h viol-t zinc zing
    - **pressing** sensation on lids: chel h1
  - **pulsating** pain: **Ars**
  - **sore**: carb-an

Head

- **Nose**; above: ...
  - **stitching** pain: agar berb camph canth$_{a1}$ chin *Coloc*$_{a1}$ kali-bi kali-c nat-m nit-ac psor ran-b rhus-t sars sep sil
  - **stunning** pain: *Acon* agath-a$_{nl2}$• ant-t asar mosch
  - **tearing** pain: aeth agar ambr chel$_{h1}$ lyc nat-c nat-m
    - **pressing** sensation on lids: chel$_{h1}$
  - **extending** to:
    - **Neck**; nape of: gink-b$_{sbd1}$•
    - **Over** the head; gradually | **delirium** and vomiting; with: cimic$_{k*}$
  - **Root**: hep ↓
    - **stitching** pain: hep$_{c1}$
- **Side** to side (See alternating sides)
- **Sides**: agar ↓ *Agn* ↓ alum ↓ am-m ↓ anac ↓ ang ↓ ant-c ↓ arg-met ↓ *Arg-n* ↓ arum-t ↓ asaf ↓ aur ↓ aur-m-n ↓ *Bell* ↓ berb ↓ bov ↓ brom ↓ bry ↓ calc ↓ calc-ar ↓ camph ↓ canth ↓ *Carb-an* ↓ caust ↓ cere-b ↓ chel ↓ chin ↓ cimic ↓ cina ↓ clem ↓ cocc ↓ cocc-s ↓ colch ↓ *Coloc* ↓ cycl ↓ dig ↓ dros ↓ euph ↓ euphr ↓ gran ↓ grat ↓ guaj ↓ hyos ↓ ign ↓ kali-i ↓ kali-n ↓ kali-s ↓ kreos ↓ lach ↓ lachn ↓ led ↓ *Lyc* ↓ lyss ↓ mag-c ↓ *Mag-m* ↓ mang ↓ *Meny* ↓ *Merc* ↓ mez ↓ nat-m ↓ nat-s ↓ nit-s-d ↓ nuph ↓ ol-an ↓ op ↓ par ↓ phel ↓ phos ↓ psor ↓ *Puls* ↓ rat ↓ ruta ↓ *Sars* ↓ seneg ↓ *Sil* ↓ **Spig** ↓ spong ↓ *Stann* ↓ staph ↓ sul-ac ↓ tarax ↓ thuj ↓ thymol ↓ til ↓ verat ↓ verb ↓ zinc ↓
  - **left**: agar ↓ agn ↓ ambr ↓ ant-c ↓ ant-t ↓ arg-met ↓ *Arg-n* ↓ asaf ↓ *Aur* ↓ *Bar-c* ↓ bov ↓ brom ↓ bry ↓ *Calc* ↓ camph ↓ cann-s ↓ caust ↓ chel ↓ chin ↓ cic ↓ cina ↓ coloc ↓ crot-t ↓ dig ↓ *Euph* ↓ gran ↓ grat ↓ ign ↓ *Iod* ↓ kali-c ↓ kali-n ↓ lyc ↓ mag-c ↓ mag-m ↓ mang ↓ *Merc* ↓ mur-ac ↓ nat-c ↓ nat-m ↓ nux-m ↓ *Nux-v* ↓ *Ph-ac* ↓ phos ↓ plat ↓ podo ↓ ran-b ↓ *Rhod* ↓ ruta ↓ sabad ↓ sabin ↓ **Sars** ↓ seneg ↓ spong ↓ squil ↓ *Stann* ↓ **Staph** ↓ sul-ac ↓ symph ↓ tarax ↓ tax ↓ teucr ↓ thuj ↓ verat ↓ verb ↓ *Zinc* ↓
    - **boring** pain: arg-met arg-n$_{a1}$ aur$_{k*}$ bov$_{a1}$ brom$_{k*}$ spong$_{h1}$
    - **pressing** pain: agn ambr ant-c$_{h2}$ ant-t arg-met asaf$_{k*}$ *Aur*$_{k*}$ camph$_{k*}$ cann-s$_{k*}$ caust cic cina coloc$_{k*}$ crot-t euph ign$_{k*}$ *Iod* kali-n mag-c merc mur-ac nat-c nat-m nux-m *Nux-v* *Ph-ac*$_{k*}$ plat podo$_{fd3.de}$• ran-b *Rhod* sabad$_{a1}$ sabin **Sars**$_{k*}$ seneg spong$_{h1}$ squil staph$_{h1}$ teucr
    - **stitching** pain: agar$_{a1}$ *Arg-n* asaf$_{a1}$ *Bar-c* bry$_{a1}$ *Calc*$_{k*}$ caust$_{h2}$ chel$_{a1}$ chin$_{h1}$ coloc dig$_{a1}$ *Euph* gran$_{a1}$ grat$_{a1}$ lyc$_{h2}$ mag-m$_{a1}$ mang$_{k*}$ phos$_{h2}$ ruta$_{tl1}$ spong$_{h1}$ *Stann* **Staph**$_{k*}$ sul-ac$_{a1}$ symph$_{fd3.de}$• tarax$_{k*}$ thuj$_{a1}$ verat$_{a1}$ verb$_{a1}$ [tax$_{jsj7}$]
    - **tearing** pain: aur euph kali-c mang$_{h2}$ *Merc* tarax$_{h1}$ *Zinc*
    - **extending** to:
      - **right**: cocc ↓ lachn ↓ squil ↓
        - **stitching** pain: cocc squil$_{k*}$
        - **tearing** pain: lachn$_{c1}$
      - **Temple**: plat ↓
        - **drawing** pain: plat$_{h2}$
  - **morning**: *Bell* ↓ carb-an ↓ mez ↓ nicc ↓ ol-an ↓ sars ↓ staph ↓
    - **8 h**: borx ↓
      - **boring** pain: borx
    - **boring** pain: *Bell*$_{k*}$ staph$_{k*}$
    - **rising** agg.; after: carb-an ↓
      - **stitching** pain: carb-an$_{k*}$
    - **stitching** pain: carb-an mez$_{k*}$ nicc$_{k*}$ sars$_{k*}$
    - **tearing** pain: ol-an
  - **forenoon**:
    - **9 h**: sil ↓
      - **stitching** pain: sil
    - **10 h**: nat-s ↓
      - **stitching** pain: nat-s
    - **11 h**: calc ↓
      - **stitching** pain: calc
  - **afternoon**: am-m ↓ phos ↓
    - **16 h**: mag-c ↓
      - **tearing** pain: mag-c
    - **stitching** pain: am-m$_{k*}$ phos$_{k*}$
  - **evening**: arg-met ↓ chel ↓ lyc ↓ nat-m ↓ phos ↓ sul-ac ↓ sulph ↓
    - **boring** pain: arg-met

- **Sides – evening**: ...
    - **stitching** pain: chel$_{k*}$ lyc$_{k*}$ nat-m$_{k*}$ phos$_{k*}$ sul-ac$_{h2}$ sulph$_{k*}$
    - **tearing** pain: sul-ac
  - **air**; in open:
    - **amel.**: carb-an ↓
      - **stitching** pain: carb-an
  - **boring** pain: arg-met *Arg-n*$_{k*}$ aur$_{k*}$ aur-m-n *Bell*$_{k*}$ brom$_{k*}$ calc$_{k*}$ cere-b$_{a1}$ cimic colch$_{k*}$ *Coloc* led$_{k*}$ mez$_{k*}$ nat-s$_{k*}$ nit-s-d$_{a1}$ *Puls*$_{k*}$ spong$_{k*}$ staph$_{k*}$
  - **burrowing**: agar$_{k*}$ clem$_{k*}$ ol-an$_{k*}$ phel$_{a1}$
  - **coryza**; during: stann ↓
    - **stitching** pain: stann$_{h2}$
  - **dinner**; after: nat-m ↓
    - **stitching** pain: nat-m$_{k*}$
  - **drawing** pain: stann$_{h2}$
  - **dull** pain: thymol$_{sp1}$
  - **hand** laying on part amel.: meny ↓
    - **pressing** pain: meny$_{h1}$
  - **laughing** agg.: glon ↓
    - **stitching** pain: glon$_{k*}$
  - **menses**; during: nat-c ↓
    - **tearing** pain: nat-c
  - **motion**:
    - **agg.**: arg-n ↓ aur ↓ euph ↓
      - **boring** pain: arg-n$_{k*}$
      - **tearing** pain: aur euph
    - **muscles**; of:
      - **agg.**: mang ↓
        - **tearing** pain: mang$_{h2}$
  - **opening** the eyes agg.: *Sil* ↓
    - **stitching** pain: *Sil*$_{k*}$
  - **pressing** pain: agar$_{k*}$ alum ang$_{h1}$ chel chin cina ign$_{k*}$ lyc$_{k*}$ ruta$_{h1}$ spig verb$_{h}$
  - **pressure**:
    - **amel.**: nat-c ↓ sul-ac ↓
      - **stitching** pain: sul-ac$_{h2}$
      - **tearing** pain: nat-c$_{h2}$ sul-ac$_{h2}$
  - **sitting** agg.: aeth ↓ calc ↓ castm ↓ merc ↓ nat-s ↓ ruta ↓
    - **stitching** pain: calc merc$_{k*}$ nat-s$_{a1}$ ruta
    - **tearing** pain: aeth castm
  - **stitching** pain: agar$_{k*}$ am-m$_{h2}$ anac$_{k*}$ ant-c$_{k*}$ asaf$_{k*}$ berb$_{k*}$ bov$_{k*}$ bry$_{k*}$ calc$_{k*}$ calc-ar canth$_{k*}$ cocc$_{k*}$ cocc-s$_{a1}$ cycl$_{k*}$ dig$_{k*}$ dros$_{k*}$ euphr$_{k*}$ gran$_{a1}$ grat$_{k*}$ hyos$_{k*}$ kali-i$_{a1}$ kali-n$_{k*}$ kali-s kreos$_{k*}$ lach$_{k*}$ mag-m$_{k*}$ mang$_{k*}$ nat-m$_{k*}$ nat-s$_{k*}$ op$_{a1}$ par$_{a1}$ phos$_{a1}$ psor$_{a1}$ rat$_{a1}$ *Sars* *Sil*$_{a1}$ **Spig**$_{a1}$ stann$_{a1}$ staph$_{k*}$ sul-ac$_{h2*}$ tarax$_{k*}$ thuj$_{k*}$ verat$_{k*}$ verb$_{k*}$ zinc$_{k*}$
    - **outward**: mag-c$_{h2}$ spong
    - **pressing** pain: dig$_{h2}$
  - **stooping** agg.: kali-n ↓ stann ↓
    - **stitching** pain: kali-n$_{k*}$
    - **tearing** pain: stann$_{h2}$
  - **tearing** pain: *Agn* arg-n arum-t aur bov camph *Carb-an* caust coloc euph grat guaj$_{h2}$ kali-i lachn *Lyc* lyss *Mag-m* mang *Meny* *Merc* mez nat-s nuph ol-an *Puls* seneg *Stann* staph til zinc
    - **intermittent**: stann$_{h2}$
    - **stitch**-like: meny$_{h1}$
  - **touch**:
    - **amel.**: chin ↓
      - **stitching** pain: chin$_{h1}$
  - **walking**:
    - **air**; in open | **after**:
      - **agg.**: calc ↓
        - **boring** pain: calc
      - **agg.**: spong ↓
        - **boring** pain: spong$_{h1}$
  - **extending** to:
    - **Back**: spong ↓
      - **pressing** pain: spong

- **Sides – extending** to: ...
  - : **Brain**, into: sul-ac ↓
    - . **stitching** pain: sul-ac
  - : **Cheek**: guaj ↓ lachn ↓
    - . **tearing** pain: guaj h2 lachn
  - : **Eye**, into: psor ↓
    - . **stitching** pain: psor
  - : **Eyebrow**: *Lyc* ↓
    - . **tearing** pain: *Lyc*
  - : **Face**: cycl ↓
    - . **stitching** pain: cycl
  - : **Jaw**: all-c ↓
    - . **stitching** pain: all-c
  - : **Nape**: arg-n ↓
    - . **boring** pain: arg-n k*
  - : **Nose**; root of: *Lyc* ↓
    - . **tearing** pain: *Lyc*
  - : **Teeth**: all-c ↓
    - . **stitching** pain: all-c
  - : **Temples**: kalm ↓ mez ↓
    - . **tearing** pain: kalm mez
  - : **Vertex**: sep ↓
    - . **tearing** pain: sep h2
  - ⁝ **right**: *Alum* ↓ anac ↓ arg-n ↓ arn ↓ *Ars* ↓ asaf ↓ *Bell* ↓ berb ↓ bov ↓ bros-gau ↓ canth ↓ *Carb-an* ↓ *Caust* ↓ **Chel** ↓ *Chin* ↓ clem ↓ coc-c ↓ *Cocc* ↓ cocc-s ↓ coloc ↓ con ↓ crot-t ↓ cycl ↓ dros ↓ dulc ↓ euph ↓ euphr ↓ ferr-i ↓ grat ↓ guaj ↓ ham ↓ hell ↓ ign ↓ iod ↓ jac-c ↓ *Kali-c* ↓ kali-i ↓ kali-n ↓ kali-s ↓ *Lyc* ↓ mag-c ↓ *Meny* ↓ merc ↓ mez ↓ mosch ↓ nat-m ↓ nat-s ↓ *Nux-v* ↓ pall ↓ par ↓ *Phos* ↓ *Plat* ↓ *Puls* ↓ rat ↓ rhus-t ↓ ruta ↓ sabin ↓ sacch-a ↓ *Sars* ↓ sil ↓ **Spig** ↓ *Squil* ↓ *Stann* ↓ *Staph* ↓ sul-ac ↓ symph ↓ tax ↓ teucr ↓ thuj ↓ valer ↓ verb ↓ viol-t ↓ zinc ↓
    - : **then** left: colch ↓
      - . **pressing** pain: colch
    - : **blow**; pain as from a: sul-ac h2
    - : **boring** pain: arg-n a1 coloc *Puls* k* ruta h1
    - : **drawing** pain: ars h2
    - : **pressing** pain: anac k* arg-n arn *Ars* k* asaf k* *Bell* k* bros-gau mrc1 *Caust* **Chel** *Chin* clem a1 coc-c con a1 (non:crot-h hs1) crot-t a1 dulc fd4.de euph k* ferr-i k* grat a1 guaj hell k* ign iod h jac-c a1 *Kali-c* kali-n h2 kali-s fd4.de meny merc mez mosch nat-s k* *Nux-v* pall a1 par phos *Plat* rhus-t ruta sabin sacch-a fd2.de• *Sars* *Spig* stann *Staph* sul-ac h2* symph fd3.de• teucr thuj k* valer verb viol-t
    - : **stitching** pain: *Alum* anac a1 bell berb a1 bov a1 canth a1 *Cocc* cocc-s a1 cycl a1 dros a1 euphr a1 ham fd3.de• kali-i a1 kali-n a1 kali-s fd4.de *Lyc* mag-c nat-m a1 nux-v *Phos* rat a1 ruta h1 sil **Spig** a1 *Squil* a1 sul-ac h2 symph fd3.de• zinc a1 [tax jsj7]
    - : **tearing** pain: *Carb-an* kali-n h2 *Lyc* *Meny* nux-v puls *Stann* sul-ac h2 thuj h1 zinc
    - : **extending** to:
      - . **left**: aesc ↓
        - **stitching** pain: aesc
      - . **left** and back to right: cycl ↓
        - **drawing** pain: cycl h1
        - **pressing** pain: cycl h1
      - . **Occiput**: kali-n ↓
        - **pressing** pain: kali-n h2
        - **tearing** pain: kali-n h2
      - . **Temple**; left: cycl ↓
        - **pressing** pain: cycl h1
- **Spot**; in a: alum h2* mang ↓ ozone sde2•
  - ⁝ **burning**: mang h2
- **Spots**; in: **Nux-m** ↓ par ↓ psor ↓ *Zinc* ↓
  - ⁝ **pressing** pain: **Nux-m** psor *Zinc*
  - ⁝ **sore**: par
- **Third** eye: agath-a nl2•
- **Upper** part: senec ↓

- **Forehead – Upper** part: ...
  - ⁝ **cutting** pain: senec bg2
- **Frontal** headache (See forehead)
- **Hair** (See Hair - painful)
- **Margin** of hair: ozone ↓
  - • **pressing** pain | **band**; as from a: ozone sde2•
- **Meninges**: petr ↓
  - • **pulling**; like: petr bg2
- **Occiput**: abrom-a ks5 *Acon* k* acon-ac ↓ acon-l ↓ act-sp ↓ *Aesc* *Aeth* k* *Agar* k* agath-a nl2• agn ↓ ail k* alf bro1 all-c a1* *All-s* k* aloe alum k* alum-p k2 alum-sil k2 alumn k* *Am-c* am-caust ↓ am-m k* am-pic br1 *Ambr* k* aml-ns ↓ ammc amp rly4• *Anac* k* androc srj1• ang ↓ *Ant-c* ↓ ant-t apeir-s mlk9.de **Apis** k* apoc-a a1 aq-mar skp7• *Arg-met* *Arg-n* arge-pl rwt5• **Arn** *Ars* k* *Ars-i* ars-s-f ↓ arum-i ptk2 arum-t ↓ arund k* asaf k* asar k* aster a1 aur aur-ar ↓ aur-i ↓ aur-m ↓ aur-m-n aur-s k2 aven br1* bac tl1 bamb-a stb2.de• bapt k* bar-c k* bar-i k2 bar-m bar-ox-suc rly4• bar-s k2 bart ↓ **Bell** k* bell-p sp1 *Benz-ac* k* berb beryl tpw5* bism borx both-ax tsm2 bov k* *Brom* **Bry** k* *Bufo* ↓ cact k* calad *Calc* k* calc-i k2 *Calc-p* calc-s calc-sil k2 calen a1 calo a1 camph k* cann-i k* cann-s cann-xyz ↓ canth caps k* *Carb-ac* k* *Carb-an* k* **Carb-v** k* **Carbn-s** carc zzh card-b a1 card-m *Carl* ↓ cassia-s ccrh1• castm ↓ **Caust** cedr k* cench k2 cent a1 cere-b a1 cham *Chel* k* chen-a ↓ chen-v ↓ **Chin** k* *Chinin-ar* chinin-s chir-fl gya2 chlol a1 chlorpr pin1• choc srj3• chord-umb rly4• *Cic* **Cimic** k* cina ↓ *Cinnb* k* clem cob k* cob-n sp1 coc-c k* coca **Cocc** k* coff ↓ *Colch* k* coli rly4• coloc colocin a1 con k* conv *Cop* k* corn k* cortico tpw7* cortiso sp1 cot a1 crat br1 croc *Crot-c* *Crot-h* k* crot-t k* *Cupr* ↓ cupr-ar k* cur a1 cycl k* cystein-l rly4• daph k* dig k* digin a1 dios k* dirc ↓ dream-p ↓ dros ↓ *Dulc* k* *Echi* *Elaps* ephe-si ↓ equis-h ↓ eran br1 ery-a a1 euon bro1 *Eup-per* k* euph k* euphr ↓ fago a1 ferr k* ferr-ar ferr-i ferr-p k* ferul ↓ fic-m ↓ **Fl-ac** flor-p ↓ form franc br1 gal-ac br1 **Gels** k* gent-l ↓ ger-i rly4• gink-b sbd1• gins bro1 **Glon** k* gnaph k* gran ↓ *Graph* k* grat guaj guat sp1 ham k* *Hell* k* helo ↓ helo-s ↓ *Helon* k* hep hera a1 hip-ac sp1 hipp ↓ hir rsj4• hist sp1 hura hydr hydr-ac k* *Hydrog* srj2• hyos k* *Hyper* *Ign* k* ind k* indg *Iod* k* *Ip* k* irid-met ↓ *Iris* jab a1 jatr-c **Jug-c** k* jug-r mrr1 kali-ar *Kali-bi* k* *Kali-br* k* *Kali-c* k* *Kali-chl* k* kali-cy a1 *Kali-i* kali-m k2 *Kali-n* k* kali-p *Kali-s* kali-sil k2 kalm a1 ketogl-ac rly4• kiss a1 kola ↓ *Kreos* lac-ac k* **Lac-c** k* lac-cp sk4• lac-d k2 lac-del hm2• lac-h sk4• lac-leo hm2• *Lach* k* lachn k* lact k* lap-la sde8.de• lappa ↓ lat-m br1 laur k* *Lec* k* led lepi a1 *Lil-t* k* limen-b-c hm2* lith-c lob k* lob-c a1 loxo-recl knl4• luna kg1• *Lyc* k* *Lycps-v* lys ↓ lyss k* m-ambo b7.de m-arct ↓ m-aust b7.de mag-c *Mag-m* mag-p ↓ mag-s k* maland jl2 malar jl2 manc mand sp1 mang k* mang-p ↓ *Med* melal-alt ↓ meny ↓ meph merc k* *Merc-c* ↓ merc-i-f k* *Merc-i-r* merl ↓ *Mez* k* mill k* morg-p pte1*• *Morph* k* *Mosch* k* *Mur-ac* k* murx k* musca-d ↓ myos-a rly4• myric k* nabal a1 nad rly4• *Naja* *Nat-ar* *Nat-c* k* nat-m k* nat-ox rly4• *Nat-p* k* *Nat-s* k* nat-sil fd3.de• nicc k* nicc-s bro1 nicotam ↓ *Nit-ac* k* nit-s-d ↓ nux-m k* **Nux-v** k* oci-sa sk4• ol-an ↓ ol-j olib-sac wmh1 olnd ↓ **Onos** k* *Op* k* oreo c1* orot-ac rly4• osm k* ox-ac oxal-a rly4• oxeod ↓ ozone sde2• paeon k* pall par pert-vc vk9 peti ↓ **Petr** k* petr-ra ↓ **Ph-ac** k* phasco-ci rbp2 phel ↓ *Phos* k* phys k* *Phyt* k* **Pic-ac** k* pieri-b mlk9.de pimp a1 pin-con oss2• pip-m pitu-gl ↓ pitu-p sp1 plac-s rly4• plan k* plat plat-m a1* *Plb* k* plect ↓ podo k2 positr ↓ prun k* psil ↓ psor k* ptel k* *Puls* k* pycnop-sa ↓ pyrid ↓ *Pyrog* k* rad-br bro1* ran-b k* ran-s k* raph k* rat ↓ retin-ac mtf11 rhod rhus-g br1* *Rhus-r* *Rhus-t* k* rhus-v ↓ ribo rly4• rumx ruta fd4.de sabad *Sabin* k* sal-al ↓ samb ↓ sang k* sanic sapin ↓ sarr a1 *Sars* sec k* sel ↓ *Seneg* k* **Sep** k* **Sil** k* *Spig* k* spira a1 *Spong* k* squil stann k* *Staph* k* staphycoc ↓ stram k* streptoc ↓ stront-c *Stry* k* suis-hep rly4• sul-ac sul-i ↓ *Sulph* k* sumb a1 suprar rly4• symph fd3.de• syph k2* *Tab* k* tarax *Tarent* k* tax ↓ tell rsj10• tep a1 teucr *Thuj* k* thymol ↓ til k* tong ↓ *Trios* rsj11• tritic-vg fd5.de trom k* ulm-c jsj8• upa ↓ urt-u k* valer vanil fd5.de vario c2* ven-m ↓ verat k* *Verat-v* k* verb k* viol-t ↓ vip fkr4.de x-ray sp1 xan k* xanth *Zinc* k* zinc-m k* zinc-p k2 zing [*Buteo-j* sej6]
  - • **one** side: puls ↓
    - ⁝ **nail**; as from a: puls
  - • **right**: anac ↓ aur ↓ calc ↓ caust ↓ chel ↓ chin ↓ chord-umb rly4• cocc ↓ colch ↓ cortico tpw7 croc ↓ dros ↓ fic-m gya1 guaj ↓ ign ↓ kali-c ↓ laur ↓ loxo-recl knl4• lyc ↓ melal-alt gya4 nat-c ↓ nat-s ↓ ph-ac ↓ phos ↓ pyrid ↓ rhod ↓ rhus-t bg2 seneg ↓ sep ↓ spig ↓ stront-c ↓ sulph ↓ tax ↓ ven-m rsj12• verb ↓ zinc ↓
    - ⁝ **burning**: nat-c b4.de* sulph b4.de*
    - ⁝ **cutting** pain: cortico sp1
    - ⁝ **drawing** pain: caust b4.de* chin b7.de* cocc b7.de* dros b7.de* laur b7.de* nat-c b4.de* rhod b4.de* spig b7.de*
    - ⁝ **dull** pain: pyrid rly4• [tax jsj7]

- **right**: ...
  - **pressing** pain: anac b4.de* aur b4.de* colch b7.de* croc b7.de* ign b7.de* lyc b4.de* nat-c bg2 nat-s bg2 ph-ac b4.de* rhod b4.de* seneg b4.de* sep b4.de* spig b7.de* verb b7.de*
    - **asunder**: calc b4.de* zinc b4.de*
  - **stitching** pain: calc b4.de* chel b7.de* ign b7.de* laur b7.de* nat-c b4.de* phos b4.de* sulph b4.de*
  - **tearing** pain: aur b4.de* chel b7.de* colch b7.de* guaj b4.de* kali-c b4.de* stront-c b4.de*
  - **extending** to | **left**: dig mez staph [tax jsj7]
- **left**: acon-ac rly4• adam skp7• agar↓ alum↓ ambr↓ androc srj1• asar↓ bar-c↓ bell↓ bism↓ carb-v↓ chel↓ chin↓ chinin-ar↓ con↓ cycl↓ cystein-l rly4• euphr↓ galeoc-c-h gms1• ger-i rly4• lap-la rsp1 lyc↓ mag-c↓ mez↓ oxal-a rly4• petr↓ phos↓ phys bg2 puls↓ sabin↓ samb↓ sars↓ sel↓ sep↓ spong fd4.de stann↓ sul-ac↓ trios rsj11• tritic-vg fd5.de verb↓ viol-t↓ zinc↓
  - **morning** | **waking**; on: sal-al blc1•
  - **burning**: chinin-ar
  - **burrowing**: agar k*
  - **cutting** pain: bell bg2
  - **drawing** pain: carb-v b4.de* chin b7.de* cycl b7.de* zinc b4.de*
  - **lancinating**: androc srj1•
  - **pressing** pain: asar b7.de* lyc b4.de* puls b7.de* sabin b7.de* sel b7a.de sep b4.de* sul-ac b4.de*
    - **asunder**: zinc b4.de*
    - **outward**: mez b4.de* stann b4.de*
  - **stitching** pain: alum b4.de* bell b4.de* chel b7.de* euphr b7.de* petr b4.de* phos b4.de* samb b7.de* sars b4.de* sul-ac b4.de* verb b7.de* viol-t b7.de*
  - **suppurating**; as if: mag-c bg2
  - **tearing** pain: agar b4.de* ambr b7.de* bar-c b4.de* bism b7.de* carb-v b4.de* con b4.de* lyc b4.de* puls b7.de* samb b7.de* stann b4.de*
  - **ulcerative** pain: mag-c
- **daytime**: aster a1 carb-v ign mag-c petr ph-ac plan k* seneg k* stry k*
- **morning**: agar *All-s* k* arum-t bov k* brucel sa3• *Bry* caust↓ cedr chinin-s cob k* colch cop dios k* dulc fd4.de euph fago a1 gels ger-i rly4• *Graph*↓ *Helon* *Jug-c* k* junc-e kali-bi↓ kali-c↓ **Lac-c** lac-h sk4• *Lach* lob lyc mag-c mag-s k* mang↓ morph *Nat-m* nit-ac nux-m *Nux-v* k* olib-sac↓ op paeon↓ petr *Ph-ac* puls *Ran-b* raph k* rhod k* rhus-r rhus-t k* ruta fd4.de sabin sanic *Sep* *Sil* spig spong fd4.de sulph k* symph fd3.de• tritic-vg fd5.de vanil fd5.de verat↓
  - **14** h; until: clem
  - **15** h; until: cob
  - **17** h; until: rhus-t
  - **bed** agg.; in: agar eupi *Jug-c* k* *Nux-v* *Ph-ac* sep
    - **lying** on back agg.: *All-s* k* *Bry* sep
  - **drawing** pain: dulc fd4.de kali-bi k* tritic-vg fd5.de
  - **pressing** pain: caust k* cedr k* dulc fd4.de *Graph* kali-bi mag-s nux-m *Nux-v* olib-sac wmh1 paeon k* *Petr* k* sil k* *Sulph* tritic-vg fd5.de
  - **rising**:
    - **agg.**: cimic cinnb dirc c1 gels kali-bi *Lyss*↓ mag-m merc-i-f *Nux-v*
      - **tearing** pain: *Lyss*
    - **amel.**: jug-c kali-p ruta fd4.de spig
  - **room** | **amel.**: bov
  - **stitching** pain: agar h2 cop a1 kali-c mang petr h2 verat k*
  - **tearing** pain: agar verat
  - **waking**; on: arg-met arn *Bry* coc-c↓ con ephe-si hsj1• fl-ac ger-i rly4• grat k* hell kali-bi k* **Lac-c** *Lach* lap-la↓ mang↓ mill *Morph* *Nat-m* op ox-ac oxal-a rly4• ozone↓ *Petr* *Ph-ac* pyrog k2 rhus-t k* sanic *Sulph* k* symph fd3.de• (non:uran-met k) uran-n verat↓
    - **amel.** at noon: *Bry*
    - **pressing** pain: coc-c hell h1 kali-bi *Sulph*
    - **stitching** pain: arn lap-la sde8.de• mang ozone sde2•
    - **tearing** pain: verat
- **forenoon**: agar k* all-c alum bov↓ *Bry* caust↓ chel k* *Chin* *Cob* cop dios k* dulc fd4.de gels indg iod↓ kali-bi↓ kali-n lact lyc nat-c op phys k* phyt k* psor rhus-t sacch-a↓ *Sep* spong sulph k* trios rsj11• tritic-vg fd5.de vanil fd5.de
- **forenoon**: ...
  - **9** h:
    - **18** h; until: pitu-gl↓
      - **dull** pain: pitu-gl skp7•
  - **11** h: bamb-a stb2.de• gels
  - **drawing** pain: sulph k*
  - **mental** exertion; after: rhus-t
  - **pressing** pain: bov caust k* dulc fd4.de iod kali-bi k* nat-c h2 sacch-a fd2.de• vanil fd5.de
  - **shaking** the head agg.; on: cann-i
  - **sitting** agg.: rhod
  - **stitching** pain: agar a1 lyc k* vanil fd5.de
- **noon**: cob k* murx k* nat-c sulph k*
  - **amel.**: **Bry**↓
    - **drawing** pain: **Bry**
- **afternoon**: aeth agar ang bov canth castm chel k* chinin-s cimic k* clem coca dios k* dirc dream-p sdj1• dulc fd4.de fago k* gent-l a1 hip-ac sp1 hydr ind iod iris kali-n mang nat-sil fd3.de• nicc↓ ol-an osm k* ph-ac phos rhus-r rhus-t rumx ruta fd4.de sacch-a↓ sapin a1 sars sep spong a1 sul-i k2 sulph tritic-vg fd5.de trom a1 vanil fd5.de
  - **13** h: mang↓ ptel
    - **pressing** pain: mang h2
  - **14** h: grat↓
    - **tearing** pain: grat
  - **15** h: suprar rly4•
  - **15**-18 h: phos
  - **16** h: cortico tpw7 gels
  - **16**.30 h: aq-mar skp7• ven-m rsj12•
    - **until** 23 h: ven-m rsj12•
  - **boring** pain: nicc k*
  - **drawing** pain: agar k* tritic-vg fd5.de
  - **pressing** pain: ang k* gent-l iod h sacch-a fd2.de• spong fd4.de tritic-vg fd5.de vanil fd5.de
  - **tearing** pain: mang h2
- **evening**: abrom-a ks5 all-c alum ambr anac↓ bar-c bell bov brom cadm-met tpw6 canth carb-an carb-v↓ carbn-s chinin-s cimic k* coc-c↓ colch dios k* dulc fd4.de form gels k* graph ham fd3.de• hyper indg jab kali-br kali-chl kali-n lac-leo hrn2• lob lyc mag-c mez mur-ac nit-ac ol-an olib-sac↓ op k* orot-ac rly4• ptel k* ran-b ran-s raph a1 rhod↓ rhus-r seneg sep sil↓ spong fd4.de stann staph stront-c sulph k* thuj k* trios rsj11• tritic-vg fd5.de (non:uran-met k) uran-n vanil↓ zinc
  - **18** h: aq-mar skp7•
  - **midnight**; until: sep↓
    - **pressing** pain: sep h2
  - **amel.**: coca sep
  - **bed** agg.; in: dulc k* graph↓ kali-n sarr k*
    - **burning**: kali-n h2
    - **drawing** pain: graph k*
  - **boring** pain: zinc k*
  - **gas** was lighted; when: zinc k*
  - **pressing** pain: anac coc-c k* dulc fd4.de olib-sac wmh1 rhod k* sep h2 spong fd4.de stann h2 staph h1 thuj k* trios rsj11• tritic-vg fd5.de vanil fd5.de
  - **shooting** pain: mag-c mur-ac h2
  - **stitching** pain: alum k* ambr k* carb-v hyper lyc mag-c h2* mur-ac k* sep k* thuj k* tritic-vg fd5.de vanil fd5.de
  - **tearing** pain: ambr carb-an hyper ran-b sil
  - **walking** in open air agg.: thuj↓
    - **pressing** pain: thuj
  - **warm** room agg.: coc-c↓
    - **pressing** pain: coc-c k*
- **night**: alum-p↓ androc srj1• benz-ac k2 borx carb-v k* carbn-s cedr k* *Chel* k* clem coli rly4• ham↓ hipp kali-n *Kali-p* lyc malar jl2 *Mez* osm ruta fd4.de sep spong fd4.de stront-c *Sulph* k* **Syph**↓ *Thuj* tritic-vg fd5.de vanil fd5.de
  - **midnight**: sep k* staphycoc rly4•
    - **before**:
      - **23** h | **amel.**: ven-m rsj12•

- **night – midnight**: ...
  - **after**: ars k2
    - **1 h**: bry rhus-t
    - **2 h**: sulph
    - **3 h**: chinin-s
    - **3-4 h**: bamb-a stb2.de• spig
  - **cutting** pain: **Syph** k*
  - **lancinating**: syph
  - **pressing** pain: alum-p k2 *Sulph*
  - **sore**: sep h2
  - **stitching** pain: ham fd3.de• lyc k*
  - **tearing** pain: lyc thuj
- **accompanied** by:
  - **hunger**: psor jl2
  - **sleeplessness**: syph jl2
  - **vertigo**: guat sp1 rad-br c11
  - **Ear**; complaints of: mur-ac bg2 onos bg2
  - **Eye**; pain in: (↗*accompanied - eye; accompanied - eye - pain)* **Nux-v**
  - **Liver**; complaints of the: *Jug-c* br1
  - **Lumbago**: rad-br c11
  - **Neck**; stiffness in: bit-ar wht1•
  - **Tibia**; pain in: carb-v
- **aching**: fic-m gya1 thymol sp1
- **air**; in open:
  - **agg.**: bov k* cob k* hydr-ac k* iod lob nux-m plect ↓
    - **pressing** pain: iod h nux-m plect
  - **amel.**: abrom-a ks5 all-c alum *Apis* carb-an *Carb-v* ↓ chlol a1 *Cimic* k* glon hydr *Kali-c* mag-m mag-s k* mez ↓ mosch pic-ac puls ↓ sep trios rsj11•
    - **opening** and shutting; as if: sep
    - **pressing** pain: *All-c* carb-an h2 *Carb-v* kali-c mag-m k* mag-s mez puls trios rsj11•
- **alternating** with:
  - **Forehead**; pain in: mosch ptel bg1
  - **Joints**; pain in: sulph
  - **Sacrum**; pain in: alum carb-v *Nit-ac*
  - **Temples**; pain in: fic-m gya1 zinc
- **anger**; after: cann-s hr1 ip petr ran-b hr1 *Staph*
  - **pressing** pain: *Petr Staph*
- **ascending** stairs agg.: *Bell Carb-v* carl ip mosch nat-s ↓ pic-ac sep k2
  - **sore**: nat-s bg1
- **bandaging** the head: calc k* gels
  - **amel.**: plb
- **bed** agg.; in: agar ↓ graph ↓
  - **drawing** pain: agar k* graph
- **bending**:
  - **head**:
    - **amel.**: bar-c ↓
      - **tearing** pain: bar-c
    - **backward**:
      - **agg.**: *Anac* bapt bg1 *Carb-v* colch ip osm k* staph tarent k*
        - **tearing** pain: anac
      - **amel.**: aeth bar-c cact chin fago k* murx ph-ac ↓ raph k* *Rhus-t* k* spig k*
        - **drawing** pain: cact k*
        - **pressing** pain: ph-ac k*
      - **must** bend head backward: chin ↓ kali-n ↓
        - **drawing** pain: chin h1 kali-n c1
    - **forward**:
      - **agg.**: staph ↓
        - **drawing** pain: staph h1
        - **pressing** pain: staph h1
- **between** vertex and occiput: ox-ac ↓
  - **pressing** pain | **inward**: ox-ac
- **binding** up hair: alum bell *Carb-v Kali-n* kali-p k2 *Nit-ac*
- **binding** up hair: ...
  - **amel.**: kali-n h2*
- **biting** pain: iod h
- **blindness**, with: *Petr*
- **blow**; pain as from a: apis bg2 bell bg1 chord-umb rly4• cimic bg1 dig h2* hell irid-met srj5• lach bg1 lappa bg1 lys bg2 *Lyss* **Naja** k* plat bg1 ran-b bg1 sabad bg1 tab bg2* tarent bg1
- **boring** pain: agar k* aml-ns bg2 *Arg-n* dig bg2 equis-h bg2 gels k* hell k* lycps-v bg2 merc k* *Mez* mosch k* nat-m k* *Nat-s* k* nicc k* nux-v bg2 ol-an k* ph-ac k* phel bg2 plan k* ran-s k* *Rhus-t* sabin k* spig k* stann k* stront-c k* stry a1 vanil fd5.de zinc k*
  - **bolt** had been driven from neck to vertex; as if a: cimic tl1
    - **pulsating**, agg. at every heartbeat: cimic
  - **sharp**: con bg2
- **breakfast** agg.; after: aster k* gels k*
- **burning**: aesc agar k* ant-c b7a.de *Apis* k* arn bg2 aur k* aur-m k* chinin-ar cupr k* dulc fd4.de *Gels* hist sp1* indg kali-c k* kali-n lyc k* mag-m k* med k* nat-c k* **Phos** k* pic-ac k* rhus-t k* sep k* *Spong* staph k* sulph k* zinc ptk1
- **burrowing**: agar k* ph-ac b4.de* phel a1 *Spig* k* til a1 zinc b4.de*
- **bursting** pain: aloe *Calc* k* *Carb-v* cassia-s ccrh1• cimic bg2* ferr flor-p rsj3• *Gels* k* *Ip* k* *Lach* k* nux-m *Nux-v Op* petr-ra shn4• podo bg2* sil bg2 spig k* spong k* staph syph xxb thuj b4a.de* zinc
  - **axe**; as if beaten with an: nux-v cp
- **chagrin** (See mortification)
- **chewing** agg.: sulph ↓
  - **drawing** pain: sulph k*
- **chill**; during: acon b7a.de eup-per k2 hell ↓ petr
  - **sore**: hell h1
- **chronic**: aloe ↓ alum ↓ arg-n ↓ ars ↓ asaf ↓ aur ↓ calc ↓ calc-p ↓ cycl ↓ kali-c ↓ kalm ↓ lach ↓ lyc ↓ nat-m ↓ phos ↓ psor ↓ sars ↓ sep ↓ sil ↓ sulph ↓ thuj ↓ zinc ↓
  - **aching**: aloe bg2 alum bg2 arg-n bg2 ars bg2 asaf bg2 aur bg2 calc bg2 calc-p bg2 cycl bg2 kali-c bg2 kalm bg2 lach bg2 lyc bg2 nat-m bg2 phos bg2 psor bg2 sars bg2 sep bg2 sil bg2 sulph bg2 thuj bg2 zinc bg2
- **closing** the eyes:
  - **agg.**: *Calc* ip *Lach* op *Stram*
    - **pressing** pain: ip
  - **amel.**: *Calc* kr cassia-s ↓ *Hell* k* *Sep*
    - **drawing** pain: cassia-s ccrh1•
- **clucking**: spig h1
- **coffee**: rhus-g tmo3•
- **coition**; after: agar bov calad calc chin graph kali-c nat-m petr sep sil staph
- **cold**:
  - **agg.**: sil tl1
  - **air**:
    - **agg.**: dulc fd4.de *Ign*
    - **amel.**: *Carb-v* euph *Lac-c*
  - **applications**:
    - **amel.**: *Acon* aloe alumn ant-t *Ars* asar *Bell* bism *Bry Calc Calc-p Caust* cham chinin-s cinnb euph ferr *Glon* ind iod *Lac-c Lach* mag-s *Mosch* myric *Nat-m Phos* psor *Puls Seneg* sep ↓ *Spig Stram Sulph* zinc
      - **opening** and shutting; as if: sep
      - **sore**: euph hr1
  - **washing** the head:
    - **amel.**: cassia-s ↓
      - **drawing** pain: cassia-s ccrh1•
- **compressed**; as if: *Acon* b7a.de am-m b7.de* cimic bg2 kali-n b4.de* mag-c b4.de* *Rhus-t* bg2 stann b4.de staph b7.de* stront-c b4.de* sul-ac b4.de* tab bg2 thuj b4.de*
- **coryza**; during: all-c tl1 sep h2
- **cough** agg.; during: alum aml-ns bg1 anac k* carb-an carb-v *Coca* coloc cortico tpw7 cupr ↓ *Ferr* k* *Ferr-m* k* *Ferr-p Glon* ign bg1 *Lach* mag-c merc k* mosch nat-m nit-ac puls bg1 pycnop-sa mrz1 pyrog k* sang sep sil *Sulph* k* tarent k* tub gk

Head

- **cough** agg.; during: ...
  - **pressing** pain: alum h2
  - **sore**: tarent
  - **stitching** pain: coloc sulph k*
  - **tearing** pain: cupr
  - **ulcerative** pain: sulph h2
- **covering** head agg.: gels ↓
  - **burning**: gels
- **cramping**: am-m *Camph* dios dulc fd4.de fl-ac a1 gels hr1 *Mosch* b7a.de nat-c b4a.de
- **cutting** pain: aesc ail k* all-c bg2 *Arg-n* k* aster *Aur-s* *Bell* k* *Bufo* *Calc* k* camph bg2 canth *Caps* k* carb-an chin k* *Con* k* *Cupr* dig dulc fd4.de gels bg2 glon med mur-ac nat-m k* sang sars stann a1 stry a1 suis-hep rly4• **Sulph** k* syph tong a1
  - **knife**; as with a: *Con* nat-m ozone sde2•
- **darkness**:
  - **agg.**: carb-an *Carb-v* lac-c onos
  - **amel.**: mag-p *Sep* *Stram*
- **deep**-seated: canth ↓ cop ↓
  - **stitching** pain: canth k* cop k*
- **dinner**; after: agar ↓ ant-t ↓ con ↓ ol-an ↓ vichy-g ↓
  - **pressing** pain: agar h2 con h2 ol-an a1 vichy-g a1
  - **stitching** pain: ant-t k*
- **drawing** pain: *Agar* k* ambr k* anac k* ang bg2* ant-t k* *Arg-met* k* arg-n k* **Arn** k* asaf k* aur-m-n k* bell k* **Bry** k* cact k* calad k* calc k* *Calc-p* k* calc-sil k2 camph cann-s k* *Carb-v* k* carbn-s *Carl* a1 cassia-s ccrh1• caust k* cere-b a1 *Chel* k* chin k* coc-c k* cocc coff b7a.de coloc k* corn k* cycl digin a1 dros *Dulc* *Ferr* k* *Gels* gins k* glon k* graph k* guaj k* hyper ip kali-bi k* kali-c *Kali-n* k* kali-p fd1.de• kali-s fd4.de laur mag-c k* mang k* meny k* merc k* mez bg2 mill k* mosch k* *Mur-ac* k* nat-c k* nat-p nat-s k* nat-sil fd3.de• nit-s-d a1 *Nux-v* k* ph-ac k* phos plat k* plect k* puls k* ran-b k* raph k* rhod rhus-t k* rhus-v a1 sabin k* sel k* *Sep* k* spig k* squil k* staph k* sulph k* *Tarax* b7a.de thuj bg2* tritic-vg fd5.de valer k* vanil fd5.de *Zinc* k* zinc-p k2
  - **alternating** with:
    - **Chest**; constriction of (See CHEST - Constriction - alternating - drawing)
    - **Temples**; pressing pain in (See temples - pressing - alternating - occiput)
    - **Thumb**; drawing pain in: arg-met
  - **wandering** pain: mez k*
- **dull** pain: *Aesc* k* alum k* alum-sil k2 ambr amp rly4• androc srj1• apis b7a.de asar bamb-a stb2.de• bry k* calc k* *Carb-v* k* cench k2 chin k* chord-umb rly4• cic k* cimic k* *Crot-h* cycl k* cystein-l rly4• dulc fd4.de *Echi* ephe-si hsj1• fl-ac k* **Gels** k* glon bg2* ham fd3.de• indg *Ip* lac-del hrn2• *Lach* mang bg2* mang-p rly4• med melal-alt gya4 meny bg2* mez bg2* musca-d szs1 nat-c k* *Nat-s* oxal-a rly4• oxeod a1 petr-ra shn4• pitu-gl skp7• pycnop-sa mrz1 ran-s k* *Rhod* k* ribo rly4• rumx ruta fd4.de sal-al blc1• samb k* *Sec* k* sep b4a.de sil b4a.de spig bg2* spong fd4.de squil bg2* staphycoc rly4• stram stront-c k* symph fd3.de• thuj k* tritic-vg fd5.de urt-u vanil fd5.de zinc bg2*
- **eating**:
  - **after**:
    - **agg.**: agar k* alum ant-t ↓ canth carb-v dios k* gels *Kali-bi* kali-p c1 kali-s ↓ mill nat-m ol-an pip-m
      - **drawing** pain: agar ant-t k* mill a1
      - **pressing** pain: carb-v k* kali-s fd4.de pip-m a1
      - **stitching** pain: alum k*
    - **amel.**: colch rsj2• psor jl2
  - **amel.**: kali-p ↓
    - **pressing** pain: kali-p
- **emotions** agg.: ars k2 benz-ac petr
- **excitement**: *Ferr* ↓
  - **bursting** pain: *Ferr*
- **exertion**:
  - **after** | **agg.**: ars k2 dulc fd4.de *Gels* limen-b-c hrn2* nit-ac k* *Ox-ac*
  - **agg.**: gels ↓
- **exertion** – **agg.**: ...
    - **drawing** pain: gels hr1
  - **amel.**: cact
    - **pressing** pain: cact
- **eyes** together; drawing the: nat-m
- **fanning** | **amel.**: *Carb-v*
- **fever**; during: *Acon* b7a.de graph h2 lyc h2 **Nux-v** rhus-t ↓ trom a1 *Verat-v*
  - **pressing** pain: rhus-t
- **foreign** body; as from a: arg-met
- **gnawing** pain: calc k* cycl h1 dros glon k* kali-m k2 led *Nat-s* nicc k* ol-an k* raph k* zinc h2*
  - **corrosive**: thuj h1
- **grasping** pain: carb-v k2 pieri-b mlk9.de
- **grief**; from: **Ph-ac**
- **hair**; unbinding (See unbinding)
- **hammering** pain: act-sp camph ferr-p gels k2 nat-m psor stram bg2
- **heart**, at every throb of: macro c1
- **heat**:
  - **during**: graph h2 lyc h2 puls ↓
    - **tearing** pain: puls
  - **stove**; of | **agg.**: *Carb-v* puls
  - **sun**; of the | **agg.**: **Acon** **Bell** brom **Bry** camph carb-v dulc fd4.de *Gels* **Glon** *Nat-c* *Ther*
- **holding** head erect amel.: spong ↓
  - **pressing** pain: spong
- **hot** applications amel.: *Gels* *Ign*
- **house**, on entering: mag-m ↓
  - **tearing** pain: mag-m
- **indigestion**, after: cann-s *Ip* petr ran-b *Staph*
- **influenza**; during: gels tl1 rad-br mrr1
- **intolerable**: vario jl2
- **irritability**; with (See MIND - Irritability - pain - occiput)
- **jar** agg.: anac **Bell** beryl tpw5 *Bry* *Calc* *Carb-v* ferr-p *Gels* **Glon** *Ip* kali-n **Led** *Mag-m* mag-s **Nit-ac** podo fd3.de• staph *Stram* ther
- **jerking** pain: acon k* *Bell* k* calc b4.de* cedr fl-ac glon kali-c mang b4.de* prun rhod b4.de* rhus-t k* *Spig* k* stann sulph thuj
  - **forward**: arg-n
  - **intermitting**: canth
- **lancinating**: aesc androc srj1• aster k* aur-s *Bufo* canth *Con* *Cupr* oxal-a rly4• plac-s rly4• *Sang* sec syph
- **laughing** agg.: zinc
  - **tearing** pain: zinc
- **laying** hand on part amel.: mang ↓
  - **pressing** pain: mang h2
- **leaning**:
  - **head**:
    - **backward**:
      - **agg.**: tarent k*
      - **amel.**: spig k*
- **light** amel.: lac-c
- **lightning**-like: bell bg2
- **liver** complaints; associated with (See accompanied - liver)
- **looking**:
  - **bright** objects; at: plb *Stram*
  - **upward** agg.: *Graph* ↓
    - **pressing** pain: *Graph*
    - **sore**: graph h2
- **lying**:
  - **abdomen**; on | **amel.**: grat
  - **agg.**: agar ambr ↓ camph canth chel **Chin** *Eup-per* euph *Gels* guat sp1* ip lachn lyss mag-s malar jl2 *Mur-ac* ↓ nux-v *Onos* *Op* pegan-ha tpi1• pip-m puls sep spig spong staph vanil fd5.de verat-v a1
    - **sore**: *Mur-ac* hr1

- **lying – agg.**: ...
  - **tearing** pain: ambr
  - **amel.**: abrom-a ks5 aeth br1 alum cassia-s ↓ *Graph Hell* hip-ac sp1 iod *Kali-s* nit-ac ph-ac spig spong fd4.de tab tritic-vg fd5.de
    - **burrowing**: *Spig* k*
    - **bursting** pain: cassia-s ccrh1•
    - **sore**: alum hell
    - **tearing** pain: spig k2
  - **back**; on:
    - **agg.**: malar jl2 plect ↓ vanil ↓
      - **pressing** pain: plect vanil fd5.de
  - **head** high; with the | **amel.**: *Gels Spig*
  - **head** low; with the | **amel.**: *Mosch*
  - **occiput**; on:
    - **agg.**: agar bufo bg1 cact carb-v bg1 cimic gk cocc br1 dulc a1 *Petr Sep* sulph h2
      - **burning**: sulph h2
      - **sore**: cimic gk sep h2
    - **amel.**: *Kali-p* ph-ac spong fd4.de
  - **side** of head; on | **amel.**: cact *Sep*
  - **side**; on:
    - **agg.**: *Carb-v*
    - **left**:
      - **agg.**: malar jl2
      - **amel.**: ars
    - **painful** side:
      - **amel.**: *Bry* ↓ plan ↓
        - **sore**: *Bry* plan
    - **right** | **agg.**: *Carb-v* petr staph
- **lying** down:
  - **after**:
    - **agg.**: **Tarax** ↓
      - **pressing** pain: **Tarax**
  - **agg.**: puls ↓
    - **stitching** pain: puls k*
  - **amel.**: cassia-s ↓
    - **drawing** pain: cassia-s ccrh1•
    - **smarting**: cassia-s ccrh1•
- **menses**:
  - **after** | **agg.**: *Carb-v*
  - **before** | **agg.**: calc calc-i k2 nat-c nit-ac
  - **during**:
    - **agg.**: bamb-a stb2.de• *Bell Bry Calc Carb-an Carb-v* ferr-p k2 *Kali-n Lac-c* mag-c mag-m k* nit-ac nux-v *Phos*
      - **contracting** the eyes: *Carb-v* k*
      - **pressing** pain: *Nux-v*
      - **scanty** flow, with: alum *Carb-v*
      - **stitching** pain: kali-n
- **mental** exertion:
  - **agg.**: abrom-a ks5 anac androc ↓ aster calc *Carb-ac* k* carb-an *Carb-v* cassia-s ↓ chin ↓ *Cimic Coc-c Colch Elaps Gels* gins ↓ ign kali-n lob *Nat-c* nat-s nat-sil fd3.de• nit-ac *Par Pic-ac* psor rhus-r rhus-t
    - **drawing** pain: *Calc* cassia-s ccrh1• chin gels hr1 gins a1
    - **pressing** pain: androc srj1• *Carb-ac Colch* nat-c rhus-r a1
  - **amel.**: cact calc calc-ar ↓
    - **pressing** pain: cact
    - **tearing** pain: calc-ar
- **mortification** | **after**: petr ran-b
- **motion**:
  - **agg.**: am-c aur *Bell* beryl tpw5 bism *Bry* k* calc *Carb-v* cassia-s ↓ chin chinin-ar chlol a1 **Cimic** ↓ coc-c colch ↓ cop ↓ *Crot-h* ↓ cupr elaps eup-per *Ferr* fl-ac k2 *Gels* k* glon *Hell Hyper* k* iod k* *Ip* k* kali-c kali-n lac-ac lac-c *Lach* lyc mag-p manc mang med k2 *Mez* k* mosch nat-s ↓ nit-ac *Nux-v Ox-ac* petr ph-ac *Sel Sep Sil* ↓ spig k* spong staph *Stram* thuj tritic-vg fd5.de
    - **cutting** pain: chin k*
    - **drawing** pain: cassia-s ccrh1• ph-ac h2*
- **motion – agg.**: ...
    - **pressing** pain: *Bism* **Bry** colch cop a1 cupr *Hyper* iod ip nat-s k* ph-ac k* spong h1
    - **smarting**: cassia-s ccrh1•
    - **sore**: **Cimic** *Crot-h Nux-v*
    - **stitching** pain: *Kali-c* kali-n k* spong tritic-vg fd5.de
    - **tearing** pain: *Aur Carb-v* ph-ac *Sil Spig*
  - **amel.**: *Agar* aq-mar skp7• arg-met ↓ carl euph pip-m *Rhus-t* stann
    - **drawing** pain: arg-met
    - **sore**: euph *Rhus-t*
  - **eyelids**; of | **agg.**: bry *Carb-v*
  - **eyes**; of | **agg.**: lac-c k2
  - **head**; of:
    - **agg.**: cact *Carb-v* colch a1 dirc c1 *Gels* glon a1 ip h1 mez ↓ nabal a1 pegan-ha tpi1• petr staph *Stram* thuj a1 tritic-vg fd5.de
      - **drawing** pain: *Cact* staph
      - **pressing** pain: mez h2 tritic-vg fd5.de
    - **forward**:
      - **agg.**: cupr ↓
        - **tearing** pain: cupr
- **nail**; as from a: *Cimic* k* con bg2 *Hep Mosch* puls tarent
- **nervousness**; with (See MIND - Excitement - nervous - pain - occiput)
- **neuralgic**: acon bg2 aesc k1 bell bg2* bry bg2* caust tl1 chel tl1 chin bg2* chinin-s bg2* mag-p bg2 nux-v bg2* puls bg2* zinc bg2 zinc-p bro1
- **noise** agg.: anac h2 *Bry* calc *Carb-v* cimic *Gels* ign ip *Nit-ac Ph-ac* plb spig k* *Stram*
  - **pressing** pain: *Carb-v Nit-ac* ph-ac k* *Spig*
  - **tearing** pain: ph-ac *Spig*
- **Occipital** protuberance: carc ↓ nit-ac ↓
  - **stitching** pain: carc fd2.de• nit-ac h2
- **opening** and shutting; as if: bell rb2 cann-i rb2 cimic rb2 *Cocc* k* sep
- **pain** in right eye; with: med c1
- **paroxysmal**: *Aesc Bell* chen-v cimic k* *Gels* **Lach** *Stram* [tax jsj7]
- **periodical**:
  - **week**; once a:
    - **spreading** over head: arg-n ↓
      - **binding** head tightly amel., followed by blindness and sore eyeballs | **dull** pain: arg-n k1
- **perspiration** | **amel.**: clem k* sep k2
- **pinching** pain: am-m k* carb-v k* chel k* hipp k* mag-m h2 meny h1 *Petr* k* ph-ac h2
- **plug**; as from a: anac bg2 *Arg-met* k* bov k* cann-xyz bg2 canth con k* hep k* mosch bg2 ph-ac bg2 puls rhod k* tarent k*
- **pregnancy** agg.; during: gels psa
- **pressing** pain: acon k* acon-l a1 aeth a1 *Agar* k* agath-a nl2• all-c *Aloe* k* *Alum* k* alum-p k2 alum-sil k2 am-caust a1 am-m k* *Ambr* k* ammc k* anac k* ang b7.de* ant-t k* apis k* *Arg-met* k* arn k* *Ars* k* *Ars-i* ars-s-f k2 asaf k* asar aur aur-ar k2 aur-i k2 aur-s k2 *Bamb-a* stb2.de• bapt k* bar-c bar-i k2 bar-s k2 *Bell* k* berb *Bism* k* borx *Bov* k* *Bry* k* cact k* *Calc* k* calc-i k2 calc-p calc-sil k2 camph k* cann-i k* cann-s k* canth k* carb-ac k* carb-an b4.de* **Carb-v** k* **Carbn-s** carc fd2.de• card-m carl a1 caust k* cedr k* cham k* *Chel* k* chen-a vml3• *Chin* k* chinin-ar cic k* cinnb k* coc-c k* cocc *Colch* k* coli rly4• coloc k* con k* cop k* croc *Crot-c* cupr k* dig k* digin a1 *Dulc* k* *Euph* k* fl-ac k* *Gels* gent-l ger-i rly4• gins k* glon k* gran k2 **Graph** k* grat guaj k* *Hell* k* *Hep* k* hydr-ac k* *Hyper Ign* k* *Iod* k* *Ip* k* jatr-c kali-bi k* *Kali-c* k* kali-m k2 kali-n k* kali-p k* kali-s fd4.de kali-sil k2 ketogl-ac rly4• kola stb3• lac-h htj1• lach lact a1 laur k* lec lil-t k2 lob k* *Lyc* k* m-aust b7.de mag-c *Mag-m* k* mag-s manc mang k* meny k* meph k* *Merc* k* merc-c b4a.de *Mez* k* mosch k* mur-ac a1 nat-ar *Nat-c* b4.de* *Nat-m* k* *Nat-p Nat-s* k* nat-sil fd3.de• nicotam rly4• *Nit-ac* k* nit-s-d a1 nux-m k* **Nux-v** k* ol-an olib-sac wmh1 *Onos Op* ox-ac paeon k* par k* **Petr** k* ph-ac k* phel *Phos* k* pip-m k* plb k* positr nl2• psil ft1 puls k* ran-b k* ran-s rhod k* *Rhus-t* ruta k* sabad k* sabin k* sars k* **Sec** sel k* seneg k* *Sep* k* **Sil** k* *Spig Spong* k* squil k* *Stann* k* *Staph* k* stram streptoc rly4• stront-c k* sul-ac sul-i k2 *Sulph* k* symph fd3.de• tab k* *Tarax* k* *Tarent* teucr k* *Thuj* k* til k* tritic-vg fd5.de valer k* vanil fd5.de verb k* zinc k* zinc-p k2 zing

- **pressing** pain: ...
  - **asunder**: aloe *Bell*$_{b4.de}$* *Bry*$_{b7.de}$* *Calc* nux-v$_{k}$* spong$_{b7.de}$* staph$_{k}$* stront-c$_{b4.de}$*
  - **band**; as from a: anac psor sulph
  - **burning**: mang$_{h2}$
  - **coryza**; as from: cic$_{c1}$
  - **downward**: hep hydr-ac laur merl$_{k}$* nat-c
  - **forward**: ant-t bov *Chel* hydr-ac mang nat-c nux-v ol-an ph-ac$_{k}$* plb sabad
  - **hard**; as from lying on something: ph-ac$_{h2}$
  - **hat**; as from a tight: *Alum*$_{k}$*
  - **intermittent**: agath-a$_{nl2}$• carb-an phel$_{k}$*
  - **inward**: bar-c$_{k}$* calc$_{k}$* ign$_{k}$* kola$_{stb3}$• mag-c meph ol-an$_{bg2}$ olnd$_{k}$* ox-ac ph-ac$_{k}$* sep$_{k}$* spig$_{k}$* stann *Staph* stront-c thuj upa$_{a1}$
  - **lying** on something hard; as from (See hard)
  - **outward**: aesc$_{bg2}$* bell berb bry$_{k}$* *Calc*$_{k}$* carb-v$_{k}$* chin$_{k}$* fago$_{a1}$ *Gels*$_{k}$* helon$_{a1}$ kola$_{stb3}$• lach$_{bg2}$ laur$_{b7a.de}$ m-arct$_{b7.de}$ mez *Nux-v*$_{bg2}$ ph-ac prun$_{k}$* ruta$_{fd4.de}$ sapin$_{a1}$ stann$_{k}$* *Staph*$_{k}$* stront-c sulph$_{ptk1}$ til$_{k}$*
  - **paroxysmal**: zinc
  - **pulsating** pain: carc$_{fd2.de}$• kali-n mosch peti sulph zinc
  - **tight** hat; as from a (See hat)
  - **upward**: all-c ambr$_{h1}$ onos puls staph$_{h1}$
  - **vise**; as if in a: am-m grat mag-c merc
  - **weight** or stone; as from a: anac arg-met$_{bg2}$ asar *Bell* bry$_{bg2}$ cann-s *Carb-v* caust *Chel* cina cocc cupr graph hell kali-n lach$_{bg2}$ laur led meny nux-v **Petr** ph-ac plat sulph
- **pressure**:
  - **agg.**: am-c calc camph carc$_{fd2.de}$• cimic↓ dios hydrog$_{srj2}$• ph-ac sanic↓ sulph$_{k}$* tab↓ ulm-c↓
    - **cutting** pain: calc$_{h2}$
    - **hat**; from pressure of a: **Carb-v** *Kali-n* lob *Nit-ac* petr sil spig$_{h1}$
    - **sore**: cimic$_{gk}$ sanic tab
      - **intermittent**: ulm-c$_{jsj8}$•
  - **amel.**: abrom-a$_{ks5}$ aeth$_{br1}$ bros-gau$_{mrc1}$ *Bry* calc *Carb-v* cassia-s↓ *Castm* chin↓ colch dios dulc$_{fd4.de}$ gels grat hydr hydrog$_{srj2}$• hyos kali-n luna$_{kg1}$• mag-c *Mag-m* *Mag-p* mang$_{k}$* *Nux-m* **Nux-v** op↓ *Plb* sabin sep spig tarent *Zinc*
    - **bursting** pain: cassia-s$_{ccrh1}$•
    - **drawing** pain: chin$_{k}$* mang
    - **pressing** pain: **Nux-v** op$_{a1}$
    - **sore**: sep$_{h2}$
- **pulled**; sensation as if hair were: arn$_{k}$* cocc$_{a1}$ kali-n$_{a1}$ kali-p laur$_{a1}$ *Nux-v*
- **pulsating** pain: acon-ac$_{rly4}$• act-sp$_{k}$* agn alum$_{k}$* am-c asar bamb-a$_{stb2.de}$• **Bell** beryl$_{tpw5}$ borx *Calc* camph$_{k}$* *Carb-v*$_{k}$* carc$_{fd2.de}$• caust *Chel* cimic con *Crot-h* dream-p$_{sdj1}$• dros dulc$_{fd4.de}$ **Eup-per** *Ferr* *Gels* *Glon* ign kali-br *Kali-n* kali-s$_{fd4.de}$ **Lach** *Led* lyss mag-m$_{k}$* mang$_{k}$* *Nat-m* nit-ac *Petr* *Phos* podo$_{fd3.de}$• psor puls$_{k}$* pyrid$_{rly4}$• ruta$_{fd4.de}$ *Sep* staphycoc$_{rly4}$• *Stram*$_{st}$ streptoc$_{rly4}$• valer vanil$_{fd5.de}$ ven-m$_{rsj12}$•
- **pulsation**, with every: *Con*↓
  - **cutting** pain: *Con*
  - **lancinating**: *Con*
  - **shooting** pain: *Con*
- **reading** agg.: carb-ac↓ helon↓
  - **pressing** pain: carb-ac$_{k}$* helon$_{a1}$
- **rheumatic**: bar-c$_{k}$* mez$_{a1}$ staph$_{h1}$
- **riding** agg.: petr phyt$_{k}$* spong$_{fd4.de}$
- **rising**:
  - **after** | **agg.**: fago$_{a1}$ gels lyss mur-ac
  - **amel.**: chin eup-per grat$_{k}$* jug-c$_{k}$* kali-p puls ruta$_{fd4.de}$
  - **bed**; from:
    - **agg.**: abrom-a$_{ks5}$ cinnb↓ *Mur-ac*
      - **pressing** pain: cinnb$_{k}$*
- **room**:
  - **closed** room agg.: abrom-a$_{ks5}$
  - **entering** a room; when: mag-m↓ nat-m↓
- **room** – **entering** a room; when: ...
  - **stitching** pain: nat-m$_{k}$*
  - **tearing** pain: mag-m$_{h2}$
- **rubbing**:
  - **amel.**: aeth$_{c1}$ canth carb-v laur ol-an op↓ ph-ac *Phos*↓ tarent
    - **pressing** pain: op$_{a1}$ ph-ac$_{k}$* *Phos*
    - **tearing** pain: laur
- **scratching** agg.; after: sulph↓
  - **burning**: sulph$_{h2}$
- **screwed** together; as if: grat mag-c merc *Rhus-t*$_{hr1}$
- **sexual** excesses; after: *Calc* **Chin** **Phos**
  - **neurasthenia**, in: gels$_{dp}$•
- **shaking** the head; on:
  - **agg.**: apis calc cann-i **Carb-v** con *Glon* *Ip* *Kali-br* mosch *Nit-ac* *Petr* staph
  - **amel.**: gels$_{k}$*
- **sharp**: *Jug-c*$_{br1}$
- **shooting** pain: acon$_{k}$* aeth$_{k}$* agar ail alum alum-p$_{k2}$ anac$_{k}$* arum-t$_{k}$* asaf bar-i$_{k2}$ bell$_{k}$* bov calc calc-i$_{k2}$ calc-sil$_{k2}$ caps$_{k}$* cedr *Chel* *Cimic*$_{k}$* cinnb$_{k}$* con dig glon grat hep *Hyper* indg iod **Jug-c** kali-bi$_{bg2}$ kali-c kali-m$_{k2}$ kali-n kali-sil$_{k2}$ lac-c laur lyc mag-c mag-m meny mur-ac naja nat-m nit-ac ol-an petr$_{c1}$ phos *Sang* sec *Sil* spong$_{fd4.de}$ stann$_{a1}$ *Sulph*$_{k}$* teucr tritic-vg$_{fd5.de}$ zinc
  - **diagonally** across: agar
  - **forward**: chel *Cinnb*
  - **upward**: ambr sep sil spong$_{fd4.de}$
- **sitting**:
  - **agg.**: *Agar* castm caust chin euph fl-ac↓ indg *Kali-br* *Kali-s* meny *Mosch* nat-sil$_{fd3.de}$• ph-ac ran-b$_{k}$* rhod spig squil$_{k}$* zinc
    - **drawing** pain: chin$_{k}$* meny$_{k}$* squil$_{k}$*
    - **pressing** pain: fl-ac
    - **stitching** pain: indg$_{k}$* squil$_{k}$*
  - **amel.**: asar *Carb-v*↓ gels ign mag-c mag-m nux-m spong$_{k2}$ vanil$_{fd5.de}$
    - **pressing** pain: nux-m
    - **tearing** pain: *Carb-v* mag-m
  - **erect**:
    - **agg.**: ign↓
      - **tearing** pain: ign
- **sleep** | **after** | **agg.**: aesc aeth agar ail alum alum-p$_{k2}$ ambr *Ars*$_{k}$* bov bry *Calc* *Carb-v* caust *Chel* chin chinin-ar *Cimic* cinnb cocc *Con* eup-per *Gels* *Graph* hep *Ip* *Kali-bi* *Kali-c* *Kali-n* **Lach** *Lyc* mang *Nat-s* nit-ac nux-m *Nux-v* *Op* ox-ac *Pall* petr ph-ac *Phos* prun ptel puls *Rhus-t* sep *Sil*
  - **amel.**: nit-ac$_{k}$* vanil$_{fd5.de}$
    - **stitching** pain: nit-ac
- **smarting**: cassia-s$_{ccrh1}$•
- **sneezing** agg.: grat lach
- **sore**: *Aesc* agar alum$_{k}$* ars$_{h2}$ aur *Bapt*$_{k}$* *Bry*$_{k}$* *Calc* camph$_{b7.de}$* cann-i carb-ac carb-an chel choc$_{srj3}$• cic **Cimic**$_{k}$* coff$_{k}$* con$_{bg2}$ crot-c crot-h dirc **Eup-per**$_{k}$* *Euph*$_{k}$* ferr ferr-p **Gels**$_{k}$* *Glon* grat *Hell*$_{k}$* helo$_{c1}$ helo-s$_{c1}$ hyos indg *Ip* kali-p m-ambo$_{b7.de}$ mag-s merc-i-f mez$_{k}$* mosch$_{b7a.de}$ *Mur-ac* nat-m nat-s nicc nit-ac$_{k}$* **Nux-v**$_{k}$* *Ph-ac* phyt$_{k}$* pip-m plan prun$_{ptk1}$ rhus-t$_{h1}$ ruta$_{fd4.de}$ sabad$_{k}$* sep$_{k}$* sil$_{bro1}$ spig **Staph**$_{k}$* sulph tab tarent zinc$_{b4.de}$*
  - **broken** loose from rest of skull; as if: chel
  - **pulsating** pain: *Eup-per*
  - **wound** were pressed; as if: sabad
- **sprained**; as if: ambr$_{ptk1}$ psor vanil$_{fd5.de}$
- **squeezed**; as if: am-m$_{b7.de}$* ambr$_{b7a.de}$ chin$_{bg2}$ graph$_{bg2}$ *Ign*$_{b7.de}$* meny$_{b7.de}$* nat-s$_{bg2}$ phel$_{bg2}$ sep$_{b4.de}$* stann$_{bg2}$ teucr$_{b7.de}$*
- **standing**:
  - **agg.**: *Carb-v* castm chin↓ *Hell* *Ip* kali-c kali-n lac-c mag-c mosch ph-ac sel↓ staph tab vanil$_{fd5.de}$
    - **drawing** pain: chin$_{h1}$* mag-c$_{k}$*
    - **pressing** pain: *Ip* kali-c sel
  - **amel.**: *Chin* nux-v plb tarax

- **standing – amel.**: ...
  - **pressing** pain: plb
  - **still**:
    - **agg.**: cham
    - **amel.**: *Tarax* ↓
      - **tearing** pain: *Tarax*
- **stepping** agg.: con ↓ kali-c ↓ sep ↓
  - **stitching** pain: con kali-c sep$_{h2}$
- **stitching** pain: acon$_{k*}$ aesc aeth$_{k*}$ aloe ambr$_{k*}$ ammc ant-c$_{b7a.de}$ ant-t$_{k*}$ arn$_{k*}$ aur-m$_{a1}$ *Bar-c*$_{k*}$ bar-i$_{k2}$ bar-m bart$_{a1}$ *Bell*$_{k*}$ bov$_{k*}$ bry$_{k*}$ *Bufo* calc calc-i$_{k2}$ calc-sil$_{k2}$ canth$_{k*}$ *Carb-an*$_{k*}$ carb-v$_{k*}$ carc$_{fd2.de}$• castm$_{sne}$ caust$_{k*}$ cham$_{k*}$ *Chel*$_{k*}$ cimic coc-c$_{k*}$ *Con* dig$_{k*}$ dulc$_{k*}$ euphr fago$_{a1}$ ferr-p ferul$_{a1}$ gels glon$_{k*}$ grat$_{k*}$ ham$_{fd3.de}$• hell$_{k*}$ *Hep*$_{k*}$ *Hyper* ign indg$_{k*}$ iod$_{k*}$ iris kali-bi$_{k*}$ *Kali-c*$_{k*}$ kali-i$_{k*}$ kali-m$_{k2}$ kali-n$_{k*}$ kali-p kali-s$_{fkr2.de}$ kali-sil$_{k2}$ ketogl-ac$_{rly4}$• kola$_{stb3}$• *Lac-c* lap-la$_{sde8.de}$• laur$_{k*}$ *Lyc*$_{k*}$ mag-c$_{k*}$ *Mag-m*$_{k*}$ mang$_{k*}$ meny$_{b7.de*}$ *Merc* *Mur-ac*$_{k*}$ nat-c *Nat-m*$_{k*}$ nit-ac$_{k*}$ nux-m ol-an$_{a1}$ olnd$_{a1}$ ozone$_{sde2}$• petr$_{k*}$ **Phos**$_{k*}$ pimp$_{a1}$ podo$_{fd3.de}$• prun$_{a1}$ puls$_{k*}$ ran-b$_{k*}$ rhus-t$_{k*}$ ruta$_{fd4.de}$ samb$_{k*}$ sars$_{k*}$ sec sel$_{b7a.de}$ *Sep*$_{k*}$ sil$_{k*}$ spig$_{k*}$ spong$_{k*}$ squil$_{k*}$ staph$_{k*}$ stront-c$_{k*}$ stry sul-ac$_{k*}$ sul-i$_{k2}$ *Sulph*$_{k*}$ *Tarax*$_{k*}$ teucr$_{k*}$ thuj tritic-vg$_{fd5.de}$ vanil$_{fd5.de}$ verat$_{k*}$ verb$_{k*}$ viol-t$_{k*}$ zinc$_{k*}$
  - **alternating** with | **Nose**; stitching pain in root of (See NOSE - Pain - root - stitching - alternating - occiput)
  - **burning**: carb-v$_{k*}$ staph$_{k*}$
  - **forward**: aeth$_{a1}$ nat-m podo$_{fd3.de}$• sars spig$_{mrr1}$
  - **pulsating** pain: *Carb-an* carc$_{fd2.de}$• *Con* cop$_{k*}$ hep$_{k*}$ kali-n$_{h2}$
  - **tearing** pain: aeth$_{k*}$ samb$_{a1}$ thuj$_{h1}$
- **stool** | **during**:
  - **agg.**: gran ↓
    - **pressing** pain: gran$_{k*}$
  - **straining** at:
    - **agg.**: *Ign* mang$_{bg1}$
    - **amel.**: asaf$_{bg1}$
- **stooping**:
  - **after**:
    - **agg.**: aloe ↓ ferr-p ↓ kali-c ↓ rhus-t ↓
      - **stitching** pain: aloe ferr-p$_{k2}$ kali-c rhus-t$_{k*}$
  - **agg.**: acon$_{k*}$ aesc aloe alum alum-p$_{k2}$ ant-t *Calc* camph carb-ac *Carb-v* chin cob colch con cupr elaps fago$_{k*}$ *Ferr* *Gels*$_{k*}$ *Hell* helon$_{k*}$ kali-c *Kali-n* lyc mag-s mang nit-ac nux-m ph-ac *Phos* prun$_{k*}$ rhus-r *Spig* staph sulph$_{k*}$ tritic-vg$_{fd5.de}$
    - **changes** to forehead; pain: carb-an
    - **cramping**: camph
    - **cutting** pain: chin$_{k*}$
    - **drawing** pain: mang
    - **pressing** pain: carb-v$_{k*}$ *Colch* nux-m ph-ac
    - **sore**: hell
  - **amel.**: ign ol-an tritic-vg$_{fd5.de}$ verat
- **straining** the eyes: lac-c$_{k2}$ mur-ac$_{k2}$
- **stunning** pain: *Ant-c*$_{b7a.de}$ ars$_{k2}$ *Cann-i*$_{k*}$ *Carb-v*$_{hr1}$ cina$_{k*}$ *Dulc* *Hell*$_{k*}$ lappa$_{bg1}$ mang$_{h2}$ *Naja* seneg$_{k*}$ spong$_{fd4.de}$ sulph$_{k*}$ syph$_{k2}$ tarent zinc$_{k*}$
- **supper** agg.; after: *Carb-v* ↓
  - **pressing** pain: *Carb-v*$_{k*}$
- **suppurating**; as if: borx$_{h2}$ mag-c$_{bg2}$ mang
- **swallowing** agg.: gels kali-c mag-c$_{bg1}$
  - **drawing** pain: mag-c$_{k*}$
- **talking** agg.: spig ↓
  - **pressing** pain: spig
  - **tearing** pain: spig$_{k2}$
- **tearing** pain: acon$_{k*}$ aeth *Agar* ail am-m$_{k*}$ ambr$_{k*}$ *Anac*$_{k*}$ arg-met *Ars*$_{k*}$ ars-s-f$_{k2}$ asaf *Aur* aur-ar$_{k2}$ aur-s$_{k2}$ bar-c bar-m bar-s$_{k2}$ bell$_{k*}$ berb bism bov$_{k*}$ calc$_{k*}$ calc-sil$_{k2}$ camph$_{k*}$ canth$_{k*}$ carb-an$_{k*}$ **Carb-v**$_{k*}$ carbn-s **Caust**$_{k*}$ chel cic$_{a1}$ colch$_{k*}$ *Con* *Cupr*$_{k*}$ form grat *Guaj*$_{k*}$ hyos$_{k*}$ *Hyper* ign$_{k*}$ indg kali-ar kali-bi$_{k*}$ kali-c$_{k*}$ kali-m$_{k2}$ kali-n$_{k*}$ kali-p kali-sil$_{k2}$ laur$_{k*}$ led$_{k*}$ *Lyc*$_{k*}$ *Lyss* mag-c$_{k*}$ *Mag-m*$_{k*}$ mang$_{k*}$ *Merc*$_{k*}$ *Merc-c*$_{k*}$ merl mez$_{b4.de*}$ mur-ac$_{k*}$ nat-s$_{k*}$ nit-ac **Nux-m**$_{k*}$ **Nux-v**$_{k*}$ *Ph-ac*$_{k*}$ phel puls$_{k*}$ ran-b$_{k*}$ sabad$_{k*}$ *Sep*$_{k*}$ **Sil** *Spig*$_{k*}$ squil$_{k*}$ stann$_{k*}$ stront-c sulph$_{k*}$ *Tarax*$_{k*}$ *Thuj*$_{k*}$ verat *Zinc*$_{k*}$ zinc-p$_{k2}$
  - **burning**: cupr
  - **forward**: aeth anac *Aur* chin merc **Sil**
  - **jerking** pain: anac$_{h2}$ mag-c$_{h2}$
  - **paroxysmal**: **Caust**
  - **pulsating** pain: kali-c mag-m mez$_{h2}$
  - **upward**: ambr berb ol-an sars **Sil**
    - **and** forward: ambr **Caust** mag-m rat
- **thinking** agg.: ign$_{k*}$ nit-ac$_{k*}$
- **throw** back head; must | **drawing** pain (See bending - head - backward - must - drawing)
- **torn**; as if: con$_{k*}$
- **touch**:
  - **agg.**: calc ↓ carc$_{fd2.de}$• chin ↓ cortico ↓ cupr gels *Kali-n* mang$_{h2}$ *Mur-ac* ↓ nat-c$_{h2}$ *Nit-ac* op petr$_{hr1}$ sep ↓
    - **cutting** pain: cortico$_{sp1}$
    - **drawing** pain: chin$_{h1*}$
    - **pressing** pain: cupr$_{k*}$ kali-n
    - **sore**: calc$_{h2}$ *Mur-ac*$_{hr1}$ sep$_{h2}$
    - **stitching** pain: kali-n$_{h2}$
    - **tearing** pain: mang
  - **amel.**: mang
  - **hair** agg.; touching the: *Carb-v* carc$_{fd2.de}$• *Kali-n* *Nit-ac*
- **turning**:
  - **eyes**:
    - **agg.**: sep
    - **upward**: arum-t ↓ **Lac-c**
      - **shooting** pain: arum-t$_{k*}$
  - **head**:
    - **agg.**: *Carb-v* mang *Op* spong$_{a1}$
      - **stitching** pain: mang *Spong*
- **twitching**: kali-n$_{h2}$
- **ulcerative** pain: am-c$_{k*}$ borx$_{h2}$ bry$_{bg2}$ chel$_{bg2}$ *Cimic*$_{bg2}$ ferr$_{bg2}$ glon$_{bg2}$ hyos$_{bg2}$ kreos mang$_{k*}$ mez$_{bg2}$ nat-s$_{bg2}$ nux-v$_{k*}$ phyt$_{bg2}$ sep$_{k*}$ spig$_{bg2}$ thuj$_{bg2}$
- **unbinding** hair | **amel.**: kali-n$_{c1}$
- **urination** | **copious** | **amel.**: *Gels*
  - **delayed**; if desire to urinate is: sep
- **vexation**; after: alum ip petr *Ran-b*$_{k*}$ staph
- **violent**: podo$_{k2}$ vario$_{jl2*}$
- **vomiting**: thuj ↓
  - **tearing** pain: thuj
- **waking** frequently: kali-p$_{k2}$
- **walking**:
  - **after**:
    - **agg.**: zinc ↓
      - **pressing** pain: zinc$_{k*}$
  - **agg.**: asar bell *Bry* *Calc* *Carb-v* *Chin* con cortico$_{tpw7}$ *Glon* *Graph*$_{k*}$ *Ip* *Kali-br*$_{k*}$ kali-c **Led** mur-ac nit-ac phys$_{k*}$ podo$_{fd3.de}$• *Spig*$_{k*}$ staph *Stram* sulph tarax tritic-vg$_{fd5.de}$
    - **cutting** pain: calc
    - **pressing** pain: *Chin*
    - **tearing** pain: con tarax
  - **air**; in open:
    - **agg.**: bov *Calc* *Caust* cina dulc$_{fd4.de}$ ferr-p mang spig staph tritic-vg$_{fd5.de}$ zinc
      - **jerking** pain: *Spig*$_{k*}$
      - **pressing** pain: staph$_{a1*}$
    - **amel.**: cimic mang rhus-t *Seneg* sulph tab
      - **pressing** pain: mang$_{h2}$
      - **slowly**: plb
  - **amel.**: chin ↓ nux-m ↓
    - **drawing** pain: chin$_{k*}$
    - **pressing** pain: nux-m

- **walking**: ...
  - **must** walk: gels k2
- **wandering** pain: nat-s k*
- **warm**:
  - **applications**:
    - **amel.**: bamb-a ↓
      - **pressing** pain: bamb-a stb2.de•
  - **clothing** agg.: ip nit-ac staph *Stram*
  - **food** | **agg.**: ip mez puls sulph
  - **room**:
    - **agg.**: *All-c Apis* bov *Bry* carb-v *Cimic* coc-c ↓ guat jl3 *Mag-m Mez* mosch *Puls Seneg* k* *Stram* sulph k*
      - **pressing** pain: *All-c Carb-v* coc-c mag-m *Mez*
      - **stitching** pain: bov k*
    - **amel.**: bov *Carb-v* ↓
      - **tearing** pain: *Carb-v*
  - **wrapping** up head | **amel.**: *Gels* ign nat-sil fd3.de• *Nux-v* **Rhus-t Sil** k*
- **warm** agg.; becoming: ars k2 *Carb-v* ip kali-c lac-c *Stram*
- **warmth** agg.:
  - **heat** agg.: cassia-s ↓ *Euph Gels* ip *Phos Puls* trios ↓
    - **drawing** pain: cassia-s ccrh1•
    - **pressing** pain: trios rsj11•
- **weather** agg.; wet: arum-i ptk2 *Bar-c* brom **Calc** *Calc-p* **Dulc** lyss *Rhus-t*
- **wine**:
  - **agg.**: zinc
  - **amel.**: gels
- **wrapping** up head:
  - **amel.**: **Sil** ↓ vichy-g ↓
    - **pressing** pain: **Sil** vichy-g a1
    - **tearing** pain: **Sil**
- **writing** agg.: carb-an cocc gels k*
  - **pressing** pain: carb-an
- **yawning**:
  - **agg.**: cocc st
  - **amel.**: staph
- ▽ **extending** to:
  - **Across**: agar ↓ sabad ↓
    - **jerking** pain: sabad
    - **stitching** pain: agar
  - **Arms**: asaf bg1
  - **Back** and chest; into:
    - **noon**: *Graph* ↓
      - **pressing** pain: *Graph*
  - **Back**; down the: *Aeth* androc srj1• cimic *Cocc* crot-h graph ip k2 *Kali-br* hr1 lil-t limen-b-c hrn2• lyss nat-m pic-ac k* podo sang sep *Stry* thuj
    - **shooting** pain: cimic
  - **Cervical** region and shoulders; upper:
    - **resting** head high on pillow, with eyes half closed amel., and with sleepiness: gels ↓
      - **drawing** pain: gels
  - **Chest**: graph
  - **Chest**; back of: eupi ↓
    - **stitching** pain: eupi
  - **Ciliary** region | **right**: arund br1
  - **Downward**: pitu-p sp1
  - **Ears**: aesc bar-c cann-s chel colch dulc fd4.de ham fd3.de• lil-t bg1 mag-m bg1 plan plb puls stry thuj bg1
    - **drawing** pain: bar-c cann-s
  - **Ears**, through: puls ↓
    - **stitching** pain: puls
  - **Eye**: cimic ↓ moni ↓ ozone ↓ sanic ↓ *Sulph* ↓
    - **shooting** pain: cimic *Sulph*
    - **stitching** pain: moni rfm1• ozone sde2• sanic

- **extending** to: ...
  - **Eyes**: androc srj1• arund bro1 atro bell bro1 carb-v bro1 chin k* cimic bro1 cystein-l rly4• dios bg1 ery-a gels k* *Glon* glyc bro1 ham fd3.de• indol bro1 lac-c bro1 **Lach** mag-m bro1 moni ↓ nat-s onos bro1 oxal-a rly4• ozone sde2• *Petr* ph-ac bro1 pic-ac k* ptel hr1 *Rhus-r* bro1 ruta fd4.de sal-fr sle1• *Sang* bro1 sanic sars k* sec a1 *Sep Sil* bro1 **Spig** k* spong fd4.de stry *Verat* zinc
    - **right** eye: *Bell* mrr1 fic-m gya1 sang k2* spong fd4.de
      - **Above**: sang hr1*
    - **left** eye: androc srj1• ham fd3.de• lac-h ↓ spig fr1*
      - **dull** pain: lac-h htj1•
    - **cutting** pain: chin k* ozone sde2•
    - **pressing** pain: *Carb-v* moni rfm1•
    - **Around** temples further to eyes: adon vh1
  - **Eyes**; behind: med ↓
    - **burning**: med ptk
  - **Face**: dulc fd4.de op k2
  - **Forehead**: ambr arg-met ↓ *Arg-n* arge-pl rwt5• arund bro1 aur *Bell* b4a.de* bell-p c1 bell-p-sp ↓ bov brom bros-gau ↓ *Calc* camph ↓ cann-i ↓ canth bg1 *Caps* ↓ *Carb-v* k* cassia-s ↓ *Chel* chin k* choc srj3• cimic bro1 *Cinnb* ↓ clem con cycl ↓ dios dirc dulc fd4.de elaps fkr8.de ferr ferr-p ↓ fl-ac **Gels** k* *Glon* glyc bro1 ham ↓ indol bro1 *Kali-bi* kali-c **Lac-c** k* *Lach* lappa bg1 mag-m bro1 mang merc mez h2 mosch mur-ac nat-c a1 *Nat-m* nat-ox rly4• nat-s nat-sil ↓ ol-j onos bro1 op ozone ↓ par bg1 *Petr* k* *Ph-ac* k* pic-ac bro1 plb podo fd3.de• ptel *Rhus-r* bro1 *Rhus-t* ruta fd4.de **Sang** k* sanic *Sars* k* *Sil* k* spig bro1 spong fd4.de sulph tarent ter thuj ↓ trios ↓
    - **right**: *Bell* mrr1
    - **cutting** pain: arg-n k* camph h1 cann-i a1 *Caps* a1*
    - **drawing** pain: arg-met h1 cassia-s ccrh1• chel chin cycl a1 nat-c h2 sars h2
    - **lancinating**: gels c1
    - **nail**; as from a: mosch [bell-p-sp dcm1]
    - **pressing** pain: ambr h1 aur h2 bros-gau mrc1 *Calc* camph h1 carb-v fl-ac ham fd3.de• mang mez h2 mur-ac h2 nat-sil fd3.de• podo fd3.de• ruta fd4.de trios rsj11•
    - **shooting** pain: *Cinnb* lac-c
    - **stitching** pain: bov chel ferr-p k* **Lac-c** nat-m h2 ozone sde2• sanic sars h2 thuj h1
    - **stunning** pain: mez h2
    - **tearing** pain: ambr *Aur* carb-v chin merc mur-ac a1
    - **waves**; in: *Sil*
  - **Forward**: aeth ambr anac aur bell-p sp1 chin kola stb3• mag-m mand sp1 mang bg1 merc nat-p fkr6.de *Ph-ac* rat sanic *Sil* spong fd4.de valer bg1
  - **Frontal** eminence: bar-c ↓
    - **stitching** pain: bar-c
  - **Head**: canth carb-v caust **Chin** eup-per k2 **Gels** *Glon* kalm mag-p merc *Mez* pic-ac *Puls* sabad sang *Sil* **Stram** vanil fd5.de
    - **Over** whole head: chin lap-la rsp1 lycpr c1 vanil fd5.de
  - **Head**, beginning in upper cervical region; over: flor-p ↓
    - **bursting** pain: flor-p rsj3•
    - **Forehead** and eyeballs; causing bursting pain in:
      - **forenoon**:
        - **10** h:
          - **lying**, with nausea; while:
            - **cold** perspiration and cold feet agg.: *Gels* ↓
              - **bursting** pain: *GelS* k*
  - **Inward**: dirc c1
  - **Jaw**: androc srj1• arg-met bg1 bar-c kali-chl nit-ac spong fd4.de
    - **Lower**: cham
  - **Mastoid**: beryl sp1
  - **Middle** of head: cob-n ↓
    - **pulling**; like: cob-n sp1
  - **Nape** of neck: berb ↓ calc ↓ kali-n ↓ kali-s ↓ mang ↓ merc ↓ mur-ac ↓ nat-c ↓ **Nux-m** ↓ **Nux-v** ↓ plect ↓ ran-b ↓ sabin ↓ stry ↓ sulph ↓
    - **drawing** pain: kali-n c1 merc nat-c plect sulph
    - **jerking** pain: calc

- **extending** to – **Nape** of neck: ...
  - **pressing** pain: kali-s fd4.de sabin c1
  - **stitching** pain: mang mur-ac stry
  - **tearing** pain: berb **Nux-m Nux-v** ran-b
  - **Neck**: agath-a↓ ambr androc srj1• aq-mar skp7• *Bell Bry* calc↓ *Carb-v* chord-umb rly4• **Cocc** dulc fd4.de glon *Graph*↓ hell hep ip k2 kali-c ketogl-ac rly4• lac-leo hrn2• laur *Lil-t* limen-b-c hrn2• lyss↓ merc↓ mur-ac↓ nat-c↓ nux-v↓ phyt plect↓ podo sal-fr sle1• sulph suprar rly4• tung-met bdx1•
    - **morning**: chinin-ar↓
      - **burning**: chinin-ar
    - **burning**: lyss c1
    - **drawing** pain: merc mur-ac h2 nat-c plect sulph
    - **pressing** pain: agath-a nl2• calc *Graph* hep laur nat-c nux-v
    - **sleep**; before going to: *Bry*↓
      - **drawing** pain: *Bry*
    - **Down** back of neck: androc srj1• arg-n bell berb bit-ar wht1• *Bry* chord-umb rly4• cimic *Cocc* com dulc fd4.de gels bg1 *Graph* hell *Hep* hydr-ac kali-c kali-cy bg1 kali-n lac-leo hrn2• laur lil-t limen-b-c mlk9.de lob mang med bg1 merc mur-ac nat-c nat-s bg1 **Nux-m Nux-v** pic-ac podo k* ran-b sabin sal-fr sle1• sep spong fd4.de sulph tarent vanil fd5.de
  - **Nose**: acon bg1 corn cystein-l rly4• lach bg1
    - **drawing** pain: corn
  - **Nose**; root of:
    - **suppressed** discharge; from: kali-bi↓
      - **shooting** pain: kali-bi bro1
  - **Scapula**: ham fd3.de• hep bg1
  - **Shoulders**: androc srj1• *Bry* carc fd2.de• caust dios dulc fd4.de *Gels* hep hydr bg1 *Ip* kali-c kali-n podo [buteo-j sej6]
    - **pressing** pain: hep ip h1
    - **while** lying on back: *Bry*
  - **Side**: asar↓
    - **pressing** pain: asar h1
  - **Sides**: kali-p fd1.de• lac-h↓
    - **right**: sil mrr1 vanil fd5.de
    - **7-11 h**: ars-s-f k2
    - **dull** pain: lac-h sk4•
  - **Skull**: kola stb3• ozone↓ sang tl1
    - **evening**:
      - **20**.30 h: ozone↓
        - **stitching** pain: ozone sde2•
    - **stitching** pain: ozone sde2•
  - **Spine**: med↓
    - **burning**: med hr1
  - **Spine** and arms, down: *Crot-h*↓
    - **shooting** pain: *Crot-h*
  - **Spine**; down (See back; down; neck)
  - **Teeth**: ferr↓ zinc bg1
    - **pressing** pain: ferr
  - **Temple**: anac↓ arn↓ sang↓
    - **drawing** pain: sang hr1
    - **tearing** pain: anac arn
  - **Temples**: anac arn bamb-a stb2.de• cann-i coca dulc fd4.de fic-m↓ *Glon* limen-b-c hrn2* lycpr c1 plb ruta fd4.de sang hr1 sars bg1 seneg sep k2 *Spig*
    - **right**: *Bell* mrr1
    - **shooting** pain: *Cann-i* fic-m gya1
  - **Throat**: hep bg1 laur
    - **tearing** pain: laur
  - **Top** of head, so severe she thinks head will burst and she will go crazy: **Calc**↓
    - **bursting** pain: **Calc**
  - **Upper** jaw, left side: cham↓
    - **stitching** pain: cham
  - **Upward**: all-c bell bg1 berb **Calc** caust cimic bg1 **Gels** glon ol-an onos bg1 ph-ac phos bg1 *Puls* samb bat1• *Sang* sars sep **Sil** spong fd4.de verat-v bg1

- **extending** to: ...
  - **Upward** from nape: ambr↓ carb-v↓ ferr↓ sep↓ staph↓
    - **drawing** pain: ambr carb-v ferr sep h2 staph h1
  - **Vertex**: ambr bov *Calc* cann-i carb-an↓ *Caust* chel↓ choc↓ **Cimic** dig *Dulc* glon hell hura ketogl-ac rly4• lac-ac lac-c lac-h↓ lyc mag-m meny↓ nat-c petr mrr1 ph-ac k2 phel rat sang tl1 sep **Sil** trios rsj11• vanil fd5.de
    - **bursting** pain: meny bg2
    - **dull** pain: choc srj3• *Cimic*
    - **nail**; as from a: *Cimic* k*
    - **neuralgic**: caust tl1 chel tl1
    - **pressing** pain: bov carb-an h2 dig glon
    - **shooting** pain | **bolt**; like a: *Cann-i Cimic Sil*
    - **stitching** pain: lac-h sk4• sep vanil fd5.de
    - **tearing** pain: ambr *Caust* mag-m rat sep h2
- **Bones**: chin↓ ph-ac↓
  - **left**: visc↓
    - **shooting** pain: visc c1
  - **drawing** pain: chin h1* ph-ac h2*
- **Cerebellum**:
  - **right**: iris↓ rhus-r↓
    - **pressing** pain: rhus-r a1
    - **stitching** pain: iris c1
- **Ears**; behind: cortiso tpw7
- **External** head: *Hell* b7a.de
  - **sore**: *Hell* b7a.de
- **Glands**: am-c↓
  - **ulcerative** pain: am-c h2
- **Protuberance**; occipital: bamb-a stb2.de• **Bry** calc sne *Calc-p* chin bg1 colch dig glon bg1 guaj bg1 kola stb3• mur-ac nat-c h2 petr bg1 podo k* *Rhus-t Sil* staph h1 (non:uran-met k) uran-n
  - **afternoon**: bamb-a stb2.de• chinin-s
    - **17** h: bamb-a stb2.de•
  - **extending** to:
    - **Eye**: mur-ac↓
      - **drawing** pain: mur-ac h2*
    - **Neck**; down: podo
    - **Shoulders**: podo
  - **hat**; from pressure of a: *Sil*
  - **motion** agg.: **Bry**
  - **touch** agg.: nat-c h2
  - **walking** in the wind agg.: mur-ac
  - **warmth** agg. | **heat** agg.: *Sil*
  - **Sides**, alternating: sep bg1
- **Sides**: acon↓ aesc k* agar↓ all-c k* alum↓ anac↓ ang↓ arg-met↓ asar↓ aster k* aur↓ aur-m-n↓ bar-c↓ bell↓ berb↓ bism↓ bov↓ bry↓ calc↓ calc-sil↓ camph↓ cann-s k* carb-an↓ *Carb-v*↓ *Carl*↓ castm↓ caust↓ cere-b↓ cham k* *Chel Chin*↓ colch k* con↓ cot a1 crot-h↓ crot-t↓ dig↓ dulc fd4.de elaps euph↓ euphr↓ **Fl-ac** glon grat↓ guaj k* ham↓ hydr-ac↓ hyos k* ign k* ind k* indg↓ iod↓ kali-bi k* kali-c↓ kali-m↓ kali-n k* kali-s↓ kali-sil↓ ketogl-ac rly4• kiss↓ *Laur*↓ led k* lyc↓ lycpr↓ mag-c mag-m↓ mag-s k* meny↓ meph mez k* mill↓ mur-ac↓ myric a1 nat-c↓ nat-m↓ nat-p↓ *Nat-s*↓ nat-sal↓ nux-v↓ ol-an k* ph-ac phel↓ phos↓ phys k* plat↓ psor↓ ptel k* puls↓ ran-b↓ rhod↓ rhus-v↓ ruta↓ sabad↓ sabin↓ samb↓ sars↓ sep k* serp a1 *Sil Spig*↓ spong fd4.de *Stann*↓ staph↓ **Stram** k* *Stront-c*↓ sul-ac↓ sulph thuj↓ verb↓ viol-t↓ zinc↓ zing↓
  - **alternating** sides: sep bg1
  - **right**: aesc k* agath-a↓ alum↓ anac↓ aster k* *Aur*↓ bism↓ both-ax tsm2 *Calc*↓ cann-s k* carb-v bg1 caust↓ chel↓ colch k* cortico sp1 dig↓ dulc fd4.de fic-m↓ guaj↓ hep ign k* ind k* *Iris* kali-bi k* kali-c↓ ketogl-ac↓ laur↓ lyc↓ mag-c↓ mag-m↓ mang↓ myric k* *Nat-c*↓ nat-s↓ nit-ac↓ ph-ac↓ phel↓ podo fd3.de• psor↓ *Rhod*↓ sang bg1* *Sanic*↓ seneg↓ sep k* serp a1 sil bg1 *Spig*↓ spong fd4.de stram k* *Stront-c*↓ sulph↓ verb↓ zinc↓
    - **boring** pain: fic-m gya1
    - **drawing** pain: alum k* caust dulc fd4.de laur a1 nat-c k* rhod spig a1 zinc h2*

- **Sides – right**: ...
  - **pressing** pain: agath-a nl2• anac k* aur h2* *Calc* carb-v caust k* colch a1 dig hep h2 lyc h2 nat-c h2* nat-s a1 ph-ac podo fd3.de• *Rhod* seneg sep h2 *Spig* verb h
    - **dislocated**; as if: psor vml
  - **stitching** pain: *Calc* k* ketogl-ac rly4• laur a1 mang h2 *Nat-c* k* nit-ac h2 phel a1 *Sanic* sulph k*
  - **tearing** pain: *Aur* bism h1 chel h1 guaj kali-c mag-c h2 mag-m h2 *Stront-c*
  - **extending** to:
    - **left**: dig *Mez* staph
      - **pressing** pain: dig
      - **stitching** pain: staph h1
    - **Eye**; left: iod
    - **Forehead**: chel ↓ sanic ↓
      - **stitching** pain: chel h1 sanic
    - **Scapulae**: hep ↓
      - **pressing** pain: hep h2
  - **left**: agar alum ↓ am-c am-m a1 androc srj1• arg-n bg1 asar ↓ bell ↓ bry bg1 calc ↓ *Carb-v* ↓ cham k* *Chel* chin ↓ con ↓ cycl ↓ dulc fd4.de guaj k* ham fd3.de• kali-p ↓ kali-s fd4.de ketogl-ac ↓ kola stb3• led k* lyc ↓ mez ↓ nat-s ↓ nat-sil fd3.de• nicotam ↓ nit-ac ↓ nuph k* ol-an k* onos bg1 petr ↓ phos ↓ phys k* ptel k* puls k* rhus-t bg1* samb ↓ sars ↓ sep bg1 *Stann* ↓ sul-ac ↓ sulph a1 thuj h1 tong ↓ verb ↓ viol-t ↓ zinc ↓ zing ↓
    - **drawing** pain: calc *Carb-v* k* *Chel* k* chin a1 cycl h1 nat-s a1 phos a1 thuj a1 zinc k*
    - **pressing** pain: androc srj1• asar a1 calc h2 *Chel* dulc h2 ham fd3.de• kali-p fd1.de• kali-s fd4.de lyc mez h2 nicotam rly4• sep h2 stann k* sul-ac k* sulph zinc zing k*
    - **sitting** agg.: *Agar*
    - **stitching** pain: alum bell *Chel* k* ham fd3.de• ketogl-ac rly4• kola stb3• nit-ac h2 petr k* samb h1 sars k* sul-ac k* tong a1 verb a1 viol-t a1
    - **tearing** pain: con lyc h2 samb h1 sep h2 *Stann*
    - **extending** to:
      - **right**: squil
        - **drawing** pain: *Squil*
      - **Eye** | **left**: spig ptk
      - **Jaw**; lower: plat ↓
        - **drawing** pain: plat h2
  - **daytime**: nuph a1 ph-ac k*
  - **morning**: agar ↓ anac ↓ bov ↓ dios k* eupi ↓ puls k* *Sil* ↓
    - **7 h**: bov ↓
      - **stitching** pain: bov
    - **stitching** pain: agar h2 bov k* eupi k*
    - **tearing** pain: anac h2 puls *Sil*
  - **forenoon**: all-c k* alum ↓ dios k* sulph ↓
    - **drawing** pain: alum k* sulph k*
  - **afternoon**: euphr ↓ petr ↓
    - **16 h**: cortico sp1
    - **stitching** pain: euphr k* petr k*
  - **evening**: carb-an ↓ mez ↓ nat-c ↓ nat-s ↓ nit-ac ↓ zing ↓
    - **20 h**: stram
    - **pressing** pain: mez h2 nat-s k* zing k*
    - **sleep**:
      - **amel.**: nit-ac ↓
        - **stitching** pain: nit-ac k*
    - **stitching** pain: carb-an k* nat-c k* nit-ac k*
    - **tearing** pain: carb-an nat-s
  - **night**: stront-c ↓
    - **boring** pain: stront-c
  - **air** agg.; draft of cold: caust ↓
    - **tearing** pain: caust
  - **bending** | **backward** | **agg.**: colch k*
    - **head**:
      - **backward**:
        - **amel.**: bar-c ↓ chin ↓
          - **drawing** pain: chin k*
          - **tearing** pain: bar-c

- **Sides**: ...
  - **blood** stagnated; as if: sulph h2
  - **boring** pain: arg-met aur-m-n k* lycpr a1 nat-sal a1 ol-an k* sabin k* stront-c
  - **breakfast**; during: nit-ac ↓
    - **stitching** pain: nit-ac k*
  - **dinner**; after: canth ↓ ol-an ↓
    - **stitching** pain: canth k* ol-an k*
  - **drawing** pain: alum k* ang a1 aur-m-n k* *Carb-v* k* *Chel* k* chin k* *Fl-ac* kali-c a1 kali-n k* kali-s kiss a1 laur k* meny h1* mez k* nat-s k* phos k* sep thuj k* zinc k*
    - **alternating** with | **Thumb**; similar sensation in the ball of: arg-met k*
    - **cramping**: kali-n plat h2 *Sulph*
    - **drawn** back, as if head would be: nat-c k*
    - **paroxysmal**: rhod k*
    - **pressing** pain: *Chel* k* *Chin* *Spig* k*
  - **hammering** pain: ign h1
  - **hands** laying on amel.: sul-ac ↓
    - **pressing** pain: sul-ac h2
  - **laughing** agg.: zinc ↓
    - **tearing** pain: zinc
  - **lying** down:
    - **amel.**: mag-s ↓
      - **pressing** pain: mag-s
  - **motion**:
    - **agg.**: *Aur* ↓
      - **tearing** pain: *Aur*
    - **head**; of:
      - **left**; to: mag-c ↓
        - **tearing** pain: mag-c
  - **pressing** pain: anac k* asar k* aur k* bov k* bry k* calc calc-sil k2 camph carb-an k* carb-v castm caust cere-b a1 *Chel* colch k* con k* crot-h crot-t k* dig k* **Fl-ac** k* glon k* hydr-ac k* ign *Laur* k* mag-s mez k* nat-c k* nat-p *Nat-s* k* nux-v ph-ac k* psor k* ruta h1 sabin k* sep *Sil* k* spig k* spong k* stann sul-ac k* sulph zinc k*
    - **asunder**: zinc h2
    - **blow**; pain as from a: dig h2
    - **outward**: ph-ac stann
    - **pulsating** pain: bell k* zing k*
  - **pressure**:
    - **agg.**: cortiso sp1 ph-ac ↓
      - **pressing** pain: ph-ac h2
    - **amel.**: hyos k* spig ↓
      - **pressing** pain: spig h1
  - **rest** agg.: nat-s ↓
    - **tearing** pain: nat-s
  - **rheumatic**: coff ↓
    - **drawing** pain: coff k*
  - **shaking** the head agg.; on: glon k*
  - **sitting** agg.: fl-ac ↓
    - **pressing** pain: fl-ac k*
  - **sneezing**:
    - **amel.**: calc ↓
      - **drawing** pain: calc h2
  - **sore**: caust euph h2 grat iod h
  - **stitching** pain: acon k* bov k* calc k* *Chel* k* grat k* guaj k* ham fd3.de• indg k* kali-bi k* kali-n k* ketogl-ac rly4• laur k* lyc k* mag-m k* mill a1 nat-c k* nat-m h2 phel a1 phos k* sars k* spig k* sul-ac k* sulph k* verb k* viol-t k*
    - **drawing** pain: chel h1
    - **pinching** pain: chel h1
    - **pressing** pain: chel h1
    - **tearing** pain: euphr h2 samb h1
    - **twitching**: cham k* mag-m k*
    - **upward**: staph h1
  - **stooping** agg.: cortiso sp1 spig ↓

· **Sides – stooping** agg.: ...
: **pressing** pain: spig h1
: **tearing** pain: agar aur bar-c berb bov camph carb-an *Carb-v* *Carl* caust colch con guaj kali-bi kali-c kali-m k2 kali-sil k2 led mag-c mag-m mur-ac *Nat-s* puls ran-b rhus-v sabad *Sil* *Stann* *Stront-c* zinc
: **intermittent**: sep h2
: **paroxysmal**: mur-ac
: **pressing** pain: lyc h2 zinc h2
: **pulsating** pain: kali-c h2
: **shooting** back and forth: carb-an
: **twitching**: bism mag-m
: **touch** agg.: thuj h1
: **turning** head agg.: ph-ac ↓
: **pressing** pain: ph-ac
: **waking** agg.; after: *Sulph* k*
: **walking**:
: **agg.**: aster k* con ↓
. **tearing** pain: con
: **air** agg.; in open: caust ↓
. **pressing** pain: caust k*
: **warm** | **bed**:
. **amel.**: caust ↓
tearing pain: caust
: **room**:
. **agg.**: zing ↓
drawing pain: zing k*
: **weather**; wet:
: **amel.**: caust ↓
. **tearing** pain: caust kl
: **extending** to:
: **Forehead**: aur ↓ *Chel* ↓ cycl ↓ mur-ac ↓
. **drawing** pain: cycl h1
. **stitching** pain: *Chel*
. **tearing** pain: aur mur-ac
: **Head**: canth ↓ sabad ↓ *Sil* ↓
. **tearing** pain: canth sabad *Sil*
: **Neck**: ambr ↓ calc ↓ *Chel* ↓ *Laur* ↓
. **pressing** pain: calc h2 *Chel* *Laur*
. **tearing** pain: ambr
: **Neck**; nape of: mur-ac ↓
. **stitching** pain: mur-ac h2
: **Side** to side: agar ↓
. **stitching** pain: agar
: **Side** he turns the head to: calc ↓
: **drawing** pain: calc h2
: **Spot**; in a: spig ↓
: **pressing** pain: spig h1
: **stitching** pain: spig h1
: **Suboccipital** region: ambr ↓ *Carb-v* ↓ iod ↓
: **pressing** pain: ambr h1 *Carb-v* iod h

· **Spot**, in a small: am-m ↓
: **cramping**: am-m

· **Spot**; in a: stront-c ↓
: **boring** pain: stront-c

· **Spots**; in: acon ↓ carb-an ↓ *Colch* ↓ glon ↓ *Lyc* ↓ meph ↓ ol-an ↓ olnd ↓ sep ↓ thuj ↓ zinc ↓
: **pressing** pain: carb-an h2 glon k* meph ptk1 ol-an k* olnd k* sep h2
: **button**; as from a: acon *Lyc* thuj zinc
: **tearing** pain: *Colch*

· **Suboccipital**: apis ↓
: **blow**; pain as from a: apis

- **Occiput** and Forehead: aeth *Alum* ambr anac aphis arn asaf aur aur-s k2 bell bry calc camph cann-i canth caps carb-v chel chin chinin-s chir-fl gya2 choc srj3• chord-umb rly4• cimic cina clem colch con corn dig dios eup-per ferr gels glon graph grat guaj hydr-ac hyos ign iod iris kali-bi kali-c kali-n lach lachn laur lyc mag-c mag-m mang merc mez mosch mur-ac nat-m ol-j onos op *Oreo* c1* pert-vc vk9 petr ph-ac prun ptel k* raph rhus-t sabad sabin sars seneg sep serp spig spong squil stry sul-ac sulph tab thuj
· **morning** | **waking**; on: kali-bi *Lach* **Onos**

- **Occiput** and Vertex: androc srj1•

- **Painful** part: *Spig* ↓
· **sore**: *Spig*

- **Parietal** bone | **chill**; during: cedr bro1

- **Periosteum**: ant-c b7.de* ruta b7.de* sabin b7.de*
· **blow**; pain as from a: ruta h1

- **Scalp**: *Acon* ↓ acon-s ↓ agar ↓ agn ↓ alum ↓ ambr b7.de* amp ↓ anac ↓ ang ↓ ant-c ↓ apis ↓ *Arg-met* ↓ *Arn* ↓ *Ars* ↓ asaf ↓ aur ↓ bar-c ↓ bell b4.de* *Bov* ↓ *Bry* ↓ calc ↓ cann-i ↓ canth ↓ caps b7a.de carb-an ↓ *Carb-v* ↓ *Caust* ↓ cham ↓ *Chin* ↓ cic ↓ *Cimic* ↓ cina ↓ *Clem* ↓ cocc ↓ colch ↓ coloc ↓ con ↓ cupr ↓ cycl ↓ daph ↓ des-ac rbp6 dig ↓ *Dros* ↓ dulc ↓ dys fmm1• euph ↓ euphr ↓ ferr b7a.de graph ↓ guaj ↓ hell ↓ helo ↓ *Hep* ↓ hist ↓ hydr ↓ hyos b7.de* ign b7.de* iod ↓ ip ↓ kali-bi ↓ kali-c ↓ kali-n b4.de* kreos b7a.de lach b7.de* laur ↓ led ↓ *Lyc* ↓ m-arct ↓ m-aust ↓ mag-m ↓ mang ↓ meny ↓ *Merc* ↓ merc-c ↓ mez b4.de* morg-g fmm1• mosch ↓ mur-ac ↓ *Nat-c* ↓ *Nat-m* ↓ nit-ac ↓ *Nux-v* b7.de* *Olnd* ↓ par ↓ petr ↓ ph-ac ↓ *Phos* ↓ phyt ↓ plat ↓ *Puls* ↓ ran-b ↓ ran-s ↓ rhod ↓ *Rhus-t* ↓ *Ruta* ↓ sabad ↓ sabin ↓ sangin-n ↓ *Sars* ↓ *Sel* ↓ sep b4a.de sil ↓ spig b7.de* spong ↓ stann ↓ staph b7.de* sul-ac ↓ *Sulph* ↓ *Thuj* b4a.de verat ↓ *Viol-t* ↓ *Zinc* ↓
· **biting** pain: agn b7.de* alum bg2 ars bg2 bar-c bg2 bry b7.de* calc b4a.de caps bg2 cham bg2 *Dros* b7.de* led b7a.de m-arct b7.de merc b4.de* mez b4.de* nux-v bg2 *Olnd* b7.de* *Puls* b7.de* ran-s b7.de* rhod b4.de* *Rhus-t* bg2 *Ruta* bg2 sep bg2 **Staph** bg2 thuj b4.de* verat bg2 *Zinc* b4.de*
· **boring** pain: alum b4.de* aur b4.de* dros b7.de* *Lyc* b4.de* phos b4.de* spong b7.de*
· **burning**: apis b7a.de arn b7.de* ars b4.de* bar-c b4.de* bell b4.de* bry b7.de* caps b7.de* carb-v b4.de* coloc b4.de* cupr b7a.de* dros b7.de* dulc b4.de* graph b4.de* helo bg2 kali-bi bg2 lyc b4.de* mang b4.de* meny b7.de* merc b4.de* mur-ac b4.de* olnd b7.de* ph-ac b4.de* phos b4.de* plat b4.de* ran-b b7.de* *Rhus-t* b7a.de ruta b7.de* sabad b7.de* *Sel* b7a.de sil b4.de* spig b7.de* spong b7.de* stann b4.de* staph b7.de* sulph b4.de* verat b7.de* viol-t b7.de* zinc b4.de*
· **chill**; during: hell b7.de
· **compressed**; as if: ruta b7.de*
· **corrosive**: agn b7.de* bar-c b4a.de caps b7.de* dros b7.de* nux-v b7.de* *Olnd* b7.de* rhus-t b7.de* ruta b7.de* staph b7.de* thuj b4.de* verat b7.de*
· **cramping**: bell b4.de* cocc b7.de*
· **drawing** pain: agar b4.de* apis b7a.de bar-c b4.de* bell b4.de* calc b4.de* canth b7.de* chin b7.de* graph b4a.de* hist sp1 ign b7.de* kreos b7a.de mag-m b4a.de* meny bg2 merc-c b4a.de nit-ac b4a.de* nux-v b7.de* par b7.de* petr b4a.de* ph-ac b4.de* *Puls* b7.de* ran-s b7.de* rhod b4a.de* rhus-t b7.de* ruta b7.de* sars b4a.de* sep b4a.de* staph b7.de* thuj b4.de* zinc b4.de*
· **gnawing** pain: bell b4.de* canth b7.de* dros b7.de* hyos b7.de* meny b7.de* nat-m bg2 par b7.de* phos bg2 ruta b7.de* spong b7.de* zinc b4.de*
· **injuries**; after: nat-m ↓
: **sore**: nat-m mtf33
· **menses**; before: sulph b4.de
· **neuralgic**: *Acon* bro1 *Cimic* bro1 hydr bro1 phyt bro1
· **pinching** pain: alum b4.de* rhus-t b7.de*
· **pressing** pain: acon-s a1 agar b4.de* alum b4a.de ambr b7.de* anac b4.de* *Arg-met* b7.de* arn b7.de* aur b4.de* calc b4.de* chin b7.de* cic b7a.de* clem b4.de* con b4.de* cycl b7.de* dig b4.de* dros b7.de* euph bg2 euphr b7.de hyos b7.de* *Lyc* b4.de* mur-ac b4.de* nit-ac bg2 *Olnd* b7.de* ph-ac b4.de* phos b4.de* rhod bg2 rhus-t b7.de* ruta b7.de* sabad bg2 sabin b7.de *Sars* b4a.de* sep b4.de* staph b7.de* *Sulph* b4.de* thuj b4.de* zinc b4.de*
: **gnawing** pain: hyos h1
· **sore**: alum b4a.de ambr b7.de* amp rly4• ang b7.de* arg-met b7.de* *Arn* bg2 *Bov* b4a.de *Bry* b7.de* calc b4.de* cann-i c1 *Chin* b7.de* *Clem* b4a.de dros b7.de* euph b4.de* graph b4.de* hell b7.de* *Hep* b4a.de ign b7.de* iod b4.de* ip b7a.de* m-aust b7.de meny b7.de* mosch b7a.de nat-m b4a.de *Nux-v* b7.de* par b7.de* petr b4a.de* ph-ac b4.de* phos b4.de* ran-b b7.de* rhod bg2 *Ruta* b7.de* sangin-n br1 staph b7.de* zinc b4.de*

Head

- **sore**: ...
  - **accompanied** by:
    - **baldness**: zinc ptk1
    - **Head**; pain in (See accompanied - scalp)
- **squeezed**; as if: arn b7.de ip b7.de par b7.de rhod b4.de* *Ruta* b7.de*
- **stitching** pain: agar b4.de* agn b7.de* alum b4.de* ang b7.de* ant-c b7.de* apis b7a.de arn b7.de* asaf b7.de* aur b4.de* bar-c b4.de* bell b4.de* calc b4.de* canth b7.de* *Caust* b4.de* chin b7.de* cina bg2 cycl b7.de* daph bg2 dig b4.de* euph bg2 euphr b7a.de guaj b4.de* hep b4.de* iod b4.de* kali-c b4.de* kreos b7a.de laur b7.de* mang b4.de* meny b7.de* merc-c b4a.de mez b4.de* *Nat-m* b4.de* nit-ac b4.de* olnd b7.de* par b7.de* ph-ac b4.de* *Phos* b4.de* ran-b b7.de* ran-s b7.de* ruta b7.de* sabad b7.de* sars b4a.de* sel b7a.de spig b7.de* staph b7.de* sulph b4.de* thuj b4.de* verat b7.de* *Viol-t* b7a.de
- **tearing** pain: agar b4.de* alum b4.de* ambr b7.de* ang b7.de* arg-met b7a.de* bar-c b4.de* bell b4.de* bry b7.de* calc b4.de* carb-an b4.de* *Carb-v* b4a.de* colch b7.de* cycl b4.de* dig b4.de* graph b4.de* guaj b4.de* laur bg2 led b7.de* *Lyc* b4.de* meny b7.de* merc b4.de* merc-c b4a.de *Nat-c* b4.de* rhod b4a.de* rhus-t b7.de* ruta b7.de* sabin b7.de* sars b4a.de* sep b4.de* staph b7.de*
- **ulcerative** pain: agar b4a.de* arg-met bg2 *Ars* b4.de* *Chin* b7.de colch bg2 graph bg2 hep b4.de kreos bg2 mang b4.de *Merc* b4.de* mur-ac b4.de* nit-ac bg2 petr bg2 ph-ac bg2 phos bg2 puls b7.de rhod bg2 rhus-t b7.de* ruta bg2 sil bg2 spig b7.de* stann bg2 sul-ac b4.de* zinc b4a.de*

- **Sides**: *Acon*↓ aesc↓ aeth↓ *Agar*↓ agath-a nl2• agn↓ all-c aloe↓ *Alum* alum-p↓ alum-sil↓ am-c↓ am-m↓ ambr↓ ammc↓ *Anac*↓ ang↓ ant-t↓ apis↓ *Arg-met*↓ *Arg-n*↓ *Arn*↓ *Ars*↓ arum-t↓ *Asaf*↓ asar atro↓ aur↓ aur-m-n↓ aur-s↓ bapt↓ bar-act↓ *Bar-c*↓ bar-i↓ bar-m↓ bar-s↓ **Bell**↓ benz-ac↓ *Berb*↓ borx↓ both-ax tsm2 bov *Brom*↓ bry↓ *Cact*↓ *Calc*↓ calc-i↓ *Calc-p* calc-s calc-sil↓ camph↓ cann-s↓ *Canth*↓ *Caps*↓ carb-ac↓ carb-an *Carb-v*↓ carbn-s↓ carl↓ castm↓ caust↓ cedr↓ *Cham*↓ *Chel*↓ chin choc↓ cic↓ cimx↓ cina↓ cinnb↓ clem↓ coc-c↓ coca↓ cocc↓ *Coff*↓ colch↓ coli rly4• *Coloc*↓ com↓ *Con*↓ cop↓ cor-r corn↓ cot↓ croc↓ crot-h↓ cupr k* cycl cystein-l rly4• daph↓ dendr-pol sk4• des-ac↓ dig dios dros↓ dulc↓ eug↓ eup-per↓ eup-pur↓ euph↓ euphr eupi↓ falco-pe nl2• *Ferr*↓ ferr-p↓ fl-ac↓ gamb↓ glon *Gran*↓ *Graph*↓ grat↓ *Guaj*↓ ham↓ *Hell*↓ **Hep**↓ heroin↓ hippoc-k szs2 hir↓ hura↓ hydr-ac↓ hydrog srj2• hyos↓ hyper↓ **Ign**↓ ind↓ indg↓ iod↓ ip↓ irid-met↓ iris↓ kali-ar↓ kali-bi *Kali-c*↓ **Kali-i** kali-m↓ kali-n↓ kali-p↓ **Kali-s**↓ kali-sil↓ kalm↓ ketogl-ac↓ kreos↓ lac-h↓ *Lach*↓ laur↓ led↓ lil-t↓ lith-c↓ lyc lyss↓ m-ambo↓ m-arct↓ m-aust↓ mag-c mag-m mag-s↓ *Mang*↓ mang-m↓ meny↓ *Merc*↓ *Merc-c* merc-i-f *Merl*↓ mez mill↓ mucs-nas rly4• *Mur-ac*↓ nat-ar↓ nat-c↓ **Nat-m**↓ nat-ox rly4• nat-p↓ nat-s↓ nat-sil↓ nicc↓ nicotam rly4• *Nit-ac*↓ nit-s-d↓ nux-m↓ **Nux-v**↓ ol-an olnd↓ orot-ac rly4• ox-ac↓ oxal-a rly4• paeon↓ paull↓ petr↓ ph-ac↓ phel↓ phos phys↓ phyt↓ pip-m↓ plac-s rly4• plan↓ plat plb b7.de* plut-n↓ podo↓ *Prun*↓ *Psor*↓ puls b7.de* rat↓ rheum↓ rhod↓ *Rhus-t*↓ rumx↓ ruta fd4.de sabad↓ *Sabin*↓ samb↓ *Sars*↓ sec↓ sel↓ *Sep*↓ *Sil*↓ **Spig**↓ spong fd4.de squil stann↓ staph↓ staphycoc↓ stront-c↓ stry↓ suis-em rly4• suis-pan rly4• sul-ac↓ sul-i↓ sulph↓ suprar↓ tab↓ tarax↓ *Tarent*↓ teucr↓ ther↓ **Thuj**↓ thymol↓ til tong↓ tritic-vg fd5.de upa↓ urt-u↓ valer↓ vanil fd5.de verat↓ verb↓ viol-t↓ **Zinc**↓ zinc-p↓
  - **both**: acon↓ aeth↓ agath-a↓ alum↓ am-m↓ arg-met↓ asar↓ bar-c↓ bell↓ bov↓ bry↓ camph↓ *Chin*↓ cic↓ com↓ gamb↓ glon↓ hell↓ kali-i↓ lac-lup↓ lam↓ mag-c↓ *Mag-m*↓ mag-s↓ medul-os-si↓ meny↓ nat-m↓ prun↓ sabad↓ sil↓ spong↓ tarax↓
    - **crushed**; as if: kali-i k2
    - **pressing** pain: acon aeth agath-a nl2• alum am-m a1 arg-met asar bar-c bell bov bry camph *Chin* cic com gamb glon hell lac-lup hrn2• lam mag-c *Mag-m* k* mag-s medul-os-si rly4• meny nat-m prun sabad sil spong fd4.de tarax
  - **one** side (= hemicrania): acon aesc aeth *Agar* agath-a nl2• agn **Alum** alum-p k2 alum-sil k2 am-c am-m ambr amn-l sp1 *Anac* androc srj1• ang k* ant-c ant-t *Apis* *Arg-met* **Arg-n** k* *Arn* *Ars* k* ars-i ars-s-f k2 arund *Asaf* *Asar* aur aur-ar k2 aur-i k2 *Aur-m-n* wbt2• aur-s k2 *Bar-c* bar-i k2 bar-m bar-s k2 *Bell* k* *Bism* borx both fne1• *Bov* *Bry* k* *Bufo* *Cact* *Calc* k* calc-i k2 calc-p calc-s k2 calc-sil k2 camph cann-i k* cann-s *Canth* *Caps* carb-an carb-v carbn-s carc fb* caust cedr bro1 *Cham* k* *Chel* chen-a hr1 *Chin* chinin-ar chinin-s chir-fl gya2 *Cic* cina cinnb clem cocc **Coff** k* colch *Coloc* k* con cop *Corn* croc crot-c sk4• crot-h cupr cycl k* dig dios dros dulc elaps elat eug eup-per euph euphr *Ferr* ferr-ar ferr-i ferr-p *Gels* gins bro1 *Glon* k* *Graph* k* *Guaj* hell hippoc-k szs2 hist sp1 hyos *Ign* k* ind

- **Sides – one** side: ...
  iod ip iris joan bro1 *Kali-ar* *Kali-bi* k* *Kali-br* **Kali-c** k* **Kali-i** kali-m k2 kali-n **Kali-p** *Kali-s* kali-sil k2 kalm kola stb3• kreos *Lac-d* *Lach* k* lact *Laur* led *Lyc* k* mag-c mag-m manc mand rsj7• mang meny *Merc* *Mez* mill moni rfm1• mosch mur-ac murx nat-ar nat-c nat-m k* nat-p nat-sil fd3.de• nicc nit-ac nux-m *Nux-v* ol-an bro1 olnd *Onos* bro1 par petr k* petr-ra shn4• **Ph-ac** *Phos* k* *Phyt* **Plat** plb *Pneu* jl2 prot jl2 prun bro1 *Psor* k* **Puls** k* ran-b ran-s rheum rhod *Rhus-t* *Rob* ruta sabad sabin samb *Sang* k* **Sars** sel seneg *Sep* k* *Sil* k* sphing kk3.fr **Spig** k* spong squil stann k* staph stict stram strept-ent jl2 streptoc jl2 stront-c **Sul-ac** sul-i k2 *Sulph* *Syph* tab tarax tarent teucr *Thuj* k* tub-d jl2 ust valer *Verat* **Verb** viol-o viol-t **Zinc** zinc-p k2 zing
    - **accompanied** by:
      - **fever** (See FEVER - Accompanied - migraine)
      - **nausea**: (↗*accompanied - nausea)* arg-n hr1 cic c1 coloc hr1 sep c1 ven-m jl1
      - **vomiting**: cocc tl1
    - **alternating** with | **Arm**; with pain in left: ptel
    - **apoplexy**; in: syph mtf11
    - **appearing** suddenly: tub-d jl2
      - **disappearing** suddenly: tub-d jl2
    - **ceases** on one side and becomes more violent on the other: *Lac-c* moni rfm1• *Nat-m*
    - **coffee**, from excessive use of: nux-v
    - **congestion**: aeth hr1
    - **duration**; variable: tub-d jl2
    - **emotional** complaints; after: arg-n br1
    - **fever**; without: tub-d jl2
    - **irregular**: tub-d jl2
    - **itching**: dig h2
    - **menses**; during: pneu jl2
    - **pressing** pain: agar b4a.de coloc b4a.de mez b4a.de
    - **extending** to:
      - **Eye**: *Asaf* brom caust croc mag-m nat-m
      - **Neck**: chir-fl gya2 guaj *Lach* lyc merc
        - **Shoulders** with stiff neck; and: chir-fl gya2 lach
      - **Shoulders**: chir-fl gya2
      - **Side** to side, through temples; from: alum chin phos plan sang
      - **Waist**: lyss
    - **Ear**; behind the: asar calc-p caust chel cortiso tpw7 fic-m gya1 onos sang spong fd4.de
      - **left**: ambr apis mrr1 kali-p sang
      - **air** agg.; in open: kali-p
      - **motion** agg.: kali-p
    - **Side** lain on (See lying - side - side lain)
    - **Spots**; in: kali-bi kalm
  - **alternating** sides: agar atis bnj1 *Aur-m-n* wbt2• bell blum-o bnj1 calc calc-ar cedr chin coch c1 colch cupr dros euon falco-pe nl2• hell hippoc-k szs2 hydr hyper *Iris* k* kali-bi kali-c bg1 **Lac-c** k* lil-t lyc nat-m nat-ox rly4• nat-p nicc *Nux-v* phos plan sal-fr sle1• samb↓ sep sil valer
    - **jerking** pain: samb
    - **stitching** pain: agar
  - **right**: acon↓ aesc↓ aeth↓ *Agar*↓ agath-a nl2• agn↓ aids↓ *Alum* alum-p↓ alum-sil k2 am-br vh1 am-c↓ am-m↓ ambr↓ amph↓ anac↓ ang↓ apis↓ arg-met arg-n k2 ars arum-d a1 arum-t↓ asaf k* asar↓ aur↓ *Aur-m-n* wbt2• bar-c↓ **Bell** k* benzol br1 *Bism* borx↓ both-ax tsm2 bov brass-n-o srj5• brom↓ bros-gau↓ *Bry* k* bufo *Cact* k* **Calc** calc-i k2 calc-sil k2 camph↓ cann-i c1 canth↓ carb-ac a1* carb-an **Carb-v** k* carc mg1.de* *Caust* *Cedr* bro1 cham *Chel* k* chen-a hr1* chin↓ chir-fl gya2 cic↓ cimic k* *Cina* cist k* *Clem*↓ coc-c coca cocc↓ coff colch a1 *Coloc*↓ com a1 *Con* cortico tpw7 croc k* *Crot-c* crot-h k* cupr↓ cycl dig↓ dream-p sdj1• dros↓ dulc fd4.de elaps fkr8.de euph k* ferr-ar ferr-p a1 fic-m gya1 fl-ac↓ galeoc-c-h gms1• gels k* gins k* gran graph grat k* guaj helodr-cal↓ *Hep* k* hipp a1 hippoc-k szs2 iber a1 **Ign** k* inul↓ iod **Iris** k* jac-c jac-g jug-c a1 kali-bi bg2* kali-c kali-s↓ kali-sil k2 kalm↓ kreos↓ lac-del↓ lac-loxod-a hrn2• lach k* lachn c1* lap-la sde8.de• laur↓ lavand-a↓ lil-t↓ limest-b↓ *Lyc* k* m-arct↓ mag-c mag-m↓ mag-s↓ mang↓ melal-alt gya4 meny k* merc merc-i-f a1 merc-i-r k* *Mez* k* mill k*

- **right**: ...
Mosch mucs-nas rly4• *Mur-ac* ↓ nat-ar k2 nat-c ↓ *Nat-m* k* nat-s ↓ nit-ac nux-m k* nux-v ↓ ol-an olib-sac wmh1 olnd ↓ ost a1 oxal-a rly4• ozone sde2• par ↓ paull ↓ petr b4.de* petr-ra shn4• *Ph-ac* ↓ *Phos* ↓ plac-s rly4• plan ↓ plat *Plb* podo ↓ pop ↓ prun mrr1 *Puls* ↓ pycnop-sa mrz1 rad-br bro1 *Ran-b* *Rat* rheum rhod k* *Rhus-t* rumx ↓ *Ruta* **Sabad** k* sabin ↓ sacch-a ↓ sal-al blc1• *Sang* k* sars ↓ sel ↓ **Sep** k* sil k* spig mrr1 spong stann ↓ staph ↓ stict a1 still a1 stront-c ↓ suis-em rly4• sul-ac ↓ sulph symph fd3.de• tab bro1 tarax tarent k* tax bro1 teucr ↓ thuj k* trios ↓ tritic-vg fd5.de urt-u valer ↓ vanil fd5.de ven-m ↓ verat verb ↓ vero-o ↓ viol-t ↓ zinc k* zinc-m a1 [bell-p-sp dcm1]
: **morning**:
: : **left** side; and | **evening**: bov
: **evening**:
: : **20**-23 h: adam skp7•
: : **bed** agg.; in: con
: **accompanied** by:
: : **Ear**:
: : . **pain** | **right**: ozone sde2•
: **aching**: vero-o rly3•
: **biting** pain: agn hr1 thuj h1
: **blurred** vision before the attack: **Iris**
: **boring** pain: anac gsy1 *Arg-n* k* arum-t k* aur bg2 bov k* bry clem coloc k* iris bg2 laur b7.de* nat-m b4.de* stann *Zinc* k*
: **burning**: ph-ac b4.de* spong h1
: **burrowing**: bry b7.de*
: **bursting** pain: zinc b4.de*
: **cough** agg.; during: am-br vh1 cortico tpw7
: **cramping**: bell k*
: **cut** off; as if: lach ptk1
: **cutting** pain: *Bell* k* bros-gau mrc1 cortico tpw7 kali-bi bg2 sel rsj9• spig ptk1
: **diet** error; after: chel mtf11
: **dimness** of left eye, with: arg-n
: **drawing** pain: alum k* ang b7.de* arg-met b7.de* arg-n k* asaf k* aur bg2* *Bell* k* calc k* camph k* caust bg2 chel bg2 cina b7.de* cocc k* dros b7.de* fl-ac k* lach k* lyc k* nat-c bg2 *Ph-ac* k* phos k* plat b4.de* rhod bg2 sars h2 spong k* sul-ac k* thuj k* valer k*
: **dull** pain: apis b7a.de lac-del hrn2• lavand-a ctl1• melal-alt gya4 rumx hr1 spong b7.de* trios rsj11•
: : **accompanied** by | **Neck**; stiffness in: lavand-a ctl1•
: **foreign** body; as from a: *Con*
: **hammering** pain: sang bg2
: **jerking** pain: acon b7.de* aeth a1 agar b4.de* calc b4.de* graph kreos lyc b4.de* plat b4.de* *Prun* puls b7.de* sabin spong b7.de* teucr b7.de*
: **lancinating**: amph a1 sang k2
: **looking** up, agg.: lil-t bg1
: **lying**:
: : **side**; on:
: : . **left** | **agg.**: adam skp7•
: : . **painful** side | **amel.**: hipp
: : . **right**:
: : . . **agg.**: mag-c
: : . . **amel.**: adam skp7•
: **nail**; as from a: *Agar* k* hep b4.de* lyc b4a.de thuj b4.de*
: **neuralgic**: chel mrr1
: **periodical**: *Cact*
: **piercing** pain: bros-gau mrc1
: **plug**; as from a: agar bg2 asaf b7.de* *Hep* b4.de* mez bg2 plat b4.de* prun bg2 thuj bg2
: **pressing** pain: agar agn anac b4.de* ang b7.de* arg-met k* arg-n k* asaf k* asar k* bar-c k* bry k* caust k* *Chel* *Clem* k* con b4.de* dream-p sdj1• dros k* euph b4.de* grat k* *Hep* k* ign k* kalm laur b7.de* lil-t limest-b es1• meny b7.de* *Mez* k* nux-m b7.de* olnd k* *Ph-ac* b4a.de plac-s rly4• plat h2 rheum b7.de* ruta fd4.de sabad k* sacch-a fd2.de• sars b4.de* spong k* tab k* thuj h1* vanil fd5.de verb h* zinc k*
: : **alternating** with | **stitching** pain in right side: anac h1*
: : **inward**: apis b7a.de calc b4.de* nat-s bg2 olnd b7.de*

- **right – pressing** pain: ...
: : **outward**: cina k* dros k* paull a1 ph-ac k* spig k* spong k* stann k* verb k* viol-t k*
: **pulsating** pain: alum bg2 bov bg2 kali-c bg2 lil-t bg2 phos bg2 sars bg2 [pop dhh1]
: **shaking** the head agg.; on: carb-v h2
: **sharp**: helodr-cal knl2• ven-m rsj12•
: **shooting** pain: lil-t k* mag-c melal-alt gya4 plan k* spong fd4.de stann k*
: **sleep** | **amel.**: adam skp7•
: **sore**: aesc k* ambr k* cortico tpw7 dros h1 merc-i-f k* mez k* nit-ac k* plat k* staph h1 zinc h2
: **squeezed**; as if: *Coloc* b4a.de *Nit-ac* b4a.de *Ph-ac* b4a.de plat b4.de*
: **stitching** pain: aeth a1 aids nl2• alum k* alum-p k2 am-c b4.de* anac k* arg-n k2 asaf b7.de* bar-c b4.de* bell b4.de* borx k* brom k* calc b4.de* camph b7.de* canth b7.de* caust k* cham b7.de* cic b7.de* cocc b7.de* cupr k* euph b4.de* grat k* guaj b4.de* inul a1 iod k* kali-bi k* kali-s fd4.de lach b7.de* laur b7.de* *Mag-c* k* mag-m b4.de* mag-s a1 mill a1 *Mur-ac* k* nit-ac k* ol-an a1 par b7.de* ph-ac k* phos a1 plb k* podo fd3.de• rat sars b4.de* sil a1 stront-c b4.de* sulph b4.de* symph fd3.de• tarent thuj k* tritic-vg fd5.de vanil fd5.de zinc b4.de*
: : **alternating** with | **pressing** pain in right side (See pressing - alternating - stitching)
: **stooping** agg.: lil-t bg1
: **stroke** of an anvil, as of: manc k*
: **stunning** pain: euph k* *Mez* k* olnd b7.de* sul-ac k* verb b7.de*
: **suppurating**; as if: agar bg2
: **tearing** pain: agar b4.de* alum k* am-m b7.de* anac k* arg-met aur b4.de* bar-c b4.de* bov k* canth b7.de* *Carb-an* k* carb-v b4.de* caust b4.de* *Chel* k* chin b7.de* cic a1 *Con* k* dig b4a.de graph b4.de* *Guaj* b4a.de ign b7.de* lyc b4.de* m-arct b7.de mag-c k* mag-m b4.de* mang k* mosch b7a.de *Mur-ac* k* nux-v b7.de* *Phos* b4.de* plb b7.de* *Puls* k* rhod b4.de* sars b4.de* stann b4.de* stront-c b4.de* sul-ac k* sulph k* teucr b7.de* thuj k* verb k* zinc b4.de*
: **then** left: anac bg1 androc srj1• arn bry colch cupr k* dig ign bg1 kalm bg1 merc-i-r k* olib-sac wmh1 phos bg1 pic-ac a1 staph tax k*
: : **pressing** pain: cupr
: **turning** in bed agg.: lil-t bg1
: **walking** agg.: cortico tpw7
: **warm** room; when entering a: *Spig* k* *Spong* k*
: **extending** to:
: : **left**: alum ↓
: : . **pressing** pain: alum h2
: : **Cervical** region: lac-loxod-a hrn2•
: : **Eye** | **right**: spig cp
: : **Forehead**: fic-m gya1
: : **Occiput**: prun mrr1
: : **Temples**: melal-alt ↓
: : . **dull** pain: melal-alt gya4

- **left**: acon ↓ aeth ↓ agar b4.de* aloe alum k* am-c ↓ am-m ↓ *Ambr* aml-ns vh1 anac bro1 ang ↓ *Ant-c* ant-t ↓ ap-g vml3• apis k1 arg-met ↓ *Arg-n* ↓ arn ↓ *Ars* k* *Ars-i* ars-met bro1 *Asaf* k* *Asar* asc-c c1 aur ↓ aur-m k2 aur-m-n wbt2• bamb-a stb2.de• *Bar-c* ↓ *Bell* k* berb ↓ bism borx ↓ *Bov* k* **Brom** k* bry k* buth-a sp1 cadm-met sp1 calad *Calc* calc-p k* cann-s canth k* *Caps* ↓ carb-an ↓ carb-v carbn-s caust *Cham* chel ↓ *Chin* chinin-ar chinin-s k* chlor a1 cic ↓ cimic k* cina *Cinnb* ↓ coca-c sk4• colch ↓ coli ↓ *Coloc* con conv cop ↓ cortiso tpw7* *Croc* k* crot-h k* crot-t ↓ cupr k* cupr-ar ↓ *Cycl* k* dendr-pol sk4• dig ↓ dios a1 dioxi rbp6 dirc a1 dros ↓ dulc fd4.de epiph bro1 erio a1 eup-pur k* *Euph* euphr a1 eupi ↓ fago a1 falco-pe ↓ *Ferr* k* *Ferr-i* fic-m gya1 fl-ac k* form a1 galla-q-r ↓ gent-c a1 *Graph* k* grat ↓ *Guaj* gymno ham k* hell ↓ helodr-cal ↓ hippoc-k szs2 hydr k* hydrog srj2• hydroph ↓ hyos ↓ ign indg ↓ inul a1 *Iod* *Kali-c* kali-p fd1.de• kali-s ↓ ketogl-ac rly4• kola stb3• lac-ac k* lac-c lac-h htj1• lac-loxod-a hrn2• *Lach* k* laur a1 led ↓ lepi ↓ lil-t k* lith-c *Lob* lyc k* m-arct ↓ m-aust ↓ *Mag-c* mag-m ↓ mag-s ↓ manc a1 mand ↓ *Mang* ↓ med medul-os-si rly4• melal-alt ↓ meny ↓ *Merc* *Merc-c* ↓ merc-i-f k* merc-i-r k* mez a1 *Mur-ac* ↓ murx k* myos-a rly4• nat-c ↓ nat-m k* nat-s ↓ neon srj5• nicc bro1 *Nit-ac* k* *Nux-m* k* nux-v bro1 ol-an ↓ olib-sac wmh1 *Olnd* *Onos* bro1 oreo bro1 osteo-a knp1• oxal-a ↓ pall *Par* paraf bro1 ph-ac ↓ phel k* *Phos* k* plac-s rly4• plan k* *Plat* plb k*

- **left**: ...
pneu jl2 polys sk4• positr nl2• ptel k* pycnop-sa mrz1 ran-b ran-s rat↓ *Rhod* *Rhus-t* ruta fd4.de sabad sal-fr sle1• *Samb* sang a1 sapin bro1 sapo bro1 *Sars*↓ sec k* *Sel* *Senec* bro1 **Sep** k* sil↓ spect↓ sphing a1 **Spig** k* stann↓ staph↓ *Stront-c*↓ suis-em rly4• suis-pan rly4• sul-ac mrr1 *Sulph* suprar↓ syc fmm1• symph fd3.de• tab k* *Tarax* tarent bg1 tax↓ tell↓ thioc-ac rly4• *Thuj* k* trios↓ tritic-vg fd5.de trom k* usn a2 vanil fd5.de ven-m rsj12• verat-v k* verb c1 viol-o viol-t x-ray sp1 xan k* *Zinc* k* zing ziz k* [bell-p-sp dcm1]
  - **morning**: adam skp7• *Arg-n* hr1
    - **waking**; on: lyss↓ sal-al blc1•
      - **burning**: lyss
  - **afternoon**: cortiso sp1
    - **16** h: adam skp7•
  - **evening** | **20** h: usn a2
  - **accompanied** by:
    - **Eye**; pain in left: apis a1* falco-pe nl2• irid-met srj5• sanguis-s hrn2•
  - **boring** pain: aur k* chin k* cop k* cycl a1 laur a1 mag-c b4.de* mag-m b4.de* mag-s k* nat-m k* nat-s k* stann b4.de* staph h1 tritic-vg fd5.de zinc k*
  - **burning**: hydrog srj2• m-aust b7.de staph b7.de*
  - **burrowing**: chin b7.de*
  - **compressed**; as if: asar b7.de*
  - **contracting**: olib-sac wmh1
  - **cough** agg.: ozone sde2•
  - **cramping**: phos thuj k*
    - **cold**, crampy: phos k*
  - **cutting** pain: *Arg-n* k* coli rly4• cupr h2 sep ptk1
  - **drawing** pain: anac k* ant-t k* apis k* arg-met arn k* bar-c k* brom k* calc bg2 canth b7.de* caps b7.de* carb-v bg2 chel bg2 cina b7.de* cinnb h1 colch k* cycl b7.de* dros b7.de* form a1 grat a1 ham fd3.de• hell b7.de* iod k* **Kali-c** k* m-arct b7.de m-aust b7.de mang h2 nit-ac k* phos bg2* plat b4.de* rhus-t k* sars k* sep k* zinc h2*
  - **dull** pain: apis b7a.de canth b7.de* *Cinnb* croc b7.de* dros b7.de* dulc fd4.de falco-pe nl2• hydroph rsj6• laur b7.de* melal-alt gya4 mez h2 olib-sac wmh1 oxal-a rly4• phos h2 polys sk4• ruta fd4.de symph fd3.de• thuj h1 trios rsj11• zinc b4.de* [bell-p-sp dcm1]
  - **exertion** agg.: adam skp7•
  - **hammering** pain: ol-an bg2
  - **jerking** pain: aeth cupr h2 nux-v b7.de* spig k*
  - **lancinating**: lepi br1 plac-s rly4• sphing kk3.fr spig kk3.fr
  - **lying**:
    - **agg.**: caust↓
      - **pressing** pain: caust
      - **redness** and bloated swelling of the cheek with nausea and vomiting; with: apis k1
    - **side**; on:
      - **left**:
        - **agg.**: ars calad kali-bi
        - **amel.**: sal-fr sle1•
      - **right** | **amel.**: brom
  - **nail**; as from a: nat-m bg2 ptel bg2
  - **neuralgic**: mand rsj7• sul-ac mrr1
  - **pain** in elbow; with: xan c1
  - **paroxysmal**: spig bg2
  - **pinching** pain: calc b4.de*
  - **plug**; as from a: nat-m bg2 ptel bg2
  - **pressing** pain: agar b4.de* am-m a1 ang b7.de* apis b7a.de arn b7.de* *Asaf* k* asar b7.de* bov k* cic a1 crot-h k* crot-t bg2 dulc fd4.de euph b4.de* fl-ac bg2* hell ign bg2 iod k* kali-s fd4.de ketogl-ac rly4• laur b7.de* mez h2 mur-ac h2 nit-ac h2 ph-ac k* rhus-t k* sars k* spig b7.de* stann b4.de* staph b7.de* *Stront-c* k* sul-ac h2 sulph k* symph fd3.de• *Thuj* k* vanil fd5.de verb b7.de* [tax jsj7]
    - **asunder**: calc b4.de*
    - **inward**: ant-t b7.de* asaf b7.de* dulc b4.de* plat b4.de*
    - **outward**: asaf k* bell k* brom bg2 calc m-arct b7.de m-aust b7.de
  - **pressure** agg.: cortiso skp7•

- **left**: ...
  - **pulsating** pain: acon tl1 am-c bg2 caps tl1 dulc fd4.de hydrog srj2• mag-m bg2 ol-an bg2 syc bka1• [spect dfg1]
  - **sharp**: helodr-cal knl2•
  - **shooting** pain: canth *Cinnb* *Ferr* rhod a1 suprar rly4• tarent tell rsj10•
  - **sore**: carb-an h2 cupr-ar laur k* lil-t k* *Mur-ac* hr1 par k* rat bg2* sulph k* [tax jsj7]
  - **spot**; in a round: pert-vc vk9
  - **squeezed**; as if: carb-v b4.de* ph-ac b4a.de thuj b4.de*
  - **stitching** pain: aeth k* am-m b7.de* anac b4.de* *Bar-c* k* berb k* borx b4a.de* calc k* calc-p k* cann-s k* canth b7.de* cham h1 chel b7.de* cic k* con b4.de* crot-h k* cycl k* euphr a1 eupi a1 ferr b7.de* fic-m gya1 galla-q-r nl2• guaj b4.de* hyos b7.de* indg a1 kali-c k* kali-s fd4.de lac-h sk4• lach k* laur b7.de* m-arct b7.de m-aust b7.de mag-c b4.de* mag-m b4.de* *Mang* k* meny b7.de* merc-c b4a.de mez b4.de* mur-ac b4.de* nat-c b4.de* nat-m h2 nux-v b7.de* ol-an a1 ph-ac b4a.de phos b4.de* *Plat* k* rhod k* sars k* sep b4.de* sil k* spig b7.de* staph b7.de* stront-c b4.de* sulph k* tab k* tarax b7.de* tritic-vg fd5.de vanil fd5.de verb b7.de*
  - **stunning** pain: *Asaf* b7.de* dulc b4.de* verb b7.de*
  - **talking** agg.: canth↓
    - **shooting** pain: canth
  - **tearing** pain: agar b4.de* am-c b4.de* ant-t b7.de* arg-met b7.de* ars aur bar-c b4.de* borx b4a.de bov b4.de* *Bry* b7.de* canth b7.de* *Caps* k* carb-v b4.de* *Caust* b4a.de *Chinin-ar* cina k* colch b7.de* *Coloc* k* croc b7.de* dig b4.de* graph k* *Guaj* k* ign b7.de* **Kali-c** k* laur k* led k* lyc b4.de* m-arct b7.de m-aust b7.de mag-m b4.de* mang b4.de* *Merc* b4.de* *Merc-c* b4a.de nat-c b4.de* *Sars* k* *Sel* k* sep b4.de* *Spig* k* staph h1 sulph b4.de* tell thuj zinc b4.de*
  - **then** right: adam skp7• aesc k2 arn beryl sp1 elaps gk euon bg1 eup-per glon k* kola stb3• lac-loxod-a hrn2• *Lac-lup* hrn2• *Nux-m* squil sulph
    - **forenoon** | **11**-14 h: adam skp7•
    - **shooting** pain: aesc eup-per k2
  - **wind** blowing on head: med c1
  - **extending** to:
    - **right**: elaps↓
      - **lancinating**: elaps hr1
    - **Forehead**: ketogl-ac rly4•
    - **Frontal** eminence: bar-c↓ guaj↓
      - **drawing** pain: guaj h2
      - **stitching** pain: bar-c k* guaj h2
    - **Jaw**: ketogl-ac rly4•
    - **Neck**: sanguis-s hrn2•
    - **Sacrum**: usn a2
  - **Head** and face:
    - **extending** to | **Neck**: guaj
- **side** to side; from: hydrog↓
  - **line**; in a: hydrog srj2•
- **daytime**: cact ferr hippoc-k szs2 hydr mag-m nicc↓ plan a1
  - **stitching** pain: nicc k*
- **morning**: aids↓ aloe alum *Ars* arum-d a1 arum-t↓ aur↓ bell bov carb-v↓ chinin-s chr-ac dios k* euphr k* fl-ac gels *Graph* ham k* hipp k* hydr k* jug-c mag-c mag-s↓ mang merc-i-r a1 nat-m↓ nicc↓ *Nux-v*↓ ost a1 phys a1 sars **Spig** k* tab k* tarent↓ thuj↓ vanil fd5.de verat-v a1
  - **7-17** h: *Puls*
  - **8** h: arg-n↓
    - **boring** pain: arg-n
  - **until** evening: nat-m↓
    - **stitching** pain: nat-m k*
  - **bed** agg.; in: graph k* nicc nux-v scut k* **Spig** k*
  - **boring** pain: arum-t k* aur k* mag-c h2
  - **cutting** pain: tarent
  - **lancinating**: tarent k*
  - **pressing** pain: carb-v h2 sars h2 vanil fd5.de
  - **rising**:
    - **agg.**: ars cact calc gels hydrog srj2• mag-s puls spig
    - **amel.**: graph merc-i-r

- **morning**: ...
  - **sore**: ars
  - **stitching** pain: aids nl2• alum k* mag-c h2 mag-s k* nat-m k* nicc k* *Nux-v* sars k* vanil fd5.de
  - **tearing** pain: mang h2 thuj
  - **waking**; on: aids ↓ arum-d a1 arum-t aur cina merc-i-r mur-ac petr-ra shn4• phos puls staph ↓ tab
    - **boring** pain: staph h1
    - **stitching** pain: aids nl2• staph h1
- **forenoon**: agar ↓ alum am-m ↓ bov ↓ cact carb-an castm euphr k* ferr-ma a1 fl-ac k* hippoc-k szs2 hydr indg jug-c k* jug-r kalm lach mag-c ↓ nat-m nicc ↓ peti plb sars stront-c vanil fd5.de verat
  - **burrowing**: agar k*
  - **pressing** pain: alum h2 vanil fd5.de
  - **sore**: bov mag-c
  - **standing** agg.: plb ↓
    - **stitching** pain: plb k*
  - **stitching** pain: alum k* am-m k* nicc k* plb k* vanil fd5.de
  - **tearing** pain: alum
  - **walking** agg.: plb ↓
    - **stitching** pain: plb k*
- **noon**: calc-p k* vanil fd5.de
- **afternoon**: aeth alum bry canth castm chinin-s coca colch ferr graph hippoc-k szs2 indg lach k* laur mag-s merc-i-r k* nat-m nicc nit-ac k* nux-m a1 nux-v k* ol-an ruta fd4.de *Sep* k* valer zinc
  - **14** h: grat ↓ laur ↓
    - **tearing** pain: grat laur
  - **15** h: mag-c ↓
    - **stitching** pain: mag-c
  - **boring** pain: mag-s k*
  - **stitching** pain: alum k* canth k* nicc k* ruta fd4.de sep k*
  - **tearing** pain: alum h2 nicc ol-an zinc
- **evening**: aloe alum-p k2 ang ↓ arg-met *Ars* bar-c bell ↓ calc-s canth carb-v ↓ caust chin chinin-ar dios k* elaps fl-ac graph ham k* hippoc-k szs2 ind k* indg kali-c kali-n lyc lyss mag-c mag-m menth-pu a1 merc-i-r mez k* mucs-nas rly4• nat-m ↓ nat-ox rly4• nicc nux-v k* pall k* phos plat ↓ *Puls* *Sep* k* sil spig sulph tab k* thuj ↓ vanil ↓ zinc k* zing k*
  - **amel**.: phos ptel k* ruta ↓ sep k*
    - **tearing** pain: ruta
  - **bed** agg.; in: arg-met ars con plat sep h2
  - **boring** pain: mag-m k* zinc k*
    - **changing** to stitching: bell
  - **bursting** pain: zinc h2
  - **drawing** pain: ang a1 phos k*
  - **pressing** pain: zinc h2
  - **sitting** agg.: phos ↓
    - **tearing** pain: phos
  - **stitching** pain: bar-c canth k* carb-v k* caust k* mag-c nat-m k* plat k* vanil fd5.de
  - **tearing** pain: graph lyc nicc phos h2 thuj
- **night**: acon alum-p ↓ arg-n ↓ cact *Caust* *Graph* k* hippoc-k szs2 kali-n mag-c k* mez nat-m nicc ol-an phos ↓ plb k* staph tarent k* vanil fd5.de
  - **midnight** | **after**: *Thuj*
  - **amel**.: mag-c
  - **drawing** pain: phos h2
  - **menses**; after: ol-an ↓
    - **stitching** pain: ol-an k*
  - **pressing** pain: alum-p k2 vanil fd5.de
  - **shooting** pain: tarent k*
  - **stitching** pain: nat-m k*
  - **tearing** pain: arg-n phos h2
- **aching**: thymol sp1
- **air** agg.; draft of cold: caust ↓
  - **drawing** pain: caust
- **air**; in open:
  - **agg**.: fago fl-ac grat ↓ mang mez rat ↓ **Sep** trom
    - **burrowing**: rat k*
- **air**; in open – **agg**.: ...
    - **drawing** pain: grat k*
  - **amel**.: aeth hr1 am-c bar-c ↓ carb-an fago hippoc-k szs2 kali-c kali-i k2 mang nat-m phos rat *Sep* sulph
    - **pressing** pain: *Kali-i*
      - **screwed** in; as if: bar-c *Kali-i*
    - **tearing** pain: kali-i k2
- **appearing** gradually: con k*
- **ascending**:
  - **agg**.: lach ↓
    - **cutting** pain: lach
  - **stairs** | **agg**.: hydr
- **bed**:
  - **in** bed:
    - **agg**.: ars iod k* thuj ↓
      - **tearing** pain: thuj
    - **amel**.: tab k*
- **bending** | **body**:
  - **right**; to:
    - **agg**.: mag-m ↓
      - **stitching** pain: mag-m h2
  - **head** | **backward**:
    - **agg**.: aur ↓
      - **boring** pain: aur k*
    - **forward**:
      - **agg**.: ang ↓
        - **pressing** pain: ang h1
- **boring** pain: agar ang k* arg-n k* arum-t k* aur k* aur-m-n k* bell h1 bov bry chin k* clem coloc k* cop k* eup-pur hep k* iris kali-i k* laur k* led mag-c mag-m k* mag-s k* mang-m mez nat-m k* nat-s k* ol-an bg2 phos h2 puls k* stann staph h1 zinc k*
  - **outward**: bell k*
  - **violent**: *Arg-n* k*
- **bowing**, on: thuj ↓
  - **stitching** pain: thuj k*
- **breakfast**; during: gels k*
- **burning**: bapt k* bar-c bell k* calc canth coloc h2 dros h1 mang k* ph-ac h2 **Phos** k*
- **burrowing**: agar k* carl k* clem phos k* rat spig h1*
- **bursting** pain: asaf bg2 asar k* bov bg2 brom k* cor-r bg2* *Glon* kali-bi bg2 nicc k* nit-ac h2 *Puls* k* zinc
- **chewing** agg.:
  - **warm** food: phos ↓
    - **pressing** pain: phos h2
- **cold**:
  - **air** agg.: bov ↓ caust ↓ ign ↓
    - **tearing** pain: bov caust ign
  - **applications** | **amel**.: acon ars k2 caust
  - **water**:
    - **agg**.: sulph ↓
      - **tearing** pain: sulph
- **cold**; after taking a: kali-c h2
- **combing** hair agg.: merc-i-f k* nat-sil fd3.de•
- **compressed**; as if: acon b7.de* aeth bg2 alum b4.de* bar-c b4.de* bell b4.de* bov b4.de* bry b7.de* calc b4.de* chin b7.de* mag-c b4.de* mag-m b4.de* meny b7.de* phel bg2 rhus-t b7.de* sabin b7.de* sars b4.de* spig b7.de* sul-ac b4.de* sulph b4.de* zinc b4.de*
- **cough** agg.; during: anac ↓ apis aur *Bry* ↓ cimic cimx ↓ dirc k* mang sulph ↓ vib
  - **boring** pain: aur k*
  - **cutting** pain: mang
  - **shooting** pain: mang k*
  - **stitching** pain: anac h2 *Bry* cimx k* mang sulph k*
- **cramping**: bell k* phos k* sars k* thuj k*

- **cutting** pain: arg-n *Arn* k* aur *Bell* k* *Calc* carb-ac a1 *Chel* cic k* cocc coli rly4• cot a1 hura iris kali-bi k* kalm a1 *Lach* k* mang nat-m k* nat-p k* rumx sep a1 spig stann a1 stry a1 tarent
  - **knife**; as with a: *Arn* k*
- **dinner**; after: bar-c↓ *Form* k* mag-c↓ mag-s↓ nit-ac ol-an↓ paeon k* phos↓ **Thuj**↓ zinc↓
  - **boring** pain: zinc k*
  - **drawing** pain: phos h2 zinc h2
  - **nail**; as from a: **Thuj**
  - **pressing** pain: zinc h2
  - **stitching** pain: bar-c k* mag-c k* zinc k*
  - **tearing** pain: mag-c h2 mag-s ol-an zinc
- **drawing** pain: *Acon* k* alum k* alum-p k2 anac k* ang k* ant-t apis *Arg-met* arg-n k* arn asaf bar-act bar-c bar-s k2 bell brom k* bry calc k* camph k* canth k* caps k* carb-v k* caust *Cham* k* chin k* cimx cina k* clem k* cocc colch coloc k* dig k* dros k* fl-ac k* gran grat k* guaj h2 hell k* indg k* iod ip *Kali-c* kali-n k* kali-p lach k* led lyc m-arct b7.de m-aust b7.de meny k* nat-s k* nit-ac nit-s-d a1 nux-v k* ph-ac phos k* plat k* rhus-t ruta h1 sars sep spong k* stann h2 suis-pan rly4• sul-ac thuj k* valer k* vanil fd5.de
  - **forward**: hell h1
  - **tearing** pain: phos h2 thuj
  - **twitching**: plat
- **dull** pain: agath-a nl2• canth croc dros ketogl-ac rly4• laur k* nat-ox rly4• oxal-a rly4• plac-s rly4• podo fd3.de• ruta fd4.de spong suis-em rly4• zinc
- **eating** | **after**:
  - **agg.**: *Ars* bar-c bell calc-s coc-c form ham kali-c lach mag-c nit-ac↓ nux-v paeon phos zinc
    - **bursting** pain: nit-ac h2
  - **amel.**: calc-p colch form ham a1 nat-m
- **exerting**:
  - **arms**: nat-s↓
    - **stitching** pain: nat-s k*
  - **eyes** and head: hyper↓
    - **stitching** pain: hyper
- **foreign** body; as from a: *Con*
- **fright** agg.: cic↓
  - **stitching** pain: cic k*
- **gnawing** pain: bell h1 phos k* *Thuj* k*
- **hammering** pain: iris
- **heat**; during: cham↓
  - **stitching** pain: cham h1
- **increases** gradually and ceases suddenly: arg-met↓
  - **drawing** pain | **torn**; as if a nerve had been: arg-met
- **internal**, while leaning head against wall: cann-s↓
  - **pressing** pain: cann-s k*
- **jar** agg.: ars k2 **Bell** *Lyc* **Spig** k*
- **jerking** pain: aeth k* alum calc h2 caust *Chin* k* graph k* kreos nat-m nicc nit-ac *Nux-v* b7.de* sabin spig spong h1
- **lancinating**: bell k* *Calc* cocc hura kali-bi k* plac-s rly4• spig staphycoc rly4• tarent k*
- **leaning** on the affected side: *Ars* k* chin k*
- **light**; from bright: cact k* spong fd4.de ziz a1
- **looking** | **intently** | **agg.**: thuj k*
  - **upward**:
    - **agg.**: caps↓
      - **pressing** pain: caps h1
      - **stitching** pain: caps k*
- **lying**:
  - **agg.**: carb-v petr petr-ra shn4• rhod sep k* spong verat-v hr1
    - **pressing** pain: spong h1
  - **amel.**: dig lyc↓ spig k2 vanil fd5.de
    - **tearing** pain: lyc spig k2
  - **must** lie down: *Con*↓
    - **tearing** pain: *Con*
- **lying**: ...
  - **side**; on:
    - **painful** side:
      - **amel.**: anac arn bry hipp ign plan puls sep
        - **sore**: plan
      - **impossible**: staph↓
        - **sore**: staph h1
    - **painless** side:
      - **amel.**: mag-c *Nux-v*
        - **sore**: nux-v
        - **stitching** pain: mag-c k*
    - **right**:
      - **hands** over head; with | **amel.**: brom
    - **Side** lain on: *Ars* bry k2* calad calc k* carb-v chel *Chin* mag-c nit-ac *Nux-m* *Nux-v* k* ph-ac puls *Spong* stann staph
    - **Side** not lain on: calc-ar k* *Graph* k* puls k*
- **menses**:
  - **after** | **agg.**: *Ferr*
  - **before**:
    - **agg.**: calc-p cinnb puls tritic-vg fd5.de
      - **stitching** pain: calc-p k*
  - **during**:
    - **agg.**: am-m ars berb calc calc-p castm chin cic colch cycl glon↓ lach↓ lob lyc mag-c mag-m nat-c nux-v puls *Sang* sep verat
      - **bursting** pain: glon lach
      - **stitching** pain: *Calc-p* mag-m k*
      - **tearing** pain: mag-c nat-c
- **mental** exertion agg.: hyper ign phos vanil fd5.de
- **milk** agg.: *Brom* k*
- **motion**:
  - **agg.**: agn arg-n ars bell calc-p k* chin dirc k* glon hipp k* mang k* *Nux-v* ph-ac phos prun sabad sil **Spig** k*
    - **boring** pain: bell h1
    - **drawing** pain: arg-n
    - **sore**: *Chin*
    - **stitching** pain: sil k*
    - **tearing** pain: **Spig**
  - **amel.**: *Agar* *Iris* kali-i k2
    - **pressing** pain: kali-i k2
    - **tearing** pain: kali-i k2
- **nail**; as from a: acon k* *Agar* carb-v bg2 chel k* *Coff* k* **Hep** k* *Ign* k* m-ambo b7.de *Nat-m* k* *Nux-v* k* plat bg2 ruta k* staph k* **Thuj**
  - **driven** outward, lying on it amel.; as if a nail were: **Ign**
- **noise** agg.: cact manc phys k* spig k2 ziz a1
  - **tearing** pain: spig k2
- **paroxysmal**: *(↗paroxysmal)* acon *Ars* kali-c k* puls sec bg2 *Sep* verat bg2
- **periodical**: *Chel*↓ *Graph* kali-bi
  - **shooting** pain: *Chel*
- **pinching** pain: calc k* crot-h k* lyc k* mez petr k* sep k* squil k* [heroin sdj2]
- **plug**; as from a: *Asaf* dulc **Hep** *Plat*
- **pressing** pain: acon k* aeth agar agath-a nl2• agn alum k* alum-p k2 am-m k* anac k* ang k* arg-met arn arum-t *Asaf* k* *Asar* k* atro a1 aur h2 *Bar-c* bar-s k2 **Bell** k* bov k* bry k* *Cact* *Calc* k* calc-i k2 cann-s k* *Caps* carb-an caust cedr k* *Chel* chin k* choc srj3• cic h1* clem k* coca coloc com con k* cor-r k* crot-h k* cupr dig k* dios dros euph fl-ac *Glon* k* grat k* guaj h2 *Hell* k* **Hep** k* hydr-ac k* ign iod kali-bi k* *Kali-i* kali-n k* kalm ketogl-ac rly4• kreos lac-h htj1• laur k* lil-t k* lyc lyss k* mag-c mag-m mang k* meny k* mez k* mur-ac k* **Nat-m** nat-s k* nat-sil fd3.de• nux-m olnd k* paeon ph-ac phos k* pip-m k* plac-s rly4• *Psor* rheum rhus-t ruta fd4.de sabad *Sabin* k* samb *Sars* k* sep k* **Spig** spong squil stann staph stront-c suis-em rly4• sul-i k2 sulph tab k* *Thuj* k* tritic-vg fd5.de vanil fd5.de verat k* verb k* viol-t zinc k* zinc-p k2
  - **all** sides, from: *Acon* tarax k*
  - **alternating** with | **stitches** in sides of head: anac h2*
  - **asunder**: *Cor-r* k* kali-bi bg2 merc b4.de* *Spig*

- **pressing** pain: ...
  - **band**; as from a: | **tied** around: dios k*
  - **behind** and before, from: nux-m spong
  - **blunt** instrument, as if from (See instrument)
  - **board**; like a heavy: eug k* irid-met srj5•
  - **burning** pain: mang h2 staph h1
  - **downward**: calc k* con k*
  - **foreign** body; as from a: con
  - **forward**: bar-c h2 hell h1 verb h
  - **hoop**; as from a: ther
  - **instrument**; as from a blunt: asaf calc h2 dulc hep olnd ruta
  - **inward**: agath-a nl2• asaf bar-c bell *Bov* calc croc dulc kali-c lyss k* mag-c nat-s k* olnd k* plat sars spong fd4.de staph h1 sul-ac sulph zinc
  - **jerking** pain: dig h2
  - **outward**: *Asaf* k* asar k* bell cina cor-r bg2* dros kreos merc nicc bg2 paull a1 ph-ac spig spong stann k* verb viol-t k*
  - **screw** behind each ear; as from a: ox-ac
  - **screwed** together; as if: am-m h2 bar-c h2 bell h1 mag-c h2 plut-n srj7• zinc h2
  - **stupefying**, as with blunt instrument: dulc h2 olnd ruta
  - **vise**; as if in a: kali-i k2
  - **weight**; as from a: con b4.de*
- **pressure**:
  - **agg.**: aesc ↓ agar ang ↓ kali-c h2 stram
    - **cutting** pain: aesc
    - **sore**: ang h1
    - **stitching** pain: kali-c h2
    - **Temples** agg.; pressure of spectacles on: lyc h2
  - **amel.**: aeth hr1 cit-ac rly4• mez plan a1 sulph **Thuj** ↓ vanil fd5.de
    - **dull** pain: mez h2
    - **nail**; as from a: **Thuj**
- **pulled**; sensation as if hair were: phos h2
- **pulsating** pain: aeth a1 arg-n k* *Ars* aur h2 bell k* *Brom* k* *Cact* k* calc-p k* carb-ac k* con k* corn a1 falco-pe nl2• hir rsj4• hura kali-c h2 laur k* nat-c h2 *Nit-ac* k* puls ruta fd4.de sec zinc k*
- **raising** head agg.: cact k*
- **reading**:
  - **agg.**: lyc h2
    - **stitching** pain: lyc k*
    - **Mastoid**: aesc ↓
      - **tearing** pain: aesc
- **rheumatic**: sep ↓
  - **drawing** pain: sep k*
- **riding** agg.: naja
- **rising**:
  - **after** | **agg.**: chin graph *Spig* k*
  - **agg.**: lyc ↓
    - **tearing** pain: lyc
  - **amel.**: carb-v dig graph k* indg merc-i-r a1 ol-an rhod tab
  - **bed**; from:
    - **amel.**: carb-v ↓
      - **pressing** pain: carb-v h2
  - **stooping**; from:
    - **agg.**: kali-c mang sul-ac
      - **pressing** pain: kali-c
      - **tearing** pain: mang
- **room**: am-m *Bov* k* euphr *Fl-ac* **Phos** sabad
  - **agg.**: am-m ↓
    - **pressing** pain: (↗ *warm - room - entering - pressing*) am-m h2
    - **stitching** pain: am-m k*
  - **amel.**: mag-s
- **rubbing** | **amel.**: chinin-ar
- **screwed** together; as if: sabad bg2
- **shaking** the head agg.; on: trom k*
- **shooting** pain: acon aesc aeth agar k* aloe alum am-c am-m anac arg-n bar-c calc k* camph canth caust cham *Chel* cocc con des-ac rbp6 *Ferr* k* fl-ac iris kali-c lach lil-t k* mag-c mag-m mang k* meny nat-m phos k* phys k* plan k* *Prun* rhod a1 rumx sabin sars spong fd4.de stann k* suprar rly4• tarent k* upa a1
- **sitting**:
  - **agg.**: am-m canth chinin-s fago k* indg mag-c nicc phos rat rhod sulph tritic-vg fd5.de
    - **boring** pain: phos h2 tritic-vg fd5.de
    - **stitching** pain: mag-c k* tritic-vg fd5.de
    - **tearing** pain: am-m mag-c phos
  - **amel.**: ars calad con
  - **must** sit: cic k2 con ↓
    - **stitching** pain: con h2
- **sitting** down agg.: rat ↓
  - **stitching** pain: rat k*
- **skull** feels smaller: grat ↓
  - **pressing** pain: grat
- **sneezing** agg.: am-m arn **Bell** grat *Spig*
- **sore**: ambr ars benz-ac bov *Chin* k* con crot-h eup-per grat ip h1 kali-ar k2 kali-i laur lil-t m-arct b7.de mag-c k* merc-i-f mez nat-m nit-ac **Nux-v** k* petr phyt plan plat rat *Rhus-t* **Ruta** k* sil staph sulph k* zinc h2
  - **wandering** pain: ind
- **sound** of talking: cact
- **squeezed**; as if: squil b7.de*
- **standing** agg.: calc canth dig kali-c mag-c mang plb vanil fd5.de zinc
  - **boring** pain: zinc h2
  - **bursting** pain: zinc
  - **stitching** pain: mag-c k* vanil fd5.de
  - **tearing** pain: mang h2
- **stepping** agg.: ars k2 calc-p k* *Lyc* **Spig** k*
  - **tearing** pain: **Spig**
- **stitching** pain: aeth k* alum k* alum-p k2 alum-sil k2 am-c am-m anac k* asaf k* aur aur-s k2 bar-c k* bar-i k2 bar-m bell *Berb* k* borx k* bov k* brom k* bry calc k* calc-i k2 calc-p k* calc-sil k2 camph cann-s k* canth k* caps k* carb-ac carb-v h2 castm caust k* cham k* chel k* chin h1 cic k* cinnb coc-c cocc con k* crot-h k* cupr k* cycl k* dig k* eup-pur euph k* euphr k* eupi k* ferr ferr-p gamb k* graph k* grat k* guaj k* hyos hyper indg k* iod k* *Kali-bi* k* kali-c k* kali-m k2 kali-p **Kali-s** kali-sil k2 lach k* laur k* *Mag-c* k* *Mag-m* k* mag-s k* mang k* meny merc-c k* mez mill k* mur-ac k* nat-c k* *Nat-m* k* nat-p nat-s nicc k* nit-ac k* *Nux-v* k* ol-an k* petr k* ph-ac k* phos k* plat k* plb k* puls k* rat k* rhod ruta fd4.de sars k* sep k* sil k* spig k* spong fd4.de staph sul-i k2 sulph tarax k* *Tarent* thuj k* tong a1 tritic-vg fd5.de urt-u a1 vanil fd5.de verb *Zinc* k* zinc-p k2
  - **alternating** with | **pressing** in sides of head (See pressing - alternating - stitches)
  - **backward**: mag-c
  - **burning**: phos h2 staph k*
  - **forward**: kali-c mag-c mag-m mang thuj h1 verb h*
  - **intermittent**: plat h2 spig h1
  - **nail**; as from a: carb-v h2 ham fd3.de•
  - **outward**: mag-c mag-m h2 staph h1
  - **pulsating** pain: aeth calc petr h2 tong a1
  - **tearing** pain: carb-v h2 con h2* sars k* spig k* thuj h1
  - **wandering** pain: *Kali-bi* tarent
- **stool** agg.; during: **Spig** k*
- **stooping**:
  - **agg.**: alum ang calc-act caps chinin-s cor-r k* dig euphr k* glon hep hipp k* indg laur k* mang ↓ phos puls sil ↓
    - **pressing** pain: caps h1 cor-r k*
    - **stitching** pain: alum k* caps k* hep k* mang h2
    - **tearing** pain: mang sil
  - **amel.**: dig iris
- **stunning** pain: asaf daph dulc euph hell h1 *Mez* olnd stann h2 sul-ac verb
- **sudden**: asaf ↓
  - **pressing** pain | **blunt** instrument; as from a: asaf

Head

- **supper**:
  - **after**:
    - **agg.**: sulph↓
      - **pressing** pain: sulph h2
    - **amel.**: sulph
- **syphilis**: kali-i k2
- **talking** agg.: canth↓ fl-ac↓ ign k* spig↓ thuj↓
  - **pressing** pain: fl-ac ign thuj
  - **stitching** pain: canth k*
  - **tearing** pain: spig k2
- **tearing** pain: aesc aeth agar alum alum-p k2 am-c am-m ambr ammc *Anac Arg-met* arg-n ars aur aur-m-n aur-s k2 bar-c k* bar-m borx bov brom bry *Canth* caps k* *Carb-an Carb-v* carbn-s castm caust *Cham Chel* chin k* cic cina coc-c colch *Coloc* con croc dig *Gran Graph* grat *Guaj* hell k* ign k* indg *Kali-c* kali-i k2 kali-m k2 kali-p kali-sil k2 laur led lith-c *Lyc* m-arct b7.de mag-c mag-m k* *Mang Merc Merl* mez mill *Mur-ac* nat-ar nat-c nat-s nicc nux-v ol-an phel k* phos plb *Puls* rat rhod ruta sars sel sep *Sil* st *Spig* stann stront-c sul-ac sulph teucr k* thuj til verb **Zinc** zinc-p k2
  - **drawing** pain: bov *Caps* mang h2 phos h2 *Zinc*
  - **forward**: indg
  - **glowing**: sulph h2
  - **intermittent**: ant-t spig h1
  - **inward**: mag-c
  - **pulsating** pain: ars
  - **stinging**: mang h2 sars
  - **twitching**: teucr
  - **upward**: phos
- **toothache** on same side, with: staph↓
  - **pressing** pain: staph h1
- **torn**; as if: nux-v k* sulph k*
- **touch**:
  - **agg.**: agar agn bar-c↓ borx cupr dirc laur merc-i-f k* nit-ac petr↓ thuj↓ vanil fd5.de
    - **nail**; as from a: thuj cp
    - **sore**: petr h2
    - **tearing** pain: bar-c h2
  - **amel.**: bry dros↓ thuj
    - **sore**: dros h1
- **turning**:
  - **eyes**:
    - **affected** side; to: con k*
    - **outward**: raph k*
    - **painful** side agg.; to the: con↓
      - **pressing** pain: con h2
      - **sore**: con
  - **head**:
    - **right** agg.; to: mag-s↓
      - **stitching** pain: mag-s k*
- **uncovering** | **amel.**: kali-n c1
- **waking**; on: thuj↓
  - **stitching** pain: thuj k*
- **walking**:
  - **about**:
    - **amel.**: *Agar*↓
      - **nail**; as from a: *Agar*
  - **agg.**: arg-met arg-n ars bell calc castm↓ clem con kali-c *Lyc* mez nat-m plb **Spig** trom k*
    - **burrowing**: clem h2
    - **pressing** pain: clem h2
    - **tearing** pain: castm **Spig**
  - **air**; in open:
    - **agg.**: agar↓ alum chinin-s grat ign kali-c↓ mag-s **Spig** thuj↓
      - **burrowing**: agar
      - **tearing** pain: kali-c h2 thuj h1*
    - **amel.**: ars k2 *Iris* kali-i k2 mang merc-i-r **Phos**
- **walking – air**; in open – **amel.**: ...
      - **pressing** pain: *Kali-i* mang h2 phos h2
      - **tearing** pain: kali-i k2
  - **rapidly** | **agg.**: sep
- **wandering** pain: nat-s k*
- **warm**:
  - **applications**:
    - **amel.**: kali-i k2 lach *Nux-v*
      - **cutting** pain: lach
      - **pressing** pain: kali-i k2
  - **bed**:
    - **amel.**: caust↓
      - **drawing** pain: caust
  - **room**:
    - **entering** a warm room; when: phos↓
      - **air**; from open: spong
      - **pressing** pain: *(↗room - agg. - pressing)* phos h2
- **warmth**:
  - **amel.**: kali-i↓
    - **tearing** pain: kali-i k2
- **weather**; wet:
  - **amel.**: caust↓
    - **tearing** pain: caust
- **writing** agg.: gels k* lyc h2* vanil fd5.de
  - **inclined** to left; with head: chinin-s
- ▽ **extending** to:
  - **Arm**: cimx fago
  - **Arm**; down: cimx↓
    - **stitching** pain: cimx
  - **Backward**: mag-c mag-s verat-v
  - **Behind** ears: caust↓
    - **drawing** pain: caust
  - **Brain**; deep into: anac↓ indg↓
    - **stitching** pain: anac indg
  - **Clavicle**: ind↓
    - **drawing** pain: ind
  - **Down** neck into face and teeth: lyc↓
    - **tearing** pain: lyc
  - **Downward**: hyper bg1 ign bg1 kali-n b4a.de lyc b4a.de mez b4a.de nat-c b4a.de stann b4a.de
  - **Ear**: ars-met chinin-s grat hura↓ lyc h2 *Merc* ruta fd4.de
    - **lancinating**: hura
    - **tearing** pain: lyc *Merc*
    - **Behind**: pic-ac
  - **Ears**: grat↓
    - **sore**: grat
  - **Eye**: (non:ars slp) ars-met slp *Asaf* brom calc caust crot-h dioxi rbp6 dulc fd4.de hura↓ mag-m nat-m *Prun*↓ ruta fd4.de tritic-vg fd5.de vanil fd5.de
    - **lancinating**: hura
    - **shooting** pain: *Prun*
    - **stitching** pain: calc mag-m k*
    - **tearing** pain: *Mag-m*
  - **Eyebrows**: chinin-s k*
  - **Eyes**: crot-h↓ dulc↓ *Lyss*↓ vanil↓
    - **pressing** pain: dulc fd4.de *Lyss* vanil fd5.de
    - **sore**: crot-h
  - **Face**: anac↓ cupr↓ kali-bi kreos↓
    - **drawing** pain: cupr
    - **stitching** pain: kali-bi
    - **tearing** pain: anac c1 kreos
  - **Forehead**: agn↓ bry↓ con↓ hydr-ac↓ iod mur-ac↓ phos↓ sars bg1 sil sul-ac↓ vanil fd5.de
    - **drawing** pain: bry phos h2 sul-ac h2
    - **pressing** pain: hydr-ac
    - **stitching** pain: agn a1 con h2 mur-ac h2 sil

- **extending** to: ...
  - **Forward**: ant-c con guaj kali-c mang verb c1
  - **Frontal** bone: con↓ guaj↓
    - **stitching** pain: con guaj
  - **Hand**:
    - **right**: phos bg1
      - **shooting** pain: phos
  - **Jaw**: ketogl-ac rly4•
  - **Jaw**; lower: hura↓
    - **lancinating**: hura
  - **Nape** of neck: elaps sars tritic-vg fd5.de vanil fd5.de
    - **stitching** pain: sars vanil fd5.de
  - **Neck**: anac↓ chel cupr cupr-act↓ *Lach* lyc *Merc* spong↓
    - **drawing** pain: *Chel* cupr-act lyc spong fd4.de
    - **tearing** pain: anac c1
  - **Nose**; root of: phos bg1
    - **shooting** pain: phos
  - **Occiput**: cic↓ clem↓ lach mag-c↓ nux-m phos tab tritic-vg fd5.de vanil fd5.de
    - **boring** pain: mag-c h2
    - **burrowing**: clem k*
    - **stitching** pain: cic h1 mag-c h2 phos tab
  - **Orbit**: mur-ac↓
    - **stitching** pain: mur-ac h2
  - **Orbits**: crot-h↓ stann↓
    - **drawing** pain: crot-h stann h2
    - **pressing** pain: stann h2
  - **Scapula**: *Chel*
  - **Shoulders**: caust *Lach*
  - **Side** to side; from: carb-v clem mag-c↓ *Nat-m* plan rhus-t
    - **line**; like a (See line)
    - **stitching** pain: carb-v mag-c h2
    - **tearing** pain: clem rhus-t
  - **Teeth**: crot-h graph iod↓ lyc h2 *Merc* nat-m↓ rhus-t↓ ruta fd4.de
    - **drawing** pain: crot-h iod nat-m h2
    - **sore**: crot-h rhus-t h1
  - **Teeth** and glands of throat: graph↓ merc↓
    - **tearing** pain: graph merc
  - **Temple**: iod↓
    - **drawing** pain: iod h
  - **Temple**, toward: iod↓ kali-n↓
    - **pressing** pain: iod h kali-n
  - **Temples**: bell hura↓ kali-bi melal-alt gya4 verat-v a1
    - **lancinating**: hura
  - **Vertex**: *Mang*↓ meny↓ spong↓
    - **stitching** pain: meny h1 spong fd4.de
    - **tearing** pain: *Mang*
  - **Waist**: lyss

○ - **Brain**: grat↓ mez↓
  - **pressing** pain:
    - **against** the bone; as if brain were pressing: mez
    - **lying** on it; as if something were: grat
- **Side** lain on: bar-c↓ carb-v↓ mag-c↓ **Nit-ac**↓ ph-ac↓
  - **drawing** pain: ph-ac
  - **pressing** pain: carb-v h2 ph-ac
  - **shooting** pain: mag-c
  - **sore**: bar-c **Nit-ac**
- **Side** not lain on: *Rhus-t*↓
  - **sore**: *Rhus-t*
- **Side** toward which he bends: chin↓
  - **pressing** pain: chin h1
- **Spot**; in a: spig↓
  - **stitching** pain: spig h1
- **Spot**; in a small: ferr-ma a1 *Kali-bi*
- **Spots**; in: agar↓ ambr↓ ang↓ ant-c↓ bar-c↓ hep↓ phos↓ plat↓ spig↓ sulph↓ zinc↓

- **Sides – Spots**; in: ...
  - **boring** pain: hep k*
  - **drawing** pain: phos k*
  - **sore**: agar ambr ang h1 ant-c plat sulph zinc h2
  - **tearing** pain: bar-c spig h1
- **Sinuses**:
  - **inflammation** of; from (See forehead - frontal; FACE - Pain - sinuses; NOSE - Pain - sinuses)
  - **suppressed** inflammation of; from: dulc mrr1
- **Skin** of head were sore: nux-v↓
  - **sore**: nux-v a1*
- **Skin**; below the: calc↓ carb-v↓ graph↓ iod↓ kreos↓ nit-ac↓ nux-v↓ petr↓ phos↓ *Rhod*↓ rhus-t↓ ruta↓ stann↓ sul-ac↓ tarax↓ zinc↓
  - **ulcerative** pain: calc b4.de* carb-v b4.de* graph b4.de* iod b4.de* kreos b7a.de nit-ac b4.de* nux-v b7.de* petr b4.de* phos b4.de* *Rhod* b4.de* rhus-t b7.de* ruta b7.de* stann b4.de* sul-ac b4a.de tarax b7.de* zinc b4.de*
- **Skull**: des-ac rbp6 hep↓ mez ptk1 pneu↓ thres-a sze7•
  - **bursting** pain: hep bg2
  - **fractured**: bell tl1 glon tl1
  - **neuralgic**: pneu jl2
- **Spot**; in a small: *Acon* bg2 agar bg2 alum h2* am-m a1 ambr h1* amp rly4• anac bg2 ant-c bg2 arge-pl rwt5• borx bg2 cann-xyz bg2* carb-v k* caust k* colch k* dulc h2* eupi k* ferr bg2* ferr-ma k* germ-met srj5• gink-b sbd1• graph k* helon k* hep k* hydr-ac k* hydrog srj2• ign bg2* irid-met srj5• *Kali-bi* k* kali-i ptk1 kali-s fkr2.de *Kalm* k* lach k* lact laur bg2 led bg2 lith-c lyc bg2 mosch bg2 nat-c bg2 nux-m *Nux-v* bg2 ol-an bg2 ox-ac k* pert-vc vk9 phos k* plan plat bg2 podo fd3.de• psil ft1 psor k* ran-b a1 ran-s k* rat sang k* sep bg2 sil bg2 sol-ni spig k* squil bg2 staph bg2 sul-ac sulph k* symph fd3.de• tell k* thuj k* vinc vip fkr4.de zinc k*

▽ - **extending** to | **All** directions: melal-alt gya4 thea br1
- **Spots**; in: acon↓ aloe↓ ambr↓ arg-n↓ ars↓ asar↓ *Bell*↓ cic↓ *Colch*↓ con↓ dig↓ dulc↓ ger-i↓ glon↓ graph↓ helo↓ helo-s↓ ictod↓ ign↓ *Kali-bi*↓ lyc↓ mang↓ meph↓ nat-s↓ nit-ac↓ nux-m↓ nux-v↓ *Ox-ac*↓ ph-ac↓ plat↓ psor↓ ran-s↓ raph↓ sang↓ *Sil*↓ sinus↓ thuj↓ zinc↓
  - **burning**: ars glon k* graph nit-ac raph
  - **gnawing** pain: nat-s bro1 ran-s bro1
  - **pressing** pain: acon arg-n bro1 asar *Bell* k* cic con h2* dig k* dulc k* ger-i rly4• glon k* ictod bro1 ign k* *Kali-bi* bro1 meph k* nit-ac nux-m c1 nux-v ox-ac ph-ac plat bro1 psor sinus rly4• thuj k* zinc
  - **sore**: ambr helo c1 helo-s c1* mang k2 *Ox-ac* k* sang hr1 *Sil*
  - **tearing** pain: aloe *Colch* lyc ph-ac
- **Spots**; in small: hist↓
  - **burning**: hist sp1
- **Sutures**:

○ - **Along**: agar bg2 **Calc-p** k* coloc h2 des-ac rbp6 **Fl-ac** k* glon bg1 kali-bi bg2 spira a1 staph ptk1
    - **Forehead** and Temporal bone | **left**: ulm-c jsj8•
  - **Coronal**: cycl↓
    - **stitching** pain: cycl a1
- **Temples**: abrom-a ks5 acet-ac↓ acon k* act-sp adam↓ aesc k* aeth agar k* *Agath-a* nl2• *Agn*↓ ail *All-c* k* aloe *Alum* alum-p k2 alum-sil k2 alumn↓ *Am-br*↓ am-c↓ am-caust↓ am-m h2* ambr **Anac** k* anan androc srj1• ang a1 ant-c↓ *Ant-t*↓ anthraq rly4• ap-g vml3• *Apis* apoc k* *Aq-mar* skp7• **Arg-met** arg-n *Arn* k* ars k* *Ars-i* k* ars-s-f↓ arum-m↓ arum-t k* *Asaf*↓ asar k* asim a1 aspar k* aster k* *Atro* k* aur k* aur-ar k2 aur-i↓ aur-m↓ aur-m-n↓ aur-s k2 bac tl1 *Bad* k* bamb-a↓ *Bapt* k* bar-act↓ bar-c bar-i k2 bar-m bar-s k2 **Bell** k* benz-ac k* berb k* *Bism*↓ *Bit-ar* wht1• blatta-o↓ bomb-pr↓ bond↓ borx bov↓ brass-n-o↓ brom k* bry k* bufo↓ buth-a sp1 cact↓ cadm-met tpw6 cadm-s↓ calad↓ calc calc-i a1* calc-met↓ calc-p k* calc-s↓ calc-sil k2 camph k* cann-i k* cann-s k* canth↓ caps k* **Carb-ac** k* carb-an k* **Carb-v**↓ carbn-s carc mlr1• card-b↓ carl a1 cartl-s rly4• casc↓ cassia-s↓ castm↓ castor-eq↓ caul↓ caust k* cedr k* cent a1 *Cham* k* *Chel* **Chin** k* chinin-ar↓ chinin-s k* chion br1 chlam-tr↓ chlol chlor↓ choc srj3• chord-umb rly4• cic k* *Cimic* hr1 cina *Cinnb* k* cit-ac↓ cit-v a1 clem k* cob k* cob-n sp1 coc-c k* coca↓ coca-c↓ *Cocc* cod↓ coff colch coli rly4• coloc k* colocin a1 com↓ con k* conch↓ cop↓ cor-r k* corn *Croc*↓ *Crot-c*↓ crot-h k* crot-t k* cupr cupr-ar k* cupr-s↓ **Cycl** k* cystein-l rly4• *Daph* k* der a1 des-ac↓ *Dig*↓ digin a1 dios k* dirc a1 dor a1 dros k* *Dulc*↓ echi elaps elat k* epiph bro1 euon a1 eup-per k* euph↓ euphr k*

Temples: ...
eupi k* fago ↓ falco-pe ↓ *Ferr* ferr-ar ferr-i *Ferr-m* k* ferr-p fic-m gya1 *Fl-ac* k* form k* franz ↓ galeoc-c-h gms1• gamb ↓ gard-j vlr2• gast ↓ *Gels* k* genist ↓ gent-c gent-ch bnj1 gent-l k* ger-i rly4• germ-met ↓ gink-b sbd1• gins a1 glon k* gran ↓ granit-m ↓ graph k* grat ↓ *Guaj* ↓ gymno haem ↓ haliae-lc srj5• ham k* helia ↓ hell k* helodr-cal ↓ hep *Hipp* k* hist sp1 hom-xyz br1 hura hydr k* hydr-ac k* hyos k* hyper k* ign k* ignis-alc ↓ *Ind* indg ↓ inul ↓ iod k* *Ip* irid-met vml3• *Iris* k* jac-c ↓ *Jatr-c* *Jug-c* jug-r ↓ *Kali-bi* k* *Kali-br* ↓ **Kali-c** k* kali-chl k* kali-cy ↓ **Kali-i** ↓ kali-m k2 kali-n ↓ kali-p kali-s kali-sil k2 kalm k* ketogl-ac rly4• kola stb3• **Kreos** k* **Lac-c** lac-d lac-del hrn2• lac-e hrn2• lac-h ↓ lac-lup ↓ *Lach* k* lachn k* lact ↓ laur k* lec led k* lepi a1 lept k* lil-t ↓ limen-b-c mlk9.de linu-c a1 lith-c lob k* lob-s ↓ lol ↓ **Lyc** k* lycps-v *Lyss* k* m-arct ↓ m-aust ↓ *Mag-c* k* *Mag-m* k* mag-s ↓ manc k* mand sp1 *Mang* med meli k* menis a1 meny ↓ *Merc* k* merc-c k* merc-i-f k* merl k* *Mez* k* mim-h ↓ mim-p ↓ moni rfm1• mosch k* mur-ac k* murx myric k* nad rly4• *Naja* k* nat-ar nat-c k* nat-m k* nat-ox rly4• nat-p nat-s nat-sil ↓ neon srj5• nept-m ↓ nicc ↓ nicotam rly4• nit-ac nit-s-d ↓ nuph k* **Nux-m** k* *Nux-v* k* oci-sa ↓ ol-an ↓ ol-j k* olib-sac ↓ olnd a1 onos k* *Op* k* oreo bro1 orig a1* orot-ac rly4• osm k* ost a1 ox-ac k* oxal-a rly4• ozone ↓ paeon ↓ pall k* pana a1 **Par** paull a1 ped ↓ peti a1 *Petr* k* petr-ra shn4• *Ph-ac* k* phasco-ci rbp2 *Phel* bro1 phos k* phys k* phyt k* pic-ac k* pieri-b mlk9.de pip-m ↓ pitu-gl skp7• plac ↓ plac-s rly4• plan k* **Plat** k* *Plb* k* plumbg a1 plut-n srj7• podo k* polys ↓ *Positr* ↓ pot-e rly4• *Prun* ↓ prun-p ↓ psor k* ptel k* **Puls** ran-b k* *Ran-s* ↓ raph k* rat ↓ rheum rhod k* *Rhus-t* k* rhus-v ↓ ribo rly4• rob k* rumx *Ruta* *Sabad* k* **Sabin** sal-ac ↓ sal-fr sle1• samb ↓ *Sang* k* sanguis-s ↓ sapin a1 *Sars* ↓ sec sel *Senec* bro1 seneg b4.de* *Sep* k* serp ↓ sil k* sin-n a1 sol-ni spig k* spira a1 spong ↓ *Squil* ↓ *Stann* k* staph k* stict ↓ still a1 stram k* streptoc rly4• stront-c ↓ stry k* succ-ac rly4• suis-em rly4• suis-pan rly4• *Sul-ac* k* sul-i k2 sulph sumb k* suprar rly4• symph ↓ syph k2* tab k* tanac ↓ **Tarax** k* *Tarent* k* tax ↓ tell rsj10• tere-la ↓ tet a1 teucr a1 thea ↓ *Ther* ↓ **Thuj** k* til ban1• tril-p ↓ *Trios* rsj11• tritic-vg fd5.de trom a1 tub al* tus-p a1 ulm-c ↓ upa a1 (non:uran-met k) uran-n usn bro1 valer ↓ vanil fd5.de verat ↓ verat-v k* **Verb** k* vichy-g a1 viol-t k* visc sp1 vit br1 x-ray sp1 xan k* xanth yuc a1 *Zinc* k* zinc-p k2 zing a1 [*Buteo-j* sej6 heroin sdj2]

- **one** side: cham ↓
  - **drawing** pain: cham h1
- **alternating** sides: hyper ip ↓ **Lac-c**
  - **bursting** pain: ip bg1
- **right**: agar ↓ agath-a nl2• agn ↓ aloe *Alum* ↓ am-c ↓ am-m ↓ anac ↓ androc srj1• ang ↓ ant-t ↓ ap-g vh1 apis apoc ↓ arg-met ↓ arg-n ↓ ars k* ars-i k* arum-t ↓ asaf ↓ aur ↓ bamb-a stb2.de• *Bapt* a1 bar-c ↓ bell k* bism ↓ borx ↓ bov ↓ *Bry* ↓ buth-a sp1 cact k* *Calc* ↓ calc-i ↓ calc-p ↓ camph ↓ cann-i ↓ canth ↓ carb-an ↓ carb-v ↓ carc ↓ casc ↓ cassia-s ↓ *Caust* k* cedr ↓ *Cham* ↓ *Chel* chin ↓ chinin-ar ↓ cic ↓ cimic ↓ *Cina* ↓ clem ↓ cocc ↓ coff ↓ colch ↓ *Coloc* k* con ↓ cop ↓ cortico ↓ crot-c ↓ crot-h ↓ *Cycl* hr1 dendr-pol sk4• des-ac rbp6 dig ↓ dream-p sdj1• dros dulc fd4.de euphr ↓ ferr-ar *Ferr-m* k* fic-m gya1 flor-p rsj3• form ↓ galeoc-c-h gms1• *Gels* glon ↓ gran ↓ grat ↓ *Guaj* ↓ hell ↓ helo-s rwt2• *Hep* ↓ heroin ↓ hyos ↓ ign ↓ ind ↓ iod ↓ *Iris* mrr1 *Jug-c* *Kali-c* ↓ kali-n ↓ kali-s fd4.de kola stb3• kreos ↓ lac-h sk4• lachn ↓ lact ↓ laur b7.de* led ↓ lyc bg1 m-arct ↓ *Mag-c* ↓ mang ↓ melal-alt gya4 meli *Merc* ↓ mosch k* mur-ac ↓ myric ↓ *Nat-ar* nat-c ↓ nat-m ↓ nat-ox rly4• nat-p ↓ nat-s ↓ nept-m ↓ nicc ↓ nicotam ↓ *Nit-ac* ↓ nux-m ↓ *Nux-v* olib-sac ↓ olnd ↓ oxal-a rly4• ozone ↓ pall k* par ↓ petr ↓ petr-ra ↓ *Ph-ac* ↓ *Phos* ↓ plat ↓ plb ↓ positr nl2• psil ft1 ptel ↓ puls ran-b ↓ rheum ↓ rhus-t k* rob a1 ruta fd4.de sabad ↓ sabal c1 *Sabin* ↓ sang hr1* *Sars* ↓ sel ↓ seneg ↓ sil ↓ sol-ni ↓ sphing kk3.fr spig kk3.fr spira a1 spong ↓ squil ↓ *Stann* ↓ staph ↓ staphycoc ↓ stram ↓ stront-c ↓ suis-em rly4• sul-ac ↓ sulfa ↓ sulph ↓ suprar rly4• *Tarax* k* tarent ↓ teucr ↓ thuj k* tritic-vg fd5.de trom k* vac ↓ valer ↓ vanil fd5.de ven-m ↓ verat-v a1* verb k* viol-t ↓ zinc ↓ ziz k* [bell-p-sp dcm1]
  - **noon** until evening: sil ↓
    - **pressing** pain: sil h2
  - **evening**: trios rsj11•
  - **alternating** with:
    - **Front** and back of head; pain between: ptel c1
    - **Knee**; pain in right: meli k* meli-a c1
  - **boring** pain: alum a1 androc srj1• bell k* coloc k* cycl bg2 *Dulc* b4.de* form a1 *Hep* k* m-arct b7.de nat-s k* ptel k* stann b4.de*
    - **inward**: alum b4.de*

- **right**: ...
  - **burning**: alum k* aur k* bar-c k* carb-an k* caust k* cimic k* con k* mang nept-m lsd2.fr rhus-t k* sulfa sp1 viol-t k*
  - **burrowing**: clem bg2
  - **bursting** pain: *Bell* k* lac-h htj1• sang k*
  - **cramping**: kola stb3• nat-m k*
  - **cutting** pain: apoc k* *Chel* nat-p c1* ptel k* puls bg2 stram k* suprar rly4• verb [heroin sdj2]
  - **drawing** pain: ant-t b7.de* arg-n bg2 ars bg2 *Bell* k* *Calc* k* casc a1 caust k* *Cina* coff k* *Coloc* a1 m-arct b7.de mang b4.de* *Merc* k* mosch b7.de* mur-ac a1 *Nit-ac* k* petr b4.de* sabad k* sabin a1 *Sars* k* squil k* stront-c b4.de*
  - **dull** pain: agar b4.de* nicotam rly4• petr-ra shn4• positr nl2• stront-c b4.de*
  - **eating**; while: verb ↓
    - **shooting** pain: verb c1
  - **gnawing** pain: sol-ni k*
  - **jerking** pain: plb bg2 spong bg2 sul-ac k*
  - **lying** on painful side agg.: stann
    - **pressing** pain: stann
  - **nail**; as from a: spira vac jl2
  - **neuralgic**: des-ac rbp6 ozone sde2•
  - **pinching** pain: crot-h k* merc k* olnd k*
  - **plug**; as from a: sul-ac b4.de*
  - **pressing** pain: agar b4.de* agn b7.de* *Alum* k* anac b4.de* ant-t b7.de* apis b7a.de arg-met b7.de* arg-n a1 ars b4.de* asaf b7.de* *Bell* k* borx h2 bov b4.de* calc b4.de* camph b7.de* canth b7.de* carc tpw2* caust k* cedr *Cham* *Chel* k* cic a1 fic-m gya1 *Guaj* k* hell b7.de* hyos b7.de* ign b7.de* *Kali-c* k* kali-n b4.de* laur b7.de* led b7.de* lyc b4.de* m-arct b7.de mosch b7.de* myric a1 nept-m lsd2.fr nit-ac h2 par k* petr b4.de* *Ph-ac* k* phos h2 positr nl2* rheum b7.de* *Rhus-t* b7.de* ruta fd4.de sabad b7.de* *Sabin* b7.de* sars b4.de* sel rsj9• sil b4.de* *Spig* k* *Stann* k* staph b7.de* sul-ac b4.de* tarax b7.de* teucr b7.de* thuj b4.de* tritic-vg fd5.de vanil fd5.de verb k* zinc b4.de
    - **asunder**: sabin b7.de* staph b7.de*
    - **inward**: cocc b7.de* dulc b4.de* sabad b7.de* sabin b7.de spig b7.de* staph b7.de* valer b7.de*
    - **outward**: canth b7.de* caust dros k* glon bg2 kali-c k* laur b7a.de mur-ac k* nat-c k* nux-m k* ph-ac k* sabad k* sabin bg2 spong k* stann k* stront-c
  - **pulsating** pain: cortico tpw7 staphycoc rly4•
  - **sharp**: fic-m gya1 ven-m rsj12•
  - **shooting** pain: *Bell* calc-p k* *Iris* lac-h sk4• oxal-a rly4• sulph k* tarent k*
  - **sore**: calc-p cop dros h1 kola stb3• nicc positr nl2•
  - **squeezed**; as if: arg-met b7.de* olnd b7.de* ph-ac b4.de* plat b4.de*
  - **stitching** pain: agar k* *Alum* k* am-m b7.de* anac b4.de* ang b7.de* bar-c b4.de* *Bell* b4.de* borx k* calc-i k2 cann-i c1 canth b7.de* cassia-s ccrh1• *Caust* chin b7.de* coff k* coloc crot-c cycl b7.de* dig b4.de* euphr b7.de* grat ign b7.de* ind bg1 kali-c b4.de* kreos b7a.de *Lyc* *Mag-c* b4.de* mang b4.de* mur-ac b4.de* nux-m b7.de* olib-sac wmh1 ozone sde2• *Ph-ac* k* *Phos* k* plb b7.de* psil ft1 rhus-t b7.de* ruta fd4.de sabad b7.de* *Sars* k* squil k* staph b7.de* stront-c k* vac jl2 *Verb* b7.de* zinc b4.de*
  - **tearing** pain: agar k* agn b7.de* alum k* am-c b4.de* am-m k* arg-met b7.de* arum-t asaf bism b7.de* bov k* *Bry* b7.de* camph k* canth b7.de* carb-v b4.de* *Chel* chinin-ar cina b7.de* colch b7.de* dig k* gran a1 iod b4.de* kali-c b4.de* kreos b7a.de lachn c1 lact laur k* mag-c b4.de* mang b4.de* mur-ac k* nat-c b4.de* nat-s ozone sde2• plb b7.de* ran-b k* rhus-t k* sang seneg b4.de* sul-ac b4.de* zinc b4.de*
  - **waking**; on: kola stb3•
  - **extending** to:
    - **left**: aesc ↓ apis ↓ glon lil-t lyc ↓ nat-ar ↓ pall plat podo fd3.de• ptel sep staphycoc rly4•
      - **boring** pain: nat-ar
      - **pressing** pain: apis lyc staphycoc rly4•
      - **stitching** pain: aesc
    - **Eye**:
      - **right**: cortico ↓
        - **pulsating** pain: cortico tpw7*

- **right – extending** to: ...
  - **Occiput**; left side of: *Iris* ↓
    - **shooting** pain: *Iris*
  - **Spots**; in small: astac ↓
    - **pressing** pain: astac kr1
- **left**: acon ↓ aesc k* aeth ↓ agar k* agn ↓ alum ↓ am-c ↓ am-m ↓ ambr ↓ *Anac* ↓ ant-c ↓ ant-t ↓ ap-g vh1 apis bg2 arg-met bg2 *Arg-n* ↓ *Arn* k* ars ↓ arum-t ↓ asaf ↓ asar k* aspar aur ↓ aur-m aur-m-n ↓ bamb-a stb2.de• bar-act bar-c ↓ bell ↓ bit-ar wht1• bov ↓ brass-n-o srj5• *Brom* ↓ bry ↓ bung-fa mtf cact ↓ cadm-met tpw6 calc ↓ canth ↓ caps ↓ carb-v ↓ carbn-s ↓ *Caust* ↓ cench k2 cham ↓ *Chel* ↓ *Chin* ↓ chir-fl ↓ cic ↓ *Cimic* k* cina ↓ *Clem* ↓ cob-n sp1 coc-c ↓ cocc ↓ colch rsj2• coli rly4• *Coloc* ↓ crot-h ↓ crot-t ↓ cupr ↓ cycl hr1 cyt-l ↓ dig digin a1 dulc ↓ euphr ↓ falco-pe nl2• ferr mrr1 genist fr1 gent-c ↓ ger-i rly4• germ-met srj5• gran ↓ graph ↓ grat ↓ guaj ↓ gymno ↓ haliae-lc srj5• ham ↓ helia ↓ hell ↓ helodr-cal knl2• ignis-alc ↓ indg ↓ iod ↓ kali-bi ↓ **Kali-c** ↓ *Kali-chl* *Kali-i* ↓ kali-n h2 kali-p fd1.de• kali-s ↓ ketogl-ac rly4• kola stb3• kreos ↓ lac-cp sk4• lac-f ↓ lac-h htj1• lac-leo hrn2• *Lach* ↓ laur ↓ led ↓ limen-b-c hrn2* lith-c bg1 luf-op ↓ lyc ↓ m-arct ↓ m-aust ↓ mag-c ↓ mag-m ↓ mang ↓ meny ↓ *Merc* k* *Merl* ↓ **Mez** ↓ mim-p ↓ mur-ac k* nad rly4• naja mrr1 nat-ox rly4• nat-p ↓ nat-s ↓ nept-m ↓ nicotam rly4• *Nit-ac* ↓ nuph k* nux-m k* nux-v ↓ ol-an ↓ olib-sac wmh1 olnd ↓ onos orot-ac rly4• ox-ac k* ozone ↓ par ↓ *Petr* ↓ petr-ra shn4• *Ph-ac* ↓ *Phos* sne pip-m ↓ plac ↓ plat ↓ plb ↓ plut-n srj7• podo ↓ positr ↓ psor ↓ *Puls* ↓ pyrid rly4• ran-b ↓ ran-s ↓ rhod k* rhus-g ↓ rhus-t ↓ ruta fd4.de sabad ↓ sabin ↓ samb ↓ sang sanguis-s hrn2• sars ↓ senec ↓ **Sep** ↓ sil k* *Spig* *Spong* ↓ stann ↓ *Staph* k* staphycoc ↓ streptoc rly4• stront-c ↓ suis-em rly4• sul-ac ↓ sulph ↓ sumb k* symph ↓ *Tarax* ↓ *Thuj* mrr1 thyr ↓ *Trios* rsj11• ulm-c jsj8• upa a1 vanil fd5.de verb ↓ viol-t k* xan ↓ *Zinc* ↓ zinc-val br1
  - **afternoon**:
    - **2.30 h**: ozone ↓
      - **stitching** pain: ozone sde2•
  - **alternating** with | **Knee**; pain in right: meli
  - **boring** pain: alum k* *Arg-n* k* aur-m-n a1 bell bg2 calc k* carb-v b4.de* *Clem* k* coloc b4a.de led a1 nat-s a1 ph-ac b4.de* psor jl2 rhod k* stann b4.de*
    - **inward**: zinc b4.de*
    - **outward**: calc b4.de*
  - **burning**: am-m k* chel k* cupr k* lac-f c1 merc k* nit-ac k* plat k* sabad k* sars k* *Spig* k* staph k* verb k*
  - **burrowing**: agar bg2 bov b4.de* calc b4.de* coloc b4.de*
  - **bursting** pain: bry bg2* kreos bg2*
  - **chewing** agg.: am-c ↓
    - **cutting** pain: am-c
    - **lancinating**: am-c
  - **compressed**; as if: asar b7.de*
  - **cramping**: agar calc b4.de* indg k* kali-c k* petr b4.de* phos bg2 plat b4a.de* sil k*
  - **cutting** pain: bar-c *Coloc* k* genist guaj ignis-alc es2• *Kali-i* onos sanguis-s hrn2• senec bg2
  - **drawing** pain: ant-c k* *Arg-met* caps colch k* cupr b7.de* cycl k* dulc k* ham fd3.de• indg a1 kali-bi bg2 kreos b7a.de* *Lach* k* mang b4.de* olnd b7.de* *Petr* k* ph-ac b4.de* plat k* *Spig* k* staph h1 staphycoc rly4• sul-ac b4.de* *Tarax* k* thuj k* zinc
  - **dull** pain: limen-b-c hrn2• mim-p rsj8•
  - **hammering** pain: ham ptk1
  - **jerking** pain: acon b7.de* anac bg2 arn b7.de* bov b4.de* cact bg2 cycl a1 ol-an bg2 stann k*
  - **Muscle**: cocc ↓
    - **cramping**: cocc h1
  - **nail**; as from a: nept-m lsd2.fr
  - **neuralgic**: zinc-val br1
  - **pecking**: nit-ac h2
  - **periodical**: spig
  - **pinching** pain: kali-c k* nat-p k* ph-ac h2 zinc h2
  - **plug**; as from a: asaf b7.de* coloc bg2 kreos b7a.de staph bg2 thyr bg2
  - **pressing** pain: alum b4.de* anac b4.de* arg-met b7.de* *Asar* k* aur k* bamb-a stb2.de• bar-c b4.de* bell b4.de* brom k* calc b4.de* *Chin* k*

- **left – pressing** pain: ...
  chir-fl gya2 cina b7.de* *Coloc* k* cupr b7.de* cycl b7.de* dulc h2 graph b4.de* guaj b4.de* ham fd3.de• kali-c b4.de* kali-s fd4.de *Kola* stb3• laur b7.de* lith-c lyc b4.de* m-arct b7.de mang b4.de* meny b7.de* merc b4.de* **Mez** k* mur-ac b4.de* nux-m b7.de* olnd b7.de* par b7.de* ph-ac b4.de* plac rzf5• plat h2* podo fd3.de• positr nl2• *Puls* k* *Rhod* k* ruta fd4.de sabad b7.de* sabin b7.de* samb b7.de* sars k* spig b7.de* sulph b4.de* symph fd3.de• vanil fd5.de *Zinc* k*
    - **asunder**: calc b4.de* mez b4.de*
    - **inward**: ant-t b7.de* asaf b7.de* bell b4.de* calc b4.de* cocc b7.de* dulc b4.de* mez b4.de* ph-ac b4.de* plat b4.de* rhod b4.de* stann b4.de* staph b7.de*
    - **outward**: asaf k* carb-v k* mez k* mur-ac k* *Phos* bg2 sabin k* verb k*
    - **weight**; as from a: *Phos* bg2
  - **pulsating** pain: falco-pe nl2• luf-op rsj5• spig suis-em rly4• [helia stj7]
  - **sharp**: cadm-met tpw6
    - **followed** by | **right**: cadm-met tpw6
  - **shooting** pain: acon bg2 aeth k* anac arum-t a1 cimic k* *Merl* *Nit-ac* rhus-g tmo3• rhus-t k* sep spig xan c1
  - **sore**: cham chir-fl gya2 gymno
  - **squeezed**; as if: calc b4.de* kali-c b4.de* plat b4.de*
  - **stitching** pain: aeth alum b4.de* am-c b4.de* am-m b7a.de ambr k* anac b4.de* *Apis* b7a.de arn b7.de* ars b4.de* asaf k* bell b4.de* *Brom* b4a.de calc canth b7.de* carbn-s *Chel* k* chin b7.de* coc-c cocc k* crot-h k* crot-t a1 cupr b7.de* cycl b7.de* cyt-l sp1 dig b4.de* euphr b7.de* gent-c graph b4.de* ham fd3.de• hell b7.de* kali-c b4.de* kali-i k2 lach b7.de* laur b7.de* mag-c k* mang b4.de* meny b7.de* nept-m lsd2.fr nit-ac b4.de* nux-m b7.de* nux-v b7.de* olib-sac wmh1 ozone sde2• par b7.de* pip-m plat k* plb b7.de* ran-b b7.de* ran-s b7.de* rhod b4.de* rhus-t b7.de* sang a1 sars b4.de* *Sep* k* *Spig* k* *Spong* b7.de* *Staph* k* stront-c b4.de* sulph b4.de* symph fd3.de• tarax k* thuj bg2 verb b7.de* viol-t b7.de* zinc b4.de*
  - **stooping** agg.: nept-m ↓
    - **stitching** pain: nept-m lsd2.fr
  - **tearing** pain: acon k* agn k* alum b4.de* am-c b4.de* ambr b7.de* *Anac* k* *Arg-met* k* arn k* *Asar* k* aur b4.de* bov b4.de* carb-v b4.de* carbn-s *Caust* b4a.de chin b7.de* cic a1 cina b7.de* dulc b4.de* gran grat guaj iod b4.de* kali-bi **Kali-c** k* kreos b7a.de laur b7.de* m-aust b7.de mag-c k* mag-m k* mang b4.de* *Merc* *Ph-ac* k* plb b7.de* podo fd3.de• *Rhod* k* samb b7.de* **Sep** k* *Spig* k* staph h1 sul-ac b4.de* sulph k* viol-t b7.de* zinc b4.de*
  - **waking**; on: kola stb3•
  - **extending** to:
    - **right**: aur-m calc cocc ↓ fl-ac hr1 hipp iod ↓ irid-met srj5• merc-i-f ol-j ptel sanguis-s ↓ sulph verb ↓
      - **cutting** pain: sanguis-s hrn2•
      - **stitching** pain: calc h2 cocc verb a1
      - **tearing** pain: aur-m iod
    - **Eye**; above left: equis-h ↓
      - **cutting** pain: equis-h a1
    - **Head**; side of: **Sep** ↓
      - **tearing** pain: **Sep**
  - **Spot**; in a: ferr mrr1
- **midnight**: agar ↓
  - **burrowing**: agar k*
- **daytime**: ars calc carl ↓ cassia-s ↓ corn a1 hell hep hydr jatr-c kali-n lyss k* mez phys a1 stann
  - **boring** pain: stann k*
  - **dull** pain: cassia-s ccrh1•
  - **pressing** pain: carl k* hep h2 *Stann* k*
  - **sore**: phys
- **morning**: all-c am-c apis bar-c bov ↓ cact camph carbn-s cham ↓ chin ↓ clem cob k* colch rsj2• coloc con ↓ cop cund cycl ↓ dios k* dirc k* dulc fd4.de equis-h *Gels* graph ham k* hep ↓ ign jac-c jac-g kali-n kali-s ↓ kola stb3• lil-t k* lith-c lyss k* mez ↓ myric a1 nat-ar nat-p k* petr-ra shn4• phos plan ↓ podo positr ↓ psor k* rhus-r rhus-t k* rumx ruta fd4.de sang k* sep k* spong fd4.de sulph tarent k* thuj k* tritic-vg ↓ vanil fd5.de

- **morning**: ...
  - **9** h: pitu-gl skp7•
  - **amel.**: coca-c ↓ mag-s
    - **pressing** pain: coca-c sk4•
  - **bed** agg.; in: graph ↓
    - **pressing** pain: graph
  - **boring** pain: apis camph k* cham k* hep lyss k* mez k*
  - **dull** pain: colch rsj2•
  - **nail**; as from a: sang k*
  - **pressing** pain: apis bov k* chin h1 cycl k* kali-s fd4.de mez k* *Phos* k* positr nl2• ruta sang a1 **Sulph** tritic-vg fd5.de vanil fd5.de
  - **rising** | **after**:
    - **agg.**: nit-ac ↓ **Sulph** ↓
      - **pressing** pain: nit-ac h2 **Sulph**
  - **agg.**: aur-m cench k2 coca *Lach* lil-t k* nat-ar nit-ac spong fd4.de sulph
  - **sore**: cob plan
  - **stitching** pain: cham k* ruta fd4.de spong fd4.de
  - **tearing** pain: am-c con
  - **waking**; on: ail *Alumn* ↓ anac apis ↓ asim atro calad calc k* camph carbn-s castor-eq cench k2 coff ferr ↓ graph ind *Lach* lith-c med mez ↓ naja nat-ar nat-p nit-ac *Nux-v* ↓ oxal-a rly4• petr-ra shn4• ph-ac ↓ positr ↓ tab zinc
    - **6** h: carbn-s k2
    - **boring** pain: apis camph a1 mez a1
    - **pressing** pain: apis calc h2 ferr k* *Nux-v* ph-ac positr nl2•
    - **shooting** pain: *Alumn* k*
- **forenoon**: alum am-m ↓ arg-n ↓ ars asar cadm-met tpw6 *Caust* cench k2 *Cham* k* clem cob k* colch rsj2• dendr-pol sk4• dios k* dulc fd4.de fago genist hep ↓ hipp hydr indg *Jug-c* k* kali-c lach lil-t lyc ↓ lycps-v mag-c ↓ mag-s myric a1 nat-ar nicc ↓ peti phyt k* podo rhus-t ruta fd4.de seneg spong fd4.de sulph k* thuj ↓ vanil fd5.de
  - **10** h: hep ↓ ozone ↓
    - **pressing** pain | **band**; as from a: ozone sde2•
    - **stitching** pain: hep
  - **10**.30 h: kalm ↓
    - **shooting** pain: kalm
  - **11** h: cassia-s ↓ lyc ↓
    - **dull** pain: cassia-s ccrh1•
    - **stitching** pain: lyc
  - **boring** pain: alum k*
  - **pressing** pain: *Cham* k* kali-c podo ruta fd4.de thuj k* vanil fd5.de
  - **sitting** agg.: nicc ↓
    - **tearing** pain: nicc
  - **sore**: nicc
  - **stitching** pain: am-m k* hep k* indg k* lyc k* mag-c mag-s k* spong fd4.de
  - **tearing** pain: alum am-m arg-n indg nicc
- **noon**: agar ↓ *Arg-n* ↓ ars calc-p ↓ dios k* dirc fago k* pall k* peti ↓ ptel k* sep ↓ sil ↓ sulph k*
  - **19** h; until: lac-cp sk4•
  - **boring** pain: *Arg-n* k*
  - **pressing** pain: agar k* fago a1 peti a1 sil k*
  - **shooting** pain: calc-p k* sep k*
- **afternoon**: aeth ↓ aloe alum bell k* bov bros-gau ↓ bry canth carbn-s castm ↓ caust cham ↓ chinin-s coca cod coloc corn k* dios k* dirc k* dulc equis-h fago k* form ↓ gamb grat guaj k* hipp iber iod k* kali-bi kola stb3• lac-c laur lyc k* mag-c ↓ mag-s myric k* nat-act nat-ar nat-c ↓ nat-m ↓ nat-s ↓ nit-ac ↓ ol-an peti plat ptel k* rumx ruta fd4.de sang k* sapin a1 sep ↓ sil stront-c sulph tritic-vg ↓ vanil fd5.de zing k*
  - **13** h: sars ↓ sep ↓ sil ↓
    - **stitching** pain: sars sep
    - **tearing** pain: sil
  - **15** h: dirc a1 *Pip-m* ↓
    - **stitching** pain: *Pip-m*
  - **16** h: caust ↓ lyc ↓
    - **tearing** pain: caust lyc
  - **17** h: bamb-a stb2.de• bry nat-ar nat-s ↓
- **afternoon – 17** h: ...
    - **boring** pain: nat-s
  - **21** h; until: adam ↓
    - **pulsating** pain: adam skp7•
  - **boring** pain: aloe nat-s k*
  - **bursting** pain: sang k*
  - **cramping**: *Plat*
  - **drawing** pain: dulc k*
  - **pressing** pain: alum h2 bros-gau mrc1 *Coloc* k* dulc h2 nat-c k* nat-m k* sang a1 sil tritic-vg fd5.de vanil fd5.de
  - **shooting** pain: form a1 sep sulph k*
  - **stitching** pain: canth k* cham k* nit-ac h2 ruta fd4.de stront-c
  - **tearing** pain: aeth castm guaj mag-c mag-s sil sulph
- **evening**: acon aloe alum alum-p k2 alumn ↓ am-c ang k* apis aran cadm-met ↓ calc ↓ calc-s k* camph castm caust *Cham* ↓ chel ↓ chin k* cinnb colch k* coloc ↓ cop crot-h dig digin ↓ dios k* dulc fd4.de equis-h fl-ac k* graph ↓ hell ↓ hydr hyper inul jac-c jac-g kali-c kali-i kali-n kreos lac-ac lach lachn ↓ led a1 lith-c mag-c ↓ *Mag-m* mez mim-p ↓ nat-c ↓ nat-m k* nat-s ↓ nept-m ↓ nit-ac nux-m k* nux-v olnd ↓ ph-ac phos ↓ pic-ac a1 plan ↓ psor k* **Puls** ran-b rhus-r rhus-t ↓ ruta fd4.de sep k* sil ↓ spong fd4.de stram stront-c sul-ac sulph tab tarent thuj k* tritic-vg fd5.de vanil fd5.de zinc zing k*
  - **18** h: kali-i ↓ sep ↓
    - **stitching** pain: kali-i sep
    - **tearing** pain: kali-i
  - **19** h: dirc a1
  - **20** h: petr-ra shn4• stram ↓
    - **stitching** pain: stram
  - **21** h: aq-mar skp7•
  - **22** h: arg-n ↓
    - **boring** pain: arg-n
  - **until** morning: kali-n ↓
    - **tearing** pain: kali-n h2
  - **amel.**: anac ↓ ozone ↓
    - **pressing** pain: anac ozone sde2•
  - **bed** agg.; in: chel glon *Mag-m* nat-c ↓ ol-an ph-ac rhus-t sep ↓
    - **stitching** pain: nat-c k* sep
  - **boring** pain: aloe alum k* coloc k* plan k*
  - **drawing** pain: alum h2 alumn k* calc dig digin a1 ran-b k* zinc
  - **dull** pain: mim-p rsj8•
  - **lying** agg.: lac-h ↓
    - **bursting** pain: lac-h htj1•
  - **lying** down agg.: mag-c ↓
    - **tearing** pain: mag-c
  - **pressing** pain: alum ang h1 calc h2 *Cham* k* chel k* colch k* dig k* dios k* hell k* nat-s k* nept-m lsd2.fr ph-ac h2 rhus-t k* ruta fd4.de spong fd4.de thuj k* tritic-vg fd5.de vanil fd5.de
  - **sharp**: cadm-met tpw6
  - **shooting** pain: nit-ac tarent k*
  - **sore**: ph-ac h2 *Puls* rhus-t
  - **stitching** pain: *Caust* dig k* graph k* hyper nat-c k* nit-ac k* phos k* sep k* sil k* stront-c tritic-vg fd5.de
  - **tearing** pain: am-c kali-c kali-n lachn led mag-c olnd *Puls* sil h2 sul-ac sulph
- **night**: alum ↓ alum-p ↓ arn ars arum-t bamb-a stb2.de• bry k* cact coca-c ↓ cop dig ferr grat kali-c lyc k* mag-s menth-pu a1 merc k2 merc-i-f k* mur-ac h2 rhus-r sang k* sapin a1 sep ↓ spong fd4.de tarent k* thuj vanil fd5.de
  - **midnight** | **before**:
    - **23** h: adam ↓
      - **pulsating** pain: adam skp7•
    - **after**:
      - **3** h: *Ferr* ↓ pitu-gl ↓
        - **stitching** pain: *Ferr* pitu-gl skp7•
  - **pressing** pain: alum alum-p k2 coca-c sk4• sep k* vanil fd5.de
  - **shooting** pain: sang *Tarent* k*
  - **sleep** agg.; during: dig ↓
    - **stitching** pain: dig k*

- **night**: ...
  - **sore**: cop
  - **stitching** pain: dig k* ferr lyc h2
  - **tearing** pain: lyc h2 thuj
- **accompanied** by:
  - **Heart** | **complaints** of the (See CHEST - Heart; complaints - accompanied - head - pain - temples)
- **air**; in open:
  - **agg.**: aur *Chin* coff coloc k* equis-h hyos k* jac-c jac-g kali-bi mang naja ol-an
    - **stitching** pain: *Mang*
    - **tearing** pain: *Mang* ol-an
  - **amel.**: abrom-a ks5 asar atro aur ↓ camph castm coloc com crot-t flor-p rsj3• glon hell hydr k* hyos k* jatr-c kola ↓ lith-c naja ↓ nuph k* olib-sac wmh1 olnd phos **Puls**
    - **drawing** pain: olnd
    - **pressing** pain: kola stb3• phos
    - **shooting** pain: naja
    - **tearing** pain: aur *Puls*
- **alternating** with:
  - **Face**; heat of: coc-c
  - **Occiput**; pain in (See occiput - alternating - temples)
- **appearing** suddenly:
  - **disappearing**; and | **suddenly**: bamb-a stb2.de•
- **ascending** stairs agg.: *Glon* kalm sulph
- **attention**, after close: hell ↓
  - **pressing** pain: hell h1
- **bandaging**:
  - **amel.**: cassia-s ↓
    - **dull** pain: cassia-s ccrh1•
- **bending**:
  - **backward**:
    - **agg.**: mang ↓
      - **boring** pain: mang k*
      - **pressing** pain: mang
  - **forward** (See stooping - agg.)
  - **head**:
    - **backward**:
      - **agg.**: *Anac Chin* mang thuj
        - **shooting** pain: anac k*
        - **tearing** pain: anac h2
      - **amel.**: thuj ↓
        - **stitching** pain: thuj h1
    - **forward**:
      - **agg.**: thuj ↓
        - **stitching** pain: thuj
- **blow**; pain as from a: *Lyc* bg2* plat ptk1 *Sul-ac* k*
- **boring** pain: *Acon* k* agar k* aloe alum k* alum-p k2 alumn ang k* ant-c k* apis k* *Arg-n* k* *Ars* aur-m-n k* bar-c bar-m bar-s k2 bell bov bufo calad calc *Camph* k* carb-an k* carb-v carbn-s cham k* clem k* *Coloc* k* cycl k* dios k* dulc k* *Ferr Ferr-ar* ferr-p fic-m gya1 form a1 grat k* *Hep* k* ip k* *Kali-i* led k* mag-m *Mang* k* mez k* mur-ac nat-ar nat-s k* nit-s-d a1 ol-an paeon k* ph-ac k* *Phos* psor k* ptel k* rhod k* sep sil stann k* stram k* sulph k* *Thuj* k*
  - **inward**: alum h2 hep
  - **outward**: ant-c k* *Dulc* k* ip b7.de*
  - **pulsating** pain: *Ferr*
  - **tearing** pain: *Rhod* k*
- **breakfast**:
  - **after**:
    - **agg.**: hyper ↓
      - **pressing** pain: hyper k*
  - **amel.**: cench k2
  - **during**: sul-ac ↓
    - **tearing** pain: sul-ac
- **breathing** agg.: anac ↓
- **breathing** agg.: ...
  - **stitching** pain: anac
- **burning**: alum k* alum-p k2 am-m k* apis k* aur k* bar-c calc k* cann-i k* carb-ac carb-an k* caust k* chel k* cimic k* cinnb k* *Coloc* k* con k* crot-t cupr lyc bg2* *Merc* k* mez bg2* nit-ac k* phel k* **Phos** k* phyt k* plat rhus-t k* sabad k* sars spig k* staph sul-ac k* verat hr1 verb k* viol-t k*
  - **blow**; pain as from a: sul-ac h2
  - **wavelike**: sul-ac h2
- **burrowing**: agar k* bar-c k* cham k* clem k* coloc mag-m b4.de* mang k*
- **bursting** pain: acon bg2* apis k* *Bell* k* brom cact caust bg2* chin bg2* chinin-s cimic k* *Cina* glon k* hell k* ign k* ind k* ip kali-bi bg2 kalm *Lach* k* lil-t merc-i-f petr-ra shn4• sabin c1 *Sang* k* sol-ni staph usn bg1*
- **ceasing** suddenly: caust ↓
  - **drawing** pain: caust
- **chewing** agg.: am-c ↓ am-m ↓ psil ft1* ptel ↓ thuj ↓
  - **drawing** pain: thuj h1
  - **pressing** pain: ptel c1
  - **stitching** pain: am-c k* am-m
- **chill**:
  - **after**: borx
  - **during**: graph ↓ hyper ↓ stann ↓
    - **stitching** pain: graph h2 stann h2
    - **tearing** pain: hyper
- **chilliness**; during: eupi ↓
  - **drawing** pain: eupi k*
- **circumscribing** temples: sabin c1
- **closing** the eyes:
  - **agg.**: sabin ↓
    - **drawing** pain: sabin k*
  - **amel.**: ip ↓
    - **boring** pain: ip h1
    - **pressing** pain: ip h1
- **cold**:
  - **agg.**: grat ↓
    - **boring** pain: grat k*
    - **tearing** pain: grat
  - **air** agg.: hyos kali-bi *Spig*
    - **shooting** pain: *Spig*
  - **amel.**: *Apis* ↓
    - **stitching** pain: *Apis*
  - **applications**:
    - **amel.**: cassia-s ↓
      - **dull** pain: cassia-s ccrh1•
  - **water** | **amel.**: aur-m coc-c k* kalm k*
- **compressed**; as if: alum b4.de* am-m b7.de* anac b4.de* ant-t b7.de* bov b4.de* bry b7.de* calc b4.de* canth b7.de* chin b7.de* cimic bg2 cocc b7.de* con b4.de* ham bg2 hell b7.de* meny b7.de* nat-m b4.de* petr bg2 ph-ac b4.de* plat b4.de* ptel bg2 ran-s b7.de* sars b4.de* stann b4.de* sul-ac b4.de* sulph b4.de* thuj b4.de* verb b7a.de*
- **contracting**: suis-pan rly4•
- **cough** agg.; during: alum ambr ant-t ars-s-f ↓ *Bry* caust *Chin* cina coca cortico ↓ kali-bi ↓ kali-c kreos **Lyc** mang moni rfm1• *Puls* rhus-t sulph tarent tax k* verb
  - **boring** pain: kali-bi
  - **bursting** pain: cina
  - **drawing** pain: *Cina*
  - **pressing** pain: ambr c1 verb
  - **pulsating** pain: cortico tpw7*
  - **shooting** pain: mang
  - **sore**: tarent
  - **stitching** pain: alum h2 ars-s-f k2 caust cina k* kali-c
  - **tearing** pain: alum puls
- **cramping**: agar k* *Calc* k* cann-s k* cina k* indg k* *Kali-c* kola stb3• nat-m k* *Petr* k* plat k* sil k* verb k* zinc k*

- **crushed**; as if: ph-ac ptk1
- **cutting** pain: acon agar ail k* alum alum-p k2 apoc k* arg-met *Arg-n* k* arum-t k* aster bapt k* bar-c **Bell** k* calc camph cann-i a1 canth k* carb-ac carbn-s *Chel* chin k* cimic k* coc-c k* *Coloc* k* *Croc* crot-c k* cupr k* cupr-ar cycl dios k* eup-per k* euphr fago a1 form genist glon k* graph guaj *Ham* hura *Hydr* k* ignis-alc es2• iris k* kali-bi k* **Kali-i** lac-c lach *Lyc* mag-c manc med merc-i-f bg2 nat-p k* *Nit-ac* onos ph-ac phos plb k* ptel k* *Puls* rhus-t sang k* sanguis-s hrn2• senec stram k* stront-c sulph suprar rly4• tanac a1 tarent k* verb xan k* xanth
  - **knife**; as with a: cycl ferr lach stram
  - **rhythmical**: calc
- **darkness** agg.: onos
- **descending** stairs agg.: merc-i-f ↓
  - **stitching** pain: merc-i-f k*
- **dinner** | **after**:
  - **agg.**: agar ↓ alum ↓ aq-mar skp7• carbn-s ↓ dios k* kali-bi k* kali-n ↓ mag-c ↓ ol-an ↓ pall k* sulph k* thuj ↓ zinc ↓
    - **burrowing**: agar k*
    - **cutting** pain: carbn-s k2
    - **pressing** pain: agar kl alum kl ol-an kl thuj kl
    - **stitching** pain: kali-n h2 mag-c k*
    - **tearing** pain: zinc h2
  - **during**:
    - **agg.**: am-c ↓ zinc ↓
      - **tearing** pain: am-c zinc
- **drawing** pain: acon k* *Agar* k* ambr ang k* ant-c k* *Ant-t* k* *Arg-met* asar aur-m k* bar-c bar-s k2 *Bell* k* borx b4a.de *Bry* k* cact *Calc* k* cann-i canth k* carb-v b4a.de carbn-s carc fd2.de• casc k* caust k* chel k* chinin-s *Cina* k* coc-c coff colch k* *Coloc* k* *Con* k* croc k* cupr k* cycl k* dulc k* eupi k* gast a1 guaj k* hep k* hipp k* indg k* kali-bi k* kreos k* *Lach* laur k* lyc k* mang k* merc k* mez k* mosch k* nit-ac k* *Nux-v* k* ol-an k* olnd k* *Petr* k* ph-ac k* phos k* phyt k* plat ran-b k* raph k* rhod k* rhus-t k* rhus-v a1 ruta k* sabad k* sabin k* sars k* seneg k* spig squil k* stann k* stront-c sul-ac k* sulph k* tab k* tarax k* thuj k* til k* upa a1 zinc zinc-p k2 zing k*
  - **pulsating** pain: staph h1
  - **worm** creeping; as from a: sulph h2
- **driving** or riding in a carriage: lith-c lyc
- **dull** pain: aesc *Agar* k* agath-a nl2• alum-sil k2 androc srj1• aq-mar skp7• bamb-a stb2.de• bit-ar wht1• calc h2 **Carb-ac** cartl-s rly4• cassia-s ccrh1• chin k* coca-c sk4• colch rsj2• coli rly4• cupr-ar echi fic-m gya1 gink-b sbd1• granit-m es1• ignis-alc es2• ind ketogl-ac rly4• laur k* limen-b-c hrn2• mim-p rsj8• nept-m lsd2.fr nicotam rly4• orot-ac rly4• oxal-a rly4• ph-ac k* phyt bg2 plac-s rly4• polys sk4• sal-fr sle1• sin-n bg2 streptoc rly4• stront-c suis-em rly4• tril-p c1 uran-n bg2 verat k*
  - **accompanied** by | **Neck**; stiffness of: bit-ar wht1•
- **eating**:
  - **after**:
    - **agg.**: alum aran calc ↓ canth castm clem con dios hydr hyos indg kali-bi k* kali-n mag-c ol-an phos ulm-c jsj8• zing k*
      - **drawing** pain: calc h2
      - **pressing** pain: calc h2 con hyos
      - **tearing** pain: con
    - **amel.**: abrom-a ks5
  - **agg.**: calc ↓
    - **drawing** pain: calc
    - **pressing** pain: calc h2
  - **amel.**: *Equis-h* c1
  - **late** agg.: *Cact* k*
  - **while**:
    - **agg.**: con ↓
      - **tearing** pain: con
- **excitement**: par ↓
  - **pressing** pain: par
- **exertion** | **after** | **agg.**: cact hell k* petr-ra shn4• psor k*
  - **agg.**: nat-c ↓
    - **pressing** pain: nat-c
- **faintness**; with: petr ↓
  - **pressing** pain: petr h2
- **fever**: sep ↓
  - **pressing** pain: sep
- **gnawing** pain: canth a1 kali-cy a1 led ran-s k* sol-ni
- **grasping** pain: mag-m b4.de*
- **grumbling** pain: sul-ac bg2
- **hammering** pain: ars k* benz-ac k* chel chin k* *Ferr* ham bg2 hep ozone sde2• psor k*
  - **accompanied** by:
    - **Eyes**:
      - **discoloration** | **redness**: ozone sde2•
- **heat** and coldness; during alternating general: borx ↓
  - **stitching** pain: borx
- **heat** of face and flickering before eyes, with: aloe ↓
  - **pressing** pain | **outward**: aloe
- **house**; in: phos ↓
  - **pressing** pain: phos k*
- **increasing** gradually: caust ↓
  - **decreasing**:
    - **gradually**: **Stann** ↓
      - **pressing** pain: **Stann**
  - **drawing** pain: caust
- **intermitting**: atro k* bad k* caust a1 clem k* iod murx k* nat-m k* nat-p k* pic-ac k* pycnop-sa mrz1 *Stann* k* stict k* sulph k*
- **jar** agg.: adam ↓
  - **pulsating** pain: adam skp7•
- **jerking** pain: acon apis k* arg-met h1 arn k* calc k* carb-ac castm *Chin* dig b4.de* glon kali-c k* lact lil-t k* lyc b4.de* mang h2 nit-ac bg2 nux-m b7.de* ox-ac k* plb k* *Puls* b7.de* rhus-t h1 *Spig* k* spong b7.de* stann k* sulph valer k*
  - **downward**: anac
  - **upward**: am-m spong
- **jerking**, with arms, on: spig ↓
  - **jerking** pain: spig h1
- **lain** on; when turning, pain moves to temple:
  - **raising**:
    - **eyes**:
      - **agg.**: puls ↓
        - **tearing** pain | **twitching**: puls k*
- **lancinating**: ail k* anan ang c1 aster k* *Bell* blatta-o bond a1 cit-ac rly4• crot-c k* *Cupr* form ger-i rly4• *Ham* hura **Kali-i** ketogl-ac rly4• lepi a1 linu-c a1 manc k* ped a1 plb k* senec k* succ-ac rly4• suis-em rly4• tarent k* tere-la rly4•
- **leaning** forward on a table:
  - **amel.**: con ↓
    - **pressing** pain: con k*
- **lemon** amel.: mag-m mrr1
- **light**; from: ap-g vh1 gels hr1* spong fd4.de
  - **agg.**: ap-g ↓ sang ↓
    - **pulsating** pain: ap-g vh1
    - **shooting** pain: sang hr1
- **looking** at light agg.:
  - **bright** light: **Nat-m** ↓
    - **stitching** pain: **Nat-m**
- **looking** at sun, at white or red color: graph ↓
  - **stitching** pain: graph h2
- **lying**:
  - **agg.**: camph clem graph kali-bi ↓ lith-c *Mag-m* spong
    - **shooting** pain: kali-bi k*
  - **amel.**: abrom-a ks5 asar benz-ac k* chel chinin-s colch ferr gels *Lach* mag-c nux-v tritic-vg fd5.de vanil fd5.de
  - **back**; on:
    - **amel.**: ign ↓
      - **pressing** pain: ign

- **lying**: ...
  - **head** high; with the:
    - **amel.**: *Spig* ↓
      - **pressing** pain: *Spig*
  - **painful** part; on:
    - **amel.**: chel ↓
      - **stitching** pain: chel
  - **side**; on:
    - **agg.**: ign ↓
      - **pressing** pain: ign
    - **left**:
      - **agg.**: asaf ↓
        - **pressing** pain: asaf$_{a1}$
- **lying** down | **after**:
  - **agg.**: camph ↓
    - **cutting** pain: camph$_{h1}$
  - **agg.**: musca-d ↓
    - **pressing** pain: musca-d$_{szs1}$
- **menses** | **before**:
  - **agg.**: *Ant-c* ↓ lach
    - **boring** pain: *Ant-c*
  - **during**:
    - **agg.**: am-m$_{k*}$ berb *Bry* ↓ calc castm lac-c **Lyc** mag-m$_{mrr1}$ nat-c nat-s nept-m$_{lsd2.fr}$ sang
      - **pressing** pain: *Bry* **Lyc**
      - **tearing** pain: am-m nat-c
- **mental** exertion:
  - **agg.**: abrom-a$_{ks5}$ anac cadm-met$_{tpw6}$ *Chin* dig gent-c hell kalm lyc ↓ manc mez nat-c nat-m nux-v ph-ac pip-m *Psor*$_{k*}$ *Puls* sil ↓ *Sulph* vanil$_{fd5.de}$
    - **plug**; as from a: *Anac*
    - **pressing** pain: dig$_{h2}$ ph-ac$_{h2}$ vanil$_{fd5.de}$
    - **sore**: ph-ac$_{h2}$
    - **stitching** pain: lyc sil sulph
  - **amel.**: calc-act
- **metrorrhagia**; during: visc ↓
  - **stitching** pain: visc$_{a2*}$
- **motion**:
  - **agg.**: agn cact calc ↓ caust *Chel* ↓ **Chin** chinin-ar ↓ cinnb cob cupr dirc *Echi* gels glon hipp hydr$_{k*}$ kali-bi kali-c ↓ **Lach** ↓ *Mez*$_{k*}$ mim-p ↓ par ↓ petr-ra$_{shn4}$• ph-ac phos phys$_{k*}$ rhod ruta ↓ sang$_{hr1}$ sil ↓ *Spig* ↓ stann ↓ tab ↓ thuj$_{k*}$ tritic-vg$_{fd5.de}$ vanil ↓ yuc$_{a1}$ zinc
    - **cutting** pain: chin$_{h1}$
    - **drawing** pain: tab$_{k*}$
    - **dull** pain: mim-p$_{rsj8}$•
    - **pressing** pain: cupr **Lach** par ph-ac phos *Spig* tritic-vg$_{fd5.de}$
    - **stitching** pain: agn$_{k*}$ calc$_{k*}$ kali-c ruta$_{fd4.de}$ stann tritic-vg$_{fd5.de}$ vanil$_{fd5.de}$
    - **tearing** pain: *Agn* *Chel* chinin-ar ph-ac$_{h2}$ sang sil$_{h2}$
  - **amel.**: carl com ferr ↓ lil-t merc$_{k2}$ *Mez* psor ↓ rhus-t$_{hr1}$
    - **pressing** pain: ferr mez psor
  - **eyes**; of | **agg.**: *Bad*$_{k*}$ chin coloc$_{k*}$ sulph
  - **jaw**; of lower:
    - **agg.**: calc ↓ kali-c ↓
      - **stitching** pain: calc$_{h2}$ kali-c
- **nail**; as from a: *Am-br* anac$_{c1}$ *Anan*$_{vh1}$ *Arn*$_{k*}$ asaf$_{k2}$ cocc$_{k*}$ dulc ham$_{k*}$ *Hep* *Ign*$_{k*}$ kali-i$_{k*}$ nept-m$_{lsd2.fr}$ sang$_{k*}$ spira$_{k*}$
- **nausea**; with: nat-ar ↓
  - **boring** pain: nat-ar$_{k2}$
- **neuralgic** | **backward**: des-ac$_{rbp6}$
- **noise** agg.: adam ↓ cact cann-s cimic *Spig* ↓ yuc$_{a1}$
  - **pressing** pain: *Spig*
  - **pulsating** pain: adam$_{skp7}$•
- **opening** the mouth agg.: ang$_{h1}$ oci-sa$_{sk4}$•
- **opera**, from attending: cact$_{k*}$
- **paroxysmal**: aesc bamb-a$_{stb2.de}$• cact$_{k*}$ lil-t
- **periodical**:
  - **two** days; every: cact ↓
    - **drawing** pain: cact
- **pinching** pain: **Arg-met** calc carb-an$_{k*}$ crot-h$_{k*}$ *Kali-c*$_{k*}$ lec merc$_{k*}$ mez$_{k*}$ olnd$_{k*}$ petr$_{h2}$ ph-ac$_{h2}$ *Sulph*$_{k*}$ **Verb**$_{k*}$ zinc$_{h2}$
  - **forceps**; as with: calc ph-ac verb
  - **pulsating** pain: rheum$_{h}$
- **plug**; as from a: *Anac*$_{k*}$ ang$_{bg2}$ *Asaf*$_{k*}$ cocc dulc hep sul-ac$_{k*}$ *Thuj*$_{k*}$
- **pressing** pain: acon$_{k*}$ aesc *Agar*$_{k*}$ agath-a$_{nl2}$• agn$_{k*}$ aloe *Alum*$_{k*}$ alum-p$_{k2}$ alum-sil$_{k2}$ *Am-br* am-caust$_{a1}$ ambr *Anac*$_{k*}$ ang$_{k*}$ *Ant-t*$_{k*}$ apis$_{k*}$ *Arg-met*$_{k*}$ *Arg-n* arn$_{k*}$ *Ars*$_{k*}$ ars-i ars-s-f$_{k2}$ arum-m$_{a1}$ *Asaf*$_{k*}$ *Asar*$_{k*}$ aur$_{k*}$ aur-ar$_{k2}$ aur-i$_{k2}$ aur-m-n$_{a1}$ aur-s$_{k2}$ bamb-a$_{stb2.de}$• bar-c bar-i$_{k2}$ bar-s$_{k2}$ *Bell*$_{k*}$ benz-ac berb$_{k*}$ *Bism*$_{k*}$ borx$_{h2}$ bov$_{k*}$ brass-n-o$_{srj5}$• brom$_{k*}$ *Bry*$_{k*}$ bufo calad$_{k*}$ *Calc*$_{k*}$ calc-i$_{k2}$ calc-sil$_{k2}$ camph$_{k*}$ cann-i$_{k*}$ *Cann-s*$_{k*}$ canth$_{k*}$ *Caps*$_{k*}$ carb-ac carb-an$_{k*}$ **Carb-v**$_{k*}$ carbn-s castor-eq caust$_{k*}$ cedr$_{k*}$ *Cham*$_{k*}$ *Chel*$_{k*}$ *Chin*$_{k*}$ chinin-ar chlor$_{a1}$ cimic$_{k*}$ cina$_{k*}$ cinnb clem$_{k*}$ cob cob-n$_{sp1}$ coc-c coca coca-c$_{sk4}$• *Cocc* cod$_{a1}$ coff$_{k*}$ colch coli$_{rly4}$• *Coloc*$_{k*}$ con$_{k*}$ conch$_{fkr1}$• cor-r$_{a1}$ *Crot-c* cupr$_{k*}$ *Cycl*$_{k*}$ *Dig*$_{k*}$ dios$_{k*}$ dros$_{k*}$ dulc$_{k*}$ echi elaps elat euon$_{k*}$ euph$_{k*}$ fago$_{a1}$ ferr$_{k*}$ ferr-ar ferr-i *Ferr-p* fl-ac$_{k*}$ galeoc-c-h$_{gms1}$• gent-c$_{k*}$ gent-l germ-met$_{srj5}$• gins$_{k*}$ **Glon**$_{k*}$ gran$_{k*}$ graph *Guaj*$_{k*}$ hell$_{k*}$ hep$_{k*}$ hipp$_{k*}$ hura hydr-ac$_{k*}$ hyos$_{k*}$ hyper$_{k*}$ ign$_{k*}$ ind$_{k*}$ inul$_{a1*}$ iod$_{k*}$ ip$_{k*}$ jac-c$_{a1}$ jatr-c kali-bi kali-br$_{a1}$ *Kali-c*$_{k*}$ *Kali-i* kali-m$_{k2}$ kali-n$_{k*}$ kali-p kali-s$_{fd4.de}$ kali-sil$_{k2}$ kalm$_{k*}$ ketogl-ac$_{rly4}$• kola$_{stb3}$• kreos$_{k*}$ lac-c lac-e$_{hrn2}$• lac-h$_{htj1}$• lac-lup$_{hrn2}$• **Lach**$_{k*}$ lachn$_{k*}$ laur$_{k*}$ lec led$_{k*}$ lith-c lob$_{k*}$ **Lyc**$_{k*}$ m-aust$_{b7.de}$ *Mang*$_{k*}$ meny$_{k*}$ *Merc*$_{k*}$ merl$_{k*}$ *Mez*$_{k*}$ mim-h$_{a1}$ *Moni*$_{rfm1}$• mosch$_{k*}$ myric$_{a1}$ naja *Nat-ar* nat-c$_{k*}$ **Nat-m**$_{k*}$ nat-p nat-s nat-sil$_{fd3.de}$• nept-m$_{lsd2.fr}$ nit-s-d$_{a1}$ *Nux-m*$_{k*}$ nux-v oci-sa$_{sk4}$• ol-an$_{k*}$ olib-sac$_{wmh1}$ olnd$_{k*}$ *Op*$_{k*}$ osm *Par*$_{k*}$ petr$_{k*}$ petr-ra$_{shn4}$• ph-ac$_{k*}$ *Phos*$_{k*}$ phys phyt$_{bg2}$ pieri-b$_{mlk9.de}$ pip-m$_{a1}$ plac$_{rzf5}$• plac-s$_{rly4}$• **Plat**$_{k*}$ plb plut-n$_{srj7}$• podo *Positr*$_{nl2}$• *Prun*$_{k*}$ prun-p$_{a1}$ psor$_{k*}$ ptel$_{k*}$ *Puls*$_{k*}$ ran-b$_{k*}$ ran-s$_{k*}$ rheum$_{k*}$ *Rhod*$_{k*}$ rhus-t$_{k*}$ ruta$_{fd4.de}$ *Sabad*$_{k*}$ *Sabin*$_{k*}$ samb$_{k*}$ sang$_{a1}$ sars$_{h2*}$ seneg$_{b4.de*}$ sep$_{b4.de*}$ sil$_{k*}$ spig$_{k*}$ spong$_{b7.de*}$ *Squil* *Stann*$_{k*}$ *Staph*$_{k*}$ still$_{a1}$ stront-c$_{k*}$ suis-em$_{rly4}$• sul-ac$_{k*}$ sul-i$_{k2}$ *Sulph* symph$_{fd3.de}$• tab$_{k*}$ tarax$_{k*}$ tax$_{k*}$ teucr$_{k*}$ ther thuj$_{k*}$ tritic-vg$_{fd5.de}$ ulm-c$_{jsj8}$• upa$_{a1}$ vanil$_{fd5.de}$ verat$_{k*}$ *Verb*$_{k*}$ viol-t$_{k*}$ *Zinc*$_{k*}$ zinc-p$_{k2}$ [helia$_{stj7}$]
  - **alternating** with:
    - **stitching** pain in temples (See stitching - alternating - pressing)
    - **tearing** pain in temples (See tearing - alternating - pressing)
    - **Occiput**; drawing pain in: bry
    - **Vertex**; drawing pain in: phos$_{h2}$
  - **asunder**: acon$_{b7.de*}$ apis$_{b7a.de}$ *Bry*$_{b7.de*}$ caust$_{b4.de*}$ chin$_{b7.de*}$ cina$_{b7.de*}$ ign$_{b7.de*}$ kreos$_{b7a.de}$ m-arct$_{b7.de}$ *Sabin*$_{b7a.de}$ stront-c$_{b4.de*}$
  - **band**; as from a: ozone$_{sde2}$•
    - **accompanied** by:
      - **weariness**: ozone$_{sde2}$•
      - **Legs** | **heaviness**: ozone$_{sde2}$•
  - **crushed**; as if: caul$_{k*}$
  - **cutting** pain: bell$_{k*}$
  - **downward**: sabad
  - **drawing** in eyes, as from strabismus: podo
  - **finger**; as from a (= digital): ambr ant-t arn asaf cham cocc dulc hell nit-ac$_{h2}$ rhus-t sep staph$_{h1}$
  - **forward**: verb
  - **intermittent**: borx$_{h2}$ ph-ac$_{h2}$ sep$_{h2}$
  - **inward**: *Acon*$_{k*}$ *Alum* alum-p$_{k2}$ *Anac*$_{k*}$ ant-c ant-t *Asaf*$_{k*}$ asar bell$_{k*}$ borx$_{h2}$ bov *Calc* cocc con dulc fl-ac hell$_{k*}$ jatr-c kali-c *Kali-i* lith-c *Lyc* mez$_{k*}$ nat-c **Nat-m** nit-ac$_{k*}$ ol-an$_{k*}$ op$_{bg2}$ *Ph-ac* *Plat*$_{k*}$ ptel$_{br}$ *Ran-s* rhod$_{k*}$ rhus-t$_{bg2}$ sabad sabin seneg sol-ni *Spig*$_{k*}$ **Stann**$_{k*}$ staph$_{k*}$ *Sul-ac* *Ther* *Thuj*$_{k*}$ ulm-c$_{jsj8}$• valer zinc$_{k*}$
  - **jerking** pain: dig$_{h2}$

- **pressing** pain: ...
  - **outward**: acon$_{k*}$ aloe$_{k*}$ anac$_{k*}$ apis$_{b7a.de}$ asaf$_{k*}$ atro$_{a1}$ berb$_{k*}$ bism$_{k*}$ bry$_{k*}$ calc$_{k*}$ canth$_{k*}$ carb-v castor-eq caust$_{k*}$ chin$_{k*}$ dros$_{k*}$ *Fl-ac*$_{k*}$ **Glon**$_{k*}$ ign$_{k*}$ indg$_{k*}$ ip$_{k*}$ kali-c kali-m$_{k2}$ kreos$_{k*}$ **Lach** lact$_{k*}$ lil-t lob *Mez*$_{k*}$ mur-ac$_{k*}$ nat-c nat-m$_{k*}$ nux-m$_{k*}$ op$_{k*}$ par$_{k*}$ ph-ac$_{k*}$ phys$_{k*}$ phyt$_{k*}$ *Prun* ran-s$_{k*}$ rhod *Sabad*$_{k*}$ sabin samb$_{k*}$ sapin$_{a1}$ senec$_{k*}$ *Spig* spong$_{k*}$ stann stront-c sulph$_{k*}$ teucr$_{k*}$ valer$_{k*}$ verb viol-t$_{k*}$
  - **paroxysmal**: *Kali-c* ptel$_{a1}$
  - **pulsating** pain: camph$_{h1}$ *Cocc Glon* grat *Hell* nux-v
  - **sharp**: mang$_{h2}$
  - **upward**: rhus-t$_{h1}$
  - **vise**; as if in a: acon anac arg-n cocc con dios ham kola$_{stb3}$• **Lyc** *Nat-m Nux-m* plat sabad
  - **wavelike**: plat$_{h2}$
  - **wedge**; as from a: *Thuj*
  - **weight**; as from a: rhus-t$_{b7.de*}$ sep$_{b4.de*}$
- **pressure**:
  - **agg.**: aspar$_{k*}$ bism castm cina coc-c↓ cop daph kali-n kali-s$_{fd4.de}$ lil-t$_{k*}$ mur-ac nat-ar nat-m ph-ac↓ *Prun* spong$_{fd4.de}$ sulph$_{h2}$ verb
    - **cutting** pain: verb
    - **drawing** pain: cina
    - **pressing** pain: bism$_{h1}$ nat-m$_{h2}$ ph-ac$_{h2}$
    - **stitching** pain: coc-c verb$_{h}$
    - **tearing** pain: bism
  - **amel.**: abrom-a$_{ks5}$ adam↓ aesc↓ aeth alum ant-c aral bros-gau↓ *Cact* calad *Calc*↓ calc-act *Chin* coc-c cop cupr-s↓ dios$_{k*}$ dirc echi *Glon* guaj hydr iod ip↓ kali-i kali-n↓ kalm kola↓ lil-t mag-c **Mag-m**$_{k*}$ meny nat-c par$_{k*}$ petr-ra$_{shn4}$• phos plan$_{k*}$ plut-n$_{srj7}$• podo ruta$_{fd4.de}$ stann thuj trios↓ vanil$_{fd5.de}$ verat
    - **boring** pain: calad ip$_{k*}$ stann
    - **drawing** pain: ant-c$_{h2}$
    - **pressing** pain: bros-gau$_{mrc1}$ dios ip$_{h1}$ kola$_{stb3}$• meny$_{h1}$ par petr-ra$_{shn4}$• *Stann*
    - **pulsating** pain: adam$_{skp7}$• trios$_{rsj11}$•
    - **shooting** pain: *Calc* cupr-s$_{a1}$
    - **stitching** pain: aesc aeth guaj thuj$_{h1}$ vanil$_{fd5.de}$
    - **tearing** pain: kali-n$_{h2}$ mag-c nat-c
  - **eyes**; on | **amel.**: mag-m$_{mrr1}$ vanil$_{fd5.de}$
  - **hard**:
    - **amel.**: cassia-s↓ mag-m$_{mrr1}$
      - **dull** pain: cassia-s$_{ccrh1}$•
  - **opposite** side amel.; on: jac-c$_{k*}$ jac-g
- **pulled**; sensation as if hair were: bry$_{h1}$
- **pulsating** pain: adam$_{skp7}$• aeth$_{a1}$ alum am-c anan anthraq$_{rly4}$• apis *Arg-n* arn$_{k*}$ aur-m$_{k*}$ *Bell* benz-ac$_{k*}$ bit-ar$_{wht1}$• borx calc-met$_{rly4}$• camph *Caps*$_{k*}$ *Carbn-s* caust$_{k*}$ cedr$_{k*}$ chel$_{k*}$ *Chin Chinin-s* chlam-tr$_{bcx2}$• cit-ac$_{rly4}$• coc-c cocc$_{c1}$ coloc corn$_{k*}$ dulc$_{fd4.de}$ *Echi* falco-pe$_{nl2}$• ferr **Glon**$_{k*}$ gymno$_{br1}$ ham$_{fd3.de}$• hep$_{k*}$ jug-r *Kali-br*$_{hr1}$ kali-n lac-c lac-d **Lach** mand$_{rsj7}$• merc-i-f$_{k*}$ nat-c$_{hr1}$ nat-s nit-ac$_{k*}$ *Phos*$_{k*}$ *Podo*$_{k*}$ pot-e$_{rly4}$• *Puls* ruta$_{fd4.de}$ sep$_{h2}$ sol-ni spig spong$_{fd4.de}$ *Stann*$_{k*}$ *Stram*$_{k*}$ streptoc$_{rly4}$• sulph$_{k*}$ suprar$_{rly4}$• thuj$_{k*}$
  - **accompanied** by:
    - **nausea**: adam$_{skp7}$•
    - **Eyes**:
      - **pain** | **In** and above eyes: adam$_{skp7}$•
- **raising** | **eyes**:
  - **agg.**: puls↓
    - **tearing** pain: puls
  - **head**:
    - **amel.**: kali-c↓
      - **stitching** pain: kali-c
- **reading** agg.: calc-act↓ carb-ac↓ carb-an↓ *Caust*↓ clem↓ coca↓ mez↓ **Nat-m**↓ par↓ phys↓ pip-m↓ sol-ecl↓ sulph↓
  - **pressing** pain: carb-an$_{k*}$ mez **Nat-m** par [sol-ecl$_{cky1}$]
  - **pulsating** pain: calc-act carb-ac clem coca mez nat-m phys pip-m sulph
  - **stitching** pain: *Caust*
- **reflecting** agg.: *Cham*↓ ph-ac↓ psor↓ *Sulph*↓
  - **pressing** pain: *Cham* ph-ac$_{k*}$ psor *Sulph*$_{k*}$
- **rest**:
  - **agg.**: dulc↓
    - **boring** pain: dulc
  - **amel.**: pert-vc$_{vk9}$
- **rheumatic**: lyc↓
  - **stitching** pain: lyc
- **rising**:
  - **after**:
    - **agg.**: fago$_{k*}$ lac-ac$_{a1}$ lycps-v nit-ac↓ vanil$_{fd5.de}$ verat
      - **pressing** pain: nit-ac$_{k*}$
  - **amel.**: calc-act rhus-t stann
  - **bed**; from | **agg.**: abrom-a$_{ks5}$
  - **lying**; from:
    - **amel.**: stann↓
      - **pressing** pain: stann$_{k*}$
  - **sitting**; from:
    - **agg.**: mang↓
      - **pressing** pain: mang$_{h2}$
- **room**:
  - **agg.**: abrom-a$_{ks5}$ jatr-c laur phos phys$_{a1}$ ran-b$_{k*}$ rhod sabad til$_{a1}$
  - **amel.**: *Chin* coff hyos ol-an zing
- **rubbing** | **amel.**: canth ol-an phos plat
- **scratching**:
  - **amel.**: plat↓
    - **stitching** pain: plat$_{h2*}$
- **screwed** together; as if: acon$_{bg2}$ cocc$_{bg2}$ coloc$_{bg2}$ lyc$_{bg2*}$
- **shaking** the head agg.; on: *Asar*↓ carbn-s chin↓ glon$_{k*}$ nat-m↓ *Nux-v*↓ pall *Sang*↓
  - **pressing** pain: *Asar* chin$_{h1*}$
  - **stitching** pain: nat-m$_{k*}$ *Nux-v*$_{k*}$
  - **tearing** pain: *Sang*
- **sharp**: fic-m$_{gya1}$ helodr-cal$_{knl2}$•
- **shivering**; during: graph↓
  - **stitching** pain: graph$_{b4a.de}$
- **shooting** pain: acet-ac$_{k*}$ acon$_{k*}$ aesc aeth$_{k*}$ agar$_{k*}$ alumn$_{k*}$ anac$_{k*}$ apis arum-t$_{k*}$ bapt *Bell*$_{k*}$ calc-p$_{k*}$ caust chel cimic$_{k*}$ coca com$_{k*}$ cupr-s$_{k*}$ cystein-l$_{rly4}$• dig echi *Form*$_{k*}$ *Gels* glon$_{k*}$ *Iris* kali-bi$_{k*}$ **Kali-c** kalm$_{k*}$ lil-t$_{k*}$ lyc merc-i-f$_{k*}$ naja nat-m$_{bg2}$ *Nit-ac* phos$_{k*}$ phys$_{k*}$ phyt$_{k*}$ pic-ac$_{k*}$ pip-m$_{k*}$ ptel rhus-t$_{k*}$ sang sep$_{k*}$ *Spig* stict$_{a1}$ *Stram* sul-i$_{k*}$ sulph$_{k*}$ suprar$_{rly4}$• *Tarent*$_{k*}$ thea verb$_{c1}$
  - **inward**: arn berb canth dirc **Kali-c** rhus-t
  - **outward**: bell dulc kali-bi rhus-t
    - **out** and in: staph
  - **pulsating** pain: acon
  - **spreading** out in a circle: *Caust*
  - **upward**: chinin-s
    - **up** and down: ang
- **singing** agg.: alum↓
  - **stitching** pain: alum$_{k*}$
- **sitting**:
  - **agg.**: am-m arg-met *Caust*↓ chin guaj↓ lil-t mang mez nicc nit-ac↓ phos staph sul-ac tarax vanil$_{fd5.de}$ verat
    - **drawing** pain: arg-met *Tarax*
    - **stitching** pain: *Caust* guaj$_{h2}$ nit-ac *Tarax*$_{k*}$
  - **amel.**: ars asar calc-act coff coloc lith-c mang merc$_{k2}$
  - **erect**:
    - **agg.**: mang↓
      - **boring** pain: mang$_{k*}$
- **sleep**:
  - **after**:
    - **agg.**: hep↓ rhus-t↓
      - **pressing** pain: hep$_{h2}$ rhus-t$_{k*}$
    - **amel.**: lac-cp$_{sk4}$•

- **sleep**: ...
  - **amel.**: sang ↓
    - **shooting** pain: sang hr1
  - **during**: mag-c k*
- **sneezing**:
  - **after**: cina ↓
    - **pressing** pain: cina
  - **agg.**: am-c cina
- **sore**: aesc agn hr1 atro calc-p castm cham cob coca cupr-ar daph dirc glon grat gymno haem ign bg2 kola stb3• lyss c1 meny h1 merl *Mez* mur-ac bg2 nicc nux-m ph-ac phys plan plb positr nl2• *Puls* *Rhus-t* k* sang k* suis-em rly4• tarent **Verb**
- **squeezed**; as if: ambr b7.de* dios ptk1 mez b4.de* rheum b7.de* zinc b4.de*
- **standing**:
  - **agg.**: ars castm chin coloc cortico tpw7 glon guaj mur-ac ↓ staph verat
    - **stitching** pain: guaj h2
    - **tearing** pain: mur-ac h2
  - **amel.**: mur-ac ↓ tarax zing
    - **drawing** pain: *Tarax* k*
    - **stitching** pain: mur-ac h2 tarax h1
- **stepping**:
  - **agg.**: aloe ↓ carbn-s coloc k* hell lyc k* sol-ni *Spig* ↓
    - **jerking** pain: *Spig*
    - **stitching** pain: aloe
  - **every** step; at: adam ↓
    - **pulsating** pain: adam skp7•
- **stitching** pain: acon k* aesc k* aeth k* agar k* agn b7.de* aloe *Alum* k* alum-p k2 alum-sil k2 am-c k* am-m k* ambr k* anac ang k* ant-c h2 ant-t k* **Apis** k* apoc k* arg-met *Arn* k* ars k* ars-i ars-s-f k2 arum-t k* asaf k* asar h1 bapt bar-c k* bar-i k2 bar-m bar-s k2 *Bell* k* berb k* bomb-pr mlk9.de borx k* bov k* *Brom* b4a.de bry k* cadm-s calad k* *Calc* k* calc-i k2 calc-s calc-sil k2 camph k* *Cann-i* k* canth k* *Carb-an* k* carb-v k* carbn-s carc fd2.de• card-b a1 carl a1 **Caust** k* *Cham* k* chel k* **Chin** k* cimic cina k* coc-c k* cocc k* coff *Coloc* cop k* crot-h k* crot-t a1 *Cupr* k* *Cycl* k* daph k* dig k* dirc a1 dulc k* euon a1 euph b4.de* euphr k* eupi k* *Ferr* ferr-ar ferr-i ferr-p franz a1 gamb k* gent-c a1 *Glon* gran k* graph grat k* *Guaj* ham fd3.de• hell hep k* hydr k* hyper ign k* iod k* iris kali-bi k* *Kali-c* k* **Kali-i** kali-m k2 kali-n k* kali-p kali-sil k2 kreos k* lach a1 laur k* lec lob a1 lob-s a1 lol a1 **Lyc** k* *Lyss* st mag-c k* mag-m k* mag-s k* manc *Mang* k* meny k* *Merc* merc-i-f merl k* mez k* mur-ac k* nat-c k* *Nat-m* k* nat-p *Nit-ac* k* nux-m k* *Nux-v* ol-an k* *Par* k* ph-ac k* *Phos* k* pieri-b mlk9.de pitu-gl skp7• plat k* plb k* psor k* ptel a1 *Puls* k* ran-b k* ran-s k* rheum k* rhod rhus-t k* rob a1 ruta k* sabad k* sal-ac sang k* *Sars* k* sel k* sep k* serp a1 *Sil* k* sol-ni *Spig* spong squil *Stann* k* *Staph* k* stram stront-c stry sul-ac sul-i k2 *Sulph* k* symph fd3.de• tab k* tarax k* tarent k* ther k* *Thuj* k* tritic-vg fd5.de vanil fd5.de verat a1 verb k* vichy-g a1 viol-t k* zinc k* zinc-p k2
  - **alternating** with | **pressing** pain: meny h1 tab k*
  - **burning**: ars bapt hr1 bar-c k* cupr phos h2 plat h2 sars h2 staph
  - **downward**: ang
  - **drawing** pain: cycl h1
  - **dull** pain: borx h2 caust h2* cycl h1 sars h2 staph h1 zinc h2
  - **intermittent**: borx h2 calc h2 stann
  - **inward**: acon arg-met arn lach rhus-t til
  - **itching**: ang h1
  - **jerking** pain: cycl h1 mang h2 rhus-t h1 squil h1
  - **needles**; as from: carc fd2.de• staph rb2 zinc h2
    - **burning**: ars
  - **outward**: bar-act berb calc dulc h2* lyc nux-m rhus-t sil sulph
  - **paroxysmal**: berb k*
  - **pulsating** pain: stann h2 staph h1
  - **rhythmical**: borx stann
  - **tearing** pain: ars h2 dig k* kali-c h2 viol-t k*
- **stool**:
  - **after**:
    - **agg.**: sil ↓
      - **pressing** pain: sil k*
- **stool**: ...
  - **before**: merc ↓
    - **pressing** pain: merc k*
  - **difficult**:
    - **during**: *Lyc* ↓
      - **cutting** pain: *Lyc* k*
        - **knife**; as with a: *Lyc*
  - **during**:
    - **agg.**: lyc ↓ merc ↓
      - **pressing** pain: merc k*
      - **shooting** pain: lyc
      - **stitching** pain: lyc
  - **straining** at | **agg.**: *Bell* nux-v *Puls* thuj k*
- **stooping**:
  - **agg.**: am-m bov *Brom* calc-act carb-ac carbn-s k2 chin coff coloc cycl dios dros fago fl-ac glon guaj hep kali-bi kali-c lach lyss mang ↓ mur-ac nat-ar nat-s nept-m ↓ *Par* ↓ phos plat *Puls* samb ↓ sol-ni *Spig* ↓ sulph thuj verat
    - **cutting** pain: chin h1
    - **pressing** pain: *Lach* phos samb h1 *Spig*
    - **stitching** pain: kali-c mang nept-m lsd2.fr *Par*
    - **tearing** pain: carbn-s samb h1
  - **amel.**: ang mang tritic-vg fd5.de verat
    - **boring** pain: mang k*
    - **pressing** pain: mang tritic-vg fd5.de
- **stretching** neck amel.: bit-ar wht1•
- **stunning** pain: acon k* ars asar k* cina k* iod k* podo k* rheum k* *Rhus-t* b7a.de sabad k* *Verb* k*
- **sun**; from exposure to: bit-ar wht1• nat-ar pert-vc vk9
- **talking**:
  - **after**: agar ↓
    - **stitching** pain: agar k*
  - **agg.**: dendr-pol sk4• glon a1 mez petr-ra shn4• phos k2
    - **pressing** pain: mez
- **tearing** pain: acon aeth agar *Agn* k* ail alum k* alum-p k2 alum-sil k2 am-c *Am-m* ambr *Anac* k* ant-c *Arg-met* k* *Arg-n* *Arn* k* arum-t asaf *Asar* aur k* aur-i k2 aur-m aur-s k2 *Bell* *Berb* bism bov bry calc k* calc-p calc-sil k2 camph canth k* carb-v carbn-s castm caust k* *Cham* k* *Chel* chin k* chinin-ar chinin-s cic cina k* cocc colch coloc con k* cop cupr cycl dig k* dulc gran grat guaj k* ham hell hyper indg iod kali-bi *Kali-c* *Kali-i* kali-m k2 kali-n kali-p kali-sil k2 kalm kreos k* lach k* lachn lact laur k* led lyc k* lyss m-aust b7.de mag-c *Mag-m* mag-s *Mang* merc k* merl mez mur-ac nat-c *Nat-m* nat-s k* nicc *Nux-m* nux-v k* ol-an olnd k* par petr ph-ac phos k* plb k* *Puls* k* ran-b k* rat rhod rhus-t k* ruta sabad sabin samb k* seneg *Sep* sil k* *Spig* k* spong stann staph h1 sul-ac sul-i k2 sulph teucr b7.de* thuj til verb viol-t **Zinc** k* zinc-p k2
  - **alternating** with | **pressing** in temples: bell h1
  - **burning**: chinin-ar lyc h2
  - **downward**: bry laur
  - **intermittent**: dulc samb h1
  - **jerking** pain: anac h2 lyc h2 mag-c h2 puls h1
  - **paroxysmal**: carb-v h2 *Kali-c* samb xxb1
  - **pulsating** pain: *Sang* staph h1
  - **stitching** pain: lyc h2 mur-ac h2 zinc h2
  - **upward**: alum h2 am-m laur mag-c h2 rhus-v *Sep*
- **thinking** of the pain agg.: **Cham** ↓
  - **pressing** pain: **Cham**
- **tickling**, with: cann-s ↓
  - **cramping**: cann-s k*
- **toothache**; with: mur-ac h2
- **torn**; as if: mur-ac k*
- **touch**:
  - **agg.**: androc srj1• *Arg-met* ↓ aur berb castm chel *Chin* con cupr daph led meny ↓ *Mez* nux-m peti sang hr1 sars ↓ staph
    - **drawing** pain: con k*
    - **pressing** pain: arg-met h1 aur h2 cupr h2 led h1 sars h2
    - **sore**: meny h1

- **touch** – **agg.**: ...
  - **stitching** pain: sars h2 staph k*
  - **tearing** pain: *Arg-met* chel cupr
  - **amel.**: ars calc ↓ calc-act *Coloc* ↓ cycl mur-ac ↓
    - **boring** pain: *Coloc*
    - **stitching** pain: ars k* *Coloc* k* cycl h1 mur-ac h2
      - **boring**: calc h2 coloc
    - **tearing** pain: mur-ac h2
  - **hair** agg.; touching the: agar ↓
    - **pressing** pain: agar
- **transient**: iris ↓ tarent ↓
  - **shooting** pain: iris tarent
- **travelling** in train or bus: adam ↓
  - **pulsating** pain: adam skp7•
- **turning**:
  - **eyes**:
    - **outward**: raph
    - **upward**: puls
- **ulcerative** pain: mur-ac k* *Puls*
- **urinate**, if the desire be not soon attended to: *Fl-ac* ↓
  - **pressing** pain: *Fl-ac*
- **vise**; as in a: kola stb3•
- **waking**; on: calad ↓ *Calc* ↓ ferr ↓ *Nux-v* ↓
  - **pressing** pain: calad k* *Calc* ferr k* *Nux-v*
- **walking**:
  - **after**:
    - **agg.**: bry ↓ tarax ↓ tell ↓
      - **stitching** pain: bry k* tarax k* tell k*
  - **agg.**: agn alum ant-t ars asar bry bufo castm chin k* cocc coff coloc con cortico tpw7 cupr dios genist glon hell kali-bi k* **Lach** ↓ lil-t lyss mang mez nat-m nat-s pall a1 petr-ra shn4• phos ptel ↓ ran-b rhod sep ↓ spig sulph
    - **drawing** pain: con k*
    - **pressing** pain: asar chin h1 hell h1 **Lach** mang h2 nat-m k*
    - **stitching** pain: ptel k* sep k*
    - **tearing** pain: castm sulph
  - **air**; in open:
    - **agg.**: arn bry coff hyos mang nat-m rhod spig tarax zing
      - **stitching** pain: tarax h1
      - **tearing** pain: arn mang
    - **amel.**: psor rhod *Sang* ↓ vanil fd5.de
      - **bursting** pain: *Sang* k*
  - **amel.**: chin guaj staph tarax vanil fd5.de
    - **drawing** pain: *Tarax*
    - **stitching** pain: guaj h2 staph k* vanil fd5.de
- **wandering** pain: acon k* *Aesc* carbn-s *Cham* k* merl k* plan k* spig k* verat-v k*
- **warm**:
  - **applications**:
    - **amel.**: kali-c ↓ vanil ↓
      - **stitching** pain: kali-c vanil fd5.de
  - **bed**:
    - **agg.**: puls ↓
      - **tearing** pain: puls
  - **room**:
    - **agg.**: cench k2 sel ↓
      - **stitching** pain: sel
- **warmth** | **agg.**:
    - **heat** agg.: cassia-s ↓ grat ↓ rhus-t ↓
      - **boring** pain: grat k*
      - **dull** pain: cassia-s ccrh1•
      - **shooting** pain: rhus-t k*
      - **tearing** pain: grat
  - **amel.** | **heat** amel.: mur-ac k* nux-m *Syph*
- **weather** agg.; cold wet: nux-m
- **wet**, getting feet: sang hr1
- **wind**, riding against the: calc-i k*
- **wine** agg.: *Cact* k* zinc
- **winking** agg.: all-c k*
- **wrapping** up head | **amel.**: mur-ac k*
- **wrapping** up with a shawl | **amel.**: abrom-a ks5
- **writing** agg.: **Nat-m** ↓ vanil ↓
  - **pressing** pain: **Nat-m** vanil fd5.de
- **yawning**:
  - **amel.**: mur-ac ↓
    - **stitching** pain: mur-ac h2
    - **tearing** pain: mur-ac
- ▽ **extending** to:
  - **Backward** over ears: arg-met cedr gymno iris bg1 nat-p syph xxb
  - **Brain**: glon ↓ psil ↓
    - **pressing** pain: glon psil ft1
    - **Into**: aloe ↓ croc ↓ ph-ac ↓
      - **stitching** pain: aloe croc ph-ac h2
    - **Through**: dig ↓
      - **stitching** pain: dig h2
  - **Brain**, into: ambr ↓ anac ↓
    - **tearing** pain: ambr anac
  - **Centre** of head: dirc
  - **Cheek**: mez ↓
    - **burning**: mez k*
  - **Chin**: gels br1 lepi ↓
    - **cutting** pain | **cut** with a razor; as if: lepi br1
  - **Ear**: atro bg1 aur aur-m ↓ bamb-a stb2.de• bov gels k* gymno bg1* hell ↓ lach bg1 nat-p ↓ puls stry bg1
    - **drawing** pain: hell h1
    - **pinching** pain: nat-p k*
    - **tearing** pain: aur-m bov
    - **To** ear; from ear: antip bro1 calc-ar bro1 mentho bro1 pall bro1 syph bro1
  - **Ears**: lach ↓
    - **pressing** pain: lach
  - **Eye**: acon-ac rly4• aloe ant-c asim berb cedr cimic lp coc-c gels gran ↓ kola stb3• lac-d kr1 nat-p petr-ra shn4• phos pip-m ruta fd4.de vanil fd5.de
    - **drawing** pain: aloe
    - **tearing** pain: gran
  - **Eyebrows**: pic-ac
  - **Eyes**: anac ↓ ant-c ↓ berb ↓ chin ↓ granit-m ↓ graph ↓ lec ↓ mang ↓ ph-ac ↓ ruta ↓ vanil ↓
    - **boring** pain: mang hr1
    - **cutting** pain: berb chin h1
    - **dull** pain: granit-m es1•
    - **pressing** pain: anac h2 ruta fd4.de vanil fd5.de
    - **stitching** pain: ant-c berb graph h2 lec ph-ac h2 vanil fd5.de
    - **Above**: alum ↓ ozone ↓
      - **pressing** pain: alum ozone sde2•
  - **Face**: alum-sil k2 am-m ant-t arg-met ↓ arg-n *Bry* graph k2 kali-c lachn puls rhus-t seneg
    - **drawing** pain: ant-t arg-met *Bry* seneg
    - **tearing** pain: am-m arg-n bry kali-c lachn seneg
  - **Forehead**: alum ↓ bell ↓ bry ↓ chinin-s ↓ lach ↓ lact ↓ lyc ↓ mang ↓ mez ↓ sabin ↓ seneg ↓ sol-ni ↓
    - **boring** pain: mang hr1
    - **drawing** pain: bell h1 chinin-s lach lact lyc sabin
    - **pinching** pain: mez h2
    - **pressing** pain: alum bry seneg sol-ni
  - **Forehead**, across: anac ↓ berb ↓ borx ↓ castm ↓ *Ferr* ↓ lyc ↓ mez ↓ ph-ac ↓ sil ↓ squil ↓ tab ↓
    - **stitching** pain: anac h2 berb a1 borx h2 *Ferr* h1 sil h2 squil h1 tab a1
    - **tearing** pain: castm lyc mez ph-ac
  - **Forehead**, over: *All-c* anac berb borx ferr glon hep lil-t lyc mez petr-ra shn4• ph-ac phos sil squil tab vanil fd5.de

- **extending** to: ...
  - **Head**: agath-a↓ ambr↓ dulc↓ hep↓ psor↓ suis-em↓
    - **boring** pain: hep
    - **drawing** pain: ambr dulc
    - **pressing** pain: agath-a nl2• ambr psor suis-em rly4•
  - **Jaw**: arg-n calc-p glon kali-c lob rhod stann
    - **cutting** pain: glon
    - **tearing** pain: arg-n kali-c
  - **Jaw**; upper: arg-n↓
    - **drawing** pain: arg-n
  - **Lower** jaw: rhus-t↓
    - **jerking** pain: rhus-t h1
  - **Malar** bone: **Bry**↓ carb-an↓
    - **boring** pain: carb-an h2
    - **drawing** pain: **Bry** h1
  - **Neck**: acon-ac rly4• bov↓ bry chel↓ fum rly4• kali-i kola stb3• pic-ac pitu-gl skp7• pot-e rly4• puls x-ray sp1
    - **pressing** pain: bov chel
    - **tearing** pain: bry kali-i
  - **Nose**: glon mez↓
    - **pinching** pain: mez h2
    - **Root** of nose: calc k2
    - **Tip**: dig↓
      - **shooting** pain: dig c1
    - **Wing**: gels br1
  - **Occiput**: carbn-s↓ cham cinnb coff iod iris kali-bi kalm kola stb3• lil-t lycps-v moni↓ ph-ac↓ pic-ac *Pip-m*↓ puls rhus-v ruta↓ sabad↓ sal-fr↓ *Spig*↓ *Stram*↓ tritic-vg fd5.de
    - **dull** pain: sal-fr sle1•
    - **pressing** pain: lil-t moni rfm1• ph-ac h2 sabad
    - **shooting** pain: kalm ruta tl1 *Spig Stram*
    - **stitching** pain: carbn-s *Cham* moni rfm1• *Pip-m* tritic-vg fd5.de
    - **tearing** pain: kali-bi rhus-v
  - **Parietal** bone: bry bg1
  - **Shoulder**, face distorted: graph
  - **Skull**: kola stb3•
  - **Teeth**: bry carb-v lachn nat-m bg1 rhus-t bg1 sars sulph *Verb*
    - **cramping**: nat-m k*
    - **jerking** pain: rhus-t h1
    - **stitching** pain: sars
    - **tearing** pain: bry carb-v lachn *Verb*
    - **Last** molar: hydr
  - **Temple** to temple; from: alumn asc-c **Bell** *Cedr* chel *Chin* chord-umb rly4• con eup-per↓ falco-pe↓ glon ham hydr kali-s fd4.de lac-c lil-t lob lyss manc menth c1 mez naja nat-ar *Phos* plan plat↓ rhod sang↓ sanguis-s↓ sep *Sulph* suprar↓ syph br*
    - **and** back again: bit-ar wht1• hydr *Lac-c* lil-t menth c1
    - **cutting** pain: asc-c c1* **Bell** *Chin* sanguis-s hrn2• *Sulph*
    - **dull** pain: falco-pe nl2• lob
    - **lancinating**: **Bell**
    - **nail**; as from a: ham
    - **pressing** pain: sulph h2
    - **shooting** pain: alumn asc-c **Bell** chel *Chin* eup-per k2 ham k2 phos plat sang suprar rly4•
    - **stitching** pain: **Chin** sang a1
  - **Throat**: croc bg1
  - **Upper** jaw: *Chin*↓
    - **jerking** pain: *Chin*
  - **Upward**: am-m bry bg1 laur rhus-v til ban1•
  - **Vertex**: am-m ambr↓ arund a1* aur-m↓ berb bg1 carbn-s↓ chel↓ coc-c cycl dioxi↓ dulc fd4.de kali-bi laur *Mang*↓ phos pieri-b mlk9.de plut-n srj7• suis-em↓
    - **drawing** pain: aur-m cycl
    - **pressing** pain: carbn-s chel dioxi rbp6 kali-bi suis-em rly4•
    - **tearing** pain: ambr hr1 laur *Mang*
  - **Zygoma**: **Bry**↓ carb-an↓ coc-c kali-c phos
    - **boring** pain: carb-an

- **Temples** – **extending** to – **Zygoma**: ...
  - **drawing** pain: **Bry**
  - **pressing** pain: **Bry**
  - **shooting** pain: *Phos*
  - **stitching** pain: kali-c
  - **tearing** pain: coc-c phos k2

○ • **Above**: hydrog↓ mang↓ mur-ac↓ positr↓ zinc↓
  - **burning**: mang a1 mur-ac h2
  - **pressing** pain: positr nl2•
  - **rising** from sitting agg.: mang↓
    - **pressing** pain: mang h2
  - **tearing** pain: zinc h2
  - **twitching**: hydrog srj2• zinc h2
- **Mastoid** process: iris↓
  - **pulsating** pain: iris
- **Side** lain on: bry xxb puls stann
  - **pressing** pain: stann
  - **tearing** pain: puls
- **Side** not lain on: graph
  - **pressing** pain: graph
- **Spots**; in: aeth↓ carb-v↓ helon↓ nept-m↓ ox-ac↓ psor↓ rat↓ sul-ac↓
  - **drawing** pain: sul-ac k*
  - **pressing** pain: helon k* nept-m lsd2.fr ox-ac k* psor
  - **tearing** pain: aeth a1 carb-v rat

- **Temples** and Forehead: agar agn ant-c ant-t aran arn *Ars* arum-t atro aur aur-ar k2 aur-s k2 bar-c *Bell* berb bit-ar wht1• bov bry *Camph* canth *Caps* hr1 cedr chel chin chinin-ar chinin-s clem coloc cor-r k* crot-t cycl dig dios dulc elat falco-pe nl2• ferr ferr-ar fl-ac galeoc-c-h gms1• gels glon gran hell hipp hura hydr-ac ind iris kali-bi kalm lachn lil-t lyc lycps-v mag-m mag-s mang merc-i-f merl mez moni rfm1• mur-ac myric naja nat-ar nat-m nat-p op ph-ac phos phys phyt pip-m psor pycnop-sa mrz1 rhod sabad sabin sel seneg **Sep** sinus rly4• spig stann sulph tab tanac verat zinc
- **Temples** and Occiput: acon aesc *Alum* bov cann-s nux-v oxal-a rly4• rhus-r spig syph jl2
- **Trigeminal** | **neuralgic** (See FACE - Pain - nerves - trigeminal)
- **Upper** half: ambr↓
  - **torn**; as if: ambr br1
- **Vertex**: acet-ac k* acon k* act-sp bro1 aesc↓ aeth k* agar k* agath-a nl2• agn alet↓ all-c↓ all-s↓ *Aloe*↓ *Alum* alum-p↓ alum-sil k2 *Alumn* k* am-c k* am-m↓ ambr aml-ns↓ amp rly4• *Anac* k* *Androc* srj1• ang↓ ant-c ant-t k* **Apis** apoc↓ arg-met↓ *Arg-n*↓ arge-pl rwt5• arizon-l nl2• arn k* ars k* ars-i ars-s-f k2 arum-t k* arund↓ asaf↓ asar↓ *Asc-t* a1 **Aur**↓ aur-ar↓ aur-i↓ aur-m-n aur-s↓ aven↓ bad bamb-a stb2.de• bapt↓ *Bar-c*↓ bar-i↓ bar-m↓ bar-s↓ bell k* *Benz-ac* k* berb↓ bism↓ bit-ar↓ borx k* bov **Brom** bros-gau↓ bry *Bufo* **Cact** k* cadm-s calc k* *Calc-ar*↓ calc-i k2 *Calc-p* k* calc-s calc-sil k2 camph↓ *Cann-i*↓ *Cann-s* k* cann-xyz↓ *Canth*↓ caps↓ carb-ac↓ **Carb-an** k* *Carb-v* k* *Carbn-s* carl a1 cartl-s rly4• castm *Caust* cedr cench k2 cent a1 cham k* *Chel* k* chen-a *Chin* k* chinin-ar chinin-s↓ choc↓ cic↓ **Cimic** k* cimx↓ *Cina*↓ *Cinnb* clem↓ cob k* coc-c coca cocc k* coff k* colch k* coli jl2* coloc↓ *Con* conv cop↓ *Corn* k* cortiso sp1 cot a1* croc↓ crot-c k* *Crot-h Cupr* cupr-s↓ *Cur* cycl h1 cypra-eg↓ cystein-l rly4• daph k* dig k* digin↓ dios dioxi↓ dirc a1 dor a1 dros k* dulc echi *Elaps* equis-h↓ ery-a↓ eug↓ euon↓ *Eup-per* k* euph k* euphr↓ eupi↓ fago↓ *Ferr* k* *Ferr-ar* ferr-i *Ferr-p* ferr-pic fic-m↓ fl-ac↓ *Form* k* *Frax*↓ fuma-ac↓ galeoc-c-h↓ *Gels* k* gent-c get↓ glon k* gran k* granit-m↓ graph grat↓ guaj↓ guare a1 ham fd3.de• hell k* helo↓ helon↓ *Hep* k* hipp↓ hir skp7• hura *Hydr* k* hydr-ac↓ *Hydrog* srj2• hyos↓ *Hyper* k* *Ign*↓ *Ind* indg↓ inul↓ iod k* ip↓ iris jab↓ jac-c↓ kali-bi k* *Kali-c*↓ *Kali-i*↓ kali-m↓ *Kali-n* a1 *Kali-p*↓ kali-s↓ kali-sil↓ kalm k* kola↓ kreos lac-ac k* lac-c lac-cp↓ lac-d lac-h sk4• *Lach* k* lachn↓ lact k* lap-la sde8.de• lappa↓ laur k* led↓ *Lil-t* limest-b↓ lipp↓ lith-c *Lyc* lyss k* *M-ambo*↓ m-arct↓ m-aust↓ *Mag-c*↓ *Mag-m*↓ mag-s↓ manc↓ mang↓ marb-w↓ med↓ melal-alt gya4 *Meny* k* *Merc* merc-c k* *Merc-i-f* k* *Merc-i-r* merl↓ *Mez* k* mill a1 morg-p pte1*• mosch k* mucs-nas rly4• mur-ac k* murx↓ myric a1 nabal a1 naja k* nat-ar *Nat-c* nat-m nat-ox rly4• nat-p *Nat-s*↓ nat-sil↓ nept-m↓ *Nicc*↓ nicotam rly4• *Nit-ac* nit-s-d↓ nuph a1 *Nux-m* k* *Nux-v* k* ol-an↓ ol-j k* olib-sac wmh1 olnd↓ op↓ orot-ac rly4• ox-ac k* pall k* pana a1 par passi↓ peti a1 *Petr*↓ petr-ra↓ *Ph-ac* k* *Phel* bro1 *Phos* k* phys k* *Phyt* k*

- **Vertex**: ...
pic-ac k* pieri-b ↓ pin-con ↓ plac-s rly4• plat bro1 plb ↓ plut-n ↓ podo k* positr nl2• propl ub1• propr ↓ psil ↓ ptel k* puls k* rad-met bro1 *Ran-b* **Ran-s** raph ↓ rat ↓ rheum rhod k* rhus-g a1 *Rhus-t* ↓ ribo rly4• rumx ruta fd4.de sabad k* sabin ↓ samb ↓ sang k* sanic sarr a1 *Sars* ↓ sedi ↓ sel rsj9• senec ↓ *Sep* k* *Sil* sol-ni sol-t-ae a1 sphing a1 *Spig* spira a1 spong k* squil stann staph stict ↓ still a1 stram k* streptoc ↓ stront-c sk4• stry a1 suis-em rly4• suis-hep rly4• suis-pan rly4• sul-ac ↓ sul-i k* **Sulph** k* suprar rly4• symph ↓ syph tab k* tarax ↓ tax ↓ tell k* tep ↓ ter ther thiam ↓ thlas ↓ thres-a ↓ *Thuj* k* til ↓ tong ↓ tritic-vg fd5.de tub ↓ upa ↓ ust valer k* vanil fd5.de ven-m rsj12• **Verat** k* verb k* vinc ↓ viol-t ↓ visc sp1 xan k* xanth yuc ↓ *Zinc* k* zinc-chr ↓ zinc-p k2 [bell-p-sp dcm1 heroin sdj2]
  - **right**: hydrog srj2• olnd ↓ prun bg1* sel rsj9• sphing ↓ spig kk3.fr tritic-vg fd5.de
    - **intermittent**: sphing kk3.fr
    - **stitching** pain: olnd b7.de*
  - **left**: aln vva1• anac bg1* dulc ↓ galeoc-c-h gms1• luf-op ↓ melal-alt gya4 phos ↓ spong fd4.de verb ↓
    - **burning**: phos b4.de*
    - **dull** pain: luf-op rsj5•
    - **plug**; as from a: anac bg2 dulc bg2
    - **stitching** pain: verb b7.de*
  - **daytime**: carbn-s ↓ *Crot-h* ↓ sep sulph tab
    - **pressing** pain: carbn-s *Crot-h*
  - **morning**: agar k* *Alumn* ↓ am-m ↓ ambr aster bar-c bov carb-ac chel ↓ cinnb k2 coc-c ↓ digin a1 dulc fd4.de graph hell ↓ hir skp7• hydr hyper k* iris lac-c luf-op ↓ merc nat-c k* nat-p ox-ac pall phos ↓ ran-b k* rhus-t ↓ ruta fd4.de spong fd4.de squil ↓ staph **Sulph** k* symph fd3.de• thuj k* tritic-vg fd5.de vanil fd5.de
    - **5** h (See night - midnight - after - 5)
    - **until** afternoon: graph ↓
      - **stitching** pain: graph h2
    - **amel.**: laur
    - **bed** agg.; in: carb-v k* hell
    - **burning**: coc-c k*
    - **bursting** pain: am-m k*
    - **drawing** pain: hell k*
    - **dull** pain: luf-op rsj5•
    - **pressing** pain: agar *Alumn* ambr k* chel coc-c k* ox-ac rhus-t ruta fd4.de squil staph h1 **Sulph** symph fd3.de• tritic-vg fd5.de vanil fd5.de
    - **rising**:
      - **agg.**: bar-act caust cimic kali-n nicc podo ruta fd4.de *Sep* spong fd4.de *Sulph*
      - **amel.**: carb-v h2 cinnb k2 ol-an
    - **sore**: bov hyper squil
    - **stitching** pain: am-m k* dulc fd4.de phos k* vanil fd5.de
    - **tearing** pain: bov ran-b
    - **waking** | **after**:
      - **agg.**: verat ↓
        - **pressing** pain: verat h1
      - **on**: alum *Alumn* ↓ bamb-a stb2.de• bar-act *Bry* bufo calc k* carb-an k* caust cedr coc-c ↓ croc hyper k* *Kali-bi* kali-p fd1.de• nat-p oxal-a rly4• puls k* *Sulph* k* symph fd3.de• tab ulm-c jsj8• vanil ↓ verat
        - **burning**: coc-c k*
        - **pressing** pain: *Alumn* calc h2 coc-c symph fd3.de• vanil fd5.de
  - **forenoon**: *Acon* ↓ *Alum* bamb-a stb2.de• bar-c borx ↓ bov bry k* calc fl-ac gamb glon kali-cy k* kali-s ↓ mag-s nat-ar nat-sil ↓ nicc nux-m k* pic-ac k* rhus-t ruta fd4.de sulph tritic-vg ↓ vanil fd5.de
    - **10** h: hydr lac-ac
    - **10**.30 h: hydr st mag-c ↓
      - **stitching** pain: mag-c
    - **11** h: hydr kali-bi ↓
      - **pressing** pain: kali-bi
    - **pressing** pain: *Acon* k* glon k* nat-sil fd3.de• ruta fd4.de vanil fd5.de
    - **sore**: nicc
    - **stitching** pain: kali-s fd4.de nicc k* tritic-vg fd5.de
    - **tearing** pain: borx
  - **noon**: manc ↓ mur-ac ↓ nat-sil ↓ *Puls-n* *Sulph* k* thuj k* tritic-vg fd5.de
    - **burning**: sulph k*
    - **pressing** pain: manc k* nat-sil fd3.de• tritic-vg fd5.de
    - **stitching** pain: mur-ac k* tritic-vg fd5.de
  - **afternoon**: alum alumn ambr androc srj1• ars bamb-a ↓ bov ↓ bufo calc-s carb-v *Cimic* k* crot-h k* dulc fd4.de graph helon k* hura hyper indg iris-foe kali-n kreos ↓ lac-ac lyc k* lyss k* mang merc-i-r mur-ac nat-ar nicc ↓ nit-ac olib-sac ↓ op ↓ osm phel phos phys k* ruta fd4.de sulph tritic-vg fd5.de tus-p a1 vanil fd5.de
    - **13**-14 h: marb-w ↓
      - **pressing** pain: marb-w es1•
    - **15** h: sabal c1
    - **15**-18 h: am-m ↓
      - **stitching** pain: am-m
    - **16**-20 h: **Lyc** ↓
      - **pressing** pain: **Lyc**
    - **17** h: stram ↓
      - **pressing** pain: stram
    - **amel.**: hir skp7•
    - **pressing** pain: alum k* bamb-a stb2.de• carb-v graph h2 olib-sac wmh1 op k* ruta fd4.de tritic-vg fd5.de vanil fd5.de
    - **sore**: nicc
    - **stitching** pain: alum k* bov k* indg k* mur-ac k* nit-ac h2 ruta fd4.de
    - **tearing** pain: kreos phos h2
    - **walking** agg.: stront-c ↓ syph ↓
      - **bursting** pain: stront-c syph bg1
  - **evening**: acon k* ambr apis borx *Calc* ↓ canth carb-an carb-v ↓ chinin-s ↓ cimic coc-c a1 coloc ↓ crot-h cycl dig ↓ dulc fago k* form glon k* *Hep* k* hyper kali-c kali-i lach k* lith-c lyc mag-c ↓ merc mur-ac nept-m ↓ nit-ac ol-an olib-sac ↓ petr positr ↓ *Ran-b* rhus-t ruta fd4.de sep sil stann stront-c *Sulph* k* thuj k* vanil fd5.de zinc
    - **18** h: hyper ↓
      - **pressing** pain: hyper
    - **19** h: lyc ↓
      - **tearing** pain: lyc
    - **bed** | **going** to bed:
      - **before**: cinnb ↓
        - **drawing** pain: cinnb
      - **in** bed | **agg.**: carb-v stann
    - **drawing** pain: borx h2 (non:bov kl) crot-h k* dulc ol-an k*
    - **jerking** pain: mur-ac a1
    - **pressing** pain: acon ambr k* carb-v h2 chinin-s coloc k* dig h2 hep h2 kali-c k* nept-m lsd2.fr olib-sac wmh1 petr h2 positr nl2• ruta fd4.de sil stann h2 *Sulph* k* vanil fd5.de
    - **sore**: mag-c sulph *Zinc*
    - **stitching** pain: *Calc* carb-an k* nit-ac k* petr h2
    - **tearing** pain: *Calc* hyper lyc
    - **twitching**: mur-ac h2
  - **night**: acon k* agar k* aln vva1• androc srj1• aster carb-an chel ↓ dulc ↓ ferr k* glon k* hipp hir skp7• iris-foe kali-n laur lyc *Merc* ↓ mez mur-ac h2 nit-ac ↓ ol-an positr nl2• rat ruta fd4.de sulph thuj ↓ tritic-vg fd5.de vanil fd5.de
    - **midnight**:
      - **before**:
        - **22**.30 h: alum ↓
          - **tearing** pain: alum
        - **23** h: luf-op ↓
          - **dull** pain: luf-op rsj5•
      - **after**:
        - **3**-4 h: *Thuj* ↓
          - **nail**; as from a: *Thuj*
        - **4** h: *Alumn* ↓
          - **pressing** pain: *Alumn*
        - **5** h: calc
          - **pressing** pain: calc
    - **amel.**: mag-c
    - **bursting** pain: carb-an
    - **pressing** pain: *Acon* agar lyc k* sulph k* vanil fd5.de

- **night**: ...
  - **sleep**; on going to | **amel.**: phyt
  - **stitching** pain: chel$_{k*}$ dulc$_{fd4.de}$ lyc$_{k*}$ nit-ac$_{h2}$
  - **tearing** pain: laur *Merc* thuj
- **accompanied** by | **nausea**: *Hir*$_{rsj4}$•
- **aching**: ign$_{ptk1}$
- **air**; in open:
  - **agg.**: ferr iris spong$_{fd4.de}$ sulph
  - **amel.**: acon ↓ carb-an cimic ferr gamb glon ind kali-n marb-w ↓ puls rat ruta ↓ tarent
    - **pressing** pain: acon marb-w$_{es1}$• ruta$_{fd4.de}$
    - **sore**: gamb
- **alternate** days: hydr
- **alternating** with | **Forehead**; pain in (See forehead - alternating with - vertex)
- **ascending**:
  - **agg.**: cimic ↓
    - **top** would fly off; as if: cimic$_{tl1}$
  - **stairs**:
    - **agg.**: ant-c cimic ferr lob meny
      - **pressing** pain: **Meny**
- **binding** head up:
  - **amel.**: **Sil** ↓
    - **bursting** pain: **Sil**
    - **pressing** pain: **Sil**
- **blow**; pain as from a: nat-m$_{bg2}$
  - **stupefying** pain, as from a blow on: valer$_{k*}$
- **blowing** the nose agg.: sulph$_{h2}$
- **boring** pain: agar$_{k*}$ ang$_{k*}$ *Arg-n* aur-s$_{k2}$ bar-c bell$_{k*}$ borx$_{b4a.de}$ caust chel$_{k*}$ chin$_{k*}$ cimic colch$_{k*}$ cycl dros$_{h1}$ kola$_{stb3}$• *Lach*$_{k*}$ led mag-s mosch$_{k*}$ mur-ac$_{k*}$ nit-ac$_{k*}$ olnd$_{k*}$ ph-ac$_{k*}$ phos$_{k*}$ puls$_{k*}$ samb$_{k*}$ spig$_{k*}$ *Sulph*$_{k*}$
  - **outward**: spig staph$_{k*}$
- **burning**: agar$_{k*}$ alumn arn ars$_{k*}$ *Aur*$_{k*}$ aur-ar$_{k2}$ aven$_{br1*}$ bapt *Bry* **Calc**$_{k*}$ *Calc-p*$_{k*}$ carb-ac carb-an$_{bg2}$ *Carb-v*$_{k*}$ carbn-s caust$_{k*}$ chinin-s$_{k*}$ cimic$_{bg2}$ coc-c$_{k*}$ *Con* *Crot-c* cupr$_{k*}$ cupr-s$_{bro1}$ daph$_{bg2*}$ dros$_{h1}$ dulc$_{k*}$ *Frax*$_{bro1}$ *Glon*$_{k*}$ **Graph**$_{k*}$ helo$_{bg2}$ helon$_{k*}$ hep$_{b4a.de}$ hyper kali-i$_{bg2}$ *Lach*$_{k*}$ laur$_{bg2}$ merl$_{k*}$ *Nat-m*$_{k*}$ nat-s$_{k*}$ peti$_{a1}$ *Ph-ac*$_{k*}$ *Phos*$_{k*}$ podo$_{k*}$ ran-s$_{k*}$ raph$_{k*}$ *Rhus-t*$_{b7a.de*}$ sabad$_{k*}$ sep$_{k*}$ stann$_{k*}$ **Sulph**$_{k*}$ tarax$_{bro1}$ thuj$_{b4a.de}$ tub$_{al}$ viol-t$_{k*}$ zinc$_{k*}$
  - **biting** pain: dros$_{h1*}$
  - **chilling** burning: caust$_{h}$
- **burrowing**: bar-c$_{b4.de*}$ bell$_{b4.de*}$ m-aust$_{b7.de}$ ol-an$_{bg2}$ phos$_{b4.de*}$ samb$_{b7.de*}$ spig$_{b7.de*}$
- **bursting** pain: alum$_{h2*}$ *Am-c* am-m$_{k*}$ bapt calc calc-sil$_{k2}$ **Carb-an**$_{k*}$ chin$_{bg2}$ *Cimic*$_{k*}$ *Ferr* glon$_{bg2}$ graph$_{k*}$ *Hyper* kali-i$_{bg2}$ lac-ac$_{k*}$ *Nat-s* nit-ac$_{k*}$ nux-v$_{bg2*}$ petr-ra$_{shn4}$• phyt$_{bg2}$ ran-b$_{bg2}$ sanic$_{ptk1}$ **Sil**$_{k*}$ spig$_{k*}$ spong stront-c$_{k*}$ syph$_{bg2*}$ xan xanth zinc$_{bg2}$
  - **blown** off; as if: cham
  - **come** off; as if top of head would: lac-d$_{c1}$
  - **fly** off; as if top would: cimic$_{k*}$
  - **forced** asunder; as if: kali-i lac-d nux-v *Sil*
  - **split** open; as if: zinc$_{h2}$
- **chewing** agg.: sulph$_{h2}$
- **chill**; during: hell ↓
  - **sore**: hell
- **cold**:
  - **air**:
    - **agg.**: *Ferr* ↓ iris ↓ ran-b ↓
      - **pressing** pain: *Ferr* ran-b$_{k2}$
      - **shooting** pain: iris
    - **amel.**: ant-c ↓ ind thuj ↓
      - **sore**: ant-c thuj
  - **applications**:
    - **amel.**: *Acon* *Alumn*$_{k*}$ sulph$_{mrr1}$
      - **burning**: sulph$_{mrr1}$
  - **water** | **agg.**: hir$_{skp7}$•
- **coldness**; during: coli$_{jl2}$ kali-n$_{h2}$
- **compressed**; as if: acon$_{bg2}$ dulc$_{b4.de*}$ graph$_{b4.de*}$ meny$_{b7.de*}$ nux-m$_{b7.de*}$ sep$_{b4.de*}$ stann$_{b4.de*}$ staph$_{b7.de*}$
- **contrariety**; after: coli$_{jl2}$
- **cough** agg.; during: agath-a$_{nl2}$• alum *Anac*$_{k*}$ apis caust con cupr kali-c sabad sanic ↓ squil sulph
  - **bursting** pain: sanic
  - **pressing** pain: *Anac*
  - **pulsating** pain: agath-a$_{nl2}$•
  - **shooting** pain: alum
  - **sore**: kali-c
  - **stitching** pain: alum$_{h2}$ con *Sabad*
  - **tearing** pain: alum$_{h2}$
- **cramping**: bell$_{bg2}$ chin$_{b7.de*}$ coloc$_{h2}$ phos$_{b4.de*}$ plat$_{k2}$
- **crushed**; as if: ip$_{bg1}$ plut-n$_{srj7}$•
- **cutting** pain: acon aur$_{h2*}$ *Bell*$_{k*}$ bov$_{bg2}$ calc$_{k*}$ *Carb-an*$_{k*}$ caust$_{bg2*}$ cimic$_{bg2}$ con dulc$_{fd4.de}$ *Lach*$_{k*}$ nat-m phos$_{bg2*}$ podo$_{bg2}$ positr$_{nl2}$• sang$_{bg2}$ senec$_{k*}$ **Thuj**$_{k*}$ verat$_{k*}$
- **dark**; while in the: sil ↓
  - **pressing** pain: sil
- **dinner**; after: calc ↓ con$_{k*}$ dirc$_{a1}$ mag-c ↓ nat-c$_{h2}$ nat-m$_{k*}$ thuj$_{k*}$
  - **pressing** pain: calc$_{h2}$ con$_{h2}$ mag-c$_{h2}$
  - **tearing** pain: mag-c
- **draw** eyes together, must: *Sulph* ↓
  - **pressing** pain: *Sulph*
- **drawing** head backward: phel ↓
  - **shooting** pain: phel
- **drawing** pain: anac$_{k*}$ ant-t$_{k*}$ arg-met$_{k*}$ *Arn*$_{k*}$ ars$_{k*}$ aur-m-n$_{a1}$ borx$_{b4a.de}$ bov$_{k*}$ *Calc*$_{k*}$ *Calc-p* caust$_{k*}$ *Chel*$_{k*}$ cinnb$_{k*}$ crot-h$_{k*}$ digin$_{a1}$ dulc$_{k*}$ grat$_{k*}$ hell$_{k*}$ indg$_{k*}$ iod$_{k*}$ *Kali-c*$_{k*}$ kali-p kali-s$_{fd4.de}$ led$_{k*}$ meny$_{b7.de*}$ myric$_{a1}$ nux-m$_{k*}$ nux-v$_{k*}$ ol-an$_{k*}$ ph-ac$_{k*}$ phos$_{k*}$ ran-b$_{k*}$ ran-s$_{k*}$ ruta$_{k*}$ sars$_{k*}$ sil$_{h2}$ spig$_{k*}$ spong$_{k*}$ stann$_{k*}$ thuj$_{h1}$ til$_{k*}$ vanil$_{fd5.de}$ zinc$_{k*}$
  - **alternating** with | **Temples**; pressing pain in (See temples - pressing - alternating - vertex)
  - **cramping**: phos$_{h2}$
  - **paroxysmal**: zinc$_{h2}$
- **driving** or riding in a carriage: lyc vanil$_{fd5.de}$
- **dull** pain: aesc$_{hr1}$ aeth agn$_{k*}$ alum-sil$_{k2}$ androc$_{srj1}$• ang ant-c$_{k*}$ asc-t$_{c1}$ *Bar-c*$_{hr1}$ caust$_{hr1}$ cench$_{k2}$ cimic$_{k*}$ coli$_{rly4}$• cystein-l$_{rly4}$• dulc$_{fd4.de}$ fic-m$_{gya1}$ gels$_{k*}$ graph$_{h2}$ *Hyper*$_{hr1}$ kali-p$_{fd1.de}$• lac-h$_{sk4}$• lach limest-b$_{es1}$• lyss$_{a1*}$ mez$_{k*}$ mill$_{hr1}$ olib-sac$_{wmh1}$ *Ox-ac*$_{hr1}$ phos$_{h2}$ ribo$_{rly4}$• ruta$_{fd4.de}$ spong$_{fd4.de}$ still$_{hr1}$ suis-em$_{rly4}$• suis-hep$_{rly4}$• suis-pan$_{rly4}$• symph$_{fd3.de}$• *Ter*$_{hr1}$ tritic-vg$_{fd5.de}$ vanil$_{fd5.de}$ zinc$_{hr1}$
- **eating** | **after**:
  - **agg.**: ambr ↓ bad calc-s castm *Cinnb* ↓ dirc inul ↓ kali-bi lyc mag-c nat-c phel rhus-t sulph tab
    - **pressing** pain: ambr$_{k2}$ *Cinnb* tab$_{a1}$
    - **tearing** pain: inul phel
  - **amel.**: carb-an ↓
    - **bursting** pain: carb-an$_{ptk1}$
- **exertion**; after strong mental: coli$_{jl2}$
- **gnawing** pain: *Ant-c* dros$_{h1}$ meny$_{k*}$ ran-b$_{bg2}$ ran-s$_{k*}$ spong$_{h1}$
- **grasping** pain: arg-n$_{bg2}$
- **grief**; from: *Calc* ↓ *Ph-ac* ↓
  - **burning**: *Calc* *Ph-ac*
  - **pressing** pain: *Ph-ac*
- **hammering** pain: hyper phos$_{k*}$
- **heat**; during: dulc$_{fd4.de}$ graph$_{k*}$
- **ice** amel.: alumn ↓
  - **pressing** pain: alumn$_{k1}$
- **increasing** and decreasing gradually: sars ↓ **Stann** ↓
  - **pressing** pain: sars **Stann**
- **inspiration** agg.; deep: *Anac*
  - **pressing** pain: *Anac*

- **jar** agg.: bell cob
- **jerking** pain: anac *Calc* gent-c k* kali-i kreos b7a.de meny mur-ac k* ran-s k* sil k* spig b7.de* spong k*
  - **paroxysmal**: *Sil*
- **lancinating**: sang k2
- **lasting** seconds: galeoc-c-h ↓
  - **sharp**: galeoc-c-h gms1•
- **laying** hand on it:
  - **agg.**: kali-n ↓
    - **pressing** pain: kali-n h2
  - **amel.**: kali-n
- **leaning** head against something:
  - **amel.**: nat-m ↓
    - **stitching** pain: nat-m h2
- **light**; from: cact ↓ sacch-a ↓
  - **pressing** pain: cact k2 sacch-a fd2.de•
- **lying**:
  - **agg.**: calc-p bg1 carb-v caust ↓ chel glon bg1 hipp kali-p fd1.de• *Lyc* ↓ mur-ac bg1 stann tritic-vg fd5.de vanil fd5.de
    - **burning**: caust h
    - **pressing** pain: *Lyc* tritic-vg fd5.de
  - **amel.**: bamb-a stb2.de• calc-p *Lyc* ↓ phos spig
    - **tearing** pain: *Lyc*
  - **back**; on | **agg.**: cinnb k2
  - **side**; on:
    - **left** | **agg.**: *Cinnb*
    - **painful** side:
      - **agg.**: nux-m ↓
        - **sore**: nux-m
    - **right** | **amel.**: cinnb k2
- **menopause**; during: **Lach** ↓ nux-v ↓ sang ↓ *Sulph* ↓
  - **burning**: **Lach** k* nux-v bro1 sang bro1 *Sulph* bro1
- **menses** | **after**:
  - **agg.**: ol-an ↓
    - **stitching** pain: ol-an k*
  - **during**:
    - **agg.**: calc k* carb-an castm ferr-p lach laur lyc mag-c nat-c ↓ nat-m nat-s k* nux-v ol-an phos rat sulph
      - **burning**: *Lach Nat-m Phos Sulph*
      - **pressing** pain: *Calc* castm ferr-p nat-c sne *Nat-s Nux-v*
      - **sore**: mag-c
      - **tearing** pain: *Laur* mag-c rat
- **mental** exertion:
  - **after**: *Cham* ↓ *Lyc* ↓ nat-s ↓ nat-sil ↓ *Nux-v* ↓ *Sep* ↓
    - **pressing** pain: *Cham Lyc* nat-s nat-sil fd3.de• *Nux-v Sep* k*
  - **agg.**: aster carb-v con *Ferr-pic* gent-c nat-m *Nux-v* k* ph-ac *Pic-ac* k* ran-b *Sep*
    - **sore**: ph-ac
- **motion**:
  - **agg.**: alum alumn aur *Bell* calc-p canth *Chin* echi *Ferr* glon ip iris lac-cp ↓ lach lob lyss mez *Ox-ac* ph-ac phyt sep spig thuj verat
    - **drawing** pain: ph-ac h2
    - **pressing** pain: aur h2 lac-cp sk4• ph-ac h2
    - **tearing** pain: aur bell
  - **amel.**: marb-w ↓ ruta ↓
    - **pressing** pain: marb-w es1• ruta fd4.de
  - **eyes**; of | **agg.**: sep
  - **head**; of | **agg.**: alum
- **nail**; as from a: euon k* form hell k* hura ign bg2 *M-ambo* b7.de* manc k* nicc k* *Nux-v* ruta fd4.de staph k* **Thuj** k*
- **noise** agg.: *Bell* ↓ *Cact* k* calc cimic ↓ ferr-p *Ferr-pic* iod spig tub bg1
  - **bursting** pain: cimic gk
  - **pressing** pain: *Bell Cact*
- **open**; as if: cimic mrr1 cypra-eg sde6.de• spig bg2
- **opening** and shutting; as if: cann-i tl1* cann-xyz bg2* cocc bg2
- **paroxysmal**: bamb-a stb2.de• chel k* *Chin* cimic k* hydr
- **periodical**: *Sil*
- **pinching** pain: mag-m h2 ph-ac h2 rheum h sep h2
- **plug**; as from a: lachn k* mez bg2
  - **bolt** had been driven from neck to vertex; as if a | **pulsating** at every heartbeat: *Cimic* k*
- **pressing** pain: (*↗Heaviness - vertex)* **Acon** k* act-sp aesc k* *Agar* k* agath-a nl2• agn k* alet vh1 all-c all-s k* *Aloe* k* alum k* alum-p k2 alum-sil k2 *Alumn* k* *Am-c* k* am-m bg2 *Ambr* k* *Anac* androc srj1• ang a1 ant-t k* apis k* arg-met b7.de* *Arg-n* arn k* *Ars* asaf k* asar b7.de* aur k* aur-i k2 aur-s k2 bamb-a stb2.de• bar-c k* bar-i k2 bar-s k2 **Bell** k* benz-ac k* bit-ar wht1• bov k* brom k* bros-gau mrc1 bry k* bufo **Cact** k* *Calc* k* *Calc-ar* calc-i k2 *Calc-p* calc-sil k2 camph k* *Cann-s* k* canth k* carb-an b4a.de* **Carb-v** k* **Carbn-s** castm *Caust* k* cedr k* cham k* *Chel* k* *Chen-a* chin k* chinin-s cic **Cimic** k* cimx k* *Cina* cinnb clem k* coc-c k* cocc k* colch k* coli rly4• coloc k* con k* cortiso tpw7 cot br1 croc k* crot-c sk4• crot-h cupr cupr-s a1 *Cycl* k* cypra-eg sde6.de• *Dig* k* digin a1 dioxi rbp6 dros k* dulc k* equis-h a1 eug eup-per euphr k* fago a1 *Ferr* k* *Ferr-ar* ferr-i *Ferr-p* k* fl-ac fuma-ac rly4• gels k* gent-c a1 **Glon** k* granit-m es1• *Graph* hell k* helon k* hep k* hipp hydr hydr-ac hyos k* *Hyper* k* ign k* indg *Iod* k* ip jac-c *Kali-bi* k* *Kali-c* k* *Kali-i* k* kali-n k* *Kali-p* kali-sil k2 kalm kreos k* lac-c lac-cp sk4• lac-h htj1*• **Lach** k* lappa ptk1 laur k* led k* lil-t k* lith-c **Lyc** k* *Lyss* k* m-aust b7.de mag-c k* mag-m k* manc mang marb-w es1• med *Meny* k* merc b4a.de merc-c b4a.de merc-i-r *Mez* k* mosch k* murx bg *Naja* nat-ar nat-c k* nat-m k* *Nat-p* nat-s nat-sil fd3.de• nept-m lsd2.fr *Nicc* k* nit-ac k* *Nux-m* k* *Nux-v* k* ol-an k* olib-sac wmh1 olnd k* op k* *Ox-ac* pall k* *Petr* k* petr-ra shn4• **Ph-ac** k* *Phel* k* *Phos* k* *Phys* k* *Phyt* k* pic-ac k* pin-con oss2• plat k* plb ptk1 plut-n srj7• podo fd3.de• *Positr* nl2• puls *Ran-b* k* ran-s k* rheum k* rhod k* rhus-t k* ribo rly4• rumx ruta fd4.de sabad k* sabin k* sang a1 *Sars* k* sedi a1 *Sep* k* **Sil** k* spig k* spong k* squil k* **Stann** k* *Staph* k* stict bg2 stram k* suis-pan rly4• sul-ac k* sul-i k2 **Sulph** k* symph fd3.de• syph tab k* thiam rly4• thres-a sze7• *Thuj* k* tong a1 tritic-vg fd5.de tub al* upa a1 valer k* vanil fd5.de *Verat* k* verb k* viol-t k* xan xanth zinc k* zinc-chr ptk1 zinc-p k2 [heroin sdj2 tax jsj7]
  - **accompanied** by | **dizziness**: petr h2
  - **asunder**: carb-an k* hyper kali-i bg2 nux-v ph-ac b4.de* ran-b k* stront-c bg2
  - **band** drawn tightly from ear to ear; as from a: ip
  - **bound**; as if: acon cycl kalm
  - **finger**; as from a: nit-ac thuj
  - **hard** body; as from a: *Ign* nux-v thuj
  - **intermitting**: chel *Cina* ph-ac h2 stann
  - **inward**: acon bg2 alum bg2 ambr bg2 aml-ns bg2 *Anac* k* arg-n bg1 asaf asar b7.de* bar-c bg2 bism bg2* *Cact* bg2 *Carb-an* b4a.de caust k* cham bg2 cina bg2* *Dulc* k* ferr glon k* hell k* hyper bg2 kali-bi bg2 kali-n bg2 lach bg2* lyc bg2* m-ambo b7.de med br1 **Meny** bg2 mosch bg2 nat-m bg2 nit-ac k* nux-m b7.de* nux-v k* ox-ac pall bg2 **Ph-ac** k* phel bg2* phos bg2 plat puls bg2* ran-s k* ruta fd4.de sep k* sil k* spig bg2* spong bg2 stann k* staph k* stict bg2 *Sulph* k* thuj bg2* tub bg2* verat bg2* zinc
    - **weight**; as from a: acon bg1 cact bg1 lach bg1 meny bg1
  - **jerking** pain: sil h2
  - **outward**: *Am-c* bell bg2 calc k* calc-p k* **Carb-an** k* cham chin bg2 **Cimic** k* *Ferr* k* glon k* helo bg2 helon a1 hydr bg2 hyper bg2 iris bg2 kali-i bg2 lac-ac bg2 *Lach* k* nat-m bg2 op k* par b7a.de ph-ac k* phys k* ran-b bg2 ruta fd4.de sep bg2 **Sil** spig stann bg2 stront-c bg2 sulph bg2 zinc bg2
    - **upward**: sep bg2
  - **paroxysmal**: chel sil h2 zinc h2
  - **plug**; as from a: **Anac**
  - **stone** were lying on it; as if a: kali-n c1
  - **turning** in a circle; as if after: calc h2
  - **upward**: **Cimic** *Ferr* glon bg1 helon k* sulph bg1
  - **vise**; as if in a: daph
  - **weight**; as from a: aloe bg2 alum b4a.de* aml-ns bg2 asar b7.de* cact bg2* cann-s b7.de* carb-v b4.de* caust b4.de* cina b7.de* cocc b7.de* cupr b7.de* graph b4.de* hell b7.de* kali-n b4.de* lach bg2 laur b7.de* led b7.de* m-ambo b7.de m-arct b7.de med bg2 meny b7.de* mosch b7a.de

- **pressing** pain – **weight**; as from a: ... nux-v b7.de* ph-ac b4.de* phel bg2* pic-ac bg2 pieri-b mlk9.de plat b4.de rhus-t a1 sep bg2 squil bg2 sulph b4.de* xanth bg2
- **pressure**:
  - **agg.**: ant-c h2 bell castm caust h2 *Chin* cina hydrog srj2• kali-c kali-n *Lach* nat-c ruta fd4.de
    - **pressing** pain: *Bell* cina h1 kali-n ruta fd4.de
    - **tearing** pain: *Bell*
  - **amel.**: alum alumn *Arg-n Cact Cina*↓ dirc k* dulc↓ eup-per k* ferr h e l l↓ lach↓ *Meny* nat-m bg1 ph-ac phys k* stann *Verat* zinc bg1
    - **drawing** pain: ph-ac h2
    - **pressing** pain: *Alumn* **Cact** k* *Cina* k* dulc fd4.de lach bg2* *Meny* k* nat-m k* stann h2 *Verat* k*
    - **sore**: hell
    - **stitching** pain: ph-ac h2
  - **hard**:
    - **amel.**: alumn↓
      - **pressing** pain: alumn k1
- **pulled**; sensation as if hair were: *Acon* alum h2* bell a1 coloc a1 eupi a1 ferr indg k* kali-n k* lachn vml3• lyc a1 *Mag-c* k* *Mag-m* k* mag-s a1 mur-ac rb2 phos bg1* spong a1 *Sulph* k*
- **pulsating** pain: aeth a1 agar k* agath-a nl2• alum amp rly4• apoc a1 a r s k* bell *Bry* k* canth carb-an k* corn a1 *Ferr* galeoc-c-h gms1• get a1 *Glon* k* helon hr1 hir rsj4• hydrog srj2• hyper inul a1 jab a1 kreos k* *Lach* *Lyc* lyss nat-c k* *Nux-v* k* phos k* pic-ac a1 propr sa3• *Sep* k* *Sil Stram* streptoc rly4• suis-pan rly4• sulph tep a1 tritic-vg fd5.de *Verat* k* [heroin sdj2]
- **reading** agg.: carb-v con k2 helon k* lyc lyss k* nat-m
  - **stitching** pain: carb-v k* lyc k*
- **reflecting** agg.: *Lyss*
- **riding** in a carriage agg.: lyc↓ vanil↓
  - **pressing** pain: lyc vanil fd5.de
- **rising**:
  - **agg.**: fic-m gya1
  - **sitting**; from | **agg.**: cob
- **room**; when entering a: *Ran-b*
- **rubbing**:
  - **amel.**: aeth a1 carb-ac phos
    - **burning**: phos k*
    - **stitching** pain: aeth
- **sharp**: galeoc-c-h gms1•
- **shooting** pain: acon aeth agar k* alum alum-p k2 am-m bar-c bar-s k2 bell berb bov bry calc caps carb-an carb-v caust cham chel chin choc srj3• cimic k* con cupr dig ery-a a1 ferr a1 hura iod ip iris kali-bi kalm lach laur lyc lyss a1 mag-c melal-alt gya4 mez mill nat-m nit-ac ph-ac phel phos phyt propr sa3• spig stram k* sul-i a1 sulph tab ter valer zinc
  - **boring** through: sil
  - **deep**: caps indg lyc staph tab
  - **forward**: cham nicc
  - **inward**: aloe lach lyc
- **sitting**:
  - **agg.**: castm lyc marb-w↓ peti phos verat viol-t
    - **pressing** pain: marb-w es1•
    - **tearing** pain: phos
  - **amel.**: con gels
- **sleep** | **after**:
  - **agg.**: ambr↓
    - **pressing** pain: ambr bg1*
  - **amel.**: calc
- **sneezing** agg.: apis bar-c nux-v sulph
- **sore**: agar h2 *Alum* am-m b7.de* ant-c apis k* arg-met aur b4a.de* bov k* bry k* bufo carb-an bg2 castm caust b4.de* chel k* *Chin* b7.de* cimic k* cinnb ferr k* ferr-p fic-m gya1 glon hyper ind iod ip bg2 kali-bi k* kali-c k* kali-n k* lac-ac *Lach* k* *Mag-c* k* mag-m k* melal-alt gya4 merc bg2* m u r - a c bg2 nat-m h2 nicc nit-ac ptk1 nux-v h1* olnd k* petr k* ph-ac k* phos k* phyt ran-s bg2 rhod k* rhus-t sabin k* sep k* sil k* spig squil sul-i **Sulph** k* thuj k* verat bg2 *Zinc* k* [bell-p-sp dcm1 heroin sdj2 tax jsj7]
- **sore**: ...
  - **pulsating** pain: caust
- **squeezed**; as if: aml-ns bg2 coloc b4.de* kali-c b4.de* ran-s b7.de* r h e u m b7.de* sep b4.de*
- **standing** agg.: alum mang ran-b sul-ac k* verat
  - **pressing** pain: alum h2 sul-ac
  - **tearing** pain: ran-b
- **stitching** pain: acon k* aesc aeth k* alum k* alum-p k2 alumn am-m k* anac k* *Bar-c* k* bar-s k2 bell k* borx bov k* *Bry* k* *Calc* k* caps k* carb-an k* carb-v k* *Caust* k* chel k* chin (non:cimic a1) cimx k* cina b7.de* *Con* k* cop k* cupr k* cycl dig k* dulc fd4.de eupi ferr k* ferr-i ferr-p graph h2 guaj k* hell k* hyper k* indg iod k* ip k* kali-i k* kali-n k* kali-s fd4.de kola stb3• lach k* laur k* lipp a1 lith-c *Lyc* k* *Mag-c* k* mag-m h2* meny k* merc-c b4a.de *Mez* k* mill k* nat-c k* *Nat-m* k* nicc k* nit-ac k* nit-s-d a1 ol-an k* olnd par b7.de* petr k* *Ph-ac* k* phel k* *Phos* k* puls ran-b bg2 raph k* rat k* ruta k* sabad k* sars k* *Sel* b7a.de sep k* sil h2 sphing a1 *Spig* k* *Stann* k* staph k* stront-c k* stry sul-i k2 sulph k* symph fd3.de• tab k* thuj k* tong a1 tritic-vg fd5.de valer k* vanil fd5.de verb k* zinc k* zinc-p k2
  - **burning**: cupr h2 phos h2 stann staph h1 zinc h2
  - **downward**: bar-c bg2 nat-m bg2
  - **intermittent**: ph-ac h2
  - **inward**: petr h2
  - **needles**; as from: dulc fd4.de staph h1
  - **outward**: spig k* staph k*
  - **paroxysmal**: *Caust* k* chel k*
  - **pulsating** pain: aeth
- **stool** agg.; during: ind iod↓ lyc k*
  - **pressing** pain: iod bg2
- **stooping**:
  - **agg.**: acon alum alumn am-m berb calc calc-p cham↓ coloc elaps glon helon indg↓ iris kreos lyc lyss meny nux-m spig↓
    - **pressing** pain: calc cham indg *Lyc* lyss spig hr1
    - **stitching** pain: alumn am-m
  - **amel.**: laur verat
- **stunning** pain: arund hr1 bov k* cycl h1 dulc k* lyss hr1 phos k* psil ft1 rheum k* valer k*
  - **alternating** with | **Forehead**; stupefying pain in (See forehead - stunning - alternating - vertex)
- **sun**:
  - **exposure** to sun; from: *Bar-c*↓
    - **stitching** pain: *Bar-c*
  - **standing** in the sun agg.: *Bar-c*↓ lac-cp↓
    - **pressing** pain: *Bar-c* lac-cp sk4•
  - **walking** in the sun | **agg.**: bar-c
- **talk** of others agg.: *Cact*↓
  - **pressing** pain: *Cact*
- **talking** agg.: iod↓ mez h2 peti↓ spig↓
  - **pressing** pain: iod mez peti spig
- **tearing** pain: act-sp agar agn k* alum alum-p k2 alum-sil k2 am-c k* *Ambr* k* anac ant-c arg-n k* **Aur** k* bar-c k* bar-i k2 bar-m *Bell* k* benz-ac borx k* bov k* *Canth* k* carb-v h2 castm caust chel k* colch k* con dulc k* hyper indg iod k* *Kali-c* k* kali-m k2 kali-n h2 kali-p kali-sil k2 kalm kreos *Lach* lachn laur k* *Lyc* k* m-aust b7.de *Mag-c* k* mag-s mang k* merc k* mez *Mur-ac* k* naja nat-c nit-ac nux-v k* ph-ac k* phel phos k* ran-b k* ran-s rat rhus-t k* ruta k* *Sars* k* sil spig k* *Stann* k* thuj k* vinc *Zinc* k* zinc-p k2
  - **jerking** pain: mag-c h2
  - **paroxysmal**: carb-v h2 zinc h2
- **thinking** about it agg.: **Cham**↓
  - **pressing** pain: **Cham**
- **top** would fly off; as if: acon bro1 bapt bg2* bell bg2 *Cann-i* bro1 cann-xyz bg2* chin bg2 cimic bg2* cinnb bg2 cob bg2 dios bg2 gels bg2 helo bg2 iris bg2* kali-bi bg2 passi bro1 syph bg2* thlas ptk1 visc bro1 xan ptk1 xanth bg2 yuc bro1
- **torn**; as if: **Carb-an** caust k* mur-ac k* thuj k* zinc k*

Head

- **touch**:
  - **agg.**: bov caust h2 chel cinnb kali-bi mez peti ph-ac ↓ phos sulph h2 zinc ↓
    - **sore**: zinc h2
    - **stitching** pain: ph-ac h2
  - **hair** agg.; touching the: *Carb-v* kreos ↓ nit-ac h2
    - **pressing** pain: *Carb-v* kreos bg1
- **transient**: indg ↓ mill ↓ nat-c ↓
  - **burning**: nat-c
  - **shooting** pain: indg mill
- **trembling**: anac ↓
  - **stitching** pain: anac h2
- **turning** head agg.: hyos ↓
  - **pressing** pain: hyos
- **ulcerative** pain: castm kreos spig b7a.de zinc
- **urinate** is not soon attended to; if desire to: *Fl-ac* ↓
  - **pressing** pain: *Fl-ac*
- **urination** agg.; after: caust
- **voices** agg.: *Ferr-pic Lyc*
- **waking**; on: kali-bi k* lyc a1 thuj k* trios rsj11•
- **walking**:
  - **agg.**: calc k* carb-an k* cedr k* chel ↓ con glon *Hep* ↓ hura peti phyt k* spong stront-c ↓ sulph vanil fd5.de
    - **bursting** pain: stront-c
    - **cutting** pain: *Carb-an* k*
    - **drawing** pain: chel k*
    - **pressing** pain: *Hep*
    - **stitching** pain: carb-an k*
  - **air**; in open:
    - **agg.**: calc vanil fd5.de
      - **pressing** pain: calc vanil fd5.de
    - **amel.**: acon aster symph fd3.de• thuj
      - **nail**; as from a: *Thuj* k*
  - **amel.**: peti sang
    - **pressing** pain: sang a1
  - **rapidly**:
    - **agg.**: chel k*
      - **pressing** pain: chel
      - **stitching** pain: chel h1
- **warm** room agg.: ran-b ↓
  - **pressing** pain: ran-b k2
- **washing**:
  - **amel.**: spig ↓
    - **stitching** pain: spig
- **weather**:
  - **change** of weather: ran-b ↓
    - **pressing** pain: ran-b k2
  - **wet**:
    - **agg.**: *Calc* ↓ *Carb-an* coli jl2
      - **bursting** pain: carb-an
      - **stitching** pain: *Calc*
- **wrinkling** of forehead; compels: *Sulph* ↓
  - **pressing** pain: *Sulph*
- **writing** agg.: gels k* nat-m ran-b
  - **tearing** pain: ran-b

▽ • **extending** to:
  - **Backward**: chel kali-bi kali-n
  - **Brain**: am-c bg1 mur-ac ↓ ox-ac bg1 spig ↓ staph ↓ sulph ↓
    - **boring** pain: mur-ac a1
    - **pressing** pain: sulph h2
    - **stitching** pain: spig h1 staph h1
  - **Downward**: kali-n h2
  - **Downward**, down limbs into abdomen and genitals: eupi ↓
    - **stitching** pain: eupi br1
  - **Ear**: agar lac-f c1 phos tritic-vg fd5.de vanil fd5.de [heroin sdj2]

- **extending** to – **Ear**: ...
    - **tearing** pain: agar phos
    - **From** one ear to the other: chel bg1 naja bg1 nit-ac bg1 pall k*
  - **Eye**: calc ↓ hydrog ↓ ruta ↓ sil ↓ vanil ↓
    - **lancinating**: hydrog srj2•
    - **pressing** pain: calc k* ruta fd4.de sil vanil fd5.de
  - **Eyebrows**: act-sp vh1 sumb bg1
  - **Eyes**: ign kali-p fd1.de• nux-m ruta fd4.de vanil fd5.de [heroin sdj2]
    - **drawing** pain: nux-m
    - **Over** the eyes: sil bg1
      - **right**: sang tl1 [tax jsj7]
  - **Face**: sacch bg1
  - **Forehead**: agar bg1 caps cartl-s rly4• *Caust* cham *Cocc* heroin ↓ hydr-ac ↓ ign ↓ led mez nat-m ↓ nicc nux-m sulph bg1
    - **drawing** pain: led
    - **pressing** pain: cham k* hydr-ac k* ign nat-m k* sulph h2 [heroin sdj2]
    - **stitching** pain: caps mez nicc
  - **Head**: chen-a ↓ dig ↓ lach ↓
    - **pressing** pain: chen-a vml3• dig h2
    - **stitching** pain: lach
    - **Centre** of: bar-c bg1 bov bg1 lach bg1 petr bg1
    - **Sides** of: hyper bg1 nit-ac bg1 pall bg1 suis-hep rly4•
    - **Through** whole: bar-c ↓
      - **stitching** pain: bar-c
  - **Malar** bones: tarent
  - **Middle** of brain: thuj ↓
    - **tearing** pain: thuj h1
  - **Neck**: calc-p *Chel* dios bg1 gels bg1 glon kalm
    - **drawing** pain: chel
  - **Nose**: plut-n ↓
    - **eating**; while: dulc
      - **drawing** pain: dulc
    - **pressing** pain: plut-n srj7•
  - **Occiput**: aloe bg1 bar-c ↓ calc-p card-b bg1 *Chel* cimic bg1 cina tl1 coloc tl1 gels indg kali-bi bg1 lil-t tl1 mag-c ↓ *Ph-ac* ↓ phys bg1
    - **pressing** pain: bar-c *Ph-ac*
    - **stitching** pain: mag-c h2
    - **tearing** pain: indg
  - **Palate**: nat-m
    - **stitching** pain: nat-m
  - **Pharynx**: cham ↓
    - **stitching** pain: cham
  - **Scapula**: lil-t bg1
  - **Shoulder**: gels ↓ lyc
    - **pressing** pain: gels
    - **tearing** pain: lyc
  - **Spine**:
    - **no** pain: benz-ac ↓
      - **pressing** pain: benz-ac k*
  - **Spine**; down: pic-ac k2
  - **Temple**: borx ↓ chel ↓
    - **drawing** pain: borx h2 chel
  - **Temples**: arg-met bg1 carb-v caust cham chel hell bg1 hipp kalm phos plut-n srj7• suis-em rly4•
    - **burning**: phos k*
    - **shooting** pain: kalm
    - **stitching** pain: carb-v phos
  - **Temples**; over: ang ↓
    - **tearing** pain: ang
  - **Throat**: cham
  - **Upward**: glon bg1
  - **Zygoma**: phos
    - **shooting** pain: phos k2
    - **tearing** pain: phos

○ • **Across**: lac-ac ↓
  - **shooting** pain: lac-ac

- **Eyes** and vertex; between: verat-v ↓
  - **aching**: verat-v ptk1
- **Here** and there: kali-i ↓
  - **jerking** pain: kali-i
- **Occiput**, then in: calc-ar ↓
  - **pressing** pain: calc-ar kr1
- **Spot**; in a small: spig ↓
  - **pressing** pain: spig
- **Spots**; in: *Arn* ↓ ars ↓ borx ↓ *Caust* ↓ chel ↓ colch ↓ *Graph* ↓ kali-bi ↓ lil-s a1 melal-alt ↓ nux-m a1 nux-v psor k* raph ↓ sol-ni spig k* sulph ↓ ulm-c ↓ vinc ↓
  - **boring** pain: borx colch k* sulph
  - **burning**: *Arn* ars k* *Graph* raph k*
  - **sore**: *Caust* melal-alt gya4 ulm-c jsj8• vinc
  - **stitching** pain: chel k* kali-bi k*

- **Vertex** and Forehead: acet-ac acon agath-a nl2• all-c aloe ambr anac androc srj1• ant-c ant-t arg-n bar-c bell berb borx bry bufo calc cann-i carb-an cartl-s rly4• castm caust cinnb corn crot-t dig dios dulc fd4.de glon graph grat helon k* hura hydr-ac ign indg kali-bi laur lyss mag-c mang meny merc mez mosch mur-ac myric naja nat-c nat-m nat-p nux-v ol-an ol-j ox-ac phel ptel puls rhus-r *Sep* sil sol-ni stann valer zinc

PARALYSIS of brain: alumn bro1 caust tl1 con bro1 cupr bro1 gels bro1 hell bro1 helo-s bnm14• lyc bro1 op bro1 phos mtf plb bro1* *Sec* bro1 zinc bro1*

- **incipient**: am-c am-m ptk1 ars carb-v hyos **Lyc** k* op phos plb zinc k*
- **sensation** as if: calc bg kola stb3• sil bg
  - **one** side: lyc b4a.de sil b4a.de
  - **ejaculations**; after: sil k*
  - **talking** agg.: calc h2
  - ○ **Forehead**: sep h2
  - **Occiput**; muscles of: dulc h1
- **threatening** | **scarlatina**; from receding: *Ail* bro1 am-c bro1 cupr-act bro1 sulph bro1 tub bro1 *Zinc* bro1
- ○ **Medulla** oblongata (= bulbar paralysis) botul br1 çanth mtf11 gels mtf11 *Gua* br1* mang-o bro1 mang-p mtf11 medul-o mtf11 naja br1 plb br1*
  - **accompanied** by:
    - **speech**; disordered: coc-c mtf11
    - **swallow**; inability to: naja vml4
    - **Throat**; constriction of: coc-c mtf11
  - **motor** nerves: gels mtf11

PERIODICITY: anac bg2 aran bg2 arn bg2 *Ars* bg2 atro bg2 aur bg2 bell bg2 cedr bg2 *Chin* bg2 chinin-s bg2 eup-per bg2 ferr bg2 ip bg2 iris bg2 kali-bi bg2 lach bg2 laur bg2 lil-t bg2 lyc bg2 mag-c bg2 mag-m bg2 mur-ac bg2 *Nat-m* bg2 nux-m bg2 nux-v bg2 phos bg2 plat bg2 puls bg2 rhus-t bg2 sabad bg2 sang bg2 sel bg2 sep bg2 sil bg2 spig bg2 stann bg2 sulph bg2 ther bg2 thuj bg2 zinc bg2

- **day**:
  - **alternate**: ambr b7.de* *Caps* b7a.de chin bg2 *Nux-v* b7.de* phos b4a.de* sulph bg2
  - **eight** to fourteen days; every: sulph bg2
  - **third** or fourth day; every: aur bg2
  - **every**: ars bg2 bell bg2 cedr bg2 *Coloc* bg2 con bg2 *Hep* bg2 *Lach* bg2 lyc bg2 *Mag-m* bg2 mang bg2 mur-ac bg2 nat-c bg2 **Nat-m** bg2 nit-ac bg2 nux-m bg2 **Nux-v** bg2 petr bg2 phos bg2 sabad bg2 seneg bg2 *Sep* bg2 **Sil** bg2 stann bg2 *Sulph* bg2 zinc bg2
  - **ten** days; every: lach bg2
  - **Sunday**; every: iris bg2 sulph bg2
    - **forenoon**: iris bg2
- **week**:
  - **second** or third week; every: arn b7a.de ferr b7.de* nux-v b7a.de
  - **every**: calc bg2* calc-ar bg2 epiph ptk1 gels bg2 iris bg2 lac-d bg2 phos bg2 sabad bg2 sang bg2 sil bg2 sulph bg2 tub bg2
  - **two** weeks; every: ars bg2 sulph bg2
  - **six** weeks; every: mag-m bg2
- **exact**: bell bg2 kali-n bg2 sel bg2

PERIOSTITIS (See Inflammation - periosteum)

PERSPIRATION:

- **amel.**: graph b4.de* mag-m b4.de* nat-m b4a.de
- **before** | **agg.**: ferr b7.de
- **during**:
  - **agg.**: ant-c b7.de arn b7.de bry b7.de *Cham* b7.de ferr b7.de rhus-t b7.de
    - **External** head: sabad b7.de*
  - **beginning** of; at the: nat-m bg2
  - ○ **External** head: sabad bg2
- **suppressed** perspiration; from: *Ars* b4a.de cham b7a.de* chin b7a.de *Nux-v* b7a.de *Puls* b7a.de

PERSPIRATION of scalp: acon b7a.de* aesc *Agar* aloe sne am-m ptk1 ambr bg2 amph a1 **Anac** k* *Ant-t* k* *Apis* k* arge-pl rwt5• ars-i bamb-a stb2.de• bar-c k* bar-i k2 *Bar-m* bar-s k2 *Bell* k* benz-ac borx k* bov k* **Bry** b7.de* bufo k* **Calc** k* calc-i k2 *Calc-p* k* *Calc-s* calc-sil k2 camph k* carb-an b4a.de* *Carb-v* k* carbn-s *Caust* k* **Cham** k* **Chin** k* cimx cina b7a.de* clem *Coloc* b4.de* cycl dig k* dulc fd4.de eup-pur gamb glon *Graph* k* grat **Guaj** k* ham bg2 hell bro1 *Hep* k* hera bro1 hyper bro1 iod ip k* ix bnm8• *Kali-c* k* kali-m k2* *Kali-p* kali-s kali-sil k2 laur k* led b7.de* *Lyc* m-ambo b7.de mag-c k* *Mag-m* k* **Merc** k* merc-c bg2 *Mez* k* mosch k* **Mur-ac** k* nat-m k* nat-sil fd3.de• *Nit-ac* k* nux-v k* ol-an olnd op k* par b7.de* *Petr* k* ph-ac k* phel **Phos** k* plb k* podo bro1 psor **Puls** k* *Pyrog* **Rheum** k* *Rhus-t* b7.de* ruta b7.de* sabad k* *Samb* bro1 *Sanic* bg2* sec b7.de* *Sep* k* **Sil** k* spig k* stann bro1 staph *Stram* stry k* suis-em rly4• sul-ac b4.de* sul-i k2 sulph k* syc fmm1• tab tarax bg2 tarent thuj k* tritic-vg fd5.de tub valer k* vanil fd5.de *Verat* b7a.de* verat-v zinc zinc-p k2 [bor-pur stj2]

- **day** and night: sulph h2
- **daytime**: ol-an stram
- **morning**: bamb-a stb2.de• *Calc* cann-s dulc hep *Mez* nat-m nux-v *Sep*
  - **rising** agg.: nat-m
- **forenoon**: mag-c tritic-vg fd5.de
- **afternoon**: bamb-a stb2.de•
- **evening**: anac bar-c h2 *Calc* mag-m h2 mur-ac h2 ruta fd4.de sep sil h2
  - **lying** down agg.; after: petr
- **night**: (↗*sleep - during)* aloe sne arum-t vh bov bry **Calc** k* calc-p mrr1 calc-sil tl1 carb-an chin coloc h2 dulc fd4.de hep h2* hydrog srj2• kali-c h2 kali-s fkr2.de med al *Merc* k* nat-m nit-ac h2 rhus-t ruta fd4.de sanic vh sep h2* *Sil* k* staph sne syc bka1• tritic-vg fd5.de tub c1
  - **midnight**: ph-ac h2 rhus-t
    - **after** | **4 h**; until: syc bka1•
- **amel.**: bov bg2 hep bg2 iod bg2
- **bed** agg.; in: bry calc-p mrr1
- **breakfast** agg.; after: par
- **chill**:
  - **after**: sulph h2
  - **during**: ars bg2 bry bg2 *Calc* bg2 *Cham* bg2 chin bg2 dig bg2 nat-m bg2 *Puls* bg2 rhus-t bg2 *Sil* bg2
- **clammy**: cham k* merc k* nux-v k*
- **cold**: acon ant-t benz-ac bry k* bufo k* *Calc* camph carb-v k2 cina k* cocc con convo-s sp1 dig k* dulc fd4.de *Hep* k* *Lob* merc k* merc-c k* *Nux-v* *Op* petr *Phos* podo stront-c sk4• tub k2 *Verat* k*
  - **air**; in open: *Calc*
  - **fever**; during: hep bg2 verat bg2
  - **room** agg.: calc k2
- **convulsions**; before epileptic: *Caust*
- **cough** agg.; during: ant-t k* calc ip merc sil tarent
- **eating**: (↗*forehead - eating - while - agg.)*
  - **after** | **agg.**: petr b4a.de
  - **while** | **agg.**: (↗*forehead - eating - while - agg.)* **Calc** sys nat-m gtr1 nit-ac a1 nux-v petr sil dx1
- **except** the head; general perspiration: *Bell* k* m-arct b7a.de merc k* mur-ac h2 nux-v k* **Rhus-t** k* **Samb** k* *Sec* k* *Sep* k* **Thuj** bg2*
- **excitement**; with (See MIND - Excitement - head; with)
- **fetid**: *Calc* *Merc* puls *Staph*
  - **one** side: *Nux-v* *Puls*
- **headache**; during: bamb-a stb2.de• calc j5.de mez h2 phys sil j5.de* **Sulph** vh

- **heat**:
  - **after** flushes of heat: *Aml-ns* vh1
  - **during**: anac bg2 bar-c bg2 *Bell* b4a.de calc bg2 *Cham* bg2* graph bg2 hep bg2 *Mag-c* bg2 **Mag-m** bg2 par bg2 puls bg2 sars bg2 sep h2 sil bg2 sulph bg2 valer bg2 verat bg2
- **honey**, smelling like: thuj k*
- **hot**: calc tl1 *Cham* k* *Cimic* con tl1 dream-p sdj1• *Glon* *Op* k* podo
- **infants**: calc mtf11
- **menses**; during: cham merc phos verat
- **mental** exertion agg.: kali-c kali-p ph-ac ran-b
- **motion**; from slight: rheum mrr1
- **musk**-like odor: *Apis* *Sulph*
- **musty**: apis ptk1 nat-m k*
- **oily**: *Bry* hera c1 *Merc*
- **only** the head●: acon *Bell* hr1 *Calc* cham k* phos k* *Puls* k* sabad k* sep k* *Sil* k* spig k* stann k*
- **painful** part: sil k2
- **profuse**: sil mtf33 stry ptk1 tarax bg2
- **reading** agg.: kali-c h2* nat-s sulph h2*
- **sensation** as if: gink-b sbd1•
- **sleep**:
  - **during**: (↗*night)* agar sne aloe sne bamb-a stb2.de• *Bry* st **Calc** k* *Calc-p* k* *Cham* k* *Cic* dys xyz60 kali-c h kali-s fkr2.de *Lyc* k* *Merc* k* *Podo* ruta fd4.de sanic *Sep* k* *Sil* k* staph sne syc pte1• thuj ser verat sne
  - **falling** asleep | **when**: graph sep k* *Sil* tarax kr1
- **soup** agg.: phos rheum
- **sour**: *Bry* calc bg2* *Cham* *Hep* *Merc* rheum k* *Sep* **Sil** k* sulph bg2
- **stool** agg.; during: ptel
- **uncovered** parts: thuj
- **waking**; on: ph-ac
- **walking** | **after** | **agg.**: *Calc* carb-v merc
  - **air** agg.; in open: borx h2 *Calc* **Chin** k* *Graph* guaj phos thuj
- **want** of perspiration: m-arct b7.de rhus-t b7.de*
- **washing** agg.; after: **Graph**

○ - **Forehead**: acet-ac k* *Acon* aeth agar aids nl2• am-c bg2 aml-ns anag k* *Ang* bg2 ant-t *Ars* ars-i asaf bapt bell h1 benz-ac bro1 *Brom* bry *Cact* *Calc* k* calc-i k2 calc-sil k2 camph **Cann-i** caps *Carb-v* k* carbn-o carbn-s cassia-s ccrh1• cham k* chel *Chin* chinin-ar cic cina k* colch con h2 croc crot-c sk4• crot-t k* cupr dig dros dulc fd4.de elaps eup-pur euph bro1 glon *Guaj* k* hell k* *Hep* hydrog srj2• iod *Ip* jab kali-ar *Kali-bi* *Kali-c* kali-p kali-sil k2 kola stb3• lac-loxod-a hrn2• lachn *Laur* **Led** k* *Lob* bro1* lyc **Merc-c** k* mosch k* *Nat-ar* **Nat-c** k* nat-m k* nat-p nat-sil fd3.de• *Nit-ac* k* nux-v k* oci-sa sk4• ol-an bg2 **Op** k* petr-ra shn4• ph-ac h2 **Phos** k* phyt podo fd3.de• psil ft1 ptel c1 pycnop-sa mrz1 ran-a *Ran-s* bg2 rheum bg2* sabad **Sars** k* sec bg2 sil sin-n k* *Stann* k* staph k* stram sul-i k2 sulph k* *Tab* tritic-vg fd5.de tub jl2 *Valer* bg2* vanil fd5.de **Verat** k* vesp *Zinc* zinc-p k2
  - **morning**: ambr ang h1 dios *Kali-c* nux-v phys stann staph
    - **6** h: nux-v
    - **8** h: dios
    - **bed** agg.; in: staph
    - **stool** agg.; during: phys
  - **noon**: nat-m valer
  - **afternoon**: dulc fd4.de ferr-i vanil fd5.de
  - **evening**: anac h2 carb-v chin dulc fd4.de ol-an puls h1 ran-b *Sars* senec
    - **18**.30 h: ol-an
    - **lying**, after: carb-v
    - **walking** agg.: chin
    - **writing** agg.: ran-b
  - **night**: bry calc k2 cann-s chin crot-t sacch-a fd2.de•
    - **midnight**:
      - **after** | **4** h: stann
    - **pain** in abdomen, during: crot-t
  - **accompanied** by:
    - **retching** (See STOMACH - Retching - accompanied - forehead)
  - **anxiety**, as from: nux-v ulm-c jsj8• *Verat*
  - **burning**: nat-c h2

- **Forehead**: ...
  - **chill**; during: *Acon* bry *Calc* *Chin* cina dig k* *Led* *Nat-s*
  - **clammy**: acet-ac acon bg2 carb-an cina cocc bg2 colch *Hep* *Op* [bell-p-sp dcm1]
  - **cold**: acet-ac k* *Acon* k* *Am-c* b7a.de ant-t k* *Ars* ars-s-f k2 asaf k* bapt bell h1 benz-ac dgt1 bros-gau mrc1 bry k* bufo *Cact* *Calc* camph k* canth bg2 caps k* **Carb-v** k* carbn-s *Chin* k* chion ptk1 *Cina* k* cist k2 cocc k* *Colch* k* croc k* cupr k* dig bg2 *Dros* k* dulc fd4.de *Gels* glon k* *Hell* k* *Hep* *Ip* k* *Kali-bi* k* kali-c k* kali-p kola stb3• *Lach* *Laur* *Lob* sne mand sp1 *Merc* merc-c k* nat-m h2* nat-sil fd3.de• nit-ac bg2 **Op** k* ox-ac petr k* phos k* *Phyt* k* *Plb* pyrog ptk2 *Rheum* b7.de* *Rhus-t* b7a.de ruta b7a.de* sabad k* *Sec* sep h2* sil k2 spong b7a.de *Staph* k* sul-ac k* sulph h2 *Tab* tung-met bdx1• **Verat** k* verat-v mrr1 vip visc sp1 zinc
    - **accompanied** by | **Intestines**; complaints of the (See ABDOMEN - Complaints - intestines - accompanied - forehead)
    - **chill**, during: bry b7.de chin cina ip bro1 *Verat* b7.de*
    - **cough**; during: *Verat* b7.de*
    - **heat**; during: dig h2 pycnop-sa mrz1
    - **icy**: lachn c1
    - **menses**:
      - **during** | **beginning** of: phos b4.de
    - **stool** | **during**: verat b7.de*
    - **trembling** anxiety, with: sep h2
    - **warm** room agg.: ambr k*
  - **cough** agg.; during: ant-t k* ars-s-f k2 chlor ip k* verat
  - **diarrhea**; during: sulph
  - **dinner** | **after**:
    - **agg.**: nat-s par ptel hr1 sars sulph
      - **nausea**; during: ptel hr1
    - **during** | **agg.**: lyc h2
  - **dream**; frightful: bell h1
  - **drinking** | **hot** water | **amel.**: chin bg2
    - **water**:
      - **agg.**: *Verat* bg2
      - **amel.**: cupr bg2 ip bg2
  - **easy**: rheum
  - **eating** | **after** | **agg.**: carb-v b4a.de card-m vml3•
    - **while** | **agg.**: (↗*eating; eating - while - agg.)* carb-v k* nit-ac nux-v sul-ac sulph tritic-vg fd5.de
  - **except** the forehead; general perspiration: tab bg2
  - **fever**; during: ant-t cann-i c1 dig h2 ip mag-s sars k* staph **Verat**
  - **greasy**: coloc hydr vh *Psor* k*
  - **hat**; from pressure of a: nat-c h2
  - **headache**; during: cist k2 glon *Kali-c* ph-ac *Phyt* sulph
  - **hot**: cham h1 chin h1* *Op* sne
  - **menses**; during: phos verat
  - **motion** agg.: valer
  - **offensive**: led sil
  - **rising** | **lying**; from | **agg.**: mag-s
    - **sitting**; from | **agg.**: *Verat*
  - **sitting** agg.: camph iris-foe
  - **sleep** agg.; during: cham h1
  - **sour**: led
  - **spots**: acet-ac c1
  - **sticky**: acon bg2 cann-i c1 cham h1 cocc k*
  - **stool** | **after** | **agg.**: crot-t ip merc nat-c h2 **Verat**
    - **during** | **agg.**: crot-t k* **Verat**
  - **storm**; during approach of a: nat-c
  - **vomiting**: ant-c h2 chion ptk1 mag-c h2 phos h2
  - **walking** in open air agg.: guaj h2 led h1 merc nux-v
  - **warm**: acon act-sp anac h2 camph cham glon *Op* sne phys psil ft1 puls

○ • **Eyes**; about: calc-p bg2 con bg2
  - **Nose**; above: (↗*NOSE - Perspiration)* rheum mtf33

- **Sides** | **left**: lac-loxod-a hrn2•
- **Head**:
  - **except** the head (See except)
  - **only** the head (See only)
- **Occiput**: anac k* ars k* bamb-a stb2.de• *Calc* k* chin k* dulc fd4.de ferr k* kali-p fd1.de• mag-c k* mosch k* nit-ac k* nux-v k* ozone sde2• **Ph-ac** k* ruta fd4.de *Sanic* k* *Sep* k* *Sil* k* spig k* stann k* **Sulph** k* tritic-vg fd5.de vanil fd5.de [calc-lac stj2 calc-met stj2 calc-sil stj2]
  - **night**: calc mtf33
  - **headache**; during: ozone sde2•
  - **sleep** agg.; during: **Calc** mrr1* kali-s fkr2.de ruta fd4.de *Sanic* k* tritic-vg fd5.de
  - **walking** agg.: ruta fd4.de sulph
- **Sides**:
  - **one** side: ambr k* *Bar-c* k* indg bg2 nit-ac h2 *Nux-v* k* **Puls** k* **Sulph** k*
    - **painless** side: aur-m-n
- **Temples**: ars-s-f k2 crot-c sk4• ol-an bg2 tritic-vg fd5.de
  - **cough** agg.: ars-s-f k2
- **Vertex**: ol-an bg2 phel bg2 ruta h1*
  - **eating**; when: all-c ptk1

PITHY feeling (See Numbness)

PLICA POLONICA (See Hair - plica)

POLLUTIONS agg.: bov b4.de* calc b4.de* chin bg2 nat-c b4.de* puls bg2 sep b4a.de sil b4a.de thuj bg2 viol-o bg2

POSITION; changing: | **amel.**: *Ign* b7a.de mag-c b4a.de*

PRESSURE:
- **left**:
  - **headache**; after | **right** side; on: ozone sde2•
- **agg.**: agar b4.de* am-c b4.de* ant-c bg2 bapt bg2 bell b4.de* bism b7.de* *Brom* b4a.de *Calc* b4.de* camph b7.de* *Cina* b7.de* kali-c b4.de* lach b7a.de* lyc b4.de* mag-c b4.de* mag-m b4.de* mur-ac b4.de* nat-c bg2 ph-ac b4a.de* prun bg2 *Stram* b7a.de sulph b4.de* teucr b7.de* ther bg2 valer b7a.de verb b7.de*
  - ○ **External** head: agar b4a.de ang b7.de* arg-met b7.de* carb-an b4a.de carb-v b4.de* kali-n b4.de* lach b7.de* led b7a.de lyc b4.de* mez b4.de* nit-ac b4a.de *Sil* b4a.de
  - **Vertex**: *Chin* ptk1 lach ptk1 phys ptk1 ther ptk1
- **amel.**: acon bg2 aloe bg2 alum b4.de* am-c bg2* anac b4.de* ant-c b7.de* apis b7a.de* *Arg-n* bg2* *Bell* b4.de* *Bry* b7.de* cact bg2* calc b4.de* camph b7.de* carb-an bg2 carb-v bg2 chel b7.de* chin b7.de* cimic bg2 cina bg2 con b4.de* dios bg2 ferr bg2* glon bg2 ip b7.de* kali-n bg2 *Lach* bg2* laur bg2 mag-c b4.de* *Mag-m* b4.de* mag-p bg2* mang b4a.de* *Meny* b7.de* merc b4.de* mez b4.de* mur-ac b4.de* nat-c b4.de* nat-m b4.de* nit-ac bg2 **Nux-m** bg2* nux-v b7.de* olnd b7.de* par b7.de* ph-ac bg2 phos b4.de* **Puls** b7.de* pyrog bg2 sabad b7.de* sabin b7.de* *Sep* b4.de* sil b4.de* spig b7.de* stann b4.de* sul-ac b4.de* sulph b4.de* thuj b4.de* verat b7.de* zinc bg2
  - ○ **External** head: calc b4.de* chin b7.de* guaj b4.de* hell b7.de*
  - **Vertex**: mag-c ptk1
- **cold** hand amel.; of: calc ptk1
- **eyes**; on | **amel.**: nat-m bg2*
- **finger** tips; as from | **Temples**: epiph ptk1
- **hand**; of:
  - **agg.**: chin bg2 teucr b7.de*
  - **amel.**: con bg2
- **hard**:
  - **amel.**: anac bg2 **Apis** b7a.de *Arg-n* bg2 chin bg2 lycps-v bg2 mag-p bg2 *Meny* bg2 nux-m bg2 *Puls* b7a.de stram bg2
    - **External** head: carb-an ptk1 *Chin* bg2 lach bg2 **Nux-m** bg2
- **nose**; on root of | **amel.**: kali-bi ptk1
- **painless** side agg.; on: cann-s b7.de*
- **vertex** agg.; on: *Chin* ptk1 lach ptk1 phys ptk1 ther ptk1

PRICKLING: abrot bg2* alum am-c bg2 am-m ammc a1 apis k* arg-n aur k* bamb-a stb2.de• bar-c calad carb-an cench k2 cham chinin-s con cupr cycl bg2* hydr-ac lachn merc mur-ac nat-m nit-ac op ph-ac k* sabad k* sep suis-hep rly4• sulph bg2 tarent thuj verb k* vinc bg2 viol-o viol-t bg2
- **forenoon**: ph-ac h2
- **debauch**, after a: *Op*

Prickling: ...
- **eating**; after: con
- **lying** agg.: merc
- **needles**; as from: agath-a nl2• con eug rhus-t thuj
- ○ **Forehead**: anthraq rly4• apis aur chinin-s ephe-si hsj1• ferr lil-t k* *Mur-ac* k* sabad sep k* thuj verat *Viol-o* k*
  - **left**: calad
  - **intermittent**: verb
  - **needles**; like: agar agath-a nl2• all-c am-c asaf caul k* hep kali-c mang nat-m sep
  - **spots**, in: apis
  - ○ **Nose**; above root of: kali-bi
- **Hair**; under: melal-alt gya4
- **Occiput**: ox-ac ptk1 ph-ac bg2*
- **Sides** | **left**: calad
- **Temples**: ail ant-c k* apis cocc cupr euphr melal-alt gya4 rhus-r tarax tarent thuj verb k*
  - **evening**: lachn
  - **needles**, as with: nicc zinc
- **Vertex**: carb-ac

PULLED backward: | **sensation** as if: chir-fl gya2 syph ptk1

PULLING a heavy load; when: mur-ac b4a.de

PULSATING: (*↗Knocking head; Knocking in; Pain - pulsating*) *Acon* k* aeth agar agath-a nl2• aids nl2• ail all-c k2 aloe alum k* alum-sil k2 am-c k* am-m *Aml-ns* k* anac k* anan ant-t k* ap-g vml3• apis k* apoc bg2 arg-n bg2* *Arn* k* *Ars* k* *Ars-i* ars-s-f k2 *Asaf* k* asar k* aster aur k* aur-ar k2 aur-m k2 bamb-a stb2.de• bar-c k* bar-m **Bell** k* beryl tpw5 bit-ar wht1• *Borx* k* bov k* brach *Brom* b4a.de *Bry* k* *Cact* k* cadm-s calc k* calc-ar calc-i k2 calc-p k* calc-s calc-sil k2 *Camph* k* *Cann-i* cann-s k* canth k* *Caps* k* carb-an *Carb-v* k* carbn-s cardios-h rly4• *Castm* *Caust* k* cedr *Cham* k* chel **Chin** k* **Chinin-s** k* chord-umb rly4• cimic cinnb clem cob cocc k* coff colch con *Croc* k* *Crot-h* k* crot-t k* cupr k* cur cycl k* cypra-eg sde6.de• daph dendr-pol sk4• dig dros k* dulc b4a.de* eug *Eup-per* k* euphr k* eupi *Ferr* k* *Ferr-ar* ferr-i ferr-p *Gels* k* **Glon** k* graph k* grat guaj guar vml3• hell hep hipp hydrog srj2• hydroph rsj6• hyos k* *Ign* k* ind indg *Iod* k* *Ip* k* *Kali-ar* kali-bi k* *Kali-c* k* kali-i k* kali-m k2 *Kali-n* kali-p *Kali-s* kali-sil k2 *Kalm* ketogl-ac rly4• *Kreos* k* lac-ac bg2 lac-d k2 lac-h sk4• lac-leo hrn2• **Lach** k* lachn lact lam *Laur* k* led k* *Lith-c* **Lyc** k* mag-c mag-m k* mag-p bg2* mag-s manc mang k* meli bg2* merc k* mez mill mucs-nas rly4• mur-ac myric nat-ar nat-c nat-m k* nat-p nat-s k2 nicc *Nit-ac* k* *Nux-m* k* nux-v k* oci-sa sk4• ol-an k* olnd k* *Op* k* par k* *Petr* k* petr-ra shn4• ph-ac k* phel *Phos* k* pic-ac *Plat* b4a.de plb k* polys sk4• psil ft1 psor *Puls* k* *Pyrog* k* *Rheum* k* rhod k* *Rhus-t* k* ruta k* sabad k* sabin k* **Sang** k* *Sarr* br1 *Sars* k* sec *Seneg* k* *Sep* k* **Sil** k* sol-ni spig k2 *Spong* k* squil k* stann staph bg3 *Stram* k* *Stront-c* sk4• suis-em rly4• sul-i k2 **Sulph** k* **Syph** hr1 tab tarent k2 ter ther k* thuj k* til tritic-vg fd5.de verat k* *Verat-v* k* visc c1 zinc k* zinc-p k2 [heroin sdj2]
- **morning**: alum k* asar aur bov *Calc* k* canth cartl-s rly4• cedr *Cob* k* gamb glon graph k* grat ina-i mlk9.de indg kali-bi lac-h sk4• lact lyc nat-c *Nat-m* nicc *Nit-ac* k* *Nux-v* plb podo polys sk4• sars sep sil spig stront-c sk4• *Sulph* k*
  - **appearing** gradually and disappearing about breakfast: *Nit-ac*
  - **increases** until evening: eup-pur sang sep
  - **rising** agg.: *Asar* caust nat-m ped a1 stront-c sk4•
  - **waking**; on: aids nl2• alum *Bry* kreos lach *Nat-m* phos k* ruta *Sulph*
- **forenoon**: alum dulc fd4.de nicc a1
- **noon** | **amel.**: stront-c sk4•
- **afternoon**: aeth k* alum k* castm caust coca glon k* graph grat guar a1 hura ind lyc mag-s k* mang k* *Merc-i-r* nat-m petr-ra shn4• phel phys sil
  - **16** h: ars-s-f k2 lac-h sk4•
  - **amel.**: polys sk4•
- **evening**: acon am-m bar-c h2 bov k* calc canth carb-v k* castm cic clem k* *Cocc* con cycl dulc fd4.de fl-ac glon guar a1 indg *Iris* kali-i lac-ac lac-leo hrn2• lyc k* mag-s *Nat-m* nit-ac k* oci-sa sk4• ox-ac *Puls* k* ruta sep h2* stram thiam rly4• zinc
  - **amel.**: stront-c sk4•
  - **bed** agg.; in: cycl k* hipp a1 lyc k* sep h2*
  - **sleep**; until going to: anac c1 castm
  - **sleep**; when falling asleep: sil h2

Head

- **night**: aloe arg-n k* ars k* *Cact* k* carb-v k* chel k* ferr glon hura hyos lyc nat-m h2 sars sep h2* sil *Sulph* k*
  - **midnight** agg.; after: *Ferr* k*
  - **appears** in the night, with nausea and vomiting: sil
  - **bed**:
    - **driving** out of bed: *Arg-n* k*
    - **in** bed | **sleep**; before: chel
  - **waking**; on: carb-v k* sulph k*
- **accompanied** by:
  - **apoplexy**: glon ptk1
  - **palpitations**: stront-c sk4•
  - ○ **Eye** | **pain**: dendr-pol sk4•
- **air**; in open:
  - **agg.**: carb-an chin k2 cocc eup-pur iris
  - **amel.**: aeth hr1 beryl tpw5 kali-bi kali-i k* mang k* nicc phos k* *Pic-ac*
- **alternating** between head and chest: bell
- **ascending**, on: alum aster k* *Bry* glon k* irid-met srj5• nat-p *Sep*
  - **fast**: glon k*
- **bathing** | **after**: castm stront-c sk4•
- **bed** agg.; in: chel con cycl graph sep k*
- **bending**:
  - **head**:
    - **amel.**: *Bell Nat-m Sil*
    - **backward** | **agg.**: aur glon **Lyc** k*
- **binding** head up | **amel.**: pic-ac sil
- **blood**, after loss of: *Chin*
- **blowing** the nose agg.: aster
- **breakfast** | **amel.**: nat-m nit-ac
- **burning**: apis coff *Rhus-t* k*
- **chewing** agg.: phos
- **chill**:
  - **after**: borx
  - **during**: acon bg ars k2 cann-i k* cham bg *Eup-per* seneg b4a.de* sep bg
- **chilliness**; with: acon bg2 borx bg2 cham bg2 seneg bg2 sep bg2 sil
- **closing** the eyes:
  - **agg.**: sep
  - **amel.**: stront-c sk4•
- **cold**:
  - **air** agg.: iris c1 stront-c sk4•
  - **bathing** | **amel.**: ars ind phos
  - **drinks**:
    - **agg.** | **overheated**; when: bry k2
- **cold**; preceding a: lach
- **cough** agg.; during: am aur aur-s k2 beryl tpw5 dirc ferr hep k* hipp *Ip* k* iris kali-c led **Lyc** k* moni rfm1• *Nat-m* nit-ac ph-ac phos seneg sep sil spong sulph
- **darkness** | **amel.**: sep
- **deep**-seated: carc tpw2* cic k* stram a1
- **dinner**; after: alum *Am-c* carb-an k* kali-bi mag-c k* nat-c ol-an plb k* zinc
- **drawing**: ars
- **drinking** agg.: acon
- **eating** | **after** | **agg.**: am-c ars k* carb-v chord-umb rly4• clem cocc sel k*
  - **before** | **agg.**: cocc
- **ending** in shooting: **Bell** k*
- **epistaxis**; after: borx
- **excitement** agg.: *Sulph*
- **exertion** agg.: gins glon k* lil-s a1
- **expiration** through nose agg.: ap-g vml3•
- **fever**; during: *Bell Eup-per*
- **gnawing**: par
- **hammers**, awakens every morning; as if from little: *Nat-m* psor
- **heat**; during: ars k2 beryl tpw5 eup-per glon k* rhus-t
  - **body**, of: nat-m h2
- **hemorrhage**; after: chin cp
- **hunger**; from: oci-sa sk4•
- **inspiration** agg.: *Carb-v*
- **intermittent**: ferr-ma verat
- **jar** agg.: *Bell* beryl tpw5 glon k* *Ther*
- **jerking**: bry ign phos
- **laughing** agg.: lyc phos k*
- **leaning** head backward, on: **Lyc** k*
- **lies** senseless with closed eyes: arg-n k*
- **light**; from:
  - **agg.**: bell k2 beryl tpw5 lac-h sk4• stront-c sk4•
  - **sunlight** | **agg.**: acon sulph
- **lying**:
  - **agg.**: aloe calc-ar glon k* lachn lyc naja phos k*
  - **amel.**: anac k* calc ferr mrr1 kali-bi marb-w es1• petr-ra shn4•
  - **back**; on | **agg.**: sep
  - **head** high; with the | **amel.**: nat-m *Spig*
  - **must** lie down: *Bell Ign* hr1 sang
  - **part** agg.; on the: *Petr*
  - **side**; on | **amel.**: beryl tpw5 nat-m sep
- **menses**:
  - **after** | **agg.**: calc-p carb-an ferr glon nat-m k*
  - **before** | **agg.**: *Bell Borx* chin *Crot-h* k* gels *Glon Lach* nat-m *Petr* k* sulph
  - **during**:
    - **agg.**: acon bell *Borx* bry cact *Calc* calc-p *Chin* croc k* eupi a1 *Glon* ign lac-d *Lach* mag-c *Nat-c* nux-m puls sang verat-v k*
      - **painless** throbbing: eupi
  - **suppressed** menses; from: *Puls*
- **mental** exertion agg.: agar *Nat-m Pic-ac* psor k* *Puls* k* *Raph* sil vib k*
- **milk** agg.: brom
- **motion**:
  - **agg.**: acon *Anac* k* *Apis* ars ars-s-f k2 aur-s k2 *Bell* k* beryl tpw5 *Bry* calc-p calc-sil k2 caust k* chin cimic *Cocc* colch dirc eupi k* ferr ferr-p *Gels Glon* k* grat k* *Iod* k* kali-bi lac-h sk4• *Lach* k* *Lyc Nat-m* k* nit-ac nux-m petr-ra shn4• *Sep* k* spig k2 *Stram* stront-c sk4• *Sulph*
    - **sudden** motion: calc-p ferr
  - **amel.**: aloe lact k*
  - **gentle** motion | **amel.**: iris vib
  - **head**; of | **agg.**: petr-ra shn4• *Sulph*
- **nausea**; with: stront-c sk4•
- **noise** agg.: alum-sil k2* lac-h sk4• spig k2 stront-c sk4•
- **odors** agg.: stront-c sk4•
- **painless**: pyrog ptk1
  - **fear** of going to sleep; with: glon k2 *Nux-m*
- **paroxysmal**: caust glon
- **periodical**: ars ferr
  - **morning**; every | **lasts** all day: *Calc*
- **perspiration** | **amel.**: ars k2 *Nat-m*
- **pressure**:
  - **agg.**: lac-h sk4•
  - **amel.**: aeth k* *Am-c* bell bry chin k2 ferr glon k* guaj a1* kali-bi kali-n k* lac-h sk4• nat-m k* petr-ra shn4• *Puls* pyrog k* stront-c sk4•
  - **hand**; of | **amel.**: apis carb-an h2 guaj
  - **upon** forehead causes beating: mag-m k*
- **raising** head suddenly agg.: nat-p squil
- **reading**, while sitting: lyc *Nat-m* k* polys sk4•
- **respiration**; during difficult: *Carb-v* k* glon k* irid-met srj5•
- **resting** head | **amel.**: kali-bi
- **riding** agg.: cocc *Glon* grat a1 phos
- **rising**:
  - **agg.**: chinin-s dirc glon phos
  - **amel.**: nat-c
  - **sitting**; from | **agg.**: bell k2 dulc fd4.de
  - **stooping**; from | **agg.**: mag-m
- **room**; when entering a: aeth k* mag-m mang k*
- **rubbing** | **amel.**: aeth
- **shaking** the head agg.; on: *Glon* k*

- **sitting**:
  - **agg.**: am-m castm guaj k* indg k* lyc ol-an k*
  - **amel.**: mag-m
- **sitting** up in bed agg.: ars calc-s k2
- **sleep**:
  - **amel.**: petr-ra shn4• sang
  - **going** to sleep; on | **agg.**: sil bg1
- **spots**, in: nux-m
- **standing**:
  - **agg.**: castm chin bg1 guaj k* plb
  - **amel.**: camph
- **stepping** agg.: alum *Phos*
- **stool** agg.; straining at: ign
- **stooping** | **after** | **agg.**: hyos h1
  - **agg.**: alum *Apis* ars-s-f k2 asar bar-c **Bell** choc srj3• colch dulc fd4.de ferr ferr-p *Glon* hydr-ac kali-bi lach *Laur* mag-m h2 nat-c nat-m *Nux-v* phos *Puls* spig k2 *Sulph*
- **stretching** limbs out, on: phos k*
- **sudden**: dendr-pol sk4•
- **synchronous** with pulse: glon k2
- **talking** agg.: acon aur *Cocc Nat-m* k* sil *Sulph*
- **thinking** agg.: ant-c
- **touch** agg.: chin k2
- **transient**, in one-half of: cham
- **turning** | **bed**; in | **agg.**: bry k2
  - **eyes** | **agg.**: sep
- **turning** around agg.: glon
- **ulcerative**: am-c bov k* castm mang
- **vertigo**; during: glon hir rsj4• nit-ac b4a.de sec
- **waking**; on: aur bell hr1 carb-v cinnb lach lyc nat-m phos k* podo ruta sulph
- **walking**:
  - **agg.**: alum aster *Bell* bry k2 calc *Glon* guaj k2 kali-bi *Nat-m* nat-s nux-v plb sars sil *Sulph*
  - **air**; in open:
    - ⁝ **agg.**: *Am-c* mag-s
    - ⁝ **amel.**: ars eup-pur *Guaj*
  - **rapidly** | **agg.**: calc h2 ferr nux-v *Puls*
- **warm**:
  - **applications** | **agg.**: beryl tpw5
  - **food** agg.: sulph
  - **room**:
    - ⁝ **agg.**: iod k* *Puls* sulph
    - ⁝ **amel.**: am-c cocc
  - **tea** | **amel.**: glon
- **wine** agg.: ox-ac
- **wrapping** head up warmly amel.: *Sil*
- **writing** agg.: kali-c k* manc
- **yawning**; after: calc k*

▽ - **extending** to:

○ · **Chest**: nat-m
  - **Ears**: [heroin sdj2]
  - **Neck**: nat-m
    - ⁝ **right**: psil ft1
    - ⁝ **amel.**: stront-c sk4•
  - **Teeth**: mez

○ - **Brain**:

○ · **Against** skull: *Ars* k* *Bell* **Chin** daph *Glon* hydr-ac laur lavand-a ctl1• mez nat-m nux-m nux-v bg2 psor rheum sep bg2 stann sul-ac *Sulph* tritic-vg fd5.de
    - ⁝ **hammers**, like little: bell k2 carb-v k2 ferr k2 glon k2 **Nat-m Psor**
    - ⁝ **waves**, as of: **Chin** dig
    - ⁝ **Middle** of brain, every morning, lasts all day; throbbing pain in: calc
  - **In** brain: *Bell Chin* cycl dig glon hyos kali-n h2 *Lyc* nit-ac op rhus-t sang k2 tritic-vg fd5.de
    - ⁝ **one** side of brain | **transient** pulsating: cham

- **Brain – In** brain: ...
    - ⁝ **deep**-seated: aloe bg2 bar-c bg2 cic
    - ⁝ **leaning** head back, on: **Lyc**
    - ⁝ **shooting**, ending in: *Bell*
- **External** head: alum b4.de* am b7.de* canth b7.de* chel b7a.de guaj b4.de* hell b7.de* phos b4.de* sulph b4.de*
- **Forehead**: acon k* aeth k* agath-a nl2• aloe alum k* alum-p k2 alum-sil k2 *Am-c* k* am-m k* amph a1 ang k* ant-t k* apis apoc k* (non:arg-met slp) arg-n k* *Ars* k* *Ars-i* ars-s-f k2 asaf asar k* aur aur-ar k2 aur-i k2 aur-m bapt bar-c k* bar-i k2 **Bell** k* borx k* brach k* bry k* *Calc* k* calc-i k2 calc-p k* calc-s a1 calc-sil k2 *Camph* k* *Cann-i* k* cann-s k* canth k* *Caps* k* carb-v k* carc syz carl a1 castm *Caust* k* cham b7a.de chord-umb rly4• cic k* cinnb k* clem k* cocc k* con h2* corn k* croc *Dig* k* digin a1 *Dros* b7a.de dulc k* euph k* eupi k* *Ferr* k* *Ferr-ar* ferr-i k2 *Ferr-p* form a1 gamb k* ger-i rly4• **Glon** k* graph k* grat k* hell k* ign k* iod k* **Iris** k* jab a1 kali-ar kali-bi bg2 kali-c k* *Kali-i* k* kali-n h2* kali-p kali-sil k2 *Kalm* k* *Kreos* k* **Lac-d** k* lac-leo hm2• laur k* lob-c a1 *Lyc* k* lyss mag-c k* *Mag-m* k* mag-s meli k* *Merc* k* *Merc-i-f* k* mez k* morph a1 nat-ar k2 nat-c k* *Nat-m* k* nat-p k* nit-ac k* *Nux-m* olnd k* op k* ox-ac k* par k* *Petr* k* petr-ra shn4• *Ph-ac* b4a.de phos k* pic-ac a1 psor al **Puls** k* ran-b rheum k* rhod k* rhus-t k* rob a1 ruta k* sabad k* sang k2 sars k* seneg k* sep k* *Sil* k* spig k* *Spong* k* stann *Stram* k* *Stront-c* sk4• ther k* thuj k* verb k* vib k* zinc k* zinc-p k2
  - **one** side: aur kali-bi ptel
  - **right**: *Ant-t* k* ars-s-f hr1 asaf b7.de* bell bg2* chin bg2 chord-umb rly4• dig bg2 ign b7.de* iris c1 lach bg2 meli bg2 *Nat-m* b4a.de ran-b b7.de* sabad b7.de* sars k* *Sep* k* spong fd4.de tarent bg2
  - **left**: acon k* aeth a1 *Arg-n* k* ars bg2 aur bg2 cann-s b7.de* chin b7.de* cimic k* cocc k* croc b7.de* dulc b4.de* glon bg2 kali-c k* *Kreos* k* nat-m bg2* nux-m k* par k* petr-ra shn4• rhod b4.de* sil bg2* spig k* sulph bg2 ther bg2 verat k* verb b7.de* zinc bg2*
  - **morning**: asar *Canth* k* grat k* *Nat-m* sil k*
    - ⁝ **rising** agg.: asar k* *Nat-m* k*
    - ⁝ **waking**; on: *Nat-m* k* ruta
  - **forenoon**: dios hr1 gamb k* lyc k*
  - **noon**: lyc k* nat-c a1
  - **afternoon**: alum k* alumn caust k* lyc k* mag-c a1 mag-s k* petr-ra shn4• sil k*
    - ⁝ **14** h: nat-m
    - ⁝ **15** h: lyc
  - **evening**: am-m k* cic k* cocc dulc fd4.de flor-p rsj3• lac-h sk4• lyc k* mag-s k* merc-i-r a1 ruta stram k*
    - ⁝ **21** h: calc caust
  - **night**: *Camph* hr1 fago k* hura *Merc* k* nat-m
  - **accompanied** by | **nausea** (See STOMACH - Nausea - accompanied - forehead - pulsating)
  - **air**; in open | **amel.**: aeth *Am-c* kali-i **Puls**
  - **ascending** stairs agg.: alum hr1 nat-p k* par k*
  - **bending** head forward agg.: nat-m
  - **cough** agg.; during: hep k* phos spong
  - **dinner**; after: *Am-c* k* kali-c zinc k*
  - **eating**; after: *Am-c* cocc inul hr1
  - **hailstones**, as from: amph a1
  - **light**; from: ars k2
  - **menses**; during: acon *Bell* borx bry cact *Calc* calc-p k* *Chin Glon Ign Lach* mag-c *Nat-c* **Puls** sang *Tarent* k*
  - **motion**:
    - ⁝ **agg.**: ars *Gels Glon* merc pic-ac
    - ⁝ **amel.**: *Puls*
  - **pressure**:
    - ⁝ **agg.**: mag-m h2
    - ⁝ **amel.**: aeth am-c nat-m
  - **reading** agg.: lyc
  - **riding**:
    - ⁝ **agg.**: *Glon* k* grat k*
    - ⁝ **cold** air; in: *Am-c* cocc
  - **rising** up in bed: ars k* glon k*

Head

- **sleep**; preventing: pyrog ptk
- **standing** agg.: kali-c
- **stooping** agg.: asar k* bar-c ost a1
- **talking** agg.: cocc
- **walking**:
  - **agg.**: *Aeth* kali-c sars
  - **air** agg.; in open: am-c sars
- **warm** room | **amel.**: *Am-c* cocc

▽ • **extending** to | **Occiput**: ars-s-f k2 bry *Con* ther

○ • **Eminence**; frontal: aesc agath-a nl2• *Arg-n* calc cocc hyos (non:iris slp) iris-foe slp lyc mez nit-ac ran-b
  - **right**: aesc calc lyc mez
  - **left**: *Arg-n* cocc verb h
  - **afternoon** | **16** h: nit-ac
  - **evening**: (non:iris slp) iris-foe slp lyc
    - **18** h: lyc
    - **20** h: iris-fl
  - **slow**: verb h
- **Eyes**:
  - **Above**: agath-a nl2• *Bell* k* carb-v bg2* digin a1 *Gels* k* glon k* gymno ham k2 ign k* *Kali-bi* k* *Lac-c* k* *Lach* k* lyc bg2* lyss k* naja bg2* *Nat-m* k* *Nux-m* k* petr-ra shn4• pic-ac a1 polys sk4• ptel *Sep* k* spig stram k* stry a1 ther vib
    - **right**: allox tpw4 xan a1*
    - **left**: digin a1 ham a1 nux-m c1 ther c1*
    - **Arteries**: caust h2
- **Root** of nose, above: *Ars* k* camph k* gamb k* glon bg2 kali-i bg2 mez phos bg2* puls
  - **forenoon**: gamb k*
  - **walking** | **amel.**: puls

- **Here** and there: acon aeth indg
- **Occiput**: *Acon* b7a.de aeth k* agar k* ail k* aloe k* *Alum* k* alum-p k2 am-c k* anac k* asar k* bapt bg2 bar-c k* bart a1 **Bell** k* berb beryl tpw5 borx k* **Bry** k* *Calc* k* *Camph* k* *Cann-i* k* cann-s cann-xyz bg2* *Carb-an* k* *Carb-v* k* carbn-s carc tpw2* caust k* *Chel* k* choc srj3• chord-umb rly4• con cop corn hr1 *Crot-h* k* *Dros* k* eup-per k* *Eup-pur* k* *Ferr* k* *Ferr-ar* ferr-p k* frax bg1 *Gels* k* *Glon* k* guare a1 ham hr1 hep k* hura ign k* indg k* kali-bi kali-br hr1* *Kali-c* k* *Kali-n* k* kali-s ketogl-ac rly4• lac-c k* *Lach* laur k* lob-c a1 lyc k* lyss k* *Mag-m* k* mang mez b4.de* mosch b7a.de* *Nat-m* k* *Nit-ac* k* *Petr* k* petr-ra shn4• **Phos** k* phys k* pic-ac k* plb *Psor* *Puls* k* ran-b k* rauw tpw8* rhus-t k* ruta k* **Sep** k* spig k* spong fd4.de *Stram* k* *Sulph* k* upa a1 *Valer* b7a.de
  - **right**: alum bg2 caust bg2 gels bg2 kali-c bg2 mang bg2 ran-b bg2 sulph bg2 zinc bg2
  - **left**: am-c bg2 bell bg2 castm bg2 eup-per bg2 hep bg2 indg bg2 kali-n bg2 laur bg2 phos bg2 plb bg2 sulph bg2
  - **daytime**: petr k*
  - **morning**: petr bg1 spong fd4.de
    - **rising** during menses; after: mag-m
  - **afternoon**: lac-h sk4• nat-m k* op a1
  - **evening**: bar-c k* kali-n puls
  - **night**: aloe lyc k*
  - **cough** agg.; during: *Ferr* ferr-p sep
  - **hammer**, like beats of: camph *Nat-m* psor
  - **lying** on back agg.: *Petr* k* spong fd4.de
  - **motion**:
    - **agg.**: **Bell** **Bry** *Eup-per* *Ferr* *Ip* *Lach* **Stram**
    - **amel.**: aloe
  - **paroxysmal**: *Glon* k*
  - **pressure** | **amel.**: alum castm kali-n k*
  - **rising**:
    - **agg.**: gels phos
    - **stooping**; from | **agg.**: mag-m
  - **rubbing** | **amel.**: caust h2
  - **shaking** the head agg.; on: kali-br k*

- **Occiput**: ...
  - **sitting**:
    - **agg.**: kali-br ran-b
    - **amel.**: mag-m
  - **standing** | **amel.**: **Camph** k*
  - **stool** agg.; during: *Ign* k*
  - **stooping** agg.: *Ferr* k* mag-m h2
  - **walking**:
    - **agg.**: kali-br k*
    - **air**; in open | **amel.**: dig
  - **warm** room agg.: mag-m

▽ • **extending** to:
    - **Forehead**: carb-v hir rsj4• sil *Spig*
    - **Forward**: bar-c lac-c op sulph
    - **Frontal** eminence: bar-c
    - **Sides** and forehead: ferr
    - **Temples**: beryl tpw5
    - **Upward**: mag-m bg2
    - **Vertex**: hura ketogl-ac rly4•
    - **Whole** head, over: mag-m

○ • **Sides**: *Alum* k* am-c k* ars bg1 castm caust k* *Eup-pur* k* indg k* kali-n k* laur k* plb k* psil ft1 ran-b k* stram k* *Sulph* k*
    - **evening** | **bed** agg.; in: kali-n k*
    - **rising** agg.: gels k*

- **Sides**: aeth k* agar alum k* alum-p k2 am-c k* ant-t arg-met bg2* arg-n ars k* aur k* aur-ar k2 aur-s k2 bar-c k* bell k* bov k* brom bg2 bry k* calc calc-p canth k* *Cham* k* chin k* coc-c bg2* coca cocc bg con k* croc k* dirc k* eup-per glon k* *Graph* k* hura indg k* iris kali-bi bg2 kali-c kali-i kali-s kalm k* laur k* lepi a1 lyc k* m-aust b7.de mag-c mag-m k* mag-s k* nat-c nit-ac ol-an k* petr k* *Phos* k* plb k* rhod rhus-t k* sars sep k* spong k* sul-ac sulph bg2 verat k* zinc
  - **right**: aeth k* agar k* alum k* anac bg2* arg-n k2 aur bov b4.de* bry b7.de* cact br1 canth b7.de* carc tpw2 con k* ferr-p k2 graph k* kali-c k* lach bg2* laur b7.de* lyc bg2* m-aust b7.de mag-c k* mag-s a1 petr-ra shn4• *Phos* k* plb b7a.de rhod k* rhus-t b7.de* sang k2 sul-ac k* zinc k*
    - **extending** to | **left**: bov indg a1
  - **left**: am-c k* bar-c k* beryl tpw5 bov b4.de* brom bg2 calc k* chin-b kr1 croc b7.de* dirc c1 dulc fd4.de glon bg2* hura kali-bi bg2* kreos b7a.de lac-h sk4• laur b7.de* mag-m k* nat-c k* *Nit-ac* k* phos k* staphycoc rly4•
    - **extending** to | **right**: beryl tpw5 nux-m
  - **morning**: aur k* bov k* *Nit-ac*
  - **forenoon**: plb k* sars k*
  - **afternoon**: alum k* graph k* lyc k*
    - **15** h: hura
  - **evening**: canth k* con k* phos k*
  - **bending** head backward agg.: aur k*
  - **cough** agg.; during: aur k* dirc k*
  - **deep**-seated: corn hr1 sars k*
  - **dinner**; after: indg a1 kali-c mag-c ol-an k*
  - **house** amel.; in: mag-s
  - **lying** on side agg.: sep k*
  - **menses**; during: nat-c k*
  - **motion**:
    - **agg.**: bell h1 *Calc-p*
    - **amel.**: kali-i k2
  - **rising** agg.; after: glon k*
  - **shaking** the head agg.; on: glon k*
  - **sitting** agg.: phos h2
  - **standing** agg.: glon a1 kali-c plb a1
  - **stooping** agg.: glon k* laur k*
  - **walking**:
    - **agg.**: kali-c plb a1
    - **air**; in open:
      - **agg.**: mag-s
      - **amel.**: kali-i k2

- **warmth** | **amel.**: kali-i k2

○ - **Side** lain on: sep k*

- **Temples**: acon k* aesc k* aeth k* agar k* all-s k* *Alum* k* alum-p k2 am-c am-m k* aml-ns bg2 androc srj1• ant-c k* ant-t k* *Apis* b7a.de arg-n k* *Ars* k* *Ars-i* *Asaf* aur-m k2 aur-m-n k* bar-c k* bar-i k2 bar-s k2 **Bell** k* bond a1 borx bov b4a.de brach a1 *Bry* k* cact k* cadm-s k* calc k* calc-i k2 calc-p calc-s camph k* *Caps* k* carb-v k* carbn-s castm *Cedr* k* cham k* *Chel* k* chin k* chinin-s chord-umb rly4• cic cocc k* *Coff* hr1 coloc k* crot-h bg2 cupr-ar k* daph k* digin a1 dulc fd4.de elae a1 ferr k* *Ferr-ar* ferr-i k2 ferr-p fl-ac *Gels* k* ger-i rly4• gins k* **Glon** k* *Grat* k* guar a1* gymno hell k* hep k* hura hyper k* *Iod* k* jug-r a1 kali-bi bg2 kali-br hr1 kali-c k* *Kali-chl* hr1 kali-i k* kali-n k* kali-p kali-s ketogl-ac rly4• kreos k* lac-ac k* *Lac-c* k* lac-d k* *Lach* k* laur k* lavand-a ctl1• lyss med k* merc-i-f hr1 mur-ac bg2* nat-ar nat-c k* nat-m k* nat-p nat-s k* *Nit-ac* k* paull a1 peti a1 petr-ra shn4• *Phos* k* phys k* pilo a1 plb k* podo k* polys sk4• pyrog jl2 *Raph* a1 rauw tpw8* rhus-t k* sabad k* *Sang* k* sapin a1 sars k* sep b4a.de sol-t-ae a1 *Spig* k* spong k* *Stann* k* *Staph* k* stram k* stront-c sk4• suis-em rly4• sul-i k* *Sulph* k* syph al tab k* thea thuj k* verat k* verat-v k* ziz a1
  - **right**: aesc k* aids nl2• alum k* am-m bg2* borx b4a.de* chel b7.de* cupr bg2 *Cupr-ar* k* fl-ac bg2* *Hep* k* hyper bg2* lac-h sk4• laur b7.de* nat-m b4a.de psil ft1 sabad b7.de* sang hr1 sars bg2* stram b7.de* stront-c sk4• sulph bg2 thuj bg2*
  - **left**: aeth bg2* am-c bg2 aml-ns k* androc srj1• ant-c b7.de* asaf b7.de* aur bg2 aur-m bg1* brach a1* chinin-s clem bg2* *Coloc* k* dig bg2 digin a1 glon bg2* hell b7.de* hyper bg2* kali-br bg2 kali-c bg2 kali-i bg1 kreos b7a.de* lach bg2 nit-ac k* petr bg2* petr-ra shn4• *Phos* k* polys sk4• rhus-t bg2* sabad b7.de* spong b7.de* stry bg2* suis-em rly4• sulph bg2
  - **midnight**: sars k*
  - **morning**: bov k* cann-s a1 lach k* *Podo* k* spong fd4.de stry k*
    - ⋮ **waking**; on: aids nl2• lach
  - **forenoon**: carl k*
  - **noon**: ars k* cham a1 thuj k*
  - **afternoon**: alum k* glon k* guar a1
  - **evening**: am-m k* bry dulc fd4.de fl-ac k* glon guar a1 kali-i k* lac-ac k*
    - ⋮ **sitting** agg.: am-m k*
    - ⋮ **walking** agg.: glon k*
  - **night**: *Cact* k* chel k* dulc fd4.de
  - **ascending** stairs agg.: glon k*
  - **chill**; before: carb-v k*
  - **cough** agg.; during: hep k*
  - **heat**; during: arg-n a1 glon k*
  - **lying** agg.: naja spong fd4.de
  - **menses**; before: *Lach* k*
  - **motion** agg.: androc srj1• caust **Chin** *Gels* *Glon* k*
  - **noise** agg.: polys sk4•
  - **paroxysmal**: glon k*
  - **pressure** | **amel.**: chin k2 dulc fd4.de pyrog jl2
  - **stooping** agg.: sul-i k*
  - **touch** agg.: chin k2
  - **vomiting** with: lac-h htj1•
  - **waking**; on: carb-v k*
  - **walking** agg.: aeth k* bar-c k* *Glon* k* nat-s k* sulph
  - ▽ **extending** to | **Occiput**: ketogl-ac rly4•
  - ○ **Carotids**: aml-ns bg2 bell bg2 chin bg2 glon bg2 meli bg2
  - **Vessels**: bell c1 chin c1 chion c1 cycl a1 mur-ac c1 oci-sa sk4• petr-ra shn4• spong fd4.de tab c1
    - ⋮ **visible**: aur mtf33

- **Vertex**: aeth agar k* *Alum* k* alum-p k2 alum-sil k2 *Aml-ns* bg2 anac k* ars k* aur ptk1 *Bell* ptk1 bry k* calc k* cann-i carb-an k* carl a1 *Caust* k* *Cham* k* *Chel* *Chinin-s* cinnb cocc k* corn *Ferr* k* *Ferr-ar* ferr-p *Glon* k* grat k* ham k* helon hr1 hura hydrog srj2• *Hyper* k* jab bg2 kali-bi bg2 kali-c k* kali-s ketogl-ac rly4• kreos k* *Lac-d* k* lach k* *Lyc* k* lyss k* manc k* *Merc-i-r* k* mucs-nas rly4• nat-ar *Nat-c* k* *Nat-m* k* nat-p *Nux-v* k* paull a1 petr petr-ra shn4• phel k* phos k* pic-ac plan k* puls k* sang k2 sars k* *Sep* k* *Sil* k* spig b7a.de *Stram* k* *Sulph* k* syph bg2* *Ter* k* thea thiam rly4• tong a1 verat k* visc bg2* xan hr1 zinc-chr ptk1 zing hr1 [heroin sdj2]

Pulsating – Vertex: ...
  - **morning**: alum k* bry k* caust k* nat-c k* *Sep* k* sulph bg1
  - **forenoon**: alum glon k*
  - **afternoon**: alum-p k2 *Hyper*
  - **evening**: lac-h sk4•
  - **ascending** steps agg.: carl k* ferr
  - **attention**, from fixing: nux-v k*
  - **bending** head back amel.: **Sil** k*
  - **dinner**; after: nat-c k*
  - **exertion** agg.: syph bg1
  - **menses**; after: ferr k* *Lach* k*
  - **mental** exertion agg.: nux-v k*
  - **motion**:
    - ⋮ **agg.**: *Bry* *Calc* *Cocc* ferr glon lach sep *Verat*
    - ⋮ **eyes**; of | **agg.**: cocc
  - **room**; in a closed: hyper br1
  - **sudden**: visc ptk1
  - **waking**; on: aids nl2• alum hr1 bry k* kreos hr1 *Lyc*
  - **walking**:
    - ⋮ **agg.**: carb-an *Sars* k*
    - ⋮ **rapidly** | **agg.**: ferr k* puls

PUSHED:
- **forward**, as if: *Canth* ferr-p k* grat k* nit-ac nux-m nux-v rhus-t staph h1
- **forward**, backward and to the right but never to the left: galla-q-r nl2•
- **into** head at expectoration; as if something were pushed: pall c1

○ - **Forehead**; sensation as if a load were pushed from occiput to pall

PUSHING: | **pressure** | **amel.**: *Arg-n*
- **sensation** of: coli rly4• croc *Nat-m* ph-ac phos

QUININE; after abuse of: | **External** head: *Bell* b4a.de

QUIVERING sensation: bov cann-s lact
- **running** and walking, while: nux-v k*
- **shaking** the head agg.; on: xan k* xanth

○ - **Brain**: bov bg2 cann-s bg2
  - **shaking** while walking; as if brain were: rhod k*

RAIN:
- **agg.**: phyt ptk1
- **amel.**: cham ptk1

RAISING: | **eyes** | **agg.**: acon bg2 arn bg2 bry b7a.de* caps b7.de* chin b7a.de lac-c bg2 lil-t bg2 m-arct b7.de* ptel bg2 puls b7.de* thuj b4a.de
- **head**:
  - **agg.**: bov bg2 calc bg2 caps b7.de* dros bg2 ign bg2 lach bg2 spong bg2 tarax b7.de*
  - **difficult** | **night**: chel k*
  - **frequently** from pillow: stram k*
  - **impossible**: bell k* carb-v h2 chel k* crot-h k2* eup-per hr1* *Lach* lap-la sde8.de* laur nux-v k* *Op* k* *Puls* k* x-ray al2
    - ⋮ **morning** | **waking**; on: *Lach*
    - ⋮ **lying** on back agg.: chel nux-v k*
    - ⋮ **stooping** agg.; after: bell k* rhus-t

RATTLING of wagons agg.: nit-ac bg2

RAW spots on scalp: bov bg2 *Calc* bg2 nit-ac bg2 sang bg2

READING:
- **agg.**: agn b7.de* apis b7a.de arg-met b7.de* arn b7.de* aur b4.de* borx b4a.de* bry b7.de* **Calc** b4.de* carb-v b4a.de* caust b4.de* cimic bg2 cina b7.de* cocc bg2 coff b7.de* ign b7.de* lyc b4.de* mez b4.de* *Nat-m* b4.de* nat-s bg2 nux-v b7.de* olnd b7.de* par bg2 sabad b7.de* *Sil* b4.de*
- **amel.**: ham ptk1 ign b7.de*
- **long** time; for a: phos bg2

Head

REFLECTING agg.: arn b7.de* asar b7.de* aur b4.de* calc bg2 cham bg2 *Chin* bg2 cina b7.de* cocc b7.de* coff b7.de* *Colch* b7.de* daph bg2 dig bg2 hell bg2 *Ign* b7.de* m-ambo b7.de m-aust b7a.de nat-m bg2 nit-ac bg2 **Nux-v** b7.de* par b7.de* ph-ac bg2 phos bg2 *Sabad* b7.de* sel b7.de* sulph bg2

RELAXATION:

○ - **Brain**:

- **alternating** with | **contraction** of brain (See Contraction - brain - alternating - relaxation)

REMOVED; as if calvarium was: arum-t k* cann-i

REST:

- **agg.**: arg-met b7.de* *Aur* b4a.de caps b7.de* cham b7.de* chin bg2 cic b7.de* coff bg2 ferr b7.de* kali-n bg2 lach bg2 lyc b4.de* mang b4.de* meny b7.de* nat-c b4.de* *Puls* b7.de* *Rhus-t* b7.de* ruta b7.de* samb b7.de* stann b4.de* staph bg2 *Thuj* b4a.de

○ · **External** head: bell b4.de*

- **amel.**: *Alum* b4a.de ant-c b7.de* *Arn* b7.de* *Brom* b4a.de **Bry** b7.de* *Chel* b7.de* *Chin* b7a.de colch b7.de* cupr b7.de* hell b7.de* hep bg2 ign b7.de* iod b4.de* kali-bi bg2 kali-c b4.de* kali-n b4.de* laur b7a.de* m-aust b7.de *Nux-v* b7.de* phos bg2 rhod b4a.de* *Sang* bg2 sars b4.de* *Sep* b4a.de *Spig* b7a.de squil b7.de* *Staph* b7.de*

RESTING, supporting head:

- **agg.**: bell b4.de*
- **amel.**: cann-s b7a.de dros b7.de* nat-m b4a.de nux-v b7.de* staph b7.de*

RESTLESSNESS: ambr k* asc-t a1 bell k* bond a1 *Calc-p* bg2 caust k* hell b7.de* jab k* merc k* phos k* pip-m k* ruta sec k* sil k* tarent k2 [buteo-j sej6]

- **forenoon**: phos k* sil k*
- **rolls** head from side to side when too weak to move body: *Ars*

○ - **Occiput**: ambr h1*

RETCHING:

- **agg.**: asar b7.de* glon bg2 ip bg2 olnd b7.de*
- **amel.**: asar a1*

REVELING agg.; night: ambr b7a.de *Bry* b7a.de* calc bg2 chin bg2 *Cocc* bg2 dulc bg2 ip b7.de* kali-n bg2 *Laur* b7.de* led b7.de* nit-ac bg2 **Nux-v** b7.de* phos bg2 *Puls* b7.de* sabin b7.de* sulph bg2

RIDING:

- **carriage**; in a:
  - **agg.**: *Cocc* b7.de* ferr b7.de* *Graph* b4.de* grat bg2 iod b4.de* *Kali-c* b4.de* lach b7.de* med bg2 meph bg2 nux-m b7.de* sulph b4.de*
  - **amel.**: bry bg2 kali-n b4.de* nit-ac bg2

RIGID feeling: *Caust* irid-met srj5• phos rheum

○ - **Brain**: phos bg2

RINSING mouth with cold water agg.: rhus-t bg2

RISING:

- **bed**; from:
  - **after**:
    - **agg.**: *Am-m* b7.de* anac b4.de* ang b7.de* bar-c bg2 bell b4.de* bry b7.de* *Calc* b4.de* camph b7.de* carb-an b4.de* cocc bg2 coloc b4.de* con b4.de* dulc b4.de* hep b4.de* ign bg2 ip b7.de* **Lach** b7a.de m-ambo b7.de m-arct b7.de mur-ac b4.de* nux-v b7.de* *Olnd* b7.de* podo bg2 *Puls* b7.de* rhod b4.de* ruta b7.de* sang bg2 sep b4.de* sil b4.de* squil b7.de*
    - **amel.**: am-c bg2 *Ambr* b7.de* ars b4.de* aur b4.de* *Bell* b4.de* carb-an b4.de* carb-v b4.de* cham b7.de* chin b7.de* ferr b7.de* graph b4a.de hep b4.de* *Ign* b7.de* kali-bi bg2 laur b7.de* m-ambo b7.de m-arct b7.de murx bg2 nit-ac b4.de* *Nux-v* b7.de* ph-ac b4.de* phos b4.de* plb b7.de* puls b7.de* *Ran-b* b7.de* rhod b4.de* rhus-t b7.de* sabin b7.de* spig b7.de thuj b4a.de verat b7.de
  - **agg.**: apis b7a.de* ars bg2 asar b7.de* aur bg2 *Calc* b4.de* caps b7.de* chel bg2 clem b4.de* dulc b4.de* glon bg2 *Graph* b4.de* hep b4.de* nux-v b7.de* petr b4.de* ph-ac b4.de* *Phos* b4.de* puls b7.de* sep bg2 staph b7.de* sulph bg2 *Verat* b7a.de
- **lying**; from:
  - **after**:
    - **agg.**: kali-n bg2 nat-c bg2 olnd bg2
    - **amel.**: kali-c bg2 kali-n bg2 nat-m bg2 stann bg2

Rising – lying; from: ...

  - **agg.**: arn bg2 daph bg2 lyc bg2 mur-ac bg2
- **sitting**; from:
  - **agg.**: chin b7.de* cob bg2 laur b7.de* mang b4.de* puls b7.de* rhus-t b7.de* verat b7.de*
  - **amel.**: arg-met b7.de* grat bg2 mang bg2 sil bg2 spig b7.de* spong b7.de* verat b7a.de
- **stooping**; from:
  - **agg.**: *Acon* b7.de* ang b7.de* arn b7.de* *Ars* b4.de* asar b7.de* bar-c b4.de* bell b4.de* bov b4.de* *Bry* b7.de* caps b7.de* cham b7.de* dros b7.de* hell b7.de* hep b4.de* ign b7.de* kali-c b4.de* laur b7.de* lyc b4.de* m-aust b7.de mag-m b4.de* mang b4.de* mur-ac b4.de* nux-v b7a.de* phos bg2 spong b7.de* *Squil* b7a.de sul-ac b4.de* tarax b7.de* verat b7.de* viol-t b7.de*
  - **amel.**: alum b4.de* ang b7.de* aur b4.de* bar-c b4.de* bry b7.de* calc b4.de* cann-s b7a.de canth b7.de* carb-v b4.de* chin b7.de* cic bg2 con b4.de* dig b4.de* ign b7.de* kali-c b4.de* laur b7.de* mag-c b4.de* nat-c b4.de* *Olnd* b7.de* *Puls* b7.de* rhus-t b7.de* spig b7.de* spong b7a.de stann b4.de* teucr b7.de*

RISING SENSATION in head: glon lac-d nat-c nux-v rhus-t thuj

- **drinking** beer, while: rhus-t
- **sinking**, and: **Bell** cob
  - **while** rest of body sinks: neon srj5•
- **walking** rapidly agg.: nux-v

○ - **Brain** raised several times in succession as if thuj

- **Scalp**: polyg-pe vml2•
- **Vertex** to forehead; sensation of something rising from: glon

ROLLING in: cupr-ar eug graph k* hura k* lys bg2 lyss bg phos bg2 phys k* plan bg2 sep k*

- **lead** ball rolled about, as if: *(↗Ball - rolling)* lyss
  - **study**, after: cupr-ar
  - **vertigo**; during: sep
  - **vomiting** agg.: eug
- **vertigo**; during: sep b4a.de

○ - **Brain** were rolled; as if arn bg2 cocc bg2 lob-e c1 plan ptk1 rhus-t bg2

- **bulk**; into a small: *Arn Coc-c*
- **skull**; about in the: chin rb2 phys rb2

ROLLING of the head (See Motions of - rolling)

ROOM:

- **agg.**: *Agn* b7a.de am-m b7.de* *Apis* b7a.de *Arn* b7a.de ars b4.de* bov b4.de* bry b7.de* camph b7.de* caust b4.de* chel b7.de* coff b7.de* con b4a.de *Croc* b7.de* *Graph* b4a.de hyos b7.de* *Laur* b7.de* lyc ptk1 m-aust b7.de mag-c b4.de* mag-m b4.de* mang b4.de* merc b4.de* mez b4.de* mosch b7.de* nat-c b4.de* *Nux-v* bg2 ph-ac b4.de* phos b4.de* plat b4.de* *Plb* ptk1 ptel bg2 **Puls** b7.de* ran-s b7.de* rhod b4.de* seneg b4.de* sep b4a.de* spong b7a.de staph ptk1 sulph b4.de* verat b7.de* verb b7.de* zinc b4.de*

○ · **External** head: meny b7.de*

- **amel.**: bell b4.de* bov b4.de* *Bry* b7.de* cham b7.de* chel b7.de* *Cocc* b7.de* **Coff** b7.de* ferr b7.de* hep b4a.de m-aust b7.de mag-c bg2 mang b4.de* meny b7.de* *Merc* bg2 nux-m b7.de* **Nux-v** b7.de* rhus-t b7.de* *Sil* b4a.de spig b7.de* staph b7.de* sulph b4.de*
- **entering** a room; when: con bg2 laur bg2 mez bg2 nat-m bg2 **Ran-b** b7.de* ran-s b7.de* rhus-t b7.de* sabad bg2 *Sel* b7a.de spong b7.de* *Verb* b7.de*

ROUGHNESS of scalp: ruta b7.de*

RUBBED; being: | **desires** head being rubbed: tarent mtf33

RUBBING:

- **against** something; rubs head (See Motions of - rubbing - against)
- **agg.**: camph k* carb-ac a1 con k* hyos k* tarent k* verat bg
- **amel.**: ars b4a.de* canth b7.de* chin ptk1 dios bg2 ham bg2 laur b7.de* ol-an bg2 op bg2 phos b4a.de* phys bg2 plb b7.de* tarent ptk1 thuj ptk1

○ · **External** head: dros b7.de*

- **forehead** | **desire** to rub: aloe sne glon k* nicc hr1* verat bg2* [tax jsj7]
- **head**: camph bg2 con bg2 hyos bg2* tarent bg2 verat k*
- **soles** of feet | **amel.**: chel bg2*

RUNNING agg.: bell b4a.de bry b7.de* nat-m b4.de* nux-v b7.de* *Puls* ptk1 spig b7a.de

SALIVATION:
- **agg.**: *Ant-c* bg2 sep bg2
- **before**: fl-ac bg2

SCALP; complaints of: alum b2.de* ambr b2.de* anac b2.de* ant-c b2.de* ant-t b2.de* arg-met b2.de* arn b2.de* **Ars** b2.de* aur b2.de* bar-c b2.de* bell b2.de* *Borx* b2.de* bov b2.de* bry b2.de* **Calc** b2.de* caps b2.de* carb-an b2.de* carb-v b2.de* caust b2.de* *Chel* b2.de* chin b2.de* cic b2.de* clem b2.de* cycl b2.de* dros b2.de* ferr b2.de* *Graph* b2.de* hell b2.de* *Hep* b2.de* kali-c b2.de* laur b2.de* led b2.de* lyc b2.de* mag-c b2.de* mag-m b2.de* **Merc** b2.de* *Mez* b2.de* mosch b2.de* mur-ac b2.de* *Nat-m* b2.de* nit-ac b2.de* nux-v b2.de* **Olnd** b2.de* par b2.de* *Petr* b2.de* *Phos* b2.de* puls b2.de* ran-s b2.de* **Rhus-t** b2.de* *Ruta* b2.de* sabad b2.de* sars b2.de* sel b2.de* *Sep* b2.de* **Sil** b2.de* spig b2.de* **Staph** b2.de* stram b2.de sul-ac b2.de* sulph b2.de* thuj b2.de* zinc b2.de*
- ○ **Forehead**: agar b2.de* alum b2.de* am-c b2.de* am-m b2.de* anac b2.de* **Ars** b2.de* bar-c b2.de* *Bell* b2.de* bism b2.de* bry b2.de* calc b2.de* carb-v b2.de* cic b2.de* con b2.de* dros b2.de* dulc b2.de* graph b2.de* *Hep* b2.de* kali-c b2.de* kreos b2.de* lyc b2.de* mag-c b2.de* mag-m b2.de* **Merc** b2.de* mez b2.de* nat-c b2.de* *Nat-m* b2.de* olnd b2.de* par b2.de* petr b2.de* *Phos* b2.de* plat b2.de* ran-b b2.de* sabad b2.de* sep b2.de* *Sil* b2.de* staph b2.de* sulph b2.de* thuj b2.de* *Viol-t* b2.de* zinc b2.de*

SCALPED; sensation as if: con bg2

SCARLET FEVER; after: *Apis* b7a.de

SCLEROSIS; cerebral: arg-n br1 arn mtf11 aur br1* bar-c mtf11

SCRATCHING head:
- **agg.**: nat-m h2
  - ○ • **External** head: caps b7a.de
- **amel.**: mang ptk1 plat b4a.de
  - ○ • **External** head: olnd bg2
- **waking**, on: calc h2*

SEDENTARY habits agg.: acon bg2 *Nux-v* b7a.de*

SENSITIVENESS: desm-g bnj1 plat k2
- **air**; draft of (See Air agg.)
- **brushing** of hair; to: *(↗Touch - hair)* **Arn** *Bell* k* *Bry* *Carb-v* carbn-s cina k* coff *Ip* *Kreos* k* lachn vml3• mang h2* nat-s ptk1* nat-sil fd3.de• *Nit-ac* olib-sac wmh1 *Rhus-t* sars h2 *Sep* **Sil** *Sulph* tub bg v-a-b jl vib bg1*
  - • **children**; in: cina mtf33
- **hat**, even to: *Bry* st1 *Carb-v* st1 chin st1 crot-t st1 hep st1 merc st1 mez st1 **Nit-ac** h2* **Sil** st1 staph st1 sulph st1
- **jar**, to the least: *(↗stepping; Pain - jar agg.)* androc srj1• **Bell** calc cob ferr-p *Glon* hep ip kali-p lac-d lyc *Mag-m* mang nat-ar **Nit-ac** ph-ac phyt raph *Sil* spig stram *Sulph* *Ther* vanil fd5.de vib
- **menses** | **before** | **agg.**: **Calc** *Carb-v* *Con* *Hyos* *Nat-m* *Phos* sil sulph h2 zinc
  - • **during** | **agg.**: bell *Calc* carb-v con gels *Hyos* ip *Kali-c* *Mag-m* *Phos* *Sil* *Zinc*
- **noise**, to (See Pain - noise - agg.; MIND - Sensitive - noise)
- **spots**; in: aloe bg2 bov bg2 nit-ac bg2
- **stepping**, to: *(↗jar; Pain - jar agg.)* **Bell** *Calc* calc-p *Carb-v* chin dros gels **Glon** *Ip* *Led* lyc *Nat-m* *Nit-ac* raph rhus-t *Spig* stann *Sulph*
  - • **ascending** agg.: *Rhus-t*
- **touch**; to: cortico tpw7 dulc fd4.de gent-ch bnj1 iod h irid-met srj5• sep h2
  - • **children**; in: lach mtf33
  - • **gentlest**, after anger: mez
  - ○ • **Bones**: kali-bi bg2
  - • **Temples**: bell bg2
  - • **Vertex**: chin bg2 ephe-si hsj1• hep bg2 nit-ac bg2 nux-v bg2 phos bg2 *Phys* bg2 sil bg2 squil bg2 sulph bg2 thuj bg2
- ○ **Brain**, of: arn br1 bamb-a stb2.de• **Bell** *Bov* brom *Bry* k* calc k* *Carb-v* k* **Chin** k* *Con* k* crot-t dros k* **Gels** k* gent-c k* germ-met srj5• **Glon** hyos k* iod k* **Ip** kali-c kali-p *Lach* k* lact led k* lyc *Mag-m* **Mez** mosch b7.de* *Nat-m* **Nit-ac** k* *Nux-v* b7a.de **Phos** k* *Phyt* pip-m a1 prost srj5• raph k* *Rhus-t* b7a.de *Sil* k* *Spig* k* *Staph* stram taosc iwa1• vib bg1 zinc k*
  - • **left**: bamb-a stb2.de•
  - • **diminished**: helo-s bnm14•

Sensitiveness – **Brain**, of: ...
  - • **electrified**; as if: bamb-a stb2.de•
- **External** head, of: *Acon* bg2 aesc bg2 agar j5.de* alum b4.de* am-c j5.de* ambr b7.de* apis b7a.de* arg-met bg2 **Ars** b4.de* asar bg2 *Bar-c* b4.de* bell b4.de* borx b4a.de* bov b4.de* *Bry* b7.de* calc b4.de* calc-p bg2 camph bg2 caps bg2 *Carb-an* b4a.de* carb-v b4.de* caust b4.de* *Cham* b7a.de chin b7.de* chinin-s j5.de cina bg2 clem bg2 cocc bg2 cop bg2 cupr bg2 *Ferr* b7a.de* ferr-p bg2 gels bg2 graph bg2 grat j5.de hell b7.de* *Hep* b4a.de* ign bg2 ip b7a.de* irid-met srj5• kali-c b4.de* kali-n b4.de* kreos b7a.de* lach j5.de* led b7a.de* lyc j5.de* mag-c j5.de* mag-m b4.de* mang b4.de* **Merc** b4.de* mez b4.de* mosch b7a.de nat-c b4.de* nat-m b4a.de* nat-s bg2 **Nit-ac** b4.de* nux-m b7a.de* nux-v b7.de* par b7.de* *Petr* b4.de* ph-ac b4.de* phos b4.de* plb bg2 puls bg2 ran-s b7.de* rhod b4.de* *Rhus-t* b7.de* sabin j5.de sars b4.de* *Sel* b7.de* sep b4.de* *Sil* b4.de* *Spig* b7.de* spong b7.de* squil b7.de* *Staph* bg2 **Sulph** b4.de* tell bg2 thuj b4.de* tong j5.de verat b7a.de* vib bg2 *Zinc* b4.de*
  - • **chill**; during: **Hell** bg2 *Hep* bg2 nux-v bg2 *Sabad* bg2 spig bg2 sulph bg2
- **Occiput**: *Hell* b7a.de
- **Scalp**, of: aloe dgt1 ars ptk1 bamb-a stb2.de• bell ptk1 bry ptk1 chin ptk1 conv br1 cop br1 der vml3• dulc fd4.de hep ptk1 *Kali-i* br1* kali-n c1 *Mag-m* h2 merc ptk1 merc-d ptk1 mez mrr1 morg-p pte1*• nit-ac ptk1 nux-v ptk1* par ptk1 sil ptk1 spig ptk1 tub ptk1
  - • **left**: bamb-a stb2.de•
  - • **electrified**; as if: bamb-a stb2.de•
  - • **motion**, to: hell h1
  - • **touch**; to: *Acon* bro1 ap-g vh* apis bro1 arn bro1 ars bro1 aza bro1 *Bell* bro1 bov bro1 bros-gau mrc1 *Bry* bro1 carb-v bro1 caust bro1 *Chin* bro1* der vml3• ephe-si hsj1• euon bro1 *Eup-per* bro1 *Gels* bro1 hell h1 *Hep* bro1 kali-bi bro1 kali-n h2 lachn bro1* meli bro1 merc bro1 mez mrr1 nat-m bro1 nit-ac bro1 nux-m bro1 *Nux-v* bro1 olnd bro1 *Par* bro1 rhus-t bro1 sep bro1 *Sil* bro1 spig cp stry bro1 sulph bro1
  - • **warm** in bed agg.; becoming: *Rhus-t* hr1
- **Vertex**: alum h2 chin bg hep bg kali-n h2 mag-c h2 mag-m h2 nit-ac bg nux-v bg phos h2* *Phys* bg sil bg squil h1* sulph h2* thuj bg zinc h2

SEPARATED:
- **body**; as if head were separated from: allox tpw3* aloe bg3* alum bg1* ant-t bg3* cann-i rb2 cann-s bg cann-xyz ptk1 cocc *Daph* k* nat-c bg3* nat-m bg3* nux-m bg3* plut-n srj7• **Psor** k* ther k*
  - • **night**: *Daph*
- **bones** were; as if: arg-n bg2* bufo bg2 kali-bi bg2 lyc bg2 ther
- ○ **Brain** from skull were; as if galla-q-r nl2• staph
- **Vertex** were; as if: sang a1 *Ther* k*
  - • **lift** it off; or she could: ther rb2

SEWING agg.: *Lac-c* ptk1 petr b4a.de*

SEXUAL DESIRE:
- **agg.**: sep bg2
- **suppression** of sexual desire agg.: con ptk1 puls ptk1

SHADOW; in: | **amel.**: **Brom** b4a.de

SHAKING sensation: *(↗Boiling; Looseness; Motions in; Surging; Swashing; Waving)* acon aeth bg aloe alum bg *Am-c* k* anac ant-c ant-t arn *Ars* asar aur k* bar-c bell k* benz-ac bov bg2 bufo k* cadm-s bg2 *Calc* k* calc-sil k2 cann-i cann-s bg cann-xyz bg2 carb-v caust k* chel cic cinnb cocc cop crot-h cub elaps eupi fl-ac glon graph grat k* hep b4a.de* *Hyos* ign indg ip bg kali-c kali-p kali-sil k2 ketogl-ac rly4• lact led lith-c *Lyc* k* *Mag-c* k* *Mag-m* b4a.de mag-p mag-s *Mang* merc mez nat-m bg nit-ac k* nux-m nux-v k* op pall petr ph-ac k* phos k* plat plb rhod rhus-t bg2 sars k* sep *Sil* k* sol-ni *Spig* stann k* stict bg stront-c sul-ac bg sulph k* tab verat verb k* viol-t zinc [heroin sdj2]
- **ascending** stairs agg.: lyc
- **chill**; during: ars k*
- **cold**:
  - • **agg.**: nux-m
  - • **air** agg.: aloe
- **cough** agg.; during: ant-t calc h2 chin cinch a1 hep k* *Lact* k* *Led* b7a.de m-arct b7.de mag-s k* rhus-t b7.de* sulph bg2
- **eating**; after: nux-m
- **heat** amel., except heat of bed: nux-m
- **laying** head down agg.: aloe
- **menses**; during: ant-c cic cinnb cub

- **motion**:
  - **agg.**: calc h2 mang h2
  - **head**; of | **agg.**: arn ars h2 cic cocc lact lyc mag-c mez h2 nux-v sol-ni *Spig*
- **rising** from stooping agg.: lyc
- **shaking** the head agg.; on: calc h2 mang h2
- **shuddering**; with: mez h2
- **sneezing** agg.: bar-c h2
- **stamping**, on: bar-c k*
- **steel** spring, as of a: grat k*
- **stepping**:
  - **agg.** | **striking** foot against anything: bar-c h2 sep sil h2
  - **every** step; at: calc h2
  - **hard** | **agg.**: led *Lyc* nux-v *Sil Spig*
- **stooping** agg.: berb k*
- **talking** agg.: cocc phos verat
- **walking**:
  - **agg.**: anac *Ars* caust h2 cic cocc hyos led *Lyc* mang nux-v rhod rb2 sep sil spig verb viol-t
  - **air** agg.; in open: caust *Nux-v*
  - **beginning** to walk: plat h2
- **warm** room | **amel.**: nux-m nux-v
- **wrapping** up warmly | **amel.**: nux-v

○ - **Against** frontal bone aur k*
- **Brain**: asar b7.de *Nux-m* b7.de*
- **Forehead**: aur h2 ketogl-ac rly4• *Merc* phos bg2 spig a1
- **Occiput**: calc h2 fl-ac a1 *Lact* a1 sulph k*
- **Scalp**: caust b4.de* sil bg2
- **Temples**: caust h2* cocc kali-c k* stront-c k*
- **Vertex**: caust bg2

SHAKING THE HEAD: (↗*Boiling; Looseness; Motions in; Surging; Swashing; Waving)*
- **causeless**: lyc ptk1
- **involuntarily**: lyc ptk1
- **slowly**, then rapidly: lyc ptk1
- **up** and down | **amel.**: chin ptk1

SHAKING THE HEAD; on:
- **agg.**: apis b7a.de asar b7.de* bar-c b4.de* *Bell* bg2* bry bg2 caust b4a.de* chin b7.de* coloc b4.de* con b4a.de* dig b4a.de *Glon* bg2* hep b4.de* kali-c b4a.de lyc b4.de* m-aust b7.de mang b4.de* nat-m b4.de* nit-ac bg2 nux-m b7.de* *Nux-v* bg2 rhus-t b7.de* sep b4a.de* *Spig* b7.de* squil b7.de* stann b4.de* staph b7.de* sul-ac b4.de*
- **amel.**: cina ptk1 gels ptk1 lach ptk1 phos ptk1

SHINY scalp: thuj bg2

SHIVERING: arg-met bg2 arn bg2 bar-c bg2 bell bg2 cann-xyz bg2 caps bg2 carb-an bg2 *Caust* bg2 cham bg2 cina bg2 *Cocc* bg2 coloc bg2 crot-h bg2 *Meny* bg2 merc bg2 mosch bg2 ol-an bg2 ph-ac bg2 plat bg2 puls bg2 ruta bg2 seneg bg2 sep bg2 *Sil* bg2 staph bg2 **Stront-c** bg2 sulph bg2 thuj bg2 *Valer* bg2 verat bg2
- **during** | **agg.**: *Acon* b7.de ant-c b7.de arn b7.de ars b4.de *Coff* b7a.de ip b7.de kali-c b4.de led b7.de phos b4.de puls b7.de *Rhus-t* b7.de
- **stool** agg.; during: staph b7.de

▽ - **extending** to | **Downward**: *Mosch* b7a.de

○ - **Occiput**: bell bg2 sil bg2 *Valer* bg2
- **Scalp**: arg-met b7.de bar-c b4.de* bell b4a.de camph bg2 caps b7.de *Caust* b4a.de cina b7.de cocc b7.de gran bg2 grat bg2 merc b4.de mosch b7.de* plat b4.de* seneg b4.de sep b4a.de *Sil* b4.de* staph b7.de stront-c b4.de sulph b4a.de thuj b4a.de verat b7.de
- **Vertex**: lyc bg2

SHOCKS (= blows, jerks): acon k* aeth k* agar *All-c* aloe bg2 alum k* alum-p k2 anac b4.de* apis bg2* *Arn* b7.de* ars k* ars-s-f k2 asaf k* aster aur b4.de* bapt k* bar-c bar-m *Bell* k* benz-ac bov k* calc k* camph k* **Cann-i** cann-s b7a.de* cann-xyz ptk1 carb-v k* carbn-s caust k* *Chin* b7a.de *Cic* k* cimic bg2* clem k* *Coca Cocc* b7.de* *Croc* k* *Crot-c* crot-h bg2 dig bg2 ferr k* ferr-ar ferr-p fl-ac *Glon* k* graph k* *Hell* k* hydr-ac hyos b7.de* ign bg2* indg ip k* *Kali-ar* kali-c k* kali-m k2 kali-p *Kali-s* kalm bg2 lach k* laur k* led k* lob *Lyc* k* lyss m-ambo b7.de m-arct b7.de m-aust b7.de mag-s manc bg2 *Mang* k* merc k* mez b4.de* mill mur-ac k* naja bg2* nat-c *Nat-m* k* nat-p nat-s nit-ac k*

Shocks: ...
nux-m bg2 nux-v k* olnd k* op bg ph-ac k* phos k* plat bg2* plb k* psor puls k* ran-b k* raph rhod bg2 rhodi br1* rhus-t k* sabad k* samb sang seneg k* *Sep* k* *Sil* k* *Spig* k* squil bg2 stann k* stict bg2 *Sul-ac* k* sulph k* tab bg2* tarent k* thea thuj valer k* verat b7.de* verat-v viol-t b7.de* zinc k*
- **morning**: phos h2
  - **bed** agg.; in: nux-v sul-ac
  - **rising**:
    - **agg.**: sep h2 tarent
    - **amel.**: nux-v
- **evening**: nit-ac h2 sul-ac
  - **bed** agg.; in: sil h2
  - **sleep**; when falling asleep: sil h2
- **night**:
  - **midnight**:
    - **after**:
      - **1 h** | **waking** him or her from sleep: psor
- **ascending**, on: ant-c arn bell meny par ph-ac
- **chewing** agg.: am-c ptk1
- **cold** air agg.: *Cic*
- **consciousness**, on regaining: cann-i
- **cough** agg.; during: ars *Calc Ip Lach* lyc mag-s mang *Nat-m* rhus-t seneg spig sul-ac sulph h2
- **drinking** cold water, on: thea
- **eating**; after: lyc
- **electric**-like: agar ail k* *All-c Alum* arn aster rb2 bar-s k2 cann-i vh carb-v carbn-s k2 *Cic* hipp kali-ar k2 lob melal-alt gya4 nat-s nux-m op *Phos* sang hr1 sul-ac k2 zinc-p k2
- **falling** asleep, while sitting: alum
- **hawking** up mucus agg.: raph
- **lying** agg.: nit-ac
- **menses**; during: borx
- **mental** exertion; after: phos
- **motion** agg.: *Am-c Cic Lyc* merc prun
- **noise** agg.: germ-met srj5• nit-ac
- **outward**: clem
- **pinching**: sep h2
- **pressure** | **amel.**: bell thuj
- **reading** agg.: carb-v
- **running** agg.: nat-m
- **shaking** the head agg.; on: mang
- **sitting** after a full meal, while: lyc
- **sleep** | **going** to sleep; on | **agg.**: nat-c phos
  - **siesta**:
    - **after**:
      - **agg.**: sep
      - **sitting**; while: alum
- **sneezing** agg.: bar-c
- **stitching**: petr h2
- **stool** agg.; during: phos
- **stooping** agg.: merc nit-ac petr h2 thuj
- **sudden**: *Cic Kali-i* plat k2
- **synchronous** with pulse: *Cimic* **Glon**
- **talking** agg.: nat-m sars ptk1
- **waking** him or her from sleep: helo-s c1 psor
- **waking**; on: cann-i k2
- **walking**:
  - **agg.**: bell mang petr h2
  - **air** agg.; in open: spig
  - **rapidly** | **agg.**: ant-c arn **Bell** nat-m h2 par ph-ac
- **writing** agg.: raph

▽ - **extending** to:

○ - **All** parts of body: mag-p ptk1
  - **Cheek**: puls
  - **Elbow** to head; from: agar
  - **Extremities**: *Ail* k* **Cic** nux-m
  - **Here** and there: zinc

○ - **Forehead**: acon k* am-c ang camph k* caust k* croc k* glon hipp kali-c k* laur k* mag-c b4.de mag-s nat-m k* olnd k* phos h2 plat k* psor rhus-t sang seneg k* sep h2 sol-ni bg2 spig k* stann sul-ac thuj zinc k*
- **right**: acon b7.de* am-m b7.de* apis bg2 m-aust b7.de spig b7.de*
- **left**: asaf b7.de croc b7.de* nat-c b4.de* *Phos* b4a.de squil b7.de* sul-ac b4.de*
- **axe**, as with an: nux-v
- **finger**, as with a: nat-m
- **motion** agg.: mag-c h2
- **painful**: sul-ac
- **sleep** agg.; during: dig
- **stool** agg.; after: spig h1
- **walking** agg.: mag-c h2
- **wavelike**: sep h2

- **Here** and there: zinc
- **Occiput**: apis bg2* arn k* bapt ptk1 bell bg2* cann-i cann-s b7a.de* cimic bg2* coloc bg2 crot-h ptk1 dig bg2 fl-ac bg2 hell k* kali-m ptk1 lach bg2* lappa bg2 lyc mang k* naja bg2* *Phos* k* plat bg2 plb k* ran-b k* sabad k* stront-c bg2 tab bg2* tarent bg2* zinc ptk1
  - **dull**, heavy, throbbing pain through head | **blow** on back of head and neck; with a sensation like a heavy: cann-i
  - **just** as he was losing himself in sleep, like a loud report: phos
  - **mental** exertion agg.: *Phos*

▽ - **extending** to | **Forehead**: clem sabad
- **Sides**: alum am-c bov chel graph kali-c kali-s laur *M-arct* b7.de mag-m nat-s phos plat plb puls sars spig sulph
  - **right**: alum b4.de bov b4.de graph k* kali-c b4.de kali-s k2 m-arct b7.de nat-m bg2 phos b4.de plb b7.de* puls b7.de* sars b4.de sulph b4.de*
  - **left**: am-c b4.de kali-bi bg2 laur b7.de* m-arct b7.de mag-m b4.de ol-an bg2 spig b7.de*
- **Temples**: agn am-c bar-c camph k* cham bg2 croc k* cycl bg2 *Iris* lach **Lyc** k* m-aust b7.de olnd ph-ac *Plat* spig sul-ac thuj k*
  - **right**: am-c b4.de* **Bell** bg2 *Croc* b7.de* ph-ac bg2 spig b7.de* stram bg2 sul-ac b4.de*
  - **left**: bar-c b4.de borx bg2 gels bg2 olnd b7.de*
  - **cough** agg.; during: **Lyc**
  - **painful**: sul-ac
  - **peg** were struck in deep, as if: sul-ac
  - **stool** agg.; during: lyc h2
  - **sudden** shock deep in, causes starting: croc k*
- **Vertex**: alum b4.de* calc k* ferr-p bg2 kali-bi bg2 lyc lyss mang nat-c k* phos k* spig b7a.de
  - **bolt** from neck to vertex, agg. at every throb of the heart; as from a: cimic
  - **electric**-like: carb-ac nat-s
  - **sleep** agg.; on going to: nat-c

▽ - **extending** to | **Forehead**: nat-m h2

SHOPPING agg.: epiph ptk1 sep ptk1

SICK HEADACHE (See Pain - accompanied - nausea)

SINGING agg.: alum b4a.de* *Calc* b4a.de *Nat-m* b4a.de ptel bg2

SINKING sensation: arg-n ptk1 bell bg2 glon k* melal-alt gya4 nux-v bg2 stram bg2
- **something** were sinking from occiput, on stooping, as if: kali-c k*

○ - **Forehead**: thuj bg2
- **Occipital** bone: (↗*Fontanelles - open - sunken - occipital)* mag-c ptk*
  - **children**; in: | **emaciated**: mag-c mtf33
- **Vertex**: sep bg2

SITTING:
- **agg.**: agar b4.de* am-m b7.de* ang b7.de* ant-c b7a.de *Ant-t* b7.de* arg-met b7.de* arn b7.de* ars b4a.de* asaf b7.de* asar b7.de* **Bell** b4a.de bism b7.de* borx bg2 bry b7.de* calc b4.de* canth b7.de* carb-an b4.de* carb-v b4a.de* caust b4.de* cham b7.de* chin b7.de* cic b7.de* cina b7.de* coff bg2 con b4.de* cycl b7.de* dros b7.de* ferr b7.de* grat bg2 lach bg2 led b7.de* lyc b4.de* m-arct b7.de mag-c bg2 mang b4.de* *Meny* b7.de* merc b4.de* mez b4.de* mosch b7.de* mur-ac b4.de* nat-c b4.de* phos b4.de* *Puls* b7.de* ran-b b7.de* rhod bg2 *Rhus-t* b7.de* *Ruta* b7.de* *Sabad* b7.de* seneg b4.de* spig b7.de* *Spong* b7.de* squil b7.de* staph b7.de* sul-ac b4.de* sulph b4.de* **Tarax** b7.de* valer b7.de* verat bg2 viol-o bg2 *Viol-t* b7.de*

○ - **External** head: dig b4.de* guaj b4.de* phos b4.de* staph b7.de*
- **amel.**: acon b7.de* ars bg2 asar b7.de* bell b4.de* *Bry* b7.de* calc b4.de* *Coff* b7.de* con b4.de* ign b7.de* kali-c b4.de* led bg2 mag-c b4.de* mag-m bg2 mang b4.de* merc b4.de* *Nux-v* b7.de* verat b7.de*
- **erect**:
  - **agg.**: arn bg2 cham bg2 glon bg2 hell bg2 ign b7.de* m-aust b7.de mang bg2 verat b7.de*
  - **amel.**: cic b7.de* gels ptk1 rhus-t b7.de* sabin b7.de
- **leaning** against something; while | **amel.**: spig b7.de*
- **still** | **amel.**: nat-m ptk1

SKULLCAP; sensation of a●: (↗*Pain - pressing pain - cap)* acon bg1 apis *Arg-n* asaf *Berb* **Carb-v** k* chinin-ar coc-c *Crot-c* **Cycl** k* *Graph* k* hell helo-s bg1* ip kali-s bg1 lach ptk1 *Lil-t* *Lyss* petr plut-n srj7• pyrid rly4• pyrog stry sulph zinc
- **afternoon** | **16** h: calc-s

SLEEP:
- **after**:
  - **agg.**: ambr b7.de* apis bg2 bov b4.de* bry b7.de* calad b7.de calc b4.de carb-v b4.de chel b7.de chin b7.de *Cocc* b7.de coff b7.de* con b4.de dig b4.de* euphr b7.de hep b4a.de* ign b7.de* m-ambo b7.de m-arct b7.de mag-c b4.de *Nicc* bg2 nux-m b7.de nux-v b7.de *Op* b7.de *Rheum* b7.de* rhus-t b7.de sabad b7.de *Sel* b7.de* sep b4a.de staph b7.de stram b7.de sulph b4.de thuj b4.de
  - **amel.**: *Arn* b7a.de epiph bg2 ign b7a.de* kreos b7a.de *Lach* b7a.de laur bg2 nux-v b7a.de onos bg2 phos b4.de* *Sang* bg2 *Sep* b4a.de thuj b4.de*
- **disturbed** | **agg.**: *Acon* bg2 canth bg2 caust bg2 **Chin** bg2 chinin-s bg2 hep bg2 kali-n bg2 mur-ac bg2 nit-ac bg2 phos bg2 plat bg2 *Sil* bg2 **Sulph** bg2
- **during**:
  - **agg.**: arg-n bg2 ars bg2 camph bg2 cham b7.de* dig bg2 ferr b7.de* led b7.de* mag-c b4a.de* nat-s bg2 nit-ac bg2 petr bg2 psor bg2 ptel bg2 ther bg2*
    - ⁝ **External** head: agn b7a.de cham b7.de* chin b7.de* rheum b7.de*
  - **amel.** | **Vertex**: calc ptk1
- **falling** asleep:
  - **agg.**: sil bg2
    - ⁝ **External** head: puls b7.de*
- **loss** of; from | **agg.**: ambr b7.de* *Colch* b7.de* *Nux-v* b7.de* *Puls* b7.de*
- **waken** from sleep | **agg.**: ars bg2

SMALLER:
- **left** half retarded in growth: fl-ac k2*
- **feels**: acon k* chel kr1* coff k* glon bg2* *Grat* k* olib-sac wmh1 pic-ac k*

○ - **Brain** feels smaller than skull acon k* glon k*
  - **too** far from skull: staph
- **Scalp** feels too small: stict c1

SMOKE in head; sensation of: rhod b4a.de sul-ac b4.de*

○ - **Brain**: arg-met b7a.de op b7a.de

SMOKING:
- **agg.**: *Acon* bg2 *Ant-c* b7.de* *Ant-t* bg2 calc b4a.de caust b4a.de* cocc b7.de* gels bg2 **Ign** b7.de* mag-c b4.de* nux-v b7.de* par b7.de* puls b7.de* spig b7.de*
- **amel.**: calc-p ptk1 carb-ac ptk1 lycps-v ptk1 naja bg2

SNAPPING vertex at every step: con h2

SNEEZING:
- **agg.**: am-m b7a.de* apis b7a.de arn b7.de* bry b7.de* carb-v ptk1 cina b7.de* *Kali-c* b4a.de* nat-m bg2* nit-ac b4a.de* *Phos* bg2* sabad b7.de* spig ptk1 sulph b4a.de*
- **amel.**: calc bg2* calc-p bg2* lil-t bg2* lyc bg2* mag-m bg2 mur-ac bg2*

○ - **External** head: mag-m b4.de*

SOFT: | **sensation** of being soft:

○ - **Vertex** | **External** head: petr bg2

○ - **Skull**: calc bro1 calc-p bro1

SOFTENING of brain: *Agar* c2* alco a1 am-c hr1 ambr k* *Arg-n* bro1* astra-e mtf11 aur bro1* bapt c2 bar-c bro1* bell-p c1* bufo c2* **Calc** hr1 calc-p tl1 cann-i bro1 *Caust* k* con bro1 crot-h hr1 fl-ac *Glon* hr1 kali-br bro1 kali-i bro1 kali-p k* kreos b7.de* lach k* lyc bro1 nux-m k* nux-v bro1 **Phos** k* pic-ac br1* plb bro1* plb-xyz c2 salam bro1 sil bg2* *Stry* ptk1 sulph syph ptk1* **Thuj** b4a.de vanad br1* *Zinc* hr1* *Zinc-p* ptk1

SOUND:
- **voice** agg.; of: bar-c bg2
- **wind** agg.; of: hell bg2

SOUR food agg.: *Bell* bg2* sel ptk1

SPICES agg.: naja bg2

SPLASHING: *(↗Swashing; Waving)* asaf bell *Carb-an* k* hep hyos nux-v rhus-t spig squil
- **walking** rapidly agg.: carb-an k*

STAGNATION of blood; sensation of: *(↗GENERALS - Stagnated)* bar-c h2* seneg b4a.de sulph bg2
○ - **Temple**, in: chel h1

STANDING:
- **agg.**: agar b4.de* alum b4.de* arg-met b7.de* arn b7.de* ars bg2 calc b4.de* canth b7.de* chin b7.de* dig b4.de* mag-c b4.de* mang b4.de* *Puls* b7.de* ran-b b7.de* rheum b7.de* *Rhus-t* b7.de* staph b7.de* sul-ac b4.de* *Tarax* b7.de* valer b7.de* verat b7.de*
- **amel.**: calc b4.de* *Chin* bg2 plb bg2 ran-b b7.de* **Tarax** b7.de*

STARING agg.: spig bg2

STEPPING HARD agg.: aloe bg2 alum bg2 ambr b7.de* *Anac* b4a.de* *Arn* b7a.de bar-c bg2 *Bell* b4.de* *Bry* b7.de* calc b4.de* calc-p bg2 *Chin* b7.de* cimic bg2 cocc b7.de* con b4.de* dros b7.de* glon bg2 *Hell* b7.de* kali-c b4.de* lach bg2 led b7.de* lyc b4.de* meny b7.de* nat-m bg2 *Nux-v* b7.de* ph-ac bg2 phos b4.de* puls bg2 *Rhus-t* b7.de* sep b4a.de* sil b4.de* sol-ni bg2 spig b7.de* spong b7.de* stann ptk1 sulph b4.de* ther bg2 viol-t b7a.de

STIFFNESS, sensation of: canth k* cardios-h rly4• *Caust* bg2* cic tl1 colch bg2* ferr k* galla-q-r nl2• gels bg2 glon k* nat-m k* nat-s k* op bg2 oxal-a rly4• phos bg phys bg plan bg2 puls bg2 rheum bg2 rhus-t bg2
- **evening** | **bed** agg.; in: sil
- **bend** head back; must: kali-n
- **hair** feels stiff: sarr a1
- **motion**:
  - **agg.**: nat-s k*
  - **head**; of | **agg.**: colch
- **waking**; on: anac k*

○ - **Brain**: phos bg2
  - **air** agg.; in open: phos
- **Occiput**, in: anac k* apoc-a a1 calc colch a1 dioxi rbp6 ferr k* fic-m gya1 gins k* helo c1 helo-s c1* kali-n k* *Mur-ac* hr1 phos k* sil k*

▽ · **extending** to | **Nose**: lach lachn k*
- **Skin** of head; on: galla-q-r nl2• rhus-t ptk1
- **Vertex**: oxal-a rly4•

STIRRED with a spoon; brain feels as if: arg-n k* iod k*

STOMACH, as if rising from (See STOMACH - Heat - extending - head; STOMACH - Pain - extending - head)

STONE; as from a (See Heaviness)

STOOL:
- **after**:
  - **agg.**: ambr b7.de sabad b7.de spig b7.de
  - **amel.**: aeth bg2 agar bg2 glon bg2 ox-ac bg2 verat-v bg2 zinc bg2
- **agg.**: manc ptk1 ther ptk1
- **amel.**: aeth ptk1 agar ptk1
- **during**:
  - **agg.**: rhus-t b7.de
    - **External** head: staph b7.de*
    - **Occiput**: crot-t bg2 hyos bg2
  - **amel.** | **Occiput**: asaf ptk1
- **hard** stool | **during**: lyc b4a.de

Stool: ...
- **urging** to:
  - **agg.**: alet bg2 apoc bg2 bry bg2 con bg2 indg bg2 iris bg2 lyc bg2* mang ptk1 nux-v bg2 ptel bg2 puls bg2 sil bg2 sulph bg2
  - **amel.**: iris bg2

STOOPING:
- **after** | **agg.**: asar b7.de* hyos b7.de* meny b7.de* viol-t b7a.de
- **agg.**: acon b7.de* alum b4.de* am-m b7.de* ang b7.de* ant-t b7.de* *Apis* b7a.de *Arn* b7.de* asar b7.de* aur b4.de* bapt bg2 bar-c b4.de* *Bell* b4.de* brom b4a.de* **Bry** b7.de* *Calc* b4.de* camph b7.de* canth b7.de* caps b7.de* carb-an b4.de* carb-v b4.de* caust b4.de* chel b7.de* chin b7.de* *Cic* b7a.de coff b7.de* colch bg2 coloc b4.de* cupr b7.de* cycl b7.de* dig b4.de* *Dros* b7.de* dulc b4.de* ferr bg2* glon bg2 hell b7.de* hep b4.de* *Ign* b7.de* ip b7.de* kali-bi bg2 kali-c b4.de* kali-n b4.de* kreos b7a.de* *Lach* b7.de* laur b7.de* lil-t bg2 lyc b4.de* mag-m b4.de* mang b4.de* merc b4.de* *Merc-c* b4a.de mur-ac b4.de* nat-c b4.de* nat-m b4a.de* nit-ac b4.de* *Nux-v* b7.de* par b7.de* petr b4.de* phos b4.de* phyt bg2 plat b4.de* *Puls* b7.de* rheum b7.de* *Rhus-t* b7.de* samb b7.de* *Sang* bg2 seneg b4.de* *Sep* b4.de* *Sil* b4.de* *Spig* b7.de* spong b7.de* stann b4.de* *Staph* b7.de* sul-ac b4a.de sulph b4.de* teucr b7.de* thuj b4.de* valer b7.de* verat b7.de*

○ · **External** head: alum b4.de* hell b7.de* kali-bi bg2 mag-m b4.de* staph b7.de*
  - **Vertex**: meny ptk1
- **amel.**: ang b7.de* bar-c b4.de* bell b4.de* cann-xyz bg2 caust b4.de* cina b7.de* con b4.de* dig b4.de* hyos bg2* *Ign* b7.de* laur b7.de* *M-aust* b7.de mang b4.de* meny ptk1 mez b4.de* nat-s ptk1 phos bg2 tarax b7.de* verat b7.de* verb b7.de* viol-t b7.de*

STOPPED up sensation: nat-c h2

STRAINING eyes agg.: | **Occiput**: onos ptk1

STRETCHING agg.: agar bg2

STRIKING:
- **against** the skull; sensation as if brain were striking●: alum k* *Ars* k* **Chin** hep bg2 laur *Nux-m* nux-v bg plat *Rhus-t* rob *Sep* stann sul-ac *Sulph* tub hr
  - **nodding** the head, on: *Sulph*
- **foot** against something; when | **agg.**: bar-c b4.de* sep b4.de* sil b4.de*
- **head**; striking: *(↗MIND - Striking - himself - head - his)* ars bg2
  - **amel.**: stram bg2
- **pain**; strikes head with fists from: ars h2
- **wall**; strikes head against the: *(↗Knocking head - wall)* bell bg2
  - **pain**; from: stram vh
  - **twitching** of lids and frontal muscles; with: mill

STROKE (See Apoplexy)

STUFFY sensation (See Heaviness; MIND - Dullness)

STUPEFACTION (See MIND - Stupefaction)

SUN:
- **exposure** to the sun: ant-c ptk1 *Bell* ptk1 *Bry* ptk1 **Glon** ptk1 *Lach* ptk1 *Nat-c* ptk1 nux-v ptk1 puls ptk1 valer ptk1
  - **agg.**: ant-c bg2 bar-c b4.de* *Bell* bg2 brom b4a.de* bry bg2 cact bg2 *Camph* bg2 chin bg2 chinin-s bg2 euphr bg2 ferr-p bg2 *Gels* bg2 **Glon** bg2 ign bg2 iod b4a.de **Lach** bg2 manc bg2 med bg2 meli bg2 *Nat-c* b4.de* nux-v bg2 puls bg2 *Sel* bg2 *Sep* b4a.de stram bg2 valer bg2 verat-v bg2 zinc bg2
  - **amel.**: graph bg2* stront-c ptk1

SUNSTROKE: *Acon* b7a.de* agar hr1* **Aml-ns** kr1* *Ant-c* hr1* apis bg2* arg-met k* arg-n *Arn* hr1* *Ars* hr1* *Bell* k* bry bro1 *Cact* hr1* cadm-s c1 *Camph* k* carb-v kr1* cit-l hr1* cortiso mtf11 crot-h c1* cyt-l mg1.de* euph-pi c1* *Gels* bg2* **Glon** k* *Hell* bg2 hydr-ac c1* hyos bg2* kalm hr1* lach bg2* lyc c1* lyss c1* meli sf1.de* **Nat-c** bg2* nat-m c1* nux-v bg2* *Op* hr1* pop-cand c1* rhus-t c1 sang tl1 sel c2 sol c1* stram k* syph c1* *Ther* k* thuj c1 usn br1* valer c1 *Verat* hr1* verat-v k*
- **accompanied** by:

○ · **Tongue** | **white** discoloration of the: *Glon* kr1*
- **ailments** after | **long** after: glon bg2 nat-c ptk1
- **prophylactic**: mate bro1
- **slept** in the sun; from having: acon k* *Bell*

SUPPORTING head:
- **agg.**: nat-m bg2
- **amel.**: alum bg2 anac bg2 am bg2 bell bg2 cimic bg2 con bg2 dros bg2 glon bg2 lac-c bg2 merc bg2 nat-m bg2 nux-v bg2 rhod bg2 staph bg2 sulph bg2

SURGING sensation: *(↗Motions in; Shaking sensation; Shaking the head; Swashing; Waving)* alum h2* coff b7.de* hyos b7a.de *Lach* bg2 merc-c b4a.de ox-ac bg2 par b7.de* petr bg2 puls bg2 sel b7a.de
- **becoming** erect amel.: alum
- **lying** agg.: ox-ac

○ - **Forehead** | **waves** rolling up and down; like: *Sep*
- **Occiput**:

▽ • **extending** to | **Forehead**: cann-i lach

SWALLOWING agg.: gels bg2 kali-c bg2 mag-c b4.de* thuj bg2

SWASHING sensation: *(↗Motions in; Shaking sensation; Shaking the head; Splashing; Surging; Waving)* acon k* am-c bg2 aphis k* *Ars* k* asaf k* *Aur* bg2 *Bell* k* carb-ac k* *Carb-an* k* chin k* cimic cina b7.de* dig k* ferr b7.de* hell ptk1 *Hep* k* *Hyos* k* indg irid-met bg2* lach bg2 lyc k* mag-m k* mag-p bg2 nux-v k* ph-ac k* plat bg2 plect bg1 *Rhus-t* k* sal-ac sne samb k* *Spig* k* squil k* sul-ac sulph bg2 thuj b4a.de viol-t k* zinc bg2
- **shaking** the head agg.; on: *Cina* hr1 *Spig* squil
- **to** and fro | **Brain**: chin ptk1 hell ptk1
- **walking** agg.: nux-v k* *Spig* k*

○ - **Brain**: hyos hr1*

SWOLLEN: am-c b4a.de **Ant-t** b7a.de apis bg2 ars b4.de* *Cupr* b7a.de guaj b4.de* *Olnd* b7.de* sulph b4.de*
- **children**; in: | **infants**: **Arn** bg2 *Rhus-t* bg2 sil bg2
- **swellings**: petr h2
- **tumor** (See Tumors - swellings)

○ - **Brain**: carc sp1
- **External** head | **chill**; during: ars bg2 cupr bg2 *Sulph* bg2
- **Forehead**: apis bg2 bell h1 cupr h2 dig h2 hell bg2 ip bg2 stann bg2
  - **pressing** on root of nose: bamb-a stb2.de•
  - **shining** swelling: phos h2
  - **sore** swellings: hell h1

○ • **Eminence**; frontal | **hard** swelling: ars h2
  - **Veins**: cub c1
- **Glabella**: fl-ac bg2* kali-c k* sel bg2* sil bro1*
- **Glands** of head: *Bar-c* *Calc* k* carb-v k2 *Merc* *Psor* **Sil** staph sne *Sulph* tub mrr1
  - **hard**: tub mrr1

○ • **Occiput**; glands of: **Bar-c** k* mag-m
- **Occiput**: bar-c ptk1
- **Scalp**: *Apis* b7a.de* **Ars** b4.de* *Bar-c* b4a.de *Bell* b4.de* calc b4a.de caust b4.de* *Cham* b7.de* crot-h bg2 cupr b7.de* *Daph* bg2 dig b4.de* euph b4.de* glon bg2 *Graph* bg2 lach b7a.de* mang bg2 merc b4a.de* *Merc-c* b4a.de mez bg2 op b7.de* petr bg2 phos b4.de* puls b7.de* **Rhus-t** b7.de* ruta bg2 sep b4.de* stram b7.de* sulph b4.de*
- **Temples**: cham b7a.de

○ • **Veins** (See FACE - Veins - temples)

SWOLLEN feeling: *(↗Enlarged; Expanded; Large)* aeth agar aids nl2• am-c k* aml-ns anac k* ant-t **Apis** k* aran hr1 *Arg-n* k* arn k* ars h2 bamb-a stb2.de• bapt k* bar-c *Bell* k* berb k* bism bov *Calc* cann-i k* caps carb-v bg2 **Cedr** k* chinin-s cimic cina cob coc-c k* coll cor-r k* cupr-act cupr-ar daph dig k* dulc eupi a1 fic-m gya1 gels gins **Glon** k* guaj h2 indg kali-i lac-lup hrn2• lach k* lachn lact k* laur lil-t k* lith-c mang k* meph k* merc k* merl k* nat-m nux-m k* **Nux-v** op k* par k* plan k* *Ran-b* k* ran-s rhus-t k* rhus-v a1 samb k* sep k* spig stront-c sulph k* tarax ther k* [lac-mat sst4]
- **entering**:
  - **house**: aeth c1
  - **room**: aeth c1
- **waking**; on: ars samb k*
- **walking** in open air agg.: aeth k* mang k*
- **washing** agg.; after: aeth

○ - **Forehead**: acon k* agar apis bg2* ars k* bamb-a stb2.de• cic k* dulc k* hell bg2* hep k* indg ip bg2 lyc k* merc mez k* nux-v k* olib-sac wmh1 phos k* pip-m plan bg2 prun mrr1 rhus-t ptk1 rhus-v k* ruta sep k* spong h1 stann bg2 tub hr1
  - **expanding**, alternating with contracting: tarax k*

Swollen feeling – **Forehead**: ...
  - **feels** broad and high: cund k*

○ • **Veins**: abrot bg1 calad bg1 camph a1 chin bg1 cub bg1* pilo a1 sulph bg1*
- **Occiput**: bry k* coc-c bg2 dulc k* pip-m puls k*
- **Sides**: caust k* nux-m k* par k*
- **Temples**: bufo calc k* cham k* euph k* par k* sang a1
  - **right**: bufo calc k* par k*
  - **left**: cham k* euph k*

○ • **Above**: sep h2
  - **Veins**: abrot k2 alco a1 ars a1 bond a1 *Carl* a1 cub a1 gent-c a1 glon a1 sulph a1 thuj a1 til a1
- **Vertex**: aids nl2• all-c k* ant-c hr1 olib-sac wmh1

TALK of others agg.: *Acon* b7a.de bar-c bg2* *Bell* b4a.de cact ptk1 lyss ptk1 mag-m ptk1 merc bg2 mur-ac ptk1 *Spig* b7a.de

TALKING agg.: *Acon* b7.de* *Arn* b7a.de aur b4.de* bry b7.de* cact ptk1 *Calc* b4a.de canth b7.de* **Chin** b7.de* **Cocc** b7.de* coff b7.de* con b4.de* *Dig* b4a.de dros b7.de* *Dulc* b4.de* hyos b7.de* *Ign* b7.de* iod b4.de* led b7.de* mag-m b4.de* mang b4.de* merc b4.de* mez b4.de* **Nat-m** bg2* nux-v b7.de* par b7.de* ph-ac b4.de* puls b7.de* rhus-t b7.de* sars b4.de* *Sil* b4.de* spig b7.de* **Sulph** b4.de* thuj b4a.de zinc bg2

○ - **External** head: cic b7.de*

TEA:
- **agg.**: *Chin* b7.de* coff bg2 lach b7.de* sel b7.de* verat b7.de*
- **hot** tea amel.: ferr-p ptk1 glon ptk1

TEARING pains in the limbs; after: | **agg.**: sars b4.de*

TEMPERATURE AGG.; CHANGE OF: carb-v bg2 *Ran-b* b7a.de *Verb* b7a.de
- **warm** to cold: carb-v b4.de* ran-b b7.de* verb b7.de*

TENSION: *(↗Constriction)*
- **fever**; during: *Sabad* b7.de*
- **waking**; on: staph b7.de*

○ - **Scalp**: acon bg2* agn b7.de* ang b7.de* ant-t bg2 *Apis* b7a.de* arg-met bg2 arn b7a.de* ars bg2 asar b7.de* *Bapt* bro1 bar-c b4.de* cact bg2 canch bro1 *Carb-an* b4a.de *Caust* b4.de* clem b4.de* hell b7.de* iris bro1 kali-br bg2 lach bg2 laur b7.de* lyc b4.de* *M-arct* b7.de* merc b4a.de* mur-ac b4.de* nit-ac b4.de* olnd b7.de* par b7.de* phos b4a.de* plat bg2 rat bro1 ruta b7.de* sabad b7.de* sel bro1 sep b4.de* spig b7.de* stann b4.de* staph b7.de* stict bro1 stront-c b4.de* tarax b7.de* thuj b4a.de *Viol-o* b7.de* viol-t b7.de*

○ • **Eyes** and ears; over: merc bg2
- **Skin**; of | **Forehead** (See FACE - Tension - forehead)
- **Vertex**: par bg2

THIN; skull seemed: *Bell* k* calc bro1 *Calc-p* k* puls k*

THINKING of complaints:
- **amel.**: camph bg2 cic bg2 ham bg2 nit-ac b4a.de pall ptk1 puls bg2 sabad bg2
- **not** thinking of complains | **amel.**: *Hell* b7a.de

THREADS around; sensation of: manc vh

THROBBING (See Pulsating)

THROMBOSIS: *(↗Cerebral hemorrhage; Cerebrovascular)* morg jl2 nux-m tl2* zinc tl2

THROWING head (See Motions of - throwing)

THUNDERSTORM agg.: *Sep* b4a.de

TICKLING in: ferr k* phos k*

○ - **Brain**: laur phos
  - **night**: hyper k*
- **Forehead**: brom k* ferr mag-c h2
- **Occiput** | **Base**: ulm-c jsj8•
- **Temples**: sep h2
- **Vertex**: ulm-c jsj8•

TIED, feels as though: colch k* desm-g bnj1 pimp a1

TIGHTNESS (See Constriction)

TINEA CAPITIS (See Eruptions - ringworm)

TINGLING: acet-ac k* acon am-c apis k* arg-met arizon-l nl2• arn aur b4.de bar-c cadm-s cartl-s rly4• caust k* chel choc srj3• chord-umb rly4• cic cocc *Colch* coli rly4• *Cupr* dulc fd4.de ger-i rly4• hydrog srj2• hyos ina-i mlk9.de kali-s fd4.de laur lil-t k2 nad rly4• nat-sil fd3.de• neon srj5• nux-m k* olib-sac wmh1 pant-ac rly4• ph-ac k* phos k* plat puls pyrid rly4• rheum *Rhus-t* k* ruta fd4.de sabad b7.de* sec sel k2 sil a1 sinus rly4• stann a1 staph h1* sulph k* symph fd3.de• tarax thuj k* verb k* *Viol-o* b7.de* [spect dfg1]
- **bell** were struck; as though a large: sars
- **speaking** aloud, on: zinc k*
- **stooping** agg.: staph h1
- **vertigo**; with: hydrog srj2•
- **walking** agg.: verb k*

○ - **Forehead**: ambr am atp rly4• aur k* carc fd2.de• cartl-s rly4• chel cic *Colch* dulc fd4.de ephe-si hsj1• ger-i rly4• ham fd3.de• indg k* kali-s fd4.de melal-alt gya4 nat-pyru rly4• ph-ac puls ruta fd4.de sabad stram k* tarax verat k* viol-o viol-t k* zinc
- **Occiput**: cartl-s rly4• coli rly4• nat-sil fd3.de• rhus-t sulph a1
  - **stupefying**, on stepping: sulph
- **Scalp** | **warm** room agg.: cadm-met tpw6
- **Temples**: borx kali-s fd4.de plat rheum stront-c sulph k*
  - **coldness** of spot, with: plat k*
- **Vertex**: aesc arizon-l nl2• calc k* cartl-s rly4• colch *Cupr* k* hyos lac-c k* nat-ox rly4• nat-sil fd3.de• pot-e rly4• sulph k* [heroin sdj2]
  - **right**: [heroin sdj2]
  - **left**: [heroin sdj2]
  - **cough** agg.; during: sulph h2
  - **menses** omitting: cupr k*

TIRED feeling●: apis k* arn bro1 bell hr1 benzol br1 carc mlr1• chinin-ar bro1 chlam-tr bcx2• con k* ferr-p bro1 iris kali-s fd4.de lach lap-la sde8.de• nat-m k* nux-m ozone sde2• **PHOS** k* *Psor* k* sil h2 zinc-val bro1 [bell-p-sp dcm1 pop dhh1]

TOUCH:
- **agg**.: *Acon* bg2 agar b4.de* agn b7.de* alum bg2 anac b4a.de apis b7a.de arg-met b7.de* ars bg2 aur ptk1 bar-c b4.de* bov bg2 bry b7.de* *Calc* b4a.de camph b7.de* canth bg2 carb-an bg2 caust b4a.de *Chin* b7.de* *Coloc* b4a.de con b4.de* cupr b7.de* daph bg2 hep ptk1 ip b7.de* kali-c bg2 kali-n b4.de* laur b7.de* led b7.de* lyc b4.de* m-ambo b7.de *Merc* b4.de* *Mez* b4a.de* nat-m bg2 nit-ac ptk1 nux-m bg2 *Nux-v* ptk1 ph-ac b4.de* phos b4.de* rhod b4.de* sars b4.de* sep b4a.de* staph b7.de* *Sulph* b4a.de

○ • **External** head: *Agar* b4a.de ambr b7.de* apis b7a.de arg-met b7.de* arn bg2 ars b4.de aur b4.de* bar-c b4.de* *Bell* b4.de* bov b4a.de bry b7.de* calc b4.de* *Cham* b7a.de *Chin* b7.de* cupr b7a.de ferr b7.de* graph b4.de* hell b7.de* *Hep* b4a.de hyos b7.de* ign b7.de* lyc b4.de* m-aust b7.de mag-m b4.de* merc b4.de* *Mez* b4a.de mosch b7a.de nat-c b4.de* nat-m b4a.de nit-ac b4.de* *Nux-m* b7a.de *Nux-v* b7.de* par b7.de* petr b4.de* ph-ac b4.de* phos b4.de* puls b7a.de rhod b4.de* *Rhus-t* b7.de* ruta b7a.de sabin b7.de* sars b4.de* sep b4.de* sil b4.de* *Spig* b7.de* *Staph* b7.de* sul-ac b4.de* sulph b4.de* tarax b7.de* thuj b4.de* zinc b4.de*
- **amel**.: ars b4.de* asaf b7a.de* bell b4.de* calc b4.de* coloc b4.de* con b4.de* cycl b7.de* mang b4.de* meny b7.de* mur-ac b4.de* phos b4.de* thuj b4.de* viol-t b7.de*

○ • **External** head: bry b7.de* dros b7.de*
- **gentle**:
  - **agg**. | **External** head: *Chin* b7.de* **Lach** bg2 nux-m bg2 *Nux-v* b7a.de
- **hair** agg.; touching the: (↗*Sensitiveness - brushing*) agar bg2 ambr b7a.de carb-v bg2 carbn-s bg2 chin b7a.de ferr b7a.de kreos bg2 *Puls* b7a.de rhus-t b7a.de

TREMBLING: agar b4a.de aloe bg2 alum b4a.de ambr k* anan k* ant-c k* *Ant-t* k* ars bg2 aur bg2 bell k* bry bg2 bufo bg2* calc k* cann-xyz bg2 carb-v k* caust k* *Chel* k* *Cic* k* cinnb k* *Cocc* k* cop k* cub k* dubo-h hs1 graph k* *Ign* k* indg k* kali-c b4a.de* kali-n bg2 kali-sil k2 kreos b7a.de *Lith-c* kl *Lyc* bg2 *Mag-p* k* merc k* mez bg2 nat-m b4a.de* *Op* k* petr k* phos b4a.de plat k* *Plb* k* sep bg2 sulph k* tab k* *Zinc* b4a.de
- **conversation**, from: ambr
- **convulsions**; before epileptic: *Caust*
- **convulsive**: cocc h1
- **cough** agg.; during: ant-t

Trembling: ...
- **exertion** agg.; after: ant-t gsy1
- **menses**; during: ant-c cic cinnb cub
- **motion** agg.: ant-t gsy1 cic k*
- **noises** in ear, with: kali-c h2
- **paroxysmal**: carb-v h2
- **talking**; after: ambr

▽ - **extending** to | **Pit** of stomach: phys k*

○ - **Brain**: bov b4.de cann-s b7.de
- **Scalp**: caust b4.de* merc b4.de

TRICKLING in head: glon bg2

TUMORS:
- **angiosarcoma**: (↗*GENERALS - Tumors - angioma*) calc-f mtf rad-br mtf sec mtf vip mtf
- **perforating** the skull: lach ptk1*
- **swellings**; tumorous: (↗*Cancer - brain*) psor al

○ • **Scalp** and skull; between | **thick**, sticky fluid; filled with a: sil k2*

○ - **Bones**: **Aur** b4.de* calc-p bg2 *Daph* bg2 merc bg2 *Phos* b4a.de sars bg2 *Sil* b4.de*
- **Brain**: (↗*Cancer - brain; GENERALS - Tumors - encephaloma; STOMACH - Vomiting - brain; STOMACH - Vomiting - cerebral*) aeth rmk1• apom bro1 arn bro1* aur-i sne *Bar-c* bro1* bell bro1* calc bro1* cham sne *Con* bro1* glon bro1* graph bro1* hydr bro1 *Kali-i* bro1* *Plb* bro1* **Plb-i** rmk1• sep bro1* sulph sne *Thuj* sne zinc-s rmk1•
  - **accompanied** by:
    - **convulsions** | **epileptic**: plb bro1*
    - **tension** in head: ap-d mtf apis mtf apom mtf hed mtf hell mtf
    - **vomiting** (See STOMACH - Vomiting - cerebral)
  - **astrocytoma**: aeth rmk1• *Bar-c* rmk1• carc rmk1• plb-i rmk1• syph mtf
  - **ependymoma**: calc mtf gels mtf plb mtf zinc mtf
  - **glioma**: bar-c mtf* carc rmk1• caust mtf plb-i rmk1•
  - **growing** rapidly: naphthoq mtf11
- **Scalp**; on: anac b4.de* anan bro1 arg-n bg2 ars bg2 aur-m bro1 calc b4a.de* *Calc-f* bro1 carb-an b4a.de caust b4.de* cupr bro1 daph bg2 fl-ac bro1 *Hecla* bro1 hell b7a.de* *Hep* b4a.de kali-c b4.de* *Kali-i* bro1 merc bro1 merc-p bro1 nux-v b7a.de* petr b4a.de* ph-ac b4.de* puls b7.de* rhus-t b7a.de* ruta b7.de* sep b4a.de* sil b4.de* still bro1
  - **cystic**: | **hairless**: *Calc* b4a.de *Graph* b4a.de
  - **encysted**: bar-c hr1
  - **painful**: kali-c ptk1*

TURNED: (↗*GENERALS - Turning - Head; GENERALS - Turning - Head - agg.*)
- **left** in convulsions; to: mygal plb
- **one** side; to: cic c1* cupr ptk1
- **right**; to: *Calc* b4a.de

TURNING:
- **bed**; in | **agg**.: lil-t bg2
- **body** | **agg**.: cham b7.de* nat-m b4.de* sil b4.de*
- **head**:
  - **agg**.: (↗*GENERALS - Turning - Head; GENERALS - Turning - Head - agg.*) arn bg2 ars bg2 bell bg2 bry bg2 calc bg2* cic bg2* con bg2 graph b4a.de hep bg2 hyos b7.de* kali-c bg2* lyc b4.de* nat-c b4.de* nat-m b4a.de* nux-v bg2 ph-ac b4.de* phos bg2 puls ptk1 sang bg2 sel bg2 *Sil* b4a.de spig bg2* spong b7.de*
    - **suddenly**: sang ptk1 spig bg2

TURNING AND TWISTING sensation: aeth k* bell k* bry k* calc k* indg iris k* **Kali-c** k* merl a1 nat-m bg2 nicc a1 petr k* plan bg2 plut-n srj7• rhus-t k* sabad k* sil k*

○ - **Brain**: bell tl1 cham tl1 *Nux-v* ptk plan ptk1
- **Occiput**: bell bg2
- **Vertex**: bell bg2

TWILIGHT agg. (See Evening - twilight - agg.)

TWISTING head: nat-m j5.de

TWITCHING: *(↗MIND - Gestures - tics)* *Agar* kl aloe kl ambr b7.de* anac b4a.de apis kl arn b7.de* bar-c kl *Bell* b4.de* bry b7.de* calc kl calc-sil k2 cann-s kl carb-v b4.de* carc fd2.de• caust b4.de* cham kl chel kl chin b7.de* *Cic* kl crot-t kl cycl b7.de* eupi kl glon kl graph kl ign b7.de* kali-c b4.de* kali-s fd4.de laur b7.de* lyc kl m-ambo b7.de m-aust b7.de mag-c b4.de* merc kl mygal kl nat-c kl nat-p kl nat-s kl nit-ac kl nux-v b7.de* *Op* tl1* petr kl *Ph-ac* b4.de* phos kl puls b7a.de* rat kl rhus-t kl sabad b7.de* *Sep* b4a.de* sil kl stann kl staph b7.de* stram kl* sulph b4.de* thuj b4a.de verat bg2
- **morning**: cham glon nux-v phos sep
- **noon**: glon
- **afternoon**: aeth borx rhus-t
- **evening**: fl-ac mur-ac nit-ac rhus-t sil
- **night**: chel rhus-t sil
- **ascending** stairs agg.: glon hell h1
- **blowing** the nose agg.: aster
- **cough** agg.; during: lyc puls
- **eating**; after: cham
- **jerking** the arms, when: spong
- **lain** on, part: rhus-t h1
- **lying** down agg.: nit-ac
- **motion**:
  - **agg.**: eupi hell h1 phos
  - **arms**; of | **agg.**: chel
- **pressure** | **amel.**: hell h1
- **pulsating**: ph-ac h2
- **sensation**: *Agar* bg2 am-m bg2 ang bg2 bry bg2 canth bg2 cham bg2 *Cic* bg2 hell h1* op bg2 phos bg2 puls bg2 rhus-t bg2
- **standing**; after: fl-ac
- **stepping** agg.: spong
- **stool** agg.; during: phos
- **stooping** agg.: berb hell h1 nit-ac petr
- **touch** agg.: chel
- **vexation** agg.: mag-c bg1
- **walking** agg.: petr *Spig*

○ - **Brain**; as if in: aster bar-c bov bry calc cann-s nit-ac h2 rat
- **Forehead**: acon *Agar* k* alumn ant-t arn k* berb borx k* bry k* caust cham k* chin k* kali-chl lach mag-m k* mez nat-sil fd3.de• phos k* *Prun* rhod sabad k* *Sep* k* sil k* spig b7a.de spong k* stann sulph thuj
  - **right**: caust b4.de* sabad b7.de* sulph b4.de*
  - **left**: mez b4.de* sabad b7.de*
  - **afternoon**: borx
    - ⁝ **lying** down agg.: hep h2
  - **evening**: alumn fl-ac nat-sil fd3.de•
  - **rising** | **amel.**: hep h2
  - **stooping** agg.: berb

▽ • **extending** to | **Brain**; into the: camph
- **Muscles**: arg-met b7.de* *Arn* bg2 colch bg2 kali-c b4.de* lach b7a.de lyc bg2 mag-c bg2
- **Occiput**: acon k* bism k* canth k* carb-an b4.de* mag-c k* *Mag-m* k* merc k* ph-ac *Puls* b7a.de rhus-t sars k* *Spig* k* sulph h2 thuj k*

▽ • **extending** to | **Forehead**: anac ph-ac h2
- **Sides**: aeth agar anac ang bar-c calc cann-i caust chin b7.de* cupr glon graph *Nit-ac* ox-ac plb valer verb
  - **right**: aeth agar bar-c k* caust k* ox-ac plb k* valer k*
  - **left**: anac k* calc cann-i cupr *Nit-ac* k* verb k*
  - **touch** agg.: bar-c h2

▽ • **extending** to:
  - ⁝ **side** to side; from: merc
  - ⁝ **Throat**: chin
  - ⁝ **Vertex**, when jerking arms and on stepping: spong
- **Temples**: acon agar k* am-c am-m anac apis arg-met arn b7a.de bar-c berb bov bry k* calc carb-an chel *Chin* k* crot-h cycl k* glon kali-c kali-s fd4.de lil-t merc ox-ac phos plb k* psor ptk1 *Puls* b7a.de *Spig* k* squil stann sul-ac valer
  - **right**: bry b7.de* cycl b7.de* kali-s fd4.de merc k* squil k* sul-ac valer verb h
  - **left**: am-m k* anac k* bar-c k* bov chel cycl b7.de* kali-c phos k* rhod b4.de* stann verb b7.de*
  - **dinner**; after: phos h2

Twitching – Temples: ...
  - **lain** on; twitching tearing in temple:
    - ⁝ **moves** to other side on turning eyes | **raising** eyes agg. (See Pain - temples - lain - raising - eyes - agg. - tearing - twitching)
  - **spots**, in: rat
  - **walking** agg.: *Spig*

▽ • **extending** to:
  - ⁝ **Brain**: camph
  - ⁝ **Jaws** or teeth: rhus-t
  - ⁝ **Vertex**: cycl
- **Vertex**: chel gent-c kreos b7a.de mag-c k* meny k* mur-ac k* petr k* phos h2 ran-s k* sil

ULCERS: ambr c1 *Anan* k* *Ars* k* *Bar-m* k* *Calc-p* k* chel k* nit-ac *Phos* k* psor k2 ruta *Sil* k* sul-ac k2 tarent thuj k*

○ - **External** head: *Ambr* b7a.de ars b4.de nit-ac bg2 ruta b7.de* tarent bg2
  - **small** ulcers: ars bg2 ruta bg2
- **Forehead** (See FACE - Ulcers - forehead)
- **Occiput**: **Sil** k*

UNCOVERING: *(↗Pain - uncovering - head - agg.)*
- **body** | **amel.**: cor-r bg2
- **head**:
  - **agg.**: *(↗Pain - uncovering - head - agg.)* acon agar ant-c arg-met arn *Ars* k* *Aur* k* aur-ar k2 *Bar-c* **Bell** k* benz-ac k* borx brom ptk1 *Calc* calc-p bg3* camph canth *Carb-v* cham chin chinin-ar cic clem cocc coff *Colch* k* *Con* k* *Graph* **Hep** k* *Hyos* k* ign kali-ar kali-bi bg3* *Kali-c* kali-p kali-sil k2 kreos *Lach* k* led mag-c k* mag-m mag-p bg3* *Merc* *Mez* naja nat-c *Nat-m* nat-p *Nit-ac* *Nux-m* k* **Nux-v** k* ph-ac *Phos* *Psor* k* puls rhod **Rhus-t** k* *Rumx* k* sabad samb k* *Sep* **Sil** k* *Squil* staph stram *Stront-c* bg2* *Thuj* k* til
  - **amel.**: acon bg2 aur bg2 borx bg2 calc bg2 glon bg2 iod bg2 *Lyc* bg2 puls bg2 sulph b4.de* verat bg2

UNSTEADY feeling: bell k* clem k* phos k* rhus-t k* sep k* *Sulph* k*
- **study** agg.; after: cupr-ar

URINATION:
- **after**:
  - **agg.**: caust bg2
  - **amel.**: agar ptk1 fl-ac ptk1 gels ptk1 ign ptk1 meli ptk1 sang ptk1 sil ptk1
- **amel.**: acon bg2 agar bg2 aml-ns bg2 fl-ac bg2 gels bg2 *Ign* bg2 kalm bg2 lith-c bg2 lyc bg2 meli bg2 mosch bg2 sang bg2 sel bg2 sil bg2 ter bg2
- **during**: acon bg2 coloc bg2* nux-v bg2* sabad bg2 tab bg2*
- **retention** agg.: fl-ac bg2* sep ptk1
- **suppressed** agg.: am-c bg2 am ptk1 con bg2 *Glon* ptk1 hyper ptk1 sang ptk1

VACANT feeling: *(↗Empty)* aq-mar skp7• *Gels* psa kali-p fd1.de• *Kola* stb3• med al nat-sil fd3.de• plut-n srj7• sec k* spong fd4.de sulph k* thioc-ac rly4•
- **sleep**; after: aq-mar skp7•

○ - **Forehead**:
  - **morning** | **waking**; after: sulph

VAULTS, cellars agg.: *Bry* b7a.de *Puls* b7a.de

VEAL; after: | **agg.**: kali-n b4.de*

VERTIGO:
- **after**: calc bg2* kali-bi bg2 phos bg2 plat bg2 plb bg2 ran-b bg2 rhus-t ptk1 sep bg2 til bg2
- **during** | **agg.**: acon b7.de ant-t b7.de* arg-met b7.de ars b4.de aur b4.de bar-c b4.de *Bry* bg2 *Calc* b4.de* canth b7.de carb-an bg2 caust bg2 cham bg2 chin bg2 chinin-s bg2 cocc bg2 con b4.de* cupr b7.de* ferr b7.de graph b4.de hell b7.de* ign b7.de *Lach* b7.de* laur b7.de* lyc bg2 nit-ac b4.de* *Nux-v* b7.de* *Phos* b4.de* *Puls* b7.de* ran-b bg2 rhus-t bg2 sep bg2 spig b7a.de *Stram* b7.de stront-c b4.de tab bg2 verb b7.de

VEXATION:
- **after**: *Acon* bg2 bry bg2 *Cham* bg2 chin bg2 cocc bg2 *Ign* bg2 mag-c bg2 *Nat-m* bg2 nux-v bg2 petr bg2 phos bg2 plat bg2 ran-b bg2 *Sep* bg2 *Staph* bg2 verat bg2

Head

- **agg.**: *Acon* b7.de ars b4a.de bov bg2 *Bry* b7.de* *Cham* b7.de* cocc b7.de *Coff* b7a.de coloc bg2 *Ign* b7.de* kali-c bg2 kreos bg2 lyc b4a.de* *M-ambo* b7.de* mag-c b4.de* nat-m b4.de* *Nux-v* b7.de* petr b4.de* phos b4.de* plat bg2 ran-b b7.de* rhus-t bg2 sep b4.de* sil bg2 staph b7.de* verat b7.de

O • **External** head: mag-c bg2

VIBRATING (See Shaking sensation)

VISOR; sensation of being pulled to like a metal: agath-a nl2•

VOICES agg.: bar-c bg2

VOMITING:

- **after**:
  - **agg.**: cham b7.de* ferr b7.de* nat-s bg2 nux-v b7.de* phyt ptk1
  - **amel.**: ang bg2 asar b7.de* *Bry* b7a.de eup-per bg2* ign bg2 iris bg2 nat-s ptk1 sang ptk1 *Sep* b4a.de stann ptk1 tab bg2
- **during** | **agg.**: *Agar* b4a.de *Apis* b4a.de* *Arn* b7a.de *Asar* b7.de* bry b7a.de caps b7a.de chin b7a.de* coloc b4a.de* con bg2 graph bg2 ip b7a.de* iris bg2 kali-c bg2 *Lach* bg2 **Lyc** b4.de* mez b4.de* mosch b7a.de* naja bg2 nat-m b4a.de* **Nux-v** b7.de* op bg2 phos b4a.de* **Puls** b7a.de* **Sang** bg2 *Sars* b4a.de **Sep** b4.de* *Sil* b4a.de *Verat* b7.de*

WAKING; on: **Agar** b4a.de alum b4a.de ambr b7.de* anac b4.de* ant-t b7.de* apis b7a.de arg-n bg2 ars b4.de* aur b4.de *Bar-c* bg2 bell b4.de* *Bov* b4.de* **Bry** b7.de* cadm-s bg2 calad bg2 *Calc* b4.de* calc-p bg2 carb-v b4.de* caust b4.de* cham b7.de* chel bg2 chin b7.de* cic b7.de* cimic bg2 cina b7.de* *Cocc* bg2 coff b7.de* con b4.de* croc b7.de* dig bg2 dros b7.de* euphr b7.de* gels bg2 *Graph* b4.de* ham bg2 hell b7.de* *Hep* b4.de* *Ign* b7.de* ip b7.de* kali-bi bg2 kali-br bg2 *Kali-c* b4.de* kalm bg2 kreos b7a.de **Lach** bg2 lyc b4a.de *M-ambo* b7.de *M-arct* b7.de mag-c b4.de* mag-m b4.de* merc bg2 murx bg2 **Nat-m** b4.de* *Nit-ac* b4.de* nux-m b7.de* **Nux-v** b7.de* op b7.de* petr bg2 *Ph-ac* b4.de* phos b4.de* puls b7.de* rheum b7.de* rhus-t b7.de* rumx bg2 ruta b7.de* sabad bg2 sel bg2 *Seneg* bg2 sep b4.de* squil b7.de* stann b4.de* staph b7.de* stram bg2 sul-ac b4.de* sulph b4.de* *Tarent* bg2 thuj b4.de* verat b7.de*

- **amel.**: cham b7.de*

WALKING:

- **after** | **agg.**: puls b7.de* rhus-t b7.de* valer b7.de*
- **agg.**: acon b7.de* alum b4.de* anac b4.de* arn b7.de* ars b4.de* asar b7.de* bar-c bg2 bell b4.de* *Bry* b7.de* *Calc* b4.de* *Caps* b7.de* carb-v b4.de* caust b4.de* chin b7.de* cic b7.de* cimic bg2 clem b4.de* cocc b7.de* con b4.de* dros b7.de* guaj b4.de* hell b7.de* hep b4a.de hyos b7.de* ign b7.de* iod b4.de* kali-bi bg2 kali-c b4.de* kali-n b4.de* *Lach* bg2 laur b7.de* led b7.de* lyc b4.de* m-arct b7.de mag-c b4.de* mang b4.de* mez ptk1 nat-m bg2 nat-s bg2 nit-ac ptk1 **Nux-v** b7.de* olnd b7.de* petr b4.de* ph-ac b4.de* phos b4.de* phyt bg2 puls b7.de* ran-b b7.de* rheum b7.de* rhus-t b7.de* sars b4.de* sep b4.de* sil b4.de* *Spig* b7.de* spong b7.de* staph b7.de* stront-c b4.de* *Sulph* b4a.de *Tarax* b7.de* tub ptk1 verat b7.de* verb b7a.de viol-t b7.de*

O • **External** head: sars b4a.de

- **air**; in open:
  - **after** | **agg.**: *Am-c* b4a.de bell b4.de* bov b4.de* *Calc* b4.de* caust b4.de* chel b7.de* chin b7.de* coff b7.de* ferr b7.de* hep b4.de* mez b4.de* nux-v b7.de* petr b4.de* puls b7.de* ran-b b7.de* ran-s b7.de* *Rhus-t* b7.de* sabad b7a.de spig b7.de* spong b7.de* thuj b4a.de zinc b4.de
  - **agg.**: acon b7.de* alum b4.de* ant-c bg2 arn b7.de* bell b4.de* *Bry* b7.de* *Calc* b4.de* caust b4a.de chin b7.de* cina b7.de* *Coff* b7.de* con b4a.de* dulc b4.de* euphr b7.de* ferr b7.de* hell b7.de* ign b7.de* kali-c b4a.de laur b7.de* lyc b4.de* m-arct b7.de m-aust b7.de mang b4.de* *Merc* b4.de* mosch b7.de* nux-m b7.de* **Nux-v** b7.de* par b7.de* plat b4.de* puls b7.de* ran-b b7.de* *Rhus-t* b7.de* sabad b7.de* sars b4.de* *Sel* b7.de* spig b7.de* spong b7.de* staph b7.de* stront-c b4.de* sul-ac b4.de* sulph b4.de* *Tarax* b7.de*
    - ⁝ **External** head: chin b7.de* led b7a.de nux-v b7.de*
  - **amel.**: alum bg2 ambr b7.de* asar b7.de* carb-an bg2 cina b7.de* croc b7.de* grat bg2 hyos b7.de* m-arct b7.de mag-m bg2 mang bg2 mosch b7a.de **Puls** b7.de* *Rhus-t* b7.de* sep bg2 sol-ni bg2 thuj bg2
- **amel.**: *Ant-c* b7.de* asar b7.de* calc b4.de* canth b7.de* *Chin* b7.de* coloc b4.de* dros b7.de* guaj b4a.de* hep b4a.de lyc b4.de* m-aust b7.de mag-c b4a.de* mang b4.de* mur-ac b4.de* nat-c b4.de* nat-m b4.de* ol-an bg2 phos b4.de* *Puls* b7.de* ran-b b7.de* *Rhus-t* b7.de* seneg b4.de* sep b4.de* spig b7.de* staph b7.de* sulph b4.de* *Tarax* b7.de* thuj b4.de*
- **rapidly** | **agg.**: *Arn* b7a.de bell b4a.de bry b7.de* calc bg2 chel b7.de* crot-h bg2 iod bg2 nat-m b4a.de nux-v b7.de* sep bg2 spig b7.de*

Walking: ...

- **wind**; in the | **agg.**: agar bg2 chin b7.de* nat-s bg2 nux-v b7.de* phos bg2 sanic bg2 sep bg2

WARBLING noise in head (See EAR - Noises - warbling)

WARM: *(↗Hat - aversion)*

- **air** agg.: *Caust* b4a.de iod b4.de*
- **applications**:
  - **agg.**: *Agn* b7a.de *Aloe* bg2 *Apis* b7a.de arg-n bg2 arn b7.de* bar-c b4.de* *Bell* b4.de* bry b7.de* *Graph* b4a.de grat bg2 iod b4.de* kalm bg2 laur b7.de* led b7.de* *Lyc* bg2 *Nat-m* b4a.de *Phos* b4a.de *Puls* b7.de* seneg b4.de* sep b4.de* spong b7a.de *Thuj* b4a.de
  - **amel.**: arg-n ptk1 *Ars* b4a.de aur ptk1 bry ptk1 gels ptk1 kali-c ptk1 *Mag-p* ptk1 *Nux-m* b7.de *Nux-v* b7.de phos ptk1 *Rhus-t* b7.de sil b4.de* staph b7.de
    - ⁝ **External** head: lach b7.de*
- **bed**:
  - **agg.**: *Bell* bg2
    - ⁝ **External** head: rhus-t bg2 *Sulph* b4a.de
- **clothes** agg.: arum-t ptk1
- **coverings** on head: *(↗Hat - aversion)*
  - **agg.**: *(↗Hat - aversion)* *Acon* k* *Apis* asar aur *Borx* bry *Calc* k* carb-an *Carb-v* cham chin *Ferr* k* glon bg2 ign **Iod** k* lach *Led* k* **Lyc** k* merc mur-ac nit-ac k* *Op* **Phos** plat **Puls** k* *Sec* seneg sep *Spig* k* staph sulph thuj *Verat*
  - **amel.**: ars bg2 mag-m bg2 *Mag-p* bg2 *Nux-m* bg2 *Nux-v* bg2 *Rhus-t* bg2 sil bg2 staph bg2 stront-c bg2
- **food** | **agg.**: *Sulph* b4a.de
- **hands** warm; keeping | **amel.**: hell bg2
- **room** | **agg.**: **Arn** bg2 bar-c bg2 bov bg2 caust bg2 laur bg2 ph-ac bg2 phos bg2 plat bg2 spong bg2
- **stove**; near a warm | **agg.**: **Arn** b7.de* bar-c b4a.de* *Puls* b7.de*

WARMTH (See Heat)

WASHING: | **face** | **amel.**: phos bg2 psor bg2

- **head**:
  - **agg.**: *Am-c* *Ant-c* *Bar-c* k* *Bell* bry *Calc* *Calc-p* *Calc-s* canth k* carb-v cham colch bg2 *Glon* led lyc merc nit-ac *Nux-m* phos *Puls* *Rhus-t* k* *Sep* spig stront-c sulph tarent ptk1 zinc-chr ptk1
  - **amel.**: ant-t bg2 ars bg2 asar b7.de* bry bg2 gnaph a2 graph bg2 stram bg2 sulph bg2* zinc bg2

WATER, sensation as of: acon bg2 am-c anan k* asaf bell k* bufo bg2 cina dig k* ferr *Hep* mag-m ph-ac h2 plat h2* samb h1*

- **bending** down; when: *Pneu* jl2
- **boiling** water; in (See Boiling - water)
- **cold**, poured on head: *Cupr* k* sabad rb2 tarent k*
- **drop** running | **Temples**: verat h1
- **dropping** on head: arn b7.de* camph bg2 cann-s k* glon bg2 sabad bg2 verat bg2*
- **head**, in the: bufo hippoc-k szs2 plat h2
- **warm** water, in: am-c peti santin
- **wrapped** up in: all-c k*

O - **Brain**: cur hr1* mag-p ptk1

WAVING sensation: *(↗Boiling; Motions in; Shaking sensation; Shaking the head; Splashing; Surging; Swashing)* acon k* alum k* ant-t bg2 aphis arg-n bg2 ars bg2 asaf bg2 aur bro1 bamb-a stb2.de• *Bell* k* calc bg2 canth bro1 caust k* chel *Chin* k* chinin-s bro1 choc srj3• *Cimic* k* cina k* cocc bg2 coff k* crot-h bg2 crot-t bg2 cupr-s dig k* dulc ferr k* fl-ac k* gels **Glon** k* graph k* grat bg2 *Hep* k* hippoc-k szs2 hydr-ac bg2 *Hyos* k* ind bro1 indg kali-c bg2 kola stb3• *Lach* k* laur k* *Lyc* lyss c1 *Mag-m* k* mag-p bro1 mang k* meli bro1* merc k* merc-c bg2 mill nat-m bg2 nux-m c1 nux-v bro1 pall bro1 par k* petr *Plat* bg2 rhus-t bro1 sars k* sel senec bro1* seneg **Sep** k* sil bg2 spig bg2 sulph k* thuj viol-t bg2 zinc bg2

- **air**; in open | **amel.**: mag-m h2
- **bending** backward agg.: dig h2
- **confusion**, with: mang h2
- **motion**:
  - **agg.**: nux-m c1
  - **amel.**: petr

- **rising** from stooping agg.: lyc
- **standing** agg.: dig
- **stooping** agg.; after: hyos lyc
- **turning** head agg.: carbn-s k2 *Glon* k*
- **water** in, as from: asaf bell cina dig ferr hippoc-k szs2 mag-m
- **wavelike** upward motion: *Glon Lach*

○ - **Brain**: cimic ptk1 croc bg2 glon ptk1 graph bg2 par bg2 phys ptk1 sars bg2 zinc bg2

- **Forehead**: asaf **Bell** k* chir-fl gya2 merc k* petr **Sep** k*
  - • **right** to left, from: glon
  - • **heavy** body swaying back and forth; like a: op
- **Occiput**: gels senec bg2 sil

▽ • **extending** to | **Forehead**: mang h2 senec ptk1*

WEAKNESS: abrot a1* alum k* *Ambr* k* anan a1 anil a1 ant-c h2 ant-t k* apis bg2 arn b7a.de ars bg2* ars-s-f k2 asaf k* aur k* bell k* benz-ac a1 bry k* canth k* carb-v k* caust k* cham k* chin k* cinnb k* cupr b7a.de dig b4a.de fago a1 ferr a1 graph b4a.de* hep k* hyper k* iod bg2* kali-c k* kali-n bg2 kreos k* lac-c bg2* *Lach* bg2 laur bg2 *Merc* k* nat-m k* nit-ac k* nux-m k* op k* ph-ac k* phos k* phyt bg2 pimp a1 plan k* psor k* ptel a1 ran-b k* raph k* rhod b4a.de rhus-t k* sars h2 sep k* sil a1 spong k* squil k* stann k* stram k* sul-ac k* sulph k* tab k* tanac k* tarent k* thuj k* viol-o b7a.de zinc k*

- **morning**: cham k* phos k* ran-b
  - • **rising** agg.; after: ph-ac k*
- **noon**: ars k* dendr-pol sk4•
- **afternoon**: sep h2
- **evening**: plan k* raph k*
- **coffee** agg.: *Cham* k*
- **cough**; after: bar-c h2 hep k*
- **dinner** | **after** | **agg.**: rhus-t h1
  - • **during** | **agg.**: sulph
- **exertion** agg.; after: hydr-ac k*
- **headache**:
  - • **after**: nat-m h2
  - • **appears**; as though: ambr iod lac-c phos stram thuj
- **heat**; after: sep k*
- **lying** on back agg.: puls k*
- **mental** exertion:
  - • **after**: cinnb k*
  - • **agg.** | **causes** mental weakness: spong k*
- **music** of piano unbearable: phos h2
- **pain**; from: ars h2 thea
- **respiration**; during deep: carb-v k*
- **standing** agg.: rhus-t k*
- **stomach**, during weakness in: ars k*
- **sun** agg.; walking in the: nat-m
- **turning**, as after much: nat-m h2
- **walking** agg.: sulph k*
- **working** in hot room, as from: glon k*

▽ - **extending** to | **Lower** limbs | **paralyzed**; as if: phys

- • **Throat**: graph k*

○ - **Side** lain on: mag-m

WEATHER:

- **change** of weather: ran-b bg2

○ • **External** head: borx bg2

- **cold**:
  - • **wet** | **agg.**: carb-an b4a.de *Rhod* b4a.de
- **foggy** agg.: bry bg2 carb-an bg2 carb-v bg2 *Glon* bg2 hyper bg2 nux-v bg2 rhod bg2
- **rainy**:
  - • **agg.**: phyt bg2
    - ⁝ **External** head: mag-c bg2
  - • **amel.**: cham bg2
- **warm**:
  - • **agg.**: nat-c ptk1
  - • **wet** | **agg.**: glon bg2 lach bg2
- **weather** agg.; stormy: bry b7a.de nux-m b7a.de nux-v b7a.de*
  - • **before** | **External** head: grat bg2

Weather – weather agg.; stormy: ...

○ • **External** head: rhod bg2

- **wet**:
  - • **agg.**: bry bg2 carb-an b4.de* carb-v bg2 *Glon* bg2* hyper bg2 nat-m b4a.de nux-v bg2 rhod b4.de*
    - ⁝ **External** head: *Mag-c* b4a.de
    - ⁝ **Temples**: borx ptk1
  - • **amel.**: carb-an b4a.de
- **windy** | **raw** wind agg.: *Chin* bg2 mur-ac bg2

WEIGHT (See Heaviness; Pain - pressing pain - weight)

WENS: agar anan hr1 *Bar-c* k* *Bell* sne *Benz-ac* bro1 *Calc* k* *Con* sne daph sne **Graph** k* *Hep* k* *Kali-c* k* *Kali-i* bro1 *Lob* lyc mez mtf11 myos-a rly4• nat-c nit-ac h2* phyt bro1* sil k* sulph j5.de

WET agg.; getting: ant-c bg2 bell b4a.de

WHIRLING in head (See VERTIGO - Turning; as - head; whirling)

WILD feeling: *(↗MIND - Wild feeling; VERTIGO - Turning; as - head; whirling)* bapt br1 cimic br1 hell mrr1 lil-t br1*

- **pain** in head; with (See MIND - Wild feeling - pain)

○ - **Vertex**: lil-t bro1

WIND (See Air)

WINE:

- **agg.**: ant-c b7.de* **Calc** b4.de* *Carb-an* b4.de* *Carb-v* b4.de* coff b7.de* lach bg2 nux-m b7.de* *Nux-v* b7.de* ox-ac bg2 puls b7.de* ran-b b7.de* *Rhod* b4.de* rhus-t b7.de* *Ruta* b7.de* sel b7.de* verat b7.de* *Zinc* b4.de*
- **amel.**: arg-n bg2

○ • **External** head: acon bg2

WIRE cage; as if wrapped in a (See Constriction; Threads)

WORK; while doing some disagreeable: chin bg2

WRAPPED (See Uncovering; Warm)

WRAPPING UP HEAD:

- **agg.**: calc b4a.de carb-v b4.de* hydr-ac bg2 iod ptk1 laur b7.de* led bg2* *Lyc* ptk1 phos ptk1 puls ptk1 sulph b4.de* valer b7.de*
  - • **tightly**: calc b4.de* sulph b4a.de
- **amel.**: *Aur* b4.de calc bg2 cor-r bg2* hep bg2* kali-c b4a.de led ptk1 mag-c bg2 mag-m b4.de* nat-m bg2 nux-v bg2* phos ptk1 rhod bg2 rhus-t bg2* *Sil* b4.de* stront-c bg2 syph bg2 tub bg2
  - • **tightly**: **Arg-n** bg2 bry b7.de* *Calc* b4a.de hep b4a.de* iod bg2 merc bg2 nit-ac bg2 *Nux-v* bg2 pic-ac bg2 puls b7a.de* *Sep* b4a.de *Sil* b4.de*

○ • **External** head: thuj b4a.de

WRINKLING FOREHEAD: *(↗FACE - Wrinkled - Forehead)*

- **agg.**: *Ars* b4a.de* mang ptk1 nat-m b4a.de* thuj bg2
- **amel.**: caust ptk1 phos bg2* sulph ptk1

WRITING:

- **agg.**: aur b4.de* borx b4a.de* *Calc* b4.de* carb-an b4a.de caust b4a.de dros b7.de* ign b7.de* ip bg2 kali-c b4.de* lyc b4.de* nat-m b4.de* ran-b b7.de* rhus-t bg2 **Sil** b4.de*
- **amel.**: ferr ptk1 ign b7.de*

YAWNING:

- **agg.**: all-c bg2 am-c bg2 bar-c b4.de* chinin-s bg2 cycl b7.de* kali-c ptk1 kreos b7a.de mag-c bg2 mur-ac b4.de* nux-m bg2 nux-v b7.de* zinc bg2
- **amel.**: m-ambo b7.de mur-ac b4a.de* nat-m bg2* staph b7.de*

BONES; complaints of: acon bg2 agn b2.de* am-c bg2 ang b2.de* ant-c b2.de* arg-met b2.de* ars b2.de* asaf bg2 **Aur** b2.de* bar-c b2.de* *Bell* b2.de* bry b2.de* *Calc* b2.de* calc-f bg2 calc-p bg2 canth b2.de* carb-v b2.de* caust b2.de* cham b2.de* *Chin* b2.de* cinnb bg2 cocc b2.de* cupr b2.de* daph bg2 fl-ac bg2 graph b2.de* guaj b2.de* *Hep* b2.de* ign b2.de* ip b2.de* kali-bi bg2 kali-i bg2 kali-n b2.de kali-p bg2 *Lyc* b2.de* *Mang* b2.de* **Merc** b2.de* *Mez* b2.de* nat-m b2.de* **Nit-ac** b2.de* nux-v b2.de* *Ph-ac* b2.de* *Phos* b2.de* puls b2.de* rhod b2.de* rhus-t b2.de* **Ruta** b2.de* sabad b2.de* sabin b2.de* samb b2.de* *Sep* b2.de* *Sil* b2.de* spig b2.de* *Staph* b2.de* *Sulph* b2.de* verat b2.de* viol-t b2.de* zinc b2.de*

Head

BRAIN; complaints of: acon ptk1 aeth br1 agar mtf33 *Alum-sil* br1 arg-n ptk1 aven br1 bell ptk1 bov ptk1 calc ptk1 diosm br1 dulc ptk1 glon br1 hyos ptk1 lach ptk1 lact-v br1 *Nux-v* ptk1 phos ptk1 pic-ac ptk1 *Stram* br1* sulfon br1 sulph ptk1 syph ptk1 thuj br1 tub ptk1 zinc br1*

- **accompanied** by:
  - **appetite**; wanting of: hell ptk1
  - **convulsions**:
    - **epileptic** convulsions (See GENERALS - Convulsions - epileptic - brain)
    - **general** convulsions (See GENERALS - Convulsions - accompanied - brain)
  - **cough**: glon ptk1
  - **hearing**; impaired: chen-a bro1 mur-ac bro1
  - **lachrymation**: dig ptk1 kali-i ptk1 zinc ptk1
  - **measles**: aeth bro1 apis bro1 *Bell* bro1 camph bro1 coff bro1 *Cupr-act* bro1 stram bro1 verat-v bro1 viol-o bro1 zinc bro1
  - **scarlet** fever: aeth bro1 ail bro1 am-c bro1 apis bro1 ars bro1 *Bell* bro1 camph bro1 cupr bro1 *Cupr-act* bro1 *Hyos* bro1 rhus-t bro1 *Stram* bro1 sulph bro1 zinc bro1
  - **strabismus**: stram ptk1*
  - **urine**; scanty: *(↗Pain - accompanied - urination - scanty)* *Apis* bell bry *Cupr* squil stram
  - **vertigo**: bell bro1 *Cocc* bro1 gels bro1 sulfon br1* tab bro1
  - **vomiting**: bell ptk1 carc mlr1• glon ptk1 kali-i ptk1 plb ptk1
  - ○ **Eyes**; rubbing the: squil ptk1
  - **Kidneys**; inflammation of (See KIDNEYS - Inflammation - accompanied - brain)
  - **Skin**; yellow discoloration of: phos mtf33
  - **Tongue**:
    - **clean** tongue: cimic kr1*
    - **Root** | **white** root of tongue: zinc kr1*
- **alternating** with | **diarrhea** (See RECTUM - Diarrhea - alternating - brain)
- **atrophic**: toxo-g jl2
- **children**; in: toxo-g jl2
- **degenerative**: bar-m br1
  - **old** people; in: | **men**; old: bar-c br1
- **dentition**; during: acon bro1 agar bro1 *Bell* bro1 *Cham* bro1 cimic bro1 cypr bro1 dol bro1 *Hell* bro1 kali-br bro1 *Podo* bro1 sol-ni bro1 ter bro1 *Zinc* bro1
- **diarrhea**; after sudden cessation of: zinc br1
- **dullness**; with (See MIND - Dullness - brain)
- **neurological**: *Arg-n* br1
- **stupefaction**; with (See MIND - Stupefaction - brain)
- **vaccination**; after: vario jl2
- **wandering** about: arg-n bg2 carb-v bg2 mang bg2 phos bg2 puls bg2 sang bg2 spig bg2 sulph bg2
- ▽ **extending** to | **Vertex**: brom bg2
- ○ **Arachnoid** | **Subarachnoid**: gels ptk1
- **Base**: helo-s rwt2•
- **Cerebrum**: cocc br1
- **Deep** in brain: **Acon** bg2* alum bg2 am-c bg2 ant-t bg2 *Arg-n* bg2* ars bg2 aur bg2 bar-c bg2 bell bg2 *Bov* bg2* brom bg2 bufo bg2 *Calc* bg2* canth bg2 *Chin* bg2 coc-c bg2 dios bg2 dulc ptk1 gels bg2 *Glon* bg2 hell bg2 hyos bg2 ign bg2 iod bg2 kali-br bg2 kali-n bg2 lach bg2* *Lyc* bg2 med bg2 mosch bg2 nat-m bg2 *Nux-v* bg2* petr bg2 **Phos** bg2* phys bg2 plat bg2 prun bg2 rhod bg2 sars bg2 spig bg2 *Stann* bg2 sulph bg2* thuj bg2 tub bg2* zinc bg2
  - ▽ **extending** to:
    - **Outward**: bov bg2 glon bg2 hep bg2
    - **Upward**: sep bg2
  - ○ **Sutures**; along: calc-p bg2 fl-ac bg2
- **Meninges**: apis bg2 *Bell* bg2 *Bry* bg2 calc bg2 cryp bg2 cupr bg2 ferr bg2 hell bg2 hydr-ac bg2 hyos bg2 merc-c bg2 stram bg2 zinc bg2

BREGMA; complaints of: ars ptk1 *Merc* ptk1 zinc-chr bg3*

FOREHEAD; complaints of: **Acon** b2.de* agar b2.de* agn b2.de* all-c bg2 aloe bg2 alum b2.de* **Am-c** b2.de* am-m b2.de* ambr b2.de* anac b2.de* ang b2.de* ant-c b2.de* *Ant-t* b2.de* *Apis* b7a.de arg-met b2.de* arg-n bg2 *Arn* b2.de* **Ars** b2.de* asaf b2.de* *Asar* b2.de* aur b2.de* bar-c b2.de* **Bell** b2.de*

Forehead; complaints of: ...
Bism b2.de* borx b2.de* bov b2.de* brom bg2 **Bry** b2.de* *Calc* b2.de* camph b2.de* cann-s b2.de* canth b2.de* *Caps* b2.de* carb-an b2.de* *Carb-v* b2.de* card-m bg2 caul bg2 caust b2.de* cedr bg2 cham b2.de* chel b2.de* **Chin** b2.de* chinin-s bg2 chion bg2 cic b2.de* cimic bg2 cina b2.de* cinnb bg2 clem b2.de* *Cocc* b2.de* coff b2.de* colch b2.de* coloc b2.de* con b2.de* croc b2.de* cupr b2.de* cycl b2.de* dig b2.de* **Dros** b2.de* *Dulc* b2.de* eucal bg2 euph b2.de* euphr b2.de* *Ferr* b2.de* gels bg2 graph b2.de* guaj b2.de* hell b2.de* *Hep* b2.de* hydr-ac bg2 *Hyos* b2.de* **Ign** b2.de* iod b2.de* ip b2.de* iris bg2 *Kali-bi* bg2 kali-c b2.de* kali-chl bg2 kali-n b2.de* kalm bg2 *Kreos* b2.de* lach b2.de* **Laur** b2.de* led b2.de* lept bg2 lil-t bg2 **Lyc** b2.de* m-ambo b2.de m-arct b2.de* m-aust b2.de* mag-c b2.de* **Mag-m** b2.de* mang b2.de* meli bg2 meny b2.de* *Merc* b2.de* merc-c b4a.de *Mez* b2.de* mosch b2.de* mur-ac b2.de* mygal bg2 myric bg2 *Nat-c* b2.de* **Nat-m** b2.de* nit-ac b2.de* nux-m b2.de* **Nux-v** b2.de* olnd b2.de* op b2.de* par b2.de* *Petr* b2.de* ph-ac b2.de* **Phos** b2.de* phyt ptk1 pic-ac bg2 *Plat* b2.de* plb b2.de* podo bg2 prun bg2* ptel bg2 *Puls* b2.de* *Ran-b* b2.de* ran-s b2.de* rheum b2.de* rhod b2.de* rhus-t b2.de* rob bg2 ruta b2.de* *Sabad* b2.de* *Sabin* b2.de* samb b2.de* sang bg2 sars b2.de* sec b2.de* sel b2.de* seneg b2.de* *Sep* b2.de* **Sil** b2.de* *Spig* b2.de* *Spong* b2.de* squil b2.de* **Stann** b2.de* *Staph* b2.de* stram b2.de* stront-c b2.de* sul-ac b2.de* **Sulph** b2.de* tarax b2.de* teucr b2.de* ther bg2 thuj b2.de* *Valer* b2.de* verat b2.de* *Verb* b2.de* viol-o b2.de* viol-t b2.de* *Zinc* b2.de*

- **alternating** sides: *Iris* ptk1 lil-t ptk1 phos ptk1 sabad ptk1
- **accompanied** by | **dullness** (See MIND - Dullness - forehead)
- **beginning** in | **Back**: lil-t bg2 pic-ac bg2 prun bg2
- ▽ **extending** to | **Face**: ip bg2 kalm bg2
- ○ **Eminence**; frontal: lycps-v bg2
- **Eyes**:
  - ○ **Above**: agar b4a.de *Apis* b4a.de arn b7a.de* *Ars* ptk1 asaf b7a.de *Bar-c* b4a.de *Bell* ptk1 bism ptk1 borx b4a.de bov b4a.de bry ptk1 calc ptk1 carb-v b4a.de* cedr ptk1 chel ptk1 *Chinin-s* ptk1 cic b7a.de colch b7a.de *Croc* b7a.de *Gels* ptk1 iris ptk1 kali-bi ptk1 *Lach* ptk1 *Lil-t* ptk1 lyc b4a.de* naja ptk1 *Nat-m* b4a.de* *Nux-m* b7a.de *Nux-v* ptk1 ph-ac b4a.de *Phos* ptk1 *Puls* ptk1 ran-b b7a.de rhus-t b7a.de sang ptk1 sel b7a.de sep b4a.de sil bg2* *Spig* ptk1 thyr ptk1 *Zinc* ptk1
    - **one** side: kali-bi bg2 nat-m bg2 phos bg2 stann bg2 ter bg2
    - **right**: bell ptk1 cact bg2 carb-ac bg2 carb-v bg2 card-m bg2 cedr ptk1 chel bg2* cimic bg2 hep bg2 ign bg2 kali-bi bg2 kalm bg2 lyc bg2* nat-m bg2* prun bg2 puls ptk1 ran-b bg2 sabad bg2 sang bg2* senec ptk1 *Sep* ptk1 sil bg2 sulph bg2 syph ptk1
      - **extending** to | **left**: aesc bg2 lac-c bg2 lyc bg2 nat-m bg2
    - **left**: arg-n bg2 ars bg2* bry bg2* caul bg2 cedr bg2 chel bg2 chin bg2 chinin-s bg2 ferr ptk1 kali-c ptk1 lach bg2 led bg2 lil-t bg2 mur-ac bg2 nux-m ptk1 sabad bg2 sel bg2* sep bg2* spig bg2* sulph bg2 ther bg2
      - **periodical**: mur-ac ptk1
      - **extending** to | **right**: caul bg2 cedr bg2 lac-c bg2 lach bg2 nux-m bg2 psor bg2 sabad bg2 *Sil* bg2 sulph bg2
  - **Behind**: acon bg2 am-m bg2 bry bg2 calc-p bg2 cann-xyz bg2 caust bg2 cimic bg2 cob bg2 fl-ac bg2 gels bg2 glon bg2 hep bg2 kali-n bg2 lach bg2 lith-c bg2 merc bg2 phyt bg2 puls bg2 *Rhus-t* bg2 sep bg2 staph bg2 sulph bg2 ther bg2
  - **Region** of: acon bg2 alum bg2 am-c bg2 ant-c bg2 ant-t bg2 **Asaf** bg2 *Bar-c* bg2 **Bell** bg2 bism bg2 borx bg2 bov bg2 carb-v bg2 caust bg2 chin bg2 cic bg2 *Cimic* bg2 *Cinnb* bg2 **Coloc** bg2 fl-ac bg2 glon bg2 hep bg2 hyos bg2 iod bg2 ip bg2 kali-bi bg2 kali-c bg2 kali-n bg2 kreos bg2 lac-c bg2 **Lach** bg2 lyc bg2 mang bg2 meph bg2 merc bg2 mill bg2 mosch bg2 *Nat-c* bg2 *Nat-m* bg2 nit-ac bg2 nux-m bg2 **Nux-v** bg2 petr bg2 ph-ac bg2 phos bg2 plat bg2 podo bg2 **Puls** bg2 ran-b bg2 sabad bg2 sel bg2 sep bg2 sil bg2 spong bg2 stann bg2 staph bg2 stront-c bg2 sul-ac bg2 sulph bg2 ther bg2 thuj bg2 valer bg2 verat bg2
    - **left**: **Ars** bg2 **Cedr** bg2 **Spig** bg2
- **Forehead** | **Nose**; above: acon b7a.de* agar b4a.de am-m b7a.de ant-t b7a.de* ars bg2 *Asar* b7a.de bar-c b4a.de *Bism* b7a.de bov bg2 camph b7a.de cupr bg2 ferr b7a.de *Hep* bg2 hyos bg2 ign b7a.de* kali-i bg2 lach bg2 *Mosch* b7a.de nux-v bg2 phos bg2 puls bg2 rhus-t bg2 staph b7a.de* ther bg2 viol-t b7a.de zinc bg2
- **Middle**: carb-ac bg2 crot-h ptk1 kali-c bg2 kali-i bg2 *Merc* bg2 merl bg2 ph-ac bg2 sil bg2
- **Upper** part: bell bg2 calc bg2 *Coloc* ptk1 rhus-t bg2

HAIR: acon b2.de* agar b2.de *Alum* b2.de* am-c b2.de* *Ambr* b2.de* ant-c b2.de* arn b2.de* *Ars* b2.de* asar b2.de* aur b2.de* *Bar-c* b2.de* **Bell** b2.de* **Borx** b2.de bov b2.de* bry b2.de* *Calc* b2.de* canth b2.de* caps b2.de* carb-an b2.de* *Carb-v* b2.de* caust b2.de* chel b2.de* *Chin* b2.de* cina b2.de cocc b2.de* colch b2.de* con b2.de* cycl b2.de* dulc b2.de* *Ferr* b2.de* **Graph** b2.de* **Hep** b2.de* ign b2.de* iod b2.de* **Kali-c** b2.de* kali-n b2.de* kreos b2.de* lach b2.de* laur b2.de* **Lyc** b2.de* mag-c b2.de* mag-m b2.de* mang b2.de* meny b2.de* *Merc* b2.de* mez b2.de* mur-ac b2.de* nat-c b2.de* **Nat-m** b2.de* *Nit-ac* b2.de* nux-v b2.de* par b2.de* petr b2.de* ph-ac b2.de* *Phos* b2.de* *Plb* b2.de* puls b2.de* *Rhus-t* b2.de* sabad b2.de* sars b2.de* sec b2.de* *Sel* b2.de* sep b2.de* *Sil* b2.de* *Spig* b2.de* spong b2.de* staph b2.de* sul-ac b2.de* **Sulph** b2.de* thuj b2.de* *Verat* b2.de* zinc b2.de*

- **baldness** (= alopecia capitis totalis): abrot tl1 all-s hr1 alumn ptk1 ambr bg2 *Anac* k* *Apis* am c2 aur k2* **Bar-c** k* *Fl-ac* k* *Graph* k* hell a hep k* lyc k* med a morg-p a* nat-m bg2 *Phos* pix a psor jl2 rosm c2 *Sep* k* *Sil* k* sulph bg2 syc a* syph a* thal c2 *Thuj* b4a.de vinc hr1 *Zinc* k*
  - **accompanied** by | **Scalp**; sore pain in (See Pain - scalp - sore - accompanied - baldness)
  - **gonorrhea**; after: kali-s ptk1*
  - **patches**: (↗*falling - spots)* *Apis* *Ars* dx1 *Calc* calc-p a* carb-an a cupr-s hr1 fl-ac a *Graph* k* *Hep* k* kali-p a *Kali-s* hr1 lyc k* morg-p a *Phos* k* psor a sep k* syph mtf tell a tub vh* vinc hr1
  - **young** people: arund vh bac a *Bar-c* k* *Sil* k* tub a
- **binding** up hair | **agg.** | **External** head: bry bg2
  - **amel.**: kali-n b4.de* sul-i ptk1
- **black** | **Roots**; at: thal-xyz srj8•
- **blond** (See GENERALS - Complexion - fair)
- **bristling**: acet-ac *Acon* k* am-c k* am k* bar-c k* bufo dgt1 calc calc-sil k2 cann-s b7.de* canth b7.de* carb-v k* carl *Cham* k* *Chel* k* cina k* coc-c cocc b7.de* dulc k* glon bg3* gran bg2* hep bg2* kali-bi bg2 lachn **Laur** b7.de* lyc k* mag-m k* mang k* meny b7.de* meph bg2* merc k* mez b4.de* *Mur-ac* k* nit-ac k* nux-v k* polyp-p bg1 puls k* *Ran-b* b7.de* seneg sil k* spig b7.de* spong k* sul-i bg2* sulph h2* tarent tub a vanil fd5.de verat k* *Zinc* k*
  - **chill**; during: acon bg2 am-c bg2 arn bg2 **Bar-c** b4a.de* canth bg2 hep bg2 laur bg2 mag-m bg2 meny b7a.de* *Puls* bg2 spong bg2 verat bg2 zinc bg2
  - **coming** in from open air: am-c k*
  - **dinner**; during: sil h2*
  - **electrified**; as if: rhod ptk2
  - **painful** part: sulph h2*
  - **seem**: acon c1
  - **sensation** of: (↗*Goose - scalp - sensation)* acon hr* am-c h2* *Ars* bg2* bar-c bg2* chel bg2* dulc bg2* irid-met srj5* *Lach* bg2* lachn c1 mez bg2* mur-ac h2* rhod ptk1 sil h2* spig h1* spong bg2* sul-i a1* vinc bg2* zinc bg2*
    - **eating**; while: sil b4a.de
    - **Occiput**: lachn c1
- **brittle**: ars k* bad bro1 bell k* borx bro1 dys fmm1• fl-ac k* graph bg2* *Kali-c* k* nat-sil fd3.de• *Plb* bro1 psor bg2* sec bro1 staph bro1 thuj bro1 wies a1 zinc ptk1*
  - **night**: psor jl2
  - **air**; in open | **amel.**: psor jl2
  - **warm** wet application | **agg.**: psor jl2
- **brown** stripe | **Edges**; at: kali-p ptk1
- **brushing** hair agg. | **External** head: arn bg2 *Puls* bg2 *Rhus-t* bg2 sil bg2 vib bg2
- **bunching** of hair (See sticks)
- **coarse**: sil mtf33
- **cold** agg.: sabad b7.de* sulph ptk1*
- **color** changes: kali-i k* sarr a1
- **combed**:
  - **cannot** be: borx mtf33 thuj mrr1
  - **uncombed**: sulph mrr1
    - **looks** as if: med mtf33
- **combing**:
  - **agg.**: bry b7.de chin bg2 kreos b7a.de
    - **External** head: bry bg2
  - **amel.**: form bg2 glon bg2 tarent bg2
- **complaints**: acon bg2 agar bg2 *Alum* bg2 am-c bg2 *Ambr* bg2 ant-c bg2 am bg2 *Ars* bg2 asar bg2 aur bg2 *Bar-c* bg2 **Bell** bg2* **Borx** bg2* bov bg2 bry bg2 *Calc* bg2* canth bg2 caps bg2 carb-an bg2* *Carb-v* bg2* caust bg2 chel bg2 *Chin* bg2 cina bg2 cocc bg2 colch bg2 con bg2* cycl bg2 dulc bg2 *Ferr* bg2 **Graph** bg2* **Hep** bg2* ign bg2 iod bg2 **Kali-c** bg2* kali-n bg2 kreos bg2 lach bg2 laur bg2 **Lyc** bg2* mag-c bg2 mag-m bg2 mang bg2 meny bg2 *Merc* bg2* mez bg2 mur-ac bg2 nat-c bg2 **Nat-m** bg2* *Nit-ac* bg2* nux-v bg2 par bg2 petr bg2 ph-ac bg2 *Phos* bg2 *Plb* bg2 puls bg2 *Rhus-t* bg2 sabad bg2 sars bg2 sec bg2 *Sel* bg2 sep bg2 *Sil* bg2 *Spig* bg2 spong bg2 staph bg2 sul-ac bg2 **Sulph** bg2* thuj bg2 ust ptk1 *Verat* bg2 zinc bg2
- **crowns**; two: calc-p a* puls a
- **curly**, becomes: mez k*
- **cutting** hair; complaints of head after: (↗*GENERALS - Hair - cutting - agg.)* bell bg2* glon bg2* led bg2 phos bg2* puls bg2 sabad bg2 sep bg2*
- **dark**: (↗*GENERALS - Complexion - dark)* **Acon** b2.de* am-m b2.de* ambr b2.de* *Anac* b2.de* ant-c b2.de* arg-met b2.de* *Arn* b2.de* *Ars* b2.de* asar b2.de* bell b2.de* bry b2.de* calc b2.de* cann-s b2.de* caps b2.de* *Carb-v* b2.de* *Caust* b2.de* chin b2.de* clem b2.de* con b2.de* dros b2.de* *Dulc* b2.de* euphr b2.de* graph b2.de* *Guaj* b2.de* hell b2.de* hep b2.de* ign b2.de* *Iod* b2.de* ip b2.de* *Kali-c* b2.de* lach b2.de* led b2.de* lyc b2.de* mag-m b2.de* merc b2.de* *Mosch* b2.de* mur-ac b2.de* nat-c b2.de* *Nat-m* b2.de* **Nit-ac** b2.de* **Nux-v** b2.de* olnd b2.de* petr b2.de* **Ph-ac** b2.de* **Phos** b2.de* **Plat** b2.de* plb b2.de* *Puls* b2.de* rheum b2.de* rhod b2.de* rhus-t b2.de* ruta b2.de* sabin b2.de* sars b2.de* **Sep** b2.de* sil b2.de* stann b2.de* *Staph* b2.de* *Sulph* b2.de* verat b2.de* verb b2.de* zinc b2.de*
- **darker**, becomes: jab c1 pilo c1 wies c1* wildb c1
- **dryness**: aloe k* alum k* *Ambr* bad k* *Calc* k* chel k* choc srj3• dream-p sdj1• dys fmm1• falco-pe nl2• *Fl-ac* k* graph bg2* hipp k* *Iod* b4a.de kali-ar hr1 *Kali-c* k* kali-s fd4.de *Med* k* nat-sil fd3.de• petr-ra shn4• ph-ac bg2* *Phos* k* *Plb* k* *Psor* k* sacch sst1• sec k* sel rsj9• sil b4a.de* *Sulph* k* **Thuj** k* [lac-mat sst4]
  - ○ **Roots**; at: phos bg2
- **electrical**: med c1
  - **combed**; when: sanic c1*
- **fair**: (↗*GENERALS - Complexion - fair)* *Agar* b2.de* am-m b2.de* ambr b2.de* *Ang* b2.de* ars b2.de* aur b2.de* bar-c b2.de* bell b2.de* *Borx* b2.de* bov b2.de* *Bry* b2.de* **Calc** b2.de* **Caps** b2.de* caust b2.de* *Cham* b2.de* cina b2.de* *Clem* b2.de* **Cocc** b2.de* coff b2.de* *Con* b2.de* croc b2.de* cupr b2.de* *Dig* b2.de* euph b2.de* ferr b2.de* **Graph** b2.de* hell b2.de* hep b2.de* **Hyos** b2.de* ign b2.de* *Iod* b2.de* ip b2.de* *Kali-bi* bg2 kali-c b2.de* *Lach* b2.de* laur b2.de* *Lyc* b2.de* mag-c b2.de* mag-m b2.de* *Merc* b2.de* *Mez* b2.de* mosch b2.de* mur-ac b2.de* nat-c b2.de* nux-v b2.de* op b2.de* *Petr* b2.de* ph-ac b2.de* *Phos* b2.de* plat b2.de* **Puls** b2.de* rheum b2.de* *Rhus-t* b2.de* ruta b2.de* *Sabad* b2.de* **Sel** b2.de* **Seneg** b2.de* sep b2.de* **Sil** b2.de* *Spig* b2.de* *Spong* b2.de* stann b2.de* staph b2.de* stram b2.de* *Sul-ac* b2.de* *Sulph* b2.de* *Thuj* b2.de* verat b2.de* viol-o b2.de*
- **falling**: (↗*SKIN - Hair - falling)* abrot br1 ail k2* all-c hr1 all-s c2 alum k* alum-p k2 *Alumn* bro1 am-c k* *Am-m* k* *Ambr* k* *Ant-c* k* ant-t k* anthraco bro1 apis k* arge-pl rwt5• am mtf11 *Ars* k* ars-i ars-s-f bg3* art-v mtf11 *Arund* k* asc-t k* **Aur** k* aur-ar k2 *Aur-m* k* aur-m-n k* aur-s bac c2* **BAR-C** k* bar-s k2 bell k* *Borx* bg2 bov k* brass-n-o srj5• bry bufo *Calc* k* calc-i k2* *Calc-p* k* calc-s k* calc-sil k2 *Canth* k* *Carb-an* k* **Carb-v** k* **Carbn-s** carl k* caust k* cean mtf11 cere-b a1 *Chel* k* chin k* chlol k* chrysar bro1 cinch a1* colch k* *Con* k* cop k* crot-c sk4• crot-h hr1* cupr-s c2 cycl b2.de* des-ac mtf11 dulc b2.de* *Elaps* *Ferr* k* ferr-ar ferr-m ferr-ma k* ferr-p k* **Fl-ac** k* *Form* k* gink-b sbd1• glon k* **Graph** k* hell k* hell-f a1* *Hep* k* hipp hr1* hippoz mtf11 hyper a1* *Ign* b2.de* iod k* jab hr1* kali-ar *Kali-bi* k* **Kali-c** k* kali-i k* kali-n k* kali-p k* **Kali-s** k* kali-sil k2 kreos k* lac-e hrn2• **Lach** k* lap-la sde8.de• lepr mtf11 lob c2 **Lyc** k* *Mag-c* k* manc k* med tl1 *Merc* k* *Merc-c* k* *Mez* k* moni rfm1• morg-g fmm1• morg-p pte1* naja nat-c k* **Nat-m** k* nat-p nat-sil fd3.de• **Nit-ac** k* nuph k* oena k* ol-j c2 op k* osm k* par b2.de* ped a1* *Petr* k* *Ph-ac* k* **Phos** k* pilo c2* pitu-p mtf11 pix br1* plb k* plut-n srj7• podo fd3.de• psor k* rad-br sze8• rein a1 rhus-t b2.de* rhus-v k* rosm mtf11 sabin b2.de* sanic sarr a1 sars k* sec k* *Sel* k* **Sep** k* **Sil** k* sphing c2* spira a1 *Staph* k* streptoc mtf11 stront-c sk4• stry-ar bro1 sul-ac k* sul-i k2 **Sulph** k* syc pte1* syph k* tab k* tax c2* tep k* test mld2 thal c1* thal-act c1* thal-met mtf11 thal-xyz srj8• **Thuj** k* thyr c2* tritic-vg fd5.de tub k* ust k* v-a-b jl vanil fd5.de vesp k* vinc c2* wies a1* x-ray sp1 *Zinc* k* zinc-p k2 [lac-mat sst4]
  - **night**; in one: ph-ac a
  - **accompanied** by:
    - **itching**: ant-c ptk1

- **accompanied** by: ...
  - **Head**; pain in (See Pain - accompanied - hair)
- **changing** color; after: kali-i ptk1
- **children**; in: nat-m ptk1
- **chronic**: *Carb-an* b4a.de *Carb-v* b4a.de
- **combing** the hair; when: canth ptk1* tritic-vg fd5.de vanil fd5.de
- **delivery**; after: *Bell* bg2 *Calc* k* *Canth* *Carb-v* k* hep bg2* **Lyc** k* *Nat-m* k* *Nit-ac* **Plat** bg2 *Puls* bg2 *Sep* k* sil bg2* **Sulph** k* verat bg2 zinc bg2
- **disease**:
  - **abdominal**; after: lyc hr1*
  - **acute** exhausting disease; following: carb-v ptk1* manc br1* thal ptk1 *Thal-met* br1
- **fevers**; after: fl-ac ptk1
- **grief**; from: caust a graph a ign a* lach a lyc a nat-m a *Ph-ac* k* staph a*
- **handfuls**, in: *Canth* bg2 carb-v ptk1 hep bg2 *Iod* bg2 lyc *Mez* k* petr bg2 **Phos** k* rein a1 sulph k* syph ptk1 thal ptk1 thal-xyz srj8• **Thuj** b4a.de
- **hard** brittle: graph mtf11
- **lactation**; during: nat-m ptk1
- **menopause**: hypoth mtf11 lyc st1 phos a *Sep* k*
- **pain** in head; with: ant-c bro1 nit-ac bro1 sil bro1
- **parturition**; after (See delivery)
- **pregnancy** agg.; during●: **Lach** k*
- **sickness**; after acute (See disease - acute)
- **spots**, in●: *(↗baldness - patches)* alum ptk1 *Apis* *Ars* k* bac a *Calc* calc-p carb-an chin-b hr1 cortiso sp1 **Fl-ac** k* graph k2* *Hep* k* ign vh* kali-p c2 lepr mtf11 lyc k2* morg-g pte1• *Nat-m* ptk1 petr a1 *Phos* k* plut-n srj7• *Psor* k* syph a tell a *Tub* mrr1
  - **emotions**; after suppressed: staph mrr1
  - **grief**; after: *Ign* vh* staph mrr1
  - **replaced** by; and is:
    - **gray** hair: vinc c1*
    - **white** hair: vinc
    - **wooly** hair: vinc ptk1*
- **typhoid** fever:
  - **after**: chloram mtf11
  - **during**: **Fl-ac** hr1
- ○ **Ears**; behind: *Phos* bg2
- **Eyebrows** (See FACE - Hair - falling - eyebrows)
- **Forehead**: ars k* bell k* *Hep* k* *Merc* k* *Nat-m* k* *Phos* k* sil k*
- **Occiput**: calc b2.de* *Carb-v* k* *Chel* k* hep b2.de* merc ptk1 *Petr* k* phos bg2* sep b2.de* sil k* staph k* sulph b2.de*
- **Sides**: ars bg1* bov k* calc bg2* *Graph* k* kali-c k* merc bg2* ph-ac k* phos bg2* *Staph* k* zinc k*
  - **left**: ars bg2
- **Temples**: calc k* croc a1 graph gk* *Kali-c* k* lyc k* merc k* *Nat-m* k* par k* sabin k*
- **Vertex**; from: **Bar-c** b2.de* calc b2.de* carb-an b2.de* **Graph** b2.de* hep b2.de* **Lyc** b2.de* *Nit-ac* b2.de* plb b2.de* sel b2.de* *Sep* b2.de* sil b2.de* thuj bg2* zinc b2.de*

- **fluffy**: med bg2 ph-ac bg2
- **gray**; becoming: ambr al2* *Ars* k* bar-c b4a.de **Bell** b4a.de bry b7a.de camph hr1 carc zzh con b4a.de graph k* hipp k* *Kali-i* kali-n k* kreos bg2 limest-b es1• **Lyc** k* moni rfm1• *Nat-m* ptk1* op k* petr-ra shn4• *Ph-ac* k* **Phos** hr1 sec k* *Sil* k* staph bg2 sul-ac k* sulph bg2 syc fmm1• thal-xyz srj8• thuj bg2 [lac-mat sst4]
  - **right**: *Lyc* mrr1
  - **grief**; after: ph-ac mrr1
  - **prematurely**: ambr al2 camph hr1 emb-r mtf11 graph lpc2 *Lyc* hr1* ph-ac a3* salv mtf11 sec bro1 sul-ac bro1* syc jl2* syph jl2
  - **spots**, in: kreos bg* *Lyc* mrr1 psor
- **greasy**: arund bg1* ben-n c2* bran bg1* brucel sa3• *Bry* k* calc vh *Caust* vh cypra-eg sde6.de• dream-p sdj1• dulc fd4.de hep a hera a1 kali-s fd4.de lac-c bg2* lyss k* *Med* vh merc bro1* *Nat-m* vh nat-p fkr6.de nat-sil fd3.de• ozone sde2• petr c1 *Ph-ac* k* plb b7.de* plut-n srj7• psor gk rheum mtf33 ruta fd4.de sulph mrr1 thuj bg2* tub a [bell-p-sp dcm1]

Hair: ...

- **growing** fast: arg-s knl• gink-b sbd1• sacch a1* thuj he1
- **hang** down; letting hair | **amel.**: bell bg2* bry bg2 cina bg2* ferr bg2* kali-m ptk1 kali-n ptk1 kali-p bg2* phos bg2*
- **hard**: *Sulph* br1*
- **lusterless**: am mtf11 astra-m br1 calc vh canth mtf11 cean mtf11 fl-ac hippoz hr1 jab mtf11 kali-n kali-s fd4.de luf-op rsj5• *Med* k* *Psor* k* sulph tl1 *Thuj* tub [tax jsj7]
- **moving** sensation: falco-pe nl2• stann h2*
- **odors**:
  - **offensive**: bufo bg2 *Lyc* bg2 staph bg2 sulph bg2 vinc bg2* viol-t bg2
  - **sour**: bufo bg2
- **oily** (See greasy)
- **painful**: anh sp1* ph-ac bg2
  - **falling** of hair; with: ant-c br1
  - **letting** hair hang down | **amel.**: bell bg1 cina bg1 dirc bg1 ferr bg1 phos bg1
  - **shivering**; during: hep b4.de
  - **touch** agg.: alum k* *Am-c* ambr k* **Apis** c1* *Ars* k* arund br1 *Asar* k* *Bell* k* bry bg2* calc k* calc-p bg2 caps b7.de* *Carb-v* k* carbn-s c1 *Carl* chel *Chin* b7.de* chinin-s *Cinnb* *Coloc* dulc fd4.de *Ferr* k* ferr-p c1 fl-ac *Hep* k* ign bg2 kali-bi bg2 *Kali-i* lac-c lach c1* mag-m k2 mez b4.de* mit c1 nat-m k* nat-s nit-ac k* *Nux-v* k* par b7.de* ph-ac bg2 phos *Puls* k* sec a1 **Sel** k* *Sep* k* spig b7.de* spira spong b7.de* stann *Sulph* k* thuj b4.de* trios rsj11• verat b7.de* vib st zinc k*
  - ○ **Roots**: acon bg2 chel bg2 chin bg2 coloc bg2* sep bg2
- **plica** polonica: ant-t bg2* bar-c bg2* borx b7a.de* carb-v b4a.de graph bg2* lyc b4a.de* merc b4a.de nat-m bg2* phos b4a.de psor bg2* sars bg2* sil b4a.de sulph b4a.de tub bg2* ust bg2 **Verat** b7a.de *Vinc* bg2* viol-o bg2* viol-t bg2*
- **pulled** out, sensation: *(↗Pain - pulled; sensation as if hair - out)* *Acon* bg2* aeth ptk1 alum bg2* *Arg-n* ptk1 canth bg2 chin bg2 iod bg2 kali-n ptk1 lach ptk1 lyc h2 mag-c bg1* phos k2* rhus-t bg2 sel bg2*
  - ○ **Vertex**: *Acon* bro1 *Arg-n* bro1 kali-n bro1 lachn bro1 mag-c bro1 *Phos* bro1
- **pulls** the: *(↗MIND - Pulling - hair - desire; MIND - Pulling - hair - desire - her)* ars bg1 **Bell** bg1* **Cupr** bg1* lil-t bg1 med bg1 mez bg1 tarent bg1 tub bg1*
- **red** (See GENERALS - Complexion - red)
- **sandy**: sil mtf33
- **soft**: borx mtf33 phos mtf33
- **splitting**: borx mtf33 thuj ptk1* **Zinc** ptk1
- **standing** on end (See bristling)
- **stand**-up spots on hair of scalp: agar ms*
- **sticks** together: *(↗tangles)* ars bg2 borx k* cic bg2 fl-ac bg2* graph bg2 lyc bg2 med bg2 **Mez** k* mill bg2 mur-ac bg2 *Nat-m* k* *Psor* k* sars bg2* sep bg2* sulph bg2* tub br *Ust* bg2 vinc bg2* viol-t bg2*
  - **combing** difficult: psor jl2
  - **ends** at: *Borx* k*
  - **hairdressing** difficult: psor jl2
  - **washing**; after: hydrog srj2•
- **stiff**: ars bg2 canth bg2 iod bg2 sel ptk1
- **stroking** hair back | **agg.**: *Puls* b7.de rhus-t b7.de*
- **tangles** easily: *(↗sticks)* ars bg2* *Borx* k* cic bg2* *Fl-ac* k* graph k* lyc bg2* *Med* bg2* mez bg2* mill bg2* mur-ac bg2 nat-m bg2* nat-sil fd3.de• *Petr* hr1 psor k* sarr a sars bg2* sep bg2* sulph bg2* tub bro1 ust bg2* verat vinc k* viol-t bg2*
- **thin**: psor jl2 sil mrr1* tub bl* vanil fd5.de [mang-sil stj2]
- **white**: apis b7a.de bell b4a.de ph-ac b4a.de
  - **patch**: psor tl1*
- **withered**: ph-ac bg2
- **yellow** | **Edges**: med ptk1

OCCIPUT; complaints of: *Acon* b2.de* agar b2.de* agn b7.de alum b2.de* am-c b2.de* am-m b2.de* *Ambr* b2.de* anac b2.de* ang b2.de* *Ant-c* b7a.de ant-t b2.de* apis b7a.de arg-met b2.de* arn b2.de* *Ars* b2.de* asaf b2.de* asar b2.de* aur b2.de* *Bapt* bg2 bar-c b2.de* *Bell* b2.de* bism b2.de* borx b2.de* bov b2.de* bry b2.de* *Calc* b2.de* camph b2.de* cann-s b2.de* canth b2.de* caps b2.de* carb-an b2.de* **Carb-v** b2.de* *Caust* b2.de* *Chel* b2.de* *Chin* b2.de* cic b2.de* cimic bg2* cina b2.de* *Cocc* b2.de* coff b2.de* colch b2.de* con b2.de* croc b2.de* cupr b2.de* cycl b2.de* dig b2.de* dros b2.de* dulc b2.de* eup-per bg2 euph b2.de* euphr b2.de* *Ferr* bg2 **Gels** bg2* graph b2.de* guaj b2.de* hell b2.de* hep b2.de* hyos b7.de **Ign** b2.de* iod b2.de* ip b2.de*

Occiput; complaints of: ...
kali-bi bg2 *Kali-c* b2.de* *Kali-n* b2.de* kreos b2.de* lach b7a.de laur b2.de* led b2.de* lyc b2.de* m-ambo b2.de m-arct b2.de* m-aust b2.de* mag-c b2.de* *Mag-m* b2.de* mang b2.de* meny b2.de* merc b2.de* *Mez* b2.de* *Mosch* b2.de* mur-ac b2.de* *Nat-c* b2.de* nat-m b2.de* nat-s ptk1 *Nit-ac* b2.de* nux-m b2.de* *Nux-v* b2.de* olnd b2.de* onos ptk1 op b2.de* par b2.de* **Petr** b2.de* ph-ac b2.de* phos b2.de* phyt bg2* pic-ac bg2 plat b2.de* plb b2.de* puls b2.de* ran-b b2.de* ran-s b2.de* rheum b7.de rhod b2.de* rhus-t b2.de* ruta b2.de* sabad b2.de* *Sabin* b2.de* samb b2.de* sang bg2 sars b2.de* sec b2.de* *Seneg* b2.de* **Sep** b2.de* *Sil* b2.de* spig b2.de* spong b2.de* squil b2.de* stann b2.de* staph b2.de* stront-c b2.de* sul-ac b2.de* *Sulph* b2.de* tarax b2.de* teucr b2.de* *Thuj* b2.de* valer b2.de* vario ptk1 verat b2.de* verat-v ptk1 verb b2.de* viol-t b2.de* *Zinc* b2.de* zinc-ar ptk1

- **alternating** sides: sep bg2*
- **right**: aur bg2 bell ptk1 carb-v bg2 chel ptk1 lach bg2 sang bg2* sil bg2

▽ • **extending** to | **Downward**: *Sang* bg2 *Sil* bg2

- **left**: arg-n bg2 bry bg2 kali-bi ptk1 lyc ptk1 nat-m ptk1 nux-v ptk1 *Onos* ptk1 rhus-t bg2 sep bg2* spig ptk1 sulph bg2*

▽ • **extending** to | **Downward**: spig bg2

- **accompanied** by:
  - **dullness** (See MIND - Dullness - occiput)
  - O **Legs**; weakness of: zinc ptk1
  - **Pupils**; dilated: verat-v ptk1

▽ - **extending** to:

O • **Downward**: bar-c bg2 calc-p ptk1 carb-v bg2 *Cimic* bg2 crot-h bg2 *Gels* bg2 glon bg2 hydr-ac bg2 lil-t bg2 mag-p bg2 par bg2 petr bg2 phos ptk1 pic-ac bg2* sars bg2 valer ptk1 zinc ptk1

- **Eyes**: *Cimic* bg2 med ptk1 petr bg2 sang bg2 sars ptk1 sil bg2 spig bg2
- **Forehead**: mosch bg2 pic-ac bg2 sars bg2
- **Forward**: sang ptk1 sil ptk1
  - **right**: bell ptk1 gels ptk1 sang ptk1 sil ptk1
  - **left**: arg-n ptk1 cimic ptk1 lach ptk1 lil-t ptk1 *Spig* ptk1 thuj ptk1
- **Nape**: bry bg2
- **Nose**; root of: sars bg2*
- **Shoulder**: kali-bi ptk1 onos ptk1 stict ptk1
- **Upward**: arg-n ptk1 *Bell* ptk1 *Calc* ptk1 carb-v ptk1 *Cimic* ptk1 **Gels** ptk1 *Glon* ptk1 *Kali-bi* ptk1 lac-c ptk1 lach ptk1 lil-t ptk1 onos ptk1 *Par* ptk1 petr ptk1 phos ptk1 sabad ptk1 **Sang** ptk1 sep ptk1 **Sil** ptk1 *Spig* ptk1 sulph ptk1 verat-v ptk1

O - **External** head: am-c b2.de* am-m b2.de* ambr b2.de* ant-c b2.de* ant-t b2.de* ars b2.de* bar-c b2.de* bell b2.de* borx b2.de* bry b2.de* *Calc* b2.de* *Carb-an* b2.de* **Carb-v** b2.de* caust b2.de* chel b2.de* chin b2.de* *Clem* b2.de* cycl b2.de* euph b2.de* graph b2.de* *Hep* b2.de* iod b2.de* *Lyc* b2.de* merc b2.de* mez b2.de* *Nat-c* b2.de* nat-m b2.de* nit-ac b2.de* olnd b2.de* **Petr** b2.de* puls b2.de* rhus-t b2.de* ruta b2.de* *Sep* b2.de* **Sil** b2.de* spig b2.de* *Staph* b2.de* *Sulph* b2.de* *Thuj* b2.de* viol-o b2.de* zinc b2.de*

- **Protuberances**: bell bg2 *Bry* bg2 calc-p bg2 chin bg2 colch bg2 coloc bg2 dig bg2 glon bg2 guaj bg2 lil-t bg2 lyc bg2 mag-m bg2 mur-ac bg2 nit-ac bg2 petr bg2 *Rhus-t* bg2 *Sil* bg2 thuj bg2 urt-u bg2 verb bg2 zinc bg2
- **Sides**: fl-ac bg2 stram bg2

SIDES; complaints of: *Acon* b2.de* agar b2.de* alum b2.de* am-c b2.de* am-m b2.de* anac b2.de* ang b2.de* ant-t b2.de* apis b7a.de arg-met b2.de* arg-n bg2 arn b2.de* ars b2.de* *Asaf* b2.de* asar b2.de* aur b2.de* *Bar-c* b2.de* bell b2.de* bism b7.de borx b2.de* *Bov* b2.de* *Bry* b2.de* calc b2.de* camph b2.de* cann-s b2.de* *Canth* b2.de* caps b2.de* carb-an b2.de* carb-v b2.de* caust b2.de* cham b2.de* chel b2.de* chin b2.de* cic b2.de* cina b2.de* clem b2.de* cocc b2.de* coff b2.de* colch b2.de* coloc b2.de* con b2.de* croc b2.de* cupr b2.de* cycl b2.de* dig b2.de* dros b2.de* dulc b2.de* euph b2.de* euphr b2.de* ferr b2.de* *Graph* b2.de* *Guaj* b2.de* hell b2.de* hep b2.de* hyos b2.de* ign b2.de* iod b2.de* kali-c b2.de* kreos b2.de* lach b2.de* *Laur* b2.de* led b2.de* lyc b2.de* m-ambo b2.de* *M-arct* b2.de* *M-aust* b2.de* mag-c b2.de* mag-m b2.de* mang b2.de* meny b2.de* merc b2.de* mez b2.de* mosch b2.de* mur-ac b2.de* nat-c b2.de* *Nat-m* b2.de* nit-ac b2.de* nux-m b2.de* nux-v b2.de* olnd b2.de* par b2.de* petr b2.de* *Ph-ac* b2.de* phos b2.de* plat b2.de* plb b2.de* puls b2.de* rheum b7.de rhod b2.de* rhus-t b2.de* ruta b2.de* sabad b2.de* sabin b2.de* *Sars* b2.de* **Sec** b7.de sep b2.de* sil b2.de* spig b7.de spong b2.de* squil b2.de* stann b2.de* staph b2.de* stront-c b2.de* sul-ac b2.de* sulph b2.de* tarax b2.de* teucr b2.de* *Thuj* b2.de* valer b2.de* *Verat* b2.de* *Verb* b2.de* viol-t b2.de* **Zinc** b2.de*

Sides, complaints of: ...

- **one** side: acon b2.de* *Agar* b2.de* agn b2.de* **Alum** b2.de* am-c b2.de* am-m b2.de* ambr b2.de* **Anac** b2.de* ang b2.de* ant-c b2.de* ant-t b2.de* apis b7a.de *Arg-met* b2.de* arg-n bg2* arn b2.de* ars b2.de* **Asaf** b2.de* asar b2.de* aur b2.de* *Bar-c* b2.de* bell b2.de* bism b2.de* borx b2.de* bov b2.de* bry b2.de* calad b7.de *Calc* b2.de* calc-act bg2 camph b2.de* cann-s b2.de* *Canth* b2.de* caps b2.de* carb-an b2.de* carb-v b2.de* caust b2.de* cham b2.de* chel b2.de* *Chin* b2.de* chinin-s bg2* cic b2.de* cimic bg2 *Cina* b2.de* clem b2.de* *Cocc* b2.de* coff b2.de* colch b2.de* **Coloc** b2.de* con b2.de* croc b2.de* cupr b2.de* *Cycl* b2.de* dig b2.de* dros b2.de* *Dulc* b2.de* eup-per bg2 euph b2.de* euphr b2.de* ferr b2.de* gels bg2 glon bg2 graph b2.de* *Guaj* b2.de* hell b2.de* hep b2.de* hyos b2.de* ign b2.de* iod b2.de* ip bg2 **Iris** ptk1 kali-bi bg2 **Kali-c** b2.de* kali-i ptk1 kali-n b2.de* kreos b2.de* lac-d bg2 lach b2.de* laur b2.de* led b2.de* lil-t bg2 lyc b2.de* m-arct b2.de* m-aust b2.de* mag-c b2.de* mag-m b2.de* *Mang* b2.de* meli bg2 meny b2.de* merc b2.de* *Mez* b2.de* mosch b2.de* *Mur-ac* b2.de* nat-c b2.de* *Nat-m* b2.de* nit-ac b2.de* nux-m b2.de* **Nux-v** b2.de* *Olnd* b2.de* onos bg2 *Par* b2.de* petr b2.de* **Ph-ac** b2.de* *Phos* b2.de* pic-ac bg2 **Plat** b2.de* plb b2.de* prun bg2 **Psor** ptk1 **Puls** b2.de* ran-b b2.de* ran-s b2.de* rheum b2.de* rhod b2.de* rhus-t b2.de* ruta b2.de* *Sabad* b2.de* *Sabin* b2.de* samb b2.de* **Sang** bg2* **Sars** b2.de* sec b7.de* sel b2.de* seneg b2.de* **Sep** b2.de* sil b2.de* *Spig* b2.de* spong b2.de* squil b2.de* stann b2.de* *Staph* b2.de* *Stront-c* b2.de* **Sul-ac** b2.de* sulph b2.de* tab bg2 tarax b2.de* ter bg2 teucr b2.de* thuj b2.de* valer b2.de* verat b2.de* **Verb** b2.de* viol-o b2.de* viol-t b2.de* vip bg2 *Zinc* b2.de*
- **alternating** sides: aesc bg2 agar bg2 aloe bg2 am bg2 *Bell* bg2 brom bg2 bry bg2 carb-v bg2 cedr bg2 *Chin* bg2 con bg2 cycl bg2 dig bg2 dulc bg2 glon bg2 ham bg2 hell bg2 hydr bg2 hyper bg2 ign bg2 *Iris* bg2 kali-c bg2 **Lac-c** bg2 lil-t bg2 lob bg2 lyc bg2 lys bg2 mez bg2 naja bg2 *Nat-m* bg2 nat-p bg2 phos bg2 pic-ac bg2 plan bg2 ptel bg2 sep bg2 sil bg2 stann bg2 staph bg2 *Sulph* bg2 thuj bg2 zinc bg2
- **right**: acon b2.de* agar b2.de* agn b2.de* *Alum* b2.de* am-c b2.de* am-m b2.de* ambr bg2 anac b2.de* ang b2.de* ant-c b7.de* ant-t b2.de* apis b7a.de* arg-met b2.de* arg-n bg2 arn b2.de* ars b2.de* asaf b2.de* asar bg2 aur b2.de* bapt bg2 bar-c b2.de* **Bell** b2.de* *Bism* b2.de* *Borx* b2.de* bov b2.de* brom bg2 *Bry* b2.de* cact ptk1 calad bg2 **Calc** b2.de* camph b2.de* *Cann-xyz* bg2 *Canth* b2.de* caps b2.de* carb-an b2.de* *Carb-v* b2.de* *Caust* b2.de* cham b2.de* *Chel* b2.de* chin b2.de* cic b2.de* *Cina* b2.de* clem b2.de* cocc b2.de* *Coff* b2.de* colch b2.de* coloc b2.de* con b2.de* croc b2.de* crot-t bg2 cupr bg2 cycl b2.de* dig b2.de* dros b2.de* *Dulc* b2.de* euph b2.de* euphr b2.de* ferr bg2 *Fl-ac* bg2 *Graph* b2.de* guaj b2.de* hell b2.de* *Hep* b2.de* hyos b2.de* **Ign** b2.de* iod b2.de* iris bg2* kali-bi bg2 kali-c b2.de* kali-n b2.de* kalm bg2* kreos b2.de* lach b7.de* laur b2.de* led b2.de* *Lyc* b2.de* m-arct b2.de* m-aust b2.de* mag-c b2.de* mag-m b2.de* mang b2.de* meny b2.de* merc b2.de* mez b2.de* mill bg2 *Mosch* b2.de* mur-ac b2.de* *Nat-c* b2.de* *Nat-m* b2.de* nit-ac b2.de* *Nux-m* b2.de* *Nux-v* b2.de* olnd b2.de* op bg2 par b2.de* petr b2.de* ph-ac b2.de* *Phos* b2.de* plat b2.de* *Plb* b2.de* prun bg2* psor bg2 puls b2.de* *Ran-b* b2.de* ran-s b7.de* rheum b2.de* rhod b2.de* *Rhus-t* b2.de* ruta b2.de* **Sabad** b2.de* *Sabin* b2.de* samb bg2 *Sang* bg2* sars b2.de* sec bg2 sel bg2 seneg b2.de* *Sep* b2.de* **Sil** b2.de* spig b2.de* spong b2.de* squil b2.de* stann b2.de* *Staph* b2.de* stram bg2 stront-c b2.de* *Sul-ac* b2.de* sulph b2.de* tarax b2.de* *Teucr* b2.de* *Thuj* b2.de* *Valer* b2.de* verat bg2 *Verb* b2.de* viol-o bg2 viol-t b2.de* zinc b2.de*

▽ • **extending** to | **left**: aesc bg2 aeth bg2 anac bg2 apis bg2 colch bg2 cupr bg2 dig bg2 dios bg2 glon bg2 ign bg2 kalm bg2 *Lach* bg2 lil-t bg2 merc-i-r bg2 mez bg2 phos bg2 ptel bg2 rhus-v bg2 sabad bg2 sep bg2 staph bg2 tarax bg2 valer bg2

- **left**: acon b2.de* agar b2.de* agn b2.de* alum b2.de* am-c b2.de* *Am-m* b2.de* *Ambr* b2.de* anac b2.de* ang b2.de* *Ant-c* b2.de* ant-t b2.de* *Apis* b7a.de* *Arg-met* b2.de* arg-n bg2 *Arn* b2.de* *Ars* b2.de* *Asaf* b2.de* *Asar* b2.de* aur b2.de* bar-c b2.de* bell b2.de* bism b2.de* borx b2.de* *Bov* b2.de* **Brom** bg2* bry b2.de* calad bg2 *Calc* b2.de* camph b2.de* cann-s b2.de* canth b2.de* *Caps* b2.de* carb-an bg2 carb-v b2.de* caust b2.de* cedr bg2 *Cham* bg2 chel b2.de* chin b2.de* chinin-s bg2* chlor bg2 *Cic* b2.de* cimic bg2 cina b2.de* clem b2.de* cocc b2.de* coff bg2 colch b2.de* *Coloc* b2.de* con b2.de* *Croc* b2.de* crot-t bg2 cupr b2.de* *Cycl* b2.de* dig b2.de* dros b2.de* dulc b2.de* *Euph* b2.de* euphr b2.de* ferr b2.de* fl-ac bg2 *Graph* b2.de* *Guaj* b2.de* hell b2.de* hep bg2 hyos b2.de* ign b2.de* iod b2.de* **Ip** bg2* *Kali-bi* bg2 *Kali-c* b2.de* kali-n b2.de* kreos b2.de* *Lach* b2.de* laur b2.de* led b2.de* *Lil-t* bg2* lith-c bg2 lyc b2.de* m-arct b2.de* m-aust b2.de* *Mag-c* b2.de* mag-m b2.de* mag-p bg2 mang b2.de* meny b2.de* **Merc** b2.de* *Mez* b2.de* mill bg2 mosch b7.de* mur-ac b2.de* naja bg2* nat-c b2.de* nat-m b2.de* **Nit-ac** b2.de* *Nux-m* b2.de* **Nux-v** b2.de* *Olnd* b2.de* onos bg2* op bg2 *Par* b2.de* petr b2.de* ph-ac b2.de* phos b2.de* *Plat* b2.de* plb b2.de* *Psor* bg2 puls b2.de* ran-b b2.de* ran-s b2.de* rheum b2.de* *Rhod* b2.de* rhus-t b2.de* rutâ bg2 sabad b2.de* sabin b2.de* *Samb* b2.de* sars b2.de*

- **Sides**; complaints of – **left**: ...
sec b2.de* *Sel* b2.de* seneg b2.de* **Sep** b2.de* sil bg2 **Spig** b2.de* spong b2.de* squil b2.de* stann b2.de* staph b2.de* stram bg2 stront-c b2.de* sul-ac b2.de* *Sulph* b2.de* *Tarax* b2.de* tarent bg2 teucr b7.de* ther bg2 thuj b2.de* valer b2.de* verat b2.de* verb b2.de* viol-o b2.de* viol-t b2.de* zinc b2.de*
▽ · **extending** to | **right**: agar bg2 arn bg2 brom bg2 calc bg2 cycl bg2 euon bg2 eup-per bg2 kali-bi bg2 laur bg2 lyc bg2 lycps-v bg2 *Nux-m* bg2 sil bg2 sin-n bg2 squil bg2 sulph bg2 zing bg2
▽ - **extending** to:
O · **Occiput**: lil-t bg2
 ⁝ **right**: lach bg2
 ⁝ **left**; diagonally from right to: phos bg2
O - **Ears**:
O · **About**: bar-c bg2 merc bg2 ph-ac bg2 puls bg2
· **Behind**: glon bg2
- **External** head: agar b2.de* ambr b2.de* ars b2.de* bar-c b2.de* *Bov* b2.de* carb-an b2.de* *Caust* b2.de* coloc b2.de* dros b2.de* *Graph* b2.de* guaj b2.de* kali-c b2.de* lyc b2.de* nit-ac b2.de* *Ph-ac* b2.de* phos b2.de* ruta b2.de* sars b2.de* *Staph* b2.de* thuj b2.de* verat b2.de* viol-t b2.de* **Zinc** b2.de*
- **Upper** part: puls bg2

SUTURES; complaints of: calc-p bg2 glon bg2

TEMPLES; complaints of: acon b2.de* *Aeth* bg2 agar b2.de* *Agn* b2.de* aloe bg2 *Alum* b2.de* am-c b2.de* am-m b2.de* ambr b2.de* **Anac** b2.de* ang b2.de* ant-c b2.de* ant-t b2.de* **Apis** b7a.de **Arg-met** b2.de* arn b2.de* ars b2.de* asaf b2.de* asar b2.de* aur b2.de* bar-c b2.de* **Bell** b2.de* bism b2.de* borx b2.de* bov b2.de* *Bry* b2.de* cact bg2 *Calc* b2.de* camph b2.de* cann-s b2.de* canth b2.de* caps b2.de* carb-an b2.de* carb-v b2.de* caust b2.de* cham b2.de* chel b2.de* *Chin* b2.de* cina b2.de* clem b2.de* *Cocc* b2.de* coff b2.de* colch b2.de* coloc b2.de* con b2.de* croc b2.de* crot-h bg2 cupr b2.de* *Cycl* b2.de* dig b2.de* dros b2.de* dulc b2.de* euph b2.de* euphr b2.de* gels bg2 glon ptk1 graph b2.de* guaj b2.de* ham bg2 hell b2.de* hep b2.de* hydr-ac bg2 hyos b2.de* ign b2.de* iod b2.de* ip b2.de* iris bg2 kali-bi bg2 *Kali-c* b2.de* kali-chl bg2 kali-n b2.de* kalm bg2 *Kreos* b2.de* lach b2.de* laur b2.de* led b2.de* lil-t bg2 lith-c bg2 lyc b2.de* m-arct b2.de* m-aust b2.de* mag-c b2.de* mag-m b2.de* mang b2.de* meny b2.de* merc b2.de* *Merc-c* b4a.de mez b2.de* mosch b2.de* mur-ac b2.de* naja bg2 nat-c b2.de* **Nat-m** b2.de* nit-ac b2.de* *Nux-m* b2.de* nux-v b2.de* olnd b2.de* op b7.de *Par* b2.de* petr b2.de* *Ph-ac* b2.de* phel bg2 phos b2.de* phyt bg2 pic-ac bg2 **Plat** b2.de* *Plb* b2.de* podo bg2 ptel bg2 *Puls* b2.de* ran-b b2.de* ran-s b2.de* rheum b2.de* rhod b2.de* *Rhus-t* b2.de* ruta b2.de* *Sabad* b2.de* *Sabin* b2.de* samb b2.de* sang bg2 sars b2.de* seneg b2.de* sep b2.de* sil b2.de* spig b2.de* spong b2.de* squil b2.de* *Stann* b2.de* staph b2.de* stram b2.de* stront-c b2.de* sul-ac b2.de* sulph b2.de* tarax b2.de* teucr b2.de* *Thuj* b2.de* uran-n bg2 valer b2.de* verat b2.de* **Verb** b2.de* viol-t b2.de* zinc b2.de*
- **right**: chel bg2 kali-bi bg2 kalm bg2 *Lyc* bg2 prun bg2 sang bg2
- **left**: arg-n bg2 ars bg2 cedr bg2 chinin-s bg2 lil-t bg2 lith-c bg2 sel bg2 spig bg2 ther bg2
▽ · **extending** to | **right**: anac bg2 aur bg2 coloc bg2 cycl bg2 hydr-ac bg2 kali-c bg2 mag-c bg2 merc-i-f bg2 psor bg2 ptel bg2 rheum bg2
- **accompanied** by | **Teeth**; complaints of (See TEETH - Complaints - accompanied - temples)
▽ - **extending** to:
O · **Canthi** | **left**: graph bg2
· **Inward**: lith-c bg2
· **Neck** and face: tarent ptk1
· **Nose**: glon bg2
· **Outward**: agn bg2
· **Temple** to temple: bell bg2 chin bg2* hyper bg2
· **Upward**: carb-v bg2
· **Vertex**: berb bg2 carb-v bg2 coc-c bg2 iris bg2 kali-bi bg2 laur bg2 phos bg2 rheum bg2 sil bg2
· **Zygoma**: agar bg2
O - **Stomach**; pain in: lith-c ptk1

VERTEX; complaints of: acon b2.de* agar b2.de* agn b2.de* alum b2.de* am-c b2.de* am-m b2.de* ambr b2.de* anac b2.de* ant-c b2.de* ant-t b2.de* apis b7a.de arg-met b2.de* arn b2.de* ars b2.de* asaf b2.de* asar b2.de* aur b2.de* bar-c b2.de* bell b2.de* borx b2.de* bov b2.de* bry b2.de* *Cact* ptk1 *Calc* b2.de* *Calc-p* ptk1 cann-s b2.de* canth b2.de* caps b2.de*

Vertex; complaints of: ...
Carb-an b2.de* carb-v b2.de* *Caust* b2.de* chel b2.de* chin b2.de* cimic ptk1 cina b2.de* clem b4.de cocc b2.de* coff b7.de colch b2.de* coloc b2.de* *Con* b2.de* croc b2.de* cupr b2.de* cycl b2.de* dig b2.de* dulc b2.de* euphr b7.de ferr b2.de* glon ptk1 graph b2.de* guaj b2.de* hell b2.de* hep b2.de* hyos b2.de* hyper ptk1 ign b2.de* iod b2.de* ip b2.de* kali-c b2.de* kali-n b2.de* kreos b2.de* *Lach* b2.de* laur b2.de* led b2.de* lith-c bg2 *Lyc* b2.de* *M-ambo* b2.de* m-arct b2.de* m-aust b2.de* mag-c b2.de* mang b2.de* meny b2.de* merc b2.de* mez b2.de* mosch b2.de* mur-ac b2.de* nat-c b2.de* nat-m b2.de* **Nit-ac** b2.de* *Nux-m* b2.de* nux-v b2.de* olnd b2.de* par b2.de* petr b2.de* ph-ac b2.de* *Phos* b2.de* plat b2.de* puls b2.de* ran-b b2.de* **Ran-s** b2.de* rheum b2.de* rhod b2.de* rhus-t b2.de* ruta b2.de* sabad b2.de* sabin b2.de* samb b2.de* sars b2.de* sep b2.de* sil b2.de* *Spig* b2.de* spong b2.de* squil b2.de* stann b2.de* staph b2.de* stram b2.de* stront-c b2.de* sul-ac b2.de* sulph b2.de* thuj b2.de* valer b2.de* **Verat** b2.de* verat-v ptk1 verb b2.de* viol-t b2.de* zinc b2.de*
- **transversely** across: chel bg2* *Ip* bg2 kali-m ptk1 naja bg2* *Nit-ac* bg2* pall bg2* phys ptk1 sabad bg2 sabal ptk1 sil ptk1
▽ - **extending** to:
O · **Forehead**: nat-m bg2
 ⁝ **right**: prun bg2
 ⁝ **left**: anac bg2
· **Jaws**: lach ptk1
· **Sides**; down: ferr-p ptk1 hyper ptk1
O - **External** head: agar b2.de* ars b2.de* *Bar-c* b2.de* bry b2.de* *Calc* b2.de* *Carb-an* b2.de* carb-v b2.de* caust b2.de* cupr b2.de* **Graph** b2.de* *Hep* b2.de* *Lyc* b2.de* meny b2.de* *Mez* b2.de* *Nit-ac* b2.de* par b2.de* phos b2.de* plb b2.de* *Ran-s* b2.de* *Sel* b2.de* sep b2.de* sil b2.de* spig b2.de* spong b2.de* squil b2.de* staph b2.de* *Verat* b2.de* *Zinc* b2.de*

DAYTIME: *Mang* b4a.de

MORNING: *Acon* b7.de* act-sp bg2 agar b4.de* alum b4.de* am-c b4.de* *Am-m* b7.de* ambr b7.de* ang b7.de* ant-c b7.de* apis b7a.de ars b4a.de bar-c b4.de* bell b4.de* borx b4a.de bry b7.de* calc b4.de* caps b7.de* carb-v b4.de* caust b4.de* cham b7.de* chel b7.de* chin b7.de* cina b7.de* con b4.de* croc b7.de* echi bg2 *Euphr* bg2 glon bg2 **Graph** b4.de* hell b7.de* hep b4.de* *Ign* b7.de* kali-bi bg2 kali-c b4.de* kali-n b4a.de* kreos b7a.de lach bg2 lyc b4.de* m-ambo b7.de m-arct b7.de m-aust b7.de mag-c b4.de* mang b4a.de merc b4.de* mur-ac b4.de* nat-c b4.de* nat-m b4.de* *Nit-ac* b4.de* **Nux-v** b7.de* par b7.de* petr b4.de* ph-ac b4.de* *Phos* b4.de* puls b7.de* ran-b b7.de* rheum b7.de* rhod b4.de* rhus-t b7.de* ruta b7.de* sars b4.de* seneg b4.de* sep b4.de* sil b4.de* *Spig* b7.de* spong b7.de* squil b7.de* staph b7.de* stram b7.de* stront-c b4.de* *Sul-ac* b4.de* **Sulph** b4.de* tarax b7.de* thuj b4.de* valer b7.de* zinc b4.de*
- **bed** agg.; in: alum bg2 am-m bg2 *Bell* bg2 **Bry** bg2 kreos bg2 lyc bg2 mag-c bg2 ph-ac bg2 rhod bg2 sep bg2 staph bg2
- **sunrise**:
  - **after** | **sunset**; until: kalm ptk1 nat-m ptk1

FORENOON: alum b4.de* ant-c b7.de* apis b7a.de *Ars* b4a.de bry b7.de* canth b7.de* cina b7.de* con b4.de* ign b7.de* kali-c b4.de* lyc b4.de* merc-c b4a.de nat-c b4.de* ph-ac b4.de* plat b4.de* plb b7.de* sabad b7.de* *Spig* b7a.de squil b7.de* sul-ac b4.de* sulph b4.de* valer b7.de* zinc b4.de*

AFTERNOON: agar b4.de* all-c bg2 alum b4.de* am-m b7.de* ang b7.de* borx b4a.de bry b7.de* calc b4.de* canth b7.de* chin b7.de* con b4.de* iod b4.de* kali-c b4.de* laur b7.de* lyc b4.de* mag-c b4.de* mur-ac b4.de* nat-c b4.de* nux-v b7.de* ph-ac b4.de* phos b4.de* plb b7.de* sil b4.de* spig b7.de* staph b7.de* sulph b4.de* valer b7.de* verat b7.de* viol-t b7.de* zinc b4.de*
- **sleep**; after | **amel.**: am-c ptk1

EVENING: agar b4.de* agn b7.de* all-c bg2 alum b4.de* *Am-c* b4.de* am-m b7.de* ang b7.de* ant-t b7.de* *Apis* b7a.de asar b7a.de* **Bell** b4a.de* borx b4a.de bry b7.de* **Calc** b4.de* carb-an b4.de* *Caust* b4.de* chel b7.de* *Chin* b7.de* cina b7.de* con b4.de* *Croc* b7.de* cupr b7a.de* daph bg2 dig b4.de* *Euphr* b7.de* ferr b7.de* graph b4.de* hep b4a.de* *Hyos* bg2 ign b7.de* iod b4a.de* kali-bi bg2 kali-c b4.de* *Lach* bg2 *Laur* b7.de* led b7.de* **Lyc** b4.de* m-ambo b7.de m-arct b7.de m-aust b7.de* mag-c b4.de* mag-m b4.de* mang b4.de* **Merc** b4.de* mez b4.de* *Mur-ac* b4.de* nat-c b4.de* **Nat-m** b4.de* *Nit-ac* bg2 nux-v b7.de* petr b4.de* ph-ac b4.de* *Phos* b4.de* plat b4.de* **Puls** b7.de* ran-b b7.de* rheum b7.de* *Rhod* b4.de* *Rhus-t* b7.de* ruta b7.de* sars b4.de* *Seneg* b4.de* *Sep* b4.de* sil bg2 spong b7.de* staph b7.de* *Sul-ac* bg2 *Sulph* b4.de* *Thuj* b4a.de valer b7.de* verat bg2 *Viol-o* b7a.de zinc b4.de*
- **bed** agg.; in: am-c bg2 calc bg2 dig bg2 nux-v bg2
- **sunset**; at | **agg.**: *Puls* b7.de*

NIGHT: acon b7.de* alum b4.de* am-c bg2 am-m b7a.de ang b7a.de apis b7a.de* arn bg2 **Ars** b4.de* bar-c bg2 bry bg2 calc b4.de* *Carb-v* b4.de* *Caust* b4a.de *Cham* b7.de* chel b7.de* chin bg2 clem bg2 cocc b7.de* *Croc* b7.de* euph b4a.de **Euphr** b7.de* gels bg2 **Hep** b4.de* **Hyos** b7.de* *Ign* b7.de* *Ip* b7a.de kali-c b4.de* lyc b4.de* merc bg2 nat-m bg2 nit-ac bg2 **Nux-v** b7.de* phos bg2 puls b7.de* ran-s bg2 rhod b4.de* rhus-t b7.de* sanic bg2 **Sep** b4.de* sil b4.de* stann b4a.de *Staph* b7.de* sulph b4.de* ter bg2 verat b7.de* zinc bg2

ABRASION: | **Cornea**: ham hr1* syph mtf11

ABSCESSES:
○ - **Canthi** | **Inner**: bry b7.de* puls bg2
- **Cornea**: calc-s bro1* *Hep* bro1 kali-s bro1 merc-c bro1 sil bro1 sulph bro1
- **Lachrymal** ducts: stann bg2

ADHESIONS:
○ - **Cornea**:
  - **Argyrol** treatment; after: kali-bi gm1
  - **atropine** treatment; after: kali-bi gm1
- **Lids** | **Eyeballs**; to: asaf bg2

AGGLUTINATED (= sticky; as if glued together): *Acon* b7.de* aeth k* *Agar* k* *All-s* *Alum* k* am-br a1 am-c b4.de* am-m b7.de* anan vh ang b7.de* ant-c b7a.de* apis k* *Arg-met* **Arg-n** k* **Ars** b4a.de* asaf ptk1 *Aur* b4a.de bamb-a stb2.de• *Bar-c* k* bar-m bar-ox-suc mtf11 bell k* borx b4a.de* bov b4.de* *Bry* k* **Calc** k* calc-s calc-sil k2 carb-an k* carb-v k* *Carbn-s* **Caust** k* **Cham** k* chel k* chlam mld2 *Clem* coc-c k* colch k* con b4.de* cortico tpw7 cortiso tpw7 croc b7.de* cycl k* *Dig* k* dros k* dulc fd4.de ery-a a1 *Euph* k* *Euphr* b7.de* ferr b7.de* gast a1 glon ptk1 **Graph** k* grat a1 guaj ptk1

Agglutinated: ...
hep b4.de* hydr *Ign* k* iod b4.de* irid-met srj5• kali-ar *Kali-bi* bg2* *Kali-c* k* kali-n k* kali-p kali-s kola stb3• **Kreos** k* lac-c laur k* led b7.de* lept k* lil-t k* limest-b es1• **Lyc** k* lyss a1 m-arct b7.de m-aust b7.de *Mag-c* k* mag-m b4.de* mang b4a.de* med jl2 *Merc* b4.de* merl a1 mez a1 mur-ac b4.de* nat-ar k* nat-c b4.de* nat-m b4.de* nat-pyru rly4• *Nat-s* k* nat-sil fd3.de• nept-m lsd2.fr nicc k* nit-ac b4.de* *Nux-m* k* *Nux-v* k* ol-an a1 olib-sac wmh1 op k* ph-ac k* **Phos** k* *Phyt* k* plat k* plb k* polys sk4• positr nl2• psor bg2* *Puls* k* rad-br sze8• ran-s a1 rheum b7.de* rhod k* rhus-t k* *Ruta* b7.de* sacch-a fd2.de• sars b4.de* seneg b4.de* **Sep** k* *Sil* k* spig k* spong *Stann* k* *Staph* k* stram b7.de* sul-ac b4.de* *Sulph* k* syph jl2* tarax b7.de* *Thuj* k* tritic-vg fd5.de (non:uran-met k) uran-n k* valer k* vanil fd5.de verat b7.de* zinc b4a.de* [buteo-j sej6]
- **left**: carb-v b4.de*
- **morning**: (↗*Opening - difficult - morning*) *Aeth* k* ail k* *Alum* k* am-br k* am-c k* am-m k* ambr androc srj1• ang k* *Arg-met* **Arg-n** k* arge-pl rwt5• *Ars* k* ars-s-f k2* atra-r skp7*• aur k* aur-ar k2 aur-m k* aur-s k* bamb-a stb2.de• bar-c bar-m k2* bar-s k2* *Bell* k* berb k* borx bov k* bros-gau mrc1 bry k* **Calc** k* calc-s *Carb-v* k* **Carbn-s** carl k* *Caust* k* *Cham* k* *Chel* k* cina h1 **Clem** con k* cop k* cortico sp1 *Dig* k* *Dios* k* dulc fd4.de erig a1 euph h2* *Euphr* gast a1 **Graph** k* *Hep* k* hydr k* hydro-v a1 hydrog srj2• ign a1 irid-met srj5• kali-ar *Kali-bi* k* *Kali-c* k* kali-n k* kali-p kali-s fd4.de* kali-sil k2* kreos a1 lac-loxod-a hm2• led k* lyc k* m-arct st *Mag-c* k* mag-m k* *Mang* **Med** k* *Merc* merl a1 mill k* mim-p skp7• mur-ac k* naja *Nat-ar* *Nat-c* k* *Nat-m* k* nat-p hr1 *Nat-s* k* nat-sil fd3.de• nicc k* nit-ac k* nux-v petr phos k* pieri-b mlk9.de plb k* plut-n srj7• polyp-p a1 positr nl2• *Psor* k* *Puls* k* pycnop-sa mrz1 raph a1 rat a1 rheum h **Rhus-t** k* ruta fd4.de sanic sars k* *Seneg* *Sep* k* sil k* sinus rly4• spong fd4.de stann staph h1* succ-ac rly4• sul-ac k* **Sulph** k* symph fd3.de• syph al* tanac a1* tarax h1* *Tarent* k* tep a1 thuj k* tritic-vg fd5.de ust a1 vanil fd5.de vesp a1* vip *Zinc* k* zinc-p k2* ziz a1
  - **accompanied** by | **photophobia**: nat-s ptk
- **afternoon**: nat-c h2* spong fd4.de
- **evening**: nat-sil fd3.de• plat h2 plb k* rhus-t a1 sep k* spong fd4.de
- **night**: aeth c1 **Alum** k* alum-p k2* alum-sil k2* am-c ang *Ant-c* k* *Apis* *Arg-n* k* ars bar-c bart a1 bell *Borx* k* *Bov* brom hr1 bry calc k* *Carb-v* **Carbn-s** cham chel cic *Croc* dig dulc fd4.de *Euph* k* *Euphr* ferr k* ferr-ar *Gamb* k* **Graph** *Hep* k* *Ign* iod h* kali-c led **Lyc** k* mag-c mag-m k* merc-n merc-ns nat-m nit-ac nux-v ol-an phos phyt bg2* plan a1 plb puls rat k* rhod *Rhus-t* k* sars **Sep** *Sil* *Spong* *Stann* k* staph stram k* sulph *Syph* tarax *Thuj* k* verat k* verat-v hr1
  - **menses**; during: calc b4.de mag-c b4.de
- **accompanied** by:
  - **pneumonia** (See CHEST - Inflammation - lungs - accompanied - lids)
  - **sneezing**: gamb br1*
- **air** agg.; in open: thuj k*
- **coryza**; during: caust b4.de*
- **inflammation**; without: *Led* b7a.de
- **menses**; during: *Calc* k* mag-c h2*
- **sensation**: carb-v h2* caust bg1 cortico tpw7* plat h2*
  - **eyeball**; as if lids stick to: asaf k2* con bg2 elaps bg2 merc bg2 nit-ac bg2 sanic c1*
- **sleep** agg.; after: borx mtf33 bros-gau mrc1 hydrog srj2• positr nl2• rheum st syph mtf33
- **sneezing**; when: gamb ptk1
- **waking**; on: (↗*Opening - difficult - morning - waking*) choc srj3• cyclosp sa3• mim-p skp7• propr sa3• ruta fd4.de tritic-vg fd5.de vanil fd5.de

○ - **Canthi**: staph b7.de*
○ • **Inner**: agar b4.de* cina b7.de* irid-met srj5• mag-c h2* nat-sil fd3.de• nicc bg2 phos b4.de* *Puls* bg2 spong fd4.de staph h1* zinc h2*
  - **Outer**: alum b4.de* ars h2 bar-c b4.de* bry bg2 colch b7.de* lyc bg2 mez bg2 nux-v b7.de* rhus-t bg2 sep h2*
- **Eyelashes**: caust bg2
- **Lid**; lower: cortiso sp1

AIR:
- **sensation** of a current of air | **passing** through eyes: thuj ptk1

AIR; IN OPEN:
- **agg.**: acon b7.de* alum b4a.de* am-c b4.de* am-m b7.de* *Asar* bg2 *Bapt* bg2 *Bell* b4.de* **Bry** b7.de* **Calc** b4.de* camph b7.de* canth b7.de* caust b4.de* *Clem* b4a.de coff b7.de* colch bg2 con b4.de* euphr bg2 graph b4.de* hell b7.de*

Eye

- **agg.**: ...
kali-c b4.de* led b7.de* **Lyc** b4.de* *Merc* b4.de* merc-c b4a.de* nat-m b4.de* nit-ac b4.de* **Nux-v** b7.de* petr b4.de* phos b4.de* *Puls* b7.de* rheum b7.de* rhod b4.de* ruta b7.de* sabad b7a.de* seneg b4.de* sep b4.de* **Sil** b4.de* staph b7.de* sul-ac b4.de* sulph b4.de* teucr b7.de* thuj b4.de*
- **amel.**: am-c b7a.de arg-n bg2 asar b7a.de coloc bg2 *Croc* b7.de* dig b4a.de *Hep* b4a.de *Lyc* b4a.de plat b4.de* *Puls* b7.de* rhus-t b7.de* sars b4.de* seneg b4.de* sep b4.de*

ALCOHOLISM agg.: calc bg2 *Chin* bg2 lach bg2 nux-v bg2 op bg2 sulph bg2

AMAUROSIS (See Paralysis - optic)

AMBLYOPIA: *(↗VISION - Dim)* acon a2* *Agar* bro1 alco mfj alum mfj alumin hsa1 ambr he1 anac hs2* anag c2 ant-t hr1 arn bro1 ars mfj atro hr1 *Aur* bro1 bapt bro1 bar-c he1* bell mfj ben-d c2* calc he1 caps hr1 carbn-s c2 caust hr1* chel hr1* *Chin* c2* *Chinin-s* mfj cic he1 cich c2 cimic hl9 cina tl1* cinch c2 cocc he1 colch bro1 con a1* crot-h c2 *Cycl* bro1 daph c2 dig a2* dros c2 elaps bro1 esin bro1 euphr hr1* fil mfj gels mfj* glon k2* hep bro1 hydr-ac bkh1 hyos a1* ign hr1* ix bnm8• *Jab* bro1 *Kali-c* bro1 kali-p bro1 lach c2 lact-v hs2 lil-t bro1 *Lith-m* bro1 lyc bro1 m-aust c1* mag-p bro1 merc hr1* merl c2 methan mfj naphtin c2* nat-m hr1* nat-sal c1 nit-ac hr1 nux-m bro1 *Nux-v* c2* onos c2* op hr1* osm bro1 ox-ac bro1 oxyt c2 *Ph-ac* c2* *Phos* c2* phos-h c2 phys bro1 picro-ac c1 pilo bro1 plb he1* *Puls* bro1 quas br1 ran-b bro1 raph c2 rhus-t he1* rob a1 *Ruta* c2* sacch c1 sacch-l c2 sal-ac hs1* *Santin* c2* seneg c2* sep he1* sil br3* spig he1 stram a1* stront-c bro1 sulfonam jl1 sulph he1 tab mfj* tarent hr1 ter hr1* thiop jl1 thuj hr1* thyr c2* titan bro1 tub c1* valer bkh1 zinc c2*
- **alcohol**; from: *(↗VISION - Dim - drunkards)* ter a2* tub al2
- **blow**; from a: ammc c1 arn hr1
- **children**; in: lyc hr1*
  - · **congenital**: calc-p br3
- **emotions** agg.: ant-t hr1*
- **eruptions**; after suppressed: cycl hr1* sil br3 sulph hr1*
- **menses**; from suppressed: cycl ll1 puls hr1*
- **old** people; in: bar-c ll1*
- **perspiration** of the feet; from suppressed: sil hr1*
- **pregnancy** agg.; during: ant-t hr1* sulph gsy2
- **rheumatism**; from: puls hr1 rhus-t he1

ANEMIA of:
○ - **Conjunctiva**: dig plb
- **Optic** nerve: alum-p k2 dig a2 kali-p k2
- **Retina**: *Agar* calc mfj (non:chin slp) chinin-s mfj1* dig k* ferr mfj lith-c k* lith-m a2 phos mfj puls mfj santin a2* sep a2* syph k2

ANXIOUS look (See FACE - Expression - anxious)

APOPLEXY:
○ - **Retina**: acon bro1 arn bro1* bell k2* both bro1 croc bro1 crot-h bro1 glon tl1 *Ham* bro1 lach a2* *Led* bro1 nat-sal bro1 phos a2* symph bro1
  - · **accompanied** by | **menses**; suppressed: bell hr1*

ARCUS SENILIS (See Opacity - cornea - arcus)

ASTHENOPIA: *(↗Weak; VISION - Dim)* agar bro1* alum bro1 am-c bro1 ammc c2* apis bro1 *Arg-n* bro1 arn bro1 art-v bro1 asar br1 atro bro1 bell bro1 carb-v c2 carbn-s bro1 *Caust* bro1 *Cimic* bro1 cina c2* con mtf11 croc c2* dub bro1 ferr ptk1 *Gels* bro1 ign bro1 jab c2* kali-c bro1 kalm bro1 lac-f bro1* lach c2 lil-t c2 lith-c br1 *Macro* bro1 mang c2 *Nat-m* bro1* nicc c2 nicc-s bro1 nicot bro1 nux-v bro1 onos bro1* par bro1 *Phos* bro1 *Phys* bro1 rhod c2* ruta bro1* santin bro1 sec c2 seneg bro1* sep bro1* stront-c bro1 thyr mtf11 vac jl2*
- **accommodative**: *(↗VISION - Accommodation - slow)* *Agar* mfj alum tl1 arg-n mfj* bell mfj calc mfj caust mfj cimic mfj con mfj croc mfj *Gels* mfj* **Jab** mfj lach bro1 lil-t mfj* merc mfj nat-m bro1 nux-m mfj op mfj par mfj phos mfj *Phys* mfj* **Ruta** mfj* spig mfj sulph mfj til bro1
- **accompanied** by:
○ · **Head** | **pain** (See HEAD - Pain - accompanied - asthenopia)
- **muscular**: *Agar* mfj **Alum** mfj calc mfj *Con* mfj **Gels** mfj **Jab** mfj kalm mfj led mfj lil-t mfj *Merc* mfj **Nat-m** mfj *Nux-v* mfj **Onos** mfj *Par* mfj *Phys* mfj rad-br mfj *Rhod* mfj *Rhus-t* mfj ruta mfj **Seneg** mfj sep mfj til br1
○ · **External** recti: cupr-act bro1 gels bro1
  · **Internal** recti: jab bro1 muscin bro1 nat-m bro1 phys bro1 pilo bro1
- **myopic**: *(↗VISION - Myopia)* esin bro1 lil-t bro1

ASTIGMATISM: gels hr1* *Lil-t* hr1* onos c1 phys hr1* pic-ac hr1 *Sep* hr1* sil a *Tub* k*

ATROPHY: *(↗Degeneration)*
○ - **Choroid**: nux-v bro1 phos bro1 *Pilo* bro1
  - · **spots**; in: alumin-p mtf aur mtf bar-m mtf both mtf calc mtf *Calc-f* mtf calc-sil mtf *Carbn-s* mtf chrysol mtf11 *Crot-h* mtf gels mtf *Ham* mtf iodof mtf **Kali-i** kr1 *Lach* mtf mag-f mtf nux-v mtf *Phos* kr1* plb mtf plb-act mtf sil mtf sulph mtf *Syph* mtf tab mtf *Verat-v* kr1
- **Conjunctiva**: arg-n bg2 aur bg2 cina bg2 hyos bg2 nux-v bg2 plat bg2 plb bg2 tab bg2
- **Optic** nerve: agar bro1 alum-p k2 *Arg-n* mfj* ars mfj atox bro1* bell bg2 carbn-s bro1 cina tl1 hyos bg2 iodof bro1 lach bg2 *Nux-v* k* **Phos** k* **Plb** mfj santin bro1 *Stry-n* bro1 stry-p mfj syph k2* *Tab* k* thal-xyz srj8• verat-v mfj zinc-p mfj
  - · **alcoholic** drinks; from: nux-v mtf11
  - · **tobacco**; from: ars nux-v mtf11
- **Retina**:
  - · **liquor**; from: nux-v mtf11
  - · **tobacco**; from: nux-v mtf11
○ · **Blood** vessels: acetan bro1

AWARENESS of: limen-b-c hrn2•

BALL in; as of a: mag-m bg2

BAND around the eyeballs; sensation of a: *Lac-d* k* laur k* limen-b-c hrn2*

BATHING agg.: clem *Sulph*

BED AGG.; IN: ambr b7.de* dig b4.de* kali-c b4.de* m-arct b7.de m-aust b7.de mag-c b4.de* nat-c b4.de* nux-v b7.de* ran-b b7.de* spong b7.de*

BENDING HEAD BACKWARD: | **amel.**: seneg ptk1

BLEEDING from eyes: acon ail k2* aloe alumn k2 am-c am-caust *Apis* b7a.de *Arn* k* bell k* **Both** k* *Calc* k* camph *Carb-v* k* *Cham* k* coff b7a.de cor-r **Crot-h** k* dig elaps euphr k* ham bg2* *Kali-chl* kali-i k2 kreos k2 **Lach** k* led bg* nit-ac **Nux-v** k* **Phos** k* plb raph ruta k* seneg bg2 **Sul-ac** bg* *Sulph* suprar bro1
- **accompanied** by | **Head**; congestion to: carb-v mtf33
- **blowing** the nose agg.: nit-ac k*
- **burning**; with: carb-v
- **cough** agg.; during: arn bg1 carb-v cham nux-v
- **trauma**, following: sul-ac br1
- **whooping** cough; in: arn h1 nux-v
○ - **Canthi**: *Graph* bg2
- **Chamber**; in: led k2
  - · **iridectomy**; after: led bro1*
- **Choroid**: ham bro1 **Lach** kr1
- **Conjunctiva**: acon mtf11 arn mtf11 both mtf11 ham mtf11 helo-s bnm14• led br1 psor jl2
- **Lids**: arn bell k* graph k2* *Hep* k* led br1 *Nat-m* k* *Nux-v* k* puls k2 **Sulph** k*
- **Retinal** hemorrhage: *(↗Inflammation - retina - hemorrhagic)* arn k* *Bell* k* both ptk1* *Crot-h* k* glon ham k* **Lach** k* led ptk1 *Merc-c* *Phos* k* *Prun* sal-ac mtf11 sul-ac br1 sulfa mtf11 *Sulph* k*
  - · **accompanied** by:
    ⁝ **Optic** nerve | **paralysis** (See Paralysis - optic - accompanied - retinal)

BLEPHARITIS (See Inflammation - lids)

BLEPHAROSPASM (See Spasms - lids)

BLINDNESS (See VISION - Loss)

BLINKING (See Winking)

BLISTERS form on eye; little (See Eruptions - cornea - blisters)

BLOATED lids (See Swelling)

BLOODSHOT (See Ecchymosis; Injected)

BLOWING in the eye; as if cold air was (See Coldness - air)

BLOWING THE NOSE: | **amel.**: aur ptk1

BLOWS: | **Eyeball** (See Ecchymosis)

BLUENESS (See Discoloration - blue)

BOILS (See Eruptions)

BREAKFAST agg.: nux-m b7.de* plb b7.de*

BRILLIANT: (↗*Glassy)* absin k* acon b7.de* *Aeth* k* ail c1 alco a1 am-caust a1 anh sp1 *Ant-t* b7a.de apis ptk1 arizon-l nl2• *Arn* b7.de* *Ars* atro k* bapt **Bell** k* ben *Bry* b7.de* **Camph** k* cann-i k* cann-s k* *Canth* bro1 cedr clem a1 coca cocc bg2 *Coff Coloc* cori-m a1 croc bg2 cupr k* cypra-eg sde6.de• diosm br1 emb-r bnj1 *Eup-per* euph k* falco-pe nl2• gast a1 *Gels Hydr-ac* bg2 hydrog srj2• *Hyos* k* *Lachn* k* lil-s a1 *Lyc Lyss* m-ambo b7.de merc-c b4a.de* mill mosch b7a.de* nux-v b7.de* *Op* k* ozone sde2• *Ph-ac* bg2 plb k* plut-n srj7• puls santa santin sec b7.de* *Spig* bg2 spira a1 *Stram* k* stroph-h ptk1 tanac k* verat b7.de* verat-v bro1 *Zinc* [tax jsj7]
- **accompanied** by | **protrusion** (See Protrusion - accompanied - brilliant)
- **chill**; during: bell bg2 *Lach* bg2 sep bg2
- **cough** agg.; during: bell bg2 kali-c b4.de* par bg2 sep b4a.de*
- **perspiration**; during: op

CAMPHOR agg.; odor of: kali-n bg2

CANCER: ars bg2 aur-m-n *Bell* bg2 **Calc** k* carb-an mrr1 con bg2 euphr sne hep bg2 **Laur** bg2 *Lyc* k* **Phos** sel sne *Sep* k* *Sil* k* thuj
- **epithelioma**: cund k* *Lach* ran-b k2

○ • **Cornea**, of: hep k* physala-p bnm7•

• **Lids**; of: con k2 hydr lach phyt ran-b c1 sep k2 thuj

⁝ **Lower**: apis cund k* thuj
- **fungus**: bell k* **Calc** k* *Lyc* k* **Phos** k* *Sep* k* *Sil* k* syph k2 thuj
- **fungus** haematodes: *Carb-an* b4a.de *Thuj* b4a.de
- **fungus** medullaris: bell k* **Calc** k* *Lyc Sil* k*

○ - **Canthi**: carb-an b4a.de *Petr* b4a.de *Phos* b4a.de *Sil* b4a.de
- **Lachrymal** glands: *Carb-an* k*

CATARACT●: acon b2.de* agar b2.de* *Am-c* k* *Am-m* k* anac b2.de* a n a g c2 ang b2.de* ant-t k* *Apis* k* arg-i c2* arn k* ars b2.de* aur b2.de* *Bar-c* k* bar-s k2 bell k* bov b2.de* bry b2.de* **Calc** k* **Calc-f** k* **CALC-P** k* calc-s calc-sil k* cann-i br1 *Cann-s* k* caps b2.de* *Carb-an* k* **CAUST** k* *Chel* k* chim k* chin k* cina b2.de* cine c1* coch c2* *Colch* k* coloc c2 *Con* k* croc b2.de* dig k* dulc b2.de* *Euph* k* euphr k* germ-met srj5• hed c2* hep k* hyos k* ign b2.de* iod bro1 *Jab* k* *Kali-c* kali-m c2* kali-s k* kali-sil k2* kreos b2.de* lac-c k* (non:lec br1) led br1* *Lyc* k* **Mag-c** k* mang b2.de* merc k* naphtin c2* nat-c b2.de* nat-m k* nat-s bg2* *Nit-ac* k* op k* *Phos* k* plat bro1 platan br1 platan-or c1* plb k* podo c2 psor *Puls* k* quas br1* rhus-t k* rubella mtf11 ruta k* sabad b7a.de sacch c2 *Santin* c2* sars b2.de* *Sec* k* seneg k* **SEP** k* **Sil** k* spig k* stann b2.de* staph b2.de* stram b2.de* **Sulph** k* tarax b2.de* tell k* thal-xyz srj8• *Thiosin* br1* valer b2.de* verat b2.de* *Zinc* k* zinc-p k2 **Zinc-s** sne
- **right**: *Am-c Kali-c Nit-ac Sil*
- **left**: merc a1 *Sulph*
- **accompanied** by:

• **menses**; absent: lyc ptk1

• **mucus**: arum-m mtf11

• **opacity** | **Corneal** (See Opacity - cornea - accompanied - cataract)
- **children**; in: mag-c mtf33
- **contusion**; from: arn *Con* k* *Symph* sne
- **dark** day; can see better on a: euph
- **gout**; with: led br1
- **hemiopia**; with vertical: caust
- **incipient**: am-c tl1* caust k* chel tl1 chim br1* halo mtf11 phos hr1 *Puls* k* sec sep k*
- **injuries**; after: con ptk1 *Symph* sne tell br1*

• **accompanied** by | **lachrymation**: euphr ptk1
- **old** people; in: calc-p *Carb-an* k* caust chol *Cine* c1* con graph kali-c lyc mag-c merc napht nat-m phos puls *Sec* k* sil sulph
- **operation**; after: **Acon** sne arn k* rhus-t hr1* *Seneg* k*
- **perspiration** of feet; after suppressed: **Sil**
- **progressive**: chim br1
- **reticularis**: caust k* plb k*
- **soft**: *Colch* k* merc k* sec k*
- **viridis** (= green): colch *Phos* k* puls k*

Cataract: ...
- **women**; in: sec ptk1 sep k*

○ - **Capsular**: *Am-m* k* colch k*
- **Conjunctiva**: arg-n mtf11
- **Cortical**: **Sulph** k*

CATARRH (= mucopus): **Acon** bg2* *Apis* bro1 *Arg-n* bro1 *Ars* bg2* **Bell** bg2* *Canth* bro1 *Cham* bg2 *Chlol* bro1 dig bg2 dub bro1 dulc bro1 euph bg2 *Euphr* bg2* *Ferr-p* bro1 guare bro1 *Hep* bg2* *Ign* bg2 kali-bi bg2 kali-m bro1 **Merc** bg2* merc-c bro1 merl bro1 morb jl2 nat-ar bro1 **Nux-v** bg2 op bro1 oscilloc jl2 pic-ac bro1 **Puls** bg2* rhus-t bro1 sep bro1 stict bro1 sulph bg2* upa bro1
- **chronic**: ars-i vh chrysar vh tub vh

• **children**; in: | **gonorrhea** in the mother; caused by: puls mtf33
- **menses** | **before** | **agg.**: euphr bro1

• **during** | **agg.**: euphr bro1

CHALAZAE (See Tumors - lids - nodules)

CHEMOSIS: *Acon* am-caust k* **Apis Arg-n** k* ars bell bry cadm-s *Con* crot-h der a1 dulc (non:euph k) *Euphr* k* *Guare* k* *Hep Ip* k* *Kali-bi* **Kali-i** *Lach* lyc bg merc merc-i-r k* mez *Nat-m* pert jl2 phyt **Rhus-t** sil syph ter thuj *Vesp* k* vesp-xyz c2
- **right**: syph vesp
- **left**: bell
- **evening** | **work**; while at: mez
- **chill**; during: bry
- **operation** for cataract; after: guare phyt
- **yellow**: am-caust k* *Merc-i-r* k*

○ - **Conjunctiva**: **Apis** bg2* guare bro1 hep bro1 *Kali-i* bro1 *Rhus-t* bg2* sul-ac bro1 *Vesp* bro1
- **Cornea**: *Hep*
- **Lids**: apis ptk1 arg-n ptk1 kali-i ptk1 lyc ptk1 rhus-t ptk1

CHILDREN; complaints of:
- **infants**: acon bg2 bell bg2 borx bg2 bry bg2 calc bg2 cham bg2 dulc bg2 *Euphr* bg2 merc bg2 nux-v bg2 puls bg2 rhus-t bg2 *Sulph* bg2
- **nurslings**: *Borx* b4a.de

CHILL; during: rhus-t b7.de

CHOREA:
- **sleep**; after | **amel**: agar tl1

CHOROIDITIS (See Inflammation - choroid)

CICATRICES:
- **injuries** or ulceration; from: *Euphr* b7.de*
- **operation**; after: graph tl1

○ - **Cornea**: *Con* b4a.de sil b4a.de

CLOSED: (↗*Open lids - sensation - wide - closed; Opening - unable)* ambr bg2 ang b7.de* *Apis* b7a.de *Ars* b4.de* **Bell** b4.de* brom bg2 *Calc* k* camph b7.de* carb-v bg2 caust bg2 **Cham** b7.de* chir-fl bnm4• *Cocc* k* coloc bg* con bg2 **Croc** b7a.de* cupr b7.de* *Grat* hell b7.de* *Hep* b4.de* hyos k* kali-c bg2 *Lachn* laur b7.de* *Merc* b4a.de* mur-ac ptk1 *Nat-m* b4.de* nit-ac bg2 nux-m ptk1 phos bg2 plb b7.de* **Rhus-t** k* sep k* sil b4a.de* spig b7.de* spong b7.de* *Staph* b7a.de* stram k* stry sulph h2* ther tl1 urt-u viol-o b7.de* viol-t b7.de* zinc h2
- **one** side (See Open lids - one)
- **evening**: nat-m h2
- **accompanied** by:

○ • **Face**; paralysis of (See FACE - Paralysis - accompanied - eyes)

• **Heart**; complaints of the (See CHEST - Heart; complaints - accompanied - eyes - closed)
- **coma**; with (See MIND - Coma - eyes - closed)
- **half** closed (See Open lids - half)
- **melancholia**; in: **Arg-n** kola stb3• sep h2
- **sensation**: sep bg2 [buteo-j sej6]

• **tight**; as if they had been closed: ambr b7.de
- **sitting** agg.: mur-ac al1*
- **sleepiness**; without: viol-o ptk1
- **spasmodic**: *Ars* ptk1 bell ptk1 cham ptk1 coloc ptk1 croc ptk1 cupr ptk1 euphr ptk1 **Hyos** ptk1 ip ptk1 kali-c ptk1 *Merc* ptk1 *Nat-m* ptk1 sil ptk1 stram ptk1

- **spoken** to; when: sep bg2*
- **swelling** of lids; from: acon k2 **Apis** mrr1

CLOSING THE EYES:

- **agg.**: agar b4.de* arn ptk1 bell b4.de* bry ptk1 calc bg2 *Canth* b7a.de carb-an ptk1 carb-v bg2 chel b7.de* clem b4.de* con b4.de* croc b7a.de* dig b4.de* hell b7.de* ign b7.de* **Lach** ptk1 lyc bg2 manc bg2 sars b4.de* sep b4.de* sil bg2 staph b7.de* stront-c ptk1 sulph b4.de* **Ther** ptk1
- **amel.**: alum b4a.de apis b7a.de aur b4.de* canth b7.de* cic b7.de* con ptk1 croc b7.de* gels ptk1 kali-c ptk1 *Lyc* b4a.de meli ptk1 nit-ac bg2 ph-ac b4.de* plat b4.de* sil ptk1 spig b7.de* tab ptk1 zinc ptk1
- **desire** to: agar k* *Agath-a* nl2• aloe bg2 alum bg2 am-m bg2 androc srj1• ant-t k* *Apis* b7a.de bar-c bg2 bell calad b7.de* *Calc* k* *Caust* *Chel* choc srj3• coff b7.de* con *Croc* b7.de* dendr-pol sk4• dios elaps gels irid-met srj5• lac-ac lac-h sk4• lyc bg2 mang bg2 *Med* op b7.de* ox-ac ph-ac bg2 plac rzf5• *Sil* sulfonam ks2 sulph bg2 *Viol-o* b7a.de [bell-p-sp dcm1]
  - **right**: querc-r svu1•
  - **morning** | **waking**; on: visc sp1
  - **evening** | **work**; while at: mez
  - **chill**; during: bry
  - **fever**; during: *(↗Photophobia - fever)* chin-b kr1
  - **walking** in open air agg.: calad k*
  - **weakness**; from: cupr
- **difficult**: aur-m borx b4a.de cadm-s carb-v caust ptk1 euph nux-m mrr1 **Nux-v** k* **Par** k* *Phos* k* *Sil* k*
  - **right**: plut-n srj7•
  - **evening**: borx h2
  - **dryness** of eyes; from: **Nux-m** c1*
  - **headache**; during: hep c lach c sulph h2
- **headache**; in: agar bg2 ant-t bg2 *Bell* bg2 *Calc* bg2 carb-an bg2 carb-v bg2 cocc bg2 hep bg2 kali-n bg2 kreos bg2 mosch bg2 nat-m bg2 nit-ac bg2 nux-m bg2 nux-v bg2 petr bg2 phos bg2 plat bg2 plb bg2 sep bg2 sulph bg2
- **involuntary**: acon k* agar b4.de* *Agath-a* nl2• alum k* am-m b7.de* androc srj1• ant-t b7.de* arg-met b7.de* ars b4.de* bamb-a stb2.de• *Bell* b4.de* bov k* bry b7.de* **Calc** b4a.de cann-s b7.de* canth b7.de* carb-an b4.de* carc mlr1• **Caust** k* cham b7a.de chel b7.de* chin k* **Chinin-s** chlor cic k* cinnb k2 cocc b7.de* **Con** k* croc b7.de* cupr b7.de* cycl b7.de* euph k* eupi ferr b7.de* *Gels* graph b4a.de* *Grat* *Hep* b4a.de hura **Hyos** b7a.de ign b7.de* ip b7a.de kali-c b4.de* kali-n b4.de* kreos b7a.de lyc b4.de* m-aust b7.de mag-s *Merc* k* mez k* *Nat-c* k* *Nat-m* b4.de* nux-m b7.de* olnd bg2 *Op* b7.de* ph-ac b4.de* phos k* plac rzf5• plat b4.de* *Puls* b7a.de *Rhus-t* k* ruta b7.de* sabad b7.de* sabin b7.de* *Sep* k* sil b4.de* *Spig* b7.de* spong k* squil b7.de* staph b7.de* sul-ac b4.de* **Sulph** k* thuj b4a.de verb b7.de* viol-o b7.de* viol-t k* zinc b4a.de
  - **afternoon**: alum
  - **accompanied** by | **vertigo** (See VERTIGO - Accompanied - eye - closing)
  - **focussed**; eyes: gels psa
  - **looking** steadily; when: gels k2
  - **sadness**; with (See MIND - Sadness - eyes)
- **menses**; during: phos
- **must** close the eyes: agar *Agath-a* nl2• arn atis bnj1 bamb-a stb2.de• calc *Canth* carb-v *Chel* croc ptk1 euph *Kali-c* *Lyc* mez petr h2 ph-ac h2 sil spig
  - **pain**; from: hep bg1 petr-ra shn4• plac rzf5•
    - **eyes**; in: ph-ac h2 plat h2 spig h1
    - **face**; in: chel ptk1
    - **head**; in: *(↗Opening - unable - headache)* carb-v h2 plat h2
- **spasmodic** closure: acon agar *Alum* apis arg-met k2 **Ars** k* *Bell* brom *Calc* cham **Coloc** *Con* cupr mtf33 hep *Hyos* k* **Merc** *Merc-c* **Nat-m** k* nux-v osm *Psor* *Rhus-t* sep sil h2 spong staph h1 stram h1
  - **morning**: hep h2 nat-m sep h2 spong h1
  - **evening**: con *Hep* nat-m sep h2
  - **night**: alum hep nat-m h2
  - **headache**; during: calc-act bg1 *Nat-m* k* sep h2*
  - **looking** agg.: *Merc*
  - **pain**; from | **abdomen**; in: coloc h2
- **will** not close; the eyes: phos bg1*

COAL gas agg.: sec bg2

COITION agg.: kali-c bg2* kali-p bg2 nat-m bg2* phos ptk1 sep ptk1

COLD:

- **agg.**: *Bell* b4a.de dig b4a.de
- **air**:
  - **agg.**: **Acon** cinnb clem *Dig* bg2 *Dulc* b4a.de *Hep* *Lac-c* lil-t bg2 merc *Puls* b7.de* rhus-t b7.de* *Sil* *Thuj*
    - **accompanied** by | **heat** in eye; sensation of (See Heat in - accompanied - cold)
    - **icy**: thuj b4a.de
    - **Lids**: **Acon**
  - **amel.**: arg-n bg2 *Asar* b7a.de
- **amel.**: arg-n bg2 *Asar* bg2 merc bg2
- **applications**:
  - **agg.**: ars ptk1 clem ptk1 *Merc* ptk1 thuj ptk1
  - **amel.**: apis ptk1 *Arg-n* ptk1 asar ptk1 bry ptk1 nux-v ptk1 phos ptk1 *Puls* ptk1 syph ptk1
- **washing** | **amel.**: apis bg2 glon bg2 kali-n bg2 thuj bg2
- **water** | **agg.**: elaps *Hep* kali-n bg2 mur-ac bg2 sep b4.de* *Sulph*

COLD; AFTER TAKING A: *Acon* b7a.de* *Ars* bg2 bell b4a.de* calc b4a.de* **Cham** b7a.de* *Dulc* b4a.de* euphr bg2 hep b4a.de* iod b4a.de kali-c b4.de* merc b4a.de* *Nux-m* bg2 nux-v b7a.de puls b7a.de* rhus-t ptk1 **Ruta** bg2 *Sulph* b4a.de*

COLDNESS: acon b7.de* aesc k* allox tpw4 alum k* am-c k* ambr k* amyg k* *Arg-n* k* asaf k* asar k* berb k* bufo *Calc* k* *Calc-p* k* *Caust* b4a.de chlor k* *Con* k* croc k* *Euphr* k* eupi k* *Fl-ac* k* form germ-met srj5• graph k* *Kali-c* k* lachn k* lith-c *Lyc* k* *M-arct* b7.de m-aust b7.de* med k* *Mez* bg2* nat-m bro1 par k* *Phyt* k* pimp a1 *Plat* k* plb psor al2 raph k* seneg k* sep k* sil k* spig spong k* squil k* stram k* sulph k* symph fd3.de• syph k* tab bg2 *Thuj* k*

- **right**: plat h2
- **left**: aesc a1 eupi a1 tarent
- **evening**: lyc k*
- **accompanied** by:
  - ○ **Forehead** | **pain** (See HEAD - Pain - forehead - accompanied - eyes - coldness)
- **air** blowing; as from cold: asaf bg2 med bg2 sulph bg2
  - ○ **Canthi**; inner: med hr1
  - **In** eyes: asaf asar h1 bell bg2 berb cinnb *Croc* k* eupi bg2 *Fl-ac* k* lac-h htj1• m-aust b7.de mang bg2 med k* mez bg2* plat bg2 sep stann bg2 staph bg2 sulph symph fd3.de• syph k* *Thuj* k* vinc bg2
  - **Under** lids: *Croc* bro1 *Fl-ac* bg2* syph bro1 thuj bro1
- **icy**: lyc bg1 m-arct bg1 m-aust bg seneg ptk1
- **painful** eye, in the: mez ptk1 *Thuj*
- **sensation** of: acon bg2 *Alum* bg2 am-c bg2 asaf bg2 *Asar* b7a.de* bell bg2 **Calc** bg2 caust bg2 *Con* bg2 croc b7.de* euphr b7a.de fl-ac bg2 graph bg2 hura bg2 kali-c bg2 lyc bg2 *M-arct* b7.de* par b7.de* ph-ac bg2 *Plat* bg2 seneg bg2 *Thuj* bg2
- **swimming** in cold water, sensation as if: squil h1*
- **walking**:
  - **air** agg.; in open: alum con sil squil symph fd3.de•
  - **wind**; in the | **cold** wind: *Squil*
- ○ **Above** eyes: graph h2
- **Back** of eyes: calc-p k*
- **Canthi**: asaf asar c1 euphr k* lith-c
  - ○ **Edges** of: kali-c
    - **closing** the eyes agg.: ph-ac
  - **Outer**: asar b7.de*
    - **left**: euphr bg2
- **Eyeballs**: ser-a-c jl2
- **Lids**: alum sne asar bg2 bell bg2 brom k* croc bro1 fl-ac bg2 graph bg2 hura *Kali-c* k* med sne ph-ac k* pip-n sne sulph sne
  - **drops** on lids; sensation of cold: scroph-n bg2
  - ○ **Between** lids and eyeballs | **drops** of cold water; as if there were: berb a1
  - **Between** margins of lids | **drops** of cold water; as if there were: berb bg2*
  - **Margins** of: croc bro1 kali-c ph-ac bro1

- **Lids – Margins** of: ...
  - ⁝ **closing** the eyes agg.: ph-ac
  - ⁝ **Inner**: *Ph-ac* b4a.de
  - · **Upper**: graph b4.de*

COMPLAINTS of eyes: abr mtf11 acon ptk1 *Agar* ptk1 apis ptk1 *Arg-n* ptk1 *Ars* ptk1 **Bell** ptk1 benzol br1 botul br1 cadm-met sp1 **Calc** ptk1 cann-i mtf11 *Carbn-s* br1 caust ptk1 cine mtf11 colch mtf11 *Com* br1 dubo-m br1 euphr ptk1 flav jl2 *Gels* ptk1 gent-l br1 germ-met srj5• graph ptk1 guare br1 helo mtf11 ilx-a br1 lith-chl mtf11 *Lyc* ptk1 **Merc** ptk1 **Nat-m** ptk1 nux-v ptk1 phos ptk1 phys mrr1* platan-oc mtf11 **Puls** ptk1 *Rhus-t* ptk1 ruta br1* santin br1 *Seneg* br1 sep ptk1 sol-ni br1 spig br1* **Sulph** ptk1 tell br1 toxi mtf2• verat ptk1 zinc ptk1 [bell-p-sp dcm1]

- **alternating** sides: acon bg2* agar ptk1 ang bg2 *Ars* ptk1 bell bg2* castm bg2 *Chin* ptk1 cupr bg2* indg bg2 lyc bg2* nat-p bg2 puls ptk1 ran-b bg2* seneg ptk1 sep bg2 sil ptk1
- **right** eye: *Acon* b7a.de* agar b4a.de* *Agn* b7a.de* *Alum* b4a.de* **Am-c** b4a.de* am-m b7a.de* ambr b7a.de* anac b4a.de* ang b7a.de* ant-c b7a.de* *Ant-t* b7a.de* apis b7a.de *Arn* b7a.de* *Ars* b4a.de* *Asaf* b7a.de* asar b7a.de* aur b4a.de* *Bar-c* b4a.de* **Bell** b4a.de* *Bism* b7a.de* borx b4a.de* *Bov* b4a.de* brom b4a.de* bry b7a.de* calad b7a.de* **Calc** b4a.de* *Camph* b7a.de* **Cann-s** b7a.de* **Cann-xyz** ptk1 *Canth* b7a.de* caps b7a.de* carb-an b4a.de* *Carb-v* b4a.de* *Caust* b4a.de* *Cham* b7a.de* chel b7a.de* chin b7a.de* *Cic* b7a.de* cina b7a.de* *Clem* b4a.de* coff b7a.de* *Colch* b7a.de* **Coloc** b4a.de* *Con* b4a.de* *Croc* b7a.de* *Cycl* b7a.de* *Dig* b4a.de* dros b7a.de* *Euph* b4a.de* *Euphr* b7a.de* *Ferr* b7a.de* **Fl-ac** bg2 *Graph* b4a.de* *Guaj* b4a.de* *Hep* b4a.de* *Hyos* b7a.de* *Ign* b7a.de* iod b4a.de* *Ip* b7a.de kali-bi bg2 *Kali-c* b4a.de* *Kali-n* b4a.de* *Kreos* b7a.de* laur b7a.de* *Led* b7a.de* **Lyc** b4a.de* m-arct b7a.de* m-aust b7a.de* mag-c b4a.de *Mag-m* b4a.de* *Mang* b4a.de* *Merc* b4a.de* mill b7a.de *Mur-ac* b4a.de* **Nat-c** b4a.de* **Nat-m** b4a.de* **Nit-ac** b4a.de* *Nux-m* b7a.de* nux-v b7a.de* olnd b7a.de* *Par* b7a.de* **Petr** b4a.de* ph-ac b4a.de* *Phos* b4a.de* **Plat** b4a.de* plb b7a.de* psor bg2 *Puls* b7a.de* *Ran-b* b7a.de* *Ran-s* b7a.de* rheum b7a.de* *Rhod* b4a.de* **Rhus-t** b7a.de* ruta b7a.de* sabad b7a.de* sars b4a.de* sel b7a.de* **Seneg** b4a.de* *Sep* b4a.de* **Sil** b4a.de* *Spig* b7a.de* spong b7a.de* squil b7a.de* stann b4a.de* *Staph* b7a.de* stram b7a.de* stront-c b4a.de sul-ac b4a.de* *Sulph* b4a.de* tarax b7a.de* *Teucr* b7a.de* thuj b4a.de* *Valer* b7a.de* *Verat* b7a.de* viol-t b7a.de* zinc b4a.de*
  - ▽ · **extending** to | **left** eye: nat-c bg2 sep bg2 spig bg2
- **left** eye: *Acon* b7a.de* *Agar* b4a.de* alum b4a.de* am-c fse1.de am-m b7a.de* ambr b7a.de* anac b4a.de* *Ant-c* b7a.de* ant-t fse1.de apis b7a.de* arg-met b7a.de *Arn* b7a.de* *Ars* b4a.de* *Asaf* b7a.de* *Asar* b7a.de* *Aur* b4a.de* bar-c b4a.de* *Bell* b4a.de* *Borx* b4a.de* bov b4a.de* brom bg2 *Bry* b7a.de* calad b7a.de* *Calc* b4a.de* camph b7a.de* canth b7a.de* caps b7a.de* *Carb-an* b4a.de* carb-v b4a.de* *Caust* b4a.de* *Chel* b7a.de* *Chin* b7a.de* cina b7a.de* *Clem* b4a.de* colch b7a.de* *Con* b4a.de* *Croc* b7a.de* *Dros* b7a.de* euph b4a.de* *Euphr* b7a.de* ferr b7a.de* fl-ac bg2 *Hell* b7a.de* **Hep** b4a.de* ign b7a.de* iod b4a.de* *Ip* b7a.de kali-c b4a.de* kali-n b4a.de* *Laur* b7a.de* *Lyc* b4a.de* *M-arct* b7a.de* *M-aust* b7a.de* *Mag-c* b4a.de* *Meny* b7a.de* *Merc* b4a.de* *Mez* b4a.de* mill b7a.de* mur-ac b4a.de* nat-c b4a.de *Nat-m* b4a.de* *Nit-ac* b4a.de* *Nux-v* b7a.de* *Olnd* b7a.de* *Op* b7a.de* par b7a.de* petr b4a.de* *Ph-ac* b4a.de* *Phos* b4a.de* plat b4a.de* *Plb* b7a.de* psor bg2 *Puls* b7a.de* ran-b b7a.de* ran-s b7a.de* *Rheum* b7a.de* rhod b4a.de* *Rhus-t* b7a.de* *Ruta* b7a.de* sabad b7a.de* *Sabin* b7a.de* sars b4a.de* *Sel* b7a.de* seneg b4a.de* *Sep* b4a.de* *Sil* b4a.de* *Spig* b7a.de* **Spong** b7a.de* *Squil* b7a.de* *Stann* b4a.de* staph b7a.de* stram b7a.de* *Stront-c* b4a.de* sul-ac b4a.de* **Sulph** b4a.de* *Tarax* b7a.de* teucr b7a.de* *Thuj* b4a.de* valer b7a.de* verat fse1.de *Viol-o* b7a.de* *Viol-t* b7a.de* *Zinc* b4a.de*
  - ▽ · **extending** to | **Vertex**: viol-o ptk1
- **accompanied** by:
  - · **coryza**: *Ars* bg2 **Bell** bg2 *Cham* bg2 **Euphr** bg2 hep bg2 *Ign* bg2 *Lach* bg2 merc bg2 *Nux-v* bg2 **Puls** bg2 staph bg2 sulph bg2
  - · **cough**: nat-m ptk1
  - · **headache** (See HEAD - Pain - accompanied - eye - complaints)
  - · **nausea**: asar b7.de*
  - · **other** parts; pain in: ars bg2 hep bg2 nit-ac bg2 sabad b7.de*
  - · **waking**; frequent: ambr b7.de*
  - · **weakness**; muscular: onos br1
  - · **worms**; complaints of: art-v sf1.de

Complaints of eyes – **accompanied** by: ...

- ○ · **Abdomen**; complaints of (See ABDOMEN - Complaints - accompanied - eyes - complaints)
- · **Ears**; complaints of: nit-ac bg2 petr bg2 phos bg2 puls bg2 viol-o ptk1
- · **Face**; pain in (See FACE - Pain - accompanied - eye - complaints)
- · **Heart** complaints (See CHEST - Heart; complaints - accompanied - eyes)
- · **Kidneys**; complaints of (See KIDNEYS - Complaints - accompanied - eyes)
- · **Liver**; complaints of (See ABDOMEN - Liver - accompanied - eyes)
- · **Mouth**; aphthae: brom ptk1
- · **Ovaries**; complaints of (See FEMALE - Ovaries - accompanied - eyes)
- · **Stomach**; complaints of: ant-c bg2 calc bg2 caps bg2 chin bg2 cocc bg2 lyc bg2 nat-m bg2 nux-v bg2 phos bg2 puls bg2 sulph bg2
- · **Throat**:
  - ⁝ **complaints** of: sep bg2 tarent bg2
  - ⁝ **tickling**: arg-n bg2

- **alternating** with:
  - · **hearing**; impaired (See HEARING - Impaired - alternating - eye)
  - · **labor**-like pain (See FEMALE - Pain - labor-like - alternating - eye)
  - ○ · **Abdomen**:
    - ⁝ **complaints** of: euphr bg2*
    - ⁝ **pain** in: *Euphr* b7a.de
  - · **Extremities**; complaints of: kreos ptk1
- ▽ - **extending** to:
  - ○ · **Cervical** region: pip-n bg2
  - · **Vertex**: lach ptk1 thlas ptk1 viol-o ptk1
- **headache**; after (See Headache)
- **nervous**: agar bg2 *Bell* bg2 caust bg2 *Chin* bg2 guaj bg2 hep bg2 *Hyos* bg2 lil-t bg2 onos bg2 par bg2 ph-ac bg2 plb bg2 **Spig** bg2 thuj bg2
- **syphilitic**: jac-g bro1 kali-i bro1 merc-i-f bro1 nit-ac bro1 thuj bro1
- ○ - **Canthi** (See Canthi)
- **Choroid**: phos ptk1
- **External** tissues: hip-ac br1
- **Eyeballs** (See Eyeballs)
- **Eyelashes** (See Hair - eyelashes - complaints)
- **Iris** (See Iris)
- **Lachrymal** ducts: apis ptk1 fago ptk1 hep ptk1 merc-d ptk1 *Petr* ptk1 plb ptk1 sil ptk1* staph ptk1
- **Lachrymal** glands (See Lachrymal glands)
- **Lachrymal** sac (See Lachrymal sac)
- **Meibomian** glands (See Meibomian)
- **Optic** nerve (See Optic)
- **Orbits** (See Orbits)
- **Retina**: coenz-q mtf11
- **Supraorbital**: viol-o br1

CONDYLOMATA (See Warts)

CONGESTION (See Discoloration - red; Hyperemia)

CONICAL cornea: calc-i mfj *Euphr* k* puls k*

CONJUNCTIVITIS (See Inflammation - conjunctiva)

CONSCIOUSNESS; agg. after return of: *Cupr* b7a.de

CONTORTED (See Distorted)

CONTRACTION:

- ○ - **Canthi** | **Inner** | **left**: agar b4.de*
  - · **Outer**: graph b4a.de
- **Ciliary** muscles: phys br1
- **Eyebrows**: bry b7.de* hell b7.de* merc-c b4a.de

Eye

- **Lids**; of: acon vh1 carc mlr1• oci-sa sp1 tab a1
  - • **coryza**; during: lyc b4.de*
  - • **headache**, with (See HEAD - Pain - accompanied - eye - contraction)
- O • **Lower**: colch ptk1

CONTRACTIVE sensation: agar k* alum b4.de* arg-n bg bell b4.de* borx b4a.de* bov brom b4a.de carb-v b4a.de chin b7.de* *Cycl* b7a.de euphr b7.de* glon a1 *Graph* b4a.de kali-c b4a.de kali-n k* kreos b7a.de lyc b4a.de *Merc* b4a.de nat-c k* *Nat-m* k* nit-ac k* *Nux-v* b7.de* olnd b7.de* petr b4a.de phos b4a.de phys bg2* plat b4.de* plb b7.de* rhod b4.de* rhus-t b7.de* sep k* sil b4a.de squil h1* stann k* staph b7.de* sul-ac b4a.de sulph b4a.de verat a1 *Viol-o* b7a.de viol-t b7.de zinc b4a.de

- **right**: hyper bg1
- **headache**; during: *Carb-v* k* kali-n c1 mag-c h2
- **reading** and writing by candlelight; while: sep h2
- O - **Canthi**; outer: graph h2
- **Eyebrows**; muscles of: hell h1
- **Lids**: agar h2 borx h2 nux-v h1 rhus-t h1 staph h1
- **Orbits**: verb b7.de*

CONVULSIONS; agg. after epileptic: cupr b7a.de

CONVULSIVE (See Movement - convulsive)

COUGH: | **before** | **agg.**: cina b7.de*

- **during** | **agg.**: acon bg2 arn bg2 bell bg2 caps bg2 carb-v bg2 cham bg2 cina b7.de* graph bg2 kali-c bg2 m-ambo b7.de nat-m bg2 nux-v bg2 phos bg2 puls b7.de* sabad b7.de* seneg ptk1 spong bg2

COVERING eyes with hand: | **amel.**: aur ptk1 thuj ptk1

CRACKS:

- O - **Canthi**; in: alum alum-p k2 *Ant-c* br1* borx bro1 calc-s k2 caust ptk1 cist k2 **Graph** k* iod **Lyc** k* merc mez k2 *Nat-m* nit-ac petr k* phos plat sep sil k* staph bro1 *Sulph* k* zinc k*
  - O • **Outer**: *Ant-c* bg2 *Nat-m* sulph zinc
- **Lids**: alum bg2 am-c k2* arn bg2 bar-c bg2 bry bg2 **Calc** bg2 carb-v bg2 caust bg2 coloc bg2 croc bg2 **Euphr** bg2 graph tl1* **Iod** bg2 kali-c bg2 **Lyc** bg2 **Nat-m** bg2 nit-ac bg2 **Nux-v** bg2 phos bg2 sep bg2 sil bg2 staph bg2 **Sulph** bg2
  - O • **Tarsi**: graph bg2

CRAMP (See Spasms)

CRAWLING: agar k* arund hr1 asar bell k* chin k* cina colch k* crot-t bg2* kali-s fd4.de kola stb3• m-arct b7.de nat-c *Nat-s* k* nux-v b7.de* plat tl1 ruta fd4.de seneg sep k* spig k* sulph k* verat

- O - **Around** the eyes: cist ptk1
- **Canthi**: plat k*
- **Eyebrows** (See FACE - Formication - eyebrows)
- **Lids**: chin b7.de* cina b7.de* kola stb3• ph-ac a1 seneg b4.de*
  - O • **Upper** lid: asar b7.de* calc-act a1 par b7.de*
    - ⁝ **Margin** of right upper lid: par a1
    - ⁝ **Under** upper lid: asar a1
- **Orbits**: plat b4.de*

CRUSTY margins of lids (See Eruptions - lids - crusts - margins)

DARK around eyes (See FACE - Discoloration - bluish - eyes)

DARKNESS:

- **agg.**: *Iod* bg2
- **amel.**: (↗*Photophobia*) con ptk1 lil-t ptk1 nux-m bg2 phos bg2

DEEP: symph fd3.de•

- **as** if too: (↗*Sunken - sensation*) ambr c1 spig gk

DEGENERATION: (↗*Atrophy*)

- O - **Cornea**: *Ars*
- **Retina**: agar mtf aur mtf dig mtf gels mtf ham bro1* kali-i mtf lith-c mtf merc mtf merc-c mtf nux-v mtf p-benzq mtf11 phos br1* plb mtf sulph mtf syph mtf
  - • **old** people; in: thiop mtf11
- **Sclera**: aur bro1 bar-m bro1 plb bro1

DENTITION agg.: bell bro1 calc bro1 ferr-p bg2 puls bro1

DESCEMETITIS (See Inflammation - descemet's)

DETACHMENT of retina: abel mtf11 acon bro1 apis **Arn** mfj* ars mfj aur k* *Aur-m* bro1 ben-d mtf11 bry mfj dig k* *Gels* k* germ-met srj5• hep mfj kali-i mfj merc mfj naphtin c2* nux-v bro1 phos k* pilo bro1 rhus-t mfj ruta ks

- **injury**: gels ptk
- **myopia**: gels ptk

DILATION (See Pupils - dilated)

DISCHARGES (= mucus; pus): *Acon* b7a.de *Agar* k* alum k* alumn k2 am-c ant-c ant-t hr1* *Apis* k* aran-sc vh1 arg-met k2 *Arg-n* ars k* arum-t k2 *Aur* k* aur-ar k2 aur-s k2 bar-m bell-p sp1 bism *Bry* *Cadm-s* **Calc** k* **Calc-s** calc-sil k2 canth k2 carb-v k* *Carbn-s* **Caust** *Cham* *Chel* *Chin* *Chlor* cist k2 cit-ac rly4• clem *Con* dig k* dream-p sdj1• dulc ery-a euph k* *Euphr* k* *Ferr* ferr-ar ferr-i k2 ferr-p flav jl2 *Graph* k* haliae-lc srj5• *Hep* k* *Hydr* ign b7.de* iod k2 *Ip* k* kali-ar kali-bi k* *Kali-c* k* *Kali-i* kali-m k2* kali-p kali-s *Kreos* lach lachn lact led b7a.de* *Lith-c* *Lyc* k* m-ambo b7.de mag-c mag-m mang-p rly4• med k2 meny b7.de* **Merc** k* merc-ns mez mill *Nat-ar* nat-c k* *Nat-m* nat-pyru rly4• nat-s nat-sil fd3.de• nit-ac k* *Nux-v* par b7.de* petr petr-ra shn4• ph-ac phos k* phys pic-ac pieri-b mlk9.de plb positr nl2• pot-e rly4• psor k2 **Puls** k* rhod b4.de* rhus-t rumx k2 ruta fd4.de *Sanic* seneg k* sep k* *Sil* k* spig h1 spong fd4.de staph stict stram *Sulph* k* **Tell** *Thuj* k* tritic-vg fd5.de vanil fd5.de

- **right** eye: lac-loxod-a hm2• musca-d szs1 propr sa3• [tax jsj7]
- **morning**: aids nl2• alum-sil k2 arg-n ars bamb-a stb2.de• cinnb dulc fd4.de kali-bi k* lac-loxod-a hm2• mag-c plb k* pot-e rly4• rad-br sze8• ruta fd4.de sang hr1 sel rsj9• sep sil spong fd4.de staph k* *Sulph* tarax h1 tritic-vg fd5.de vanil fd5.de
  - • **waking**; on: samb bat1•
- **evening**: brucel sa3• kali-p phos h2
- **night**: alum atra-r skp7*• positr nl2•
- **abundant** (See copious)
- **acrid**: am-c ars k* ars-i ars-s-f k2 arum-t bro1 bell-p sp1 calc canth k2 *Carbn-s* *Cham* coloc k* *Euphr* k* fl-ac *Graph* *Hep* iod k2 kali-ar k* kola stb3• kreos k2 merc k* merc-c bro1 nit-ac psor bro1 rhus-t bro1 staph a1 *Sulph*
  - • **water**: **Clem** k*
- **bland**: all-c k2* euph tl1 puls mtf33
  - • **accompanied** by | **Nose**; excoriated discharge of (See NOSE - Discharge - excoriating - accompanied - eyes)
  - • **coryza**; during (See NOSE - Coryza - accompanied - eyes - discharge)
- **bloody**: **Arn** bg2 ars ars-s-f k2 asaf *Bell* bg2 bry k2 *Calc* b4a.de* canth k2 carb-v *Carbn-s* *Caust* cham k* clem b4a.de *Crot-h* bg2 *Euphr* b7.de* *Hep* *Kali-c* kreos lach k* lyc *Merc* mez nat-m **Nux-v** b7.de* petr ph-ac phos k* *Puls* rhus-t ruta b7.de* seneg bg2 sep *Sil* **Sul-ac** bg2 sulph thuj
  - • **watery**: canth tl1
    - ⁝ **children**; in: | **newborns**: cham ptk1*
- **burning**: verb c1
- **copious**: *Arg-n* br1 atra-r skp7*• euphr k2* kali-i k2 puls mtf33 rhus-t k2 verb c1
- **egg** white; like: nat-m mtf33
- **excoriating** (See acrid)
- **fetid**: psor k2
- **frothy** | **Lids**: berb bg2
- **gray**: arg-met k2
- **green**: calc-sil k2 kali-i k2* kali-m k2 kali-s k2 merc k2 nat-s k2 psor k2 puls mrr1
- **hanging** over eyes which must be wiped away; sensation of discharge: croc *Puls*
- **mucus** (See Discharges)
- **offensive**: asaf k2 led h1 par bg2
- **opening** the eyes forcibly; when: ferr-i k2
- **purulent**: ail alum-p k2 alumn k* ant-t bro1 *Arg-met* **Arg-n** k* ars b4.de* aur-ar k2 bar-c h2 bell h1 bry b7.de* **Calc** k* *Calc-s* bro1 calen bro1 *Carb-v* *Carbn-s* *Caust* *Cham* *Chlor* cist k2 con b4a.de dig b4a.de dulc k2* ery-a euph k* *Euphr* b7a.de ferr bg2 ferr-i *Graph* *Grin* **Hep** k* kali-bi bg2 kali-c b4.de* *Kali-i* kola stb3• *Lach* *Led* k* **Lyc** *Lyss* mag-c k* mag-m mang b4.de* **Merc** k* *Merc-d* bro1 nat-c nat-m bro1 *Nat-p* bro1 nat-s bro1 nat-sil fd3.de• nit-ac *Nux-v* b7.de* par b7.de* petr k* ph-ac phos pic-ac bro1 plac rzf5• *Propr* sa3• psor k2 **Puls** k* *Rhus-t* k* *Ruta* b7.de* *Sep* k* sil bro1 sinus rly4• spong stann bro1 *Sulph* k* syph k2* tarax b7.de* tell zinc h2

- **purulent**:...
  - **daytime**: phos
  - **morning**: ars h2 bapt bar-c h2 cham h1 nat-sil fd3.de•
  - **Anterior** chamber: hep bro1 sil bro1
- **sensation** as if: arge-pl rwt5•
- **serous** | **Cornea**: apis bro1
- **sticky**: lac-loxod-a hm2• sel rsj9•
- **stringy**: agar bg2 am-br bg2 hydr bg2 kali-bi bg2* lyc bg2 petr-ra shn4•
- **suppressed** | **agg.**: chin bg2 euphr bg2 hep bg2 lyc bg2 puls bg2 sil bg2 sulph bg2
- **thick**: alum alum-sil k2 arg-n ars k2 atra-r bnm3• bapt hr1 calc-s k* calc-sil k2 *Chel* dulc k2 *Euphr* fuma-ac rly4• *Hep Hydr Kali-bi* kali-i k2 kali-s fd4.de kali-sil k2 *Lyc* medul-os-si rly4• nat-c k2 *Nat-m* k* petr-ra shn4• pic-ac k2 *Puls* k* sep *Sil* spong fd4.de sulph thuj zinc-p k2
- **thin**: acon k2 ars k2 bell-p sp1 canth k2 euphr mrr1 *Graph* sil k2
- **viscid**: hydr k2 kola stb3• oci-sa sk4• petr-ra shn4• polys sk4•
- **warm**: verb c1
- **watery**: acon k2 aids nl2• bell-p sp1 cortiso gse dulc k2 euphr k2 kali-s fd4.de nat-m mtf33
  - **cough** agg.; during: cassia-s ccrh1•
- **white**: alum ant-t k2 atra-r skp7*• hydr kola stb3• lachn nat-m mtf33 nat-pyru rly4• *Petr* petr-ra shn4• plb k* tung-met bdx1• [tax jsj7]
  - **milk**-white: atra-r skp7*• kali-chl kali-m k2
- **yellow**: *Agar* aids nl2• alum alum-p k2 alumn k2 *Arg-n* ars ars-s-f k2 atra-r bnm3• aur aur-ar k2 aur-s k2 bapt hr1 bar-ox-suc rly4• *Calc Calc-s* k* calc-sil k2 carb-v carbn-s caust cham k2 chel dream-p sdj1• dulc k2 *Euphr* hydr k2 hydrog srj2• *Kali-bi* kali-c kali-chl kali-m k2 kali-s kali-sil k2 kreos lac-loxod-a hm2• *Lyc Merc* nat-c k2 nat-p olib-sac wmh1 ozone sde2• podo fd3.de• psor k2 **Puls** k* *Rhus-t* hr1 sel rsj9• *Sep* **Sil** spong fd4.de *Sulph Thuj* tritic-vg fd5.de vanil fd5.de
- **Canthi**: agar b4a.de am-br vh1 ant-c bell berb *Bism* k* dig dulc fd4.de euph k* euphr h2 guaj h2 kali-bi lachn c1 nat-c nat-m k* nat-pyru rly4• *Nux-v* pic-ac psor ribo rly4• ruta fd4.de spong fd4.de zinc-p k2
  - **morning**: ant-c calc-p *Cham* ruta
  - **dry** discharge in: alum bg2 calc caust cham euphr grat *Hell* lyc bg2 nit-ac olib-sac wmh1 spong fd4.de viol-t
    - **morning**: lyc spong fd4.de
  - **greasy**: kreos bg2
  - **hard** discharge in: dig guaj *Hep Ip* k* kali-s fd4.de nux-v *Petr* ruta fd4.de sabad sil a1 vanil fd5.de
    - **forenoon**: coff
    - **night**: seneg
  - **pus**: aur b4a.de bry b7a.de *Calc* b4a.de cham k* cina b7.de* *Graph* k* *Kali-bi* k* kali-c k* kali-i led lyc b4a.de nat-c b4a.de nit-ac b4a.de **Nux-v** k* petr b4a.de *Ph-ac* phos b4a.de puls b7.de* ran-b sil b4a.de stann b4a.de staph b7.de* *Zinc* k*
    - **yellow**: mim-p skp7•
  - **Inner**: agar k* ant-c b7.de* apis b7a.de euphr b7a.de* hyos b7.de* kali-bi bg2 kali-s fd4.de mag-s nat-pyru rly4• nicc nux-v b7.de* petr hr1 phos **Puls** ruta b7.de* spong fd4.de staph *Stram* streptoc rly4• thuj h1 *Verat-v Zinc*
    - **morning**: bamb-a stb2.de• hell h1 kali-s fd4.de nicc phos **Puls** spong fd4.de staph zinc
    - **dry** discharge in: hell h1 kali-s fd4.de ruta fd4.de staph h1
    - **menses**; during: mag-c
    - **purulent**: euphr mrr1
  - **Outer**●: ant-c k* bar-c bry chin h1 dulc fd4.de *Euphr* b7a.de ip h1 lyc m-arct b7.de mez nux-v k* rhus-t ruta b7.de* sep
    - **morning**: nux-v rhus-t sep
    - **night**: bar-c *Lyc*
    - **hard** discharge in: euph *Hep Ip* nux-v sabad
    - **purulent**: euphr mrr1 nux-v
    - **sticky**: agar b4a.de *Nat-m* b4.de*
- **Eyelashes** | **mucus**: *Hep* b4a.de *Seneg* b4a.de
- **Lachrymal** sac, from: (*↗Lachrymation)* ars arum-t k* *Con* k* *Hep* k* iod *Merc* k* *Nat-m* k* **Petr** k* *Puls Sil* k* stann k* *Sulph* k*
- **Lids**:
  - **moisture**: led b7.de*

Discharges – Lids: ...

  - **mucus**: *Acon* b7a.de agar b4a.de *Apis* b7a.de cham b7a.de *Euphr* b7.de* ferr b7.de* graph b4a.de ign b7.de* *Nux-v* b7.de* *Plb* b7a.de *Puls* b7.de* rhus-t b7.de* *Sulph* b4a.de
  - **pus** | **dried** up: *Graph* b4a.de
- **Meibomian** glands: chel tl1

DISCOLORATION:

- **blue**: ferr-i k2 gaert fmm1• [am-br stj2]
  - **Canthi**: aur ham sars
    - **Inner**: aur b4.de* sars b4.de*
  - **Conjunctiva** (See sclera)
  - **Cornea**: *Euphr* b7a.de
    - **turbid**: *Calc* b4a.de *Hep* b4a.de
  - **Lids**: apis bg2 ars bg2 *Dig* k* dros k* *Kali-c* k* morph bro1 naja k* op bg2 phyt bg2 zinc k*
    - **Blood** vessels: *Ign* b7a.de
    - **Tarsi**: bad ptk1 bov ptk1 phyt ptk1
  - **Margins**: *Bad Bov* dig bro1 morph bro1 *Phyt* verat
  - **Sclera** or conjunctiva: ars h2* bell calc gk calc-p mrr carbn-o **Carc** fb* cupr sst3* med mrr plb stram tub bn* verat b7.de*
    - **children**; in: **Carc** mrr1* cupr mtf33 tub mtf33
- **brownish** | **Lids**: *Cina* b7a.de
- **earthy**:
  - **Canthi**: plb b7.de*
  - **Sclera**: plb b7.de*
- **gray** | **Cornea**: apis b7a.de *Calc* b4a.de cann-s b7a.de
- **gray-white** | **Cornea**: helo-s bnm14•
- **green**: canth k* cupr-act k*
  - **ring** | **Around** eye (See FACE - Discoloration - greenish - eyes)
  - **Cornea**: puls b7a.de
  - **Iris**: hydrog srj2•
- **pale**:
  - **Lids**: graph tl1
  - **Optic** disks: acetan bro1
- **pink**: euphr ptk1
- **red**: abrot absin k* acet-ac achy-a bnj1 **Acon** k* act-sp bg2 aesc k2* aeth **Agar** k* ail k* **All-c** k* allox tpw3* aloe k* alum k* alum-p k2 alum-sil k2 alumn k2 am-c am-caust a1 am-m b7a.de* ambr k* aml-ns k* anac androc srj1• ang b7.de* *Ant-c* k* ant-t b7.de* **Apis** k* apoc arg-met b7.de* **Arg-n** k* *Arn* k* **Ars** k* ars-h ars-i arund-d a1 *Asaf* asar k* astac a1 aster atra-r skp7• atro a1 *Aur* k* aur-ar k2 aur-i k2 aur-m aur-s k2 bad bapt bg2* *Bar-c* k* bar-i k2 **Bar-m** bar-s k2 **Bell** k* *Berb* bism k* bism-sn a1 blum-o bnj1 bond a1 bov k* brom bg bros-gau mrc1 bry k* bufo buth-a sp1 calad *Calc* k* calc-i k2 *Calc-p Calc-s* calc-sil k2 camph k* **Cann-i** k* canth b7a.de* *Caps* k* *Carb-an* carb-v bg carbn-h *Carbn-s* card-m cassia-s ccrh1• *Caust* k* cere-b a1 cham k* *Chel* k* *Chin* k* chinin-s chlf a1 *Chlol* k* chord-umb rly4• *Cimic Cinnb* hr1* *Clem* k* cob coff k* *Colch* coloc con k* cop cot a1 croc bg *Crot-h Crot-t* k* *Cupr* k* cycl k* der desm-g bnj1 *Dig* k* dor dros dulc bro1* elaps **Euphr** k* fago k* *Ferr* k* *Ferr-ar* ferr-i *Ferr-p* galeoc-c-h gms1• gels k2* ger-i rly4• gins a1 **Glon** k* gran *Graph* k* grin a1 haem a1 *Ham* k* *Hell Hep* k* hir rsj4• hist sp1 hura hydro-v a1 hygroph-s bnj1 *Hyos* k* *Ign* k* iod *Ip* k* *Iris* jab jug-c *Kali-ar* k* *Kali-bi* k* *Kali-br* k* *Kali-c* k* kali-chl *Kali-i* k* kali-ox a1 *Kali-p* **Kali-s** kali-sil k2 ketogl-ac rly4• kreos k* lac-del hm2• lac-lup hm2• *Lach* k* lact laur b7a.de* led k* *Lith-c* k* lol a1 *Lyc* k* lyss m-arct b7.de *Mag-c* k* *Mag-m* k* manc mand rsj7• mang k* med c1 *Meph* k* merc k* *Merc-c* k* merc-cy a1 merc-d a1 merc-i-r ptk1 *Merl Mez* mill k2 mim-p rsj8• morph a1* *Mur-ac* myric a1 *Nat-ar* **Nat-m** k* nat-p *Nat-s* k* nicc *Nit-ac* k* **Nux-v** k* oena olnd *Op* k* osm k* ozone sde2• paeon k* parth vml3• peti a1 petr k2 petr-ra shn4• ph-ac phos k* phyt pic-ac k* pip-m a1 pitu-a vml2• pitu-gl skp7• *Plb* k* podo k* positr nl2• prot jl2 *Psor* puls k* rad-br ptk1 ran-s b7.de* *Rhus-t* k* rhus-v ric a1 ros-d wla1 *Ruta* k* sabin a1 sacch-a fd2.de• salin a1 santin sapin a1 sec k* *Seneg* k* *Sep* k* *Sil* k* sol-ni *Spig* k* *Spong* k* stann b4.de* *Staph* k* **Stram** k* stront-c b4.de* stry k* sul-ac k* sul-i k2 sulfon bro1 **Sulph** k* syph tab k* tarent k* ter *Teucr* k* thal a1 thal-xyz srj8• *Thuj* k* trios rsj11• tritic-vg fd5.de upa a1 urol-h rwt• *Vac* jl2 vanil fd5.de *Verat* k* verat-v bro1 verin a1 vesp k* viol-o b7.de* vip vip-t j2 visc a1 xan xanth zinc k* ziz k*
  - **right**: cassia-s ccrh1• petr-ra shn4•
  - **left**: atra-r skp7• cassia-s cdd7*• elaps hr1 luf-op rsj5• psil ft1

- **daytime**: *Sulph*
- **morning**: acon bg1 act-sp bg1 am-br k* apoc bry caps dios dulc fd4.de eug bg1 fago galeoc-c-h gms1• ham fd3.de• *Mez* nat-ar raph *Rhus-t* ruta fd4.de sang sep spig h1 **Sulph** tritic-vg fd5.de urol-h rwt• valer
  - **9-15 h**: meny
- **afternoon**: pitu-gl skp7•
- **evening**: apoc atra-r skp7• dig flav jl2 *Hyos* kali-chl lyc spong fd4.de urol-h rwt•
- **night**:
  - **midnight**:
    - **after** | **4** h: hyper
- **accompanied** by:
  - **hiccough** (See STOMACH - Hiccough - accompanied - eyes)
  - **pain**; burning (See Pain - burning - accompanied - red)
  - **palpitations**: iber c1
  - **protrusion** (See Protrusion - accompanied - red)
  - **styes** (See Styes - accompanied - red)
  - **vision**; yellow: aloe br1*
  - **vomiting** (See STOMACH - Vomiting - accompanied - eyes)
  - **Head**; complaints of (See HEAD - Complaints - accompanied - eyes - red)
  - **Prostate** gland; enlargement of (See PROSTATE - Swelling - accompanied - eyes)
- **air**; in open:
  - **agg.**: cassia-s ccrh1•
  - **amel.**: **Arg-n**
- **blood**-red: ars bg2 thuj bg2
- **bluish**: plb ptk1
- **cold** applications | **amel.**: apis mrr1 phos k2
- **congestive**: stram bg2
- **coryza**; during: verat b7.de*
- **cough** agg.; during: cassia-s ccrh1•
- **dark** red: *Acon* b7a.de
  - **Canthi**: rhus-t ptk1
- **eating**; while: sulph h2
- **fever**; during: cassia-s ccrh1• *Hyos* b7.de*
- **headache**:
  - **before**: phos sulph
  - **during**: (↗*migraine - during*) arg-met h1 bamb-a stb2.de• bell carb-an hr1 *Cimic* gels hr1 glon k* *Kali-br* sne kola stb3• kreos sne lach hr1 mez hr1 ozone sde2• sang hr1 spig h1* spong fd4.de sulph
- **inflamed**; as if: *Acon* bro1 ant-c bro1 arg-n bro1 ars bro1 aur-m bro1 *Bell* bro1 caust bro1 clem bro1 *Euphr* bro1 ferr-p bro1 hep bro1 indol bro1 ip bro1 jac-c bro1 lyc bro1 merc bro1 nat-m bro1 rhus-t bro1 sangin-n bro1
- **injuries**; after: **Acon** *Arn Euphr Hep Sil*
- **megrim** (See migraine)
- **menses** | **before** | **agg.**: dros k2 glon
  - **during** | **agg.**: acon bell cham dros k2 euphr glon hep ign merc nux-v puls zinc
- **migraine** | **during**: (↗*headache - during*) *Kali-br* hr1 *Spig* hr1
- **neuralgia**, with: aml-ns hr1 chel hr1 mag-p hr1 nat-m hr1
- **pale** red | **Canthi**: apis ptk1
- **raw** beef; like: arg-n bro1* crot-t bro1 kali-i ptk1 lyc hr1*
- **reading** agg.: ammc **Arg-n** k* lact *Merl* *Nat-m* k* pitu-gl skp7• rad-br ptk1 ruta ptk1
- **scarlet**: arg-n bg2
- **sewing**●: **Arg-n** k* **NAT-M** k ●* rad-br ptk1 *Ruta* k*
- **sexual** excesses; after: **Staph** k*
- **spot**: arg-n mrr1 kali-bi bg2
  - **Sclera**: puls bg2
- **streaks**: acon bg2 bell bg2 kali-bi bg2 nux-v bg2 sars bg2 spig bg2

- **red**: ...

○ • **Canthi**: agar k* *Apis* b7a.de **Arg-n** k* ars b4.de* *Asar* b7a.de *Aur* aur-s c1 bell k* bism b7.de* *Borx* bov k* brach bry k* *Calc-s* cinnb bro1 crot-h gran graph bro1 ina-i mlk9.de iris kali-bi kali-n *Mag-c* *Nat-m* nux-v *Puls* b7a.de ruta fd4.de sil **Sulph** k* tab teucr k* tritic-vg fd5.de upa zinc k*
  - **Inner**: acon bg2 aids nl2• alum bg2 arg-n k* aur k* calc-p calc-sil k2 chel *Graph* mag-c k* nat-ar ph-ac b4a.de podo rhus-t k* ruta fd4.de tritic-vg fd5.de valer b7.de*
  - **Outer**: **Ant-c** carbn-s nux-v k* positr nl2• ran-b k* *Sulph* k*
    - **right**: propr sa3•
- **Carunculae**: kali-c
- **Conjunctiva**: arg-n bg2 *Bell* b4a.de *Calc* b4a.de parathyr jl2 tub jl2 v-a-b jl2 vac jl2 zinc b4a.de
- **Cornea**: helo-s bnm14•
  - **hot**: glon tl1 sanic tl1
  - **pale** red margin around: con b4a.de
  - **stripes**; red: arg-n bg2 sars b4.de* sulph b4a.de
  - **Margin**: *Puls* b7a.de
- **Eyeballs**: atra-r bnm3•
  - **left**: atra-r bnm3•
  - **evening**: atra-r bnm3•
- **Lids**: *Acon* k* agar bro1 am-br bro1 **Ant-c** k* antip vh1 **Apis** k* *Arg-met* k* **Arg-n** k* *Ars* k* ars-i ars-s-f k2 *Aur* k* aur-ar k2 *Aur-m* aur-s k2 bamb-a stb2.de• bar-c bar-i k2 bar-m *Bell* k* berb bism b7.de* bomb-chr a1 *Bry* k* *Calc* k* calc-i k2 calc-sil k2 cann-s k* canth b7a.de carb-v b4.de* *Carbn-s Caust* k* cham k* chel *Chinin-s* cinnb k* clem bro1 *Cocc* colch k* com *Crot-t* cupr *Dig* b4a.de* elaps **Euphr** k* *Ferr* k* *Ferr-ar* ferr-i ferr-p **Gels** gink-b sbd1• granit-m es1• *Graph* k* hell b7.de* *Hep* k* iod k* irid-met srj5• *Kali-ar* kali-bi k* *Kali-c* **Kali-i** kola stb3• kreos b7a.de* *Lac-d* lac-leo hrn2• lat-m bnm6• **Lyc** k* mag-m h2 **Merc** k* *Merc-c* bro1 *Merc-i-f* *Mur-ac* k* myric ptk1 *Nat-m* k* nicc nux-v k* *Olnd* b7a.de par b7.de* **Petr** k* ph-ac bg2 plb k* podo psor k* *Puls* k* ran-b c1 rhod k* *Rhus-t* k* rhus-v ruta tl1* sabad b7.de* sanic *Sep* k* sil stram b7.de* sul-i k2 *Sulph* k* syph jl2 **Tell** teucr tritic-vg fd5.de tub tl1 *Tub-a* jl2 upa vac jl2 vinc zinc zinc-p k2
  - **right**: caust b4.de* phos b4.de*
  - **morning**: bry kali-s fd4.de **Sulph**
  - **noon**: bamb-a stb2.de•
  - **night**: cench k2 **Merc**
  - **bluish** red: ars bg2 ferr-i k2 phyt bg2
  - **coryza**; during: sabad b7.de*
  - **menses**; before: aur
  - **spots**: berb camph b7.de* sel rsj9•
  - **styes** are going to be formed; as if: psor jl2
  - **Lower**: arg-met b7.de* bry b7.de* cham bg2 chel bg2 *Dig* b4.de* glon ptk1 indg bg2 lach b7.de* nat-m b4.de* ph-ac b4.de* puls b7a.de* ven-m rsj12•
    - **spots**: sil b4.de*
  - **Margins** of: *Acon* bg2 agar bg2* am-br bro1 *Ant-c* bro1 apis bro1 *Arg-met* k* *Arg-n* k* **Ars** k* aster bell bg2* *Borx* *Bufo* calc k* carb-v h2 **Carbn-s** cench k2 *Chel* k* cinnb bro1 clem bro1 coff k* *Colch* k* *Coloc* *Con* dig br1* **Eup-per** *Euph* bg2 **Euphr** k* ferr bg2 *Ferr-m* *Gels* **Graph** k* hep bro1 hura hydr k2 *Ip* irid-met srj5• *Kali-bi* k* *Kali-c* k* kali-i bg2 kreos *Lil-t* lyc bro1 *Med* merc bro1* *Merc-c* k* *Nat-m* k* nux-m k* nux-v ozone sde2• par k* *Ph-ac* *Puls* k* *Rhus-t* k* sabad k* sanic sep ptk1 stram k* **Sulph** k* syph tritic-vg fd5.de upa valer b7a.de zinc zinc-p k2
  - **Upper**: *Acon* b7a.de ang bg2 arg-met b7.de cassia-s ccrh1• hep b4.de* merc b4.de* teucr b7.de*
- **Orbit** | **left**: arum-t mrr1
- **Sclera**: hedy a1*
  - **stripes**; red: nux-v b7.de*
- **Veins**: *Acon* k* aesc k2* aeth all-c *Alumn Ambr Ant-t Apis* k* *Arg-n* k* *Ars* ars-s-f k2 aur-m k2 bar-m *Bell* k* blum-o bnj1 borra-o oss1• *Calc-p* calc-sil k2 *Camph Carbn-s Caust Clem* con *Crot-t* dig c1 elaps *Euphr* k* ferr-ar k2 *Graph Hep* ign irid-met srj5• kali-ar *Kali-bi* kali-c *Kali-i Kali-s* kali-sil k2 *Lach Lyc* mag-c h2 mag-m h2 meph *Merc Merc-c* **Nat-ar Nat-m** nat-p onos ph-ac k* phos *Sang* sil spig k* *Stram Sulph* ter vanil fd5.de

- **smoky**:

○ • **Cornea**: apis b7a.de
- **Pupils** | **Background** of: **Apis** b7a.de **Chin** b7a.de

- **yellow**: acon k* agar k* am-caust a1 *Ambr* b7.de* anan ant-c b7.de* *Ars* k* ars-h k* ars-i k* astac k* *Aur* b4a.de *Aur-m-n* sne bell b4.de* *Bry* b7.de* calc-s *Canth* k* carb-an *Carb-v* b4a.de *Card-m* k* caust *Cham* k* chel k* **Chin** k* *Chion* clem k* cocc k* con k* corn k* **Crot-h** k* cupr-act cur *Dig* k* *Dios* elat hr1 *Eup-per* k* *Ferr* k* ferr-ar k* ferr-i k* ferr-p k* *Gels* k* graph guat sp1 *Hep* k* hip-ac sp1 *Hydr* k* hygroph-s bnj1 ign b7.de* *Iod* k* *Ip* kali-ar k* *Kali-bi* k* **Lach** k* loxo-recl knl4• lyc k* *Mag-m* k* malar jl2 **Merc** bg2 myric k* nat-c nat-p k* *Nat-s* k* nit-ac k* **Nux-v** k* op k* ph-ac k* phel *Phos* k* phyt bg2* pic-ac k* *Plb* k* *Podo* k* psor al2 puls b7.de* querc-r c1 rhus-t b7.de* sabad b7a.de *Sang* k* sec k* **Sep** k* *Sil* b4a.de spig bg* stram bg2 sul-i k2 sulph b4.de* *Verat* k* vip k*
  - **perspiration**; during: ars b4.de*
  - **rings**; yellow brown | **Around** the eyes: nit-ac
  - **spot** on eye: agar k* ph-ac k* spig gk
  - ○ **Conjunctiva**: glycyr-g cte1• loxo-lae bnm12• oscilloc jl2
    - ⁝ **spots**: ph-ac ptk1
  - **Lower** part; of: nux-v k*
  - **Sclera**: brass bro1 cham bro1 chel bro1* *Chin* bro1 crot-h bro1* dig bro1 euon-a bro1 iod bro1 kali-bi tl1 lach bro1 merc bro1 myric bro1 nat-p bro1 nat-s bro1 physala-p bnm7• plb bro1 *Podo* bro1 sep bro1

○ - **Around** eyes (See FACE - Discoloration - bluish - eyes - around)
- **Iris**: *Aur* coloc *Euphr* hydrog srj2• kali-i merc-i-f *Nat-m* spig syph
  - **allergic**: nat-m mrr1
  - **blue**: carc mlr1•
  - **brown**: carc mlr1•
  - **green**: hydrog srj2• rhus-t hr1

DISTENDED feeling: acon bg2 ant-t b7.de* asar b7.de* **Bell** bg2 bism b7.de* bov bg2 **Bry** bg2 calc-p bg2 cann-xyz bg2 caust b4.de* con b4a.de gels bg2 guaj b4.de* hep b4.de* hyos b7.de* mag-c b4a.de merc bg2 mez b4a.de nat-c b4.de* *Nat-m* bg2 **Nux-v** bg2 op b7a.de* par b7.de* ph-ac b4a.de* phyt bg2 plb b7.de* prun bg2 rhus-t bg2 seneg b4.de* sep b4a.de **Spig** b7.de* staph bg2 sulph b4a.de tarax bg2 thuj b4.de* zinc bg2

DISTORTED: *Acon* k* *Agar* alco a1 ang b7.de* *Arn* b7.de* *Ars* k* **Bell** k* bry b7.de* cadm-s calc-p *Camph* k* canth k* carb-ac carb-v k* *Cham* k* *Chel* *Chin* choc srj3• *Cic* k* cocc k* colch k* con conin a1 crot-h *Cupr* k* dig k* hell b7.de* *Hydr-ac* k* *Hyos* k* kali-s k* *Lach* k* *Laur* k* *Merc* merc-c b4a.de *Mosch* k* olnd k* op k* petr k* ph-ac k* *Plat* k* plb k* puls k* ran-s k* santin sec k* *Sil* k* spig b7.de* *Stann* b4.de* *Stram* k* sul-ac k* *Sulph* k* tarent k* *Thuj* b4a.de verat k* verat-v
- **evening**: bry k* caust k*
- **accompanied** by | **pneumonia**: chel hr1 chol hr1
- **convulsions**; during: sil ptk1
- **sleep** agg.; during: aeth k* chin cocc cupr k* hyper k* ph-ac h2

○ - **Iris**: apis *Merc* k* merc-i-f hr1 rhus-t k*
  - **ragged**: thuj mtf33
- **Lids**:
  - **spasmodic**: cham b7.de* rheum b7.de* *Ruta* b7.de* *Stram* b7.de*
  - ○ **Lower**: seneg b4.de*

DRAWING together of the eyes; sensation of (See Drawn together - sensation)

DRAWN BACKWARD; eyes are: | **sensation** as if eyes were drawn backward (See Pain - drawing - backward)

DRAWN DOWNWARDS: (↗*Turned - downward)*

○ - **Lids**; upper: apis bg2 *Cann-s* b7a.de carb-an b4.de* *Cham* b7a.de *Op* b7.de* *Sep* b4.de* *Spig* b7.de* squil b7.de* *Sulph* b4a.de *Zinc* b4a.de
  - **right**: alum b4a.de caust b4.de*
  - **left**: chel b7.de*

DRAWN INWARD: | **Lids**: ruta bg2

DRAWN OUTWARD: aloe bg2 crot-c bg2 lach bg2 med bg2

○ - **Lids**: croc b7.de* ip b7.de*

DRAWN TOGETHER; eyes are: *Merc* a1
- **pain**; from: *Coloc* a1 lyc a1 *Sep* a1 *Sulph* a1
- **sensation** as if eyes were drawn together: *Coloc* bg2 grat bg2* lach bg3* lyc bg2* merc bg2* **Nat-m** k* op bg2* sep k* *Sulph* k* zinc bg2*

DRAWN UPWARDS:

○ - **Eyebrows** and lids are lachn c1
- **Lids**: acon bg2 lach bg2 plb bg2 rhus-t bg2

DROOPING lids (See Paralysis - lids)

DROWSINESS (See Sleepy)

DRYNESS: (↗*Xerophthalmia)* **Acon** k* agar k* *Aids* nl2• allox tpw4 aln vva1• **Alum** k* alum-p k2 alum-sil k2 ammc a1* androc srj1• ang c1 anh sp1 arg-met *Arg-n* arge-pl rwt5• arizon-l nl2• *Arn* **Ars** k* ars-s-f k2 *Asaf* k* *Asar* k* aur-m k* bamb-a stb2.de• bar-c k* bar-s k2 bart a1 **Bell** k* berb k* bit-ar wht1• bry k* calc bg2 carb-v k* carc sst• cardios-h rly4• *Caust* k* cedr k* *Cham* k* chin chlam-tr bcx2• choc srj3• chord-umb rly4• chr-ac a1 cina *Clem* k* cocc k* colch a1 cop cortiso tpw7* *Croc* k* crot-h *Cycl* k* cystein-l rly4• daph a1 dioxi rbp6 dros dulc a1 *Elaps* euph a1 *Euphr* k* fago k* franz a1 gamb k* gels a1 gink-b sbd1• glon k2* *Graph* k* grat k* haliae-lc srj5• ham fd3.de• hep hist sp1* ign bg* irid-met srj5• kali-ar kali-bi k* kali-c k* kali-n k* kali-p kali-s kali-sil k2 ketogl-ac rly4• kola stb3• lac-c mtf11 lac-d k2 lac-e hrn2• lach k* lachn k* laur k* lec lepr mtf11 limest-b es1• lith-c k* *Luf-op* rsj5• luna kg1• **Lyc** k* *Mag-c* k* mag-m k* manc k* *Mang* k* *Med* k* medul-os-si rly4• melal-alt gya4 *Meny* vh merc k* merc-c k* *Merl* k* **Mez** k* moni rfm1• musca-d szs1 nat-ar k* nat-c k* nat-m k* nat-ox rly4• nat-p *Nat-s* k* neon srj5• nicc nicotam rly4• **Nux-m** k* *Nux-v* k* *Olib-sac* wmh1 **Op** k* orot-ac rly4• paeon k* pall pant-ac rly4• *Petr* petr-ra shn4• phel phos k* pic-ac plan a1 plb k* plut-n srj7• podo c1 pot-e rly4• **Puls** k* *Rhod* k* *Rhus-t* k* rumx ruta fd4.de sacch sst1• sal-fr sle1• *Sang* k* sanic k* sars *Seneg* k* *Sep* k* sil k* sinus rly4• spig k* spong fd4.de *Staph* k* stict bro1 suis-em rly4• suis-pan rly4• **Sulph** k* tep a1 tere-la rly4• thuj k* tritic-vg fd5.de **Verat** k* verat-v hr1 *Viol-o* b7a.de **Zinc** k* zinc-p k2 [buteo-j sej6 spect dfg1]
- **morning**: acon arge-pl rwt5• berb *Caust* k* chord-umb rly4• dioxi rbp6 graph k* lachn c1* (non:lyc kl) mag-c k* mag-m h2 *Nux-v* *Puls* *Sil* k* spong fd4.de tritic-vg fd5.de **Zinc** k*
  - **lachrymation**; after: **Sulph**
  - **waking**; on: arg-n k* elaps lyc kl melal-alt gya4 phos k* plut-n srj7• sanic spong fd4.de *Staph* k*
- **afternoon**: caust h2 chlam-tr bcx2• *Nat-s*
  - **sleep**; after: mag-m h2
- **evening**: aln vva1• *Alum* k* *Caust* k* cina coloc k* dioxi rbp6 graph h2 *Lyc* mang nat-s nicc pall k* *Puls* sang k* sep sil *Staph* k* suis-pan rly4• tritic-vg fd5.de **Zinc** k*
  - **going** to bed; on: op
  - **looking** at fire: mag-m h2
- **night**: ham fd3.de• lyc sanic bg1 spig h1 sulph h2*
- **exertion** of eyes; as from: lith-c ptk1
- **fever**; during: *Spig* b7.de*
- **light**; from artificial: ars pic-ac
- **looking** at bright light: **Mang** k*
- **menses**; during: mag-c k*
- **reading** agg.: aur cina graph k* hyos nat-m phos h2
- **sensation** of: asaf b7.de* asar b7.de* bar-c b4a.de* caust b4a.de* chin b7.de* cina b7.de* *Croc* b7.de* graph bg2 **Nux-m** b7.de* sil b4a.de verat b7.de* *Viol-o* b7a.de *Zinc-s* bg2
  - **accompanied** by | **lachrymation**: staph ptk1*
- **waking**; on: arg-met chord-umb rly4• elaps phos puls sanic staph *Verat*
- **warm** room agg.: **PULS** k ● **Sulph** k ●

○ - **Canthi**: acon-l a1 *Alum* k* arg-met asar h1 berb k* nat-m k* **Nux-v** k* thiam rly4• *Thuj* k*
  - **evening**: nat-m k*
  - ○ **Inner**: alum bg2 ang b7a.de des-ac rbp6 *Nux-v* b7.de* rhus-t b7.de*
    - ⁝ **right**: *Alum* b4.de* euph b4a.de thiam rly4•
    - ⁝ **morning**: nux-v a
  - **Outer**: thuj h1
    - ⁝ **left**: thuj b4.de*
- **Chiasma**: anh sp1
- **Conjunctiva**: hist sp1
- **Inner**: anh sp1
- **Lachrymal** duct:
  - **right**: sel rsj9•
    - ⁝ **followed** by | **left**: sel rsj9•

Eye

- **Lids**: *Acon* b7.de* alum b4.de* am-c vh1 ang b7.de* anh sp1 arn b7.de* ars b4.de* *Asaf* bg2 asar h1 *Bar-c* b4a.de *Bell* bro1 bry b7.de* carb-v b4.de* cham b7.de* chin b7.de* cina b7.de* cocc b7.de* cortiso sp1 cycl b7.de* dulc c1 euph b4.de* euphr bg2* graph b4.de* ip b7.de* irid-met srj5• kali-bi bg2 lith-c bro1 m-ambo b7.de m-arct b7.de *M-aust* b7.de mag-m h2* mand rsj7• mang b4.de* nux-m b7.de* nux-v bro1 petr h2* puls b7.de* **Rhus-t** b7.de* sal-fr sle1• sars b4.de* seneg bro1 sep bro1 sil b4a.de *Staph* b7a.de sulph b4.de* verat b7.de* *Viol-o* b7a.de zinc h2*
  - **chill**; during: rhus-t b7.de*
  - **sensation** of: ign b7.de* laur b7a.de m-ambo b7.de m-arct b7.de m-aust b7a.de rhus-t b7.de* *Verat* b7.de*
  - O **Lower**: petr b4.de*
  - **Margins** of: *Acon* bro1 alum bro1 ars h2* *Bell* bro1 cham b7a.de* cortiso tpw7 euphr bg2 ferr-p bg2 *Graph* bro1 lith-c bro1 nux-v bro1 puls bro1 seneg bro1 sep bg2* sulph h2* thuj mtf33 zinc bro1
    - **sensation** of: pall c1
- **Orbits**: ignis-alc es2•
- **Papillae**: anh sp1
- **Sclera**: anh sp1

DULLNESS: abrot k* acet-ac bro1 acon k* aesc k* aeth **All-c** k* androc srj1• ang k* ant-c br1* **Ant-t** k* arg-n bg2 arn k* ars k* ars-s-f k2 asaf b7.de* asar k* asc-t c1 atro k* aur hr1 *Bapt* k* *Bar-c* b4.de* basil a1 bell k* berb k* bism bro1 bov k* bry k* bufo caj a1 calc k* *Calc-ar* calc-i k2 camph k* cann-s b7.de* carb-ac bg carb-an b4.de* *Carb-v* carbn-s caust b4.de* *Cedr* *Chel* k* chin k* *Chinin-s* *Chlor* cimic cina b7.de* clem b4.de* *Cocc* b7a.de coloc k* com k* con k* croc b7.de* cupr k* cycl k* cyt-l a1* daph diph bro1 *Dulc* b4a.de ery-a a1 fago a1 ferr k* ferr-ar k2 gels k* *Glon* graph b4.de* grat hell k2 hyos k* iod k* ip bro1 kali-bi k* *Kali-br* k* kali-c k* kali-i a1 kali-p *Kalm* kreos k* lach k* lepr mtf11 *Lyc* lycpr bro1 *Merc* k* merc-c k* mez k* mit a1 mosch k* myric a1 nat-c b4.de* *Nit-ac* k* nux-m a1 **Nux-v** k* *Oena* bro1 olnd b7a.de onos bro1 op k* ozone sde2• petr-ra shn4• ph-ac k* phos k* phyt bg2 plb k* podo pycnop-sa mrz1 rheum k* rhus-t k* rhus-v a1 rumx sabad b7.de sabin k* sang k* *Santin* bro1 sec bro1 seneg b4.de* sep bro1 spig k* spong k* squil k* stann k* *Staph* k* stram k* sul-ac sul-i k2 *Sulph* k* sumb a1 tab bro1 trif-p k13 valer k* verat k* zinc k* zinc-p k2 zinc-s [tax jsj7]
- **morning**: sep h2
- **exertion** agg.; after: ferr
- **menses**; during: mag-c h2
- **sexual** excesses: **Staph**
- O **Iris**: colch a1 ip a1 kali-bi k* kali-i k* sulph k* syph k*

DUST in the eyes; sensation of (See Pain - dust)

EATING:
- **after**:
  - **agg.**: ambr b7.de* croc b7.de* nux-v b7.de* ruta b7.de* valer b7.de* verat b7a.de
  - **amel.**: meny b7.de*

ECCHYMOSIS (= black eye): *Acon* k* aeth allox tpw3 am-c arg-n k* *Arn* b7.de* **Ars** *Bell* k* **Cact** k* calc bg2 cham k* *Chlol* k* *Con* *Crot-h* k* *Cupr-act* der a1 erig flor-p rsj3• *Glon* *Ham* k* hydrog srj2• irid-met srj5• kali-bi k* *Kali-chl* kreos lac-h htj1• *Lach* k* laur b7a.de **Led** k* loxo-recl knl4• **Lyc** k • lyss merc-c bg2 mill k2 mim-p rsj8• nat-p hr1 *Nux-v* k* olib-sac wmh1 *Phos* phys ptk1 plb k* positr nl2• ruta k* sal-fr sle1• sang hr1 sel rsj9• *Seneg* bg2 staph gk *Sul-ac* k* symph tl1 ter thuj ptk1 xan c1 [bell-p-sp dcm1 spect dfg1]
- **right**•: brucel sa3• *Con*
- **morning**: brucel sa3•
- **cough** agg.; during: *Arn* bell
- **debauchery**; after: nux-v hr
- O **Canthi**; inner: hydrog srj2•
- **Lids**: *Arn* k* led sol-t-ae a1
- **Sclera**: *Arn* bro1 bell bro1 cham bro1 ham bro1 lach bro1 *Led* bro1 nux-v bro1 seneg bro1

ECTROPION (See Eversion)

ELONGATION; sensation of: | **Lids**: alum bg2

EMBOLISM of arteria retina: *(↗GENERALS - Embolism)* aml-ns nta1 croc br1 op cp*

ENLARGED:
- **cough** agg.; during: chin vml
- O **Cornea**: calc-p bro1

Enlarged: ...
- **Lens**: colch k*
- **Retina**:
  - O **Blood** vessels:
    - **accompanied** by | **Optic** disks; hyperemia of (See Hyperemia - optic - accompanied - retina)
- **Veins**: *Acon* b7.de* aesc tl1 *Ambr* b7.de* *Ars* b4a.de* **Bell** b4a.de* dig ptk1 *Ign* bg2 *Kali-br* a1* lach bg2 **Merc** bg2 ph-ac b4a.de* spig b7.de* sulph bg2

ENLARGEMENT, sensation of: **Acon** k* agar bg2* alum bg2 alum-sil k2 ant-c **Arg-n** bg2* *Ars* *Aur* bg2 *Bell* bg2* ben-n *Bism* b7a.de bufo-s calad calc-p caps caust chel k* chlol k* chlor cimic k* colch coloc bg2* *Com* k* con *Daph* gels bg2 *Glon* bg2* *Guaj* bg* hyos k* irid-met srj5• kali-ar kola stb3• lach laur b7.de* luf-op rsj5• *Lyc* k* meli ptk1 *Mez* k* nat-ar k* **Nat-m** k* onos *Op* k* ox-ac bro1 **Par** k* ph-ac k* *Phos* k* *Plb* k* *Pulx* bg1* pycnop-sa mrz1 rhus-t k* ruta bg2* sanic bg2* sarr bro1 seneg k* **Spig** k* stram tril-p k*
- **right**: com bg2 phos bg2
- **right** feels larger than left: **Com** *Phos* vh*
- **left**: arg-n bg2* psil ft1*
- **morning**: nat-ar
- **evening**: am-br brucel sa3•
- **night**: chr-ac
  - **gaslight**; from: sulph
- **accompanied** by | **Head**; pain in (See HEAD - Pain - accompanied - eye - enlarged)
- **closing** eyes; when: kola stb3•

ENTROPION (See Inversion)

EPISTAXIS: | **amel.**: brom bg2

ERUPTIONS:
- **eczema**: *Bry* bg2 petr-ra shn4• sep bg2
  - O **Lids**: petr-ra shn4•
- **herpes** (See Herpes)
- **petechiae**: *Arn* b7a.de nux-v b7.de* ruta b7.de*
- **pustules**: *Coloc* bg2 kali-bi bg2 **Merc** bg2 *Sep* bg2 sulph bg2
- **suppressed** | **after**: *Ars* bg2 *Bell* bg2 **Bry** bg2 calc bg2 **Camph** bg2 *Carbn-o* bg2 cham bg2 *Graph* bg2 hep bg2 hyos bg2 *Lach* bg2 *Merc* bg2 nat-m bg2 nit-ac bg2 *Puls* bg2 rhus-t bg2 sel bg2 sep bg2 **Sulph** bg2 zinc bg2
- O **About** the eyes: agn k* ant-c ptk1 ant-t bro1 apis ptk1 arn *Ars* k* ars-s-f k2 aur-m-n wbt2• bar-c ptk1 calc k* carbn-s *Caust* k* clem k2 con k* crot-h crot-t bro1 euphr k* *Graph* guaj bro1 *Hep* k* ign k* kali-c *Kali-s* mag-m mtf33 med c1 **Merc** k* merc-c olnd k* petr k* psor al *Rhus-t* k* *Sel* sil k* spong k* **Staph** k* staphycoc rly4• suis-pan rly4• **Sulph** k* *Syph* thuj
  - **boils**: *Sil*
  - **crusts**: chrysar br1 **Merc** bg2 sep bg2 spong bg2
    - **pus** underneath; with: chrysar br1 mez br1
  - **dry**: *Chrysar* br1
  - **eczema**: kali-sil k2
  - **fine**: euphr k*
  - **herpes**: *(↗cornea - herpes; lids - herpes; Herpes)* alum bry *Caust* *Con* hep ptk1 kreos lach olnd spong sulph
  - **maculae** (= syphilitic): calc tl1
  - **pimples**: guaj ptk1 **Hep** mag-m k2 merc petr h2 staph h1
  - **rash**: sulph
  - **scabby** (See crusts)
  - **scaly**: *Chrysar* br1
  - **tetters**: sulph b4a.de
  - **vesicular**: clem k2
- **Above** the eyes: cystein-l rly4• ran-b
  - **left**: musca-d szs1 [bell-p-sp dcm1]
    - **boils**: nat-m ptk1
  - **bluish** black vesicles: ran-b
- **Below** eyes (See FACE - Eruptions - eyes - below)
- **Canthi**: lacer a1* lact k* syph k*
  - O **External**: ant-c c1 tax
  - **Inner** | **crusts**: clem lacer a1*

- **Cornea**:
  - **blisters**; small: am-m b7a.de *Aur* b4a.de bell b4a.de bufo br1 *Euphr* b7a.de **Rhus-t** b7a.de *Sulph* b4a.de syph jl2
  - **herpes**: *(↗about - herpes; lids - herpes; Herpes)* *Graph* *Hep* ign ran-b br1*
  - **pustules**: aeth c1 aethi-a bwa3 ant-c br1 arg-n bg2 calc tl1 kali-bi bg2 kali-m ptk1 merc bg2 syph jl2*
    - **accompanied** by | **measles** (See SKIN - Eruptions - measles - accompanied - cornea)
  - **vesicles**: *Agar* k* am-m b7a.de ars *Aur* k* bar-c k* bell b4.de* bufo k2 *Calc* k* cann-s k* *Euphr* k* *Hep* k* ip k* *Kali-bi* k* *Kali-chl* k* kali-m k2 *Merc* k* *Merc-c* k* *Nat-c* k* *Nat-m* k* *Nit-ac* k* petr k2 psor k* *Puls* k* ran-b k2* *Rhus-t* b7a.de sulph k*
- **Eyebrows** (See FACE - Eruptions - eyebrows)
- **Lids**: ant-t aur-m-n wbt2• bell bg2 *Bry* carbn-s crot-t k* *Euphr* bg2 **Graph** k* guaj **Hep** k* kali-bi bg2 kali-s kreos *Mag-m* med c1 merc bg2 *Mez* *Nat-m* nit-ac bg2 petr-ra shn4• physala-p bnm7• positr nl2• *Psor* puls rhus-t k* *Sars* *Seneg* bg2 sep bg2 sil *Spong* bg2 **Staph** bg2 sulph k* **Thuj** k*
  - **blotches**: aur bry calc ran-s staph thuj
  - **boils** (See pustules)
  - **burning**: carbn-s k2
  - **crusts**: ant-c *Arg-n* k* *Ars* bro1 *Aur* berb borx bro1* bufo calc k* dig *Dulc* b4a.de *Graph* k* hep kali-m bro1 lyc bro1 *Merc* b4a.de olib-sac wmh1 positr nl2• *Psor* *Sanic* seneg bro1 sep k* *Sulph*
    - **Margins** of lids: arg-n bro1 *Ars* bro1 borx bro1 calc bro1 *Dulc* hr1 *Graph* bro1 kali-m bro1 lyc bro1 seneg bro1 *Sep* bro1 tub jl2
      - **morning**: borra-o oss1• olib-sac wmh1
  - **eczema**: bac bro1* borx mtf11 **Bry** bg2 chrysar bro1 clem **Graph** k* *Hep* kreos ptk1 *Mez* k* *Petr* bro1 psor jl2 rhus-t bg2 sep bg2 sil mtf11 staph bro1* sulph bro1* tell k* **Thuj** tub cp v-a-b jl2
    - **crusts**; covered with: graph tl1
    - **moist**: graph tl1
    - **red**: *Graph* tl1 *Sulph* tl1
    - **scabby**: graph mtf11
    - **Margins** of lids: bac c1* chrysar bro1 *Graph* bro1 *Petr* bro1 staph bro1 sulph bro1 tell bro1 tub ptk1*
  - **herpes**: *(↗about - herpes; cornea - herpes; Herpes)* bry corn *Graph* kreos *Psor* *Rhus-t* *Sep* sulph tarent tub al*
  - **itching**: carbn-s k2 nit-ac h2 *Sars*
  - **pimples**: alum k* aur a1 bell bg2 bry a1 canth a1 chel guaj **Hep** k* *Lyc* k* merc-c mosch b7a.de* nat-m k* nit-ac h2* petr b4.de* positr nl2• rhus-t k* sel k* *Seneg* k* sil bg2 sulph b4.de* tarent a1 [bell-p-sp dcm1]
    - **Lower**: croc b7.de* nat-m b4.de* *Rhus-t* b7a.de seneg b4.de*
      - **left**: alum b4.de*
    - **Upper**: hep b4.de* nit-ac b4a.de
      - **right**: canth b7.de* lyc b4.de* mosch b7a.de
      - **left**: chel b7.de* mosch b7a.de
  - **pustules**: *Ant-c* k* arg-met calc-p a1 carbn-s hep bro1 hydrog srj2• jug-c vml3• lyc k* *Merc* puls k2 sep *Sil* sulfonam ks2 *Sulph* **Tell** upa a1
    - **yellow**: sulfa sp1
    - **Canthi**: bell bry calc kali-c *Lach* lyc nat-c petr puls sil
      - **Inner** | **left**: stann
    - **Margins**: ant-c bro1* *Arg-met* hep bro1 hydrog srj2• irid-met srj5• puls sep
    - **Under** lids | **right** lid: pall c1
  - **rash**: sulph
  - **recurrent**: physala-p bnm7•
  - **scales**: ars k* borx bro1 cob a1 plut-n srj7• *Psor* **Sep** k* tell bro1 thuj bro1
    - **Margins**; on: ars ptk1 *Graph* ptk1 mag-m ptk1 med ptk1 merc ptk1 *Sep* ptk1 thuj mtf33
  - **scaly** herpes: *Chel* kreos *Nat-m* **Psor** sep
    - **Margins**: *Apis* arg-n *Aur* aur-m *Dulc* **Graph** *Kali-chl* *Kali-s* med c1 *Merc* *Tub*
  - **scurfy**: arg-n bg2 ars bg2 berb bg2 *Graph* bg2 lyc b4.de* mag-m bg2 *Merc* b4.de* *Mez* nat-m bg2 **Petr** **Sep** k* tub
    - **Margins**: *Merc* b4a.de *Sep* b4a.de
  - **spots**: camph k* sil

Eruptions – Lids – spots: ...
    - **red**: camph kl orot-ac rly4• sil kl
  - **tetters**:
    - **dry**, burning, itching: *Bry*
    - **Lower**: *Rhus-t* b7a.de
    - **Upper**: *Bry* b7.de* *Kreos* b7a.de *Olnd* b7a.de rhus-t b7.de* sep b4.de* sulph b4a.de
  - **tubercles**: aur bry k* calc ran-s k* *Staph* k* *Thuj*
    - **Lower**: aur b4.de *Calc* b4.de sulph b4a.de thuj b4.de
  - **vesicles**: berb bomb-chr a1 canth bro1 *Cimic* *Crot-t* k* kali-bi bg2 kali-p fd1.de• kali-s fkr2.de lachn a1 m-arct b7.de mez k* *Nat-s* bro1 pall k* *Psor* rhus-t k* rhus-v k* *Sars* sel k* sep bro1 *Thuj* bro1
    - **yellow**: dulc *Psor* rhus-t k*
    - **Margins**; on: aur pall psor jl2 *Sel* urt-u
  - ○ **Lower**: croc bg2
  - **Upper** lids:
    - **right**: canth bg2
    - **left**: chel bg2
- **Orbital** arch; on:
  - **boils** (See pustules)
  - **pustules**: phos h2
- **Sclera**:
  - **pimples**: bar-c b4.de*
  - **vesicles**: am-m h2 rhus-t mtf11
    - **accompanied** by | **photophobia**: syph mtf11

ERYSIPELATOUS (See Inflammation - erysipelatous)

ESOPHORIA (See Paralysis - eyeballs - muscles - external)

EVERSION of lids: alum *Apis* k* **Arg-met** k* **Arg-n** k* ars bg2 bell k* benz-ac dgt1 *Calc* k* caps bg2* graph k* *Ham* hep *Lyc* k* *Merc* k* *Merc-c* mez **Nat-m** k •* *Nit-ac* k* petr c1 psor k* puls bg2 sil b4a.de* spig ptk1 *Staph* k* *Sulph* k* thiosin br1* zinc
- **eruptions**; after suppressed: mez
- **nitrate** of silver; after: nat-m
- ○ **Lower**: *Apis* k*

EXCORIATION:
- **painful**: aeth a1
- **sensation** of: alum b4.de* *Am* bg2 *Ars* bg2 bar-c b4a.de borx b4a.de clem b4.de* croc bg2 *Hep* b4a.de kali-bi bg2 mag-m b4.de* ran-b bg2 rhus-t bg2 stann b4a.de zinc b4a.de
- ○ **Canthi**: alum k* ant-c b7.de* apis k* **Ars** k* borx euph *Graph* bg2 hell b7.de* kali-c h2 nat-m h2 *Petr* bg2
  - ○ **Inner**: alum bg2
  - **Outer**: ant-c h2 borx h2 zinc h2
    - **left**: *Borx* b4a.de *Kali-c* b4.de* phos b4a.de
- **Lids**: am-c k2 apis k* **Arg-n** **Ars** ars-s-f k2 *Calc* graph *Hep* kreos k2 led b7.de* *Med* **Merc** *Merc-c* *Nat-m* *Sulph*
  - ○ **Lower**: sec b7a.de
  - **Margins** of: *Borx* b4a.de

EXCRESCENCES (See Condylomata)

EXERTION:
- **agg.**: apis b7a.de bar-c b4a.de *Bell* b4a.de *Carb-v* b4a.de cina b7a.de *Euphr* b7a.de ferr b7a.de mang b4a.de merc b4a.de nat-c bg2 phos bg2 plat b4a.de rheum b7a.de rhod b4a.de *Ruta* b7a.de seneg b4a.de staph b7a.de sul-ac b4a.de
- **amel.**: aur k*

EXERTION OF THE EYES agg.: *Bell* bg2 **Nat-m** bg2 ph-ac bg2 *Ruta* bg2

EXOPHORIA (See Paralysis - eyeballs - muscles - internal)

EXOPHTHALMOS (See Protrusion - exophthalmos)

EXOSTOSIS: | **Orbits**: merc bg2

EXPRESSIONLESS (See Dullness)

EYE GUM: *Agar* b4.de* alum k* am-c k* ant-c k* *Arg-n* k* bism k* borx b4a.de *Calc* k* caust k* cham b7.de chin b7.de coff bg1 con k* cystein-l rly4• dig b4.de* dros b7.de dulc fd4.de euph b4.de* euphr ptk1 graph k* guaj b4.de* hep b4.de* ip k* kali-bi ptk1 lyc b4.de nat-c b4.de nit-ac b4.de* nux-v k* ph-ac b4.de

Eye gum: ...
positr nl2• pot-e rly4• *Psor* k* rheum b7.de rhus-t b7.de* *Seneg* k* sil b4.de* spig b7.de spong fd4.de staph k* succ-ac rly4• sulph b4.de tarax b7.de thuj k* tritic-vg fd5.de

- **dry**: borx h2 cystein-l rly4• pot-e rly4•
- **sticky** (See Eye gum)

○ - **Canthi**●: aeth k* *Agar* k* alum bg2 *Am-c* b4a.de* *Ant-c* k* arg-n bg2 ars-s-f a1* bism k* borx b4a.de *Calc* k* caust b4.de* cham bg2 chin bg2 coff b7.de* con bg2 cystein-l rly4• dig b4.de* dros bg2 dulc fd4.de *Euph* k* euphr b7.de* graph b4.de* guaj b4.de* hep b4a.de* ip b7.de* kali-bi ptk1 lyc bg2* nat-ar nat-c h2* *Nat-m* k* nit-ac h2* nux-v k* ph-ac bg2 rheum bg2 rhus-t bg2 seneg b4.de* sil h2* spig bg2 spong fd4.de staph k* *Sulph* k* tarax bg2 thuj b4.de*

○ · **Inner**: agar b4.de* euphr b7.de* hell b7.de* par b7.de* rhus-t b7.de* sil b4.de* staph b7.de*
  ⁝ **right**: cystein-l rly4• nat-c b4.de*

  · **Outer**: ars h2* chin k* coloc b4a.de dulc fd4.de euph k* hep b4a.de ip b7.de* kali-c k* nat-ar nat-m h2* sabad b7.de* staph b7.de*

- **Eyelashes**: agar bg2 bar-ox-suc rly4• graph bg2 mag-m k2
- **Lids**; on: *Agar* k* am-c k* ars borx ptk1 dros b7.de* dulc fd4.de ferr b7.de* **Graph** k* kali-s fd4.de led b7.de* mag-m k2 psor ptk1 rheum b7.de* rhus-t b7.de* seneg k* staph b7.de* tarax b7.de* tritic-vg fd5.de
  · **morning**: alum amp rly4• berb con *Phos* seneg

FALLING:

- **out**; as if eyes were falling: acet-ac bg2 acon bg2 all-c bg2 alum bg2 brom bg2* carb-an bg2* cham bg2 coloc bg2* crot-c k* glon bg2* guaj ptk1 hell bg2* ign bg2* lap-la sde8.de• lyc bg2* nux-v bg2 *Puls* bg2* sep b4a.de* tril-p bg2*
  · **stooping** agg.: brom kr1 coloc kr1

○ - **Lids**; of: (↗*Paralysis - lids*) acon alco a1 *Alum* ant-t apis apoc k* arg-n hr1 arn k* *Bell* k* both tsm2 both-ax tsm2 bros-gau mrc1 bung-fa tsm2 cann-i k* carbn-s *Caust* cham chel chlol a1 con k* croc crot-c tsm2 crot-h dendr-pol tsm2 der a1 fago a1 **Gels** k* ger a1* graph helo-s rwt2• kali-br k* kali-p lach bg1 *Lyc* merc k* morph a1 naja nat-c nux-m k* nux-v *Op* k* oxyum-sc mcp1• ozone sde2• phel phos k2 sep k* sil spig spong stram a1 sul-ac k* sulph syph xxb tax k* thal-xyz srj8• vanil fd5.de viol-o *Viol-t* vip k* zinc k*
  · **morning** | **waking**; after: bell h1
  · **evening**: am-br k* am-m h2 bar-c h2 bov a1 vanil fd5.de
  · **coma**; with (See MIND - Coma - eyelids)
  · **headache**; during: *Sep*
  · **reading** agg.: mez h2
  · **sleepiness**; with: plat h2
  · **walking** in open air agg.: graph h2

FAT in eye; sensation of: calc h2* paraf bro1

FEVER; during: ail bg2 canth b7.de puls bg2

FIERY eyes: bell b4a.de canth b7.de* cham bg2 coloc b4a.de dulc bg2 hyos bg2 kreos bg2 sep bg2

FILMY: agath-a nl2• arge-pl rwt5• cann-s bg chel bg *Euphr* bg lyc k* nat-c h2 positr nl2• puls bg

FIRE agg.; looking into: acon bro1 canth bro1 glon bro1 *Merc* k* nat-s

FISSURE, Canthi (See Cracks - canthi)

FISTULA:

- **lachrymalis**: agar k* *Apis* k* *Arg-n* aur b4a.de *Aur-m* k* *Bell* bg2 *Brom* k* **Calc** k* calc-f mfj caust b4a.de* chel k* **Fl-ac** k* graph bg2* hecla mfj *Hep* k* kali-c b4a.de kreos bg2* *Lach* k* *Lyc* k* merc mfj merc-c bro1 mill k* nat-c k* *Nat-m* k* *Nit-ac* k* **Petr** k* phos bro1 phyt k* **Puls** k* ruta b7.de* **Sep** b4a.de **Sil** k* *Stann* k* staph b7.de* *Sulph* k* zinc b4a.de
  · **accompanied** by | **Face**; eruptions on: lach ptk1
- **pressure**; discharging pus on: nat-m ptk1 **Puls** k* *Sil* k* *Stann* k*
- **suppurating**: *Calc* k* **Puls**

○ - **Cornea**: *Sil*

FIXED look (See Staring)

FOCUS: | **difficult** to: luf-op rsj5• musca-d szs1 [bell-p-sp dcm1]

FOREIGN BODY; sensation of a (See Pain - foreign)

FRIGHTFUL look (See FACE - Expression - frightened)

FRINGE were falling over the eyes; sensation as if a: *Con* k*

FULLNESS, sensation of: *Aloe* bg2 apis k* *Arg-n* k* bell k* caust cub k* dulc euph ferr k2 gels ger k* *Guaj* gymno k* hep lac-ac k* lyc k* morph nat-m k* *Nux-m* k* nux-v hr1 olnd k* phys plb podo c1 rhus-t hr1 sapin a1 *Seneg* sep spig bg2 stach a1 sulph k* thuj verat k* verat-v a1

○ - **Lids**: gels c1

FUNGUS oculi (See Cancer - fungus)

GANGRENE: canth k2

GLASSY appearance: (↗*Brilliant*) acon k* am-m amyg a1 arn k* ars k* ars-s-f k2 *Bell* k* ben-n bry k* camph k* cedr chlor k* *Cic* cic-m a1 cina k2 coc-c k* cocc k* cod a1 com k* croc k* cupr k* daph elaps eup-per fago k* gels k2 *Glon* *Hell* hydr-ac k* hyos k* iod k* *Kali-ar* ketogl-ac rly4• *Lach* k* *Lyc* lyss merc merc-c b4a.de mosch k* nux-v a1 **Op** k* ox-ac k* petr k* **Ph-ac** k* *Plat* podo c1 psor puls sang sec k* sep k* spig k* *Stram* k* sulph tab *Thuj* b4a.de tritic-vg fd5.de ulm-c jsj8• verat-v a1 vesp k2

- **morning**: sep tritic-vg fd5.de
- **chill**; during: bell k* cocc
- **coma**; with (See MIND - Coma - eyes - glassy)
- **convulsions**; during: cina k2
- **fever**; during: bell k* bry glon iod k* op
- **perspiration**: bell cocc puls

GLAUCOMA: acon bro1* arec br1 arn mfj ars mfj* asaf mfj atro a1* aur bro1* *Bell* bro1* berb ptk1 bry hr1* calc mrr1 camph st1 caust bro1* cedr c2 cham mfj (non:cinnb br1) *Clem* cocain bro1 cocc k* colch st coloc c2* com bro1* con mfj cortico sp1 cortiso mtf11 croc br1* crot-h hr1* crot-t mfj diph-t-tpt jl2 esin c2* gels br1* germ-met srj5• *Glon* st grin c2 ham mfj ictod ks kali-c st1 kali-i st lac-c hr1* lach br1* lyc j5.de macro mfj mag-c bro1* merc mfj* mez bg* nat-pyru mtf11 nux-v bro1* op bro1 *Osm* bg2* par mtf11 *Phos* b4a.de* *Phys* kr1* pipe c2 plb ks* pot-a ks prun k* *Puls* b7a.de* rhod mtf11 *Rhus-t* hr1* sil j5.de *Spig* k* streptoc mtf11 sulph st* suprar bro1 syph k* tell *Ter* st thuj k* wies c2

- **accompanied** by:
  · **vision**; iridescent: osm ptk1
○ · **Eye**; pain in: acon bg2* mez k* *Phos* k* rhod st1
  · **Lids** | **heaviness** of: allox sp1 cob-n sp1 eys sp1
- **chronic**: saroth mtf11
- **glimmering**; with sensation of: hed sp1
- **injuries**; after: phys ptk1

GLAZED: cupr k* hyos k* ix bnm8• op k* ph-ac bro1 podo k* zinc bro1

GLISTENING (See Brilliant; Glassy)

GONORRHEA; AFTER SUPPRESSED: *Acon* bg2 *Clem* b4a.de merc bg2 nit-ac bg2 **Puls** bg2 sulph bg2 thuj bg2

GRANULAR:

○ - **Canthi**; outer: ant-t
- **Conjunctiva**: thuj bro1
- **Lids**: abr c2* acon bg alco a1 *Alum* k* ant-t *Apis* k* *Arg-n* k* **Ars** k* ars-s-f k2 *Aur* aur-ar k2 aur-m bg* bar-c bell *Borx* k* *Calc* bg* *Carbn-s* *Caust* cinnb bro1 dulc k2* *Euphr* k* fago k* **Graph** k* hep bro1 *Kali-bi* k* kali-m bro1 **Lyc** k* *Merc* bg *Merc-c* *Merc-i-f* *Merc-i-r* k* merl bro1 mez morg-p pte1*• *Nat-act* nat-ar c2* *Nat-m* nat-p k2 *Nat-s* k* *Nit-ac* bg *Nux-v* ol-j petr phos bg phyt k* psor k2 *Puls* k* rheum rhus-t *Sang* k* *Sep* k* *Sil* staph bg *Sulph* k* tab a1 *Thuj* k* *Zinc* k* zinc-s c2*
  · **evening**: *Nux-v*
  · **cold** applications | **amel.**: *Apis Puls*
  · **summer**: nux-v
  · **water** agg.: *Sulph*

GREENISH (See Discoloration - green)

GRITTY sensation (See Pain - sand)

HAGGARD (See FACE - Expression - haggard)

HANGING down; Lids (See Paralysis - lids)

HARDNESS: cann-i c1 coloc graph k2 marb-w es1• phos bg1 plb a1

- **marble**; sensation as if hard as: cann-i coloc st1 mez st1

- **sensation** of | **Eyeballs**: coloc bg2 *Phos* bg2

O - **Lids**: (↗*Thickening - lids*) *Acon* arg-met bar-c k2 bry b7.de* *Calc* k* *Con* med *Merc* b4a.de *Merc-c* *Nit-ac* *Phyt* psor ran-s k* sep *Sil* *Spig* k* **Staph** b7.de* *Thuj* k*

O . **Upper**: med ptk1

⋮ **sensation** of: *Acon* b7a.de spig b7.de* staph b7.de*

⋮ **Sides**: med jl2

- **Meibomian** glands, of: *Bad* *Lith-c* staph

HEADACHE; after: cocc bg2

HEAT: | **during** | **agg.**: asar b7.de* *Hyos* b7.de kreos b7a.de lac-lup hrn2• op b7.de spig b7.de symph fd3.de• valer b7.de

- **fire**; of:

. **agg.**: *Ant-c* ptk1 arg-n ptk1 merc ptk1 phos bg2*

. **amel.**: fl-ac ptk1

HEAT agg. (See Warm - agg. - heat)

HEAT in: *Acon* k* acon-l a1 aesc k* agar k* allox tpw3 aloe k2 alum bg2 am-c bg2 am-m bg2 ambr bg2 ammc a1 anan androc srj1• ang k* apis bg2 aran k* *Arg-n* arn bg2 *Ars* k* *Asaf* bg2 asar bg2 aster aur aur-ar k2 aur-s k2 bar-c b4.de* **Bell** k* benz-ac berb k* borx bg2 *Bov* k* brom ptk1 bry bg2* calc k* calc-p k2 calc-s a1 *Canth* k* caps bg2 carb-an bg2 carb-v k* *Carbn-s* *Carl* a1 caust b4.de* **Cham** k* *Chel* k* **Chin** k* chlol cic b7.de* cimic ptk1 *Clem* k* coloc bg2 con k* cor-r k* croc bg2 crot-c sk4• *Cycl* k* dig k* eucal a1 euphr bg2* eupi a1 fago a1 ferr bg2 *Glon* k* *Graph* k* haliae-lc srj5• *Hep* b4a.de* *Ign* k* indol bro1 irid-met srj5• *Jab* kali-ar *Kali-bi* k* **Kali-c** k* kali-p ptk1 kali-sil k2 *Kreos* k* lac-leo sk4• lach k* laur b7a.de* *Lil-t* k* **Lyc** k* lyss a1 m-arct b7.de mag-c bg2 mag-p br1* mang k* med meph k* *Merc* k* merc-c ptk1 *Mez* k* mim-p rsj8*• morph a1 nat-ar nat-c k* nat-m k* *Nat-s* k* neon srj5• nicc *Nit-ac* k* nux-m bg2 nux-v bg2 onos *Op* k* par b7.de* petr k* petr-ra shn4• ph-ac k* *Phos* k* pieri-b mlk9.de plat k* plb bg2 plut-n srj7• *Psor* puls b7.de* ran-b raph a1 rhod b4.de* rhus-t k* rumx ptk1 **Ruta** k* sabin k* sapo bro1 sel rsj9• *Sep* k* sil k* *Spig* k* spong bg2 staph b7.de* stram bg2 stry bro1 sul-ac bg2 **Sulph** k* *Tab* k* tarax bg2 tarent k* tell k* thuj k* trios rsj11• ust a1 valer bg2 *Verat* k* verb k* viol-o k* zinc k* zinc-p k2 [spect dfg1]

- **right**: bov bg2 choc srj3• dig bg2 mag-c bg2 sulph bg2 thuj bg2
- **left**: pip-n bg2
- **daytime**: *Ars* k* phos k*
- **morning**: apoc k* fago a1 *Hep* *Mez* sep k* sulph k*
- **forenoon**: con k*
- **afternoon**: chin a1 petr h2 spig a1
- **evening**: con h2 dios fago a1 kali-bi k* nat-m k* nicc psor *Puls*

. **candlelight**; by: graph

. **hot** air streamed out; as if: dios k*

- **night**: *Crot-t* nat-c k* zinc
- **accompanied** by | **cold** air; sensitiveness of eye to: clem bro1 cor-r bro1
- **chill**; after: petr h2
- **choroiditis**: *Coloc*
- **closing** the eyes:

. **agg.**: *Cor-r* echi ptk1 manc ptk1 ust

. **amel.**: mim-p rsj8•

- **cold**; after taking a: kali-c h2
- **cold** air agg.: zinc
- **cough** agg.; during: sulph bg2
- **eating**; after: caust
- **exertion** agg.: aur k* jab **Ruta**
- **exertion** of the eyes agg.: aur jab **Ruta**
- **fever**; during: *Sep* k*
- **flushes**: *Gels* phos sep
- **iritis**, in: *Arg-n* hr1 *Arn* puls
- **painful**: naja ptk1
- **radiating**: gent-ch bnj1
- **steaming** out; sensation of: **Cham** k* *Clem* k* dios k* eug vml3• nat-s
- **streaming** through: aloe bg2
- **walking** in open air agg.; after: lyc h2
- **weather** agg.; wet: aran bro1

O - **Around** the eyes: cic h1 sulph bg2 ulm-c jsj8•

- **Canthi**: agar bg2 alum bg2 am-m bg2 aur bg2 bar-c bg2 *Calc* bg2 carb-v k* clem bg2 nat-m bg2 nux-v bg2 par bg2 *Ph-ac* bg2 phos k* psor k* puls bg2 sep bg2 sil bg2 staph bg2 stront-c bg2 *Sulph* bg2 thuj k*

Heat in – **Canthi**: ...

O . **Outer**: cann-s k* glon k* thuj k*

- **Eyebrows**: all-c bg2 apis bg2 bell bg2 coloc bg2 dig bg2 dros bg2 kali-c bg2 merc bg2 spig bg2 sulph bg2 thuj bg2
- **Lids**: acon k* *Apis* bg2 *Ars* bg2 arum-d a1 *Bell* b4.de* benz-ac k* bomb-chr a1 *Bry* bg2 *Calc* k* calc-p k* caust bg2 chel k* cimic k* cinnb clem bg2 con bg2 euph a1 *Gels* *Glon* *Graph* k* hist vml3• kali-ar a1 lil-t k* lyc bg2 *Med* merc bg2 nux-v bg2 olnd bg2 par b7.de* ph-ac bg2 phos bg2 pic-ac a1 plut-n srj7• rhus-t bg2 seneg bg2 sep k* spig bg2 stry a1 *Sulph* bg2 syph upa k* viol-o bg2

O . **Lower**: polyg-h bg2

. **Margins** of: ars bg2 nat-m bg2 par k* phyt *Sep* k* *Sulph*

. **Upper** | **Margins** of: **Calc** bg2

- **Orbits**: clem bg2 cob ptm1•

HEAVINESS: abrom-a ks5 *Aesc* *Agath-a* nl2• alet vh1 all-c k* all-s allox tpw3* **Aloe** k* ambr c1 amyg a1 anan anders bnj1 androc srj1• apis k* aq-mar rbp6 *Arn* k* ars-i ptk1 ars-met ars-n arum-t asc-t a1 bapt bro1 bell h1* bit-ar wht1• caj a1 cann-i a1 *Carb-v* k* carbn-s cartl-s rly4• caust b4.de* cent a1 cere-b a1 chel a1 chir-fl gya2 choc srj3• cimic a1 *Com* conin c2 croc b7.de* crot-t a1 ery-a a1 falco-pe nl2• fic-m gya1 flor-p rsj3• gard-j vlr2• gels a1* gins a1 glon bg2 ham a1 hell b7.de* helo-s rwt2• hep hipp k* hydrog srj2• hydroph rsj6• influ jl2* irid-met srj5• iris c1 kali-bi bg2* kali-p fd1.de* lac-ac a1 lac-h sk4• lach lavand-a ctl1• lil-t a1 lob-s a1 luf-op rsj5• lyc k* lycpr bro1 lycps-v bg2 mag-s a1 malar jl2 manc k* mand rsj7• marb-w es1• melal-alt gya4 meli bro1 mim-p rsj8• mit a1 myric a1 nat-sil fd3.de• nux-m a1 *Onos* bro1 op bro1 par bro1 parth bro1* peti a1 petr-ra shn4• phys a1 pic-ac a1 pieri-b mlk9.de pitu-gl skp7• plb k* plut-n srj7• podo k* positr nl2• pot-e rly4• *Propr* sa3• ptel c1 pycnop-sa mrz1 rhus-v a1 rumx ruta fd4.de sacch-a fd2.de• sal-fr sle1• sel rsj9• *Sep* b4a.de* sinus rly4• sol-t-ae a1 spong fd4.de stach a1 stram k* stront-c sk4• sulfon bro1 *Sulph* k* suprar rly4• tab a1 tarent a1 thuj mlk1 trif-p a1 trios rsj11• tritic-vg fd5.de vanil fd5.de verat a1 vib zinc a1 [bell-p-sp dcm1 buteo-j sej6 sol-ecl cky1 *Spect* dfg1]

- **left**: propr sa3•
- **daytime**: granit-m es1•
- **morning**: malar jl2 propr sa3•
- **noon**: petr-ra shn4•
- **afternoon** | **14**-16 h: sel rsj9•
- **accompanied** by:

. **head**; pain in: aloe bro1 pitu-gl skp7•

. **vertigo** (See VERTIGO - Accompanied - eye - heaviness)

- **closing** the eyes | **amel.**: bit-ar wht1• propr sa3•
- **menses** | **before** | **agg.**: lac-d *Nat-m*

. **during** | **agg.**: carb-an k* lac-d *Nat-m*

- **motion** agg.: propr sa3•
- **room** agg., stuffy: gard-j vlr2•
- **stooping** agg.: propr sa3•
- **warm** room agg.: gard-j vlr2•

O - **Eyeballs**: carb-v ptk1 croc bg2 pic-ac bg2 sulph bg2

- **Eyebrows**: abrom-a ks5 arg-n bg2 cact bg2 chin bg2 kali-c bg2 lith-c bg2 manc bg2

. **right**: abrom-a ks5

. **air**; in open | **amel.**: abrom-a ks5

. **closing** the eyes | **amel.**: abrom-a ks5

- **Lids**: abrom-a ks5 absin k* acon k* adam srj5• agar alum ptk1 anan apis k* arum-t k* arund k* asaf atro vh1 bamb-a stb2.de• bapt bg2 bar-c k2 bell k* berb k* bit-ar wht1• brom k* bros-gau mrc1 bufo caj k* *Calc* k* calc-sil k2 cann-i k* carb-v br1 carbn-s cassia-s ccrh1• *Caul* k* **Caust** k* cent a1 cham k* chel k* chinin-m c1 chir-fl gya2 chlam-tr bcx2• chlol k* choc srj3• cimic k* cina cinnb *Cocc* k* coloc a1 **Con** k* corn k* croc br1 crot-c k* cupr cypra-eg sde6.de• dirc a1* dream-p sdj1• eucal a1 euph b4.de* euphr b7.de* *Ferr* k* ferr-p bg2 *Form* k* fum rly1*• galla-q-r nl2• **Gels** k* gins a1 glon bg2 *Graph* k* haem a1* ham fd3.de• *Hell* k* helo bro1 helo-s rwt2• *Hydr* jab a1 *Kali-bi* k* kali-p k* kola stb3• *Lac-c* *Lac-d* lac-h sk4• lachn lil-t bg2* *Lyc* k* mag-m h2 mag-p bg2 manc ptk1* *Merl* k* mim-p rsj8*• naja k* nat-ar *Nat-c* k* *Nat-m* k* nat-p k* *Nat-s* k* nat-sil fd3.de• nicot a1 nit-ac k* *Nux-m* k* *Nux-v* k* ol-j a1 *Olib-sac* wmh1 onos op k* oreo br1 ozone sde2• peti a1 petr bg2 petr-ra shn4• ph-ac k* phel *Phos* phys k* pic-ac k* pieri-b mlk9.de pitu-gl skp7• plat bg2 plb a1 plumbg a1 podo bg2 positr nl2• pot-e rly4• psil ft1 pyrid rly4• **Rhus-t** k* ruta fd4.de sal-fr sle1• *Sep* k* sil k* spig b7.de* spira a1 spirae a1 *Spong* k* streptoc rly4• sul-i a1* sulfonam ks2 *Sulph* suprar rly4• symph fd3.de• syph ptk1 tarent thuj k* tung-met bdx1•

- **Lids**: ...
vanil fd5.de verat a1* *Verat-v* k* vero-o rly4*• viol-o k* visc c1 *Zinc* [bell-p-sp dcm1 heroin sdj2 tax jsj7]
  - **right**: abrom-a ks5 caust ptk1
  - **left**: bar-c ptk1 bufo ptk1 coloc ptk1 kali-p ptk1 lyc bg2 thuj ptk1
  - **morning**: chel bg1 daph k* ferr k* glon bg1* ham fd3.de• lachn vml3• myric k* nat-sil fd3.de• phos sacch-a fd2.de• *Sep* symph fd3.de• *Upa* k*
    - **open**; as if could not be held: lachn c1* nat-sil fd3.de• nit-ac *Sep*
    - **waking**; on: flav jl2 *Kali-bi* ozone sde2• positr nl2• sacch-a fd2.de• *Sep*
  - **evening**: bufo cinnb dig k* kola stb3• pic-ac k* pieri-b mlk9.de sulph k* vanil fd5.de
    - **reading** by light | **lamplight**: *Nat-s* k*
  - **accompanied** by:
    - **glaucoma** (See Glaucoma - accompanied - lids)
    - **leukorrhea** (See FEMALE - Leukorrhea - accompanied - lids)
  - **bending** head backward | **amel.**: seneg ptk1
  - **closing** the eyes | **amel.**: abrom-a ks5
  - **cold** air | **amel.**: abrom-a ks5 cassia-s ccrh1•
  - **dinner**:
    - **after** | **immediately**: aq-mar skp7•
  - **headache**; during: bell bro1 caust sne gels br1*
    - **Forehead**; in (See HEAD - Pain - forehead - accompanied - eyes - heaviness)
  - **lying** agg.: nat-m ptk1
  - **numbness** of lids; with: neon srj5•
  - **painful**: manc ptk1
  - **pressed** down; as if: alet vh1 chir-fl gya2
  - **using** the eyes: nat-c *Nat-m*
  - **warm** room; in: bamb-a stb2.de•
  - O **Lower**: plut-n srj7•
  - **Upper**: alum-p k2 apis bg2 bell b4.de* bry bg2 *Cann-s* b7a.de caust b4.de* *Cham* b7.de* croc b7.de* **Gels** bg2 germ-met srj5• *Graph* b4a.de* hell b7.de* lyc bg2 nat-m bg2 *Nux-m* bg2 *Nux-v* b7.de* *Sep* b4.de* spig b7.de* spong b7.de* sulph b4a.de thuj bg2 verat b7.de*

HEMORRHAGE (See Bleeding)

HERPES ZOSTER OPHTHALMICUS: *(↗Eruptions - about - herpes; Eruptions - cornea - herpes; Eruptions - lids - herpes)* ars mfj canth mfj **Crot-t** mfj graph mfj merc mfj puls mfj **Ran-b** mfj rhus-t mfj

HIGHER: | **one** eye is higher than the other; sensation as if: bell bg2

HIPPUS: anh sp1

HORDEOLUM (See Styes)

HYPEREMIA: **Acon** bg2 alum bg2 apis bg2 *Arn* bg2 aur bg2 **Bell** bg2 brom bg2 bry bg2 **Calc** bg2 carb-v bg2 cham bg2 clem bg2 coff bg2 con bg2 croc bg2 euphr bg2 hep bg2 lach bg2 laur bg2 lyc bg2 merc bg2 nat-m bg2 *Nux-v* bg2 phos bg2 plb bg2 *Puls* bg2 *Rhus-t* bg2 ruta bg2 seneg bg2 *Sep* bg2 sil bg2 **Spig** bg2 stram bg2 **Sulph** bg2 thuj bg2 verat bg2

- O **Choroid**: agar bro1 phos bro1 rhod bro1 ruta bro1 *Santin* bro1
- **Conjunctiva**: *Acon* bro1 all-c bro1 ars bro1 *Bell* bro1 ip bro1 lat-m bnm6• *Nux-v* bro1 rhus-t bro1 sulph bro1 *Thuj* bro1
- **Optic** disks:
  - **accompanied** by | **Retina**; enlarged blood vessels of: bell bro1 onos bro1
- **Retina**; of: acon bro1 *Aur* bro1 *Bell* bro1 carbn-s bro1 *Dub* bro1 ferr-p bro1 gels bro1 phos bro1 puls bro1 *Santin* bro1
  - **accompanied** by:
    - **neuroretinitis** (See Inflammation - retina - neuroretinitis - accompanied - hyperemia)
    - **Heart**; complaints of (See CHEST - Heart; complaints - accompanied - retina)
  - **exertion** of eyes; from: *Ruta* bro1 santin bro1
  - **light**; from bright: glon bro1
  - **menses**; from suppressed: bell bro1 puls bro1

HYPERESTHESIA:

- O **Retina**: *(↗Touch - agg.)* acon mfj ant-t mfj ars mfj *Bell* mfj* chin mfj cimic bro1 *Con* k* crot-h gels mfj haliae-lc srj5• hep mfj hyos mfj **Ign** k* lac-ac lil-t br1* macro mfj* *Merc* mfj **Nat-m** *Nux-v* k* ox-ac bro1* phos bro1 puls mfj rhus-t mfj sep mfj stry bro1 sulph mfj
  - **right**: haliae-lc srj5•

HYPERPHORIA (See Paralysis - eyeballs - muscles - superior)

HYPERTROPHY: | **Conjunctiva**: apis

HYPOPYON: crot-t bro1 *Hep* bro1 merc bro1 merc-c bro1 plb bg2* *Sil* bro1

IMMOBILITY (See Staring)

INDENTED SPOTS: | **Cornea**: *Ip* b7a.de

INDURATION (See Hardness)

INFANTS; eye complaints of (See Inflammation - children - infants)

INFILTRATION (See Hardness; Thickening)

INFLAMMATION (= ophthalmia/ophthalmitis): abr mtf11 abrot hr1* achy-a bnj1 **Acon** k* *Act-sp* aethi-a bwa3 aethi-m br1 *Agar* k* albz-f bta1• alco a1 **All-c** allox sp1 *Alum* k* alumn k2 am-c k* *Am-m* c2 *Ambr* k* ant-ar br1 *Ant-c* k* *Ant-t* k* **Apis** k* aran-sc vh1 arg-met *Arg-n* k* **Arn** k* **Ars** k* ars-i ars-s-f k2 *Asaf* k* asar k* asc-t a1 *Aur* k* aur-ar k2 aur-i k2 aur-m aur-s k2 *Bad* k* *Bar-c* k* *Bar-m* **Bell** k* benz-ac beryl sp1 *Borx* k* bov b4.de* brom k* *Bry* k* cact bg2 cadm-met sp1 cadm-s k* *Cain* calad **Calc** k* *Calc-p* **Calc-s** k* calen c2 camph k* cann-s k* *Canth* k* caps k* caps-f jsx1.fr carb-v b4.de* carbn-s *Caust* k* cent c2 *Cham* k* chel b7a.de* *Chin* k* chinin-ar chlol a1 cic c1* cimic *Cinnb* k* cist k2 *Clem* k* *Cocc* b7a.de coff k* *Colch* k* *Coloc* k* *Con* k* convo-d c2 conyz-sm jsx1.fr cop *Cortiso* tpw7* croc crot-h bg2 crot-t k* cupr k* daph k* der c2 dig k* dor a1 dros k2 dulc k* elaps ery-a k* eug k* *Eup-per* *Euph* k* **Euphr** k* fago a1 ferr k* ferr-ar ferr-p k* fl-ac a1 *Form* gamb c2 *Gels* k* *Glon* k* gonotox jl2 gran a1 *Graph* k* *Grin* *Ham* k* *Hep* k* hip-ac sp1* hist sp1 *Hydr* hydro-v c1* hyos k* *Ign* k* *Iod* k* *Ip* k* irid-met srj5• *Iris* jac-c a1 jac-g c2 kali-ar *Kali-bi* k* *Kali-c* k* *Kali-chl* *Kali-i* k* kali-n a1 kali-ox c2 kali-p k* kali-s kali-sil k2 *Kalm* k* kreos k* lac-f wza1• *Lach* k* *Led* k* lil-t k2 *Lith-c* **Lyc** k* *Lyss* k* *Mag-c* k* mag-m k* manc c2 mand sp1* med c1* meph **Merc** k* *Merc-c* k* *Merc-i-r* k* *Merl* *Mez* k* morph mur-ac h2* muru a1 myric a1 nat-ar c2 nat-c k* **Nat-m** k* nat-p *Nat-s* nat-sil fd3.de• *Nit-ac* k* *Nux-v* k* olnd a1 op k* oxal-c jsx1.fr paeon a1 paull a1 *Petr* k* ph-ac k* *Phos* k* phos-pchl c1 *Phyt* k* pic-ac a1 plan a1 plb k* plb-xyz c2 plumbg a1* podo a1* prim-o c2 priva-l bta1• **Psor** k* **Puls** k* ran-b k* ran-r c2 rat **Rhus-t** k* ruta tl1* sabad b7.de samb b7a.de sang sec bg2 sel a1 seneg mrr1 **Sep** k* **Sil** k* sinus rly4• sol-cp bta1• *Spig* k* spong fd4.de staph k* still a1 *Stram* k* *Sul-ac* k* sulfa sp1 **Sulph** k* syph tab bg2 tarax k* tarent k* tell c2 *Ter* k* teucr k* *Thuj* k* tritic-vg fd5.de tub tl1 *Urin* c1 ust a1 valer bg2 vanil fd5.de verat k* vip a1 x-ray sp1 xan c1 xime-c bta1• yuc a1 *Zinc* k* [rubd-met stj2 ruth-met stj2 stront-m stj2]

- **morning**: nat-ar k2 ruta fd4.de
- **afternoon** | **16 h**: *Ars*
- **evening**: choc srj3•
- **accompanied** by:
  - **lachrymation**; profuse: crot-t bg2
  - **pneumonia**: ant-t gsy1
- **acute**: *Acon* k* ant-c bg2 **Apis** arn bg2 *Ars* aur-m *Bell* k* borx bg2 *Bry* **Calc** canth bg2 *Cham* k* *Dulc* bg2 *Euphr* k* *Ferr-p* *Hydr* ign bg2 kali-i k2 kola stb3• lach bg2 med c1 *Merc* k* nit-ac bg2 *Nux-v* k* **Puls** k* *Sep* spig bg2 sul-ac bg2 **Sulph** k* syph mtf33 verat bg2
  - **left**: med vh
  - **bee** sting, after: sep h2
  - **injuries**; after: *Acon* *Arn*
- **alternating** with:
  - O **Feet**; swelling of: *Ars*
  - **Joints** | **rheumatic** pain in: bry k2
  - **Throat**; sore: par
- **arthritic**● (= gouty and rheumatic): acon bro1 *Ant-c* **Ant-t** *Apis* *Ars* arum-m bell k* *Borx* *Bry* k* cact **Calc** k* caust bro1 *Cham* *Chin* k* clem bro1 *Cocc* *Colch* k* *Coloc* dig *Euphr* k* **Form** *Graph* *Hep* ilx-a c1* *Kali-bi* bro1 kali-i k2 *Kalm* *Led* k* lith-c bro1 **Lyc** k* med c1 *Merc* k* merc-c bro1 *Mez* nat-m sne *Nux-v* k* **Phyt** k* *Psor* *Puls* **Rhus-t** k* **Sep** sil bro1 spig k* *Staph* *Sulph* k*

- **burns** agg.: **Canth**
- **catarrhal**: *Acon* bro1 am-m bro1 ant-t tl1 apis bro1 arg-n tl1 ars bro1 asaf tl1 bell bro1 cham bro1 dulc bro1 *Euphr* bro1 gels bro1 *Kali-bi* bro1 merc bro1 merc-c bro1 nux-v bro1 *Puls* bro1 sulph bro1
  - **air** agg.; in open: alum-sil k2
  - **cold**; from: **Acon** act-sp **All-c** alum alum-sil k2 alumn ant-c ant-t *Apis Arg-met Ars* ars-i *Arund Aur* aur-ar k2 aur-i k2 aur-s k2 bapt **Bell** *Bry* cadm-s k2 **Calc** *Calc-p Carbn-s Cham* chel *Chlol* com con *Dig* **Dulc Euphr** gamb *Graph Hep Hydr* iod ip *Iris* kali-ar *Kali-bi* kali-c *Lyc* **Merc** *Merc-c Mez Nux-v Petr Phyt* **Psor Puls** *Sang Sep Staph* sul-i k2 *Sulph Thuj*
    - **morning**: hep kali-bi *Mez*
    - **night**: all-s *Cinnb Dulc* **Merc** *Rhus-t*
      - **midnight**:
        - **after** | **1** h: chinin-ar
  - **read**; when trying to: all-s
- **children**; in: ant-c mtf33 bar-c br1 ip mtf33
  - **infants**: *Acon* k* alumn **Apis** *Arg-met* **Arg-n** arn **Ars** arund *Bell* k* borx *Bry* k* **Calc** k* *Cham* k* *Dulc* k* *Euphr Hep Ign Lyc Merc* k* *Merc-c* **Nit-ac** k* *Nux-v* k* **Puls** k* *Rhus-t Sulph* k* syph k2 **Thuj** zinc
  - **newborns**: acon vh1 arn lmj kali-s ptk2 merc-c ptk2 puls br1* thuj lp
- **chill**; during: acon bg2 bell bg2 kreos bg2 rhus-t bg2
- **chronic**: *Alum* bg2* ant-c bg2* arg-n bro1 **Ars** bg2* bar-c bg2 *Borx* bg2 **Calc** bg2 caust bg2 chin bg2 coloc bg2 con bro1 dig bg2 dulc bg2 **Euphr** bg2* ferr bg2 graph bg2* **Hep** bg2 hyos bg2 kali-bi bro1 *Lach* bg2 *Lyc* bg2* *Nit-ac* bg2 petr bg2 **Phos** bg2 psor bro1* rhus-t bg2 sep bg2* **Sil** bg2 *Spig* bg2 *Sulph* bro1 *Thuj* bg2 verat bg2 zinc bro1
  - **children**; in: ant-c mtf33
- **cold**:
  - **agg.**: *Ars Dulc* hr1 nat-ar k2 sil
  - **amel.**: apis **Arg-n** *Asar Bry* caust phos k2 **Puls** *Sep*
  - **bathing** | **agg.**: syph pd
  - **washing** | **amel.**: asaf c1
  - **water** | **agg.**: sep h2
- **croupous**: kali-bi
- **dentition**: | **agg.**: ferr-p bg1
- **dust**; from: acon c1
- **eruptions**; after suppressed: mez
- **erysipelatous**: *(↗FACE - Erysipelas - eye)* *Acon Anac* **Apis** k* *Bell* k* com *Graph Hep Led Merc Merc-c* **Rhus-t** k* vesp k*
  - **bites** of insects; from: led
  - ○ **Lids**: *Hep* bg2
- **fire**:
  - **agg.**: **Ant-c** apis k2 *Arg-n* k* **Merc**
  - **being** over; cold air and cold applications | **amel.**: **Arg-n**
- **foreign** bodies: **Acon** k* **Arn** *Calc* k* *Puls* **Sil** k* sulph k*
- **gonorrheal**: acon bro1* ant-c *Ant-t* apis bro1 *Arg-n* bro1 *Bell* bro1 calc-s bro1 cann-s br1* chin clem h2* cor-r cub hedy c1* *Hep* bro1 ip bro1 kali-s bro1 med k* *Merc* k* *Merc-c* bro1 *Merc-pr-r* bro1 nat-m gm1 **Nit-ac** k* **Puls** k* rhus-t bro1 *Spig Sulph* k* syph bro1* *Thuj* k*
- **headache**; during: apis bry k2 lach k2 led med c1 spig hr1 verat
  - **during** three days: med c1
- **heat** | **fire**; of: phos bg1
- **injuries**; after: acon lp1 *Arn* calc hr1 calen br1 *Ham Hep Puls* sil hr1* *Sulph*
- **light**; from:
  - **gaslight** | **agg.**: *Merc*
  - **reflected**: acon lp1
  - **sunlight** | **agg.**: calc k2
- **looking** | **steadily**: calc k2
- **measles**; after: arg-met *Carb-v* crot-h euphr *Puls* k*
- **menses**:
  - **before** | **agg.**: puls bro1
  - **during** | **agg.**: *Ars Puls* b7a.de* **Zinc** k*
  - **suppressed** menses; from: *Apis* b7a.de *Puls* k*
- **mercurial**: *Asaf Hep Mez*
  - **air**; in open | **amel.**: asaf c1 *Asar* **Puls**
- **old** people; in: alum bro1
- **panophthalmitis**: acon mfj apis mfj ars mfj asaf mfj bell mfj **Hep** mfj* *Iod* mfj merc mfj *Phyt* mfj **Rhus-t** mfj* sil mfj sulph mfj
- **periodical**: puls b7a.de
- **perspiration**; from suppressed: rhus-t k2
- **purulent**: apis bro1 arg-n bro1* calen bro1 grin bro1 *Hep* bro1 merc-c bro1 merc-pr-r bro1 nat-s bro1 plb bro1 puls bro1 *Rhus-t* bro1
- **recurrent**● (See GENERALS - History - eye)
- **sand** and dust agg.: sulph
- **scrofulous**: acon c1 *Aeth* a1* *Aethi-a* c1* *Aethi-m* bro1 alumn am-br c2 *Ant-c Apis* k* *Arg-met* arg-n bro1 arn bro1 **Ars** ars-i k* arund **Aur** k* aur-ar k2 aur-i k2 aur-m bro1 **Aur-m-n** aur-s k2 *Bad Bar-c* k* bar-i bro1 **Bar-m** *Bell* k* *Cadm-s* **Calc** k* calc-i k2* *Calc-p* **Calc-s** cann-s k* **Carbn-s Caust** *Cham* chin chinin-ar *Cinnb Cist* k* clem bro1 *Coch* bro1 colch bro1 *Con* k* dig *Dulc Euphr* k* ferr ferr-ar ferr-i c2 *Fl-ac* **Graph** k* **Hep** k* *Hyos Iod* k* ip *Kali-bi* k* *Kali-i* kali-sil k2 lach mtf11 *Lith-c Lyc Mag-c* **Merc** *Merc-c* k* merc-d bro1 merc-n bro1 merc-pr-r bro1 *Nat-m* k* *Nat-p Nat-s* k* **Nit-ac** k* *Nux-v* ol-j k* **Petr Phyt Psor** k* **Puls** k* *Rhus-t* k* *Sars* scroph-n bro1 **Sep Sil** k* solid c2 *Spig Sul-ac* **Sulph** k* *Tell* thuj bro1 *Viol-t* k* *Zinc* zinc-s bro1
  - **children** disposed to scald-head and with inflammation of external ear; in: ars k1
- **smallpox**; after: merc bro1 sulph bro1
- **snow** and sun; in: acon bg*
- **storm**; after exposure to: sil kr1
- **summer**: *Sep*
- **sympathetic** ophthalmia: *Arg-n* bro1 bell mfj* bry mfj* calen bro1 euphr bro1 kali-i mfj merc mfj* puls bro1 rhus-t mfj* sil mfj*
- **syphilitic**: apis bro1 arg-met arg-n *Ars* ars-i k2 **Asaf** k* *Aur* aur-ar k2 aur-i k2 aur-m aur-m-n aur-s k2 *Cinnb Clem* gels bro1 *Graph Hep* **Kali-i** k* **Merc Merc-c** k* *Merc-cy Merc-i-f* k* **Nit-ac** k* **Phyt** sil k2 *Staph Syph* thuj zinc bg1
- **vaccination**; after: thuj
- **warm** | **bed** | **agg.**: **Merc**
  - **covers** | **amel.**: *Hep*
- **warmth** agg. | **heat** agg.: **Apis Bad Bell** *Bry* **Glon** *Kali-i* med *Merc* still
- **washing**:
  - **agg.**: **Sulph**
  - **amel.**: puls k2
- **weather**:
  - **change** of weather: cadm-s k2
  - **cold**:
    - **wet** | **agg.**: calc k2 **Dulc Rhus-t** *Sil*
- **wet**:
  - **becoming**, agg.: *Calc* dulc *Rhus-t*
  - **feet** getting wet: calc k2 *Chel*
- **wind**:
  - **dry**, cold: **Acon** k* nat-ar k2
  - **riding** in: calc k2
- **wounds**: arn calad **Staph**
- ○ **Canthi**: acon b7.de* alum b4.de* am-c k* ant-c bg* apis k* **Arg-n** k* ars b4.de* *Borx* k* bufo *Calc* k* calc-s cham b7.de* clem *Euphr* b7.de* *Graph* k* ign b7.de* kali-c lil-t a1 mag-c k* merc nat-c k* nux-v b7.de* phos b4.de* puls b7.de* ruta fd4.de sulph k* vanil fd5.de zinc k*
  - **morning**: *Nux-v*
  - **ulceration**; with: *Apis* bufo *Kali-c* zinc
  - ○ **Inner**: *Agar* k* allox sp1 *Borx* k* *Clem* k* cortiso tpw7* mag-c h2 merc b4.de* nat-c h2* *Nat-m* b4a.de *Nux-v* petr rhus-t a1 ruta fd4.de vanil fd5.de zinc br1*
    - **right**: petr b4.de* *Sil* b4a.de
    - **left**: bell b4.de* calc b4.de*
  - **Outer**: *Borx* k* calc b4.de* **Graph** k* *Kali-c* lyc bg2 syph al
    - **ulceration**; with: *Calc-act* upa
- **Caruncles**: bell k* berb k* cann-i k*
- **Chorioretinitis**: **Gels** kr1 **Kali-m** kr1 **Phos** kr1 **Puls** kr1
- **Choroid**: acon mfj *Ars* k* asaf k2 *Aur* aur-s k2 *Bell* k* **Bry** k* *Cedr* k* cina tl1 *Coloc* crot-h mfj *Dub* mfj ferr-p mfj *Gels* k* *Hep* mfj iod mfj *Ip* k* jab *Kali-chl Kali-i* k* kali-m mfj kalm mfj lach mfj *Merc* k* *Merc-c Merc-d* merc-i-r bro1 naphtin bro1 *Nux-v* phos k* *Phyt Prun* k* psor puls *Rhus-t* c2* ruta santin bro1 *Sil Spig Sulph* tab bro1 tell bro1 *Thuj* k* tub jl2 verat-v mfj viol-o c2
  - **atrophic**: nux-v bro1 phos bro1 *Pilo* bro1

- **purulent**: hep bro1 rhus-t bro1
  - **extending** to:
    - **Iris**: kali-i bro1 *Prun* bro1 sil bro1
    - **Retina**: aur bro1 *Kali-i* bro1 kali-m bro1 merc-c bro1 *Merc-i-r* bro1
- **syphilitic**: aur bro1 *Kali-i* bro1 kali-m bro1 merc-c bro1 *Merc-i-r* bro1

- **Conjunctiva** (= conjunctivitis): abr mtf11 achy-a bnj1 **Acon** k* act-sp aethi-a ll1 ail **All-c** ptk1 **Alum** k* alum-p k2 am-br vh1 ant-c ant-t k* **Apis** k* **Arg-n** k* am ptk1 **Ars** k* ars-i ars-s-f k2 asaf k2 asc-t aur k2 aur-i k2 bamb-a stb2.de• bar-i k2 bar-ox-suc rly4• bar-s k2 **Bell** k* beryl sp1 bomb-chr a1 brom k* bry k* **Calc** k* *Calc-f* calc-i k2 *Calc-p* **Calc-s** k* cann-i cann-s k2 *Canth* **Carbn-s** cedr k* *Cham* chin k* chlam-tr bcx2• *Chlol* k* chrys-ac c1 chrysar bwa3* *Cinnb* *Clem* k* coc-c k* colch tl1 conyz-sm jsx1.fr cortico mtf11 cortiso tpw7* crat br1 crot-h *Crot-t* cupr-s c2 des-ac mtf11 *Dig* k* dys pte1* ery-a c2 **Euphr** k* ferr-i *Ferr-p* ferr-p-h c1* flav jl2 gels k2 gonotox jl2 *Graph* mrr1 grat a1 grin c2 guare a1 *Ham* *Hep* k* hist sp1 *Hydr* influ jl2* *Iod* *Ip* k* kali-ar a1 *Kali-bi* k* kali-chl kali-m k2 kali-p kali-s k2* kali-sil k2 lap-la sde8.de• lat-h bnm5• lat-m bnm6• led leptos-ih jl2* lil-t k2 *Lyc* lyss mtf11 med k2* *Merc* k* merc-c mtf11 merc-d c2 merl c2 mez k2 morg-p pte1* myric c2 *Nat-ar* nat-p k* *Nat-s* k* *Nit-ac* h2* *Nux-v* oscilloc jl2 oxal-c jsx1.fr paeon c1 parat-b mtf11 penic mtf11 peti c2 *Petr* k* physala-p bnm7• pic-ac k* pieri-b mlk9.de plac rzf5• propr sa3• psor jl2 *Puls* k* **Rhus-t** k* ruta fd4.de sang hr1 sanic c2 sec a1 ser-a-c jl2 spira a1 *Staph* sul-i k2 sulfa sp1 **Sulph** k* sumb k* syc pte1* syph k2* tell c2* tep thal c2 thal-xyz srj8• *Thuj* thyr mtf11 tub c1* tub-a jl2 v-a-b jl2* vac jl2* *Zinc* k* [bor-pur stj2]
  - **right** eye: propr sa3•
  - **accompanied** by:
    - **coryza**: stict c1
    - **influenza**: influ jl2 oscilloc jl2 tub-a jl2
    - **menses**; absent: euphr ptk1
    - **Cornea**; ulceration of (See Ulceration - cornea - accompanied - conjunctiva)
  - **acute**: euphr mtf11
  - **allergic**: cortiso mtf11 equis-h mtf11 puls mrr1
  - **catarrhal**: stict br1 v-a-b jl2*
  - **chronic**: *Alum* bro1 *Ant-c* bro1 arg-n bro1* *Ars* bro1 *Aur-m* bro1 bell bro1 euphr bro1 graph mrr1* guare mtf11 *Kali-bi* bro1 merc bro1 oxyte-chl mtf11 pic-ac bro1 psor bro1 *Puls* bro1 sil mtf11 sulph bro1* syph mtf11 thuj bro1 zinc bro1
  - **cold** agg.; after becoming: *Dulc* mrr1
  - **croupous**: acet-ac k* apis bro1 guare bro1 iod bro1 kali-bi k* merc *Merc-cy* bro1
  - **follicular** (See membrana - granular)
  - **gonorrheal**: *Acon* bro1 ant-t bro1 apis bro1 arg-n bro1* calc-hp bro1 *Hep* bro1 kali-bi bro1* *Merc* bro1 merc-c bro1 nit-ac ptk1 *Puls* bro1* rhus-t bro1 verat-v bro1
  - **granular**: *(↗trachoma)* abr bro1 acon vh1 *Apis* k* **Arg-n** k* ars bro1* aur bro1 *Aur-m* bro1 calc-i bro1 crot-t bro1 *Ery-a* *Euphr* *Ham* kali-bi bg* *Merc* nat-m bro1 nat-s *Petr* *Phyt* k* psor puls bro1 rhus-t sang hr1 sep *Sil* *Sulph* *Thuj* k* zinc-s bro1
    - **cold** applications | **amel.**: *Apis* asar *Puls*
  - **injuries**; after: *Acon* bro1 *Arn* bro1 bell bro1 *Calen* bro1 canth bro1 euphr bro1 *Ham* bro1 led bro1 symph bro1
  - **menses**; with absent: euphr ptk2
  - **purulent**: abr mtf11 alum bg2 am-c bg2 *Arg-n* bro1 bell bg2 calc bg2 calc-hp bro1 calc-s mtf33 caust bg2 chin bg2 *Dig* bg2 **Euphr** bg2 ferr-i mtf11 *Graph* bg2 guaj bg2 hep bg2* lyc bg2 **Merc** bg2* *Merc-c* bro1 nit-ac bg2 **Puls** bg2* *Rhus-t* bro1 *Seneg* bg2 sil bg2* spig bg2 *Sulph* bg2 thuj bg2
  - **pustular**: abr bro1 *Aeth* agar ant-c *Ant-t* bro1 **Apis** arg-n bro1 ars k* aur bar-c **Calc** k* calc-i calc-s mfj cann-s mfj *Cham* *Chlol* **Clem** coloc bg *Con* *Crot-t* *Euphr* k* **Graph** k* hep k* *Ip* *Kali-bi* k* **Kali-chl** *Kali-i* kali-m k2 *Lach* *Merc* *Merc-c* k* *Merc-d* *Merc-i-f* merc-n bro1 *Nat-c* *Nat-m* *Nat-s* *Nit-ac* **Petr** **Psor** **Puls** k* *Rhus-t* k* **Sec** **Sep** *Sil* **Sulph** *Syph* k* tell *Thuj* zinc
    - **phlyctenous**: ars ptk1 calc-i mtf11 graph ptk1
  - **wet**; after getting: *Rhus-t* hr1

- **Cornea**: *(↗Xerophthalmia)* acon bro1 *Apis* k* arg-n a2 *Ars* k* ars-i bro1* ars-s-f k2 aur-ar k2 *Aur-m* k* *Bell* k* **Calc** k* *Calc-p* cann-s bro1 chrysar bwa3* *Cinnb* *Con* k* *Crot-h* crot-t *Euphr* k* fl-ac lp* *Graph* k* *Hep* k* ilx-a bro1 *Kali-bi* lp* *Kali-chl* kali-m k2* *Kalm* *Lyc* lyss a1 **Merc** k* *Merc-c* lp* *Merc-i-f* k* morg-p pte1*•

- **Cornea**: ...
  nit-ac lp* nux-v bro1 phos bro1 plat k* plb *Psor* *Puls* *Rhus-t* k* sang bro1 *Sep* sil lp* spig k* **Sulph** k* syph al* **Thuj** k* tub mtf11 vario al2
  - **right**: *Tub* jl2
  - **arthritic**: clem bro1 colch bro1 coloc bro1
  - **chronic**: syph jl2*
  - **cold** bathing | **amel.**: syph ptk1
  - **herpetic**: *Apis* bro1 *Ars* bro1 calc-p bro1 euphr bro1 ran-b br1* tell bro1
  - **interstitial**: tub jl2 v-a-b jl2
    - **syphilitic**: aur bro1 *Aur-m* bro1 cann-s bro1 merc-c bro1 merc-cy bro1
  - **keratoconus** (See Conical)
  - **pannus**: acon vh1
  - **parenchymatous**: apis mfj ars mfj **Aur** mfj *Aur-m* bro1 bar-i mfj calc-hp bro1 calc-p mfj *Cann-s* mfj ferr-p mfj hep mfj kali-i mfj* **Kali-m** mfj* merc mfj* sep mfj **Sulph** mfj* syph jl2
  - **phlyctenular**: *Apis* bro1 bell bro1 calc bro1 *Calc-f* bro1 calc-p bro1 con bro1 *Graph* bro1 hep bro1 ip bro1 *Merc-c* bro1 puls bro1 rhus-t bro1 syph bro1* thuj bro1
  - **pustular**: aethi-a bwa3 *Ant-c* bro1 calc bro1 con bro1 crot-t bro1 euphr bro1 *Hep* bro1 kali-bi bro1 kali-i bro1 merc-n bro1 morg-p mtf11 nit-ac bro1 pyrog mtf11 syph jl2 vac jl2*
  - **recurrent** (See GENERALS - History - cornea)
  - **scrofulosa**: aethi-a ll1
- **Descemet's** membrane: ars mfj aur mfj calc mfj **Gels** mfj hep mfj **Kali-bi** mfj merc mfj
- **Episclera** and sclera: *(↗sclerae)* acon mfj* aur mfj bell bro1 bry bro1 cinnb mfj cocc mfj kali-i bro1 **Kalm** mfj *Merc* mfj merc-c bro1 nux-m mfj puls mfj rhus-t bro1 *Sep* mfj spig mfj sulph mfj ter bro1 terebe mfj **Thuj** mfj*
- **Follicular**: abr bro1 aur-m bro1 euphr bro1 *Puls* bro1 sulfa sp1
- **Iridochoroiditis**: apis mfj ars mfj asaf mfj aur mfj *Bell* mfj *Bry* mfj **Gels** mfj *Hep* mfj kali-i mfj* merc mfj *Merc-c* mfj prot mfj prun mfj* sil mfj* sulph mfj thuj mfj
- **Iris** (= iridocyclitis): acon mfj* *Apis* k* *Arg-n* k* **Arn** k* *Ars* k* *Ars-i* ars-s-f k2 *Asaf* k* *Aur* aur-ar k2 aur-i k2 aur-s k2 *Bell* k* **Bry** bg2* calc calc-hi mfj *Cedr* k* *Chin* chinin-m kr1* *Cinnb* k* *Clem* k* *Colch* k* *Coloc* k* *Com* con mfj crot-h *Crot-t* dub bro1 *Dulc* *Euphr* k* ferr-p bro1 gels bg2* grin c2* ham mfj *Hep* k* iod k* *Kali-bi* k* *Kali-i* k* kalm mrr1 lepr mtf11 *Merc* k* **Merc-c** k* merc-i-f merc-pn mfj mez morg-p pte1* *Nat-m* k* nat-sal mfj *Nit-ac* k* nux-v mfj petr phyt mrr1 plb k* *Puls* k* **Rhus-t** k* sabal c2 sal-ac c2 *Seneg* k* *Sil* k* spig k* *Staph* k* sul-i k2 *Sulph* k* *Syph* k* tell bro1 *Ter* k* thuj k* toxo-g jl2* vac jl2* zinc k*
  - **night**: *Ars* *Dulc* **Kali-i** k* **Merc** **Merc-c** *Nit-ac* *Rhus-t* *Staph* *Sulph* zinc
  - **accompanied** by | **Prostate**; complaints of: sabal c1*
  - **adhesions**, with: *Calc* k* *Clem* k* graph bg *Merc-c* k* *Nit-ac* k* sil k* spig k* staph *Sulph* k* *Ter* k*
  - **chronic**: absin mtf11 asaf mtf11 lac-f mtf11 lar-d mtf11
  - **hypopyon**, with: ant-s-aur c1 grin c1 **Hep** k* *Merc* k* *Merc-c* **Sil** k* sulph *Thuj*
  - **injuries**; after: acon bro1 *Arn* bro1 bell bro1 *Ham* bro1 led bro1 nat-sal bro1 rhus-t bro1
  - **plastic**: *Acon* bro1 bry bro1 cinnb bro1 hep bro1 *Merc-c* bro1 rhus-t bro1 thuj bro1
  - **rheumatic**: arn k* *Ars* *Bry* k* clem bro1 *Colch* k* coloc *Dulc* echi sne *Euphr* k* form bro1 grin c1 *Kali-bi* k* kali-i *Kalm* k* led bro1 merc-c bro1 nat-m sne **Rhus-t** k* sol-t c2 *Spig* k* syph *Ter* k* *Thuj* bro1
  - **serous**: apis bro1 *Ars* bro1 bry bro1 cedr bro1 *Gels* bro1 merc bro1 merc-c bro1 spig bro1
  - **syphilitic**: *Arg-n* *Ars* *Asaf* k* *Aur* k* *Aur-m* *Cinnb* k* clem bro1 *Hep* iod bro1 kali-bi bro1 **Kali-i** k* kalm mtf11 *Merc* **Merc-c** k* merc-cy bro1 *Merc-i-f* k* **Nit-ac** k* petr sil k2 *Staph* k* sul-i k2 sulph bro1 syph *Thuj* k* zinc
    - **accompanied** by:
      - **bursting** pain | **Eyeball**, temple and side of face; in: **Staph**
    - **bursting** pain in eyeball, temple and side of face: **Staph**
  - **tubercular**: *Ars* bro1 bar-i kali-bi bro1 sulph bro1 syph bro1 tub k*
- **Keratoconjunctivitis**; phlyctenular: aethi-a bwa3* *Ant-c* mfj *Ant-t* mfj* apis mfj ars mfj aur mfj bar-c mfj bar-i mfj calc mfj* calc-hp mfj calc-i mfj calc-pic mfj* calc-s mfj cham mfj con mfj* crot-t mfj euphr mfj* graph mfj* *Hep* mfj ign bro1 *Ip* mfj kali-bi mfj lach mfj lister mtf11 merc mfj merc-c mfj* merc-d mfj *Merc-n* mfj

- **Keratoconjunctivitis**; phlyctenular: ...
  merc-pn mfj morb jl2 morg-p mtf11 *Nat-m* mfj nux-v mfj puls mfj* pyrog mtf11 **Ran-b** mfj rhus-t mfj* *Sep* mfj sil bro1 sulph mfj* thuj mfj vac mtf11
- **Lachrymal** ducts: acon apis arg-n hs2 *Calc Fl-ac* k* graph c2 hep iod ptk1 kali-bi k* *Nat-m* nit-ac k* **Petr** k* **Puls** *Sil* k* *Stann*
  - **children**; in: | **newborns**: **Sil** mrr1
- **Lachrymal** glands: acon mfj *Ant-c* apis *Cupr* fl-ac hep iod mfj **Puls** rhus-t mfj **Sil**
- **Lachrymal** sacs (= dacryocystitis): apis k* arum-t fl-ac bro1 *Graph* hep k* hip-ac mtf11 iod br1* *Merc* k* nat-c **Petr** k* **Puls** k* **Sil** k* *Stann* bro1
- **Lids** (= blepharitis): *Acon* k* act-sp aethi-a tl1 am-c k2 anac androc srj1• **Ant-c** k* **Apis** k* **Arg-met Arg-n** k* *Ars* k* ars-s-f k2 arund asar he1* asc-t a1 atro a1 bac tl1 bar-c k* bar-s k2 bell k* berb k* borx b4a.de bry b7.de* *Calc* b4.de* **Calc-s** cann-s b7a.de canth k2 *Carb-an* carb-v b4.de* **Carbn-s** caust b4.de* cham b7.de* chrysar bwa3* cimic a1 *Cinnb* clem b4a.de* *Cocc* k* com k* con crot-t *Dig* k* dream-p sdj1• dulc bro1 dys pte1* euph b4.de* euphr k* gaert fmm1• gels k2 granit-m es1• **Graph** k* *Hep* k* hip-ac mtf11 hist mtf11 *Hydr* hyos k* ign b7.de* influ jl2* irid-met srj5• *Iris* kali-ar kali-bi k* *Kali-c* k* kali-s kali-sil k2 kreos k* lach k* lat-m bnm6• lil-t **Lyc** k* m-ambo b7.de m-aust b7.de mag-c a1 **Med** k* meph **Merc** k* merc-i-f bro1 *Merc-pr-r* bro1 *Mez* morg-g pte1* morg-p fmm1• nat-ar k* *Nat-c* k* *Nat-m Nit-ac* nux-v b7.de* olnd a1 **Petr** k* *Ph-ac* b4a.de phos podo a1* *Psor* k* puls k* **Rhus-t** k* rumx hr1 ruta tl1* sabad b7a.de *Sang Sanic* sarr sars k* *Seneg* k* *Sep* k* *Sil Spig* k* spong b7.de* stann **Staph** k* stram k* sul-ac a1 **Sulph** k* syph al **Tell** *Ter* thal-xyz srj8• *Thuj* k* tub tl1* tub-a jl2* upa bro1 (non:uran-met k) *Uran-n* k* v-a-b jl2* vac jl2 *Valer* b7a.de vario br1 verat k* zinc k* zinc-p k2
  - **right**: phos b4.de*
  - **chronic**: *Alum* bro1 ant-c bro1 *Arg-n* bro1 aur bro1 bar-c bro1 *Borx* bro1 calc bro1 clem bro1 euphr bro1 *Graph* bro1 hep bro1 jug-c bro1 merc-c bro1 merc-pr-r bro1 petr bro1 psor bro1 sep bro1 *Sil* bro1 *Staph* bro1 *Sulph* bro1 *Tell* bro1
    - **children**; in: ant-c tl1
  - ○ **Inner** side: *Ars* b4a.de *Bell* b4a.de dig b4a.de hep b4a.de merc b4a.de merc-c b4a.de *Rhus-t* b7a.de sep b4a.de *Sulph* b4a.de *Thuj* b4a.de
  - **Lower**: *Ars* b4.de* bell b4.de* cham b7a.de hip-ac sp1 mag-c b4.de* puls b7a.de *Rhus-t* b7a.de ruta fd4.de sulph h2
    - **right**: ina-i mlk9.de
  - **Margins** of: *Acon* bro1 *Aeth* k* ant-c vh1 apis bro1 *Arg-met Arg-n* k* ars k* *Aur-m* bell k* *Borx* k* *Bov Cham* k* **Clem** k* *Dig* k* dulc bro1 euphr k* **Graph** k* *Hep* k* *Hydr* irid-met srj5• jatr-c c2 kreos bro1 lach lyc b4a.de med c1* merc k* *Merc-c* k* merc-i-f bro1 *Merc-pr-r* bro1 mez h2 nat-ar k* *Nat-m* nat-s nux-v ozone sde2• petr bro1 ph-ac b4a.de *Plb* b7a.de psor mrr1 *Puls* k* *Rhus-t* b7a.de* **Sanic** k* sel b7a.de *Seneg* sil b4a.de* *Spig* b7a.de *Staph* k* stram k* *Sulph* b4a.de* syph alj1 **Thuj** b4a.de upa bro1 uran-n bro1 *Valer* b7a.de zinc b4a.de
    - **chronic**: *Alum* bro1 ant-c bro1 *Arg-n* bro1 aur bro1 bar-c bro1 *Borx* bro1 calc bro1 clem bro1 euphr bro1 *Graph* bro1 hep bro1 jug-c bro1 merc-c bro1 merc-pr-r bro1 petr bro1 psor bro1 sep bro1 *Sil* bro1 *Staph* bro1 *Sulph* bro1 *Tell* bro1
  - **Tarsi**: *Borx* bg2 clem bg2* *Euphr* bg2 **Graph** bg2* mag-m ptk1 *Nat-m* bg2 *Petr* bg2* **Puls** bg2* sanic ptk1 sep bg2 *Staph* bg2 *Sulph* bg2*
  - **Upper**: *Acon* b7a.de graph b4a.de hep b4a.de ign b7a.de *Puls* b7a.de thuj b4a.de
    - **right**: spong fd4.de zinc h2
- **Meibomian** glands: *Bell* b4a.de cham *Colch Dig* k* *Euphr Hep* k* indg k* kreos *Merc* b4a.de phos psor al2 puls *Staph* stram sulph
  - **suppurative**: *Con Phos*
- **Membrana** nictitans | **granular**: ars-i vh
- **Optic** nerve (= papillitis): *Apis* bro1 ars bro1 *Bell* k* carbn-s bro1 diph-t-tpt jl2 germ-met srj5• kali-i bro1 merc k2 *Merc-c* bro1 morb jl2* nux-v bro1 *Phos* k* pic-ac bro1 plb k* *Puls* k* rhus-t bro1 santin bro1 sulfa sp1* tab k* thal-xyz srj8• thyr bro1 toxo-g jl2*
  - **accompanied** by | **Optic** disk; swelling of: bell bro1 bry bro1 dub bro1 gels bro1 hell bro1 nux-v bro1 puls bro1 verat-v bro1
  - **descendens**; neuritis (See retina - neuroretinitis)
- **Orbit**:
  - **caries**; with: asaf mfj aur mfj calc mfj calc-hp mfj *Fl-ac* mfj *Hecla* mfj kali-i mfj lyc mfj merc mfj mez mfj nit-ac mfj petr mfj phos mfj **Sil** mfj sulph mfj symph mfj

Inflammation – Orbit: ...

  - **cellulitis**; orbital: acon mfj apis mfj* ars mfj bell mfj bry mfj **Hep** mfj* **Iod** mfj kali-i mfj* lach mfj merc mfj **Phyt** mfj* **Rhus-t** hr1* **Sil** mfj* sulph mfj
  - **necrosis**; with: asaf mfj aur mfj calc mfj calc-hp mfj *Fl-ac* mfj *Hecla* mfj kali-i mfj lyc mfj merc mfj mez mfj nit-ac mfj petr mfj phos mfj **Sil** mfj sulph mfj symph mfj
- **Orbits** | **Periosteum** of orbit: asaf mfj* aur mfj* calc mfj calc-hp mfj *Fl-ac* mfj *Hecla* mfj kali-i hr1* lyc mfj merc mfj* mez mfj nit-ac mfj petr mfj phos mfj **Sil** mfj* sulph mfj symph mfj
- **Retina**: *Ars* asaf aur k* bell k2* ben-d c2* bry bro1 *Calc* cina tl1 crot-h *Dub* bro1 *Gels* k* germ-met srj5• kali-p bg *Kalm Lach Merc* k* *Merc-c* k* *Phos* k* pic-ac bro1 plb ptk1 *Prun* puls k* santin bro1 sec *Sulph* k* toxo-g jl2*
  - **albuminuria**: apis mfj ars mfj crot-h bro1 gels mfj* hep mfj kali-i mfj **Kalm** mfj* **Merc-c** mfj* nat-sal bro1 phos lp* plb mfj* sal-ac bro1
    - **pregnancy** agg.; during: kalm ptk1
  - **apoplectic**: glon bro1 lach bro1
  - **chronic**: crot-h bro1 gels bro1 kalm bro1 *Merc-c* bro1 nat-sal bro1 phos bro1 *Plb* bro1 sal-ac bro1
  - **commotio** retinae: *(↗Injuries)* **Apis** mfj **Arn** mfj gels mfj **Hyper** mfj
  - **diabetic**: sec ptk1
  - **hemorrhagic**: *(↗Bleeding - retinal)* arn mfj **Bell** mfj **Crot-h** mfj **Dub** mfj **Lach** mfj **Merc-c** mfj* **Phos** mfj
  - **leukemic**: nat-s bro1 thuj bro1
  - **neuroretinitis**: ars bro1 cupr bro1 merc-c bro1 vanad br1
    - **accompanied** by | **hyperemia** of retina: acon mfj ars mfj aur mfj **Bell** mfj bry mfj cact mfj chinin-s mfj con mfj **Dub** mfj ferr-p mfj **Gels** mfj kali-i mfj kali-m mfj lach mfj merc mfj napht mfj nux-v mfj **Phos** mfj puls mfj sec mfj spig mfj sulph mfj verat-v mfj
  - **overexertion** of eyes; after: sulph ptk1*
  - **pigmented**: lyc mfj nux-v mfj* phos mfj*
  - **pregnancy** agg.; during: gels bro1
  - **punctata** albescens: bell bro1 kali-i bro1 merc-c bro1 merc-i-r bro1 napht mfj naphtin bro1 sulph bro1
  - **rapid**: kali-i bro1 thuj bro1
  - **syphilitic**: *Asaf* mfj *Aur* mfj iod bro1 *Kali-i* mfj* merc mfj **Merc-c** mfj nit-ac mfj
- **Retrobulbar**: alco mfj ars mfj cann-i mfj chinin-s bro1 ferr-p mfj iodof mfj* kali-p mfj nitrob mfj *Nux-v* mfj plb mfj stram mfj tab mfj terebe mfj
- **Sclerae**: *(↗episclera)* acon k* ars bg2* aur bg2 aur-m bro1 bar-c bg2 bell bg2 bry bg2 chinin-m c2 *Cocc* ery-a c2* hep bg2* hura kali-i bg2 *Kalm* k* *Merc* k* merc-c bro1* plb bg2 *Psor* rhus-t k* sep bg2* spig k* ter bg2 *Thuj* k*
  - **rheumatic**: chinin-m kr1
  - **stitches** and aversion to sunlight; with: nux-v
- **Tenon's** capsule: bry mfj kali-i mfj **Kalm** mfj puls mfj rhus-t mfj
- **Trachoma**: *(↗conjunctiva - granular)* acon bg2* alum mfj alumn hr1* apis tl1 *Arg-n* mfj ars bg2* *Aur* mfj aur-m bg2 bell bg2* calc bg2* chinin-m c2* cupr mfj cupr-s c2 euphr bg2* kali-bi bg2* merc bg2* merl c2 *Nat-m* mfj *Nit-ac* bg2 nux-v mfj phos bg2 puls mfj rhus-t bg2* sang hr1 sep mfj staph bg2 sulfa sp1 sulph bg2* thuj b4a.de*
- **Uvea** (= uveitis): arn mfj **Aur** mfj **Bry** mfj **Gels** mfj hep mfj **Kali-bi** mfj kali-i mfj merc mfj **Rhus-t** mfj sil mfj streptoc jl2 toxo-g jl2*

INGROWING EYELASHES (See Hair - ingrowing)

INJECTED: acon bg3* aesc k2 all-c k* androc bnm2• ant-t apis bg3* arg-n bg3* *Arn* bg3* astac aur-m k2 bapt hr1 bar-m k2 bar-ox-suc rly4• *Bell* k* bry k2 bufo camph cedr *Clem* con cub c1 cycl a1 ferr ferr-ar ferr-m ferr-p **Glon** k* *Hep Kali-bi* led bg3* mang-p rly4• meph a1 *Merc* k* merc-i-r a1 mill k2 nat-m bg3* *Nux-v* bg3* phasco-ci rbp2 podo fd3.de• symph fd3.de• tere-la rly4• verat-v hr1 vesp k2

○ - **Canthi**:

○ - **Inner**: ammc vml3• euphr k2 laur nat-p symph fd3.de•
  - **Outer**: sars h2
- **Conjunctiva**: apom vh1
  - **dark** vessels; full of: aesc k2 alumn k2 *Apis* arg-n ars ars-h bar-m *Bell Calc Calc-p Camph* cann-i cann-s k2 *Carbn-s Chinin-s Chlol* clem *Con Cop Crot-c Crot-t Euphr Ferr Graph Ham Hep Ip* kali-ar *Kali-bi* kali-c *Kali-i* kali-p kali-s *Lach* lyss merc *Merc-c Mez* morph *Morph-s* hr1 *Nat-ar*

- **Conjunctiva** – **dark** vessels; full of: ...
  Nat-m *Nux-v Op* phos podo sang sec sep *Sil* spig stram stry sul-ac k2 *Sulph* tarent thuj visc c1
  ⁝ **morning**: *Mez*
  ⁝ **headache**; during: *Bell* bro1 glon kr1* meli bro1 nux-v bro1 sang hr1
  ⁝ **menses**; before: puls
- **Cornea**: **Aur** k* *Graph* k* hep *Ign* k* ip *Merc* k* plb

INJURIES; after: (↗*Inflammation - retina - commotio)* acon k* *Arn* k* art-v br1 *Bry* b7a.de calc k* calc-s calc-sil gm1 calen bro1 canth bro1 cic bg2 *Cine* br1 coc-c st coch bro1 con b4a.de* erig ptk1 *Euphr* k* ham k* hep h2* hyper st1* kali-bi gm1 *Led* k* nit-ac bg2 petr bg2 phys c2* puls b7a.de* *Rhus-t* bro1 ruta bg2 sil k* *Staph* k* sul-ac k* sulph k* *Symph* k* thuj gm1
- **bloodshot** (See Ecchymosis)
- **blunt** instrument; from: *Arn* mrr1
- **contusions**: *Acon* b7a.de *Arn* b7a.de *Euphr* b7a.de puls b7a.de
- **foreign** body; from: **Acon** b7a.de* *Arn* b7a.de* *Calc* b4a.de coc-c st *Hep* b4a.de *Sil* hr1 *Sulph* b4a.de
- **incisions**: staph bro1*
- **lacerations**: asar gm1 hyper mrr1 staph bro1*
  - **painful**: asar gm1
- **penetration**: hyper mrr1
- **stitch**; from a: *Con* b4a.de

○ - **Bone** (See orbits)
- **Conjunctiva**: acon bro1 *Arn* bro1 *Ham* bro1 lach bro1 led bro1 nux-v bro1
- **Cornea**: acon b7a.de arn b7a.de con b4a.de euphr b7a.de
- **Orbits**: acon bro1 arn bro1* ham bro1 led mrr1 ruta bg2* symph bro1*
- **Retina**: acon bro1 *Arn* bro1 bell bro1 *Ham* bro1 lach bro1 led bro1 phos bro1

INSENSIBILITY: ars b4a.de carbn-o carbn-s chen-a a1 cic k2 crot-h k* dig b4a.de hyos k* kali-br kali-p bro1 op k* *Stram*
- **coma**; with (See MIND - Coma - eyes - insensibility)

○ - **Eyeball** | **right**: chen-a c1
- **Lids**: plb b7.de*

INTOXICATED appearance (See FACE - Expression - intoxicated)

INTOXICATION; after: | **agg.**: nux-v b7.de* spong b7.de*

INVERSION of lids: (↗*Hair - ingrowing)* anan *Arg-n* mfj (non:*Bor-pur* mrr1) *Borx* k* *Calc Graph* k* lyc hr *Merc* k* *Merc-c* mfj *Nat-m* k* *Nit-ac* psor bg* puls bg2* *Sil* bg2* *Sulph* k* tell bro1* zinc

IRITIS (See Inflammation - iris)

IRRITATION: amyg-p c2* apis arge-pl rwt5• *Ars* k* atis bnj1 bar-ox-suc rly4• canth mrr1 carbn-dox knl3• cardios-h rly4• *Caust* con k* cortiso tpw7* **Euphr** mrr1 fago k* ign k* iod k* irid-met srj5• ketogl-ac rly4• *Luna* kg1• lyc mang-p rly4• med c1 merc-i-f nat-ar pant-ac rly4• petr-ra shn4• puls k* ran-s k* rhus-t k* ruta sang sinus rly4• *Trios* rsj11• vanad br1
- **right**: mand rsj7•
- **left**: mand rsj7•
- **daytime** only: iod k*
- **morning**: apoc k*
- **afternoon**: bad k*
  - **13-15** h: sal-al blc1•
- **evening**: iod k* lyc *Ruta*
  - **candlelight**; from: lyc
  - **reading** by light | **lamplight**: *Apis*
- **burn**; after: canth mrr1
- **eyelashes** in it; as if: chlam-tr bcx2•
  - **morning**: chlam-tr bcx2•
- **light**; from artificial: colch rsj2•

○ - **Canthi**:
  - **right** eye: propr sa3•

○ • **Inner**: allox tpw3
  ⁝ **left** eye: *Propr* sa3•
- **Conjunctiva**: *Acon* bro1 *Arg-n* mrr1 sulph bro1
- **Lids**: allox tpw3 borx mrr1 *Trios* rsj11•
  - **right**: trios rsj11•
  - **air**; in cold | **amel.**: coff
  - **lachrymation**; from: gard-j vlr2•

Irritation – **Lids**: ...

○ • **Margins** of: nat-m bg2 **Sulph** mrr1
- **Optic** nerve: (non:phos k*) phos-h a1*
- **Orbits**:
  - **right**: bac jl2

○ • **Below**:
  ⁝ **extending** to | **Axilla**: bac jl2

ITCHING: absin acon *Agar* k* agath-a nl2• *Agn* br1* *Aids* nl2• *All-c* k* allox tpw3* *Alum* k* alum-sil k2 am-c b4.de* am-m k* ambr b7.de* anan *Ant-c* k* ap-g br *Apis* k* *Arg-met* k* *Arg-n* arge-pl rwt5• arizon-l nl2• ars b4.de* ars-met bro1 arund asaf b7.de* asc-t aspar aur aur-m k* bamb-a stb2.de• *Bar-c* k* bar-i k2 *Bar-m* st bar-s k2 bell k* berb *Bit-ar* wht1• borx k* bov b4.de* bry k* bufo cadm-met sp1 *Calc* k* calc-p calc-s calc-sil k2 cann-s canth k* carb-an k* *Carb-v* k* carbn-s k2 cardios-h rly4• casc *Caust* k* chel b7.de* chim chin chord-umb rly4• cist k2 clem coli rly4• coloc k* con b4.de* cop cortiso gse croc bro1 cupr k* cycl k* diosm br1 dulc fd4.de elaps eug *Euphr* k* fago k* ferr k* ferr-i fuma-ac rly4• galeoc-c-h gms1• gamb bro1 gels ger-i rly4• germ-met srj5• grat k2 hep hura hydro-v a1 hygroph-s bnj1 ign k* iod irid-met srj5• *Kali-bi* k* kali-c h2 kali-n kali-s *Kalm* kola stb3• kreos k* lac-h htj1• lach k* lachn lap-la sde8.de• laur b7.de* lob *Luna* kg1• *Lyc* lyss m-ambo b7.de* m-arct b7.de m-aust b7.de mag-c k* *Mag-m* k* *Manc* bg2 mand rsj7• mang b4.de* mang-p rly4• meph *Merc* k* merc-c k* *Mez* mim-p rsj8• *Moni* rfm1• mosch k* *Mur-ac* k* *Nat-c* k* *Nat-m* k* nat-p nat-pyru rly4• nat-s k* nat-sil fd3.de• nicc nit-ac *Nux-v* k* ol-an olib-sac wmh1 olnd b7.de* osm ozone sde2• paeon pall pant-ac rly4• parth vml3• *Petr* k* petr-ra shn4• ph-ac *Phel Phos* k* phyt pin-con oss2• plat b4.de* podo fd3.de• *Positr* nl2• pot-e rly4• psor al **Puls** k* pycnop-sa mrz1 ran-b k* rhod k* rhus-t k* ros-d wla1 ruta sacch-a fd2.de• sal-fr sle1• samb bat1• sang bg2 sars sep k* sil k* *Sin-a* bg *Sin-n* bg2 spig k* spong fd4.de squil b7.de* stann k* staphycoc rly4• stram stront-c k* succ-ac rly4• **Sulph** k* tarent tell br1* tere-la rly4• thres-a sze7• trios rsj11• tritic-vg fd5.de tung-met bdx1• urol-h rwt• vanil fd5.de verat h1 vesp viol-t k* *Zinc* k* [buteo-j sej6 heroin sdj2 *Spect* dfg1]
- **right**: germ-met srj5• irid-met srj5• nat-pyru rly4• positr nl2• stront-c sk4•
- **left**: *Aids* nl2• bit-ar wht1• melal-alt gya4 spong fd4.de stront-c sk4• symph fd3.de• vanil fd5.de

▽ • **extending** to | **right**: cench k2
- **morning**: agar k* am-c arge-pl rwt5• borra-o oss1• *Brucel* sa3• calc-s k2 caust h2 chinin-m kr1 chord-umb rly4• dios dulc fd4.de fago irid-met srj5• meph nat-c h2 *Nat-m Nat-s* podo fd3.de• ruta fd4.de spong fd4.de stront-c sk4• *Sulph* tritic-vg fd5.de vanil fd5.de
  - **rising** agg.; after: nat-m
  - **waking**; on: *Brucel* sa3•
- **forenoon**: ruta fd4.de *Sulph* tritic-vg fd5.de
  - **11** h: nat-c
- **evening**: *Acon* bamb-a stb2.de• brucel sa3• calc calc-p *Cupr* dios dulc fd4.de erig eug euph ferr *Gamb* mag-c meph *Merc-c* nat-sil fd3.de• pall phos plat h2 podo fd3.de• **Puls** ruta fd4.de sil spong fd4.de **Sulph** tritic-vg fd5.de vanil fd5.de vesp
  - **rubbing** | **not** amel.: pall
- **night**: ars galeoc-c-h gms1• stront-c sk4• sulph
  - **bed**; before going to: brucel sa3•
- **air**; in open:
  - **agg.**: dulc fd4.de staph bg1
  - **amel.**: **Puls**
- **biting** from rubbing: ruta h1
- **cold**:
  - **applications** | **amel.**: kola stb3• *Puls* k*
  - **bathing** | **amel.**: bit-ar wht1•
  - **water** | **amel.**: stront-c sk4•
- **corrosive**: ars h2
- **coryza**; during: caps *Gels* lp moni rfm1• ros-d wla1 tritic-vg fd5.de
- **cough** agg.; during: cassia-s ccrh1•
- **dinner**; after: mag-c
- **exertion** of the eyes agg.: *Rhus-t*
- **fever**; during: cedr bg2*
- **gnawing** (See Pain - gnawing - itching)
- **house**; in: ran-b
- **lachrymation**; with: bit-ar wht1•
  - **rubbing**; from: nat-c h2 ruta h1

- **light**; from:
  - **agg.**: anan
  - **gaslight** | **agg.**: *Phyt*
- **moistening** eye amel.: nat-c h2
- **pressure** upward amel.: bell h1
- **reading** agg.: carbn-s k2
- **rubbing**:
  - **agg.**: agath-a nl2• irid-met srj5• *Kalm* kreos melal-alt gya4 sulph
  - **amel.**: agar k* agath-a nl2• am-c h2 bit-ar wht1• brucel sa3• *Caust* dulc fd4.de euph h2 *Euphr* galeoc-c-h gms1• mag-c mag-m h2 nat-c *Nux-v* ol-an phos h2 podo fd3.de• ruta fd4.de spig h1 spong stann h2 stram sulph tritic-vg fd5.de vanil fd5.de zinc
- **stool** agg.; after: carbn-s k2
- **waking**; on: *Brucel* sa3•
- **warm** | **bathing** | **agg.**: *Mez*
  - **room** | **agg.**: *Puls Sulph*

○ - **About**: agn apis ars h2 aur-s k2 berb *Carb-v* con lach lyc olib-sac wmh1 pall sars spong fd4.de til
- **Around** the eyes: colch rsj2•
- **Below**: nat-m h2 spong h1
- **Canthi**: aeth a1 agar agath-a nl2• aln vva1• **Alum** k* *Ant-c* ap-g bro1 apis b7a.de **Arg-met** k* *Arg-n* arge-pl rwt5• arn k* ars bro1 asc-t *Aur* k* aur-s bg* bell k* benz-ac berb borx **Calc** k* carb-v k* *Caust* k* cina k* cinnb clem *Con* k* crot-c dulc fd4.de *Euph* k* *Euphr* ferr-ma *Fl-ac* k* galeoc-c-h gms1• *Gamb* k* graph k2 hell b7.de* *Hep* bro1 hyos b7.de* iod k* kali-bi bg2 kali-s fd4.de kola stb3• led k* *Lyc* k* m-ambo b7.de mag-c bg2 *Mosch Mur-ac* k* *Nat-m* k* nux-v k* orot-ac rly4• petr ph-ac h2 phos bro1 plat b4.de* plb bg2 prun psor al *Puls* k* ruta k* sep spong fd4.de staph k* *Stront-c* k* succ-ac br1* *Sulph* k* tritic-vg fd5.de trom vanil fd5.de zinc k*
  - **evening**: aln vva1• mag-c ph-ac h2 puls
    - **air**; in open:
      - **agg.**: staph
      - **amel.**: gamb

○ - **Inner**: agath-a nl2• **Alum** k* alum-p k2 ap-g br *Apis* k* *Aur* bell b4.de* borx k* calc carb-v *Caust* k* chel chlol c1 cimic gk cina *Cinnb* clem *Con* k* cycl dulc fd4.de fl-ac k* galeoc-c-h gms1• *Gamb* k* *Graph* grat guare mtf11 ham fd3.de• hyos kali-s fd4.de lach laur led b7.de* *Lyc* k* m-ambo b7.de m-arct b7.de mag-c k* **Mag-m** melal-alt gya4 mez mur-ac h2 nat-ar bg2 *Nat-m* nat-sil fd3.de• nit-ac k* nux-v b7.de* ol-an bg2 olib-sac wmh1 osm ph-ac h2* phos *Psor* k* *Puls* k* pyrid rly4• rhus-t bg2* *Ruta* k* sep k* spong fd4.de stann k* staph k* *Stront-c* k* *Sulph* syph tab tritic-vg fd5.de trom vml3• vanil fd5.de verat bg2 *Zinc* k* [ambro stj]
    - **right**: alum b4.de* aur b4a.de benz-ac bg2 calc bg2 caust b4.de* cina bg2 cycl bg2 grat bg2 mag-m b4.de* manc bg2 phel bg2 phys bg2 sulph b4.de* tab bg2 trom bg2
    - **left**: agar bg2 aids nl2• aln vva1• apis b7a.de* carb-v b4.de* caust b4.de* dios bg2 galeoc-c-h gms1• hyos bg2 kali-n bg2 lach bg2 lachn a1 laur b7.de* lob bg2 mez bg2 nat-c b4.de nat-m bg2 osm bg2 prun bg2 sil bg2
      - **Upper** lid: galeoc-c-h gms1•
    - **morning**: sep
    - **evening**: dios fl-ac ham fd3.de• nat-sil fd3.de• *Puls* spong fd4.de vanil fd5.de
  - **Outer**: agath-a nl2• ant-c k* aur-m benz-ac bry k* carb-v cina b7.de* cinnb com euph b4.de* euphr fago form hyos b7.de* kali-p fd1.de• m-ambo b7.de* mez mosch b7a.de *Nat-m* prun puls b7.de* rhus-t sep k* spong fd4.de squil b7.de* *Sulph* tarent tax tritic-vg fd5.de upa vanil fd5.de
    - **right**: calc b4.de* carb-v b4.de* mur-ac b4.de* rhus-t b7.de*
    - **left**: alum b4.de* bry b7.de* calc b4.de* euph b4.de* nat-m b4.de* sep bg2 squil b7.de*
- **Eyebrows** (See FACE - Itching - eyebrows)
- **Lids**: agar h2* agath-a nl2• agn b7.de* aids nl2• alum k* alum-p k2 ambr k* ambro br1* anag ang h1 apis k* **Arg-met** arg-n ptk1 ars b4.de* asaf asc-t aur aur-m aur-s k2 bamb-a stb2.de• bell k* berb bit-ar wht1• bros-gau mrc1 bry k* bufo cadm-met tpw6 *Calc* k* camph b7.de* carb-an h2 carb-v b4.de* carbn-s *Caust* k* chin b7.de* cina b7.de* cocc b7.de* con croc k* *Crot-t* cycl k* dros k* dulc fd4.de euph k* *Euphr* k* gal-ac c1 gamb bro1* *Graph* k* helo c1 helo-s c1* *Hep* k* iod h* kali-ar *Kali-bi* k* kreos b7a.de led h1* lob lyc b4.de* m-ambo b7.de m-arct b7.de m-aust b7.de mag-m h2 mand rsj7• melal-alt gya4 *Merc* b4a.de *Mez* k* *Morph* bro1 nat-c b4.de* nat-p nux-v k* olnd b7.de* paeon pall par b7.de* *Petr Ph-ac Phos* k* podo fd3.de• positr nl2• psor a1 **Puls** k* **Rhus-t** k* ruta h1

Itching – **Lids**: ...

sal-fr sle1• *Sep* k* sil h2 sin-n spong k* staph b7.de* streptoc rly4• succ-ac br1* **Sulph** k* tarent **Tell** k* ter mrr1 tritic-vg fd5.de verat b7.de* vesp vinc zinc k* zinc-p k2
  - **right**: *Apis* b7a.de bros-gau mrc1 croc b7.de* kali-c b4.de* nat-c b4.de* phos b4.de* psor jl2
  - **left**: aids nl2• apis b7a.de chin b7.de* hydroph rsj6• nat-c b4.de* positr nl2• tritic-vg fd5.de
  - **daytime** only: *Phos* **Sulph**
  - **morning**: carb-v dulc fd4.de nat-c h2 nux-v ruta fd4.de
  - **evening**: *Mez* phos h2 **Puls** ruta fd4.de tritic-vg fd5.de
  - **rubbing**:
    - **agg.**: plac rzf5•
    - **amel.**: agath-a nl2• staph h1

○ - **Lower**: carb-v b4a.de caust b4.de* lach b7.de* petr b4.de* petr-ra shn4• ruta b7.de* sul-ac b4.de*
    - **left**: alum b4.de* euph b4.de*
  - **Margin**: agar bro1 agath-a nl2• alum bro1 am-c *Ambro* bro1 asaf bar-c h2 bry *Calc* k* *Carb-v* chin con dulc fd4.de euphr fago *Gamb* bro1 graph bro1 grat jatr-c kali-bi kali-c kreos lyc bro1 mez k* *Morph* bro1 nat-ar nat-p *Nat-s* nux-v k* phos plac rzf5• plut-n srj7• prun **Puls** k* pycnop-sa mrz1 rhus-t bro1 sel k* *Sep* **Staph** k* succ-ac bro1 *Sulph* k* tell bro1 zinc k*
    - **right**: olib-sac wmh1
  - **Tarsi**: calc bg2* clem bg2 kali-bi bg2 mez bg2 puls ptk1 sabad ptk1 sel bg2 sep bg2 staph bg2*
  - **Upper**: agn b7.de* ang b7.de* bar-c b4.de* bros-gau mrc1 carb-an b4.de* cassia-s ccrh1• cina b7.de* con b4a.de croc b7.de* *Lyc* b4a.de sil b4.de* staph b7.de*
    - **right**: alum b4.de* apis b7a.de laur b7.de* rhus-t b7.de*
    - **left**: bry b7.de* mag-m b4.de* olnd b7.de* plb b7.de* zinc b4.de*
    - **cold** applications | **amel.**: cassia-s ccrh1•
    - **sunlight** agg.; from: cassia-s ccrh1•
- **Orbital** arch: kali-n h2 nat-m bg2

JERK in right lid; burning: sulph h2

JERKING of the muscles of the eyes (See Movement - convulsive)

KEEP the eyes open; difficult to (See Opening - difficult - keep)

KERATITIS (See Inflammation - cornea)

KERATOCONUS (See Conical)

LACHRYMATION: (↗*Discharges - lachrymal; Tears*) absin acet-ac achy-a bnj1 *Acon* k* acon-ac rly4• act-sp aesc *Agar* k* agath-a nl2• agn b2.de* aids nl2• *Ail* **All-c** k* all-s aloe *Alum* k* am-c k* am-m k* ambr k* *Ambro* br1* amph a1 anac k* androc srj1*• ant-t b2.de* antip bro1* *Apis* k* apom vh1 aran-sc vh1 *Arg-n* k* arge-pl rwt5• arist-cl sp1 arn k* *Ars* k* ars-i ars-met bro1 ars-s-f k2 art-v arum-t arund *Asar* k* atra-r bnm3• *Aur* k* aur-ar k2 aur-i k2 aur-s k2 bamb-a stb2.de• bapt hr1 bar-c b2.de* bar-s k2 **Bell** k* berb borx k* bov b2.de* *Brom* k* bros-gau mrc1 bry k* buth-a sp1 cadm-s **Calc** k* calc-i k2 calc-p camph b2.de* *Cann-s* b7a.de canth b2.de* *Caps* k* *Carb-ac* carb-an k* *Carb-v* k* *Carbn-s Cardios-h* rly4• caul *Caust* k* cench k2 *Cham* *Chel* k* chin k* chinin-ar chlam-tr bcx2• chlol chlor k* cimic cina k* cinnb clem k* coc-c coff b2.de* *Colch* k* coli rly4• coloc k* *Com Con* k* cor-r bg2 cortiso gse *Croc* k* *Crot-c Crot-h Crot-t* cupr-ar cyclosp sa3• cystein-l rly4• daph dig k* dios diosm br1 dulc fd4.de *Elaps* eug k* *Eup-per Euph* k* **Euphr** k* *Ferr* k* ferr-ar *Ferr-i Ferr-p* **Fl-ac** k* formal br1 fuma-ac rly4• gamb gels ger-i rly4• germ-met srj5• gink-b sbd1• glon bg2* *Granit-m* es1• *Graph* k* grat guare bro1 *Ham* hell b2.de* helo c1 helo-s c1* *Hep* k* hydr hydro-v a1 *Hydrog* srj2• hygroph-s bnj1 *Ign* k* *Iod* k* ip k* irid-met srj5• jab br1 kali-ar *Kali-bi* k* *Kali-br* hr1 *Kali-c* k* *Kali-i* k* kali-n b2.de* kali-p k* kali-s ketogl-ac rly4• kola stb3• kreos k* *Lach* k* lachn lap-la sde8.de• lat-m sp1* laur b2.de* *Led* k* lil-t br1 limest-b es1• **Lyc** k* *M-ambo* b2.de* m-arct b2.de* m-aust b2.de* *Mag-c* k* mag-m h2 mag-p br1 mag-s mand rsj7• mang-p rly4• meny b2.de* **Merc** k* *Merc-c* b4a.de* *Merl* k* *Mez* mill moni rfm1• morb jl2 mosch k* mur-ac b2.de* muscin a1 naja narc-ps c1* nat-ar k* *Nat-c* k* **Nat-m** k* nat-p *Nat-s* k* nat-sil fd3.de• nept-m lsd2.fr nicc **Nit-ac** k* nux-m k* *Nux-v* k* ol-an *Olib-sac* wmh1 olnd k* **Op** k* osm *Par* k* parth vml3• pert jl2 petr k*

Lachrymation: ...
petr-ra shn4• ph-ac k* phasco-ci rbp2 **Phos** k* phyt k* pitu-p sp1 plat b2.de* plut-n srj7• positr nl2• *Psor* **Puls** k* ran-b k* ran-s k* rheum k* *Rhod* k* rhus-g tmo3• **Rhus-t** k* rosm lgb1 *Ruta* k* *Sabad* k* sabin k* *Sang* k* sangin-n br1* sanic mrr1 sars b2.de* sec b2.de* sel k* *Seneg* k* *Sep* k* *Sil* k* sin-n sinus rly4• *Sol-ni* sphing kk3.fr *Spig* k* *Spong* k* squil k* stann k* staph k* stict bro1 *Stram* k* stront-c b2.de* stry succ br1* succ-ac rly4• *Sul-ac* k* **Sulph** k* sumb symph fd3.de• syph al* taosc iwa1• *Tarax* k* tax c2* tell k* teucr k* thiam rly4• thres-a sze7• *Thuj* k* trios rsj11• tritic-vg fd5.de tub-a jl2 ust valer b2.de* vanil fd5.de *Verat* k* verat-v a1 viol-o b2.de* visc c1* xan c1 *Zinc* k* [bell-p-sp dcm1 heroin sdj2]

- **right**: acon bg2* aids nl2• ars bg2 brom k* calc calc-sil k2 cassia-s cdd7*• chin h1 chlam-tr bcx2• dulc fd4.de fic-m gya1 fuma-ac rly4• graph k2 haliae-lc srj5• ham fd3.de• hydrog srj2• *Hyos* k* irid-met srj5• kali-n h2 lyc h2 mag-c h2 mand rsj7• nit-ac h2 olib-sac wmh1 podo fd3.de• sang hr1* sep bg2* spig bg2* spong fd4.de stram a1 ulm-c jsj8• vanil fd5.de verb k* vesp k*
  - **alternating** with | **Mouth**; dry sensation in: ulm-c jsj8•
- **left**: abrom-a ks5 *Aids* nl2• arum-t k2 bros-gau mrc1 calc-s hr1 carb-ac k* carb-v h2 cench k2 chin-b hr1 clem *Coloc* k* cyclosp sa3• dios k* elaps hr1 gink-b sbd1• *Ign* k* irid-met srj5• kali-s fd4.de kola stb3• mag-c h2 nat-sil fd3.de• olib-sac wmh1 phys hr1 plut-n srj7• ruta fd4.de sel rsj9• sin-n k* symph fd3.de• thuj h1* (non:uran-met k) uran-n vanil fd5.de
- **daytime** only: **Alum** k* bry tl1 lyc k* sars k* sep tl1 zinc k*
- **morning**: alum am-m h2 arge-pl rwt5• bell h1 borx h2 bung-fa mtf *Calc* k* carb-an dulc fd4.de granit-m es1• ham fd3.de• irid-met srj5• kali-n k* kali-p fd1.de• kreos lachn limest-b es1• mag-c merc nat-ar k2 nat-c nat-m k* nat-sil fd3.de• nicc oci-sa sk4• petr-ra shn4• phel phos podo fd3.de• **Puls** k* rat rhus-t ruta fd4.de sacch-a fd2.de• *Sep* k* spong fd4.de staph stront-c sk4• **Sulph** k* symph fd3.de• tritic-vg fd5.de vanil fd5.de zinc k*
  - **early**: calc bro1* *Puls* ptk1 *Sulph* ptk1
  - **rising** agg.: plut-n srj7•
  - **waking** | **after** | **agg.**: alum h2 dulc fd4.de ham fd3.de• podo fd3.de• ruta fd4.de spong fd4.de vanil fd5.de
    - **on**: irid-met srj5• marb-w es1• nat-ar plut-n srj7• ruta fd4.de sep symph fd3.de• tritic-vg fd5.de zinc h2
- **forenoon**: ham fd3.de• nat-c k* squil vanil fd5.de
- **afternoon**: arge-pl rwt5• dulc fd4.de kali-p fd1.de• lyc h2 spong fd4.de vanil fd5.de
  - **14** h: cyclosp sa3•
  - **17** h: chinin-m kr1
- **evening**: acon k* all-c k* asar bung-fa mtf calc k* cystein-l rly4• dulc fd4.de eug k* euphr br1 gink-b sbd1• kali-s fd4.de mag-m k* merc nicc k* olib-sac wmh1 phos k* podo fd3.de• *Rhus-t* k* *Ruta* *Sep* k* ter k* tritic-vg fd5.de vanil fd5.de **Zinc** k*
- **night**: acon all-s am-c h2* am-m h2* *Apis* k* am bg1 ars bg1 bar-c bg1 chin h1 dulc fd4.de gels bg1 hep c1 nit-ac ptk1 phos h2 psor a1 ran-s bg1 tritic-vg fd5.de vanil fd5.de **Zinc** k*
- **abundant** (See profuse)
- **accompanied** by:
  - **blurred** vision (See VISION - Blurred - accompanied - lachrymation)
  - **dryness**; sensation of (See Dryness - sensation - accompanied - lachrymation)
  - **measles** (See SKIN - Eruptions - measles - accompanied - coryza)
  - **sneezing**: just ptk1 nat-m ptk1 sabad ptk1
  - **stricture** of lachrymal duct (See Stricture)
  - **swelling** | **Lachrymal** glands (See Swelling - lachrymal - accompanied - lachrymation)
  - **vomiting** (See STOMACH - Vomiting - accompanied - lachrymation)
  - ○ **Head**:
    - **complaints** of (See HEAD - Complaints - accompanied - lachrymation)
    - **pain** in (See HEAD - Pain - accompanied - lachrymation)
  - **Heart**; complaints of (See CHEST - Heart; complaints - accompanied - lachrymation)
- **air**; in open:
  - **agg.**: ail alum alum-p k2 arn bapt a1 bar-c bell bry **Calc** k* camph *Canth* carbn-s *Caust* chel chlor *Clem* cob coc-c *Colch* k* dios dulc euph *Graph* hyos lyc h2* mang-p rly4• merc nat-ar *Nat-m* k* nat-sil fd3.de• nit-ac petr phel **Phos** k* phyt podo fd3.de• *Puls* rheum *Rhus-t* *Ruta* *Sabad* k* sacch-a fd2.de• sanic bro1 senec seneg *Sep* **Sil** k* staph **Sulph** symph fd3.de• **Thuj** tritic-vg fd5.de trom vml3• ust vanil fd5.de verat vesp ptk2 zinc zinc-p k2
  - **amel.**: agath-a nl2• all-c bro1 chinin-s *Croc* phyt k* plat h2 prun ptk1
- **amel.**: prun ptk1
- **bending** head backward | **amel.**: seneg ptk1
- **breathing** deep agg.: graph ptk1
- **chill**; during: **Apis** b7a.de* bell bg2 elat euphr k2 kreos bg2 *Mez* b4a.de* rhus-t bg2 sabad ptk1
- **closing** the eyes agg.: berb bg2* spong bg2*
- **cold**:
  - **air** agg.: acon bro1 ars-i k2 calc-sil k2 chlam-tr bcx2• chord-umb rly4• cob dig k* echi elaps gk euphr eupi c1 kali-sil k2 kreos lyc nat-sil fd3.de• phos **Puls** ruta k2 sanic c1* *Sep* *Sil* sul-i k2 sulph gt1 thuj
  - **applications**:
    - **agg.**: sanic bro1*
    - **amel.**: *Puls* mrr1
- **contraction** of upper lid, from: spig h1
- **copious** (See profuse)
- **coryza**; during: acon agar agn bg2 **All-c** k* alum k* *Anac* k* anan *Arg-n* k* ars k* ars-i bry k2 calc-s hr1 calc-sil k2 carb-ac k* *Carb-an* hr1 **Carb-v** k* cench k2 cham k2 *Chin* k* *Dulc* k* euph tl1 **Euphr** k* iod jab kali-bi bg2 *Kali-c* lac-c tl1 lach k* lyc moni rfm1• nat-sil fd3.de• **Nux-v** k* petr-ra shn4• *Phos* *Phyt* k* *Puls* k* pyrid rly4• ran-s k* *Sabad* *Sang* k* sin-n *Spig* k* squil b7.de* staph k* **Tell** k* tritic-vg fd5.de vanil fd5.de verat b7.de* *Verb* k*
  - **amel.**: lach bg2
  - **discharge**; with | **amel.**: lach bg2
- **cough**; with: acon k* *Agar* k* *All-c* bg2* aloe arg-n bg2 am bg2* *Bell* bg2 brom bry k* calc caps bro1 carb-ac carb-v k* cench chel k* choc srj3• cina k* cupr ptk1 cycl k* *Eup-per* k* euph **Euphr** k* *Graph* k* hep k* hydrog srj2• ip irid-met srj5• kali-c kali-m kali-perm kali-s fkr2.de kreos m-ambo b7.de merc moni rfm1• **Nat-m** k* nat-sil fd3.de• op k* ozone sde2• phel bg2 *Phyt* k* **Puls** k* rhus-t k* *Sabad* k* sil k* **Squil** k* staph sulph tritic-vg fd5.de tub xxb
  - **profuse** lachrymation, with every paroxysm of cough: am k1
  - **whooping** cough: all-c hr1 *Caps* k* *Graph* k* *Nat-m* k*
- **dreams**; during: plan ptk1
- **eating**; while: ol-an c1* vanil fd5.de zinc ptk1*
- **epiphora** (See profuse)
- **fever**; during: acon ail bg1 apis bell calc cham eup-per gels ign lyc petr *Puls* k* sabad bro1 spig spong stram ptk1 sulph
- **followed** by | **salivation**: atra-r bnm3•
- **gushing**: am-c ptk1 aur bg2* chinin-ar bg2* eug bg1 ip ptk1 rhus-t ptk1
- **headache**; during: *(↗HEAD - Complaints - accompanied - lachrymation)* adam skp7• agar apis ptk1 arg-n asar bell bov carb-an carb-v chel k* com con cypra-eg sde6.de• dulc fd4.de eug euphr k2 ham fd3.de• hep *Ign* k* ind kali-c k* kali-i kali-s fd4.de kola stb3• lac-c lach bg1 lil-t merc mez ptk1 nat-m bg1 osm phel bro1* *Plat* k* *Puls* k* rhus-g tmo3• rhus-r rhus-t bro1 ros-d wla1 ruta fd4.de spig bro1 spong stann hr1 stram sulph k2 symph fd3.de• tax k* tritic-vg fd5.de vanil fd5.de
- **itching**: ars ptk1 senec ptk1
  - **morning**: *Granit-m* es1•
- **laughing** agg.: carb-v h2 nat-m k* phos ptk1 symph fd3.de• tritic-vg fd5.de vanil fd5.de
- **light**; from:
  - **agg.**: **Con** mrr1 dig dulc fd4.de kreos puls spong symph fd3.de•
  - **bright** light | **agg.**: ail arist-cl sp1 chel *Chinin-s* dig ptk1 *Kreos* *Mag-m* k* sabad spong
  - **sunlight** | **agg.**: agath-a nl2• bros-gau mrc1 bry dulc fd4.de eug vml3• graph ign sang a1 staph k*
- **looking**:
  - **fire**; at the: ant-c chel *Mag-m* k* *Merc* k* sabad
  - **steadily**: *Apis* chel k* cinnb echi euph euphr k* gink-b sbd1• ign ip hr1 kali-c kreos j5.de nat-ar osm plat h2 psor c1* *Seneg* spong tab
  - **sun** agg.; at: staph ptk1

- **lying** agg.: euphr ptk1
- **menses** | **before** | **agg.**: euphr bro1
  - **during** | **agg.**: calc k* euphr bro1 phyt bg3* zinc k*
- **music**; hearing: graph ptk1
- **nose**:
  - **biting** pain in; from: aur h2
  - **itching**; from: kali-p fd1.de• mag-m h2 nat-sil fd3.de• plat h2
- **opening** the eyes:
  - **agg.**: *Kali-bi* k* **Rhus-t** hr1
  - **forcibly** agg.: acon k2 *Apis* k* *Con* k* *Ip* k* *Merc-c* k* *Rhus-t* k*
- **pain**; from: chel ptk1 cinnb ptk1 lach ptk1 mez ptk1 nat-m ptk1 plan ptk1 puls ptk1 ran-b ptk1 sabad ptk1
  - **eye**, in: aml-ns vh1 aphis br1 calc chel cimic hr1 *Coloc* ferr gels hr1 gink-b sbd1• hep h2 ip c1 lac-d k2 lac-f c1 lap-la sde8.de• mag-c h2 mag-m h2 meny h1 nat-c h2 petr-ra shn4• rheum h spig gk stann k2 sulph h2 thuj h1
    - **lid**; right: xan c1
  - **face**; in: bell j5.de* ip bro1 lach j5.de nux-v bro1 plan bro1* puls bro1* spig j5.de verb bro1
  - **nose**, in: anac h2 aur h2 hydrog srj2• mag-m h2 olib-sac wmh1
  - **other** parts of body; in: acon h1 ferr *Sabad*
  - **supraorbital** region; in: mez c1
  - **throat**, in: sep k*
- **peppery** sensation in throat and mouth; from: hydrog srj2•
- **profuse**: abrom-a ks5 all-c k2* atra-r bnm3• calc bro1 dulc fd4.de **Euphr** br1* graph bro1 hep bro1 ignis-alc es2• lat-m bnm6• med tl1 merc bro1* *Merl* bro1 *Nat-m* bro1 plb mtf33 sil bro1 squil bro1 tong bro1
  - **accompanied** by:
    - **inflammation** of eye (See Inflammation - accompanied - lachrymation)
    - **photophobia** (See Photophobia - accompanied - lachrymation)
- **reading** agg.: *Am-c* k* arist-cl sp1 *Carbn-s* *Croc* k* elaps gk grat hera c1 ign irid-met srj5• nat-ar nat-m mrr1 nit-ac olib-sac wmh1 olnd k* phos ruta *Seneg* k* sep still stront-c ptk1 sul-ac k*
- **rising** agg.: visc sp1
- **room** agg.: agn a1 asar bamb-a stb2.de• caust *Croc* dig k* phos podo fd3.de• syph br
- **rubbing**; after: nat-c h2 ph-ac h2 ruta h1 sep h2
- **sensation** of: ars bg2 chlam-tr bcx2• nit-ac bg2 phasco-ci rbp2 spig b7.de*
  - **asleep**; when falling: phasco-ci rbp2
- **side**, affected●: lach bg3 nat-m bg3 nux-v bg3 puls bg3 spig bg3
- **sleep**; during | **Canthi**; outer: psil ft1
- **snow**; from: acon bro1
- **stinging** | **morning**: *Granit-m* es1•
- **stool** agg.; during: **Phos** vh
- **sun** agg.; in: bry ptk1
- **suppressed**: sec ptk1
- **swallowing** agg.: arg-n bg1*
- **tickling** larynx; from: chel ptk1
- **tiredness**; from: visc sp1
- **urination**:
  - **before**: *Dulc* b4a.de
  - **during**: *Clem* hr1 **Phos** vh
- **vomiting**:
  - **before**: apom br1
  - **with** (See STOMACH - Vomiting - accompanied - lachrymation)
- **walking** in open air agg.: bapt a1
- **warm** room agg.: *All-c* bamb-a stb2.de• *Phos*
- **weakness**; from: visc sp1
- **weather** agg.; wet: crot-h graph
- **wind** agg.●: calc vml1.nl* dulc fd4.de **Euphr** k* kali-p fd1.de• ketogl-ac rly4• lac-h htj1• lyc *Nat-m* k* nat-sil fd3.de• phos k* plut-n srj7• **Puls** k* rhus-t ruta k2 sanic k* sep gk *Sil* sulph *Thuj*

Lachrymation: ...

- **writing**:
  - **after**: ferr
  - **agg.**: *Calc* k* ol-an k* staph h1 vanil fd5.de
- **yawning** agg.: abies-n vh ammc kr1 ant-t arge-pl rwt5• bar-act a1 bar-c bg bell h1 calc-p ferr h1* hell bg hydrog srj2• ign k* kali-c kreos mag-p ptk meph *Nux-v* k* ph-ac h2* plat h2 rhus-t *Sabad* k* sars staph k* tub xxb viol-o

○ - **Affected** side agg.: lach ptk1 nat-m ptk1 nux-v ptk1 puls ptk1 spig ptk1

- **Canthi**: *Nat-m* b4a.de petr b4.de* thuj b4.de*

○ • **Outer**: sil b4.de*

- **sleep**; during (See sleep - canthi)

LARGE; feels too: *Ars* b4a.de *Guaj* b4a.de *Mag-c* b4a.de *Mez* b4a.de *Ph-ac* b4a.de plb tl1 *Seneg* b4a.de sep b4a.de sulph b4a.de thuj b4a.de

○ - **Eyeballs**: nat-m tl1

LENS after cataract surgery; to absorb: seneg mtf11

LIGHT; from:

- **agg.**: (↗*Photophobia)* acon b7.de* all-c bg2 apis b7a.de arg-n bg2 *Ars* bg2 asar b7a.de* bell b4a.de* **Calc** bg2 carb-an b4.de* clem b4.de* colch b7.de* dig b4a.de* **Euphr** b7.de* ip b7a.de kreos bg2 lyc b4.de* mag-m b4.de* mang b4.de* merc-c bg2 mur-ac b4.de* nit-ac b4.de* **Nux-v** b7.de* phos b4.de* *Puls* b7a.de *Rhus-t* b7a.de sars b4.de* staph b7.de* sulph bg2 thuj b4.de*
- **amel.**: *Am-m* b7.de*
- **artificial** light | **agg.**: ars ptk1 calc bg2 calc-p bg2 carb-an bg2 cina bg2 croc bg2 *Dros* bg2 **Euphr** bg2 glon bro1 graph bg2 hep bg2 jab bro1 *Lach* bg2 laur bg2 lyc bg2 mag-m bg2 mang bg2 *Merc* bg2 mez bg2 nat-s bg2 nux-m bg2 petr bg2 ph-ac bg2 phos bg2 phyt bg2 pic-ac ptk1 plat bg2 podo bg2 **Puls** bg2 *Ruta* bg2 sars bg2 seneg bg2 **Sep** bg2 sulph bg2
- **bright** light | **agg.**: clem ptk1
- **candlelight** | **agg.**: agn b7a.de *Bell* b4a.de *Calc* b4a.de carb-an b4.de *Caust* b4a.de *Cina* b7.de* *Croc* b7.de* graph b4.de kali-c b4a.de laur b7.de *Lyc* b4.de* mang b4.de* merc b4.de nux-m b7.de petr b4.de *Ph-ac* b4.de* phos b4.de plat b4.de *Ruta* b7.de* sars b4.de* *Seneg* b4.de* *Sep* b4a.de sulph b4.de
- **daylight** | **agg.**: ant-c b7.de* calc b4a.de *Con* bg2 *Dros* bg2 *Euphr* bg2 **Graph** b4a.de* *Hep* b4a.de* mag-c b4.de* mang b4.de* **Merc** bg2 nit-ac b4.de* **Nux-v** bg2 petr b4.de* **Ph-ac** bg2 phos b4.de* rhod b4.de* sars b4.de* **Sep** b4.de* *Sil* bg2 *Sulph* b4.de* thuj b4a.de
- **moonlight** | **amel.**: (↗*MIND - Moonlight)* *Aur* k*
- **sunlight** | **agg.**: aml-ns bg2 *Asar* b7a.de* *Bell* bg2 *Bry* b7a.de* calc b4a.de *Euphr* bg2 graph b4.de* *Ign* b7a.de* m-arct b7.de mag-m b4.de* *Nat-c* b4.de* ph-ac b4a.de puls b7a.de* stram bg2 *Sulph* b4.de* zinc b4.de*

LINE:

- **fine** line under margin of lower lid: asaf vh3 lil-t vh3 mosch vh3 nat-m vh3*
- **transverse** line through middle of upper lid | **children**; in: **Nat-m** mrr1

LONG lashes (See Hair - eyelashes - long)

LOOKING: (↗*VISION - Exertion of)*

- **distance**, agg.; into: dig euphr ruta
- **downward**:
  - **agg.**: acon b7.de* alum b4a.de* bell bg2 nat-m ptk1 stann bg2
  - **amel.**: bar-c bg2* sabad b7.de*
- **fire**; at the: apis ptk1 mag-m b4.de* *Merc* b4.de* nat-s ptk1
- **intently**:
  - **agg.**: anac b4.de* aur b4.de* bar-c b4.de* *Bell* b4a.de calc bg2 canth b7.de* *Carb-v* b4.de* chel b7.de* chin b7a.de cina b7.de* croc b7.de* dros b7.de* graph b4.de* kreos bg2 lach bg2 laur b7.de* lyc b4.de* *Merc* bg2 nat-m b4.de* petr bg2 phos b4.de* plat b4.de* ran-b b7.de* rhod b4.de* rhus-t b7.de* *Ruta* b7.de* seneg b4.de* spong b7.de* staph b7.de* stront-c b4.de* sul-ac b4.de* sulph bg2 valer b7.de*
  - **amel.**: petr k*
- **light**; at:
  - **bright** light: am-m b7.de* apis b7a.de *Ars* b4a.de *Bry* b7a.de calc bg2 chel b7a.de graph b4.de* ign b7.de* kreos b7a.de* mag-m b4.de* mang bg2 *Nux-v* b7a.de* *Ph-ac* bg2 sabad b7.de*
  - **sun**; into the: *Apis* ptk1 graph b4.de* *Lyc* ptk1 seneg b4.de*
- **long** time at something; for a: kreos b7a.de rheum b7.de* ruta b7.de*
- **momentary** agg.: ars bg2 puls bg2 sabin bg2

Eye

- **one** eye only; with: phos b4.de* til bg2
- **paper**; at pieces of | **agg.**: calc-s ptk1
- **sideways** agg.: bar-c bg2 bell b4a.de mag-m bg2
- **steadily**: (↗*VISION - Exertion of)* agar apis cadm-s calc k2 caust croc *Merc Ruta* k* spong thuj
- **upward**:
  - **agg.**: alum b4.de* *Ars* k* bell carb-v k* *Chel* k* colch puls b7.de* sabad b7.de* sabin b7.de* sars bg2 sulph
  - **amel.**: alum bg2
  - **cannot**: arund c1
- **white** objects agg.; at: apis k* graph b4.de* *Lyc* ptk1

LOOSE, sensation as if: all-c bg2 bell bg2 *Bry* bg2 camph bg2 *Carb-an* k* carb-v bg2 caust bg2 con bg2 dros bg2 guaj bg2 ign bg2 kali-bi bg2* **Lach** bg2 laur bg2 led bg2 ph-ac bg2 ran-b bg2 rhod bg2

LOOSENED:

○ - **Conjunctiva**: *Apis* b7a.de arg-n bg2 *Bell* b4a.de* brom b4a.de* dig bg2 gels bg2 *Lyc* b4a.de *Merc* b4a.de *Puls* b7a.de *Seneg* bg2 sil b4a.de **Sulph** b4a.de* *Thuj* b4a.de
- **Lids**: bell b4a.de *Sulph* b4a.de

○ • **Inner** side: **Rhus-t** b7a.de

LOSS of vital fluids agg.: anac bg2 calc bg2 *Chin* bg2 *Cina* bg2 nat-c bg2 nat-m bg2 nux-v bg2 ph-ac bg2 sep bg2 sulph bg2

LUMP:
- **sensation** of a lump | **Canthi**; outer: sul-ac hr1*

LUPUS:

○ - **Eyebrows** (See FACE - Cancer - lupus - eyebrows)
- **Lids**: alumn kali-chl phyt

○ • **Lower** lid: *Apis*

LUSTERLESS (See Dullness)

LYING:
- **agg.**: ars bg2 carb-v bg2 con bg2 gels bg2 iod bg2 led b7.de* phos bg2 zinc bg2
- **bed**; in | **agg.**: merc-c b4a.de
- **side**; on:
  - **painful** side | **agg.**: syph bg2

LYING DOWN:
- **agg.**: carb-v b4.de m-ambo b7.de zinc b4.de
- **amel.**: *Ars* bg2 **Merc** bg2

MACULAR DEGENERATION (See Atrophy - choroid; Inflammation - choroid)

MASTURBATION agg.: *Cina* bg2

MELANOSIS: *Aur* k*

MELT away; feel as would: ham st1

MEMBRANE drawn over eyes; sensation as if: apis caust k* croc bg daph *Kola* stb3• puls rat

MENSES:
- **after** | **agg.**: calc bg2 cinnb bg2 phos bg2
- **agg.**: aur bg2 bell bg2 cic bg2 cocc bg2 con bg2 mag-c bg2 nat-m bg2 nux-v bg2 phos bg2 plat bg2 puls bg2 rhus-t bg2 sep bg2 stram bg2 sulph bg2
- **before** | **agg.**: *Apis* b7a.de *Ars* bg2 aur bg2 bell bg2 brom bg2 cinnb bg2 cycl bg2 ign bg2 lyc bg2 merc bg2 nat-m bg2 nux-v bg2 sil b4.de* zinc bg2
- **during** | **agg.**: acon bg2 alum bg2 am-c bg2 apis bg2 *Ars* bg2 *Bell* bg2 bov b4.de* brom bg2 **Calc** b4.de* cann-xyz bg2 carb-an bg2 *Castm* bg2 caust bg2 cedr bg2 cham bg2 chel bg2 chin bg2 cic bg2 cimic bg2 cinnb bg2 colch bg2 croc ptk1 crot-t bg2 cycl bg2 elaps bg2 euph bg2 gels bg2 glon bg2 graph bg2 hep bg2 hyper bg2 ign bg2 kali-c bg2 lyc bg2 **Mag-c** b4.de* mag-m bg2 merc bg2 mosch bg2 naja ptk1 nat-m bg2 *Nit-ac* bg2* nux-m bg2 nux-v bg2 phos bg2 phyt bg2 plat bg2 *Puls* bg2 rhod bg2 sep bg2 verat-v bg2 *Zinc* bg2

MENTAL EXERTION agg.: cina b7.de* ign b7.de* nux-v b7.de*

MOISTENING the eyes: | **amel.**: staph b7.de*

MOONLIGHT; eye symptoms amel. by (See Light - moonlight - amel.)

MOTION:
- **agg.**: agar bg2 **Bry** bg2 chin b7.de* *Gels* bg2 influ jl2* kali-bi bg2 led b7.de* *Nux-v* bg2 plb b7.de* ran-b b7.de* spig b7a.de
- **eyelids**; of:
  - **agg.**: *Ars* b4a.de *Colch* b7a.de coloc ptk1 m-aust b7.de
  - **amel.**: asar b7.de* stann b4.de*
  - **difficult**: arn b7a.de nux-m b7a.de rhus-t b7.de* *Verat* b7a.de
  - **impossible**: meny b7.de* rhus-t b7a.de spig b7.de*
  - **spasmodic** | **to** and fro: ruta b7.de*
- **eyes**; of | **agg.**: acon b7.de* *Arn* bg2 **Ars** b4.de* bapt bg2 bell bg2 *Brom* b4a.de *Bry* b7a.de* calc bg2 camph b7.de* cham b7.de* **Chin** b7.de* clem b4.de* con b4.de* cupr b7a.de *Hep* b4.de* ign b7.de* kali-c bg2 lach bg2 led bg2 mag-m bg2 mang b4.de* merc b4.de* nat-m b4.de* nux-v bg2 phos bg2 puls b7.de* ran-b bg2 ran-s b7.de* rhus-t b7.de* *Spig* b7.de* spong b7.de* stann b4.de* stront-c b4.de* **Sulph** b4.de* valer b7.de*
- **face** agg.; of muscles of: puls b7.de*

MOVEMENT:
- **one** side: apoc ptk1 phyt bg2*
- **constant**: agar k* arg-n br1* *Bell* k* ben-n caust ptk1 cham ptk1 cupr ptk1 hyos ptk1 *Iod* kali-br ptk1* kali-i ptk1 mag-p ptk1 phys lp sil *Stram* k* thal-xyz srj8•
  - **closed** lids, under: ben-n cupr bg2* zinc bg2*
- **convulsive**: acon k* *Agar* k* **Bell** k* bufo canth k* *Cham* b7.de* chinin-s cic ptk1 cocc c1 coff cupr b7.de* hyos b7.de* ign k* *Kali-br* hr1 kali-cy *Lach* b7a.de m-arct b7.de* *Mag-p* spig b7a.de sulph verat zinc
  - **delivery**; during: chinin-s hr1
  - **light**; from: bell
  - **menses**; during: chin b7a.de
  - **sleep** agg.; during: hell op ph-ac
  - **waking**; on: coff
- **cyclophoria** (See rotary)
- **difficult**: am-c b4a.de ang b7a.de arn b7a.de borx b4a.de *Hep* b4a.de lach b7a.de laur b7.de* loxo-lae bnm12• *Spig* b7.de*
- **direction**; in every (See constant)
- **easy** (= increased mobility): bell b4.de* *Camph* b7a.de con b4a.de cupr b7.de* *M-arct* b7.de* *Merc-c* b4a.de ph-ac b4.de*
- **involuntary** (= nystagmus): *Agar* k* atra-r bnm3• bell mtf33 ben-n c2* bufo mtf33 *Calc* canth k* carbn-h bro1 caust mtf33 *Cic* bro1 cupr k* gels c2* hyos b7a.de* iod bro1 ix bnm8• kali-i c2* lach b7a.de m-arct b7a.de *Mag-p* k* meny mtf11 *Nux-v* oxyum-sc mcp1• phys bro1 spig b7.de* stram b7.de* sulph syph jl2 zinc mtf33
  - **lateral**: atra-r bnm3•
  - **staring** ahead; when: ph-ac
- **irregular**: agar k2
- **pendulum** like, from side to side: **Agar** k* amyg *Ars* k* *Bell* mfj ben-n benz-ac ptk1 *Carbn-h* cic cocc bg2* con h2 *Cupr* k* elaps ptk1 *Gels* k* hyos mfj ign mfj jab mfj kali-c bg1 kali-i bg2 mag-p mfj* nux-v mfj phys mfj puls bg2* sabad stram mfj sulph zinc bg2*
- **rapid**: plut-n srj7•
- **restless**: iod bg2
- **rolling**: (↗*rotary; Turned)* aeth *Agar* k* amyg apis bg2 arg-n *Bell* k* ben-n *Bufo* k* camph *Caust* k* cham *Cic Cocc* k* colch con h2 cori-m a1 *Cupr* k* *Euphr Gels* hell *Hyos* k* kali-br kali-i lach ptk1* lyss merc merc-c nat-ar op petr raph bg1 santin sec *Stram* stry tarent ter tub ust *Verat Zinc* k*
  - **closed**; with eyes: cocc tl1* cupr bro1* stict ptk1
  - **convulsions**; during: zinc bro1
  - **drink**, at sight of: bell
  - **sideways**: *Ben-n* bro1 spig h1 zinc bro1
  - **sleep**:
    - **during**: aeth mtf33 *Apis* ol-an puls h1
    - **going** to sleep; on | **agg.**: aeth c1*
  - **up** and down: benz-ac sulph thal-xyz srj8•
  - **upward**: *Acon* amyg anan *Apis* bell bro1 *Bufo* camph *Cic* bro1 cina *Cupr* hell bro1 *Lact Laur* mur-ac bro1 oena bro1 plat ter *Verat*
- **rotary** motion of the eyeball: (↗*rolling)* colch bg2 rat bg2 seneg mfj verat bg2

- **sensation** of: calc b4a.de
- **sleep**:
  - **amel.**: agar k2 [tax jsj7]
  - **during**: aeth ptk1 apis ptk1

O - **Lids** | **irregular**: bell bg2

MYDRIASIS (See Pupils - dilated)

NARROWING of intervals between lids: *Agar* k* ant-c b7.de* arg-n k* *Arn* b7.de* canth b7.de* croc bg2 crot-h bg2 dig h2 euphr nat-m nux-v rhus-t squil b7.de*
- **left**: squil vl1.nl
- **necessary**: aloe bg2

NAUSEA; during (See Complaints - accompanied - nausea)

NEAR the eyes; bringing objects: | **aversion** to: fl-ac k* mang

NEURALGIA (See Pain - neuralgic)

NODULES in lids (See Tumors - lids - nodules)

NUMBNESS: asaf bg2

O - **Around** the eyes: **Asaf** k* haliae-lc srj5•
- **Eyebrows**: *Asaf* bg2
- **Lids**:
  - **looking** upward: ulm-c jsj8•

O
  - **Lower**:
    - **right**: ulm-c jsj8•
      - **extending** to | **left**: ulm-c jsj8•
  - **Upper**: asaf b7.de* naja bg2
- **Mucous** membranes: *Kali-br* br1
- **Retina**: cina tl1

NYSTAGMUS (See Movement - involuntary)

OBSTRUCTION: | **Lachrymal** canal (See Stricture)

ONYX: *Hep* k* *Merc* k* rhus-t k*

OPACITY:

O - **Conjunctiva**: zinc k2
- **Cornea**: *(↗Spots; Spots - cornea)* *Acon* b7a.de agn ang b7.de* *Apis* k* **Arg-n** k* asaf tl1 atra-r bnm3• *Aur* k* *Aur-m* k* *Aur-s* k2 bar-c k* *Bar-i* bar-s k2 *Bell* b4a.de* *Bov* b4a.de **Cadm-s** k* **Calc** k* calc-f k* calc-hp bro1 calc-i bro1 calc-p k* calc-sil k2 *Cann-s* k* **Cann-xyz** ptk1 caps b7.de* *Caust* k* *Cham* b7a.de *Chel* k* *Chin* k* *Cina* bro1 cine c1* *Cinnb Cocc Colch* k* **Con** k* *Crot-t* k* *Dig* b4a.de dulc b4a.de euph k* *Euphr* k* helo-s br1* *Hep* k* *Hydr Kali-bi* k* *Kali-c* k* kali-m bro1 *Kali-s* kali-sil k2 *Lach* k* lepr mtf11 *Lyc Mag-c* k* *Merc* k* merc-c k* *Merc-i-f Naphtin* bro1* **Nat-m** b4a.de *Nit-ac* k* op k* phos b4a.de* plb b7.de* podo bg2 puls k* rhus-t ruta b7.de* sacch c2* *Seneg* k* *Sil* k* *Stann* b4a.de **Sulph** k* tarax b7.de* *Tarent* k* thiosin br1* tub al* *Zinc* k* **Zinc-s** c2* zing c1
  - **right**: *Lyc Sil*
  - **left**: *Hep Sulph*
  - **accompanied** by | **cataract**: cine mtf11
  - **arcus** senilis: acon ars calc ptk1 *Cocc Coloc Kali-bi* kali-c bg3* **Lyc** ●* *Merc* k* merc-c mosch ox-ac bg2 phos bg3* **Puls** k* **SULPH** k ●* vanad bg2 vario ptk1 zinc
  - **diffuse**: calc-p mtf33
  - **dust**; as if covered with: sulph b4a.de
  - **punctuated**: kali-bi kali-chl kali-i
  - **smallpox**; after: *Sil* k*
  - **smoky**, cloudy: **Apis** b7a.de *Chin* b7a.de
  - **spots**; in: calc-f ptk1
  - **white** hue; like a: **Con** b4a.de
  - **wounds**; from: *Euphr* k*

O
  - **Vitreous**: chlol c2 chol br1 colch *Gels* k* ham bro1* hep bro1* kali-i bro1* kali-n br1 merc-c bro1* *Merc-i-f* merc-i-r bro1* morg-g pte1* *Phos* k* prun k* psor k* seneg k* *Sulph* k* syc pte1* thuj bro1*
    - **turbid**: chlol bro1 chol ptk1 *Kali-i* bro1* phos bro1* prun bro1* *Seneg* bro1* sol-ni bro1 sulph bro1*

OPEN lids: *(↗MIND - Prostration)* acon bg *Ang* bg ant-t apis aur bg *Bell* bg camph bg *Caust* k* *Cocc* crot-h *Cupr Dol* **Guaj** hydr-ac *Hyos* k* **Iod** k* *Laur* **Lyc** naja nat-m bg nux-m bg nux-v k* olnd k* *Onos Op* k* *Phos* bg phys bro1 plb bg rhus-t bg sol-ni squil *Stram* k* tanac a1 thuj mtf33
- **one** side: ant-t gsy1* chin bg2* ign bg2* verat bg2*
- **right** eye | **more** open than the other: staph h1
- **accompanied** by | **apoplexy**: bell bg2 ip bg2 op bg2 stram bg2 thuj bg2
- **attack**; before an: *Laur*
- **coma**; with (See MIND - Coma - eyes - open)
- **delirium**; with: *Crot-h* k* op bg2 **Stram** k*
- **half** open: *Agar* alum bg2 amyg *Ant-t* k* *Apis* arn b7a.de* *Ars* k* ars-s-f k2 *Art-v* bapt k* **Bell** k* *Bry* k* cadm-s cann-i *Canth* caps k* *Carbn-h Cham* k* chin bg2 *Cocc Coff Colch* k* *Coloc* k* *Crot-c Crot-h* **Cupr** k* *Dig* ferr k* ferr-ar k2 ferr-m ferr-p *Gels Hell* k* *Hydr-ac* k* ign b7.de* *Ip* k* *Kreos Lach* laur k* *Lyc* k* mag-m h2 *Merc Morph Nat-m Oena* **Op** k* ph-ac k* phel *Phos* k* plb podo k* *Rhus-t* samb k* *Stram* k* *Sulph* k* ter thuj bg2* verat k* *Zinc* k* zinc-p k2
  - **left**: arn ptk1 fl-ac ptk1 squil a1*
  - **coma**; with (See MIND - Coma - eyes - open - half)
  - **convulsive**: op bro1
  - **diarrhea**; during: sulph mtf33
  - **one** eye half open, the other closed | **sleep**; during: chin bg2 ign bg2
  - **sleep**; during: ant-t b7a.de* arn bg2 ars bg2 bell bg2* bry b7a.de* caps bg2 *Cham* bro1 chin bg2 coloc bg2 ferr b7.de* hell b7.de* hyos bro1 ign bg2 ip b7.de* laur bg2 lyc bg2 *Op* b7.de* ph-ac bg2 podo bg2* *Samb* b7.de* stram b7.de* sulph bg2 thuj bg2 verat b7.de* zinc bg2*
- **hard** to keep open (See Opening - difficult - keep)
- **must** keep the eyes open: *(↗Opening - desire)* arn br1
  - **and** look into the light: puls
- **sensation** as if open: bell bg2
  - **wide** open: *Brucel* sa3• carb-v choc srj3• fl-ac rb2 ger-i rly4• haliae-lc srj5• lac-lup hrn2• marb-w es1• onos pip-m tung-met bdx1•
    - **closed** lids are wide open: *(↗Closed; Opening - unable)* phos sep
- **sleep**; during: ant-t apis gsy1 ars k* *Bell* k* bry cadm-s k* calc h2* chin *Cocc* coloc b4a.de con h2 cupr cur a1 dat-f c1 diph ptk1 ferr ferr-p c1 fuma-ac rly4• gard-j vlr2• hyos gl1.fr• ip *Lyc* k* op k* ph-ac k* phos sne puls h1* samb stram k* sulph k*
- **spasmodic**: acon b7.de* aeth ang k* apis arn k* aur bg2 **Bell** k* camph k* *Caust Cocc* crot-h bg2* dol euph b4.de* *Guaj* hyos k* **Iod** k* *Ip* k* laur k* lyc lyss naja nat-m b4.de* nux-m bg2 **Nux-v** k* op k* *Phos* b4.de* plb bg2 rhus-t bg2 squil b7.de* **Stram** k* *Stry* tarent k2*
  - **delirium**; during: *Op Stram*
- **unable** to open the eyes (See Opening - unable)
- **unconsciousness**; during: cic hr1 *Op* k* ter sne
- **wide** open: plb a1 stram mtf33
  - **delirious** speech; with (See MIND - Speech - delirious - eyes)

OPENING the lids (= raising lids):
- **agg.**: acon b7.de* alum bg2 *Ars* b4a.de *Bell* b4a.de borx b4a.de canth b7.de* *Clem* b4a.de croc b7.de* euph b4.de* ign b7.de* *Ip* b7a.de kali-bi bg2 mag-m b4.de* *Nux-v* b7.de* phos b4.de* *Spig* b7.de*
- **aversion** to open them, fears it will agg. the headache: phys
- **closing** in quick succession; and: agar chlf hr1 mygal hr1*
- **desire** to keep the eyes wide open: *(↗Open lids - must)* onos
- **difficult**: **Acon** b7.de* *Agar* k* alum k* ambr k* anan k* ang bg *Arg-met* arg-n **Ars** k* **Bell** b4.de* *Borx* k* bov b4.de* bry b7.de* **Calc** b4.de* caps b7.de* carb-v b4.de* **Caust** k* **Cham** b7.de* *Chel* k* *Cina* b7.de* cocc b7.de* *Con* k* croc b7.de* cupr k* dig b4a.de elaps euph b4.de* *Ferr* k* ferr-ar *Fl-ac* **Gels** k* germ-met srj5• granit-m es1• hell b7.de* hep b4.de* hydr-ac hyos k* ign b7a.de *Ip* b7a.de kali-ar kali-c k* lac-h sk4• lach b7.de* *Lyc* mag-c b4.de* *Mag-m* k* *Merc* k* merl (non:nat-act kl) *Nat-c* b4a.de* nat-m *Nit-ac* k* nux-m b7.de* *Nux-v* k* petr b4.de* *Phos* k* puls b7.de* rhus-t b7.de* samb sep k* *Sil* b4a.de spig k* spong b7.de* stann hr1 sul-ac k* thuj b4a.de verat b7.de* *Viol-o* b7a.de viol-t b7.de* visc c1
  - **right**: plut-n srj7•
  - **left**: alum b4.de*

- **difficult**: ...
  - **morning**●: (*↗Agglutinated - morning)* ambr bar-c borx bov *Caust* con cortiso gse hep bg1 luf-op rsj5• *Lyc* mag-c h2 mag-m med jl2 nicc *Nit-ac Petr Ph-ac* psor rhus-t **Sep** k ● sul-ac
    - **waking**; on: (*↗Agglutinated - waking)* atra-r skp7• *Cocc* k* kali-c plut-n srj7•
  - **night**: carb-v h2 chel *Cocc* mag-m nat-m rhus-t **Sep** k ●
  - **dryness** of eyes; from: nux-m mrr1
  - **face**; during pain in: chel ptk1
  - **keep** the eyes open; hard to: ars bapt *Borx* bufo caust fum rly1• **Gels** helo c1 helo-s c1* hyos lavand-a ctl1• naja nat-ar ph-ac pic-ac
  - **sneezing**; after: *Graph* ptk1
  - **swallowing** | **amel.**: ter ptk1
- **shutting** involuntarily; and: musca-d szs1
- **sneezing**; causes: **Graph**
- **unable** to: (*↗Closed; Open lids - sensation - wide - closed)* abrot *Alum* k* alum-p k2 am-c anan *Arg-met* ars ars-s-f k2 *Aur* aur-ar k2 bufo cadm-s carb-v *Cham Chel Con* gels hell hyos kali-n h2 lach lyc mag-c merl nat-ar k* nat-sil fd3.de• **Nux-m** *Nux-v* oena op petr ph-ac sil staph sul-ac syph k2 *Tarent* thuj
  - **morning**: *Lyc* mag-m nat-sil fd3.de• petr ph-ac staph thuj
    - **pressure** in forehead; from: ph-ac
  - **night**: ars carb-v cinnb *Cocc*
    - **sleeplessness**; during: nat-c h2
    - **waking**; on: *Merl* verat hr1
  - **headache**; during: (*↗Closing - must - pain - head)* euph h2 nat-m ptk1 nux-v h1 petr h2 ph-ac a1 *Tarent* k*
  - **heaviness** in forehead; from: *All-s* vh1
  - **menses**; during: *Cimic* k*
  - **sleeplessness**; with: nat-c h2
  - **swelling** around the eyes; from: **Apis** mrr1
  - **waking**; on: am-c h2 *Merl* nat-sil fd3.de•

OPENNESS; spasmodic (See Open lids - spasmodic)

OPERATION; after: *Acon* bro1 alum ptk1 arn bro1 asaf ptk1 asar bro1 bry bro1 croc bro1 ign bro1 *Led* bro1 mez ptk1 rhus-t bro1 seneg bro1 staph ptk1 stront-c bro1 thuj bro1 zinc ptk1

OPHTHALMIA (See Inflammation)

ORBITAL CELLULITIS (See Inflammation - orbit - cellulitis)

PAIN: (*↗Stiffness)* *Abel*↓ abrom-a↓ absin achy-a↓ *Acon* k* act-sp↓ adam skp7• aegle-m↓ aesc k2 aeth agar k* *Agath-a* nl2• **Agn**↓ aids↓ ail↓ alf↓ *All-c* allox tpw4 *Aloe* k* *Alum* alum-p↓ alum-sil k2 alumn k2 am-br↓ *Am-c* am-m k* *Ambr* ammc↓ amph↓ *Anac* anan androc↓ ang↓ anh↓ ant-c↓ ant-t aphis↓ *Apis* k* *Apoc*↓ arag↓ aran↓ *Arg-met*↓ *Arg-n* arge-pl↓ arist-cl↓ *Arn* k* *Ars* ars-i ars-met↓ ars-s-f↓ arum-t↓ arund↓ *Asaf* asar asc-t aspar aster↓ *Atro* **Aur** aur-ar k2 aur-i k2 aur-m aur-m-n↓ aur-s↓ bad k* *Bamb-a* stb2.de• bapt *Bar-c* k* bar-i↓ bar-m bar-s↓ **Bell** k* bell-p-sp↓ benz-ac↓ benzol↓ *Berb* beryl↓ *Bism*↓ bit-ar↓ blum-o↓ *Borx* bov k* brom bros-gau mrc1 **Bry** k* bufo bufo-s↓ bung-fa↓ cadm-s↓ cain↓ calad *Calc* k* calc-i k2 *Calc-p Calc-s* calc-sil k2 *Camph*↓ cann-i↓ *Cann-s*↓ canth b7.de* *Caps*↓ *Carb-ac* carb-an carb-v k* *Carbn-s* carc↓ card-m cardios-h↓ *Carl* cartl-s↓ cassia-s ccrh1• *Caul*↓ *Caust Cedr* cench↓ cephd-i↓ *Cere-b*↓ **Cham** *Chel* k* *Chen-a* chim↓ **Chin** chin-b↓ chinin-ar chinin-m↓ *Chinin-s*↓ chion bro1 chlam-tr↓ *Chlol*↓ chlor choc↓ chord-umb↓ chr-o c2 cic *Cimic* k* cina k* *Cinnb Cist*↓ *Clem* k* cob↓ cob-n↓ *Coc-c*↓ coca↓ *Cocc* coff↓ *Colch* k* *Coloc Com Con* cop cor-r *Corn*↓ cortico tpw7 cortiso↓ *Croc* k* crot-c *Crot-h Crot-t Cund*↓ *Cupr Cur*↓ *Cycl*↓ cystein-l rly4• daph dendr-pol↓ *Dig* k* dios↓ dioxi↓ dirc↓ dor↓ dros↓ dulc fd4.de echi *Elaps* ephe-si↓ ery-a↓ esin↓ eug↓ eup-per k* *Euph*↓ *Euphr* k* eupi↓ fago↓ falco-pe↓ ferr *Ferr-ar* ferr-i ferr-m↓ *Ferr-p* fic-m↓ fl-ac form↓ fum↓ galeoc-c-h gms1• galla-q-r nl2• gamb gard-j vlr2• *Gels* k* ger-i↓ germ-met↓ gink-b sbd1• *Glon* k* glycyr-g↓ gran↓ *Granit-m*↓ *Graph* grat↓ grin c2 *Guaj*↓ *Guar Guare* gymne gymno haliae-lc srj5• *Ham* hed↓ hedy a1 hell *Hep* k* heroin↓ hir↓ hist↓ hom-xyz↓ hura↓ *Hydr* hydr-ac↓ hydrc hydro-v↓ hydrog↓ hydroph↓ hyos hyper iber↓ *Ign* k* ignis-alc↓ ilx-a↓ ind↓ indg↓ indol↓ iod k* ip irid-met srj5• jab jug-c↓ jug-r↓ juni-v↓ *Kali-ar* kali-bi *Kali-c* kali-chl↓ kali-i kali-m↓ *Kali-n*↓ *Kali-p* kali-s kali-sil k2 **Kalm** k* ketogl-ac↓ kola↓ kreos *Lac-ac Lac-c*

Pain: ...
lac-d k2 lac-del hrn2• lac-e↓ lac-f↓ lac-h↓ lac-lup↓ *Lach* lachn↓ lact↓ lact-v↓ lap-la↓ laur↓ *Lec*↓ led lept↓ lil-t limen-b-c↓ limest-b↓ lith-c lob *Luf-op*↓ *Luna* kg1• **Lyc** k* lycps-v↓ *Lyss* m-ambo↓ m-arct b7.de m-aust↓ mag-c mag-m *Mag-p* mag-s c2 malar↓ manc mand↓ mang k* marb-w↓ *Med* medul-os-si↓ melal-alt↓ meli↓ mentho↓ meny↓ meph **Merc** *Merc-c* k* merc-i-f merc-i-r *Merl Mez* k* mill k2 mim-p↓ moni↓ mosch↓ *Mur-ac*↓ muru↓ myos-a↓ myric↓ nabal↓ naja naphtin↓ nat-ar k* nat-c b4.de* **Nat-m** k* nat-ox↓ nat-p nat-pyru rly4• *Nat-s*↓ nat-sil fd3.de• nept-m↓ *Nicc*↓ nicc-s↓ **Nit-ac** k* *Nux-m*↓ *Nux-v* oena↓ ol-an↓ *Olib-sac*↓ olnd b7.de* onos↓ *Op*↓ orot-ac↓ osm ox-ac ozone↓ paeon↓ pall par parth↓ passi↓ *Petr* k* petr-ra shn4• *Ph-ac* phel *Phos* k* *Phos-pchl*↓ *Phys* physala-p bnm7• *Phyt* pic-ac *Pieri-b*↓ pilo↓ pin-con oss2• pitu-a↓ pitu-gl skp7• plac-s↓ *Plan Plat* k* *Plb* k* plut-n↓ podo polys↓ positr↓ pot-e rly4• *Propr*↓ *Prot*↓ *Prun* psil ft1 *Psor Ptel Puls* k* pycnop-sa↓ pyrog↓ rad-br sze8• rad-met↓ **Ran-b** k* ran-r↓ ran-s b7.de* raph↓ rauw↓ rheum↓ *Rhod Rhus-t* k* rhus-v ribo rly4• rob↓ ros-d↓ rumx **Ruta** k* sabad sabin b7.de* sacch-a↓ sal-al↓ *Sal-fr*↓ samb bat1• **Sang** sangin-n br1 santin *Sars* k* scroph-n↓ scut↓ sec *Sel Senec*↓ **Seneg** *Sep* k* *Sil* k* sin-a↓ *Sin-n*↓ sinus↓ sol-ecl↓ sol-ni↓ **Spig** k* *Spong* squil↓ *Stann* k* *Staph* k* stict↓ stram *Stront-c*↓ stry suis-em↓ suis-hep↓ suis-pan rly4• **Sul-ac**↓ sul-i↓ *Sulph* sumb↓ suprar↓ symph c2 syph k2* tab tarax *Tarent* tax↓ tax-br↓ tell↓ tep↓ *Ter* tetox↓ *Teucr*↓ *Ther* k* thiam↓ thres-a↓ *Thuj* til↓ tril-p↓ *Trios* rsj11• tritic-vg fd5.de tub k* ulm-c↓ upa↓ urt-u usn↓ ust valer k* vanil fd5.de verat k* verat-v↓ verb↓ vesp vib↓ viol-o↓ viol-t↓ vip↓ xan↓ xanth↓ xero↓ *Zinc* k* zinc-p k2 zing

- **one** side: syph jl2
  - ▽ **extending** to:
    - **Other** side: **Chin**↓ nat-c↓ syph jl2
      - **burning**: **Chin** nat-c
- **alternating** sides: *Chin*↓ lac-c k2 nat-c↓
  - **burning**: *Chin* nat-c k13
- **right**: abrom-a↓ *Agath-a* nl2• ambr↓ amph↓ anag vh1 anan aphis br1 *Apis* apoc↓ arg-n↓ ars↓ bapt↓ **Bell** k* bell-p-sp↓ bit-ar wht1• bov↓ bry↓ calc-ar cann-i↓ **Carb-ac** card-m cedr bro1 celt↓ *Chel* bro1 choc srj3• cic↓ coc-c colch↓ *Coloc*↓ **Com** k* cortiso↓ croc↓ crot-c↓ crot-h dios↓ dol dulc↓ ephe-si↓ erig *Ferr*↓ fl-ac a1 germ-met↓ gran↓ haliae-lc↓ ham↓ hydrog srj2• ign↓ ina-i mlk9.de *Kali-c* kali-p↓ kali-s↓ kali-sil k2 *Kalm* k* ketogl-ac↓ kola stb3• lac-h↓ mag-c↓ *Mag-p* bro1 mand rsj7• med medul-os-si↓ *Nat-m* nat-sil↓ nept-m lsd2.fr olib-sac↓ ozone↓ pall petr-ra↓ phys↓ plut-n↓ podo fd3.de• propr sa3• *Prun* k* psor a1 puls↓ pyrog↓ *Ran-b* k* rhus-t↓ ruta bro1* sal-fr↓ **Sang** k* **Sep**↓ *Sil Spig*↓ spong↓ *Sulph*↓ suprar↓ symph↓ tarent tell c1 thuj↓ til↓ trios rsj11• tritic-vg fd5.de uran-n sne verat-v a1 vero-o rly3• zing↓ [tax jsj7]
  - **evening**: cortiso↓
    - **sore**: cortiso sp1
  - **aching**: bit-ar wht1• sal-fr sle1• [bell-p-sp dcm1]
  - **burning**: *Agath-a* nl2• ambr a1* ars cp bry cp germ-met srj5• ketogl-ac rly4• lac-h sk4• nat-sil fd3.de• petr-ra shn4• sang hr1 suprar rly4• symph fd3.de•
    - **cold** iron pierced through eye; as from a: til a1*
  - **bursting** pain: sang mrr1
  - **cutting** pain: *Coloc* psor jl2 *Sulph*
  - **drawing** pain: thuj bg2
  - **foreign** body; as from a: agath-a nl2• cortiso tpw7 sulph
  - **lying** on left side agg.: lac-f
  - **neuralgic**: sang tl1 thuj tl1
  - **pressing** pain: apoc k* cann-i a1 *Coloc* com bg2 crot-c ephe-si hsj1• *Ferr* k* *Fl-ac* ign bg2 kali-s fd4.de kalm nat-m olib-sac wmh1 podo fd3.de• propr sa3• psor jl2 puls bg2 ruta fd4.de sang bg2 *Spig* k* spong fd4.de symph fd3.de• tritic-vg fd5.de zing bg2
    - **outward**: apoc vh1
  - **sand**; as from: abrom-a ks5 amph a1 dulc fd4.de ephe-si hsj1• kali-p fd1.de• nat-sil fd3.de• **Sep** k* symph fd3.de•
  - **sore**: *Chel* choc srj3• *Com* haliae-lc srj5• medul-os-si rly4• plut-n srj7• pyrog k2 symph fd3.de•
  - **stitching** pain: arg-n sne bapt hr1 celt a1 cic h1 cortiso tpw7 dios ham fd3.de• kali-p fd1.de• kola stb3• nat-m olib-sac wmh1 ozone sde2• phys podo fd3.de• rhus-t symph fd3.de•

- **tearing** pain: ambr bov colch croc gran mag-c *Prun*
- ▽ **extending** to:
  - **left**: bad germ-met↓
    - **burning**: germ-met srj5•
  - **Forehead**: kalm podo fd3.de•
  - **Occiput**: sang hr1 tub xxb
- ○ **Around** right eye; in and: ambr↓
  - **tearing** pain | **short** jerks; in: ambr a*

- **left**: acon↓ agar aids↓ alum↓ *Anac* arist-cl↓ *Ars Asar* asc-t *Aur* aur-m bamb-a↓ borx↓ brass-n-o srj5• *Bry*↓ calc-s↓ camph↓ carb-an↓ *Caust* chel tl1 chim↓ chin↓ chin-b↓ cimic↓ cist↓ *Coloc*↓ *Croc*↓ cystein-l↓ diaz sa3• *Elaps* elat↓ falco-pe nl2• galeoc-c-h gms1• germ-met↓ gymno↓ *Hep* hydroph rsj6• indg↓ irid-met srj5• kali-p fd1.de• kola stb3• lac-d k2 lac-f *Lach* lavand-a ctl1• limen-b-c↓ luf-op↓ lyc h2 mag-c↓ mag-m mand rsj7• melal-alt gya4 mentho bro1 *Mur-ac*↓ naja nat-p↓ nicc↓ onos k* ox-ac k2 pall c1 pic-ac pitu-gl skp7• podo↓ *Propr*↓ psil ft1 psor↓ *Puls*↓ pyrog↓ ruta fd4.de sanguis-s hm2• sep↓ sinus rly4• **Spig** bro1* spong fd4.de stann k2 stram↓ suis-pan rly4• *Sulph* symph↓ syph k2 tell↓ ther bro1* *Thuj*↓ *Trios* rsj11• tritic-vg fd5.de verat-v hr1 xan↓ zinc zing↓ [heroin sdj2]
  - **night**: lavand-a ctl1•
  - **accompanied** by:
    - **photophobia**: mand rsj7•
    - **Head**; pain in left side of (See HEAD - Pain - sides - left - accompanied - eye)
  - **aching**: acon h1 *Agar* aids nl2• galeoc-c-h gms1• luf-op rsj5•
  - **burning**: alum bg2 hydroph rsj6• *Propr* sa3•
  - **bursting** pain: mag-c bg2
  - **cutting** pain: *Asar* borx calc-s hr1 caust lac-f nat-p c1
  - **foreign** body; as from a: alum bg2 carb-an bg2 kola stb3• tritic-vg fd5.de
  - **grinding** pain: xan c1
  - **jerking** pain: agar lac-f
  - **lying** on left side agg.: lac-f↓
    - **stitching** pain: lac-f
  - **neuralgic**:
    - **accompanied** by:
      - **Upper** limbs:
        - **right** | **numbness** of (See EXTREMITIES - Numbness - upper limbs - right - accompanied - eye - left - pain)
  - **pressing** pain: agar alum bg2 bamb-a stb2.de• *Bry* bg2 calc-s camph bg2 *Coloc* cystein-l rly4• gymno bg2 indg kola stb3• limen-b-c hrn2* podo fd3.de• *Puls* ruta fd4.de spong bg2* stram bg2 sulph h2 symph fd3.de• tritic-vg fd5.de zinc h2 zing
    - **outward**: anac bg2 bamb-a stb2.de• kola stb3• thuj bg2
  - **sore**: aids nl2• bamb-a stb2.de• germ-met srj5• podo c1 pyrog c1 [heroin sdj2]
  - **splinter**; as from a: elat c1
  - **stinging**: arist-cl rbp3• germ-met srj5•
  - **stitching** pain: aids nl2• bamb-a stb2.de• borx hr1 chim chin chin-b c1 cimic cist *Croc* falco-pe nl2• kola stb3• lac-f *Mur-ac* podo fd3.de• psor a1* ruta fd4.de sep h2 *Spig* spong fd4.de suis-pan rly4• symph fd3.de• tell c1 *Thuj* tritic-vg fd5.de verat-v hr1 zinc
    - **followed** by | **itching** and tears: chin-b c1
  - **tearing** pain: agar h2 caust *Chel* coloc nicc sulph thuj
  - ▽ **extending** to:
    - **right**: croc↓ lach k2 mur-ac↓
      - **burning**: mur-ac k2
      - **stitching** pain: croc mur-ac
      - **washing**:
        - **amel.**: mur-ac↓
          - **burning**: mur-ac hr1*
    - **Ear**; left: aesc↓ tub xxb
      - **stitching** pain: aesc vh1
    - **Vertex**: phos↓ phyt↓
      - **stitching** pain: phos phyt
  - ○ **Orbits**: **Spig** mrr1

- **daytime**: cimic↓
  - **stitching** pain: cimic
- **daytime** only: am-c↓ ammc caust cob *Hep* **Kalm** k* lyc mang nat-c↓ phos **Sang** sep sulph↓
  - **burning**: am-c hep *Mang* nat-c phos sulph
  - **drawing** pain: *Kalm*
  - **pressing** pain: caust lyc sep
  - **reading** agg.: sul-ac↓
    - **burning**: sul-ac
  - **sore**: sulph
- **morning**: agar↓ *Alum*↓ am-c↓ am-m↓ *Ambr* apoc↓ arg-n ars-met asar *Aur* aur-ar k2 bell↓ borx cadm-met↓ calc↓ calc-s↓ caps↓ carb-an↓ carbn-s↓ caust↓ chel chinin-m kr1 cimic con↓ croc↓ *Crot-h*↓ dios↓ dulc fd4.de elaps euphr fago↓ falco-pe nl2• *Ferr*↓ form granit-m↓ graph grat↓ ham↓ hep↓ hura↓ ign↓ *Kali-bi*↓ kali-c kali-n↓ kali-p↓ kali-s↓ lachn↓ lyc↓ mag-c↓ mag-m↓ mag-s↓ meph *Mur-ac*↓ myric↓ naja *Nat-ar* nat-c nat-m *Nat-s*↓ nat-sil↓ nicc *Nit-ac*↓ *Nux-v* olib-sac↓ paeon phel↓ phos phys↓ podo polys↓ positr nl2• *Puls* rat↓ rhod↓ rhus-t ruta fd4.de sars↓ seneg *Sep* st sil c1 sol-ni↓ **Spig** spong fd4.de stann stront-c↓ stry sulph symph↓ syph↓ tarent thlas↓ thuj tritic-vg fd5.de valer vanil fd5.de zinc
  - **6** h: arg-met↓ hir↓
    - **burning**: hir skp7•
    - **stitching** pain: arg-met
  - **7** h: *Puls*
  - **8**-9 h: *Chin*
  - **aching**: arg-n a1 *Form Graph* podo polys sk4• spig stry sulph
  - **begins** in morning, increases till noon and ceases in evening: **Kalm** *Nat-m*
  - **burning**: *Alum* am-c am-m calc calc-s caps h1 carb-an carbn-s *Chel* dios elaps fago *Ferr* granit-m es1• graph ham fd3.de• hep *Kali-bi* kali-n kali-s fd4.de lachn c1 lyc mag-m meph *Mur-ac* nat-ar **Nat-m** *Nat-s* nicc *Nit-ac* **Nux-v** phel phys podo fd3.de• rat rhod ruta sars *Seneg Sep* sil spong fd4.de stront-c **Sulph** symph fd3.de• thuj vanil fd5.de **Zinc**
  - **contracting**: stry
  - **cutting** pain: hura
  - **drawing** pain: grat sep
  - **dust**; as from: thlas mtf11
  - **foreign** body; as from a: *Sulph*
  - **opening** the eyes; on: form ph-ac
  - **pressing** pain: agar bell h1 borx calc caust h2 con dulc fd4.de euphr graph ham fd3.de• kali-p fd1.de• meph *Nux-v* olib-sac wmh1 phos rhus-t ruta fd4.de seneg *Sep* symph fd3.de• thuj *Valer* **Zinc**
  - **rising** | **after** | **agg.**: sep spong fd4.de sulph thuj
    - **agg.**: ars-met↓ fago↓ ham↓ kali-p↓ nat-c↓ nat-m↓ *Sulph*↓ symph↓ thuj↓
      - **burning**: ars-met fago ham fd3.de• kali-p fd1.de• nat-c nat-m *Sulph* symph fd3.de• thuj
  - **sand**; as from: apoc k* dulc fd4.de kali-p fd1.de• lyc **Nat-m** k* nat-sil fd3.de• ruta fd4.de *Sil* sol-ni *Sulph* syph jl2 thuj
  - **sore**: cadm-met tpw6 dios fago myric nat-ar ruta fd4.de sars
  - **stitching** pain: arg-n croc *Crot-h* fago falco-pe nl2• ign kali-p k2 lyc h2 nit-ac *Nux-v* ruta fd4.de *Sil* spong fd4.de tarent thuj
  - **tearing** pain: *Crot-h* mag-c mag-s
  - **twilight**; in the: am-m
  - **waking** | **after**:
    - **agg.**: hell↓
      - **stitching** pain: hell
    - **on**: agar↓ alum↓ alum-p↓ am-c↓ arg-n↓ bell-p-sp↓ bry chel↓ elaps↓ falco-pe nl2• ferr *Form* hir↓ iod↓ irid-met srj5• kali-p kali-s↓ lac-cp sk4• *Lach* marb-w↓ nat-ar↓ nat-m nicc↓ **Nux-v** ol-an↓ podo↓ positr nl2• rat↓ ruta fd4.de sal-fr↓ sars↓ *Sep* spong fd4.de staph↓ sulph sumb↓ symph↓ thuj↓ upa
      - **5** h | **pressing** pain (See night - midnight - after - 5 - pressing)
      - **aching**: nat-ar sumb

Eye

- • **waking – on**: ...
  - : **burning**: alum alum-p$_{k2}$ am-c$_{h2}$ arg-n$_{a1}$ chel elaps hir$_{skp7}$• iod kali-s$_{fd4.de}$ nicc ol-an podo$_{fd3.de}$• rat ruta$_{fd4.de}$ sars sep spong$_{fd4.de}$ *Sulph* symph$_{fd3.de}$•
  - : **pressing** pain: agar$_{h2}$ bry nat-m ruta$_{fd4.de}$ *Sep* staph$_{h1}$ symph$_{fd3.de}$• thuj upa
  - : **sore**: marb-w$_{es1}$• sal-fr$_{sle1}$• [bell-p-sp$_{dcm1}$]
- • **walking** agg.: anac↓ puls
  - ⁝ **tearing** pain: anac
- • **washing**:
  - ⁝ **agg.**: kali-n↓ *Mur-ac*↓ *Sulph*↓
    - : **burning**: kali-n$_{h2}$ *Mur-ac*$_{k}$* *Sulph*
  - ⁝ **amel.**: alum↓ am-m↓ mur-ac↓ nicc↓
    - : **burning**: alum$_{h2}$ am-m$_{h2}$ mur-ac$_{hr1}$* nicc$_{k}$*
- • **working** amel.: *Form*

- **forenoon**: am-m↓ apis↓ chel↓ cimic↓ con↓ dios↓ dulc↓ ery-a↓ gels↓ ham↓ kali-bi kali-n↓ kreos↓ lach limen-b-c↓ lyc nat-c nat-sil↓ phys↓ phyt plat podo rumx ruta$_{fd4.de}$ spong$_{fd4.de}$ sulph tritic-vg$_{fd5.de}$ ust↓ valer↓ vanil↓ zinc
  - • **10** h:
    - ⁝ **10**-14 h: diaz$_{sa3}$•
    - ⁝ **noon**; until: *Chin* stann
  - • **11** h: jac-g phys
  - • **aching**: cimic sulph
  - • **burning**: dios gels ham$_{fd3.de}$• kali-bi nat-c nat-sil$_{fd3.de}$• phys *Sulph* tritic-vg$_{fd5.de}$ ust valer vanil$_{fd5.de}$
  - • **drawing** pain: podo
  - • **foreign** body; as from a: am-m dios sulph
  - • **pressing** pain: dulc$_{fd4.de}$ kali-n$_{h2}$ lach limen-b-c$_{mlk9.de}$ lyc plat spong$_{fd4.de}$ tritic-vg$_{fd5.de}$
  - • **sand**; as from: chel con$_{k}$* dulc$_{fd4.de}$ kali-n$_{h2}$
  - • **stitching** pain: apis ery-a
  - • **tearing** pain: kreos
- **noon**: cham *Chinin-s* dulc↓ gymno↓ ign kali-c↓ sulph valer verat
  - • **12**.30 h: nat-m↓
    - ⁝ **burning**: nat-m
  - • **burning**: dulc$_{fd4.de}$ gymno *Sulph*
  - • **pressing** pain: cham ign kali-c$_{h2}$ valer verat
  - • **tearing** pain: chinin-s
- **afternoon**: all-c$_{bg1}$* ars-met borx↓ bry↓ calc↓ caust↓ *Cham* chin *Cimic* coloc↓ com↓ dig↓ dios↓ dulc$_{fd4.de}$ fago↓ gamb↓ grat ham↓ jug-c↓ kalm↓ lachn lyc↓ merc-i-f↓ *Nat-c*↓ nat-m↓ *Nat-s*↓ nicc↓ petr ph-ac↓ phos↓ phys phyt pitu-gl↓ rhod↓ rhus-t ruta$_{fd4.de}$ sang seneg sep sil sin-n↓ spong$_{fd4.de}$ staph stry↓ *Sulph*↓ *Thuj*↓ tritic-vg$_{fd5.de}$ vanil$_{fd5.de}$ **Zinc**↓
  - • **13** h: ars
  - • **14** h: dios lyc↓ phys pitu-gl↓ sep
    - ⁝ **burning**: pitu-gl$_{skp7}$•
    - ⁝ **nap**; after a: euphr↓
      - : **pressing** pain: euphr
    - ⁝ **siesta**; after: euphr
    - ⁝ **tearing** pain: lyc sep
  - • **15** h: mag-c
  - • **15** or 16 h: *Com*
  - • **16** h: caust gent-l hura **Lyc** sil
    - ⁝ **16**-20 h: **Lyc**
    - ⁝ **beer**; after: sulph
    - ⁝ **pressing** pain: sil
    - ⁝ **sore**: lyc
  - • **16**-18.30 h: aq-mar↓
    - ⁝ **burning**: aq-mar$_{skp7}$•
  - • **17** h: chinin-m$_{kr1}$ mag-c nat-ar petr-ra↓ thuj
    - ⁝ **burning**: petr-ra$_{shn4}$•
  - • **18** h: euph phys
  - • **aching**: staph

- **afternoon**: ...
  - • **burning**: borx$_{h2}$* caust$_{h2}$ corn dulc$_{fd4.de}$ gamb ham$_{fd3.de}$• jug-c kalm merc-i-f *Nat-c* *Nat-s* nicc ph-ac pitu-gl$_{skp7}$• rhod stry *Sulph* *Thuj* vanil$_{fd5.de}$ **Zinc**
  - • **closing** the eyes agg.: cimic
  - • **drawing** pain: phys
  - • **menses**; during: nicc↓
    - ⁝ **burning**: nicc
  - • **pressing** pain: borx$_{h2}$ *Cham* chin coloc dulc$_{fd4.de}$ grat lachn phyt ruta$_{fd4.de}$ sil spong$_{fd4.de}$
  - • **rolling** upward or outward agg.: sang
  - • **sand**; as from: bry dulc$_{fd4.de}$ ruta$_{fd4.de}$ vanil$_{fd5.de}$
  - • **siesta**: | **amel.**: am-c$_{ptk2}$
  - • **sitting** agg.: phos↓
    - ⁝ **stitching** pain: phos
    - ⁝ **tearing** pain: phos$_{h2}$
  - • **sore**: dios fago nat-m
  - • **stitching** pain: caust$_{h2}$ dig sin-n spong$_{fd4.de}$ tritic-vg$_{fd5.de}$ vanil$_{fd5.de}$
  - • **tearing** pain: borx calc lyc phos sep
  - • **walking** agg.: bell↓
    - ⁝ **stitching** pain: bell
- **evening**: acon↓ agar↓ aloe alum alum-p↓ alum-sil↓ am-br↓ am-c↓ am-m↓ ang↓ ant-t↓ apis↓ *Ars*↓ ars-met ars-s-f$_{k2}$ bamb-a↓ bapt↓ borx↓ bov *Calc* *Calc-s* camph cann-s↓ carb-an *Carb-v* *Carbn-s* carc↓ *Caust*↓ cedr *Chel*↓ chr-ac↓ cinnb↓ coloc com↓ con↓ con cor-r↓ croc *Crot-h*↓ cycl↓ daph dig dios dream-p↓ dulc$_{fd4.de}$ erig↓ eug↓ euphr fago↓ ferr gamb↓ *Gels*↓ glon↓ graph ham↓ hep hura↓ hyper↓ ind kali-ar↓ kali-bi↓ kali-c↓ kali-chl kali-s↓ *Kalm* kola$_{stb3}$• laur↓ led↓ lyc lycps-v↓ mag-c↓ mag-m mag-s↓ meph↓ merc mur-ac myric↓ nat-ar↓ nat-c nat-m nat-p↓ *Nat-s*↓ nat-sil↓ nicc↓ nit-ac op orot-ac↓ osteo-a↓ ox-ac↓ paeon↓ pall$_{c1}$ *Petr* petr-ra↓ ph-ac↓ phos↓ phys pic-ac↓ plat podo↓ positr$_{nl2}$• psor↓ **Puls** ran-b↓ rat↓ rheum↓ rhus-t **Ruta** sal-fr↓ sars seneg **Sep**↓ sil↓ spong$_{fd4.de}$ *Stann*↓ *Staph* stry suis-hep↓ **Sulph** symph↓ tarent thuj↓ tritic-vg$_{fd5.de}$ vanil$_{fd5.de}$ verat verat-v↓ viol-o↓ **Zinc** zinc-p↓
  - • **18**-20 h: caust↓
    - ⁝ **burning**: caust
  - • **19** h: *Cedr* glon
  - • **20** h: ham lac-ac stry
  - • **aching**: dios ferr merc myric orot-ac$_{rly4}$• paeon petr **Puls** rhus-t ruta **Sulph** verat-v
  - • **air** agg.; in open: glon kali-bi
    - ⁝ **burning**: kali-bi
    - ⁝ **pressing** pain: glon kali-bi
  - • **amel.**: chel ruta$_{fd4.de}$
    - ⁝ **aching**: chel
  - • **bed** | **going** to bed:
    - ⁝ **after**: op↓ upa↓
      - . **burning**: op
      - . **pressing** pain: upa
    - ⁝ **in** bed:
      - : **agg.**: hipp↓
        - . **stitching** pain: hipp
  - • **burning**: acon agar$_{k}$* *Alum* alum-p$_{k2}$ alum-sil$_{k2}$ am-br am-c am-m ang$_{h1}$ ant-t ars bamb-a$_{stb2.de}$• bapt cann-s carbn-s *Caust* con cycl$_{hr1}$ dios dream-p$_{sdj1}$• dulc$_{fd4.de}$ erig eug fago gamb graph ham$_{fd3.de}$• hura kali-ar kali-bi kali-s$_{fd4.de}$ kola$_{stb3}$• laur led$_{h1}$ lyc$_{h2}$ mag-c mag-s meph$_{a1}$ mur-ac$_{h2}$ nat-ar nat-c **Nat-m** *Nat-s* nat-sil$_{fd3.de}$• nicc osteo-a$_{knp1}$• ph-ac phos pic-ac podo$_{fd3.de}$• psor **Puls** ran-b$_{k2}$ rat **Ruta** seneg **Sep** sil spong$_{fd4.de}$ *Sulph* thuj tritic-vg$_{fd5.de}$ vanil$_{fd5.de}$ viol-o **Zinc** zinc-p$_{k2}$
  - • **candlelight**; by: calc↓ calc-caust↓ carb-an↓ graph↓ ol-an↓ *Petr*↓ ph-ac↓ **Ruta**↓ seneg↓
    - ⁝ **burning**: calc calc-caust$_{c1}$ graph ol-an ph-ac **Ruta**
    - ⁝ **pressing** pain: carb-an *Petr* seneg
  - • **constricting** pain: rat
  - • **contracting**: agar euphr glon rhus-t

- **coryza**; during: sep ↓
  - **stitching** pain: sep
- **cutting** pain: calc chr-ac
- **drawing** pain: bov phys
- **foreign** body; as from a: rheum h *Sulph* tritic-vg fd5.de vanil fd5.de
- **gaslight**; by: *Calc* carb-an petr phyt ↓ *Ruta* seneg
  - **burning**: phyt
- **light**; from: carb-an ↓ petr ↓ *Ruta* ↓
  - **aching**: carb-an petr *Ruta*
- **looking**:
  - **fire**; at the: mag-m ↓ *Nat-s* ↓ phyt ↓
    - **burning**: mag-m *Nat-s* phyt
  - **light**; at:
    - **agg.**: amph **Lyc** ↓ plat
      - **stitching** pain: **Lyc**
- **lying** down:
  - **after**:
    - **agg.**: *Carb-v* ↓ chel ↓ cocc ↓
      - **aching**: *Carb-v*
      - **tearing** pain: chel cocc
  - **agg.**: *Carb-v* fl-ac zinc
  - **amel.**: nat-c ↓
    - **burning**: nat-c
- **pressing** pain: aloe alum h2 ang ant-t *Calc* *Calc-s* camph carb-an carbn-s carc fd2.de• coloc con croc dulc fd4.de euphr graph hep *Kalm* led h1 lycps-v mag-m mur-ac *Nat-m* nat-s k* nit-ac *Petr* rhus-t ruta fd4.de sars *Seneg* spong h1 *Staph* suis-hep rly4• **Sulph** tritic-vg fd5.de *Zinc*
- **reading**:
  - **agg.**: agn ↓ alum ↓ ars-s-f ↓ *Calc* caust ↓ *Graph* ↓ mill *Nat-m* ↓ *Nat-s* phys pic-ac ↓ **Ruta** spong ↓ sul-ac ↓
    - **burning**: agn ars-s-f k2 *Graph* *Nat-m* **Ruta** sul-ac kl
    - **pressing** pain: alum h2 mill *Nat-s*
    - **stitching** pain: caust mill pic-ac spong fd4.de
  - **light**; by: mez h2 sars h2
    - **pressing** pain: sars h2
- **sand**; as from: *Ars* *Calc* cor-r hr1 ferr kali-bi ox-ac petr *Puls* ruta fd4.de vanil fd5.de **Zinc** k*
- **sewing**: apis mez **Ruta**
- **sitting** agg.: chinin-s
- **sore**: am-br calc-s cinnb com dios *Gels* lyc h2 nat-p positr nl2• ruta fd4.de sal-fr sle1• stry symph fd3.de• zinc
- **splinter**; as from a: petr-ra shn4•
- **stitching** pain: borx *Caust* *Crot-h* hep *Kalm* kola stb3• **Lyc** *Merc* pic-ac spong *Stann* tarent thuj
- **sunset** to sunrise: syph k2
- **tearing** pain: calc *Chel* coloc crot-h hyper kali-c nat-c h2 nat-m thuj
- **twilight**; in the: am-m k* nat-m stram ↓ sul-ac ↓
  - **burning**: am-m k* stram sul-ac h2
  - **pressing** pain: *Nat-m*
- **walking** agg.; after: **Sep** ↓
  - **sore**: **Sep**
- **walking** and driving: plan
- **writing** agg.: *Nat-m* ↓ sel wildb
  - **burning**: *Nat-m*

- **night**: acon alum ↓ am-m *Apis* ↓ ars k* *Asaf* k* *Aur* aur-ar k2 *Bry* calc ↓ canth carc ↓ cardios-h ↓ *Caust* ↓ chel *Chin* chinin-ar cimic cinnb k2* cob cocc coloc *Con* k* croc ↓ *Crot-t* cycl dios ↓ dulc fd4.de eug ↓ euphr bro1 fago ↓ gels ↓ ham ↓ *Hep* k* ilx-a ↓ kali-ar kali-bi ↓ *Kali-c* ↓ *Kali-i* k* kola ↓ *Led* lyc k* **Merc** k* **Merc-c** k* merc-i-f nat-sil ↓ nept-m ↓ nit-ac lp* *Nux-v* *Plb* propr ↓ **Prun** puls bro1 *Rhus-t* hr1* ruta fd4.de sanic ↓ *Sep* k* *Spig* k* *Staph* stry ↓ sulph ↓ symph ↓ *Syph* k* *Tarent* ↓ thuj k* til ↓ tritic-vg fd5.de vanil fd5.de vesp **Zinc** ziz
  - **midnight**: merc
    - **before**:
      - **22** h: arg-met ↓
        - **stitching** pain: arg-met

- **night – midnight – before**: ...
      - **23** h: euphr nat-m
        - **pressing** pain: euphr nat-m
    - **at**: ars ↓ merc
      - **stitching** pain: ars
    - **after**: ars sulph
      - **2** h | **2-5** h: syph c1
      - **3** h: spig
      - **4** h | **waking**; on: *Nux-v*
      - **5** h: stann
        - **pressing** pain: stann
      - **burning**: **Sulph**
  - **aching**: *Bry* cob coloc merc merc-i-f
  - **air** agg.; in open: aur-m ↓
    - **pressing** pain: aur-m
  - **bed** agg.; in: arn cimic **Merc** ↓ ruta fd4.de sil
    - **tearing** pain: **Merc**
  - **burning**: alum am-m **Ars** asaf carc fd2.de• cardios-h rly4• *Con* *Crot-t* dulc fd4.de eug fago ham fd3.de• ilx-a c1 kali-ar kali-c merc nept-m lsd2.fr **Ruta** sanic stry sulph *Tarent* vanil fd5.de
    - **balls** of fire; like: **Ruta**
  - **bursting** pain: staph
  - **closing** the eyes:
    - **agg.**: bell ↓
      - **aching**: bell
    - **amel.**: nit-ac ↓ pic-ac ↓
      - **aching**: nit-ac pic-ac
  - **cutting** pain: *Merc*
  - **drawing** pain: lyc
  - **neuralgic**: plb hr1
  - **pressing** pain: alum h2 chel *Cocc* croc cycl propr sa3• ruta fd4.de *Sep* *Staph*
  - **reading** in bed, while: cycl ↓
    - **burning**: cycl
  - **sand**; as from: calc kali-bi nat-sil fd3.de• symph fd3.de• **Zinc** k*
  - **sore**: *Bry* *Cocc* dios gels ruta fd4.de
  - **stitching** pain: acon *Apis* asaf k2 *Caust* *Coloc* *Con* *Euphr* ham fd3.de• hep kola stb3• **Merc** prun rhus-t ruta fd4.de *Spig* tarent thuj til
  - **tearing** pain: coloc *Kali-c* **Merc** nux-v *Plb* rhus-t
  - **throbbing**: *Asaf*
  - **waking** him or her from sleep: *Nux-v* ↓
    - **tearing** pain: *Nux-v*
  - **waking**; on: chel cycl
    - **pressing** pain: chel cycl

○ - **Around** the eyes: *Acon* ↓ coloc ↓
    - **tearing** pain: *Acon* coloc
- **abdominal** suffering, increases with: arg-n c1
- **accompanied** by:
  - **glaucoma** (See Glaucoma - accompanied - eye)
  - **myopia**: viol-o mtf11
  - **vertigo** (See VERTIGO - Accompanied - eye)

○ - **Ear** | **inflammation** of: plan br1
  - **Eyeballs** | **dryness** of: melal-alt gya4 **Sulph**
  - **Head**:
    - **complaints** (See HEAD - Complaints - accompanied - eyes - pain)
    - **pain** (See HEAD - Pain - accompanied - eye - pain)
  - **Teeth**; pain in (See TEETH - Pain - accompanied - eyes)

- **aching**: abrom-a ks5 achy-a bnj1 **Acon** aesc k* *Agar* k* ail alf bro1 allox tpw3* aloe bro1 androc srj1• ant-t apis *Arg-met* arg-n br1* am k* *Ars* ars-s-f k2 aur aur-ar k2 *Bad* bapt k* bar-c bar-i k2 bar-s k2 *Bell* benzol br1 bov brom *Bry* k* *Calc-p* *Calc-s* cann-s c1 caps tl1 carb-v *Carbn-s* *Carl* caul cench k2 *Cere-b* cham chel chin chinin-s **Cimic** k* *Cina* cob coc-c coca colch coloc cop cortico tpw7* cupr dig dios dulc h1 ery-a esin bro1 **Eup-per** k* euphr bro1 ferr

- **aching**: ...
ferr-ar ferr-i k2 ferr-p form gels k* *Glon Graph* grat *Ham* bro1 hell *Hep* hir rsj4• hydr-ac hydrc iod ip kali-bi kali-n *Kali-p* ketogl-ac rly4• lac-d k2 lach laur led k* lept k* lob luf-op rsj5• *Luna* kg1• lyc lyss mag-m mang marb-w es1• *Med* mentho bro1 merc merc-i-r *Mez* mim-p rsj8• myric naja nat-ar *Nat-m* k* nat-p nicc-s bro1 *Nit-ac* k* *Nux-v* onos k* osm k2 paeon par petr ph-ac phel *Phos* *Phyt* k* pic-ac *Plan Podo* k* psor **Puls** rad-met bro1 ran-b c1 *Rhus-t* k* rhus-v ribo rly4• rumx *Ruta* k* sal-fr sle1• sang scut c1 sep k* sil **Spig** k* staph stront-c stry *Sulph* sumb suprar rly4• syph tep thiam rly4• thuj til ust valer verat verat-v xan xanth zinc [bell-p-sp dcm1]
- **air**:
  - **agg.**: *Chel* ↓
    - **sore**: *Chel*
- **air** agg.; draft of: hist sp1* mim-p vml3•
  - **burning**: mim-p skp7•
- **air**; in open:
  - **agg.**: aur-m benz-ac berb clem euphr k2 glon graph ↓ *Hep* ↓ kali-bi kali-p ↓ *Kalm Merc* ↓ merc-c nat-ar ↓ ol-an ↓ phel ↓ seneg *Sil* ↓ *Spig* k* sul-ac ↓ verat ↓
    - **burning**: graph kali-bi *Merc* merc-c nat-ar ol-an sul-ac h2 verat
    - **pressing** pain: aur-m *Clem* glon kali-bi seneg sul-ac h2
    - **stitching** pain: *Hep* kali-p fd1.de• kalm phel *Sil* spig
  - **amel.**: abrom-a ↓ **Arg-n** ars **Asaf** cortiso ↓ *Gamb* ↓ gink-b sbd1• hir ↓ lac-c k2 *Lil-t* limest-b ↓ nat-m *Phos* *Phyt* ↓ pieri-b mlk9.de *Puls* sars ↓ *Seneg* ↓ sep spong fd4.de
    - **aching**: limest-b es1• *Seneg*
    - **burning**: asaf k2 *Gamb* hir skp7• *Phyt* **Puls** spong fd4.de
    - **drawing** pain: sep
    - **pressing** pain: *Asaf Phos Puls*
    - **sand**; as from: abrom-a ks5 sars
    - **stitching** pain: **Asaf** cortiso sp1 *Puls* sars h2
- **alternating** with:
  - **complaints**; other: *Euphr* b7a.de
  - O **Abdomen**:
    - **complaints** of: *Euphr* b7a.de
  - **Arm**; pain in left: plb ptel c1
  - **Ear**; pain in (See EAR - Pain - alternating with - eyes)
  - **Ovary**; pain in: sulph
- **anger**; after: coloc k2
- **appearing** suddenly:
  - **disappearing**; and:
    - **suddenly**: bamb-a ↓
      - **stitching** pain: *(↗sudden - stitching)* bamb-a stb2.de•
- **bathing** the eyes:
  - **agg.**: *Mur-ac* ↓ *Sulph*
    - **burning**: *Mur-ac* sulph
  - **amel.**: am-m ↓ aur mur-ac nicc thuj
    - **burning**: am-m h2 mur-ac k2 nicc
  - **cold** water; in | **amel.**: *Apis Asar Phos Puls* syph c1
- **bed** agg.; in: arn ↓ mag-c ↓ mag-s ↓ **Merc** ↓
  - **stitching** pain: arn
  - **tearing** pain: arn mag-c mag-s **Merc**
- **bending** | **forward** | **agg.**: cassia-s ccrh1• *Coloc*
  - **head** | **downward**:
    - **agg.**: chel ↓
      - **sore**: chel
    - **forward** | **agg.**: hist sp1
- **biting** (See burning)
- **blinking** (See winking)
- **blow**; from a: **Arn Symph**
  - **sore**: **Symph**
- **blowing** the nose:
  - **agg.**: nit-ac h2 tritic-vg fd5.de
  - **amel.**: aur
- **blunt** instrument; as from a: *(↗dull)* carb-v b4.de cina b7.de
- **boring** pain: apis k* arg-n asaf k* *Aur* k* aur-m bism k* borx a1 calc bg2 chinin-s coff *Coloc* bro1 *Crot-h Crot-t* bro1 elaps form hell k* hep bg2* kali-c k* *Merc* merc-c bro1 merc-i-f nat-m k* *Nux-m* phos bg2 puls k* ruta fd4.de spig k* stry tab bg2 thuj k*
- **breakfast**:
  - **after**:
    - **agg.**: *Sulph* ↓
      - **burning**: *Sulph*
    - **amel.**: naja
      - **aching**: naja
- **bruised** (See sore)
- **burn**; after: canth mrr1
- **burning** (= smarting; biting): **Acon** k* aesc *Aeth Agar* k* *Agath-a* nl2• agn k* ail **All-c** k* allox tpw3* aloe **Alum** k* alumn am-c k* *Am-m* k* ambr k* ammc bro1 anan ang k* anh sp1 ant-t b7.de aphis **Apis** k* arag br1 aran *Arg-n* arge-pl rwt5• arist-cl sp1 arn k* **Ars** k* ars-met bro1 arum-t arund *Asaf* k* asar k* aur k* aur-ar k2 aur-m k* bamb-a stb2.de* bapt k* bar-c k* bar-i k2 bar-m bar-s k2 **Bell** k* berb bism b7.de* bit-ar wht1• blum-o bnj1 borx k* bov b4.de* brom k* *Bry* k* bufo bufo-s bung-fa mtf cain calad k* **Calc** k* calc-i k2 calc-s calc-sil k2 camph cann-i a1 cann-s b7.de *Canth* k* *Caps* k* carb-ac carb-an k* **Carb-v** k* **Carbn-s** card-m cardios-h rly4• *Carl* cassia-s ccrh1• *Caust* k* *Cedr* k* cephd-i bnj1 cham k* *Chel* **Chin** k* chin-b c1 *Chinin-ar Chlol* choc srj3• chord-umb rly4• cic b7.de* *Clem* k* cob coc-c coff *Colch* k* *Coloc* k* **Con** k* cop cortico sp1 croc k* *Crot-h Crot-t* cupr k* *Cycl* k* cystein-l rly4• dendr-pol sk4• *Dig* k* dios dros k* dulc fd4.de elaps ephe-si hsj1• eug *Euph* k* **Euphr** k* eupi fago k* ferr k* ferr-ar ferr-i ferr-p k* fl-ac form *Gamb* gels k* ger-i rly4• germ-met srj5• glon glycyr-g cte1• gran *Granit-m* es1• *Graph* k* gymno k* ham fd3.de• hedy a1* hell k* *Hep* k* hir rsj4• hist sp1 *Hydr* hydro-v a1 hydroph rsj6• hyos hyper *Ign* k* ilx-a bro1 indol bro1 *Iod* k* ip k* irid-met srj5• jab br1* jug-r *Kali-ar Kali-bi* k* **Kali-c** k* *Kali-i* k* kali-m k2 kali-n kali-p *Kali-s* kali-sil k2 kalm ketogl-ac rly4• kola stb3• kreos k* *Lac-c* lac-del hm2• lac-h sk4• lac-lup hm2• *Lach* k* lachn lact lact-v hr1 laur k* led b7.de* lept br1* lil-t *Luf-op* rsj5• *Lyc* k* lyss m-ambo b7.de m-arct b7.de *Mag-c* k* *Mag-m* k* mag-p bro1 malar jl2 manc ptk1 mand rsj7• mang k* medul-os-si rly4• melal-alt gya4 meph *Merc* k* *Merc-c* k* merc-i-f *Merc-i-r Mez* mim-p skp7*• moni rfm1• mosch k* *Mur-ac* k* muru a1 myos-a rly4• nat-ar k* *Nat-c* k* **Nat-m** k* nat-ox rly4• nat-p *Nat-s* nat-sil fd3.de• *Nicc Nit-ac* k* nux-m k* *Nux-v* k* ol-an *Olib-sac* wmh1 olnd k* *Op* k* orot-ac rly4• osm ozone sde2• paeon k* par k* parth vml3• *Petr* k* petr-ra shn4• **Ph-ac** k* phel *Phos* k* phys *Phyt* k* pic-ac *Pieri-b* mlk9.de pilo bro1 pitu-a ft pitu-gl skp7• plat k* plb k* podo polys sk4• pot-e rly4• *Propr* sa3• *Prot* jl2 psor **Puls** k* rad-br ptk1 **Ran-b** k* ran-r c2 *Ran-s* k* raph rauw sp1 rheum b7a.de *Rhod* k* *Rhus-t* k* rhus-v ros-d wla1 **Ruta** k* sabad k* sabin k* sacch-a fd2.de• *Sang* k* sars k* sel rsj9• *Seneg* k* *Sep* k* sil k* *Sin-n* k* sinus rly4• sol-ni *Spig* k* spong k* *Stann* k* staph k* stict stram b7.de* *Stront-c* k* *Stry* suis-em rly4• suis-pan rly4• *Sul-ac* k* **Sulph** k* suprar rly4• symph fd3.de• syph tab tarax b7.de* *Tarent* tell rsj10• tep tetox pin2• *Teucr* k* thres-a sze7• *Thuj* k* til trios rsj11• tritic-vg fd5.de tub jl2 ulm-c jsj8• valer k* vanil fd5.de verat k* verb b7a.de* vesp vib viol-o k* viol-t k* vip fkr4.de **Zinc** k* zinc-p k2 zing [bell-p-sp dcm1]
  - **accompanied** by:
    - **red** discoloration of eyes: stront-c ptk1
    - **sneezing**: com ptk1
    - **Teeth**; pain in (See TEETH - Pain - accompanied - eyes - burning)
    - **Throat**; pain in: petr-ra shn4•
  - **alternating** with | **pressing** pain (See pressing pain - alternating - burning)
  - **dry** burning: arum-t ptk1 croc ptk1
  - **itching** pain: calc h2 *Kali-bi Lyc* moni rfm1• olib-sac wmh1 **Puls**
  - **pepper**; as from: eug vml3•
  - **salt**; as from: nux-v cp
  - **sand**; as from: agar ambr **Caust** k* con ign iod mag-m merc *Nat-m* k*
  - **smoke**; as from: aeth *All-c* alum-sil k2 ars bg2 *Croc* k* lyc h2 mosch nat-ar nat-m k* nit-ac bg2 petr k* petr-ra shn4• ran-b bg2 thuj bg2 valer bg2
  - **weeping**; as from: croc ptk1
- **burrowing**: bism b7.de* calc b4.de* colch b7.de* phos b4.de* *Spig* b7.de*
- **bursting** pain: am-br bro1 asar bell bg2 bry bro1 choc srj3• *Cimic* bro1 *Com* bro1 daph *Gels Glon* juni-v lac-ac k* mag-c par bro1 phos bg* **Prun** k* puls *Seneg* spig k* *Staph* k* stram k* **Sulph** bg2*

- **bubble**, like a: puls
- **orbits**; as if bursting out of: kola stb3• usn a2*

- **changing** | **dark** to light, and light to dark; from: *Stram*
- **chill**:
  - **before**: rhus-t↓
    - ⁝ **burning**: rhus-t
  - **during**: **Acon** k* apis bg2 bell bg2 *Borx* b4a.de* calad bg2 calc bg2 canth k* caps bg2 cham bg2 coloc bg2 croc↓ kreos bg2 lach bg2 led bg2 lyc bg2 mez bg2 rhod bg2 rhus-t bg2 seneg k* *Sep* bg2 *Tub*↓
    - ⁝ **burning**: borx bg2 cham bg2 croc bg2 seneg bg2 sep bg2
    - ⁝ **pressing** pain: kreos b7a.de* lyc bg2 *Rhus-t* b7.de* sep bg2
    - ⁝ **sore**: *Tub* k*
    - ⁝ **stitching** pain: acon bg2 apis bg2 borx bg2 *Coloc* bg2 rhus-t bg2
  - **with**: chinin-m kr1
- **chronic** | **children**; in: ant-c mtf33
- **ciliary** neuralgia (See ciliary body - neuralgic)
- **clawing** pain: am-m
- **cleaning** eyes: ph-ac↓
  - **burning**: ph-ac h2
- **closed**; when: med↓ trios↓
  - **pulled** out; as if being: med
  - **sore**: trios rsj11•
- **closing** the eyes:
  - **agg.**: agar↓ allox↓ am-m↓ arg-n↓ *Bell* calc↓ canth *Carb-v* cimic clem con eug↓ fago ham↓ hell↓ hir↓ irid-met srj5• kola stb3• lac-ac lyc↓ manc bg1 petr-ra↓ pitu-gl↓ psil↓ sars↓ sep↓ sil k* staph stront-c↓ sumb symph↓
    - ⁝ **burning**: agar k* am-m arg-n vml3• calc carb-v *Clem* eug vml3• ham hir skp7• lyc *Manc* k* pitu-gl skp7• psil ft1 sars sil stront-c sk4• symph fd3.de•
    - ⁝ **drawing** pain: carb-v
    - ⁝ **foreign** body; as from a: allox tpw4
    - ⁝ **pressing** pain: *Bell* con k* sep h2 *Staph* k* symph fd3.de•
    - ⁝ **sand**; as from: allox tpw4 sep h2
    - ⁝ **stitching** pain: *Cimic* clem hell h1 petr-ra shn4• sars h2
    - ⁝ **tearing** pain: sil
  - **amel.**: allox sp1 arg-n br1 *Chel* cortico tpw7 cystein-l↓ germ-met srj5• *Lac-d* nit-ac ph-ac pic-ac plac rzf5• plat propr↓ sin-n tritic-vg↓
    - ⁝ **aching**: allox tpw3 cortico tpw7
    - ⁝ **burning**: allox tpw3 cortico tpw7* germ-met srj5• tritic-vg fd5.de
    - ⁝ **pressing** pain: cystein-l rly4• propr sa3•
  - **forcibly**: sulph↓
    - ⁝ **sore**: sulph h2
  - **must** close the eyes: *Aur* bar-c *Calc* *Mang* hr1 spig↓
    - ⁝ **burning**: spig c1
    - ⁝ **press** them in; with a sensation as if she should: calc h2
- **closing** the eyes; on: cimic↓
  - **stitching** pain | **needles** thrust into eyeball; as if: cimic ptk
- **coition**; after: bart nat-m bg1
- **cold**:
  - **air**:
    - ⁝ **agg.**: *Acon* asar bro1* chel cinnb *Clem* k* cob **Hep** k* mag-p kr1* nit-ac k2 rhus-t hr1 **Sil** *Spig* thuj↓ zinc↓
      - ⁝ **sore**: chel *Sil* zinc
      - ⁝ **stitching** pain: thuj h1
    - ⁝ **amel.**: *Arg-n* k* asar k* gink-b sbd1• hist sp1* puls bro1
    - ⁝ **breathing** | **nose**; through: cor-r br1
  - **applications**:
    - ⁝ **amel.**: aegle-m↓ aq-mar↓ arg-n mrr1 cassia-s↓ chel↓ petr-ra shn4• *Puls* mrr1 ruta fd4.de spig k2 sulph↓
      - ⁝ **burning**: aegle-m zzc1• aq-mar skp7• cassia-s ccrh1•
      - ⁝ **sore**: chel *Puls* sulph
  - **bathing**:
    - ⁝ **amel.**: *Apis*↓ ars↓ *Aur*↓ hir↓ nicc↓ parth↓ pitu-gl↓ *Puls*↓ *Sep*↓ stront-c↓ thuj↓
- **cold** – **bathing** – **amel.**: ...
      - ⁝ **burning**: *Apis* ars k2 *Aur* hir skp7• nicc parth vml3• pitu-gl skp7• *Puls* *Sep* stront-c sk4• thuj
  - **washing**:
    - ⁝ **amel.**: *Apis*↓ *Asar*↓ *Phos*↓ *Puls*↓
      - ⁝ **pressing** pain: *Apis* *Asar* *Phos* *Puls*
  - **water** | **amel.**: acon *Apis* *Asar* *Aur* *Form* hist vml3• irid-met srj5• lac-d nat-ar nit-ac *Phos* pic-ac pot-e rly4• *Puls* staph hr1 syph bg1
- **combing** hair agg.: nux-v bg1
- **compressed**; as if: arg-met b7.de* lyc bg2 nit-ac bg2 sabin b7.de spig b7a.de* *Verat* b7.de* viol-o b7.de*
- **congestion**; as from: nit-ac h2
- **constricting** pain: acon amph cham chlor elaps lyc naja nit-ac
- **contracting**: agar k* arg-met bg2 bism b7.de* borx k* bov b4.de* *Brom* b4a.de crot-c dulc a1 euphr k* gink-b sbd1• glon bg2 hyper bg2 kali-i bg2 *Kali-n* k* kali-p fd1.de• m-aust b7.de merc-c b4a.de nat-c k* nit-ac b4.de* phys bg2 plb k* rhus-t b7.de* sep b4.de* sil bg2 spig b7.de* squil b7.de* tritic-vg fd5.de *Verat* k*
- **convulsions**; from: dros k2
- **corrosive**: kreos b7a.de ox-ac bg2 *Ran-s* b7a.de rheum b7.de*
- **coryza**:
  - **during**: *Bell*↓ lyc↓ sep b4.de* vanil↓
    - ⁝ **burning**: *Bell* b4a.de
    - ⁝ **pressing** pain: lyc h2 vanil fd5.de
  - **suppressed**: kali-c k2
- **cough** | **during**:
    - ⁝ **agg.**: bry k2 cassia-s ccrh1• kali-chl↓ kali-m↓ lach bg2 pyrog jl2 seneg sul-ac
      - ⁝ **pressing** pain | **outward**: kali-chl c1 kali-m c1
      - ⁝ **stitching** pain: *Seneg* k*
  - **with**: agar↓ bol-la↓ chin↓
    - ⁝ **burning**: agar bol-la chin
- **covering** the eyes:
  - **hands** amel.; with the: *Aur-m* *Thuj*
    - ⁝ **tearing** pain: aur-m k*
  - **lightly** amel.: hep c1
- **cramping** (See Spasms)
- **crushing**: acon k* asaf bro1 aur-m bro1 **Bry** k* chin bro1 clem bro1 crot-t bro1 cupr bro1 euphr bro1 hep bro1 mentho bro1 nit-ac bro1 olnd bro1 *Par* bro1 *Ph-ac* bro1 phos bro1 **Prun** k* ran-b bro1 rhus-t bro1 *Ruta* bro1 sang bro1 sep bro1 *Spig* bro1
- **cutting** pain: act-sp agath-a nl2• am-c k* *Apis* k* *Asaf* k* asar atro aur aur-s k2 *Bell* k* borx k* bry k* bufo cadm-s *Calc* k* calc-sil k2 canth b7.de* carbn-s caust *Chel* k* *Chin* k* cic *Cimic* k* *Colch* k* *Coloc* k* con crot-c *Cund* dros k* echi *Euphr* k* ferr-i graph hep bg2 ind iod kali-c bg2 lac-f *Lach* k* lyc bg2 *Merc* k* mosch bg2 mur-ac k* nat-p *Nux-v* k* ol-an petr k* phyt plb bg puls k* rhus-t k* sang sil sinus rly4• spig bg2 staph bg2 *Sulph* k* tarent tub jl2 verat k* viol-t k* zinc
  - **inward**: acon act-sp *Asaf* bry *Coloc*
  - **outward**: cadm-s *Lach* sulph
- **darkness**:
  - **agg.**: ph-ac↓
    - ⁝ **pressing** pain: ph-ac h2
  - **amel.**: bell *Chin* con bro1 *Euphr* lil-t bro1 luna kg1• *Nux-m* staph
    - ⁝ **pressing** pain: *(↗light - agg. - pressing)* *Bell* euphr staph
- **darting** (See stitching)
- **digging** pain: bell bism colch phos h2 sep spig
- **dinner**; after: agar carb-v↓ kali-bi↓ mag-m↓ mez nat-c↓ ol-an↓ phos seneg thuj↓ zinc↓
  - **burning**: carb-v h2 kali-bi mag-m nat-c thuj zinc h2
  - **drawing** pain: agar
  - **pressing** pain: agar mez phos seneg
  - **stitching** pain: nat-c k* ol-an
- **dragging**: apis *Caust* sep
- **drawing** pain: *(↗Pulling)* *Agar* k* apis am k* *Ars* k* ars-s-f k2 asar b7.de* bell k* borx c1 bov calc-p *Camph* cann-s k* canth k* carb-v carbn-s *Caust* k* cham *Chel* cic cina b7.de* *Colch* k* con cop croc b7.de* crot-c *Cur* *Glon* *Graph* hell *Hep* k* hyos jug-c kali-ar kali-bi kali-c kali-p **Kalm** kreos k* lac-d lach lil-t lith-c lyc lyss m-ambo b7.de med *Naja* **Nat-m** nit-ac h2 oena **Par** mrr1 petr

- **drawing** pain: ...
  phos b4.de* *Phys* plat k* plb b7.de* podo k* puls b7.de* ran-s rhod b4.de* **Ruta** sabad b7.de* *Seneg* k* sep sil *Spig* stront-c k* sulph symph fd3.de• syph al tab thuj til *Zinc* zing
  - **accompanied** by | **Occiput**; pain in: *Carb-v*
  - **backward**: agar aster k* aur-m bell bg2 bov k* bry bg2* carbn-s cham k* *Crot-t* k* cupr gels bg2 *Graph* k* grin ptk1 *Hep* k* ignis-alc es2• *Lach* k* *Mez* k* nicc-s bg1 olnd bg2* **Par** k* petr bg2 phos bg2* plb k* podo bg2 prun ptk1 *Puls* k* rad-br ptk1 rhod *Rhus-t* ptk1 seneg ptk1 sep k* sil k* spig ptk1 stry sulph k* zinc
  - **downward**: aeth br1
  - **outward**: aloe bg1 cop crot-c med phos bg1
  - **sticking** pain: *Lach*
  - **string** to back of head or into the brain; as with a: *Crot-t* k* hep *Lach* **Par** k* plb mrr1 ruta rb2 sil
- **dull** pain: *(↗blunt)* apis b7a.de carb-v bg2 cina bg2 croc b7.de* dioxi rbp6
- **dust**; as from: ail bg2 ambr bg2 arge-pl rwt5• bar-c bg2 beryl tpw5 cocc bg2 dig bg2 euphr k2 ign bg2 kali-n bg2 lach bg2 lachn vml3• lyc bg2 mag-m bg2 op bg2 rheum b7a.de* rhus-t bg2 sulph b4a.de zinc bg2
  - **penetrating**: *Sulph* bg2
- **eating** | **after**:
  - ⁝ **agg.**: ambr ↓ dig lyc h2 sulph
    - **pressing** pain: sulph
    - **stitching** pain: ambr a1* dig
  - **while**:
    - ⁝ **agg.**: meny ↓ podo ↓
      - **pressing** pain: meny h1 podo fd3.de•
- **exertion** of the eyes:
  - **after**: staph ↓
    - ⁝ **stitching** pain: staph
  - **agg.**: *(↗writing; Strained)* aegle-m zzc1• *Arg-n* k* *Arn* k* aur-s k2 bar-c bar-m k2 bar-s k2 **Bry** k* *Calc* canth carb-v *Chel* cimic bro1 con dros ↓ dulc fd4.de euphr bro1 graph k2 ign jab ↓ kalm bro1 *Lach* *Mang* k* meph a1 merc ↓ *Merl* mur-ac naja **Nat-m** k* nat-s ↓ *Nux-m* *Nux-v* onos k2* *Petr* ↓ phos phys bro1 *Phyt* plat *Psor* *Puls* *Rhus-t* k* **Ruta** k* seneg mrr1 sil *Spig* k* *Staph* stram k2 tritic-vg fd5.de vanil fd5.de
    - ⁝ **burning**: bar-c bar-s k2 dros h1 dulc fd4.de jab br1 **Nat-m** *Petr* **Ruta** staph tritic-vg fd5.de vanil fd5.de
    - ⁝ **bursting** pain: staph
    - ⁝ **cutting** pain: merc petr
    - ⁝ **fine** work; from: *Carb-v* cina k2 coloc *Con* *Jab* merc mur-ac *Nat-m* **Ruta** k* seneg sulph symph fd3.de•
    - ⁝ **pressing** pain: dulc fd4.de nat-s k2 ruta fd4.de
- **exertion** of the eyes; as from: gink-b sbd1• graph h2
- **fever**:
  - **before**: arn ↓ bell b4a.de bry ↓ nat-c b4a.de rhus-t ↓ spig ↓
    - ⁝ **burning**: arn b7a.de bry b7a.de rhus-t b7a.de spig b7a.de
  - **during**:
    - ⁝ **agg.**: acon bg2 apis bg2 ars bg2 bell bg2 borx b4a.de* calc bg2 *Canth* b7.de* carb-an bg2 carb-v bg2 cic bg2 *Coloc* b4a.de* dig bg2 dulc ↓ hep bg2 hyos bg2 ip bg2 kali-c ↓ lac-del hrn2• lach bg2 *Led* b7.de* **Lyc** b4.de* nat-c bg2 *Nat-m* b4a.de* nux-v bg2 op bg2 ph-ac bg2 puls bg2 *Rhod* b4.de* rhus-t bg2 ruta bg2 sabad bg2 seneg bg2 sep bg2 spig bg2 stram bg2 sulph bg2 thuj ↓ **Valer** bg2 verat bg2
      - **pressing** pain: dulc fd4.de kali-c nat-c h2 sep thuj
- **fine** work; during: arn ↓ *Con* ↓ *Ruta* ↓
  - **pressing** pain: *Con* *Ruta*
  - **sore**: arn br1
- **followed** by | **sneezing** agg.: aml-ns vh1
- **foreign** body; as from a: *Acon* k* agar bg2 agath-a nl2• allox tpw4 alum k* alum-p k2 am-m ambr b7.de* *Anac* k* **Apis** k* arn k* ars b4.de* asaf b7.de* *Aur* k* bar-c b4.de* *Bell* k* borx k* *Bov* k* *Bry* b7.de* *Calc* k* **Calc-p** k* calc-s *Caps* k* carb-an k* carb-v b4.de* caul *Caust* k* *Chel* k* *Chin* b7.de* cina b7.de* cinnb *Cist* coc-c k* cocc b7.de* con b4.de* cortiso tpw7 croc b7.de* dig b4a.de dios ptk1 euph b4.de* *Euphr* k* ferr b7.de* *Fl-ac* k* *Gels* graph b4a.de* *Hep* k* hyos k* *Ign* k* iod b4.de* kali-bi k* kali-n b4.de* kali-p fd1.de• kali-s fd4.de kola stb3• *Lyc* k* m-arct b7.de mag-m b4.de* med meny b7.de* meph *Merc* k* *Nat-m* k* nit-ac b4.de* olnd b7.de* petr b4.de* petr-ra shn4• ph-ac b4.de* phos k* plat b4.de*

- **foreign** body; as from a: ...
  plb k* plut-n srj7• *Psor* puls k* pycnop-sa mrz1 ran-b b7.de* rheum b7.de* rhus-t k* ruta sang sars k* seneg b4.de* sep k* *Sil* k* spig b7.de* stann k* *Staph* k* stram stront-c b4.de* sul-ac bg2* *Sulph* k* teucr b7.de* *Thuj* k* tritic-vg fd5.de upa vanil fd5.de viol-t b7.de*
  - **cotton**; as from a piece of: rad-br ptk1
  - **grains**; as from little: kali-s fd4.de lith-c sars sep
  - **hair**; as from a: *Coc-c* sang
  - **penetrating** the eye: *Acon* bg2 **Sul-ac** bg2 *Sulph* bg2
- **frowning**:
  - **amel.**: petr-ra ↓
    - ⁝ **burning**: petr-ra shn4•
- **glaucoma**; in (See Glaucoma - accompanied - eye)
- **gnawing** pain: agn ars berb kali-c h2 ox-ac *Plat*
  - **itching** pain: **Agn** br1
- **grinding** pain: xan xanth
- **hay** fever; during: ran-b ↓
  - **burning**: ran-b tl1
- **headache**:
  - **after**: gels ↓
    - ⁝ **stitching** pain: gels
  - **during**: adam ↓ ail ↓ aran ↓ bamb-a ↓ bapt ↓ bry ↓ carb-v ↓ carbn-s ↓ cimic ↓ cocc ↓ *Coff* ↓ cypra-eg ↓ dulc ↓ *Eug* ↓ fic-m ↓ granit-m ↓ hep ↓ hipp ↓ hom-xyz ↓ nux-v ↓ ozone ↓ petr-ra ↓ phos ↓ ran-b ↓ *Ros-d* ↓ sacch-a ↓ sal-fr ↓ sang ↓ *Sel* ↓ seneg ↓ spig ↓ sulph ↓ thuj ↓ vanil ↓
    - ⁝ **burning**: adam skp7• ail aran bapt a1 bry k2 carb-v k2 carbn-s *Coff* cypra-eg sde6.de• dulc fd4.de *Eug* granit-m es1• hep petr-ra shn4•
    - ⁝ **pressing** pain: bamb-a stb2.de• carb-v h2 dulc fd4.de fic-m gya1 ran-b c1 *Ros-d* wla1 sacch-a fd2.de• *Sel* seneg sulph h2 vanil fd5.de
      - **outward**: nux-v hr phos h2 sang hr1 spig hr1 vanil fd5.de
    - ⁝ **pulled** out; as if being: carb-v h2 cocc h1
    - ⁝ **sore**: bamb-a stb2.de• cimic k2 hom-xyz br1 sal-fr sle1•
    - ⁝ **stitching** pain: hipp thuj
    - ⁝ **tearing** pain: ozone sde2•
- **heart**, at each beat of: atro
- **heat**:
  - **during**: bros-gau ↓ cassia-s ↓ cedr ↓ chin ↓ *Guar* *Guare* hep kali-c *Led* **Lyc** *Nat-m* *Nux-v* *Petr* ↓ petr-ra shn4• ph-ac puls rhod rhus-t *Sep* *Stram* sul-ac ↓ thuj **Valer**
    - ⁝ **burning**: bros-gau mrc1 cassia-s cdd7*• cedr chin lyc h2 *Petr* k* rhod sul-ac
    - ⁝ **stitching** pain: *Kali-c* lyc h2
  - **sun**; of the:
    - ⁝ **agg.**: abrom-a ks5
      - **aching**: abrom-a ks5
      - **sand**; as from: abrom-a ks5
- **house**; in: phel ↓
  - **stitching** pain: phel
- **increased** | **pressing** pain (See Glaucoma)
- **increasing** until noon: **Kalm** *Nat-m* *Puls* *Stann*
- **indoors**: rumx ↓
  - **burning**: rumx ptk1
- **influenza**; during: bapt ↓ bry ↓ eup-per ↓ gels ↓ tub ↓
  - **sore**: bapt gk bry st1 eup-per st1 gels st1 tub gk
- **intermitting** (See paroxysmal)
- **iritis**, in: *Asaf* ↓ **Merc** ↓ **Rhus-t** ↓ *Thuj* ↓
  - **stitching** pain: *Asaf* **Merc** **Rhus-t** *Thuj*
- **jar** agg.: spig mrr1
- **jerking** pain: agar ars bg2 *Asar* lac-f staph h1 sulph bg2
- **jumping** out; as if: gels c1
- **lachrymation**:
  - **amel.**: petr-ra ↓ prun ↓
    - ⁝ **burning**: petr-ra shn4•
    - ⁝ **bursting** pain: prun br1
  - **during**: aegle-m ↓ chin ↓ com ↓ dream-p ↓ gink-b ↓ hedy ↓ ignis-alc ↓ nat-s ↓ nux-m ↓ sulph ↓ tax ↓

- **during**: ...
  - **burning**: aegle-m zzc1• chin h1 com ptk1 dream-p sdj1• gink-b sbd1• hedy a1* ignis-alc es2• nat-s tl1 nux-m c1 sulph h2 [tax jsj7]
- **lancinating** (See cutting)
- **light**; from:
  - **agg.**: allox sp1 ammc↓ *Apis Ars* asar gm1 asc-t atro aur-ar k2 *Aur-m* **Bar-c** bar-i k2 bar-s k2 *Bell Calc* calc-sil k2 *Chel* **Chin** cob cocc-s kr1 **Con** cortico tpw7 *Cupr* ery-a↓ euphr ferr-i graph k2 ham↓ *Hep* iod irid-met srj5• *Lac-d* lycpr c1 mag-m↓ mang k* *Merc* nat-ar *Nat-m Nux-m Nux-v* petr *Phos Phyt* pin-con oss2• pycnop-sa mrz1 ros-d↓ sep *Sil Staph* sulph syph thuj
    - **burning**: ammc vml3• calc cob ery-a ham fd3.de• iod ros-d wla1 staph h1
    - **bursting** pain: staph
    - **foreign** body; as from a: allox tpw4
    - **pressing** pain: (↗*darkness - amel. - pressing*) aur-m *Bell Con* euphr mag-m h2 *Phos* sep *Staph* sulph
    - **sand**; as from: allox tpw4
    - **sore**: *Chel*
  - **artificial** light:
    - **agg.**: allox↓ *Calc Calc-p* carb-an *Chel* cina croc ip irid-met srj5• *Lith-c* luna kg1• lyc mang nat-ar *Nat-m* k* nux-v k* petr pic-ac plat sars *Seneg* sep staph
      - **foreign** body; as from a: allox tpw4
      - **sand**; as from: allox tpw4
  - **bright** light:
    - **agg.**: amph↓ arist-cl↓ cob↓ cortico↓ ery-a↓ euphr↓ graph↓ ham↓ *Hep*↓ hir↓ iod↓ *Kali-c*↓ *Kreos*↓ lyc↓ *Mag-m*↓ *Merc*↓ petr↓ phyt↓ *Puls*↓ *Rhod*↓ ruta↓ thuj↓
      - **aching**: cortico tpw7* *Hep* petr phyt ruta thuj
      - **burning**: arist-cl sp1 ery-a ham fd3.de• hir skp7• *Kreos Mag-m Rhod*
      - **sand**; as from: arist-cl sp1
      - **stitching** pain: amph cob euphr graph iod *Kali-c* lyc *Merc Puls* thuj
    - **amel.**: am-m↓
      - **burning**: am-m
  - **candlelight**:
    - **agg.**: *Calc*↓ calc-caust↓ carb-an↓ *Colch*↓ cor-r↓ croc↓ graph↓ mag-s↓ mang↓ ol-an↓ petr↓ ph-ac↓ pic-ac↓ *Seneg*↓ *Sep*↓ staph↓ sulph↓
      - **burning**: *Calc* calc-caust c1 cor-r graph mag-s ol-an ph-ac pic-ac sulph
      - **cutting** pain: *Calc*
      - **pressing** pain: carb-an croc mang petr *Seneg* staph
      - **stitching** pain: *Colch Sep*
    - **amel.**: am-m↓
      - **burning**: am-m
  - **change** of light: stram↓
    - **pressing** pain: stram h1
  - **daylight**:
    - **agg.**: am-c ammc k* brom a1 gink-b sbd1• hell hep lac-ac mag-c↓ *Merc* psor al sars *Sil*
      - **burning**: mag-c h2
  - **dim** light: am-m *Apis* sars *Stram*
    - **burning**: am-m stram
  - **fire**; of the: asar bro1 con bro1 **Merc** k* phos mtf11 sil mtf11
  - **lamplight**:
    - **agg.**: syph↓
      - **drawing** pain: syph
  - **strong** light:
    - **agg.**: *Asar* com *Hep Mang* nat-ar nat-c k2 petr phos pic-ac ruta *Sil Sulph* thuj
    - **amel.**: stram k2
  - **sunlight**:
    - **agg.**: aml-ns asar bro1 calc *Clem* dulc fd4.de *Graph*↓ *Hep Kali-p Mang* merc bro1 merc-sul c1 *Nat-ar Nat-m Puls*↓ ribo rly4• sulph
      - **aching**: *Nat-ar* ribo rly4•
- **light**; from – **sunlight** – **agg.**: ...
      - **cutting** pain: *Graph*
      - **stitching** pain: *Calc* graph *Puls*
- **linear**: syph jl2
- **looking**:
  - **agg.**: acon anac *Apis* k* caust ham fd3.de• **Nat-m** k* ph-ac *Phos* plac rzf5• rheum *Ruta* sars sulph tab
    - **pressing** pain: acon anac caust **Nat-m** ph-ac *Phos* rheum
  - **bright** objects; at: hist vml3•
  - **downward**:
    - **agg.**: nat-m bro1 [pop dhh1]
    - **amel.**: bar-c h2
      - **pressing** pain: bar-c h2
  - **fire**; at the: *Apis*↓ mag-m↓ *Merc*↓ *Nat-s*↓ phyt↓
    - **burning**: *Apis* mag-m *Merc Nat-s* phyt
  - **fixedly**: arund↓ lac-f↓
    - **stitching** pain: arund lac-f
  - **inward**:
    - **agg.**: mang↓
      - **pressing** pain: mang h2
  - **light**; at:
    - **agg.**: *Ars*↓ *Aur-m*↓ *Mag-m*↓ nux-v↓
      - **burning**: *Mag-m* k* nux-v
      - **tearing** pain: *Ars Aur-m*
    - **candlelight**: euphr graph k2 staph
      - **pressing** pain: *Euphr* staph
  - **near** objects; at: ph-ac↓
    - **pressing** pain: ph-ac h2
  - **one** point; at: bar-c↓ *Nat-m*↓
    - **pressing** pain: bar-c *Nat-m*
  - **sharply**:
    - **agg.**: bar-c↓ *Carb-v*↓ castm↓ *Chel*↓ coloc↓ mag-m↓ merc↓ nat-ar↓ **Nat-m**↓ *Psor*↓ rhod↓ *Rhus-t*↓ **Ruta**↓ sul-ac h2 symph↓
      - **aching**: *Carb-v Chel* coloc merc nat-ar **Nat-m** *Psor Rhus-t* **Ruta**
      - **burning**: bar-c castm mag-m *Nat-m* psor rhod sul-ac h2 symph fd3.de•
      - **pressing** pain: sul-ac h2
    - **near** objects; at: *Mang*↓
      - **aching**: *Mang*
  - **sideways** agg.: bar-c mag-s↓ pyrog k2
    - **pressing** pain: bar-c
      - **outward**: mag-s c1
  - **snow**; at: apis k2
  - **steadily**:
    - **agg.**: anac↓ *Apis Ars Arund* calc k2 *Carb-v Caust Chel Cina* ham fd3.de• nat-ar nat-c **Nat-m** plat *Psor* rheum h *Rhus-t Ruta Seneg*
      - **pressing** pain: anac h2 caust *Nat-m* rheum h rhus-t h1
    - **near** objects; at: echi *Mang*
  - **upward**:
    - **agg.**: alum↓ ars bar-c *Carb-v Chel* k* con kali-c h2 mang plb pyrog k2 sabad sulph
      - **aching**: *Chel*
      - **burning**: alum
      - **pressing** pain: ars h2 bar-c mang sabad
  - **white** or red, or at the sun; at anything: **Lyc**↓
    - **stitching** pain: **Lyc**
- **lying**:
  - **agg.**: bell bro1 *Carb-v* cedr con bg1 *Gels* nux-v *Phos* ruta fd4.de zinc bg1
    - **bursting** pain: *Gels*
  - **amel.**: chel *Cimic*
  - **back**; on | **amel.**: puls bro1
  - **side**; on:
    - **left**:
      - **agg.**: lac-f↓
        - **cutting** pain: lac-f

Eye

- • **side**; on – **left**: ...
  - : **amel.**: nat-ar
  - : **painful** side:
    - : **agg.**: syph bg1
    - : **amel.**: lach zinc
- **lying** down:
  - • **agg.**: dig ↓ *Nux-v* ↓ psor ↓ ruta ↓
    - : **burning**: *Nux-v*
    - : **pressing** pain: psor jl2
    - : **stitching** pain: dig ruta fd4.de
  - • **amel.**: cassia-s ↓ cimic ↓ propr ↓
    - : **burning**: cassia-s ccrh1•
    - : **pressing** pain: propr sa3•
    - : **stitching** pain: cimic
- **masturbation**; after: *Cina*
  - • **aching**: *Cina*
- **menses**:
  - • **after**:
    - : **agg.**: nat-m ↓
      - : **sore**: nat-m bro1
  - • **before**:
    - : **agg.**: merc ↓ nicc ↓ sil ↓
      - : **burning**: nicc bro1
      - : **pressing** pain: merc b4.de sil b4.de
  - • **during**:
    - : **agg.**: **Calc** b4.de* carb-an cassia-s ↓ castm ↓ *Coloc* croc mag-c b4.de nat-p ↓ nicc ↓ *Nit-ac* ↓ *Zinc* ↓
      - : **burning**: cassia-s ccrh1• castm mag-c nicc k* *Nit-ac*
      - : **pressing** pain: carb-an *Croc* nat-p
      - : **sore**: *Zinc*
      - : **stitching** pain: calc
      - : **tearing** pain: *Coloc*
- **moistening** eye:
  - • **amel.**: nat-c ↓
    - : **burning**: nat-c h2
- **motion**:
  - • **agg.**: **Acon** ↓ allox ↓ *Asaf* ↓ bamb-a ↓ bell-p-sp ↓ berb ↓ brom ↓ *Bry* ↓ carbn-s ↓ cassia-s ↓ caust ↓ *Cupr* ↓ gels ↓ ind ↓ **Kalm** ↓ *Nat-m* ↓ propr ↓ *Prun* ↓ *Puls* ↓ rhus-t ↓ *Spig* ↓ sulph ↓ viol-t ↓
    - : **burning**: berb cassia-s ccrh1• caust h2 propr sa3• [bell-p-sp dcm1]
    - : **cutting** pain: bry ind
    - : **drawing** pain: **Kalm** *Nat-m* *Puls*
    - : **foreign** body; as from a: allox tpw4
    - : **sand**; as from: allox tpw4 propr sa3•
    - : **sore**: bamb-a stb2.de• carbn-s *Cupr*
    - : **stitching** pain: **Acon** *Asaf* brom *Bry* k* gels *Prun* rhus-t *Spig* sulph viol-t
  - • **amel.**: *Coloc* ↓ dros ↓ **Dulc** ↓ phys ↓ thuj ↓
    - : **stitching** pain: *Coloc* dros **Dulc** phys thuj
  - • **eyelids**; of:
    - : **agg.**: **Bry** ↓ carbn-s k2 glon ↓ nat-ar ↓
      - : **sore**: **Bry** glon nat-ar
    - : **amel.**: stann h2
  - • **eyes**; of:
    - : **agg.**: acon ↓ agar apis arg-n arn *Ars* k* ars-s-f k2 astac aur-s k2 bad *Bapt* ↓ bell k2 *Berb* brom **Bry** k* camph *Carb-v* *Carbn-s* caust chel *Chin* cimic k* clem com cor-r k* cortico tpw7 crot-h crot-t bro1 *Cupr* desm-g bnj1 *Gels* glon grin k* haliae-lc srj5• *Hep* hipp c1* hir ↓ indol bro1 ip tl1 kali-ar kali-c kali-p *Kalm* k* *Lac-d* lach limen-b-c ↓ lyc k* mand rsj7• *Mang* med meph merc nat-ar *Nat-m* par phos phys phyt pic-ac **Prun** *Puls* pyrid rly4• pyrog ↓ ran-b ↓ *Ran-s* rauw ↓ **Rhus-t** k* sang a1 sep sil *Spig* k* spong fd4.de stann *Stict* ↓ *Sulph* sumb symph fd3.de• trios rsj11• tritic-vg fd5.de tub k2*
      - : **aching**: acon h1 *Bad* **Bry** chel cortico tpw7 *Gels* *Hep* nat-ar phyt pic-ac
      - : **burning**: hir skp7• stict ptk1

- **motion** – **eyes**; of – **agg.**: ...
  - : **pressing** pain: agar brom **Bry** camph *Carb-v* chel clem crot-h glon *Hep* *Lach* limen-b-c mlk9.de *Mang* merc *Spig* stann tritic-vg fd5.de
  - : **rapid**: ran-s stram
  - : **sore**: agar *Bapt* **Bry** *Carb-v* *Carbn-s* *Com* *Crot-t* *Cupr* gels haliae-lc srj5• nat-ar *Nat-m* phos *Phys* pic-ac pyrog k2 ran-b c1 rauw tpw8 **Rhus-t** *Stict* **Tub** k*
  - : **stitching** pain: stann h2
  - : **amel.**: dulc kali-i bro1 op rhod k2
    - : **pressing** pain: op
  - : **side** to side; from:
    - : **agg.**: cortico tpw7 rauw ↓
      - . **aching**: rauw sp1
- **nail**; as from a: abel vh1 hell hist sp1*
- **nausea**; with: ruta ↓ symph ↓ thuj ↓
  - • **aching**: ruta fd4.de symph fd3.de• thuj
- **neuralgic**: *Ars* bro1 asaf bro1 bell bro1 *Cedr* bro1 chin bro1 chinin-s bro1 *Cimic* bro1 *Cinnb* bro1 coloc bro1 com bro1 crot-t bro1 *Gels* bro1 glon tl1 kali-i bro1 kalm bro1 mag-p bro1 meli bro1 mez bro1 osm bro1 phos bro1 phys bro1 *Prun* bro1 rhod bro1 *Spig* bro1 thuj tl1
  - • **palpebral** neuralgia (See lids - neuralgic)
- **noise** agg.: spig mrr1
- **opening** the eyes:
  - • **agg.**●: agar ↓ alum ↓ ars *Bry* ↓ caust ↓ cephd-i bnj1 croc desm-g bnj1 *Graph* h2 *Hydr* kali-bi *Led* mag-m ↓ *Nat-m* ph-ac sil ↓ upa
    - : **burning**: agar a1 **Ars** *Kali-bi* mag-m
    - : **cutting** pain: *Bry*
    - : **pressing** pain: alum h2 caust h2 croc sil a1* upa
    - : **sore**: sil
    - : **stitching** pain: **Ars**
  - • **impossible**: alum ↓ kali-s ↓
    - : **pressing** pain: alum h2 kali-s fd4.de
- **operation**; after: asar gm1 mez ↓ *Staph* ↓ *Zinc* ↓
  - • **burning**: asar c1 *Staph* *Zinc*
  - • **neuralgic**: mez ptk1
- **otitis** media; with (See accompanied - ear - inflammation)
- **palpitations**:
  - • **during**: iber ↓
    - : **pressing** pain | **outward**: iber vml3•
- **paroxysmal**: ars **Bad** *Chin* *Chinin-s* hep h2 nicc plat puls sil tell c1 tritic-vg fd5.de
- **perfume**; reaction to: lac-del ↓
  - • **burning**: lac-del hrn2•
- **periodical**: ars bro1 asaf bro1 aur-m *Cedr* k* *Chin* k* chinin-m kr1 *Chinin-s* k* *Coloc* *Euphr* *Gels* *Nat-m* **Prun** ran-s ↓ *Spig* bro1
  - • **alternate** day: ars h2
  - • **burning**: asaf
  - • **pressing** pain: aur-m ran-s
  - • **tearing** pain: aur-m chinin-s
- **perspiration**; during: *Acon* bg2 arn bg2 ars bg2 **Bell** bg2 *Bry* bg2 *Calc* bg2 canth bg2 caust bg2 cham bg2 *Hep* bg2 led bg2 **Lyc** bg2 merc bg2 nat-c bg2 nux-v bg2 phos bg2 puls bg2 rhod bg2 **Rhus-t** bg2 sep bg2 sil bg2 **Spig** bg2 *Sulph* bg2 thuj bg2 verat bg2
- **piercing** (See stitching)
- **pinching** pain: arn croc b7.de* euph h2 kali-c nit-ac k*
- **pressing** apart: *Asar* b7a.de* prun bg2*
- **pressing** **pain** (= pressure; as from): acon k* aeth *Agar* k* agath-a nl2• aloe *Alum* k* alum-p k2 alum-sil k2 *Am-c* k* *Ambr* k* *Anac* k* ang k* ant-t k* *Apis* k* arg-n arn k* ars k* ars-s-f k2 *Asaf* k* asar k* *Aur* k* aur-ar k2 aur-i k2 aur-s k2 bamb-a stb2.de• bapt bar-c k* bar-i k2 bar-m bar-s k2 *Bell* k* benz-ac berb bism k* borx k* bov bros-gau mrc1 **Bry** k* bufo cain calad **Calc** k* calc-s calc-sil k2 camph cann-i cann-s canth k* caps k* carb-an k* *Carb-v* k* *Carbn-s* card-m *Carl* *Caul* *Caust* k* cere-b **Cham** k* *Chel* k* **Chin** k* chinin-ar cic cimic cina k* cinnb *Clem* k* coc-c coca *Cocc* k* coff b7.de colch k* *Coloc* *Com* *Con* k* croc k* crot-c crot-h bg2 *Crot-t* *Cupr* k* *Cycl* cystein-l rly4• daph *Dig* k* dros b7.de dulc k* euph b4a.de* *Euphr* k* fago *Ferr* b7.de* ferr-m fic-m gya1 fl-ac gels *Glon* *Graph* k* grat gymno ham hell *Hep* k* hydr *Ign* k* ind indg iod k* *Ip* b7a.de kali-ar *Kali-bi* *Kali-c* k* kali-chl kali-i kali-m k2 kali-n k* kali-p kali-s kali-sil k2 kalm

- **pressing** pain: ...
  kreos k* lac-ac *Lac-c* *Lach* k* lachn laur k* *Led* k* lil-t limen-b-c hrn2* **Lyc** k* lyss m-aust b7.de *Mag-c* k* mag-m k* manc mang k* med meny k* meph **Merc** k* *Merc-c* k* merc-i-f merc-i-r *Mez* k* mosch k* mur-ac k* naja nat-ar nat-c k* **Nat-m** k* nat-p *Nat-s* nicc **Nit-ac** k* nux-m b7.de *Nux-v* k* ol-an olib-sac wmh1 olnd k* op paeon par b7.de* *Petr* k* *Ph-ac* k* *Phos* k* phys *Phyt* *Plat* k* *Plb* k* positr nl2• *Prun* psil ft1 *Psor* *Puls* k* **Ran-b** k* ran-s k* raph rheum b7.de* *Rhod* k* *Rhus-t* k* *Ruta* k* sabad b7.de* samb b7.de sang santin *Sars* k* sec k* sel k* **Seneg** k* *Sep* k* *Sil* k* **Spig** k* *Spong* k* *Stann* k* *Staph* k* *Stram* k* stront-c k* stry suis-hep rly4• sul-ac b4.de* sul-i k2 *Sulph* k* symph fd3.de• tab *Ther* *Thuj* k* tritic-vg fd5.de tub valer k* vanil fd5.de verat k* viol-o vip *Zinc* k* zinc-p k2 zing
  - **alternating** with | **burning**: sars
  - **backward**: *Bism* h1* limen-b-c hrn2*
  - **contracting**: euphr h2
  - **downward**: anac h2 aur k* bry cain carb-an h2 carb-v coloc *Hell* b7a.de kali-s fd4.de *Seneg* b4a.de sulph h2
  - **finger**, as from a: nit-ac h2
  - **hair**; as from a: kali-n h2
  - **hard** substance in it; as from a: olnd
  - **inward**: agar k* anac k* *Aur* k* aur-m bro1 bamb-a stb2.de• bapt bell k* bism b7.de* borx k* bry b7.de* **Calc** k* cann-s b7.de* caust k* chel b7.de* *Chin* b7a.de* cor-r a1* *Crot-t* bro1 daph bg2* hep b4a.de* kali-c b4.de* kola stb3• limen-b-c hrn2* olnd bro1 *Par* bro1 ph-ac k* *Spig* b7.de* spong fd4.de symph fd3.de• zinc k*
  - **looking** at sun; as from: nit-ac
  - **outward**: *Acon* b7.de* agar agath-a nl2• arg-n bg2 *Asaf* k* asar k* aur b4.de* bapt bg2 bar-c b4a.de bell k* berb k* *Bry* k* calc b4.de* camph k* *Cann-s* k* canth b7.de* card-m k2 caul caust b4a.de* cedr ptk1 cham k* cimic k* *Cocc* bro1 coloc bro1 com bro1 con b4.de* crot-c daph dros bg2 dulc a1 eupi fago ferr a1* *Fl-ac* *Glon* k* guaj k* guare k* gymno ptk1 *Ham* k* hell b7.de* iber bg1 ign k* ip k* kali-bi bg2 kali-m ptk1 kali-n b4.de* kola stb3• *Lac-c* lach k* laur b7.de* **Led** k* lyc b4a.de* lycps-v k* m-arct b7.de mag-c h2 med c1 *Merc* k* merc-c k* merl *Mez* b4a.de nat-m h2* *Nat-s* nit-ac bg2 nux-m bg2 **Nux-v** k* op par k* passi bro1 ph-ac k* *Phos* k* *Phyt* prun ptk1 *Psor* puls k* ran-b b7.de* rhus-t b7.de* sabad bg2 sabin c1 *Sang* k* *Seneg* k* sep gk *Sil* **Spig** k* staph b7.de* sulph h2 ther bro1 thuj k* tril-p c1 tritic-vg fd5.de usn bg2 valer b7.de* vanil fd5.de
  - **plug**; as from a: *Anac* k* asar bg2 irid-met srj5• *Ran-b*
  - **sand**; as from: *Calc* b4a.de *Caust* b4a.de euph b4a.de *Hep* b4a.de iod b4a.de *Phos* b4a.de *Sulph* b4a.de *Thuj* b4a.de
  - **sleep**; as from loss of: chin
  - **stye** on lid, as from: stann
  - **upward**: *Bism* h1* irid-met srj5•
- **pressing** throat; when: **Lach** ↓
  - **pressing** pain | **outward**: **Lach** k*
- **pressing** together: op bg1 symph fd3.de•
- **pressure**:
  - **after**: bar-act
    - **aching**: *Bar-act*
  - **agg.**: arn brom bry k2 cassia-s ↓ choc srj3• cortiso ↓ dros eup-per k2 ham petr ↓ plan sars spig ↓
    - **burning**: cassia-s ccrh1• spig k2
    - **stitching** pain: brom cortiso sp1 petr h2
  - **amel.**: abrom-a ks5 arg-n br1* *Asaf* k* bapt bry *Calc* *Caust* chel k* chinin-s k* choc srj3• cic ↓ cimic coloc k* con k* cystein-l ↓ eup-per ↓ ham hyos ↓ kali-p sne lac-d c1 lil-t bro1 luna kg1• mag-m *Mag-p* mur-ac phys sne pic-ac prot jl2 pycnop-sa mrz1 spig ↓ tarent sne verat ↓
    - **aching**: abrom-a ks5 cic h1 pic-ac
    - **burning**: pic-ac spig k2
    - **cutting** pain: *Bry* coloc
    - **pressing** pain: *Asaf* *Caust* cystein-l rly4• *Ham* mur-ac
    - **sore**: *Chel* eup-per k2 hyos verat h1
    - **stitching** pain: *Bry* *Coloc* kali-p phys tarent
  - **slight** | **agg.**: hip-ac sp1
  - **upward**:
    - **amel.**: bell ↓
      - **burning**: bell h1
- **pricking** (See stitching)
- **protruding** tongue: syph xxb
- **pulled** out; as if being: agar bg bell h1 com mtf11 *Glon* med sel bg
- **pulsating** pain: *Ars* *Asaf* k* *Bell* bro1 bry bro1 cartl-s rly4• *Chel* cimic bro1 *Hep* bro1 mand rsj7• merc bro1 ozone sde2• petr petr-ra shn4• rheum h rhus-t stront-c sk4• symph fd3.de• ther bro1
- **radiating**: mez ptk1 sec a1 spig ptk1
- **reading**:
  - **agg.**: (↗*writing*) *Agar* agn ↓ allox sp1 alum alum-p k2 ammc *Apis* *Arg-n* arist-cl ↓ *Arn* *Ars* ars-i ars-met ars-s-f k2 asar aur aur-ar k2 aur-s k2 bapt bar-c ↓ *Bry* cadm-met ↓ *Calc* calc-p cann-i *Carb-v* ↓ *Carbn-s* ↓ caust cic cina a1 cob ↓ **Con** *Croc* ↓ cycl ↓ des-ac ↓ **Dulc** *Echi* *Graph* ↓ ham ↓ ign *Jab* kali-ar *Kali-bi* ↓ *Kali-c* *Kali-p* kola stb3• lac-ac *Lac-c* *Lac-d* k* lac-f ↓ *Lach* lil-t ↓ *Lith-c* lyc h2 *Mang* merc *Merl* mur-ac myric ↓ *Nat-ar* k* nat-c **Nat-m** k* nat-p nat-s nat-sil ↓ nit-ac *Nux-v* ol-j olnd *Onos* petr ph-ac ↓ phel *Phos* phys phyt pic-ac pitu-gl skp7• psor ↓ *Puls* *Rhod* **Ruta** sars sel ↓ *Seneg* **Sep** spong fd4.de *Staph* sul-ac ↓ sulph symph fd3.de• thuj tritic-vg fd5.de vanil fd5.de zinc ↓
    - **aching**: allox tpw3 cann-i **Dulc** *Jab* nat-ar ol-j olnd *Puls* **Ruta** staph
    - **burning**: agn allox tpw3 arist-cl sp1 *Ars* asar bar-c cadm-met tpw6 *Calc* *Carb-v* *Carbn-s* cob *Con* *Croc* cycl *Graph* ham fd3.de• kali-ar *Kali-c* kola stb3• lil-t myric *Nat-ar* *Nat-c* **Nat-m** nat-sil fd3.de• *Olnd* petr phos pic-ac psor *Puls* rhod *Ruta* *Seneg* sep *Staph* sul-ac h2 *Sulph* thuj tritic-vg fd5.de vanil fd5.de zinc
    - **bursting** pain: asar staph
    - **cutting** pain: *Calc* *Merc* petr phyt
    - **drawing** pain: lac-d k2
    - **pressing** pain: *Agar* alum asar cic cina a1 *Con* dulc ign *Kali-c* mang merl k* mur-ac *Nat-m* *Nat-s* *Nux-v* pic-ac *Ruta* sars staph symph fd3.de•
    - **sand**; as from: arist-cl sp1
    - **sore**: *Croc* des-ac rbp6 *Kali-bi* nat-ar nat-p
    - **stitching** pain: *Apis* carbn-s caust *Kali-c* lac-f nat-c ph-ac phyt pic-ac rhod sel *Sulph*
  - **light**; by: kali-c h2
    - **artificial**: calc-p k2
    - **candlelight**: benz-ac *Cina* lach mang nat-m nux-v staph
      - **pressing** pain: mang h2
  - **other** eye; with: kalm bg1
  - **small** print: ind ↓ mur-ac ↓ nat-m ↓ onos vml3• psor ↓ *Ruta* ↓
    - **burning**: ind mur-ac nat-m psor *Ruta*
- **redness**; without: caust ↓
  - **burning**: caust b4a.de
- **rest**:
  - **agg.**: *Coloc* dros dulc merc-i-f mur-ac thuj
    - **cutting** pain: mur-ac
  - **amel.**: agath-a nl2• asaf bro1 berb bry bro1 cimic bro1 pic-ac spong fd4.de tritic-vg fd5.de
    - **pressing** pain: berb pic-ac
- **rheumatic**: **Acon** bg2 anac h2 *Apis* *Ars* bg2 bell bg2 *Bry* bg2 cham bg2 clem *Dulc* euphr bg2 ign bg2 kali-bi k2 kali-c *Led* k* lyc bg2 **Merc** bg2 *Mez* nux-v bg2 *Phyt* *Puls* bg2 rhus-t bg2 *Spig* bg2 **Sulph** bg2 verat bg2
  - **stitching** pain: bry *Merc* *Rhus-t*
- **riding** agg.: verat ↓
  - **aching**: verat
- **ring**; as from a: sep
- **rising** agg.: ars cere-b fago
- **rubbed**; as if | **woolen** towel; with a: stann h2
- **rubbing**:
  - **agg.**: agn ↓ ars ↓ carb-an ↓ carb-v caust h2 *Con* ↓ euphr kali-c kalm ↓ melal-alt gya4 *Puls* ↓ ros-d ↓ sep spong fd4.de vanil fd5.de
    - **burning**: carb-an carb-v *Con* kalm *Puls* sep h2 vanil fd5.de
    - **pressing** pain: ars bg1 sep
    - **sand**; as from: ros-d wla1 sep h2
    - **stitching** pain: agn a1
  - **amel.**: agn a1 allox sp1 am-c ↓ art-v ptk2 borx ↓ *Caust* gink-b ↓ mag-c ↓ *Ran-b* ruta fd4.de spig ↓ tritic-vg fd5.de zinc
    - **burning**: am-c h2 gink-b sbd1• mag-c h2 tritic-vg fd5.de zinc

Eye

- **amel.**: ...
  - **foreign** body; as from a: allox tpw4 spig h1
  - **pressing** pain: borx h2 *Caust Ran-b* ruta fd4.de
  - **sand**; as from: allox tpw4
- **must** rub: **All-c** ↓ chin ↓ chin-b ↓ **Puls** ↓
  - **burning**: **All-c** chin chin-b kr1 **Puls**
  - **pressing** pain: chin h1

- **sand**; as from: abrom-a ks5 *Acon* bro1 agar k* allox tpw4 alum k* alum-p k2 alum-sil k2 am-br k* am-c vh1 ambr k* *Apis Apoc* vh1 arg-n arge-pl rwt5• **Ars** k* asaf k* asc-t k* *Aur* k* aur-ar k2 aur-s k2 bar-c k* bar-i k2 bar-s k2 bell k* berb k* borx b4a.de* bry k* **Calc** k* calc-sil k2 cann-s k* *Canth* b7a.de caps k* *Carb-v* k* carbn-s cassia-s ccrh1• **Caust** k* *Chel* k* **Chin** k* chinin-m c1 chlam-tr bcx2• cina k* *Clem* bg2 cob k* cob-n sp1 coc-c bro1 cocc k* con k* *Cor-r* k* cortico tpw7* *Croc* bg2 cystein-l rly4• *Dig* k* dios hr1 dulc fd4.de elaps euph k* *Euphr* k* *Ferr* k* ferr-ar ferr-i ferr-p k* **Fl-ac** k* form germ-met srj5• graph k* grat k* ham fd3.de• hed sp1 *Hep* k* hist sp1 hura c1 hydrog srj2• hyos b7a.de* *Ign* k* iod k* irid-met srj5• kali-ar kali-bi k* kali-c h2 kali-chl k* kali-i k2 kali-m k2 kali-n bg2 kali-p kali-s fd4.de kali-sil k2 kola stb3• kreos k* lac-d k* lac-h htj1• lach lachn k* *Led* k* lith-c luna kg1• *Lyc* k* m-arct b7a.de mag-m k* *Med* k* merc k* mosch b7a.de* myric **Nat-m** k* nat-p k* nat-sil fd3.de• nit-ac k* ol-an *Op* k* ox-ac paeon parth vml3• petr k* ph-ac k* phos k* *Phyt* k* pic-ac k* plat k* plut-n srj7• pot-e rly4• *Propr* sa3• *Psor* k* *Puls* k* rhus-t k* ros-d wla1 ruta fd4.de sacch-a fd2.de• sal-al blc1• sars k* seneg bg2 *Sep* k* *Sil* k* sol-ni *Spig* k* stram stront-c k* sul-ac bg2 **Sulph** k* sumb symph fd3.de• syph k* tarax b7a.de tarent tax-br oss1• teucr b7a.de *Thuj* k* trios rsj11• tritic-vg fd5.de upa urt-u k* vanil fd5.de viol-t k* xan c1 xero bro1 *Zinc* k* zing hr1*
  - **accompanied** by | **Head**; pain in: lac-d ptk1
  - **penetrated** by sand; as if: *Sulph* bg2
- **scraped** with a knife; as if: lyc bg2 puls b7.de* rhus-t bg2
- **scratching** pain: *Daph* bg2
- **sewing**, while: *Apis* ars-met *Cina* dig lyc h2 mang k2 mez
  - **fine** work; on: carb-v coloc *Con* merc *Nat-m* **Ruta**
- **shaking** the head agg.; on: lyc h2 nit-ac h2 puls ↓
  - **stitching** pain: puls
- **shooting** (See stitching)
- **sitting** agg.: chinin-s merc phos
  - **drawing** pain: merc
- **sleep**:
  - **after**:
    - **agg.**: alum ↓ canth euphr gels
      - **burning**: alum canth
    - **amel.**: cassia-s ↓ chel ↓
      - **burning**: cassia-s ccrh1• chel
  - **amel.**: am-c chel irid-met srj5• **Phos** ruta fd4.de spong fd4.de
  - **before**: *Con* **Phos**
    - **agg.**: *Con* ↓
      - **aching**: *Con*
  - **going** to sleep; on:
    - **agg.**: **Phos** ↓
      - **stitching** pain: **Phos**
- **sleep**; loss of:
  - **after**: kali-c ↓
    - **pressing** pain: kali-c h2
- **sleepiness**; with | **burning** (See SLEEP - Sleepiness - eyes - burning)
- **smarting** (See burning)
- **smoke** agg.: petr-ra ↓ spig mrr1 vanil fd5.de
  - **burning**: petr-ra shn4•
- **smoking** agg.: calad dulc fd4.de ran-b ↓
  - **pressing** pain: calad ran-b br1
- **sore** (= bruised, tender): *Acon* aesc *Agar* agath-a nl2• agn a1 allox tpw4* alum k* alum-p k2 alum-sil k2 alumn k2 am-br androc srj1• ang bg2 ant-c k* ant-t k* *Apis* k* arg-met arg-n *Arn* k* *Ars* ars-i ars-s-f k2 *Aur* aur-ar k2 aur-m bro1 bad bamb-a stb2.de• *Bapt* k* bar-c k* bar-i k2 *Bell* **Bry** k* cain calad calc calc-i k2 *Calc-p Calc-s* calc-sil k2 camph canth k* *Carb-v* k* *Carbn-s* carc sp1* caust cedr cham k* *Chel* chin bg2 chion ptk1 *Cimic* k* clem cocc k* *Colch Com* k* cor-r *Corn* cortiso sp1 *Croc* k* *Cupr* k* dios dirc dor dros bg2 **Eup-per** k* euphr b7a.de* fago

- **sore**: ...
Gels k* *Glon* granit-m es1• gymno haliae-lc srj5• **Ham Hep** k* hir rsj4• hom-xyz br1 hura hyos *Hyper* ign bg2 iod k* kali-bi kali-c bg2 kali-i k2 kali-p *Lach* lec *Led* bg2 lil-t limest-b es1• lith-c luf-op rsj5• *Luna* kg1• *Lyc* k* lyss mag-m a1 mag-p ptk1 manc mang k2 medul-os-si rly4• *Merc* k* mim-p rsj8• naphtin nat-ar nat-c nat-m k* nat-p *Nit-ac* k* *Nux-v* k* onos k* ox-ac phos k* *Phos-pchl* c1 *Phys* phyt k* pic-ac plan plut-n srj7• podo positr nl2• **Prun** psor *Puls* k* pyrog k2 *Ran-b* k* rauw tpw8 **Rhus-t** k* rob rumx k* *Ruta* k* sal-al blc1• *Sal-fr* sle1• sang k* sars scroph-n br1 sel rsj9• *Sep* k* *Sil* k* sin-n *Spig* k* spong fd4.de stann staph bg2 stry sul-ac sul-i k2 sulph k* *Symph* ter thiam rly4• thuj k2 *Tub* k* urt-u ust valer bg2 verat b7.de* vib **Zinc** [heroin sdj2 sol-ecl cky1]
  - **alternating** with | **Throat**; inflammation of (See THROAT - Inflammation - alternating with - eyes)
  - **foreign** body; as from a: gels hura
  - **itching** pain: aids nl2•
  - **smoke**; as from: ran-b br1
- **sparks**; as from: petr-ra shn4• tarent
- **spectacles**, from wearing: borx ↓
  - **burning**: borx hr1
- **splinter**; as from a: apis bro1 aur bro1 *Hep* bro1 med k* merc bro1 nit-ac k* par bg2 petr-ra shn4• sil bg2 sulph bro1 tarent thuj bro1
- **sprained**; as if: lil-t ptk1
- **standing** agg.: merc-sul ↓
  - **drawing** pain: merc-sul
- **stepping** | **every** step; at: hep
- **sticks**; as from: med hr1
- **stiff** sensation, in muscles: **Nat-m** ↓
  - **drawing** pain: **Nat-m**
- **stinging**: *Agath-a* nl2• androc srj1• **Apis** k* arge-pl rwt5• bufo bg2 *Calc Caust* chlam-tr bcx2• *Crot-t* euphr bro1 *Ferr* hr1 fum rly1*• *Granit-m* es1• hep bro1 hist vml3• hydrog srj2• irid-met srj5• kali-c bro1 ketogl-ac rly4• lac-e hm2• *Luna* kg1• mag-s mand rsj7• melal-alt gya4 meph nabal a1 nat-c nept-m lsd2.fr nit-ac plac-s rly4• podo fd3.de• *Puls* k* spong tarent thuj k*
- **stitching** pain: *Abel* vh1 *Acon* k* aegle-m zzc1• aesc agar k* agn b7.de* all-c alum alum-p k2 alum-sil k2 am-c k* anac anan ang ant-c k* **Apis** k* aran *Arg-met Arg-n* arn k* ars k* ars-i ars-s-f k2 asaf k* aspar aur k* aur-ar k2 aur-i k2 aur-m aur-m-n aur-s k2 bamb-a stb2.de• bapt bell k* *Berb* borx k* *Brom* k* *Bry* k* bufo bg2 calad *Calc* k* calc-sil k2 canth k* caps b7.de* carb-an k* carb-v h2 carbn-s *Caust* k* *Cham* k* *Chel* chim bro1 chin k* cic b7.de* *Cimic* k* cinnb k* cist clem bro1 cob cocc coloc k* con k* cortiso sp1 croc b7.de* crot-t cycl k* *Dig* k* dios dros k* *Dulc* eup-per *Euphr* k* eupi fago falco-pe nl2• ferr k* ferr-i ferr-p form *Gels* k* *Glon Graph* k* ham fd3.de• *Hell* k* *Hep* k* hist sp1 *Hyos* hyper ign k* iod k* *Ip* k* irid-met srj5• *Kali-bi* **Kali-c** k* kali-chl kali-i kali-m k2 kali-n *Kali-p* kali-s fd4.de kali-sil k2 *Kalm* k* kola stb3• lac-f *Lach* k* laur k* *Lec* led limest-b es1• *Lith-c Lyc* k* lyss m-ambo b7.de m-arct b7.de m-aust b7.de mag-c k* *Mag-m* k* mag-p bro1 manc mang med k2* meny b7.de* *Meph* *Merc* k* merc-c b4a.de* merc-i-r merl mill k2* mosch bg2 *Mur-ac* k* naja nat-ar *Nat-c* k* *Nat-m* k* nat-p k* nat-pyru rly4• nat-s k* nept-m lsd2.fr *Nit-ac* k* *Nux-m* *Nux-v* k* ol-an *Par* k* *Petr* k* petr-ra shn4• ph-ac k* *Phos* k* phys k* phyt pic-ac plan k* plb b7.de* positr nl2• **Prun** k* psor *Puls* k* rauw sp1 rhod bro1 **Rhus-t** k* rhus-v ruta fd4.de sang sars b4.de* sec sel k* *Senec* seneg k* *Sep* k* *Sil* k* sin-a **Spig** k* spong k* stann k* staph k* stram stront-c k* stry suis-pan rly4• sul-i k2 **Sulph** k* symph fd3.de• tab tarax k* *Tarent* ter *Thuj* k* til tritic-vg fd5.de valer bg2* vanil fd5.de verat k* viol-t b7.de* *Zinc* k* zinc-p k2
  - **alternating** with | **pulsation**: calc
  - **backward**: bell berb cinnb graph hyper lac-f rhus-t sep **Spig**
  - **burning**: *Euphr* stann h2 tarax h1
  - **downward**: carb-an h2 hell
  - **forward**: spig
  - **inward**: arn b7.de* *Asaf* **Bell** b4.de* *Caust Cimic* cinnb *Coloc* k* graph h2 lac-f phos k* phyt **Prun Rhus-t Spig** k* stram syph
  - **itching**: cycl h1
  - **jerking** pain: staph h1
  - **needles** thrust into eyeball; as if: caust bg2 cimic ptk1 kola stb3• nicc bg2 positr nl2• rhod ptk1 spig c1*
    - **hot** needles: kola stb3• rhod ptk1
  - **outward**: **Asaf** *Bell* cadm-s calc b4.de* *Camph* cocc k* dros k* *Kali-bi* *Mur-ac* k* *Nat-c* k* rhod senec sil b4.de* *Spig* sulph b4.de* *Thuj* viol-t b7.de*

  - **presses** lids down: spig$_{h1}$
  - **pulsating** pain: *Ars* calc rhus-t
  - **radiating** from the eyes: **Spig**
- **stool** | **after**:
    - **agg.**: carbn-s ↓ nat-c
      - **burning**: *Nat-c*$_{k*}$
      - **stitching** pain: carbn-s
  - **during** | **agg.**: calc-sil$_{k2}$ *Crot-t*
- **stooping** agg.: berb bov brom ↓ *Coloc* dros ↓ ferr-p$_{tl1}$ fl-ac lac-ac ↓ merc merl ↓ pycnop-sa$_{mrz1}$ seneg spig$_{k*}$ verat-v ↓
  - **aching**: coloc
  - **burning**: bov
  - **bursting** pain: lac-ac
  - **cutting** pain: coloc
  - **pressing** pain: *Coloc* fl-ac merl$_{k*}$ seneg
  - **stitching** pain: brom coloc dros$_{h1}$ verat-v$_{a1}$
- **storm**:
  - **before**: *Cedr* **Rhod**$_{k*}$ *Sil*
    - **stitching** pain: *Cedr Rhod Sil*
  - **during**: **Rhod** sep *Sil*
- **strained**; as if: allox$_{tpw4}$ androc$_{srj1}$• bell$_{bg2}$ graph$_{h2}$ *Guaj*$_{bro1}$ jab$_{bro1}$ *Kalm*$_{bro1}$ med$_{bro1}$ *Mez* *Nat-m*$_{bro1}$ olnd$_{b7a.de}$ onos$_{bro1}$ petr-ra$_{shn4}$• rhus-t$_{bro1}$ **Ruta**$_{k*}$
- **straining** eyes: mur-ac ↓ nat-m ↓ *Ruta* ↓ seneg ↓ symph ↓
  - **pressing** pain: mur-ac nat-m$_{k*}$ *Ruta*$_{k*}$ seneg$_{tl1}$ symph$_{tl1}$
- **string**; as if drawn with a (See drawing - string)
- **sudden**: sil ↓
  - **stitching** pain: *(↗appearing - disappearing - suddenly - stitching)* sil
- **sunrise** until sunset: *Kalm*$_{k*}$ *Nat-m*$_{k13*}$
- **swallowing** agg.: tarent
  - **stitching** pain: tarent
- **talking** agg.: bry ↓
  - **stitching** pain: bry
- **tearing** pain: acon aeth agar all-c alum$_{b4.de*}$ am-m$_{k*}$ ambr$_{k*}$ *Anac*$_{k*}$ ant-t$_{k*}$ apis *Arn*$_{k*}$ *Ars*$_{k*}$ ars-s-f$_{k2}$ asaf$_{bg2*}$ asar$_{k*}$ aur aur-ar$_{k2}$ aur-m$_{k*}$ bar-c bar-s$_{k2}$ *Bell*$_{k*}$ berb borx$_{k*}$ bov$_{k*}$ bry$_{k*}$ cadm-s *Calc*$_{k*}$ calc-sil$_{k2}$ canth$_{k*}$ carb-v carbn-s caust *Cham*$_{k*}$ *Chel*$_{k*}$ chin$_{bg2}$ *Chinin-s* cic cob *Cocc* *Colch*$_{k*}$ *Coloc*$_{k*}$ con$_{k*}$ croc *Crot-h* crot-t$_{bro1}$ dros$_{k*}$ *Euphr*$_{b7a.de}$ gran graph$_{h2}$ grat guare$_{bro1}$ *Hyos* hyper *Ip*$_{k*}$ kali-ar *Kali-c*$_{k*}$ kali-n kali-p kali-s kali-sil$_{k2}$ kalm$_{k2}$ kreos led$_{k*}$ *Lyc*$_{k*}$ m-ambo$_{b7.de}$ mag-c$_{k*}$ med **Merc**$_{k*}$ merc-c$_{k*}$ *Mez*$_{k*}$ nat-c$_{b4.de*}$ nat-m$_{bg2}$ nat-s nicc *Nux-v*$_{k*}$ paeon par$_{k*}$ *Phos*$_{k*}$ plb$_{k*}$ *Prun* **Puls**$_{k*}$ rhus-t ruta$_{k*}$ *Seneg*$_{bg2}$ sep$_{k*}$ *Sil*$_{k*}$ spig$_{b7a.de*}$ spong$_{k*}$ squil$_{k*}$ sulph$_{k*}$ tax thuj valer$_{k*}$ *Verat*$_{k*}$ zinc$_{k*}$ zinc-p$_{k2}$
  - **outward**: sil$_{h2}$
  - **paroxysmal**: chinin-s nicc *Sil*
- **thinking** of it agg.: cortiso ↓
  - **stitching** pain: cortiso$_{sp1}$
- **thinking** of the pain agg.: *Lach Spig*
- **thread** were drawn through eye; as if a: bufo$_{bg2}$ ign$_{bg2}$ lach$_{bg2}$ mur-ac$_{bg2}$ par$_{b7.de*}$ plat$_{bg2}$ valer$_{bg2}$
- **throat** symptoms, with: tarent$_{bg1}$
- **throbbing** in temples, after: glon ↓
  - **pressing** pain: glon
- **thunderstorm**; during: dulc$_{fd4.de}$ sep
- **toothache**; with: plan$_{c1*}$
- **torn** out; as if: *Ars*$_{b4a.de}$ bamb-a$_{stb2.de*}$ bell$_{b4.de*}$ *Calc*$_{b4.de*}$ caps$_{bg2}$ carb-v$_{b4.de*}$ chel$_{bg2}$ *Cocc*$_{b7.de*}$ nat-c$_{bg2}$ ph-ac$_{b4.de*}$ puls$_{bg2}$ *Sil*$_{b4.de*}$
- **touch**:
  - **agg.**: *Agar* aids$_{nl2}$• allox$_{sp1}$ arg-n asaf aur bamb-a$_{stb2.de}$• *Bell* borx ↓ *Bry*$_{k*}$ calc-s$_{k2}$ *Caust* chin clem$_{h2}$ cupr dig dirc$_{c1}$ eup-per$_{k2}$ **Hep**$_{k*}$ hip-ac$_{sp1}$ lach$_{k2}$ mag-p melal-alt$_{gya4}$ *Merc* nat-c$_{h2}$ phos$_{bro1}$ plan$_{bro1}$ positr ↓ psor pyrog$_{k2}$ sang$_{hr1}$ scut$_{c1}$ sil$_{h2}$ spig$_{k2*}$ sulph$_{h2}$ thuj tub$_{k2}$ vero-o$_{rly4*}$• x-ray$_{sp1}$
    - **aching**: bry$_{k2}$ dig$_{k*}$
    - **burning**: agar$_{h2}$ *Caust* thuj
    - **cutting** pain: *Asaf*$_{k*}$

- **touch** – **agg.**: ...
    - **pressing** pain: *Aur Caust* cupr psor
    - **sore**: borx$_{h2}$ bry$_{k2}$ calc-s$_{k2}$ hep$_{h2}$ positr$_{nl2}$• spig$_{c1}$ sulph$_{h2}$ thuj$_{k2}$ tub$_{k2}$
  - **throat** agg.; touching: lach$_{k2}$
    - **pressing** pain: lach$_{k2}$
- **turning**:
  - **eyes**:
    - **agg.**: ars ↓ **Spig** ↓ tub ↓
      - **pressing** pain: **Spig** tub
      - **stitching** pain: ars$_{h2}$
    - **right**; to: dig$_{h2}$ sep
      - **pressing** pain: sep
    - **sideways**: bad bar-c *Bry* carc$_{fd2.de}$• cimic$_{mtf11}$ *Crot-t Cupr* **Kalm** lyc$_{h2}$ *Med* phys *Rhus-t Sil* **Spig** *Stict* tarent **Tub**$_{k*}$ ust
      - **drawing** pain: **Kalm**
    - **upward**: ars bar-c *Carb-v* carc$_{fd2.de}$• *Chel* con mang plb sabad *Sulph*
  - **head**:
    - **agg.**: lac-ac ↓
      - **bursting** pain: lac-ac$_{k*}$
- **ulcerative** pain: dros$_{bg2}$ kali-c$_{bg2}$ nit-ac$_{bg2}$
- **unbearable**: zinc$_{h2}$
- **urination**; copious | **amel.**: acon ferr-p *Gels Ign Kalm* petr-ra$_{shn4}$• sang sil ter verat
- **violent**: symph$_{jl2}$
- **walking**:
  - **after**:
    - **agg.**: anac bell con euphr pall puls sep
      - **pressing** pain: con (non:euphr$_{kl}$)
  - **agg.**: anac dulc$_{fd4.de}$ merc-sul ↓ puls symph$_{fd3.de}$•
    - **drawing** pain: merc-sul
  - **air**; in open:
    - **agg.**: benz-ac carb-v ↓ euphr ↓ pall ↓ plan sep ↓ sulph zinc
      - **aching**: pall zinc
      - **pressing** pain: carb-v$_{h2}$ euphr$_{kl}$ sep$_{h2}$ sulph zinc
    - **amel.**: arn carb-v nat-m symph$_{fd3.de}$•
      - **pressing** pain: arn nat-m symph$_{fd3.de}$•
  - **warm** room; in a:
    - **amel.**: *Coloc*
      - **burning**: *Coloc*
      - **cutting** pain: *Coloc*
      - **stitching** pain: *Coloc*
- **warm**:
  - **air** agg.: sinus$_{rly4}$•
  - **applications**:
    - **agg.**: arg-n$_{bro1}$ arn *Chel Com*$_{bro1}$ kali-sil$_{k2}$ lac-d$_{k2}$ mag-p$_{tl1}$ merc mez nat-m *Puls*$_{k*}$ sulph$_{bro1}$ thuj$_{bro1}$
    - **amel.**: **Ars**$_{k*}$ aur-ar$_{k2}$ *Aur-m Dulc* ery-a **Hep**$_{k*}$ kali-ar *Lac-d Mag-p*$_{k*}$ *Nat-ar* nat-c rhod$_{k2}$ seneg *Sil* spig *Thuj*$_{k*}$
      - **pressing** pain: nat-c seneg
  - **bed**:
    - **agg.**: cinnb$_{k2}$ *Merc* ↓
      - **burning**: *Merc*
    - **amel.**: nat-c ↓
      - **pressing** pain: nat-c
  - **room**:
    - **agg.**: abrom-a ↓ aeth ↓ *Apis* **Arg-n** cadm-met ↓ *Con* parth ↓ *Puls* symph ↓
      - **burning**: aeth **Apis** cadm-met$_{tpw6}$ *Con* parth$_{vml3}$• **Puls** symph$_{fd3.de}$•
      - **pressing** pain: *Apis*
      - **sand**; as from: abrom-a$_{ks5}$
  - **stove** agg.: *Apis Com*$_{k*}$ merc$_{k2}$
- **warmth**:
  - **agg.**: anac ↓ *Arn* ↓

- **agg.**: ...
  - ⁝ **stitching** pain: *Arn*
  - ⁝ **tearing** pain: anac arn
- **amel.**: ery-a ↓ galeoc-c-h ↓ *Hep* ↓ *Ign* ↓ *Sil* ↓ thuj ↓
  - ⁝ **aching**: ery-a galeoc-c-h$_{gms1}$• *Hep*
  - ⁝ **stitching** pain: *Hep Ign Sil* thuj
  - ⁝ **tearing** pain: thuj$_{k2}$
- **dry** warmth:
  - ⁝ **amel.**:
    - ⁝ **dry** heat amel.: ars ↓
      - **burning**: ars$_{k2}$

- **washing**:
  - **agg.**: *Mur-ac* ↓
    - ⁝ **stitching** pain: *Mur-ac*
  - **amel.**: alum ↓ kali-n ↓ *Mur-ac* ↓
    - ⁝ **burning**: alum$_{gk}$ kali-n$_{h2}$* *Mur-ac*$_{hr1}$
- **weakness**, causing: glon ↓ staph ↓
  - **pressing** pain: glon staph
- **weariness**; with: bamb-a ↓ tritic-vg ↓
  - **burning**: bamb-a$_{stb2.de}$• tritic-vg$_{fd5.de}$
- **weather**:
  - **change** of weather: cadm-s$_{bg1}$
  - **warm**:
    - ⁝ **agg.**: sulph
      - ⁝ **stitching** pain: *Sulph*
  - **wet**:
    - ⁝ **agg.**: *Calc Dulc* kali-p$_{fd1.de}$• *Merc* merc-c$_{bro1}$ *Rhus-t*$_{k}$* *Spig*$_{k}$* verat ↓
      - ⁝ **stitching** pain: rhus-t
      - ⁝ **tearing** pain: *Merc* verat$_{hr1}$
- **weeping**; after: berb positr$_{nl2}$• tab
- **weeping**; as after: lap-la$_{rsp1}$ stann$_{h2}$
- **wind**:
  - **agg.**: ars-met asar symph$_{fd3.de}$•
  - **cold**:
    - ⁝ **agg.**: cortico$_{sp1}$* **Sep** ↓
      - ⁝ **burning**: cortico$_{tpw7}$ **Sep**
- **wine**; after a glass of: zinc
- **winking**: kali-i$_{k2}$*
  - **amel.**: bar-c$_{h2}$
  - **obliged** to wink: staph$_{h1}$*
- **working**; while: graph ↓ nat-c ↓ symph ↓
  - **burning**: graph nat-c symph$_{fd3.de}$•
  - **sun**; in the: dulc ↓ sulph ↓
    - ⁝ **pressing** pain: dulc$_{fd4.de}$ sulph$_{h2}$
- **writing** agg.: (↗ *exertion of the eyes - agg.; reading - agg.)* alum ↓ *Calc-f* cann-s ↓ canth ↓ cob ↓ coff con euphr lac-f ↓ lact ↓ *Lil-t* ↓ lyc ↓ *Merl* *Nat-ar*$_{k}$* nat-c **Nat-m** nat-sil ↓ phyt rhod ↓ *Seneg* ↓ sep staph ↓ symph ↓ vanil$_{fd5.de}$ zinc ↓
  - **aching**: *Calc-f*
  - **burning**: cob lact *Lil-t* nat-ar nat-c *Nat-m* nat-sil$_{fd3.de}$• rhod *Seneg* staph$_{h1}$ symph$_{fd3.de}$• vanil$_{fd5.de}$ zinc
  - **cutting** pain: cann-s canth phyt
  - **pressing** pain: alum$_{h2}$ con
  - **stitching** pain: cob lac-f$_{c1}$ lyc *Phyt*
- **yawning** agg.: agar ruta$_{fd4.de}$
  - **burning**: agar$_{k}$*

▽ - **extending** to:

- ○ **All** directions: spig$_{k2}$
- **Arm**: rumx
- **Backward**: *Aur* bapt$_{k2}$ cimic colch coloc *Com* crot-h hep irid-met$_{srj5}$• lach lil-t mag-p$_{bg2}$ mez nat-m *Par* phos phys *Rhus-t* *Spig*$_{k}$* syph$_{br}$ tarent *Thuj*
  - ⁝ **Brain**, into: grin$_{c1}$
- **Brain**: *Thuj* ↓

- **extending** to – **Brain**: ...
  - ⁝ **tearing** pain: *Thuj*
- **Chiasma**; optic: anh$_{sp1}$
- **Downward**: arg-met$_{bg2}$ *Aur*$_{k}$* bry cain cann-xyz$_{bg2}$ carb-v coloc$_{k}$* *Gels*$_{k}$* hell$_{bg2}$ lach$_{bg2}$ nat-m$_{bg2}$ olnd$_{bg2}$ par$_{bg2}$ puls$_{bg2}$ ran-b$_{bg2}$ sin-n$_{bg2}$
- **Ear**: bar-c$_{h2}$ fago mang$_{k2}$ petr tub$_{xxb}$
  - ⁝ **drawing** pain: petr
- **Eyebrows**: ambr ↓
  - ⁝ **pressing** pain: ambr$_{k2}$
- **Face**, over side of: acon$_{bg2}$* lyc$_{k}$* op$_{k}$*
- **Forehead**: agar croc hura kali-s ↓ kalm ran-b ruta$_{fd4.de}$ symph$_{fd3.de}$•
  - ⁝ **drawing** pain: agar
  - ⁝ **pressing** pain: agar croc kali-s$_{fd4.de}$ ran-b ruta$_{fd4.de}$
  - ⁝ **Across**: cedr lac-ac tritic-vg$_{sna6}$
- **Forehead** and cheeks: lyc ↓
  - ⁝ **tearing** pain: lyc
- **Forward**: spig$_{vml}$
- **Frontal** sinus: anh$_{sp1}$ **Spig**$_{k}$*
- **Head**: coloc ↓ euphr ↓ *Graph* ↓ *Hep* ↓ lach ↓ nat-m ↓ psil$_{ft1}$ *Rhus-t*$_{a1}$ spig$_{c1}$
  - ⁝ **cutting** pain: coloc euphr$_{k2}$
  - ⁝ **drawing** pain: *Graph* lach
  - ⁝ **pressing** pain: hep nat-m
  - ⁝ **sore**: *Hep*
- **Head**; top of: cimic ↓ *Lach* ↓ phyt ↓
  - ⁝ **stitching** pain: cimic *Lach* phyt
- **Inward**: spig$_{br1}$
- **Nose**: camph$_{bg2}$* nicc$_{bg2}$ podo$_{fd3.de}$•
- **Nose**; root of: coloc ↓
  - ⁝ **stitching** pain: coloc$_{h2}$
- **Occiput**: *Bell* ↓ *Bry* cic ↓ cimic$_{bg2}$ coc-c$_{k}$* colch com$_{k}$* crot-t dios gels$_{bg2}$* *Ign* ↓ kali-p lac-f ↓ lach *Naja* ↓ *Nat-ar* onos$_{bg2}$ pic-ac prun$_{bg2}$ rhus-t ↓ ruta$_{fd4.de}$ sil spong$_{fd4.de}$ tab$_{bg2}$ tub$_{xxb}$ uran-n ↓
  - ⁝ **drawing** pain: *Lach Naja*
  - ⁝ **stitching** pain: *Bell* cic$_{h1}$ dios *Ign* lac-f *Lach Prun* rhus-t (non:uran-met$_{k}$) uran-n
  - ⁝ **tearing** pain: colch
- **Outward**: *Asaf* aster hydr-ac
- **Side** of head: tarent ↓
  - ⁝ **stitching** pain: tarent
- **Teeth**: *Chel* ↓
  - ⁝ **tearing** pain: *Chel*
- **Temple**: cic ↓ crot-c ↓
  - ⁝ **drawing** pain: cic$_{hr1}$ crot-c
- **Temples**: anac bad bar-c$_{h2}$ chel coc-c ip kali-p ↓ *Lach* ↓ phys
  - ⁝ **stitching** pain: kali-p *Lach*
  - ⁝ **tearing** pain: anac$_{k}$* chel ip
- **Upper** jaw: agar ↓ vanil ↓
  - ⁝ **stitching** pain: agar$_{h2}$ vanil$_{fd5.de}$
- **Upward**: am-m$_{bg2}$ bell$_{bg2}$ bism$_{bg2}$
- **Vertex**: cimic$_{k}$* *Croc*$_{k}$* kreos$_{bg2}$* lach$_{k}$* phyt$_{k}$*
  - ⁝ **drawing** pain: *Lach*
- **Zygoma**: *Chel* ↓
  - ⁝ **tearing** pain: *Chel*

○ - **About** the eyes: acon ↓ aesc ↓ aeth ↓ aids ↓ ant-c ↓ borx ↓ cinnb ↓ coloc ↓ hura ↓ spig ↓ spong ↓

- **eating**; after: ambr ↓
  - ⁝ **stitching** pain: ambr$_{a1}$
- **encircles**: cinnb ↓
  - ⁝ **stitching** pain: cinnb
- **stinging**: aesc spong
- **stitching** pain: acon aeth aids$_{nl2}$• ant-c$_{h2}$ borx$_{b4a.de}$ cinnb coloc hura spig$_{k2}$

- **Around** the eye; in and: ambr↓
  - **tearing** pain | **short** jerks; in: ambr$_{a1}$
- **Around** the eyes: acon↓ ars$_{bro1}$ aur$_{hr1}$ borx↓ canth↓ chlor↓ cic↓ *Cimic*$_{bro1}$ *Cinnb* clem$_{bro1}$ colch↓ *Gels* granit-m↓ *Ign* iod↓ kali-n↓ kali-p↓ lyc↓ mag-c↓ **Mag-m** manc↓ merc merc-c mez↓ nat-c↓ nat-sil$_{fd3.de}$• neon$_{srj5}$• nit-ac nux-v$_{bro1}$ pall par$_{bro1}$ phos↓ phyt pin-con$_{oss2}$• plat↓ puls ruta$_{fd4.de}$ **Spig**$_{k}$* spong↓ stann$_{k2}$ staph↓ sulph ter thuj$_{bro1}$ vanil$_{fd5.de}$
  - **right**: cortiso$_{tpw7}$* phase-vg↓
    - **afternoon**: cortiso$_{tpw7}$*
    - **burning**: phase-vg$_{a1}$
    - **pressure** agg.: cortiso$_{tpw7}$*
    - **warm** room agg.: cortiso$_{tpw7}$*
  - **left**:
    - **extending** to | **Beyond** right eyebrow: pall$_{c1}$
  - **burning**: canth chlor cic manc nat-c$_{h2}$ phos spig$_{k2}$ spong staph$_{h1}$
  - **drawing** pain: plat$_{h2}$
  - **pressing** pain: borx$_{h2}$ kali-n$_{h2}$ kali-p$_{fd1.de}$• mag-c$_{h2}$ mez$_{h2}$ phyt$_{a1}$* ruta$_{fd4.de}$ staph$_{h1}$
  - **sore**: colch$_{rsj2}$• granit-m$_{es1}$•
  - **tearing** pain: acon$_{vh1}$ iod$_{h}$ lyc$_{h2}$
  - **wrinkling** forehead agg.: phase-vg$_{a1}$
- **Behind** the eyes (See HEAD - Pain - forehead - eyes - behind) allox↓ form↓
  - **burning**: allox$_{tpw3}$ form
  - **pressing** pain (See HEAD - Pain - forehead - eyes - behind - pressing)
- **Below** the eyes: nat-m↓ rhus-t↓ sil↓ spong↓
  - **right**:
    - **night**: ars↓
      - **pressing** pain: ars$_{h2}$
  - **left**: bell↓
    - **drawing** pain: bell$_{h1}$
  - **pinching** pain: sil$_{h2}$
  - **stitching** pain: nat-m$_{h2}$ rhus-t$_{h1}$ spong$_{h1}$
- **Between** eye and nose: mang
  - **afternoon**: kalm
- **Between** frontal bones: cimic$_{a1}$
- **Between** the eyes: (↗*HEAD - Pain - forehead - eyes - between*) agath-a$_{nl2}$• arund$_{mrr1}$ asc-c carbn-h caust cimic$_{a1}$ dios gymno
  - **drawing** pain: caust$_{h2}$
- **Canthi**: acon↓ aesc↓ *Agar*$_{b4.de}$* alum↓ alum-p↓ alum-sil↓ *Am-m*↓ anan↓ ang↓ *Ant-c*↓ ant-t↓ *Apis*↓ arg-met↓ arg-n↓ *Asaf*↓ *Asar*↓ *Aur*↓ aur-s$_{k2}$ bar-c↓ bar-s↓ bell↓ berb↓ borx↓ brom↓ **Bry**↓ cact↓ *Calc*↓ carb-an↓ *Carb-v*↓ *Carbn-s*↓ *Caust*↓ *Cham*↓ chel↓ chin cinnb↓ *Clem*↓ *Colch*↓ coloc↓ con↓ cortiso↓ cycl↓ dig↓ euphr fl-ac↓ galeoc-c-h$_{gms1}$• gels↓ gran↓ **Graph**↓ grat↓ hell↓ hyos↓ hyper↓ iris↓ kali-bi↓ *Kali-c*↓ kali-m↓ kali-n↓ lach lact↓ laur↓ m-arct↓ mag-c↓ mag-m↓ meny↓ mez↓ *Mur-ac*↓ nat-c↓ nat-m *Nux-v*↓ par↓ petr↓ ph-ac↓ phos↓ plb *Puls*↓ ran-b↓ *Ran-s*↓ rhod↓ *Rhus-t*↓ ruta↓ sanic↓ **Sep**↓ sil$_{b4.de}$* spig↓ spong↓ squil↓ stann↓ *Staph*↓ stront-c↓ *Sulph*↓ sumb↓ symph↓ tab↓ tarax↓ teucr↓ ther↓ thuj↓ tril-p↓ verat↓ *Zinc*↓
  - **left**: agar↓ sil↓
    - **foreign** body; as from a: agar$_{b4.de}$*
    - **pressing** pain: sil$_{b4.de}$*
  - **morning**: am-m↓ carb-an↓ ham↓ rhod↓ sil↓ stront-c↓ sulph↓
    - **burning**: am-m$_{k}$* carb-an$_{h2}$ ham$_{fd3.de}$• rhod sil$_{h2}$ stront-c sulph
    - **waking**; on: sep↓
      - **burning**: sep
  - **afternoon**:
    - **17 h**: mag-c↓
      - **burning**: mag-c
  - **evening**: ang↓ mur-ac↓ sulph↓ thuj↓
    - **burning**: ang mur-ac$_{a1}$ sulph thuj
  - **night**: **Bry**↓
    - **burning**: **Bry**
  - **aching**: galeoc-c-h$_{gms1}$• mag-m

- **Canthi**: ...
  - **boring** pain: thuj$_{b4.de}$*
  - **burning**: aesc *Agar*$_{k}$* alum$_{k}$* alum-p$_{k2}$ alum-sil$_{k2}$ *Am-m*$_{k}$* ant-t$_{k}$* *Apis* *Asaf* *Aur* bar-c bar-s$_{k2}$ bell berb **Bry**$_{k}$* cact *Calc* carb-an *Carb-v*$_{k}$* *Carbn-s* *Caust* cinnb *Clem* coloc con$_{k}$* euphr fl-ac gels gran *Graph* hell$_{h1}$ hyper iris kali-bi$_{k}$* *Kali-c* kali-m$_{k2}$ kali-n lact mag-c mez$_{b4a.de}$* *Mur-ac*$_{k}$* nat-c$_{h2}$ nat-m nux-v$_{k}$* par petr ph-ac$_{k}$* phos$_{k}$* ran-b$_{k}$* *Ran-s*$_{k}$* rhod *Rhus-t* ruta$_{k}$* sanic *Sep*$_{k}$* sil$_{k}$* spig squil$_{b7a.de}$ stann$_{b4.de}$* *Staph*$_{k}$* stront-c *Sulph*$_{k}$* symph$_{fd3.de}$• tab teucr ther thuj tril-p zinc$_{k}$*
    - **itching** pain: alum euphr
  - **closing** the eye; on: ign symph$_{fd3.de}$•
  - **coryza**; during: carb-v↓
    - **burning**: carb-v$_{b4.de}$*
  - **cutting** pain: bell brom
  - **digging** pain: anan
  - **drawing** pain: *Aur* **Sep**
  - **foreign** body; as from a: alum cortiso$_{sp1}$
  - **pressing** pain: agar$_{b4.de}$* alum$_{b4a.de}$* calc *Carb-v*$_{k}$* *Colch* cycl grat hell$_{b7.de}$* lach sil stann$_{b4a.de}$ staph$_{b7.de}$* tarax$_{b7a.de}$
  - **raw**: ant-c$_{ptk1}$
  - **sand**; as from: acon alum$_{b4a.de}$* dig sumb tarax$_{c1}$ thuj
  - **scratching** pain: laur$_{b7.de}$*
  - **sore**: ang$_{b7a.de}$ *Ant-c*$_{bro1}$ *Apis*$_{k}$* arg-n borx$_{bro1}$ *Carb-v*$_{k}$* *Cham*$_{k}$* **Graph**$_{k}$* *Nat-m* *Nux-v*$_{k}$* petr$_{bro1}$ phos plb$_{b7.de}$* *Sil*$_{bro1}$ staph$_{bro1}$ *Zinc*$_{b4a.de}$*
  - **stinging**: alum$_{bg2}$ *Apis* asar carb-an ran-s spong squil$_{h1}$
  - **stitching** pain: agar alum$_{k}$* ant-t$_{k}$* arg-met *Asar*$_{b7a.de}$ bar-c berb brom calc$_{k}$* chel *Clem*$_{b4a.de}$ con$_{k}$* laur m-arct$_{b7.de}$ mur-ac$_{a1}$ nat-m$_{k}$* petr$_{b4.de}$* ph-ac phos$_{b4a.de}$ *Puls* ruta stann$_{b4.de}$* staph$_{b7.de}$* sulph verat$_{k}$*
  - **tearing** pain: chin hyos$_{b7.de}$* meny$_{b7.de}$* nat-m
  - **washing**:
    - **after**:
      - **agg.**: am-m↓
        - **burning**: am-m$_{k}$*
      - **amel.**: am-m↓
        - **burning**: am-m$_{h2}$*
  - **writing** agg.: kali-bi↓
    - **burning**: kali-bi

○ **Inner**: acon↓ agar↓ *Alum* alum-sil↓ ammc$_{vml3}$• amph$_{a1}$ anac↓ ang↓ ant-t↓ apis↓ arg-met↓ arg-n↓ arn↓ asar↓ asc-t *Aur*↓ aur-m-n$_{vml3}$• bar-c↓ bell$_{b4.de}$* berb↓ brom↓ bry↓ *Calc*↓ calc-caust↓ calc-s↓ canni-i↓ carb-an↓ carb-v↓ *Caust*↓ chel↓ cic↓ cina↓ *Cinnb*↓ clem↓ coloc↓ *Con*↓ cycl↓ dig$_{b4.de}$* dios↓ elaps↓ elat↓ eug↓ **Euphr**↓ *Fl-ac* galeoc-c-h$_{gms1}$• gamb↓ *Graph* grat↓ ham↓ hell↓ hydr-ac↓ indg↓ iod↓ kali-c↓ kali-n↓ *Lach* laur↓ led↓ lyc↓ m-aust↓ mag-c↓ mag-m↓ mag-s↓ med↓ meny↓ mez↓ mosch↓ mur-ac↓ nat-c↓ nat-m↓ nat-p↓ nat-s↓ nicc↓ *Nux-v*↓ ox-ac↓ ozone↓ par↓ *Petr*↓ ph-ac↓ *Phos*↓ phyt↓ plan↓ podo↓ *Propr*$_{sa3}$• *Puls*↓ rat↓ rhod↓ *Rhus-t*↓ sang↓ sep↓ *Sil*↓ sol-ni spig↓ *Stann*↓ staph$_{k}$* *Sulph*↓ symph$_{fd3.de}$• syph tarax↓ teucr↓ thiam↓ *Thuj*↓ tril-p↓ valer↓ verat↓ **Zinc**↓
  - **right**: anac↓ ant-t↓ arg-n↓ aur↓ bell↓ brom↓ bry↓ carb-v↓ caust$_{b4.de}$* chel↓ cic↓ clem↓ coloc↓ eug↓ fl-ac↓ grat↓ hell↓ ind↓ iris↓ kali-bi↓ led↓ lyc↓ mag-c↓ mag-m↓ mag-s↓ mur-ac↓ nat-m↓ nux-v↓ petr-ra↓ *Propr*$_{sa3}$• puls↓ rhod↓ sep↓ sil↓ sol-ni↓ spig↓ stann↓ staph↓ sulph↓ tarax↓ thuj↓ zinc↓
    - **burning**: ant-t$_{b7.de}$* aur$_{b4a.de}$ carb-v$_{b4.de}$* clem$_{b4.de}$* coloc$_{b4.de}$* iris$_{c1}$ mag-c$_{b4.de}$* mur-ac$_{b4.de}$* sep$_{b4.de}$* sil$_{b4a.de}$ sulph$_{b4.de}$* tarax$_{b7.de}$* zinc$_{b4.de}$*
    - **pressing** pain: anac$_{b4.de}$* carb-v$_{b4.de}$* cic$_{b7.de}$* hell$_{b7.de}$* rhod$_{b4a.de}$ stann$_{b4.de}$* staph$_{b7.de}$*
    - **sore**: bry$_{bg2}$ kali-bi$_{bg2}$ nux-v$_{bg2}$ puls$_{bg2}$ staph$_{bg2}$ zinc$_{bg2}$
    - **stitching** pain: arg-n$_{bg1}$ brom$_{bg1}$ chel$_{b7.de}$* coloc$_{bg1}$ eug$_{bg1}$ fl-ac$_{bg1}$ grat$_{bg1}$ ind$_{bg1}$ led$_{bg1}$ mag-m$_{b4.de}$* mag-s$_{bg1}$ nat-m$_{b4a.de}$ petr-ra$_{shn4}$• sol-ni$_{bg1}$ spig$_{bg1}$ thuj$_{b4.de}$*
    - **tearing** pain: bell$_{b4.de}$* lyc$_{b4.de}$*

• **Inner**: ...
⁝ **left**: agar↓ alum↓ arg-met↓ asar↓ *Aur*↓ aur-m-n vml3• calc↓ cann-s↓ carb-an↓ carb-v↓ clem↓ elat↓ *Euphr*↓ galeoc-c-h gms1• laur↓ nat-c↓ nat-m↓ nat-s↓ nit-ac↓ *Propr*↓ rhus-r↓ spong↓ stann↓ thuj↓ vac↓
: **aching**: galeoc-c-h gms1•
: **burning**: asar b7.de* carb-an b4.de* carb-v b4.de* *Propr* sa3•
: **pressing** pain: *Euphr* b7.de* laur b7a.de stann b4.de*
: **stitching** pain: agar bg1 alum b4.de* arg-met bg1 *Aur* b4.de* aur-m-n bg1 calc b4.de* cann-s bg carb-an b4.de* clem b4.de* elat bg1 nat-c b4.de* nat-m bg2* nat-s bg1 nit-ac bg2* rhus-r bg1 spong bg1 stann bg1 thuj b4.de* vac jl2
: **tearing** pain: galeoc-c-h gms1•
⁝ **morning**: calc-s↓ carb-an↓ con↓ eug↓ ham↓ **Nux-v**↓ phos↓
: **air** agg.; in open: phos↓
. **stitching** pain: phos
: **burning**: calc-s ham fd3.de• **Nux-v**
: **stitching** pain: carb-an con h2 eug phos
⁝ **evening**: mag-c↓ *Puls*↓ sulph↓
: **burning**: mag-c h2
: **stitching** pain: *Puls* sulph
⁝ **aching**: acon cic h1 galeoc-c-h gms1• mosch *Puls* rhus-t stann
⁝ **burning**: agar b4.de* alum k* alum-sil ang b7.de* ant-t k* apis b7a.de asar b7.de* aur b4.de* bar-c b4.de* bell b4.de* bry k* calc b4.de* calc-s carb-an h2 carb-v *Caust* cina b7.de* coloc h2 *Con* k* dig b4.de* dios graph k* ham fd3.de* hell b7.de* kali-c b4.de* laur b7.de* m-aust b7.de mag-c b4.de* mez k* mur-ac h2 nat-m b4.de* nicc nux-v k* ox-ac ozone sde2• par b7.de* *Petr* ph-ac b4.de* *Phos* k* phyt *Puls* k* rhod b4.de* *Rhus-t* a1* sep sil stann h2 *Staph* k* *Sulph* k* symph fd3.de• teucr k* tril-p c1 *Zinc*
: **biting** pain: ozone sde2•
⁝ **cutting** pain: petr b4a.de *Sil* b4a.de
⁝ **foreign** body; as from a: agar berb tarax b7.de*
⁝ **looking** steadily agg.: ph-ac↓
: **pressing** pain: ph-ac h2
⁝ **pressing** pain: anac bell b4.de* carb-an b4.de* *Caust* cic cycl **Euphr** gamb hell hydr-ac iod lach k* laur lyc mag-m h2 mosch b7a.de nat-m petr ph-ac puls k* rhod k* rhus-t a1 *Stann* staph tarax h1 zinc
⁝ **sand**; as from: ozone sde2• tarax h1
⁝ **sore**: bry k* *Nux-v* k* podo *Puls* k* sep k* thiam rly4• valer b7.de* **Zinc** k*
⁝ **stitching** pain: agar alum ant-t k* arg-met arg-n arn k* *Aur* aur-m-n bar-c *Bell* k* brom *Calc* k* cann-i carb-an chel *Cinnb* clem k* *Con* k* elaps elat eug fl-ac *Graph* k* grat indg laur b7.de* led mag-m mag-s med c1 meny b7.de* nat-c h2 nat-m nat-p nat-s *Petr* ph-ac b4.de* phos k* plan *Puls* k* sang sol-ni spig k* stann h2 staph k* sulph *Thuj* verat b7.de* **Zinc** k*
⁝ **tearing** pain: bell h1 calc-caust kali-n meny h1 nat-c nicc rat
⁝ **waking**; on: ther↓
: **burning**: ther c1
⁝ **warm** water:
: **amel.**:
. **hot** water: galeoc-c-h↓
aching: galeoc-c-h gms1•
⁝ **extending** to:
: **Eyebrows**; around: cinnb
. **Ears**; to: cinnb br1
: **Forehead**: cinnb mrr1
: **Outer**: nat-c h2
⁝ **Above**: thuj↓
: **boring** pain: thuj h1

• **Outer**: am-m↓ amph↓ anac↓ **Ant-c**↓ apis↓ arg-n↓ aur↓ aur-m↓ aur-m-n↓ bar-c↓ borx↓ brom↓ bry↓ calc↓ calc-act↓ camph↓ carb-an↓ carb-v↓ cham↓ chin h1 cina↓ cinnb↓ colch↓ con↓ crot-c↓ dig↓ dios↓ euph↓ *Euphr*↓ fago↓ form↓ *Hep*↓ ign irid-met↓ kali-bi↓ *Kali-c*↓ kali-i↓ kali-n↓ kola stb3• lachn↓ laur↓ lyc↓ m-arct↓ mang↓ *Mez*↓ mur-ac↓ nat-c↓ nat-m↓ nicc↓ *Nit-ac*↓ nux-v↓ ol-an↓ op↓ petr↓ ph-ac↓ phos↓ ran-b k2 ran-s↓ rhus-t↓ ruta↓ sep↓ spig↓

- **Canthi – Outer**: ...
spong↓ squil↓ staph↓ stront-c↓ *Sul-ac*↓ sulph symph↓ *Thuj*↓ verat↓ *Zinc*↓ zinc-s↓
⁝ **right**: carb-v↓ colch↓ kali-c↓ mur-ac↓ nat-c↓ ran-b↓ ran-s↓ stann↓ staph↓ sul-ac↓ sulph↓
: **burning**: carb-v b4.de* colch b7.de* nat-c b4.de* ran-b b7.de* ran-s b7.de* stann b4.de* staph b7.de* sulph b4.de*
: **foreign** body; as from a: sul-ac b4.de*
: **stitching** pain: kali-c b4.de* mur-ac b4.de* ran-s b7.de* stann b4.de* staph b7.de*
⁝ **left**: anac↓ bry↓ chel↓ chin↓ laur↓ mur-ac↓ nit-ac↓ spong↓ squil↓ tarax↓ thuj↓
: **burning**: bry b7.de* chel b7.de* laur b7.de* mur-ac b4.de* tarax b7.de* thuj b4.de*
: **pressing** pain: anac b4.de thuj b4.de
: **stitching** pain: chel b7.de* nit-ac b4.de* spong b7.de* squil b7.de* tarax b7.de*
: **tearing** pain: chin b7.de*
⁝ **aching**: chin dios lyc
⁝ **burning**: **Ant-c** apis b7a.de arg-n aur-m bry camph k* carb-an b4.de* carb-v h2 cina b7.de* colch k* dig *Hep* k* ign k* kali-bi k* kali-c b4.de* kali-n b4.de* lyc m-arct b7.de mang k* mur-ac nux-v k* phos k* *Ran-b* ran-s ruta sep b4.de* spig b7.de* squil b7.de* staph h1 stront-c b4.de* sulph k* thuj h1 zinc zinc-s bg2
: **itching** pain: cina h1
⁝ **cutting** pain: brom hep k* kali-i
⁝ **drawing** pain: spong h1
⁝ **foreign** body; as from a: apis bar-c k* con k* *Euphr* ign k* kola stb3• nit-ac b4.de* phos *Sul-ac*
⁝ **lips**; with denuded: cham↓
: **sore**: cham h1
⁝ **pinching** pain: euph b4.de*
⁝ **pressing** pain: anac h2 bar-c b4.de* calc b4.de* (non:carb-an kl) carb-v h2 chin k* con h2 lachn *Mez* op ph-ac b4.de* staph b7.de* sul-ac k* symph fd3.de• thuj h1
⁝ **sand**; as from: bar-c con crot-c *Nit-ac* staph sulph
⁝ **sore**: **Ant-c** k* borx calc b4.de* calc-act cham k* fago form ign b7.de* *Kali-c* *Ran-b* k* rhus-t sep k* verat hr1 *Zinc*
⁝ **stitching** pain: amph a1 aur-m-n bar-c k* cinnb euphr ign b7.de* irid-met srj5• kali-c laur mur-ac nat-c h2 nat-m nicc ol-an op petr spong staph *Sulph* k* *Thuj*
⁝ **tearing** pain: am-m b7a.de* aur h2 ign b7.de* staph b7.de*
⁝ **extending** to:
: **Inner** canthi: petr↓
. **stitching** pain: petr h2
: **Inward**: caust bg1

- **Caruncle**: bell↓
• **burning**: bell h1
• **pressing** pain: bell h1

- **Chiasma**: anh↓
• **burning**: anh sp1

- **Ciliary** body: acon↓ amylam↓ arn↓ ars↓ *Asaf*↓ bad↓ *Bell*↓ cedr↓ chel↓ chen-a↓ chin↓ chinin-m↓ chr-o↓ cimic↓ **Cinnb**↓ *Coloc*↓ com↓ croc↓ crot-t↓ *Flav* jl2 gels↓ *Hyper*↓ ign↓ ip↓ kali-p↓ lach↓ *Mag-p*↓ mez↓ nat-m↓ nat-sal↓ par↓ phos↓ phyt↓ *Plan*↓ **Prun**↓ rad-br↓ rhod↓ sang↓ sapo↓ *Sil*↓ **Spig**↓ terebe↓ thuj bg2
• **right**: *Flav* jl2 prun↓
⁝ **neuralgic**: prun mtf11
• **left**: **Spig**↓
⁝ **neuralgic**: **Spig** mrr1
• **exertion** of the eyes agg.: prun↓
⁝ **neuralgic**: prun mtf11
• **neuralgic**: acon mfj amylam mfj arn mfj ars bg2* *Asaf* mfj bad mfj *Bell* mfj cedr bg2* chel bg2* chen-a bro1 chin bg2* chinin-m mfj chr-o bro1 cimic mfj* **Cinnb** bg2* *Coloc* bg2* com bg2* croc bg2* crot-t bg2* gels bg2* *Hyper* mfj ign mfj ip mfj kali-p mfj lach bro1 *Mag-p* mfj mez bg2* nat-m bg2* nat-sal mfj par bg2* phos bg2* phyt mfj *Plan* mfj* **Prun** bg2* rad-br mfj rhod bg2* sang mfj sapo bro1 *Sil* hr1* **Spig** bg2* terebe mfj thuj bg2*
• **storm**; before: rhod↓

- **storm**; before: ...
  - ⁝ **neuralgic**: rhod tl1
- **Conjunctiva**: ser-a-c jl2

○ · **Under**: tab↓
  - ⁝ **foreign** body; as from a: tab
- **Cornea**: haliae-lc srj sil bg2
- **Eyeballs**: *Acon* bro1 agar↓ alf bro1 am-br bro1 apis bg2 ars bg2 asaf bro1 atra-r skp7*• aur bro1 aza bro1 bad↓ bapt bro1 *Bell* bro1 *Bry* bro1 buteo-j↓ cassia-s↓ cedr bg2* cham↓ chel bro1 chim bro1 chion br1 cimic bg2* *Clem* bro1 cocc bro1 coloc bro1 *Com* bro1 con bro1 crot-t bro1 esin bro1 eup-per bg2* *Euphr* bro1 *Gels* bro1 granit-m↓ grin bro1 guare bro1 hep bro1 indol bro1 jab bro1 kali-i bro1 kali-s↓ kalm bro1 lach↓ lith-c bg2 *Lycps-v* bro1 med jl2 mentho bro1 *Merc-c* bro1 mim-p↓ nat-m bro1 nicc-s bro1 olnd bro1 onos bro1 osm bro1 par bro1 passi bro1 ph-ac bro1 phos bro1 phys bro1 pitu-gl↓ plat bro1 prun bg2* *Puls* bro1 rhod bro1 rhus-t bg2* *Ruta* bro1 sang bro1 ser-a-c jl2 spig bg2* staph bro1 stry↓ suis-hep↓ syc bka1*• symph bro1 syph bro1 ter bro1 tetox pin2• ther bro1 thuj bro1 tritic-vg fd5.de tub↓ upa bro1 vac↓ viol-o bro1
  - **one** side: phos bg2
  - **right**: coloc↓ merc↓ suis-hep↓ thuj↓
    - ⁝ **evening**: cortiso↓
      - : **sore**: cortiso skp7•
    - ⁝ **cutting** pain: coloc bg2 merc bg2
    - ⁝ **pressing** pain: suis-hep rly4• thuj bg2
  - **left**: atra-r skp7*• lach↓
    - ⁝ **foreign** body; as from a: lach bg2
  - **afternoon**:
    - ⁝ **17** h:
      - : **amel.**: pitu-gl↓
        - . **tearing** pain: pitu-gl skp7•
  - **bursting** pain: vac jl2
  - **closing** the eyes:
    - ⁝ **amel.**: cassia-s↓
      - : **dull** pain: cassia-s ccrh1•
  - **cough** agg.; during: pyrog jl2
  - **cutting** pain: agar bg2 apis bg2 sang bg2 stry bg2
  - **dull** pain: cassia-s ccrh1•
  - **menses**; during: cassia-s↓
    - ⁝ **burning**: cassia-s ccrh1•
    - ⁝ **drawing** pain: cassia-s ccrh1•
  - **neuralgic**: bad mrr1
  - **pressing** pain: ars bg2 cham tl1 granit-m es1• kali-s fd4.de lach tl1 mim-p rsj8• ruta fd4.de suis-hep rly4• thuj bg1 tritic-vg fd5.de
  - **pressure** agg.: anth↓
    - ⁝ **sore**: anth vh1
  - **pushed** forward; as if: atra-r skp7*• [buteo-j sej6]
  - **reading** agg.: mand rsj7•
  - **sore**: symph tl1 tub tl1
  - **tearing** pain: pitu-gl skp7•
  - **touch** agg.: plan↓
    - ⁝ **sore**: plan br1

▽ · **extending** to:
    - ⁝ **Cervical** region: pitu-gl↓
      - : **tearing** pain: pitu-gl skp7•
    - ⁝ **Forehead**: bad↓
      - : **neuralgic**: bad mrr1
    - ⁝ **Temples**: pitu-gl↓
      - : **tearing** pain: pitu-gl skp7•

○ · **Center** of eyeballs: agath-a nl2• cimic coloc tl1 mand rsj7• ph-ac tl1
  - **Muscles**: carb-v bro1 cimic bro1 *Onos* bro1
  - **Upper** half: ars bg2
    - ⁝ **motion** of eyes agg.: acon↓
      - : **sore**: acon vh1
- **Eyebrows**: acon aeth agn↓ am-m↓ ambr↓ ang↓ apis b7a.de *Arn*↓ **Ars**↓ asaf bro1 *Asar*↓ **Bell**↓ bov↓ *Brom*↓ *Bry* bro1 **Calc**↓ camph↓ cann-s↓ canth↓ carb-ac bro1 **Carb-v**↓ caust↓ *Cedr* bro1 *Chel* chin↓ *Chinin-s* bro1

- **Eyebrows**: ...
chir-fl↓ cic↓ *Cinnb* bg2 *Cocc*↓ **Coloc**↓ con **Croc**↓ *Crot-h*↓ cupr dig↓ dros dub bro1 elaps *Euph*↓ ferr fl-ac *Gels* bro1 guaj↓ ham↓ hell h1 hyper ign↓ ip↓ irid-met srj5• kali-bi bg2* *Kali-c*↓ kali-n↓ kali-s↓ *Lach*↓ laur↓ lith-c **Lyc**↓ lyss m-arct↓ mag-m↓ mag-p bro1 mang↓ meli bro1 mentho bro1 **Merc**↓ merc-c bro1 mez↓ mosch↓ mur-ac↓ naja nat-c↓ nux-v b7.de olnd↓ par↓ petr↓ **Ph-ac**↓ phos↓ plan↓ plat bro1 podo fd3.de• ran-b↓ rhus-t ruta bro1* sal-fr↓ scroph-n↓ sep↓ *Spig* bro1 spong↓ sulph↓ tarax↓ thuj k* viol-t↓ zinc↓
  - **right**: *Chel* dig c1 hyper lyss olib-sac↓
    - ⁝ **stitching** pain: olib-sac wmh1
    - ⁝ **touch** agg.: nux-v h1
  - **left**: *Asar*↓ olib-sac↓
    - ⁝ **burning**: *Asar* bg2
    - ⁝ **coughing**; when: rumx bg2
    - ⁝ **stitching** pain: olib-sac wmh1
  - **night**: hyper lyss
  - **blow**; as if from a: plat b4.de*
  - **boring** pain: mez bg2
  - **burning**: **Acon** bg2 am-m bg2 apis b7a.de arn bg2 **Ars** bg2 asaf b7.de* *Asar* bg **Bell** b4a.de* brom bg2 **Bry** bg2 **Calc** bg2 **Carb-v** bg2 **Coloc** b4a.de* **Croc** bg2 *Crot-h* bg2 dig b4.de* dros b7.de* *Euph* bg2 kali-bi bg2 kali-n bg2 *Lach* bg2 laur bg2 **Lyc** bg2 mag-m bg2 **Merc** b4.de* mur-ac bg2 nat-c bg2 nux-v bg2 **Ph-ac** bg2 phos bg2 rhus-t bg2 sep bg2 spig b7.de spong bg2 sulph b4a.de* tarax bg2
  - **burnt**; as if: chir-fl gya2
  - **corrosive**: agn b7.de* par b7.de*
  - **drawing** pain: asaf b7.de* *Bell* b4.de* caust b4.de* cic h1 dros b7.de* hell b7.de* laur b7.de* m-arct b7.de *Rhus-t* b7.de*
  - **lifting** agg.: ptel↓
    - ⁝ **pressing** pain: ptel c1
  - **pressing** pain: ambr b7.de* *Arn* b7.de* camph b7.de* canth b7.de* chin b7.de* dig b4.de* ign b7.de* mosch b7.de* par b7.de* ran-b b7.de*
    - ⁝ **downward**: cann-s b7.de*
  - **reading** agg.: ferr-p
  - **sore**: apis b7a.de *Bell* bg2 dig bg2 dros h1* guaj h2 *Kali-c* k* nux-v bg2 olnd b7.de* plan bg2 plat bg sal-fr sle1• thuj bg2
  - **stitching** pain: ang b7.de* apis b7a.de arn b7.de* bov k* *Brom* b4a.de cic h1 ham fd3.de• hell b7.de* ip b7.de* kali-s fd4.de mang k* par bg2 petr k* scroph-n bg2* thuj k* viol-t b7.de* zinc k*
  - **tearing** pain: am-m b7.de* arn b7.de* bell k* caust b4a.de *Cocc* *Coloc* b4a.de euph k* kali-c k* laur b7.de* *Rhus-t* b7.de* *Thuj* k* zinc k*
  - **ulcerative** pain: dros b7.de* kali-c b4.de
  - **walking** agg.; after: lyss

○ · **Above**: sulph↓
    - ⁝ **left**: ambr↓ camph↓ sul-ac↓
      - : **pressing** pain: ambr h1* camph h1 sul-ac h2
    - ⁝ **pressing** pain: sulph h2
  - **Between**: propr sa3•
  - **Bones** below eyebrows: *Bell* b4a.de
- **Eyes**, forehead and face concentrate in tip of nose: *Kali-n*↓
  - **contracting**: *Kali-n* k*
- **Infraorbital**: arg-n↓ ars↓ bell↓ caust↓ colch↓ dys↓ kalm↓ mag-p↓ mez↓ nux-v↓ phos↓ plat↓ sil↓ thuj↓
  - **neuralgic**: arg-n bg2* ars mfj bell bg2* caust bg2 colch bg2 dys fmm1• kalm mfj mag-p bg2* mez bg2* nux-v bg2* phos bg2* plat bg2 sil bg2 thuj bg2
- **Lachrymal** ducts: all-c k* fago ptk1 psor al
  - **stitching** pain: all-c k*

▽ · **extending** around eye to temple: cinnb br1
- **Lachrymal** glands: staph↓
  - **pressing** pain: staph h1
  - **tearing** pain: staph k*
- **Lens**: meny bg2

- **Lids**: *Acon*↓ agar↓ *Agn*↓ all-c↓ allox↓ alum bg2 am-c↓ am-m↓ ambr↓ ang↓ anh sp1 *Ant-c*↓ *Apis*↓ arg-n↓ arn↓ ars b4.de* arund↓ asar↓ *Aur*↓ bapt↓ bar-c↓ *Bell*↓ benzol br1 bomb-chr↓ borx↓ **Brom**↓ *Bry*↓ calc b4.de* camph↓ cann-s↓ canth↓ caps↓ carb-v↓ *Caust* cham↓ chel chim↓ chin k* cic↓ cimic tl1 cina↓ clem↓ cob↓ colch↓ coloc↓ **Con**↓ croc↓ cupr↓ cycl↓ dig↓ dios↓ dros↓ euph↓ *Euphr*↓ form↓ gal-ac↓ graph h2 hell↓ *Hep*↓ hist↓ ign k* iod↓ irid-met↓ kali-act↓ kali-bi↓ kali-c↓ kali-i↓ kali-n↓ kali-p↓ kalm↓ kreos↓ laur↓ led↓ lith-c↓ *Lyc* m-arct b7.de *M-aust*↓ mag-c↓ mand↓ mang b4.de* med↓ *Merc*↓ merc-c↓ mez mim-p↓ mur-ac↓ myric↓ nat-c h2 nat-m↓ nat-p↓ nat-pyru↓ nat-sil↓ nit-ac↓ nux-m↓ *Nux-v*↓ olnd↓ par↓ *Petr*↓ petr-ra shn4• ph-ac h2 phos b4.de* *Phys*↓ phyt↓ pic-ac↓ plat↓ plb↓ *Psor*↓ *Puls*↓ ran-b↓ ran-s↓ rat↓ rheum↓ *Rhus-t*↓ ruta tl1 sabad↓ sal-fr sle1• sars b4.de* seneg↓ sep *Sil* b4.de* spig b7.de* spong↓ stann↓ *Staph*↓ staphycoc↓ stict↓ stram↓ sul-ac↓ *Sulph* symph↓ tarax↓ tarent↓ thuj↓ urol-h↓ valer b7.de* vanil↓ verat hr1 vesp *Viol-o*↓ xan xanth zinc b4.de*
  - **right**: carb-v↓ mand↓ merc↓ nat-pyru↓ sulph↓ xan c1
    - **burning**: merc b4.de* sulph b4.de*
    - **drawing** pain: carb-v b4.de*
    - **jerking** pain: sulph b4.de*
    - **sore**: mand rsj7•
    - **stitching** pain: nat-pyru rly4•
  - **left**: alum↓ anac↓ asar↓ cassia-s↓ caust↓
    - **burning**: alum b4.de* asar b7.de* caust b4.de*
    - **cold** applications:
      - **amel.**: cassia-s↓
        - **stitching** pain: cassia-s ccrh1•
    - **stitching** pain: cassia-s ccrh1•
    - **tearing** pain: anac b4.de*
  - **morning**: calc lyc nux-v sep sulph
    - **waking**; on: lac-h↓
      - **aching**: lac-h sk4•
  - **afternoon**: cimic
    - **13 h**: ars
  - **evening**: sulph↓ thuj zinc k*
    - **17-19 h**: rhus-t hr1
    - **candlelight**; by: cina↓
      - **burning**: cina h1
    - **pressing** pain: sulph h2
  - **night**: kali-c↓
    - **sore**: kali-c h2
  - **aching**: allox sp1
  - **burning**: *Acon* b7a.de agar bro1 all-c bro1 allox tpw4* alum h2* am-m k2 ambr b7.de* *Apis* b7a.de* *Ars* b4.de* arund bro1 asar b7.de* aur h2 *Bell* b4.de* bomb-chr a1 *Bry* b7.de* calc b4a.de* camph b7.de* canth b7a.de caps b7.de* carb-v b4.de* caust b4.de* cham b7a.de* cina b7.de* clem b4.de* colch rsj2• coloc ptk1 con b4.de* croc b7a.de* dig b4a.de dros h1 *Euphr* bro1 gal-ac c1* graph b4.de* hist sp1 ign b7.de* kali-bi bg2* kali-c b4.de* kali-i bro1 kali-n b4.de* kali-p fd1.de• kreos b7a.de laur b7a.de lyc b4a.de* *M-aust* b7.de *Merc* b4a.de* merc-c b4a.de mez bro1 mim-p rsj8• nat-m bro1 nat-sil fd3.de• nit-ac bg2 *Nux-v* b7.de* olnd b7.de* par b7a.de *Petr* bg2* petr-ra shn4• ph-ac b4.de* phos h2 phyt ptk1 puls bro1 ran-b tl1* ran-s b7.de* rhus-t b7.de* sabad bro1 sars b4.de* seneg b4.de* sep b4a.de* sil b4.de* spig b7.de* spong h1 stann b4.de* *Staph* bg2 stict ptk1 sulph b4.de* tarax h1 thuj b4a.de urol-h rwt• *Valer* b7a.de *Viol-o* b7a.de zinc b4a.de*
  - **chill**; during: acon↓ apis↓ bell↓ kreos↓ rhus-t↓
    - **burning**: acon bg2 apis bg2 bell bg2 kreos bg2 rhus-t bg2
  - **closing** the eyes:
    - **agg.**: cimic dig↓ manc↓ phyt rhus-t sang↓
      - **burning**: manc ptk1 sang a1
      - **sore**: dig h2 phyt rhus-t
    - **amel.**: allox↓
      - **sore**: allox tpw3
  - **cold air agg.**: rhus-t↓
    - **sore**: rhus-t
  - **corrosive**: *Agn* b7.de* caust h2 puls b7.de
  - **cutting** pain: calc b4.de* coloc h2 *Merc* b4a.de staph h1

- **Lids**: ...
  - **drawing** pain: caust bg2 colch b7.de* graph h2 *M-arct* b7.de nux-v b7.de* ph-ac b4.de* plat b4.de* *Puls* b7a.de rheum b7.de* seneg b4a.de
  - **gnawing** pain: agn bg2 ign b7.de* puls bg2
  - **motion** of eyelids agg.: *Mang* a1
  - **neuralgic**: verat c2
  - **paralytic**: graph b4.de* plb b7.de* *Rhus-t* b7.de*
  - **paralyzed**; as if: graph h2
  - **pressing** pain: alum b4.de* am-c h2 ambr b7.de* borx h2 bry b7.de* cann-s b7.de* cham b7a.de cic a1 croc b7.de* cupr b7.de* cycl b7.de* euph b4.de* graph b4.de* hep b4a.de* kali-c b4.de* laur b7a.de lyc h2 nat-m b4.de* nit-ac h2 nux-m b7.de* nux-v b7.de* ph-ac h2 ran-b tl1 rheum b7.de* sars b4.de* seneg b4.de* sep h2 sil b4.de* spig b7.de* spong b7.de* stann b4.de* staph b7a.de* stram b7.de* sulph b4a.de* vanil fd5.de zinc h2
    - **downward**: zinc h2
    - **outward**: **Con** bg2 seneg bg2
    - **upward**: rat bg2
  - **reading** agg.: allox↓ zinc↓
    - **pressing** pain: zinc h2
    - **sore**: allox tpw3
  - **sand**; as from: *Graph* b4a.de med jl2
  - **sore**: allox tpw3 ang b7.de* *Ant-c* bro1 arg-n br1* ars b4.de* bar-c b4a.de bell borx bro1 *Calc* b4a.de canth b7.de* caust b4a.de cham k* chim cimic bg2 cob colch bg* coloc h2 croc b7.de* dig b4.de* dios dros h1* *Euphr* k* form *Graph* bro1 *Hep* b4a.de* ign bg irid-met srj5• kali-act kali-bi kali-c b4.de* kalm led bg lith-c lyc mand rsj7• merc merc-c bro1 myric nat-p *Nux-v* b7.de* petr bro1 ph-ac b4a.de phos bg *Phys* phyt pic-ac plb psor puls bg ran-b c1 rhus-t b7a.de* sil k* spig b7.de* *Staph* bg staphycoc rly4• stram bg sulph b4.de* symph fd3.de• valer b7.de* verat k* zinc b4a.de*
    - **denuded**; as if: (non:cham kl) *Psor*
    - **rubbed**; as if: verat
    - **splinter**; as from a: med nit-ac tarent
  - **squeezed**; as if: *Hep* b4a.de
  - **sticks**; as from: med hr1*
  - **stinging**: *Apis* *Aur* petr-ra shn4• tarax h1
  - **stitching** pain: alum h2 ang h1 apis b7a.de arg-n bg2 arn b7.de* aur h2 bapt hr1 bar-c h2 **Brom** b4a.de camph b7.de* cic a1 cimic bg2 cycl b7.de* hell b7.de* ign b7.de* kali-bi bg2 lyc b4a.de m-arct b7.de m-aust b7.de mang h2 *Merc* b4a.de mez h2 mur-ac a1 nat-pyru rly4• ph-ac b4.de* sil h2 spig b7.de* stann b4a.de* sul-ac h2 sulph b4a.de tarax b7.de* thuj bg2 *Valer* b7a.de zinc h2
  - **tearing** pain: alum h2 bar-c h2 bry b7.de* cann-s b7.de* cic a1 colch b7.de* iod b4.de* kali-c h2 mag-c b4.de* nat-c h2 nux-v b7.de* plb b7.de* zinc b4.de*
  - **touch** agg.: lyc h2 mang hr1
  - **ulcerative** pain: dros b7.de* *Hep* b4a.de
  - **using** eyes, when: cob
  - ○ **Behind**: meny↓ *Merc*↓ spig↓ stann↓ *Staph*↓
    - **foreign** body; as from a: meny h1 *Merc* spig h1 stann *Staph*
  - **Inner side**: *Ars*↓ caust↓ chin↓ con↓ *Ph-ac*↓ *Thuj*↓
    - **burning**: *Ars* b4a.de caust b4a.de con b4a.de *Ph-ac* b4a.de *Thuj* b4a.de
    - **crawling**: chin h1
  - **Lower**: alum↓ anh↓ bry↓ calc↓ colch↓ croc↓ dros↓ kali-bi↓ kali-p↓ laur↓ mez↓ nat-m↓ olnd↓ ran-b↓ rhus-t↓ sabin↓ spig↓ stann↓ sul-ac↓ vanil fd5.de
    - **right**: apis↓ canth↓ coloc↓ laur↓ nat-c↓ nat-m↓ ph-ac↓ ran-b k2 stann↓ zinc↓
      - **burning**: coloc b4.de* laur b7.de* ran-b b7.de* stann b4.de*
      - **cutting** pain: coloc b4.de*
      - **pressing** pain: ph-ac b4.de*
      - **sore**: nat-m b4.de* ran-b k2
      - **stitching** pain: apis b7a.de canth b7.de* stann b4.de* zinc b4.de*
      - **tearing** pain: nat-c b4.de*
    - **left**: caust↓ m-aust↓ merc↓ ph-ac↓ sep↓ spong↓ stann↓ zinc↓
      - **burning**: caust b4.de* merc b4.de* sep b4.de* spong b7.de* stann b4.de*

- **Lower – left**: ...
  - : **pressing** pain: m-aust b7.de ph-ac b4.de* zinc b4.de*
  - : **burning**: calc b4.de* kali-bi bg2 kali-p fd1.de• laur bg2 olnd b7.de* ran-b bg2 rhus-t b7a.de* stann bg2
  - : **cutting** pain: spig b7.de*
  - : **pressing** pain: bry b7.de* croc b7.de*
  - : **sand**; as from: anh sp1
  - : **sore**: colch bg dros b7.de* nat-m bg ran-b b7.de*
  - : **stitching** pain: alum b4.de* croc b7.de* mez b4.de* sabin b7.de* sul-ac b4.de*
  - : **Margins** of: zinc ↓
    - : **pressing** pain: zinc h2
- **Margins** of: *Acon* ↓ agar ↓ all-c ↓ alum-sil ↓ alumn ↓ ambr ↓ *Ant-c* ↓ *Apis* ↓ arg-n ↓ arn ↓ **Ars** ↓ ars-s-f ↓ arum-d ↓ arund ↓ asaf ↓ asar ↓ aur ↓ aur-m-n ↓ bell ↓ *Borx* ↓ brom ↓ bry ↓ bufo ↓ calc ↓ camph ↓ cann-i ↓ carbn-s ↓ carc ↓ card-m ↓ caust ↓ cham ↓ cina ↓ clem ↓ coc-c ↓ *Colch* ↓ con ↓ croc ↓ crot-h ↓ *Dig* ↓ **Euphr** ↓ fago ↓ ferr-i ↓ ferr-p ↓ gins ↓ *Graph* ↓ hell ↓ hep ↓ hura ↓ jatr-c ↓ kali-bi ↓ kali-i ↓ kali-p ↓ kali-s ↓ kalm ↓ kreos ↓ *Lach* ↓ *Led* ↓ lyc ↓ manc ↓ med ↓ meph ↓ merc ↓ *Merc-c* ↓ mez ↓ nat-m ↓ nat-p ↓ *Nat-s* ↓ *Nux-v* ↓ *Olnd* ↓ petr ↓ phos h2 psil ↓ puls ↓ ran-s ↓ sabad ↓ sang ↓ sanic ↓ sel ↓ sep ↓ sol-ni ↓ spig ↓ *Sulph* ↓ thuj *Valer* ↓ zinc
  - : **daytime** only: nat-m ↓ *Sulph* ↓
    - : **burning**: nat-m *Sulph*
  - : **morning**: *Gamb* ↓ *Nat-s* ↓ *Nit-ac* ↓ *Nux-v* ↓ seneg ↓ **Sulph** ↓ valer ↓ *Zinc* ↓
    - : **burning**: *Gamb Nat-s Nit-ac Nux-v* seneg **Sulph** *Zinc*
    - : **reading** agg.: carbn-s ↓ ign ↓
      - . **burning**: carbn-s k2 ign
    - : **sore**: nux-v *Sulph* valer
    - : **waking**; on: agar ↓ euphr ↓ kali-bi ↓ sulph ↓
      - : **burning**: agar euphr kali-bi sulph
  - : **forenoon**: sulph ↓
    - : **burning**: sulph
  - : **afternoon**: kali-bi ↓ *Sang* ↓ *Sulph* ↓
    - : **burning**: kali-bi *Sang Sulph*
  - : **evening**: **Ars** ↓ thuj k* zinc
    - : **burning**: **Ars** *Thuj Zinc*
  - : **burning**: agar bro1 all-c bro1 (non:alum bro1*) alum-sil k2 alumn slp ambr k2 *Apis* k* **Ars** k* ars-s-f k2 arum-d arund bro1 asaf asar h1 aur aur-m-n bell bro1 brom bry bufo calc k* camph cann-i carbn-s card-m k* caust b4a.de* cham bro1 cina h1 clem coc-c *Colch* k* con k2 croc bro1 crot-h *Dig* k* **Euphr** k* fago ferr-i k2 ferr-p gins graph bro1 hell hura jatr-c kali-bi k* kali-i bro1 kali-p kali-s fkr2.de kreos *Lach Led* lyc bro1 manc med meph merc bro1 *Merc-c* k* mez k* nat-m bg2* nat-p k2 *Nat-s* nux-v k* *Olnd* psil ft1 puls bro1 ran-s k* sabad bro1 sang hr1 sanic sel b7a.de sep b4a.de* sol-ni spig h1 *Sulph* k* thuj bg2
  - : **cutting** pain: spig h1 sulph bg2
  - : **pressing** pain: sel b7a.de
  - : **sore**: *Acon Ant-c* bro1 *Apis* k* arg-n bro1 arn b7a.de ars bro1 *Borx* k* carc mg1.de* dig b4a.de* euphr bro1 *Graph* bro1 hep bro1 kalm merc-c bro1 *Nux-v* k* petr bro1 spig sulph b4a.de* *Valer* b7a.de zinc bro1
  - : **Glands**: rheum ↓
    - : **burning**: rheum h
    - : **pressing** pain: rheum h
- **Tarsi**: ars ↓ clem ↓ euphr ↓ mez ↓
  - : **burning**: ars ptk1 clem bg2 euphr ptk1 mez bg2
- **Under**: berb ↓ kola stb3•
  - : **foreign** body; as from a: berb ptk1 kola stb3•
- **Upper**: *Acon* ↓ ang ↓ arn ↓ bell ↓ borx ↓ cadm-met ↓ calc ↓ camph ↓ cann-s ↓ carb-an ↓ carb-v ↓ carc ↓ cassia-s ↓ caust ↓ cham ↓ chel ↓ *Chin* ↓ cina ↓ clem ↓ graph ↓ hell ↓ hep ↓ kali-bi ↓ lach ↓ laur ↓ *Lyc* ↓ m-arct ↓ mang ↓ merc-c ↓ nat-c ↓ par ↓ ph-ac ↓ phos ↓ rheum ↓ sang ↓ sil ↓ spig ↓ stann ↓ staph ↓ sulph ↓ vanil ↓ verat ↓
  - : **right**: alum ↓ bar-c ↓ cassia-s ↓ chel ↓ clem ↓ coloc ↓ cycl ↓ hep ↓ hyos ↓ nat-c ↓ olib-sac ↓ olnd ↓ rhus-t ↓ spig ↓ stann ↓ tarax ↓ thuj ↓ zinc ↓
    - : **daytime**:
      - . **amel.**: cassia-s ↓

- **Lids – Upper – right – daytime – amel.**: ...
  - **pulsating** pain: cassia-s ccrh1•
  - : **night**: cassia-s ↓
    - **pulsating** pain: cassia-s ccrh1•
  - : **burning**: clem b4.de* coloc b4.de* olnd b7.de* rhus-t b7.de* spig b7.de* stann b4.de*
  - : **closing** the eyes:
    - . **amel.**: cassia-s ↓
      - **pulsating** pain: cassia-s ccrh1•
  - : **lying** down:
    - . **amel.**: cassia-s ↓
      - **pulsating** pain: cassia-s ccrh1•
  - : **motion** of the lids:
    - . **agg.**: cassia-s ↓
      - **pulsating** pain: cassia-s ccrh1•
  - : **pressing** pain: chel b7.de* hep bg2 hyos b7.de nat-c b4.de* rhus-t b7.de* tarax b7.de* thuj b4.de*
  - : **pulsating** pain: cassia-s ccrh1•
  - : **sore**: zinc b4.de*
  - : **stitching** pain: cycl b7.de* olib-sac wmh1 spig b7.de* stann b4.de*
  - : **tearing** pain: alum b4.de* bar-c b4.de*
  - : **touch** agg.: verat ↓
    - . **stitching** pain: verat c2
  - : **left**: ars ↓ asaf ↓ asar ↓ aur ↓ bar-c ↓ *Brom* ↓ bry ↓ chel ↓ kali-n ↓ merc ↓ olnd ↓ spig ↓ zinc ↓
    - : **burning**: aur b4.de* bry b7.de*
    - : **cutting** pain: merc b4.de*
    - : **pressing** pain: ars b4.de* asaf b7.de* asar bg2 chel b7.de* kali-n a1
    - : **stitching** pain: bar-c b4.de* *Brom* b4a.de olnd b7.de* spig b7.de* zinc b4.de*
  - : **burning**: *Acon* b7a.de cadm-met tpw6 calc b4.de* cina b7.de* clem bg2 kali-bi bg2 lach bg2 laur bg2 *Lyc* b4a.de m-arct b7.de merc-c b4a.de ph-ac b4.de* phos b4.de* rheum b7.de* spig b7.de*
  - : **cutting** pain: staph b7.de*
  - : **opening** the eyes agg.: borx ↓
    - : **pressing** pain: borx a1
  - : **pressing** pain: borx b4a.de camph bg2 cann-s b7.de carb-v b4.de* caust b4.de* cham b7.de* graph h2 hep b4.de* lyc b4.de* nat-c h2 ph-ac h2 phos b4.de* rheum b7.de* sil b4.de* spig b7.de* stann b4.de* staph b7.de* sulph b4.de* verat b7.de*
    - : **downward**: carb-an bg2 chel b7.de* *Chin* b7.de* hell b7.de* par b7.de* spig b7.de*
  - : **sore**: arn b7.de*
  - : **stinging**: carc mg1.de*
  - : **stitching** pain: ang b7.de* bell bg2 cassia-s ccrh1• hep b4.de* m-arct b7.de mang b4.de* sang a1 sil b4.de* spig b7.de* vanil fd5.de verat b7.de*
  - : **sunlight**: cassia-s ↓
    - : **stitching** pain: cassia-s ccrh1•
  - : **warm** applications:
    - : **amel.**: cassia-s ↓
      - **stitching** pain: cassia-s ccrh1•
  - : **Under**: berb ↓ coc-c ↓ cortico ↓ ferr-p ↓
    - : **foreign** body; as from a: berb ptk1 coc-c ptk1 ferr-p ptk1
    - : **sand**; as from: cortico tpw7*
    - : **left**: ammc ↓
      - . **foreign** body; as from a: ammc a1*
    - : **right**: calc-caust ↓
      - . **foreign** body; as from a: calc-caust c1
- **Orbital** arch: alum ↓ nat-m ↓ petr ↓
  - **sore**: nat-m h2 petr a1
  - **tearing** pain: alum h2
- **Orbits**: aloe bro1 alum ↓ am-pic bro1 anac ↓ ang ↓ ant-c ↓ *Apis* ↓ *Arn* ↓ ars ↓ *Asaf* bro1 aur bro1 *Bell* b4a.de *Bism* ↓ bov ↓ bry ↓ calc ↓ camph ↓ carb-v ↓ caust ↓ cedr ↓ chel bro1 chin b7.de* chinin-s ↓ cimic bro1 cina ↓ cinnb bro1 cocc ↓ con ↓ crot-t bro1 cupr ↓ dulc ↓ gels bro1 *Hell* ↓ hep ↓ hyos ↓ ign ↓ ilx-a bro1 iod b4.de* kali-bi ↓ kali-c ↓ *Kali-i* bro1 kalm ↓ lach b7.de* laur b7.de* led ↓ m-ambo ↓ mag-c ↓ mentho bro1 meny ↓ *Merc* b4.de*

- **Orbits**: ...
merc-c b4a.de mez ↓ mur-ac ↓ nat-m ↓ nuph ↓ nux-v ↓ olnd ↓ par ↓ ph-ac ↓ *Phos* bro1 plat ↓ plb ↓ puls b7.de* rhod ↓ rhus-t ↓ ruta bro1 sars ↓ sel b7.de* seneg ↓ sep ↓ *Spig* b7.de* spong ↓ stann ↓ stront-c ↓ sul-ac ↓ *Sulph* ↓ symph ↓ ther bro1 thuj ↓ *Upa* bro1 vac jl2 *Valer* ↓ verat ↓ verb ↓
  - **boring** pain: *Bism* b7a.de calc b4.de* hep b4.de*
  - **burning**: carb-v b4a.de meny b7.de* sulph b4.de*
  - **burnt**; as if: bry b7.de*
  - **coition** agg.: cedr ↓
    ⁝ **neuralgic**: cedr ptk1
  - **compressed**; as if: spig b7.de*
  - **constricting** pain: verb c1
  - **cutting** pain: chin b7.de*
  - **drawing** pain: spong b7.de* stann b4.de* thuj bg2 valer b7.de*
  - **fever**; during: valer b7.de
  - **gnawing** pain: hyos b7.de*
  - **jerking** pain: m-ambo b7.de stann b4.de*
  - **lying** down agg.: atra-r bnm3•
  - **menses**; during: bov b4.de
  - **neuralgic**: ars ptk1 cedr ptk1 chinin-s ptk1 kali-bi ptk1 kalm ptk1 nat-m ptk1 spig ptk1 stann ptk1
    ⁝ **accompanied** by | **Testes**; neuralgic pain of: lycps-v ptk1
  - **pinching** pain: ph-ac h2
  - **pressing** pain: anac b4.de* ang b7.de* ant-c b7.de* *Apis* b4a.de *Arn* b7.de* ars b4.de* *Asaf* b7.de* aur b4.de* bell b4.de* bov b4.de* carb-v b4a.de caust h2 chel b7.de* cina b7.de* cocc b7.de* con b4a.de* dulc fd4.de *Hell* b7.de* hyos b7.de* ign b7.de* kali-c h2 laur b7.de* led b7.de* mez b4.de* nuph vml3• olnd b7.de* par b7.de* ph-ac b4.de* phos b4.de* plb b7.de* rhod b4.de* ruta b7.de* seneg b4.de* sep b4.de* spig b7.de* spong fd4.de stann b4.de* stront-c b4.de* *Sulph* b4.de* symph fd3.de• thuj bg2 *Valer* b7.de* verat b7.de*
  - **reading** agg.: flor-p ↓
    ⁝ **pressing** pain: flor-p rsj3•
  - **sore**: apis b4a.de cupr b7a.de nux-v bg2 plat b4.de* rhus-t b7.de*
  - **stitching** pain: ant-c b7.de* aur b4.de* bov b4.de* calc b4.de* camph b7.de* caust bg2 ph-ac b4.de* rhod b4.de* rhus-t b7.de* spong b7.de* valer b7.de*
  - **tearing** pain: alum b4.de* anac b4.de* aur b4.de* bism b7.de* bov bg2 calc b4.de* kali-c b4a.de mag-c b4.de* mur-ac b4.de* phos b4.de* sep b4.de* spig b7.de* stann b4a.de sul-ac b4.de*
  - **thrust**; as from a: sars b4.de* stann b4.de*
  - **torn** out; as if: *Bell* b4.de* phos bg2

▽ · **extending** to | **Outward**: bar-c bg2 *Cimic* bg2

O · **Around**: apis bro1 *Asaf* bro1 aur bro1 bell bro1 *Cinnb* bro1 hep bro1 hydrc bro1 ilx-a bro1 plat bro1 plb bro1 spig bro1
  - **Below**: ser-a-c jl2
    ⁝ **right**: bac jl2
    ⁝ **left**: atra-r bnm3•
  - **Bones**: apis b4a.de bov b4a.de cupr b7a.de par b7a.de phos b4a.de sulph ↓ syph ↓
    ⁝ **drawing** pain: sulph h2
    ⁝ **suppurative**: syph bg2
  - **Deep** in: *Aloe* bro1 gels bro1 merc-c bro1 phos bro1 phyt bro1 plat bro1 ruta bro1 sarr bro1 *Spig* bro1 stann bro1 upa bro1
  - **Lower** part: bapt hr1 sars ↓
    ⁝ **sore**: sars h2
  - **Margins**: hell ↓ kali-bi ↓
    ⁝ **right**: sang hr1
    ⁝ **nail**; as from a: hell b7a.de
    ⁝ **stitching** pain: kali-bi bg2

- **Pannus**, in: *Apis* ↓
  - **stitching** pain: *Apis*
- **Papillae**: anh ↓
  - **burning**: anh sp1
- **Postorbital**: caust ↓ colch ↓ con ↓ kali-c ↓ phos ↓

Pain – Postorbital: ...
  - **neuralgic**: caust bro1 colch bro1 con bro1 kali-c bro1 phos bro1
  - **vaccinations**; from: thuj ↓
    ⁝ **neuralgic**: thuj tl1
- **Pupils**: calc-p tl1 caps tl1 cimic tl1
- **Sclera**: anh ↓
  - **burning**: anh sp1
- **Sockets** | **constricting** pain (See orbits - constricting)
- **Spots**; in: nat-m ↓ petr-ra ↓ *Phos* ↓
  - **burning**: nat-m h2 petr-ra shn4• *Phos*
- **Supraorbital**: arg-n ↓ *Asaf* ↓ **Cedr** ↓ chel ↓ chin ↓ chinin-s ↓ cimic ↓ **Cinnb** ↓ dys ↓ ign ↓ *Kali-bi* ↓ kalm ↓ *Mag-p* ↓ morph ↓ nat-m ↓ nux-v ↓ ran-b ↓ sep ↓ *Spig* ↓ stann ↓ tetox ↓ thein ↓ tong ↓ viol-o ↓
  - **neuralgic**: *(↗HEAD - Pain - forehead - eyes - above - neuralgic)* arg-n bro1 *Asaf* mfj* **Cedr** mfj* chel mfj* chin mfj chinin-s mfj* cimic bro1 **Cinnb** mfj dys fmm1• ign mfj *Kali-bi* bro1 kalm mfj *Mag-p* mfj* morph bro1 nat-m mfj nux-v mfj* ran-b bro1 sep mfj *Spig* bro1 stann bro1 tetox pin2• thein bro1 tong bro1 viol-o bro1
- **Surface**; on: *Stront-c* ↓
  - **pressing** pain: *Stront-c* b4a.de

PALE: alco br1

PANNUS: alum mfj *Apis* k* **Arg-n** k* *Aur* k* aur-m bro1* *Bar-c* k* *Calc* k* cann-s mfj *Caust* chinin-m kr1* *Euphr* k* *Graph* k* *Hep* k* kali-bi k* kali-c k* merc *Merc-i-f* k* *Merc-i-r* k* merl k* *Nit-ac* k* petr k* puls hr1 rhus-t k* sep sil k* *Sulph* k*

PARALYSIS: cocc tl1
- **sensation** of | **right**: caust bg2

O - **Accommodative** muscles (See VISION - Accommodation - defective)
- **Extrinsic** ocular muscles: acon mfj *Alum* mfj arn mfj aur mfj **Caust** mfj chel mfj *Con* mfj cupr-act mfj **Gels** mfj* hyos mfj kali-i mfj merc-pn mfj nat-m mfj nux-v mfj par mfj phos mfj* rhus-t mfj **Seneg** mfj spig mfj sulph mfj
- **Eyeballs**:

O · **Muscles**: *(↗Strabismus)* *Acon* mfj alum k2 arg-n bro1 arn mfj aur mfj bar-ox-suc mtf11 bell bro1 bufo k2 **Caust** k* chel mfj cocc k2 *Con* k* cupr-act mfj *Euphr* k* **Gels** k* hyos k2* kali-i lach bro1 merc-i-f merc-pn mfj *Nat-m* **Nux-v** k* oxyt bro1* par mfj phos k2* phys br1* *Rhus-t* k* ruta k2* santin bro1 *Seneg* k* spig mfj syph k2* thal-xyz srj8•
    ⁝ **accompanied** by | **Throat** muscles; paralysis of: gels hr1
    ⁝ **cold** agg., becoming: **Rhus-t** hr1*
    ⁝ **diphtheria**; after: phys br1*
    ⁝ **wet**; getting feet: *Rhus-t* hr1
    ⁝ **Ciliary** muscles: *Acon* alum k2 *Arg-n* cocc k2 *Con* *Dub* gels graph kali-br lil-t br1 nat-m nux-v par k* phys **Ruta** seneg
    ⁝ **External** recti (= esophoria): **Caust** k ●* chel gels kali-i rhod *Ruta* sulph syph mtf33
    ⁝ **Internal** recti (= exophoria): *Agar* k* alum *Con* graph *Jab* lil-t merc-i-f **Morph** **Nat-m** k* phos rhod *Ruta* *Seneg*
    ⁝ **Superior** oblique (= hyperphoria): *Arn* cupr *Seneg* k* *Syph* k*
- **Iris**: **Arn** hr1 (non:ars hr1*) kali-bi *Par* k*
- **Lids**, of: *(↗Falling - lids)* *Acon* bg2 *Alum* k* arn bg2 *Ars* k* bapt bar-m bell k* bufo k2 *Cadm-s* caul bro1 **Caust** b4a.de* *Cocc* k* *Con* k* dulc bro1 **Gels** bg2* *Graph* k* *Guare* haem bro1 helo bro1 hydr-ac *Kalm* bg2* lach bg2 lat-m bnm6• *Merc-i-f* *Morph* bro1 naja bro1 nat-ar k* nat-c k2 nit-ac k* nux-m bro1 nux-v bro1 op k* oxyum-sc mcp1• phos bro1 *Plb* k* puls *Rhus-t* b7.de* **Sep** k* **Spig** k* stram k* sulfon bro1 syph bro1 thal-xyz srj8• upa bro1 *Verat* k* verat-v hr1 vip zinc k* zinc-p k2
  - **right**: caust ptk1 nept-m lsd2.fr
  - **left**: bar-c ptk1 bufo ptk1 coloc ptk1 graph bg2 kali-p ptk1 thuj ptk1
  - **night**: ars bg2
  - **coal** gas; from: sec ptk1
  - **vertigo**; with: bapt hr1

O · **Lower**: graph bg2 phyt bg2
  - **Upper**: *Acon* mfj *Alum* k* alum-p k2 anh vh1 apis arn *Ars* k* bar-m k2 *Bell* b4a.de botul br1* bufo *Cadm-s* calc gk *Cann-s* b7a.de **Caust** k* chlol cina cinnb k2 *Cocc* k* *Con* k* crot-c crot-h cur dig b4a.de *Dulc* k* euph ferr tl1 **Gels** k* germ-met srj5• *Graph* hydroph rsj6• kali-c mrr1 kalm mfj *Led*

- **Lids**, of – **Upper**: ...
lyss Mag-p k* Med k* Merl morb mtf11 Morph naja k* nat-ar nat-c nat-s tl1 **Nit-ac** k* Nux-m op k* Phos k* Plb k* **Rhus-t** Sec **Sep** k* **Spig** k* stann Syph k* thuj b4a.de Verat k* vip mtf11 Zinc k*
  - **one** side: syph jl2
  - **right**: alum k* Apis k* caust bg2 Cur gins bg1 mag-p med bg2* nat-m bg2* nit-ac bg2 phys plut-n srj7• rad-br bg2 rhus-t sulph
  - **left**: ars bg2* bar-c bg1 bar-m bg2 caust bg1 coloc bg2* elaps gk graph bg2 kali-p bg2* lyc bg2 nux-v plb thuj bg2* verat bg2
  - **morning**: Nit-ac
  - **accompanied** by | **Face**; pain in: gels bro1
  - **cold**; from: **CAUST** k ● **Rhus-t** k*
  - **cough** agg.; during: nit-ac tl1 sep tl1
  - **injuries**; after: Led
  - **periodical** | **week**; every: stann hr1*
  - **sleepy**; patient seems: syph jl2
  - **Exterior**: con bg med ptk
- **Optic** nerve (= amaurosis): Acon b2.de* agar b2.de* alum b2.de* am-c b2.de* am-m b2.de* ambr b2.de* anac k* anan ang b2.de* ant-c b2.de* ant-s-aur c1* ant-t b2.de* apis bro1 Arg-met arg-n arn b2.de* Ars k* ars-s-f k2 asaf b2.de* aur k* aur-ar k2 Aur-m k* Aur-m-n aur-s k2 bar-c k* bar-s k2 **Bell** k* ben-n c2 borx b2.de* both k* Bov k* bry k* bufo Calc k* calc-sil k2 camph b2.de* cann-s b2.de* canth b2.de* caps k* carb-an b2.de* carb-v b2.de* card-b c2 Caust k* cench c2 cham b2.de* Chel k* Chin k* chinin-s k* cic k* cocc k* **Con** k* croc k* cycl b2.de* daph c2 dig k* dros k* dulc k* Elaps k* euphr k* Ferr k* ferr-ar ferr-ma c2 fl-ac **Gels** k* graph b2.de* guaj k* Hep b2.de* Hyos k* ign b2.de* iod b2.de* kali-ar kali-c k* **Kali-i** k* kali-p Kali-s kali-sil k2 kreos b2.de* laur k* led b2.de* Lyc k* m-ambo b2.de m-arct b2.de mag-c b2.de* manc bro1 mang b2.de* Meny k* Merc k* mez b2.de* mom-b bro1 naphtin bro1 nat-ar nat-c k* **Nat-m** k* nat-p nit-ac k* nux-m bro1 Nux-v k* olnd k* Op k* oxyt bro1* par b2.de* petr k* Ph-ac k* **Phos** k* Plb k* Plb-act bro1 plb-xyz c2 Psor **Puls** k* Rhus-t k* Ruta k* sabad b2.de* sabin b2.de* santin bro1 sars b2.de* **Sec** k* seneg b2.de* Sep k* **Sil** k* sol-ni c2 sol-t c2 spig k* staph k* **Stram** k* stront-c b2.de* stry bro1 stry-xyz c2 **Sulph** k* syph Tab c2* thal-xyz srj8• Thuj k* upa c2 vanad bro1 verat k* verat-v hr1* verb b2.de* vib zinc b2.de* zinc-p k2
  - **right**: Bov
    - **stool** | **amel.**: apis ptk2
    - **then** left: Chin
  - **accompanied** by:
    - **Kidneys**; inflammation of (See KIDNEYS - Inflammation - accompanied - optic)
    - **Pupils**; contracted: Sep b4a.de Zinc b4a.de
    - **Retinal** hemorrhage: both mtf11
  - **delivery**; during: aur-m c1
  - **headache**; with severe: iris mrr1 zinc br1
  - **incipient**: Ant-t b7.de* aur b4.de* Caps b7a.de Caust b4.de* Chin b7.de* dulc b4.de* hyos b7.de* Merc b4a.de Nat-m b4.de* **Puls** b7.de* Rhus-t b7a.de Ruta b7a.de sep b4a.de* Sil b4a.de Spig b7a.de Sulph b4.de*
  - **masturbation**: gels c1
- **Retina**: hyos mtf11

PENDULUM of a clock; sensation as from the: m-ambo b7.de

PERIODICITY: cedr bg2 chin bg2 cinnb bg2 coloc bg2 gels bg2 nat-m bg2 prun bg2 spig bg2

PERSPIRATION on eyebrows and lids: calc-p hr1* mag-c ptk1

PHOTOMANIA: *(↗MIND - Darkness - agg.; MIND - Light - desire)* Acon k* am-m k* **BELL** k ●* calc cann-s bg cann-xyz bg2 carb-ac bg carb-an bg2 ferr-p k2 **Gels** k* grin bg2 Lac-c nat-m bg phos bg2 plb bg2 ruta sanic bg2 **Stram** k* tarent bg2 valer
- **delirium**; with: calc k*

PHOTOPHOBIA: *(↗Darkness - amel.; Light - agg.; MIND - Light - aversion; MIND - Light - aversion - shuns; MIND - Sensitive - light)* **Acon** k* acon-ac rly4• aeth k* aethi-a mtf11 aethyl-s-d dp1.fr agar k* agath-a nl2• Agn k* Ail k* All-c k* Alum k* alum-p k2 alum-sil k2 am-c k* am-m k* ammc vh1* anac k* Anan k* ange-s oss1• ant-c k* Ant-t k* Apis k* arg-met vh **Arg-n** k* Arn k* **Ars** k* ars-met bro1 Arum-t k* arund Asar k* asc-t k* aster k* atis bnj1 atis-r gsb1 atp rly4• Aur k* aur-ar k2 Aur-m k* aur-s bapt **Bar-c** k* bar-i k2 Bar-m bar-s k2 **Bell** k* benzol br1* berb k* bit-ar wht1• borx k* brom k*

Photophobia: ...
bros-gau mrc1 brucel sa3• Bry k* bufo buth-a sp1 cact **Calc** k* calc-f sp1 Calc-p k* calc-s calc-sil k2 camph k* cann-i carb-ac carb-an b2.de* **Carbn-s** carc sst• castm k* Caust k* cedr k* cere-b Cham k* Chel **Chin** k* Chinin-ar Chinin-s chlam-tr bcx2• chlf hr1 chlol c1 chrysar br1 Cic k* cimic k* cina k* cinnb k* Clem k* Coff k* colch b2.de* coli rly4• coloc k* **Con** k* Croc k* Crot-h k* Crot-t k* cupr b2.de* dendr-pol sk4• Dig k* dirc a1* dros k* dulc fd4.de dys pte1• elaps k* ery-a a1* Eup-per k* Euph hr1 **Euphr** k* falco-pe nl2• ferr br1 ferr-i fum rly4• gal-ac c1* galeoc-c-h gms1• gamb Gels k* Glon k* **Graph** k* guat sp1 haliae-lc srj5• Ham hr1* Hell k* Hep k* hir rsj4• hydro-v a1 Hyos k* Ign k* iod bg2 ip k* irid-met srj5• ix bnm8• Jab hr1 Kali-ar Kali-bi k* Kali-c k* Kali-chl hr1 kali-i k* kali-m k2 Kali-n k* Kali-p k* kali-s k2 ketogl-ac rly4• kreos bg2 Lac-ac **Lac-c** k* Lac-d k* lac-del hrn2• Lach k* laur b2.de* Led leptos-ih jl2 Lil-t k* Lith-c luf-op rsj5• luna kg1• **Lyc** k* lyss k* m-arct b2.de* mag-c k* mag-m h2 Mag-p k* mag-s mang b2.de* marb-w es1• med c1 **Merc** k* Merc-c k* Merc-i-f k* Merl morb jl2 mosch mur-ac k* Nat-ar Nat-c k* **Nat-m** k* nat-p **Nat-s** k* nicc nit-ac k* Nit-s-d hr1 nux-m k* **Nux-v** k* **Op** k* ozone sde2• petr petr-ra shn4• ph-ac k* phel bg2* Phos k* phys lp* Phyt k* plac rzf5• plac-s rly4• plb b7a.de* Plut-n srj7• podo fd3.de• positr nl2• Propr sa3• psil ft1 Psor k* ptel c1 Puls k* ran-b br1 retin-ac mtf11 **Rhus-t** k* ribo rly4• ros-d wla1 ruta fd4.de sabad bg2 sal-fr sle1• Sanic k* sars b2.de* scroph-n bro1 sec k* seneg k* Sep k* Sil k* sol-ni Spig k* spong fd4.de staph k* Stram k* suis-em rly4• sul-ac k* **Sulph** k* Sumb syc pte1*• syph al* Tab tarax k* Tarent k* tell rsj10• thal-xyz srj8• ther k* thres-a sze7• thuj b4a.de* tritic-vg fd5.de Tub k* vanil fd5.de Verat Viol-o b7a.de vip fkr4.de visc sp1 Zinc k* ziz k* [heroin sdj2 spect dfg1 tax jsj7]
- **morning**: am-c am-m Ant-c k* bros-gau mrc1 Calc k* hydro-v a1 kali-n Nat-s **Nux-v** k* phyt propr sa3• rhus-t hr1 sil tritic-vg fd5.de verat
  - **rising** agg.: ant-c h2 calc k*
  - **waking**; on: dirc c1 Lach nat-s ptk rhus-v tritic-vg fd5.de
- **afternoon**: dulc fd4.de petr-ra shn4• zing
  - **17** h: chinin-m kr1
- **evening**: arund borx **Calc** carb-an Caust k* eug Euphr Lyc Merc ph-ac ribo rly4• sil stram sumb Zinc zing k*
  - **18-20** h: **Caust**
- **night**: con gels olib-sac wmh1
  - **midnight**:
    - **after** | **3** h; until: chinin-ar
- **accompanied** by:
  - **coryza** (See NOSE - Coryza - accompanied - photophobia)
  - **disorders**; chronic eye: sil mtf11
  - **focusing**; difficult: hir rsj4•
  - **formation** of phlyctenula (See Eruptions - sclera - vesicles - accompanied - photophobia)
  - **lachrymation**; profuse: seneg bg2
  - **pain**:
    - **left** eye; in (See Pain - left - accompanied - photophobia)
    - **Face**; in (See FACE - Pain - accompanied - photophobia)
  - ○ **Head**; complaints in (See HEAD - Complaints - accompanied - photophobia)
- **chill**; during: acon k* apis k* ars k* **Bell** k* borx k* cham k* hep k* kreos bg2 lyc k* nux-v rhus-t k* seneg bg2 sep k*
- **chronic**: aeth k* Nat-s Sil k* tritic-vg fd5.de
- **coition**; after: apis calc Chin Graph **Kali-c** kali-p phos sep sil
- **convulsions**; after: hyos tl1
- **coryza**; during: Ars bg2 Euphr b7a.de **Merc** bg2 Puls b7.de*
- **crusts** are torn from nose, if: Kali-bi
- **dinner**; after: Calc
- **driving**; while: falco-pe nl2• sal-fr sle1•
- **eating**; after: sil h2
- **fever**; during: *(↗Closing - desire - fever)* acon bg2 bell b4a.de* con b4a.de* ferr-p mrr1 Hep b4a.de* sulph bg2
- **glistening** objects: lyss mrr1
- **headache**:
  - **before**: Kali-bi mrr1
  - **during**: agath-a nl2• Ferr-p Kali-br hr1 kali-c bg kali-p luf-op rsj5• mim-p skp7*• moni rfm1• **Nat-s** k* ozone sde2• puls bg sep bg syph al tarent k*

Eye

- **inflammation**:
  - **except** during inflammation: kali-bi$_{bg2}$
  - **slight** inflammation; with only: con$_{bg2}$
  - **without**: agn$_{b7a.de}$ *Am-c*$_{b4a.de}$ *Am-m*$_{b7a.de}$ anac$_{b4a.de}$ borx$_{b4a.de}$ carb-an$_{b4a.de}$ cic$_{b7a.de}$ *Cina*$_{b7a.de}$ *Coff*$_{b7a.de}$ colch$_{b7a.de}$ **Con**$_{k}$* croc$_{b7a.de}$ *Cycl*$_{b7a.de}$ *Dros*$_{b7a.de}$ *Graph*$_{b4a.de}$ hell$_{k}$* **Ign**$_{b7a.de}$ kali-n$_{b4a.de}$ laur$_{b7a.de}$ m-arct$_{b7a.de}$ mang$_{b4a.de}$ mur-ac$_{b4a.de}$ *Nat-c*$_{b4a.de}$ nux-m$_{b7a.de}$ *Puls*$_{b7a.de}$ sil$_{b4a.de}$ *Spig*$_{b7a.de}$
- **light**; from:
  - **artificial** light | **agg.**: agar *Arg-n*$_{k}$* aster borx bros-gau$_{mrc1}$ *Calc* calc-p$_{k}$* castm chel choc$_{srj3}$• coff *Con* *Crot-h*$_{k}$* cupr dros$_{k}$* *Euphr*$_{k}$* galeoc-c-h$_{gms1}$• gels$_{k}$* hydrog$_{srj2}$• *Ip*$_{k}$* irid-met$_{srj5}$• *Lac-d*$_{k}$* lith-c *Merc*$_{k}$* *Nat-m*$_{k}$* phos plut-n$_{srj7}$• *Puls* stram$_{k}$* *Sulph* tung-met$_{bdx1}$•
  - **blue** light | **agg.**: tab
  - **bright** light | **agg.**: glon$_{tl1}$ merc$_{tl1}$
  - **candlelight** | **agg.**: borx$_{c1}$ gels$_{c1}$ hep$_{c1}$
  - **daylight**:
    - **agg.**: *Acon* androc$_{srj1}$• ant-c **Ars** bell berb *Bry* camph castm *Caust* **Chin** *Cic* *Clem* *Con* *Euphr* **Graph** hell *Hep* *Ign* kali-ar *Kali-bi* *Kali-c* kali-s kali-sil$_{k2}$ ketogl-ac$_{rly4}$• lac-c *Lith-c* *Lyc* *Merc* merc-c merc-sul *Nat-ar* nat-c nit-ac nux-v petr ph-ac *Phos* plac-s$_{rly4}$• psor ros-d$_{wla1}$ *Sars* sep sil stram suis-em$_{rly4}$• *Sulph* *Zinc*
    - **desires** lamplight: stram
    - **gaslight**; more than: *Graph* kali-bi
    - **only**: *Kali-bi* nit-ac
  - **fire**; of the: euphr$_{k2}$ mag-m$_{bg2}$ **Merc**$_{k}$*
  - **gaslight** | **agg.**: asc-t *Calc-p* dirc$_{a1}$* *Graph* *Med* **Merc** *Sulph*
  - **sunlight** | **agg.**: **Acon** agath-a$_{nl2}$• androc$_{srj1}$• *Ars* ars-s-f$_{k2}$ *Asar* berb bros-gau$_{mrc1}$ *Bry* calc camph castm **Chin** *Cic* *Clem* *Euphr* gels$_{hr1}$ **Graph** *Hep* *Ign* irid-met$_{srj5}$• *Kali-ar* *Lac-c* *Lith-c* *Merc* merc-c *Merc-sul* mim-p$_{skp7}$• petr ph-ac *Phos* pitu-a$_{vml2}$• pycnop-sa$_{mrz1}$ ros-d$_{wla1}$ **Sulph** zinc zinc-p$_{k2}$
- **masturbation**; after: cina$_{k}$*
- **menses**; during: ferr-p ign$_{k}$*
- **operation**; after: stront-c$_{ptk1}$
- **perspiration**; during: acon$_{bg2}$ am$_{bg2}$ *Ars*$_{bg2}$ *Bell*$_{bg2}$ bry$_{bg2}$ *Calc*$_{bg2}$ *Cham*$_{bg2}$ chin$_{bg2}$ graph$_{bg2}$ hep$_{bg2}$ lyc$_{bg2}$ *Merc*$_{bg2}$ **Nux-v**$_{bg2}$ phos$_{bg2}$ puls$_{bg2}$ **Rhus-t**$_{bg2}$ *Sep*$_{bg2}$ stram$_{bg2}$ sulph$_{k}$*
- **rage**; during: *Acon* ars **Bell** hyos merc nux-v phos puls **Stram**
- **snow**; from: ant-c apis$_{gsd1}$ **Ars** cic$_{br1}$ merl$_{a1}$ sacch-a$_{fd2.de}$•
- **spring**; in: cob$_{bg3}$*
- **straining** the eyes, after: **Arg-n**$_{k}$*
- **vertigo**; with: scut$_{c1}$ verat-v$_{a1}$
- **walking**:
  - **air**; in open:
    - **agg.**: *Clem*$_{k}$* *Psor*$_{k}$*
    - **amel.**: *Gamb*
- **warm** room agg.: **Arg-n**$_{k}$*
- **weather**:
  - **change** of weather: calc$_{tl1}$
  - **cloudy** weather: | **agg.**: ammc$_{vml3}$•
  - **foggy**: cic
  - **warm** | **agg.**: sulph

POLLUTIONS; after: kali-c$_{bg2}$

POLYPUS (See Tumors - canthi - outer - polypus)

PRESSURE:
- **agg.**: *Aur*$_{bg2}$ cina$_{b7.de}$* dros$_{b7.de}$* hep$_{bg2}$ nat-c$_{bg2}$ nat-m$_{bg2}$ rhus-t$_{b7.de}$*
- **amel.**: am-m$_{b7.de}$* apis$_{b4a.de}$* asaf$_{ptk1}$ bell$_{bg2}$ bry$_{b7.de}$* caust$_{ptk1}$ chel$_{ptk1}$ pic-ac$_{ptk1}$ puls$_{b7.de}$* verat$_{b7.de}$*
- **throat** agg.; on: lach$_{b7a.de}$
- **upward** | **amel.**: bell$_{b4.de}$*

PRESSURE IN THE EYEBALL:
- **decreased**: apisin$_{bro1}$ cedr$_{bro1}$ esin$_{bro1}$ nat-m$_{bro1}$* osm$_{bro1}$ prun$_{bro1}$ ran-b$_{bro1}$ rhod$_{bro1}$

Pressure in the eyeball: ...
- **increased** (See Glaucoma)

PRICKLING: agar$_{bg2}$ arg-n$_{bg2}$ hedy$_{a1}$* lyc$_{h2}$ nat-pyru$_{rly4}$• sep$_{b4a.de}$* zinc$_{h2}$

○ - **Lids**: *Canth*$_{b7a.de}$
- **Orbits** | **left**: nat-m$_{bg2}$

PROJECTING (See Protrusion)

PROTRUDING tongue agg.: syph$_{ptk1}$

PROTRUSION: acet-ac *Acon*$_{k}$* *Aeth* agn$_{bg2}$ aloe$_{k}$* ang$_{b2.de}$* anh$_{sp1}$ apis$_{bg2}$ arn$_{k}$* *Ars*$_{k}$* *Ars-i* ars-s-f$_{k2}$ *Aur*$_{k}$* aur-ar$_{k2}$ aur-i$_{k2}$ aur-s$_{k2}$ *Bar-c* bar-i$_{k2}$ bar-s$_{k2}$ **Bell**$_{k}$* borx$_{b2.de}$* brom$_{k}$* bufo$_{k2}$ *Cact* calc calc-i$_{k2}$ calc-p$_{k}$* calc-s$_{hr1}$ *Camph* *Canth*$_{k}$* caps$_{k}$* cedr *Cham* chin$_{k}$* chlor$_{k}$* *Cic*$_{k}$* *Clem* *Cocc*$_{k}$* colch *Coloc* **Com**$_{k}$* *Con*$_{k}$* crot-h cupr$_{k}$* cupr-n$_{a1}$ dig dor *Dros*$_{k}$* dulc *Ferr*$_{k}$* *Ferr-ar* **Ferr-i**$_{k}$* *Ferr-p* fl-ac$_{k}$* *Glon*$_{k}$* **Guaj**$_{k}$* gymno hed$_{sp1}$ helo-s$_{br1}$* *Hep*$_{k}$* hydr-ac *Hyos*$_{k}$* *Ign* *Iod*$_{k}$* jab$_{ptk1}$ kali-ar kali-c$_{k2}$ kali-i$_{k}$* kali-m$_{k2}$ kali-n$_{bg2}$* kara$_{c1}$ *Kreos*$_{k}$* lac-ac lac-c *Lach*$_{k}$* *Laur*$_{k}$* lycps-v$_{ptk1}$ m-arct$_{b2.de}$* *Merc*$_{b2.de}$* merc-c$_{b4a.de}$* morph mosch$_{k}$* **Nat-m**$_{k}$* *Nux-v*$_{k}$* oena *Op*$_{k}$* *Phos*$_{k}$* *Plat* plb$_{bg2}$ *Puls* rhus-t$_{k}$* sang *Sangin-t*$_{c1}$ santin spig$_{k}$* *Spong*$_{k}$* squil$_{b2.de}$* *Stann*$_{k}$* staph$_{b2.de}$* **Stram**$_{k}$* stry sul-ac sul-i$_{k2}$ sulph$_{k}$* tab thuj *Verat*$_{k}$* vip
- **right**: am$_{h1}$
  - **more** than left: arn$_{ptk1}$ **Com**$_{k}$*
- **accompanied** by:
  - **brilliant** eyes: aeth$_{ptk1}$
  - **red** discoloration of eyes: apis$_{ptk1}$
  - **trembling**: meph$_{ptk1}$
- **coryza**; during: spig$_{b7a.de}$*
- **cough** agg.; during: caps$_{ptk1}$ dros$_{ptk1}$*
- **epilepsy**; during (See GENERALS - Convulsions - epileptic - during - eyes - protruding)
- **exophthalmos**: aml-ns$_{k}$* ars atra-r$_{bnm3}$• *Aur*$_{k}$* bad *Bar-c*$_{k}$* bell$_{k}$* cact *Calc*$_{k}$* calc-i$_{k2}$ clem$_{bro1}$ com$_{bro1}$ con crot-h dig digin$_{c2}$ diph-t-tpt$_{jl2}$ dros$_{tl1}$ **Ferr**$_{k}$* **Ferr-i** ferr-p$_{bro1}$ glon$_{bro1}$ helo$_{bro1}$ helo-s$_{br1}$* *Ign*$_{k}$* **Iod**$_{k}$* kali-ar$_{c2}$ *Lycps-v*$_{k}$* *Nat-m*$_{k}$* nat-n$_{mtf11}$ par$_{bro1}$ passi$_{c2}$ *Phos*$_{k}$* pyrog$_{mtf11}$ sangin-t$_{c1}$* sapin$_{c2}$ sapo$_{bro1}$ scut$_{c2}$ **Sec** *Spong*$_{k}$* stel$_{bro1}$ *Stram*$_{bro1}$ stry$_{bro1}$ stry-xyz$_{c2}$ thuj$_{mtf33}$ thyr$_{bro1}$* thyreotr$_{mtf11}$
  - **accompanied** by:
    - **trembling**: meph$_{ptk1}$
    - **tumor** behind eyeball (See Tumors - eyeballs - behind - accompanied - exophthalmos)
  - **exophthalmic** goitre (See EXTERNAL - Goitre - exophthalmic)
- **fever**; during: *Spig*$_{b7.de}$*
- **injuries**; after: led$_{ptk1}$
- **mania**; during: camph$_{ptk1}$
- **measles**; during: dros$_{ptk1}$
- **sensation** of: bell$_{k}$* bry con$_{bg2}$ daph ferr-p$_{k2}$ guaj$_{h2}$* ham *Med*$_{k}$* **Par**$_{k}$* scut$_{c1}$ spong$_{ptk1}$ tung-met$_{bdx1}$•
  - **right**: com$_{a1}$
  - **left**: atra-r$_{jl1}$* [tax$_{jsj7}$]

○ · **Canthi**: euphr

○ - **Conjunctiva**: nit-ac$_{ptk1}$
- **Cornea**: colch$_{mtf11}$
- **Iris** protruding through cornea: ant-s-aur$_{c1}$* phys$_{bro1}$
- **Pupil**; a membrane protrudes into the: colch$_{hr1}$

PTERYGIUM: *Am-br*$_{k}$* apis$_{bro1}$ *Arg-n*$_{k}$* *Ars*$_{k}$* *Ars-met* *Aur*$_{sne}$ bell$_{lb}$ cadm-met$_{sp1}$ *Calc*$_{k}$* cann-i$_{mfj}$ *Cann-s*$_{bro1}$ cann-xyz$_{ptk1}$ chim$_{k}$* *Euphr*$_{k}$* *Form*$_{k}$* guare$_{c2}$* *Lach*$_{k}$* lyc$_{lb}$ merc$_{lb}$ *Nux-m*$_{k}$* nux-v$_{c1}$ *Psor*$_{k}$* *Puls*$_{bg2}$ *Rat*$_{k}$* rhus-t$_{mtf11}$ spig$_{k}$* *Sulph*$_{k}$* teil$_{k}$* *Thuj*$_{sne}$ *Zinc*$_{k}$* zinc-s$_{ptk1}$
- **pink** color; of: *Arg-n*$_{k}$*
- **recurrent**: psor$_{jl2}$

○ - **Cornea**; over: nux-m$_{ptk1}$
- **Lids**: arg-n$_{bg2}$ lach$_{bg2}$

PTOSIS (See Paralysis - lids - upper)

PUCKERED conjunctiva (See Wrinkled)

PULLING sensation: *(↗Pain - drawing)* carneg-g rwt1• con tl1 crot-t mur-ac raph sacch-a fd2.de• sep

PULSATION: allox tpw3 bell ptk1
- **night**: asaf ptk1 merc ptk1
- ○ - **Around** the eyes: *Ars* luna kg1•
- **Canthi**: calc b4.de*
- **Eyebrows**: *(↗in - superciliary)* *Bell* b4a.de cina b7.de* petr b4.de* scroph-n bg2
- **In** the eyes: acon bg2 ammc k* apis *Ars* k* asaf asar k* aur-ar k2 aur-s k* **Bell** k* benz-ac k* berb bg2* brom bry k* bufo cact k* *Calc* k* calc-sil k2 cham bg2 *Chel* k* clem k* cocc bg2 *Coloc* *Croc* b7a.de dig bg2 *Gels* k* glon *Hep* k* *Hyos* k* ign bg2 kola stb3• kreos bg2 lil-t k* lith-c lyss k* m-arct b7.de m-aust b7.de mang k* *Merc* k* *Merc-i-f* k* *Nux-v* k* petr k* phos bg2 phys k* pic-ac k* rheum k* seneg *Sil* k* stann bg2 stram k* tarent k* ter k* ther k* vanil fd5.de
  - **midnight** | **after**: *Ars* k*
  - **morning**: *Nux-v* k*
    - ⁝ **lying** down agg.: nux-v k*
  - **evening**: cycl k* kreos k*
  - **night**: ars k* **Asaf** **Merc** k* *Merc-i-f* k*
  - **alternating** with | **stitching** pain: calc
  - **motion** agg.: cortico tpw7
  - **paroxysmal**: calc *Sil* k*
  - **reading** agg.: ammc
  - ○ **Superciliary** muscle: *(↗eyebrows)* cina a1*
- **Lids**:
  - ○ **Lower**: bell b4.de* seneg b4.de*
  - **Upper**: cassia-s cdd7• cina bro1 mang h2 stry
    - ⁝ **right**: mang b4.de*
- **Orbits**: dig b4.de* spig b7a.de

PUSTULES on the cornea (See Eruptions - cornea - pustules; Inflammation - conjunctiva - pustular)

QUIVERING: *(↗Twitching; Winking)* **Agar** bg2 alum k* alum-p k2 *Am-m* k* *Apis* k* aran k* bell b4a.de* carb-v chin b7.de* con k* fl-ac k* *Glon* k* *Hyos* k* iod bg2* petr k* *Phos* plat b4a.de* plb b7.de* *Rat* rhus-t k* sars *Seneg* k* sil b4a.de spong fd4.de stann k* sulph b4a.de* zinc k*
- **right**: sars
- **left**: alum k*
- **evening**: alum k*
- **night**: *Apis* berb
- **looking** downward agg.: alum
  - **steadily**: *Seneg*
- **rubbing** | **amel.**: am-m h2 spong fd4.de
- ○ - **Canthi**: phos stann h2
  - ○ **Inner** | **right**: phos b4a.de stann b4.de*
  - **Outer** | **left**: fl-ac bg2 phos b4a.de seneg b4.de*
- **Eyebrows** (See FACE - Quivering - eyebrows)
- **Lids**●: aesc k* **Agar** k* alum am-m ambr b7.de* *Anan* vh1 ang b7.de* aran-sc st1 ars b4.de* asaf k* **Bell** k* berb **Calc** k* carb-an carb-v k* *Carbn-s* *Carl* k* *Caust* k* **Cic** *Cocc* k* con croc k* *Crot-c* crot-h k* cupr k* *Cur* dys xyz60 grat hell b7.de* *Iod* k* kali-bi bg2 kreos b7a.de* lyc h2 *Meny* b7.de* merc k* mez b4.de* mur-ac b4a.de *Nat-m* k* nat-p k* nux-v b7.de* *Ol-an* k* op b7.de* par k* petr k* phel *Phos* k* *Plat* k* puls b7.de* *Rat* rhod k* rhus-t k* sabin k* sars k* schin st sel b7a.de sep k* sil k* spong fd4.de stann b4.de* stront-c k* *Sulph* k* *Verat* k* zinc
  - **right**: bell k* nat-p k* nit-ac h2 petr h2* sars k*
  - **left**: ant-c b7.de* carb-v b4.de* lyc h2
  - **chill**; during: calc bg2 *Rhus-t* b7.de*
  - **painful**: bell
  - **reading** by candlelight: berb
  - ○ **Lower**: *Am-m* b7.de* *Calc* b4a.de cic b7.de* graph b4.de* m-ambo b7.de merc b4.de* seneg b4.de* sep b4.de* sulph b4.de*
    - ⁝ **right**: agar b4.de* canth b7.de*
    - ⁝ **left**: am-m b7.de* colch b7.de* zinc b4.de*

Quivering – Lids: ...
  - **Under** | **painful**: caps hr1
  - **Upper**: ars b4.de* asaf b7.de* bry b7.de* *Calc* b4a.de camph b7.de* chel bg2 con b4.de* croc b7.de* sabin b7.de* stram b7.de* verat b7a.de*
    - ⁝ **right**: alum k* bell k* calc k* colch b7.de* cycl a1 nat-m k* par b7.de* plb b7.de* sacch-a gmj3 sars h2
    - ⁝ **left**: **Arum-t** k* berb k* *Croc* k* jatr-c bg2 mez h2 mur-ac b4.de* rhod b4.de* sacch-a gmj3 stront-c b4.de*
- **Orbits**: alum bg2

READING:
- **agg.**: agar bg2 agn b7.de* alum b4a.de* ang b7.de* apis b7a.de asar b7.de* **Calc** b4.de* canth b7.de* carb-v bg2 *Cic* bg2 cina b7.de* coff b7.de* con b4.de* croc b7.de* *Dros* b7.de* dulc b4.de* *Graph* b4.de* ign bg2 *Ip* b7a.de kali-c b4.de* **Lach** bg2 lil-t bg2 lith-c bg2 lyc b4.de* m-arct b7.de mez bg2 nat-c b4.de* *Nat-m* bg2 nit-ac b4.de* olnd b7.de* petr b4.de* ph-ac bg2 phos b4.de* puls b7.de* rhod b4.de* **Ruta** b7a.de* sars b4.de* seneg b4.de* **Sep** bg2 **Sil** b4.de* sul-ac b4.de* sulph bg2 valer b7.de*
- **light**; by:
  - **artificial**: agn b7a.de *Calc* b4.de* *Caust* b4a.de cina b7.de* kali-c b4a.de *Lyc* b4a.de mang b4.de* mez b4.de* nat-m ptk1 nux-m b7.de* *Ph-ac* b4a.de ruta b7a.de sars b4a.de *Seneg* b4a.de
  - **twilight**: sul-ac b4.de*
- **unaffected** eye agg.; with: kalm bg2
- **writing** agg.; and: chin ptk1 phyt ptk1

REDNESS (See Discoloration - red)

RELAXATION:
- ○ - **Lids**: *Op* b7a.de spig b7.de* *Sulph* b4a.de
  - ○ **Inner** side: nat-ar bg2 rhus-t bg2 thuj bg2

REST:
- **agg.**: mur-ac b4.de*
- **amel.**: *Brom* b4a.de

RESTLESS eyes: *(↗Unsteady)* bell *Chinin-s* k* cupr bg iod bg kali-p lyss ph-ac bg *Stram* k* stry valer *Verat* k*

RETINITIS (See Inflammation - retina)

RIDING a carriage: | **agg.**: nat-m b4.de*

RISING:
- **bed**; from:
  - **after**:
    - ⁝ **agg.**: am-m b7.de* ant-c b7.de* cina b7.de* par b7.de*
    - ⁝ **amel.**: bell b4.de* *Nux-v* b7.de* phos b4.de* *Ran-b* b7.de* rhus-t b7.de*

RISING; sensation of something: am-m b7.de*

ROLLING (See Movement - rolling)

ROOM:
- **agg.**: agn b7.de* am-c b4.de* *Arg-n* bg2 *Asar* b7a.de caust b4.de* croc b7.de* dig b4.de* led b7.de* petr b4.de* phos b4.de* plat b4.de* *Puls* b7.de* ran-b b7.de*
- **amel.**: alum bg2 con b4.de* *Ruta* b7a.de sul-ac b4.de* zinc b4.de*
- **entering** a room; when: *Ran-b* b7.de* sel b7a.de

ROUGH cornea: ferr-p bg2 kali-bi bg2 sil k* tarent bg2
- **sensation** on winking: ail bell

RUBBING:
- **agg.**: apis bg2 ars bg2 borx bg2 carb-an b4.de* caust b4.de* *Con* b4.de* croc bg2 fl-ac bg2 kali-bi bg2 mez bg2 op bg2 puls b7.de* sanic bg2 seneg bg2 sep b4.de* spig b7.de* squil bg2 stann b4.de* stront-c b4.de* sulph bg2
- **amel.**: agar b4.de* agn b7.de* alum b4.de* am-c b4.de* am-m b7.de* *Apis* b7a.de bell b4.de* borx bg2 calc b4.de* canth b7.de* carb-an b4.de* caust b4.de* chin b7.de* cina bg2* croc bg2* guat sp1 laur b7a.de mag-c b4.de* mag-m b4.de* mosch b7a.de nat-c b4.de* nat-s bg2 nux-v b7.de* phos b4.de* plb b7.de* puls bg2* ran-b b7.de* rhus-t b7.de* spig b7.de* staph b7.de* sulph b4.de* zinc b4.de*

RUBBING the eyes: all-c ptk1 gamb ptk1 gymno ptk1 ign ptk1 sanic ptk1 seneg ptk1 squil ptk1
- **desire** to: agar h2 all-c apis ars bg* bamb-a stb2.de• borx carb-ac *Caust* chin-b kr1 cina vml1.nl *Con* *Croc* fl-ac gamb bg gymno k* irid-met srj5• kali-bi kali-c sne kola stb3• limest-b es1• *Mez* morph nat-c nat-p c1* nat-sil fd3.de• olib-sac wmh1 *Op* ozone sde2• plb podo fd3.de• psor al *Puls* pyrid rly4• rat sacch-a fd2.de• sanic bg1* seneg bg1 *Squil* *Sulph* symph c1

Eye

- **desire** to: ...
  - • **children**; in: | **waking**; on: sanic mtf33
- **measles**; during: squil ptk1

○ - **Brain**; complaints of (See HEAD - Brain; complaints of - accompanied - eyes)

RUPTURE: | **Cornea**: *Sep* b4a.de

SAND in eye:
- **agg.**: *Calc* b4a.de hep b4a.de *Sulph* b4a.de*
- **sensation** of (See Pain - sand)

SARCOMA (See Tumors - conjunctiva - sarcoma; Tumors - lids - sarcoma)

SCARLATINA; after: *Apis* b7a.de

SCROFULOUS affections: aeth *Am-br* *Apis* ars k* *Aur* k* aur-s k2 *Bar-c* bg2 bell k* **Calc** k* *Cann-s* cann-xyz bg2 **Caust** k* *Cham* k* chin bg2 *Chinin-ar* cist *Clem* bg2 *Con* k* dig bg2 *Dulc* k* **Euphr** k* ferr k* **Graph** k* *Hep* k* **Ign** bg2 iod bg2 kali-bi bg2 lyc bg2 mag-c k* merc k* nat-m k* *Nux-v* k* petr bg2 *Phos* bg2 **Puls** k* rhus-t k* scroph-xyz c2 sep bg2 **Sulph** k* zinc
- **children**; in: calc-i mtf11

SEASONS:
- **spring** agg. | **Conjunctiva**: cob ptk1 nux-v ptk1

SENSITIVE: apoc vh1 cit-ac rly4• suis-hep rly4• [sol-ecl cky1]
- **accompanied** by | **vertigo** (See VERTIGO - Accompanied - eye - sensitive)
- **brilliant** objects: **Bell** bufo *Canth* **Lyss** *Stram*
- **headache**; during: cina k2
- **heat**: *Apis* *Arg-n* caust clem con *Merc* puls
- **light**; to (See Photophobia)
- **painfully** sensitive (See Pain)

○ - **Conjunctiva**: ser-a-c jl2
- **Eyeballs**: nat-m bg2
- **Lids**: carb-an b4.de* m-arct b7.de merc b4.de*
  - • **right** upper: zinc h2

SEWING agg.: mang ptk1

SHAKING:

○ - **Head** | **agg.**: cham b7.de* com bg2 puls b7.de* spig b7.de*

SHINING eyes (See Brilliant; Glassy)

SHIVERING; during: | **agg.**: sabad b7.de

SHORT; sensation as if too:

○ - **Lids**: *Guaj* b4.de* sep bg2
- **Muscles**: sabin c1

SHRINKING (See Atrophy)

SICKLY look around the eyes: *(↗FACE - Discoloration - bluish - eyes - around; FACE - Expression - sickly)* **Cina** k* guare vanil fd5.de

SITTING:
- **agg.**: *Mur-ac* b4a.de *Nat-c* b4.de* phos b4.de*
- **amel.**: led b7.de*

SLEEP:
- **after** | **agg.**: ambr b7.de* cham b7.de* chin b7.de* rheum b7.de* verat b7.de*
- **before** falling asleep | **agg.**: rheum b7.de*
- **during** | **agg.**: apis bg2 *Bell* b4a.de bry b7a.de chin b7.de* ferr b7.de* hell b7.de* ign b7.de* ip b7.de* ol-an bg2 *Op* b7.de* ph-ac b4a.de puls b7.de* rheum b7.de* *Samb* b7.de* stram b7.de* sulph b4a.de verat b7.de*

SLEEPINESS agg.: *Con* b4a.de hep b4a.de *Rhod* b4a.de

SLEEPY feeling of eyes: acon b7a.de *Ant-t* b7a.de asaf b7a.de borx b4a.de* euphr b7.de* ferr b7.de* *Gels* bg2 malar jl2 phos h2 plb b7a.de staph b7.de* thuj h1* *Viol-o* b7a.de *Viol-t* b7a.de

SMALLER; sensation as if: alum st bell bg2* bry b7a.de* calc b4a.de croc b7.de* grat bg2 kreos b7a.de* lach bg* lappa bg2 merc-c b4a.de* merl st nat-m b4a.de* phos hr1 rhod bg sep bg* squil bg2*
- **right**: sep bg2
- **left**: nat-m bg2 rhod bg2

SMOKE agg.: *Euphr* b7a.de

SMOKE; sensation of: croc ptk1

SNEEZING:
- **agg.**: sabad bg2
- **amel.**: lil-t ptk1

SNOW; ailments from exposure to: acon bro1* cic bro1* symph fd3.de•

SPARKLING (See Brilliant)

SPARKS on the lids; sensation of many burning: sulph h2

SPASMODIC (See Movement - convulsive)

SPASMS: ambr bg2 ang bg2 bell bg2 brom bg2 bufo bg2 cann-xyz bg2 *Cham* bg2 cocc bg2 croc bg2 **Hep** bg2 **Hyos** bg2 **Merc** bg2 *Nat-m* bg2 ruta bg2 *Sil* bg2 *Staph* bg2 viol-o ptk1

○ - **Ciliary** muscles: agar k* *Arg-n* aur aur-m caust cic bro1 esin c2* gels hyosin c2 ip bro1 *Jab* k* lil-t bro1 *Morph* nat-m nit-ac *Nux-v* phys k* pilo bro1 puls *Ruta* spig stry bro1 sulph tab
- **Eyebrows**: agar bg2 am b7.de* asaf b7.de* cina tl1 hell b7.de*
- **Eyes**: ambr b7.de* ang b7.de* bell b4a.de* *Brom* b4a.de cann-s b7.de* rhus-t b7a.de sil h2 *Verb* b7.de*
- **Lids**: agar k* alum k* ambr b7.de* ang b7.de* ars b4a.de* atro bro1 *Bell* k* *Calc* k* calc-p k* camph cann-s b7a.de *Cham* b7a.de* chel c1 chinin-ar cic bro1 *Cocc* bg2 *Cod* bro1 con b4a.de croc k* *Cupr* der vml3• esin bro1 *Euphr* k* gels bro1 guaj bro1 **Hep** b4a.de* hyos b7.de* hyper bg1 ign b7a.de* *Ip* bg2 jab mtf11 lob-p bro1 *Mag-p* k* meny b7.de* *Merc* bg2 *Merc-c* k* nat-c k2 *Nat-m* k* nicot bro1 nit-ac b4a.de *Nux-v* k* petr b4a.de phys bro1 plat *Plb* positr nl2• *Puls* k* rheum b7a.de rhod b4.de* *Rhus-t* b7a.de ruta k* seneg b4.de* sep k* sil k* *Staph* bg2 stry bro1 sul-ac bro1 vanil fd5.de verat b7a.de verb b7.de* *Viol-o* b7.de*
  - • **right**: crot-t bg2
  - • **left**: positr nl2•
  - • **night**: alum croc *Merc-c*

○ • **Lower**: ruta b7.de* vanil fd5.de
  - • **Upper**: *Stram* b7a.de
    - ⁝ **right**: agar b4.de*
- **Orbicularis** palpebrarum: chinin-ar der vml3• *Mez* verat c2
- **Orbits**: *Plat* b4a.de

○ • **Margins**: plat bg2
- **Retina** | **Arteries**: nux-v bro1

SPECTACLES; wearing: | **agg.**: borx b4a.de

SPOTS, specks, etc.: *(↗Opacity - cornea)*

○ - **Cornea**; on: *(↗Opacity - cornea)* agar alumn ant-s-aur c1* **Apis** k* arg-n bg2 *Ars* k* ars-s-f k2 *Aur* k* aur-s k2 bar-c bell k* *Cadm-s* **Calc** k* *Calc-f* k* *Calc-p* calc-sil k2 cann-s k* *Caust* k* *Chel* k* cina k* *Clem* hr1 coch c2 *Colch* **Con** k* cupr *Euphr* k* *Form* graph bg2 *Hep* k* hydr bg2 kali-ar kali-bi bg2 *Kali-c* kali-s kali-sil k2 lach bg2 lyc k* mag-c b4a.de* *Merc* k* *Nat-m* k* *Nit-ac* k* nux-v k* phos psor *Puls* k* rhus-t *Ruta* k* *Seneg* k* sep k* *Sil* k* spig bg2 spong *Sulph* k* *Syph* tarax b7a.de thuj zinc bg2
  - • **bluish**: *Colch*
  - • **brown**: agar kali-bi bg1 thuj hr1
  - • **humid** spots, painful if perspiration touches them | **Outer** canthi; in: *Ant-c*
  - • **scars**: *Apis* *Ars* cadm-s *Con* euphr kali-chl *Merc* *Sil*
  - • **white** spots | **Canthi**; in: colch
  - • **yellow** spots:
    - ⁝ **White** of eyes; in: agar chel tl1 ph-ac spig gk
      - : **marked** by a network of blood vessels on cornea: **Aur** k*
- **Sclera**; on | **brown**: kali-bi bg2

SQUEEZING the eyes: | **must** squeeze the eyes: aeth bg2 aloe bg2 cocc bg2 gels bg2

SQUINT (See Paralysis - eyeballs - muscles; Strabismus)

STAPHYLOMA: *Alumn* k* *Apis* k* *Aur-m* k* bar-m k* calen hr1 *Caust* k* *Chel* k* colch mtf11 *Euph* ptk1 *Euphr* k* *Hep* k* ilx-a c1* *Lyc* k* *Nit-ac* k* puls ptk1 sil k* *Thuj* k*
- **inflammation**; after suppurative: *Apis* bro1 euphr bro1 ilx-a bro1 phys bro1

STARING: *(↗MIND - Insanity - staring; MIND - Staring)* *Acon* k* *Aeth* k* *Agar* k* alum bg2 am-c k* *Anac* k* ang b2.de* *Ant-t* k* *Arn* k* *Ars* k* *Ars-i* *Art-v* k* asar k* atra-r bnm3• atro k* aur k* aur-ar k2 bar-c bg2 **Bell** k* ben-n borx k* *Bov* k* brom k* bry k* *Calc* k* *Camph* k* cann-i k* *Canth* k* carb-ac k* carb-v *Carbn-s* cass a1 caust k* *Cham* k* chin k* *Chinin-s* *Chlor* k* *Cic* k* cic-m a1 cina k* clem k* coc-c bg2 coca *Cocc* k* *Colch* k* con b2.de* *Croc* k* crot-c k* *Cupr* k* dig b2.de* dor k* eup-per k* gels k* *Glon* k* grat k* (non:guaj k*) guar a1* *Hell* k* *Hep* k* hipp a1 hydr-ac k* hydrog srj2• **Hyos** k* *Hyper* k* *Ign* k* **Iod** k* ip k* ix bnm8• jab br1 kali-ar k* kali-br k* kali-c k* *Kali-cy* k* *Kali-i* k* kali-n k* kali-p k* kali-sil k2 kalm k* kola stb3• *Kreos* k* lac-loxod-a hrn2• lach k* lachn k* *Laur* k* **Lyc** k* lyss k* m-ambo b2.de* m-arct b2.de* mag-p tl1 manc k* med **Merc** k* merc-c k* *Merc-cy* a1* *Mez* k* morph k* mosch k* mur-ac k* *Naja* k* nat-ar nat-c k* nat-m bg2 nat-p nitro-o a1 *Nux-m* k* *Nux-v* k* oena k* olnd k* **Op** k* ozone sde2• paeon k* petr k* *Ph-ac* k* phos k* *Phyt* k* pisc bro1 plat k* plb k* plb-c a4 plb-chr a1 positr nl2• puls k* ran-b rhus-t k* ribo rly4• ruta k* sang k* sangin-t c1 santin **Sec** k* seneg k* sep b2.de* sil k* sol-ni spig b2.de* *Spong* k* *Squil* k* **Stram** k* *Stry* k* sul-ac sul-i k2 sulph k* tab k* tarent k* ter k* *Verat* k* verat-v hr1* vip k* visc sp1 *Zinc* k* zinc-p k2

- **morning** | **open** air; in: nux-v k*
- **evening**: chin k*
  - **bed** agg.; in: sil k*
  - **convulsions**; during: ars k*
  - **waking**; on: *Ip* k*
- **night**: corn k* eup-pur
  - **sleep** agg.; during: ant-t k* corn k* op k*
- **accompanied** by:
  - **sleeplessness**: eup-pur
  - **stupor**: ars k* *Hell*
- **chill**; during: *Acon* b7.de* bell bg2 *Calc* **Cic** bg2 hyos bg2 lach bg2
- **cold** agg.; after becoming: cic k*
- **convulsions**; during: *(↗GENERALS - Convulsions - epileptic - during - pupils - dilated)* aeth bro1* ign k2 *Kali-br* hr1
- **fever**; during: *Op* b7a.de
- **frightened**; as if: zinc ptk1
- **headache**; during: **Bell** k* **Glon** k* *Spig* bg **Stram** k*
- **involuntary**: cic a1
- **menses**; before: puls k*
- **music**, on listening to: tarent k*
- **object**, the head inclines forward; at: cic c1
- **pain**:
  - **forehead**, with pain in: spig
  - **occiput**; in: *Carb-v*
- **persons** who talk to him; to: merc-c ptk1
- **point**; at one: bov ptk1 *Cic* b7.de* *Cocc* b7.de* *Hell* b7a.de kali-c b4a.de ruta b7.de* seneg b4a.de squil b7.de* **Stram** b7.de* *Sulph* b4a.de verat b7a.de
- **sensation** as if: med k* positr nl2•
- **sleep**; during: ant-t b7a.de
- **stupid**: hell ptk1
- **sunstroke**: *Glon* k*
- **thoughtless**: guaj ptk1
- **unconsciousness**: aeth hr1 caust k* cic a1* hyos sfa*
- **vacantly**: bov ptk1
- **vertigo**; during: hep h2 mosch b7a.de
- **waking**; on: *Arn* bell k* ip k* stram *Zinc* k*
  - **suddenly**: sec k* *Zinc*
- **walking** in open air agg.; after: alum h2
- **wildly**: petr a1

STEPPING HARD agg.: hep b4a.de*

STICKY lids (See Agglutinated)

STIFFNESS: *(↗Pain)* asar bro1 aur bro1 *Kalm* bro1 med bro1 nat-ar bro1 rhus-t bro1

○ - **Eyeballs**: agar alum bg ars k* bar-c bg bar-m k* *Bell* bg calc calc-p camph caust k* cham bg chin bg cic bg *Cocc* bg crot-c *Cupr* bg cupr-s k* hep hyos bg *Ign* bg **Kalm** k* lach bg laur bg merc bg mosch bg *Nat-ar* **Nat-m** k* nux-v bg onos k* op bg phos k* rhus-t bg ruta mrr1 *Sec* bg seneg sil bg1 spig k* *Stram* bg stry k* *Verat* bg

Stiffness: ...

- **Lids**: **Apis** k* ars bg2 arum-d k* camph carb-v bg2 caust bro1 dios bg2 gels k* **Kalm** k* lach bg2 meny b7.de* nat-ar nat-m ptk1 *Nux-m* k* onos ptk1 plb bg2 rat ptk1 *Rhus-t* k* ruta mrr1 *Sep (non:*spig b7.de*) spig-m a1* sulph bg2 *Verat* k*
  - **spasmodic**: meny bg2
  - ○ **Margins** of: *Ars* b4a.de sulph b4a.de
  - **Upper**: **Rhus-t** b7.de* *Spig* b7.de* verat b7.de*
- **Muscles** about the eyes: agar ery-a a1 **Kalm** k* *Nat-m* nux-v a1 ruta mrr1

STONES, as if full of little: kali-n h2* lac-d bg1

- **headache**; during: lac-d ptk1

STOOL agg.: nat-c ptk1

STOOPING:

- **agg.**: *Brom* b4a.de coloc bg2 com bg2 dros b7.de* ip bg2 seneg b4.de* valer b7.de*
- **amel.**: acon bg2

STRABISMUS: *(↗Paralysis - eyeballs - muscles)* acon bg2 aeth bg2 agar k* *Alum* k* alumn k* androc srj1*• ant-t k* **Apis** k* apoc bro1 *Arg-n* k* arn bg2* ars k* **Bell** k* ben-d bro1 ben-n k* bufo k* *Calc* k* calc-p k* cann-i k* cann-s bg cann-xyz bg2 *Canth* k* carb-an c2 caust bg2* *Chel* k* *Chinin-s* **Cic** k* *Cina* k* *Con* k* cupr bg2* cupr-act c2* **Cycl** k* *Dig* hr1 ery-a c2 esin mfj *Gels* k* *Hell* k* *Hyos* k* jab k* kali-bi ptk1 *Kali-br* k* *Kali-i* k* kali-p k* lac-loxod-a hrn2• *Lyc* lyss k* *Mag-p* k* meny k* *Merc* k* *Merc-c* k* morph k* nat-ar nat-c b4a.de *Nat-m* k* nat-p k* nat-sal a1 *Nux-v* k* olnd c2 op k* oxyurn-sc mcp1• phys bg2 pin-s c2 plb k* podo c2* psor puls k* rhus-t bg2 ruta k2 *Santin* bro1 sapin c2 scor a1* sec b7.de* **Seneg** mfj sil bg2 *Spig* k* staph mrr1 *Stram* k* sulph k* syph c2* *Tab* k* tanac a1 thal-xyz srj8• thuj b4a.de* tub k* verat k* verat-v hr1 *Zinc* k* [arg-met stj1]

- **right** turned in: alumn k*
- **left** turned in: *Calc* *Cycl* k*
- **night**: spig vh spig-m vh teucr vh
- **accompanied** by:
  - **menses** | **irregular**: cycl ptk1
  - **worms**; complaints of: bell bro1 cina bg2* cycl bro1 hyos bro1 merc bro1 *Santin* bro1 spig bro1
  - ○ **Brain**; complaints of (See HEAD - Brain; complaints of - accompanied - strabismus)
  - **Meninges**; inflammation of (See HEAD - Inflammation - meninges - accompanied - strabismus)
- **brain** disease:
  - **after**: kali-p ptk1*
  - **during** (See HEAD - Brain; complaints of - accompanied - strabismus)
- **congenital**: *Syph* mrr1
- **convergent**: alum bg2* art-v bg2* calc b1* *Camph* hr1 carb-v bg chel hr1 **Cic** k* cina k* **Cycl** k* jab k* lil-t k2 *Lyc* hr1 mag-p nux-v k* op hr1 spig hr1* syph hr1*
- **convulsions**:
  - **after**: cycl hr1*
  - **during**: stram ptk1
- **dentition**; during: alum bg3* gels mtf11 hell mtf11 stram mtf11 tub mtf11
- **diarrhea**; from suppressed: podo k2 stram ptk1
- **divergent**●: *Agar* k* alum k* *Camph* hr1 *Coloc* k* *Con* k* dig bg2 graph k* hyos bg2* *Jab* k* lil-t merc-i-f morph a1* morph-s hr1 **NAT-M** k ●* nat-sal c2* oxyurn-sc mcp1• phos k* rhod ruta seneg spig vml sulph hr1 syph mtf33 tab bg2 zinc hr1 [arg-met stj1]
- **emotions** agg.: *Cic* *Nux-m* stram
- **epilepsy**, during paroxysms: bell bro1 *Cic* bro1 hyos bro1 tarent gt1
- **fear**; from: *Cic* *Nux-m* stram k*
  - **night** (See MIND - Fear - terror - night - followed - children)
- **fever**; during: *Apis* b7a.de*
- **injuries**; after: cic k2*
- **measles**; after: cycl hr1
- **one** eye amel; looking with: kali-bi ptk1
- **operation**; after: jab ptk1
- **painless**: buth-a sp1
- **periodical**: chin *Chinin-s* **Cic** jab *Nux-v* thuj bg1

Eye

- **periodical**: ...
  - **day** | **alternate**: *Chinin-s* k*
  - **injuries**; after: cic br1
- **reading** agg.: tab
- **sensation** of: bell bg2 calc ptk1 *Con* bg2 meny h1* nat-m bg2 op bg2 podo bg2 puls b7.de*
- **touch** agg.: cic k2
- **upward**: benz-ac mtf11 jab mtf11

STRAINED: *(↗Pain - exertion of the eyes - agg.)* bell bg2 phys mrr1 **Ruta** br1* seneg mrr1 tere-la rly4• [sol-ecl cky1]
- **accompanied** by | **Head**; complaints of (See HEAD - Eyes - exertion)
- **sewing**; from: arg-n br1
- **warm** room agg.: arg-n br1

STRICTURE of lachrymal duct: **Abrot** vn1.fr *Arg-met* k* calc k* euphr *Fl-ac* graph hep k* med merc-d ptk1 **Nat-m** k •* **Puls** k •* **Rhus-t** k • **SIL** k •* thiosin bc
- **children**; in: nat-m mtf33 sil mtf33
  - **newborns**: **Sil** mrr1
- **cold**; after exposure to: calc bro1

STRING: | **drawing** backwards; sensation of a string (See Pain - drawing - string)

STYES: adeps-s mtf11 aegle-m zzc1• agar bro1 allox tpw4* alum k* alum-p k2 alum-sil k2 am-c k* ambr b7.de* ant-t st1 *Apis* k* ars b4a.de* *Aur* k* aur-m-n bro1 bar-c k2 bar-ox-suc mtf11 bor-ac mtf11 bry k* cain calc b4a.de calc-f bg2* *Calc-pic* bro1 **Carbn-s** carc tpw2* caust k* *Chel* k* coch c1 colch k* **Con** k* cortiso sp1 cupr cypr k* *Dig* b4.de* dulc fd4.de dys pte1• elaps *Euphr* b7a.de fago c2 *Ferr* k* ferr-p k* gaert pte1• **Graph** k* hep k* *Jug-c* k* *Jug-r* kali-br ctd kali-p kola stb3• kreos bg2* lac-f c1* lach bg2 lap-a c1 lappa c1* **Lyc** k* m-aust k* mand sp1 med st1 meny k* *Merc* k* morg-g pte1• morg-p pte1• nat-m k* osteo-a jl2 petr b4a.de *Ph-ac* k* phos k* pic-ac c2 *Psor* k* **Puls** k* *Rhus-t* k* sacch-l c2 sanguis-s hrn2• seneg k* **Sep** k* *Sil* k* sol-o c2 stann k* **Staph** k* staphycoc mtf11 sulfa sp1 sulfonam ks2 **Sulph** k* *Thuj* k* tub al uran-n c2* valer k* viol-o c1* zinc bg* ziz c2
- **right** eye: am-c k* (non:cupr k*) cypr k* dulc fd4.de ferr-p k* musca-d szs1 *Nat-m* k* tub al*
- **left** eye: *Bar-c* k* colch k* elaps hydr k* *Hyper* k* kola stb3• nept-m lsd2.fr sanguis-s hrn2• staph k* sulph bg1
- **accompanied** by:
  - **red** discoloration of eyes: sep ptk1
  - ○ **Face**; swelling of: kola stb3•
- **appearing** gradually (= slowly): penic mtf11
- **chronic**: lappa mtf11 psor jl2 pyrog jl2
- **closing** the eyes agg.: allox tpw4
- **crops**: anthraci br1 lappa br1*
- **eating** fat, greasy, rich food or pork: puls al staph al
- **induration** from: *Calc* k* *Con* k* **Sep** *Sil* **Staph** k* *Thuj*
- **infected**: pyrog jl2
- **light**; from:
  - **agg.**: allox tpw4
  - **artificial** light | **agg.**: allox tpw4
- **motion** agg.: allox tpw4
- **recurrent**• (See GENERALS - History - eyes - recurrent styes)
- **rubbing** | **amel.**: allox tpw4
- ○ **Canthi**:
  - ○ **Inner**: aur-ar k2 bar-c k* **Nat-m** k • stann k* sulph b4.de*
    - **right**: nat-m b4.de*
    - **toward**: kali-c *Lach* *Lyc* k* **Nat-m** k • petr puls sil
  - **Outer**: aur-s
    - **sensation** of a stye in left: abies-c c1
- **Lid**: carc mlr1• cortiso tpw7 lyc tl1 pyrog jl2 staphycoc jl2
  - **left**: hydroph rsj6•
  - ○ **Lower**: *Apis* b7a.de *Bry* b7a.de *Colch* cypr k* *Dig* b4a.de elaps *Ferr* b7a.de ferr-p *Graph* *Hyper* kali-p kola stb3• ozone sde2• *Phos* puls *Rhus-t* k* seneg *Sep* b4a.de
    - **right**: ferr-p bg2 flor-p rsj3•

Styes – Lid – Lower: ...
- **left**: caust bg2 glycyr-g cte1• sulfa sp1 sulph bg2
- **Upper**: alum b4.de* am-c bell caust b4.de* dulc fd4.de ferr k* merc k* petr-ra shn4• *Ph-ac* k* **Puls** k* pyrog al staph sulph b4.de*
  - **right**: bell bg2 cassia-s ccrh1•
  - **left**: cassia-s ccrh1• osteo-a jl2

SUFFUSED (See Lachrymation)

SUGGILLATIONS (See Ecchymosis)

SUNKEN: *Abrot* bg2* acet-ac k* *Aeth* agar agar-cps a1 am-c am-caust a1* ambr b2.de* ammc a1 amyg a1 *Anac* k* ant-c k* **Ant-t** k* ap-g bro1 arg-n k* *Arn* k* *Ars* k* ars-h vh ars-i ars-s-f k2 aster astra-m br1 bar-m k* bell k* *Berb* k* bov bg2 *Bufo* buth-a sp1 cadm-s calc k* calc-i k2 *Camph* k* *Canth* k* *Carb-v* *Carbn-s* *Cedr* cent a1 chel k* **Chin** k* chinin-ar chinin-s chlor k* chr-ac a1 cic k* cimic **Cina** k* clerod-i bnj1 coc-c k* coca *Cocc* b7a.de *Colch* *Coloc* k* crot-h k* *Cupr* k* *Cur* *Cycl* k* cyt-l a1 *Dros* k* ferr k* ferr-ar ferr-p *Glon* k* gran a1* *Graph* haem k* hell k* hyos b2.de* ign bg2 iod k* ip bro1 *Iris* k* kali-ar kali-bi bg2 *Kali-br* *Kali-c* k* *Kali-i* kali-p *Kreos* lach k* laur b7.de lith-c *Lyc* k* *Merc* k* merc-c k* merc-cy ptk1 merc-n c1 morph k* naja nat-c bro1 nit-ac k* nux-v k* oena k* olnd k* *Op* k* ox-ac petr k* *Ph-ac* k* *Phos* k* phyt k* *Plat* k* plb plumbg a1 podo k* psor jl2 **Puls** k* pycnop-sa mrz1 raph k* rhus-t bg2 rob k* sacch-a fd2.de* sang k* **Sec** k* sep k* sil mtf33 **Spig** bg2* *Spong* k* *Stann* k* *Staph* k* stram stront-c bg2 stry sul-i k2 *Sulph* k* syph jl2 tab k* ter k* teucr k* thuj til k* upa k* valer bg2 *Verat* k* vip k* visc c1* zinc k* zinc-m a1 zinc-p k2 [spect dfg1]
- **morning**: elaps zinc
- **forenoon**: lyc k* ox-ac k*
- **afternoon**: iod k*
- **air** agg.; in open: kali-c h2
- **coma**; with (See MIND - Coma - eyes - sunken)
- **menses** | **before** | **agg.**: cycl bro1 ip bro1 verat bro1
  - **during** | **agg.**: *Cedr* k* cycl bro1 ip bro1 verat bro1
- **sensation**: *(↗Deep - as)* ambr bg2* ap-g bg1* aur bg2* chin bg2* cinnb bg2* iod bg2 lac-f bg1 led bg1 limest-b es1• lyc bg2* spig gk teucr bg2* zinc bg2* [spect dfg1]
- **stool** agg.; during: *Ars* b4a.de
- ○ **Cornea**: aeth c1*

SUNSET; at (See Evening - sunset)

SUPPRESSION:
- **bloody** discharges agg.; of: bell bg2 calc bg2 lyc bg2 nux-v bg2 phos bg2 puls bg2 sep bg2 sulph bg2
- **coryza** agg.; of: **Bell** bg2 cham bg2 *Euphr* bg2 hep bg2 *Ign* bg2 *Lach* bg2 merc bg2 *Nux-v* bg2 **Puls** bg2 sulph bg2

SUPPURATION: *Aur* b4a.de bell bg2 brom bg2 bry bg2 **Caust** b4.de* **Euphr** bg2 graph bg2 hep bg2 kali-bi bg2 kali-c b4.de* *Kreos* bg2 merc bg2 *Nit-ac* b4.de* plat b4.de* puls bg2 sulph bg2
- ○ **Canthi**: kali-c b4.de* zinc b4a.de
  - ○ **Outer**: lyc b4.de*
- **Lids**: *Am-c* b4a.de ign b7.de* rhus-t b7.de* ruta b7.de* staph b7.de* tarax b7.de*

SWALLOWING agg.: arg-n bg2* tarent ptk1

SWELLING: achy-a bnj1 *Acon* k* aids nl2• alum-p k2 **Anac** **Apis** k* *Ars* k* atra-r bnm3• atro aur-i k2 bapt bar-c k* bell b4a.de* bros-gau mrc1 *Bry* k* bufo cann-i canth b7a.de carb-v k* card-m cardios-h rly4• *Cedr* *Cham* **Chlol** chord-umb rly4• cob ptm1• coloc croc desm-g bnj1 dulc ery-a k* fago ferr k* ferr-ar fum rly1*• gels **Guaj** k* *Hep* k* hura *Ign* k* *Ip* jug-c kali-bi bg2 *Kali-c* k* kali-i kali-p kali-s fd4.de lach led b7.de* lyc *Mag-c* k* mand rsj7• mang k* medus c1* merc mur-ac b4a.de *Nat-ar* nat-s k2 nat-sil fd3.de• *Nit-ac* *Nux-v* k* oena ol-j par petr-ra shn4• phos k* phys pieri-b mlk9.de pitu-gl skp7• plac-s rly4• plb k* psor puls pyrog raph **Rhus-t** k* rumx bg ruta b7.de* sars **Sep** k* spig spong fd4.de *Stram* k* stry sulph b4.de* thuj b4a.de til tritic-vg fd5.de vanil fd5.de vesp k*
- **right**: bar-ox-suc rly4• dulc fd4.de ephe-si hsj1• lac-h sk4• *Lyc* k* symph fd3.de•
- **left**: aids nl2• ars bg2 carb-v h2 *Coloc* k* dulc fd4.de trios rsj11•
- **morning**: bar-c bry **Cham** cocc *Crot-h* cupr dulc fd4.de flav jl2 ignis-alc es2• kali-s fd4.de myric naja nat-sil fd3.de• rumx ptk1 ruta fd4.de sarr **Sep** sil spong fd4.de **Sulph** tub c1 (non:uran-met k) uran-n vanil fd5.de
  - **headache**; after: (non:coc-c kl) cocc h1*

- **morning**: ...
  - • **waking**; on: aids nl2• chel dulc fd4.de flav jl2 kali-bi mag-c nat-ar nicc vanil fd5.de
- **forenoon**: bry *Euphr* myric ruta fd4.de
- **evening**: *Hep* sep
- **night**: *Hep* symph fd3.de•
- **accompanied** by:
  - • **vertigo**: pitu-gl skp7•
  - • **Head**:
    - ⁝ **pain**: pitu-gl skp7• sep h2
- **edematous**: kali-i ptk1 lat-m bnm6• medus br1

○ • **Retina**: apis ptk1 kali-i ptk1

- **sensation** of: acon b7.de* ant-t bg2* apis b7a.de arg-n bg2* bapt bar-ox-suc rly4• bell bg2* calc calc-p cann-i caust chel bg2* choc srj3• coloc bg2* com ptk1 con rb2 croc b7.de* digin rb2 dulc fd4.de **Guaj** k* ham ip b7.de* lach bg2 mag-c k* mez ptk1 nat-ar *Nat-m* ptk1 nux-m b7.de* olib-sac wmh1 op bg2* par b7.de* phos rb2 phys prun ptk1 *Rhus-t* k* rumx ptk1 sarr seneg ptk1 sol rb2 spig b7a.de* spong ptk1 sulph bg2 symph fd3.de• thlas rb2 thuj k* tritic-vg fd5.de vanil fd5.de [buteo-j sej6]
  - • **right** eye: agar bg2 rhus-t bg2

○ • **Eyeballs**: sulph bg2

  - • **Lids**: acon b7.de* am-br bro1 am-c vh1 apis b7a.de* arg-n bro1 *Ars* bro1 ars-met bro1 arum-t rb2 aur-m bro1 bell bro1 calc bro1 carbn-s rb2 *Caust* k* chel chin bg1 cimic cinnb bg2 coc-c *Croc* k* *Cycl* k* dig bro1 euph-l bro1 euphr bro1* fago rb2 graph bro1 guaj hep bro1 kali-bi bg2 *Kali-c* bro1 kali-i bro1 lact rb2 mag-m h2 meny b7.de* merc-c bro1 nat-ar bro1 nat-c bro1 phos bro1 psor puls bro1 rhus-t b7.de* rhus-v bro1 sabad bro1 sacch-l rb2 sep bro1 stram rb2 sumb rb2 tarax k* *Thuj* valer b7.de*
    - ⁝ **Lower**: arum-t rb2 coloc rb2 nat-ar rb2
    - ⁝ **Upper**: viol-o b7.de

○ - **Above** the eyes (See FACE - Swelling - eyes - above)

- **Around** the eyes (See FACE - Swelling - eyes - around)
- **Canthi**: agar k* *Arg-n* bro1 aur bell bry **Calc** k* cinnb bro1 dulc fd4.de graph bro1 merc petr sars k* sil k* stann zinc bro1
  - • **sensation** of: rhus-t b7.de*

○ • **Inner**: aids nl2• arg-n br1 bell b4.de* calc-p dulc fd4.de kali-c ptk1* merc b4.de* petr puls ptk1 sars sep

  - ⁝ **right**: petr b4.de* sars b4.de* *Sil* b4a.de
  - • **Outer**: *Merc* b4a.de ran-b b7.de*
- **Caruncles**; lachrymal: agar **Arg-n** k* cann-i *Kali-c* *Petr* b4a.de *Sil* b4a.de zinc
  - • **left**: agar b4.de* nat-m bg2 sil bg2
- **Conjunctiva**: antip vh1 *Apis* k* *Arg-n* k* *Ars* bell bry k* cadm-s cedr cham *Chel* chlol euph *Graph* *Ip* kali-c mrr1 led medul-os-si rly4• mez k2 nat-ar *Nat-c* nat-m nux-v *Rhus-t* hr1* sep
  - • **allergic**: kali-c mrr1
  - • **baglike**: apis ptk1 ars ptk1
  - • **dermoid**: *Calc* k* *Nat-c* k* *Nat-m* k* nit-ac ptk1 thuj

○ • **Gland**: *Agar* anan *Graph* kali-i **Sil**

  - • **Lachrymal** ducts: apis bell brom *Calc* graph bro1 *Nat-m* **Petr** *Sil* k*
  - • **Lachrymal** sacs: nat-c h2 nat-m h2 **Puls** **Sil**
- **Eyebrows**: apis b7a.de kali-c b4.de*
- **Lachrymal** glands: carb-an b4a.de *Nat-m* b4a.de phos b4a.de *Sil* b4a.de
  - • **right**: sil tl1
  - • **accompanied** by | **lachrymation**: brom mtf33
- **Lens**: colch mtf11
- **Lids**: absin *Acon* k* agar h2* *All-c* alum alum-sil k2 am-br vh1 anac k* androc srj1• ant-c b7a.de antip vh1 **Apis** k* aran-sc vh1 *Arg-met* k* **Arg-n** k* arge-pl rwt5• arn k* **Ars** k* ars-i ars-s-f k2 aur k* aur-ar k2 aur-s k2 bamb-a stb2.de• bar-c k* bar-i k2 *Bar-m* bar-s k2 *Bell* k* berb bry k* cadm-s c1 *Calc* k* calc-i k2 calc-sil k2 *Carbn-s* card-m *Carl* carneg-g rwt1• *Caust* k* cham k* chin bg2* *Chinin-s* chord-umb rly4• *Cic* bg2 cinnb cob-n sp1 cocc b7.de* colch k* com *Con* k* *Crot-t* k* cupr *Cycl* k* *Dig* k* dream-p sdj1• dulc fd4.de euph k* **Euphr** k* *Ferr* k* *Ferr-ar* *Ferr-i* *Ferr-p* gels *Graph* k* *Guaj* bg2 ham hell b7.de* *Hep* k* hip-ac sp1 hydro-v a1 hyos k* ign k* iod k* *Ip* *Kali-ar* *Kali-bi* k* *Kali-c* k* **Kali-i** k* kali-p kali-s kali-sil k2 kola stb3• **Kreos** k* lac-leo hrn2• lach lat-m bnm6• loxo-lae bnm12• *Lyc* k* mag-c b4.de* mag-m manc mang k*

- **Lids**: ...

med k2* **Merc** k* merc-c merc-i-f mez *Moni* rfm1• *Mur-ac* k* naja bg2 **Nat-ar** **Nat-c** k* *Nat-m* nat-p nat-s nat-sil fd3.de• **Nit-ac** k* nux-m *Nux-v* k* oci-sa sk4• *Olnd* b7a.de op petr petr-ra shn4• ph-ac bg2 *Phos* k* phys bg2 physala-p bnm7• *Phyt* k* plac-s rly4• plb plut-n srj7• *Psor* *Puls* k* rheum h* rhod b4.de* **Rhus-t** k* **Rhus-v** ruta k* *Sanic* sars bg2 sec k* *Seneg* k* *Sep* k* sil spig b7a.de spong k* squil k* stram k* sul-ac sul-i k2 sulfa sp1 *Sulph* k* syph k* *Tell* ter *Thuj* k* tritic-vg fd5.de tub c1* urt-u v-a-b jl2 valer k* vario jl2 verat vesp vip zinc-p k2

- • **right**: cassia-s ccrh1• caust b4.de* lach bg2 lyc b4.de* mand rsj7• phos b4.de*
- • **left**: agar b4.de* ars bg2 carb-v b4.de* mez bg2 phos b4.de* rhus-t bg2 sel rsj9• sulfa sp1
- • **morning**: arge-pl rwt5• bamb-a stb2.de• bar-c h2 cham h1 crot-h hr1 dulc fd4.de ham fd3.de• irid-met srj5• kali-s fd4.de petr-ra shn4• podo fd3.de• ruta fd4.de sep h2 tritic-vg fd5.de
  - ⁝ **waking**; on: cyclosp sa3•
- • **accompanied** by | **coryza**: bamb-a stb2.de•
- • **bite** of dog; after: lyss c1
- • **chill**; during: apis bg2 ferr bg2 *Rhus-t* bg2
- • **dark**: **Rhus-t** bg2
- • **edematous**: am-be mtf11 anac **Apis** k* *Arg-n* *Arn* **Ars** k* ars-i bamb-a stb2.de• bros-gau mrc1 cham tl1 colch *Crot-t* *Cycl* *Ferr* hr1* *Graph* *Iod* k* *Kali-ar* *Kali-bi* k* **Kali-c** *Kali-i* kali-p kola stb3• lat-m bnm6• medus br1 *Merc-c* *Nat-ar* *Phos* *Phyt* k* *Psor* puls raph **Rhus-t** **Tell** urt-u vesp zinc
  - ⁝ **sack**-shaped: kali-c mtf11
- • **hard** and red: acon thuj
- • **menses** | **during** | **agg.**: apis cycl kali-c
  - ⁝ **suppressed** menses; from: acon arg-n *Ars* *Calc* cycl *Kali-c* merc nux-v rhus-t sulph
- • **purple** color: phyt
- • **sensation** of (See sensation - lids)
- • **waking**; on: tub jl2
- • **watery**, white: *Iod*

○ • **Inner** side: *Rhus-t* b7a.de thuj b4a.de

- • **Lower**: apis bro1* arg-met b7.de* arg-n mtf33 arge-pl rwt5• arn ptk1 *Ars* b4.de* aur k* bamb-a stb2.de• bell b4.de* bros-gau mrc1 bry b7.de* cain calc h2* **Cham** b7a.de colch b7.de* crot-c *Dig* k* *Euphr* b7a.de **Ferr** b7a.de glon bg2* ham fd3.de• hip-ac sp1 **Kali-ar** k* kali-c mrr1 lach b7.de* m-aust b7.de mag-c b4.de* merc-i-f ptk1 moni rfm1• op k* ozone sde2• petr-ra shn4• ph-ac b4.de* *Phos* k* podo fd3.de• raph rhus-t b7.de* ruta fd4.de sep b4.de* spong fd4.de xero bro1 zinc bg2
  - ⁝ **right**: carb-an bg2 eupi bg2 nat-ar bg2 ven-m rsj12•
  - ⁝ **left**: calc k* colch bg2 lyc bg2 merc k* ruta fd4.de sep bg2
  - ⁝ **morning**: bamb-a stb2.de• calc h2 ozone sde2• podo fd3.de•
  - ⁝ **water** bags; like: apis mtf11
  - ⁝ **Margins** of: puls b7a.de
- • **Margins** of: alum ptk1 arg-met b7.de* arum-t k* calc ptk1 *Chel* coc-c k* *Con* dig hr1* euph bg2 **Euphr** k* *Graph* k* *Hep* k* kali-bi k2 *Kali-c* *Kreos* k* lach bg2 med mtf33 merc ptk1 *Merc-c* nicc bg2 nux-m k* ph-ac *Phos* psor puls k* sulph syph tell ptk1 valer k*
- • **Under** the lids: (*↗FACE - Swelling - eyes - under)* **Apis** **Ars** k* dream-p sdj1• *Hep* **Kali-c** k* med k* merc mtf33 nux-v mtf33 ph-ac h2 **Phos** st puls mtf33 tritic-vg fd5.de
- • **Upper**: acon b7.de* alum b4.de* **Apis** k* arg-met b7.de* arg-n mtf33 *Arn* b7a.de asar b7.de* bamb-a stb2.de• bell b4a.de* bor-ac bg2 bry k* caust b4.de* *Con* k* *Cycl* k* dulc fd4.de germ-met srj5• ham fd3.de• hep b4.de* hydrog srj2• *Ign* k* kali-bi bg2 **Kali-c** k* kali-i kali-s fd4.de kola stb3• lac-leo hrn2• *Med* k* merc b4.de* moni rfm1• nat-ar k2 *Nat-c* k* nat-sil fd3.de• nit-ac b4a.de nux-m bg2* ozone sde2• *Petr* petr-ra shn4• phos b4a.de* plut-n srj7• podo fd3.de• **Puls** b7a.de rhus-t b7a.de* sep b4.de* sil b4.de* spong fd4.de *Squil* k* sulph b4.de* *Syph* k* teucr k* thuj b4.de* zinc h2 [tax jsj7]
  - ⁝ **one** side: *Coli* jl2
  - ⁝ **right**: acon bg2 bry bg2 *Caust* k* cimic bg2 coli jl2 crot-t bg2 dulc fd4.de eupi bg2 kali-bi bg2 kali-c b4.de* lac-h sk4• lac-leo hrn2• naja bg2 nat-c k* nat-sil fd3.de• phos k* rhus-t bg2 sep h2* thuj bg2 vesp bg2*
  - ⁝ **left**: ars bg2 asar k* cain coli jl2 euph bg2 kali-s fd4.de kola stb3• tell

Eye

- **Upper**: ...
  - **morning**: bamb-a stb2.de• dulc fd4.de ozone sde2• spong fd4.de
  - **headache**; during: stront-n vh
  - **sensation** of: viol-o bg2
- **Meibomian** glands: *Aeth* k* bad bro1 borx *Clem* k* *Colch Con* dig bro1 graph bro1 hep k* merc nicc *Phyt* puls bro1 *Rhus-t* hr1* sil *Staph Sulph* thuj
- **Optic** disks: arn mtf ars mtf nat-s mtf perh mtf
  - **accompanied** by | **Optic** nerve; inflammation of (See Inflammation - optic - accompanied - optic)
- **Orbital** arch: apis bg2 merc bg2 phos bg2
  - **right**: cob ptm1•
  - **temporal**: spig h1
- **Retina**: *Apis* bro1 bell bro1 canth bro1 *Kali-i* bro1 phos bro1
- **Under** the eyes (See FACE - Swelling - eyes - under)

SWOLLEN (See Swelling)

SYMPATHETIC OPHTHALMIA (See Inflammation - sympathetic)

SYPHILIS: aur bg2 lyc bg2 *Merc* bg2 *Nit-ac* bg2 phos bg2 thuj bg2

TALKING about complaints agg.: sep bg2

TEARS: (↗*Lachrymation)* acon bg2 all-c bg2 alum bg2 am-c bg2 apis bg2 ars bg2 ars-i bg2 aur bg2 bell bg2 brom bg2 calc bg2 carb-v bg2 caust bg2 cham bg2 chel bg2 chin bg2 clem bg2 com bg2 con bg2 croc bg2 crot-t bg2 cycl bg2 *Euphr* bg2 ferr-p bg2 graph bg2 iod bg2 ip bg2 kali-c bg2 kali-i bg2 kreos bg2 merc-c bg2 mez bg2 nat-m bg2 phel bg2 puls bg2 rhus-t bg2 ruta bg2 sabad bg2 sang bg2 seneg bg2 sep bg2 sil bg2 spig bg2 staph bg2 sulph bg2 thuj bg2 uran-n bg2 verb bg2 zinc-s bg2
- **daytime** | **agglutination** at night; and: ign hr1
- **acrid**: abrom-a ks5 all-s apis bro1 **Ars** k* ars-s-f k2 *Aur* b4a.de bell k* bry k* *Calc* k* *Caust* k* cedr k* clem k* *Colch* k* *Coloc* k* cypra-eg sde6.de• dig k* eug k* *Euph* **Euphr** k* fl-ac gamb k* gard-j vlr2• graph k* *Ham* k* *Ign* k* iod irid-met srj5• kali-ar kali-bi bg2 kali-c bg2 *Kali-i* bro1 kali-n h2 kiss a1 *Kreos* k* *Led* k* *Lyc* k* m-ambo b7.de *Merc* k* **Merc-c** k* naphtin bro1 *Nat-m* k* *Nit-ac* k* nux-v b7.de* ol-an bg2 ph-ac pic-ac k* plb k* puls k* rhus-t k* sabin sec b7a.de spig k* staph **Sulph** k* syph k* teucr uran-n bg2
  - **night**: *Merc*
  - **acid**; sensation as if tears are: gard-j vlr2•
- **biting**: acon b7.de* *Ars* b4a.de bell b4.de* *Calc* b4.de* carb-v b4.de* con b4.de* dig b4.de* *Euph* b4a.de **Euphr** b7.de* graph b4.de* ham fd3.de• *Ign* b7a.de kreos b7a.de* *Led* b7.de* lyc b4.de* m-ambo b7.de nat-m b4 de* nux-v bg2 ph-ac b4.de* *Plb* b7a.de rhus-t b7.de* sabad bg2 *Sabin* b7.de* sec b7a.de seneg bg2 *Spig* b7.de* staph b7.de* sulph b4.de* teucr b7.de*
- **bland**: **All-c** k* gink-b sbd1• *Puls* bro1
- **bloody** | **newborn**; in: cham ptk1
- **brine**; like: bell ptk1
- **burning**: **Apis** k* *Arn* k* *Ars* k* *Ars-i Aur* bell k* brom bg2 bros-gau mrc1 cadm-s k* *Calc* k* canth carb-v bg2 cedr bro1* **Chin** k* chinin-ar chlol a1 clem bg2 con bg2 croc b7a.de dios k* eug k* **Euphr** k* graph bro1* irid-met srj5• kali-c bg2 *Kali-i* bro1 kreos k* led c1 *Lyc* k* m-ambo b7.de mang-p rly4• *Merc* k* *Merc-c* bro1 naphtin bro1 nat-m bg2* nat-p hr1* *Nat-s* k* *Nit-ac* k* nux-v k* ph-ac h2 phel bg2 phos h2* *Phyt* k* plb k* podo c1* psor k* puls ptk1 **Rhus-t** k* *Sang* k* seneg bg2 *Sil* k* spig staph k* stict k* stront-c **Sulph** k* syph al* *Verb* k* zinc k*
  - **sun**; looking at the: sang ptk1 staph ptk1
- **cold** agg.: lach k* squil b7a.de staph b7a.de
- **copious**: syph dgt
- **excoriating**: led b7.de* *Spig* b7a.de
- **gushing**: aur bg2
- **hot**: apis b7a.de* arg-n sne **Arn** sne ars sne bell sne bry sne cadm-s sne calc sne carb-v sne chinin-ar sne clem sne con sne cycl sne dios sne *Euphr* sne graph sne kali-c sne kreos b7a.de* *Merc* sne *Merc-c* sne *Merc-i-r* sne nat-m bg2* phel sne phos sne phyt sne plb sne* podo sne *Psor* vml* *Rhus-t* sne sang sne seneg sne sil sne spig sne staph sne* zinc sne
- **itching**: ars bg2 nux-v bg2 senec bg2
- **milky**: atra-r bnm3•
- **oily**: atra-r bnm3• sulph k*
- **salty**: bell irid-met srj5• *Kreos* k* nux-v rhus-t b7.de*
- **sensation** as from: cassia-s ccrh1• cor-r a1 eupi k* fago a1 hyos k* ign h1 lil-t k* merc k* nit-ac k* (non:pyrog slp) pyrus slp sep k* sil h2 spig h1 spirae a1 staph h1 sulph h2
  - **cold** air | **amel**.: cassia-s ccrh1•

Tears: ...
- **sticky**: plat bg2*
- **thick**: ruta fd4.de tarent bg2*
- **varnish** mark; leave: euphr ptk1 graph ptk1 nat-m ptk1 petr ptk1 *Rhus-t* ptk1 thuj ptk1

TENONITIS (See Inflammation - tenon's)

TENSION: acon bg2 agar k* allox sp1 alum b4.de* ang b7.de* apis asaf k* *Aur* k* bar-c b4.de* bell bg2 berb k* *Calc* k* camph k* carb-v carl k* caust chin choc srj3• colch k* *Coloc* k* cop croc k* dros h1 dulc k* euphr k* *Gels* k* glon k* hyper k* iod b4.de* *Ip* k* jab c2 kreos k* lach k* led k* *Lith-c* lyc bg2 med k2 merc k* merl k* mez *Nat-m* k* *Nux-m* k* *Nux-v* k* onos *Par* k* *Phos* k* phys k* plat k* puls b7.de* **Ruta** k* sabad k* sabin b7.de* seneg k* sep k* *Sil* k* sol-ni spig k* stann k* stram b7.de* streptoc jl2 *Sul-ac* bg2 *Sulph* b4a.de tab k* til k* viol-t b7.de*
- **right**: zinc h2
- **left**: lyc h2
- **morning**: ang k* merc k* merl k* thuj
  - **waking**; on: sulph h2
- **closing** ● the eyes:
  - **agg.**: phys k*
  - **amel.**: aur
- **coition**; after: agar *Calc* phos sep *Sil*
- **cough** agg.; during: lach b7a.de
- **fixing** eyes agg.: aur k*
- **looking** upward: sulph h2
- **motion** of eyes agg.: nit-ac h2 spig vml
- **pain** in occiput, with: carb-v
- **reading** agg.: calc caust
- **turning** the eyes: *Calc*
- ○ **Around** the eyes: alum limest-b es1• *Nux-m Nux-v* par spong
- **Behind** the eyes: hydrog srj2•
- **Canthi**: olnd b7.de*
  - ○ **Inner**: bar-c h2 kali-cy
  - **Outer**: spong b7.de* staph b7.de*
- **Eyebrows**: bov k* dros b7.de* hell b7.de* par b7.de*
- **Lids**: acon k* *Ars* b4.de* canth b7.de* dros h1 dulc fd4.de hyper merl nit-ac k* *Nux-m* k* olnd k* ph-ac phys ptk1 plat *Puls* b7a.de staph b7.de* stram b7a.de sul-ac k* sulph b4.de*
  - **right**: carb-v olnd a1
  - **morning**: sulph h2
  - **closing**, on (See closing - agg.)
  - **reading** agg.: calc caust olnd a
  - ○ **Lower** lid: arum-t
- **Orbits**: cob ptm1• meny b7.de* nux-m b7a.de plat b4.de* spig b7.de* thuj bg2

THICKENING:
- **sensation** of: lach bg2
- ○ **Conjunctiva**; of: apis st aur-m k2 cadm-s k2 kali-m k2 zinc k2
- **Cornea**; of: *Apis* k* *Arg-n* asar bell haliae-lc srj *Nit-ac* sil
- **Eyebrows**; skin of: par b7.de
- **Lids**: (↗*Hardness - lids)* **Alum** k* apis **Arg-met** k* **Arg-n** k* aur-m k2 bar-c k2* borx k2 calc bro1 *Carbn-s* coloc *Euphr Graph* k* hep bro1 **Merc** k* *Nat-m Phyt Psor Puls* sal-fr sle1• *Sulph* **Tell** k* zinc k2
  - ○ **Margins** of: hydr k2 ozone sde2•
- **Mucous** membranes: petr k2
- **Tissues** around the eyes: lach k2

THINKING of eyes agg.: lach ptk1 spig ptk1

THINNED; eyebrows (See FACE - Thin - eyebrow)

THREAD (See Hair - sensation)

THROMBOSIS: | **Retinal** vein; central: bacls-7 mtf11 ham bro1* phos bro1*

TICKLING: | **Periosteum** around the eyes: phos h2

TINGLING: allox tpw3 clem k* ozone sde2• *Phyt* k* pic-ac k* spig c1
- **left**: cench k2
- **closing** the eyes | **amel**.: allox tpw3
- **reading** agg.: allox tpw3
- ○ **Bones**: phos bg1

- **Canthi**; inner | **right**: coloc b4.de*
- **Orbits**: phos bg2

TIRED EXPRESSION: *(↗FACE - Expression; FACE - Expression - tired)* arizon-l nl2• clem h2 cupr h2 *Cycl* hr1 dream-p sdj1• dulc fd4.de kali-c h2 kali-s fd4.de lap-la sde8.de• nat-sil fd3.de• sacch-a fd2.de• tritic-vg fd5.de

TIRED SENSATION●: abies-c oss4• allox tpw3* aln vva1• am-m androc srj1• ang bg2 ant-t bg2* arg-n br1 arge-pl rwt5• arizon-l nl2• *Arn* bg2 ars k* asar bg2 aur-m-n wbt2• bar-c h2* *Bell* bg2 bit-ar wht1• bov bg2 *Bry* bg2 cadm-met tpw6* *Cann-xyz* bg2 carb-an bg2 caust bg2 *Chin* bg2 chlam-tr bcx2• choc srj3• cina bg2 clem bg2 colch rsj2• con bg2 cortico tpw7* cortiso tpw7* croc bg2 cycl bg2 flav jl2 *Graph* k* haliae-lc srj5• hydrog srj2• hydroph rsj6• iod k* irid-met srj5• jab lac-h htj1• lac-loxod-a hrn2• lac-lup hrn2• lach bg2 luf-op rsj5• *Luna* kg1• **Lyc** ●* mag-p br1 mand rsj7• mang mrr1 mim-p rsj8• myos-a rly4• nat-ar k* nat-c bg2 nat-m k* nicotam rly4• nit-ac bg2 olib-sac wmh1 onos mrr1 op bg2 ozone sde2• petr h2 petr-ra shn4• ph-ac bg2 **Phos** k ● plac rzf5• plat b4a.de plut-n srj7• positr nl2• psor k* pyrid rly4• rauw tpw8* rheum bg2 *Ruta* k* sabad bg2 sel rsj9• seneg bg2 **Sep** k ●* *Spig* bg2 squil bg2 stann k* stram k* streptoc jl2 suis-em rly4• sulph taosc iwa1• thres-a sze7• thuj b4a.de *Trios* rsj11• tritic-vg fd5.de tub jl2 valer bg2 vanil fd5.de *Verat* bg2 *Zinc* k* [bell-p-sp dcm1 heroin sdj2]

- **left**: bit-ar wht1•
- **morning**: cadm-met sp1
- **afternoon**: chlam-tr bcx2•
- **evening**: flav jl2 psor jl2 trios rsj11•
- **closing** the eyes | **amel.**: bit-ar wht1• mim-p rsj8•
- **motion** from side to side agg.: rauw sp1
- **neon** light: pneu jl2
- **reading** agg.: psor jl2 ruta tl1 sulph h2
- **rubbing** | **amel.**: cortico tpw7*
- **sight**-seeing, moving pictures, etc.; after: am br1*
- **waking**; on: cadm-met tpw6
- ○ **Lids**: adox a1* cortiso sp1

TOBACCO agg.: dig br1

TOUCH:

- **agg.**: *(↗Hyperesthesia - retina)* *Acon* bro1 agar b4.de* aids nl2• allox tpw3 ant-t b7.de* am bro1 ars bro1 *Aur* b4.de* **Bell** b4.de* borx b4a.de *Bry* bro1* caust b4.de* chel b7.de* *Chin* bg2 cimic bro1 clem b4.de* cupr b7.de* dig b4.de* dros b7.de* eup-per bro1 *Ham* bro1 hell b7.de* **Hep** b4.de* kali-bi bg2 lach k2 lept bro1 lyc bg2 merc b4.de* *Nat-c* b4.de* *Nux-v* b7.de* olnd b7.de* par b7.de* petr b4.de* phos b4.de* rhus-t bro1 seneg b4.de* sep b4.de* sil bro1 *Spig* bro1 suis-hep rly4• *Sulph* b4.de* thuj bro1
- **amel.**: bry bg2 spong b7.de* thuj b4.de*

TRACHOMA (See Inflammation - trachoma)

TREMULOUS (See Quivering)

TRICHIASIS (See Hair - ingrowing)

TUMORS:

- ○ **Canthi**:
  - ○ **Outer** canthus | **polypus**: *Lyc* k*
- **Conjunctiva**:
  - **polypus**: *Kali-bi* *Staph* thuj
  - **sarcoma**: iod
- **Eyeballs**: symph mtf11
  - ○ **Behind**: thuj mtf33
    - **accompanied** by | **exophthalmos**: thuj ptk1*
- **Iris** | **cystic**: syph jl2
- **Lids**: arg-n sne aur *Bar-c* sne *Benz-ac* c2 *Calc* caust chion sne *Con* graph *Hep* hydr sne hydrc kali-bi lyc *Nat-m* nat-s sne *Nit-ac* *Phos* *Puls* *Sil* *Staph* k* sulph teucr k* *Thuj* k*
  - **right**:
    - **Lower**: zinc
    - **Upper**: zinc
  - **cystic**: *Benz-ac* bro1 *Calc* k* calc-f bro1* con b4a.de ferr-p ptk1 *Graph* iod bro1 kali-c b4a.de kali-i c2* *Merc* k* morg-g pte1*• platan-oc bro1 prot jl2 *Sil* k* staph k* sulph b4a.de thuj k*
    - **tarsal** cysts: *(↗tarsal)* ferr-p c2 ferr-py c2* kali-i c2 morg-p pte1*• syc pte1*• zinc mtf11

Tumors – Lids: ...

- **epithelioma**: con tl1 sep ptk1
- **nodules** in the lids: *(↗meibomian; tarsal)* *Alum* vh1 ant-t bro1 calc mfj* caust mfj* *Con* k* ferr-py bro1 graph bg3* hep mfj *Kali-i* bro1 **Platan-oc** mfj* puls k2 *Sil* k* **Staph** k* sulph *Thuj* k* tub c1 zinc mfj*
  - **styes**; after: con bro1 staph bro1 thuj bro1
  - **Lower** lids: aur bg2 *Calc* bg2 thuj bg2
  - **Margins**: aur h2 *Calc* *Con* *Sep* sil **Staph** thuj
- **polypus**: | **Lid**; under surface of upper: *Kali-bi*
- **sarcoma**: iod *Phos*
- **sensitive**: staph k2
- **tarsal** tumors: *(↗cystic - tarsal; meibomian; nodules)* ant-t bro1 arg-n bg2 bar-c calc bg2* caust k* *Con* bro1 ferr-py bro1* hep bg2 hydr bg2 *Kali-i* bro1 nat-s bg2 *Platan-oc* br1* *Puls* k* sanic c2 *Sep* k* *Sil* k* *Staph* k* sulph mtf33 teucr ptk1 *Thuj* k* **Zinc** k*
  - **children**; in: platan-oc br1
  - **recurrent** (See GENERALS - History - lids)
  - **repeated** styes; after: **Sep**
- **wens**: *Graph*
- ○ **Meibomian** glands: *(↗nodules; tarsal)* alum st bad **Staph** *Thuj*
  - **cysts**: *Benz-ac* bro1 calc bro1 *Calc-f* bro1 graph mtf11 hep mtf11 iod bro1 *Kali-i* bro1 kreos mtf11 merc bro1 platan-oc bro1 prot jl2* staph bro1* staphycoc mtf11 thuj mtf11
  - **inflamed**: lol st1
- **Orbits**: kali-i bro1

TURN; sensation as if they would: petr h2 phos h2

TURNED: *(↗Movement - rolling)* bell k* caust h2 con k* hipp meph k* nicc phos bg2* **Spig** k*

- **right**: camph *lp*
- **left**: amyg bufo dig k* hydr-ac phos ptk1
- **convulsions**; during: aeth j5.de
- **downward**: *(↗Drawn downwards)* (non:aeth bg2*) *Aether* slp canth k* cham k* *Hyos* bro1*
  - **convulsions**; during: *(↗GENERALS - Convulsions - epileptic - during - eyes - downwards)* aeth bro1*
- **inward**: arg-n bell ben-n *Calc* plb rhod ruta
- **outward**: bell k* camph *Crot-h* k* dig k* glon morph k* op phos k* plb bg2* stry k* sul-ac verat zinc k*
- **sideways**: dig b4.de*
- **sleep**; during: anac b4a.de chin b7.de* hell b7.de* op b7.de* ph-ac b4a.de puls b7.de*
- **upward**: acet-ac k* acon k* agar (non:am-c k*) am-caust a1* anan ant-t k* arn k* ars k* art-v bell k* *Bufo* k* *Camph* k* carb-ac carb-an h2 cham sne chin chlol cic k* cina cocc cub c1 *Cupr* k* euph k* *Glon* k* *Hell* k* hyos ign sne jatr-c kali-cy k* kalm lach k* mez bg2 morph k* mosch k* nux-v k* olnd k* *Op* k* stry k* tab k* thal-xyz srj8• verat k* zinc sne
  - **right**, to: camph plb gk stry
  - **left**, to: amyg bufo kr1 dig hydr-ac
    - **convulsions**; before: bufo kr1
  - **bending** head forward; when: bufo gk cic br1
  - **convulsions**; during: atro vh cham sne hydr-ac kr1 ign sne op bro1 plb a1 zinc mtf33 [art-v stj]
  - **fever**; during: hell k*
  - **inclining** head: cic br1
  - **sleep**; when falling asleep: mez k*

TURNING THE EYES: acon bg2 bry bg2 *Cupr* b7a.de* *Gels* bg2 lyc b4.de* meph bg2 nux-v bg2 puls b7.de* **Rhus-t** b7.de* sang ptk1 sep b4.de* *Sil* b4a.de* **Spig** b7.de* tub ptk1

TWILIGHT; in the:

- **agg.**: am-m b7.de* nat-m b4.de* puls b7.de* sul-ac b4.de*
- **amel.**: *Bry* b7a.de *Rhus-t* b7a.de

TWISTED sensation: chin bg2* petr bg2* phos bg2* phys bg2* pop-cand bg2* spong k*

TWITCHING: (↗*Quivering; MIND - Gestures - tics)* acon k* aesc k* **Agar** k* alum k* am-m k* apis k* arn b7.de* *Ars* k* **Arum-t** sne *Asar* b7a.de bar-c *Bell* bg2 calc k* camph bg2 carb-ac k* carb-an k* carb-v bg2 carbn-s carc mrr1 caust bg2 cedr *Cham* b7.de* chin k* cina tl1 croc b7a.de* *Crot-t* k* cupr tl1 dulc b4a.de* fuma-ac rly4• gels k* *Glon* k* hyos b7.de* iod h* juni-v c2 kali-n k* kali-p kali-s fd4.de kalm k* kola stb3• kreos b7a.de* *Lachn* k* limen-b-c hrn2* lith-c lyc bg2 mag-p k2 mang b4.de* merc-c b4a.de mez k* nat-m k* nat-sil fd3.de• nicc k* **Nux-v** bg2 ozone sde2• petr k* phys lp* phyt k* pieri-b mlk9.de plat k2 plb b7.de* *Positr* nl2• puls k2 rat k* rhus-t k* ruta fd4.de sel k* spong fd4.de *Stann* k* suis-pan rly4• sul-i k2 sulph bg2 ust k* vanil fd5.de vesp k* xan c1 zinc bg2*

- **right**: androc srj1• falco-pe nl2• fic-m gya1 nat-m bg2 nat-sil fd3.de• rat k* sel rsj9• ther k*
- **left**: apis carc fd2.de• hydrog srj2• iod bg2 mez k* positr nl2• sel k* spong fd4.de
- **daytime**: aloe k* nat-m k* sal-fr sle1•
- **accompanied** by dim vision: allox sp1
- **cold** water | **amel**.: agar
- **looking** fixedly agg.: lach bg1
- **painful**: agar rhus-t hr1
- **paroxysms**: ars calc
- **reading** agg.: agar
- **rubbing** | **amel**.: am-m h2
- **weather** | **thunderstorm**; before: agar mtf33

○ - **Around** the eyes: luna kg1• ruta fd4.de

- **Canthi**: agar k* indg a1 kali-chl k* lachn k* nat-sil fd3.de• rhus-t vanil fd5.de
  - **right**: lachn c1
  - ○ **Inner**: *Carl* k* chel k* kali-chl k* kali-m k2 kali-s fkr2.de nat-sil fd3.de• rat k* stann k* sul-ac k* symph fd3.de• vanil fd5.de
    - **right**: chel b7.de* kali-c bg2 rat bg2 rhus-t bg2 stann bg2 sul-ac b4.de*
  - **Outer**: am-c k* bar-c b4.de* camph k* *Cann-i* k* ind a1* mez k* nat-m k* nat-sil fd3.de• nicc k* *Phos* k* positr nl2• seneg k* vanil fd5.de
    - **right**: seneg bg2
    - **left**: ind c1 nat-m b4.de* nicc bg2 phos bg2 positr nl2•
    - **chewing** agg.: kali-n ptk1
- **Eyebrows**: carc tpw2* caust k* cic cina k* dulc fd4.de echi ptk1 grat k* hell h1* kali-c k* kali-p fd1.de• kali-s fd4.de ol-an k* pieri-b mlk9.de (non:puls k*) puls-n slp ruta k* sin-n k* stront-c k* vanil fd5.de zinc k*
  - **left**: caust bg2 ol-an bg2
  - **staring** at any object; when: cina mtf33
- **Lids**: acon a1 aesc k* **Agar** k* allox tpw4* alum k* alum-p k2 anac k* ant-c k* *Apis* arge-pl rwt5• *Ars* k* ars-i ars-s-f k2 **Arum-t** sne arund k* asar k* aster k* atp rly4• bad k* bar-c h2 bell k* benzol br1 berb k* bomb-chr mlk9.de calc k* calc-i k2 calc-s k* calc-sil k2 camph k* canth k* carb-v k* carbn-s carc mg1.de* card-b a1 *Caust* k* cedr k* *Cham* k* chel k* chin h1 **Cic** k* cina bg2 *Cocc* k* cod vml3• colch b7.de* coloc ptk1 croc k* *Crot-t* k* *Cupr* k* cupr-s a1 cypra-eg sde6.de• dulc k* dys fmm1• euphr k* *Gels* bg2 grat k* guar c2* hell k* hist sp1* hydr-ac hyos k2* *Ign* k* ind indg k* *Iod* k* *Ip* k* jab br1 jatr-c kali-bi k* kali-p k2 kali-s fd4.de kreos k* *Lach* k* lachn k* lil-t k2 lyc k* *M-arct* b7.de* mag-c k* *Mag-p* k* meny k* merc k* merl k* *Mez* k* nat-c h2 *Nat-m* k* nat-ox rly4• nat-sil fd3.de• nit-ac k* nitro-o a1 *Nux-v* k* ol-an k* olib-sac wmh1 oreo br1 par k* petr k* *Ph-ac* b4a.de *Phos* k* **Phys** k* pieri-b mlk9.de *Plat* k* plut-n srj7• positr nl2• *Puls* k* *Rat* k* **Rheum** k* rhod k* rhus-t k* *Ruta* bg2 sabin sal-fr sle1• sel k* seneg k* sep k* *Sil* k* spig spong fd4.de staph mrr1 stront-c k* suis-pan rly4• sul-i k2 **Sulph** k* vanil fd5.de verat-v k* zinc bg2
  - **right**: alum chin k* coloc k* corian-s knl6• falco-pe nl2• form k* *Lach* k* medul-os-si rly4• nat-m k* par k* sacch-a fd2.de• sal-fr sle1• staphycoc rly4• sulph bg1 syph k* trios rsj11• vanil fd5.de
  - **left**: aloe arum-t mrr1* bad k* bry cp carb-v bg2 carc tpw2* *Caust* k* cench k2 chinin-s c1 croc k* lac-leo sk4• merl k* *Mez* k* olib-sac wmh1 ozone sde2• phos bg2 plut-n srj7• positr nl2• puls k* rhus-g tmo3• stront-c suis-pan rly4• vanil fd5.de
  - **evening**: trios rsj11•
  - **accompanied** by:
    - **convulsions** (See GENERALS - Convulsions - epileptic - during - lids - twitching)
    - **respiration**; asthmatic (See RESPIRATION - Asthmatic - accompanied - lids)
    - **trigeminal** neuralgia (See FACE - Pain - nerves - trigeminal - accompanied - lids)
    - **vertigo**: chinin-s ptk1

Twitching – Lids: ...

- **children**; in: androc bnm2•
- **closed**; when: allox tpw4 cupr-s k* lachn k* merc k* polyg-h ptk1
- **cold** air agg.: dulc k*
- **convulsions**; before epileptic: agar gt1
- **eating**; while: meny k*
- **light**; from:
  - **agg**.: allox tpw4
  - **artificial** light | **agg**.: allox tpw4
- **lying** agg.: polyg-h ptk1
- **menses**; before: *Nat-m* k*
- **motion** agg.: allox tpw4
- **opening** the eyes agg.: kali-bi k*
- **painful**: coloc ptk1
- **persistent**: cod vml3• guar vml3• kreos ptk1
- **rapid**: mygal ptk1 rat ptk1
- **reading**:
  - **agg**.: agar berb ptk1 kali-bi (non:puls slp) puls-n slp ruta fd4.de
  - **light**; by | **lamplight**: berb
- **rubbing** | **amel**.: allox tpw4
- **sleep** agg.; during: rheum k*
- **thunderstorm**; before: *Agar*
- ○ **Lower**: allox tpw3 am-c aran-sc c1* carc tpw2* coc-c k* graph hir rsj4• *Iod* k* kali-i k* lyc h2* mag-c b4.de* nat-m nat-sil fd3.de• ph-ac b4.de* phos bg2 positr nl2• ruta ptk1* sel rsj9• seneg k* spong fd4.de sulph k* vanil fd5.de zinc k*
  - **right**: asaf bg2 asar b7.de* laur b7.de* rhus-t b7.de*
  - **left**: am-m h2 canth b7.de* chin b7.de* lyc b4.de* mag-c b4.de* nat-sil fd3.de• positr nl2• sinus rly4•
- **Upper**: alum k* amph a1 ars *Aur* k* bry cp *Calc* k* camph b7.de* cedr k* chin kr1 coloc bg2 iod bg2 kali-s fd4.de lac-ac k* lachn k* mag-c mtf33 mag-m h2* mang b4.de* *Merl* k* *Mez* k* mur-ac k* nat-m k* ozone sde2• positr nl2• rat k* rhod bg2 sacch-a fd2.de• spong fd4.de stram k* stront-c
  - **right**: apis b7a.de bar-c b4.de* canth b7.de* par b7.de* phos bg2 rhod b4.de seneg b4.de*
  - **left**: amph c1 asaf bg2 asar b7.de* carc fd2.de• jatr-c c1 kali-p fd1.de• kali-s fd4.de mag-c b4.de* mez b4.de* mill bg2 nat-m bg2 nicc bg2 ol-an bg2 petr-ra shn4• podo fd3.de• positr nl2• rhus-t b7.de spong fd4.de stront-c b4.de

- **Muscles**: hist sp1
- **Orbits**: am-m b7.de* bar-c b4.de* calc b4.de* cypra-eg sde6.de• nat-m bg2

ULCERATION:

○ - **Canthi**: calc *Graph* bg2 phos k*

- **left**: *Petr* b4a.de *Sil* b4a.de
- ○ **Outer**: *Ant-c* bg2 borx calc b4.de* *Kali-c* sep bg2

- **Conjunctiva**: **Alum** k* alumn k2 arg-n vh cadm-s k2 **Caust** k* coloc k* *Crot-t* k* hippoz hr1 *Hydr* k* *Lyss* nit-ac psor k2 sul-ac k2 syph k2
- **Cornea**: *Acon* b7a.de aethi-a bro1 *Agar* k* ambr b7.de* **Apis** k* *Arg-n* k* am b7.de* *Ars* k* ars-s-f k2 *Asaf* atro vh1 *Aur* k* aur-ar k2 aur-m bro1 aur-s k2 *Bar-c* k* bar-m bell bg2* **Brom** b4a.de bufo **Calc** k* calc-f calc-hp bro1 calc-i bro1 *Calc-p* k* *Calc-s* k* calc-sil c2* *Cann-s* k* caps b7.de* carbn-s k2 carc mlr1• caust b4a.de cedr cham b7.de* *Chin* k* chinin-ar chinin-m kr1 chlol k* cimic k* *Clem* k* *Con* k* cortico sp1* crot-c *Crot-t* *Cund* k* **Euphr** k* *Form* k* *Graph* k* ham k2 *Hep* k* hippoz hydr k2 iod k2 *Ip* k* kali-ar *Kali-bi* k* *Kali-c* k* kali-chl k* kali-m bg* kali-s kali-sil k2 kreos *Lach* k* *Led* b7a.de lyc b4.de* *Lyss* med k2 *Merc* k* *Merc-c* k* merc-d k* *Merc-i-f* k* merc-i-r bg2 morg-g pte1* nat-ar *Nat-c* k* *Nat-m* k* *Nit-ac* k* petr b4a.de* phos b4.de* podo k* *Psor* k* *Puls* k* *Rhus-t* k* ruta k* *Sang* k* *Sanic* k* sep b4a.de *Sil* k* *Sin-n* bg2 spong b7.de* stann b4a.de staph b7.de* *Sulph* k* syph al* *Thuj* k* tub c1* x-ray sp1 zinc bg2*
  - **alternating** sides: *Ars*
  - **right**:
    - **extending** to | **left**: **Con** k*
  - **accompanied** by:
    - **conjunctiva**; inflammation of: med mtf33
    - **typhoid** fever: apis bro1 ip bro1
  - **air**; in open | **amel**.: asaf k2

- **Cornea**: ...
  - **children**; in: bac tl1 calc-i mtf11
    - **newborns**: arg-n k2
  - **deep**: ars bro1 euphr bro1 *Kali-bi* bro1 *Merc-c* bro1 merc-i-f bro1 merc-i-r bro1 sil bro1
  - **destructive**: *Arg-n* bg2 *Ars* bg2 asaf bg2 **Caust** bg2 con bg2
  - **indolent**: calc bro1 *Kali-bi* bro1 *Sil* bro1 sulph bro1
  - **pain** and photophobia, without: kali-bi ptk1
  - **painful**: *Merc-c Nat-c* hr1
    - **midnight**:
      - **after** | **3h**; until: chinin-ar
  - **perforating**: apis ptk1
  - **pulsating**: kali-bi k2
  - **scars**; from: cadm-s *Euphr* sil
  - **superficial**: ars bro1 asaf bro1 euphr bro1 kali-m bro1 merc bro1 nit-ac bro1
  - **syphilitic**: carbn-s gm1
  - **vascular**: aur bro1 calc k* cann-s hep k* merc-c merc-i-f plb bg2 *Sil*
  - ○ **Edges**: kali-m bg2
- **Lachrymal** ducts: anan
- **Lids**: anan ang bg2 *Apis* arg-met k2 arg-n k2* *Ars* k* aur b4a.de *Bar-m* bell bg2 carbn-s k2 *Caust* bro1 cham bg2 *Clem* k* colch b7.de* *Con* b4a.de croc b7.de* **Euphr** bg2* *Graph* k* *Hep* k* ign b7.de* kali-bi k* kali-c bg2 kali-i lappa bro1 led k* **Lyc** k* *Merc* k* *Merc-c* k* nat-m k* nat-p nux-v b7.de* phos k* plb bg2 psor puls b7.de* rhus-t k* sep sil b4.de* *Spig* k* *Staph* b7.de* *Stram* k* *Sulph* k* tell c1* thuj b4a.de verat bg2 *Zinc* k*
  - **malignant**: phyt
  - ○ **Canthi** (See canthi)
  - **Lower**: **Apis** b7a.de colch b7.de* nat-m b4.de* rhus-t b7a.de sec b7a.de
  - **Margins** of: *Anan* vh1 arg-n br1* *Ars* bro1 bufo calc *Caust* bro1 **Clem** k* *Colch* b7a.de crot-t *Euphr* k* *Graph* k* hep k2* lappa br1* lyc bro1 *Merc* k* *Nat-m* psor puls k* **Sanic** k* sel b7a.de spig b7a.de* staph *Sulph* b4a.de* *Tell* bro1
  - **Surfaces**; under: **Ars** bell merc nux-v phos puls rhus-t sil sulph
  - **Tarsi**: *Clem* bg2* sanic ptk1
  - **Upper**: *Hep* b4a.de
- **Meibomian** gland: *Colch*

UNSTEADY look: (↗*Restless*) aloe anan k* arg-n bro1 *Bell* k* camph k* cedr k* cupr hydrc c1 *Lach* k* **Morph** k* par k* sabad b7.de* *Stram* k*

URINATION: | **amel.**: gels ptk1 ign ptk1 kalm ptk1

UVEITIS (See Inflammation - uvea)

VACANT look (See FACE - Expression - vacant)

VACILLATE (See Unsteady)

VARICOSE veins: | **Lids**: carb-v bg2 plb bg2 *Puls* bg2

VEINS (See Discoloration - red - veins)

VESICLES: bell bg2 sulph h1*
- ○ **Cornea**; on the (See Eruptions - cornea - vesicles)
- **Sclera**; on the (See Eruptions - sclera - vesicles)

VIVID: *Coff* b7a.de m-aust b7.de

VOMITING:
- **after**: agar bg2
- **hiccough**; and | **agg.**: apis ptk1 arn ptk1 asar ptk1 bry ptk1 chin ptk1 lyc ptk1 nux-v ptk1 puls ptk1 sep ptk1 sil ptk1 verat ptk1

WAKING; on: alum bg2 *Ambr* b7.de* **Bell** b4.de* **Bry** b7.de* chin bg2 croc b7.de* euph b4.de euphr bg2 hell b7.de* hep b4.de* ign b7.de* kali-bi bg2 kali-c b4.de* kreos b7a.de lyc bg2 m-ambo b7.de m-arct b7.de mag-c b4.de* nux-v b7.de* phos b4.de* **Puls** bg2 rheum b7.de* rhod b4.de* sars b4.de* sep b4.de* staph b7.de* tarax b7.de* zinc b4.de*

WALKING:
- **agg.**: *Cic* bg2 hep b4a.de kali-bi bg2 *Nat-m* bg2 sep bg2

Walking: ...
- **air**; in open:
  - **agg.**: *Alum* b4a.de anac b4.de* ars b4.de* borx b4a.de bry b7.de* carb-v b4.de* *Con* b4.de* euphr b7.de* guaj bg2 merc bg2 nat-m bg2 nux-v b7.de* sabad b7.de* staph b7.de* sul-ac b4.de* sulph b4.de* thuj b4.de* zinc b4.de*
  - **amel.**: ambr b7.de* hyos b7.de* puls b7.de*
- **amel.**: ol-an bg2
- **wind**; in the | **agg.**: *Puls* b7a.de

WANDERING (See Unsteady)

WARM: bry bg
- **agg.** | **heat**: *Apis* k* *Arg-n* k* cann-i a1 caust clem *Coff* k* gels psa hep c1 **Merc** k* **Puls** k ●* til *Zinc* k*
- **air** agg.: *Sulph* b4a.de
- **applications** | **agg.**: am-c b4a.de bry b7.de*
- **covering** | **amel.**: *Fl-ac* bg2
- **room** | **agg.**: arg-n bg2
- **sensation** of warmth (See Heat in)

WARTS: *Ars* b4a.de arund *Calc* k* cinnb dulc fd4.de *Merc Nit-ac* k* phos sil kr staph **Thuj**
- ○ **Canthi**: calc k* *Lyc* b4a.de nit-ac (non:psor al2)
- **Cornea**: arg-n bg2 ars h2
- **Eyebrows**: anan k* *Caust* k* nit-ac bg2 *Thuj* k*
- **Eyes**; about: caust bg2 sulph bg2
- **Iris**: *Cinnb* k* **Merc** k* staph thuj k*
- **Lids**: *Calc* b4a.de *Caust* k* cinnb *Dulc* b4a.de *Nit-ac* k* sulph **Thuj** k*
  - **bleeding** when touched: nit-ac
  - ○ **Lower** | **right**: *Nit-ac* k* *Thuj* b4a.de
  - **Upper**: nit-ac b4a.de*
- **Sclerae**: arund

WASHING:
- **agg.**: am-m b7.de* *Kali-n* b4a.de mur-ac b4.de* *Sep* b4a.de
- **amel.**: alum b4.de* am-m b7.de* chel b7.de* form bg2 laur b7.de* mag-c b4.de* mur-ac b4.de*

WATER; sensation of: ars bg2 chin bg2 cinnb bg2 ign bg2 nat-s bg2 nit-ac bg2 rob bg2 sil bg2 squil bg2
- **cold** water; as from: berb bg2 bufo bg2 squil b7.de* staph b7a.de

WATERY (See Lachrymation)

WEAK: (↗*Asthenopia; VISION - Weak*) *Agar* k* alum h2 am-c h2 ammc a1 *Anac* ant-t k* *Apis* ars k* asc-t k* *Aur* bamb-a stb2.de• bapt k* bar-c k* blum-o bnj1 bov k* calc k* calc-i k2 calc-sil k2 cann-i k* *Cann-s* k* caps *Carb-an* k* *Carb-v* carbn-o *Carbn-s* carc tpw2* caust k* cench k2 cham k* chel chin chlol a1* (non:chlor k*) cic cina cinnb k* cob k* **Con** k* croc k* crot-t k* cupr k* cycl k* daph k* dig k* dios k* dor k* dros k* ery-m a1 *Euphr* k* eupi k* *Ferr* k* ferr-i gels k* *Graph* k* haliae-lc srj5• ham k* hep hura hyos hyper k* ign br1 iod k* kali-bi k* *Kali-c* k* kali-n h2 kali-p kali-sil k2 kalm k* kreos k* lach k* lact k* *Lil-t* k* lyc k* lycps-v lyss k* mang meph k* merc k* merc-i-r k* morph k* naja nat-ar *Nat-m* k* nat-s nicc k* nit-ac k* nux-m *Op* k* osm k* ox-ac k* par ped a1 petr k* *Phos* k* *Phys* k* plat plb *Propr* sa3• ran-b c1 raph k* rhod k* rhus-t **Ruta** sabad k* sang a1 sec **Seneg** k* sep *Sil* sin-n k* spig k* staph stram stront-c stry k* sulph k* tab k* tarent k* *Thuj* k* urt-u k* ust k* verat k* zinc k*
- **daytime**: stann k*
- **morning**: ars k* bry k* cina dig k* dios k* phos sang k* upa k*
- **forenoon**: ph-ac k* squil k* sulph k* valer k*
- **noon**: cinnb k*
- **afternoon**: sin-n k*
- **evening**: alum h2 carb-an k* nicc k* psor k*
  - **bed**; after going to: op
  - **light**; by: lyc sep
- **candlelight**; from: bell
- **coition**; after: **Kali-c** k* kali-p bg1
- **dinner**; after: valer k*
- **emissions** agg.; after: jab kali-c lil-t nat-m puls sep
- **fever**; during: carb-v b4a.de* *Nat-m* b4.de* sep b4a.de*
- **light**: aster k* gins k* merc k* nat-p

- **looking**:
  - • **intently**:
    - ⁝ **agg.**: *Lyc*
    - ⁝ **long** time agg.; for a: alum h2
- **measles**; after: *Kali-c* *Puls* k*
- **menopause**; at: tril-p c1
- **menses**; during: *Cinnb* k*
- **reading**:
  - • **after**: am-c gsy1
  - • **agg.**: agar *Ammc* k* anders bnj1 bell calc bro1 cina bro1 *Jab* bro1 kali-i lyc myric nat-ar k2* *Nat-m* k* phos bro1 phys **Ruta** k* **Seneg** *Sep* k* sulph bro1
- **sensation**: alum bg2 aur b4.de* bell bg2 cann-s b7.de* chin b7.de* rheum b7.de* stann b4.de* verat b7.de*
- **sexual** excesses; after: *Calc* *Chin* gels upa k*
- **sun**; in the: *Propr* sa3•
- **weeping**; as after: cycl bg1
- **work**; from fine: carb-v k2
- **writing** agg.: anders bnj1 bell carl *Nat-m* *Sep*

○ - **Behind** the eyes | **indoors**: lavand-a ctl1•

- **Ciliary** muscles (See Asthenopia; Asthenopia - accommodative)
- **Lids**: alum b4.de* caust b4.de* cina b7.de* con bg2 kali-c bg2 kali-p bg2 *Lyc* bg2 *Onos* bg2 *Ruta* bg2 seneg bg2 sep bg2
  - • **right**: agar bg2

WEATHER:

- **change** of weather: cadm-s bg2 ran-b bg2
- **dull**, not clear weather | **amel.**: *Bry* b7a.de
- **stormy** | **before**: agar bg2 nat-c bg2

WEEPING:

- **agg.**: borx b4a.de canth b7.de* croc b7.de* lach b7.de* m-arct b7.de *Puls* b7a.de stann b4.de* *Teucr* b7a.de
- **sensation** as if from: bell bg2 croc b7.de* cycl bg2 kreos b7a.de lach bg2 stann bg2 tab bg2 *Teucr* b7.de*

WET APPLICATIONS agg.: cham b7a.de

WHIRLING sensation: | **Orbits**: bov b4.de*

WILD look: acet-ac aeth dgt1 ail k* *Alumn* k* *Anac* k* anan k* arg-n k* *Ars* k* ars-i **Bell** k* *Camph* k* cann-i k* *Canth* sne *Carb-v* *Cimic* k* con k* *Cupr* k* *Glon* k* hydr-ac *Hyos* k* iod k* kali-br sne kali-i *Lach* k* lil-t ptk1 **Lyss** k* *Nit-ac* k* **Nux-v** k* op k* plb k* sec k* *Stram* k* stry tab valer k* verat hr1 verat-v ptk1 vesp k2 vip

- **delirium**; during: verat-v ptk1

WIND:

- **agg.**: *Asar* b7a.de *Bell* b4a.de *Calc* b4a.de *Euphr* b7a.de lyc b4.de* nat-ar bg2 nat-m bg2 *Phos* b4.de* puls b7.de* thuj b4.de*
- **cold** wind blowing in eye (See Coldness - air)

WINE agg.: *Gels* k* **Zinc** k*

WINKING: (↗*Quivering; MIND - Gestures - tics*) acon bg2* agar k* all-c dgt1 am-c k* anan *Apis* arg-n k* aster k* bamb-a stb2.de• **Bell** k* bit-ar wht1• calc bg2* carc tpw2* *Caust* k* chel k* chin k* con k* *Croc* k* cycl k* **Euphr** k* *Fl-ac* k* glon k* hep b4a.de* hydrog srj2• *Ign* iod b4.de* kalm lac-cp sk4• lac-leo sk4• merc gl1.fr• merc-d ptk1 *Mez* k* nat-c a1 nit-ac k* *Nux-v* k* op k* petr k* ph-ac h2* plat k* positr nl2• *Spig* k* staph bg2 sulph k* sumb k* syc bka1*• tub jl2

- **air** agg.; in open: merl
- **amel.**: asaf bell ptk1 croc k* *Euphr* k* olnd k* stann
- **children**; in: carc tpw*
- **convulsions**; during epileptic: kali-bi k*
- **frequent**: carc gk6
- **headache**; during: all-c dgt1
- **looking** at bright objects: acon k* acon-c a1 apis
- **must** wink: fl-ac ptk1
- **rapidly**: *Aster* ptk1 merc-d ptk1
- **reading** agg.: *Calc* k* *Croc* k* merl
- **sunlight**: *Merl* k*
- **writing**; after: hep k*

WIPE, inclination to: agar k* alum k* arg-n k* *Calc* k* carb-an k* *Croc* k* euphr bg* kreos lac-c lyc k* *Nat-c* k* nat-m ptk1 petr-ra shn4• phos bg2 plb k* *Puls* k* rat seneg ptk1 sep sulph bg

WIPING: | **amel.**: *Calc* ptk1 cina ptk1 cycl ptk1 euphr ptk1 *Nat-c* ptk1

WRINKLED conjunctiva: arg-n bg2* ars ptk1 brom k* nat-ar

WRITING agg.: alum bg2 apis b7a.de calc-f ptk1 canth b7.de* carb-v bg2 ferr b7.de* graph b4.de* hep b4a.de* kali-bi bg2 mez b4.de* nat-c b4.de* nat-m b4.de* ph-ac bg2 phyt ptk1 rhod b4.de* seneg b4.de* *Sep* bg2 *Sil* bg2 staph b7.de* valer b7.de verat bg2 zinc b4.de*

XEROPHTHALMIA: (↗*Dryness; Inflammation - cornea; GENERALS - Sicca*) brass-n-o srj5• lepr mtf11 pert-vc vk9

YAWNING agg.: agar ptk1 ant-t b7.de* arn b7.de* ferr b7.de* ign b7.de* nux-v b7.de* ph-ac b4.de* *Sabad* b7.de* sars b4.de* staph b7.de* viol-o b7.de*

YELLOWNESS (See Discoloration - yellow)

CANTHI; complaints of: acon b2.de* **Agar** b2.de* **Alum** b2.de* am-c b2.de* am-m b2.de* anac b2.de* ang b2.de* ant-c b2.de* ant-t b2.de* arg-met b2.de* **Arg-n** bg2 arn b2.de* ars b2.de* asar b2.de* *Aur* b2.de* bar-c b2.de* **Bell** b2.de* bism b2.de* *Borx* b2.de* bov b2.de* *Bry* b2.de* **Calc** b2.de* camph b2.de* carb-an b2.de* **Carb-v** b2.de* *Caust* b2.de* cham b2.de* chel b2.de* chin b2.de* cic b2.de* cina b2.de* clem b2.de* coff b2.de* colch b2.de* coloc b2.de* con b2.de* dig b2.de* *Euph* b2.de* *Euphr* b2.de* *Graph* b2.de* guaj b2.de* hell b2.de* hep b2.de* hyos b2.de* ign b2.de* iod b2.de* ip b2.de* kali-c b2.de* kali-n b2.de* lach b2.de* laur b2.de* led b2.de* lyc b2.de* m-ambo b2.de m-arct b2.de m-aust b2.de mag-c b2.de* mag-m b2.de* meny b2.de* *Merc* b2.de* mez b2.de* mosch b2.de* mur-ac b2.de* nat-c b2.de* **Nat-m** b2.de* nit-ac b2.de* **Nux-v** b2.de* olnd b2.de* par b2.de* *Petr* b2.de* ph-ac b2.de* **Phos** b2.de* plat b2.de* plb b2.de* **Puls** b2.de* *Ran-b* b2.de* ran-s b2.de* rhod b2.de* rhus-t b2.de* ruta b2.de* sabad b2.de* sars b2.de* seneg b2.de* *Sep* b2.de* sil b2.de* spig b2.de* spong b2.de* squil b2.de* *Stann* b2.de* **Staph** b2.de* stront-c b2.de* sul-ac b2.de* **Sulph** b2.de* tarax b2.de* teucr b2.de* *Thuj* b2.de* valer b2.de* verat b2.de* zinc b2.de*

- **alternating** sides: indg bg2
- **right**: arg-n bg2 brom bg2 coloc bg2 fl-ac bg2 grat bg2 led bg2 sol-ni bg2 spig bg2
- **left**: agar bg2 alum bg2 arg-met bg2 aur bg2 calc bg2 cann-xyz bg2 carb-an bg2 clem bg2 nat-c bg2 nat-m bg2 nat-s bg2 nit-ac bg2 rhus-t bg2 spong bg2 stann bg2

▽ - **extending** to:

○ • **Inward**: caust bg2

• **Nose**:

⁝ **External** | **right**: caust bg2

○ - **Canthi**:

○ • **Inner**: **Agar** b2.de* *Alum* b2.de* anac b2.de* ang b2.de* ant-c b2.de* *Ant-t* b2.de* arn b2.de* asar b2.de* *Aur* b2.de* bar-c b2.de* **Bell** b2.de* borx b2.de* bry b2.de* **Calc** b2.de* carb-an b2.de* *Carb-v* b2.de* *Caust* b2.de* chel b2.de* cic b2.de* cina b2.de* *Clem* b2.de* coloc b2.de* *Con* b2.de* dig b2.de* euphr b2.de* fl-ac bg2 graph b2.de* hell b2.de* hyos b2.de* lach b2.de* laur b2.de* led b2.de* lyc b2.de* m-ambo b2.de m-arct b2.de m-aust b2.de *Mag-c* b2.de* mag-m b2.de* meny b2.de* merc b2.de* mez b2.de* mosch b2.de* mur-ac b2.de* nat-c b2.de* nat-m b2.de* nit-ac b2.de* *Nux-v* b2.de* par b2.de* *Petr* b2.de* ph-ac b2.de* *Phos* b2.de* *Puls* b2.de* rhod b2.de* rhus-t b2.de* ruta b2.de* sars b2.de* sep b2.de* *Sil* b2.de* spig b2.de* stann b2.de* **Staph** b2.de* stront-c b2.de* sul-ac b2.de* sulph b2.de* tarax b2.de* teucr b2.de* thuj b2.de* valer b2.de* verat b2.de* *Zinc* b2.de* zinc-s bg2

• **Outer**: agar b2.de* alum b2.de* anac b2.de* ant-c b2.de* asar b2.de* *Bar-c* b2.de* borx b2.de* bry b2.de* **Calc** b2.de* camph b2.de* carb-an b2.de* carb-v b2.de* cham b2.de* chel b2.de* chin b2.de* cina b2.de* colch b2.de* con b2.de* *Euph* b2.de* euphr b2.de* *Graph* b2.de* hep b2.de* hyos b2.de* *Ign* b2.de* ip b2.de* kali-bi bg2 kali-c b2.de* kali-n b2.de* laur b2.de* lyc b2.de* m-ambo b2.de m-arct b2.de merc b2.de* mosch b2.de* mur-ac b2.de* nat-c b2.de* *Nat-m* b2.de* nit-ac b2.de* *Nux-v* b2.de* petr bg2 ph-ac b2.de* phos b2.de* plat bg2 puls b2.de *Ran-b* b2.de* ran-s b2.de* rhus-t b2.de* ruta b2.de* sabad b2.de* sars b2.de* seneg b2.de* sep b2.de* sil b2.de* spig b2.de* spong b2.de* **Squil** b2.de* stann b2.de* *Staph* b2.de* stront-c b2.de* sul-ac b2.de* **Sulph** b2.de* tarax b2.de* thuj b2.de*

CONJUNCTIVA; complaints of: **Acon** b2.de* agar b2.de *All-c* ptk1 alum b2.de am-c b2.de am-m b2.de ambr b2.de* ang b2.de ant-c b2.de* ant-t b2.de* **Apis** bg2* arg-met b2.de* **Arg-n** ptk1 arn b2.de* **Ars** b2.de* *Asar* b2.de* aur b2.de* bar-c b2.de* **Bell** b2.de* bism b2.de borx b2.de brom bg2 bry b2.de* calc b2.de*

Conjunctiva; complaints of: ...
camph b2.de cann-s b2.de canth b2.de caps b2.de carb-v b2.de caust b2.de* cham b2.de* chel b2.de* chin b2.de* clem b2.de* cocc b2.de coff b2.de coloc b2.de con b2.de* croc b2.de cupr b2.de dig b2.de* dulc b2.de* euph b2.de **Euphr** b2.de* ferr b2.de* gels bg2 graph b2.de* hep b2.de* hyos b2.de ign b2.de* iod b2.de ip b2.de kali-c b2.de* **Kali-i** bg2 kreos bg2 lach b2.de led b2.de* **Lyc** b2.de* m-arct b2.de mag-c b2.de mag-m b2.de* **Merc** b2.de* merc-n bg2 mez b2.de nat-m b2.de nit-ac b2.de nux-v b2.de* op b2.de* petr b2.de ph-ac b2.de phos b2.de* plb b2.de* **Puls** b2.de* ran-b b2.de ran-s b2.de **Rhus-t** b2.de* sabad b2.de samb b2.de sep b2.de* **Sil** b2.de* spig b2.de* stann b2.de staph b2.de stram b2.de* stront-c b2.de sul-ac b2.de* **Sulph** b2.de* tarax b2.de teucr b2.de thuj b2.de verat b2.de* viol-o b2.de zinc b2.de

CORNEA; complaints of: acon b2.de* am-c b2.de am-m b2.de ang b2.de ant-t b2.de *Apis* bg2 arn b2.de* *Ars* b2.de* aur b2.de bar-c b2.de bell b2.de* bov b2.de* bry b2.de **Calc** b2.de* **Cann-s** b2.de* *Cann-xyz* ptk1 caps b2.de caust b2.de* chel b2.de* chin b2.de* con b2.de* cupr b2.de dig b2.de dulc b2.de euph b2.de **Euphr** b2.de* ferr b2.de graph b2.de* haliae-lc srj **Hep** b2.de* hyos b2.de kali-bi bg2 kreos b2.de lach b2.de* lyc b2.de mag-c b2.de* **Merc** b2.de* merc-i-f ptk1 mosch b2.de nat-c b2.de nat-m b2.de* **Nit-ac** b2.de* nux-v b2.de op b2.de* phos b2.de plb b2.de **Puls** b2.de* rhus-t b2.de* ruta b2.de* sars b2.de seneg b2.de* sep b2.de* sil b2.de* spig b2.de* spong b2.de squil b2.de stann b2.de* stram b2.de **Sulph** b2.de* tarax b2.de thuj bg2 valer b2.de verat b2.de

EYEBALLS; complaints of: **Acon** b2.de* agar b2.de agn b2.de alum b2.de* am-c b2.de am-m b2.de ambr b2.de* anac b2.de ang b2.de ant-c b2.de ant-t b2.de apis bg2 arg-met b2.de* arn b2.de* ars b2.de* asaf b2.de asar b2.de* aur b2.de* bar-c b2.de* **Bell** b2.de* bism b2.de borx b2.de* bov b2.de bry b2.de* calad b2.de **Calc** b2.de* camph b2.de cann-s b2.de canth b2.de* caps b2.de carb-an b2.de carb-v b2.de* caust b2.de* cham b2.de* chel b2.de chin b2.de* cic b2.de cina b2.de clem b2.de* cocc b2.de coff b2.de colch b2.de coloc b2.de con b2.de* croc b2.de* cupr b2.de cycl b2.de dig b2.de* dros b2.de dulc b2.de euph b2.de **Euphr** b2.de* ferr b2.de graph b2.de* guaj b2.de hell b2.de **Hep** b2.de* hyos b2.de ign b2.de* iod b2.de ip b2.de kali-c b2.de* kali-n b2.de kreos b2.de* lach b2.de laur b2.de led b2.de* lyc b2.de* m-ambo b2.de m-arct b2.de m-aust b2.de mag-c b2.de* mag-m b2.de mang b2.de meny b2.de merc b2.de* mez b2.de mosch b2.de mur-ac b2.de nat-c b2.de* nat-m b2.de* nit-ac b2.de* nux-m b2.de nux-v b2.de* olnd b2.de op b2.de par b2.de* petr b2.de* ph-ac b2.de* phos b2.de* plat b2.de* plb b2.de* puls b2.de* ran-b b2.de* ran-s b2.de rheum b2.de rhod b2.de rhus-t b2.de* ruta b2.de* sabad b2.de sabin b2.de samb b2.de sars b2.de sec b2.de sel b2.de seneg b2.de* sep b2.de* sil b2.de* **Spig** b2.de* spong b2.de squil b2.de stann b2.de* staph b2.de* stram b2.de* stront-c b2.de* sul-ac b2.de* **Sulph** b2.de* tarax b2.de teucr b2.de thuj b2.de* valer b2.de verat b2.de* verb b2.de viol-o b2.de viol-t b2.de zinc b2.de*

○ - **Behind**: bad ptk1 bell bg2 bry bg2* chel ptk1 cimic bg2* gels ptk1 *Lach* ptk1 lith-c bg2* manc ptk1 merc ptk1 podo bg2* puls ptk1 rhus-t bg2* sep ptk1 ther ptk1 thlas bg2

EYEBROWS; complaints of: agar b2.de* *Agn* b2.de* alum b2.de* am-m b2.de* ambr b2.de* ang b2.de* *Arn* b2.de* ars b2.de* asaf b2.de* bar-c b2.de* **Bell** b2.de* bov b2.de* bry b2.de* camph b2.de* cann-s b2.de* canth b2.de* **Caust** b2.de* chin b2.de* cina b2.de* clem b2.de* coloc b2.de* croc b2.de* cupr b2.de* dig b2.de* *Dros* b2.de* euph b2.de* guaj b2.de* *Hell* b2.de* ign b2.de* ip b2.de* *Kali-bi* bg2 **Kali-c** b2.de* laur b2.de* m-arct b2.de mag-m bg2 mang b2.de* merc b2.de* mosch b2.de* nat-m b2.de* nux-v b2.de* olnd b2.de* **Par** b2.de* petr b2.de* plat b2.de* plb b2.de* ran-b b2.de* rhod b2.de* rhus-t b2.de* ruta b2.de* **Sel** b2.de* sep b2.de* sil b2.de* *Spig* b2.de* spong b2.de* stann b2.de* stram b2.de* stront-c b2.de* sulph b2.de* tarax b2.de* *Thuj* b2.de* viol-t b2.de* zinc b2.de*

EYELASHES (See Hair - eyelashes)

EYELIDS; complaints of (See Lids)

HAIR:

- **combing** hair agg.: nux-v bg2*
- **falling**:

○ · **Eyebrows**; from (See FACE - Hair - falling - eyebrows)

· **Eyelashes**; from●: alum k* *Apis* *Ars* k* aur aur-ar k2 borx bg2* bufo *Calc* b4a.de *Calc-s* *Chel* chlol *Euphr* graph bg2 kali-c st1 lepr mtf11 med k* *Merc* k* nat-m bg2* petr br1* ph-ac psor **Rhus-t** k* *Sel* k* sep sil *Staph* k* *Sulph* k* thal-xyz srj8•

- **ingrowing** eyelashes: (↗*Inversion*) bell bg2 borx b4a.de* graph mtf33 merc bg2 nat-m bg2 *Puls* bg2 sil b4a.de*

○ · **Lids**; upper: *Puls* b7a.de

Hair: ...

- **sensation** of hair in eye●: bry bg2 calc-f st *Coc-c* bg2* euphr bg2* irid-met srj5• kali-n h2* m-aust b7.de mag-p st nat-c h2* olib-sac wmh1 plan **Puls** k●* *Ran-b* b7.de* sang k* sil st tab til bg2
  · **afternoon**: sang

○ - **Eyebrows** | **white** (See FACE - Hair - white - eyebrows)

- **Eyelashes**:
  · **complaints** of: alum bg2 borx bg2 graph bg2 sel bg2 stann-i bg2
  · **fine**; are: calc-p dgt phos mtf33 **Tub** mrr1
  · **long**; are: calc-p vml1.nl* carc mrr* gaert fmm1• phos ptk2* syc fmm1• tub dgt*
    ⁝ **curved**; and: phos ptk1*
  · **stiff**, pointing to nose: nit-ac ptk1

IRIS; complaints of: bell ptk1 clem bg2 **Merc** bg2* *Merc-c* ptk1 nit-ac ptk1 seneg bg2 **Sulph** bg2*

LACHRYMAL GLANDS; complaints of: arg-n bg2 *Bell* bg2 brom ptk1 bry bg2 **Calc** bg2 *Chel* bg2 nat-c bg2 petr bg2 phos bg2 puls bg2 ruta bg2 sabad br1* sil bg2 stann bg2 staph bg2

LACHRYMAL SAC; complaints of: *Apis* bg2 arg-met bg2 arg-n bg2 aur bg2 calc-f bg2 con bg2 fl-ac bg2 hep bg2 iod bg2 lach bg2 led bg2 lyc bg2 merc bg2 nat-c bg2 nat-m bg2 nit-ac bg2 petr bg2 phos bg2 phyt bg2 puls bg2 ruta bg2 sil bg2 stann bg2 staph bg2 sulph bg2

○ - **Lower**: apis bg2
- **Upper**: kali-c bg2

LENS; complaints of: euphr ptk1 *Puls* ptk1 *Sil* ptk1 *Sulph* ptk1

LIDS; complaints of: **Acon** b2.de* agar b2.de* agn b2.de* alum b2.de* am-m b2.de ambr b2.de* anac b2.de ang b2.de ant-c b2.de* ant-t b2.de* apis ptk1 arg-met b2.de arn b2.de* **Ars** b2.de* asaf b2.de asar b2.de aur b2.de bar-c b2.de **Bell** b2.de* borx b2.de* bov b2.de brom bg2 **Bry** b2.de* **Calc** b2.de* camph b2.de cann-s b2.de* canth b2.de caps b2.de carb-an b2.de carb-v b2.de* **Caust** b2.de* **Cham** b2.de* chel b2.de* chin b2.de* cic b2.de cina b2.de clem b2.de cocc b2.de colch b2.de* coloc b2.de con b2.de **Croc** b2.de* cupr b2.de cycl b2.de* **Dig** b2.de* dros b2.de dulc b2.de euph b2.de* euphr b2.de* ferr b2.de* *Graph* b2.de* guaj b2.de hell b2.de **Hep** b2.de* hyos b2.de* *Ign* b2.de* iod b2.de kali-c b2.de* kali-n b2.de *Kreos* b2.de* lach b2.de laur b2.de led b2.de **Lyc** b2.de* m-ambo b2.de m-arct b2.de m-aust b2.de mag-c b2.de* mag-m b2.de mang b2.de meny b2.de* **Merc** b2.de* mez b2.de mosch b2.de mur-ac b2.de *Nat-c* b2.de* nat-m b2.de* nit-ac b2.de* nux-m b2.de **Nux-v** b2.de* olnd b2.de* op b2.de par b2.de* petr b2.de **Ph-ac** b2.de* phos b2.de* plat b2.de plb b2.de* **Puls** b2.de* ran-b b2.de ran-s b2.de rheum b2.de* rhod b2.de* **Rhus-t** b2.de* ruta b2.de sabad b2.de sabin b2.de sars b2.de sec b2.de sel b2.de seneg b2.de* **Sep** b2.de* sil b2.de* **Spig** b2.de* spong b2.de* squil b2.de stann b2.de* staph b2.de* stram b2.de* stront-c b2.de sul-ac b2.de **Sulph** b2.de* tarax b2.de* teucr b2.de thuj b2.de valer b2.de* verat b2.de* verb b2.de viol-o b2.de* viol-t b2.de zinc b2.de* [bell-p-sp dcm1]

- **alternating** sides: alum bg2

○ - **Eyelashes** (See Hair - eyelashes - complaints)

- **Inner** surface of: *Acon* b2.de* agar b2.de* *Arg-n* ptk1 **Ars** b2.de* *Bell* b2.de* borx b2.de* bry b2.de* calc b2.de* canth b2.de* caust b2.de* cham b2.de* con b2.de* dros b2.de* hep bg2 ign b2.de* *Merc* b2.de* nat-m b2.de* *Nux-v* b2.de* par b2.de* *Phos* b2.de* *Puls* b2.de* **Rhus-t** b2.de* sep b2.de* sil b2.de* *Sulph* b2.de*
- **Lower**: agar b2.de alum b2.de* am-m b2.de* arg-met b2.de ars b2.de* asar b2.de aur b2.de bell b2.de* **Bry** b2.de* **Calc** b2.de* canth b2.de* carb-v b2.de caust b2.de* cham b2.de chin b2.de cic b2.de colch b2.de* *Coloc* b2.de* croc b2.de* dig b2.de* dros b2.de euph b2.de euphr b2.de ferr b2.de graph b2.de iod b2.de lach b2.de* laur b2.de lyc b2.de m-aust b2.de mag-c b2.de* merc b2.de* mez b2.de nat-c b2.de nat-m b2.de* olnd b2.de petr b2.de **Ph-ac** b2.de* puls b2.de* ran-b b2.de rhus-t b2.de* **Ruta** b2.de* sabin b2.de sec b2.de **Seneg** b2.de* sep b2.de* sil b2.de spig b2.de stann b2.de* sul-ac b2.de* sulph b2.de zinc b2.de*
- **Margins** of lids: arg-met b2.de* arn b2.de* *Ars* bg2 *Bell* b2.de* **Borx** b2.de* bry bg2 calc b2.de* canth b2.de* **Cham** b2.de* *Clem* b2.de* colch b2.de* *Dig* b2.de* **Euphr** b2.de* graph b2.de* *Hep* b2.de* kreos b2.de* lyc b2.de* **Merc** b2.de* mez b2.de* *Nux-v* b2.de* ph-ac b2.de* **Puls** b2.de* rhus-t b2.de* sabad b2.de* seneg b2.de* *Sep* b2.de* sil b2.de* *Spig* b2.de* **Staph** b2.de* stram b2.de* **Sulph** b2.de* *Valer* b2.de* zinc b2.de
- **Meibomian** glands (See Meibomian)
- **Outer** surface of: *Acon* bg2 bell bg2 *Hep* bg2 sulph bg2

Eye

- **Upper**: acon b2.de agar b2.de agn b2.de alum b2.de* ang b2.de arg-met b2.de arn b2.de* ars b2.de asaf b2.de* asar b2.de* aur b2.de bar-c b2.de* bell b2.de* borx b2.de **Bry** b2.de* calc b2.de* camph b2.de cann-s b2.de* canth b2.de carb-an b2.de carb-v b2.de **Caust** b2.de* cham b2.de* chel b2.de* chin b2.de cina b2.de clem b2.de colch b2.de coloc b2.de con b2.de* croc b2.de* cycl b2.de* dulc b2.de ferr b2.de* **Gels** bg2* graph b2.de hell b2.de hep b2.de* hyos b2.de *Ign* b2.de* kali-c b2.de* kalm ptk1 kreos b2.de laur b2.de *Lyc* b2.de* m-arct b2.de mag-c b2.de mag-m b2.de mang b2.de* merc b2.de* mez b2.de mosch b2.de mur-ac b2.de nat-c b2.de* nat-m b2.de nit-ac bg2 *Nux-v* b2.de* olnd b2.de* op b2.de par b2.de* ph-ac b2.de* phos b2.de* plb b2.de* puls b2.de* rheum b2.de rhod b2.de rhus-t b2.de* sabin b2.de seneg b2.de **Sep** b2.de* sil b2.de* *Spig* b2.de* spong b2.de squil b2.de stann b2.de* staph b2.de* stram b2.de* sulph b2.de* tarax b2.de teucr b2.de thuj b2.de verat b2.de* viol-o b2.de zinc b2.de*

MEIBOMIAN GLANDS; complaints of: aeth bg2 bad bg2 *Dig* bg2 graph bg2 hep bg2 led bg2 **Puls** bg2 rhus-t bg2 sil bg2 staph bg2 sulph bg2

OPTIC nerve; complaints of: arg-n bg2* aur bg2 bell bg2 chin bg2 cina bg2 dig bg2 fil bg2 lach bg2 lycpr mtf11 nux-v bg2 onos bg2 plat bg2 plb bg2* tab bg2

ORBITS; complaints of: alum b2.de* am-m b2.de* anac b2.de* ang b2.de* ant-c b2.de* *Apis* ptk1 arn b2.de* ars b2.de* asaf b2.de* aur b2.de* bar-c b2.de* *Bell* b2.de* bism b2.de* bov b2.de* bry b2.de* calc b2.de* camph b2.de* chel b2.de* chin b2.de* cinnb bg2* cocc b2.de* coloc b2.de* con b2.de* cupr b2.de* dig b2.de* hell b2.de* hep b2.de* hyos b2.de* ign b2.de* iod b2.de* kali-bi bg2* lach b2.de* laur b2.de* led b2.de* lyc b2.de* m-ambo b2.de mag-c b2.de* meny b2.de* merc b2.de* merc-i-f ptk1 mez b2.de* mur-ac b2.de* nit-ac b2.de* nux-m b2.de* *Nux-v* bg2 olnd b2.de* par b2.de* ph-ac b2.de* phos b2.de* *Plat* b2.de* plb b2.de* puls b2.de* rhod b2.de* rhus-t b2.de* ruta b2.de* sars b2.de* sel b2.de* seneg b2.de* sep b2.de* **Spig** b2.de* spong b2.de* *Stann* b2.de* stront-c b2.de* sul-ac b2.de* sulph b2.de* syph ptk1 **Valer** b2.de* verat b2.de* verb b2.de* zinc-s ptk1

○ - **Region** of: viol-o br1

PUPILS:

- **alternately** contracted and dilated in the same light: acet-ac k* *Acon* k* aesc bg2 agar bg2 am-c k* anac k* arn bg2* ars k* *Bar-c* k* cann-s k* *Carb-ac* k* cham h1* chin b7.de* chlol a1 cic k* cocc bg2 con bg2 cycl k* dig k* dros k* dulc k* gels bg2 *Hell* k* hyos bg2 ign b7.de* *Lach* k* mur-ac a1 oena k* op bg2 *Phys* k* puls bg2 sol-ni stann bg2 staph bg1 stram bg2 stroph-h bg2* zinc k*
- **angular**: acon bar-c *Cocc* k* hyos k* merc-c
- **contract**, difficult to: nit-ac
- **contracted** (= miosis): *Acon* k* aesc k* agar k* alco a1 am-caust a1 amyg a1* *Anac* k* ang b2.de* ant-t k* *Apis* k* arec br1 arg-met arg-n bg2* *Arn* k* *Ars* k* atra-r bnm3• *Aur* k* aur-ar k2 aur-s k2 bar-c bg2 *Bell* k* *Calc* k* calc-sil k2 *Camph* k* canth k* caps k* carb-ac k* carbn-s cham k* *Chel* k* chin b2.de* *Chinin-s* *Chlf* hr1 chlor a1 cic k* cina b2.de* cinch a1 clem a1 cocc k* con croc b2.de* crot-t k* cub a1* cycl a1 cyt-l a1 *Daph* k* *Dig* k* digin a1 dros k* dubo-h a1* esin a1* euph a1 *Euphr* k* ferr hr1 fl-ac k* gamb k* gels k* *Gins* gran a1 guat sp1 haem *Hell* k* hydr-ac a1 *Hyos* k* ign k* iodof bro1 ip b7a.de* jab k* kali-bi k* *Kali-br* hr1 *Kali-chl* hr1 kali-i k* laur b2.de* led k* lon-x bro1 lyss hr1 m-arct b2.de* mag-p hr1 mang k* meny b2.de* *Merc* k* *Merc-c* k* *Mez* k* morph a1* mosch b2.de* *Mur-ac* k* muscin a1 narc-ps a1* narcot a1 nat-c h2 *Nat-m* k* nit-s-d hr1 *Nux-m* k* nux-v k* oci-sa sp1 oena a1 ol-an olnd b2.de* **Op** k* oxyt bro1* paeon c1 petr a1 ph-ac k* phos k* *Phys* k* phyt k* pilo bro1 *Plb* k* podo k* *Puls* k* rheum k* rhod b2.de* *Rhus-t* k* rob a1 russ a1 ruta b2.de* sabad k* sal-ac hr1 samb k* sec k* seneg k* *Sep* k* sil k* sol-ni k* squil k* *Stann* k* staph b2.de* stram k* sul-ac k* sulph k* tab k* tarax b2.de* *Ter* hr1 **Thuj** k* tub upa a1 vario hr1* *Verat* k* verat-v hr1 viol-o b2.de* viol-t b2.de* vip a1 visc a1 *Zinc* k* zinc-m a1 zinc-p k2 [heroin sdj2]
  - **right**: anac h2 *Arg-n* k* atro hr1 onos verat-v k*
  - **left**: *Arg-met* *Tarent*
    - **accompanied** by:
      - **Eye** | **dilatation** of the right eye: colch lyss rhod *Tarent*

Pupils – contracted: ...

- **accompanied** by:
  - **apoplexy** (See GENERALS - Apoplexy - accompanied - pupils - contracted)
  - **mental** symptoms (See MIND - Mental symptoms - accompanied - pupils)
- **alternating** with dilatation (See alternately)
- **chill**; during: *Acon* bg2* bell caps k* cham bg2 dig bg2 gins a1 nux-v sep k* sil k* sulph k* *Verat* bg2
- **coma**; with (See MIND - Coma - pupils - contracted)
- **convulsions** during: cic kr1 *Op* kr1 phyt kr1
- **fever**; during: acon bg2
- **followed** by | **dilatation**: cic b7.de mur-ac a1 puls b7.de stann h2 stram b7.de
- **headache**; during: bell h1
- **heat**; during: acon arn ars bell cham cocc digin a1 *Gels* hyos mur-ac nux-v phos sec stram verat
- **one** eye: colch hr1 gels br1 phys hr1 rhod tarent k* zinc hr1
  - **accompanied** by | **dilatation** of the other eye: *(↗dilated - one)* anac b4a.de cadm-s colch bg2* gels bg2* mang b4a.de nat-p bg2 ph-ac b4a.de phys hr1 plb bg2 rhod k* tarent k* zinc hr1
- **perspiration**: bell camph bg2 caps bg2 cham k* cocc k* mez k* mur-ac k* phos k* puls k* sep k* sil k* sulph k* thuj k* verat k*
- **pinpoint**; to a: atra-r bnm3• cub c1 **Op** sne [heroin sdj2]

- **dilated** (= mydriasis): absin a1 acet-ac k* acetan br1* *Acon* k* aesc k* *Aeth* k* *Agar* k* agar-ph a1 *Agn* k* *Ail* k* alumn k* am-caust a1* amyg hr1 *Anac* k* androc srj1• ang b2.de* anh sp1* anthraci vh1 *Apis* k* **Arg-n** k* *Arn* k* ars k* ars-i art-v hr1 arund k* asaf b2.de* asar bg2 astac k* atro a1* aur b2.de* bapt bg2 bar-c k* bar-i k2 *Bar-m* k* **Bell** k* bell-p c2* benzol br1 brom k* bry a1* bufo k* cadm-s cain **Calc** k* calc-i k2 calen hr1 *Camph* k* *Cann-s* b7a.de canth b2.de* caps k* carb-ac c1 *Carb-an* k* carbn-s cass a1 caust k* *Cedr* k* *Chel* k* **Chin** k* *Chinin-s* chlf hr1 *Cic* k* cimic k* *Cina* k* cinch a1 cloth tsm2 coca *Cocain* bro1 *Cocc* k* *Coff* k* *Colch* k* *Coloc* k* *Con* k* convo-s sp1 *Cor-r* k* cori-m a1 *Croc* k* crot-c crot-h k* crot-t cupr b2.de* *Cycl* k* cypra-eg sde6.de• cyt-l a1* *Dig* k* dor hr1 dros k* dub c2* dubo-h a1* dubo-m br1 dulc k* euph b2.de* falco-pe nl2• **Gels** k* ger a1 *Glon* k* gran a1 *Grat* hr1 *Guaj* k* guare a1* *Hell* k* helo-s bnm14• hep k* hippoz hr1 hydr-ac k* **Hyos** k* *Hyper* k* ign k* *Iod* k* *Iodof* bro1 ip k* ix bnm8• jasm a1 kali-bi bg2* *Kali-br* k* kali-cy a1 *Kali-i* k* kali-n kali-ox a1 kola stb3• kreos b2.de* lac-ac k* lach k* lachn k* lact k* lact-v hr1 lat-m bnm6• *Laur* k* *Led* k* lobin a1 loxo-recl knl4• lyc k* lyss k* m-ambo b2.de* m-arct b2.de* m-aust b2.de* mand sp1* **Mang** k* meny b2.de* *Merc* k* merc-c b4a.de *Merl* k* mez b2.de* *Mosch* k* mur-ac b2.de* narc-ps a1* nat-ar *Nat-c* k* nat-f sp1 *Nat-m* hr1 *Nat-p* nat-sal a1 *Nit-ac* k* nit-s-d bg nitro-o a1 nux-m k* *Nux-v* k* oena hr1* ol-an bg olnd b2.de* *Op* k* oxyurn-sc mcp1• par b2.de* past a1 ped a1 petr b2.de* *Ph-ac* k* phase-vg a1 *Phos* k* phys k* phyt k* pic-ac k* pilo bg pitu-p sp1 plb b2.de* psil ft1 *Puls* k* ran-b k* raph rheum b2.de* rhod k* rhus-t b2.de* samb k* *Sang* k* sangin-t c1* sars k* scor a1* **Sec** k* sol-ni sol-ps c2 *Spig* k* squil k* stann b2.de* staph k* **Stram** k* *Stry* k* sul-i k2 sulph k* suprar bwa3 tarax b2.de* tarent a1* thal-xyz srj8• thuj b2.de* thyr br1 valer k* *Verat* k* verat-v bg2* verb h* vib k* vip bg2* visc a1* xan c1 zinc k* zinc-m a1 zinc-p k2 zinc-s a1
  - **one** side: *(↗contracted - one - accompanied - dilatation)* cadm-s br1 nat-p k2*
  - **right** more than left: colch a1 cycl h1 mang *Merc-i-f* hr1 *Ph-ac* plb sil *Tarent*
  - **left** more than right: *Art-v* hr1 atra-r bnm3• nat-ar urt-u
  - **accompanied** by:
    - **diarrhea** (See RECTUM - Diarrhea - accompanied - pupils)
    - **nausea**: cimic tl1 glon tl1
    - **respiration**:
      - **complaints** of (See RESPIRATION - Complaints - accompanied - pupils)
    - **vertigo** (See VERTIGO - Accompanied - pupils)
    - **Head**; complaints of (See HEAD - Complaints - accompanied - pupils)
  - **catalepsy**; during: gels c1

• **chill**; during: aeth apis k* **Bell** bg2* calc k* carb-an k* cham cic k* croc bg2 hyos k* ign bg2 ip k* lach mez b4a.de* nux-m op stram k*
• **cold** wet weather; in: *Rhus-t* hr1
• **coma**; with (See MIND - Coma - pupils - dilated)
• **convulsions** | **before** | **epileptic**: *(↗GENERALS - Convulsions - epileptic - aura - pupils)* **Arg-n** *Bufo* k*
⁝ **during** | **epileptic**: aeth mtf33 *Bell* kr1 carb-ac kr1 cic kr1 *Cina* kr1 cocc kr1 ign hr plb kr1 verat-v kr1
• **fever**; during: *Apis* bg2 bell mtf33 *Cina* b7a.de*
• **heat**; during: ail apis k* ars atro vh **Bell** bufo chin cic cina k* cocc colch hell hyos lyc merc nux-v
• **horizontally**: *Apis* b7a.de
• **insensible** to light: *(↗insensible)* aeth bwa1 am-m hs1 amyg a1 apis nh8 arg-n a1 arn hs1 atro a1 bar-s k2 bell a1 ben vml4 camph a1 carb-ac a1 chlf c1 cina hs1 cocc ll1 cupr hs1 dat-f a2 dig hr1 gels a1 hep hr1 hydr-ac a1* hyos k2 ix bnm8• kali-cy a1 kali-i cda1 merc-c a1 nitro-o a1 op a1 phase br1 phos a1 plb a1 sang a1 santin a1* stram a1 tab a1
⁝ **epilepsy**; before (See GENERALS - Convulsions - epileptic - aura - eyes - dilated)
• **meningitis**: gels c1
• **menses** | **before** | **agg.**: lyc k*
⁝ **during** | **agg.**: glon
• **perspiration**; during: acon bell k* bufo calc k* cina k* cocc hell hep k* hyos k* op k* spig bg2 stram k*
• **reading** agg.: *Ph-ac* k*
• **reprimands**; after: *(↗MIND - Admonition - agg.)* **Stram** kr1*
• **reproaches**; at: stram a1
• **spasmodic**: *Stram* bg2
• **stupor**; during: sec k*
• **toothache**; during: mang k*

- **dull**: bell b4a.de calc b4a.de *Nat-m* b4a.de sil b4a.de*
- **grown** together: *Calc* b2.de* graph b2.de* merc-c b4a.de *Nit-ac* b2.de* sil b2.de* sulph b2.de*
- **insensible** to light: *(↗dilated - insensible)* acon b2.de* aeth k* agar k* agar-pr a1 alco a1 amyg a1 arg-n **Arn** k* ars k* atra-r bnm3• aur-m *Bar-c* k* *Bar-m* **Bell** k* benzol bro1 bufo k* cain *Camph* k* carb-ac carb-an carb-v k* cedr k* cham b2.de* *Chel* chin k* *Cic* k* cic-m a1 *Colch* **Cupr** k* der a1 *Dig* k* dub k* euph k* ferr b2.de* gels k* *Hell* k* hep k* hydr hydr-ac k* hydrc a1 **Hyos** k* jab br1 kali-bi k* *Kali-br* kali-cy a1 *Kali-i* k* lach bg2 laur k* m-arct b2.de* *Merc* *Merc-c* k* morph a1 naja nit-ac k* nit-s-d a1 nux-m nux-v sne oena a1 **Op** k* ox-ac k* oxyt ptk2 par phase-vg a1 phos k* pilo bro1 *Plat* plb b2.de* ran-b k* rhus-t seneg b2.de* sol-ni spig b2.de* *Stram* k* sul-ac k* sulph tab k* ter *Tub* visc a1* *Zinc* bro1
  • **convulsions**; before: bufo mtf33
  • **daylight**: benzol br1
  • **fever**; during: op bro1
- **irregular**: acon aur hr1* bar-c k* chlor k* cinnb dig br1* dub k* hyos k* merc bg2* merc-c bg2 nit-ac plb sec bg2 sil k* sulph k* tab k* tub al
- **large** (See dilated)
- **sluggish**: acon-f a1 *Ail* hr1* alco a1 *Arg-n* hr1 bell k* carbn-s cench a1 cham k* *Chin* hr1 croc br1 cupr cyt-l a1 dig k* *Gels* hr1 gran a1 *Hell* k* ip k* ix bnm8• jatr-c merc k* naja nit-ac **Op** hr1 phos k* rhod hr1 rumx sec k* seneg k* sul-ac k* tab k* tax k*
- **small** (See contracted)
- **staring** (See Staring)
- **unequal**●: absin br1 bell cadm-s cann-i chlor colch k* cypra-eg sde6.de• cyt-l sp1 dig digin a1 hyos bg3* lyss mang merc-c merc-i-f hr1 morph k* nat-p plb rhod sulph *Syph* jl2 tarent k* zinc h2
  • **coma**; with (See MIND - Coma - pupils - unequal)
- **weak**: spig k*

Eye

DAYTIME: am-m b7a.de ant-c b7a.de hell b7a.de *Mang* b4a.de nux-v b7a.de stram b7a.de *Sulph* b4a.de verat b7a.de

MORNING: am-c b4.de* am-m b7.de* ang b7.de* borx b4a.de bov b4.de* b r y b7.de* calc b4.de* caps b7.de* carb-an b4.de* carb-v b4.de* caust b4.de* c h a m b7.de* chel b7a.de dros b7.de* kali-bi bg2 kali-c b4.de* *Lach* b7a.de mag-c b4.de* nat-m b4.de* *Nux-v* b7.de* phos b4.de* puls b7.de* seneg b4.de* s e p b4.de* stram b7.de* sul-ac b4.de* verat b7.de* zinc b4.de*

FORENOON: alum b4.de* am-m b7.de* carb-an b4.de* nux-v b7.de* p h - a c b4.de* puls b7.de* sep b4.de*

AFTERNOON: agar b4.de* alum b4.de* am-m b7.de* calc b4.de* con b4.de* dig b4.de* ign b7.de* iod b4.de* kali-c b4.de* lyc b4.de* mag-c b4.de* mang b4.de* merc b4.de* nux-v b7.de* sep b4.de* sulph b4.de* thuj b4.de* zinc b4.de*

- **15** h or 16 h: bufo bg2

EVENING: alum b4.de* am-m b7a.de *Anac* b4a.de borx b4a.de calc b4.de* carb-an b4.de* cham bg2 cina b7.de* cinnb bg2 *Croc* b7.de* cupr b7a.de dros b7.de* ferr b7.de* *Hep* b4.de* ign b7.de* kali-c b4.de* kali-n b4.de* laur b7.de* **Lyc** b4.de* m-ambo b7a.de petr b4.de* ph-ac b4.de* phos b4.de* puls b7.de* rhod b4.de* rhus-t b7.de* sars b4a.de *Sep* b4.de* *Staph* b7a.de sulph b4.de* tab bg2 valer b7.de* verat b7.de* *Viol-o* b7a.de

- **sunset**:
  - **after** | **agg.**: *Bell* bg2 sil bg2 sulph bg2

NIGHT: am-c b4.de* bar-c b4.de* chel b7.de* chin bg2 *Hyos* b7.de* lyc bg2 phos bg2 puls b7a.de ruta b7.de* staph b7.de* *Verat* b7.de*

ACCOMMODATION:

- **action** too great: phys
- **contours** appear stronger: ozone sde2•
- **defective**: *Agar* k* ail k* alum bro1 androc srj1• *Arg-n* k* atra-r bnm3• aur-m bapt-c c2 **Bell** mfj bit-ar wht1• calc k2 caust mfj cocc k2 con k2* diphtox jl2 *Dub* mfj elae c2 **Gels** mfj germ-met srj5• *Haliae-lc* srj5• *Hydr* ip bro1 lach bro1 limen-b-c hrn2* *Morph* k* *Nat-m* k* nit-ac nitro-o a1 nux-v hr olib-sac wmh1 onos k* *Phys* k* plut-n srj7• ruta k2* spig k* tritic-vg fd5.de tung-met bdx1•
  - **diphtheria**; after: phys br1
  - **headache**; causing (See HEAD - Pain - vision)
  - **moving** objects: cocc k2
  - **overexertion**: (non:nux-v hr1)
- **diminished**: duboin nh3 morph olib-sac wmh1 phys tab visc sp1
  - **children**; in: lac-d mtf11
- **slow**; too: (*↗EYE - Asthenopia - accommodative*) *Aur-m* *Cocc* **Con** **Gels** k* hippoc-k szs2 kola stb3• *Nat-m* *Onos* *Plat* propr sa3• *Psor*
- **tension**: *Jab* k*

ACUTE: (*↗MIND - Senses - acute*) acon k* agath-a nl2• anac c1 ang k* ant-c b7.de* *Apis* b7a.de arge-pl rwt5• aspar k* bamb-a stb2.de• *Bar-c* b4a.de **Bell** k* borx b4a.de *Bufo* k* camph b7a.de* carb-an bg2 *Chin* k* c h o c srj3• chrysar bro1 cic a1 coff b7.de* colch k* coli rly4• *Con* b4a.de* conch fkr1• *Cupr* b7a.de cycl k* falco-pe nl2• fic-m gya1 fl-ac k* galla-q-r nl2• haliae-lc srj5• hell b7.de* hyos k* ign b7.de* lac-del hrn2• lac-loxod-a hrn2• lac-lup hrn2• lach luna kg1• m-arct b7.de *Nux-v* k* ozone sde2• ph-ac k* *Plut-n* srj7• positr nl2• ribo rly4• sal-al blc1• sanguis-s hrn2• sars k* seneg k* spig b7.de* suis-pan rly4• suprar rly4• thres-a sze7• tung-met bdx1• valer bg2* viol-o k* visc sp1 [*Buteo-j* sej6 spect dfg1 tax jsj7]

- **daytime**: choc srj3• suprar rly4•
- **morning**: bamb-a stb2.de• positr nl2•
- **night**:
  - **hysterical** persons; in: *Ferr* k*
  - **night** vision: ferr tl1 plut-n srj7• sanguis-s hrn2•
- **air**; in open: coff mp1•
- **alternating** with | **dim** vision (See Dim - alternating - clear)
- **clear**, bright and lucid (See Acute; Bright)
- **darkness**; seems to see even in the (See night - night)
- **details**; for: (*↗objects*) sanguis-s hrn2•
- **movement**; for: [*Buteo-j* sej6]
- **objects**; for small: (*↗details*) calc b4.de* *Coff* b7.de* *Hep* b4.de* lac-del hrn2• m-aust b7.de
- **reading** of small print; easier: **Coff** ptk1*
- **rubbing**; after: *Cina* mp1•
- **urination** agg.; after: eug bg2

AIR; IN OPEN:

- **agg.**: alum b4.de* coff b7.de* con b4.de* laur b7.de* lyc b4.de* meny b7.de* nat-m b4.de* *Phos* b4a.de puls b7.de* sep b4.de* staph b7.de* thuj b4.de*
- **amel.**: croc bg2 mur-ac b4.de* phos b4a.de sabin b7.de*

ALCOHOL agg.; abuse of: aur bg2

AMAUROSIS (See EYE - Paralysis - optic)

AMBLYOPIA (See EYE - Amblyopia)

APPROACH and then recede; objects seem to: (*↗VERTIGO - Objects - approach*) *Cic* k* nit-ac h2

- **movies**; looking at: cadm-met gm1

ASTHENOPIA (See EYE - Asthenopia)

ASTIGMATISM (See EYE - Astigmatism)

AURA:

- **people**; of: plut-n srj7• [lac-mat sst4]
- **trees**; of: [lac-mat sst4]

BALLS: (*↗Colors*) act-sp bg2 caust b4.de* kali-c b4.de* stram bg2 verat-v

- **fire**, of: plut-n srj7• stram k*
- **floating**: kali-c k*
- **luminous**: cycl k* plut-n srj7•

BATHING agg.: ant-c bg2

BENDING HEAD BACKWARD: | **amel.**: seneg b4.de*

BLACK SPOTS; floating (See Colors - black - spots - floating)

BLINDNESS (See Loss)

BLOW agg.; from a: *Con* b4a.de

BLOWING THE NOSE agg.; after: alum b4.de* caust b4.de* n a t - m bg2 nat-s bg2

BLURRED: (*↗Dim; Objects - blurred; Run; Weak*) acon acon-ac rly4• aeth agath-a nl2• all-c hr1 am-br vh1 am-m hr1 arg-n br1 arge-pl rwt5• arn *Ars* k* atra-r bnm3• *Aur* aur-ar k2 bamb-a stb2.de• bell bg2 benzol br1 bit-ar wht1• both tsm2 both-ax tsm2 botul br1 bung-fa tsm2 cact k* c a l c k* calc-f k* calc-p k2 caps br1 cardios-h rly4• cartl-s rly4• cassia-s ccrh1• chel chin cic j *Con* k* conch fkr1.de corv-cor bdg• *Crot-c* k* crot-h tsm2 cycl bg cypra-eg sde6.de• cystein-l rly4• dendr-pol tsm2 dros dulc fd4.de elaps tsm2 euphr k2 fago k* falco-pe nl2• flor-p rsj3• fuma-ac rly4• **Gels** k* *Glon* k* haliae-lc srj5• hipp jl2 hippoc-k szs2 irid-met srj5• iris ix bnm8• jab k* kali-n br1 kali-p kali-s fd4.de ketogl-ac rly4• kola stb3• **Lac-c** lat-m bnm6• *Lil-t* k* l i m e n - b - c hrn2* luf-op rsj5• lyc mag-p br1 malar jl2 mang-p rly4• med k* melal-alt gya4 meph br1 merl k* mim-p skp7• naja tsm2 nat-ar **Nat-m** k* nat-ox rly4• nat-s k* nicotam rly4• *Nux-v* k* onos k* oxyurn-sc mcp1• pant-ac rly4• phos k* *Phys* k* *Plat* podo fd3.de• positr nl2• *Psor* k* pycnop-sa mrz1 rauw sp1 *Rhus-t* *Ruta* sec k* sel rsj9• sil h2 spong fd4.de stram streptoc jl2 symph fd3.de• ter hr1 *Teucr* k* thal-xyz srj8• thuj k* tril-p tritic-vg fd5.de urol-h rwt• vanil fd5.de ven-m rsj12• xan c1 [bell-p-sp dcm1 s o l - e c l cky1]

- **one-half** of vision, in: zinc br1
- **left** eye: hydroph rsj6•
- **morning**: merl k* nat-s k* podo fd3.de• spong fd4.de symph fd3.de• urol-h rwt• vanil fd5.de
- **afternoon**: bamb-a stb2.de• ruta fd4.de sel rsj9• spong fd4.de
- **evening**: podo fd3.de• ruta vanil fd5.de
- **night**, after fine work: pic-ac mp1•
- **accompanied** by:
  - **lachrymation**: bamb-a stb2.de• con mtf11 granit-m es1• positr nl2•
  - **vertigo** (See VERTIGO - Accompanied - vision - blurred)
- **body** arose, as if, which impeded sight: am-m mp1•
- **closing** the eyes | **amel.**: calc-f k*
- **confused** spots: **Con** mp1•
- **deafness**, after: *Glon* mp1•
- **distant** objects: chel jab positr nl2• ruta fd4.de
- **emissions** agg.; after: *Calc* *Chin* *Lil-t* k* **Phos**
- **endless** strings of globules were in eye: upa mp1•
- **figures**: ail k*
- **glasses** adjusted; even after having: gels br1

Vision

- **headache**:
  - **after**: podo fd3.de• xan c1
  - **before**: *Gels* hyos **Iris** k* *Kali-bi* lac-d bg1* nat-m mrr1 podo psor bg1 *Sep Sulph* vh tub xxb
  - **during**: anac tl1 carc zzh coll tl1 conch fkr1• crot-h tl1 ip tl1 iris tl1 nat-p tl1 ptel tl1 ruta fd4.de tritic-vg fd5.de [bell-p-sp dcm1]
- **irritated**; when: con
- **large** objects seem: lac-del hm2•
- **letters**: ail k* arg-met arg-n k* *Ars Bell* cann-i mp1• cann-s mp1• carb-ac k* *Chel* chlol hr1 cina cob k* cund hr1 dros hr1 ferr mp1• graph k2 jab kali-c lyc meph k* nat-m mp1• olib-sac wmh1 ox-ac k* oxal-a kr1 ozone sde2* phys plut-n srj7• *Ruta* sil mp1• staph mp1• stram k* sulph k* symph fd3.de• thlas mp1•
- **light**; from:
  - **agg.**: calc
  - **artificial** light | **agg.**: olib-sac wmh1
  - **gaslight** | **agg.**: calc
- **looking** a short time: nat-ar
- **menses**; during: cassia-s ccrh1•
- **milky** layer; as through a: ozone sde2•
- **muscae** volitantes, with: *Lil-t* mp1•
- **only** noticed when looking to left: *Kali-i* mp1•
- **outlines** of objects not sharp: phos mp1•
- **overheated**; when: *Nux-v* k*
- **paralysis** of accommodation: arg-n mp1•
- **parenchymatous** metritis, in: lac-c mp1•
- **pressure** | **amel.**: calc-f k*
- **prolapsus** uteri, in: *Lil-t* mp1•
- **reading** | **after** | **sudden**: phos mp1•
  - **agg.**: musca-d szs1
- **rubbing** | **amel.**: thuj mp1•
- **slightly**: mim-p skp7•
- **turning** the eyes: gels k*
- **vexation**; after: con ptk
- **waking**; on: granit-m es1•
- **winking**, wiping amel.: euph mp1•
- **writing** agg.: calc-f k* nicotam rly4• [tax jsj7]

BRIGHT: agath-a nl2• alum b4a.de* anan a1* anh sp1 *Ars* h2 chel k* falco-pe nl2• olnd k* [tax jsj7]

- **as** if someone had turned up the lights: falco-pe nl2•
- **colors** seem bright: tung-met bdx1•
- **objects** seem brighter: agar k* alum bg2 am-c bg2 am-m bg2 *Anh* bro1 *Ant-t* bg2 ars bg2 *Aur* bg2* bar-c bg2 *Bell* bg2* *Borx* bg2 bry bg2 *Calc* bg2 camph b2.de* cann-xyz bg2 carb-an k* caust bg2 chel bg2 chin bro1 chlor bg2 cic bg2* coloc bg2 con b2.de* croc bg2 *Cycl* bro1 dig k* dros bg2 dulc bg2 euphr bg2 falco-pe nl2• graph bg2 hyos k* ign bg2 iod bg2 irid-met srj5• *Kali-c* bg2 kola stb3• lyc bg2 mang bg2 meny bg2 mez bg2 *Nat-m* bg2* nit-ac bg2 nux-v k* olnd bg2 op bg2 ph-ac bg2 plat bg2 *Plut-n* srj7• puls bg2 rhus-t bg2 sabin bg2 sec bg2 seneg bg2 sep bg2* *Sil* bg2 *Spig* bg2 stront-c bg2 suis-pan rly4• *Valer* b2.de* verat bg2 viol-o bg2 xanth bg2 zinc bg2
  - **evening**: ulm-c jsj8•

CAMPHOR; odor of: | **agg.**: kali-n b4.de*

CHANGING: (↗*Moving*) gels

CHILL: | **after** | **agg.**: cic b7.de

- **during**: cham b7.de

CIPHERS: (↗*MIND - Delusions - seven*) irid-met srj5• *Ph-ac* k* phos sulph k*

CIRCLES: (↗*Colors; Rings*) calc bg3 *Calc-p Carb-v* caust elaps bg3 falco-pe nl2• ham fd3.de• hell iod *Kali-c* phos bg3 plb *Psor* ruta fd4.de stront-c zinc

- **bright**: nat-m b4a.de
- **brighter** field; around an internal: carb-v
- **candles**; around: cic c1
- **colored**: falco-pe nl2•
  - **bands**: con
  - **bright** center; around a: ammc
  - **white** objects; around: hyos

Circles: ...

- **fiery** (See Fiery - circles)
- **heat**; during: (non:dig k*) digin a1*
- **letters** seem: bell h1*
- **light**; about: cycl
- **objects**:
  - **around**: cic c1 dig mrr1
  - **moving** in a circle: chel ptk1 cic a1 cycl ptk1 nat-m ptk1
    - **closing** the eyes; on: hep k*
- **reading** agg.: kali-c k*
- **semicircles**: **Con** ●*
- **turning** agg.: *Kali-c* k* ruta fd4.de
- **yellow** and white rays, with: kali-c k*
- **zigzags**: irid-met srj5• viol-o k*
  - **colored**: (↗*Zigzags - circles*) sep viol-o k13
  - **flickering**: ign k* irid-met srj5•

CLAIRVOYANCE (See MIND - Clairvoyance)

CLARITY of (See Acute)

CLEAR (See Acute)

CLEARER than before (See Acute)

CLOSER; objects seem (See Nearer)

CLOSING THE EYES:

- **agg.**: alum b4a.de arn b7a.de ars bg2 *Bell* bg2* *Bry* bg2* calc bg2* caust bg2 chin bg2 dig b4.de* fl-ac bg2 kali-c b4a.de *Lach* bg2 mang b4.de* nat-m bg2 phos ptk1 sec bg2 spong bg2 stram bg2 tarent bg2 thuj bg2* verat-v ptk1 xanth bg2
- **amel.**: *Apis* b7a.de seneg b4.de*
  - **one** eye; closing: bell bg2
  - **partly**; closing the eyes: nat-m bg2

CLOUDY (See Foggy)

COBWEBS before eyes: (↗*Foggy*) *Arn* b7a.de *Bell* b4a.de calc b4a.de m-arct b7.de nit-ac b4a.de

COITION: | **agg.**: kali-p bg2

COLD; AFTER TAKING A: *Ars* b4a.de calc b4.de* *Dulc* b4a.de *Sulph* b4a.de

COLD AGG., HEAD BECOMING: calc bg2

COLD AIR agg.: puls b7.de* *Rhus-t* b7.de*

COLORS before the eyes: (↗*Balls; Circles; Moving; Spots - colored*) acon bg2 agar k* alum-p k2 am-c k* am-m b7a.de* ambr bg2 anac k* anh c1* arn k* ars bg2 arund asaf bg2 aur k* bar-c k* *Bell* k* borx bg2 *Bry* k* *Calc* k* calc-i k2 calc-sil k2 *Camph* k* cann-s b7.de* canth b7.de* caps b7.de* carb-v bg2 caust k* cham bg2 chin k* chinin-s *Cic* k* *Cina* cocc k* coli rly4• **Con** k* croc b7.de* cupr bg2 *Cycl Dig* k* dros bg2 euph euphr bg2 falco-pe nl2• ferr bg2 *Fl-ac* bg2 graph bg2 hep k* hyos b7.de* *Iod* k* ip kali-ar *Kali-bi Kali-c* k* kali-n kali-p kali-sil k2 laur bg2 lyc bg2 mag-c k* *Mag-p* manc vh mang bg2 meny bg2 merc k* mosch bg2 mur-ac bg2 nat-c k* *Nat-m* k* nat-p nit-ac k* nux-v bg2 olnd bg2 op bg2 osm bg petr bg2 ph-ac k* phos k* plb bg2 psor puls k* ruta k* sabad b7.de* sars sec bg2 sep k* sil k* spig b7.de* spong squil bg2 staph b7.de* stram k* stront-c k* sulph k* thuj k* tritic-vg fd5.de valer bg2 vanil fd5.de verat bg2 verb bg2 viol-o bg2 zinc bg2

- **left**: olib-sac wmh1
- **evening**: agar kali-n sars
- **accompanied** by | **Head**; pain in: med mrr1 psil ft1
- **black**: acon b2.de* agar k* am-m b2.de* anac bg2 *Arn* k* *Atro* bro1 aur b2.de* bar-c b2.de* *Bell* b2.de* calc b2.de* caps b2.de* carb-v b2.de* *Carbn-s* bro1 caust bg2 *Chin* b2.de* cic b2.de* cina k* *Clem* k* cocc b2.de* con bg2 cycl a1* dig bro1 euphr b2.de* falco-pe nl2• ferr k2 *Kali-c* b2.de* kali-p fd1.de• *Lach* k* lyc b2.de* mag-c b2.de* mag-p bro1 mang b2.de* melal-alt gya4 *Merc* k* mosch b2.de* nat-c bg2 **Nat-m** k* nit-ac b2.de* nux-v b2.de* petr b2.de* ph-ac b2.de* *Phos* k* phys bro1 ruta b2.de* sec b2.de* **Sep** b2.de* **Sil** b2.de* staph b2.de* *Stram* b2.de* stront-c bg2* sulph bg2 *Tab* bro1 thuj bg2* valer b2.de* verat b2.de* zinc bg2*
  - **animals**: nat-ar
  - **balls**: *Bell* cund k* *Kali-c* k*

· **circles** (See rings)
· **disk**: elaps
· **figures**: anh sp1 bell bg2 cocc k* mosch b7a.de petr k*
: **floating** before eyes: cocc k*
· **flickering**: **Lach** k*
· **flies**, floating: *(↗spots - floating)* agar k2 asaf k2 bar-s k2 kali-sil k2 ruta fd4.de sulph k*
· **floating**: aur-s k2 calc-f sp1 *Chel* chin chlf k* cop daph k* gins ign gk led petr k* **Phos**
· **halo**: caust bg2 ph-ac b4a.de phos k*
· **horns**: cund k*
· **letters** change to points: *Calc-p*
· **lightning**: sec b7a.de staph k* *Valer* b7a.de
· **looking** downward agg.: *Kalm*
· **motes**: agar hr1 arg-n hr1 merc-i-f k*
· **moving**: thuj
· **objects**: caps k* *Cic* k* falco-pe nl2• melal-alt gya4 sol-ni stram k* sul-ac k*
: **turning** agg.: cocc k* sarr k*
· **outlines**; and white: chir-fl gya2
· **plate**: kali-bi k*
· **points**: *Am-c* b4a.de am-m b7a.de anan k* ant-c bell b4a.de calc k* *Caust* chin k* chlf a1 con k* dig b4.de* elaps *Gels* jatr-c *Kali-c* k* *Merc* k* mez a1 mosch k* nat-c b4.de* nat-m k* nit-ac k* *Nux-v* k* petr b4.de* *Phos* k* *Ruta* b7a.de *Sep* b4a.de sol-ni sulph b4.de* tab k* ter a1 thuj k* *Valer* b7a.de vanil fd5.de
: **morning**: bell k*
: **candlelight**; by: carb-an k*
: **dinner**; before: thuj k*
: **reading** agg.: calc k* *Kali-c*
· **reading** agg.: cic k* kali-c k* sol-ni
: **accompanying** letter: calc k*
· **rings**, circles: elaps bg3* hell bg1 nit-s-d bg1 pitu-gl skp7• psor ruta fd4.de sal-al blc1• sol-ni
: **bright** centre; with a: caust b4a.de
: **floating**: dig k* digin a1
: **headache**; before: *Psor*
: **heat**; during: dig k* digin a1
: **reading** agg.: kali-c k*
: **waving**: dig k*
· **rising** | **bed**; from | **agg.**: cina k2
: **stooping**; from | **agg.**: carc fd2.de• mez podo fd3.de•
· **serpents**: *(↗Snake)* cund k*
· **sparks**: mang h2* stry k*
· **spots**: acon b7.de* agar k* am-c k* am-m b7a.de ammc hr1 arg-n asc-t k* *Aur* k* *Bar-c* k* bar-s k2 bell k* *Calc* k* *Camph* k* carb-an h2* carb-v b4.de* chel k* chinin-s chlf k* chlor *Cimic* k* cocc k* *Con* k* cupr-ar k* cur k* daph hr1 dulc k* elaps gels k2 **Glon** k* hell k* hydrog srj2• hyos mtf11 *Kali-c* b4.de* *Lil-t* *Lyc* k* *Mag-c* k* mang b4.de* med k* meli k* nat-c k* **Nat-m** *Nit-ac* k* petr k* ph-ac b4a.de *Phos* k* *Psor* k* ruta fd4.de sec b7a.de **Sep** k* *Sil* k* stram k* stront-c symph fd3.de• syph tab k* thuj vanil fd5.de verat k* [bell-p-sp dcm1]
: **morning** | **waking**; on: dulc
: **closed**; when eyes are: *Con* elaps
: **eating**; after: lyc k*
: **exertion** agg.: *Calc* k*
: **floating**: *(↗flies)* acon aesc *Agar* k* am-c am-m b2.de* anac c1 anan ant-t k* *Arg-n* arn asaf *Aur* k* *Bar-c* *Bell* k* *Calc* k* cann-s b2.de* *Carb-v* *Carl* *Caust* k* chel **Chin** k* *Chinin-s* bg2 chlf c2 chlol cob **Cocc** k* coff k* *Con* k* croc mtf11 *Crot-h* cupr-ar cur c2 *Cycl* *Daph* dig k* dulc b2.de* dys mtf11 *Gels* glon hep b2.de* hyos k* ign gk itu c2 *Kali-c* k* kali-p kali-s kali-sil k2 lact lact-v hr1* *Lil-t* *Lyc* mag-c k* med gk *Merc* k* mez morph nat-c **NAT-M** k ●* **Nit-ac** k ●* *Nux-m* *Nux-v* k* op b2.de* ozone sde2• par paraf c2 petr mtf11 **PHOS** k ●* **Phys** k* plb b2.de* *Psor* k* puls b2.de* *Rhus-t* k* *Ruta* b2.de* sal-al blc1• sec b2.de* **SEP** k ●* **Sil** k* sol-ni spig b2.de* *Stram* k* **Sulph** k* *Tab* k* ter thuj k* vanil fd5.de verat zinc k*

- **black – spots – floating**: ...
: **right**: chinin-s ptk1 cimic ptk1 sel ptk1 *Sil* ptk1
: **left**: agar ptk1 calc ptk1 *Caust* ptk1 merc ptk1 *Sulph* ptk1
: **eating**; after: lyc *Phos*
: **fixing** the eye on an object amel.: aesc k1
: **reading** agg.: choc srj3• *Kali-c*
: **sewing**, after: am-c
: **walking** in open air agg.: ter
: **writing** agg.: *Nat-c*
: **headache**:
: **before**: phos ptk *Psor*
: **during**: *Glon* k* **Meli** k* psil vml3•
: **moving** in all directions: *Chinin-s* med c1 *Sep* k* stram k*
: **reading**:
: **after**: cocc *Cur*
: **agg.**: med c1
: **rising** from sitting agg.: verat k*
: **sewing**:
: **after**: am-c kl*
: **while**: (non:am-c kl)
: **turning** quickly: *Glon* k*
: **vertigo**; with: *Con* k* *Glon* k*
: **writing** agg.: *Nat-c* k*
· **stripes**: aids nl2• con k* galla-q-r nl2• ph-ac k* *Sep* sol-ni sulph
: **morning**: bell k*
: **coming down**: aids nl2•
: **reading** agg.: kali-c sol-ni
· **swirling** void: falco-pe nl2•
· **veil**: aur k*
: **right** eye; before the: *Phos*
· **white** outlines; and (See outlines)
- **blindness** for (See Loss - colors)
- **blue**: acon k* act-sp k* agar mfj aids nl2• aml-ns bg2* ars bg2 *Aur* k* *Bell* k* *Bry* k* **Chin** **Cina** k* coff bg2* *Crot-c* k* crot-h bro1 cycl k* dig bg2* elaps galla-q-r nl2• glon bg2 jab bg1 jatr-c bg2 kali-c k* kreos bg2* *Lach* k* *Lyc* k* nicc k* phos k2 positr nl2• *Stram* k* stront-c k* sulph b2.de* symph fd3.de• thuj bg2* tril-c bro1 tril-p k* tritic-vg fd5.de *Tub* k* valer bg2* xan c1 zinc k* *Zinc-chr* ptk1 [heroin sdj2]
· **right** eye: nicc k*
· **evening**: am-br k* olib-sac wmh1
· **blindness** for: carbn-s
· **borders** of objects: stront-c b4.de*
· **circles**: zinc k*
· **closed**; when eyes are: thuj
· **dark** blue: cycl k* kreos k*
· **distance**, in the: *lod*
· **flashes**: positr nl2• xan c1
: **headache**; during: positr nl2•
· **halo** around candle: *Hipp* k* *Ip* *Lach* k* [heroin sdj2]
· **haze**: *Bry* k*
· **increased**: anh sp1
· **lace**; as through blue: xan c1
· **letters**: bell h1*
· **light**: plut-n srj7•
: **around**: *Lach* k*
: **candlelight**: hipp k*
· **points**: androc srj1• sec
· **reading** agg.: bell k* irid-met srj5•
· **rubbing** agg.: stront-c
· **sparks**: ars k*
· **spots**: acon k* *Kali-c* k*
: **morning** | **rising** agg.: aids nl2• thuj k*
: **night** | **lying** on right side in a dark room; when: stram k*
: **dark** room; in a: hep stram

Vision

- **squares**: aids nl2•
- **stars**: psor
  - **headache**; during: _Psor_
- **stripes**: aids nl2• tritic-vg fd5.de

- **bright**: aloe alum k* am-c k* _Ant-t_ k* ars k* _Aur_ k* aur-ar k2 aur-i k2 bar-c k* _Bell_ k* _Borx_ k* bry k* _Camph_ k* cann-s k* caust k* chel k* chlol hr1 cic k* **Cina** coloc k* _Con_ k* croc k* _Dig_ k* digin a1 dros k* dulc k* euphr k* fl-ac k* _Graph_ k* hydrog srj2• _Hyos_ k* ign k* _Iod_ k* _Ip_ irid-met srj5• _Kali-bi_ _Kali-c_ b2.de* _Lyc_ k* m-ambo b2.de* mang k* meny k* mez k* nat-c ptk1 nat-m k* **Nux-v** k* olnd k* op k* ph-ac b2.de* phos plat k* _Puls_ k* rhus-t k* sabin k* sec k* seneg k* spig k* stram k* stront-c k* _Valer_ k* verat k* viol-o k* zinc k* [spect dfg1]
  - **appear** brighter; colors (See Acute)
  - **dark** room agg.; in a: valer ptk1
  - **spots**: ol-an bg2
- **brown**: agar bg2* bell bg2 lac-c bg2* med bg2* spong fd4.de
  - **dark** brown | **spots**: agar b4.de*
  - **spot**: med jl2 spong fd4.de
    - **closing** other eye: agar h2
    - **floating**: agar ptk1
    - **weather**; in gloomy: agar h2
- **changing**: galla-q-r nl2•
- **dark**: acon k* agar k* am-m k* ambr k* _Anac_ k* arn k* ars k* ars-s-f k2 asaf k* _Aur_ bg2 _Bar-c_ bg2 _Bell_ k* berb _Calc_ k* calc-sil k2 carb-v k* _Caust_ k* cham k* _Chin_ k* cic b2.de* _Cocc_ k* _Con_ k* cupr k* dig k* dros k* _Euphr_ k* ferr k* hep k* _Kali-c_ k* kali-p kali-s kali-sil k2 laur k* lyc k* mag-c k* mang k* meny k* _Merc_ k* mosch k* mur-ac k* nat-ar nat-c k* nat-m k* nat-p _Nit-ac_ k* nux-v k* olnd k* op k* petr k* ph-ac k* _Phos_ k* plb k* ruta k* sabad k* sec k* _Sep_ k* _Sil_ k* squil k* staph k* _Stram_ k* **Sulph** k* thuj k* verat k* verb k*
  - **circles**: caust b4.de* hell bg2 _Iod_ k* kali-c k*
    - **bright** centre; with: _Calc_ b4a.de carb-v b4.de* kali-c b4.de* thuj bg2
    - **points** of light; with: caust k*
  - **clouds**: coca lac-ac k* ol-an k* tarent
  - **cough** agg.; during: coff b7.de* kali-c bg2 lach bg2 sulph bg2
  - **objects**: ant-t ign lac-c hr1 _Nat-m_ phos k* sulph
    - **moving**: carbn-h lac-c hr1
    - **seem** dark: bell k* berb caps a1 hep k* nit-ac olib-sac wmh1 thuj k*
  - **points**: am-m b7a.de chlf k* cic k* _Con_ hyos b7.de* **Sulph** k*
    - **floating**: aur cann-s a1 hyos k* phos h2*
  - **serpent**-like waves: phys k*
  - **specks**: _Calc_ k* cimic bg2 con cupr-ar _Kali-c_ k* mag-c nat-m nit-ac **Phos** k* sep **Sil** k* sulph
  - **spots**: agar anac h2* asc-t cact carb-ac k* carb-an k* chlf a1 chlol k* _Cimic_ k* _Cocc_ con k* elaps euon a1 fl-ac hell k* jatr-c _Kali-c_ med _Merc_ _Phos_ k* spong fd4.de **Sulph** k* thuj k*
    - **morning**: cassia-s ccrh1•
    - **floating**: agar cocc k* phos h2* **Sulph** k*
    - **reading** agg.: fl-ac _Kali-c_ _Lach_ k* lachn
    - **white** margins, with: con k*
  - **stripes**: cic k* ph-ac b4a.de **Sulph** k* zinc k*
  - **worms**: phys k*
- **glistening**: _Bell_ b4a.de
- **golden**: bell b4.de* hyos b7.de*
  - **chain** dangling before eyes: _Chin_
  - **everything** looks: hyos k* irid-met srj5•
  - **letters** seem: bell k*
- **gray**:
  - **black** objects seem gray: arg-n bg2 ars bg2 brom bg2 calc-p bg2 elaps bg2 lachn bg2 nit-ac bg2 nux-v b7.de* **Phos** bg2 sep bg2* **Sil** bg2 _Stram_ k*
  - **bluish** gray circle around light: lach
  - **borders** of objects: stram b7.de
  - **circles**: lachn k*
  - **cover** before the eyes; a gray: _(↗veil)_ phos k* sil b4.de*
  - **fog**: cic k*
  - **halo**: phos k* sep k*
- **gray**: ...
  - **letters**: stram k*
    - **change** to round gray spots: calc-p k*
  - **margin** on objects: stram bg2
  - **objects** seem: ammc bg1 arg-n bg1* _Ars_ brom bg1 calc-p bg1 **camph** conv bro1 elaps bg1 guare k* lachn bg1 nit-ac k* _Nux-v_ k* phal k* _Phos_ k* sep k* _Sil_ k* _Stram_ k*
  - **point** before right eye moving with eye: brom k*
  - **points**: _Nux-v_ k*
  - **reddish** gray border around white things: _Stram_ k*
  - **serpent**-like bodies: **Arg-n** k*
  - **spots**: _Arg-n_ k* calc-p k* chlf k* cic k* conv br1 lachn k* nit-ac b4.de* symph fd3.de•
    - **distance**, at a: nit-ac
    - **square**; about three inches: conv br1
  - **veil**: _(↗cover)_ _Apis_ k* elaps k* nept-m lsd2.fr phos hr1* sil c1
- **green**: aids nl2• aml-ns bg2* **Ars** k* bry bg2* calc cann-i k* cann-s b7a.de* canth carbn-s caust bg2* chin bg2 **Cina** k* cupr bg2 _Cycl_ k* _Dig_ k* hep bg2* kali-ar kali-c k* _Lac-c_ mag-m k* merc k* nit-ac bg2 osm bro1* **Phos** k* phyt ptk1 _Ruta_ k* sal-fr sle1• **Santin** k* sep k* stram k* _Stront-c_ k* stry k* sulph k* tab a1* tritic-vg fd5.de (non:tub slp*) ulm-c jsj8• vario ptk1 verat bg2 verat-v bg1 zinc k* zinc-p k2
  - **left**: ulm-c jsj8•
  - **blindness** for: carbn-s
  - **circles**: zinc k*
    - **light**; around: verat-v
  - **dinner**; during: mag-m k*
    - **eructations** | **amel.**: mag-m
  - **fever**; during: _Chin_ bg2
  - **halo** around light: ammc bg1 anag bg1 atro bg1 bell bg2 calc cann-xyz bg2 _Caust_ k* chin bg2* com bg2* dig b4a.de* mag-m k* **Osm** br1 ozone sde2• **Phos** k* ruta k* _Sep_ k* sil k* _Sulph_ k* verat bg2 verat-v bg2 zinc k*
  - **increased**: anh sp1
    - **metallic** taste; produces (See MOUTH - Taste - metallic - green)
  - **letters**: canth k*
  - **lights**; sees green: plut-n srj7•
  - **objects** appearing green: aml-ns vh1
    - **red** and foggy; then: carbn-s c1
  - **pea** green, on looking in the glass; saw herself: cina
  - **radiation**: bell bg2* con bg2* ign bg2* ph-ac bg2*
  - **rising**:
    - **agg.**: vario ptk1
    - **bed**; from | **agg.**: vario jl2
  - **sparks**: kali-c
  - **spots**: _Caust_ _Kali-c_ k* _Lac-c_ nit-ac k* stram stront-c k*
    - **walking** in the dark, while: _Stront-c_ k*
  - **stripes**: lac-loxod-a hrn2• thuj k* tritic-vg fd5.de
  - **vomiting**: tab k*
  - **yellow**-green: aids nl2• santin
- **halo** of colors:
  - **letters** while reading; around the: alum cic
  - **light**; around the: alum alum-p k2 _Anac_ bar-c **Bell** k* _Bry_ _Calad_ **calc** _Carb-v_ cham chim chlol bro1 _Cic_ k* colch bg2 _Cycl_ _(non:dig b4a.de*)_ _Digin_ a1* euph b4a.de gels _Hep_ hyos bro1 _Ip_ irid-met srj5• kali-c k* kali-n k* kali-p kali-s _Lach_ mag-m merl nat-p _Nicc_ nit-ac **Osm** _Ph-ac_ **Phos** **Puls** ran-b _Ruta_ _Sars_ _Sep_ stann _Staph_ **Sulph** k* _Tub_ k* zinc zinc-p k2
    - **bluish** green and red border: osm bg2
    - **red** and green: sil bg2
  - **objects**; around: dig mrr1
  - **pulsating** to the rhythm of music (See Illusions - colorful - pulsating)
- **increased**: anh sp1

- **jewel** like: falco-pe nl2•
- **motions**; when making fast: stram
- **one** color; everything is as if: anh sp1
- **pale**: dig b4.de*
- **prismatic** (See rainbow - all)
- **purple**: cund a1 haliae-lc srj5• melal-alt gya4 *Verat-v* ptk1
- **rainbow**: irid-met srj5•
  - **right**: haliae-lc srj5•
  - **all** the colors: *Bell* k* *Bry* k* calc bg2 cic b2.de* *Con* k* dig k* digin a1* euph b2.de euphr bg2 haliae-lc srj5• ip k* kali-c b2.de* kali-n b2.de* osm bg2 *Ph-ac* b2.de* *Phos* b2.de* puls stann b2.de* stram b2.de* sulph b2.de*
  - **beaming** light of: bell
  - **circles**: bry vh1 dig digin a1* ip k*
  - **halo** around light: kali-n b4.de* osm bg2 *Phos* b4a.de stann b4a.de
  - **striped** | **closing** one eye; on: bry k*
- **red**: antip bro1 apis bro1 **Bell** k* bry bg2* *Cact* k* calc mfj cann-s b2.de* carbn-s caust mfj cedr k* com bg2* **Con** k* croc k* cund bg1* *Dig* k* dream-p sdj1• *Dub* bro1 elaps k* fl-ac bg2* *Hep* k* *Hyos* k* iodof bg1 ip b7a.de* *Kali-bi* lac-c mag-m k* *Nux-m* nux-v bg2* onos bg2 **Phos** k* plut-n srj7• positr nl2• ruta bg3* sabad b2.de* sars k* sep k* spig b2.de* spong stram b2.de* *Stront-c* k* *Sulph* k* symph fd3.de• tarent *Thuj* b4a.de verat bg2 verat-v bg3* zinc bg2*
  - **evening** | **reading** by candle-light: sars h2
  - **night**: cedr k* chin elaps mag-m spong
    - **and** yellow during day: cedr
  - **blindness** for: carbn-s
  - **blood**-red: positr nl2•
  - **borders** of objects: stram b7.de stront-c b4.de*
  - **circles**: cact k*
    - **light** seems to be: *Sulph* k*
    - **rubbing**; on: stront-c
  - **closing** the eyes agg.: elaps
  - **decreased**: anh sp1
  - **dinner**; during: mag-m h2*
  - **flashing** buttons: plut-n srj7•
  - **halo**: *Bell* ●* com *Ip* osm bg2 sars b4a.de sil k* stront-c b4a.de *Sulph* b4a.de verat-v k*
    - **lamplight**; around the: com
  - **letters** seem: *Phos* bg2*
  - **luminous** appearance: *Phos* spong k*
  - **margin** on objects: stram bg2
  - **masses**: spig k*
  - **objects** seem: atro k* **Bell** k* carbn-s **Con** k* *Dig Hep Hyos* k* iod k* iodof k* *Nux-m* k* **Phos** spong fd4.de *Stront-c* k*
  - **obstructions** on looking at the light: cund k*
  - **paper** looks red: croc k* sars h2*
  - **points**: *Bell* b4a.de elaps
  - **sparks**: fl-ac k* stry k*
  - **spots**: dub bg1 elaps hipp a1 hyos lac-c lyc ozone sde2• verat-v ptk1 [bell-p-sp dcm1]
    - **fiery**: elaps
    - **floating**: *Dubo-m* br1
  - **wheel**, candlelight seems to be a red: sulph h2
- **rubbing**; after: stront-c
- **stripes**; colored: *(↗Stripes)* *Am-c* k* am-m b2.de* bell k* cham b2.de* **Con** k* iod b2.de* kali-c b2.de* m-ambo b2.de merc bg2 *Nat-m* k* phos b2.de* puls k* *Sep* k* sol-ni bg1 sulph bg2* thuj [tax jsj7]
- **swirling**: falco-pe nl2• positr nl2•
- **variegated**: *Bell* k* *Bry* calc bro1 *Cic* k* **Con** k* croc bro1 dig k* euph b2.de* falco-pe nl2• galla-q-r nl2• *Ip* b7a.de kali-c k* kali-n k* kali-s mag-p k* merc bro1 nicc *Ph-ac* k* *Phos* k* *Puls* bro1 ruta bro1 *Sep* staph bro1 stram k* sulph k*
  - **borders** of objects: hyos b7a.de
  - **circles**: hyos b7a.de kali-n b4.de*
  - **stripes**: *Con* b4a.de
  - **wheels**: kali-n h2
- **violet**: cann-i a1 **Cina** k*
- **vivid** | **appear** more vivid; colors (See Acute)
- **white**: alum b2.de* am-c k* apis bg2* ars bg2* bell k* cann-s b2.de* caust b2.de* chel b2.de* chlf bg1 chlol bro1* coca bg2 *Dig* k* elaps grat k* *Kali-c* k* nept-m lsd2.fr *Ph-ac* k* positr nl2• ruta fd4.de sulph b2.de* thuj bg2* ust bg2*
  - **blindness** for: carbn-s
  - **bottles** of water: thuj bg2*
  - **candlelight** seems: dig k*
  - **clouds** wandering from left to right: bell h1*
  - **drops** on looking at snow; falling: *Kali-c* k*
  - **flames**: chlf k*
  - **flickering**: *Ign* k* sep k*
  - **flies**: bell bg2 dig bg2*
  - **globules**: upa k*
  - **green**; white objects look: grat
  - **lines**: positr nl2•
  - **margin**: con bg2
    - **letters**; around: *Chin*
  - **pale**, faces appear white: dig k* ind k*
  - **points**: ars k* cann-s a1 rat ust
  - **rays**, flaming: cann-s k*
  - **serpents**: *(↗Snake)* ign bg2*
  - **sparks**: rat bg2* stry k* ust bg2*
  - **spots**: acon k* alum b4.de* am-c b4.de* ars k* *Caust* coca con k* gins k* jab br1* mez k* ruta fd4.de sol-ni *Sulph* k* ust k* [bell-p-sp dcm1]
    - **floating**: jab ptk1 ust ptk1
    - **then** green: *Caust*
    - **waving**: dig k* ruta fd4.de
  - **stars**: alum k* am-c k* bell k* calc bg2* caust k* kali-c k* nat-c k*
    - **blowing** the nose agg.: alum k*
    - **sneezing** agg.: am-c h2
    - **writing** agg.: kali-c k*
  - **stream** of light with a black streak in it: galla-q-r nl2•
  - **stripes**: sol-ni [tax jsj7]
  - **swirling**: positr nl2•
  - **wheels**: kali-c h2*
  - **zigzags** in a circle: ign k*
- **yellow**: agar k* aids nl2• aloe k* alum k* am-c b4a.de* am-m b2.de* aml-ns bg2* apis bg2 ars k* aur bg2* *Bell* k* bry bg2* calen bg2* cann-i k* cann-xyz bg2 *Canth* k* carb-an bg2 cedr bg2* chin bg2* **Cina** k* coff bg2* colch bg2 coli rly4• coloc bg2* *Crot-h Cycl* k* *Dig* k* digox bro1 falco-pe nl2• hyos b2.de* ind irid-met bg1 kali-ar *Kali-bi* k* *Kali-c* k* kali-s kali-sil k2 lac-c lachn bg2* mang b2.de* merc bg2 nat-s bg2 osm bg2* petr bg2* phos bg2* plb k* santin k* *Sep* k* sil k* stront-c k* sulph k* tab bg2* tritic-vg fd5.de zinc k* [erech stj]
  - **day**: cedr k*
    - **and** red at night: cedr
  - **blindness**; after attacks of: bell ptk1
  - **blue**; surrounded by: aml-ns bg2
  - **border** around all objects: bell k*
  - **circles**: aloe bg2 kali-c b4.de* mang b4.de* zinc b4.de*
    - **light**; around the: alum gsy1 *Kali-c Osm* zinc
    - **moving**: *Aloe*
  - **cloud**: kali-c k*
  - **crescent**-shaped bodies floating obliquely upwards: *Aur*
  - **decreased**: anh sp1
  - **fiery**: *Bell* b4a.de ph-ac b4.de*
  - **flames**: santin thuj
  - **halo**:
    - **light**; around the: **Alum** k* sarr sulph b4a.de
    - **objects**; around: dig mrr1
  - **letters**: canth k*
  - **looking** long at same point: lachn vml3•
  - **objects** seem yellow: aml-ns vh1 ars-s-f k2 dys bh* kali-bi tl1 phasco-ci rbp2

Vision

- **objects** seem yellow: ...
  - **accompanied** by | **red** discoloration of eyes (See EYE - Discoloration - red - accompanied - vision)
- **points**: carb-an k* tritic-vg fd5.de
- **red** things look yellow: bell
- **shiny** tremulous mist: kali-c
- **spots**: agar am-c k* am-m k* carb-an h2* lachn c1 ph-ac bg2 plb k*
  - **before** left eye: agar k*
    - **looking** at white objects: am-c k*
    - **reading** agg.: phos
  - **reading** agg.: lachn a1
- **veil**: kali-bi k*
- **vomiting**; while: tab k*
- **wheels**: kali-c h2* zinc h2*
- **white** objects look yellow: [erech stj]

COMPLAINTS of vision: arg-n ptk1 aur ptk1 **Bell** ptk1 *Con* ptk1 cycl ptk1* *Gels* ptk1 haliae-lc srj5• *Hyos* ptk1 jab ptk1 lil-t mrr1 *Lyc* ptk1 med jl2 **Nat-m** ptk1 nux-v ptk1 op ptk1 *Phos* ptk1 puls ptk1 ruta ptk1 sarr br1 sep ptk1 *Sil* ptk1 *Stram* ptk1 **Sulph** ptk1 tub jl2 vac jl2 [bell-p-sp dcm1]

- **accompanied** by:
  - **nausea**: ars bg2 dig bg2 kalm bg2
  - **palpitation** (See CHEST - Palpitation - accompanied - vision)
  - **sleepiness**: thuj b4a.de zinc bg2
  - **vertigo**: con bro1 *Gels* bro1 pilo bro1
  - **worms**; complaints of: *Hyos* b7a.de
  - ○ **Kidneys**; complaints of: kali-p bg2
  - **Throat**; tickling in: acon bg2
- **head**; pain in:
  - **after**: caust ptk1 con ptk1 *Lach* ptk1 *Phos* ptk1 sil ptk1 *Sulph* ptk1
  - **before**: anh bro1 bell bro1 *Cycl* bro1 epiph bro1 gels bro1* glon ptk1 graph ptk1 ign bro1 iris bro1* **Kali-bi** bro1* kali-c bro1 lac-c bro1 *Lac-d* bro1 lach ptk1 *Nat-m* bro1* nicc bro1 nux-v bro1 *Phos* ptk1 pic-ac bro1 podo bro1* **Psor** bro1* *Sang* bro1 *Sep* ptk1 sil bro1* spig bro1 *Sulph* ptk1 ther bro1* *Tub* ptk1 *Zinc-s* bro1
  - **during**: anh bro1 bell bro1* *Cycl* bro1 epiph bro1 *Gels* bro1 ign bro1 iris bro1* *Kali-bi* bro1 kali-c bro1 lac-c bro1 *Lac-d* bro1 *Nat-m* bro1 nicc bro1 nux-v bro1 ph-ac ptk1 pic-ac bro1 podo bro1* psor bro1 *Puls* ptk1 *Sang* bro1 sil bro1 spig bro1 *Ther* bro1 zinc ptk1 *Zinc-s* bro1
- **tension** of eyes; from: aur tl1

CONDYLOMATA; after: *Caust* b4a.de

CONFUSED: acon aeth atro *Aur* bapt bell cann-i cann-s c1 cedr cic k2 cocc c1 *Con* k* croc dig eug **Gels** *Glon* graph b2.de* hep c1 ign k2 iod b2.de* kali-bi k* led b2.de* lil-t lyc k* **Nat-m** nat-s c1 *Phos* b4a.de *Phys* pic-ac *Plat* k* *Psor* *Rhus-t* ruta fd4.de sec sil b2.de* stram k* stry ther tl1 tub-r jl2

- **alternating** with | **Head**; pain in (See HEAD - Pain - alternating - vision - confusion)
- **pressure** under nose amel.: gels psa*
- **stool** agg.; after: gels a1
- **wine** agg.; red: gels a1

CONTRACTED: | **visual** field: acetan br1* ben-d mtf11 mang-act br1 titan mtf11 [tax jsj7]

CONTRAST increased: anh sp1

CONTUSIONS agg.; after: *Con* b4a.de sul-ac b4a.de

COUGH agg.: coff b7.de* ign ptk1 kali-c b4.de* kali-m ptk1 kali-n bg2 nux-v bg2 par b7.de*

CROOKED:

- **lines**, while reading: *Bell*
- **objects** appear: *Bell* k* bufo k* nux-m ptk1 stram ptk1

DANCING: all-c *Bell* calc k* *Cic* *Glon* k* nux-m *Psor* santin

- **headache**; before: *Psor*

DARKENING of: arist-cl sp1 cypra-eg sde6.de• euphr b7a.de mand sp1 psor ptk1 stram ptk1 sulph ptk1 ulm-c jsj8•

- **evening**: ulm-c jsj8•

Darkening of: ...

- **rising** agg.: arist-cl sp1

DARKNESS:

- **agg.**: bar-c b4.de* staph b7.de* stront-c b4.de* valer b7.de*
- **amel.**: ferr bg2

DAY BLINDNESS (See Dim - daytime; Loss - daytime)

DAZZLING: acon am-m anan ant-c ars **Bar-c** k* bell k* *Calc* k* calc-sil k2 *Camph* k* carb-an b2.de* caust b2.de* chel b2.de* cic b2.de* **Con** k* crot-c dig b2.de* **Dros** k* *Euphr* k* **Graph** b2.de* hyos b2.de* ign b2.de* irid-met srj5• **Kali-c** k* kali-s kali-sil k2 lach *Lyc* k* mang b2.de* *Merc* k* nat-c k* nat-m tl1 nit-ac b2.de* nux-v b2.de* olnd k* ph-ac k* *Phos* k* plat h2 plb plut-n srj7• psil ft1 *Psor* k* *Seneg* k* sep k* **Sil** k* spong fd4.de stram k* *Sulph* k* *Valer* k* verat-v

- **morning**: sulph h2*
- **candlelight**: lyc
- **darkness** | **amel.**: ferr bg1
- **distant** objects: all-c k*
- **looking** long: **Sulph** k*
- **near** objects: ph-ac h2*
- **reading** agg.: seneg
- **snow**: ant-c *Ars* olnd sep
- **spot** before eyes: am-m b7a.de *Chel* k*
- **sunlight**: euphr lith-c *Sep* spong fd4.de *Stram*
- **urination** agg.; after: eug
- **walking** in the street; when: psor jl2

DELIRIUM agg.; during: crot-h bg2 op bg2 stram bg2

DIM: (*↗Blurred; Weak; EYE - Amblyopia; EYE - Asthenopia*) absin k* acon b2.de* aesc-g hr1 **Agar** k* ail k* alet hr1 allox tpw3* *Alum* k* alum-p k2 alum-sil k2 alumn k* *Am-c* k* am-m b2.de* ambr k* aml-ns vh1 *Ammc* k* amyg hr1 *Anac* k* ang b2.de* ant-t b2.de* *Apis* k* *Arg-met* k* *Arg-n* k* arn b2.de* *Ars* k* *Ars-i* ars-s-f k2 *Arum-t* k* arund k* asaf k* *Asar* k* astac k* atro k* **Aur** k* aur-ar k2 aur-i k2 *Aur-m* aur-s k2 bamb-a stb2.de• bapt-c c2 *Bar-c* k* bar-i k2 *Bar-m* bar-s k2 **Bell** k* berb k* bism k* bism-sn a1 borx b2.de* bov b2.de* brach hr1 bry k* bufo *Cact* k* cadm-s calad bg2 **Calc** k* *Calc-f* k* calc-i k2 calc-s calc-sil k2 camph k* cann-i k* **Cann-s** k* **Cann-xyz** ptk1 canth k* caps k* carb-ac k* *Carb-an* k* *Carb-v* k* **Carbn-s** **Caust** k* cedr k* cench k2 *Cham* k* *Chel* k* **Chin** k* *Chinin-ar* *Chinin-s* k* chlf a1 *Chlol* k* chlor hr1 *Cic* k* *Cimic* k* *Cina* k* *Cinnb* *Clem* k* clerod-i bnj1 cob k* cob-n sp1 *Cocc* k* coch hr1 coff b2.de* *Colch* k* *Coloc* k* *Com* k* **Con** k* cop hr1 *Croc* k* *Crot-c* *Crot-h* k* *Crot-t* cupr b2.de* cupr-ar k* cupr-s hr1 **Cycl** k* cypra-eg sde6.de• daph bg2* dig k* *Dros* b2.de* *Dulc* k* elae c2 *Elaps* eucal hr1 **Euph** k* euphr k* fago k* ferr b2.de* ferr-ar *Form* k* **Gels** k* gent-ch bnj1 gink-b sbd1• *Glon* k* graph k* guaj bg2 haem a1 ham k* hell k* helon k* **Hep** k* hura *Hydr* k* hydr-ac hr1 *Hyos* k* hyper *Ign* k* *Iod* k* *Ip* k* iris bg2 jab k* *Kali-ar* k* *Kali-bi* k* *Kali-br* k* *Kali-c* k* kali-cy k* *Kali-i* k* kali-m k2 *Kali-p* kali-s kali-sil k2 *Kalm* k* *Kreos* k* *Lac-c* k* *Lac-d* k* **Lach** k* lachn k* lact-v hr1 lap-la sde8.de• *Laur* k* lavand-a ctl1• *Led* k* *Lil-t* k* *Lith-c* lol bg2 **Lyc** k* lyss k* m-arct b2.de m-aust b2.de* *Mag-c* k* *Mag-m* k* mag-p hr1 mand rsj7• *Mang* k* med k2 melal-alt gya4 meny b7.de* meph k* **Merc** k* merc-i-f hr1 *Merl* mez b4.de mim-h a1 mosch b2.de* *Mur-ac* k* *Nat-ar* *Nat-c* k* *Nat-m* k* nat-p k* *Nat-s* k* nicc k* **Nit-ac** k* nux-m k* *Nux-v* k* oena k* ol-an k* olib-sac wmh1 olnd k* onos **Op** k* osm k* ox-ac bg2 oxyt ptk2 par k* *Petr* k* **Ph-ac** k* phel k* **Phos** k* *Phys* k* *Phyt* k* pic-ac k* pieri-b mlk9.de plat b2.de* *Plb* k* prot fmm1• *Psor* **Puls** k* ran-b b2.de raph rat bg2 rheum b2.de* rhod k* *Rhus-t* k* rhus-v k* **Ruta** k* *Sabad* k* sabin b2.de sacch br1 sang k* sangin-t c1* sarr hr1 *Sars* k* *Sec* k* sel k* *Seneg* k* **Sep** k* **Sil** k* sol-ni *Spig* k* spira c2 spong hr1 stann b2.de* *Staph* k* *Stram* k* stront-c b2.de* stry k* suis-pan rly4• *Sul-ac* k* sul-i k2 **Sulph** k* sumb k* tab k* tarax b2.de* *Tarent* k* tax k* *Teucr* thal-xyz srj8• *Ther* *Thuj* k* til k* tritic-vg fd5.de upa k* uran-n bg2 valer b2.de* vanil fd5.de *Verat* k* *Verat-v* k* verb k* vinc bg2 viol-o k* viol-t k* vip k* zinc k* zinc-p k2 [buteo-j sej6]

- **right**: agar k* chel k* form k* iris vh *Kali-c* k* kalm k2 nept-m lsd2.fr osm k* plut-n srj7• *Puls* k* rhod k* ruta symph fd3.de• tarent teucr thal-xyz srj8•
- **left**: borx *Com* dulc fd4.de podo fd3.de• sars h2 symph fd3.de•
  - **headache**; with right-sided: arg-n
- **daytime**: (*↗Loss - daytime*) apis both *Mang* h2* *Phos* nifj sep stram mfj
- **morning**: ammc vml3• asar bry h1 calc caps h1* carb-an k* *Carb-v* *Caust* k* cham chel k* *Croc* cycl k* daph elaps gels hell k* *Hep* *Kali-c* k* mag-s k* nat-m k* *Nux-v* k* ozone sde2• petr a1 *Puls* ruta stram k* sul-ac k* valer k*
  - **7 h** | **7 -10 h**: tarent

• **amel.**: *Chin Phos* k*
• **rising** agg.; after: ammc a1* ang h1*
• **waking**; on: *Caust* k* *Dulc* k* *Kali-c* mag-c k* raph k* zinc k*
• **washing** | **amel.**: caust k*
- **forenoon**: carb-v k* sulph k* *Tarent*
• **11 h**: *Sulph*
• **reading** agg.: op k*
- **noon**: bell h1* nat-ar
• **rising** from sitting agg.: nat-ar
- **afternoon** | **reading** agg.: ol-an
- **evening**: alum k* *Ammc* k* anac h2* *Apis* asar aur-m k2 borx brom a1 carbn-s c1 choc srj3• *Euphr* k* ind k* *Kalm* lachn marb-w es1• merl nat-c hr1 nicc k* nit-ac *Puls* k* *Ruta* sulph k* tarent
• **21 h**: stram k*
• **light**; from | **artificial** light | **agg.**: aur-m k2
⁝ **fire**; of the: merc
• **lying** down | **amel.**: sep k*
• **menses**; during: *Sep* k*
• **reading**:
⁝ **agg.**: **Apis** croc k* *Hep* (non:mez kl) rhod k* *Ruta*
⁝ **light**; by: mez h2
: **artificial**: nux-m c1
• **room** after walking; when entering a: dros k*
• **twilight**; in the: arg-n
⁝ **amel.**: phos k2
• **walking**:
⁝ **agg.**: kali-bi k* *Puls*
⁝ **rapidly** | **agg.**: **Puls**
• **warm** from exertion, when: **Puls**
- **night**: (↗*Loss - night*) alum-sil k2 anac anders bnj1 **Chin** hell *Hyos* positr nl2• *Puls* *Ran-b* retin-ac mtf11 *Stram* k* zinc
• **better** at night than by day: apis ferr ptk1
• **menses**; during: *Puls*
- **accompanied** by:
• **vertigo** (See VERTIGO - Accompanied - vision - dim)
○ • **Abdomen**; complaints of (See ABDOMEN - Complaints - accompanied - vision)
• **Head**; complaints of (See HEAD - Complaints - accompanied - vision - dim)
- **air**; in open:
• **agg.**: alum asar con ferr c1 merl **Puls** thuj upa
• **amel.**: *Asar* nat-s
- **alcohol**; from habitual use of: (↗*stimulants*) **Nux-v** hr1
- **alternating** with:
• **clear** vision: anac h2 bell bg2 euphr h2 nept-m lsd2.fr
• **cramps** in hands and feet: bell h1*
• **deafness**: cic
• **dullness** (See MIND - Dullness - alternating - vision)
• **hearing** impaired (See HEARING - Impaired - alternating - obscuration)
- **amblyopia** potatorum (See drunkards)
- **anxiety**, during: chel k*
- **blowing** the nose agg.: *Caust* k*
- **center** of objects; for: ign b7a.de
- **chill**; during: bell k* **Cham** b7.de* chin k* cic bg2 dig bg2 gels k2 **Kreos** b7a.de* lach bg2 laur bg2 lyc bg2 nat-m k* sabin k*
- **coition**; after: *Chin* **Kali-c** k* *Kali-p* nat-p **Phos** **Sep** *Sil*
- **cold** | **applications** | **amel.**: cassia-s ccrh1•
• **bathing** | **amel.**: **Asar** glon k* nicc k*
- **cold** agg.; head becoming: *Calc* k*
- **cough** agg.; during: coff k*
- **dark** day amel.: (non:euph k*) sep
- **darkness** | **amel.**: mur-ac k2
- **descending** stairs agg.: phys k*
- **dilatation** of pupils, holding hand before eyes amel.; with: ph-ac h2
- **dinner**; after: bell h1* calc peti k*
- **diphtheria**; after: apis gels **Lach** nux-v phys **Phyt** *Sil*
- **distant** objects: *Cact* k* camph hr1 euphr k* *Gels* k* *Jab* mang k* nat-ar nat-c k* nat-m k* nat-p ol-an k* ph-ac k* phos k* phys k* rat k* spong **Stram** k* *Sulph* k* tritic-vg fd5.de [tax jsj7]
- **drunkards**; in: (↗*EYE - Amblyopia - alcohol*) *Kali-br* hr1 **Nux-v** ter c2 tub al
- **eating** | **after** | **agg.**: arg-n sne *Calc* k* *Kali-c* hr1 *Nux-v*
• **while** | **agg.**: bufo nat-s *Nux-v*
- **ejaculation**; after: kali-c *Lil-t* nat-m **Sep**
- **emotions**; after: ant-t vh
- **epistaxis**; with: indg c1
- **eruptions**; after suppressed: cycl hr1
- **exertion** agg.: *Calc* **Puls**
- **exertion** of the eyes agg.: alum-sil k2 aur-s k2 bar-s k2 *Calc* calc-f k2 mang *Nat-m* nit-ac *Petr*
- **fainting** | **during**: calc pd lach pd lyc pd nux-v pd
- **fever**; during: sabin c1
- **fine** work; during: agar *Calc* nat-c h2 *Nat-m* **Ruta**
- **glass**; as if looking through a dim: nat-m h2
- **glasses**; in spite of: allox sp1
- **headache**:
• **right** side: chen-a hr1
• **after**: *Lach* c1 *Sil*
• **before**: aur-m-n wbt2• elaps gk *Gels* hyos **Iris** *Kali-bi* k* *Lac-d* k* lyc gk *Nat-m* k* nux-v hr podo k* *Psor* k* puls gk *Sep* stram h1*
• **during**: am-c bg androc srj1• anh c1 *Arg-n* hr1 *Ars* asar aster *Bell* bov bg bry bg carb-an bg caul hr1 *Caust* k* chen-a hr1 chim-m hr1 croc bg crot-h bg **Cycl** k* dulc fd4.de elaps gk ferr bg ferr-p gels k* hyos bg1 ign bg1* **Iris** lac-c br1 lil-t mag-m bg* mur-ac bg* nat-c bg* *Nat-m* nit-ac h2* nux-v bg ol-an bg *Petr* *Phos* *Psor* **Puls** bg sarr kr1 sars bg sep bg *Sil* *Stram* **Sulph** k* tritic-vg fd5.de tub c1 verat-v k* *Zinc*
- **heat**; during: asar bell h1
- **increasing** suddenly: (↗*sudden*) mosch k2 santin mtf11
• **decreasing** | **suddenly**: cadm-s caust hr1 euphr *Lyc*
- **light**; from:
• **artificial** light | **agg.**: nat-m ptk1
• **bright** light | **agg.**: bell caust h2* positr nl2• sol-ni
• **candlelight** | **agg.**: all-c *Arg-n* k* aur-m bar-c *Euphr* *Hep*
• **fire**; of the: *Merc* *Nat-s*
• **sunlight** | **agg.**: agar asar *Both* cic *Merc*
- **looking**:
• **fixedly**: chinin-s c1
• **long**: agar mang nat-ar
• **steadily** | **amel.**: *Aur* mang
• **white** objects, at: cham h1 ther ptk1
- **measles**; after: *Caust* k* *Euphr* **Kali-c** *Puls*
- **menses** | **before** | **agg.**: agn bell k* cinnb *Graph* hr1 nat-m bg1 ph-ac b4a.de puls k2
• **during** | **agg.**: cycl *Graph* k* mag-c b4.de nat-m *Puls* k* *Sep* k* *Sil* k*
- **mental** exertion agg.: arg-n *Nux-v* hr1
- **momentary** spells (See increasing - decreasing - suddenly)
- **motion**, from uneven: cic bg1 con
- **moving** objects: cocc tl1 con k* *Gels* k*
- **mucus**, as if covered with: nat-m h2* tab a1
- **nausea**; with: kalm bg1 mygal hr1* ozone sde2• verat-v hr1
- **occasional** dimness of vision: prot pte1•
- **occiput** extending to eye; with pain in: ery-a verat-v ptk1
- **old** people: *Ambr* vh1 *Bar-c*
- **overheating**; from: *Nux-v*
- **pain**; with | **stomach**; in: gels a1
- **periodical**: iris ptk1
- **perspiration** | **suppressed** perspiration of feet; after: bell bg2 calc bg2 caust bg2 con bg2 hep bg2 hyos bg2 *Merc* bg2 **Nat-m** bg2 phos bg2 puls bg2 **Sil** k* **Stram** b7.de* sulph bg2
- **pregnancy** agg.; during: ant-t vh gels c1

- **reading** agg.: agar k* alum am-c *Apis* *Arg-met* *Asar* k* atro k* brom a1 bry h1 calc *Carb-v* *Caust* cina h1 cocc c1 colch ptk1 *Croc* k* daph elaps gk gels *Hep* k* *Ign* k* jab kola stb3• malar jl2 merl k* **Nat-m** **Nit-ac** k* op ph-ac k* *Phos* podo fd3.de• rhod k* rhus-v k* **Ruta** **Seneg** sep **Sil** **Sulph** k* symph fd3.de• tritic-vg fd5.de vinc k*
  - **small** letters: cadm-s ptk1 mang ptk1 meph ptk1 nat-c ptk1
- **recurrent**: cact
- **rheumatism**; during: puls
- **rising**:
  - **bed**; from | **agg.**: ars sec
  - **sitting**; from | **agg.**: con laur verat-v
  - **stooping**; from | **agg.**: nat-m
- **room** | **amel.**: alum con
- **rubbing**:
  - **agg.**: caust k*
  - **amel.**: caps h1* cina dulc fd4.de nat-ar k2 ph-ac h2* *Puls* sulph
- **sadness**, during (See MIND - Sadness - vision)
- **sideways**: cham h1* ruta h1
  - **only** see objects when looking sideways at them; can: *Chinin-s* k* lil-t bg1 olnd ptk
- **sitting** erect agg.: *Verat-v* k*
- **sleep** | **after** | **agg.**: cassia-s ccrh1•
  - **siesta**:
    - **after** | **agg.**: lyc bg1
- **small** print is impossible; reading: iod b4.de* *Nat-c* b4.de* *Petr* b4.de*
- **smoking** agg.: asc-t k*
- **standing** agg.: (non:dig k*) digin a1* verat-v
- **stimulants**, from: *(↗alcohol)* kali-br **Nux-v** *Sil* hr1*
- **stitching** in eye; with: thuj h1
- **stool** agg.; during: hyos bg2
- **straining** eyes: agar *Calc* **Ruta**
- **sudden**: *(↗increasing)* **Bell** ptk1 caps ptk1 cic ptk1 *Con* ptk1 cycl ptk1 glon ptk1 graph ptk1 hyos ptk1 merc ptk1 *Nat-m* ptk1 olnd ptk1 *Phos* ptk1 *Puls* ptk1 sep ptk1 sil ptk1 *Stram* ptk1 sulph ptk1
- **thinking**, from: arg-n k*
- **twilight**; in the | **amel.**: bry bg1* lyc bg1* *Phos* psor al2
- **uncovering** head agg.: *Calc*
- **urination** | **amel.**: eug vml3• *Gels* k*
- **vertigo**:
  - **before**: stram h1*
  - **during**: *(↗VERTIGO - Accompanied - vision - dim)* *Acon* act-sp aesc-g hr1 agar k* amyg k* *Anac* k* ant-t apis arg-met arg-n k* ars k* asaf *Bell* k* calc *Camph* k* canth carb-an cassia-s ccrh1• caul hr1 cham k* chin bg cic k* cimic coff bg coff-t hr1 *Cupr* cupr-s hr1 **Cycl** k* dulc euon k* **Ferr** **Gels** k* gins k* *Glon* k* *Gran* graph gymno hell k* hep hyos *Kali-bi* k* kali-p lp kalm lach lact laur lil-t bg *Merc* mosch mur-ac h2* nat-m bg *Nit-ac* **Nux-v** olnd ozone sde2• par k* phel bg *Phos* *Phyt* puls raph k* sabad k* *Sabin* sang hr1 seneg sep lp *Stram* *Stront-c* *Sulph* tep k* ter til tub al vanil fd5.de verat bg zinc
- **vexation** agg.: iris vh
- **vomiting**; after: cycl a1
- **waking**; on: allox tpw3* **Cycl** k* **Lach** hr1 *Puls*
- **walking**:
  - **agg.**: dor k* gels k* *Puls* sanic sin-a k*
  - **air**; in open:
    - **agg.**: agar con h2 gels nat-m h2 sulph h2 til
    - **amel.**: lachn
- **warmth** agg.: calc **Puls**
- **washing** agg.; after: kali-c
- **water**, as if full of: chin ld staph b7a.de [bell-p-sp dcm1]
- **weather** | **cloudy** weather: | **amel.**: nux-v hr
  - **wet** | **agg.**: *Calc* crot-h
- **white** objects, when fixing eyes upon: cham k*
- **winking** amel.: anac h2* anan *Euphr* k* kali-p fd1.de• tub-r jl2
- **wiping** the eyes | **amel.**: *Alum* k* arg-n carl k* *Cina* croc k* *Euphr* k* *Lyc* *Nat-ar* *Nat-c* plb b7a.de *Puls* k* *Sil*
- **writing** agg.: aloe calc-f k* chel k* con lyc k* **Nat-m** ol-an k* phys rhod k* sep k* thuj k* zinc

DIPLOPIA: aeth k* *Agar* k* alum bg2* *Alumn* k* am-c k* anh sp1* apis arag br1* *Arg-n* k* arn *Ars* b4a.de art-v k* atro k* **Aur** k* aur-i k2 aur-s k2 bamb-a stb2.de• bar-c k* bar-i k2 *Bell* k* botul br1* bry calc k* calc-s k2 cann-i k* cann-s carbn-s *Caust* k* cham b2.de* *Chel* k* chlf k* chlol a1 *Cic* k* cimic bg2* clem k* cob-n sp1 *Con* k* crot-h k* cupr *Cycl* k* *Daph* k* *Dig* k* eug k* euph k* **Gels** k* ger k* gins bro1 *Graph* k* **Hyos** k* *Iod* k* iodof c2 ix bnm8• kali-bi k* kali-c k* *Kali-cy* k* kali-i k* kali-m k2 *Lach* b7a.de led b2.de* *Lyc* k* *Lyss* k* m-aust b2.de* mag-p k* med k* merc k* *Merc-c* k* mez b4a.de *Morph* k* **Nat-m** k* *Nicc* k* **Nit-ac** k* nux-m *Nux-v* k* *Olnd* k* onos c2* op k* oxyurn-sc mcp1• par k* petr k* phos bro1* phys k* phyt k* *Plb* k* plb-xyz c2 podo ptk1 pop-cand c1 psor *Puls* k* raph k* rhus-t k* sec k* *Seneg* k* sep *Spong* k* stann *Stram* k* stroph-h c2 sul-i k2 sulfon bro1 *Sulph* k* syph k* tab k* ter k* ther k* *Thuj* k* ust k* vanil fd5.de *Verat* k* verat-v bg* zinc k*

- **one** side: cham b2.de
- **morning**: cycl gels
- **evening**: agar k* con k* nit-ac phyt k*
- **night**: bamb-a stb2.de• nit-ac
- **accompanied** by:
  - **nausea**: crot-t ptk1
  - **vertigo** (See VERTIGO - Diplopia)
  - ○ **Uterus**; complaints of: sep ptk1
- **alternating** with | **deafness**: cic ptk1
- **below** the other; one image seen: haliae-lc srj5• syph c1
- **bending** head backward | **amel.**: seneg bg3*
- **blowing** the nose; on: caust ptk1
- **candlelight**; from: alumn k2
- **chill**; before: gels k2
- **convulsions**; with: *Bell* cic *Hyos* *Nux-v* *Stram*
- **diphtheria**; after: lach ptk1
- **distant** objects: am-c k* bell nit-ac plb
- **fever**; during: gels hr1
- **glass**; as if looking through frosted: lavand-a ctl1•
- **headache**:
  - **before**: gels mrr1 tub xxb
  - **during**●: *Gels* k* stroph-h c1 tub xxb
- **hearing**; with impaired: cic c1
- **hemorrhage** of retina, from: arn br1
- **horizontal**: *Lach* b7a.de *Olnd* b7a.de puls b7a.de
- **horizontal** objects, of: gels c1 mag-p c1 **Nit-ac** k* olnd k*
- **inclining** head to either side: gels
- **injuries**; after: arn br1
- **linear**: sulph bg2
- **looking**:
  - **downward**: *Arn* k* olnd k*
  - **intensely**: am-c con gins k* vanil fd5.de
    - **amel.**: eug vml3•
  - **light**; at | **agg.**: ther
  - **sideways**: gels k*
    - **right**: caust dig
      - **amel.**: caust bg3*
  - **upward**: *Caust*
- **lying** down | **amel.**: spong k*
- **masturbation**; from: cina ptk1 sep ptk1
- **measles**; after: caust ptk1 *Kali-c* ptk1
- **menses** | **before** | **agg.**: gels bro1
  - **during** | **agg.**: gels bro1
- **near** objects: aur bell cic con nit-ac phyt stann verat-v
- **overwork** at the desk: *Agar* k*
- **paralysis** of muscles, from: arn br1 gels mrr1
- **pregnancy** | **during**●: bell cic *Gels* k*
- **reading** agg.: agar ant-t arg-n *Camph* *Graph* lyss mtf11 stram thuj vanil fd5.de
- **riding** in the cars, after: (non:cupr c1) cupr-act k*
- **rising** from stooping agg.: gels psa
- **rubbing** eye | **amel.**: carb-an ptk1
- **sexual** excesses; after: sep ptk1
- **shifted** in relation to the other; one picture is: *Stram* b7.de*
- **sleep** agg.; after: chlol gels
- **standing** erect and looking down: olnd k*

- **strength** of will amel.: gels$_{psa*}$
- **turning** eyes to right, on: dig$_{k*}$
- **vertical**: atro$_{bg3*}$ cic$_{h1*}$ haliae-lc$_{srj5\bullet}$ kali-bi$_{bg3*}$ lith-c$_{ptk1}$ rhus-t$_{bg3*}$ seneg$_{bg3*}$ staph$_{gk}$ stram$_{bg3*}$ syph$_{bg3*}$
- **vertigo**; after: bell$_{k*}$ olnd$_{ptk1}$
- **weakness** of muscles; from (See paralysis)
- **writing** agg.: cob-n$_{sp1}$ coca *Graph*$_{k*}$ vanil$_{fd5.de}$ [tax$_{jsj7}$]

DISTANT, objects seem: *(↗MIND - Distances - inaccurate)* *All-c*$_{k*}$ *Anac*$_{k*}$ atro$_{k*}$ *Aur* bell$_{k*}$ calc$_{k*}$ cann-i cann-s$_{b7a.de*}$ carb-an$_{k*}$ *Carbn-s* carneg-g$_{rwt1\bullet}$ cic$_{b2.de*}$ **Gels**$_{k*}$ glon hyos$_{bg2}$ melal-alt$_{gya4}$ merc-c$_{k*}$ nat-c$_{bg2}$ nat-m$_{k*}$ *Nux-m*$_{k*}$ ox-ac$_{k*}$ *Phos*$_{k*}$ *Plat*$_{bg2}$ *Plb*$_{k*}$ puls$_{bg2}$ *Stann*$_{k*}$ *Stram*$_{k*}$ **Sulph**$_{k*}$ ther$_{bg2}$ thuj$_{bg2}$ xan$_{c1}$
- **darkness** agg.: nux-m
- **waking**; on: anac
- **yawning**; on: all-c$_{ptk1}$

DISTORTED: *(↗MIND - Schizophrenia - paranoid)* anh$_{mg1.de*}$ atra-r$_{bnm3\bullet}$ bell$_{bg2*}$ flor-p$_{rsj3\bullet}$ hydroph$_{rsj6\bullet}$ melal-alt$_{gya4}$ nux-v$_{bg2*}$ plat$_{tl1}$ ruta$_{fd4.de}$ stram$_{bg2*}$ suis-pan$_{rly4\bullet}$

DOUBLE vision (See Diplopia)

DROPS before eyes: kali-c$_{h2*}$
- **raindrops**; like: bell$_{b4a.de}$

DRUNKARDS; in: *Nux-v*$_{b7a.de}$

EATING: | **after** | **agg.**: bar-c$_{bg2}$ *Calc*$_{b4.de*}$ dig$_{b4.de*}$ gels$_{bg2}$ grat$_{bg2}$ lyc$_{bg2}$ nux-v$_{b7.de*}$ phos$_{b4.de*}$ sil$_{b4.de*}$ sulph$_{bg2}$ thuj$_{b4.de*}$ zinc$_{bg2}$
- **while** | **agg.**: hep$_{b4a.de}$ iod$_{b4.de*}$ nat-s$_{bg2}$ olnd$_{b7.de*}$

EMOTIONS agg.: puls$_{bg2}$

EXERTION:
- **agg.**: am-c$_{bg2}$ chin$_{bg2}$ helo$_{bg2}$ lyc$_{bg2}$
- **amel.**: *Aur*$_{k*}$

EXERTION OF THE EYES agg.: *(↗EYE - Looking; EYE - Looking - steadily)* agar agn$_{bg}$ alum alum-p$_{k2}$ alum-sil$_{k2}$ *Am-c* am-m anac ang$_{bg}$ *Apis* arg-met **Arg-n**$_{k*}$ arn$_{bg}$ *Asaf* asar *Aur* bar-c bar-m bell$_{k*}$ borx bry **Calc**$_{k*}$ calc-sil$_{k2}$ cann-i canth carb-an$_{bg}$ *Carb-v*$_{k*}$ *Caust* cham$_{bg}$ chel$_{bg}$ chin$_{bg}$ chlol *Cic* **Cina** cocc coff con **Croc**$_{k*}$ cupr dros dulc ferr *Gels*$_{bg}$ *Graph* hep ign *Jab* **Kali-c**$_{k*}$ kali-p kali-s kali-sil$_{k2}$ kreos *Lach*$_{bg}$ laur$_{bg}$ led lith-c$_{bg2}$ **Lyc** mag-c mag-m mang meny$_{bg}$ merc mez mur-ac *Naja* nat-ar *Nat-c* **Nat-m**$_{k*}$ *Nat-p* nicc nit-ac nux-m *Nux-v* olnd **Onos** orot-ac$_{rly4\bullet}$ par petr *Ph-ac* *Phos*$_{k*}$ phys *Phyt* pic-ac$_{bg2}$ plat$_{bg}$ puls ran-b **Rhod** *Rhus-t* **Ruta**$_{k*}$ sabad *Sars* sel **Seneg** *Sep* **Sil**$_{k*}$ *Spig*$_{k*}$ *Spong* staph stram stront-c sul-ac sulph ther thuj valer verb viol-o zinc zinc-p$_{k2}$

FADE away, then reappear; objects: gels$_{k*}$

FAR-SIGHTED (See Hypermetropia)

FASTING agg.: calc$_{bg2}$

FEATHERY: *Alum*$_{k*}$ *Calc*$_{k*}$ kreos$_{k*}$ **Lyc**$_{k*}$ mag-c$_{k*}$ *Merc* *Nat-c*$_{k*}$ nat-m$_{k*}$ seneg$_{k*}$ spig$_{k*}$

FIELD of vision; complaints of: fl-ac$_{ptk1}$ hep$_{ptk1}$ mang$_{ptk1}$ phos$_{ptk1}$ thuj$_{ptk1}$

FIERY: act-sp$_{bg2}$ am-c$_{b2.de*}$ arg-n$_{bg2}$ ars$_{b2.de*}$ *Aur*$_{b2.de*}$ bar-c$_{b2.de*}$ **Bell**$_{k*}$ brom$_{bg2}$ *Bry*$_{k*}$ calc$_{b2.de*}$ cann-s$_{b2.de*}$ carb-v$_{b2.de*}$ *Caust*$_{b2.de*}$ cham$_{b2.de*}$ cinnb$_{ptk1}$ coca$_{ptk1}$ coloc$_{b2.de*}$ con$_{b2.de*}$ *Croc*$_{b2.de*}$ cycl$_{ptk1}$ *Dig*$_{k*}$ *Dulc*$_{b2.de*}$ fl-ac$_{bg2}$ glon$_{bg2}$ graph$_{b2.de*}$ *Hyos*$_{k*}$ ign$_{ptk1}$ iod$_{k*}$ kali-bi$_{bg2}$ **Kali-c**$_{k*}$ *Lach*$_{k*}$ **Lyc**$_{bg2}$ m-ambo$_{b2.de}$ m-arct$_{b2.de}$ mang$_{b2.de*}$ merc$_{b2.de*}$ mez$_{b2.de*}$ *Nat-c*$_{b2.de*}$ *Nat-m*$_{k*}$ *Nux-v*$_{k*}$ olnd$_{b2.de*}$ op$_{b2.de*}$ par$_{bg2}$ petr$_{b2.de*}$ ph-ac$_{b2.de*}$ *Phos*$_{k*}$ plb$_{bg2}$ *Psor* **Puls**$_{b2.de*}$ sec$_{b2.de*}$ *Sep*$_{k*}$ sil$_{b2.de*}$ **Spig**$_{k*}$ staph$_{b2.de*}$ stram$_{k*}$ stront-c$_{b2.de*}$ sulph$_{b2.de*}$ thuj$_{bg2}$ valer$_{b2.de*}$ verat$_{b2.de*}$ viol-o$_{k*}$ zinc$_{k*}$
- **balls**: act-sp$_{bg2*}$ *Cycl*$_{k*}$ plut-n$_{srj7\bullet}$ stram$_{k*}$ verat-v$_{hr1}$
- **bodies**: arg-n$_{k*}$ zinc
- **circles**: anan$_{k*}$ calc-p$_{k*}$ *Camph*$_{k*}$ carb-v ip$_{k*}$ *Puls*$_{k*}$ *Zinc*$_{k*}$
  - **semicircles**: viol-o$_{b7.de*}$
- **closing** the eyes agg.: spig$_{hr1}$
- **disks**: thuj
- **perspiration**; during: *Bell*$_{bg2}$ caust$_{bg2}$ kali-c$_{bg2}$ nat-m$_{bg2}$ *Nux-v*$_{bg2}$ puls$_{bg2}$ spig$_{bg2}$
- **points**: *(↗spots)* ammc$_{k*}$ *Aur*$_{k*}$ *Cycl*$_{hr1}$ merc$_{k*}$ merl *Nat-m*$_{k*}$ petr sec zinc

Fiery – points: ...
  - **falling** points: ph-ac$_{h2*}$
  - **moving** with the eyes: am-c ammc$_{k*}$ nat-m$_{h2*}$
- **rays** about the light: *Kali-c* **Lach**$_{k*}$
- **rising** from sitting agg.: verat$_{k*}$
- **shimmerings**: *Calc-p*
- **showers**: plb$_{k*}$
- **specks** (See points)
- **spots**: *(↗points)* *Alum*$_{k*}$ coca elaps$_{k*}$ psor$_{tl1}$ sep$_{tl1}$ *Zinc*$_{b4a.de}$
  - **menses** | **before** | **agg.**: cycl$_{bro1}$ sep$_{bro1}$
  - **during** | **agg.**: cycl$_{bro1}$ sep$_{bro1}$
- **surface**: ph-ac$_{h2*}$
- **wheels** of fire: *Hyos*$_{b7a.de}$ puls$_{b7a.de}$
- **zigzags**●: con$_{k*}$ *Graph*$_{k*}$ ign **Nat-m**$_{k*}$ *Sep*$_{k*}$
  - **around** objects: graph$_{k*}$ *Nat-m*

FIRE:
- **blue**: [heroin$_{sdj2}$]
- **closing** the eyes; a sea of fire on: **Phos** spig

FLAMES: **Bell**$_{k*}$ bry$_{c1}$ calc cann-s$_{k*}$ *Carb-v* chin-b *Chinin-s* cycl dulc myric *Puls* santin spong staph$_{k*}$ ther$_{k*}$ *Thuj*
- **night**:
  - **bed** agg.; in: spong staph
  - **waking**; on: cycl$_{k*}$
- **chill**; during: bell$_{bg2}$ hyos$_{bg2}$
- **various** colored flames: *Crot-h* *Phos* thuj

FLASHES: *(↗Sparks; Stars)* agar$_{bro1}$ alco$_{a1}$ aloe$_{bro1}$ androc$_{srj1\bullet}$ anh$_{sp1}$ **Bell**$_{k*}$ ben-n brom calc calc-f$_{bro1}$ carbn-s caust$_{k*}$ *Cedr* chlf$_{k*}$ clem$_{bro1}$ coca *Croc* cycl$_{k*}$ dig digin$_{a1}$ falco-pe$_{nl2\bullet}$ fl-ac *Glon*$_{k*}$ hep$_{bro1}$ iber$_{a1}$ ign$_{bro1}$ *Iris*$_{bro1}$ kali-p$_{fd1.de\bullet}$ lat-m$_{bnm6\bullet}$ lyc$_{bro1}$ maias-l$_{hrn2\bullet}$ menth$_{c1}$ merc merc-i-f *Nat-c*$_{k*}$ nux-v$_{hr}$ op$_{k*}$ **Phos**$_{k*}$ **Phys**$_{k*}$ plut-n$_{srj7\bullet}$ positr$_{nl2\bullet}$ *Puls*$_{k*}$ rauw$_{sp1}$ sec$_{k*}$ seneg$_{bro1}$ *Sil* spong staph$_{h1}$ stram$_{k*}$ sulph tab$_{k*}$ tarent$_{k*}$ *Valer* verat-v$_{hr1}$ viol-o$_{bro1}$
- **morning**: lat-m$_{bnm6\bullet}$
  - **dark**; in the: arg-n
  - **waking**; on: *Nat-c*
- **evening** | **sleep**; when falling asleep: kali-p$_{fd1.de\bullet}$ nat-c$_{h2}$ phos$_{mrr1}$
- **awake**; while: *Nat-c*$_{kl}$
- **bending** head downward agg.: androc$_{srj1\bullet}$
- **closing** the eyes agg.: ail androc$_{srj1\bullet}$ atro$_{a1}$ falco-pe$_{nl2\bullet}$ melal-alt$_{gya4}$ *Nat-c* phos sep spong sulph
- **cough** agg.; during: kali-c kali-chl
- **darkness** agg.●: arg-n$_{k*}$ **Phos** stram$_{k*}$ *Valer*
- **electric** shocks, like: *Croc*
- **motion**; sudden: androc$_{srj1\bullet}$
- **sleep** agg.; on going to: des-ac$_{rbp6}$ falco-pe$_{nl2\bullet}$ *Phos*
- **streaks**: nat-c nux-v
- **waking** agg.; after: (non:nat-c$_{kl}$)

FLICKERING: acon$_{k*}$ acon-f$_{a1}$ *Aesc*$_{k*}$ *Agar*$_{k*}$ alco$_{a1}$ all-c$_{k*}$ allox$_{tpw3}$ aloe alum$_{k*}$ alum-p$_{k2}$ *Am-c*$_{k*}$ am-m$_{bg2}$ anac$_{k*}$ anh$_{sp1}$ *Ant-t*$_{k*}$ *Aran*$_{k*}$ arn$_{b7a.de*}$ *Ars*$_{k*}$ *Ars-i* ars-s-f$_{k2}$ bar-c$_{k*}$ bar-i$_{k2}$ bar-m **Bell**$_{k*}$ bell-p$_{sp1}$ *Borx*$_{k*}$ bry calc$_{k*}$ calc-f$_{k*}$ calc-s calc-sil$_{k2}$ camph$_{k*}$ cann-i$_{k*}$ cann-s$_{k*}$ caps$_{k*}$ *Carb-v*$_{k*}$ carbn-o **Carbn-s** carl$_{k*}$ *Caust*$_{k*}$ *Cham*$_{k*}$ *Chel*$_{k*}$ *Chin*$_{k*}$ chinin-ar chlf$_{k*}$ clem$_{k*}$ coca$_{k*}$ coff *Colch*$_{bg2}$ con$_{k*}$ croc cupr-act **Cycl**$_{k*}$ dig$_{k*}$ dros$_{b2.de*}$ dulc$_{fd4.de}$ euphr$_{b7a.de}$ form$_{hr1}$ *Gels*$_{k*}$ **Graph**$_{k*}$ hell$_{k*}$ *Hep*$_{k*}$ *Hyos*$_{k*}$ *Ign*$_{k*}$ *Iod*$_{k*}$ *Kali-c*$_{ptk1}$ kali-sil$_{k2}$ *Kalm*$_{k*}$ kola$_{stb3\bullet}$ **Lach**$_{k*}$ *Led*$_{k*}$ lipp$_{a1}$ luf-op$_{rsj5\bullet}$ *Lyc*$_{k*}$ m-ambo$_{b2.de*}$ med$_{k*}$ meny$_{k*}$ merc$_{k*}$ merl mez$_{k*}$ moni$_{rfm1\bullet}$ mur-ac$_{k*}$ nat-ar nat-c **Nat-m**$_{k*}$ nat-p *Nux-v*$_{k*}$ ol-an$_{bg}$ olnd$_{b2.de*}$ op$_{k*}$ paeon$_{k*}$ *Petr*$_{k*}$ ph-ac$_{k*}$ **Phos**$_{k*}$ phys$_{k*}$ *Plat*$_{k*}$ plb$_{k*}$ plect$_{a1}$ plut-n$_{srj7\bullet}$ *Psor*$_{k*}$ *Puls*$_{k*}$ salin$_{a1}$ santin sars$_{k*}$ sec$_{k*}$ *Seneg*$_{k*}$ **Sep**$_{k*}$ *Sil*$_{k*}$ sol-ni *Spig*$_{ptk1}$ *Staph*$_{k*}$ stram$_{k*}$ stront-c$_{k*}$ stroph-h$_{bg}$ sul-i$_{k2}$ **Sulph**$_{k*}$ sumb$_{k*}$ syph$_{bg}$ tab$_{k*}$ ther$_{k*}$ *Thuj*$_{k*}$ tritic-vg$_{fd5.de}$ vanil$_{fd5.de}$ verat$_{b2.de*}$ *Zinc*$_{k*}$ zinc-p$_{k2}$
- **right**: bry$_{k*}$ kola$_{stb3\bullet}$ lach tritic-vg$_{fd5.de}$
- **left**: *Chinin-ar* dig$_{a1}$ nat-p olib-sac$_{wmh1}$
- **daytime**: anac$_{k*}$ phos$_{k*}$
- **morning**: am-c$_{k*}$ *Borx* calc ign$_{gk}$ kali-c
  - **5 h** (See night - midnight - after - 5)
  - **headache**; during: **Cycl**$_{k*}$

- **morning**: ...
  - • **rising** agg.: carb-v k* **Cycl** k* nat-p k*
  - • **waking**; on: calc k* dulc k* ign gk
  - • **writing** agg.: _Borx_
- **afternoon** | **nap**; after: _Lyc_
- **evening**: kola stb3• merc k* merl plat h2* til k*
  - • **read**; on attempting to: _Cycl_
- **night**: cycl k*
  - • **midnight**:
    - ⁝ **after** | **5** h: nat-p
- **around** outside the range of vision: _Graph_ nux-v hr
- **ascending** stairs agg.: dig k*
- **black** borders; with: cimic ptk1
- **breakfast** agg.; after: sulph k*
- **candlelight**: bar-c k*
- **chill**: cham k* led k* lyc k* sep k* ther
- **circles**: calc-p k* ign a1
- **closing** eyes, when: nat-ar ther k* vanil fd5.de
- **colors**, various: **Cycl** k*
- **coughing**; while: ign ptk1
- **dinner** | **after** | **agg.**: bry k*
  - • **during** | **agg.**: _Thuj_ k*
- **eating** | **amel.**: phos k*
- **entering** a house: dig k*
- **exertion** agg.; after: dig k*
- **fainting** with: nux-v c1*
- **fever**; during: sep b4.de*
- **headache**:
  - • **before**●: aran k* aur-m-n wbt2• _Graph_ iris _Nat-m_ k* _Plat_ _Psor_ k* _Sars_ sep st1 _Sulph_ ther a1
  - • **beginning** of: _Sars_
  - • **during**: caps hr1 **Chin** chinin-ar chinin-s _Coloc_ k* con **Cycl** k* graph k* _Lach_ k* **Nat-m** k* _Phos_ k* sars k* _Sil_ _Sulph_ tritic-vg fd5.de
- **looking**:
  - • **intently**: led k* tab k* tritic-vg fd5.de
  - • **light**; at | **agg.**: anac h2* dig a2 phos mtf _Sep_ k*
  - • **long**: caust k* ph-ac k* psor
- **lying** agg.: _Cham_ k*
- **moving** to the right: borx
- **paroxysmal**: _Ther_ k*
- **perspiration**; during: caust bg2 _Cham_ bg2 graph bg2 lyc bg2 _Nux-v_ bg2 **Sep** bg2 staph bg2
- **reading**:
  - • **agg.**: aran k* arn k* cob _Cycl_ k* merc k* ph-ac k* _Seneg_ k*
  - • **light**; by: ph-ac h2
- **rising** agg.: acon ant-t a1 verat h1
- **sewing**, while: iod k*
- **sleep** agg.; on going to: lyc k*
- **stooping**; while: ther ptk1
- **sudden**: zing k*
- **vertigo**; with: alum k* am-c bg2 ant-t b7a.de* aran ptk1 _Bell_ k* _Calc_ chel a1 _Cycl_ mrr1 dig k* _Glon_ k* ign b7a.de* mez b4a.de* olnd b7a.de* ozone sde2• _Stram_ k* thuj k* vinc k*
- **weather** agg.; wet: aran bro1
- **wiping** eyes agg.: seneg k*
- **writing** agg.: agar k* _Aran_ k* arn k* _Borx_ nat-m _Seneg_ k*

FLOATING, luminous undulating object: arund c1 dys fmm1•

FOCAL distance:
- **changes** while reading: agar k* carb-ac jab lyc
- **unequal**: _Chin_ k*

FOGGY: (↗_Cobwebs_) acon k* _Agar_ k* agath-a nl2• all-c bg1 _Alum_ k* alum-p k2 alum-sil k2 am-c k* am-m k* ambr k* ammc k* anac bg2 ang b7.de* anh sp1 _Ant-t_ k* _Apis_ aran k* _Arg-met_ k* _Arg-n_ k* arge-pl rwt5• arn b7a.de* **Ars** k* _Ars-i_ ars-s-f k2 arum-t k* arund k* asaf k* atro k* _Aur_ k* aur-ar k2 aur-i k2 _Aur-s_ k2 bamb-a stb2.de• _Bar-c_ k* bar-i k2 bar-s k2 _Bell_ k* berb k* bism k* bov b4.de* bruc k* bry k* bufo cain calad bg1 **Calc** k* calc-f k* calc-i k2 _Calc-p_ k* calc-s calc-sil k2 _Camph_ k* cann-i k* cann-s b7.de* carb-an k* carbn-s carl k*

Foggy: ...
Castm vh **Caust** k* cedr k* _Cham_ k* _Chel_ k* **Chin** k* _Chinin-s_ _Cina_ k* clem k* cob-n sp1 _Cocc_ k* coff-t k* coloc k* _Con_ k* **Croc** k* crot-h bg2 crot-t k* cund k* **Cycl** k* dig k* dream-p sdj1• _Dros_ k* _Dulc_ k* elaps euph b4.de* euphr k* eupi k* falco-pe nl2• form k* gamb k* **Gels** k* gent-c k* _Glon_ k* _Graph_ k* grat k* haem k* helo-s rwt2• _Hep_ k* hydr-ac k* _Hyos_ k* _Ign_ b7.de* _Iod_ k* ip k* jab k* kali-ar kali-bi bg2 _Kali-c_ k* _Kali-i_ k* kali-n c1 kali-p kali-s kalm k* ketogl-ac rly4• _Kola_ stb3• _Kreos_ k* lac-ac k* _Lac-d_ hr1 lac-del hrn2• lach k* lachn c1 lact bg1* _Laur_ k* _Lil-t_ k* limest-b es1• _Lith-c_ luf-op rsj5• _Lyc_ k* m-aust b7.de mag-c k* melal-alt gya4 meny ptk1 **Merc** k* merl k* _Mill_ k* _Mom-b_ bro1 _Morph_ k* mosch bg1 nat-ar nat-c bg2 _Nat-m_ k* nat-ox rly4• nat-p k* nat-sil fd3.de• nit-ac k* nux-m k* oci-sa sp1 ol-an k* olib-sac wmh1 op k* osm k* ox-ac bg1 ozone sde2• par b7.de* _Petr_ k* _Ph-ac_ k* **Phos** k* phys bro1 pic-ac k* plan k* _Plat_ k* _Plb_ k* podo k* positr nl2• psor **Puls** k* _Ran-b_ k* raph _Rhod_ k* _Rhus-t_ k* _Ruta_ k* sabad sabin b7.de* sang k* sangin-t c1 _Sars_ k* _Sec_ k* seneg bg2 _Sep_ k* _Sil_ k* sol-ni spig k* staph k* _Stram_ k* stry k* sul-i k2 **Sulph** k* symph fd3.de• tab k* _Tarent_ k* _Ther_ k* _Thuj_ k* til k* upa k* vac jl2 vanil fd5.de verb b7.de* vinc bg1 viol-t b7.de* visc sp1 **Zinc** k* zinc-p k2 [heroin sdj2]
- **daytime**: bar-c k*
- **morning**: alum h2* am-m k* ang c1 _Bar-c_ k* bov k* bry k* caust _Lyc_ k* merl hr1 nat-sil fd3.de• nicc k* nit-ac stram k* vac jl2 vanil fd5.de zinc k*
- **forenoon** | **10** -15 h: nat-m
- **afternoon**: _Cycl_ k* mag-c k* nat-m k* nat-sil fd3.de• ol-an hr1
  - • **15**-16 h: bufo
  - • **16** h | **sleep**; after: cain lyc
- **evening**: alum k* cina euphr k* ind k* lachn hr1 lyc k* nept-m lsd2.fr phos k* rhus-t k* ruta fd4.de **Sulph** k* tab k* vanil fd5.de
  - • **22** h: marb-w es1•
  - • **candlelight**: sulph
- **accompanied** by:
  - • **glaucoma**: _Chin_ b7a.de
  - ○ • **Face**; pain in: til bro1
- **air** agg.; in open: alum h2* am-m k* thuj
- **albuminuria**, in: _Ars_ mp1•
- **candlelight**; around: osm tell
- **chill**; during: bell bg2 croc bg2 _Laur_ bg2
- **circles**: merl
- **closing** the eyes | **amel.**: nit-ac h2* [heroin sdj2]
- **colors**; caused by: tarent
- **dark** clouds, pass: lac-ac mp1•
- **dinner**; after: bar-c lyc k*
- **distant** objects: mill c1 phos k*
- **driving**; while: nept-m lsd2.fr positr nl2•
- **eating**; after: _Bar-c_ k* calc zinc h2*
- **faintness**; with: petr h2*
- **fever**: sep
- **followed** by | **Occipital** protuberances; fleeting pain in: podo
- **headache**; during: aster _Cycl_ k* dream-p sdj1• gels k2 sulph k*
  - • **mist** before eyes: podo st
- **hemiopia**, in: **Aur** k*
- **incipient** cataract: bar-c k2 _Caust_
- **itching** in inner canthi, with: _Zinc_ mp1•
- **lachrymation** amel.: calc h2*
- **light**; from:
  - • **bright** light | **agg.**: agath-a nl2• am-m
  - • **gaslight** | **agg.**: nat-p k2
  - • **sunlight** | **agg.**: agath-a nl2• am-m _Tarent_
- **looking** intently agg.: calc h2
- **lying** on left side agg.: merc-i-f k*
- **menorrhagia**, during: _Cycl_ hr1
- **menses** | **before** | **agg.**: bell mp1• puls k2
  - • **during** | **agg.**: cassia-s ccrh1•
- **motion**:
  - • **agg.**: con
  - • **eyes**; of | **amel.**: nit-ac h2
- **myelitis**; in (See spinal)
- **periodical**: bell mtf11 cact mtf11 glon mtf11
- **reading** agg.: arn _Ars_ calc h2* camph cina croc k* gent-c k* grat k* _Kali-c_ k* lyc k* nat-m k* ph-ac k* ruta fd4.de _Sulph_ k* vanil fd5.de vinc k*

- **rising** from sitting agg.: puls k*
- **room** agg.: lac-ac k* osm k*
- **rubbing**:
  - • **agg.**: caust h2 spig h1
  - • **amel.**: cina h1 **Puls** h1
- **seminal** emissions, after: sars k*
- **sewing**: ph-ac
- **shivering**; during: laur b7.de
- **sitting** down agg.: lachn hr1
- **sitting** for a long time agg.; after: sars
- **sleep** agg.; after: stram k*
- **spinal** cord; with inflammation of: stram mp1•
- **standing** agg.: *Caust* k* nat-m k*
- **tremulous**: kali-c k*
- **walking**:
  - • **agg.**: phys k* puls k* vinc k*
  - • **air** agg.; in open: caust h2
  - • **amel.**: lachn hr1
- **washing** | **amel.**: alum h2* am-m k* caust
- **white**: ars h2 *Con* b4a.de *Sulph* b4a.de
- **writing** agg.: asaf k* calc-f k* grat k* lyc k* ol-an hr1 ph-ac k*

FOREIGN body; from: *Sulph* b4a.de

FURRY: *Daph* bg2

GAUZE (See Foggy)

GLIMMERING (See Flickering)

GLITTERING objects: aran k* ars bg2 arund k* *Bell* b4a.de *Calc-p* k* *Camph* k* chel rb2 con bg2* *Cycl* k* falco-pe nl2• *Graph* ptk1 ign rb2 iod ptk1 kali-c b4a.de kali-i bg2 lach ptk1 nat-m bg2 nat-s rb2 *Nux-v* k* ol-an ptk1 phos bg2* seneg bg2 stroph-h ptk1 sul-i bg2 syph ptk1 *Ther* k* verat bg2
- **bodies** on blowing nose: alum nat-s
  - • **bright**, luminous appearances: calc *Hep Phos*
  - • **outside** the range of vision: *Nux-v*
- **candlelight**; by: anag k*
- **circles**: calc-p k* falco-pe nl2•
- **gaslight**, in: aur k*
- **needles**: **Cycl** k*
- **points**: chel k*
- **reading** agg.: aran k*
- **spots**: ol-an bg2 seneg b4.de*
- **stars**: con k*
- **vertigo** with: calc k*
- **zigzags**: ign k*

HAIR hung before the sight and must be wiped away; as if a: alum k* ars-h colch con bg2 cund xyz61 dig *Euphr* k* kali-c bg2 lach bg2* plan bg3* sang spig k* staph

HALO around the light: abrot mtf11 alum b2.de* anac b2.de* **Bell** b2.de* calc b2.de* *Cham* b7a.de chim ptk1 cic b2.de* *Cocc* bg2 cycl bg2 *Dig* b2.de* euph b2.de euphr bg2 ferr bg2 kali-c b2.de* *Kali-n* b2.de* kali-s k2 *Lach* bg2* nat-p k2 osm ptk1 ph-ac b2.de* **Phos** b2.de* **Puls** b2.de* **Ruta** b2.de* sars b2.de* *Sep* b2.de* stann b2.de* staph b2.de* stront-c b2.de* **Sulph** b2.de* zinc b2.de*
- **evening**: alum h2 anac h2
- **bright**: calc b4.de*
- **dark**: *Phos* b4a.de

HEAT: | **during** | **agg.**: puls b7.de
- **fire**; of | **agg.**: phos bg2

HEMERALOPIA (See Dim - daytime)

HEMIOPIA: *Ars* k* *Aur* k* aur-ar k2 aur-m aur-s k2 *Bov* cain *Calc* k* calc-s k* cann-s caust k* chin bg2* chinin-s c1 chion bg* cic *Cocc* cycl k* dig k* ferr-p bg2 gels k* *Glon* k* hep bro1* hyos bg2* iod bg2 lach bg* *Lith-c* k* lob k* *Lyc* k* morph k* mur-ac k* nat-ar nat-c *Nat-m* k* onos bg2 plb k* psor ran-b bg2* rhus-r a1 rhus-t k* *Sep* k* staph *Stram* k* sulph syc pte1*• *Titan* br1* titan-xyz c2 tub ptk1 verat bg2* verat-v bro1 zinc
- **right** half lost●: borx a *Calc* k* *Cocc* k* cycl k* glon ind mfj iod **Lith-c** k* *Lyc* k*
- **left** half lost●: calc k* cic k* lith-c bro1 lyc bro1 nat-c k*
- **evening**: am-br vh1 calc-s k* dig digin a1

Hemiopa: ...
- **accompanied** by:
  - • **vertigo**: titan br1
  - ○ • **Head**; complaints of: onos bg2
- **head**; before pain in: nat-m ptk1
- **hemicrania**, with: **Lyc** ●*
- **horizontal**●: **Ars** k* *Aur* k* *Lith-c* vh *Lyc* vh nit-ac b4a.de sep sulph titan mfj *Tub* k*
- **lower** lost●: *Aur* k* cain dig bro1 podo fd3.de• sulph k*
- **menses**; during: lith-c k*
- **pregnancy** agg.; during: ran-b k2*
- **upper** lost●: am mfj *Ars* k* **Aur** k* aur-ar k2 aur-s k2 *Camph* k* *Dig* k* digin a1 gels k* verat-v hr1
- **vertical**●: aur bov k* calc k* *Caust* k* cic ferr-p bro1 gels glon **Lith-c** k* *Lyc* k* morph k* *Mur-ac* k* *Nat-m* k* op plb seneg b4a.de syc mtf11 titan br1* tub mtf11 [*Lith-f* stj2 *Lith-s* stj2]
  - • **looking** too long at something; from: *Bell* b4a.de
- **walking** agg.: dig k* digin a1

HIGH; objects seem too (See Large - objects - raises)

HYPERMETROPIA: acon k* *Aesc* alum k* alum-sil k2 am-c b2.de* androc srj1• **Arg-n** k* *Bell* k* bry k* **Calc** k* calc-sil k2 *Carb-an* k* caust k* chel k* *Chin* coff bg2 *Coloc* k* *Con* k* *Dros* k* grat k* *Hyos* k* jab c2* *Lil-t* k* *Lyc* k* mag-m k* meph bg2 mez k* morph k* *Nat-c* k* *Nat-m* k* *Nux-v* k* *Onos Petr* k* phos k* phys k* phyt k* psor raph k* ruta bro1* sang **Sep** k* **Sil** k* spig k* stram k* sulph k* symph fd3.de• tab k* valer k*
- **evening**: hyper k* ruta fd4.de
- **eating**; after: mez h2*
- **headache**; during: choc srj3•
- **overuse** of eyes in fine work: *Arg-n*
- **suddenly**: arg-n c1

ILLUSIONS: (↗*MIND - Delusions - visions)* absin a1 acon b7.de* aesc k* *Agar* k* am-c hr1 am-m b7.de* ambr b7.de* anac hr1 ang b7.de* ant-t b7.de* arg-met b7.de* *Asaf* b7.de* bell k* benzol br1 bism b7.de* bit-ar wht1• bov a1 bry b7.de* camph k* cann-s b7.de* carbn-s cham b7.de* chel k* cina b7.de* *Cocc* b7.de* *Croc* b7.de* cycl b7.de* dig k* digin a1* dros b7.de* eup-per eup-pur k* *Euphr* b7.de* galv c2 glon k2 hyos k* *Ign* b7.de* kali-bi kali-br k* kola stb3• lact k* laur b7.de* m-ambo b7.de m-arct b7.de m-aust b7.de med k2 *Merc* k* morph c2 nux-v b7.de* olnd b7.de* *Onos Op* b7.de* par b7.de* past a1 **Phos** plb k* psil ft1 *Puls* b7.de* ran-b b7.de* rhus-t b7.de* *Ruta* b7.de* sabin b7.de* *Samb* b7.de* (non:sang k*) *Sec* b7.de* seneg a1* sep ptk1 spig b7.de* spong fd4.de staph b7.de* stram k* sulph k* thres-a sze7• thuj k* tritic-vg fd5.de valer b7.de* verat b7.de* verb b7.de* viol-o b7.de* viol-t b7.de*
- **one** eye: cham bg2
- **animals**, bugs: *Hyos* bg2 *Stram* bg2
- **clouds**: *Alum* b4a.de bell b4.de* con b4.de* dig b4.de* rhus-t b7.de* sabin b7.de*
- **colorful**: (↗*MIND - Delusions - visions - colorful)* anh br1 visc sp1
  - • **pulsating** to the rhythm of music; halo of color: (↗*HEARING - Illusions - sounds - melody)* anh br1
- **flies**: streptoc jl2
- **insects**: agar b4a.de *Am-m* b7a.de caust k* cocc b7.de coff b7a.de dig k* merc k* stram b7.de
- **objects**: *Coc-c* bg2
  - • **passing**: glon k*
- **operation**; after: stront-c ptk1
- **points** at the margin; objects seem to have sharp: *Hyos* b7a.de
- **shooting** stars that are falling down: m-ambo b7.de m-arct b7.de
- **sleep**; when falling asleep: melal-alt gya4 **Phos**
- **straws** hanging down; like: merc b4.de*
- **water**; bubbling, seething: *Puls* b7a.de
- **wheels**; of: kali-n b4a.de zinc bg2
  - • **fire**; of (See Fiery - wheels)

IMAGES too long retained: alum anan k* falco-pe nl2• gels bg3* hydrog srj2• jab k* *Lac-c* k* *Nat-m* k* nicc st1 phos bg3 spong fd4.de tab k* tub k*
- **lasting** all day: anh sp1
- **lasting** an hour: anh sp1

IMPAIRED (See Dim)

INFLAMMATION of eyes; from: *Puls* b7a.de

INJURIES agg.; from: *Con* b4a.de sul-ac b4a.de

INVERTED, objects seem: bell k* gels hr1 guare k* kali-c k*

JUMP when reading; words: bell k* hyos k2 irid-met srj5• lyss

LARGE:
- **light**; flame of: dig hyos k2 osm
- **objects** seem large: *(↗MIND - Size - incorrect)* aeth anh sp1 apis atro berb k* bov bro1 cann-i cann-s caust bg3* con conin c1 *Cycl* b7a.de euph k* hep br1* **Hyos** k* kreos bg2* *Laur* k* nat-m k* *Nicc* k* **Nux-m** k* nux-v bro1 *Onos* k* op k* ox-ac k* *Phos* b2.de* phys psor al2 staph b2.de* verb k*
  - **cerebral** congestion: aeth
  - **elongated**: bell bro1 ox-ac ptk1 zinc
  - **raises** his foot unnecessarily high in stepping over small objects when walking: agar bg1 euph **Onos**
  - **rising** from sitting agg.: staph
  - **twilight**; in the: *Berb* k*

LARGE FIELD of vision: choc srj3• fl-ac stry

LETTERS:
- **dancing**: bell ptk1 lyss ptk1
- **disappear** while reading: cic bro1* cocc bro1*
- **double** while writing: graph ptk1
  - **red**: phos ptk1
- **smaller**; appear: glon ptk1

LIGHT: calc k* *Caust Chinin-s* helo-s bnm14• limest-b es1• *Phos* spong
- **beams** (See Rays)
- **insensibility** to (See EYE - Pupils - insensible)
- **points**: irid-met srj5• kali-s fd4.de nat-m k* *Plut-n* srj7•
  - **dark** circle; in a: caust
- **spots**: con k* hydrog srj2•
- **streaks** of: am-c b4a.de* *M-ambo* b7.de* **Nat-m** k* *Sep* b4a.de
  - **pass** downward; seen to one side of eye in dark: thuj k*
- **waves** of: borx k*

LIGHT; from:
- **agg.**: hyos ptk1
- **amel.**: gels ptk1 stram ptk1
- **artificial** light:
  - **agg.**: aur ptk1 lyc ptk1 nat-m ptk1
  - **amel.**: *Con* b4a.de
- **bright** light | **agg.**: *Bar-c* b4a.de *Calc* b4a.de *Phos* b4a.de
- **candlelight** | **agg.**: am-m b7a.de *Anac* b4a.de *Bar-c* b4a.de *Bell* b4a.de borx b4a.de calc b4.de* *Caust* b4a.de cina b7.de* *Con* b4a.de croc b7.de* dros b7.de* hep b4.de* ign b7.de* ip b7a.de *Kali-c* b4.de* laur b7.de* *Lyc* b4.de* mang b4.de* merc b4.de* nit-ac b4a.de ph-ac b4.de* *Phos* b4.de* *Puls* b7.de* *Ruta* b7.de* *Seneg* b4a.de sep b4.de* *Sil* b4.de* staph b7.de* sulph b4.de*
- **daylight** | **agg.**: am-m b7a.de *Ant-c* b7a.de caust b4.de* *Con* b4.de* dros b7.de* *Euphr* b7a.de *Graph* b4.de* *Hell* b7.de* *Hyos* b7a.de kali-c b4.de* mag-c b4.de* merc b4.de* nit-ac b4.de* **Nux-v** b7.de* petr b4.de* phos b4.de* samb b7.de* sep b4.de* *Sil* b4.de* stram b7.de*
- **fire**; of the: **Merc** b4.de*
- **moonlight** | **amel.**: *(↗MIND - Moonlight) Aur*
- **sunlight** | **agg.**: acon b7.de* *Ant-c* b7a.de *Ars* b4.de* *Bry* b7a.de *Chin* b7.de* con b4.de* dulc b4.de* *Euphr* b7a.de graph b4.de* ign b7.de* m-arct b7.de *Nux-v* b7a.de seneg b4.de* stram b7.de* sulph b4.de* zinc b4.de*

LIGHTNING: *Bell* k* brom k* *Caust* croc k* cycl k* dig k* fl-ac *Glon* k* *Kali-c* k* m-ambo b2.de m-arct b2.de *Nat-c* k* *Nux-v* k* olnd k* op ozone sde2• *Phos* k* phys plut-n srj7• *Puls* k* santin sec k* sep *Sil Spig* k* staph k* stram *Sulph* b4a.de thuj b4a.de* valer zinc k*
- **noon**: dig k*
- **night**:
  - **23 h** | **distant** sheet lightning in the dark; a: coca
- **black** (See Colors - black - lightning)
- **dark**; in●: olib-sac wht1• *Phos* stram k* valer
- **sheet** lightning: kali-c b4a.de *Nux-v* b7a.de sec b7a.de
- **sleep**; when falling asleep: nat-c **Phos** sulph
- **vertigo**; during: thuj b4a.de
- **waking**; on: *Nat-c*

LINE seems above the upper; lower: kali-c h2*

LINEN; as if looking through coarse: agar b4.de anac b4a.de *Bar-c* b4a.de **Caust** b4.de stram b7.de*

LOOKING:
- **concentrated**, focused:
  - **agg.**: agar b4.de* agn bg2 alum b4.de* am-c b4.de* am-m b7a.de* anac bg2 ang bg2 arg-met bg2 **Arg-n** bg2 arn bg2 *Asaf* bg2 asar bg2 *Aur* bg2 bar-c bg2 bell bg2 borx bg2 bry bg2 **Calc** b4a.de* canth bg2 carb-an bg2 *Carb-v* b4.de* *Caust* bg2 cham bg2 chel bg2 chin bg2 *Cic* bg2 **Cina** b7.de* cocc bg2 coff bg2 *Con* bg2 **Croc** bg2 cupr bg2 dros b7.de* dulc bg2 ferr bg2 gels bg2 laur bg2 led b7.de* **Lyc** b4.de* mag-c b4.de* mag-m bg2 mang bg2 meny bg2 merc bg2 mez bg2 mosch bg2 mur-ac bg2 *Nat-c* bg2 **Nat-m** b4a.de* nit-ac b4.de* nux-m bg2 nux-v bg2 *Olnd* bg2 **Onos** bg2 par bg2 petr bg2 ph-ac b4.de* *Phos* b4.de* plat bg2 puls bg2 ran-b bg2 rheum bg2 **Rhod** bg2 rhus-t bg2 **Ruta** b7.de* sabad bg2 *Sars* bg2 sel bg2 **Seneg** b4.de* *Sep* bg2 **Sil** bg2 *Spig* b7.de* *Spong* bg2 staph bg2 stram bg2 stront-c bg2 sul-ac bg2 sulph b4.de* thuj bg2 valer bg2 verb bg2 viol-o bg2 zinc bg2
  - **amel.**: petr b4.de* ph-ac b4.de*
  - **one** eye; with | **amel.**: kali-bi ptk1 phos bg2* phys ptk1
- **distance**; into the | **agg.**: euphr b7.de* *Ruta* b7a.de
- **downward** | **agg.**: kali-c ptk1 olnd b7.de* stann ptk1 verat ptk1
- **fire**; at the: merc ptk1
- **light**; at | **bright** light: caust b4a.de colch b7.de* *Kali-c* b4a.de *Ph-ac* b4a.de *Phos* b4a.de sep b4.de* zinc b4a.de
- **long** at something | **agg.**: bell bg2 caust bg2 cic b7.de* rheum b7.de* ruta b7.de* spig b7a.de
- **sideways**:
  - **agg.**: bell b4a.de gels bg2 olnd b7.de* seneg b4.de sep bg2
  - **amel.**: chinin-s bg2 lil-t bg2 *Olnd* b7a.de
- **straight** ahead:
  - **agg.**: *Olnd* b7a.de
  - **amel.**: olnd b7.de*
- **upward** | **agg.**: ars bg2 *Zinc* b4a.de
- **white** (snow); on something | **agg.**: *Am-c* b4a.de *Am-m* b7a.de cham b7.de* cic bg2 graph b4.de* kali-c b4.de* nat-m b4.de* stram b7.de*

LOSS OF VISION (= blindness): **Acon** k* aconin c2 *Agar* k* agath-a nl2• all-c alum am-c b2.de* ambr b7.de* anac b2.de* ant-c k* ant-t k* antip vh1 apis k* arg-met arg-n arn k* ars k* asaf b7.de* asar b7a.de* aster atra-r bnm3• *Aur* k* aur-ar k2 *Aur-m* aur-s k2 bar-c b2.de* *Bell* k* berb *Both* k* *Bov Bry* b7.de* bufo cact *Calc* k* camph k* cann-i cann-s b2.de* caps k* carb-an k* carbn-o *Carbn-s* k* *Caust* k* cent c2 cham k* chel k* *Chin* k* *Chinin-s* k* chlf chlol cic k* cimic bg2 clem cocc b2.de* *Con* k* croc k* crot-c crot-h crot-t cupr b7a.de cupr-act cycl k* *Dig* k* diph-pert-t mp4• dros b2.de* dulc b2.de* elaps eug eup-per euph b2.de* *Euphr* k* eupi ferr k* ferr-p fil c2 flor-p rsj3• *Gels* k* glon *Graph* b2.de* guaj b2.de* hell hep b2.de* hura k* hura-c c1* hydr-ac **Hyos** k* iod b2.de* ip jug-c c2 kali-ar kali-bi k* kali-br kali-c b2.de* kali-cy *Kali-i* kali-n k* kali-sil k2 kalm k* kreos k* lac-ac lac-v c2 lach k* lact lam laur b2.de* led k* lil-t bg2 *Lith-c* k* *Lyc* k* *Lyss* mag-c b2.de* mag-m b4.de manc c2* mang b4.de* meny k* meph k* **Merc** k* merc-c b4a.de mom-b bro1 morph mosch k* mur-ac bg2 naja naphtin bro1 nat-c b2.de* *Nat-m* k* nat-p k2 nit-ac k* nux-m k* *Nux-v* k* olnd k* *Op* k* ourl jl2 ox-ac k2 petr b2.de* ph-ac k* *Phos* k* phyt bg2 pitu-p sp1 plat b2.de* *Plb* k* *Plb-act* bro1 psor bg2 **Puls** k* ran-b b7.de raph rhus-t k* rhus-v russ c2 *Ruta* b2.de* sabad b7.de* sang bg2 santin bro1 sars k* *Sec* k* seneg b2.de* *Sep* k* **Sil** k* sol-ni spig k* spiros-af oss• squil b7a.de staph b2.de* **Stram** k* stront-c b2.de* stry bro1 stry-n mtf11 suis-pan rly4• *Sulph* k* syph ptk1 *Tab* k* thal-xyz srj8• *Ther* thuj k* valer b2.de* vanad br1* vanil fd5.de verat k* *Verat-v* verb b7.de* vesp br1 viol-o b2.de* vip zinc k* zinc-m
- **one** side: apoc vh1 cham b7a.de tab bg2
- **right**: carbn-s bg2 mag-c bg2
- **left**: ulm-c jsj8• [bell-p-sp dcm1]
- **daytime**: *(↗Dim - daytime)* acon b7a.de* anac b4a.de ant-c b7.de* both c2* castm bro1* chin bg2 con k* dig b4a.de hyos bg2 kali-n b4a.de* lyc bg2* merc bg2 nux-v b7a.de* *Phos* b4.de* puls b7a.de ran-b c1* ran-s bg2 *Sec* b7a.de *Sil* k* **Sol-ni** b7a.de *Staph* b7a.de **Stram** k* sulph k* *Verat* b7.de*
  - **light**; by: castm br1 merl nit-ac *Phos* sep
- **morning**: arg-n hr1 bell k* ign k* sulph k*
  - **fasting**: *Calc* k*
  - **rising** agg.: puls

- **forenoon**: thuj k*
- **noon**: am-c k*
  - **eating**; before: dulc
- **afternoon**: indg k*
  - **16** h: *Lyc*
  - **pain** in head and eyes; after: *Con*
  - **rising** after sleep, on: ferr k*
  - **stooping** agg.: apis
- **evening**: ammc a1* bell k* borx a1 calc k* camph ferr k* nat-c k* phos k* psor sulph hr1 til k*
  - **light**; by: **Lyc** mang thuj
  - **menses**; during: *Sep* k*
  - **reading** agg.: brom k*
  - **sitting** down during vertigo, on: coloc k*
  - **sunset**, at: bell k*
  - **twilight**; in the●: both st1 **LYC** k ● psor verat hr1
    - ⁝ **amel.**: psor a1
- **night**: *(↗Dim - night)* achy-a bnj1 arg-n bg2 bell k* cadm-s k* chel k* **Chin** k* chinin-s bg2 *Dig* b4.de* hell k* hep bro1 *Hyos* k* **LYC** k ●* meph merc k* *Nit-ac* k* nux-v k* petros k* phos bg2 phys bg* positr nl2• psor puls k* *Ran-b* k* ruta b7.de* sil bg1 stram k* stry bro1 stry-xyz c2 sulph b4a.de* vanil fd5.de verat k* zinc
  - **flickering** by day, blind at night: anac k*
- **abdominal** pain, with: crot-t k* plb k*
- **accompanied** by:
  - **hemorrhage**: chin bro1* ferr bro1 phos bro1
  - **vertigo** (See VERTIGO - Accompanied - vision - loss)
  - ○ **Brain**; inflammation of | **Medulla** oblongata (See HEAD - Inflammation - brain - medulla - accompanied - vision)
  - **Head** pain (See headache - beginning; headache - during)
  - **Heart**; complaints of the (See CHEST - Heart; complaints - accompanied - vision)
- **air**; in open:
  - **agg.**: nit-ac k*
  - **amel.**: merc k* phos k*
- **alcohol**; from: ter ptk1
- **alternating** with | **Head**; pain in (See HEAD - Pain - alternating - vision - loss)
- **ascending** stairs agg.: coca
- **bleeding**; from: chin tl1
- **bright** objects; by (See looking - object - bright)
- **camphor**; at odor of: kali-n h2
- **causeless**: tab ptk1
- **chill**; during: *Bell* b4a.de* cann-i k* chin bg cic b7a.de* dig bg hyos bg2 kreos b7a.de* lach bg2 m-aust b7a.de nat-m bg2 ol-j a1 **Sabin** b7a.de*
- **cold**; after taking a: acon k*
- **colors**; for: bell k* ben-d c2* carbn-s k* chlol k* cina k* onos c2* phys bro1 santin k* tab c2 thal-xyz srj8•
- **convulsions**:
  - **after**: dig h2* sec k*
  - **before**: *Cupr* k*
- **delirium**; during: phos k*
- **delivery**; during: aur-m caust cocc cupr k*
- **dinner** | **after** | **agg.**: *Calc* zinc
  - **during** | **agg.**: gels a1
- **eating** | **after** | **agg.**: *Calc* k* *Crot-t* sil k*
  - **soup** | **agg.**: nat-s k*
- **electric** shocks | **after**: phos k2
- **emotions** agg.; sudden: jug-c
- **exerting** eyes: (non:chin slp) cinch slp helon lyc nat-m
  - **sewing**, in: berb *Nat-m* *Ruta*
- **eyes**; from inflammation of: manc ptk1
  - **exertion**; from: crot-h ptk1
- **fainting**:
  - **after** sudden fainting: plb hr1*
- **fainting**: ...
  - **as** from fainting: *Agar* aur bell brucel sa3• *Calc* k* *Caust* chel k* *Chen-a* *Cic* cycl dros ferr ferr-p *Graph* hep *Hyos* kali-n manc hr1 *Mang* merc *Nat-m* olnd *Phos* *Puls* *Sep* spig stram verat-v a1
- **fever**; during: *Carb-v* bg2 *Nat-m* b4a.de* *Puls* b7.de* sep bg2
- **fixing** eyes: ant-t k* euphr k* kali-bi k* lachn a1 mag-c k* *Nat-m* nit-ac k* spig k*
- **grief**; from: crot-h ptk1
- **head**:
  - **rush** of blood; during: grat
  - **turning** agg.: chir-fl gya2 sec
- **headache**:
  - **after**: *Arg-n* hr1 sil k*
  - **before**: gels hr1* *Iris* bro1 kali-bi al* lac-d bro1 nat-m bro1 psor al2
  - **beginning** of; at: kali-bi k* nat-m hbh sars
  - **during**: atro hr1 *Bell* b4a.de* *Caust* hr1* *Chen-a* hr1 cupr hr1 *Ferr-p* hr1 *Gels* hr1 *Kali-bi* mrr1 *Lac-d* hr1 lil-t k2 **Meli** hr1 *Nat-m* hr1 petr hr1* *Sep* b4a.de* *Stram* hr1 vanil fd5.de *Zinc* hr1 [bell-p-sp dcm1]
- **hemorrhage**; after: chin hr1
- **hysterical**: gels kr1 phos bro1* plat bro1* sep bro1*
- **incipient**: agar bg2 aur bg2 *Bell* bg2 *Calc* bg2 caps bg2 *Caust* bg2 *Chin* bg2 *Cic* bg2 cina bg2 *Con* bg2 dig bg2 dros bg2 dulc bg2 euphr bg2 guaj bg2 *Hyos* bg2 kali-c bg2 lach bg2 lyc bg2 *Merc* bg2 nat-c bg2 *Nat-m* bg2 *Nit-ac* bg2 nux-m bg2 **Op** bg2 *Phos* bg2 plb bg2 *Puls* bg2 rhus-t bg2 sec bg2 *Sep* bg2 *Sil* bg2 *Sulph* bg2 verat bg2 zinc bg2
- **increasing** and decreasing suddenly: calc-ar k2
- **injuries**; after:
  - **eye**; to the: *Arn*
  - **head**; to the: arn mrr1
- **light**; by: agath-a nl2• calc k* *Graph* k* mang k* phos k*
  - **artificial** light: aur-m chin k* *Lyc* mang *Nux-m* phos k*
  - **entering** light from darkness: dig k*
  - **sunlight**: *Lith-c* k*
- **lightning**; after a stroke of: phos k*
- **looking**:
  - **downward**: kalm k*
  - **object**; looking at an: nux-m br1
    - ⁝ **before** him: med jl2
    - ⁝ **bright** objects; at: grat ph-ac
    - ⁝ **long** time; for a: mang
    - ⁝ **near** objects; at: mag-m
  - **sideways**: olnd k*
  - **upward**: *Cupr* k*
- **lying** down:
  - **agg.**: cham bg1
  - **amel.**: cina phos sep
- **masturbation**; from: gels lp ph-ac ptk1*
- **meningitis**; after: phos hr1
- **menses**:
  - **amel.**: *Sep* k*
  - **before** | **agg.**: cycl bro1 ph-ac b4a.de puls bro1 sep bro1
  - **during** | **agg.**: cycl hr1* *Graph* k* *Ign* b7a.de lyc **Puls** k* *Sep* k*
  - **suppressed** menses; during: chen-a hr1
- **mental** exertion agg.: arg-n meny k*
- **momentary** (See increasing)
- **moonlight**: bell ptk1
- **motion** agg.: grat
- **nausea**; during: *Sep* k*
- **object** (See looking - object)
- **optic** nerve; from atrophy of: syph ptk1
- **paroxysmal**: acon arg-n bg calc bg chel bg chin bg con dig bg euphr bg hyos bg kali-n mang mosch k2 nit-ac h2* nux-v phos k* sil k* stram sulph
- **passive**: aur bg2 caps bg2 caust bg2 chin bg2 dros bg2 dulc bg2 nat-c bg2 nat-m bg2 op bg2 ph-ac bg2 plb bg2 sec bg2 verat bg2

Vision

- **periodical**: acon b2.de* am-c b2.de* anac b2.de* ant-c b2.de* *Ant-t* k* bar-c b2.de* bell b2.de* calc b2.de* caust b2.de* *Chel* k* chin k* con b2.de* croc b2.de* *Dig* k* *Euphr* k* graph b2.de* hyos k* kali-n b2.de* lyc b2.de* merc k* nat-c b2.de* *Nat-m* k* nux-v b2.de* petr b2.de* *Phos* k* plb b2.de* *Puls* k* rhus-t b2.de* ruta b2.de* sec b2.de* *Sep* k* *Sil* k* spig b2.de* staph b2.de* stram b2.de* *Sulph* k* verat b2.de*
- **reading**:
  - **agg.**: agar k* arg-n k* aur-m caust k* clem k* crot-h k* dros haem k* lachn k* lyc k* nat-c k* nat-m h2* *Phos* k* staph k*
  - **small** print: cadm-s c1
  - **standing** agg.; while: glon
- **retinal** hemorrhage; from: both ptk1 crot-h ptk1
- **rising**:
  - **agg.**: cedr k* glon k* *Hep* olnd
  - **bed**; from | **agg.**: bell *Cina* colch com sec verat-v hr1
  - **eating** agg.; rising after: merc
- **scarlet** fever; from: aur-m k2
- **shivering**; during: bell b4.de m-aust b7.de *Sabin* b7.de*
- **sitting**:
  - **agg.**: kalm k* lyss hr1 merc k* phos k*
  - **bent** forward | **after**: *Hep* k*
- **sleep** | **amel.**: calc grat k*
- **sleeping** in the sun, after: con k*
- **snow**, by: cic k* *Kali-chl* hr1 *Merl* hr1
- **standing**:
  - **agg.**: colch
  - **amel.**: merc
- **stool** | **after** | **agg.**: petr h2
  - **amel.**: apis ptk1*
- **stooping** agg.: bell k* *Calc* hr1 coff k* com ferr-p k* graph k* nat-m h2* phos k* upa
- **sudden**: acon c1* arg-n bg2 aur-m k* calc k* chel bg2 chin k* chinin-s br1 cupr dig bg2 euphr bg2 gels c1 hyos bg2 mosch *Nat-m* k* nux-v bg2 phos k* psor k* puls bg2 sec k* sep bg2 *Sil* bg2 *Sulph* bg2
  - **cold** weather: acon vh1
  - **fright**; from: acon vh1*
  - **hot** weather: acon vh1
  - **shock**; after: acon mrr1
- **sunlight**, sleeping in: con k*
- **sunset** | **at**: bell bg1
- **syphilis**; from: aur-m k2
- **tobacco**: ars nux-v k* phos k* pilo bro1 plb-act bro1
- **transient**: kali-c h2 merc h1 phos h2
- **turning** head suddenly agg.: helon
- **vanishing** of sight: acon b2.de* *Agar* b2.de* alum b2.de* ambr b2.de* anac b2.de* ang b7a.de ant-t k* *Apis* b7a.de *Arg-met* k* *Arg-n* *Arn* b2.de* ars b2.de* asaf b2.de* asar b2.de* *Aur* b2.de* bar-c b4.de **Bell** b2.de* borx b2.de* bry b2.de* *Calc* b2.de* camph b2.de* cann-s b2.de* canth b7.de* caps b2.de* carb-an b2.de* carb-v b4.de *Carbn-s* *Caust* b2.de* cham b2.de* *Chel* k* *Chen-a* *Chin* b2.de* *Cic* k* cina b2.de* clem b2.de* *Con* b2.de* croc b2.de* *Crot-t* cupr b2.de* *Cycl* k* dig b2.de* *Dros* b2.de* dulc b2.de* euphr b2.de* *Ferr* b2.de* *Gels* graph k* *Grat* *Hep* b2.de* *Hydr-ac* bg2 **Hyos** b2.de* iod b2.de* kali-bi k* *Kali-c* k* kali-n b2.de* *Lach* b2.de* *Laur* k* led b2.de* lyc b2.de* lyss m-aust b2.de* mag-c b2.de* mag-m b2.de* *Mang* b2.de* meny b2.de* **Merc** b2.de* mez b2.de* mosch b2.de* mur-ac b2.de* *Nat-m* k* nit-ac b2.de* *Nux-m* k* **Nux-v** k* **Olnd** b2.de* *Op* b2.de* *Ox-ac* petr b2.de* **Phos** b2.de* plat b2.de* plb b2.de* *Puls* k* ran-b b2.de* ruta b2.de* sabad b2.de* sabin b2.de* sec b2.de* seneg b2.de* *Sep* k* *Sil* k* spig k* squil b2.de* staph b2.de* **Stram** b2.de* sulph b2.de* *Tab* bg2 tarax b2.de* thuj b2.de* verat b2.de* viol-t b2.de* *Zinc* k*
  - **cough**; from inability to: sulph h2
  - **menses**; during: *Graph* k*
  - **pregnancy** agg.; during: *Sil* hr1
  - **rising** | **sitting**; from | **agg.**: hep
    - **stooping**; from | **agg.**: *Kali-bi*
  - **uterine** complaints; with: *Sil* hr1
  - **writing** agg.: arg-n a1 *Kali-c* k*

Loss of vision: ...

- **vertigo** | **caused** by vertigo with pain in eyes: bell ptk1 gels ptk1 *Nux-v* ptk1 ther hr1*
- **waking**; on: bell k* *Dulc* hr1 oena k*
- **walking**:
  - **agg.**: cic hr1 dor ferr hell lachn nat-m h2 sulph *Verat-v*
  - **air** agg.; in open: merc
- **warm** room agg.: merc k* *Puls* hr1
- **weather** agg.; wet: crot-h
- **white** objects, looking at: graph k* tab k*
- **writing** agg.: arg-n k* grat k* kali-c k* nat-m h2* phys k* zinc k*

LUMINOUS: dig h2 irid-met srj5•

- **dark**; in: valer ptk1
- **objects** are jumping, on covering the eyes: dig a1 irid-met srj5•
- **operation**; after: zinc ptk1

LYING agg.: cham bg2

MASTURBATION agg.: cina b7a.de

MENSES:

- **after** | **agg.**: bell bg2
- **before** | **agg.**: agn bg2 bell bg2 cinnb bg2 dict bg3* nat-m bg2 verat bg2
- **during** | **agg.**: cycl bg2* graph bg2* mag-c bg2 puls b7.de* sep bg3*

MENTAL EXERTION agg.: arg-n bg2 gels bg2

MERCURY; after abuse of: *Carb-v* b4a.de hep b4a.de *Nit-ac* b4a.de

MIRAGE: lyc ptk1

MIST (See Foggy)

MISTAKES: adam srj5• bell k* bov k* euph k* *Hyos* b2.de* kali-c k* *Plat* k* spig ptk1 stram b2.de*

- **form**, size and distance; regarding: camph b7.de* cann-xyz ptk1 carb-an ptk1 *Cic* b7.de* hyos b7.de* laur b7.de* m-aust b7.de *Olnd* b7.de* onos ptk1 *Puls* b7.de* *Sec* b7.de* staph b7.de* **Stram** b7.de* valer b7.de* verat b7.de* verb b7.de*
  - **confused**: *Bell* bg2 led b7.de* stram b7.de*

MOTION:

- **agg.**: calc b4.de* *Nat-m* b4.de* *Phos* b4a.de
  - **uneven** motion: cic bg2 con bg2
- **head**; of | **agg.**: mosch b7.de*

MOVING: (↗*Changing; Colors*) **Acon** bg2 *Agar* k* *Aloe* am-c k* *Am-m* bg2 apis b7a.de **Arg-n** aur bg2 bapt bg2 *Bell* k* *Borx* *Calc* k* calc-p *Cann-i* **Chin** bg2 *Cic* k* cocc bg2 coff bg2 *Con* k* dulc bg2 *Euphr* k* *Glon* hyos b2.de* ign k* *Lach* laur k* lyc k* m-ambo b2.de* meny k* merc k* mosch k* nat-m bg2 **Nit-ac** bg2 *Nux-v* k* *Olnd* k* par k* petr k* **Phos** bg2 *Psor* k* rhus-t bg2 ruta bg2 sabad k* *Sep* k* **Sil** h2* stram k* *Sulph* bg2

- **evening** | **reading** agg.: merc
- **chill**; during: cic bg2 lyc bg2 *Sabad* bg2
- **letters**: *Agar* k* am-c h2* cic c1 con k* *Hyos* iod merc k* phys k*
  - **towards** noon: am-c k*
- **objects** seem to be moving: bapt carb-ac con euphr hydr-ac hydrog srj2• ign kola stb3• nux-m petr h2 psor rhus-g tmo3•
  - **backward**: *Bell* calc cic sep
    - **forward**; and: carb-ac *Cic*
    - **slowly**: sep
  - **car** in rain seems to be moving: hydrog srj2•
  - **dancing**: *Arg-n* ptk1 *Bell* ptk1 cic ptk1 cocc ptk1 con ptk1 glon ptk1 psor ptk1
    - **colors**; with changing: stront-c ptk1
  - **fine** motion: petr
  - **floating** (See Swimming - objects)
  - **jumping**: irid-met srj5• meny h1
  - **left**; to: ulm-c jsj8•
  - **looking** sideways: rhus-g tmo3•
  - **revolving**: *Bell* squil b7a.de
  - **right**; to the: kola stb3• nat-sal ptk1
  - **side** to side: cic plut-n srj7•

- **objects** seem to be moving: ...
  - **to** and fro: cic b7.de* euphr b7.de laur b7.de* m-ambo b7.de meny b7.de* mosch b7.de* par b7.de*
    - **noon**; towards: elaps
  - **up** and down: ars *Cocc* con sil spong
    - **pulsation** in ear; from: sil h2
- **something** moving: lyss k* psor k* spong fd4.de
  - **fingers** before eyes; as if one was playing with: psor a1*
  - **shivering**; during: sabad b7.de

MULTIPLIED; objects seem (See Diplopia; Polyopia)

MUSCAE volitantes (See Colors - black - spots - floating)

MYOPIA: *(↗EYE - Asthenopia - myopic)* acon bro1 *Agar* k* *Am-c* k* *Anac* k* androc srj1• ang b2.de* *Ant-t* b2.de* apis k* arec c1* *Arg-n* k* ars k* aur-m bro1 bac jl2 bell bro1 *Calc* k* *Carb-v* k* carbn-s k* *Chin* k* cimic k* coff-t k* *Con* k* *Cycl* k* dig k* diphtox jl2 euph b2.de* *Euphr* k* form bg2 *Gels* k* *Graph* k* grat k* haliae-lc srj5• hep b2.de* *Hyos* k* *Jab* k* kali-s fd4.de kola stb3• *Lach* k* lil-t br1* *Lyc* k* *Mang* k* *Meph* k* mez k* nat-ar *Nat-c* k* *Nat-m* k* nat-p nat-sil fd3.de• *Nit-ac* k* ol-an mtf11 *Petr* k* petr-ra shn4• *Ph-ac* k* **Phos** k* **Phys** k* *Pic-ac* k* pilo c2* *Plat* b2.de plb k* podo fd3.de• positr nl2• psor **Puls** k* raph k* retin-ac mtf11 *Ruta* k* sel k* spong k* *Stram* k* *Sul-ac* k* *Sulph* k* symph fd3.de• syph k* *Thuj* k* *Tub* *Valer* k* verb k* viol-o k* viol-t k*

- **accompanied** by | **Eyes**; pain in (See EYE - Pain - accompanied - myopia)
- **candlelight** than by daylight; sight worse by: arg-n
- **children**; in: bar-ox-suc mtf11
- **exerting** the eyes, after: *Carb-v* k*
- **looking** away from work amel.: ph-ac k*
- **myopic** astigmatism: lil-t br1
- **reading** agg.: agar k* grat k* lyc k* podo fd3.de• symph fd3.de•
- **turning** head sideways to see clearly: lil-t ptk1

NARROW: | **field** of vision: stram b7.de*

NEARER, objects seem: *(↗MIND - Distances - inaccurate)* arg-n bg2 bell bg2 berb bg2 *Bov* k* cann-xyz bg2 cham bg2 *Cic* b2.de* coli rly4• dros bg2 euph bg2 falco-pe nl2• gels bg2 **Hyos** bg2 laur bg2 mosch bg2 nat-c bg2 nat-m bg2 nit-ac bg2 nux-m bg2 osm bg2 phos bg2 phys k* rhus-t k* staph bg2 stram k* sulph bg2 tub bg2 valer ptk1 verb bg2

- **to** each other: *Nux-m* k*
- **yawning** agg.: all-c ptk1

NET before eyes: anac b4a.de* bell bg2 *Carb-an* k* *Chinin-s* k* hyos k* stram bg2 thuj a1

- **swimming**: *Carb-an* k* thuj a1

NIGHT BLINDNESS (See Dim - night; Loss - night)

NYCTALOPIA (See Loss - night)

OBJECTS:

- **beside** field of vision; sees objects: arizon-l nl2• calc bg2* camph bg3* cann-s bg3 cann-xyz ptk1 coloc bg3* graph bg3* ign bg3* lac-c bg3* nux-m bg3* nux-v bg3* sinus rly4• stram bg3* thuj bg3*
- **blurred**; outlines of objects: *(↗Blurred)* phos kr1
- **borders**; with colored: hyos ptk1
- **colored**; colorless objects appear: anh sp1
- **deformed** objects appear: anh sp1
- **half** in light, half in dark: glon ptk1
- **ill** defined: bell hr1 kali-bi hr1 phos hr1 **Sulph** kr1
- **indistinct**: *Agar* bg am-m bg anac tl1 ang bg aur bg bell bg* bry bg calc-p tl1 *Cann-s* bg canth bg *Caps* bg carb-v bg cham bg cic bg cina tl1 cocc tl1 coff bg croc bg dig bg *Dros* bg *Euphr* bg gels tl1 hyos bg *Ign* bg kali-bi kr1 laur bg led bg *Merc* bg par bg plb bg rhus-t bg sars bg sec bg spig bg stram bg *Sulph* bg verat bg verb bg
- **whirling** around each other: sabad ptk1

OBLIQUITY: *Nux-m* k* *Stram* k*

OBSCURATION of vision (See Dim)

PAIN:

- **head**; in:
  - **after**: caust bg2 cic b7.de* con bg2 form bg2 gels bg2 kali-bi bg2 lach bg2 phos bg2 plb bg2 sep bg2 sil bg2 stram bg2

Pain – head; in: ...

  - **before**: aran bg2 canth bg2 coca bg2 gels bg2 glon bg2 graph bg2 hyos bg2 *Iris* bg2 **Kali-bi** bg2 lach bg2 *Nat-m* bg2 *Phos* bg2 podo bg2 psor bg2 rhus-t bg2 sars bg2 *Sep* bg2 stram bg2 ther bg2
    - **during**; and: gels bg2 glon bg2 iris bg2 kali-bi bg2 ther bg2
  - **during**: acon b7.de* ant-t bg2 arg-n bg2 *Bell* b4a.de* bry b7.de* chinin-ar bg2 cic bg2 cimic bg2 *Cycl* b7.de* dig bg2 epiph bg2 gels bg2 hydr-ac bg2 *Hyos* bg2 ign b7.de* iris bg2 lach bg2 lil-t bg2 meny bg2 mur-ac b4a.de* nat-c bg2 *Nat-m* b4.de* nux-m bg2 ol-an bg2 olnd bg2 *Ph-ac* b4a.de psor bg2 sars bg2 sil bg2 *Stram* bg2 **Sulph** b4.de* tab bg2 thuj bg2 verat-v bg2 zinc bg2
  - **violent** pains; during: *Chin* bg2 **Iris** bg2 *Ph-ac* bg2 phos bg2 podo bg2 **Puls** bg2 *Zinc* bg2

PALE: agar b4.de* carb-v b4a.de *Chin* b7.de* croc b7.de* *Dros* b7.de* petr b4.de* puls b7.de* rhus-t b7.de* *Sil* b4.de*

- **objects** become pale after looking long: *Agar* k* rhus-t a1

PERSPECTIVE; distorted: anh sp1 kali-p ptk1

PERSPIRATION; during: | **agg.**: stram b7.de

POINTS:

- **floating**: *Am-m* b7a.de ruta b7.de*
- **half**: viol-o b7.de*

POLLUTIONS agg.; after: *Kali-c* b4a.de

POLYOPIA: anh sp1 gels kl iod h

PRESSURE:

- **cheek** agg.; pressure on: bell b4.de*
- **eye**; on | **agg.**: bar-c b4.de* bell b4a.de

PROPORTION; out of: anh sp1

QUIVERING (See Trembling)

RAIN, seems looking through rain: nat-m k*

RAINBOW (See Colors - halo; Colors - rainbow)

RANGE of vision changes while reading (See Focal - changes)

RAYS: bell b4.de* cham b7.de* iod b4.de* kali-c b4.de* lach bg2 plut-n srj7• [heroin sdj2]

- **around** light: kali-c h2*
- **broken** up into rays; light seems: bell
- **curved**, shooting from visual axis: iod k*

READING: | **agg.**: agar b4.de* alum b4.de* *Am* b7a.de ars bg2 *Asaf* b7.de* asar b7.de aur bg2 bar-c b4a.de bry b7.de* *Calc* b4.de* carb-v b4.de* caust b4.de* *Chin* bg2 cina b7.de* con b4.de* croc b7.de* *Dros* bg2 dulc b4.de* *Graph* b4.de* hep b4a.de* ign b7.de* kali-c b4.de* lith-c bg2 lyc b4.de* meny b7.de* merc b4.de* nat-c b4.de* **Nat-m** b4.de* ox-ac bg2 petr b4.de* phos b4.de* rhod b4.de* *Ruta* b7.de* seneg b4.de* sep b4.de* *Sil* b4.de* staph b7.de* stram b7.de* *Sulph* b4a.de thuj b4.de* viol-o b7.de*

RECEDING (See Moving)

REFLECTING agg.: meny b7.de*

RINGS: *(↗Circles)* anh sp1 calc h2* calc-p ptk1 carb-v h2* elaps bg3* falco-pe nl2• kali-c ptk1 phos h2* psor ptk1

- **turning** agg.: kali-c ptk1

RISING:

- **bed**; from:
  - **agg.**: ang b7.de* carb-v b4.de* cina bg2 puls b7.de* stram b7.de*
  - **amel.**: carb-v b4.de*
- **sitting**; from | **agg.**: ambr b7.de* ant-t b7.de* laur b7.de* puls b7.de* verat b7.de*
- **stooping**; from | **agg.**: hep bg2 olnd b7a.de

RISING BODY is obscuring vision: am-m h2*

ROOM:

- **agg.**: *Con* b4a.de dros b7.de* dulc b4.de* mur-ac b4.de* puls b7.de* sabin b7.de*
- **amel.**: alum b4.de* am-m b7.de* con b4.de* meny b7.de*

ROUND objects pass before eyes while lying: caust k*

Vision

RUBBING:
- **agg.**: caust b4.de* spig b7.de* *Stront-c* b4a.de
- **amel.**: art-v bg2 caps b7.de* cina b7.de* ph-ac b4.de*

RUN together: (↗*Blurred)* anh sp1
- **letters**: *Agar* bro1 arg-n k* *Am* b7a.de *Art-v* k* atro k* bell k* berb bry k* calc k* calc-ar k* *Camph* k* **Cann-i** k* *Cann-s* bg *Cann-xyz* bg2* carb-ac a1* *Chel* k* *Chin* k* cina bro1 clem k* coca *Con* k* cund a1 *Daph* bg2 *Dros* k* elaps k* euphr k* *Ferr* k* gels gins k* *Graph* k* hyos b2.de* iris *Lac-c* k* lach bg2 *Lil-t* bg2 *Lyc* k* lycpr c1 meph k* *Merl* k* **Nat-m** k* op k* osm k* phos bg2 **Ruta** k* *Seneg* k* **Sil** k* **Staph** k* **Stram** k* thlas bg2* *Tub* viol-o k*
  - **morning**: bry k*
  - **evening**: merl k*
    - **reading** in bed, while: bell k*
  - **after** a little while: *Con*
  - **exertion** of vision at fine work, from: nat-c h2*
  - **mental** exertion; after: *Arg-n*
  - **writing** agg.: carb-ac k* *Chel* k* clem k* *Ferr* k* gels lyc *Merl* op k* *Sil*
- **objects**: berb k* *Calc* hr1 sil k*
  - **sewing**, while: berb k* *Calc*
  - **stitches** while sewing: **Nat-m** k*

SCINTILLATIONS (See Flickering; Sparks)

SCOTOMA: abel jl1 agar mtf11 aloe calc-f vh1 carbn-s ign gsd1 tab k* thal-xyz srj8•
- **right** eye | **injuries**; after: merc hr1
- **accompanied** by | **Head**; pain in (See HEAD - Pain - morning - accompanied - scotoma)
- **central**: aur mp1• ben-d c1 carbn-s k* iodof mp1• plb a1* tab k* thal vml3• thyr br1

SEMINAL EMISSIONS agg.: ph-ac bg2

SEXUAL EXCESSES agg.: chin bg2 kali-c bg2

SHADE amel.: con bg3* phos bg3*

SHADING eyes: | **amel.**: phos b4.de*

SHADOWS: calc b4.de* nat-m bg2 *Ruta* k* *Seneg* k*
- **objects** appear as if shaded: *Seneg* k*
- **side** of objects; at one: *Calc* k*

SHARPER (See Acute)

SHIVERING; during: | **agg.**: laur b7.de* sabad b7.de* sabin b7.de*

SITTING ERECT agg.: kalm ptk1

SITTING UP in bed agg.: *Bell* b4a.de hep b4a.de

SIZE; objects increase and decrease in: anh sp1

SKIN or membrane over the eyes; illusion as of a: *Apis* b7a.de cann-s b7.de* caust b4.de* chel b7.de* **Con** b4a.de croc b7.de* *Euphr* b7.de* lyc bg2 ol-an ptk1 puls b7.de* *Ruta* b7.de* sulph b4a.de
○ - **Canthi**; from inner: *Ars* b4a.de

SLEEP:
- **after**:
  - **afternoon**: lyc bg2 puls b7a.de
  - **agg.**: con b4.de* ign b7.de*
  - **amel.**: cham b7a.de
- **falling** asleep; before | **agg.**: rhus-t b7.de*

SMALL, objects seem: (↗*MIND - Delusions - small - things - appear; MIND - Size - incorrect)* *All-c* anh sp1 *Aur* ben-d bro1 camph carb-v *Glon* k* *Hyos* k* *Kali-chl* *Lyc* med k* *Merc* *Merc-c* k* nicot bro1 nit-ac nux-m c1 op petr h2 *Plat* k* *Plb* psor al2 stram k* thuj k*

SMOKY (See Foggy)

SNAKE are moving before the eyes; bodies in the shape of a: (↗*Colors - black - serpents; Colors - white - serpents)* arg-n k* *Gels* k* kola stb3• phys a1 viol-o bg2

SNEEZING agg.: am-c b4.de* nat-c bg2

SNOW:
- **morning**:
  - **waking**; on | **objects** seem covered with snow: dig k*
- **exposure** to snow agg.: *Acon* ptk1 cic ptk1
- **falling**: kali-s fd4.de plb k*
- **flakes**: bell k* jab k* kali-s fd4.de plb rb2
- **surface**: ph-ac h2*

SPARKS: (↗*Flashes; Stars)* acon k* allox tpw4 am-c k* ammc k* ant-t k* arn k* ars k* ars-i ars-s-f k2 *Aur* k* aur-ar k2 aur-i k2 aur-s k2 *Bar-c* k* bar-i k2 bar-s k2 **Bell** k* bol-s a1 *Bry* b7.de bufo calc k* *Calc-f* k* calc-i k2 calc-sil k2 *Camph* k* *Caust* k* *Chel* **Chin** k* chinin-ar *Chinin-s* chlf k* choc srj3• coff coloc b4.de* con k* croc b7.de* cupr cupr-ar *Cycl* k* *Dig* b4.de* dulc k* ferr-i *Glon* k* hyos k* iod k* kali-ar *Kali-bi* k* *Kali-c* k* kali-m ptk1 kali-s kali-sil k2 *Lach* lyc k* lyss *M-ambo* b7.de mag-p k* mang b4.de *Merc* k* mez k* naphtin bro1 nat-ar nat-c k* nat-p nit-ac k* *Nuph* k* *Nux-v* k* *Op* k* petr k* phos k* pic-ac k* *Plat* *Psor* k* sec k* *Sep* k* *Sil* k* sol-ni *Spig* k* staph k* stram k* stront-c k* stry k* sul-i k2 *Sulph* k* thuj k* valer k* vanil fd5.de verat k* zinc
- **daytime**: croc k*
- **morning**: calc k* ferr-i
  - **waking**; on: *Calc*
- **noon**: dig k* verat k*
- **evening**: ammc k*
  - **rays**, like: mang
- **night**: *Am-c* k* *Staph*
  - **sleep**; when falling asleep: **Phos**
  - **waking**; on: *Am-c* *Calc*
- **air**, open, on going into: con k* lyc k*
- **black**, when looking at light: mang h2 mang-act h1
- **blowing** the nose agg.: alum cod k* nat-s bg1*
- **breakfast** agg.; after: ferr-i
- **chains** of light | **right** eye: moni rfm1•
- **closing** the eyes agg.: *Hydr* k* mang h2*
- **cough** agg.; during: bell kali-c k* kali-chl c1 kali-m k2 nuph k* par k*
- **darkness**●: *Bar-c* k* bell ptk1 calc k* lyc k* *Phos* k* thuj valer
- **dinner**; during: thuj k*
- **epileptic** fit, before: *Hyos*
- **fever**; during: bell b4a.de* *Op* b7.de*
- **fiery**: allox sp1 anh sp1
- **glowing** sparks: *Nux-v* b7.de*
- **headache**:
  - **before**: carb-ac chinin-s coca cycl eug lach nat-m mrr1 phos *Plat* psor sars spong sulph k2 viol-o
  - **during**: am-c ars k* *Chel* k* **Mag-p** k*
- **mental** exertion agg.: *Aur*
- **motion** of eyelids agg.: bell h1
- **outside** either side of the field of vision: thuj k*
- **rest** agg.; during: dulc
- **sewing**, while: iod
- **sitting** agg.: hura
- **sneezing** agg.: kali-chl c1 kali-m k2
- **streaks**, after writing; in: *Carl*
- **vertigo**; during: ars k* bell c1 *Camph* k* ign ptk1 psor k* vanil fd5.de
- **walking**:
  - **agg.**: hura
  - **air** agg.; in open: con h2
- **white**: alum ptk1
- **winking**, on: *Caust* k*
- **writing** agg.: borx c1 kali-bi k*

SPIRALS: falco-pe nl2•

SPOTS: acon b2.de* act-sp k* agar b2.de* allox sp1 alum k* am-c b2.de* **Am-m** b2.de* anac b2.de* arg-n br1 art-v ptk2 asc-t c1 *Atro* bro1 *Aur* b2.de* *Bar-c* b2.de* *Bell* b2.de* **Calc** b2.de* calc-sil k2 cann-s b2.de* carb-v b2.de* carbn-s *Caust* k* chel b2.de* chin b2.de* cocc b2.de* colch k* *Con* k* **Cycl** k* cypr bro1 dig b2.de* dros b2.de* elaps euon a1 euphr b2.de* fl-ac bg2 hyos b2.de* *Jab* kali-bi k* **Kali-c** k* lach bg2 lyc b2.de* *Mag-c* b2.de* mang b2.de* meli bro1 **Merc** b2.de* morg-p fmm1• mosch b2.de* nat-c b2.de* *Nat-m* b2.de* nat-pyru rly4• *Nit-ac* b2.de* *Nux-v* bro1 petr b2.de* ph-ac b2.de* **Phos** k* phys bro1 plut-n srj7• ruta b2.de* scroph-n br1 sec b2.de* seneg b2.de*

Spots: ...
Sep b2.de* sil k* sol-ni spong fd4.de stront-c b2.de* **Sulph** k* symph fd3.de• tab bro1 thuj b2.de* valer b2.de* vanil fd5.de verat bg2 verat-v
- **bright**: con b4.de* kali-bi tl1 vanil fd5.de
- **closing** the eyes agg.: *Hydr* vanil fd5.de
- **colored**: *(↗Colors)* astac
- **fiery** (See Fiery - spots)
- **floating**: am-m k* calc-sil k2 cann-i k* dig k* dioxi rbp6 hell k* hydrog srj2• phos k* plut-n srj7• ruta h1 symph fd3.de• zinc-p k2
- **headache**:
  - **before**: **Psor** k ●
  - **during**: cycl
- **jumping** up and down: *Croc*
- **looking** steadily agg.: act-sp k*
- **luminous**: *Hyos*
- **reading** agg.: astac cic a1 *Jab* kali-c k*
- **round**: dig k*
- **waking**; on: **Cycl** k*
- **wooly**: dys fmm1•
- **writing** agg.: kali-bi k*
- **yellow**: nat-pyru rly4•

STANDING ERECT agg.: puls b7.de*

STARS: *(↗Flashes; Sparks)* alum *Ammc* atro *Aur* aur-s k2 *Calc* castm con hyos *Kali-c* kali-p fd1.de• nat-c puls sec sulph k2 tarent vanil fd5.de verat-v
- **right** side of field of vision: *Calc*
- **dancing**: croc k* psil ft1
- **falling** stars: alum bg2 con bg2 xanth bg2
- **halo** of stars round light: puls k*
- **headache**; before: sulph k2
- **light**; in artificial: puls
- **periphery** of vision: plut-n srj7•
- **sneezing** agg.: nat-c bg1
- **white** (See Colors - white - stars)
- **writing** agg.: *Kali-c*

STEREOSCOPIC, hyper-acute: anh sp1

STOOPING: | **after** | **agg.**: hep b4a.de
- **agg.**: *Calc* b4.de* elaps ptk1 ferr-p bg2* *Graph* b4.de* *Nat-m* b4.de* phos b4.de* ther ptk1

STRIPES: *(↗Colors - stripes)* **Con** k* mand sp1 *Sep* k* *Sulph* k* thuj k*

SUN agg.: sulph bg2

SWIMMING of:
- **letters**: bell k* coca olib-sac wmh1 symph fd3.de•
- **objects**: anag k* carb-ac k* *Carl* k* coloc conin c1 euphr bg2 hyos bg2 lyss merl mez k* **Nat-m** k* nux-m k* olnd bg2 par k* phos bg2 positr nl2• puls bg2 stram bg2 sumb k* thuj k* til k* zinc k* [heroin sdj2]
  - **17 h**: thuj

THREAD before: choc srj3• con b4.de*
- **right** eye; before: con h1
- **bright**: anh sp1
- **hanging** down: sulph b4a.de

TREMBLING objects: *(↗Vibration - heated)* acon bg2 alum k* aml-ns bg2 apis b7a.de bell k* camph *Cann-i* carb-v ptk1 carbn-s chlor bg2 *Con* k* *Cur* dig b4.de* dros b7.de* kali-c k* kali-s fd4.de led b2.de* *Lyc* k* m-ambo b7.de morph bg2 nat-m bg2 *Nux-v* b7.de* *Petr* k* ph-ac k* *Phos* k* phys *Plat* k* plb *Psor* k* sabad k* sabin b2.de* seneg b2.de* stram b2.de* sumb thuj b2.de* verat-v bg2 viol-o k*
- **morning** | **waking**; on: phos k*
- **evening** | **light**; by: **Lyc** k* petr
- **chill**; during: led bg2 lyc bg2 sabad bg2 sabin bg2
- **dark**; then become: psor ptk1
- **light**; in artificial: **Lyc**
- **yellow** shining tremulous mist: *Kali-c* k*

TRIPLOPIA: *Bell* k* **Con** ●* sec k*
- **turning** eyes to right: dig k*

TWILIGHT; in the:
- **morning** | **amel.**: phos h2

Twilight: ...
- **agg.**: *Bell* bg2 dig b4.de* nat-m bg2
- **amel.**: bry b7a.de* lyc bg2 phos b4a.de* *Rhus-t* b7a.de

TWO-DIMENSIONAL objects become multi-dimensional: anh sp1

UNOBSTRUCTED field of vision: | **desire** for: brass-n-o srj5•

UNSTEADILY: spig ptk1

URINATION; during: | **amel.**: cann-xyz bg2

VANISHING of sight (See Loss - vanishing)

VARIEGATED colors (See Colors - variegated)

VEIL; as through a (See Foggy)

VERTIGO; during: | **agg.**: *Acon* b7.de* ant-t b7.de* arg-met b7.de* asaf b7.de* canth b7.de* carb-an b4.de* **Cham** b7.de* *Cic* b7.de* cina b7.de* croc b7.de* dulc b4.de* *Ferr* b7.de* hyos b7.de* laur b7.de* mosch b7.de* nat-m b4.de* nit-ac b4.de* *Nux-v* b7.de* olnd b7.de* op b7.de* phos b4.de* *Puls* b7.de* sabad b7.de* sabin b7.de* sec b7.de* squil b7.de* *Stram* b7.de* sulph b4.de* zinc b4.de*

VIBRATION:
- **heated** air; as of: *(↗Trembling)* *Lyc* *Puls* b7a.de
- **luminous** vibration before eyes: ther br1

VISIONS (See MIND - Delusions - visions)

VOMITING: | **hiccough** agg.; or: apis bg2 am bg2 asar bg2 bry bg2 chin bg2 lyc bg2 nux-v bg2 puls bg2 sep bg2 sil bg2 verat bg2

WAKING; on: calc b4.de* *Dros* b7.de* nat-c bg2 phos b4.de* zinc b4.de*

WALKING:
- **agg.**: *Nat-m* b4.de* sep b4.de*
- **air**; in open | **after** | **agg.**: dros b7.de*
  - **agg.**: agar b4.de* cic b7a.de con b4.de* euphr b7.de* m-aust b7.de merc b4.de* nux-v b7.de* psor bg2
- **amel.**: lach bg2
- **beginning** to walk: puls b7.de*

WARM: | **air** agg.: *Sulph* b4a.de

WARM AGG.; BECOMING: nux-v bg2 puls b7a.de*

WASHING:
- **agg.**: kali-c b4a.de
- **amel.**: am-m b7.de* caust b4a.de chel b7.de* phos b4a.de
- **eyes** | **amel.**: nat-s bg2

WAVERING: aml-ns vh1 bell chlf bg1 chlor bg cic c1 con cycl a1 cystein-l rly4• kali-s fd4.de kola stb3• limen-b-c hrn2* lyc k* manc k* morph bg1* *Nat-m* k* rhus-r a1 santin sumb k* *Verat-v* k* zinc-chr ptk1

WAVING, luminous openings, he sees: arund k*

WEAK: *(↗Blurred; Dim; EYE - Weak)* acet-ac acon *Agar* k* alum k* *Am-c* k* am-m bg2 ambr bg2 *Anac* k* ang b7.de* *Apis* k* *Arg-met* k* *Arg-n* k* arge-pl rwt5• *Ars* k* ars-i k* art-v bg2 asaf *Asar* k* aur b4a.de* *Aur-m* *Bapt-c* c1 bar-c k* bar-i k2 bar-s k2 bell k* borx b4a.de* bry b7a.de* cact k* *Calc* b4.de* cann-i cann-s k* canth b7a.de* *Caps* b7.de* carb-an b4a.de* carb-v b4.de* *Caust* k* cham b7.de* chel k* **Chin** k* *Chinin-ar* cic k* cimic bg2 *Cina* k* *Cinnb* coc-c cocc bg2 coff bg2 coloc bg2 **Con** k* croc b7.de* *Crot-h* k* dig k* *Dros* b7.de* dulc b4.de* *Euph* b4.de* *Euphr* bg2 gels k* glon bg2 graph b4.de* *Ham* hep b4.de* hura hyos k* hyper *Ign* b7.de* *Iod* k* jab bg2 jug-c c2 kali-ar kali-bi kali-br *Kali-c* k* kali-i *Kali-p* k* kali-s kali-sil k2 *Kalm* kreos b7a.de* *Lach* k* lact laur bg2 *Led* k* *Lil-t* k* *Lith-c* k* *Lyc* k* mag-c b4.de* malar jl2 *Mang* k* meph k* *Merc* k* merl mez bg2 *Morph* *Morph-s* hr1 nat-ar nat-c b4.de* *Nat-m* k* *Nat-s* nicc k* nit-ac b4.de* *Nux-m* c2 *Nux-v* k* olib-sac wmh1 **Op** k* par k* *Petr* k* *Ph-ac* k* **Phos** k* phys bg2 plat b4a.de* plb k* positr nl2• prun bg2 *Puls* k* raph rheum b7.de* rhod b4.de* rhus-t k* **Ruta** k* sabad b7.de* sal-ac sars b4a.de* sec k* *Seneg* k* *Sep* k* *Sil* k* sol-ni *Spig* k* spong fd4.de stann *Staph* b7.de* *Stram* k* stront-c b4.de* sul-ac *Sulph* k* tab *Tarent* thuj k* til uran-n bg2 vanil fd5.de verat k* verb bg2 zinc b4.de* zing [tax jsj7]
- **morning** | **eyes** were strained; as if: melal-alt gya4 ruta
- **evening**: euphr k* tarent k*
  - **candlelight**; by: bar-c *Hep* k*
  - **exertion** of the eyes agg.: **Apis**

- **evening**: ...
  - **twilight**; in the: arg-n k*
- **accompanied** by:

O • **Head**:
  - **complaints** of (See HEAD - Complaints - accompanied - vision - weak)
  - **pain**: zinc ptk1
- **coition** agg.: kali-c bro1* lil-t mrr1
- **exertion** of the eyes agg.: agar alum *Am-c* **Apis** *Arg-met Carb-v* caust crot-h ptk gels *Jab* **Nat-m** par *Phos* **Ruta Seneg** spong fd4.de sulph
- **fever**; during: *Nat-m* b4a.de
- **grief**; from: crot-h ptk
- **hysterical**: gels br1
- **light**; from bright: bell positr nl2• sol-ni
- **long** distances, for: gels psa nat-ar
- **masturbation**; from: *Cina* hr1*
- **smoking** a very little | **after**: asc-t c1
- **thinking** agg.: gels psa

WEATHER:
- **dull**, not clear weather:
  - **agg.**: agar b4.de*
  - **amel.**: *Bry* b7a.de

WHIRLING: apis k* atro k* aur-m a1 eug k* *Glon* k* kali-c merc h1* pic-ac k* plut-n srj7• ust k* verat

WHITE glistening points falling: ph-ac h2

WINDSHIELD wipers; sensation of: anh sp1

WINE; red: | **agg.**: gels psa

WINKING:
- **agg.**: caust b4.de*
- **amel.**: asaf b7.de* croc b7.de*

WIPING:
- **agg.**: seneg b4.de*
- **amel.**: alum b4.de* caps b7a.de carb-an b4.de* cina b7.de* croc b7.de* euphr bg2 lyc bg2 plb b7.de* puls b7.de*

WRITING: | **agg.**: *Asaf* b7.de* borx b4a.de canth b7.de* carb-v b4.de* graph b4.de* kali-c b4.de* lyc b4.de* nat-c b4.de* nat-m b4.de* petr b4.de* rhod b4.de* seneg b4.de* sep b4.de* zinc b4.de*

YAWNING agg.: merc-c bg2

YELLOW: | **objects** appear yellow (See Colors - yellow - objects)

ZIGZAGS: cann-s b7.de* coca bg2 coloc bg1 con bg2* falco-pe nl2• fl-ac bg2* *Graph* k* ham fd3.de• ign k* kali-bi bg2* kola stb3• lach bg2* lyc bg2* **Nat-m** k* ozone sde2• phos bg2* podo fd3.de• puls gk *Sep* k* spong fd4.de *Sul-i* bg* sulph k2 thuj b4a.de viol-o b7.de*
- **circles** of colors●: *(↗Circles - zigzags - colored)* ham fd3.de• **Sep** k ● viol-o k*
- **eating**; after: ign sne sulph k2
- **fiery**●: con h2 graph h2 ign h1 nat-m h2 sep h2
- **flickering**: *Graph* ign k* irid-met srj5• *Lach* k* phos k*
- **fluttering**: thuj k*
- **headache**:
  - **before**: nat-m k2 psor k2 sulph k2
  - **during**: anh kr1 podo fd3.de•
- **outside** the range of vision: flor-p rsj3• *Graph*
- **walking** agg.: hura c1
- **wavy**: kola stb3• thuj k*
- **writing** agg.: thuj k*

DAY AND NIGHT: hell b7a.de

MORNING: alum b4.de* ambr b7.de* arg-met b7.de* aur b4.de* bell b4.de* borx b4a.de calc b4.de* caust b4.de* cocc b7.de* ferr b7.de* fl-ac bg2 graph b4.de* lach b7.de* lyc b4.de* merc b4.de* mez b4.de* nat-m b4.de* nux-m b7.de* *Nux-v* b7.de* plat b4.de* puls b7.de* rhod b4.de* sars b4.de* sil b4.de* stann b4.de* verat b7.de* zinc b4.de*

FORENOON: asaf b7.de* carb-an b4.de* lyc b4.de* mang b4.de* nat-c b4.de* nux-m b7.de* petr b4.de* phos b4.de* plb b7.de* rhod b4.de* sabad b7.de* sars b4.de*

AFTERNOON: alum b4.de* am-c b4.de* am-m b7.de* ambr b7.de* ant-c b7.de* carb-an b4.de* carb-v b4.de* laur b7.de* lyc b4.de* mur-ac b4.de* petr b4.de* phos b4.de* plb b7.de* puls b7.de* rhus-t b7.de* sars b4.de* zinc b4.de*

EVENING: alum b4.de* apis b7a.de bar-c b4.de* bell b4.de* borx b4a.de bry b7.de* calc b4.de* canth b7.de* caps b7.de* carb-an b4.de* carb-v b4.de* caust b4.de* cham b7.de* croc b7.de* *Graph* b4.de* hep b4.de* hyos b7.de* kali-c b4.de* lach b7.de* lyc b4.de* mag-c b4.de* mang b4.de* merc b4.de* nat-c b4.de* nat-m b4.de* nit-ac b4.de* nux-v b7.de* par b7.de* petr b4.de* plat b4.de* plb b7.de* *Puls* b7.de* *Ran-b* b7.de* ran-s b7.de* rhod b4.de* sabin b7.de* sel b7a.de sep b4.de* sil b4.de* spig b7.de* spong b7.de* stann b4.de* staph b7.de* sul-ac b4.de* *Sulph* b4.de* tarax b7.de* thuj b4.de* valer b7.de* zinc b4.de*

NIGHT: am-c b4.de* am-m b7.de* bar-c b4.de* carb-an b4.de* *Cham* b7.de* dulc b4.de* **Graph** b4.de* kali-n b4.de* mag-c b4.de* mag-p bg2 nux-v b7.de* puls b7.de* rhus-t b7.de* sep b4.de* sil b4.de*

ABSCESS: *(↗Discharges - purulent; Eruptions - boils; Suppuration)* alum bg2 bov bg2 bry bg2 calc-pic ptk1 camph bg2 kali-c bg2 *Merc* bg2* *Puls* bg2 *Ruta* bg2 *Spong* bg2 stann bg2 syph ptk1
- ○ - **Behind** the ears: *(↗Eruptions - behind - boils)* anan **Aur** *Bar-m* brom k2 *Caps* carb-an kali-c *Nit-ac* phyt **Sil**
  - **periodical** | **weeks** ear gathers and discharges; every two: iris
- - **Below** the ears: caps k2 nat-hchls
- - **Mastoid**: caps k2
- - **Meatus**: **Calc-s** crot-h **Hep** *Mag-c* *Puls* **Sil**
  - **menses**; during: puls
- - **Middle** ear: syph mtf33

ADHESIONS in middle ear: *(↗Stopped - middle)* dulc mrr1 *Graph* kr1 iod k* iris mp1• puls mrr1 thiosin c1
- - **accompanied** by | **hearing** impaired (See HEARING - Impaired - adhesions)
- - **noises** in ear; with: thiosin c1
- - **tinnitus**; with: thiosin c1

AGGLUTINATION of auricle to head: olnd k*

AIR:
- - **drawing** in air through nose | **agg.**: teucr b7.de*
- - **sensation** of air:
  - **before** ear; fanning: calc mang nit-ac
  - ○ **In** ear: dulc bg2 graph k* hir skp7• *Mez* k* puls b7.de* til bg2
    - **bubble** of air: hura rb2 *Nat-m*
    - **cold**: caust dulc kali-c ptk1 *Mez* k* mill ptk1 plat staph vinc
    - **distending** the meatus; as if air were: mez c1 **Puls** b7.de*
      - **evening**: mez
  - **Into** ear; rushing: amph a1 *Fl-ac* b4a.de lachn mang mez staph
    - **blowing** nose; when: puls h1 sulph
    - **drawing** jaw to other side; on: sarr
    - **eructations**, during: caust graph
  - **Out** of ear; rushing: *(↗Opening sensation - air)* aphis rb2 *Chel* k* stram rb2*
    - **cold** air: mill
- - **sensitive** to open air: *(↗Wind - sensitive)* ars bro1 bell bro1 *Borx* bro1 caps bro1 caust **Cham** k* ferr-p bro1 **Hep** bro1* **Lach** merc bro1 *Mez* k* nux-v bro1 petr bro1 tell bro1 [*Mang* stj1]
- - **streaming** into (See sensation - into)

AIR; IN OPEN:
- - **agg.**: agar b4.de* am-m b7.de* bry b7a.de carb-an b4.de* *Con* b4.de* euph b4.de* lyc b4.de* mang b4.de* spig b7.de*
- - **amel.**: cic b7.de* mag-c b4a.de puls b7.de*

ALIVE in ear; sensation of something: rhus-t b7.de* sil c1*

ANGER; after: sulph b4a.de

ANIMAL in ear; as if having a small: propr sa3•

AUDITORY vertigo (See VERTIGO - Ménière)

AURAL vertigo (See VERTIGO - Ménière)

BALD spot above: phos k*

BENDING:
- - **backward** | **agg.**: *Fl-ac* b4a.de

BITING teeth together agg.: *Anac* b4a.de

BLEEDING (See Discharges - blood)

BLOW; after a: calc-s ptk1

BLOWING sensation in: ail k* rhus-t k* *Sel*
- - **right**: ail k* rhus-t k*
- - **headache**; during: *Sel*
- - **pulsative**, at night: sep k*

BLOWING THE NOSE:
- - **agg.**: act-sp ptk1 alum b4.de* *Am* b7a.de bar-c b4.de* calc b4.de* caust b4.de* con b4.de* dios bg2* hep b4.de* *Lach* b7a.de lyc b4.de* *Mang* b4a.de* meny b7.de* ph-ac b4.de* puls b7.de* spig b7.de* stann b4.de* sulph ptk1 teucr b7.de*
- - **amel.**: *Mang* b4a.de* *Merc* b4a.de *Sil* b4a.de stann b4.de*

BOARD; sensation of a:
- ○ - **Before** ear: arg-n k*
  - **left** ear: arg-n k*

BODY; sensation of a hard: | **Behind** ear: graph h2*

BORING fingers in: *(↗GENERALS - Boring; GENERALS - Boring - amel.)* agar k* arund mp1• borx b4a.de* chel k* cina bro1* colch a1 hipp a1 lach mp1• mang sne mez k* mill k* nat-m mtf33 phys k* psor bro1* rheum mp1• rhus-t h1* ruta k* sal-ac sel b7a.de *Sil* k* spig mp1• suis-pan rly4• thuj
- - **amel.**: *(↗Itching - meatus - boring - amel.)* aeth ptk1 agar a1 *Anac* b4a.de chel k* coloc bg2* lach k* *Mez* k* nat-c br1* par k* psor bg2 rheum k* rhus-t b7.de* spig k*
- - **children**; in●: **Arund** k ● *Cina* k* nat-m mtf33 *Psor* k* *Sil* k*
- - **sleep** agg.; during: *Sil* k*

BREATH came from ear; sensation as if: psor k*

BUBBLING sensation, as if bubbles were moving about: bar-c b4.de* graph b4.de* kreos b7a.de* lyc b4.de* petr b4.de* rheum b7.de* sil b4.de*

CALCAREOUS deposit on tympanum: *Calc-f* k* syph k*

CANCEROUS affections: | **Nerve**; auditory: calc mtf calc-sil mtf kali-sil mtf sil mtf staph mtf

CARIES, threatened: *Asaf* **Aur** *Calc* *Calc-f* *Calc-s* fl-ac k2 nat-m **Sil** sulph
- ▽ - **extending** to | **Meninges**: *Stram* k2
- ○ - **Mastoid**: anthraci sne ars sne *Asaf* bg2 **Aur** k* aur-ar k2 bapt mrr1 *Bell* sne calc-s mrr1* *Canth* sne **Caps** k* carb-an k* chin sne crot-h sne **FERR-P** sne *Fl-ac* k* *Gels* sne *Hecla* sne *Hep* k* *Lach* *Merc* sne *Nit-ac* k* paro-i sne pyrog sne sec sne **Sil** k* *Staph* bg2 stram k2 syph k2* thuj sne
  - **accompanied** by | **burning** pain: caps mrr1
  - **influenza**; from: bapt mrr1
- - **Ossicula**: asaf bro1 *Aur* bro1 calc bro1 caps bro1 fl-ac bro1 hep bro1 iod bro1 *Sil* bro1 syph bro1
- - **Petrous** portion temporal bone: calc-f br1* **Caps**

CATARRH: *(↗Discharges)*
- - **accompanied** by | **Ear**; noises in: euph mtf11
- ○ - **Eustachian** tubes: *(↗Swelling - eustachian; GENERALS - Inflammation - sinuses)* alf bro1 alum k* *Ars* bnt ars-i k2 arum-d a1 **Asar** k* aur bnt bar-c mtf11 bar-m k2* *Cal-ren* bro1 **Calc** k* *Calc-act* bro1 *Calc-ar* bro1 *Calc-br* bro1 *Calc-caust* bro1 *Calc-cn* bro1 *Calc-f* bro1 *Calc-hp* bro1 calc-i k2* *Calc-lac* bro1 *Calc-lp* bro1 *Calc-m* bro1 *Calc-ox* bro1 calc-p k2* *Calc-pic* bro1 calc-s k* *Calc-sil* bro1 *Calc-st-s* bro1 caps k* *Caust* k* cench k2 cham bnt chin k2 coc-c sne dulc c1* ery-a h1 ferr-i bro1 **Ferr-p** k2* gels k* *Graph* bro1 helo-s rwt2•

Ear

- **Eustachian** tubes: ...
  hep bro1 *Hydr* k* ign bnt *Iod* k* *Kali-bi* k* *Kali-chl* k* *Kali-i* kali-m c1* **Kali-s** k* kola stb3• lach k2* *Lap-a* bro1 lob-c bro1 lob-s c2 *Mang* k* melal-alt gya4 mentho br1* *Merc* k* *Merc-d* k* mez k2 morg-p xyz60 *Nat-m* k* *Nit-ac* k* pen bro1 **Petr** k* *Phos* phyt k* **Puls** k* rhus-t c1* ros-d bro1* *Sang* k* sangin-n c2* sanic c1 **Sil** k* *Sulph* hr1 thiosin mp1• tub-a jl2 visc bro1
- **Middle** ear: ars-i k2* cham mtf11 dulc mrr1 euph mtf11 kali-m k2 merc-d br1
  - • **chronic**: nat-chl br1

CERUMEN (See Discharges - earwax)

CHEWING agg.: alum b4a.de* am-c bg2 anac ptk1 apis ptk1 arg-met b7.de* calc b4a.de cann-s b7.de* *Graph* bg2 hep b4.de* *Meny* b7a.de nat-m bg2 nit-ac b4a.de* nux-m bg2 nux-v b7.de* seneg b4a.de* sulph ptk1

CHILBLAINS: (*↗Itching - meatus - burning)* agar bro1 *Apis* bro1 bell bro1 rhus-t bro1

CHILDREN; in: bar-ox-suc mtf11 bell mp1• calc mp1• calc-p mp1• caust mp1• *Cham* k* *Hep* mp1• kali-m mp1• lyc mp1• *Merc* mp1• phos mp1• *Puls* k* sil mp1• thuj mp1• *Zinc* k* [*Mang* stj]

CHILL; during: acon b7.de *Asar* b7.de* m-aust b7.de puls b7.de ran-b b7.de

CHILLINESS: calc b4.de* *Ip* bg2 kali-c bg2 lach bg2 meny bg2 *Merc* bg2 plat bg2 seneg bg2 staph bg2 verat bg2

CICATRICES: | **otitis**: syph jl2

CLOSED sensation (See Stopped)

COITION; after: | **agg.**: carb-v bg2

COLD:

- **agg.**: caps ptk1 *Hep* ptk1 sil ptk1
- **air** agg.: agar b4.de* bell bg2 nit-ac b4.de* rhus-t b7.de*
- **amel.**: bell ptk1
- **applications** | **amel.**: merc b4.de* phos b4.de*
- **heat** and cold agg.: cic ptk1

COLD; TAKING A:

- **after**: acon b7.de* aran bg2 *Bell* b4a.de *Cham* b7a.de* *Chin* bg2 *Dulc* b4a.de* ferr-p ptk1 hep bg2 kali-m ptk1 led bg2 merc b4a.de* merc-d ptk1 *Nux-v* b7.de* phos ptk1 **Puls** b7.de* sulph b4a.de* urt-u bg2 visc bg2
  - • **agg.**: *Bell* b4a.de led b7a.de puls b7a.de

COLDNESS: aeth agath-a nl2• amyg k* ars k* bapt k* berb k* *Calc* k* *Calc-p* k* carb-v k* *Chel* k* chin c1 cic k* dulc b4.de* ham fd3.de• ip k* kali-ar *Kali-c* k* *Lach* k* lyc k* *Mang* k* meny k* merc k* mez bg2* *Nit-ac* paeon k* *Petr* k* *Plat* k* psor k* pyrog c1 ran-s k* seneg k* stann b4.de* stram k* ter k* thea vanil fd5.de *Verat* k* verat-v k* zinc bg2

- **one** side: ign bg2 kali-c bg2
- **right**: chel a1 hydrog srj2• *Kali-c* lyc mang h2* plat h2* psor a1 verat a1
  - • **burning**; and | **left** ear; of: nat-n
- **afternoon** | **17** h: paeon
- **evening**: mez k* paeon vanil fd5.de
  - • **warm** bed agg.: merc
- **accompanied** by | **Teeth**; pain in (See TEETH - Pain - accompanied - ears)
- **alternating** with | **heat** of ears: berb k* *Cic* k* verat k*
- **burning** hot yet cold to touch: bapt k* nat-n
- **draft**, as from a: agath-a nl2• mang k* stann
- **during** | **agg.**: cham b7.de
- **heat**; during: *Ip* k* *Lach* k* stram sne
- **one** cold the other hot: chel k* ign *Kali-c* hr1 nit-ac paeon a1
- **pregnancy** agg.; during: berb ptk merc ptk2
- **sensation** of: bros-gau mrc1 calc bg2 *Ip* b7a.de* meny b7.de* plat bg2 staph b7.de* verat b7.de* verat-v a1
  - • **air** blowing on it; as if: hydrog srj2•
    - ⁝ **left**: mosch bg2
  - ○ • **External** ears: lachn nat-n
- **warm** bed agg.: merc bg1
- **water**:
  - • **into** ear; as if cold water had got: meny
  - • **out** of ear; as if cold water had run: merc
- ▽ - **extending** through: seneg k*
- ○ - **About** the ears: aeth bry form a1*

Coldness: ...

- **Above** the ears: indg k* lac-ac k*
- **Behind** right ear: *Form*
- **Below** the ears: aeth
- **Internally**: ars bg2 berb bg2 calc bg2 dulc bg2 lach bg2 lyc bg2 merc bg2 mez bg2 psor bg2 sel bg2 ter bg2
- **Meatus**: caust *Merc* *Mez* *Plat* staph vanil fd5.de
  - • **wind**; as from: caust mang *Mez* sanic staph

COMPLAINTS of ears: agra br1 aur ptk1 *Bell* ptk1 *Calc* ptk1 caust tl1 cham ptk1 elaps br1 **Ferr-p** ptk1 *Graph* ptk1 hep ptk1 kali-s tl1 lyc ptk1 mang ptk1 med tl1* **Merc** ptk1 mez mrr1 mur-ac tl1 nat-sal br1 petr ptk1 ph-ac ptk1 phos ptk1 plan ptk1 propr sa3• *Psor* ptk1 puls tl1* **Sil** ptk1 **Sulph** ptk1 tell br1* verb br1 viol-o br1 zinc-chr ptk1 [bell-p-sp dcm1 *Mang-act* stj2 *Mang-i* stj2 *Mang-m* stj2 *Mang-met* stj2 *Mang-n* stj2 *Mang-p* stj2 *Mang-s* stj2 *Mang-sil* stj2]

- **alternating** sides: arn bg2 bell bg2* *Bry* ptk1 cann-xyz bg2 *Caps* bg2* caust bg2* chel bg2* cocc bg2* ferr-p ptk1 glon ptk1 hep bg2 kali-c bg2* laur bg2 lil-t bg2 mag-m bg2* med ptk1 mez bg2 mosch ptk1 nit-ac bg2* plan bg2 sulph bg2* thuj bg2
- **right**: *Acon* b7a.de* agar b4a.de* *Alum* b4a.de* *Am-c* b4a.de* *Am-m* b7a.de* ambr b7a.de* anac b4a.de* *Ang* b7a.de* *Ant-c* bg2 apis b7a.de* arg-met b7a.de* arn b7a.de* ars b4a.de* asaf b7a.de* asar b7a.de* bar-c b4a.de* **Bell** b4a.de* borx b4a.de* bov b4a.de* brom b4a.de* bry b7a.de* calad b7a.de* *Calc* b4a.de* cann-s b7a.de* *Canth* b7a.de* *Carb-an* bg2 carb-v b4a.de* caust b4a.de* cham b7a.de* *Chel* b7a.de* chin b7a.de* cic b7a.de* clem b4a.de* cocc b7a.de* colch b7a.de* coloc b4a.de* con b4a.de* croc b7a.de* cupr b7a.de* cycl b7a.de* dig b4a.de* dros b7a.de* dulc b4a.de* euph b4a.de* euphr b7a.de* ferr b7a.de* **Fl-ac** b4a.de* graph b4a.de* hell b7a.de* *Hep* b4a.de* hyos b7a.de* **Iod** b4a.de* ip b7a.de* **Kali-c** b4a.de* **Kali-n** b4a.de* kreos b7a.de* lach b7a.de* laur b7a.de* led b7a.de* *Lyc* b4a.de* m-arct b7a.de mag-c b4a.de* mag-m b4a.de* mang b4a.de* meny b7a.de* merc b4a.de* mez b4a.de* mill b7a.de* mur-ac b4a.de* nat-c b4a.de* nat-m b4a.de* **Nit-ac** b4a.de* nux-m b7a.de* **Nux-v** b7a.de* par b7a.de* petr b4a.de* ph-ac b4a.de* *Phos* b4a.de* **Plat** b4a.de* *Plb* b7a.de* psor bg2 *Puls* b7a.de* ran-b b7a.de* *Ran-s* b7a.de* rheum b7a.de* rhod b4a.de* *Rhus-t* b7a.de* ruta b7a.de* sabad b7a.de* sabin b7a.de* samb b7a.de* *Sars* b4a.de* sel b7a.de* seneg b7a.de* sep b4a.de* **Sil** b4a.de* spig b7a.de* **Spong** b7a.de* squil b7a.de* stann b4a.de* staph b7a.de* *Sul-ac* b4a.de* *Sulph* b4a.de* tarax b7a.de* teucr b7a.de* *Thuj* b4a.de* valer b7a.de* verat b7a.de* verb b7a.de* zinc b4a.de*
  - • **followed** by | **left**: bar-c bg2 lyc bg2
- **left**: acon b7a.de* agar b4a.de* agn b7a.de* alum b4a.de* *Am-c* b4a.de* am-m b7a.de* ambr b7a.de* **Anac** b4a.de* ang b7a.de* ant-c b7a.de* *Apis* b7a.de* arg-met b7a.de* *Arn* b7a.de* ars b4a.de* **Asaf** b7a.de* asar b7a.de* *Aur* b4a.de* bar-c b4a.de* bell b4a.de* bism b7a.de* **Borx** b4a.de* *Brom* b4a.de* *Bry* b7a.de* calad b7a.de* calc b4a.de* *Camph* b7a.de* cann-s b7a.de* canth b7a.de* caps b7a.de* carb-an b4a.de* carb-v b4a.de* caust b4a.de* chel b7a.de* chin bg2 cic b7a.de* clem b4a.de* colch b7a.de* coloc b4a.de* con b4a.de* croc b7a.de* cupr b7a.de* cycl b7a.de* dig b4a.de* dros b7a.de* *Dulc* b4a.de* euph b4a.de* euphr b7a.de* ferr b7a.de* fl-ac bg2 **Graph** b4a.de* **Guaj** b4a.de* hep b4a.de* **Ign** b7a.de* iod b4a.de* kali-c b4a.de* kali-n b4a.de* kreos b7a.de* lac-c bg2 lach b7a.de* *Laur* b7a.de* lyc b4a.de* mang b4a.de* meny b7a.de* *Merc* b4a.de* *Mez* b4a.de* *Mill* b7a.de* mur-ac b4a.de* nat-c b4a.de* nat-m b4a.de* nit-ac b4a.de* nux-m b7a.de* **Olnd** b7a.de* par b7a.de* petr b4a.de* ph-ac b4a.de* phos b4a.de* pip-n bg2 plat b4a.de* plb b7a.de* *Psor* bg2 puls b7a.de* ran-b b7a.de* ran-s b7a.de* rheum b7a.de* rhod b4a.de* rhus-t b7a.de* sabad b7a.de* sabin b7a.de* sars b4a.de* sel b7a.de* seneg b7a.de* sep b4a.de* sil b4a.de* spig b7a.de* spong b7a.de* squil b7a.de* stann b4a.de* *Staph* b7a.de* sul-ac b4.de* sulph b4a.de* tarax b7a.de* teucr b7a.de* thuj b4a.de* valer b7a.de* verat b7a.de* *Verb* b7a.de* **Viol-o** b7a.de* viol-t b7a.de* zinc b4a.de*
  - • **followed** by | **right**: aesc bg2 arn bg2 brom bg2 calc-p bg2 graph ptk1 merc bg2 mur-ac ptk1
- **accompanied** by:
  - • **coryza** (See NOSE - Coryza - accompanied - ear)
  - • **head**; pain in: acon bg2 aur bg2 coff bg2 gels bg2 ign b7.de* kali-n b4.de* merc b4a.de phos b4a.de phyt bg2 puls b7.de* ran-s b7a.de sil bg2 spig bg2
  - • **nausea**: onos bg2

- **accompanied** by: ...
  - **pain** (See GENERALS - Pain - accompanied - ears)
  - ○ **Eyes**; complaints of (See EYE - Complaints - accompanied - ears)
  - **Kidneys**; complaints of (See KIDNEYS - Complaints - accompanied - ears)
  - **Occiput**; pain in (See HEAD - Pain - occiput - accompanied - ear)
  - **Parotid** gland:
    - **induration** of the: sil k2
    - **swelling** of: ail ptk1 sil ptk1
  - **Teeth**; pain in: glon ptk1 plan ptk1 *Rhod* ptk1
  - **Tonsils**; enlarged: *Aur* bg2 merc bg2 *Nit-ac* bg2 *Staph* bg2
- **alternating** with:
  - ○ **Abdomen**; complaints of: rad-br ptk1
  - **Teeth**; complaints of: plan ptk1
- **followed** by | **Eyes**; complaints of: propr sa3•
- **paroxysmal**: mag-p bg2
- **scarlet** fever; after: bell bro1 carb-ac bro1 carb-v bro1 gels bro1 *Hep* bro1 *Merc* bro1 sil bro1 sulph bro1
- **sudden**: plb b7a.de sec b7a.de
- ▽ **extending** to:
  - ○ **Backward**: mur-ac bg2
  - **Forward**: eupi bg2 form bg2 lach bg2 puls bg2
  - **Neck**; down the: tarax ptk1
  - **Outward**: agar ptk1 calc ptk1 canth ptk1 chel bg3* merc ptk1 psor ptk1
  - **Parotid** glands: bell bg2 sep bg2
  - **Vertex**: mur-ac ptk1
- ○ **Behind** the ears: acon b2.de* alum b2.de* am-c b2.de* am-m b2.de* ambr b2.de* anac b2.de* *Ang* b2.de* ant-c b2.de* arg-met b2.de* *Arn* b2.de* ars bg2 asaf bg2 asar b2.de* aur b2.de* **Bar-c** b2.de* *Bell* b2.de* borx b2.de* bry b2.de* *Calc* b2.de* cann-s b2.de* **Canth** b2.de* *Caps* b2.de* carb-ac bg2 carb-an b2.de* carb-v b2.de* **Caust** b2.de* cham b2.de* chel b2.de* chin b2.de* cic b2.de* cina b2.de* cocc b2.de* colch b2.de coloc b2.de* *Con* b2.de* crot-h bg2 dig b2.de* dros b2.de* *Ferr-p* bg2 glon bg2* **Graph** b2.de* hell b2.de* *Hep* b2.de* kali-c b2.de* kali-n b2.de* *Lach* b2.de* *Lyc* b2.de* mag-c b2.de* mag-p bg2 mang b2.de* meny b2.de* merc b2.de* *Mez* b2.de* *Mur-ac* b2.de* nit-ac b2.de* **Olnd** b2.de* onos bg2 **Petr** b2.de* *Ph-ac* b2.de* **Phos** b2.de* plat b2.de* plb b2.de* psor ptk1 *Puls* b2.de* pyrog bg2 rhod b2.de* rhus-t b2.de* ruta b2.de* *Sabad* b2.de* sabin b2.de* sanic ptk1 sars b2.de* sel b2.de* *Sep* b2.de* **Sil** b2.de* spong b2.de* squil b2.de* stann b2.de* **Staph** b2.de* *Sulph* b2.de* tarax b2.de* tell bg2 ther bg2 thuj b2.de* verat b2.de* verb b2.de* viol-o b2.de* viol-t b2.de* zinc b2.de* zinc-chr ptk1
- **Below** the ears: alum b2.de* arg-met b2.de* asar b2.de* aur b2.de* *Bar-c* b2.de* **Bell** b2.de* *Calc* b2.de* carb-an b2.de* carb-v b2.de* *Chel* b2.de* *Chin* b2.de* cina b2.de* cocc b2.de* dros b2.de* iod b2.de* mang b2.de* nat-c b2.de* nit-ac b2.de* *Olnd* b2.de* *Phos* b2.de* puls b2.de* *Ruta* b2.de* *Sars* b2.de* *Sep* b2.de* *Sil* b2.de* *Sulph* b2.de* verat b2.de* zinc b2.de*
- **Between** the ears: plan ptk1*
- **Bones**: asaf bg2 aur bg2 benz-ac bg2 calc bg2 calc-s bg2 caps bg2 fl-ac bg2 hep bg2 merc bg2 nit-ac bg2 phos bg2 pic-ac bg2 sil bg2 sulph bg2 thuj bg2
- **Cochlea** (See Cochlea)
- **Eustachian** tube (See Eustachian)
- **External** ears: acon b2.de* aethi-a mtf11 **Alum** b2.de* am-c b2.de* am-m b2.de* ambr b2.de* *Anac* b2.de* *Ang* b2.de* ant-c b2.de* *Arg-met* b2.de* *Arn* b2.de* ars b2.de* asaf b2.de* asar b2.de* aur b2.de* *Bar-c* b2.de* *Bell* b2.de* bism b2.de* *Borx* b2.de* bov b2.de* *Bry* b2.de* *Calc* b2.de* camph b2.de* cann-s b2.de* canth b2.de* caps b2.de* carb-an b2.de* carb-v b2.de* caust b2.de* cham b2.de* *Chel* b2.de* *Chin* b2.de* cic b2.de* cina b2.de* clem b2.de* cocc b2.de* coenz-q mtf11 colch b2.de* coloc b2.de* con b2.de* cupr b2.de* dig b2.de* *Dros* b2.de* dulc b2.de* ferr b2.de* graph b2.de* guaj b2.de* hell b2.de* hep b2.de* hyos b2.de* iod b2.de* **Kali-c** b2.de* **Kreos** b2.de* laur b2.de* lyc b2.de* m-ambo b2.de m-aust b2.de mal-ac mtf11 mang b2.de* meny b2.de* *Merc* b2.de* mur-ac b2.de* nat-c b2.de* nat-m b2.de* nit-ac b2.de* nux-v b2.de* olnd b2.de* par b2.de* *Petr* b2.de* **Ph-ac** b2.de* *Phos* b2.de* plat b2.de* plb b2.de* puls b2.de* rhus-t b2.de* *Ruta* b2.de* *Sabad* b2.de* sabin b2.de* *Sars* b2.de* *Sep* b2.de* *Sil* b2.de* **Spig** b2.de* *Spong* b2.de* squil b2.de* stann b2.de* staph b2.de* sulph b2.de* tarax b2.de* tell mtf11 thuj b2.de* verat b2.de* verb b2.de* viol-o b2.de* viol-t b2.de* zinc b2.de*

Complaints of ears: ...

- **Front** of ears; in: arg-met b2.de* bry b2.de* calc b2.de* carb-v b2.de* mur-ac b2.de* olnd b2.de* sars b2.de* *Sep* b2.de* sil b2.de* verb b2.de* *Zinc* b2.de*
- **Internal** ear: *Calc* ptk1 caust ptk1 graph ptk1 kali-c ptk1 mang ptk1 *Nux-v* ptk1 *Phos* ptk1 *Psor* ptk1 *Puls* ptk1 *Sep* ptk1 *Spig* ptk1
- **Labyrinth** (See Labyrinth)
- **Meatus** (See Meatus)
- **Nerves**; auditory: chen-a br1 nat-sal br1 phos mtf11 sulph mtf11 syph mtf11
- **Vestibulo**-cochlear: phos mtf11 sulph mtf11 syph mtf11

CONGESTION of blood (See Fullness)

CONSCIOUS of ear: chen-a vml3•

CONSTRICTION of: thuj

CONTRACTION: anac k* asar b7.de* bry b7.de* caust k* croc b7.de* dig b4.de* dros b7.de* lach k* merc b4.de* *Puls* b7a.de sars k* spig b7.de* spong b7.de* thuj b4.de*

- **sensation** of: graph h2* sars h2*
  - **sleeping** on that side; evening after lying down and agg. when: caust
- **spasmodic**:
  - **afternoon** | **sitting** agg.: aeth k*
- ○ **Below** the ears: aeth dulc h2 zinc h2
- **Front** of ears; in: zinc h2
- **Meatus**: anac arg-n bry

CORYZA amel.: lach bg2

COUGH agg.: calc bg2* caps b7.de* chel b7.de* dios ptk1 nux-v b7.de* sep bg2

CRACKS behind ear (See Eruptions - behind - cracks)

CRAWLING (See Formication)

DEGENERATION: | **tympanic** membrane: mez k2

DILATATION of meatus, sensation of: mez k*

- **evening**: mez k*

DISCHARGES: (↗*Catarrh)* absin k* aeth k* aethi-a c1* aethi-m br1 agra br1* aids nl2• *All-c* k* *Alum* k* *Alumn* k* am-c k* am-m k* anac k* anan k* *Ant-c* k* ap-g c2* *Apis* *Ars* k* *Ars-i* k* arund k* *Asaf* k* *Aur* k* aur-ar k2 aur-s k2 bar-c bar-i k2 **Bar-m** k* *Bell* k* *Borx* k* bov k* brom k* *Bry* k* bufo **Calc** k* *Calc-f* calc-i k2 **Calc-p** k* **Calc-s** k* calen bg1 caps k* *Carb-an* k* **Carb-v** k* **Carbn-s** castm **Caust** k* *Cham* k* cheir br1 chin k* cic k* **Cist** k* coc-c colch k* **Con** k* cop k* croc b2.de* *Crot-c* *Crot-h* k* crot-t k* cur k* dulc k2 *Elaps* k* ery-a k* ferr k* ferr-ar ferr-p k* *Fl-ac* k* *Gels* hr1 **Graph** k* hed sp1 **Hep** k* hipp k* *Hydr* k* iod k* jug-r k* *Kali-ar* **Kali-bi** k* **Kali-c** k* *Kali-chl* hr1 kali-i a1 kali-p k* **Kali-s** k* kali-sil k2 kino bg1 kreos lac-c al* *Lach* k* lachn k* **Lyc** k* m-ambo b2.de mang k2 meny k* meph k* **Merc** k* *Merc-c* k* *Merc-d* hr1 mez k2 mosch b2.de* *Nat-m* k* *Nat-s* *Nit-ac* k* ol-j hr1 op gk **Petr** k* *Phos* k* **Psor** k* **Puls** k* *Rhus-t* k* sal-ac k* *Sang* k* sarr a1 *Sel* k* *Sep* k* **Sil** k* spig k* sul-i k2 **Sulph** k* syc bka1• syph k* tarent **Tell** k* tep teucr hr1* thuj k* tritic-vg fd5.de tub br1 vanil fd5.de vesp k* vinc c1 viol-o lp* visc c2 zinc k*

- **right**: aeth ars st dulc fd4.de elaps eucal-r br1 *Lyc* *Merc* h1* merc-i-f vh nat-s k2 nept-m lsd2.fr *Nit-ac* polys sk4• *Sil* *Thuj* tritic-vg fd5.de tub xxb
- **left**: atra-r skp7*• cheir c1 dulc fd4.de *Ferr* k* *Graph* k* nat-s hr1 *Psor* k* *Puls* h1* sil h2* sulph mrr1 trios rsj11• tritic-vg fd5.de ulm-c jsj8• vanil fd5.de zinc h2*
- **night**: *Merc* hr1 neon srj5• sep k*
  - **warm** bed agg.: merc
- **accompanied** by:
  - **deafness** (See HEARING - Lost - accompanied - ear - discharge)
  - **polypus**: kali-s ptk1
  - ○ **Head**; pain in: psor ptk1
  - **Mastoid**; swelling of: carb-an ptk1
- **alternating** with | **hearing**; impaired (See HEARING - Impaired - alternating - otorrhea)
- **birth**, from: viol-o ptk1
- **black**: naja ptk1*
- **blood**: *Adren* br1 am-c k* *Arn* k* ars bg2 arund k* asaf bar-c bg2 bar-s k2 *Bell* k* **Both** bry k* bufo *Calc* b2.de* calc-sil k2 cann-xyz bg2 cary a1 caust bg2 *Chin* k* *Cic* k* colch con k* **Crot-h** k* *Elaps* k* ery-a k* **Ferr-p** sne *Graph* b2.de* *Ham* k*

Ear

- **blood**: ...
kali-sil k2 **Lach** b2.de* lyc b2.de* merc k* mosch k* *Nit-ac* b2.de* *Op* k* *Petr* k* **Phos** k* puls k* *Rhus-t* k* rob a1 sep b2.de* sil b2.de* sul-ac k2 *Sulph* b2.de* tell k* zinc b2.de* zinc-p k2
  - **morning**: merc k*
  - **cough** agg.; during: bell k*
  - **hematoma**: bell mtf11
  - **menses**; instead of: *Bry* k* *Phos* k*
  - **sensation** of: plut-n srj7•
  - **suppuration**; after prolonged: *Chin*
- **bloody**: am-c am bg ars k* arund asaf tl1 bar-c bell bry k* *Calc* **Calc-s** cann-s *Carb-v* *Carbn-s* caust k* *Chin* k* cic k* con k* *Crot-h* k* elaps ery-a k* ferr-p bro1 *Graph* k* ham k* *Hep* k* kali-ar kali-c kali-i a1* kali-p kali-s kino bg1 *Lach* lyc **Merc** k* merc-i-r mosch k* *Nit-ac* *Petr* k* phos k* **Psor** k* *Puls* k* rhus-t k* sarr a1 sep **Sil** k* skook bro1 *Sulph* *Tell* k* zinc
- **brownish**: *Anac* k* carb-v k* *Kali-s* k* lach sne nit-ac k2 *Psor* k* tarent k* tritic-vg fd5.de
- **caries** threatening: *Asaf* k* **Aur** k* *Calc* k* *Calc-f* k* *Calc-s* caps nat-m k* **Sil** k* sulph

▽ • **extending** to | **Meninges** (See Caries - extending - meninges)

- **cheesy**: *Hep* k* **Sil**
- **children**; in: *Psor* jl2
- **chronic**: aur bg2* bar-c bg2 borx bg2 cadm-met gm1 calc bg2* calc-f dgt1 calc-i bg2 *Calc-s* mrr1 **Graph** mrr1 hydr mrr1 **Kali-bi** bg2* kali-i bg2 kali-p mrr1 *Lap-a* sne lyc mtf11 merc hr1 petr bg2 psor jl2* *Puls* hr1 sil bg2* sulph bg2* tell mrr1 tub mtf33
  - **right**: tub xxb
  - **left**: aur st *Graph* mrr1 *Puls* st
- **clear**: bry k* **Tell** sne
- **cold**; sensation of: merc bg2*
- **copious**: *Bar-m* k* caust mtf33 *Fl-ac* hr1 *Kali-bi* hr1 kali-i k2 *Lach* hr1 *Merc* hr1 psor al **Puls** hr1 skook br1 *Sulph* hr1 tarent k2 tell hr1*
- **dentition**; during: cheir bro1
- **earwax**: am-m anac carb-v bro1 caust bro1 *Con* bro1 dulc fd4.de elaps bro1 graph bro1 hep kali-c lach bro1 lyc marb-w es1• merc mosch nat-m nit-ac phos puls k* sep bro1 spong bro1
  - **right**: *Acon* fse1.de *Agar* fse1.de *Alum* fse1.de am-c fse1.de *Am-m* fse1.de ambr fse1.de anac fse1.de *Ang* fse1.de *Ant-c* fse1.de arg-met fse1.de arn fse1.de ars fse1.de asaf fse1.de *Asar* fse1.de *Bar-c* fse1.de **Bell** fse1.de borx fse1.de *Bov* fse1.de bry fse1.de *Calad* fse1.de *Calc* fse1.de *Cann-s* fse1.de *Canth* fse1.de *Carb-an* fse1.de carb-v fse1.de *Caust* fse1.de *Cham* fse1.de *Chel* fse1.de chin fse1.de *Cic* fse1.de clem fse1.de *Cocc* fse1.de *Colch* fse1.de coloc fse1.de *Con* fse1.de croc fse1.de *Cupr* fse1.de *Cycl* fse1.de dig fse1.de dros fse1.de dulc fse1.de euph fse1.de euphr fse1.de ferr fse1.de graph fse1.de *Hell* fse1.de *Hep* fse1.de *Hyos* fse1.de **Iod** fse1.de *Ip* fse1.de *Kali-c* fse1.de *Kali-n* fse1.de kreos fse1.de *Lach* fse1.de laur fse1.de *Led* fse1.de *Lyc* fse1.de *M-arct* fse1.de *Mag-c* fse1.de *Mag-m* fse1.de mang fse1.de meny fse1.de merc fse1.de mez fse1.de mur-ac fse1.de nat-c fse1.de nat-m fse1.de *Nit-ac* fse1.de *Nux-m* fse1.de **Nux-v** fse1.de par fse1.de *Petr* fse1.de *Ph-ac* fse1.de *Phos* fse1.de **Plat** fse1.de *Plb* fse1.de *Puls* fse1.de *Ran-b* fse1.de *Ran-s* fse1.de rheum fse1.de rhod fse1.de *Rhus-t* fse1.de ruta fse1.de sabad fse1.de sabin fse1.de *Samb* fse1.de *Sars* fse1.de sel fse1.de *Seneg* fse1.de *Sep* fse1.de **Sil** fse1.de spig fse1.de **Spong** fse1.de squil fse1.de stann fse1.de staph fse1.de *Sul-ac* fse1.de *Sulph* fse1.de tarax fse1.de teucr fse1.de *Thuj* fse1.de valer fse1.de *Verat* fse1.de verb fse1.de zinc fse1.de
  - **left**: *Acon* fse1.de agar fse1.de agn fse1.de alum fse1.de *Am-c* fse1.de am-m fse1.de *Ambr* fse1.de **Anac** fse1.de ang fse1.de ant-c fse1.de arg-met fse1.de *Arn* fse1.de *Ars* fse1.de **Asaf** fse1.de asar fse1.de *Aur* fse1.de bar-c fse1.de bell fse1.de *Bism* fse1.de **Borx** fse1.de *Bry* fse1.de calad fse1.de *Calc* fse1.de *Camph* fse1.de cann-s fse1.de canth fse1.de *Caps* fse1.de carb-an fse1.de *Carb-v* fse1.de *Caust* fse1.de chel fse1.de chin fse1.de cic fse1.de cina fse1.de clem fse1.de colch fse1.de coloc fse1.de con fse1.de croc fse1.de cupr fse1.de cycl fse1.de dig fse1.de dros fse1.de *Dulc* fse1.de euph fse1.de euphr fse1.de ferr fse1.de **Graph** fse1.de **Guaj** fse1.de hep fse1.de **Ign** fse1.de iod fse1.de kali-c fse1.de kali-n fse1.de *Kreos* fse1.de lach fse1.de *Laur* fse1.de lyc fse1.de mang fse1.de meny fse1.de *Merc* fse1.de *Mez* fse1.de *Mur-ac* fse1.de nat-c fse1.de nat-m fse1.de *Nit-ac* fse1.de nux-m fse1.de **Olnd** fse1.de *Par* fse1.de petr fse1.de ph-ac fse1.de *Phos* fse1.de plat fse1.de plb fse1.de *Puls* fse1.de ran-b fse1.de ran-s fse1.de rheum fse1.de *Rhod* fse1.de *Rhus-t* fse1.de sabad fse1.de *Sabin* fse1.de

- **earwax – left**: ...
sars fse1.de sel fse1.de seneg fse1.de *Sep* fse1.de sil fse1.de *Spig* fse1.de spong fse1.de squil fse1.de *Stann* fse1.de *Staph* fse1.de sul-ac fse1.de *Sulph* fse1.de tarax fse1.de teucr fse1.de thuj fse1.de valer fse1.de verat fse1.de *Verb* fse1.de **Viol-o** fse1.de viol-t fse1.de zinc fse1.de
- **egg** white; like: nat-m mtf33
- **eruptions**; after suppressed: aur-s k2 cist mez k* *Sulph*
- **excoriating**: aethi-a bro1 alum k* am-c k2 ars k* *Ars-i* k* asaf bro1 aur bro1 borx bro1 **Bov** lp *Calc* bro1 calc-i bro1 *Calc-p* k* *Calc-s* bro1 caps bro1 carb-an bg2 *Carb-v* k* cist bro1 elaps bro1* ferr-p bro1 *Fl-ac* k* graph bro1 *Hep* k* *Hydr* hr1* iod bg2* kali-bi bro1 *Kali-s* bro1 kino bro1 *Lyc* k* *Merc* k* merc-pr-r bro1 *Nat-m* k* paro-i sne petr bg2 psor bro1 puls k* *Rhus-t* k* *Sil* bro1 **Sulph** k* *Syph* k* **Tell** k* thuj bro1 tub bro1
- **fetid**: aethi-a bro1 aids nl2• *Ars* k* *Ars-i* k* ars-s-f k2 asaf k2* **Aur** k* aur-ar k2 aur-i k2 aur-s k2 *Bar-m* hr1 borx bro1 *Bov* k* *Calc* k* *Calc-s* bro1 caps bro1 *Carb-ac* k* *Carb-v* k* carbn-s *Caust* hr1 *Chin* hr1 **Cist** k* cub *Elaps* k* ery-a hr1 ferr-p bro1 graph bro1 *Hep* k* *Hydr* hr1* *Kali-ar* *Kali-bi* k* kali-c k* kali-i k2 kali-p sne *Kali-s* hr1* kino bro1 **Lyc** hr1* meph k* **Merc** k* *Merc-c* k* merc-pr-r bro1 nat-m bro1 *Nit-ac* k* ol-j hr1 **Psor** k* puls hr1* *Rhus-t* hr1 rob a1 sal-ac k* sep k* *Sil* bro1 **Sulph** k* syph bg1 **Tell** k* thuj k* tub bro1 vanil fd5.de zinc k*
  - **diarrhea**; with watery, offensive: *Psor* hr1*
- **flesh**-colored: *Carb-v* bg2* kali-c bg2* zinc bg2*
- **green**: *Elaps* *Hep* k* *Kali-i* kali-s k2 **Lac-c** k* lyc *Merc* k* polys sk4•
  - **morning**: elaps
  - **odorless**: lac-c k*
- **head**; after pain in: absin ptk1
- **ichorous**: am-c **Ars** k* calc-p *Carb-an* k* *Carb-v* **Lyc** k* *Nit-ac* k* **Psor** k* sep *Sil* k* skook br1 *Tell*
- **malaria**; after: carb-v k2
- **measles**; after: *Bov* cact *Carb-v* colch *Crot-h* *Lyc* merc *Nit-ac* psor al2 **Puls** k* *Sulph*
- **moisture**: asaf b2.de* carb-an b2.de* *Caust* b2.de* colch b2.de* kreos b2.de* m-ambo b2.de* meny b2.de* *Merc* b2.de* nat-m b2.de* nit-ac b2.de* phos b2.de* spig b2.de*
- **mucous**: aethi-a bro1 alum b2.de* ars-i bro1 asaf bro1 aur bro1 bell b2.de* borx b2.de* bov bg2* *Calc* b2.de* *Calc-s* bro1 caps bro1 carb-v bg2* elaps bro1 ferr-p bro1 graph b2.de* hep bg2* *Hydr* hr1* kali-bi hr1* kali-chl hr1 *Kali-s* bro1 kino bro1 *Lyc* b2.de* m-ambo b2.de* **Merc** b2.de* merc-pr-r bro1 nat-m bg2* phos b2.de* psor bro1 **Puls** b2.de* sil bg2* *Sulph* b2.de* tarent bg2* *Tell* bro1 thuj bro1 tub bro1
- **offensive**: aethi-a c1 aids nl2• *Ars* k* ars-br vh ars-s-f k2 asaf k* **Aur** k* aur-ar k2 aur-s k2 *Bar-m* k* *Bell* b4a.de borx bg2 *Bov* k* *Calc* k* calc-s calc-sil k2 *Carb-v* k* *Carbn-s* *Caust* k* *Chin* k* **Cist** k* con bg2 crot-h k* elaps ery-a k* ferr-ar *Fl-ac* k* *Graph* k* *Hep* k* *Hydr* k* hyos bg2 *Kali-ar* *Kali-bi* k* kali-c k* *Kali-p* k* *Kali-s* k* kali-sil k2 kreos lach bg2 limest-b es1• **Lyc** k* mang meph k* **Merc** k* *Merc-c* k* *Nit-ac* k* ol-j k* **Psor** k* puls k* pyrog bg2 rob a1 sanic mrr1 sep k* **Sil** k* sul-ac *Sulph* k* syph bg2 *Tell* k* *Thuj* k* *Tub* zinc k*
  - **cadaverous** smelling: *Ars* k* skook br1
  - **cheese**; like rotten: *Bar-m* *Hep*
  - **chronic**: tub mtf33
  - **fish**-brine, like: *Graph* k* naja ptk1* sel ptk1 **Tell** k*
  - **meat**; like putrid: **Kali-p** **Psor** k* *Thuj* k*
  - **sour**: *Sulph* k*
- **painful**: *Calc-s* ferr-p mang k2 **Merc** k*
  - **stinging**: merc mtf33
- **pappy**: calc bg2
- **periodical** | **every** seventh day: *Sulph*
- **purulent**: (*↗Abscess; Eruptions - boils; Suppuration*) acon bg2* aeth k* aethi-a bro1 *All-c* k* *Alum* k* alum-p k2 alum-sil k2 *Alumn* k* *Am-c* k* am-m anan k* arn k* ars bg2 ars-i bro1 *Arund* k* *Asaf* k* *Aur* k* aur-ar k2 aur-i k2 aur-s k2 bar-c bg2 *Bar-m* k* bell k* *Borx* k* *Bov* k* bry bg2 bufo k* **Calc** k* calc-i mtf11 **Calc-s** k* calc-sil k2 cann-xyz bg2 *Caps* k* carb-an k* *Carb-v* k* *Carbn-s* *Caust* k* cham *Chin* k* *Cist* k* clem bg2 coc-c bg2 *Con* k* cop k* crot-h bg2 cur k* dys fmm1• elaps bro1 ery-a a1 ferr-p k* gels k* *Graph* k* **Hep** k* *Hydr* k* jug-r a1 **Kali-bi** k* **Kali-c** k* kali-i a1 kali-m bg2 *Kali-p* k* **Kali-s** k* kali-sil k2 kino k* *Lach* k* **Lyc** k* **Merc** k* *Merc-c* k* merc-pr-r bro1 *Nat-m* k* nat-s k2 *Nit-ac* k* oscilloc jl2 *Petr* k* phos k* polys sk4• **Psor** k* **Puls** k* pyrog bg2 rhus-t k* rob a1 sacch sal-ac k* *Sep* k* **Sil** k* sulph k* syc fmm1• syph k* tell k* tep k* thuj k* *Tub* k* tub-a jl2 *Zinc* k* zinc-p k2
  - **accompanied** by | **hearing**; difficult: calc-i mtf11

- **bloody**: *Rhus-t* hr1*
- **eczema**; with: *Calc Hep Lyc Merc Sulph*
- **mercury**; after abuse of: *Asaf* k* *Aur* k* **Hep** k* **Nit-ac** k* *Sil* k* *Sulph*
- **pus**-like: bry bg1
- **sulphur**, after abuse of: *Calc* merc *Puls*

- **putrid**: kali-p mtf11 psor bg2 thuj bg2
- **scarlet** fever; after: *Apis Asaf* k* *Asar Aur* k* *Bar-m* k* *Bell* hr1 *Bov* brom calc-s **Carb-v** colch hr1 *Crot-h* k* *Graph* k* *Hep* k* *Kali-bi* k* **Lyc** k* *Merc* k* *Nit-ac* k* **Psor** k* *Puls* k* sil hr1 *Sulph* k* tell k* *Verb*
- **scrofulous**: aethi-a c1
- **sensation** of a: acon bg2* agar b4.de* calc bg2* chr-ac bg1 cimic bg2 cinnb bg1 dirc bg1 dulc fd4.de gink-b sbd1• graph bg2* merc b4.de* nat-m bg2* sil bg2* tell bg2*
- **sequelae** (See GENERALS - Convalescence - ear)
- **serous**: elaps *Kali-bi* hr1 psor mtf33 tarent k* *Tell*
- **sticky**, gluey: caust mtf33 **Graph** k* nat-m sanic tl1 tritic-vg fd5.de
- **suppressed**: (↗*GENERALS - History - discharges - suppressed*) alum asaf **Aur** k* *Bell* bg2 bry bg2 *Calc* **Carb-v** k* *Castm* **Chinin-m** sne dulc bg2 *Graph* k* *Hep* k* lach bg2 led bg2* **Merc** k* nux-v bg2 petr *Puls* k* rhus-t sne stram k2 sulph k* vinc c1 viol-o c2 zinc k*
  - **followed** by | **meningitis** (See HEAD - Inflammation - meninges - ear discharge)
- **thick**: aur-ar k2 borx hr1 **Calc Calc-s** calc-sil k2 *Caps* sne *Carb-v* k* caust mtf33 dulc fd4.de ery-a k* graph mrr1 hep k2 **Hydr** k* **Kali-bi** k* *Kali-chl* k* kali-i k2 kali-sil k2 limest-b es1• *Lyc* k* merc k2 nat-m k* psor k2 **Puls** k* sarr a1 sep **Sil** tarent k*
- **thin**: ars asaf hr1 cham elaps *Graph* k* kali-c h2* **Kali-s** k* merc k* petr k* *Psor* k* *Sep* k* *Sil* k* *Sulph*
- **tough**: caust mtf33
- **warm**; as if: aeth c1*
- **watery**: ars bg2 asaf bg2 bry bg2 calc k* calc-sil k2 *Carb-v Cist* k* *Elaps* k* *Graph* k* *Hydr* sne *Kali-bi* hr1 **Kali-s** k* kreos bg2 *Merc* k* nat-m mtf33 phos h2* podo fd3.de• puls hr1 ser-a-c jl2 **Sil** k* spong bg2* staphycoc rly4• sulph bg2 *Syph* k* **Tell** k* thuj k* ulm-c jsj8• vanil fd5.de
- **white**: *Calc* hr1* ery-a k* *Hep* k* *Kali-bi* hr1 *Kali-chl* k* merc sne **Nat-m** k*
  - **milky**: **Kali-chl** kali-m k2
- **yellow**: aeth k* aids nl2• anan a1 *Ars* k* aur-ar k2 bov lp *Calc Calc-s* calc-sil k2 *Caps* hr1* *Crot-h* dulc mrr1 *Hydr Kali-ar* **Kali-bi** k* *Kali-c* k* kali-i a1 **Kali-s** k* kali-sil k2 limest-b es1• *Lyc* k* *Merc* k* *Nat-s* k* petr k* phos k* polys sk4• psor al* **Puls** k* sarr a1 sep k2 *Sil* tritic-vg fd5.de
  - **brownish**: *Psor* jl2
- **yellowish** green: ars-i k2 calc-sil k2 *Cinnb Elaps Kali-chl* k* *Kali-s Merc* k* **Puls** k* sil gk tell hr1

DISCOLORATION:

- **amber**; deep | **Tympanum**: ser-a-c jl2
- **blue**: nitro-o a1 santin **Tell** k*
- **brown** spots: cop k*
- **livid**: carbn-o op k* ran-s hr1
- **pale**: calc k2 petr hr1
- **redness**: acon k* **Agar** k* ail *Alum* k* alum-p k2 *Ant-c* k* **Apis** k* arizon-l nl2• arn asaf k* astac k* *Aur Aur-m* k* aur-s k2 *Bell* k* bry k* calc-p k* *Camph* k* canth b7.de* *Caps Carb-v* k* *Carbn-s Caust* k* *Cham* k* **Chin** k* choc srj3• cit-v k* der a1 dulc fd4.de *Elaps* fuch br1 gink-b sbd1• *Glon* k* graph k* ham fd3.de• hep k* *Hydr* k* *Ign* k* ind k* jab k* jug-r k* *Kali-bi* k* *Kali-c* k* kali-n k* *Kreos* k* lac-del hrn2• lyc k* *Mag-c* k* manc k* meph k* *Merc* k* *Nat-m* k* nat-p k* *Nit-ac* k* nitro-o a1 *Nux-v* b7a.de oena a1 olib-sac wmh1 op ozone sde2• peti a1 petr b4.de* *Phos* k* plan plat k* psil ft1 *Psor* k* **Puls** k* pyrog tl1* raph a1 rauw tpw8* *Rhod* b4a.de *Rhus-t* k* rhus-v a1 samb k* *Sang* k* sec b7a.de sep b4.de* spira a1 spirae a1 spong b7.de* *Sulph* k* tab k* tarent a1 *Tell* trom k* vanil fd5.de vesp a1
  - **one** side: alum k* ant-c bg2* carb-v k* chin h1 choc srj3• *Ign* k* ind *Kali-c* kreos bg2* meph a1 nat-m bg2* nat-p sep bg2* tab tell bg2*
  - **right**: bry hr1 calc k* *Cham* hr1 ham fd3.de• ind a1* kali-n h2* lac-lup hrn2• meph a1 ozone sde2• samb hr1
  - **left**: dulc fd4.de hir rsj4• jug-r a1 peti a1 raph a1 sep k*
  - **afternoon**: astac a1 nat-m k*
  - **evening**: *Alum* k* *Carb-v* k* elaps ham fd3.de• oena k* raph k* rhus-t rhus-v a1 sep k* spirae a1 tab k* tarent k* trom k* vanil fd5.de vesp k*
  - **chilblains**: **Agar** k*

Discoloration – redness: ...
  - **children**; in: sulph mtf33
  - **chill**; during: bell bg2 puls bg2
  - **erysipelatous** (See Inflammation - erysipelatous)
  - **hot**; and | **Lobes**: camph ptk1
  - **menses**; during: agar
  - **touched** or scratched, when: ail
  - **wine**; after: gink-b sbd1•
  - ○ **About** the ears: arn k*
  - **Behind** the ears: acon-l ant-s-aur canth b7a.de *Hydr* moni rfm1• *Nit-ac* olnd b7a.de *Petr* k* ptel rhus-v tab
    - **left**: tell rsj10•
    - **spots**: cocc b7.de*
  - **Conchae**: arn k* nat-m k* vanil fd5.de
  - **External** ears: *Acon* ptk1 agar ptk1 apis ptk1 caust ptk1 chin ptk1 ip ptk1 nat-p ptk1 *Puls* ptk1 pyrog ptk1 sulph ptk1
    - **left**: ant-t ptk1 carb-v ptk1 kreos ptk1
  - **Lobes**: caj a1 camph b7a.de* caps a1 *Cham* k* chin k* cit-v a1 kali-n h2* merc h1* puls hr1
  - **Meatus**: *Acon Cham* k* *Graph* hr1 *Mag-c* k* merc ptk1 *Pic-ac* k* **Puls** k* *Sulph* ptk1
  - **Tympanum**: **Acon** bgt bell mrr1 *Dulc* bgt **Ferr-p** bgt* hydr sne mang bgt *Sil* sne
    - **children**; in: oscilloc jl2
- **white**: rhus-t a1
  - ○ **Tympanum**: (↗*Tympanum - white*) *Carb-v* sne graph ptk1 *Ign* sne **Kali-m** sne lach sne mez k2

DISTANCE between right ear and right shoulder; as if more:

agath-a nl2•

DISTENSION:

- **blowing** nose; on: *Puls*
- **sensation** of distension in ear: (↗*Fullness*) bell kali-i laur *Mez* k* nat-s k2 nit-ac *Puls* k*
- **veins**; of: dig c1*

DRINKING:

- **agg.**: con b4.de*
  - **rapidly**: nat-m b4.de*
- **water** in sips | **amel.**: bar-m ptk1

DRIVING: | **agg.**: ars-i bg2

DRYNESS: aeth k* arn k* aur k* aur-s k2 berb k* bufo bg2 *Calc* k* *Carb-v* k* carbn-s castm bg2 castor-eq *Cham* b7a.de* colch k* cortiso tpw7 fago bg1 **Graph** k* hydrog srj2• iod bg2 iodof a1* kali-s k2 *Lach* k* mag-c st1 neon srj5• nit-ac k* *Nux-v* k* *Onos Petr* k* phos k* podo bg2 positr nl2• psor al *Puls* k* *Sulph* k* tetox pin2•

- **sensation** of: lac-del hrn2• petr k* phos k*
- ○ - **Lobes**: hydrog srj2•
- **Meatus**: aeth bg2 alum bg2 calc-pic bro1 carb-v bro1 ferr-pic bg2* graph bg2* iod bg2 *Kali-m* sne *Lach* sne nux-v hr1* petr bg2* phos bg2* psor al sil k* verb bg2*

EARACHE (See Pain)

EARDRUM (See Tympanum)

EARWAX (See Discharges - earwax; Wax)

EATING:

- **after**:
  - **agg.**: canth b7.de* carbn-s bg2 cina bg2 con bg2 mag-c bg2 op b7.de* plb b7.de* sil bg2 zinc bg2
  - **amel.**: nux-v b7.de*
- **agg.**: con bg2 graph b4.de* mag-c b4.de* sul-ac b4.de* sulph b4a.de verb b7.de* zinc b4.de*
- **before** | **agg.**: sil bg2

ECCHYMOSIS:

○ - **Behind** ear | **coma**; with (See MIND - Coma - ear)

EFFUSION into labyrinth:

- **bloody**: chen-a bro1*
- **serous**: chen-a bro1*

ELONGATION; from: | **Tonsils**; of: aur b4a.de merc b4a.de nit-ac b4a.de *Staph* b7a.de

ENLARGED; sensation as if: | **right**: agath-a nl2•

EQUALIZING of pressure is difficult: bit-ar wht1•

ERUCTATIONS agg.: bell b4.de* graph ptk1 sulph b4.de*

ERUPTIONS: agar k* alum alum-p k2 am-c am-m k* ant-c k* apis ars k* ars-s-f k2 **Bar-c** k* *Bar-m* bov k* bry k* calad k* *Calc* k* calc-p k* calc-pic mtf11 calc-s bro1 cann-s carb-v caust k* chin k* chord-umb rly4• *Cic* k* *Cist* k* com k* con b4a.de cop k* elaps k* *Fl-ac* *Graph* k* hep k* *Hyper* hr1 jug-c hr1 jug-r a1 kali-ar *Kali-bi* k* kali-c k* kali-p kali-s kreos k* lach bg2* *Lyc* k* merc b4a.de* mez k* mosch k* mur-ac k* nat-m k* nat-p k* *Olnd* k* *Petr* k* *Phos* k* **Psor** k* ptel k* puls k* rhus-t k* rhus-v k* ruta fd4.de *Sep* k* sil b4.de* spong k* staph k* *Sulph* k* tell k* teucr k* thiam rly4• thuj tritic-vg fd5.de vanil fd5.de verb

- **alternating** sides: carc fb*
- **acne**: calc-s bro1
- **after** eruptions agg.: bell bg2 bry bg2 carb-v bg2 *Colch* bg2 hep bg2 lyc bg2 *Meny* bg2 merc bg2 **Puls** bg2 *Rhus-t* bg2 sulph bg2
- **blisters**: camph k* *Kreos* meph k* nicc a1 ptel a1* rhus-t hr1
- **blotches**: berb bry bg2* calc bg2* *Carb-an* bg2* caust bg2* dros lach merc nicc phos spong staph
- **boils**: (↗*Abscess; Discharges - purulent; Suppuration*) arge-pl rwt5• bov hr1* carc fb* kali-c k* morg-g pte1• nat-m bg pic-ac hr1* ptel hr1 sil k* spong k* *Sulph* syph tritic-vg fd5.de
  - **left**: oci-sa sk4•
  - ○ **External** ears: merc ptk1
- **burning**: anan k* *Cic* k* *Kali-bi* hr1 merc a1 mosch k* puls k* sars k*
- **confluent**: cop k* *Psor* k*
- **cracked** and desquamating a substance like powdered starch: *Com* k*
- **cracks**: *Calc* bg2* chel bg2 graph bro1 m-ambo b7.de mag-c bg2 sep bg2 teucr b7.de*
- **desquamating**: *Anac* bry k* *Com* k* cop k* *Graph* k* merc k* phos *Psor* k* ptel a1* rhus-t a1 teucr a1
- **discharge** from ear; caused by: *Tell* bg2
- **discharging** (See moist)
- **dry**: *Chrysar* br1
- **eczema**: *Bov* c2 *Hydr* sne *Kali-bi* k* *Kali-s* k* **Lyc** hr1* petr tl1* *Psor* k* sars mtf11 *Scroph-n* br1*
- **excoriating**: ang bg dros bg *Graph* hr1 **Kali-bi** k* kali-c kali-s *Lach* bg *Merc* k* ol-an bg *Petr* k* *Sulph*
- **herpes**: am-m caust k* cist k* graph k* kreos k* mag-m k* *Olnd* k* phos k* *Psor* al* ptel hr1 rhus-t bro1 sars a1 sep k* tell bro1 teucr k*
- **itching**: *Agar* bro1 am-m h2* ars bro1 hep bro1 *Kali-bi* k* merc h1* *Mez* k* mosch k* nat-m k2 nat-p bro1 neon srj5• pall k* *Psor* k* puls ruta fd4.de sars k* *Staph* k* *Sul-i* bro1 tub bro1 vanil fd5.de
- **moist**: ant-c k* bov k* *Calc* k* **Graph** k* *Hep* hr1* *Hydr* sne *Kali-bi* k* kreos k* *Lyc* k* *Merc* k* mez k* nat-m k2 nat-p k2 otit-m-xyz mtf11 petr k* *Psor* k* ptel k* puls h1* rhus-t a1 *Rhus-v* hr1 sanic bro1 staph k*
- **painful**: aethi-a bwa3 anthraq rly4• graph bro1 petr bro1 sulph bro1 tritic-vg fd5.de vanil fd5.de
- **pimples**: agar am-c am-m b7.de* berb k* calad k* *Calc-p* k* calc-s hr1 *Camph* hr1 cann-s k* chord-umb rly4• cic clem b4.de* coff ind a1* kali-c k* *Kali-s* *Kreos* k* m-ambo b7.de mang b4.de* merc k* merc-c *Mur-ac* k* nat-m k* nat-sil fd3.de• petr k* phos k* *Psor* k* ruta fd4.de sabad k* sel k* spong staph *Sulph* k* tritic-vg fd5.de vanil fd5.de
  - **itching**: mur-ac h2*
- **purulent**: ars bro1 cic k* cycl gast a1 *Hep* hr1* *Kreos* **Lyc** hr1 **Psor** k* ptel a1* sep k* *Sulph* k*
  - **itching**: mur-ac h2
  - **stitching**: phos h2
- **red** | **swollen**; and: *Acon* bro1 *Agar* bro1 anac bro1 apis bro1 *Bell* bro1 chin bro1 graph bro1 hep bro1 kali-bi bro1 medus bro1 merc bro1 puls bro1 *Rhus-t* bro1 scroph-n bro1 sulph bro1
- **scabby**: aethi-a bwa3 anan k* bar-c b4.de* bov b4.de* bry chrysar br1* elaps graph k* hep b4a.de* *Hydr* k* iod k* lach k* lyc k* mur-ac k* nat-p k* *Psor* k* ptel a1* *Puls* k* rad-br ptk1 sanic sarr a1 sars k* sep b4a.de sil k* spong k* sulph bg2 vanil fd5.de
  - **pus** underneath; with: chrysar br1 mez br1
- **scaly**: *Chrysar* br1 cop k* hydr k2 kali-m sne neon srj5• *Petr* k* psor k* teucr k*

Eruptions – scaly: ...

- ○ **Lobes**: hydrog srj2•
  - **Meatus**: calc-pic bro1
- **scurfy**: aur-m k* bar-c ptk1 bov k* calc cinnb hr1 com k* graph hep k* hyper hr1 *Iod* k* *Lach* **Lyc** k* mur-ac k* nat-m k2 **Psor** k* puls k* sars k* sil k*
  - **right** ear: cinnb k*
  - ○ **Behind** the ears: *Bar-c* b4a.de calc b4a.de *Graph* b4.de* *Hep* b4a.de* *Lyc* b4a.de* mez b4a.de petr b4a.de *Puls* b7.de* sep b4a.de sil b4a.de *Staph* b7.de*
- **suppressed** eruptions; ear complaints after (See Discharges - eruptions)
- **suppressions**; after: ant-c bg2 caust bg2 graph bg2 lach bg2 sulph bg2
- **tetters**:
  - ○ **Behind** the ears: am-m b7.de* graph b4a.de *Nux-v* b7a.de
  - **Front** of ears; in: olnd b7a.de
  - **Lobes**: *Apis* b7a.de caust b4a.de *Graph* b4a.de *Kreos* b7a.de rhus-t b7a.de *Sep* b4a.de teucr b7.de*
- **touch**; sensitive to: am bro1 *Bell* bro1 bry bro1 *Caps* bro1 *Chin* bro1 ferr-p bro1 *Hep* bro1 psor bro1 sanic bro1 sep bro1
- **vesicles**: alum k* ars k* meph k* nat-m k2 *Olnd* k* phos k* *Psor* al* ptel k* rhus-t a1* rhus-v k* sep k* *Tell*
  - **coalescing**: ars k*
  - **discharging** water: ptel k*
  - **gangrenous**: ars k*
  - **purulent**: ptel k*
  - **serum**, filled with: rhus-v k*
  - **surrounded** by inflamed base: ars k*
  - **transparent**: alum k*
  - **white**: ptel k*
    - **red** base; on: ptel
- ▽ **extending** to:
  - ○ **Face**: *Graph* psor al *Sep*
  - **Scalp**: hep psor al
- ○ **About** the ears: ant-c b7.de* calc-p k2 *Camph* hr1 caust bg2 chrysar br1 *Cic* k* *Cist* k* graph bg2 hep *Hydr* k* *Hyper* lach k* mag-c b4.de* *Mez* mur-ac b4.de* nat-p k* nat-sil fd3.de• olnd k* petr b4.de* phos b4.de* *Sulph* k*
  - **eczema**: *Ars* bro1 arund bro1 bov bro1 chrysar bwa3* *Clem* bro1 crot-t bro1 *Graph* bro1 hep bro1 kali-m bro1 *Mez* bro1 olnd bro1 petr bro1 psor bro1 *Rhus-t* bro1 sanic bro1 scroph-n br1* tell bro1
  - **extending** to | **Scalp**: hep
  - **herpetic**: olnd k* psor tl1
  - **moist**: ant-c mtf33 kreos
  - **rash**: *Ars* k*
  - **scabby**: chrysar br1
- **Above** the ears | **pimples**: cop mur-ac
- **Antitragus**: am-m h2 spong
- **Behind** the ears: alum b4a.de anac bg2* ang bg2 ant-c k* ars ars-s-f k2 arund **Bar-c** k* bar-s k2 bufo k* **Calc** k* calc-s canth b7.de* caps bg2 carb-v *Carbn-s* **Caust** k* chin b7.de* chord-umb rly4• **Cic** k* cocc cur bg2 dros bg2 **Graph** k* guare *Hep* k* jug-c vml3• jug-r kali-c kali-i *Kali-s* lach k* limest-b es1• **Lyc** k* mag-m mag-s med gk *Merc* *Mez* k* morb jl2 morg-p fmm1• *Mur-ac* bg2* nat-m *Nit-ac* bg2* ol-an bg2 *Olnd* k* **Petr** k* **Psor** k* *Puls* k* rhus-t b7a.de ruta b7a.de* *Sabad* b7.de* sanic scroph-n br1 sel k* *Sep* k* **Sil** k* **Staph** k* **Sulph** k* tell teucr tub al* vanil fd5.de vinc *Viol-t* k*
  - **right**: chord-umb rly4•
  - **left** then right: *Graph*
  - **blotches**: anac vh bry *Calc* carb-an caust chin vh graph k2 *Mur-ac* vh *Nit-ac* vh *Sabad* vh staph
  - **boils**: (↗*Abscess - behind*) *Ang* bry *Calc* carc fb *Con* nat-c *Phyt* *Sulph* *Thuj*
    - **right**: neon srj5•
  - **burning**: viol-t
    - **scratching**; after: mag-m
  - **cracks**: bufo gk calc gk chel **Graph** k* *Hep* *Hydr* *Lyc* k* med gk morg-p pte1*• nit-ac gk *Petr* k* *Sep* k* sil mrr1 *Sulph* k* syc bka1•
  - **crusts**: graph mtf11

- **Behind** the ears: ...
  - **eczema**: ars bro1 arund bro1 aur-m k2 bac jl2 bov bro1 **Calc** chrysar br1* **Graph** k* *Hep* bro1 jug-r bro1 kali-m bro1 **Lyc** k* med gk *Mez* bro1 *Olnd* k* *Petr* bro1 **Psor** k* rhus-t bro1 sanic bro1 scroph-n br1* sep bro1 staph bro1 stront-n c2 sulph tell k* tub al*
  - **excoriating**: **Graph** kali-c nit-ac **Petr** **Psor** k* sanic sulph
  - **flaky** (See scurfy)
  - **herpes**: am-m bufo *Caust* cist con *Graph* *Mag-m* mez *Olnd* *Sep* k* teucr
  - **itching**: bufo *Graph* mag-m mag-s mez h2 morg-p pte1• nat-m h2 *Petr* psor mrr1 staph viol-t
  - **moist**: am-m ant-c aur *Calc* carb-v caust **Graph** k* kali-c *Lyc* k* *Mez* nit-ac *Olnd* k* **Petr** k* phos **Psor** k* ptel *Rhus-t* rhus-v sanic *Sep* sil *Staph* k* thlas bro1 tub al*
    - **scratching** agg.; after: *Graph*
    - **sticky**: **Graph** sanic
  - **oozing**: mez tl1
  - **pimples**: alum calad calc cann-s canth caust dros graph ham mez nat-m nicc *Pall* puls rhus-t ruta fd4.de sabad sel staph a1 sulfonam ks2 sulph
    - **left**: sulfonam ks2
    - **burning** on touch: canth
    - **itching**: rhus-t ruta fd4.de
  - **pustules**: bac jl2 berb cann-s carb-v castor-eq crot-h phyt *Psor* ptel **Puls** spong sumb
    - **right**: *Vac* jl2
  - **rash**: ant-c nat-m
  - **scabby**: aur-m *Bar-c* **Graph** hep c1 kali-c lach **Lyc** **Sil** tell thuj
    - **exuding** a glutinous moisture, sore on touch: thuj
    - **herpes**: kali-i
  - **scurfy**: hep k* kali-sil k2 **Psor** k* puls sars mtf11 *Sil* staph thlas mtf11
  - **sore**: *Graph* k* kali-c nit-ac **Petr** **Psor**
  - **spots**: morb jl2
    - **extending** to | **Body**; whole: morb jl2
  - **vesicles**: am-m calc caust chin nat-m phos *Psor* *Rhus-t* *Rhus-v* tell
    - **extending** to | **Face**: *Graph* sep
- **Below** the ears: calc mrr1 vanil fd5.de
  - **boils**: *Calc* k*
  - **cracks**: syc bka1*•
  - **vesicles**: mag-c h2 ptel k*
    - **discharging** water: ptel k*
- **Conchae**: am-m h2* ars k* chin h1* mosch a1 phos k*
  - **crusts**: mur-ac nat-p podo fd3.de•
  - **pimples**: agar a1 kreos a1* mur-ac h2* psor a1
    - **left**: psor jl2
      - **breaking** into four parts: psor jl2
  - **scurfy**: iod h*
  - **vesicles**: ars k* phos k*
- **Front** of ears; in: berb cic olnd sep ter
  - **boils**: bry carb-v hir rsj4• laur sulph
  - **herpes**: olnd
  - **pimples**: ant-c h2 nat-c h2 verb h
  - **pustules**: mag-c
  - **vesicles**: cic
- **Inside** (See meatus)
- **Lobes**, on: bar-c k* caust k* hydrog srj2• puls sars k* *Sep* bg2 spong fd4.de tell teucr k* tritic-vg fd5.de vanil fd5.de
  - **boils**: nat-m
  - **cracks**: graph mtf33
  - **eczema**: graph mtf33
    - **discharging**: graph mtf33
    - **inflamed**: graph mtf33
  - **herpes**: caust cist *Sep* k* teucr
  - **lupus**: nit-ac st1

Eruptions – Lobes, on: ...
  - **menses**; during: mag-c
  - **moist**: musca-d szs1
  - **pimples**: lach merc tritic-vg fd5.de vanil fd5.de
    - **right**: sulfonam ks2
  - **scabs**: sars
  - **scurfs**: sars
    - **burning** and itching: sars h2
  - **vesicles**, caused by the discharge: **Tell**
- **Margins** | **moist**: sil k*
- **Meatus**: *Graph* bro1 kreos *Nit-ac* petr bro1 *Psor* k* thiam rly4• vanil fd5.de verb br1
  - **boils**: bell bg2* bov *Calc-pic* bg2* carc gk6 crot-h ferr-pic bg2 hep bro1 kali-c bg2 **Merc** k* morg-g fmm1• morg-p pte1*• **Pic-ac** k* puls pyrog jl2 rhus-t sil bg2* **Sulph** k*
    - **alternating** ears: carc gk6
    - **right** ear: oci-sa sp1
  - **eczema**: bac jl2 borx bg2 graph bg2 kreos bg2 morg-p pte1*• nit-ac petr bg2 *Psor*
  - **herpes**: merc
  - **pimples**: jug-r kali-p vanil fd5.de
  - **pustules**: castor-eq pic-ac k2
  - **scurfy**: all-s **Lyc** *Psor*
  - **vesicles**: nicc
- **Tragus**: mur-ac k* *Puls* k* sulph k*
- **Tympanum**:
  - **scaly**: graph k*
    - **white**, thin scales: graph bro1
  - **vesicles**: tell c1

ERYSIPELAS (See Inflammation - erysipelatous)

EVERYTHING affects the ears: cann-xyz ptk1 gels ptk1 mang ptk1 plan ptk1

EXCORIATION: all-c ptk1 *Ars* ptk1 graph bg2 *Kali-bi* ptk1 kali-c b4.de* *Lach* bg2 *Merc* b4.de* petr b4.de* **Psor** ptk1 sep b4a.de sulph bg2* tell ptk1

○ - **Behind**: *Graph* b4a.de kali-c b4a.de* nit-ac b4a.de* petr b4a.de*
  - **sensation** of: cic c1

EXERTION agg.: mag-c bg2

EXERTION OF THE EYES agg.: spig bg2

EXOSTOSIS: puls

○ - **Meatus**: calc-f bro1 *Hecla* bro1 kali-i bro1

EXUDATION, serous on Tympanum: jab ptk1

FAVUS agg.: lyc b4a.de

FEVER:
- **during** | **agg.**: *Calad* b7.de*
- **intermittent** fever:
  - **after**: *Calc* bg2 carb-v bg2 hep bg2 nux-v bg2 *Puls* bg2 sulph bg2
  - **suppressed**; after: *Calc* b4a.de
- **nervous** fever; after: arn b7a.de *Dulc* b4a.de ph-ac b4a.de phos b4a.de verat b7a.de

FLAPPING in the ears (See Noises - flapping)

FOREIGN BODY in; sensation of a: anan hr1 ang h1* **Asar** hr1 astac a1 bell bg2 calc bg2 cann-xyz bg2 dulc fd4.de ol-an bg2 phos h2* plan ptk1 sarr a1 sil h2* tub jl2
- **rough** body: nux-m b7a.de

○ - **Between** ears: plan ptk1
- **Eustachian** tube; in: nux-m bg2*

FORMICATION: agath-a nl2• alum b4.de* am-c k* ambr k* ant-c k* *Arg-met* ars k* ars-s-f k2 arund k* bar-c k* bar-s k2 calc k* carb-v b4.de* caust k* chel ptk1 chin k* colch k* coloc k* cop k* der a1 dros k* dulc b4.de* grat k* kali-c k* lachn k* laur k* mang b4.de* med hr1 merc k* mill k* nat-m k* nit-ac h2* nux-v k* osm phys k* pic-ac a1 plat k* prun-p a1 psor al rat k* rhus-t b7.de* samb k* sep k* spig k* spong b7.de* stry sul-ac k* sulph k* tong a1 zinc k*
- **morning**: zinc k*

Ear

- **eating**; while: lachn k*

▽ - **extending** to:

O • **Lower** jaw: am-c k*

• **Outward**: chel bg3*

O - **About** the ears: calad k* hydrog srj2• nit-ac h2*

- **Behind** the ears: bry k* prun-p a1

- **Meatus**: am-c ambr k* ant-c k* calc caust kali-n laur k* mang a1 med k* plat k* puls k* samb k* sulph k*

FREEZING easily: zinc k*

FROZEN; as if●: **AGAR** k ●* colch k* crot-h k* **PETR** k ● **PULS** k ● sacch-l rb2

FULLNESS, sensation of: (↗*Distension - sensation; Pain - pressing pain)* acon bg2 aesc agar bg2 agn bg2 *Alum* bg2 anac bg2 ant-c bg2 *Arg-n* k* arge-pl rwt5• arn bg2 ars-s-f hr1* ars-s-r hr1 arum-d k* *Aur* bg2 bell k* berb k* bond a1 borx bg2 both-ax tsm2 bry bg2 *Calc* bg2 camph bg2 **Cann-i** k* cann-xyz bg2 canth bg2 carb-v k* *Caust* bg2 cham chel k* chin bg2 choc srj3• cinnb k* cocc bg2 colch bg2 com k* *Con* bg2 *Crot-h* k* cur dig a1 dros bg2 eup-per eup-pur k* ferr k* *Ferr-p* bg2 *Fl-ac* bg2 form a1 galla-q-r nl2• gels bg2 ger-i rly4• *Glon* k* granit-m es1• *Graph* bg2 hep k* ign bg2 ina-i mlk9.de iod k* iodof k* irid-met srj5• jug-r k* *Kali-c* bg2 kali-i kali-n bg2 kali-p k* kreos bg2 lac-c k* laur k* led bg2 loxo-recl knl4• lyc b4.de* mag-c bg2 mag-m bg2 mang k* *Merc* k* **Mez** nat-c k* *Nat-m* bg2 nat-p k* nat-s k* nit-ac k* *Nux-v* bg2 oci-sa sk4• *Op* k* pen k* petr bg2 phos k* phys k* plat bg2 positr nl2• *Puls* k* rheum bg2 rhod bg2 rhus-t bg2 ruta tl1* sec bg2 sel bg2 **Sep** bg2 sil bg2 **Spig** bg2 spong bg2 staph bg2 stram bg2 stry k* suis-hep rly4• suis-pan rly4• sul-ac bg2 sulph k* *Thuj* k* vanil fd5.de verat bg2 verat-v k* viol-o bg2 x-ray sp1 [bell-p-sp dcm1]

- **right**: galla-q-r nl2• propr sa3• vanil fd5.de
- **left**: luf-op rsj5• melal-alt gya4
- **morning**: ham k* thuj k*
- **afternoon**: stry k* vanil fd5.de
  - **13** h: com
- **evening**: mez nat-p k* orot-ac rly4• vanil fd5.de
- **accompanied** by | **impaired**; hearing: granit-m es1•
- **alternating** with | **popping** of ears (See Noises - explosion - alternating - fullness)
- **blowing** the nose agg.: culx vml3• mang k* *Puls* k*
- **boring** in, amel.: mez
- **eating**; while: *Nat-c* k*
- **excitement** agg.: dig k*
- **stitching** pains, after: iod iodof k*
- **swallowing** agg.: arum-d k* *Mang* k*

O - **Behind** the ears: ther c1*

- **Tympanum**: ser-a-c jl2

FUNGOUS excrescences: *Calc* b4a.de *Merc* k* sep mtf11

GANGRENE: sec b7a.de

GLUE ear (See Adhesions)

HAIR cutting agg.: led b7a.de* puls b7a.de*

HAMMERING: chel a1 ferr-p bg2 kali-c h2* thuj b4.de*

HAND over ears; passing: | **agg.**: teucr b7.de*

HARDNESS of glands about ear (See FACE - Indurations - parotid)

HAWKING: | **agg.**: hyos b7.de*

HEAT: **Acon** k* aeth k* agar bg2 agath-a nl2• agn k* aloe *Alum* k* alum-p k2 alum-sil k2 alumn k* aml-ns anan k* ang k* ant-c k* ant-t a1* apis bg2 *Arg-met* arn k* *Ars* k* ars-i ars-s-f k2 ars-s-r hr1 arum-d a1 arund asaf k* asar k* astac hr1* aur-m-n k* *Bell* k* berb k* borx bov brom k* *Bry* k* **Calc** k* calc-i k2 *Calc-p* k* calc-sil k2 *Camph* k* cann-s canth k* *Caps* k* *Carb-v* k* carbn-s carc fd2.de• *Carl* k* casc k* *Cham* k* chel k* chin k* choc srj3• chord-umb rly4• *Cic* k* cinnm hr1 clem k* coc-c k* cocc b7.de coloc k* com k* crot-h k* cycl b7.de der a1 dulc fd4.de *Elaps* fago k* form a1* gast a1 gran k* *Graph* k* ham fd3.de• hep k* hir rsj4• hyos k* *Hyper* k* *Ign* k* iod iodof k* jac-c k* jac-g jatr-c kali-ar *Kali-bi* k* *Kali-c* k* kali-m k2 kali-n k* kali-p kali-s fd4.de kali-sil k2 kiss a1 kola stb3• kreos k* lach k* lob-s a1 luf-op rsj5• *Lyc* k* lyss k* m-ambo b7.de m-arct b7.de mag-c bg2 mag-m k* manc k* mang k* meny k* meph k* *Merc* k* merc-sul a1* mur-ac k* nat-ar *Nat-m* k* nat-n k* nat-p k* nat-s k* *Nit-ac* k* nitro-o a1 nux-m k* nux-v b7a.de oena k* ol-an k* olib-sac wmh1 olnd h1* op k*

Heat: ...

paeon k* par k* paull a1 peti a1 petr k* petr-ra shn4• ph-ac k* *Phos* k* phys k* pip-m k* plat k* polys sk4• positr nl2• psil ft1 psor k* *Puls* k* ran-b b7.de raph k* rauw tpw8 rhod b4a.de* rhus-t bg2 rob a1 ruta h1 sabad bg2 sabin k* samb hr1 sang k* sarr a1 seneg k* sep k* sil k* spig bg2 spira a1 *Spong* k* stry suis-pan rly4• sul-ac k* sul-i k2 *Sulph* k* tab k* taosc iwa1• tarent k* ter k* thuj k* til k* tritic-vg fd5.de vanil fd5.de verat zinc bg2 zing k* [bell-p-sp dcm1 heroin sdj2]

- **one** side: agath-a nl2• alum k* asar carb-v k* chin h1 ign k* kali-c bg2 nat-m h2 nat-p puls h1 ruta fd4.de
  - **sensation** as if one ear were hot, which it is not: arn h1 mang h2 petr-ra shn4•
- **right**: aeth hr1 arizon-l nl2• asar bry hr1 com k* crot-h a1 dulc fd4.de irid-met srj5• *Kali-c* k* lyss k* *Nat-s* k* ozone sde2• plut-n srj7• positr nl2• psor a1 samb k* sep h2* ter k* vanil fd5.de [heroin sdj2]
  - **red** and hot:
    - ⁝ **left** ear | **pale** and cold: *Kali-c* k* phos gk
- **left**: agath-a nl2• arn h1* *Asaf* k* calc bg2 carb-v h2* cinnm hr1 cycl h1* dulc fd4.de fago a1 *Graph* k* ham fd3.de• jac-c k* kali-p fd1.de• kola stb3• *Kreos* a1* mang h2* merc hr1 nat-m h2* peti a1 pip-m a1 plut-n srj7• podo fd3.de• raph a1* ruta fd4.de sep h2* ulm-c jsj8• vanil fd5.de
  - **accompanied** by:
    - ⁝ **Face**; heat in | **left**: ulm-c jsj8•
    - ⁝ **Head**; pain in: kola stb3•
    - ⁝ **Shoulder**; heat in | **left**: ulm-c jsj8•
  - **then** right: mur-ac k* nat-n a1
- **morning** | **bed** agg.; in: cocc
- **afternoon**: cann-s k* spong fd4.de tritic-vg fd5.de vanil fd5.de
  - **13** h: com
  - **coffee**; after: nat-m
- **evening**: *Alum* k* bry k* *Caps* k* *Carb-v* k* cycl h1* dulc fd4.de ham fd3.de• lyc h2* nat-m k* nat-n k* *Nat-s* k* oena a1 psor jl2 ruta fd4.de sabin k* sanic sil k* vanil fd5.de
  - **22** h: stry
  - **bed**; when going to: hyper
  - **lying** agg.: ars h2*
  - **sleep**; before: ph-ac h2*
- **night**: alumn k* ham fd3.de• meph a1 sulph k* vanil fd5.de
  - **midnight**: alumn k*
- **alternating** with | **coldness** of ears (See Coldness - alternating - heat)
- **chill**; during: acon k* alum k* ars k* bell k* dig bg2 merc k* puls k* rhus-t k*
  - **back**; in: asaf
- **cold**:
  - **body**; with coldness of: acon
    - ⁝ **lying** agg.: (non:ars h2)
  - **touch**; yet cold to: ail dgt2 ambr dgt2 apis dgt2 ars dgt2 bapt bry dgt2 calc dgt2 calc-caust dgt2 calc-i dgt2 caust dgt2 cench dgt2 chel dgt2 cinnb dgt2 con dgt2 cor-r dgt2 elaps dgt2 fl-ac dgt2 grat dgt2 hep dgt2 ign dgt2 ip dgt2 lach dgt2 lec dgt2 lyc dgt2 mag-c dgt2 mag-m dgt2 med dgt2 meph dgt2 morg-g dgt2 nat-n nit-ac dgt2 nux-v dgt2 phos dgt2 plb dgt2 plut-n srj7• ptel dgt2 rumx dgt2 sang dgt2 sep dgt2 sil dgt2 sul-ac dgt2 sul-i dgt2 sulph dgt2 vip dgt2
- **during** | **agg.**: calad b7.de *Ip* b7a.de nux-v b7.de
- **eating**; after: *Asaf* k*
- **escaping**, sensation of: aeth k* calc k* *Canth* k* caust bro1* clem k* *Kali-c* k* mur-ac k* ol-an k* par k* rob a1 sul-ac h2*
  - **water** were running out of right; as if hot: cham
- **exertion** agg.: polys sk4•
- **flushes**: arg-met chord-umb rly4• **Lyc** k* propr sa3•
  - **vertigo**; during: cassia-s ccrh1•
- **lying** down agg.: ars h2
- **pressure** in occiput, during: gran k*
- **redness** of one ear, with: alum tab ulm-c jsj8•
- **sensation** of: alum b4.de* arn b7.de* galla-q-r nl2• kali-c b4.de* lap-la sde8.de• m-ambo b7.de m-arct b7.de mag-m b4.de* mang b4.de* par b7.de* plat b4.de* pyrog tl1 rauw sp1 seneg b4.de* sul-ac b4.de* verat b7.de*
  - **right**: galla-q-r nl2•
  - **left**: petr-ra shn4•

- **sensation** of: ...
  - **evening**: olib-sac$_{wmh1}$
  - **alternating** with | **coldness** (See Coldness - alternating - heat)
- **swallowing** agg.: arum-d$_{k}$*
- **talking** agg.: polys$_{sk4}$•
- **touch** agg.: rauw$_{tpw8}$

▽ - **extending** to:

○ · **Hand**: plut-n$_{srj7}$•
  - **Head**; half of: chel
  - **Occiput** to nape of neck; from: spong
  - **Pharynx**:
    - **evening** | **riding** agg.: nux-m
  - **Skull**: psor$_{jl2}$

○ - **Auricle** (See external)
- **Behind** the ears: merc$_{bg2}$
- **External** ears: acon$_{bg2}$ *Alum*$_{bg2}$ ang$_{bg2}$ arn$_{bg2}$ bry$_{bg2}$ camph$_{bg2}$ carb-an$_{bg2}$ caust$_{bg2}$ chin$_{bg2}$ kali-c$_{bg2}$ kali-n$_{bg2}$ kreos$_{bg2}$ merc$_{bg2}$ *Sabad*$_{bg2}$ sil$_{bg2}$
  - **chill**; during: acon$_{bg2}$ alum$_{bg2}$ kreos$_{bg2}$ merc$_{bg2}$
  - **touch** agg.: rauw$_{sp1}$
- **Inside** (See meatus)
- **Lobes**, of: alum$_{h2}$* ang$_{b7.de}$* arn$_{b7.de}$* bry$_{b7.de}$* camph$_{b7.de}$* chin$_{b7.de}$* hyos$_{b7.de}$* kali-c$_{h2}$ kali-n$_{h2}$ merc$_{bg2}$ nat-m$_{h2}$ olnd$_{b7.de}$* petr-ra$_{shn4}$• sil$_{h2}$
  - **moaning**; with: alum$_{kr1}$
- **Meatus**: acon$_{k}$* agn$_{bg2}$ alum$_{bg2}$ anan$_{a1}$ ang$_{bg2}$ arn$_{bg2}$ *Ars*$_{bg2}$ asar$_{k}$* bell$_{h1}$* bry$_{bg2}$* *Calc*$_{k}$* calc-p$_{k}$* canth$_{k}$* caps$_{bg2}$ carb-v$_{bg2}$ casc$_{k}$* caust$_{bg2}$ chel$_{k}$* chin$_{bg2}$ cocc$_{bg2}$* com$_{k}$* cycl$_{bg2}$ euphr$_{k}$* hep$_{bg2}$ ign$_{bg2}$ irid-met$_{srj5}$• *Kali-c*$_{bg2}$ kali-n$_{bg2}$ kreos$_{bg2}$ *Lyc*$_{k}$* m-ambo$_{bg2}$ m-arct$_{b7a.de}$ meny$_{bg2}$ *Merc*$_{bg2}$ mur-ac$_{bg2}$ nat-m$_{bg2}$ nux-v$_{bg2}$ par$_{bg2}$ petr$_{bg2}$ ph-ac$_{bg2}$ plut-n$_{srj7}$• puls$_{k}$* ran-b$_{bg2}$ rhod$_{bg2}$ rob$_{a1}$ sabin$_{bg2}$ *Sep*$_{bg2}$ sil$_{bg2}$ spong$_{bg2}$* succ-ac$_{rly4}$• suis-pan$_{rly4}$• sul-ac$_{bg2}$ vanil$_{fd5.de}$ zinc$_{bg2}$
  - **right**: ham$_{bg2}$
- **Pinna** (See external)

HEAVINESS: | **Front** of ears; in: carb-v$_{br1}$

HEMATOMA (= othematoma): bell$_{ptk1}$

HICCOUGH; after: | **agg.**: bell$_{b4.de}$*

HOLLOWNESS, sensation of: aur-m$_{k}$* loxo-recl$_{knl4}$• *Nux-v*$_{k}$* symph$_{fd3.de}$•
- **morning** | **dinner** amel.; after: nux-v

HUMMING (See Noises - humming)

HYDROPS: | **Middle** ear (See Swelling - edematous - middle)

INDURATION: *Con*$_{bg}$ rhus-t$_{bg}$ sil$_{bg}$

○ - **Tympanic** membrane sulph$_{k2}$

INFLAMMATION: acon$_{k2}$ *Apis* bamb-a$_{stb2.de}$• *Bell* borx bov brom$_{k2}$ *Bry* *Cact*$_{k}$* cadm-s *Calc* canth caps$_{tl1}$ cur$_{c2}$ dys$_{fmm1}$• eug$_{c2}$ ferr-p$_{tl1}$* *Fl-ac* flav$_{jl2}$ guaj$_{c2}$ influ$_{jl2}$ kali-bi kali-c$_{k}$* kali-i *Kreos* led$_{c2}$ mag-c **Merc**$_{k}$* **Merc-c**$_{k}$* mez$_{mtf11}$ morb$_{jl2}$ morg-g$_{fmm1}$• morg-p$_{fmm1}$• mur-ac$_{tl1}$ nat-n$_{c2}$ nux-v$_{k2}$ parathyr$_{jl2}$ phos$_{ptk1}$* *Pic-ac*$_{k}$* *Plan*$_{c2}$ pneu$_{jl2}$ podo$_{fd3.de}$• prot$_{jl2}$ **Puls**$_{k}$* *Rhus-t* sil$_{bg}$ streptoc$_{jl2}$ sulph$_{bg}$* syc$_{fmm1}$• tell$_{ptk1}$ ter thuj$_{lp}$ tub$_{jl2}$ verat [chr-met$_{stj2}$ mag-sil$_{stj2}$ plb-m$_{stj2}$ zinc-n$_{stj2}$]
- **alternating** sides: caps$_{ptk2}$
- **right**: physala-p$_{bnm7}$•
- **left**: bamb-a$_{stb2.de}$• graph$_{mtf33}$ ozone$_{sde2}$•
- **acute**: strept-ent$_{jl2}$ streptoc$_{jl2}$
- **airplane**; from changes of atmospheric pressure in an: arn$_{mtr}$
- **barotrauma** (See airplane)
- **blow** on ear | **after**: calc-s$_{hr1}$*
- **chronic**: *Mucor*$_{jl2}$ parathyr$_{jl2}$ psor$_{jl2}$ strept-ent$_{jl2}$ streptoc$_{jl2}$ tub$_{jl2}$
- **erysipelatous**: *Apis*$_{k}$* ars bell$_{k}$* calc-p *Carb-v* *Crot-h*$_{k}$* graph$_{gk}$ jug-c$_{hr1}$ *Kali-bi* *Lach* meph$_{k}$* *Merc* *Petr* **Puls**$_{k}$* *Rhus-t*$_{k}$* *Rhus-v*$_{k}$* samb$_{k}$* *Sep* *Sulph*$_{k}$* tell tep$_{k}$*
- **recurrent**: flav$_{jl2}$
- **rheumatic**: lob-c$_{bnt}$
- **scarlatina**; after: apis$_{c1}$
- **scrofulous** | **About** the ears: aethi-a$_{bwa3}$

Inflammation: ...
- **serous**: **Sil**$_{mrr1}$
- **suppurative**: am caps moni$_{rfm1}$• psor$_{jl2}$ syph$_{jl2}$ tub$_{jl2}$

○ - **Conchae**: arund$_{hr1}$ ham$_{fd3.de}$• jug-r$_{a1}$ nat-m$_{k}$* psor$_{a1}$* rhus-t$_{hr1}$ sil$_{k}$*
- **Eustachian** tubes (= salpingitis): am-m **Calc**$_{k}$* ery-a$_{k}$* ferr$_{mtf11}$ *Gels*$_{k}$* *Iod*$_{k}$* kali-chl$_{k}$* kali-m$_{c1}$ **Kali-s**$_{k}$* *Mang*$_{k}$* *Merc* *Nat-m*$_{k}$* nit-ac petr$_{k}$* *Phyt*$_{k}$* **Puls**$_{k}$* *Sang*$_{k}$* **Sil**$_{k}$* sul-i$_{k2}$ *Sulph* teucr
  - **right**: melal-alt$_{gya4}$
  - **accompanied** by | **Head**; noises in: **Hydr**$_{vh}$ **Merc**$_{vh}$
  - **painful**: bell$_{bro1}$ caps$_{bro1}$
- **External** ears: bamb-a$_{stb2.de}$• *Bell*$_{bg2}$ borx$_{bg2}$ calc$_{bg2}$* cinnb$_{mtf11}$ **Graph**$_{mrr1}$* influ$_{mp4}$• mag-c$_{bg2}$ merc$_{bg2}$* **Puls**$_{bg2}$ rhus-t$_{bg2}$ sil$_{bg2}$ sulph$_{bg2}$ tell$_{mtf11}$
  - **left**: graph$_{mtf33}$
  - **chronic**: borx$_{mtf11}$ sulph$_{tl1}$
- **Inside** (See meatus)
- **Labyrinth**: aur$_{bro1}$ kali-i$_{bro1}$ merc-i-r$_{bro1}$
- **Lobes**: kali-n$_{b4a.de}$* sars$_{b4a.de}$ vanil$_{fd5.de}$
  - **right**: carc$_{tpw2}$* kali-n$_{c1}$
- **Margin**: sil$_{k}$*
- **Mastoid** (= mastoiditis): *Am-pic*$_{bro1}$ *Ars*$_{sne}$ asaf$_{bro1}$ aur$_{bro1}$* aur-i$_{mtf11}$ *Bell*$_{bro1}$ benz-ac$_{bro1}$ calc-p$_{ptk1}$ canth$_{bro1}$* caps$_{hr1}$* coenz-q$_{mtf11}$ ferr-p$_{ptk1}$ hep$_{bro1}$* kali-m$_{bro1}$ lach$_{ptk1}$ mag-p$_{bro1}$ mentho$_{bro1}$ morg-g$_{fmm1}$• onis$_{bro1}$ *Onos*$_{bro1}$ oscilloc$_{jl2}$ pert$_{jl2}$ phos$_{ptk1}$* plan$_{mtf11}$ prot$_{jl2}$ pyrog$_{jl2}$* sil$_{ptk1}$ streptoc$_{jl2}$ tell$_{bro1}$ thuj$_{sne}$ tub-a$_{jl2}$
  - **right** side: mag-p$_{mtf11}$
  - **chronic**: streptoc$_{jl2}$
- **Meatus**: *Acon*$_{k}$* apis$_{bro1}$ *Arn*$_{b7a.de}$* ars$_{bg2}$ ars-i$_{bro1}$ arund$_{k}$* *Bar-c*$_{k}$* *Bar-m*$_{k}$* **Bell**$_{k}$* borx$_{k}$* bov brach$_{bro1}$ bry$_{k}$* *Cact*$_{k}$* **Calc**$_{k}$* *Calc-pic*$_{bro1}$ **Calc-s**$_{k}$* *Camph*$_{b7a.de}$ cann-xyz$_{ptk1}$ canth$_{k}$* *Caps*$_{k}$* carb-v$_{k}$* carbn-s carc$_{tpw2}$* *Caust*$_{k}$* **Cham**$_{k}$* chel$_{hr1}$ chin$_{b7a.de}$ coenz-q$_{mtf11}$ *Con* cur$_{k}$* ferr-p$_{k}$* **Graph**$_{k}$* **Hep**$_{k}$* *Kali-bi*$_{k}$* *Kali-c*$_{k}$* *Kali-chl*$_{k}$* *Kali-i*$_{k}$* *Kali-m*$_{bro1}$ kali-n$_{b4.de}$* kino kreos$_{b7a.de}$* *Lach* led$_{k}$* **Lyc**$_{k}$* m-aust$_{b7.de}$ *Mag-c*$_{k}$* mag-m mal-ac$_{mtf11}$ **Merc**$_{k}$* *Merc-c*$_{k}$* mez$_{k}$* *Nat-s* *Nit-ac*$_{k}$* **Nux-v**$_{b7.de}$* *Petr*$_{k}$* *Ph-ac*$_{b4.de}$* phos$_{k}$* *Pic-ac*$_{k}$* *Psor*$_{k}$* *Puls*$_{k}$* *Rhus-t*$_{k}$* *Sang*$_{k}$* sep *Sil*$_{k}$* spig spong$_{b7.de}$* **Sulph**$_{k}$* tell$_{bro1}$* ter$_{k}$* ther *Thuj* verat-v verb zinc

○ · **Wall** of: carc$_{sp1}$*
- **Media** (= otitis media): all-c$_{k2}$* *Apis* *Arn* aur-m-n$_{wbt2}$• *Bar-c* *Bell*$_{k}$* *Borx* **Calc**$_{k}$* **Calc-s**$_{k}$* *Caps* *Carb-v* carbn-s$_{k2}$ carc$_{cd}$ *Caust* **Cham**$_{k}$* chen-vg$_{mtf11}$ cina$_{mrr1}$ cleom-g$_{jsx1.fr}$ cur dros$_{gk}$ *Dulc* ferr$_{mtf11}$ *Ferr-p*$_{k}$* gels$_{k}$* graph$_{vh}$* **Hep**$_{k}$* hydr$_{k}$* kal$_{jsx1.fr}$ **Kali-bi** *Kali-c* *Kali-chl* *Kali-i* kali-m$_{mtf11}$ kali-p$_{mtf11}$ kali-s$_{mrr1}$* kali-sil$_{k2}$ lach$_{mrr1}$* lap-a$_{br1}$ **Lyc**$_{k}$* mang$_{mrr1}$ med$_{mrr1}$ **Merc**$_{k}$* **Merc-d**$_{k}$* myris$_{br1}$ *Nat-c*$_{k}$* *Nat-m* op$_{wbt}$• petr$_{mrr1}$ phos$_{gk}$ plan$_{mtf11}$ *Psor*$_{k}$* **Puls**$_{k}$* rhus-t sanic$_{mrr1}$ **Sil**$_{k}$* skook$_{br1}$* spig$_{mrr1}$ **Sulph**$_{k}$* *Tell* terebe$_{ktp9}$ thiosin$_{br1}$ *Thuj*$_{k}$* tub$_{ih}$* tub-a$_{vs}$* tub-m$_{vs}$* *Verat-v*$_{a1}$ zinc
  - **right**: *Bell*$_{mrr1}$ **Merc**$_{st1}$ merc-i-f$_{mrr1}$
  - **left**: med$_{mrr1}$ spig$_{mrr1}$ sulph$_{mrr1}$
  - **acute**: *Acon*$_{bro1}$ ars$_{bg2}$ *Bell*$_{bro1}$ caps$_{mtf11}$ cham$_{bro1}$ *Ferr-p*$_{bro1}$ gels$_{bro1}$ hep$_{bro1}$ *Kali-m*$_{bro1}$ *Merc*$_{bro1}$ *Puls*$_{bro1}$ rhus-t$_{bro1}$ sil$_{bro1}$
  - **catarrhal**: tell$_{mtf11}$ tub-a$_{jl2}$
  - **children**; in: bell$_{mtf33}$ **Cham**$_{mrr1}$* dros$_{k2}$ dulc$_{k2}$ ign$_{mtf11}$ puls$_{mtf33}$
  - **chronic**: acon$_{mtf11}$ agar$_{bro1}$ ars$_{bro1}$ *Bar-m*$_{bro1}$ *Calc*$_{bro1}$ calc-f$_{cr}$ *Caust*$_{bro1}$ *Cham*$_{mrr1}$ chin$_{bro1}$ graph$_{bro1}$ *Hydr*$_{bro1}$ *Iod*$_{bro1}$ jab$_{bro1}$ kali-bi$_{bro1}$ kali-i$_{bro1}$ kali-m$_{c1}$* *Kali-s*$_{mrr1}$ kreos$_{mtf11}$ mang$_{mrr1}$ med$_{mrr1}$ merc$_{mrr1}$* *Merc-d*$_{bro1}$ moni$_{rfm1}$• nit-ac$_{bro1}$ phos$_{bro1}$ psor$_{mrr1}$ *Puls*$_{mrr1}$ sabal$_{c1}$ sang$_{bro1}$ *Sil*$_{mrr1}$ teucr$_{bro1}$ thuj$_{mtf33}$ thymul$_{mtf11}$ tub$_{mtf11}$*
    - **accompanied** by:
      - **hearing** | **loss** of (See HEARING - Lost - accompanied - ear - inflammation)
  - **followed** by | **meningitis**: *Crot-h*$_{hr}$
  - **painful**: *Hep*$_{mrr1}$
  - **recurrent**: calc$_{mrr1}$ flav$_{mtf11}$ psor$_{mtf33}$ sil$_{mrr1}$ thymul$_{ttm}$ tub$_{mrr1}$
  - **subacute**: thiosin$_{br1}$
  - **vaccination**; after: sil$_{mrr1}$
  - **wind**; from exposure to cold, dry: acon$_{vml2}$*

Ear

- **Petrous** portion temporal bone: aur ptk calc-p ptk canth ptk caps k* ferr-p ptk hep ptk lach ptk *Phos* ptk sil ptk
- **Tragus**: bamb-a stb2.de•
- **Tympanum**: *Acon* bro1 atro bro1 bell bro1 bry bro1 chin bro1 *Hep* bro1

INJURY: arn b7a.de

○ - **Tympanum**: tell ptk1

INSENSIBILITY: *Mur-ac* bg2

INSPIRATION agg.: *Bar-c* bg2

ITCHING: acon b7.de* agar b4.de* allox sp1 alum b4.de* am-c b4.de* am-m b7.de* ambr b7.de* *Anac* bg2 ant-c b7.de* apis vh1 arg-met b7.de* arge-pl rwt5• ars b4.de* atp rly4• aur bg2* bar-c b4.de* bell b4.de* borx b4a.de* bov b4.de* calc b4.de* canth b7.de* caps b7.de* carb-v b4.de* caust b4.de* chel b7.de* chin b7.de* chord-umb rly4• *Chrysar* br1 cit-ac rly4• coloc b4.de* con b4.de* cortico tpw7* cupr bg2 dioxi rbp6 dros b7.de* flor-p rsj3• graph b4.de* hep b4.de* hippoc-k szs2 ign b7.de* kali-bi bg2 *Kali-c* b4.de* kali-n b4.de* kola stb3• kreos b7a.de* lac-loxod-a hrn2• lach b7a.de laur b7.de* lyc b4.de* m-ambo b7.de mag-c b4.de* mag-m b4.de* mang b4.de* meny b7.de* mez b4.de* mosch b7a.de mur-ac b4.de* myos-a rly4• nat-c b4.de* nat-m b4.de* nat-p bg2 neon srj5• nit-ac b4.de* nux-v b7.de* ol-an bg2 orot-ac rly4• petr b4.de* ph-ac b4.de* phos b4.de* plat b4.de* pot-e rly4• psor jl2 puls b7.de* rheum b7.de* rhod b4.de* *Rhus-t* b7.de* rumx bg2 ruta b7.de* *Sabad* b7.de* samb b7.de* sars b4.de* sel b7.de* sep b4.de* sil b4.de* spig b7.de* stann b4.de* suis-em rly4• suis-pan rly4• sul-ac b4.de* sul-i bg2* *Sulph* b4.de* suprar rly4• tarax b7.de* *Tell* bg2 thiam rly4• ven-m rsj12• viol-t b7.de* zinc b4.de* [bell-p-sp dcm1 spect dfg1 tax jsj7]

- **alternating** sides: chel bg2
- **right** ear: arge-pl rwt5• bros-gau mrc1
- **left** ear: fic-m gya1 [bell-p-sp dcm1]
- **accompanied** by:
  - • **coryza** (See NOSE - Coryza - accompanied - ear - itching)
  - • **earwax**; increased: cycl ptk1
  - • **hay** fever (See NOSE - Hay - accompanied - ears)
- **burning**: agar bg2 calc bg2
- **scratching** | **amel.**: bros-gau mrc1 [bell-p-sp dcm1]

▽ - **extending** to | **Jaw**: bov bg2 lyc bg2 phel bg2 spig bg2

○ - **About** the ears: phel

- • **evening**: phel
- **Above** the ear:
  - • **left** ear: anis c1 zinc-val ptk1
    - ⁝ **touch** | **amel.**: anis c1
- **Antitragus**: coc-c k*
- **Behind** the ears: *Agar* alum aur aur-m brom calc calc-s k2 carb-v fago **Graph** k* hura hydrog srj2• lyc mag-c mag-m merc-i-f *Mez* *Mosch* bg2* **Nat-m** k* *Nit-ac* olnd bg2 *Petr* puls bg2 *Rhod* bg2* rhus-t bg2 rhus-v *Ruta* h1* sabad bg2 sep bg2 staph bg2 sulph k* ther k* til vanil fd5.de ven-m rsj12• verat verat-v
  - • **right**: petr-ra shn4•
  - • **noon**: fago
  - • **evening** | **bed** agg.; in: merc-i-f sulph
  - • **night**: *Aur-m* mag-c mag-m merc-i-f ruta
  - • **followed** by | **burning**: nat-m ven-m rsj12•
  - • **scratching** | **amel.**: brom mag-c mag-m ruta
- **Below** the ears: ars caust kola stb3• mag-c ol-an spong fd4.de verat
  - • **scratching** | **amel.**: mag-c
- **Conchae**: agar k* ant-c h2* arg-met bry a1 calc k* chel k* ham fd3.de• kali-n a1 paeon k* ped a1 phel a1 raph k* spig k* spong fd4.de sulph k* symph fd3.de• wies a1
- **Eustachian** tubes: agar arg-met bell bg2 *Calc* k* caust coc-c k* coloc ign bg2* *Kali-m* bg2* nat-p a1* **Nux-v** k* *Petr* k* senec bg2* **Sil** k*
  - • **coughing**; compels: gels bro1 nux-v bro1 sil bro1
  - • **swallow**; must: gels bro1 **Nux-v** k* sil bro1
- **External** ears: **Agar** k* aids nl2• *Alum* am-m ant-c k* apis k* *Arg-met* k* ars-s-f k2 bamb-a stb2.de• berb k* brom a1 calc-p k* *Calc-s* *Carb-v* chel a1 *Coloc* *Con* k* cortico tpw7 fago k* *Graph* ham fd3.de• hep a1* kali-bi k2 *Kali-c* k* mag-m manc k* med jl2 meph a1 mez a1 mosch b7a.de nat-c k* nat-m k* nat-p a1 ol-an a1 *Petr* ph-ac pic-ac k* plat **Puls** k* rhod k* **Rhus-t** k* rhus-v a1 sil h2* spig b7.de* spira a1 spong fd4.de stry **Sulph** k* **Tell** k* trom verat zinc

Itching – External ears: ...

- • **rubbing** | **amel.**: cortico tpw7
- • **touch** | **amel.**: anis c1
- **Front** of ears; in: alum h2 ol-an spong fd4.de
  - • **left** ear:
    - ⁝ **touch** | **amel.**: anis c1
- **Lobes**: agar k* alum k* *Arg-met* k* asc-t a1 bry h1 caust k* graph k* hydrog srj2• kali-bi k* kali-c h2* laur k* nat-c h2* nat-m k* nat-sil fd3.de• nux-v petr-ra shn4• ph-ac h2* *Rhus-t* a1 ros-d wla1 sabad k* sulph symph fd3.de• verat b7.de*
  - • **night**: nux-v
- **Meatus**: acon aeth *Agar* k* allox tpw4 alum k* alum-p k2 alum-sil k2 *Am-c* am-m ambr k* *Anac* k* anag ant-c arg-met k2 *Ars* ars-s-f k2 arund c1 **Aur** aur-ar k2 bamb-a stb2.de• **Bar-c** k* bar-m bar-s k2 bell bg benz-ac borx *Bov* brach br1 *Calad* *Calc* k* *Calc-s* calc-sil k2 canth bg *Caps* k* *Carb-v* *Carbn-s* *Caust* k* chel k* chin bg cinnb *Cist* coc-c k* *Colch* *Coloc* con bg crot-h crot-t cupr *Cycl* dros bg dulc fd4.de *Elaps* k* ferr-ar ferr-p k2 *Fl-ac* form galla-q-r nl2• *Graph* grat k2 ham **Hep** k* hyper *Ign* irid-met srj5• *Kali-ar* *Kali-bi* k* **Kali-c** k* kali-n *Kali-p* *Kali-s* kali-sil k2 kreos bg lach lachn *Laur* *Lyc* mag-c mag-m manc k* **Mang** k* med meny *Merc* merc-d a1 merc-i-f merc-i-r k* *Mez* mill mur-ac nat-ar nat-c k* nat-m nat-p nat-s nat-sil fd3.de• neon srj5• nit-ac **Nux-v** k* ol-an bg olib-sac wmh1 **Petr** k* petr-ra shn4• petros ptk1 ph-ac *Phos* pin-con oss2• plat bg podo fd3.de• *Psor* k* puls b7a.de* pycnop-sa mrz1 rat rheum b7a.de* rhod *Rhus-t* bg *Ros-d* wla1 rumx ruta k* sabad k* sacch-a fd2.de• samb b7a.de* *Sars* sel bg **Sep** k* **Sil** k* *Spig* stann sul-ac sul-i **Sulph** k* syc pte1*• symph fd3.de• tab tarax h1* tarent *Tell* k* tritic-vg fd5.de tub-a br1 vanil fd5.de viol-o bro1 viol-t bg zinc zinc-p k2
  - • **alternating** sides: chel bg1
  - • **right**: carb-ac cassia-s ccrh1• chel cinnb meny merc-i-r mez nat-m nat-p olib-sac wmh1 podo fd3.de• psor rat rumx ruta fd4.de symph fd3.de• tarent [tax jsj7]
  - • **left**: **Anag** androc srj1• anis c1 benz-ac calc caust cist coc-c form ham kali-p fd1.de• lachn hr1 mang mur-ac nat-c k* nat-s nat-sil fd3.de• olib-sac wmh1 petr h2 petr-ra shn4• phel rhus-t ruta fd4.de sars stann sulph symph fd3.de• *Tell* verat-v zinc
  - • **daytime**: cench k2
  - • **morning**: am-c arg-met choc srj3• kali-n nat-c nat-sil fd3.de• podo fd3.de• sacch-a fd2.de• sars h2 symph fd3.de• tritic-vg fd5.de vanil fd5.de
  - • **afternoon**: agar laur ol-an puls tritic-vg fd5.de vanil fd5.de
  - • **evening**: acon borx calad calc-p dulc fd4.de elaps graph grat mag-c nat-m nat-sil fd3.de• podo fd3.de• psor puls ruta fd4.de tritic-vg fd5.de vanil fd5.de
    - ⁝ **21** h: phel
    - ⁝ **walking** agg.: borx
  - • **night**: cench k2 ham fd3.de• *Merc-i-r* nat-sil fd3.de• podo fd3.de• ruta fd4.de sep stry tritic-vg fd5.de vanil fd5.de
  - • **alternating** with:
    - ⁝ **Anus**; itching in: sabad k*
    - ⁝ **Teeth**; pain in (See TEETH - Pain - alternating with - ear)
  - • **boring** with finger:
    - ⁝ **amel.**: (↗*Boring - amel.)* aeth agar *Bov* k* coc-c *Coloc* k* fl-ac kola stb3• lachn laur mag-m mill ol-an zinc k*
    - ⁝ **not** amel.: agar *Carb-v* laur mang ruta h1
  - • **burning**: (↗*Chilblains)* **Agar** alum arg-met k2 *Arn* **Ars** arund bad **Bry** calc calc-p carb-an carb-v carl c1 *Caust* corn lach *Lyc* *Mur-ac* nat-p *Nit-ac* *Nux-v* **Petr** *Phos* puls stry *Sulph* thuj zinc
    - ⁝ **scratching**; after: *Fl-ac*
    - ⁝ **warm** room agg.: calc-p
  - • **corrosive**: *Arg-met*
  - • **cough** agg.: lach
  - • **deaf** ear; of: sep h2
  - • **eating**; while: lachn
  - • **fleas** jumping about; sensation of: zinc b4.de*
  - • **frozen**, as if: **Agar** k* colch crot-h hipp **Petr**

- Meatus: ...
  - **laughing** agg.: mang ptk1
  - **lying** agg.: kali-p
  - **menses**; during: agar
  - **moving** jaws, when: ph-ac
  - **riding**; after: calc-p
  - **rising**, soon after: arg-met trom
  - **rubbing**:
    - **agg.**: alum
    - **amel.**: cortico tpw7 mez h2 ol-an phel
    - **not** amel.: zinc
  - **scratching**:
    - **agg.**: bamb-a stb2.de•
    - **amel.**: caust mag-c nat-c
    - **must** scratch until bleeding: alum *Arg-met* k* nat-p k* nat-sil fd3.de•
    - **not** amel.: am-m *Arg-met* cist k2 fl-ac hydrog srj2• *Sars*
  - **sleep** agg.; during: *Lyc* ros-d wla1
  - **sneezing** agg.: cycl br1*
  - **stitching**: lach
  - **stooping** agg.: lepi
  - **swallowing**:
    - **agg.**: mang *Sil*
    - **must** swallow: carb-v **Nux-v** k*
  - **talking** agg.: mang ptk1 vanil fd5.de
  - **touch** | **amel.**: hyper mur-ac h2 nat-m
  - **walking** agg.: borx
  - **warm**:
    - **room**:
      - **agg.**: calc-p coc-c
      - **entering** a warm room; when | **cold** air; from: *Coc-c*
  - **yawning** agg.: acon
  - ▽ **extending** to:
    - **Body**; whole: am-c
    - **Mouth**: coc-c bg1
    - **Throat**: elaps gk
  - ○ **Deep** in meatus; very: ros-d wla1
- **Tragus**: mur-ac k*

JUMPING in ear; sensation of something: spig b7.de*
- **fleas**; like: mosch b7a.de

LAUGHING agg.: mang b4.de*

LIGHT of the fire; from: *Zinc* b4a.de

LIGHTNING-LIKE sensation: | **swallowing** agg.: psor jl2

LUMPS; hard: | **Behind** ear: cinnb

LUPUS on the lobe: nit-ac k*

LYING:
- **agg.**: aloe bg2 ant-c b7.de* calc b4.de* carb-v b4.de caust b4.de* ferr-p bg2 graph b4.de* nat-m b4.de* rhod b4.de* rhus-t b7.de* sulph b4.de* thuj b4.de*
- **amel.**: *Bell* b4a.de ph-ac bg2
- **bed**; in | **agg.**: cocc b7.de* croc b7.de* nux-v b7.de* puls b7.de* sel b7a.de spong b7.de* valer b7.de*
- **ear**; on the | **agg.**: am-c b4.de* am-m b7.de* arg-n bg2 bar-c b4.de* hep b4a.de kali-n b4.de* spong b7.de*
- **face**; on the | **amel.**: rad-br ptk1

LYING DOWN agg.; after: hep b4a.de sulph b4.de*

MEASLES; after: carb-v b4a.de puls b7a.de* sulph b4a.de

MÉNIÈRE'S disease (See VERTIGO - Ménière)

MENSES:
- **before** | **agg.**: ferr b7.de nat-c bg2

Menses: ...
- **during**:
  - **agg.**: agar bg2 aloe bg2 ars bg2 asar bg2 borx bg2 cact bg2 calc bg2 cann-xyz bg2 chin bg2 crot-h bg2 graph bg2 hyper bg2 ign bg2 **Kali-c** b4.de* **Kreos** bg2 mag-c bg2 mang bg2 mosch bg2 **Petr** b4.de* *Verat* b7.de*
  - **beginning** of menses | **agg.**: mang bg2 merc bg2
- **suppressed** menses; from | **agg.**: *Puls* bg2

MERCURY; after abuse of: asaf b7a.de* aur bg2 carb-v b4a.de* hep b4a.de* *Nit-ac* b4a.de* petr bg2 sil bg2 *Staph* b7a.de* *Sulph* bg2

MOISTURE: arg-n bg2 *Calc* bg2 *Graph* bg2* *Hep* hr1 kali-c h2* *Lyc* bg2 *Merc* h1* olnd bg2 petr bg2* phos h2* sep h2* spig a1
- ○ **Behind** the ears: calc k* carb-v caust **Graph** k* hep k* kali-c k* lyc k* nit-ac k* *Olnd* k* *Petr* k* phos *Psor* ptk1 puls bg2 rhus-v a1 sep b4a.de sil k* *Sulph* b4a.de
- **Conchae**: sil k* sulph k*
- **Margin**: sil k*
- **Meatus**: bell bg2

MOON:
- **full** moon | **agg.**: graph b4a.de *Sil* b4a.de*

MOTION:
- **agg.**: puls b7.de* verat bg2
- **amel.**: sil b4.de*
- **head**; of | **agg.**: graph b4.de* puls b7.de* sep b4.de* sil b4.de* staph b7.de*
- **jaw**; of lower | **agg.**: ant-c b7a.de nux-m b7.de* ph-ac bg2 stann b4.de*

MOVING in ear; sensation of something:
- **swallowing** agg.: nat-c ptk1
- **wood** were moving about; as if a piece of: ruta b7.de*

MUMPS (See FACE - Inflammation - parotid - mumps)

MUSIC agg.: ph-ac ptk1 tab ptk1
- **organ** music: lyc b4a.de

NARROW sensation: asar a1 lyc h2*

NECROSIS: | **Mastoid**: aur bro1

NODES:
- ○ **Auricle**, on: berb ptk1* tritic-vg fd5.de
- **Behind** the ears: bar-c k* bry b7.de* *Calc* bg2 carb-an b4.de* caust b4.de* dros b7.de* dulc fd4.de ph-ac k* staph b7.de*
- **Conchae**: spong bg2
- **External** ears; on: apis b7a.de nat-m bg2 spong b7.de*
  - **arthritic** or gouty nodosities:
    - **accompanied** by | **tearing** pain: berb bro1
  - **copper**-colored nodes: arg-met dros h1 graph h2 merc staph h1
- **Front** of ears; in: bry b7.de*
- **Lobes**: merc b4.de*

NOISE:
- **agg.**: acon b7.de* am bg2 *Bell* ptk1 calad b7.de* carb-an b4a.de *Cham* b7a.de chin b7.de* coff b7.de* colch b7.de* *Con* bg2* *Iod* b4a.de kali-p bg2 lyc b4a.de nux-v b7.de* **Op** ptk1 ph-ac b4.de* puls b7.de* sil bg2 spig b7.de* *Sulph* bg2* *Ther* ptk1
  - **slight** noise: cimic ptk1
- **amel.**: calen ptk1 graph bg2* jab ptk1 nit-ac ptk1

NOISES in: acon k* acon-c a1 aconin c2 act-sp adam skp7• adren bro1 *Aesc* agar k* agath-a nl2• *Agn* k* ail all-c k* aloe alum k* am-c k* am-m k* *Ambr* k* anac k* anag anan hr1 ang anis ant-c k* ant-t antip br1* aphis br1* *Arg-n* arist-cl sp1 *Arn* k* *Ars* k* *Ars-i* arund k* asaf k* *Asar* k* aster atp rly4• atro *Aur* k* aur-ar k2 *Bar-c* k* bar-i k2 *Bar-m* k* bar-s k2 **Bell** k* benz-ac bg2 berb k* bism bit-ar wht1• bol-s a1 *Borx* k* bov k* brom k* bros-gau mrc1 *Bry* k* **Cact** k* cadm-met tpw6 cadm-s cain calad k* **Calc** k* calc-i k2 calc-p k* *Calc-s* calc-sil k2 camph k* canch bro1 **Cann-i** k* cann-s k* canth k* carb-ac carb-an k* *Carb-v* k* carbn-h carbn-o *Carbn-s* k* card-b a1 *Carl* k* castm **Caust** k* *Cedr* cham k* *Chel* k* chen-a c2* **Chin** k* chin-b hr1 chinin-ar **Chinin-s** k* chinin-sal c2* chlf k* chlor a1* *Cic* k* cimic k* cinch a1 *Cinnb* a1* cit-d bro1 cit-v a1 clem k* cob a1* cob-n sp1 *Coc-c* k* coca cocc k* coff k* coff-t a1* colch k* coloc k* com *Con* k* convo-s sp1 cop k* croc k* crot-t k* *Cupr* k* cupr-act cur k* cycl k* daph k* *Dig* k* dios k* dirc dros k* dulc k* elaps k* ery-a k* euon eup-per k* *Eup-pur* k* euph b2.de* euphr a1* fago a1

Ear

Noises in: ...
falco-pe nl2• ferr k* ferr-ar ferr-i k* ferr-p k* ferr-pic c2* ferr-s hr1 ferul a1 fl-ac k* form k* gad a1 gamb k* gast a1 *Gels* a1* *Glon* k* gran a1 **Graph** k* guar a1 guare k* ham a1* hed sp1 hell k* hell-v a1 helo-s bnm14• hep k* hippoc-k szs2 hura hydr k* hydr-ac k* hydrc a1 hyos k* hyper k* iber a1* *Ign* k* indg k* *Iod* k* irid-met srj5• iris mtf11 jab bro1 jac-c a1 jal a1* jatr-c kali-ar kali-bi k* kali-br k* *Kali-c* k* kali-chl k* **Kali-i** k* *Kali-m* bro1 kali-n k* *Kali-p* k* *Kali-s* kali-sil k2 kalm k* kiss a1* kola stb3• *Kreos* k* lac-ac k* *Lac-c* k* *Lach* k* lachn k* lact k* lact-v c1* lap-la sde8.de• lat-h bnm5• laur k* lec bro1 led k* lepi k* linu-c a1 lipp a1 lith-m bro1 lob-d c2 lol a1 **Lyc** k* *Lyss* m-ambo b2.de m-arct b2.de m-aust b2.de mag-c k* mag-m k* mag-s k* manc k* mang k* med hr1 meny k* *Merc* k* merc-c k* merc-cy a1 merc-d bg2* merc-i-r a1 merc-n a1 mez k* mill a1* mim-h a1 morg-p pte1*• morph k* mosch k* mur-ac k* murx a1 myric k* naja narcot a1 nat-ar nat-c k* *Nat-m* k* *Nat-p* k* *Nat-s* k* *Nat-sal* c2* nicc k* *Nit-ac* k* nitro-o a1 nux-m k* *Nux-v* k* oci-sa sp1 ol-an a1 olnd k* *Op* k* osm k* paeon k* *Par* k* parth bro1 paull a1 ped a1 pen a1 peti a1 **Petr** k* petros hr1 **Ph-ac** k* phel k* *Phos* k* phys a1 pic-ac k* pieri-b mlk9.de pilo bro1 pimp c2 pin-s k* pitu-p sp1 plan k* *Plat* k* *Plb* k* plb-chr a1 plect a1 pot-e rly4• **Psor** k* ptel k* **Puls** k* puls-n c2 rat a1* rauw sp1 rheum k* *Rhod* k* rhus-r a1 rhus-t k* ric a1 ros-d wla1 ruta k* sabad k* sabin k* sacch-a fd2.de• *Sal-ac* k* salin a1* **Sang** k* sangin-n c2* sarr k* sars k* *Sec* k* sel a1 seneg k* *Sep* k* *Sil* k* sphing a1* **Spig** k* spong k* stann k* *Staph* k* staphycoc rly4• stram k* stront-c stry k* sul-ac k* sul-i c2 sulfon c2* **Sulph** k* *Tab* k* tanac ptk2 tarax tarent k* tep k* ter hr1 teucr k* thea ther thiosin c2* thuj k* thymol sp1 til trios rsj11• tritic-vg fd5.de **Tub** valer k* vanil fd5.de verat k* verat-n c2 verat-v a1 viol-o b2.de* visc sp1 x-ray sp1 xan xanth zinc k* [bell-p-sp dcm1 heroin sdj2 spect dfg1]

- **right**: aesc ail ang bar-c k2 borx brom bros-gau mrc1 bry a1 calc-p k* castm cham chin-b hr1 chlor k* colch k* con k* euph h2* falco-pe nl2• ferr k* fl-ac a1 gad a1 kali-s fd4.de lac-c al loxo-recl knl4• lyc k* mag-c h2* mag-m h2* meny k* merc k* merc-c k* mez k* mill k* mur-ac k* *Nat-s* k* nat-sil fd3.de• ozone sde2• phel a1 phos k* phys a1 plat h2* podo fd3.de• positr nl2• rat a1* rheum rhod k* rhus-v k* sep k* spong stront-c sulph a1 symph fd3.de• tarent a1* tritic-vg fd5.de tub vanil fd5.de [heroin sdj2]
- **left**: agar anac *Berb* bit-ar wht1• bov bry k* carbn-s chel k* chin-b hr1 cic k* cob k* coc-c k* coff k* ery-a k* gamb hr1 glon a1* graph k* hydrc a1 hyper a1 irid-met srj5• kali-s fd4.de lac-ac a1* lap-la sde8.de• mag-c h2* mag-s k* merc h1* merc-c h1* mill a1* myric k* nat-m k* nat-s a1 ol-an a1 paeon a1 paull a1 phos h2* pot-e rly4• sars k* spong fd4.de stann staph ter hr1 zinc
- **daytime**: ph-ac k* sulph k*
- **morning**: alum k* alum-p k2 ant-c k* arg-n k* ars k* aur k* bell k* calc k* carb-v carbn-s caust k* clem k* *Coff* hr1 *Cupr* h2* dios k* dros dulc k* gamb a1 *Graph* k* *Lach* k* mag-c k* mag-m h2* mang h2* merc k* mez k* naja nat-ar nat-c k* nat-m k* *Nat-s* nat-sil fd3.de• *Nux-v* h1* ph-ac k* phel k* phos h2* plat k* ptel a1 puls k* rhod k* ruta fd4.de sil k* spong fd4.de sulph k* tab k* teucr k* vanil fd5.de zinc k*
  - **after**: alum ars calc nux-v sil spong fd4.de
  - **amel.**: rhod ptk1
  - **bed** agg.; in: arg-n k* aur k* graph k* ham fd3.de• mag-c k* nat-m k* puls k* sulph k*
    - **motion** of lower jaw agg.: graph
  - **rising** agg.: mez spong fd4.de
  - **waking**; on: hyper k* **Lach** k* *Naja* nat-m k* podo fd3.de• rhod k* tarent
- **forenoon**: ars h2* carb-v k* chinin-s dulc fd4.de fl-ac k* hura mag-c k* *Nat-m* k* rhod k* spong fd4.de vanil fd5.de
  - **9** h: euphr hura
  - **11** h: mag-c *Nat-m*
- **noon**: cedr k* fago k* glon k* sars h2* thuj a1
- **afternoon**: all-c k* *Ambr* k* *Ant-c* k* *Bad* a1* carb-v k* carl a1 cham k* dios k* dulc fd4.de elaps gamb k* hydr k* kalm k* lac-ac a1* mag-c k* murx a1 nit-ac h2* nux-v h1* ptel puls k* rhus-t k* sacch-a fd2.de• sars h2* spig spong fd4.de sulph thuj k* tritic-vg fd5.de vanil fd5.de verat verat-v k*
  - **14** h: hydr verat verat-v
  - **15** h: elaps fago mag-c
  - **16** h: dios *Lyc* puls
  - **17** h: ol-an sulph
  - **18** h: ol-an
- **evening**: acon alum k* alum-p k2 arge-pl rwt5• bad a1* bar-c k* borx calc k* canth *Carbn-s* *Caust* k* cinnb k* cit-ac rly4• *Coc-c* hr1 *Con* hr1 croc k* gamb k* glon k* *Graph* k* ham a1 hydr k* kali-n k* kali-s fd4.de lach k* lact k* linu-c a1
- **evening**: ...
  Lyc k* mag-c k* *Merc* k* *Merc-i-r* k* murx nat-ar nat-m k* nat-sil fd3.de• nicc k* *Nux-v* k* op k* petr k* ph-ac k* plat k* plb k* ptel k* *Puls* k* rhod k* sel k* sep k* *Sil* k* spig k* stann k* sul-ac h2* *Sulph* k* sumb k* tab k* tarent a1 thuj k* tritic-vg fd5.de valer k* vanil fd5.de zinc k* zinc-p k2
  - **19** h: mag-c phys
  - **20** h: ham
  - **21** h: hydr
  - **22** h: nat-ar
  - **bed** agg.; in: croc *Graph* lact *Merc* phos rhod sel **Sulph** valer
- **night**: agar am-c k* am-m k* androc srj1• bar-c k* carb-an k* carbn-s k2 cham chin chin-b hr1 chinin-s cinch a1 coc-c k* con k* cycl k* *Dulc* k* elaps euph k* *Graph* k* kola stb3• lac-c al* lil-t k* lyss k* mur-ac k* *Nat-m* hr1 nicc k* *Nux-v* k* ph-ac k* rat k* sars a1 sep k* *Sil* k* spong k* sulph ther k* tub vanil fd5.de zinc k* zinc-p k2
  - **midnight**: am-c k* rat k*
    - **2** h: chinin-s
    - **lying** on the ear: am-c k*
    - **waking**; on: rat k*
  - **headache**; during | **agg.**: cycl
  - **waking**; on: con k* hydr k* rat a1
- **accompanied** by:
  - **catarrh** (See Catarrh - accompanied - ear)
  - **hearing**; impaired (See HEARING - Impaired - accompanied - noises)
  - **hemorrhage** (See GENERALS - Hemorrhage - accompanied - ear)
  - **mental** symptoms (See MIND - Mental symptoms - accompanied - ear)
  - **nausea**: acon bg2 gink-b sbd1• naja ptk1
  - **pain** in ear (See Pain - accompanied - noises)
  - **respiration**; complaints of (See RESPIRATION - Complaints - accompanied - ears)
  - **vertigo** (See VERTIGO - Accompanied - ear - noises)
  - ○ **Head**:
    - **complaints** (See HEAD - Complaints - accompanied - ear - noises)
    - **pressing** pain in (See HEAD - Pain - pressing pain - accompanied - ear)
- **air**; in open:
  - **agg.**: agar k* carb-an k* graph tab k*
  - **amel.**: ars k* cic k* *Coff* hr1 puls k* thuj k*
- **anxiety** agg.: act-sp melal-alt gya4
- **bagpipe**, as from distant: nat-c k*
- **bats**; sounds as from: mill
  - **night**: ph-ac
- **beating**: kali-s fd4.de pyrog jl2 spong fd4.de
  - **door**; someone beating a: ant-c
  - **rising**:
    - **amel.** | **distant** sounds: mez
- **bed**; driving out of: mag-c h2* sil h2*
- **bees**, sound of (See buzzing)
- **bell** of a clock: agath-a nl2• mang k*
- **bells**: (↗*ringing)* agath-a nl2• alum b4.de* ambr b7a.de ant-c b7.de* ars k* arund c1 aur bg2 borx b4a.de *Calc* b4.de* calc-f bg2 chin *Chinin-s* k* clem k* coff bg2 *Con* b4a.de croc b7.de* crot-h hyos b7.de* kali-c b4.de* kali-n b4a.de *Led* b7.de* lyc b4.de* mag-c b4.de* mang k* meny b7.de* merc b4a.de merc-d bg2 mez bg2 *Nat-m* b4a.de nat-s k* *Petr* ph-ac phos b4.de* psil ft1 pyrog ptk1 rhod b4.de* sars k* *Sil* b4.de* *Spig* sul-ac k* sulph b4.de* valer k* zinc b4.de*
  - **morning**: mang k*
- **blood** to the head; caused by rush of: am br1
- **blowing**: bell bg2 chel bg2 hydr-ac hydrc k* mez bg2 mosch b7a.de* ox-ac k* *Phos* *Sel* sep h2* spig b7.de* stann bg2 stram bg2 *Verat* b7a.de
- **blowing** the nose agg.: bar-c k* *Calc* k* *Carb-an* k* *Hep* k* kali-chl k* lyc k* mang k* meny k* ph-ac k* spong fd4.de stann k* teucr k*
- **boring** into ear | **amel.**: aeth c1 lach k* meny k* nicc k*

- **breakfast**; during: carb-v nit-ac k* zinc
- **breathing** agg.: bar-c *Iod* nat-s
- **bubbling**: bell k* berb ptk2 card-b a1 con k* dulc k* euphr k* graph k* hura kali-c k* kali-n kreos k* lim a1 lyc k* *Nat-c* k* nat-m k* petr h2* rheum sil k* sulph h2* thuj k* vanil fd5.de
- **bursting** of a bubble: aloe bg2 bar-c b4.de* cic b7.de* graph b4.de* hep b4a.de mosch bg2 *Nat-c* hr1* nat-sil fd3.de• nept-m lsd2.fr rhus-t b7.de* sabad b7.de* sulph h2 symph fd3.de• tritic-vg fd5.de
- **buzzing**: abrom-a bnj1 abrot k* achy-a bnj1 acon k* agar k* *Aids* nl2• alco a1 all-c k* aloe alum k* alum-p k2 *Am-c* k* ambr anac c1* anis c1 ant-c antip bro1 *Arg-met* **Arg-n** k* *Arn* k* *Ars* k* *Ars-i* ars-s-f k2 *Aur* k* aur-ar k2 aur-i k2 *Aur-m* k* aur-s k2 *Bar-c* k* bar-i k2 *Bar-m* k* bar-s k2 *Bell* k* *Berb* k* bit-ar wht1• borx *Cact* k* cain calad *Calc* k* calc-i k2 calc-s *Camph* k* canch a1* **Cann-i** k* carb-ac a1* carb-an *Carb-v* k* carbn-s carc mlr1• cardios-h rly4• carl k* castm *Caust* k* cedr k* chel k* chen-a a1* **Chin** k* chinin-ar **Chinin-s** k* chlf k* choc srj3• *Cic* hr1 cimic k* coc-c coca mrr1 cocc *Coff* k* coff-t a1 *Con* k* cop k* croc crot-c k* cypra-eg sde6.de• dig k* dios k* dros *Dulc* k* *Elaps* *Eup-per* k* euph k* fago a1 ferr c1 *Ferr-p* k* ferr-pic *Form* k* gamb k* gard-j vlr2• gent-ch bnj1 glon k* graph bro1 guare hr1 *Ham* k* hep hydr mtf11 hydr-ac k* *Hyos* k* *Iod* k* iris bro1* kali-ar **Kali-c** k* kali-i k* kali-m k2* kali-p k* kali-s kalm k* *Kreos* k* *Lac-c* k* *Lach* k* lact *Laur* **Lyc** k* lyss k* *Mag-c* k* mag-m k* merc k* merl mim-p skp7• mosch ptk1 *Mur-ac* k* murx a1 *Nat-m* k* nat-s a1 nicc k* nit-ac k* nitro-o a1 *Nux-m* k* **Nux-v** k* olnd k* *Op* k* *Petr* k* ph-ac h2 *Phos* k* phys a1 *Pic-ac* k* **Plat** k* plb k* polys sk4• pot-e rly4• *Psor* k* puls k* rhod k* rhus-t k2 ric a1 sabad k* sabin k* sal-ac k* sang a1 sarr a1* sars h2 sec sel *Sep* k* *Spig* k* stront-c sul-ac k* *Sul-i* k* *Sulph* k* *Tarent* k* tell rsj10• term-a bnj1 ther thuj k* trios rsj11• tub jl2 vanil fd5.de ven-m rsj12• verat h1* x-ray sp1 zinc zinc-p k2 [*Buteo-j* sej6 spect dfg1]
  - **one** ear and then the other: dulc fd4.de *Sulph*
  - **right**: cann-i a1 cassia-s ccrh1• dulc fd4.de elaps *Euph* hr1 fago a1 lac-c k* lyss a1* mag-c h2* mag-m mur-ac k* phys a1 plut-n srj7• sul-ac hr1 sulph k* thuj a1 vanil fd5.de
  - **left**: *Aur-m* hr1 *Berb* bit-ar wht1• *Coff* k* glon a1 kali-c h2 merc h1 podo fd3.de• rhod a1
    - **bending** neck to left agg.: bit-ar wht1•
  - **morning**: dios k* mag-m k* sil hr1 vanil fd5.de
    - **waking**; on: nat-m
  - **forenoon**: ant-c dulc fd4.de rhod k*
  - **noon**: cedr k* fago k* sars h2 thuj a1
  - **afternoon**: gamb k* murx a1 nux-v h1*
  - **evening**: *Bar-c* k* gamb k* murx nux-v h1* sel *Spig* sul-ac
    - **bed** agg.; in: lact
  - **night**: aids nl2• am-m **Dulc** k* *Euph* ignis-alc es2• lac-c k*
  - **alternating** with | **whistling** (See whistling - alternating - buzzing)
  - **chill**; during: *Ars* bg2 glon k* m-aust b7.de puls bg2
  - **convulsions**; after epileptic: *Caust*
  - **descending** stairs, while: crot-c k*
  - **eating**; while: choc srj3•
  - **headache**; during: dios k*
  - **intermittent**, in: *Ars* k*
  - **leaning** on head amel.: kali-c
  - **menses** | **before** | **agg.**: *Kreos* k*
    - **during** | **agg.**: coca al *Kreos* k*
  - **mental** exertion; after: ferr-pic
  - **perspiration**; during: **Ars**
  - **side** lain on: mag-m k*
  - **sitting** agg.: am-m bell h1*
  - **sleep**; during | **amel.**: cassia-s ccrh1•
  - **stool** | **after** | **agg.**: *Calc-p* k*
    - **during** | **agg.**: lyc k*
  - **swallowing** agg.: rhod k*
  - **vertigo**; with: alum bg2 *Arg-n* k* arn bg2 *Ars* bell hr1* benz-ac bg2 cann-i a1 carb-v bro1 chen-a bro1 chin bg2 **Chinin-s** k* *Cic* k* euph bg2 *Gels* bro1 *Glon* k* kreos bg2 laur nat-s k* ph-ac bg2 pic-ac bro1 sal-ac bg2* seneg b4.de* sil bg2 *Stry* bro1 tab bg2 ther bg2 valer bro1 zinc
- **buzzing**: ...
  - **whistling** agg.: rhod k*
- **cannonading**: aphis br1 bad chel chen-a c1* chin-b c1 mosch
  - **distant**: bad a1* chel a1* plat k*
- **cascade**; sound of a (See rushing - waterfall)
- **cat**, like a spitting: calc *M-aust* b7.de nit-ac k* plat k* sil b4.de* spig b7.de*
  - **afternoon**: nit-ac k*
- **chewing** agg.: (↗*eating; motion - jaw - agg.*) aloe alum k* bar-c bar-i k2 bar-m k* bros-gau mrc1 *Calc* k* carb-v k* *Graph* k* *Iod* k* **Kali-s** k* mang k* meny k* nat-m k* **Nit-ac** k* nux-v *Petr* k* sil k* sulph
- **chill**; during: cedr chinin-s k* glon k* nat-m h2* puls rhus-t *Tub*
- **chirping**: agar bry k* calad k* carb-v k* *Carbn-s* *Caust* k* cedr k* euph k* ferr k* kali-m bg2 kali-s lach *Lyc* k* meny k* mur-ac k* *Nat-s* nat-sil fd3.de• nicc k* *Nux-v* k* ozone sde2• podo fd3.de• *Puls* k* rat k* *Rhus-t* k* sal-ac sne *Sil* k* stann a1 sulph tarax k* teucr sne *Tub* vanil fd5.de
  - **right**: euph h2* (non:hep h2) nicc a1 rat k*
  - **morning** | **bed** agg.; in: podo fd3.de• puls k*
  - **evening**: *Carbn-s* lyc k* nat-s nat-sil fd3.de•
  - **night**: carb-v mur-ac k* nat-sil fd3.de• nux-v k* rhus-t
  - **blowing** the nose; on: ozone sde2•
  - **intermittent**, during: *Lyc* *Nat-s* nux-v *Puls* *Rhus-t* tub
  - **valve**; as if opening and shutting: goss c1 *Graph* c1* xan c1
- **clashing**: *Mang* sabad sil
- **closing** the eyes agg.: chel k*
- **clucking**: agar k* *Bar-c* k* cadm-s *Elaps* *Graph* k* ham fd3.de• kali-c k* lyc k* petr k* rheum sep k* sil spong fd4.de tritic-vg fd5.de
  - **left** ear; while lying on: bar-c
  - **rising** from stooping, when: graph k* sep k*
  - **stooping** agg.: graph spong fd4.de
- **coition**:
  - **after**: carb-v k* dig k* graph ptk1
  - **during**: graph k*
- **cold** drinks agg.; after: kali-c
- **convulsions**:
  - **after**: *Ars* k* caust ptk1
    - **epileptic**: *Caust*
  - **before**: hyos mrr1
    - **epileptic**: *Hyos* hr1*
- **cough** agg.; during: kali-m ptk1 nux-v k* sil
- **covering** eyes with hands amel.: spig h1*
- **cracking**: agar aloe bg2 alum b4.de* aur-ar k2 *Bar-c* k* *Brom* b4a.de bry bg2* *Calc* k* carbn-s *Caust* b4a.de coc-c k* cocc k* *Coff* k* *Com* k* con hr1 dig hr1 dulc ery-a k* *Form* k* glon k* *Graph* k* hep k* kali-ar k2 **Kali-c** k* kali-chl k* *Kali-m* bg2* kali-s kalm k* *Lach* k* lachn a1 mang k* meny k* *Merc* b4a.de mosch k* mur-ac k* nat-c k* *Nat-m* k* nat-sil fd3.de• **Nit-ac** k* nux-v b7.de* ol-an k* ped a1 **Petr** k* *Psor* k* *Puls* k* rhod k* *Rhus-t* bg2* sabad b7.de sang a1 stry k* sulph k* tarent k* thuj k* zinc k*
  - **right**: *Hep* bg2* kali-s fd4.de lachn a1 nat-c h2* nat-sil fd3.de• ped a1 sang a1 tarent a1
  - **left** ear; in | **headache**; during: form br1
  - **morning**: *Coff* hr1 nat-c k* nat-sil fd3.de•
    - **bed** agg.; in: *Graph* k*
    - **moving** jaw: *Graph* k* rhus-t h1*
  - **evening**: petr k*
    - **eating**; while: *Graph* k* petr
  - **night**: bar-c sne *Mur-ac* k*
  - **blowing** the nose agg.: ambr bro1 aphis bro1 *Bar-c* bro1 *Bar-m* bro1 calc bro1 chen-g bro1 form bro1 gels bro1 *Graph* bro1 hep k* kali-c k* kali-chl k* kali-m k2* lach bro1 mang k* *Nit-ac* bro1 ozone sde2• petr bro1 puls bro1 sil bro1 thuj bro1 [bell-p-sp dcm1]
  - **breakfast** | **after** | **agg.**: zinc k*
    - **during**: **Nit-ac** k*
  - **burst** during sleep; as if drum had: (non:lach a1) *Rhus-t* a1
  - **chewing** agg.: aloe alum k* ambr bro1 aphis bro1 bar-c k* *Bar-m* bro1 brom bg2 *Calc* k* calc-sil k2 chen-g bro1 cocc bg2 form bro1 gels bro1

Ear

- **chewing** agg.: ...
Graph k* kali-c bg2* *Kali-m* bro1 *Kali-s* lach bg2* meny k* *Nat-m* k* **Nit-ac** k* *Petr* k* puls bro1 rhus-t h1* sabad bg2 sil k* sulph thuj bro1
- **cough** agg.; during: nux-v k*
- **intermittent**: petr k*
- **lying** | **amel.**: bar-c
- **motion** of body agg.: puls h1
- **moving**:
  - **Head**: graph k* *Puls* k*
  - **Jaw**: aloe *Carb-v* sne *Graph*
- **nap**; during: dig br1
- **opening** the mouth: dulc k* glon bg1
- **reading** aloud: aloe
- **sleep** agg.; during: dig k* *Lach*
- **sneezing** agg.: ambr bro1 aphis bro1 *Bar-c* k* *Bar-m* bro1* bry k* calc bro1 chen-g bro1 form bro1 gels bro1 *Graph* k* kali-c bro1 *Kali-m* bro1 lach bro1 *Nit-ac* bro1 petr bro1 puls bro1 sil bro1 thuj bro1
- **stroking** cheek: sang k*
- **swallowing** agg.: agar alum ambr bro1 aphis bro1 *Bar-c* k* *Bar-m* bro1* *Calc* k* chen-g bro1 cic k* coc-c k* coca der k* *Elaps* form bro1 gels bro1 graph h2* kali-c bro1 kali-chl k* kali-m k2* lach bro1 mang k* nat-m k* *Nit-ac* bro1 petr bro1 puls bro1 sil k* thuj k*
- **turning** head agg.: *Caust* k*
- **walking** rapidly agg.: *Bar-c* k*
- **yawning** agg.: cocc k*
- ○ **Joints**; in: nat-m bg2
- **Tympanum**; in: alum bg2

- **crackling**: acon agar alum k* ambr k* ars atp rly4• aur k* aur-s k2 *Bar-c* k* bar-s k2 borx calc k* cann-i carb-v carneg-g rwt1• coc-c k* con cypra-eg sde6.de• dulc k* *Elaps* k* eup-pur k* glon k* *Graph* k* ham fd3.de• hep k* hipp a1 hippoc-k szs2 kali-ar kali-c k* kali-i kali-s lach k* m-arct b7.de meny merc-c b4a.de mosch k* nit-ac puls k* rheum k* sabad k* sep k* spig k* sulph teucr k* thuj bg2*
  - **left**: visc c1
  - **evening**: acon borx
  - **blowing** the nose agg.: hep ozone sde2• teucr k*
  - **breakfast**; during: carb-v
  - **chewing** agg.: (↗*motion*) alum k* carb-v k*
  - **lying** upon ear: bar-c k*
  - **motion** of jaws: (↗*chewing*) carb-v
  - **opening** the mouth agg.: dulc k*
  - **sneezing** agg.: bar-c
  - **swallowing** agg.: alum k* bar-c k* elaps eup-pur k* graph hep kali-i kali-s fd4.de
  - **synchronous** with pulse: coff k* puls k*
  - **walking** agg.: bar-c meny puls h1*
- **crashing**: aloe bar-c con dig *Graph* phel vml3• zinc
  - **night**: bar-c k*
    - **sleep**; when falling asleep: *Dig* zinc
  - **breaking** of a pane of glass; as from: aloe dig zinc
- **creaking**: agar k* ambr graph k* mosch puls b7.de* rhus-t h1 stann k* thuj k*
  - **morning**:
    - **bed** agg.; in | **motion** of lower jaw agg.: graph k*
  - **evening**: stann k*
    - **bed** agg.; in: graph kl
    - **eating**; while: (non:graph kl)
  - **swallowing** agg.: agar k* graph k* *Thuj* k*
- **crickets** (See chirping)
- **croaking** like frogs:
  - **sitting** agg.: mag-s
  - **walking** agg.: mang
- **cymbals** and drums, sounds of: lob lol k*
- **dentition**; during: aloe bg1 caust bg1 *Mang* bg1* *Nit-ac* bg1* phos bg1 *Thlas* bg1*
- **din** | **stepping** hard; when: *Lyc*
- **dinner** (See chewing)
- **distorted**: [bell-p-sp dcm1]
- **drumming**: bell k* borx k* canth k* *Cupr* k* *Dros* k* dulc k* *Lach* k* manc k* rob a1
  - **morning**: lach
    - **waking**; on: lach
  - **distant**: *Cupr* k* dros k* mez k*
  - **dull**: borx
  - **lain** on, rising up amel.; in ear: *Cupr*
  - **walking** agg.: manc k*
- **eating**: (↗*chewing*)
  - **after** | **agg.**: agar canth cinnb k* con k* mag-c k* nat-s a1 op k* sil k* sulph hr1
  - **while** | **agg.**: con *Graph* nat-m petr sil sulph zinc
- **echoes** (See reverberating)
- **excited**, when: melal-alt gya4 nat-sil fd3.de• sulph
- **explosion**, like an: (↗*reports*) aloe ptk1 ars ptk1 bar-c ptk1 cann-i dig k* glon ptk1 graph k* hep h2 hippoc-k szs2 kali-c ptk1 mosch ptk1 nat-c k* nit-ac ptk1 ozone sde2• peti a1 petr ptk1 *Phel* ptk1 phos k* *Rhus-t* ptk1 sabad ptk1 sil ptk1 vero-o rly3• zinc ptk1
  - **alternating** with | **fullness**; sensation of: granit-m es1•
  - **blowing** the nose; on: hep c1 ozone sde2• [bell-p-sp dcm1]
  - **breaking** glass; as from: aloe dig zinc
  - **sleep** agg.; during: dig k* mag-c stann
  - **swallowing** agg.: cic hr1
  - **yawning**; on: aids nl2•
- **fever**; during: *Ars* ptk1 lach k* *Nux-v* ptk1 puls hr1 *Tub* k*
- **fibrous** bands; from: thiosin c1
- **flapping**: alum-p k2 aur-ar k2 bar-c k2 bar-i k2 calc bg2* calc-sil k2 carbn-s k2 kali-s k2 kali-sil k2 nat-s k2 spig bg2 *Sulph* bg2
  - **bird** is flapping; sensation as if a (See fluttering - bird)
- **fluttering** sounds: acon k* agar alum k* alum-p k2 alum-sil k2 ant-c b2.de* ant-t a1* ars ars-i aur k* aur-s k2 *Bar-c* k* bar-i k2 bar-s k2 *Bell* k* berb k* borx k* *Calc* k* calc-sil k2 *Carbn-s* carl k* caust k* cham k* chin k* cocc k* con k* cupr k* dros k* dulc k* *Graph* k* hep k* iod jac-c a1* kali-c k* kali-i *Kali-p* *Kali-s* lach k* laur k* *Lyc* k* m-ambo b2.de m-arct b2.de m-aust b2.de mag-c k* *Mag-m* k* mang k* meny k* *Merc* k* merc-d a1* mosch k* nat-m k* nat-s nit-ac k* olnd k* petr k* *Ph-ac* k* phos k* **Plat** k* psil ft1 *Psor* *Puls* k* rheum k* rhod k* sabad k* sel k* sep k* sil k* **Spig** k* spong k* stann k* staph *Sulph* k* tab a1 toxo-g jl2 zinc k* zinc-p k2
  - **right**: mag-c k* mag-m k* nat-s plat h2* tab a1
  - **morning**: bell k* plat h2
    - **waking** agg.; after: bell k*
  - **afternoon** | **17** h: sulph
  - **evening**: mag-c k* mang plat h2 tab k*
  - **bird**, as of a: ant-t a1* *Calc* vh* cham k* jac-c c1 mag-c k* mang k* mosch h1* *Ph-ac* k* plat h2* spig h1*
  - **breathing** agg.: *Bar-c*
  - **butterfly**, as of a: jac-c k* jac-g nat-m k*
  - **dinner**; during: nat-m k*
  - **eructations**; with: caust graph k*
  - **lying** | **amel.**: *Bar-c* *Ph-ac*
  - **rhythmical**: sil k*
  - **swallowing** agg.: ars
- **gong**; like a | **lying** agg.: sars
- **gout**; from: ferr-pic br1
- **guns**, sound of: am-c cann-i k* graph spong k*
  - **night**: spong k*
  - **swallowing** agg.: graph
- **gurgling** in ears as of air bubbles: *Lyc* k* nat-c ptk1
- **hammering**; sounds of: spig k* thuj b4a.de
- **headache**; during: acon-c k* arist-cl sp1 carbn-s caust k13 **Chin** k* *Cocc* hr1 cycl k* dios k* erig hr1 euphr k* ferr-s hr1 form ptk1 gels k* glon a1* hydr-ac a1 *Kali-c* hr1 *Lyc* hr1 mand sp1 *Naja* k* narcot a1 *Nux-v* h1* onos vml3• phos hr1 *Plat* hr1 plb-chr a1 *Puls* k* sep h2* *Sil* k* staph h1 sulo-ac a1 vanil fd5.de

- **hissing**: acon k* aeth br1* agar alum k* anis bar-c bar-m bg2 benz-ac k* borra-o oss1• bry k* cain *Calc* k* calc-hp ptk1 *Cann-i* k* caust chin k* chinin-s bg2* **Dig** k* dros k* ferr-pic gamb hr1 glon *Graph* k* hep k* kali-n k* kali-s fd4.de kreos k* *Lach* lyc k* m-arct b7.de mag-m med k* merc-i-r bg2 mur-ac k* nat-s k* *Nux-v* k* *Pic-ac* k* plut-n srj7• rhod bg2 sep h2* sil k* sulph k* sumb k* teucr k* thuj k* valer k*
  - **morning**:
    - **side** lain on: mag-m h2
    - **snuffing** and eructation; with: teucr
  - **evening**: calc k* hep
  - **accompanied** by | **Head**; bursting pain in (See HEAD - Pain - bursting - accompanied - ear - noises)
  - **boiling** water, as from: *Bar-c* bry k* *Cann-i* k* cann-xyz ptk1 chlf a1 *Dig* k* lyc k* mag-m k* sulph k* thuj k*
  - **clock**; near: ph-ac h2
  - **convulsions**; after epileptic: *Caust*
  - **synchronous** with pulse: bamb-a stb2.de• benz-ac k* borra-o oss1• sep h2*
  - **talking** agg.: teucr k*
- **horn**; like blowing of a: *Kalm* k*
- **howling**: sep h2
- **humming**: abrot k* *Acon* k* act-sp agar k* all-c k* all-s k* aloe *Alum* k* alum-p k2 alum-sil k2 *Am-c* k* am-m k* aml-ns amyg a1 *Anac* k* anag ant-c *Arg-n* k* *Arn* k* *Ars* k* ars-i ars-s-f k2 *Aur* k* aur-ar k2 aur-i k2 aur-m-n hr1 aur-s k2 *Bell* k* bry k* calc k* calc-i k2 calc-s calc-sil k2 cann-xyz ptk1 *Canth* k* carb-ac k* carb-an k* carb-v k* *Carbn-s* card-b k* cardios-h rly4• *Carl* k* casc castm *Caust* k* cham chel k* **Chin** k* chin-b hr1* chinin-ar *Chinin-s* k* cinch a1 cob k* *Con* k* convo-s sp1 cop k* *Croc* k* crot-t cur a1 *Cycl* k* daph k* der a1 dirc *Dros* k* *Dulc* k* falco-pe nl2• *Ferr* k* ferr-ar ferr-i ferr-p k* ferul a1 galeoc-c-h gms1• gels k* glon k* *Graph* k* hep k* hyos k* iod k* jal a1* kali-ar kali-c k* kali-m k2* kali-p k* kali-s k* kalm k* kola stb3• kreos k* lact k* laur **Lyc** k* mag-c b4a.de* mag-m k* meny k* merc k* merc-c k* mez k* mosch ptk1 *Mur-ac* k* nat-ar nat-c k* *Nat-m* k* nat-p nicc k* *Nit-ac* k* nitro-o a1 nux-m ptk1 *Nux-v* k* olnd ptk1 *Op* k* *Petr* k* *Ph-ac* h2* **Phos** k* plat ptk1 plb a1 *Psor* k* *Puls* k* rauw sp1 rhod k* rhus-t k2 ric a1 rob a1 sabad k* sang k* sec k* seneg k* **Sep** k* sil k* *Sphing* k* *Spig* k* stann h2* *Stry* k* sul-ac b4.de* sul-i k2 *Sulph* k* symph fd3.de• tab k* ter hr1* tetox pin2• thuj b4.de* tritic-vg fd5.de verat verat-v k* zing k* [*Buteo-j* sej6 heroin sdj2]
  - **alternating** sides: sulph h2*
  - **left**: anac a1 bry a1* chin-b hr1 cob a1* merc a1 merc-c h1 sphing a1* ter hr1
    - **extending** to | **Occiput**: sphing kk3.fr
  - **morning**: *Alum* k* carbn-s symph fd3.de•
    - **rising** agg.; after: alum h2 ars sil
    - **waking**; on: nat-m k* rhod k*
  - **forenoon** | **11** h: zing
  - **evening**: alum nicc k* *Ph-ac* hr1 rhod a1 sep k* spig symph fd3.de• tritic-vg fd5.de
    - **supper** agg.; after: canth
  - **night**: agar chin-b hr1 *Nux-v*
  - **air**; in open:
    - **agg.**: tab
    - **amel.**: *Ars*
  - **anxiety** agg.; mental: act-sp
  - **bells**, as from: alum h2*
  - **chewing** agg.: *Iod*
  - **chill**; during: *Ars* puls
  - **heat**; during: *Ars* *Nux-v*
  - **internally**: galeoc-c-h gms1•
  - **lying**:
    - **agg.**: all-c k* rhod a1
    - **ear**; on the | **agg.**: mez
  - **menses** | **before** | **agg.**: borx bry *Kreos* k*
    - **during** | **agg.**: *Kreos* k*
  - **motion** agg.: *Puls* k*
  - **noises** agg.; loud: ol-an tab

- **humming**: ...
  - **resting** head on table amel.: ferr k*
  - **room** agg.; in: tab
  - **sitting** agg.: bell
  - **sleep** agg.; after: act-sp
  - **synchronous** with pulse: carl k* puls k*
  - **talking** agg.: op k*
  - **vertigo**; with: alum bg2 arg-n bg2* arn bg2 bell h1* benz-ac bg2 chin bg2 chinin-s bg2 euph bg2 kreos bg2 *Ph-ac* bg2* sal-ac bg2 seneg bg2 sep k* sil bg2 tab bg2 ther bg2
  - **warm** room agg.: *Ars* *Ph-ac* hr1
  - **world** is humming: galeoc-c-h gms1•
  - ○ **Body**; whole: galeoc-c-h gms1•
- **inspiration** agg.: bar-c *Iod* teucr ptk1
- **leaning** head on table | **amel.**: ferr c1*
- **loose**, as if: *Calc* bg2* *Graph* bg2*
- **lying**:
  - **agg.**: agar all-c cann-i con *Cupr* *Ferr-act* vh ferr-p bg1* kola stb3• lil-t *Mag-c* merc nat-c nat-m phos plat puls sil *Sulph* *Tarent* trios rsj11• tritic-vg fd5.de vanil fd5.de
  - **amel.**: *Bar-c* k* bell nat-c nat-s **Ph-ac** k*
  - **ear**; on the | **agg.**: am-c bar-c cupr kali-s fd4.de mag-m mez rhus-r sep spong
- **machinery**, sound of: bell bg2 falco-pe nl2• ferr-p bg2 hydr k* kola stb3•
  - **14** h: hydr
- **menopause**; during: sang ptk1
- **menses**:
  - **after** | **agg.**: chin k* ferr k* kreos k*
  - **before** | **agg.**: *Borx* k* bry k* cann-xyz bg2 chin bg2 ferr k* *Ign* bg2* *Kreos* k* nux-v bg2 phys bg1 verat bg2
  - **during** | **agg.**: ars *Borx* chin *Ferr* k* *Ign* hr1 kreos k* lac-c al* mosch *Petr* k* *Verat* k*
  - **suppressed** menses; from: calc graph puls
- **mental** exertion agg.: *Caust* con k* ferr-pic
- **mice**, sound of: rhus-t k* teucr hr1
  - **twittering** like young mice: (↗*squeaking)* rhus-t b7.de* teucr bg2
- **mill**, sound of: bry k* cit-v k* iod k* mez k* naja nux-v k* plat hr1
  - **morning** | **waking**; on: naja
  - **distance**, at a: bry mez
- **motion**:
  - **agg.**: nat-c nux-v *Puls* staph sulph
  - **head**; of: (↗*Turning)*
    - **agg.**: *Graph* nat-c bg1 puls staph
  - **jaw**; of lower | **agg.**: (↗*chewing)* ant-c *Carb-v* dulc *Graph*
- **murmuring**: borx c1 puls b7.de*
- **music**:
  - **agg.**: *Acon* bro1 ambr bro1 bufo bro1 viol-o bro1
  - **amel.**: aur *Aur-m*
- **music**, he seems to hear: ail k* bell calc k* *Cann-i* k* cann-xyz ptk1 dulc fd4.de kalm lyc k* *Merc* k* nat-c k* phos k* plb k* puls k* sal-ac k* sarr k* stram k* sulph
  - **evening**: lyc k* puls k*
    - **lying** down agg.: puls
  - **piping**: *Borx*
  - **rest** agg.: nat-c k*
  - **shrill**: coff k* symph fd3.de•
  - **whimpering** tune: ant-c
- **musical** instrument; as from a | **left** ear: lavand-a ctl1•
- **nails** driven into a board at a distance, sound of: agar k*
- **nervous** exhaustion; from: kali-p k2
- **noise** agg.: coloc kali-p ol-an k* phos plat k* tab k*

Ear

- **occiput**; in (See HEAD - Noises - occiput)
- **opening**:
  - **mouth** (See motion - jaw - agg.)
  - **valve** were opening and shutting; as if a: goss st1 graph b4.de* xan bg1
- **pain**; with every attack of: *Ars* k* lach k*
- **perspiration**; with: **Ars** ign
- **popping** (See explosion)
- **pressure**:
  - **amel.**: thlas bg1
  - **ear**; from pressure in: diosm br1
- **pulsating**, throbbing: allox tpw4 bell ptk1 calc b4a.de* cann-xyz ptk1 caust bro1 *Ferr-p* bro1* *Glon* bro1 hep b4a.de* hydrobr-ac bro1 lach bro1 lap-la sde8.de• mag-m b4a.de merc bro1 *Morph* bro1 nit-ac b4a.de* phos b4a.de* puls bro1* tritic-vg fd5.de
- **quinine**; after: kali-ar k2
- **rain**, sound of: bov a1 chinin-s sne coff-t hr1 kali-i rhod k* rhus-r k*
- **rattling**: bar-c bg2* m-arct b7.de *Rhus-t* bg1* rhus-v bg2 *Sep* b4.de*
- **re**-echoes (See reverberating)
- **remedies** fail to act; well selected: (↗*GENERALS - Remedies - fail)* ergot mtf11
- **reports** in: (↗*explosion)* aloe k* am-c aster *Bad* *Bar-c* k* bell bg2 **Calc** cann-i chel *Chin* cic cocc bg2 dig eup-pur graph k* hep itu c2 kali-c k* *Mang* b4a.de* mosch k* nat-c k* nat-m bg2 neon srj5• nit-ac nux-v bg2 petr bg2 phos plat rhus-t k* sabad k* sil b4.de* staph k* zinc k*
  - **morning**: nat-c k* zinc
  - **afternoon** | **sleep**; on going to: rhus-t
  - **night**: bar-c *Spong*
  - **blowing** the nose agg.: hep mang atr ozone sde2•
  - **breakfast** agg.; after: zinc
  - **breaking** of glass, like the: aloe dig k* zinc k*
  - **distant** shots, as of: am-c k* bad k* chel *Dig* plat k*
  - **drops** of blood, with: mosch k*
  - **menses**; during: mosch
  - **sleep**:
    - **during**: dig k*
    - **going** to sleep; on | **agg.**: dig rhus-t zinc
  - **swallowing** agg.: *Cic* mang atr
  - **violent** in ears: aster
- **reverberating**●: ant-c bg2 *Bar-c* k* *Bar-m* bro1 bar-s k2 bell bg2* bit-ar wht1• cadm-s k* carb-v bg2 *Carbn-s* **CAUST** k ●* *Cic* *Coff* b7a.de coloc br1* cop cypra-eg sde6.de• *Dig* b4a.de *Graph* hep hydr-ac iod b4a.de* *Kali-br* k* kali-c kali-m k2 *Kali-p* kola stb3• lac-c *Lach* k* lat-m bnm6• **Lyc** k* merc k* mosch mur-ac nat-c nat-s **Nit-ac** k ●* *Nux-v* k* *Ph-ac* k* **PHOS** k ●* pin-con oss2• plat k* pot-e rly4• *Puls* k* *Rhod* k* sabad b7.de *Sars* k* sec **Sep** k* sil spig k* sulph ter bro1 zinc
  - **morning**: *Caust* k* *Nux-v* k* phos k*
  - **forenoon**: *Nux-v* k*
  - **afternoon** | **16** h: *Lyc*
  - **blowing** the nose agg.: *Bar-c* k* bar-m sne hep
  - **breakfast**; before: ant-c
  - **every** sound: anh br1 *Caust* *Lyc* k* ph-ac h2* phos k*
    - **difficult** hearing; with: **Caust** *Lyc* merc h1
  - **loud** sounds reverberate long: rhod c1
  - **own** voice: bell ptk1 *Caust* k* *Graph* hr1 kali-c a1 lac-c k* nat-s *Nit-ac* k* nux-v k* ph-ac k* *Phos* k* sars h2* *Spig* bg2* ter ptk1 zinc bg2*
  - **painful**: cop k* kola stb3• nit-ac
  - **sneezing**; on: bar-c ptk1
  - **sounding** board; like: caust bg2 graph bg2 iod bg2 phos bg2 puls bg2 sabad bg2 tab bg2 thuj bg2
  - **swallowing** agg.: *Cic*
  - **waking**; on: puls k*
  - **walking**:
    - **agg.**: verb c1
    - **amel.**: cop
- **ringing**: (↗*bells)* **Acon** k* acon-c a1 *Aesc* k* *Agar* k* agath-a nl2• agn k* aids nl2• ail k* alco a1 *All-c* k* aloe alum k* alum-p k2 alum-sil k2 alumn am-c k* am-m b2.de* ambr k* anac b4.de* anan ang k* anis ant-c k* apis apoc bg2* *Arg-n* k* arge-pl rwt5• arn k* *Ars* k* ars-i ars-s-f k2 arund k* asaf k* asar b2.de* atro k* *Aur* k* aur-ar k2 aur-i k2 aur-m k* aur-s k2 *Bar-c* k* bar-i k2 bar-m bar-s k2 **Bell** k* berb k* *Borx* k* brom k* brucin a1 bry k* **Cact** k* **Calc** k* calc-f bro1 calc-i k* **Calc-s** k* calc-sil k2 *Camph* k* **Cann-i** k* cann-s k* cann-xyz ptk1 *Canth* k* carb-an k* **Carb-v** k* *Carbn-o* *Carbn-s* k* carc mlr1• card-b a1 *Carl* k* **Caust** k* *Cham* k* *Chel* k* chen-a k* **Chin** k* chin-b hr1* chinin-ar **Chinin-s** k* chlf k* chlol k* chlor k* cic k* cinch a1 cinnb hr1 cit-ac rly4• cit-d br1 *Cit-v* k* *Clem* k* coc-c k* coca *Cocc* k* cod a1 (non:coff slp) coff-t a1* colch k* coloc k* com k* *Con* k* corn hr1 croc k* crot-h (non:cupr slp) cupr-act slp *Cycl* k* *Dig* k* dios k* dream-p sdj1• *Dulc* k* elaps ery-a k* *Euph* k* euphr k* fago a1 *Ferr* k* ferr-ar ferr-i ferr-p k* *Ferr-s* hr1 *Fl-ac* k* *Form* k* gamb k* gast a1 *Glon* k* *Gran* k* *Graph* k* guare k* haliae-lc srj5• *Ham* k* *Hell* k* hell-v a1 helo-s c1* hep k* hippoc-k szs2 hura *Hydr* k* hydr-ac k* hydrc k* *Hydrog* srj2• hyos k* *Ign* k* iod k* *Ip* k* irid-met srj5• iris bro1 kali-ar kali-bi k* kali-br hr1 **Kali-c** k* kali-cy k* **Kali-i** k* kali-m k2 kali-n k* kali-p **Kali-s** k* kali-sil k2 kalm k* kiss a1 kreos k* lac-c k* lac-h htj1• lach k* lachn k* laur hr1 lec led k* loxo-recl knl4• **Lyc** k* m-ambo b2.de m-arct b2.de* m-aust b2.de* *Mag-c* k* mag-s k* manc k* mang k* *Meny* k* *Merc* k* merc-cy k* merc-n a1* *Mez* k* mill k* morph k* mur-ac k* musca-d szs1 myric k* nat-ar nat-c k* *Nat-m* k* nat-p *Nat-s* k* nat-sal a1* nat-sil fd3.de* nicc a1 nit-ac *Nux-m* k* *Nux-v* k* ol-an a1 olnd k* op k* *Osm* k* paeon k* *Par* k* pen a1 **Petr** k* petros hr1 *Ph-ac* k* phel k* *Phos* k* phys a1 plac-s rly4• plan k* **Plat** k* plb k* plb-chr a1 positr nl2• **Psor** k* *Ptel* k* **Puls** k* rat k* *Rhod* k* rhus-t b2.de* rhus-v k* rumx ruta k* sabad k* sal-ac k* salin a1 *Sang* k* sars k* sel k* **Sep** k* *Sil* k* sinus rly4• sol-t-ae k* *Spig* k* spong k* *Stann* k* staph k* staphycoc rly4• stram k* suis-em rly4• suis-hep rly4• suis-pan rly4• sul-ac k* sul-i k2 sulfa sp1 sulo-ac a1 **Sulph** k* tab k* tanac a1 tarax b2.de* tarent k* tax-br oss1• tell rsj10• ter k* tere-la rly4• teucr k* thuj k* thymol sp1 thymu br1 til k* tritic-vg fd5.de urol-h rwt• valer k* verat k* verat-v a1 vero-o rly4*• vinc k* viol-o k* xan k* xanth bg2 zinc k* zinc-p k2 [bell-p-sp dcm1]
  - **right**: *Aesc* k* ail k* ang k* apoc a1 ars h2* borx brom k* caust h2* cham k* chin a1 chlor k* colch k* coloc k* con k* erig hr1 *Ferr* k* fl-ac a1 helo-s rwt2• *Lac-c* k* loxo-recl knl4• lyc k* mag-c h2* meny k* mez a1 mill k* nat-m a1 nat-s k* osm k* phys a1 plat h2* plut-n srj7• positr nl2• psor jl2 puls hr1 *Rhod* rhus-t h1* rhus-v k* spong k* taosc iwa1• teucr a1* thuj k* xan k* zinc a1*
    - **alternating** with | **left**: psor jl2
  - **left**: agar k* androc srj1• arn k* bry a1 caust k* chin-b hr1 cic k* coc-c k* coca-c sk4• ery-a k* fago a1 *Gamb* k* germ-met srj5• glon a1 graph k* hydrc a1 kali-c h2* kali-n h2* mag-c h2* mag-s k* mez h2* myric k* nat-m h2* nat-s a1 nicc a1 *Nux-v* k* ol-an a1 olnd h1* paeon a1 par k* petr-ra shn4• ph-ac h2* phos h2* sars k* stann k* staph k* vinc hr1 [tax jsj7]
    - **followed** by | **right**: androc srj1•
  - **daytime**: sulph k*
  - **morning**: clem k* loxo-recl knl4• mang k* nux-v phel sulph k* tarent k2 [bell-p-sp dcm1]
    - **bed** agg.; in: arg-n mag-c sulph
    - **dressing**, after: mez h2*
    - **rising** agg.: alum mez *Nux-v*
  - **forenoon**: carb-v k* fl-ac k*
    - **9** h: euphr
    - **11** h: nat-m
  - **noon**: glon k* sars h2* tritic-vg fd5.de
  - **afternoon**: carb-v k* carl a1 kali-n kalm k* sars h2*
    - **14** h: verat-v
    - **15** h: fago
    - **16** h: dios
    - **18** h: ol-an
  - **evening**: bar-c caust k* cinnb hr1 croc k* kali-n k* *Merc* k* rhod k* sil k* tritic-vg fd5.de valer k*
    - **19** h: phys
    - **20** h: ham
    - **bed** agg.; in: croc *Merc* phos rhod valer
  - **night**: carb-an k* chin-b hr1 cycl k* ph-ac k* sulph zinc k*

- **night**: ...
  - **midnight**:
    - **before**:
      - **23** h | **sudden** ringing: limest-b es1•
    - **after** | **2** h: chinin-s
    - **waking**; on: rat k*
  - **rise** and walk about; must: sil
- **air** agg.; in open: carb-an k*
- **blowing** the nose agg.: *Carb-an* k* teucr k*
- **boring** with finger in ear: chel h1*
  - **amel.**: meny nicc
- **chill**; during: cedr chin k* **Chinin-s** graph k* rhus-t k* *Sep*
- **closing** the eyes agg.: chel k*
- **coition**; after: *Dig* k*
- **cold** water | **amel.**: euphr k*
- **coldness**; during: graph k*
- **cough**; with: sil k*
- **dinner** | **after** | **agg.**: cinnb k* mag-c k* thuj a1
  - **during** | **agg.**: *Sulph* k*
- **distant**: all-c k* arg-n k* coca *Spig* k*
- **epileptic** fit, before: **Hyos** k*
- **excitement** agg.: mag-c melal-alt gya4
- **faint**, as if going to: sol-t-ae vml3•
- **followed** by | **sleep**: anis c1
- **headache**; during: acon-c carbn-s caust **Chin** k* coca hr1 cycl dios euphr hydrog srj2• *Naja* *Puls* sul-ac c1
- **hemorrhage**; after: chin hr1
- **lying** down | **after** | **agg.**: croc
  - **agg.**: sulph k*
- **menses** | **before** | **agg.**: *Ferr* k* *Ign* k* kreos b7a.de
  - **during** | **agg.**: borx b4a.de coca al **Ferr** k* *Ign* hr1 petr b4.de verat k*
- **motion**:
  - **agg.**: *Nux-v* k*
  - **head**; of | **agg.**: staph k*
- **one** ear ringing, burning in the other: kali-c
- **rest** | **amel.**: nux-v k* staph k*
- **rising** | **amel.**: tarent k*
- **rubbing** | **amel.**: meny k*
- **sitting** agg.: ars k* merc-cy k* *Sulph* k*
- **sneezing** agg.: euph k*
- **stool** | **after** | **agg.**: apoc k*
  - **during** | **agg.**: *Lyc* k*
- **stopping** up ear with finger does not amel.: croc
- **talking** agg.: spig k*
- **turning** head agg.: nat-c k*
- **vertigo**; with: acon-c a1 alum carb-v k* chin c1 cocc k* coff-t hr1 com *Dig* k* lith-c ptk1 merc-cy a1 myric k* nat-m k* petr hr1 ph-ac k2* ptel a1* *Puls* hr1 sil h2 tritic-vg fd5.de
- **waking**; on: arg-n carb-an b4.de* mag-c rat k* sulph tarent k* tere-la rly4•
- **walking**:
  - **agg.**: chel manc nicc rhus-t
  - **air** agg.; in open: agar carb-an
- **yawning**; with: acon

- **rising**:
  - **agg.**: acon mez *Phos*
  - **amel.**: ham fd3.de• nat-c tarent vanil fd5.de
  - **sitting**; from | **agg.**: lac-ac *Verat*
  - **stooping**; from | **agg.**: mang sep
- **roaring**: *Acon* k* acon-c a1 aconin a1 agar k* *Agn* k* alco a1 all-c k* alum k* alum-p k2 alum-sil k2 am-c k* am-m k* *Ambr* k* ammc hr1 *Anac* k* anis ant-c k* ant-t k* apom a1 aran bg2 arg-n arn k* *Ars* k* *Ars-i* *Asar* k* atro k* *Aur* k* aur-ar k2 aur-i k2 *Aur-m* k* aur-s k2 bapt k* **Bar-c** k* bar-i k2 *Bar-m* bar-s k2 **Bell** k* benz-ac bg2 berb k* bism k* **Borx** k* bov k* brom k* *Bry* k* cact cain calad k*

- **roaring**: ...
Calc k* calc-i k2 *Calc-s* calc-sil k2 *Camph* k* canch a1 cann-s k* *Canth* k* carb-ac k* carb-an k* **Carb-v** k* *Carbn-h* **Carbn-s** card-b a1 *Carl* k* castm **Caust** k* cedr *Cham* k* chel k* chen-a k* **Chin** k* *Chinin-ar* **Chinin-s** k* chlf k* chlol hr1 cic k* cimic cinch a1 *Cinnb* k* cit-v a1 clem k* cob-n sp1 coc-c k* coca *Cocc* k* coff k* coff-t a1 *Colch* k* *Coloc* k* *Con* k* cop croc k* crot-h hr1 crot-t k* cub a1 cupr k* cur a1 *Cycl* k* daph k* dig k* dirc k* *Dros* k* dulc k* *Elaps* k* euon k* euph k* falco-pe nl2• ferr k* ferr-ar *Ferr-i* k* ferr-p k* fl-ac bg2 *Gels* k* gran a1 **Graph** k* guare a1 *Hell* k* hell-v a1 helo-s bnm14• *Hep* k* hippoc-k szs2 hydr k* hydr-ac k* hyos k* hyper a1 iber a1* ign k* indg k* *Iod* k* jatr-c kali-ar kali-bi a1 kali-br k* *Kali-c* k* kali-chl k* kali-i k* kali-m k2 kali-n k* kali-p k* *Kali-s* kali-sil k2 kiss a1 *Kreos* k* lac-ac k* lac-c *Lach* k* lact k* lat-h bnm5• *Laur* k* *Led* k* lepi a1* lipp a1 lol a1 **Lyc** k* m-ambo b2.de m-arct b2.de* m-aust b2.de* *Mag-c* k* *Mag-m* k* mag-s a1 manc k* mang k* mela a1 meny k* *Merc* k* *Merc-c* k* merc-d bro1 merl mez k* morph k* mosch k* mur-ac k* murx bg2 narcot a1 nat-ar nat-c k* *Nat-m* k* *Nat-p* *Nat-s* nat-sal bro1 nat-sil fd3.de• nicc k* *Nit-ac* k* **Nux-v** k* ol-an k* olnd k* *Op* k* paeon k* paull a1 ped a1 *Petr* k* **Ph-ac** k* *Phos* k* pimp a1 pin-s a1 *Plat* k* plb k* plect a1 psor k* ptel k* **Puls** k* rheum k* *Rhod* k* rhus-t k* rumx ruta b2.de* sabad b2.de* *Sal-ac* k* sang k* *Sec* k* seneg k* *Sep* k* **Sil** k* sphing a1 **Spig** k* spong k* stann b2.de* *Staph* k* stram k* stront-c k* stry k* *Sul-ac* k* sul-i k2 **Sulph** k* symph fd3.de• tab k* tanac a1 tarent a1 tell hr1 tep k* ter teucr k* thea *Ther* k* thuj k* thymol sp1 til k* tritic-vg fd5.de vanil fd5.de verat k* *Verat-v* k* viol-o k* wies a1 zinc k* zinc-p k2 zinc-s a1
  - **right**: am-m k* bar-c k* castm caust k* cham a1 colch a1 con k* falco-pe nl2• mag-c k* merc-c k* mez a1 mur-ac k* nat-s nicc a1 ph-ac h2* phos k* plat h2* rheum sep h2* *Sil* stront-c vanil fd5.de
  - **left**: agar k* all-c hr1 ars a1 asar hr1 borx bov k* bry k* coc-c k* *Coloc* k* con h2* graph k* hep h2* hyper a1 lac-ac a1* lach a1 laur a1 mag-c a1 mag-s a1 mela a1 meny h1* *Nat-c* k* nat-m k* nit-ac h2* *Nux-v* hr1 paull a1 sal-ac sne sil h2* sul-ac a1 thuj k* tritic-vg fd5.de
  - **daytime**: calad hr1 caust h2* ph-ac k* sulph
  - **morning**: alum k* calc k* carbn-s lach a1 mag-m k* merc k* nat-s ph-ac k* plat k* ptel a1 tab k* vanil fd5.de
    - **bed** agg.; in: *Aur* k* mag-m a1 nat-m k*
    - **rising** agg.; after: alum calc k* nat-s *Nux-v* k*
    - **waking**; on: hyper k* lach a1
  - **forenoon**: vanil fd5.de
    - **11** h: mag-c
  - **afternoon**: all-c k* *Ambr* k* *Ant-c* k* cham k* lac-ac a1* mag-c a1 thuj a1
    - **15** h: elaps mag-c
    - **16** h: **Lyc**
    - **air**; when coming in from open: thuj
    - **rising** agg.: lac-ac k*
  - **evening**: alum k* alum-p k2 calc k* *Carbn-s* caust k* cinnb k* coc-c hr1 graph hydr k* lach a1 mag-c k* op k* ped a1 petr k* ph-ac k* plat k* plb k* ptel k* rhod hr1 spig k* sul-ac k* **Sulph** k* thuj k* vanil fd5.de
    - **19** h: mag-c
    - **21** h: hydr
    - **bed** agg.; in: hep h2 sulph h2
    - **waking**; on: hydr
  - **night**: am-c k* (non:chin slp) cinch a1* coc-c k* con k* elaps euph k* **Graph** k* *Hydr* k* *Kali-br* k* nicc k* nux-v k* sep k* *Sil* k* vanil fd5.de zinc
    - **waking**; on: con k* hydr k*
  - **air**; in open | **amel.**: *Cic* puls thuj
  - **alternating** with | **whistling** (See whistling - alternating - roaring)
  - **bed**; driving out of: mag-c h2*
  - **blowing** the nose agg.: meny k*
  - **boring** with finger in ear amel.: castm lach k*
  - **cattle**: thuj h1*
  - **coition**:
    - **after**: carb-v dig k*
    - **during**: graph
  - **cold**, from feet becoming: *Sil*
  - **convulsions**; after epileptic: *Caust*

- **coryza**; during: acon bg2 ars bg2 bell bg2 hep bg2 lach bg2 *Merc* bg2 nux-v bg2 **Puls** bg2 rhod b4.de* sep b4.de* sulph bg2
- **dinner**; after: cinnb con
- **eating**:
  - **after** | **agg.**: cinnb k* op k* sil k*
  - **before** | **agg.**: sil h2*
  - **while** | **agg.**: con k* sil
- **fever**:
  - **after**: lach b7a.de
  - **before**: ars b4a.de
  - **during** | **agg.**: *Ars* b4a.de* lach k* nat-m bg2 *Nux-v* b7.de* puls hr1
- **headache**; during: *Aur* bg1* borx a1 chen-a hr1 *Chin* bro1 *Chinin-s* bro1 ferr bro1 gels k* *Lyc* hr1 narcot a1 phos hr1 *Plat* hr1 puls hr1 sang bro1 *Sil* staph h1* sulfon bro1 vanil fd5.de
- **heat**; during: *Ars* k* *Nux-v* k*
- **holding** hand over eyes amel.: spig k*
- **inspiration** agg.: bar-c
- **jerking**: staph h1*
- **lying**:
  - **agg.**: con graph *Mag-c* merc plat **Sulph** vanil fd5.de
  - **amel.**: *Ph-ac* k*
  - **ear**; on the:
    - **agg.**: mag-m spong
    - **amel.**: phos
- **menses**:
  - **before** | **agg.**: borx
  - **during** | **agg.**: *Ars* borx k* chin b7a.de kreos k* *Petr* k* *Verat* k*
  - **suppressed** menses; from: graph
- **mental** exertion agg.: con k*
- **motion** agg.: nat-c k*
- **music** | **amel.**: ign bro1*
- **pain**:
  - **ear**; with pain in: petr h2*
  - **every** attack of; with: *Ars* lach
- **painful**: ant-c h2*
- **perspiration**; during: ars k* bell bg2 *Calc* bg2 *Caust* b4a.de* graph bg2 hep bg2 ign lyc bg2 m-aust b7.de **Nux-v** b7.de* puls bg2 sabad bg2 *Sep* bg2 **Sulph** bg2
- **reading** agg.: acon vanil fd5.de
- **rhythmical**: *Coloc* k* *Kali-br* k* sep k* *Sul-ac* k*
- **rising**:
  - **agg.**: acon *Phos*
  - **sitting**; from | **agg.**: verat
- **room** agg.; in: cic mag-c
- **sitting** agg.: con nat-m phos h2 sulph
- **sitting** up in bed | **amel.**: mag-c op
- **sneezing** agg.: mag-c
- **sound**; at every: coloc k* ol-an k*
- **stool**:
  - **painful** and bloody; with: kali-chl c1
  - **straining** at | **agg.**: lyc
- **stooping** | **after** | **agg.**: mang k*
  - **agg.**: croc
- **supper** agg.; after: canth k*
- **swallowing** | **amel.**: rheum
- **talking** agg.: nat-c k*
- **vertigo**; with: alco a1 *Bell* k* calc k* carb-v k* cocc crot-t k* gran k* hell k* nat-c k* *Op* k* petr k* *Phos* k* *Psor* k* puls b7a.de* sel b7a.de seneg a1 stry
- **walking** agg.: colch k* cycl k* ferr k* nat-m k*
- **waterfall**, on opening mouth during dinner; as from a: sul-ac
- **wind**; as if from: asar rb2 caust rb2 chel rb2 con rb2 croc rb2 led rb2 mag-c rb2 petr rb2 sulph rb2 verat rb2

- **roaring**: ...
  - **yawning** agg.: verat k*
- **rolling** sound: am-m b7.de* *Graph* k* *Plat* k*
  - **morning**: *Plat* k*
- **rubbing** | **amel.**: meny k*
- **rumbling**: (↗*thundering)* apis *Asar* bry k* chlf hr1 *Elaps* equis-h gast a1 merc hr1 *Plat* k* sel k* sep k* tarent a1 thuj a1
  - **left**: elaps gk
  - **evening** | **bed** agg.; in: sel k*
  - **foreign** body; as from a: ruta b7.de*
  - **tornado**, like a distant: *Asar* k*
- **running**; as of something: am-c b4.de*
- **rushing**: abrot k* *Acon* b7.de* agar k* *Agn* b7a.de alco a1 alum b4.de* am-c k* *Am-m* b7a.de ambr b7a.de anac b4.de* ant-t b7.de* *Arn* k* ars k* ars-s-f k2 asar b7.de* aster k* *Aur* k* aur-ar k2 aur-s k2 bar-c k* bell b4.de* bit-ar wht1• borx k* bov k* brom k* *Bry* b7.de* calc k* canth b7.de* *Carb-an* b4.de* *Carb-v* b4.de* carbn-s k2 caust k* cham b7.de* *Chel* k* chin b7.de* *Chinin-s* cinnb k* *Cocc* k* *Coloc* k* con k* croc b7a.de *Cupr* b7.de* cypra-eg sde6.de• dulc k* euph h2* (non:euphr slp) ferr b7.de* ferr-p bro1 *Gels* k* glon k* *Graph* k* ham fd3.de• hep k* hydr-ac *Hyos* k* *Iod* b4a.de kali-ar **Kali-c** k* kali-cy k* kali-n k* *Kali-p* *Kali-s* *Lach* k* lap-la sde8.de• *Led* k* lil-t k* **Lyc** k* lyss k* m-ambo b7.de m-aust b7.de mag-c k* mag-s k* mang k* merc k* merc-c b4a.de mez k* mosch k* mur-ac b4a.de* nat-ar nat-c k* **Nat-m** k* nat-p k* nat-sil fd3.de• **Nit-ac** k* nitro-o a1 nux-v k* op b7.de* ox-ac **Petr** k* **Phos** k* phyt k* pieri-b mlk9.de plat k* *Puls* k* rhod b4.de* rhus-r a1 rhus-t k* ruta b7.de* sec b7.de* *Sel* sep k* sil k* spig k* spong fd4.de stann k* staph stront-c b4.de* *Sul-ac* k* *Sulph* k* symph fd3.de• tab k* ther k* vanil fd5.de verat k* viol-o k* zinc b4.de*
  - **right**: brom a1 *Mag-c* bg1* nat-ar plat h2 spong fd4.de
  - **morning**: dulc k* merc k* spong fd4.de
  - **evening**: bar-c caust mag-c k* petr k* sep k* symph fd3.de•
  - **night**: am-c k* caust con k* euph k* ham fd3.de• lil-t k* nux-v k* ther k* vanil fd5.de
    - **midnight** | **lying** on the ear: am-c
  - **breathing** agg.: bar-c k2
  - **coition**; during: graph k*
  - **distant**: brom k*
  - **eructations** agg.: caust
  - **headache**; during: tub c1
  - **lying**:
    - **agg.**: agar con lil-t merc nat-m
    - **ear**; on the | **agg.**: am-c
  - **menses** | **before** | **agg.**: borx *Kreos* b7a.de verat b7.de
    - **during** | **agg.**: borx h2* kreos k*
  - **mental** exertion agg.: con k*
  - **rising** from sitting agg.: verat
  - **room** agg.: mag-c
  - **steam** escaping, like: glon k* sil
  - **synchronous** with pulse: bit-ar wht1• **Puls** k* sil spong fd4.de
  - **water**; as of: aster **Cham** k* *Cocc* k* kali-n kola stb3• mag-c mag-s nitro-o rb2 petr *Puls* k* rad-br ptk1 spong fd4.de ther ptk1
    - **16** h; after: *Puls*
  - **waterfall**; like a: ars k* aster aur bry k* cann-i k* caust k* chel k* chinin-s cob-n sp1 con k* lyss k* mag-c k* nat-p k* petr k* rhus-t k* sul-ac k* ther k*
    - **accompanied** by | **hearing**; impaired (See HEARING - Impaired - accompanied - noises - rushing)
    - **opening** the mouth agg.: sal-ac sul-ac k*
  - **wind**, rushing out of ears; sound of: abrot rb2 mosch rb2 sulph rb2
- **rustling**: aloe *Bell* borx brom k* carb-v k* caust cham h1* mang merc mosch a1 phos puls rhus-v a1 sil stann a1 ther viol-o
  - **bird**, like a: cham h1*
  - **blowing** the nose agg.: sil h2*
  - **motion** of lower jaw agg.: aloe carb-v
- **scratching** like a bird: cham b7.de*
- **shrieking**: ph-ac b4a.de stann b4.de*
  - **blowing** nose; on: ph-ac c1 stann

- **shuddering** (See trembling)
- **singing**: acon$_{k}$* am-m$_{k}$* arg-met arn$_{k}$* *Ars*$_{k}$* asar$_{k}$* atro$_{k}$* bell$_{k}$* bry cact$_{k}$* *Calc*$_{k}$* calc-p$_{k}$* calc-s$_{k}$* calth$_{br1}$ *Camph*$_{k}$* cann-i$_{k}$* cann-s$_{k}$* carb-v$_{b4.de}$* carbn-o *Carbn-s Caust*$_{k}$* cedr$_{k}$* cer-s$_{a1}$ cham$_{k2}$ chel$_{k}$* **Chin**$_{k}$* *Chinin-ar* chinin-s$_{bg2}$* chlf$_{k}$* chlor$_{k}$* cimic$_{k}$* coff$_{k}$* coff-t$_{a1}$ coloc$_{k}$* *Con*$_{k}$* cot$_{a1}$ croc cupr-act dig$_{bg2}$* erig$_{a1}$ ery-a$_{k}$* ferr$_{k}$* ferr-ar ferr-m ferr-p fl-ac$_{k}$* gast$_{a1}$ gels$_{psa}$ gink-b$_{sbd1}$• glon$_{k}$* *Graph*$_{k}$* *Hyos*$_{k}$* iod$_{b4a.de}$ kali-bi$_{k}$* **Kali-c**$_{k}$* kali-i$_{k}$* kali-m$_{k2}$ *Kali-p* lac-ac$_{k}$* *Lach*$_{k}$* lachn$_{k}$* linu-c$_{a1}$ *Lyc*$_{k}$* mag-m$_{b4a.de}$ merc-i-r$_{k}$* morg-g$_{pte1}$*• mur-ac$_{k}$* nat-ar *Nat-c*$_{k}$* nat-m$_{k}$* nat-p *Nit-ac*$_{b4a.de}$ nitro-o$_{a1}$ *Nux-v*$_{k}$* ol-an$_{k}$* olib-sac$_{wmh1}$ olnd$_{k}$* onos op$_{k}$* pen$_{a1}$ petr$_{k}$* petros$_{hr1}$ ph-ac$_{k}$* phel$_{k}$* phos$_{k}$* phys$_{k}$* *Psor*$_{k}$* ptel$_{c1}$ puls$_{bro1}$ rhus-t$_{k}$* *Sang*$_{k}$* sec$_{k}$* sep$_{k}$* *Stram*$_{k}$* sul-ac$_{b4a.de}$ sul-i$_{k}$* sulph$_{b4a.de}$ sumb$_{k}$* ter$_{k}$* thuj$_{a1}$ verb vichy-g$_{a1}$ [heroin$_{sdj2}$]
  - • **right**: arn$_{a1}$ asar$_{k}$* calc-p$_{k}$* cer-s$_{a1}$ erig$_{a1}$ lach$_{a1}$ lachn$_{k}$* *Nat-c*$_{k}$* phel$_{a1}$ sumb$_{a1}$ visc$_{c1}$
  - • **left**: bry cann-i$_{a1}$ cot$_{a1}$ ery-a$_{a1}$* lac-ac$_{a1}$* lachn$_{a1}$ linu-c$_{a1}$ nat-m$_{h2}$* ol-an$_{a1}$ olnd$_{h1}$* tarent
  - • **morning**: phel$_{k}$*
  - • **afternoon**:
    - ⁝ **17** h: ol-an
    - ⁝ **walking** in open air agg.: lachn
  - • **evening**: linu-c$_{a1}$ merc-i-r$_{k}$* sumb$_{k}$*
  - • **night**: mur-ac$_{k}$* nux-v$_{k}$*
    - ⁝ **lying** down agg.; after: *Phys*$_{k}$*
  - • **closing** the eyes agg.: chel$_{k}$*
  - • **locusts**, like: nux-v$_{k}$* rhus-t$_{k}$*
  - • **lying** agg.: cann-i$_{k}$* ph-ac$_{k}$* *Phos*$_{k}$*
  - • **menses**:
    - ⁝ **after** | **agg.**: *Chin*$_{k}$* *Ferr*$_{k}$*
    - ⁝ **before** | **agg.**: ferr$_{k}$*
    - ⁝ **during** | **agg.**: petr$_{k}$*
  - • **periodical**: *Cann-i*$_{k}$*
  - • **resting** head on table amel.: ferr$_{k}$*
  - • **sitting** agg.: ars
  - • **steam** escaping: phys$_{k}$*
  - • **teakettle**, like a: *Lach* tarent
  - • **vertigo**; with: *Camph*$_{k}$* *Sang*$_{k}$* stram
  - • **walking** in open air agg.: lachn$_{k}$*
- **sitting** agg.: am-m ars bell con lap-la$_{sde8.de}$• mag-s merc-cy nat-c nat-m op sulph tritic-vg$_{fd5.de}$ vanil$_{fd5.de}$
- **sleep**; when falling asleep: dig$_{k}$* zinc
- **slipping**; as of something: cham$_{b7.de}$*
- **snapping**: ambr$_{k}$* aq-pet$_{a1}$ ars-s-f$_{k2}$ bar-c borx *Dulc*$_{k}$* *Graph*$_{k}$* hep$_{k}$* *Kali-c* kali-m$_{k2}$ lac-ac$_{k}$* (non:puls$_{slp}$) puls-n$_{slp}$ tarent$_{k}$*
  - • **evening**: tarent$_{k}$*
  - • **blowing** the nose agg.: hep
  - • **electric** sparks, like: ambr$_{k}$* *Calc*$_{k}$* dulc *Hep*$_{k}$* rheum sabad
  - • **eructation**, after every: *Graph*$_{k}$*
  - • **opening** the mouth agg.: dulc$_{k}$*
  - • **swallowing** agg.: bar-c
  - • **synchronous** with pulse: ars-s-r
  - • **turning** head agg.: *Caust*$_{k}$*
- **sneezing** agg.: bar-c$_{k}$* bar-m$_{ptk1}$ bry$_{a1}$ euph$_{k}$* graph$_{k}$* mag-c spong$_{fd4.de}$
- **squashing**: borx$_{b4a.de}$ calc$_{b4.de}$* mang$_{b4a.de}$
  - • **swallowing** agg.: **Calc**
  - • **yawning** agg.: mang$_{atr}$
- **squeaking**: *(↗mice - twittering)* eup-pur lyc$_{b4.de}$* teucr$_{b7.de}$
- **standing** | **amel.**: bell$_{k}$*
- **startling**: mill$_{k2}$
- **steam** escaping, like: caust chinin-s$_{sne}$ glon$_{k}$* lach$_{k}$* phys$_{k}$* tarent
- **stool** | **after** | **agg.**: apoc$_{k}$* calc-p$_{k}$*
  - • **during** | **agg.**: *Con*$_{hr1}$ lyc$_{k}$* spong$_{fd4.de}$
- **stooping** agg.: croc$_{k}$* *Graph*$_{bg1}$* *Mang*$_{bg1}$* spong$_{fd4.de}$
- **stretched** sounds: musca-d$_{szs1}$
- **stupefying**, stunning noise: bar-c$_{h2}$* olnd$_{b7.de}$*
- **swallowing**:
  - • **agg.**: agar alum ars *Bar-c*$_{k}$* bar-m benz-ac$_{k}$* *Calc*$_{k}$* *Cic*$_{k}$* coc-c coca *Elaps Eup-pur* graph hep kali-chl kali-i kali-s$_{fd4.de}$ lepi mag-c mang nat-m rhod sil thuj
  - • **amel.**: rheum
- **swashing**: androc$_{srj1}$• ant-c$_{b7a.de}$* calc$_{b4.de}$ graph$_{ptk1}$ mang$_{bg2}$ merc$_{ptk1}$ sarr$_{k}$* spig$_{k}$* **Sulph**$_{k}$*
  - • **motion** of lower jaw agg.: ant-c
- **swishing** (See hissing)
- **synchronous** with pulse●: am-m ars-s-r$_{hr1}$ benz-ac$_{hr1}$ *Bufo*$_{hr1}$ carl$_{a1}$ chen-a$_{c1}$* coff$_{k}$* coloc glon$_{kr1}$ kali-br$_{k}$* lyc$_{gk}$ merc$_{h1}$* (non:merc-c$_{k}$*) **Nux-v**$_{k}$ ●* op$_{h1}$* **Puls**$_{k}$ ●* pyrog$_{ptk2}$ **Rhus-t**$_{k}$ ● sarr$_{a1}$ **Sep**$_{k}$ ●* sil$_{k}$* spong$_{fd4.de}$ sul-ac urol-h$_{rwt}$•
- **talking** agg.: nat-c$_{k}$* op$_{k}$* sars$_{hr1}$ spig$_{k}$* teucr$_{k}$* vanil$_{fd5.de}$
- **teething**, while (See dentition)
- **throbbing** (See pulsating)
- **thundering**: *(↗rumbling)* am-m$_{k}$* *Calc*$_{k}$* carbn-o caust$_{b4.de}$* chel$_{k}$* *Graph*$_{k}$* *Lach* lob$_{bg2}$ mosch$_{bg2}$ ol-an petr *Plat*$_{k}$* rhod sil
  - • **morning**: *Plat*
  - • **night**: am-m$_{k}$*
  - • **sitting** agg.: am-m$_{k}$*
- **ticking** sound: bell$_{bg2}$ *Chin*$_{k}$* *Graph*$_{k}$* mag-s$_{k}$* nat-m$_{k}$* petr$_{k}$* sil$_{bg2}$ ter$_{k}$* zinc-val$_{bg2}$
  - • **evening**: nat-m$_{k}$*
- **tick**-tack sound: calad gad$_{k}$*
- **tinkling**: agn aloe am-c am-m atro$_{k}$* bar-c bell$_{k}$* berb carb-v *Caust*$_{k}$* cham chin *Con* ferr graph hippoz$_{hr1}$ kali-c kali-m$_{k2}$ lyc mag-c$_{k}$* meny mur-ac$_{k}$* nat-m nat-s$_{k}$* nux-v ol-an olnd op par petr *Puls*$_{k}$* sars$_{k}$* stann staph sulph ter valer viol-o
- **touch**, unexpected: mag-c$_{c1}$
- **trembling** sounds: sabin$_{b7.de}$*
  - • **right**: bit-ar$_{wht1}$•
- **trumpets**, din like: bell$_{k}$* chin-b$_{hr1}$ gast$_{a1}$
- **turning** head agg.: *(↗motion - head)* *Caust*$_{k}$* nat-c$_{k}$*
- **twanging**:
  - • **harp** string; a: lyc sulph
  - • **wire**; a loose: phel
- **twittering** (See chirping)
- **valve** were opening and shutting; as if a (See opening - valve)
- **vertigo**:
  - • **before**: chin$_{bg}$ lachn sep
  - • **with** (See VERTIGO - Accompanied - ear - noises)
- **vibrating** sounds: bell$_{b4.de}$ con$_{b4.de}$ dulc$_{b4.de}$ laur$_{b7.de}$ merc-c$_{b4a.de}$ *Olnd*$_{b7.de}$* petr$_{b4.de}$* phos$_{b4.de}$ *Plat*$_{b4.de}$* *Rhod*$_{b4.de}$* sel$_{b7a.de}$ spig$_{b7.de}$ spong$_{b7.de}$ zinc$_{b4.de}$
- **voices**; as if confused: benz-ac$_{ptk1}$ ulm-c$_{jsj8}$•
- **waking**; on: *Ars*$_{hr1}$ bell$_{k}$* con$_{k}$* hydr$_{k}$* hyper$_{a1}$ lach$_{k}$* lap-la$_{sde8.de}$• naja nat-m$_{k}$* puls$_{k}$* rat$_{k}$* rhod$_{k}$* tarent$_{k}$*
  - • **start**; with a: dig zinc
- **walking**:
  - • **agg.**: bar-c chel colch cycl ferr manc mang meny nat-m nicc rhus-t spig verb$_{c1}$
  - • **air** agg.; in open: agar carb-an lachn
  - • **amel.**: bell cop
  - • **rapidly** | **agg.**: bar-c
- **warbling**, of birds: bell$_{k}$* bry$_{k}$*
- **warm** room agg.: ars cic$_{k}$* mag-c$_{k}$* *Ph-ac*$_{hr1}$ thuj
- **watch**; like when winding a: ambr
- **water**:
  - • **boiling**; sound of: bry$_{k}$* cann-i cann-xyz$_{bg2}$ chlf$_{rb2}$ dig$_{k}$* lyc$_{bg2}$* m-ambo$_{b7.de}$ m-arct$_{b7.de}$ sulph$_{k}$* thuj$_{k}$*
  - • **in** the ear; as if water were: adam$_{skp7}$• nit-ac spong$_{fd4.de}$
- **waterfalls** (See rushing - waterfall)
- **wheezing**: sang$_{bg2}$
- **whimpering**: ant-c$_{b7a.de}$
- **whirling**: calc$_{b4.de}$* kali-c lact lyc meny$_{b7.de}$* merc-c$_{k}$* nux-v$_{k}$* puls$_{k}$*
  - • **evening** | **bed** agg.; in: lact

Ear

- **rhythmical**: merc-c a1*
- **whispering**: am-c dulc med hr1 rhod k*
  - **morning**: dulc
  - **evening**: rhod k*
- **whistling**: aeth k* alum k* *Ambr* k* aur k* bell k* borx b4a.de* carb-an k* caust k* chel k* chin-b hr1* cur k* dulc fd4.de elaps ferr k* ferul a1 graph ham fd3.de• hep k* hura ina-i mlk9.de kali-s fd4.de kola stb3• kreos lap-la sde8.de• lyc k* m-ambo b7.de mag-c k* manc k* merc k* mur-ac k* nat-sil fd3.de• *Nux-v* k* podo fd3.de• puls k* ros-d wla1 ruta fd4.de sarr k* sars sep k* sil k* spong fd4.de symph fd3.de• teucr k* vanil fd5.de verat k* vinc k* zinc
  - **right**: chin-b hr1 dulc fd4.de ham fd3.de• *Hep* h2 kali-s fd4.de lap-la rsp1 mur-ac h2* podo fd3.de• puls a1 tell rsj10• verat a1 [tax jsj7]
  - **left**: caust h2* dulc fd4.de lap-la rsp1 nat-sil fd3.de• ruta fd4.de thres-a sze7• vinc hr1
    - **followed** by | **right**: plut-n srj7•
  - **forenoon**: ham fd3.de• hura vanil fd5.de
    - **9** h: hura
  - **afternoon**: *Ambr* k* dulc fd4.de kali-s fd4.de spong fd4.de vanil fd5.de
  - **evening**: dulc fd4.de ham fd3.de• lyc k* sep k* symph fd3.de• vanil fd5.de
  - **alternating** with:
    - **buzzing**: mag-c k*
    - **roaring**: mag-c
  - **blowing** the nose agg.: carb-an k* hep k* lyc k* ozone sde2• ph-ac spong fd4.de
  - **light**; from: lap-la rsp1
  - **walking** agg.: manc k*
  - **writing** agg.: sep k*
- **whistling**, while: op k* ped a1
- **whizzing**: agar alum k* alum-p k2 alum-sil k2 am-c *Arg-n* k* bar-m bro1 bell k* berb k* brom calc calc-sil k2 *Caust* k* chel *Hep* k* hura kali-c k* kali-m k2* kali-p kali-s kreos ptk1 *Lach* k* laur k* led k* **Lyc** k* *Mag-c* k* *Mang* k* merc k* mim-h a1 mosch ptk1 *Mur-ac* k* naja nat-c k* nat-p nicc nit-ac k* nux-m ptk1 nux-v hr1 olnd k* op ptk1 ped a1 **Petr** k* ph-ac k* phos k* *Plat* k* plb k* podo fd3.de• puls ptk1 rhod bro1 rhus-t sang k* sep k* sil sol-t-ae a1 sphing a1* spig h1* spong fd4.de sul-ac *Sulph* k* tab tarent k* thuj k* zinc k* zinc-p k2
  - **daytime**: ph-ac k*
  - **morning**: plat k*
  - **forenoon** | **11** h: mag-c
  - **evening**: ph-ac k* spig h1* sul-ac zinc k*
    - **lying** down agg.; after: plat k*
    - **writing** agg.: sep k*
  - **night**: am-c podo fd3.de•
    - **bed** amel.; while in: phos plat
  - **blowing** the nose agg.: hep
  - **painful**: kola stb3•
- **wind**, sound of: abrot k* am-c *Bar-c* h2* bell h1* calc carbn-s *Chel* k* con bg2 dulc bg2 ign laur bg2 *Led* k* mag-c k* mosch k* olnd bg2 **Petr** k* *Phos* k* plat k* *Puls* k* rhod bg2 *Sep* k* spig k* spong bg2 stry a1 sulph k* verat h1* vinc zinc bg2
  - **afternoon**: mag-c k* puls k*
  - **night**: sep k*
  - **noise** agg.: plat k*
  - **storm**: caust h2 con h2 mag-c h2
  - **tree**; in: visc c1
  - **whirlwind**: croc k*
- **wings**; of (See fluttering - bird)
- **writing** agg.: carl k* dulc fd4.de sep k*
- **yawning** agg.: acon cocc k* mang k* mez k* verat k*

NUMBNESS: agar bg2 bros-gau mrc1 calc-i k* carb-ac hr1 fl-ac k* gels k* irid-met k* lach k* mag-c bg2* manc k* nux-m *Plat* k* sarr a1 sulph thuj k* *Verb* k*
- **left**: arizon-l nl2• tarax thuj *Verb*
- ○ **About** ear: calad hr1 *Fl-ac* k* lach k*
- **Behind** the ears: ox-ac bg2*
  - **teeth** together; on pressing: all-s vh1
- **Conchae**: lach k*

Numbness: ...
- **Front** of ears; in: sulph
- **Mastoid**; in: **Plat**
- **Meatus**: lach mur-ac k*

OBSTRUCTION (See Stopped)

ODORS: *Aur* bg2 *Borx* bg2 **Carb-v** bg2 graph k* *Hep* bg2 olnd bg2 **Psor** bg2
- **offensive**: *Calc* ptk1 carb-v ptk1 *Caust* ptk1 *Graph* b4a.de hep ptk1 kali-p ptk1 nat-c ptk1 **Psor** ptk1 *Sil* ptk1 *Sulph* ptk1 thuj ptk1
  - ○ **Behind** the ears: olnd b7a.de
  - **Margin**: *Ars* b4a.de *Carb-v* b4a.de sulph b4a.de
- ○ **Behind** the ears: *Olnd* bg2

OPEN; meatus seems: aur-m mez k*
- **morning**: mez

OPENING, sensation of: mez bg2 vero-o rly4•
- **air** penetrates on opening and closing the mouth; through which the: (↗*Air - sensation - out*) thuj
- **closing** like a valve; and: *Am* bg2 *Bar-c* k* borx k* goss st1 *Graph* k* *Iod* k* iris-foe a1 *Nat-s* k* *Psor* k* ruta bg2 verat bg2 xan bg1 xanth bg2
  - **stepping** | **every** step; at: graph
- ▽ **extending** to | **Ear** to ear: alet bg2*

OPENING THE MOUTH:
- **agg.**: dulc bg2 sul-ac b4.de* thuj bg2
- **amel.**: nat-c b4.de*

OPERATION; complaints after: | **Mastoid**: caps ptk1

OTITIS; external (See Inflammation - external)

OTORRHEA (See Discharges)

OTOSCLEROSIS: med jl2 syph jl2

PAIN (= otalgia): *Acon* k* acon-ac ↓ act-sp aesc aeth agar agath-a nl2• aids ↓ ail *All-c* k* allox sp1 aln ↓ aloe alum alum-p ↓ alum-sil k2 alumn ↓ am-c am-m am-pic ↓ ambr aml-ns ↓ *Anac* anac-oc ↓ anag hr1 anan ↓ androc ↓ *Ang* k* anh sp1 *Ant-c* k* ant-t anthraq ↓ antip bro1 *Apis* k* apoc ↓ aran k* arg-met *Arg-n* arge-pl rwt5• arist-cl sp1 arizon-l ↓ *Arn* *Ars* k* ars-i ars-s-f k2 arum-d a1 arum-t arund k* asaf k* *Asar* astac ↓ aster ↓ *Aur* aur-ar k2 aur-i ↓ aur-m aur-m-n aur-s k2 *Bamb-a* stb2.de• *Bapt* ↓ *Bar-c* bar-i ↓ *Bar-m* bar-s ↓ **Bell** k* benz-ac ↓ berb beryl tpw5 bism k* *Borx* k* bov k* brach k* brom k* bros-gau mrc1 bry k* bufo ↓ cact cadm-met tpw6 cadm-s calad k* *Calc* k* calc-caust ↓ calc-f calc-i k2 *Calc-p* k* *Calc-s* calc-sil ↓ camph k* canch ↓ *Cann-i* k* cann-s cann-xyz ↓ canth *Caps* k* carb-ac hr1 carb-an *Carb-v* k* *Carbn-s* carc ↓ card-m hr1 cardios-h rly4• carl k* cassia-s ccrh1• castm *Caust* k* celt ↓ cench ↓ **Cham** k* *Chel* k* chim hr1 chim-m hr1 chin k* chinin-ar chinin-s k* chlf k* *Chr-ac* hr1 cic k* *Cimic* k* *Cina* ↓ cinnb k* cist hr1 cit-v a1 clem k* cob k* coc-c k* coff bro1 colch k* coli ↓ coloc k* colum-p sze2• com con k* *Cop* ↓ cortico sp1 croc k* crot-c ↓ crot-h k* crot-t k* *Cupr* k* cupr-ar k* *Cur* k* cycl k* cystein-l rly4• daph ↓ der k* des-ac ↓ desm-g bnj1 dig k* dios k* diph-pert-t mp4• dol hr1 *Dros* k* *Dulc* k* echi ↓ elaps ery-a k* erythr-ca bta1• euph k* euphr k* eupi k* fago k* falco-pe ↓ ferr k* ferr-ar ferr-i k* ferr-m ferr-ma a1 ferr-p k* ferr-s hr1 *Fl-ac* k* *Form* k* gamb k* gast a1 *Gels* k* genist a1 gent-c a1 gink-b sbd1• glon k* gran a1 granit-m ↓ *Graph* k* grat a1 *Guaj* k* guare ↓ haliae-lc srj5• ham k* hed sp1 hell k* hell-f a1 helo ↓ helo-s ↓ **Hep** k* hir ↓ hist sp1 hura hydr k* hydr-ac ↓ hydrc a1 hydrog ↓ hyos k* hyper k* ign k* ina-i ↓ indg k* inul a1* iod k* iodof a1* ip k* irid-met srj5• iris ↓ iris-fl ↓ jac-c ↓ jatr-c jug-r a1 kali-ar *Kali-bi* k* *Kali-c* k* kali-chl k* kali-i k* kali-m bg* kali-n k* *Kali-p* *Kali-s* kali-sil k2 *Kalm* k* ketogl-ac ↓ kola ↓ kreos k* lac-ac k* lac-c k* **Lach** k* lachn a1* lact k* lap-la sde8.de• lat-m sp1 laur k* led ↓ lepi a1 lil-t k* limen-b-c mlk9.de lipp a1 lith-c lob k* lob-e c1 lob-s k* luna kg1• **Lyc** k* lycps-v ↓ lyss k* m-ambo b7.de m-arct ↓ m-aust ↓ mag-c k* mag-m k* *Mag-p* k* mag-s k* *Mang* k* marb-w ↓ med k* melal-alt ↓ menth ↓ mentho bro1 meny hr1 meph k* **Merc** k* merc-c k* *Merc-d* ↓ *Merc-i-f* k* *Merc-i-r* k* merc-sul ↓ merl k* *Mez* k* *Mill* k* mim-p ↓ mit a1 morph k* mosch k* mucs-nas rly4• *Mur-ac* k* muru a1 murx hr1 musca-d ↓ nad ↓ naja bro1 nat-ar nat-c k* *Nat-m* k* nat-n a1* *Nat-p* k* nat-pyru rly4• *Nat-s* k* nat-sil ↓ neon srj5• nept-m ↓ nicc k* nicotam rly4• *Nit-ac* k* nit-s-d a1 nux-m k* *Nux-v* k* oci-sa sp1 ol-an a1* ol-j olib-sac ↓ olnd k* onis a1 op k* oscilloc ↓ osm k* ost a1 ox-ac k* ozone ↓ paeon a1 pall a1* par k* paull a1 *Petr* k* petr-ra shn4• **Ph-ac** k* *Phel* k* **Phos** k* phys k* phyt k* pic-ac a1* pin-con oss2• pin-s a1 pip-m a1 plac-s rly4• *Plan* k* *Plat* k* *Plb* k* plect a1 plumbg a1 pneu jl2 podo ↓ positr ↓ pot-e rly4• *Propl* ub1• prot jl2 prun k* *Psor* k* ptel k* **Puls** k* pycnop-sa ↓ pyrid rly4• pyrog ↓ ran-b a1*

Pain: ...
ran-s k* raph k* rat ↓ rheum ↓ *Rhod* k* rhodi ↓ rhodi-o-n c2 *Rhus-t* k* rhus-v ↓ ribo rly4• rob ↓ *Ros-d* ↓ rumx ruta k* sabad k* sabin k* sacch-a ↓ sal-ac a1* sal-fr ↓ samb k* *Sang* k* sanguis-s hrn2• sarr k* **Sars** k* sec hr1 sel ↓ seneg k* *Sep* k* *Sil* k* *Sphing* ↓ *Spig* k* *Spong* k* squil *Stann* staph stram k* streptoc jl2 stront-c stry ↓ suis-em rly4• suis-hep rly4• suis-pan ↓ sul-ac k* sul-i ↓ **Sulph** suprar rly4• symph ↓ syph k* tab tarax tarent k* tax ↓ tell tep ↓ ter hr1* tere-la ↓ teucr k* *Thuj* til trios ↓ tritic-vg fd5.de trom *Tub* k* tub-a ih tung-met ↓ upa ↓ ust v-a-b ↓ valer k* vanil fd5.de verat **Verb** k* vero-o rly4*• vesp ↓ viol-o bro1 viol-t ↓ visc c2* xan xanth *Zinc* k* zinc-p k2 zing [bell-p-sp dcm1 spect dfg1]

- **one** side: alum ↓ cham ↓ chin ↓ ign ↓
  - **burning**: alum bg2 cham bg2 chin bg2 ign bg2
- **alternating** sides: ang ↓ aphis ↓ nit-ac ↓
  - **drawing** pain: ang vh1
  - **pressing** pain | **plug**; as from a: nit-ac
  - **tearing** pain: aphis c1
- **right**: acon sne acon-ac ↓ aeth agar ↓ *Agath-a* nl2• aids nl2• all-c ↓ aln ↓ am-c ↓ *Am-m* ambr amp ↓ anag hr1 ant-c ↓ anthraq rly4• aran ↓ arg-n ars-s-f k2 arum-t ↓ asaf k* aur-m *Aur-m-n* wbt2• bamb-a stb2.de• *Bar-c* *Bar-m* bar-s k2 **Bell** k* berb bov ↓ brom k* bros-gau ↓ brucel ↓ bry calc-p ↓ cann-i a1 *Canth* ↓ carb-an ↓ *Carb-v* hr1 **Carbn-s** ↓ carc ↓ card-m hr1 cassia-s ↓ *Caust* chel k* chim k* chim-m hr1 chin choc ↓ clem ↓ coc-c ↓ cocc hr1 colch k* *Coloc* con ↓ crot-c ↓ cupr cupr-ar ↓ *Cycl* k* dios a1 dros k* dulc fd4.de *Echi* vh *Elaps* euphr h2* eupi k* fago a1 ferr ↓ ferr-p a1* **Fl-ac** k* flav jl2 form hr1 galla-q-r ↓ gamb ↓ gels k* germ-met srj5• gink-b sbd1• *Glon* a1* ham a1 hell a1 helo-s rwt2• hir skp7• hura hydr a1 hydrog srj2• hyper k* ina-i ↓ iod ↓ ip h1 *Kali-c* k* kali-i ↓ kali-n ↓ kali-s fd4.de kali-sil k2 *Kalm* k* ketogl-ac ↓ kola stb3• kreos ↓ *Lac-c* k* lac-h ↓ lach k* laur ↓ lipp a1 *Lyc* k* lycps-v ↓ lyss a1* mag-c k* mag-m k* mag-p ↓ mang ↓ med ↓ melal-alt gya4 *Merc* k* merc-i-f k* merc-i-r c1 mez ↓ mim-p ↓ mit ↓ mosch ↓ mur-ac k* mygal ↓ myos-a ↓ nat-c ↓ nat-m ↓ nat-n a1 nat-p k2 *Nat-s* k* nicc ↓ nicotam ↓ **Nit-ac** k* *Nux-v* ozone sde2• paeon a1 petr k* petr-ra shn4• phys a1 phyt ↓ plac-s ↓ plat ↓ plb ↓ podo ↓ positr ↓ pot-e ↓ propr ↓ prun k* psor k* *Puls* k* pycnop-sa ↓ ran-b k2 ran-s a1 raph ↓ rat a1* rhod ↓ rhus-t ↓ rosm ↓ ruta fd4.de sabad ↓ sacch-a fd2.de• sal-al blc1• sal-fr ↓ samb h1* sanguis-s hm2• sars ↓ seneg k* sep k* sil ↓ spig ↓ spong fd4.de stann ↓ staph ↓ stram ↓ stront-c suis-hep ↓ suis-pan ↓ sulph k* symph fd3.de• syph al* tab taosc iwa1• tarent k* tax ↓ *Tell* k* ter hr1 thuj til ↓ trios ↓ tritic-vg fd5.de trom ↓ tung-met bdx1• urol-h rwt• vanil fd5.de verat ↓ verb vero-o rly4*• vesp ↓ zinc ↓ zing ↓ [bell-p-sp dcm1]
  - **accompanied** by:
    - ⁝ **Head**:
      - ⁝ **pain** | **right** (See HEAD - Pain - sides - right - accompanied - ear - pain - right)
  - **aching**: asaf k* berb k* brom k* choc srj3• crot-c sk4• euphr a1 ham k* hell a1 hydrog srj2• ip h1 ketogl-ac rly4• lac-c al lach hr1 merc-i-r a1* mit a1 mygal hr1 myos-a rly4• nat-p k* nicotam rly4• petr-ra shn4• plac-s rly4• plat h2* podo c1 psor k* pycnop-sa mrz1 ran-s a1 rhod hr1 suis-hep rly4• suis-pan rly4• [bell-p-sp dcm1]
  - **biting** pain: plat bg2
  - **boring** pain: am-m bar-c cann-i carb-an carbn-s caust chel colch coloc cupr-ar gels hell mag-m mez nicc plb stann stront-c
  - **burning**: am-c arum-t k* bov calc-p k* carb-an carb-v chel k* cycl k* dros k* ham k* lycps-v lyss k* mag-c k* merc a1 nat-m k* nat-p k* sabad k*
  - **burrowing**: am-m k* hell k*
  - **cramping**: petr h2 samb stann thuj
  - **cutting** pain: rosm lgb1 trios rsj11•
  - **digging** pain: am-m k* colch k* *Gels* k* nat-m h2* plat h2
  - **drawing** pain: ant-c aur-m bry *Caust* coc-c *Cycl* dros dulc fd4.de gamb glon ina-i mlk9.de lac-h sk4• mosch nat-m nit-ac petr h2 podo fd3.de• sep sil spong
  - **dull** pain: propr sa3•
  - **gnawing** pain: mur-ac k* tab k*
  - **lacerating**: tarent k*
  - **lying** on it amel.: *Lach*
  - **neuralgic**: mag-p bg2
  - **piercing** pain: bros-gau mrc1 glon k* *Nat-s* k*
- **right**: ...
  - **pinching** pain: nat-c thuj
  - **pressing** pain: acon-ac rly4• aran hr1 asaf a1 berb k* brucel sa3• chel k* chim-m hr1 *Dros* hr1 dulc fd4.de eupi k* fl-ac a1 glon a1 ham fd3.de• hyper iod a1 kola stb3• kreos a1 lach a1 laur a1 lyss a1* mur-ac k* nat-s k* plac-s rly4• podo fd3.de• positr nl2• pot-e rly4• prun k* rhod k* seneg k* spong fd4.de symph fd3.de• vanil fd5.de verat k* [tax jsj7]
  - **pulled** out; as if: nat-m bg2
  - **pulsating** pain: cassia-s ccrh1•
  - ○ **Round** back of head to left ear: helo-s rwt2•
  - **stitching** pain: acon *Aeth* agar all-c aln vva1• amp rly4• **Bell** lp brom **Carbn-s** carc fd2.de• *Caust* clem h2 dros dulc fd4.de *Echi* vh ferr ferr-p galla-q-r nl2• gink-b sbd1• glon ham fd3.de• hell hyper ina-i mlk9.de kali-n h2 kali-s fkr2.de kalm kreos lac-h sk4• *Lyc* lyss med mim-p skp7• nat-c nat-m *Nat-s* nit-ac ozone sde2• phys phyt podo fd3.de• ran-b k2 raph rat rhus-t ruta fd4.de sal-fr sle1• samb xxb1 sars sep spong fd4.de staph symph fd3.de• tarent thuj trom vanil fd5.de vesp zinc
  - **tearing** pain: aeth agar am-m ambr arg-n bamb-a stb2.de• cann-i *Canth* carb-v con cupr eupi iod *Kali-c* kali-i *Lyc* lyss mang plb rat rhod sars spig stram stront-c tab *Tarent* til zing
  - **then** left: *Arg-n* ↓ bar-c bell ↓ calc hr1 cassia-s ccrh1• laur ↓ *Lyc* merc-i-f hr1 propr sa3• sulph ↓
    - ⁝ **pinching** pain: bell
    - ⁝ **pressing** pain: bar-c k*
    - ⁝ **stitching** pain: *Arg-n* laur sulph
    - ⁝ **extending** to | **Head**; back of: helo-s rwt2•
  - **twinging**: anag k* arg-n coloc dulc k* form a1 kreos k*
    - ⁝ **followed** by | **left**: visc c1
  - **writing** agg.: phys a1*
  - **yawning** agg.: ozone sde2•
  - ▽ **extending** to:
    - ⁝ **left**: arn bg1 *Ars* vh helo br1 laur ↓ sulph ↓
      - ⁝ **tearing** pain: laur sulph
    - ⁝ **External** throat; pain in: propr sa3•
  - ○ **External**: dros ↓
    - ⁝ **pecking** | **burning**; and: dros h1
- **left**: *Abel* ↓ acon k* acon-ac ↓ aesc ↓ agar ↓ agath-a nl2• aids ↓ am-c ↓ anac ↓ androc srj1• ang ↓ ant-c ↓ apis ↓ arg-met ↓ arge-pl rwt5• arn ↓ *Ars* ↓ arum-t ↓ arund hr1 asaf k* asc-c ↓ aur ↓ aur-m ↓ bamb-a stb2.de• bar-c ↓ bell sne bism ↓ *Borx* ↓ bry ↓ calad ↓ calc ↓ calen k* camph k* canth ↓ carb-ac ↓ carb-an ↓ carb-v ↓ carbn-s ↓ carc ↓ cassia-s ccrh1• caust ↓ cench k2 chel ↓ choc ↓ cob a1* coc-c ↓ coch k* colch ↓ coli ↓ con ↓ cop ↓ *Crot-t* hr1 dig ↓ dros ↓ *Dulc* k* elaps ↓ erig ery-a euphr h2* eupi a1 fago a1 fl-ac a1 form k* gard-j ↓ gast ↓ genist a1 gran a1 *Graph* k* grat a1 guaj k* ham ↓ hir ↓ *Hydrog* ↓ hydroph rsj6• hyper a1 ina-i ↓ indg a1 inul a1* iodof ↓ irid-met srj5• jac-c ↓ jug-r ↓ **Kali-bi** ↓ kali-i ↓ kali-n ↓ kali-p ↓ kali-s ↓ ketogl-ac ↓ kola stb3• kreos ↓ *Lac-c* k* lac-h ↓ lach k* laur ↓ lavand-a ↓ limen-b-c ↓ lob a1 lob-s a1 luf-op ↓ mag-c h2* mag-m ↓ mag-s k* mang k* med ↓ merc h1* merc-c ↓ merc-d ↓ merc-i-f a1* merl ↓ mez k* mill ↓ morph a1 mucs-nas rly4• mur-ac k* muru a1 nad rly4• nat-c h2 nat-m k* nat-pyru ↓ nat-sil ↓ neon srj5• nept-m ↓ nicc ↓ nit-s-d a1 olib-sac ↓ olnd ↓ ost a1 osteo-a ↓ ozone ↓ pall ↓ petr k* petr-ra shn4• plac-s ↓ plan a1 plat ↓ plumbg ↓ plut-n srj7• podo ↓ positr nl2• propl ub1• prun a1 psor ↓ ptel ↓ puls h1* pyrid ↓ rhod ↓ rhus-t ↓ rob a1 ruta fd4.de sabad ↓ sabin ↓ sal-al ↓ sal-fr sle1• samb ↓ sang ↓ sep k* sil ↓ spig k* spong fd4.de *Staph* ↓ stram k* stry ↓ suis-em rly4• sul-ac ↓ **Sulph** ↓ symph fd3.de• tarax **Tell** ↓ teucr ↓ til ↓ trios rsj11• tritic-vg fd5.de ulm-c jsj8• urol-h ↓ v-a-b ↓ valer ↓ vanil fd5.de ven-m rsj12• verat ↓ *Verb* zinc [bell-p-sp dcm1 heroin sdj2 spect dfg1]
  - **morning** | h: sal-al blc1•
  - **accompanied** by | **Throat**; sore: gink-b sbd1•
  - **aching**: acon-ac rly4• androc srj1• bell k* choc srj3• coli rly4• ery-a k* guaj k* iodof a1* ketogl-ac rly4• lac-c al* lac-h htj1• laur a1 lob a1 mez k* nat-m k* plumbg a1 pyrid rly4• rob a1 sep h2 sil k* sulph k* tell rsj10• urol-h rwt• v-a-b jl [bell-p-sp dcm1]
  - **biting** pain: caust bg2* psor k*
  - **boring** pain: agar canth mag-s med merc-c merc-i-f stry

- **burning**: acon am-c ant-c k* arum-t k* bry cop k* fago k* hir rsj4• jac-c a1* jug-r a1 kreos a1* laur a1 merc h1* olnd h1* osteo-a knp1• pall hr1 petr-ra shn4• rhus-t a1 stry k* **Tell** k*
- **cramping**: agar mur-ac nat-m k* spong zinc
- **cutting** pain: arg-met *Hydrog* srj2• petr plut-n srj7•
- **digging** pain: jac-c a1* merc-c k* stry k*
- **drawing** pain: ang vh1 arn chel con dig dulc fd4.de hyper ina-i mlk9.de mez mill plat spig spong fd4.de til valer *Verb*
- **dull** pain: trios rsj11•
- **gnawing** pain: kali-i bg2
- **griping** pain: carbn-s
- **lancinating**: v-a-b jl2
- **piercing** pain: nat-pyru rly4•
- **pinching** pain: carb-an carb-v dulc staph
- **plug**; as from a: aur-m bg2
- **pressing** pain: asaf k* bism hr1 carb-ac hr1 chel hr1 dig k* dulc fd4.de fl-ac a1 gast a1 ham fd3.de• nat-sil fd3.de• plac-s rly4• podo fd3.de• ruta fd4.de sep k* sil h2* spig k* spong fd4.de symph fd3.de• tarax tritic-vg fd5.de vanil fd5.de
  - ⋮ **plug**; as from a: aur-m bg2
- **sore**: aids nl2• luf-op rsj5•
- **stitching** pain: *Abel* h2 aesc arg-met asc-c hr1 bar-c *Borx* k* bry calad carb-an carc fd2.de• coc-c colch cop dros dulc fd4.de eupi form gard-j vlr2• graph ina-i mlk9.de irid-met srj5• **Kali-bi** kali-n h2 kali-p kali-s fd4.de* ketogl-ac rly4• kola stb3• lac-h htj1• lavand-a ctl1• limen-b-c hrn2* mag-c mag-m mag-s merc-c merc-i-f mill nat-sil fd3.de• nept-m lsd2.fr nicc olib-sac wmh1 ozone sde2• podo fd3.de• psor ptel *Puls* rhod ruta fd4.de sabad sal-al blc1• samb sang sep sil spong fd4.de *Staph* k* suis-em rly4• **Sulph** vanil fd5.de verat verb
  - ⋮ **accompanied** by | **headache** (See HEAD - Pain - accompanied - ear - stitches)
- **tearing** pain: *Acon* anac apis *Ars* aur hr1 bamb-a stb2.de• bar-c calc camph carb-an caust coc-c elaps *Graph* grat mag-c merl mez puls sabin sul-ac *Sulph* teucr *Verb*
- **then** right: aesc aloe ↓ arn borx ↓ brom calc-p ↓ kola stb3• lach sne merc k* podo fd3.de• spong fd4.de staph ↓ symph fd3.de•
  - ⋮ **aching**: brom k* calc-p bg1 merc hr1
  - ⋮ **pressing** pain: arn k* spong fd4.de
  - ⋮ **stitching** pain: aloe borx kola stb3• staph h1
- **twinging**: coc-c k* crot-t k* merc-d a1 prun k* staph k*
- **ulcerative** pain: psor jl2
- **walking** agg.: mez ↓
  - ⋮ **cramping**: mez
- ▽ **extending** to:
  - ⋮ **right**: aloe ↓ androc srj1• atra-r ↓ calc-p indg ↓ sal-fr sle1•
    - ⋮ **gnawing** pain: indg
    - ⋮ **tearing** pain: aloe atra-r skp7•

- **day** and night: hell k*
- **daytime**: nat-m k* rhod k*
  - **amel.**: acon bro1
- **morning**: all-c alum ambr ↓ ars bamb-a ↓ borx bry sne carb-v k* cham sne dulc fd4.de ferr k* form k* ham ↓ hep sne hydr a1 hydrog srj2• kali-bi a1 kali-c h2* lach sne lyss k* *Mang* k* merc merc-i-f mez a1 *Nat-ar* nat-c k* nat-s k* nept-m ↓ nux-m k* nux-v k* psor a1 rhod a1* rumx ruta fd4.de sanguis-s hrn2• sars k* sep k* spong fd4.de symph ↓ tarent k* tritic-vg fd5.de trom vanil fd5.de verat zinc ↓
  - **8** h: dios nat-c
    - ⋮ **tearing** pain: nat-c
  - **9** h: rosm ↓
    - ⋮ **cutting** pain: rosm lgb1
  - **bed** agg.; in: carb-v ↓ ferr ↓ form ↓ merc-i-r ↓ *Nux-v* ↓
    - ⋮ **aching**: merc-i-r
    - ⋮ **stitching** pain: *Nux-v*
    - ⋮ **tearing** pain: carb-v
    - ⋮ **twinging**: ferr form k*
  - **boring** pain: alum

- **morning**: ...
  - **jerking** pain: mang k*
  - **lancinating**: tarent k*
  - **pinching** pain: nat-c
  - **pressing** pain: dulc fd4.de ham fd3.de• nat-s k* nux-m k* ruta fd4.de spong fd4.de symph fd3.de• tritic-vg fd5.de vanil fd5.de verat k*
  - **rising** agg.: ferr ↓ form ↓
    - ⋮ **aching**: ferr form k*
  - **stitching** pain: all-c ars borx *Ferr* form kali-c nept-m lsd2.fr *Nux-v* ruta fd4.de sars tritic-vg fd5.de vanil fd5.de
  - **tearing** pain: ambr a1 bamb-a stb2.de• mang sars zinc
  - **waking**; on: borx ↓ daph ↓ dulc fd4.de gink-b sbd1• nit-ac sne nux-v ↓ podo fd3.de• sanguis-s hrn2• sep k* vanil fd5.de *Verb*
    - ⋮ **pressing** pain: sep *Verb*
    - ⋮ **screwing** pain: daph k* nux-v h1
    - ⋮ **stitching** pain: borx gink-b sbd1• vanil fd5.de
  - **washing** in cold water, when: borx ↓
    - ⋮ **stitching** pain: borx
- **forenoon**: chinin-s elaps ↓ fago a1 gamb a1 genist a1 ham ↓ hydr k* indg a1 kali-bi a1 kali-i a1 *Mag-c* k* mag-s ↓ mang h2* nat-ar ↓ nat-c a1 nat-m k* nux-m k* paeon ↓ phos ↓ plan a1 plb k* plect a1 ruta fd4.de sars k* tritic-vg fd5.de vanil fd5.de
  - **9** h: elaps nat-s
    - ⋮ **going** out; after: tell
    - ⋮ **pressing** pain: nat-s
    - ⋮ **tearing** pain: elaps
  - **10** h: mag-s
    - ⋮ **stitching** pain: mag-s
  - **10**.30 h: hydr
    - ⋮ **pressing** pain: hydr
  - **11** h: dios hydr petr-ra shn4•
  - **boring** pain: mag-c
  - **pressing** pain: vanil fd5.de
  - **sitting** agg.: nat-m h2* phos k*
  - **standing** agg.: plb k*
  - **stitching** pain: chinin-s ham fd3.de• kali-bi kali-i mag-c mag-s nat-ar nat-m nux-m paeon sars tritic-vg fd5.de vanil fd5.de
  - **tearing** pain: elaps kali-i mag-c phos plb
- **noon**: aloe carc ↓ chinin-s dulc fd4.de gels k* kali-bi a1 limen-b-c ↓ nat-p a1 psor k* ruta fd4.de stry ↓ sulph
  - **burning**: stry k*
  - **stitching** pain: carc fd2.de• chinin-s dulc fd4.de gels limen-b-c hrn2* psor
  - **tearing** pain: sulph
- **afternoon**: aeth agath-a nl2• alum aran bov brom bry carbn-s castm ↓ *Chel* k* chinin-s clem ↓ dios k* dulc fd4.de euphr k* fago a1 form k* gels k* ham a1 hir skp7• hydr a1 indg a1 kali-bi a1 lyss k* *Merc-c* k* nat-ar nat-s ↓ nat-sil ↓ nept-m ↓ ol-an a1 ox-ac a1 paull a1 plect a1 rumx ruta fd4.de sars ↓ sep ↓ spong fd4.de stry sulph k* tarent k* tritic-vg fd5.de trom vanil fd5.de [bell-p-sp dcm1]
  - **13** h: graph
    - ⋮ **stitching** pain: graph
  - **14** h: chinin-s
  - **15** h: agath-a nl2• phys trom ↓
    - ⋮ **stitching** pain: phys trom
  - **16** h: kalm nat-c
    - ⋮ **stitching** pain: kalm nat-c
  - **17** h: bamb-a stb2.de• berb dios ↓ ham ↓ merc sne sep ↓
    - ⋮ **aching**: dios ham sep
    - ⋮ **stitching** pain: berb
  - **aching**: euphr k* sep a1 [bell-p-sp dcm1]
  - **boring** pain: alum gels indg merc-c
  - **burning**: stry k*
  - **digging** pain: gels k* merc-c k*
  - **gnawing** pain: indg k*

- **pinching** pain: aran
- **stitching** pain: aeth bry carbn-s chinin-s clem dulc fd4.de form merc-c nat-ar nat-s nat-sil fd3.de• nept-m lsd2.fr ruta fd4.de spong fd4.de tritic-vg fd5.de trom vanil fd5.de
- **tearing** pain: aeth bov castm *Chel* indg sars
- **twinging**: aran k*

- **evening**: acon acon-ac rly4• aloe alum am-c ↓ *Ars* ars-s-f k2 berb borx brom bry sne carb-v carbn-s carc ↓ caust chinin-s clem ↓ cob k* coc-c ↓ daph ↓ dios k* dulc fd4.de fago a1 *Ferr-p* sne graph k* ham k* hyos k* hyper k* indg k* inul a1* kali-ar *Kali-bi* k* kali-c k* kali-i k* kali-n a1 kali-s kola stb3• lach k* lyc k* lyss hr1 mag-c ↓ mang k* merc mez ↓ mim-p vml3• mur-ac h2* nat-c k* nat-m k* nat-s ↓ nat-sil ↓ nux-v k* ol-an ↓ osm ↓ ox-ac k* par k* phel ↓ phos ↓ phys ↓ psor k* puls hr1* ran-b k* ran-s ↓ rhus-r ruta fd4.de sep k* spong fd4.de staph still ↓ sulph k* symph ↓ tarent thuj tritic-vg fd5.de tung-met bdx1• vanil fd5.de verb zinc zing ↓
  - **18** h: phys ↓
    - **stitching** pain: phys
  - **19** h: bamb-a stb2.de• mag-c ↓ phys zing
    - **tearing** pain: mag-c zing
  - **19**.30 h: fago
  - **20** h: nat-s
    - **stitching** pain: nat-s
  - **20**-22 h: phel
    - **biting** pain: phel
    - **burning** | **electric** sparks; like: phel
    - **stitching** pain: phel
  - **21** h: carbn-s dios
    - **stitching** pain: carbn-s
  - **aching**: berb k* brom k* kali-bi k* lyc k* nat-m k* osm a1 sep k*
  - **air** agg.; in open: acon ↓ sep ↓
    - **aching**: sep
    - **burning**: acon
  - **bed** | **going** to bed:
    - **when**: ferr-p ↓
      - **stitching** pain: ferr-p
    - **in** bed:
      - **agg.**: caust ↓ kali-c ↓ kali-i ↓ *Nux-v* ↓ spong ↓ thuj ↓
        - **burning**: caust
        - **stitching** pain: caust kali-c kali-i *Nux-v* spong thuj
        - **tearing** pain: thuj
      - **amel.**: mang ↓
        - **tearing** pain: mang h2
  - **biting** pain:
    - **electric** sparks, like: phel k*
    - **itching** pain: caust phel k*
  - **boring** into ear with finger agg.: phel ↓ phle ↓
    - **biting** pain | **itching** pain: phel phle
  - **boring** pain: phys ran-s
  - **burning**: ars k* brom k* ham k* ol-an k* ran-b a1 still hr1 zinc k*
  - **cramping**: ran-b thuj
  - **cutting** pain: lach
  - **drawing** pain: coc-c kl (non:crot-c kl) ran-s
  - **eating**; after: graph ↓
    - **stitching** pain: graph
  - **gnawing** pain: mur-ac k*
  - **jerking** pain: mang k*
  - **lancinating**: nux-v ruta fd4.de
  - **lasting** through the night: mim-p vml3•
  - **lying**:
    - **agg.**: mang ↓
      - **tearing** pain: mang h2
    - **bed**; in:
      - **after**:
        - **amel.**: mang ↓

- **evening** – **lying** – **bed**; in – **after** – **amel.**: ...
        - **jerking** pain: mang
    - **side**; on:
      - **painful** side:
        - **agg.**: kali-n ↓
          - **stitching** pain: kali-n
  - **lying** down agg.: mang ↓
    - **jerking** pain: mang
  - **pinching** pain: am-c
  - **pressing** pain: berb k* dulc fd4.de hyper kali-bi k* mang h2* ruta fd4.de sep spong fd4.de symph fd3.de• tritic-vg fd5.de vanil fd5.de *Verb*
  - **pressure**:
    - **amel.**: ham ↓
      - **burning**: ham k*
  - **rubbing**; after: grat ↓
    - **burning**: grat
  - **sore**: borx
  - **stitching** pain: *Alum Ars* berb borx carc fd2.de• chinin-s clem daph dulc fd4.de graph hyper kali-c kali-i kali-n merc nat-m nat-sil fd3.de• ox-ac phos psor ran-b ruta fd4.de spong fd4.de staph sulph tarent thuj tritic-vg fd5.de vanil fd5.de
  - **tearing** pain: alum *Ars* indg kali-i mag-c nat-s thuj zinc zing
  - **twinging**: aloe carb-v k* mez k*

- **night**: *Acon* bro1 alum am-m ars bro1 aur sne aur-m ↓ bamb-a stb2.de• bar-c *Bell* bro1* bros-gau ↓ *Bry* calc-p bro1 carbn-s ↓ carc ↓ cassia-s ccrh1• *Cham* bro1 cimic a1 cop ↓ cycl **Dulc** k* ferr sne ferr-p bro1 gran a1 hell k* *Hep* k* ina-i mlk9.de kali-ar *Kali-bi* k* kali-c k* kali-i bro1 kali-n k* kalm ↓ lac-c k* *Lach* k* mang k* melal-alt gya4 **Merc** k* merc-i-f k* mim-p ↓ *Nat-m* hr1 nat-sil ↓ nit-ac sne nux-v petr ↓ phos h2* **Puls** k* *Rhus-t* k* ruta fd4.de sal-fr ↓ sep k* *Sil* spong fd4.de stry tell thuj ↓ tritic-vg fd5.de *Tub* vanil fd5.de vib
  - **22** h: form ↓ nat-sil ↓
    - **stitching** pain: form nat-sil fd3.de•
  - **23** h: mim-p ↓
    - **stitching** pain: mim-p skp7•
  - **midnight**: kali-c
    - **before** | **22** h: form
    - **after**: sep
      - **aching**: sep k*
      - **bed**; driving out of: *Mygal*
      - **walking**:
        - **wind**; in the:
          - **after**: sep ↓
            - **aching**: sep
          - **agg.**: sep
  - **aching**: *Dulc* k* *Lach* k* rhus-t hr1 sep h2*
  - **boring** pain: am-m mang
  - **burning**: aur-m hr1 stry k*
  - **burrowing**: hell a1 mang h2
  - **cold**; after taking a: glon ↓
    - **drawing** pain: glon
  - **digging** pain: am-m k* mang k*
  - **drawing** pain: alum bar-c dulc fd4.de ina-i mlk9.de *Sil*
  - **gnawing** pain: mang k*
  - **griping** pain: carbn-s
  - **lying** on it: am-m ↓
    - **digging** pain: am-m k*
  - **piercing** pain: bros-gau mrc1
  - **pinching** pain: bry
  - **sleep**; before: still ↓
    - **burning**: still
  - **stitching** pain: *Alum Ars* carc fd2.de• cop cycl dulc fd4.de hell ina-i mlk9.de *Kali-bi* kalm mim-p skp7• nat-sil fd3.de• *Phos* sal-fr sle1• thuj vanil fd5.de
  - **tearing** pain: am-m petr hr1
  - **toothache**; with: hell ↓

Ear

• **toothache**, with: ...
⁝ **stitching** pain: hell
• **waking**; on: carbn-s ↓
⁝ **griping** pain: carbn-s
⁝ **stitching** pain: carbn-s
- **accompanied** by:
• **coryza**: tub jl2
• **noises** in ear: arist-cl sp1 oci-sa sp1
○ • **Head**; complaints of (See HEAD - Complaints - accompanied - ear - pain)
- **aching**: acon-ac rly4• aids nl2• all-c aloe *Ambr* bg anac bg *Arn* bg ars bg asaf asar bg bell brom calc-s k2 cann-i *Caps* k* carb-v bg caust **Cham** k* chin bg chlf *Cimic* clem colch coli rly4• coloc *Con* crot-c sk4• cur cystein-l rly4• dros bg **Dulc** k* ery-a euphr ferr-p bg* form guaj k* ham hell bg hyos iod ip jatr-c jug-r kali-c *Kali-s* kali-sil k2 ketogl-ac rly4• lach lact laur lyc mang meny h1* meph merc bg* merc-i-r mez mosch mur-ac bg musca-d szs1 nat-c bg nat-m nat-p nicotam rly4• nit-ac nux-m nux-v k* olnd osm par bg *Phos* phyt ptk1 plac-s rly4• plan ptk1 plat bg podo c1 psor **Puls** k* ran-b ran-s bg *Rhod* bg rhus-t ribo rly4• sabad bg seneg sep sil *Spig* bg spong stann bg suis-em rly4• suis-hep rly4• suis-pan rly4• sul-i k2 **Sulph** k* tab tarent **Tell** k* teucr bg thuj tub c ust verb bg [bell-p-sp dcm1]
• **accompanied** by | **Teeth**; pain in (See TEETH - Pain - accompanied - ears - pain)
- **acute**: aloe bg2 *Ambr* b7.de* anac b4.de* *Ang* b7a.de *Arn* b7.de* ars b4.de* asar b7.de* *Bell* b4.de* bry b7a.de calc b4a.de cann-s b7a.de carb-v b4.de* caust b4.de* *Cham* b7.de* chin b7.de* cina b7.de* clem b4.de* colch b7.de* coloc b4.de* con b4.de* croc b7.de* dros b7.de* dulc b4.de* euph b4.de* guaj b4.de* hell b7.de* *Hep* b4a.de iod b4.de* kali-c b4.de* kreos b7a.de laur b7.de* lyc b4.de* m-arct b7.de m-aust b7.de mang b4.de* meny b7.de* merc b4.de* mez b4.de* mur-ac b4.de* nat-c b4.de* nit-ac b4.de* nux-m b7.de* **Nux-v** b7.de* par b7.de* petr b4a.de phos b4.de* plat b4.de* **Puls** b7.de* *Ran-b* b7a.de ran-s b7.de* rheum b7.de* *Rhod* b4.de* rhus-t b7.de* sabad b7.de* sep b4.de* sil b4a.de *Spig* b7.de* spong b7.de* stann b4.de* *Sulph* b4.de* tab bg2 teucr b7.de* thuj b4.de* valer b7a.de verb b7.de* *Zinc* b4a.de
- **ague**; after suppression of: *Puls*
- **air** | **amel.**: *Phos*
- **air** agg.; draft of: act-sp bg1 bell sne camph *Dulc* *Hep* hir skp7• *Lyc* *Mez* mim-p vml3• ruta fd4.de staph dtp valer br1
• **stitching** pain: *Camph* mim-p skp7•
- **air**; in open:
• **agg.**: acon bry con dulc fd4.de euph k* *Hep* k* hir skp7• *Lyc* k* *Mang* k* mez par a1 *Sep* k* sulph tab
⁝ **aching**: euph k* *Lyc* k* sep a1
⁝ **burning**: acon
⁝ **stitching** pain: acon sulph tab
• **amel.**: acon bro1 aur bro1 cic ferr-p bro1 *Puls* k* sep sne
• **going** into; when: bry ↓ con ↓ mang ↓
⁝ **cutting** pain: mang
⁝ **stitching** pain: bry con h2
- **airplane**; from changes of atmospheric pressure in an.: cham mtf kali-m mtf
- **alternating** with:
○ • **Abdomen**; pain in: rad-br c11
• **Eyes**; pain in: bell
- **appearing** suddenly | **disappearing** suddenly: crot-c sk4•
- **bell** agg.; from the stroke of the: mag-m ph-ac k*
• **stitching** pain: mag-m ph-ac
- **bending** body:
• **right** agg.; to: mag-m ↓
⁝ **stitching** pain: mag-m h2
⁝ **tearing** pain: mag-m
- **biting** pain: caust k* lyc k* phel k* plat h2* psor k*
- **biting** teeth together: anac h2
- **blow**; pain as from a: am-c k* anac k* arn k* bell k* cham b7.de* cic b7.de* cina k* con k* nat-m k* nux-v k* paeon plat k* ruta b7.de* spig k*
- **blowing** the nose agg.: act-sp alum alum-p k2 bar-c *Bar-m* sne *Calc* k* caust con dios k* hep k* lap-la sde8.de• lyc k* ph-ac k* puls k* sil k* spig spong fd4.de stann teucr tritic-vg fd5.de trom
- **blowing** the nose agg.: ...
• **aching**: ph-ac hr1 sil k*
• **pressing** pain: sil h2 tritic-vg fd5.de
• **stitching** pain: *Calc* con hep lyc spong fd4.de trom
- **boring** into ear:
• **agg.**: agar ↓ mez ↓ phys ↓
⁝ **boring** pain: agar mez phys
• **amel.**: aeth ↓ *Coloc* ↓ mur-ac ↓ ph-ac ↓ psor ↓
⁝ **boring** pain: aeth c1
⁝ **stitching** pain: aeth *Coloc* mur-ac ph-ac psor
- **boring** pain: agath-a nl2• alum k* alum-p k2 alum-sil k2 am-c am-m k* am-pic bro1 ant-c *Arund* bg1* *Asaf* bro1 aur k* aur-m-n *Bar-c* k* *Bell* k* cann-i canth *Caps* bro1 carb-an k* carbn-s caust k* chel *Cina* coc-c colch coloc *Cupr* cupr-ar euph euphr k* gels hell k* *Hep* b4a.de hydr-ac indg irid-met srj5• kali-c *Kali-i* k* kali-s kali-sil k2 lach b7a.de lact laur k* mag-c k* mag-m k* mag-s mang **Merc** merc-c *Merc-i-f* mill nat-m *Ol-an* k* phel *Phos* plat k* plb k* ran-s k* rhod k* *Ruta* sil k* *Spig* k* stann k* stront-c k* stry sulph thuj zinc bg2
• **acute**: merc-i-f
• **sticking** pain: mag-m
• **tickling**: nicc
- **boring** with finger: borx ↓
• **agg.**: anac k* mur-ac h2* ruta sep h2* *Tarent* zinc
⁝ **pressing** pain: anac h2* ruta
⁝ **tearing** pain: anac
• **amel.**: agar k* *Coloc* k* fl-ac k* lach k* mez k* mur-ac k* ph-ac k* phys psor k*
⁝ **cutting** pain: *Coloc*
⁝ **pressing** pain: fl-ac k*
• **sore**: borx h2
- **breathing** agg.: mang k*
- **bruised** (See sore)
- **burning**: acon k* aesc k* agar b4a.de* all-c k* alum k* alum-p k2 alumn am-c am-m k* aml-ns anac bg anac-oc hr1 ang k* ant-c k* ant-t *Apis* k* arg-met arn k* *Ars* k* ars-s-f k2 arum-t k* arund k* asaf k* **Aur** k* aur-ar k2 aur-m hr1 aur-s k2 bell k* berb brom k* bry k* calad hr1 calc b4.de* calc-p hr1 camph k* cann-i k* cann-s bg canth b7a.de* *Caps* k* carb-an k* carb-v **Caust** k* chel k* chin k* chinin-ar cic clem b4.de* con k* cop k* cycl k* daph k* dig k* *Dros* k* fago k* grat a1 ham a1 hir rsj4• *Ign* k* irid-met srj5• jac-c k* jatr-c jug-r a1 kali-ar kali-bi k* kali-c bg2 kali-n k* kreos k* lach b7a.de* laur k* lob-s k* lyc k* lycps-v lyss k* m-ambo b7.de mag-c k* mag-m k* *Mang* k* **Merc** k* merc-sul k* merl mit a1 mur-ac k* naja **Nat-m** k* nat-p k* ol-an k* olnd b7.de* op k* ph-ac k* phel k* phos k* pic-ac k* plat k* positr nl2• prot jl2 pyrog bg2 ran-b b7.de* rhus-t b7.de* rhus-v a1 sabad k* sabin a1* **Sang** k* sarr a1 sars b4.de* sep b4a.de* spig k* spong k* staph k* suis-pan rly4• sulph k* tab k* tarax b7.de* **Tell** k* teucr bg til k* upa zinc k* zinc-p k2 [bell-p-sp dcm1]
• **accompanied** by | **Mastoiditis** (See Caries - mastoid - accompanied - burning)
- **burrowing**: am-c am-m k* ant-c k* coc-c colch bg2 hell k* *Mang* bg2 merc-c b4a.de plat b4.de*
- **bursting** pain: aml-ns bg2 bell bg2 calc-caust *Caust* k* *Clem* *Dulc* glon a1 *Guaj* hell k* hep k2 indg a1 lyc k* *Merc* *Mur-ac* nit-ac k* par bg2 *Phos* k* **Plat** psor k* spig bg2 spong fd4.de *Stann* *Viol-o* bg2 [bell-p-sp dcm1]
- **catarrh**; suppressed: calc k2
- **causeless**: cham mtf11
- **centering** at the ear, hard pains: mang k*
- **chewing** agg.: aloe *Anac* *Apis* arg-met bell cann-s hep lach k* nux-m k* nux-v k* ozone sde2• seneg k* verb
• **pressing** pain: seneg
• **stitching** pain: cann-s nux-v
- **children**; in: acon st1 all-c k2* *Bell* sne cham k2* **Dulc** hr1 **Ferr-p** sne puls k2* spong fd4.de ter hr1 *Verb* hr1 *Zinc* hr1
• **infants**: ser-a-c jl2
- **chill**:
• **after**: merc-sul ↓
⁝ **burning**: merc-sul c1
• **during**: acon k* apis k* asar bg2 calad bg2 calc k* dig bg2 gamb k* graph k* mez bg2 *Nux-v* k* phos bg2 psor ↓ puls k* sulph k*
⁝ **pressing** pain: asar b7.de*

- • **during**: ...
    - ⁝ **stitching** pain: gamb graph k* psor puls k*
- **chilliness**, on beginning of: gamb ↓
    - • **stitching** pain: gamb
- **chronic**: syph jl2
- **cleaning**: sulph h2
- **closing** the ear lightly | **amel.**: mim-p skp7•
- **closing** the eyes:
    - • **amel.**: calc ↓
        - ⁝ **stitching** pain: calc
- **closing** the mouth agg.: nat-c ↓
    - • **stitching** pain: nat-c
- **cold**:
    - • **air**:
        - ⁝ **agg.**: agar *Ars* bry calc-p k2* caps bro1 *Cham* bro1 colch *Dulc* gard-j ↓ graph k2 *Hep* k* kali-ar k2 kali-m bro1 kali-s ↓ lach *Lyc* mag-p bro1 merc *Mez* nat-c par ruta fd4.de sang bro1 *Sep* symph fd3.de• valer br1 [*Mang* stj]
            - ⁝ **stitching** pain: gard-j vlr2• graph k2 kali-ar kali-s fd4.de
            - ⁝ **tearing** pain: agar
        - ⁝ **amel.**: hist sp1 phos ↓
            - ⁝ **pressing** pain: phos
    - • **amel.**: merc ↓
        - ⁝ **stitching** pain: merc
    - • **applications**:
        - ⁝ **agg.**: aur sne borx bufo calc k* cham sne dulc k* **Hep** merc sne sep *Sil*
        - ⁝ **amel.**: ars-s-r hr1 aur k2 merc k* puls k*
    - • **drinks** | **amel.**: bar-m k*
    - • **washing**:
        - ⁝ **agg.**: mag-p br1
        - ⁝ **face** and neck agg.: *Mag-p* br1*
- **cold**; after taking a: *Bell* calc k2 *Dulc* *Gels* *Kalm* led *Merc* *Puls* sep
- **cold** agg.; feet becoming: stann
    - • **boring** pain: stann
- **corrosive**: ang b7.de *Arg-met* b7a.de dros b7.de plat b4a.de rhod b4a.de sulph b4a.de
- **coryza**; during: am b7.de* *Bell* bg2 *Cycl* b7a.de lach b7.de* *Merc* bg2 **Puls** b7.de*
- **cough**:
    - • **during**: *Calc* *Caps* k* dios eug hr1* ferr-p sne kali-bi nux-v k* sep bg1 thuj tung-met bdx1•
        - ⁝ **agg.**: *Caps* ↓ nux-v ↓
            - ⁝ **bursting** pain: caps
            - ⁝ **pressing** pain: *Caps* k*
            - ⁝ **stitching** pain: nux-v
- **cramping**: agar k* aloe k* *Anac* k* anan ang b7.de* ars k* bell b4.de* bry bufo bg2 calc k* carb-an k* *Cina* k* colch k* croc k* crot-t dig dros b7.de* *Glon* bg2* graph k* kali-c k* kali-n k* kali-p kali-sil k2 kreos k* mang k* *Merc* k* mur-ac k* nat-m nit-ac k* nux-v b7.de* olnd k* petr k* **Ph-ac** k* *Plat* k* ran-b k* samb k* *Sars* k* *Sil* k* spig k* spong k* stann k* staph k* thuj k* valer k* zinc
- **crawling**: bar-c h2*
- **cutting** pain: acon k2 anac arg-met k* cadm-s canth b7.de* caust *Coloc* k* cur dros ferr bg2 *Ferr-i* *Form* k* *Hydr* bg1* *Hyos* bg2* kali-bi bg2 kali-i kali-s lach mang mur-ac k* musca-d szs1 *Nit-ac* bg2* nux-m petr k* plb bg2 *Puls* bg2* *Syph* k* tarent bg2 trios rsj11• vero-o rly3• *Zinc* k*
- **darting** (See stitching)
- **deafness**, then: caps ptk2
- **descending** stairs agg.: bad chinin-s
    - • **stitching** pain: chinin-s
- **digging** pain: am-m k* anan k* ant-c bg colch k* gels k* hell bg kali-i k* mang k* merc-c k* nat-m k* plat k* *Ruta* sep h2* stry k*
    - • **insect** had got into them; as if an: kali-i
- **dinner**; after: agar k* ant-c k* bov carb-an indg a1 ol-an a1 phel ↓ plb k*
    - • **boring** pain: plb
    - • **drawing** pain: ant-c
    - • **tearing** pain: bov carb-an phel
- **discharges** | **amel.**: calc k2
- **dragging**: cann-xyz bg2 caust bg2 euphr bg2 merc b4.de* sabin bg2 staph bg2
- **drawing** pain: acon aloe ambr c1 anac k* ang k* ant-c k* arg-met k* arn k* ars ars-s-f k2 asaf k* asar k* aur sne aur-m *Bar-c* bar-m bar-s k2 *Bell* k* berb bism b7.de* bov k* bry calc k* calc-sil k2 caps sne carb-an k* *Cham* chel coc-c colch coloc b4.de* *Con* k* croc b7.de* crot-h *Cycl* k* dros k* dulc k* ferr-ma ferr-p guaj b4a.de hell k* kali-ar kali-bi *Kali-c* k* kali-m k2 kali-n kali-p kali-sil k2 kalm kreos k* lact lyc m-arct b7.de mag-m k* mag-s mang b4.de* merc mez k* mill mosch k* mur-ac k* *Nat-m* k* nicc *Nit-ac* k* nux-v b7.de* ol-an olnd k* op petr k* **Ph-ac** k* *Phos* k* *Plat* k* puls ran-s k* rhod k* rhus-t b7.de* sabin b7.de* sars k* *Sep* k* *Sil* k* *Sphing* k* *Spig* b7.de* spong k* squil b7.de* *Stann* k* staph k* sul-ac k* sulph k* *Tarax* k* teucr b7.de* til tritic-vg fd5.de valer k* verat b7.de* *Verb* k* viol-o b7.de* zing
    - • **downward**: berb
    - • **outward**: con b4a.de
    - • **paroxysmal**: alum *Ph-ac*
    - • **thread** were drawn through ear; as if a: rhus-t h1*
- **drinking** agg.: (↗*swallowing - agg.*) con dulc fd4.de
    - • **pinching** pain: con h2
    - • **stitching** pain: con
- **dull** pain: anthraq rly4• ketogl-ac rly4• nat-pyru rly4• pot-e rly4•
- **eating**:
    - • **after**:
        - ⁝ **agg.**: graph k* mang nat-m hr1
        - ⁝ **amel.**: acon ↓
            - ⁝ **burning**: acon
    - • **agg.**: apis carb-an carbn-s cassia-s ccrh1• cinnb phel verb
    - • **amel.**: mag-c
    - • **while**:
        - ⁝ **agg.**: verb ↓
            - ⁝ **stitching** pain: verb
            - ⁝ **tearing** pain: verb
- **electric** shocks; as from: m-ambo b7.de
- **eructations** agg.: bell h1 bry sne phys c1 sulph tarent k*
    - • **drawing** pain: sulph
    - • **stitching** pain: bell h1
    - • **throat** along Eustachian tube to middle ear; from: phys a1*
- **excoriating** (See burning)
- **exertion** of vision, after: sil
- **face**; with pain in: **Bell** merc ph-ac
- **fainting** with pain in ear: cur k* *Hep* *Merc* k*
- **fall**; as from a: *Arn* b7.de *Ruta* b7.de* verat b7.de
- **forcing** out (See pressing out)
- **foreign** body; as from a: ang h1* bell bg calc bg cann-s bg ol-an bg phos k* *Puls* sne sil h2
- **full** moon, during: (↗*MIND - Moonlight*) sil k*
- **gnawing** pain: arg-met b7.de* dros k* indg a1 kali-c k* kali-i k* led k* mang k* mur-ac k* phos b4.de* plat h2 *Ran-s* b7a.de sulph k* tab k*
- **griping** pain: carbn-s colch a1 kali-c h2
- **hammer**, from sound of: sang k*
- **headache**; during: (↗*HEAD - Complaints - accompanied - ear - pain*) antip vh1 borx ↓ caps ↓ cassia-s ccrh1• dulc fd4.de ham k* *Kali-bi* ↓ kali-n ↓ lach k* merc phos psor k* puls ran-s k* rhus-t ↓ sang k*
    - • **burning**: rhus-t bro1
    - • **stitching** pain: borx c1 caps bro1 dulc fd4.de *Kali-bi* kali-n
- **heart** beat; with each: aml-ns ↓
    - • **bursting** pain: aml-ns
- **heat**; during: calad k* calc chinin-s dulc fd4.de graph k* ran-b ↓
    - • **burning**: ran-b k*
    - • **stitching** pain: calc dulc fd4.de
- **hiccough** agg.: bell tarent ptk1
    - • **pinching** pain: bell
- **increasing** gradually and decreasing suddenly: sul-ac k2
- **intermittent**: arn nat-c k* nat-m k* tarent a1
- **itching** pain: *Caps* hr1

- **jerking** pain: all-c k* am-m bg2 anac ang k* *Calc* k* calc-p k* calc-sil k2 cann-s carb-v h2* caust *Cina* k* clem h2* dig k* fl-ac k* *Hep* k* m-aust k* mag-m k* mang k* mur-ac k* nux-v h1* paeon petr k* ph-ac k* phos h2* **Plat** k* *Puls* k* rhod k* rhus-v a1 sabad k* sil k* spig k* valer k* zinc
- **lacerating**: bell cadm-s **Merc** hr1 **Sulph** tarent k*
- **lancinating**: acon bro1 aeth k* *Agath-a* nl2• all-c bro1 alum am-m anac androc srj1• anthraq rly4• arg-met *Asaf* aster aur-s k* bamb-a stb2.de• *Bell* k* berb cadm-s caps bro1 caust cham hr1* chin bro1 cit-v k* cur k* der k* ferr-i k* ferr-p bro1 gamb k* hura kali-bi hr1 kali-c bro1 kali-i k* lepi a1 *Mag-p* bro1 melal-alt gya4 menth c1 meny nad rly4• nat-c h2 nit-ac bro1 nux-v plb k* *Puls* bro1 raph k* rob a1 ros-d wla1 ruta fd4.de sarr a1 sil bro1 *Spig* bro1 suis-pan rly4• sulph tl1 tarent k* tere-la rly4• teucr k* v-a-b jl verb c1 vero-o rly4• viol-o bro1 zinc
  - **acute**: v-a-b jl2
  - **intermittent**: *Asaf* tere-la rly4•
  - **inward**: hydrog srj2• ruta fd4.de
  - **outward**: aeth a1 *Asaf*
- **laughing** agg.: mang k*
  - **stitching** pain: *Mang*
- **leaning** on hand: arn kali-c kali-n lac-c lach
- **lying**:
  - **agg.**: cassia-s ccrh1• cham sne kali-p ↓
    - **stitching** pain: kali-p
  - **bed**; in | **agg.**: acon sne *Bell* mrr1 *Caust* kali-i *Kali-p* nux-v sang sep gk *Sulph* thuj tritic-vg fd5.de
  - **ear**; on the:
    - **agg.**: agar am-c h2 am-m *Bar-c* bar-m chin coc-c ↓ cortico tpw7 hep h2 kali-n lac-c med podo fd3.de• sanguis-s hrn2• vanil fd5.de
      - **pressing** pain: bar-c coc-c
      - **stitching** pain: kali-n
      - **tearing** pain: agar am-m
    - **amel.**: bry sne cortico tpw7 *Hep* sne lach
  - **must** lie down: cur k*
  - **side**; on:
    - **affected** side | **amel.**: cortico sp1
    - **left**:
      - **agg.**: merc ↓ streptoc jl2
        - **stitching** pain: merc
    - **right**:
      - **agg.**: merc sne mim-p vml3• ptel
        - **stitching** pain: mim-p skp7• ptel
- **lying** down agg.; after: sang ↓ sulph ↓
  - **aching**: sang k*
  - **drawing** pain: sulph
- **menopause**; during: sang bro1
- **menses**:
  - **during**:
    - **agg.**: agar k* aloe *Kali-c* k* kreos k* mag-c k* merc k* petr
      - **aching**: aloe
      - **burning**: agar
      - **pressing** pain: kreos k*
      - **stitching** pain: kali-c k*
      - **tearing** pain: *Merc*
    - **beginning** of menses | **agg.**: merc b4.de
  - **suppressed** menses; from: am-c puls sulph
- **mercury**; after abuse of: asaf nit-ac petr hr1 staph
- **motion**:
  - **agg.**: bry ↓ cassia-s ccrh1• chel ↓ mentho bro1 *Sil* stann [mang stj1]
    - **stitching** pain: bry tl1 chel tl1
  - **amel.**: aur bro1 *Cham* k* *Ferr* sne kali-i sne *Psor* puls k2*
  - **head**; of | **agg.**: am-c
  - **jaw**; of lower:
    - **agg.**: caust ↓ *Con* ↓ *Euphr* ↓ melal-alt gya4 nux-m ph-ac stann sul-ac ↓ verb
      - **cutting** pain: nux-m
      - **drawing** pain: stann verb
        - **outward**: caust *Con* *Euphr* sul-ac h2
- **motion – jaw**; of lower – **agg.**: ...
      - **pressing** pain: nux-m
      - **stitching** pain: *Nux-m* ph-ac
      - **tearing** pain: *Nux-m* stann
- **music**:
  - **agg.**: *Ph-ac* ↓ tab ↓
    - **stitching** pain: *Ph-ac* tab
  - **amel.**: aur-m c1
  - **from**: *Acon* sne ambr cham kreos *Ph-ac* tab
- **nail** were thrust through; as if a: berb kr1
- **nausea**; with: *Dulc* k*
- **neuralgic**: acon bg2 all-c bg2 bell bg2 caps bg2 cham bg2 chin bg2 ferr-p bg2 kali-c bg2 kali-p bg2 mez bg2 plan bg2 puls bg2 rhodi br1 sil bg2 spig bg2 verb bg2
- **noise** agg.: *Acon* sne am-c k* anh sp1 arn *Bell* k* carb-v cham bro1 chin k2 **Con** k* ferr sne gad k* kali-s fd4.de kola stb3• mur-ac k* *Op Phos* plan br1 psor al *Sang* k* *Sil* k* **Sulph** k* symph fd3.de• [tax jsj7]
  - **deaf** ear; in the: am-c
  - **loud**: kali-s fd4.de spig h1*
  - **menopause**; during: sang hr1
  - **tearing** pain: **Sulph**
- **onion** on ear | **amel.**: all-c tl1 puls tl1
- **opening** the mouth:
  - **agg.**: melal-alt gya4 *Petr* ↓
    - **stitching** pain: *Petr*
  - **amel.**: nat-c
    - **stitching** pain: nat-c
- **paroxysmal**: alum anac *Cham* k* crot-t k* dulc fd4.de ferr-p guaj hr1* **Merc** sne merc-i-f kr1* mim-p vml3• petr-ra shn4• *Ph-ac* k* ruta fd4.de sacch-a fd2.de• stront-c tarent k* verb bg2
- **pecking**: dros b7.de* m-arct b7.de
- **periodical**: arn *Gels* k* nat-c k* *Nat-m* k*
- **perspiration**; during: **Acon** b7.de* bell bg2 **Calad** bg2 *Calc* bg2 caust bg2 cham sne **Graph** bg2 ign lyc bg2 merc bg2 nat-m bg2 nit-ac bg2 puls bg2 **Sep** bg2 sulph bg2 thuj bg2
  - **burning**: acon k*
- **piercing** pain: androc srj1• berb k* calc k* canch k* celt a1 cench con k* glon k* kali-i *Nat-c* k* nat-pyru rly4• *Nat-s* k* petr-ra shn4• pycnop-sa mrz1 rat a1 tung-met bdx1•
  - **inward**: *Nat-s* k*
  - **outward**: berb k* glon k*
- **pinching** pain: am-c ang aran arg-n bg *Arn* bg asar *Bell* k* bry k* carb-an carb-v k* caust **Cham** bg clem bg colch *Con* k* crot-t der **Dros** bg dulc k* ferr-ma guaj bg kali-c kreos laur mang h2 meny *Merc* k* *Mur-ac* k* nat-c nit-ac nux-m bg nux-v phos bg plat bg pot-e rly4• **Puls** bg ran-s bg *Rhod* bg sabad bg sabin k* *Spig* spong bg stann k* staph k* **Sulph** bg teucr thuj k* verb bg
- **plug**; as from a: anac b4a.de* des-ac rbp6 spig b7.de*
- **pressing** on ear: raph ↓
  - **drawing** pain: raph
- **pressing** out, as if something must be torn from within: *Con* lil-t k* nat-s k*
- **pressing** pain: *(↗Fullness)* acon k* aesc **Anac** k* androc srj1• aran k* arn k* ars-s-f k2 asaf k* *Asar* k* aur k* *Bell* k* berb k* bism k* bry k* calc k* calc-i k2 calc-p k* camph k* cann-s cann-xyz bg2 *Caps* k* carb-ac hr1 carb-v k* carbn-s carl k* *Caust* k* **Cham** k* *Chel* k* chim-m hr1 chin k* *Clem* coc-c coloc b4.de* con k* crot-h hr1 crot-t *Cupr* k* dig k* *Dros* k* *Dulc* k* eupi k* fl-ac k* form k* gast a1 gink-b sbd1• glon k* granit-m es1• *Graph* k* *Guaj* ham fd3.de• hell k* hep k2 hydr-ac k* hyper k* ign b7.de* ina-i mlk9.de indg k* iod k* ip k* kali-bi bro1 kali-c k* kali-m k2 kali-n k* kali-p kali-s kreos k* lach k* laur k* lyc k* lyss k* mang k* **Merc** k* merc-i-r k* merl k* mosch k* *Mur-ac* k* nat-c k* *Nat-m* k* *Nat-s* k* nat-sil fd3.de• nit-ac k* nux-m k* *Nux-v* k* olib-sac wmh1 olnd k* op a1 osm a1 ozone sde2• *Par* k* petr k* *Ph-ac* k* *Phos* k* phys a1 pin-con oss2• pip-m a1 plac-s rly4• *Plat* k* podo fd3.de• positr nl2• pot-e rly4• prun k* **Puls** k* rheum k* rhod k* ruta k* sabad k* sabin b7.de* **Sars** k* seneg k* sep k* *Sil* k* *Spig* k* spong k* *Stann* staph b7.de* sul-i k2 sulph k* suprar rly4• symph fd3.de• tarax *Thuj* k* trios rsj11• tritic-vg fd5.de vanil fd5.de verat k* [bell-p-sp dcm1 tax jsj7]

- **alternating** with | **tearing** pain (See tearing - alternating - pressing)
- **asunder**: cann-s b7.de* caust b4a.de con b4.de* graph b4.de* hell b7.de* kreos b7a.de* m-aust b7.de nit-ac b4.de* *Par* b7.de* puls b7.de* rhod b4a.de spig b7.de* spong b7.de*
- **finger**; as from a: rheum h
- **forward** in ear: *Cann-s* caust nat-s nux-v par *Puls* spong
- **hot** pressure: ruta h1
- **intermittent**: arn
- **inward**: bell b4.de* *Merc-d* sne nit-ac b4.de* olnd b7.de* rheum b7.de* ruta b7.de* sep h2* spig b7.de* spong fd4.de tarax b7.de* viol-t b7.de* [tax jsj7]
  - **alternating** with | **tearing** out pain (See tearing - outward - alternating - pressing)
- **outward**: aml-ns bg2 ars-s-f k2 astac calc-caust *Caust* k* chel k* *Con* falco-pe nl2• graph guare k* helo c1 helo-s c1* hist sp1 hydr k* iris kali-n kreos k* lyc *Merc* k* mur-ac k* nat-m k* *Nat-s* k* nit-ac *Nux-v* k* par hr1 prun **Puls** k* sep k* vanil fd5.de [tax jsj7]
- **plug**; as from a: *Anac* k* *Spig* k*
- **rhythmical**: mur-ac k*
- **tickling**: ruta h1

- **pressing** teeth close together: anac ↓
  - **ulcerative** pain: anac c1
- **pressing** teeth together: anac c1
- **pressure**:
  - **agg.**: alum ↓ caps k2 cina lac-c mentho bro1 mim-p skp7*• ozone sde2• raph spong
    - **boring** pain: alum
  - **amel.**: alum bism cann-i a1 carb-an caust *Gels* sne gink-b sbd1• ham ruta fd4.de
    - **aching**: ham k*
    - **pressing** pain: bism h1*
    - **stitching** pain: alum h2
  - **forehead** agg.; on: nit-ac k*
    - **stitching** pain: nit-ac
  - **hand**; of:
    - **amel.**: alum ↓ bism ↓ carb-an ↓ hyos ↓
      - **tearing** pain: alum bism carb-an hyos
  - **meatus** agg.; on the external: ros-d wla1
- **pricking** pain: agath-a nl2• **Aur** k* brach k* carc fd2.de• dulc k* irid-met srj5• lepi a1 merc k* petr-ra shn4• psor jl2 raph a1 sil k* tritic-vg fd5.de vanil fd5.de
  - **itching** pain: spig k*
- **prosopalgia**; during: ars hs1 bell hr1 calc hr1 coff br1
- **pulled** inward; as if: dros bg2 verb b7.de*
- **pulled** out; as if: merc bg2
- **pulsating** pain: acon bro1 allox sp1 *Bell* bro1* bufo cact bro1 calc bro1 carb-ac hr1 cardios-h rly4• dulc fd4.de *Ferr-p* bro1 gamb a1 glon a1* indg a1 kali-bi k* lepi a1 mag-c hr1 mag-m a1 *Merc* hr1* merc-c bro1 ol-an a1 petr-ra shn4• plac-s rly4• plan a1 ptel a1 **Puls** hr1* rhus-t k* ruta fd4.de spong fd4.de symph fd3.de• *Tell* k* tere-la rly4•
- **reason**; pain which almost deprived him of: merc *Puls*
- **rest** agg.: phos ↓ psor ↓
  - **stitching** pain: phos psor
- **rheumatic**: arn bg2 *Bell* bg2 chin bg2 hep bg2 *Merc* bg2 nux-v bg2 **Puls** bg2 rhus-t bg2
- **rhythmical**: mur-ac k*
- **rising**:
  - **agg.**: acon sne
  - **bed**; from:
    - **amel.**: coc-c ↓
      - **stitching** pain: coc-c
  - **sitting**; from:
    - **agg.**: nit-ac sne *Sil*
      - **drawing** pain: *Sil*
- **rising**: ...
  - **stooping**; from:
    - **agg.**: mang
      - **tearing** pain: mang
    - **amel.**: carb-v
- **room**; when entering a: nux-v
- **rubbing**:
  - **amel.**: aeth indg ↓ lepi a1 mang k* merc hr1 ol-an k* petr-ra shn4• phos k*
    - **gnawing** pain: indg k*
    - **pinching** pain: mang h2
    - **stitching** pain: mang
    - **tearing** pain: aeth phos
- **scraping** pain: lyc a1 ruta
- **scratching**:
  - **after**: ol-an ↓
    - **burning**: ol-an k*
  - **agg.**: mang ↓
    - **stitching** pain: mang h2
- **screwing** pain: bell k* daph k* *Hep* b4a.de nux-v b7.de
- **shaking** the head; on:
  - **amel.**: kali-c ↓
    - **stitching** pain: kali-c h2
- **shivering**; during: graph b4a.de
- **shooting** (See stitching)
- **singing** agg.: ph-ac
  - **stitching** pain: ph-ac
- **sitting**:
  - **agg.**: berb gels indg lach nat-c nat-m ↓ phos
    - **stitching** pain: gels nat-m phos
    - **tearing** pain: indg nat-c phos
  - **long** time agg.; for a | **after**: *Sil*
- **sleep** | **amel.**: sep k*
- **smarting**: cann-s b7.de*
- **sneezing**:
  - **after**:
    - **amel.**: mag-m ↓
      - **drawing** pain: mag-m
  - **agg.**: act-sp calc ph-ac phos *Puls* ↓ *Sulph*
    - **bursting** pain: *Puls* k*
    - **pressing** pain: phos k* *Sulph* k*
    - **stitching** pain: calc
  - **amel.**: mag-m
- **sore**: acon bg aids nl2• anac b4.de* *Arn* *Aur* sne *Bapt* hr1 bell bg borx k* bry k* *Calc-p* k* caps bg *Caust* k* chel a1 *Chin* k* cic k* crot-h a1 cupr-ar k* des-ac rbp6 ery-a k* fago k* falco-pe nl2• ferr bg form bg graph bg jug-r k* kali-bi *Lac-c* k* lyc b4.de* m-aust b7.de mag-c k* mag-s k* *Mang* k* *Merc* k* merc-i-f k* *Mur-ac* nat-p hr1 nat-pyru rly4• ol-an a1 phos k* pic-ac hr1 psor al* ptel k* puls bg *Ruta* sars bg sel k* sep k* spong k* stry *Sulph* k* symph fd3.de• teucr b7.de* zinc [bell-p-sp dcm1]
- **sore** throat, with: **Apis** *Bar-m* *Cham* **Lach** k* *Merc* k* **Nit-ac** k* *Par* k* petr-ra shn4•
- **sounds**, sharp: **Con** *Cop* k* *Sil*
- **spasmodic**: chin croc bg merc k* murx k* ol-an ran-b k* rob a1 sarr a1 spig *Thuj*
- **spoken** to; when being | **loudly**: ter hr1*
- **squeezed**; as if: arg-n bg2 *Arn* b7.de* **Bell** bg2 bry bg2 carb-v bg2 **Cham** bg2 chel b7.de* cic b7a.de clem bg2 colch bg2 con bg2 crot-h bg2 **Dros** bg2 *Dulc* bg2 guaj bg2 mur-ac bg2 nux-m bg2 **Nux-v** b7.de* phos bg2 plat bg2 **Puls** bg2 ran-s bg2 *Rhod* bg2 ruta b7.de* sabad bg2 sabin bg2 *Spig* b7.de* spong bg2 stann bg2 staph bg2 **Sulph** bg2 thuj bg2 verb bg2
- **stabbing** (See stitching)
- **standing** agg.: mag-s nat-c plb
  - **stitching** pain: mag-s
  - **tearing** pain: nat-c plb

Ear

- **stinging** (See stitching)
- **stitching** pain: *Acon* k* aesc *Aeth* agar *Agath-a* nl2• all-c aln wa1• aloe *Alum* k* alum-p k2 alum-sil k2 am-c k* *Am-m* k* anac k* anan ang k* ant-c k* apis k* apoc arg-met k* *Arg-n* arge-pl rwt5• arizon-l nl2• *Arn* k* *Ars* k* ars-i ars-s-f k2 arum-d *Asaf* aur aur-ar k2 aur-i k2 aur-m aur-m-n aur-s k2 *Bar-c* k* bar-m k* bar-s k2 **Bell** k* benz-ac *Berb* *Borx* k* *Bov* k* brom *Bry* k* bufo calad *Calc* k* *Calc-p* calc-s calc-sil k2 *Camph* k* cann-s k* canth k* *Caps* k* *Carb-an* k* carb-v k* **Carbn-s** carc fd2.de• **Caust** k* **Cham** k* chel k* **Chin** k* *Chinin-ar* *Chinin-s* cimic *Cinnb* clem b4.de* coc-c *Colch* k* *Coloc* k* com **Con** k* crot-c cupr cycl desm-g bnj1 dol *Dros* k* **Dulc** k* echi euph eupi *Ferr* k* ferr-ar ferr-p k* fl-ac form gamb *Gels* k* gink-b sbd1• glon gran **Graph** k* ham fd3.de• hell k* *Hep* k* hist sp1 hura hyos hyper ign k* indg ip b7.de* iris-fl jatr-c *Kali-ar* *Kali-bi* k* **Kali-c** k* **Kali-i** k* kali-m k2 *Kali-n* k* kali-p *Kali-s* kali-sil k2 *Kalm* ketogl-ac rly4• kola stb3• *Kreos* k* *Lach* lact laur k* limen-b-c hm2* lob lyc k* lyss m-arct b7.de m-aust b7.de mag-c k* *Mag-m* k* mag-s *Mang* k* marb-w es1• med k2 meny k* *Merc* k* *Merc-c* k* merc-i-f mez k* mill mim-p skp7• mur-ac k* *Nat-ar* *Nat-c* k* *Nat-m* k* *Nat-p* *Nat-s* k* nat-sil fd3.de• nept-m lsd2.fr nicc *Nit-ac* k* *Nux-m* k* *Nux-v* k* ol-an olnd oscilloc jl2 paeon *Petr* k* *Ph-ac* k* *Phos* k* *Phyt* pic-ac plan k* *Plat* k* *Plb* k* prot jl2 psor ptel **Puls** k* ran-b k* ran-s k* raph rat rhod k* *Rhus-t* rhus-v *Ros-d* wla1 ruta k* sabad k* sal-fr sle1• samb k* sang sarr *Sars* k* sep k* *Sil* k* spig k* spong k* squil b7.de* stann k* *Staph* k* stront-c k* stry suis-em rly4• sul-ac k* sul-i k2 **Sulph** k* symph fd3.de• syph k2* tab tarax k* tarent tep teucr k* *Thuj* k* til tritic-vg fd5.de tub xxb valer vanil fd5.de verat b7.de* verb k* vesp viol-o k* *Zinc* k* zinc-p k2
  - **backward**: mur-ac h2
  - **cold** stitches: ferr-ma
    - **ice**-cold needle; as from (See needles - cold)
  - **insects**; as from stings of: berb kr1
  - **intermittent**: plat h2
  - **inward**: aeth a1 alum am-m b7.de* arg-met k* arg-n arn b7.de* canth b7.de* carb-v k* dros b7.de* dulc a1 hyos b7.de* kali-bi mag-c h2 meny k* ruta fd4.de vanil fd5.de
  - **itching**: mez h2 mur-ac h2 ph-ac h2
  - **needles**; as from | **cold** needles: agar k1
  - **outward**: *Alum* k* am-m b7.de* *Ars* *Asaf* berb calc h2 calc-caust cann-s b7.de* canth *Con* k* dulc h2 kali-c k* laur b7.de* mang k* *Nat-c* k* psor al rhod b4a.de sep *Sil* k* spong b7.de* stront-c k* *Sulph* b4a.de tarax b7.de* viol-o b7.de*
  - **paroxysmal**: caust dulc fd4.de kola stb3•
  - **picking** pain: clem h2
- **stool** | **after**:
  - **agg.**: carbn-s ↓
    - **stitching** pain: carbn-s
  - **during**:
    - **agg.**: sep
      - **pressing** pain: sep k*
- **stooping** | **after** | **agg.**: mang h2
  - **agg.**: bry *Cham* graph kreos m-arct h1 merc h1 merc-c ↓ phos h2 rheum h
    - **pressing** pain: cham kreos
    - **stitching** pain: **Cham** *Merc* merc-c
- **stretched**; as if: viol-o b7.de*
- **swallowing**:
  - **agg.**: *(↗drinking)* ail alum alum-p k2 anac **Apis** *Bar-m* sne benz-ac beryl tpw5 bov *Calc* carb-an *Carbn-s* coc-c *Con* k* cypra-eg sde6.de• dros k* *Elaps* fago k* ferr-m ferr-ma k* gels k13* hep sne jug-c k* kali-bi hr1 kali-s ↓ kola stb3• *Lac-c* al* **Lach** k* lyc k* mang k* *Merc* merc-i-f k* mur-ac nat-i k13 nat-m k* nat-pyru ↓ **Nit-ac** k* **Nux-v** k* ozone sde2• *Par* k* *Petr* k* phos *Phyt* k* plb k* pot-e rly4• ruta fd4.de sars k* *Sulph* k* thuj tritic-vg fd5.de trom vanil fd5.de vip fkr4.de
    - **right** ear: brom ozone sde2• pyrid rly4• [pop dhh1]
    - **left** ear: carbn-s fago a1 kali-bi mang ruta fd4.de tritic-vg fd5.de vanil fd5.de
    - **aching**: con k* dros hr1 fago k* gels ptk1
    - **drawing** pain: alum ferr-ma
    - **pressing** pain: nux-v k* phos k* *Sulph* k* tritic-vg fd5.de vanil fd5.de
    - **sore**: nat-pyru rly4•
- **swallowing – agg.**: ...
    - **stitching** pain: anac con *Gels* kali-s fd4.de lach lyc *Mang* nat-m **Nux-v** *Petr* **Phyt** thuj trom vanil fd5.de
    - **tearing** pain: anac
    - **ulcerative** pain: anac h2* sulph h2
  - **amel.** | **left** ear: rhus-t
- **talking** agg.: mang k* nux-v spig teucr
  - **stitching** pain: *Mang*
- **tearing** pain: *Acon* k* aeth *Agar* k* all-c k2 *Alum* k* alum-p k2 alum-sil k2 am-c am-m k* *Ambr* k* *Anac* k* ang b7.de* ant-c bg2 apis bg2 aran bg2 *Arg-n* arn k* *Ars* ars-i ars-s-f k2 arum-t asaf bg2 aur k* aur-s k2 bamb-a stb2.de• *Bar-c* k* bar-i k2 bar-m bar-s k2 **Bell** k* berb bism k* borx k* bov k* brom bry bg2 calc k* calc-i k2 calc-p calc-sil k2 camph k* cann-i *Canth* k* *Caps* k* carb-an k* *Carb-v* k* carbn-s **Caust** k* **Cham** k* *Chel* k* **Chin** k* *Chinin-ar* coc-c coff bg2 colch k* *Con* k* cupr k* cycl k* dros b7.de* *Dulc* k* elaps ery-a eupi ferr-p bg2 gamb gels bg2 gran *Graph* k* grat *Guaj* k* hep bg2* hyos k* indg iod k* kali-ar kali-bi k* **Kali-c** k* kali-i k* kali-m bg2 kali-n k* kali-p k* kali-s kali-sil k2 kalm kola stb3• kreos bg2 *Lach* lachn laur k* **Lyc** k* *Lyss* m-arct b7.de m-aust b7.de *Mag-c* k* *Mag-m* k* mag-p bg2 *Mang* k* meny b7.de* meph **Merc** k* merl *Mez* k* mur-ac k* nat-ar nat-c k* *Nat-p* nicc *Nit-ac* k* *Nux-m* nux-v k* par k* petr k* *Ph-ac* k* phel *Phos* k* plan bg2* *Plat* k* *Plb* k* psor **Puls** k* raph rat *Rhod* k* rhus-t bg2 sabin *Sars* k* *Sep* sil k* spig k* *Squil* k* *Stann* k* staph bg2 stram stront-c k* *Sul-ac* k* sul-i k2 **Sulph** k* tab tarax k* tarent tell bg2 teucr k* *Thuj* k* til verat b7.de* *Verb* k* *Zinc* k* zinc-p k2 zing
  - **alternating** with | **pressing** pain: bell h1
  - **downward**: **Bell** verb
  - **intermitting**: nat-c psor
  - **outward**: ars h2 bell ↓
    - **alternating** with | **pressing** pain inward: bell h1*
  - **paroxysmal**: bamb-a stb2.de• stront-c
  - **violent**: ferr-p bg2
- **thrust**; as if from a: am-c bg2 anac b4.de* *Arn* bg2 bell b4.de* cham bg2 cic bg2 cina bg2 con b4.de* nat-m b4.de* nux-v b7.de* plat bg2 *Ruta* bg2 spig b7.de*
- **thunderstorm**; before: rhod k*
  - **aching**: rhod k*
- **tickling**: dros ↓
  - **stitching** pain: dros h1
- **tobacco**; from: raph k*
- **toothache**:
  - **after**: mang h2*
  - **with**: ammc hr1 calc-caust c1 chim-m hr1 chr-ac hr1 clem h2* dulc fd4.de *Glon* k* hydrog srj2• meph k* *Merc* h1* merl k* mur-ac h2* ph-ac *Plan* k* *Puls* hr1 **Rhod** k* sep k*
- **torn** out; as if: bell b4.de* cann-s b7.de* *Caust* b4a.de nat-m bg2 par b7.de*
- **touch**:
  - **agg.**: bamb-a stb2.de• bell sne caust h2* *Cham* mrr1 chin k* cop k* cortico tpw7* gast a1 **Hep** sne hydrog srj2• **Kali-l** sne *Lach* k* mag-c h2* mang k* merc gk merc-i-f c1* *Mur-ac* k* *Nit-ac* sne plut-n srj7• rauw ↓ sal-al blc1• teucr a1
    - **burning**: cop k* rauw tpw8
  - **amel.**: mur-ac ↓ sars ↓
    - **stitching** pain: mur-ac h2 sars h2
- **traumatic** causes: arn
- **turning** | **eyes** | **outward**: raph
  - **head**:
    - **agg.**: *Carb-v* chinin-s coc-c **Mag-p** meph
      - **stitching** pain: chinin-s
- **twinging**: aloe anac anag aran arg-n asar *Bar-c* berb k2 carb-v caust coc-c coloc *Crot-t* dulc ferr graph kali-n kreos merc mez par plan prun staph suis-pan rly4•
  - **spasmodic**: crot-t k*
- **twisting**, evening: nux-v ↓
  - **screwing** pain: nux-v k*
- **ulcerative** pain: acon bg2 anac k* ant-t rb2 bell bg2 borx bg2 bry bg2 calc caps b7.de* caust b4.de* cic b7.de* ferr k* form bg2 graph b4.de* kali-c k* mag-c k* mang k* merc bg2 mur-ac k* nat-c h2* phos bg2 psor a1 puls b7a.de* sars k* sep k* spong b7.de* sulph rb2

- **undulating** (See waves)
- **urination**; copious: **Thuj**
- **vexation**; after: sulph
- **violent**: cham mtf11
- **waking**; on: acon-ac rly4• *Form*↓ hydrog srj2• nit-ac sne propr↓ sep k* spong↓ tarent *Tub* ven-m rsj12•
  - **dull** pain: propr sa3•
  - **stitching** pain: *Form* spong
- **walking**:
  - **agg.**: am-c arg-n↓ borx bry con gels sne kali-bi *Lach* mang merl↓ rumx
    - **stitching** pain: arg-n borx kali-bi *Mang* k* merl
  - **air**; in open:
    - **agg.**: am-m benz-ac bry *Chin* con dulc fd4.de *Mang* nat-c par *Sep* spong
      - **boring** pain: am-m
      - **burning**: am-m k*
      - **cramping**: mang spong
      - **pressing** pain: mang k*
      - **stitching** pain: am-m bry con
    - **amel.**: am-m
  - **slowly** | **amel.**: puls k2
- **warm**:
  - **agg.**: acon bro1 borx bro1 calc-p bro1 *Cham* bro1 dulc bro1 *Merc* bro1 nux-v bro1 *Puls* bro1*
  - **amel.**: *Bell* bro1 caps bro1 cham bro1 dulc bro1 hep bro1 *Mag-p* bro1
  - **applications**:
    - **amel.**: cham↓ kali-sil k2
      - **stitching** pain: cham k2
  - **bed**:
    - **agg.**: **Merc** merc-i-f *Nux-v* phos puls
      - **and** wrapping up amel.: *Cham* *Dulc* **Hep** irid-met srj5• kali-ar lach *Mag-p* mur-ac rhod k2 rhus-t *Sep* stram
      - **boring** pain: **Merc**
      - **stitching** pain: **Merc**
  - **room**:
    - **agg.**: *Nat-s* *Nux-v* phos positr nl2• *Puls*
      - **pressing** pain: phos k* *Puls*
      - **tearing** pain: *Nux-v*
    - **amel.**: bell sne sep
    - **entering** a warm room; when: *Nat-s*↓ *Nux-v*↓
      - **amel.**: sep↓
        - **aching**: sep
      - **cold** air; from: graph dgt kali-n↓ *Nat-s*
        - **burning**: kali-n
      - **stitching** pain: *Nat-s* *Nux-v*
- **warmth** agg.; dry: bry
  - **burning**: bry
- **washing** | **after** | **agg.**: taosc iwa1•
  - **agg.**: cortico tpw7*
- **waves**; in: bamb-a stb2.de•
- **weather**:
  - **change** of weather: calc k2 dulc fd4.de gels sne hep sne *Mang* nit-ac sne rhod *Rhus-t* *Sil*
  - **cold** agg.: asar calc k2 calc-p↓ dulc mrr1 ferr-p sne
    - **pressing** pain: asar dulc fd4.de
    - **tearing** pain: calc-p k2
  - **rainy** | **agg.**: nux-v
  - **wet**:
    - **agg.**: *Calc* *Calc-p* *Dulc* k* ferr-p sne gels sne mang k2 *Merc* sne *Nat-s* *Nux-m* bg1* *Petr* bg1* *Puls* sne *Sil*
      - **stitching** pain: *Nat-s*
- **wedge**; as from a: par b7.de*
- **wind**: *Cham* mrr1 nux-v vanil fd5.de [*Mang-act* stj2 *Mang-m* stj2 *Mang-n* stj2 *Mang-p* stj2 *Mang-s* stj2 *Mang-sil* stj2]
  - **cold** | **agg.**: acon k2 ars-i dulc fd4.de irid-met srj5• *Lac-c* k* positr nl2• **Sep** k●* spong
- **writing** agg.: phys k* phyt↓
  - **aching**: phyt ptk1
- **yawning** agg.: acon aids nl2• cocc hep ozone sde2• podo fd3.de• rhus-r verat
  - **burning**: acon k*
  - **stitching** pain: acon podo fd3.de•

▽ - **extending** to:

○ · **Above** the ear: psil ft1

- **All** directions: bamb-a↓
  - **lancinating**: bamb-a stb2.de•
- **Arm**: agath-a nl2•
  - **left**: staph
- **Behind** the ear: psil ft1
- **Brain**: arg-met↓ chin↓
  - **stitching** pain: arg-met h1 chin h1
- **Brain**; base of: arg-met c1
- **Cheek**: kali-p↓ spig↓ sul-ac↓
  - **stitching** pain: kali-p k2 spig hr1
  - **tearing** pain: sul-ac h2
- **Chest**: stram
- **Chin**: bell
  - **stitching** pain: bell h1
- **Downward**: agath-a nl2• **Bell** k* cur verb
- **Eustachian** tube: ant-c carb-an irid-met srj5• med k2 pot-e rly4•
  - **drawing** pain: ant-c
- **Eye**: arn bg2 glon hura indg bg2 *Puls* spig k*
  - **left**: hura
  - **stitching** pain: puls h1 spig hr1
- **Face**: anac *Bell* cann-s melal-alt gya4 *Merc* nux-v puls bl1 stram thea
- **Fingers** | **Tips**: ham
- **Forehead**: bell bg2* dig nux-v k* ptel k* spig bg2*
- **Gums**: limen-b-c hrn2•
  - **left**: limen-b-c hrn2•
- **Head**: aeth a1 *Sulph*
  - **tearing** pain: sulph h2
- **Inward**: arg-met arn bry *Calc* carb-an carb-v dros hyos kali-bi kali-i lob lyss med nat-s nux-v rhus-t thuj verb
- **Jaw**: androc srj1• bov cypra-eg sde6.de• lyc bg1 merl phel ruta fd4.de sal-fr sle1• spig tung-met bdx1•
  - **stitching** pain: spig hr1
  - **Lower**: am-c asar com kali-bi plut-n srj7• ruta fd4.de symph fd3.de•
  - **Upper**: agar
- **Legs**: cur
- **Lobule**: phos
  - **stitching** pain: phos h2
- **Malar** bone: sphing↓ spig
  - **drawing** pain: sphing kk3.fr spig kk3.fr
  - **pressing** pain: spig h1
- **Mouth**; roof of (See palate) kali-bi↓
  - **stitching** pain: kali-bi
- **Mucous** membrane: limen-b-c hrn2•
  - **left**: limen-b-c hrn2•
- **Neck**: agath-a nl2• ars bg2* bapt hr1 **Bell** k* coc-c bg2* *Crot-h* bg2* dulc fd4.de *Haem* bg1* **Kali-bi**↓ *Kreos* bg2* lith-c k* *Lyc* bg2* mur-ac bg2 *Nat-m* bg2* neon srj5• positr nl2• sil k* tarax k* *Ther* bg2* tung-met bdx1• *Zinc* bg2*
  - **side** of: *Carb-v* cocc dulc fd4.de kali-bi *Mag-p* meph *Nat-m*
    - **right**: psil ft1
    - **Clavicular** region and to last back teeth and side of occiput; and: coc-c
  - **drawing** pain: bell h1 dulc fd4.de
  - **stitching** pain: agath-a nl2• **Kali-bi** sne nat-m
  - **And** shoulders: *Nat-m*↓
    - **drawing** pain: *Nat-m*

Ear

- **Nose**: sil
- **Nostril**; left: jac-c ↓ lac-c ↓
  - **boring** pain: lac-c
  - **digging** pain: jac-c k* lac-c
- **Occiput**: ambr k* *Bell* bg2* fago *Mur-ac* bg2* podo fd3.de• [tax jsj7]
  - **Side** of: coc-c
  - **tearing** pain: ambr h1
- **Other** ear: chel *Hep* laur menth ↓ plan br1 thuj bg1
  - **stitching** pain: *Hep* menth c1
- **Outward**: aeth am-c *Am-m* *Ars* asaf bg2 bar-c *Bell* bg2 berb calc-p cann-s carb-v con k* dulc glon gran *Kali-c* k* kali-i lyc *Merc* bg2 merc-i-f nat-m *Nat-s* nicc ol-an bg2 *Puls* k* *Sep* *Sil* k* thuj til
- **Palate**: *Kali-bi* k*
- **Parietal** bone: indg ran-b
- **Parotid** gland and mastoid process: *Kali-bi* sep
- **Shoulder**: agath-a nl2• *Ars* bg2* cann-s cann-xyz bg2 *Kreos* bg2* lach bg2 *Nat-m* rumx ruta bg2
  - **left**: nat-m
  - **stitching** pain: agath-a nl2• nat-m
- **Spine**: agath-a nl2• ptel
- **Teeth**: bell cassia-s ccrh1• chel limen-b-c hrn2* lyss menth c1 mosch ol-an k* plan br1 *Spig* xan
  - **right** teeth; tearing from right ear to: chel ↓
    - **tearing** pain: chel
  - **left** lower: limen-b-c hrn2•
  - **drawing** pain: bell
  - **pressing** pain: spig h1
  - **stitching** pain: spig hr1
  - **tearing** pain: chel
- **Temple**: sars ↓
  - **pressing** pain: sars h2
- **Temples**: eupi form indg lac-c lach *Nux-v* puls sars sil ↓ sul-ac ↓ tarent tung-met bdx1• vanil fd5.de
  - **stitching** pain: *Nux-v* sil a1
  - **tearing** pain: lach *Nux-v* sul-ac h2
- **Throat**: all-c ptk1* carb-an k* carc ↓ chel k* fago k* kali-bi kola stb3• *Merc-i-f* k* pip-n bg2 puls bl1 *Spig* k* sulph ↓ tung-met bdx1• vanil fd5.de
  - **stitching** pain: carc fd2.de• spig hr1 sulph vanil fd5.de
- **Upper** jaw: agar ↓ anac ↓ mag-c ↓
  - **tearing** pain: agar anac mag-c
- **Vertex**: arn k* chel k* mur-ac hr1 ol-an bg2* phos ↓ psor bg2* sars bg2*
  - **tearing** pain: phos h2
- **Zygoma**: hyper spig

○ - **About** the ears: aeth ↓ agar ↓ am-c ↓ am-m arg-n arn ↓ asaf ↓ asar astac a1 aur-m-n ↓ bell bry k* *Calc* ↓ *Calc-p* ↓ canth ↓ cench k2 chel a1 clem ↓ coc-c *Con* ↓ daph ↓ dol hr1 dulc k* ery-a hr1 fago a1 glon k* grat ham a1 indg a1 kali-bi ↓ kali-c k* kali-s fd4.de lac-c al lepi a1 meph hr1 merc-i-f k* mez mur-ac h2* nat-c h2* nat-m ↓ nat-s ↓ nit-ac k* osm a1 ox-ac k* *Petr* k* phos ↓ plb a1 psor ↓, *Puls* rhod k* sabad a1 sabin tell tritic-vg fd5.de viol-o ↓

- **morning** | **rising** agg.; after: arg-n brom
- **afternoon**: clem ↓
  - **drawing** pain: clem k*
- **boring** pain: am-m k* aur-m-n a1 bell k* rhod k*
- **burning**: agar k2 *Calc* k* daph hr1 ham a1
- **drawing** pain: asaf k* grat k* nit-ac k*
- **pinching** pain: glon
- **pressure**:
  - **amel.**: grat ↓
    - **drawing** pain: grat k*
- **sore**: calc-p k* coc-c psor al
- **stitching** pain: arn br1 asaf k* *Calc-p* hr1 clem k* con k* fago k* kali-bi a1 nat-c h2* nat-m k* phos h2* viol-o
- **tearing** pain: aeth am-c canth *Con* ery-a grat kali-c mur-ac h2 nat-s phos h2 plb rhod
- **walking** agg.; after: pall

- **About** the ears: ...

○
- **Bones**: canth br1
- **Glands**: calc-p bg2 phys bg2

- **Above** the ears: *Arg-met* arg-n ars ↓ asaf k* aur-m aur-m-n brom camph cann-i carb-v cedr k* chel k* chinin-s coc-c ↓ coloc dios k* dulc *Eup-per* hr1 hura hydr a1 indg a1 irid-met srj5• kali-c h2* lach led a1 lepi a1 lil-t ↓ lyss hr1 mag-c h2* merc k* mez k* mur-ac a1 nat-s k* nux-m k* osm a1 ox-ac k* pall hr1 plan ↓ plumbg a1 *Puls* k* rhod sabin k* sep h2* sil tell ther ↓ tritic-vg fd5.de vanil fd5.de verat
- **right**: chel ↓
  - **tearing** pain: chel
- **left**: arg-met ↓
  - **tearing** pain: arg-met
- **16** h: merc ↓
  - **stitching** pain: merc
- **morning**: brom
  - **pressing** pain: brom
- **evening**: chel ↓ chinin-s dios k* lyss hr1
  - **tearing** pain: chel
- **aching**: dulc k* lil-t a1 lyss hr1 mez k* tell k*
- **bed** agg.; in: chel ↓
  - **drawing** pain: chel
- **boring** pain: arg-n cann-i k* rhod
- **cutting** pain: carb-v k*
- **drawing** pain: asaf k* chel k* coloc k* lach k* mez k* verat k*
- **pinching** pain: carb-v h2
- **pressing** pain: arg-met aur-m-n brom camph k* cedr k* dulc k* hura lil-t a1 mez k* nux-m k* osm a1 ox-ac k* *Puls* k* sabin k* ther c1 tritic-vg fd5.de
- **scar**; in an old: lach ↓
  - **drawing** pain: lach
- **stitching** pain: ars k* asaf k* coc-c k* indg k* kali-c k* mag-c k* merc k* mur-ac k* plan k* sep k*
- **stool** agg.; during: ox-ac
  - **pressing** pain: ox-ac
- **tearing** pain: *Arg-met* camph chel nat-s sil
- **walking** agg.: ars ↓
  - **stitching** pain: ars k*

▽
- **extending** to:
  - **Crown**: lach ↓
    - **drawing** pain: lach k*
  - **Teeth**; upper back: chel k*

- **Antitragus**: anac ↓ berb ↓ mur-ac k*
- **tearing** pain: anac berb
- **touch** agg.: coc-c ↓ kreos ↓ sep ↓
  - **stitching** pain: coc-c k* kreos k* sep h2*

- **Base** of ears; at the: hist ↓
- **pressing** pain: hist sp1

- **Behind** the ears: acon aesc aeth ↓ agar alet all-c aloe alum am-c am-m ↓ *Ambr* anac anan ↓ androc srj1• ang ↓ arg-met arg-n *Arn* ↓ ars ars-s-f k2 arum-d asaf asar atra-r ↓ *Aur* aur-ar k2 aur-m ↓ *Aur-m-n* aur-s ↓ bar-c bar-m ↓ bar-s k2 *Bell* berb ↓ borx brom ↓ bry cadm-s calc ↓ calc-act ↓ *Calc-p* *Calc-s* cann-i a1 cann-s canth *Caps* carb-ac bg1 carb-an ↓ carb-v cardios-h rly4• castm caul ↓ *Caust* cedr cham ↓ *Chel* chin cic cina ↓ coc-c colch *Coloc* con cop ↓ croc *Crot-h* *Cupr* cupr-ar ↓ dig dios dulc ↓ euphr ↓ fl-ac gels ↓ gent-c ↓ germ-met srj5• *Glon* **Graph** ↓ grat ↓ ham hell ↓ *Hep* hura hydrog srj1• ign indg ip ↓ irid-met srj5• kali-ar kali-bi *Kali-c* kali-i kali-m k2 kali-n *Kali-p* kali-sil k2 kalm kola stb3• *Lach* lachn ↓ laur led lith-c lyc lyss ↓ mag-c ↓ manc mang meny ↓ merc merc-i-f merl mez mosch mur-ac murx ↓ myric nat-ar nat-c nat-m nat-p ↓ nat-s *Nit-ac* nux-v ol-an ↓ onis ↓ oscilloc jl2 ox-ac k2 paeon par *Petr* ↓ ph-ac ↓ phel phos phys phyt pic-ac plac-s ↓ plan ↓ *Plat* ↓ plb ↓ plect ↓ pot-e ↓ *Prun* ↓ *Psor* ↓ ptel *Puls* ↓ pycnop-sa ↓ ran-s rhod ↓ rhus-t rhus-v ↓ rumx ruta fd4.de sabad ↓ sabin sanic ↓ sars sep **Sil** spig spong ↓ squil ↓ stann stry suis-hep ↓ *Sulph* tab tarax ↓ ter ↓ thea ther *Thuj* trios rsj11• tritic-vg fd5.de verat ↓ verat-v verb viol-o viol-t ↓ xan xanth ↓ zinc zinc-p k2

- **right**: aesc agar↓ arum-d$_{ptk2}$ bapt$_{hr1}$ bar-c↓ berb↓ calc-caust↓ calc-p↓ cann-i↓ canth↓ chel$_{c1}$ coloc↓ euphr↓ grat↓ kalm↓ mag-c↓ marb-w↓ mez↓ nat-m↓ nat-s↓ onis↓ plect↓ plut-n↓ ran-s↓ sars↓ thuj↓ tritic-vg$_{fd5.de}$
  - **boring** pain: cann-i$_{k*}$ coloc$_{k*}$ mez$_{a1}$ nat-s$_{a1}$ onis$_{a1}$ ran-s$_{k*}$
  - **burning**: calc-p$_{k*}$ grat$_{k*}$ nat-m$_{k*}$ plut-n$_{srj7}$• thuj$_{k*}$
  - **stitching** pain: berb$_{k*}$ canth euphr$_{k*}$ kalm$_{a1*}$ mag-c$_{h2*}$ marb-w$_{es1}$• plect$_{a1}$ sars$_{h2*}$ thuj
  - **tearing** pain: agar bar-c calc-caust
- **left**: am-m↓ *Ambr*↓ anac↓ androc$_{srj1}$• atra-r↓ **Aur** bell↓ caps↓ caust↓ coloc↓ graph↓ helo↓ helo-s↓ kali-p *Lach* mur-ac↓ ph-ac↓ rumx↓ ruta$_{fd4.de}$ sabad↓ tell↓ viol-t↓
  - **boring** pain: **Aur**$_{k*}$ caust$_{k*}$ *Lach*$_{k*}$ rumx$_{bg2}$ sabad$_{a1}$
  - **drawing** pain: atra-r$_{bnm3}$•
  - **pressing** pain: anac bell$_{h1}$ coloc$_{h2}$ graph$_{h2}$ helo$_{c1}$ helo-s$_{c1*}$ ph-ac$_{h2}$
  - **sore**: tell$_{rsj10}$•
  - **stitching** pain: am-m viol-t$_{a1}$
  - **tearing** pain: *Ambr* atra-r$_{skp7*}$• caps$_{h1}$ mur-ac$_{a1}$
    - **followed by** | **right**: atra-r$_{bnm3}$•
- **daytime**: kali-n↓
  - **drawing** pain: kali-n$_{k*}$
- **morning**: calc↓ dios ptel sulph
  - **stitching** pain: calc$_{k*}$
- **forenoon** | **11** h: ham
- **afternoon**: calc↓ caust↓ ham iris lyss↓ nat-c↓ ph-ac↓ phel↓ ptel rat↓ sars↓ sil↓
  - **13** h: nat-c sil
    - **stitching** pain: nat-c
    - **tearing** pain: nat-c sil
  - **15** h: mag-c↓ phel
    - **stitching** pain: mag-c
    - **tearing** pain: phel
  - **16** h: caust grat
    - **tearing** pain: caust
  - **stitching** pain: calc lyss$_{hr1}$ nat-c$_{k*}$ ph-ac$_{k*}$
  - **tearing** pain: caust nat-c phel sars sil
    - **upward**: rat sars
  - **waking**; on: ptel
- **evening**: bell↓ berb↓ canth↓ carb-an↓ ham nat-m nit-ac↓ ran-s ruta$_{fd4.de}$ sulph↓ thuj↓
  - **21** h: alum↓
    - **tearing** pain: alum
  - **boring** pain: ran-s$_{k*}$
  - **pressing** pain: nat-m
  - **sitting** up in bed:
    - **amel.**: alum↓
      - **tearing** pain: alum
  - **stitching** pain: bell$_{h1*}$ berb$_{k*}$ carb-an nit-ac$_{h2*}$ sulph$_{k*}$
  - **tearing** pain: canth nit-ac$_{h2}$ thuj
- **night**: aur-m↓
  - **burning**: aur-m$_{k*}$
- **aching**: arum-d caust cedr con glon hydrog$_{srj2}$• lyc mang mosch nat-m stry suis-hep$_{rly4}$• viol-o
- **air** agg.; in open: *Kali-p* mang
  - **aching**: mang
- **biting** pain: lyc$_{k*}$ ol-an$_{k*}$ *Puls*$_{hr1}$
- **boring** pain: am-m *Aur*$_{k*}$ aur-m-n$_{k*}$ cann-i$_{k*}$ caust$_{k*}$ coloc$_{k*}$ *Cupr*$_{k*}$ *Lach*$_{hr1}$ mez$_{k*}$ mosch$_{k*}$ nat-s$_{k*}$ onis$_{a1}$ ran-s$_{k*}$ rumx sabad$_{k*}$ *Sep*$_{vh}$ spig
- **burning**: aur$_{k*}$ aur-m$_{k*}$ calc-p$_{k*}$ *Cic*$_{bg}$ grat$_{k*}$ lyc$_{h2}$ nat-m$_{k*}$ rhus-v$_{k*}$ sabad$_{k*}$ spong$_{k*}$ thuj$_{k*}$ verat$_{bg}$
- **cough**; with: phos↓
  - **sore**: phos
- **cramping**: calc-act$_{h1}$ mang murx
- **cutting** pain: bell$_{a1}$ carb-v$_{a1}$ ox-ac$_{a1}$ sil$_{h2*}$
- **cutting** pain: ...
  - **downward**: sil$_{h2}$
- **dinner**; after | **amel.**: bapt$_{hr1}$
- **drawing** pain: aloe anac$_{k*}$ arg-met ars asaf$_{k*}$ atra-r$_{bnm3}$• bar-c bar-s$_{k2}$ canth chel$_{k*}$ chin$_{k*}$ coloc$_{k*}$ crot-h dig dulc$_{fd4.de}$ gent-c$_{a1}$ kali-bi$_{k*}$ kali-c$_{k*}$ kali-n$_{k*}$ kali-sil$_{k2}$ laur$_{k*}$ mang$_{k*}$ merc$_{k*}$ merl$_{a1}$ mur-ac$_{k*}$ ol-an$_{a1}$ petr$_{k*}$ *Prun*$_{k*}$ sars$_{h2}$ sil$_{k*}$ sulph$_{k*}$ thuj$_{k*}$ zinc$_{k*}$
  - **downward**: arg-met
- **drinking** rapidly: nat-m↓
  - **pressing** pain: nat-m$_{h2}$
- **gnawing** pain: kali-i$_{k*}$
- **jerking** pain: kali-c mang merc mez$_{h2}$ sil
- **lancinating**: kali-c pycnop-sa$_{mrz1}$
- **lying** on it: coc-c
  - **pressing** pain: coc-c
- **motion**:
  - **agg.**: bapt$_{hr1}$ nat-m↓ *Prun*↓
    - **drawing** pain: *Prun*$_{k*}$
    - **stitching** pain: nat-m$_{k*}$
  - **head**; of:
    - **agg.**: am-c hydrog$_{srj2}$• *Kali-p*
      - **tearing** pain: am-c
- **paroxysmal**: aesc
- **pinching** pain: lyc merc paeon pot-e$_{rly4}$• sabin
- **pressing** pain: acon$_{b7.de*}$ aloe$_{bg2}$ *Arn*$_{b7a.de}$ asar$_{k*}$ *Bell*$_{k*}$ borx$_{k*}$ cadm-s cann-s canth$_{k*}$ caps$_{sne}$ *Caust*$_{k*}$ cina$_{b7.de*}$ coc-c coloc *Crot-h* hell$_{b7.de*}$ ip$_{h1}$ kali-bi led manc merl mez mur-ac nat-m nat-s ox-ac plac-s$_{rly4}$• *Plat*$_{k*}$ ruta$_{b7.de*}$ stann$_{k*}$ ther *Thuj*$_{k*}$ verb$_{k*}$ viol-o$_{k*}$
- **pressure**:
  - **agg.**: mur-ac$_{h2}$ oscilloc$_{jl2}$
  - **amel.**: mag-c↓ nat-c↓
    - **stitching** pain: mag-c$_{k*}$ nat-c$_{h2*}$
- **pulsating** pain: germ-met$_{srj5}$• hura
- **reading** agg.: aesc spig
  - **boring** pain: spig
  - **tearing** pain: aesc
- **rest** agg.: arg-met sabin↓
  - **drawing** pain: arg-met
  - **stitching** pain: sabin$_{k*}$
- **screwing** pain: ox-ac$_{ptk1}$
- **shaking** the head agg.; on: glon
  - **aching**: glon
- **sitting**:
  - **amel.**: asar mang↓
    - **pressing** pain: asar mang$_{h2}$
- **sitting** up in bed | **amel.**: alum
- **sore**: anac borx *Bry* calc-p **Caps** chel cic$_{k*}$ cupr-ar **Graph** ham$_{bg2}$ kali-c lachn lyc merc mur-ac nit-ac *Petr*$_{k*}$ *Psor* ruta sanic$_{tl1}$ *Sil* verat$_{k*}$
- **spasmodic**: murx$_{k*}$
- **stitching** pain: aeth$_{k*}$ agar$_{k*}$ *Arn*$_{k*}$ ars-s-f$_{br1}$ aur$_{k*}$ aur-s$_{k2}$ bar-c$_{h2*}$ bell$_{k*}$ berb$_{k*}$ brom$_{k*}$ calc$_{k*}$ calc-p cann-s$_{k*}$ canth$_{k*}$ carb-an$_{k*}$ *Caust*$_{k*}$ cham$_{b7.de*}$ cina$_{k*}$ con$_{k*}$ cop$_{k*}$ dig$_{k*}$ dios euphr$_{k*}$ gels$_{k*}$ hell$_{b7.de*}$ hep$_{b4.de*}$ *Kali-c*$_{k*}$ kali-m$_{k2}$ *Kali-n*$_{k*}$ kali-p$_{k*}$ *Kalm*$_{k*}$ lyc$_{k*}$ lyss$_{hr1}$ mag-c$_{k*}$ meny$_{k*}$ mur-ac$_{k*}$ nat-ar$_{k2}$ nat-c$_{k*}$ nat-m$_{k*}$ nat-p nit-ac$_{h2*}$ ph-ac$_{k*}$ phos$_{k*}$ plan$_{a1}$ plect$_{a1}$ ptel$_{k*}$ sabad$_{k*}$ sabin$_{k*}$ sars$_{k*}$ stry sulph$_{k*}$ tab$_{k*}$ tarax$_{k*}$ ter$_{bg2}$ thuj$_{k*}$ tritic-vg$_{fd5.de}$ verat$_{k*}$ verb$_{k*}$ viol-o$_{k*}$ viol-t$_{b7.de*}$ xan$_{k*}$ xanth
- **tearing** pain: agar alum$_{k*}$ am-c$_{k*}$ *Ambr*$_{k*}$ anan ang$_{b7.de*}$ arg-met$_{k*}$ arg-n ars atra-r$_{bnm3}$• *Bar-c*$_{k*}$ bar-m bell$_{k*}$ berb brom calc$_{k*}$ canth$_{k*}$ *Caps*$_{k*}$ carb-v caul *Caust* chel$_{k*}$ coc-c colch$_{k*}$ *Con*$_{b4a.de}$ dig indg kali-c kali-m$_{k2}$ kali-n$_{k*}$ kali-sil$_{k2}$ laur lyc mang meny$_{b7.de*}$ mez$_{h2}$ mur-ac nat-ar$_{k2}$ nat-c nit-ac$_{h2}$ nux-v petr phel plb$_{b7.de*}$ rhod$_{b4.de*}$ rhus-t$_{k*}$ rhus-v sars$_{k*}$ *Sep*$_{k*}$ **Sil**$_{k*}$ squil$_{k*}$ tab tarax$_{h1}$ thuj zinc
  - **intermittent**: petr
- **touch** agg.: bar-c$_{h2}$ mang merc↓ sil

• **touch** agg.: ...
⁝ **aching**: mang
⁝ **drawing** pain: merc$_{h1}$* sil$_{k}$*
⁝ **tearing** pain: bar-c$_{h2}$
• **turning** head agg.: bar-c$_{h2}$ irid-met$_{srj5}$•
• **walking**:
⁝ **agg.**: asar mez↓
: **boring** pain: mez$_{a1}$
: **pressing** pain: asar
⁝ **air** agg.; in open: mang
: **pressing** pain: mang$_{h2}$
⁝ **bent** | **must** walk bent: irid-met$_{srj5}$• lyc
• **warm** bed agg.: coc-c
• **writing** agg.: spig
⁝ **boring** pain: spig
▽ • **extending** to:
⁝ **Arm**, left: staph
⁝ **Clavicle**: petr↓
: **tearing** pain: petr
⁝ **Eye**: apis$_{mrr1}$ **Prun**
: **stitching** pain: **Prun**$_{k}$*
⁝ **Jaw**: *Zinc*↓
: **drawing** pain: *Zinc*
⁝ **Jaws**: kali-n↓ lyc↓
: **stitching** pain: kali-n$_{k}$* lyc$_{k}$*
⁝ **Mastoid** process: atra-r↓ chin↓
: **drawing** pain: atra-r$_{bnm3}$• chin
⁝ **Neck**: agath-a$_{nl2}$• chel↓ lith-c mur-ac↓ nat-m↓ plut-n$_{srj7}$• sil↓ tarax↓
: **cutting** pain: mur-ac$_{bg1}$ sil$_{bg1}$
: **stitching** pain: nat-m$_{k}$*
: **tearing** pain: chel tarax
: **Nape** of neck: mur-ac↓
. **drawing** pain: mur-ac$_{h2}$
. **tearing** pain: mur-ac
⁝ **Shoulder**: ars↓
: **drawing** pain: ars$_{h2}$
: **tearing** pain: ars
⁝ **Temple**: apis$_{mrr1}$ cedr
⁝ **Temples**: cedr↓
: **aching**: cedr
⁝ **Vertex**, occiput, nape and shoulder, moving head agg.: am-c↓
: **tearing** pain: am-c
- **Below** the ears: acon$_{k}$* aloe alum am-c antip$_{br1}$ apis↓ arg-met↓ asar bapt$_{hr1}$ *Bar-c* bry↓ caps$_{k}$* caust chel$_{k}$* coc-c↓ crot-t↓ dig↓ dulc$_{fd4.de}$ hell↓ hell-f$_{a1}$ iod↓ kali-s$_{fd4.de}$ mag-c$_{a1}$ mag-s$_{a1}$ *Merc*$_{k}$* nat-p$_{k}$* nit-ac↓ ol-an$_{k}$* olnd$_{k}$* petr$_{h2}$* phos$_{k}$* ptel↓ sars$_{h2}$* sep$_{k}$* sil$_{k}$* sul-ac↓ tab↓ tarent↓ viol-o↓ xan↓ xanth↓ zinc
• **right**: gink-b$_{sbd1}$• ol-an$_{a1}$ sil$_{a1}$
• **left**: crot-c$_{sk4}$•
• **boring** pain: caust$_{k}$*
• **burning**: mag-c
• **drawing** pain: arg-met$_{h1}$ dig$_{h2}$* dulc$_{fd4.de}$ petr$_{h2}$* sul-ac$_{h2}$*
• **lancinating**: tarent
• **menses**; during: mag-c↓
⁝ **burning**: mag-c
• **motion** of head agg.: am-c
⁝ **tearing** pain: am-c
• **nail** were thrust through; as if a: olnd$_{b7.de}$*
• **pressing** pain: asar dulc$_{fd4.de}$ iod$_{h}$ sep zinc
• **rubbing**:
⁝ **amel.**: ol-an$_{a1}$ phos$_{k}$*
: **tearing** pain: *Phos*
• **sitting** agg.: phos$_{k}$*
- **Below** the ears – **sitting** agg.: ...
⁝ **tearing** pain: *Phos*
• **sore**: **Bar-c** ptel sars zinc
• **stitching** pain: apis bar-c bry$_{k}$* coc-c$_{k}$* crot-t$_{k}$* hell$_{h1}$* kali-s$_{fd4.de}$ mag-s$_{k}$* nit-ac$_{h2}$* sars$_{k}$* viol-o$_{k}$* xan$_{k}$* xanth
• **swallowing** agg.: nat-hchls
• **tearing** pain: acon alum am-c caust iod$_{h}$ nit-ac$_{h2}$ ol-an phos sil tab zinc
▽ • **extending** to | **Jaw**; lower: *Merc*
- **Cartilages**: arn↓
• **lying** on it; when: med$_{hr1}$
⁝ **aching**: med$_{hr1}$
• **sore**: arn$_{br1}$
- **Conchae**: ant-c↓ arund↓ asaf↓ bell↓ bism↓ bov↓ canth↓ *Caps*↓ carb-v↓ caust↓ chin↓ cupr↓ dros↓ dulc↓ guaj↓ hyos↓ iod↓ ip$_{h1}$ kali-bi↓ kali-c$_{h2}$* kola$_{stb3}$• *Kreos*↓ laur$_{a1}$ lyc$_{k}$* lyss↓ mag-c$_{a1}$ mag-s$_{a1}$ mang↓ merc↓ mez↓ mosch↓ mur-ac$_{h2}$* nat-c↓ nat-m↓ op↓ ph-ac↓ phos$_{h2}$* plb↓ plut-n$_{srj7}$• podo$_{fd3.de}$• ran-s↓ rhus-t$_{a1}$ rhus-v↓ ruta↓ sars$_{h2}$* spig spong↓ stann↓ staph↓ sulph↓ symph$_{fd3.de}$• thuj↓ tritic-vg↓ wies↓ zinc↓
• **left**: elat↓
⁝ **stitching** pain: elat$_{hr1}$
• **night**: phos$_{h2}$*
• **burning**: caust kali-bi$_{k}$* lyss$_{hr1}$ merc$_{k}$* mur-ac$_{k}$* nat-m$_{k}$* op$_{k}$* phos$_{k}$* spig$_{k}$* staph$_{h1}$* wies$_{a1}$
• **cramping**: staph$_{h1}$
• **drawing** pain: asaf$_{a1}$ dulc$_{fd4.de}$ sars$_{h2}$* stann$_{h2}$* tritic-vg$_{fd5.de}$
• **pressing** pain: bell$_{h1}$* bism$_{h1}$* cupr$_{h2}$* iod$_{a1}$ lyc$_{k}$* mez$_{a1}$ mosch$_{a1}$ sars$_{h2}$* staph$_{h1}$* symph$_{fd3.de}$• tritic-vg$_{fd5.de}$
• **pressure**:
⁝ **amel.**: bism↓
: **pressing** pain: bism$_{a1}$
• **sore**: ruta$_{h1}$ spong$_{k}$* zinc$_{k}$*
• **stitching** pain: ant-c$_{h2}$* arund$_{c1}$ dulc$_{fd4.de}$ kola$_{stb3}$• *Kreos*$_{b7a.de}$ nat-c$_{k}$* plb$_{a1}$ ran-s$_{b7a.de}$ rhus-t rhus-v$_{a1}$ stann sulph$_{k}$* symph$_{fd3.de}$• thuj$_{k}$*
• **tearing** pain: bell$_{h1}$ bism$_{h1}$ bov canth$_{b7.de}$* *Caps* carb-v$_{b4.de}$* chin cupr dros$_{b7.de}$* guaj hyos kali-c lyc mag-c$_{h2}$ mang mur-ac$_{a1}$ ph-ac sars$_{h2}$ thuj
○ • **Anterior** part: anh$_{sp1}$
⁝ **pressing** pain: anh$_{sp1}$
• **Margin**: ant-c↓ caust↓
⁝ **stitching** pain: ant-c$_{h2}$* caust$_{h2}$*
- **Deaf** ear, in the: lac-h↓ *Mang*↓ sep↓
• **stitching** pain: lac-h$_{sk4}$• *Mang* sep$_{h2}$
- **Deep** in ear: carb-v↓
• **stitching** pain: carb-v$_{bg2}$
- **Ear** to ear: lil-t↓
• **pressing** pain | **band**; as from a: lil-t$_{bg2}$
- **Earring** hole:
• **left**: med↓
⁝ **sore**: med$_{hr1}$
- **Eustachian** tubes: agar↓ alum↓ ant-c$_{br1}$ coloc↓ gels↓ med$_{jl2}$ nat-m↓ *Nux-m*↓ ruta$_{fd4.de}$ sal-ac↓ staph↓
• **chewing** agg.: arg-met↓
⁝ **cutting** pain: arg-met
• **foreign** body; as from a: *Nux-m*$_{k}$*
• **pressing** pain: nat-m$_{bg2}$
• **stitching** pain: agar$_{k}$* alum$_{bg2}$ coloc$_{h2}$* gels$_{bg2}$ sal-ac$_{a1}$* staph$_{bg2}$
○ • **Extending** to | **Tympanum**:
: **boring** with finger:
. **amel.**: carl↓
stitching pain: carl$_{c1}$
⁝ **Upward** Eustachian tube and out of the ears: med$_{hr1}$*

- **External** ear:
  - **tearing** pain:
    - **accompanied** by | **arthritic** or gouty nodosities (See Nodes - external - arthritic - accompanied - tearing)
- **External** ears: *Acon*↓ **Agar**↓ agath-a nl2• alum↓ *Ars*↓ bell↓ bry↓ *Calc-p*↓ caust↓ celt↓ cham↓ chin↓ *Clem*↓ dros↓ ferr-p↓ form↓ ign↓ jug-r↓ kreos↓ lyss↓ *Mang*↓ merc↓ mur-ac↓ nat-p↓ ol-an↓ petr ptk1 pic-ac↓ psor↓ puls↓ rauw↓ *Rhus-t*↓ sang↓ sulph↓ **Tell**↓ upa↓ vib↓ *Zinc*↓
  - **burning**: acon bg2 **Agar** k* alum bg2 *Ars* k* bell bg2 caust bg2* cham bg2 chin bg2 *Clem* k* dros h1* ferr-p bg2 ign bg2 jug-r a1 kreos k* lyss hr1 merc bg2 ol-an a1 pic-ac k* puls bg2 rauw tpw8 *Rhus-t* k* sang bg2* sulph k* **Tell** k* upa a1
  - **piercing**; from: celt↓
    - **sore**: celt a1
  - **sore**: *Acon* k* bry k* *Calc-p* k* celt a1 form k* *Mang* k* mur-ac k* nat-p hr1 psor al vib *Zinc*
- **Front** of ears; in: anac ang arg-met↓ arg-n aur-m-n *Bar-c* bov *Calc*↓ *Calc-p* *Carb-v*↓ caust↓ *Cham*↓ colch *Cupr* dig↓ dios dros↓ dulc fd4.de grat↓ indg kali-c↓ kali-i lach↓ laur↓ mag-c mag-m merc-i-f nat-ox↓ nat-p ol-an *Phos* plan↓ ptel↓ ran-s↓ rat sars↓ senec↓ sep stront-c sul-ac sulph↓ tab *Thuj*↓ tritic-vg fd5.de verb↓ zinc
  - **right**: brass-n-o srj5•
    - **extending** to | **Forehead**: choc srj3•
  - **afternoon**:
    - **15** h: dios↓
      - **aching**: dios
  - **evening**: con↓ mag-c↓ ran-s↓
    - **stitching** pain: con mag-c ran-s
    - **tearing** pain: con h2
  - **aching**: anac cupr dios merc-i-f nat-ox rly4•
  - **bending** | **body**:
    - **right**; to:
      - **agg.**: mag-m↓
        - **boring** pain: mag-m h2
    - **head**:
      - **right** agg.; to | **boring** pain: (non:mag-m h2*)
  - **boring** pain: arg-n aur-m-n *Bar-c* laur
  - **bursting** pain: dros
  - **cutting** pain: arg-met
  - **drawing** pain: *Bar-c* dig h2 sulph
  - **gnawing** pain: sulph h2
  - **jerking** pain: dros
  - **pressing** pain: aur-m-n caust h2 *Cupr* dios *Phos* sep verb h zinc
  - **sore**: *Calc* ptel senec zinc
  - **stitching** pain: arg-met aur-m-n caust h2 *Cham* laur mag-c mag-m plan ran-s sars stront-c *Thuj* tritic-vg fd5.de verb zinc
  - **tearing** pain: ang k* *Bar-c* bov *Carb-v* colch dros h1 grat indg kali-c h2 kali-i lach tl1 mag-c mag-m nat-p ol-an rat stront-c sul-ac tab verb h zinc
  - **warm** room agg.: *Phos*↓
    - **pressing** pain: *Phos*
  - ▽ **extending** to:
    - **Cheek**: sul-ac↓
      - **tearing** pain: sul-ac
    - **Temples**: kali-i↓ sul-ac↓
      - **tearing** pain: kali-i sul-ac
- **Inside** (See meatus)
  - **spasmodic** (See meatus - spasmodic)
- **Lobes**: ambr↓ ars↓ bamb-a stb2.de• carb-an↓ *Carb-v*↓ cham chel↓ chin↓ crot-h↓ dros ham fd3.de• kali-n↓ kali-p fd1.de• mur-ac h2 nat-c↓ nat-m ph-ac phos plat↓ plb psor↓ *Rhus-t*↓ sabad sabin↓ sars↓ sil↓ stann↓ tab **Tell**↓ vanil fd5.de verat↓ zinc
  - **left**: ars↓ mur-ac↓
    - **tearing** pain: ars mur-ac
- **Lobes**: ...
  - **burning**: carb-an k* carb-v h2* chel k* kali-n k* *Rhus-t* a1 sabad k* sabin a1 sil b4a.de **Tell**
  - **corrosive**: plat h2
  - **cramping**: zinc
  - **drawing** pain: ars h2 *Cham* dros kali-p fd1.de• phos sars h2
  - **pressing** pain: phos h2
  - **pressure**:
    - **amel.**: nat-c↓
      - **stitching** pain: nat-c h2*
  - **rubbing**:
    - **amel.**: nat-c↓
      - **stitching** pain: nat-c h2*
  - **sore**: chel h1 crot-h mur-ac
  - **stitching** pain: nat-c h2* nat-m k* ph-ac k* phos k* plb k* psor a1 sabad k* tab k* zinc
  - **tearing** pain: ambr ars carb-an *Carb-v* cham chin mur-ac stann h2 verat h1 zinc
  - **ulcerative** pain: mur-ac h2
  - ○ **Behind** the ear: arg-met↓ mag-c↓
    - **drawing** pain: arg-met
    - **sore**: mag-c h2
- **Mastoid**: am-pic br1 bapt hr1 bell↓ *Canth*↓ caps k2 caust↓ con↓ hir rsj4• mang↓ mur-ac↓ plat↓ **Ruta**↓ sars↓
  - **left**: hydroph rsj6•
  - **cutting** pain: bell h1 caust con mur-ac
  - **pressing** pain: caps sne mur-ac h2 plat h2
  - **pressure** | **amel.**: bapt hr1
  - **sore**: **Ruta**
  - **stitching** pain: sars h2
  - **tearing** pain: *Canth* sne mang h2
  - ▽ **extending** to:
    - **Forehead**: sars↓
      - **drawing** pain: sars h2
      - **stitching** pain: sars h2
    - **Neck**: lith-c↓
      - **cutting** pain: lith-c ptk2
      - **Nape** of: mur-ac↓
        - **cutting** pain: mur-ac ptk2
    - **Orbit**: bapt hr1
    - **Teeth**: mez↓
      - **drawing** pain: mez h2
  - ○ **Below**: *Cina*↓
    - **pressing** pain: cina tl1
    - **stitching** pain: *Cina* a1*
  - **Region** of: hist↓
    - **compressing**: hist sp1
- **Meatus**: abies-n br1 absin *Acon* bro1 aeth↓ agar agath-a nl2• aids↓ allox↓ aloe alum *Anac* anan↓ androc srj1• ang ant-c apis k* apoc arg-met arn ars↓ ars-i bro1 arund *Asaf* *Asar* *Aur* aur-m-n aur-s k2 bar-c *Bar-m* **Bell** k* berb bism borx k* bov brach bro1 brom bry *Calc* *Calc-p* *Calc-pic* bro1 *Canth* k* caps k* carb-an carb-v *Caust* cench k2 **Cham** k* chel chin cic coc-c colch croc crot-t↓ cycl tl1 dig dros *Dulc* ferr ferr-p k* *Fl-ac* gamb *Graph* haem slp (non:ham slp) hell **Hep** k* ign indg jatr-c↓ kali-bi bro1 *Kali-c* *Kali-m* bro1 kali-n kali-sil k2 kreos **Lach** *Lyc* mag-c↓ malar↓ mang meph *Merc* k* *Merc-i-f* *Mez* *Mur-ac* *Nat-m* nat-p nat-s nept-m lsd2.fr *Nit-ac* k* *Nux-v* olnd op ox-ac par petr **Ph-ac** phel *Phos* phys pic-ac↓ *Plat* plb psor k* **Puls** k* ran-b ran-s rheum rhod rhus-t bro1 rumx ruta fd4.de samb sang↓ sars sep *Sil* *Spig* *Spong* stann stry sul-ac *Sulph* sumb tab tarax tarent *Tell* k* *Thuj* tritic-vg fd5.de upa valer vanil fd5.de verat viol-t *Zinc*
  - **right**: brom↓
    - **burning**: brom
  - **evening**: psor↓
    - **pricking** pain: psor jl2

Ear

- **burning**: aeth bg2 anan ars bg2* arund k* aur-s berb ptk1 borx brom canth caps bg2* caust crot-t jatr-c mag-c *Merc* olnd sang bg2* sep spong stry k* sulph ptk1
- **cramping**: *Ang* b7a.de croc b7a.de mur-ac b4a.de petr b4a.de ph-ac b4a.de *Plat* b4a.de ran-b b7a.de samb b7a.de thuj b4a.de valer b7a.de
- **drawing** pain: *Cycl* b7a.de malar jl2 valer b7a.de
- **frequent**: psor ↓
  ⁝ **pricking** pain: psor jl2
- **pricking** pain: psor jl2
- **recurrent**: psor ↓
  ⁝ **pricking** pain: psor jl2
- **rest** agg.: psor ↓
  ⁝ **pricking** pain: psor jl2
- **scratching**; after:
  ⁝ **amel.**: psor ↓
  ⁝ **pricking** pain: psor jl2
- **sore**: aids nl2• allox sp1 merc h* pic-ac hr1
- **spasmodic**: anac *Ang Caust* croc ferr kreos merc mur-ac petr *Ph-ac Plat* puls ran-b samb thuj valer

O • **Inside**: allox ↓
  ⁝ **sore**: allox tpw4

- **Middle** ear | **right**: lat-m sp1
- **Nerves** | **trigeminal** neuralgia: lith-c mtf11 sin-a mtf11
- **Petrous** bone | **touch** agg.: caps bro1 onos bro1
- **Processus** styloideus: agar ↓ con ↓
  - **stitching** pain: agar h2 con h2
- **Side** lain on: am-m ↓
  - **boring** pain: am-m
  - **burrowing**: am-m
- **Spots**; in: calc-p ↓
  - **burning**: calc-p k*
- **Tragus**: anac ↓ cham ↓ fago k* lach a1 *Mur-ac* ↓ nit-ac a1 ph-ac ↓ puls ↓
  - **burning**: *Mur-ac* puls h1*
  - **drawing** pain: mur-ac h2* ph-ac h2*
  - **pressing** pain: mur-ac k* ph-ac h2*
  - **stitching** pain: cham k* lach a1
  - **tearing** pain: anac nit-ac
- **Tympanum**: anac ↓ ang ↓ calc-act ↓ caust ↓ germ-met ↓ kola stb3• nat-s ↓ nit-ac ↓ olib-sac ↓ ran-b ↓ rhod ↓ ser-a-c jl2 tritic-vg fd5.de viol-t ↓
  - **burning**: ang k*
  - **cramping**: olib-sac wmh1
  - **eating**:
    ⁝ **amel.**: germ-met ↓
    ⁝ **pressing** pain: germ-met srj5•
  - **pressing** pain: anac bg2 calc-act bg2 nat-s bg2 nit-ac bg2 viol-t bg2
    ⁝ **airplane**; as if taking off in an: germ-met srj5•
    ⁝ **pressed** out; as if: kola stb3•
  - **tearing** pain: caust bg2 ran-b bg2 rhod bg2

PARALYSIS: | **Auditory** nerve: *(↗HEARING - Impaired - auditory)* acon b2.de* alum b2.de* am-c b2.de* ambr b2.de* anac b2.de* ang b2.de* ant-c b2.de* am b2.de* ars b2.de* asar b2.de* aur b2.de* bar-c b2.de* **Bell** b2.de* borx b2.de* bry b2.de* *Calc* b2.de* cann-s b2.de* caps b2.de* carb-v b2.de* *Caust* b2.de* cham b2.de* *Chel* b2.de* chin b2.de* *Cocc* b2.de* *Con* b2.de* cycl b2.de* dros b2.de* *Dulc* b2.de* *Graph* b2.de* **Hyos** b2.de* ign b2.de* iod b2.de* kali-c b2.de* kali-n b4a.de* led b2.de* *Lyc* b2.de* m-ambo b2.de m-arct b2.de m-aust b2.de mag-c b2.de* mang b2.de* *Merc* b2.de* mur-ac bg2 nat-c b2.de* nat-m b2.de* *Nit-ac* b2.de* *Nux-v* b2.de* olnd b2.de* op b2.de* *Petr* b2.de* ph-ac b2.de* phos b2.de* *Puls* b2.de* rhod b2.de* rhus-t b2.de* ruta b2.de* sabad b2.de* *Sec* b2.de* sep b2.de* *Sil* b2.de* spig b2.de* staph b2.de* sulph b2.de* syph mtf33 verat b2.de*

PEPPERY sensation: hydrog srj2•

PERFORATION:

O - **Tympanum**: aur bg2* calc bg2* calc-i bg2 calc-p sne caps bg2* *Elaps* sne ferr-p sne hep ptk1* *Hydr* bg2* *Kali-bi* bg2* *Kali-p* hr1* lach sne lap-a mtf11 *Lyc* sne merc bg2* merc-c ptk1 *Sil* bg2* sul-i bg2 *Sulph* bg2* tell bg2* *Tub* bg2*

Perforation – Tympanum: ...
  - **air** passing through when snuffing: *Tell* kr1
  - **cavity** filled with thick yellow pus: *Caps* hr1*
  - **edges**; with ragged: *Tub* br1*
  - **threatened** in otitis media: **Merc** kr1 *Puls* kr1

PERIODICITY: aran bg2 plat bg2 sec b7a.de* spig b7a.de* sulph bg2
- **day**; every | **coughing**; when: rhod bg2

PERSPIRATION: act-sp bg2* calc bg2 olnd bg2 puls k* zinc bg2*
- **agg.**: acon b7.de m-aust b7.de nux-v b7.de

O - **Behind** the ears: cimic

POCKS agg.; after: *Merc* b4a.de

POLYPUS: alum bro1 anac k* **Calc** k* calc-i k* calc-p bro1 caust form bro1 *Hep* c2 hydr hr1 kali-bi k* kali-chl kali-i bro1 *Kali-m* bro1 *Kali-s* k* *Lach* k* *Lyc* k* *Merc* k* *Nit-ac* bro1 petr k* *Phos* k* puls lp sang k* sil bg2* staph k* sulph tax c2 *Teucr* k* *Thuj* k*
- **accompanied** by | **discharge** from ear (See Discharges - accompanied - polypus)
- **bleeding**: calc k* merc k* thuj k*
  - **soft** polypus, bleeding easily: *Calc Merc* **Thuj** k*

O - **Meatus**: kali-s tl1

PREGNANCY agg.; during: caps tl1*

PRESSING teeth together: | **agg.**: aloe bg2 anac bg2 nux-v b7.de*

PRESSURE:
- **agg.**: cina b7.de* hyos b7.de* spong b7.de*
- **amel.**: bism b7.de* caust b4.de* thlas bg2

PRESSURE; sensation of (See Fullness; Pain - pressing pain)

PRICKLING: dulc h2

PUFFING in ears from pulsation of temporal arteries: benz-ac k*

PULSATION: acon bg2 aln vva1• aloe alum k* alum-p k2 alum-sil k2 alumn am-c k* am-m k* aml-ns anac k* anan k* ars-s-f k2 ars-s-r atis bnj1 *Aur* b4a.de bar-c k* bar-m bar-s k2 **Bell** k* benz-ac k* berb k* bov b4.de* brom k* bry h1 *Cact* k* calad k* **Calc** k* calc-p k* *Calc-s* calc-sil k2 **Cann-i** k* cann-s k* carb-ac k* carb-an *Carb-v* k* *Carbn-o* carbn-s *Caust* k* cham bg2 chel k* chin k* chord-umb rly4• cob k* coc-c k* coca *Coloc* k* *Con* k* crot-h dig k* dulc fd4.de ferr-m ferr-ma k* ferr-p bg2* gamb k* *Glon* k* graph k* *Hep* k* hydrc k* hydrog srj1• ign k* ind a1* indg k* kali-bi k* kali-c k* kali-i bg2 kali-n k* kali-p kali-s kali-sil k2 kola stb3• *Lach* k* lec br1 lyc k* *Mag-m* k* *Med* k* *Merc* k* *Merc-c* k* merc-i-f k* mez k* *Mur-ac* k* nat-c k* *Nat-m* k* nat-p **Nit-ac** k* ol-an k* onis a1 op k* petr-ra shn4• **Phos** k* phys k* plan k* psor al ptel k* *Puls* k* pyrog jl2 rheum k* rhod k* *Rhus-t* k* rumx sang k* sel k* sep k* *Sil* k* spig k* spong sulph k* syph al *Tell* k* thuj k* visc sp1 zinc k* zinc-p k2
- **right**: am-m k* cact k* calad k* chord-umb rly4• glon k* hydrc k* kali-c h2* lec mag-m k* ol-an k* petr-ra shn4• phos k* plut-n srj7• ptel k* sel k* sep sne sil k*
- **left**: am-c k* *Bar-c* k* berb k* carbn-o cob k* dulc fd4.de gamb k* indg a1 kali-n a1 *Merc-c* k* nat-c k* plan k* rhod k* spig k*
- **morning**: dulc fd4.de graph k*
- **forenoon**: coca dulc fd4.de
  - **11 h**: petr-ra shn4•
- **evening**: cob k* dulc fd4.de hep a1 ind k* indg phys k* zinc
  - **bed** agg.; in: hep thuj
  - **sleep**; when falling asleep: sil
- **night**: am-m k* dig k* *Kali-bi* **Puls** *Rhus-t* k* sep k*
  - **lying** on the ear, when: am-c k* *Bar-c* k* kali-c k* lec sil k*
  - **warm** in bed agg.; becoming: *Merc*
- **accompanied** by | **Head**; pain in (See HEAD - Pain - accompanied - ear)
- **air**; exposure to | **agg.**: ptel
- **breakfast** agg.; after: zinc
- **dinner**; after: carb-an k* indg k*
- **eating** agg.: graph k*
- **lying** | **ear**; on the | **agg.**: am-c bar-c chord-umb rly4• kali-c nat-hchls sil *Spong*

- **lying**: ...
  - **side**; on | **agg.**: bar-c nat-hchls
- **pressure** | **amel.**: carb-an k*
- **rheumatic** pains; after: dig bro1
- **rubbing** | **amel.**: petr-ra shn4•
- **sitting** agg.: am-m k* indg k*
- **standing** agg.: cann-s
- **stooping**:
  - **agg.**: graph rheum zinc
  - **amel.**: cann-s
- **walking** agg.; after: phos k*
- **wavelike**: spig h1*
- **writing** agg.: rheum zinc k*

○ - **Above** the ears: plut-n srj7•
- **Arteries**; of: pyrog jl2
- **Behind** the ears: *Aml-ns* anan ang b7.de* calc-p caust dulc fd4.de glon kali-c kali-m k2 lach mez phos pic-ac rhus-t zinc-chr ptk1*
  - **right**: marb-w es1•
  - **cold** air | **amel.**: rhus-t
  - **lying** on affected side: rhus-t
  - **motion** of head agg.: kali-c
  - **walking** | **amel.**: rhus-t
  - **warmth** agg.: rhus-t
- **Below** the ears: sang
- **Front** of ears; in: bar-c calad hep lyc
  - **morning**: lyc
  - **evening**: lyc
  - **lying** | **ear**; on the | **agg.**: bar-c
    - **side**; on:
      - **left** | **agg.**: choc srj3•
  - **lying** down agg.; after: hep
- **Lobes**: ferr-m ferr-ma k* phos k*
- **Meatus**: coc-c bg2 rumx bg2

QUININE; after abuse of: *Calc* bg2 carb-v bg2 hep bg2 nux-v bg2 *Puls* bg2 sulph bg2

QUIVERING (See Trembling)

RAWNESS behind (See Eruptions - behind)

READING agg.: bry b7.de* verb b7.de*

REDNESS (See Discoloration - redness)

RELAXATION tympanum, sensation of: rheum h*

REST:
- **agg.**: ant-c b7.de*
- **amel.**: staph b7.de*

RESTING, supporting: | **head** | **agg.**: anac b7a.de am b7a.de
- **head** on table | **amel.**: ferr b7.de*

RETRACTED, Tympanum: merc-d ptk1

RETRACTION, sense of: verb k*

REVERBERATIONS (See Noises - reverberating)

RIDING in a car: | **amel.**: graph b4a.de* **Nit-ac** ptk1 puls bg2*

RISING:
- **bed**; from:
  - **after** | **agg.**: arg-met b7.de* nux-v b7.de*
- **sitting**; from | **agg.**: *Phos* bg2 verat b7.de*
- **stooping**; from | **agg.**: cann-s b7.de* *Nux-v* b7a.de

ROLLING to and fro in ear on shaking head; as if something is: ruta

ROOM agg.: bry b7.de* cic b7.de* colch b7.de* m-ambo b7.de *Mag-c* b4a.de phos b4.de* *Puls* b7a.de

ROUGH epidermis:

○ - **Front** of ears; in: olnd b7a.de
- **Meatus**: olnd

RUBBING agg.: *Cina* hr1

RUSH of blood to right ear: **Lyc** h2* lyss ozone sde2• puls h1*

SCARLATINA; after: *Bar-c* b4a.de *Bell* b4a.de *Hep* b4a.de *Lyc* b4a.de *Merc* b4a.de mur-ac ptk1 *Nit-ac* b4a.de sulph ptk1

SCLEROSIS: calc-f mtf11 coenz-q mtf11 cortico mtf11 mand mtf11 syph mtf11 thiosin mtf11 thyr mtf11

○ - **Ossicula**: thyr ptk1
  - **and** petrous portion of temporal bone: calc-f bro1
    - **deafness**, ringing and roaring; with: calc-f br1

SCRATCHING sensation: mang h2* plb b7.de* ruta k* tere-la rly4•

SENSIBILITY:

○ - **External** ear:
  - **diminished**: mur-ac k*
  - **increased**: bit-ar wht1• cortico sp1 kali-i kali-p fd1.de• *Lach* k* merc k* mur-ac h2* valer zinc
    - **deaf** ear; in | **painful**: *Am-c*

SENSITIVE: *Lach* b7.de*
- **air**; to open (See Air - sensitive)
- **touch**; to | **Meatus**: ars bro1 bell bro1 *Borx* bro1 caps bro1 *Cham* bro1 ferr-p bro1 *Hep* bro1 merc bro1 mez bro1 nux-v bro1 petr bro1 tell bro1
- **wind**; to (See Air - sensitive; Wind - sensitive)

○ - **Lobes**: phos h2*
- **Mastoid**: aur bg2 bell bg2 caps bg2 chin bg2 ferr-p bg2 form bg2 hep bg2 lach bg2 mag-c bg2 mang bg2 phos bg2 plb bg2 psor bg2 tell bg2 ther bg2
- **Meatus**: kali-c bg2 lach bg2 tell bg2

SHAKING THE HEAD; on:
- **agg.**: ruta b7.de*
- **amel.**: lach b7a.de

SHOCKS on swallowing: con

SILENCE: | **agg.**: *Ant-c* b7a.de

SINGING agg.: ph-ac ptk1

SITTING agg.: am-m b7.de* bell b4.de* kali-c b4.de* nat-m b4.de* phos b4.de* sulph b4.de*

SLEEP:
- **falling** asleep; when | **agg.**: calad b7.de* rhus-t b7.de* zinc bg2

SNEEZING agg.: *Bar-c* b4a.de euph b4.de*

STANDING: | **amel.**: bell b4a.de

STEATOMA (See Tumors - steatoma)

STENOSIS (See Contraction)

STEPPING agg.: spig b7.de*

STOOL agg.; during: lyc b4.de* sep b4.de*

STOOPING:
- **agg.**: bry b7.de* cham b7.de* croc b7a.de* graph b4.de* m-arct b7.de mang b4.de* merc b4.de* merc-c bg2 phos b4.de* rheum b7.de* stann b4.de
- **amel.**: *Am* b7a.de cann-s b7.de*

STOPPED sensation: acon k* aeth k* agar k* agath-a nl2• agn bg2 alet alum alum-p k2 alum-sil k2 *Anac* k* anag k* androc srj1• ang b2.de* ant-c k* arg-met k* *Arg-n* k* arizon-l nl2• ars k* ars-i ars-s-f k2 **Asar** k* aur-m bamb-a stb2.de• *Bar-c* bar-i k2 bell bg2 berb k* bism k* bit-ar wht1• borx k* brom bros-gau mrc1 bry k* bufo calad k* calc k* calc-s calc-sil k2 cann-i cann-xyz bg2 canth bg2 **Carb-v** k* *Carbn-s* k* carc tpw2* carl a1 *Caust* k* cham k* *Chel* k* chen-v hr1 *Chin* k* chinin-s chlf k* choc srj3• chord-umb rly4• cinnb k* coc-c k* cocc k* cod a1 *Colch* k* coli rly4• coloc k* **Con** k* crot-h k* cycl k* cypra-eg sde6.de• des-ac rbp6 dig k* dios k* dream-p sdj1• dulc fd4.de falco-pe nl2• galla-q-r nl2• gard-j vlr2• gast a1 *Glon* k* *Graph* k* *Guaj* k* guare k* ham a1* hell-v a1 helo-s rwt2• hep k2 hippoc-k szs2 hura hydr k* hydrc k* hydrog srj2• hyos bg2 indg k* *Iod* k* jac-c k* jac-g kali-bi k* kali-c k* kali-m bg* kali-p kali-s kali-sil k2 ketogl-ac rly4• kola stb3• lac-del hrn2• lac-h sk4• *Lach* k* lachn k* *Led* k* lepi a1 lim a1 lob k* lol bg2 **Lyc** k* lyss k* m-ambo b2.de mag-m k* manc k* *Mang* k* marb-w es1• melal-alt gya4 *Meny* k* **Merc** k* merc-c k* merc-i-f k* merl k* *Mez* k* *Mill* k* nat-ar *Nat-c* k* nat-m k* nat-ox rly4• nat-p *Nat-s* neon srj5• *Nit-ac* k* nit-s-d a1 *Nux-m* k* ol-an k* op k*

Stopped sensation: ...
ozone sde2• par bg2 petr k* *Phos* k* phys k* phyt k* plac rzf5• plac-s rly4• plat k* plect a1 podo fd3.de• psil ft1 psor k* **Puls** k* pyrid rly4• raph k* rheum bg2 rhus-t k* rumx ruta fd4.de sabad k* *Sang* sanic sec k* *Sel* k* seneg k* sep k* **Sil** k* sinus rly4• *Spig* k* spong k* stann k* streptoc rly4• succ-ac rly4• suis-em rly4• *Sul-ac* k* sul-i k2 *Sulph* k* symph tab k* tell k* tep k* teucr k* thuj k* til k* tritic-vg fd5.de tub upa k* urol-h rwt• vanil fd5.de *Verat* k* *Verb* k* [bell-p-sp dcm1 heroin sdj2 tax jsj7]

- **alternating** sides: cocc podo fd3.de•
- **right**: aeth ant-c k* arg-met astac c1 brom a1 cann-i caust k* chen-v hr1 colch k* crot-h k* cycl k* dioxi rbp6 dream-p sdj1• dulc fd4.de ham a1* kali-c h2* lach a1 lim a1 lob hr1 merc-i-f a1 nat-c k* *Nat-s* nept-m lsd2.fr ol-an a1 oxal-a rly4• podo fd3.de• propr sa3• *Puls* a1 rhus-t k* spong fd4.de succ-ac rly4• tell k* teucr a1 thuj k* til k* tritic-vg fd5.de *Tub*
- **left**: acon k* agar k* arizon-l nl2• aur-m berb k* cartl-s rly4• coc-c k* des-ac rbp6 falco-pe nl2• ham fd3.de• hydr k* hydrc k* hydrog srj2• irid-met srj5• jac-c k* jac-g kali-bi k* ketogl-ac rly4• lepi a1 melal-alt gya4 merl a1 nat-c a1 nat-p fkr6.de neon srj5• nit-s-d a1 ozone sde2• plac-s rly4• podo fd3.de• rumx ruta fd4.de sel k* spig k* spong fd4.de stann k* ulm-c jsj8• [bell-p-sp dcm1 tax jsj7]
  - **then** right: *Verb* k*
  - **morning**: ozone sde2•
- **morning**: ant-c k* brom caust k* dulc fd4.de ruta fd4.de sil k* spong fd4.de tell c1 teucr thuj k* *Tub* vanil fd5.de
- **forenoon**: ham a1 nat-m podo fd3.de• psor k* ruta fd4.de tell k* vanil fd5.de
- **afternoon**: agath-a nl2• mill k* nat-m k* podo fd3.de• spong fd4.de vanil fd5.de
  - **15** h: jac-g
  - **amel.**: nat-m k*
- **evening**: ant-c k* dulc fd4.de ham k* kali-c k* lim a1 ruta fd4.de spig thuj k* vanil fd5.de
  - **20** h: bamb-a stb2.de• dios
  - **bed** agg.; in: sel k*
  - **sitting** agg.: kali-c k*
- **accompanied** by:
  - **cough**: chel b7.de* sil bg2
  - **hearing**; impaired (See HEARING - Impaired - accompanied - obstruction)
  - **voice**; complaints of: *Meny* bg2 puls bg2
- **air** agg.; in open: spig
- **alternating** with:
  - **clear** ears (See intermittent)
  - **open** sensation: hist vml3•
- **blocked** and unblocked on movement of jaws: melal-alt gya4
- **blowing** the nose:
  - **agg.**: alum k* bamb-a stb2.de• calc *Con* k* *Mang* k* spig *Sulph* k* vanil fd5.de
  - **amel.**: coli rly4• kola stb3• *Merc* k* spong fd4.de stann k* vanil fd5.de
- **boring** with finger | **amel.**: arizon-l nl2• lob k* mag-m k* sel k* spig vanil fd5.de
- **breakfast**; after | **amel.**: ant-c
- **breathing** deeply through nostrils | **amel.**: melal-alt gya4
- **chewing** agg.: sulph ptk1
- **chronic**: petr mrr1
- **cotton**; as from: hippoc-k szs2
- **cough**; after: chel
- **dinner**; after: chinin-m c1 mill
- **eating**; while: *Sulph*
- **excitement** agg.: dig k*
- **hawking** up mucus agg.: hyos k*
- **intermittent**: *Calc* bg2 hist sp1* *Nit-ac* bg2 sulph bg2
- **lying**:
  - **agg.**: coc-c
  - **ear**; on the | **after**: sel
- **menses**; during: mag-m k*
- **moon**; full: graph ptk1
- **plug**; as from a: asar ptk1 led ptk1
- **reading** aloud: verb k*
- **report**; ears open with loud: *Sil*

Stopped sensation: ...

- **rhythmically**: coloc k* vanil fd5.de
- **rising** | **amel.**: stann
- **suddenly**: borx a1 dios rb2 ruta fd4.de tanac br1
- **swallowing**:
  - **agg.**: ars hydrog srj2• vanil fd5.de
  - **amel.**: alum calc merc k* *Sil* k* vanil fd5.de
- **talking** agg.: meny k*
- **valve**; as if by a: *Bar-c* k* borx graph *Iod* k* *Nat-s* k* vanil fd5.de
- **walking** agg.: colch k*
- **washing** hair; from | **right** ear: limest-b es1•
- **weather** agg.; cold: mang k2
- **wool**: cycl bg2 lol bg2 puls bg2 sil bg2
- **writing** agg.: raph k*
- **yawning** | **amel.**: bit-ar wht1• nat-m k* *Sil* k*
- ○ **Eustachian** tubes: *Agra* sne alf br1 ars-i sne bit-ar wht1• elaps sne **Hydr** sne hydrog srj2• *Kali-bi* sne **Kali-m** ptk1* *Lach* sne *Merc* sne *Merc-d* ptk1* *Nit-ac* sne petr ptk1 phyt a1* puls sne sang sne sil sne vanil fd5.de
  - **night**: alf br1
- **Middle** ear: *(↗Adhesions)* dulc mrr1 vanil fd5.de

STRICTURE: | **Eustachian** tubes: lach k2*

STROKES, blows in ears: am-c bg anac bg arn bell bg cham bg cic bg con bg nat-m nux-v paeon plat spig bg

SULPHUR; after abuse of: *Merc* bg2 **Puls** bg2

SUPPURATION: *(↗Abscess; Discharges - purulent; Eruptions - boils)* borx b4a.de merc b4a.de thiosin br1

- **chronic**: kali-bi tl1
- ○ **Behind** the ears: kali-c *Nit-ac* phyt
- **External** ears: alum bg2 **Am-c** bg2 *Carb-v* bg2 kali-c bg2 merc bg2 puls bg2 ruta bg2 spong bg2 stann bg2
- **Front** of ears; in: *Merc*
- **Middle** ear: *Acon* bro1 am-c ars bro1 ars-i bro1 bar-c *Bell* bro1 borx bro1 **Bov** lp* *Calc* k* **Calc-s** k* *Caps* k* carb-an *Carb-v* *Caust* k* *Cham* bro1 *Ferr-p* bro1 gels bro1 guaj bro1 **Hep** k* hydr **Kali-bi** k* kali-m bro1 *Kali-p* k* lap-a vs lyc k* **Merc** k* myris br1* nat-m k* olnd *Plan* bro1 psor k2 *Puls* k* **Sil** k* *Spong* stann sulph thiosin bro1
  - **chronic**: *Aethi-m* bro1 alum bro1 *Ars-i* bro1 aur bro1 bar-m bro1 *Calc* bro1 calc-f bro1 *Calc-i* bro1 caps bro1 *Caust* bro1 chen-a bro1 elaps bro1 *Hep* bro1 hydr bro1 iod bro1 *Kali-bi* bro1 kali-i bro1 kali-m bro1 kali-p bro1 *Kali-s* bro1 kino bro1 lap-a bro1 lyc bro1 *Merc* bro1 naja bro1 nit-ac bro1 *Psor* bro1 *Puls* bro1 *Sil* bro1 *Sulph* bro1 tell bro1 *Thuj* bro1 viol-o bro1

SURGING: kali-p k*

SWALLOWING:

- **agg.**: alum b4.de* anac b4a.de apis ptk1 *Arn* b7a.de ars b4.de* bar-c b4.de* bar-m bg2 bell bg2 bov b4.de* *Calc* b4.de* cic b7.de* con b4.de* dros b7a.de* gels bg2* graph b4.de* lach ptk1 mang b4a.de* nit-ac ptk1 *Nux-v* b7a.de* petr bg2 phos bg2 *Phyt* bg2* plb b7.de* *Puls* b7a.de rhod b4.de* spig b7.de*
- **amel.**: alum b4a.de merc b4a.de rheum b7.de*

SWELLING: *Acon* agar bg2 alum k* alum-p k2 anac k* anac-oc hr1 ant-c k* *Apis* k* arn ars k* *Bell* k* borx k* bry k* bufo k2 **Calc** k* calc-ar k2 calc-p k* *Carb-v* k* caust k* chlol k* cist k* com bg2 dys pte1*• ery-a k* glon k* **Graph** k* hep bg2 hydr k2 ign bg2 iod b4a.de jug-c hr1 jug-r k* kali-ar *Kali-bi* k* *Kali-c* k* kali-n b4.de* kali-p kali-s fd4.de kreos k* lach b7a.de lyc k* med hr1 medus a1* *Merc* k* *Nat-m* k* nit-ac k* *Nux-v* b7a.de *Petr* k* ph-ac k* phos k* pic-ac k* podo fd3.de• psor k* ptel k* **Puls** k* *Rhus-t* k* rhus-v k* samb k* sec b7a.de *Sep* k* *Sil* k* spong k* *Tell* k* tep tritic-vg fd5.de urt-u k* zinc k* zinc-p k2

- **right**: bry hr1 calc k* crot-c k* glon k* jug-c hr1 jug-r kali-s fd4.de ptel k* sulph k2
- **left**: ant-c k* ery-a k* graph k* jug-r a1 kreos a1* nit-ac k* rhus-t k* spong fd4.de *Tell* k*
- **edematous**: medus br1 tell ptk1
  - ○ **Middle** ear: jab mtf11
- **piercing**; from: celt a1
- **sensation** of: lach b7.de*
- **sudden**: calc-p mtf33 dys fmm1•
- ○ **About** the ears: arn k* form k* *Phyt* k* puls k2

- **About** the ears: ...
  - ○ · **Glands**; of: *Bar-c* k* bar-m bell bro1 *Calc* k* caps bro1 carb-an h2 con k2 dig h2 graph bro1 iod bro1 kali-m ptk2 *Merc* k* mur-ac tl1 *Nit-ac* tub xxb
- **Antitragus**: kreos k* spong k*
- **Behind** the ears: ant-s-aur *Aur* *Bar-c* bar-m benz-ac berb bry k* calc k* *Calc-s* **Caps** k* *Carb-an* k* caust cist colch dig *Graph* *Hep* kali-c *Lach* lyc *Nit-ac* ozone sde2• ph-ac puls rhus-t rhus-v *Sil* tab tub al
  - · **hard** and red: tab
  - · **knotty** swelling: *Bar-c* *Graph*
  - · **shiny**: con lyc rhus-v
  - · **warm** bed | **amel.**: nit-ac
  - ○ · **Lymphatic** glands: apis *Bar-c* carc gk dig h2 kola stb3• *Nit-ac*
  - · **Periosteum**: caps *Carb-an* k* *Puls* bg2
- **Below** the ears: all-c **Bar-c** berb *Caps* cist glon br hura nat-hchls ptel samb sars tub al [pop dhh1]
  - ○ · **Glands**: am-c **Bar-c** *Cist* dig *Graph* kali-c k2 *Nit-ac* ptel *Rhus-t* hr1 sars tell hr1
- **Bones**: puls b7a.de
- **Conchae**: ant-c h2* arn k* nat-m k* phos k* **Puls** hr1 sil k* tep k* tritic-vg fd5.de
- **Eustachian** tubes: *(↗Catarrh - eustachian)* ars-i br1*
- **Front** of ears; in: anthraci bry k* *Calc* cist iod *Merc* *Sep* b4a.de
  - ○ · **Glands**: puls h1
- **Inside** (See meatus)
- **Lobes**: chin br1 kali-n k* puls k* *Rhus-t* k* spong fd4.de
- **Mastoid**: caps hr1*
  - · **accompanied** by | **discharge** from ear (See Discharges - accompanied - mastoid)
- **Meatus**: acon bry **Calc** calc-p calc-sil k2 cann-s *Caust* *Cist* *Cupr* graph kali-bi bg2 kali-c h2 lach mag-c merc bg2 mez nat-m k* *Nit-ac* *Petr* ph-ac **Puls** *Sep* k* *Sil* spong bg2 streptoc rly4• *Tell* thuj zinc zinc-p k2
  - · **evening**: mez
- **Parotid** gland (See FACE - Swelling - parotid)
- **Tympanum**: bell mrr1 oscilloc jl2

TALKING:

- **agg.**: aloe bg2 *Arn* b7a.de ars b4a.de caust bg2 *Dig* b4a.de *Iod* b4a.de mang b4.de* nit-ac bg2 nux-v b7.de* *Ph-ac* b4a.de phos bg2 spig b7.de* teucr b7.de* thlas bg2
- **loudly** agg.: mang ptk1 ter ptk1

TENSION: alum k* ambr k* apis asar b7.de* aur bg2* bamb-a stb2.de• carl a1 cham bg2 colch b7.de* dros b7.de* euphr b7.de* glon a1 graph k* kreos k* lach lact a1 lyc k* *M-arct* b7.de* mag-c h2* nux-v k* plb a1 spong b7.de* staph b7.de* thuj k* verat b7.de* viol-o b7.de*

- **painful**: bamb-a stb2.de•
- ○ **Behind**: am-c k* apis b7a.de ars-s-f k2 asar b7.de* caust k* *Con* k* glon a1 *Kali-n* k* lyc k* mag-c h2* mez b4.de* nit-ac k* plat h2* plb b7.de* verb b7.de* *Zinc* b4a.de
- **Below**: *Graph* h2* petr h2* thuj h1*
- **Conchae**: bov k*
- **External** ears: thuj b4.de*
  - · **right** | **skin** stretched over ear; sensation as if: asar hr1*
- **Inside** (See meatus)
- **Meatus**: alum b4.de* *Asar* k* aur k* bamb-a stb2.de• bov b4.de* cham dig k* euphr k* kali-n b4.de* lact k* *Merc*

THICKENING: *Hydr* hr1 rhus-t a1 rhus-v a1

- ○ **Cartilages**: arg-met k2
- **Tympanum**: ars-i bg2* graph bg2 iod bg2 merc-d bro1* mez ptk1 thiosin bro1

THROBBING (See Pulsation)

TICKLING (See Itching)

TINGLING: agar k* am-c am-m ambr anac k* ant-c k* arg-met k2 arn ars ars-s-f k2 ars-s-r hr1 asaf aur-m-n bar-c bar-m *Bell* k* brach k* *Calc* k* camph cann-s carb-ac hr1 carb-an *Carb-v* caust cent a1 cham chel *Chin* hr1 *Chinin-s* cic *Colch* k* con k* dig dulc ferr-ma k* *Graph* ham fd3.de• hell ign kali-ar kali-c kali-m k2 kali-n kalm lachn k* *Laur* k* lol a1 lyc mag-c mill k* *Mur-ac* k* nat-m k* neon srj5• nux-v olib-sac wmh1 plat podo fd3.de• puls k* rhus-t rob a1 salin a1 sarr a1 sars k* *Sep* k* stann stry k* suis-hep rly4• sul-ac sul-i k* *Sulph* k* thuj k* tritic-vg fd5.de vanil fd5.de verat

- **right**: anac c1 salin a1
- **left**: dulc fd4.de ham fd3.de• nat-m h2 sars h2 suis-hep rly4• [tax jsj7]

Tingling – left: ...

  - · **music** agg.: choc srj3•
- **morning** | **bed** agg.; in: sulph
- **noon**: stry k*
- **night**: carb-an tritic-vg fd5.de
- **boring** with finger | **amel.**: lachn a1* mill a1
- **menses**; before: ferr c1
- **sitting** agg.: sulph
- **sneezing** agg.: euph
- **turning** head agg.: nat-c
- **walking**:
  - · **agg.**: rhus-t
  - · **air** agg.; in open: carb-an
- ○ **Meatus**: alum k* dulc fd4.de ham fd3.de•

TINNITUS (See Noises)

TOUCH:

- **agg.**: calc b4.de* calc-p bg2 caust b4.de* chin b7.de* colch b7.de* hep bg2 kreos b7a.de mur-ac b4.de* phos b4.de* rhod b4.de* sep b4.de* sil b4.de* spong b7.de* teucr b7.de* zinc b4.de*
- **amel.**: ant-c b7.de* mang b4.de* ph-ac b4.de*

TREMBLING in: bov k* kali-c k* kali-i a1 spig b7.de*

- **sad** news; after: *(↗MIND - Ailments - bad)* kali-c k* sabin k*
- ○ **Tympanum**:
  - · **right**: propr sa3•
  - · **morning** | **waking**; on: propr sa3•
  - · **evening**: propr sa3•

TUBERCLE, hard:

- ○ **Behind** the ear:
  - · **right** ear: graph ph-ac kl
  - · **left** ear: nicc
- **Lobe**; on the: merc (non:ph-ac kl)
  - ○ · **Posteriorly**: nit-ac h2

TUMORS:

- **cystic**: *Nit-ac* k* ribo rly4•
  - ○ · **Lobes**: nit-ac b4a.de*
- **fungous** (See Fungous)
- **nodes** (See Nodes)
- **small** tumors: | **Behind** the ears: berb bry caust *Con*
- **steatoma**: calc k* nit-ac
  - ○ · **Lobes**: *Nit-ac* bg2
- **wart**-like (See Wart-like)
- **wens**:
  - ○ · **Behind** the ears: merc-i-r verb
  - · **Lobe**; on: nit-ac
- ○ **Behind** the ears: berb ptk1 olnd
- **Front** of ears; in: bry *Calc*
- **Lobes**:
  - ○ · **Below**: *Calc*
  - · **On**: merc *Nit-ac*

TURNING HEAD agg.: carb-v ptk1 *Mag-p* ptk1 seneg b4.de*

TURNING in ear; sensation of something: nux-v b7.de*

TWITCHING: act-sp k* aeth k* *Agar* k* all-c hr1 am-c k* am-m k* anac k* ang b7.de* ant-t k* bar-c k* bar-m bar-s k2 borx bov k* *Calc* k* calc-act calc-p k* calc-sil k2 cann-i k* cann-s b7.de* caust k* chin cina b7.de* clem k* dig k* dros b7.de* fl-ac hep k* kali-c k* kali-m k2 kali-p kreos b7a.de lyc h2* mag-m k* manc k* mang k* merc k* merc-c b4a.de mez k* *Mur-ac* k* nat-m k* nicc k* nit-ac k* nux-v k* op a1 petr k* ph-ac k* phos k* pieri-b mlk9.de plat k* *Puls* k* rhod k* sars k* sil k* spig k* sul-ac k* thuj k* valer b7.de* vanil fd5.de zinc k* zinc-p k2

- **right**: ant-t k* calc k* mag-m k* *Mang* k* nat-m k* nicc a1 nit-ac k* petr h2* plat h2* sul-ac k* thuj k*
- **left**: am-c k* bar-c k* bov k* phos h2* sil k*
- **morning**: ant-t k* mang k* nux-v k*
  - · **6 h**: nat-m
  - · **waking**; on: nux-v k*

Ear

- **evening**: ant-t hr1 mez nux-v k*
- **blowing** the nose agg.: act-sp k*
- **rising** agg.: kali-c k*
- **sneezing** agg.: act-sp k*

▽ - **extending** to:

○ • **Eye** and lower jaw: spig
• **Lower** jaw: nit-ac
• **Mouth**: thuj
• **Outward**: caust
• **Throat**: spig

○ - **Behind** the ears: am-m b7.de* bar-c h2 kali-c h2
- **Below** the ears: elaps
- **Conchae**: agar k* ant-t hr1 calc-act h1 cina b7a.de ph-ac k* spig k* upa k*
- **External** ear | **cramp**-like: cina h1
- **Front** of ears; in: ang b7a.de* dros h1 mag-m
- **Lobe**; in: kali-n h2 nat-c b4a.de ph-ac sars
  • **visible**: sars
- **Meatus**: am-m anac k* carb-v k* lyc k* nit-ac k* valer k* vanil fd5.de

TYMPANITIS (See Inflammation - media)

TYPHOID fever; after: arn bg2 ph-ac bg2 *Phos* bg2 verat bg2

ULCERATION: alum b4.de* am-c b4a.de* *Anac* k* *Bell* b4a.de bov k* bry k* bufo *Calc* k* *Camph* k* carb-v bg2* *Caust* b4a.de graph k* hep kali-bi k* kali-c b4.de* kali-sil k2 *Kreos* b7a.de *Lyc* b4a.de* merc k* mur-ac k* *Olnd* k* *Petr* k* ph-ac b4a.de psor k2 **Puls** b7.de* *Ruta* b7.de* sarr a1 sars k* sep *Spong* b7.de* stann b4.de* sul-ac b4a.de sulph k*
- **right**: bov k*
- **left**: camph graph k* mur-ac k* sars k*
- **swallowing**; painful: anac k* bov a1

○ - **About** the ears: calc-p k* olnd hr1
- **Front** of ears; in: carb-v merc
  • **fistulous** opening: *Calc*
- **Inside** (See meatus)
- **Lobes** | **Hole** for earrings; in: *Ars* b4a.de kali-m ptk1 kola stb3• *Lach* k* med k* *Pitu-a* a sil gk stann k*
- **Meatus**: bov *Calc* k* *Camph* k* *Carb-v* k* *Hep* kali-bi k* kali-c *Lyc* k* *Merc* merc-c ptk1 nit-ac ptk1 *Puls* k* sep *Sil* k* sulph k* tell k*
- **Tympanum**: *Calc* k* hep k2 *Iod* k* *Kali-bi* k* *Kali-p* k* lach sne *Lyc* sne **Merc** k* **Merc-d** hr1* mez k2 *Psor* k* puls k2 *Sil* k*

ULCERS (See Ulceration)

UNCOVERING HEAD agg.: led b7a.de *Nux-v* b7.de* puls b7a.de

URINATION agg.; copious: thuj ptk1

VALVE (See Opening, sensation - closing)

WAKING; on: bell b4.de* borx b4a.de* carb-an b4.de* kali-bi bg2 nux-v b7.de* puls b7.de* rhod b4.de*

WALKING:
- **agg.**: am-m b7.de* bar-c b4.de* *Brom* b4a.de chel b7.de* colch b7.de* mang b4.de* phos b4.de* rhus-t b7.de*
- **air** agg.; in open: am-m b7.de* bry b7a.de par b7.de* spong b7.de*
- **amel.**: bell b4.de*
- **room** agg.; in a: *Colch* b7a.de

WARM:
- **applications**:
  • **agg.**: cham bg2 merc b4.de* phos b4.de*
  • **amel.**: lach b7.de* mag-p bg2 rhus-t b7.de*
- **bed** | **agg.**: puls bg2

WARM; BECOMING:
- **agg.**: kali-c bg2
- **amel.**: nit-ac b4.de*

WARMTH: | **external** | **amel.** (See Warm - applications - amel.)
- **sensation** of (See Heat - sensation)

WART-LIKE growth, inflamed and ulcerated:

○ - **Behind** the ears: calc
- **External** ears; on: bufo

WASHING ear: | **cold** water; with: borx b4a.de*

WATER; sensation of:
- **in** ear: ant-c bry gk carneg-g rwt1• chel sne falco-pe nl2• graph hippoc-k szs2 kola stb3• lach sne meny nept-m lsd2.fr podo fd3.de• pot-e rly4• psil ft1 spig h1 *Sulph* k* [tax jsj7]
  • **right** ear; comes and disappears suddenly in: chr-ac rb2
  • **left**: acon a1* carneg-g rwt1• graph kola stb3• lach sne
  • **drop** of water: acon ptk1
  • **warm** water agg.: acon ptk1 calad cham ptk1
- **into** ears; rushing: adam skp7• hippoc-k szs2 petr rb2 puls rb2 rhod k* sulph rb2
- **out** of ears; running: calc cypra-eg sde6.de• spig sulph
  • **cold** water: merc k*
  • **hot** water:
    ⁝ **right** ear: cham
    ⁝ **left** ear: acon

WAX:
- **balls**; like small: dios ptk1
- **black**: elaps k* *Mang* sne **Puls** k*
  • **hardened**: elaps ptk1
- **brown**: calc-s k* irid-met srj5•
  • **red** or dark: *Mur-ac* k*
- **dark**, flowing: calc-s ptk1*
- **dry**: alum bg2 *Elaps* graph bg2 *Ing* sne lac-c *Lach* k* mur-ac k* petr k*
  • **desquamating** in scales: *Mur-ac*
- **flowing**: am-m bg2 anac bg2 *Kali-c* bg2 *Lyc* bg2 *Merc* bg2 mosch bg2 *Nat-m* bg2 *Nit-ac* bg2 *Phos* bg2 *Puls* bg2
- **foul**: aur bg2 bov bg2 *Carb-v* bg2 caust bg2* hep bg2 lach bg2 zinc bg2
- **hardened**: all-s k* con elaps bg2 lach k* mur-ac hr1 **Puls** k* sel k*
- **increased**: agar k* aloe sne am-m k* ammc hr1 anan k* arist-cl rbp3• bar-ox-suc mtf11 bell k* *Calc* k* calc-sil k2 *Carb-v* bg2 **Caust** k* chin-b kr1 *Con* k* cycl k* dios k* *Elaps* helo c1 helo-s rwt2• *Hep* k* iod b4a.de irid-met srj5• kali-c k* *Lach* bg2 *Lyc* k* *Mang* sne merc bg2 merc-i-r k* merl mosch k* mur-ac petr k* sedi a1 sel k* sep k* sil k* succ-ac rly4• sulph k* syc pte1*• tarent k* thuj k* wies a1 zinc k*
  • **accompanied** by | **itching** (See Itching - accompanied - earwax)
- **mushy**: chel bg2 con bg2 lach b7.de*
- **pale**: **Lach** k* wies a1
- **paper**:
  • **chewed**; like: con b4a.de* lach ptk1
  • **rotten**; like: con
- **purulent**: con k* sep k*
- **red**: **Con** k* mur-ac k* *Psor* k*
  • **blood** red: con b4.de*
  • **dark** red: con bg2 mur-ac bg2
- **reddish**: *Psor* k*
- **removal** of | **amel.**: bry b7.de* con b4a.de
- **scanty**: aur-s k2 lach ptk1
- **slimy**: con b4a.de
- **soft**: petr hr1 sil k* wies a1
- **sour**: act-sp bg2
- **spoiled**: con bg2 *Lach* bg2
- **sticky**: calc bg2 lach bg2 sil bg2
- **thick**: chel k* irid-met srj5• *Petr* k* suis-pan rly4•
- **thin**: am-m k* arizon-l nl2• *Cham* hr1 *Con* k* *Hep* k* iod k* *Kali-c* k* lach k* *Merc* k* mosch k* *Petr* k* sel k* *Sil* k* sulph k* *Tell* k* tung-met bdx1• wies a1
- **troublesome**: con mrr1
- **wanting**: aeth anac k* *Calc* k* *Carb-v* k* *Cham* k* *Graph* b4a.de *Lach* k* mur-ac k* *Petr* k* psor al sil sne
- **whitish**: chel k* con **Lach** k* sep k*
  • **mush**; like: chel
- **yellow**: arizon-l nl2• *Carb-v* k* irid-met srj5• *Kali-c* k* lach suis-pan rly4•

WEATHER:
- **change** of weather: *Mang* b4a.de* nux-m b7a.de
- **cold**:
  • **wet** | **agg.**: calc bg2 dulc bg2 mang b4a.de* merc bg2 puls bg2 *Rhod* b4a.de sil bg2

- **wet** | **agg.**: calc bg2 calc-p bg2 calen bg2 croc bg2 dulc bg2 mang bg2 merc bg2 nat-s bg2 nux-m b7.de* petr bg2 sil bg2

WENS (See Tumors - wens)

WET:
- **getting**:
  - **feet** | **agg.**: dulc bg2

WHISTLING agg.: rhod b4a.de

WIND:
- **agg.**: act-sp bg2 *Cham* ptk1 dulc bg2 hep bg2 lac-c bg2 lach b7.de* lyc bg2 mez bg2 nat-c b4.de* sep bg2 spig b7.de* [mang stj1 *Mang-n* stj2]
- **sensation** of wind:
  - **left**: psor bg2
  - **into** ear or upon it; wind blowing: *Caust* k* *M-aust* b7a.de mang meny mez c1 mosch nat-m bg2 plat rhus-t b7.de* stann staph k*
    - **cold** wind blowing against meatus of right ear: *Caust* mang sanic staph
    - **warm** wind: m-aust b7.de psor bg2
    - **extending** to | **Throat**: mez c1
  - **out** of ears: aeth bg2 bell b4a.de* calc bg2 canth b7.de* chel b7.de* *Fl-ac* b4a.de meny bg2 mill bg2 stram b7.de*
    - **cold** and warm alternating: verat bg2
    - **hot** air; sensation of: bufo bg2 canth b7.de* par b7.de*
    - **passing** out of ears: abrot *Aeth* vh *Bell* *Calc* vh canth *Chel* meli *Mill* vh psor vh stram
      - **putting** finger in ear amel.: chel
    - **puffing** out of ears: agar bg2 aml-ns bg2 borx bg2 meli seneg bg2 sep bg2 sil k*
      - **swallowing** agg.: meli rb1
  - ○ **In** the ear: *Bell* carbn-s *Caust* *Chel* eupi led mag-c mang *Mez* k* mosch plat puls stann stram streptoc jl2 vinc
    - **right**: streptoc jl2
    - **left**: carbn-s mag-c mosch stann
- **sensitive** to: *(↗Air - sensitive)* ars bg2 bov bg2 caust **Cham** k* **Hep** bg2* ina-i mlk9.de kali-p fd1.de• **Lach** *Lyc* mag-c dgt mag-m dgt *Mez* k* nux-v bg2 petr bg2 podo fd3.de• [*Mang* stj1]
- **sound** of (See Noises - wind)

WORMS, sensation of: acon k* calc k* coloc k* guare k* med k* mur-ac hr1 nux-v h1* pic-ac k* puls k* rhod k* rhus-t h1 ruta k* sep h2*

WRITING agg.: rheum b7.de* sep bg2

YAWNING:
- **agg.**: cocc b7.de* hep b4.de* mang b4a.de verat b7.de*
- **sensation** like when yawning: olnd b7.de*

COCHLEA; complaints of: chinin-ar mtf11 chinin-s mtf11 sal-ac mtf11

EUSTACHIAN TUBE; complaints of: alum bg2 *Bar-m* bg2* fago ptk1 *Ferr-p* ptk1 gels bg2 hydr bg2 kali-m bg2* merc-d bg2* nux-m bg2 nux-v ptk1 pen br1 petr bg2* ros-d mtf11 sil bg2* staph bg2
- **right**: hydr ptk1
- **left**: sang ptk1
- **accompanied** by | **hay** fever: ros-d br1

GLANDS about ear; complaints of: bell ptk1 cham ptk1 con ptk1 lach ptk1 *Merc* ptk1 rhus-t ptk1 sil ptk1

LABYRINTH; complaints of: chen-a mtf11 chinin-ar mtf11 nat-sal br1 sal-ac mtf11

LOBES; complaints of: alum b2.de* ambr b2.de* ang b2.de* arg-met b2.de* arn b2.de* **Bar-c** b2.de* bry b2.de* camph b2.de* carb-v b2.de* **Caust** b2.de* chel b2.de* **Chin** b2.de* colch b2.de* graph b2.de* hyos b2.de* *Kali-c* b2.de* *Kali-n* b2.de* **Kreos** b2.de* merc b2.de* *Nat-m* b2.de* nit-ac b2.de* olnd b2.de* *Ph-ac* b2.de* phos b2.de* plat b2.de* puls ptk1 *Sabad* b2.de* *Sars* b2.de* *Sep* b2.de* stann b2.de* teucr b2.de* verat b2.de*

MASTOID; complaints of:
▽ - **extending** to | **Neck**: lith-c ptk1 mur-ac ptk1

MEATUS; complaints of: acon b2.de* aethi-a mtf11 agar b2.de* *Alum* b2.de* ambr b2.de* *Anac* b2.de* ang b2.de* ant-c b2.de* arg-met b2.de* arn b2.de* ars b2.de* asaf b2.de* *Asar* b2.de* aur b2.de* bar-c b2.de* bell b2.de* bism b2.de* *Borx* b2.de* bov b2.de* bry b2.de* **Calc** b2.de* camph b2.de*

Meatus; complaints of: ...
cann-s b2.de* canth b2.de* caps b2.de* carb-an b2.de* carb-v b2.de* *Caust* b2.de* cham b2.de* chel b2.de* chin b2.de* cic b2.de* cina b2.de* clem b2.de* coenz-q mtf11 colch b2.de* coloc b2.de* con b2.de* croc b2.de* cupr b2.de* cycl b2.de* dig b2.de* *Dros* b2.de* *Dulc* b2.de* euph b2.de* euphr b2.de* ferr b2.de* *Graph* b2.de* guaj b2.de* hell b2.de* hep b2.de hyos b2.de* ign b2.de* iod b2.de* ip b2.de* kali-bi bg2 **Kali-c** b2.de* kali-m bg2 *Kreos* b2.de* lach b2.de* *Laur* b2.de* **Lyc** b2.de* m-ambo b2.de m-arct b2.de m-aust b2.de mag-c bg2 mal-ac mtf11 **Mang** b2.de* meny b2.de* *Merc* b2.de* mez b2.de* mur-ac b2.de* nat-c b2.de* *Nat-m* b2.de* *Nit-ac* b2.de* nux-v b2.de* olnd b2.de* par b2.de* *Petr* b2.de* *Ph-ac* b2.de* phos b2.de* *Plat* b2.de* plb b2.de* puls b2.de* ran-b b2.de* rheum b2.de* rhus-t b2.de* ruta b2.de* sabad b2.de* sabin b2.de* samb b2.de* sars b2.de* seneg b2.de* **Sep** b2.de* sil b2.de* **Spig** b2.de* spong b2.de* squil b2.de* stann b2.de* staph b2.de* stram b2.de* sul-ac b2.de* sulph b2.de* tarax b2.de* tell mtf11 teucr b2.de* thuj b2.de* valer b2.de* verat b2.de* *Verb* b2.de* viol-o b2.de* zinc b2.de*

TYMPANUM:
- **adhesions** (See Adhesions)
- **calcareous** (See Calcareous)
- **catarrh** (See Discharges)
- **congested**: *Ferr-p* kr1
  - **capillaries**; distended: *Graph* kr1
  - ○ **Mastoid** periostitis; in: sil kr1
- **inflammation** (See Inflammation - media)
- **perforation** (See Perforation - tympanum)
- **pressing** quickly with a blunt instrument; as if someone were: carbn-s kr1
- **red** (See Discoloration - redness - tympanum)
- **stitches** | **insect** (See Pain - stitching)
- **swelling** (See Swelling - tympanum)
- **thickened**: graph kr1 mez ptk2
  - **white** and opaque | **eruption** on hairy scalp; after a suppressed: mez hr1*
- **thin** and transparent: *Graph* hr1*
- **ulceration** (See Ulceration - tympanum)
- **white**: *(↗Discoloration - white - tympanum)*
  - **right** whiter then left: phos kr1
  - **coating** after scarlatina; covered with: *Graph* kr1

Ear

ACUTE: (↗*MIND - Senses - acute)* **Acon** k* adam srj5• agar k* alco a1 aloe alum k* alum-p k2 alum-sil k2 am-c k* *Anac* k* ang k* anh sp1 apis arizon-l nl2• arn k* ars k* ars-i *Asar* atro k* *Aur* k* aur-ar k2 aur-i k2 aur-s k2 bar-i k2 **Bell** k* borx bry k* bufo k2 cact k* calad k* calc k* calc-i k2 calc-sil k2 calen hr1* *Cann-i* k* carb-v k* carbn-s cham k* **Chin** k* chinin-ar choc srj3• *Cic* cimic *Cocc* k* **Coff** k* coff-t hr1 *Colch* k* **Con** k* cop cupr k* falco-pe nl2• germ-met srj5• gink-b sbd1• *Graph* k* haliae-lc srj5• *Hep* k* hippoc-k szs2 hydrog srj2• ina-i mlk9.de *Iod* k* irid-met srj5• kali-ar k2 *Kali-c* k* kali-m k2 *Kali-p* *Kali-s* *Kola* stb3• lac-del hrn2• **Lach** k* *Lyc* k* lyss hr1 m-aust b2.de mag-c k* mand a1 med hr1* merc k* mur-ac k* *Nat-ar* **Nat-c** k* *Nat-m* *Nat-p* nitro-o a1 *Nux-m* k* **Nux-v** k* olib-sac wmh1 **Op** k* petr k* *Ph-ac* k* *Phos* k* phys k* phyt k* *Plan* k* plb k* plut-n srj7• positr nl2• psor al ptel k* *Puls* k* sal-al blc1• sang k* sanguis-s hrn2• sarr a1 sec k* seneg k* *Sep* k* **Sil** k* *Spig* k* staph k2 stram k* *Stry* k* *Sulph* k* **Tab** k* *Ther* k* thuj k* valer k2 vanil fd5.de *Verat* k* viol-o zing k* [bell-p-sp dcm1 *Buteo-j* sej6 heroin sdj2 tax jsj7]

- **right**: aesc bg2 ferr bg2 hep bg2 lac-c bg2 mag-c bg2 nat-c bg2 nat-s bg2 rhod bg2 sil bg2
- **left**: berb bg2 caust bg2 coloc bg2 gamb bg2 graph bg2 nux-v bg2 zinc-val bg2
- **morning**: *Fl-ac* k*
- **evening**: coca rhod k*
  - **bed** agg.; in: *Kali-c*
  - **sleep**; when falling asleep: calad calc lac-del hrn2•
- **night**: atro k*
- **bed** agg.; in: kali-c
- **chill**; during: arn **Caps**
- **cracking** in ears, preceded by: graph k* mur-ac h2*
- **deafness**, precedes: **Sulph** mp1•
- **deep** resonant tones; to: choc srj3•
- **discharge** of moisture, after: spig h1*
- **distant** sounds: calen ptk1 haliae-lc srj5• nux-m c1*
- **dull**, followed by: cic ptk1 *Iod* mp1•
- **headache**; during: acon bg1 bry mp1• coff bg1 gels psa phyt bg1 spig hr1
- **heat**; during: acon bell calc **Caps** k* **Con** k* ip lyc nux-v
- **labor** pain; during●: cimic
- **menses**; during: *Hyper* k* mag-c nux-v
- **music**, to: **Acon** aloe ambr bufo *Cact* carb-v hr1 *Cham* *Coff* *Lyc* *Nat-c* **Nux-v** ph-ac *Sep* sulph *Tab* taosc iwa1• viol-o
  - **amel.**: **Aur** aur-m
  - **menses**; during: *Nat-c*
  - **organ**: lyc
  - **piano**: phos h2 sabin sulph
  - **violin**: viol-o
- **noise**; to: (↗*MIND - Sensitive - noise)* **Acon** k* aloe am-c anh bro1 apis arn *Ars* *Asar* bro1 **Aur** k* aur-ar k2 aur-i k2 aur-s k2 bar-c **Bell** k* bit-ar wht1• borx k* bry bufo calad *Calc* cann-i c1 caps caust k* cham ptk1 chen-a k* *Chin* k* *Cic* cimic bro1 *Cocc* k* *Coff* k* **Con** k* crot-h k* elaps gk *Ferr* k* ferr-p k* fl-ac k* *Gels* k* graph tl1 hippoc-k szs2 hydrog srj2• *Ign* k* *Iod* k* *Ip* k* *Kali-c* kali-m k2 *Kali-p* k* kali-sil k2 *Kola* stb3• lac-c **Lach** k* lat-m bnm6• **Lyc** k* mag-c k* mag-m k* mill k* **Mur-ac** k* *Nat-ar* *Nat-c* k* *Nat-p* k* *Nat-s* **Nit-ac** k* nux-m k* **Nux-v** k* ol-an k* **Op** k* petr bro1 *Ph-ac* k* phos bro1 phys a1 plan a1* plb k* plut-n srj7• positr nl2• psil ft1 psor al ptel a1* puls bro1 sabal ptk1 *Sang* k* sarr a1 sec k* *Sep* k* *Sil* k* *Spig* k* stann staph k2 sul-i k2 *Sulph* tab k* taosc iwa1• ter bro1 **Ther** k* tritic-vg fd5.de *Tub* vanil fd5.de verat-v a1 **Zinc** k*
  - **hammer**; sounds of a: sang
  - **high**-pitched: chen-a br1*
  - **nausea**, cause: *Cocc* *Ther*
  - **painful**: coff k2
  - **perspiration**; during: **Caps**
  - **retained**; long: lyc phos
  - **rumpling** of paper●: *Asar* sf1.de *Borx* k* calad k* ferr lyc k2 *Nat-c* k* *Nat-s* k* tarax h1* zinc
  - **scratching** on linen and silk●: **Asar** k*
  - **slightest** noise: cimic br
    - ⁝ **louder** noises; not so much disturbed by: borx br1
  - **teeth**, affect the: *Lach* *Ther*
  - **vehicles**, though deaf to voices; of: *Chen-a* k*
  - **watch**; ticking of one's: chen-a c1 hydrog srj2•
  - **water** running: **Lyss**

Acute: ...

- **perspiration**; during: acon arn hr3 bell calc **Caps** hr3 **Cham** chin hr3 *Coff* **Con** ip lyc nat-c **Nux-v** sabad hr3 zinc
- **ringing**; to: lat-m bnm6•
- **sleep** agg.; during: (↗*SLEEP - Semi-conscious - hears)* alumn *Calad*
- **sleepless** from distant sounds: **Op** mp1•
- **stepping** | **every** step; at●: **Coff** k* *Nux-v*
- **typhoid** fever; during: lyc mp1•
- **vision**, with loss of: stram mp1•
- **voices** and talking: acon bro1 *Agar* am-c anh bro1 ars *Asar* bro1 aur bro1 *Bell* bro1 *Borx* bro1 cact carb-v chen-a bro1 *Chin* bro1 cimic bro1 *Cocc* *Coff* k* con ferr-p bro1 *Ign* k* iod bro1 *Kali-c* kali-p lach bro1 mag-m bro1 *Mur-ac* *Nat-c* bro1 nit-ac bro1 nux-m bro1 *Nux-v* bro1 *Op* k* petr bro1 ph-ac k* phos bro1 plan bro1 ptel puls bro1 sang bro1 sep bro1 *Sil* bro1 spig bro1 ter bro1 *Ther* bro1 verat **Zinc** k*
  - **her** own: bell ptk1* op
    - ⁝ **loud**; seems very: (↗*MIND - Sensitive - noise - voices - own)* *Caust* k* hippoc-k szs2
  - **waking**; on: carb-v puls

AURA: bell bg2 cic bg2 hyos bg2 sulph bg2

AUTOPHONY (See Acute - voices - her)

CLAIRAUDIENCE (See MIND - Clairaudient)

DIFFICULT (See Impaired)

DISTANT: (↗*MIND - Distances - inaccurate)*

- **sounds** seem: (↗*Impaired - distance - all; MIND - Distances - inaccurate)* all-c k* bit-ar wht1• cann-i k* cann-s b7a.de* carb-an bg2 cham k* coca k* coli rly4• eupi k* hippoc-k szs2 irid-met srj5• **Lac-c** k* nat-sil fd3.de• nux-m k* peti pieri-b mlk9.de sabal ptk1 sol-ni thuj a1 [bell-p-sp dcm1]
- **voices** seem: cann-i k* cann-s c1 cob-n sp1 coca nitro-o k* pop-cand c1 sabal ptk1 [bell-p-sp dcm1]
  - **his** own voice: aran jl arn cann-i cann-s c1

ILLUSIONS: (↗*MIND - Delusions - hearing; MIND - Delusions - hearing - illusions; MIND - Delusions - noise - hearing)* absin k* am-c anac c1 atro *Bell* ptk1 cact ptk1 *Calc* ptk1 cann-xyz ptk1 carb-v carbn-o carbn-s *Caust* ptk1 **Chin** ptk1 *Chinin-s* ptk1 cimic ptk1 coff k2 con conin c1* corv-cor bdg• crot-h dulc fd4.de elaps eup-pur graph ptk1 hyos kali-ar *Kali-i* ptk1 kali-p fd1.de• lyc ptk1 mang ptk1 med k* petr ptk1 ph-ac ptk1 psor ptk1 *Puls* ptk1 rad-br ptk1 rhodi-o-n c2 sang ptk1 spig ptk1 spong ptk1 stram *Sulph* ptk1 thea thres-a sze7• thyr ptk1 tub ptk1 valer ptk1

- **bellowing**: am-m bg2 aur bg2 bell bg2 bry bg2 *Caust* bg2 con bg2 lach bg2 lyc bg2 nat-c bg2 *Nat-m* bg2 nux-v bg2 puls bg2 sabad bg2 sep bg2 spig bg2 sulph bg2
- **boiling**, bubbling: kreos bg2 nat-c bg2 thuj bg2
- **bursting** like bubbles: nat-m bg2 sulph bg2
- **chiming**: nat-m bg2
- **cracking**: ars ptk1 coff ptk1 dig ptk1 glon ptk1 *Phel* ptk1
- **crying** for help: streptoc jl2
- **drums** which proclaim his execution: verat kr1
- **own** ears; as if he was not hearing with his: psor a*
- **sleep**; during: canth b7.de* carb-v b4.de* cham b7a.de sulph bg2
- **sounds**: (↗*MIND - Delusions - hearing - sounds)*
  - **left** side when they really come from the right; sounds seem to come from: *Nat-c* k*
  - **melody** surrounded by a halo of light; each note upon the piano becomes a center of: (↗*VISION - Illusions - colorful - pulsating)* anh br1
  - **proper** sound; nothing seems to have its: bit-ar wht1• coloc a1
  - **remained** longer: ptel a1*
- **tickling**: chin ptk1 graph ptk1 zinc-val ptk1
- **voice**; his own | **changed**; seems (See MIND - Delusions - strange - voice)
- **world**; as if tone came from another: **Carb-an**

IMPAIRED: abrom-a bnj1 achy-a bnj1 acon b2.de* aeth k* agar k* agn k* *Agra* bro1 alco a1 alet *All-c* k* alum b2.de* alum-p k2 alum-sil k2 *Am-c* k* *Am-m* k* *Ambr* k* *Anac* k* androc srj1• *Ang* k* ant-c k* ap-g vh1 *Apis* k* arg-met k* arg-n k* *Arn* k* *Ars* k* ars-i k2* ars-s-f k2 asaf k* *Asar* k* aster k* *Aur* k* aur-ar k2 aur-i k2 aur-m k* aur-s k* bacls-7 fmm1• *Bapt* k* **Bar-c** k* bar-i k2 *Bar-m* k* bar-s k2 **Bell** k* borx k* *Bov* k* *Bry* k* bufo cact k*

Impaired: ...
cadm-met gm1 caj hr1 calad k* **Calc** k* calc-f bro1 calc-i k2 *Calc-p* k* calc-sil k2 calen bro1 cann-i k* cann-s b2.de* canth b2.de* caps k* **Carb-an** k* **Carb-v** k* carbn-o **Carbn-s** k* **Caust** k* cedr k* cham k* cheir bro1 *Chel* k* *Chen-a* bg2* **Chin** k* chin-b hr1 chinin-ar chinin-s k* chlf k* *Chlor* hr1 *Cic* k* cimic bg2 cist cit-v a1 clem k* coc-c k* *Cocc* k* coff k* colch k* coli rly4• coloc k* com k* *Con* k* conin a1 cor-r k* croc k* crot-c crot-h k* *Crot-t* k* **Cupr** k* *Cycl* k* cypra-eg sde6.de• der a1 dig k* diosm bro1 *Dros* k* dulc k* *Elaps* k* euph b2.de* *Euphr* hr1 *Ferr* k* ferr-ar *Ferr-i* ferr-p k* ferr-pic bro1 *Fl-ac* k* *Form* k* gad a1 galla-q-r nl2• gamb k* gaul a1 *Gels* k* *Glon* k* **Graph** k* grat guaj guar k* guare *Hell* br1 *Hep* k* hippoc-k szs2 hippoz hr1 *Hydr* k* hydr-ac k* hydrobr-ac bro1 **Hyos** k* iber a1* ign k* *Iod* k* iodof a1* *Ip* k* irid-met srj5• jatr-c kali-ar bro1 *Kali-bi* k* *Kali-br* k* *Kali-c* k* kali-chl k* kali-i k* kali-m bg2* kali-n k* kali-p k* kali-s k* kali-sil k2 kalm k* kola stb3• *Kreos* k* *Lach* k* lachn k* *Lact* *Laur* k* *Led* k* lepi a1 lil-t bg2 lob bro1 **Lyc** k* m-ambo b2.de* m-arct b2.de m-aust b2.de *Mag-c* k* *Mag-m* k* mag-p k* *Mang* k* mang-act bro1 med k* meny k* meph k* *Merc* k* merc-c b4a.de *Merc-d* bg2* merc-i-r k* merl k* mez k* mim-p skp7• mosch k* *Mur-ac* k* nat-ar *Nat-c* k* **Nat-m** k* *Nat-p* *Nat-sal* bro1 nicc k* nicot a1 **Nit-ac** k* nux-m k* *Nux-v* k* ol-j hr1 olnd k* onos op k* oscilloc jl2 par k* peti a1 **Petr** k* petr-ra shn4• **Ph-ac** k* **Phos** k* phys k* physala-p bnm7• phyt a1 plat k* *Plb* k* podo fd3.de• positr nl2• psil ft1 *Psor* k* **Puls** k* ran-b b2.de* rham-cal bro1 rheum k* rhod k* *Rhus-t* k* rhus-v a1 rob a1 *Ruta* k* *Sabad* k* *Sabin* k* *Sal-ac* k* salin a1 *Sang* hr1 sangin-n bro1 sarr k* sars k* **Sec** k* sel k* *Sep* k* **Sil** k* *Spig* k* *Spong* k* squil k* stann k* *Staph* k* *Stram* k* *Sul-ac* k* sul-i k2 **Sulph** k* syc bka1*• symph fd3.de• syph al* tab k* tarax k* tarent k* *Tell* k* tep k* teucr b2.de* ther k* *Thiosin* bro1 thuj k* tritic-vg fd5.de tub-a ih valer k* vanil fd5.de vario jl2 *Verat* k* verat-v ptk1 **Verb** k* viol-o k* wies a1 zinc k* zinc-p k2 [spect dfg1]

- **one side**: *Ambr* b7a.de
  - **noises** in other: ambr ptk1
- **right**: ant-c tl1 *Arn* *Calc* k* cocc cycl k* *Ham* k* iber a1 ip h1 *Kali-s* k* *Led* k* merc k* nat-c a1* petr-ra shn4• phys k* propr sa3• puls hr1 thuj a1 [heroin sdj2]
  - **then** left: elaps
- **left**: all-s vh1 anac k* ap-g vh *Arg-n* k* borx bry k* *Calc* hr1 chel k* cit-v a1 coc-c k* hydroph rsj6• jac-c k* mag-m k* nat-c k* ol-j hr1 op k* podo fd3.de• *Sal-ac* sne vanil fd5.de visc c1
  - **accompanied** by | **buzzing** in head: acon vh1
  - **then** right: aloe hr sulph
- **morning**: calc k* clem k* gamb k* merc-i-r k* rob a1 sil k* stann k*
  - **amel.**: rhod ptk1
- **forenoon**: asaf k* clem *Ham* k* mag-c k* phys k* tritic-vg fd5.de
  - **11** h: mag-c
  - **11**-20 h: phys
- **afternoon**: elaps sil k*
  - **ear**; with pain in the: ign
- **evening**: anan ant-c h2* cham ham a1 kali-c k* merc-c k* nicc k* plb k* rob a1 tarax
  - **21** h: phys
- **night**: *Cedr* k* elaps k*
- **accompanied** by:
  - **coryza**: *Cham* b7a.de *Nux-v* b7a.de
  - **discharge** from ears: *Calc* b4a.de caust b4a.de *Lyc* b4a.de *Puls* b7a.de sulph b4a.de
    - **purulent**: *Arn-c* b4a.de *Anac* b4a.de **Lyc** b4a.de *Nit-ac* b4a.de *Phos* b4a.de
  - **dryness** in ears: *Petr* b4a.de
  - **fullness** in the ear; sensation of (See EAR - Fullness - accompanied - impaired)
  - **gout**: *Ferr-pic* bro1* ham bro1* kali-i bro1* led bro1* sil bro1* sulph bro1* visc bro1*
  - **hardened** earwax: mur-ac b4a.de
  - **heat** in ears: mur-ac b4a.de
  - **noises**●: *Agra* sne am-c b4a.de *Anac* b4a.de arg-n ptk1 bar-c b4a.de borx b4a.de *Calc* b4a.de caust b4a.de* cimic ptk1 cocc h1 con b4a.de* dig b4a.de* *Graph* b4a.de *Hep* b4a.de kali-c b4a.de lyc b4a.de* mag-c b4a.de* mang b4a.de merc b4a.de* nit-ac b4a.de* petr b4a.de* ph-ac b4a.de* *Phos* b4a.de *Rhod* b4a.de sal-ac tl1 sec a1 sep b4a.de* sil b4a.de* staph sne sulph b4a.de*
- **accompanied** by – **noises**: ...
    - **constant** noises: chin k2
    - **ringing**: led b7a.de
    - **rushing**: ant-c b7a.de *Arn* b7a.de cocc b7a.de dros b7a.de rheum b7a.de
      - **waterfall**; like a: ther br1
  - **obstruction** of ears: *Asar* b7a.de cann-s b7a.de cham b7a.de chel b7a.de cycl b7a.de led b7a.de puls b7a.de *Spig* b7a.de stann b7a.de verat b7a.de
    - **mucus**; with: *Nit-ac* b4a.de
  - **rheumatism**: *Ferr-pic* bro1* ham bro1* kali-i bro1* led bro1* sil bro1* sulph bro1* visc bro1*
  - ○ **Brain**; complaints of (See HEAD - Brain; complaints of - accompanied - hearing)
  - **Tonsils**; swelling of (See THROAT - Swelling - tonsils - accompanied - hearing)
- **adenoids**; from: staph ptk1*
- **adhesions** in middle ear, from: iod ptk1*
- **air**; in open:
  - **agg.**: calc
  - **amel.**: mag-c merc
- **alternating** with:
  - **acuteness** of hearing: aur bg2 bell bg2 calc bg2 chen-a ptk1 coff bg2 hippoc-k szs2 lyc bg2 positr nl2• sep bg2 sil bro1 spig bg2
  - **obscuration** of sight: cic k*
  - **otorrhea**: puls
  - ○ **Eye** symptoms: guare k* manc bg2
- **anger**; after: mosch k2
- **apoplexy**; after: chen-a vml3•
- **auditory** nerve; from paralysis of the: *(↗EAR - Paralysis - auditory)* *Bar-c* *Bell* calc *Caust* k* chel *Chen-a* bro1 dulc *Glon* k* graph *Hyos* k* kali-n c1* kali-p k* lyc merc nit-ac nux-v *Op* petr *Ph-ac* *Puls* sec *Sil* k*
- **band** over ear; as if caused by: m-arct mp1•
- **bending** head backward | **amel.**: *Fl-ac* k*
- **blowing** the nose:
  - **agg.**: sulph tl1*
  - **amel.**: hep *Mang* k* merc k* *Sil* k* stann
- **bone** conduction; due to deficient or absent: *(↗sclerosis)* chen-a bro1*
- **burning** and stinging, after: caps
- **catarrh** of eustachian tube: all-s vh1 ars-i br1* **Asar** k* bacls-7 fmm1• *Cal-ren* bro1 **Calc** k* *Calc-act* bro1 *Calc-ar* bro1 *Calc-br* bro1 *Calc-caust* bro1 *Calc-cn* bro1 *Calc-f* bro1 *Calc-hp* bro1 *Calc-i* bro1 *Calc-lac* bro1 *Calc-lp* bro1 *Calc-m* bro1 *Calc-ox* bro1 *Calc-p* bro1 *Calc-pic* bro1 *Calc-s* bro1 *Calc-sil* bro1 *Calc-st-s* bro1 caps k* caust bro1* chin k2 dulc mp1• gels k* graph bro1* hep bro1* hydr bro1* ign sne *Iod* k* kali-bi bro1* *Kali-l* sne **Kali-m** bro1* **Kali-s** k* kali-sil k2 lach k* *Lap-a* bro1 *Mang* k* mang-act bro1 mentho bro1* merc bro1 merc-d br1* merc-sul mp1• mez mp1• morg mp1• morg-p fmm1• nit-ac k* **Petr** k* *Phos* **Puls** k* rhus-t sf1.de ros-d bro1* *Sang* k* sep bro1* *Sil* k* sulph gk thiosin br1*
- **changing** the linen agg.: *Sil* k*
- **children**; in: calc c1 med mtf33
  - **nutritional** disturbances; from: calc bro1 merc-i-r bro1
- **cholera**; after: sec ptk1
- **clock**, near: ph-ac h2
- **cold**; after taking a: ars bell *Elaps* ferr-p ptk1 gels ptk1 kali-m ptk1 lach *Led* mag-c k* merc merc-d ptk1 phos ptk1 **Puls** sil k*
  - **menses**; during: ferr-p ptk1
- **cold**; exposure to: acon bro1 kali-m bro1 visc bro1
- **cold** sensation in abdomen; with: ambr ptk1*
- **concussions**, from: **Arn** k* chinin-s k* croc kl* hell mp1• nat-s mp1•
- **confusion** of sounds: alco a1 **Carb-an** k* coli rly4• dulc fd4.de germ-met srj5• *Ph-ac* b4a.de plat k* sec k*
- **congenital**: meph mp1• tub mp1•
- **convulsions**; after: sec ptk1
- **coryza**; during: *Puls* b7a.de
- **cotton** in ear; as from: cycl tl1 hippoc-k szs2 kola stb3• led ptk1 mang sne ozone sde2• [heroin sdj2]
  - **motion** of jaw | **amel.**: ozone sde2•
- **cough**:
  - **amel.**: *Sil* k*

- during: chel k* puls seneg bg2
- **delusions**; during: hyos mp1•
- **dentition**; during: cheir bro1
- **dinner**; after: **Nux-v** hr1 sulph k*
- **direction** of sound, cannot tell: arg-n vn* *Carb-an* k* kali-bi vn* ter c1
- **discharge**:
  - **amel.**: cadm-met gm1
  - **suppressed**; after: lob bro1*
- **distance**:
  - **all** sounds seem far off: *(↗Distant - sounds)* cann-i cann-s k2 lac-c k* nux-m
  - **amel.**: calen br1* gamb ph-ac br1
  - **when** at a: ph-ac k*
- **dressing** agg.: sil gln1.de
- **drunkards**; in: *Kali-br* hr1*
- **dull**; everything sounds: cham b7.de* lyc b4a.de
- **earwax**; after removal of | **amel.**: *Con*
- **eating** agg.: sil k* spig **Sulph** k*
- **eczema**; after a suppressed: lob br1* mez sne
- **eructations** agg.: petr h2*
- **eruptions**; after suppressed: *Ant-c* b7a.de lob ptk1 mez ptk1
  - **head**; about the: *Mez* k*
- **fever** | **intermittent** fever; suppressed: *Calc* *Chinin-s*
- **fog** in front of ears; as from: spig b7.de*
- **foreign** body in the ear; as from a: phos b4a.de sep b4a.de sil b4a.de
- **fright**; after: mag-c
- **headache** in occiput, with: ign h1
- **heat**; during: *Euphr* hr1 rhus-t
- **hiccough**; after: bell h1*
- **humiliation**, after: ign mp1•
- **increasing** | **slowly**:
  - ⁝ **decreasing** | **slowly**: kali-c h2
  - **suddenly**: dig *Elaps* *Gels* *Mag-c* br1 mosch k2 nicc nit-ac h2 *Plb* sec sep *Sil*
- **infectious** disease; from: am bro1 *Bapt* bro1 *Gels* bro1 hep bro1 lyc bro1 petr bro1 phos bro1 puls bro1
- **inflammation** middle ear; from (See catarrh; cold sensation)
- **injury** to membrana tympani: tell ptk1
- **intermittent**: mag-m k* sil k*
- **leaf** or membrane before the ear; like a: acon k* agar agn b7.de alum am-c ang b7a.de ant-c k* *Arg-n* *Arn* b7a.de asaf *Asar* k* bell k* calad k* *Calc* cann-s k* carb-v b4.de chel *Chin* k* cocc k* *Cycl* k* *Graph* hyos b7.de iod b4a.de kali-i kola stb3• led k* m-arct b7.de* *Mag-m* k* mang med meny b7.de nit-ac k* par k* *Phos* k* rheum b7.de rhus-t b7.de sabad k* sel k* spig b7.de *Sul-ac* k* sulph b4a.de tab verat k* **Verb** k*
  - **shaking** head and boring in ear amel.: sel k*
- **low** toned sounds: chen-a br1*
- **malaria**; after: carb-v mtf33
- **measles**; after: arg-n asar *Carb-v* k* cheir c1 kali-chl hr1 *Merc* k* nit-ac ptk1* **Puls** k* *Sil* spig *Sulph* k* ter c1
- **mechanical** injuries (See concussions)
- **membrana** tympani thickened, retracted: mez mp1•
- **menses**:
  - **before** | **agg.**: ferr ferr-pic bro1 *Kreos* k* scroph-n c1
  - **during** | **agg.**: *Calc* k* ferr-p ptk1 *Kreos* k* mag-m k* scroph-n c1
  - **suppressed** menses; from: *Cub* bg1* nat-c ptk1
- **mercury**; after abuse of: *Asaf* k* aur bg *Carb-v* k* chin bg hep bg* merc-d sne *Nit-ac* k* *Petr* k* *Staph* *Sulph*
  - **syphilitic**: nit-ac tl1
- **moon** full agg.: sil h2
- **mortification**; from: ign k*
- **nervous**: *Ambr* bro1 anac bro1 aur bro1* *Bell* bro1 caust bro1 chin bro1 chinin-s bro1 *Gels* bro1 *Ign* bro1 jab bg3* *Lach* bro1 ph-ac bro1 phos bro1 plat bro1 puls bkh1 sil hr1 syph ptk1 tab bro1 *Valer* bro1
- **nitric** acid, abuse of: petr k*
- **noises**:
  - **amel.**●: calen bro1* **GRAPH** k ●* jab ptk1 mag-c c1 nit-ac bro1*
  - **with** (See accompanied - noises)
  - **without**: *Sep* b4a.de **Sil** b4a.de *Sulph* b4a.de
- **old** people: bar-c k* *Cic* k* kali-chl bg3 kali-m bg3* mag-c c1 merc-d h1* *Petr* k* phos bro1
- **overheated**, from becoming: merc merc-i-f
- **pain** in ear:
  - **after**: caps ptk1 nat-c ptk1
  - **with**: cham mp1• cycl h1*
- **paralysis** of auditory nerve (See auditory)
- **periodical**: caps mp1• sec k* *Spig* k*
- **plug**, as from a: sep h2*
- **pocks**; after: *Merc* b4a.de *Sulph* b4a.de
- **pregnancy** agg.; during: caps
- **pressing** on ear | **amel.**: *Phos* k*
- **pressure** in ear; from: diosm br1
- **quinine**, after abuse of: *Calc* k* carb-v bg hep bg nux-v bg puls bg sulph bg
- **rapid**: phos mp1•
- **reading** aloud, while: verb k*
- **receding**: syph jl2
- **report**:
  - **amel.**: graph hep k* *Mang* bg2 mur-ac *Sil* k* tarent
  - **loud** | **deafness**; followed by: sep
- **riding**:
  - **carriage**; in a:
    - ⁝ **agg.**: graph tl1 nit-ac tl1
    - ⁝ **amel.**: calen bro1* *Graph* k* **Nit-ac** k* *Puls* k*
- **ringworm**; from suppurating: mez tl1
- **room** agg.: mag-c k*
- **rubbing** | **amel.**: *Phos* k*
- **scarlet** fever; after: *Am-c* b4a.de asaf hr1 bell b4a.de* **Carb-v** k* *Crot-h* k* *Graph* k* *Hep* k* *Lach* k* **Lyc** k* *Nit-ac* *Puls* k* *Sil* **Sulph** k*
- **sclerosis** of ossicula: *(↗bone)* calc-f st1 ferr-pic bro1 thiosin bro1
- **scrofulous**: *Aethi-m* bro1 calc bro1 merc bro1 mez bro1 sil bro1 *Sulph* bro1
- **sensation** of: plut-n srj7•
- **sexual** excesses: *Petr* k*
- **singing** agg.: apoc
- **stooping**:
  - **agg.**: *Croc* merc merc-c zzl
  - **amel.**: croc ptk1
- **storm**; before: croc pd nux-m k*
- **street**; in | **amel.**: mag-c c1
- **suddenly**: elaps ptk1 gels ptk1 *Mag-c* ptk1 plb ptk1 sep ptk1 sil ptk1
- **swallowing**:
  - **agg.**: ars aur phos
  - **amel.**: alum merc k*
- **syphilitic**: kreos bro1 lac-c ptk1
- **tired**; when: sabin c1*
- **tonsils**:
  - **enlarged**: *Agra* br1 aur bar-c mp1* calc mtf33 calc-i mp1• calc-p mp1• calc-s mp1• hep ptk1 *Kali-bi* k* lyc mp1• med c1* *Merc* k* *Nit-ac* k* plb mp1* psor mp1• *Staph* k* sul-i mp1•
  - **hypertrophy** of: *Agra* bro1 aur bro1 *Bar-c* bro1 calc-p bro1 *Hep* bro1 lyc bro1 merc bro1 nit-ac bro1 plb bro1 psor bro1 staph bro1
  - **induration**: nit-ac tl1
- **transient**: sep h2* sulph h2*
- **typhoid** fever; after: *Apis* k* *Arg-n* k* *Ars* k* *Nit-ac* k* *Ph-ac* k*
- **voice**, the human●: *Ars* k* bell bg2 bov k* bufo calc bro1 *Carb-an* k* *Chen-a* k* dulc fd4.de *Fl-ac* k* hippoc-k szs2 ign bro1 iod kali-p led bg lyc h2 mag-c st1 mur-ac k* nit-ac b4a.de onos **PHOS** k ●* rhus-t k* *Sil* k* **SULPH** k ●*
  - **except** for: ign k*
- **walking**:
  - **agg.**: chinin-s k* verat-v ptk1
  - **amel.**: merc-i-r ptk1
  - **wind**; in the | **agg.**: phos
- **warm**:
  - **room**:
    - ⁝ **agg.**: kali-s
    - ⁝ **amel.**: *Puls* k*

Hearing

- **warm**; becoming:
  - **walking**; from:
    - **agg.**: merc
    - **amel.**: merc-i-r k* puls sne
- **washing** agg.: calc-s sne sil k*
- **water** in ear; from getting: limest-b es1• verb c1*
- **weather**:
  - **changes** of weather agg.: mang sabin c1*
  - **cold**:
    - **wet** | **agg.**: acon mp1• dulc kali-m mp1• *Mang* k* *Merc* *Puls* *Sil* visc mp1•
  - **foggy**: sabin c1
  - **wet** | **agg.**: anan calen bg1* *Mang* mang-act bro1 sabin c1
- **working** in water: *Calc* k* calc-s sne
- **worms**, with infection of: chen-a vml3•
- **worry**, but noises are intensified; from: ign c1
- **yawning** | **amel.**: sil k*

LOST: acon aconin c2 *Agar* k* agra c2* all-s c2 alum am-c k* *Ambr* k* *Anac* ant-c k* ant-t *Arg-n* k* arn k* ars *Ars-i* k* asaf k2 *Asar* aur aur-ar k2 *Aur-m* k* aur-s k2 bar-c k* *Bar-m* k* **Bell** k* borx bry caj hr1* *Calc* k* calc-f bro1* calen c2* cann-s caps k* carb-an bro1 *Carb-v* k* *Carbn-s* k* carl **Caust** k* cham cheir c1* *Chel* b7a.de* chen-a hr1* chin bg2* chinin-s k* chinin-sal c1* chlor k* *Cic* k* cob-n sp1 coca k* cocc k* colch bg2 colum-p sze2• con k* cortico sp1 croc crot-t k* cupr dig bro1 dros dulc k* *Elaps* k* ferr-p bro1 ferr-pic bg2* form a1* gels k* *Glon* k* *Graph* k* gua br1 **Hep** k* hippoz hr1 hydr bro1 hydr-ac k* hydrobr-ac bro1 *Hyos* k* iod hr1* ip c2 jatr-c kali-ar k* kali-bi bg2 kali-br a1 kali-c k* kali-i mtf11 kali-m bro1* *Kali-n* k* kali-p k* kali-s bg2 kara a1* kreos bg2 lac-c al* lach k* lachn k* lam a1 laur led k* lepi a1 lob c2* lob-e c2 lol a1 **Lyc** k* *Lyss* *M-arct* b7.de mag-c k* mag-m k* mag-p hr1 mang k* mang-act bro1 med k* meny meph hr1 merc k* merc-c k* merc-d c2* mez k2* mosch k* *Mur-ac* b4a.de nat-c k* nat-m k* nat-p nat-s nat-sal br1* nicc k* nit-ac k* **Nux-v** hr1 ol-an ol-j hr1 olnd k* ourl jl2 peti a1 petr k* ph-ac k* phos k* pilo c2 *Plat* k* plb k* positr nl2• psor k* *Puls* k* puls-n c2 querc-r-g-s br1 raph rham-cal bro1 rheum k* rhod k* rhus-t k* rhus-v a1 rob a1 ros-d mtf11 sabad sal-ac a1* salin a1* sang c2 sangin-n c2* sarr a1* scroph-xyz c2 *Sec* k* sep k* sil k* solid c2 sphing a1* **Spig** k* spong stann k* *Stram* k* **Sulph** k* syc pte1• syph k* tell bg2* ther bg2 *Thiosin* bro1 thymol sp1 ulm-c c2 vanil fd5.de verat k* verb b7.de* vib-t c2 viol-o lp* vip k* visc c2 zinc [bell-p-sp dcm1 gal-met stj2]

- **left**: all-s k* lepi a1 ol-j hr1 puls hr1 visc a1
- **morning**:
  - **rising** agg.; after: stann k*
    - **long** after rising: rhod bg3
- **afternoon**: sil k*
- **evening**:
  - **21 h** | **lying** down agg.: merc-c
- **accompanied** by:
  - **acne** punctata: nat-c c1
  - **diarrhea**; chronic: oxyte-chl mtf11 penic mtf11 streptom mtf11
  - **fever**: oxyte-chl mtf11 penic mtf11 streptom mtf11
  - **vertigo**: merc-c b4a.de* nux-v b7.de* puls b7.de*
  - ○ **Ear**:
    - **discharge** from: asaf ptk1 elaps ptk1 lyc ptk1
    - **inflammation** of; chronic: mang mrr1
  - **Head**:
    - **complaints** of: bell bg2 chinin-s bg2 cupr bg2 dulc bg2 ign bg2 sep bg2
    - **noises** in: querc-r-g-s br1
    - **pain**: chinin-s bro1 verb bro1
- **alternating** with | **vision**; dim (See VISION - Dim - alternating - deafness)
- **anemia**; after: lob-e c1
- **apoplexy**; after: arn bro1 bell bro1* caust bro1 hyos al1* rhus-t bro1
- **blowing** the nose agg.: spig k*
- **boring** finger amel.: spig k*
- **bull**-necked boys, in: scroph-n c1
- **catarrh** in middle ear; from: acon bg2 ars bg2 bell bg2 calc bg2 caust bg2 cham bg2 coff bg2 euph mtf11 hep bg2 lach bg2 led bg2 merc bg2 nit-ac bg2 puls bg2 sulph bg2
- **causeless**: syph mtf33

Lost: ...

- **chill**; during: *Cham* b7.de* chin bg2 puls bg2 *Rhus-t* bg2
- **congestion**; from: anac bg2 aur bg2 bell bg2 bry bg2 calc bg2 caust bg2 graph bg2 lyc bg2 merc bg2 mur-ac bg2 nux-v bg2 phos bg2 puls bg2 sep bg2 sil bg2 spig bg2 sulph bg2
- **convulsions**; after: sec k*
- **dinner**; during: sulph k*
- **eruptions**; after suppressed: ant-c bg2 caust bg2 graph bg2 lach bg2 mez k* sulph bg2
- **exanthema**; after: bell bg2 carb-v bg2* meny bg2 merc bg2 phos bg2 puls bg2 sulph bg2
- **fever**; during: *Rhus-t* b7a.de*
- **gout**; from: ferr-pic br1
- **influenza**; after: sal-ac br1*
- **injury** to head; after: arn mrr1
- **leaflet** before, sensation of: ant-c k*
- **loss** of fluids; from: bell bg2 hep bg2 lach bg2 led bg2 merc bg2 puls bg2
- **loud** sounds, followed by: sep
- **measles**; after suppressed: puls hr1
- **memory**; with loss of (See MIND - Memory - loss - hearing)
- **menses** | **before** | **agg.**: kreos bro1
  - **during** | **agg.**: kreos bro1 lyc k*
- **mercury**; after abuse of: asaf bg2 aur bg2 carb-v bg2 chin bg2 hep bg2 nit-ac bg2 petr bg2 staph bg2 sulph bg2
- **moving** quickly; from: verat-v ptk1*
- **nervous**: acon bg2 am-c btw2 ambr btw2* *Anac* bg2 ant-c bg2 arg-n bg2 arn bg2 ars bg2 asar bg2* aur bg2 bar-c bg2 **Bell** bg2 borx bg2 bry bg2 *Calc* bg2 caps bg2 **Caust** bg2 chel bg2 chin bg2 chinin-s bwa3 cocc bg2 con bg2 dros bg2 dulc bg2 ferr-pic c1 gels ll1 *Graph* bg2 hyos bg2 ign bg2 kali-c bg2 led bg2 levo mtf11 *Lyc* bg2 mag-c bg2* *Merc* bg2 mur-ac bg2 nat-c bg2 nat-m bg2 *Nit-ac* bg2 nux-v bg2 op bg2 *Petr* bg2 ph-ac bg2 phos bg2* plat a2 **Puls** bg2 rhus-t bg2 sal-ac c1 sec bg2 sep bg2 **Sil** bg2 spig bg2 streptom mtf11 **Sulph** bg2 syph ptk2* tab br1 verat bg2
  - **noise** amel.: jab bg3*
- **otorrhea**; after: lob-e c1 lyc tl1
- **oversensitiveness**; preceded by: sulph tl1
  - **human** voice; to: sulph tl1
- **quinine**; after abuse of: calc bg2 carb-v bg2 hep bg2 nux-v bg2 puls bg2 sulph bg2
- **rheumatic**: *Visc* br1
- **riding** in a wagon amel.: *Graph* k*
- **scarlet** fever; after: *Graph* hr1 *Lach* hr1 **Lyc** k* mur-ac bro1
- **singing**; after: mang-act c1 nit-ac a2*
- **stooping** agg.; after: mang h2*
- **stopped** sensation, with: calad k* limest-b es1• luna kg1• *Mang* k* peti a1 *Sep* k* sphing k* spig
- **temporarily**: thymol sp1
- **tonsillectomy**; after: lob-e c1
- **tonsils**; from swelling of: aur bg2 merc bg2 nit-ac bg2 staph bg2
  - **children**; in: kali-bi ptk1
- **typhoid** states; after: arn bg2 ph-ac bg2 phos bg2 verat bg2
- **vomiting**:
  - **after**: ant-c hs2*
  - **before**: raph a1*
- **waking**; on: oena k*
- **wisdom** teeth, from cutting: cheir c1* ferr-pic c1 mag-c c1*

MUFFLED: hippoc-k szs2

- **loud**; while her own voice seems: hippoc-k szs2

STRANGE, her own voice sounds strange in her ears: *Galeoc-c-h* gms1• tanac c1*

UNNATURAL; one's own voice sounds: ter ptk1*

ALTERNATING SIDES: phyt bg3 sin-n bg3a* sulph bg3

MORNING: agar b4.de* agn bg2 all-c bg2 aloe bg2 *Am-c* b4a.de ambr b7.de* apis b7a.de bar-c b4.de* bell b4.de* borx b4a.de bov bg2 bry b7.de* calc b4.de* caps b7.de* carb-an b4.de* carb-v b4.de* caust b4.de* chin b7.de* coff b7.de* cycl bg2 dros b7.de* ham bg2 hep b4.de* kali-c b4.de* kreos b7a.de lach bg2 mag-c b4.de* mag-m b4a.de meny b7.de* nat-c b4.de* nit-ac b4.de* *Nux-v* b7.de* petr b4.de* phos b4.de* rhus-t b7.de* sars b4.de* sep bg2 sil b4.de* stann b4.de* sulph b4.de* thuj b4.de* zinc b4.de*
- **evening**; and: mag-c bg2

FORENOON: carb-v b4.de* *Nit-ac* b4a.de tarax b7.de*

AFTERNOON: agar b4.de* alum b4.de* ant-t bg2 arg-met b7.de* benzol br1 calc-p bg2 carb-an b4a.de carb-v b4.de* chel b7.de* graph b4.de* kali-bi bg2 kali-c b4.de* laur b7.de* lyc b4.de* *M-arct* b7.de phos b4.de* sulph b4.de* zinc b4.de*

EVENING: aloe bg2 alum b4.de* ant-c b7a.de* bell b4.de* borx bg2 caps b7.de* chin b7.de* coff b7.de* colch b7.de* coloc b4.de* dros b7.de* ferr b7.de* graph b4.de* kali-bi bg2 kali-n b4.de* lach bg2 lyc b4.de* mang b4.de* nux-v b7.de* phos b4.de* puls b7.de* sep b4.de* sul-ac b4.de* *Sulph* b4a.de*

NIGHT: aloe bg2 arn bg2 *Bell* b4.de* bry b7.de* calc b4.de* caps bg2 carb-an b4.de* carb-v b4.de* graph b4.de* kali-bi bg2 kali-c b4.de* lach bg2 lyc b4a.de merc b4.de* nat-m b4.de* nat-s bg2 nit-ac bg2 rhus-t b7.de* verat b7a.de*

ABSCESS: cadm-s k2 *Calc* k* **Hep** k* *Lac-c* k* lach *Merc* k* **Sil** k* still k*
- ○ - **Root**; at: *Puls* k*
- **Septum**: acon bro1 *Bell* bro1 calc bro1 *Hep* bro1 sil bro1
- **Tip**: acon bg3* am-c ptk1 anan bg3

ADENOIDS: *Agra* c2* bar-c br1* calc c2* calc-f c2* calc-i br1* calc-p br1* carc mlr1• chr-ac br1* gonotox jl2 *Iod* br1* kali-s br1* lob-s c2* *Merc* ptk1 mez br1* mucor jl2 **Nat-m** sne osm c2 psor c2* sangin-n c2* *Spig* c2 *Staph* c2 *Sulph* c2* syc bka1* *Thuj* br1* tub k2*
- **children**; in: *Carc* mlr1• syc fmm1• tub mtf33
- **enlarged**: agra mtf11 bac mtf11 bar-i mtf11 bar-m mtf11 calc-i mtf11 calc-p mtf11 syc fmm1• tub mtf11
- **removal**; after: carc mlr1• kali-s ptk1
  - **children**; in: carc mlr1•
- **swelling**: calc-f sp1
- ○ - **Posterior** nares: mez ptk1

AGGLUTINATION of nostrils: *Agath-a* nl2• **Aur** k* bar-c k* carb-an kola stb3• lyc k* phos k*
- **morning**: *Agath-a* nl2• lyc k*
- **sensation** of: bar-c h2 kola stb3• phos spong fd4.de
- **suppuration**; by: aur bg2 bar-c bg2 lyc bg2 merc bg2 nit-ac bg2 phos bg2 thuj bg2

AIR:
- **blowing** on it; sensation as if air was: *(↗current)* spig b7.de*
- **current** passing over the dorsum; as of a light: *(↗blowing)* spig
- **inspired** air; sensitive to: acon bg2* *Aesc* k* alum bro1 alum-sil bro1 am-c k* *Ant-c* k* aral bro1 ars k* *Arum-t* bro1 aur bg2* aur-m bro1 bell bro1 brach brom bg2* bufo k* calad bg2 calc bro1 camph bg3* *Cimic* bg2* cist bg2* cor-r bg2* echi fago bg1 gins **Hep** k ●* hydr k* *Ign* k* kali-bi bg2* kali-i bg1 kreos lith-c k* mag-s med k* *Merc* bro1 nat-ar nat-m bro1 **Nux-v** ●* osm k* ox-ac bg1 **Phos** k ●* psor k* *Ran-b* k* rumx bg2* sep k* sil bro1 syph xxb thuj zinc bg2
  - **feels** cold: cor-r br1 lith-c ptk1
  - ○ **Frontal** sinus: zinc h2
  - **Posterior** nares: kreos

AIR AGG.; DRAFT OF: dulc bg2 elaps bg2 graph bg2 merc bg2 nat-c bg2 nux-v bg2

AIR; IN OPEN:
- **agg.**: aloe bg2
- **amel.**: acon ptk1 *All-c* ptk1 *Aur* b4.de* hydr ptk1 iod ptk1 kali-c bg2 nux-v ptk1 *Puls* ptk1 tell ptk1

ANOSMIA (See Smell - wanting)

APHTHAE: *(↗MOUTH - Aphthae)* nat-c mrr1

ATROPHY: | **accompanied** by | **catarrh**; chronic: kali-bi bg2 **Teucr** br1
- ○ - **Inside**: lem-m br1

BALL; sensation as if a: agar bg2

BED; in: | **amel.**: mag-m bg2

BLACK (See Discoloration - black; Sooty)

BLEEDING (See Epistaxis)

BLISTERS bursting, sensation: sars h2

BLOOD, congestion of (See Congestion - nose)

BLOWING:
- **wind instruments** | **agg.**: rhus-t bg2

BLOWING THE NOSE:
- **agg.**: am-c b4.de* *Ambr* b7a.de arg-met b7.de* arn bg2 *Aur* b4.de* *Bar-c* b4a.de bell b4.de* bry b7.de* carb-v b4.de* chin b7.de* euphr b7.de* hep b4a.de *Iod* b4.de* lach bg2 led b7.de* mag-m b4a.de merc b4.de* nat-m b4.de* ph-ac bg2 phos bg2 sars b4.de* spong b7.de* sulph b4.de* thuj b4.de*
- **inability** to blow the nose in children: am-c st*
- **inclination** to blow the nose; constant: agar am-c bro1 *Am-m* k* ambr tsm1 bar-c bar-s k2 *Borx* k* bov calc h2 carb-an echi hep *Hydr* k* iodof a *Kali-bi* k* lac-c bro1 lyc ptk1 mag-c mag-m bro1 mang ptk1 nat-m nat-ox rly4• phos psor rumx k2 **Stict** k* sulph k* **Teucr** k* ther tritic kr1* vanil fd5.de
  - **evening**: lith-c
  - **amel.**; but does not: *(↗Obstruction - blowing the - not)* *Stict* mrr1
  - **body** in nose; sensation of a large: am-m gsy1 **Teucr**
  - **without** discharge; but (See Dryness - inside - blowing)

BOILS: *(↗FACE - Eruptions - boils - nose)*
- ○ - **Septum**: anthraci ptk1

BORING in nose with fingers: *(↗Picking - nose; GENERALS - Boring; GENERALS - Boring - amel.; MIND - Gestures - hands - grasping - nose)* anac bg3* androc srj1• apis bg2 arg-n bg2 **Arum-t** k* aur k* bacls-10 ptj• bell bg2 borx bg2 bov bg2 bufo k* carb-v bg3* caust bg3* **Cina** k* con k* hell bg2* hep bg3* lil-t bg2 lyc bg3* merc bg3* nat-c dx1 *Nat-m* bg3* nat-p bg2* op bg2 petr-ra shn4• ph-ac k* phos k* psor rumx mg sabad bg* sabal bg3 *Santin* bro1 sel k* **Sil** bg2* spig bg2* stict stront-c ptk1 sulph bg3* tarent bg2 teucr bro1* thuj bg3* tritic-vg fd5.de verat *Zinc* k*
- **agg.**: *Cina* b7.de*
- **bleeds**; until: arum-t bg2 cina bg2* phos bg2 spig bg2
- **catarrhal** symptoms; with: hep c1 tritic-vg fd5.de
- **convulsions**; with: verat bg2
- **headache**; during: hep c1

BROAD and flat: syph al

BUBBLING sensation: sars k* sulph k*

CANCER: alumn k* apis sne *Ars* k* **Aur** k* *Aur-m* k* aur-s gm1 *Calc* k* carb-ac k* *Carb-an* k* caust sne cund k* eucal gm1 euphr c2 gal-met sne hecla c1 **Jug-c** sne kali-bi sne *Kali-c* b4a.de *Kreos* k* merc nat-m sne *Nit-ac* sne *Phos* b4a.de *Phyt* k* *Sep* k* *Sil* bg2 sulph k* symph gm1 syph mrr1* tab b7a.de thuj sne *Zinc* b4a.de
- **epithelioma**: *Ars* ars-i k13* aur k2 *Carb-ac* k* con k2* cund k* *Hydr* kali-bi sne **Kali-s** k* *Kreos* k* nit-ac sne
  - ○ **Wings**: med k2
- **flat**: euphr ptk1
  - **right** side; on: euphr k*
- ○ - **Antrum**: aur bro1 symph bro1*
  - **right**: symph c1
- **Posterior** nares: chr-ac mtf11

CARIES: *(↗Necrosis; Ozena)* *Alum* b4a.de anthraq rly4• **Asaf** k* **Aur** k* aur-ar k2 *Aur-m* k* aur-m-n cadm-s k* calc calc-s k2 con b4a.de fl-ac *Hecla* *Hep* k* *Hippoz* *Kali-bi* bro1 kali-i lyc k2 *Merc* bg2* merc-c b4a.de merc-i-r k* nit-ac ptk1 petr b4a.de *Phos* k* *Phyt* **Sil** k* *Still* syph k2*
- **syphilitic**: *(↗Ozena - syphilitic)* hecla c1 *Kali-bi* k* *Sil* k*
- ○ - **Septum**: hecla *Hippoz* *Kali-bi* k* syph jl2

CATARRH: *(↗Coryza; Discharge; Inflammation)* abrom-a ks5 acet-ac k* achy-a mtf11 *Acon* k* aesc *Agar* k* agath-a nl2• agra br1 ail all-c tl1 all-s br1 allox tpw4 aloe *Alum* k* alum-p k2 alum-sil k2 *Alumn* k* am-c k* *Am-m* am-n mtf11 ambr k* *Anemps* br1 *Ant-c* *Ant-s-aur* ant-t k* *Apis* *Arg-met* *Arg-n* k* arge-pl rwt5• **Ars** k* *Ars-i* k* *Arum-t* k* *Asaf* asar aspar **Aur** k* aur-ar k2 aur-i k2 *Aur-m* k* aur-s k2 aza mtf11 bacls-10 pte1*• bapt k* *Bar-c* k* bar-i k2 *Bar-m* k*

Nose

Catarrh: ...
bar-s k2 **Bell** berb k* *Borx* *Bov* **Brom** k* bry cadm-s k2 calad **Calc** k* calc-ar calc-f k2 calc-i k2 *Calc-p* k* *Calc-s* calc-sil k2 camph canth caps *Carb-ac* k* *Carb-an* **Carb-v** **Carbn-s** *Castm* caust cean-tr br1 cham k* chel k* chin chinin-ar cic cimic cina cinnb *Cist* k* clem coc-c cocc coff k* colch coloc *Con* k* cop k* cor-r k* crot-h k* crot-t cub c1* cupr cycl cystein-l rly4• diph-pert-t mp4• dream-p sdj1• dros dulc k2* elaps **Eup-per** k* euph *Euphr* k* fab br1 *Ferr* k* *Ferr-ar* *Ferr-i* k* ferr-ma a1 ferr-p *Fl-ac* k* flor-p rsj3• *Form* k* formal br1 fuma-ac rly4• gaert pte1*• gels k* **Graph** k* guaj hed mtf11 helia br1* hell k* **Hep** k* *Hippoz* k* *Hydr* k* *Hydrog* srj2• hydroph rsj6• ign k* influ c1* *Iod* k* jal *Kali-ar* **Kali-bi** k* *Kali-c* k* *Kali-chl* k* *Kali-i* k* kali-m k2 *Kali-p* kali-s k* kali-sil k2 kreos k* lac-ac k* *Lac-c* k* lac-d lac-del hrn2• lac-h sk4• *Lach* k* laur k* led lem-m k* lith-c mtf11 luf-op mtf11 **Lyc** k* mag-c *Mag-m* k* *Mang* k* *Med* mentho br1 meny **Merc** k* **Merc-c** *Merc-i-f* k* *Merc-i-r* k* *Mez* k* morb jl2 morg-g pte1*• morg-p pte1*• mosch mur-ac musca-d szs1 naja **Nat-ar** k* *Nat-c* k* nat-cac mtf11 **Nat-m** k* nat-p k* *Nat-s* k* *Nicc* k* **Nit-ac** k* *Nux-m* k* **Nux-v** k* oci-sa sp1 *Ol-j* k* oscilloc jl2 *Osm* k* oxal-a rly4• par k* **Petr** k* ph-ac *Phos* k* phyt k2 pin-con oss2• plac-s rly4• plat k* plb k* positr nl2• **Psor** k* **Puls** k* quill br1 ran-b ran-s k* rhod **Rhus-t** *Rumx* *Sabad* *Samb* k* *Sang* k* *Sars* **Sel** seneg k* **Sep** k* **Sil** k* sinus rly4• solid br1 *Spig* k* spong *Squil* stann *Staph* k* *Stict* k* still stront-c suis-pan rly4• sul-ac sul-i k2 **Sulph** k* *Syc* pte1*• tab tarent k2 *Teucr* k* *Ther* k* *Thuj* k* titan br1 toxo-g jl2 trom c2 *Tub* k* (non:uran-met k) uran-n urol-h rwt• ust verat visc sp1 zinc k* zinc-p k2 [heroin sdj2 *Spect* dfg1]

- **one** side: hippoz kali-c nat-c phos phyt
- **right**: *Lyc* rhus-g tmo3• sang hr1
- **left**: kali-s iach k* luf-op rsj5• sep sinus rly4• teucr
- **morning**: arge-pl rwt5• *Ferr-i* kali-c k2 petr k2 urol-h rwt• [spect dfg1]
- **evening**: all-c tl1 ars tl1 hydrog srj2• *Mang* k* *Puls* k*
- **accompanied** by:
  - **constipation**: aur-m-n c1 hydr c1
  - **mucus**; thick: nat-c mtf11
  - **urticaria**: all-c bro1 dulc bro1
  - ○ **Eustachian** tube; complaints of: bar-m bg2
  - **Head**:
    - **fullness** (See HEAD - Fullness - accompanied - catarrh)
    - **pain**: nat-ar br1
  - **Mucous** membrane; dryness of: stict mtf11
  - **Nose**:
    - **fullness** of: anemps br1
    - **obstruction** of: anemps br1
- **acute** (See Catarrh)
- **air**; in open:
  - **agg.**: dulc tl1
  - **amel.**: abrom-a ks5 androc srj1• *Aur* *Bry* carb-v hydroph rsj6• *Mag-m* **Puls** k*
- **alternating** with:
  - **leukorrhea** (See FEMALE - Leukorrhea - alternating - nasal)
  - **rheumatic** disease (See EXTREMITIES - Pain - rheumatic - alternating - catarrh)
  - ○ **Teeth**; pain in (See TEETH - Pain - alternating with - catarrh)
- **bloody**: ars bg2 graph bg2 kali-bi bg2 lem-m mtf11 puls bg2
- **children**; in: med jl2
- **chill**; during: merc bro1
- **chronic**: alum bg2* am-br bro1 am-i mtf11 *Am-m* bro1 anac bg2 *Ant-s-aur* br1 ars-i br1* aur-m bro1 bals-p bro1 bar-ox-suc mtf11 brom bro1 *Calc* bg2* calc-p bro1 caps tl1 carb-v bg2 carc fb caust bg2 chel tl1 cist tl1 *Coll* br1 con bg2 cub bro1 elaps bro1 *Eucal* bro1 *Graph* bg2 *Hep* bro1 *Hippoz* bro1 *Hydr* bro1 *Kali-bi* bro1 kali-br tl1 kali-c bro1* kali-i bro1 kreos bro1 lem-m bro1 lyc bg2 med bro1* merc bro1* merc-i-r bro1 *Nat-c* bg2* nat-m bg2* nat-s bro1* nit-ac bg2* petr a1 phos bro1 psor bro1 *Puls* bg2* sabad bro1 sang bro1 sangin-n bro1 sep bg2* sil bg2* spig bro1 stict bro1 *Sulph* bg2 *Teucr* br1* ther bro1 thuj hr1* zinc bg2
  - **accompanied** by | **atrophy** (See Atrophy - accompanied - catarrh)
- **constipation** (See accompanied - constipation)
- **crusty**, scabby: lem-m mtf11
- **dry**, chronic: *Carb-v* k* cor-r br1 *Dulc* k* limen-b-c hrn2* mang-act br1 morg-g pte1*• *Nat-m* k* **Sil** k* *Spong* k* **Stict** k* *Sulph*
- **epistaxis**; with: bar-c bg2 ip bg1 kali-bi bg1
- **eruption**; from retrocession of: mez *Sep*
- **followed** by: (↗*Coryza - followed*)
  - ○ **Antrum**; complaints of: berb kali-c kali-i merc
  - **Chest**; complaints of: bry
  - **Downward**; complaints of air passages travelling: sang mtf11
  - **Frontal** sinuses; complaints of: (↗*Coryza - followed - frontal; GENERALS - Inflammation - sinuses)* abies-c vml3• ammc bro1 *Ars* aur-m-n wbt2• berb bry *Calc* calc-sil k2 *Cupr* ferr fuma-ac rly4• ign bro1 iod bro1 *Kali-bi* k* kali-c mrr1 *Kali-chl* *Kali-i* k* **Lyc** k* mentho bro1 **Merc** merc-i-f k* *Moni* rfm1• nat-m bro1 *Nux-v* k* ozone sde2• propl ub1• *Puls* sabad bro1 *Sang* **Sep** sne **Sil** k* spig mrr1 stict k* *Thuj* k* verb
  - **Maxillary** sinuses; complaints of: ozone sde2•
    - **right**:
      - **extending** to | **left**: ozone sde2•
    - **chronic**: ozone sde2•
- **infantile**: calc tl1
- **measles**, scarlatina and variola; after: *Thuj*
- **menses** | **before** | **agg.**: euphr bro1
  - **during** | **agg.**: euphr bro1
- **mercury**; after abuse of: asaf kali-chl k*
- **nitrate** of silver, abuse of: *Nat-m*
- **offensive** (See Discharge - offensive; Ozena)
- **old** people; in: *Alum* k* am-c bar-c eup-per ictod kali-s k* *Kreos* k* merc-i-f
- **portal** congestion; from: coll br1
- **purulent**: tub-a jl2 visc sp1
- **recurrent**: abrot bg2 carc mlr1• cinnb bg2 coloc bg2 dulc bg2 kali-bi bg2 lach bg2 nux-v bg2 puls bg2 sil bg2 sulph bg2
- **room**; in a closed: abrom-a ks5
- **scabby** (See crusty)
- **scrofulous**: bov bg2 carb-v bg2 graph bg2 lyc bg2
- **seaside** agg.: nat-m
- **syphilitic**: aur-m k2
- **thick**: luf-op rsj5• sang hr1
- **violent**: lyc tl1
- **warm** | **application** on nose | **amel.**: dulc tl1
  - **room** | **agg.**: all-c tl1
- **watery**: visc sp1
- **weather**:
  - **cold** agg.: *Ars* carc mlr1• dulc tl1
  - **wet** | **agg.**: dulc tl1 kali-bi k2 *Nux-m*
- **white**: luf-op rsj5•
- **wine**; from sour: ant-c k2

▽ - **extending** to: (↗*Coryza - extending)*
  - ○ **Downward** (See followed - downward)

○ - **Postnasal**: (↗*Discharge - posterior)* acon aesc *Alum* alum-sil k2 alumn androc srj1• ant-s-aur ap-g c2* *Arg-n* *Aur* k* aur-m bar-c k* bar-m bg2 bry *Calc* calc-f c1* calc-i k2 *Calc-s* calc-sil k2 *Canth* caust chin-b c1 choc srj3• cinnb *Cor-r* k* dulc k2 euphr fago br1 *Ferr* **Ferr-p** fuma-ac rly4• graph k2 helo-s rwt2• **Hep** *Hydr* k* hydrog srj2• *Iod* **Kali-bi** k* *Kali-c* k* *Kali-chl* *Kali-i* kali-sil k2 kreos lac-h sk4• lith-c lob-s c2 *Lyc* mag-s *Manc* *Mang* med melal-alt gya4 *Merc-i-f* *Merc-i-r* k* *Merl* *Mez* morg-g pte1*• morg-p pte1*• nat-ar k* **Nat-c** k* **Nat-m** nat-p c2 nat-s neon srj5• *Nit-ac* ovi-p c2 oxal-a rly4• pen c2* petr k* phos *Phyt* plac-s rly4• *Plb* **Psor** pycnop-sa mrz1 rhus-g tmo3• *Rhus-t* sang sangin-n c2 *Sel* **Sep** k* *Sil* sin-n c2 spig k* staph stict c2 suis-pan rly4• syc pte1*• syph k2 tell c2 *Ther* thuj k* ven-m rsj12• wye c2 yuc c2 zinc zing c2 [buteo-j sej6]
  - **forenoon**: ven-m rsj12•
  - **evening** | **amel.**: ven-m rsj12•
  - **night**: cop br1
  - **accompanied** by | **epistaxis**: bar-c br1
  - **chronic**: pen br1
  - **green**: ven-m rsj12•
  - **heat**: ven-m rsj12•
  - **sudden**: ap-g vml3•
  - **temperature**; change of: ven-m rsj12•
  - **watery**: lac-del hrn2•

- **Sinus**; from frontal: ammc br1 dulc mrr1 Kali-i hr1* nat-m c2 thuj c2

CHAPPED: arum-t k* carb-an k*

○ - **Nostrils**: aur k* graph h2*
- **Tip** of | **menses**; during: carb-an b4.de

CHILL: | **after** | **agg.**: eup-per bg2 hep bg2
- **during**: Acon bro1 bapt bro1 Camph bro1 caps bro1 ferr-p bro1 Gels bro1 merc-i-r bro1 Nat-m bro1 nux-v bro1 phyt bro1 Quill bro1 sapo bro1

COBWEBS; sensation of (See FACE - Cobweb - sensation)

COFFEE agg.: nux-v bg2 sul-ac bg2

COLD:
- **air**:
  - **agg.**: (↗Coldness - inside - inspiration) aloe bg2 camph dw1 dulc dw1 hydr ptk1 kali-bi dw1 **Phos** ●* **Rumx** ●* stict dw1 sulph ptk1
  - **inspiration** agg.: cist bg2
- **applications** | **agg.**: Calc b4a.de
- **washing**:
  - **after** | **head** with cold water agg.; after washing: bell b4a.de Sep b4a.de
- **water** | **amel.**: bell bg2

COLD AGG.; BECOMING: chinin-s bg2

COLDNESS: aloe k* am-c vh1 anan k* ant-c bg2 apis b7a.de* arn k* Ars k* ars-h k* ars-s-f k2 bell k* brom k* calc-p k* **Camph** k* cann-i k* cann-xyz bg2 Caps ptk1 **Carb-v** k* Carbn-o bg2 Carbn-s cench k2 chel bg2 Chin k* cist k* cocc k* colch k* cortico tpw7 Crot-h k* cycl k* dros k* euph bg2 gink-b sbd1• hir skp7• ictod Ign k* iod k* kali-bi bg2 kali-c bg2 kali-n bg2* **Lac-c** k* laur bg2* luf-op rsj5• mang meny bg2* merc bg2 murx k* nat-m bg2 Nux-v k* op k* ozone sde2• ph-ac k* Plb k* polyg-h bg2 polyp-p bg1 Puls ruta fd4.de sep k* Sil k* Spong k* stram k* sulph k* symph fd3.de• tab k* tarax k* thuj bg2 ven-m rsj12• **Verat** k* verat-v k* zinc k* [bell-p-sp dcm1 heroin sdj2 lac-mat sst4]
- **evening** | **20** h: ruta fd4.de tarax c1
- **accompanied** by | **Hand**; perspiration of (See EXTREMITIES - Perspiration - hand - accompanied - nose)
- **chill**; during: ant-c apis bol-la cedr chel colch iod meny sil sulph Tarax
- **fever**; during: cedr bg2 Colch b7a.de* tarax bg2
- **headache**; before: lac-f c1
- **icy** coldness: Cedr k* laur bg2 ruta fd4.de symph fd3.de• Verat k*
- **knees**; with hot (See EXTREMITIES - Heat - knee - accompanied - nose)
- **perspiration**; during: nux-v bg2 ph-ac bg2 Verat bg2
- **sensation** of: anac b4a.de* **Ant-c** bg2 cortico sp1 ign bg2 meny bg2 murx bg2 v-a-b jl2

○ - **Inside**: ant-c b7.de* camph bg2 chel bg2 cist bg2 fl-ac bg2 Ign b7a.de kali-bi bg2
  - **Root**: aq-mar skp7•
- **warm** applications | **amel.**: ars-h vh

○ - **Inside**: Aesc bro1 Camph bro1 Cist bro1 cor-r bro1 hydr bro1 kali-bi bg2 lith-c bro1 ruta fd4.de verat bro1
  - **blowing**, after: Cist
  - **cold air agg.**: **Cist** mrr1
  - **icy** coldness: **Cist** mrr1
  - **inspiration** agg.: (↗Cold - air - agg.) Aesc alum-sil k2 anan Ant-c Ars brom camph k* chel bg2* cimic Cist k* **Cor-r** k* hipp k* Hydr ign bg2 kali-bi k* lith-c menth gg
  - **menthol**; as if had smelled: (↗Open - nostrils; Open - sensation - nostrils) limen-b-c hrn2•
  - **walking** in a room agg.: Camph
- **Posterior** nares: cist bg2 verat bg2
- **Root**: aq-mar skp7• cinnb k2 lac-f c1
- **Tip** of: aloe k* anac bg2* ant-c bg2* **Apis** k* arizon-l nl2• Arn k* Ars k* bros-gau mrc1 Calc-p k* Camph bro1 carb-v bro1 Cedr k* Chin bro1 choc srj3• crot-c sk4• crot-h hell bro1 kali-c h2* Lach k* lob k* med k* meny bg2* phyt bg2 polyp-p bg1 Tab bro1 verat br1* [tax jsj7]
  - **icy** coldness: verat mtf33
- **Wings**, both: laur k*

COMEDONES (See FACE - Eruptions - comedones)

COMPLAINTS of nose: acon ptk1 aesc ptk1 alum ptk1 Ars ptk1 Aur ptk1 calc ptk1 elaps br1 flav jl2 graph ptk1 hep ptk1 hydr ptk1 ign ptk1 iod ptk1 **Kali-bi** ptk1 Kali-i ptk1 Lyc ptk1 Merc ptk1 merc-i-f ptk1 nat-c mtf1 Nat-m ptk1 nit-ac ptk1 nux-v ptk1 phos ptk1 **Puls** ptk1 sabad ptk1 Sep ptk1 **Sil** ptk1 spig ptk1 Sulph ptk1 teucr br1 zinc-chr ptk1
- **one** side: am-m ptk1 hep ptk1 ign ptk1 nux-v ptk1 phos ptk1 phyt ptk1 Sabad ptk1 sil ptk1 sin-n ptk1
- **alternating** sides: kali-i ptk1 lac-c ptk1 lach ptk1 mez ptk1 nux-v ptk1 Phos ptk1 phyt ptk1 rhod ptk1 Sin-n ptk1 sulph ptk1
- **right** side: Acon b7a.de* agar b4a.de Agn b7a.de* Alum b4a.de* am-c b4a.de* am-m b7a.de* Ambr b7a.de* anac b4a.de* ant-c b7a.de* Ars b4a.de Asaf b7a.de* Aur b4a.de* Brom b4a.de* Bry b7a.de* Calad b7a.de* Calc b4a.de* Canth b7a.de* carb-an b4a.de* carb-v b4a.de* caust b4a.de* Chel b7a.de* Cic b7a.de* cocc b7a.de* Colch b7a.de* **Con** b4a.de* Croc b7a.de* dros b7a.de* Fl-ac b4a.de* Graph b4a.de* hep b4a.de* Iod b4a.de* kali-bi bg2 Kali-c b4a.de* Kali-n b4a.de* laur b7a.de* Lyc b4a.de* M-arct b7a.de* Mang b4a.de* merc b4a.de* Nat-c b4a.de* nat-m b4a.de* Nit-ac b4a.de* Nux-v b7a.de* petr b4a.de* Ph-ac b4a.de* Phos b4a.de* plat b4a.de* Psor bg2 Puls b7a.de* Ran-b b7a.de* Ran-s b7a.de* Rhus-t b7a.de* sabin b7a.de* sars b4a.de* sep b4a.de* Sil b4a.de* **Spig** b7a.de* stann b4a.de* sul-ac b4a.de* Sulph b4a.de* tarax b7a.de* Teucr b7a.de* Thuj b4a.de* Verat b7a.de* Viol-o b7a.de* viol-t b7a.de* zinc b4a.de*
- **left** side: Agar b4a.de* alum b4a.de Am-c b4a.de* Am-m b7a.de* anac b4a.de* ant-c b7a.de* apis b7a.de* Ars bg2* Asar b7a.de* Aur bg2* Bell b4a.de* Borx b4a.de* Bov b4a.de* brom bg2 Bry b7a.de* Calc b4a.de* canth b7a.de* Caps b7a.de* carb-an b4a.de* **Carb-v** b4a.de* Caust b4a.de* chel b7a.de* Chin b7a.de* Cina b7a.de* cocc b7a.de* Coff b7a.de* Coloc b4a.de* dros b7a.de* Dulc b4a.de* ferr bg2 fl-ac bg2 graph b4a.de* Hell b7a.de* Hep b4a.de* kali-c b4a.de* laur b7a.de* lyc b4a.de* m-arct b7a.de* Mag-c b4a.de* Mag-m b4a.de* Merc b4a.de* nat-c b4a.de **Nat-m** b4a.de* nit-ac b4a.de* Nux-m b7a.de* Nux-v b7a.de* Olnd b7a.de* petr b4a.de* Phos bg2* Plat b4a.de* psor bg2 puls b7a.de* **Rhod** b4a.de* Rhus-t b7a.de* sabin b7a.de* Sars b4a.de* **Sep** b4a.de* Sil b4a.de* Spong b7a.de* stann b4a.de* Staph b7a.de* Sulph bg2* tarax b7a.de* teucr b7a.de* Thuj b4a.de* viol-t b7a.de* zinc b4a.de*
- **accompanied** by:
  - **fainting**: croc b7a.de
  - **vexation** (See MIND - Irritability - nose)

○ - **Extremities**; pain in: acon bro1 bry bro1 Eup-per bro1 Gels bro1
- **scrofulous**: asaf bg2 Aur bg2 bry bg2 **Calc** bg2 **Hep** bg2 lach bg2 Merc bg2 phos bg2 puls bg2 **Sulph** bg2

▽ - **extending** to:

○ - **Ear**: elaps ptk1
  - **swallowing** agg.: elaps ptk1

○ - **Bones** of nose (See Bones)
- **Dorsum**: alum b2.de* calc b2.de* canth b2.de* chin b2.de* con b2.de* olnd b2.de* **Ph-ac** b2.de* ruta b2.de* samb b2.de* spig b2.de* spong b2.de* thuj b2.de*
- **External** nose: acon b2.de* alum b2.de* ambr b2.de* ant-c b2.de* arn b2.de* **Aur** b2.de* bar-c b2.de* bell b2.de* borx b2.de* bov b2.de* bry b2.de* Calc b2.de* cann-s b2.de* canth b2.de* caps b2.de* carb-an b2.de* **Carb-v** b2.de* Caust b2.de* cham b2.de chel b2.de* chin b2.de* cic b2.de cina bg2 clem b2.de cocc bg2 Coff b2.de* colch b2.de Coloc bg2 con b2.de dros b2.de* dulc b2.de* euphr b2.de fl-ac bg2 graph b2.de* hell b2.de* hep b2.de* hyos b2.de iod b2.de kali-c b2.de* laur b2.de* lyc b2.de* m-arct b2.de mag-c b2.de* mag-m b2.de* meny b2.de Merc b2.de* mez b2.de **Nat-c** b2.de* **Nat-m** b2.de* nit-ac b2.de* Nux-m bg2 nux-v bg2 olnd bg2 petr b2.de* **Ph-ac** b2.de* phos b2.de* Plat bg2 Plb b2.de psor bg2 puls b2.de* rheum b2.de **Rhod** b2.de* rhus-t b2.de* ruta b2.de sabin bg2 samb b2.de sars b2.de* **Sep** b2.de* sil b2.de* **Spig** b2.de* spong b2.de* staph b2.de* sul-ac b2.de* sulph b2.de* tarax b2.de* teucr bg2 Thuj b2.de* verat b2.de* viol-o b2.de* viol-t b2.de* zinc b2.de*
- **Internal** nose: acon b2.de* agar b2.de* alum b2.de* am-c b2.de* am-m b2.de* ambr b2.de* anac b2.de* ang b2.de* **Ant-c** b2.de* ant-t b2.de* arg-met b2.de* arn b2.de* ars b2.de* asar b2.de* **Aur** b2.de* Bell bg2 borx b2.de* bov b2.de* Bry b2.de* **Calc** b2.de* camph b2.de* Canth b2.de* caust b2.de* cham b2.de* chel b2.de* chin b2.de* cic b2.de* cina b2.de* cocc b2.de* coff b2.de* Colch b2.de* coloc b2.de* con b2.de* cycl b2.de* dros b2.de* euph b2.de* **Graph** b2.de* guaj b2.de* hep b2.de* hyos b2.de* Ign b2.de* iod b2.de* Kali-c b2.de* kali-n b2.de* Kreos b2.de* lach b2.de* laur b2.de* led b2.de* lyc b2.de* m-ambo b2.de m-arct b2.de mag-c b2.de* mag-m b2.de* mang b2.de* meny b2.de* Merc b2.de* mez b2.de* mur-ac b2.de* nat-c b2.de* nat-m b2.de* nit-ac b2.de* nux-v b2.de* petr b2.de* ph-ac b2.de* phos b2.de* plb b2.de* Puls b2.de*

Nose

- **Internal** nose: ...
  Ran-b b2.de* ran-s b2.de* rhus-t b2.de* ruta b2.de* Sabad b2.de* sars b2.de* sel b2.de* seneg b2.de* sep b2.de* **Sil** b2.de* **Spig** b2.de* Squil b2.de* stann b2.de* Staph b2.de* sulph b2.de* Teucr b2.de* thuj b2.de* verat b2.de* zinc b2.de*
- **Maxillary** Sinus (See FACE - Complaints - jaws - joints; FACE - Complaints - maxillary)
- **Nasopharynx** (See THROAT - Complaints - nasopharynx)
- **Nostrils**: lem-m br1 lyc ptk1 thuj ptk1
- **Root** of nose: acon b2.de* agar b2.de agn b2.de* am-m b2.de* ant-t b2.de* am b2.de* ars ptk1 arum-t bg2 Asar b2.de* bar-c b2.de* bell b2.de* Bism b2.de* borx bg2 Calc b2.de* Camph b2.de* cann-s b2.de* caps bg2 carb-v b2.de* caust b2.de* chin bg2 chion ptk1 cimic ptk1 cina b2.de* cinnb bg2 colch b2.de* coloc b2.de* con b2.de* cupr ptk1 ferr b2.de* gels ptk1 hell b2.de* hep b2.de* **Hyos** b2.de* ign b2.de* iod bg2* Kali-bi bg2* kali-c b2.de* kali-i ptk1 lach bg2 laur b2.de* meny b2.de* merc b2.de* mosch b2.de* mur-ac bg2 nat-m b2.de* olnd b2.de* par ptk1 petr b2.de* phos bg2* Puls b2.de* ran-b b2.de* rheum b2.de* rhus-t bg2 Ruta b2.de* sang ptk1 sars bg2* sep bg2 staph b2.de* stict bg2* ther bg2 viol-t b2.de* Zinc bg2
- **Septum** of nose (See Septum)
- **Tip** of nose: aur b2.de* bell b2.de* borx b2.de* bry b2.de* Calc b2.de* canth b2.de* **Carb-an** b2.de* **Carb-v** b2.de* **Caust** b2.de* chel b2.de* clem b2.de* colch b2.de* con b2.de* kali-n b2.de* m-arct b2.de meny bg2 merc b2.de* mosch b2.de* murx bg2 Nit-ac b2.de* ph-ac b2.de* rheum b2.de* Rhus-t b2.de* samb b2.de* **Sep** b2.de* Sil b2.de* spong b2.de* sul-ac b2.de* Sulph b2.de* viol-o b2.de*

COMPRESSING nose: | **agg.**: chin b7.de*

CONDYLOMATA (See Warts)

CONGESTION: (↗Obstruction) **Acon** bg2 agar bg2 alum h2* am-c k* ambr bg2 anac bg2 ant-c bg2 apis bg2 arg-met bg2 Arn bg2 ars bg2 **Aur** bg2 bar-c bg2 **Bell** bg2 bit-ar wht1• borx bg2 **Bry** bg2 calc k* cann-xyz bg2 canth bg2 caps bg2 carb-an bg2 carb-v bg2 cartl-s rly4• Caust bg2 cham bg2* Chin bg2 chord-umb rly4• cina bg2 coca-c sk4• coff bg2 colch bg2 coli rly4• con bg2 cortico sp1 **Croc** bg2 **Cupr** k* Dros bg2 dulc bg2 euphr bg2 falco-pe nl2• Ferr bg2 Graph bg2 helo-s rwt2• hep h2* hippoz jl2 hyos bg2 influ mp4• iod bg2 Ip bg2 **Kali-c** bg2 **Kali-n** bg2 ketogl-ac rly4• kreos bg2 lach bg2 Led bg2 Lyc bg2 mag-c bg2 mag-m bg2 mang-p rly4• medul-os-si rly4• meli br1 Merc bg2 morg fmm1• **Mosch** bg2 mucs-nas rly4• Nat-c bg2 nat-m bg2 nat-pyru rly4• nicotam rly4• **Nit-ac** bg2 Nux-v bg2 oci-sa sp1 osm a1* pant-ac rly4• petr bg2 Ph-ac bg2 phos bg2 plac-s rly4• positr nl2• pot-e rly4• **Puls** bg2 pyrid rly4• ran-b bg2 rauw sp1 **Rhus-t** bg2 ribo rly4• ruta bg2 sabad bg2 sabin bg2 samb k* sars bg2 Sec bg2 sep bg2 **Sil** bg2 sinus rly4• Spig bg2 spong bg2 stann bg2 suis-em rly4• suis-hep rly4• suis-pan rly4• Sul-ac bg2 sulph k* tarax bg2 Thuj bg2 Verat bg2 x-ray sp1 [bell-p-sp dcm1]

- **night**: Flav jl2
  - **sleep**; during: am-c mrr1
- **children**; in: Morg fmm1•
- **chronic**: psor jl2
- **eating**; while: helo-s rwt2•
- **lying** agg.: lac-del hrn2•
- **menses**; during: am-c mrr1
- **stooping** agg.: am-c
- ○ **Bones** | **Turbinated** bones: Syc fmm1•
- **Mucous** membranes: hippoz jl2 morg fmm1•
- **Nose**; to: am-c b4.de* bell bro1 cham bg2 cupr bg2* fic-m gya1 hep b4a.de* Meli bro1 sulph bg2
  - **sensation** as if: am-c bg2
- **Root** of nose; to: medul-os-si rly4• nit-ac h2 x-ray sp1
- **Sinuses**: adren br1 fum rly1•
- **Tip**: am-c bro1

CONSTRICTION: acon bg2 agar bg2 arg-n hr1 graph hell k* kali-c bg2 kali-n nat-m nit-ac bg2 oena bg2 sang bg2 verat bg2

- **alternating** with | **expansion**: bism hr1
- ○ **Nasopharynx**: nux-v bg2

CONTRACTION: anac b4a.de bism b7.de* caps b7.de* graph b4.de* hell b7.de* hep b4a.de* kali-n b4.de* lyc h2 nat-m bg2 nit-ac h2 phys bg2 sabad b7.de* spong bg2

- ○ **Root**; at: hist vml3•

CONVULSIVE motion (See Twitching)

CORYZA: (↗Catarrh) Acon k* acon-ac rly4• Aesc k* aeth k* agar k* agath-a nl2• Aids nl2• ail k* **All-c** k* all-s k* allox sp1 aloe alum k* alum-sil k2 am-br c2 Am-c k* Am-m k* **Ambr** k* ammc k* amp rly4• Anac k* anan Androc srj1• anis ant-c k* ant-t k* antho c2 anthraq rly4• aphis k* apis Apoc k* aq-mar skp7• aran k* Arg-met k* Arg-n k* arist-cl sp1 arn k* **Ars** k* Ars-i k* ars-met c2 arum-m c2 Arum-t k* **Arund** k* asaf k* Asar k* asc-t k* Aspar k* astac atp rly4• Aur k* aur-ar k2 Aur-m k* aur-s Aven br1* Bad k* Bamb-a stb2.de• bapt bar-c k* bar-m k* **Bell** k* bell-p sp1 Benz-ac k* Berb k* beryl sp1 Borx bov k* Brom k* bros-gau mrc1 Bry k* bufo Cact k* cadm-s k2 cain calad Calc k* calc-ar calc-f calc-p k* calc-s k* camph k* canth Caps k* Carb-ac Carb-an **Carb-v** k* **Carbn-s** carc sp1 cassia-s cdd7*• castor-eq Caust k* Cean k* cench k2 cent c2 Cham k* **Chel** k* Chin k* chin-b c2 chinin-ar Chlor k* chord-umb rly4• Cic cimic k* cimx Cina Cinnb k* cist k2 clem k* coc-c k* cocc k* coenz-q mtf11 coff Colch k* coli gmj1 coloc con k* cop br1 Cor-r k* corn cortiso sp1 croc crot-h crot-t cupr k* Cycl k* cystein-l rly4• daph dendr-pol sk4• dig k* dioxi rbp6 dros k* dulc k* dys pte1*• ephe-si hsj1• eucal k* eug c2 **Eup-per** k* eup-pur euph **Euphr** k* Ferr k* Ferr-ar ferr-i c2* **Ferr-p** k* fl-ac k* formal br1 Gels k* glon glyc bro1 Graph k* guaj haliae-lc srj5• hed sp1 helia br1* **Hep** k* hom-xyz c2 Hydr k* hydr-ac bro1 ign k* ina-i mlk9.de influ jl2* Iod k* ip k* Jab k* jac-c k* jal c2 jug-c c2 Just bro1 Kali-ar Kali-bi k* Kali-c k* Kali-chl k* kali-chls c2 **Kali-i** k* kali-m k2 kali-n k* kali-p Kali-s k* kali-sil k2 Kalm k* ketogl-ac rly4• kola stb3• kreos lac-ac Lac-c k* lac-del hrn2• lac-h sk4• lac-loxod-a hrn2• Lach k* lap-la rsp1 lat-m sp1 laur lob-s c2 Luna kg1• Lyc k* lycpr c2 lyss Mag-c k* Mag-m k* mag-s k* mand sp1 mang k* med k* mentho bro1 meph **Merc** k* Merc-c k* Merc-i-f hr1 Merc-i-r k* merc-sul Mez k* morb jl2 mur-ac k* myric k* myrt-c c2 Naja naphtin br1 narc-ps c1* **Nat-ar** k* Nat-c k* nat-i c2 Nat-m k* nat-ox rly4• nat-p nat-pyru rly4• nat-s k* nicc Nit-ac k* nux-m mrr1 **Nux-v** k* nymph c2 oci-sa sp1* ol-an c2 ol-j c2 orot-ac rly4• Osm k* ovi-p c2 oxal-a rly4• oxyg c2 ozone sde2• par pen c2* Petr k* petr-ra shn4• Ph-ac k* phel k* **Phos** k* Phos-pchl c2 Phyt k* plac-s rly4• plat plb pop-cand c2 positr nl2• propl ub1• prot fmm1• psil ft1 psor k* **Puls** k* quill br1* ran-b tl1 ran-s c2 rhod k* rhodi br1* rhus-r **Rhus-t** k* rob c2 Ros-d wla1 Rumx k* Sabad k* sal-ac c2 sal-fr sle1• Samb bg2* Sang k* sangin-n c2* sanguis-s hrn2• sanic c2 Sapo br1 sars k* sec a1 sel k* Senec k* seneg k* Sep k* **Sil** k* sin-n k* sinus rly4• skook br1 solid bro1 spig spira c2 Spong k* Squil k* stann k* **Staph** k* Stict k* still suis-pan rly4• sul-ac k* sul-i c2 **Sulph** k* syc fmm1• syph k2* tarent k* tell k* ter k* tere-la rly4• Teucr k* ther bro1 thuj k* til tritic-vg fd5.de trom bro1 tub c* tub-d jl2 upa c2 vac vanil fd5.de ven-m rsj12• verat verb k* vichy-g a1 wye k2 yuc c2 zinc k* zinc-o c2 [calc-br stj1 heroin sdj2]

- **one** side: alum am-m h2 aur-m bell calc-s k2 calen vml3• hep kali-c lac-h htj1• nux-v k* petr-ra shn4• **Phos** k* Phyt k* plat rhod stann staph
- **alternating** sides: lac-c mrr1 sin-n mrr1
- **right**: **Ars** k* brom Calc-s k* chir-fl gya2 cystein-l rly4• euphr k* kali-bi kali-i vh mang-p rly4• merc-i-r k* positr nl2• Sang k* sars suis-pan rly4• tarent tritic-vg fd5.de
  - **bathing**; after: calc-s k*
  - ▽ **extending** to | **left**: androc srj1• (non:borx h2*) **Brom** a1* Carb-v chel euphr lyc
- **left**: agar aids nl2• All-c k* alum h2* **Arum-t** k* bad k* berb cist cop cystein-l rly4• gels mrr1 jug-c k* ketogl-ac rly4• mang petr-ra shn4• plac-s rly4• plut-n srj7• psil ft1 Sin-n mrr1 sinus rly4• thlas thuj zinc k* [heroin sdj2]
  - ▽ **extending** to | **right**: agar all-c androc srj1•
- **day** and night: ign b7a.de
- **daytime**: carb-v k* caust k* cimic k* euphr k* merc nat-c hr1 Nux-v k* stann k* suis-pan rly4•
- **morning**: aeth k* agar b4.de* all-c alum k* ant-c ars-met Arum-t k* asc-t k* Bar-c k* bov b4.de* bry b7.de* bufo Calc k* calc-ar calc-p camph b7.de* canth b7.de* carb-an b4.de* Carb-v k* caust b4.de* cina b7.de* clem b4.de* coff b7.de* coloc b4.de* con k* corn k* cycl k* dig k* dros b7.de* euphr k* ferr-i hell b7.de* iod k* kali-bi k* kali-c k2 kola stb3• Kreos b7a.de lach k* laur b7.de* lyc b4.de* m-aust b7.de Mag-c k* mag-m bg2 merc b4.de* myric k* Nat-c b4.de* nat-m k* nit-ac b4.de* nux-m b7.de* **Nux-v** k* onos ozone sde2• par b7.de* petr a1 phos b4.de* puls pyrid rly4• Rhod b4.de* rhus-t b7.de* sars k* sep k* spig b7.de* spong fd4.de Squil k* streptoc rly4• sulph b4.de* sumb k* thuj b4.de* zinc b4.de* [heroin sdj2 spect dfg1]
  - **9 h**: kali-c bg2
  - **evening**; and: mag-c bg1
    - **waking**; on: ars Aster carb-v h2 dulc
  - **amel.**: stict

- **rising**:
  - **agg**.: all-c bg2 hell b7.de* nat-ar bg2 **Nux-v** mrr1 par b7.de* rhus-t b7.de*
  - **amel**.: m-arct b7.de nux-m b7.de* *Nux-v* b7.de* ozone sde2• ran-b b7.de*
- **waking**; on: agar bg2 am-c bg2 am-m bg2 ars k* *Aster* k* bov bg2 carb-v h2* *Dulc* hr1 graph bg2 kali-bi bg2 nat-ox rly4• **Nux-v** mrr1 oci-sa sk4• ozone sde2• petr-ra shn4• sabad bg2 spong fd4.de staphycoc rly4• suis-pan rly4•

- **forenoon**: carb-an b4.de* mag-c b4.de* mur-ac b4.de* phos b4.de* rhod b4.de* sabad b7.de* sars b4.de* squil b7.de* zinc b4.de*
- **noon**: cina
  - **until** noon: oci-sa sk4•
- **afternoon**: agar alum k* am-c b4.de* ant-t b7.de* apis b7a.de lach laur b7.de* lyc k* mag-c b4.de* mang b4.de* mur-ac b4.de* nux-v b7.de* phos b4.de* plb b7.de* sin-n staph b7.de* stict sulph b4.de* zinc b4.de*
  - **16** h: apis
- **evening**: *All-c* k* alum b4.de* anac k* ant-c b7.de* aphis *Apis* arn k* calad b7.de* calc-s a1 camph b7.de* *Carb-an* k* *Carb-v* k* chlor k* cina b7.de* coff b7a.de dulc k* euphr k* glyc bro1 iod k* kali-bi k* kali-c b4.de* lach k* lith-c m-ambo b7.de mag-c k* mag-m b4.de* mang k* nad rly4• nit-ac b4.de* petr b4.de* phos k* *Puls* k* ran-b b7.de* *Rumx* sabad b7.de* sel k* sin-n staph b7.de teucr b7.de* ther k* thuj b4.de* trom k* *Zinc* k* zinc-p k2 [spect dfg1]
  - **19**-20 h: stront-c sk4•
  - **fluent** | **dry** in morning; and: apis k* kali-bi bg2
  - **lying** down agg.; after: zinc
- **night**: alum k* am-c b4.de* am-m b7.de* ant-c k2 bov b4.de* bry k* *Calc* *Carb-an* carb-v k* cassia-s ccrh1• caust cham k* euphr ferr k* *Hyos* b7a.de kali-bi bg2 lac-c ptk2 *Lyc* b4.de* m-arct b7.de mag-m k* **Merc** k* naja *Nat-c* k* nat-s k* nicc *Nit-ac* k* *Nux-v* k* phos k* pitu-gl skp7• rumx sang sep b4.de* squil b7.de* thuj k*
  - **midnight**:
    - **before**: acon k2
    - **after** | **3** h: am-c
  - **air** agg.; in open: *Aeth* calc-p calc-s nat-c
- **accompanied** by:
  - **anemia** (See GENERALS - Anemia - accompanied - coryza)
  - **bruised** pain (See GENERALS - Pain - sore - accompanied - coryza)
  - **complaints**; other: acon b2.de* alum b2.de* *Am-m* b2.de* ambr b2.de* anac b2.de* ant-t b2.de* arn b2.de* ars b2.de* bar-c b2.de* bell b2.de* borx b2.de* bov b2.de* bry b2.de* calad b2.de* *Calc* b2.de* camph b2.de* canth b2.de* caps b2.de* carb-an b2.de* *Carb-v* b2.de* caust b2.de* **Cham** b2.de* chin b2.de* cic b2.de* cina b2.de* cocc b2.de* coff b2.de* cupr b2.de* dig b2.de* dulc b2.de* euph b2.de* euphr b2.de* *Graph* b2.de* hell b2.de* **Hep** b2.de* ign b2.de* ip b2.de* kali-c b2.de* kali-n b2.de* kreos b2.de* *Lach* b2.de* laur b2.de* *Lyc* b2.de* m-arct b2.de m-aust b2.de mag-c b2.de* mag-m b2.de* mang b2.de* *Merc* b2.de* mez b2.de* mosch b2.de* mur-ac b2.de* nat-c b2.de* nat-m b2.de* nit-ac b2.de* nux-m b2.de* **Nux-v** b2.de* par b2.de* petr b2.de* ph-ac b2.de* phos b2.de* plat b2.de* **Puls** b2.de* rhod b2.de* rhus-t b2.de* *Sabad* b2.de* samb b2.de* sars b2.de* seneg b2.de* *Sep* b2.de* sil b2.de* *Spig* b2.de* spong b2.de* squil b2.de* stann b2.de* staph b2.de* sul-ac b2.de* sulph b2.de* teucr b2.de* thuj b2.de* verat b2.de* zinc b2.de*
  - **congestion**: all-c tl1
  - **conjunctivitis** (See EYE - Inflammation - conjunctiva - accompanied - coryza)
  - **cough**; hacking (See COUGH - Hacking - accompanied - coryza)
  - **diarrhea**: ars bg2 bell bg2 calc bg2 carb-v bg2 *Cham* bg2 **Chin** bg2 chlor hr1 dulc bg2 hep bg2 *Ip* bg2 **Merc** bg2 nit-ac bg2 **Puls** bg2 **Sang** bg2 sep b4.de* staph bg2 *Sulph* bg2
    - **night**: sang hr1
    - **summer**; in: dulc ptk1
  - **diphtheria** (See THROAT - Membrane - accompanied - coryza)
  - **dryness** in nose: *Bell* b4a.de *Bry* b7a.de *Cann-s* b7a.de verat b7a.de

- **accompanied** by: ...
  - **epistaxis**: acon bg2 ambro vh1 ant-t bg1 ars b4a.de* bell bg2 bry bg2* chin bg2 elaps bg2 graph h2* ip mtf33 kali-bi bg1 kreos k2 *Merc* bg2 mosch b7a.de nit-ac h2 *Nux-v* bg2 puls b7a.de* rhus-t bg2 senec ptk1 sil ptk1 sulph h2*
  - **excitement**; nervous (See MIND - Excitement - nervous - coryza)
  - **fever** (See FEVER - Accompanied - coryza)
  - **hawking** up mucus: colch b7a.de
  - **hearing**; impaired (See HEARING - Impaired - accompanied - coryza)
  - **heat**; general sensation of (See GENERALS - Heat - sensation - accompanied - coryza)
  - **hemorrhage** (See GENERALS - Hemorrhage - accompanied - coryza)
  - **measles** (See SKIN - Eruptions - measles - accompanied - coryza)
  - **moaning** (See MIND - Moaning - coryza)
  - **nausea** (See STOMACH - Nausea - accompanied - coryza)
  - **neuralgia** (See GENERALS - Pain - neuralgic - accompanied - coryza)
  - **obstruction** (See Obstruction - accompanied - coryza)
  - **odor** from nose; bad: bell bg2
  - **photophobia**: all-c bro1 ars bro1 bell bro1 *Euphr* bro1
  - **respiration**:
    - **asthmatic** (See RESPIRATION - Asthmatic - accompanied - coryza)
    - **complaints** of: bov b4a.de *Calc* b4a.de kali-c b4a.de
    - **difficult** (See RESPIRATION - Difficult - accompanied - coryza)
  - **salivation**: **Arund** mrr1 *Calc-p* kr1* cupr-ar kr1* kali-i ptk1
  - **smell**; loss of: am-m b7.de* ant-t b7.de* arn b7.de* **Ars** bg2 bov bg2 *Bry* bg2 calc bg2 carb-an b4a.de* cina b7.de* cocc b7.de* *Cycl* b7a.de graph bg2 hell b7.de* **Ip** b7a.de* kali-c bg2 kali-n b4a.de* mag-m b4a.de* mang b4.de* med ptk1 mez b4a.de* *Nat-m* b4a.de* *Nux-v* b7.de* **Puls** b7.de* rhod b4.de* sabad b7.de* spig b7.de* squil b7.de* staph b7.de* sul-ac b4a.de* sulph bg2
  - **sneezing** (See Sneezing - coryza - with)
  - **sour** food; desire for (See GENERALS - Food and - sour food - desire - accompanied - coryza)
  - **urination**:
    - **burning**: ran-s ptk1
    - **profuse** (See URINE - Copious - coryza)
  - **vertigo** (See VERTIGO - Accompanied - coryza)
  - **voice**; complaints of: ars bg2 carb-v bg2 caust bg2 **Cham** bg2 **Dig** bg2 *Dulc* bg2 euphr bg2 graph bg2 *Ign* bg2 kali-c bg2 *Lach* bg2 *Merc* bg2 *Nat-c* bg2 *Nit-ac* bg2 *Petr* bg2 **Puls** bg2 *Sang* bg2 *Sep* bg2 **Spig** bg2 *Sulph* bg2 *Thuj* bg2
  - **weeping** (See MIND - Weeping - coryza)
  - ○ **Cervical** region | **pain** (See BACK - Pain - cervical - accompanied - coryza)
  - **Chest**:
    - **oppression** of chest (See CHEST - Oppression - accompanied - coryza)
    - **pain** in (See CHEST - Pain - accompanied - coryza)
  - **Ear**:
    - **complaints**: sil mtf33
    - **itching**: cycl bg2
    - **pain** (See EAR - Pain - accompanied - coryza)
  - **Eyes**:
    - **complaints** (See EYE - Complaints - accompanied - coryza)
    - **discharge**:
      - **acrid**: all-c tl1
      - **bland**: euph tl1

Nose

- **Eyes**: ...
  - **red**: ozone sde2•
  - **tears** (See EYE - Lachrymation - coryza)
- **Face**:
  - **eruptions** on (See FACE - Eruptions - accompanied - coryza)
  - **pain** in (See FACE - Pain - coryza - during)
- **Forehead**; pain in (See HEAD - Pain - forehead - coryza)
- **Head**; pain in (See HEAD - Pain - coryza - during)
- **Heart**; anxiety in (See CHEST - Anxiety - heart - accompanied - coryza)
- **Jaw**; pain in (See FACE - Pain - jaws - coryza)
- **Knees**; hot: ign ptk1
- **Lids**; swelling of (See EYE - Swelling - lids - accompanied - coryza)
- **Limbs**; aching in (See EXTREMITIES - Pain - accompanied - coryza)
- **Lips**; eruptions on: ars bg2 **Bell** bg2 *Hep* bg2 lach bg2 **Merc** bg2 mez b4a.de* nux-v bg2 sulph bg2
- **Occiput**; pain in (See HEAD - Pain - occiput - coryza)
- **Root** of nose; pressing pain at (See Pain - root - pressing - accompanied - coryza)
- **Skin**; complaints of: ars bg2
- **Stomach** complaints (See STOMACH - Disordered - accompanied - coryza)
- **Teeth**; pain in (See TEETH - Pain - coryza)
- **Throat**:
  - **burning** pain in (See THROAT - Pain - burning - accompanied - coryza)
  - **pain** in (See THROAT - Pain - accompanied - coryza)
  - **red** discoloration of (See THROAT - Discoloration - redness - accompanied - coryza)
- **Tongue** | **white** discoloration of the: **Kali-i** kr1*

- **acrid**: *(↗Discharge - excoriating)* *All-c* tl1* beryl sp1 cassia-s ccrh1•
  - **dry** in warm room, fluent in open air: hydr
- **acute**: aven br1 influ mp4• pop-cand br1 sapo br1
- **agg.**: am-c b4.de* am-m b7.de* ant-t b7.de* am b7.de* bell b4.de* calc b4.de* carb-v b4.de* cina b7.de* cocc b7.de* hell b7.de* lyc b4.de* nit-ac b4.de* *Nux-v* b7.de* phos b4.de* *Puls* b7.de* spig b7.de* squil b7.de* staph b7.de* zinc b4.de*
- **air** | **hot** | **inhaling** (See warm - air - inspiration - amel. - hot)
  - O **Posterior** nares sensitive to: kreos
- **air** agg.; draft of: carb-v k2 *Dulc Elaps* lap-la sde8.de• med c1 *Merc Nat-c* k* nit-ac tritic-vg fd5.de
- **air**; in open:
  - **agg.**: *(↗Discharge - watery - air - agg.)* *Aeth* k* agar bg2 allox sp1 alumn ars-i *Calc-p* k* calc-s kr1 caps bg2 carb-ac carbn-s *Cocc* b7.de* coloc *Dulc* euphr *Graph* hydr iod k* irid-met bg2* *Kali-bi* k* kali-i k2 lach bg2 lith-c lycpr c1 merc merc-c b4a.de* nat-ar nat-c k* **Nit-ac** bg2* nux-v b7.de* *Phos* plat k* positr nl2• psor al2* **Puls** k* rhod bg2 sabad k* sal-ac bg2 sanguis-s hrn2• squil bg2 sulph k* tarax teucr k* thuj k* trom vml3•
    - **cold** (See cold - air)
  - **amel.**: *Acon* k* *All-c* k* arist-cl sp1 ars bro1 aur-m k2 bry k* calc-p ptk1 *Calc-s* k* chinin-ar crot-c sk4• *Cycl* euphr vh ham fd3.de• hed sp1 ina-i mlk9.de iod b4.de* kola stb3• mag-m merc merc-i-r k* **Nux-v** k* ol-an c1 petr-ra shn4• phos k* *Puls* k* ran-b b7.de* rhod b4.de* rhus-t b7.de* stict k* tell thuj k* tritic-vg fd5.de vanil fd5.de
    - **while**; after a: tell
- **alcoholic** drinks agg.: fl-ac bg2
- **alternating** with:
  - **cough**: colch a1
  - **obstruction** (See Obstruction - alternating with - discharge)
  - O **Abdomen**; cutting pain in (See ABDOMEN - Pain - cutting - alternating - coryza)
- **amel.** general symptoms: thuj bg2*
- **annual** (See Hay)
- **autumn** agg.: merc ptk1
- **bathing**: ant-c bg2 sulph k2
  - **sea**; in the | **amel.**: med hr1* tritic-vg fd5.de
- **beer**; after: fl-ac bg2
- **beginning** of: *Quill* br1 *Sapo* br1
- **bloody** coryza: ars bg2 graph bg2 kali-bi bg2 puls bg2
  - **children**; in: | **infants**; in: calc-s ptk1*
- **breathing** obstructed (See Dryness - inside - breathing - mouth; Obstruction)
- **catarrhal**: ign b7a.de spig b7a.de
- **children**; in: dulc fd4.de merc-i-r br1* **Nux-v** hr1 oci-sa sp1
  - **newborns**: dulc br1*
- **chill**; during: am-c bg2 ant-t b7.de* arg-n bg2 ars bg2 *Aur* b4.de* bry b7.de* calad k* caps b7.de* *Carb-v* bg2 cham bg2 elat *Kali-c* bg2 lach bg2 lyc bg2 merc bg2 mur-ac b4.de* nat-c bg2 *Nux-v* b7.de* puls bg2 rhus-t bg2 sabad bg2 spong b7.de* sulph bg2 thuj bg2
- **chilled**; from becoming:
  - **overheated**; while: **Ars** *Carb-v Puls Sil*
  - **snow** or ice; from: ant-c ptk1 dros ptk1 iod ptk1 laur ptk1 puls ptk1 seneg ptk1 verat ptk1 verb ptk1
- **chilliness**; with: *Acon* k* ant-t b7.de* aphis arg-n k* *Ars* k* *Bry* k* calad b7.de calc-p k* *Camph* br1 caps b7.de carbn-s caust k* *Cham* b7.de* *Gels* bg2 graph k* ham fd3.de• hep b4a.de* lach bg2 mag-c bg3* **Merc** k* nat-c k* nit-ac **Nux-v** k* *Puls* k* *Sarr Sil Spig* k* *Spong* k* *Sulph* k*
  - O **Back**, in: aphis
- **chronic**: *(↗obstinate; Ozena)* ail alum k* am-c k* anac k* ant-c k2 *Apis* ars-i aur-m-n wbt2• bar-c sne berb **Brom** k* bry *Calc* k* calc-i bro1 calc-p calc-sil k2 *Canth* carb-v bg2 carc fb* caust bg2 cist k* coch *Colch* coloc con bg2* *Cycl* elaps hr1 eucal fl-ac graph k* hep bro1* hydr influ jl2* kali-bi bro1* kali-c mtf33 kali-i bro1 kreos *Lyc* k* mang nat-ar nat-c k* nat-m k* nit-ac bg2 ol-j phos psor puls k* sabad ptk1 *Sang* sars k* sep h2* *Sil* k* spig spong sul-i k2 *Sulph* k* *Teucr Tub* k* zinc bg2
  - **left**: *Berb*
  - **accompanied** by | **respiration**; asthmatic (See RESPIRATION - Asthmatic - accompanied - coryza - chronic)
- **cold**:
  - **air**:
    - **agg.**: aesc tl1 aral vh1 ars vh bar-i mtf11 *Calc-p* cist tl1 coff cor-r kkb *Dulc* k* euphr st1 graph hyos *Kali-ar* k* kali-c mtf11 kali-p k2 lac-e hrn2• lap-la sde8.de• mang **Merc** nat-c mtf11 nat-ox-act mtf11 **Ph-ac** phos tl1 rumx tl1
    - **amel.**: all-c bg2 lac-e hrn2•
  - **bathing** | **amel.**: calc-s k* hed sp1
  - **dry** | **air**: carc fd2.de• hyos
- **cold**; after taking a: acon b7.de* alum bg2 am-c bg2 aral bg2 *Ars* bg2 bar-c bg2 **Bell** bg2 bry b7.de* calc b4a.de* camph bg2 carc mlr1• caul bg2 cham b7.de* *Dulc* bg2 euphr bg2 ferr-p bg2 gels bg2 graph bg2 **Hep** bg2 ign bg2 *Ip* bg2 kali-bi bg2 kali-c bg2 kali-i bg2 **Lach** bg2 **Merc** bg2 nat-c b4a.de* nat-m bg2 nit-ac bg2 **Nux-v** b7.de* petr-ra shn4• phos bg2 psor bg2 *Puls* b7.de* *Rhus-t* b7.de* sep bg2 spig bg2 sulph bg2* tub bg2
- **cold** agg.; becoming: acon b7.de* ars-i k2 benz-ac cocc b7.de* dulc b4a.de* graph k* *Hep* b4a.de *Kali-ar* kali-i m-ambo b7.de *Merc* k* nat-c b4.de* *Nit-ac* b4a.de nux-m b7.de* nux-v k* petr h2 rhus-t b7.de* sacch-a gmj3 tritic-vg fd5.de
- **company**; with desire for (See MIND - Company - desire - coryza)
- **constant**: bar-c brom tl1 calc calc-i mtf11 carbn-s graph hep mtf11 hydr mtf11 kali-n kali-sil k2 ketogl-ac rly4• kola stb3• nat-c petr-ra shn4• sanguis-s hrn2• sil sul-ac mtf11
- **cough**:
  - **after**: *Bell* b4a.de *Hep* b4a.de kali-n h2
  - **with**: *(↗COUGH - Sneezing - with)* acon k* adam skp7• agar ptk1 *All-c* k* alum k* alum-p k2 alum-sil k2 am-c ambr k* *Ars* ars-i bad bar-c k* bar-i k2 bar-s k2 **Bell** k* bry bg2* *Calc* k* calc-sil k2 canth k* carb-an carb-v k* carbn-s *Caust Cham* k* cimx *Colch* con *Cupr* b7.de* dig b4a.de* dros bro1 **Euphr** k* *Ferr-p Gels Graph* hed sp1 hep *Hydrog* srj2• ign k* iod **Ip** k* *Just* bro1 *Kali-bi* k* kali-c kali-chl *Kali-i* kali-m k2 kali-n h2 kali-p lach k*

- **with**: ...
  Lyc k* mag-c mag-s meph merc k* nat-ar nat-c k* *Nat-m* nat-p k2 *Nit-ac* k* **Nux-v** b7.de* ph-ac k* *Phos* **Puls** b7a.de* *Rhus-t* k* rumx *Sang* k* sarr sars h2 *Seneg* sep sil sin-n bro1 spig *Spong* k* *Squil* k* staph stict bro1 sul-ac sul-i k2 *Sulph* k* *Tell* *Thuj* k* tritic-vg fd5.de
  - **daytime**: adam skp7•
  - **night** | **amel.**: adam skp7•
- **croup**, with: *Acon* k* *Am-caust* bro1 apis bro1 *Ars* k* cub k* echi bro1 *Hep* k* *Kali-bi* bro1 lach bro1 merc bro1 *Nit-ac* k* *Spong* k*
- **cutting** the hair, from: *Bell* k* **Nux-v** k* puls *Sep* k* sil h2*
- **diarrhea**; with (See accompanied - diarrhea)
- **dinner**; after: nat-c h2* **Nux-v** hr1
- **diphtheria**; during (See THROAT - Membrane - accompanied - coryza)
- **discharge**, with (= fluent): *Acon* k* *Aesc* k* aeth *Agar* k* agra bro1 ail k* **All-c** k* alum k* **Am-c** k* *Am-m* k* am-p bro1 ambr b2.de* *Ambro* bro1 anac k* anan androc srj1• ant-c k* *Ant-t* k* aphis apis aq-mar skp7• aral bg2* **Arg-met** k* **Ars** k* *Ars-i* k* ars-s-f k2 *Arum-t* k* asaf k* asar b2.de* *Asc-t* *Aspar* aur k* aur-ar k2 aur-i k2 aur-m aur-s k2 bad k* bamb-a stb2.de• *Bar-c* k* bar-i k2 bar-m bar-s k2 **Bell** k* benzol br1 berb beryl tpw5 *Borx* k* *Bov* k* *Brom* k* bros-gau mrc1 *Bry* k* bufo cact cain calad k* **Calc** k* *Calc-ar* calc-f calc-i k2 *Calc-p* *Calc-s* *Camph* k* canth b2.de* caps b2.de* carb-ac *Carb-an* k* *Carb-v* k* carbn-s carc fd2.de• castm castor-eq *Caust* k* *Cham* k* *Chel* k* *Chin* k* chinin-ar chlor k* cic b2.de* cimic cimx cina k* cinnb clem k* coc-c cocc b2.de* coff k* colch k* *Coloc* k* *Con* k* cop *Cor-r* cortiso gse crot-t *Cupr* k* *Cycl* k* dig diphtox jl2 *Dros* k* *Dulc* k* *Elaps* eucal bro1 *Eup-per* k* eup-pur euph k* **Euphr** k* fago br1 ferr b2.de* ferr-i ferr-p bg2* *Fl-ac* form *Gels* k* *Glon* graph k* guaj k* ham fd3.de• hell b2.de* *Hep* k* *Hydr* k* *Hydrog* srj2• **Ign** k* ina-i mlk9.de *Iod* k* *Ip* b7a.de* jac-g *Just* bro1 **Kali-ar** *Kali-bi* k* kali-br bg2 *Kali-c* k* *Kali-chl* k* **Kali-i** k* kali-m k2 kali-n *Kali-p* kali-s kalm ketogl-ac rly4• kreos k* **Lac-c** lac-h htj1• *Lach* k* lap-la sde8.de• laur b2.de* led b2.de* lil-t lim mtf11 *Lyc* k* m-ambo b2.de* m-arct b2.de* m-aust b2.de* mag-c k* *Mag-m* k* *Mag-s* *Mang* k* med k* meny k* meph k* **Merc** k* **Merc-c** k* merc-i-r merc-sul *Mez* k* mosch b2.de* mur-ac k* naja k* narc-po bro1 *Nat-ar* k* **Nat-c** k* **Nat-m** k* nat-p *Nat-s* **Nit-ac** k* **Nux-v** k* ol-j op bg2 *Osm* ox-ac ozone sde2• par k* *Petr* k* petr-ra shn4• ph-ac k* phasco-ci rbp2 phel a1 phos k* *Phyt* plac rzf5• plat k* plb k* prot pte1*• psil ft1 **Puls** k* pycnop-sa mrz1 *Quill* bro1 *Ran-b* k* ran-s k* rhod b2.de* rhodi br1 rhus-r rhus-t k* rumx k* ruta bg2 **Sabad** k* *Sang* k* *Sangin-n* bro1 sarr sars k* sel k* seneg b2.de* *Sep* k* *Sil* k* sin-n sinus rly4• sol-ni bro1 *Spig* k* *Spong* k* squil k* stann b2.de* staph k* stict bg2 stront-c b2.de* sul-ac k* sul-i k2 **Sulph** k* *Syph* tab bg2 **Tell** teucr b2.de* **Thuj** k* trif-p bro1 trios rsj11• tritic-vg fd5.de vanil fd5.de verat b2.de* xan *Zinc* k* zinc-p k2 [buteo-j sej6 spect dfg1]
  - **one** side: alum b4a.de* am-m b7a.de bell b4a.de* *Hep* b4a.de lac-c bg2 m-arct b7.de nux-v b7.de* puls b7.de* rhod b4a.de* staph b7a.de* ter bg2
  - **alternating** sides: androc srj1• dulc fd4.de **Lac-c**
  - **daytime**: *Bar-c* b4a.de carb-v caust cimic dig k* euphr k* meny b7a.de merc nat-c **Nux-v** k* stann vanil fd5.de
  - **morning**: *Acon* alum b4a.de* ant-c k* *Ars* b4a.de bar-c b4a.de calc-p carb-v caust coloc k* *Cycl* dros k* *Euphr* k* ferr-i k2 kali-c k2 mag-c nit-ac b4a.de **Nux-v** k* ozone sde2• puls k* sars k* *Sep* k* *Squil* k* *Sulph* thuj k*
    - **bed** agg.; in: carb-v
    - **cough** and expectoration; with: **Euphr**
    - **dry** in afternoon: mag-c
    - **rising** agg.; after: calc-sil k2 caust **Nux-v** k*
  - **forenoon**: calc-p cimic cina b7a.de* dulc fd4.de merc-i-r nat-c
    - **10** h: med
    - **11** h: *Tell*
    - **dry** | **afternoon**: *Puls* b7a.de
  - **noon**: *Cina* dulc fd4.de
  - **afternoon**: alum h2 **Arum-t** calc-p dulc fd4.de kali-c mag-s plb k* staph b7a.de sulph trom wye
    - **amel.**: nat-c
  - **evening**: agar **All-c** aphis *Apis* bufo *Carb-an* k* *Carb-v* k* coff dulc fd4.de fl-ac iod bg2 kali-c k* kali-s fd4.de lach b7a.de* mez nat-ar *Nux-v* b7a.de phos b4a.de *Puls* *Rumx* sel k* sil bg2 sulph ther thuj trom ven-m rsj12• *Zinc*
    - **18** h: pitu-gl skp7•
  - **night**: aur-m caust bg2 fl-ac iod *Kali-bi* merc *Nat-c* *Rumx* tritic-vg fd5.de
  - **accompanied** by | **urine**; burning: ran-s ptk1
- **discharge**, with: ...
  - **air**; in open:
    - **agg.**: arg-n bg2 *Ars* calc-s calc-sil k2 *Carb-ac* *Coloc* dulc euphr hydr *Iod* k* nat-m bg2 **Nit-ac** plat k* **Puls** sabad sul-i k2 *Sulph* k* tell teucr bg2 *Thuj* k* trom vanil fd5.de zinc zing
      - **room**; but without discharge in a: hydr bg2 iod bg2 plat bg2 puls bg2 thuj bg2
    - **amel.**: androc srj1• ars-i *Calc-s* carb-v choc srj3• cycl trios rsj11•
  - **alternating** with:
    - **dry** (See discharge, without - alternating - fluent)
    - **Chest**; oppression of (See CHEST - Oppression - alternating - coryza)
  - **chill**; during: ant-t bg2 *Ars* bg2 aur bg2 *Bry* b7.de* *Carb-v* bg2 cham bg2 kali-c bg2 lach bg2 merc bg2 nat-c bg2 *Puls* bg2 *Rhus-t* bg2 sulph bg2 thuj bg2
  - **cold** | **room** | **agg.**: *Calc-p* *Carb-ac* *Merc*
    - **water** | **agg.**: fl-ac
  - **cough** agg.; during: *Euphr* b7a.de *Ign* b7a.de *Merc* b4a.de
  - **fever**; during: kali-c b4a.de
  - **followed** by coryza without discharge: zinc h2
  - **lying** agg.: *Spig* trios rsj11•
    - **flows** into fauces and rattle while breathing: phos k*
  - **obstruction**; with: *Ars* b4a.de
  - **periodical**: sep bg2
  - **room** agg.: all-c ptk1 calc-p ptk1 *Nux-v* b7a.de*
  - **stooping** agg.: agar *Merc*
  - **warm** room agg.: **All-c** k* androc srj1• cycl kali-c k2 *Merc* *Nux-v* **Puls**
  - **weather**; windy: euphr hep k2
- **discharge**, without: *(↗Obstruction)* *Acon* k* aesc bg2 agar k* agn b2.de* all-c all-s alum k* alum-p k2 alum-sil k2 *Am-c* k* *Am-m* k* ambr k* ambro bro1 *Anac* k* *Ant-c* k* apis k* arg-met b2.de* *Ars* k* arum-t bg2* asar k* asc-t aur k* aur-ar k2 aur-i k2 aur-s *Bamb-a* stb2.de• bar-c b2.de* *Bell* k* bov k* *Brom* bg2 *Bry* k* *Cact* **Calad** b2.de* **Calc** k* calc-i k2 calc-s *Camph* k* cann-s b2.de* canth b2.de* *Caps* k* *Carb-an* k* *Carb-v* k* *Carbn-s* **Caust** k* cham k* chel k* **Chin** k* *Chinin-ar* cic b2.de* cina b2.de* cist bro1 coff k* *Con* b2.de* cor-r k* croc k* cupr k* cycl dig k* dros k* *Dulc* k* elaps bro1 euph b2.de* falco-pe nl2• ferr-p bg2 glyc bro1 *Graph* k* guaj b2.de* hep k* hydr bg2 hyos b2.de* *Ign* k* *Iod* k* *Ip* k* kali-ar *Kali-bi* bg2* *Kali-c* k* kali-chl kali-i bg2 kali-m bg2* kali-n k* kali-p kola stb3• kreos k* lach k* laur b2.de* *Lyc* k* m-ambo b2.de* m-arct b2.de* m-aust b2.de* *Mag-c* k* mag-m k* *Mang* k* mentho bro1 meny b2.de* merc k* mez k* mosch k* mur-ac b2.de* naja bg2 *Nat-ar* *Nat-c* k* *Nat-m* k* nat-s k* *Nit-ac* k* nux-m b2.de* **Nux-v** k* ol-an ol-j olib-sac wmh1 op k* osm bro1 ozone sde2• *Par* k* petr k* ph-ac b2.de* phasco-ci rbp2 **Phos** k* *Plat* k* plb b2.de* psor k* *Puls* k* ran-b b2.de* rat *Rhod* b2.de* *Rhus-t* b7a.de sabad b2.de* sabin k* sacch **Samb** k* sang bg2* sars k* sel b2.de* seneg b2.de* *Sep* k* *Sil* k* sin-n bro1* *Spig* k* *Spong* k* squil k* stann k* staph b2.de* **Stict** k* stram b2.de* *Sul-ac* k* *Sulph* k* teucr k* *Thuj* k* tub bg2 (non:uran-met k) uran-n vanil fd5.de verat b2.de* verb k* *Zinc* k*
  - **one** side: alum b4a.de* am-m b7a.de* bell bg2 bry bg2 *Hep* bg2 ign bg2 lach bg2 m-arct b7.de nat-m bg2 *Nux-v* b7.de* *Phos* bg2 phyt bg2 plat b4a.de* pyrog bg2 rhod bg2 sabad bg2 sin-n bg2 stann b4a.de* staph bg2 sul-ac bg2 sulph bg2
  - **left**: calc-caust *Sep* sin-n mrr1
  - **daytime**: carb-an k* caust bg2
  - **morning**: *Apis* bov b4a.de calc k* *Carb-an* k* carb-v k* con k* dig k* iod k* kali-c lach k* laur lyc b4a.de mag-m b4a.de mag-s nat-m k* nux-v k* *Phos* b4a.de sep b4a.de *Sil* k*
    - **fluent**:
      - **daytime**; during: *Sil*
      - **evening**; during: apis
    - **rising** | **after** | **agg.**: bov
      - **amel.**: carb-an
  - **forenoon**: sars b4a.de ven-m rsj12•
  - **afternoon**: mag-c mang b4a.de nat-c b4a.de
  - **evening**: calad b7a.de* calc carb-an b4a.de carb-v carbn-s caust bg2 cimic euphr iod k* kali-c b4.de* lach mag-m b4a.de mang k* nicc nux-v k* puls k* rhod b4a.de *Sulph*
    - **bed** agg.; in: kali-c

Nose

- **evening**: ...
  - ⋮ **discharge** during the day; with: cimic dig euphr *Nux-v*
- **night**: alum k* am-c k* bamb-a stb2.de• bov b4a.de calad b7a.de calc *Caust* k* dig k* euphr lach *Lyc* b4a.de *Mag-c* k* mag-m k* nat-c k* nicc nit-ac k* **Nux-v** k* *Puls* b7a.de sep b4a.de*
  - ⋮ **fluent** during the day: caust dig euphr merc nat-c nicc **Nux-v** k*
- **accompanied** by:
  - ⋮ **obstruction** (See Obstruction - accompanied - coryza - discharge)
  - ⋮ **respiration**; impeded: m-arct b7.de
- **air** agg.; in open: calc-p naja **Nux-v** k*
- **alternating** with | **fluent**: alum k* alum-p k2 alum-sil k2 am-c bro1 ant-c ant-t *Apis Ars* k* bell k* cund euphr k* kali-c k2 kali-n h2 kola stb3• *Lac-c* bro1 lach k* mag-c *Mag-m* k* *Mang* k* *Nat-ar* k* *Nat-c* k* *Nat-m* k* nit-ac **Nux-v** k* ozone sde2• par k* *Phos* k* psor k2 **Puls** k* quill bro1 sang *Sil* k* *Sin-n* bro1 sol-ni bro1 spong bro1 sul-ac *Sulph* tritic-vg fd5.de zinc zinc-p k2
- **children**; in: carb-v b4a.de dulc b4a.de
  - ⋮ **nurslings**: nux-v b7a.de samb b7.de*
- **chronic**: *Bry* b7a.de *Ip* b7a.de
- **cold** air agg.: dulc b4a.de
- **eating** | **after** | **agg.**: nit-ac b4a.de sep b4a.de sil b4a.de sulph b4a.de zinc b4a.de
  - ⋮ **agg.**: spig
- **followed** by fluent: asc-t cor-r plat
- **perspiration**; during: *Bry* bg2 calad bg2 calc bg2 dulc bg2 *Ip* bg2 kali-c bg2 *Lyc* bg2 nat-m bg2 nit-ac bg2 **Nux-v** bg2 phos bg2 *Rhod* bg2 rhus-t bg2 *Samb* bg2 sil bg2
- **room** agg.: *Thuj* b4a.de thyr ptk1
- **shivering**; during: kali-c b4.de
- **sleep**; during: *Lyc* b4a.de
- **warm** room agg.: *Ars* calc-p k2 *Coloc* hydr *Iod* plat psor al2 *Puls Sulph Thuj* zing

- **eating**:
  - **after** | **agg.**: carb-an bg2 clem bg2* fl-ac bg1 **Nux-v** k* *Plb* bg2* puls bg2 sanic bg2* spig sulph b4a.de* trom bg2 *Zinc*
  - **agg.**: *(↗Discharge - eating; Discharge - eating - while - agg.)* aq-mar jl arge-pl rwt5• calc sne carb-an k* graph sne hydrog srj2• nux-v ptk1 sanic bg3* trom k*
  - **amel.**: chir-fl gya2 oci-sa sk4•
- **epistaxis**; with (See accompanied - epistaxis)
- **excitement** amel.: fl-ac k*
- **exhausting**: arg-met bg2* arg-n bg1
- **fever**:
  - **before**: bell b4a.de hep b4a.de
  - **with**: *Acon* k* all-c am-c b4.de am-m bg2 anac k* ant-t b7a.de* arn b7a.de *Ars* k* *Aur* b4.de* bapt bro1 bar-m k* *Bell* k* **Bry** k* calad b7a.de calc bg2 camph b7.de* *Carb-v* b4a.de* caust b4a.de cham b7.de* *Chin* b7a.de chlor coff b7.de* con bg2 euphr bg2 gels k* graph k* *Hep* k* iod k* jab k* **Kali-c** b4.de* kreos b7a.de lac-del hrn2• lach k* lyc b4.de* **Merc** k* *Merc-c* b4a.de *Mez* bg2 mur-ac b4.de nat-c k* nit-ac k* nux-m b7.de nux-v b7.de* phos bg2 **Puls** bg2 **Rhus-t** b7.de* sabad b7.de* *Sel* bg2 *Seneg* k* sep b4.de* sil bg2 spig k* sulph bg2 *Tarent* k* **Thuj** b4a.de
    - ⋮ **east** winds; due to cold: acon mtf11
    - ⋮ **menses**; during: graph b4.de*
- **flowers**: *(↗odors - roses)* **ALL-C** k ● sabad k* sang k*
  - **chamomile**: wye vh
- **followed** by: *(↗Catarrh - followed)*
  - **diarrhea**: alum ptk1 calc bg3* *Sang* k* sel k* tub bg3*
  - **fever**; intermittent: psor jl2
  - **sneezing** agg.: naja ptk1
  - **voice**; complaints of: **Carb-v** bg2 *Caust* bg2 **Dros** bg2 *Mang* bg2 *Phos* bg2 rhus-t bg2 sil bg2 sulph bg2
  - ○ **Air** passages; complaints of: am-br bg2 am-c bg2 just bg2 kali-c bg2
- **followed** by: ...
  - **Chest**; complaints of: *All-c* am-c st am-m vh1 aral vh ars-i vh brom mtf33 *Bry* mrr1 carb-v euphr ign mtf33 iod mtf33 *Ip* kali-c mtf33 lac-c mtf33 lap-a st lyc mtf33 mang ptk1 *Merc* nux-v *Phos* mrr1* sang mrr1 sep mtf33 sil ptk2 stict c1 sulph mtf33
  - **Downward**; complaints of air passages travelling: ars ptk1 bry ptk1 carb-v ptk1 iod ptk1 kali-c ptk1 kali-i ptk2 lyc ptk1 phos ptk1 stict ptk1 sulph ptk1 tub ptk1
  - **Frontal** sinuses; complaints of: *(↗Catarrh - followed - frontal; GENERALS - Inflammation - sinuses)* *Ars* atro vh calc-p cimx fuma-ac rly4• *Kali-i* pyrid rly4• samb bat1• *Sil Stict*
  - **Head**; pain in: ant-c ptk1
  - **Larynx**; complaints of: all-c mrr1 carb-v k2 graph k2 rhus-t k2
  - **Throat**; complaints of: ars k2 carb-v k2 pyrid rly4•
  - **Upward**; complaints of air passages travelling: arum-t ptk1 *Brom* ptk1 lac-c ptk1 merc ptk1 sep ptk1
- **hay** fever (See Hay)
- **headache**, with (See HEAD - Pain - coryza - during)
- **hunger**; with: all-c ars-i ptk1 hep *Sul-ac*
- **inflammation**; with:
  - ○ **Eyes**; of: cain c1
  - **Larynx**; of: acon alum am-m *Ars* ars-met bar-c *Benz-ac* **Bry** calc *Calc-p* calc-s **Carb-v** carbn-s **Caust** cham *Dig* dulc eup-per ferr-p graph *Hep Kali-bi* kali-c *Kalm Mag-m* mag-s **Mang Merc** *Merc-i-r* nat-ar *Nat-c* nat-m *Nit-ac Petr* phel **Phos** puls *Ran-b Rumx Seneg Sep Spig Spong* sul-ac sulph *Tell* thuj zinc
- **influenza**; from: influ jl2*
- **intermittent**: nat-c k*
- **lachrymation**; with: acon bro1 *All-c* bro1 am-p bro1 ambro bro1 aral bro1 arg-n br1 *Ars* bro1 ars-i bro1 camph bro1 cham bro1 *Cycl* bro1 eup-per bro1 *Euphr* bro1 *Gels* bro1 ip bro1 *Just* bro1 kali-chl bro1 *Kali-i* bro1 mentho bro1 merc bro1 naphtin bro1 *Nat-m* bro1 *Nux-v* bro1 quill bro1 *Sabad* bro1 sin-n bro1 solid bro1 squil bro1 stict bro1
  - **copious**: all-c tl1 euphr tl1
- **light**; from | **strong** light | **agg.**: *Puls*
  - **sunlight** | **agg.**: agar bg2 aml-ns bg2 aur bg2 hydr bg2
- **lying**:
  - **agg.**: am-c bg2 caust bg2 chinin-ar euphr k* kali-bi bg2 mag-m nux-m b7.de* puls bg2 sep bg2 sin-n spig k*
  - **amel.**: arg-n bg2 graph bg2 merc k* psor k2
- **lying** down agg.: puls b7.de
- **menses**:
  - **before**:
    - ⋮ **agg.**: graph k* *Mag-c* k* mag-m bg2 nat-act mtf **sep** bro1 tarent k*
      - ⋮ **cough** and hoarseness; with: *Graph*
  - **during**:
    - ⋮ **agg.**: acon bg2 agar bg2 alum k* *Am-c* k* am-m ambr bg2 bar-c ptk1 **Bry** bg2 carb-an bg2 dulc bg2 *Graph* k* *Kali-c* k* kali-n h2* lach bg2* mag-c k* nat-s bg2 nux-v bg2 phos bg3* senec ptk1 *Sep* b4a.de* *Sulph* bg2 verat bg2 zinc bg3*
    - ⋮ **beginning** of menses | **agg.**: mag-c b4.de
  - **suppressed** menses; from: seneg
- **milk** agg.: lac-d ptk1
- **motion**:
  - **agg.**: nux-v k2 petr-ra shn4•
  - **amel.**: *Ars* b4a.de *Dulc* nux-m b7.de nux-v bg2 phos *Puls* b7.de* *Rhus-t* thuj
- **nervous**: kali-p bg2 lach bg2 sabad bg2 sel bg2 sil bg2 sumb bg2
- **obstinate**, with soreness beneath nose and on margin of nose: *(↗chronic)* **Brom** iod
- **odors**:
  - **agg.**: ozone sde2• sang bg2
  - **peaches** agg., of: **All-c** k*
  - **roses** agg. of: *(↗flowers)* *All-c Sabad Sang Tub* wye
- **old** people: am-c k* anac br1 ant-c ptk1 camph ptk1
  - **palpitations**; with: anac bro1*

- **opening** the eyes | **amel.**: graph bg2
- **overheated**, from becoming: acon k* ars bry k* *Carb-v* cham bg2 *Ip* b7.de **Nux-v** b7.de* *Puls* k* *Rhus-t* bg2 *Sep* sil sulph k2
- **paper**; when handling: bros-gau mrc1
- **periodical**: (↗ *GENERALS - Cold; taking - Tendency)* ars bro1 *Brom* ptk1 chin bro1 chinin-ar k2 *Graph* k* nat-m bro1 sang bro1 sil k*
  - • **day**:
    - ⁝ **alternate**: aran *Nat-c* k*
    - ⁝ **every** day: graph bg2
    - ⁝ **fourth**; every: iod
  - • **week** | **three** weeks; every: ars-met
  - • **month** | **August**: all-c tl1
  - • **year**; every (See Hay)
- **perspiration**:
  - • **after**:
    - ⁝ **agg.**: cham b7a.de
    - ⁝ **amel.**: *Cham* b7.de* nat-c k* nat-m *Nux-v* b7.de*
  - • **night**: hep b4a.de *Merc* b4a.de
  - • **with**: am-m bg2 ant-t bg2 *Ars* bg2 **Bell** bg2 calc bg2 carb-v bg2 caust bg2 **Cham** bg2 *Cycl* bg2 eup-per euphr bg2 jab *Lach* bg2 *Merc* k* mez bg2 nat-c bg2 *Puls* bg2 **Rhus-t** bg2 *Sel* bg2 sil bg2 *Squil* bg2 **Sulph** bg2 thuj bg2
- **reading** out loud: verb b7.de*
- **recurrent** (See GENERALS - History - coryza)
- **scarlatina**; during: **Ail** *All-c* *Am-c* **Arum-t** *Caps* *Mur-ac* *Nit-ac* phos phyt rhus-t
- **seasons**:
  - • **spring**; in: gels k* lach k* naja
  - • **summer**; in: brom mrr1 dulc ptk1 *Gels* k* sang mrr1
    - ⁝ **accompanied** by | **diarrhea** (See accompanied - diarrhea - summer)
  - • **winter**; in: am-c bg2 ars bg2 cist bg2
- **sensation** of: agar b4.de* am-m b7.de* ambr b7.de* ant-c b7.de* apis b7a.de arg-met b7.de* bell bg2 bov b4.de* bry b7.de* cann-s b7.de* carb-an b4.de* carb-v b4.de* chel b7.de* cic b7.de* coff b7.de* ign b7.de* ip b7.de* *Kreos* b7a.de laur b7.de* mag-c b4.de* mag-m b4.de* meny bg2 merc b4.de* mur-ac b4.de* nit-ac b4.de* nux-m b7.de* phos b4.de* plb bg2 sabin b7.de stram bg2 teucr b7.de* thuj b4.de* verb bg2
- **short**: graph h2* nit-ac h2* sep h2* sulph h2*
- **singing**; from: all-c ptk1
- **sitting** on a cold surface agg.: nux-v
- **sitting** up in bed | **amel.**: carb-an bg2 mag-m nux-m b7.de* puls b7.de* sin-n
- **sleep**:
  - • **during**: fl-ac ptk1 lac-c ptk1 puls b7.de*
  - • **fluent** during sleep: *Fl-ac*
- **sleeplessness**; with: ars k* *Calc-ar* cham bro1
- **smoke**; from: petr-ra shn4•
- **sneezing**; after: nux-v b7a.de
- **snow** air agg.: *Puls* *Rhus-t*
- **sore** throat, with (See THROAT - Pain - sore - accompanied - coryza)
- **spasmodic**: flav jl2 mucor jl2
- **stomach**; from disordered: *Bry* b7.de* **Puls** b7.de* staph b7.de*
- **stool** | **after** | **agg.**: hep bg2
  - • **during** | **agg.**: sep bg2 thuj k*
- **stooping** agg.: laur k*
- **sudden** attacks: agar alum apis aven vml3• bar-c h2* cycl fl-ac k* *Iod* k* *Plan* k* spig k* staph k* sulph h2* syph ptk1 *Thuj* k* tub-d jl2 *Zinc* k*
  - • **evening** | **lying** down agg.; after: *Zinc* k*
- **sun**; walking in the | **amel.**: aral vh1
- **suppressed**: *Acon* k* am-c ambr k* *Ars* k* *Arum-t* ptk1 **Bell** k* brom ptk1 *Bry* k* *Calc* k* carb-v k* cham k* *Chin* k* *Cina* k* *Dulc* b4a.de euphr bg2 graph hep bg2 ign bg2 ip bg2 kali-bi k* kali-c **Lach** k* *Lyc* k* *M-aust* b7.de merc bg2 *Nit-ac* ptk1 *Nux-v* k* par puls k* rhus-t bg2 sep k* *Sil* k* *Sulph* bg2 teucr ptk1
  - • **cold** air; from least contact of: dulc
  - • **sensation** of suppressed coryza: osm ptk1
- **swallowing** agg.: carb-an k*
- **talking** agg.: acon kali-bi bg2 nat-c b4.de* petr-ra shn4•
- **tea** | **amel.**: aq-mar skp7*•
- **temperature**; change of: aids nl2• all-c ptk1 ars bg2 gels ptk1 kali-i bg2 nux-v bg2 rumx mtf11 sabad bg2
- **uncovering**; from: nux-v k2 pyrog bg2
  - • **head**; the: *Hep* *Nat-m*
- **violent** attacks: alum alum-sil k2 **Ars** k* **Arum-t** k* *Bry* *Calc* *Carb-v* chlor cina a1 cocc cycl kali-n c1 **Lyc** k* mag-c mang a1 mez nat-c nit-ac petr a1 ph-ac h2* psil ft1* rhus-t k2 sil *Staph* thuj
- **waking**; on: kali-c bg2
- **walking**:
  - • **agg.**: cassia-s ccrh1•
  - • **air**; in open | **after** | **agg.**: op b7.de*
    - ⁝ **agg.**: *Ant-c* b7a.de tarax b7.de*
  - • **amel.**: *Dulc* merc-i-r k* phos *Puls* *Rhus-t*
- **warm**:
  - • **air**:
    - ⁝ **agg.**: ant-c *Apis* **Merc**
      - ⁝ **yet** dreads cold: apis *Merc*
    - ⁝ **inspiration**:
      - ⁝ **amel.** | **hot** air: sabad k2
  - • **bed** | **agg.**: merc k2 nux-v k2
  - • **drinks** | **amel.**: petr-ra shn4• sabad mrr1
  - • **room**:
    - ⁝ **agg.**: **All-c** k* *Ant-c* ars bro1 aur-m k2 carb-v cycl iod k2 kali-i k2 laur b7.de* *Merc* *Merc-i-r* k* *Nux-v* k* op b7.de* phos k* psil ft1* puls b7.de* ran-b b7.de* rhus-t b7.de* sep spig b7.de* spong bg2 sulph bg2 verb b7.de*
    - ⁝ **amel.**: *Ars* k* calc-p coloc *Dulc* k* kali-i mrr1 psor k2 *Sabad* k*
  - • **water** | **nose** amel.; in: ars k2
- **warm** from walking; becoming | **amel.**: aral vh merc-i-r
- **warmth**:
  - • **agg.**: *Nux-v* b7a.de
  - • **amel.**: *Ars* b4a.de sabad mrr1
- **washing**:
  - • **after** | **agg.**: fl-ac
  - • **amel.**: calc-s k* phos k*
  - • **head**:
    - ⁝ **after** | **agg.**: *Bell* b4a.de *Sep* b4a.de
- **water** through the nose; drawing in | **amel.**: merc-c b4a.de
- **weather**:
  - • **changeable**, in: ars k2 calc mtf33 gels k* hep kali-i k2 petr-ra shn4• sulph k2
  - • **cold**:
    - ⁝ **wet** | **agg.**: *All-c* br1 dulc mrr1
  - • **dry** cold: nux-v
  - • **warm** | **agg.**: brom k2
  - • **wet** | **agg.**: all-c dulc k* hep kali-i ptk1 mang k* *Merc* *Puls* sin-n
  - • **windy**, in: euphr
- **wet**; after getting: ant-c bg2 cassia-s ccrh1• nat-c hr1 *Puls* bg2 sep k*
  - • **head**: *Rhus-t* hr1
- **whooping** cough; in: all-c hr1 alum bro1 lyc bro1 nat-c bro1
- **wind**:
  - • **cold**:
    - ⁝ **dry** | **agg.**: **Acon** *Spong*
    - ⁝ **west**: *Kali-bi*
    - ⁝ **wet**: all-c k2
  - • **dry** | **east** wind: *Spong* b7.de*
  - • **north** east wind; after: **All-c**
- **wine**:
  - • **agg.**: fl-ac bg2
  - • **amel.**: fl-ac bg2
- **yawning**; with: bry b7.de* carb-an k* cupr k* hell b7.de* laur b7.de* lyc k*

Nose

▽ - **extending** to: *(↗Catarrh - extending)*

○ · **Chest** (See CHEST - Inflammation - bronchial - coryza)

· **Downward** (See followed - downward)

· **Upward** (See followed - upward)

○ - **Choanae** (See posterior)

- **Posterior** nares (= choanae): *Cist* br1 staph bg2
- **Root**; at: aq-mar jl1*

COUGH agg.; during: acon b7.de* caps bg2 carb-v bg2 dros bg2 lach bg2 merc b4.de* nat-m b4.de* nux-v bg2 *Puls* b7.de*

COVERING: | **suffocation**; covering nose produces (See RESPIRATION - Difficult - covering)

CRACKLING noise in: acon k* sulph

CRACKS: agar bg2 ant-c b7.de* arum-t ptk1 bell bg2 carb-an bg2* caust tl1 graph bg2 merc bg2 morg-p fmm1• nit-ac bg2 petr bg2 sulph bg2

○ - **Corners** of: *Graph* k* merc morg-p pte1*• syc pte1*• thuj mtf33

- **Nostrils**; in: agath-a nl2• **Ant-c** k* anthraco k* arge-pl rwt5• *Aur* *Aur-m* *Graph* k* merc ptk1 nit-ac *Petr* k* plut-n srj7• thuj ptk1

○ · **Corners** of: acon-ac rly4• ant-c bg2

- **Septum**: merc
- **Tip**: **Alum** k* carb-an k* *Graph* bro1 petr bro1 succ-ac rly4•
  - · **menses**; during: carb-an
- **Wings**: alum bro1 *Ant-c* bro1 *Arum-t* bro1 aur bro1 aur-m aur-m-n bro1 bov bro1 *Calc* bro1 caust k* cor-r bro1 cund bro1 *Graph* bro1 hep ign bro1 *Kali-bi* bro1 kali-c bro1 lac-c mtf33 lyc bro1 *Merc* k* *Nit-ac* bro1 *Petr* bro1 sil sulph bro1 syc bka1• ter bro1 *Thuj* k* vanil fd5.de

CRAMPS of nose: ambr b7.de* lyc h2* phys bg2 sulph h2

○ - **Wings**: ambr h1

CRAWLING in (See Formication; Itching)

CREEPING (See Tingling)

CRUSTS (See Discharge - crusts)

CRYING; after: nit-ac b4a.de*

DENTED in (See Sunken)

DEPIGMENTATION: | **Wings**: stram ptk1

DESQUAMATION: ars k* aur k* aur-m k* canth k* carb-an k* crot-t mez bg2 *Nat-c* k* *Nat-m* k* nit-ac bg3* phos bg3* samb vh sep bg2 sumb bg1

○ - **Septum**, of: crot-t kali-bi

- **Tip**, of: carb-an nat-c

DILATED nostrils: *(↗Motion; Motion - wings)* *Ant-t* k* *Ars* k* cupr ptk1 hell k* iod ptk1 *Lyc* k* op h1 ox-ac phos phys *Spong* k*

- **expiration** agg.; during: *Ferr* k*
- **inspiration**, at each: *Merc-i-f*
- **sensation** of: iod k* olib-sac wmh1

DINNER; after: kali-bi bg2

DIPHTHERIA in: *Am-c* k* am-caust bro1 **Apis** ptk1 *Ars* ptk1 brom ptk1 *Diph* ptk1 *Hydr* *Kali-bi* k* kali-chl ptk1 kali-i ptk1 *Lac-c* ptk1 **Lach** ptk1 *Lyc* k* merc-c merc-cy k* *Merc-i-f* ptk1 merc-i-r ptk1 mur-ac ptk1 nit-ac k* *Petr* *Phos* ptk1 *Phyt* ptk1 *Rhus-t* ptk1 spong ptk1 sul-ac ptk1

- **begins** in: lyc merc-c merc-cy

▽ - **extending** to | **Lips**: am-c

○ - **Posterior** nares: lac-c lach

DIRTY (See Sooty)

DISCHARGE: *(↗Catarrh; Inflammation)* beryl tpw5 cassia-s ccrh1• flav jl2 gink-b sbd1• hir skp7• jab br1 med jl2 melal-alt gya4 nicotam rly4• olib-sac wmh1 petr-ra shn4• ros-d wla1 streptoc jl2 *Vac* jl2

- **one** side: agath-a nl2• alum bg2 bell bg2 calc-s k* calen bro1 hippoz hydrog srj2• lac-c bg2 phyt c1* puls bg2 rhus-t bg2 staph bg2 symph fd3.de•
- **right**: chir-fl gya2 crot-c k* kali-bi kali-c kali-p lac-h htj1• lyc melal-alt gya4 pitu-gl skp7• positr nl2• puls rhus-g tmo3• sal-fr sle1• sang
- **left**: aids nl2• all-c anth vh aq-mar skp7• arum-t k2 bad vh chir-fl gya2 hydrog srj2• kali-s ketogl-ac rly4• lach pitu-gl skp7• positr nl2• pyrid rly4• sep streptoc rly4• symph fd3.de• teucr [tax jsj7]
  - · **then** right: olib-sac wmh1
- **daytime**: arum-t caust nat-c

Discharge: ...

- **morning**: amp rly4• apoc vml3• berb coli rly4• dulc fd4.de ephe-si hsj1• gink-b sbd1• granit-m es1• ham fd3.de• helo-s rwt2• *Hydrog* srj2• ignis-alc es2• kali-c k2 kali-p kali-s fd4.de ketogl-ac rly4• mang ozone sde2• petr-ra shn4• phos podo fd3.de• puls ruta fd4.de sacch-a fd2.de• sal-fr sle1• squil streptoc rly4• suis-hep rly4• tritic-vg fd5.de vanil fd5.de
  - · **waking**; on: petr-ra shn4•
- **forenoon**: erig k* sacch-a fd2.de• tritic-vg fd5.de vanil fd5.de
- **noon** | **12** h: brucel sa3•
- **afternoon**: lyc olib-sac wmh1 tritic-vg fd5.de vanil fd5.de
- **evening**: abrom-a ks5 aids nl2• dulc fd4.de kali-s fd4.de puls ruta fd4.de tritic-vg fd5.de vanil fd5.de ven-m rsj12•
  - · **21** h: pitu-gl skp7•
  - · **amel.**: galeoc-c-h gms1•
- **night**: agath-a nl2• cassia-s ccrh1• crot-c k* kali-bi **Lac-c** k* nat-s ptk1 **Nit-ac** vanil fd5.de
  - · **midnight**:
    - ⁝ **after** | **5** h: *Ars*
- **accompanied** by:
  - · **expectoration**; copious (See EXPECTORATION - Copious - accompanied - nose)
  - · **obstruction** of nose (See Obstruction - accompanied - discharge)
  - · **vertigo** (See VERTIGO - Accompanied - nose - discharge)

○ · **Face**; pain in (See FACE - Pain - accompanied - nose)

- **acrid** (See excoriating)
- **air**; in open:
  - · **agg.**: allox tpw4
  - · **amel.**: beryl tpw5 chir-fl gya2 hydr bg1
- **albuminous**: *(↗egg)* aesc bro1 am-caust a1 *Aur* k* calc bro1 calc-sil k2 camph bro1 coli gmj1 graph bro1 hippoz hydr bro1 hydrog srj2• *Iod* kali-bi bro1 kali-i bg2* *Kali-m* bro1 lac-c bro1 mag-p bg2 mentho bro1 **Nat-m** k* *Nat-s* phos bg2* positr nl2• ruta fd4.de
- **alternating** with obstruction (See Obstruction - alternating with - discharge)
- **biting** (See excoriating)
- **bitter**: ars ph-ac
- **black**: atra-r skp7*• *Thuj* b4a.de
- **bland**: anthraq rly4• arg-n bg2 *Calc* cassia-s ccrh1• chir-fl gya2 cycl bg2 **Euphr** k* jug-c bro1 kali-i bro1 kali-s bg2 lac-h htj1• melal-alt gya4 plan positr nl2• **Puls** k* sal-fr sle1• *Sep* k* *Sil* staph stront-c sk4•
- **blood**-streaked: ham fd3.de• mez lp phos bg2* ribo rly4• sinus rly4• vanil fd5.de
- **bloody**: acon k* act-sp k* *Agar* k* agath-a nl2• **Ail** k* **All-c** **Alum** k* alum-p k2 alum-sil k* **Am-c** k* *Am-m* ambr k* androc srj1• ant-t k* *Apis* arg-met k* arg-n k* arn bg2 **Ars** k* ars-h k* *Ars-i* ars-s-f k2 *Arum-t* k* asar k* atp rly4• *Aur* k* aur-ar k2 aur-i k2 *Aur-m* k* *Aur-m-n* k* aur-s k2 bamb-a stb2.de• bapt k2 bar-c k* bar-i k2 bar-s k2 **Bell** k* borx k* bov bg2 brom bg2* bry k* bufo calad k* *Calc* k* **Calc-s** k* calc-sil k2 canth k* caps k* carb-ac k* *Carb-v* k* carbn-s cardios-h rly4• carneg-g rwt1• cartl-s rly4• *Caust* k* cench k2 chel k* **Chin** k* **Chinin-ar** cimic cinnb clem k* *Cocc* k* coli rly4• *Con* k* cop cortico tpw7* *Croc* k* *Crot-c* crot-h k* cupr k* cypra-eg sde6.de• daph bg2 dros k* dulc fd4.de echi bro1 euphr k* *Ferr* k* *Ferr-ar* ferr-i ferr-p k* fl-ac bg2 gels k* get a1 glycyr-g cte1• *Graph* k* ham fd3.de• **Hep** k* hippoz k* *Hydr* k* hydrog srj2• hyos a1 ind k* iod k* ip k* *Kali-ar* *Kali-bi* k* *Kali-c* k* kali-chl bg2 kali-cy a1 **Kali-i** k* kali-n k* kali-p kali-s kali-sil k2 kreos k* *Lac-c* k* *Lach* k* laur k* led k* *Lyc* k* mag-c k* mag-m k* *Mang* k* med k2* **Merc** k* merc-c bro1 *Merc-i-r* k* *Mez* k* mur-ac k2 myric nat-c b4.de *Nat-m* k* **Nit-ac** k* nux-m k* *Nux-v* k* op k* par k* pen bro1 petr k* ph-ac k* phasco-ci rbp2 *Phos* k* phyt plan a1 podo fd3.de• **Psor** k* puls k* ran-b k* rhus-t k* ribo rly4• ros-d wla1 sabad k* sabin k* sangin-n bro1 sanic sarr k* sel k* *Sep* k* *Sil* k* *Sin-n* spig k* spong k* *Squil* k* *Stict* stront-c b2.de* succ-ac rly4• sul-ac k* sul-i k2 *Sulph* k* symph fd3.de• *Thuj* k* tritic-vg fd5.de *Tub* vanil fd5.de zinc k* zinc-p k2
  - · **one** side, from: asc-t bros-gau mrc1 coli rly4• ham fd3.de• ribo rly4• spong fd4.de
  - · **left**: olib-sac wmh1
  - · **morning**: agath-a nl2• *Am-c* arum-t k* calc cartl-s rly4• digin a1 dulc fd4.de fago a1 ham fd3.de• kali-bi gk kali-c *Lach* lyc k* petr phos k2 plan a1 sol-t-ae a1 spig h1* sulph k* tritic-vg fd5.de vanil fd5.de

- **morning**: ...
  - **blowing** the nose agg.: androc srj1• calad caust chel dulc fd4.de graph ham fd3.de• lach lap-la sde8.de• meny h1 nit-ac phos h2 puls sep h2 sulph symph fd3.de• thuj zinc
- **evening**: sul-ac k2 vanil fd5.de
- **night**: sulph h2*
- **blowing** the nose; when: bros-gau mrc1
- **children**; in: calc-s k2*
- **coryza**; during: sulph h2*
- **cough** agg.; during: caps k*
- **crusts**; forms: am-m b7a.de *Ambr* b7a.de
- **trickles**; in: bros-gau mrc1
- **watery**: rhus-t bg2
- ○ **Posterior** nares: *Hep* k* nux-v h1* puls h1* ribo rly4• sabad ptk1 tell k*

- **blowing**; soon after | **amel.**: cist tl1
- **blue**: am-m k* arund k* *Kali-bi* k* *Nat-ar*
  - **children**; in: am-m ptk1
- **brownish**: bamb-a stb2.de• cench k2 hydrog srj2• *Kali-s* nit-ac k2 rhus-g tmo3• sin-n hr1 thuj
- **burning**: *Acon* bg2* aesc tl1 agar **All-c** k* alum *Am-c* k* am-m aphis aq-mar skp7• *Ars* k* *Ars-i* k* *Ars-met* ars-s-f k2 arum-t k* bell bg2 brom calad k* calc k* canth k* carb-an k* *Caust* k* *Cham* bg2 chel k* chord-umb rly4• cina k* *Cinnb* k* con k* cupr-act br1 euph graph bg2 ham k* iod k* *Kali-ar* kali-bi kali-c k* kali-i k* kali-s kreos k* lach bg2 lyc bg2 m-arct b2.de* merc k* mez k* mosch k* nat-m bg2* par bg2 phos bg2 **Puls** k* rhus-t bg2 seneg bg2 spong bg2 sul-ac k* *Sulph* k* *Tub* jl2 wye k2 zinc bg2
- **changeable**: calc staph a1*
- **chronic**: anac bg2 phos bg2
- **clear**: *(↗watery)* *Acon* acon-ac rly4• agar aids nl2• am-m androc srj1• anth vh asar atp rly4• atra-r bnm3• aur bamb-a stb2.de• bell k2 calc carbn-s cardios-h rly4• castm cedr chir-fl gya2 choc srj3• chord-umb rly4• con cystein-l rly4• dulc fd4.de ephe-si hsj1• falco-pe nl2• galeoc-c-h gms1• ger-i rly4• germ-met srj5• graph helodr-cal knl2• hydr *Hydrog* srj2• *Iod* ketogl-ac rly4• kola stb3• lac-ac *Lac-h* htj1• mag-c mang melal-alt gya4 merc-i-r a1 moni rfm1• *Nat-m* nat-pyru rly4• nat-sil fd3.de• oxal-a rly4• ozone sde2• phos plac-s rly4• plut-n srj7• podo fd3.de• positr nl2• pot-e rly4• pyrid rly4• ribo rly4• sal-al blc1• sal-fr sle1• spong fd4.de squil k2 staphycoc rly4• suis-hep rly4• sulph suprar rly4• symph fd3.de• tritic-vg fd5.de vanil fd5.de [bell-p-sp dcm1 *Spect* dfg1]
  - **left**: anth vh
  - **hot** water: acon
  - ○ **Posterior** nares; from: all-c bro1 *Kali-m* bro1 lycpr bro1 nat-m bro1
- **cold** agg.: ambro bg2* diphtox jl2 ichth ptk1 kali-i ptk1 lach bg2* phos bg2 pitu-gl skp7•
- **constant**: agar all-c k2 hydr iod kali-bi lac-c mim-p vml3• phos puls mtf33 teucr
- **copious**: abrom-a ks5 acon aeth agar ail k* **All-c** k* alum alum-p k2 *Alumn* am-m bro1 ammc vh1 anac anan aral br1* arg-met b7.de* arg-n bg2 **Ars** k* *Ars-i* k* arum-t k* aspar bals-p bro1 bamb-a stb2.de• bar-c k* bar-i k2 bar-m bar-s k2 berb borx k* bov b4.de* brom bg2 *Bry* calc k* calc-f calc-i bro1 calc-sil k2 canth k* carb-v b4.de* carbn-s cardios-h rly4• cassia-s ccrh1• caust cedr cench k2 chel b7.de* chlor choc srj3• chord-umb rly4• cic k* cina b7.de* coc-c coff k* con b4.de* cop cor-r crot-c cupr cycl k* dros ephe-si hsj1• ery-a eup-pur k* euph euphr k* ferr-i *Fl-ac* mrr1 *Galeoc-c-h* gms1• gels bg2 granit-m es1• *Graph* k* guaj helo-s rwt2• hep k2* hydr k* hydrog srj2• ignis-alc es2• ina-i mlk9.de *Iod* k* irid-met vml3• kali-bi k2* kali-c kali-chl **Kali-i** k* kali-m k2 ketogl-ac rly4• lac-ac lac-c lach b7.de* lem-m br1 lyc m-ambo b7.de mag-m k* merc b4a.de* moni rfm1• mur-ac k* *Nat-ar* *Nat-c* **Nat-m** k* nat-ox rly4• nat-s *Nit-ac* nux-v k* pen br1 petr b4.de* **Phos** k* phyt bg2 plac rzf5• plan plat k* plb b7a.de *Puls* k* pyrid rly4• ran-b b7.de* ran-s b7a.de rein a1 rhod k* rhus-t b7.de* *Rumx* *Sabad* k* sang bro1 sangin-n bro1 *Sel* b7.de* *Senec* *Sep* k* sil b4.de* skook br1 *Spig* k* squil b7.de* staph *Stict* suis-hep rly4• sul-i k2 *Sulph* teucr thuj bro1 *Tub* k* verat-v verb c1 wye k2 *Zinc* k* zinc-p k2
  - **left**: plut-n srj7•
  - **morning**: ephe-si hsj1• puls k2
    - **rising** agg.; after: *Rhus-t* h1
  - **air** agg.; in open: hydr
  - **coryza**; without: agar ptk1 caust bg2 cycl bg2 mag-c bg2 mag-m h2 phos h2 *Rhus-t* bg2* sabad bg2 sel bg2 spig bg2 squil bg2 ter ptk1
  - **dripping**: fic-m gya1
- **copious**: ...
  - **faucet**; runs like a: fl-ac mrr1
  - **sneezing**; on: solid ptk1
  - **stuffing** of head; with: *Acon* agar *Arum-t* *Calc* **Kali-i** *Nit-ac* *Nux-v* phos h2 spig h1
    - **morning**: *Arum-t*
  - ○ **Posterior** nares; from: carb-v chord-umb rly4• **Cor-r** euph ketogl-ac rly4• nat-ox rly4• plac rzf5• *Spig*
  - **Sinus**; from frontal: verb c1
- **corrosive**: am-m b7.de* *Ars* b4a.de *Cham* b7a.de kali-bi bg2 lyc bg2 merc bg2 nit-ac bg2 *Nux-v* b7.de* sil bg2 squil bg2 sulph bg2
- **coryza**; without: agar ptk1 ter ptk1
- **cough** agg.; during: agar bg2* caps bg1 lach bg2* nat-m ptk1 nit-ac bg3* plac-s rly4• sal-ac bg1 sil bg2 *Squil* ptk1 sul-ac vh sulph bg1* thuj bg1*
- **creamy**: cench k2 *Hippoz* bg1
- **crusts**, scabs, inside: *(↗Scurfy; Scurfy - nostrils)* *Agar* aids nl2• ail *Alum* k* alum-p k2 *Alum-sil* k* *Alumn* am-m b7a.de ant-c k* ant-t b7.de apis arg-n k* arn b7.de *Ars* ars-s-f k2 *Arum-t* bro1 arund *Aur* k* aur-ar k2 *Aur-m* k* aur-s bamb-a stb2.de• bar-c bar-s k2 bell b4a.de* *Borx* k* **Bov** k* *Brom* k* bry k* cadm-s c2* *Calc* k* calc-f bro1 calc-p bg2 *Calc-s* calc-sil k2* canth b7.de *Carb-an* k* carbn-s caust k* cench k2 *Cham* b7.de* chr-ac br1 chr-met dx cic k* coc-c *Cocc* b7.de* con cop k* cor-r kkb crot-t culx daph *Diphtox* jl2 dulc bro1* *Elaps* k* fago c2* *Ferr* k* ferr-ar *Ferr-i* ferr-p flav jl2 galeoc-c-h gms1• **Graph** k* ham fd3.de• helo-s rwt2• *Hep* k* *Hippoz* hydr k* hydrog srj2• hyos b7.de hyper *Ign* b7.de* *Iod* **Kali-bi** k* *Kali-c* k* kali-i k2 kali-n b4.de* kali-p kali-s fd4.de kali-sil k2 lac-c *Lach* k* lem-m c1* lith-c *Lyc* k* mag-c k* *Mag-m* k* *Merc* k* *Merc-i-f* k* merc-i-r *Mez* k* morg-g pte1*• *Nat-ar* k* *Nat-c* k* *Nat-m* k* nat-p nat-s *Nit-ac* k* nux-v k* ozone sde2* petr k* petr-ra shn4• ph-ac b4.de* *Phos* k* *Phyt* pip-n sne plac rzf5• positr nl2• pot-e rly4• psor k* *Puls* k* ran-b k* rat rhod rhus-r rhus-t b7a.de* ruta fd4.de sangin-n bro1 *Sanic* k* sars k* sel b7.de **Sep** k* *Sil* k* spig b7.de* spong fd4.de squil b7.de* staph k* **Stict** k* streptoc jl2 stront-c suis-pan rly4• *Sulph* k* syc pte1*• symph fd3.de• syph k* teucr k* ther bro1 **Thuj** k* tritic-vg fd5.de trom **Tub** k* vanil fd5.de vinc xan zinc-chr ptk1 zinc-i ptk1 [helia stj nat-n stj1 spect dfg1]
  - **right**: *Alum* *Aur* aur-s k2 dulc fd4.de hep *Iod* kali-p k2 lith-c nit-ac sars *Sil* *(non:uran-met k)* uran-n xan
  - **left**: aids nl2• cob kali-s fd4.de nat-p ruta fd4.de
  - **adhere** tightly: kali-bi mrr1 phos syph jl2
  - **alternating** with | **fluent**: ozone sde2•
  - **black**: calc falco-pe nl2• rhod
  - **bloody**: allox tpw4 am-c k* am-m ambr k* calc dulc k2 falco-pe nl2• ferr bg2 gink-b sbd1• hydr bg2* *Kali-bi* k* nat-ar nux-v bg2 *Phos* k* puls ruta fd4.de sep spong fd4.de stront-c k* succ-ac rly4• thuj bg2*
  - **branny**: sulph bg2*
  - **brown** crusts: gink-b sbd1• *Kali-c* *Thuj* vinc
  - **cold** agg.; parts becoming: chinin-s bg1
  - **dark** colored: galeoc-c-h gms1•
  - **detach** | **easy** to detach:
    - **soreness** at root; but if pulled away to soon, they cause | **photophobia**; with: **Kali-bi**
    - **hard** to detach | **raw** and sore spot; leave a: *Ars* *Bov* **Kali-bi** nit-ac *Phos* phyt psor puls k2 stict *Thuj*
  - **detached**; when:
    - **bleeding**; cause: *Arg-n* aur-m k2 *Kali-bi* k* kali-c k2 lac-c *Nat-ar* nat-c k2 *Nit-ac* puls k2 suis-pan rly4• tritic-vg fd5.de
    - **pain** and soreness; cause: arg-n a1 *Kali-bi* nit-ac teucr *Thuj* [nat-n stj1]
    - **raw** and bleeding until other crusts form; leaving nostrils: *Ars* brom *Nit-ac*
    - **reform**; crusts: *Ars* borx k* **Kali-bi** lac-c *Psor*
  - **dry**: borx mtf33 cob-n sp1 syc bka1• syph jl2 ulm-c jsj8•
  - **elastic** plugs: **Kali-bi** *Lyc* *Stict* mrr1
  - **gray**: ail bros-gau mrc1 hippoz kali-c
  - **green**: *Nat-s* sne podo fd3.de• tritic-vg fd5.de vanil fd5.de
    - **morning**, every: bros-gau mrc1 *Nit-ac* k*
    - **masses**: alum k2 *Elaps* **Kali-bi** *Phos* **Sep** *Teucr*
  - **greenish**, seem to come from an ulcer: *Nat-s*

Nose

• **hard**: bamb-a stb2.de•
⁝ **plugging** the nose: _(↗hard - plugging)_ mur-ac vh
• **large**: teucr br1
• **offensive**: teucr br1
• **orange**: limest-b es1•
• **painful**: bamb-a stb2.de• graph mag-m a1 _Sil Thuj_
⁝ **large**, must discharge through posterior nares: alum _Sep_
• **recurrent**: syph jl2
• **rhinitis**; in atrophic: calc-f br1
• **sensation** of: olib-sac wmh1
• **shining**: lith-c
• **thick**: helia br1 kali-bi mrr1
• **watery** on eating (See watery - eating)
• **whitish**: kali-bi podo fd3.de•
• **yellow**: aur aur-m _Calc Cic Iod Kali-bi_ kali-br a1 kali-c kali-p k2 mag-m ozone sde2• puls k2 rhod
• **yellow** orange:
⁝ **coryza**, in: _Bar-c_ brom _Kali-c_
⁝ **dry**: aur-m
⁝ **thick**, heavy, high up: crot-t
○ • **Bones** | **Turbinated** bones: cop br1
• **High** up: arum-t calc-sil k2 crot-t nit-ac k2 _Sil_ staph
⁝ **discharge** of a large scab from gathering high up beyond the nasal bones: arum-t k1
• **Margins** of nose: ant-c ptk1 borx ptk1 calc-s k2
• **Posterior** nares (See posterior - crusty)
• **Septum**: anac _Kali-bi Lac-c_ ph-ac _Psor_ sel _Sil_ **Thuj** k*
⁝ **right**: _Lac-c (non:_uran-met k) uran-n
- **dark**: cinnb ptk1 merc-d ptk1
- **dries** quickly, forming scabs: cench k2 psor _Stict_
- **drinking** agg.; after: caust b4a.de
- **dripping**: acon bg2 agar bg2 _Agath-a_ nl2• _All-c_ bg2* am-c ptk1 _Ars_ bg2* ars-i bg3* arum-t bg3* calc bg2* cham bg2 chin bg2 chir-fl bnm4• con bg2 eup-per ptk1 euph bg2 euphr bg3* graph bg3* _Hep_ bg2* kali-bi bg2 kali-i k* lavand-a ctl1• lyc bg2 mag-c bg2 mag-m bg2 merc bg2 merc-c bg2 nat-m bg2 nit-ac bg2* nux-v bg3* petr-ra shn4• phos k* pin-con oss2• psor jl2 rhod bg2 _Rhus-t_ bg2* sabad bg3* sang bg2 sep bg2 sil bg2 squil ptk1 _Sulph_ bg2* tab k* vanil fd5.de
• **cold** agg.: lach bg2
• **eating** agg. (See eating)
• **sensation** as if: nat-m bg2 phos bg2
- **drying**: agar bg2 lach bg2 lyc bg2 merc-c bg2 sin-n bg2
- **eating**: _(↗watery - eating; Coryza - eating - agg.)_
• **after**:
⁝ **agg.**: caust b4a.de trom ptk1
⁝ **amel.**: aq-mar skp7•
• **while** | **agg.**: _(↗watery - eating; Coryza - eating - agg.)_ carb-an bg3* clem bg3* nux-v bg3* plb bg3* sanic bg3* sulph bg3* trom bg3*
- **egg** white; like: _(↗albuminous) Aur_ hydrog srj2• **Nat-m** k*
- **excoriating**: _(↗Coryza - acrid; Excoriation)_ agar _Ail_ k* **All-c** k* aloe sne _Alum_ k* alum-p k2 alum-sil k2 _Am-c_ k* am-caust bro1 **Am-m** k* _Ambro_ bro1 anac k* ant-c k* ant-t apis aral bg2* **Ars** k* _Ars-h_ **Ars-i** k* ars-met ars-s-f k2 **Arum-t** k* atp rly4• _Aur-m_ bamb-a stb2.de• bell bro1 bell-p sp1 beryl tpw5 borx k* _Brom_ k* bry bg2 cact k* cain calad _Calc_ k* calc-i k2 _Calc-s_ k* calc-sil k2 cann-s k* canth k* carb-an k* _Carb-v_ k* _Carbn-s_ carc mg1.de* castm _Caust_ cedr k* _Cham_ k* chin k* chlor k* cinnb _Con_ k* cupr-act br1 eucal bro1 eup-pur euph b2.de* euphr _Ferr_ k* ferr-ar **Ferr-i** ferr-p fl-ac _Gels_ k* glyc bro1 **Graph** k* ham k* _Hep_ k* _Hippoz_ k* _Hydr_ k* ign k* **Iod** k* kali-ar _Kali-bi_ k* kali-br bg2 _Kali-c_ k* _Kali-i_ k* kali-m k2 kali-n kali-p kali-s ketogl-ac rly4• **Kreos** k* _Lac-c_ _Lach_ k* _Lyc_ k* m-arct b2.de mag-c k* _Mag-m_ k* mag-s mang k* **Merc** k* _Merc-c_ k* _Merc-i-f_ merc-i-r bg2 _Mez_ k* _Mur-ac_ k* _Naja_ k* naphtin bro1 _Nat-ar_ bro1 nat-c bg2 nat-m k* **Nit-ac** k* **Nux-v** k* par bg2 petr bg2 ph-ac k* _Phos_ k* _Phyt_ k* puls k* _Ran-b_ k* _Rhus-t_ ribo rly4• sabad bro1* _Sang_ k* _Sangin-n_ bro1 seneg bg2 sep k* _Sil_ k* _Sin-n_ k* spig k* spong bg2 _Squil_ k* stann staph k* stict k* sul-ac k* _Sul-i Sulph_ k* thuj k* trif-p bro1 (non:uran-met k) uran-n wye k2 _Zinc_ k* zinc-p k2 [calc-br stj1]
- **excoriating**: ...
• **right**: kali-bi sang
• **left** nostril, from: **All-c**
• **daytime**: cain
• **morning**: ars-met _Squil_
• **forenoon** | **11** h: ars-met
• **night**: **Nit-ac** k*
• **accompanied** by | **Eyes**; bland discharge from: **All-c** k*
• **air** agg.; in open: kali-s
• **cold** washing | **amel.**: calc-s k*
• **menses**; during: am-c k*
• **reddening** upper lip: ars-i bg3*
○ • **Corners** of nose: chinin-ar sulph k2
• **Lips**: sulph k2
• **Posterior** nares; from: ars-i bro1
- **fetid** (See offensive - fetid)
- **fish**-brine, smelling like: elaps k* thuj ptk1
- **flocculent**: am-c _Ars_ carb-v ferr hydrog srj2• puls sep sil sulph
- **foamy** (See frothy)
- **frothy**: acon bg2 am-m bg2 ammc a1 ant-c bg2* arund bg2* carb-ac bg2* chir-fl bnm4• cic bg2 cic-m a1 dios bg2 hydrog srj2• kali-cy bg2* lac-ac bg2* lach bg2 merc bg2* oena bg2* op bg2* plb bg2 sil bg3*
• **yellow**: merc bg2
- **gelatinous**: arg-met bg2 bar-c bg2 chin bg2 coc-c k2 _Dig_ bg2 ferr bg2 hep _Laur_ bg2 sabad bg2 sel k* spong fd4.de
- **glairy**: alum cund hr1 _Petr_ k*
- **glassy**: cedr k* iod k*
- **glue**-like: dulc fd4.de ham fd3.de• hep bg1* _Kali-bi_ ptk1 _Merc-c_ k* _Psor_ sel stict _Sulph_
○ • **Posterior** nares; from: _Merc-c_ ozone sde2• sumb
- **gray**: **Ambr** k* anac k* ars k* asim k* bell bg2 carb-an k* cardios-h rly4• chin k* hippoz k* kali-c k* kreos k* **Lyc** k* mang k* med nux-v k* ozone sde2• rhus-t k* sang k* seneg k* sep k* thuj k*
- **grayish** white: sang
- **greenish**: acon-ac rly4• adam skp7• _Alum_ alum-p k2 alum-sil k2 anan k* anthraq rly4• am ars k* _Ars-i_ k* ars-s-f k2 arund k* asaf k* aur k* aur-ar k2 aur-i k2 aur-m k* aur-s k2 bac jl2 bamb-a stb2.de• _Berb_ k* _Borx_ k* bov k* _Bry_ k* bufo calc k* _Calc-f_ calc-i k2 calc-sil k2 calen vml3• cann-s k* carb-an k* _Carb-v_ k* carbn-s cimic k* colch k* coli rly4• conch fkr1* cop k* cortico sp1 culx dros k* dulc fd4.de ferr k* ferr-ar _Ferr-i_ flav jl2 graph hep hippoz k* hydr-ac k* _Hydrog_ srj2• hyos k* ind k* iod k* kali-ar **Kali-bi** k* _Kali-c_ k* **Kali-i** k* kali-p kali-s k* kali-sil k2 kreos k* **Lac-c** k* led k* lyc k* lyss m-aust b2.de mag-c bg2 mang k* marb-w es1• **Merc** k* _Nat-c_ k* nat-s k2* _Nit-ac_ k* nux-v k* orot-ac rly4• ozone sde2• par k* petr-ra shn4• _Phos_ k* pitu-gl skp7• plb k* plut-n srj7• psil ft1 **Puls** k* _Rhus-t_ k* ruta fd4.de sanic **Sep** k* _Sil_ k* spig k* spong fd4.de squil a1 stann k* _Stict_ suis-em rly4• _Sul-i_ k* sulph k* symph fd3.de• syph k* _Teucr_ k* _Ther_ k* _Thuj_ k* _Trios_ rsj11• tritic-vg fd5.de tub al* tung-met bdx1• vanil fd5.de [kali-n stj1]
• **morning**: dulc fd4.de gink-b sbd1• ruta fd4.de
• **evening** | **amel.**: ven-m rsj12•
• **blood**-streaked: **Phos**
• **light**; on exposure to: _Nat-s_
- **greenish** black: **Kali-i**
- **greenish** brown: _Hydr-ac_
- **greenish** yellow (See yellowish green)
- **gummy**: _Agath-a_ nl2• sumb k*
- **gushing** fluid: agar h2* all-c bg2 apis bg2 ars bg2 bad vh chlor bg2 con bg2 dulc ptk1 euphr h2* fl-ac bg2* hydr bg2* kali-bi bg2* lach bg2* lyc bg2 _Nat-c_ bg2* _Nat-m_ bg2* phos bg2* sel bg2* sil bg2 spig bg2 squil ptk1 staph bg2* _Thuj_ bg2* zinc bg2
• **left**: bad vh
• **morning**: squil ptk1
- **hard**, dry: agar k* _Alum_ k* alum-sil k2 **Alumn** ant-c k* ars arund **Aur** aur-i k2 _Aur-m_ aur-s k2 bar-c bar-i k2 bar-s k2 _Borx_ k* brom _Bry_ k* calc carbn-s cere-b a1 coc-c a1 _Con_ k* elaps galeoc-c-h gms1• _Graph_ guare k* hydr-ac _Iod_ k* **Kali-bi** k* kali-c k2 _Lach_ k* limest-b es1• lyc k* _Merc_ merc-i-f mez _Nat-ar Nat-c_ k* nat-s petr phos k* phyt bg2 sec **Sep** k* **Sil** k* sin-n a1 staph k* **Stict** stront-c k* sul-i k2 _Sulph_ k* symph fd3.de• tell teucr br1 thuj k* xan

- **morning**: *Arum-t* a1 asim **Sil**
- **bloody**: kali-c bg2 phos bg2 sep bg2
- **menses**; during: sep h2*
- **plugging** nose: (↗*crusts - hard - plugging*) kali-bi tl1 mur-ac bg1
- ○ **Posterior** nares: *Merc*

- **hot**: acon *All-c* bro1 am-caust bro1 *Am-m* bro1 *Ambro* bro1 *Aral* bro1 *Ars* bro1 ars-i bg3* ars-met arum-t bro1 bamb-a stb2.de• bell bro1 carb-v bro1 cham bro1* eucal bro1 *Gels* bro1 glyc bro1 iod k* kali-i bg1* kreos bro1 lach bro1 lyc merc bro1 *Merc-c* bro1 mur-ac bro1 naphtin bro1 *Nat-ar* bro1 *Nat-m* bro1 nit-ac bro1 *Rhus-t* k* *Sabad* bro1 sang bro1 *Sangin-n* bro1 sin-n mrr1 squil bro1 sulph bro1 trif-p bro1
- **ichorous**: **Ail** all-c k* ars arum-t k* aur-m-n k* *Lyc* merc *Nit-ac* *Rhus-t* rhus-v a1
  - **singing** agg.: all-c k*
- **irritating**: syph jl2
- **light**-colored: am-m b7.de* sabad b7.de*
- **lumpy**: alum ptk1 cinnb bg3* kali-bi bg2* mag-p bg2 mang k2 merc-d bg3* mur-ac bg2 petr h2* phos bg2* sel b7.de* sep bg2* *Sil* bg2* solid bg3* teucr ptk1 zinc-i bg3*
  - ○ **Posterior** nares; from: *Alum* sne calc ptk1 cimic ptk1 merc-i-f bg3* osm c1* sep ptk1 syph ptk1 teucr bro1* zinc h2
- **membranous**: *Am-caust* bro1 echi bro1 hep bro1 *Kali-bi* bro1 lach bg2 phos bg2 sep bg2
  - **isinglass**: merc-c bg2
- **mucous**: acon b2.de* agar b2.de* agn b2.de* alum b2.de* am-c b2.de* *Am-m* b2.de* ambr b2.de* anac b4a.de* ant-c b2.de* ant-t b2.de* *Arg-met* b2.de* **Ars** b2.de* asar b2.de* aur b2.de* bar-c b2.de* *Bell* b2.de* **Borx** b2.de* bov b2.de* *Bry* b2.de* calad b2.de* *Calc* b2.de* calc-p bg2 cann-s b2.de* canth b2.de* caps b2.de* carb-an b2.de* carb-v b2.de* caust b2.de* cham b2.de* **Chin** b2.de* chlor bg2 *Cina* b2.de* cocc b2.de* coloc b2.de* con b2.de* crot-h bg2 dig b2.de* dros b2.de* dulc b2.de* euph b4.de* euphr b2.de* *Ferr* b2.de* graph b2.de* guaj b2.de* hep b2.de* hyos b2.de* iod b2.de* ip b2.de* kali-n b2.de* kreos b2.de* *Laur* b2.de* lyc b2.de* m-ambo b2.de* m-aust b2.de *Mag-c* b2.de* mag-m b4.de* mang b2.de* *Merc* b2.de* *Mez* b2.de* mur-ac b2.de* *Nat-m* b2.de* nit-ac b2.de* nux-m b2.de* nux-v b2.de* op b2.de* par b2.de* petr b2.de* ph-ac b2.de* **Phos** b2.de* plb b2.de* *Puls* b2.de* ran-b bg2 ran-s bg2 rhod b2.de* rhus-t b2.de* *Sabin* b2.de* samb b2.de* sars b2.de* sel b2.de* *Seneg* b2.de* **Sep** b2.de* *Sil* b2.de* spig b2.de* *Spong* b2.de* **Squil** b2.de* *Stann* b2.de* *Staph* b2.de* sul-ac b2.de* *Sulph* b2.de* ther bg2 thuj b2.de* verat b2.de* **Zinc** b2.de*
  - **air** agg.; in open: rhod bg2
  - **bloody**: graph bg2 kali-bi bg2 kali-c bg2 lach bg2 mag-m bg2 phos bg2
  - **chronic**: anac bg2 phos bg2
  - **coryza**; without: par b7a.de ran-b b7a.de ran-s b7a.de rhus-t b7a.de
  - **increased**: alum bg2 ant-c bg2 bar-c bg2 euphr bg2 iod bg2 phos bg2 plb bg2 ran-s bg2 rhod bg2 sabad bg2 spig bg2
  - **menses**; during: alum b4a.de sep b4a.de
  - ○ **Posterior** nares:
    - **coppery**: cimic bg2
    - **tenacious**: aesc bg2 am-m bg2 arg-n bg2 cimic bg2 cinnb bg2 cist bg2 coc-c bg2
- **musty**: nat-c ptk1
- **offensive**: abrom-a ks5 agar alum k* alum-p k2 alum-sil k2 anan aq-mar skp7• am bg2 ars k* ars-i bg2* ars-s-f k2 **Asaf** k* asim **Aur** k* aur-ar k2 aur-i k2 *Aur-m* aur-s k2 bals-p bro1 bapt k2 *Bar-c* bar-s k2 bell k* berb k* bufo k* cadm-s bg2 **Calc** k* *Calc-f* k* *Calc-s* calc-sil k2 canth bg2 *Carb-ac* k* carb-v bg2 carbn-s caust k* cham bg2 chin k* chr-met dx con k* cop crot-h bg2 cub cupr bg2 cur dig b2.de echi bro1 *Elaps* k* eucal bro1 ferr bg2 fl-ac *Graph* k* guaj k* ham **Hep** k* hip-ac sp1 *Hippoz* hydr bg2* ign bg2 *Iod* k* kali-ar k2 **Kali-bi** k* kali-br bg2 *Kali-c* k* *Kali-i* k* kali-n a1 *Kali-p* *Kali-s* kali-sil k2 kreos k* lac-c bg2 *Lach* k* led k* *Lyc* k* m-aust b2.de *Mag-m* k* mang bg2 **Merc** k* *Merc-c* b4a.de merc-i-f k* merc-i-r bg2 mez bg2* nat-ar **Nat-c** k* nat-s *Nit-ac* k* nux-v k* petr k* ph-ac k* *Phos* k* phyt **Psor** k* **Puls** k* pyrog jl2 rhus-t k* sabin k* sang k* sarr k* *Sep* k* **Sil** k* sol-o a1 spig stann k* stram k* **Sulph** k* syph k* tell teucr k* *Ther* k* *Thuj* k* tub bro1* ust vanil fd5.de
  - **burnt**: berb
  - **catarrh**; like old: *Puls* b7.de*
  - **cheese**; like: hep merc k* *Thuj* b4a.de **Tub** k*
  - **fetid**: *Agar* alum b4a.de* anthraci apis *Aq-mar* jl ars bro1 ars-i bro1 arum-t bro1 *Asaf* **Aur** k* aur-ar k2 *Aur-m-n* k* bac jl2 *Bals-p* bro1 berb
- **offensive – fetid**: ...
  bufo bg1 *Calc* k* calc-i k2* calc-s bro1 *Carb-ac* caust *Con* b4a.de cop cur diphtox jl2 *Dulc* bro1 eucal k* *Graph* k* *Hep* k* hippoz jl2 *Hydr* bro1 *Iod* kali-bi bro1* *Kali-c* kali-i bro1 *Kali-n* *Kali-s* bro1 *Kreos* led lyc k* mag-m med bro1 *Merc* k* *Myric* nat-c k* *Nat-s* bro1 *Nit-ac* k* ozone sde2• pen bro1 petr phos bro1 *Puls* k* rhus-t sangin-n bro1 sil k* tell *Ther* k* thuj k* tub al* vanil fd5.de
  - **herring** pickle: *Elaps*
  - **menses** | **during**: *Graph* sep h2*
  - **pungent**: berb
  - **putrid**: agar arund asaf bufo **Carb-ac** *Elaps* graph psil ft1 **Psor**
  - **sickly**, sweetish: nit-ac k*
  - **sour**: alum hep
  - **urine**; like: graph k* puls ptk1*
- **oily**: *Thuj* b4a.de
- **orange** colored: hydrog srj2• puls ptk1*
  - **crusts** (See crusts - orange)
- **plugs**: *Con* b4a.de merc-c b4a.de *Sep* b4a.de *Sil* b4a.de
- **profuse** (See copious)
- **purulent**: acon b2.de* acon-l a1 ail *Alum* k* alum-p k2 alum-sil k2 am-c k* anac anan arg-met k* *Arg-n* k* ars k* *Ars-i* arund a1 *Asaf* k* asar k* **Aur** k* aur-ar k2 aur-i k2 *Aur-m* aur-m-n aur-s k2 bac jl2 *Bar-m* bell k* *Berb* k* brom bg2 bry bg2 **Calc** k* calc-i k2 **Calc-s** calc-sil k2 *Carb-v* bg2 *Carbn-s* cham k* chin k* chinin-ar cic k* cina k* cinnb bg2 *Cocc* k* *Coloc* **Con** k* cop cor-r bg2 cur dros k* dulc bg2 eucal euph euphr *Ferr* k* *Ferr-ar* *Ferr-i* *Ferr-p* flav jl2 *Graph* k* guaj k* **Hep** k* *Hippoz* *Hydr* k* ign k* *Iod* ip k* ipom-p kali-ar **Kali-bi** k* *Kali-c* k* *Kali-i* kali-m bg2* kali-n k* *Kali-p* **Kali-s** k* kali-sil k2 kreos k* lac-c **Lach** k* laur b2.de led k* **Lyc** k* mag-c k* *Mag-m* k* **Merc** k* merc-c b4a.de merc-i-f k* mur-ac *Nat-ar* *Nat-c* k* *Nat-m* k* *Nat-p* *Nat-s* *Nit-ac* k* nux-v k* oscilloc jl2 *Petr* k* *Ph-ac* k* *Phos* k* plb b2.de* **Psor** k* *Puls* k* *Rhus-t* k* ruta bg2 sabin k* samb k* *Sang* sec bg2 *Sep* k* ser-a-c jl2 **Sil** k* stann k* staph k* *Stict* still streptoc jl2 sul-i k2 *Sulph* k* symph fd3.de• *Thuj* **Tub** k* (non:uran-met k) *Uran-n* vac jl2 zinc k* zinc-chr ptk1 zinc-p k2
  - **right**: *Kali-c* *Puls*
  - **left**: symph fd3.de• (non:uran-met k) uran-n
  - **morning**, early | **blowing** the nose; on: am-c
  - **forenoon**: ail
  - **bending** head forward agg.: ser-a-c jl2
  - **bloody**: arg-met b7a.de syph bg2
  - **excoriating**: merc b4.de*
  - **green**: asaf b7a.de nux-v b7a.de rhus-t b7a.de
  - **offensive**: asaf b7a.de nux-v b7a.de rhus-t b7a.de
  - **sudden**: aur-m
  - **weather**:
    - **cold**:
      - **wet** | **agg.**: ser-a-c jl2
  - **weekly**: kali-s
  - **yellow**: *Alum* b4a.de **Calc** b4.de* cic b7.de* *Con* b4.de* mag-m b4.de* nat-c b4.de* sulph b4.de*
  - ○ **Posterior** nares; from: **Kali-bi** mrr1
- **reading** loud; when: verb ptk1
- **reddish**: bry bg2 kali-cy a1 par k* squil bg2
- **reddish** yellow: calc hydrog srj2•
- **retarded**, late: **Calc** b4.de*
- **salty**: ambr vh1 aral bg3* cimic bg3* germ-met srj5• kali-i sne nat-m bg2* tell bro1
  - ○ **Posterior** nares: kali-i bg2
- **scanty**: alum-sil k* astac hr1 bell k2 coli rly4• kali-bi mag-c melal-alt gya4 nat-p k2 petr-ra shn4• sin-n
  - **room** agg.: hydr
- **singing**; when: all-c ptk1
- **sleep**; after | **amel.**: aq-mar skp7•
- **slimy** (See mucous)
- **starch**, like boiled: *Arg-n* k* *Nat-m* k* nat-s
- **sticky**: atra-r skp7*•
  - ○ **Posterior** nares: caps ptk1 kali-bi ptk1
- **stiffening** the linen: bell bg2

Nose

- **stool** agg.; during: thuj b4a.de*
- **stooping** agg.: am-c k*
- **stringy**: *Kali-bi* br1

○ • **Posterior** nares: *Get* br1

- **sudden**: apis calc chlor coff cycl h1* plan k* tung-met bdx1•
  - **disappearing**: tub-d jl2
  - **gushing** (See gushing)
- **suppressed**: (↗*GENERALS - History - discharges - suppressed*) *Acon* bg2 ail alum am-c am-m ambr *Arg-n Ars* k* *Aur* aur-ar k2 *Bell* bg2 **Bry** k* **Calc** k* *Carb-v* k* *Carbn-s* caust cham k* *Chin* k* cina k* cinnb bg2 con *Dulc* k* euphr bg2 *Graph Hep* k* ign bg2 *Ip* k* *Kali-bi* k* *Kali-c Kali-i Lach* k* *Lyc* k* mag-c mang **Merc** k* *Nat-ar Nat-c Nat-m Nit-ac* k* *Nux-v* k* *Petr* ph-ac bg2 *Phos* **Puls** k* rhod bg2 rhus-t bg2 samb sars *Sep* k* *Sil* k* spong bg2 stann sulph k* thuj zinc bg2
- **talking** agg.: kali-bi ptk1 nat-c ptk1
- **tallow**, like, leaving grease spots on linen: *Cor-r* k* lyc
- **thick**: abrom-a ks5 acon k* aesc a1 aeth k* agar aids nl2• all-c *Alum* k* alum-p k2 alum-sil k2 am-br bro1 *Am-m* k* ambr k* androc srj1• ant-c k* ant-t a1 apis apoc k* aq-mar jl* arg-met b2.de* arg-n k* **Ars** k* *Ars-i* ars-met ars-s-f k2 *Arum-t* arund asaf bg2 asim atra-r skp7*• *Aur* k* aur-ar k2 aur-i k2 aur-m k2 aur-s k2 *Bad* bamb-a stb2.de• bapt k* *Bar-c* k* bar-i k2 *Bar-m* bar-s k2 bell bg2 borx k* bov k* *Calc* k* *Calc-f* calc-i k2 **Calc-s** calc-sil k2 caps *Carb-v* k* *Carbn-s* carc gk6* cardios-h rly4• cartl-s rly4• caust k* choc srj3• cinnb cist k* *Coc-c* colch cop cor-r croc dig k* dulc k* ery-a k* euphr ferr-i k* gal-ac a1* glycyr-g cte1• graph k* *Hep* k* hip-ac sp1 *Hippoz* **Hydr** k* *Hydrog* srj2• iod k* ip k* *Kali-ar* **Kali-bi** k* kali-br *Kali-c* k* *Kali-i* k* kali-m bg2* **Kali-p** *Kali-s* k* kali-sil k2 ketogl-ac rly4• kola stb3• kreos k* lac-ac **Lac-c** k* lac-h sk4• lach lat-m sp1 led a1 lob-s a1 lyc k* lyss mag-c k* mag-m k* mang k* med k* *Merc* k* merc-c b4a.de* merc-i-f k* *Mur-ac* k* *Nat-ar Nat-c* k* *Nat-m* k* *Nat-p* **Nat-s** k* nicotam rly4• nit-ac k* nux-v ol-an a1 olib-sac wmh1 op k* par k* pen bro1 petr petr-ra shn4• ph-ac *Phos* k* pin-con oss2• pitu-gl skp7• plac-s rly4• plan a1 plb psor k2* **Puls** k* *Ran-b* k* *Rhus-t* ribo rly4• *Ruta* bg2 *Sabad* k* sal-al blc1• samb k* *Sang* sangin-n bro1 sanic sars k* sel k* *Sep* k* **Sil** k* sin-n *Spong* k* *Stann* k* *Staph* k* *Stict* bro1 suis-em rly4• suis-hep rly4• *Sul-ac* k* *Sul-i* k* *Sulph* k* suprar rly4• syph k* teucr *Ther* k* *Thuj* k* *Trios* rsj11• tritic-vg fd5.de **Tub** k* tung-met bdx1• ust a1 vanil fd5.de ven-m rsj12• zinc k* zinc-p k2 ziz a1
  - **daytime**: abrom-a ks5 *Arum-t* k* sulph a1 sumb a1
  - **accompanied** by | **catarrh** (See Catarrh - accompanied - mucus)
  - **air**; in open | **amel**.: abrom-a ks5
  - **clear**, headache if it ceases: *Kali-bi* k*
  - **room**; closed warm: abrom-a ks5
  - **then** thin: staph h1*

○ • **Posterior** nares; from: alum h2* am-br bro1 ant-c h2* calc-sil bro1 *Carb-an* cor-r bro1 *Hydr* k* *Kali-bi* k* lem-m bro1 med mtf33 mentho bro1 merc-i-f bro1 nat-c bro1 *Nat-p Nat-s* k* orot-ac rly4• petr petr-ra shn4• *Phyt* prot jl2 pyrid rly4• sangin-n bro1 sep bro1 sil mrr1 spig bro1 thuj mrr1

- **thin**: abrom-a ks5 acon-ac rly4• aesc ail k2 all-c tl1 aphis ars tl1* arum-t aur-m k2 beryl tpw5 bov calc-sil k2 camph b7.de* caps b7.de* carb-v k2 cassia-s ccrh1• cench k2 chord-umb rly4• coc-c colch crot-c eup-pur a1 euphr mrr1 form a1 *Graph* helo-s rwt2• hep hippoz hydr hydrog srj2• ind **Iod** ip b7a.de kali-s ketogl-ac rly4• lac-c lach laur b7.de* lil-t m-arct b7.de mez *Mur-ac* k* naja *Nat-c* k* nit-ac k2 *Phyt* rhod rhus-t b7.de* ribo rly4• *Sabad* k* sin-n staph b7.de* staphycoc rly4• *Sulph* tere-la rly4• trif-p a1 [bell-p-sp dcm1]
  - **morning**: abrom-a ks5
    - **rising** agg.: camph h1
  - **evening**: abrom-a ks5
    - **bed**; when going to: camph h1
  - **air**; in open | **amel**.: abrom-a ks5
  - **heat** of the sun agg.: abrom-a ks5
  - **relieving** the burning: psor k*
  - **room** agg.; closed: abrom-a ks5
- **transparent**: aur bg2 bell bg2 merc-c bg2 sabad b7.de*
- **viscid**, tough: acon b2.de* aeth a1 agar agn b2.de* aids nl2• alum k* alum-p k2 am-m b2.de* ant-c b2.de* ant-t b2.de* arg-n arge-pl rwt5• ars k* bamb-a stb2.de• bar-c b2.de* bell bg2 borx b2.de* **Bov** k* brom k* bry b2.de* calc b2.de* *Cann-s* k* *Canth* k* carb-an carb-v b2.de* carbn-s k2 cartl-s rly4• *Caust* k* **Cham** k* chin b2.de* chord-umb rly4• cinnm coc-c cocc b2.de* *Colch* k*
- **viscid**, tough: ... conch fkr1• croc dros dulc b2.de* euph b4.de euphr b2.de* ferr bg2 gal-ac bro1 gran *Graph* k* hep hip-ac sp1 *Hippoz* **Hydr** k* hydrog srj2• ina-i mlk9.de iod b2.de* **Kali-bi** k* kali-c b2.de* **Kali-i** kali-m k2 kali-p k2 **Kali-s** ketogl-ac rly4• kola stb3• kreos bg2 lac-ac lac-h sk4• *Lach* bg2 lyc bg2* m-ambo b2.de mag-c bg2 mag-m b2.de* merc bg2 *Mez* k* mur-ac myrt-c bro1 *Nat-ar* nat-c k* nat-m bg2 nat-sil fd3.de• nux-v b2.de* olib-sac wmh1 *Par* k* petr b2.de* petr-ra shn4• ph-ac b2.de* *Phos* k* *Plb* k* podo fd3.de• *Psor* puls b2.de* *Ran-b* k* rhod b4.de rhus-g tmo3• rhus-t bg2 *Sabad* k* sabin b2.de* *Samb* k* sanic sel seneg b2.de* *Sep* k* *Sil* k* spig k* *Spong* k* squil b2.de* **Stann** k* staph b2.de* *Stict* bro1* sul-ac *Sulph* k* sumb bro1 suprar rly4• tritic-vg fd5.de verat b2.de* zinc b2.de*

○ • **Posterior** nares; from: alum h2 bell k2 calc canth **Caps** *Carb-an* dulc fd4.de *Hydr* k* **Kali-bi** k* kola stb3• lyss sne *Nat-ar Nat-p* ozone sde2• *Phyt* plb psor staph sumb symph fd3.de• vip fkr4.de

- **warm** room agg.: beryl tpw5
- **watery**: (↗*clear*) abrom-a ks5 abrot *Acon* k* acon-ac rly4• aesc k* *Agar* k* ail **All-c** k* aloe alum k* alum-sil k2 am-br k* am-c k* am-caust k* am-m k* ambr k* *Ambro* bro1 anag androc srj1• ant-c k* ant-t k* anth br1 antip vh1 ap-g vh1 aphis apis aq-mar jl* *Aral* bro1 arg-met k* arg-n bg2 arist-cl sp1* **Ars** k* *Ars-i* k* **Arum-t** k* arund k* asar k* aur-ar k2 *Aur-m* bad bamb-a stb2.de• bell k* bell-p sp1 berb beryl sp1 botul jl2 bov k* *Brom* k* *Bry* k* bufo cain *Calc* k* calc-i k2 calc-p calc-s k* calc-sil k2 carb-an k* *Carb-v* k* carbn-s k2 carc fd2.de• cassia-s ccrh1• castm k* cedr a1 cench k2 **Cham** k* chel *Chin* k* chinin-ar k* chlor k* cinnb clem k* cob k* cob-n sp1 coc-c coca coff k* colch coloc con k* cortiso gse crot-h bg2 crot-t a1 cub cupr cupr-ar *Cycl* k* cypra-eg sde6.de• daph bg2 dios k* diphtox jl2 dros *Dulc* k* elaps eucal bro1 eup-pur k* euph k* **Euphr** k* fago a1 ferr k* ferr-ar *Ferr-i Fl-ac* k* flor-p rsj3• gels k* glyc bro1 granit-m es1• **Graph** k* guaj k* ham k* hep k2 *Hydr* k* *Hydrog* srj2• ign k* ignis-alc es2• ind k* **Iod** k* irid-met vml3• *Kali-bi* k* kali-br bg2 *Kali-i* k* kali-n k* *Kali-p* kali-s fd4.de kola stb3• kreos k* lac-c lac-h sk4• lach k* lil-t limest-b es1• luna kg1• lyc bg2 lyss m-arct b2.de* mag-c k* mag-m k* mag-s k* mang-p rly4• marb-w es1• med jl2 melal-alt gya4 meny b2.de* **Merc** k* merc-c bg2* merl a1 mez k* mim-p skp7*• moni rfm1• mur-ac k* *Naja* k* naphtin bro1 **Nat-ar** k* nat-c k2 *Nat-m* k* nat-s nat-sil fd3.de• **Nit-ac** k* **Nux-v** k* olib-sac wmh1 oscilloc jl2 osm ox-ac k* pall k* par k* petr petr-ra shn4• phos k* *Phyt* k* pitu-a vml2• **Plan** plb k* podo fd3.de• propl ub1• puls k* ran-s k* rhus-t b2.de* ribo rly4• rumx k* *Sabad* k* sacch-a fd2.de• *Sang* k* *Sangin-n* bro1 *Seneg* k* sep k* *Sil* k* sin-n spig k* spira a1 spong fd4.de squil k* stann b2.de* *Staph* k* stront-c sk4• sul-ac k* *Sulph* k* symph fd3.de• tab a1 **Tell** k* ter teucr thres-a sze7• thuj k* trif-p bro1 tritic-vg fd5.de tub-a jl2 tub-d jl2 vanil fd5.de ven-m rsj12• verb bg2 wies a1 yuc a1 zinc zing a1 [bell-p-sp dcm1 calc-m stj1 nat-n stj1]
  - **right**: alum calc-s k* *Kali-bi* melal-alt gya4 nit-ac olib-sac wmh1 petr-ra shn4• pitu-gl skp7• podo fd3.de• sol-ni br1 ven-m rsj12• [tax jsj7]
    - **daytime**: calc-s
  - **left**: am-br androc srj1• anth vh chlor lach a1 olib-sac wmh1 ozone sde2• spong fd4.de
    - **night**: calc-s
  - **daytime**: cassia-s ccrh1•
  - **morning**: abrom-a ks5 amp rly4• bamb-a stb2.de• olib-sac wmh1 spong fd4.de tritic-vg fd5.de
  - **evening**: abrom-a ks5
  - **night**: calc-s a1 cassia-s cdd7• dulc fd4.de nat-s bg3 nit-ac k2 phasco-ci rbp2
    - **midnight**:
      - **after** | **5** h: *Ars*
  - **accompanied** by:
    - **obstruction** (See Obstruction - accompanied - discharge - watery)
    - **Head**; pain in: pitu-gl skp7•
  - **air**; in open:
    - **agg.**: (↗*Coryza - air; in - agg.*) *Ars* calc-s k* carb-ac k* choc srj3• dulc euphr hydr *Iod* nat-m **Nit-ac** *Phos* podo fd3.de• **Puls** sabad *Sulph* tell thuj vanil fd5.de zinc
    - **amel**.: abrom-a ks5
  - **chorea**, with: *Agar*
  - **cold** | **room** | **agg**.: carb-ac
    - **washing** | **amel**.: calc-s
  - **coryza**, without: *Agar* k* alum am-c dulc fd4.de kali-n ter ptk1
  - **drinking** agg.; after: caust vanil fd5.de

- **eating**; while: *(↗eating; eating - while - agg.)* plb bg1* sulph h2 *Trom* vh
- **epistaxis**; after: agar
- **excoriating**: am-c b4.de* am-m b7.de* *Ars* b4.de* lach b7.de* lyc b4.de* m-arct b7.de mag-m b4a.de *Merc* b4a.de mez b4a.de mur-ac b4.de* *Nux-v* b7.de* sil b4.de* squil b7.de* *Sulph* b4a.de
- **followed** by | **thick** discharge: ven-m rsj12•
- **heat** of the sun agg.: abrom-a ks5
- **menses**; during: am-c
- **pain** in eye, during: mag-c h2*
- **perspiration** | **amel**.: aq-mar skp7•
- **room** agg.; closed: abrom-a ks5
- **sudden** copious from eyes, nose and mouth: **Fl-ac**
- **walking** agg.: cassia-s ccrh1•
- **warm**:
  - ⁝ **room**:
    - : **agg**.: abrom-a ks5
    - : **amel**.: calc-s carb-ac

- **whey** like: am-c b2.de* *Ars* b2.de* carb-v b2.de* ferr k* puls b2.de* sep b2.de* sil b2.de* *Sulph* b2.de*
- **white**: *Acon* bg2 agar k* am-br a1 am-c a1 am-m bg2 ambr bg2 androc srj1• apis aq-mar skp7• *Arg-met* bg2 *Arg-n* ars-s-f k2 ars-s-r arund *Aspar* aur-m bg2 bamb-a stb2.de• bell a1* berb borx k2 bov a1 brom a1 bry a1 carb-an bg2 **Carb-v** bg2 carc fd2.de• chin bg2 chir-fl bnm4• choc srj3• cimic a1 cina bg2 coc-c a1 cupr bg2 dulc fd4.de elaps *Euphr* b7a.de fago a1 ferr bg2 graph k* ham fd3.de• hippoz *Hydr* *Hydrog* srj2• kali-bi k2 *Kali-chl* kali-m k2 kali-p ketogl-ac rly4• kola stb3• *Kreos* bg2 lac-ac a1 **Lac-c** lac-h sk4• lach bg2 luf-op rsj5• lyc k* med k2* merc **Nat-m** nux-v ozone sde2• petr-ra shn4• ph-ac bg2 *Phos* bg2 **Puls** bg2 rhus-t bg2 *Sabad* k* sanic senec a1 *Sep* bg2 sil bg2 sin-n spig k* spong fd4.de **Sulph** bg2 thiam rly4• tritic-vg fd5.de vanil fd5.de
  - **left**: graph k*
  - **daytime**: cimic
  - **air**; in open | **amel**.: abrom-a ks5
  - **egg** white (See egg)
  - **lumpy** | **Posterior** nares; from: zinc h2
  - **milky**: *Kali-chl* kali-m k2 kola stb3• **Sep**
  - **room** | **warm** closed: abrom-a ks5
- **yellow**: abrom-a ks5 acon k* *Alum* k* alum-p k2 alum-sil k2 am-c b2.de* am-m k* anag k* androc srj1• ang bg2 ant-c k* *Arg-n* *Ars* k* *Ars-i* *Ars-met* ars-s-f k2 **Arum-t** k* atra-r skp7*• **Aur** k* aur-ar k2 aur-i k2 *Aur-m* k* aur-s k2 *Bad* bamb-a stb2.de• *Bar-c* k* bar-i k2 *Bar-m* bar-s k2 bell b2.de* *Berb* k* borx b2.de* bov k* brom k* bros-gau mrc1 **Bry** b2.de* bufo **Calc** k* calc-i k2 calc-p a1 **Calc-s** k* calc-sil k2 carb-an b2.de* **Carb-v** b2.de* carbn-s k2 carc fb* cardios-h rly4• cench k2 cham b2.de* chinin-ar chlor k* *Cic* k* cinnb *Cist* k* coc-c *Con* k* *Cop* k* cortico sp1 cupr *Daph* bg2 dig b2.de* *Dros* bg2 dulc k2* ery-a k* *Ferr-i* *Graph* k* **Hep** k* hip-ac sp1 **Hydr** k* *Hydrog* srj2• *Hyper* ign b2.de ind k* *Iod* k* kali-ar **Kali-bi** k* *Kali-c* k* kali-chl **Kali-i** k* kali-m k2 **Kali-p** **Kali-s** k* kali-sil k2 kola stb3• kreos b2.de* lac-ac *Lach* k* lap-la sde8.de• lat-m sp1 lil-t k* limest-b es1• luna kg1• **Lyc** k* mag-c b2.de* *Mag-m* k* mag-s k* malar jl2 mang k* med k2* merc b2.de* *Mez* k* moni rfm1• mur-ac k* *Nat-ar* *Nat-c* k* *Nat-m* nat-ox rly4• *Nat-p* *Nat-s* k* nat-sil fd3.de• **Nit-ac** k* nux-v b2.de* olib-sac wmh1 op a1 ozone sde2• petr k2 petr-ra shn4• ph-ac b2.de* *Phos* k* plac-s rly4• plan k* pib b2.de* psor k2* **Puls** k* rhus-g tmo3• rhus-t ribo rly4• rumx k2 *Ruta* bg2 sabad b2.de* sabin k* sang sanic sel k* seneg k* **Sep** k* *Sil* sin-n spig k* *Spong* b2.de* stann k* *Staph* b2.de* *Stram* suis-hep rly4• sul-i k2 **Sulph** k* sumb a1 syph k2* teucr *Ther* *Thuj* k* tritic-vg fd5.de **Tub** k* tung-met bdx1• vanil fd5.de verat b2.de* wies a1 [bell-p-sp dcm1 spect dfg1]
  - **right**: plan
  - **left**: bros-gau mrc1 calc-s k* kali-bi k* sumb k*
  - **daytime**: abrom-a ks5 *Arum-t* k*
  - **morning**: apoc ptk berb bros-gau mrc1 dulc fd4.de **Kali-bi** kali-p *Lach* *Mang* nat-sil fd3.de• petr-ra shn4• phos k* **Puls** k* sulph k* vanil fd5.de
  - **afternoon**: bad
  - **evening**: calc-s k* **Puls** sulph h2*
  - **amel**.: hydrog srj2•
  - **bloody**: lach bg2 ozone sde2• phos bg2
  - **dirty**: olib-sac wmh1 teucr

Discharge – yellow – dirty: ...

- ⁝ **Posterior** nares; from: cinnb
- **gray**: sabad bg2
- **honey**, like: **Ars-i**
- **waking**; on: choc srj3•
- **watery**: mez b4.de* sep b4.de*

○ • **Posterior** nares; from: ant-c h2 ars sne calc sne *Calc-s* carb-v sne cench sne cinnb coli rly4• ferr-p sne **Hydr** **Kali-bi** k* kali-s mrr1 kola stb3• malar sne mang sne meny merc-i-f merc-i-r sne nat-ar sne *Nat-p* *Nat-s* k* petr-ra shn4• *Rumx* sep wt sin-n sne spig h1 stann sne sul-ac sne sumb tell sne thyr sne

- **yellow** orange: kali-bi bg2* *Kali-p* bg2 puls mtf33 ulm-c jsj8•
- **yellowish** green: *Alum* k* alum-p k2 alum-sil k2 arge-pl rwt5• *Ars* b4a.de* ars-i bro1 arum-t bro1 arund atp rly4• aur b4a.de* *Aur-m* *Bals-p* bro1 borx b4a.de bufo *Calc* bro1 *Calc-f* calc-i bro1 *Calc-s* k* calc-sil k2 carb-v k2 caust choc srj3• cop cortico tpw7 dendr-pol sk4• *Dulc* bro1 elaps br eucal bro1 *Hep* k* **Hydr** k* hydrog srj2• **Kali-bi** k* *Kali-c* k* *Kali-i* k* *Kali-s* bro1 kola stb3• lac-c limest-b es1• *Lyc* bro1 *Mang* k* med bro1 **Merc** k* *Nat-c* k* *Nat-s* k* nat-sil fd3.de• nicotam rly4• nit-ac bg2* ozone sde2• par pen bro1 petr-ra shn4• *Phos* k* plan psor **Puls** k* rhus-t k* sabad k* sangin-n bro1 sarr k* **Sep** k* *Sil* k* syph k* *Ther* k* *Thuj* k* **Tub** c1* [spect dfg1]
  - **morning**: gink-b sbd1•
  - **night** | **staining** pillow: lac-c k*
  - **bloody**; and: sep b4.de*
  - **eating**; while: plb bg
- **yellowish** white: calc merc-i-r k* suis-em rly4•

○ - **Posterior** nares: *(↗Catarrh - postnasal)* acon-ac rly4• *All-c* k* alum bg2* *Alumn* am-c bg2 anac k* androc srj1• *Ant-c* k* aq-mar skp7• *Arg-n* k* arn h1* ars h2* arum-t bamb-a stb2.de• bar-c bar-i k2 bell bg2 bry k* bufo bg2* *Calc* k* calc-f sp1 *Calc-s* *Canth* **Caps** k* carb-ac *Carb-an* carb-v k* caust bg2* chin k* chord-umb rly4• cinnb k* coc-c ptk1 colch bg2 coli rly4• cop **Cor-r** k* crot-c sk4• cystein-l rly4• dios bg2 dulc k2 elaps euph k* euphr k* *Ferr* ferr-i k2 ferr-p bg2 galeoc-c-h gms1• ger-i rly4• gran ham fd3.de• hep k* hydr k* hydrog srj2• iod **Kali-bi** k* *Kali-chl* kali-m k2 kali-s fd4.de lac-ac lach k* lem-m br1 mag-c ptk1 *Mang* med melal-alt gya4 *Merc* k* merc-c k* merc-i-f k* *Merc-i-r* mez k* *Nat-ar* **Nat-c** k* **Nat-m** k* *Nat-p* k* *Nat-s* nat-sil fd3.de• *Nit-ac* k* nux-v bg2 osm k* oxal-a rly4• paeon *Petr* ph-ac *Phos* k* *Phyt* k* plac rzf5• plac-s rly4• *Plb* podo fd3.de• psil ft1 *Psor* k* rhus-t k* ribo rly4• rumx k* sabad k2 *Sel* sep k* sin-n k* *Spig* k* spong fd4.de staph staphycoc rly4• *Stict* k* suis-em rly4• sulph k* symph fd3.de• syph ptk1 tell k* tere-la rly4• ther ptk1 thiam rly4• thuj k* tritic-vg fd5.de *Tub* k* vanil fd5.de *Zinc* k* zinc-p k2 zing
  - **morning**: aq-mar skp7• aur cartl-s rly4• coli rly4• *Mang* *Nat-m* nat-sil fd3.de• petr sacch-a fd2.de• spong fd4.de symph fd3.de• tell
  - **forenoon**: *Arg-n*
  - **night**: cop br1 nat-p c1 plac rzf5•
  - **bitter**: ph-ac bg2
  - **chronic**: *Alum* bro1 am-br bro1 ant-c bro1 ars-i bro1 aur bro1 calc-sil bro1 cist mrr1 *Cor-r* bro1 echi bro1 glyc bro1 *Hydr* bro1 irid-met bro1 *Kali-bi* bro1 kali-m bro1 *Lem-m* bro1 med mrr1 merc-i-r bro1 nat-c bro1 nat-s mrr1 *Pen* bro1 *Phyt* bro1 *Sangin-n* bro1 sin-n bro1 spig bro1 stict bro1 syph mrr1 teucr bro1 ther bro1 wye bro1
  - **coryza**; without: par b7a.de ran-b b7a.de ran-s b7a.de rhus-t b7.de* sabad b7.de sel b7.de spig b7.de squil b7.de
  - **crusty**: alum k2 alumn *Bar-c* bufo vh calc-ar caust vh culx elaps fago br1 galeoc-c-h gms1• hydr kali-c k2 *Sep* syph k2
  - **dripping**: all-c bg2* cor-r bg2 hydr bg2* merc-c bg2* nat-c bg2 spig ptk1
  - **involuntary**: *Rhus-t* b7.de*
  - **plugs**: kali-bi bg2 psor bg2 ruta bg2 sep bg2 sil bg2
  - **salty**: nat-s k2
  - **sweetish**: kali-bi bg2
  - **waking**; on: hydr st

DISCOLORATION:

- **black**: *(↗Sooty)* merc k*
  - **pores**: sabin c1 sulph mtf33

○ • **Wings**: ant-t ptk1

- **bluish**: agar k* ars bg2 aur k* calc b4a.de Carl a1 chir-fl bnm4• crot-h cypra-eg sde6.de• Lach k* merc-c b4a.de phos bg2 sec bg2 sil b4a.de verat bg2 verat-v k*
  - **coppery**: carb-v bg2
  - ○ **Root**: calc
  - **Tip**: agar k* carb-an bg2* Crot-h Dig bro1
  - **Wings**: hydr-ac tub-a jl2
- **brown**: Aur k*
  - **red** in spots: Aur
  - ○ **Across**: Carb-an ptk1 Lyc ptk1 op ptk1 sanic ptk1 Sep ptk1* sulph ptk1 Syph ptk1
- **copper**-colored spots: ars cann-s
- **pale**:
  - ○ **Tip**: apis bro1 Ars bro1 calc-p bro1 Camph bro1 carb-v bro1 Chin bro1 hell bro1 Tab bro1 Verat bro1
  - **Wings**:
    - **accompanied** by | **Face**; red discoloration of: stram c1
- **redness**: act-sp a1 Agar bg2* aloe k* Alum k* alum-p k2 am-caust vh1 am-m bg2* anan anthraci Apis k* Ars k* ars-i arund Aur k* aur-ar k2 aur-i k2 aur-m k* aur-s c1* bamb-a stb2.de• bar-c bar-i k2 Bell k* bond a1 Borx k* both-ax tsm2 bov b4.de* Calc k* calc-i k2 cann-s k* cann-xyz ptk1 canth k* caps b7.de* carb-an k* carb-v carbn-s caust k* chel bg2* Chin k* Clem b4a.de coc-c a1 cycl cypra-eg sde6.de• fago a1 ferr bg2* ferr-m st ferr-p bg2* fl-ac graph k* ham fd3.de* Hep k* hippoz k* iod k* Kali-bi k* kali-br a1* Kali-c k* kali-i k* kali-n h2* Lach k* led lith-c k* m-arct b7.de mag-c k* Mag-m k* mag-p mang k* Merc k* Merc-c k* morg-g pte1*• Nat-ar Nat-c k* nat-m k* Nit-ac bg1* ox-ac bg2 petr bg2 ph-ac b4.de* phel a1 Phos k* Plb k* psor k* ran-b k* rhus-t k* rhus-v a1* ruta bg2 sarr k* Sep bg2 sil h2* spong fd4.de Stann k* stram bg2* sul-ac bg2 sul-i k2 Sulph k* thuj k* Tub jl2 vinc bg2* yuc a1* Zinc k* zinc-p k2
  - **right** side: aur k* lith-c ox-ac
    - **extending** to | **Cheek**: anthraci
  - **left** side: aur-m nat-m
  - **afternoon**: kali-c sulph a1
  - **evening**: mag-c h2* mang a1 oena a1 ox-ac a1
  - **air**, in cold open: aloe Sulph
  - **anger**; after: vinc k*
  - **bright**: Sulph bg2
  - **chill**; during: bell bg2 rhus-t bg2 sep bg2
  - **coppery**: Ars bg2 calc bg2 Cann-s b7a.de Carb-an bg2 carb-v bg2 con bg2 kreos bg2 mez bg2 rhus-t bg2 ruta bg2 Verat bg2
  - **drunkards**; in: agar Ars bg2 Aur sne bell bg2 Calc bg2 crot-h k* hep bg2 Lach k* led k* merc bg2 Puls bg2 Sulph bg2
  - **eating**; while: Sil h2*
  - **erysipelatous**: Apis Rhus-v
    - **left** side: lac-ac
  - **excitement**; after: vinc
  - **exertion** agg.; after: sil h2*
  - **fever**; during: sulph bg2
  - **freezing**, after: Zinc
  - **injuries**; from: arn bg2
  - **mercury**; after abuse of: lach
  - **painful** to touch: alum bg2 bell k* bry bg2 calc bg2 Carb-an Hep bg2 Merc bg2 phos bg2 rhus-t bg2 sulph bg2
  - **shining**: borx k* canth merc Ox-ac Phos k* sep bg2 sil bg2
    - **Tip**: bell borx k* caps tl1 Phos sulph
    - **Wing** | **right**: canth
  - **spots**, in: aur k* calc Iod k* manc a1 ph-ac k* rhod k* Sars sep bg2* sil k* sulph bg2 thuj bg2 verat k*
    - **right** side: euphr
    - **tender** to touch: aur calc rhod
    - **Septum**: alum h2* berb lil-t sars
  - **sudden**: bell borx
  - **women**; young: borx hr1*

Discoloration – redness: ...

- ▽ **extending** to | **Frontal** sinuses; over nose to (See FACE - Discoloration - red - nose - extending)
- ○ **Inside**: acon act-sp ail apis Ars bar-c bell k* bry carb-an coc-c k* cocc gels hep ip k2 kali-bi kali-c Kali-i lach **Merc** nux-v petr phel phos polyg-h stann **Sulph**
  - **right**: aur
  - **left**: Nat-m plut-n srj7• stann
  - **bloody**: Kali-c
  - **Posterior** nares: alum bg2 Arg-n phyt
  - **Septum**: alum borx bov Lil-t
- **Saddle**: ictod thal-xyz srj8•
- **Tip**: agar alum Aur k* bar-c b4a.de Bell k* borx k* Calc k* caps k* **Carb-an** k* Carb-v k* Carbn-s chel clem k* con Crot-h der a1 Kali-c kali-i k2* kali-n br1* lac-h sk4• **Lach** k* led m-arct b7a.de m-aust merc nat-m nicc k* Nit-ac k* ozone sde2• phos psor al2 rhus-g tmo3• Rhus-t k* sal-n bro1 sep sil k* **Sulph** k* vinc bg2*
  - **evening**: caps k*
  - **anger**; after: vinc k*
  - **begins** at tip and spreads: Ox-ac
  - **drunkards**: agar k* carb-an k* Crot-h hr1 lach k* Led k*
  - **dyspnea**; during: ph-ac c1
  - **menses**; during: carb-an k*
  - **purple**, in cold air: aur both-ax tsm2 phos
  - **stooping** agg.: Am-c
- **Wings** (= alae nasi): agar bro1 all-c aur h2* bell bg2 Caj calc k* chinin-ar clem a1 crot-h a1 ham fd3.de* Kali-bi Kali-c Mag-m k* merc bro1 ozone sde2• peti a1 ph-ac k* Phos k* plb b7a.de* plb-act bro1 sabin **Sin-n** sulph bg2*
  - **right**: canth gins mag-m k*
  - **left**: calc a1 gink-b sbd1• nat-m k* stann h2* zinc
  - **edges**: coc-c Gels lach bg2* ph-ac k*
  - **Corners** of: benz-ac plb
- **spots**: canth b7.de* m-arct b7.de rhus-t b7.de* trios rsj11• verat b7.de*
  - **brown**: aur bg2
  - **yellow**: Sep bg2
- **white** (See Depigmentation)
- **yellow**: *(↗FACE - Discoloration - yellow - saddle; FACE - Saddle)*
  - **patch**: *(↗FACE - Discoloration - yellow - nose)* cadm-s mtf11
  - **saddle**: *(↗FACE - Discoloration - yellow - saddle)* carb-an k* chel bg2 lyc bg3 op bg3 sanic k* **Sep** k* sulph bg3 syph mrr1* tril-p bg2
  - **spots**: sep k*
- ○ **Wings**; of: sanic mtf33

DISTENSION: lyc h2

DOUBLE; feels as if she had two noses (See MIND - Delusions - nose - double)

DRAINAGE; increased (See Discharge - copious)

DRAWN INWARD by a string; as if root of nose was: brom ptk1 par c1*

DRAWN UP by a string; as if tip of nose was: crot-c k*

DRINKING agg.: caust bg2

DRIPPING nose (See Discharge - dripping)

DRYNESS:

- **night**: nux-v bg2 sil bg2
- **air** agg.; in open: ant-c bg2
- **burning**: kali-bi bg2
- ○ **Anterior** part (See FACE - Dryness - nose - anterior)
- **External** (See FACE - Dryness - nose)
- **Inside**: abrot k* Acon k* aesc k* Agar k* agar-ph a1 agath-a nl2• agn b7.de* ail k* All-c k* aloe k* alum k* alum-sil k2 alumn k* am-c k* am-m k* Ambr k* anac ant-c b7a.de* ant-t k* Apis k* aq-pet a1 arge-pl rwt5• **Ars** k* **Ars-i** k* ars-s-f k2 arum-t k* Arund k* atro k* aur k* aur-i k2 aur-s k2 bamb-a stb2.de• **Bar-c** k* bar-i k2 bar-m bar-s k2 **Bell** k* Berb k* bism k* bond a1 borx k* brom k* bros-gau mrc1 Bry k* bufo Cact k* **Calc** k* calc-i k2 Calc-s k* calc-sil k2 Camph bro1 Cann-s k* canth b7.de* carb-an bg2* **Carb-v** k* **Carbn-s**

- **Inside**: ...
cardios-h rly4• cartl-s rly4• *Caust* k* *Cham* k* *Chel* k* chin k* chin-b hr1 chinin-ar chlor k* chord-umb rly4• cic k* cimic *Cimx* k* clem k* cob k* cob-n sp1 *Coc-c* k* *Colch* k* coll a1 coloc bg2* con k* cop k* cor-r k* cortiso tpw7 crot-t k* cund *Cycl* k* des-ac rbp6 *Dig* k* digin a1 dios k* dros k* dulc k* eup-per k* euph bg2 *Euphr* k* fago a1 falco-pe nl2• ferr-i k* flav jl2 flor-p rsj3• gamb k* gink-b sbd1• glyc bro1 gran **Graph** k* hipp hist sp1 hydr k* hydr-ac k* *Hyos* k* hyper k* ign k* *Iod* k* ip k* jug-c a1* kali-ar **Kali-bi** k* *Kali-c* k* kali-i bro1 kali-m k2 kali-n k* kali-p *Kali-s* kali-sil k2 kreos b7a.de lac-ac a1 lac-c lach lact k* laur lec oss• lem-m bro1 lil-t k* lith-c lob-s a1 **Lyc** k* m-arct b7.de mag-c b4.de* *Mag-m* k* manc k* *Mang* k* mang-act br1 med jl2 meli k* menis a1 meny bg2 meph k* *Merc* k* merc-c b4a.de* *Merc-i-f* k* *Merc-i-r* k* merl k* *Mez* k* morg-p fmm1• mur-ac k* naja k2 nat-ar *Nat-c* k* **Nat-m** k* nat-ox rly4• *Nat-s* k* neon srj5• nicc k* *Nit-ac* k* **Nux-m** k* *Nux-v* k* ol-an olib-sac wmh1 onos c2* op k* oxal-a rly4• ozone sde2• pant-ac rly4• *Petr* k* ph-ac k* **Phos** k* pimp a1 plan a1 plb bg2* podo fd3.de• pot-e rly4• propr sa3• *Psor* puls k* *Quill* bg1* rad-br sze8• ran-b b7.de* rat k* rauw sp1 rhod k* rhus-g a1 *Rhus-t* k* rhus-v k* ribo rly4• ros-d wla1 *Rumx* k* ruta fd4.de sabad k* sabin bg2 sacch sst1• sal-fr sle1• **Samb** k* sang k2* sangin-n bro1 sec bg2* senec k* *Seneg* k* *Sep* k* **Sil** k* sin-n k* spig k* **Spong** k* **Stict** k* stram k* succ-ac rly4• **Sulph** k* sumb a1 syc pte1*• symph fd3.de• syph k2* tab k* tanac a1 tarent k2 tell k* tep a1 *Ther* k* **Thuj** k* thyr ptk1 til k* trif-p a1 trom k* ulm-c jsj8• ust k* *Verat* k* vinc k* *Wye* xan k* *Zinc* k* zinc-i ptk1 zinc-p k2 zing k* [spect dfg1]
- · **alternating** sides: sin-n
- · **right**: gamb k* kali-bi k* petr k*
- · **left**: calc-s k* chel k* cist cob k* merl k* oxal-a rly4• ribo rly4• *Sep* k* sin-n k*
- · **morning**: apis bros-gau mrc1 *Calc* cassia-s ccrh1• cycl hr1 ferr-i kali-bi gk kali-s fd4.de *Lyc* k* mag-c k* olib-sac wmh1 plect a1 ruta fd4.de spong fd4.de symph fd3.de•
  - ⁝ **bed** agg.; in: aloe paeon k*
  - ⁝ **waking**; on: am-c *Calc* carb-an hydrog srj2• kali-bi lyc mag-c k* spong fd4.de sulph symph fd3.de• thuj k*
  - ⁝ **walking** agg.: hydr k*
- · **forenoon**: calc-s a1 ust a1
  - ⁝ **air** agg.; in open: *Sulph*
- · **afternoon**: cortico tpw7 op a1 phys a1 stram a1
  - ⁝ **15** h: *Sulph*
- · **evening**: apis cur dulc k* graph k* kali-bi k* paeon podo fd3.de• tell thuj k* trom yuc a1
- · **night**: agath-a nl2• am-m *Borx* cact *Calc* k* calc-s k* kali-ar k2 lyc k* mag-c merc-d a1 nux-v phos *Sil* spig h1* thuj
  - ⁝ **moist** during day: calc k*
  - ⁝ **sleep**, prevents: *Borx*
  - ⁝ **wakes** her: agath-a nl2• ammc mag-c
- · **accompanied** by:
  - ⁝ **catarrh** (See Catarrh - accompanied - mucous)
  - ⁝ **cough**: nux-m b7.de*
  - ⁝ **respiration**; complaints of (See RESPIRATION - Complaints - accompanied - nose)
  - ⁝ **Head**; pain in (See HEAD - Pain - accompanied - nose - dry)
  - ⁝ **Mouth**; dryness of: ulm-c jsj8•
    - ⁝ **sensation** of: ulm-c jsj8•
  - ⁝ **Throat**; dryness of: ulm-c jsj8•
- · **air**; in open | **amel.**: ozone sde2• rad-br gk1 *Thuj* v-a-b jl2
- · **alternating** with:
  - ⁝ **discharge** (See Coryza - discharge, without - alternating - fluent)
  - ⁝ **obstruction** (See Obstruction - alternating with - dryness)
- · **blowing** nose, but without discharge; compels●: agar amp rly4• cench k2 cimic **KALI-BI** k ● lac-c *Lach* mag-c naja nat-ox rly4• *Psor* **Stict** **Teucr**
  - ⁝ **dry** sensation, when: bar-c k*
- · **breathing** | **mouth**; must breath through: meli ptk1
- · **chill**; during: bell bg2 calc bg2 *Rhod* bg2 sabad bg2 sil bg2
- · **chronic**: am-c ambr caust *Sil*

Dryness – Inside: ...
- · **cold** air | **amel.**: kali-bi v-a-b jl2
- · **coryza**; during: mur-ac a1 nit-ac h2* ros-d wla1
- · **discharge**, after: bar-c h2*
- · **fever**; during: apis bg2 ars bg2 *Bell* bg2 calc bg2 dros bg2 graph bg2 merc bg2 nat-m bg2 phos bg2 *Rhod* b4.de* sep bg2 sil bg2 *Spig* b7.de* sulph bg2
- · **heat**; with: *Bell* a1* cann-s k* clem k* *Rhod* a1
- · **indoors**: nux-v ptk1 thyr ptk1
- · **inspiration** agg.: olib-sac wmh1
- · **obstruction**; without: *Sep* b4.de*
- · **painful**: agath-a nl2• alum-p k2 bamb-a stb2.de• bar-c c1 calc **Graph** k* kali-bi *Phos* k* sep *Sil* k* *Stict* succ-ac rly4• (non:sulph k*)
  - ⁝ **coryza**; during: sulph h2*
- · **perspiration**:
  - ⁝ **during**: bell bg2 *Calc* bg2 graph bg2 nat-m bg2 nit-ac bg2 phos bg2 sil bg2
  - ⁝ **suppressed** perspiration of feet; after: **Sil**
- · **sensation** of: anac b4a.de* *Bell* hr1 cann-s b7.de* con b4a.de* iodof hr1 ip b7.de* kali-bi bg2 kola stb3• *Lyc* hr1 merc-c b4a.de mez k* nat-m h2* *Petr* k* phos k* psor al2 sabad b7.de* seneg k* **Sil** k* stram b7.de* verat b7.de* zing hr1
  - ⁝ **discharge**; with: mur-ac a1
- · **sleep**; during: *Sil* b4a.de
- · **swallowing** | **amel.**: sin-n k*
- · **walking** in open air agg.: ant-c kali-c k2 lyc sal-fr sle1• sulph
- · **warm**:
  - ⁝ **air** agg.: calc-p kali-bi
  - ⁝ **room** | **agg.**: *Kali-bi* *Kali-s* *Thuj* v-a-b jl2
- · **weather** agg.; cold: kali-bi k2
- **Nostrils**: agar mtf33 brucel sa3• luf-op rsj5• rad-br c11
- **Posterior** nares: *Acon* k* *Aesc* k* alum bg2 alumn k* bell bg2* calc-p carb-ac carb-an bg2 carb-v k* chinin-s bg2 *Cinnb* cist bg2 *Coc-c* k* colch bg2 cop br1 cor-r bg2 fago graph h2* lem-m br1 **Lyc** k* mag-m bg2 merc b4a.de* merc-c k* mur-ac b4a.de nat-c h2* *Nat-m* k* neon srj5• nux-m k* onos petr bg2 phos bg2 plb bg2 rhod b4a.de rumx k* sabad b7.de* sang bg2 seneg bg2 *Sep* k* *Sil* k* sin-n k* spong fd4.de stram k* tub mtf33 verat bg2 *Wye* zinc k* zinc-i ptk1 zing sf1.de
  - · **morning**: carb-ac nat-m
  - · **night**: cinnb
  - · **air** agg.; in open: nat-c h2
  - · **sensation** as if: dros bg2 nux-m bg2 tarax bg2
  - ▽ · **extending** to | **Larynx**: visc c1
- **Tip** (See FACE - Dryness - nose - tip)
- **Turbinated** bones (See FACE - Dryness - nose - turbinated)
- **Wings**: chlor bro1 hell bro1 *Sangin-n* bro1

DUST in nose; sensation of: olib-sac wmh1

DYSPNEA in nose: am-c tl1 *Ars* bg2* euphr bg1 hell bg1 kreos bg2* lach bg2* merc bg1* phos bg1* *Puls* bg2* sabad bg3* sulph bg2*

EATING: | **after** | **agg.**: am-c b4a.de arg-met b7.de zinc b4.de
- **while** | **agg.**: arg-met bg2 cann-xyz bg2 clem bg2 fl-ac bg2 jatr-c bg2 kali-bi bg2 lach b7.de* *Nux-v* bg2 plb bg2 sanic bg2 sil bg2 spong b7.de* sulph bg2 zinc bg2

ECCHYMOSES: *Arn* b7a.de

EDEMA: **Apis** bapt k* bros-gau mrc1

ENLARGED: am-c bg2
- **sensation** as if: *(↗MIND - Delusions - enlarged - nose)* cann-s k*

EPISTAXIS: abel vh1 abrot k* acet-ac k* **Acon** k* adel a1 *Adren* br1 *Agar* k* *Aids* nl2• ail k* alco a1 *All-c* k* allox tpw4 aloe k* alum k* *Alumn* k* **Am-c** k* am-caust a1 am-m k* **Ambr** k* ambro c2* anac k* anag k* anan ang b2.de* **Ant-c** k* ant-s-aur k* ant-t k* antip c2 apis k* aran k* *Arg-met* k* arg-n arist-cl rbp3• **Arn** k* *Ars* k* *Ars-i* ars-s-f k2 arum-t k2 asaf asar k* astac k* aster k* aur k* aur-ar k2 aur-i k2 bals-p c2 bamb-a stb2.de• *Bapt* k* *Bar-c* k* *Bar-m* bar-ox-suc rly4• **Bell** k* bell-p sp1 benz-ac k* *Berb* k* beryl sp1 bism k*

Nose

Epistaxis: ...
bit-ar wht1• blum-o bnj1 borx k* **Both** **Bov** k* *Brom* k* *Bry* k* *Bufo* **Cact** k* cadm-s k* **Calc** k* calc-i k2 **Calc-p** k* **Calc-s** k* calc-sil k2 camph k* *Cann-s* k* canth k* *Caps* k* *Carb-an* k* **Carb-v** k* **Carbn-s** carc mlr1• card-m k* cardios-h rly4• *Carl* a1 **Caust** k* cer-s a1 cere-s c2 *Cham* k* chel c2 **Chin** k* chinin-ar chinin-m c1 *Chinin-s* chlf a1 choc srj3• cic k* *Cina* k* cinch c2 *Cinnb* k* cinnm k* clem k* cob-n sp1 cocc k* coff k* coff-t a1 colch k* coloc k* *Con* k* conv br1 *Cop* k* cor-r k* **Croc** k* crot-c k* **Crot-h** k* *Cupr* k* cycl a1 cyn-d zzc1• cyt-l sp1 der a1 *Dig* k* diph br1 *Diphtox* jl2 *Dros* k* *Dulc* k* echi *Elaps* k* elat a1 *Erig* k* euphr k* eupi k* *Ferr* k* ferr-act bro1 *Ferr-ar* k* ferr-m k* *Ferr-p* k* **Ferr-pic** c1* fic-r bro1 gal-ac a1* gamb k* gels k* *Glon* k* glycyr-g cte1• gran bg2* *Graph* k* **Ham** k* *Hecla* helia c2* hell a1 *Hep* k* hepat c2 hir rsj4• *Hydr* k* hydrc a1 **Hyos** k* ign k* ind a1* indg k* *Iod* k* **Ip** k* kali-ar *Kali-bi* k* *Kali-c* k* kali-chl k* **Kali-i** k* kali-m k2 *Kali-n* k* kali-p k* kali-s kola stb3• *Kreos* k* *Lac-ac* k* **Lach** k* lachn k* lap-la sde8.de• lapa c2 *Led* k* leptos-ih jl2 lil-s a1 lil-t lob k* lol a1 luf-op rsj5• *Lyc* k* *Lyss* k* m-ambo b2.de* m-arct b2.de* *Mag-c* k* mag-m k* mag-s k* maias-l hrn2• **Med** k* **Meli** k* meli-xyz c2 *Meny* bg2* meph k* **Merc** k* *Merc-c* k* merc-cy bg2* merl bg1 *Mez* k* **Mill** k* morg-g pte1* morg-p pte1*• *Mosch* k* mur-ac k* naja bg2 nat-ar *Nat-c* k* nat-hchls *Nat-m* k* nat-n bg2* *Nat-p* k* nat-s k* nat-sal br1* nicc a1 nicotam rly4• **Nit-ac** k* *Nux-m* k* *Nux-v* k* oena k* onis bro1 onon c2 op k* orig a1 osm bro1 ox-ac oxal-a rly4• oxyurn-sc mcp1• par k* parathyr jl2 pert jl2 *Petr* k* *Ph-ac* k* **Phos** k* phys a1 phyt k2 pic-ac k* pimp a1* pin-s a1 plat k* plb k* plut-n srj7• positr nl2• *Prun* bg2* psil ft1 **Puls** k* pyrog bg2* ran-b k* raph c2 *Rat* k* rauw sp1 *Rhod* k* rhus-g c2* **Rhus-t** k* rob a1 ros-d wla1 *Rumx* k* ruta k* sabad k* **Sabin** k* sal-ac tl1 sal-fr sle1• samb k* *Sang* k* santin c2 sarr k* *Sars* k* **Sec** k* sel b2.de* senec k* seneg k* *Sep* k* *Sil* k* sin-n k* sol-t-ae c2 spig k* spira a1 *Spong* k* squil k* *Stann* k* staph k* stict k* stram k* stront-c k* *Sul-ac* k* **Sulph** k* sumb a1 syc pte1*• symph fd3.de• syph k2 tab a1 tarax k* *Tarent* k* tep a1* *Ter* k* teucr k* thlas bro1* *Thuj* k* til k* *Tril-p* k* trios rsj11• tritic-vg fd5.de **Tub** k* urt-u mtf11 *Ust* vac k* valer k* vanil fd5.de *Verat* k* vinc k* viol-o k* vip k* visc sp1 wies c2 zinc k* [buteo-j sej6 erech stj]

- **one** side: ozone sde2•
- **right**: am-c k* arg-n k* brom a1 bry k* calc k* cham a1 cic k* con k* cor-r a1 cupr k* dulc fd4.de echi ptk2 eupi a1 gamb gins a1 ind indg k* kali-bi k* kali-c k* kali-chl k* kola stb3• mag-c merc-c lp mez a1 phys a1 pic-ac a1 ruta fd4.de sars k* sil a1 spong fd4.de streptoc rly4• succ-ac rly4• symph fd3.de• *Verat* k*

▽ • **extending** to | **left**: coca cor-r

- **left**: aids nl2• am-c k* am-m k* aml-ns asaf hr1 asc-t a1* bapt k* bar-ox-suc rly4• berb k* bry a1 caust k* chel a1 chlf a1 cor-r a1 del a1 dios k* dulc eupi a1 *Ferr* bg2* ferr-act lp glycyr-g cte1• ham fd3.de• hydr k* ignis-alc es2• kali-bi a1 *Kali-n* bg2* kola stb3• lach a1 maias-l hrn2• merc k* phys a1 plut-n srj7• rhod k* rhus-g a1 sars k* *Sep* h2* spong fd4.de tarax h1* tarent k* thiam rly4• thuj a1 [helia stj7]
  - • **bathing**; after: calc-s

▽ • **extending** to | **right**: ham

- **morning**: acon agar k* *Agn* bg2* aids nl2• aloe am-c k* **Ambr** k* ant-c k* apis am k* ars sne *Arum-t* k* astac a1 bell k* berb k* borx **Bov** k* *Bry* k* bufo *Calc* k* *Calc-s* canth k* caps k* **Carb-an** k* *Carb-v* k* *Carbn-s* *Caust* k* *Chin* k* coff k* colch k* croc dios hr1 dros k* *Ferr* k* ferr-p flav jl2 *Graph* k* **Ham** k* hep k* hipp k* hyos indg a1 kali-bi k* *Kali-c* k* kali-n bg2 kali-p kali-s kreos k* *Lac-ac* k* *Lach* k* lap-la sde8.de• *Mag-c* k* maias-l hrn2• *Meny* bg2* merc *Nat-c* k* *Nat-m* k* nat-n bg2 nat-p a1 **Nit-ac** k* *Nux-v* k* olib-sac wmh1 *Petr* bg2* *Phos* k* puls k* rhus-r *Rhus-t* k* sabin sal-fr sle1• sec *Sep* k* sol-t-ae a1 spong fd4.de *Stann* k* succ-ac rly4• **Sulph** k* thiam rly4• thuj k* tritic-vg fd5.de trom a1 urol-h rwt•
  - • **6** h: sal-al blc1•
    - ⁝ **6**-7 h: aids nl2• *Chin* bg1*
  - • **8** h: *Bry* bg1* sal-al blc1•
  - • **bed**:
    - ⁝ **in** bed:
      - ⁝ **agg.**: aloe ptk1 ambr k* bar-c k* bov *Caps* k* *Carb-v* k*
      - ⁝ **amel.**: mag-m bg1
    - ⁝ **waking**; in bed on: aids nl2• aster k* bell k* *Bry* k* lap-la sde8.de• mag-c stann k*
  - • **rising** agg.; after: agar k* aloe bro1 ambr bro1 berb k* both-ax tsm2 bov bro1 **Bry** k* cham a1 **Chin** k* coff k* ferr ferr-p sne kali-bi a1 lach bro1 *Nux-v* bro1 sep k* stann k* thuj k*
  - • **stooping** agg.: *Ferr* k*
- **forenoon**:
  - • **9** h: kali-c
  - • **10**-12 h: carb-v
- **noon**: kali-bi k* tarax k*
- **afternoon**: *Ant-t* bg2* *Calc-p* k* carb-an k* cham k* dulc fd4.de indg k* kali-m k2 kali-n k* lach a1 *Lyc* k* m-arct *Nat-s* k* spong fd4.de *Sulph* bg2* tab k* thuj k* trom k*
  - • **15** h: *Sulph*
  - • **16** h: *Lac-c* *Lyc*
- **evening**: *Ant-c* k* borx bufo *Carbn-s* *Coff* bg2* *Colch* k* dios hr1 dros k* dulc fd4.de *Ferr* k* gamb k* *Graph* k* ham fd3.de• indg a1 kali-bi k* kali-m k2 *Lach* k* *Lyc* k* mez k* nat-s k2 *Ph-ac* *Phos* k* phys a1 *Puls* ruta fd4.de sars k* *Sep* k* *Sul-ac* k* *Sulph* k* thuj k* til k*
  - • **18** h: coff
- **night**: aloe bg2* ant-c arg-met am k* *Bell* k* bry calc k* caps bg2* carb-an k* **Carb-v** k* con k* cor-r k* croc graph k* hyos kali-bi bg2* kali-chl k* mag-m k* mag-s k* *Merc* merc-c lp mill k* nat-m k* nat-s k* **Nit-ac** k* olib-sac wmh1 *Puls* *Rhus-t* k* sars k* spong fd4.de sulph ptk1 *Verat* k*
  - • **midnight** | **before**:
    - ⁝ **22** h: graph
      - . **flushing** of heat; preceded by: graph c1
    - ⁝ **after** | **3-4** h: bry c1
  - • **morning** | **towards**: apis mag-c h2
- **accompanied** by:
  - • **catarrh** | **Posterior** nares (See Catarrh - postnasal - accompanied - epistaxis)
  - • **complaints**; other: carb-v b4.de
  - • **coryza** (See Coryza - accompanied - epistaxis)
  - • **cough** (See COUGH - Accompanied - epistaxis)
  - • **gastric** complaints: *Bry* b7a.de
  - • **goose** flesh: camph bro1*
  - • **hemorrhoids** (See RECTUM - Hemorrhoids - accompanied - epistaxis)
  - • **nausea**: ars b4a.de
  - • **odors**; imaginary: kali-s tl1 puls tl1
  - • **pain**:
    - ⁝ **pressing** | **Root** of nose: ham bro1 ruta ptk1
  - • **scarlatina** (See SKIN - Eruptions - scarlatina - accompanied - epistaxis)
  - • **swelling** and dryness of nose: phos tl1
  - • **vertigo** (See VERTIGO - Accompanied - epistaxis)
  - • **weakness** (See GENERALS - Weakness - epistaxis)
  - • **worms**; complaints of: *Cina* bg2 merc bg2

○ • **Chest**; complaints of (See CHEST - Complaints - accompanied - epistaxis)

  - • **Face**:
    - ⁝ **congestion** of: *(↗HEAD - Congestion - epistaxis - with)* bell bro1 bufo br1 cact mrr1 coff bg2 erig mrr1 meli bro1* nux-v bro1
    - ⁝ **pale**: carb-v bg2* chin bg1 ferr bg1 *Ip* bg1* puls bg1 verat bg1
  - • **Head**:
    - ⁝ **constriction** (See HEAD - Constriction - accompanied - epistaxis)
  - • **Liver** and region of liver; complaints of (See ABDOMEN - Liver - accompanied - epistaxis)
  - • **Teeth**; pain in (See TEETH - Pain - accompanied - nose - epistaxis)
  - • **Uterus**; complaints of (See FEMALE - Complaints - uterus - accompanied - epistaxis)
  - • **Varicose** veins (See GENERALS - Varicose - accompanied - epistaxis)
- **agg.**: *Ham* bg2
- **alcoholics**; in: *Acon* bg2 bell bg2 bry bg2 *Carb-v* k* hyos bg2* *Lach* k* nux-v bg2* **Sec** k*
- **alternating** with | **blood**; spitting of: **Ferr** k*

- **amel.**: brom bg2* bry bg2 elaps ptk1 ferr-p bg2 kali-chl bg2 meli bg2* psor bg2* rhus-t bg2* tarent ptk1
- **amenorrhea**, with: both-ax tsm2 *Bry* *Cact* con ham lach ol-j *Phos* *Puls* sep bg1
- **anemia**, with: bry bg2* chin bg2* ferr bg2* hydr bg2* kali-c bg2* nat-m sf1.de *Puls* bg2*
- **anger**; after: *Ars*
- **bathing**, after (See washing)
- **bleeders**, in: bov bg2 crot-h bg2 lach bg2
- **bleeding**; with general: crot-h bg1 lach bg1
- **blood**:
  - **acrid**: kali-n k* nit-ac k* sil k*
  - **bright**: *Acon* k* aids nl2• am-c k* ant-t k* arn k* ars k* bapt k* bar-c k* **Bell** k* bit-ar wht1• borx k* bov b2.de brom a1 bry k* calc k* calc-sil k2 canth k* *Carb-ac* k* carb-an k* carb-v k* cham a1 *Chin* k* cic k* *Crot-c* k* cyn-d zzc1• dig k* dios k* dros k* *Dulc* k* *Elaps* erech br1* *Erig* k* eupi a1 ferr k* *Ferr-p* k* gins a1 graph k* hydr a1 **Hyos** k* indg a1 **Ip** k* kali-bi a1 kali-n k* kreos k* *Lach* k* laur k* *Led* k* mag-m k* maias-l hrn2• merc k* mez k* *Mill* k* nat-ar nat-c k* nat-s k* nux-m k* *Ph-ac* **Phos** k* puls k* *Rhus-t* k* sabad k* *Sabin* k* sec k* sep k* sil k* stram k* streptoc rly4• stront-c k* sulph k* *Tril-p* bro1 *Tub* zinc k*
  - **clotted**, coagulated: acon agar bg2 aids nl2• ambr c1 *Arg-n* *Arn* b2.de* bapt **Bell** k* bry k* calc bg2 cann-i canth k* carb-an k* *Carbn-s* caust k* **Cham** k* **Chin** k* con k* *Croc* k* dig dios dulc *Ferr* k* *Ferr-m* glycyr-g cte1• ham k2 hep hyos k* ign k* **Ip** k* kali-n kola stb3• kreos k* *Lach* bg2* lyc lyss mag-c mag-m b2.de* *Merc* k* nat-hchls k* *Nat-m* *Nit-ac* k* nux-v k* ph-ac k* *Phos* **Plat** k* *Puls* k* **Rhus-t** k* sabin k* **Sec** k* sel k2 sep k* stram k* stront-c k* *Sulph* *Tarent* k* *Tub*
    - **continually** full of; nose is: ferr
    - **liver**; looking like: sabin bg1
    - **quickly**: croc bg1 merc nit-ac puls bg1 rhus-t bg1
    - **slowly**: blum-o bnj1 ham bg2* lach bg2* loxo-lae bnm12•
  - **dark**, black: acon k* agar bg2 am-c k* ant-c k* *Arn* k* asar k* *Bapt* k* *Bell* k* bism k* bry k* calc canth k* **Carb-v** k* *Carbn-s* caust bg2 *Cham* k* chin k* *Cina* cinnb cocc k* con k* **Croc** k* *Crot-h* k* cupr k* dig k* dros k* *Elaps* ferr k* graph k* *Ham* k* ign k* jug-r vml3• *Kali-bi* *Kali-n* k* *Kreos* k* **Lach** k* led k* lyc k* mag-c k* mag-m k* *Merc* k* merc-cy mtf11 mill bg1 *Mur-ac* k* nat-hchls *Nit-ac* k* *Nux-m* k* **Nux-v** k* *Ph-ac* k* phos k* plat k* *Puls* k* rhus-t bg2 **Sec** k* sel k* *Sep* k* *Stram* k* sul-ac sulph k* *Tarent* verat bg1* *Vip* st1
    - **and thin**: arn bro1 carb-an *Carb-v* **Crot-h** k* **Ham** k* *Lach* k* mur-ac bro1 *Nit-ac* **Sec** k* *Sul-ac*
  - **fluid**: am-c k2 arn *Carb-v* **Crot-h** *Erig* eupi a1 *Ham* *Kreos* lp maias-l hrn2• phos mrr1 **Sec** *Sul-ac* ter til a1
  - **hot**: acon bg1 *Bell* bg1*
  - **offensive**: *Sec*
  - **pale**: abrot bg2 acon bg2 am-c b2.de* ant-t b2.de* arn k* ars b2.de* bar-c k* bell k* borx b2.de* bov b2.de* bry b2.de* calc b2.de* canth b2.de* *Carb-ac* carb-an bg1 *Carb-v* k* chin b2.de* crot-h k* dig k* dros b2.de* dulc k* erig bg2 *Ferr* b2.de* *Graph* k* hyos k* ip b2.de* kali-n b2.de* *Kreos* b2.de* lach lachn k* laur b2.de* led k* mag-m b2.de* merc b2.de* mill bg2 nat-c b2.de* nat-s a1 nux-m b2.de* phos k* puls k* rhus-t k* *Sabad* b2.de* sabin k* sars a1 sec k* sep b2.de* sil b2.de* stram b2.de* stront-c b2.de* *Sulph* b2.de* ter til a1 tril-p bg2 zinc b2.de*
  - **putrid**: *Mur-ac* hr1
  - **stringy**: bapt **Croc** k* crot-h bg2* *Cupr* k* kali-bi *Kreos* bg1* *Lach* bg1* mag-c k* *Merc* k* naja bg1 *Sec* k* sep k* verat bg1
  - **uncoagulable**: ars bro1 bry bro1 carb-v bro1 crot-h bro1* ham bro1 ip bro1 *Lach* bro1 *Phos* bro1 thlas bro1 tril-p bro1
  - **warm**: dulc k*
  - **watery** (See pale)
- **blow**; from a: acet-ac k* **Arn** k* *Elaps* *Ham* k* mill bro1 *Sep* k*
- **blowing** on wind instruments agg.: *Rhus-t* bg2*
- **blowing** the nose agg.: *Agar* k* alum k* alum-p k2 alum-sil k2 *Alumn* am-c k* am-m k* ambr k* anac ant-c k* arg-met k* arg-n k* **Arn** k* asar k* asc-t aur k* *Aur-m* k* aur-s k2 bamb-a stb2.de• bapt *Bar-c* k* bar-i k2 bar-s k2 borx k* *Bov* k* brom *Bry* bufo *Calad* calc calc-p k* calc-sil k2 canth k* caps k* carb-ac *Carb-an* *Carb-v* k* **Carbn-s** caust k* chin cinnb *Croc* *Crot-h* cupr k* dros k* elaps ferr k* ferr-i ferr-p *Graph* k* ham fd3.de• hep k* hir rsj4• indg iod kali-c k*
- **blowing** the nose agg.: ...
  kali-p kali-s kali-sil k2 kola stb3• **Lach** k* lap-la sde8.de• led k* lyc k* mag-c k* mag-m k* meny k* merc k* mez k* nat-ar nat-c k* *Nat-m* k* nat-p nat-s nit-ac k* *Nux-v* k* pant-ac rly4• par k* petr b2.de* **Ph-ac** k* **Phos** k* plut-n srj7• *Puls* k* ran-b k* rhus-t k* ruta k* sabad k* sal-al blc1• sars *Sec* bro1 *Sep* k* sil k* spig k* spong k* stront-c k* **Sulph** k* symph fd3.de• teucr *Thuj* k* tritic-vg fd5.de vanil fd5.de zinc k* zinc-p k2
  - **right**: arg-n
  - **left**: am-c bapt ham fd3.de• kali-n sars
  - **morning**: *Agar* arn borx *Bov* *Caust* kali-s k2 **Lach** nat-c nit-ac *Puls* sulph h2 thuj tritic-vg fd5.de vanil fd5.de
  - **evening**: borx graph ham fd3.de• sep vanil fd5.de
  - **night**: arg-n graph nit-ac
- **boring** with finger: *Ferr-m* bg3 *Ferr-ma* a1 *Lach* bg3 ruta fd4.de *Sil* h2*
- **children**; in●: abrot c1* arn bro1 aur-m-n wbt2• bell k* calc bro1* chinin-s cop ptk2 *Croc* k* diphtox jl2 **Ferr** k* *Ferr-p* k* ferr-pic st1 *Ham* k* ip mtf33 lach sne merc nat-m ih* nat-n ih1.de phos k* *Puls* b7a.de *Sil* vh *Ter* k*
  - **boys**: abrot br1* cop hr1*
  - **girls**: croc ptk1
  - **infants**: sil ptk1
  - **nurslings**: sil mtf33
  - **scrofulous**: calc bg1 sil bg1
- **chill**:
  - **after**: *Eup-per* bg2* *Hep* k*
  - **during**: acon bg2 arn bg2 ars bg2 bell k* bry k* calc k* cham bg2 chin bg2 dig bg2 ferr bg2 hyos bg2 ip bg2 kali-n bg2 kreos k* lyc bg2 merc bg2 puls k* rhus-t k* sabad bg2 stram bg2 sulph bg2 thuj ptk1 verat bg2
  - **instead** of: nat-m
- **chronic**: *(↗several)* bry tl1 *Vip* tl1
- **clotted** (See blood - clotted)
- **coffee** agg.: nux-v bg2*
- **cold**; after taking a: *Bry* b7a.de dulc bg2
- **congestion** of face, with (See accompanied - face - congestion)
- **convulsions**:
  - **during**: caust st op a1 plb a1
  - **with**: caust ptk1 *Mosch* bg1*
- **coryza**; during (See Coryza - accompanied - epistaxis)
- **cough**, with (See COUGH - Accompanied - epistaxis)
- **crying**; after: nit-ac bg2*
- **diarrhea**; from suppressed: abrot k2*
- **dinner** | **after** | **agg.**: am-c k* arg-met hydr a1 spong zinc k*
  - **during** | **agg.**: kali-bi k* sil a1 spong k*
- **diphtheria**; in: ars k* *Carb-v* *Chin* k* *Crot-h* k* diph br1* *Hydr* k* *Ign* k* *Kali-chl* k* lac-c hr1 *Lach* k* *Merc-cy* k* *Mur-ac* hr1 *Nit-ac* k* phos k*
  - **detachment** of membrane; after: *Phos*
- **drink** the blood; desire to: plut-n srj7•
- **drunkards**; in: sec a1
- **ear** noises, with: bell bg2* *Chin* bg2* graph bg2* nux-v bg2*
- **easily** | **amel.**: maias-l hrn2•
- **eating** | **after** | **agg.**: am-c k* arg-met bg2* arg-n vh kali-bi bg2 kali-c bg1 spong bg2 *Zinc* bg2*
  - **amel.**: tarax bg2*
- **emotions** agg.: carb-v hr1
- **exertion** agg.: *Arn* k* bry bg2 calc bg2 carb-v k* *Croc* lap-la rsp1 puls bg2 *Rhus-t* k* sulph bg2
- **expectoration**; during: dros ptk1
- **fever**:
  - **amel.**: crot-h bg1 lach bg1
  - **during** | **agg.**: acon bg2 arn bro1 bell bg2 bry bg2* carb-v bg2* cham bg2 chin bg2 erig bg2* ferr gk ferr-p k* ham k* ign bg2 ip bro1 lach bg2* lyc bg2 meli k* nux-v bg2 op bg2 ph-ac bg1 phos bro1 pyrog k2 rhus-t bg2* sep bg2 sil bg2 squil bg2 stram bg2 sulph bg2 thuj ptk2 verat bg2
- **flushes** of heat; after: ferr bg1 graph c1
- **followed** by | **vertigo**: carb-v h2*
- **gushing** out: **Acon** bg2 *Arn* bg2 bell bg2 **Chin** bg2 *Merc* bg2 puls bg2 rhus-t bg2 sec bg2
- **habitual**: nat-n sf1.de sil sf1.de
- **hawking**: rhus-t h1*

- **headache**:
  - **after**: am-c bg1 ant-c k* bell bg1 carb-an croc lach k* meli k* nux-v k* sabin **Sep** k*
  - **during**: **Acon** k* **Agar** k* alum k* am-c ambr aml-ns bro1 ant-c bro1 asaf bell *Bry* k* cadm-s c1 carb-an k* cham bg1 chin bg1 *Cinnb* k* crot-h bg1 dig bg1 dulc k* ferr k2 ferr-p ham bro1 kreos bg1 lach k* lap-la sde8.de• mag-c bg1 **Meli** bro1* mill bg1 nux-v bg1 parathyr jl2 phys a1 rhus-t bg1 tub c1* verat bg2
    - **left** nostril; bleeding from: ant-c bg2
- **heated** if: thuj h1* thyr bg1
  - **sun**: cyn-d zzc1•
- **hemoptysis**, with: *Ham* bg1*
- **hemorrhoids**:
  - **suppressed**; from: kali-bi sne *Nux-v* k* sulph bg1
  - **with** (See RECTUM - Hemorrhoids - accompanied - epistaxis)
- **hot** weather: **CROC** k •*
- **injuries**; from (See blow; from)
- **itching**:
  - **after**: am-m bg1
  - **followed** by: *Hydr* bg1*
  - **with**: arg-met bg1 *Arg-n* vh *Arn* bg1* bell bg1 *Carb-v* bg1* kali-bi bg1 lach bg1 *Rhus-t* bg1*
- **jarring**, from: *Carb-v* k* sep ptk1
- **lifting** agg.: *Rhus-t* bg1*
- **light**; from: bell bro1
- **lying**:
  - **agg.**: hura puls k*
  - **side**; on:
    - **right** | **agg.**: sulph ptk1
- **masturbation**; from: lach ptk1
- **measles** agg.: acon bro1 bry bg1* ip bro1 puls bg1 sabad bg1
- **mechanical** causes; from: arn tl1
- **menopause**•: arg-n bell bg2* bry bg2* *Ham* bg2* **Lach** k* nux-v bg2* *Puls* bg2* *Sep* bg2* *Sul-ac* k* *Sulph* k*
- **menses**:
  - **after** | **agg.**: calc b4a.de sulph k*
  - **before** | **agg.**: acon bro1 *Bar-c* k* *Bry* b7a.de* *Con* b4a.de dig bro1 gels bro1 hydr hr1 *Ip* bg1* **Lach** k* *Nat-s* k* nux-v bg1 *Phos* b4a.de *Puls* sep bro1 *Sulph* k* thuj b4a.de *Verat* k* vib
  - **during**:
    - **agg.**: acon bg2* agar bg2 alum bg2 *Am-c* bg2 **Ambr** k* bov bg2 bry k* carb-an bg2 dig bro1 dulc bg2 ferr k2 gels bro1 **Graph** bg2* ham k2* *Kali-c* bg2 lach b7a.de* *Mag-c* bg2 nat-c bg1 nat-m bg2 *Nat-s* k* nux-v bg2 puls k* *Sep* k* *Sulph* k* verat bg2*
      - **profuse** menses: acon k* ambr calc bg2* *Croc* bg2* meli ptk1 sabin bg2*
      - **scanty**: *Bry* bg2* graph bg1 *Phos* puls bg2* sec bg2* sep bg2* [corn xyz62]
    - **intermits**; when flow: *Eupi* k* nat-c bg1
  - **instead** of: apis ptk1 both-ax tsm2 *Bry* k* carb-an ptk1 cham ptk1 dulc bg3* erig vml3• eupi c1 ferr ptk1 graph *Ham* k* *Lach* k* lyc ptk1 nat-s bro1 phos bro1* *Puls* bro1* senec ptk1 sep bro1 sil ptk1
  - **suppressed** menses; from: acon bell both-ax tsm2 **Bry** k* *Cact* k* calc carl c1 *Con* k* *Croc* dulc bg2 *Gels* k* ham hyos kali-i **Lach** k* nit-ac ol-j *Phos* k* **Puls** k* *Rhus-t* *Sabin* senec c1 *Sep* k*
- **motion** agg.: bell bro1 carb-v bg1 *Rhus-t* bg1*
- **noise** agg.: bell bro1
- **nursing** the child: vip ptk1
- **old** people: *Agar* k* aur bg2 bar-c b4a.de* bov bg2 *Carb-v* k* chin bg1 con bg2 ferr-p bg1 ham k* phos bg2 **Sec** k* sil bg2 sul-ac k* verat bg1
- **oozing**: aloe k2 *Bapt* hr1 chin mtf33 crot-h ham k* phos plb a1 *Sul-ac* hr1
- **operation**; after: thlas bro1*
- **overheating**; from: sep k* thuj k*
- **ozena**, in: sang bg1*
- **pale** face, with (See accompanied - face - pale)
- **passive** flow: ham bg2
- **periodic** (See GENERALS - History - epistaxis)
- **periodical** | **day**; every: carb-v bro1
- **persistent**: camph bro1 *Carb-v* carc mlr1• *Croc* *Crot-h* *Ferr* bg1* led bg1* mill bg1 mur-ac **Phos** *Sulph* k*
- **perspiration**; with: bry bg2* caust bg2* con bg2* nux-v bg2* op bg2* **Phos** k* tarax bg2* thuj bg2*
  - **forehead**; on: crot-h bg1
- **plethoric** patients: (↗*GENERALS - Plethora - constitution)* abrot bg1 *Acon* nux-v
- **pregnancy**:
  - **during**: bry ptk2 cocc hr1 *Sep* hr1* thlas mrr1
    - **whole** pregnancy: erig zr
- **profuse**: *Acon* b7.de* aids nl2• bell b4a.de cact br1 cann-s b7.de* *Chin* b7a.de con b4.de* croc b7.de* crot-h tl1 erig bg2 ham k2 ip mtf33 *Led* b7.de* meli ptk1 merc-cy ptk1 mill bg2 plut-n srj7• rhus-t b7.de* sabin b7.de* sec a1
  - **short**; but: cact ptk1 positr nl2•
- **puberty**; in: abrot bg2* croc bg2 ferr bg2 ferr-p bg2 graph bg2 ham bg2 kali-c bg2* nat-m bg2 phos bg2* puls bg2 sil bg2
- **purpura** hemorrhagica, with: *Crot-h* k* *Ham* k* *Lach* k* **Phos** k* rhus-t k* ter hr1
- **recurrent** (See GENERALS - History - epistaxis)
- **relaxation** of blood vessels; from: *Agar* b4a.de
- **rubbing**; after: phos h2*
- **salivation**; with: hyos bg1*
- **scarlatina**; after: mur-ac bro1
- **scrofula**; with: calc-s bg2 sil bg2
- **sensation** as if: cina wd2 cupr rb2 eucal wd2 lac-ac rb2* lil-t wd2 meli rb2 phys wd2 plut-n srj7• xan wd2
  - **fever**; during: sep bg2
- **sepsis**; with: lach bg2 naja bg2 pyrog bg2
- **several** days: (↗*chronic)* cop ptk2
- **singing**; after: hep k*
- **sitting** agg.: carb-an bg1 sul-ac bg1
- **sleep** agg.; during: bell bg1 bov k* *Bry* k* *Crot-c* graph kali-bi a1 **Merc** k* *Merc-c* bg1* nat-s k* *Nit-ac* k* *Nux-v* k* pitu-a vml2• puls k* spong fd4.de sulph k* *Verat* k*
- **smell**, lost: *Ip* bg1*
- **sneezing**:
  - **after**: ham fd3.de• indg hr1 zinc h2*
  - **agg.**: aids nl2• am-c bg1 bapt *Bov* k* *Con* k* ferr-p k2 *Indg* *Mag-c* bg1* rumx *Sabad* bg2*
- **spring**, in the: con
- **standing** agg.: sul-ac bg1
- **stool** | **during** | **agg.**: bry b7a.de carb-v k* coff k* phos k* rhus-t k* symph fd3.de•
  - **straining** at:
    - **after**: *Carb-v*
    - **agg.**: *Coff* k* *Phos* *Rhus-t*
- **stooping** | **after** | **agg.**: carb-v
  - **agg.**: dros *Ferr* k* *Nat-m* k* *Nux-v* ol-j *Rhus-t* k* sil
- **sudden**: cob-n sp1
- **swallowing** agg.: lac-c mtf33
- **talking** agg.: lac-c k*
- **tendency** to (See Epistaxis)
- **touch** agg.; slight: cic k* hydr ind k* ruta fd4.de *Sec* sep ptk1*
- **typhoid** fever; during: *Acon* bro1 **Arn** k* ars bg1 **Bapt** k* *Bry* k* carb-v bg1 *Chinin-s* croc bro1 **Crot-h** k* gels *Ham* bro1 *Ip* bro1 kali-p **Lach** k* meli bro1 *Ph-ac* k* phos bg1 *Rhus-t* k* *Ter*
- **vertigo**:
  - **after** (See VERTIGO - Followed - epistaxis)
  - **before** (See followed - vertigo)
  - **with** (See VERTIGO - Accompanied - epistaxis)
- **vicarious**: *Bry* k* graph k13 **Ham** k* *Lach* k* **Phos** k* *Puls* k* sec k2
- **vision**; with loss of: indg ox-ac k*
- **vomiting**:
  - **after**: ars h2*
  - **with**: ox-ac ptk1 sars bg1*
- **waking**; on: am-c ptk1

- **walking**:
  - **agg.**: elaps k* lach a1 nat-s a1
  - **air** agg.; in open: bry lyc bg1 nat-c k* taosc iwa1•
- **warm** agg.; becoming: carb-v bg1
- **warm** room agg.: *Puls* sep
- **washing**; from: *Am-c* bro1 *Ant-s-aur* bro1 am bro1 calc-s bg kali-c bro1 mag-c bro1

○ • **Face**: am-c k* ambr ptk1 ant-s-aur **Arn** k* bry ptk1 *Calc-s Dros* dulc fd4.de kali-bi *Kali-c* k* onis bro1 phos gm1 symph fd3.de• tarent tritic-vg fd5.de
  - **Feet**: carb-v bg1*
  - **Hands**: am-c k2*
- **watery** discharge, after: agar
- **weakened** by (See GENERALS - Weakness - epistaxis)
- **weeping**; while: *Nit-ac* k*
- **wet**; after getting: *Dulc* k* *Puls Rhus-t*
- **whooping** cough●: **Arn** k* bell bro1 *Bry* cer-ox bro1 *Cina Cor-r* k* *Crot-h Cupr* bro1 **Dros** k* *Ind* bro1 *Iod* bro1 **Ip** k* *Led* k* *Merc* k* *Mur-ac Nux-v* k* spong stram
  - **paroxysm**; after: cina indg
- **wine** agg.: ars k*
- **wiping** nose; when: sec a1
- **young** women: abrot ptk1 phos k* **Sec** k*

○ - **Posterior** part: ail bg2 cor-r ptk1 ferr-p bg2 spig ptk1

ERUPTIONS (See FACE - Eruptions - nose)

ERYSIPELAS (See FACE - Erysipelas - nose)

EXCORIATION: (↗*Discharge - excoriating; Pain - raw*)
agar b4.de* *All-c* ptk1 alum bg2 am-m b7.de* ang b7a.de* ant-c b7.de* *Ars* b4a.de* ars-i ptk1 arum-t bg2* borx bg2 bov b4.de* brom b4a.de* calc bg2 calc-p bg2 caust b4.de* euphr b7a.de* *Fl-ac* bg2 gels ptk1 graph bg2* hell bg2 ign b7a.de* iod ptk1 kali-bi bg2 kali-c bg2 kali-i bg2* kreos ptk1 lach b7.de* m-arct b7.de mag-m b4a.de* mang bg2 merc bg2* merc-c ptk1 mez b4a.de* nat-m b4a.de* *Nit-ac* b4a.de* *Nux-v* b7.de* petr bg2 *Phos* b4.de* puls b7.de* *Rhus-t* b7a.de sil b4.de* sin-n ptk1 *Spig* b7.de* squil b7.de* staph bg2 sulph bg2 verat bg2 zinc b4a.de*
- **coryza**; during: am-m b7a.de ant-t b7a.de *Cham* b7.de* cocc b7a.de *Puls* b7a.de *Squil* b7a.de *Staph* b7a.de

○ - **Inside**: graph b4a.de
- **Nostrils** | **coryza**; during: am-m b7.de* ant-t b7.de* **Ars** b4a.de* **Brom** b4a.de bry b7.de* calc b4.de* **Cham** b7a.de* chlor bg2 cocc b7.de* *Gels* bg2 graph bg2 hep bg2 ign b7.de* kali-bi bg2 *Lach* b7.de* lyc b4.de* m-arct b7.de mag-m bg2 mang bg2 **Merc** b4.de* mez bg2 mur-ac bg2 nit-ac bg2 *Nux-v* b7.de* par bg2 petr b4.de* phos bg2 *Puls* b7.de* sang bg2 sars b4.de* seneg bg2 sil bg2 *Spig* b7.de* spong bg2 squil b7.de* stann b4.de* staph b7.de* *Sulph* bg2 zinc bg2

EXERTION agg.: kali-bi bg2

EXHALATIONS fetid, putrid (See Discharge - offensive - fetid)

EXOSTOSIS: *Aur* br1 merc phos

EXPANSION; sensation of: asaf bg2 bar-c bg2 bism b7.de* cor-r bg2 mez bg2 nit-ac bg2 *Nux-v* bg2 prun bg2 puls bg2

○ - **Nasal** passage while walking in open air carb-ac carb-an
- **Posterior** nares: *Fl-ac* k*

EXPIRATIONS fetid, putrid (See Discharge - offensive - fetid)

FALL; after a: *Sep* b4a.de

FAN-LIKE motion (See Motion - wings - fan-like)

FLAPPING: | **Wings**: morb jl2 pyrog jl2

FLUIDS (See Liquids)

FLUIDS; from loss of: *Chin* b7a.de

FOOD; sensation of:

○ - **Posterior** nares: *Nit-ac* k* petr *Sil* k*
  - **swallowing** agg.: *Nit-ac* petr h2 *Sil* k*

FOREIGN body; sensation of a: agar bg2* am-m k* calc calc-p bg2* con k* hep h2* ign bg2 irid-met srj5• kali-bi k* merc bg2 nat-c k* nat-m bg2 olib-sac wmh1 psor bg2* ruta bg2* sep bg2* sil bg2 spig b7.de* stann bg2*
- **hard**; of something hard: nat-c b4.de*

○ - **Root**: spig h1*
- **Upper** part: am-m ptk1

FORMICATION: (↗*Itching*) aesc agar b4.de* am-c b4.de* ambr b7.de* arg-met k* arg-n bg2 arn k* aur b4.de* bar-c bg2 bell b4.de* borx b4a.de* bry b7.de* *Calc* b4a.de camph bg2 caps b7.de* carb-v b4.de* cham bg2 cic b7.de* *Cina* b7.de* coff bg2 colch b7.de* coloc b4a.de con b4.de* des-ac rbp6 dros b7.de* fl-ac bg2 gran bg2 hep b4a.de* hydrog srj2• ign b7.de* kali-bi bg2 kali-n b4.de* lach b7.de* *M-aust* b7.de mang b4.de* merc b4.de* mez b4.de* mosch b7.de* nat-m b4.de* nat-s bg2 nit-ac b4.de* nux-m b7.de* *Nux-v* b7.de* petr bg2 ph-ac b4.de* phos bg2 plat b4.de* psor bg2 **Ran-b** b7.de* ran-s b7.de* rheum b7.de* rhod b4a.de* rhus-t b7.de* sabad b7.de* sep b4.de* sil bg2 spig b7.de* spong b7.de* sul-ac b4a.de *Sulph* k* teucr b7.de* thuj k* zinc b4.de*
- **accompanied** by:
  - **coryza**: borx b4a.de *Carb-v* b4a.de
  - **sneezing**: carb-v bg2 plat bg2 teucr bg2

○ • **Throat**; scratching in: kola stb3•
- **insects**; sensation as if from running: rhus-t b7.de

○ - **Dorsum**: con
- **Inside**: am-c arg-met b7a.de aur caps h1* carb-v cench k2 con hep h2* mang a1 med c1 mez ozone sde2• ran-b b7a.de ran-s b7a.de *Sabad* b7a.de spig b7a.de teucr b7a.de
- **Nostril**; inside: arg-met bg2 aur-m bg2 carb-v bg2 *Cina* bg2 *Ran-b* bg2 ran-s bg2 sabad bg2 spig bg2 teucr bg2
- **Root**: *Teucr*
- **Tip**: con kali-n h2* mosch b7a.de* rheum b7a.de*

FRECKLES: lyc a1 **Phos** k ●* **SULPH** k ●*

FROSTBITTEN: *Agar* k* m-aust b7a.de zinc bg2
- **easily**: *Zinc*

FULLNESS, sense of: aesc agar k* all-c alum-sil k2 am-c bg2 anemps br1 asaf **Bapt** k* beryl tpw5* bit-ar wht1• calc bg2 *Cham* k* coca-c sk4• cupr bg2 cystein-l rly4• echi *Gels* bg2 glon bg2 hep bg2 hip-ac sp1 kali-bi bg2 **Kali-i** k* ketogl-ac rly4• lac-ac *Lac-c* lac-del hrn2• laur k* merc bg2 nicotam rly4• par k* pen br1 *Phos* k* puls samb bg2 *Senec* k* sulph bg2
- **evening**: beryl tpw5
- **accompanied** by | **catarrh** (See Catarrh - accompanied - nose - fullness)
- **air**; in open:
  - **agg.**: beryl tpw5
  - **amel.**: beryl tpw5*
- **sinuses**; from inflammation of frontal: cystein-l rly4• *Kali-bi* k*
- **warm**:
  - **room**:
    - **agg.**: beryl sp1
    - **amel.**: beryl tpw5

○ - **Around** the nose: calc k*
- **Nostril**:
  - **left** | **high** up: phos
- **Posterior** nares: puls k2
- **Root**: aesc bell bg2 bit-ar wht1• cann-i cund *Gels* haliae-lc srj5• ham bg2 *Kali-bi* k* lac-c nat-p *Par* phos sang **Stict** k*

▽ • **extending** to | **Neck** and clavicle: gels

FUMES agg.; acrid: ant-c b7a.de

GANGRENE: *Ars* hippoz sec a1

GRANULAR:
- **posterior** nares: fago br1
  - **accompanied** by | **itching**: fago br1

HAIR; sensation of: bros-gau mrc1 coc-c bg2 kali-bi bg2* spig bg2 sulph bg2

HARDNESS: aur-m-n bro1 calc k* calc-f bro1 canth carb-an ptk1 con bro1 **Kali-c** k* sep bg2 sulph bg2 thuj bg2
- **mucous** surface, of: iod

Nose

O - **Wings**, of: aur-m aur-m-n bro1 *Calc-p* bro1 guar bro1 rhus-r bro1 *Thuj* k*
- **left**: alum *Thuj*

HAWKING: | **agg.**: coff b7.de* *Rhus-t* b7.de*

HAY FEVER: *(↗Smell - acute - flowers; GENERALS - Allergic)* acon-ac mtf11 adren br1 **Agar** vh1* agath-a nl2• ail **All-c** k* am-c mrr1 ambro c1* anac vh1 antho c1* *Antip* vh1 aral hr1* **Ars** k ●* *Ars-i* k* arum-m mtf11 *Arum-t* k* **Arund** k* asc-c c1* *Aur-m-n* wbt2• bad k* benz-ac bro1* *Brom* bros-gau mrc1 calc rb2* *Calc-ln* c1 calc-sil k2 camph c1 *Carb-v* carc gk6* chin br1 chinin-ar bro1* cocain bro1* con rb2 cortiso sp1 cumin mtf11 cupr-act br1* cycl dioxi rbp6 *Dulc* k* dys pte1*• euph bg2* euph-pi bro1* *Euphr* k* fuma-ac mtf11 galph mtf11 **Gels** k ●* graph kl grin kl hep bro1* ichth br1 iod k* ip bg2* just br1 kali-bi k* *Kali-i* k* *Kali-p* k* kali-s mha* kali-s-chr c1* ketogl-ac mtf11 lach k* lec oss• linu-u c2* lob-s c2 **Lyc** ●* lycpr br1 mag-m mrr1 malar c2 mang-p rly4*• med bg1 meph j5.de merc rb2 merc-i-f bro1* merc-k-i c1* moni rfm1• *Naja* k* napht c1* naphtin br1* nat-ar mrr1 nat-c k2* nat-i c2* **NAT-M** k ●* nat-p mrr1 nat-s fs nat-sil fd3.de• nux-m mrr1 nux-v k* phle bg1* phos rb2* *Pin-con* oss2• poll bro1* **Psor** k* **Puls** k ●* pycnop-sa mrz1 *Ran-b* k* rhus-t k1 ros-d c2* **Sabad** k* *Sang* k* sangin-n c2* senec bg2* seneg c2 sep rb2* *Sil* k* sin-a c1* **Sin-n** k* skook c1* solid bro1 *Stict* k* succ-ac bg1* succ-xyz c2 sul-ac mrr1 sul-i k2 *Sulph* rb2* suprar bro1 syc pte1*• teucr thres-a sze7• thuj mrr1 trif-p bro1* tritic-vg fd5.de **Tub** al2* *Wye* k* [lith-i stj2 mang-i stj2 mang-n stj2]
- **accompanied** by:
  - **stuffed** up nose (See Obstruction - accompanied - hay)
  - O **Ears**; itching in: *Agar* mrr1
  - **Eustachian** tube; complaints of (See EAR - Eustachian - accompanied - hay)
  - **Eyes**; burning (See EYE - Pain - hay - burning)
  - **Palate**; itching in: *Agar* mrr1 dioxi rbp6
- **asthmatic** breathing; with: *(↗RESPIRATION - Asthmatic - hay; from)* agath-a nl2• ambro ll **Ars** k ●* *Ars-i* arum-t ptk1 *Bad* bit-ar wht1• *Carb-v* *Carc* mlr1• chinin-ar st chlor ptk1 *Dulc* *Euphr* k* **Iod** k* kali-i lach linu-u kr1 *Naja* k* **Nat-s** k ● **Nux-v** k ●* op kl *Sabad* k* sang k* sep ptk1* sil *Sin-n* stict
- **August**; in: **All-c** ambro vh1 dulc k* gels naja
  - **until** fall: sin-n st
- **autumn** agg.: *Dulc* mrr1 psor k2
- **beginning**: ros-d br1
- **chronic**: carc fb
- **dust** agg.: *(↗GENERALS - Dust - agg.)* lycpr br1
- **eating**; after | **amel.**: dioxi rbp6
- **frequent**: carc fb*
- **goldenrod**; from: solid br1
- **grass**; newly mown: dulc k1
- **grief**; from: nat-m gk
- **hands** in warm water agg.: dioxi rbp6
- **periodical** | **year**; every: *Bamb-a* stb2.de•
- **prophylaxis**: ars bro1* kali-p ptk1 psor bro1*
- **spring**; in: *All-c* *Gels* lach naja sabad k1 sang k1* tub kr1
- **sun**; exposure to: dioxi rbp6
- **temperature** agg.; change of: dioxi rbp6
- **warm** room | **amel.**: lec oss•

HEADACHE: | **after** | **agg.**: alum b4a.de ant-c b7.de* carb-an b4a.de dulc b4a.de mag-c b4a.de
- **during** | **agg.**: *Acon* b7a.de coff b7.de* m-arct b7.de phos bg2

HEAT in: *(↗Smell - acute - flowers)* aesc a1 agar bg2 aloe bg2 alum bg2 am-m bg2 anis bg1 ant-c bg2 *Apis* arn k* **Ars** bg2* asar bg2 aur bg2 bar-c bg2 bar-m *Bell* k* bov bg2 brom a1 calad k* cann-i cann-s k* canth k* caps b7.de* *Carb-an* bg2* caust bg2* *Cham* k* chel bg2* **Chin** k* *Cina* b7.de* cinnb a1 clem k* coff b7.de* colch k* cor-r k* crot-c sk4• crot-h cycl a1 daph k* dios a1 eup-pur euphr fago a1 gran a1 *Graph* k* guare hell k* *Hep* k* hyos k* iod bg2 *Kali-bi* k* kali-c k* kali-cy a1 kali-i ptk1 *Kali-n* bg2 *Led* bg2 lepi a1 lyc h2* m-ambo bg2 m-arct b7.de mag-m k* *Merc* bg2* merc-i-r k* *Mez* bg2 mosch bg2 naja nat-c bg2 nat-m bg2 nit-ac bg2 *Nux-v* k* op a1 petr bg2 **ph-ac** bg2 phos bg2* phys a1* phyt bg2 podo bg2 psor k* ptel a1 **Puls** bg2 rheum b7.de* rhod bg2 rhus-g a1 rhus-r rhus-t bg2 ruta k* sabad ptk1 sang k* sars bg2 sil bg2* sin-n mrr1 spig bg2 stann bg2 stront-c k* sulph bg2 thuj k* verat k* vinc k* zinc bg2
- **right**: *Merc-i-r* k*
- **left**: cina coff k* nat-m sin-n mrr1
- O **Below**: rhus-t h1*
- **air** feels hot; expired: **Kali-bi** k* *Rhus-t* h1* sulph bg2

Heat in: ...
- **bleed**; as if it would: *(↗RESPIRATION - Asthmatic - hay; from)* cann-s sep wd1
- **breath** seems hot: allox tpw4 **Kali-bi** petr-ra shn4• ptel *Rhus-t* k*
- **chill**; during: bell bg2 rhus-t bg2
- **cold** to touch: am
- **coryza**; during: nux-v b7.de
- **fever**; during: am ptk1
- **inspiration** agg.: allox sp1
- **sensation** of: canth bg2 coff bg2 colch bg2 rheum bg2 thuj bg2
- **sneezing**; when: anis c1 com ptk1
- **streaming** from nose; as if: kali-bi bg2 rhus-t bg2 sabad bg2 stront-c bg2

O - **Inside**: bamb-a stb2.de•
- **Nostrils**: cina gsy1
  - **catarrh**; with: *Acon* vh1
- **Posterior** nares: *Acon* ptk1 aesc bg2* arg-n bg2 colch bg2 lyc ptk1 phos bg2 sep ptk1 zinc-i ptk1
- **Root**: carc fd2.de• **Kali-bi**
- **Tip**: aesc vh1 bell caps k* con m-arct k* *Nat-m*
  - **evening**: *Caps* sin-n
  - **weather**; in warm: bell

HEATED; FROM BECOMING: bry b7a.de sep b4a.de *Thuj* b4a.de

HEAVINESS: alum bg2 am-c k* carb-v k* *Caust* *Cham* k* colch k* *Crot-h* euphr *Ind* bg1* kali-bi bg2* merc k* *Phyt* bg1* samb k* *Sang* sil k* *Stann* k* [heroin sdj2]
- **stooping** agg.: am-m k* sil k*
- **weight** hanging down; sensation of a: *Kali-bi* k* merc
- O **Bones**: colch

O - **Bones**: colch bg2
- **Dorsum** (= Bridge): glon bg2
- **Root**: bism k* cinnb glon bg2 *Kali-bi* mrr1 kali-i mrr1 melal-alt gya4 *Sang* stann staph h1 stict bg2 ther
- **Sinuses**: stann h2*

HOLLOW sensation in nose: galeoc-c-h gms1•

INFLAMMATION: *(↗Catarrh; Discharge)* acon bro1 agar b4.de* allox sp1 alum am-c mrr1 *Apis* bro1 *Arn* k* *Ars* k* *Asaf* asar *Aur* k* aur-m k* *Bell* k* borx k* brom mrr1 *Bry* k* cadm-s *Calc* k* cann-s k* *Canth* k* carb-ac mrr1 carb-an bro1 *Caust* cist k* coch *Con* k* *Crot-h* cystein-l rly4• diphtox jl2 dulc fd4.de euph b4a.de euphr bg2 ferr-i bro1 *Ferr-pic* bro1 *Fl-ac* k* graph bro1* hed sp1 *Hep* k* *Hippoz* k* ip k2 *Kali-i* bro1* kali-n b4.de* **Lach** k* lat-m bnm6• manc mrr1 mang k* mangi br1 med k* medus bro1 *Merc* k* merc-c bro1 *Merc-i-r* k* mez bg2 mucor jl2 naphtin bro1 *Nat-c* k* *Nat-m* k* *Nit-ac* bro1 nux-v k* oscilloc jl2 parathyr jl2 phel **Phos** k* plb k* *Puls* k* rad-br sze8• ran-b k* rat *Rhus-t* k* sacch-a fd2.de• samb mrr1 *Sep* k* sil bg2* spong fd4.de stann b4a.de* stict mrr1 **Sulph** k* titan br1 tub-a jl2 ust c2 vac jl2 verat k*
- **one side**: nat-m b4a.de
- **right**: **Aur** cystein-l rly4• dulc fd4.de merc-i-r k*
- **left**: cist goss ham fd3.de• *Nat-m* sacch-a fd2.de•
- **acute**: streptoc jl2
- **allergic**: cortiso mtf11 galph mtf11 graph mrr1 *Kali-i* mrr1
- **atrophic** (See Ozena)
- **chronic**: aesc bg2 alum bg2 arg-n bg2 ars bg2 arum-t bg2 bar-c bg2 brom bg2 carb-v bg2 caust bg2 cinnb bg2 *Cist* bg2* coc-c bg2 diphtox jl2 graph bg2 hep bg2 hippoz br1* hydr bg2 kali-m bg2 lach bg2 lyc bg2 *Med* mrr1 merc bg2* nat-c bg2 petr bg2 prot jl2 psor mtf33 puls bg2 rumx bg2 sang bg2 seneg bg2 sep bg2 strept-ent jl2 streptoc jl2 toxo-g jl2 v-a-b jl2*
- **coryza**; during: *Calc* b4a.de hep b4a.de lyc b4.de* mang b4.de* merc b4.de* ph-ac b4a.de stann b4.de*
- **drunkards**; in: *Ars* bell *Calc* hep *Lach* merc *Puls* *Sulph*
- **purulent**: penic mtf11 psor jl2 strept-ent jl2 vac mtf11
  - **children**; in: alum bro1 arg-n bro1 *Calc* bro1 cycl bro1 hep bro1 iod bro1 *Kali-bi* bro1 *Lyc* bro1 nat-c bro1 nit-ac bro1
- **spasmodic**: flav jl2 psor jl2

O - **Bones**: anan k* asaf k* **Aur** *Aur-m* **Hep** still k*
- **Ethmoid** bone: syph jl2
- **Inside**: *Agar* k* *Alum* bg2 am-m h2* ars k2 asaf bg2 **Aur** bg2 *Bell* borx *Bry* k* *Calc* k* canth k* carb-v bg2 caust bg2 cham chel cic bg2 cist cocc k* con k* goss graph bg2 *Hep* *Kali-bi* k* kali-c bg2 *Kali-i* *Lach* bg2 lyc bg2 mag-c bg2 mag-m bg2 mang k* merc k* mez bg2 nat-c bg2 *Nat-m* nit-ac bg2 *Nux-v* k* petr k2 **Phos** k*

- **Inside**: ...
polyg-h psor bg2 *Puls* bg2 ran-b k* rhus-t k* sabad k2 sacch-a fd2.de• sep bg2 sil k* stann *Sulph* k* thuj bg2 verat k*
  - **right**: allox tpw4
  - **left**: allox tpw4
- **Margins** of: bar-c mez k* spong fd4.de
- **Nasopharynx** (See THROAT - Inflammation - nasopharynx)
- **Periosteum**: asaf bro1 *Aur* bro1 merc bro1 *Phos* bro1
- **Posterior** nares: alum bg2 bar-m bg2 bell bg2 colch bg2 gels bg2 graph bg2 ign bg2 lach bg2 lyc bg2 merc bg2 nux-v bg2 phyt bg2 sang bg2 wye bg2
- **Septum**: alum h2* psor k* sars
- **Sinus** (See Sinuses; GENERALS - Inflammation - sinuses)
- **Tip**: *Aur* bell k* borx k* bry *Carb-an* **Caust** cist bro1 crot-h euph bro1 kali-c *Kali-n* k* *Lach* lyc merc k* nicc k* *Nit-ac* k* phos *Rhus-t* k* *Sep* k* sulph k*
- **Wings**: nit-ac h2* sacch-a fd2.de• sulph h2*
  - **left**: gink-b sbd1•

INSPIRATION:
- **agg.**: ant-c bg2 chin b7.de* ign b7.de* kreos bg2 sep b4.de*
- **nose** agg.; through: *Ant-c* b7.de* ign b7.de

IRRITATION: bell-p sp1 *Kali-perm* br1 petr-ra shn4• vanad br1 vero-o rly3•
○ - **Nostrils**:
  - **accompanied** by | **sneezing** (See Sneezing - accompanied - nostrils - irritation)

ITCHING: *(↗Formication)* acon bg2 acon-ac rly4• *Agar* k* agath-a nl2• agn b7.de* *Aids* nl2• ail k* alum k* alum-p k2 alum-sil k2 am-c k* am-m k* ang bg2 apis k* arg-met b7.de* *Arg-n* k* arge-pl rwt5• arn k* ars bg2 ars-met **Arum-t** k* arund k* asar b7.de* asc-t k* *Aur* k* aur-ar k2 aur-m k* aur-s bamb-a stb2.de• bar-c bell k* berb k* borx k* *Bov* k* brach k* brom k* bros-gau mrc1 bry b7.de* *Calc* k* *Calc-p* k* *Calc-s* camph k* cann-s b7.de* canth bg2* caps k* carb-ac k* carb-an b4.de* *Carb-v* k* carbn-s card-m **Caust** k* cench k2 cere-b a1 *Cham* *Chel* k* chin k* chord-umb rly4• **Cina** k* cinnb k* cinnm c1 cob cob-n sp1 coc-c k* colch k* coloc b4.de* com k* con k* *Crot-c* cystein-l rly4• dulc fd4.de euphr bg2* fago a1 falco-pe nl2• ferr a1 ferr-i a1 ferr-m k* fil bro1 fl-ac germ-met srj5• gran bg2 grat k* hell k* hep b4a.de* hipp a1 hist sp1 hydr k* ign k* iod bro1 ip k* jatr-c kali-ar kali-bi bg2* *Kali-c* k* kali-m k2 *Kali-n* k* kali-p kali-s ketogl-ac rly4• lac-c lac-loxod-a hrn2• lach b7.de* lat-m bnm6• laur b7.de* lepi a1 lipp a1 lob-s a1 *Lyc* k* lyss k* mag-c b4.de* *Mag-m* k* med k* menis a1 *Merc* k* merc-sul merl k* *Mez* k* moni rfm1• morph a1* mosch b7a.de* mur-ac b4.de* napht c1 narcot a1 nat-c b4.de* nat-ox rly4• nat-p bg2* nat-sil fd3.de• neon srj5• *Nit-ac* k* *Nux-v* k* ol-an a1* olib-sac wmh1 olnd k* op bg2* pen a1 *Ph-ac* k* phos k* phyt bg2 pin-s a1* plat b4.de* plb b7.de* podo bg2 puls k* rat k* rhod b4a.de* rhus-t bg2* rhus-v a1 ribo rly4• *Ros-d* wla1 ruta fd4.de *Sabad* b7.de* samb k* sanic sars b4.de sel b7.de* seneg b4.de* sep k* *Sil* k* sinus rly4• *Spig* k* spong fd4.de squil staph k* stront-c b4.de* stry k* succ-ac br1 sul-ac b4a.de sul-i k2* **Sulph** k* sumb a1 syph jl2 tarent a1 *Teucr* k* ther k* thres-a sze7• thuj k* til c1 tritic-vg fd5.de tub k* (non:uran-met k) uran-n urt-u k* vanil fd5.de verat bg2 vinc k* viol-t b7.de* zinc k* zing a1* [helia stj7]
- **right**: cystein-l rly4• fl-ac k* gins hydr merl *Nux-m* vh **Nux-v** bg1* sars spig h1* *Teucr*
- **left**: aids nl2• bad carb-v h2* cench k2 chel k* cob k* dulc fd4.de falco-pe nl2• grat hell *Hydr* hr1 ignis-alc es2• laur mag-c a1 nat-m h2* nat-sil fd3.de• pall plb a1 rhus-r sacch-a fd2.de• sars k* staph
  - **feather**; as from a: ros-d wla1
  - **hair**; as from a: kali-bi ptk2
- **evening**: carb-v h2* coloc k* kali-n h2* lach k* phys a1 puls k* sil k* spong fd4.de sulph a1
- **night**: am-m bg1 arg-n bg1* cystein-l rly4• *Gamb* bg1* ham fd3.de• hydr a1
- **accompanied** by cough (See COUGH - Accompanied - nose - itching)
- **alternating** with | **Anus**; itching in: sabad ptk1
- **burning**: *Agar* *Aur* falco-pe nl2•
- **chill**; during: *Cina* bg2 sil bg2 spig bg2
- **eating**; while: jatr-c k* lach k*
- **epistaxis**; before: am-m h2* arg-met h1
- **feather**; as from a: bamb-a stb2.de•
- **fever**; during: *Cina* b7a.de*
- **menses**; after: *Sulph* k*

Itching: ...
- **painful**: mag-c h2*
- **perspiration**; during: *Cina* bg2 lach bg2 merc bg2 *Sel* bg2 sil bg2
- **rubs**: agar h2* aloe sne arg-n bell h1 borx h2* caust bg3 **CINA** k ● hell ptk2 lyc bg2 med pc sabad bg3 seneg bg2 sil staph sne teucr bg2
  - **attacks**, before: bufo hr1
  - **children**; in:
    - **starts** out of sleep and rubs nose; child: lyc k*
    - **waking**; on: sanic mtf33
  - **constantly**: arg-n k* bell mtf33 borx bg1* caust mtf33 **Cina** k* med pc napht c1 sil k*
- **scratch** until raw; must: lat-m bnm6• limest-b es1•
- **worms**; from: *Santin* br1 spig c1

○ - **Bones**: spong h1*
- **Dorsum**: alum h2* chin h1* con h2* samb h1* spig h1*
- **External** nose: agar bg2 bov bg2 calc bg2 caust bg2 nat-m bg2 phos bg2 staph bg2
- **Inside**: acon-ac rly4• *Agar* k* *Agn* bro1 all-c bro1 am-c k* am-m k* ambr h1* anac *Arg-met* *Arg-n* k* arn *Ars* k* ars-h ars-i bro1 **Arund** k* asar h1* asc-t a1 *Aur* k* aur-m k* aur-s k2 bamb-a stb2.de• bar-m bell benz-ac berb k* bit-ar wht1• borx k* brach k* brom k* bufo *Calc* calc-p calc-s k2 camph k* *Caps* k* carb-ac c1 *Carb-v* card-m **Caust** k* *Cham* chel *Cina* k* *Colch* colum-p sze2• con k* corn k* cupr cystein-l rly4• eug k* euphr fago a1* ferr bg2* gamb glyc bro1 gran graph grat a1 *Hep* *Hydr* bro1 hydrog srj2• hyper ign kali-ar *Kali-bi* kali-c kali-n h2* *Kali-s* kali-sil k2 kalm ketogl-ac rly4• lac-c laur *Lyc* k* lyss k* mag-c k* mag-m h2* med k* menis a1 *Merc* merl k* mosch mur-ac k* nat-c h2* *Nat-m* k* nit-ac **Nux-v** k* ol-an ozone sde2* petr h2* ph-ac phos plat h2* podo fd3.de• psil ft1 *Puls* pyrid rly4• *Ran-b* k* ran-s rat k* rhod k* ros-d bro1 rumx k2 *Sabad* k* sang k* *Santin* bro1 *Sel* k* seneg k* sep k* *Sil* k* sin-n *Spig* spong fd4.de staph bg2 *Stict* stram *Stront-c* k* sul-ac mrr1 **Sulph** k* syph k* tab *Teucr* k* ther k* *Thuj* k* tritic-vg fd5.de (non:uran-met k) uran-n urt-u ust vanil fd5.de wies a1 *Wye* bro1* *Zinc* k* zinc-p k2 zing [spect dfg1]
  - **right**: *All-c* am-c bit-ar wht1• card-m con h2* cystein-l rly4• dros h1* hydr kali-c kali-n nat-m *Teucr* zinc
    - **then** left: aur-m card-m verat-v
  - **left**: acon-ac rly4• androc srj1• arg-met asc-t bell benz-ac brom calc camph carb-v card-m caust cob coloc grat kali-bi kola stb3• lachn a1 mag-c h2* mang med ol-an plut-n srj7• rhus-r sars spong syph k* tung-met bdx1• zinc h2*
    - **then** right: brom
  - **coryza**; during: am-m b7.de* caps b7.de* carb-v b4.de* hep b4a.de mag-c b4.de* mosch b7a.de *Nux-v* b7.de* plat b4a.de *Puls* b7.de* sabad b7.de* sep b4.de* spig b7.de* staph b7.de* *Teucr* b7a.de

▽ • **extending** to:
    - **Ear**: wye mrr1
    - **Pharynx**: tritic-vg fd5.de
- **Nostrils**: arund br1 brach hr1 carb-v h2* caust h2* chord-umb rly4• con h2* ketogl-ac rly4• lac-h sk4• nat-sil fd3.de• ol-an hr1 olib-sac wmh1 ph-ac h2* plat h2* rad-br c11 ros-d wla1 spong fd4.de *Syph* hr1* tell rsj10• [heroin sdj2]

○ • **Inside**: arund mrr1 brach br1 cob-n sp1
- **Posterior** nares: ail bg2* fago br1 kali-p ptk1 lac-h htj1• nux-v ptk1 ran-b ptk1 *Wye* br1
  - **accompanied** by | **granular** appearance (See Granular - posterior - accompanied - itching)
- **Root**: asc-t a1 con inul merc olnd
- **Septum**: asc-t a1 benz-ac k* bry *Iod* k* *Kali-bi* k* sel a1
- **Tip**: agn k* anag vh1 ars-met brucel sa3• calc-p k* calc-s k2 cann-s a1 carb-an k* carbn-s **Caust** k* *Chel* k* choc srj3• *Cina* bro1 colch *Con* k* hydrc a1* kali-n h2* laur k* med c1* merc *Morph* bro1 mosch mur-ac ol-an k* paeon *Petr* k* petr-ra shn4• ph-ac psor a1 rat k* rheum rhus-v ros-d wla1 *Santin* bro1 *Sep* k* *Sil* k* stront-c bg2 sulph h2* symph fd3.de• vanil fd5.de [heroin sdj2 tax jsj7]
- **Wings** (= alae nasi): agar k* alum aur calc cann-s carb-v bro1 carneg-g rwt1• **Caust** k* *Cina* bro1 merc nat-m nat-p bro1 *Nat-s* k* nat-sil fd3.de• olib-sac wmh1 ros-d wla1 *Santin* bro1 sars k* sel k* sil k* sulph k* tritic-vg fd5.de [tax jsj7]
  - **right**: fl-ac laur spig staph thuj tritic-vg fd5.de
  - **left**: ars-met bad k* bell hell h1* laur mag-c nat-m h2* nat-sil fd3.de• olib-sac wmh1 pall hr1 staph h1*

JERKING at root of nose; sudden: *Hyos* a1*

Nose

KNOBBY: *Ars* ptk1 aur bg2*
O - **Tip**: *(↗Swelling - knotty)* *Aur* k* calc bg2

LACERATION: calen

LIFTING agg.: *Rhus-t* b7a.de

LIPOMA: *Sulph*

LIQUIDS:
- **come** out through the nose on attempting to swallow: *(↗LARYNX - Paralysis - larynx; THROAT - Liquids; THROAT - Paralysis)* anan **Arum-t** k* aur *Bar-c* bell k* bism *Borx* b4a.de canth k* *Carb-ac* caust k* cocc ptk1 cupr cur diph br1* gels k* hyos k* ign kali-bi *Kali-perm* k* **Lac-c** k* **Lach** k* **Lyc** k* *Merc* k* *Merc-c* *Merc-cy* *Nat-m* op k* petr k* **Phos** b4a.de* *Phyt* *Plb* puls sil *Sul-ac* k* *Sulph* b4a.de

O - **Sinuses** on attempting to swallow; pass into merc b4a.de *Petr* b4a.de *Phos* b4a.de

LONG:
- **pointed**; and (See Pointed)
- **sensation** as if elongated: choc srj3•

LOOSENESS; sensation as if: | **Bones**: kali-bi bg2 sulph bg2

LUMP: | **Posterior** nares: aesc ptk1 cist bg3* hydr bg3* kali-bi bg3* *Lach* bg3* nat-m bg3* phos bg3* positr nl2• sep bg3* spig bg3* stict bg3* sulph bg3* teucr bg3* zinc bg3*

LUPUS: alumn k* am-caust vh1 ars bg2* *Aur-m* k* calc bro1 *Caust* k* cic bro1 graph bg2 hydr bro1 *Hydrc* bro1 *Kali-bi* k* kali-chl **Kreos** k* merc bg2* nat-m bg2 nit-ac bg2 *Phyt* k* rhus-t bro1 sep bg2 sil bg2 staph bg2 sulph bg2* thuj k* tub bro1 x-ray bro1
- **left** side: caust *Kreos* k*
- **exedens**: cist k* *Hydrc* k* jug-c k* kali-bi k2 phyt k* thuj k*

O - **Wing**, on: *Aur-m* *Hydrc*

LYING:
- **agg.**: puls bg3*
- **bed**; in | **agg.**: caps b7.de*

MEMBRANE, mucous: mim-p skp7• morg-p pte1• petr k2 psor jl2
- **atrophy**: ambr k2
- **destroyed**: am-m
- **detached**: *Elaps*
- **gangrenous**: *Ars*

MENOPAUSE; during: bell bg2 bry bg2 ham bg2 *Lach* bg2 nux-v bg2 puls bg2 sep bg2 sul-ac bg2 sulph bg2

MENSES:
- **absent** agg.: sep bg2
- **after** | **agg.**: sulph bg2
- **before** | **agg.**: bar-c bg2 bry bg2 con bg2 dig bg2 hydr bg2 *Lach* bg2 nat-c bg2 nat-s bg2 nux-v bg2 phos bg2 sulph bg2 verat b7.de*
- **during**:
  - **agg.**: carb-an b4.de* nat-s bg2 sep b4.de*
  - **beginning** of menses | **agg.**: mag-c bg2
- **suppressed** menses; from: *Bry* b7a.de *Puls* b7a.de

MERCURY; after abuse of: asaf bg2 **Aur** b4a.de* bell bg2 con b4a.de *Hep* bg2 *Lach* bg2 sil b4a.de sulph bg2

MOIST after eating: caust h2*

MOROSENESS agg.; after: ars bg2

MOTION: *(↗Dilated)*
- **agg.**: nux-v b7.de*

O - **Wings**; of: *(↗Dilated)*
  - **constant**: *Ammc* diph bg3
  - **fan**-like: ammc *Ant-t* k* ars ptk1 bapt bg1* bell ptk1 *Brom* k* *Chel* k* chlf bg1 cupr ptk1 diph ptk1 ferr c1 gad bro1 *Iod* k* kali-bi bg1 kali-br bro1 **Lyc** k* merc-i-f ol-j bg1 *Phos* k* phys bg2 pyrog k* rhus-t ptk1 *Spong* k* sul-ac k* zinc k* [calc-br stj1 mag-br stj1]
    - **asthma**; in: **Lyc** mrr1
    - **nervous**: phos mtf33
    - **palpitation**, with: lyc ptk1
    - **pneumonia**, in: *Ammc* *Ant-t* k* chel c1 *Kreos* **Lyc** k* *Phos* *Sulph* k*

NECROSIS: *(↗Caries)* aur bro1 kali-bi bro1 *Phos*

NODOSITIES: *Alum* b4a.de **Ars** k* **Aur** bar-m k* cann-s b7.de* lyc bg2 merc-i-r k* nat-c h2 *Sulph*
- **surrounded** by red swelling like acne rosacea: cann-s

O - **Internal** nose: ars bro1
- **Root** | **painless**: sep

NOISES: alum bg2 sabad bg2
- **blowing** the nose; on: mez bg2

NOSTRILS drawn in: aeth ptk1 cina bg3*

NUMBNESS: acon bg3* ars bg2 ars-h k* ars-met asaf k* bell bg3* cadm-s k* ferr k* jug-c a1* kali-bi bg2* lyc med k* nat-c bg1 nat-m bg2* nux-m olnd k* phys k* plat k* pyrid rly4• ran-b bro1 sabad bro1 samb k* sang bro1 sil bro1 spig bg2* *Stict* bro1 viol-o b7.de*
- **one** side: *Nat-m* k*
- **accompanied** by | **Head**; pain in (See HEAD - Pain - accompanied - nose - numbness)
- **epistaxis**; with: acon ptk1 bell ptk1 med ptk1
- **snuff**; from: nat-m b4.de* spig b7.de*

O - **Bones**, of: aml-ns k* am k* *Asaf* bg1*
  - **right**: plat
- **Inside**: bamb-a stb2.de• nat-m k*
- **Tip**, of: gels k* viol-o k*

OBSTRUCTION: *(↗Congestion; Coryza - discharge without)* abrom-a ks5 acon k* acon-ac rly4• aeth k* *Agar* k* *Agath-a* nl2• agra br1 aids nl2• ail k* *All-c* k* allox tpw4 *Alum* k* alum-sil k2 am-br k* *Am-c* k* am-caust *Am-m* k* *Ambr* k* ambro bro1 anac k* androc srj1• anemps br1 ant-c k* anthraq rly4• apeir-s mlk9.de apis apoc k* arg-met k* *Arg-n* k* arge-pl rwt5• **Ars** k* **Ars-i** k* ars-met ars-s-f k2 **Arum-t** k* asaf k* atra-r bnm3• **Aur** k* aur-ar k2 aur-i k2 *Aur-m* k* *Aur-m-n* bro1* aur-s k2 bad k* *Bamb-a* stb2.de• bapt k* bar-c k* *Bar-m* bar-s k2 bell b4.de* *Borx* k* *Bov* k* brass-n-o srj5• brom k* bros-gau mrc1 bry k* bufo cact k* cadm-s k* calad **Calc** k* calc-i k2 calc-p a1 *Calc-s* k* camph bro1 cann-s k* **Caps** k* *Carb-ac* k* *Carb-an* k* **Carb-v** k* **Carbn-s** *Cardios-h* rly4• carneg-g rwt1• cassia-s cdd7• castm **Caust** k* cench k2 *Cham* k* chel k* *Chin* k* chinin-ar chlor k* choc srj3• chord-umb rly4• cic k* cimic cina k* clem a1 cob k* coc-c k* coff colch k2 coli gmj1 *Coloc* k* **Con** k* cop k* cor-r k* cortico tpw7 crot-c sk4• crot-t k* *Cupr* k* dendr-pol sk4• *Dig* k* dios k* dream-p sdj1• dros k* *Dulc* k* echi *Elaps* k* ephe-si hsj1• eucal bro1 eup-per ferr-i ferr-ma a1 fl-ac k* *Form* bro1 galeoc-c-h gms1• gard-j vlr2• gels k* glyc bro1 **Graph** k* grat k* haliae-lc srj5• *Ham* helia c2* *Hell* helo-s rwt2• *Hep* k* hippoc-k szs2 *Hydr* k* *Hydrog* srj2• ign k* ina-i mlk9.de *Iod* k* *Ip* k* *Kali-ar* **Kali-bi** k* *Kali-c* k* *Kali-chl* *Kali-i* k* kali-m k2 kali-n k* *Kali-p* kali-s kali-sil k2 kalm k* ketogl-ac rly4• kola stb3• kreos lac-ac lac-c k* lac-h sk4• *Lach* k* lap-la sde8.de• lat-m sp1 laur k* lec oss• lem-m br1* limen-b-c hrn2* limest-b es1• lob mrr1 *Luf-op* rsj5• luna kg1• **Lyc** k* m-arct b7.de mag-c k* *Mag-m* k* *Mang* k* mang-act br1 mang-p rly4• med k* mentho bro1 *Merc* k* *Merc-c* *Merc-cy* hr1 *Mez* k* mill k* mosch k* *Mur-ac* k* musca-d szs1 *Nat-ar* k* **Nat-c** k* **Nat-m** k* nat-ox rly4• nat-p *Nat-s* k* nat-sil fd3.de• nauf-helv-li elm2• *Nicc* **Nit-ac** k* *Nux-m* k* **Nux-v** k* oci-sa sp1* ol-an op k* orot-ac rly4• oscilloc jl2 ozone sde2• par k* pen bro1 *Petr* k* petr-ra shn4• ph-ac phel **Phos** k* phys br1 *Phyt* k* pic-ac k* pieri-b mlk9.de plac rzf5• plat k* plb k* plut-n srj7• pot-e rly4• *Propr* sa3• prot pte1* psil ft1 *Psor* k* **Puls** k* rad-br bro1 ran-b k* raph k* rat *Rhod* k* *Rhus-t* k* *Ros-d* wla1 *Rumx* ruta fd4.de *Sabad* k* sal-al blc1• sal-fr sle1• **Samb** k* *Sang* k* *Sangin-n* bro1 sapo bro1 sars k* sec sel k* *Seneg* *Sep* k* **Sil** k* *Sin-n* bro1 sinus rly4• spig k* *Spong* k* *Stann* k* staph k* *Stict* k* stram k* *Sul-ac* k* *Sulph* k* *Sumb* k* syph k* tab tell k* **Teucr** k* ther mrr1 thioc-ac rly4• thuj k* til a1 tritic-vg fd5.de tub ser tub-a jl2 *Tung-met* bdx1• v-a-b jl *Vac* jl2 vanil fd5.de verb k* vinc k* *Zinc* k* zinc-p k2 zing k* [bell-p-sp dcm1 buteo-j sej6 heroin sdj2 nat-caust stj2]
- **one** side: agath-a nl2• alum k* alum-p k2 **Am-m** lp asar b7.de* bell chel k* chlor bg2 coc-c bg1 ferr-ma flav jl2 *Hep* b4a.de* ign k* kreos sne lac-c lac-h sk4• *Lach* bg2* *Lyc* b4a.de m-ambo b7.de m-arct b7.de mez nux-m b7a.de* *Nux-v* petr-ra shn4• phos k* phyt k* plat h2 *Pyrog* bg1* ran-b b7.de* raph bg2 *Rhod* k* sabad k* *Sep* b4a.de *Stann* b4a.de *Staph* k* stront-c sk4• sul-ac k* *Sulph* k* symph fd3.de• teucr til bg2 vinc
  - **coryza**; during: staph b7a.de
- **alternating** sides: acon bro1 am-c bro1 aur-m-n wbt2• bamb-a stb2.de• borx bro1 bros-gau mrc1 *Gels* bg1* hydrog srj2• *Kali-bi* bg1* **Lac-c** k* mag-m bro1 manc bg1 mez nux-v k* ozone sde2• *Phos* k* phyt bg1* plat rhod k* sabad k* sin-n sulph ptk1 thuj bg2 vanil fd5.de

- **right**: abrom-a ks5 aids nl2• alum *Aur-m-n* wbt2• bamb-a stb2.de• bapt k* *Borx* brom k* camph k* carb-v chel h1* chord-umb rly4• croc dulc fd4.de ferr-ma a1 *Gels* k* gink-b sbd1• kali-bi kali-c h2* kali-n h2* kali-s fd4.de* lac-c lac-h sk4• lil-t k* mag-c *Merc* bg1* nat-ar nicc ozone sde2• petr-ra shn4• phyt podo fd3.de• ruta fd4.de *Sars* k* sep spong fd4.de stict stront-c sk4• *Sulph* bg1* symph fd3.de• **Teucr** k* thuj tritic-vg fd5.de xan k* ziz hr1 [heroin sdj2]
  - • **fluent**, left: alum
  - • **then** left: aq-mar skp7*• *Borx* brom k* bros-gau mrc1 chel stront-c sk4•
  - • **waking**; on: samb bat1•
- **left**: alum k* am-c anac apeir-s mlk9.de aq-mar jl* *Arum-t* k* asar k* bamb-a stb2.de• brucel sa3• carb-an carb-v cassia-s ccrh1• chinin-ar chlor choc srj3• cimic dulc fd4.de ham fd3.de• hydrog srj2• kali-s fkr2.de lac-h htj1• mag-c *Mag-m* mag-s nit-ac nux-m olib-sac wmh1 orot-ac rly4• petr-ra shn4• phasco-ci rbp2 plut-n srj7• podo fd3.de• propr sa3• rhod k* ruta fd4.de sec k* sep k* *Sin-n* k* spong fd4.de stann stram k* stront-c sk4• thioc-ac rly4• tritic-vg fd5.de ulm-c jsj8• (non:uran-met k) uran-n [heroin sdj2]
  - • **followed** by | **right**: bros-gau mrc1
  - • **uncovering** any part of the body: stront-c sk4•
  - • **waking**; on: samb bat1•
  - • **water** dropping out; with: bov dulc fd4.de
- **daytime**: caust bg2 mag-c *Naja* *Nux-v* b7a.de tritic-vg fd5.de
  - • **amel.**: cassia-s ccrh1•
- **morning**: aeth *Agath-a* nl2• apoc am arum-t k* bamb-a stb2.de• bell bov *Calc* k* calc-sil k2 *Carb-an* k* carb-v bg2 carneg-g rwt1• con k* dig dulc fd4.de ferr-i gink-b sbd1• ham fd3.de• *Hep* k* iod bg2 *Kali-bi* k* kali-i kali-s fkr2.de lach k* lith-c *Lyc* k* mag-c h2* *Mag-m* marb-w es1• merc-i-r a1 *Nat-ar* nat-m bg2 nat-sil fd3.de• nit-ac *Nux-v* bg2 ozone sde2• par k* petr-ra shn4• *Phos* k* puls k2 rhod k* sacch-a gmj3 sep *Sil* k* spong fd4.de symph fd3.de• tritic-vg fd5.de trom vanil fd5.de
  - • **amel.**: flav jl2
  - • **fluent** during day: *Sil* k*
  - • **rising**:
    - ⁝ **agg.**: lac-h sk4•
    - ⁝ **amel.**: ozone sde2•
  - • **waking**; on: aeth aids nl2• apoc *Aur-m-n* wbt2• *Calc* carb-an carc fd2.de• chord-umb rly4• dioxi rbp6 haliae-lc srj5• ham fd3.de• hydrog srj2• kali-bi *Kali-i* lac-h htj1• nat-ar k2 nit-ac ozone sde2• pant-ac rly4• petr-ra shn4• phyt propr sa3• sal-fr sle1• sil stront-c sk4• symph fd3.de• tritic-vg fd5.de tung-met bdx1• vanil fd5.de [heroin sdj2]
- **forenoon**: carb-an h2* podo fd3.de• sars spong fd4.de vanil fd5.de
- **afternoon**: dulc fd4.de mag-c h2* ruta fd4.de spong fd4.de
- **evening**: ant-c k* calad b7a.de* *Carb-v* k* cimic *Cina* k* dulc fd4.de euphr k* galeoc-c-h gms1• ham fd3.de• *Iod* k* *Kali-bi* *Kali-c* kali-s fd4.de kalm *Lyc* *Mag-m* pitu-a vml2• **Puls** k* *Ran-b* k* sep staph k* symph fd3.de• *Teucr* k* *Thuj* tritic-vg fd5.de vanil fd5.de
- **night**: *Agar* agath-a nl2• **Am-c** k* am-m k* ambr ptk1 ant-c k2 arg-n *Ars* k* ars-i k2 bamb-a stb2.de• bar-i k2 *Bov* bry k2 *Calc* k* calc-sil k2 cassia-s ccrh1• *Caust* k* cheir c1* cortiso gse cycl k2 *Ferr-i* glon hydrog srj2• iod k2 ip kali-bi k2 *Kali-p* kola stb3• **Lyc** k* *Mag-c* *Mag-m* k* *Nat-ar* *Nat-c* k* nat-s k2 nat-sil fd3.de• nicc k* nit-ac **Nux-v** k* oxal-a rly4• phel phos h2* pitu-gl skp7• podo fd3.de• puls k2 ruta fd4.de *Samb* sec sep sil spong fd4.de stict k* stront-c sk4• syph k2* tell tritic-vg fd5.de vanil fd5.de zinc-i bg3* [bell-p-sp dcm1]
  - • **bed** agg.; in: lyc mrr1 vanil fd5.de
  - • **sleep**; during: am-c mrr1
  - • **uncovering** head during day; from: *Nat-m*
  - • **wakes** him: ammc vml3• bamb-a stb2.de• kola stb3• *Mag-c* k* nit-ac *Phyt* k* stict k*
    - ⁝ **3 h**: *Phyt*
- **accompanied** by:
  - • **catarrh** (See Catarrh - accompanied - nose - obstruction)
  - • **coryza**: *Ars* bg2* arum-t bg2 bov bg2 brom bg2 cham bg2 chin bg2 graph bg2 kali-i bg2 kali-n b4a.de *Nux-v* bg2 par b7a.de rhod b4a.de* staphycoc rly4•
    - ⁝ **discharge**; without: mang ptk1
  - • **discharge**: carc fd2.de• dulc fd4.de kali-s fd4.de nauf-helv-li elm2•
    - ⁝ **watery**: am-m bg1 ars bg2* calc bg1 dulc fd4.de mag-m bg1 nauf-helv-li elm2• nit-ac bg1 nux-v bg2 psil ft1 zinc bg2
  - • **hay** fever: ran-b tl1
- **accompanied** by: ...
  - • **sneezing**: aesc bg2 teucr bg2
  - ○ • **Head**; pain in (See HEAD - Pain - accompanied - nose)
- **air** agg.; draft of: dulc vg
- **air**; in open:
  - • **agg.**: arg-n bg1 beryl tpw5 calc bg2 dulc ptk1 naja bg2 *Nat-m* bg1* *Nux-v* bg2 psor k2 *Rhod* bg1* *Rhus-t* bg1* *Sulph* bg1*
  - • **amel.**: arg-n ephe-si hsj1• hydrog srj2• kali-c ptk1 olib-sac wmh1 ozone sde2• petr-ra shn4• **Phos** k •* pic-ac psor mtf33 puls ptk1 rhod rhus-t h1* **Sulph** k •* tritic-vg fd5.de v-a-b jl
- **alternating** with:
  - • **discharge**: *Ars* bell h1 hippoc-k szs2 mag-c mang nat-m olib-sac wmh1 ozone sde2• sal-fr sle1• sang *Sil* sin-n mrr1 tritic-vg fd5.de urol-h rwt•
  - • **dryness**: kali-c k2
  - ○ • **Cheeks**; pain in (See FACE - Pain - cheeks - alternating - nose)
  - • **Throat**; complaints of (See THROAT - Complaints - alternating with - nose)
- **bending** the head forward: ozone sde2•
- **blood** pressure, from high: iod ptk1
- **blowing**:
  - • **agg.**: carb-v a1
  - • **amel.**: ferr-i k2
- **blowing** the nose | **not** amel.: (*↗Blowing the - inclination - amel.)* bamb-a stb2.de• brass-n-o srj5• **Stict** mrr1 tritic-vg fd5.de
- **breathing** | **mouth**; must breath through: am-c ptk1 kali-c ptk1* lyc ptk1 mag-c ptk1 mag-m ptk1* nux-v ptk1 samb ptk1
- **children**; in: (*↗Snuffling - children - newborns)* am-c k* ambr ptk1 apoc ptk1 *Ars* asc-t aur ptk1 carb-v bg2 cham b7a.de* dulc bg2 kali-bi ptk1 *Lyc* ptk1 mag-m mtf33 med ptk1 **Nux-v** b7a.de* osm ptk1 phos ptk1 *Samb* b7a.de* *Syph* ptk1
  - • **nursing** infants•: *Aur* k* *Kali-bi* k* **Lyc** k* **Nux-v** k* *Samb* k*
    - ⁝ **nurse**; child is unable to: samb mrr1
- **chill**; during: bry bg2 calad bg2 *Kali-c* bg2 lyc bg2 nat-c bg2 nux-v bg2 rhus-t bg2 sulph bg2
- **chronic**: bry **Calc** k* calc-s mrr1 *Con* k* fl-ac k* *Kali-s* mrr1 mag-m mtf11 nat-c mrr1 puls mrr1 rauw mtf11 sars k* sel k* serp mtf11 *Sil* k* *Stict* mrr1 *Sulph* k*
- **cold**:
  - • **air**:
    - ⁝ **agg.**: cassia-s ccrh1• dulc bg2 hep br1 kali-s mrr1 petr-ra shn4•
    - ⁝ **amel.**: beryl tpw5 kali-c k2
- **cold**, after every: rhus-t k2 *Sil* k*
- **coryza**:
  - • **amel.**: sil h2*
  - • **discharge**; with | **amel.**: *Lach* bg2
- **cough** agg.; during: ozone sde2•
- **dentition**; during: cheir bro1
- **diphtheria**; in (See THROAT - Membrane - accompanied - nose)
- **discharge**:
  - • **mucus**; of: cic c1
  - • **not** amel.: kali-bi k2 lach k2 naja k2 psor k2 stict k2
  - • **watery**; with (See accompanied - discharge - watery)
  - • **with**: ars bg3 **Arum-t** lp* atp rly4• bros-gau mrc1 bry bg3 calc bg3 chin bg3 cic bg3 graph bg3 hydrog srj2• kali-bi bg3 *Lach* bg3 lap-la sde8.de• *Lyc* lp mag-m bg3 merc bg3 nit-ac bg3 nux-v bg3* osm bg3 puls bg3 sil bg3
  - • **without**: iod mrr1 lem-m mrr1 *Propr* sa3• sil mrr1
- **drink**, inability to: lach
- **eating**; after: nat-c spig
- **epistaxis**; with: acon bg1 calc bg1 puls bg1
- **exertion** | **amel.**: cor-r kkb
- **fever**; during: *Am-c* bg2 bell bg2 bry bg2 *Calad* bg2 calc bg2 dulc bg2 hep bg2 ip bg2 **Lyc** bg2 mur-ac bg2 nat-m bg2 nit-ac bg2 **Nux-v** bg2 petr bg2 phos bg2 puls bg2 rhod bg2 samb bg2 sep bg2 **Sil** bg2 spig bg2 *Sulph* b4a.de*
- **followed** by | **watery** discharge: cassia-s ccrh1•

Nose

- **hay** fever; during (See accompanied - hay)
- **headache**; with (See HEAD - Pain - accompanied - nose)
- **heat** (See warmth)
- **lachrymation**; with: borx k*
- **leaflet**, as from a: bar-c bg2* ign k* kali-i k* mur-ac k*

○ • **Root** of nose: kali-i rb2

- **lying**:
  - **abdomen**; on | **agg.**: bamb-a stb2.de• nat-sil fd3.de•
  - **agg.**: bamb-a stb2.de• bov bg3* bros-gau mrc1 caust k* chinin-ar nat-sil fd3.de• *Nux-m* k* puls bg3 tritic-vg fd5.de vanil fd5.de
  - **side**; on | **agg.** | **side** lain on; of: calc bg2* carb-v bg2 cypra-eg sde6.de• *Rhus-t* bg1* staph bg2*
    - **amel.**: bros-gau mrc1
- **menses** | **before** | **agg.**: *Mag-c* k*
  - **during**:
    - **agg.**: am-c mrr1
    - **beginning** of menses | **agg.**: mag-c b4.de
- **overheated**; when: kali-s mrr1
- **perspiration**:
  - **during**: nux-v b7a.de
  - **suppressed** perspiration; from | **feet**; of: **Sil**
- **pus**, with: aur b4.de* *Calc* k* chinin-ar lach led *Lyc* k* nat-c puls sep **Sil** k*
  - **night**: **Lyc** k*
- **reading** aloud, while: teucr k* verb k*
- **riding** in a carriage agg.: asaf k* aur-m-n k2 *Phyt* k*
- **rising**:
  - **bed**; from:
    - **agg.**: beryl tpw5 vanil fd5.de
    - **amel.**: ham fd3.de• nux-m ozone sde2• tritic-vg fd5.de
- **room**:
  - **agg.**: arg-n bg2 prot jl2 psor mtf33 sulph bg2
  - **amel.**: dulc ptk1
- **sauna** agg.: ozone sde2•
- **sensation** of: agar agath-a nl2• am-m b7.de* ars bg2 arum-t **Aur** k* *Aur-m* k* bar-c k* bit-ar wht1• cann-s *Cham* k* cob k* cop br1 cupr k* dulc fd4.de eucal k* ferr-i graph bg2 *Ham* k* *Hydr* hydrog srj2• kali-bi k* kreos b7a.de lach bg2 laur k* mag-m k* meny k* merc-c k* nat-ar nat-c nat-s k* nux-m b7.de* **Nux-v** k* par b7a.de petr bg2 *Phos* bg2* plb b7.de* podo fd3.de• puls bg2 stann stram k* teucr b7.de* thuj k* verb b7.de* zinc k* zing k*
  - **watery** discharge; with: **Ars** arum-t bov brom chin *Cupr* graph kali-i *Merc-c* nux-v sec sin-n

○ • **Nostril** | **right**: aq-mar skp7• aur corian-s knl6• teucr

  - **Posterior** nares: hydr lac-ac
  - **Sinuses**: haliae-lc srj5• stann h2*
- **sitting** | **amel.**: bamb-a stb2.de•
- **sleep** agg.; during: *Am-c* k* ars k* bamb-a stb2.de• **Lyc** k* nit-ac k2 nux-v bro1 samb bro1 staphycoc rly4• *Stict*
- **sneezing**:
  - **after**: brom a1* carb-v h2* phos h2* spong fd4.de sul-ac h2*
    - **amel.**: flav jl2 naja mtf33
  - **agg.**: luf-op rsj5• ulm-c jsj8•
    - **Nostrils** stick together: carb-an
- **stool** | **after** | **agg.**: hep b4a.de*
  - **during** | **agg.**: (non:hep h2)
- **stooping** agg.: agar k* ozone sde2•
- **sudden**: aeth a1 sep
- **suffocating**; with sensation as if: coli gmj1 lob mrr1
- **swelling**, from: cadm-s tritic-vg fd5.de

○ • **Inside**: lem-m br1* tritic-vg fd5.de

- **syphilitic**: phyt
- **talking**:
  - **agg.**: nat-c sil
  - **loudly** agg.: kali-bi ptk1 sil ptk1 teucr ptk1 verb ptk1
- **temperature**; change of: abrom-a ks5
- **walking** in open air | **amel.**: *Kali-c* k* *Puls*

Obstruction: ...

- **warm**:
  - **room**:
    - **agg.**: abrom-a ks5 **Ant-c** k* arg-n *Ars-i* beryl tpw5 calc-p carb-v choc srj3• cycl *Hydr* bg1* **Iod** kali-c **Kali-i** kali-s tl1 nux-v k2 olib-sac wmh1 op **Phos** k ● pic-ac plat **Puls** k* ran-b k* sabad **Sulph** k ● *Thuj* bg1* v-a-b jl
    - **amel.**: cassia-s ccrh1• olib-sac wmh1 psor k2
    - **entering** a warm room; when | **cold** air; from: carc zzh
  - **wet** application | **amel.**: dulc ptk1
- **warmth**:
  - **agg.**: ant-c mrr1
  - **amel.**: cassia-s ccrh1• dulc k2
- **weather**:
  - **cold**:
    - **agg.**: kali-s mrr1
    - **wet** | **agg.**: dulc mrr1 lem-m mrr1
  - **warm**:
    - **wet** | **agg.**: *Kali-bi*
  - **wet** | **agg.**: calc bg1 *Dulc* elaps lem-m bg1* *Mang*
- **wisdom** teeth; from irritation of cutting: cheir c1*

○ - **Anterior** part: arg-met b7.de* *Spig* b7.de*

○ • **Nostril**:
    - **right**: pitu-gl skp7•
    - **forenoon**:
      - **10 h** | **amel.**: pitu-gl skp7•

- **High**, in: nat-m ptk1
- **Posterior** nares: anac k* *Calc-s* elaps ptk1 graph b4a.de hydr k* iris k* kali-i k* lyc b4a.de med k* nat-ar petr k* puls *Rhod* b4a.de sep b4a.de sin-n hr1 *Stann* b4a.de staph k* zing
- **Root**, at: arg-n st **Ars** elaps hr1 kali-bi *Kali-i* lith-c *Lyc* med mur-ac h2* nat-s hr par k* sin-n stict sulph h2*
  - **hawking** thick grayish mucus followed by bloody mucus | **amel.**: med c1
  - **painful**: arg-n bg1* kali-bi
- **Sinuses**: dulc mrr1

ODORS; imaginary and real: agn b2.de* alum b2.de* am-m bg2 ambr tsm1 *Anac* b2.de* apoc-a bro1 ars b2.de* *Aur* b2.de* **Bell** b2.de* benz-ac k2 **Calc** b2.de* canth b2.de* chin b2.de* cina k2 con b2.de* cor-r bro1 corv-cor bdg• dig b2.de* dios bro1 *Graph* b2.de* hep b2.de* ign bro1 kali-bi bg2* kreos b2.de* laur b2.de* lyc b2.de* *M-ambo* b2.de *M-arct* b2.de mag-m bro1 manc ptk1 *Meny* b2.de* merc b2.de* mez b2.de* mosch k2 *Nit-ac* b2.de* *Nux-v* b2.de* **Par** b2.de* ph-ac b2.de* phos b2.de* plb b2.de* *Puls* b2.de* sang bro1 *Seneg* b2.de* sep b2.de* sil b2.de* spong fd4.de *Sulph* b2.de* tritic-vg fd5.de valer b2.de* vanil fd5.de *Verat* b2.de* zinc-chr ptk1

- **acid** (See sour)
- **acrid**, pungent: sulph b4a.de
- **agreeable**: *Agn* k* anh vh1 olib-sac wmh1 positr nl2• puls k*
- **almonds**, bitter: asaf bg2 laur k*
- **animals**: corv-cor bdg•
  - **back** part of nose; in: (non:con h2)
- **bad**:
  - **morning**: kreos puls
  - **coryza**; during (See Coryza - accompanied - odor)
  - **waking**; on: maias-l hrn2•
- **beer**, sour: *Bell* thuj k*
- **blood**, of: nux-v k* psor k* sil k*
  - **cold**; during: trios rsj11•
- **books**; of musty: allox tpw4*
- **brandy**: aur k*
- **bread** | **foul**: par b7a.de
- **brimstone** (See sulphur)
- **broth**: olib-sac wmh1
- **burning**:
  - **clothes**: taosc iwa1•
  - **something**: anac k* aur k* bapt bg2 berb bg2 calc b2.de* graph k* nux-v k* puls bg2 sulph k* vanil fd5.de [tax jsj7]

- **burning**: ...
  - **tinder** in the morning: anac k*
- **burnt**:
  - **feathers**: bapt ptk1
  - **hair**: graph k* positr nl2• sulph k* tritic-vg fd5.de
  - **horn**: puls bg2 sulph
  - **sponge**: anac k*
  - **wood**: haliae-lc srj5• tritic-vg fd5.de
- **cabbage**, of: benz-ac k*
- **cadaverous**: *Bell* b4a.de chin k* vichy-g c1
- **cancer**; like: cadm-s lyc b4.de* sulph
- **catarrh**; as of: graph ptk1 puls ptk1 sulph ptk1
  - **old** catarrh: androc srj1• ars *Graph* k* merc k* **Puls** k ●* **SULPH** k ●*
- **chalk**, food smells like: sulph h2
- **cheese**, of: *Nux-v* k*
- **chemical**: bamb-a stb2.de• musca-d szs1 plut-n srj7•
  - **toxic**: plut-n srj7•
- **chicken** dung: anac
- **clothes**; like old: m-ambo b7.de*
- **coffee**; of: ozone sde2• **Puls** k ●* spong fd4.de
- **coppery**: antip vh1
- **corpse**; like a (See cadaverous)
- **coryza** in posterior nares; as if from: con h2*
- **cucumbers**, like: vichy-g c1
- **drinks** smell putrid: *Nux-v*
- **dung**; as of: manc ptk1
- **dust**, of: benz-ac k* m-arct b7.de*
- **earth**; as of: anac b2.de* *Calc* b2.de* m-ambo b2.de m-arct b2.de sulph b2.de* *Verat* b2.de*
- **feces**, of: *Chel* bg2* crot-t bg2 dios bg2 m-arct b7.de sulph bg2 vanil fd5.de
- **fermented** beer, of: agn bell thuj
- **fetid**: ail k2 arg-n asaf *Aur* k* **Bell** k* benz-ac ptk1 *Calc* k* *Carbn-s* *Chel* chlor chr-ac crot-t cub br1 elaps *Graph* k* iod **Kali-bi** k* kali-s fd4.de kreos lac-c meny k* merc nit-ac k* nux-v **Par** k* petr k2 ph-ac k* **Phos** k* *Plb* psor al2 *Puls* k* sarr *Sep* sil **Sulph** k* valer bg2 verat
  - **blowing** the nose agg.: aur
  - **breathing** through nose, when: nit-ac
- **fish**-brine, of: agn *Bell* colch cypra-eg sde6.de• elaps thuj k*
  - **blowing** the nose agg.: bell
- **flowers**: sulph bg2
- **food**; of: nat-m h2
- **foul** (See fetid)
- **fruit**: musca-d szs1
- **garlic**, sensitive to: sabad k* tritic-vg fd5.de
- **grave**; like in a: olib-sac wmh1
- **gunpowder**: *Calc* k* manc ptk1
- **haunting**: positr nl2•
- **herring** brine; like: *Bell* b4.de* thuj b4a.de*
- **herring**; like: agn b7.de* bell bg2
- **hollow** teeth, from: mez h2
  - **lying** down agg.: nit-ac
- **honey**, everything smells like: *Apoc-a* br1*
- **horse**-radish: raph
- **hospital**: taosc iwa1•
- **lavender**: bamb-a stb2.de•
- **lime** and whitewash: calc bg2 m-arct k* sulph b4.de*
- **lobster**, when expectorating: lyc
- **manure**, of: anac k* bry *Calc* k* m-ambo b7.de* mag-c puls k2 verat k*
- **milk** | **spoiled**: par b7a.de
- **mouse** excrement: haliae-lc srj5•
- **musk**: agn k* *Puls* b7a.de sul-ac bg2
- **musty**: kali-n bg2 *M-ambo* b7.de* nat-c bg2
  - **discharge**: nat-c
- **nauseating**: canth falco-pe nl2• meny
  - **milk**, of: bell h1
    - **mother's** milk: lac-h sze9•

Odors; imaginary and real: ...
- **offensive**: agar alum bg2 ambr tsm1 anac aq-mar skp7• ars k* ars-s-f k2 asaf k* **Aur** b4a.de* aur-s k2 *Bell* b4.de* benz-ac *Calc* k* *Calc-s* carc fd2.de• caust bg2 *Chel* *Cina* con b4a.de* dig b4a.de* dios bg2 dros elaps k* *Graph* b4a.de* ham hep bg2 *Kali-bi* bg2 kali-s fd4.de kreos b7a.de lem-m mrr1 lyc bg2 mag-c mag-m bg2 manc bg2 meny b7.de* merc b4a.de* mez h2 nat-c bg2 nat-p *Nit-ac* k* nux-v b7.de* par k* ph-ac b4a.de* *Phos* k* plb b7a.de puls bg2* rhus-t bg2 sang bg2 sep k* **Sulph** k* thuj bg2 valer b7.de* vanil fd5.de verat
  - **morning**: kreos nat-p puls
  - **evening**: nit-ac
  - **blowing** the nose agg.●: *Aur* kali-bi **Sulph**
  - **coryza**; during: *Bell* b4a.de
  - **lying** down agg.: nit-ac
  - ○ **Tip** of nose: borx b4a.de *Rhus-t* b7a.de
  - **Within** nose: aur bg2 bell bg2 calc bg2 canth bg2 con bg2 kali-bi bg2 nit-ac bg2 nux-v bg2 phos bg2 plb bg2 puls bg2 sulph bg2
- **old** catarrh (See catarrh - old)
- **onions**: cor-r *Manc* plat bg1 sang bg2 spong fd4.de
  - **roasted**: sang k*
- **peaches**: musca-d szs1
  - **ripe** | **remedy**: musca-d szs1
- **peas**, soaked: sulph k*
- **pigeon** dung: anac k*
- **pine**-smoke: *Bar-c*
- **pitch**: ars k* cact bg2 con k*
- **pus**, of: *Arg-n* k* gamb seneg k* sulph k*
  - **night**: arg-n
- **putrid**: anac b2.de* anthraci asaf aur k* bell k* calc k* canth b2.de* chin b2.de* cob con b2.de* dig b2.de* graph k* interf sa3• *Kali-bi* k* kali-s fd4.de kreos k* lem-m br1 m-ambo b2.de m-arct k* meny k* merc k* mez b2.de* *Nit-ac* k* nux-v b2.de* par k* ph-ac b2.de* phos k* plb b2.de* **Puls** seneg k* sep k* sulph b2.de* valer b2.de* verat k*
  - **morning** | **waking**; on: kreos
  - **blowing** the nose agg.: *Aur* kali-bi
  - **bread** and milk smell: par
  - **cheese**; like spoiled: nux-v b7.de*
  - **eggs**, of: aur bell k* *Calc* k* hep bg2 kali-bi k* m-arct k* meny k* merc nit-ac bg2 nux-v k* par bg2 phos sep k* *Sulph*
  - **food** and milk smell: *Nux-v* par
  - **food** smells putrid: sulph h2
  - **meat**; like spoiled: par b7.de*
- **repulsive**: canth b7a.de* meny b7.de* mez b4.de* nux-v b7.de* plb b7.de*
- **sickly**: aur cench k2 cob nit-ac *Nux-v* sil
- **smoke**; of: (↗*Smoke; as*) bar-c k* cor-r *Sulph* k* taosc iwa1• vanil fd5.de verat
  - **wood**; of: taosc iwa1•
- **smoked** ham: colch
- **snuff**: graph **Sulph**
- **soot**, of: graph k*
- **sour**: alum k* bell k*
  - **morning**, early: alum
  - **bread** smells: bell h1
- **sulphur**; like: anac k* *Ars* k* calc k* graph k* musca-d szs1 *Nux-v* k* plb k* sulph x-ray sp1
- **sweetish**: aur k* nit-ac b2.de* nux-v b2.de* sil b2.de*
- **syrup**, dislikes: sang
- **tallow**: valer k*
- **tar**: ars con k*
  - **back** part of nose; in: con h2*
- **tinder**: anac k* nux-v
- **tobacco**: puls k*
- **ulcer**; like an: cadm-s seneg k*
- **urine**; like: graph b4a.de
- **whiskey**: aur k*

OEDEMA (See Edema)

OILY: calc k* *Hydr* k* iris bg2* merc bg2 mez bg2 puls

OPEN:
- **sensation** as if:
  ○ • **Nostrils** feel as if he had smelled menthol: *(↗Coldness - inside - menthol)* limen-b-c hrn2•
  • **Posterior** nares; sensation as if open: fl-ac bg2 iris bg2 lob bg2 xanth bg2
    ⋮ **walking** in open air agg.: fl-ac k*
○ - **Nostrils** are wide: *(↗Coldness - inside - menthol)* iod bg2* merc bg2 nux-v bg2 op b7.de* phys bg2
  • **sensation** as if: kali-bi bg2

OPERATION; after: ferr-p ptk1

OZENA: *(↗Caries; Coryza - chronic)* all-c tl1 all-s k* *Alum* k* *Am-c* k* *Arg-n* *Ars* k* ars-i bro1 **Asaf** k* **Aur** k* aur-ar k2 **Aur-m** k* *Aur-m-n* k* aur-s k2 bac jl2* cadm-s c1* **Calc** k* *Calc-f* k* *Calc-p* k* calc-s k2 calc-sil k2 *Carb-ac* k* *Carb-an* k* *Carbn-s* chr-ac k* chr-met dx *Con* k* crot-h k* *Cur* k* der a1* diph bro1 *Elaps* k* euph mtf11 ferr-i bro1 fl-ac k* gonotox jl2 *Graph* k* **Hep** k* *Hippoz* k* *Hydr* k* *Hydrin-m* c2* influ jl2 *Iod* c2* **Kali-bi** k* kali-c bro1 kali-chr bro1 **Kali-i** k* *Kali-p* k* kali-perm c2 *Kali-s* k* kreos bro1 lac-c br1 *Lach* k* lem-m c1* luf-op mtf11 mag-m k* **Merc** k* *Merc-c* k* *Merc-i-f* k* merc-pr-r bro1 mez k* *Myric* k* *Nat-ar* *Nat-c* k* *Nat-m* k* nat-p *Nat-s* k* *Nit-ac* k* nux-v ptk1 oci-sa sp1 ol-j k* *Petr* k* *Ph-ac* k* phos k* *Phyt* k* *Psor* c2* **Puls** k* *Sang* k* sanic c2 **Sep** k* **Sil** k* skook c2 *Stict* k* strept-ent jl2 *Sulph* k* *Syph* k* *Teucr* k* *Ther* k* thuj c2* *Trios* bro1 zing c2
- **acrid**: lyc ptk1 mag-m ptk1
- **chronic**: *Alum* bro1 am-c bro1 aur bro1 *Calc-f* bro1 cinnb bro1 elaps bro1 fl-ac bro1 graph bro1 *Hep* bro1 *Kali-bi* bro1 kali-i bro1 kali-s-chr bro1 *Lem-m* bro1 *Lyc* bro1 merc bro1 sabal bro1 *Sep* bro1 *Stict* bro1 *Sulph* bro1 teucr bro1 wye bro1
- **crusty**: mag-m ptk1
- **itch**; after suppressed: calc
- **menses**; during: graph ptk1
- **syphilitic**: *(↗Caries - syphilitic)* *Asaf* k* **Aur** k* *Aur-m* k* crot-h k* fl-ac k2* **Hep** k* **Kali-bi** hr1* *Kali-i* k* *Lach* hr1 *Merc* *Merc-c* hr1 mez hr1 *Nat-s* hr1 **Nit-ac** k* *Phyt* k* **Sil** k* still hr1* *Syph* k*

PAIN: acon act-sp ↓ aesc k* aeth ↓ agar k* agn k* aids ↓ ail ↓ *All-c* ↓ allox ↓ aloe ↓ alum alum-p ↓ alum-sil ↓ *Am-c* ↓ am-m ↓ ambr ↓ anac k* anan ↓ ang ↓ anis ↓ ant-c b7.de* ant-t k* aphis ↓ apis b7a.de aq-mar ↓ aral ↓ *Arg-met* *Arg-n* k* *Arn* ↓ *Ars* k* ars-h ↓ ars-i ars-met ars-s-f ↓ *Arum-t* arund asaf k* asar asc-t ↓ aspar **Aur** k* aur-ar k2 aur-i k2 *Aur-m* k* aur-m-n ↓ aur-s ↓ bamb-a ↓ bapt ↓ bar-c k* bar-i k2 bar-m ↓ bell k* benz-ac berb ↓ bism ↓ blum-o ↓ *Borx* bov ↓ brach ↓ brom k* bry ↓ bufo cadm-s ↓ calad ↓ *Calc* k* calc-p ↓ calc-sil ↓ camph ↓ cann-i cann-s ↓ canth b7.de* caps ↓ carb-an carb-v k* carbn-s card-b ↓ card-m ↓ **Castm** ↓ caul ↓ caust b4.de* cedr ↓ cench k2 cham ↓ chel ↓ chin k* chlor ↓ choc ↓ chr-ac ↓ cic ↓ cimic k* *Cina* ↓ *Cinnb* *Cist* ↓ clem ↓ coc-c ↓ cocc b7.de* coff k* *Colch* k* coli rly4• coloc k* *Con* ↓ conv ↓ cop ↓ cor-r crot-c ↓ *Crot-h* *Crot-t* ↓ cupr-ar ↓ cycl des-ac ↓ dios ↓ dulc fd4.de dys fmm1• echi ↓ *Elaps* euph ↓ *Euphr* k* fago ↓ falco-pe ↓ ferr-i ↓ fl-ac k* gamb ↓ *Gels* ↓ ger-i ↓ glon gran ↓ **Graph** k* grat k* guaj ham ↓ hell **Hep** k* hist ↓ *Hydr* ↓ *Hydrog* srj2• hyos ↓ hyper ↓ ign ignis-alc ↓ ind ↓ indg ↓ *Iod* k* ipom-p ↓ kali-ar **Kali-bi** k* *Kali-c* ↓ **Kali-i** k* kali-n k* kali-p ↓ kali-s kali-sil k2 kalm k* kola ↓ lac-c ↓ lac-h ↓ lach k* lachn ↓ laur lec ↓ led b7.de* lith-m ↓ lyc k* lyss k* m-ambo ↓ m-arct ↓ mag-c k* mag-m k* mag-s ↓ mang k2 *Med* ↓ *Merc* k* merc-c b4a.de *Merc-i-f* k* merc-i-r ↓ merl ↓ *Mez* ↓ mosch ↓ mur-ac ↓ naja ↓ nat-ar nat-c ↓ nat-m k* nat-ox ↓ nat-s nat-sil ↓ nept-m ↓ nicc ↓ *Nit-ac* k* nux-m ↓ *Nux-v* ↓ ol-an ↓ olib-sac ↓ olnd pall ↓ pen ↓ petr petr-ra shn4• ph-ac ↓ phel ↓ phos k* phys ↓ phyt k* plat ↓ plb b7.de* podo ↓ polyg-h ↓ prun psor ↓ **Puls** k* ran-b k* ran-s ↓ rat ↓ rheum rhod ↓ rhus-t b7.de* rumx k2 ruta *Sabad* ↓ samb ↓ sang sars k* sec ↓ senec ↓ *Seneg* ↓ *Sep* k* **Sil** k* sin-n ↓ **Spect** ↓ spig spong fd4.de squil ↓ stann b4.de* *Staph* ↓ stront-c ↓ stry ↓ suis-em rly4• sul-ac ↓ *Sul-i* ↓ *Sulph* k* suprar ↓ syc ↓ symph ↓ syph ↓ tab ↓ tarent ↓ teucr thlas ↓ *Thuj* tritic-vg fd5.de vanil fd5.de verat viol-o ↓ viol-t ↓ zinc ↓
- **right**: aesc ↓ alum ↓ am-m aur-s k2 brom camph card-m ↓ crot-t ↓ dulc fd4.de hydr ↓ ign ↓ kali-bi ↓ kali-n ↓ lyc ↓ mez k* nat-c ↓ plat ↓ psor spig ↓ sulph ↓ zinc ↓
  • **blowing** the nose: kali-bi ↓
    ⋮ **stitching** pain | **rubbed** together; as if bones: kali-bi
  • **boring** pain: camph k* psor k* spig k*
  • **breathing** agg.: hydrog ↓ op ↓ ox-ac ↓
    ⋮ **stitching** pain: hydrog srj2• op ox-ac
  • **burning** pain: card-m crot-t hydr kali-bi kali-n

Pain –**right**: ...
  • **cramping**: ign bg2
  • **drawing** pain: aesc lyc nat-c zinc k*
  • **jerking** pain: zinc k*
  • **pressing** pain: lyc h2* plat h2*
  • **smarting**: lyc bg2
  • **stitching** pain: psor k* sulph
  • **tearing** pain: alum k* zinc k*
▽ • **extending** to:
    ⋮ **left**: euphr k*
    ⋮ **Forehead**:
      ⋮ **blowing** nose; on: sulph ↓
        . **stitching** pain: sulph
- **left**: alum am-c ↓ arg-met ars-met arum-m k* aur ↓ aur-m ↓ bell calc ↓ camph ↓ caps ↓ carb-ac ↓ carneg-g rwt1• cench k2 chin ↓ cina ↓ cist ↓ coff ↓ dulc fd4.de *Gels* ↓ grat ↓ irid-met ↓ kali-c ↓ mang ↓ medul-os-si ↓ nat-p k2 ol-an ↓ petr-ra ↓ psil ↓ ruta fd4.de *Sep* ↓ spong fd4.de stann
  • **burning** pain: caps cina cist coff *Gels* grat kali-c petr-ra shn4• ruta fd4.de *Sep*
  • **contracting**: caps k*
  • **cutting** pain: medul-os-si rly4•
  • **drawing** pain: bell camph k*
  • **inspiration** agg.: chin ↓
    ⋮ **stitching** pain: chin
  • **jerking** pain: caps k*
  • **raw**; as if: psil ft1 *Sep*
  • **stitching** pain: arg-met calc carb-ac chin k* grat irid-met srj5• *Spong*
  • **tearing** pain: am-c k* aur aur-m mang k* ol-an k*
- **morning**: ham ↓ mag-m ↓ petr-ra ↓
  • **burning** pain: ham fd3.de• mag-m petr-ra shn4•
  • **raw**; as if: mag-m
- **forenoon**: dulc fd4.de phos h2*
- **evening**: alum ars-met bamb-a ↓ cycl des-ac rbp6 dulc fd4.de ferr-p a1 lyc ↓ pall ↓ ran-b k2 ruta fd4.de spong fd4.de
  • **bed** agg.; in: lyc ↓
    ⋮ **cutting** pain: lyc
  • **burning** pain: bamb-a stb2.de• pall ruta fd4.de spong fd4.de
  • **cutting** pain: lyc k*
  • **raw**; as if: des-ac rbp6
  • **sore**: alum k*
- **night**: am-m h2* **Aur** aur-s k2 bell cor-r *Crot-h* ↓ hep ↓ lach phos
  • **boring** pain: **Aur** phos k*
  • **drawing** pain: *Crot-h* k* hep k*
  • **sleeplessness**; with: cor-r
- **accompanied** by | **Head**; complaints of (See HEAD - Complaints - accompanied - nose)
- **aching**: asar k* cench k2 cimic k* dulc ptk1 *Elaps* merc-i-f k*
- **air** agg.; in open: kali-c ↓ spong ↓
  • **burning** pain: kali-c spong fd4.de
- **beating** (See pulsating)
- **biting** pain: ambr k* ang k* arg-met b7.de* am k* *Aur* k* bar-m berb k* bry k* calc-p k* *Carb-v* k* chin k* euph k* grat k* hell hep h2* kali-c k* kali-n lach k* led b7a.de lyc mez k* olnd b7.de* plat k* ran-b b7.de* ran-s k* rhus-t bg2 *Sabad* k* sil bg2* spig k* squil b7.de* teucr thuj
  • **suffocative**: euph b4a.de*
- **blowing** the nose:
  • **after**: aesc ↓ ant-c ↓ cist ↓ *Hep* ↓ nat-ar ↓ *Nit-ac* ↓
    ⋮ **raw**; as if: aesc ant-c cist k* *Hep* nat-ar *Nit-ac*
    ⋮ **thick** mucus; blowing out: aesc ↓ ant-c ↓ cist ↓ nat-ar ↓ *Nit-ac* ↓
      : **burning** pain: aesc ant-c cist nat-ar *Nit-ac*
  • **agg.**: aur bamb-a stb2.de• carb-v ↓ euphr h2* **Graph** *Hep* hydrog ↓ **iod** kali-bi kali-c kali-i kali-n ↓ *Led* k* mag-s ↓ mang h2* *Nat-m* nit-ac sars ↓ *Sil* sul-i ↓ sulph ↓ teucr
    ⋮ **burning** pain: bamb-a stb2.de• carb-v graph kali-n sars sul-i k2

- • **agg.**: ...
  - ⋮ **contracting**: kali-c
  - ⋮ **raw**; as if: *Hep*$_{k*}$ hydrog$_{srj2\bullet}$
  - ⋮ **sore**: *Aur* **Graph**$_{k*}$ led$_{k*}$ mag-s *Nat-m* *Sil*
  - ⋮ **stitching** pain: *Kali-bi*$_{k*}$ kali-c *Nit-ac* sulph
- **boil**; as from a: hep
- **boring** pain: arum-t$_{tl1}$ asaf$_{bro1}$ **Aur**$_{k*}$ aur-ar$_{k2}$ aur-i$_{k2}$ bism$_{b7.de*}$ brom$_{bro1}$ camph$_{bg2*}$ cina$_{b7a.de*}$ *Kali-i*$_{k*}$ led$_{bg2}$ merc-i-r$_{bro1}$ mez$_{bg2}$ nat-m$_{k*}$ ph-ac$_{bg2*}$ phos$_{bg2*}$ psor$_{bg2*}$ ruta sil$_{bg2}$ spig$_{k*}$ sulph$_{k*}$
- **breathing** strongly, while: am-c borx op
- **bruised** (See sore)
- **burning** pain: *Aesc*$_{k*}$ aeth *Agar*$_{k*}$ aids$_{nl2\bullet}$ *All-c* aloe alum$_{k*}$ alum-p$_{k2}$ alum-sil$_{k2}$ *Am-c* ambr anan ang ant-c$_{k*}$ aphis apis *Arg-met* *Arg-n* arn$_{b7.de}$ **Ars**$_{k*}$ *Ars-i*$_{bro1}$ ars-s-f$_{k2}$ arum-t$_{k2*}$ *Arund* aur$_{k*}$ aur-ar$_{k2}$ aur-m aur-s$_{k2}$ bamb-a$_{stb2.de\bullet}$ bar-c$_{k*}$ *Bell*$_{k*}$ berb borx bov$_{k*}$ brach brom$_{k2}$ bufo calad$_{k*}$ *Canth*$_{k*}$ caps$_{k*}$ *Carb-an*$_{k*}$ *Carb-v* card-m *Caust* chel chlor chr-ac$_{bro1}$ cimic cina$_{k*}$ *Cist*$_{k*}$ clem coc-c coff$_{b7.de}$ coli$_{rly4\bullet}$ *Coloc* *Con* cop crot-c *Crot-t* dulc$_{fd4.de}$ gamb *Gels* ger-i$_{rly4\bullet}$ gran graph$_{b4.de*}$ grat ham$_{fd3.de\bullet}$ hell$_{b7.de}$ *Hep*$_{k*}$ *Hydr* iod$_{b4.de*}$ kali-ar *Kali-bi* *Kali-c*$_{k*}$ **Kali-i**$_{k*}$ *Kali-n*$_{k*}$ kali-p kali-s kali-sil$_{k2}$ *Lach*$_{bro1}$ led$_{k*}$ lyc m-ambo$_{b7.de}$ *Mag-m*$_{k*}$ *Med* merc$_{k2}$ *Merc-c*$_{k*}$ merl *Mez*$_{k*}$ mosch$_{b7a.de}$ nat-ar *Nat-m* nat-ox$_{rly4\bullet}$ *Nat-s* nicc *Nit-ac* ol-an olib-sac$_{wmh1}$ pall petr$_{k*}$ petr-ra$_{shn4\bullet}$ ph-ac$_{k*}$ phel *Phos* phys plat psor *Puls*$_{b7.de*}$ rat ruta$_{fd4.de}$ sabad sang$_{hr1*}$ sars$_{k*}$ sec$_{k2}$ senec *Seneg* **Sil**$_{k*}$ sin-n spig$_{bg2}$ spong$_{fd4.de}$ stann$_{k*}$ stront-c$_{b4a.de}$ stry sul-ac$_{mrr1}$ *Sulph*$_{k*}$ syc$_{pte1*\bullet}$ syph$_{k*}$ tab tarent$_{k2}$ *Thuj*$_{b4a.de}$ vanil$_{fd5.de}$
  - • **drop** of hot grease, like a: bar-c
  - • **pepper**; as from: calad cench$_{k2}$ choc$_{srj3\bullet}$ hydrog$_{srj2\bullet}$ ignis-alc$_{es2\bullet}$ lac-h$_{htj1\bullet}$ nept-m$_{lsd2.fr}$ *Seneg*
- **burnt**; as if: bry$_{b7.de*}$
- **burrowing**: calc$_{b4.de*}$ coloc$_{k*}$ kali-bi$_{bg2}$ kali-n$_{k*}$ sil$_{bg2*}$
- **bursting** pain: asaf$_{k*}$ bar-c hydr$_{bg2}$ kali-bi$_{k*}$ sars$_{bg2}$
  - • **bubble**; as from a bursting: sars$_{bg2}$ sulph$_{bg2}$
- **chill**; during: camph ↓
  - • **pressing** pain: camph$_{bg2}$
- **clawing** pain: arg-n$_{k*}$ kali-n$_{k*}$
- **cold**:
  - • **air** agg.: aesc ↓ bufo ↓ cist ↓ kali-c ↓ led ↓
    - ⋮ **burning** pain: aesc$_{bg1}$ bufo cist$_{k*}$ kali-c$_{k2}$ led$_{ptk}$
  - • **room** | **agg.**: dulc$_{k2}$
- **compressed**; as if: acon$_{b7a.de}$ verat$_{b7.de*}$
- **compressing** (See pressing)
- **compressing** wings, when: arg-n ↓ colch ↓ nat-m ↓
  - • **sore**: arg-n$_{k*}$ colch nat-m
- **contracting**: anac$_{k*}$ caps$_{k*}$ fago$_{bg1}$ graph$_{k*}$ hell$_{k*}$ hep$_{k*}$ *Kali-n* lyc$_{h2}$ nit-ac$_{h2}$ sabad vanil$_{fd5.de}$
- **corrosive**: agn$_{b7.de*}$
- **coryza**; during: *Acon*$_{bg2}$ *Aesc* ↓ ail ↓ *All-c* ↓ aloe ↓ *Am-c* ↓ am-m$_{b7.de*}$ *Ambr* ↓ ant-c ↓ arn ↓ **Ars** ↓ **Bell**$_{bg2}$ **Brom** ↓ calad ↓ calc ↓ carb-v ↓ caust$_{bg2}$ chin ↓ *Cina* ↓ cypra-eg ↓ dulc$_{bg2}$ euph ↓ *Gels* ↓ ham ↓ *Hep*$_{bg2}$ *Lach*$_{bg2}$ mang ↓ **Merc**$_{bg2}$ mez ↓ mosch$_{b7a.de}$ mur-ac ↓ nit-ac$_{bg2}$ nux-v$_{bg2}$ pall ↓ pen ↓ ph-ac$_{bg2}$ phos$_{bg2}$ puls$_{bg2}$ *Senec* ↓ *Seneg* ↓ sep ↓ *Sil* ↓ staph ↓ sulph$_{bg2}$ syph ↓ *Teucr* ↓ uva ↓
  - • **biting** pain: carb-v$_{b4.de*}$ euph$_{b4.de*}$
  - • **burning** pain: *Aesc*$_{k*}$ *All-c* aloe *Am-c* arn$_{b7.de*}$ **Ars**$_{k*}$ *Bell*$_{b4a.de}$ calad$_{k*}$ *Caust* *Cina*$_{b7a.de}$ cypra-eg$_{sde6.de\bullet}$ *Gels* ham$_{fd3.de\bullet}$ mez$_{k*}$ pall$_{c1}$ puls$_{b7.de*}$ *Senec* *Seneg* *Sulph* syph$_{jl2}$ *Teucr*$_{b7a.de}$
  - • **raw**; as if: aesc$_{k*}$ ail$_{k*}$ all-c$_{k2*}$ ant-c **Ars** pen$_{br1}$ sep *Sil* uva
  - • **scratching** pain: nux-v$_{b7.de*}$
  - • **sore**: *Ambr*$_{b7a.de}$ *Ars*$_{b4a.de}$ **Brom**$_{b4a.de}$ calc$_{b4a.de}$ chin$_{b7.de*}$ mang$_{b4.de*}$ **Merc**$_{b4a.de}$ mez$_{b4.de*}$ mur-ac$_{b4a.de}$ nit-ac$_{b4.de*}$ nux-v$_{b7.de*}$ sil$_{b4a.de}$ staph$_{b7.de*}$
- **cough**:
  - • **during**:
    - ⋮ **agg.**: nit-ac
      - : **stitching** pain: *Nit-ac*$_{k*}$
    - ⋮ **amel.**: hydrog ↓
      - : **stitching** pain: hydrog$_{srj2\bullet}$
- **cramping**: arn$_{b7.de*}$ bell$_{bg2}$ hyos$_{b7a.de}$ laur$_{bg2}$ nux-m plat$_{k*}$ sabad$_{bro1}$ sulph$_{k*}$ zinc$_{bg2}$
- **cutting** pain: arn bry cadm-s$_{bg2}$ caust$_{k*}$ hydrog$_{srj2\bullet}$ *Kali-bi*$_{k*}$ kali-i nit-ac$_{ptk1}$ sulph$_{bg2}$ zinc$_{k*}$
- **darting** (See stitching)
- **digging** pain: *Coloc*$_{k*}$ kali-n
- **discharge**:
  - • **amel.**: hydrog ↓
    - ⋮ **stitching** pain: hydrog$_{srj2\bullet}$
- **distending** pain: bar-c$_{k*}$
- **drawing** pain: agar anac ant-c$_{k*}$ aur-m-n$_{a1}$ bapt$_{k*}$ bell$_{k*}$ camph$_{k*}$ canth$_{k*}$ carb-v$_{b4.de*}$ caul$_{k*}$ caust chel$_{b7.de*}$ clem$_{k*}$ colch$_{k*}$ crot-h$_{k*}$ crot-t$_{k*}$ guaj$_{b4.de*}$ *Hep*$_{k*}$ ign$_{b7.de*}$ kali-bi$_{bg2}$ kali-c$_{bg2}$ *Kali-n* lach$_{k*}$ laur$_{k*}$ lyc$_{bg2}$ mang$_{bg2}$ mez$_{k*}$ nat-c$_{b4.de*}$ nat-m$_{bg2}$ nat-s phyt$_{bg2}$ psor$_{bg2}$ rheum$_{b7.de*}$ sil$_{k*}$ thuj$_{b4.de*}$ zinc$_{b4.de*}$
- **dryness**, from: calc **Graph** *Kali-bi* *Phos* *Sep* *Sil* *Stict* sulph
- **dull** pain: aq-mar$_{skp7\bullet}$
- **epistaxis**; with: hydr ↓ led ↓ mill$_{bg1}$ rumx$_{bg1}$
  - • **burning** pain: hydr$_{bg1}$ led$_{bg1}$
- **excoriated**; as if: lyc$_{h2*}$
- **fever**; during: rhod$_{b4a.de*}$
- **fleabites**; like: asc-t$_{k*}$
- **foreign** body; as from a: calc-p con
- **gnawing** pain: aur$_{bg2}$ berb$_{bg2}$ bufo$_{bg2}$ *Calc*$_{b4.de*}$ card-b$_{a1}$ fago$_{bg1}$ merc$_{k*}$ **Sil**$_{k*}$ thlas$_{bg2}$
- **griping** pain: kali-n$_{b4.de*}$ nux-m$_{b7.de}$ nux-v$_{bg2}$ stront-c$_{bg2}$
- **headache**; during: **Agar** ferr glon hep merc mez
- **healing** slowly: allox ↓
  - • **raw**; as if: allox$_{sp1}$
- **hot** (See warm)
- **inspiration** agg.: *Aesc* agar ↓ alum-sil$_{k2}$ am-c *Ant-c* brach bufo cist ↓ coli ↓ gins *Hep* hydr kali-i ↓ mag-m ↓ mag-s med$_{k2}$ olib-sac$_{wmh1}$ osm ox-ac phos *Psor* sep symph$_{fd3.de\bullet}$ thuj tritic-vg$_{fd5.de}$ vanil$_{fd5.de}$
  - • **burning** pain: aesc$_{ptk1}$ ant-c$_{k2}$ cist$_{k2*}$ coli$_{rly4\bullet}$ kali-i$_{mrr1}$ mag-m med
  - • **raw**; as if: *Aesc* agar *Ant-c* cist$_{k2}$ *Sep*
- **itching** pain: aur-m$_{h2*}$
- **jerking** pain: con$_{k*}$
- **lacerating**: *(↗tearing)* cadm-s
- **lancinating** (See stitching)
- **lying** agg.: *Borx* ↓
  - • **pressing** pain: *Borx*
- **lying** down:
  - • **agg.**: *Borx*
  - • **amel.**: cupr
- **menses** | **before** | **agg.**: con$_{k*}$
  - • **during**:
    - ⋮ **agg.**: alum$_{b4a.de}$ carb-an ↓
      - : **burning** pain: carb-an
- **motion** agg.: cupr lyc$_{h2*}$
- **paroxysmal**: plat zinc
- **perspiration**; during: caust$_{bg2}$ *Merc*$_{bg2}$ ph-ac$_{bg2}$ puls$_{bg2}$ **Rhod**$_{bg2}$ *Rhus-t*$_{bg2}$ thuj$_{bg2}$
- **pinching** (See pressing)
- **pressing** pain: acon$_{k*}$ aeth$_{a1}$ agar$_{k*}$ agn$_{k*}$ alum$_{h2*}$ arn$_{b7.de*}$ asaf$_{k*}$ *Aur-m*$_{k*}$ bell$_{b4.de*}$ *Borx* brom$_{bg2}$ calc$_{k*}$ cann-s$_{b7.de*}$ carb-v$_{b4.de*}$ chin$_{b7.de*}$ *Cinnb*$_{k*}$ *Colch*$_{k*}$ coloc$_{k*}$ con$_{h2*}$ *Cor-r*$_{k*}$ cycl grat hyos$_{b7.de*}$ *Kali-bi*$_{k*}$ kali-c$_{h2*}$ kalm laur$_{k*}$ lyc$_{b4.de*}$ mag-c$_{k*}$ mag-m$_{k*}$ merc$_{k*}$ nat-sil$_{fd3.de\bullet}$ olnd$_{k*}$ ph-ac$_{b4.de*}$ phos$_{k*}$ plat$_{bg2}$ prun puls$_{k*}$ ran-b$_{k*}$ ruta$_{b7.de*}$ samb$_{b7.de}$ *Sep*$_{bg2}$ *Sil*$_{b4.de*}$ *Sulph*$_{k*}$ suprar$_{rly4\bullet}$ symph$_{fd3.de\bullet}$ teucr tritic-vg$_{fd5.de}$ vanil$_{fd5.de}$ verat$_{k*}$ viol-t$_{b7.de*}$ zinc$_{b4.de*}$
  - • **alternating** with | **sticking** in nose (See stitching - alternating - pressure)
  - • **brain** were forcing its way out; as if: am-c *Borx*
  - • **downward**: borx$_{tl1}$ mag-c$_{bg2}$ mag-s$_{k*}$ merc$_{k*}$
  - • **glasses**; as from: cinnb$_{bg2}$ zinc$_{bg2}$
  - • **outward**: asaf$_{b7a.de}$
  - • **together**: lachn$_{bg2}$ verat$_{bg2}$
  - • **upward**: ran-b$_{c1}$

Nose

- **pressure**:
  - **agg**.: alum-p k2 aur-m k2 chin con k* cupr-ar led lyc bg1 spong fd4.de
  - **amel**.: agn k* alum ↓ kali-bi bg1 sulph ↓
    - **tearing** pain: alum k* sulph
- **pricking** (See stitching)
- **pulling**; sensation in left side as if a hair were: plat
- **pulsating** pain: ars bell bro1 borx *Coloc Hep* bro1 kali-bi *Kali-i* k* ph-ac plat
- **raw**; as if: (↗*Excoriation*) *Aesc* k* ail k* all-c k2 allox tpw4 aral ptk1 ars k* ars-h **Arum-t** k* bar-m calc k* canth bg2 caust ptk1 conv br1 cop des-ac rbp6 dulc fd4.de echi graph k2 *Hydr* k* kali-ar kali-bi bg2 kola stb3• *Lach* k* lec mag-m k* merc bg2* *Merc-c* k* *Mez* k* nat-ar k2 nat-m h2* pen br1 petr-ra shn4• phos bg2 polyg-h bg2 sabad k2 sang k2 *Sep* k* *Sil Sul-i* k* sulph bg2
- **rubbing**:
  - **amel**.: bell nat-c
    - **drawing** pain: nat-c
- **saddle**; like a: cinnb bg2* kali-bi bg2 **Sep** bg2 thuj bg2*
- **scarlatina**; after: mur-ac bro1
- **scraping** pain: ferr-i a1* hyper a1 nux-v k*
- **scratching** pain: bell bg2 nux-v b7.de* ruta b7.de* teucr bg2
- **smarting**: arg-n bg2 *Ars* bg2 aur bg2 bell bg2 cedr bg2 crot-c bg2 dios bg2 kali-bi bg2 nit-ac b4.de* phos bg2 phyt bg2 ran-b bg2 ran-s bg2 staph b7.de* sulph bg2
- **sneezing** agg.: *Nit-ac* senec ↓
  - **burning** pain: senec ptk1
  - **stitching** pain: *Nit-ac* k*
- **sore** (= bruised, externally): act-sp agar aids nl2• alum-sil c2 am-c b4.de* am-m ambr b7.de* anac b4.de* ang b7.de* ant-c b7.de* arg-n k* *Arn* k* *Ars* k* asaf bg2 **Aur** k* bell k* benz-ac bov b4.de* brach *Brom* k* *Calc* k* camph b7.de* carb-an bg2 caust b4.de* chin b7.de* cic k* *Cina* k* coff b7.de* colch b7.de* coli rly4• coloc con k* crot-t cupr-ar dulc fd4.de fago c2 falco-pe nl2• *Graph* b4a.de *Hep* k* hist sp1 ign b7.de* iod *Kali-bi* k* kali-n kali-s fd4.de lac-c led lith-m c2 lyc b4.de* lyss m-arct b7.de mag-c b4.de* mag-m b4.de* mang b4.de* mez b4.de* naja bg2 *Nat-m* k* nat-sil fd3.de• nit-ac b4.de* *Nux-v* b7.de* *Petr* k* *Phos* k* podo c1 *Puls* rhod b4.de* rhus-t b7.de* sep b4.de* **Sil** k* spig b7.de* spong fd4.de squil b7.de* staph b7.de* sulph b4.de* symph fd3.de• tritic-vg fd5.de vanil fd5.de viol-o k* zinc k* [**Spect** dfg1]
- **spectacles** agg.: cinnb bg1 lyc bg1
- **splinter**; as from a: *Aur* bro1 *Hep* bro1 kali-bi bro1 *Nit-ac* k*
- **squeezed**; as if: arg-n bg2 *Arn* b7.de* bell b4.de* cic b7a.de colch b7.de* hyos b7.de* kali-c b4.de* lyc bg2 plat b4.de* viol-o b7a.de zinc b4.de*
- **sticks**; full of: alum k2
- **stinging**: sep bg1
  - **fleabites**; like (See fleabites)
- **stitching** pain: *Aesc* agar b4.de* anan k* anis ant-c b7.de* **Apis** k* arn b7.de* ars b4.de* asc-t k* *Aur* k* bamb-a stb2.de• bar-m bell k* berb k* blum-o bnj1 calc k* calc-p calc-sil k2 camph k* canth b7.de* caps k* cham bg2 chin b7.de* cic b7.de* cina bg2 con euph euphr fl-ac bg2 ipom-p kali-bi k* *Kali-c* k* kali-n b4.de* lach b7.de* laur b7.de* led bg2 mez bg2 mur-ac k* nat-m bg2 **Nit-ac** k* nux-m k* olnd phyt bg2 psor bg2* puls *Sang* k* sep bg2 sil bg2 spig k* spong b7.de* squil b7.de* sul-ac b4.de* tarent teucr k* thuj vanil fd5.de
  - **alternating** with | **pressure** in nose: laur k*
- **stupefying**: acon b7a.de* olnd b7a.de rheum b7a.de*
- **sudden**:
  - ○ **Root**: hyos ↓
    - **jerking** pain: hyos k*
- **talking** agg.: canth bg1
- **tearing** pain: (↗*lacerating*) alum k* alum-sil k2 am-c b4.de* ant-t bg2 arn k* bry b7.de* cadm-s *Calc* k* carb-an b4.de* **Castm** lp caust b4.de* chel k* *Chin* k* colch k* con bg2 euphr ind indg k* kali-bi k* kali-c b4a.de kali-i lach lyc k* mag-c k* mag-m k* mang k* merc bg2 merc-c bg2 mez bg2 nat-c b4.de* nat-s k* nicc k* plb b7.de* *Sep* k* sil k* spong k* *Sulph* k* teucr b7.de* zinc k*
- **through** right side: *Borx* ↓
  - **pressing** pain | **downward**: *Borx* k*
- **thrust**; as if from a: *Arn* b7.de* cic b7.de* viol-o b7.de*
- **thrust** transversely through the nose: ruta ↓
  - **plug**; as if from: ruta b7.de
- **touch** agg.: aesc bro1 aids ↓ alum k* alum-p k2 alum-sil bro1 am-m bg2 anac ↓ *Ant-c* bro1 aral bro1 ars bro1 *Arum-t* bro1 *Aur* k* aur-m bro1 aur-s k2 bar-m bell k* bry calc bro1 camph bro1 canth carb-an caust cic k2 cinnb c1 colch con ↓ crot-t ↓ dulc ↓ euphr ↓ graph k2 *Hep* k* ictod ↓ kali-bi k* kali-i ↓ kali-n lachn ↓ led lith-m ↓ lyc lyss ↓ *Mag-m* mag-s *Mang* ↓ **Merc** k* nat-c *Nat-m* k* **Nit-ac** osm bro1 petr petr-ra shn4• ph-ac *Phos* rhus-t sabin sec ↓ *Sil* k* stann sulph thuj ↓ zinc ↓
  - **burning** pain: kali-n mag-m phos
  - **coryza**; during: calc b4.de* chin b7.de* hep b4a.de *Lyc* b4a.de *Nux-v* b7.de*
  - **sore**: aids nl2• *Alum* k* am-m anac **Aur** k* *Aur-s* bell k* bry k* *Calc* k* carb-an h2* caust cic *Cinnb* bro1 colch con bro1 crot-t a1 dulc fd4.de euphr graph k* *Hep* k* ictod *Kali-bi* k* kali-i lachn bro1 lith-m bro1 lyss *Mag-m* k* *Mang* k* *Merc* k* *Nat-m Nit-ac* k* **Phos** rhus-t bro1 sec a1 *Sil* k* sulph thuj zinc
  - **splinter**; as from a: *Nit-ac Sil*
  - **stitching** pain: calc **Nit-ac** k* *Sil* zinc
  - **ulcerative** pain: am-m **Aur** bry mag-s c1 petr *Sil* k*
- **ulcerative** pain: aeth am-c bg2 am-m b7.de* ant-c bg2 arg-n bg2 arn k* aur bg2 aur-ar k2 aur-s k2 bell bg2 borx bg2 brom bg2 bry b7.de* calc bg2 calc-p bg2 camph b7.de* canth b7.de* caust bg2 chin bg2 chlor bg2 cocc b7.de* colch bg2 dulc b4.de* fl-ac bg2 graph b4.de* *Hep* k* ign k* kali-bi bg2 *Kali-c* k* kali-n b4.de* lach bg2 mag-m bg2 mag-s mur-ac b4.de* naja bg2 nat-m bg2 nit-ac bg2 *Nux-v* b7.de* petr b4.de* phos bg2 phyt bg2 podo bg2 *Puls* k* *Rhus-t* b7.de* sep bg2 sil b4a.de* spig bg2 squil bg2 *Staph* k* thuj bg2 verat b7.de* zinc bg2
- **warm**:
  - **air**:
    - **inspiration**:
      - **amel**. | **hot** air: merc k2
- **wiping**; with: brom k2
- ▽ **extending** to:
  - ○ **Brain** | **rays**; like: *Sil*
  - **Chin**: chin
  - **Downward** from above: arn hyos ↓
    - **jerking** pain: hyos
  - **Ear**: merc-c ↓ phyt ↓
    - **stitching** pain: merc-c bro1 phyt bg2
  - **Ears**: berb bg1 fago bg1 lem-m c1 psor bg1 tritic-vg fd5.de
    - **swallowing** agg.: elaps k*
  - **Eye**: zinc ↓
    - **contracting**: zinc
    - **left** to above left eye; from: caps ↓
      - **contracting**: caps
  - **Eyebrows**: inul
  - **Eyes**: **Hep** lyc symph fd3.de•
    - **drawing** pain: hep k*
    - **Canthus** of left eye; from root along orbital arch to outer: kali-bi
  - **Forehead**: bufo calc kali-bi k2 kali-i nat-s sabal c1* sil
  - **Head**: alum-sil k2 kali-bi kali-i
  - **Head**; top of: tarent ↓
    - **stitching** pain: tarent
  - **Malar** bone: kali-bi rhus-t a1 thuj bg1
  - **Neck**: gels
  - **Occiput**: acon bg1 agar bg1 kali-c
    - **blowing** nose; on: cic ↓ kali-c ↓
      - **stitching** pain: cic h1 kali-c
    - **contracting**: kali-c
  - **Posterior** nares: bapt
  - **Root** of nose: *Coloc* sang
  - **Root**; from left side to: *Coloc* ↓
    - **digging** pain: *Coloc* k*
  - **Side**: chin ↓
    - **pressing** pain: chin k*
  - **Temples**: kali-bi mag-c
  - **Throat**: kola ↓
    - **raw**; as if: kola stb3•

○ - **Above** nose: ambr↓ cupr↓
- **changing** to tearing, followed by dullness in back of head | **pressing** pain: ambr cupr

- **Around** the nose: phos↓
- **burning** pain: phos h2

- **Behind** the nose: plut-n↓
- **burning** pain: plut-n srj7•

- **Bones**: *Aesc* k* agar↓ anan↓ arg-n k* arn↓ *Ars* k* *Asaf* bro1 **Aur** k* aur-ar k2 *Aur-m*↓ aur-m-n k* aur-s k2 bell↓ benz-ac k* bufo↓ cadm-s k2 *Calc* b4a.de *Carb-an* k* carb-v↓ castor-eq cench k2 cham↓ chel↓ *Cina*↓ cinnb bro1 clem↓ colch k* *Con*↓ cor-r k* cupr-ar↓ cycl k* gamb↓ graph k2 guaj k* **Hep** k* hyos b7.de indg k* jab↓ **Kali-bi** k* *Kali-i* k* kali-n k* kali-sil k2 *Kalm*↓ *Lac-c*↓ lach k* laur a1 led k* lyc↓ merc k* merc-c b4a.de merc-i-f↓ merl↓ mez k* mosch k* nat-m k* onos phos k* prun↓ *Puls* k* rhus-t ptk1 ruta fd4.de **Sil** k* spira a1 spong↓ *Staph* b7a.de *Sulph* k* symph↓ teucr↓ thuj k* verat k*
- **right**: aesc k* aur laur↓ plat↓
  ⋮ **cramping**: laur k* plat k*
  ⋮ **sore**: **Aur**
- **left**: aesc↓ anac↓ arg-n↓ cench k2 marb-w es1• nat-m↓ spong↓
  ⋮ **sore**: aesc k* anac arg-n nat-m
  ⋮ **stitching** pain: spong
- **daytime**: *Sulph*
- **evening**: sulph↓
  ⋮ **pressing** pain: sulph k*
- **night**: *Aur* br1 phos↓
  ⋮ **boring** pain: phos k*
- **aching**: bell k* castor-eq colch bg2 cycl k* laur a1 mosch k* sulph k*
- **boring** pain: **Aur** k* aur-m-n k* led k* mez k* nat-m k* phos k*
- **burning** pain: **Kali-i** kali-n h2 *Mez* nat-m phos
- **cutting** pain: indg *Kali-bi* *Kali-i* merc-i-f teucr
- **dragging**: merl k*
- **drawing** pain: clem k* *Colch* k* lach k* mez k*
  ⋮ **like** a saddle: thuj h1*
- **gnawing** pain: bufo **Kali-i**
- **nausea**; with: *Kalm*↓
  ⋮ **tearing** pain: *Kalm*
- **pressing** pain: agar k* arn bell h1* carb-v k* cinnb k* *Cycl* k* **Kali-bi** k* lyc h2* merc k2 ruta fd4.de *Sulph* k* verat k*
  ⋮ **pressed** asunder: colch cor-r k* laur k* prun *Puls*
- **pressure** agg.: merc k2
- **pulsating** pain: anan **Kali-i**
- **sore**: arg-n k* **Aur** k* *Aur-m* k* *Aur-s* bell a1 chel cupr-ar graph k2 guaj *Hep* k* jab kali-i k2 *Lac-c* k* lach k2 merc k* *Nat-m* k* *Sil* k* symph fd3.de•
- **stitching** pain: ars k* calc k* cham k* *Cina* kali-bi kali-i k* lach k* led k* spong k* teucr
- **tearing** pain: *Aur-m* k* *Con* k* gamb k* indg k* *Kalm* k* merc k2 mez k*

▽ • **extending** to:
  ⋮ **Forehead**: *Kali-i*↓
    : **boring** pain: *Kali-i* k*
  ⋮ **Root** of nose: *Coloc*↓
    : **boring** pain: *Coloc*

○ • **Turbinated** bones: cop↓
  ⋮ **cutting** pain: cop br1

- **Cartilage**: mang↓
- **pressure** agg.: calc
- **sore**: mang k2

○ • **Junction** of: **Kali-bi** mang k2

- **Corners** of: camph↓ nux-v↓
- **stitching** pain: camph
- **ulcerative** pain: camph nux-v k*

- **Dorsum**: agn k* bar-c↓ canth chin *Cinnb*↓ coloc↓ *Hep* kali-bi k* kalm *Nat-c*↓ nat-sil fd3.de• *Petr*↓ *Phos* *Sil*↓ symph↓ vanil fd5.de
- **right** side: con↓ inul↓
  ⋮ **stitching** pain: con inul

- **Dorsum**: ...
- **morning**: canth↓
  ⋮ **aching**: canth
- **aching**: agn k* canth
- **burning** pain: bar-c h2 coloc
- **pressing** pain:
  ⋮ **glasses**; as from: *Cinnb*
  ⋮ **stone**; like a: agn coloc kalm symph fd3.de•
- **pressure**:
  ⋮ **amel.**: agn↓
    : **pressing** pain: agn
- **sore**: **Hep** k* *Kali-bi* *Nat-c* *Petr* k* **Phos** *Sil*
- **tearing** pain: *Chin* k*

- **Inside**: acon↓ *Aesc*↓ agar↓ all-c↓ allox↓ *Alum*↓ alum-p↓ alum-sil↓ *Am-m*↓ ambr↓ anac↓ ang↓ anis↓ ant-c↓ aphis↓ arn↓ *Ars*↓ *Ars-i*↓ **Arum-t**↓ **Aur**↓ aur-ar↓ aur-m↓ aur-s↓ bapt↓ bar-c↓ bar-m↓ bell↓ beryl↓ borx↓ *Bov*↓ *Brom*↓ bry↓ bufo↓ *Calc*↓ *Calc-p*↓ calc-sil↓ camph↓ caps↓ carb-an↓ carbn-s↓ cartl-s rly4• caust↓ cench↓ cham↓ chel↓ cic↓ cocc↓ colch↓ coli↓ *Con*↓ conv↓ cop↓ crot-t↓ dios↓ *Euphr* hr1 gels↓ ger-i rly4• **Graph** k* *Hep*↓ *Hydr*↓ hydr-ac↓ *Hyper*↓ *Ign*↓ jab↓ **Kali-bi**↓ *Kali-c*↓ **Kali-i**↓ *Kali-n*↓ kali-p↓ kali-s↓ kali-sil↓ lac-c↓ *Lach*↓ lact↓ led↓ lith-c↓ loxo-recl↓ *Mag-m*↓ mag-s↓ **Mang**↓ med↓ merc mtf33 merc-c↓ *Mez*↓ mur-ac↓ nat-ar k2 *Nat-m*↓ nat-ox↓ nat-p↓ nat-s↓ nat-sil↓ nicc↓ **Nit-ac**↓ *Nux-v*↓ ol-an↓ pen↓ *Petr*↓ phos↓ podo↓ psor↓ ptel↓ puls↓ ran-b↓ rheum c2 rhod↓ rhus-t k2 sabad↓ *Sang*↓ sangin-n↓ sars↓ sec↓ sep↓ **Sil**↓ sin-n↓ stann↓ staph↓ sulph↓ symph fd3.de• syph↓ teucr↓ *Thuj*↓ tritic-vg fd5.de *Tub*↓ uran-n↓ verat↓ *Zinc*↓ zinc-p↓
- **right**: allox↓ *Alum*↓ am-c↓ ant-c↓ **Aur**↓ calc↓ colch↓ *Graph*↓ kali-bi↓ *Kali-c*↓ *Kali-n*↓ kali-p↓ lac-c↓ mag-c↓ *Sil*↓ *Thuj*↓
  ⋮ **sore**: allox tpw4 *Alum* am-c ant-c *Aur* calc colch kali-bi *Kali-n* k* kali-p lac-c mag-c *Sil* *Thuj* k*
    : **followed** by | **left**: allox tpw4
  ⋮ **ulcerative** pain: **Aur** *Graph* *Kali-c* thuj
- **left**: agn↓ am-m↓ **Arum-t**↓ cench↓ coc-c↓ cocc↓ coff↓ fl-ac↓ ictod↓ med↓ nat-p↓ puls↓ staph↓
  ⋮ **sore**: agn k* **Arum-t** k* cench k2 coff k* fl-ac ictod med k* nat-p k* staph
  ⋮ **ulcerative** pain: am-m k* coc-c cocc puls staph
- **burning** pain: acon bro1 aesc bro1 all-c br1* alum-sil bro1 am-m bro1 *Ars* bro1 *Ars-i* bro1 arum-t bro1 bar-c bro1 brom bro1 caps bro1 cop bro1 hep bro1 *Hydr* bro1 *Merc* bro1 merc-c bro1 pen bro1 sabad bro1 *Sang* bro1 sangin-n bro1 sin-n bro1
- **inspiration** agg.: ant-c↓ symph↓ tax↓ tritic-vg↓
  ⋮ **sore**: ant-c h2 symph fd3.de• tritic-vg fd5.de [tax jsj7]
- **sore**: *Aesc* agar allox tpw4* *Alum* k* alum-p k2 alum-sil k* *Am-m* k* ambr k* anac ang k* anis bg1 ant-c k* aphis arn *Ars* **Arum-t** k* **Aur** k* aur-ar k2 aur-s k2 bapt k* bar-c k* bar-m beryl sp1 borx *Bov* *Brom* k* *Calc* k* *Calc-p* calc-sil k2 camph carb-an k* carbn-s caust k* cench k2 cham chel k* cic cocc colch coli rly4• *Con* k* conv br1 cop crot-t dios k* *Euphr* k* gels **Graph** k* hep k* *Hyper* k* *Ign* k* jab k* **Kali-bi** k* *Kali-c* k* **Kali-i** *Kali-n* k* kali-p kali-s kali-sil k2 lac-c k* *Lach* k* lact led bg1 lith-c loxo-recl knl4• *Mag-m* k* mag-s **Mang** med k* *Merc* merc-c k* *Mez* k* mur-ac k* nat-ar *Nat-m* k* nat-ox rly4• nat-p nat-s k* nat-sil fd3.de• nicc k* **Nit-ac** k* *Nux-v* k* ol-an k* *Petr* k* phos k* podo k* psor ptel k* puls k* ran-b rhod k* *Rhus-t* k* sars sec sep k* **Sil** k* stann k* staph k* sulph k* symph fd3.de• syph k* teucr *Thuj* k* tritic-vg fd5.de *Tub* k* (non:uran-met k) uran-n *Zinc* zinc-p k2
- **stitching** pain: bufo calc *Con* hydr-ac merc-c mur-ac sang k*
- **ulcerative** pain: *Am-m* k* ars k* **Aur** aur-m bg2 bell k* borx k* bry k* *Hep* k* ign *Kali-bi* *Nit-ac* *Nux-v* k* puls *Sil* k* verat k*

▽ • **extending** to | **Ear**:
  : **blowing** nose; on: calc↓
    . **stitching** pain: calc
  ⋮ **Forehead**: bufo↓ *Kali-bi*↓ *Kali-i*↓
    : **stitching** pain: bufo *Kali-bi* *Kali-i*

- **Margins** of: am-m↓ arn↓ calc↓ *Calc-p*↓ chel↓ kali-bi↓ nux-v↓ squil↓ sulph↓ sumb↓ thuj↓
- **burning** pain: arn chel sulph thuj

- **raw**; as if: sulph k*
- **sore**: am-m calc k* *Calc-p* k* kali-bi k* nux-v k* squil sumb k* thuj k*

- **Nostrils**: aesc↓ *Ail*↓ alum↓ ant-c↓ ars↓ *Arum-t*↓ aur↓ aur-m↓ bar-c↓ bell h1 **Bov**↓ **Brom**↓ cact↓ calc↓ *Calc-p*↓ canth↓ caps↓ caust↓ con↓ corian-s↓ dulc fd4.de euph↓ graph↓ hep↓ hepat↓ hydr↓ hydrog srj2• iod↓ *Kali-bi*↓ kali-c↓ **Lach**↓ lachn↓ lap-la↓ led↓ luna kg1• lyc↓ *Mag-m*↓ med↓ merc↓ merc-c↓ nit-ac↓ phos↓ phys↓ rhus-t↓ ruta fd4.de sang↓ *Sep*↓ spong fd4.de stann↓ suis-em rly4• sulph↓ vanil fd5.de
  - **right**: abrom-a ks5 dulc fd4.de lach↓ lyc h2* olib-sac↓ psor↓ vanil fd5.de
    - **cutting** pain: lyc k*
    - **digging** pain | **tensive**: lach
    - **drawing** pain: olib-sac wmh1
    - **perforating**: psor jl2
    - **sore**:
      - **followed** by | **left**: allox sp1
    - **extending** to | **Shoulder**; over the head and down the right neck to the: brass-n-o srj5•
  - **left**: bell h1* lac-h↓ olib-sac↓ ruta fd4.de spong fd4.de suis-em rly4•
    - **evening**: chin↓
      - **biting** pain: chin k*
    - **drawing** pain: olib-sac wmh1
    - **pressing** pain: lac-h sk4•
    - **stitching** pain: olib-sac wmh1
    - **Anterior** angle: cocc h1* coff k*
    - **Interior** angle: coff
  - **morning**: aq-mar skp7•
  - **breathing** through: med↓ ptel↓
    - **burning** pain: med c1 ptel hr1
  - **burning** pain: aesc bg2 alum bg2 ars bg2 arum-t bg2 aur-m bg2 bell bg2 canth bg2 caps h1 caust con h2 corian-s knl6• dulc fd4.de euph bg2 hep bg2 hydr bg2 kali-bi bg2 kali-c h2 lap-la rsp1 led bg2 mag-m h2* med al2 merc bg2 nit-ac bg2 phys br1 ruta fd4.de sang bg2 spong fd4.de stann bg2 sulph bg2
  - **corrosive**: lyc h2*
  - **ear**; like a string from nostril to: lem-m br1*
  - **pressing** pain | **pinched**; as if: *Kali-bi* lachn spong
  - **raw**; as if: *Ail* k* *Arum-t* bar-c **Bov Brom** cact calc *Calc-p* graph k2 iod **Lach** *Mag-m* merc merc-c k* phos rhus-t *Sep* sulph k2
  - **sore**: ant-c tl1* aur tl1 calc tl1 hepat br1 med tl1 merc tl1
  - **touch** agg.: abrom-a ks5
  - ○ **Inside**: ger-i↓ merc↓ ruta↓ spong↓
    - **burning** pain: ger-i rly4• merc k2* ruta fd4.de spong fd4.de

- **Outer** part: plat↓
  - **gnawing** pain | **acrid**; as of something: plat k*

- **Posterior** nares: *Acon*↓ *Aesc*↓ agar↓ ail↓ alum↓ am-m↓ ang↓ aral↓ arg-n↓ arum-m↓ *Arum-t*↓ bapt↓ bell↓ caps↓ carb-v↓ caust↓ chlor↓ *Cist*↓ colch↓ cop↓ crot-t↓ des-ac rbp6 dig↓ *Elaps* hydr↓ irid-met↓ iris↓ *Kali-bi*↓ kali-n↓ kali-perm kreos↓ lac-ac↓ lac-del↓ lec↓ lyc↓ mag-c↓ mag-s↓ *Merc-i-r*↓ mez↓ nux-v↓ ox-ac↓ par↓ pen↓ petr↓ ph-ac↓ phos↓ *Quill*↓ rhod↓ sang↓ seneg↓ sep↓ spong fd4.de staph↓ verat↓ zinc↓
  - **left**: *Gels*↓
    - **burning** pain | **scalding** water; like: *Gels*
  - **morning**: chlor↓ dig↓
    - **raw**; as if: chlor dig h2*
    - **sore**: dig
  - **afternoon**: nat-ar↓
    - **raw**; as if: nat-ar
  - **evening**: dig↓
    - **raw**; as if: dig h2*
  - **air** streamed in on coughing or talking; as if: mag-s
  - **blowing** the nose agg.: *Carb-v* k*
  - **burning** pain: *Aesc* k* arg-n arum-m bg2 bell bg2 caps bg2 carb-v bg2 *Cist* colch bg2 crot-t *Kali-bi Merc-i-r* petr bg2 phos sang bg2 verat bg2
  - **chill**: des-ac rbp6
  - **cough** agg.; during: *Carb-v* k*
    - **sore**: carb-v

- **Posterior** nares: ...
  - **eructation**, after: sulph h2*
  - **inspiration** agg.: *Ferr-p*↓ kreos↓
    - **raw**; as if: *Ferr-p* kreos
  - **pressing** pain: lac-del hrn2• lyc h2*
  - **raw**; as if: *Acon* agar bg2 ang bg2 aral bg2 *Arum-t* carb-v k* caust bg2 chlor *Cist* dig h2* hydr irid-met bg2* iris *Kali-bi* kali-n k* lac-ac *Merc-i-r* mez bg2 pen br1* *Quill* bg1* sep k*
  - **sand**; as from: cist bg2
  - **scratching** pain: ail bg2 mez bg2 nux-v bg2 rhod bg2 seneg bg2 sep bg2 staph k* zinc bg2
  - **snoring**; from: des-ac rbp6
  - **sore**: acon ptk1 am-m h2* aral vh1 bapt k* carb-v bg2* cop dig bg2 kali-n ptk1 kreos lec mag-c k* ox-ac k* par k* ph-ac k* sep ptk1 spong fd4.de
  - **splinter**; as from a: alum bg2
  - **stitching** pain: *Aesc*
  - **swallowing** agg.: *Carb-v* k*
  - **tearing** pain: zinc
  - **ulcerative** pain: bapt bg2 carb-v bg2 dig bg2 mag-c bg2 ox-ac bg2 ph-ac bg2

- **Posteriorly**: ferr-p↓ hydr↓ iris↓
  - **smarting**: ferr-p bg2 hydr bg2 iris bg2

- **Root**: abrom-a↓ *Acon* k* acon-ac rly4• aesc↓ agar↓ agath-a nl2• agn k* all-c↓ all-s↓ aloe↓ *Alum* k* alum-p k2 alum-sil k2 am-c↓ ammc↓ anan↓ androc srj1• *Ant-t* arg-n arn↓ *Ars* k* *Arum-t* arund k* asar↓ aspar *Bapt* k* bar-c↓ bar-i k2 bell↓ benz-ac↓ bism↓ *Brom*↓ calc calc-act↓ calc-sil k2 cann-i k* cann-s k2 cann-xyz bg2 caps↓ carb-an↓ *Carb-v* k* castm↓ caust↓ chel↓ *Chin* chion↓ cimic↓ cimx↓ cinnb colch↓ coloc bg2 *Con* crot-t cund↓ *Cupr* k* *Cycl*↓ *Dig* k* *Dulc*↓ dys pte1*• *Elaps* euphr *Ferr* ferr-p bg1 *Gels* k* *Glon* k* granit-m↓ grat↓ ham↓ hell k* **Hep** k* heroin↓ hipp↓ hydrog srj2• hyos bg2 *Ign* inul↓ *Iod*↓ **Kali-bi** k* *Kali-c*↓ kali-chl↓ kali-i bg1* *Kali-p*↓ *Kalm*↓ kola stb3• lac-cp sk4• lac-d k2 lach bg1 lyc↓ mag-s↓ malar jl2 manc↓ *Mang*↓ meny↓ *Merc* k* *Merc-c*↓ *Merc-i-f* k* merl↓ *Mez* mill k2 *Nat-ar* k* *Nat-m* k* *Nat-s* nicc↓ *Nit-ac*↓ *Nux-v*↓ olib-sac↓ olnd↓ onis↓ ozone↓ *Par*↓ parth gm1 *Petr* k* *Phos* k* *Phyt* plat propr sa3• prun↓ ptel↓ *Puls* k* *Ran-b*↓ raph↓ rheum↓ *Rhus-t*↓ rhus-v↓ ruta bg2 *Sang* k* *Sangin-n*↓ sarr k* *Sep* k* ser-a-c jl2 *Sil* k* sol-t-ae↓ spong↓ *Stict* mrr1 streptoc rly4• sul-i↓ sulph k* symph fd3.de• *Teucr*↓ ther k* thuj k* tritic-vg fd5.de *Tub-a* jl2 viol-t bg2 zinc bg2
  - **right**: aur↓ kali-c↓ lachn↓
    - **boring** pain: aur mrr1
    - **burning** pain: lachn
    - **cramping**: kali-c
  - **left**: agar↓ kali-c↓
    - **burning** pain: kali-c h2
    - **stitching** pain: agar
  - **7-12 h**: hep↓
    - **boring** pain: hep
  - **morning**: *Hep*↓
    - **boring** pain: *Hep* k*
  - **aching**: agn k* asar k* bapt chin hell *Hep Kali-bi* k* nat-ar phos bg2 puls sang sulph k*
  - **boring** pain: agar bism k* *Hep* k* nat-m k* phos k* sulph k*
  - **burning** pain: *Kali-bi* mrr1 kali-i mrr1 [heroin sdj2]
  - **bursting** pain: ham bg2 ign bg2 mez bg2
  - **catarrhal** symptoms or headache; with: hep↓
    - **boring** pain: hep c1
  - **cramping**: *Acon* k* arn k* bapt k* bell k* colch hyos k* kali-c *Mang* k* *Plat* k* zinc k*
  - **crushing**: anan k*
  - **cutting** pain: *Kali-c Teucr*
  - **drawing** pain: *Calc* k* *Carb-v* k* caust bg2 kali-chl k* lach bg2 nat-m k* petr *Phyt* k* rheum *Sil* k*
    - **upward**: nat-m h2
  - **falls** with vertigo; before he: *Kali-c*↓
    - **stitching** pain: *Kali-c*

- **gnawing** pain: (non:calc slp) calc-act slp merc k* raph k*
- **headache**; during: **Agar** carc fd2.de• *Cupr* k* dulc a1 ferr glon hep *Merc Merc-i-f* k* *Mez* ozone sde2• stict c1*
- **menses**; before: *Con* k*
- **operation**; after: ferr-p ↓
  - **sore**: ferr-p ptk1
- **paroxysmal**: arn hyos zinc
- **pressing** pain: abrom-a ks5 acon k* acon-ac rly4• aesc k* agar k* agn k* all-c k* all-s k* aloe bg2 alum bro1 am-c ammc vh1 anan k* *Ant-t* arum-t bro1 asar bg2 aspar k* *Bapt* k* bar-c k* benz-ac k* bism *Brom* calc k* cann-s k* cann-xyz bg2 caps bro1 carb-v k* chel *Chin* k* chion br1 cimic bg3 cimx *Cinnb* k* coloc k* cund k* *Cycl Dulc* k* *Gels* k* glon bg2* granit-m es1• grat k* ham fd3.de• hell h1* hep bro1 hipp *Hyos* k* ign bg2 *Iod* k* **Kali-bi** k* *Kali-c* kali-i bro1 *Kali-p* kalm k* kola stb3• *Lac-d* k* lach bg2 lyc h2* mag-s manc k* mang meny bro1 *Merc* k* merl a1 mez k* *Nat-ar* k* *Nat-m* k* nit-ac bg2 *Nux-v* bro1 olib-sac wmh1 olnd onis bro1 ozone sde2• *Par* bro1 phos k* plat bro1 prun ptel hr1* *Puls* k* *Ran-b* k* raph k* rhus-v ruta k* *Sangin-n* bro1 sarr k* *Sep* k* sil bg2 sol-t-ae vml3• spong stict k* sul-i k2 ther k* *Thuj* k* tritic-vg fd5.de *Zinc* k*
  - **accompanied** by:
    - **coryza**: ran-b bg2 zinc bg2
    - **epistaxis** (See Epistaxis - accompanied - pain - pressing - root)
    - **vertigo** (See VERTIGO - Accompanied - nose - pressing - root)
  - **followed** by:
    - **epistaxis**: bry bg1 *Dulc* bg1* kali-bi bg1 *Ruta* bg1*
    - **vertigo**: *Zinc*
  - **stupefying**: acon cann-s olnd zinc h2*
- **pressure**:
  - **amel.**: *Kali-bi* ↓
    - **pressing** pain: *Kali-bi*
- **pulsating** pain: kali-bi sarr k*
- **reading** agg.: *Nat-ar* mrr1
- **sneezing** agg.: nit-ac ↓
  - **stitching** pain: nit-ac k*
- **sore**: *Ant-t* k* carb-an k* kali-bi k* nicc k* *Nit-ac* k* raph k*
- **stitching** pain: acon inul *Kali-bi* k* merc-i-f k* mill nat-m k* nicc *Nit-ac* k* *Phos Rhus-t* sil k* teucr
  - **alternating** with | **Occiput**; stitching in: acon
- **stooping** agg.: puls ↓
  - **ulcerative** pain: puls
- **tearing** pain: castm k* chin coloc k* *Kalm* k* *Mang* k* *Merc-c* k* nicc k* *Phos* k*
- **touch** agg.: petr ↓
  - **ulcerative** pain: petr h2
- **vomiting**; after: dig c1*
- ▽ **extending** to:
  - **Canthus** of eye; external: *Kali-bi* ↓
    - **stitching** pain: *Kali-bi*
  - **Ear**: elaps ↓
    - **burning** pain: elaps
  - **Ears** | **swallowing** agg.: elaps
  - **Forehead**: elaps hr1 hep k2 merc k2 *Mez Nat-m* ↓ ozone sde2• sabal c1
    - **tearing** pain: *Nat-m*
  - **Forehead**; side of: chin ↓ ozone ↓
    - **pressing** pain: chin ozone sde2•
  - **Malar** bones: *Rhus-t* ↓
    - **burning** pain: *Rhus-t* hr1
  - **Occiput**: ferr-i ↓
    - **cutting** pain: ferr-i
  - **Tip**: camph ↓ rheum ↓
    - **drawing** pain: rheum
    - **stitching** pain: camph k*
- ○ **Behind**: trios ↓

- **Root – Behind**: ...
  - **dull** pain: trios rsj11•
- **Inside**: carbn-s ↓ *Kali-bi* ↓ lap-la ↓ nat-m ↓
  - **burning** pain: carbn-s *Kali-bi* lap-la rsp1 nat-m
- **Spot**; in a small: ozone ↓
  - **pressing** pain: ozone sde2•

- **Septum**: alum alum-sil k2 aphis ↓ asar ↓ aur ↓ borx ↓ *Bov* ↓ calc ↓ caust k* chin ↓ cina ↓ *Cinnm* ↓ *Colch* ↓ con ↓ crot-t ↓ dulc fd4.de hep ↓ *Hydr* ↓ *Iod* ↓ kali-bi k* kali-s ↓ *Lac-c* ↓ lyc ↓ *Mag-m* ↓ *Merc-i-f* ↓ mez ↓ *Mur-ac* ↓ nat-m ↓ petr-ra ↓ plb sel k* sep ↓ *Sil* k* spong fd4.de *Staph* ↓ *Sulph* ↓ thuj ↓ tritic-vg fd5.de
  - **right**: lac-c ↓ lyc ↓ *Merc-i-f* ↓
    - **pimple**, from a: calad ↓
      - **sore**: calad
    - **sore**: lac-c k* lyc h2* *Merc-i-f* k*
  - **left**: cina ↓ dulc ↓ helodr-cal ↓ spong ↓
    - **boring** pain: helodr-cal knl2•
    - **burning** pain: cina dulc fd4.de spong fd4.de
    - **inspiration** agg.: agar ↓
      - **cutting** pain: agar
  - **morning**: *Sulph* ↓
    - **burning** pain: *Sulph*
  - **biting** pain: asar
  - **burning** pain: aphis cina dulc fd4.de *Kali-bi* mez sil spong fd4.de *Sulph*
  - **cutting** pain: lyc k* merc-i-f k*
  - **raw**; as if: dulc fd4.de lac-c *Mag-m* petr-ra shn4•
  - **sore**: *Alum* k* borx *Bov* k* calc caust k* *Colch* k* con crot-t a1 dulc fd4.de hep k* *Hydr* k* **Kali-bi** k* kali-s *Lac-c* k* *Mag-m Merc-i-f* k* *Mur-ac* nat-m petr-ra shn4• sep k* *Sil Staph* k* *Sulph* k* thuj k* tritic-vg fd5.de
  - **stitching** pain: aur k* chin *Cinnm* k* con k* *Iod* k* *Sil*
  - **tearing** pain: plb k*
  - **touch** agg.: con ↓ sil ↓ staph ↓ zinc ↓
    - **burning** pain: sil staph
    - **sticking**: zinc
    - **stitching** pain: con h2 sil zinc
    - **ulcerative** pain: staph
  - ○ **Upper** part: lyc ↓
    - **cutting** pain: lyc k*

- **Sides**: aeth ↓ alum ↓ carb-an ↓ carb-v ↓ graph ↓ petr ↓ rhodi ↓ sil ↓ sul-ac ↓
  - **right**: lyc ↓
    - **tearing** pain: lyc h2*
  - **left**: mag-c ↓
    - **tearing** pain: mag-c h2*
  - **burning** pain: aeth alum h2 graph h2 petr h2 sil h2
  - **neuralgic**: rhodi br1
  - **stitching** pain: aeth alum h2* sil sul-ac h2*
  - **tearing** pain: carb-an carb-v h2*
  - ▽ **extending** to:
    - **Eye**: lyc ↓
      - **tearing** pain: lyc h2
    - **Temple**: mag-c ↓
      - **tearing** pain: mag-c h2

- **Sinuses**: (↗*Sinuses; FACE - Pain - sinuses)* anh sp1 gels ↓ ign ↓ iod ↓ kali-bi ↓ *Kali-i* ↓ merc ↓ nux-v ↓ pseuts-m oss1• sang ↓ sil ↓ *Stict* ↓ tritic-vg ↓
  - **right** | **night**: am-m c1
  - **burning** pain: kali-i ptk1
  - **inspiration** agg.: syph ptk1
  - **pressing** pain: gels bro1 ign bro1 iod bro1 kali-bi bro1* *Kali-i* bro1 merc bro1 nux-v bro1 sang bro1 *Stict* bro1 tritic-vg fd5.de
  - **pressure** | **amel.**: lob mrr1
  - **pulsating** pain: kali-i ptk1 sil h2*
  - **ulcerative** pain: sil h2*
  - ○ **Maxillary** sinus (See FACE - Pain - sinuses - maxillary)

- **Skin**: *Mez* ↓

- **biting** pain: *Mez* k*
- Spots; in: bar-c ↓ graph ↓ iod ↓ merc-i-f ↓
  - **burning** pain: bar-c graph iod k*
  - **sore**: merc-i-f k*
- **Tip**: anis ↓ bar-c k* bell k* berb ↓ *Borx* ↓ calc ↓ caps ↓ carb-an k* carb-v bg3 carbn-s ↓ caust bg3 *Cist* k* *Con* ↓ hep ↓ kali-bi ↓ kali-c ↓ kali-n h2* lact ↓ *Lith-c* ↓ loxo-recl ↓ lyc k* merc-sul ↓ nicc ↓ ol-an ↓ op ↓ ox-ac ↓ plb *Rhus-t* a1* sars ↓ sep bg3 sil a1 stront-c ↓ tax ↓
  - **burning** pain: bell k* borx bro1 caps *Carb-an* k* carbn-s nicc ol-an ox-ac bro1 rhus-t bro1 sil
  - **burrowing**: sil k*
  - **cramping**: stront-c
  - **gnawing** pain: berb k*
  - **griping** pain: kali-n h2*
  - **menses**; during: carb-an
    - **burning** pain: *Carb-an*
  - **pressing** pain: lact k*
  - **raw**; as if: calc carbn-s
  - **sore**: bell *Borx* k* calc k* carb-an cist k* *Con* k* hep kali-bi k* *Lith-c* k* loxo-recl knl4• lyc k* merc-sul k* op k* *Rhus-t* k* sil k* tax k*
  - **stitching** pain: anis bell k* *Con* kali-c kali-n k* sars h2* sep sil k*
  - **touch** agg.: borx bro1 *Hep* bro1 *Menth* bro1 *Rhus-t* a1* sep ↓ sulph h2*
    - **stitching** pain: sep
  - ▽ **extending** to:
    - **Forehead**: sil ↓
      - **stitching** pain: sil k*
- **Upper** part: teucr ↓
  - **stitching** pain: teucr
- **Wings** (= alae nasi): all-c ↓ am-m ↓ ant-c ↓ aphis ↓ ars ↓ aur ↓ aur-m-n ↓ bar-c brom ↓ calc k* calc-p ↓ calc-s ↓ caps ↓ caust ↓ chel ↓ clem ↓ coc-c ↓ gels hep iod ↓ kali-bi ↓ kali-c ↓ kali-n ↓ lyc bg3 *Nat-m* ↓ nept-m ↓ *Nit-ac* ↓ nux-v ↓ plat ↓ plb ↓ rhus-t ↓ *Sangin-n* ↓ seneg ↓ sil ↓ sin-n ↓ stram sulph ↓ syph ↓ thuj bg3 vanil fd5.de zinc ↓
  - **right**: ambr ↓ arg-n k* asaf ↓ caust ↓ cic ↓ daph ↓ falco-pe ↓ hydr ↓ mez ↓ vanil fd5.de
    - **bursting** pain: asaf
    - **cramping**: ambr k*
    - **cutting** pain: caust
    - **motion** agg.: calc
    - **sore**: cic daph falco-pe nl2• hydr k* mez
    - **tearing** pain: caust
    - **touch** agg.: mag-m
  - **left**: ail ↓ alum h2* calc ↓ gink-b sbd1• laur ↓ med ↓ nat-m ↓ plat ↓ sil ↓ thuj ↓ zinc k*
    - **cramping**: plat
    - **cutting** pain: zinc
    - **desire** to rub; with: carb-ac ↓
      - **electric** sparks; sensation of: carb-ac
    - **just** above: lach
    - **sore**: ail vh1 calc med nat-m h2*
    - **tearing** pain: sil k* thuj
    - **touch** agg.: alum h2* stann h2*
    - **ulcerative** pain: laur
  - **evening**: nux-v ↓
    - **ulcerative** pain: nux-v k*
  - **biting** pain: aphis aur-m-n a1
  - **burning** pain: all-c aphis k* ars bro1 caps h1 chel clem coc-c kali-c kali-n nept-m lsd2.fr *Nit-ac* *Sangin-n* bro1 seneg bro1 sin-n bro1 sulph k* syph
  - **cramping**: kali-n plat zinc
  - **cutting** pain: caust stram zinc k*
  - **drawing** pain: caust plb a1
  - **griping** pain: kali-n h2*
  - **motion** agg.: nux-v ↓
    - **ulcerative** pain: nux-v k*

Pain – Wings: ...

  - **raw**; as if: all-c k2
  - **rubbing**:
    - **amel.**: nept-m ↓
      - **sore**: nept-m lsd2.fr
  - **sore**: am-m ant-c ptk1 aur h2* brom calc calc-p calc-s gels iod kali-bi *Nat-m* nept-m lsd2.fr nit-ac k* nux-v ptk1 rhus-t
  - **stitching** pain: kali-c stram vanil fd5.de
  - **tearing** pain: caust sil k* stram k*
  - **touch** agg.: *Alum* bro1 *Ant-c* bro1 ars bro1 *Arum-t* bro1 aur-m bro1 calc bro1 cop bro1 cor-r bro1 fago bro1 *Graph* bro1 *Hep* bro1 *Kali-bi* bro1 mag-m merc bro1 *Merc-c* bro1 *Nit-ac* bro1 petr bro1 squil bro1 stann k* uran-n bro1
  - **ulcerative** pain: nux-v k*
  - ○ **Edges**: sulph ↓
    - **right**: sulph ↓
      - **evening**: alum ↓
        - **burning** pain: alum
      - **burning** pain: sulph
    - **left**: hell ↓ sulph ↓
      - **burning** pain: hell sulph
    - **burning** pain: sulph bg1
  - **Inner** surface: *Mag-m* ↓ med ↓ nat-m ↓
    - **raw**; as if: *Mag-m* med nat-m h2
  - **Junction** of face; with: all-s ↓
    - **left** side: all-s ↓
      - **stitching** pain: all-s
    - **stitching** pain: all-s

PARCHMENT, sensation as if nose were: *Kali-bi* k* sulph k*

PEELING of (See Desquamation)

PERFORATED: | **Septum**: alum kl *Kali-bi* br1* kali-br bg3 kali-i bg3* merc bg3* merc-c bg3* sil ptk1* syph ptk1*

PERSPIRATION on: *(↗FACE - Perspiration - offensive; HEAD - Perspiration of - forehead - nose)* bac bn bell k* calc sne chin bg2 cimx cina k* cinnb dp• hell bg2 ign h lap-la sde8.de• laur k* **Nat-m** k ●* rheum k* ruta k* suis-pan rly4• teucr bg2* **Tub** k ●* [heroin sdj2]

- **morning**: cimx
- **cold**: *Cina* a1
  - ○ **Around** nose: **Chin** k* rheum h

PICKING: rumx bg2

- **affected** parts; the: mag-m
- ○ **Nose**: *(↗Boring)* **Arum-t** k* aur-m a bacls-10 ptj• bell sne carb-v bg3 caust bg3 **Cina** k* *Con* cop hell hyper ign sne lac-c limest-b es1• **Lyc** bg1* merc bg3 nat-m bg3 nat-p nit-ac bg3 nux-v petr bg petr-ra shn4• ph-ac *Phos* bg3* pip-n sne sabal c1 sil bg3 sulph bg3 sumb c1 tarent mtf33 **Teucr** thuj bg* zinc
  - **bleeds**, until it: **Arum-t** **Cina** *Con* *Lach* *Phos* bg1* pip-n sne *Sil* bg1* zinc mtf33
  - **constant** desire: *(↗MIND - Gestures - tics)* *Con* lil-t rumx stict symph ter
    - **brain** affections; in: **Cina** k* *Con* *Hell* **Sulph** k*

PINCHED: ant-t k2 aur-m k2 *Camph* k* canth k2 cina bg2* hyos bg2 *Kali-bi* k* kali-c bg2* lachn a1 *Lyc* k* op a1 podo a1 sep a1 *Spig* k* spong k* verat k* verat-v k* zinc bg2

- **as** if: hist vml3• *Kali-bi* ptk1 spong ptk1
  - ○ **Root** of nose: hist sp1 lachn br1 vac jl2
    - **breakfast** agg.; after: vac jl2
    - **epistaxis**; before: vac jl2

POINTED: anan k* *Ant-t* k* apis bro1 *Ars* k* calc-p bro1 **Camph** k* *Carb-v* k* chin b7.de* cocc k* *Cupr* k* *Hell* k* kali-cy a1 *Lach* k* laur b7.de* morph a1 myos-a k* nux-v k* op bg2 *Ph-ac* k* plb podo bg2 raph a1 rhus-t k* sec b7.de* spong *Staph* k* *Tab* bro1 **Verat** k*

POLYPUS: *All-c* k* alumn k* *Apis* arg-met jl arist-cl sp1 arum-m k* aur k* aur-m bg2 aur-s k2 bell k* bell-p sp1 blum-o bnj1 cadm-s bg2* **Calc** k* calc-i k* *Calc-p* k* *Calc-s* calc-sil k2 *Carbn-s* caust bro1 *Con* k* form k* gaert pte1*• gonotox jl2 *Graph* k* hecla hep hip-ac jl hydr influ jl2* *Kali-bi* k* *Kali-i* bg1*

Polypus: ...
Kali-n k* *Lem-m* k* lyc k* med c1* merc k* merc-aur bg2 merc-c *Merc-i-r* k* merc-k-i c2 morg-g pte1*• nat-m b4a.de nit-ac k* nux-v sne petr b4a.de ph-ac b4a.de *Phos* k* *Psor* k* puls k* reser jl rob a **Sang** k* sangin-n br1* *Sep* k* *Sil* k* staph k* sul-ac b4a.de sulo-ac jl *Sulph* k* syc pte1*• **Teucr** k* *Thuj* k* tub k13* tub-a jl2 v-a-b jl2 vac jl2 visc jl wye bro1 zinc-chr kl*
- **right**: *Caust* vh *Kali-n* k*
- **left**: alumn k* apis calc merc-i-r k*
- **bleeds** easily: calc calc-p k* *Phos* k* thuj
- **pedunculated**; large: calc-p tl1

○ - **Posterior** nares: *Teucr* k*

PRESSURE:
- **agg.**: am-m bg2 kali-bi bg2 led b7.de* lyc bg2 sil bg2
- **amel.**: agn b7.de*
- **glasses**; of:
  - **agg.**: arg-n bg3* chin bg3* cinnb bg3* con bg3* cupr-ar bg3* fl-ac ptk1 kali-bi bg3* *Merc* bg3* phos bg3*
  - **amel.**: fl-ac bg2

PRICKLING (See Tingling)

PROTUBERANCES: *Iod* k* *Nit-ac* k* syph

PUFFINESS: *(↗Swelling)* bell caust kali-c merc nat-c ph-ac plb puls rhus-t sep

PULLED, as if: *Nat-c* bg1*

PULSATION: *Agar* k* all-c arg-met k* **Ars** k* bell bg2 borx k* bov bg2 canth b7.de* *Coloc* k* cor-r k* hydrog srj2• kali-bi k2 **Kali-i** k* mag-m k* ph-ac b4.de* sil k*
- **right**: kali-bi bg2
- **left**: arg-met

○ - **Root**: ars bg2 borx camph bg2 **Kali-bi** k* phos h2* sarr k* zinc bg2
- **Tip**: hydrog srj2• ph-ac
- **Wings**: acon bro1 brom bro1

QUIVERING: agar k* chel k* kali-bi bg2 mosch stront-c k*
- **left** side: am-c k*

○ - **Root**:
  - **visible**: mez k*

▽ - **extending** to | **Cheek**: calc-s k*

RATTLING: *(↗RESPIRATION - Rattling)* alum h2* am-c h2*

RED (See Discoloration - redness)

RESPIRATION noisy (See RESPIRATION - Loud)

RHINITIS (See Inflammation)

RISING: | **after** | **agg.**: *Bry* bg2 carb-v bg2 phos bg2
- **bed**; from | **agg.**: stann b4.de* thuj b4.de*

ROOM agg.: *Aur* b4.de* bell bg2 puls b7.de*

ROUGHNESS inside: carb-v bg2 kola stb3• mez
- **night**: carb-v

▽ - **extending** to | **Pharynx**: kola stb3•

○ - **Posterior** nares: am-m h2 gal-ac hyper irid-met vml3• staph

RUBBING:
- **amel.**: bell b4.de* nat-c b4.de* phos b4.de* plb b7.de* sulph b4.de* thuj b4.de* zinc b4.de*
- **sensation** as if: kali-bi bg2

RUBS nose (See Itching - rubs)

SCABS (See Discharge - crusts)

SCARLET FEVER; after: arum-t bro1 *Aur* b4a.de aur-m bro1 mur-ac bro1 sulph bro1

SCRAPING: nat-c h2* **Nat-m** nat-s

○ - **Posterior** nares: *Kali-bi* k* *Kali-chl* *Kali-p* nat-c h2* **Nat-m** nat-s

SCURFY: *(↗Discharge - crusts)*

○ - **Nostrils**: *(↗Discharge - crusts)* *Alum* am-m *Ant-c* k* arge-pl rwt5• **Aur** borx **Bov** brom k2 **Calc** carb-an chel cic crot-t ferr **Graph** *Hep* *Hippoz* *Iod* *Kali-bi* *Kali-c* **Lach** *Lyc* mag-m *Merc* *Merc-c* *Nat-m* *Nat-s* *Nit-ac* *Petr* *Phos* **Puls** rat sars **Sep** **Sil** *Sulph* *Thuj*

Scurfy – Nostrils: ...

○ • **Side** of nostrils: petr h2
- **Tip** of nose: nit-ac ptk1

SEASONS:
- **winter**; in | **agg.**: am-c k* ars k* cist bg2 sulph ptk1

SENSITIVE: agar b4.de* am-m b7a.de* *Ant-c* b7a.de aur b4.de* canth b7.de* chin b7.de* *Hep* b4a.de ign b7.de* kreos bg2 led b7.de* merc-c b4a.de nat-c b4a.de* nux-v b7.de* psor bg2 rhus-t b7.de* sabad b7.de* *Sep* b4a.de sil b4a.de* sulph bg2 thuj bg2 *Zinc* b4.de*
- **air**; to:
  - **cold** air (See Cold - air - agg.)
  - **inspired** air (See Air - inspired)
- **touch**; to (See Pain - touch)

○ - **Inside**: agar bg2 am-c bg2
- **Nostrils**:
  - **accompanied** by | **voice**; loss of (See LARYNX - Voice - lost - accompanied - nostrils)
- **Tip**: kali-bi bg2

SENSITIVE to odors (See Smell - acute)

SHINY: ambr vh1 aur-m-n k* *Calc* bg1* canth k* *Hydr* bg1* *Iris* bg1* merc k* *Mez* bg1* ox-ac k* peti a1 **Phos** k* rhus-v a1

○ - **Tip**: *Bell* k* borx *Phos* k* *Sulph* k*
- **Wing** | **right**: canth

SHRIEKING; complaints from: *Arn* b7a.de

SINGING; after: hep b4a.de

SINUSITIS (See Sinuses; GENERALS - Inflammation - sinuses)

SITTING: | **agg.**: carb-an b4a.de

SLEEP agg.; during: bry b7.de* merc b4.de* verat b7.de*

SMELL:
- **acute**: *(↗MIND - Senses - acute; MIND - Sensitive - odors)* **Acon** k* adam srj5• *Agar* k* alum k* alum-sil k2 am-c b2.de* ambr tsm1 *Anac* k* ant-c k* aran bg3 aran-ix sp1 arist-cl rbp3• arizon-l nl2• am k* *Ars* k* ars-s-f k2 asar k* **Aur** k* aur-ar k2 aur-s k2 bamb-a stb2.de• *Bar-c* k* bar-s k2 **Bell** k* bry k* *Calc* k* calc-sil k2 canth k* caps carb-ac k* carb-v bro1 *Carbn-s* *Cham* k* **Chin** k* choc srj3• cimic gk cina k* *Cocc* k* **Coff** k* *Colch* k* *Con* k* cupr k* cycl k* der a1 dig b2.de* dream-p sdj1• dulc fd4.de ephe-si hsj1• falco-pe nl2• galla-q-r nl2• granit-m es1• **Graph** k* haliae-lc srj5• ham k* *Hep* k* hippoc-k szs2 hydrog srj2• hyos k* *Hyper* k* **Ign** k* ip b2.de* kali-ar kali-bi bg2* kali-c k* kali-p kali-s kali-sil k2 *Kalm* k* ketogl-ac rly4• kola stb3• lac-ac k* lac-cp sk4• lach lavand-a ctl1• limen-b-c hm2* **Lyc** k* *Lyss* k* m-arct b2.de mag-c k* mag-m bro1 marb-w es1• merc bg2 mez k* mur-ac tl1 musca-d szs1 nat-ar nat-c k* nat-p nat-sil fd3.de• neon srj5• *Nux-m* k* **Nux-v** k* *Olib-sac* wmh1 **Op** k* oxal-a rly4• ozone sde2• par vml3• petr k* petr-ra shn4• ph-ac k* **Phos** k* pieri-b mlk9.de *Plat* k* *Plb* k* plumbg a1 plut-n srj7• podo fd3.de• positr nl2• psor al2 puls k* ruta fd4.de sabad k* sang bg2* sel k* senec a1 **Sep** k* sil k* spig b2.de* spira a1 spong fd4.de stann staph k2 succ-ac rly4• sul-i a1 *Sulph* k* tab k* thuj k* tritic-vg fd5.de valer k* vanil fd5.de viol-o k* zinc k* zinc-p k2 [heroin sdj2 spect dfg1 tax jsj7]
  - **aromatic** drinks | **agg.** (See GENERALS - Food - aromatic - agg. - smell)
  - **beer** agg. (See GENERALS - Food - beer - agg. - smell)
  - **blood**: haliae-lc srj5•
  - **broth**: **Colch** olib-sac wmh1 sep k2
  - **cheese**: tritic-vg fd5.de
    - ⁝ **agg.** (See GENERALS - Food - cheese - agg. - smell)
  - **chlorine**: hippoc-k szs2 ozone sde2•
  - **coffee**: *(↗GENERALS - Food - coffee - agg. - smell)* arg-n lach sul-ac tub al2 vanil fd5.de
    - ⁝ **menopause**; during: **Lach** st *Sul-ac* kr1*
  - **cooking** food: *(↗food)* ars k2* chin k* cocc tl1* **Colch** k* *Dig* k* *Eup-per* falco-pe nl2• ip tl1* kali-s fd4.de kola stb3• merc-i-f ptk1 psor stx1 sanic stx1 *Sep* k* stann k* syc stx1 thuj tl1 tritic-vg fd5.de
  - **coryza**; during: *Bell* b4a.de kalm ptk1*
  - **delighted** by smells: positr nl2•

Nose

- **acute**: ...
  - **eggs**: (↗*GENERALS - Food - eggs - agg. - smeli)* **Colch** k* upa c1
  - **everything** smells too strong (See acute)
  - **exhaust** gas in city: ozone sde2•
  - **fat**: *Colch* b7a.de
  - **fish**: *Colch* k*
    - **foul**: par ptk1
  - **flowers**: (↗*Hay; Heat in; MIND - Sadness - flowers)* all-c k* chin k* choc srj3• galla-q-r nl2• **Graph** k* hyos kali-s fd4.de *Lac-c* k* lem-m c1 limen-b-c hrn2• lyc k* nat-sil fd3.de• **Nux-v** k* **Phos** k* sabad k2* sang k*
  - **food**: (↗*cooking; GENERALS - Food - food - agg. - smell; GENERALS - Food - food - aversion - smell)* ant-c k2 arg-n k* **Ars** k* bamb-a stb2.de• chin stx1 *Cocc* **Colch** k* eup-per falco-pe nl2• *Ip* lach ruta fd4.de sang stx1 **Sep** k* stann syc stx1 sym-r stx1 tritic-vg fd5.de upa stx1
  - **foul** | **agg.**: anthraci ptk1 kreos ptk1 par ptk1 pyrog ptk1
  - **fruit**: choc srj3•
  - **fuel**: ozone sde2•
  - **garlic**: (↗*GENERALS - Food - garlic - agg. - smell)* sabad b7a.de*
  - **gas** causes vertigo: **Nux-v Phos**
  - **headache**; during: dulc fd4.de moni rfm1• ozone sde2• **Phos** k* sang hr1
  - **meat**: falco-pe nl2•
    - **agg.** (See GENERALS - Food - meat - agg. - smell)
  - **mice**: sabad k*
  - **peaches**: (↗*GENERALS - Food - peaches - agg. - smell)* all-c k*
  - **perfumes**: (↗*MIND - Perfume - aversion)* ephe-si hsj1• falco-pe nl2• nat-sil fd3.de• phos mrr1* ruta fd4.de sabad mrr1 spong fd4.de symph fd3.de• tritic-vg fd5.de
  - **petrol**: petr-ra shn4•
  - **pork** | **agg.** (See GENERALS - Food - pork - agg. - smell)
  - **pregnancy** agg.; during: *Sep* mrr1 stann k*
  - **sensitive** to odors (See acute)
  - **soot**: bell k*
  - **sour** odors: alum bg2* bell bg2 dros k*
  - **stool**: dios ptk1 **Sulph** k*
  - **strange** odors: hippoc-k szs2 ozone sde2•
  - **strong** odors: *Acon* k* *Agar* k* anac k* asar k* **Aur** k* bar-c k* **Bell** k* bry k* cact bg2 calc k* canth k* carbn-s *Cham* k* *Chin* k* *Cocc* k* **Coff** k* **Colch** k* *Con* k* cupr k* **Graph** k* *Hep* k* hippoc-k szs2 **Ign** k* kali-c k* **Lyc** k* *Lyss* mag-c k* moni rfm1• musca-d szs1 nat-c k* nat-m **Nux-v** k* petr k* petr-ra shn4• **Phos** k* plb k* puls k* sabad b2.de* sabin sang bg2 sel k* *Sep* k* spig k* stann bg2 *Sulph* k* suprar rly4• ther bg2 valer k* [spect dfg1]
  - **sweets**: arg-n ptk1 aur bg2* nit-ac bg2* sil bg2*
  - **syrup**: sang bg2*
  - **tobacco**●: bamb-a stb2.de• *Bell* k* chin hippoc-k szs2 *Ign* kali-s fd4.de kola stb3• lyss nat-sil fd3.de• *Nux-v* phos podo fd3.de• *Puls* ruta fd4.de
  - **unpleasant** odors●: *Acon* all-c falco-pe nl2• hippoc-k szs2 kali-s fd4.de olib-sac wmh1 pall phos h2 podo fd3.de• **SULPH** k ●
  - **urine** | **cat**; from: limen-b-c hrn2•
  - **vinegar**: agar *Agar-em* c1 hydrog stx1
  - **water**: agath-a nl2•
  - **wine**: agar kr1 tab
  - **wood**: graph b2.de*
- **complaints** of: aur ptk1 **Bell** ptk1 calc ptk1 *Colch* ptk1 graph ptk1 hep ptk1 lyc ptk1 nat-m ptk1 **Nux-v** ptk1 **Phos** ptk1 *Puls* ptk1 *Sep* ptk1 *Sil* ptk1 **Sulph** ptk1
- **diminished**: *Alum* k* alum-sil k2 am-m bg2 **Anac** k* anh vh1 ant-t bg2 *Arg-n* k* arist-cl sp1 asaf aur b4a.de* **Bell** k* benz-ac k* bry bg2 bung-fa mtf **Calc** k* calc-s ptk1 calc-sil k2 *Caps* k* carb-an bg2 caust bg2 chel bg2 *Cocc* k* *Coloc* con k* *Cycl* k* diphtox jl2 dream-p sdj1• gink-b sbd1• graph bg2 *Hell* k* *Hep* k* **Hyos** k* *Ip* bg2 kali-bi bg2* kali-br k* kali-c k* kali-sil k2 kola stb3• laur k* *Lyc* k* *Mag-m* b4.de* mang b4.de* mentho bro1 *Merc* ptk1 *Merc-c* b4a.de *Mez* k* morg-p fmm1• mur-ac h2* nat-ar **Nat-m** k* nit-ac k* *Nux-v* k* olnd k* op k* osm a1 *Phos* b4a.de* plb k* *Positr* nl2• *Puls* k* rhod k* rhus-t k* ruta k* sang bg2* sec k*

Smell – diminished: ...
sel bg2 **Sep** k* **Sil** k* stram bg2 sul-ac b4.de* sulph h2* syc fmm1• tab k* teucr ptk1 verat bg2 zinc k* zinc-p k2 [spect dfg1]
  - **accompanied** by:
    - **epilepsy**: plb ptk1
    - **taste**; loss of: anac ptk1 ant-t bg2 crot-t ptk1 hyos bg2 just bg2* mag-m bg2* nat-m bg2* *Puls* bg2* rhod bg2 sil ptk1
  - **catarrh**; from: alum bg2 calc bg2 hep bg2 mez bg2 nat-m bg2 *Nux-v* bg2 *Puls* bg2 sep bg2 sil bg2 sulph bg2
  - **coryza**; after: mag-m ptk1
  - **leaflet** at root; with sensation of a: kali-i
  - **paralysis** of nerves of smell; from: bell bg2 caust bg2 *Hyos* bg2 lyc bg2 nat-m bg2 *Nux-v* bg2 op bg2 plb bg2 sep bg2
- **illusions** (See Odors)
- **increased**; sense of smell (See acute)
- **wanting** (= lost): (↗*MOUTH - Taste - wanting loss)* ail *Alum* k* alum-p k2 alum-sil k2 *Am-m* k* amyg-p br1* *Anac* k* *Ant-c* ant-s-aur br1 *Ant-t* k* apoc-a bro1 arg-n bg2* *Ars Ars-i* ars-s-f k2 arund asaf bg2 aspar *Aur* k* aur-ar k2 aur-i k2 aur-s k2 **Bell** k* *Bry* k* bufo **Calc** k* calc-i k2 **Calc-s** calc-sil k2 camph *Caps* k* carb-an k* *Carbn-s* card-m *Caust* k* *Cham* chel b2.de* chlor cocc b2.de cod con b2.de *Cupr* cycl k* dulc fd4.de *Elaps Graph* k* **Hep** k* *Hyos* k* *Ign* k* *Iod* k* *Ip* k* just bro1 *Kali-bi* k* *Kali-c* b2.de* *Kali-i* kali-n h2* kali-p *Kali-s* kali-sil k2 lach laur b2.de lem-m br1* *Lyc* k* m-ambo b2.de m-arct b2.de *Mag-m* k* mag-p mang k* med k* **Merc** *Mez* k* morg-p pte1• *Nat-ar Nat-c* **Nat-m** k* nit-ac b2.de* *Nux-m Nux-v* b2.de* olnd b2.de *Op* k* phel **Phos** k* **Plb** k* positr nl2• *Psor* k* **Puls** k* rhod k* *Rhus-t* k* ruta b2.de* *Sang* k* *Sarr* sec k* **Sep** k* **Sil** k* spig stram k* *Sul-ac* k* sul-i k2 *Sulph* k* syc pte1*• *Syph* jl2 *Teucr* k* tub-a jl2 verat k* *Zinc* k* zinc-m bro1
  - **coryza**; during (See Coryza - accompanied - smell)
  - **injuries**; after: | **head**; of: thala mtf11

SMOKE; as if complaints were caused by: (↗*Odors - smoke; of)* olnd b7.de*

SMOKE; sensation as if from (See Odors - smoke; of)

SNEEZING: abrom-a ks5 *Acon* k* acon-ac rly4• acon-f a1 aegle-f bnj1 *Aesc* k* aeth k* *Agar* k* agar-em a1 agath-a nl2• agn b2.de* *Aids* nl2• ail k* *All-c* k* allox tpw4* aloe alum k* alum-sil k2 alumn am-c b2.de* *Am-m* k* ambr k* ambro bro1* ammc k* *Anac* k* anag androc srj1• anis ant-c b2.de* *Ant-t* k* anth ptk2 aphis apis k* apoc a1 aq-mar skp7• *Aral* bro1 *Arg-met* k* *Arg-n* k* arge-pl rwt5• arist-cl sp1 arn k* **Ars** k* ars-h a1 *Ars-i* k* ars-s-f k2 ars-s-r arum-d arum-t k* *Arund* k* asaf b2.de* asar k* asc-t a1* aspar k* atra-r bnm3• atro a1 *Aur* k* aur-ar k2 aur-i k2 aur-m a1 aur-m-n a1 aur-s a1* *Bad* k* *Bamb-a* stb2.de• bapt k* *Bar-c* k* bar-i k2 bar-m bar-s k2 *Bell* k* benz-ac k* benzol br1 berb k* bit-ar wht1• borx k* bov b2.de* brach k* *Brom* k* bros-gau mrc1 **Bry** k* bufo buth-a sp1 cadm-met tpw6* cadm-s k2 caesal-b bnj1 calad b2.de* *Calc* k* *Calc-ar* calc-f a1 calc-i k2 *Calc-p* k* *Calc-s* k* calc-sil k2 *Camph* k* cann-i a1 cann-s b2.de* canth b2.de* *Caps* k* carb-ac k* *Carb-an* k* **Carb-v** k* carbn-dox knl3• **Carbn-s** card-b a1 *Cardios-h* rly4• *Carl* a1 cartl-s rly4• cassia-s ccrh1• castm *Caust* k* cench k2 cent a1 cere-b a1 cham bg2* chel k* *Chin* k* *Chinin-ar Chinin-s* chir-fl gya2 chlor k* choc srj3• chord-umb rly4• *Cic* k* cimic k* cimx a1 **Cina** k* *Cist* cit-ac rly4• clem k* cob k* cob-n sp1 **Coc-c** k* cocc k* coch coff b2.de* colch k* coli rly4• coloc a1 *Con* k* cop k* cortiso sp1 *Croc* b2.de* crot-c sk4• crot-h k* crot-t cupr k* *Cycl* k* cypra-eg sde6.de• cystein-l rly4• delphin a1 dig k* digin a1 dios a1 dream-p sdj1• *Dros* k* *Dulc* k* erio a1 **Eup-per** k* eup-pur euph k* *Euphr* k* falco-pe nl2• ferr *Ferr-ar* ferr-i ferr-ma a1 *Ferr-p* fl-ac bg2 flav jl2 flor-p rsj3• form fum rly1*• fuma-ac rly4• galeoc-c-h gms1• *Gamb* k* gels k* gent-c a1 germ-met srj5• gins a1 glon k* glycyr-g cte1• *Graph* k* grat k* ham k* hell k* hell-v a1 helodr-cal knl2• hep k* hist sp1 hydr k* *Hydrog* srj2• hyos a1 hyper k* ichth bro1 ign ptk1 *Ind* k* *Indg* k* *Iod* k* *Ip* k* ipom-p irid-m rb iris jac-c k* *Kali-ar Kali-bi* k* kali-c k* kali-chl k* *Kali-i* k* kali-m k2 kali-n b2.de* kali-p k* kali-s *Kalm* k* ketogl-ac rly4• kola stb3• *Kreos* k* lac-ac *Lac-c* lac-cp sk4• lac-h htj1*• lac-leo hrn2• *Lach* k* lact a1 laur b2.de* led a1 lil-t lim a1 linu-c a1 lipp a1 lob bg2* lob-c a1* lob-s a1 *Luf-op* rsj5• *Lyc* k* lyss k* m-ambo b2.de* m-arct b2.de* m-aust b2.de* mag-c b2.de* mag-m k* mag-s a1 mand sp1 mang b2.de* mangi br1 mela a1 melal-alt gya4 menis a1 mentho bro1 meny a1 meph k* **Merc** k* merc-i-f merc-i-r a1* merc-sul mez k* mim-p skp7• mosch b2.de* mur-ac k* myos-a rly4• naja k2 napht bro1 narz a1 *Nat-ar* nat-br a1 *Nat-c* k* *Nat-m* k* nat-ox rly4• *Nat-p* nat-pyru rly4• *Nat-s* nat-sil fd3.de• nicc nicotam rly4• *Nit-ac* k* *Nux-m* k* **Nux-v** k* oci-sa sp1* ol-an a1 ol-j olib-sac wmh1

Sneezing: ...
olnd k* op a1 orot-ac rly4• oscilloc jl2 *Osm* k* ox-ac k* ozone sde2• pant-ac rly4• par b2.de* *Petr* k* petr-ra shn4• *Ph-ac* k* phasco-ci rbp2 *Phos* k* phys k* plac rzf5• plac-s rly4• *Plan* plb b2.de* positr nl2• prun k* psor k* ptel k* **Puls** k* pyrid rly4• pyrog bg2 quill br1 ran-s k* raph a1 rat k* rhod b2.de* *Rhus-r* **Rhus-t** k* ribo rly4• rob a1 *Ros-d* bro1* *Rumx* k* ruta b2.de* **Sabad** k* sabin a1 sacch *Sal-ac* k* sal-fr sle1• samb bat1• **Sang** k* *Sangin-n* bro1 sanic sapin a1 sapo bro1 sars k* sec *Senec* k* *Seneg* k* senn a1 *Sep* k* *Sil* k* sin-n a1* sinus rly4• sol-t-ae a1 spig b2.de* *Spong* k* *Squil* k* stann b2.de* *Staph* k* stict k* stram a1 stront-c b2.de* stry a1 succ-ac bro1 suis-hep rly4• suis-pan rly4• sul-ac b2.de* sulfa sp1 **Sulph** k* sumb a1 suprar rly4• symph fd3.de• tab a1 *Tarax* k* tarent k* tet a1 *Teucr* k* ther k* thiam rly4• thres-a sze7• thuj k* til a1 tritic-vg fd5.de upa a1 urt-u a1 v-a-b jl2 valer b2.de* vanil fd5.de ven-m rsj12• verat k* verat-v a1 verin a1 vichy-g a1 wies a1 x-ray sp1 zinc k* zinc-p k2 zing k* ziz a1 [bell-p-sp dcm1 buteo-j sej6 calc-n stj1 helia stj7 heroin sdj2 mag-n stj2 spect dfg1 tax jsj7]

- **daytime**: cartl-s rly4• gamb k* hydrog srj2• merc a1 *Nit-ac* a1 petr a1 ther tritic-vg fd5.de urol-h rwt•
- **morning**: abrom-a ks5 agar k* *All-c* alum h2* **Am-c** k* ap-g vh1 arge-pl rwt5• aspar benz-ac k* bov bry k* calc k* calc-ar camph bro1* carneg-g rwt1• **Caust** k* chlor k* *Cimx* *Cist* clem k* cortiso tpw7 dulc fd4.de eupi a1 falco-pe nl2• fl-ac k* *Gels* k* granit-m es1• hell k* hydrog srj2• hyper a1 *Kali-bi* k* kali-n h2* kali-p fd1.de• kali-s fd4.de *Kreos* k* lac-h sk4• laur lyc k* lyss *Mag-c* k* menis a1 merc mez *Nat-m* k* nat-sil fd3.de• nicc a1 nit-ac k* nux-m a1* *Nux-v* k* oci-sa sk4• ol-an a1 onos ozone sde2• petr-ra shn4• phos psil vml3• *Puls* k* ruta fd4.de sars k* *Sep* k* sil bro1* sin-n spong fd4.de stict streptoc rly4• stront-c sk4• suis-pan rly4• **Sulph** symph fd3.de• taosc iwa1• thuj bg1* tritic-vg fd5.de urol-h rwt• vanil fd5.de zinc h2*
  - **6** h: *Sep*
  - **7** h: bamb-a stb2.de• sal-al blc1•
  - **8-9** h | **amel.**: arist-cl sp1
  - **evening**; and: lac-h sk4• nit-ac bg1 sulph bg1
  - **bathing** | **amel.**: cortiso tpw7
  - **bed** agg.; in: agar **Am-c** k* aspar bamb-a stb2.de• **Nux-v** k* *Puls* k* *Sep* k*
  - **early**: caust bg2 kreos bg2 puls bg2
  - **fasting**: hell k*
  - **rising**:
    - **after**: agar a1 all-c bov bg1 caust k* hell nux-v k* rhod k* sacch-a gmj3 sars k*
    - **when**: nat-m bg2
  - **talking**, prevents: rhus-t
  - **waking**; on: agar a1 **Am-c** k* aq-mar skp7*• ars k* aster k* bov k* calc cench k2 chin chin-b c1 graph k* hydr bg1 hydrog srj2• kali-c h2* lap-la rsp1 nat-sil fd3.de• **Nux-v** mrr1 oci-sa sk4• petr-ra shn4• psil ft1 sal-fr sle1• spig staphycoc rly4•
  - **washing** amel.: cortiso sp1*
- **forenoon**: arum-t vh bros-gau mrc1 bry a1 cimx dulc fd4.de mez a1 nat-sil fd3.de• nicc a1 olib-sac wmh1 spong fd4.de tritic-vg fd5.de
- **afternoon**: *Arum-t* a1 bad bros-gau mrc1 chord-umb rly4• cimic a1 cystein-l rly4• digin a1 dream-p sdj1• dulc fd4.de fl-ac k* ham a1 laur mur-ac h2* peti a1 podo fd3.de• sil a1 spong fd4.de tritic-vg fd5.de zinc h2*
  - **16** h: dendr-pol sk4•
- **evening**: abrom-a ks5 aids nl2• all-c k* bar-c bar-ox-suc rly4• bry a1 calc-p a1 carc fd2.de• cham a1 *Cist* coc-c a1 coff a1 dulc fd4.de eupi a1 glon a1 glyc bro1 hydrog srj2• *Iod* kali-p fd1.de• lac-leo hm2• lyss mag-c k* mur-ac h2* nat-sil fd3.de• nit-ac k* ozone sde2• petr h2* petr-ra shn4• phos k* *Puls* k* rumx ruta fd4.de spong fd4.de stann a1 sul-i k2 **Sulph** ther k* thuj a1 tritic-vg fd5.de vanil fd5.de zinc a1
  - **bed**; when going to: bufo
  - **undressing**: nat-m bg2
- **night**: am-c mrr1 ars a1 *Arum-t* k* bamb-a stb2.de• carb-v k* dream-p sdj1• dulc fd4.de *Elaps* ferr-i hep a1 kola stb3• petr petr-ra shn4• rhus-t rob a1 *Rumx* sin-n k* tong a1 tritic-vg fd5.de
  - **midnight**:
    - **before**:
      - **22** h: brucel sa3•
      - **23** h: brucel sa3• conch fkr1•
- **night – midnight**: ...
    - **after**:
      - **2** h: kali-p k*
      - **5** h: nicc
  - **lying** down agg.: sin-n
- **accompanied** by:
  - **crawling** (See Formication - accompanied - sneezing)
  - **dry** nose: ambr kl chin kl graph kl staphycoc rly4•
  - **obstruction** (See Obstruction - accompanied - sneezing)
  - ○ **Eyes**:
    - **agglutinated** (See EYE - Agglutinated - accompanied - sneezing)
    - **pain** in; burning (See EYE - Pain - burning - accompanied - sneezing)
  - **Head**; throwing backward of (See HEAD - Motions of - throwing - backward - accompanied - sneezing)
  - **Hypochondria**; pain in (See ABDOMEN - Pain - hypochondria - accompanied - sneezing)
  - **Larynx**; irritation of (See LARYNX - Irritation - larynx - accompanied - sneezing)
  - **Neck**; pain in (See BACK - Pain - cervical - nape - accompanied - sneezing)
  - **Nostrils** | **irritation** in both nostrils: cassia-s ccrh1•
- **air** agg.; draft of: aral br1 dulc fd4.de lac-h sk4• nit-ac k2
- **air**; in cold (See cold air)
- **air**; in open:
  - **agg.**: alumn bamb-a stb2.de• *Kali-bi* nat-sil fd3.de• puls mrr1 sabad tarax
  - **amel.**: abrom-a ks5 *All-c* calc-i calc-s phos puls rauw sp1
- **ascending** | **agg.**: sol-t-ae bg1
- **bathing**; after: cassia-s ccrh1•
- **blowing** nose | **agg.**: carb-v bg1* eupi c1
- **burning** in mouth and throat; with: sabal c1
- **cannot** sneeze with relief (See ineffectual)
- **chalk**, from: *Nat-p* vh
- **chill**; during: bell bg2 calc bg2 *Carb-v* bg2 cham bg2 *Cina* bg2 des-ac rbp6 hydrog srj2• lach bg2 merc bg2 puls bg2 *Rhus-t* bg2 *Sabad* bg2 staph bg2 sulph bg2 teucr bg2
- **chronic**: sil bro1
- **cold**; after taking a: *Camph* br1
- **cold** agg.; becoming: dulc fd4.de hep vh kali-s fd4.de spong fd4.de symph fd3.de• tritic-vg fd5.de vanil fd5.de
- **cold** air agg.: amp rly4• anan ars bro1 bamb-a stb2.de• cassia-s ccrh1• cist mrr1 des-ac rbp6 dulc fd4.de hep bro1 hydrog srj2• kali-s fd4.de kola stb3• lac-h sk4• nat-sil fd3.de• nit-ac k2 sabad bro1* vanil fd5.de
- **combing** or brushing the hair, from: sil k*
- **concussive**: castm *Puls* b7a.de *Sabad* b7.de* sulph
- **constant**: agath-a nl2• all-c anac *Antip* vh1 ars k* *Dulc* gamb *Indg* iris kali-i k2 merc k* mez a1 mim-p skp7• nat-c k* nat-m bg2 oci-sa sk4• ozone sde2• puls bg2 sabad k2 sil bg2 skook br1 squil k* sul-ac a1 sulph k2 thyr st1 tub-a jl2
  - **morning**: lac-h sk4•
  - **forenoon**: cimx
  - **night**: carb-v rhus-t
  - **desire**: aml-ns vh1
- **coryza**:
  - **with**: all-c tl1 ant-t b7a.de* arg-met b7a.de* arg-n bg2 ars bg2 calad b7a.de* calc b4a.de* carb-an b4a.de* chin b7a.de* cob-n sp1 cycl b7a.de* dros b7a.de* ephe-si hsj1• *Gels* bg2 germ-met srj5• kali-c bg2 kreos bg2 lach bg2 nat-m b4a.de* nux-v bg2* oxal-a rly4• pitu-gl skp7• puls tl1 rhus-t tl1 sep b4a.de* squil b7a.de* staph b7a.de* suis-hep rly4• tere-la rly4• tritic-vg fd5.de tub jl2 vanil fd5.de
    - **evening** | **18** h: pitu-gl skp7•
  - **without**: acon aesc *Agar* k* alum k* alum-sil k2 *Am-m* ars k* **Calc** k* *Carb-v* k* caust k* cic k* cist con k* dig dros k* dulc fd4.de euph b4.de* *Euphr* hell hyos k* iod k* kali-c *Kreos* b7a.de lac-h sk4• lyc k* melal-alt gya4 meny k* *Merc* k* mur-ac nat-c k* nicc *Nit-ac* k* ozone sde2• petr h2 phos k* psor jl2 *Rhus-t* b7a.de *Sep* sil stann k* staph k* sulph *Teucr* k* ther c1 zinc k*

Nose

- **cough**:
  - **after●**: **Agar** *Arg-n* k* bad k* *Bell* k* bry k* caps k* *Carb-v* k* hep lyc nit-ac a1 oena br1 psor rhus-t hr1 *Rumx* lp seneg k* *Squil* stict c1 sulph h2*
  - **before**: *Ip* bg1* nat-m bg2
  - **between** the coughs: bry
  - **during**: agar k* bad ptk1 bell k* just ptk1* psor k* *Squil* k*
    - ⁝ **morning** (See COUGH - Sneezing - with - morning)
- **crawling** in nose; after: (↗*tingling*) ambr b7.de* carb-v b4.de* colch b7.de* dros b7.de* hep b4a.de mur-ac b4.de* nit-ac b4.de* **Puls** b7.de* seneg b4.de* spig b7.de* teucr b7.de* zinc b4.de*
- **difficult**: phos b4.de* sulph b4.de*
- **dinner**:
  - **after**: agar k* dulc fd4.de kali-bi a1 phel a1 phos k* zinc
  - **during**: grat k*
- **discharge** amel.: senec vml3•
- **dry**: agn a1 ambr chin k* graph
- **dust** causes: aids nl2• benz-ac bg1 brom hist vml3• lyss sal-al blc1• spong fd4.de
- **eating** agg.: helodr-cal knl2• kali-p bg1 zinc bg1
- **epistaxis** | **amel**.: astac kr1
- **eructations**, with: ham bg1 lob bg1 *Phos* bg1*
- **eyes** closed; with: gamb ptk1
- **flowers**: sabad k2 sang mrr1
- **followed** by | **cough** (See COUGH - Sneezing - preceded)
- **frequent**: acon agar agath-a nl2• *All-c* alum k* alum-p k2 alum-sil k2 am-c **Am-m** ambr ammc vml3• anac ant-t bg2 apis bg2 arg-met arn **Ars** asaf aspar *Aur* bar-c k* bar-m *Bell* k* *Brom* brucel sa3• *Bry* k* buth-a sp1 calc k* calc-p a1 carb-an h2* **Carb-v** **Carbn-s** castm *Caust* k* chinin-s cic cist k* cob-n sp1 **Coc-c** coff a1 con cor-r k* cortiso gse crot-h cupr *Cycl* dig h2* dream-p sdj1• *Dros* *Dulc* euph gink-b sbd1• gins graph k* gymno *Hep* hydrog srj2• hyos h1* ind a1 kali-ar *Kali-bi* bg2* *Kali-c* kali-i k* kali-n h2* kali-p kali-sil k2 kalm *Kreos* k* lact laur lil-t *Lyc* k* mag-c k* mag-m k* mag-s mang h2* **Merc** k* mez k* mosch mur-ac k* nat-ar *Nat-c* k* nat-m *Nit-ac* nux-m **Nux-v** olib-sac wmh1 petr k* *Phos* *Plan* propl ub1• prun k* psor **Puls** fs ran-s *Rhus-t* k* ruta *Sang* k* scor a1* sep *Sil* spig k* spong fd4.de *Squil* k* stann staph k* *Stict* stront-c **Sulph** k* ther tritic-vg fd5.de vanil fd5.de verat *Zinc* k*
  - **accompanied** by | **Head**; pain in (See HEAD - Pain - accompanied - sneezing)
- **hay** asthma, with: agath-a nl2• *Ars* *Carb-v* *Dulc* *Euphr* lach *Naja* *Nat-s* nat-sil fd3.de• *Nux-v* sin-n stict tritic-vg fd5.de
- **hay** fever; in: lach bg2
- **heat**:
  - **before**: arn b7a.de cham b7a.de chin b7a.de* cina b7a.de sabad b7a.de
  - **during**: arn bg2 bell bg2 bry bg2 **Carb-v** bg2 caust bg2 *Cham* bg2 *Chin* bg2 **Cina** bg2 cycl bg2 merc bg2 puls bg2 *Rhus-t* bg2 **Sabad** bg2 senn c2 sil bg2 staph bg2 teucr bg2
- **ineffectual** efforts: acon k* aeth k* alum k* anac a1 ars bg2* asar k* benz-ac bov a1 calc k* **Calc-f** k* canth k* **Carb-v** k* caust k* cocc k* colch culx st1 euph k* guare k* hell k* hydrog srj2• indg k* *Kali-i* k* laur k* lyc k* mang a1 *Mez* k* mur-ac k* *Nat-m* k* *Nit-ac* k* nux-v bg2* osm k* phos k* *Plat* k* plb k* positr nl2• *Sabad* ptk1 sal-fr sle1• sars k* sep a1 **Sil** k* sul-ac k* sulph k* zinc k* zing a1
  - **air** agg.; in open: cocc h1*
- **inspiration** agg.: brom
- **itching**, with: dulc fd4.de nat-sil fd3.de• *Stry* bg1* tritic-vg fd5.de
- ○ • **Ears**; in: cycl ptk1*
- **larynx**; from irritation in: *Agar* *Arg-n* *Carb-v* k*
- **looking** at shining objects: lyss
- **loud** (See violent)
- **lying**:
  - **agg**.: kali-bi bg1
  - **amel**.: merc
- **menses**, during: mag-c h2*
- **nausea** | **after**: sang hr1 sulph c1
- **odors**:
  - **agg**.: nat-sil fd3.de• ozone sde2• phos ptk1* podo fd3.de• sabad mrr1 vanil fd5.de
  - **juice** agg.; of: cycl a1
  - **strong** odors agg.: petr-ra shn4•
- **opening** the eyes agg.: am-c bg1* *Graph* k* sangin-n bg1
- **painful**: acon b7.de* aids nl2• bar-c b4a.de bell b4a.de borx b4a.de carb-an cina dros k* kali-i mez a1 stict bg2
- ○ • **Throat**, in: phos ptk2
- **paroxysmal**: *Agar* agath-a nl2• arn bell k* calc carc sst• cist mrr1 coc-c a1 con dulc fd4.de *Gels* k* glon ham k* hell *Ip* kali-bi bg2* *Kali-i* lac-h sk4• lach lyss morph a1 mosch a1 *Nat-m* nat-sil fd3.de• nux-v oci-sa sk4• ozone sde2• phos k* puls bg2 pycnop-sa mrz1 *Rhus-t* k* ribo rly4• *Ros-d* wla1 ruta fd4.de *Sabad* k* sep bg2 sil spong fd4.de staph *Stram* k* stront-c sk4• succ-ac br1 sul-ac h2* *Sulph* k* symph fd3.de• tab hr1 ther thiam rly4• tritic-vg fd5.de vanil fd5.de
  - **morning**: gels hr1 nat-sil fd3.de•
  - **prolonged** paroxysms: nux-v ros-d wla1 sabad mrr1
    - ⁝ **lasting** 4 to 6 hours with sinking of strength: petr
- **peaches**; handling: all-c bro1
- **perfumes**; from: sabad mrr1 vanil fd5.de
- **periodical**:
  - **minutes**; every five: cob-n sp1
  - **hour** | **two** hours; every: granit-m es1•
- **perspiration**; during: ant-t bg2 **Bell** bg2 carb-v bg2 **Cham** bg2 cina bg2 *Cycl* bg2 lach bg2 puls bg2 *Rhus-t* bg2 *Sabad* bg2 sil bg2 staph bg2 **Sulph** bg2
- **rapid** and continued: verat-v ptk1
- **rising**:
  - **after**: nauf-helv-li elm2• psil ft1 [heroin sdj2]
  - **bed** agg.; from: all-c bro1 stach bg1 symph fd3.de•
- **room**; in a closed: abrom-a ks5
- **sleep**:
  - **during**: bar-m k* *Nit-ac* k* petr-ra shn4• puls k* vanil fd5.de
  - **wakes** him from: **Am-m** k* vanil fd5.de
- **sleepiness**, with: *Petr* bg1*
- **stomach**, as from: *Dig* bg1*
- **sudden**: glon ind a1 rumx seneg c2 tritic-vg fd5.de
- **sulfur** vapor; with sensation of: x-ray sp1
- **sunshine** agg.; in the: agar k* agath-a nl2• aur bg1* dulc fd4.de hydr bg1 *Merc* bg1* merc-sul k* *Nat-m* sne *Sang* bg1* sel sne
- **talking**, prevents: rhus-t k*
- **temperature**; from a slight change of: rumx vh
- **tickling**; from:
  - ○ • **Ears**; in: *Trios* rsj11•
  - **Nose**; in: *Trios* rsj11•
  - **Trachea**; in: caps k*
- **tingling** in nose: (↗*crawling*) arg-n a1 borx carb-v dulc fd4.de ferr *Hydrog* srj2* kali-bi melal-alt gya4 paeon plat rumx senec pd stict teucr tritic-vg fd5.de vanil fd5.de
- **uncovering**, from: **Hep** k* *Merc* nat-m bg1 nux-v ptk1 pyrog ptk1 *Rhus-t* k* sil ptk1
  - **hands**: **Hep** pyrog rhus-t tub jl2
- **unsatisfactory**: ars-i ptk1
- **urging** to: ozone sde2• [bell-p-sp dcm1]
- **vapor** in throat; as from: sal-ac bg1 thuj bg1
- **violent**: acon k* agar ptk1 all-c k* am-c k* anac k* anag *Antip* vh1 aphis arg-met *Ars* k* ars-h asaf asar k* aspar *Bar-c* k* brom k* brucel sa3• *Bry* k* calad canth caps k* carb-v cench k2 chin k* chlor *Cina* k* cist k* coc-c con k* croc crot-h k* crot-t bg2 cycl b7a.de* dig ephe-si hsj1• euph bg2 fl-ac *Gamb* gels k* gymno ictod *Ind* k* indg k* *Ip* k* kali-ar kali-bi bg2* *Kali-c* k* *Kali-i* k* kali-n b4.de* kali-p kali-sil k2 lach a1 laur k* lim a1 lyc mag-c melal-alt gya4 merc k* mez a1 moni rfm1• mosch k* mur-ac a1 *Nat-ar* *Nat-c* k* nat-m k* nat-s bg2 nicc k* nit-ac nux-v k* olnd k* op tl1 par b7.de* petr-ra shn4• puls k* pycnop-sa mrz1 *Rhus-t* k* rumx k* sabad k* seneg k* sil k* sin-n mrr1 *Squil* k* sulph k* teucr b7.de* ther *Thuj* tritic-vg fd5.de valer b7.de* verat k* verin a1 vero-o rly4*•
  - **August**; in: all-c tl1
  - **lasting** 5 minutes: seneg
- **walking** in open air agg.: bamb-a stb2.de• cocc k* kali-p fd1.de• nat-sil fd3.de• plat k* tarax k*

- **warm** room:
  - **agg.**: *All-c* k* **Puls** k*
    - ⁝ **going** from a cold into a warm room: am-br vh1
  - **entering** a warm room; when: all-c bg2*
- **water**, immersing hands in: lac-d bro1 phos bro1*
- **weather** | **changeable**: ars k2 tritic-vg fd5.de
- **wet** agg.; getting the feet: oci-sa sk4•
- **wind** | **cold** wind; from every: hep k2* kali-p fd1.de•
- **yawning**, with: astac bry k* cycl bg1* hell bg2 laur bg2 lob bg1* mag-c h2*

SNEEZING; from: | **agg.**: *Am* b7a.de canth b7.de* con b4.de* mag-m b4a.de

SNUBBED: aur mtf33

SNUFFLING: allox tpw4 alum bg1 am-c apoc bg1* ars bg1 arund c1 *Asc-t Aur* aur-m cist br1 cupr bg1 dulc k2 elaps ger-i rly4• iodof mtf11 kali-bi bg3* kali-i bg1 **Lyc** k* *Med* bg3* merc bg1* nat-m bg1 **Nux-v** k* olib-sac wmh1 osm bg3* phasco-ci rbp2 phos bg3 puls sabad bg3 **Samb** k* sep b4.de* syph mtf11* tub gk vib bg3* [bell-p-sp dcm1]
- **children**; in: med mtf33
  - **newborns**; in●: *(↗Obstruction - children)* acon bro1 *Am-c* bro1 bell bro1 calc-lac bc *Cham* bro1 *Dulc* k* elaps bro1 *Hep* bro1 **Lyc** k* *Merc* bg1* merc-i-f bro1 **Nux-v** k* *Puls* k* **Samb** k* stict bro1 sulph bro1 syph mtf33
- **constantly**, but no discharge: iodof
  - **talking** agg.: kali-bi
  - **weather**; warm wet: *Kali-bi*

SOOTY nostrils: *(↗Discoloration - black)* *Ant-t* k* *Chlor* k* *Colch* k* crot-h bg3* falco-pe nl2• *Hell* k* *Hyos* k* *Lyc* med br1* merc ptk1* *Zinc*

SORENESS (See Pain - sore)

SPARKS at left wing; sensation of electric: carb-ac k*

SPASMS in muscles: lyc

○ - **Wings**; in: ambr

SPOTS (See Discoloration - spots)

SQUEAKING sensation: nat-c k* teucr k*

STIFFNESS: arg-n bg2 phos h2*
- **sensation** as if | **Nostrils**: arg-n bg2 ferr bg2 kali-bi bg2 phos bg2 sulph bg2

STOOPING:
- **agg.**: am-c b4a.de* *Bell* b4a.de *Bry* b7a.de cinnb bg2 dros b7.de* ferr b7.de* nat-m b4.de* puls b7.de* *Rhus-t* b7.de* sil b4.de*
- **amel.**: rhus-t b7.de*

STUFFED UP (See Obstruction)

SUNKEN nose: ant-t k2 *Aur* k* hep merc k13 *Psor* k* sil
- **children**, infants; in: *Aur-m*

SWELLING: *(↗Puffiness)* acon b2.de* agath-a nl2• agn b2.de all-c bg2 *Alum* k* alum-p k2 alum-sil k2 am-c k* am-m k* ambr b2.de* anan ant-c b2.de* anthraci antip bro1 **Apis** k* **Arn** k* **Ars** k* **Ars-i** k* **Ars-met** ars-s-f k2 asaf k* **Aur** k* aur-ar k2 aur-i k2 **Aur-m** k* aur-s k* *Bapt* **Bar-c** k* bar-i k2 bar-s k2 *Bell* k* borx k* bov k* brom k* bry k* cadm-s **Calc** k* calc-i k2 *Calc-p Calc-s* calc-sil k2 cann-s k* *Canth* k* caps b2.de* *Carb-an* k* carb-v b2.de* *Carbn-s Cardios-h* rly4• caust k* cham k* chel b2.de* chin b2.de* cic b2.de* cist **Coc-c** cocc k* con b2.de* cor-r croc b2.de* crot-h dulc b2.de* euph b2.de* *Ferr-i* fl-ac *Graph* k* *Guaj* hell b2.de* **Hep** k* hippoz k* hir rsj4• hyos b2.de* ictod ign k* *Iod* k* *Kali-ar Kali-bi* k* kali-br a1* **Kali-c** k* kali-chl *Kali-i* k* kali-n k* *Kali-p* kali-s kali-sil k2 kreos bg2 *Lach* k* *Lem-m* bro1 lith-c **Lyc** k* mag-c k* *Mag-m* k* medus br1 meph **Merc** k* *Merc-c* k* merc-i-r k* mez b2.de* *Naja* nat-c b2.de* *Nat-m* k* nicc nit-ac k* *Nux-v* b2.de* petr k* *Ph-ac* k* **Phos** k* *Plb* b2.de* *Puls* k* ran-b k* rat rhod b2.de* *Rhus-t* k* *Rhus-v* ruta b2.de* sabad bro1 samb b2.de* sang bro1 sarr k* sars ptk1 **Sep** k* *Sil* k* sol-ni *Spig* b2.de* spong b2.de* stann b2.de* staph b2.de* stram b2.de* sul-i k2 **Sulph** k* thuj k* tritic-vg fd5.de *Tub* k* urt-u verat b2.de* *Zinc* k* zinc-p k2
- **one** side: brom b4a.de* cocc k* croc k* hippoz nat-m b4a.de* *Phos* k* *Zinc* k*
- **right**: *Aur* aur-m k* cocc cor-r *Kali-bi Lith-c Merc-i-f Merc-i-r Mez* ox-ac tritic-vg fd5.de zinc
  - **sensation** of: kali-n rat
- **left**: *Alum* am-m *Aur-m* k* brom k* *Calc* cist *Hydr* lach merc *Nat-m* sep h2* stann thuj

Swelling – left: ...
  - **pressed**, when: brom
- **morning**: agath-a nl2• aur caust
- **evening**: agath-a nl2• alum mag-c h2* *Puls*
  - **amel.**: caust
- **accompanied** by | **Teeth**; complaints of (See TEETH - Complaints - accompanied - nose - swelling)
- **cold** agg.: ph-ac k*
- **coryza**; during: bar-c mtf33 *Bell* b4a.de bry b7.de* cham b7.de* *Lach* b7a.de *Merc* b4a.de nit-ac bg2 phos h2* puls b7.de* rhus-t b7.de* spig b7.de*
- **edematous**: medus br1 rhus-t k2
- **hard**: alum aur-m-n calc thuj
- **headache**; during: gels c1
- **hypertrophy**: lach bg2
- **knotty**: *(↗Knobby - tip)* **Ars** k* **Aur**
  - **ridge**, on: calc
- **pustulous** | **alcoholics**; in: alum gl1.fr• caust gl1.fr• hep gl1.fr•
- **red**: lith-c ptk1 mag-m ptk1
  - **saddle**; like a: ictod
- **room**, after walking in open air; in: aur
- **sensation** of swelling: apis b7a.de* bamb-a stb2.de• bar-c b4.de* calc b4a.de canth b7.de* cob-n sp1 coloc bg2 dulc fd4.de kali-bi bg2 rat bg2 rhus-t bg2 sep bg2
- **shining**: *Aur-m-n* k* borx lith-c ox-ac k* sulph k*
  - **red**: borx merc ox-ac k* phos sulph k*
    - ⁝ **right** side to tip: ox-ac k*
    - ⁝ **left**: aur-m k*
- **spongy**, vascular, distending it: kali-bi
- **spot** which throbs | **Lachrymal** bone; on right: kali-bi k*
- **throbbing**: cor-r kali-bi
- **touch**, painful to: alum *Calc* k* hippoz *Nat-m Phos*
- **walking** in open air agg.; after: aur

○ - **Below** the nose: kali-bi bg2
  - **sensation** of: rhus-t h1*
- **Bones**: anan arg-met k2 asaf *Aur* b4.de* **Hep** *Hydr* ictod **Kali-i** *Merc* k* *Merc-c* b4a.de *Merc-i-r* **Phos** k* sulph k*

○ - **Turbinated** bones: *Lem-m* br1
    - ⁝ **Inferior** of: hip-ac sp1
- **Cavities**: am-c bg2 bell bg2 canth bg2 cocc bg2 kali-n bg2 lach bg2 zinc bg2
- **Dorsum** (= Bridge): *Alum* b4a.de calc k* ictod bg2 kali-bi *Ph-ac* k* rat k*
- **Inside**: *Acon* am-c arg-met k2 ars-i k2* aspar bell k* beryl sp1 cadm-s *Calc* canth k* carb-ac cist cob-n sp1 cocc k* *Euphr* k* hip-ac sp1 *Ign Kali-bi Kali-c* kali-n k* kali-sil k2 *Lach* lem-m br1 *Merc* mez k2 *Nat-m* petr k2 prot jl2 rhus-t ruta fd4.de sang **Sep** *Sil* stann *Teucr* zinc k*
  - **sensation** of: kali-n h2* kreos b7a.de mag-c h2*
- **Posterior** nares: bell bg2 bry k* ham bg2 hydr kali-i bg2 lach bg2 petr k2 ph-ac k* rumx k2 sang bg2 spig bg2
- **Root**: bry b7a.de *Calc* k* hippoz *Kali-bi* k* merc k* *Nit-ac Petr* sarr k* sars bg3*
  - **appearing** and disappearing: *Calc*
- **Septum**: *Alum* k* caust elaps ham k* merc k* *Merc-i-f* k* tritic-vg fd5.de
- **Sinuses**: | **left**: vult-gr sze5•
- **Tip**: agath-a nl2• alum a1 aur-s k2 *Bell* k* *Borx* k* *Bry* k* calc k* **Caust** k* *Chel* k* clem k* *Crot-h* k* *Kali-c* k* lyc k* merc merc-sul k* nicc k* ox-ac psor al2 *Sep* k* *Sulph* k*
  - **weather**; in warm: bell
- **Wings**: aloe bg2 alum bg2 aur h2* brom k* calc bg2 cann-s cann-xyz bg2 carb-an cham bg2 cocc bg2 hydr-ac kali-bi k* *Kali-c* k* lach k* mag-m k* merc bg2 naja bg2 *Nat-m* k* *Nit-ac* k* ox-ac k* phel phos rhus-t bg2 stann *Sulph* k* thuj k*
  - **right**: aloe bg2 arg-n k* calc k* cocc bg2 hydr kali-bi bg2 *Mag-m* k* merc-i-f mez k*
  - **left**: *Alum* k* lach bg2 merc nat-m k* stann h2* thuj zinc k*
    - ⁝ **spot**: calc zinc h2*

SYPHILITIC: asaf bg2* **Aur** bg2* aur-m bro1 *Cinnb* bro1 fl-ac bro1 hep bg2 *Kali-bi* bro1 *Kali-i* bro1 *Lach* bg2 **Merc** bg2 merc-c bro1 *Nit-ac* bg2 sil bro1 sulph bg2 thuj bg2

TALKING agg.: canth b7.de*

TENDERNESS (See Pain - sore)

TENSION: *(↗FACE - Tension)* *Acon* k* ant-t bg2 asaf k* borx k* cadm-s k* canth b7.de* caps k* carb-ac bg2 carb-an k* caust bg2 cham bg2 chel b7.de* chin b7.de* graph b4.de* ham bg2* hist sp1 kali-bi kali-i ptk1 meny b7.de* merc k* *Petr* k* ph-ac k* ran-b k* rhus-t bg2 sarcol-ac sp1 senec ptk1 spong bg2 sulph k* symph fd3.de• *Thuj* k* viol-o b7.de*
- **painless** over nasal bones: asaf

○ - **Above** the nose: *Glon* k* hep k*
- **Across**: eucal hr1 ham hr1 merc petr hr1
- **Below**: rhus-t h1*
- **Bones**: thuj k*
- **Dorsum**: ph-ac symph fd3.de•
- **Inside**: cadm-s canth k* graph k* *Lac-d* k*
- **Nostrils**: caps h1
- **Root**: *All-c* k* *Ant-t* k* cadm-s k* carb-ac k* caust bg2 cupr cupr-s hr1 *Graph* bg1* ham hep bg2 hist sp1 *Kali-bi* k* *Kali-i* k* lac-d meny k* merc nat-p petr spong

○ • **Above** root: all-c ptk1 ant-t ptk1 kali-bi ptk1 kali-i ptk1
  ⋮ **band**; as from a: ant-t
  ⋮ **saddle**; as from a: thuj h1
- **Skin**: acon arg-met *Petr* k* *Phos* k*
- **Tip**: *Carb-an* k*
- **Wings**: thuj k*

THICK: agar bg2 arg-met k2 aur bg2 bar-c bg2 bell bg2 calc bg2 carb-an bg2 carb-v bg2 *Ferr-i* graph bg2 kali-bi bg2 kali-c k* kali-i bg2 lach bg2 mez bg2 sulph bg2

THROBBING (See Pulsation)

TICKLING (See Itching)

TINGLING: aesc agar k* all-c k* am-c ambr k* arg-met k* arg-n bg2 arn k* arum-t k2* asar bg2 bamb-a stb2.de• bell bg2 berb brom bg2 calc canth caps k* colch k* corn dros k* dulc fd4.de gels bg2 gran ham fd3.de• ip bg2 kali-s fd4.de lach laur b7.de* mag-c melal-alt gya4 nat-p nat-pyru rly4• nit-ac bg2 ol-an podo bg2 ran-b bg2* ran-s b7.de* rhus-r rumx bg2 ruta fd4.de sabad bg2* sal-al blc1• sal-fr sle1• sang bg2 sep bg2 sinus rly4• sul-ac symph fd3.de• vanil fd5.de vero-o rly3• [bell-p-sp dcm1 tax jsj7]
- **right**: plut-n srj7•
- **accompanied** by | **Head**; pain in (See HEAD - Pain - accompanied - nose - numbness)

○ - **Bones**: cinnb corn spong
- **Inside**: agar aids nl2• *All-c* k* am-c ambr k* antip vh1 arg-met **Arn** k* bamb-a stb2.de• bell k2 berb borx *Caps* k* carb-ac carb-v cham *Colch* k* *Con* k* crot-c sk4• daph *Gels* k* gent-ch bnj1 hep hist sp1 hydr-ac *Hydrog* srj2• kali-s fd4.de kola stb3• laur mag-c melal-alt gya4 nat-p nat-pyru rly4• nit-ac k* ol-an olib-sac wmh1 ozone sde2• ph-ac plat *Ran-b* k* ran-s k* rat *Rumx* ruta fd4.de *Sabad* k* sang a1 sep k* sinus rly4• spig stict mrr1 stry k* sul-ac sulph tab *Teucr* k*
  • **right**: agar *All-c* k* ars-s-r k* mag-c melal-alt gya4 sinus rly4• *Stict* k* sul-ac
  • **left**: arg-met carb-v dros hep nat-p
  • **evening**: carb-v
  • **blowing** the nose agg.: agath-a nl2• hep
  • **cobweb**; as from: brom ptk1
  • **epistaxis**; before: arg-met h1
  • **spreading** to whole body: sabad ptk1
  • **sudden**, sharp, followed by sneezing: *Rumx*
- **Nostrils**: phys br1 ruta fd4.de sal-fr sle1• vanil fd5.de
- **Posterior** nares: arg-n mag-c h2* ran-b rumx k2
- **Root**: ambr olib-sac wmh1
- **Septum**: ozone sde2•
  • **blowing** the nose; when: bry
- **Tip**: aesc bell k* berb con kali-n lach *Morph* bro1 mosch paeon plut-n srj7• ran-b a1 ran-s rheum ruta fd4.de sars vanil fd5.de [bell-p-sp dcm1 helia stj7 heroin sdj2]
  • **rubbing** | **amel.**: bell
- **Wings**: carb-ac dulc fd4.de [tax jsj7]

TORPOR, sense of: asaf plat samb viol-o

TOUCH agg.: agar bg2 asaf bg2 aur b4.de* *Bell* b4.de* *Bry* b7a.de* canth b7.de* cina b7.de* clem b4a.de cocc b7.de* colch b7.de* dros bg2 **Hep** b4.de* kali-bi bg2 kali-n b4.de* led b7a.de* mag-m b4a.de* mang bg2 *Merc* bg2 merc-c b4a.de nat-m b4a.de* nit-ac b4a.de* petr b4.de* *Phos* b4.de* plat b4.de* rhod b4.de* *Rhus-t* b7.de* ruta bg2 sil b4.de* stann b4.de* sulph b4.de*

TREMBLING: carb-v bg2 chel b7.de*

TREMULOUS sensation at tip: *Bry* ptk1 chel k*

TUMOR:
- **left** side: merc-i-r
- **hard**: ars
- **malicious** sarcoma:

○ • **Maxilla** | **right**: symph c1

○ - **Inside**: ars kali-bi thuj sne
- **Postnasal**: chr-ac br1* osm bro1
- **Root**: bell
- **Tip**: anan k* carb-an k* sulph k*

TURNING back on itself; sensation as if nose was: plut-n srj7•

TWITCHING: *(↗FACE - Twitching)* agar b4.de* agn bg2 am-c bg2* ambr bg2* arg-n bg2 arn b7.de* aur b4.de* brom bg2 bry k* calc k* caps b7.de* carb-v bg2 *Chel* bg3* choc srj3• con k* *Glon* bg2* *Hyos* b7.de* *Kali-bi* bg2* *Lyc* b4a.de* mez bg2 mosch nat-m ptk1 nat-pyru rly4• phys k* *Plat* k* puls k* stront-c b4a.de* zinc bg2*
- **right** side: brom k* con bg2 glon bg2 hyos bg2 mez bg2 mosch bg2 phos bg2 zinc h2*
- **left** side: am-c k* irid-met srj5• nat-m
  • **draw** up the wing; seems to: am-c
- **creeping**:

○ • **Skin**; under | **left** side: arg-n

○ - **Nostrils**:
  • **involuntary** (= myoclonic):
  ⋮ **children**; in: androc bnm2•
- **Root**: hyos ptk1 mez ptk1 phos h2* plut-n srj7•
  • **left** side: nat-m
  • **visible**: carb-v h2* con k* glon k* *Hyos* k* *Mez* k* nat-m
- **Septum**: aur
- **Tip**: *Bry* k* chel k*
- **Wings**: glon bg2
  • **right**: lyc k*
  • **left**: kali-bi k* plat

ULCERS: alum bg2 alum-p k2 alum-sil k2 anac bg2 anan k* ant-c bg2 ant-t bg2 *Anthraco* arg-met bg2 arg-n bg2 arn bg2 ars bg2* ars-s-f k2 aur bg2* aur-ar k2 aur-i k2 aur-m-n k* aur-s k2 bell bg2 bov bg2 brom bg2 bry k* cadm-s bg2 calc bg2 calc-sil k2 caust k* cham bg2 chr-met dx cocc k* cor-r k* *Fl-ac* k* graph bg2 hep bg2 hydr bg2* hyos bg2 ign bg2 *Kali-bi* k* *Kali-c* k* kali-n bg2 kali-sil k2 kreos bg2 lach bg2 lyc bg2 mag-m bg2 *Merc* k* merc-c bg2 mez bg2* morg-g fmm1• *Nat-c* k* nat-m bg2* nit-ac bg2* nux-v bg2 petr bg2 phos bg2 psor k2 puls k* ran-s c2 sabad k2 sang bg2 sep bg2 spig bg2 *Squil* bg2 *Staph* bg2 sulph bg2* syph k2* *Thuj* bg2
- **right**: cor-r gamb k*
- **left**: *Aur-m* bell borx bry calc lyc
- **bleeding**: bov bg2
- **burning**: *Ars* k* *Sil*
- **malignant**: carb-an kali-bi k*
- **menses**; instead of: euphr ptk1
- **painful**: aur mtf33 cor-r br1 **Sil** k*
- **perforating**: fl-ac hippoz hr1* *Kali-bi* k* merc *Merc-c* k*
- **phagedenic**: ars k2 hep k2 merc-c k2
- **small** ulcers | **Inside**: arg-n bg2
- **yellow**, crusted: arg-n

○ - **Bones**: asaf bro1 *Hecla* bro1 hep bro1 kali-bi bro1
- **External** nose: cham b7a.de cor-r bg2 **Puls** b7.de* *Staph* b7a.de
- **Inside**: all-c bro1 *Alum* k* alum-sil k2 anan k* ang k* **Ant-c** k* ant-t k2 *Arg-n* k* *Arn* k* *Ars* k* *Ars-i* k* arum-t bro1 asaf k2 **Aur** k* **Aur-m** k* **Aur-m-n** k* *Borx* k* brom k* bry k* bufo cadm-s *Calc* k* calc-p carb-ac c1 carb-an *Carbn-s* *Cham* k* chr-ac br1 *Crot-c* k* ferr-i *Fl-ac* k* *Graph* k* *Hep* bro1 *Hippoz* k* hydr k2* hyos h1* ign k* *Iod* k* jatr-c **Kali-bi** k* kali-c k* *Kali-i* k* kali-n h2* kali-p kreos bro1 lac-h sze9• lyc k* *Mag-m* k* *Merc* k* *Merc-c* k* morg-g pte1• *Nat-c* k* **Nit-ac** k*

- **Inside**: ...
  Petr k* *Phos* k* puls k* ran-s bro1 sang **Sep** k* **Sil** k* spong k2 *Squil* k* staph k* sul-i k2 *Sulph* k* syph k* tab k* **Thuj** k* *Vinc* bro1
  - **right**: aur bry gamb k* kali-n k* *Sil* k* thuj
    - **High** up: *Nat-c* k* *Sil* k* *Thuj*
  - ○ **High** up: *Kali-c* b4a.de *Sil* b4a.de
- **Nostrils**: alum h2* am-c b4a.de am-m b7a.de anac b4.de *Ant-c* b7.de* ant-t b7.de arn b7.de* *Ars* b4a.de aur b4.de* bell k* borx b4a.de* *Brom* b4a.de bry b7.de* bufo cadm-s calc b4.de* *Cham* b7.de* *Cic* b7a.de *Cocc* k* con b4a.de *Cor-r* k* *Graph* b4.de* hep b4.de* hyos b7.de ign b7.de* kali-bi bg2 kali-c k* kali-n bg2 *Kreos* b7a.de lach b7.de lyc b4.de* *Mag-m* h2* merc k* mur-ac b4a.de* nat-c b4.de* nat-m b4a.de nit-ac k* nux-v b7.de petr b4a.de* phos k* puls b7.de* *Rhus-t* b7a.de ruta b7a.de **Sep** k* sil b4.de* spig b7.de *Squil* b7.de* *Staph* b7.de* sulph b4a.de* syph k2 thuj b4.de
  - **left**: tub jl2
- **Outer** angle: bell h1
- **Posterior** nares: ail bg2 arg-n k* arum-m bg2 arum-t kali-bi bg2 lach bg2 merc-c bg2 nit-ac bg2 phyt bg2 syph k2
- **Septum**: alum bg2* arg-n br1 arn bg2 aur bg2* bar-c bg2 bov bg2 brom bro1 calc bro1 carb-ac bro1 crot-t bg2 fl-ac bro1 hippoz bro1 *Hydr* bro1 **Kali-bi** bg2* kali-i bro1 merc-c bro1 mez bg2 nat-m bg2 nit-ac bg2* petr-ra shn4• sep bg2 sil bro1* thuj mrr1 vinc bro1
  - **round** ulcers: alum bg1 *Aur* calc-p cop *Fl-ac* *Hippoz* **Kali-bi** *Kali-i* merc *Merc-c* *Nat-c* nit-ac bg1 sars *Sep* **Sil** syph **Thuj**
  - **syphilitic**: *Aur* bro1 aur-m bro1 cor-r bro1 kali-bi bro1 *Kali-i* bro1 lach bro1 merc-aur bro1 *Nit-ac* bro1
- **Tip**: *Borx* k* *Bry* k* **Caust** k* rhus-t bro1
- **Under** nose: arund k*
- **Wings**: kali-c k* psor **Puls** k* *Sanic* thuj
  - **right**: *Ars* k* cor-r
  - **left**: dulc k* fl-ac kali-bi kali-c
  - **borders**: *Kali-bi* k* mag-m

UNEASY feeling around: ail ptk1

VAPOR rising into the nose; as if: ol-an bg2 phos bg2 sul-ac bg2

VEINS, varicose: (↗*FACE - Veins*) aur *Caps* mrr1 carb-an bg2* *Carb-v* k* *Crot-h* k* mez
○ - **Tip**: carb-v bg2

VERTIGO: | **after** | **agg.**: carb-an b4a.de
- **during** | **agg.**: *Acon* b7.de* *Ant-c* b7.de*

VOMITING: | **agg.**: ars bg2

WAKING; on: aloe bg2 kali-bi bg2 mag-c bg2 stann b4.de*

WALKING IN OPEN AIR agg.: m-arct b7.de

WARM: | **applications** | **agg.**: *Aur* b4.de*
- **room** | **agg.**: kali-s tl1

WARMTH; sensation of (See Heat in)

WARTS: **Caust** k* *Nit-ac* k* **Thuj** k*
○ - **Inside** nose: caust bro1 nit-ac k* *Thuj* bro1
- **Tip** of nose: caust k2*

WASHING:
- **face** | **agg.**: am-c b4a.de* am-m bg2 dros bg2 kali-bi bg2 kali-c bg2

WATER; sensation as if:
- **dripping** from nose: nat-m bg2 phos bg2
- **hot**, was flowing from: gels ptk1
- **running** down the nose and stopping at the tip; a drop: bros-gau mrc1
○ - **Posterior** nares; had passed through bapt hr1

WEATHER agg.; changing: ars ptk1

WEIGHT (See Heaviness)

WET:
- **agg.**: kali-bi bg2 rhus-t bg2
- **becoming** wet agg.: dulc bg2
- **sensation** in nose: pen br1
  - **blowing** nose does not amel.: pen bro1

Wet – **sensation** in nose: ...
  - **discharge**; but no: hist sp1
○ - **Posterior** nares: pen br1

WHISTLING: alum h2*

WINTER agg. (See Seasons - winter - agg.)

WRAPPING UP head: | **amel.**: nat-m bg2

WRINKLED skin: cham k*
○ - **Above** the nose: cham bg2

YELLOW (See Discoloration - yellow)

BONES; complaints of: anac b2.de* arg-n bg2 arn b2.de* ars b2.de* **Aur** b2.de* calc b2.de* carb-an b2.de* colch b2.de* con b2.de* hep b2.de* hyos b2.de* kali-bi ptk1 kali-n bg2 lach b2.de* **Merc** b2.de* nat-m b2.de* petr b2.de* phos ptk1 plat b2.de* rhus-t ptk1 *Sil* b2.de* spong b2.de* thuj b2.de* verat b2.de*

DORSUM; complaints of (See Complaints - dorsum)

HAIR:
- **falling** | **Nostrils**: calc k* *Caust* k* *Graph* k* iod sil b2.de*

SEPTUM; complaints of: alum bg2 aur b2.de* bry b2.de* caust b2.de* cina b2.de* colch b2.de* con b2.de* iod b2.de* *Kali-bi* bg2 lyc b2.de* merc b2.de* petr b2.de* ruta b2.de* sil b2.de* staph b2.de* sulph bg2

SIDES; complaints of nose in alternating (See Complaints - alternating)

SINUSES; complaints of: (↗*Pain - sinuses; GENERALS - Inflammation - sinuses*) ars bro1 *Asaf* bro1 aur bro1 bell bro1 bit-ar wht1• calc bro1* camph bro1 carc mtf33 cinnb bg3* *Coch* br1 cot c2 eucal bro1 helodr-cal knl2• hep bro1 *Hydr* bg2* iod bg2* kali-bi bg2* kali-c mrr1 *Kali-i* bro1* kali-m bro1 kali-n mrr1 lac-f wza1• lach bg3* lob mrr1 lyc bro1 merc bg2* *Merc-i-f* bro1 mez bro1 morg-g pte1• olib-sac wmh1 ph-ac bro1 phos bg2* scolo-v vs sep mrr1 sil c2* spig bro1* stict bro1* strept-ent jl2 sulph bg2* syph bg3* teucr bro1 thuj mrr1 [heroin sdj2]
- **right**: lob mrr1
- **syphilitic**: aur bro1 *Kali-i* bro1 nit-ac bro1

○ - **Frontal** sinuses: (↗*FACE - Pain - sinuses - frontal*) ars-i bg2 asaf bg2 aur bg2 bell bg2 calc bg2 cinnb bg2 hep bg2 hydr bg2 iod bg2* kali-bi bg2* kali-i bg2 lyc bg2 merc bg2 nat-m bg2 nit-ac bg2 phos bg2 puls bg2 sabad bg2 sil bg2* spig mrr1 stict mrr1 teucr bg2 thuj bg2 verb bg2
- **Maxillary** sinuses (See FACE - Complaints - jaws - joints; FACE - Complaints - maxillary)

TIP of nose; complaints of (See Complaints - tip)

TURBINATED bones; complaints of: ail bg2 alum bg2 ant-c bg2 aral bg2 iod bg2 kali-i bg2 rumx bg2 spig bg2 zing bg2

WINGS; complaints of (= alae nasi): alum b2.de* ambr b2.de* *Aur* b2.de* canth b2.de* carb-v b2.de* caust b2.de* con b2.de* dulc b2.de* euphr b2.de* hell b2.de* kali-c b2.de* mag-m b2.de* merc b2.de* nat-c b2.de* *Nat-m* b2.de* phos b2.de* plb b2.de* puls b2.de* rhus-t b2.de* *Sil* b2.de* spig b2.de* staph b2.de* **Thuj** b2.de* viol-t b2.de* zinc b2.de*

DAYTIME: *Lyc* b4a.de

MORNING: ambr b7.de* ang b7a.de apis bg2 aur bg2 bell b4.de* bov b4a.de bry b7.de* chin b7.de* con b4.de* croc b7.de* guaj b4.de* hell b7.de* hep b4.de* ign b7.de* kali-c b4.de* lyc b4.de* m-ambo b7.de m-arct b7.de merc b4.de* *Nux-v* b7.de* *Olnd* b7a.de petr b4.de* phos b4.de* plat b4.de* puls b7.de* rhus-t b7.de* sabad b7.de* sars b4.de* sep b4.de* spig b7.de* sulph b4.de* thuj bg2 verat b7.de* verb b7.de* zinc b4.de*

FORENOON: alum b4.de* am-m b7.de* kali-bi bg2 merc b4.de* nat-c b4.de* phos b4.de* sabad b7.de* sars b4.de* sulph b4.de* valer b7.de*

AFTERNOON: alum b4.de* anac b4.de* *Asaf* b7a.de bov b4.de* canth b7.de* caps b7.de* carb-an b4.de* carb-v b4.de* cham b7a.de chin b7.de* hep b4.de* kali-bi bg2 laur b7.de* lyc b4.de* m-arct b7.de nat-c b4.de* nat-m b4.de* nux-v b7.de* petr b4.de* phos b4.de* rhus-t b7.de* sep b4.de* spig b7.de* stront-c b4.de* sulph b4.de* viol-t b7.de* zinc b4.de*

EVENING: acon b7.de* am-m b7.de* ambr b7.de* *Ang* b7a.de ant-t b7.de* apis b7a.de arn b7.de* ars b4.de* *Bry* b7.de* caps b7.de* carb-v b4.de* con b4.de* graph b4.de* hep b4.de* ign b7.de* kali-bi bg2 kali-c b4.de* laur b7.de* lyc b4.de* *M-ambo* b7.de* m-arct b7.de meny b7.de* merc b4.de* mez b4.de* nux-v b7.de* par b7.de* phos b4.de* plat b4.de* puls b7.de* ran-b b7.de* ran-s b7.de* rhus-t b7.de* sabad b7.de* sep b4.de* spong b7.de* stann b4.de* stront-c b4.de* sulph b4.de* thuj b4.de* valer b7.de* verat b7.de* verb b7.de* viol-t b7.de* zinc b4.de*

NIGHT: ant-c bg2 ant-t b7.de apis b7a.de ars b4.de* bell b4.de* calad b7.de* cham b7.de* chin b7.de* con b4a.de* dig b4.de* dros b7.de* graph b4.de* hep b4.de* ign b7.de* led b7.de* mag-c b4a.de* mag-p bg2 mang b4.de* nat-c b4.de* nit-ac b4.de* nux-m b7.de* petr b4.de* *Phos* b4a.de puls b7.de* rheum b7.de* rhod b4.de* sep b4.de* *Sil* b4.de* sulph b4.de* thuj bg2

- **midnight**:
  - **before**: chin b7.de* phos b4a.de
  - **after**: dros b7.de* nit-ac bg2

ABSCESS: anan *Bell* **Hep** *Kali-i* **Merc** *Phos Sil*

○ - **Antrum**: kali-i k* lyc *Merc* mez k* **Sil**
- **Jaws**: ars hecla mrr1 phos
  - **dental** origin; of (See TEETH - Abscess - extending - jaw)
- **Lip**: *Anthraci* k*

○ - **Upper**: *Bell* k*
- **Parotid** glands: **Ars** k* *Lach* lyc *Phos* k* phyt *Rhus-t* k* **Sil** k*
- **Sublingual** gland: bar-c mtf33
- **Submaxillary** glands: bar-c mtf33 *Calc* hippoz k* *Kali-i* k* *Lach* k* *Phos Sil* sulph k2 tub-m jl2
- **Submental** glands: staph ptk1

ACRIDITY (See Pain - corrosive)

ADHESION of skin to forehead: sabin k*

AIR: | **blew** upon face; as if cold: coloc k* m-arct b7.de *M-aust* b7a.de mez k* olnd b7.de* thuj bg2*

AIR AGG.; DRAFT OF: *Acon* b7.de* *Phos* b4a.de verb b7.de*

AIR; IN OPEN:
- **agg.**: alum b4.de* ars b4.de* berb bg2 borx b4a.de carb-an b4.de* *Cocc* b7.de* guaj b4.de* kali-bi bg2 kali-c b4.de* laur b7.de* merc b4.de* mur-ac b4.de* phos b4.de* plat b4.de* puls b7.de* sars b4.de* *Spig* b7a.de sulph b4.de* thuj b4.de* valer b7.de*
- **amel.**: am-m b7.de* hep b4.de* rhus-t b7.de*

ANEMIC (See Discoloration - pale)

ANGER; after: *Staph* b7a.de

ANGIOMA: abrot br1*

APHTHAE: (↗*GENERALS - Aphthae*) cystein-l rly4• thiam rly4•

○ - **Cheek**:
  - **right**: brucel sa3•
  - **left**: *Brucel* sa3•
- **Lips**; on: *Ant-t* cadm-s chin-b c1 cub c1* graph k2 hep st1 *Hydr* k* ip k* *Jug-r* st1 *Kali-c* st1 **Merc-c** hr1* *Merc-cy* hr1 *Mur-ac* st1 nicotam rly4• ozone sde2• pot-e rly4• ruta fd4.de sanic c1 spong fd4.de sulph hr1 tritic-vg fd5.de vanil fd5.de

APPEARANCE (See Expression)

ASCENDING STAIRS agg.: sabad b7.de*

BARBER'S ITCH (See Eruptions - beard - folliculitis)

BEARD falling (See Hair - falling - whiskers)

BEER; after: merc-c b4a.de

BELL'S PALSY (See Distortion - one; Paralysis - one)

BIRTHMARKS (See SKIN - Nevi)

BITING:
- **agg.**: bell b4.de* dig b4.de* graph b4.de* spong b7.de* verb b7.de*
- **teeth** together; biting | **agg.**: verb b7.de*

○ - **Lips** (See MOUTH - Biting - lips)

BLEEDING of lips: aloe am-c k* androc srj1• *Ars* k* **Arum-t** k* bapt ptk1 *Bell* b4a.de *Brom* k* *Bry* k* calc k2 carb-an k* *Cham* k* chlol k* chlor cist k2 cob k* com a1 gins a1 hyos k2 *Ign* k* kali-c k* kreos k2* *Lach* k* merc bg2 nat-m k* nit-ac k2 petr-ra shn4• ph-ac k* phos k2 pip-n bg2 plat k* rhus-t k2 sal-fr sle1• sep k2 sol-t-ae a1 stram k*

○ - **Lower** lips: ars b4.de* bry b7.de*
- **Upper** lips: kali-c b4.de*

BLOATED: (↗*Congestion; Swelling*) **Acon** k* aeth bro1 agar ail k2 alum b2.de *Am-be* bro1 am-c b2.de am-m b2.de *Ant-t Apis* k* *Apoc* arn k* **Ars** k* arum-t lp* asaf k2 *Aur* k* aur-i k2 bapt k2 bar-c k* *Bell* k* bor-ac bro1 borx b2.de both bro1 bov b2.de *Bry* k* *Bufo Cact* calc k* calc-ar k2 *Camph* canth b2.de caps b2.de carb-an b2.de carb-v b2.de carbn-s caust b2.de *Cedr* cench k2 cham k* chel b2.de *Chin* k* chlor cic b2.de *Cina* k* *Cocc* k* *Colch* k* coloc b2.de con k* cop cori-m a1 *Crot-c Crot-h* cupr b2.de dig k* dirc dor dros k* *Dulc* k* elaps euph b2.de ferr k* ferr-i k2 glon graph k* guaj b2.de guare haliae-lc srj5• hell k* hep b2.de *Hippoz* hura hydr-ac hyos k* hyper iod b2.de ip k* kali-bi *Kali-c* k* kali-s fd4.de kreos b2.de *Lach* k* laur k* led k* *Lyc* b2.de m-arct b2.de mag-c b2.de mag-m b2.de manc medus bro1 merc k* *Merc-c* bro1 mosch b2.de *Nat-c* k* *Nat-m* k* nit-ac b2.de* nux-m b2.de nux-v k* oena olnd b2.de *Op* k* petr b2.de ph-ac b2.de *Phos* k* plb k* puls k* rheum b2.de rhus-t b2.de ruta b2.de sabin b2.de *Samb* k* sang sec b2.de senec sep k* sil b2.de sol-ni *Spig* k* spong k* stann b2.de staph b2.de stram k* sul-ac b2.de sulfonam ks2 sulph k* tarent mtf33 tax bro1 teucr b2.de thuj verat b2.de* *Verat-v* br1 vesp vinc xero bro1
- **morning**: crot-h k* dirc k* kali-c hr1 kali-s fd4.de nat-c h2*
  - **waking**; on: agar hura *Spig*
- **chill**; during: lyc bro1
- **fever**; during: sil h2*
- **glossy**, and: aur k*
- **lying** agg.: apoc k*
- **menses**; before: bar-c *Graph Kali-c Merc Puls*
- **speaking** in company: carb-v h2

○ - **Eyes**:

○ - **About**: *Am-be* bro1 *Apis Ars* k* bor-ac bro1 colch elaps k* *Ferr* kali-s fd4.de merc *Merc-c* bro1 nat-c bro1 (non:nit-ac kl) phos k* rhus-t k* thlas bro1 xero bro1
  - **morning**: nit-ac h2
  - **Between** the: lyc
  - **Over** the: cench k2 ruta sep
  - **Under**: apis apoc k2 *Ars Aur* bry cench k2 kali-c merc nux-v olnd phos puls
- **Lids** and eyebrows; between: cench **Kali-c** k* lyc bg2
- **Lips**: chin mtf33 mur-ac ptk1

○ - **Lower**: mur-ac
- **Side** lain on: phos h2*

BLOCKED sinuses (See Obstruction - sinuses)

BLOOD to face; rush of: acon b7.de* alum b4a.de *Bar-c* b4a.de *Bell* b4a.de bov b4.de* calc b4a.de caust b4.de* chin b7.de* clem b4a.de **Ferr** b7.de* graph b4a.de merc-c b4a.de sil b4a.de *Stram* b7.de*

BLOW as of a thrust (See Pain - blow; pain)

BLOWING THE NOSE:
- **agg.**: staph bg2
- **amel.**: lach bg2

BROAD; sensation of becoming: (↗*Enlarged - sensation*) coll

Face

BUBBLING sensation, as if bubbles were moving about: rheum b7.de*
○ - **Jaws** | **Lower**: *(↗Clucking)* bell b4.de*

BURNT look: | **Lips**: ars bg2 hyos b7.de*

BURNT; sensation as if:
○ - **Lips**: arge-pl rwt5• sabad b7.de*
○ · **Upper**: bar-c b4.de* plat b4.de* sulph bg2

CACHECTIC (See Expression - sickly)

CANCER: **Ars** k* *Aur Carb-an* k* cist bro1 *Con* k* *Graph* b4a.de **Jug-c** sne *Kali-ar* kali-c k* kali-i k* lach nit-ac k* *Phos* sil sulph symph tl1 syph k2 zinc
- **epithelioma**: **Ars** k* aur-ar k2 cic con k* *Cund* sne hydr kali-ar **Kali-s** k* *Lach* lap-a lob-e bro1 *Phos* k* ran-b k2 rumx-act mtf11 *Sep* sil
  · **accompanied** by | **crusts**: kali-s mtf11
○ · **Forehead**: morg-g pte1•
  · **Lips**: acet-ac br1 *Ars* c2 ars-s-f k2 aur k2 aur-ar k2 aur-s k2 *Cic* k* com sne *Con* k* *Hydr* kali-m k2 *Kreos* c2 lap-a med k2 **Phos** sne sep k* thuj sne
    ⁝ **Lower**: *Ars* clem *Dulc* vh *Merc-i-f* nit-ac sne *Phos* k* *Sep Sil* thuj sne
  · **Nose**; near wing of: *Aur* sep k2
- **lupoid**: *Hep* kali-m k2
- **lupus**: *(↗GENERALS - Cancerous - lupus; SKIN - Lupus)* alum bg2 alumn k* *Arg-n* k* **Ars** k* aur-m bac bn carb-ac k* *Carb-v* k* cist k* graph bg2* **Hydrc** kali-ar *Kali-bi* k* kali-chl kreos lach mag-c bg2 nat-c bg2 phos bg2 *Psor Sep Sil* k* staph bg2 sulph bg2 syph k2
  · **exedens**; lupus (See lupus)
○ · **Eyebrows**: alum alumn anan
  · **Upper** jaw; left: bac vh
- **noli** me tangere: cist graph sne jug-c k* kali-bi sne phyt thuj
○ · **Nose**; on: bry sne cist graph sne jug-c k* kali-bi sne phyt thuj
- **scirrhus**: *Bell* bg2 *Carb-an* k* sil k*
○ · **Lips**: *Bell* bg2 *Sil* bg2
○ - **Cheeks**: con tl1
- **Jaws**:
  · **right**: *Ant-c* vh arg-n vh ars vh aur vh calc vh fl-ac vh graph vh rhus-t vh
  · **left**: *Ars* vh hecla sne hep sne lap-a sne merc vh phos vh* sil vh symph sne
○ · **Bones**; of: hecla gm1 symph gm1
- **Lips**: *(↗Ulcers - lips - cancerous)* acet-ac bro1 ant-m c2 *Apis* b7a.de *Ars* k* ars-i bro1* aur k* *Aur-m Bell* b4a.de* bry b7.de* camph *Carb-an* caust *Cic* k* *Cist* k* clem k* com bro1 **Con** k* cund k* *Hydr* c2* kali-bi sne kali-chl kali-cy sne kali-s *Kreos* k* *Lach Lyc* k* mez b4a.de nit-ac sne phos k* phyt k* *Sep* k* *Sil* k* sulph k* tab c2* thuj bro1
  · **pressure** of pipe: aur-m-n sne *Con* k* sep k* thuj sne
  · **tobacco**; from: con mrr1
○ · **Lower**: ant-m k* *Ars* aur sne aur-m-n sne caust bg2 *Cist* k* *Clem* k* *Con Dulc* bc1* kreos sne *Lyc* nit-ac sne *Phos* k* sabad bg2 *Sep Sil* k* thuj sne
  · **Upper**: ant-c bg2 calc bg2 ph-ac bg2 sabad bg2 sil c1 stront-c bg2
- **Malar** bone | **right**: syph c1
- **Parotid** glands: *Phyt* rmk1•
- **Submaxillary** glands: *Anthraci* vh calc-s vh carb-an vh ferr-i vh tub-m jl2

CAPILLARIES; nets of: plat bg2

CARBUNCLES on the chin (See Eruptions - carbuncles - chin)

CARIES of bone: **Aur** k* aur-m cist bro1 fl-ac bro1 hecla bro1 kali-s *Merc-c* b4a.de *Phos Sil* b4a.de
○ - **Jaws**:
○ · **Joints**: caust mrr1
    ⁝ **right**: caust mrr1
  · **Lower**: amph bro1 ang bro1 asaf *Aur Aur-m Aur-m-n Cist* k* *Con Fl-ac Kali-i Merc* k* mez *Nit-ac Phos* k* *Phyt Sil* k* staph

CHAFED (See Excoriation)

CHAPPED: *(↗Cracked)* *Arum-t* k* cench k2 choc srj3• *Graph* k* kali-c h2* *Lach* k* mur-ac h2 nicc hr1* olnd mrr1 *Petr* k* *Sil* k* suis-pan rly4•
○ - **Lips**: *(↗Cracked - lips)* acon-ac rly4• act-sp hr1 aeth a1 agar k* **Alum** k* am-m k* amp rly4• *Ant-t* k* apis arn k* ars **Arum-t** k* bar-ox-suc rly4• beryl tpw5* bov k* **Calc** k* caps tl1 **Carb-v** cham k* chel k* chin chr-ac hr1 *Colch* k* *Cor-r* k* dioxi rbp6 fl-ac *Graph* k* guare k* hep hydrog srj2• *Kali-bi* k*

Chapped – Lips: ...
Kali-c k* *Kali-chl* hr1 kali-i k* kali-s fd4.de kreos *Mag-m* k* mang-p rly4• mez cp mono a1 nat-c h2 **Nat-m** ol-an k* ph-ac *Phos* sel staph staphycoc rly4• **Sulph** tab tarax tere-la rly4• zinc

CHEWING motion of the jaw: *(↗Motion of lower; MIND - Biting; TEETH - Grinding)* *Acon* k* aml-ns bg2* asaf aster st *Bell* k* **Bry** k* *Calc* k* canth bg2 caust st cham k* cic k* cimic bg2 cina bg2* cupr bg2* fl-ac gels *Hell* k* ign k* lach k* lat-m bnm6• *Lyc* ptk1 *Merc* mosch k* nat-m k* *Phos* plb podo k2 ruta st sec st sep sol-ni *Stram* k* strych-g br1 *Sulph* bg2 thal-xyz srj8• verat k* *Verat-v* bg2*
- **accompanied** by | **meningitis**: bry mtf11
- **agg.**: acon b7.de* alum b4.de* am-c b4a.de* *Am-m* b7a.de *Am* b7a.de bell b4.de* bry b7.de* calc b4.de* euphr b7.de* graph b4.de* ign bg2 lyc b4a.de* mag-p bg2 meny b7a.de* *Nat-m* b4.de* nit-ac b4.de* phos bg2 puls bg2* rhus-t b7a.de sep b4.de* sil b4.de* spig b7.de* staph ptk1 thuj bg2 verat b7.de* verb b7a.de
- **amel.**: cupr ptk1
- **brain** affections; in: bry ptk1 hell mrr1
- **children**; in: | **teeth**; before child has: cina mtf33
- **chill**; during: nat-m
- **chorea**, in: asaf ptk1
- **convulsions**; before epileptic: *Calc* k*
- **difficult**: ozone sde2•
- **food** escapes from mouth during: arg-n ptk1
- **forward** and backward: lyc h2*
- **involuntary**: strych-g br1
- **loud**: plb ptk1*
- **meningitis**; in (See brain)
- **saliva**; with frothy: asaf ptk1
- **sideways**: bry k2
- **sleep** agg.; during: aloe sne aml-ns bg2 bry bg2* **Calc** k* chel dgt cina bg2* ign bg2* podo sep k* zinc k*
  · **swallows**; and: calc ptk1 cina ptk1 ign ptk1

CHILBLAINS: agar bro1 *Colch* b7a.de

CHILLINESS: acon b7.de* ang h1* arn bg2 ars h2* ars-h hr1 bar-c bg2 berb k* brach k* *Calc* bg2 camph b7.de* **Caust** k* *Cham* bg2 chin b7.de* cina bg2 coloc h2* dros bg2 ign b7.de* laur bg2 *Lyc* bg2 merc bg2 merc-c bg2 mosch bg2 *Nux-v* b7.de* ph-ac bg2 phos bg2 *Plat* bg2 puls bg2 ran-b bg2 *Rheum* bg2 rhod k* ruta bg2 sabin bg2 sep bg2 spig bg2 stront-c bg2

CHLOASMA: *(↗SKIN - Discoloration - chloasma)* ant-c hr1 *Ars* hr1 cadm-s mtf11 card-m ptk1 caul ptk1 coch hr1 guar ptk2 kali-p ptk1 lyc bg3* merc-i-r hr1 nux-v bg3* plb hr1 raph mgm• rob ptk1 sep bg3* sul-ac hr1 *Sulph* hr1 syph dgt
- **pregnancy** agg.; during: caul bg2 *Con* bg2 ferr bg2 nit-ac bg2 **Sep** bg2
- **sun** and wind agg.; exposure to: cadm-s br1*

CHLOROTIC: *Acet-ac* alet k2 **Ars** ars-s-f k2 bar-c *Bell* **Calc** k* **Calc-p** carb-an *Carb-v* k* **Carbn-s** caust *Chin* k* chinin-ar **Cocc** *Con Crot-h Cycl* dig **Ferr** k* ferr-ar k2 *Ferr-i* **Ferr-m** ferr-p **Graph** k* *Hell Helon* k* ign kali-ar **Kali-c** kali-p *Kali-s* lach k2 **Lyc** *Mang* merc **Nat-m** k* **Nit-ac** *Nux-v* k* olnd ph-ac *Phos* k* **Plat** plb **Puls** sabin **Senec** **Sep** k* spig staph sul-ac **Sulph** k* valer zinc

CHOREA (See Distortion; Twitching)

CICATRICES: *(↗SKIN - Cicatrices)* mez k2
- **deep** scars; full of: glycyr-g cte1•
- **eruptions**; from | **Eyes**; around: mez k2

CLENCHED jaw: *(↗Lockjaw)* acet-ac k* acon k* agar k* am-caust a1 ars k* atra-r bnm3• bamb-a stb2.de• **Bell** k* camph k* carb-ac c1 carbn-dox knl3• carbn-h k1 carl c1 cic k* cit-ac rly4• colch k* (non:crot-h k1) cupr k* dig digin a1 dios k* *Glon* hydr-ac k* *Hyos* k* ign k* laur k* lyc ptk1 *Merc* k* morph c2 nux-v k* *Oena* k* *Op* k* ox-ac k* phos k* *Phyt* ptk1 plac-s rly4• podo ptk1 positr nl2• pot-e rly4• (non:sil k1) staph k* *Stram* k* streptoc rly4• sulph k* syph mrr1 tarent k* vanil fd5.de *Verat* k* vip k*
- **left** side: positr nl2•
- **night**: positr nl2•
- **accompanied** by | **sleepiness**: positr nl2•
- **chewing** agg.: alum ptk1
- **coma**; with (See MIND - Coma - jaw)
- **dentition**; during: cic bro1 phyt bro1 podo bro1
- **grinding** of teeth; with: canth ptk1 cic ptk1
- **sunstroke**; from: glon ptk1

○ - **Lower** jaw; beneath sang hr1*

CLOSING:

○ - **Jaws** | **involuntary**: acon bg2 cob ptk1 dios bg2 ign bg2 iod bg2 merc bg2 plat bg2 plb bg2 stram bg2

CLOSING THE MOUTH agg.: mez b4.de*

CLUCKING: *(↗Bubbling - jaws - lower)*

○ - **Jaws** | **Lower**: bell h1*

COBWEB:

- **sensation** of: *(↗Hair - sensation)* alum k* alumn kr1 arg-n bg2 bar-act br1 *Bar-c* k* bor-ac rb2 borx k* *Brom* k* bry k* calad k* calc k* carbn-s carl k* chin bg con k* euph bro1 **Graph** k* lath wd laur k* *Mag-c* k* mez k* morph k* petr ptk1 ph-ac k* phos bg plb *Ran-s* k* rat bg2* *Sangin-n* bg1* *Sul-ac* k* sulph sumb k* wies a1 [calc-br stj1 mag-br stj1]
  - **right** side: borx c1*
  - **evening**: ran-s k*
    - ⁝ **22** h | **bed** agg.; in: sumb
  - ○ **Chin**: alum bg2
- **tension** as from: *(↗Tension - one - drawn)* Bar-c

COFFEE agg.: nux-v bg2

COLD:

- **air**:
  - **agg.**: *Acon* b7.de* agar b4.de* arn bg2 bell bg2 *Coloc* b4a.de dulc b4a.de* *Kali-bi* bg2 mag-p bg2 merc b4.de* nat-s bg2 rhus-t b7.de* sanic bg2
  - **amel.**: arg-n ptk1
- **applications** | **amel.**: kalm bg2 *Phos* b4a.de
- **water**:
  - **mouth**; holding cold water in | **amel.**: clem ptk1

COLD; AFTER TAKING A: coloc b4a.de *Phos* b4a.de*

COLDNESS: abrot k* acon k* agar am-c k2 aml-ns anh sp1 *Ant-t* k* *Apis* **Ars** k* *Ars-i* ars-s-f k2 asar b7.de* *Bar-c* k* bar-i k2 bar-s k2 bell k* berb k* bism k* bry k* *Cact* k* *Calc* k* calc-i k2 *Camph* k* cann-i k* canth k* caps k2* **Carb-v** k* carbn-s cass a1 cedr *Cham* k* chel k* *Cic* k* cimic k* **Cina** k* clem a1 *Cocc* k* colch k* *Coloc* k* crot-t k* *Cupr* k* cyt-l a1* dig dros k* *Graph* k* *Ham* k* *Hell* k* *Helo-s* rwt2• *Hep* hydr-ac k* *Hyos* k* ign k* *Iod* k* ip k* iris jal br1 kali-bi k* *Kreos* k* lach k2 lil-t k* lyc k* meny bg2 merc k* merl hr1 mez k* morph k* mosch bg2 naja nat-c h2* nit-ac b4a.de* *Nux-v* k* oena k* op k* ox-ac k* petr k* ph-ac **Plat** k* plb k* *Puls* k* ran-s k* rheum bg2 rhus-t k* *Ruta* sabin k* *Sec* k* sep k* spong fd4.de *Stram* k* stry sul-ac k* sul-i k2 sulph k* ter k* til bg upa **Verat** k* verat-v k* zinc k* [bell-p-sp dcm1]

- **one** side: kali-c bg2 ph-ac puls
  - **other** hot and pale; one side cold and red: ip st *Mosch*
  - **other** painful: dros ptk1 polyg-h ptk1
- **right**: gels k* ph-ac h2* **Plat** k* polyg-h
  - **pain** is most severe in left; when: polyg-h polyg-pe vml2•
- **left**: ars bg1 dros k* **Graph** k* hydrog srj2• lob ruta spong fd4.de
- **morning**: cedr petr k*
- **forenoon**: phos k*
  - **10** h: petr
- **afternoon**: ars k*
  - **14** h: grat
  - **17** h: ars
- **night**: *Lyc* k*
- **accompanied** by:
  - ○ **Hands**; coldness of: cic c1
  - **Occiput**; pain in: *Carb-v*
- **alternating** with | **heat** of face: *Calc* chel lyc k* merc tub jl2
- **and** coldness of hands (See accompanied - hands)
- **burning**; with: bar-c h2* grat nat-m
- **children**; in: | **obese** children: iod ptk1
- **chill**; with: ant-t bg2 asar h1* bell bg2 bism bg2 *Camph* bg2 canth bg2 carb-v bg2 cham bg2 chel cic bg2 **Cina** k* *Dros* k* *Hyos* bg2 ign bg2 *Ip* b7a.de* *Lyc* k* nat-c k* nit-ac bg2 *Petr* k* *Plat* k* puls k* rheum bg2 *Rhus-t* k* sec *Stram* **Verat** k*

Coldness: ...

- **cholera**: ant-t k* **Camph** k* *Carb-v* *Cupr* iris **Verat** k*
- **dinner**; after: cann-i k*
- **drops** were spurting in face when going into open air; sensation as if: berb k*
- **dry**; and: *Camph* *Carb-v*
- **fever**; during: calc bg2 carb-v bg2 chin bg2 *Cina* bg2 **Cycl** bg2 hyos bg2 **Ip** b7a.de* lyc bg2 nit-ac bg2 plat bg2 ran-s bg2 **Rheum** b7a.de* *Spong* b7.de* verat bg2
- **followed** by | **pain** in face: *Dulc* k*
- **headache**; during: ars k* *Carb-v* ip lac-d k2
- **heat**; with:
  - **internal**: nat-m h2
  - ○ **Body**; of: spong
    - ⁝ **cold** hands; and: puls a1
  - **Forehead**; of: thuj h1
- **hydrocephalus**, in: agar arg-n **Camph** hell *Lyc* hr1 *Verat*
- **icy** coldness: *Agar* k* *Arg-n* hr1 **Camph** hr1 *Cupr* hr1 *Hell* hr1 helo-s rwt2• lyc h2* **Verat** hr1*
  - **moustache** of ice; as if had: lach hr1*
- **menses**; during: nat-m h2*
- **pain**:
  - **followed** by (See followed - pain)
  - ○ **Occiput**; with pain in (See accompanied - occiput)
- **painful**: lyc plat h2*
- **palpitations**; with: *Camph* k*
- **paroxysmal**: sulph h2*
- **perspiration**; during: camph bg2 cham bg2 *Cina* bg2 hyos bg2 *Lyc* bg2 **Verat** bg2
- **sensation** of: abrot hr1* acon k* *Agar* bro1 *Ant-t* bro1 arn b7.de* bar-c b4.de* berb bg2 bros-gau mrc1 **Calc** b4a.de* camph bg2* carb-v bro1 caust b4a.de* chin bg2 *Cina* bg2 dros bro1 hell bg2 *Helo* bro1 ign bg2 *Lyc* bg2 *Merc* k* merc-c b4a.de* mosch b7.de* nux-v bg2 **Ph-ac** bg2* phos b4.de* *Plat* k* *Ran-b* bg2 ran-s k* rheum bg2 rhod b4.de* stront-c b4.de* thuj bg2 verat bro1
  - **side**; on one: ph-ac *Plat*
- **sleep** agg.; during: ign k*
- **spots** in: *Agar*
- **water**; as from: sulph h2*
- **wind** | **as** from cold wind: ph-ac

▽ - **extending** to | **Back**: berb

○ - **Cheeks**: *Bell* bg2 cham b7a.de* coloc ptk1 rheum bg2
  - **left** | **burning** pain in face; from: sul-ac h2*
  - **accompanied** by:
    - ⁝ **Face** | **heat** of: *Bell* b4a.de
  - **fever**; during: bell bg2 *Colch* b7a.de* nat-c bg2
  - **perspiration**; during: bell bg2 cham bg2
- **Chin**: aeth k* chin c1* chinin-s kali-n ptk1 stram tell rsj10• verat k*
  - **sensation** of: aeth a1 **Plat** k*
- **Forehead** (See HEAD - Coldness - forehead)
- **Jaws**:
  - ○ **Lower**: **Plat** k*
    - ⁝ **sensation** of: plat b4.de
- **Lips**: amyg a1 anh sp1 apis k* ars k* *Cedr* k* cupr flor-p rsj3• plat k* sang hr1 sep bg2 verat
  - **menses**; during: cedr k*
  - **sensation** of: *Plat* b4.de* sep b4a.de*
  - ○ **Upper**: sel rsj9•
- **Malar** bones: *Plat* mrr1
- **Mouth**:
  - ○ **Above**: hydrog srj2•
  - **Corners** of: aeth c1*
- **Nose** (See NOSE - Coldness)

COLLAPSED (See Sunken)

COMEDONES (See Eruptions - comedones)

COMPLAINTS of face: acon ptk1 ant-c ptk1 apis ptk1 ars ptk1 *Bell* ptk1 bry ptk1 caust ptk1 cham ptk1 chin ptk1 ferr ptk1 hyos ptk1 lyc ptk1 mag-p ptk1 *Merc* ptk1 *Nux-v* ptk1 *Rhus-t* ptk1 stram ptk1 *Sulph* ptk1 verat ptk1

Face

- **one** side: *Acon* bg2 am-c bg2 am-m bg2 arg-n bg2 caust bg2 cham bg2 colch bg2 **Coloc** bg2 **Con** bg2 gels bg2 kreos bg2 mez bg2 *Nat-m* bg2 **Nux-v** bg2 *Phos* bg2 *Plat* bg2 **Spig** bg2 staph bg2 verat bg2
- **alternating** sides: chin ptk1 lyc ptk1 phos ptk1 staph bg2
- **right** side: acon b7a.de* *Agar* bg2* *Agn* b7a.de* *Alum* bg2* am-c bg2* *Am-m* b7a.de* *Anac* bg2* ant-c b7a.de* ant-t b7a.de* apis b7a.de* *Arg-met* b7a.de* arn b7a.de* *Ars* bg2* asaf b7a.de* asar bg2* *Aur* bg2* *Bar-c* bg2* **Bell** bg2* *Bism* b7a.de* borx bg2* brom bg2 *Bry* b7a.de* cact ptk1 **Calc** bg2* camph b7a.de* cann-s b7a.de* **Canth** b7a.de* caps b7a.de* carb-an bg2* carb-v bg2* *Caust* bg2* cham b7a.de* *Chel* b7a.de* *Chin* b7a.de* cina b7a.de* *Cocc* b7a.de* *Colch* b7a.de* coloc bg2* *Con* bg2* cupr b7a.de* *Cycl* b7a.de* dig bg2* *Dros* b7a.de* *Dulc* bg2* euphr b7a.de* *Fl-ac* bg2 *Graph* bg2* *Guaj* bg2* *Hep* bg2* hyos b7a.de* iod bg2* *Kali-c* bg2* *Kali-n* bg2* *Kalm* bg2* *Kreos* b7a.de* *Lach* b7a.de* laur b7a.de* led b7a.de* **Lyc** bg2* m-arct b7a.de* *Mag-c* bg2* mag-m bg2* mag-p bg2 *Mang* bg2* *Meny* b7a.de* *Merc* fse1.de *Mez* fse1.de mill b7a.de* *Mosch* b7a.de* **Nat-c** bg2* *Nat-m* bg2* *Nit-ac* bg2* *Nux-m* b7a.de* **Nux-v** b7a.de* olnd b7a.de* par b7a.de* petr bg2* ph-ac bg2* *Phos* bg2* plat bg2* *Plb* b7a.de* *Psor* bg2 *Puls* b7a.de* ran-b b7a.de* ran-s b7a.de* *Rheum* b7a.de* *Rhus-t* b7a.de* sabad b7a.de* sabin b7a.de* *Sang* ptk1 *Sars* bg2* *Sep* bg2* *Sil* bg2* *Spig* b7a.de* spong b7a.de* stann bg2* *Staph* b7a.de* stram b7a.de* stront-c bg2* sul-ac bg2* *Sulph* bg2* *Tarax* b7a.de* *Teucr* b7a.de* *Thuj* bg2* *Valer* b7a.de* verat b7a.de* *Verb* b7a.de* zinc bg2*
  - **extending** to | **left**: graph ptk1
- **left** side: acon b7a.de* alum bg2* alumn a1 *Am-c* bg2* anac bg2* *Ant-c* b7a.de* ant-t b7a.de* apis b7a.de* arg-met b7a.de* *Arn* b7a.de* ars bg2* *Asaf* b7a.de* *Asar* b7a.de* aur bg2* *Bar-c* bg2* *Bell* bg2* *Borx* bg2* *Bov* bg2* *Brom* bg2 *Bry* b7a.de* *Calc* bg2* **Cann-s** b7a.de* canth b7a.de* *Caps* b7a.de* *Carb-an* bg2* *Carb-v* bg2* *Caust* bg2* cedr bg2 cham b7a.de* chel b7a.de* chin b7a.de* *Chinin-s* bg2 *Cic* b7a.de* *Cina* b7a.de* *Clem* bg2* cocc b7a.de* *Coff* b7a.de* colch b7a.de* **Coloc** bg2* **Con** bg2* *Cupr* b7a.de* *Dig* bg2* dros b7a.de* *Dulc* bg2* *Euph* bg2* *Euphr* b7a.de* fl-ac bg2 *Graph* bg2* guaj bg2* *Hell* b7a.de* hep bg2* *Hyos* b7a.de* *Ign* b7a.de* iod bg2* ip b7a.de* kali-c bg2* kali-n bg2* kreos b7a.de* *Lach* b7a.de* laur b7a.de* *Led* b7a.de* lyc bg2* **M-ARCT** b7a.de* mag-c bg2* mag-m bg2* mang bg2* meny b7a.de* *Merc* bg2* **Mez** bg2* mill b7a.de* mosch b7a.de* **Mur-ac** fse1.de nat-c bg2* *Nat-m* bg2* nit-ac bg2* *Nux-m* b7a.de* *Nux-v* b7a.de* *Olnd* b7a.de* *Par* b7a.de* petr bg2* *Ph-ac* bg2* phos bg2* *Plat* bg2* plb b7a.de* *Psor* bg2 *Puls* b7a.de* ran-b b7a.de* *Rhod* bg2* *Rhus-t* b7a.de* *Ruta* b7a.de* *Sabad* b7a.de* *Sabin* b7a.de* *Samb* b7a.de* *Seneg* bg2* *Sep* bg2* *Sil* bg2* *Spig* b7a.de* *Spong* b7a.de* stann bg2* *Staph* b7a.de* stram b7a.de* stront-c bg2* sul-ac bg2* *Sulph* bg2* tarax b7a.de* teucr b7a.de* *Thuj* bg2* valer b7a.de* *Verat* b7a.de* *Verb* b7a.de* *Viol-o* b7a.de* *Viol-t* b7a.de* zinc bg2*
- **accompanied** by | **Head**; pain in (See HEAD - Pain - accompanied - face - complaints)
- **paroxysmal**: con bg2
- **weeping**; with (See MIND - Weeping - face - complaints)

▽ - **extending** to:

○ · **Ear**: bell bg2 caust bg2 coloc bg2 kali-bi bg2 sulph bg2
  - **Forehead**: phos bg2
  - **Head**: coloc bg2
  - **Occiput**: sep bg2
  - **Teeth**: kali-bi bg2 merc bg2 mez bg2
  - **Temples**: carb-an bg2 sanic bg2

○ - **Antrum**: chel br1 kali-i br1 til br1
- **Bones**: *Mez* br1
  - **menses**; before: stann bg2
- **Cheeks**: acon b2.de* agn b2.de* alum b2.de* am-c b2.de* am-m b2.de* ambr b2.de* anac b2.de* ang b2.de* ant-c b2.de* arg-met b2.de* *Arn* b2.de* ars b2.de* asaf b2.de* asar b2.de* aur b2.de* *Bell* b2.de* *Borx* b2.de* bov b2.de* bry b2.de* *Calc* b2.de* cann-s b2.de* canth b2.de* carb-an b2.de* *Carb-v* b2.de* **Caust** b2.de* cham b2.de* chel b2.de* chin b2.de* cina b2.de* clem b2.de* cocc b2.de* coloc b2.de* con b2.de* cycl b2.de* dig b2.de* dros b2.de* dulc b2.de* euph b2.de* euphr b2.de* ferr b2.de* graph b2.de* guaj b2.de* hep b2.de* hyos b2.de* ign b2.de* ip b2.de* kali-c b2.de* kali-n b2.de* kreos b2.de* lach b2.de* laur b2.de* lyc b2.de* m-ambo b2.de *M-arct* b2.de m-aust b2.de mag-m b2.de* mang b2.de* meny b2.de* merc b2.de* mez b2.de* nat-m b2.de* nit-ac b2.de* *Nux-v* b2.de* olnd b2.de* par b2.de* ph-ac b2.de* phos b2.de* plat b2.de* *Puls* b2.de* **Rhus-t** b2.de* ruta b2.de* sabad b2.de* sabin b2.de* samb b2.de* sars b2.de* sep b2.de* sil b2.de* spig b2.de* *Spong* b2.de* *Stann* b2.de* **Staph** b2.de* stront-c b2.de* sul-ac b2.de* sulph b2.de* tarax b2.de* thuj b2.de* valer b2.de* verat b2.de* verb b2.de* viol-t b2.de*
- **Cheeks**: ...
  - **accompanied** by | **Teeth**; complaints of (See TEETH - Complaints - accompanied - cheeks - complaints)
- **Chin**: *Agar* b2.de* agn b2.de* alum b2.de* am-c b2.de* am-m b2.de* ambr b2.de* anac b2.de* *Ant-c* b2.de* asaf b2.de* aur b2.de* *Bell* b2.de* borx b2.de* bov b2.de* bry b2.de* calc b2.de* cann-s b2.de* *Canth* b2.de* carb-v b2.de* **Caust** b2.de* chel b2.de* cic b2.de* clem b2.de* cocc b2.de* coloc bg2 con b2.de* cupr b2.de* dig b2.de* dros b2.de* dulc b2.de* euph b2.de* euphr b2.de* graph b2.de* *Hep* b2.de* hyos b2.de* kali-c b2.de* *Kreos* b2.de* *Laur* b2.de* led b2.de* lyc b2.de* *M-ambo* b2.de* m-aust b2.de mag-c b2.de* mag-m b2.de* mang b2.de* *Merc* b2.de* mez b2.de* nat-c b2.de* nat-m b2.de* nit-ac b2.de* nux-m b2.de* nux-v b2.de* olnd b2.de* op b2.de* par b2.de* ph-ac b2.de* phos b2.de* **Plat** b2.de* plb b2.de* puls b2.de* ran-b b2.de* *Rhus-t* b2.de* sabin b2.de* *Sars* b2.de* sep b2.de* **Sil** b2.de* spig b2.de* *Spong* b2.de* squil b2.de* stann b2.de* staph b2.de* stram b2.de* *Stront-c* b2.de* *Sulph* b2.de* tarax b2.de* thuj b2.de* *Verat* b2.de* verb b2.de* *Zinc* b2.de*
- **Eyes**:

○ · **Around**: asaf ptk1 chel bg2 cimic bg2 cinnb bg2* hep ptk1 ign ptk1 kali-bi ptk1 merc ptk1
  - **Below**: iris bg2 nux-v bg2 ruta bg2
- **Jaws**:

○ · **Bones**: phos ptk1 sil ptk1
  - **Joints**: (↗*Pain - sinuses - maxillary*) acon b2.de* alum b2.de* am-c b2.de* am-m b2.de* *Ang* b2.de* arn b2.de* asaf b2.de* *Asar* b2.de* **Bell** b2.de* bry b2.de* calc b2.de* *Camph* b2.de* canth b2.de* caust b2.de* cham b2.de* *Cic* b2.de* cocc b2.de* *Colch* b2.de* con b2.de* cupr b2.de* dros b2.de* euphr b2.de* graph b2.de* hyos b2.de* **Ign** b2.de* kali-c b2.de* lach b2.de* laur b2.de* m-ambo b2.de *M-arct* b2.de mang b2.de* meny b2.de* **Merc** b2.de* mur-ac b2.de* nat-c b2.de* nat-m b2.de* nit-ac b2.de* nux-m b2.de* *Nux-v* b2.de* op b2.de* petr b2.de* ph-ac b2.de* phos b2.de* plat b2.de* plb b2.de* **Rhus-t** b2.de* sabad b2.de* sabin b2.de* sars b2.de* sec b2.de* sep b2.de* sil b2.de* *Spig* b2.de* *Spong* b2.de* stann b2.de* staph b2.de* stram b2.de* sul-ac b2.de* sulph b2.de* thuj b2.de* verat b2.de* verb b2.de*
  - **Lower**: acon b2.de* *Agar* b2.de* agn b2.de* alum b2.de* *Am-c* b2.de* am-m b2.de* ambr b2.de* anac b2.de* ang b2.de* ant-t b2.de* arg-met b2.de* arn b2.de* asaf b2.de* asar b2.de* *Aur* b2.de* bar-c b2.de* **Bell** b2.de* borx b2.de* bov b2.de* *Bry* b2.de* calc b2.de* camph b2.de* cann-s b2.de* **Canth** b2.de* caps b2.de* carb-an b2.de* *Carb-v* b2.de* **Caust** b2.de* **Cham** b2.de* chel b2.de* *Chin* b2.de* cic b2.de* cina b2.de* clem b2.de* cocc b2.de* coff b2.de* colch b2.de* coloc b2.de* con b2.de* *Cupr* b2.de* dig b2.de* dros b2.de* dulc b2.de* euph b2.de* euphr b2.de* graph b2.de* guaj b2.de* *Hecla* br1 hell b2.de* hep b2.de* hyos b2.de* ign b2.de* kali-bi bg2 kali-c b2.de* kali-n b2.de* kreos b2.de* lach ptk1 **Laur** b2.de* led b2.de* lyc b2.de* m-ambo b2.de **M-arct** b2.de* mag-c b2.de mag-m b2.de* mang b2.de* meny b2.de* merc b2.de* mez b2.de* mur-ac b2.de* **Nat-c** b2.de* nat-m b2.de* nit-ac b2.de* nux-m b2.de* nux-v b2.de* olnd b2.de* op b2.de* par b2.de* petr b2.de* ph-ac b2.de* *Phos* b2.de* plat b2.de* **Plb** b2.de* *Puls* b2.de* ran-b b2.de* ran-s b2.de* rheum b2.de* rhod b2.de* *Rhus-t* b2.de* ruta b2.de* sabad b2.de* *Sabin* b2.de* *Sars* b2.de* sel b2.de* seneg b2.de* sep b2.de* *Sil* b2.de* spig b2.de* spong b2.de* squil b2.de* stann b2.de* **Staph** b2.de* stront-c b2.de* sul-ac b2.de* sulph b2.de* teucr b2.de* thuj b2.de* valer b2.de* *Verat* b2.de* verb b2.de* viol-o b2.de* viol-t b2.de* **Zinc** b2.de*
    - **accompanied** by | **Teeth**; pain in (See TEETH - Pain - accompanied - jaw - complaints)
    - **extending** to:
      - **Ear**: coloc bg2 spig bg2
      - **Head**: nat-s bg2
      - **Temples**: mang ptk1
  - **Upper**: acon b2.de* *Agar* b2.de* *Alum* b2.de* **Am-c** b2.de* am-m b2.de* ambr b2.de* ang b2.de* arn b2.de* asar b2.de* *Aur* b2.de* *Bell* b2.de* borx b2.de* bov b2.de* bry b2.de* *Calc* b2.de* canth b2.de* carb-an b2.de* **Carb-v** b2.de* caust b2.de* cham b2.de* chel b2.de* **Chin** b2.de* clem b2.de* coff b2.de* colch b2.de* com bro1 con b2.de* cycl b2.de* dulc b2.de* euph b2.de* euph-a bro1 euphr b2.de* graph b2.de* guaj b2.de* *Hecla* br1 hell b2.de* hep bro1 hyos b2.de* *Kali-c* b2.de* *Kali-i* bro1 *Kali-n* b2.de* kali-s bro1 **Kreos** b2.de* lyc b2.de* m-ambo b2.de m-arct b2.de m-aust b2.de mag-c b2.de* mag-m b2.de* mang b2.de* meny b2.de* merc b2.de* merc-c bro1 *Mez* b2.de* mur-ac b2.de* *Nat-c* b2.de* *Nat-m* b2.de*

- **Upper**: ...
Nit-ac b2.de* nux-m b2.de* nux-v b2.de* par bro1 ph-ac b2.de* *Phos* b2.de* plat b2.de* puls b2.de* *Ran-s* b2.de* rheum b2.de* rhod b2.de* rhus-t b2.de* sabad b2.de* samb b2.de* sars b2.de* seneg b2.de* sep b2.de* sil b2.de* *Spig* b2.de* spong b2.de* stann b2.de* staph b2.de* stront-c b2.de* *Sul-ac* b2.de* sulph b2.de* teucr b2.de* *Thuj* b2.de* til bro1 verat b2.de* verb b2.de* **Zinc** b2.de* [*Buteo-j* sej6]

- **Lips**: acon b2.de* agar b2.de* alum b2.de* am-c b2.de* *Am-m* b2.de* ang b2.de* ant-c b2.de* *Arn* b2.de* **Ars** b2.de* arum-t ptk1 asaf b2.de* **Bar-c** b2.de* *Bell* b2.de* borx b2.de* bov b2.de* **Bry** b2.de* **Calc** b2.de* cann-s b2.de* canth b2.de* caps b2.de* carb-an b2.de* carb-v b2.de* *Caust* b2.de* cham b2.de* chin b2.de* cic b2.de* clem b2.de* *Con* b2.de* croc b2.de* cycl b2.de* dig b2.de* dulc b2.de* graph b2.de* *Hell* b2.de* *Hep* b2.de* hyos b2.de* *Ign* b2.de* ip b2.de* **Kali-c** b2.de* *Kreos* b2.de* laur b2.de* lyc b2.de* m-ambo b2.de mag-c b2.de* mag-m b2.de* *Merc* b2.de* *Mez* b2.de* mur-ac b2.de* *Nat-c* b2.de* **Nat-m** b2.de* nit-ac b2.de* nux-v b2.de* olnd b2.de* op b2.de* *Par* b2.de* *Ph-ac* b2.de* *Phos* b2.de* *Plat* b2.de* *Puls* b2.de* rhod b2.de* **Rhus-t** b2.de* sabad b2.de* **Sep** b2.de* sil b2.de* spig b2.de* spong b2.de* squil b2.de* **Staph** b2.de* stram b2.de* stront-c b2.de* **Sulph** b2.de* tarax b2.de* thuj b2.de* valer b2.de* verat b2.de* zinc b2.de*

○ - **Lower**: agar b2.de* alum b2.de* am-c b2.de* am-m b2.de* arn b2.de* ars b2.de* asaf b2.de* aur b2.de* bar-c b2.de* bell b2.de* *Borx* b2.de* bov b2.de* **Bry** b2.de* *Calc* b2.de* caps b2.de* carb-v b2.de* caust b2.de* cham b2.de* chin b2.de* clem b2.de* con b2.de* dros b2.de* euph b2.de* graph b2.de* hep b2.de* hyos b2.de* **Ign** b2.de* kali-c b2.de* laur b2.de* lyc b2.de* m-ambo b2.de m-arct b2.de mag-c b2.de* mang b2.de* merc b2.de* *Mez* b2.de* mur-ac b2.de* nat-c b2.de* nat-m b2.de* nux-v b2.de* olnd b2.de* op b2.de* par b2.de* *Ph-ac* b2.de* phos b2.de* plat b2.de* **Puls** b2.de* ran-s b2.de* rheum b2.de* rhod b2.de* rhus-t b2.de* sabad b2.de* sabin b2.de* samb b2.de* sars b2.de* **Sep** b2.de* sil b2.de* spig b2.de* spong b2.de* stann b2.de* staph b2.de* sulph b2.de* teucr b2.de* valer b2.de* zinc b2.de*

- **Middle**: puls ptk1

- **Upper**: acon b2.de* agar b2.de* am-c b2.de* am-m b2.de* ant-c b2.de* arg-met b2.de* arn b2.de* *Ars* b2.de* **Bar-c** b2.de* *Bell* b2.de* borx b2.de* bov b2.de* bry b2.de* calc b2.de* canth b2.de* caps b2.de* *Carb-v* b2.de* caust b2.de* chel b2.de* chin b2.de* cic b2.de* coff b2.de* colch b2.de* con b2.de* cycl b2.de* dig b2.de* dulc b2.de* *Graph* b2.de* hell b2.de* hep b2.de* ign b2.de* **Kali-c** b2.de* *Kreos* b2.de* laur b2.de* led b2.de* lyc b2.de* m-ambo b2.de m-arct b2.de mag-c b2.de* mag-m b2.de* *Merc* b2.de* mez b2.de* mosch b2.de* mur-ac b2.de* *Nat-c* b2.de* nat-m b2.de* nit-ac b2.de* nux-v b2.de* olnd b2.de* *Par* b2.de* petr b2.de* ph-ac b2.de* phos b2.de* plat b2.de* plb b2.de* puls b2.de* rheum b2.de* rhus-t b2.de* *Sabad* b2.de* sars b2.de* sel b2.de* seneg b2.de* sep b2.de* sil b2.de* spig b2.de* squil b2.de* *Staph* b2.de* *Stront-c* b2.de* sul-ac b2.de* **Sulph** b2.de* tarax b2.de* *Thuj* b2.de* valer b2.de* verat b2.de* *Zinc* b2.de*

- **Malar** bones: acon b2.de* aeth bg2 agar b2.de* *Alum* b2.de* am-m b2.de* ambr b2.de* anac b2.de* ang b2.de* ant-c b2.de* ant-t b2.de* *Arg-met* b2.de* arn b2.de* ars b2.de* *Ars-i* ptk1 asaf b2.de* *Aur* b2.de* bar-c b2.de* *Bell* b2.de* bism b2.de* borx b2.de* bov bg2 *Bry* b2.de* *Calc* b2.de* calc-p bg2 cann-s b2.de* canth b2.de* caps b2.de* carb-v b2.de* caust b2.de* chel b2.de* *Chin* b2.de* cina b2.de* cocc b2.de* *Colch* b2.de* coloc b2.de* *Con* b2.de* *Dig* b2.de* *Dros* b2.de* ferr b2.de* glon bg2* graph b2.de* guaj b2.de* hell b2.de* *Hep* b2.de* hyos bg2 ign b2.de* kali-bi bg2* *Kali-c* b2.de* kali-i ptk1 kali-n bg2 lach bg2 laur b2.de* led b2.de* lyc b2.de* mag-c b2.de* *Mag-m* b2.de* mang b2.de* **Merc** b2.de* *Mez* b2.de* mosch b2.de* mur-ac b2.de* nat-c b2.de* *Nat-m* b2.de* nat-s bg2 nit-ac b2.de* *Nux-v* b2.de* ol-an bg2* *Olnd* b2.de* par b2.de* **Phos** b2.de* *Plat* b2.de* plb b2.de* puls b2.de* rheum bg2 rhus-t b2.de* ruta b2.de* sabad b2.de* sabin b2.de* samb b2.de* sang bg2 *Sep* b2.de* sil bg2 **Spig** b2.de* spong b2.de* **Stann** b2.de* **Staph** b2.de* stront-c b2.de* *Sul-ac* b2.de* sulph b2.de* tab bg2 teucr bg2 thuj b2.de* tub ptk1 valer b2.de* verat b2.de* **Verb** b2.de* *Viol-o* b2.de* zinc b2.de*

- **Maxillary** sinuses: (*↗Pain - sinuses - maxillary)* aur mtf11 calc mtf33 chr-ac mtf11 cist mtf11 *Coch* br1 jug-r mtf11 kali-bi mrr1 sil mrr1 symph mtf11

- **Mouth**:

○ - **Angles** (See corners)

- **Around**: aeth bg2 ars ptk1 *Bell* bg2 bry ptk1 cic bg2 *Cina* bg2* ip bg2 kali-n ptk1 *Kreos* ptk1 merc bg2 nat-m ptk1 phos bg2 podo bg2 rhus-t ptk1 sep ptk1 staph ptk1 *Stram* bg2 *Sulph* ptk1 tarent bg2

- **Corners** of: am-m b2.de* ambr b2.de* **Ant-c** b2.de* arn b2.de* asaf b2.de* bar-c b2.de* **Bell** b2.de* bov b2.de* bry b2.de* *Calc* b2.de* cann-s b2.de* canth b2.de* carb-v b2.de* *Caust* b2.de* chel b2.de*

Complaints – Mouth – Corners of: ...
coloc b2.de* dros b2.de* *Graph* b2.de* hell b2.de* *Hep* b2.de* *Ign* b2.de* ip b2.de* kreos b2.de* laur b2.de* lyc b2.de* *M-arct* b2.de* *Mang* b2.de* **Merc** b2.de* mez b2.de* nat-c b2.de* nat-m b2.de* nux-v b2.de* olnd b2.de* op b2.de* par b2.de* *Petr* b2.de* **Phos** b2.de* ran-b b2.de* ran-s b2.de* rheum b2.de* rhod b2.de* rhus-t b2.de* seneg b2.de* sep b2.de* *Sil* b2.de* stront-c b2.de* sul-ac b2.de* sulph b2.de* tarax b2.de* verat b2.de* zinc b2.de*

- **Inner** side (See MOUTH - Complaints)

- **Muscles**; masseter: ang mtf11 hydr-ac ptk1 ign ptk1
- **Salivary** glands: *Iris* br1
- **Side** lain on: phos b4a.de
- **Temples** (See Temples)
- **Uncovered** part: *Thuj* b4a.de

COMPRESSION malar bones: fl-ac bg2

CONDYLOMATA: | **Mouth**; corners of: sulph brm

CONGESTION: (*↗Bloated; Heat)* acet-ac ptk1 acon k* agar k* all-c bro1 alum bg2 **Aml-ns** k* ang bg2 *Ant-c* bg2 ant-t *Apis* k* apoc ptk1 aran bro1 arg-met bg2 arg-n k* *Arn* bg2 ars bg2* **Aur** k* *Bapt* mrr1 bar-c k* bar-i k2 **Bell** k* borra-o oss1• bov bg2 *Bry* k* *Cact* k* calad bg2 *Calc* k* camph bg2 cann-s cann-xyz bg2 canth bg2 *Caps* bg2* carb-v bg2 caust k* *Cedr* bro1 **Cham** bg2* chel bg2 chin k* chinin-ar bro1 *Chinin-s* bro1 cic bg2 cimic bro1 clem bg2 coc-c *Cocc* bg2 *Coff* bg2* coloc k* con bg2 cop croc bg2 crot-h ptk1 *Cupr* bg2 dig bg2 *Dros* bg2 dulc bg2 equis-h eup-per euphr bg2 ferr bg2* *Ferr-p* bg2 *Gels* k* **Glon** k* graph bg2* ham bg2 hecla bro1 *Hep* bg2 hydr-ac hyos k* ign k* ind *Iod* kali-bi bg2 kali-br bg2 kali-c bg2 *Kali-i* bg2* kali-n bg2 kali-p bro1 kalm bro1 kreos bg2 lac-ac *Lach* k* lat-m bnm6• laur bg2* led lil-t *Lyc* bg2* mag-c bg2 *Mag-p* bro1 malar jl2 manc ptk1 meli k* mentho bro1 meny bg2 merc bg2* merc-c k* merc-d ptk1 mez bg2* mit morph mosch bg2 mur-ac bg2 nat-c bg2 *Nat-m* bg2 nit-ac bg2 nit-s-d bro1 nux-m bg2 **Nux-v** bg2* oena op k* paeon *Ph-ac* bg2 *Phos* k* *Plan* bro1 plat bg2* psil ft1 psor ptk1 **Puls** k* rad-br bro1 ran-b bg2 rhod bro1 *Rhus-t* bg2* sabad bg2 sabin samb bg2* *Sang* bg2* sec bg2 sep bg2 *Sil* bg2* spig bg2* *Spong* bg2* squil bg2 stann bg2* **Stram** k* *Stront-c* bg2 *Stry* sul-ac bg2 sulph bg2* tanac tarax bg2 tarent ptk1 thuj k* til bro1 tub-d jl2 ust valer bg2 verat bg2 verat-v ptk1 *Verb* bro1 zinc-p bro1 *Zinc-val* bro1 ziz

- **afternoon**, 15 h: sulph
- **accompanied** by | **apoplexy** (See GENERALS - Apoplexy - accompanied - face - congestion)
- **air** agg.; in open: phos k*
- **dinner**; after: cor-r br1
- **eating** | **after** | **agg.**: ignis-alc es2•
  - **while** | **agg.**: *Cop* k*
- **exertion** agg.; slight: *Spong* br1
- **flushes** (See Heat - flushes)
- **hurrying**, during: ign k*
- **prosopalgia**: plat j
- **rubbing**; after: aesc k*
- **sensation** of: samb b7.de*
- **spots**; in irregular: ail vh1
- **stool** agg.; during: aloe
- **walking** agg.; after: caust k*

▽ - **extending** to:

○ - **Body**; whole: malar jl2
  - **Head**: malar jl2

CONSTRICTION: | **Beneath** lower jaw: sang a1

CONSTRICTION of jaw (See Clenched)

CONTORTION (See Distortion)

CONTRACTION: (*↗Distortion)* acon alum b4.de* ars asar b7.de* *Bell* calc b4a.de cann-s *Cham* chin b7.de* choc srj3• con dulc b4.de* gels irid-met srj5• kali-i kali-n b4.de* laur lyc *Merc* morph nicotam rly4• nit-ac b4.de* phos phys phyt plb positr nl2• rhus-t k* sars sec sep b4.de* spong b7.de* stann b4.de* suis-pan rly4• tab verb bg2 zinc zinc-s

- **right**: eup-per k* sars h2* stann h2*
- **sensation** of: plac rzf5•

○ - **Lips**: arg-met bg2
- **sudden** | **Cheeks**: eup-per ptk1

○ - **Forehead** (See HEAD - Contraction - forehead)
- **Jaws**: nicotam rly4•

Face

- **Jaws**: ...
  - ○ · **Lower** jaw: cupr bg2 *Nux-m* b7.de* nux-v b7.de* puls b7.de* sil b4a.de stann b4.de*
- **Lips**: am-m b7a.de* calc b4.de* coc-c bg2 (non:cocc a1) sec b7.de*
  - ○ · **Lower**: coc-c a1 hipp jl2
- **Malar** bones: coloc a1 nit-ac h2*
- **Masticator** muscles: convo-s sp1
- **Mouth**; around: gels bg*
- **Muscles**; masseter: meny ptk1 merc ptk1
- **Parotid** glands: mang b4.de*
- **Salivary** glands (See MOUTH - Contraction - salivary)
- **Skin**; of: cann-i c1
- **Submaxillary** glands: lyc a1 sil k*

CONVULSIONS, spasms: acon agar k* ambr amyg anan ant-t k* arg-n k* *Ars* atro bar-c bar-m k2 **Bell** k* bism *Bov* brom *Bufo* calc k* camph k* canth k* carbn-s *Caust* *Cham* k* **Cic** k* *Cocc* con crot-c **Cupr** k* dig k* dulc bg2 gels bg2 *Glon* *Hep* hydr-ac *Hyos* *Ign* k* iod tl1 *Ip* k* kali-n *Laur* k* *Lyc* k* *Lyss* merc-c k* morph nat-c k* nit-ac nux-v *Oena* k* ol-an *Op* k* phos k* *Phys* plb *Puls* bg2 *Ran-b* ran-s rheum b7.de* rhus-t sec k* *Sil* bg2 **Stram** k* stry k* sul-ac sulph k* tab verat vip *Zinc* ziz

- **one** side: dig plb
- **right**: agar bell mrr1
- **left**: dig c1
- **beginning** in face (See GENERALS - Convulsions - begin - face)
- **chill**; during: ars k* bell k* calc bg2 cham k* cic k* ign k* op k* stann bg2 stram k*
- **menses**; before: puls
- **talking** agg.: ign mtf33 plb
- **tonic**: ambr b7.de* *Camph* b7.de* cann-s b7.de* carb-v b4.de* cham b7.de* cocc b7.de* cupr b7.de* dig b4.de* guaj b4.de* hep b4.de* laur b7.de* m-arct b7.de op b7.de* sep b4.de* stram b7.de* *Verat* b7a.de
  - ○ · **Lips**: ambr b7.de* ang b7.de* ran-b b7.de*
- ▽ - **extending** to | **Limbs**: cic k2 santin sec
- ○ - **Chin**: bell b4.de*
- **Eyes**; around: cic k2
- **Jaws**: agar aids nl2• ars asaf atra-r bnm3• *Bell* carb-an cic k2 coloc crot-c hydr-ac ign kali-c mang oena op ran-b stram sulph
  - ○ · **Joints**: caust mrr1 colch kali-c nicc ol-an rhus-t sil spong stann *Stry* mrr1
    - ⁝ **right**: caust mrr1
  - · **Lower**: ign b7.de* laur b7.de plb b7.de* stram b7.de* tab ptk1 *Verat* b7.de*
- **Lips**: (↗*Cramp - lips*) *Ambr* k* bell b4a.de cadm-s c1 caust cham b7.de* crot-c *Ign* b7a.de ip b7.de* kali-c lyc b4a.de naja gm1 olnd b7.de* op b7.de* ran-b k* stram b7.de*
  - ○ · **Lower** lips: ambr h1*
- **Mouth**: ant-c vh1 bell cham dulc ign *Ip* *Lyc* merc nit-ac h2 olnd op stram
- **Muscles**: bell tl1
  - ○ · **Masseter** muscles: ambr ang cic k2 cocc cupr laur br1 mang nux-v

COUGH:

- **after** | **agg.**: cina b7.de* croc b7.de*
- **before** | **agg.**: croc b7.de*
- **during** | **agg.**: am-c bg2 cina b7.de* ip b7.de* kali-bi ptk1 op b7.de* samb ptk1 *Spong* b7.de* verat b7.de*

CRACKED: (↗*Chapped*) bufo bg2 sil b4.de* *Sulph* b4a.de

- ○ - **Lips**: (↗*Chapped - lips*) acon-ac rly4• *Agar* k* *Ail* k* allox tpw4* aloe k* alum k* alum-p k2 *Am-c* k* *Am-m* k* ambr k* amp rly4• androc srj1• ant-c bg2* ant-t k* apis b7a.de* aral vh arist-cl sp1 *Arn* k* *Ars* k* ars-s-f k2 **Arum-t** k* aur aur-ar k2 aur-s k2 bac wz *Bapt* k* bar-c k* bar-s k2 bell k* beryl tpw5* bism *Bov* k* **Bry** k* bung-fa mtf **Calc** k* calc-p ptk1 *Calc-s* calc-sil k2 *Cann-s* b7.de* *Caps* k* carb-ac k* *Carb-an* k* **Carb-v** k* **Carbn-s** k* caust k* cench k2 *Cham* k* chel k* **Chin** k* chinin-ar cimic k* cist k2 *Clem* bro1 colch k* con cop cor-r k* *Croc* k* crot-t a1 *Cund* bro1 cupr dros k* dys pte1*• echi bro1 fago a1 gink-b sbd1• glyc bro1 **Graph** k* guare ham k* *Hell* k* hep b4a.de* hyos k2 *Ign* k* ina-i mlk9.de iris jatr-c kali-ar kali-bi k* kali-c k* kali-i k* kali-p kali-s kali-sil k2 kalm k* *Kreos* k* lac-lup hm2• **Lach** k* lap-la sde8.de• lat-m sp1 luna kg1• lyc bg2 mag-m k* mang bg1 meny b7.de* *Merc* k* *Merc-c* k* merc-pr-r bro1 *Mez* k* moni jl2 mur-ac h2* musca-d szs1 nat-ar nat-c k* **Nat-m** k* nicc nit-ac k* nux-v k* ol-an bg2 ozone sde2• par k* petr h2* ph-ac k* *Phos* k* plac rzf5• *Plat* k* plb k* positr nl2• pot-e rly4• *Prot* jl2 ptel c1 puls k* rauw sp1 *Rhus-t* k* sabad k* sabin bg2 sacch-a fd2.de• sal-fr sle1• sel k* sep bg2* *Sil* k* spig k* spong fd4.de

Cracked – Lips: ...

squil k* staph b7.de* *Stram* k* stront-c b4.de* **Sulph** k* syc pte1*• symph fd3.de• syph k2 tab k* tarax k* ter k* tere-la rly4• *Thuj* b4a.de tritic-vg fd5.de tub-m vs tub-r vn* vanil fd5.de *Verat* k* vip fkr4.de visc sp1 vit-b-x mtf11 *Zinc* k* zinc-p k2

- · **accompanied** by:
  - ⁝ **burning** pain: beryl tpw5
  - ⁝ **hoarseness**: **Arum-t** mrr1
- · **coryza**; during: *Cham* b7.de* hell b7.de* staph b7.de*
- · **cough** agg.; during: *Bell* b4a.de
- ○ · **Lower**: anag vh apis k* arag br1 borx bg2 bry b7.de* cham k* chin b7.de* cimic dros b7.de* graph b4.de* hep b4a.de lap-la sde8.de• mez b4.de* *Nat-c* k* nat-m b4.de* *Nit-ac* nux-v b7.de* ozone sde2• pert-vc vk9 ph-ac b4.de* *Phos* k* plat b4.de* positr nl2• *Puls* b7.de* rauw tpw8* sacch-a fd2.de• **Sep** k* sulph b4.de* thuj b4a.de trios rsj11• zinc h2
  - ⁝ **right** side: positr nl2•
  - ⁝ **Middle** of●: agar k* *Am-c* k* apoc vh1 aq-mar skp7• aur-m calc bg1* *Cham* k* *Chin* h1* dros k* graph bro1* haliae-lc srj5• *Hep* k* iyc xyz61 mag-m gk meny gk **Mez** gk *Nat-c* bg2* **Nat-m** k ●* *Nux-v* h1* *Ph-ac* h2* *Phos* h2* pip-n bg2 *Puls* k* *Sep* bg1* spong fd4.de
- · **Upper**: agar b4.de* am-c b4.de* androc srj1• bar-c bell bg2 *Bry* b7a.de calc h2* caust b4.de* cimic hr1 (non:hell b7a.de*) *Kali-c* k* kali-s fd4.de kreos b7a.de* nat-c *Nat-m* k* par b7.de* ph-ac b4.de* sabad b7.de* sel b7.de* (non:tarax b7.de*) tub-r jl2 vanil fd5.de zinc h2
  - ⁝ **Middle**●: bar-ox-suc rly4• *Calc* ptk1* carc fd2.de• *Cham* ptk1 *Chin* vh hell kl *Hep* k* kali-s fd4.de mag-m dgt *Nat-c* vh *Nat-m* k* neon srj5• *Nux-v* vh *Ph-ac* vh *Phos* ptk1* *Puls* ptk1 *Sel* *Sep* ptk1* sulph bg2 tarax kl
  - ⁝ **Third** external part: tub-r jl2
- **Mouth**; corners of: (↗*Excoriation - mouth; Ulcers - mouth - corners*) allox tpw3* am-c am-m bro1 ambr k* *Ant-c* k* apis arist-cl sp1 ars bro1 **Arum-t** k* arund bro1 bov bro1 calc caust cinnb **Cund** k* echi bro1 elaps gk eup-per k* gink-b sbd1• **Graph** k* *Hell* k* *Hep* bro1 *Hydr* hydrog srj2• ign lp ind k* *Iod* bg1* kola stb3• lac-c mtf33 lac-h htj1*• limen-b-c hm2* luf-op rsj5• mag-p bg2* *Merc* k* merc-c ptk1* *Mez* k* morg-g fmm1• morg-p pte1• *Nat-ar* *Nat-m* k* nat-sil fd3.de• **Nit-ac** k* petr bro1 plac rzf5• propl ub1• prot pte1*• psor ptk1* ptel gk rhus-t bro1* sec bro1 *Sep* k* **Sil** k* sulph k2 syc pte1*• syph xxb thal-xyz srj8• *Thlas* bg1* tritic-vg fd5.de ulm-c jsj8• v-a-b jl vanil fd5.de verat b7.de* vip fkr4.de *Zinc* k* [heroin sdj2]
  - · **right**: acon-ac rly4• kola stb3• kreos k2 loxo-recl knl4• *Lyc* bg1* merc ptk1 nat-sil fd3.de• tritic-vg fd5.de
  - · **left**: abrom-a ks5 corian-s knl6• [heroin sdj2]
  - · **indurated**: sil mtf33
  - · **menses**; during: kreos k2
  - · **painful**: **Cund** br1

CRACKING in articulation of jaw: aloe bg2 am-c b4a.de* *Arn* b7a.de brom bg2 carb-v bg2 coc-c bg2 gran bg2 haliae-lc srj5• lach bg2 *Meny* b7a.de mez bg2 nit-ac b4.de* ol-an bg2 rhus-t b7.de* ruta fd4.de sabad b7.de* sel bg2 sep bg2 sulph bg2 thuj b4a.de* tritic-vg fd5.de vanil fd5.de

- **chewing** agg.: *Am-c* k* brom chinin-s *Cor-r* bg1* cypra-eg sde6.de• *Gamb* bg1* gran kka1.de* ign sne kali-c dgt ketogl-ac rly4• *Lac-c* k* *Lach* *Meny* *Mez* **Nit-ac** k* ol-an **Rhus-t** k* sabad sel spong *Stry* bg1* sulph *Thuj* vanil fd5.de
- **opening** mouth wide; when: podo fd3.de• sabad k* thuj tritic-vg fd5.de
- **would** crack; as if it: petr h2* sep h2*
- **yawning** agg.: sabad b7.de*

CRAMP: anac bg2 *Ang* b7a.de bell b4.de* *Calc* b4a.de cina b7.de* cocc b7.de* *Coloc* b4a.de* dig b4.de* dulc b4.de* fl-ac bg2 hyos b7.de* kali-c b4.de* mag-m b4.de* meny b7.de* *Mez* b4.de* nit-ac b4.de* par bg2 plat b4.de* *Rhus-t* b7.de* sep b4a.de spong b7.de* stann b4.de* thuj b4.de* valer b7.de* *Verb* ptk1

- **accompanied** by:
  - ○ · **Lips** | **retraction** of: *Ang* b7a.de
- **eating** | **after** | **agg.**: atro vh1 mang h2
  - · **agg.**: (non:mang h2) spong
- ○ - **Chin**: bell h1*
- **Jaws**: kali-c ptk1 plat ptk1 tab ptk1 verat ptk1
  - · **eating**; after: mang h2 verat ptk1
  - ○ · **Joints**: ang a1* asaf asar k* *Bell* k* carbn-h coloc bg3 crot-h k* dig h2* fl-ac kali-c k* kali-i k* mang hr1 mez bg3 nicc c1 nit-ac k* ox-ac plat rhus-t sep sil *Spong* k* sulph *Verb* bg3

- **Jaws**: ...
  - **Lower**: acon bg2 agar bg2 alum b4.de* *Ang* b7.de* arg-n bg2 arn b7.de* asaf b7.de* asar b7.de* **Bell** b4.de* bry bg2 bufo bg2 calc bg2 *Camph* bg2 cann-xyz bg2 *Canth* bg2 caust bg2 cham b7.de *Cic* bg2 cocc b7.de* colch b7.de* con bg2 cupr bg2 cur bg2 dig bg2 dulc bg2 gels bg2 *Hyos* bg2 hyper bg2 *Ign* b7.de* ip bg2 kali-br bg2 kali-c b4.de* *Lach* bg2 laur bg2 lyc bg2 m-ambo b7.de *M-arct* b7.de mag-p bg2 mang b4.de* *Merc* b4.de* merc-c b4a.de mur-ac b4.de* nux-v b7.de* ol-an bg2 **Op** bg2 phos bg2 phys bg2 phyt bg2 *Plat* b4.de* plb bg2 **Rhus-t** b7.de* sec bg2 sil bg2 spig b7.de* spong b7.de* stann b4.de* **Stram** bg2 stry bg2 *Sulph* b4.de* tab bg2 **Verat** bg2 verb b7.de* zinc bg2
- **Lips**: *(↗Convulsions - lips)* ambr b7.de* ang b7.de* bell b4.de* caust b4.de* kali-c b4.de* merc b4.de* plat b4.de* ran-b b7.de*
  - ○ **Lower**: ambr h1*
- **Malar** bones: ang b7.de* ars bg2 cina b7.de* cocc b7.de* coloc bg2 gran bg2 hyos b7a.de mag-m bg2 meny h1 mez bg2 nit-ac bg2 olnd bg2 *Plat* bg2 ruta b7.de* sep bg2 **Spig** bg2 valer b7a.de*
  - **left**: spong bg2
  - **yawning** agg.: arn h1
  - ○ **Below**: dig h2
- **Muscle** below left mastoid | **must** turn head to right: mang h2
- **Muscles**; masseter: *Ang* b7a.de cocc b7a.de

CRAWLING (See Formication)

CREAKING noise in maxillary joints: *Arn* b7a.de *Rhus-t* b7.de*

CREEPING (See Formication)

DANDRUFF: | **Eyebrows**: sanic ptk1* sulph mrr1

DENTITION agg.: *Bry* b7.de* *Hyos* b7.de*

DESQUAMATION:
- ○ **Lips** (See Peeling)
- **Skin** (See Eruptions - desquamating)

DISCOLORATION: *(↗Spots - colored)* bros-gau mrc1
- **ashy**: *Ars* k* *Bad* k* brom k2* *Chlor* k* *Cic* k* *Ferr* k* kali-bi k* kali-br a1 *Lach* hr1 *Lyc* hr1 morph k* *Phos* k* *Plb* k* sec k* sulph k* vanil fd5.de verat k* verat-v hr1
- **black**: alco a1 camph k* canth k2 **Chin** k* *Cor-r* k* crot-h k* hydr-ac k* *Lach* k* *Oena* k* op k* stry k* *Tarent* k*
  - **alternating** with red | **cough**; during (See red - alternating with - blackness - cough)
  - **blue** spots; and: arn crot-h *Lach* phos rhus-t **Sul-ac** *Tarent*
  - **cough** agg.; during: samb
  - **pores**: sabin c1*
  - **spots**: *Glycyr-g* cte1•
    - **acne**; from suppressed: glycyr-g cte1•
    - **Eyes**; around: psor mtf33 [sol-ecl cky1]
  - ○ **Lips**: acon k* amyg a1 ant-t **Ars** k* *Bell* b4a.de bry k* bufo carb-ac k* *Carb-v* k* *Chin* k* *Chlor* k* colch con der a1 fago a1 *Hyos* k* kali-ar *Kali-c* k* *Lach* k* *Merc* k* *Merc-c* k* merc-sul k* ph-ac k* *Phos* k* *Psor* k* rhus-t sal-fr sle1• squil k* *Sul-ac* b4a.de *Verat* k* vip bro1
    - **spots**: ars b4.de*
  - **Mouth**, around the: ars h2*
- **bluish**: absin bro1* acon k* *Agar* k* agar-ph a1 *Ail* alum-p k2 alum-sil k2 am-c bg2* aml-ns androc srj1• ang b2.de* ant-c b7a.de ant-t k* *Apis* k* *Arg-n* k* **Ars** k* *Ars-i* ars-s-f k2 **Asaf** k* asar b2.de* asim k* *Aur* k* aur-ar k2 bad **Bapt** k* **Bell** k* borx k* both k* brom k* **Bry** k* bufo *Cact* k* cadm-met sp1 calc k* calc-p k* **Camph** k* **Cann-i** *Canth* k* *Carb-an* k* **Carb-v** k* *Carbn-s* carl *Caust* k* *Cedr* k* *Cench* k* *Cham* k* chinin-ar chlf hr1 *Chlol* *Chlor* k* *Cic* k* cimic k* *Cina* k* cinnb bro1 *Cocc* k* colch k* **Con** k* cor-r croc crot-h k* crot-t k* **Cupr** k* *Cupr-act* bro1 cypra-eg sde6.de• cyt-l a1 **Dig** k* *Dros* k* *Dulc* k* ferr bro1 frag a1 gels k2 *Glon* k* helo-s bnm14• *Hep* k* hydr-ac k* **Hyos** k* ign k* indg br1 iod k* **Ip** k* jal br1 *Kali-c* k* kali-cy k* *Kali-i* k* kali-m k2* kali-p kali-sil k2 *Kreos* k* **Lach** k* lachn k* *Laur* k* loxo-lae bnm12• *Lyc* k* mag-p k* meph k* merc k* merc-c k* merc-cy mez b2.de mill k2 **Morph** k* mosch k* nat-ar *Nat-m* k* nat-p k* nitro-o a1 *Nux-v* oena bro1 **Op** k* ox-ac k* petr phenac bro1 phos k* *Phyt* k* plb prun psor k* *Puls* k* rhus-t k* russ a1 *Samb* k* sang sars k* sec k* sil spig k* *Spong* k* *Staph* k* *Stram* k* *Stry* k* succ-ac rly4• sul-ac k* *Sulph* k* *Tab* k* *Tarent* tub k2 **Verat** k* **Verat-v** k* vesp k* *Vip* visc sp1 zinc k* zinc-p k2
  - **morning**: bamb-a stb2.de• phos h2*

Discoloration – bluish: ...
- **alternating** with:
  - **redness** | **cough** agg.; during: bell bg2 con bg2 kali-c bg2 lach bg2
- **angry**, when: *(↗MIND - Abusive - scolds; MIND - Anger)* mosch k2* *Staph* k*
- **asthma**, in: *Aur* hr1 *Crot-h* hr1 cupr bg1* samb mrr1 *Stram* k* tab k*
- **chill**; during: ars bg2 asar h1* bry *Cact* k* camph bg2 con bg2 cupr bg2 hyos bg2 lach k* nat-m **Nux-v** k* *Op* bg2 petr **Stram** k* sulph k* *Tub* verat bg2
- **cholera**; during: *Camph* **Cupr** k* **Verat** k*
- **convulsions**; with: absin hr1* agar hr1* atro hr1* *Bell* hr1* *Cic* k* cina kr1 crot-h hr1 **Cupr** k* *Hyos* ign j5.de *Ip* nux-v hr1* *Oena* k* op kr1 phys plb hr1* stry *Verat* hr1*
- **cough** agg.; during: acon bg2 *Apis* bell k* caust **Cina** bg2 *Coc-c* con bg2 *Cor-r* cupr h2* **Dros** k* **Ip** k* kali-c bg2 *Mag-p* nux-v b7a.de* op b7.de* samb k* sil bg2 *Verat* k*
  - **whooping** cough: ars *Coc-c* *Cor-r* crot-h cupr tl1* *Dros* k* *Ip* k* meph br1 *Nux-v* samb ptk1
- **croup**; in: brom k* *Carb-v* k*
- **dyspnea**, with: *Arg-n* hr1 brom k2 bry *Dros* gk *Op* *Stram* sulph gk
- **eruption**; suppressed: abrot br1
- **headache**; during: cact *Op*
- **heart** trouble: *Apis* *Cact* k* laur br1
- **heat**; during: lach bg1
- **laughing** agg.: **Cann-i** cann-xyz ptk1
- **maniacal** rage: acon ars bell con hyos lach merc *Op* puls verat
- **menses**:
  - **before** | **agg.**: *Puls* k*
  - **close** of; at: verat
  - **during**:
    - **agg.**: verat b7.de*
    - **amel.**: puls k2
- **newborn** infant: laur br1
- **pale** | **accompanied** by | **apoplexy** (See GENERALS - Apoplexy - accompanied - face - bluish)
  - **diarrhea**; during: tub br1*
- **pregnancy** agg.; during: *Phos* k*
- **purple**: ail tl1 *Anil* br1 ant-t tl1 borra-o oss1• carb-v tl1 glon tl1 lach tl1* led bg *Op* mrr1* tub xxb vario jl2
  - **coma**; with (See MIND - Coma - face - purple)
  - **cough** agg.; during: cor-r br1
  - **epilepsy**; during (See GENERALS - Convulsions - epileptic - during - face - purple)
  - **urination** agg.; before: *Dulc* b4a.de
  - **veins**: asaf tl1
  - **Cheeks** | **Center** of cheeks: diph ptk1
  - **Lips**: am-c fr3* ant-t tl1 arn tl1 *Op* a1 tub-r jl2
- **purple**-red: acon bg2 *Bapt* bg2 bar-c bg2 phyt bg2
  - **Lips**: bar-c b4a.de*
- **red**: *(↗red - bluish)* *Aur* hr1 bell hr1 bry hr1 carb-v bg1 *Caust* hr1 *Cedr* hr1 **Dig** hr1 *Dulc* hr1 hydr-ac a1 *Hyos* hr1 *Ip* hr1 *Lach* hr1 *Op* hr1 phos a1 tub jl2 verat hr1
  - **evening**: phel ptk1
  - **Eyelashes**; above: *Tub* jl2
    - **Hairs**; at the roots of: *Tub* jl2
- **retching**; from: bell h1*
- **spasm** of glottis: *Bell* *Coff* **Lach** *Mosch*
- **speaking** in company: carb-v h2
- **spots**: ail apis ars k* aur k* *Bapt* crot-h ferr k* hura kali-br kali-p lach led mur-ac *Thuj* b4a.de
  - **following** eruptions: ant-t ferr **Lach** thuj
- **stool** | **after** | **agg.**: rhus-t
  - **during** | **agg.**: rhus-t
- **urination** agg.; during: aspar k*

Face

- **vexation**; after: verat
- **white**:
  - **Lips** | **spots**: merc b4.de*
- ○ **Cheeks**: cham k*
- **Chin**: plat k*
- **Eyes**: *Ip* bg2
  - **Around**; circles: (↗*EYE - Sickly)* abrot k* *Acet-ac* k* acon k* agar ail alum-sil k2 *Anac* k* androc srj1• ant-c bro1 ant-t k* ap-g bro1 *Aran* arge-pl rwt5• *Arn* b7a.de **Ars** k* ars-i ars-s-f k2 bad bamb-a stb2.de• *Bell* k* **Berb** k* *Bism* k* cadm-s br1 *Calc* k* *Calc-ar* calc-p *Camph* k* *Canth* carb-an cench k2 cham k* chel **Chin** k* chir-fl gya2 *Cic* k* cimic *Cina* k* cinnb *Cocc* k* corn *Crot-h* k* *Cupr* k* cycl k* dulc fd4.de fago *Ferr* k* ferr-ar ferr-p glon k2 gran bro1 *Graph* k* ham hell k* *Hep* k* hura hydrog srj2• *Ign* b2.de* *Indg* *Iod* **Ip** k* *Iris* jatr-c kali-ar kali-bi k* kali-c k* *Kali-i* k* kali-p kola stb3• kreos lac-d k2 lach k* luf-op rsj5• **Lyc** k* mag-c manc bg2 merc k* merc-c b4a.de merc-i-f ptk1 mez k* *Naja* **Nat-ar** **Nat-c** k* *Nat-m* k* nat-ox rly4• *Nat-p* nit-ac k2 **Nux-m** k* **Nux-v** k* *Oena* bro1 **Olnd** k* op ozone sde2• pall petr *Ph-ac* k* *Phos* k* *Phyt* pin-con oss2• plat plb plut-n srj7• psil ft psor k* *Puls* pycnop-sa mrz1 pyrog jl2 raph **Rhus-t** k* rhus-v *Sabad* k* sabin k* *Santin* bro1 **Sec** k* *Sep* k* spig b2.de* *Stann* k* *Staph* k* stram k* sulph k* symph fd3.de• tab k* taosc iwa1• tarent ter thuj ptk1 upa k* *Verat* k* visc c1* zinc k* zinc-p k2
    - **fever**; during: *Cina* b7.de*
    - **menses** | **after** | **agg.**: *Phos* b4a.de
      - **before** | **agg.**: tub xxb
  - **Under** the eye: ferr ptk1 hep b4a.de lachn c1 psil ft1 sep ptk1 spong fd4.de thuj ptk1
- **Forehead**: apis rhus-t hr1
- **Lips**: **Acet-ac** k* *Acon* k* agar k* alum k* alumn k* am-c k* amyg k* ang b7.de* anil br1 **Ant-t** k* *Apis* k* *Apoc* k* **Arg-n** k* arn tl1 *Ars* k* ars-i *Aur* k* *Bar-c* bar-i k2 berb k* *Bry* b7a.de *Cact* calc calc-sil k2 **Camph** k* carb-an bg2* carb-v bro1 carc sp* caust k* *Cedr* k* *Chin* k* *Chinin-s* k* chir-fl bnm4• chlol k* chlor cic bg2 cina b7.de* *Colch* k* con k* *Crot-h* cub c1 **Cupr** k* cupr-ar hr1 cupr-n a1 cupr-s bro1 cur k* cyt-l a1 *Dig* k* *Dros* k* dulc fd4.de eup-pur ferr-p bg2 gels bg2 glon bg2 hell bg2 helo-s bnm14• *Hep* k* **Hydr-ac** k* hyos bg2 *Iod* k* *Ip* k* ix bnm8• kali-ar *Kali-i* k* kreos k* **Lach** k* lachn k* laur mrr1 **Lyc** k* merc k* merc-c b4a.de merc-cy mosch k* naphthoq mtf11 *Nat-m* k* nitro-o a1 **Nux-v** k* *Op* k* ox-ac a1* *Phos* k* plan plb bg2 *Prun* psor k* rhus-t hr1 samb k* sec k* sil b4a.de *Spig* b7a.de spong ptk1 stram k* *Stry* k* tab bg2 tub-r jl verat k* vip k* *Zinc* bro1
  - **chill**; during: *Ars* k* *Chinin-s* eup-per bro1 eup-pur k* *Ip* k* meny bro1 **Nat-m** k* *Nux-v* k* *Sec* verat bro1
  - **cholera**; in: cupr mtf33
  - **coma**; with (See MIND - Coma - lips)
  - **convulsions**; during: cupr mtf33 dulc fd4.de **Nux-v** k*
  - **menses**; during: *Arg-n* k* *Cedr* k* verat tl1
  - **scolding**, from: *Mosch* k*
  - **whooping** cough: cupr k* dros k* ip *Nux-v*
- **Mouth**; about the: acon bg2 agar bg2 ars k* **Cina** k* *Cupr* k* kreos *Lach* b7a.de nit-ac k2 ph-ac sabad stram sulph syph xxb verat k*

- **bronzed**: ant-c bro1 ars-h k* bufo bg2 nit-ac bro1 sec bro1 spig bro1
- **brown**: acon-l a1 *Arg-n* ars ars-i *Bapt* bry k* calc-p bg2 carb-ac carb-v b2.de* carc sp1* caust con crot-h gels hyos k* *Iod* k* kreos b2.de* lyss k* mag-m *Nit-ac* k* op k* puls k* rhus-t k* samb sars sec b2.de* *Sep* k* staph k* stram k* *Sulph* k*
  - **angry**, when: (↗*MIND - Anger)* *Staph* k*
  - **coffee** with milk: carc mlr1•
  - **reddish**: *Apis* b7a.de bry k* hyos k* iod bg2 kreos b7a.de* nit-ac k* *Op* k* puls samb k* sec b7.de* *Sep* stram k* sulph
    - **Eyes**; around: lach bg2 merc bg2
  - **sleep** agg.; during: *Stram* k*
  - **spots**: ambr anan ant-c ars ars-i benz-ac cadm-s *Calc* *Carb-an* k* *Carbn-s* carc gk6 caul c1* caust *Colch* con ferr ferr-p k2 glycyr-g cte1• hyos iod *Kali-c* kali-i kali-p *Laur* k* *Lyc* nat-ar *Nat-c* nat-p nat-s k2 *Nit-ac* ozone sde2• petr petr-ra shn4• phos *Sep* k* *Sulph* k* sumb thuj
    - **acne**; from suppressed: glycyr-g cte1•
    - **coffee** with milk: carc fb*
    - **delivery**; after: crot-h

- **brown – spots**: ...
    - **sun** agg.: cadm-s br1
    - **wind** agg.: cadm-s br1
  - **yellowish**: phos vac k*
  - ○ **Cheek**:
    - **spots**:
      - **dark** brown: guat sp1
      - **small**: guat sp1 trios rsj11•
  - **Eyes**:
    - **Around**: *Lach* bg1* ozone sde2• sep ctc•
    - **Below**: *Puls* b7a.de *Sulph* b4a.de
  - **Forehead**: kali-p phos
    - **spots**: *Caul* *Nat-c* nit-ac k2 *Sep* trios rsj11• vanad ptk1*
      - **accompanied** by | **leukorrhea** (See FEMALE - Leukorrhea - accompanied - forehead)
      - **dark** brown: guat sp1
  - **Lips**: ant-t apis b7a.de *Ars* k* ars-h bry k* *Carb-v* chlor k* *Hyos* olnd k* op k* *Phos* k* *Psor* k* rhus-t ptk1 squil k* staph k* sul-ac k* *Verat*
    - **spots** | **Upper** lip: nat-c k* sep b4a.de sulph b4.de*
    - **streak**:
      - **Lower** lip; along: *Ars*
      - **Upper**: ars b4.de*
  - **Mouth**; below: phos h2
- **brownish** yellow forehead at edges of hair: caul bg3 kali-p bg3 med bg3 nat-m bg3
- **changing** color: *Acon* k* agn b2.de* *Alum* k* apis b7a.de ars k* asaf b2.de* aur b2.de* **Bell** k* bism b2.de* borx bov k* bry bg2 camph *Caps* k* carb-an b2.de* *Cham* k* chin k* *Cina* k* croc k* cycl b2.de* *Ferr* k* glon bg2 graph b2.de* hyos k* **Ign** k* iod h* kali-c k* lach b7a.de laur k* led k* lyc b2.de* *Mag-c* k* mag-s mur-ac b2.de* nat-c b2.de* nat-m b2.de* nux-v k* olnd k* *Op* k* ph-ac k* **Phos** k* **Plat** k* puls k* *Sec* k* sep bg2* spig k* squil k* stann bg2 staph bg2 stram b2.de* *Sul-ac* k* *Sulph* b2.de* til a1 valer b2.de* verat k* zinc k*
  - **rest**, when at: ign al*
  - ○ **Lips**: sulph ptk1
- **chloasma** (See Chloasma)
- **coffee** colored spots (See brown - spots)
- **copper** colored: alum k* *Ars* k* ars-h k* calc k* *Calc-p* k* cann-s b2.de* *Carb-an* k* cupr *Kreos* k* led k* nit-ac bro1 *Rhus-t* k* *Ruta* k* stram k* verat k*
  - **spots**: *Benz-ac* k* *Carb-an* bro1 *Graph* lyc bro1 nit-ac bro1
  - ○ **Cheeks**: alum h1*
- **cyanotic**: (↗*GENERALS - Cyanosis)* anan androc bnm2• **Ant-t** mrr1 **Ars** k* atra-r bnm3• *Aur* borx mtf33 both fne1• *Cact* carb-v mrr1* *Cupr* k* hydr-ac k* ix bnm8• lat-m bnm6• laur mrr1 lyss merc-cy **Nat-m** ox-ac mrr1 physala-p bnm7• psor jl2 russ a1 spig hr1 vesp
  - **accompanied** by:
    - **pneumonia** (See CHEST - Inflammation - lungs - accompanied - face - cyanotic)
    - **respiration**; complaints of (See RESPIRATION - Complaints - accompanied - face)
  - **cough** agg.; during: ip mrr1
  - ○ **Lips**: androc bnm2• atra-r bnm3• loxo-lae bnm12•
    - **accompanied** by | **respiration**; complaints of (See RESPIRATION - Complaints - accompanied - face)
    - **children**; in: androc bnm2• loxo-lae bnm12•
    - **About**: ant-t mrr1
- **dark**: *Ail* k* alum ptk1 am-c k2 ant-t ptk1* *Apis* k* arg-n bg2 ars k* asaf k2 bacls-10 fmm1• bacls-7 fmm1• **Bapt** k* bell k2 bit-ar wht1• both k* cact k2 calc-p bg2 canth k2 carb-an bg2 *Carb-v* k* *Carbn-s* **Carc** mrr1 chin bg2 colch ptk1 croc bg2 crot-h bg2* cub c1 cupr k* dub k* elaps *Gels* k* glon k2 hell ptk1 hura hydr-ac k* iod ptk1* kali-i k* lach k* morph k* mur-ac ptk1 nat-m mtf33 **Nit-ac** k* *Op* k* ox-ac k* parth vml3• *Phos* bg1* plan a1 plb k* psor k2* stram ptk1 *Sulph* k* thuj bg1 tub ptk1 vanil fd5.de verat k* verat-v bg2 zinc bg2
  - **coma**; with (See MIND - Coma - face - dark)
  - **fever**; during: carb-v b4a.de lach bg2 nat-m b4a.de
  - **menopause**; during: morg fmm1•
  - ○ **Eyes**; circles under: chinin-s mrr1 cina mtf33 cycl mrr1 ger-i rly4• psor mtf33 sep ptk2* spong fd4.de taosc iwa1• thuj mtf33 tritic-vg fd5.de vanil fd5.de

- **Lips** | **stripes**: ars b7a.de
- **Mouth**; around: ars bg2 phos bg2

- **deathly**: ars tl1
- **dirty** looking: *Apis* **Arg-n** k* borx mtf33 *Bry* b7.de calc-p k2 *Caps* card-m *Chel* k* chlor hr1 *Cupr* k* *Ferr* b7.de guat sp1 iod k* kali-br a1 *Kali-c* hr1 kali-p *Lach* hr1 **Lyc** k* *Mag-c* k* *Merc* k* nat-m mtf33 phos k* **Psor** k* *Sanic* sec k* sep hr1 spong fd4.de **Sulph** k* thuj tub mtf33
- **dusky** (See dark)
- **earthy**: *Acet-ac* bro1 *Aeth* hr1 *Ant-t* k* anthraci ptk1 *Arn* k* *Ars* k* ars-h k* *Ars-i* ars-met ars-s-f k2 *Aster* k* aur bapt bg2 bell k* *Berb* k* bism k* *Borx* k* *Brom* k* *Bry* k* *Calc* k* calc-i k2 *Calc-p* k* calc-sil k2 camph bro1 canth b2.de* carb-ac a1 *Carb-an* k* *Carb-v* k* **Carc** mrr1 *Caust* bro1 chel bro1 **Chin** k* chinin-ar *Cic* k* cimic *Cina* cocc k* con k* *Croc* k* crot-h a1 der k* diosm br1 euph b2.de* **Ferr** k* *Ferr-ar* **Ferr-i** **Ferr-p** k* glyc bro1 gran k* **Graph** *Helon* hr1 hydr bro1 hydr-ac k* hyos b2.de* *Ign* k* iod k* ip k* kali-ar kali-bi k* kali-chl k* kali-p kreos k* *Lach* k* *Laur* k* *Lyc* k* *Mag-c* k* *Mag-m* k* mag-s k* *Med* **Merc** k* merc-c bro1 *Mez* k* mosch k* nat-ar nat-c k* *Nat-m* k* nat-p *Nit-ac* k* *Nux-v* k* ol-an k* **Op** k* pall *Ph-ac* k* *Phos* k* pic-ac bro1 plb k* psor k* *Puls* k* samb k* *Sanic* bro1 sec k* **Sep** k* *Sil* k* spig bg2* *Staph* bro1 sulph k* syph jl2 tarent k* ter k* thuj k* *Verat* bg2* vip k* zinc k* zinc-p k2
  - **chill**; during: ars bg2 chin bg2 ferr bg2 nat-m bg2 nux-v bg2 sil bg2
  - **fever**; during: *Lach* bg2
  - **yellow**: lycps-v ptk1
- **florid** complexion (See GENERALS - Complexion - florid)
- **ghastly** (See pale)
- **grayish**: arg-met bg2 arg-n bg2 *Ars* k* *Berb* k* *Brom* k* *Bufo* *Cadm-s* *Carb-v* k* *Chel* k* **Chin** k* *Chlor* *Cocc* b7a.de *Colch* k* *Cupr* k* gels *Hydr-ac* k* kali-bi bg2 kali-c k* kreos k* *Lach* k* laur k* **Lyc** k* mag-s sp1 med mtf33 *Mez* k* oena phos k* plut-n srj7• tab k* tarent k* tub-r vn* vanil fd5.de *Verat* hr1
  - **accompanied** by:
    - **vomiting** (See STOMACH - Vomiting - accompanied - face)
    - **Tongue**; gray discoloration of the: kali-c kr1*
  - **yellow**: *Ars* hr1 *Carb-v* k* chel k* *Kali-c* k* kreos k* **Lyc** k*
    - **fever**; during: *Lach* b7a.de
- **greenish**: *Ars* k* berb **Carb-v** k* **Chel** k* cocc k2 crot-h cupr dig k* *Ferr* ferr-ar *Iod* k* kreos lach-h sze9• *Med* meny bg2 merc merc-c k* nux-v *Puls* verat k*
  - **heat**; during: lach vh
  - **spots**: ars k*
  - ○ **Eyes**; about the: *Verat* k*
- **greenish** yellow: ars b4a.de carb-v b4.de*
- **lead**-colored: *Apoc* hr1 **Arg-n** k* ars k* ben-n camph tl1 carb-an k* carbn-o chr-ac hr1 coca cocc k* cori-m a1 crot-h k* *Kali-i* k* lach k* merc k* *Mez* b4a.de *Nat-m* k* nit-ac k* *Oena* op k* phos b4a.de *Plb* k* thuj verat k* zinc hr1
- **liver** spots (See brown - spots)
- **livid**: dros bg2 merc-cy br1 tab bg2 *Verat-v* br1
  - ○ **Lips**: ars mtf33
- **mahogany**-colored (See red - mahogany)
- **marbled**: merc mrr1 phos sabad
- **mottled**: *Ail* *Bapt* *Bell* k* bry k2 calc-p k2 *Cench* *Crot-h* *Dor* k* gels k2 helo-s bnm14• *Lach* k* lachn bg1 led mrr1 op k2* psor k2 puls k2 *Rhus-t* k* spig k2 sulph k2
  - ○ **Lips**: cact k2
- **pale**: abrot hr1* absin k* *Acet-ac* k* acetan br1 *Acon* k* adam srj5• *Aesc* k* *Aeth* k* agar k* agav-a br1 ail k* alet k2 all-s k* aloe k* alum k* alum-p k2 alumn k* *Am-c* k* *Am-m* k* ambr k* aml-ns ammc k* amyg k* **Anac** k* anan k* androc srj1• ant-c k* **Ant-t** k* anth vh1 *Apis* k* apoc k* apom vh1 **Arg-met** *Arg-n* k* *Arn* k* **Ars** k* ars-h k* *Ars-i* ars-s-f k2 ars-s-r hr1 arund hr1 *Aspar* k* *Aster* k* atra-r bnm3• *Aur* k* aur-ar k2 aur-i k2 aur-m bg2* aur-m-n k* aur-s k* bacls-10 fmm1• bacls-7 fmm1• *Bad* k* bamb-a stb2.de• *Bar-c* k* bar-i k2 bar-m k* bar-s k2 *Bell* k* ben ben-n **Berb** k* bism k* boerh-d bnj1 *Borx* k* bov k* brom k* bros-gau mrc1 *Bry* k* *Bufo* *Cact* k* cadm-s caesal-b bnj1 **Calc** k* *Calc-ar* k* calc-i k2 **Calc-p** k* *Calc-s* k* calc-sil k2 **Camph** k* cann-i k* cann-s k* *Canth* k* caps k* *Carb-ac* k* *Carb-an* k* **Carb-v** k* carbn-h carbn-o **Carbn-s** carc mlr1• *Caust* k* cedr k* cench k2 *Cham* k* *Chel* k* chen-a vml3• **Chin** k* chinin-ar **Chinin-s** chir-fl gya2 chlf k* chlol k* *Chlor* k* *Cic* k* cimic k* **Cina** k* **Clem** k* *Cocc* k* cod k* coff coff-t a1* *Colch* k* coleus-a bnj1 *Coli* jl2 *Coloc* k* *Con* k* cop k* crat br1 *Croc* k* crot-h k* crot-t **Cupr** k* cupr-ar k* *Cycl* k* cyt-l br1* der k* **Dig** k* dirc k* dor k* *Dros* k* dubo-h hs1 dubo-m br1 *Dulc* k* dys fmm1• emb-r bnj1

- **pale**: ...
Eup-per k* euph k* euphr k* fago k* **Ferr** k* *Ferr-act* bro1 ferr-ar **Ferr-i** ferr-m k* ferr-ma a1 **Ferr-p** k* ferr-r bro1 fl-ac k* gaert fmm1• *Gels* k* *Glon* k* gran k* granit-m es1• **Graph** k* grat k* haem a1 ham k* *Hell* k* helo-s bnm14• *Hep* b2.de* hipp jl2 hura *Hydr* k* *Hydr-ac* k* *Hydrog* srj2• hygroph-s bnj1 *Hyos* k* *Ign* k* ignis-alc es2• *Iod* k* *Ip* k* irid-met srj5• jab k* jatr-c *Kali-ar* k* *Kali-bi* k* kali-br k* *Kali-c* k* *Kali-chl* k* *Kali-i* k* kali-m k2 kali-n k* *Kali-p* k* kali-s kali-sil k2 kali-sula a1* *Kalm* k* *Kreos* k* *Lac-d* k* *Lach* k* lachn lact k* lap-la sde8.de• lat-h bnm5• *Laur* k* lec k* *Led* k* lept k* limest-b es1• **Lob** k* loxo-lae bnm12• loxo-recl bnm10• **Lyc** k* lyss k* m-ambo b2.de* m-arct b2.de* *Mag-c* k* *Mag-m* k* *Mag-p* mag-s k* maland jl2 manc k* **Mang** k* **Med** k* meli k* *Merc* k* *Merc-c* k* *Merc-cy* k* *Merc-d* k* merc-n c1 *Merc-sul* k* *Mez* k* morg-g pte1*• morg-p fmm1• morph k* mosch k* *Mur-ac* k* naja **Nat-ar** **Nat-c** k* **Nat-m** k* nat-n k* **Nat-p** k* nat-s k* nicc *Nit-ac* k* nuph k* *Nux-m* k* *Nux-v* k* oena k* ol-an k* olib-sac wmh1 olnd k* **Op** k* opun-s a1 orot-ac rly4• oscilloc jl2 *Ox-ac* k* ozone sde2• *Par* k* parathyr jl2 *Petr* k* **Ph-ac** k* *Phos* k* phys k* physala-p bnm7• *Phyt* k* *Plat* k* **Plb** k* plut-n srj7• podo k* prot jl2* *Psor* k* ptel k* *Puls* k* *Pyrog* k* raph k* *Rheum* k* *Rhus-t* k* rhus-v k* rob hr1 sabad k* sabin k* sacch sst1• *Samb* k* *Sang* k* santin k* sarr hr1 **Sec** k* sel k* senec k* **Sep** k* *Sil* k* *Spig* k* *Spong* k* squil hr1 *Stann* k* staph b2.de* *Still* hr1 *Stram* k* stry k* *Sul-ac* k* **Sulph** k* sumb k* syc pte1*• syph xxb **Tab** k* tarent k* tax k* tep k* *Ter* k* *Teucr* k* thea ther k* thuj k* thyr br1 til k* tritic-vg fd5.de **Tub** k* tub-a jl2 tub-m dp* tub-r vn* tub-sp vn* tung-met bdx1• ulm-c jsj8• urin c1 ust bg2* v-a-b jl2 valer vanil fd5.de **Verat** k* verat-v k* verb k* vero-o rly4*• vesp k* vinc k* vip k* yohim bwa3 **Zinc** k* zinc-p k2* ziz a1* [spect dfg1 zinc-i stj2 zinc-m stj2 zinc-n stj2]
  - **one**-sided: acon arn bell *Cham* k* coloc ign ip *Mosch* nux-v tab verat
    - **one** side pale and hot, the other side red and cold: *Mosch* k*
  - **morning**: aloe *Bov* k* cod k* con h2* lyc k* mag-c k* nat-m k* *Nat-s* hr1 olnd k* op k* **Sec** k* sep k*
    - **rising** agg.; after: *Bov* k* graph k* olnd h1* ph-ac k*
    - **waking**; on: nat-s k*
  - **noon**: kali-c h2* ox-ac k* phos k* sulph k* *Verat* k*
  - **afternoon**: dulc fd4.de hura mag-c k* nat-m k*
    - **14** h: verat-v
    - **waking**; on: spig k*
  - **evening**: caust k* kali-c h2* lyc k* merc k* olnd k* ozone sde2• *Phos* k* sep k*
    - **19** h: phos
    - **walking** agg.: phos k*
  - **night**: carb-v k* mang k* merc merc-c k*
  - **accompanied** by:
    - **heat** of face: cimic ptk1 cina ptk1 croc ptk1 hyos ptk1 op ptk1
    - **leukorrhea** (See FEMALE - Leukorrhea - accompanied - face; FEMALE - Leukorrhea - accompanied - face - pale)
    - **mental** symptoms (See MIND - Mental symptoms - accompanied - face - pale)
    - **palpitations** (See CHEST - Palpitation - accompanied - face)
    - **pneumonia** (See CHEST - Inflammation - lungs - accompanied - face - pale)
    - **red** face in open air; pale face in house but (See red - air - pale)
    - **sleepiness** (See SLEEP - Sleepiness - accompanied - face - pale)
    - **swelling** (See Swelling - accompanied - pale)
    - **thin** (See Emaciation - accompanied - pale)
    - **vertigo** (See VERTIGO - Accompanied - face - pale)
    - **vomiting** (See STOMACH - Vomiting - accompanied - face - pale)
    - **Abdomen**:
      - **complaints** (See ABDOMEN - Complaints - accompanied - face - pale)
      - **pain** in (See ABDOMEN - Pain - accompanied - face)

Face

- **accompanied** by: ...
  - **Head**:
    - **complaints** (See HEAD - Complaints - accompanied - face - discoloration - pale)
    - **pain** in (See HEAD - Pain - accompanied - face - pale)
  - **Stomach**; pain in (See STOMACH - Pain - accompanied - face)
  - **Teeth**; pain in (See TEETH - Pain - accompanied - face)
- **air**; on going into:
  - **damp** | **agg.**: *Nux-m*
  - **fresh** | **amel.**: cann-i caust *Gels*
  - **open**: kali-c h2
- **alternating** with | **redness** (See red - alternating with - paleness)
- **anger**; after: (↗*MIND - Anger*) ars gl• carb-v gl• *Con* **Nat-m** st petr gl• plat gl• **Staph** st
- **ascending**, on: dirc k*
- **children**; in: abrot mtf33 aeth mtf33 androc bnm2• borx mtf33 brom mtf33 calc mtf33 calc-p mtf33 *Carb-v* mtf33 cham mtf33 chin mtf33 chir-fl bnm4• dros mtf33 ferr mtf33 hyos mtf33 kali-c mtf33 loxo-lae bnm12• med mtf33 nat-m mtf33 psor mtf33 sacch sst1• sep mtf33 sil mtf33 sulph mtf33 thuj mtf33 tub mtf33 verat mtf33
  - **running**; on: sil ptk2
- **chill**:
  - **before**: ars cina ferr
  - **during**: ant-t b7.de* arg-n k* bell k* **Bry** k* **Camph** k* canth k* *Caps* b7a.de *Chin* k* chinin-s cic bg2 **Cina** k* cocain bro1 cocc bg2 coff k* croc k* *Dros* k* *Hep* k* ign k* ip k* *Lyc* k* *Merc* b4.de* mez bg2 *Mosch* b7a.de* *Nux-m* k* nux-v k* ph-ac k* phos k* *Puls* k* *Rhus-t* k* *Sec* sep k* sil bg2 *Sulph* k* **Verat** k* zinc k*
- **circumscribed**: cina mtf33
- **cold** air | **entering** cold air agg.: nux-m
- **coma**; with (See MIND - Coma - face - pale)
- **congestion** of head, with: *Cycl* hr1
- **convulsions**; during: cic kr1 cupr hr1* glon hr1 hyos hr1 ip kr1 kali-i kr1 kali-p kr1 lach hr1* nux-v hr1 op hr1 plb a1 puls hr1 sil kr1 sulph kr1 *Verat* kr1 zinc kr1*
- **cough** agg.; during: ars b4a.de *Chin* b7a.de cina b7.de* *Ferr* b7a.de mez b4a.de sulph bg2
- **dentition**; during: ars bro1 kreos bro1
- **dinner**; during: mag-m nat-m nit-ac phel
- **eating**; after: *Kali-c* k* mag-c k* nit-ac b4a.de thuj k*
- **emotions**; from: ferr mtf33
- **epistaxis**, with (See NOSE - Epistaxis - accompanied - face - pale)
- **exertion** | **after** | **agg.**: nit-ac h2 spong ptk1
  - **agg.**: ferr mtf33
    - **children**; in: sil ptk1
- **flushes** easily: agath-a nl2• **Ferr** k*
- **headache**, with (See HEAD - Pain - accompanied - face - pale)
- **heat**; during: acon b7a.de* ant-t bro1 *Ars* k* bell b4.de* borx bg2 **Cina** k* cocc k* **Croc** k* *Ferr* hr1 glon k2 *Hep* bg1* **Hyos** bg2* *Ip* k* *Lyc* k* nat-m k* op bg2 *Ph-ac* b4a.de puls k* rhus-t k* sep k* spong k* thuj k* verat k* visc c1
  - **head**; of: hell h1
- **heated**; when: hep h2*
- **hemorrhage**; after a little: erig zr
- **lying**:
  - **agg.**: *Bell* thea
  - **amel.**: petr k*
- **maniacal** rage, with: anac ars croc merc phos puls *Verat*
- **menses**:
  - **absent**: lob ptk1
  - **after** | **agg.**: *Nat-m* k* puls verat k*

- pale – **menses**: ...
  - **before** | **agg.**: am-c k* cycl bro1 ip bro1 mang k* verat bro1
  - **during** | **agg.**: am-c k* apis *Ars* k* castm *Cedr* k* *Cocc* hr1 cycl bro1 *Ferr* k* graph k* **Ign** k* *Ip* k* lyc k* *Mag-c* k* *Mag-m* k* ph-ac b4a.de puls k* sep b4a.de sil b4a.de stann k* verat k*
- **pain**; from: *Ferr* k*
  - **abdomen**; in (See ABDOMEN - Pain - accompanied - face)
- **palpitations**, during (See CHEST - Palpitation - accompanied - face - pale)
- **perspiration**; during: ars bg2 bell bg2 chin bg2 **Cina** bg2 *Lyc* bg2 mosch nux-v bg2 *Puls* bg2 *Rhus-t* bg2 **Sel** b7a.de* sep k* *Sulph* bg2 **Verat** b7.de*
- **pregnancy** agg.; during: glon tl1
- **puffy**; and (See Swelling - accompanied - pale)
- **reading** agg.: graph k* sil h2*
- **red** in spots: *Aur-m* k* bamb-a stb2.de• *Ferr* k* *Sulph*
- **rising** agg.: *Acon* k* *Puls* *Verat* k* *Verat-v* k*
- **shivering**; during: camph b7.de verat b7.de
- **sitting** up in bed agg.: acon h1*
- **sleep** | **after** | **agg.**: bov hr1 spig k*
  - **during**: rheum
- **spots**, in: (↗*white; white - spot*) bell k* calc k* helo-s bnm14• sil k*
- **standing** agg.: chin k* petr k* rumx
- **stool** | **after** | **agg.**: coloc k* *Crot-t* k* ferr-ma k*
  - **during** | **agg.**: ars bg2 bros-gau mrc1 *Calc* k* crot-t k* ip k* *Kali-c* k* *Rheum* k* verat k*
- **streak** down center of: *Cina* hr1
- **sudden**: *Cimic* k* graph k* phos h2*
- **vexation**; after: (↗*MIND - Ailments - reproaches*) *Ars*
- **walking** in open air agg.: plb k2
- **warm**:
  - **room**:
    - **agg.**: am-c h2* apis
    - **amel.**: nux-m k*
- **weather** agg.; wet: aloe nux-m
- **yellow** (See yellow - pale)
- ○ **Cheek** | **alternating** with:
  - **redness**: tub jl2
    - **menses**; during: am-c b4.de
  - **hot**; and: mosch bg2
- **Eyes**; about: pitu-a vml2• ptel bg1
- **Lips**: aeth k2 ant-t k* *Apis* *Aran* k* **Ars** k* *Calc* k* carb-ac k* caust k* coca *Colch* k* cupr *Cycl* k* dig k* **Ferr** k* *Ferr-ar* *Ferr-p* **Hydr-ac** k* ip k* **Kali-ar** k* kali-c k* kali-s k2 *Lac-d* k* *Lyc* k* manc k* *Mang* **Med** k* *Merc-c* k* nat-p *Op* k* ph-ac k* phos h2* pic-ac k* *Puls* k* sec k* *Senec* k* sep k2 spig k* sulph k* thuj k* valer k* verat k* verat-v k* visc c1 xan k*
  - **menses** | **during** | **agg.**: cycl k* *Ferr* k*
    - **suppressed** menses; from: ars chin cycl k* *Ferr* ph-ac rhus-t *Senec* *Sep* sulph
  - **Upper**: aeth c1
- **Middle** down: phos bg2
- **Mouth**; around: aeth bg2* arum-t ptk1 *Bell* b4a.de* *Carb-ac* *Caust* b4a.de cic bg2* **Cina** k* *Cupr* b2.de ip bg2 lyc b4a.de merc-c bg2* *Mez* b4a.de nat-p k2 *Phos* b4a.de* podo bg2 **Stram** k* tarent bg2
  - **rest** of face dusky red: carb-ac
- **Nose**; around: cina mtf33 nat-p k2 phos mtf33

- **pink** spots: carb-an k*
- **purple** (See bluish - purple)
- **red**: abies-n br1 acet-ac k* **Acon** k* adel a1 aegle-f bnj1 aeth k* *Agar* k* agar-ph a1 agath-a nl2• agn b2.de* *Ail* k* alco a1 aloe k* alum k* alum-p k2 am-br a1 am-c k* am-caust a1 am-m b2.de* ambr b2.de* *Aml-ns* k* amyg a1 *Anac* k* ang b2.de* *Ant-c* k* *Ant-t* k* *Antip* vh1 **Apis** k* apoc a1 arg-met k* *Arg-n* k* arizon-l nl2• *Arn* k* *Ars* k* ars-h k* ars-i ars-s-f k2 arum-d a1 arum-t k* *Asaf* k* asar b2.de* *Astac* *Aster* k* atro k* aur k* aur-i k2 *Aur-m* k* aur-s k2 *Bad* k*

- **red**: ...
bamb-a stb2.de• **Bapt** k* *Bar-c* k* bar-i k2 bar-m k* bar-s k2 **Bell** k* berb k* borra-o oss1• borx k* *Bov* k* brach brass-n-o srj5• brom k* **Bry** k* cact k* calad k* calc k* calc-f sp1 calc-i k2 *Camph* k* cann-i k* cann-s k* *Canth* k* **Caps** k* carb-ac k* carb-an b2.de* carb-v k* carbn-h carbn-o carbn-s *Carl* k* castm *Caust* k* *Cedr* k* cench k2 **Cham** k* **Chel** k* **Chin** k* *Chinin-s* k* chir-fl gya2 chlam-tr bcx2• chlf a1 chlol a1* chlor k* choc srj3• **Cic** k* cimic k* **Cina** k* cinnm hr1 clem k* cob-n sp1 *Coc-c* k* *Cocc* k* cod k* *Coff* k* colch hr1 coll a1 *Coloc* k* com k* con k* cop k* cori-r a1 cortiso sp1 cot a1 *Croc* k* crot-c k* *Crot-h* k* *Crot-t* k* cub k* cund hr1 *Cupr* k* cupr-act bro1 cupr-s a1* cur k* cycl b2.de* cyt-l sp1 der a1 *Dig* k* digin a1 dirc c1 dor k* dream-p sdj1• *Dros* k* dub k* *Dulc* k* echi *Elaps* epil a1* *Erig* hr1 eryt-j a1 *Eup-per* k* eup-pur k* euph b2.de* euphr k* fago k* falco-pe nl2• **Ferr** k* *Ferr-ar* **Ferr-i** k* ferr-m k* *Ferr-ma* k* ferr-p k* *Gamb* hr1 gels k* *Glon* k* gran bg* graph k* *Grat* k* gua br1 *Guaj* k* guar a1* ham fd3.de• helia a1 *Hell* k* *Hep* k* hippoz hist sp1 *Hura* hydr-ac a1 hydrog srj2• hygroph-s bnj1 **Hyos** k* hyosin a1 *Hyper* k* iber a1 *Ign* k* ind k* indg k* iod k* ip k* irid-met srj5• iris *Jab* k* jug-c k* jug-r k* kali-act kali-bi k* kali-br k* kali-c k* kali-chl k* kali-cy a1 *Kali-i* k* kali-m k2 kali-n k* kali-ox a1 kali-p kali-s k* kali-sil k2 kali-sula a1* kalm k* keroso a1 ketogl-ac rly4• kreos k* lac-ac a1 *Lac-c* hr1 **Lach** k* lachn bg1* lap-la sde8.de• laur k* led k* lil-t k* linu-c a1 lob k* lob-s a1 lol a1 lon-x a1 *Lyc* k* lyss k* m-ambo b2.de* m-arct b2.de* m-aust b2.de mag-c k* mag-m k* mag-s k* *Maias-l* hm2• mand sp1 mang k* melal-alt gya4 **Meli** k* meny k* *Merc* k* *Merc-c* k* merc-cy a1 merc-d a1 merc-i-r k* merc-n a1* merl k* **Mez** k* mill k* mim-p rsj8• mom-b a1 morg-p pte1• morph k* mosch b2.de* *Mur-ac* k* mygal k* myris a1 *Naja* narcot a1 nat-ar *Nat-c* k* *Nat-m* k* nat-ox rly4• nat-p k* nat-s k* nat-sal a1 neon srj5• nicc k* nit-ac k* nitro-o a1 nux-m k* **Nux-v** k* oci-sa sp1 oena k* ol-j a1 olib-sac wmh1 olnd k* **Op** k* opun-f bnj1 ox-ac k* paeon k* par b2.de* ped a1 *Petr* k* ph-ac k* phel k* **Phos** k* phys k* phyt k* pieri-b mlk9.de pilo a1 plac-s rly4• *Plan* k* *Plat* k* *Plb* k* plb-chr a1 plut-n srj7• podo k* polyp-p a1 positr nl2• pot-e rly4• psor k* ptel k* *Puls* k* *Pyrog* k* ran-a a1 *Ran-b* k* ran-s b2.de* raph k* rheum b2.de* rhod b2.de* **Rhus-t** k* rhus-v k* rumx ruta k* *Sabad* k* sabin k* *Samb* k* **Sang** k* santin sarr k* sars b2.de* sec k* sel b2.de* *Senec* seneg b2.de* *Sep* k* *Sil* k* sol-a a1 sol-ni sol-t-ae k* *Spig* k* spig-m a1 spira a1 spirae a1 *Spong* k* squil k* *Stann* k* staph k* **Stram** k* *Stront-c* k* stry k* suis-em rly4• *Sul-ac* k* sul-h a1 sul-i k2 *Sulph* k* *Tab* k* tanac a1 *Tarax* k* tarent hr1* tart-ac a1 tell c1 tep k* *Ter* k* teucr b2.de* ther *Thuj* k* thymol sp1 til k* tritic-vg fd5.de trom a1 tub k2* tub-a jl2 tub-d jl2 upa a1 uva vac hr1* valer k* vario hr1 *Verat* k* **Verat-v** k* verb hr1 vesp k* vib viol-o b2.de* viol-t b2.de* vip a1 wies a1 yuc a1 zinc k* zinc-m a1 zing k* ziz a1* [spect dfg1]
  - **one** side: acon k* ant-t *Arn* k* ars bg1* bar-c b4a.de* bell k* borx b4a.de* calc bg1 cann-s k* canth b7.de* **Cham** k •* *Chel* k* chin b7.de* cina bg2* coff bg2 coloc k* dros bg2* **Ign** k •* ip k* kali-c bg2 lac-c ptk1 lach bg2 *Lyc* bg2* m-arct b7.de merc ptk1 *Mosch* k* *Nat-m* bg1 nit-ac gk nux-v k* ph-ac b4a.de *Phos* b4a.de* *Plb* bg1* **Puls** k •* *Ran-b* bg2* rheum k* *Rhus-t* bg1* sang k* seneg bg2 sep bg3 spig bg3* stram b7a.de sul-ac b4a.de sulph bg2* tab bg2* thuj bg2 verat k* viol-t bg2
    - **accompanied** by | **pain** of that side (See Pain - one - accompanied - red)
    - **chill**; during: acon bg2 arn bg2 **Cham** bg2 ip bg2 **Mosch** bg2 nux-v bg2 *Rheum* bg2 rhus-t bg2 thuj bg2
    - **pale**, the other red; one side: acet-ac *Acon* k* cann-s k2 caps **Cham** k* *Cina* ign hr **Ip** k* *Lach* *Mosch* *Nux-v* k* *Puls* rheum k* sulph
  - **alternating** sides: chel bg2* lach bg2* nat-p bg2* *Phos* bg2*
  - **right**: arizon-l nl2• ars bg2* *Calc* ptk1 cham h1* choc srj3• elaps lachn ptk1 mag-c h2* merc bg2* mosch ptk1 nat-c bg2* nicc hr1 puls sang ptk1 sep hr1 sul-ac h2* tab ptk1
    - **left**:
      - **paleness** of the left with heat, right without heat: mosch
      - **waxy**-yellow: canth
  - **left**: *Acet-ac* k* aesc k* agar ptk1 alumn k* am-c h2* ambr ptk2 apis ptk1 arum-t mrr1 asaf borx h2* cann-s hr1 cham ptk1 chel *Graph* hr1 ham fd3.de• inul hr1 lac-ac hr1 lac-c lyc k* merc h1* murx nat-m k* ol-an ph-ac phos bg2* rhus-t bg2* spig stram ptk1 *Sulph* ptk1 thuj h1* verat ptk1
    - **right** | **pale**: cann-s upa a1
    - **followed** by | **right** side: ign bg2
    - **stool** agg.; during: rhus-t bg2*
  - **morning**: ail k* dirc k* kali-c k* lyc k* phos h2* *Podo* rhus-t *Sep* hr1 sulph k2 yuc a1
    - **8** h: myric
    - **until** 15 h: stront-c
  - **morning**: ...
    - **waking**; on: kali-cy a1 nat-m k* **Sulph** hr1
  - **forenoon**: dulc fd4.de lyc k*
    - **9** h: lyc
    - **11** h: nat-c sol-ni zing
  - **noon**: apis bamb-a stb2.de• bell h1* lyc k* mag-c k* nat-m k* phos k* sep h2* sil k* spig h1*
  - **afternoon**: calc h2* luf-op rsj5• lyc a1 meli k* nat-c h2* phos h2* phys k* sang senec k* thuj a1 **Tub**
    - **14** h: cench k2 nat-m
    - **15** h: coff meli
    - **16** h: agar puls-n sil
    - **17** h: chel mag-c
    - **17**-19 h: mag-c
    - **17**-21 h: plat
    - **18** h: cann-s sarr
  - **evening**: ars-h hr1 bamb-a stb2.de• bar-c k* bell h1 calc h2* carb-an h2* *Croc* k* elaps ham fd3.de• **Ign** k* iod k* kali-c h2* luf-op rsj5• lyc k* mag-c h2* mag-m h2* naja nat-m k* nux-v k* oena k* ox-ac k* plan k* plat h2* plb hr1 puls k* rumx scut k* sep k* sulph k* thuj h1* trom k* upa a1 verat h1* zinc h2*
    - **21** h: phos
  - **night**: aloe cedr cic k* cocc-s hr1 plb hr1 viol-t hr1
    - **midnight**:
      - **after** | **1**-8 h: lachn c1
  - **accompanied** by:
    - **anemia** (See GENERALS - Anemia - accompanied - face)
    - **apoplexy** (See GENERALS - Apoplexy - accompanied - face - red)
    - **epistaxis** (See NOSE - Epistaxis - accompanied - face - congestion)
    - **flabby** constitution (See GENERALS - Relaxation - physical - accompanied - face - discoloration)
    - **hemorrhage**: aml-ns ptk1
    - **hypertension** (See GENERALS - Hypertension - accompanied - face)
    - **meningitis** (See HEAD - Inflammation - meninges - accompanied - face)
    - **menses** | **painful** (See FEMALE - Menses - painful - accompanied - face)
    - **mental** symptoms (See MIND - Mental symptoms - accompanied - face - red)
    - **pale** face in house; red face in open air but (See air - pale)
    - **palpitations** (See CHEST - Palpitation - accompanied - face - red)
    - **respiration**; impeded (See RESPIRATION - Difficult - accompanied - face)
    - **sleepiness** (See SLEEP - Sleepiness - accompanied - face - red)
    - **stool**; complaints of (See STOOL - Complaints - accompanied - face)
    - **vomiting** (See STOMACH - Vomiting - accompanied - face - red)
    - **Body**; coldness of: arn br1 plut-n srj7•
      - **accompanied** by heat of head (See HEAD - Heat - accompanied - face - redness - coldness)
    - **Head**:
      - **complaints** (See HEAD - Complaints - accompanied - face - discoloration - red)
      - **pain** (See headache)
    - **Heart**; palpitation of (See CHEST - Palpitation - accompanied - face - red)
    - **Lungs**; inflammation of (See CHEST - Inflammation - lungs - accompanied - face - red)

- **accompanied** by: ...
  - **Teeth**; complaints in (See TEETH - Complaints - accompanied - face - red)
- **air** agg.; in open: valer k2
  - **pale** in house; but: nat-m bg2
- **alcohol**; after: (*↗wine)* aloe sne bamb-a stb2.de• bapt sne carb-v gm1 sulph mrr1
- **alternating** with:
  - **blackness** of face | **cough** agg.; during: dros bg2
  - **bluish** | **cough**; during (See bluish - alternating - redness - cough)
  - **chill**: am-c bg2 bell bg2 ferr bg2 ign bg2 ip bg2 phos bg2 plat bg2 rhus-t bg2 verat bg2
  - **paleness**: **Acon** k* alum k* alum-p k2 am-c am b7a.de ars k* aur bg1 bell k* *Borx* bov k* brom *Bry* bg2 *Camph* k* caps k* cham k* *Chin* k* cimic bg1 cina k* croc k* cub **Ferr** k* ferr-p k* gins *Glon* k* graph bg2 *Hell* hyos k* *Ign* k* kali-c k* kola stb3• **Lac-c** k* lach b7a.de *Led* k* lyc mag-c k* merc k* mur-ac k* nat-c k* nat-p nit-ac nux-v k* olnd k* op b7.de* ph-ac k* phos k* plat k* puls k* *Rhus-t* k* sep bg1 spong k2 squil k* stann bg2 staph bg2 stram b7a.de* stront-c ptk1 sul-ac k* *Sulph* bg2* tab k* til c1 tub jl2 verat k* zinc k*
    - **headache**; during: kola stb3•
    - **menses**; during: zinc k*
    - **Cheeks**: tub jl2
    - **Nose**: tub jl2
- **anger**; after: (*↗MIND - Anger; MIND - Anger - face - red - face)* aster vh bell mtf33 *Bry* hydrog srj2• staph
- **asthma**, with: caps ptk1
- **blood** red: *Hyos* bg2 stram bg2
- **blotches**: iod ptk1 kreos k2* mim-p rsj8• nat-p k2* oena ptk1 *Tell* rsj10• [pop dhh1]
- **bluish** red: (*↗bluish - red)* *Acon* k* agar k* **Ang** b2.de* *Ant-c* b7a.de *Ant-t* k* *Apis* k* *Ars* k* asar k* aur k* **Bell** k* **Bry** k* camph k* **Cann-i** carb-ac carb-v bg2* carl a1 *Caust* hr1 *Cedr* hr1 cham k* cic k* cina k* *Con* k* cor-r *Crot-c* *Cupr* k* dig k* dros k* *Dulc* b4a.de* gels k2 grin *Hep* k* hydr-ac k* hyos k* ign k* ip k* kali-chl *Lach* k* lyc k* meli merc k* merc-c b4a.de morph k* nux-v bg2 *Op* k* *Ox-ac* petr k* phel phos k* puls k* *Samb* k* sang spong k* staph k* stram k* stry a1 verat k* verat-v
  - **chill**; during: bell bg2 bry bg2 cupr bg2 lach bg2 op bg2 sulph bg2
  - **perspiration**; during: apis bg2 bell bg2 bry bg2 **Lach** bg2 op bg2 samb bg2
  - **Eyes**; under: lach bg2
  - **Lips**: petr a1
- **bright** red: *Bell* bg2 lach mtf33 stram bg2
  - **eating**; after: ignis-alc es2•
  - **spots**: calad hr1 chel a1* sep hr1 teucr b7.de*
- **brownish** red: *Caps* bg2
  - **fever**; during: *Caps* b7a.de
- **burning** | **Cheeks** (See glowing)
- **children**; in: puls mtf33 sulph mtf33
- **chill**:
  - **before**: cedr chin h1*
  - **during**: acon k* aeth k* agar bg2 all-s k* alum k* *Am-m* k* anac bg2 apis k* *Arn* k* *Ars* k* *Bell* k* *Bry* k* *Calc* k* *Cann-s* b7a.de* **Cham** k* *Chin* k* coc-c k* cocc b7.de* coff bg2 coloc bg2 con bg2 cycl bg2 dig b4a.de* dros bg2 **Ferr** k* *Ferr-ar* glon hyos k* *Ign* k* *Ip* k* kali-n k* kreos k* lach b7a.de* *Led* k* lyc k* mang bg2 merc k* merl mur-ac k* nat-c bg2 *Nux-v* k* *Olnd* bg2 op bg2 ox-ac k* plb k* puls k* ran-b b7.de* *Rhus-t* k* ruta b7a.de* seneg bg2 *Sep* k* sil bg2 spong bg2 *Staph* bg2 **Stram** k* *Sulph* k* thuj k* *Tub* verat b7a.de* zinc k*
- **circumscribed**: acon k* ambr c1 *Ant-t* k* *Arg-n* k* *Ars* k* ars-i ars-s-f hr1* aur-m k2 bar-c k* bar-i k2 benz-ac k* bry k* calc k* calc-sil k2 *Camph* hr1 carb-v k* chel **Chin** k* chinin-ar *Cina* k* clem a1 *Colch* k* con k* croc k* crot-h bg2 dol k* dros k* *Dulc* k* **Ferr** k* *Ferr-i* ferr-m bro1 ferr-p k* hep k* iod k* *Kali-c* k* kali-n k* kali-p kali-s kali-sil k2 kola stb3• *Kreos* k* *Lach* k* lachn k* laur k* led k* **Lyc** k* m-arct b2.de* merc k* mez hr1 nat-m k* nit-ac k* nux-v k* op ph-ac k* **Phos** k* *Puls* k* pyrog rhus-t hr1
- **circumscribed**: ... sabad samb k* *Sang* k* seneg k* sep k* sil k* spong k* *Stann* k* stram b2.de* sul-i k2 **Sulph** k* **Tab** thuj k* **Tub** k* tub-m dp* wies a1
  - **fever**; during: **Acon** bg2 bry bg2 *Calc* bg2 **Chin** bg2 croc bg2 dros bg2 dulc bg2 *Ferr* bg2 iod bg2 *Kali-c* bg2 *Kreos* bg2 lach bg2 led bg2 *Lyc* bg2 nux-v bg2 ph-ac bg2 *Phos* bg2 *Puls* bg2 samb bg2 sep bg2 stann bg2 stram bg2 *Sulph* bg2
  - **heart** disease; with: aur-m k2
  - **tubercular**: tub mrr1
- **cold**; and: asaf bro1* caps k* chin kr1 *Ferr* k* mosch bg2* ol-an k* phos psor
  - **chill**; during: ferr bg2 mosch bg2
  - **Cheeks** | **one** side: mosch ptk1
- **coma**, with (See MIND - Coma - face - red)
- **contradiction**, from: ign
- **convulsions**; during: (*↗GENERALS - Convulsions - epileptic - during - face - red)* aeth kr1* *Bell* kr1 bufo camph kr1 caust h2* **Cic** kr1 cina kr1 cocc c1 *Cupr* kr1* **Glon** k* ign kr1 ip kr1 lyc kr1 nux-v kr1 *Oena* **Op** k* stram kr1
- **cough**:
  - **deathly** pale when not coughing: *Nit-ac*
  - **during**: acon am-c h2 **Bell** bry cadm-s caps k* *Carb-v* chr-ac *Coc-c* con cor-r *Cupr* *Dros* eup-per ferr ferr-p sne *Graph* hep hyos iber br1 *Ip* kali-bi *Kali-c* lach lyc mag-p mur-ac nit-ac pert c1* sabad samb **Sang** sil squil staph stram sulph tub bg*
- **dark** red: *Acon* hr1 *Ail* bro1 alum ant-t k* antip vh1 apis bro1 *Arn* hr1 ars-h hr1 ars-met bro1 asaf k2 aur-m hr1 **Bapt** k* *Bar-c* k* **Bell** k* berb hr1 both bro1 **Bry** k* *Camph* k* carb-ac bro1 cench k2 *Chel* k* chlol gm1 cimic tl1 clem a1 *Coloc* k* *Cupr* hr1 *Dig* hr1 diph bro1 *Gels* k* **Glon** hr1 *Graph* hr1 *Hep* hr1 *Hyos* k* jab br1 kali-c hr1 kola stb3• kreos *Lach* hr1* *Lyss* hr1 *Merc* hr1 merl hr1 *Morph* bro1 *Mur-ac* hr1 *Nux-m* sne nux-v bro1 oena hr1 **Op** k* ph-ac h2* plat hr1 *Rhus-t* hr1* *Sang* *Sec* k* sil h2* **Spig** hr1 spong hr1 squil bg2 stann stram bg2* *Sulph* *Tarent* vario jl2 *Verat* k* *Verat-v* bg2 vesp bg2*
  - **cough** agg.; during: agar bg2 bar-c bell ptk1 cor-r kali-c ph-ac h2 sang ptk1 sil h2 squil stram tub ptk1
    - **otherwise** pale: kali-c
- **delirium**; during: lachn c1
- **dinner**; after: cedr k* cor-r br1 grat k* hell k* lob-s a1 nat-c k* par k*
- **dysmenorrhea**, during: ferr-p hr1 **Xan**
- **easily**: ferr br1 ferr-p br1 sulph br1
- **eating** | **after** | **agg.**●: alum bro1 arum-t caps ptk1 carb-an bro1 carl k* caust k* choc srj3• coff k* cor-r bro1 cycl k* *Ignis-alc* es2• **Lyc** k ●* merc k* nit-ac k* nux-v k* petr h2* puls sil k* stront-c bro1 sulph h2* upa a1 vesp k*
  - **agg.**: sep
- **epistaxis** | **amel.**: bapt bg1 bell bg1 erig bg1 ferr bg1 meli bg1 nux-v bg1
- **erysipelatous**: **Acon** k* am-c k* *Apis* k* ars k* bar-c k* **Bell** k* borx k* bry k* calc k* camph k* canth k* carb-an k* *Cham* k* chel hr1 clem k* **Euph** k* **Graph** k* **Hep** k* *Hydr* hr1 lac-ac hr1 *Lach* k* lyc k* merc k* nat-c k* ph-ac phos k* puls b2.de* **Rhus-t** k* ruta k* samb k* sep k* sil k* stram k* sulph k* thuj k*
  - **Forehead**: ruta b7a.de
  - **Lower** half: *Arn* b7a.de
  - **Upper** half: *Graph* b4a.de
- **erythema**: (*↗SKIN - Eruptions - erythema)* ars-i bro1 *Bell* bro1 cund bro1 echi bro1 euph bro1 gels c1 graph c2* nux-v bro1 syc pte1•
- **excitement**: (*↗GENERALS - Orgasm - emotions; MIND - Blushing; MIND - Confidence - want; MIND - Excitement; MIND - Timidity; MIND - Timidity - bashful)* acon bro1 *Am-m* vh1 ambr bro1 *Aml-ns* bro1* androc bnm2• atra-r bnm3• bar-s zr carb-an bro1 carl bro1 cimic gk *Coca* bro1 *Coff* **Ferr** k* *Ferr-p* mrr1* graph tl1 ign bro1 ix bnm8• loxo-recl knl4• meli bro1 *Morg* fmm1• op mrr1 phos physala-p bnm7• positr nl2• *Puls* mrr1 ruta fd4.de sep spig gk *Stram* bro1* sulph k* *Trios* rsj11• tritic-vg fd5.de [sol-ecl cky1]
  - **air**; in open | **amel.**: trios rsj11•
  - **erythrophobia**, in: ambr st ruta fd4.de
- **exertion** agg.; after: **Ferr** k* ferr-p sne nux-v h1* squil k*

- **fever** | **during** | **agg.**: **Acon** b7.de* agar b4.de* alum b4.de* am-m b7a.de* apis bg2 arg-met b7.de* arn b7a.de* ars b4.de* **Astac** hr1 bamb-a stb2.de• bar-m hr1* **Bell** k* brom *Bry* b7.de* calc h2* camph b7.de* canth b7.de* caps b7a.de* carb-an carb-v b4.de* *Cedr* k* *Cham* b7.de* chel **Chin** k* cina k* *Cocc* k* coff k* con b4.de* **Croc** b7.de* cycl b7.de* dig k* dulc b4a.de* **Eup-per** k* euphr bg2* ferr k* ferr-p k* gels hell k* **Hep** bg2 hura hydrog srj2• hyos bg2* ign b7.de* ip **Kreos** bg2 *Lach* b7a.de* lyc k* merc k* merc-c b4a.de* nat-c bg2 nat-m h2* *Nux-v* k* **Op** b7.de* par b7.de* phos k* *Plb* bg2 *Psor* *Puls* b7.de* rhus-t k* *Ruta* bg2 sang k* **Sep** k* sil k* spig b7.de* *Spong* b7.de* squil b7a.de* **Stram** b7.de* sulph k* *Tub* valer b7.de* *Verat* k* **Viol-t** b7.de* zinc b4.de*
  - **without**: **Caps Ferr** ol-an phos psor
- **flushes**: aml-ns ptk1 coca ptk1 stroph-h ptk1 tell ptk1
  - **Roots** of hair to neck and chest; from: chlol gm1
- **followed** by:
  - **blue** discoloration: *Acon* bg2 caps bg2 *Cham* bg2 chin bg2 *Cina* bg2 croc bg2 hyos bg2 *Ign* bg2 *Led* bg2 op bg2 squil bg2 verat bg2
  - **white** discoloration: hist sp1
- **glowing** red: *Acon* k* *Apis* *Arg-n* hr1 arn b7.de **Astac** k* aur k* bamb-a stb2.de• **Bell** k* bry b7.de* *Calc* *Camph* k* cann-s b7.de **Canth** b7.de* *Caps* b7.de* *Carb-v* k* cham b7.de chin b7.de* **Cina** k* cocc k* coff b7.de* croc k* euph h2* *Ferr* k* ferr-s hr1 *Glon* k* hell b7.de *Hep* k* ign b7.de inul hr1 kali-c h2* kola stb3• *Lyc* k* m-arct b7.de marb-w es1• mur-ac k* nat-c h2* *Nux-v* b7.de olnd b7a.de *Op* b7.de* *Phos* hr1 *Plat* k* *Ran-b* b7.de* ruta b7.de *Sabad* k* *Samb* b7.de* sil *Stram* k* sulph k2 tab *Thuj* k* *Valer* b7.de* [bell-p-sp dcm1]
  - **Cheeks**: **Acon** bg2 agar b4a.de alum bg2 arn bg2 *Bell* b4.de* bov bg2 *Bry* bg2 cann-xyz bg2 canth bg2 caps bg2 carb-an b4.de* cham bg2 *Chin* bg2 cina bg2 *Cocc* bg2 coff bg2 *Dulc* b4.de* *Euph* b4a.de hell bg2 *Hep* b4a.de ign bg2 kali-c b4.de* *Kali-n* b4a.de *Lyc* b4.de* mang b4.de* merc b4.de* merc-c b4a.de mur-ac b4a.de* *Nit-ac* b4a.de *Nux-v* bg2 *Op* bg2 *Phos* b4a.de plat b4.de* pyrog bg2 ran-b bg2 ruta bg2 *Sabad* bg2 samb bg2 sil bg2 stann b4.de* *Stram* bg2 thuj b4a.de* valer bg2 zinc bg2
- **headache**; during: acon k* agar k* ail alum h2* aml-ns bro1 *Arg-n* hr1 aur **Bell** k* bov bry *Bufo* *Cact* *Calc* k* calc-sil k2 camph cann-s canth cham bro1 *Cic* *Coff* *Croc* cycl k* equis-h a2 *Ferr* k* *Ferr-p* k* gels bro1 **Glon** k* gua br1 guar vml3• hydrog srj2• ign ind indg k* ip *Kali-br* hr1 kali-i *Kalm* k* kola stb3• kreos *Lach* k* led k* lyc lyss mag-c mag-m mag-p k* mag-s c1 **Meli** k* mur-ac naja bro1 nat-c *Nat-m* k* *Nux-m* k* *Nux-v* k* *Op* phos plat plb podo bro1 *Psor* ptel k* puls k* rhus-t sang hr1* sep kr1* sil spong stront-c sulph syph k2* tarax thuj k* zinc
- **heart**, with shocks at: phos h2*
- **heat**:
  - **fire**; during heat of: **Ant-c** nat-m
  - **with**: acet-ac bro1 acon bg2* agar bro1 aml-ns bg2* *Aster* bro1 aur bg2 bamb-a stb2.de• bapt bg2* *Bell* bg2* bry bg2 canth bro1 caps bro1 cham bg2 chin bg2 coff bg2 eup-per mrr1 ferr bg2 *Ferr-p* bro1 gels bg2* glon bg2* glyc bro1 iod bg2 kola stb3• kreos bro1 lac-lup hrn2• meli bg2* mygal bro1 nux-v bg2 op bg2* querc bro1 rham-cal bro1 sang bg2* spong bg2 stram bg2* sulph bro1 verat-v bg2* vip bg2
  - **without** internal: agar mtf33 asaf bg2 bamb-a stb2.de• caps bg2 ferr bg2 mill c1
- **hemorrhage**; before: meli bro1
- **homesickness**; with: caps k2
- **hot**; and:
  - **air**; in open | **Cheeks**: positr nl2• valer ptk1*
- **influenza**; during: bapt tl1
- **lying**:
  - **agg.**: acon lob-c verat
    - **becomes** pale on rising: *Acon* k* *Puls* *Verat* k* *Verat-v*
  - **back**; on | **agg.**: chlol
  - **side**; on:
    - **left** | **agg.**: *Calc*
- **mahogany** red: *Ail* k* *Arn* carb-v tl1 eup-per *Gels* op br1
- **maniacal** rage, with: acon ars **Bell** *Camph* sne cic h1 *Cupr* *Hyos* lyc meli sne merc nux-v *Op* plat puls *Stram* *Verat*
- **menopause**; during: *Graph* *Kali-bi* **Lach** lyc *Phys* vh *Sang* vh **Sul-ac** sulph k2 ter
- **menses** | **before** | **agg.**: *Bell* bro1 calc-p bro1 ferr bro1 *Ferr-p* bro1 gels bro1 *Sang* bro1
  - **during**:
    - **agg.**: *Bell* b4a.de* calc-p bro1 ferr b7a.de* *Ferr-p* bro1 gels bro1 ind k* *Puls* *Sang* bro1 xan
    - **amel.**: puls k2
- **metrorrhagia**; during: *Ferr* b7a.de
- **motion**, at least: nux-v h1 squil h1
- **mottled**: *Bell* hr1 ferr irid-met srj5• *Lach*
- **music** agg.: ambr
- **pain**; when in●: bell caps cham cimic bg1 **Ferr** k* ferr-p spig bg2* ter bg1
- **perspiration**; during: acon bg2 agar bg2 alum bg2 *Am-m* bg2 ars bg2 bell bg2 bry bg2 *Cham* bg2 **Chin** bg2 coff bg2 con bg2 ferr bg2 hep bg2 hyos bg2 **Ign** bg2 lyc bg2 merc bg2 *Nux-v* bg2 *Op* b7a.de* phos bg2 puls bg2 rhus-t bg2 ruta bg2 sabad bg2 *Samb* bg2 **Sep** bg2 **Sulph** bg2 *Verat* bg2 zinc bg2
- **purple**-red (See bluish - purple-red)
- **riding**:
  - **agg.**: ferr
  - **air**; in open: sulph k2
- **rising** agg.: naja phys k* sulph k2 verat bg1
- **scarlet**: *Am-c* b4a.de **Bell** b4.de* glon bg2
- **scratching** agg.; after: sulph k*
- **shivering**, while: **Arn** k* plut-n srj7•
- **sitting** agg.: **Bell** ferr-p k2 ign sne merc a1 phos k* tell hr1 thuj a1
- **sitting** up in bed agg.: mag-s k*
- **sleep** agg.; during: *Arum-m* bell chlol meny op b7.de* stram b7.de* viol-t k*
- **spidery**: med hr1
- **spots**: (↗*SKIN - Discoloration - red - spots)* acon ptk1 aeth k* ail alum k* alum-p k2 **Am-c** k* ambr k* *Anan* ars k* ars-s-f k2 aur k* aur-ar k2 aur-s k2 bamb-a stb2.de• **Bell** k* berb *Bry* k* calc ptk1 canth k* *Caps* k* carb-an k* *Carbn-s* *Chin* ptk1 cimic ptk cortiso sp1 croc k* cycl cypra-eg sde6.de* elaps ptk1 *Euphr* b7a.de *Ferr* k* fic-m gya1 gels k2 hura hydrog srj2• ictod iod ptk1 kali-bi kali-c ptk1 kreos ptk1 *Lac-c* lach *Lyc* k* m-arct b7.de* merc k* mosch b7a.de nat-m nux-m b7.de* nux-v b7.de* *Oena* k* olib-sac wmh1 op k* ox-ac par b7.de* ph-ac ptk1 **Phos** k* plac-s rly4• propl ub1• puls ptk1 *Rhus-t* b7a.de rhus-v **Sabad** k* samb k* *Sang* ptk1 sars b4a.de *Sil* k* spong fd4.de stann ptk1 stroph-h ptk1* sul-ac k2 **Sulph** k* sumb symph fd3.de• tab tarax tell rsj10• tub ptk1 visc sp1 zinc b4.de* [pop dhh1]
  - **burning**: *Chel* *Croc* tab
  - **circumscribed** (See circumscribed)
  - **eating**; after: lyc h2* sil h2*
  - **eruptions**, after: dig h2*
  - **fright**; after: am-c
  - **hot**: bry luf-op rsj5•
  - **painful**: alum h2*
  - **vexation**; after: am-c k*
  - **washing** agg.; after: *Aesc* k* *Am-c* *Kali-c* phos k* spong fd4.de
  - **women**; in young: cimic ptk
  - **Cheeks**: cortiso tpw7 rhus-t ptk1
- **stimulating** food agg.: carb-v k2
- **stool**:
  - **before**: *Caust* b4a.de* manc k*
  - **during** | **agg.**: caps bg2 caust ptk1 *Cham* b7a.de ind vml3•
- **stooping** agg.: *Bell* *Canth* k*
- **stripes**: apis b7a.de*
- **sudden**: acon bg2 alum h2* *Aml-ns* bg2 *Bell* k* calc bg1 clem k* euphr h2* ferr bg2* *Mur-ac* k* phos bg2* puls h1* sep bg2 sulph bg2 thuj k*
- **supper** agg.; after: carb-v h2*
- **swelling**; with: agar mtf33 cic c1
- **talking** agg.: squil h1*
- **tea** agg.: plan

Face

- **toothache**; with: *Acon* k* **Bell** k* **Cham** k* *Coff* *Ferr-p* merc nux-m phos puls rhus-t sulph verat hr1
- **unconsciousness**, during: canth kr1 glon k* *Kali-br* hr1 *Mur-ac* kr1*
- **urination** agg.; before: coc-c bg2
- **vertigo**; during: anan k* *Bell* k* *Cact* k* *Cocc* k* *Ferr* hr1* *Glon* hr1 kalm ptk1 *Lyc* hr1 **Nux-v** hr1 *Stram* k*
- **waking**; on: choc srj3• cimic k* **Cina** hura
- **walking**:
  - **agg.**: phos ptk1 stront-c
  - **air** agg.; in open: mur-ac sulph
- **warm** room agg.●: am-m hr1 apis mrr1 ferr-p sne ferr-s hr1 grat pneu jl2 *Sulph*
- **washing**; after: *Aesc* *Am-c* bry xxb dulc fd4.de *Kali-c* phos spong fd4.de
- **weather**:
  - **cold** agg.: sulph k2
  - **wet** | **agg.**: sulph k2
- **weeping**; with (See MIND - Weeping - face - redness)
- **wine**, the pale face becomes red after: (↗*alcohol*) *Carb-v* cypra-eg sde6.de• *Ferr* tax nb [ferr-i stj1 ferr-m stj1 ferr-p stj1 ferr-s stj1]
- **yellowish** red: *Chel* ptk1 gels ptk1 lach bg2* nux-v bg2*
- ○ **Affected** side: ter bg2
- **Cheeks**: *Acon* ptk1 arn ptk1 bell ptk1 brom bro1 *Caps* bro1 **Cham** ptk1 chin ptk1 cic bro1 coff bro1 colch bro1 cypra-eg sde6.de• euph bro1 euphr bro1 *Ferr* ptk1 *Ign* ptk1 lac-lup hrn2• *Lyc* ptk1 *Meli* bro1 morg-p fmm1• mosch ptk1 nux-v ptk1 olib-sac wmh1 phos ptk1 *Puls* ptk1* *Sang* br1* sulph ptk1 *Tub* jl2 vanil fd5.de
  - **one** side: *Acon* bro1 *Cham* bro1 cina bro1 dros bro1 ip bro1 *Nux-v* bro1 sep ptk1
    - **accompanied** by | **Head**; complaints of (See HEAD - Complaints - accompanied - cheeks - red - one)
    - **chill**; during: acon b7.de* am-m b7a.de arn b7a.de *Cham* b7a.de
    - **coryza**; during: *Cham* b7.de* nux-v b7.de*
  - **left**: verat ptk1*
    - **fever**; during: acet-ac bro1
  - **accompanied** by:
    - **Abdomen**; cramping pain in: cham ptk1
    - **Head**; complaints of (See HEAD - Complaints - accompanied - cheeks - red)
    - **Teeth**; pain in (See TEETH - Pain - accompanied - cheeks)
  - **blotches**: tell rsj10•
    - **right**: tell rsj10•
  - **burning** (See glowing)
  - **children**; in: calc-s lmj **Caps** lmj *Ferr* lmj *Iod* lmj ol-an phos lmj psor lmj *Sulph* lmj
  - **chill**; during: acon b7.de* alum b4a.de **Bry** b7.de* *Cham* b7.de chin b7a.de *Ign* b7a.de* ip bg2 kreos b7a.de lyc b4a.de mosch bg2 nux-v b7.de*
  - **fever** | **during** | **agg.**: *Acon* b7.de* chin b7.de cocc b7.de ferr b7.de *Hyos* b7.de iod bro1 kreos b7a.de nux-v b7.de rhus-t b7.de
    - **without** fever: calc-s lmj **Caps** lmj *Ferr* lmj *Iod* lmj ol-an lmj phos lmj psor lmj *Sulph* lmj
  - **shivering**; during: acon b7.de ign b7.de nux-v b7.de rhus-t b7.de
  - **stool** agg.; during: caps b7.de*
- **Chin**: ail canth k* colch k* merc k* (non:nat-m k*) spira a1 sul-i c1 zinc k*
  - **spots**: anac k* *Caust* crot-t k* dig k* nat-m h2* sep h2* sulph k* sumb k* zinc
- **Eyebrows** | **Above**: fl-ac bg2
- **Eyes**:
  - **Around**: apis bg2* borx h2* chinin-ar ptk1 elaps bg2* fic-m gya1 lappa bg2* maland bg1* *Psor* jl2 *Puls* bg2* rumx ptk1 sil bg2*
    - **weeping**; when: borx h2
  - **Between**: plut-n srj7•
- **Forehead**: calc k* cypra-eg sde6.de• hura laur k* lil-t k* merc-i-r k* mez k* rhus-v k* stram k* vac k* verat k*
  - **accompanied** by:
    - **Cheeks** | **pale**: bell b4a.de

- **red – Forehead**: ...
  - **spots**, in: aesc k* berb k* caps k* cycl k* mosch k* sars h2* sulph k* *Tell* k*
- **Lips**: all-c aloe k* *Apis* k* ars bg2* arum-t k* *Aur-m* bar-c k* *Bell* k* beryl tpw5 bry k* calc-caust c1 carb-v chin mtf33 chlol cund sne dulc fd4.de kreos k2* lac-c *Lach* lachn merc merc-c k* morg-p pte1*• mur-ac bg2 op mrr1 ozone sde2• phos bg2* psor k2 puls k* rhus-t sacch-a fd2.de• *Sang* sep b4a.de spig k* spong fd4.de stram k* sul-ac bg2* **Sulph** k* thyr ptk1 *Tub* k* tub-m vn vanil fd5.de verat
  - **accompanied** by:
    - **respiration**:
      - **complaints** of (See RESPIRATION - Complaints - accompanied - lips)
      - **difficult** (See RESPIRATION - Difficult - accompanied - lips - red)
  - **bright**: **Sulph** bg2
  - **dark**: aloe bro1 bar-c bell gins mez *Sulph* bro1 tub bro1 tub-m jl2
  - **scarlet**: stroph-h ptk1
  - **spot**: caust h2* nat-m h2* sulph h2*
  - **warmth** agg. | **heat** agg.: beryl tpw5
  - **Lower**: sep ptk1 *Sulph* ptk1
    - **spots**: mez b4.de*
      - **Below** | **right** lip: chlam-tr bcx2•
  - **Middle** of the lips | **dark**: tub-m jl2
  - **Upper**: ars-i ptk1 calc ptk1 nat-m ptk1 *Tub* jl2
    - **spot** | **Above** the upper lip red: caust h*
- **Lower** half of face: *Arum-t* mrr1
- **Malar** bones: dulc fd4.de phos h2
  - **left**: arum-t mrr1
- **Mouth**:
  - **Around**: ars bg2 *Arum-t* mrr1 *Ign* bg2 ip k* lac-lup hrn2• op bg2
    - **cold** weather agg.: lac-lup hrn2•
    - **eating** agg.: lac-lup hrn2•
  - **Corners** of: ars
- **Nose**:
  - **extending** to frontal sinuses; over nose and: am-caust a1*
  - **Nostrils**: ars tl1 mez tl1
    - **left**: arum-t mrr1
- **Parotid** glands: *Bell* b4a.de
- **Roots** of hair to neck and chest; from: chlol gm1
- **Uncovered** side | **fever**; during: thuj bg2 *Viol-t* bg2

- **rosy**: (↗*GENERALS - Complexion - florid*) arn ptk1 caps tl1 ferr ptk1 lach mtf33
  - **spots**: *Carb-an* b4a.de
- **sallow**: ail k* alum k* alumn k* ant-c mtf33 ant-t ptk1 *Apis* *Arg-met* k* **Arg-n** k* *Arn* k* *Ars* k* ars-h k* ars-i k* ars-s-f k2 *Bapt* k* berb k* *Calc* k* *Calc-p* k* *Carb-ac* k* **Carb-v** k* carl k* caust br1* cench k2 **Chel** k* *Coc-c* k* cocc k* *Coloc* k* con k* *Corn* k* *Croc* k* *Crot-c* *Crot-h* dulc k2 *Eup-per* *Ferr* k* ferr-ar *Ferr-i* ferr-p k* *Helon* k* hydr k* hydr-ac k* ind k* *Iod* k* kali-c k* kalm k* *Lac-d* k* *Lach* k* lept lyc tl1* mag-c k2 **Med** k* *Merc* k* myric k* naphtin **Nat-m** k* *Nat-s* k* nit-ac k2 *Nux-v* k* op k* *Pall* k* pic-ac br1 plan k* **Plb** k* podo k* puls k* rhus-t a1 *Sep* k* spong fd4.de stann k2 sul-i k2 **Sulph** k* syc pte1• syph xxb
  - **accompanied** by | **Stomach**; pain in (See STOMACH - Pain - accompanied - face - sallow)
  - **apyrexia**; during: nat-m bro1
  - **diarrhea**; with: corn br1
  - **headache**; during: kali-bi tl1
- **sickly** color: acet-ac aesc k* alet k2 aloe alum alum-p k2 alumn k* am-c ant-t k2* apis *Arg-met* *Arg-n* k* **Ars** k* ars-h k* *Ars-i* *Bapt* k* bism k* borx brach k* brom k2* **Calc** calc-ar k2 calc-s *Carb-v* carbn-s *Caust* k* *Chel* k* *Chin* k* chinin-ar *Cina* *Clem* k* cocc k2 con k* *Crot-c* *Crot-h* dig k* dulc k2 eup-per k* **Ferr** *Ferr-ar* *Ferr-i* graph k2 hydr k2 *Iod* k* ip k2 *Kali-c* k* kali-chl k* kali-n kali-p kali-s *Kreos* k* lac-d k2 lachn k* **Lyc** k* mag-c *Mag-m* k* *Mang* **Med** k* *Merc* k* mez k2 nat-m mtf33 nat-s k* *Nit-ac* *Nux-v* k* petr k2 *Ph-ac* k* *Phos* k* podo psor k* ptel c1 puls k2 pyrog k2 rhus-t sil *Spig* k* spong fd4.de *Staph* k* sul-ac k2 *Sulph* k* tab tarent k2 teucr ther k2 thuj k* til **Tub** k* zinc zinc-p k2

- **spots**: acon ptk1 aeth ptk1 ars ptk1 carb-an ptk1 *Kali-bi* ptk1 lach ptk1 manc ptk1 mur-ac a1 *Rhus-t* ptk1 sil ptk1 sulph ptk1
  - **elevated**: carb-an b4a.de
- **tanned** (See bronzed)
- **white**: (↗*pale - spots)* cyt-l sp1 mand sp1
  - **chalk**; like: | **children**; in: calc br1
  - **dirty**: *Caust* br1*
  - **itching**: sulph h2
  - **pearly** white | **Mouth**; around: aeth bro1 *Cina* bro1 santin bro1
  - **powdery** | **Lips**: ars bg2
  - **spot**: (↗*pale - spots)* ars k* calc b4a.de merc k* nat-c k* pip-m mtf11 sil b4a.de* sulph h2 tor mtf11
  - ○ **Lips**: ferr b7a.de valer b7.de*
    - **accompanied** by | **nausea** (See STOMACH - Nausea - accompanied - lips)
    - **Lower**: calc b4.de* merc-c b4a.de
  - **Mouth**; around: *Cina* b7.de*
- **yellow**: acal vh1 acon k* aesc agar k* ail alumn k* *Ambr* k* anan k* ant-ar ant-c b2.de* aphis a1* apis **Arg-met** **Arg-n** k* arn k* **Ars** k* *Ars-h* k* *Ars-i* ars-s-f k2 asaf b2.de* asc-t k* aur b2.de* *Bapt* k* *Bell* k* berb bro1 blatta-a bro1 blatta-o *Bry* k* caj k* **Calc** k* calc-i k2 **Calc-p** k* cann-s b2.de* *Canth* k* carb-an k* *Carb-v* k* *Carbn-s* **Card-m** k* **Caust** k* cedr k* *Cham* k* cheir c1 **Chel** k* *Chin* k* chinin-ar *Chinin-s* *Chion* k* chlor k* cimic cina k* clem a1 coc-c cocc k* **Con** k* *Corn* k* *Croc* k* *Crot-c* *Crot-h* k* cupr k* *Dig* k* *Dios* hr1 dol dulc b2.de* *Elaps* euph b2.de* **Ferr** k* *Ferr-ar* **Ferr-i** *Ferr-p* *Gels* k* gran granit-m es1• *Graph* k* *Hell* k* *Hep* k* hura hydr k* ign b2.de* *Iod* k* *Ip* k* kali-bi k* kali-br k* *Kali-c* k* kali-i bg2 kali-p kali-s kali-sil k2 kreos bg2* **Lach** k* lachn k* laur k* *Lept* loxo-lae bnm12• loxo-recl bnm10• **Lyc** k* lyss k* *Mag-c* k* *Mag-m* k* malar jl2 manc k* mang *Med* k* **Merc** k* merc-c k* *Merc-d* bro1 mez k* *Myric* k* naja nat-ar nat-c k* *Nat-m* k* nat-p k* **Nat-s** k* **Nit-ac** k* **Nux-v** k* oena hr1 ol-j bro1 *Op* k* ox-ac k* *Petr* k* ph-ac b2.de* *Phos* k* *Phyt* k* pic-ac bg2* **Plb** k* *Podo* k* psor k* ptel k* *Puls* k* ran-b b2.de* raph k* rheum b2.de* rhus-t k* ruta b2.de* sabad b2.de* samb k* *Sars* k* *Sec* k* **Sep** k* *Sil* k* spig k* spong fd4.de stann b2.de* stram sul-ac k* sul-i k2 **Sulph** k* tarax b2.de* tarent hr1 tub jl2 upa k* verat k* yuc bro1 zinc hr1
  - **morning**: raph k*
  - **afternoon**: gels k*
  - **night**: plb k*
  - **accompanied** by:
    - **leukorrhea** (See FEMALE - Leukorrhea - accompanied - face - yellow)
    - **stool**; watery: berb ptk1
  - **anger**; after: (↗*MIND - Anger)* nat-s
  - **chill**; during: arn bg2 ars bg2 *Chin* bg2 con bg2 dig bg2 ferr bg2 *Hell* bg2 ign b7a.de* lach bg2 nat-m bg2 nit-ac bg2 nux-v bg2 phos bg2 puls b7a.de rhus-t bg2 sep bg2 sulph bg2
  - **convulsions**; during: cic kr1 plb kr1
  - **heat**; during: *Ars* b4a.de* *Chin* b7a.de cina c1 *Ferr* lach k* *Nat-m* b4a.de* nux-v k* *Rhus-t* b7.de*
  - **hemorrhage**; during: kali-c h2
  - **intermittent**, in: am-c *Chinin-s* *Con* ferr k* nat-c nat-m *Nux-v* **Sep** *Tub*
  - **menses**; during: *Caust* k*
  - **pale**: bry bg2 chin bg2 crot-h bg2 kali-bi bg2* kreos bg2 merc bg2
    - **spots**: nat-m bg2
    - **Forehead**: chel bg2 phos bg2
    - **Nose**: agar bg2 kali-bi bg2 nux-v bg2 *Sep* bg2
    - **Temples**: *Caust* bg2
  - **perspiration**; during: **Chin** bg2 con bg2 ferr bg2 **Nat-m** bg2 nux-v bg2 *Rhus-t* bg2 *Sep* bg2 *Sulph* bg2
  - **rage**; during: (↗*MIND - Rage)* *Acon* canth lach lyc merc *Nux-v* phos puls verat
  - **saddle** across cheeks: (↗*Saddle; NOSE - Discoloration - yellow; NOSE - Discoloration - yellow - saddle)* carb-an bg2 lyc bg2 **Sep** k* sulph bg2
  - **shivering**; during: hell b7.de

Discoloration – yellow: ...

  - **spots**: ambr b7a.de* ars-i k2 calc b4.de* carb-an bg2 caust bg2 *Colch* b7a.de* *Ferr* b7a.de* hell b7.de* kali-i a1 laur b7a.de* lyc b4.de* nat-c b4.de* nat-m b4a.de *Nit-ac* bg2 nux-v bg2 phos b4.de* rhus-t bg2 sep b4a.de* sulph bg2 sumb a1
  - **sun** and wind stain yellow on nose and cheeks; exposure to: cadm-s br1
  - **syphilis**: **Lach** k* merc-c nit-ac
  - **vexation**; after: (↗*MIND - Ailments - reproaches)* *Kali-c* k*
  - ○ **Cheek** | **spots**: cadm-s br1
  - **Eyes**; around: coll bg3* irid-met srj5• mag-c bg2* med hr1 *Nit-ac* k* nux-v k* spig k*
    - **perspiration**; during: ars b4.de*
  - **Forehead**: chel k* kali-p ptk1 nat-c k2 phos k* sep ptk1
    - **spot**: kali-c h2 nat-c h2
  - **Lips**: merc-c b4a.de *Nat-c* b4a.de *Nux-v* bg2 sep b4a.de*
    - **spots**: vip bg2
    - **streaks** on: stram b7.de*
    - **Upper** lip:
      - **spots** on: nat-c b4.de*
      - **streak** on: (non:stram kl)
  - **Margins** of hair: med hr1
  - **Mouth**; around: act-sp hydrc mag-m h2* nux-v k* *Sep* k*
  - **Nose**; around: (↗*NOSE - Discoloration - yellow - patch)* mag-m bg2 nux-v k* sep k*
  - **Temples**: *Caust* k* *Kali-c* b4a.de
  - **Whiskers**; around: *Con* b4a.de

DISLOCATION of jaws:

- **easy**: caust st* *Ign* b7.de* m-arct b7.de mez h2 petr b4.de* ph-ac b4.de* phos bg2 rheum h *Rhus-t* b7.de* staph k* vanil fd5.de
  - ○ **Lower** jaw (See easy)
- **sensation** of: gran a1 *Ign* hr1 petr k* ph-ac c1 podo fd3.de• rhus-t k* *Rob* hr1 spong hr1
  - **painful**: ulm-c jsj8•
    - **left**: ulm-c jsj8•
    - **eating** agg.: ulm-c jsj8•

DISTORTION: (↗*Contraction)* absin k* acon k* agar b4a.de* am-c b2.de* am-caust a1 am-m k* ambr b2.de* *Ang* b2.de* ant-t k* apis *Ars* k* art-v bro1 atro vh bar-m k* *Bell* k* bism k* bry b2.de* *Bufo* calc b2.de* *Camph* k* cann-i k* cann-s b2.de* canth b2.de* carb-v b2.de* caust k* *Cham* k* **Chin** bg2 choc srj3• *Cic* k* cic-m a1 cina cocc k* *Colch* b2.de* *Coloc* k* crot-c *Crot-h* k* cupr k* *Cupr-act* bro1 dig b2.de* dulc k* gels bg2 glon a1 *Graph* k* guaj b2.de* *Hell* k* hep b2.de* *Hydr-ac* k* **Hyos** k* **Ign** k* iod b2.de* ip k* kali-c b2.de* kali-i k* kali-s k* *Lach* k* lact k* lat-m bnm6• *Laur* k* lol a1 lyc k* lyss m-ambo b2.de m-arct b2.de *Merc* b2.de* *Merc-c* k* mill mosch b2.de* nat-c b2.de* *Nux-m* k* **Nux-v** k* olnd b2.de* **Op** k* petr k* *Ph-ac* b2.de* phos k* phyt plat k* plb k* puls b2.de* ran-b b2.de* ran-s b2.de rheum b2.de* rhus-t k* samb b2.de* *Sec* k* sep b2.de* *Sil* k* sol-ni **Spig** b2.de* spong b2.de* squil k* staph b2.de* **Stram** k* **Stry** k* sul-ac k* sulph b2.de* *Syph* mrr1 tab k* tarent k* tell br1* verat k* vip k* zinc bg2

- **one** side: agar mrr1 cadm-s mrr1* chlorpr mtf11 tell bg1
- **morning**: *Mygal* olnd k* *Spig* k*
- **accompanied** by | **Teeth**; complaints in (See TEETH - Complaints - accompanied - face - distorted)
- **chill**; during: ars bg2 bell bg2 cann-s k* cic bg2 op bg2 stram bg2
- **congenital**: *Syph* mrr1
- **convulsions**; during: **Cic** mrr1 stram tl1
- **frightful**: **Cic** br1*
- **maniacal** rage, with: ars *Bell* lach nux-v sec **Stram** *Verat*
- **pain**:
  - **abdomen**; from pain in: coloc h2
  - **from**: lat-m bnm6•
  - **with**: cham ptk1* coloc tl1 phos h2
- **sensation** as if distorted: nit-ac bg2
  - **excitement**; sensation as if he had to distort the face after excessive: lyc h2
- **sleep** | **after** | **agg.**: cic

Face

- **sleep**: ...
  - **during**: ph-ac b4.de* til k*
- **storm**; at approach of: rhod tl1
- **supper** agg.; after: lyc h2*
- **swallowing** agg.: **Nit-ac**
- **talking** agg.: caust c1 *Ign* k* stram tl1
- **toothache**: staph h1 tarent
- **vomiting**; while: *Verat* k*
- **waking**; on: crot-h ptk1
- **wind** agg.: acon mrr1 cadm-s mrr1 caust mrr1

○ - **Lips**: ars a1 *Art-v* bro1 cadm-s bro1 *Cic* bro1 *Cupr-act* bro1 cur bro1 stram bro1
- **Mouth**: agar ars b4a.de* *Bell* k* bry k* cadm-s br1 camph k* *Cocc* *Con* k* *Cupr* k* cur *Dulc* k* *Graph* k* hydr-ac a1 ign k* kali-n k* lach k* *Laur* *Lyc* k* merc k* nux-m b7a.de* **Nux-v** k* op k* ph-ac plat k* **Plb** puls k* *Ran-b* b7a.de sec k* stram k* stry k* sulph tarent k*
  - **one** side: acon vh1 *Dulc* k* graph
  - **alternating** sides: cham lyc h2 nit-ac
  - **right** corner, outward: bell h1
  - **drawing** up to a point: conin c1
  - **left**; drawn to: phos ptk1 verat-v ptk1
  - **sleep** agg.; during: bry cupr k*
  - **talking**:
    - **agg.**: caust tell br1
    - **beginning** to talk agg.: agar mrr1

DRAWN: *Acon* k* **Aeth** k* agar k2 am-c k* ambr k* androc srj1*• *Ang* b2.de **Ant-c** k* ant-t b2.de *Arg-n* k* **Ars** k* *Ars-h* k* ars-i bar-c k* bar-i k2 **Bell** k* bism k* brom dgt1 *Bry* k* calc k* *Camph* k* cann-s k* *Canth* k* *Carb-v* k* carbn-h carbn-s *Caust* k* *Cham* k* ch *Cic* k* cocc k* colch k* crot-h k* *Cupr* k* dig k* dulc k* gels k* glon bg2 *Gran* k* *Graph* k* guaj k* hell helo-s rwt2• hep k* hydr-ac hydrog srj2• *Hyos* k* *Ign* k* iod k* *Ip* k* kali-bi k* kali-c k* kali-s kali-sil k2 lach k* laur k* **Lyc** k* m-ambo b2.de m-arct b2.de *Merc* k* *Merc-c* k* *Mez* mosch k* nat-ar k2 nat-c k* nit-ac k* nux-m k* nux-v k* olnd k* **Op** k* ph-ac k* *Phos* k* *Plat* k* plb k* plut-n srj7• puls k* ran-b k* ran-s k* rheum k* *Rhus-t* k* samb k* **Sec** k* sep k* sil k* spig k* spong k* *Squil* k* *Stann* staph k* **Stram** k* sul-i k2 *Sulph* k* **Tab** k* **Verat** k* vip k* [spect dfg1 thal-met stj2]
- **cough** agg.; during: *Spong* b7.de*
- **lines**, in: ars k* dulc fd4.de lyc k* spong fd4.de vanil fd5.de
- **point**, to a: *Agath-a* nl2• bism ptk1 brom bg2* kali-n ptk1
- **sleep** agg.; during: tab k*

○ - **Jaws**:

○ • **Lower**:
  - **backward**; drawn: bell b4.de* ign bg2 m-arct bg2 rhus-t bg2
  - **down**: spong b7.de*
- **Lips**: ant-t ptk1 bry b7.de* *Camph* ptk1 cupr b7.de* ign b7a.de ip b7a.de nux-v b7.de* op b7.de* phyt ptk1 puls b7.de* *Ran-b* b7a.de *Sec* b7.de* *Stram* b7a.de tab ptk1
  - **sideways**: acon bg2 ars b4a.de *Bell* b4.de* bry bg2 caust b4a.de cupr bg2 *Dulc* b4a.de graph b4.de* lyc b4a.de* merc b4.de* nux-v b7.de* op bg2 puls bg2 *Sec* b7.de* sil b4a.de sulph b4a.de
    - **sensation** as if: kreos b7a.de

○ • **Upper**:
  - **exposing** teeth; drawn up: acon bg1 ant-t bg1 **Camph** *Phyt* bg1*
  - **laughing**; drawn up while: mag-m dgt sil dgt
- **Masseter** and temporal muscles: glon bg2

DRAWN DOWN: | **Mouth**; corners of: ox-ac bg2

DRAWN UPWARD: | **Mouth**; corners of: camph bg2 nux-v bg2 phyt bg2

DRINKING: | **after** | **agg.**: cham b7.de* cocc b7.de*
- **agg.**: ang bg2 rhus-t b7.de*

DROPPING: (↗*MOUTH - Open*)

○ - **Jaws**: (↗*MOUTH - Open*) acet-ac apis *Am* k* *Ars* k* *Bapt* bufo k2 *Carb-v* *Chel* cimic colch cupr gels k* glon *Hell* k* hydrog srj2• *Hyos* k* *Kali-i* **Lach** k* **Lyc** k* merc-cy **Mur-ac** k* *Nux-v* k* **Op** k* ph-ac *Phos* podo sec *Stram* k* **Sulph** k* suprar rly4• tab vario verat-v zinc
  - **left**: nux-v ptk
- **Lips**: bar-c ptk1 merc ptk1 nux-v ptk1

○ • **Lower**: ars bg2* calc bg2 glon bg2 manc bg2* op b7.de*

Dropping – Lips – Lower: ...
  - **sensation** of: calc h1* glon a1

DRUNKARDS; complaints of: led b7a.de

DRYNESS: (↗*SKIN - Dry*) abrot br1 acon-ac rly4• allox sp1 anh sp1 arizon-l nl2• **Ars** bamb-a stb2.de• beryl sp1 cadm-met sp1 choc srj3• cimic coli rly4• cortico tpw7* cypra-eg sde6.de• cystein-l rly4• dioxi rbp6 dulc fd4.de eup-per hydr-ac hydrog srj2• *Iod* irid-met srj5• jug-c kali-c kali-s fd4.de lac-h htj1• limest-b es1• m-aust b7.de mag-m mrr1 mand rsj7• merc-c mim-p rsj8• morg-p pte1• oci-sa sp1 olib-sac wmh1 pant-ac rly4• petr-ra shn4• positr nl2• rauw tpw8* rhus-t b7.de* ribo rly4• sal-fr sle1• spong fd4.de suis-em rly4• sul-i k2 sulph suprar rly4• tax nb tell rsj10•

○ - **Cheeks**: coli rly4• euph h2* spong fd4.de
- **Lips**: (↗*MOUTH - Dryness - lips - lower*) abrom-a ks5 *Acon* k* acon-ac rly4• aesc agar k* all-s allox tpw3* aloe k* alum k* alum-p k2 *Am-c* k* *Am-m* k* ambr b7.de* *Aml-ns* k* ammc vh1 anac k* anan androc srj1• ang k* anis c1 **Ant-c** k* *Ant-t* k* anth vh1 *Apis* k* apoc k* *Aq-mar* jl* aral vh1 *Arg-n* k* arizon-l nl2• arn b7.de* *Ars* k* ars-met ars-s-f k2 *Arum-t* vh asar atro vh1 bamb-a stb2.de• bapt bg2 *Bar-c* k* bar-m bar-ox-suc rly4• bar-s k2 *Bell* k* berb k* beryl tpw5* *Bit-ar* wht1• brach **Bry** k* cadm-met tpw6* calad k* *Calc* *Calc-act* *Calc-ar* calc-sil k2 cann-i k* cann-s k* *Canth* k* carb-ac c1 carb-an b4.de* carb-v h2* *Carbn-s* carc fd2.de• card-m cassia-s ccrh1• caust h2* cench k2 cham b7.de* chel k* *Chin* k* chion bro1 chlf br1 choc srj3• chr-ac k* cimic k* cocc coli rly4• con k* cop croc b7.de* *Crot-t* k* cub cycl k* cystein-l rly4• *Dig* k* digin a1 dios dream-p sdj1• dros k* dulc fd4.de dys pte1*• euon bro1 *Ferr* k* ferr-ar ferr-p k* flor-p rsj3• galeoc-c-h gms1• gard-j vlr2• *Gels* k* glyc bro1 *Graph* k* ham k* *Hell* k* helo-s rwt2• *Helon* k* *Hydr* hydrog srj2• **Hyos** k* hyper k* *Ign* k* iodof irid-met srj5• iris jal kali-ar *Kali-bi* k* *Kali-c* kali-i k* kali-m k2 kali-p kali-s fd4.de kali-sil k2 *Kalm* kola stb3• *Kreos* k* *Lac-c* lac-lup hrn2• *Lach* k* lap-la sde8.de• loxo-recl knl4• luna kg1• *Lyc* k* mag-c b4.de* mag-s k* malar jl2 mand rsj7• mang k* meny b7.de* *Merc* k* *Merc-c* k* *Merc-cy* merc-i-f k* mez k* moni jl2 morg-p pte1*• *Mur-ac* k* nat-c h2* *Nat-m* k* nat-s nat-sil fd3.de• neon srj5• *Nit-ac* **Nux-m** k* *Nux-v* k* oci-sa sp1 olib-sac wmh1 olnd k* ozone sde2• petr bg2 ph-ac k* *Phos* k* phyt k* pieri-b mlk9.de pin-con oss2• pip-n bg2 plac rzf5• plat k* *Positr* nl2• *Psor* k* ptel **Puls** k* pycnop-sa mrz1 rauw tpw8* *Rhod* k* rhodi br1* **Rhus-t** k* ribo rly4• ruta sabad k* sacch-a fd2.de• sal-fr sle1• sang k* senec k* *Sep* k* *Sil* spig spong fd4.de squil b7.de* *Stram* k* suis-em rly4• sulfonam ks2 **Sulph** k* sumb a1 suprar rly4• syc pte1*• symph fd3.de• tab k* taosc iwa1• tell rsj10• tere-la rly4• thres-a sze7• thuj b4.de* thyr ptk1 *Trios* rsj11• tritic-vg fd5.de tub al* tub-m vn* v-a-b jl2 vanil fd5.de *Verat* k* **Verat-v** k* vib vinc k* zinc k* zinc-p k2 [bell-p-sp dcm1]
  - **morning**: apoc vh1 carb-an h2* chen-a vml3• mag-c h2* mang h2* rein a1
  - **evening**: cench k2 crot-t a1 mag-s k* positr nl2•
  - **night**: ant-c aq-mar jl* calad k* cham k*
  - **accompanied** by:
    - **itching**: bit-ar wht1•
    - **thirst** (See STOMACH - Thirst - accompanied - lips)
    - **thirstlessness** (See STOMACH - Thirstless - accompanied - lips)
    - **Stomach**; emptiness of (See STOMACH - Emptiness - accompanied - lips)
  - **air** agg.; in open: mang
  - **chill**; during: acon bg2 ars bg2 bell bg2 bry bg2 chin bg2 con bg2 ign bg2 *Nux-v* bg2 ph-ac bg2 phos bg2 rhus-t bg2
  - **heat**; during: ars bg2 beryl tpw5 cench k2 chin bg2 nux-v b7.de* phos b4.de* *Rhus-t* b7.de* verat bg2
  - **licks** them frequently: (↗*MOUTH - Wetting*) aloe dgt1 puls br1 symph fd3.de•
  - **menses**; during: nux-v b7.de
  - **perspiration**; during: acon bg2 arn bg2 ars bg2 bell bg2 *Bry* bg2 chin bg2 ferr bg2 merc bg2 **Nux-v** bg2 *Phos* bg2 rhus-t bg2 *Sep* bg2 verat bg2
  - **sensation** of: acon b7.de* arn b7.de* asar b7.de* nat-s bg2 nux-v b7.de* ulm-c jsj8•
  - **waking**; on: ambr k* apoc vh1 calad coca

○ • **Lower**: bit-ar wht1• merc b4.de* mez b4.de* sabin b7.de*
  - **Upper**: am-c b4.de* con b4a.de plat b4.de* sulph b4.de*
- **Nose**: acon-ac rly4• carb-an k* *Caust* dioxi rbp6 spong fd4.de

○ • **Anterior** part: merl a1 spig b7.de*

- **Nose**: ...
  - **Tip**: carb-an h2*
  - **Turbinated** bones: cop br1
- **Sinus**; maxillary: anh sp1
- **Skin** (See Dryness)

EATING: | **after** | **agg.**: am-c bg2 am-m bg2 anac b4.de* *Asaf* b7.de* caps b7.de* caust bg2 cham b7.de* ign b7.de* kali-c bg2 lyc bg2 m-aust b7.de mang b4a.de merc b4.de* mez bg2 **Nux-v** b7.de* petr b4a.de* sars b4.de* sil b4a.de* staph bg2 sulph bg2 viol-t b7.de* *Zinc* b4a.de

- **while**:
  - **agg.**: euphr b7.de* laur b7.de* lyc bg2 mez ptk1 *Nat-m* b4a.de nux-v b7.de* *Phos* bg2* *Rhod* b4a.de spong b7.de* verat b7.de*
  - **amel.**: kalm ptk1 rhod ptk1

EDEMA (See Swelling - edematous)

EGG WHITE; sensation of (See Cobweb - sensation; Tension - egg)

EMACIATION: (↗*Thin; GENERALS - Emaciation)* acet-ac k* agar alum ptk1 anac ars k* ars-i bar-c bar-i k2 *Calc* k* *Carb-v* ptk1* cench k2 chinin-s k* coff mrr1 cupr *Ferr* bg2* *Guaj* hell k2 hura iod k* kali-bi kali-br a1 kali-i *Lac-d* lyc k2 merc-c mez k* naja nat-c nat-m ptk1* nat-p nux-m ph-ac k2 plb k* *Psor* k* sec k2 *Sel* k* *Sep* k* sil stann k2 staph ptk1 sul-ac k2 sulph sumb tab k* *Tarent* bg1* verat bg1*

- **accompanied** by | **pale** discoloration of face: abrot bg2 ars bg2 borx bg2 *Calc-p* bg2 iod bg2 merc bg2 *Nat-m* bg2 *Plb* bg2 sec bg2 sulph bg2
- **and** hands; of face: grat sel k*
- **neuralgia**, after: plb k*

EMOTIONS agg.: aml-ns bg2 staph bg2

EMPYEMA:

○ - **Sinuses**: | **Maxillary**: arn br1

ENLARGED: *(↗Swelling)*

- **sensation** as if the face were larger: *(↗Broad; Swelling - sensation)* **Acon** k* alum k* arg-met glon k*
  - **dinner**; after: alum

○ - **Eyebrow**; sensation as if plut-n srj7•

- **Jaws**: hecla irid-met srj5• *Phos*
- **Parotid** gland (See Swelling - parotid)
- **Submaxiliary** glands (See Swelling - submaxillary)

EPISTAXIS: | **amel.**: meli bg2

ERODED sensation (See Excoriation - sensation)

ERUPTIONS: *(↗SKIN - Eruptions)* agar k* agath-a nl2• agn b2.de* ail *Alum* k* *Am-c* k* *Am-m* k* ambr k* anac b4.de **Ant-c** k* *Ant-s-aur* *Ant-t* apis k* arg-met k* arg-n arn k* *Ars* k* ars-i k* ars-s-f k2 asc-t *Aur* k* aur-ar k2 aur-i k2 aur-m aur-s k2 bamb-a stb2.de• *Bar-c* k* bar-i k2 *Bar-m* bar-s k2 *Bell* k* berb borx k* *Bov* k* brom bros-gau mrc1 brucel sa3• *Bry* k* cadm-s **Calc** k* *Calc-f* *Calc-p* *Calc-s* calc-sil k2 cann-s b2.de* canth k* caps k* carb-an k* *Carb-v* k* *Carbn-s* **Caust** k* cham k* chel k* chinin-s chord-umb rly4• *Cic* k* cinnb *Cist* clem k* cocc b2.de* colch b7.de coli rly4• coloc k* com *Con* k* crot-h k* *Crot-t* k* cystein-l rly4• dig b2.de* **Dulc** k* elaps eug euph k* *Fago* ferr bg2 ferr-ma *Fl-ac* fuma-ac rly4• galeoc-c-h gms1• gels ger-i rly4• *Graph* k* guaj hell k* *Hep* k* hydr hyos b2.de* ign k* iod ip kali-ar *Kali-bi* k* **Kali-br** k* **Kali-c** k* kali-chl *Kali-i* kali-m k2 kali-n b2.de* kali-p *Kali-s* kali-sil k2 **Kreos** k* lac-ac lac-c *Lach* k* lappa br1 laur b2.de* **Led** k* lith-c bg2 *Luna* kg1• *Lyc* k* m-arct b2.de mag-c k* *Mag-m* k* mang k* med k* melal-alt gya4 **Merc** k* merc-c **Mez** k* morb jl2 morg-p pte1*• morph *Mur-ac* k* *Nat-ar* *Nat-c* k* **Nat-m** k* nat-p nat-pyru rly4• nat-s nat-sil fd3.de• neon srj5• nicc nicc-met sk4• *Nit-ac* k* nux-m b7.de nux-v k* olnd b2.de* orot-ac rly4• oxal-a rly4• pall par k* **Petr** k* petr-ra shn4• *Ph-ac* k* phenac c2 *Phos* k* phyt pic-ac plan plb b7.de plut-n srj7• pneu jl2 **Psor** k* **Puls** k* **Rhus-t** k* *Rhus-v* ruta k* sabad b2.de* sabin b2.de* sang sars k* sel k* seneg **Sep** k* *Sil* k* spong k* stann b4.de *Staph* k* stront-c b2.de* suis-hep rly4• suis-pan rly4• sul-ac b2.de* sul-i k2 **Sulph** k* suprar rly4• tarax b2.de* tarent ter thuj k* tritic-vg fd5.de urt-u valer vanil fd5.de *Verat* k* *Viol-o* *Viol-t* b2.de* zinc k* [spect dfg1]

- **both sides** | **symmetrical**: nept-m lsd2.fr
- **night**: *Ars* *Mag-m*
  - **warm** room agg.: mag-m
- **accompanied** by | **coryza**: mez ptk1

Eruptions: ...

- **acne**: *(↗SKIN - Eruptions - acne)* agar st ail c2 ambr bro1* *Ant-c* k* ant-s-aur c1* *Ant-t* bro1 anthraci c2* arge-pl rwt5• arist-cl sp1 *Ars* k* *Ars-br* c2* *Ars-i* k* ars-s-f k2 ars-s-r c2* asim bro1 *Aster* c2* **Aur** aur-m k2 aur-s wbt2• bac jl2 bar-c k* bar-s k2 bell k* bell-p c2* berb hr1 *Berb-a* bro1 bov bro1* brom dgt1* bros-gau mrc1 bufo gk *Calc* calc-f sp1 calc-p bro1* *Calc-pic* bro1 *Calc-s* k* **Calc-sil** k* carb-ac c1* **Carb-an** k* **Carb-v** k* **Carbn-s** k* carc mg1.de* **Caust** k* chel k* chim c2 chir-fl gya2 chlorpr mtf11 chord-umb rly4• cic bro1* cimic bro1 clem bro1 cob bro1 *Con* k* *Cop* k* cortico tpw7* cortiso sp1* *Crot-h* k* crot-t bro1 des-ac rbp6 dios c2 dulc st echi bro1 *Eug* k* **Fl-ac** st foll mtf11 glon br1* *Glycyr-g* cte1• gran bro1 **Graph** c2* hed sp1 **Hep** k* hir st *Hydrc* bro1 ign c2 ind bro1 indg c2 ins br1 iod k* *Jug-c* c2* *Jug-r* c2* **Kali-ar** bro1* **Kali-bi** a1* **Kali-br** k* kali-c bro1* *Kali-i* hr1* kali-m c2* *Kreos* k* lac-e hm2• *Lach* k* lappa c2* led k* limen-b-c hm2• **Lyc** bro1* mag-c st mag-m st maland c2 med k* *Merc* st* moni rfm1• morg-p pte1• mur-ac st nabal bro1 nat-br bro1 nat-c st **Nat-m** k ●* nat-p st nept-m lsd2.fr nicc-met sk4• *Nit-ac* k* nux-m c1 **Nux-v** k* olnd bro1 ozone sde2• *Ph-ac* k* **Phos** st pic-ac c2 pin-con oss2• pix c2 pseuts-m oss1• *Psor* k* **Puls** k ●* querc-r svu1• rad-br bro1 (non:rad-met) **Rhod** st **Rhus-t** st *Ros-d* wla1 sabin k* sanic k* **Sars** st sel k* **SEP** k ●* **Sil** k* staph bro1 sul-i k* sulfa sp1 **Sulph** k ●* sumb c2* **Syph** st* tere-la rly4• **Teucr** st *Thuj* k* tritic-vg fd5.de *Tub* k* tub-r vn* (non:uran-met k) uran-n urin c1* urol-h rwt• vac jl2 vinc c2 x-ray sp1 **Zinc** st
  - **left** more than right: pitu-a ft
  - **accompanied** by | **diabetes** (See GENERALS - Diabetes mellitus - accompanied - acne)
  - **cachexia**; in: ars bro1 carb-v bro1 nat-m bro1 sil bro1
  - **cheese**; from: nux-v k2*
  - **chronic**: merc mrr1
  - **coffee** agg.: psor al1
  - **constipation**; with: calc-sil vh
  - **cosmetics**; from: bov br1*
  - **cystic**: nit-ac mrr1
  - **drunkards**; in: ant-c bro1 ars j bar-c bro1 carbn-s k2 kreos j lach j *Led* bro1 *Nux-v* bro1 puls j rhus-r mp1• rhus-t bro1 sulph j*
  - **fair** women: kreos c1
  - **fat** | **agg.**: psor al1
  - **fire**, near a: *Ant-c*
  - **gastric** complaints; with (See stomach)
  - **girls**; in anemic: ars-br j aster j bar-c j calc j calc-p bro1 graph j hep j kali-c j nat-c j nat-m j sabin j sel j sulph j thuj j
  - **glands**; with swelling of: brom bro1 calc-s bro1 merc bro1
  - **heated**; from becoming: *Caust*
  - **indurated**: eug br1
  - **intestinal** decomposition; from: skat br1
  - **kalium** iodide; from abuse of: aur bro1
  - **masturbation**; from: crot-h ptk1 ph-ac ptk1
  - **meat** agg.: psor al1
  - **menses**:
    - **after** | **agg.**: med ptk1
    - **before** | **agg.**: arist-cl mg graph bg* mag-m ptk1 ozone sde2• petr-ra shn4• pitu-a ft* psor ptk1 sep hr1*
    - **delayed**: crot-h ptk1
    - **during**:
      - **agg.**: cycl kr1 dulc kr1 kali-br gk mag-m k13 psor al1* sang mha
        - **scanty**: sang ptk1
    - **irregular**: aur-m-n bro1 bell bro1 bell-p bro1 berb bro1 *Berb-a* bro1 calc bro1 *Cimic* bro1 con bro1 eug bro1 *Graph* bro1 kali-br bro1 kali-c bro1 kreos bro1 nat-m bro1 psor bro1 *Puls* bro1 *Sang* bro1 sars bro1 thuj bro1 verat bro1
  - **mercury**; from abuse of: kali-i bro1 mez bro1 nit-ac bro1
  - **painful**: arn ptk eug br1
  - **papules**; with indurated: agar bro1 arn bro1 ars-i bro1 berb bro1 bov bro1 brom bro1* *Carb-an* bro1 cic tl1 cob bro1 con bro1 *Eug* bro1 iod bro1 *Kali-br* bro1 *Kali-i* bro1 nat-br bro1 nit-ac bro1 rob bro1 *Sulph* bro1 thuj bro1
  - **persistent**: bac jl2 hir st
  - **pregnancy** agg.; during: *Bell* bro1 sabin bro1 sars bro1 sep bro1

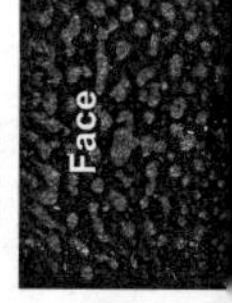

- **puberty**; at: podo fd3.de•
- **punctata**; acne: *(↗comedones)* ars hr1* aster vs* bell rwp2 calc hr1 carb-an cp1* dios hl1* grat hr1* hep hr1* hydr hr1* kali-br hs1* nat-c c1* nat-m hr1* nit-ac tt1* ph-ac he1* rhus-t sne sul-i c1 sulph j2* sumb hr1*
- **pustular**: berb ptk1 kali-br tl1 merc mrr1 morg-g pte1• sul-i ptk1 vac jl2 vario jl2
- **rheumatism**; with: led bro1 rhus-t bro1
- **rosacea**: agar kr1* alum b2.de* *Ars* k* *Ars-br* bro1* ars-i c2* aur k* aur-ar k2 *Aur-m* k* aur-s k2 bell bro1 bufo bg2 *Calc* b2.de* *Calc-p* k* **Calc-sil** cann-s b2.de* canth k* *Caps* k* carb-ac k* **Carb-an** k* **Carb-v** k* carbn-s **Caust** k* chel chrysar bwa3* *Cic* k* clem k* cortico mtf11 **Eug** k* euphr bg2 guare hr1 hep mrr1 *Hydr-ac* k* *Hydrc* c2* iris kali-bi bg2 kali-br k* kali-c bg2 kali-i bro1* *Kreos* k* **Lach** k* lap-la sde8.de• led k* *Mez* k* morg-p pte1*• nit-ac bg2 nux-v c2* ov c2* *Petr* k* ph-ac bg2 phos bg2 plb k* **Psor** k* *Rad-br* k* (non:rad-met k) rhus-r bro1 **Rhus-t** k* *Ruta* k* sars xyz61 *Sep* k* *Sil* k* sul-ac k* *Sul-i* bro1 sulo-ac c1* *Sulph* k* syc pte1*• thuj bg2 *Tub* tub-m jl2 *Verat* k* viol-o k* *Viol-t* k*
  - **bluish**: *Lach Sulph*
  - **groups**, in: **Caust** k*
  - **Nose**, on: ars-br br1 calc-p calc-pic vh cann-s carb-an h2* **Caust** kali-i bg3* *Psor* rhus-t bg3* sars ptk1
- **sadness**; with (See MIND - Sadness - acne)
- **scars**; with: carb-an ptk1 cop ptk1 kali-br ptk1 merc mrr1 *Sil* mrr1 thuj mrr1
  - **red**: bell mrr1
  - **unsightly**: carb-an bro1* cop hr1* kali-br bro1*
- **scrofulous** persons; in: bar-c bro1 brom bro1 *Calc* bro1 calc-p bro1 con bro1 *Iod* bro1 merc bro1 mez bro1 sil bro1 *Sulph* bro1
- **sexual** excesses; with: *Aur* bro1 calc bro1 eug j kali-br bro1 *Ph-ac* bro1 rhus-t bro1 sep bro1 thuj bro1
- **spring** agg.; in: ars-br vh
- **stomach** complaints; with: *Ant-c* bro1 *Carb-v* bro1 cimic bro1 lyc bro1 *Nux-v* bro1 puls bro1 rob bro1
- **sugar** agg.: psor al1
- **symmetrical** distribution; with a: arn bro1
- **syphilis**; from: aur bro1 *Kali-i* bro1 merc bro1 nit-ac bro1
- **tubercular** | **children**; in: tub bro1
- **tuberous**: tub-r jl2
- **vaccination**; from: thuj tl1
- **wet** cold | **agg.**: bell-p tl1
- **young** people; in fleshy: tub jl2 vac jl2
  - **coarse** habits and bluish, red pustules on face, chest and shoulders; with: kali-br bro1

○ • **Chin**: bros-gau mrc1 chir-fl gya2 *Hydr* jug-r vml3• limen-b-c hrn2* prot dx1* sanic mrr1 sulfa sp1 thuj sp verat *Viol-t* k*
  - **delivery**; after: sep bro1
- **Forehead**: acon-ac rly4• agar sne ant-c *Ars* k* aur aur-ar k2 bamb-a stb2.de• bar-c bell *Calc* calc-pic dx1 *Caps* **Carb-an** **Carb-v** **Carbn-s** **Caust** chir-fl gya2 *Cic* clem ger-i rly4• **Hep** *Hydr* hr1 kali-bi a1 *Kali-br* a1* kola stb3• *Kreos* k* led moni rfm1• *Nat-m* *Nit-ac* **Nux-v** k* *Ph-ac* **Psor** **Rhus-t** ros-d wla1 **Sep** **Sil** k* streptoc rly4• sulfonam ks2 **Sulph** k* thuj sne tritic-vg fd5.de viol-t
  - **sticking** pain; with: led br1
- **Lips**: aids nl2• borx mp1• cadm-s caps hydr psor mp1• sars mp1• sul-i mp1•
  - **Lower**: aids nl2•
    - **left**: aids nl2•
- **Nose**: am-c mp1• ars bro1* ars-br bro1* aster bro1* borx bro1* calc-p cann-s caps **Caust** k* chord-umb rly4• clem bro1* elaps bro1* ger-i rly4• graph kali-br bro1* nat-c bro1* petr-ra shn4• ros-d wla1 sel sep mp1• sil bro1* *Sulph* k* thuj mp1• zing bro1*
  - **Below**: caps hr1
  - **Tip**: am-c bro1 caust bro1 sep bro1

- **acrid** (See excoriating)
- **air**; in open | **amel.**: sel rsj9•
- **angioedema**: *(↗SKIN - Eruptions - angioedema)* apis mrr1*
- **biting**: bry merc nat-m plat sil vanil fd5.de
- **blackish**: ars spig
- **bleeding**:
  - **scratched**; when: *Dulc* hr1 lach k2 *Merc Mez* par *Petr Rhus-t Sulph*
  - **touched** on nose; when: aids nl2• *Brom Merc* tritic-vg fd5.de
- **blisters**: canth k2

○ • **Forehead**: bit-ar wht1•
- **blotches**: alumn ant-t hr1 apis arg-n ars bar-c *Berb-a* bro1 calc canth *Carb-an* carb-v chel chlol hr1 con cop k* cund hr1 dig dulc elaps *Fl-ac* k* *Graph* k* *Guaj* hell *Hep* iod *Kali-bi* k* kali-c k* *Kali-i* k* lach lat-h bnm5• *Led* k* *Lyc* k* mag-c mag-m k* med hr1* merc nat-c nat-p hr1 nux-v k* op k* *Phos* k* phyt k* podo fd3.de• puls rhus-g tmo3• rhus-r *Rhus-t* k* sabin k* sep k* sulph sumb viol-t
  - **night**: *Mag-m* k*
  - **itching**: graph k* sep h2*
  - **menses** agg., before: mag-m
  - **warm** bed agg.: mag-m
  - **washing** agg.; after: am-c phyt k* podo fd3.de•

○ • **Chin**: bry carb-an euph hep mag-m olnd rhus-g tmo3•
  - **Forehead**: arn a1 ars a1 *Mag-m* hr1 nat-c
  - **Jaws** | **Lower**: stann staph
  - **Lips**: arg-met ars bar-c caust con hep kali-i mag-m nat-c sep sil sulph
  - **Mouth**:
    - **Corner**:
      - **left**: cassia-s ccrh1•
        - **itching**: cassia-s ccrh1•
  - **Nose**: bell brass a1 iod rhus-g tmo3•
    - **Root**: cassia-s ccrh1•
- **boils**: alum k* am-c k* anan k* ant-c k* arn k* bar-c k* bar-i k2 bar-s k2 *Bell* k* bell-p sp1 brom b4a.de* bry k* *Calc* k* *Calc-p* c2* calc-s k* calc-sil k2 carb-an b4.de carb-v k* chin k* cina k* coli rly4• coloc k* *Hep* k* hyos k* iod k* iris kali-ar k* kali-br **Kali-i** k* *Lappa* laur b7.de* led k* mand sp1 med bro1 *Mez* k* mur-ac k* nat-c k* nat-m k* nat-pyru rly4• nit-ac k* pic-ac bg2 rhus-t bg2 rhus-v k* sars k* *Sil* k* suis-hep rly4• sul-i k2 *Sulph* k* suprar rly4• tub a1 ven-m rsj12• [bell-p-sp dcm1]
  - **blood** boils, small: alum k* iris *Sil* k*
  - **menses**; during: med br1
  - **painful**: *Hep*
  - **repeating**: alum h2
  - **small** | **menses**; during: med ptk1

○ • **Cheeks**: suis-hep rly4•
  - **right**: luf-op rsj5• sel rsj9•
- **Chin**: am-c k* caust bg2 cob k* hep k* lap-la sde8.de• lyc nat-c h2* nat-pyru rly4• nit-ac k* sil k* suis-hep rly4• suprar rly4•
  - **right** side of: cob k* nat-c a1
  - **Under**: carb-v
- **Forehead**: alum a1 am-c k* bar-c h2* carb-an h2* lac-h sk4• led k* mag-c k* phos k* ptel c1 rhus-v a1 sep
  - **Eyes**; above the: calc-s nat-m
- **Jaws** | **Lower**: carb-v b4a.de
- **Lips**: *Hep* k* *Lach* k* nat-c petr
- **Mouth**; corner of: am-c **Ant-c**
- **Nose**: *(↗NOSE - Boils)* acon k* alum k* am-c k* anan cadm-s k* carb-an coli rly4• con cur bro1 *Hep* k* mag-m k* phos sars sil k* tub a1*
  - **pus**; with greenish: tub jl2
  - **small** | **crops**: tub mtf33
  - **Inside**: alum am-c apis ptk1 *Borx* a1 carb-an k* coli rly4• phys a1 pic-ac a1 sep sil k* *Tub* k* vinc bro1
  - **Nostrils**: bac jl2* hir rsj4•
    - **left**: hir rsj4•
  - **Tip**: acon k* am-c k* anan k* apis borx k* carb-an tub al
- **Temples**: mur-ac
  - **right** temple: mur-ac
  - **left** temple: adam skp7•
- **brownish**: dulc k* ruta fd4.de tritic-vg fd5.de vanil fd5.de
- **burning**: alum am-c am-m k* *Anac* ant-c apis *Ars* k* bamb-a stb2.de• bar-c h2* calc *Caust* chinin-s *Cic* euphr graph kali-c led mag-m merc nat-m olib-sac wmh1 phos rat *Rhus-t* ruta fd4.de samb h1* *Sars* seneg *Sep* staph sulfa sp1 sulph k*

- **air** agg.; in open: *Led*
- **scratching** agg.: nat-s sars
- **sleep** without cold applications; cannot: am-m
- **touch** agg.: canth k2
- **warmth**:
  - **amel.** | **heat** amel.: sulfa sp1
- **wet**, when: euphr k*
- **Forehead**: granit-m es1•
- **Lips**: am-c aur bov caust graph mag-m mur-ac nat-m h2* nicc plat rat ruta fd4.de seneg *Staph* sulph
  - **Upper**: hir rsj4•
- **Nose**: alum apis caust graph nat-c nat-m ol-an phos

- **cancerous**: *Rhus-t* b7a.de
- **carbuncles**: | **Chin**; on: *Lyc*
- **cold** air agg.: *Ars* dulc kali-c bg2*
- **comedones**: (↗*acne - punctata*) *Abrot* k* **Ant-c** bg2 *Ars* k* aster vh aur k* aur-ar k2 aur-s k2 bar-c bg2* *Bell* k* brom bg2 *Bry* k* *Calc* k* calc-sil k2* *Carb-v* k* **Carbn-s** chel cic bro1 *Coloc* b4a.de dig k* dios hl1 dros k* *Eug* k* **Graph** k* grat hr1 *Hep* k* hydr k* jug-r bro1* kali-bi bg2 **Kali-br** bg2 kali-c bg2 *Lach* bg2 **Lyc** bg2 mez bg2* *Nat-ar* *Nat-c* k* *Nat-m* k* *Nit-ac* k* **Petr** bg2 plb b2.de* **Psor** bg2 *Sabad* k* sabin k* **Sel** k* *Sep* k* *Sil* k* *Sul-i* bg2 **Sulph** k* sumb k* thuj k* *Tub* k*
  - **ulcerating**: dig k* *Sel* *Tub*
  - **Chin**: dros k* jug-r vml3• sulph b4a.de *Tub*
    - **and** upper lip: sulph k*
  - **Forehead**●: **Sulph**
  - **Lips**; upper: sulph b4a.de
  - **Mouth**:
    - **Corners** | **left**: brucel sa3•
  - **Nose**: aur b4a.de dros k* *Graph* k* mez bg2* *Nit-ac* k* *Sabad* b7a.de sabin k* sel k* **Sulph** k ●* sumb **Tub** k ●*
- **confluent**: carb-v cic sarr hl1
- **coppery**: *Ars* **Ars-i** *Aur* aur-ar k2 benz-ac calc **Carb-an** k* *Graph* *Hydr* *Hydrc* *Kali-i* *Lyc* merc *Psor* rhus-t ruta syph k2 verat
  - **spots**; in: carb-an bro1 lyc bro1 *Nit-ac* bro1
  - **Chin**; about: verat k*
  - **Forehead**: *Carb-an* *Lyc*
  - **Nose**: *Carb-an*
- **corrosive**: dig
- **cracks** (See fissures)
- **crusty**, scabby: aethi-a c1 *Anan* *Ant-c* k* **Ars** k* aur-s k2 bar-c bar-m bar-s k2 **Calc** k* calc-i k2 *Carbn-s* *Caust* *Chel* *Cic* k* *Cist* k* *Clem* *Con* cory br1 **Dulc** k* elaps fl-ac *Graph* k* *Hep* k* hyper *Ign* b7a.de jug-c *Kali-bi* lach k2 lappa *Led* *Lith-c* *Lyc* *Merc* merc-i-r **Mez** k* *Mur-ac* nit-ac k2 **Petr** ph-ac *Psor* k* **Rhus-t** k* sars spong fd4.de sul-ac sul-i k2 *Sulph* syph thuj vac *Viol-t* zinc
  - **areola**; with: nit-ac bro1
  - **black**: *Ars*
  - **greenish** yellow: calc h2 *Merc* k* *Petr* k*
  - **offensive**: *Psor* *Rhus-t* hr1
  - **old** people; in: cory br1
  - **saddle**; like a: bufo bg2
  - **serpiginous**: sulph
  - **syphilitic**: kali-bi bg2
  - **thick**: calc mtf33 cic mrr1
  - **white**: calc mtf33 *Mez*
  - **yellow**: *Ant-c* *Calc* *Cic* k* **Dulc** *Hyper* *Merc* *Mez* ph-ac sulph *Viol-t*
  - **Cheeks**: *Ant-c* dulc k2 lith-c ptk1 *Lyc*
  - **Chin**: ant-c br1 *Cic* **Dulc** *Graph* *Mez* *Sep* *Sil* *Sulph* syph
    - **scabs**; elevated white: *Mez*
  - **Eyebrows**: mez mrr1 sep b4a.de
  - **Forehead**: agar b4a.de *Ars* *Calc* carb-v b4a.de clem b4a.de *Dulc* hep b4a.de *Mur-ac* nat-m b4a.de phos b4a.de sulph b4a.de viol-t b7a.de
  - **Lips**: ail bg2 alum h2 am-c tl1 *Apis* *Ars* k* *Arum-t* bg2* berb bry *Cinnb* *Con* kali-p *Merc* merc-c moni jl2 *Mur-ac* k* nat-c h2 nat-m ptk1 *Nux-v* petr k2 **Ph-ac** k* *Phos* b7a.de* *Rhus-t* k* sep bg1* **Sil** k* squil k* staph ptk1 sulph k2* *Ter* valer k* verat vh

- **crusty**, scabby – **Lips**: ...
  - **brown** crusts:
    - **accompanied** by | **blue** and pale spots of mucous membrane of mouth: ars k*
  - **yellow**: cic bg2
  - **Lower** | **Below**: sang hr1
  - **Upper**: arum-t tl1 borx c1 maland jl2 sanic tl1 tub jl2
  - **Margin** of hair: mez mrr1
  - **Mouth**:
    - **Around**: **Graph** hyper *Led* *Merc* *Mez* *Nat-m* **Nit-ac** petr k2 rhus-v
      - **honey**-like: mez tl1
    - **Corners** of: ant-c bov ptk2 **Graph** k* guare kali-p lac-v c1 lap-la sde8.de• merc ptk1 nat-m nit-ac k* *Rhus-t* rhus-v *Sars* thuj ptk1 tub-m jl2
  - **Nose**: ail *Alum* k* am-m bg2 ant-c bg2 ant-t bg2 arg-n bg2 arn bg2 ars bg2 arum-t mtf11 *Aur* k* aur-m-n aur-s k2 bar-c b4.de* bell bg2 borx mtf11 bov b4.de* brom bg2 bry bg2 *Calc* canth bg2 carb-an k* carb-v k* carbn-s *Caust* k* *Cham* bg2 chin *Cic* k* cocc bg2 graph k* hep b4a.de* hyos bg2 hyper ign bg2 *Iod* k* *Kali-bi* bg2 kali-c bg2 lach bg2 *Led* *Lyc* k* mag-c b4.de* *Mag-m* k* mang k* **Merc** k* *Merc-i-r* mez bg2 *Nat-m* k* *Nit-ac* k* *Nux-v* bg2 ph-ac k* phos bg2 psor bg2 puls bg2 ran-b k* rat sangin-n mtf11 sars k* sel bg2 *Sep* k* *Sil* k* *Spig* bg2 spong *Squil* bg2 *Staph* k* stict bg2* stront-c bg2 sul-i k2 *Sulph* k* syph teucr bg2 thuj bg2 tub bg2
    - **extending** to | **Down** lip with deep fissure, very sore and sensitive to touch: *Hep*
    - **Around**: led
    - **Below**: *Ars* b4a.de bar-c k* *Kali-c* k* *Rhus-t* sars k* *Sil* spong fd4.de sulph k*
    - **Inside** and on: *Ant-c* aur borx **Bov** carb-an h2 chel cic crot-t cypra-eg sde6.de• **Graph** *Hep* *Kali-c* **Lach** *Lyc* mag-m *Merc* *Merc-c* *Nat-s* phos **Puls** rat sars **Sep**
    - **Margins**: *Calc-s* kali-bi nit-ac phos sulph
      - **bloody** crusts on margins of nostrils: *Phos*
    - **Tip**: *Carb-an* k* carb-v k* **Caust** k* kali-n b4.de* *Nit-ac* k* sep k* *Sil* k* *Zinc* b4a.de
    - **Under** nose (See below)
    - **Wing**, near the: aur bar-c ptk *Merc-i-r* *Nit-ac* petr rhus-t h1
  - **Temples**: agar b4a.de alum b4a.de* anac b4a.de bar-c b4a.de carb-v b4a.de dros b7a.de *Dulc* *Mur-ac* nat-m b4a.de nux-m b7a.de viol-t b7a.de
  - **Zygoma**: ars *Cist* mag-m
- **desquamating**: am-c bg2 apis k* *Ars* k* *Bell* k* canth k* chinin-s hydr k* hydrog srj2• *Kali-ar* k* kali-s k2 lach k* *Merc* k* nat-m k2 ol-an k* phos k* *Psor* puls k* *Rhus-t* k* rhus-v k* sol-t-ae a1 *Sulph* k* thuj k*
  - **yellow** spot: kali-c h2*
  - **Chin**: sphing kk3.fr
  - **Whiskers**: sphing kk3.fr
- **discharging** | **ichorous**: *Rhus-t* b7a.de
- **dry**: acon-ac rly4• arist-cl sp1 **Ars** bar-ox-suc rly4• choc srj3• chrysar br1 cory br1 kali-i led *Lyc* mim-p rsj8• orot-ac rly4• psor *Sep* spong fd4.de
  - **old** people; in: cory br1
  - **Forehead**: granit-m es1•
- **eczema**: alum alum-p k2 *Anac* k* *Ant-c* k* arist-cl sp1 **Ars** k* ars-i k2 *Aur-m-n* wbt2• bac bro1 bar-c k* bar-s k2 bell-p sp1 *Borx* k* **Calc** k* calc-ar k2 *Calc-s* calc-sil k2 *Carb-ac* bro1 *Carb-an* bg2 carb-v cassia-s ccrh1• *Caust* *Chel* bg2 chin cr **Cic** k* cist k2 clem coloc bro1 *Con* bg2 corn bro1 **Crot-t** k* cur cycl dros gk **Dulc** k* ferr-i *Fl-ac* **Graph** k* **Hep** k* hom-xyz mgm• hyper bro1* *Iris* *Kali-ar* k* kali-sil k2 *Kreos* bg2* lac-d c1* *Lach* bg2 lec br1 led bro1 *Lyc* k* *Merc* k* merc-i-r merc-pr-r bro1 *Mez* k* mur-ac k* nat-m k* nat-s k2 oci-sa sp1 oxyte-chl mtf11 parth vml3• *Petr* *Ph-ac* bg2 phos k* podo fd3.de• **Psor** k* ran-b **Rhus-t** k* **Sars** k* *Sep* k* sil k* staph k* sul-ac *Sul-i* bro1 **Sulph** k* syc fmm1• *Syph* vinc k* *Viol-t* k* x-ray sp1
  - **accompanied** by | **impetigo**: bac mtf11
  - **bleeding**: alum *Ars* dulc *Hep* *Lyc* *Merc* *Petr* psor sep *Sulph*
  - **burning**: *Cic* *Viol-t*
  - **children**; in: graph mtf33
    - **infants**: dulc k2 *Morg* fmm1• morg-p fmm1* nat-hp mtf11 syc pte1*•
    - **scrofulous** children; in: cur mtf11

Face

- **dry**: cassia-s ccrh1•
- **fetid**: lyc
- **heat** of stove agg.: **Ant-c**
- **honey**, like dried: *Ant-c* **Cic** mez
- **itching**: carb-ac mtf11 cassia-s ccrh1• pix mtf11
- **moist**: *(↗SKIN - Eruptions - eczema - discharging)* **Calc** mtf33 *Cic* **Graph** kali-sil k2 **Lyc** *Petr Psor Rhus-t*
- **nursing** mothers; in: sep
- **weeping**: bell-p sp1

○ • **Beard**, of: ars-i ptk1
  - **washing** agg.: ars-i ptk2
- **Cheeks**: cic k2 dros gk ger-i rly4•
- **Chin**: borx *Cic* graph kali-sil k2 *Merc-i-r* k* morg-p pte1*• phos rhus-t sep
- **Ear**; spreading from: ars
- **Forehead**: hydr bg morg-p pte1*• nat-p k2 nit-ac k13 sulph k13
- **Lips**: *Ant-c* bro1 aur-m bro1 bov bro1 calc bro1 graph bro1 kali-sil k2 lyc bro1 *Mez* bro1 *Rhus-v* bro1
- **Margins** of hair: hydr ptk1 nat-sil fd3.de• **Sulph**
- **Mouth**:
  - **Around**: ant-c br1 kali-sil k2 led tl1 *Mez* mur-ac *Nat-m*
    - **cough**; causing: led tl1
  - **Corners** of: *Arund Graph Hep* lyc *Rhus-t* sil
- **Nose**: *Ant-c* bals-p bro1 caust *Cist* k* iris bro1 kali-sil k2 nit-ac bg2 rhus-t k* sars bro1 *Sep* k* spig bg2 sulph k*
  - **fissure** of right wing: *Thuj*
  - **Wings**; on: ant-c bro1* bals-p bro1 bar-c bro1 *Graph* bro1 *Petr* bro1
- **Occiput**; spreading from: *Lyc* sil

- **edges** raised: cortiso sp1
- **elevations**: bell cic cop nat-ar pic-ac
  - **indurated**: rhus-v
  - **reddish**: phos h2* pic-ac rhus-v
  - **vesicles** | **elevated** vesicles in nursing infants with aphthous stomatitis; with: corn br1
- **erythema** (See Discoloration - red - erythema)
- **excoriating**: calc-f gm1 dulc fd4.de *Graph* hell **Merc** *Mez* **Petr** *Phos Psor Sulph* viol-t

○ • **Cheeks**: bros-gau mrc1
- **Chin**: ant-c bros-gau mrc1 hep mang verat
- **Nose**: agar bov caust graph phos sil

- **fine**: aur ptk1* con h2*

○ • **Forehead**: aur mtf33
- **Lips**: aur mtf33

- **fissures**: calc **Graph** *Merc* mim-p rsj8• nicc nit-ac *Petr Psor Sil* k* sulph
  - **bleeding**: petr

○ • **Nose**: beryl sp1

- **furfuraceous** | **Whiskers**; in: kali-ar
- **granular**: kreos b7a.de
  - **yellow**: ant-c b7a.de
- **hard**: anac crot-h dulc fd4.de falco-pe nl2• mag-c puls verat
- **herpes**: aeth mrr1 *Agar* agath-a nl2• alum k* *Am-c* am-m k* anac anac-oc bro1 *Anan* androc srj1• apis bro1 arn br1 *Ars* k* *Bar-c* bar-s k2 bell *Bov* bry bufo *Calc* calc-f k* *Calc-s* calc-sil k2 canth bro1 caps k* *Carb-an Carb-v Carbn-s* caust k* chel *Cic* clem bro1 coloc *Con* k* crot-t cycl hr1 diph-t-tpt jl2 *Dulc* k* dys pte1*• elaps euph bro1 gink-b sbd1• *Graph Hep* kali-ar *Kali-bi Kali-c Kali-i* k* kali-s kali-sil k2 kola stb3• kreos lac-e hrn2• **Lach** k* **Led** lim bro1 *Lyc* k* *Merc* morg-g fmm1• *Nat-ar Nat-c* k* **Nat-m** k* *Nat-s* nicc *Nit-ac* k* petr ph-ac phos plac rzf5• *Psor* ran-b bro1 **Rhus-t** k* ruta fd4.de sabad k* sarr k* **Sep** k* *Sil* spig gk spong *Sulph* k* syc pte1*• tarent k* thal-xyz srj8• thuj tritic-vg fd5.de vanil fd5.de
  - **left**: morg-g pte1*•
  - **burning** and itching; with: *Mez* vh
  - **circinatus**: anag bar-c calc k* cinnb clem dulc *Graph* hell kali-chl lith-c lyc med k2 *Nat-c Nat-m* phos *Sep* sulph tarent *Tell* k* **Tub**
  - **cough**; with spasmodic: arn br1*

- **herpes**: ...
  - **mealy**: **Ars** bry cic kreos *Lyc* merc nit-ac sulph thuj
  - **neuralgia**; with facial: *Kalm* vh
  - **scurfy**: anac anan calc *Graph* kreos led lyc phos *Rhus-t* sep *Sulph*
  - **tonsurans**: calc bg2 cic bg2 *Graph* bg2 sep bg2 sul-i bg2

○ • **Cheeks**: alum am-c ambr anac ant-t bov carbn-s k2 caust chel **Con** k* dulc graph hep kali-i kreos lach merc nat-m nicc ph-ac psor tl1 sars sil *Spong* staph stront-c thuj
- **Chin**: am-c ars bro1 *Bov* carb-v caust bro1 chel dulc graph bro1 mez bro1 *Nat-m* k* nux-v ph-ac sars k* *Sil* k* spong fd4.de
- **Forehead**: agar hr1 ars-br vh bad k* bar-c borx caps k* dulc tarent k*
- **Lips**: *Ars* ptk1 dulc ptk1 manc ptk1 **Nat-m** ptk1 phos ptk1 *Rhus-t* ptk1 sep ptk1 sul-i ptk1
  - **About**: *(↗vesicles - lips - fever)* agar k* *Agath-a* nl2• aids nl2• allox tpw4* anac arist-cl sp1 *Ars* k* asc-t bell-p sp1 borx k* brom bros-gau mrc1 *Calc-f* k* canth *Caps* bro1 carb-v caust chel choc srj3• cit-ac rly4• colch rsj2• conv br1 crot-t *Dulc* k* elaps gk frax bro1 *Graph* k* *Hep* k* hyos h1* ip kali-p kola stb3• lac-c lac-h htj1• lach mand sp1 *Med* k* melal-alt gya4 mim-p rsj8• moni rfm1• musca-d szs1 nat-ar nat-c k* **Nat-m** k* *Nicc* nit-ac gk ozone sde2• *Par* petr k2 ph-ac plac rzf5• podo fd3.de• *Propl* ub1• ptel gk **Rhus-t** k* rhus-v bro1 sal-fr sle1• sars **Sep** k* sil spig gk spong sul-i bro1 sulph k* tell rsj10• thuj mrr1* tritic-vg fd5.de *Tub* k* ulm-c jsj8• upa bro1 urol-h rwt• urt-u [bell-p-sp dcm1 heroin sdj2]
    - **black**: tub ptk1
    - **children**; in: tub jl2
    - **hard** small: calc-f ptk1
    - **menses** | **before** | **agg.**: germ-met srj5•
      - **during** | **agg.**: sars ptk1
    - **recurrent**: med jl2
  - **Above**: phos h2*
  - **Inner** side: med ptk1
  - **Lower**: musca-d szs1
  - **Margins**: kola stb3•
  - **Upper**: agar aids nl2• aur sne carc gk6* gink-b sbd1• kali-p fd1.de• podo fd3.de• sars symph fd3.de• tritic-vg fd5.de vanil fd5.de [heroin sdj2]
    - **right** | **painful**: med c1
- **Mouth**:
  - **Around**: am-c anac ars aur sne *Borx* k* cic con *Hep Hydr* sne kreos mag-c med nat-c **Nat-m** k* olib-sac wmh1 *Par* parathyr jl2 petr k2 phos *Rhus-t* k* *Sep* k* spig gk sulph thuj mtf11
    - **cutting**: phos h2*
    - **stitching**: phos h2*
  - **Corners** of: bros-gau mrc1 carb-v choc srj3• dioxi rbp6 *Hydr* sne lac-e hrn2• *Lyc* med musca-d szs1 nat-m mrr1 ph-ac phos h2* samb bat1• sep spong fd4.de *Sulph*
    - **Below**: *Calc-f Nat-m*
- **Nose**: acon-l bro1 **Aeth** k* agath-a nl2• aloe alum bro1 aur bell bro1 bell-p sp1 *Calc* carc gk6* chel conv br1 gins graph iod lyc morg-g pte1*• mur-ac bro1 *Nat-c Nat-m* k* *Nit-ac* ph-ac phys br1 *Rhus-t Ros-d* wla1 *Sep* k* sil spig sulph k*
  - **itching**: nit-ac h2*
  - **Across** nose: sep *Sulph*
    - **saddle**; like a: sulph c1
  - **Corners** of: nat-m mrr1
  - **Nostrils**: phys br1
  - **Tip** of: aeth c1* clem bro1 conv bro1 dulc bro1 nat-m bro1
  - **Wings** of: dulc bro1 leptos-ih jl2 nat-m bro1 *Nit-ac* phys bro1 sil bro1
    - **menses**; during | **beginning** of menses: gink-b sbd1•
- **Temples**: *Alum* k* cadm-s *Psor* k*
- **Whiskers**: agar calc lach *Nat-m* k* *Nit-ac* k* sil

- **herpes** zoster: apis mrr1 mez mrr1
  - **left** side: *Apis* mrr1
- **impetigo**: **Ant-c** k* ars **Calc** *Cic Con Crot-t Dulc Graph Hep Kali-bi* kreos *Lyc Merc Mez Nit-ac Rhus-t* k* sep vac jl2 *Viol-t*

• **accompanied** by | **eczema** (See eczema - accompanied - impetigo)
○ • **Cheeks**: ferr-i br1
• **Forehead**: ant-c kreos led *Merc* k* *Rhus-t* sep sulph *Viol-t*
• **Lips**; around: tarent
- **irritating**: aethi-a c1
- **itching**: agar aium-p k2 am-c *Anac Ant-c Ars* bufo *Calc Calc-s* caps *Carbn-s* cassia-s ccrh1• *Caust* chel chinin-s *Cic* con dig euphr flor-p rsj3• granit-m es1• *Graph Jug-c Kali-bi Kali-c Kali-i* k* led luna kg1• *Lyc* k* *Mag-m* marb-w es1• *Merc* **Mez** k* mim-p rsj8• nat-c *Nat-m* nat-pyru rly4• nat-s k2 nicc *Nit-ac Olnd* orot-ac rly4• parth vml3• *Petr Phos* k* psor k* **Rhus-t** k* ruta fd4.de sanic *Sars* **Sep** squil h1* stann h2* staph k* stram **Sulph** teucr thuj vanil fd5.de *Viol-t* zinc
• **night**: *Mez Sulph Viol-t*
• **scratching**, unchanged by: am-c
• **warmth** agg.: *Ant-c* euphr *Mez Psor Sulph* teucr
○ • **Chin**: dulc lyc mag-m h2* nat-c nat-m nux-v par sars sep sulph k2 thuj zinc
• **Eyebrows**: mez mrr1
• **Forehead**: caps h1* granit-m es1• ruta fd4.de *Sars*
⁝ **menses**; during: eug bro1 psor bro1 sang bro1 sars bro1
• **Lips**: am-c calc graph h2* mag-m h2* nit-ac h2* sil h2* vanil fd5.de
• **Malar** bones: nat-pyru rly4•
• **Margin** of hair: mez mrr1
• **Mouth**; around: borx c1
• **Nose**: apis carb-v iod lyc h2* nat-c nit-ac pall phel sil squil *Sulph*
⁝ **Below**: nat-pyru rly4• sars h2*
• **Temples**: zinc h2*
- **leprous** spots: alum bg2 *Ant-t Graph* mag-c bg2 phos **Sec**
○ • **Chin**, on: calc hir rsj4•
- **menses** | **before** | **agg.**: dream-p sdj1• dulc k2* *Mag-m* **Nat-m** ●* nux-m sf1.de sapin a1 sars k* **Sep** ●*
• **during** | **agg.**: am-c ptk1 calc dream-p sdj1• dulc k* eug graph k* kali-c gt1 nux-m gt1 psor sang sars gt1*
- **menstrual** complaints; with: sang c1
- **miliary**: ail anan k* ars bell k* cham k* *Euph* bg2 euphr hep k* hura ip *Lach* b7.de* manc k* par phos h2* rheum b7.de* sarr tab tarent k* teucr b7.de* verat k*
○ • **Forehead**: plut-n srj7•
- **moist**: ant-c k* *Ars* ars-br vh *Ars-i Calc* k* *Carb-v Carbn-s* carc xxb caust cham cic k* *Clem* k* con **Dulc** k* **Graph** k* *Hep* k* kreos **Lyc** k* *Merc* **Mez** k* nat-ar nat-c k* nat-m k2 nit-ac olnd *Petr* ph-ac *Psor* k* **Rhus-t** k* sars *Sep Sil* squil *Sulph* k* *Thuj* vinc *Viol-t* k*
• **fetid**: ars-br vh cic merc
• **scratching** agg.; after: *Kali-c Sars* sulph h2*
• **yellow**: lyc rhus-t *Viol-t*
○ • **Eyebrows**: mez mrr1
• **Forehead** | **menses**; before: sars h1*
• **Margin** of hair: mez mrr1
• **Nose**: aur-m-n carb-v **Graph** nat-c thuj
⁝ **Septum**: vinc
⁝ **Wings**: thuj
- **mottled**: *Calc* bg2 *Merc* bg2 *Nat-c* bg2
- **nodular**: bry *Chel* k* cic irid-met srj5• kali-ar rhus-t
○ • **Forehead**: ars h2* caust ptk1 *Cocc* hr1 rhus-t hr1
• **Nose**: bar-m nat-m
- **painful**: (↗*smarting*) aethi-a c1 alum apis *Bell* berb calc cic k* clem eug falco-pe nl2• hydrog srj2• kali-br a1 led luna kg1• petr-ra shn4• phos k* plat ruta fd4.de sep staph k* **Sulph** vanil fd5.de
• **night**: viol-t
• **spots**: luna kg1•
• **touch** agg.: ant-c bell cic a1 *Hep* hydrog srj2• irid-met srj5• lach led nat-c h2 nit-ac par petr-ra shn4• sabad sep h2* stann staph a1 sulph h2* valer vanil fd5.de
○ • **Chin**: **Sulph**
• **Lip**; upper: clem h2*
• **Nose**: calad caps cassia-s ccrh1• cor-r mag-c phos sel sep

- **painful** – **Nose**: ...
⁝ **cold** applications | **amel.**: cassia-s ccrh1•
⁝ **stinging**: apis kl squil kl
⁝ **touch** agg.: chin clem kali-c petr petr-ra shn4• ph-ac
- **papular**: allox tpw3* aur borx *Calc* carb-v *Crot-h* cub c1 dig h2* dulc h2* galeoc-c-h gms1• *Gels Hydrc Kali-c Kali-i Lyc* ol-an k* *Petr Pic-ac* plut-n srj7• sabal c1 sep sil staph a1 sulfa sp1 syph zinc
• **hard**: glycyr-g cte1•
⁝ **menses**; before: glycyr-g cte1•
• **painful**: *Calc*
• **roseolous** papules without fever or itching: cub c1
○ • **Cheeks**: borx hr1*
• **Chin**: allox tpw3 borx hr1* calc caust *Crot-h Lyc* merc nit-ac prot jl2 *Sars*
• **Forehead**: cycl a1 mur-ac a1
• **Lip**, upper: prot jl2 zinc
• **Nose** | **Tip**: galeoc-c-h gms1•
• **Nostril**:
⁝ **right** | **Inside**: chen-a hr1
- **patches**: calc *Graph* hydrog srj2• *Kali-bi* k* lac-c k* *Merc Nux-m* k* phos k* puls sec sep stram k* sumb
• **menses**; during: nux-m hr1*
○ • **Cheek**:
⁝ **red**:
: **bed**; when going to: cortiso tpw7
: **heat**: cortiso tpw7
: **scratching** agg.: cortiso tpw7
: **washing** agg.: cortiso tpw7
- **pimples**: agar k* agath-a nl2• aids nl2• alum k* alum-p k2 am-m ambr k* anac b4.de* anan *Ant-c* k* apis arg-met b7.de* *Ars* k* *Ars-i* ars-s-f k2 arum-t aster *Aur* k* aur-ar k2 aur-i k2 aur-s k2 bamb-a stb2.de• bar-c k* bar-i k2 bar-m bar-s k2 *Bell* k* berb borx k* *Bov* k* **Calc** k* *Calc-p* k* *Calc-s* calc-sil k2 caps b7.de* **Carb-an** k* *Carb-v* k* *Carbn-s* **Caust** k* *Chel* k* *Cic* k* clem k* cocc b7.de* coli rly4• coloc *Con* k* crot-h cub vh cycl hr1 cystein-l rly4• dioxi rbp6 dream-p sdj1• dros k* dulc fd4.de **Eug** k* fuma-ac rly4• gels k* ger-i rly4• *Glon* granit-m es1• **Graph** k* ham fd3.de* *Hep* k* hir rsj4• hura hydr *Hydrc* k* indg k* iod k* jug-r *Kali-ar* k* **Kali-c** k* kali-chl kali-m k2 kali-n k* kali-s kali-sil k2 kola stb3• **Kreos** lac-d kr1* lach k* lappa br1 *Led* k* **Lyc** k* lyss k* mag-c b4.de* *Mag-m* mang-p rly4• melal-alt gya4 meny meph **Merc** mosch k* *Mur-ac* k* nat-ar *Nat-c* k* **Nat-m** k* *Nat-p* nat-pyru rly4• *Nat-s* **Nit-ac** k* **Nux-v** k* ol-an k* olib-sac wmh1 pall pant-ac rly4• par k* petr k* petr-ra shn4• *Ph-ac* k* phasco-ci rbp2 *Phos* k* *Psor* puls k* *Rhus-t* k* ruta fd4.de sabin sacch-a fd2.de• sanic *Sars* k* *Sep* k* *Sil* k* sol-t-ae k* spong fd4.de stann b4.de* *Staph* k* suis-hep rly4• sul-ac b4.de* sul-i k2 **Sulph** k* suprar rly4• symph fd3.de• syph tarax k* tarent k* tell c1 tere-la rly4• thuj k* til k* tritic-vg fd5.de *Tung-met* bdx1• vanil fd5.de verat b7.de* vero-o rly4*• vinc k* zinc k* zinc-p k2 [bell-p-sp dcm1]
• **night**: *Mag-m*
• **areola**; with: kali-i bro1
• **blind**: dioxi rbp6
• **bluish**: lyss
• **burning**: aphis *Cic* graph h2* kali-c h2* nat-c h2* sars h2*
⁝ **touch** agg.: coloc h2 nat-s
• **cold** air agg.: *Ars*
• **confluent**: *Cic Psor* tarent k*
• **copper** colored: kali-i k*
• **elevated** margins: verat k*
• **greenish**: cupr k*
• **inflamed**: bry k* *Chel* dulc fd4.de nat-sil fd3.de• podo fd3.de• sacch-a fd2.de• sars h2* spong fd4.de stann k* sulph k* tritic-vg fd5.de vanil fd5.de
• **insects**; pimples as from: ant-c
• **itching**: agar h2* *Ant-c* k* asc-t calc h2* *Caust* clem hr1 *Con* dulc a1 ephe-si hsj1• **Graph** *Hep Mur-ac* ol-an k* pall *Psor* sars h2* *Sep* stann h2* staph h1* *Til* zinc
⁝ **moist** after scratching: **Graph**
⁝ **stitching**: staph h1*
⁝ **summer**: *Mur-ac* hr1

Face

- **itching**: ...
  - **warm**; when: *Ant-c* cocc *Til*
- **liver** spot, on: con h2*
- **menses** | **before** | **agg.**: dulc gt1 *Mag-m* [sol-ecl cky1]
  - **during** | **agg.**: dulc eug graph kali-c gt1
- **painful**: caps a1
  - **touch**; to: bamb-a stb2.de• petr a1
- **pink**: mim-p rsj8•
- **purplish** halo; with: **Merc**
- **red**: aids nl2• coli rly4• ephe-si hsj1• *Kreos* bg2 *Lach* bg2 led ptk1 ph-ac h2* phos h2* tritic-vg fd5.de zinc h2*
- **scratching** agg.; after: alum h2*
- **small**: mim-p rsj8• [bell-p-sp dcm1]
- **warm** room agg.: *Mag-m*
- **washing** agg.: nux-v k* *Sulph*
- **white**: agath-a nl2• aids nl2• coloc h2* graph h2* mag-m h2* sinus rly4• tritic-vg fd5.de zinc h2*
- ○ **Chin**: alum k* ambr amp rly4• ant-c arg-n a1 *Ars* b4a.de aster bamb-a stb2.de• bell b4.de borx calc b4.de* carc fd2.de• caust b4.de* *Chel* *Clem* k* coli rly4• con k* crot-h dulc k* ferr-m fuma-ac rly4• helo-s rwt2• *Hep* k* hydrog srj2• kali-chl kali-p fd1.de• kali-s fd4.de *Lyc* k* mag-c b4.de* mag-m a1 merc k* nat-c b4.de* nat-pyru rly4• nat-s nept-m lsd2.fr nit-ac k* *Nux-v* h1* par pegan-ha tpi1• ph-ac propr sa3• *Psor* *Rhus-t* k* sars k* *Sep* k* sil k* spong fd4.de succ-ac rly4• suis-hep rly4• sulph b4.de symph fd3.de• thuj k* tritic-vg fd5.de vanil fd5.de zinc k* [bell-p-sp dcm1]
- **Forehead**: acon-ac rly4• agar k* alum k* alum-p k2 am-c am-m *Ambr* k* anac ars k* aur aur-ar k2 aur-s k2 bamb-a stb2.de• bell k* berb hr1 *Bov* k* bry k* calc k* *Calc-p* k* canth carb-v k* carc fd2.de• chel k* chin bg1 cic hr1 *Clem* k* con k* cycl k* dioxi rbp6 ferr-m gels hr1 gran k* ham fd3.de• hep k* hura hyper hr1 indg k* kali-bi k* kali-br k* kali-chl k* kola stb3• kreos k* lac-d hr1 lac-h sk4• lach k* lachn c1 *Led* k* mag-m k* meph k* mez k* *Mur-ac* k* nat-c k* nat-m k* *Nat-p* nat-sil fd3.de• nept-m lsd2.fr nit-ac k* nux-v a1 olnd k* ozone sde2• par k* *Ph-ac* k* phos k* positr nl2• *Psor* k* puls k* *Rhod* rhus-v k* sabin hr1 *Sep* k* sol-ni suis-hep rly4• *Sulph* k* suprar rly4• tab k* tarent k* tritic-vg fd5.de vanil fd5.de zinc k* zinc-p k2 zing hr1 ziz k*
  - **burning**: ars h2* bell k* canth k* cic hr1
  - **itching**: alum k* calc k* mag-m h2* *Sulph* k* ziz k*
    - **rubbing** agg.: mag-m h2*
  - **painful**: ambr h1* bamb-a stb2.de• clem h2* galeoc-c-h gms1• indg k* kola stb3• melal-alt gya4 nept-m lsd2.fr sep h2* staph k* *Sulph* h2*
  - **red**: ambr h1* anac bell k* carb-v k* led br1 nat-c h2* nat-m k* nept-m lsd2.fr nux-v a1 sep h2* sol-ni
  - **sore** to touch: ambr h1* galeoc-c-h gms1• hell h1* led br1 melal-alt gya4 ph-ac k* zinc h2*
  - **stinging** on rubbing: sulph h2*
  - **suppurating**: bamb-a stb2.de•
  - **thick**: bamb-a stb2.de•
  - **washed**, smarting when: nux-v k*
  - **white**: carb-v k* kali-br k* sulph zinc
  - **wine** agg.: zinc k*
- **Jaws** | **Lower**: ars h2 coli rly4• dioxi rbp6 *Lac-lup* hrn2• meph a1 par *Sil* tritic-vg fd5.de
- **Lips**: *Agar* k* am-m apis b7a.de arn aur k* bell h1* berb k* borx *Bov* k* bry b7a.de bufo calc cann-s b7.de* caps b7.de* *Carb-v* chin b7.de* dulc b4.de* ferr-m galeoc-c-h gms1• *Graph* k* guaj *Hep* hyos b7.de* ip b7.de* *Kali-c* k* kali-chl k* kali-p m-ambo b7a.de mag-m b4.de* *Merc* *Mur-ac* k* *Nat-c* k* nit-ac h2* nux-v k* pall par petr k* ph-ac k* positr nl2• *Rhus-t* b7.de* ruta k* *Sep* k* spig h1* spong b7.de* staph b7a.de* thuj k* tritic-vg fd5.de vanil fd5.de
  - **left**: galeoc-c-h gms1•
  - **burning**: aur hep h2* ph-ac h2* staph h1*
    - **itching**: aur kali-c h2*
  - **itching**: am-m h2* kali-c h2* nit-ac h2* thuj h1*
  - **sensation**; as if: arge-pl rwt5•
- **Lips**: ...
  - **Lower**: *Apis* b7a.de bell b4.de* *Bry* b7.de* calc b4.de* caps b7.de* caust b4.de* galeoc-c-h gms1• hep b4a.de ign b7.de* kali-chl c1 mang b4.de* merc b4.de* mur-ac b4.de* nat-c b4.de* nicc nit-ac h2* pall *Rhus-t* b7.de* samb b7.de* sil b4.de* spig b7.de* sulph bg2 teucr b7.de* vanil fd5.de zinc h2*
  - **Upper**: acon b7.de* am-m k* amph a1 ant-c k* **Ant-t** b7a.de arn k* *Bar-c* b4a.de bell b4.de* bufo calc b4.de* caps b7.de* *Carb-v* k* caust b4.de* cench k2 *Cic* b7a.de clem h2* dig b4.de* dulc fd4.de hep b4a.de kali-c b4.de* led b7.de* lyc b4.de* m-ambo b7.de m-arct b7.de mag-m b4.de* mang nat-c a1 nat-sil fd3.de• nux-v b7.de* par b7.de* positr nl2• *Puls* b7a.de rhus-t b7.de* ruta fd4.de sars b4.de* sep b4.de* sil b4.de* spig k* squil b7.de* staph b7.de* stront-c b4.de* *Thuj* k* tritic-vg fd5.de vanil fd5.de *Zinc* k*
    - **burning**: aphis graph h2*
    - **itching**: graph h2* lyc h2*
    - **red**: positr nl2• zinc h2*
    - **sore** to touch: zinc
    - **Above**: petr a1
    - **Middle**: cassia-s ccrh1•
      - **painful**: cassia-s ccrh1•
- **Malar** bones: hura br1
- **Mouth**:
  - **Around**: agar h2* ant-c ptk1 aster ptk1 *Bar-c* bov calc h2* *Dulc* hydrog srj2• kali-c h2* *Mag-c* *Mur-ac* ozone sde2• phos *Rhus-t* sep *Sil* vanil fd5.de zinc
  - **Corners**, of: ant-c b7.de* arg-n a1 bar-c k* bell b4.de* calc b4.de* cann-s b7.de* canth b7.de* caust b4.de* coloc b4.de* dulc fd4.de galeoc-c-h gms1• lyc h2 m-arct b7.de mag-m h2* mang b4.de* merc bg2 mur-ac bg2 nat-c bg2 nat-m h2 ozone sde2• petr k* phos b4.de* rhod b4.de* rhus-t b7.de* sil bg2 spong fd4.de tarax k* tritic-vg fd5.de *Verat* b7.de*
- **Nose**: agar alum k* **Am-c** k* *Anac* k* ant-c bg2* arum-d asc-t a1 aur k* bamb-a stb2.de• bar-c k* *Bell* k* berb a1 borx bov b4.de* brom k* **Calc** k* calc-p tl1 cann-s k* cann-xyz bg2 canth bg2* caps k* carb-an k* carb-v **Caust** k* clem k* cob a1 coc-c a1 cocc a1 coli rly4• con b4.de* cub bg1 dulc k* euph bg2 euphr k* *Fl-ac* k* *Graph* k* guaj k* *Kali-c* k* kali-i k* kali-n b4.de* kola stb3• lach k* led bg2 *Lyc* k* m-arct mag-m b4.de* mag-s a1 mang k* *Merc* k* *Nat-c* k* *Nat-m* k* nat-sil fd3.de• nicc a1 ol-an k* ox-ac pall petr k* *Ph-ac* k* *Phos* k* plan plb k* podo *Psor* rat a1 rhus-t sars k* sel *Sep* k* *Sil* k* spong fd4.de stram bg2* stront-c b4.de* suis-hep rly4• sul-ac bg2* *Sulph* k* **Syph** *Teucr* thuj tritic-vg fd5.de vanil fd5.de zinc b4.de*
  - **burning**: alum aphis canth k* kali-n h2* ol-an a1
    - **touch** agg.: canth
  - **oozing**: ol-an
  - **painful**: bamb-a stb2.de• spong fd4.de tritic-vg fd5.de vanil fd5.de
  - **red**: ant-c aur calc-p kali-c ptk1 lach ptk1 pegan-ha tpi1• ph-ac h2* plan psor ptk1 sulph a1
  - **white**: carb-v galeoc-c-h gms1• kali-c *Nat-c* k* nat-m h2*
  - **About** nose: carb-v h2* nat-m h2* pall a1 par k* plan a1 sep a1 (non:tarax k*) vanil fd5.de
  - **Below** nose: caps h1* dig h2* dulc fd4.de oxal-a rly4• par a1 vanil fd5.de
  - **Corners**, in: dulc h2* rhus-g tmo3• tarax h1*
  - **Dorsum**; on | **inflamed** base; with: fl-ac
  - **Inside**: arn k* calad calc k* carb-an chin h1* graph guaj kali-c ox-ac petr h2* phos k* rat sep h2* sil tub
  - **Nostrils**: chin h1 kola stb3• sep h2 vanil fd5.de
    - **right**: aphis ox-ac phos rat
    - **left**: acon-ac rly4• calc dulc graph kali-c
      - **Below**: dig h2
    - **painful** only when muscles of face and nose are moved: calc
  - **Root**: bell h1* caust k* cench k2 clem a1 elaps fkr8.de *Led* k*
  - **Septum**: arg-n k* asc-t k* calad k* chin k* nat-m ol-an k* podo fd3.de• *Teucr* vip fkr4.de
    - **oozing**: ol-an
    - **Below**: nat-m h2*
  - **Side**: aster sil

- Nose – Side: ...
  - right: alum euphr lach ox-ac sars
  - left: caps h1* hir rsj4• nat-c h2*
  - small and hard: agar k*
  - Tip: am-c k* asaf bomb-chr mlk9.de **Caust** k* cench k2 clem a1 coc-c k* cund k* galeoc-c-h gms1• *Lyc* nit-ac pall k* pegan-ha tpi1• ph-ac k* podo fd3.de• spong vanil fd5.de
    - bleeding when pressed: pall
    - sore: *Lyc*
  - Wings: anac a1 bamb-a stb2.de• bar-c k* chel a1 chin k* dulc fd4.de nat-m k* phos h2* tarax k* tritic-vg fd5.de vanil fd5.de zing
    - left: dulc fd4.de fl-ac
    - perforation size of a pea: fl-ac
    - recurrent (See GENERALS - History - nose)
- Temples: arg-met carb-v h2* cocc hr1 ham fd3.de• helo-s rwt2• *Mur-ac* *Nit-ac* k* sacch-a fd2.de• symph fd3.de• tritic-vg fd5.de
- Whiskers: *Agar* ambr k* calc k* calc-s graph lach *Mez* b4a.de nit-ac k* pall sulph

- pocks: ant-c b7a.de arn b7.de* hyos b7.de* petr bg2
  - ○ Chin: hyos b7.de*
- psoriasis: ars b4a.de *Aur* b4.de calc b4a.de lyc b4a.de rhus-t b7.de sulph b4a.de
  - ○ Eyebrows; of: *Phos* k*
- purulent:
  - ○ Mouth | Corner of mouth; below right: germ-met srj5•
- pustules: am-c k* *Anac* **Ant-c** k* ant-t arn *Ars* k* ars-i k2 ars-s-f k2 **Aur** aur-ar k2 aur-s k2 **Bell** k* bov *Calc* k* calc-p calc-s k* *Carb-v* carbn-s *Caust* k* chel k* **Cic** k* cimic k* clem *Con* *Crot-t* k* cund cycl a1 dros k* dulc eug eup-per k* graph k* grat k* grin mtf11 *Hep* k* *Hydr* hyos k* ind k* *Iris* jug-c k* *Kali-bi* k* *Kali-br* k* kali-c h2* *Kali-i* k* kali-n h2* kreos lach k* lyc k* mag-c mag-m mag-s *Merc* k* *Mez* k* morg-p pte1• nat-c h2 *Nat-p* k* *Nit-ac* k* nux-m pall petr a1 petr-ra shn4• ph-ac k* phos k* propl ub1• psor k* puls **Rhus-t** ruta fd4.de sars k* sulph syph k2 tarax thal-xyz srj8• thuj tritic-vg fd5.de **Tub** vanil fd5.de verat *Viol-t* zinc
  - confluent: *Cic*
  - disappear before fully developed: chin-b kr1
  - itching: euph h2* grin mtf11 ph-ac h2* sars h2*
  - menses; during: am-c h2*
  - sanious: iris
  - ulcers, terminating in: crot-t
  - ○ Cheeks: am-c calc carb-an h2* chin-b kr1 choc srj3• iris *Kali-bi* lyc h2* pall sacch-a fd2.de•
    - menses; during: am-c h2*
  - Chin: am-c anthraq rly4• camph caust k* *Clem* *Graph* k* hyos k* *Kali-bi* kali-i mang k* merc k* *Mez* nit-ac k* nux-m olnd k* petr h2* petr-ra shn4• plat bg2 prot jl2 *Psor* rhus-t ruta fd4.de sabin bg2 sars *Tub* *Viol-t* *Zinc*
    - hard red borders; with: nux-m c1
    - itching: zinc a1
    - painful if touched: rhus-t h1
  - Forehead: am-c k* anac aq-mar skp7• ars carb-an chel chin bg1 clem cycl dulc fd4.de eup-per euph h2* *Hydr* hr1 *Kali-bi* kali-c k* kali-p lyc h2* *Lyss* hr1 *Merc* mur-ac k* nat-c h2* *Nat-m* k* nat-sil fd3.de• psor hr1 rhod sacch-a fd2.de• sars k* spig hr1 sulfa sp1 tritic-vg fd5.de vanil fd5.de
    - painful: sil tl1
    - ulcers; join to form: sil tl1
    - variola-like: sil tl1
    - Eyelashes; above the: tub jl2
      - oozing: tub jl2
  - Lips: ant-c *Anthraci* aur bell berb *Calc* *Cinnb* clem *Hep* iris mag-c h2* mur-ac h2* petr-ra shn4• samb h1* sep h2* *Viol-t* zinc
    - black: **Anthraci** *Lach*
    - Lower: petr-ra shn4•
    - Upper: ant-c *Anthraci* arg-n a1 calc carb-v h2* mag-c h2* mur-ac a1 prot jl2 sul-i c1 *Viol-t* zinc
      - Middle: cassia-s ccrh1•
  - Mouth:
    - Around: nat-c h2 ruta fd4.de
    - Corners of: ant-c h2 bar-c coloc h2 phos h2 tarax h1

- pustules: ...
  - Nose: *Am-c* k* ant-c ars-br vh asc-t bell k* bov brom bg2 bufo canth bg2 clem k* cocc crot-h bg2 euphr k* fl-ac bg2 *Hep* bro1 hippoz hir rsj4• *Iris* kali-n bg2 mag-c merc k* nat-c nit-ac petr k* ph-ac h2* *Phos* plb k* podo k* psor bro1 sars k* sil bro1 sulph bg2 symph fd3.de• tarax *Tub*
    - right: con cund fl-ac mag-c mang sars
    - left: kali-n nat-c
    - Corner: mang h2* sacch-a fd2.de•
    - Inside: arn hippoz *Tub*
    - Ridges: sulfa sp1
    - Root: clem
    - Septum: am-c *Anac* hippoz lycps-v petr psor
      - right: anac sars tarax
      - perforation, with: hippoz
    - Tip: am-c clem kali-br k* lyc mag-c pall c1
    - Under: arn h1 borx bov mag-c h2 squil
    - Wings: anac h2* euphr mang nat-c h2 tarax
      - right: petr
      - left: nat-c h2*
  - Temples: lyc h2* mag-m h2*
    - right: sulfa sp1
- rash: *Acon* aids nl2• *Ail* anan *Ant-c* ant-t k* *Ars* ars-s-f k2 **Bell** *Bry* carbn-s caust *Cham* coff con crot-c sk4• *Euphr* germ-met srj5• *Graph* *Hep* hydr k* *Ip* k* jab kali-br lac-h htj1• lach *Merc* *Mez* *Nat-m* nit-ac phos **Puls** **Rhus-t** k* *Stram* k* **Sulph** k* tab tarent tell rsj10• teucr k* thal-xyz srj8• verat
  - left:
    - extending to | right: germ-met srj5•
  - bluish: *Lach* *Phos* sulph
  - burning: germ-met srj5• teucr k*
  - itching: caust h2* mim-p rsj8• teucr k*
    - Forehead: rheum h1* teucr a1*
  - menses amel.: lac-h htj1•
  - purple: hyos k* sep k*
  - scratching agg.; after: alum h2*
  - sun agg.: germ-met srj5•
  - syphilitic: syph
  - warmth agg.: aids nl2• *Euphr* kali-i vh teucr
  - washing agg.; after: glon
  - water agg.: germ-met srj5•
  - ○ Chin: aids nl2• am-c anthraq rly4•
  - Forehead: ail k* arn k* calc-caust dgt1 indg k* *Ip* hr1 lil-t k* rheum teucr k*
- red: aids nl2• alum h2* ant-c k* anthraq rly4• aq-mar skp7• aur k* bamb-a stb2.de• bar-ox-suc rly4• calc calc-p carb-an h2* carbn-s carc xxb caust k* cham cic euphr fago falco-pe nl2• hyper *Lac-c* *Led* k* marb-w es1• nit-ac olib-sac wmh1 par *Petr* phos k* psor sep sulph tere-la rly4• vanil fd5.de
  - spots: aq-mar rbp6 *Berb-a* bro1 euph bro1 kali-bi bro1 *Kali-c* bro1 oena bro1 orot-ac rly4• petr bro1
  - ○ Cheeks: aids nl2• borx c1 vanil fd5.de [heroin sdj2]
    - erythema: physala-p bnm7•
  - Chin: borx c1 bros-gau mrc1 caust h2* mag-m h2* vanil fd5.de verat h1*
    - erythema: prot jl2*
  - Eye:
    - Under | left: plut-n srj7•
  - Forehead: nat-s k2
  - Lips; upper | erythema: prot jl2*
  - Mouth; around: vanil fd5.de verat h1*
  - Nose, on: aids nl2• androc srj1• aur bell carbn-s crot-t lach lap-la sde8.de• ph-ac samb h1* syph thuj
- rhus poisoning: **Anac** apis mrr1 *Bry* *Crot-t* k* *Graph* *Rhus-t* *Rhus-v* sep sulph
- rosy: diosm br1
  - accompanied by | discoloration of face; earthy: diosm br1
- rough: alum k* anac bar-c *Berb-a* bro1 granit-m es1• kali-c k* kalm k* led nat-m k* *Petr* bro1 puls rhus-t k* rhus-v k* sep k* stram k* sulph k* teucr

- **morning**: nat-m
- **red**: phos h2* sep sulph
- **summer**: kalm k*

○ • **Chin**: hir rsj4• hydrog srj2•
- **Forehead**; on: pall rhus-t sars sep sulph teucr
  - **spots**: sars
- **Lips**: lap-la sde8.de• merc sulph tab
- **Mouth**; around: anac ars

- **rupia** | **Cheeks**: syph k2
- **scabby** (See crusty)
- **scabies**: mez b4a.de *Sars* b4a.de
- **scaly** (See scurfy)
- **scorbutic**: kali-bi bg2
- **scurfy**: aloe bg2 alum anac **Ant-c** ant-t **Ars** k* *Ars-i* ars-s-f k2 aur k* aur-ar k2 aur-s k2 bamb-a stb2.de• **Bar-c** k* bell k* *Bry* b7.de* *Bufo* k* *Calc* k* calc-s calc-sil k2 carb-an carb-v b4.de carbn-s **Caust** k* chinin-s chrysar br1 *Cic* k* coli rly4• coloc k* cory br1 crot-t k* dulc k* euph bro1 granit-m es1• *Graph* k* *Hep* k* *Kali-ar* kali-s k2 kreos **Lach** k* led k* *Lyc* k* mag-m h2* *Merc* k* merc-i-f *Mez* k* mim-p rsj8• mur-ac k* nat-m k2 nit-ac k* *Nux-v* k* parth vml3• *Petr* k* *Ph-ac* k* *Phos* k* *Phyt* plat **Psor** k* rauw sp1 rhus-t k* rhus-v k* ruta fd4.de sars k* **Sep** k* *Sil* k* spong fd4.de suis-pan rly4• sulph k* thuj k* vanil fd5.de verat *Viol-t* k* zinc k*
  - **old** people; in: cory br1
  - **sensation** of: bell bg2
  - **white**: anac *Ars*
  - **yellow**: cic hr1 *Merc*

○ • **Cheeks**: anac bell calc *Cic* coli rly4• kreos lach *Lyc* ruta fd4.de
- **Chin**: am-c *Ars* b4a.de caust h2* *Cic* k* coli rly4• crot-t a1 dulc *Graph* k* hydrog srj2• kreos k* merc *Mez* b4a.de rhus-t b7a.de sep k*
- **Forehead**: *Ars* hr1 calc dulc granit-m es1• graph hr1 kali-p fd1.de• mag-c h2* mur-ac ruta fd4.de spong fd4.de sulph hr1
  - **Temples**; and: dulc mur-ac k*
- **Lids** (See EYE - Eruptions - lids - scurfy)
- **Lips**: ant-t **Ars** k* bar-c k* bell berb borx *Bry* b7.de* calc *Cann-s* b7.de* caps a1 cham k* *Cic* k* *Graph* b4a.de *Hep* ign k* *Kali-c* k* kali-s fd4.de merc k* mur-ac k* *Nat-ar* nat-m b4a.de nux-v k* ozone sde2• petr k* ph-ac k* phos plan rhus-t *Sep* k* *Sil* k* squil staph k* sulph k*
  - **Lower**: alum b4.de* calc b4.de* *Caust* b4a.de nat-m b4.de* ph-ac b4.de* sulph b4.de* *Thuj* b4a.de
  - **Upper**: *Ars* b4.de* **Bar-c** b4a.de borx b4a.de cic b7.de* kali-bi bg2 kali-c b4.de* merc b4.de* petr b4.de* *Sars* b4a.de sep b4a.de sil b4.de* staph b7.de* *Sulph* b4.de* *Thuj* b4a.de
- **Mouth**:
  - **Around**: am-c anac calc *Cic* gaert pte1• *Graph* *Mur-ac* k* *Petr* sep
  - **Corners** of: calc b4.de* graph b4.de* hep b4a.de ign k* lyc h2* petr k* sil b4.de*
    - **Below**: hep h2*
- **Nose**: ant-c br1 aur-m-n *Caust* bro1 iod nat-m sil h2* vanil fd5.de
  - **bleeding**: hir rsj4• kali-n h2*
  - **Dorsum**: phos h2*
  - **Tip**: caust k* kali-n h2* nat-c bro1 nit-ac k* sep
  - **Under**: bar-c mag-c h2* ph-ac h2*
- **Whiskers**: calc k* lach k*

- **small**: pneu jl2 *Vac* jl2
- **smarting**: (↗*painful)* cic ip rhod spong fd4.de verat
- **sore** (See painful)
- **spots**: acon alum am-c ambr ars bar-c bell berb bry *Calc* carb-an carb-v colch croc ferr ferr-m hyos h1* irid-met srj5• luna kg1• lyc *Merc* *Nat-c* nit-ac par phos podo fd3.de• propl ub1• samb sars **Sep** sulph symph fd3.de• tub vanil fd5.de vip zinc

○ • **Chin**: bros-gau mrc1

- **spring** agg.; in: ars-br vh
- **stinging**, painful: clem dulc h2* led plat squil h1* staph
- **sun** agg.: parth vml3•
- **suppurating**: **Ant-c** *Cic* lyc *Psor* *Rhus-t* sacch-a fd2.de• vanil fd5.de
- **syphilitic**: *Ars-i* *Aur* *Cinnb* *Fl-ac* k* *Hep* *Kali-bi* **Kali-i** kreos *Lach* *Lyc* k* **Merc** **Merc-c** *Nit-ac* *Phyt* sep *Sil* *Sulph* **Syph** k*
- **tetters**: am-c b4.de* bar-c b4.de* bov b4.de* calc b4.de* carb-v b4.de* caust b4.de* chel b7.de* *Con* b4a.de dulc b4a.de* *Graph* b4.de* *Kreos* b7a.de lach b7a.de *Led* b7.de* nat-c b4.de* nit-ac b4.de* *Petr* b4.de* phos b4.de* *Rhus-t* b7.de* sabad b7.de* sep b4.de* sil b4.de* *Sulph* b4a.de *Thuj* b4a.de

○ • **Cheeks**: am-c b4a.de ambr b7.de* anac b4.de* bar-c b4.de* *Bov* b4.de* bry b7.de* caust b4.de* *Kreos* b7a.de merc b4.de* ph-ac b4a.de
- **Chin**: am-c b4a.de ars b4a.de *Bov* b4.de* *Chel* b7.de* mez b4a.de nat-m b4.de* nux-v b7.de* *Rhus-t* b7a.de sil b4.de* sul-ac b4a.de thuj b4a.de
- **Forehead**: *Bry* b7a.de caps b7.de* *Nux-v* b7a.de *Sep* b4a.de
- **Lips**: anac b4.de* ars b4.de borx b4a.de caust b4a.de *Kreos* b7a.de nat-c b4a.de *Nat-m* b4a.de *Par* b7.de* ph-ac b4a.de rhus-t b7.de* sars b4a.de *Sep* b4.de*
  - **Lower**: *Sep* b4.de*
  - **Upper**: *Bar-c* b4a.de *Kali-c* b4a.de phos b4.de *Sars* b4a.de *Sep* b4.de*
- **Mouth**:
  - **Around**: *Am-c* b4a.de *Anac* b4a.de *Mag-c* b4a.de *Nat-c* b4a.de *Nat-m* b4a.de phos b4a.de *Sep* b4a.de
  - **Corners** of: carb-v b4.de phos b4.de* sep b4.de sulph b4a.de
- **Nose**: *Calc* b4a.de mez b4a.de *Nat-m* b4a.de nit-ac b4a.de *Rhus-t* b7.de* *Sars* b4a.de spig b7.de* *Sulph* b4a.de
  - **About**: rhus-t b7a.de sulph b4a.de
  - **Across**: *Nat-c* b4a.de
- **Temples**: *Alum* b4.de*
- **Whiskers**: nit-ac b4a.de

- **tubercles**: *Alum* k* ant-c *Ars* asaf bar-c calc carb-an bro1 *Carb-v* cic con dulc *Fl-ac* k* *Graph* hep *Kali-bi* kali-c *Kali-i* kali-n c1 lach *Led* lyc mag-c mag-m merc *Nat-c* nit-ac olnd phyt puls sil sumb syph k2 thuj k* zinc
  - **itching**: kali-n h2*
  - **painful**: sep h2*
  - **suppurating**: *Fl-ac* nat-c *Sil*

○ • **Cheeks** | **small** tubercles: asaf ptk1
- **Chin**: carb-an euph hep mag-m olnd
- **Forehead**: ant-c h2* *Fl-ac* *Led* k* lyc h2* olnd k* sep h2* sulph h2*
- **Jaws** | **Lower**: graph nat-c staph verat
- **Lip**; upper | **white** tubercles; small: graph h2*
- **Mouth**; about: ars bar-c bry caust con mag-m sep sil sulph
- **Mouth**; corners of: mag-c h2
- **Nose**:
  - **Root** of; at | **painless** tubercle: sep h2
  - **Side** of; at right | **painless** tubercle: nat-c h2
  - **Wings** of: hippoz

- **urticaria**: *Am-c* anan k* *Ant-c* k* **Apis** k* **Ars** astac vh *Bell* k* *Calc* *Chel* *Chinin-s* **Chlol** k* **Cop** k* crot-t k* dulc h2* *Gels* k* *Hep* k* hydr hydrc k* *Kali-i* k* lach k* *Led* mag-m h2 mez *Nat-m* nit-ac h2* *Rhus-t* k* *Sep* sil **Sulph** *Urt-u* [heroin sdj2]
  - **morning**: chin k*
  - **air**; in open | **amel.**: calc
  - **seasons** | **winter**: *Kali-i*
  - **symmetrical**: crot-t a1
- **variola** | **Nose**: canth b7.de
- **vesicles**: acon bg2 aeth k* *Agar* k* alum k* am-c k* am-m k* anac k* *Ant-c* k* ant-t *Ars* k* ars-s-f k2 bar-c b4.de* benz-ac borx k* calc-s canth k* carb-an k* *Carbn-s* caust k* cham b7a.de cic k* cist *Clem* k* **Crot-t** k* *Dulc* *Euph* k* ferr-i *Graph* k* grin mtf11 hep indg kali-ar k* kali-bi k* *Kali-i* kali-n k* lach *Mag-c* k* **Manc** k* mang k* medus br1 *Merc* k* merc-c b4a.de mez k* mur-ac h2* nat-ar *Nat-c* k* **Nat-m** k* *Nat-s* *Nit-ac* k* ol-an k* *Petr* k* petr-ra shn4• ph-ac phos k* plb k* plect a1 prot jl2 **Psor** k* ran-b **Rhus-t** k* rhus-v k* ruta fd4.de samb sars b4a.de **Sep** k* *Sil* k* spong fd4.de stram stront-c k* *Sulph* k* syph tritic-vg fd5.de valer k* zinc k* zinc-p k2
  - **acrid**: caust k* rhus-t k*
  - **blood**; filled with: lach k2 ruta fd4.de
  - **burning**: agar *Anac* aur caust k* cic grin mtf11 hep h2* nat-c h2* *Nat-m* nat-s hr *Ran-b*
    - **touch** agg.: nat-s hr
  - **cold** air agg.: *Dulc*

- **confluent**: crot-t k* mez a1 ran-b rhus-t k* *Sulph*
- **itching**: *Anac* ant-c k* *Ars* cic grin mtf11 mang h2* *Mez* prot jl2 sars h2* sep k*
- **purulent**: *Ars* b4a.de *Clem* b4a.de merc b4.de *Olnd* b7.de* *Rhus-t* b7a.de sabin b7.de sars b4a.de sil b4a.de zinc b4.de
  - **Lips**: carb-v b4a.de
- **varioloid**, like: ant-c k*
- **white**: clem hell mez h2* nat-c h2* sulph valer
- **yellow**: *Agar* ant-c ars k* cic com crot-t *Dulc Euph Euphr* kreos *Manc* k* *Merc* mur-ac h2* nat-c ph-ac **Rhus-t** k* *Rhus-v* k* sep
- ○ **Chin**; on: agar anac *Ars* b4a.de canth *Cic* crot-t hep k* *Manc Nat-c* **Nat-m** *Nat-s Nit-ac Sanic Sars* k* *Sil* b4a.de
- **Forehead**: am-c k* arn k* borx canth k* kali-i k* mag-c h2* mez k* nat-m k* nat-sil fd3.de• plb k* *Psor* k* rhus-v k* stront-c
- **Jaws**: hydrog srj2•
  - **Lower** jaw: mur-ac a1
- **Lips**: acon b7.de* agar k* ail allox tpw4 *Alum* k* am-c b4.de* am-m k* ant-c b7.de* ant-t arn b7.de* **Ars** b4a.de* asc-t aur bar-c b4.de* *Bell* b4.de* berb borx k* bov k* **Bry** b7.de* *Calc* b4a.de* calc-s cann-s b7.de* canth b7.de* caps b7.de* *Carb-an* k* *Caust* b4.de* chel k* chin b7.de* chinin-s k* cic cina bg2 cit-ac rly4• *Clem* k* coloc b4.de com *Con* k* dig b4a.de dulc b4.de* graph bg2 hell k* hep k* hyos b7.de* *Ign* b7.de* ip b7.de* kali-bi bg2 kali-c b4.de* kali-p kali-s kreos bg2 lac-ac lac-c lach bg2 laur b7.de* led b7.de lyc b4a.de m-ambo b7.de* m-arct b7.de *Mag-c* k* *Mag-m* k* mang k* merc k* mur-ac b4.de* nat-c k* **Nat-m** k* nat-s k* *Nit-ac* k* nux-v b7.de* par k* petr b4a.de* plat k* positr nl2• rhod k* **Rhus-t** b7.de* ruta b7a.de* samb b7.de* sang *Sanic* seneg k* *Sep* b4a.de* sil k* spig b7.de* spong b7.de* squil b7.de* *Staph* b7.de* **Sulph** b4.de* tarax b7.de* teucr b7.de thuj b4a.de tritic-vg fd5.de valer verat b7.de* zinc b4.de*
  - **fever** blisters: (↗*herpes - lips - about*) ars bg2* brom hr1* *Calc-f* hr1* canth hr1* *Crot-h* kr1 *Crot-t* hr1 frax br1 *Graph* hr1* hep bro1 hyos h1* ign bg2 *Lac-c* hr1* med hr1* melal-alt gya4 *Nat-m* bg2* nux-v bg2 phos bg3 **Rhus-t** bg2* sep hr1 spong fd4.de sulph bg2 tritic-vg fd5.de urt-u hr1*
    - **Lower** lip: melal-alt gya4
  - **Lower**: agar ail am-c b4.de* aur k* bell b4.de* bry b7.de* carb-v b4.de* clem b4.de* com hep b4a.de *Hyos* b7a.de kali-bi bg2 kali-c b4.de* lac-c mtf33 laur b7.de* mag-c h2* mag-m mang a1 melal-alt gya4 mur-ac b4.de* **Nat-m** b4.de* nat-s k* par k* petr-ra shn4• phos b4.de* plat b4.de* rhod b4.de* ruta fd4.de sang hr1 sars b4.de* *Sep* b4.de* staph b7.de* sulph b4.de* tritic-vg fd5.de
    - **left**: olib-sac wmh1
    - **itching**: clem h2*
    - **white**: phos h2*
    - **yellow**: mur-ac a1
    - **Below**: hep h2* sang hr1
    - **Inside** (See MOUTH - Eruptions - vesicles - lips - lower - inside)
  - **Upper**: *Agar* alum k* am-m k* *Ars* b4.de* carb-v b4.de* cic k* con b4.de* graph b4.de* hell b7.de* kali-n h2* kali-p laur b7.de* mag-c h2* mag-m b4.de* mag-p mang k* mur-ac b4.de* nat-c a1 phos bg2 plat b4.de* rat *Rhus-t* b7a.de rhus-v seneg k* sep bg2 sil b4.de* spong fd4.de stront-c b4.de* tritic-vg fd5.de valer k* zinc
    - **blood** blisters: *Nat-m* k*
- **Mouth**:
  - **Around**: am-c h2* am-m h2 *Borx Hell* mag-c h2* nat-c h2* **Nat-m** *Nat-s* sacch-a fd2.de•
    - **fever**; during: nat-m k2
    - **pearls**; like: *Nat-m* hr1*
  - **Corners** of: agar am-c h2* carb-v bg2 caust k* *Cic* glycyr-g cte1• graph bg2 laur b7.de* lyc bg2 mag-c h2* mez k* nat-c h2* phos b4a.de* positr nl2• ros-d wla1 seneg k* senn sep bg2 verat h1*
    - **Below**: mang h2*
- **Nose**: am-c ant-c b7.de* arn bg2 ars bg2 canth bg2 carb-an b4.de* clem crot-t ham fd3.de• *Hell* b7a.de lac-ac *Lach* k* *Mag-c* k* mag-m k* merc bg2 *Mez* k* nat-c *Nat-m* k* nit-ac k* petr k* phel phos k* *Plb* k* **Rhus-t** sabin b7.de* sep bg2 sil k* verat k*

- **vesicles – Nose**: ...
  - **menses**; before: mag-c h2*
  - **Around**: phos h2*
  - **Centre**, on: *Carb-ac*
  - **Inside** | **right**: ars bg1 **Carb-an** lach phos
  - **Nostril**, under: sil h2*
  - **Root**: cassia-s ccrh1• nat-m
    - **cold** applications | **amel.**: cassia-s ccrh1•
    - **pain**; with prickling: cassia-s ccrh1•
  - **Septum**: am-c crot-h thuj
  - **Side** | **bloody**: sep h2
  - **Tip**: nit-ac
  - **Wings**: chel **Nat-m** sil thuj
    - **right**: nat-c
- **warmth**:
  - **agg.**: euphr mez psor sel rsj9• sulph teucr
  - **amel.**: *Ars*
- **washing** agg.: nux-v podo fd3.de• sulph
- ○ **Beard**: *Calc* bg2 cic bg2 *Hep* c2 lach bg2 nit-ac bg2
  - **folliculitis** (= barber's itch): am-m bg2 *Ant-c* bg2* *Ant-t* bro1 anthraco bro1 arg-n bg2 *Ars* bg2* *Aur* bro1 calc bro1* calc-s bro1 carb-an bg2 carb-v bg2 chrysar bro1 cic bg2* cinnb bro1 clem bg2 cocc bro1 con bg2 dulc bg2 graph bg2* *Hep* bg2 *Kali-bi* bro1 kali-m bro1 kreos bg2 led bg2 lith-c bro1* *Lyc* bro1 mag-p ptk1 med bro1 *Merc-pr-r* bro1 mez bg2* nat-s bro1* *Nit-ac* bro1 olnd bg2 petr bro1 phyt ptk1* plan bro1 *Plat* bro1 rad-br mtf11 rhus-t ptk1 sabin bro1 sars bg2 scop ptk1 sep bg2* **Sil** bg2* spig bg2 staph bg2* staphycoc jl2 stront-c bro1 *Sul-i* br1* *Sulph* bg2* tell bro1* thuj bg2*
- **Cheeks**: agar k* agn b2.de* aids nl2• alum k* alum-p k2 am-c k* ambr b2.de* anac k* ang b2.de* **Ant-c** k* aq-mar jl* arn b2.de* asaf b2.de* bar-c b2.de* *Bell* k* borx b2.de* *Bov* k* bros-gau mrc1 bry k* *Calc* k* calc-sil k2 canth b2.de* carb-an carb-v b2.de* carc fd2.de• *Caust* k* cham k* chel b2.de* chord-umb rly4• cic k* cina b2.de* **Clem** b4a.de con k* cycl b2.de* dig k* *Dulc* k* **Euph** k* **Euphr** k* ferr-ma graph b2.de* hep b2.de* hyos b2.de* ip b7.de *Kali-chl* kali-i kali-m k2 kali-n b2.de* **Kreos** k* *Lach* k* laur k* *Led* bro1 *Lyc* mag-m k* merc k* merc-i-r mez k* nat-c k* *Nat-m* k* nit-ac k* nux-v b2.de* olnd b2.de* orot-ac rly4• petr-ra shn4• phos k* **Rhus-t** k* ruta b2.de* sabad b2.de* sabin b2.de* sars b2.de* *Sep* k* *Sil* k* spong k* **Staph** k* stront-c k* symph fd3.de• tarax b2.de* thal-xyz srj8• thuj b2.de* tritic-vg fd5.de valer b2.de* *Verat* k* verb k* viol-t k* [heroin sdj2]
  - **right**: limest-b es1• [heroin sdj2]
    - **malignant**: syc fmm1•
  - **left**: aids nl2• aq-mar rbp6 bac jl2 coca-c sk4• lac-h sk4• tub c*
    - **spots**: bac jl2
- **Chin**: agn b2.de* alum k* alum-p k2 am-c k* am-m bg2 ambr k* amp rly4• anac k* *Ant-c* k* anthraq rly4• aq-mar skp7• arg-n *Ars* b4a.de aster bro1 bell b2.de* borx k* *Bov* k* bros-gau mrc1 *Calc* k* calc-sil k2 canth b2.de* carb-an bg2 carb-v k* *Carbn-s* caust k* *Chel Cic* k* clem k* cob *Coloc* b4a.de con k* crot-h crot-t dig k* dioxi rbp6 dros b2.de* *Dulc* k* ferr-ma ferr-p bg2 *Graph* k* *Hep* k* hydr *Hydrog* srj2• hyos b2.de* kali-bi kali-c k* kali-i kali-p fd1.de• *Kreos* k* *Lach* k* laur b2.de* led bg2 *Lyc* k* m-ambo b2.de* m-aust b2.de* mag-c k* manc *Merc* k* merc-i-r *Mez* k* nat-c k* **Nat-m** k* nat-p nat-s nit-ac k* nux-m k* *Nux-v* k* olnd k* *Par* k* ph-ac k* phos k* plat b2.de* prot jl2 *Psor* puls k* **Rhus-t** k* sabin b2.de* sars k* **Sep** k* *Sil* k* sinus rly4• spig k* spong b2.de* squil b2.de* stront-c b2.de* sul-i c2* **Sulph** k* *Syph* tarax b2.de* thuj k* tritic-vg fd5.de tung-met bdx1• verat k* verb b2.de* viol-t zinc k*
  - **left** side: aq-mar skp7•
  - **desquamating**: prot jl2
  - **dry**: prot jl2
  - **painful**: aq-mar skp7• merc rhus-t sars **Sulph**
    - **pressure** agg.: aq-mar skp7•
  - **points**; small honey yellow: ant-c b7.de* rhus-t b7a.de
  - ○ **Lip**; between chin and: kali-chl c1*
- **Eyebrows**: guaj b4a.de kali-c b4a.de mez mrr1 musca-d szs1 nat-m b4a.de par b7a.de sel b7a.de sep b4a.de sil b4a.de *Spong* b7a.de stann b4a.de thuj b4a.de
  - **painful** touch: musca-d szs1

○ • **About**: ars b2.de* bar-c b4a.de* *Caust* k* clem k* cupr b7.de* ferr-ma guaj b4.de* hell b2.de* irid-met srj5• *Kali-c* k* mez k2 **Nat-m** k* par k* *Phos* rhus-t b2.de* *Sel* k* sep k* sil k* spong b7.de* stann k* staph k* suis-pan rly4• sulph k* tarax b7.de* thuj k*

⁝ **boils**: *Sulph* b4a.de

⁝ **crusty**: anan fl-ac nat-m sep spong h1

⁝ **eczema**: kali-sil k2

⁝ **itching**: morg-p fmm1• **Nat-m**

⁝ **pimples**: fl-ac bro1 guaj h2 kali-c nept-m lsd2.fr podo fd3.de• ros-d wla1 sil bro1 stann h2 tarax h1 thuj bro1

⁝ **burning**: stann h2

⁝ **psoriasis**: **Phos** k ●

⁝ **scaly**: morg-p fmm1•

⁝ **spongy**: fl-ac nat-m

⁝ **yellow**: fl-ac nat-m rhus-t spong h1

• **Above | pimples**: propr sa3•

• **Between | pustules**: thuj h1

- **Eyes | About | inflamed**: spig h1

• **Below**: dulc guaj hep b4a.de sel thuj vanil fd5.de

- **Forehead**: agar k* agn b2.de* ail k2 alum k* alum-p k2 am-c k* am-m k* ambr k* anac b2.de* **Ant-c** k* *Apis* b7a.de aq-mar skp7• arg-met k* arn b2.de* ars k* aur k* aur-s k2 bad bar-c k* bar-m bar-s k2 bell k* bit-ar wht1• *Bov* k* bry k* cadm-s *Calc* k* *Calc-p* calc-sil k2 canth b2.de* caps k* carb-an k* carb-v k* carc fd2.de• caul *Caust* k* cham k* chel b2.de* chin bg1 cic k* clem k* cocc b2.de* con b2.de* cycl dig b2.de* dros b7a.de dulc k* euph b2.de* ferr-ma galeoc-c-h gms1• ger-i rly4• graph b2.de* hell b2.de* *Hep* k* hura iod b4a.de ip b7.de kali-c b2.de* **Kreos** k* lac-h sk4• laur b2.de* **Led** k* lol bg2 *Lyc* k* mag-c b2.de* mag-m k* melal-alt gya4 merc b2.de* mez b2.de* mur-ac k* musca-d szs1 nat-ar nat-c k* **Nat-m** k* nat-ox rly4• nat-p nat-sil fd3.de• nit-ac k* **Nux-v** k* olnd b2.de* *Par* k* petr-ra shn4• *Ph-ac* k* *Phos* k* pneu jl2 *Psor* k* puls b2.de* rheum b7.de rhod b2.de* **Rhus-t** k* rhus-v ruta b2.de* sabad b2.de* *Sars* k* **Sep** k* sil k* spig b7a.de staph k* sul-ac b2.de* **Sulph** k* tritic-vg fd5.de urol-h rwt• valer b2.de* verat b2.de* viol-t k* zinc b2.de*

• **menses**; before: mag-m hr1 positr nl2• sars b4a.de*

• **touch** agg.: galeoc-c-h gms1•

- **Jaws | Lower**: anthraq rly4• canth b7.de* graph bg2 mur-ac a1 par b7.de* pip-n bg2 rhus-t b7.de* sulph bg2 verat b7.de*

- **Lips**: agar ail alum k* *Am-c* k* am-m ant-c ant-t apis arg-n arge-pl rwt5• arn **Ars** k* asc-t aur-m bell berb *Borx* k* bov brom bry k* cadm-s *Calc* k* calc-f calc-s calc-sil k2 cann-s h1* canth caps carb-an carb-v carbn-s caust k* cham chel chinin-s cic cinnb *Clem Com Con Crot-t* dig k* ferr-m galeoc-c-h gms1• *Graph* k* guaj hed sp1 hell *Hep* k* hydr ign ip kali-c kali-chl kali-m k2 kali-s lac-c lach lyc k* *Mag-c* k* *Mag-m* mang med melal-alt gya4 merc k* merc-c mez b4.de *Mur-ac* k* nat-ar *Nat-c* k* **Nat-m** k* nat-p nat-s nicc *Nit-ac* nux-v pall par petr k* ph-ac phos plat k* psor bro1 rhod **Rhus-t** ruta sang sars k* seneg **Sep** k* *Sil* k* spong *Squil* staph staphycoc rly4• *Sul-i* bro1 sulph k* tarent ter k* thuj k* tritic-vg fd5.de urt-u valer viol-t

• **accompanied** by | **coryza** (See NOSE - Coryza - accompanied - lips)

• **blisters**: ven-m rsj12•

⁝ **black**: tub ptk1

• **chill**; during: *Ars* bg2 bry bg2 caps bg2 ign bg2 *Nat-m* bg2 *Nux-v* bg2 rhus-t bg2

• **fever**; during: *Ars* b4a.de *Ign* b7a.de *Nat-m* b4.de* nux-v b7.de*

• **perspiration**; during: ant-c bg2 *Ars* bg2 *Bry* bg2 calc bg2 caust bg2 *Ign* bg2 ip bg2 lyc bg2 **Nat-m** bg2 *Nux-v* bg2 rhus-t bg2 *Sep* bg2 sil bg2

○ • **Above | right**: vero-o rly3•

• **Around** lips | **licking**; from: agar zr

• **Lower**: alum b2.de* borx k* **Bry** k* *Calc* k* caust k* cham b2.de* clem b2.de* galeoc-c-h gms1• *Ign* b2.de* mez b2.de* *Nat-c* k* *Nat-m* k* *Ph-ac* k* phos k* rhod b2.de* **Sep** k* *Sulph* tritic-vg fd5.de

⁝ **left**: galeoc-c-h gms1•

⁝ **inflamed**: borx a1

• **Upper**: acon b2.de* aids nl2• amph a1 ant-c b2.de* arg-n a1 arn b2.de* **Ars** k* *Bar-c* k* bell k* borx h2 canth b2.de* *Carb-v* k* caust b2.de* *Cic* k* cinnb con b2.de* dig h2* graph k* hell b2.de* hep b2.de* **Kali-c** k* **Kreos** k* *Lyc* k* m-ambo b2.de mag-c k* mag-m k* mang merc b2.de* *Nat-c* k* *Nat-m* k* nit-ac k* *Par* k* petr b2.de* phyt plat b2.de* prot jl2 *Rhus-t* k*

- **Lips – Upper**: ...
sabad b2.de* *Sars* b4a.de *Sep* k* *Sil* k* spig b2.de* squil **Staph** k* sul-i c2 **Sulph** k* *Thuj* k* tritic-vg fd5.de vero-o rly4• viol-t zinc b2.de*

⁝ **desquamating**: prot jl2

⁝ **dry**: prot jl2

- **Margin** of hair: mez mrr1

- **Mouth**:

○ • **Angles** (See corners)

• **Around**: acon b2.de* *Agar* k* alum b2.de* am-c k* am-m b2.de* anac k* ant-c b2.de* **Ant-t** arn b2.de* **Ars** k* bar-c b2.de* bell k* *Borx* k* *Bov* k* **Bry** b2.de* *Cadm-s Calc* k* calc-f calc-sil k2 cann-s b2.de* canth b2.de* caps b2.de* carb-an b2.de* (non:carb-v k*) carbn-s *Caust* k* (non:cham k*) (non:chel k*) chin b2.de* (non:chinin-s kl) choc srj3• *Cic* b2.de* clem b2.de* cocc b2.de* coloc b2.de* con b2.de* crot-h kl dig b2.de* dream-p sdj1• dulc b2.de* galeoc-c-h gms1• **Graph** k* *Hell* k* *Hep* k* hydr hyos b2.de* *Hyper* ign k* ip b2.de* kali-ar *Kali-bi Kali-c* k* **Kali-chl** kali-i kali-m k2* **Kreos** k* lach laur k* *Led* k* *Lyc* k* m-ambo b2.de m-arct b2.de *Mag-c* k* *Mag-m* k* mang k* *Merc* k* *Merc-c Mez* k* *Mur-ac* k* **Nat-ar Nat-c** k* **Nat-m** k* nat-p nat-s **Nit-ac** k* *Nux-v* k* *Par* k* *Petr* k* ph-ac b2.de* *Phos* k* plat b2.de* rhod b2.de* **Rhus-t** k* rhus-v ruta b2.de* sabad b2.de* samb b2.de* **Sep** k* *Sil* k* spig b2.de* spong b2.de* squil b2.de* **Staph** k* **Sulph** k* tarax k* thuj b2.de* verat b2.de* zinc k*

⁝ **coryza**; during: mez ptk1

⁝ **tettery** (See itching - mouth)

• **Corners** of: **Am-m** bg2 *Ant-c* k* arn b2.de* *Ars* bro1 ars-br vh aster bro1 **Bell** k* bov k* **Calc** k* calc-f cann-s h1* carb-v k* caust b2.de* *Cic* coloc b2.de* *Cund* echi bro1 galeoc-c-h gms1• **Graph** k* hell b2.de* **Hep** k* hydrog srj2• *Ign* k* iris *Kreos* k* *Lyc* k* m-arct b2.de *Mang* k* **Merc** k* mez k* mur-ac bro1 naphtin bro1 nat-c k* *Nat-m* k* **Nit-ac** k* nux-v k* *Petr* k* ph-ac *Phos* k* psor rhod b2.de* rhus-t seneg k* **Sep** k* *Sil* k* tab tritic-vg fd5.de tung-met bdx1• verat k* zinc b2.de*

⁝ **right**: bell bg1 cassia-s ccrh1• hep bg1 merc bg1 sep bg1 til bg1

⁝ **left**: corian-s kni6• galeoc-c-h gms1• tritic-vg fd5.de

⁝ **curving** upwards: mur-ac a1

⁝ **Below**: caust h2 graph h2 hep h2

- **Nose**: agar k* agn k* aids nl2• *Alum* k* alum-p k2 am-c k* am-m k* amp rly4• anac k* ant-c k* arn k* ars k* ars-i arum-t *Aur* k* aur-ar k2 aur-i k2 aur-m-n aur-s k2 bar-c k* bar-i k2 bar-m bar-s k2 bell k* bond a1 borx k* both-ax tsm2 bov k* brom k* bry k* cadm-s calc k* calc-sil k2 cann-s b2.de* canth k* caps k* *Carb-an* k* *Carb-v* k* carbn-s **Caust** k* cham k* chel k* chin k* chord-umb rly4• cina k* *Cist Clem* k* coloc b2.de* con k* crot-t cystein-l rly4• dulc k* *Elaps* euphr k* fl-ac bg2 graph k* guaj k* hell b2.de* hep k* ign k* iod k* iris kali-ar *Kali-br* c2 *Kali-c* k* kali-i bg2 kali-n k* kali-s lach k* lap-la sde8.de• laur k* *Led* lyc k* m-arct b2.de* mag-c k* mag-m k* mang b2.de* meny *Merc* k* mez k* mur-ac k* *Nat-ar* **Nat-c** k* nat-m k* **Nat-p** nicc k* *Nit-ac* k* nux-v k* olnd k* orot-ac rly4• par petr k* **Ph-ac** k* phos k* plat k* plb k* *Puls* k* ran-b rhod b2.de* *Rhus-t* k* sabad b2.de* sabin b2.de* sal-fr sle1• samb b2.de* sars k* sel k* seneg b2.de* **Sep** k* **Sil** k* *Spig* k* spong b2.de* staph k* stront-c k* sul-ac k* **Sulph** k* syph tarax k* tax c2 thuj k* tritic-vg fd5.de tung-met bdx1• vanil fd5.de verat k* viol-t k* zinc k* zinc-p k2

○ • **Around**: alum k* am-c k* *Ant-c* k* ars bg2 bar-c k* bov k* calc k* *Caust* k* choc srj3• dulc k* elaps m-arct b2.de* mag-m k* *Nat-c* k* par k* **Rhus-t** k* *Sep* k* sil k* sul-ac k* sulph k* tarax k* zinc k*

• **Below**: *Bar-c* bg2 caps b7a.de* *Cic* b7a.de fl-ac bg2 lach bg2 *Sars* bg2 sil bg2 squil b7a.de* sulph bg2 teucr b7.de*

• **Corners**, of: anac carb-v h2* dulc k* euphr k* led mang merc-c b4a.de mill plb k* rhus-g tmo3• *Rhus-t* k* sil b4a.de thuj k*

• **Dorsum**: *Alum* b4a.de *Fl-ac* b4a.de

• **Fossa**: staphycoc jl2

• **Inside**: acon-ac rly4• am-m k* ant-c b7.de* arn b7.de* canth b7.de* carb-an bg2 cic b7.de* cocc b7.de* graph bg2* guaj b4.de* kali-bi bg2 kali-n b4.de* *Kreos* b7a.de mag-c k* petr bg2 phel phos b4a.de phyt a1 podo ran-b b7.de* sars k* sel k* sil k* spig b7.de*

⁝ **right**: calc carb-an dulc gamb kali-n lach medul-os-si rly4• spig a1

⁝ **left**: bell borx calc cob cystein-l rly4• dendr-pol sk4• graph a1 podo fd3.de• sars k*

• **Root** of: bell bg2 cassia-s ccrh1• caust h2 clem bg2

⁝ **spots**: cassia-s ccrh1•

• **Septum**: am-c bg2 bar-c bov calad caps crot-t kali-bi bg2 ol-an podo fd3.de• psor k* teucr thuj k* vinc

- • **Tip**: acon *Aeth* k* am-c k* anan asaf calc bg2 carb-an k* carb-v k* *Caust* k* clem k* con bg2 galeoc-c-h gms1• kali-n h2* lyc mag-c bg2 nat-c bg2* nit-ac k* pall ph-ac k* podo fd3.de• rhus-t mrr1 *Sep* k* sil k* s p o n g k* vanil fd5.de
- • **Under** nose: arn borx bov irid-met srj5• lyc k2 petr-ra shn4• sars squil
- • **Wings**, on: ant-c mtf33 ars aur-m carb-v caust ptk1 chin k* cor-r dulc euphr k* fl-ac hipp *Merc-i-r* naja bg2 nat-m k* *Nit-ac* k* petr rhus-t k* sep *Sil* spig k* thuj k* tritic-vg fd5.de vanil fd5.de
  - ⁝ **left**: limest-b es1•
- **Temples**: *Alum* k* ambr b2.de* anac b2.de* *Ant-c* k* arg-met k* arn b2.de* asar b7a.de bar-c b2.de* bell k* bry k* calc k* carb-v k* caust k* chel b7a.de cocc b2.de* *Dulc* lach k* lyc k* *Mur-ac* k* *Nat-m* k* nept-m lsd2.fr nit-ac k* sabin k* spig k* sulph k* symph fd3.de• thuj k* tritic-vg fd5.de
  - • **right**: sulfa sp1
- **Whiskers**: agar b4a.de ambr k* *Calc* k* cic k2 graph k* hep bro1 lach nat-c b4a.de nat-m b4a.de nit-ac k* plb b7a.de sil b4a.de

ERYSIPELAS: *(↗Gangrene)* acon bg2 agn hr1 ail k* am-c bg2 a n a c - o c k* anan k* *Anthraci* **Apis** k* arg-n bg2 arn k* ars k* *Astac* *Aur* k* aur-ar k2 aur-m bar-c bg2 **Bell** k* *Borx* k* bry bg2 bufo calc k* *Camph* k* *Canth* k* *Carb-an* k* *Carb-v* k* carbn-s *Caust* *Cham* k* *Chel* k* *Chin* k* cic k2 cinnb cist k* clem bg2 com crot-h k* crot-t k* *Cupr* k* diph-t-tpt jl2 dor k* *Echi* *Euph* k* ferr-m bro1 gels **Graph** k* gymno k* *Hep* k* hippoz k* *Hydr* hr1 *Jug-c* k* kali-ar kali-c kali-i k* **Lach** k* *Led* k* lyc bg2 meph merc bg2 *Mez* k* morg-p pte1*• naja nat-c bg2 nat-s k* *Nit-ac* k* phos k* phyt k2 plb k* psor al2 *Puls* k* **Rhus-t** k* *Rhus-v* ruta bg2 samb bg2 sarr sep k* sil bg2 sol-ni bro1 s o l - t - a e k* stram k* *Sul-ac* *Sulph* k* tep k* ter k* thuj k* verat-v bro1

- **one** side: apis borx cham k2 nux-v k* sep *Stram* k*
- **right**: arund k* *Bell* k* stram k* sulph k2
  - ▽ • **extending** to | **left**: apis arund **Graph** lyc sulph
- **left**: agn k* *Borx* k* *Cham* k* lach k* *Stram* hr1
  - ▽ • **extending** to | **right**: lach **Rhus-t**
- **accompanied** by:
  - ○ • **Scalp**; erysipelas on: *Lach*
  - • **Tongue** | **red** discoloration of the tongue | **fiery** red: *Canth* kr1*
    - ⁝ **smooth**: rhus-t kr1*
- **bites** of insects, from: *Led* k*
- **edematous**: **Apis** ars chin crot-t hell lyc merc *Rhus-t* sulph thuj
- **erratic**: arn k* bell k* mang k* **Puls** k* rhus-t sabin k* sulph k*
- **gangrenous**: **Ars** k* camph k* **Carb-v** k* chin k* *Hippoz* **Lach** k* mur-ac k* *Rhus-t* k* **Sec** k* sil k*
- **nursing** the child agg.; when: borx
- **periodical**: **Apis** *Crot-h*
- **phlegmonous**: *Acon* k* anthraci bro1 *Apis* *Arn* k* *Ars* bro1 *Bell* k* both bro1 b r y k* bufo carb-an k* carbn-s cham k* *Crot-h* k* ferr-p bro1 *Graph* k* *Hep* k* *Hippoz* k* **Lach** k* led k2 merc k* phos k* puls k* **Rhus-t** k* sep k* *Sil* k* *Sulph* k* *Tarent-c* bro1 verat-v bro1
- **pregnancy** agg.; during: *Borx*
- **rays**, spreading like: graph
- **spot**: *Apis*
- **vesicles**:
  - • **with**: *Ars* bell camph canth chin cist com **Euph** *Graph* hep lach puls ran-b **Rhus-t** *Rhus-v* sep sulph tep
  - • **without**: chin c1
- ▽ **extending** to:
  - ○ • **Body**: *Graph*
  - • **Ear**: *Jug-c*
  - • **Head**: agn hr1 *Chel* op k* puls k2
- ○ **Cheeks** | **menses**; after: stram b7.de
- **Ear**; beginning in right: sulph
- **Eye**; around: *(↗EYE - Inflammation - erysipelatous)* acon anac **Apis** ars bell com *Graph* *Hep* *Led* *Merc* *Merc-c* **Rhus-t** vesp
- **Forehead**: apis kali-i k* ruta sulph
  - • **spots**: kali-i k* sulph
- **Lip**; lower:
  - ▽ • **extending** to | **Face**: *Anthraci* apis
- **Nose**: agn hr1 am-m *Apis* arn bg2* *Aur* bell bro1 cadm-s *Calc* k* *Canth* k* graph hippoz lach bg2 plb k* rhus-t k* stram k*

EVERTED lips: **Apis** k* *Bell* bg2 bry xyz61 camph k* merc bg2 phyt k*

Everted lips: ...

- **swollen**: **Merc-c** k*
- ○ **Upper**: *Merc* b4a.de merc-c b4a.de

EXCORIATION: *Graph* b4a.de

- **menses**; during: kreos bg1*
- **sensation** of: agn bg2 ambr bg2 cham bg2 dig bg2 olnd bg2 ph-ac bg2 plat bg2 rhod bg2 ruta bg2 staph bg2
- ○ **Jaws** | **Lower**: mang b4.de*
- **Lips**: all-c k2 aloe sne am-c k2 am-m k* ant-t **Ars** k* **Arum-t** k* borx bg2 b r o s - g a u mrc1 calc k* canth k* *Caust* k* cham k* cop cupr k* *Graph* k* ham *Hell* ign bg2 *Iod* kali-c k* *Kali-p* kreos k2 lac-c **Lach** lyc k* mang merc mez k* *Mur-ac* nat-m k* *Nit-ac* ph-ac b4a.de phos *Sep* stram sulph k2
  - • **coryza**; during: am-m b7.de* *Cham* b7.de*
  - • **pollution**; after: nux-v bg2
  - • **saliva**; from acrid: am-c k2* arum-t k2 **Nit-ac** k* sulph k2
  - ○ • **Inside**: cupr h2 ruta fd4.de sep h2
  - • **Lower**: *Ars* b4a.de ign b7.de* *Sep* b4.de*
  - • **Upper**: *All-c* mrr1 brom bg2 mag-c h2 mag-m b4a.de mang a1 symph fd3.de•
- **Mouth**; corners of: *(↗Cracked - mouth)* ant-c k* *Ars* **Arum-t** k* arund br1 bamb-a stb2.de• bell bov brach *Caust* k* *Cocc* *Cund* dios eup-per form *Hell* k* ign br1 ind ip kreos k2 **Lyc** k ●* **Merc** k* mez k* mur-ac bg2 nat-c h2 nat-m k* pall phos k* *Psor* sul-ac bg2 **Sulph** k ● thuj b4a.de zinc b4.de*
- **Nose**; corners of: chinin-ar

EXERTION:

- **agg.**: nux-v b7.de* *Rheum* b7a.de spong b7.de*
- **before**: chin bg2

EXOSTOSIS: *Aur-m* fl-ac bro1 *Hecla* k* phyt

- ○ **Jaws**: hecla br1*
  - • **dental** origin; of: hecla mrr1
  - ○ • **Lower**: **Ang** k* **Calc-f** k* *Hecla* st1* *Hep* k*
- **Malar** bones: aur ptk1
  - • **right**: *Aur-m*

EXPRESSION: *(↗EYE - Tired expression)*

- **absent**: camph bg1 falco-pe nl2• graph bg1 mang bg1 positr nl2•
- **alert**: ozone sde2•
- **anxious**: *(↗MIND - Anxiety)* **Acon** k* **Aeth** k* agar **Ail** all-c k* aloe am-c k* am-m k* ant-c bg2 *Ant-t* k* *Apis* k* apoc k2 **Arg-n** sne *Arn* b7a.de **Ars** k* ars-h k* ars-s-f k2 *Aspar* hr1* *Aur* sne *Bapt* k* bar-m k* *Bell* k* **Borx** k* *Cact* k* *Calc* k* **Camph** k* cann-i k* canth k* *Carb-v* carbn-o carbn-s *Chel* k* chin bro1 chinin-ar **Chinin-s** chlol k* cic k* cina bro1 coff k* colch k* *Coloc* k* *Crot-h* k* *Cupr* k* cupr-ar k* *Cur* k* *Dig* k* dulc k* dys fmm1• eup-per k* ferr-m k* hell mrr1 hydr sne hyos bg2 ign hr iod bro1 ip k2 iris kali-ar k* kali-bi k* kali-br a1* kali-ox a1 *Kalm* k* kreos bro1 **Lac-c** k* lach k2 *Lat-m* *Lyc* k* lyss k* merc k* merc-c k* merc-sul c1 morph k* mygal k* naja nit-ac k* *Nux-v* k* op gk phos a1* *Plb* k* sec bg2 sol-ni *Spig* k* *Spong* k* staph hr1 *Stram* k* *Stry* k* sul-ac k* *Sulph* k* *Tab* bro1 **Verat** k* vesp k* vip k* zinc k*
  - • **cradle**, when child is lifted from●: calc k*
  - • **downward** motion; during●: *(↗MIND - Fear - falling)* **Borx** k* gels
  - • **menopause**; during: *Tril-p* k1
- **astonished**: acon k* bell k* cann-s k* carbn-s plb k* stram
- **besotted**: ail k* arn bg2* ars bg2 *Asaf* tl1 **BAPT** k ●* bell k* *Bry* k* *Bufo* k* calc bg2 *Carbn-s* mrr1 cench *Cocc* k* *Crot-c* *Crot-h* k* **Gels** k ●* hyos ptk1 **Lach** k●* led merc bg2 mur-ac nat-m bg2 **Nux-m** k ●* op k* sol-ni *Stram* k*
  - • **influenza**; during: bapt tl1
- **bewildered**: *(↗MIND - Confusion; MIND - Disconcerted; MIND - Forgetful)* *Aesc* *Bry* carbn-s glon *Lyc* nux-m k* *Ph-ac* bg1* phos a1 plb k* *Stram* k* zinc
- **bright**: ozone sde2•
- **cachectic** (See sickly)
- **cadaverous**: ars k2 canth b7.de* carb-v k2* colch tl1 lach b7a.de laur b7.de* *Plb* b7a.de sec b7.de* tab bg2 thuj ptk1 verat b7.de*
- **changed**: *Acon* bg3* aeth alum b2.de* ant-c b2.de* ant-t bg2 apis bg3* arg-n bg3* arn bg2 ars k* bell b2.de* bism b2.de* bry b2.de* bufo calc b2.de* *Camph* k* canth b2.de* caust k* *Cham* k* *Chin* b2.de* choc srj3• colch k* coloc b2.de* *Cupr* k* dros bg2 *Ferr* bg2 gels bg3* graph b2.de* *Hell* k* hyos b2.de* ign k* iod b2.de* lach b2.de* laur b2.de* lyc k* mag-c b2.de* mang bg2*

Face

- **changed**: ...
merc-c b4a.de nux-v b2.de* olnd b2.de* *Op* k* ph-ac b2.de* phos bg2* plat bg2 *Plb* b2.de* puls b2.de* ran-s b2.de* rheum b2.de* *Rhus-t* b2.de* sec k* sep b2.de* sil b2.de* spig b2.de* spong b2.de* squil k* stann bg2 *Staph* bg2 *Stram* k* verat k* viol-o b2.de* zinc b2.de*
- **changing**: squil h1
  - **rapidly**: stram mtf33
- **childish**: *Anac* k* nux-m k*
- **cold**, distant: *(↗MIND - Mood - repulsive)* falco-pe nl2• puls k*
- **confused**: *(↗MIND - Confusion; MIND - Disconcerted; MIND - Forgetful)* *Aesc* *Ars* k* *Bufo* *Camph* b7a.de cupr-act hyos k* lach b7a.de **Lyc** nat-m k* *Olnd* b7.de* op b7.de phos k* plb k* stram b7.de* *Verat* b7.de zinc b4a.de*
- **dazed**: bry k2
- **deathly** (See cadaverous)
- **deformed**: verat bg2
- **despair**; of: canth b7a.de*
- **diabolic** grin: nux-m c1
- **discontented**: *(↗MIND - Discontented)*
  - **children**; in: | **sick**; when: aeth br1
- **distressed**: *(↗suffering; MIND - Discomfort)* *Ail* k* am-c **Ars** k* *Arum-t* lp *Aspar* k* **Cact** *Crot-t* k* cupr cupr-n a1 gels k2 *Iod* k* lach k2 *Nux-m* k* nux-v k* phos k* spong k2 *Stram* k* stry k* zinc-p k2
  - **children**; in: | **sick**; when: aeth br1
- **disturbed**: camph b7.de* *Cupr* b7.de* olnd bg2 op b7.de* sec b7.de* *Stram* b7.de* *Verat* b7.de*
- **don't** bother me (See sullen)
- **dreamy** (See sleepy)
- **dull** (See sleepy)
- **embarrassed**: ambr ptk1
- **emotions** strongly; shows: *Calc* b4a.de
- **excited**: neon srj5•
- **fierce**: *(↗MIND - Rage)* **BELL** k ● hydr-ac k* merc-i-r k* op k* [tax jsj7]
- **foolish**: *(↗MIND - Childish; MIND - Foolish; MIND - Frivolous; MIND - Grimaces)* absin k* acon k* arg-n k* *Bar-c* k* **BUFO** k ●* kali-br k* *Lyc* k* *Nux-m* k* *Phos* k* *Stram* k*
  - **accompanied** by | **trembling**; nervous: both mtf11
  - **children**; in: bar-c mtf33 bufo mtf33 lyc mtf33 phos mtf33 stram mtf33
- **friendly**: ant-c mrr1 *Stram* b7.de* verat b7.de
- **frightened**: *(↗MIND - Ailments - fright)* **Acon** k* apis k* arg-n sne ars k* atro k* *Bapt* k* bell k2 cact k2 *Canth* k* cimic cocc k* cupr bg1* hyos b7.de* kali-ar k* kali-br a1 lac-c tl1 lyss k* op bg2* sol-ni *Spong* b7a.de* **Stram** k* stry tab k* tarent k* *Ter* sne verat b7a.de* vip k* zinc k*
  - **aroused**, when: *Ail*
- **frowning** (See Wrinkled; Wrinkled - forehead)
- **gloomy**, sinister: *Alum* b4.de* cham b7.de stram b7.de zinc b4.de*
- **haggard**: *(↗MIND - Anxiety; MIND - Cares full; MIND - Prostration)* am-c androc bnm2• ant-c ptk1* **Ars** k* bell k* *Camph* k* canth k* *Caps* k* *Carb-v* colch k* cupr k* elec c1 *Graph* hr1 *Hydr* k* *Hyos* k* kali-ar **Kali-c** k* kali-p k* *Lach* k* merc k* morph k* naja *Nat-m* k* nit-ac op k* ox-ac k* *Phos* k* plb k* sang k* *Sangin-t* c1 sec k* *Sil* spong fd4.de staph k* stram sul-i k2 tab k* *Verat-v* k* zinc-p k2
- **happy**: *Apis* *Ars* irid-met srj5• **Op** k ●* stram bg2 verat bg2
- **hard**: sep mrr1
- **idiotic**: *(↗MIND - Idiocy)* **Agar** k* bry k2 *Calc* cann-i k2 cic mrr1 kali-br k* *Lach* k* *Laur* k* *Lyc* plb k* sec k* stram k* tarent k* thuj k*
- **intoxicated**: *(↗MIND - Stupefaction)* bapt k2 bry k2 *Bufo* cann-i k* cench k2 chlf k* chlol *Cocc* dor k* eug *Gels* hydr hydrc a1 hyos k* kali-i k* *Lach* *Led* merc k* merl mur-ac naja gm1 *Nux-v* *Op* psor jl2 ruta *Stram*
- **looks** in a glass to see his expression: nat-m bg1 spong fd4.de tritic-vg fd5.de vanil fd5.de
- **magical**: agar dgt1
- **mask**; immobile like a: atra-r bnm3• botul br1* lycps-v ptk1 mang ptk1 mang-act bro1 tritic-vg fd5.de
  - **weakness** of facial muscles; from: botul br1
- **miserable** (See wretched)
- **morose**: mag-c b4a.de
  - **cough** agg.; during: spong h1*
- **old** looking: *(↗Shrivelled; GENERALS - Old - premature)* *Abrot* k* aeth vh1* *Alum* ptk1 *Ambr* *Anthraci* vh1 *Arg-met* vh1 **Arg-n** k* *Ars* k* *Ars-h* k* *Ars-i* *Aur-m* k* *Bar-c* k* borx bg2 brom k2 bry hr1 **Calc** k* carc sst• chlor k* coca bg2 con k* *Fl-ac* k* glycyr-g cte1• **Guaj** k* hydr-ac k* hydrog srj2• *Iod* k* kali-bi bg2 *Kreos* k* lyc bg2* mag-m mrr1 merc bg2* merc-c **Nat-m** k* ol-j **Op** k* ph-ac k2* plb k* *Plut-n* srj7• *Pulx* br1 *Samb* hr1* sanic ptk1 *Sars* k* sec mrr1 *Sep* k* sil stj2* spong fd4.de staph *Sulph* k* syph c1* *Ter* st1 tritic-vg fd5.de tub ptk1* vanil fd5.de vip bg2 zinc mrr1 [calc-sil stj2 ferr-sil stj2 mag-sil stj2 mang-sil stj2 nat-sil stj2 sil-met stj2]
  - **children**; in: abrot mtf33 aeth mtf33 arg-n mtf33 ars mtf33 bar-c mtf33 calc mtf33 iod mtf33 lyc mtf33 nat-m mtf33 op mtf33 sars gm1 sep mtf33 sil tl1* sulph mtf33 syph mtf33 tub mtf33
    - **newborns**: op ptk1
    - **nurslings**: op ptk1
  - **prematurely**: arg-n br1 iod mtf33
  - **sallow**, wrinkled●: arg-n bg2 calc bg2 fl-ac bg2 pulx ptk1 *Sep* vanil fd5.de zinc mrr1* [zinc-i stj2 zinc-m stj2 zinc-n stj2 zinc-p stj2]
- **painful**: *Colch* b7a.de *Puls* b7a.de ser-a-c jl2 stram b7a.de
- **pinched**: *Acon* k* *Aeth* k* ant-t ptk1 **Ars** ptk1 *Ars-i* hr1 camph hr1* carb-an k* *Carb-v* k* chin ptk1 *Cina* cocc k* coff mrr1 *Cupr* k* *Dig* hr1 ferr k* *Ferr-p* hr1 *Iod* k* kali-ar k2 kali-n k* lyc h2* merc merc-c k* nat-m mrr1 phos k* rhus-t hr1 *Sec* k* sil mtf33 staph k* sul-ac hr1 *Tab* k* vanil fd5.de *Verat* k* verat-v k* zinc k*
- **pleading**: hell mrr1
- **plethoric** (See Congestion)
- **questioning**: hell mrr1
- **reactive** to every sensation: lyc k2
- **ridiculous** during sleep: hyos b7.de*
- **sad**: *Ant-c* b7a.de colch b7.de* cupr b7a.de* ign b7.de* stram b7a.de
- **sardonic** grin (See Risus)
- **scowling** (See sullen)
- **serene**: laur b7.de* op b7.de*
- **serious**: merc mrr1 nat-m mrr1 rumx bg2 tritic-vg fd5.de
- **shy**: stram b7a.de
- **sickly**: *(↗EYE - Sickly)* acon k* aesc k* aloe k* alum b4a.de alumn k* am-c b4a.de* *Anac* k* ant-t b7.de* *Apis* arg-met k2 *Arg-n* k* **Ars** k* **Ars-h** k* *Ars-i* ars-s-f k2 bamb-a stb2.de• bar-c k2 *Berb* k* bism k* *Borx* k* *Bry* b7.de* *Calc* k* *Calc-p* cann-i canth b7.de* carb-ac carb-an k* *Carb-v* carbn-s carl k* *Caust* k* *Chel* k* *Chin* k* chinin-s **Cina** k* *Clem* k* coff mrr1 colch k* con k* cop k* corn k* crot-h k* cund cupr k* *Dig* k* dulc fd4.de *Eup-per* k* *Ferr* ferr-ar k2 ferr-i glon k* *Gran* k* hura *Iod* k* *Kali-ar* k* kali-bi k* kali-br a1 *Kali-c* k* kali-chl k* kali-m k2 kali-n k* kali-p kali-s kali-sil k2 kreos k* **Lach** k* lact k* **Lyc** k* mag-c mrr1 *Mag-m* k* *Mang* k* *Merc* k* *Merc-c* b4a.de mez b4.de* naja *Nat-m* k* nat-s k* nit-ac k* nux-m k* nux-v k* ol-j hr1 op k* petr b4a.de *Ph-ac* k* *Phos* k* phyt k* *Plb* k* psor k* ptel k* puls b7.de* *Rhus-t* k* *Sec* b7.de* sel k2 sep k* *Sil* k* *Spig* k* spong fd4.de *Stann* k* *Staph* k* stram k2 sul-ac k2* sul-i k2 *Sulph* k* tab k* teucr b7.de* thuj k* til k* tritic-vg fd5.de *Tub* k* vanil fd5.de *Verat* b7.de* zinc k* zinc-p k2
  - **morning**: dulc fd4.de sep h2*
  - **evening**: dulc fd4.de phos h2
- **sleepy**: **Cann-i** k* gels mrr1 laur k* **Nux-m** k ● **OP** k ●* phos k* phys k* psor jl2
- **smiling**: ars bg2 bell bg2
- **soft**: gels mrr1
- **solemn** on waking: stram h1
- **sour**: mag-m mrr1
- **stiff** (See Stiffness)
- **stony**: positr nl2•
- **stupid**: *(↗MIND - Dullness; MIND - Stupefaction)* agath-a nl2• ail k2* apis bro1 *Arg-n* k* *Arn* k* *Ars* k* ars-h k* asc-c a1 aster k* *Bapt* bg2* *Bar-c* bg2* bell k* **Bufo** mrr1* camph k* **Cann-i** k* cann-s k* cann-xyz ptk1 chinin-s con bg2 *Crot-c* cupr *Ferr* k* *Ferr-p* sne *Gels* k* glon k2 *Hell* k* hura *Hydr* *Hyos* k* kali-br k* kreos ptk1 lil-t lyss hr1 merc k* *Nux-m* k* op k* ox-ac k* phos k* phyt k* plb k* rhus-t bro1 rhus-v sec k* *Sep* tl1 *Stram* k* sulph tab k*
- **suffering**: *(↗distressed)* *Acon* k* aeth alum vh1 *Am-c* k* *Anac* *Ant-t* k* apoc vh arg-n k* **Ars** k* ars-s-f k2 aur-ar k2 *Borx* *Bry* sne **Cact** k* *Calc-ar* *Canth* k* caps fkm1• *Carb-v* carbn-s caust k* cench k2 *Cham* sne *Chel* k* *Chinin-s* k* *Cocc* *Colch* k* coloc k* cupr k* *Dig* hr1 dulc fd4.de ferr-ar k2 helon k* hyper k* kali-ar kali-br k* **Kali-c** k* kali-m k2 kali-p kali-s kali-sil k2* *Kreos* k* *Lach* k* lyc sne **Lyss** k* mag-c k* *Mag-m* k* **Mang** k* *Mez* k* nat-m k* nat-sil fd3.de• nit-ac k* *Nux-m* k* ozone sde2• ph-ac k* phase-vg a1 *Phos* k* *Phyt* k* plat k* plb k* *Puls* k* raph k* sec k* **Sil** k* spong fd4.de stram stry k* sul-ac k* **Sulph** k* wies a1

- **sullen**: *(↗MIND - Discontented; MIND - Frown; MIND - Morose; MIND - Sulky)* alum k* falco-pe nl2• lac-loxod-a hrn2• mag-c h2* nux-v k*
- **suspicious**: *(↗MIND - Suspicious)* lach k2
- **tired**: *(↗EYE - Tired expression)* acetan vh1 acon adam srj5• aeth a1 *Anthraci* vh1 arg-met k2 *Ars* chlam-tr bcx2• cimic dulc fd4.de gels mrr1 hell ptk1 kali-br a1 kali-s fd4.de mag-c mrr1 mag-m mrr1 ozone sde2• *Plut-n* srj7• sec mrr1 sep mrr1 spong fd4.de stram tritic-vg fd5.de
- **troubled**: mag-c bg2 zinc bg2
- **unhealthy** (See sickly)
- **vacant**: *(↗MIND - Absorbed; MIND - Dream; as; MIND - Dullness; MIND - Ennui; MIND - Introspection; MIND - Meditating; MIND - Prostration; MIND - Stupefaction)* *Anac* k* anan arn bg1 *Bell* k* *Camph* k* cann-i k2 carbn-s cic k* *Cocc* k* *Ferr* k* *Ferr-p* sne gels ptk1 *Hell* k* hyos irid-met srj5• ix bnm8• *Kali-br* k* *Lach* k* lycps-v ptk1 *Mez* op k* ozone sde2• *Ph-ac* *Phos* bg1* plb psor k2 ruta fd4.de sanic sil *Stram* k* sul-ac bg1 tritic-vg fd5.de zinc k*
- **wild** (See EYE - Wild)
- **wretched**: ars bg2 berb bg2 iod mtf33 nat-m bg1 ozone sde2• ruta fd4.de spong fd4.de sul-ac bg2 sulph bg2 zinc ptk1
- **young**: bell gl1.fr• bry gl1.fr• nat-m gl1.fr• sulph gl1.fr• tub xxb

FALLING of hair (See Hair - falling)

FEELING face before attack: bufo c1

FEVER: | **before** | **agg.**: chin b7.de
- **during** | **agg.**: *Chin* b7.de coff b7.de nux-v b7.de verat b7.de

FISTULA: | **Parotid** glands: calc ptk1

FLAPPING cheek with difficult respiration: chen-a c1*

FLUSHED (See Congestion; Discoloration - red; Discoloration - red - anger; Discoloration - red - excitement; Discoloration - red - glowing)

FORMICATION: *(↗SKIN - Formication)* *Acon* k* acon-f agar bro1 agn k* alum k* ambr b7.de* apis k* arg-n a1 arn b7.de* arund aster bar-c k* bell b4.de* berb brom cadm-s calad k* calc camph cann-s b7.de* chin b7.de* coc-c k* *Colch* b7.de* con crot-c *Crot-t* k* ferr bg2 grat k* gymno k* helo bro1 helo-s rwt2• hist sp1 kola stb3• lach b7a.de* lachn lact lap-la rsp1 *Laur* k* lyss mag-m myric k* nux-v k* ol-an k* ph-ac k* **Plat** k* pycnop-sa mrz1 ran-b b7.de* *Rhus-t* b7.de* sabad b7a.de **Sec** k* sul-ac b4.de* sulph tab k* thuj k* til urt-u verat b7.de
- **right** side: alum k* *Plat*
- **left**: arg-n bg1* cench k2
- **children**; in: androc bnm2•
- **following** pain: euph h2*
- **tingling**: apis ptk1

○ - **Chin**; on: kreos b7a.de ran-b b7.de* stram
- **Eyebrows**: arn b7a.de croc b7.de* ran-b b7.de*
  - **left**: croc a1
- **Hair**; margin of: ham bg2
- **Jaws**:

○ • **Lower**: acon b7.de* alum h2 alumn k* bufo-s *Fl-ac* b4a.de grat ol-an **Plat** *Ran-b* b7a.de
  ⁝ **right** side: alum a1
- **Lips**: ant-c *Arn* b7.de* *Ars* b4a.de berb k* borx k* calc carc fd2.de• caust k* graph k* lap-la rsp1 nat-c h2* nat-m k* ph-ac k* **Sabad** b7.de* stront-c
  - **bugs** running over lips; as if: borx b4a.de* graph tl1
  - **menses**; during: graph k*

○ • **Lower**: ars b4a.de* borx bg2 caust b4.de* sabad b7.de*
  - **Upper**: ant-c b7.de* calc b4.de* ph-ac b4.de* sabad b7.de* stront-c b4.de*
- **Parotid** glands: con b4.de*
- **Zygoma** towards: thuj h1

FRECKLES: *Alum* bg2 *Am-c* k* *Ant-c* k* ant-t b2.de* bry b2.de* *Calc* k* carb-v b2.de* carc mlr1• coch hr1 con b2.de* dros b2.de* *Dulc* k* *Graph* k* hyos b2.de* iod b2.de* iris-g br1* *Kali-c* k* lach b2.de* laur b2.de* **Lyc** k* med hr1* merc b2.de* merc-i-r hr1 mez b2.de* mur-ac k* *Nat-c* k* nat-m b4a.de *Nit-ac* k* *Nux-m* k* petr b2.de **Phos** k* plb b2.de *Puls* k* *Sep* k* sil k* stann b2.de* **Sulph** k* tab br1* thuj k*
- **summer** agg.: phos dgt sulph dgt

FRIGHT agg.; after: hep b4a.de

FROSTBITE; after: agar b4a.de

FROTHY: | **Lips**: cina bg2 op bg2

FROWNING (See Wrinkled)

FULLNESS: aeth k* apis arn br1 cub k* ferr k* glon k* kreos k* lac-ac k* lac-c merc-c k* nat-m k* nat-pyru rly4• ox-ac k* petr-ra shn4• phos k* plan k* puls k2 sang k* sulph k2 syph hr1 tanac a1 ziz a1*
- **mental** exertion; after: phos k*

○ - **Lips** (See Thick - lips)

FUNGUS growth:

○ - **Jaws** | **Lower**: *Hep* *Phos* thuj

FUR; sensation as if covered with: cocc b7a.de

FUR-like in hemiplegia: caust hr1

FURROWS (See Wrinkled)

GANGRENE: *(↗Erysipelas)* *Merc* sul-ac

GLOWING (See Discoloration - red - glowing)

GREASY: *(↗Shiny - oily)* agar k* *Am-m* bro1 apis hr1 arg-n k* ars h2* aspar st aur k* *Aur-m-n* wbt2• *Bar-c* k* *Bry* k* bufo k* calc k* carc fd2.de• caust k* *Chin* k* con h2* cortico mtf11 des-ac mtf11 dulc fd4.de ferr-ar hr1 fl-ac ptk1 ger-i rly4• germ-met srj5• graph bro1 *Hep* gk hydr hr1* iod h* iris ptk1 kali-br bro1 *Kali-c* bro1 kali-p ptk1 kali-s bro1* lyc h2* *Mag-c* k* maland ptk1 mand sp1 med k* medul-os-si rly4• *Merc* k* mez bro1 **Nat-m** k •* nat-p fkr6.de nat-sil fd3.de* nux-v mtf33 ol-an ptk1 olnd mrr1 ozone sde2• petr-ra shn4• phos h2* *Plb* k* *Psor* k* puls ptk1 raph br1* **Rhus-t** k •* ruta fd4.de sanic bro1 sars bro1 *Sel* k* sep h2* sil h2* spong fd4.de staph bro1 stram k* suis-hep rly4• sulph hr1* syc pte1*• thuj k* *Tub* k* tung-met bdx1• valer ptk1 vanil fd5.de *Vinc* bro1 [bell-p-sp dcm1]

○ - **Forehead**: dulc fd4.de *Hydr* k* kali-s fd4.de nat-sil fd3.de• *Psor* k* ruta fd4.de spong fd4.de symph fd3.de• vanil fd5.de
- **Lips**: am-m k*

GUSHING sensation:

○ - **Jaws** | **Lower**: rheum b7.de*

HAGGARD (See Expression - haggard)

HANGING down:

○ - **Cheeks**; of: apis ptk1
- **Jaw**; of (See Dropping - jaws)
- **Lips**: verat ptk1

HARDNESS (See Indurations)

HEADACHE agg.; during: alum bg2 bov bg2 calc bg2 cann-xyz bg2 carb-an bg2 carb-v bg2 croc bg2 ign bg2 lyc bg2 merc bg2 zinc bg2

HEAT: *(↗Congestion)* acet-ac k* *Acon* k* *Aesc* k* *Aeth* k* *Agar* k* agn k* *Ail* k* *All-c* k* aloe k* *Alum* k* alum-p k2 *Am-c* k* *Am-m* k* ambr b7.de* *Aml-ns* k* amph a1 *Anac* k* ang b7.de* *Ant-c* k* *Ant-t* k* *Apis* k* aran k* *Arg-met* k* arg-n k* arge-pl rwt5• arizon-l nl2• *Arn* k* ars k* ars-s-f hr1* ars-s-r hr1 asaf k* asar k* aspar hr1 astac hr1 atro k* aur k* aur-ar k2 *Bapt* k* bar-c k* bar-m bar-s k2 **Bell** k* benz-ac k* berb k* *Bism* bg2 bit-ar wht1• borx b4a.de* *Bov* k* brach hr1 **Brom** k* **Bry** k* calad k* *Calc* k* calc-ar k* *Calc-p* k* calc-s k* calc-sil k2 camph k* cann-s k* *Canth* k* *Caps* k* *Carb-an* k* carb-v k* carbn-s card-b a1 card-m k* caust b4.de* cedr k* **Cham** k* *Chel* k* *Chim* hr1 *Chin* k* chin-b hr1 *Chinin-s* chir-fl gya2 chlam-tr bcx2• chlol k* choc srj3• chord-umb rly4• chr-ac hr1 cic b7a.de cimic k* **Cina** k* *Cinnb* k* cinnm hr1 cist k* cit-ac rly4• *Clem* k* coc-c k* *Cocc* k* *Coff* k* colch k* coli rly4• coloc k* *Con* k* *Cor-r* k* corn k* cortico tpw7* *Croc* k* crot-t k* cupr k* cycl k* cyt-l sp1 daph hr1 dendr-pol sk4• dig k* digin a1 *Dros* k* dulc k* *Elaps* equis-h eup-per eup-pur k* euph k* euphr k* fago k* *Ferr* k* ferr-ar ferr-ma k* *Ferr-p* k* *Fl-ac* k* form k* *Gels* k* *Glon* k* gran k* **Graph** k* *Grat* k* *Guaj* k* *Gymno* ham fd3.de• hell k* **Hep** k* hipp k* hist sp1 hura hydr k* hydr-ac a1 hydrog srj2• hygroph-s bnj1 hyos k* hyper k* iber hr1 *Ign* k* ind k* indg k* inul k* *Ip* k* irid-met srj5• jab k* jatr-c *Kali-ar* *Kali-bi* k* kali-br a1 kali-c k* kali-i k* kali-m k2 kali-n k* kali-p kola stb3• *Kreos* k* lac-c hr1 lac-d k2 *Lach* k* lact k* lap-la sde8.de• lat-m sp1 laur k* *Led* k* lil-t k* limest-b es1• lob hr1 *Lyc* k* lyss k* m-ambo b7.de *M-arct* b7.de m-aust b7.de mag-c k* mag-m b4.de malar jl2 manc k* *Mang* k* medul-os-si rly4• melal-alt gya4 meny k* *Merc* k* merc-c k* merl hr1 *Mez* k* mill c1 morg-p pte1• morph k* mosch k* mur-ac k* mygal bg2 myric k* naja narcot k* nat-ar *Nat-c* k* *Nat-m* k* nat-p nicc-met sk4• *Nit-ac* k*

Face

Heat: ...
nit-s-d hr1 *Nux-m* k* **Nux-v** k* ol-an hr1 olib-sac wmh1 olnd k* **Op** k* *Ox-ac* k* ozone sde2• paeon k* pant-ac rly4• par k* ped a1 *Petr* k* *Ph-ac* k* phel k* *Phos* k* *Phyt* k* pin-s k* plan k* *Plat* k* plb k* plut-n srj7• positr nl2• pot-e rly4• psil ft1 psor k* ptel k* **Puls** k* pyrog k2 ran-b k* ran-s b7.de* rat k* rauw sp1 rheum b7.de *Rhod* k* *Rhus-t* k* *Rhus-v* k* ribo rly4• rumx ruta k* sabad k* *Sabin* b7.de* sal-fr sle1• samb k* *Sang* k* sarr hr1 sars k* seneg k* sep b4.de* *Sil* k* spig k* spirae a1 spong k* squil k* *Stann* k* staph b7.de* **Stram** k* *Stront-c* k* stry suis-em rly4• suis-pan rly4• *Sul-ac* k* sul-i k2 *Sulph* k* *Tab* k* *Tarax* k* tarent k* tell c1 teucr b7a.de *Thuj* k* til k* tritic-vg fd5.de **Tub** k* *Urt-u* k* *Valer* b7.de* vanil fd5.de *Verat* k* verat-v hr1 vib hr1 vinc hr1 viol-o b7a.de* viol-t b7.de* wies a1 *Xan* k* zinc k* zing hr1 [bell-p-sp dcm1 heroin sdj2 neon stj2]

- **one** side: acon mrr1* arizon-l nl2• arn k* asaf kr1 asar h1 bar-c h2 benz-ac cham mrr1 chin h1 cimic coff hist vml3• ign k* ip mrr1 kali-c *Lac-d* vh murx phos h2 spong stann sulph h2 viol-t k*
  - **other** side; with coldness of: cham ptk1 dros ptk1 ip ptk1
- **right**: alum h2* cham h1* chir-fl gya2 crot-t a1 dros hr1 dulc fd4.de kali-s fkr2.de lyss k* nat-m nicc puls sinus rly4• sul-ac h2*
  - **sensation** of: olib-sac wmh1
  - **then** left: brom k*
- **left**: alum h2* alumn k* arg-n k* arn h1* borx euphr h2* inul k* *Lac-d* vh *Olnd* k* ph-ac h2* phyt hr1 positr nl2• raph k* staphycoc rly4• ulm-c jsj8• verat k*
  - **accompanied** by:
    - **Ear**; heat in left (See EAR - Heat - left - accompanied - face - left)
    - **Shoulder**; heat in | **left**: ulm-c jsj8•
- **daytime**: petr k* sulph h2
- **morning**: ail k* bar-c chel k* coc-c a1 croc k* cycl k* ferr k* hep k* kali-c k* kali-n h2* lyss hr1 nit-ac k* nux-v k* ph-ac h2* phos k* *Sep* k* sil a1 sulph k* til k* verat k*
  - **8** h: asaf myric
  - **15** h; until: stront-c
  - **rising** agg.: coloc k* lyc k* nux-v k* rhod k*
- **forenoon**: dulc fd4.de lact k* lyc k* nux-m k* ox-ac puls hr1 zinc k*
  - **9** h: asaf lyc
    - **9-16** h: lyc
  - **11** h: equis-h sol-ni
- **noon**: caps h1* lyc k* mag-c k* ped a1 ruta fd4.de sep k* *Spig* k*
- **afternoon**: agar k* alum anac k* arg-n a1 **Arum-t** k* bar-c h2* berb k* cann-s k* *Carb-an* k* carbn-s cench k2 chel k* chinin-s coli rly4• com k* dig digin a1 gels k* graph k* grat k* hyper k* ip h1* kali-bi k* luf-op rsj5• lyc k* mag-c mag-m k* mag-s k* nat-m h2* nit-ac k* ped a1 petr k* ph-ac k* phos h2* phys k* phyt *Rhus-t* k* ruta stront-c zing k*
  - **13** h: equis-h
  - **14** h: cench k2 *Chel* grat lyc phys
  - **14.30** h: gels
  - **14-15** h: phos h2
  - **15** h: chin sol-ni
  - **16** h: agar anac h2 coli rly4• sol-t-ae
  - **17** h: coli rly4• kali-bi *Rhus-t* zing
  - **20** h; until: psil ft1
- **evening**: *Acon* k* agar k* *All-c* hr1 alum k* anac h2* *Ang* k* ant-t k* apis *Arn* k* ars h2* aur h2* bry k* *Calc-p* k* carb-an h2* carbn-s *Cham* chinin-s coc-c a1 con k* croc k* dig digin a1 dulc fd4.de euphr k* fago k* fl-ac k* gran k* graph k* *Guaj* k* ham fd3.de• **Hep** k* hura ip h1* lob k* luf-op rsj5• lyc k* mag-c k* mez k* naja nat-c k* nat-m k* nat-p nit-ac k* nux-v k* oena k* ph-ac k* phos k* plat k* positr nl2• puls k* ran-b hr1 ran-s k* rhus-t k* rumx sabad k* sep k* sil k* spong fd4.de *Sulph* k* thuj k* verat k* zinc h2* zinc-s k*
  - **18** h: cann-i cedr chinin-s ferr-p
    - **18-19** h: phos h2
  - **19** h: ars a1 *Hep*
    - **19-20** h: ars h1*
  - **20** h: (non:ars kl) ham fd3.de•
    - **20-21** h: ars h1*
  - **21** h: ars hura
  - **22** h: *Chr-ac*
  - **bed** agg.; in: sep h2 spong fd4.de
  - **chilliness**; during: apis graph k*
- **evening**: ...
  - **lying**, after: am-m k* asar k* nux-v k* sep h2* viol-t hr1
  - **sleep**; before: dulc fd4.de ph-ac h2*
- **night**: aloe alumn a1* brass-n-o srj5• cocc-s hr1 cortico tpw7 **Hep** k* *Mez* ph-ac k* rhus-v k* ruta fd4.de sars k*
  - **midnight**: alum nat-m sulph
    - **after**: sulph h2
  - **waking**; on: am-c k* tarax h1*
- **accompanied** by:
  - **mental** symptoms (See MIND - Mental symptoms - accompanied - face - heat)
  - **respiration**; complaints of (See RESPIRATION - Complaints - accompanied - face - heat; RESPIRATION - Difficult - accompanied - face - heat)
  - **sleepiness** (See SLEEP - Sleepiness - accompanied - face - heat)
  - **vomiting** (See STOMACH - Vomiting - accompanied - face - heat)
  - ○ **Abdomen** | **complaints** (See ABDOMEN - Complaints - accompanied - face - heat)
  - **Head**:
    - **complaints** of (See HEAD - Complaints - accompanied - face - heat)
    - **heat** of (See HEAD - Heat - accompanied - face - heat)
  - **Teeth**; pain in (See TEETH - Pain - accompanied - face - heat)
- **air**; at the side exposed to: ph-ac viol-t k*
- **air**; in open:
  - **agg.**: (non:dig slp) digin slp hep mur-ac sulph h2 valer
  - **amel.**: am-m phos h2 stann
- **alternating** with:
  - **chilliness**: caust h2*
  - **cold** body: stram k*
  - **coldness** of face (See Coldness - alternating - heat)
  - ○ **Temples**; pain in (See HEAD - Pain - temples - alternating with - face)
- **anxiety**, during: *(↗MIND - Anxiety)* *Acon* j5.de arg-n j5.de bell j5.de **Carb-v** k* graph k* merc j5.de puls a1
- **bed**:
  - **in** bed:
    - **agg.**: nux-v k* sep verat
    - **amel.**: alum k*
- **blowing** the nose | **amel.**: acon bg1
- **burning**: acon am-m k* ant-t k* apis aran k* arn bg2 *Ars* hr1 *Bapt* k* **Bell** k* benz-ac hr1 borx h2 *Bry* k* camph caps k* carb-ac c1 *Cham* bg1* chel **Cina** cist *Clem* cocc k* croc k* cypra-eg sde6.de• dulc a1 grat k* hyos h1* ign k* iod irid-met srj5• *Kali-bi* hr1 kola stb3• mag-c h2* mang h2* merc-sul hr1 mosch hr1 *Nat-c* k* nat-p nux-v k* olib-sac wmh1 paeon petr h2* phos h2* plan hr1 plat k* plut-n srj7• psor hr1 ptel k* *Puls* bg1 rhus-t k* ruta fd4.de sabad k* samb k* *Sang* k* sep h2* spig hr1 stront-c k* sulph k* tab thuj k* urt-u hr1 verat k*
  - **fire**; like: olib-sac wmh1
  - **redness** of left side; and: alum asaf lac-c murx nat-m ol-an ph-ac spig
- **chill**:
  - **after**: ars h2* graph hr1 merc-sul hr1 petr h2* sep h2* staph h1* sulph h2*
  - **before**: calc k* chin h1* lyc meny staph sulph
  - **during**: acon k* agar k* alum k* ambr k* anac k* *Apis* k* **Arn** k* ars b4a.de* asar b7.de aur h2* bar-c bg2 bell k* bov b4.de* brom bg2 *Bry* k* *Calc* k* *Calc-p* k* *Cann-s* b7.de* canth b7.de* carb-v bg2 carbn-s cedr **Cham** k* chin k* cina cocc b7.de **Coff** k* coloc k* con h2* dig b4.de* *Dros* k* *Euph* b4a.de* **Ferr** k* gels k* graph k* hell k* hep bg2 *Hyos* k* ip b7a.de* jatr-c kreos k* lach k* led k* lyc k* mang b4a.de* *Merc* k* mez k* mosch bg2 *Mur-ac* k* nat-c k* nat-m h2* nat-p **Nux-v** k* **Olnd** k* ph-ac k* *Phos* k* plat b4.de* *Puls* k* ran-b k* *Rhus-t* k* ruta k* sabad k* sabin b7.de* samb k* sars h2* *Sel* b7a.de seneg k* spig bg2 spong b7.de* squil b7.de stann bg2 staph k* *Stram* k* stront-c bg2 sulph k* tarax bg2 thuj b4.de* tub verat b7a.de*

- **chilliness**:
  - **after**: kali-c h2*
  - **during**: alum k* asar k* bov k* dig h2* dros bro1 ferr k* gels k* *Hell* k* ign bro1 inul hr1 *Kali-bi* hr1 kali-c k* **Merc** k* *Nux-v* k* ol-an k* plut-n srj7• ran-b k* sabad a1* sabin hr1 samb h1* squil h1*
- **coffee** agg.: chinin-s c1 lyss k*
- **cold**:
  - **agg.**: melal-alt gya4
  - **room** | **agg.**: *Cocc* nat-c
  - **touch**; to: spig h1
  - **washing** | **after** | **agg.**: euph bg1 phos sil
    - **desire** for cold washing; with: *Fl-ac*
  - O **Back**: asaf tl1
  - **Body**, with: *Arn* k* ars mrr1 berb dgt1 *Calc-p* k* cann-s carneg-g rwt1• *Cham* k* *Chin* k* dig h2* *Led* k* melal-alt gya4 nit-ac phyt bro1 sal-fr sle1• *Stram* k* tab k* trom k*
  - **Cheek** cold and red, the other hot and pale; one: acon tl1 arn tl1 *Cham* tl1 *Mosch* k*
  - **Feet**, with: acon k* ars h2* aur h2* bell h1* caps h1* chin bro1 ferr br1* gels k* graph h2* ign k* kali-c h2* mag-c h2* meny hr1 nat-c h2* petr h2* phos h2* puls bro1 sabin hr1* samb k* sel rsj9• *Sep* sil h2* **Stram** k* verat h1*
  - **Fingers**: ferr mtf11
    - **Tips**: thuj h1
  - **Hands**: **Arn** k* ars asaf k* aur h2* camph h1* caps h1* chin h1* con k* cycl *Dros* k* euph euphr h2* ferr br1 graph h2* hyos ign kali-n h2* m-ambo al2 meny hr1 nat-c h2* nit-ac h2* nit-s-d a1 phos h2* plat h2* ruta sabin k* *Sep* hr1 sil h2* spig h1 **Stram** k* sumb k* thuj k*
    - **and** feet (See EXTREMITIES - Coldness - hands - feet - face)
  - **Limbs**: *Arn* k* bell h1* *Calc-p* cham k* chin k* dros k2 hell *Sabad* hr1 *Stram* k*
  - **Nose**, with: arn k*
  - **Side** cold, the other hot; one: *Acet-ac* *Acon* **Cham** **Ip** *Kali-c* *Lach* *Mosch* *Nux-v* spong c1
- **coryza**; during: ars-met **Arum-t** croc k* graph h2* **Nux-v** k* rhod b4.de* vanil fd5.de
- **cough** agg.; during: am-c b4.de* bell b4.de* *Cham* hr1 *Con* b4a.de *Guaj* hr1 *Hyos* b7a.de ip b7.de* *Mur-ac* hr1 sulph b4.de*
- **delivery**; during: *Arn* k* *Bell* k* *Coff* k* *Ferr* k* *Gels* k* *Op* k*
- **dinner** | **after** | **agg.**: am-c k* *Am-m* k* anac a1 asaf hr1 calc hr1 calen hr1 caps h1* carb-an k* *Cor-r* k* grat k* hell k* hura mag-m k* phyt k* ran-b k* tell k*
  - **during** | **agg.**: am-c k* am-m mag-m a1*
- **drinking** agg.: **Cham** cocc
- **eating** | **after** | **agg.**: am-c k* am-m k* anac k* *Asaf* k* *Calc* k* calen hr1 caps h1* carb-an b4a.de carl k* caust k* **Cham** k* *Coff* k* cor-r k* ignis-alc es2• *Lyc* k* merc k* nat-m h2* nit-ac k* nux-v k* paull br1 *Petr* k* phos k* phyt sep k* sil k* sulph viol-t k*
  - **agg.**: am-c k* carb-an b4a.de nat-c
- **eruptions**; before: nat-m h2*
- **exertion** agg.: am-c k* nux-v h1* spig k* spong k* squil k*
- **faintness**; with: petr h2*
- **fever**:
  - **before**: calc b4a.de
  - **during** | **agg.**: *Acon* b7.de* aza bro1 calc b4a.de cham bro1 *Chin* b7.de coff b7.de dros b7.de puls bro1 samb b7.de* spig b7.de spong b7.de staph b7.de tarax b7.de valer b7.de
- **fire**; of | **agg.**: *Euph* b4a.de
- **flushes**: *Acon* adam srj5• *Aesc* agar agn c1 alum *Ambr* *Apis* mrr1 *Arg-met* arge-pl rwt5• arizon-l nl2• ars asaf bamb-a stb2.de• bapt a1 bell tl1 bufo *Cact* calc h2 calc-s camph carb-ac carb-an **Carbn-s** carl caust ptk1 cedr cench k2 cham *Chel* chir-fl gya2 cic cimic *Cist* cit-ac rly4• clem coc-c *Cocc* k* coff colch crot-c crot-h cub dig dros dulc a1 ferr k* ferr-ar ferr-p fic-m gya1 gels tl1 *Glon* k* **Graph** helo c1 helo-s c1* hep hydr ignis-alc es2• inul irid-met srj5• *Kali-bi* kali-br a1 kali-c kali-chl kali-m k2 kali-p kali-s kalm k2 *Kreos* lac-h htj1• **Lach** k* lat-m bnm6• limen-b-c hrn2• lob **Lyc** lyss c1 maias-l hrn2• mang h2 med melal-alt gya4 meny h1 mez k2 mill k2 morg fmm1• nit-ac h2 nux-v orot-ac rly4•

- **flushes**: ...
oxal-a rly4• *Petr* petr-ra shn4• ph-ac *Phos* plb podo propr sa3• *Psor* ptel c1 puls k2* ran-s rauw tpw8 rhus-t ribo rly4• sabad sabin samb xxb1 sang tl1* seneg **Sep** *Sil* spig h1 spong *Stann* streptoc rly4• stront-c k* *Sul-ac* **Sulph** tarent tell *Ter* teucr *Thuj* til tub bg valer vanil fd5.de visc c1 yohim c1* [heroin sdj2 spect dfg1]
  - **left**: *Lac-d* k* sulph h2
  - **morning**: lyc h2 sulph k2
  - **forenoon**: flor-p rsj3•
  - **noon**: bamb-a stb2.de•
  - **afternoon**: cedr seneg
  - **evening**: alum arn bamb-a stb2.de• cedr nit-ac nux-v petr
    - **18** h: cedr
      - **18**-20 h: rauw tpw8*
  - **accompanied** by:
    - **anemia** (See GENERALS - Anemia - accompanied - face)
    - **faintness**: sulph tl1
    - **Heart**; weakness of (See CHEST - Weakness - heart - accompanied - face)
  - **alternating** with | **chills**: cedr petr
  - **bathing** amel.: bufo k2
  - **chilliness**; with: ambr c1 nit-ac petr puls h1 sulph h2
  - **cold** air | **amel.**: bufo k2
  - **cough** agg.; during: petr
  - **drinking** agg.; after: cocc c1
  - **epistaxis**; with: bufo br1
  - **excitement** agg.: *(↗MIND - Excitement - face - heat)* *Aml-ns* vh1 sulph k2 yohim br1*
  - **headache**, on side of: sang kr1
  - **heat** of stove agg.: bufo k2
  - **hemorrhage**; after: chin br
  - **menopause**; during: aml-ns apis mrr1 carc fb* glon al *Graph* *Kali-bi* *Kali-br* hr1 **Lach** *Lyc* *Psor* sang mrr1 **Sul-ac** sulph k2* *Ter*
  - **motion** agg.: *Stann* streptoc rly4•
  - **shivering**; with: **Sulph**
  - **sudden**: bamb-a stb2.de• mang
  - **warm** room agg.: bufo k2 sulph k2
  - **wine** agg.: coff k2 ferr-i mrr1 [tax jsj7]
- **flying** heat in the face: alum b4a.de* ambr b7.de* arn b7.de asaf b7.de bry b7.de carb-an b4.de cocc b7.de* graph b4.de* kali-c b4a.de* lyc b4.de* m-arct b7.de meny b7.de nit-ac b4.de nux-v b7.de petr b4.de phos b4a.de* plb b7.de sabad b7.de sabin b7.de sulph b4.de teucr b7.de* thuj b4.de* valer b7.de
- **followed** by:
  - **leukorrhea**: kreos b7a.de
  - **perspiration**: cassia-s cdd7•
- **headache**; during: *Acon* k2* agar k* aloe aml-ns br1* ang h1* aran k* *Bell* bro1 calc h2* cham bro1 **Chinin-s** k* cop k* ferr hr1 ferr-p k2* gels psa* *Glon* k* grat k* indg hr1 lac-ac c1 lact br1 lap-la sde8.de• lith-c mag-p bro1 *Meli* bro1 naja bro1 nat-m h2* nux-v hr1* phys hr1 podo bro1 ptel hr1 puls hr1 rumx ruta h1 *Sang* bro1 sep bro1 *Spong* k* til a1 viol-t k* zing k*
- **heart**, constriction of: hydrc
- **internal**: chin h1* con h2* nit-s-d a1 peti a1 sep a1 squil h1*
- **lying** agg.: mang petr phos plb spong fd4.de
- **lying** down agg.; after: am-m asar *Cham* nux-v
- **maniacal** rage, with: *Acon* **Bell** kali-c lach lyc merc op puls *Verat*
- **menopause**; during (See flushes - menopause)
- **menses** | **before** | **agg.**: alum k* lyc h2*
  - **during** | **agg.**: nat-m k*
- **mental** exertion agg.: agar *Am-c* k* lyc lyss k*
- **motion** | **after** | **agg.**: **Spong** k*
  - **agg.**: chin k* nux-v h1* spig h1* squil h1*
- **movements** of the child; at first: sulph h2
- **nose** amel.; blowing (See blowing - amel.)
- **painful** part: spig
- **pains**, with: ars h2*

- **palpitation**; during (See CHEST - Palpitation - accompanied - face - heat)
- **periodical**: aloe phos
- **perspiration**; during: acon bg2 bell bg2 **Calc** bg2 cham bg2 chin bg2 coff bg2 **Con** b4.de* ferr bg2 ign bg2 **Nux-v** b7.de* sabad bg2 sil bg2 stram bg2 *Tarax* b7.de* *Valer* b7.de*
- **prickly**: bell h1 morg-p fmm1•
- **reading** agg.: arg-met
- **redness** without: adren st equis-h c1 olnd st
- **rising** from sitting agg.: nat-c k*
- **room**:
  - **agg.**: am-m kali-n h2
  - **entering** a room; when | **open** air; from: **Chin** k*
- **sensation** of: *Agar* bro1 agav-t jl1 agro bro1 ang k* ant-c bro1 arn b7.de *Ars* bro1 arum-t bro1 asaf b7.de* asar b7.de* bar-act a1 bar-c b4.de *Bell* k* *Brom* b4a.de bry b7.de calc-s a1 camph b7.de cann-s b7.de* canth b7.de* *Caps* bro1 *Cham* bro1 chin b7.de* chir-fl gya2 cocc b7.de* coff b7.de* *Croc* b7.de* cycl b7.de cypra-eg sde6.de• dros b7.de *Euph* bro1 euphr k* helo-s c1 *Hep* b4a.de hydrog srj2• hyper ip b7.de kali-c bro1 kali-n b4.de* lap-la sde8.de• laur b7.de* led b7.de lyss hr1 m-arct b7.de m-aust b7.de mag-m k* mang h2* *Merc* k* merc-c b4a.de mosch b7a.de nat-c bro1 nit-ac h2* nux-v b7.de olib-sac wmh1 olnd b7.de par b7.de petr k* ph-ac b4.de* plat k* puls b7.de* pyrid rly4• rheum b7.de rhus-t b7.de* ruta b7.de* sabad b7.de samb b7.de* sang bro1 sarr rb2 seneg b4.de* sil bro1 spong b7.de squil b7.de stram b7.de stront-c k* *Sulph* bro1 symph fd3.de• tarax k* thuj k* valer b7.de* viol-t bro1 yohim mp4• ziz a1*
  - **night** | **bed** agg.; in: cortico sp1
  - **cold** to touch; when: chin grat plut-n srj7• rhus-t hr1
  - **fire**; face were on: sarr rb2
- **shivering**; during: acon b7.de arn b7.de cham b7.de cina b7.de coff b7.de dros b7.de hyos b7.de nux-v b7.de olnd b7.de puls b7.de rhus-t b7.de *Ruta* b7.de* *Sabad* b7.de staph b7.de verat b7.de
- **shuddering**; with: ars k* plut-n srj7• thuj k*
- **sitting** agg.: calc k* carb-v h2* con k* ferr-p k* nit-s-d a1 phos k* **Valer** k* viol-t k*
- **sleep** agg.; during: meny k* op b7.de*
- **smoking** agg.: *Calad*
- **sneezing** agg.: nux-v rhod k*
- **standing** agg.: mang k*
- **stool** | **after** | **agg.**: caust b4.de* trom hr1
  - **during** | **agg.**: gran k* hep k* merc k*
- **stooping** agg.; after: rhus-t k*
- **sudden**: alum h2* euphr h2* petr a1 rhus-t h1
- **supper** agg.; after: alum h2* anac h2* ang h1* carb-v k* chinin-s
- **talking**; after: fl-ac k* sep k* squil
- **vexation**; after: *Cham Phos*
- **waking**; on: alum k* bry bg1 chin bg1 *Hep* hr1 nit-ac sulph
- **walking**:
  - **after** | **agg.**: sep k*
  - **agg.**: mang nux-v stront-c *Sulph* tarax
  - **air** agg.; in open: mur-ac hr1 ph-ac h2 tarax h1
  - **amel.**: sabad
- **warm** | **drinks** | **agg.**: sabad
  - **room** | **agg.**: hyos *Puls*
- **weakness**; with: hydrog srj2• spong fd4.de
- **weeping**; with (See MIND - Weeping - face - heat)
- **wine** agg.: fl-ac k* ruta fd4.de
- **writing** agg.: chinin-s
- **yawning**; after: calc k*

▽ - **extending** to | **Body**; whole: chir-fl gya2

○ - **Cheeks**: **Acon** bg2 agar bg2 alum bg2 ang h1* *Ant-c* b7a.de* arizon-l nl2• arn bg2 ars bg2 asar bg2 **Aur** bg2 bamb-a stb2.de* **Bell** bg2 **Bov** bg2 brucel sa3• **Bry** bg2 *Calc* bg2 cann-xyz bg2 canth bg2 *Caps* bg2 carb-an bg2 carb-v bg2 caust bg2 **Cham** bg2 **Chin** b7a.de* chir-fl gya2 cina bg2 clem bg2 **Cocc** bg2 coff bg2 coloc bg2 croc bg2 dros bg2 *Dulc* bg2 *Euph* bg2 *Ferr* bg2 hell h1* hep h2* *Hyos* bg2 **Ign** bg2 iod bg2 ip bg2 irid-met srj5• **Kali-c** bg2 kali-n bg2 **Kreos** bg2 lach bg2 *Led* bg2 *Lyc* bg2 mang h2* medul-os-si rly4• **Merc** bg2 *Merc-c* bg2 mosch bg2 mur-ac bg2 nat-sil fd3.de• *Nit-ac* bg2 *Nux-v* bg2 olib-sac wmh1 olnd b7a.de* *Op* bg2 ph-ac bg2 *Phos* bg2 **Plat** bg2 plb bg2 pot-e rly4• puls bg2 ran-b bg2 rheum h rhod bg2 **Rhus-t** b7a.de* *Ruta* bg2 *Sabad* bg2 *Samb* bg2 sang ptk1 **Sep** bg2 sil h2*

Heat – Cheeks: ...
sinus rly4• spig bg2 **Stann** bg2 staph h1* **Stram** bg2 suis-pan rly4• sulph bg2 symph fd3.de• tab ptk1 *Thuj* bg2 til ban1• ulm-c tl1* *Valer* b7a.de* vanil fd5.de *Viol-t* bg2 zinc bg2 [bell-p-sp dcm1]

- **one** side: *Arn* bg2 bar-c bg2 *Bell* bg2 borx bg2 *Cann-xyz* bg2 canth bg2 **Cham** bg2 chin bg2 coloc bg2 *Dros* bg2 **Ign** bg2 ip bg2 kali-c bg2 *Mosch* bg2 nux-v bg2 ph-ac bg2 *Phos* bg2 plb bg2 puls bg2 *Ran-b* bg2 rheum bg2 stram bg2 sul-ac bg2 thuj bg2 verat bg2 *Viol-t* bg2
  - **accompanied** by | **coldness** of other cheek: kali-c bg2
- **right**: crot-h bg2 laur bg2
- **left**: *Acon* bg2 merc bg2
- **accompanied** by | **Teeth**; pain in (See TEETH - Pain - accompanied - cheeks - heat)
- **chill**; during: *Bry* b7a.de *Calc* b4.de cham b7.de* lyc b4.de *Mur-ac* b4a.de *Nat-c* b4a.de
- **eating**; while: ulm-c jsj8•
- **flying** heat: cocc b7a.de
- **sensation** of: olib-sac wmh1
- **uncovered**: *Thuj* bg2 viol-t bg2

○ - **Affected** side: tub ptk1

- **Chin**: canth k* euphr k* nat-m k*
  - **sensation** of: agar bg2 anac bg2 ant-c bg2 apis bg2 *Ars* bg2 bell bg2 bov bg2 *Caust* bg2 clem bg2 euphr b7.de* kreos bg2 mang bg2 merc bg2 mez bg2 plat bg2 *Rhus-t* bg2 sep bg2 *Sil* bg2 spong bg2 sulph bg2 thuj bg2 verat bg2 zinc bg2
- **Jaws** | **Lower**: acon bg2 bov b4.de* canth bg2 **Caust** bg2 cham bg2 kola stb3• nat-c bg2 par bg2 phos bg2 puls bg2 rhus-t bg2 *Staph* bg2 zinc bg2
- **Lips**: *Acon* k* aesc agar bg2 aloe am-c bg2 am-m bg2 ambr k* ang apis b7a.de* arn k* **Ars** bg2 ars-met asaf bg2 bapt bg2 bell b4.de* borx bg2 brom b4a.de* *Bry* bg2 canth b7.de* caps bg2 carb-an b4.de* card-b a1 caust bg2 cench k2 chin bg2 cic bg2 cina bg2 clem bg2 coll a1 fl-ac a1 gels k* hep b4.de hyos bg2 *Hyper* k* *Kali-chl* kreos b7a.de* lach a1 *Merc* k* **Mez** b4.de* mur-ac bg2 nat-m bg2 *Nit-ac Nux-v* bg2 oena a1 ph-ac bg2 phos bg2 puls bg2 rhod bg2 *Rhus-t* bg2 sabad k* senec a1 sep b4.de* sil a1 spig bg2 *Staph* b7a.de* sulph h2* sumb a1 thuj bg2 verat bg2
  - **burning** heat: acon bro1 ammc vh1 anis bro1 arn k* *Ars* bro1 arum-t bro1 *Bry* bro1 caps bro1 nat-m bro1 phos bro1 rhus-t bro1 *Sulph* bro1 taosc iwa1• thyr bro1

○ - **Upper**: *Apis* borx h2 *Carb-v* k* *Kali-bi* mez h2* sep bg2*

- **Mouth**:

○ - **Around**: ulm-c jsj8•

  - **Corners** of: arn bg2 dros bg2 mez bg2 nat-c bg2 zinc bg2
    - **right**: coloc bg2 crot-h bg2
- **Nose**; around: rheum h
- **Parotid** glands: brom
- **Side**:
  - **not** lain on: ph-ac k* viol-t k*

○ - **Affected** side: tub ptk1

HEATED; FROM BECOMING: acon b7a.de *Hep* b4a.de *Staph* b7a.de

HEAVY feeling: acon bg2* alum k* cham cupr bg2 gels bg2 hell bg2 iod kali-i ketogl-ac rly4• nicc k* op bg2 osteo-a knp1• petr-ra shn4• phos bg2 positr nl2•

○ - **Jaws**:

○ - **Joints**: spong h1

  - **Lower**: cham bg2 kali-i bg2 nux-v bg2 sabin b7.de* spong b7.de*
- **Lips**: anh sp1 graph b4.de* mur-ac b4.de*

○ - **Lower**: *Graph* k* *Mur-ac* k*

  - **Upper**: caust k*
- **Muscles** | **chewing** agg.: anh sp1

HEMORRHAGE:

○ - **Eyes**:

○ - **Orbits** | **Around**: helo-s bnm14•

HIPPOCRATIC: (↗*Sunken*) acon k* **Aeth** k* agar *Am-c Ant-c* **Ant-t** k* arn bro1 **Ars** k* asc-t berb bro1 *Camph* k* canth k* **Carb-v** k* carbn-h **Chin** k* chlor cic *Colch Cupr* k* cypr bro1 dig ferr ferr-ar ferr-i ferr-p hell bro1 iod kali-bi kali-n *Lach* k* laur b7.de* lyc merc merc-c k* merc-cy bro1 mez

Hippocratic: ...
nux-m *Nux-v* bg2 op ox-ac *Ph-ac* k* *Phos* k* phyt *Plb* k* puls k2 pyrog bro1 rhus-t bg2 rhus-v **Sec** k* stann staph k* stry sul-ac sul-i k2 **Tab** k* **Verat** k* vip zinc k*
- **children**; in: aeth mtf33 ars mtf33 *Carb-v* mtf33 chin mtf33
  - **newborns**: abrot mrr1 aeth mrr1

HOLE; sensation of a: | **Mouth** to eyebrow; from: plut-n srj7•

HUMMING sensation:
○ - **Jaws** | **Lower**: mur-ac h2*

HYPERESTHESIA: | **left**: trios rsj11•

INDURATIONS: am-c h2* ars k* *Bell* bg2 bry k* clem k* cob k* *Con* bg2 *Graph* k* led mag-c *Merc-c* hr1 olnd puls rhus-t k* sep k* **Sil** k* sulph k* viol-t hr1 zinc hr1
- **red**, hard lumps: *(↗Nodosities)* cob k*
○ - **Cheeks**: am-c h2* *Antip* bro1* caust ptk1 *Cham* k* merc
- **Forehead**: cic con led olnd
  - **lumps** like grit under the skin; small: plut-n srj7•
- **Jaws**:
○ • **Lower**: staph b7.de*
  ⁝ **Periosteum**: aur-m-n graph staph
- **Lips**: ars bg2 aur-m k* bell k* bov b4a.de *Bry* b7a.de calc-p k* chin k* cic bg2* clem bg2 *Con* k* cund bg2 dulc b4a.de graph bg2 hydr bg2 hydrog srj2• phos b4a.de rhus-t b7.de* sep k2 sil k* thuj bg2
  - **sense** of: cycl
○ • **Fold** of lips: cob-n sp1
  - **Glands**: con b4.de* sulph b4.de* zinc b4.de*
  - **Upper**: calc-p k*
    ⁝ **sensation** of: cycl b7.de* *Euphr* b7a.de
- **Mouth**, corners: am-c h2* aur-m nat-ar sil k*
- **Nose**, below: thuj h1*
- **Parotid** glands: *Am-c* k* anthraci jl2 arum-t k2 bar-c k2 *Bar-m* brom k* *Calc* *Carb-an* k* **Carb-v** b4a.de cist k2 *Clem* *Con* k* *Cupr* ign *Kali-c* kali-sil k2 merc k* *Merc-i-f* nat-c k2 *Nat-m* k* petr k2 *Phyt* psor k2 **Rhus-t** k* **Sil** k* sul-i k2
  - **right**: anthraci jl2 ign kali-c
  - **accompanied** by | **Ear** complaints (See EAR - Complaints - accompanied - parotid)
  - **hot**: brom ptk1
- **Submaxillary** glands: anthraci jl2 arum-t k2 **Bar-c** **Bar-m** brom k2* *Carb-v* *Cocc* *Con* *Cupr* graph k* kali-n k* *Merc-i-f* nat-c k2 nat-m k* petr k2 *Psor* *Rhus-t* k* sul-i k2 tub-m jl2
  - **right**: anthraci jl2
- **Submental** gland: anthraci ptk1 *Staph*
- **Temples**: thuj

INFLAMMATION: *Acon* b7a.de *Apis* b7a.de arn b7a.de bry b7a.de *Staph* b7a.de
- **follicular** (See Eruptions - beard - folliculitis)
- **sensation** of: gard-j vlr2•
○ - **Bone**, of: **Aur** k* bufo bg2 *Calc* k* *Fl-ac* k* *Merc* hr1 merc-c b4a.de *Mez* k* *Nit-ac* k* *Ph-ac* k* *Ruta* *Sil* k* *Staph* k* *Still* k* symph k*
- **Chin**: caust b4a.de
- **Jaws**:
○ • **Joints**: bry mtf11
  - **Lower**: calc-f ptk1 phos mtf11 symph mtf11
  - **Upper**: bamb-a stb2.de•
    ⁝ **left**: bamb-a stb2.de•
- **Lips**: *Acon* k* anan k* arn bg2 **Bell** k* canth b7a.de* crot-t bg2 **Merc** k* merc-c bg2 mez h2* mono a1 ph-ac rhus-t bg2 staph
○ • **Upper**:
    ⁝ **left**: mang
    ⁝ **coryza**; during: calc b4a.de lyc b4.de* *Mag-m* b4a.de mang b4.de* *Mez* b4a.de
- **Maxilla** (See jaws - upper)
- **Maxillary** sinuses: achy mtf11 morg-p fmm1•
- **Mouth**; corners of: ant-c mrr1 sil ptk1
- **Nerves**: ars tl1

Inflammation: ...
- **Parotid** glands (= parotitis; parotiditis): acon c1 *Am-c* k* anthraci jl2 *Ars* k* *Arum-t* *Aur* k* aur-ar k2 bar-act bro1 **Bar-c** k* *Bar-m* **Bell** k* *Brom* bg2 *Calc* k* calc-sil k2 *Carb-an* **Carb-v** k* *Cham* k* chinin-s c2 **Cist** k* coc-c k* cocc k* *Con* k* *Crot-h* k* dios c2 dor k* euphr c2 *Ferr-p* graph c2 *Hep* k* hippoz k* hyos bg2* *Iod* bro1 jab hr1* kali-ar *Kali-bi* k* *Kali-c* k* kali-chl hr1 kali-p kali-sil k2 *Lach* k* *Lyc* mang c2 **Merc** k* merc-i-r c2 musca-d szs1 myris br1 *Nat-m* k* nit-ac b4a.de *Nux-v* b7a.de* *Phos* phyt k* **Puls** k* **Rhus-t** k* sal-p c2 sars *Sil* k* sol-ni c2 sulph b4a.de* [calc-br stj1 calc-m stj1]
  - **right**: *Bar-m* *Calc* k* *Hep* hr1 *Kali-bi* k* *Kali-c* k* **Merc** k*
    ⁝ **then** left: **Lyc**
  - **left**: **Brom** k* *Lach* k* **Rhus-t** k*
  - **epidemic**: parot mtf11
  - **fistula**; with: phos k2
  - **gangrenous**: anthraci k*
  - **meningitis**; threatening: gels bnt jab bnt
  - **metastasis** to:
    ⁝ **Brain**: apis bro1 bell bro1 hyos c1
    ⁝ **Mammae**●: abrot k2 carb-v k2 con bro1 jab bro1 **Puls** k*
    ⁝ **Ovaries**: con bro1 jab bro1 puls bro1
    ⁝ **Testes**●: abrot k2 *Ars* k* aur bro1 *Carb-v* k* *Clem* bro1 *Ham* bro1 jab k* **Merc** bg2 nat-m k* nux-v bg2 ourl jl2 plb ptk1 **Puls** k* **Rhus-t** k ●* staph bro1* thuj k2
  - **mumps**: acon c2* ail c2* am-c bro1 ant-t bro1 anthraci bro1 aur-m bro1 bapt c2 *Bar-c* bro1 bar-m c2* *Bell* c2* brom br1* calc bro1 carb-an bro1 carb-v c2* cham c2* cist bro1 con ptk1* dulc bro1 euphr bro1 fago c2 ferr-p c2* hep bro1 jab c2* kali-bi c2* kali-m c2* lach c2* mag-p bro1 merc c2* *Merc-c* c2* merc-cy bro1 merc-i-f bro1 merc-i-r bro1 ourl jl2 pancr c2 phyt c2* pilo c2* pilo-m mtf11 *Puls* c2* *Rhus-t* bro1* sil bro1* sul-i bro1 sulph bro1 trif-p c2* trif-r c2*
    ⁝ **accompanied** by | **salivation**: *Hydr* st1 musca-d szs1 *Nat-m* kr1*
    ⁝ **prophylaxis** for mumps: trif-p ptk1* trif-r bro1
    ⁝ **terminal** period: ourl jl2
  - **scarlatina**:
    ⁝ **after**: bar-c hr1
    ⁝ **in**: **Am-c** hr1* *Calc* ll* *Phos* hr1 phyt bro1 **Rhus-t** hr1*
  - **suppuration**, with: **Ars** k* **Brom** k* *Bry* k* **Calc** k* *Con* k* **Hep** k* *Lach* **Merc** k* *Nat-m* k* *Phos* k* **Rhus-t** k* **Sil** k* sul-ac
- **Periosteum** (= periostitis): **Aur** k* *Calc* k* *Fl-ac* k* *Merc* k* merc-c *Mez* k* **Nit-ac** k* **Ph-ac** k* **Phos** phyt *Ruta* sil k* *Spig* bg2 *Staph* k* still k* symph k*
○ • **Lower**, jaw: ang bg2 *Merc* *Ph-ac* *Phos* ruta
- **Skin**: streptoc jl2
- **Sublingual** gland: kalm **Merc** psor sil k2
- **Submaxillary** glands: aln bro1 anthraci jl2 ars ars-s-f k2 *Arum-t* bro1 asim bro1 *Bar-c* bro1 **Bar-m** *Bell* brom bro1 calc bro1 calen bro1 cham bro1 chin cist bro1 clem bro1 crot-t *Dulc* graph k* iod bro1 kali-ar *Kali-bi* bro1 kali-c *Kali-i* kali-m bro1 kali-s kalm k* *Lach* lyc k* mag-c mag-p bro1 **Merc** k* merc-cy bro1 *Merc-i-r* bro1 nat-m bro1 nit-ac petr bro1 *Phyt* k* pin-s bro1 *Psor* *Puls* **Rhus-t** k* sep *Sil* k* spong staph bro1 stram *Sul-ac* k* *Sulph* k* tarent trif-p bro1 trif-r bro1 tub-m jl2 *Verat-v*

INJURIES: symph ptk1

INVERTED lips: camph b7.de* cund hr1

INVOLUNTARILY, mouth opens: *(↗MIND - Gestures - tics)* *Ther* k*

IRRITATION:
- **alternating** with | **Pharynx**; sore pain in (See THROAT - Pain - pharynx - sore - alternating - face)

ITCHING: *(↗SKIN - Itching)* acon *Agar* k* *Agath-a* nl2• *Agn* k* *Alum* k* alum-p k2 am-c k* ambr k* *Anac* anac-oc anan ant-c k* *Apis* *Apoc-a* *Arg-met* k* arn *Ars* ars-s-f k2 aur b4.de* bell k* berb k* bov b4.de* brach *Brom* *Bry* bg1* bufo bg2 bufo-s cadm-met tpw6* **Calc** k* *Calc-s* cann-s k* caps k* carb-ac carb-v b4.de* carbn-dox knl3• carbn-s carneg-g rwt1• **Caust** k* chel k* chinin-s cist k2 clem b4.de* cod colch k* coli rly4• coloc b4.de* colum-p sze2• com con k* cortico tpw7 cycl dol dulc b4.de* euph ferr-ma *Fl-ac* gels k* glon gran *Graph* k* grat ham fd3.de• hydr indg irid-met srj5• kali-ar kali-bi k* kali-br k* *Kali-c* k* kali-i kali-n k* kali-p kali-s kali-sil k2 ketogl-ac rly4• kola stb3• lach k* lachn *Laur* limest-b es1• lyc k* mag-c b4.de* malar jl2

Face

Itching: ...
mand sp1 meph merc *Mez* bro1 mim-p rsj8• morph myric bro1 nat-ar *Nat-c* k* nat-m k* nat-p *Nat-s* k* nicc nux-v k* *Olib-sac* wmh1 op k* pall par petr k* ph-ac k* *Phos* k* pieri-b mlk9.de plan plat b4.de* plb b7.de* podo fd3.de• positr nl2• rhodi br1* *Rhus-t* k* **Rhus-v** ribo rly4• *Ros-d* wla1 ruta k* sabad b7.de* *Sars* k* *Sep* k* *Sil* k* spong fd4.de stram k* stront-c k* stry a1 suis-hep rly4• sul-ac *Sulph* k* symph fd3.de• tarent thres-a sze7• thuj b4.de* til trios rsj11• tritic-vg fd5.de *Urt-u* vanil fd5.de ven-m rsj12• verat k* visc sp1 zinc k* zinc-p k2

- **right**: kali-p olib-sac wmh1 positr nl2•
- **forenoon**: tritic-vg fd5.de
  - **9** h: ven-m rsj12•
  - **10** h: mag-c
  - **11** h: iod
- **afternoon**: *Chel* k* dulc fd4.de fago k* podo fd3.de• ruta fd4.de spong fd4.de tritic-vg fd5.de
- **evening**: berb hr1 dulc fd4.de gink-b sbd1• olib-sac wmh1 ph-ac h2* podo fd3.de• rhus-v k* sabad k* *Sulph* k* tritic-vg fd5.de zinc k*
  - **19** h: fago
- **night**: ail bg1* *Dig* h2* ham fd3.de• kalm k* *Lach* k* *Mez* k* *Puls* bg1* rhus-v k* spong fd4.de stry k* ven-m rsj12• *Zinc* bg1*
- **beard** on the face (See whiskers)
- **biting**: *Agar* agn alum arn a1 calc *Caust Euph* hell h1* *Lach Lyc Merc Nat-c* nat-m nat-p petr ph-ac phos rhus-t hr1 sep sil *Sulph* urt-u zinc
- **burning**: caps a1* kali-c h2* sil h2* spong fd4.de
  - **rubbing**; after: con h2
- **eating**; while: hep b4a.de
- **following** pain: agn hr1 euph
- **frostbitten**, as if: *Agar Arg-met*
- **rubbing** | **amel.**: malar jl2 rhus-v
- **scratching** | **amel.**: *Agath-a* nl2• *Apis* carneg-g rwt1• con h2 grat mag-c h2 malar jl2 nat-c podo fd3.de•
- **spot**: gels bg2 luna kg1• positr nl2• ruta fd4.de spong fd4.de sulph h2* tell rsj10• visc sp1
- **stinging**: agn **Apis** arn ars *Calc Calc-s Caust* con h2* *Graph Kali-c* kali-s melal-alt gya4 merc nat-c *Nat-m* nat-p *Rhus-t* sars h2* *Sep Sil Sulph* urt-u bg verat-v bg
- **touch** agg.: psor k*
- **wandering**: (↗*SKIN - Itching - wandering*) cadm-met tpw6 tritic-vg fd5.de vanil fd5.de
  - **scratching**; on: berb hr1 sars k*
- **warm** agg.; becoming: *Mez* k* (non:puls slp) puls-n slp
- **writing** agg.: chinin-s
- ○ **Cheeks**: agar k* agath-a nl2• agn k* alum k* anan k* ang k* ant-c k* asaf k* bell k* berb k* bufo bg2 chel b7.de* con b4.de* cycl b7.de* dig b4.de* dulc h1* *Euph* hr1 galla-q-r nl2• graph b4.de* ham fd3.de• hep b4a.de hyper k* kali-p ketogl-ac rly4• lach b7.de* laur b7.de* mag-m k* malar jl2 nat-m k* olnd b7.de* orot-ac rly4• puls k* rhus-t k* ruta k* sabad b7.de* sil b4.de* spong k* staph b7.de* *Stront-c* k* sulph k* thuj k* tritic-vg fd5.de vanil fd5.de viol-t k* zinc hr1 zing hr1
  - **left**: *Agath-a* nl2•
  - **dinner**; during: hep h2*
  - **scratching** | **amel.**: malar jl2
- **Chin**: agn b7.de* alum k* am-c k* benz-ac k* berb k* calc h2* carb-an k* *Chlol* k* *Chlor* cob hr1 con k* dig b4.de* gamb k* ham fd3.de• *Kali-c* k* laur b7.de* *Lyc* k* mag-c b4.de* meph a1 nat-c k* nat-m k* nit-ac b4a.de op b7.de* ozone sde2• phos k* plat b4.de* positr nl2• puls b7.de* ros-d wla1 sars b4.de* spig b7.de* squil b7.de* *Stront-c* k* suis-hep rly4• **Sulph** k* tarax b7.de* ther thuj b4.de* til a1 tritic-vg fd5.de trom k* vanil fd5.de zinc k*
  - ○ **And** lips; between: hydr-ac c1
  - **Under**: alum h2* ruta fd4.de tarax h1* vanil fd5.de
- **Eyebrows**: agar k* agn k* all-c alum k* apis b7a.de ars arund berb bry caust k* chin b7.de* com con ferr fl-ac irid-met srj5• laur k* m-arct b7.de manc mez nat-m k* pall par k* rhod k* rhus-t b7a.de sel k* sil k* spig k* **Sulph** k* thuj b4a.de verat viol-t k*
  - **morning**: nat-m
  - **evening**: all-c
- **Eyes** | **Under**: agn b7.de* apis *Con* k* dulc fd4.de olnd b7.de* rhus-t b7a.de spong b7.de*
- **Forehead** (See HEAD - Itching - forehead)
- **Jaws**: melal-alt gya4

Itching – Jaws: ...

- ○ **Lower**: cycl a1 laur b7.de* nat-m bg2 par b7.de* phos h2 squil b7.de*
  - **biting** and burning: arg-met nat-c h2 par
  - **Under** the lower jaw: mang a1
- **Lips**: alum b4.de* am-c b4.de* ap-g vml3• *Apis* k* arge-pl rwt5• ars k* arum-t k* asc-t k* aur-m k* bac hr1 berb k* calc b4.de* caust b4.de* ferr-ma a1 glon bg2 hep b4a.de kali-bi bg2 kali-c b4.de* laur b7.de* manc bg2 mang b4.de* melal-alt gya4 nat-c h2 *Nit-ac* k* ol-an k* rhus-v a1 sabad k* tub k*
  - **coryza**; during: hell b7.de*
  - **rub** them with teeth, desire to: ap-g vml3•
  - **spot**: sulph h2*
  - ○ **Lower**: anag hr1 bry b7.de* irid-met srj5• laur b7.de* sabad b7.de* sil k*
  - **Margins** of lips: kali-c h2
  - **Upper**: arn b7.de* ars b4.de* bar-c calc-act h1 calc-ar k* chel b7.de* con b4.de* fago a1 graph b4.de* hell b7.de* interf sa3• mag-c b4.de* nat-c b4.de* nit-ac h2* phos h2* rhus-v a1 ros-d wla1 sabad b7.de* sal-fr sle1• sulph b4.de* thuj b4.de* vinc k* zinc k*
    - **left**: sal-fr sle1•
    - **coryza**; during: hell b7.de*
- **Malar** bones: hura br1
- **Mouth**:
  - ○ **Around**: anac k* calc h2* caust h2* ham fd3.de• *Hep* kali-s fd4.de kreos b7a.de nat-p bg2 rhus-t k* sil h2* spong fd4.de zinc
  - **Below**: mang h2*
  - **Corners**, of: alum h2 chel b7.de* hell h1 ruta bg2
- **Nose** (See NOSE - Itching)
- **Parotid** glands: con b4.de* nit-ac h2*
- **Temple**: ars h2* vanil fd5.de
- **Whiskers**: agar k* ambr k* arg-met *Calc* k* cob k* kali-bi k* kali-n bg2 kali-p maias-l hm2• mez **Nat-c** k* nat-m k* nat-s k2 sil k* trom hr1* zing hr1
- **Zygoma**: alum h2* hep h2* thuj h1*

JAR agg.: pip-n bg2

JAUNDICE (See Discoloration - yellow)

JERKING (See Twitching)

LARGE: | **Lower** jaw: bufo mtf33

LARGER; sensation as if the face was (See Enlarged - sensation)

LAUGHING agg.: *Borx* b4a.de* mang b4.de*
○ - **Jaws** | **Joints**: tab ptk1

LEATHER; like: | **Lips**: hyos bg2

LICKING:

- **agg.**: bell bg2
- **lips**: agar bg2* aloe bg2* am-m bg2 ars bg2* bell bg2 chin bg2 choc srj3• kali-bi bg2 kreos ptk1 *Lyc* bg2* *Nat-c* bg2 nat-m ptk1 phys ptk1 pip-n bg2 *Puls* bg2* *Stram* bg2* sulph bg2
  - **heat**; during: *Puls* hr1

LINEA nasalis: aeth k* ant-t ptk1 carb-ac ptk1 cina bg2* ip ptk1 merc mtf33 merc-cy ptk1 *Phos* ptk1 spong fd4.de *Stram* ptk1 tarent ptk1 thuj mtf33 vanil fd5.de

- **white**: ip mtf33

LOCKJAW: (↗*Clenched*) absin k* *Acon* k* aconin c2 aeth k* agar k* agar-ph c2 alum k* alumn am-m b7a.de ambr hr1 amyg k* androc srj1• ang b7.de* ant-t k* anthraci k* apis b7a.de *Arg-n* k* arn k* art-v k* asaf bg2 asar bg2 aster k* aur k* aur-m-n k* bapt k* bar-c mrr1 **Bell** k* ben-n c2 both fne1• bry k* bufo bg2 calc k* *Camph* k* cann-xyz bg2* *Canth* k* carbn-h br1 carbn-o c2* carbn-s c1 castor-eq *Caust* k* *Cedr* k* cham b7a.de* chinin-s chlf k* chr-o c2 **Cic** k* cina cob k* cocc b7a.de* colch k* con k* cori-m a1 *Crot-c* crot-h k* *Cupr* k* cur bg2* dig b4.de* dios k* dulc bg2* *Gels* k* *Glon* k* graph b4a.de *Hep* k* hydr-ac k* hydroph rsj6• *Hyos* k* **Hyper** k* ign k* *Ip* k* kali-br bg2 kali-c bg2 kali-p mtf11* lach k* lat-h bnm5• lat-m bnm6• *Laur* k* linu-u c2* *Lyc* k* m-arct b7.de* mag-p k* mang bg2 *Merc* k* merc-c b4a.de merc-i-f ptk1 morph a1* *Mosch* k* mur-ac bg2 naja *Nux-m* k* **Nux-v** k* *Oena* k* ol-an bg2 olnd br1 **Op** k* ph-ac k* phos k* phys k* phyt bg2 *Plat* k* *Plb* k* plb-xyz c2 podo k* puls k* rhus-t k* scor c1 *Sec* k* sil k* sol-ni k* sol-t c2 spig b7.de* spong k* stann bg2 *Stram* k* strept-ent jl2 **Stry** k* sulph k* tab bg2* tarent ter k* ther k* *Verat* k* verat-v k* verb bg2 zinc bg2

- **morning**: ther ptk1
  - **waking**; on: *Ther* k*
- **children**; in: bell mtf33 nux-v mtf33 op hpc2*
  - **newborns**; in: ambr ptk1* ang c1* camph ptk1 merc c1
- **injuries**; after: all-c gsy1
- **lips** separated, displaying teeth: ang c1*
- **menses**; during: hyos k*
- **prophylaxis**: hyper hr1*
- **toothache**; from: staph h1*
- **yawning** agg.: ang b7.de* *Ign* b7.de* *M-arct* b7.de **Rhus-t** b7.de* *Staph* b7.de*

LONG:
- **sensation** as if elongated: choc srj3• stram k*
  - **one** side: *Rhus-t* b7.de*
  - ○ **Chin**: glon k*
  - **Nose** (See NOSE - Long - sensation)

LOOSE sensation:
- ○ **Lower** jaw: ozone sde2•
  - ○ **Joints**: sabad bg2

LUMPS (See Nodosities)

LUPUS (See Cancer - lupus)

LYING:
- **agg.**: ambr b7.de* chel b7.de* graph b4.de* hep b4.de* ign b7.de* *Mag-c* b4a.de petr b4a.de *Phos* b4a.de plat b4.de* sulph b4.de*
- **bed**; in | **agg.**: nux-v b7a.de spong b7.de* verb b7.de* viol-t b7.de*
- **face**; on the:
  - **agg.**: acon b7.de* chin b7.de*
  - **amel.**: viol-t b7.de*
- **side**; on:
  - **affected** side | **amel.**: kreos bg2

LYING DOWN agg.: nux-v b7.de*

MAGNETIC attraction; sensation of a: | **Between** upper and lower jaws: plut-n srj7•

MALFORMATION: | **Lower** jaw: bufo mtf33

MARBLED skin (See Veins - nets)

MEMBRANE on:
- ○ **Lips**: ars-i arum-t bry
- **Mouth**; corners of: ars-i arum-t bry iod kali-bi

MENSES:
- **after** | **agg.**: dig bg2 nat-m bg2 phos bg2 spig bg2 stram bg2
- **before** | **agg.**: acon bg2 alum bg2 am-c b4.de* bar-c bg2 bell bg2 caust bg2 *Coloc* b4a.de dulc bg2 ferr bg2 gels bg2 graph bg2 ign b7.de* kali-c bg2 lach bg2 mag-c bg2 *Mag-m* bg2 mang b4.de* nat-m bg2 phos bg2 sars bg2 senec bg2 sep bg2 stann b4.de* stram bg2 *Sulph* bg2 sumb bg2 thuj bg2 verat-v bg2
- **during** | **agg.**: acon bg2 agar bg2 am-c b4.de* anac bg2 apis bg2 bar-c bg2 bell bg2 berb bg2 cact bg2 calc bg2 castm bg2 caust b4.de* cedr bg2 *Cham* bg2 chel bg2 chin bg2 cic bg2 crot-h bg2 cycl bg2 elaps bg2 **Ferr** bg2 glon bg2 graph b4.de* *Helo* bg2 hyos bg2 ip bg2 kreos bg2 lach bg2 lyc b4.de* mag-c b4.de* mag-m b4.de* mang bg2 merc bg2 mez bg2 mosch bg2 nat-m bg2 nux-m bg2 phos bg2 plat bg2 **Puls** bg2 *Sang* bg2 sars bg2 senec bg2 sep b4.de* sil b4.de* stann b4.de* stram bg2 *Sulph* bg2 verat b7.de* verat-v bg2 zinc b4.de*

MOTION:
- **agg.**: alum bg2 am-m bg2 bell b4.de* borx bg2 bry b7.de* dig b4.de* ign b7.de* ip b7.de* kali-n b4.de* kreos bg2 *Lyc* b4a.de m-ambo b7.de mang bg2 nat-m bg2 nux-v b7.de* phos bg2 *Spig* b7.de* squil b7.de* verb bg2
- **amel.**: meny b7.de* valer b7.de*
- **downward** motion | **agg.**: borx bg2
- **jaw**; of lower | **agg.**: borx bg2 bry b7.de* ign b7.de* m-arct b7.de* *Mez* bg2 rhus-t b7.de*

MOTION OF FACIAL MUSCLES:
- **agg.**: bry b7.de* olnd b7.de* stann bg2
- **constant** motion: fl-ac bg2*
  - ○ **Lips**: chin b7.de* ign b7.de*

Motion of facial muscles – **constant** motion – **Lips**: ...
- ⁝ **continued** motion: atra-r bnm3•
- ⁝ **delirium**; during: *(↗MIND - Delirium - lips)* hell k2 stram sne
- ⁝ **involuntarily**: atra-r bnm3•
- ⁝ **smoking**; as if: plb hr1
- **Mouth**; around the: cocc zr
- **difficult**:
  - ○ **Lips**; of the:
    - ⁝ **accompanied** by | **swallowing**; difficult (See THROAT - Swallowing - difficult - accompanied - lips)

MOTION OF LOWER JAW: *(↗Chewing)*
- **amel.**: ang b7a.de
- **rapidly**: ars bg2 bry bg2

MUCUS:
- ○ **Lips**: bell bg2 hydr-ac bg2 kali-bi bg2 kali-i k* lyc bg2 merc-i-r bg2 stram zinc k*
- **Mouth**; corners of: par b7.de*

MUMPS (See Inflammation - parotid - mumps)

MUSTACHE in women (See Hair - growth - women - lips)

NECROSIS of:
- ○ **Bones**; of: hep bro1 mez bro1 sil bro1
- **Jaws**:
  - ○ **Lower**: *Hep* merc merc-c ptk1 **Phos** k* *Sil*
  - **Upper**: *Merc-c*

NEVI:
- **flat**:
  - ○ **Temples**:
    - ⁝ **right** | **children**; in: fl-ac bro1

NODOSITIES: *(↗Indurations - red)* *Alum* b4.de* ant-c b7.de* *Ars* k* bar-c b4.de* bry k* calc b4.de* canth b7.de* carb-v b4.de* chel b7.de* cic k* cund dig b4.de* dulc b4.de* graph b4.de* hecla br1 hell b7.de* *Hep* k* iod b4.de* kali-c b4.de* kali-s fd4.de lach b7.de* led b7.de* lyc b4.de* m-arct b7.de *Mag-c* k* mag-m b4.de* merc k* *Merc-i-r* nat-c b4.de* nux-v b7.de* olnd b7.de* op b7.de* puls b7.de* still vh thuj b4a.de tritic-vg fd5.de viol-t b7.de* zinc b4.de*
- ○ **Chin**: bry b7.de* euph k* *Hep* b4a.de olnd b7.de* *Sil* b4a.de
  - ○ **Below**: phos b4a.de
  - **Glands**: *Bell* b4a.de graph b4a.de *Hep* b4a.de merc b4a.de phos b4a.de sulph b4a.de
- **Forehead**: con b4a.de led mtf11 sep b4a.de still vh
- **Jaws** | **Lower**: bry b7.de* *Graph* k* kali-c k2 nux-v b7.de* staph b7.de* verat b7.de*
- **Lips**: bell k* caust k* *Con* k* *Hep* b4a.de *Sep* k* sil k* sulph k* tritic-vg fd5.de
  - ○ **Lower**: *Bell* b4a.de borx b4a.de *Con* b4a.de ign b7.de* phos b4a.de *Sep* b4.de*
  - **Upper**: ars b4.de* bar-c b4.de* bell b4a.de graph b4.de* m-ambo b7.de tritic-vg fd5.de
- **Mouth**, corner of: bry b7.de* *Mag-c* sil stront-c b4.de*
- **Nose** wings: hippoz jl2
- **Temples**: calc b4a.de *Thuj* b4a.de

NODULES:
- ○ **Glandular**: *Bry* bg2
- **Subcutaneous**: psor jl2

NOISE agg.: ang bg2 pip-n bg2 spig ptk1

NUMBNESS: acon k* agar bg2 anac b4.de* ang b7.de* anh sp1 *Asaf* k* asar bamb-a stb2.de• bapt k* bell k* benz-ac k* caj a1 *Caps* b7a.de *Caust* k* c h a m bg2* chel bg2* cocc k* coll a1 coloc bg2 fl-ac bg2 gels k* *Glon* tl1 gran bg2 helodr-cal knl2• hist sp1 kali-bi sne kalm ptk1 *Mez* k* *Nux-v* olnd b7.de* **Plat** k* querc-r svu1• rauw sp1 *Ruta* b7.de* samb k* sang gk sep ptk1 spong fd4.de suis-em rly4• tab bg2* thuj k* tritic-vg fd5.de urt-u a1* verb bg2*
- **one** side: acon vh1* hist sp1*
  - **multiple** sclerosis; in: nat-m lp
- **right**: *Chel* k* *Gels* k* **Plat** k* querc-r svu1• sinus rly4• tritic-vg fd5.de
  - **chill**; during: **Plat**
- **left**: des-ac rbp6 dream-p sdj1• graph k* ruta fd4.de
- **affected** side: bell *Caust* k* *Nux-v* k* *Plat* k* puls

- **alternating** with | **neuralgic** pain (See Pain - neuralgic - alternating - numbness)
- **headache**; before: nat-m mrr1
- **waking**; on: marb-w es1•

○ - **Bones**: *Asaf* hr1* ruta h1
- **Cheeks**: asaf *Caps* k* *Mez* k* nad rly4• nat-ox rly4• *Nux-v* k* *Olnd* k* *Plat* k* plb pyrid rly4• ruta fd4.de samb h1* sinus rly4• suis-em rly4•
  - **following** pain: *Caust* k* kali-chl c1 *Mez*
- **Chin**: *Asaf* k* helodr-cal knl2• olib-sac wmh1 *Plat* k* *Spong* k*
- **Jaws**: choc srj3• fl-ac k* gran k* hura nad rly4• phos suis-em rly4•

○ • **Lower**: plat k2 ruta b7.de* suis-em rly4• ther tl1 valer b7.de*
- **Lips**: *Acon* k* ambr k* anis c1 calc k* caust vh cic *Crot-h* k* cycl b7a.de echi bro1 glon k* hydrog srj2• irid-met srj5• lath br1 lyc bg2 nad rly4• **Nat-m** k •* olnd bg2* phos bg1 plat k* ros-d wla1 sal-fr sle1• suis-em rly4•
  - **morning** | **waking**; on: ambr k*
  - **accompanied** by | **Head**; pain in (See HEAD - Pain - accompanied - lips)
  - **headache**; before: nat-m mrr1

○ • **Lower**: calc k* *Glon* k* helodr-cal knl2• phos bg2 [tax jsj7]
  - **Upper**: anh sp1 cycl k* *Euphr* b7a.de glon bg2 hydrog srj2• kali-p fd1.de• olnd k* samb bat1•
    - **extending** to:
      - **Chin**: samb bat1•
      - **Lower** lip: samb bat1•
      - **Nose**:
        - **Dorsum** of nose; moving over: samb bat1•
        - **Tip** of: samb bat1•
- **Malar** bones: marb-w es1• plat ptk1 sep ptk1
- **Mouth**; around: aids nl2• choc srj3• irid-met srj5• plat spong fd4.de
- **Nose**; below: des-ac rbp6
- **Zygoma**: fl-ac bg1 **Plat** k*

OBSTRUCTION:

○ - **Sinuses**: [bell-p-sp dcm1]
  - **accompanied** by | **neuralgia** (See Pain - neuralgic - accompanied - sinuses)

OEDEMA (See Swelling - edematous)

OILY (See Greasy; Shiny - oily)

OLD looking (See Expression - old)

OPEN mouth (See MOUTH - Open)

OPENING THE MOUTH agg.: *Am-m* b7a.de ang b7.de* cham b7.de* cocc b7.de* dros b7.de* hep b4a.de* merc b4.de* *Phos* b4a.de sabad b7.de* spong b7.de* thuj b4.de* verat b7.de*

○ - **Jaws**; lower: hep ptk1

PAIN (= aching/prosopalgia): abrom-a ks5 abrot acet-ac ↓ **Acon** k* acon-c ↓ *Aconin* ↓ act-sp ↓ aesc ↓ aeth ↓ *Agar* agath-a nl2• *Agn* ↓ all-c all-s ↓ aloe ↓ alum alum-p k2 alum-sil k2 am-c k* am-m ambr amph ↓ *Anac* anac-oc ↓ anan anh ↓ ant-c ↓ *Ant-t* ↓ apeir-s mlk9.de apis apoc ↓ apoc-a ↓ aran ↓ arg-met *Arg-n* *Arn* **Ars** k* *Ars-i* *Ars-met* ars-s-f ↓ arum-t ↓ arund asaf asar aspar ↓ astac ↓ **Aur** k* aur-ar k2 aur-i k2 aur-m aur-m-n ↓ aur-s k2 bamb-a stb2.de• bapt ↓ bar-c k* bar-i k2 bar-m ↓ bar-s k2 **Bell** k* benz-ac *Berb* beryl ↓ bism borx bov brach brom ↓ *Bry* k* bufo ↓ cact *Cadm-s* calad ↓ **Calc** k* calc-ar ↓ calc-i k2 *Calc-p* calc-s calc-sil ↓ camph k* cann-s ↓ canth ↓ *Caps* k* carb-ac ↓ *Carb-an* k* *Carb-v* k* carbn-s casc castor-eq ↓ **Caust** k* **Cedr** k* cench ↓ *Cham* k* *Chel* k* *Chin* k* chinin-ar *Chinin-s* chir-fl ↓ *Chlol* chord-umb rly4• cic ↓ *Cimic* *Cina* *Cinnb* ↓ cist cit-v ↓ clem coc-c *Coca* ↓ *Cocc* cocc-s ↓ *Coff* *Colch* **Coloc** k* com ↓ *Con* cop ↓ cor-r corn ↓ croc ↓ crot-h *Crot-t* ↓ *Cupr* *Cupr-ar* cycl ↓ cypra-eg ↓ cystein-l rly4• dendr-pol ↓ der ↓ desm-g bnj1 dig dios ↓ dros *Dulc* dys ↓ echi elaps ↓ eug ↓ euon eup-pur ↓ *Euph* euphr falco-pe nl2• ferr ↓ ferr-ar ferr-m ferr-ma ↓ ferr-p fic-m ↓ fl-ac ↓ **Gels** k* germ-met ↓ *Glon* graph grat *Guaj* guar ↓ ham k2 hecla ↓ hell ↓ helodr-cal ↓ *Hep* hir ↓ hist ↓ hura hydrc *Hyos* *Hyper* *Ign* *Ind* ↓ indg ↓ iod irid-met srj5• *Iris* jac-g ↓ jug-c ↓ *Kali-ar* *Kali-bi* *Kali-c* kali-chl ↓ kali-cy gm1 *Kali-i* kali-m k2 *Kali-n* ↓ *Kali-p* *Kali-s* kali-sil ↓ kalm k* kola ↓ kreos lac-c lac-del hrn2• *Lach* lachn ↓ lat-h ↓ laur ↓ led lepi *Lith-c* lob lob-c ↓ *Lyc* k* *Lyss* ↓ m-ambo b7.de m-arct ↓ m-aust ↓ *Mag-c* *Mag-m* **Mag-p** k* mag-s ↓ *Manc* ↓ mang melal-alt ↓ mentho ↓ meny ↓ *Merc* *Merc-c* merc-i-f merc-sul ↓ *Mez* k* morg-g ↓ morph mosch ↓ mur-ac ↓ murx ↓ myric ↓ naja nat-ar *Nat-c*

Pain: ...
nat-hchls **Nat-m** k* nat-ox rly4• nat-p nat-pyru rly4• nat-s nat-sil ↓ nicc nit-ac k* nit-s-d ↓ nux-m ↓ **Nux-v** k* ol-an *Olnd* ↓ onos op b7.de* osteo-a ↓ oxal-a ↓ *Paeon* pall ↓ par ↓ petr ↓ petr-ra ↓ ph-ac **Phos** k* *Phyt* *Plan* **Plat** k* plb plut-n ↓ positr ↓ pot-e rly4• prun ptk1 psil ↓ psor ptel ↓ *Puls* pyrid rly4• rad-br ↓ ran-b ran-s raph ↓ rauw ↓ rham-cal br1 *Rhod* *Rhodi* ↓ rhus-g ↓ *Rhus-t* k* rhus-v rob ↓ ruta sabad sabin sal-fr ↓ *Samb* ↓ sang sanic sars sec senec ↓ seneg ↓ *Sep* k* *Sil* k* sol-t-ae **Spig** k* spong **Stann** k* **Staph** k* staphycoc ↓ stict ↓ still ↓ **Stram** k* stront-c *Stry* ↓ suis-pan rly4• sul-ac sul-i k2 sulfa ↓ *Sulph* syc ↓ syph k2 tab ↓ tarax tarent ↓ tep ↓ ter teucr ↓ thal ↓ *Thuj* til ↓ tong ↓ tritic-vg fd5.de tung-met ↓ ust ↓ valer vanil fd5.de *Verat* **Verb** k* vero-o ↓ vesp ↓ vinc ↓ viol-o viol-t ↓ visc c1 zinc zinc-p ↓ *Zinc-val* ↓ zing ↓ ziz ↓ [ang stj4]
- **one** side: acon am-c am-m ↓ caps *Caust* cham colch euon grat hist ↓ *Kali-bi* kalm kreos led h1 mag-c br1 mez nux-v ol-j phos puls spig vml verat verb x-ray ↓
  - **accompanied** by | **red** discoloration of that side: spig bg2
  - **burning**: hist sp1
  - **dull** pain: x-ray sp1
  - **neuralgic**: am-m b7a.de colch b7a.de verat b7a.de
- **alternating** sides: lac-c k2
- **right**: agar k* agath-a nl2• am-c k* *Am-m* k* anac k* anag ↓ aran bro1 arg-met ↓ arizon-l ↓ arn k* arund ↓ *Aur* k* aur-m-n wbt2• aur-s k2 **Bell** k* brach ↓ bry *Cact* k* *Calc-p* camph k* caps bro1 *Carb-v* k* *Caust* k* cedr k* **Chel** k* *Chin* ↓ *Chinin-s* *Cist* k* *Cit-v* ↓ *Clem* k* coff k* colch bro1 *Con* ↓ cupr ↓ *Cur* k* dor *Ferr* *Guaj* ↓ ham ↓ hir ↓ hom-xyz hyper bro1 indg k* *Iris* kali-chl ↓ *Kali-i* k* kali-m k2 *Kali-p* k* *Kalm* k* lachn ↓ led ↓ lil-t k* *Lyc* k* lyss k* *Mag-c* ↓ *Mag-p* k* med c1 melal-alt gya4 *Merc* k* mez j5.de* nat-p ↓ nat-sil fd3.de• nit-ac ↓ nux-v onos ↓ op j5.de pall ↓ phos j5.de *Plat* k* psor **Puls** k* rhod k* *Rhus-t* vh* ruta fd4.de sanic sars ↓ *Sep* k* *Spig* k* spong k* stram j5.de stront-c sul-ac k* *Sulph* k* syph ter k* thuj ↓ urt-u k* verat j5.de *Verb* k* zinc k*
  - **boring** pain: *Camph* k* *Plat* k* stront-c
  - **burning**: arund k* chin k* ham k* lachn hr1 *Merc* nux-v pall k* psor k* puls k* *Rhus-t* bg2
  - **cutting** pain: **Bell**
  - **drawing** pain: agar k* am-c anac arg-met *Caust* k* kali-chl bg1 lyc bg1 lyss nit-ac h2* sars h2* ter k* thuj verat h1*
  - **gnawing** pain: *Lyc*
  - **jerking** pain: am-m carb-v
  - **lancinating**: *Agar* k* brach k* *Guaj* *Mag-p* verb
  - **menses**; during: bamb-a stb2.de•
  - **neuralgic**: cact mrr1 *Caust* mrr1 *Cit-v* br1* hir rsj4• kalm mrr1 lyc mrr1 *Mag-p* mrr1
  - **pressing** pain: arizon-l nl2• chel iris kalm psor spong verb
  - **stinging**: sars
  - **stitching** pain: agath-a nl2• am-m *Bell* cist *Clem* cupr h2* *Guaj* k* ham *Kali-i* lyss k* *Mag-p* nat-p onos *Phos* sars h2* *Sep* *Spig* spong verat h1* verb zinc
  - **tearing** pain: agar am-c am-m anac anag arg-met *Bell* *Carb-v* **Chel** *Chin* *Con* *Kalm* led h1* *Lyc* *Lyss* *Mag-c* *Mag-p* phos *Plat* psor sars h2* spig spong stram *Sulph* thuj

▽ • **extending** to | **left**: calc-p lyc nat-m
- **left**: *Acon* k* aesc ↓ all-c ↓ am-c ↓ apis ↓ aq-mar mgm• arg-n bro1 *Ars* k* arund k* *Asaf* ↓ asar k* *Aur* ↓ *Bamb-a* stb2.de• bapt ↓ bell j5.de camph ↓ *Carb-v* ↓ *Caust* ↓ *Cedr* cench ↓ cham j5.de *Chel* k* *Chin* k* *Chinin-s* colch ↓ *Coloc* k* *Con* ↓ cor-r k* dros ↓ *Dulc* k* echi glon k* gran ↓ graph ↓ *Guaj* k* ham fd3.de• hell k* hir ↓ *Hydr* ↓ hydrc bro1 hydrog srj2• hydroph rsj6• indg ↓ irid-met srj5• *Kali-bi* k* kali-chl j5.de kali-i ↓ kola stb3• lac-c ↓ lach j5.de* lepi ↓ **Lob** k* lyc h2* *Mag-c* k* mag-s ↓ *Mang* ↓ merc-c k* merc-i-f ↓ mez j5.de murx ↓ nat-c hr1 nat-hchls *Nat-m* ↓ nux-v j5.de ol-an ↓ osm k* osteo-a knp1• par bro1 ph-ac ↓ *Phos* k* plan k* plat bro1 polyg-h puls k* *Rhus-t* ↓ *Rhus-v* ↓ ruta fd4.de sabad k* sal-fr ↓ sang hr1 sapo bro1 sars ↓ senec bro1 sep k* **Spig** k* spong ↓ stann k* staph k* stict ↓ stram j5.de *Sulph* ↓ syc ↓ *Thuj* k* valer ↓ **Verb** k* vesp k* zinc ↓ zinc-val bro1 zing ↓
  - **boring** pain: aur *Thuj*
  - **burning**: arg-n k* *Asaf* bg2 asar k* bapt k* cench k2 **Coloc** k* *Hydr* k* lac-c bg2 murx k* ol-an bg2 ph-ac bg2 *Rhus-t* *Rhus-v* hr1 *Spig* k* thuj
  - **cutting** pain: bell k* senec

- **drawing** pain: arg-n bg1* *Aur* chel k* irid-met srj5• nat-hchls ol-an a1 ph-ac h2* puls hr1 sal-fr sle1• *Sulph* bg1* *Verb* zing
- **lancinating**: chinin-s lepi br1 sulph
- **neuralgic**: hir rsj4• *Lach* bg2 lob mrr1 mag-c mrr1 nat-m mrr1 **Spig** bg2* syc bka1•
- **pressing** pain: bamb-a stb2.de• **Verb**
- **stitching** pain: aesc all-c apis asar k* bamb-a stb2.de• camph k* chel k* **Coloc** k* *Con* dros h1* *Guaj* indg *Kali-bi* kali-i *Mag-c* *Mang* merc-i-f k* nat-c a1 *Nat-m* par *Plan* puls *Sang* senec sep h2* stict *Sulph* valer
- **tearing** pain: am-c ars *Aur* bamb-a stb2.de• *Carb-v* *Caust* colch a1 **Coloc** k* gran graph *Guaj* *Lach* mag-c k2 mag-s *Mez* plan sars *Spig* spong staph *Thuj* zinc
- ▽ **extending** to:
  - **right**: cench ↓ *Chin*
    - **burning**: cench k2
  - **Ear**:
    - **left**: *Coloc* ↓
      - **stitching** pain: *Coloc* k*

- **daytime**: calc cedr br1* *Cimic* kalm mag-p manc ↓ plan bro1 puls **Spig** k* *Stann* sulph ↓ thuj
  - **burning**: manc k* sulph k*
- **morning**: agar *Chin* *Chinin-s* corn ↓ *Cupr* dulc fd4.de kali-bi ↓ kali-cy gm1 kalm k2 lyc ↓ mez k* nat-hchls nat-sil fd3.de• *Nux-v* k* rumx sars k* spong fd4.de sulph ↓ thuj k* verat verb k*
  - **5** h (See night - midnight - after - 5)
  - **7** h:
    - **7-8** h: rhus-t
    - **7-12** h: *Chinin-s*
    - **7-14** h: plan br1
  - **9-16** h: lyc ↓
    - **burning**: lyc
  - **15** h; until: stront-c ↓
    - **burning**: stront-c
  - **burning**: corn k* lyc
  - **drawing** pain: kali-bi k* sulph
  - **increases** till noon, then decreases: mag-c
  - **lancinating**: verb
  - **rising** agg.: guaj ↓
    - **drawing** pain: guaj h2
  - **sore**: sars
  - **tearing** pain: *Mez* k* *Nux-v* thuj k*
  - **until** sunset: *Spig* ↓
    - **tearing** pain: *Spig*
  - **waking**; on: agar hydrog srj2• *Iris* kali-cy gm1 sars k* sep k* sulph
    - **sore**: sars
- **forenoon**: *Chinin-s* lach nat-m k* plat k* tritic-vg fd5.de vanil fd5.de
  - **9** h: *Caust* kali-bi lac-c nux-v sul-ac *Verb*
  - **9.30** h: verb
  - **9-16** h: *Verb*
  - **10** h: *Chinin-s* gels nat-m
  - **11** h: mag-p nux-v puls
  - **11-14** h: mag-p
- **noon**: nat-m spig k* stram sulph verb
- **afternoon**: alum ↓ calc cimic *Cocc* k* euphr ↓ fago ↓ hyper k* kalm lac-c lyc ↓ mez a1 nux-v *Phos* ↓ ruta fd4.de spong fd4.de sulph k* ter tritic-vg fd5.de vanil fd5.de verb
  - **13** h: ars coff
  - **14** h: mag-p
  - **15** h: calc *Chinin-s* pip-m
  - **16** h: chinin-s coloc verb
    - **16** h lasting all night: merc-c
    - **16-20** h: **Lyc**
  - **burning**: fago k* *Phos* k* spong fd4.de vanil fd5.de

- **afternoon**: ...
  - **drawing** pain: alum h2* euphr lyc k* sulph
  - **tearing** pain: alum calc ruta fd4.de tritic-vg fd5.de
- **evening**: acon ↓ am-m k* anac ↓ aq-mar ↓ *Ars* bro1 bamb-a ↓ borx ↓ caps k* carb-an ↓ carb-v ↓ cham ↓ *Chinin-s* cist k* cocc k* com ↓ dulc fd4.de guaj hyper k* ign kali-s lach ↓ mag-c bro1 mag-s merc bro1 *Mez* k* nat-sil fd3.de• nit-ac ol-an ↓ *Phos* pip-m *Plat* polys sk4• ptel ↓ *Puls* k* rhus-t k* ruta fd4.de sep k* spong stram k* *Sulph* *Thuj* k* tritic-vg fd5.de *Verb* yuc ↓ *Zinc*
  - **18** h till morning: *Guaj*
  - **19-20** h: **Cedr**
  - **20** h: *Guaj* ↓ *Puls* ↓
    - **tearing** pain: *Guaj* *Puls*
  - **21** h: sul-ac urt-u zinc ↓
    - **drawing** pain: zinc
  - **21-3** h: sulph
  - **amel.**: kali-bi spig stann sulph verat
  - **bed** agg.; in: kali-n ↓
    - **tearing** pain: kali-n h2
  - **burning**: acon tl1 aq-mar skp7• borx cham k* com k* mag-c h2* ptel tl1 spong fd4.de yuc a1
  - **drawing** pain: anac cist k* ol-an a1 thuj tritic-vg fd5.de
  - **lying** down agg.; after: stram
  - **pressing** pain: ruta fd4.de tritic-vg fd5.de *Verb*
  - **stitching** pain: bamb-a stb2.de• guaj lach k* zinc
  - **tearing** pain: am-m carb-an carb-v h2* cist mag-s phos **Puls** rhus-t thuj h1* tritic-vg fd5.de zinc
- **night**: *Acon* agar aran *Ars* bro1 bamb-a ↓ brach a1 brass-n-o ↓ *Calc-p* caps bro1 *Caust* k* cench ↓ chel k* chin ↓ clem ↓ *Cocc* *Con* *Glon* *Guaj* kali-p fd1.de• *Lach* led *Mag-c* k* *Mag-p* **Merc** k* merc-c *Mez* k* nicc olib-sac ↓ phos *Phyt* plan k* plat puls k* rhus-t bro1 *Sep* *Sil* k* spong k* staph k* *Sulph* k* syph ↓
  - **midnight** | **before** | **22** h: chinin-s coloc ign
    - **after**:
      - **2** h: spig
      - **3** h: *Sulph* **Thuj**
      - **4** h: kali-cy gm1
      - **5** h: caj
  - **amel.**: cupr *Staph*
  - **bed**; driving out of: *Mag-c* *Mag-p* *Rhus-t*
  - **boring** pain: *Mag-c* *Mez* *Plat* *Sil*
  - **burning**: brass-n-o srj5• cench k2 chin *Lach* k* *Mez* olib-sac wmh1
  - **neuralgic**: syph mrr1
  - **prickling** pain: olib-sac wmh1
  - **rest** agg.: *Mag-c* mag-p
  - **stitching** pain: bamb-a stb2.de• clem *Guaj* *Mag-c*
  - **tearing** pain: chin *Cocc* *Con* *Lach* led h1* *Mag-c* k* rhus-t
- **accompanied** by:
  - **appetite**; ravenous: dulc bro1
  - **catarrh** (See GENERALS - Catarrh - accompanied - face)
  - **indigestion**: tarent tl1
  - **paralysis** | **Lids**; of upper (See EYE - Paralysis - lids - upper - accompanied - face)
  - **photophobia**: nit-s-d bro1 plan bro1
  - **salivation**: bell j *Mez* j* plat kr1* verb j zinc j
  - **twitching** in face (See Twitching - accompanied - pain)
  - **vision**; foggy (See VISION - Foggy - accompanied - face)
  - ○ **Eye** | **complaints** of: coloc ptk1
  - **Head** | **complaints** (See HEAD - Complaints - accompanied - face - pain)
  - **Neck**; stiffness of: mez bro1
  - **Nose**; discharge from: spig ptk1
  - **Teeth** | **chattering**: sul-ac ptk1*
- **aching**: fic-m gya1

Face

- **accompanied** by | **Teeth**; pain in (See TEETH - Pain - accompanied - face - pain - aching)
- **acids**, from: kali-c bro1
- **agg.**: thuj bg2
- **ague**; after suppressed: **Nat-m** sep *Stann*
- **air** | **change** of air agg.: staph verb mrr1
- **air** agg.; draft of: bell calc-p caps chin coff gink-b sbd1• hep kali-p *Mag-c* k* mag-m br1 *Mag-p* *Merc* *Nux-v* *Sil* *Stram* sulph *Verb*
  - **drawing** pain: *Verb*
  - **stitching** pain: kali-p k2 mag-c
- **air**; in open:
  - **agg.**: alum alum-p k2 alum-sil k2 amph a1 *Ars* ars-s-f k2 *Bell* calc carb-an chin chinin-ar cocc guaj *Hep* kali-ar *Kali-c* *Kali-p* kreos laur mag-c mag-p *Merc* merc-c *Phos* plat puls *Rhus-t* sars sep sil spig k* spong **Sulph** thuj valer
  - **amel.**: all-c am-m hep kali-bi *Kali-i* *Kali-s* lac-c k* nat-m nat-s *Puls* *Sulph* thuj bro1
    - **burning**: kali-i
- **alone** agg.: pip-m
- **alternating** with:
  - ○ **Chest**; oppression in: cocc-s c1
  - **Coeliac** region; pain in: coloc ptk1
  - **Limbs**; pain in: *Kali-bi*
  - **Shoulder**; pain in: mag-p
  - **Stomach**; pain in: bism bro1*
- **anger**; after: cham k2
- **bathing**:
  - **after**: con ↓
    - **sore**: con h2*
  - **agg.**: am-c coff con h2*
- **bed** agg.; in: carb-v *Mag-c* *Mag-p* puls *Sil* spong verb viol-t
- **bending**:
  - **forward**:
    - **agg.**: lac-c
    - **head** to floor amel.; with: *Sang* ↓
      - **neuralgic**: sang tl1
      - **stitching** pain: *Sang* k*
- **binding** tightly amel.: kali-c h2* sep h2*
- **biting** pain: apis b7a.de berb hr1 cann-s b7.de* *Carb-an* hr1 grat hr1 lyss a1 m-ambo b7.de nat-pyru rly4• plat h2* rhus-t a1 sep h2* spig b7.de* zinc hr1
- **blow**; pain as from a: *Arn* b7.de* asar b7.de* cina b7.de* cupr b7a.de euph b4.de* hep bg2 mang h2* plat b4.de* ruta b7.de* stann b4.de*
- **blowing** the nose agg.: **Merc**
- **boring** pain: apis bg2 arg-n k* **Aur** k* bar-c k* bell k* bov k* *Calc* k* calc-sil k2 camph k* carb-v k* chel bg2 *Cocc* dros bg2 dulc k* euph b4.de* hep ptk1 *Ign* k* indg m-ambo b7.de *Mag-c* k* merc bg2 *Mez* k* nat-s bg2 **Plat** k* ruta fd4.de sabad bg2 sil stront-c b4.de* *Thuj* k* tritic-vg fd5.de ziz a1
- **breakfast**:
  - **after**:
    - **agg.**: *Iris*
    - **amel.**: caj
- **bruised** (See sore)
- **burning**: (↗*warmth*) acon k* aeth *Agar* k* all-c alum am-m b7.de* anac k* anac-oc *Apis* k* apoc bg2 aran *Arg-met* k* arg-n *Arn* k* **Ars** k* ars-s-f k2 arum-t bg2 *Asaf* b7.de asar k* aspar astac aur b4a.de bapt *Bell* k* berb k* beryl sp1 brom *Bry* k* calad b7.de* calc h2* camph k* cann-s canth b7.de* *Caps* k* carb-v b4.de* carbn-s *Caust* k* cedr k* cench k2 *Cham* k* chel k* *Chin* k* chinin-ar cic b7.de* cimic k* cist clem k* cocc coloc k* com con bg2 cop corn croc bg2 *Crot-t* k* cupr bg2 cycl b7.de* dig k* dios bg2 dros b7.de* dulc k* elaps k* eup-pur bg2 *Euph* k* euphr fl-ac bg2 germ-met srj5• graph k* grat bg2 guar hir skp7• hist sp1 hyos b7.de* hyper ign b7.de* jac-g jug-c *Kali-ar* kali-bi k* kali-c b4.de* *Kali-i* k* *Kali-n* k* kali-s fd4.de *Kreos* k* lach k* laur k* led b7.de* **Lyc** k* *M-ambo* b7.de* m-arct b7.de mag-c b4.de* manc mang b4.de* meny b7.de* merc k* merc-c merc-sul *Mez* k* mosch k* mur-ac murx bg2 myric nat-c b4.de* nat-m bg2 nat-p nux-v k2 olnd k* osteo-a knp1• pall par b7.de* petr b4a.de* petr-ra shn4• *Ph-ac* k* phos b4.de* *Plat* k* plb b7.de* psor k* ptel tl1 puls k* raph rhod b4.de* **Rhus-t** k* rhus-v ruta h1* sabad b7.de* samb b7.de* sang bg2 sars b4.de* sil k* *Spig* k* spong b7.de* *Stann* k* staph k* *Stront-c* k* sul-ac b4.de*
- **burning**: ...
  sul-i k2 sulfa sp1 **Sulph** k* teucr b7.de* *Thuj* k* til k* tritic-vg fd5.de ust k* vanil fd5.de verat k* vesp zinc b4a.de*
  - **burrowing**: coloc h2*
  - **chemical**; like: chir-fl gya2
  - **cutting** pain: chin
  - **frostbitten**; as if: agar k*
  - **glowing** iron; like a: mag-c bg2
  - **needles**; as from: **Ars** k* *Caps* spig k*
- **burnt**; as if: nux-v b7.de* plut-n srj7•
- **burrowing**: *Bell* b4a.de bov b4.de* chel b7.de dros b7.de euph b4.de* *Mag-c* b4a.de *Thuj* b4a.de
- **bursting** pain: bell bg2 bov bg1 *Thuj* bg1*
- **caries**, in: **Aur** ↓
  - **burning**: **Aur** k*
- **change** of temperature: mag-c ↓
  - **stitching** pain: mag-c
- **chewing**:
  - **agg.**: acon aloe ptk1 alum alum-p k2 alum-sil k2 am-m anac ang bro1 anh sp1 arg-n *Bell* *Bism* *Bry* calc caust ↓ *Cham* cocc bro1 coff coloc bg1 cur desm-g bnj1 dulc fd4.de euphr graph hell bro1* hep bro1 kali-chl ptk1 lach mez bro1 *Nat-m* nit-ac osm phos plat puls k* sep sil spig *Staph* k* verat verb k*
    - **sore**: caust h2* *Nat-m* k*
  - **amel.**: cupr cupr-act bro1
- **chill**; during: acon k* *Caust* k* chin k* dros ↓ lach k* mez k* nux-v k* rhus-t k* spig k*
  - **stitching** pain: **Caust** dros
- **chilliness**:
  - **after**: merc-sul ↓
    - **burning**: merc-sul k*
  - **during**: *Caust* ↓ mur-ac ↓
    - **burning**: *Caust* k* mur-ac k*
- **chilliness** with the pain: *Caust* coloc bro1* dulc bro1 *Mez* bro1 *Puls* bro1 rhus-t bro1*
- **closing** the eyes agg.: cimic med
- **coffee**:
  - **abuse** of coffee agg.: **Nux-v**
    - **tearing** pain: *Nux-v*
  - **agg.**: spig
- **cold**:
  - **agg.**: ruta ↓
    - **neuralgic**: ruta mrr1
  - **air**:
    - **agg.**: *Acon* aeth ↓ *Agar* **Ars** aur-s k2 *Bell* *Carbn-s* *Colch* *Dulc* kali-ar kali-c kali-p *Mag-c* **Mag-p** *Merc* phos *Rhod* **Rhus-t** ruta spig ↓ sulph verb
      - **drawing** pain: kali-p k2
      - **stitching** pain: kali-p k2
      - **tearing** pain: aeth kali-p k2 *Rhus-t* spig hr1
    - **amel.**: *All-c* **Kali-s** nat-hchls ↓ nicc *Puls*
      - **drawing** pain: all-c nat-hchls
  - **applications**:
    - **agg.**: aesc *Bell* con *Ferr* *Hep* *Mag-c* **Mag-p** *Phos* *Rhod* **Rhus-t** sanic **Sil** stann
      - **neuralgic**: mag-p mrr1
    - **amel.**: apis arg-met ars-met asar *Bism* k* *Bry* *Caust* chin *Clem* bro1 **Coff** k* ferr k2* *Ferr-p* fl-ac *Kali-p* k* *Lac-c* nicc phos bro1 *Puls* k* sabad sep
      - **tearing** pain: **Puls**
  - **bathing**:
    - **agg.**: ferr ptk1 mag-c ptk1
    - **amel.**: caust ptk1

- **exposure** to | **agg.**: *(↗weather; wind)* acon k* *Agar* k* arn *Bell* *Calc* *Calc-p* calc-sil k2 *Caust* coff bro1 *Dulc* *Gels* *Graph* *Hep* kali-cy gm1 *Kalm* k* *Mag-c* k* *Mag-p* k* *Merc* nit-s-d bro1 *Phos* *Rhod* *Rhus-t* ruta *Sep* **Sil** *Sulph* verb
- **heat** agg.; exposure to cold or: merc plan sul-ac
- **washing** agg.; after: sil ↓
  - **burning**: sil h2
- **water**:
  - **amel.**: *Ars-met* ↓
    - **burning**: *Ars-met*
  - **mouth**; holding cold water in | **amel.**: bism hr1 clem ptk1
- **wet** places; from exposure to cold: coloc bro1 *Dulc* bro1 mag-m bro1 rhus-t bro1 *Sil* bro1 *Spig* bro1 thuj bro1

- **cold** agg.; becoming: calc-s mag-p ptk1
- **cold** in stormy weather; after taking a: nit-s-d c1
- **coldness**; during: grat ↓ nat-m ↓
  - **burning**: grat k* nat-m k*
- **compressed**; as if: *Cina* b7.de* olnd b7.de* *Verat* b7.de*
- **contradiction**, from: *Bell*
- **corrosive**: *Agn* b7.de* ambr b7.de* cham b7.de dig b4.de* lyc b4a.de olnd b7.de ph-ac b4.de plat b4.de *Puls* b7a.de rhod b4.de ruta b7.de* staph b7.de
- **coryza**:
  - **during**: all-c tl1 am-m ↓
    - **tearing** pain: am-m b7a.de
  - **suppressed** coryza; from: kali-bi ↓
    - **neuralgic**: kali-bi mrr1
- **cough**:
  - **during**: *Kali-bi*
    - **agg.**: carb-v ↓ ip ↓
      - **cramping**: ip mrr1
      - **drawing** pain: carb-v h2
- **cramping**: ang bro1 bism bro1 bry bro1 *Cact* bro1 calc h2 *Cocc* k* coloc bro1* cystein-l rly4• hyos *Mag-m* *Mag-p* mang mez bro1* mur-ac h2 plat k* thuj bro1 verat bro1 *Verb* bro1*
  - **burning**: stann h2
- **crushing**: sul-ac bg2 sulph bg2 verb bg2 zinc bg2
- **cutting** pain: acon bro1 amph bro1 arg-met k* arg-n k* ars bg1* aur bro1 *Bell* k* calc-s caust bro1 *Cham* bro1 chin k* clem k* *Coloc* bro1 con k2 dulc bro1 hyper bro1 mag-c k2 mag-p bro1 merc bro1 mez bro1 nux-v bro1 phos bro1 *Puls* bro1 rhod bro1 rhodi bro1 rhus-t k* sabin senec bro1 sil bro1 *Spig* bro1 staph k* thuj bg2 til visc c1
- **darting** (See stitching)
- **digging** pain: aur-m bov cupr euph h2* *Kali-bi* *Mag-c* *Plat* sep *Thuj* tritic-vg fd5.de
- **dinner**; after: carb-an ↓ grat ↓
  - **burning**: grat k*
  - **tearing** pain: carb-an
- **diversion** of the mind amel.: pip-m k*
- **draft** agg. (See air agg.)
- **dragging**: canth b7.de* staph b7.de*
- **drawing** pain: abrot k* acon acon-c k* *Agar* k* aloe *Alum* k* alum-p k2 alum-sil k2 am-c anac k* ang bg2* ant-t k* arg-met k* arg-n bg2* **Ars** k* ars-s-f k2 asaf *Aur* k* aur-ar k2 aur-m-n k* aur-s k2 bar-c bar-m k* bar-s k2 bell k* bism b7.de* *Bry* k* *Cact* bro1 cadm-s *Calc* calc-sil k2 cann-s b7.de* *Carb-v* k* carbn-s *Caust* k* cham k* *Chel* k* cit-v k* clem b4.de* cocc k* coff b7a.de *Colch* k* *Coloc* k* *Con* **Dig** k* dros k* dulc b4.de* euon k* euphr k* graph k* guaj b4.de* hep k* hist vml3• hyper k* *Ign* k* kali-ar kali-bi k* *Kali-c* k* kali-chl k* kali-m k2 *Kali-n* kali-p kali-s kali-sil k2 kreos k* *Lach* led k* lob-c lyc k* m-arct b7.de mag-m k* mang k* **Merc** *Mez* k* nat-c b4.de* nat-hchls nat-m k* *Nux-v* k* *Ol-an* k* petr b4.de* ph-ac k* *Phos* k* *Plat* k* puls k* ran-s k* rhod k* *Rhus-t* k* rhus-v k* *Sars* seneg b4.de* *Sep* k* *Sil* k* *Spig* k* *Stann* k* *Staph* k* *Sul-ac* b4a.de sulph k* tep k* ter k* thuj k* tritic-vg fd5.de valer k* vanil fd5.de *Verat* k* *Verb* k* viol-o b7.de* viol-t b7.de* zinc b4.de* zing k*
  - **paroxysmal**: *Caust* cocc nat-hchls sep
  - **thread** pulled the cheek; as if a: sal-fr sle1•
  - **tighter** and tighter and then suddenly let loose: *Puls* k*
  - **upward**: *Ol-an*
- **drinking** agg.: bism bro1 iris bro1 *Mez* bro1
- **dull** pain: fic-m gya1 hell b7.de* olnd b7.de* spig b7.de*
- **eating**:
  - **after**:
    - **agg.**: agar chin iris mang nux-v *Phos* spig ↓ zinc k*
      - **burning**: spig
      - **cramping**: mang
    - **amel.**: chin kali-p *Kalm* spig
  - **agg.**: bism bro1 bry coloc bro1 gels iris bro1 kali-chl c1 mag-p *Mez* k* phos k* plan positr nl2• spig spong syph verb bro1
    - **neuralgic**: mez tl1
    - **tearing** pain: phos
  - **amel.**: caj k* chin c1 kalm ptk1 phos ↓ rhod k*
    - **burning**: chin
    - **tearing** pain: chin phos h2* rhod
  - **while**:
    - **agg.**: *Mez* ↓ phos ↓ psor ↓
      - **stitching** pain: *Mez* phos psor al2
- **electric** shock; as from an: *Con* b4a.de psil ft1 sep b4a.de
- **eroding**: dig h2*
- **eruptions**; after suppressed: *Dulc* k* *Kalm* *Mez* thuj
  - **neuralgic**: mez mrr1
  - ○ **Face**; in: dulc ↓
    - **neuralgic**: dulc mrr1
- **excitement**: ang c1 cact cham k2 *Coff* k* coloc k2 cupr lyc sep *Staph*
  - **agg.**: coff ↓
    - **neuralgic**: coff mrr1
  - **amel.**: kali-p pip-m
- **exertion**:
  - **agg.**: **Bry** *Cact* k* calc-p kreos ↓ lac-c k* merc
    - **burning**: kreos k*
  - **amel.**: iris sep
- **fasting** agg.: *Cact*
- **fever**; during: cocc ↓ dulc ↓ mez bg2 *Spig* b7.de*
  - **burning**: cocc bg2 dulc bg2
- **gnawing** pain: ambr a1 arg-met k* arn b7.de* aur-m hr1 bamb-a stb2.de• bar-c k* berb k* *Cham* b7.de* eug euph k* *Glon* indg kali-bi bg2 lyc k* lyss k* ph-ac k* *Puls* b7a.de *Ran-s* b7a.de samb b7.de* stann k* sulph k* thuj bg2
- **gonorrhea**; after suppressed: thuj hr1
- **gouty**: *Caust* bg2 ruta b7.de*
  - ○ **Jaws** | **Lower**: caust h*
- **headache**; during: stront-c ↓
  - **burning**: stront-c
- **heat** (See warmth)
  - **during**: olnd ↓
    - **stinging**: olnd h1*
  - **stove**; of | **amel.**: *Mez* **Sil**
- **increasing**:
  - **gradually** | **ceasing**:
    - **suddenly**: *Arg-met* ↓
      - **tearing** pain: *Arg-met*
    - **decreasing**:
      - **gradually**: *Plat* k* **Stann** k*
      - **suddenly**: arg-met bro1 *Bell* bro1 puls k* sul-ac
  - **suddenly**:
    - **decreasing** | **suddenly**: **Bell** mez ptk *Spig* *Sulph*
- **inflammatory**: *(↗GENERALS - Inflammation - sinuses)* *Acon* k* *Agar* bro1 all-c bro1 aran bro1 arg-n bro1 arn k* *Ars* bro1 *Aur* b4a.de* *Bar-c* k* **Bell** k* *Bry* k* cact k* *Caps* bro1 caust bro1 *Cedr* bro1 *Cham* bro1 *Chin* bro1 chinin-ar bro1 *Chinin-s* bro1 cimic bro1 coff bro1 *Coloc* bro1 ferr bro1 *Ferr-p* k* *Gels* bro1 glon k* hecla bro1 *Kali-i* bro1 kali-p bro1 kalm bro1 *Lach* k* *Mag-p* bro1 mentho bro1 **Merc** k* merc-c bro1 *Mez* bro1 nit-s-d bro1 phos k* *Plan* bro1 plat k* puls bro1 rad-br bro1 rhod bro1 *Rhus-t* bro1 ruta fd4.de sang bro1 sep b4a.de sil bro1 *Spig* bro1 stann bro1 **Staph** bg2 sulph bro1 thuj k* til bro1 verat k* *Verb* bro1 zinc-p bro1 *Zinc-val* bro1

Face

- **intermittent** (See paroxysmal)
- **irritability**; with (See MIND - Irritability - pain - face)
- **jar** agg.: *Arn* **Bell** k* chin *Cocc* ferr-p bro1 *Mag-c* *Spig* k*
  - **stitching** pain: *Chin*
- **jerking** pain: acon bro1 am-m amph bro1 *Ars* bro1 aur bro1 **Bell** bry **Carb-v** k* caust bro1 *Cham* k* chin bg2* cina k* *Cocc* k* colch k* *Coloc* bro1 dulc bro1 euph b4.de* gels *Glon* hyper bro1 indg m-ambo b7.de mag-p bro1 mang k* merc bro1 mez bg2* **Nux-v** bg2* phos bg2* puls k* rhod k* rhodi bro1 senec bro1 *Sep* k* sil bro1 spig k* stann b4.de* stront-c k* sul-ac thuj h1* valer *Zinc*
- **joy**; from excessive: coff k2
- **kneeling** and pressing head firmly against ground: | **amel.**: sang bro1*
- **lancinating**: acet-ac *Agar* k* alum k* arg-n bro1 ars bro1 *Asaf* aur *Bell* bro1 bufo *Chin* k* cocc k* *Coloc* bro1 gels bro1 graph bro1 *Guaj* hep bro1 *Kali-i* bro1 *Kalm* kreos bro1 **Mag-p** k* *Nux-v* bro1 phos bro1 *Plan* k* *Rhodi* bro1 sang bro1 senec sil *Spig* bro1 *Stry* bro1 sulph thal dx verb zinc bro1
- **laughing** agg.: aq-mar ↓ borx mang tab
  - **burning**: aq-mar skp7•
  - **jerking** pain: mang h2*
- **light**; from: *Ars* k* *Bell* k* *Cact* k* *Chel* k* cocc-s hr1 *Con* k* mag-p k* spig k*
  - **agg.**: chin ↓
    - **stitching** pain: chin
- **line** of pain coursing along the nerve; a fine: all-c bro1* caps bro1*
- **lying**:
  - **agg.**: ail ambr arn bell carbn-s cham chel *Chin* *Coloc* *Ferr* k* gels graph hep ign kalm lac-c *Mag-c* phos pip-m plat plb *Puls* ruta sil spig sulph syph *Verb*
    - **burning**: chin plb
    - **drawing** pain: chel k*
    - **neuralgic**: ruta mrr1
    - **tearing** pain: ail k* *Chin* **Mag-c** phos *Puls*
  - **amel.**: *Cact* k* calc-p chinin-s coff *Nux-v* sep spig
    - **tearing** pain: nux-v
  - **back**; on:
    - **agg.**: *Arg-met* ↓
      - **tearing** pain: *Arg-met*
  - **face**; on the:
    - **amel.**: spig
      - **tearing** pain: spig
  - **head** low; with the | **agg.**: *Puls*
  - **quietly** | **amel.**: bry sep
  - **side**; on:
    - **affected** side:
      - **agg.**: acon arn chin *Clem* puls spig syph
      - **amel.**: bry cupr ign kali-n ↓ sul-ac
        - **tearing** pain: kali-n h2
    - **painful** side:
      - **amel.**: kreos ↓
        - **burning**: kreos
    - **unaffected** side | **agg.**: kreos bro1
- **malaria**; after suppressed: nat-m ↓
  - **neuralgic**: nat-m mrr1
- **menses**:
  - **after**:
    - **agg.**: spig
      - **tearing** pain: spig
  - **before** | **agg.**: am-c coloc b4a.de mang *Stann* zinc
  - **during**:
    - **agg.**: am-c bamb-a stb2.de• caust graph lyc mag-c mag-m *Nat-m* sep sil k* stann k* zinc k*
      - **sore**: stann k*
  - **scanty**; with: caust ptk1 lob ptk1 mez ptk1
  - **suppressed** menses; from: stann wt
- **mental** exertion agg.: am-c bry calc-p *Coff* ign k* kali-c bro1 kalm lac-c *Nux-v* spig k2 staph
  - **burning**: spig
- **mental** exertion agg.: ...
  - **tearing** pain: spig k2
- **mercury**; after abuse of: *Aur* kr1 aur-m carb-v k* chin k* **Hep** k* kali-chl hr1 **Kali-i** k* mez bro1 *Nit-ac* k* *Sulph* k*
  - **stitching** pain: kali-i
- **motion**:
  - **agg.**: *Acon* arge-pl rwt5• ars bro1 **Bell** k* **Bry** *Cact* k* calc calc-p *Chin* k* chinin-ar chinin-s bro1 *Colch* *Coloc* k* *Ferr-p* *Gels* kali-c bro1 kreos bro1 lac-c k* mez **Nux-v** k* phos k* rhod sep **Spig** k* squil staph *Valer* *Verb* k*
    - **burning**: spig
    - **stitching** pain: chin spig k2
    - **tearing** pain: **Bell** *Colch* coloc k* *Nux-v* *Spig*
  - **amel.**: agar *Bism* k* ferr iris kali-p lyc *Mag-c* k* mag-p meny *Plat* k* *Puls* *Rhod* **Rhus-t** k* ruta thuj bro1 *Valer*
    - **tearing** pain: **Mag-c** **Rhus-t**
  - **eyes**; of | **agg.**: bry kali-c
  - **face** agg.; of muscles of: stann h2
    - **cutting** pain: stann h2*
    - **pressing** pain: stann h2*
  - **jaw**; of lower:
    - **agg.**: alum alum-p k2 am-c androc srj1• borx bry cham cocc *Coloc* bg1* cor-r ign kali-c m-arct mag-p mang *Merc* nat-ar nat-m osteo-a knp1• phos rhus-t sabad spig spong thuj verat *Verb*
    - **amel.**: phos ↓ *Rhod*
      - **tearing** pain: phos h2
- **music** agg.: *Cact* k* nux-v ph-ac
  - **drawing** pain: ph-ac
- **nervous** origin; of: *Caps* ↓ chin ↓ *Verb* ↓
  - **neuralgic**: *Caps* b7a.de chin b7a.de *Verb* b7a.de
- **neuralgic**: ***(↗nerves)*** *Acon* b7.de* *Aconin* bro1 agar b4a.de* all-c bro1 alum b4.de* *Am-m* b7a.de anan c2* *Ang* b7a.de apoc-a c2 aran bro1 *Arg-met* b7a.de arg-n bg2* arn b7a.de* *Ars* b4a.de* asaf b7.de* aur b4.de* bar-c b4.de* *Bell* b4.de* *Bism* b7a.de *Borx* b4a.de *Bry* b7.de* cact bg2* *Calc* b4.de* *Caps* b7.de* carb-ac bg2* *Carb-v* b4a.de carbn-s mtf11 *Caust* bro1* *Cedr* bg2* *Cham* bg2* chel b7a.de* **Chin** b7.de* chinin-ar bro1 chinin-s bg2* cimic bg2* cina b7.de* cit-v br1 cocc bg2* cocc-s c2* *Coff* bg2* colch b7.de* **Coloc** b4.de* *Con* b4.de* cupr bro1 cypra-eg sde6.de• dendr-pol sk4• der c2 dig b4a.de* *Dros* b7a.de* dys fmm1• ferr b7a.de* gels bg2* glon bro1 graph b4.de* guaj b4a.de* hecla bro1 helodr-cal knl2• hep b4a.de* hyos bg2 iris bg2 **Kali-c** b4.de* kali-chl c2* kali-i bg2* kali-p bro1 *Kalm* bro1* led b7a.de* lob mrr1 *Lyc* b4.de* mag-c b4a.de* *Mag-m* b4.de* mag-p c2* mang b4.de* mentho bro1 **Merc** bg2* merc-c bro1 *Mez* b4.de* morg-g fmm1• mur-ac b4.de* *Nat-c* b4a.de nat-m b4a.de* nat-s bro1 *Nit-ac* b4.de* nit-s-d bro1 **Nux-v** b7.de* *Olnd* b7a.de **Phos** b4.de* *Plan* bro1 **Plat** bg2* *Plb* b7a.de **Puls** b7a.de* rad-br bro1 rhod bro1 **Rhus-t** bg2* *Ruta* b7a.de* sabad b7a.de *Samb* b7a.de sang bro1* sep b4.de* sil bg2* *Spig* b7.de* spong fd4.de stann b4.de* **Staph** b7.de* *Stram* bg2 *Stront-c* b4a.de *Stry* bro1 *Sulph* b4a.de* syc fmm1• syph mrr1 tab bg2 *Thuj* b4a.de* til bro1 tong c2 valer b7.de* *Verat* b7.de* **Verb** b7.de* *Viol-o* b7a.de *Zinc* b4a.de* zinc-p bro1 *Zinc-val* br1*
  - **accompanied** by:
    - **headache**: dulc bro1 iris tl1
    - **menses**; suppressed: *Gels* bro1
    - **Liver** complaints (See ABDOMEN - Liver - accompanied - face)
    - **Sinuses**; obstructed: cadm-met gm1
  - **alternating** with | **numbness**: plat mrr1
- **noise** agg.: *(↗MIND - Sensitive - noise)* acon arn ars bro1 calc-p *Chin* k* chinin-s bro1 *Cocc* *Coff* k* *Nux-v* sep k* **Spig** k*
  - **neuralgic**: coff mrr1 spig mrr1
  - **stitching** pain: chin
  - **tearing** pain: *Spig*
- **numbness**; with: acon k* asaf bg2 *Caps* bg2 **Cham** *Kalm* mentho bro1 *Mez* k* nux-v hr *Olnd* bg2 *Plat* k* rhus-t bro1 verb bg2
- **odors** agg.: sep k*
- **opening** the eyes agg.: bry
- **opening** the mouth agg.: alum ang aq-mar ↓ cham **Cocc** dros hydrog srj2• mag-p k* mang-p rly4• merc ozone sde2• phos sabad spong thuj verat
  - **burning**: aq-mar skp7•

- **opening** the mouth agg.: ...
  - **cramping**: cham h1
  - **pressing** pain: *Cocc* dros h1
- **overheated**; when: *Ferr*
- **paralysis**; with: *Caust* k* *Cur* k* *Gels* k* kali-chl k* **Nat-m** k*
- **paralyzed**; as if: agn b7.de* cina b7.de* ign b7.de* sabin b7.de*
- **paroxysmal**: acon arg-n bro1 ars bro1 *Bell* k* *Caust* *Cedr* k* *Cham* *Chin* chinin-s cocc k* *Coloc* k* dulc gels bro1 graph bro1 guaj k2 hep bro1 *Kali-i* bro1 kreos bro1 mag-p bg2* *Nux-v* bro1 phos bro1 plan bro1 plat *Rhodi* bro1 sabad k* sang bro1 sep k* sil bg2 *Spig* bro1 stann stram *Stry* bro1 thuj *Verb* k* zinc bro1
- **periodical**: *Ars* ars-s-f k2 *Cact* k* *Cedr* k* *Chin* k* chinin-ar *Chinin-s* k* *Coloc* bro1 glon k* graph bro1 *Guaj* k* kali-ar *Mag-p* k* mez j5.de **Nat-m** k* nux-v j5.de plan bro1 **Spig** k* thuj k* verat j5.de* verb bro1
  - **tearing** pain: guaj *Spig*
- **perspiration**; during: bry bg2 calc bg2 mez bg2 nux-v bg2 *Sep* bg2 **Spig** bg2 thuj bg2
- **pinching** pain: anac b4.de* arn b7.de* cina b7.de* phos b4.de* rhod b4a.de ruta b7.de* sul-ac b4.de* verat b7.de* verb b7.de*
- **plug**; as from a: nat-s bg2 verat bg2
- **pregnancy** agg.; during: *Ign* k* mag-c ptk1 *Sep* k* stram k*
- **pressing** pain: acon acon-c a1 agar b4.de* *Anac* k* ang bro1 ant-t b7.de* arg-met k* arg-n k* asaf k* bamb-a stb2.de• bar-c b4.de* bell b4.de* bism b7.de* bry k* *Cact* bro1 calc b4.de* cann-s b7.de* caps b7a.de* chin b7.de* *Cina* k* *Coca* cocc k* coloc bro1 *Dig* k* dros k* dulc b4.de* ferr-p k* graph b4.de* hyos b7.de* ign b7.de* iod b4.de* kali-bi bg2 kali-c h2* kola stb3• lac-del hrn2• laur bg2 lyc b4.de* mang b4.de* merc k* *Mez* b4a.de* mosch b7.de* nat-c nat-m k* nit-s-d a1* nux-m b7.de* *Olnd* b7.de* oxal-a rly4• par b7.de* petr b4.de* ph-ac b4.de* phos k* plat b4.de* positr nl2• rhus-t k* ruta fd4.de sabad b7.de* sabin b7.de* samb b7.de* *Sep* k* **Spig** b7.de* spong b7.de* *Stann* k* staph b7.de* sul-ac h2* sulph bg2 tarax k* teucr b7.de* thuj bro1 tritic-vg fd5.de vanil fd5.de verat b7.de* **Verb** k* viol-o b7.de* viol-t b7.de* zinc k*
  - **asunder**: colch b7.de* kali-bi bg2
  - **benumbing**: *Mez* bg2
  - **compressed**; as if: tung-met bdx1•
  - **finger**; as from a: sul-ac h2*
  - **inward**: agath-a nl2•
  - **outward**: asaf b7a.de* dros b7.de* kali-i merc
  - **pulsating** pain: anh sp1
- **pressing** teeth together agg.: verb bro1
- **pressure**:
  - **agg.**: *Bell* calc-p k2 *Caps* k* caust ↓ *Cina* *Coloc* cupr dros k* euph ↓ gels kali-cy gm1 *Mag-c* merc-i-f k* nux-v petr h2* *Verb*
    - **pressing** pain: *Cina* k* verb
    - **sore**: caust h2* euph h2*
  - **amel.**: ail am-c ↓ aur h2* *Bry* k* carb-an ↓ chin bro1 coloc k* cupr *Dig* guaj kali-c ↓ kali-n ↓ lepi *Mag-c* mag-m br1* **Mag-p** k* *Merc* ↓ *Mez* *Rhod* bro1 *Rhus-t* ↓ sang sep k* spig spong fd4.de stann staph syph
    - **boring** pain: *Merc* *Mez*
    - **jerking** pain: am-c
    - **neuralgic**: mag-c mrr1 mag-m mrr1 *Mag-p* mrr1
    - **pressing** pain: aur h2*
    - **tearing** pain: aur h2 *Bry* carb-an h2 kali-c h2 kali-n h2 **Mag-c** **Mag-p** *Rhus-t*
  - **hard** | **amel.**: bell k* *Bry* chin *Chinin-s* *Rhus-t* spig
- **prickling** pain: agath-a nl2• lyc h2* staphycoc rly4•
- **pulsating** pain: **Acon** k* arg-met *Arn* bamb-a stb2.de• *Cact* cupr-ar k* *Ferr-p* *Glon* *Mag-c* merc-i-f nit-ac *Plat* puls k* sabad sep k* spig k* staph
- **quiet** in a dark room amel.: *Mez* k*
- **quinine**; after: ars bro1 chin bro1 *Hep* k* ip bro1 **Nat-m** k* *Nux-v* k* *Puls* k* *Stann*
  - **neuralgic**: nat-m mrr1
- **radiating**: arg-n bro1 ars bro1 *Bell* bro1 cocc bg2* *Coloc* bro1 ferr bg2 gels bro1 graph bro1 hep bro1 *Kali-i* bro1 kreos bro1 mag-p bg2* mez bg2 *Nux-v* bro1 phos bro1 plan bro1 ptel bg2 *Rhodi* bro1 sang bro1* spig bg2* *Stry* bro1 zinc bro1
- **rest** agg.: *Mag-c* ↓
  - **boring** pain: *Mag-c*
- **rheumatic**: **Acon** k* act-sp k* **Ars** k* **Bry** k* *Calc-p* k* **Caust** k* cham bro1 *Chin* k* *Cimic* k* *Colch* k* *Coloc* k* *Dulc* bro1 gels k* *Hell* *Hep* hr1 *Kali-ar* kali-bi *Kalm* k* lach k* *Lith-c* mag-c k* med k2 *Merc* k* merc-i-f mez k* nat-c h2 nux-v k* phos k* *Phyt* k* *Puls* k* rhod k* *Rhus-t* k* *Sil* *Spig* k* sul-ac ↓ verat k*
- **rheumatic**: ...
  - **drawing** pain: caust sul-ac h2*
  - **tearing** pain: sul-ac h2
  - ○ **Jaws** | **Joints**: rhus-t tl1
- **rising**:
  - **bed**; from | **after**:
    - **agg.**: nat-m ↓
      - **burning**: nat-m k*
    - **agg.**: chin olnd rhus-t spig
  - **up** again:
    - **agg.**: chin
    - **amel.**: hep
- **room** agg.: am-m chin hell m-aust *Puls* ran-s
- **rubbing** | **after**:
  - **agg.**: kali-c ↓ rhus-v ↓ sep ↓
    - **burning**: kali-c h2* rhus-v a1 sep h2*
  - **amel.**: acon bro1 alum ↓ ant-c *Caust* nat-c ↓ **Phos** plat k* plb *Rhus-t* valer
    - **pressing** pain: phos
    - **stitching** pain: nat-c h2*
    - **tearing** pain: alum h2 nat-c h2 *Phos* *Rhus-t*
- **salivation**, with (See accompanied - salivation)
- **scratching** pain: par b7.de*
- **shaving**; after: aur-m carb-an h2*
  - **burning**: aur-m k*
- **shocks** in rapid succession: coff
- **shooting** (See stitching)
- **sitting** | **agg.**: am-m canth graph guaj kreos bro1 *Mag-c* *Phos* rhus-t thuj
- **sitting** up in bed | **amel.**: bell *Ferr* hep mag-c h2 *Puls* sulph
- **sleep**:
  - **amel.**: mag-p **Phos** sep k*
  - **from**: mez k* verb
  - **going** to sleep; on | **agg.**: *Caps* lach
- **smoking** amel.: clem
- **sneezing** agg.: chin ham fd3.de• mag-c h2* *Verb* k*
- **sore** (= bruised): alum b4.de* anac b4.de* ant-t bg1 *Arn* k* **Aur** beryl sp1 *Bry* b7.de* canth b7.de* carbn-s caust k* chir-fl gya2 con k* cor-r k* cupr cupr-ar a1 dros b7.de* graph ham k* *Ign* kali-bi k* *Kali-c* bg1* **Lach** lat-h bnm5• lyss a1* mag-m b4.de* *Manc* bg1* *Merc-i-f* k* mez bg1 *Nat-m* k* nat-sil fd3.de• nit-ac bg2 *Phos* bg1* plan k* *Plat* bg1* positr nl2• puls k* rauw sp1 *Ruta* k* sars sil b4.de* spig b7.de* stann k* sul-ac b4.de* sulfa sp1 sulph k* thuj til *Verat* bg1* vero-o rly4• zinc k*
- **splinter**; as from a: agar k*
- **spring**: *Lach* *Nux-v*
  - **tearing** pain: *Lach* *Nux-v*
- **standing** agg.: chin guaj nux-v k* spig
  - **burning**: chin
  - **cutting** pain: chin
- **stinging**: all-s k* ant-c tl1 **Apis** am k* **Ars** k* asar k* berb k* caps tl1 caust k* *Chin* k* *Cinnb* k* *Clem* k* **Coloc** k* con k* dros k* *Euph* k* *Ferr-p* k* *Graph* k* *Ind* k* *Kali-c* k* kalm merc-i-f k* rhus-g tmo3• sars spong k* vesp k* zing
- **stitching** pain: *Acon* k* aesc k* aeth k* agar k* agath-a nl2• agn b7.de* alum k* alum-p k2 alum-sil k2 am-c k* am-m k* amph bro1 ang k* ant-c k* ant-t b7.de* apeir-s mlk9.de apis k* arg-met b7.de* ars k* arund k* *Asaf* k* asar k* **Aur** k* aur-ar k2 aur-m k* aur-s k2 bamb-a stb2.de• bar-c k* **Bell** k* berb k* bry b7.de* calad k* calc k* calc-sil k2 camph k* canth b7.de* caps k* *Carb-an* k* carb-v h2* carbn-s castor-eq *Caust* k* cedr *Cham* k* chin k* chinin-s *Cist* clem k* *Cocc* k* *Coloc* k* con k* cupr-ar k* cycl b7.de* *Dig* k* dros b7.de* dulc bro1 euphr k* ferr-ma k* ferr-p fl-ac *Gels* k* *Graph* k* *Guaj* k* *Ham* k* hyper bro1 *Ign* k* indg k* kali-ar *Kali-bi* k* *Kali-c* k* kali-chl k* *Kali-i* k* kali-m k2 *Kali-n* k* kali-p kali-s kali-sil k2 *Kalm* kreos b7a.de* lach k* lyc b4.de* lyss k* *M-ambo* b7.de* m-arct b7.de m-aust b7.de *Mag-c* k* mag-m b4.de* *Mag-p* k* manc k* *Mang* k* meny b7.de* *Merc* k* merc-c merc-i-f k* mez k* naja nat-c b4.de* nat-hchls nat-m k* nat-p k* nit-ac k* nux-v k2* olnd b7.de* par k* petr b4.de* *Phos* k* plan k* *Plat* k* plb b7.de* psor **Puls** k* *Rhod* k* rhodi bro1 *Rhus-t* k* ruta fd4.de sabad b7.de* sabin k* *Sang* k* senec k* **Sep** k* *Sil* k* *Spig* k* spong k* *Stann* k* *Staph* k* stict k* still k* stront-c k* *Stry* sul-ac b4.de* *Sulph* k* tarax b7.de* tarent k* thuj k* valer k* verat b7.de* verb k* vesp k* *Zinc* k*

Face

- **burning**: stann h2*
  - ⁝ **needles**; as from: **Ars** k* *Aur* caps *Spig*
- **intermittent**: *Asaf*
- **itching**: aur h2* cycl h1* plat h2* stann h2* staph h1*
- **jerking** pain: zinc h2*
- **needles**; as from: agar bg2 ars bg2 melal-alt gya4 nit-ac bg2 petr-ra shn4•
  - ⁝ **cold**: agar br1*
  - ⁝ **warm** (See burning - needles)
- **outward**: **Asaf**
- **rhythmical**: bamb-a stb2.de•
- **upward**: clem sul-ac h2*

- **stool** agg.: spig verb c1
- **stooping** agg.: ang c1 *Bell* bro1* bry canth carc zzh coloc ferr-p k* gels kali-c nux-v petr puls *Spig* k*
  - **drawing** pain: nux-v k*
- **storm**; before: *Rhod* ↓
  - **tearing** pain: *Rhod*
- **stretched**; as if: ambr bg2 cina b7.de* rhus-t bg2
- **stunning**: cocc b7.de* *Mez* k* olnd b7.de* *Plat* k* stann h2* verb k*
- **stupefying** (See stunning)
- **sudden**: *Ign* k* kalm valer k*
- **sun**:
  - **comes** and goes with the sun: kali-bi *Kalm* *Nat-m* *Spig* k* *Stann* *Verb*
  - **exposure** to sun; from: germ-met ↓
    - ⁝ **burning**: germ-met srj5•
- **swallowing** agg.: bell bg1 kali-n phos staph
  - **tearing** pain: phos
- **talking**:
  - **agg.**: *Bry* chel euphr kali-chl c1 kreos bro1 mag-c h2* *Mez* phos k* puls rhod spig squil verb k*
    - ⁝ **burning**: kreos k*
    - ⁝ **stitching** pain: mez *Phos* verb
    - ⁝ **tearing** pain: phos
  - **amel.**: kali-p
- **tea** agg.: sel bro1 *Spig* k* thuj bro1
- **tearing** pain: acon bro1 act-sp aeth *Agar* k* agn b7.de* *Alum* k* alum-p k2 alum-sil k2 am-c k* *Am-m* b7.de* ambr k* amph bro1 *Anac* *Ant-t* *Arg-met* k* arg-n bg2 *Ars* k* ars-s-f k2 asaf bg2 **Aur** k* aur-ar k2 aur-s k2 bamb-a stb2.de• **Bell** k* berb borx k* bry k* *Calc* k* calc-ar calc-sil k2 caps carb-an k* **Carb-v** k* carbn-s **Caust** k* *Cham* bro1 *Chel* k* *Chin* k* chinin-ar cina b7.de* cist *Cocc* *Colch* k* **Coloc** k* *Con* k* *Cupr* bg2 dig b4.de* dulc b4.de* euon euph b4.de* gels k* *Graph* k* grat k* guaj b4.de* hep k* hyper bro1 ign k2 indg kali-ar kali-bi k* *Kali-c* k* kali-chl kali-m k2 *Kali-n* k* kali-p kali-s kali-sil k2 *Kalm* kreos b7a.de **Lach** lachn led k* **Lyc** k* *Lyss* m-ambo b7.de **Mag-c** k* mag-m b4.de* **Mag-p** k* mag-s meny b7.de* **Merc** k* *Merc-c* b4a.de *Mez* k* mur-ac k* nat-c b4.de* nat-m b4a.de *Nat-s* k* *Nit-ac* k* **Nux-v** k* *Phos* k* *Plat* plb k* **Puls** k* *Rhod* k* rhodi bro1 *Rhus-t* k* ruta k* sars k* senec bro1 seneg b4.de* *Sep* k* *Sil* k* *Spig* k* spong k* stann b4.de* staph k* stram *Stront-c* k* sul-ac k* *Sulph* k* tab teucr k* thuj k* tritic-vg fd5.de *Verat* k* vinc viol-o k* zinc k*
  - **asunder**: colch b7.de* nit-ac b4.de* nux-v b7.de*
  - **jerking** pain: agar am-m *Carb-v* euph h2* *Puls* rhod
  - **paroxysmal**: **Caust** *Coloc* nux-v puls
  - **wandering** pain: colch k* puls
- **teeth**:
  - **carious** or after extraction of; from: coff-t bro1* hecla bro1* merc bro1 merc-sul xyz61 mez bro1* staph bro1*
    - ⁝ **decayed**: thuj hr1
- **temperature**; change of: mag-c *Verb* k*
- **thinking**:
  - **agg.**: spig ↓
    - ⁝ **stitching** pain: spig k2
  - **tearing** pain (See mental exertion - tearing)
- **thinking** of the pain: aur bro1
- **tobacco**; from: ign sep k* spig mrr1
- **toothache**; with: nept-m ↓ sil ↓ *Staph* ↓
  - **burning**: nept-m lsd2.fr sil h2* *Staph* hr1
- **torn** out; as if: phos bg2
- **touch**:
  - **agg.**: acon bro1 arn aur bad c1 bamb-a ↓ **Bell** k* *Bry* k* canth ↓ *Caps* k* *Chel* *Chin* k* chinin-s cina *Clem* hr1 cocc **Coff** *Coloc* k* cor-r cupr k* dig dros k* **Hep** k* kali-c h2* kali-chl c1 kali-cy gm1 **Lach** lyc mag-c k* mag-m ↓ mag-p k* merc-i-f c1 *Mez* bro1 nat-m *Nux-v* par k* ph-ac *Phos* k* positr nl2• puls k* rhus-g ↓ *Sep* k* spig k* spong staph k* sulph h2* verb k* zinc k*
    - ⁝ **burning**: canth k2 *Chin* **Coloc** hr1
    - ⁝ **stinging**: rhus-g tmo3•
    - ⁝ **stitching** pain: *Chin* chinin-s cupr kl (non:mag-c k*) mag-m h2* nat-m kl *Phos* sep h2* staph *Verb*
    - ⁝ **tearing** pain: *Chin* **Coloc** k* *Mag-p* staph
    - ⁝ **ulcerative** pain: bamb-a stb2.de•
  - **amel.**: am-c am-m asaf chin euphr kali-p olnd thuj
    - ⁝ **boring** pain: *Thuj* k*
- **ulcerative** pain: acon b7.de* bamb-a stb2.de• chin h1* hep b4a.de mag-c h2* mang h2* *Nat-m* b4a.de rhus-t b7.de* staph b7.de*
- **urination**:
  - **frequent**; with: calc ptk1
  - **profuse** | **amel.**: acon ferr-p **Gels** ign kalm sang sil ter verat
- **vexation**:
  - **after**: *Coloc* ↓
    - ⁝ **tearing** pain: *Coloc*
  - **agg.**: *Coloc* kalm nat-hchls ↓ staph
    - ⁝ **stitching** pain: nat-hchls
- **waking**; on: croc hell hep kali-p k2 *Lach* nux-v puls sabad sep spig verb
- **walking**:
  - **after** | **agg.**: ran-s
  - **agg.**: ang c1 guaj laur mang merc mur-ac petr thuj
  - **air**; in open:
    - ⁝ **agg.**: ham ↓ nat-c nux-v thuj ↓
      - **jerking** pain: thuj h1*
      - **pressing** pain: nat-c
      - **stitching** pain: ham fd3.de• thuj h1*
    - ⁝ **amel.**: asar *Coloc* *Mag-c*
  - **amel.**: agar ail ↓ *Mag-c* k* sulph
    - ⁝ **stitching** pain: *Mag-c*
    - ⁝ **tearing** pain: ail **Mag-c**
  - **slowly** | **amel.**: chin *Ferr* *Puls*
- **wandering** pain: acon arg-n a1 *Colch* **Gels** graph h2* kali-bi bg2 *Mag-p* **Puls** rob bg2
- **warm**:
  - **applications**:
    - ⁝ **agg.**: cedr vh
    - ⁝ **amel.**: dulc hr1 lac-c k2
  - **bed**:
    - ⁝ **agg.**: clem glon *Merc* *Mez* plat *Puls* verat
      - **stitching** pain: clem
  - **drinks** | **agg.**: cham
  - **food** | **agg.**: mez *Puls* sep
  - **hand**; warm:
    - ⁝ **amel.**: kali-p ↓
      - **stitching** pain: kali-p k2
  - **room**:
    - ⁝ **agg.**: am-c **Kali-s** k* *Mez* k* nat-hchls ↓ **Puls** k*
      - **stitching** pain: *Mez* nat-hchls
    - ⁝ **amel.**: *Calc* *Hep* lac-c laur *Sep* k* staph
      - **pressing** pain: sep k*
- **warm** from walking agg.; becoming: plan k* **Puls**
- **warmth**: *(↗burning)*
  - **agg.**: cham bro1 glon bro1 kali-s bro1 merc bro1 mez bro1 *Puls* bro1
    - ⁝ **heat** agg.: cedr chin ferr ptk1 glon *Phos* rhod
    - ⁝ **tearing** pain: *Puls*

- **amel.**: **Ars**$_{k}$* ars-s-f$_{k2}$ *Calc*$_{k}$* *Calc-p* calc-sil$_{k4}$ caust *Cham* chinin-s coloc$_{k}$* cupr cupr-act$_{bro1}$ *Dulc*$_{hr1}$ gink-b$_{sbd1}$• **Hep** kali-p lac-c$_{k2}$ lach mag-c↓ mag-m$_{bro1}$ **Mag-p**$_{k}$* *Mez*$_{k}$* phos rhod *Rhus-t* sanic **Sil** spig sul-ac sulph thuj$_{bro1}$
  - ⁝ **drawing** pain: **Ars** *Caust Coloc*
  - ⁝ **heat** amel.: calc-p$_{k2}$ gink-b$_{sbd1}$• kali-ar$_{k4}$
  - ⁝ **neuralgic**: mag-c$_{mrr1}$ mag-m$_{mrr1}$ *Mag-p*$_{mrr1}$ mez$_{tl1}$
  - ⁝ **tearing** pain: *Coloc*$_{k}$* **Mag-p** *Rhod* **Rhus-t**

- **washing** | **cold** water; in (See cold - applications)
- **waves**; in: spig$_{ptk1}$
- **weather**: (↗*cold - exposure - agg.)*
  - **change** of weather: dulc$_{fd4.de}$ kali-cy$_{gm1}$ *Rhod*
    - ⁝ **tearing** pain: *Rhod*
  - **cold** agg.: kali-cy$_{gm1}$
  - **stormy**:
    - ⁝ **agg.**: *Caust* phos **Rhod Sil** spig verb
    - ⁝ **before**: *Rhod* sep *Sil*
  - **wet**:
    - ⁝ **agg.**: amph$_{a1}$ *Calc Calc-p* chinin-s dulc mag-c$_{br1}$ *Merc Nat-s Rhod*↓ *Rhus-t*↓ *Sep Sil* spig$_{k}$* verat
      - ⁝ **tearing** pain: *Merc Rhod Rhus-t* verat
- **wind**: (↗*cold - exposure - agg.)*
  - **agg.**: *Caust Dulc* irid-met$_{srj5}$• lac-c mag-p phos pot-e$_{rly4}$• *Rhod Sep*
    - ⁝ **neuralgic**: caust$_{mrr1}$ mag-p$_{mrr1}$
    - ⁝ **tearing** pain: *Rhod*
  - **cold**:
    - ⁝ **dry**:
      - ⁝ **agg.**: **Acon** bell$_{k2}$ *Caust* **Hep** lac-c **Mag-p** rhod
        - **neuralgic**: acon$_{mrr1}$
  - **south**, warm, moist: ip *Kali-s Puls*
- **wine** agg.: bell *Cact*$_{k}$*
- **wrapping** up head:
  - **amel.**: gink-b$_{sbd1}$•
    - ⁝ **night**: phos$_{k2}$
- **writing** agg.: chinin-s
- **yawning** agg.: aloe$_{ptk1}$ arn$_{k}$* ign mag-c$_{h2}$* op rhus-t sabad staph$_{k}$*

▽ - **extending** to: kola$_{stb3}$•

○ • **Arms**: kalm lyc↓
    - ⁝ **tearing** pain: *Kalm* lyc$_{h2}$
  - **Chest**: sil
  - **Chin**: phos↓
    - ⁝ **drawing** pain: phos
  - **Ear**: *Acon*↓ *Bell*↓ *Carb-an*↓ colch↓ **Coloc**↓ irid-met↓ kali-bi↓ **Lach**↓ *Lyss*↓ mur-ac↓ plan↓ **Puls**↓ *Sep*↓
    - ⁝ **stitching** pain: *Acon Bell Carb-an Coloc*$_{k}$* irid-met$_{srj5}$• kali-bi mur-ac$_{h2}$*
    - ⁝ **tearing** pain: colch$_{a1}$ **Coloc**$_{k}$* **Lach** *Lyss* plan **Puls** *Sep*
  - **Ear**; into: *Acon*↓ *Caust*↓ con↓ ph-ac↓
    - ⁝ **drawing** pain: *Acon Caust* con ph-ac$_{h2}$
  - **Ears**: **Bell** *Calc* carb-an *Caust* cocc-s$_{kr1}$ *Coloc Hep* irid-met$_{srj5}$• **Lach** lyc *Mez*$_{k}$* plan **Puls** sang *Sep* spig thuj
  - **Eyes**: ang↓ chel$_{mrr1}$ chin↓ clem↓ kalm$_{mrr1}$ naja↓ sang$_{hr1}$
    - ⁝ **chewing** agg.: bell↓
      - ⁝ **stitching** pain: bell
    - ⁝ **cramping**: ang$_{c1}$
    - ⁝ **pressure** agg.: mur-ac↓
      - ⁝ **stitching** pain: mur-ac$_{h2}$
    - ⁝ **stitching** pain: chin clem naja
  - **Fingers**: cocc$_{ptk1}$ *Coff* lyc↓
    - ⁝ **tearing** pain: lyc$_{h2}$
  - **Forehead**: nat-c↓ zinc↓
    - ⁝ **stitching** pain: nat-c$_{h2}$*
    - ⁝ **tearing** pain: zinc$_{h2}$
  - **Head**: all-c$_{k2}$ colch↓ *Coloc*↓ sang$_{hr1}$
    - ⁝ **tearing** pain: colch$_{a1}$ *Coloc*$_{k}$*
  - **Neck**: *Bell Coloc Guaj* lyc$_{bg1}$ nat-hchls↓ *Puls* sang *Spig*

- **extending** to – **Neck**: ...
    - ⁝ **stitching** pain: bell nat-hchls
    - ⁝ **tearing** pain: *Puls*
  - **Nose**: puls$_{k2}$ sang$_{hr1}$ *Spig*
    - ⁝ **Root** of: kola$_{stb3}$• phos
  - **Occiput**: sep↓
    - ⁝ **tearing** pain: sep$_{h2}$
  - **Other** parts: calc-p *Cocc*
  - **Parietal** bone: chin↓
    - ⁝ **tearing** pain: chin
  - **Pubis**: arund$_{br1}$
  - **Shoulders**: arund$_{br1}$
  - **Teeth**: chel$_{mrr1}$ *Hist*↓ kalm$_{mrr1}$ melal-alt$_{gya4}$ merc$_{bg1}$
    - ⁝ **dull** pain: *Hist*$_{sp1}$
  - **Temple**: alum↓ chin↓ mez↓ naja↓ nat-hchls↓
    - ⁝ **stitching** pain: alum chin mez naja nat-hchls
  - **Temples**: ang↓ berb hep med$_{c1}$ *Mez*$_{k}$* phos plan$_{br1}$* spig zinc↓
    - ⁝ **cramping**: ang$_{c1}$
    - ⁝ **tearing** pain: zinc$_{h2}$

○ - **Bones**: aeth agar$_{b4a.de}$ alum$_{bro1}$ amp$_{rly4}$• anan *Arg-met*$_{b7a.de}$ arg-n$_{bro1}$ asaf$_{b7.de}$* astra-m$_{c2}$* aur$_{k}$* bamb-a$_{stb2.de}$• bufo$_{bg2}$ *Calc*$_{b4a.de}$ *Caps*$_{k}$* *Carb-an*$_{b4a.de}$* carb-v$_{h2}$* caust$_{bro1}$ chel$_{b7.de}$* *Chinin-s Cimic* colch$_{k}$* cupr-ar↓ dulc$_{bro1}$ graph$_{h2}$* hell$_{k}$* *Hep*$_{k}$* hydrog$_{srj2}$• *Kali-bi*↓ kali-c$_{b4a.de}$* kali-n lyc↓ mag-m$_{b4a.de}$* mag-s↓ mang-p$_{rly4}$• *Merc*$_{k}$* *Merc-c*$_{b4a.de}$ merc-i-f$_{k}$* merc-i-r nat-c$_{k}$* nat-m nat-s↓ nit-ac$_{k}$* nit-s-d$_{bro1}$ nux-m$_{b7.de}$* nux-v olnd$_{b7.de}$* onos phos$_{b4a.de}$* *Phyt*$_{k}$* *Plb*$_{b7a.de}$ rad-br$_{sze8}$• rhus-t$_{mtf11}$ ruta$_{b7.de}$* samb$_{b7.de}$* sang$_{a1}$ sil$_{h2}$* spig$_{b7.de}$* staph$_{b7.de}$* sulph$_{bg1}$ symph$_{fd3.de}$• tab↓ tarent↓ valer$_{b7.de}$* zinc$_{k}$*
  - **left**: bamb-a$_{stb2.de}$• ruta$_{fd4.de}$
  - **accompanied** by | **Teeth**; pain in (See TEETH - Pain - accompanied - face - pain - bones)
  - **boring** pain: kali-bi$_{bg2}$
  - **chewing** agg.: nat-m$_{h2}$*
  - **drawing** pain: kali-bi$_{bg2}$
  - **gnawing** pain: arg-met$_{b7a.de}$ samb$_{b7a.de}$
  - **pinching** pain: kali-c$_{bg2}$
  - **sore**: bufo$_{k}$* *Carb-v*$_{k}$* cupr-ar$_{k}$* hep$_{a1}$ *Kali-bi*$_{k}$* *Merc-i-f*$_{k}$* nat-m rhus-t$_{k2}$ tarent zinc$_{bg2}$
  - **tearing** pain: kali-bi$_{bg2}$ lyc$_{bg2}$ mag-s$_{sp1}$ merc-c$_{bg2}$ nat-s$_{bg2}$ tab$_{bg2}$
    - ⁝ **torn** out; as if: phos$_{h}$*
- **Cheekbones** (See malar bones)
  - **pressing** pain (See malar bones - pressing)
  - **stitching** pain (See malar bones - stitching)
- **Cheeks**: acon$_{k}$* agar$_{bro1}$ alum-sil$_{k2}$ *Ang*$_{k}$* asar↓ bamb-a$_{stb2.de}$• *Bell Bism*$_{k}$* bry$_{k}$* *Caps Caust*$_{k}$* *Chel*$_{k}$* *Chinin-s* chord-umb$_{rly4}$• cimic *Cina* clem↓ cocc *Coloc*$_{k}$* dig$_{k}$* dulc$_{k}$* euph↓ ferr-p↓ ham$_{fd3.de}$• *Hep* hyos *Kali-bi Kali-i*$_{k}$* *Mag-c*$_{k}$* *Mag-m*$_{k}$* medul-os-si$_{rly4}$• *Merc*$_{k}$* merc-i-f$_{k}$* merc-i-r$_{a1}$ mez$_{k}$* nat-m nit-s-d↓ olib-sac↓ onos ph-ac↓ phel↓ phos↓ *Plat*$_{k}$* polys$_{sk4}$• psor pyrog↓ rhus-t$_{k}$* ruta sep$_{k}$* spong$_{fd4.de}$ *Stann*$_{k}$* sul-ac↓ sulph↓ valer vanil$_{fd5.de}$ verat$_{bro1}$ **Verb**$_{k}$* [**Spect**$_{dfg1}$]
  - **right**: *Chel* dulc$_{fd4.de}$ guaj$_{k2}$ nat-p$_{k2}$ nept-m$_{lsd2.fr}$ ozone$_{sde2}$• thuj↓
    - ⁝ **afternoon** | **15** h: dendr-pol$_{sk4}$•
    - ⁝ **cramping**: thuj$_{h1}$
  - **left**: phasco-ci$_{rbp2}$ stann↓
    - ⁝ **cramping**: stann$_{h2}$
  - **daytime**: cimic
  - **accompanied** by | **Teeth**; complaints of (See TEETH - Complaints - accompanied - cheeks - pain)
  - **alternating** with | **Nose**; obstruction of: ozone$_{sde2}$•
  - **burning**: agar$_{b4a.de}$* asar$_{b7a.de}$ caust$_{b4a.de}$ clem$_{b4a.de}$ euph$_{bro1}$ ferr-p$_{bro1}$ nit-s-d$_{bro1}$ olib-sac$_{wmh1}$ ph-ac$_{b4a.de}$* phel$_{bg2}$ phos$_{bro1}$ pyrog$_{jl2}$ rhus-t$_{b7a.de}$ sulph$_{bro1}$ vanil$_{fd5.de}$
  - **cough** agg.; during: *Ars*↓ *Kali-bi*
    - ⁝ **stitching** pain: *Ars*$_{b4a.de}$
    - ⁝ **extending** to | **Head**: thuj

- **coughing**; when: carb-v ↓
  - **drawing** pain: carb-v b4.de*
- **pinching** pain: ruta h1 sul-ac h2
- **splinter**; as from a: agar ptk1
- **stitching** pain: plat bg2
- **warmth** | **amel.**: ozone sde2•

- **Chin**: acon ↓ agar ↓ agn ↓ am-m ↓ anac ↓ ant-c ↓ apis ↓ *Ars* ↓ asaf ↓ aur ↓ aur-m-n ↓ bamb-a ↓ bell ↓ berb ↓ bov ↓ cann-s ↓ canth ↓ *Caust* ↓ chinin-s ↓ con ↓ cupr ↓ dulc ↓ euphr ↓ fl-ac ↓ hyper ↓ lact ↓ laur ↓ m-aust ↓ maias-l hm2• mang k* merc ↓ mez ↓ nat-c ↓ nux-m k* ol-an ↓ olnd ↓ phos ↓ plat ↓ rhus-t ↓ ruta fd4.de *Sil* ↓ spong ↓ stann ↓ staph ↓ stront-c ↓ sulfa ↓ sulph ↓ tell ↓ verat ↓ *Verb* ↓ zinc ↓
  - **right**: kali-n ↓
    - **tearing** pain: kali-n h2
  - **biting** pain: plat h2* stront-c b4.de*
  - **burning**: anac k* ant-c b7.de* apis k* *Ars* b4a.de berb k* bov k* canth k* caust k* mang k* merc k* mez k* nat-c k* ol-an k* rhus-t k* sil b4a.de spong k* sulph k2
    - **sparks**; as from hot: ant-c
  - **compressed**; as if: cann-s b7.de*
  - **corrosive**: agn b7.de* plat b4.de*
  - **cutting** pain: caust k* stann k* staph bg2
    - **glass** were cutting outward; as if a piece of: caust h2*
  - **drawing** pain: agar k* aur-m-n k* caust k* chinin-s cupr k* hyper olnd k* stront-c k* *Verb*
  - **dull** pain: plat b4.de*
  - **gnawing** pain: laur b7.de*
  - **pinching** pain: dulc b4.de* phos b4.de*
  - **pressing** pain: acon a1 agar k* anac k* asaf k* bov k* fl-ac k* plat k*
  - **scratching** agg.; after: sulph ↓
    - **burning**: sulph k*
  - **smarting**: mang b4.de* verat b7.de*
  - **sore**: ant-c b7.de* m-aust b7.de spong b7.de* sulfa sp1 tell rsj10•
  - **stitching** pain: agar k* am-m k* ant-c b7.de* apis b7a.de bamb-a stb2.de• bell k* bov bg2 canth b7.de* con h2* euphr k* lact laur b7.de* nux-m b7.de* ruta fd4.de *Sil* b4.de* stann b4.de* zinc h2*
  - **tearing** pain: agar k* am-m b7a.de* aur k* *Caust* k* plat k* zinc h2
  - ○ **Between** the chin and lower lip: mag-c ↓
    - **burning**: mag-c h2*
    - **pressing** pain: mag-c h2*
  - **Skin**: nux-m b7.de*
  - **Under** the chin: bar-c ↓
    - **pressing** pain: bar-c h2
- **Eye** | **left**: arg-n coloc k2 **Spig** mrr1
- **Eyebrows**: rhod ↓
  - **coryza**; during: ars ↓
    - **pressing** pain: ars b4a.de
  - **pinching** pain: rhod b4a.de
- **Eyes**:
  - ○ **Around**: m-aust ↓
    - **night**: plb ↓
      - **neuralgic**: plb hr1
    - **sore**: m-aust b7.de
  - **Below** (= infraorbital): *Acon* *Arg-n* *Ars* aur-m-n *Bell* carc zzh cham j5.de *Chin* c1 colch bro1 coloc dros ↓ *Gels* hydrc iris k* lap-la rsp1 mag-p k* mang h2 mez k* *Nux-v* k* phos j5.de* plat puls j5.de ruta fd4.de *Sil* spig k* sulph tritic-vg fd5.de verb k* zinc
    - **right**: bac jl2 *Iris* mrr1 samb bat1• visc c1
    - **burning**: dros b7a.de
    - **extending** to | **Axilla**: bac jl2
  - **Below** eye up through to vertex: tarent ↓
    - **lancinating**: tarent
- **Inner** side: cob-n ↓
  - **sore**: cob-n sp1

- **Jaws**: acon bro1 agar bro1 agath-a nl2• *Aids* nl2• all-c k2 allox sp1 alum bro1 *Alumn* ↓ am-c k* am-m bro1 am-pic bro1 ambr amph c2* anac ↓ androc srj1• ang bro1 anh sp1 arge-pl rwt5• arum-t bro1 aster bro1 aur bro1 bapt-c bro1 berb ↓ bov ↓ bry ↓ calc ↓ calc-caust bro1 carb-ac ↓ carb-an bro1 carb-v h2* **Caust** k* cham ↓ cimic cimx ↓ cina ↓ clem k2 coff k2 con crot-h cystein-l ↓ daph ↓ dol c2 dulc fd4.de falco-pe nl2• fl-ac ↓ ham ↓ heroin ↓ hydrog srj2• irid-met srj5• kali-p k2 kali-s fd4.de kalm ↓ lac-h ↓ lach lap-la sde8.de• lyc h2* lyss ↓ med tl1 merc k* merc-c merc-i-r k* mez ↓ morg-p fmm1• mur-ac ↓ naja ↓ nat-c h2 nat-m ↓ nat-s ↓ nit-ac nux-m ↓ *Nux-v* ↓ op ↓ oxyt ptk2 ph-ac ↓ phos k* phyt ↓ plan ↓ positr ↓ puls ↓ pyrid rly4• rhus-t bro1 *Rhus-v* ↓ rumx ruta fd4.de sabad ↓ sang hr1* sars ↓ seneg sil ↓ *Sphing* bro1 spig bro1 spong fd4.de suis-pan rly4• sulph ↓ symph fd3.de• thuj ↓ til ↓ tritic-vg fd5.de vanil fd5.de verat ↓ vip xan bro1 zinc ↓
  - **right**: petr-ra shn4•
    - **Lower** part: lavand-a ctl1•
  - **left**: aids nl2• guaj k2 hydroph rsj6• ruta fd4.de suis-pan rly4•
  - **evening**: nat-c ↓ ruta ↓
    - **pressing** pain: nat-c h2* ruta fd4.de
  - **night**:
    - **midnight**:
      - **after**:
        - **4 h**: bamb-a ↓
          - **stitching** pain: bamb-a stb2.de•
  - **aching**: merc ptk1 phyt ptk1
  - **bending** head backward agg.: sars ↓
    - **aching**: sars ptk1
  - **boring** pain: ruta fd4.de
  - **burning**: anac bov caust daph fl-ac
  - **chilliness**; during: sep ↓
    - **drawing** pain: sep h2*
  - **clenching** in sleep; from: merc-i-f ↓
    - **aching**: merc-i-f ptk1
  - **cold**:
    - **water**:
      - **mouth**; holding cold water in | **amel.**: clem k2
  - **coryza**; during: all-c tl1
  - **cough** agg.; during: am-c h2
  - **cramping**: con h2 cystein-l rly4• nit-ac h2
  - **dislocated**; as if: lac-h htj1•
  - **drawing** pain: acon k* agar a1 *Alumn* k* anac ang h1* *Aur* k* bry k* calc k* carb-ac a1 **Carb-v** k* caust cham *Con* lyc k* mez mur-ac k* nat-c nat-s k* nit-ac *Nux-v* k* ph-ac k* phos k* puls *Rhus-v* k* sabad k* sil k* sulph k* til a1 vanil fd5.de vip fkr4.de zinc k*
    - **cramping**: sulph h2*
  - **dull** pain: arge-pl rwt5•
  - **gnawing** pain: naja nat-m
  - **heat** agg. (See warmth - agg. - heat)
  - **lying** | **night**: cench k2
  - **pressing** pain: dulc fd4.de ruta fd4.de symph fd3.de• tritic-vg fd5.de vanil fd5.de
  - **screwed** together or asunder; as if being: ambr b7.de* nux-m b7.de*
  - **sore**: *Caust* crot-h lyss c1 phos plan positr nl2• sars h2
  - **stitching** pain: acon agath-a nl2• aids nl2• ambr arge-pl rwt5• berb carb-an cimx ham fd3.de• kalm op thuj verat zinc [heroin sdj2]
  - **tearing** pain: cina a1
  - **waking**; on: hydrog srj2•
  - **warm** bed agg.: clem k2
  - **warmth**:
    - **agg.** | **heat** agg.: clem k2 glycyr-g cte1•
  - ▽ **extending** to:
    - **Ear**: bell ↓ *Cham* ↓ **Sep** ↓
      - **stitching** pain: bell *Cham* **Sep**
    - **Neck**: zinc ↓
      - **stitching** pain: zinc

- **extending** to: ...
  - **Teeth**: *Cham* ↓
    - **stitching** pain: *Cham*
  - **Temple**: alum ↓ mang ↓
    - **stitching** pain: alum mang h2*
- **Condyles**: **Psor**
- **Joints**: acet-ac k* agar k* alum k* alumn k* am-m hr1 anac ↓ ang mrr1 *Arum-t* k* asaf k* asar *Bapt* hr1 bell ↓ brom k* *Bry* ↓ calc k* *Caust* k* *Cham* ↓ cimic k* cist coloc ↓ cor-r k* cycl ↓ dendr-pol sk4• dream-p sdj1• dros k* dulc fd4.de fl-ac k* glon k* gran ↓ hep ↓ hydrog srj2• hyper k* kali-n ↓ kali-s fd4.de lac-e hrn2• laur k* mang k* nat-c a1 nat-m ↓ nicc k* nit-ac ↓ op k* paeon ↓ pin-con oss2• psil ft1 *Rhus-t* k* sep ↓ sphing a1* spig k* spong k* staph ↓ *Stry* k* sul-ac tab ↓ til c1 tritic-vg fd5.de tung-met bdx1• verb br1 vesp k* xan c2
  - **right**: caust mrr1 dulc fd4.de hydrog srj2•
  - **left**: cor-r br1 kali-s fd4.de mang-p rly4• podo fd3.de• ulm-c ↓ v-a-b jl2
    - **stitching** pain: ulm-c jsj8•
    - **Temples**; near: v-a-b jl2
  - **morning**: vesp
  - **burning**: op
  - **burrowing**: dros h1
  - **chewing** agg.: acon k* alum k* am-c am-m k* bar-c bg2 bell calc k* coc-c k* cor-r k* dulc fd4.de kali-s fd4.de sil spig ↓ v-a-b jl2 zinc ↓
    - **sore**: sil
    - **tearing** pain: spig h1 zinc h2
  - **cramping**: *Rhus-t* a1
  - **cutting** pain: asar h1
  - **motion** agg.: kali-n ↓ rhus-t ↓ verat ↓ zinc ↓
    - **pressing** pain: kali-n h2*
    - **sore**: rhus-t
    - **stitching** pain: kali-n h2* verat a1 zinc
  - **opening** the mouth agg.: alum k* am-c am-m k* **Caust** cor-r dros dulc fd4.de hep nicc sabad verat zinc ↓
    - **stitching** pain: verat h1* zinc
  - **pinching** pain: *Bry* coloc gran
  - **pressing** pain: asaf k* dros h1* dulc fd4.de kali-n k* nat-m h2* op k* paeon k* verb k*
  - **pressure** | **amel.**: rhus-t hr1
  - **rest** agg.: *Rhus-t*
  - **rheumatic**: caust tl1 dys fmm1• *Rhus-t*
  - **shutting** mouth: *Bar-c* k*
  - **stitching** pain: agar bell *Cham* hep kali-n h2* nat-m nit-ac staph h1* tab
  - **swallowing** agg.: *Arum-t* kali-n ↓ ozone sde2•
    - **pressing** pain: kali-n h2*
    - **stitching** pain: kali-n h2*
  - **tearing** pain: anac h2 cycl a1 nat-c h2 sep h2
  - **warmth** | **amel.**: rhus-t hr1
  - **yawning** agg.: cor-r k* ign rhus-t k* staph k*
  - **extending** to:
    - **Ears**: ozone sde2•
    - **Face**: verb c1
      - **stitching** pain: verb c1
    - **Nose**: ozone sde2•
    - **Teeth**; into: lac-e hrn2•
  - **Behind**: tarax ↓
    - **pressing** pain: tarax h1*
- **Lower**: acon k* aeth ↓ agar k* agath-a nl2• *Agn* ↓ aids ↓ allox tpw3 aloe alum ↓ am-c b4.de* *Am-m* b7a.de ambr amph a1* *Anac* ↓ ang ↓ ant-t ↓ *Anthraci* ↓ apis ↓ arg-met arg-n ↓ arn ↓ *Ars* k* asaf ↓ asar ↓ **Aur** ↓ aur-m-n ↓ aur-s ↓ bar-c ↓ *Bell* ↓ berb ↓ *Bov* ↓ brom ↓ *Bry* ↓ calad ↓ calc bro1 calc-ar ↓ cann-s ↓ cann-xyz ↓ canth ↓ caps h1* *Carb-an* ↓ *Carb-v* k* carbn-s ↓ *Caust* k* cham k* chin k* chinin-s bro1 cimic k* cina ↓ clem ↓ coc-c ↓ *Cocc* ↓ coff k2 *Colch* ↓ *Coloc* ↓ con ↓ cor-r ↓ cupr ↓ cupr-ar k* dig ↓ dros bg2 *Dulc* echi euphr ↓ eupi ↓ falco-pe nl2• fl-ac ↓ *Gels* ↓ graph k* grat guaj ham ↓ hell ↓ hep ↓ heroin ↓ hyos ↓ ign b7.de* ind ↓ indg ↓ iod k* irid-met ↓ kali-bi ↓ kali-c ↓ kali-chl ↓ kali-i ↓ kali-n ↓ kali-p *Kalm* ↓ kola stb3• kreos ↓ *Lach* k* lact ↓ lap-la sde8.de• laur ↓

- **Lower**: ... led ↓ lob ↓ lyc b4.de* lyss k* *M-ambo* ↓ *M-arct* ↓ mag-c ↓ mag-m ↓ mang k* melal-alt ↓ *Meny* b7a.de meph ↓ *Merc* k* merc-c k* merc-i-f ↓ merc-i-r k* *Mez* mur-ac ↓ nat-c ↓ *Nat-m* ↓ nat-p k2 nat-s bg2 nit-ac k* nit-s-d bro1 nux-m ↓ *Nux-v* ↓ op k* ox-ac ↓ pall k* par ↓ petr b4.de* ph-ac k* *Phos* k* phys k* *Plat* k* plb ↓ psor ↓ puls ↓ rad-br bro1 ran-b ↓ *Rat* ↓ rheum ↓ rhod k* *Rhus-t* rhus-v ↓ rob ↓ rumx ruta ↓ sabad b7.de* sabin b7.de* *Sars* ↓ *Sel* ↓ seneg b4.de* sep k* *Sil* k* *Spig* k* spong b7.de* squil ↓ stann ↓ staph b7.de* stram k* stront-c ↓ stry k* sul-ac sulph k* symph fd3.de• tab ↓ tarent k* *Thuj* ↓ til ↓ tritic-vg ↓ tung-met ↓ verat ↓ *Verb* ↓ viol-o ↓ viol-t ↓ vip bg2 xan bro1 zinc k* zinc-val bro1 zing ↓
  - **right**: aur ↓ brom ↓ coloc ↓ elaps ↓ indg ↓ led ↓ nat-p ↓ nat-s ↓ sabin ↓
    - **night**: chin ↓
      - **pressing** pain: chin h1
      - **tearing** pain: chin h1
    - **boring** pain: aur brom coloc elaps indg led nat-s bg2
    - **drawing** pain: sabin c1
    - **sore**: nat-p k2
  - **left**: glycyr-g cte1• kali-n ↓ mez ↓ musca-d szs1 plb ↓ positr ↓ sabad ↓
    - **boring** pain: mez plb sabad
    - **sore**: positr nl2•
    - **tearing** pain: kali-n h2
  - **morning**: kali-p ↓ sulph ↓ thuj ↓ zinc ↓
    - **drawing** pain: sulph
    - **sore**: zinc
    - **stitching** pain: kali-p fd1.de• thuj
  - **afternoon**: euphr ↓ sulph ↓
    - **drawing** pain: euphr sulph
  - **evening**: anac ↓ berb ↓ falco-pe nl2• ham ↓ merc ↓ nat-c ↓ nit-ac k* phos ↓ *Plat* sulph ↓ symph fd3.de• thuj ↓
    - **drawing** pain: anac h2 thuj h1
    - **stitching** pain: berb ham fd3.de• symph fd3.de•
    - **tearing** pain: merc k* nat-c phos sulph h2 thuj h1
  - **night**: graph ↓ *Mez* ↓ sil ↓ symph ↓ zinc ↓
    - **boring** pain: *Mez*
    - **drawing** pain: sil h2
    - **menses**; during: sul-ac ↓
      - **tearing** pain: sul-ac k*
    - **pressing** pain: graph h2 sil
    - **stitching** pain: sil h2* symph fd3.de• zinc
  - **accompanied** by | **Head**; complaints of (See HEAD - Complaints - accompanied - jaw - pain)
  - **aching**: nat-c bg2 op bg2
  - **blow**; pain as from a: m-ambo b7.de ruta b7.de*
  - **boring** pain: aur aur-m-n bov k* brom *Cocc* coloc indg kali-bi *Lach* led mag-c *Mez* plat ptk1 plb k* sabad k* symph fd3.de•
  - **break**; as if it would: ph-ac rhus-t b7.de* sars bg2 tung-met bdx1•
  - **burning**: acon b7.de* agn bg2 ars bov b4.de* caust k* *M-arct* b7.de* mang par b7.de*
  - **burrowing**: ang b7.de* *Bell* b4a.de bry b7.de* caust b4.de* cocc b7.de* dros b7.de* kali-bi bg2 *M-arct* b7.de*
  - **chewing** agg.: bar-c bg2 luf-op rsj5• ph-ac ↓ positr ↓ verat ↓
    - **sore**: positr nl2• verat h1
    - **tearing** pain: ph-ac h2
  - **cold** applications agg.: glycyr-g cte1•
  - **corrosive**: par b7.de*
  - **cough** agg.; during: am-c b4a.de
  - **cramping**: agar b4a.de ang b7.de* carb-v h2* *Caust* b4a.de dig b4.de* nit-ac bg2 nux-m b7.de* plat b4.de* sars b4.de* sep h2* sil b4a.de spong b7.de* stann b4.de* zinc bg2
  - **cutting** pain: asar b7.de* *Bell* b4a.de
  - **digging** pain: cocc *Plat*
  - **dinner**; during: euphr ↓
    - **stitching** pain: euphr h2*
  - **dislocated**; as if: cor-r bg2* *Ign* b7.de* *M-ambo* b7.de* *M-arct* b7.de* op bg2 petr bg2 *Rhus-t* b7.de* rob bg2 spig b7.de* spong b7.de* staph b7.de*

Face

- **Lower**: ...
  - **drawing** pain: agar k* alum b4.de* am-m anac ant-t b7.de* apis b7a.de arg-met b7.de* arg-n asaf b7.de* aur b4.de* bell bry k* calad calc cann-s b7.de* carbn-s caust b4.de* cham b7a.de* chin k* clem b4.de* con b4.de* cupr b7.de* dig b4.de* euphr eupi fl-ac guaj k* indg kali-bi k* kali-n kreos b7a.de lach led lob lyc m-ambo b7.de m-arct b7.de mang b4.de* mez b4.de* nat-c b4.de* nat-m k* nat-s nux-m b7.de* nux-v b7.de* ox-ac k2 petr h2 ph-ac b4a.de phos k* plat b4.de* puls b7.de* rheum b7.de* rhus-t b7.de* sabad b7.de* sabin b7.de* sars b4.de* *Sil* b4.de* stann stront-c b4.de* sulph tab thuj k* til viol-t zing k*
  - **drinking** agg.; after: con ↓
    - **drawing** pain: con h2
  - **dull** pain: spig b7.de*
  - **excoriating**: bry bg2 canth bg2 plb bg2
  - **gnawing** pain: bar-c k* canth b7.de* fl-ac ind kali-i par k*
  - **gouty**: caust h2*
  - **jerking** pain: cina a1 lyss
  - **laughing** agg.: mang ↓
    - **stitching** pain: mang h2*
  - **lying** agg.: phos ↓
    - **tearing** pain: phos h2
  - **mental** exertion agg.: lyss
  - **pecking**: cann-xyz bg2
  - **pinching** pain: bry b7.de* nat-m h2 verb h
  - **pressing** pain: agn b7.de* ambr k* ang b7.de* arn b7.de* asar b7.de* aur k* berb bry b7.de* chin b7.de* coff b7.de* cupr k* dros b7.de* guaj b4.de* ign b7.de* kali-n b4.de* led k* lyss *M-arct* b7.de* mag-m k* merc-c b4a.de petr h2 phos k* sabin b7.de* *Sars* k* sil spig k* stront-c k* *Sul-ac* b4a.de tritic-vg fd5.de verat b7.de* *Verb* k*
    - **backward**: lyc
    - **inward**: led
  - **pressure**:
    - **agg.**: petr a1
    - **amel.**: nat-c ↓
      - **sore**: nat-c h2
  - **shivering**; during: puls b7.de
  - **smarting**: mang b4.de* verat b7.de*
  - **sore**: agar aids nl2• arn b7.de* **Aur** k* bry b7.de canth b7.de cham bg2 coc-c hyos bg2 *Lach* laur b7.de* lyss mang h2 merc-i-f mur-ac nat-c k* *Nat-m* nat-p k* nit-ac bg2 puls bg2 rhus-t b7.de* sabad sars h2 sil k* spong verat b7.de* zinc k*
  - **splinter**; as from a: agar
  - **stitching** pain: acon k* agar b4.de* agath-a nl2• ambr b7.de* aur k* bar-c *Bell* k* berb *Carb-an* k* *Caust* *Cham* k* chin k* cina k* clem b4.de* *Cocc* colch *Coloc* cupr b7.de* dig dros k* euphr k* *Gels* graph b4.de* guaj b4.de* ham fd3.de• hell b7.de* hep b4a.de irid-met srj5• kali-chl kali-i kali-n b4.de* kali-p fd1.de• kalm lact laur b7.de* *M-arct* b7.de* **Mang** k* melal-alt gya4 nat-c b4.de* nat-m b4.de* nat-p op bg2 phos b4.de* plb k* psor rhus-t b7.de* rhus-v sabin k* *Sars* k* sep sil k* spig b7a.de squil b7.de* staph k* symph fd3.de• *Thuj* k* verat b7.de* zinc [heroin sdj2]
    - **itching**: mang h2*
  - **stooping** agg.: petr a1
  - **sweets** agg.: allox tpw3*
  - **tearing** pain: aeth k* *Agar* k* *Agn* k* am-m k* *Anac* k* *Anthraci* arg-met arn b7.de* *Aur* k* aur-s k2 bar-c k* bell k* berb k* *Bov* k* *Bry* k* calc k* calc-ar canth k* carb-an k* carb-v k* *Caust* k* *Cham* k* chin b7.de* cocc b7.de* coff b7.de* *Colch* k* *Dros* k* graph k* ign bg2 indg k* kali-c h2 kali-i k* kali-n k* *Kalm* k* kreos b7a.de *Lach* laur k* led lyc *Lyss* *M-arct* b7.de* mag-m k* meph *Merc* k* mez k* nat-c h2* nat-m h2 *Nux-v* k* *Phos* k* plb k* puls k* ran-b b7.de* *Rat* k* rhus-v sars b4.de* *Sel* k* sep k* spig k* stann b4.de* stront-c k* sul-ac k* *Sulph* k* thuj a1 viol-o k* zinc k*
    - **jerking** pain: lyc h2
  - **torn** out; as if: ph-ac b4a.de rob bg2 spig b7.de*
  - **touch** agg.: nat-m h2* spong h1*
  - **ulcerative** pain: caps b7.de* mag-c b4.de* nat-c b4.de*
  - **waking**; on: luf-op rsj5•
  - **walking** agg.: euphr ↓ zinc ↓
    - **stitching** pain: euphr zinc

- **Lower**: ...
  - **whirling**: ran-b b7a.de
  - **extending** to:
    - **Angle** of lower jaw: ph-ac ↓
      - **drawing** pain: ph-ac h2
    - **Chin**: phos ↓ thuj ↓
      - **drawing** pain: phos
      - **pressing** pain: phos
      - **tearing** pain: phos k* thuj k*
    - **Ear**: am-c ↓ cham ↓ choc srj3• elaps ↓ ham ↓ lyc k* *Lyss* ↓ mag-m ↓ ol-an k* petr ↓ sep ↓ sol-ni **Spig** ↓ viol-o ↓
      - **boring** pain: elaps
      - **pressing** pain: petr
      - **stitching** pain: ham fd3.de• sep h2
      - **tearing** pain: am-c cham h1 *Lyss* mag-m h2 **Spig** k* viol-o k*
      - **Nape**: spig ↓
        - **tearing** pain: spig vml
      - **Out** of: sulph ↓ thuj ↓
        - **stitching** pain: sulph h2 thuj h1
    - **Ear** and head: con ↓
      - **drawing** pain: con h2
    - **Forehead**: phos ↓
      - **stitching** pain: phos h2
    - **Head**: kali-n ↓
      - **tearing** pain: kali-n h2
    - **Head**; side of: viol-t ↓
      - **drawing** pain: viol-t
    - **Malar** bones: sabin ↓
      - **lancinating**: sabin c1
    - **Nape**: petr ↓
      - **pressing** pain: petr
    - **Temples**: mang ↓
      - **stitching** pain: mang h2
  - **Angles**: mang ↓ ph-ac ↓ sang bg2 sil ↓ spig ↓ tarent c1*
    - **right**: rad-br c11
    - **pressing** pain: ph-ac h2 sil h2 spig h1
    - **stitching** pain: mang h2
    - **Behind** angles of lower jaw: sang c1*
  - **Glands** of (See submaxillary)
  - **Middle**: ser-a-c jl2
  - **Rami**: agar ↓ *Kali-bi* ↓ merc-i-f ↓ sul-ac ↓
    - **boring** pain: agar merc-i-f
    - **digging** pain: *Kali-bi*
    - **gnawing** pain: sul-ac
- **Point** of | **left**: acet-ac br1
- **Upper**: acon ↓ agar ↓ *Amph* bro1 anh sp1 arg-met ↓ ars ↓ aster k* astra-m bro1 aur ↓ aur-m-n ↓ bamb-a stb2.de• berb ↓ bism bro1 brom k* calc ↓ calc-act ↓ *Calc-ar* ↓ *Calc-caust* bro1 *Calc-p* k* *Calc-s* k* carb-an ↓ carb-v k* caust ↓ *Cham* bro1 chel k* chin ↓ cimic k* clem ↓ coloc bro1 cycl k* dros ↓ dulc bro1 euph bro1 *Euph-a* bro1 euphr ↓ fl-ac k* graph bro1 ham fd3.de• hydrog srj2• iod k* iris bro1 *Kali-bi* ↓ kali-chl ↓ *Kali-cy* bro1 *Kali-i* bro1 kali-n k* kali-p fd1.de• kalm bro1 *Kreos* bro1 lach ↓ lap-la sde8.de• led k* *Lyc* ↓ mang k* meny ↓ merc ↓ merc-i-r k* merl k* mez bro1 mur-ac ↓ nat-m ↓ olnd k* op k* ozone sde2• par bro1 phos k* phyt k* plb ↓ podo fd3.de• polyg-h bro1 pyrid rly4• rhus-v ↓ ruta ↓ sacch-a fd2.de• samb ↓ sang bro1 sep ↓ *Spig* bro1 *Spong* ↓ stann k* stront-c ↓ sulph ↓ symph fd3.de• thuj bro1 vanil ↓ *Verb* bro1 zinc k* zing ↓
  - **right**: dioxi rbp6 ozone sde2• x-ray ↓
    - **night**: chin ↓ lyc ↓
      - **pressing** pain: chin h1
      - **tearing** pain: chin h1* lyc h2*
    - **dull** pain: x-ray sp1
  - **left**: bamb-a stb2.de• foen-an ↓ pyrid rly4• ruta ↓ vanil ↓
    - **pressing** pain: foen-an a1 ruta fd4.de vanil fd5.de
  - **morning**: carb-v ↓
    - **tearing** pain: carb-v k*

- **Upper**: ...
  - **afternoon**: indg ↓
    - **stitching** pain: indg
  - **evening**: sulph ↓
    - **bed** agg.; in: spong ↓
      - **stitching** pain: spong
    - **tearing** pain: sulph k*
  - **night**: cassia-s ↓
    - **lying** agg.: phos ↓
      - **tearing** pain: phos h2*
    - **sleep**; preventing: cassia-s ↓
      - **stitching** pain: cassia-s ccrh1•
    - **stitching** pain: cassia-s ccrh1•
  - **boring** pain: aur aur-m-n led *Mez* rhus-v thuj
  - **burning**: chin h1*
  - **cramping**: spong h1
  - **drawing** pain: acon agar chel dros euphr graph nat-m rhus-v sulph thuj vanil fd5.de zing k*
  - **extending** to:
    - **Ear**: kali-bi ↓ phos ↓ spong ↓
      - **stitching** pain: kali-bi phos spong h1
    - **Ears**: *Act-sp* bro1 arg-n bro1 ars bro1 bell bro1 bism bro1 *Cham* bro1 clem bro1 *Coff* bro1 *Coloc* bro1 dulc bro1 *Kali-cy* bro1 *Mez* bro1 phos bro1 plan bro1 rhod bro1 sang bro1 *Spig* bro1 thuj bro1 *Verb* bro1
    - **Eyes**: *Act-sp* bro1 arg-n bro1 ars bro1 bell bro1 bism bro1 *Cham* bro1 clem bro1 *Coff* bro1 *Coloc* bro1 dulc bro1 *Kali-cy* bro1 *Mez* bro1 phos bro1 plan bro1 rhod bro1 sang bro1 *Spig* bro1 thuj bro1 *Verb* bro1
    - **Malar** bones: *Act-sp* bro1 arg-n bro1 ars bro1 bell bro1 bism bro1 *Cham* bro1 clem bro1 *Coff* bro1 *Coloc* bro1 dulc bro1 *Kali-cy* bro1 *Mez* bro1 phos bro1 plan bro1 rhod bro1 sang bro1 *Spig* bro1 thuj bro1 *Verb* bro1
    - **Teeth**: *Act-sp* bro1 arg-n bro1 ars bro1 bell bro1 bism bro1 *Cham* bro1 clem bro1 *Coff* bro1 *Coloc* bro1 dulc bro1 *Kali-cy* bro1 *Mez* bro1 phos bro1 plan bro1 rhod bro1 sang bro1 *Spig* bro1 thuj bro1 *Verb* bro1
    - **Temples**: *Act-sp* bro1 arg-n bro1 ars bro1 bell bro1 bism bro1 *Cham* bro1 clem bro1 *Coff* bro1 *Coloc* bro1 dulc bro1 *Kali-cy* bro1 *Mez* bro1 phos bro1 plan bro1 rhod bro1 sang bro1 *Spig* bro1 thuj bro1 *Verb* bro1
    - **Vertex**: spig ↓
      - **stitching** pain: spig h1*
  - **gnawing** pain: kali-n h2 samb h1 thuj h1
  - **pressing** pain: acon ars aster calc h2 chel graph h2 iod h kali-bi lach podo fd3.de• ruta fd4.de symph fd3.de• vanil fd5.de zinc h2
  - **sore**: mang h2
  - **stitching** pain: chel clem coloc k* *Kali-bi* kalm meny h1* merc rhus-v *Spong*
    - **synchronous** with pulse: clem h2*
  - **tearing** pain: agar k* arg-met berb calc-act h1 *Calc-ar* k* carb-an h2 *Carb-v* k* caust cycl a1 kali-chl k* *Lyc* k* meny k* merl k* mur-ac k* plb k* rhus-v k* sep k* stront-c sulph k* thuj k*
  - **Angles**: **Bell** ↓ kali-n ↓ laur ↓ thuj ↓
    - **tearing** pain: **Bell** kali-n laur thuj k*
- **Joints**: am-m ↓ bell ↓ daph ↓ nat-c ↓ *Rhus-t* ↓ sars ↓ tritic-vg ↓ verb ↓
  - **drawing** pain: am-m bell daph nat-c h2 *Rhus-t* sars tritic-vg fd5.de verb
  - ▽ **extending** to:
    - **Ear**: agar ↓ ol-an ↓
      - **drawing** pain: agar ol-an
- **Lips**: *Acon* ↓ agar ↓ *All-c* ↓ am-c k* *Am-m* ↓ anac ↓ anan k* anis ↓ ant-c ↓ ant-t ↓ apis ↓ arg-n ↓ arizon-l ↓ arn ↓ ars ↓ ars-met arum-t bg2 asaf ↓ aur ↓ aur-ar ↓ aur-m ↓ aur-m-n ↓ aur-s ↓ bar-c ↓ bell ↓ berb ↓ beryl ↓ borx ↓ bov ↓ bry calc ↓ caps ↓ carb-ac ↓ *Carb-an* ↓ carbn-s ↓ caust ↓ chel ↓ chin ↓ chlf ↓ cic k* clem ↓ con ↓ cor-r k* *Crot-t* ↓ flor-p ↓ *Glon* ↓ *Graph* ↓ *Ham* ↓ hell ↓ *Hep* k* heroin ↓ hyos ↓ ign ↓ ip ↓ kali-bi ↓ *Kali-c* k* kali-p ↓ kali-s ↓ lac-c ↓ lach ↓ lap-la ↓ lyc ↓ lyss ↓ mag-s maland ↓ manc ↓ merc k* mez k* moni ↓ *Mur-ac* k* nat-c ↓ nat-m ↓ nat-s ↓ **Nit-ac** ↓ *Nux-m* ↓ *Nux-v* ↓ par ↓ petr ↓ petr-ra ↓ *Ph-ac* ↓ *Phos* ↓ plat ↓ plb k* podo ↓ positr ↓ psor k* ptel ↓ *Puls* ↓ ran-s ↓ rauw ↓ rhod ↓ rhus-t ↓ *Rhus-v* ↓ ruta fd4.de *Sabad* ↓ sacch-a ↓ sal-fr ↓ sep k* sil ↓ spig ↓ spong fd4.de stann ↓ *Staph* ↓ *Sulph* ↓ symph ↓ tab ↓ tell ↓ thuj ↓ thyr ↓ tub ↓ vanil fd5.de zinc ↓

- **Lips**: ...
  - **air** agg.; in open: plat ↓
    - **burning**: plat h2
  - **biting** pain: hell b7.de* ip b7.de* maland bg2
  - **burning**: *Acon* k* agar b4.de* *All-c* *Am-c* k* *Am-m* k* anac k* ant-t apis k* arg-n arizon-l nl2• arn k* ars k* **Arum-t** k* asaf k* aur k* aur-ar k2 aur-m k2 aur-m-n aur-s k2 bar-c h2* bell k* berb k* beryl tpw5* borx bry k* caps k* carb-ac k* *Carb-an* k* carbn-s chel k* chin k* chlf *Cic* k* con *Crot-t* *Glon* k* *Ham* hyos b7.de* kali-c b4.de* kali-p fd1.de• kali-s fd4.de lac-c lach k* lap-la sde8.de• lyss mag-s k* *Merc* k* *Mez* k* moni jl2 *Mur-ac* k* nat-s k* *Nux-m* k* *Nux-v* b7.de petr-ra shn4• *Ph-ac* *Phos* k* plat h2* podo fd3.de• *Psor* k* rhod k* rhus-t b7.de ruta fd4.de *Sabad* k* sacch-a fd2.de• spig k* spong fd4.de *Staph* k* *Sulph* k* symph fd3.de• tab k* tell c1 thuj k* thyr ptk1 tub tl1 vanil fd5.de zinc
    - **accompanied** by | **cracked** lips (See Cracked - lips - accompanied - burning)
  - **corrosive**: plat b4a.de *Puls* b7a.de ran-s b7a.de
  - **cramping**: bell caust kali-c *Merc* plat
  - **cutting** pain: manc bg2 staph b7.de*
  - **drawing** pain: bell h1* calc h2* *Sep* spig
  - **excoriated**; as if: caust h2 [heroin sdj2]
  - **fever**; during: chin ↓
    - **burning**: chin b7.de
  - **fire**; like: am-m ↓
    - **burning**: am-m ptk1
  - **gnawing** pain: *Puls* b7a.de ran-s b7a.de
  - **neuralgic**: apis ptk1
  - **pinching** pain: rhus-t b7.de*
  - **rubbing**; after: phos h2*
  - **smokers**; in: bry ↓
    - **burning**: bry ptk1
  - **sore**: anis bro1 ant-c b7.de* ars bg2 *Arum-t* bro1 bell bg2 beryl sp1 borx bro1 calc bro1 caust h2* flor-p rsj3• ign b7a.de* ip b7a.de* kali-bi bg2 kali-c b4.de* lyc ptk1 mur-ac k2* nat-m bro1 ph-ac b4.de* *Phos* b4.de* plat b4.de* podo bg2 positr nl2• ptel c1 puls b7.de* rauw tpw8* rhus-t b7.de* *Rhus-v* bro1 sabad b7a.de* sal-fr sle1• sep bro1 sil bg2
  - **splinter**; as from a: bov k* ign k* **Nit-ac** k* par phos k* *Sep* k*
  - **squeezed**; as if: apis b7a.de
  - **stinging**: agar am-m ant-c ars asaf caust *Graph* kali-c merc nit-ac petr ph-ac phos sil stann staph sulph thuj
  - **stitching** pain: ant-c h2* apis bg2 asaf bell bov k* caust h2* clem h2* con k* kali-c h2* nat-c h2* nit-ac k* ph-ac h2* phos h2* podo fd3.de• ruta fd4.de sabad sep spong stann h2* staph sulph h2* thuj h1* zinc k*
  - **tearing** pain: agar b4.de* caust b4.de* stann h2*
  - **touch** agg.: bry *Hep* merc k* mez
    - **burning**: merc ptk1 mez h2
  - **warmth** agg.:
    - **heat** agg.: beryl ↓
      - **burning**: beryl tpw5
  - ▽ **extending** to:
    - **Face**:
      - **touch** agg.: staph ↓
        - **stitching** pain: staph
  - ○ **Around**: chlam-tr ↓
    - **burning**: chlam-tr bcx2•
    - **sore**: chlam-tr bcx2•
  - **Lower**: aeth ↓ agar ↓ alum ↓ am-c ↓ am-m ↓ anac ↓ asaf ↓ bar-c ↓ bell ↓ borx ↓ bov ↓ *Bry* ↓ calc ↓ canth ↓ caust ↓ chin ↓ *Clem* ↓ coloc ↓ euph ↓ graph ↓ ham ↓ hep ↓ *Ign* ↓ kali-c ↓ m-arct ↓ mag-c ↓ *Mez* ↓ *Mur-ac* ↓ *Nat-m* ↓ nux-v ↓ olnd ↓ *Ph-ac* ↓ phos ↓ *Puls* ↓ *Rhod* ↓ sabad ↓ sacch-a ↓ sang ↓ sep ↓ spong ↓ stann ↓ teucr ↓ *Thuj* ↓ ulm-c ↓ valer ↓ zinc ↓
    - **right**: ph-ac tl1
    - **left**: chin ↓ hir ↓ ven-m ↓
      - **sore**: chin h1* hir rsj4• ven-m rsj12•

Face

- **Lower**: ...
  - **evening**: borx ↓
    - **burning**: borx h2
  - **burning**: am-c am-m b7.de anac asaf b7.de* bar-c b4.de* bell b4.de* borx k* bov b4.de *Bry* b7.de* caust b4a.de* clem k* coloc k* graph b4.de* ham fd3.de• hep b4a.de* *Ign* bg2 kali-c b4.de* *Mez* k* *Mur-ac* k* *Nat-m* k* olnd b7.de* *Ph-ac* k* phos b4.de *Puls* bg2 sabad b7.de* sacch-a fd2.de• sang k* sep k* spong fd4.de *Thuj* bg2 ulm-c jsj8•
  - **cutting** pain: canth b7.de* *Clem* h2* phos k*
  - **drawing** pain: calc b4.de*
  - **pressing** pain: valer b7.de*
  - **sore**: am-m b7.de* borx b4a.de* chin b7.de* euph b4.de* ign b7.de* mez b4.de* nux-v b7.de* *Rhod* b4a.de sep b4.de* teucr b7.de*
  - **stitching** pain: agar b4.de* asaf b7.de* bov b4.de* bry b7.de* caust b4.de* clem b4.de* *Ign* b7.de* m-arct b7.de* nux-v b7.de* spong b7.de* stann b4.de*
  - **tearing** pain: aeth a1 alum b4.de* caust b4a.de mag-c b4.de* stann b4.de* zinc h2*
  - **touch** agg.: mez ↓ mur-ac ↓
    - **burning**: mez h2 mur-ac a1
  - **ulcerative** pain: chin b7.de ign b7.de
  - **Below** left half of:
    - **16** h; from | **midnight**; until: mur-ac hr1
- **Upper**: am-m ↓ ant-c ↓ ars aur ↓ bar-c ↓ bell ↓ beryl ↓ borx ↓ brom ↓ *Calc-p* hr1 caust ↓ chin ↓ cic ↓ colch ↓ graph ↓ ham ↓ ign ↓ kali-c ↓ kali-s ↓ kreos ↓ lach ↓ lyc ↓ lycps-v ↓ m-ambo ↓ mag-c ↓ maland ↓ mang ↓ merc ↓ *Mez* ↓ mur-ac ↓ nat-c ↓ nat-m ↓ nit-ac ↓ *Nux-v* ↓ par ↓ ph-ac ↓ phos ↓ plb ↓ plut-n ↓ rhus-t ↓ sabad ↓ sel ↓ *Sep* ↓ sil ↓ spig ↓ squil ↓ staph ↓ sul-ac ↓ sulph ↓ thuj ↓ vanil fd5.de verat ↓ zinc ↓
  - **right**: chin ↓
    - **sore**: chin h1*
  - **morning**:
    - **bed** agg.; in: borx ↓
      - **burning**: borx h2
  - **air** agg.; in open: plat ↓
    - **burning**: plat h2
  - **burning**: ant-c b7.de* ars k* aur bg2 bar-c k* bell bg2 borx k* brom k* *Calc-p* k* caust b4.de* cic b7a.de* graph b4.de* ham fd3.de• kali-c bg2 kali-s fd4.de kreos b7a.de* lach bg2 lycps-v bg2 mag-c b4.de* merc b4.de* *Mez* k* mur-ac h2* nat-c b4.de* nat-m h2* phos h2* plut-n srj7• rhus-t b7.de* sabad b7.de sep b4.de* spig b7.de* staph b7.de* sulph k* thuj bg2 vanil fd5.de verat b7.de*
  - **corrosive**: mang h2*
  - **cutting** pain: colch b7.de* lyc k* nit-ac k* *Sep* k*
  - **discharges**; from: all-c ↓
    - **burning**: all-c tl1
  - **drawing** pain: bell b4.de* plb b7.de*
  - **jerking** pain: zinc h2
  - **pressing** pain: sul-ac b4.de*
  - **sore**: beryl tpw5 caust b4.de* chin b7.de* kreos b7a.de m-ambo b7.de mang h2* mez b4a.de* sabad b7.de* sel rsj9• sil bg2 squil bg2
  - **stinging**: am-m maland jl2
  - **stitching** pain: am-m b7.de* ant-c b7.de* bell b4.de* graph b4.de* ign b7.de* kali-c b4.de* merc b4.de* nat-c b4.de* nat-m b4.de* *Nux-v* b7.de* par b7.de* ph-ac b4.de* phos b4.de* sabad b7.de* staph b7.de* thuj b4.de* zinc b4.de*
  - **tearing** pain: caust colch b7.de* kali-c b4.de* zinc b4.de*
  - **touch**:
    - **amel.**: anis ↓
      - **stinging** | **blood** would press out; stinging sensation as if: anis c1
  - **extending** to:
    - **Ear**: nat-m ↓
      - **stitching** pain: nat-m h2
      - **tearing** pain: nat-m h2*

- **Malar** bones: aesc ↓ *Aeth* ↓ agar ↓ agn ↓ alum ↓ alum-p ↓ am-c ↓ *Am-m* ↓ amp ↓ anac ↓ ang bro1 ant-t ↓ arg-met bro1 arge-pl rwt5• ars ↓ ars-i ↓ *Aur* k* aur-m-n ↓ aur-s ↓ bamb-a ↓ *Bell* ↓ berb ↓ *Bism* ↓ borx ↓ bov ↓ bry ↓

- **Malar** bones: ...
  Calc ↓ calc-caust c2* *Calc-p* caps k* *Carb-an* ↓ **Carb-v** ↓ caust chel chin ↓ cic ↓ cimic bro1* *Cina* ↓ cinnb cist ↓ cocc ↓ *Colch* ↓ coloc bro1 con ↓ cor-r ↓ cypra-eg ↓ des-ac rbp6 dig ↓ dros ↓ euon ↓ gels ↓ ger-i ↓ glon ↓ graph ↓ grat ↓ guaj k2 ham ↓ hep ↓ hydrc bro1 hyos ↓ indg ↓ *Kali-bi* kali-c k2 kali-chl ↓ *Kali-i* ↓ kali-n ↓ kali-p ↓ lac-loxod-a hrn2• lec bro1 **Lyc** ↓ mag-c bro1 *Mag-m* ↓ mag-s ↓ malar jl2 mang h2 melal-alt gya4 mentho bro1 **Merc** ↓ merc-i-f ↓ merc-i-r ↓ mez bro1 mur-ac ↓ nat-c ↓ nat-m ↓ *Nat-s* ↓ neon srj5• nit-ac ↓ nux-v ↓ ol-an bro1 *Olnd* ↓ oxal-a ↓ ozone ↓ par bro1 petr-ra ↓ *Phos* ↓ phyt ↓ *Plat* bro1 polyp-p c2 positr nl2• psor pycnop-sa ↓ rhus-t bro1 ruta fd4.de sabin ↓ samb ↓ sep ↓ sil ↓ *Sphing* bro1 *Spig* bro1 *Stann* ↓ staph ↓ *Stront-c* ↓ stry bro1 stry-xyz c2 sul-ac ↓ sulph ↓ symph fd3.de• tab ↓ teucr ↓ thuj bro1 tritic-vg fd5.de tub bg valer ↓ vanil fd5.de verb k* viol-o ↓ zinc bro1 [**Spect** dfg1]
  - **right**: agn ↓ calc-caust ↓ *Chel* ↓ *Merc-i-f* ↓ ozone ↓ sulph ↓ zinc ↓
    - **pressing** pain: ozone sde2•
    - **sore**: *Merc-i-f* k* sulph k* zinc k*
    - **tearing** pain: agn calc-caust *Chel*
  - **left**: caust ↓ cor-r ↓ des-ac rbp6 germ-met srj5• kali-n ↓ lac-loxod-a hrn2• lyc ↓ ol-an ↓ *Plat* ↓ positr ↓ sul-ac ↓ vanil fd5.de
    - **cramping**: ol-an *Plat*
    - **sore**: cor-r k* positr nl2• sul-ac k*
    - **tearing** pain: caust h2 kali-n h2 lyc k13 sul-ac h2
    - **extending** to:
      - **Lower** jaw: stann ↓
        - **tearing** pain: stann h2
  - **morning**: ozone ↓
    - **pressing** pain: ozone sde2•
  - **afternoon**:
    - **amel.**: ozone ↓
      - **pressing** pain: ozone sde2•
  - **evening**: lyc h2 positr nl2• tritic-vg fd5.de
  - **night**: kali-c h2 mang ↓ nat-m ↓
    - **amel.**: cimic ptk
      - **neuralgic**: cimic ptk1
    - **boring** pain: nat-m h2
    - **pressing** pain: mang h2
  - **blowing** the nose agg.: *Merc* ↓
    - **pressing** pain: *Merc*
  - **boring** pain: aur-m-n bov indg *Mag-c* *Mez* nat-m h2 ruta fd4.de *Stront-c* *Thuj* k* tritic-vg fd5.de
  - **burning**: *Aur* bg2 caust k* chel a1 cic cist gels bg2 glon bg2* grat nat-m ol-an k* par k* spig k* staph k* sulph h2* thuj
  - **bursting** pain: cimic bg2
  - **chewing** agg.: nat-m ↓
    - **sore**: nat-m h2*
    - **warm** food: phos ↓
      - **pressing** pain: phos h2
  - **coryza**; from suppressed: kali-c k2
  - **cramping**: *Ang* cina cocc *Coloc* dig hyos *Mag-m* mez nit-ac h2 ruta sep valer
  - **digging** pain: *Mag-c* mang h2 petr-ra shn4• *Psor* *Thuj* tritic-vg fd5.de
  - **drawing** pain: am-c anac ant-t b7a.de arg-met h1 carb-an h2 *Caust* k* *Chel* k* *Colch* k* dros h1 hep c1 kali-chl nat-c h2 nat-m h2 *Plat* k* *Rhus-t* a1 sil stann staph b7a.de* tritic-vg fd5.de valer b7a.de *Verb* k* viol-o b7a.de
  - **growing** up into malar bone; as if teeth: des-ac rbp6
  - **jerking** pain: **Carb-v** cina k* colch k* mang spig k* stann h2 stront-c
  - **lancinating**: alum cimic *Guaj* melal-alt gya4
  - **menses** | **before** | **agg.**: stann bro1
    - **during** | **agg.**: stann bro1
  - **neuralgic**: stann ptk1
  - **opening** and shutting mouth amel.: ang ↓
    - **cramping**: ang h1
  - **picking** pain: chin h1

- **pressing** pain: agar h2 am-c anac k* ant-t k* arg-met k* *Bell* berb *Bism* k* *Caps* k* chel cic a1 *Cina* cocc colch *Coloc* cypra-eg sde6.de• dros h1 ger-i rly4• ham fd3.de• hyos k* kali-chl *Kali-i* kali-p fd1.de• mang h2 *Merc* *Mez* k* nat-c h2 nat-m h2 *Olnd* k* oxal-a rly4• ozone sde2• phos h2 *Plat* k* pycnop-sa mrz1 sabin k* samb k* sep spig k* *Stann* k* staph k* sulph teucr k* tritic-vg fd5.de vanil fd5.de **Verb** k* viol-o k*
  - ⁝ **cramping**: stann h2
  - ⁝ **intermittent**: bism h1 mang h2 *Verb*
- **running** about:
  - ⁝ **amel.**: bism ↓
    - : **neuralgic**: bism ptk1
- **sore**: ars-i ptk1 aur ptk1 chel a1 cor-r k* glon ptk1 mang h2* merc-i-f k* merc-i-r ptk1 nat-m k* nit-ac h2* phyt ptk1 positr nl2• *Rhus-t* stann sul-ac k* sulph k* tub ptk1 verb ptk1 zinc k*
- **stitching** pain: aesc aeth agar alum amp rly4• arg-met h1 ars bamb-a stb2.de• berb *Carb-an* con des-ac rbp6 euon guaj *Kali-bi* kali-c k2 *Kali-i* melal-alt gya4 merc mez h2 par k* phos psor sabin k* sil stann h2 staph k* verb k*
- **tearing** pain: *Aeth* agar agn k2 alum alum-p k2 am-c *Am-m* k* *Ang* b7a.de ant-t *Arg-met* aur aur-s k2 berb borx bry *Calc* *Carb-v* *Chel* cina k* *Colch* *Coloc* graph hep c1 indg kali-c kali-n **Lyc** k* *Mag-c* mag-s **Merc** k* mez h2 mur-ac *Nat-s* nit-ac nux-v k* *Phos* *Rhus-t* ruta k* sep sil h2 *Spig* k* stann h2 staph k* stront-c sul-ac sulph h2 tab teucr k* tritic-vg fd5.de *Zinc*
- **toothache**; with: mur-ac h2
- **warm** room; when entering a: phos ↓
  - ⁝ **pressing** pain: phos h2
- ▽ **extending** to:
  - ⁝ **Eye**:
    - : **left**: *Coloc* ↓
      - . **cramping**: *Coloc*
  - ⁝ **Forehead** and side of head: merc-i-f ↓
    - : **sore**: merc-i-f k*
  - ⁝ **Teeth**: nat-m ↓
    - : **pressing** pain: nat-m h2

\- **Mental** foramen: *Mez*

- ▽ **extending** to | **Ear**: calc

\- **Mouth**:

- ▽ **extending** to:
  - ⁝ **Nose**: thuj ↓
    - : **drawing** pain: thuj h1*
- ○ **Around**: plat ↓ puls ↓ sulph ↓
  - ⁝ **burning**: sulph h2*
  - ⁝ **gnawing** pain: puls
  - ⁝ **opening** the mouth agg.: nat-m ↓
    - : **sore**: nat-m h2
  - ⁝ **sore**: plat h2*
- **Corners** of: ambr ↓ androc ↓ ant-c ↓ arn ↓ bell ↓ borx ↓ calc ↓ carb-an ↓ carb-v ↓ cassia-s ↓ caust ↓ cob ↓ coloc ↓ **Dros** ↓ graph ↓ hep ↓ ip ↓ kali-chl ↓ kreos ↓ m-arct ↓ mang ↓ mang-act ↓ merc ↓ mez ↓ nat-c ↓ nat-m ↓ nat-s ↓ ozone ↓ ph-ac ↓ phos ↓ ran-b ↓ rhus-t ↓ sul-ac ↓ ven-m ↓ zinc ↓
  - ⁝ **night**: nat-s ↓
    - : **burning**: nat-s hr
  - ⁝ **burning**: ambr androc srj1• arn b7.de borx carb-an h2 cob coloc b4.de* **Dros** k* hep b4a.de ip kali-chl kreos b7a.de mez k* nat-c b4.de* nat-s ph-ac zinc k*
  - ⁝ **drawing** pain: carb-v b4.de*
  - ⁝ **sore**: androc srj1• ant-c b7a.de* bell b4.de* calc b4.de* cassia-s ccrh1• caust b4.de* graph b4.de* ip b7.de* m-arct b7.de mang b4.de* merc b4.de* nat-c bg2 nat-m b4.de* ozone sde2• rhus-t bg2* sul-ac b4.de* ven-m rsj12•
  - ⁝ **stitching** pain: bell bg2 phos b4.de* ran-b b7.de*
  - ⁝ **tearing** pain: bell h1* carb-v h2*
  - ⁝ **ulcerative** pain: borx h2 m-arct b7.de mang a1 mang-act a1

\- **Muscles**: anac bro1 ang bro1 cocc bro1 colch bro1 glon ↓ ox-ac bg2 oxyt bro1 sabin bro1

\- **Muscles**: ...

- **gnawing** pain: glon bg2
- ○ **Masseter** muscles: ang ↓ cocc ↓ colch ↓ cupr ↓ hydr-ac ↓ kali-bi ↓ *Nux-v* ↓ sabin ↓ *Sars* ↓ stram ↓ stry ↓ thuj ↓ verb ↓
  - ⁝ **left**: ulm-c ↓
    - : **cramping**: ulm-c jsj8•
  - ⁝ **cramping**: ang c1* cocc ptk1 cupr ptk1* hydr-ac ptk1 stram ptk1 stry ptk1
    - : **accompanied** by | **opisthotonos** (See BACK - Opisthotonos - accompanied - masseter)
  - ⁝ **drawing** pain: kali-bi a1 *Nux-v* a1 sabin br1 *Sars* k* thuj a1 verb k*
    - : **extended** horizontally; as if: colch b7a.de
  - ⁝ **pressure** agg.: ulm-c ↓
    - : **cramping**: ulm-c jsj8•

\- **Nerves**: (↗*neuralgic*) apoc-a c2 caps h1* ruta fd4.de tong c2

- ○ **Trigeminal** neuralgia (= trifacial neuralgia): *Acon* bro1 all-c bro1 aml-ns bro1 anh vh1 aran bro1* *Arg-n* bro1 *Ars* bro1 arund bro1 bell a1* bell-p sp1 cact bro1 cedr bro1 *Cham* bro1 *Chel* bro1 chin bro1 chlorpr mtf11 *Cimic* bro1 cocc-s mtf11 colch bro1 coloc dh1* ferr bro1 *Gels* bro1 glon bro1 gnaph mtf11 hed sp1 hydrc mtf11 iris bwa1 kali-cy mp4• *Kalm* bro1 lach br1 lob mrr1 mag-c mrr1 mag-p bro1* merc bro1 mez bwa1* nat-s bro1 nux-v hr1* phos bro1 plan mtf11 plat hr1 puls bro1 rad-br c11 rhus-t bro1 sabal bro1 sal-ac mtf11 sang bro1 spig bg3* stann bro1 syph jl2* thuj bro1 tong bro1 verat bro1 verb bro1* zinc bro1 *Zinc-val* bro1
  - ⁝ **left**: anh vh1 lob mrr1 mag-c mrr1 verb mrr1
  - ⁝ **morning** | 7h: nat-m tl1
  - ⁝ **accompanied** by | **Lids**; twitching of: mag-p mtf11

\- **Nose** (See NOSE - Pain)

\- **Nose** and eyes, between: mang ↓

- **tearing** pain: mang

\- **Parotid** glands: agn ↓ ail ↓ am-m ↓ apis aran arg-met arum-t k2 asaf ↓ *Aur* k* aur-ar k2 *Aur-m* ↓ aur-s k* bapt bar-c h2* *Bell* bry ↓ calc k2 calc-act calc-p k* calc-s ↓ carb-an ↓ cham chin ↓ coc-c k* con ↓ cop ↓ dios k* dros ↓ *Dulc* ↓ elaps fago k* ferr-p hippoz jl2 ign ↓ *Kali-bi* ↓ kali-c k2 kali-n ↓ kalm ↓ lac-ac k* lyc ↓ lycps-v mang *Merc* k* *Merc-i-r* k* nat-c ↓ nat-m k* nit-ac ↓ ourl jl2 phos ↓ phyt plb k* podo ↓ psor k2 puls b7.de* *Rhus-t* sabad k* *Sep* ↓ sil ↓ spong ↓ sulph k* wies ↓

- **right**: bar-c h2 bar-m fr2 bell calc-s k2 coc-c k* cocc merc k* merc-i-r a1 sulfonam ks2
  - ⁝ **sore**: calc-s
- **left**: agn ↓ arum-t ↓ coloc podo fd3.de• rhus-t
  - ⁝ **drawing** pain: agn k*
  - ⁝ **sore**: arum-t k*
- **afternoon**: dios k*
  - ⁝ **dinner**; after: sulph k*
- **evening**:
  - ⁝ **20**.30 h: merc-i-r
  - ⁝ **22** h: dios
- **boring** pain: sabad k*
- **burning**: apis *Bell* b4a.de merc k* phos k*
- **chewing** agg.: arg-met ↓
  - ⁝ **cutting** pain: arg-met
- **clawing**: sabad
- **cold**:
  - ⁝ **air**:
    - : **agg.**: kali-c
    - : **amel.**: merc ↓
      - . **burning**: merc
  - ⁝ **applications** | **amel.**: merc
- **cutting** pain: arg-met k*
- **digging** pain: sulph k*
- **dinner**; after: sulph ↓
  - ⁝ **digging** pain: sulph
- **drawing** pain: agn k* *Arg-met* mang
- **drinking** agg.: nat-m ↓
  - ⁝ **tearing** pain: nat-m k*

Face

- **lancinating**: carb-an k*
- **pinching** pain: aran nat-m
- **pressing** pain: aur b4a.de mang b4.de* merc b4.de* podo fd3.de•
- **smarting**: con b4.de*
- **sore**: ail k* arum-t k* aur k* *Aur-m* bry k* calc-p k* calc-s cop k* dros kali-n k* merc k2 merc-i-r k* nat-c k* phos k* wies a1
- **squeezed**; as if: aur b4a.de sabad b7.de*
- **stinging**: apis merc
- **stitching** pain: am-m k2 asaf **Bell** k* bry k* calc cham k* chin k* con b4.de* *Dulc* k* ign k* *Kali-bi* k* kali-c kalm k* lyc k* merc k* nat-c k* nit-ac b4.de* phos puls k* *Sep* k* sil k* spong sulph k*
- **swallowing** agg.: *Chin* ign ↓ spig ↓
  - **stitching** pain: ign spig h1
- **tearing** pain: bell k* nit-ac b4.de*
- **touch** agg.: arum-t k2 *Aur* k* merc-i-r a1 phos h2* sulfonam ks2
- ▽ **extending** to:
  - **Ear**: lac-ac c1
  - **Eye**: coloc

- **Sinuses**: *(↗NOSE - Pain - sinuses)*
  - **right**: *Trios* rsj11•
  - **cold**; during a catarrhal: *Trios* rsj11•
  - **pressure** | **amel.**: lob mrr1
  - ○ **Antrum** of Highmore (See maxillary)
  - **Ethmoidal**: anh sp1 ser-a-c jl2 [bell-p-sp dcm1]
  - **Frontal**: *(↗HEAD - Pain - forehead - frontal; NOSE - Sinuses - frontal)* anh sp1 *Bell* mrr1 hed sp1 iod mtf33 kali-bi mrr1 kali-c mrr1 kali-i br1 pneu jl2 sang tl1 sil mrr1 spig mrr1 [bell-p-sp dcm1]
  - **Maxillary**: *(↗Complaints - jaws - joints; Complaints - maxillary)* anh sp1 arizon-l ↓ arn pe1 aur pe1 bamb-a stb2.de• *Bell* mrr1 chel c1 com a1* flav jl2 hecla hr1* hep pe1 *Kali-bi* mrr1 kali-i hr1* kali-s c1 lac-del ↓ mag-c a1* merc k2* merc-c c1 mez hr1* oscilloc jl2 petr ↓ phos bro1 puls pe1 pyrid rly4• sil pe1* spig bro1 spong ↓ syc bka1• zinc-val br1
    - **left**: bamb-a stb2.de• germ-met srj5• propr sa3•
    - **pressing** pain: arizon-l nl2• lac-del hrn2• petr h2 spong fd4.de
    - **pressure** | **amel.**: galeoc-c-h gms1•
    - **stitching** pain: bamb-a stb2.de•
- **Skin**: sabad b7.de* sabin b7.de*
- **Spot**; in a: ph-ac ↓ verb
  - **burning**: ph-ac h2
- **Spot**; in a small: spig mrr1
- **Sublingual** glands: calc k2
- **Submaxillary** glands: agath-a nl2• am-m ↓ ambr *Arg-met* ↓ *Ars* ars-s-f k2 arum-t k2 *Aur* aur-ar k2 aur-i k2 *Aur-m* aur-s k2 **Bar-c** bar-i k2 **Bar-m** bar-s k2 bell k2 brom bry calc h2* calen ↓ carbn-s **Chin** cina clem cob ↓ coc-c cop ↓ *Cor-r* *Crot-t* cycl ↓ *Dulc* fago ↓ graph hippoz jl2 hyper ↓ ign kali-c ↓ kali-i ↓ kali-m k2 kali-n led lyc mag-c merc ↓ merc-c ↓ mez nat-m *Nit-ac* nux-v ↓ ph-ac ↓ *Phos* plan ↓ plb psor k2 puls *Rhus-t* ruta fd4.de sabad sep *Sil* *Spong* ↓ *Staph* k* *Stram* *Sul-ac* *Sulph* verat verat-v ↓ vesp ↓
  - **night**: nat-m
    - **boring** pain: nat-m k*
  - **boring** pain: led k* lyc nat-m k* puls k* sabad k*
  - **chewing** agg.: *Calc*
  - **coryza**; during: graph b4.de*
  - **cutting** pain: arg-met h1
  - **digging** pain: *Rhus-t* k*
  - **drawing** pain: am-m k* *Arg-met* cob k* cycl h1* ign k* lyc k* *Sil* k*
  - **eating**; after: lyc ↓
    - **drawing** pain: lyc
  - **lancinating**: am-m hyper a1
  - **motion** of lower jaw agg.: mag-c h2
  - **pinching** pain: verat h1
  - **pressing** pain: ars h2 aur h2 chin h1 cina a1 cycl h1 graph h2 nit-ac h2 rhus-t h1 spong h1
  - **pressure** agg.: ars h2 mag-c h2

- **Submaxillary** glands: ...
  - **sore**: ars h2* arum-t k2 calen a1 chin a1 clem a1 cop k* crot-t k* fago a1 graph k* kali-c k* lyc k* mag-c k* merc-c k* nat-m *Nit-ac* k* plan a1 psor k* puls k* sep k* *Sil* k* *Spong* k* *Staph* *Sulph* k* verat-v a1 vesp
  - **squeezed**; as if: nat-m h2 staph h1
  - **stinging**: am-m kali-i k*
  - **stitching** pain: agath-a nl2• am-m k* arg-met bell *Calc* k* merc *Mez* k* nat-m gk nux-v k* ph-ac k* sep h2* sil k* *Sul-ac* k* *Sulph* k*
  - **stooping** agg.: nat-m h2
  - **swallowing** agg.: chin kr1 cor-r nux-v ↓ *Rhus-t* ↓ stram
    - **stinging**: nux-v
    - **stitching** pain: nux-v *Rhus-t*
  - **swelling**:
    - **sensation**: nat-m h2 staph sul-ac h2
    - **with**: ambr k1 staph h1
  - **touch** agg.: sep h2 sil h2
  - ▽ **extending** to | **Tongue**: sul-ac h2
- **Temples**:
  - ○ **Skin**: anh ↓
    - **pressing** pain: anh sp1
- **Trigeminus** (See nerves - trigeminal)
- **Zygoma**: agar ↓ alum ↓ am-m ↓ *Arg-met* ↓ arg-n ↓ *Aur* bamb-a stb2.de• berb ↓ borx ↓ calc ↓ *Calc-p* camph ↓ caps k* carb-an ↓ **Carb-v** ↓ carc ↓ caust chel cinnb con ↓ cor-r ↓ dig ↓ dros ↓ dulc ↓ euph ↓ gins ↓ *Graph* ↓ hell ↓ ign ↓ *Kali-bi* lec br1 led ↓ lycpr ↓ mag-m a1 mang h2* merl ↓ mur-ac ↓ nat-c ↓ nat-s ↓ nit-ac ↓ petr-ra ↓ phos ↓ *Plat* ↓ polys sk4• positr ↓ psor ptel c1 rhus-t ↓ ruta ↓ sabin ↓ sphing a1* spig kk3.fr spong fd4.de staph ↓ sul-ac ↓ sulph ↓ symph ↓ thuj ↓ verb *Zinc* ↓
  - **right**: arg-met ↓ *Chel* ↓ *Lyss* ↓ nat-c ↓ spig ↓ spong ↓
    - **gnawing** pain: *Lyss*
    - **jerking** pain: chel
    - **tearing** pain: arg-met *Chel* nat-c a1 spig a spong
  - **left**:
    - **Front** of ear; in: carb-v ↓
      - **jerking** pain: carb-v k*
  - **left** then right: arg-n ↓
    - **tearing** pain: arg-n
  - **evening**: am-m ↓ caps ↓ *Carb-v* ↓ con ↓ lyc h2*
    - **jerking** pain: am-m *Carb-v* k*
    - **pressing** pain: caps k* con h2*
  - **night**: kali-c h2*
  - **boring** pain: *Aur* k* *Psor* thuj h1*
  - **burrowing**: mang h2 thuj h1
  - **corrosive**: bamb-a stb2.de•
  - **cough** agg.; during: *Hep* ↓
    - **blow**; pain as from a: *Hep* b4a.de
  - **drawing** pain: calc h2* camph a1 chel k* con a1 dig h2* gins a1 kali-bi a1 mag-m a1 staph h1 sulph a1 thuj a1
  - **eroding**: bamb-a stb2.de•
  - **jerking** pain: am-m **Carb-v** k* chel
  - **lying** agg.: chel ↓
    - **drawing** pain: chel
  - **menses** | **before** | **agg.**: stann b4.de
    - **during**:
      - **agg.**: stann ↓
        - **blow**; pain as from a: stann b4.de
  - **pressing** pain: agar a1 caps *Cinnb* dulc h1* euph h2* hell a1 ign a1 lec led a1 lycpr a1 nat-s a1 *Plat* positr nl2• rhus-t a1* sabin c1 symph fd3.de• *Verb* k*
    - **outward**: dros h1*
  - **sore**: cor-r sul-ac zinc
  - **stitching** pain: arg-n a1 aur carc fd2.de• nat-c h2 petr-ra shn4• rhus-t h1* sphing a1* staph h1 verb *Zinc*

- **tearing** pain: alum am-m k* *Arg-met* arg-n **Aur** k* berb borx carb-an h2* **Carb-v** k* chel con k* *Graph* k* mag-m h2* merl mur-ac h2* nat-c h2* nit-ac h2* phos h2* ruta fd4.de spig k* spong staph h1
- **touch** agg.: caps ↓
  - ⁝ **pressing** pain: caps k*
- **twitching**: cina ↓
  - ⁝ **cramping**: cina h1
- **walking** agg.: *Aur* ↓
  - ⁝ **boring** pain: *Aur* k*

▽ • **extending** to:
  - ⁝ **Head**: mag-m ↓
    - ⁝ **tearing** pain: mag-m h2*

PARALYSIS: *Acon* bg2* aethi-m bro1 *Agar* all-c k* alum bro1* *Am-p* c2* anac *Apis* b7a.de *Bar-c* k* bell k2* botul jl2 *Cadm-s* k* calc-i mtf11 carc fb* **Caust** k* *Cocc* k* crot-h *Cupr* *Cur* k* *Dulc* k* form k* *Gels* bg2* *Graph* k* hyper bro1* *Ign* mp1• iod ix bnm8• *Kali-chl* k* kali-i bro1* kali-m k2 kali-p merc ptk1* merc-k-i c2 nat-m bro1* *Nux-v* ol-an c2 op k* oxyurn-sc mcp1• petr k* phys mp1• physal-al bro1 plat mp1* plb k* puls rhus-t b7a.de* ruta k* seneg k* sep bg2 solid mp1• stram br1 stry syph k* tub jl2 zinc zinc-pic c2*

- **one** side: acon vh* agar mrr1 *Bar-c* cadm-s k* **CAUST** k ●* chlorpr mtf11 *Cocc* con k2 dulc vh *Graph* k* ign vh *Kali-chl* kali-p phos vh plat vh* puls sil hr1 syph mp1•
  - • **grief**; from: ign vh
- **right**: apis gsy1* *Arn* bell bro1 *Caust* k* hep kali-chl kali-p *Phos* plb sil zinc-p k2
  - • **eye** closed; with right: apis hr1*
- **left**: *All-c* alum tl1 cadm-s k* *Cur* form graph *Nux-v* k* seneg bro1 spig sulph
- **accompanied** by:
  - • **speech | difficult**: cadm-s ptk1* dulc vh* syph ptk1*
  - • **swallowing**; difficult: cadm-s ptk1*
  - ○ • **Eyes**; closed: apis ptk1
  - • **Muscles**; twitching of: kali-m ptk1*
- **bathing** agg.: graph
- **chewing**, with difficult: syph ptk1*
- **close** eye; cannot: cadm-s ptk1
- **cold**; from●: acon c1 *Cadm-s* **Caust** k* *Dulc* merc vml ruta k*
- **distortion** of muscles, with: graph ptk1*
- **eruptions** in face; from suppressed: bac bn18 caust k2*
- **goitre**; from suppression of: iod ptk1
- **injuries**; after: hyper fyz6
- **opening** the mouth agg.: caust ptk1*
- **pain**; after: kali-chl k* kali-m mp1•
- **painless**: plat mrr1
- **riding** in the wind: acon mp1* bell mp1• *Cadm-s* **Caust** k ●* ign mp1•
- **sensation** of: ol-an bg2 seneg b4.de*
- **unilateral** (See one)
- **urination**; with copious: all-c
- **wet**; after getting: **CAUST** k ●*

○ - **Jaws**:
  - • **left**: lacer c1
  - • **sensation** as if: nux-m tl1*

○ • **Lower**: arn b7.de* ars k* bapt bg1 carb-v bg1 caust b4a.de cocc b7.de* colch bg1 crot-h dulc k* *Hell* bg1* *Hyos* bg1* lach k* *Lyc* bg2* *Mur-ac* bg1* naja bg2 nux-m c1 *Nux-v* **Op** bg2* *Phos* bg1* ran-b *Sec* bg1* *Stram* bg1* *Sulph* bg1* *Zinc* bg1*
  - ⁝ **evening**: ran-b
  - ⁝ **sensation** as if: phyt bg2
- **Lips**: anac bro1 bar-c bro1 *Bell* bro1 caust bro1 cocc bro1 con bro1 gels bro1 mang-o bro1 naja br1 nux-v bro1 olnd bro1 plb bro1
  - • **left** side | **breathing** agg.: acon vh1

○ • **Upper**: cadm-s graph
  - ⁝ **conversation**; prolonged: gels c1
- **Mouth** drop; corners of: agar ptk1
  - • **saliva** runs out; and: agar op zinc
- **Muscles | chewing** agg.: anh sp1
- **Trigeminal** nerve: nat-m hr1*

PARCHMENT; sensation as if covered with: ars bro1 bar-act bg2*

PEAKED (See Pointed)

PEELING off of lips: acon k* allox tpw4 aloe k* alum k* am-m k* anac bg2 ant-t b7.de* aphis c1 apis b7a.de* ars bg2 arum-t k* bell b4.de* berb brom bg2 camph canth k* caps b7.de* cham k* choc srj3• cob coli rly4• con k* iod *Kali-c* k* kali-chl kreos k* lac-c k* mang bg2 merc-c b4a.de mez k* mosch k* nat-c bg2* nat-m k* nat-s neon srj5• nit-ac bg1* *Nux-v* k* petr-ra shn4• plat b4.de* plb k* puls k* rhus-t bg2 sep k* sil bg2 spig b7a.de stram k* sul-ac k* sulph h2* symph fd3.de• thuj k* thyr ptk1

○ - **Lower**: kali-c b4.de* mez b4.de* nat-m b4.de* thuj b4a.de
- **Upper**: con b4a.de sulph b4.de*

PERIODICITY: *Ars* bg2 bell bg2 cedr bg2 *Chin* bg2 chinin-s bg2 ip bg2 iris bg2 nat-m bg2 sep bg2 valer bg2 verb bg2

PERSPIRATION: acet-ac br1* acon k* acon-l a1 act-sp hr1 aesc k* aeth k* *Agar* k* *Alum* k* alum-p k2 am-c bg1 *Am-m* k* ambr k* aml-ns bro1 amyg k* **Ang** b7.de* ant-t k* aphis c1 apom a1 arg-met k* *Arg-n* k* *Arn* k* *Ars* k* ars-h k* asaf b7.de* atra-r bnm3• aur k* aur-ar k2 aur-s k2 bamb-a stb2.de• *Bapt* k* **Bell** k* benz-ac k* berb hr1 borx k* *Bry* k* *Bufo* **Cact** hr1 **Calc** k* *Calc-p* k* calc-s calc-sil k2 **Camph** k* cann-s b7.de* canth a1 *Caps* k* *Carb-ac* k* carb-an k* **Carb-v** k* *Carbn-s* cassia-s cdd7*• cham k* *Chin* k* chin-b hr1 chinin-ar chion c1 *Chlf* br1 cic k* **Cina** k* cit-l hr1 *Cocc* k* *Coff* k* colch k* coloc k* con k* croc b7.de* crot-h *Cupr* k* cupr-s k* *Dig* k* digin a1 *Dros* k* dulc k* elaps euph bro1 ferr k* ferr-ar ferr-p fl-ac k* *Glon* k* guaj k* ham fd3.de• *Hell* k* hep k* hydr-ac k* *Hyos* k* iber a1* **Ign** k* *Ip* k* jab k* *Kali-ar* *Kali-bi* k* kali-c k* kali-i k* kali-m k2 kali-p kali-s kali-sil k2 kreos k* *Lach* k* lachn k* lap-la rsp1 lat-m bnm6• laur k* led b7.de* linu-c a1 *Lob* bro1 **Lyc** k* lyss hr1* *M-ambo* b7.de m-arct b7.de m-aust b7.de mag-c k* med k* **Merc** k* *Merc-cy* hr1 mez k* morph k* mosch k* mur-ac k* nat-c b4.de* *Nat-m* k* *Nat-s* k* nitro-o a1 **Nux-v** k* ol-an k* **Op** k* ox-ac k* ozone sde2• par k* ped a1 *Petr* k* petr-ra shn4• *Phos* k* pilo a1 plat b4.de* plb bg2* *Psor* k* **Puls** k* ran-s b7.de* rheum k* rhus-t k* ribo rly4• ruta b7.de* sabad k* *Samb* k* *Sars* k* *Sec* k* *Sep* k* **Sil** k* sin-n bro1 spig k* spirae a1 **Spong** k* *Stann* k* staph k* *Stram* k* stry k* suis-hep rly4• sul-ac k* *Sulph* k* *Tab* k* tarent k* tell k* *Thuj* k* til k* tritic-vg fd5.de **Valer** k* vanil fd5.de **Verat** k* verat-v k* viol-t b7.de* vip k* wies a1

- **one** side: alum k* *Ambr* k* *Bar-c* k* **Nux-v** k* **Puls** k* sulph k*
- **right**: alum puls k*
- **morning**: ars k* bamb-a stb2.de• chin k* nit-ac h2* puls k* ruta h1 sulph k* verat k*
- **forenoon**: phos k* ruta fd4.de
- **noon**: cic k*
- **afternoon**: bamb-a stb2.de• com k* ign k* samb k*
  - • **16** h: bamb-a stb2.de•
- **evening**: ham fd3.de• hura iber a1 psor k* puls k* sars spong k* yuc a1
  - • **house**; in: mez k*
- **night**: dros h1* hep h2* olib-sac wmh1 puls ruta fd4.de til ban1•
  - • **midnight**: plat h2* rhus-t k*
    - ⁝ **after | 2** h: ars
- **accompanied** by:
  - • **mental** symptoms (See MIND - Mental symptoms - accompanied - face - perspiration)
  - • **vomiting** (See STOMACH - Vomiting - accompanied - perspiration - face)
  - ○ • **Head**; complaints of (See HEAD - Complaints - accompanied - face - perspiration)
- **amel.**: rhus-t bg2
- **anxiety**; with: iber vml3• nat-c h2
- **bee** stings; from: sep h2
- **children**; in: med jl2
- **chill**; during: *Ars* bg2 calc bg2 **Coff** bg2 euph bg2 lach bg2 led bg2 **Lyc** bg2 *Nux-v* bg2 *Puls* bg2 sabad bg2 sulph bg2 thuj bg2
- **cold**: acon k* aeth agar a1 ant-c *Ant-t* k* am k* **Ars** k* ars-s-f k2 *Aur* k* aur-ar k2 aur-s k2 bell k* benz-ac k* berb hr1 *Bry* k* **Cact** k* cadm-s *Calc* k* *Calc-p* k* calc-s **Camph** k* caps k* carb-ac k* carb-an **Carb-v** k* *Carbn-s* *Chin* k* chinin-ar **Cina** k* coc-c k* *Cocc* k* croc bg2 crot-h *Cupr* k* *Dig* k* *Dros* k* elaps euph bro1 euph-l br1 ferr k* *Glon* hell k* hep k* hura iber hr1* ign hr1 *Ip* k* *Kali-bi* k* kali-cy a1 kali-ox a1 *Lach* k* lachn k* *Lob* k* *Lyc* k* *Merc* k* **Merc-c** k* *Merc-cy* hr1 morph k* mur-ac nat-m k* *Nux-v* k* *Op* k* ox-ac k* phos hr1* plat k* plb hr1 *Puls* k* pyrog *Rheum* k* rhus-t k* ruta k* sabad k* *Samb* k* *Sec* k* sep k* spig k* **Spong** k* staph k* *Stram* k* stront-c sk4• sul-ac k* *Sulph* k* *Tab* k* **Verat** k* verat-v k* zinc-m bro1

Face

- **cold**: ...
  - **diarrhea**, in: apoc ptk1
  - **fever**; during: *Ant-t* bg2 ars bg2 **Caps** bg2 carb-v bg2 cina bg2 *Dig* bg2 ip bg2 lach bg2 spong bg2 sulph bg2 valer bg2 verat bg2
  - **waking**; on: puls b7.de verat b7.de
  - ○ **Forehead** (See HEAD - Perspiration of - forehead - cold)
  - **Lips** | **Upper**: chin mrr1
  - **Mouth**, around: **Chin** rheum
- **convulsions**; during: *Bufo* k* *Cocc* k*
- **cough** agg.; during: ip b7.de* tarent k*
- **dinner** | **after** | **agg.**: sulph k* tritic-vg fd5.de
  - **during** | **agg.**: carb-an k*
- **drinking** agg.; after: *Cham* k*
- **eating**:
  - **after** | **agg.**: alum k* carb-an b4a.de **Cham** k* ign ptk1 *Nat-m* ptk1 nat-s k* psor k* sulph ptk1 tritic-vg fd5.de viol-t k*
  - **agg.**: carb-an b4a.de *Ign* k* kali-p fd1.de• *Nat-m* k* *Sulph* k*
  - **warm** food agg.: mag-c bl1 sep k*
- **eructations**; during: cadm-s c1
- **except** the face; general perspiration: *Rhus-t* k* *Sec* k*
- **exertion** | **after** | **agg.**: sil k2
  - **agg.** | **slightest** exertion: bamb-a stb2.de• sulph h2
- **fever**; during: cassia-s ccrh1•
- **flatus**, when passing: *(↗PERSPIRATION - Flatus)* kali-bi
- **heat**; during: alum h2* **Am-m** bg2 *Ant-t* bg2 ars h2* bell h1* carb-v bg2 *Cham* k* *Chel Dros* dulc k* ign bg2 *Lach* lyc bg2 op bg2 *Psor* k* **Puls** k* samb bg2 sep h2* spong k* valer k*
- **hot**: *Cham* bg2* op bg2 stram bg2
- **motion**:
  - **agg.**: psor hr1 valer k*
  - **slight** motion | **agg.**: rheum mrr1
- **offensive**: *(↗NOSE - Perspiration) Puls*
- **only** face: calc k2 con vh ign k* phos vh
- **palpitation**: ars
- **shivering**; during: *Coff* b7a.de
- **sitting** agg.: calc k* nat-s a1 spong a1
- **sleep**:
  - **before**: calc h2*
  - **during**: med k* prun k* sep k* tab k*
  - **going** to sleep; on | **agg.**: sil
- **spots**; on | **eating**; while: ign bro1*
- **standing** agg.: eupi k*
- **stool** agg.; after: com k*
- **supper**; during: calc k*
- **vomiting**; when (See STOMACH - Vomiting - accompanied - perspiration - face)
- **waking**; on: bamb-a stb2.de• ham fd3.de• puls h1*
- **walking**:
  - **agg.**: borx h2 valer verat h1
  - **air** agg.; in open: guaj k2
- **warm** food and drink: sep k* sul-ac k*
- ○ **Chin**: con ptk1
- **Eyes** | **Under**: con bg1*
- **Forehead** (See HEAD - Perspiration of - forehead)
- **Lids** and eyebrows:
  - **sleep** | **during** (See EYE - Perspiration)
- **Lips**:
  - ○ **Lower**: rheum k*
  - **Upper**: acon k* coff k* ham fd3.de• ign mrr1 kali-bi k* kali-c k* med bg2* nux-v k* petr-ra shn4• rheum k* ribo rly4• sin-n thuj st1
- **Mouth**; around: chin bg2 lac-h sk4• rheum ptk1*
- **Scalp** and: puls k* valer verat
- **Side** lain on: *Acon* k* act-sp k* chin
- **Side** not lain on: sil thuj

PICKING: chin b7.de* lach
○ - **Chin**; picking point of arund c1

Picking: ...
- **Lips**: *(↗MIND - Delirium - picking; MIND - Gestures - hands - grasping - nose - lips)* apis *Am* bg1* ars bg2* **Arum-t** k* **Bry** k* cina k* cob con hell k* kali-br ptk1 lac-c sne *Lach* bg1* med gk nat-m sne *Nit-ac* k* *Nux-v* k* ph-ac phos mtf33 rheum *Stram* bg2* tarent ptk1* thuj mtf33 zinc
  - **bleed**; until they: *Arum-t* c1* hell bro1 zinc bro1*
  - ○ **Upper**: acon kali-bi sanic pc
- **Malar** bones: chin h2

PLETHORIC (See Congestion)

POINTED (= peaked): agath-a nl2• **Ars** bg2 **Chin** bg2 *Nux-v* bg2 *Ph-ac* bg2 rhus-t bg2 sep gsd1* **Staph** bg2* **Verat** bg2
○ - **Lips**: stram bg2

PRESSING sensation, being pulled in: *Agath-a* nl2•

PRESSURE:
- **agg.**: cina b7.de* cupr b7.de* *Dros* b7a.de sabin b7.de* spig b7.de* verb b7.de*
- **amel.**: bry b7.de* chin b7.de* *Coloc* bg2 dig b4.de* mag-p bg2 pip-n bg2 rhus-t b7.de*
- **pipe** agg.; of: kreos b7a.de

PRICKLING (See Tingling)

PROGNATHISM: bufo gk

PROJECTS lower jaw: lac-lup hrn2•

PROMINENT CHEEKBONES (See Protrusion - malar)

PROTRUDING tongue agg.: hyos ptk1 syph ptk1

PROTRUSION:
○ - **Jaw**; of upper: calc-f c1
- **Malar** bones: *Bac* bn

PUFFED (See Congestion; Swelling)

PULLED UPWARD; sensation as if: agar bg2 ol-an bg2 sel bg2

PULSATION: acon *Agar* k* am-m b7a.de *Arg-met* k* arg-n bg2 arn k* ars bell k* bry k* bufo *Calc* k* cann-s k* carb-an h2* caust k* cham k* clem k* croc k* *Ferr-p* hell b7.de* hura hyos bg2 iris bg2 kola stb3• kreos k* m-arct b7.de mag-c k* merc bg2 *Mur-ac* myric nit-ac petr b4.de* *Plat* bg2 pot-e rly4• rumx sabad k* spong staph k* suis-pan rly4• sulph
- **agg.**: petr bg2
- **heartbeat**; with: mur-ac bg2* pip-n bg2
- ○ **Chin**: stry
- **Jaws**:
  - ○ **Lower**: bov k* cann-s b7.de* carb-an cham cupr-ar ind *Lach* k* nat-c k* nat-m ptk1 petr h2 plat stram
    - **evening**: ind
  - **Upper**: *Phos* ptk1
- **Lips**: arge-pl rwt5• berb bg1 beryl tpw5
  - **night** | **waking**; on: arge-pl rwt5•
  - **warmth** agg. | **heat** agg.: beryl tpw5
- **Malar** bones: calc h2 carb-an h2 mag-c merc-i-f sulph
- **Parotid** glands: hyos gt1
- **Submaxillary** glands: am-m k* cham k* clem h2* ign a1 iod bg2 lach bg2 lyc k* stram k* tarent k*

QUIVERING: agar k* ambr b7.de* bar-c b4.de* caps b7.de* chin cocc k2 coloc k* *Gels* hell b7.de* *Kali-c* k* lyss mag-m merc bg2 mez b4a.de nux-v bg2* op b7.de* phel plb k* puls b7.de* sec bg2 stram bg2 stront-c k* thuj k* valer b7.de*
○ - **Chin**: coloc b4.de* gels c1* m-ambo b7.de mag-m b4.de*
- **Eyebrows**: alum k* ang b7.de* caust k* crot-c bg2 hell b7.de* kali-c k* ol-an k* ruta k* stront-c k*
  - ○ **Between**: ang ptk1
    - **reading** agg.: ang h1
- **Jaws** | **Lower**: agar nat-c
- **Lips**: ars berb *Carb-v* castm crot-h lact sulph k2 til c1
  - **talk**; on attempting to: lach k2 phos k2 stram k2 zinc k2
  - ○ **Upper**: *Carb-v* nat-c h2*

REDNESS (See Discoloration - red)

RELAXED: camph bg2 coloc b4a.de* cupr bg2 merc-c b4a.de nat-m bg2 neon srj5• *Op* b7a.de* suprar rly4•

REST agg.: ang b7a.de *Mag-c* b4a.de meny b7.de* *Plat* bg2 rhus-t b7.de* spig b7.de*

RETRACTION of lips (= showing the teeth): ang b7.de* ant-t ptk1 camph b7.de* hydr-ac bg2 hyos bg2 *Nux-v* bg2 phyt bg2 plb bg2 sec bg2 tab bg2

RISING:
- **amel.**: hep b4.de*
- **bed**; from | **after** | **agg.**: chin b7.de* olnd b7.de* rhus-t b7.de* spig b7.de*
  - **agg.**: guaj b4.de*
- **stooping**; from | **agg.**: *Acon* b7a.de* chin b7.de* naja bg2 verat bg2

RISUS sardonicus: **Bell** k* camph sf* cann-i a1 *Caust* k* *Cedr* hr1 cic h1* *Colch* k* con k* croc a1 *Cupr* hr1 cupr-act bro1 hydr-ac hr1* *Hyos* k* ign k* med hr1* nux-m k* *Oena* k* op bro1 phyt sf plb k* ran-b hr1 ran-s k* *Sec* k* sol-ni *Stram* k* stry k* tarent k13 tell bro1 verat k* zinc zinc-ox j5.de

ROOM:
- **agg.**: am-m b7.de* chin b7.de* hell b7.de* m-aust b7.de puls b7.de* ran-s b7.de*
- **amel.**: laur b7.de*

ROUGH skin: alum b4a.de* anac bg2 ars bg2 *Bar-c* bg2 berb-a c2 bov bg2 *Caps* bg2 cortiso tpw7* *Graph* bg2 kali-s fd4.de merc bg2 nit-ac bg2 *Petr* c2 phos bg2 rhus-t b7.de* sars b4a.de* *Sep* b4a.de* spong fd4.de sulph b4a.de*
- **left**: bell bg2
- **raw**; as if: *Graph* bg2 *Sulph* bg2
- ○ - **Forehead**: sep h2*
- **Mouth**; around: anac bg2 ars bg2 phos h2 spong fd4.de
- **Nostril** | **left**: mim-p rsj8•
- **Temples**: nat-m h2*

RUBBING:
- **agg.**: *Cina* hr1
  - **cough**; face and eyes with fist during: caust ptk1 puls ptk1 *Squil* bro1*
- **amel.**: ant-c b7.de* nat-s bg2 phos b4.de* plat b4.de* plb b7.de* valer b7.de*

SADDLE across the nose: (*↗Discoloration - yellow - saddle; NOSE - Discoloration - yellow*) *Carb-an* k* sanic **Sep** k* syph xxb tril-p bg1

SALIVA; sensation of:
- ○ - **Mouth**:
  - ○ • **Corner** | **left**: phasco-ci rbp2

SCARLATINA; after: *Merc* b4a.de

SEALED; sensation as if lips are (See Sticking - lips - together - sensation)

SENSITIVE: acon bufo bg2 carb-an k* *Carbn-s* caust bg2 chinin-s cod *Kali-bi* bg2 kali-chl kola stb3• *Lach* melal-alt gya4 nux-v ph-ac bg2 phos bg2 *Puls* k* *Rhus-g* tmo3• *Spig* b7.de* teucr b7.de* thuj bg2 vanil fd5.de *Zinc*
- **air**, to: colch kali-i kola stb3• pyrid rly4•
- **neuralgia**; after: cod bro1
- **noise**; to: plut-n srj7•
- **shaving** agg.: carb-an k* colch rsj2• nat-sil fd3.de• ox-ac k* vanil fd5.de
- ○ - **Bones**: aur bro1 bufo bg2 *Carb-v* *Hep* bro1 *Kali-bi* k* *Merc* *Merc-i-f* mez bro1 sulph
  - • **accompanied** by | **typhus** fever (See FEVER - Typhus - accompanied - bones)
- **Chin**; under: nux-m bg2
- **Lips**: arge-pl rwt5• hep kali-c lach k2 *M-ambo* b7.de* mag-c merc nat-m nux-v b7a.de puls b7.de* vanil fd5.de
  - ○ • **Lower**: nat-m b4.de* op b7.de* puls b7.de*
  - • **Upper**: hep b4.de* kali-c b4.de* mag-c b4.de* merc b4.de* puls b7.de* thuj bg2
- **Submaxillary** glands: *Ars* kali-ar a1 *Lyc* k* *Merc-c* k* *Merc-cy* phys a1 *Psor* vesp a1

SENSUAL: | **Lips**: (*↗MIND - Sensual*) **Bufo** mrr1* plat mrr1*

SHAVING:
- **agg.**: aur-m ptk1 carb-an k* ox-ac bg2 ph-ac bg2 phos bg2 *Puls* bg2
- **amel.**: brom bg*

SHINY: (*↗Waxy*) acon agar bg2 **Apis** k* arg-n ars ptk1 *Aur* k* bry bg2 card-m bg2 caust chin bg2 coff cupr der eup-pur k* glon k2 hyos *Lyc* k* *Mag-c* bg2 med k* merc bg2 merc-c bg2 *Nat-m* k* op *Plb* k* psor k* rheum rhus-t k* sel k* stram bg2 thuj k*
- **oily**; as if: (*↗Greasy*) *Nat-m* k* *Plb* k* psor mtf33 syc fmm1• thuj
  - • **perspiration**; during: nat-m bg2 *Rhus-t* bg2 sel bg2
- **spots** after eruptions: nat-m
- ○ - **Lips**: am-m b7a.de cub c1 stram bg2

SHIVERING: acon b7.de* ang bg2 **Arn** b7a.de* bry bg2 calc bg2 *Caust* bg2 *Cham* b7.de* ign b7.de* laur b7.de* merc bg2 ph-ac bg2 **Puls** b7.de* *Rhod* b4.de* ruta bg2 staph b7.de* stram bg2
- **accompanied** by:
  - ○ • **Head** | **complaints** (See HEAD - Complaints - accompanied - face - shivering)
- **stool**; after every: ang c1
- ○ - **Chin**: stram b7.de*
- **In** face and spreading from: caust k* mag-m h2

SHOCKS followed by burning: *Thuj*

SHORTENED, lower jaw seems: alum k*

SHRIVELLED: (*↗Expression - old; Wrinkled*) ant-t apis choc srj3• crot-t dulc fd4.de merc nat-c ptk1 op plb rob sec k2 sin-n spong fd4.de sulph k2* ter tritic-vg fd5.de vanil fd5.de zinc-s
- **children**; in: sulph mtf33
- ○ - **Eyes**; around: choc srj3• spong fd4.de
- **Lips**: am-m k* ant-t k2* ars k2 chin k* mang h2* ox-ac bg2 sul-ac bg2 sulph bg2 vanil fd5.de *Verat* b7.de* zinc k2

SICKLY (See Discoloration - sickly; Expression - sickly)

SITTING:
- **agg.**: am-m b7.de* canth b7.de* graph b4.de* phos b4.de*
- **erect** | **agg.**: rhus-t b7.de*

SLEEP:
- **after** | **agg.**: cina b7.de* spig b7.de*
- **during** | **agg.**: bry b7.de* cham b7.de* ign b7.de* meny b7.de* nat-c bg2 puls b7.de* rheum b7.de* samb b7.de*
- **falling** asleep | **when**: ars bg2 asar bg2 *Caps* b7.de* verb b7.de*

SLIMY lips: kali-i k* *Lyc* lp stram k* zinc k*

SMACKING lips: aml-ns bg2* nux-m mrr1

SMALL FACE: bac bn

SMUTTY: *Ant-t*

SNATCHING about with hands: hyos b7.de*

SNEEZING agg.: chin b7.de* lyc bg2

SORDES on the lips: (*↗MOUTH - Sordes - lips*) arn sne **Ars** k* atro sne bapt tl1* chlol hr1* *Colch* k* hippoz sne *Hyos* k* iod sne kali-cy sne led sne merc-i-f sne merc-k-i sne merc-meth sne mur-ac sne ph-ac sne *Phos* k* plb sne rhus-t k2 **Stram** k* syph sne tart-ac sne

SPASMS (See Convulsions; Distortion)

SPIDER WEB sensation (See Cobweb - sensation)

SPLIT:
- ○ - **Lip** | **Upper** lip: *Tub-r* jl2

SPOTS:
- **colored**: (*↗Discoloration*) *All-s* alum b2.de* am-c b2.de* ambr b2.de* **Ars** b2.de* aur bg2 aur-m bg2 bell b2.de* benz-ac bry b2.de* *Calc* k* cann-s b2.de* canth b2.de* **Carb-an** k* colch b2.de* croc b2.de* dor **Ferr** b2.de* flor-p rsj3• *Guaj* hell b2.de* hydroph rsj6• kali-chl kreos b2.de* laur b2.de* led b2.de* *Lyc* k* m-arct b2.de merc b2.de* morb jl2 mosch b2.de* *Nat-c* k* nux-m k* nux-v b2.de* op b2.de* par b2.de* phos b2.de* **Rhus-t** k* ruta b2.de* sabad k* samb b2.de* sars b2.de* sec b2.de* sep b2.de* **Sil** k* sul-ac *Sulph* b2.de* syph tell rsj10• teucr b2.de* ven-m rsj12• verat b2.de* verb zinc b2.de [spect dfg1]
- **painful** sensation (See Pain - spot; in a)
- **ulcerating**: nat-c staph

STANDING agg.: chin b7.de*

STICKING:

○ - **Lips**: arg-n bg2 bell bg2 chin b7.de* con bg2 *Hyos* b7a.de merc-i-r bg2* nux-m b7.de* ran-b b7.de* rhus-t bg2 stram b7.de* zinc b4a.de*
- **moisture** on lips; sticky: zinc b4.de*
- **together**: am-c bg2 arg-n bg2 bapt bg2 bry bg2 cann-i c1* *Cann-xyz* bg2* cham bg2 chin bg2 con bg2 *Helon* bro1 hyos bg2 kali-c bg2 kali-i bg2 lyc bg2 mez bg2 nux-m bg2* pin-con oss2• rhus-t bg2 stann bg2 stram b7.de* sulph bg2 zinc mtf33
  - ⁝ **sensation** as if: plut-n srj7•

STIFFNESS: anac bg2 anh sp1 arn bg2 ars bg2 bry bg2 euphr b7a.de* ham bg2 ip bg2 kali-bi bg2 lach bg2 nux-v bg2 plan bg2 *Rhus-t* bg2* sang bg2 sars bg2 thuj bg2 tritic-vg fd5.de verat bg2

- **paralytic**: botul jl2 carc gk6

○ - **Jaws**:
- **left**: lacer c1
- ○ **Joints**: carb-an bg2 sang hr1
- **Lower**: absin bro1 acet-ac acon k* aml-ns bg2 anthraci apis b7a.de* arn bro1 ars-met (non:ars-n kl) arum-t bg2 bad bell k* bit-ar wht1• calc k* camph b7.de* cann-i cann-xyz bg2 carbn-o bro1 carbn-s carc tpw2* **Caust** k* cham bro1 chim cic bg1* cocc k* colch b7a.de crot-h *Cupr* bro1 *Cupr-act* bro1 cur bro1 daph dios dulc bro1 euphr k* falco-pe nl2• form k* *Gels* k* glon k* graph k* helo-s rwt2• hydr-ac bro1 hydrog srj2• hyos k* *Hyper* bro1 *Ign* bg1* irid-met bg2 *Kali-i* k* lac-h sze9• *Lach* k* lyss med *Merc* k* *Merc-c* k* *Merc-i-f* *Mez* *Morph* bro1 nat-ar *Nat-c* b4a.de nat-s k* nicot bro1 nux-m k* **Nux-v** k* oena bro1 olnd bro1 op k* petr k* phos k2 phys bro1 *Phyt* bg1* pin-con oss2• positr nl2• **Rhus-t** k* sang k* sars k* sep k* *Sil* b4a.de sol-ni bro1 spig b7a.de stram bro1 **Stry** k* sulph sumb *Ther* thuj k* tung-met bdx1• *Verat* k* vip bg2 [tax jsj7]
  - ⁝ **morning**: falco-pe nl2• *Ther*
    - ⁝ **rising** agg.; after: nat-s
    - ⁝ **waking**; on: falco-pe nl2•
  - ⁝ **chewing** agg.: euphr h2
  - ⁝ **swallowing** agg.: *Arum-t*
  - ⁝ **talking** agg.: euphr h2
- **Lips**: *Aml-ns* **Apis** k* crot-h dulc fd4.de *Euphr* k* kalm k* *Lach* k* morg-p fmm1• tritic-vg fd5.de
  - **morning**: morg-p pte1*•
- ○ **Upper**: aml-ns bg2 apis bg2 *Euphr* k* kalm bg2 sep bg2
  - ⁝ **wood**; as if made of: cycl b7a.de *Euphr* b7a.de
- **Muscles**: absin bro1 acon bro1 agar k* anac arn bapt bro1 bry *Caust* bro1 dulc fd4.de gels bro1 ham helo bro1 ip med k2 *Nux-v* k* phos k2 plan rhus-t bro1 sang staph stry k* *Verat*
  - **cough** agg.; during: **Ip** k*
  - **pain**; during: nit-ac bg1
  - ⁝ **Occiput**; in: staph
- ○ **Masseter** muscles: ign ptk1 pin-con oss2• sars h2* thuj h1*

STOOL: | **during** | **agg.**: caps b7.de* verat b7.de*

- **urging** to | **agg.**: caust bg2

STOOPING:

- **agg.**: apis b7a.de canth b7.de* nux-v b7.de* petr b4.de*
- **amel.**: rhus-t b7.de*

SUCKING; motion as from: bell ptk1

SUN:

- **exposure** to the sun | **agg.**: stann b4.de*

SUNBURN: *Thuj* bg1*

- **agg.**: *Clem* b4a.de

SUNKEN: (*↗Hippocratic)* acon *Aeth* k* *Agn* hr1 aloe androc srj1• *Ant-c* k* **Ant-t** k* apis *Arg-n* k* *Arn* k* **Ars** k* ars-h k* *Ars-i* hr1 ars-s-f k2 asc-t hr1 bar-i k2 bell k* **Berb** k* *Brom* hr1 **Bufo** mrr1 *Calc* k* calc-i k2 **Camph** k* cann-i k2 cann-xyz bg2 canth k* **Carb-v** k* *Carbn-s* *Cham* k* *Chel* k* **Chin** k* chlor k* cina k* *Cocc* b7a.de* *Colch* k* *Coloc* hr1 con k* corn hr1 crot-h bg2 *Cub* k* cupr k* cupr-ar hr1 **Dig** k* dirc dros k* dulc fd4.de eup-per k* *Ferr* k* *Ferr-ma* ferr-p gels k* gran *Ham* hr1 hell k* hydr k2* hydr-ac k* hyos k* **Ign** k* iod *Ip* k* *Kali-ar* k* kali-bi bg2 *Kali-c* k* *Kali-i* hr1 kali-m k2* kali-n k* kali-p k* kali-s kali-sula a1* *Lach* k* laur k* *Lyc* k* **Mang** k* *Merc* k* merc-c k* mez k* morph *Mur-ac* k* *Myos-a* hr1 *Nat-s* k* *Nit-ac* k* nux-v k* ol-an olnd k* **Op** k* ox-ac par ptk1 petr *Ph-ac* k* *Phos* k* phyt k* pic-ac hr1 *Plat* k* *Plb* k* psor k2 puls k2

Sunken: ...
pyrog bg2* *Rhus-t* k* sabad k* *Samb* k* **Sec** k* *Sel* hr1 sep k* sin-n spong fd4.de squil k* *Stann* k* *Staph* k* sul-ac k* sul-i k2 *Sulph* k* *Tab* k* ter k* teucr b7.de* **Verat** k* wies a1 *Zinc* k* zinc-p k2

- **morning**: lyc nat-m ol-an olnd hr1
- **dinner**; after: nat-m
- **rage**; during: *Ars* canth cupr lach nux-v phos sec verat
- **sensation** as if: *Agath-a* nl2•
- **stool** agg.; after: crot-t hr1 ferr-m

○ - **Cheeks**: dros tl1 plb mtf33 verat tl1

SUPPURATION: *Rhus-t* bg2

○ - **Chin** | **old** boils: anac h2

- **Jaws** | **Lower**: aur bg2 cist bg2 merc bg2 phos k* sil bg2
- **Mouth** closed by ulceration; corner of: calc b4.de*
  - **right**: calc h1

SWALLOWING agg.: kali-n b4.de* phos ptk1 staph b7.de*

SWELLING: (*↗Bloated; Enlarged)* **Acon** k* act-sp bg2 aesc aeth k* agar k* ail k* all-c bro1 aloe k* alum k* alum-p k2 am-c k* am-m k* ambr b7.de amyg k* anac k* anac-oc k* anan k* ant-ar bro1 *Ant-t* k* antip bro1 ap-g br1 **Apis** k* apoc *Arn* k* **Ars** k* ars-met bro1 ars-s-f k2 *Arum-t* asaf k2 asim br1 *Aur* k* aur-ar k2 *Aur-m* bacls-7 fmm1• bapt bg2 *Bar-c* k* bar-i k2 bar-s k2 **Bell** k* boerh-d bnj1 borra-o oss1• borx k* both fne1• **Bov** k* **Bry** k* *Bufo* k* *Cact* **Calc** k* *Calc-ar* calc-f sp1 *Camph* *Canth* k* caps k* carb-an b2.de* *Carb-v* k* carbn-h *Carbn-s* caust b2.de* **Cham** k* chel k* *Chin* k* chinin-ar chlor k* choc srj3• cic k* *Cina* k* *Cocc* k* *Colch* k* coli rly4• *Coloc* k* *Com* k* *Con* k* convo-s sp1 cop cortiso sp1 *Crot-h* k* crot-t k* cub k* cupr k* dig k* dol dor k* dros k* *Dulc* b2.de* *Elaps* *Euph* k* fago k* **Ferr** k* *Ferr-ar* ferr-i ferr-m k* *Ferr-p* gels k* ger-i rly4• germ-met srj5• glon k* *Graph* k* *Guaj* k* guare k* gymno hell k* helon k* **Hep** k* hir rsj4• hura hydr-ac k* hydrc k* hyos k* hyper iod b2.de* ip k* irid-met srj5• kali-ar k* kali-bi k* *Kali-c* k* kali-chl k* *Kali-i* k* kali-m k2 kali-p kali-s fd4.de kali-sil k2 kreos b2.de* lac-c k* lac-d ptk1 *Lach* k* lachn k* lat-h bnm5• lat-m sp1* laur k* led k* loxo-recl bnm10• **Lyc** k* lycps-v ptk1 m-arct b2.de mag-c k* mag-m b2.de* mag-p bg2* manc k* medus br1 **Merc** k* *Merc-c* k* *Mez* k* mosch b2.de* muru a1 *Nat-ar* *Nat-c* k* *Nat-hchls* **Nat-m** k* nat-pyru rly4• nicc k* *Nit-ac* k* *Nux-m* k* *Nux-v* k* *Oena* k* olnd b2.de* **Op** k* ox-ac k* petr b2.de* ph-ac b2.de* *Phos* k* plan k* *Plat* k* plb k* podo bg2 psor k* puls k* rheum b2.de* **Rhus-t** k* *Rhus-v* k* ruta b2.de* sabin k* *Samb* k* sang k* sec k* sel k* senec seneg k* *Sep* k* sil b2.de* sol-ni *Spig* k* spong k* *Stann* k* staph b2.de* *Stram* k* stry k* sul-ac b2.de* sul-i k2 sulph k* syc fmm1• tab k* tarax k* tarent ptk1 tax k* ter k* teucr b2.de* thuj tritic-vg fd5.de urin c1 vac k* vanil fd5.de *Verat* k* *Verat-v* ptk1 vesp k* vinc k* vip k* *Zinc* b4a.de zinc-s k* ziz a1* [astat stj2 pop dhh1 tung-met stj2]

- **one** side: am k* *Ars* *Aur* bar-c h2 bell k* borx h2 bry k* canth k* *Cham* k* graph h2 kola stb3• *M-arct* b7a.de *Merc* k* *Merc-c* ptk1 nux-v k* phos b4a.de phyt k2 plb k* puls sep k* spig ptk1 stann sne staph
- **right**: act-sp bg1 am ptk1 *Ars* bg1* *Calc* bg1* elaps merc merc-i-f ptk1 moni rfm1• nicc k* *Plb* bg1* polyg-h ptk1 rumx bg1 sang ptk1 spong fd4.de stann sne
- **left**: anac k* arg-met k1 arg-n k* *Com* k* *Kali-c* k* kola stb3• **Lach** k* lat-h bnm5• lyss k* nat-m h2* *Phyt* k* zinc k*
  - **heat** and burning, with: arg-met a1*
- **morning**: **Ars** k* aur calc crot-h dirc graph h2* *Hep* bg1* kali-c *Kali-chl* bg1* kali-s fd4.de *Kalm* bg1* *Lyc* bg1* manc k* merc k* nat-pyru rly4• *Nit-ac* *Phos* bg1* *Sep* bg1* *Spig* bg1* sulph h2* syc pte1*• tritic-vg fd5.de
  - **waking**; on: agar hura nat-ar rhus-t spig
- **afternoon**: *Ars* bell bg1 phos k*
- **evening**: ars bg1 lyc bg1 rhus-t k* sulph bg1
- **night**: *Lach* k* tritic-vg fd5.de
- **accompanied** by:
  - **pale** discoloration: apis bg2* *Ars* bg2* *Calc* bg2* graph bg2* hell ptk1 kali-c bg2 lyc ptk1
  - ○ **Eyes** | **styes** (See EYE - Styes - accompanied - face)
  - **Teeth**; pain in (See TEETH - Pain - accompanied - face - swelling)
- **bee** stings; from: apis mrr1 *Carb-ac* *Lach* *Led*
- **bladder**-like: borx bg2
- **chill**; during: am-m bg2 am bg2 ars bg2 bell bg2 cham bg2 ferr bg2 lach bg2 *Lyc* bg2 sil bg2
- **coryza**; during: *Nux-v* b7.de* staph b7.de*

- **cough** agg.; during: samb b7a.de
- **eating** | **after** | **agg.**: merc h1*
  - **agg.**: sep h2
- **edematous**: aeth am-be mtf11 ant-ar k* *Ant-t Antip* vh1 **Apis** *Apoc* **Ars** k* ars-h *Ars-met* asaf k2 boerh-d zzc1• brass-n-o srj5• bros-gau mrc1 bry k2 *Cact* **Calc** calc-ar k2 carbn-s *Chel Chin* chinin-ar k2 *Colch Crot-h* cupr-ar *Dig Dulc* euph *Ferr Ferr-p* **Graph** ham *Hell* irid-met srj5• kali-ar lach k2 lat-m bnm6• **Lyc** medus br1* *Merc Merc-c* morg-g pte1*• *Nat-ar Nat-c Nat-m* ozone sde2• *Phos Plb* puls k2 rauw sp1 *Rhus-t* streptoc jl2 thuj tub al* urt-u bg1 *Vesp Xan*
  - **sudden**: morg-g fmm1•
- **erysipelatous** (See Erysipelas)
- **fever**; during: *Am-m* b7a.de* apis bg2 ars b4.de* dig b4a.de* ferr bg2 **Lyc** b4a.de*
  - **intermittent**: ars chin lyc nat-m
- **hard**: am-c k* *Arn* ars bell borx calc-f br1 dulc fd4.de hecla mrr1 **Hep** k* *Merc* k* *Sil*
- **hot**: borx h2 rhus-t h1* tritic-vg fd5.de
- **itching**: irid-met srj5• moni rfm1• rhus-t h1*
- **lying** agg.: apoc k*
- **menses**:
  - **before** | **agg.**: bar-c k* *Graph* k* *Kali-c* k* *Merc* k* *Puls*
  - **during** | **agg.**: aeth cham b7.de* *Sulph* k*
  - **instead** of: *Kali-c* h2*
- **mercury**; after abuse of: *Hep* hr1 *Kali-i* k*
- **nodular**: alum k*
- **pale**: *Bov* b4a.de calc b4a.de graph b4a.de sep b4a.de sulph b4a.de
- **perspiration**; during: **Am-m** bg2 apis bg2 ars bg2 bell bg2 bry bg2 *Cham* bg2 **Lyc** bg2 *Merc* bg2 nux-v bg2 rhus-t bg2 *Sep* bg2
- **pregnancy** agg.; during: jab hr1 *Merc-c Phos* k*
- **prosopalgia**, during: bell j5.de coloc j5.de phos j5.de plat j5.de spig j5.de verb j5.de zinc j5.de
- **red**: *Acon* ptk1 *Arn* k* ars bell borx chin ptk1 cic coloc euph ferr ptk1 guaj h2* *Kali-c* k* lach k* merc k* moni rfm1• nat-c k* nux-v olnd op ptk1 rhus-t k* sang a1 stram ptk1 sulph verat h1*
- **scarlet** fever: **Apis Arum-t** k* *Calc* k* *Hell* k* *Kali-s Lyc* k* zinc k*
- **sensation** of swelling: (*↗Enlarged - sensation)* acon b7.de* *Aesc* bg1* aeth alum k* ambr b7.de* apis b7a.de apisin wd2 *Aran* ars-met bamb-a stb2.de• bar-act wd1 bar-c k* *Bell* bg1* *Bov* b4a.de calc k* *Chel* daph rb2 dulc fd4.de euph rb2 *Ferr* k* ger-i rly4• glon bg2 *Grat Gymno* irid-met srj5• kola stb3• *Lil-t* bg1* *Mez* bg1* nat-ar k2 *Nat-m* bg1* nicc *Nux-m* k* phos k* pip-m puls k* samb b7.de* spig b7.de* *Staph* stram *Sul-ac* k* tritic-vg fd5.de vanil fd5.de
  - **left**: nux-m c1 stram rb2
  - **air** agg.; in open: phos h2
  - **coryza**; during: ars-met rb2
  - **entering** house; on: aeth
  - ○ **Cheeks** (See cheeks - sensation)
  - **Malar** bones (See malar - sensation)
- **shining**: apis arn aur spig
- **toothache**: all-c k* am-c h2* *Ant-c* k* aur h2* *Bell* bro1 borx h2 *Calc* k* *Calc-s* k* **Cham** k* coff bro1 colch k* *Euph* k* graph h2* *Hep* iod h* kali-bi gk *Kali-c* k* **Lach** k* lyc h2* *Mag-c* k* **Merc** k* nat-c h2 nat-m h2* nit-ac h2* nux-v k* petr a1* phos h2* samb k* **Sep** k* **Sil** *Spig* k* staph h1* stront-c sulph gk *Thuj* bg1* *Verat* k*
- **washing** agg.; after: *Aesc* k*
- **white**: apis bg2 rhus-t bg2

○ - **Bones**: aur b4a.de bufo bg2 mag-c b4a.de merc-c b4a.de ph-ac b4a.de sil b4.de* spig b7.de*
  - **Cheeks**: *Acon* bro1 am-c k* am-m k* ambr h1 *Ant-c* b7a.de apis k* *Arn* k* ars k* *Aur* k* aur-s k2 bar-c b2.de* bell k* borx b2.de* bov k* bry k* *Calc* b2.de* *Calc-f* bro1 canth b2.de* caps h1* carb-an h2* carb-v k* caust k* *Cham* k* chin b2.de* dig k* dulc fd4.de euph b2.de* euphr ferr b2.de* graph b2.de* *Guaj* hr1 hep b2.de* iod b2.de* kali-ar kali-bi gk *Kali-c* k* *Kali-i* k* kali-m bro1 kali-sil k2 *Lach* b2.de* lyc b2.de* *M-arct* b2.de* *Mag-c* k* mag-m b2.de* **Merc** k* merc-c k* nat-c k* nat-m b2.de* nept-m lsd2.fr nit-ac k* *Nux-m* b7a.de nux-v k* petr b2.de* ph-ac b2.de* phos b2.de* *Plan* bro1 plat bro1 positr nl2• puls k* rhus-t b2.de* samb b2.de* sep k* *Sil* k* spig b2.de* *Spong* k* *Stann* k* staph k* sulph k* *Tub* jl2 vanil fd5.de
    - **one** side: **Arn** bg2 **Bell** bg2 *Bry* bg2 canth bg2 **Cham** bg2 **Merc** bg2 **Nux-v** bg2 plb bg2 puls bg2 *Sep* bg2
  - **Cheeks**: ...
    - **left**: spig bg2 sul-ac h2*
    - **morning**: nat-c h2*
    - **hard**: am-c h2* calc-f ptk1
    - **hot**: **Cham** bg2
    - **menses**:
      - **after** | **agg.**: phos b4.de*
      - **before** | **agg.**: apis bro1 graph bro1 phos h2*
      - **during** | **agg.**: apis bro1* graph k* sep k*
    - **pale**: **Merc** bg2
    - **red**: sulph h2*
    - **sensation** of swelling: acon aran rb2* bamb-a stb2.de• calc h2 *Chel* echi wd1 kali-c wd1 nat-ar k2* nux-m wd2 samb spig h1 staph rb2* tritic-vg fd5.de
  - **Chin**: borx b4a.de carb-v k* caust k* *Nit-ac* b4a.de rhus-t b7.de* spig b7.de* spong fd4.de *Thuj* b4a.de
    - **left**: chinin-ar vh
    - ○ **Under**: am-c bg2 caust bg2 staph bg2
  - **Eyes**:
    - **morning**: dulc fd4.de ignis-alc es2• nat-sil fd3.de• sep k1 vanil fd5.de
    - ○ **Above**: aur-m-n vml3• cench c2* chin bg1 **Kali-c** k* lach k2 *Lyc* k* nat-ar puls bg2* ruta k* sep k* symph fd3.de• [pop dhh1]
      - **left**: aur-m-n vml3•
      - **coughing**; when: kali-c k2
      - **edematous**: *Tub* jl2
        - **Hair**; at the roots of: *Tub* jl2
      - **Between** eyebrows and lids: kali-c b4a.de*
    - **Around**: all-c **Apis** k* *Ars* k* bell bg2 calc-ar k2* chin k* colch coli rly4• cupr k* cycl mrr1 cypra-eg sde6.de• dulc fd4.de elaps *Ferr* k* gels bg2 ger-i rly4• germ-met srj5• ham fd3.de• irid-met srj5• **Kali-c** k* kali-i ptk1 lach bg2 lat-h bnm5• lat-m bnm6• merc k* nat-pyru rly4• nit-ac k* *Phos* k* puls b2.de* rheum b2.de* **RHUS-T** k ●* ribo rly4• ruta bg2 sang k* sep bg2 spig h1* spong fd4.de stram k* tritic-vg fd5.de urt-u bg1 vanil fd5.de
      - **right**: ail bg1 *Rhus-v* bg1*
      - **morning**: ars h2* coli rly4• dulc fd4.de nit-ac h2* symph fd3.de• tritic-vg fd5.de vanil fd5.de
      - **fever**; during: *Ferr* b7.de*
      - **menses**; during: puls k2
    - **Between**: lyc
    - **Under**: (*↗EYE - Swelling - lids - under)* **Apis** k* apoc arn ptk1 **Ars** k* *Aur* k* aur-m-n wbt2• borx bg2 bry k* calc h2* *Calc-ar* cench k2 cham b2.de* cinnb coloc xyz61 dulc fd4.de *Fl-ac* k* ham fd3.de• hep b4a.de ignis-alc es2• iod k2* **Kali-c** *Kali-i* kali-p fd1.de• kali-s fd4.de med k* merc k* merc-i-f ptk1 nat-c h2* nat-pyru rly4• nat-sil fd3.de• nit-ac k* nux-v k* olnd k* oxal-a rly4• phos k* plut-n srj7• puls k* *Raph* bg1* rhus-t bg2 ruta fd4.de sep bg2 sil b4a.de stram bg2 syc fmm1• symph fd3.de• *Thlas* bg1* tritic-vg fd5.de vanil fd5.de
      - **right**: carb-ac bg1 merc bg2 merc-i-f ptk1 polyg-h ptk1 tritic-vg fd5.de
      - **left**: colch bg1 dulc fd4.de ruta fd4.de sulph bg1
      - **morning**: syc bka1•
      - **cough** agg.; during: kali-c k2
      - **purple**: ter mrr1
  - **Forehead**: abrot bg2 apis bg1 ars bg1 bell b4a.de calad bg2 camph bg2 chin bg2 coli rly4• cupr bg2 fl-ac bg2 hell bg1 lol bg2 lyc bg1 *Nux-v* bg1 phos bg2* puls bg2 rhus-t bg1 ruta b7.de* sep b4a.de* sulph bg2
  - **Ganglions** | **Chin**; under the: psor jl2
  - **Glands** in general: am-c am-m arn *Ars Ars-i* **Arum-t** asaf aur aur-m aur-s k2 bad *Bar-c Bar-m* **Bell** bov brom bry calad **Calc** k* calc-sil k2 camph *Carb-an Carbn-s* cham chin cic clem cocc con cor-r crot-t dulc graph **Hep** **Iod** k* jab *Kali-c* kali-i kali-m k2 *Lach* led *Lith-c Lyc* **Merc** *Mur-ac Nat-c Nat-m* nat-p *Nit-ac* nux-v ozone sde2• petr *Phos* plb puls **Rhus-t** *Sep* **Sil** spig spong stann *Staph Sul-ac* **Sulph** thuj verat
    - **hard**, painful: bar-c *Bell* calc hell iod mur-ac nat-m ozone sde2• petr *Rhus-t* **Sil** staph *Sulph*
    - **under** jaw (See submaxillary)
  - **Jaws**: amph bro1 *Calc-f* bro1 hecla bro1 plb bro1 thuj bro1

Face

○ • **Lower**: acon k* alum b4a.de* amph a1* ang b7a.de *Anthraci* arn b7.de* ars k* *Aur* aur-m-n bro1 bar-i k2 calc k* *Calc-f* calc-s caust k* *Crot-h* *Fl-ac* *Kali-c* k* **Lach** k* lyc bg2 mag-c h2* merc k* *Merc-c* b4a.de *Nit-ac* k* ol-an k* petr k* **Phos** k* *Rhus-t* b7a.de *Sil* k* spong fd4.de staph b7.de* sulph symph bro1 vanil fd5.de verat b7.de* zinc

⋮ **right**: anthraci vh1

⋮ **morning**: zinc

⋮ **accompanied** by:

: **Head**; complaints of (See HEAD - Complaints - accompanied - jaw - swelling)

: **Teeth**; pain in (See TEETH - Complaints - accompanied - jaw - swelling)

⋮ **chill**; during: kali-c b4.de

⋮ **hard**: anthraci ptk1

⋮ **sensation** of: sabad b7.de*

⋮ **Angle**; hard: lyc h2

⋮ **Bone**: **Ang** b7a.de *Aur* b4a.de *Hep* b4a.de kali-bi bg2 **Merc-c** b4a.de ph-ac b4a.de phos bg2 *Rhus-t* b7a.de *Sil* b4.de*

⋮ **Periosteum**: aur-m-n br1

• **Upper**: alum *Nit-ac* k* phos stann

- **Lips**: acon *Agath-a* nl2• ail k* alum k* alum-p k2 am-m bg2 anan ant-t antip bro1 **Apis** k* ara-maca sej7• arg-met k* arg-n arge-pl rwt5• arn k* *Ars* k* **Arum-t** k* asaf k* *Aur* k* aur-ar k2 *Aur-m* aur-s k2 bac hr1 bar-c k* **Bell** k* beryl tpw5 *Bov* k* brach **Bry** k* cadm-s calad *Calc* k* canth k* *Caps* k* *Carb-an* k* *Carb-v* k* caust b2.de* chin k* cic bg2 *Clem* con b2.de* *Cor-r* *Crot-h* cub c1 dig k* gels glon graph b2.de* hell k* hep k* hydrog srj2• kali-ar *Kali-c* k* kali-chl kali-m k2 kali-p kali-s kali-sil k2 *Kalm* *Lach* k* lachn lyc k* m-ambo b2.de* med brl medus br1* *Merc* k* *Merc-c* k* mez k* mono a1 mosch b2.de* mur-ac b2.de* *Nat-c* k* **Nat-m** k* **Nit-ac** k* *Nux-m* k* olnd b2.de* op k* *Par* k* petr b2.de* ph-ac phel *Phos* k* plb *Psor* k* puls k* rhus-t k* *Rhus-v* c2* sang sec b7a.de **Sep** k* *Sil* k* spong fd4.de staph k* stram k* *Sulph* k* thuj k* tub urt-u vanil fd5.de *Vip* bro1 zinc k* zinc-p k2

• **morning**: apis bg2 aur bg2 lyc h2* sep bg2

• **accompanied** by | **Teeth**; pain in (See TEETH - Complaints - accompanied - lips)

• **angioedema**: *(↗SKIN - Eruptions - angioedema)* apis mrr1*

• **chill**; during: *Ars* bg2 bry bg2 rhus-t bg2

• **edematous**: medus br1

• **fever**; during: *Ars* b4a.de*

• **perspiration**; during: apis bg2 *Ars* bg2 *Bry* bg2 calc bg2 con bg2 mez bg2 nat-m bg2 *Sulph* bg2

• **sensation** of: acon bg2 agath-a nl2• apis b7a.de* bar-c bg2 brom bg2 calc-f sp1 coloc bg2 dulc fd4.de glon bg2 hyos b7a.de lact lact-v bg2 olnd b7.de* rhus-t b7.de* sabad bg2 [bell-p-sp dcm1]

• **warmth** agg. | **heat** agg.: beryl tpw5

○ • **Lower**: agath-a nl2• alum k* am-caust c1 arn bg1 **Asaf** k* borx h2* *Bry* b7a.de calc k* *Caust* k* *Clem* com crot-c mre1.fr *Kali-bi* *Kali-c* kali-s lach bg2* *L,* k* *Merc* ptk1 *Merc-c* mez k* *Mur-ac* k* *Nat-c* h2* **Nat-m** k* nept-m lsd2.fr nit-ac h2* physala-p bnm7• puls k* sang hr1 *Sep* k* sil k* stram *Sul-ac* b4a.de *Sulph* k*

⋮ **right**: ros-d wla1

⋮ **morning**: *Sep* h2*

⋮ **sensation** of: glon rb2*

• **Upper**: **Apis** k* arg-met k* arg-n bg2 arge-pl rwt5• ars k* **Bar-c** k* **Bell** k* *Bov* k* *Bry* k* **Calc** k* *Calc-p* k* canth k* *Carb-v* k* cimic bg2 con b2.de* dulc b4a.de graph k* grat guare k* **Hep** k* interf sa3• jug-r a1 kali-bi bg2 *Kali-c* k* kali-p *Lach* k* lat-h bnm5• *Lyc* k* mang *Merc* k* merc-c k* merc-i-f *Mez* k* moni rfm1• mosch b7a.de *Nat-c* k* **Nat-m** k* nept-m lsd2.fr **Nit-ac** k* nux-m bg2 par b2.de* petr b2.de* phel k* *Phos* k* *Psor* k* rhus-t k* *Rhus-v* a1 sil b2.de* spig bg2 **Staph** k* **Sulph** k* thuj b2.de* *Tub* k* vanil fd5.de vinc k* zinc b2.de* [heroin sdj2]

⋮ **right**: psor jl2

⋮ **morning**: *Calc* k* grat k* phos h2*

⋮ **evening**: sulph h2

⋮ **coryza**; during: bar-c c1*

⋮ **pale**: bov b4a.de dulc b4a.de sil b4a.de

- **Lips – Upper**: ...

⋮ **sensation** of: ephe-si hsj1• psor jl2

- **Malar** bones: kali-bi bg2 nat-ar bg1

• **sensation** of swelling: spig h1

⋮ **right** malar bone: chel rb2

- **Mouth**:

○ • **Around**: carb-an ham fd3.de• nux-v olnd h1*

• **Corners** of: asaf b7.de* clem olnd b7.de* vinc

- **Nasal** bones (See NOSE - Swelling - bones)

- **Nose**; under (See NOSE - Swelling - below)

- **Parotid** glands: *Ail* *Am-c* k* am-m bg2* anth k* anthraci jl2 apis k* *Arn* k* *Ars* **Arum-t** *Aur* k* aur-ar k2 *Aur-m* aur-s k2 **Bapt** hr1* **Bar-c** k* bar-i k2 *Bar-m* bar-s k2 **Bell** k* **Brom** k* *Bry* k* bufo *Calc* k* calc-p k2 *Calc-s* calc-sil k2 *Carb-an* k* *Carb-v* k* *Carbn-s* **Cham** k* **Chin** k* *Chinin-ar* chlol *Cinnb* *Cist* coc-c *Cocc* k* *Con* k* *Crot-h* dig k* *Dulc* k* euph b4a.de fago *Ferr-p* *Graph* *Hep* k* hippoz k* hyos k* *Ign* k* *Iris* kali-ar *Kali-bi* k* *Kali-c* k* *Kali-i* kali-m k2 kali-p kali-sil k2 lac-c *Lach* *Lyc* mag-c b4a.de mang k* **Merc** k* *Merc-cy* *Merc-i-r* merc-sul c1 **Mez** b4a.de *Mur-ac* nat-ar nat-c k* **Nit-ac** k* nux-v k* ourl jl2 petr k2 *Phos* k* phys bg2 *Phyt* plb propl ub1• *Psor* puls k* **Rhus-t** k* sarr *Sep* k* **Sil** k* staph stram *Sul-ac* sul-i k2 sulfonam ks2 sulph k* sumb thuj b4a.de vip [calc-br stj1]

• **right**: am-c anthraci jl2 **Bar-c** *Bar-m* **Bell** calc-s k2 carb-an graph *Kali-bi* kali-c *Merc* nit-ac plb sep stram sulfonam ks2

⋮ **then** left: **Lyc**

• **left**: **Brom** k* con *Lach* **Rhus-t** *Sul-ac* k* symph fd3.de•

• **accompanied** by:

⋮ **cough** (See COUGH - Touched - parotid)

⋮ **typhus** fever (See FEVER - Typhus - accompanied - parotid)

⋮ **Ear**; complaints of (See EAR - Complaints - accompanied - parotid - swelling)

• **cold** air | **amel.**: *Merc*

• **eruption**, after: anthraci *Arn* *Bar-c* **Brom** *Carb-v* dulc iod kali-bi mag-c sulph

• **hard**: am-c **Bar-m** **Brom** *Merc* sil h2* sul-ac

• **menses**; during: kali-c

• **mumps**; after: sul-i ptk1

• **sensation** of: trif-p br1

- **Salivary** glands (See MOUTH - Swelling - salivary)

- **Side** lain on: phos bg1

- **Sinuses**: | **Maxillary**: phos bro1 spig bro1

- **Sublingual** gland: brom k2 calc k2 *Canth* con k2 kalm led ptk1 **Merc** petr k2 plb k2 psor staph h1*

- **Submaxillary** glands: am-c k* *Am-m* k* ambr k* *Anan* *Anthraci* k* *Arg-met* arn bg2 *Ars* k* **Ars-i** ars-s-f k2 **Arum-t** k* asim k* aur aur-ar k2 *Aur-m* k* aur-s k2 **Bar-c** k* bar-i k2 **Bar-m** bar-s k2 bell k* bov k* **Brom** k* bufo calad k* **Calc** k* calc-i k2 *Calc-p* *Calc-s* calc-sil k2 *Camph* h1* *Carb-an* carbn-s **Cham** k* **Chin** k* chinin-ar chinin-s chlol cic bg2* clem k* *Cocc* k* *Con* k* cop a1 *Cor-r* k* *Crot-h* *Crot-t* k* der a1 dros tl1 *Dulc* bg2 fago a1 *Ferr-i* *Graph* k* *Hep* hippoz k* ign k* *Iod* k* jab a1 *Jug-c* k* *Kali-ar* *Kali-c* k* **Kali-i** kali-n k* kali-p kali-s kali-sil k2 *Kreos* bg2 *Lac-c* k* *Lach* led k* **Lyc** k* mag-m med *Merc* k* *Merc-c* k* merc-cy k* *Merc-i-f* *Merc-i-r* k* mit a1 *Mur-ac* **Nat-c** k* *Nat-m* k* nat-p *Nat-s* **Nit-ac** k* *Nux-v* ozone sde2• *Petr* k* ph-ac bg2 phos h2* phys a1 *Phyt* k* pin-s a1* *Plb* k* *Psor* k* puls bg2 **Rhus-t** k* ruta fd4.de *Sep* k* **Sil** k* spong k* stann k* *Staph* k* stram *Sul-ac* k* sul-i k2 *Sulph* k* syph tab k* tarent thuj bg2 tub-m jl2 vanil fd5.de verat k* verat-v a1 vesp a1 vip a1 zinc k* [bell-p-sp dcm1 calc-br stj1]

• **right**: anthraci jl2 bufo kali-br sep spong k* stram *Sulph*

• **left**: ars h2* arum-t **Brom** *Cor-r* ruta fd4.de sul-ac mrr1 vanil fd5.de vesp

• **evening**: ars h2*

• **accompanied** by | **Teeth**; pain in (See TEETH - Pain - accompanied - submaxillary)

• **fever**; during: calad b7.de* kali-c bg2 merc bg2

• **hard**: ars h2* **Brom** **Calc** *Graph* *Kali-c* *Merc* **Rhus-t** syph

• **painful**: am-m arum-t aur aur-m **Bar-c** *Bar-m* bell h1* bufo **Calc** calc-f sp1 cic c1 clem h2* *Graph* merc-i-r *Nit-ac* petr a1 ruta fd4.de **Sil** stann h2* sul-ac h2* *Sulph*

⋮ **night**: bell h1*

- **painful**: ...
  - ⁝ **swallowing** agg.: chin h1*
- **perspiration**; during: calad bg2 *Kali-c* bg2
- **salivation**; with: der vml3•
- **Submental** gland: am-c bar-i k2 con k2 glech bg1 graph h2* led h1* staph
  - **painful**: am-c
- **Zygoma**: con h2*

TALKING agg.: bry ptk1 euphr b7.de* kali-chl ptk1 mez ptk1 *Phos* bg2 puls ptk1 sep ptk1 squil b7.de* tell ptk1

TEETH; pain in: | **after**: *Arn* b7a.de ars b4.de* bov b4.de* calc b4.de* caust b4.de* graph b4.de* kali-c b4.de* mag-c b4.de* mag-m b4.de* nat-c b4.de* nat-m b4.de* nit-ac b4.de* petr b4.de* ph-ac b4.de phos b4.de* sep b4.de* sil b4.de* sulph b4.de*

TEMPERATURE:
- **change** of | **agg.**: acon bg2 puls bg2 verb b7a.de*

TENSION of skin: *(↗NOSE - Tension)* acon k* *Alum* k* am-c k* ambr k* ang b7.de* ant-t k* apis b7a.de arn b7.de* *Asaf* k* *Aur* b4.de* bamb-a stb2.de• *Bar-c* k* bar-m k* benz-ac k* berb k* borx b4a.de bov k* brom a1 bry b7.de* calc b4.de* cann-i k* cann-xyz ptk1 canth k* carbn-s k2 **Caust** bg2 chel b7.de* choc srj3• colch k* *Coloc* b4a.de* con b4.de* *Euph* k* gard-j vlr2• *Gels* k* graph k* *Grat* k* hep k* hist sp1 hyper k* irid-met srj5• kali-bi bg2* kali-c kali-chl k* kali-m k2 kali-n k* kali-p kreos b7a.de* *Lach* k* laur k* *Led* b7.de* lyc k* *M-arct* b7.de* m-aust b7.de *Mag-c* k* mag-m k* *Merc* k* merc-c bg2 merl k* *Mez* k* mosch k* nat-c b4.de* *Nat-m* nat-sil fd3.de• nit-ac h2* nux-v b7.de* olnd b7.de* par b7.de* petr b4.de* *Ph-ac* k* phel k* *Phos* k* plat b4.de* plut-n srj7• *Puls* k* rheum k* *Rhus-t* k* sabad k* samb k* sars b4a.de sep b4.de* spong b7.de* squil k* stann h2* staph h1* *Stront-c* b4a.de sul-ac b4.de* teucr b7.de* tritic-vg fd5.de verat k* verb b7.de* viol-o k* viol-t k*
- **one** side: benz-ac coloc h2 mag-c h2 phos k*
  - **drawn** to one side; as if muscles were: *(↗Cobweb - tension)* cist
- **right**: am-c h2* verat h1*
- **morning**: nit-ac h2*
  - **waking**; on: am-c k*
- **evening**: alum k* sacch-a fd2.de•
- **night**: apis sacch-a fd2.de•
  - **1-4** h: apis
- **acid**; as if the tears were: gard-j vlr2•
- **alternating** with constriction of occiput (See HEAD - Constriction - occiput - alternating)
- **chill**; during: acon bg2 **Bar-c** b4a.de* con bg2 lyc bg2 phos bg2 puls bg2 rhus-t bg2
- **egg** white were dried on the face; as if: *Alum* k* alum-p k2 *Bar-c* k* calad galla-q-r nl2• graph k* *Lec* *Mag-c* k* nat-m bg1 ol-an bg3* ph-ac k* sul-ac k* sulph k*

○ • **Lips**: ol-an ptk1 ph-ac ptk1
- **prosopalgia**, before: ign hr1
- **varnished**, as if: *Lec*
- **washing** agg.; after: lec oss•
- **white** of egg (See egg)

○ - **Cheek**; as from swelling of ambr a1*
- **Chin**: *Alum* k* cann-i a1 caust b4a.de* plat k* staph a1 verb b7.de*

○ • **Below**: staph h1*
- **Eyes**, below: nux-v k* viol-o k*
- **Forehead**: *(↗HEAD - Constriction - forehead)* am-c bell hr1 cann-i a1 cortico tpw7 dioxi rbp6 nat-sil fd3.de• *Nit-ac* k* par bg2 phos bg2 tritic-vg fd5.de *Viol-o* a1* viol-t b7a.de*
  - **drawing** upward of skin of forehead: carb-an merc bg3 phos k2
  - **frowning**; when: phasco-ci rbp2
- **Jaws**: arge-pl rwt5• meny h1* sacch-a fd2.de• suis-hep rly4• suprar rly4• tritic-vg fd5.de
  - **morning**: lyc

▽ • **extending** to | **Ear**: bell

○ • **Joints**: alum h2* colch k* *Merc* k* nat-m k* *Pin-con* oss2• sars h2* spig h1* *Stry* mrr1 verb hr1
  - ⁝ **chewing** agg.: alum h2* am-m h2*

Tension of skin – **Jaws** – **Joints**: ...
  - ⁝ **opening** the mouth agg.: alum h2* am-m h2*
  - **Lower**: alum k* *Am-m* b7a.de ang b7.de* apis b7a.de aur k* bar-c k* *Bell* k* bry b7.de* carbn-s **Caust** k* choc srj3• coca-c sk4• ign bg1 kali-bi bg2 lach lyc k* meny b7.de* merc k* mucs-nas rly4• nux-v bg2 op petr h2* *Phos* k* sars k* seneg k* spig b7.de* staph b7.de* stram k* *Stry* sulph tritic-vg fd5.de verb b7.de* [spect dfg1]
- **Lips**: am-c h2* apis choc srj3• crot-t a1 hep c1 kali-p fd1.de• lachn k* plan a1 sacch-a fd2.de• sal-fr sle1• spig k* sulph h2*

○ • **Lower**: apis b7a.de kreos bg2 ph-ac k* plan k* puls k* sacch-a fd2.de• sep k*
  - **Upper**: apis k* **Bell** k* *Hep* k* kreos b7a.de* mag-c k* mur-ac k* rhus-t k* sabad k* spig k* thuj k*
- **Malar** bones: aur k* bar-act a1 *Chel* b7a.de lec lyc h2* mag-m h2* *Phos* k* plat h2* tritic-vg fd5.de verat-v ptk1 verb h*
- **Mouth** and nose, around: nux-v k*
- **Muscles**; masseter: ang c1 bamb-a stb2.de• cyclosp sa3• kali-bi a1 ketogl-ac rly4• *Nux-v* k* sars h2* verb h
- **Parotid** glands: phos b4.de* sabad b7.de* sil b4.de*
  - **stooping** agg.: phos h2
  - **turning** head agg.: sep h2

THICK:
- **spots**: carb-an

○ - **Jaws** | **Lower**: hecla ptk1 hep bg2 sil bg2
- **Lips**: bar-c ptk1 bufo gk* calc ptk1 graph ptk1 med ptk1 merc ptk1 mez h2* nat-m ptk1 op mrr1 plat mrr1 psor ptk1 syph ptk1* zinc mrr1
  - **fleshy**, sensual: plat mrr1*
  - **mouth** breathing; from: med br1*
- **Skin**: bell k* parth vml3• rhus-v a1 viol-t k*

THIN: *(↗Emaciation)*

○ - **Eyebrow**; thinned | **left**: tell rsj10•
- **Lips**: dulc fd4.de

○ • **Upper**: bov zr sil zr
- **Skin** | **sensation** of a thin skin: *(↗SKIN - Thin - sensation)* bamb-a gm1

THINKING OF THE PAIN agg.: aur ptk1 spong b7.de*

TIC: *(↗MIND - Gestures - tics; MIND - Tourette's)* agar mrr1 der vml3• lyc h2 stram mrr1 zinc mrr1

TIC DOULOUREUX (See Pain - neuralgic)

TICKLING: *Bell* b4.de* cann-s b7.de* coloc b4.de* laur b7.de* phos b4.de* stront-c b4.de*
- **perspiration**; from: psor bg2

TIGHTNESS (See Clenched)

TINGLING: *Acon* k* alum ambr k* amph a1 apis k* arund atra-r bnm3• aur bamb-a stb2.de• bar-c bell cadm-met tpw6 calc k* cann-i caust k* *Colch* k* coli rly4• con bg2 crot-h cycl k* dros b7.de* dulc fd4.de *Ferr-ma* fuma-ac rly4• grat helodr-cal knl2• hep k* hist sp1 *Hydr* hr1 hydrog srj2• hyper k* irid-met srj5• kali-p fd1.de• kali-s fd4.de ketogl-ac rly4• kola stb3• lach lachn lact laur lyc k* lyss c1 melal-alt gya4 nad rly4• nat-pyru rly4• nat-sil fd3.de• nux-m k* nux-v ol-an k* olnd k* orot-ac rly4• ozone sde2• paeon plat pot-e rly4• ran-b rhus-g tmo3• rhus-t ruta fd4.de sabad sars bg2 *Sec* k* spong fd4.de stront-c k* suis-em rly4• suis-pan rly4• sul-ac symph fd3.de• thuj tritic-vg fd5.de
- **right**: aur dulc fd4.de elaps gymno oxal-a rly4• sinus rly4•
- **left**: bapt a1 euon hydrog srj2• kali-s fd4.de ruta fd4.de spong fd4.de zinc h2* [tax jsj7]
  - **followed** by | **right**: bamb-a stb2.de•
- **sides** are separated; as if: bamb-a stb2.de•
- **warm** room agg.: cadm-met tpw6

▽ - **extending** to | **Nose**: [heroin sdj2]

○ - **Beard**: ambr vh1
- **Cheeks**: *Acon* bro1 choc srj3• dulc fd4.de *Hyper* hr1 oxal-a rly4• plat bro1 ruta fd4.de sinus rly4• spong fd4.de suis-pan rly4• tritic-vg fd5.de [helia stj7]
  - **and** lips: agn *Arn* ars berb dros
- **Chin** and nose: ran-b verat
- **Eyes**:

○ • **Around**: ambr c1 kali-s fd4.de plut-n srj7•
  - **Under** eyes: ketogl-ac rly4•

Face

- **Forehead** (See HEAD - Tingling - forehead)
- **Jaws** | **Lower**: caust h2 mur-ac nad rly4•
- **Lips**: *Acon* k* apis k* arge-pl rwt5• arizon-l nl2• arn h1* arum-m ptk2 arum-t k2* chir-fl gya2 dulc fd4.de echi ferr-ma fuma-ac rly4• hydrog srj2• irid-met srj5• lyc bg2 *Nat-m* k* neon srj5• *Pic-ac* k* plac-s rly4• plut-n srj7• rhus-t bg2 sabad k* sal-fr sle1• stram bg2 streptoc rly4• suis-em rly4• suprar rly4• symph fd3.de• trios rsj11• [helia stj7]
  - **accompanied** by | **Head**; pain in (See HEAD - Pain - accompanied - lips)
  - ▽ **extending** to | **Vertex**: plut-n srj7•
  - O **Lower**: melal-alt gya4 plac-s rly4• plut-n srj7•
  - **Upper**: brucel sa3• hydrog srj2• olib-sac wmh1 paeon plut-n srj7• symph fd3.de•
- **Masseter** muscles:
  - **waking**; on:
    - **night**:
      - **midnight**:
        - **after** | **3** h: cyclosp sa3•
- **Mouth** | **Above**: dulc fd4.de hydrog srj2• tritic-vg fd5.de
- **Parotid** glands: phos
- **Whiskers**: ambr

TIRED FEELING: ozone sde2•

O - **Jaws**: *(↗Weakness - jaw)* alum cham iod nicc nit-ac tarent k* vip

TOUCH:

- **agg.**: *Acon* b7.de* ang bg2 ant-c b7.de* apis b7a.de ars b4.de* aur b4.de* bell b4.de* **Bry** b7.de* canth b7.de* *Caps* b7.de* *Cham* b7.de* *Chin* b7.de* *Cina* b7a.de coloc b4.de* cupr b7.de* dig b4.de* dros b7a.de* hell b7.de* *Hep* b4.de* ip b7.de* lappa ptk1 lyc b4.de* m-ambo b7.de *Merc* b4.de* merc-c b4a.de mez b4.de* nit-ac b4.de* *Nux-v* b7.de* op b7.de* petr b4.de* *Ph-ac* b4.de* *Phos* bg2 *Puls* b7.de* rhus-t b7.de* *Sabin* b7.de* sars b4.de* sil b4.de* *Spig* b7.de* spong b7.de* stann b4.de* *Staph* b7.de* *Zinc* b4a.de
  - O **Lips**: cadm-s ptk1
- **amel.**: am-c b4.de* am-m b7.de* asaf b7.de* chin b7.de* euphr b7.de* olnd b7.de* thuj b4.de*
- **hair** of the beard agg.; touching the: ign b7.de*
- **tongue** agg.; touching: bell bg2

TREMBLING: *Ambr* k* maias-l hrn2• merc k* *Op* k* plb k* sabad sec k*

- **right** then left: *Plb* bg1*
- **nervous**: thyr br1
- **spasmodic**: ambr k* sec k*
- **talking** agg.: merc k*
- O **Chin**: agar ptk1 *Ant-t* ptk1 gels ptk1 m-ambo b7.de
  - **accompanied** by | **Tongue**; trembling of (See MOUTH - Trembling - accompanied - chin)
- **Jaws**:
  - O **Lower**: aeth bg2* agar k* alum bro1 *Ant-t* bg2* apis b7a.de cadm-s k* carb-v k* *Cocc* k* *Gels* bg2* ign bg2* nat-c b4.de* nux-v bg2 op k* phos k* stry k* [arg-met stj1 zinc stj1]
    - **yawning** agg.: olnd c1*
- **Lips**: absin a1 *Agar* k* agar-ph a1 aloe k* *Ambr* b7a.de aml-ns bg2 *Arg-n* arn k* ars bg2 *Bell* k* benz-ac k* cann-i k* cann-xyz bg2 cit-v a1 crot-h k* *Gels* bg1* graph bg2 hep b4a.de iod k* lach k* lact k* nat-c bg2 *Nux-v* bg1* op k* ran-s k* *Stram* k* *Sulph* k* *Ter* bg1* *Zinc* bg1
  - **eating**; while: arn ptk1
  - **talking** agg.: arg-n ptk1
  - O **Lower**: ant-t bg1 arn k* bry k* con k* *Gels* bg1* kali-bi bg2 op bg2 plb k* puls b7.de* *Ran-s* bg2* sulph
    - **eating**; while: arn ptk1
    - **sensation** of trembling in lower lip: arn bg2 bry bg2 con bg2 kali-bi bg2 op bg2 plb bg2 puls bg2 *Ran-s* b7.de*
  - **Upper**: ars k* bell k* *Carb-v* ptk1 graph b4.de* hep k* nat-c b4.de ox-ac k*
    - **internal**: germ-met srj5•
- **Mouth**:
  - O **About**: ign ptk1 *Op* ptk1 senec ptk1* thuj ptk1
  - **Corners** of | **sensation** of: ran-s b7.de*

TRIGEMINAL NEURALGIA (See Pain - nerves - trigeminal)

TRISMUS (See Lockjaw)

TUMOR:

- **cystic** tumor: *Calc* b4a.de *Fl-ac* b4a.de *Graph* b4a.de
  - O **Cheek**; on: graph k* thuj ptk1*
  - **Lips**; on: ars sne *Con* kreos sep sil sne
    - **Lower**: ars sne phos sil sne
  - **Malar** bones: mag-c ptk
  - **Parotid** gland | **right**: bar-c sne bar-m sne calc k* calc-f sne con sne
- **hard**:
  - **walnut**; as a | **Cheeks**: hep hr1*
- O **Cheek**; on: thuj mtf33
- **Jaw**; on: astra-e jl1*
  - O **Upper** jaw: hecla bro1
- **Maxillary** bones; on: astra-e jl1 mag-c ptk1

TURNING HEAD agg.: *Bry* b7.de*

TWITCHING: *(↗MIND - Gestures - tics; MIND - Tourette's; NOSE - Twitching)* acon k* **Agar** k* agn b7a.de am-m k* *Ambr* k* aml-ns bg2 ant-c k* *Ant-t* k* arg-met b7.de arg-n bro1 arn k* *Ars* k* *Ars-i* ars-s-f k2 atra-r bnm3• atro aur-m bamb-a stb2.de• bar-c bar-s k2 bell k* bism bg2 borx b4a.de brom k* bry b7.de* bufo calc k* calc-i k2 calc-p mtf camph k* cann-s k* carb-ac carb-v k* carc fb* *Caust* k* *Cham* k* chel chlol cic k* *Cina* k* cocc colch k* *Con* crot-c cupr bro1* cupr-ar cyt-l sp1 cytin bro1 dros b7.de* dubo-h hs1 dys pte1• gels bg2* glon graph ham fd3.de• *Hell* hep b4.de* hist sp1 *Hyos* k* *Ign* k* *Iod* k* *Ip* k* kali-ar kali-c *Kali-chl* kali-i kali-m k2 kali-n kali-s lach bg2 *Laur* k* **Lyc** k* lyss m-ambo b7.de mag-c h2* mag-p bg2* maias-l hrn2• mang b4a.de meny k* merc bg2 merc-c b4a.de *Mez* k* *Mygal* k* nat-ar nat-c h2* *Nat-m* k* nat-sil fd3.de• nit-ac k* nux-v k* *Oena* k* olnd k* **Op** k* ox-ac k* petr-ra shn4• *Phos* k* plb k* puls k* ran-s k* rauw sp1 rheum b7.de* rhus-t b7.de* ruta fd4.de sang santin sec k* **Sel** k* senec ptk1 sep k* sil b4.de* spig k* spong b7.de* stann b4.de* staph mrr1 stram k* *Stront-c* k* stry *Sul-ac* k* sul-i k2 sulph k* syc fmm1• syph k* tell br1* thuj k* tub c1 valer k* verat k* verat-v visc bro1 **Zinc** k* zinc-p k2 ziz a1

- **right**: **Agar** bg2 calc bg2 *Caust* choc srj3• glon bg2 kali-n bg2 mez bg2 plb mtf33 puls spig bg2
  - **followed** by | **left**: aml-ns bg2
- **left**: agar arg-met bg2 arn bg2 *Calc* vh ham fd3.de• kali-c bg2 phos bg2 stront-c bg2 tell br1 valer bg2
  - **followed** by | **right**: bry bg2
- **morning**: *Nux-v* sulph
- **evening** | **lying** down agg.; after: ambr *Nux-v*
- **night**:
  - **sleep** | **during**: nat-c
- **accompanied** by:
  - **pain** in face: agar bro1 bell bro1 *Colch* bro1 kali-c bro1 nux-v bro1 thuj bro1 *Zinc* bro1
  - O **Feet** up to knees; cold and clammy: laur ll1*
- **asthma**: | **before**: bov ptk1
- **children**; in: androc bnm2•
- **cough** agg.; during: **Ant-t** k* kali-m ptk1
- **flatulence**; from: nat-c h2*
- **mercury**; after abuse of: *Kali-chl* *Nit-ac*
- **motion** of head, on: sul-ac h2*
- **pregnancy** agg.; during: *Hyos*
- **pressure** | **amel.**: am-c am-m h2* nux-m
- **protruding** tongue; when: hyos ptk1*
- **rest** agg.: meny
- **rubbing** | **amel.**: phos h2*
- **sleep** agg.; during: ars bg2 bry k* nat-c k* rheum h* viol-t b7a.de
- **talking** agg.: kali-m ptk1 plb sep k* sil til
- **thunderstorm**; before: agar mrr1*
- ▽ **extending** to | **Body**; whole: sec a1
- O **Cheek** muscles: mez tl1
  - **right**: mez ptk1
- **Chin**: m-ambo b7.de mag-m a1 nat-sil fd3.de• plat h2* sulph h2*
  - **children**; in: androc bnm2•

- **Eyes**; below: choc srj3• cic a1 nit-ac h2 ruta fd4.de spong fd4.de
  - **right**: rat c1 ther c1
  - **left**: aml-ns a1 cupr-ar c1 ruta fd4.de
- **Jaws**:

○ · **Lower**: acon b7.de* agar bg2 alum k* ant-t ptk1 arn b7.de* bell k* bry b7.de* cadm-s ptk1 canth b7.de* carb-v k* *Cham* b7a.de chin k* cina b7.de* cocc ptk1 con k* gels ptk1 ign b7.de* kali-chl lach m-ambo b7.de **M-arct** b7.de* mang k* merc-i-r mill nat-c a1 ol-an k* petr-ra shn4• phos h2* rhus-t b7.de* sabin b7.de* staph b7a.de *Sulph* valer b7.de*
  - **right**: nit-ac h2
  - **left**: sulph h2
  - **evening**: lyc
  - **night**: sil
  - **sleep**; when falling asleep: sulph
  - **walking** agg.: sabin
  - **Along**: stict bg2
- **Lips**: *Agar* bro1 *Ambr* b7a.de anac b4a.de ars b4.de* *Art-v* bro1 atra-r bnm3• bell bry b7.de* *Carb-v* k* *Cham* k* cimic bro1 dulc k* *Gels* bro1 ign br1* ip k* lact k* lact-v hr1 mygal bro1 nicc bro1 ol-an bg2* olnd b7.de op bro1 ran-b sabad b7.de senec bg2* sep h2* sil h2* squil stry bro1 *Sulph* k* tell ptk1 **Thuj** k* valer b7.de vip ptk1
  - **one** side: nat-c bg2 thuj bg2 zinc bg2
  - **morning**:
    - **bed** agg.; in: plat h2
    - **sleep**; during: ol-an
  - **children**; in: androc bnm2•
  - **cold** air agg.: dulc k*
  - **convulsions**; during: sil ptk1
  - **sleep** | **during** | **agg.**: anac
    - **falling** asleep | **when**: **Ars**
  - **talking** agg.: arg-n ptk1

○ · **Below**: choc srj3•
  - **Lower**: bry b7.de* cann-i a1 carc fd2.de• crot-c sk4• hipp ind bg1 plut-n srj7• *Puls* bg1* *Thuj* bg1* valer b7.de*
  - **Upper**: *Agar* k* *Ars* **Carb-v** k* *Graph* hep b4a.de* irid-met srj5• nat-c b4.de* nat-sil fd3.de• nicc ozone sde2• plat b4.de* plut-n srj7• sabad b7.de* stront-c b4.de* symph fd3.de• *Thuj* k* *Zinc* k*
    - **left** side: gink-b sbd1•
    - **extending** to:
      - **Eye** | **left**: ptel c1
- **Malar** bones: glon bg2
  - **left**: glon a1
- **Molars**; upper (See TEETH - Twitching - molars - upper)
- **Mouth**: cub c1
  - **sleep** agg.; during: anac k*

○ · **Around**: aeth a1 borx bg2 bry bufo dgt1 *Chel* guare *Ign* k* mag-p mosch nat-sil fd3.de• olnd bg2 **Op** phys plat *Rheum* k*
  - **Corners** of: anac ant-c k* *Bell* b4a.de borx *Bry* *Chel* *Ign* k* mag-p olnd k* *Op* k* ozone sde2• petr-ra shn4• rheum k* zinc
    - **left** corner:
      - **night**:
        - **midnight**:
          - **after** | **4** h: coch c1
- **Zygoma**: kali-n h2* phos h2* spig h1* sulph h2*
  - **toward**: thuj h1

ULCERS: anan ant-t apis b7a.de **Ars** k* aur b4a.de aur-m-n bamb-a stb2.de• *Bry* b7.de* *Con* k* cund *Graph* b4a.de *Hep* iod k* *Kali-ar* kali-bi *Kali-chl* *Kali-i* kali-m k2 *Kreos* b7a.de *Lach* merc k* mez k2 nat-m *Nit-ac* *Phos* k* *Phyt* *Psor* sep b4a.de *Sil* b4a.de* thuj vesp
- **bluish**: *Glycyr-g* cte1•
- **burning**: hep h2* nux-v
- **cold** applications | **amel.**: glycyr-g cte1•
- **eating** agg.: *Ars* *Con* k* nux-v *Phos*
- **hard** edges: *Kali-bi*
- **induration**, surrounded by: cina a1
- **putrid**: merc
- **rodent** ulcers: con bro1 cund c2 ferr-pic c2 jug-c c2 mill c2 phyt c2

Ulcers: ...
- **sensitive** to air: **Hep**
- **serpiginous**: caust kali-bi sne *Staph*
- **small** sized: *Glycyr-g* cte1•
- **wart**-like: **Ars** k*

○ - **Cheeks**: ant-c ant-t calc iod nat-m phos psor k2
  - **right**: hir skp7•
  - **painful** | **eating** agg.: hir skp7•
- **Chin**: *Ars* b4a.de **Cund** k* hep k* merc *Nat-m* k* *Nit-ac* k* sep syph k2
- **Forehead**: *Sil* hr1
- **Jaws** | **Lower**: *Ang* b4a.de* *Hep* b4a.de *Rhus-t* b7a.de *Sil* b4a.de
- **Lips**: agath-a nl2• am-m k* anan ant-c bg2 antip vh1 arg-n bg2 **Ars** k* ars-s-f k2 *Aur* bg2 aur-ar k2 *Aur-m* k* aur-s k2 bamb-a stb2.de• bell k* beryl vk1 borx bg2* bov k* *Bry* k* *Caps* k* carbn-s *Caust* *Cham* k* chin k* chinin-ar *Cic* k* *Clem* *Con* k* dulc b4.de* flor-p rsj3• *Graph* k* hep k* *Kali-ar* *Kali-bi* k* *Kali-c* k* kali-chl kali-m k2 kali-p kali-sil k2 lyc k* *Mag-c* mand rsj7• mang bg2 *Merc* k* *Mez* k* mim-p rsj8• musca-d szs1 nat-ar *Nat-c* k* *Nat-m* k* **Nit-ac** k* nux-v k* *Ph-ac* k* *Phos* *Phyt* *Psor* sep k* **Sil** k* staph k* **Stram** k* sulph k* syph k2 thuj bg2 tub jl2 *Zinc* k* zinc-p k2
  - **acrid** saliva from: *Nit-ac*
  - **air** agg.; in open: ars h2
  - **burning**: *Caust* chin h1* *Cic* nux-v staph sulph h2*
  - **cancerous**: *(↗Cancer - lips)* *Ars* k* aur sne *Aur-m* carb-an *Clem* **Con** cund sne *Kali-bi* k* lyc *Phos* phyt
  - **crusty**: staph h1*
  - **itching**: chin k* staph h1*
  - **lardaceous** base: caps k2
  - **painful** on motion: ars h2* caps h1*
  - **phagedenic**: *Ars* caps k2 *Con*
  - **serpiginous**: borx kali-bi sne
  - **splinter**, with sensation of a: bov **Nit-ac**
  - **touch** agg.: ars h2*

○ · **Glands**: ign b7.de*
  - **Lower**: *Ars* b4a.de bamb-a stb2.de• borx b4a.de bry b7.de* calc-sil k2 caps b7.de* cassia-s ccrh1• *Caust* *Clem* ign b7.de* *Lyc* k* m-ambo b7.de merc b4.de* nux-v b7.de* ph-ac k* *Phos* k* puls b7.de* sep k* sil k* staph b7.de* sulph zinc k*
    - **Inner** surface (See MOUTH - Ulcers - lips - lower)
  - **Middle**: nat-m bg2
  - **Upper**: agath-a nl2• *Ars* b4a.de *Bar-c* b4a.de caps b7.de* caust k* kali-c k* merc k* *Mez* k* *Sars* b4a.de sep b4a.de sil b4a.de staph b7.de* *Zinc*
- **Mouth**:
  - **itching**: sil h2

○ · **Around**: agath-a nl2• dulc h2* *Nat-c* k* *Nit-ac*
  - **Corners** of: *(↗Cracked - mouth)* ail *Am-m* k* anan ant-c k* arn k* ars bro1 *Arum-t* bro1 arund bro1 aur-m-n *Bell* k* borx b4a.de *Bov* k* **Calc** k* carb-an carb-v k* chin-b c1 *Cocc* cund bro1 echi bro1 eup-per bro1 glycyr-g cte1• **Graph** k* hell b7.de* *Hep* k* ign k* ip *Kreos* b7a.de lyc bg2 *Mang* k* **Merc** k* mez k* *Nat-m* k* **Nit-ac** k* nux-v k* petr bg2* ph-ac b4a.de *Phos* k* *Psor* **Rhus-t** k* sec bro1 *Sil* k* *Staph* k* *Sulph* thuj k* zinc k* zinc-p k2
    - **extending** into | **Cheek**; inner: glycyr-g cte1•
- **Parotid** glands: bar-c calc-p rhus-t sars sil
- **Submaxillary** glands: *Kali-i*
- **Zygoma**: phos

VARICOSE veins (See Veins - varicose)

VEINS distended: *(↗NOSE - Veins)* acon bg2 ambr bg2 ars bg2 *Aur* sne bapt *Bar-c* bg2 *Bell* b4a.de* both-ax tsm2 bov bg2 calc bg2 *Caps* mrr1 caust bg2 **Chin** k* clem bg2 cupr bg2* dig ptk1 *Ferr* k* gels bg2 *Glon* k* graph bg2 **Lach** k* maias-l hrn2• nat-c bg2 nat-m bg2 *Op* k* ph-ac bg2 phos bg2 psor sang k* sars spig b7a.de* *Stram* bg2 sulph bg2 syph k2 tab bg2* thuj k*
- **children**; in: puls mtf33
- **nets** as if marbled: *Calc* caps k2 *Carb-v* k* *Caust* b2.de *Crot-h* **Lach** k* lyc k* *Plat* b2.de thuj k*
- **spider** nevi: *(↗SKIN - Nevi)* carb-v ptk1 lach ptk1 maias-l hrn2* *Plat* ptk1 sep ptk1 thuj ptk1
- **varicose**: crot-h mrr1 lach gk puls gk

○ - **Cheeks**: sulph mrr1
- **Chin**: *Plat* k*
- **Forehead**: abrot bg1* calad bg1 camph bg1 chin bg2* cub bg1 jab bg2 *Sulph* bg3*

○ · **Eyes**:
⁝ **Above** | **left**: dig ptk1
- **Lips**: *Crot-h* *Dig* k* lach gk puls gk
- **Nose**: both-a rb3 sulph mrr1
- **Temples**: abrot vh1 acet-ac k* aml-ns bg2 *Ars* k* aur bg2 bapt a1 **Bell** bg2 cact bg2* calc hr1 cedr bg2 **Chin** k* *Chinin-s* cub bg2* cupr bg2 *Ferr* k* *Glon* k* guaj k2 jab bg2 ph-ac h2* podo bg2 psor hr1* *Sang* k* stry sulph bg2* tab bg2 thuj k*. til a1 vanil fd5.de xan
  - · **accompanied** by | **Head**; pain in: carl bro1 gels bro1
  - · **menses**; during: *Croc*

VOMITING agg.: *Sulph* b4a.de

WAKING; on: ambr bg2 apis bg2 bov bg2 croc b7.de* hell b7.de* hep b4.de* m-arct b7.de nux-v b7.de* par bg2 puls b7.de* sabad b7.de* spig b7.de* verb b7.de*

WALKING:
- **agg.**: borx b4a.de guaj b4.de* laur b7.de* mang b4.de* merc b4.de* mur-ac b4.de* petr b4.de* sulph b4.de* thuj b4.de*
- **air**; in open:
  - · **after** | **agg.**: ran-s b7.de*
  - · **agg.**: mur-ac bg2 *Nux-v* b7.de*
  - · **amel.**: asar b7.de*
- **wind**; in the | **agg.**: *Puls* b7a.de

WARM:
- **agg.**: cham bg2 kali-c bg2 mag-c bg2 mez bg2 puls bg2
- **applications**:
  - · **agg.**: *Coloc* b4a.de
  - · **amel.**: coloc bg2 mag-p bg2 rhod bg2 rhus-t bg2
- **food**:
  - · **agg.**: *Mez* b4a.de
  - · **amel.**: rhod bg2 rhus-t b7.de*
- **room** | **agg.**: am-c b4.de* hep b4.de* *Mez* b4a.de

WARM AGG.; BECOMING: sabad b7.de* spig b7a.de

WARMTH:
- **amel.** | **heat** amel.: pip-n bg2

WARMTH; sensation of (See Heat - sensation)

WARTS: *Ars* b4a.de aur b4a.de *Calc* k* calc-s bro1 carb-an bro1 castm bro1 **Caust** k* **Dulc** k* kali-bi dg2 kali-br tl1 *Kali-c* k* lyc k* *Mag-c* b4a.de *Nit-ac* k* ruta fd4.de *Sep* k* sulph k* *Thuj* k*

○ - **Chin**●: *Lyc* k* *Sep* hr1 **Thuj** k*
- **Forehead**: castm bro1 castor-eq c1* ruta fd4.de
- **Lips**: calc b4a.de* *Caust* k* *Con* sne cupre-l sne kali-p sne kali-s **Nit-ac** k* sulph sne thuj k*

○ · **Lower**: dulc b4a.de
- **Mouth**; around: cund k* *Psor* k* *Sep* hr1

WASH in cold water, desire to: *(↗GENERALS - Cold - Bathing - desire)* *Apis* k* *Asar* k* aster vh bamb-a stb2.de• *Fl-ac* k* mez sabad

WASHING:
- **agg.**: con b4.de* ph-ac b4a.de sil b4.de* stann b4.de* *Thuj* b4a.de
- **amel.**: apis b7a.de ars bg2 *Phos* b4a.de sabad b7.de*

WATER:
- **sensation** of | **running** down face: verat b7.de*

WAXY: *(↗Shiny)* *Acet-ac* k* **Apis** k* apoc bg2 **Ars** k* *Aspar* *Calc* calc-p bg2* carb-v colch k2 con dulc k2 ferr bro1* *Ferr-ar* graph k2 hydr k2 kali-ar k2 lach bro1 mag-c k2* mang k2 **Med** k* merc-c bro1 mez k2 nat-c bro1 nat-m k* nit-ac ph-ac *Phos* k* psor jl2 sel ptk1 senec *Sep* k* *Sil* k* stann b4a.de* thuj k2* zinc

WEAKNESS:
- **right** side: atra-r bnm3•

○ - **Jaw**; of lower: *(↗Tired - jaws)* cham bg2 gels bg2 kalm bg2 nit-ac h2* ran-b bg2 vip bg2

Weakness – Jaw; of lower: ...
  - · **eating**; after: *Bar-c* k* cham bg1
- **Lips**; upper: card-m ptk1
- **Muscles**; of: botul br1

WEATHER:
- **cloudy** weather: | **agg.**: aloe bg2

WETTING: | **amel.**: mez b4.de*

WHISKERS (See Eruptions - whiskers; Hair - complaints - whiskers; Hair - falling - whiskers; Itching - whiskers; Tingling - whiskers)

WHITE of egg; sensation of (See Cobweb - sensation; Tension - egg)

WIND:
- **agg.**: chel bg2 sanic bg2
- **blowing** upon the face; as if wind (See Air)

WINE:
- **agg.**: acon b7a.de bell bg2 sabad b7.de*
- **from** wine; complaints as if: bell b4.de

WITHERED: kali-c b4a.de

WOOD agg.; smell of: graph b4a.de

WRAPPING part: | **amel.**: mez bg2 thuj bg2

WRINKLED: *(↗Shrivelled)* *Abrot* k* aeth agath-a nl2• alco a1 alum bg3* ant-t anthraci vh apis arg-met k2 arg-n bro1* *Ars* k* bar-c k* bell k* borx bro1 **Calc** k* calc-p bro1 carbn-h cham ptk1 con bro1 crot-t *Fl-ac* bro1 graph bg2 *Hell* k* hyos ptk1 iod bro1* kreos bro1 *Lyc* k* mag-m mrr1 merc k* nat-m k* nit-ac op k* ozone sde2• plb k* *Psor* bro1 *Pulx* br1* rheum bg2* rob *Sanic* bro1 *Sars* k* sec bg1* *Sep* b2.de* sil bro1 sin-n stram k* sulph bro1* syph ptk1* taosc iwa1• tarent mtf33 ter verat ptk1* zinc k* zinc-s
- **children**; in: abrot mtf33 arg-n mtf33 ars mtf33 bar-c mtf33 iod mtf33 op mtf33 sep mtf33 syph mtf33 tarent mtf33 zinc mtf33
  - · **newborns**: abrot mrr1 aeth mrr1
- **fine** superficial wrinkles: calc mtf33 gels mrr1
- **sensation** of: thuj bg2
- **sun**; after exposure to: pert-vc vk9

○ - **Cheeks**: **Lyc** mrr1 plb mrr1
- **Eyebrows**: **Hell** mrr1 **Lyc** mrr1 ox-ac *Rheum* bg1* stram k* ther viol-o bg1*
- **Eyes**; wrinkled around: choc srj3•
- **Forehead**●: *(↗HEAD - Wrinkling; MIND - Frown)* acet-ac k* agar bg2 alum k* am-c b2.de* brom k* bry b2.de* calc-p bg2 *Caust* k* *Cham* k* *Cycl* equis-h a1 *Graph* k* grat k* *Hell* k* hyos ptk1 kali-c dgt lachn c1 **LYC**● k* mang k* merc k* merc-c bg2 nat-m **Nux-v** b2.de* ox-ac phos puls dgt2 rheum k* rhus-t k* *Sep* k* *Stram* k* *Sulph* bg2 *Syph* bg1* taosc iwa1• verat ptk1 viol-o b2.de* zinc k*
  - · **accompanied** by | **Head**; complaints of (See HEAD - Complaints - accompanied - forehead)
  - · **headache**; during: aster *Caust* k* grat k* hell h1* hyos nat-m petr-ra shn4• phos **Stram** k* sulph verat ptk1 viol-o
  - · **meningitis**; in (See brain)
  - · **sensation** of: agath-a nl2• *Bapt* bro1 *Bell-p* bro1 *Graph* k* grat bro1 *Hell* bro1 phos bro1 prim-v bro1 thuj k*
  - · **straining** eyes; from: petr-ra shn4•
  - · **think**; when trying to: hell mrr1
  - · **vertical**: aur mtf lyc mtf

○ · **Brain** symptoms, in: grat ptk1 *Hell* k* **Stram** k*
  - · **Chest** symptoms, with: **Lyc** k*
- **Lips**: am-c bg1 *Verat* bg2

YAWNING agg.: ang b7.de* apis b7a.de arn b7.de* cocc bg2 *Ign* b7.de* *M-arct* b7.de* op b7.de* **Rhus-t** b7.de* sabad b7.de* *Staph* b7.de*

BLOOD vessels: | **Veins** distended (See Veins)

FOREHEAD; complaints of: agar b2.de* agn b2.de* alum b2.de* am-c b2.de* am-m b2.de* *Ambr* b2.de* anac b2.de* *Ant-c* b2.de* arg-met b2.de* arn b2.de* ars b2.de* aur b2.de* bar-c b2.de* bell b2.de* *Bov* b2.de* bry b2.de* *Calc* b2.de* canth b2.de* caps b2.de* carb-an b2.de* *Carb-v* b2.de* *Caust* b2.de* *Cham* b2.de* chel b2.de* chin b2.de* cic b2.de* *Clem* b2.de* cocc b2.de* colch b2.de* coloc b2.de* con b2.de* croc b2.de* dig b2.de* *Dros* b2.de*

Forehead; complaints of: ...
dulc b2.de* euph b2.de* graph b2.de* guaj b2.de* hell b2.de* **Hep** b2.de* iod b2.de* ip b2.de* kali-c b2.de* *Kreos* b2.de* laur b2.de* **Led** b2.de* lyc b2.de* mag-c b2.de* mag-m b2.de* mang b2.de* meny b2.de* merc b2.de* mur-ac b2.de* nat-c b2.de* *Nat-m* b2.de* nit-ac b2.de* nux-v b2.de* olnd b2.de* *Par* b2.de* **Ph-ac** b2.de* *Phos* b2.de* puls b2.de* rheum b2.de* rhod b2.de* **Rhus-t** b2.de* ruta b2.de* sabad b2.de* samb b2.de* sars b2.de* **Sep** b2.de* sil b2.de* spig b2.de* squil b2.de* *Staph* b2.de* sul-ac b2.de* **Sulph** b2.de* teucr b2.de* valer b2.de* verat b2.de* verb b2.de* viol-o b2.de* viol-t b2.de* zinc b2.de*

HAIR:

- **complaints** of:
  - ○ **Beard**: agar bg2 ambr bg2 *Calc* bg2 *Graph* bg2 *Mez* bg2 nat-c bg2 nat-m bg2 nit-ac bg2 plb bg2 sil bg2
  - **Margin** of hair: calc b2.de* hydr ptk1 kali-p ptk1 med ptk1 merc bg2 mez bg2 *Nat-m* b2.de* nit-ac bg2 olnd ptk1 petr bg2* *Sep* b2.de* *Sulph* ptk1 tell bg2* zinc bg2
  - **Whiskers**: agar b2.de* ambr b2.de* *Calc* b2.de* graph b2.de* *Mez* b2.de* nat-c b2.de* nat-m b2.de* nit-ac b2.de* plb b2.de* sil b2.de*
- **falling** of hair:
  - ○ **Beard**: *(↗whiskers)* agar dx calc dx *Caps* hr1 graph dx nat-m dx psor vh sphing mtf9 thal dx tub a*
  - **Chin**: graph ptk1
  - **Eyebrows**●: *Agar* k* ail alum k* *Anan* aur-m *Bell* b2.de* borx bro1 caust b2.de* hell k* kali-c k* med hr1* merc bro1 mill *Nit-ac* bro1 par b2.de* ph-ac k2* plb k* plb-act bro1 sanic bro1 sel k* sil k* sulph thal-xyz srj8• thuj b4a.de
    - ⁝ **Lateral** half: lach a thal dx thal-xyz srj8• **Thuj** a*
  - **Mustache**: bar-c k* kali-c k* nat-m bg2 plb k* sel k* tub mrr1*
    - ⁝ **left** side: tub xxb
  - **Whiskers**: *(↗beard)* agar k* alum k2 ambr k* *Anan* k* aur-m *Calc* k* carb-an *Graph* k* *Kali-c* k* *Nat-c* k* *Nat-m* k* nit-ac k* *Ph-ac* plb k* ran-b b7a.de sanic sel b7a.de* sil k* sphing c1* verat b7a.de
    - ⁝ **grief**; after: *Ph-ac*
- **fuzzy**: calc bg2 caust ptk1 nat-m bg2 psor bg2*
  - **hysteria**; in: nat-m ptk1* psor ptk1
- **gray**; becomes:
  - ○ **Beard**: *Lyc* mrr1
    - ⁝ **right**: *Lyc* mrr1
    - ⁝ **spots**; in: *Lyc* mrr1
- **growth** of hair: morg-p fmm1• syc bka1*•
  - **children**; in: calc nat-m ol-j k* psor sulph thyr c1
  - **women**; in: *(↗GENERALS - Hair - distribution)* stram mrr1
    - ⁝ **Chin**: ign vh ol-j ptk1
    - ⁝ **Lips**; upper: cortico sp1 hydrog srj2• nat-m kl ol-j pd* sep kl syc pte1*• thuj k13 thyr c1
    - ⁝ **Whiskers**: calc zr calc-s zr ign zr nat-m zr
  - ○ **Beard**: plut-n srj7•
  - **Eyebrows**:
    - ⁝ **thick**, bushy: med mtf **Sulph** mrr1
    - ⁝ **Between**: kali-n dgt phos dgt
- **painful** | **Beard**: nux-v b7.de*
- **sensation** of a: *(↗Cobweb - sensation)* carl k* chlol *Graph* laur k* led bg2 sulph vh sumb ptk1
  - ○ **Chin** | **right**: germ-met srj5•
- **white** | **Eyebrows**: ars-h k*

MARGIN OF HAIR (See Hair - complaints - margin)

PAROTID GLAND; complaints of:
am-c b2.de* arg-met b2.de* arn b2.de* ars bg2 aur b2.de* bar-c b2.de* **Bell** b2.de* brom bg2 *Bry* b2.de* *Calc* b2.de* calc-f ptk1 calc-i bg2 caps b2.de* *Carb-an* b2.de* *Carb-v* b2.de* caust b2.de* **Cham** b2.de* chin b2.de* clem bg2 cocc b2.de* **Con** b2.de* dig b2.de* dulc b2.de* euph b2.de* graph b2.de* hep b2.de* hyos b2.de* *Ign* b2.de* iod bg2* *Kali-c* b2.de* lyc b2.de* mag-c b2.de* mang b2.de* **Merc** b2.de* mez b2.de* nat-c b2.de* nit-ac b2.de* nux-v b2.de* petr b2.de* ph-ac b2.de* phos b2.de* phys bg2 phyt bg2* *Puls* b2.de* **Rhus-t** b2.de* *Sabad* b2.de* sep b2.de* *Sil* b2.de* staph b2.de* *Sulph* b2.de* thuj b2.de*

Parotid gland; complaints of: ...
- **accompanied** by | **rheumatic** complaints (See EXTREMITIES - Pain - rheumatic - accompanied - parotid)

TEMPLES; complaints of:
alum b2.de* ambr b2.de* *Anac* b2.de* **Ang** b2.de* ant-c b2.de* *Arg-met* b2.de* arn b2.de* asar b2.de* bar-c b2.de* bell b2.de* bry b2.de* *Calc* b2.de* carb-v b2.de* caust b2.de* chel b2.de* *Chin* b2.de* cocc b2.de* cycl b2.de* dros b2.de* ign b2.de* *Kali-c* b2.de* *Kreos* b2.de* lach b2.de* **Lyc** b2.de* mang b2.de* *Merc* b2.de* *Mur-ac* b2.de* **Nat-m** b2.de* nit-ac b2.de* *Par* b2.de* petr b2.de* ph-ac b2.de* phos b2.de* plat b2.de* **Puls** b2.de* rhus-t b2.de* sabad b2.de* *Sabin* b2.de* sep b2.de* sil b2.de* spig b2.de* sul-ac b2.de* sulph b2.de* *Thuj* b2.de* *Verb* b2.de* zinc b2.de*

- ○ **Veins**: ars ptk1 cupr ptk1 fl-ac ptk1 glon ptk1 ham ptk1 puls ptk1 sang ptk1 vip ptk1 zinc ptk1

Face

MORNING: acon b7.de* aloe bg2 alum b4.de* am-c b4.de* am-m b7.de* ambr b7.de* ant-c b7.de* *Apis* b7a.de arg-met b7.de* arn b7.de* ars b4.de* arum-t bg2 bar-c b4.de* bell b4.de* bov b4.de* bry b7.de* calc b4.de* calc-p bg2 camph b7.de* cann-s b7.de* canth b7.de* caps b7.de* carb-an b4.de* carb-v b4.de* caust b4.de* cham b7.de* chin b7.de* chinin-s bg2 clem b4.de* cocc b7.de* colch b7.de* coloc b4.de* croc b7.de* cupr b7.de* dig b4.de* fl-ac bg2 graph b4.de* hell b7.de* hep b4.de* hyos b7.de* ign b7.de* iod b4.de* kali-bi bg2 kali-c b4.de* kali-n b4.de* lach bg2 lyc b4.de* *M-ambo* b7.de* m-arct b7.de *M-aust* b7.de* mag-c b4.de* mag-m b4.de* mang b4.de* nat-c b4a.de* *Nat-m* b4.de* nit-ac b4.de* *Nux-v* b7.de* par b7.de* petr b4.de* phos b4.de* plat b4.de* plb b7.de* *Puls* b7.de* ran-s b7.de* rheum b7.de* rhod b4.de* rhus-t b7a.de sabad b7.de* sabin b7.de* sars b4.de* *Sel* b7a.de seneg b4.de* sep b4.de* sil b4.de* spig b7.de* spong b7.de* stann b4.de* stront-c b4.de* sul-ac b4.de* *Sulph* b4.de* tarax b7.de* valer b7.de* verat b7.de* verb b7.de* *Zinc* b4.de*

- **waking**; on: bar-c bg2 calc-p bg2 caust bg2 graph bg2 lach bg2 nat-c bg2

NOON: kali-bi bg2

NIGHT:

- **midnight** | **after**: nux-v bg2 puls bg2 rhus-t bg2

ABSCESS: *(↗Suppuration)*

○ - **Gums**; of: *(↗Boils; Fistula - gums; Pustules - gums; Suppuration - gums; Ulcers - gums)* alum am-c aur bell ptk1 bros-gau mrc1 *Bufo* calc-f ptk1 caust h2* cham k2 echi ptk1 euph *Hecla* k* helodr-cal knl2• *Hep* k* jug-r kali-bi gk lach merc k* petr phos plb *Sil* k* staph gk sul-ac h2

- • **painful**: borx br1
- • **recurring** frequently: *Bar-c* calc **Caust** k* *Hep* *Lyc* med gk *Nux-v* *Sil* k* *Sulph*
- • **sensation** of: am-c

- **Palate**: phos ptk1

○ • **Hard** palate: phos mtf33

- **Tongue**: calc hr1*
- • **accompanied** by | **pricking** pains: merc kr1*
- • **sublingual** abscess, opening externally: hippoz kr1*

○ • **Tip**: am-c bg2* dros bg2*

ADHERES to roof of mouth; tongue: *(↗Dryness - tongue; Sticky - tongue)* alum k* arg-met k* bell k* *Bry* k* caust k* hydrog srj2• kali-p kr1* laur bg2 nit-ac k* **Nux-m** k* sanic k* spong fd4.de sulph h2 syc pte1*•

AIR: | **drawing** in air | **agg.**: mez b4.de*

- **filled** with; as if: acon

AIR AGG.; DRAFT OF: ambr b7.de* chin b7.de*

AIR; IN OPEN:

- **agg.**: merc b4.de* merc-c b4a.de stann b4.de*
- **amel.**: bell bg2 kali-bi bg2

ANGER; after: *Staph* b7a.de

APHTHAE: *(↗Discoloration - white - patches; Thrush; Ulcers; GENERALS - Aphthae; NOSE - Aphthae)* acet-ac achy-a vk1 *Aeth* k* agar k* all-s allox sp1 alum alum-sil k2 amp rly4• anac-oc hr1 anan k* *Anis* vk1 ant-c br1* ant-t bg2* apis k* aral vh arg-met arg-n br1 arge-pl rwt5• **Ars** k* *Ars-i* ars-s-f k2 *Arum-t* k* asim k* astac kr1 atp rly4• aur k* aur-ar k2 aur-i k2 aur-m k* aur-s **Bapt** k* bell b4a.de *Berb* k* **Borx** k* brom k* bros-gau mrc1 *Brucel* sa3• b r y k* cadm-met tpw6 *Calc* k* calc-i k2 calc-sil k2 *Camph* hr1 canth k* caps k* *Carb-ac* k* *Carb-an* k* *Carb-v* k* carbn-s carc mlr1• cardios-h rly4• caul k* cean cham k* *Chel* b7a.de chin k* *Chin-b* c1 chinin-ar chlor cic cinnb bg2 clem k* cocc k* corn cub k* cystein-l rly4• der a1 *Dig* k* dulc k* elaps gk eucal a1 *Eup-a* br1* *Ferr* ferr-s hr1 ferul a1 gamb k* gink-b sbd1• *Hell* k* *Hep* k* hippoz hydr k* *Hydrin-m* bro1 ina-i mlk9.de *Iod* k* *Ip* b7.de* *Jug-c* k* *Kali-ar* *Kali-bi* k* *Kali-br* k* *Kali-c* k* **Kali-chl** k* kali-i k* *Kali-m* bg2* kali-s kali-sil k2 *Kreos* k* *Lac-ac* k* lac-c lac-d lac-del hrn2• *Lac-e* hrn2• lac-h sk4• *Lach* k* *Lyc* k* *Mag-c* k* mand sp1 med c1* **Merc** k* **Merc-c** k* *Merc-cy* hr1* *Merc-d* hr1 *Moni* jl2 **Mur-ac** k* *Myric* k* *Nat-ar* k* nat-c k* nat-hchls *Nat-m* k* nat-ox rly4• *Nit-ac* k* nux-m k* **Nux-v** k* oci-sa sp1* olib-sac wmh1 ox-ac k* oxyg c2 ozone sde2• pant-ac rly4• petr k2 petr-ra shn4• *Phos* k* phyt k* pin-con oss2• plac-s rly4• plan k* *Plb* k* pneu jl2 podo fd3.de• pot-e rly4• propl ub1• prot jl2 psil ft1 psor k2* ran-b bg2 ran-s k* *Rhus-g* bro1* rhus-t bg2 ribo rly4• *Ros-d* wla1 ruta fd4.de sal-ac k* sanic *Sars* k* sec k* *Semp* c1* sep bg2 sil k* sin-n mrr1 s p o n g fd4.de *Staph* k* succ-ac rly4• suis-pan rly4• **Sul-ac** k* sul-i k2 **Sulph** k*

Aphthae: ...
tarent vk1 ter k* thiam rly4• thioc-ac rly4• thuj k* tritic-vg fd5.de tub c1* urol-h rwt• vanil fd5.de vinc k* zinc b4a.de

- **accompanied** by:
- • **eruptions**; vesicular: corn br1
- • **noise**; sensitivity to (See MIND - Sensitive - noise - aphthae)
- • **salivation**: der vml3• *Hell* kr1* kali-c mtf33 **Merc** kr1* **Merc-c** kr1* *Nat-m* kr1*

○ • **Tongue**; cracked (See Cracked - tongue - accompanied - aphthae)

- **black**: bapt k2
- **bleeding**:
- • **easily**: **Borx** *Lac-c* psil ft1*
- • **ichor**; bloody, offensive: *Sul-ac*
- **bluish**: **Ars** k*
- **burning**: ars mrr1 chinin-ar *Kali-c* hr1 *Nat-m* k* psil ft1 sulph
- **chewing** gums; from: merc ptk1
- **children**; in: ars lmj *Asim* hr1* *Bapt* k2* **Borx** k* bry hr1* **Calc** vh* casc hep lmj hydr k2 *Kali-br* hr1* *Kali-chl* k* kali-m c1* lac-ac mp1• med c1* **Merc** k* *Mur-ac* k* nat-m lmj* *Nux-m* k* *Nux-v* k* oxal-s bta1• *Plan* k* psor lmj sacch k* sil lmj* *Staph* hr1 **Sul-ac** k* sulph k* viol-o hr1 viol-t st1
- • **infants**: borx mp1• *Bry* st1 calc mp1* *Corn* bg2 merc bg2 nux-v bg2 *Sul-ac* bg2 sulph bg2
- ⁝ **recurrent**: calc mtf33
- • **nurslings**: bapt ptk1 borx mtf33 corn br1 *Nat-m* sne **Phos** sne phyt sne sil mtf33 *Staph* sne sul-ac k2 sulph mtf33
- ⁝ **eruption**; with vesicular | **face**; in: corn br1
- **complaints**; with: brom dgt1
- **diarrhea**, with lienteric: hell ptk1*
- **eruption**; with vesicular (See accompanied - eruptions)
- **gangrenous**: *(↗Stomatitis - gangrenous)* *Ars* carb-ac cocc k* lach merc-d plb
- **infants** (See children - infants)
- **influenza**: *Ant-t* st1 nat-m mp1•
- **mercury**; from: **Carb-v** bg2 chin bg2 dulc bg2 *Hep* bg2 iod bg2 nat-m bg2 *Nit-ac* bg2 staph bg2 sulph bg2
- **nursing**:
- • **infants** (See children - nurslings)
- • **mothers**: bapt k2* eup-a sne helon sne hydr k2* kali-m c1* *Lach* sne nat-c sne sul-ac k2 *Sulph* sne
- **offensive**: bapt k2
- **periodical**: sul-ac mrr1
- **pregnancy** agg.; during: helon ptk2 kreos ptk1
- **salt**; abuse of: borx ptk1 carb-v bg2
- **small** and sore: med ptk1*
- **white**: *Ars* k* *Borx* k* *Hell* b4a.de ozone sde2• *Sul-ac* k* vanil fd5.de
- • **red** edges; with: ozone sde2•
- **yellowish** base: *Staph* k*

▽ - **extending** to | **Intestinal** tract; through: *(↗Thrush - extending - gastrointestinal)* ars mrr1 borx mrr1 sul-ac mrr1 *Ter* k*

○ - **Gums**: amp rly4• colch cub hr1* *Hep* k* maias-l hm2• **Nat-m** k* petr-ra shn4• spong fd4.de *Sul-ac* k*

○ • **Incisors**; between: oci-sa sk4•

- **Lips**:

○ • **Inner** side of:

- ⁝ **Lower**: nept-m lsd2.fr
- ⁝ **Upper**: lac-h sk4• nept-m lsd2.fr oci-sa sk4•

- **Palate**: agar k* agav-a bro1* aral vh1 borx b4a.de* *Calc* *Hell* b4a.de *Hep* kali-bi ptk1* lac-e hm2• *Merc* b4a.de *Nux-m* k* phasco-ci rbp2 *Phos* k* sars k* semp st1* spong fd4.de sul-ac b4a.de*
- • **mercurial**: agar aur sars a1 sulph

○ • **Hard** palate: borx bg2 carb-v bg2 sars bg2

- **Tongue**: aeth k* agar k* amp rly4• *Anis* k* aran-ix vk1 ars k* ars-s-f k2 arum-d k* arum-t k2 atp rly4• aur k* aur-s k2 **Borx** k* camph k* *Carb-v* b4a.de* carbn-s k2 caul kr1* caust vk1 cham vk1 *Dulc* b4a.de gink-b sbd1• graph k2 hell b4a.de* hydr k* iod k2 *Jug-c* k* kali-chl ptk1 *Lac-ac* vk1 *Lach* k* mand sp1* m e d c1* *Merc* k* *Merc-cy* k* *Mur-ac* k* *Nat-m* k* nux-v k* ox-ac k* ozone sde2• parathyr jl2 *Phos* k* plac-s rly4• plb k* raja-s vk1 sars k* *Sul-ac* k* *Sulph* k* tarent k* thuj k* tub c1

Mouth

- **Tongue**: ...
  - **accompanied** by:
    - **diphtheria** (See THROAT - Diphtheria - accompanied - tongue - aphthae)
    - **scabs**:
      - **thick**: merc-cy kr1*
      - **white** | **yellowish** white: merc-cy kr1*
    - **speech**; impeded (See Speech - difficult - accompanied - tongue - aphthae)
    - **stomatitis** (See Stomatitis - accompanied - tongue - aphthae)
    - **tuberculosis**; beginning (See CHEST - Phthisis - incipient - accompanied - tongue)
    - **typhus** fever (See FEVER - Typhus - accompanied - tongue - aphthae)
  - **bleeding**: **Borx** raja-s vk1
  - **burning**: *Nat-m* kr1*
  - **large** aphthae: *Jug-c* kr1*
  - **mercury**; after abuse of: *Agar* kr1* *Sars* kr1*
  - **painful**: merc-cy kr1* sul-ac mrr1
    - **nursing**; prevents child from: **Borx** kr1* cean vk1 merc vk1 nux-v vk1 sul-ac vk1 sulph vk1
  - **patches**; in: *Phos* kr1*
  - **salt** agg.; eating: [*Moly-met* stj2]
  - **scabs**; with (See accompanied - scabs - thick)
  - **sensitive**: **Borx**
  - **small** | **dirty** yellow: agar kr1* iod vk1 sulph vk1
  - **sore** points: *Thuj* kr1*
  - **spots**, in: *Phos* kr1* *Sul-ac* k*
  - **tender** (See painful)
  - **ulcers**; forming: merc-cy kr1*
  - ○ **Below**: gink-b sbd1• med c1 streptoc rly4•
  - **Edges**: anis kr1* arg-n ptk1 bov hr1*
  - **Tip**: agar k* anthraq rly4• atp rly4• *Bry* k* graph k2 *Ham* k* kali-i mrr1 *Lach* k* med c1 phasco-ci rbp2 raja-s vk1

ASCENDING STAIRS agg.: nux-v b7.de*

ASLEEP (See Prickling)

ASTRINGENT sensation: chin h1*

ATROPHY:

- ○ **Gums**: kali-c k* *Merc* k* musca-d szs1 plb k*
- **Tongue**: mur-ac b4a.de* plb bg2
  - **accompanied** by | **cancer** of tongue and speaking with a thick hoarse voice (See Cancer - tongue - accompanied - atrophy of tongue and)
  - ○ **Papillae**: arg-n bg2

BATHING:

- **sea**; in the | **agg.**: nat-m bg2 zinc bg2

BEER agg.: merc-c b4a.de

BENDING:

- **head**:
  - **backward**:
    - **agg.**: chin b7.de*
    - **amel.**: *Cham* b7.de*

BITING: (↗*MIND - Biting)*

- **glass** when fed: ars bg1 bell bg1 cham bg1 *Cina* bg1* *Cupr* bg1* *Puls* bg1* *Verat* bg1*
- ○ **Cheeks**: carb-an h1* cardios-h rly4• caust bg2 *Ign* b7.de* nit-ac bg2
  - **sleep**; during: rhus-g tmo3•
  - **talking** or chewing; when●: (↗*lips - lower - eating; tongue - chewing)* *Aur-m-n* wbt2• bufo ptk1 carb-an k* **Caust** k ●* *Cic* ptk1 dulc fd4.de hyos ptk1 **IGN** k ●* nat-sil fd3.de• **Nit-ac** k* ol-an c1* petr-ra shn4• phos sne sal-fr sle1• spong fd4.de vanil fd5.de [heroin sdj2]

Biting: ...

- **Lips**: anac sne **Arum-t** vh1* benz-ac sne choc sne ham fd3.de• kali-n sne sep sne spong fd4.de symph fd3.de• tritic-vg fd5.de vanil fd5.de
  - **chewing** lips: choc srj3•
  - ○ **Lower** lip: aur-m-n wbt2• benz-ac ham fd3.de• kali-p fd1.de• nat-sil fd3.de• podo fd3.de• symph fd3.de• tritic-vg fd5.de vanil fd5.de
    - **eating**; when: (↗*cheeks - talking)* benz-ac hr1* tritic-vg fd5.de vanil fd5.de
- **Nails** (See MIND - Biting - nails)
- **Tongue**: absin k* acet-ac k* acon vk1 agar k* alum k* anis bro1* *Arn* vk1 ars vk1 *Asar* bg2* **Bell** vk1 **Bufo** k* carb-ac k* *Caust* k* *Cham* bg2* *Chin* vk1 *Cic* k* colch k* *Coloc* vk1 *Croc* vk1 *Cupr* b7a.de dig k* dios k* *Dros* vk1 dulc fd4.de gink-b sbd1• glon k* *Hydr* bro1* *Hyos* k* **IGN** k ●* iod a1 ip vk1 jal kr1* kola stb3• lach k* merl k* mez k* nat-c a1* *Nat-m* k* *Nit-ac* k* oena bg2* *Ol-an* vk1 *Op* vk1 petr k* petr-ra shn4• *Ph-ac* k* plb b7.de* *Puls* k* ran-s vk1 ruta fd4.de sec k* sep vk1 stram k2 sulph k* teucr vk1 ther bg2* thuj k* tritic-vg fd5.de vanil fd5.de verat k* vip bg2* zinc vk1
  - **morning**: art-v k*
  - **night** | **sleep**; in: alum k* apis k* *Cic* k* med k* mez k* *Mygal* vh *Ph-ac* k* phos ptk2 ther k* zinc k* [tax jsj7]
  - **accompanied** by:
    - **typhoid** fever (See FEVER - Typhoid - accompanied - tongue - biting - sleep)
    - **Brain**; concussion of (See HEAD - Concussion - accompanied - tongue)
  - **bitten**; as if (See Pain - tongue - bitten)
  - **chewing** agg.: (↗*cheeks - talking)* dulc fd4.de **Ign** kr1* *Nit-ac* kr1* ruta fd4.de
  - **convulsions**; during: absin c1 *Art-v* k* *Bufo* k* camph k* *Caust* k* *Cic* vk1* cocc k* *Cupr* k* lach vh nit-ac h2* *Oena* k* *Op* k* plb a1 sec k* stram k2 tanac c1 tarent k* valer k*
    - **epileptic** (See GENERALS - Convulsions - epileptic - during - tongue - biting)
    - **hysterical**: *Cic* kr1*
  - **drinking** agg.; when not: dios kr1*
  - **easily**; biting (See tongue)
  - **eating** agg.; when not: dios kr1*
  - **followed** by | **unconsciousness**: *Oena* kr1*
  - **shock** in head; caused by: agar kr1*
  - **spasms**; in (See convulsions)
  - **swelling** of tongue; from: thuj mtf33
  - **talking**; when: *Hyos* kr1* **Ign** kr1*
  - ○ **Sides**:
    - **night** | **sleep**; in: *Ph-ac* vk1
  - **Tip**: bell bg2* *Puls* kr1* ther ptk1 vanil fd5.de
    - **sleep**; during: med kr1* ther kr1*

BITING sensation: acon am-m ambr asar aur-m cham h1* cupr-s

BLEEDING: *Acon* k* *Adren* br1 ail bg2 alum-p k2 alumn hr1 am-c am-caust a1 *Arn* k* *Ars* k* ars-h a1 ars-i *Arum-t* bapt k2* bar-m *Bell* k* borx b4a.de* bry bg2* but-ac sp1* calc b4a.de canth k* *Carb-v* *Carbn-s* *Chel* **Chin** k* chinin-ar cina k* cop bg2 *Cor-r* k* **Crot-h** k* cupr dros k* eug hr1 *Ferr* k* ferr-ar ferr-p gamb a1 ham hed sp1 **Hep** k* *Hyos* bg2 *Ip* k* irid-met srj5• ketogl-ac rly4• *Kreos* k* *Lach* k* led k* lyc k* mag-m b4.de* manc k* *Merc* k* *Merc-c* k* nat-m bg2 *Nit-ac* bg2 nux-m k* *Nux-v* k* oxyurn-sc mcp1• ozone sde2• **Phos** k* phyt c1 plb bg2 positr nl2• rhus-g a1 *Rhus-t* k* ruta fd4.de *Sec* k* spong fd4.de stram bg2* succ-ac rly4• *Sul-ac* k* sulph bg2 ter k* tril-p tritic-vg fd5.de vanil fd5.de vario

- **forenoon**: chel
- **accompanied** by | **cough**: **Dros** bg2 *Ip* bg2 nux-v bg2
- **blood**:
  - **black** blood: *Carb-v* *Crot-h* k* *Lach* k*
  - **clotted**: canth *Caust* k* coch k* vac hr1
  - **red**; bright: dros mtf33
- **continuous**, does not coagulate: anthraci crot-h
- **convulsions**; during: bufo k2
- **cough** agg.; during: *Dros* b7a.de

- **easily**: **Hep** k* lach **Phos** k*
- **oozing** of blood: ail k* anthraci ars-h a1 *Chel* k* crot-h lach k* merc-c k* *Phos* k* rhus-t k* stram k2 *Sul-ac* ter k*
- **scarlet** fever; during: **Arum-t** k*
- **whooping** cough; in: *Cor-r* k* dros k* ip k* *Merc* hr1 nux-v k*

○ - **Cheek** | **spot** inside: mag-c h2

- **Gums**: *Agar* k* agav-a br1 ail k* *Alum* k* alum-p k2 alum-sil k2 alumn hr1* *Am-c* k* ambr k* anac k* *Ant-c* k* ant-t k* apis k* arg-met k* *Arg-n* k* arn bg2* ars k* ars-h a1 ars-s-f k2 arum-m k* arum-t arund k* asc-t a1* aur k* aur-i k2 aur-s a1* bapt k* **Bar-c** k* bar-i k2 bar-m k2 bar-s k2 *Bell* k* berb k* bit-ar wht1• borx k* **Bov** k* bufo **Calc** k* calc-sil k2 carb-an k* **Carb-v** k* carbn-s carl a1 cary a1 *Caust* k* cedr k* *Chel* k* chinin-s cist k* colch con k* crot-c **Crot-h** k* crot-t k* cyclosp sa3• der a1 dros gk erig k* euphr k* fago a1 ferr ferr-ar ferr-i k* ferr-ma k* ferr-p k* *Graph* k* *Ham* k* *Hep* k* hippoz k* hir rsj4• hyos k2 *Iod* k* irid-met srj5• kali-ar kali-bi k* kali-br hr1 kali-c k* kali-chl k* kali-i bg2 kali-m k2 kali-n k* *Kali-p* k* kali-s kali-sil k2 ketogl-ac rly4• kreos k* lac-c k* lac-h htj1*• **Lach** k* lob-s a1 lyc k* mag-c *Mag-m* k* **Merc** k* **Merc-c** k* merc-n a1 mez k* mim-h a1 *Moni* jl2 mur-ac k* musca-d szs1 *Myric* k* nat-ar nat-c k* **Nat-m** k* nat-p nat-sil fd3.de• **Nit-ac** k* *Nux-m* k* *Nux-v* k* olib-sac wmh1 ox-ac k* oxal-a rly4• ozone sde2• petr k* petr-ra shn4• *Ph-ac* k* **Phos** k* pin-con oss2• plan k* plb k* positr nl2• propl ub1• psil ft1 *Psor* k* *Puls* b7a.de ran-s k* rat k* rhus-g tmo3• rhus-t b7a.de* rob k* ruta k* sacch-a fd2.de• sal-ac tl1 *Sang* k* *Sec* k* sel rsj9• **Sep** k* *Sil* k* sin-n k* sphing k* spig k* spong fd4.de *Staph* k* *Sul-ac* k* sul-i k2 *Sulph* k* tab bg2 tarax tarent hr1 tell k* tep a1 *Ter* k* tetox pin2• thuj k* tril-p tritic-vg fd5.de tub jl2 tub-r jl2 vanil fd5.de visc c1 *Zinc* k* zinc-p k2 [heroin sdj2]
  - **morning**: ham fd3.de• ruta fd4.de sep h2* tritic-vg fd5.de vanil fd5.de
  - **afternoon**: chel a1 plan a1
    - **15 h**: ferr-i
  - **night**: calc h2 graph
  - **accompanied** by:
    - **indigestion**: kali-p mrr1
    - **sour** taste: graph ptk1
  - **black** blood: but-ac sp1 graph h2*
    - **oozes** out: bov kreos
    - **teeth** are extracted; when: *Ars*
  - **cleaning** them, when: am-c *Anac* bung-fa mtf calc-s k* *Carb-v* k* carc fd2.de• dream-p sdj1• *Graph* ham fd3.de• *Hir* rsj4*• irid-met srj5• kali-chl kali-p fd1.de• kali-s fd4.de *Lyc* k* olib-sac wmh1 ox-ac ozone sde2• ph-ac *Phos* mp1• plac rzf5• podo fd3.de• positr nl2• ruta sacch-a fd2.de• sep spong fd4.de *Staph* k* symph fd3.de• *Ter* k* tritic-vg fd5.de vanil fd5.de [heroin sdj2 pop dhh1]
  - **coagulates** quickly; blood: kreos
  - **copious**: ambr a1* ruta fd4.de
  - **easily**: *Agav-a* bro1 alum k* *Am-c* k* ambr bro1 *Anac* *Ant-c* k* apis arg-met c1 *Arg-n* k* *Arn* bro1 ars k* ars-h a1 ars-i k2 arum-m k* asc-t k* aur k* aur-ar k2 bapt bro1 bar-c br1 benz-ac bro1 berb k* borx bro1 *Bov* k* calc bro1 calc-i k2 *Carb-an* k* **Carb-v** k* **Caust** hr1* *Cist* k* con k* **Crot-h** k* echi bro1 gran *Ham* k* **Hep** k* hippoz hr1 hydrog srj2• *Iod* k* *Kali-chl* k* *Kali-p* k* **Kreos** k* lac-e hrn2• **Lach** k* luna kg1• lyc *Mag-m* k* *Merc* k* **Merc-c** k* *Merc-i-f* hr1 **Nat-m** k* nit-ac k2* *Ph-ac* k* **Phos** k* plan hr1* rob k* ruta scroph-n c1 *Sep* k* sil bro1 staph bro1 *Sul-ac* k* sulph bro1 tell k* tub xxb *Zinc* k*
  - **extraction** of teeth; profuse after: alumn **Arn** k* ars bro1 bov bro1 *Calen* br1* chin bro1 *Ham* k* *Kreos* k* **Lach** mill k2* **Phos** k* tril-p c1*
  - **fever**; during: carb-v bg2 graph bg2 phos bg2 *Staph* b7.de*
  - **menses** | **during**:
    - **agg.**: *Cedr* k*
      - **Around** decayed tooth: bell k*
    - **suppressed** menses; from: *Calc* k*
  - **pain**; with: agar
  - **perspiration**; during: ars bg2 carb-v bg2 merc bg2 nat-m bg2 *Sep* bg2 **Staph** bg2 sulph bg2
  - **pressing** with finger; large quantity oozes when: *Bapt* k* graph k* staph h1
  - **scanty**: but-ac sp1*
  - **scurvy**: *(↗Scorbutic)* ant-t k* **Ars** k* carb-ac mtf11 *Carb-an* k* cit-l mtf11 coch mtf11 hydr mtf11 kali-perm mtf11 merc-i-r mtf11 *Mur-ac* k* *Nat-m* k* *Nux-v* k* *Sulph* k*

Bleeding – Gums: ...

  - **sucking** them; on: *Am-c* *Bov* k* **Carb-v** k* kali-bi *Nit-ac* *Rat* rosm lgb1 ruta fd4.de tritic-vg fd5.de zinc
  - **thick**: but-ac sp1*
  - **touch** agg.: carb-v k2 fic-m gya1 *Hep* lyc k* **Merc** k* *Nat-c* k* ph-ac k* **Phos** k* plb k* *Sep* k* sol-t-ae a1 sul-ac k* zinc k*
- **Palate**: crot-h ptk1 lach ptk1 phos ptk1
  - **oozing** purpura: *Crot-h* *Lach* *Phos* ter

○ - **Hard** palate: plut-n srj7•

- **Tongue**: anan k* arg-met k* ars k* **Arum-t** k* bapt k2 bell vk1 **Borx** k* bry k* bufo vk1 cadm-s k* calc k* caps k* *Carb-v* mtf33 cham k* chin vk1 chlol k* clem k* cocc vk1 colch vk1 *Crot-h* vk1 cupr vk1 cur k* dig vk1 guare k* hyos k2 kali-bi k* kali-chl k* kali-p k2 lac-ac k* *Lach* k* *Lept* vk1 lyc k* med k* *Merc* k* mur-ac vk1 nat-m k* nat-p k* nit-ac k* nux-v k* *Op* vk1 phos k* plb vk1 *Podo* k* rhus-t k2* sabad vk1 sars k* sec k* sep k* spig k* spong vk1 stram vk1 sulph vk1 ter k* vanil fd5.de **Verat** vk1
  - **accompanied** by:
    - **cancer** of tongue (See Cancer - tongue - accompanied - hemorrhage)
    - **dysentery** (See RECTUM - Dysentery - accompanied - tongue - bleeding)

○ - **Below**: ter kr1*

  - **Tip**: lach k* phos k* vanil fd5.de
    - **accompanied** by | **cracked** tongue (See Cracked - tongue - accompanied - bleeding - tip)

BLISTERS (See Eruptions - vesicles)

BLOTCHES:

○ - **Palate**: *Elaps* *Fl-ac* k* *Syph* zinc

- **Tongue** | **Under** the tongue; like vegetable growths: ambr k*

BLOWING: *(↗RESPIRATION - Blowing)*

- **bubbles**: bufo mtf33 ign mtf33 merc mtf33
  - **weeping**; when: graph mtf33 lach mtf33

BLOWING THE NOSE agg.: carb-v b4a.de

BOILS at gums: *(↗Abscess - gums)* agn k* anan k* arn aur borx h2* carb-an k* *Carb-v* k* caust chel k* euph hecla mtf11 jug-r *Kali-chl* k* *Kali-i* k* lac-c k* *Lyc* k* *Merc* k* mill k* *Nat-m* k* nat-p k* nat-s *Nux-v* k* *Petr* k* petr-ra shn4• ph-ac *Phos* k* plan k* plb sanic c2 **Sil** k* staph strept-ent jl2 sulph fs

- **right** upper molar: bung-fa mtf
- **small**, painful to touch | **Upper** canine; near left (= near left eyetooth): *Agn* k* cassia-s ccrh1•

BRANDY: | **agg.**: *Rhus-t* b7a.de

BREAD agg.: ran-s b7.de*

BREAKFAST: | **amel.**: croc b7.de*

BREATH (See Odor; RESPIRATION - Coldness; RESPIRATION - Hot)

BREATHING agg.: arg-met b7.de* chin b7.de* hep b4.de* kali-n b4.de* mez b4a.de

BROAD TONGUE: cas-s br1 chion br1* conv bwa2* cory br1 *Kali-bi* hr1* mag-m ptk1 merc ptk1 *Nat-m* hr1* plb a1 *Podo* hr1 puls cda1* vib hr1 ziz hr1

- **sensation** as if: *(↗Enlarged - tongue - sensation)* bell bg2 conv vml3• *Kali-bi* k* **Nat-m** k* par k* plb k* *Podo* k* positr nl2• **Puls** k* vib k* ziz k*
  - **accompanied** by:
    - **Tongue**; discoloration of | **Center**; a pasty coat in the: podo vk1

BRUXISM (See TEETH - Grinding)

BUBBLING sensation, as if bubbles were moving about: | **Gums**: nux-v b7.de

BURNS: *(↗GENERALS - Burns)*
○ - **Tongue**:
- **sensation** as if tongue has been burnt (See Pain - tongue - burnt)

○ • **And** lips: ham k*

BUTTERFLIES: | **Tongue**; sensation of butterflies on the: olib-sac wmh1

CANCER: *(↗Tumors)* **Aur-m** rmk1• carc sne cic sne hecla sne merc-c sne syph mrr1
○ - **Gums**: beryl mtf cob mtf graph mtf hecla mtf iod mtf kreos mtf merc mtf phos mtf staph mtf syph mtf thuj mtf
- **Palate**: aur hydr k*
  - **hard**: scolo-v gm1
- **Tongue**: *Alumn* k* *Apis* k* arg-cy gm1 *Ars* k* ars-h sne ars-met sne *Aur* k* *Aur-m* k* aur-m-n bro1* benz-ac k* calc k* *Calc-f* sne *Carb-an* k* carc sne caust k* chr-ac br1 cit-ac mtf11 *Con* k* crot-h k* cund k* eos sne gali c1* guaj mtf11 *Hydr* k* kali-chl k* kali-cy k* *Kali-i* k* *Lach* k* lyc sne *Merc* sne *Mur-ac* k* *Nit-ac* k* *Phos* k* *Phyt* k* rad-br sne* sang sne semp bro1* sep k* *Sil* k* *Strych-g* bro1* sulph k* tarent sne thuj k* *Vib-p* c2*
  - **left**: *Mur-ac* vk1
  - **accompanied** by:
    - **atrophy** of tongue: merc vk1 *Mur-ac* k*
    - **atrophy** of tongue and speaking with a thick hoarse voice: *Mur-ac* kr1*
    - **blue** discoloration: *Mur-ac* kr1*
    - **hemorrhage**; tendency to: crot-h kr1*
  - **epithelioma**: *Ars* bro1* carb-ac bro1* chr-ac br1* **Hydr** bro1* kali-chl sne *Kali-cy* bro1 kali-i sne mur-ac bro1 nit-ac sne *Thuj* bro1
  - **hard**, indurated, ulcerated, warty growths: *Mur-ac* kr1*
  - **painful**: cit-ac sne cit-l kr1*
  - **scirrhus** carcinoma: alum kr1* alumn br1 cob mtf iod mtf kali-cy mtf semp br1 staph mtf

CANCRUM oris (See Stomatitis - gangrenous)

CANDIDA ALBICANS (See Thrush)

CANKER sores (See Ulcers - canker)

CARIES:
○ - **Gums**: calc
- **Palate**: **Aur** k* guare hippoz k* *Merc* merc-cy bro1 *Nit-ac* k* syph k2

CHEWING agg.: aloe bg2 **Bell** b4.de* borx b4a.de ign b7.de* kali-bi bg2 nat-c b4.de* *Ph-ac* b4.de*
○ - **Palate**: borx ptk1

CHEWING motion (See FACE - Chewing)

CHOREA, tongue: cina h1

CLAMMY: bell ptk1 brass-n-o srj5• bufo *Dios* k* gamb k* gels glon jac-c k* lac-d k* *Lach* k* merc-sul k* naja nat-s *Onos* k* plb sang
- **waking**; on: *Cycl* k* *Puls*

CLEAN Tongue: *(↗Smooth)* abrom-a vk1* *Aeth* bg2* **Ars** bg2* **Asar** bg2* bism bg2* *Chin* bro1* **Cina** bg2* cocc kr1* **Cory** br1* cund sne *Dig* bg2* elaps kr1* *Glycyr-g* cte1• hell-o c1 *Hyos* bg2* ign bg2* **Ip** b7a.de* *Mag-p* bg2* nat-m bg2* *Nit-ac* bro1* oena kr1* **Pyrog** bro1* **Rhus-t** bro1* sec bg2* *Sep* bro1* sulph bg2* zinc bg2*
- **accompanied** by:
  - **bitter** taste: chinin-s kr1*
    - **women**; in old: *Carb-v* kr1*
  - **cholera** (See RECTUM - Cholera - accompanied - tongue - clean)
  - **constipation** (See RECTUM - Constipation - accompanied - tongue - clean)
  - **dryness** of tongue | **Tip** of tongue: sec kr1*
  - **fever**; during: ars bro1 cina bro1 *Ip* b7a.de

Clean Tongue – **accompanied** by: ...
  - **headache** (See HEAD - Pain - accompanied - tongue - clean)
  - **lepra** (See GENERALS - Lepra - accompanied - clean)
  - **nausea** (See STOMACH - Nausea - accompanied - tongue - clean)
  - **nephritis**; acute: apis kr1*
  - **smooth** tongue (See Smooth - accompanied - clean)
  - **typhoid** fever (See FEVER - Typhoid - accompanied - tongue - clean)
  - **urination**; copious: solid ptk1
  - **vomiting** (See STOMACH - Vomiting - accompanied - tongue)

○ • **Brain** complaints (See HEAD - Brain; complaints of - accompanied - tongue - clean)
  - **Root** of tongue:
    - **coated** (See Discoloration - tongue - white - root - accompanied - clean)
    - **slimy** coating (See Mucus - tongue - root - accompanied - clean)
  - **Stomach**; pain in (See STOMACH - Pain - accompanied - tongue - clean)
  - **Tip** of tongue | **red** discoloration (See Discoloration - tongue - red - tip - accompanied - clean; Discoloration - tongue - red - tip - accompanied - clean - sides)
- **menses**; during: *Sep* ptk1*
  - **dirty** tongue after menses; and: sep bro1
- **spot** in the centre; clean: diph bg2 rham-cal bg2*

○ - **Centre**:
  - **accompanied** by | **white** discoloration of the tongue (See Discoloration - tongue - white - accompanied - centre - clean)
- **Sides**: arg-n ptk1 mangi vk1
  - **accompanied** by:
    - **indigestion** (See STOMACH - Indigestion - accompanied - tongue - sides)
    - **liver**; hardness of (See ABDOMEN - Hard - liver - accompanied - tongue - clean - tip)
    - **tongue**; discoloration of:
      - **black** (See Discoloration - tongue - black - accompanied - sides - clean)
      - **cream**-like (See Discoloration - tongue - cream-like - accompanied - clean)
      - **red** tip (See Discoloration - tongue - red - tip - accompanied - clean - sides)
      - **white** (See Discoloration - tongue - white - accompanied - edges - clean)
- **Tip**:
  - **accompanied** by:
    - **Liver**; hardness of (See ABDOMEN - Hard - liver - accompanied - tongue - clean - tip)
    - **Tongue**; white discoloration of (See Discoloration - tongue - white - accompanied - tip - clean)

CLEFT palate: *Syph* mrr1

CLOSED: amyg ant-t *Cic* cob ptk1 cupr mtf33 *Stram* k* sulph h2*

CLOSING mouth: | **difficult**: *Sil* b4a.de

CLUMSY: | **Tongue**: *(↗Enlarged - tongue)* merc k2

COATED (See Discoloration; Discoloration - tongue - white; Membrane)

COLD:
- **air**:
  - **agg.**: bell bg2 dulc bg2 *Merc* b4.de* nux-v bg2
  - **drawing** in cold air | **agg.**: *Nux-v* b7.de*

- **drinks** | **agg.**: *Bell* b4a.de* dulc bg2
- **water** | **amel.**: asar b7.de* kali-bi bg2 merc-c bg2 sep b4.de*

COLD; AFTER TAKING A: *Acon* bg2 bar-c b4a.de* **Bell** b4a.de* bry b7.de* *Cham* b7.de* *Coff* bg2 **Dulc** b4a.de* hyos b7.de* ign bg2 *Lach* bg2 **Merc** bg2 *Nux-v* b7.de* puls bg2 sulph bg2

COLD AGG.; BECOMING: *Dulc* b4a.de

COLDNESS:
- **breath**; of (See RESPIRATION - Coldness)
- **sensation** of coldness: acon k* *Ars* k* bit-ar wht1• bol-la *Camph* k* cann-xyz bg2 carb-an *Carb-v* k* caust b4.de* chlf *Cist* mrr1 clem colch bg2 cupr bg2 eupi kali-bi bg2 kali-n k* *Lac-c* bg1* *Lach* bg1* lyss olib-sac wmh1 plat rhus-t k* tell k* thuj bg2 ven-m rsj12• *Verat* k*
  - **convulsions**; after: eupi
  - **icy**: cocc-s
  - **peppermint**; as from: *Camph* *Lyss* k* rhus-t tell verat k*
  - **warm** tea seems cold: camph k*
  - ▽ **extending** to | **Stomach**: kali-n
  - ○ **Gums**: cocc-s bro1 phos bg1
    - **Upper**: sil
  - **Lips** | **lower**: bit-ar wht1•
  - **Palate**: acon bg2 caust h2* verat b7.de*
  - **Tongue**: acon k* anag k* ant-t k* ars-h bell bit-ar wht1• **Camph** **Carb-v** k* carbn-s k2 cist k* guare k* helo helo-s rwt2• hydr-ac k* iris bg1 kali-chl k* laur k* *Verat* k* zinc
    - **right**: *Gels*
    - **left**: aloe bg1
    - **air**; sensation of cold: *Acon*
    - **peppermint**; as from: lyss
    - **Frenum**, near: anag
    - **Tip**: bell k* cupr k*
- ○ **Tongue**: acet-ac k* acon aloe bg2 am-c anh sp1 *Ars* k* bar-c bell k* calc **Camph** k* *Carb-v* k* carbn-s cist bro1* *Colch* k* cupr b7.de* cupr-ar *Cupr-s* helo c1* helo-s c1* hydr bg2 hydr-ac bro1 *Ip* bg2 *Iris* k* kali-br kali-chl bg2* *Laur* k* merc naja k* *Nat-m* op *Ox-ac* *Ph-ac* sec k* **Verat** k* zinc k*
  - **right**: gels bg2
  - **left**: aloe bg2
  - **morning**: zinc
  - **accompanied** by:
    - **Tongue** | **white** discoloration of the tongue: *Calc* kr1*
  - **icy**: ars cocc-s hr1 zinc
  - **sensation** of: acon bg2 bell b4.de* colch bg2 *Cupr* bg2 kreos bg2 laur b7.de* m-aust b7.de mez b4.de* verat b7a.de*

COMPLAINTS of mouth (= buccal cavity in general): *Acon* b2.de* agar b2.de* agn b2.de* *Alum* b2.de* am-c b2.de* am-m b2.de* ambr b2.de* anac b2.de* ang b2.de* ant-c b2.de* ant-t b2.de* arg-met b2.de* arn b2.de* ars b2.de* asaf b2.de* asar b2.de* aur b2.de* bar-c b2.de* **Bell** b2.de* bism b2.de* *Borx* b2.de* bov b2.de* bry b2.de* calad b2.de* *Calc* b2.de* camph b2.de* cann-s b2.de* *Canth* b2.de* *Caps* b2.de* carb-an b2.de* *Carb-v* b2.de* caust b2.de* *Cham* b2.de* chel b2.de* *Chin* b2.de* cic b2.de* cina b2.de* cocc b2.de* coff b2.de* colch b2.de* coloc b2.de* con b2.de* croc b2.de* cupr b2.de* cycl b2.de* dig b2.de* dros b2.de* dulc b2.de* euph b2.de* ferr b2.de* graph b2.de* guaj b2.de* hell b2.de* hep b2.de* hyos b2.de* *Ign* b2.de* iod b2.de* ip b2.de* kali-c b2.de* kali-n b2.de* kreos b2.de* *Lach* b2.de* laur b2.de* led b2.de* lyc b2.de* m-ambo b2.de m-arct b2.de m-aust b2.de mag-c b2.de* mag-m b2.de* mang b2.de* meny b2.de* **Merc** b2.de* *Merc-cy* br1 *Mez* b2.de* mosch b2.de* mur-ac b2.de* nat-c b2.de* nat-m b2.de* *Nit-ac* b2.de* nux-m b2.de* **Nux-v** b2.de* olnd b2.de* op b2.de* par b2.de* petr b2.de* ph-ac b2.de* **Phos** b2.de* plat b2.de* plb b2.de* *Puls* b2.de* ran-b b2.de* ran-s b2.de* rheum b2.de* rhod b2.de* rhus-t b2.de* ruta b2.de* *Sabad* b2.de* sabin b2.de* samb b2.de sars b2.de* sec b2.de sel b2.de* seneg b2.de* *Sep* b2.de* sil b2.de* spig b2.de* spong b2.de* squil b2.de* stann b2.de* staph b2.de* *Stram* b2.de* stront-c b2.de* sul-ac b2.de* sulph b2.de* tarax b2.de* teucr b2.de* thuj b2.de* valer b2.de* *Verat* b2.de* viol-o b2.de* *Zinc* b2.de*
- **right**: *Alum* bg2* *Am-c* bg2* ant-c b7a.de* ars bg2* aur bg2* *Bell* bg2 bov bg2* brom bg2 *Calc* bg2* *Carb-v* bg2* *Caust* bg2* *Chin* b7a.de* *Coloc* bg2* *Dros* b7a.de* *Fl-ac* bg2 graph bg2* iod bg2* *Kreos* b7a.de* lach b7a.de* *M-arct* b7a.de* **Merc** bg2* mill b7a.de *Nat-m* bg2* nit-ac bg2* *Nux-v* b7a.de* *Petr* bg2* plat bg2* *Plb* b7a.de* psor bg2 *Ran-b* b7a.de* rhus-t b7a.de* *Sabad* b7a.de* *Sep* bg2* sil bg2* *Spig* b7a.de* *Stann* bg2* *Sulph* bg2* teucr b7a.de* *Thuj* bg2* zinc bg2*
- **left**: *Acon* b7a.de* alum bg2* *Ang* b7a.de* ant-c b7a.de* *Ant-t* b7a.de* *Apis* b7a.de* *Aur* bg2* *Bar-c* bg2* **Bell** bg2* bov bg2* calc bg2* *Carb-an* bg2* carb-v bg2* *Caust* bg2* *Colch* b7a.de* *Croc* b7a.de* *Cupr* b7a.de* dros b7a.de* euph bg2 *Euphr* fse1.de fl-ac bg2 *Graph* bg2* *Hep* bg2* iod bg2* kali-bi bg2 *Kali-c* bg2* kreos b7a.de* **Lach** b7a.de* *Lyc* bg2* *M-aust* b7a.de* *Meny* b7a.de* *Merc-i-r* bg2 *Mez* bg2* mill b7a.de nat-m bg2* *Nit-ac* bg2* *Nux-m* b7a.de* *Nux-v* b7a.de* olnd b7a.de* ph-ac bg2* *Phos* bg2* plat bg2* *Puls* b7a.de* *Rhod* bg2* *Rhus-t* b7a.de* *Sabad* b7a.de* *Sabin* b7a.de* *Seneg* bg2* **Sep** bg2* *Sil* bg2* *Spig* b7a.de* spong bg2 *Sulph* bg2* *Tarax* b7a.de* *Teucr* b7a.de* *Thuj* bg2* *Verat* b7a.de* *Zinc* bg2*
- **accompanied** by:
  - **respiration**; difficult (See RESPIRATION - Difficult - accompanied - mouth)
  - ○ **Gums**; complaints of: *Alum* bg2 lach bg2
  - **Head**; pain in (See HEAD - Pain - accompanied - mouth)
  - **Larynx**; complaints of (See LARYNX - Larynx - accompanied - mouth)
- ○ **Corners** | **Inner** side: sep bg2
- **Gums** (See Gums)
- **Inner** side (See Complaints)
- **Palate**: *Aur* ptk1 bell ptk1 crot-h ptk1 *Merc* ptk1 *Nux-v* ptk1 phos ptk1
- **Salivary** glands: abrot bg2 acon bg2 arum-t bg2 aur bg2 bar-c bg2 brom bg2 calc bg2 calc-f bg2* carb-v bg2 cham bg2* cist bg2 clem bg2 cocc bg2 *Coch* br1 con bg2 ham bg2 iod bg2* jab bg2 kali-bi bg2 kali-m bg2 kali-n bg2 lach bg2 lyc bg2 merc bg2* nit-ac ptk1 phyt bg2* puls bg2* rhus-t bg2 sil bg2 sul-ac bg2 sul-i bg2 sulph bg2 thuj bg2
- **Tongue** (See Tongue-tie)

CONDYLOMATA:
- ○ **Palate**: arg-n
- **Tongue**: aur *Aur-m* aur-m-n lyc mang staph

•**CONGESTION** of gums: graph h2* helia br1 strept-ent jl2

CONSCIOUSNESS; after return of: *Cupr* b7a.de

CONSTRICTION: lach k* lob-s k* nit-ac k* phos k* plb k* sulph k*
- **accompanied** by | **hiccough**: cupr bg2
- ○ **Palate**: acon bg2* fago bg2 nux-v bg2 tarent bg2
- **Tongue**: iod bg2 lach bg2 valer bg2

CONTRACTION: *(↗Shrivelled; Wrinkled)* alum b4.de* arg-n bg2 asar b7.de* chin b7.de* cocc b7.de* gels bg2 nit-ac b4.de* par b7.de* phos b4.de* plb b7a.de seneg b4.de* sulph b4.de*
- **sensation**: aesc alum k* asar k* fl-ac k* gast a1 plac rzf5• seneg k*
- **spasmodic**: acon *Ars* asar h1* *Bell* bufo calc k* cupr hyos mosch sep
- ○ **Gums**: staph b7.de*
- **Palate**: am b7a.de cham bg2 glon bg2
- **Salivary** glands: ambr b7.de* chin h1*
- **Tongue**: agar bg2 *Carb-v* k* cina bg2 crot-t bg2 ip bg2 laur b7.de* *Merc-c* k* nux-v bg2
  - **alternating** with | **swelling**: xan bg1 xanth bg2
  - **cylindrical**: cina k*
    - **spasmodically** forced through lips; which is: cina hr1

CONVULSIONS (See Spasms)

CORRUGATED Tongue: nat-ar k*

COTTON; sensation of: *(↗Velvet)* bell bg2 berb bg2
- ○ **Tongue**: bell bg2

COUGH: | **after** | **amel.**: stann b4.de*
- **agg.**: *Acon* b7a.de am-c b4.de* *Arg-met* b7a.de arg-n bg2 ars bg2 arum-t bg2 bell bg2 caps b7.de* carb-an b4.de* carb-v b4a.de* caust b4.de* ham bg2 hep b4a.de* ign b7a.de kali-c b4.de* lyc b4.de* meny b7.de* mur-ac b4.de* nat-m b4.de* nit-ac b4.de* ph-ac b4.de* *Phos* b4.de* puls bg2 sep b4.de* sulph b4.de* tarent bg2

COVER:
- **hand**; covers mouth with: am-c ptk1 arg-n ptk1 cor-r ptk1 cupr ptk1 ip bg1* kali-bi bg1* *Lach* bg1* **Rumx** bg1* thuj ptk1

- **suffocation**; covering mouth produces (See RESPIRATION - Difficult - covering)

CRACKED: ambr arum-t bg3 bell bg3 bism bry k2 bufo *Cocc* k* cund c2 eup-per c2 hydr k2 kali-bi bg3 lach k* lat-m bnm6• merc k2 merc-c bg2 morg-g fmm1• *Ph-ac* k* *Phos* k* prot fmm1• syc fmm1• thal-xyz srj8•

O - **Corners** of mouth (See FACE - Cracked - mouth)

- **Gums**: plat k*
- **Tongue** fissured: **Ail** k* alco a1 anan k* *Apis* k* **Ars** k* **Ars-i** k* ars-s-f k2 **Arum-t** k* arund br1* atro k* aur k* aur-ar k2 aur-s k2 *Bapt* k* bar-c k* bar-i k2 bar-m k* bar-s k2 *Bell* k* *Benz-ac* k* bor-ac bro1* *Borx* k* both-ax tsm2 *Bry* k* bufo k* calad bg2* *Calc* k* calc-f br1* calc-i k2 calc-p k* calc-s k* *Camph* k* carb-ac k* *Carb-v* k* carbn-s k* *Cham* k* chel k* *Chin* k* chinin-ar k* chlorpr vk1 cic k* clem k* cob k* *Crot-h* k* cupr k* cur k* der a1 *Dulc* b4a.de fago a1 **Fl-ac** k* gaert pte1*• *Glycyr-g* cte1• hell bg2* **Hyos** k* iod k* *Kali-bi* k* kali-c k2 kali-i bg1* *Lach* k* *Leon* bro1* *Lyc* k* *Mag-m* k* *Merc* k* mez k* moni jl2 *Mur-ac* k* myris a1* *Nat-ar* k* nat-m bro1* **Nit-ac** k* nux-v k* ph-ac k* **Phos** k* *Phyt* bg2* pic-ac hr1 plat k* *Plb* k* plb-act bro1* *Podo* k* psor al2 puls k* *Pyrog* k* raja-s vk1 ran-s k* raph k* **Rhus-t** k* rhus-v k* ruta fd4.de sacch k* sec b7.de* semp bro1* *Sin-n* bg2* sol-t-ae c2 **Spig** k* stram k* sul-i k2 *Sulph* k* syc pte1*• syph c1* *Tub* k* vanil fd5.de *Verat* k* *Zinc* k* zinc-p k2 zinc-s a1
  - **accompanied** by:
    - **aphthae**: **Borx** kr1*
    - **black** tongue: *Lyc* kr1*
    - **bleeding** tongue: arum-t ptk1
      - **Tip**: lach kr1*
    - **burning** pain (See Pain - tongue - burning - accompanied - tongue)
    - **burns**: calen kr1*
    - **diabetes** (See GENERALS - Diabetes mellitus - accompanied - tongue - cracked)
    - **dysentery** (See RECTUM - Dysentery - accompanied - tongue - cracked)
    - **influenza** (See GENERALS - Influenza - accompanied - tongue - cracked)
    - **pneumonia** (See CHEST - Inflammation - lungs - accompanied - tongue - cracked)
    - **rheumatism** (See EXTREMITIES - Pain - rheumatic - accompanied - tongue - cracked)
    - **scarlatina** (See SKIN - Eruptions - scarlatina - accompanied - tongue)
    - **tobacco** poisoning (See GENERALS - Tobacco - agg. - nicotinism - accompanied - tongue)
    - **typhoid** fever (See FEVER - Typhoid - accompanied - tongue - cracked)
    - **typhus** fever (See FEVER - Typhus - accompanied - tongue - cracked)
    - **yellow** fever (See FEVER - Yellow - accompanied - tongue - cracked)
  - **deep**: benz-ac kr1* fl-ac bg2* glycyr-g cte1• kali-i bg2*
  - **directions**; in all: **Fl-ac** k* mag-m k2 **Nit-ac** k*
    - **accompanied** by | **ulcer** in the centre: *Fl-ac* kr1*
  - **moistened**; as if it would crack if not: pic-ac kr1*
  - **one** deep red furrow:
    - **accompanied** by:
      - **Tongue**:
        - **pale**: raph kr1*
        - **purple**: raph kr1*
  - **sensation** as if: nat-c bg2 sulph bg2
  - **typhoid** fever; after: *Merc* kr1*

O • **Across**: acet-ac bg3 asar bg3 cob k* kali-p bg3 merc ptk1
  - **Anterior** part: nat-ar kr1*
  - **Centre**: bapt k* bufo k* *Cob* k* cub k* glycyr-g cte1• lept k* *Mez* k* *Nit-ac* k* raph k* rhus-t vk1 *Rhus-v* k* ruta fd4.de sin-n k* syph ptk1 vanil fd5.de
    - **Across**: cob k* lach bg1 merc bg1 vanil fd5.de
  - **Down** median line: sin-n kr1*

Cracked – **Tongue** fissured – **Down** median line: ...
    - **two** deep cracks running lengthwise parallel to median line: syph kr1*
  - **Edges**: anan k* ars sne clem k* fago a1 ferr-p bg2* *Lach* k* *Nux-v* k* thuj bg2
    - **left**: *Bar-c* k*
    - **accompanied** by | **hard** tongue | **Edges**: clem vk1
      - **typhoid** fever (See FEVER - Typhoid - accompanied - tongue - cracked - edges)
    - **nursing** woman: lach vk1
    - **painful** with hard edges: clem
  - **Lengthwise**: glycyr-g cte1• merc bg2* pip-m vk1 pip-n bg2 ruta fd4.de syph br
    - **deep**: syph mtf33
    - **Upper** part: *Merc* bro1*
  - **Tip**: bar-c h2* lach k*

CRACKLING of gums on pressure: daph k*

CRAMPS (See Spasms)

CRAWLING: acon alum k* bamb-a stb2.de• *Carb-v* ptk1 colch b7.de* dulc fd4.de *Kali-c* ptk1 kali-m ptk1 lach ptk1 merl k* nux-m pieri-b mlk9.de sacch-a fd2.de• tritic-vg fd5.de vanil fd5.de *Zinc* k*

O - **Cheeks**; inner side of: zinc h2*
- **Gums**: am k* graph k* kali-c k* kola stb3• **Merc** b4a.de rhus-t b7.de* **Sec** k*
- **Lips**; around:
  - **forenoon** | **10**h: lap-la rsp1
- **Palate**: acon ars ptk1 carb-v k* caust h2* colch bg2 grat k* lach b7a.de lap-la rsp1 phos ptk1 polyg-h ptk1 ran-b ptk1 sabad k* sil ptk1 symph fd3.de• tritic-vg fd5.de
  - **morning** | **8**h: lap-la rsp1
- **Tongue**: acon b7.de* alum b4.de* bamb-a stb2.de• dulc b4.de* kali-n b4a.de* kali-s fkr2.de merc b4.de* nat-m b4.de* pieri-b mlk9.de *Plat* k* podo fd3.de• puls b7.de* *Sec* b7.de* seneg b4.de* vanil fd5.de *Zinc* b4.de*

O • **Anterior** part: anh sp1

CRUSTS: myric ptk1
- **dry**, scaly: gaert fmm1• *Myric* phos k2
- **ulcerated**: arg-n

O - **Palate**:
  - **dry**, scaly: myric plb sec sul-ac
  - **white**: ox-ac

O • **Uvula**; behind the base of the: *Bar-c*
- **Tongue** (See Discoloration - tongue - crusts)

CUT on the edges; sensation as if tongue was (See Pain - tongue - edges - cutting - cut)

DARTING out: | **Tongue** (See Protruding - tongue)

DENTAL FISTULA (See Fistula - gums)

DENTITION agg.: apis bg2 asar bg2 borx bg2 mag-c bg2 merc bg2

DENUDED spots: | **Tongue**; on: ran-s k*

DEPAPILLATED (See Papillae - absent)

DESQUAMATION:

O - **Cheek**; inside: sulph h2
- **Palate** | **sensation** of: phos h2

DETACHED from teeth; gums: *(↗Protruding - gums; Scorbutic)* alumn k2 *Am-c* *Ant-c* k* arg-met *Arg-n* k* *Ars* b4a.de* *Aur-m-n* *Bapt* bar-c k* bar-i k2 bar-s k2 bov k* brom bufo *Calc* *Camph* k* caps k* **Carb-v** k* *Carbn-s* caust k* chin b7a.de *Cist* k* colch cupr k* *Dulc* k* gink-b sbd1• gran *Graph* k* hep b4a.de* *Iod* k* kali-bi bg2 *Kali-c* k* kali-chl ptk1 *Kali-i* **Kali-p** k* kola stb3• *Kreos* k* lac-c lach **Merc** k* *Merc-c* k* mez mur-ac ptk1 nat-c k* *Nat-s* k* nit-ac *Nux-v* b7a.de *Par* bg1* *Ph-ac* k* *Phos* k* plb k* psor k* rhus-t k* sep k* **Sil** vh *Staph* k* sul-i k2 *Sulph* k* ter thuj bg2 tritic-vg fd5.de wies a1 *Zinc* k*
- **and** bleed easily●: ant-c **Carb-v** k* *Phos* k* sulph mtf33
- **sensation** as if loose: arg-n bg2 par b7.de*

DIRTY sensation: | **drinking** amel.: bit-ar wht1•

DIRTY tongue (See Discoloration - tongue - dirty)

DISAGREEABLE sensation: | **Palate**: ant-t b7.de*

DISCHARGE:

- **brown** ichor on making incision near second molar; stinking: anthraci
- **offensive**:
  ○ · **Gums**; from | **menses**; during: but-ac sp1
- **putrid**: *(↗Pyorrhea)* **Carb-ac** hr1

DISCOLORATION:

- **black**: ars k2 carb-ac hr1
  · **bluish** black | **spots**: *Plb* b7a.de
- **blue**: cic b7.de* cina tl1 *Gymno* br1 loxo-recl bnm10• merc k* plb tab bg2
  · **accompanied** by:
    ⁝ **brown** crusts on lips (See FACE - Eruptions - crusty - lips - brown - accompanied - blue)
    ⁝ **pale** spots: ars k*
  ○ · **Gums** | **Margin**: *Carb-v* b4a.de *Nat-m* b4a.de
- **brown**: bry k2
  · **pale**: choc srj3•
  · **red**: lyc ptk1
  · **stool** agg.; during: *Ars* b4a.de
  · **yellow** | **Middle**: sec a1
- **pale**: acet-ac carb-v k2 *Chinin-s* eup-per ferr kali-c k2 mang merc *Nat-m*
  · **accompanied** by | **blue** spots (See blue - accompanied - pale)
- **purple** blotches: merc k2 plb sars k2
- **red**: am-c *Apis* k* ars aur-s c1 bell k* bell-p sp1 beryl sp1 *Borx* k* calad *Canth* k* chlol chord-umb rly4• convo-s sp1 *Cupr-act* *Cycl* ferr-i fuch br1 *Hydr* *Hyos* ign k* ip k2 kali-ar k2 *Kali-bi* k* kali-br a1 *Kali-chl* kreos *Merc* k* merc-c merc-cy merc-i-r merc-sul nat-ar *Nat-c* *Nit-ac* oci-sa sp1 pitu-gl skp7• psor k2 rhus-v sal-ac
  · **left** side: pitu-gl skp7•
  · **fiery**: apis bg2
  · **spots**: ozone sde2• plb
  ○ · **Cheek**; inside of: nat-hchls vk1
- **reddish** blue: ars
  · **spots**: berb sars
- **spots**: ars b4a.de zinc b4a.de
- **white**: *Bell* b4a.de *Borx* b4a.de cina tl1 dios br1 kreos bg2 *Lac-c* med k2 *Merc* b4.de* moni jl2 mur-ac a1* *Sul-ac* k* tub jl
  · **bluish** white spots | **Lips**; inside of: merc h*
  · **patches**: *(↗Aphthae; Leukoplakia)* merc k2 *Morb* jl2 *Mur-ac* a1 phos k2 sal-ac sulph k2
- **yellow**: plb b7a.de*
  · **fever**; during: *Plb* b7a.de*
  · **patches**: *Nit-ac* visc c1
  · **red**: lyc ptk1
  · **spots**: lac-c lach lyc
- ○ **Cheek**; inside of:
  · **red**: *Mur-ac* a1 nat-hchls vk1
  · **reddish** blue spot: mag-c h2*
  · **white** patches: morb jl2
- **Fauces** | **red**: *Arg-n* bg2 kali-bi bg2 merc bg2 mur-ac bg2
- **Gums**:
  · **black**: agar-ph a1 ars b4a.de carb-v k2 cary a1 chin b7a.de *Merc* k* merc-c b4a.de merc-sul hr1 plb k*
    ⁝ **sooty**: hippoz k*
  · **blue** line on margin: merc k2 **Plb** k* plut-n srj7• thal-xyz srj8•
  · **bluish**: acon-l a1 aur-m k* borx bg2 *Cocc* b7a.de con bg2 ferr-p bg2 kali-bi bg2 **Kreos** hr1* *Lach* k* lyc k* merc k* merc-sul hr1 nux-v b7a.de olnd k* *Plb* k* psor sabad k*
  · **bluish** red: con k* **Kreos** lach
  · **bluish** white: olnd k*
  · **brown**: chel *Colch* *Phos* k* *Plb* k*

Discoloration – **Gums**: ...

  · **changed** color: ars b4a.de *Caps* b7a.de carb-v b4a.de *Dulc* b4a.de *Merc* b4a.de *Nux-v* b7a.de *Sulph* b4a.de
  · **dirty**: *Alum* *Alumn* k* merc
  · **gray**, dirty gray: *Alum* alumn k2 plb b7a.de*
  · **greenish** tint | **Border**; along free: cupr-s k*
  · **pale**: ars-h a1 asc-t k* aur bg2 bar-c b4a.de *Bell* b4a.de camph hr1 carb-an b4.de* carb-v b4a.de *Chel* k* clem a1 *Cycl* k* **Ferr** k* iod a1 med k* **Merc** b4.de* **Merc-c** k* nit-ac k* nux-v k* olnd b7a.de* phos **Plb** k* rat hr1 sabin b7.de* senec k* *Staph* k* tab a1 zinc b4a.de*
    ⁝ **Upper**: bar-c b4.de*
  · **purple**: *Bapt* k* cupr bg2 *Lach* k* **Merc-c** k* **Plb** k* thal-xyz srj8•
    ⁝ **thin** border nearest teeth: **Plb**
  · **red**: am-c k* ant-t *Apis* arund *Aur* k* aur-i k2 *Bell* k* berb borx hr1 calad calc k* canth *Carb-an* k* *Cham* chord-umb rly4• crot-h *Dol* *Dulc* eup-per ferr-p **Hep** bg2 hydr *Iod* k* iris a1 kali-ar kali-c k* kali-chl kali-n b4.de* kali-p **Kreos** k* *Lach* mag-c k* **Merc** k* *Merc-c* k* merc-i-r mur-ac *Nat-m* bg2 *Nat-s* *Nit-ac* nux-v k* phel phos bg2 psor jl2 ran-s k* *Sep* k* sil bg2 **Sulph** bg2
    ⁝ **dark**: *Aur* k* **Bapt** *Borx* hydr sep
    ⁝ **dirty**: berb
    ⁝ **line** or seam: *Ant-c* bro1 apis bro1 *Cham* bro1 kali-p bro1 *Puls* bro1 rhus-t bro1
    ⁝ **spots**: canth b7.de* chord-umb rly4• plut-n srj7•
    ⁝ **Margins**: bar-c b4a.de
      ⁝ **pale**: bar-c kali-chl
      ⁝ **red**, bright: *Crot-h* *Merc*
  · **violet** border: merc-cy k*
  · **white**: acet-ac k* ars k* aur-m k* *Crot-h* k* *Ferr* k* *Kali-bi* k* kali-s a1 **Merc** k* mur-ac a1 *Nit-ac* k* nux-v k* olnd b7a.de *Ph-ac* k* sabin b7a.de spong k* *Staph* k* zinc k*
  · **yellow**: asc-t k* *Carb-v* k* *Merc* k*
- **Palate**:
  · **bluish**: merc-sul k* phos b4a.de *Phyt* k*
    ⁝ **red**: acon ptk1 apis ptk1 cham ptk1 phos k* sulph k*
  · **brown** | **Soft** palate: canth b7.de*
  · **coppery**: *Kali-bi* k* *Merc* k*
  · **grayish**: lac-c rhus-t
  · **purple**: phyt k*
  · **red**: **Acon** k* aeth k* agn b7.de* ant-t k* **Apis** k* arg-n k* aur bro1 *Bapt* k* bell k* berb k* beryl sp1 canth b7.de* *Caps* k* *Caust* k* **Cham** k* cimic k* coc-c k* *Colch* k* cop *Cupr* hr1 *Daph* *Dulc* hr1 fago a1 *Fl-ac* k* gent-c a1 *Graph* k* *Kali-bi* k* *Kali-i* k* lac-c hr1 *Lach* k* *Merc* k* **Merc-c** hr1* *Merc-cy* hr1 merl k* morph k* *Mur-ac* k* *Nit-ac* k* nux-m b7.de* op ox-ac a1 ozone sde2• *Par* b7a.de phos hr1 phys a1 *Phyt* k* puls streptoc jl2 sul-ac ziz k*
    ⁝ **cough** agg.; during: beryl tpw5
    ⁝ **dark** red: bell tl1
    ⁝ **patches** | **right**: brucel sa3•
    ⁝ **Soft** palate: acon bg2 *Bell* b4.de* berb bg2 canth bg2 nux-m bg2
    ⁝ **Velum**: acon hr1 aeth k* agn k* *Alum* k* am-caust a1 *Apis* *Arg-n* k* **Bapt** hr1 *Bell* *Calc* *Cedr* k* *Cham* k* chen-a cop cupr-act der a1 hydrc a1 kali-bi *Merc* *Mur-ac* k* nux-m k* *Petr* k* *Puls* k*
  · **spots**, as if ulcers would form | **Forepart**; in: kali-bi
  · **white**: alum bg2 am-caust k* bond a1 cycl hr1 *Ferr* k* lac-c *Merc* k* **Nat-p** k* rhus-t sil tarent a1
    ⁝ **patches**: *Mur-ac* a1
  · **yellow**: plb b7a.de
    ⁝ **creamy**: **Nat-p** k*
  ○ · **Soft** palate | **red** spots: sulfonam ks2
- **Tongue**:
  · **berry** color (See Papillae - reddened)
  · **black**: *(↗dark)* aeth k* *Arg-n* k* arn ptk1 *Ars* k* ars-h hr1* *Bapt* bro1* bar-c k* bell bg2 bry b7.de* bufo k* cadm-s k* camph bro1* *Carb-ac* k* **Carb-v** k* **Chin** k* *Chinin-ar* k* chlol k* *Chlor* k* chloram vk1 choc srj3• cocc bg2 colch b7a.de* crot-h bg2* cupr k* dig bg2* elaps k* gymno ptk1

- **black**: ...
hippoz k* hyos k* kali-bi bg2 *Kali-c* k* *Lach* k* *Lept* bg2* lol a1 *Lyc* k* **Merc** k* *Merc-c* k* *Merc-cy* k* merc-d a1* merc-sul k* mur-ac bg2 nit-ac bg2 *Nux-v* k* *Op* k* **Phos** k* plb k* rad-br ptk1 *Rhus-t* b7a.de* sabad bg2 *Sec* k* sin-n k* spong bg2 stram k* sul-ac k2 sulph b4a.de* vario hr1* *Verat* k* vip k*
  - **accompanied** by:
    - **constipation** (See RECTUM - Constipation - accompanied - tongue - black)
    - **cracked** tongue (See Cracked - tongue - accompanied - black)
    - **diphtheria** (See THROAT - Diphtheria - accompanied - tongue - black)
    - **dryness** (See Dryness - tongue - accompanied - black)
    - **dysentery** (See RECTUM - Dysentery - accompanied - tongue - black)
    - **scarlet** fever (See FEVER - Scarlet - accompanied - tongue - black; SKIN - Eruptions - scarlatina - accompanied - tongue - black)
    - **typhoid** fever (See FEVER - Typhoid - accompanied - tongue - black)
    - **typhus** fever (See FEVER - Typhus - accompanied - tongue - black)
    - **yellow** fever (See FEVER - Yellow - accompanied - tongue - black)
    - **Abdomen**; cramping pain in (See ABDOMEN - Pain - cramping - accompanied - tongue - black)
    - **Edges** | **red**: **Merc** k* nux-v k*
    - **Root** | **yellow**: ars vk1
    - **Sides** | **clean**: ars vk1
  - **bluish** black: *Alum* vk1 ars bro1 bufo k* cupr-s bro1 *Dig* bro1 *Gymno* bro1 *Lach* vk1 *Lyc* vk1 *Merc* vk1 merc-cy bro1 *Morph* bro1 mur-ac bro1 op bro1 *Phos* vk1 *Sec* bro1 *Verat* bro1 vip bro1
    - **spots**; in: plb b7a.de
  - **crusts**: *Phos* k*
  - **gangrenous**: bism ptk1
  - **medial** line; along: chlol vk1 *Phos* vk1
  - **purplish** black: *Op* k*
  - **red** edges; with (See accompanied - edges - red)
  - **sooty** black: *Chlor* kr1* hippoz kr1*
  - **Centre**: chlol k* lept k* *Merc* k* **Phos** k* sec k*
    - **streak** like ink: chlol k* lept k* raja-s vk1
      - **accompanied** by:
        - **white** tongue and liver disease (See ABDOMEN - Liver - accompanied - tongue white)
        - **Sides** | **red**: raja-s jl3*
  - **Posterior** part (See root)
  - **Root**: *Verat* k*
  - **Sides**:
    - **accompanied** by | **grayish** yellow centre of tongue (See yellow - grayish - centre - accompanied - sides - black)
- **bloodless** (See pale)
- **blue**: *Agar* k* ambr bg1 **Ant-t** k* arg-met vk1 arg-n a1 **Ars** k* benz-ac k* bufo k* *Carb-v* k* colch k* cupr-s k* **Dig** k* gymno bg1* helo-s bnm14• *Iris* k* *Merc-cy* vk1 **Morph** vk1 *Mur-ac* k* op k* *Plat* k* *Podo* k* *Sabad* vk1 *Sec* vk1 spig k* tab k* thuj k* **Verat** vk1 *Vip* vk1
  - **accompanied** by:
    - **cancer** of tongue (See Cancer - tongue - accompanied - blue)
    - **cholera** (See RECTUM - Cholera - accompanied - tongue - blue)
    - **cyanosis** (See GENERALS - Cyanosis - accompanied - tongue - blue)
    - **dysentery** (See RECTUM - Dysentery - accompanied - tongue - blue)
  - **lead** colored: *Ars* kr1* *Carb-v* kr1*
  - **reddish** blue: ars k* raph k*
  - **spots**, in: arg-n k* *Plb* b7a.de sars k*
- **bluish**: arg-n bg2 ars b4.de* benz-ac bg2 bufo bg2 carb-v tl1 *Cocc* b7a.de colch b7a.de* cupr-s bro1* **Dig** b4.de* **Gymno** bg2* merc tl1 merc-cy bro1* **Morph** bro1* mur-ac b4.de* op bg2* podo bg2 sabad b7.de* **Sec** bro1* tab bg2 (non:vario) **Verat** bro1* vip bro1*
- **bluish** black (See black - bluish)
- **bluish** white (See white - bluish)
- **brown**: *Acon* b7.de* aesc k* **Ail** k* *Am-c* bro1* ant-t k* *Anthraci* k* *Apis* k* arg-n a1 *Arn* k* **Ars** k* ars-i k* ars-s-f k2 atro k* aur k* aur-ar k2 aur-i k2 **Bapt** k* *Bell* k* both-ax tsm2 **Bry** k* cact hr1 *Cadm-s* k* *Carb-ac* k* *Carb-v* k* cassia-s ccrh1• *Chel* k* *Chin* k* **Chinin-ar** k* *Chlor* hr1 coc-c k* cocc hr1 *Colch* k* *Crot-h* k* *Cupr* k* *Cupr-ar* bro1* *Dig* k* dios k* dor k* *Echi* bro1* elat k* *Eup-pur* hr1 gels k* glon bg2* guaj k* *Ham* hr1 *Hep* k* **Hyos** k* iod k* *Ip* hr1 joan vk1 *Kali-bi* k* kali-br k* **Kali-p** k* kali-t a1 *Lac-c* k* **Lach** k* *Lyc* k* mag-p bg2 med k* *Merc* k* merc-cy bro1* *Merc-i-f* k* morph bro1* mur-ac bro1* mygal hr1 myric bg2* nat-s bro1* *Nux-v* k* *Op* k* ox-ac k* par b7.de* ph-ac k* **Phos** k* phyt k* **Plb** k* podo hr1 ptel k* *Pyrog* k* **Rhus-t** k* rumx k* sabad kr1* sabin k* **Sec** k* *Sep* k* *Sil* k* spig bg2* *Spong* k* sul-ac k2 *Sulph* k* tarax b7.de* tarent k* *Tart-ac* a1 tax a1 ter k* thuj b4a.de verat vk1 verb k* vib hr1 vip bro1* *Zinc* hr1
  - **morning**: *Bapt* k* dios a1 **Rhus-t** k* sumb a1 tarax h1*
  - **accompanied** by:
    - **chorea** (See GENERALS - Chorea - accompanied - tongue - brown)
    - **consumption** (See CHEST - Phthisis - accompanied - tongue - brown)
    - **convulsions** | **puerperal** (See GENERALS - Convulsions - puerperal - accompanied - tongue - brown)
    - **delirium** (See MIND - Delirium - tongue - brown)
    - **diarrhea** (See RECTUM - Diarrhea - accompanied - tongue - brown)
    - **diphtheria** (See THROAT - Diphtheria - accompanied - tongue - brown)
    - **dryness** (See Dryness - tongue - accompanied - brown)
    - **dysentery** (See RECTUM - Dysentery - accompanied - tongue - brown)
    - **influenza** (See GENERALS - Influenza - accompanied - tongue - brown)
    - **phthisis** (See CHEST - Phthisis - accompanied - tongue - brown)
    - **pneumonia** (See CHEST - Inflammation - lungs - accompanied - tongue - brown)
    - **scarlatina** (See SKIN - Eruptions - scarlatina - accompanied - tongue - brown)
    - **typhoid** fever (See FEVER - Typhoid - accompanied - tongue - brown)
    - **typhus** fever (See FEVER - Typhus - accompanied - tongue - brown)
    - **vomiting**; chronic (See STOMACH - Vomiting - chronic - accompanied - tongue - brown)
    - **water** brash (See STOMACH - Eructations; type - water brash - accompanied - tongue - brown)
    - **yellow** fever (See FEVER - Yellow - accompanied - tongue - brown)
    - **Prostate**; induration of (See PROSTATE - Induration - accompanied - tongue - brown)
    - **Root** | **green**: *Nat-s* kr1*
    - **Sides** and tip; red: *Lyc* k* rhus-t k*
    - **Sides**; red: *Lyc* rhus-t *Sep* a1*
    - **Throat** | **ulcers** (See THROAT - Ulcers - accompanied - tongue - brown)
    - **Tip** and sides; red (See sides and)
    - **Urethra** | **stricture** (See URETHRA - Stricture - accompanied - tongue - brown)
  - **dark** brown: *Bry* kr1* carb-ac hr1* *Crot-h* kr1* dor kr1* rhus-t tl1
    - **Centre**: nat-p kr1* sanic tl1

• **brown** – **dark** brown: ...
: **Root**:
. **accompanied** by | **measles** (See SKIN - Eruptions - measles - accompanied - tongue - brown)
: **earth**; brown like: *lp* kr1*
: **greenish** brown: nat-s k*
: **heavily** coated: auran kr1* *Bapt* kr1* *Colch* kr1* *Gels* kr1* med kr1* podo kr1*
: **accompanied** by:
. **Bladder**; catarrh of (See BLADDER - Catarrh - accompanied - tongue - brown - heavily)
. **Stomach** complaints (See STOMACH - Complaints - accompanied - tongue - brown - heavily)
: **red** tip and sides (See accompanied - sides and)
: **reddish** brown: ox-ac a1 rhus-t a1 rumx k* sul-ac k* *Zinc* k*
: **accompanied** by | **typhoid** fever (See FEVER - Typhoid - accompanied - tongue - brown - reddish)
: **thick**: med br1
: **yellowish** brown: ant-t k* bapt k* brom *Carb-v* k* choc srj3• cina crot-h k* dios k* merc-i-f k* nat-s bg2 phos a1 pyrog tl1 rumx *Verat* hr1 verb k*
: **accompanied** by:
. **diphtheria** (See THROAT - Diphtheria - accompanied - tongue - brown - yellowish)
. **dryness** of tongue (See Dryness - tongue - accompanied - brown - yellowish)
. **pneumonia** (See CHEST - Inflammation - lungs - accompanied - tongue - brown - yellowish)
. **remittent** fever (See FEVER - Remittent - accompanied - tongue - brown - yellowish)
. **typhoid** fever (See FEVER - Typhoid - accompanied - tongue - brown - yellowish)
. **typhus** fever (See FEVER - Typhus - accompanied - tongue - brown - yellowish)
. **vomiting** during pregnancy (See STOMACH - Vomiting - pregnancy - accompanied - tongue - brown - yellowish)
. **Sides**; smooth: bapt k*
: **Centre**: *Bapt* hr1 bry mrr1
: **Root**: *Kali-bi* kr1*
: **Base**, at: lyss vh pyrog bg1 tor bg1
: **Centre**: ail hr1 *Arn* k* ars k* bapt hr1* *Bry* k* canth k* *Colch* k* *Crot-h* k* *Eup-pur* k* hyos k* hyosin a1 iod k* *Lac-c* k* nat-p k* *Phos* k* *Plb* k* pyrog k* vib k* wies a1
: **morning** | **rising**; on: rhus-t k*
: **accompanied** by:
. **typhoid** fever (See FEVER - Typhoid - accompanied - tongue - brown - centre)
. **Sides**:
moist: *Apis* k*
white: arn k* iod kr1* malar jl2 nat-p k*
: **Root**: pyrog bg2 verb c1
: **yellowish** brown: penic vk1
: **Sides**: *Kali-bi* k* phyt alj
: **accompanied** by:
. **Centre** | **red** discoloration: *Kali-bi* kr1*
: **Tip**: sec a1 term-c vk1
: **accompanied** by:
. **papillae**; red elevated (See Papillae - reddened - elevated - accompanied - tip - brown)
. **scarlatina** (See SKIN - Eruptions - scarlatina - accompanied - tongue - brown - tip)

• **changing** color: sec b7a.de

• **cream**-like: mez vk1
: **accompanied** by:
: **clean** sides: mez vk1

• **cream**-like – **accompanied** by: ...
: **salivation** (See Salivation - accompanied - tongue - cream-like)
: **Anterior** half | **one** side: tub vk1
: **Root**: tub vk1

• **crusts**: bry k2 chin b7.de*

• **cyanotic** (See blue)

• **dark**: (↗*black*) arn k2 ars k2 *Bapt* hr1* bell bg2* bry k2 carb-v k2 kali-bi k2 lach k2 mur-ac bg2* nit-ac k2 ph-ac k2 phos bg2* rhus-t k2 sec k2 sul-ac bg2* verat-v bg2*
: **accompanied** by | **cough** (See COUGH - Accompanied - tongue - dark)
: **streaks**:
: **Edges**: petr ptk1
. **accompanied** by | **Centre**; white (See white - accompanied - edges - dark)
: **Centre**: arn bg2* bapt bg2*
: **streak** in centre; dark: *Arn* bro1* *Bapt* bro1* *Mur-ac* bro1*

• **dirty**: **Acon** b7.de* all-c k* **Ant-c** b7.de* anthraco k* arg-n k* arn b7.de* *Ars* b4a.de bry b7a.de* calc k* *Camph* k* carb-v k* cean bg2* **Chin** k* conv br1 croc k* cub c1 hydr ptk1 hyper bg2* *Kali-chl* k* lac-c k* lyc b4a.de* *Mag-m* hr1 merc mtf33 merc-i-f bg2* morg fmm1• morg-g pte1*• **Nat-s** k* olnd b7a.de* syph k* thuj bg2 valer hr1 verb b7.de zinc k*
: **accompanied** by:
: **angina** (See THROAT - Inflammation - accompanied - tongue - dirty)
: **metrorrhagia** (See FEMALE - Metrorrhagia - accompanied - tongue - dirty)
: **pneumonia** (See CHEST - Inflammation - lungs - accompanied - tongue - dirty)
: **typhoid** fever (See FEVER - Typhoid - accompanied - tongue - dirty)
: **typhus** fever (See FEVER - Typhus - accompanied - tongue - dirty)
: **urine** | **suppressed** (See BLADDER - Retention - accompanied - tongue - dirty)
: **Liver** complaints (See ABDOMEN - Liver - accompanied - tongue; dirty)
: **heavily** coated: **Chin** kr1* conv br1 valer kr1*
: **Root** of tongue: **Nat-s** kr1*
: **Centre**: *Lac-c* kr1*
: **Root**: *Lac-c* kr1* **Nat-s** kr1*

• **foul** (See dirty)

• **gray**: *Ambr* k* anan k* ant-t k* *Arg-n* bg2* ars bg2* ars-h k* *Bell* bg2* bry k* *Chel* k* *Cupr* bg2* cupr-act k* ery-a a1 ferr bg2* hyper a1 *Kali-c* k* kali-m ptk1 kali-s fd4.de lac-c k* *Merc-cy* k* nat-s mrr1 ox-ac a1 ozone sde2• ph-ac k* *Phos* k* phyt k* puls k* ribo rly4• tub xxb [tax jsj7]
: **accompanied** by:
: **diphtheria** (See THROAT - Diphtheria - accompanied - tongue - gray)
: **grayish** complexion; pale (See FACE - Discoloration - grayish - accompanied - tongue)
: **indigestion** (See STOMACH - Indigestion - accompanied - tongue - gray)
: **nausea** and pain in head (See HEAD - Pain - accompanied - nausea and gray)
: **Head**; pain in (See HEAD - Pain - accompanied - tongue - gray)
: **Root** | **green**: **Nat-s** kr1*
: **greenish** gray: **Nat-s** k*
: **whitish** gray: *Kali-c* kr1* ph-ac kr1*
: **Centre**: phos k*
: **accompanied** by | **sides**; yellow (See yellow - sides - accompanied)
: **Root**: *Kali-m* br1

- **gray**: ...
  - **Sides**:
    - **accompanied** by | **yellow** discoloration of tongue (See yellow - accompanied - sides - gray)
- **grayish** yellow (See yellow - grayish)
- **green**: ars bg2 ars-met k* calc-caust k* caps bg1 chion bg1 cupr k* guare kr1* iod bg1 **Mag-c** bg2* mag-m bg2* **Nat-s** k* *Nit-ac* k* *Plb* k* plb-act bro1* propr sa3• *Rhod* k*
  - **accompanied** by:
    - **malaria** (See GENERALS - Malaria - accompanied - tongue - green)
    - **salivation** (See Salivation - accompanied - tongue - green)
  - **Root**: caps ptk1 chion ptk1 cop bg2
    - **accompanied** by:
      - **brown** discoloration (See brown - accompanied - root - green)
      - **gray** tongue (See gray - accompanied - root - green)
- **greenish** brown (See brown - greenish)
- **greenish** gray (See gray - greenish)
- **greenish** yellow (See yellow - greenish)
- **leather**, looks like burnt: hyos k*
- **orange**: choc srj3•
- **pale**: agar b4.de* *Ail* k* ant-c b7a.de ant-t k* *Ars* k* boerh-d bnj1 brass-n-o srj5• caesal-b vk1 *Chel* k* *Colch* b7a.de *Cupr* hr1 cupr-s bro1 *Dig* bro1 emb-r bnj1 *Ferr* k* *Gymno* bro1 hydr k* *Ip* k* kali-br k* *Kali-c* k* kreos b7a.de* *Lyss* k* **Merc** k* merc-cy bro1 *Morph* bro1 mur-ac bro1 nat-c k* *Nat-m* k* op bro1 ph-ac hr1* phos k* raph k* rhus-t hr1 sec b7a.de* *Sep* k* stram hr1 sul-ac b4a.de *Verat* k* vip bro1 xan k*
  - **accompanied** by:
    - **anasarca** (See GENERALS - Dropsy - external - accompanied - tongue - pale)
    - **cardialgia** (See STOMACH - Heartburn - accompanied - tongue - pale)
    - **chlorosis** (See GENERALS - Chlorosis - accompanied - tongue - pale)
    - **cholera** (See RECTUM - Cholera - accompanied - tongue - pale)
    - **diarrhea** | **chronic** (See RECTUM - Diarrhea - chronic - accompanied - tongue - pale)
    - **diphtheria** (See THROAT - Diphtheria - lips - accompanied)
    - **flabby** tongue: acet-ac k*
    - **furrow** on tongue; one deep red (See Cracked - tongue - one - accompanied - tongue - pale)
    - **heartburn** (See STOMACH - Heartburn - accompanied - tongue - pale)
    - **indigestion** (See STOMACH - Indigestion - accompanied - tongue - pale)
    - **intestinal** catarrh (See ABDOMEN - Catarrh - intestinal - accompanied)
    - **phthisis** (See CHEST - Phthisis - accompanied - tongue - pale)
    - **scarlatina** (See SKIN - Eruptions - scarlatina - accompanied - tongue - pale)
  - **Edges**: chinin-s k*
  - **Root**:
    - **accompanied** by | **yellow** tongue (See yellow - accompanied - root - pale)
  - **Tip**:
    - **accompanied** by | **sides**; livid: *Ail* kr1*
- **pasty** coat (See white)
- **purple**: borra-o oss1• *Cact* k* hydr k* *Kali-chl* k* *Lach* k* *Op* k* *Petr* k* raph k* stry k*
- **purple**: ...
  - **accompanied** by:
    - **diphtheria** (See THROAT - Diphtheria - accompanied - tongue - purple)
    - **enlarged** tongue (See Enlarged - tongue - accompanied - purple)
    - **epithelioma** (See GENERALS - Cancerous - epithelioma - accompanied - tongue - purple)
    - **furrow** on tongue; one deep red (See Cracked - tongue - one - accompanied - tongue - purple)
    - **hypertrophy** of the tongue (See Enlarged - tongue - accompanied - purple)
  - **black**: op k*
  - **spots**: sars k2
- **raspberry** color: scarl jl2
- **red**: acet-ac k* *Acon* k* adam skp7• aloe k* ant-c k* ant-t k* **Apis** k* arg-n k* arn b7a.de **Ars** k* ars-s-f k2 arum-t k* aur k* aur-ar k2 *Aur-m* k* bac bn *Bapt* k* **Bell** k* bell-p sp1 *Bism* k* *Bor-ac* bro1 borra-o oss1• borx vk1 bry k* cain k* *Calc* k* *Calc-s* k* calen k* *Camph* k* *Canth* k* carb-ac k* *Carb-v* k* *Cham* k* *Colch* k* coloc k* *Crot-c* k* *Crot-h* k* crot-t k* *Cupr* k* *Cupr-act* vk1 cur k* cypra-eg sde6.de• *Diph* br1* diphtox jl2 elaps k* eos br1 *Ferr-p* k* fl-ac k* *Gels* k* glon k* *Hydr* k* *Hyos* k* ictod k* *Iod* b4a.de ip tl1* *Kali-bi* k* kali-br hr1 *Kali-c* k* kali-m k2 kali-n br1 lac-ac k* lac-c k* *Lach* k* loxo-lae bnm12• *Lyc* k* *Mag-m* k* **Merc** k* *Merc-c* k* merc-sul vk1 *Mez* bro1* moni jl2 mosch b7a.de mur-ac k* nat-ar k* nat-m k* *Nat-s* k* **Nit-ac** k* *Nux-v* k* oci-sa sp1* ox-ac k* paeon a1 pall k* ped a1 *Ph-ac* b4a.de **Phos** k* *Plb* k* podo k* psil ft1 *Pyrog* k* ran-s k* **Rhus-t** k* rhus-v k* sang k* sars k* spong k* stann k* stram k* *Sulph* k* syph k* tarax bro1 tarent k* *Ter* k* *Tub* k* tub-m vn *Verat* k* verb k* vesp a1*
  - **accompanied** by:
    - **abscess** (See GENERALS - Abscesses - accompanied - tongue - red)
    - **diabetes** (See GENERALS - Diabetes mellitus - accompanied - tongue - red)
    - **diphtheria** (See THROAT - Diphtheria - accompanied - tongue - red)
    - **dryness** of tongue (See Dryness - tongue - accompanied - red)
    - **respiration**; complaints of (See RESPIRATION - Complaints - accompanied - tongue)
  - **brick** dust coating: anan kr1*
  - **bright** red: *Bell* kr1* *Colch* kr1* pyrog jl2 ter kr1* terebe ktp9
    - **accompanied** by:
      - **diabetes** (See GENERALS - Diabetes mellitus - accompanied - tongue - red - bright)
      - **dropsy** (See GENERALS - Dropsy - external - accompanied - tongue - red - bright)
      - **scarlet** fever (See FEVER - Scarlet - accompanied - tongue - red - bright)
  - **cherry** red: kali-c kr1*
  - **dark** red: bell tl1 bry b7a.de hyos mtf33 rhus-t b7a.de
    - **Tip**: diph ptk1
  - **fiery** red: **Apis** k* *Bell* k* calc-s k* *Canth* k* pyrog ptk1 sang ptk1*
    - **accompanied** by:
      - **heartburn** (See STOMACH - Heartburn - accompanied - tongue - red - fiery)
      - **Face**; erysipelas in (See FACE - Erysipelas - accompanied - tongue - red - fiery)
    - **Tip**: fl-ac k* *Phyt* k*
  - **glistening**: (↗*Smooth)* apis k* *Canth* bro1 com k* crot-h bro1 crot-t k* glon k* jal bro1 **Kali-bi** k* *Lach* k* *Nit-ac* bro1 *Phos* k* pyrog bg2* rhus-t hr1* stram bg2 *Ter* k*
  - **meaty**: arum-t bg2
  - **painted**; clean as if: *Calc* kr1*
  - **spots**: apis k* choc srj3• manc k* *Merc* k* ox-ac a1 *Ran-s* bro1* raph k* syph k2 *Tarax* bro1* ter k* verat k*
    - **small**: stram ptk1
    - **Sides** | **right**: sulfonam jl3*

- **red**: ...
  - **strawberry** (See Papillae - erect - strawberry)
  - **stripes**: ant-t k* arg-met k* ars tl1 pert-vc vk9
    - **Down** centre; stripe●: ant-t k* arg-met k* *Arg-n* k* arn bg1 *Ars* k* *Bapt* bg1 *Bell* k* **Caust** k* *Cham* k* colch bg1 crot-h bro1 *Crot-t* vk1 iris bg1 *Kali-bi* k* lach bg1 merc-c k* osm k* pall k* *Ph-ac* k* *Phos* k* *Plb* bg1* *Pyrog* bg1* *Rhus-t* bg1* *Rhus-v* kr1* *Sang* k* symph fd3.de• *Tub* k* verat k* **Verat-v** k*
      - **accompanied** by:
        - **grayish** yellow centre of tongue (See yellow - grayish - centre - accompanied - centre - red)
        - **pneumonia** (See CHEST - Inflammation - lungs - accompanied - tongue - red - centre)
        - **white** tongue (See white - accompanied - centre - red - stripe)
      - **sore**: osm k*
    - **Edges**; along: nat-m mtf33
  - **yellowish** red | **Under** tongue: *Kali-bi* kr1*
  - **Anterior** half: lach k*
  - **Centre**: *Ant-t* bg2* *Ars* bg2* *Bapt* bg2* caust bro1* cham k* crot-h bro1 kali-bi k* merc-c bg2 nit-ac bro1 oci-sa sp1 *Phos* k* *Rhus-t* k* *Rhus-v* hr1 sulph k* symph fd3.de• **Verat-v** bg2*
    - **accompanied** by:
      - **Sides** | **brown** discoloration (See brown - sides - accompanied - centre - red)
    - **spots**: raph kr1*
  - **Root**: bry ptk1 *Nux-v* kr1*
  - **Sides**: acon k* amyg-p bro1* ant-c k* ant-t k* apis ptk1 **Ars** k* *Bapt* k* bar-c k* bell k* bell-p vk1 bry k* *Canth* k* carb-an k* card-m k* **Chel** k* colch k* conv k* cop k* *Crot-h* k* cupr k* cypra-eg sde6.de• echi bro1 *Fl-ac* k* *Gels* k* helon k* hydr bg2* ictod k* *Iris* k* *Kali-bi* k* kali-p k* lac-c k* lac-del hrn2• *Lach* k* lyc bg lyss k* **Merc** k* merc-c k* merc-cy k* *Merc-i-f* k* mur-ac k* *Nit-ac* k* nux-v k* oci-sa vk1 op k* ox-ac k* pert-vc vk9 *Phos* k* *Plb* k* podo bro1* raph k* *Rhus-t* k* rhus-v k* ruta k* sec k* sep k* stram k* sul-ac k* **Sulph** k* tarax bro1 verat-v k* vip k*
    - **left**: sulfonam ks2
    - **accompanied** by:
      - **black** discoloration of tongue (See black - accompanied - edges - red)
      - **brown** discoloration of tongue (See brown - accompanied - sides; red)
      - **brown** tongue and red tip (See brown - accompanied - sides and)
      - **mucus** on tongue; yellow (See Mucus - tongue - yellow - accompanied)
      - **typhoid** fever (See FEVER - Typhoid - accompanied - tongue - red - sides)
      - **white** tongue and moist edges (See white - accompanied - edges - moist)
      - **yellow** tongue (See yellow - accompanied - sides - red)
      - **Centre**:
        - **black** (See black - centre - streak - accompanied - sides - red)
        - **white** (See white - centre - accompanied - sides - red)
        - **yellow** (See yellow - centre - accompanied - sides - red)
  - **Tip**: amyg-p bro1* ant-t bg2* *Apis* k* **Arg-n** k* **Ars** k* bell bg2* bell-p sp1* card-m k* chel k* chinin-ar k* com k* conv k* crot-h k* cycl k* cypra-eg sde6.de• eupi k* ferr k* *Fl-ac* k* helon k* hipp k* hyos bg1 ictod k* ip ptk1 *Lach* k* *Lyc* k* merc-c bg2* merc-i-f k* merc-i-r bg2* mez k* morph k* *Nit-ac* k* oena k* op bg2* ox-ac k* pert-vc vk9 **Phyt** k* plb k* podo fd3.de• **Rhus-t** k* **Rhus-v** k* rob k* sars k* sec k* stram k* sul-ac k* sul-i k* **Sulph** k* symph fd3.de• thuj kr1* verat bg2 verat-v k* vip k*

- **red** – **Tip**: ...
  - **accompanied** by:
    - **albuminuria** (See URINE - Albuminous - accompanied - tongue - red - tip)
    - **brown** tongue and red sides (See brown - accompanied - sides and)
    - **clean**:
      - **Sides**: mangi vk1
      - **Tongue**: sec kr1*
    - **diphtheria** (See THROAT - Diphtheria - accompanied - tongue - red - tip)
    - **sides** and brown tongue; red (See brown - accompanied - sides and)
  - **painful**: arg-n k* cycl k* symph fd3.de•
  - **triangular**●: arg-n ptk1 **Rhus-t** k* sep ptk1
  - **Under**: adam skp7•
- **reddish** blue (See blue - reddish)
- **reddish** brown (See brown - reddish)
- **rosy**: coli jl2
  - **median** band from the root to the point; with: coli jl2
- **strawberry** (See Papillae - erect - strawberry)
- **stripe** | **Centre**; down: ant-t bg2 arn bg2 bapt bg2 card-m bg2 caust bg2 colch bg2 osm bg2 phos bg2 stann bg2 *Verat-v* bg2
- **white**: *Acon* k* adam skp7• *Aesc* k* aeth c1 agar k* *Agn* k* ail k* alco a1 all-s k* alum k* alum-p k2 alum-sil k2 am-c k* am-m k* ambr k* anac k* androg-p vk1 ang k* **Ant-c** k* *Ant-i* c1 *Ant-t* k* anth c1 *Apis* k* apoc kr1* aran-ix vk1 *Arg-n* k* *Arn* k* **Ars** k* ars-br vh ars-h hr1* *Ars-i* k* *Ars-met* k* ars-s-f kr1* asaf k* asar k* asc-c k* atro k* *Atro-s* kr1* *Aur* b4a.de aur-m-n k* *Bapt* k* bar-c k* bar-m k* bar-s k2 **Bell** k* berb k* *Bism* k* boerh-d bnj1 bol-la k* borx k* bov k* **Bry** k* cact k* caesal-b vk1* cain k* caj a1 **Calc** k* calc-p k* calc-sil k2 cann-i k* cann-s k* *Canth* b2.de* caps kr1* *Carb-ac* k* *Carb-v* k* carbn-s k* **Card-m** vk1 cassia-s cdd7*• caul k* caust k* *Cham* k* *Chel* k* *Chin* k* chinin-ar k* chinin-s k* chlol a1 cic k* *Cimx* k* *Cina* k* cinnb k* clem k* clerod-i bnj1 cob k* coc-c k* *Coca* vk1 *Cocc* k* coch k* *Colch* k* coli jl2* coll k* *Coloc* k* cop k* cor-r k* corn hr1* croc k* crot-c sk4• crot-t k* cub hr1* cupr k* cupr-ar k* cupr-n a1 cupr-s a1* cycl k* der a1 *Dig* k* dios k* dirc c1 dulc b4a.de* echi k* elaps k* *Elat* hr1 *Enteroc* jl2 equis-h c2 *Eup-per* k* euph k* *Ferr* k* ferr-ar k* ferr-p k* *Fl-ac* k* gard-j vlr2• *Gels* k* ger-i rly4• get br1 gins a1 *Glon* k* gnaph k* *Graph* k* guaj k* haliae-lc srj5• ham k* *Hedeo* vk1 hell k* hep bg2* hipp jl2 hir rsj4*• hydr k* hydr-ac k* hydrog srj2• **Hyos** k* *Hyper* k* hypoth vk1 ign k* iod k* ip k* iris k* ix bnm8• jug-r k* just vk1 *Kali-ar* k* **Kali-bi** k* kali-br k* kali-c k* *Kali-chl* k* *Kali-i* k* *Kali-m* bg2* *Kali-n* k* *Kali-p* k* kali-s a1 kali-sil k2 *Kalm* k* *Kreos* k* kurch bnj1 lac-ac k* lac-c k* *Lac-d* al lac-h sze9• *Lach* k* lact k* lact-v hr1 lat-h bnm5• lat-m sp1* laur k* lec k* lob-p br1 lol a1 luf-op rsj5• *Lyc* k* lyss kr1* m-arct b2.de* mag-c k* mag-m k* malar jl2 manc k* mand sp1 mang k* mangi vk1 **Merc** k* *Merc-c* k* merc-d a1 *Merc-i-f* k* merc-sul k* merl a1* *Mez* k* mill kr1* mim-p rsj8• morg-p fmm1• *Mur-ac* k* *Myric* vk1 myris a1* naja k* *Nat-ar* k* *Nat-c* k* *Nat-m* k* nat-n bg2* *Nat-s* k* **Nit-ac** k* nuph k* *Nux-m* k* *Nux-v* k* nyct br1 olnd k* *Op* k* orot-ac rly4• oscilloc jl2 osm kr1* ox-ac k* ozone sde2• par k* parathyr jl2 *Petr* k* *Ph-ac* k* *Phos* k* phys a1 phyt k* plan a1 *Plb* k* *Podo* k* prun bg2 *Psor* k* ptel k* **Puls** k* pyrog jl2* ran-b k* ran-s k* raph k* rheum b2.de* *Rhus-t* k* rhus-v a1 rob kr1* *Rumx* k* ruta b2.de* *Sabad* k* sabin k* samb xxb1 sang k* sars k* sec b2.de* sel k* senec kr1* *Seneg* k* *Sep* k* *Sil* k* skat br1 **Spig** k* spong fd4.de *Stann* k* staph b2.de* still a1* stram bg2* strept-ent jl2 *Stront-c* b2.de* sul-ac k* **Sulph** k* sumb a1 symph fd3.de• *Syph* k* tab a1 tanac a1 **Tarax** k* tarent bg2* tell k* thuj b2.de* trios rsj11* tritic-vg fd5.de tub jl2 tung-met bdx1* vac kr1* valer k2 vanil fd5.de *Ven-m* rsj12• verat k* verat-v k* verb k* vib hr1* viol-t k* zinc k* zinc-m a1 zinc-p k2 ziz a1* [nat-p stj1]
  - **morning**: agar k* *All-c* kr1* benz-ac k* calc-p k* cann-i a1 carbn a1 **Chin** k* cinnb k* dig k* dulc fd4.de echi k* elaps k* *Hell* k* hyper hr1 kali-c h2* *Mag-m* k* mang a1 mur-ac h2* nat-c h2* nat-p kr1* *Nit-ac* k* phos h2* plan a1 **Puls** k* ran-s k* sel k* seneg k* sil a1 still kr1* sulph h2* sumb a1 symph fd3.de• tritic-vg fd5.de vanil fd5.de zinc a1
  - **afternoon**: bism kr1*
  - **evening**: bism k*

Mouth

- **white**: ...
  - **accompanied** by:
    - **bad** taste (See Taste - bad - accompanied - tongue - white)
    - **cholera** (See RECTUM - Cholera - accompanied - tongue - white)
    - **cholera**; morbus (See RECTUM - Cholera - morbus - accompanied - tongue - white)
    - **cholera**-infantum (See RECTUM - Cholera - infantum - accompanied - tongue)
    - **cholerine** (See RECTUM - Cholera - beginning - accompanied - tongue - white)
    - **chorea** (See GENERALS - Chorea - accompanied - tongue - white)
    - **coldness** of tongue (See Coldness - tongue - accompanied - tongue - white)
    - **colic** (See ABDOMEN - Pain - cramping - accompanied - tongue - white)
    - **constipation** (See RECTUM - Constipation - accompanied - tongue - white)
    - **coryza** (See NOSE - Coryza - accompanied - tongue - white)
    - **delirium** tremens (See MIND - Delirium tremens - tongue - white)
    - **diabetes** (See GENERALS - Diabetes mellitus - accompanied - tongue - white)
    - **diarrhea** (See RECTUM - Diarrhea - accompanied - tongue - white)
    - **diphtheria** (See THROAT - Diphtheria - accompanied - tongue - white)
    - **dryness** of tongue and endocarditis (See CHEST - Inflammation - heart - endocardium - accompanied - tongue)
    - **dysentery** (See RECTUM - Dysentery - accompanied - tongue - white)
    - **endocarditis** and dry tongue (See CHEST - Inflammation - heart - endocardium - accompanied - tongue)
    - **erysipelas** (See SKIN - Erysipelas - accompanied - tongue - white)
    - **flatulence** (See ABDOMEN - Flatulence - accompanied - tongue - white)
    - **flatulent** indigestion (See ABDOMEN - Flatulence - accompanied - tongue - white; STOMACH - Indigestion - accompanied - tongue - white)
    - **gastric** affections (See STOMACH - Complaints - accompanied - tongue - white)
    - **giddiness** (See VERTIGO - Accompanied - tongue)
    - **greasy** sensation of tongue: *Iris*$_{kr1}$*
    - **head**; pain in (See HEAD - Pain - accompanied - tongue - white discoloration)
    - **heartburn** (See STOMACH - Heartburn - accompanied - tongue)
    - **hemorrhoids** (See RECTUM - Hemorrhoids - accompanied - tongue - white)
    - **hiccough** (See STOMACH - Hiccough - accompanied - tongue - white)
    - **hysteria** (See MIND - Hysteria - tongue - white)
    - **indigestion** (See STOMACH - Indigestion - accompanied - tongue - white)
    - **influenza** (See GENERALS - Influenza - accompanied - tongue - white)
    - **insanity** (See MIND - Insanity - tongue - white)

- **white – accompanied** by: ...
    - **intussusception** (See ABDOMEN - Intussusception - accompanied - tongue)
    - **jaundice** (See SKIN - Discoloration - yellow - accompanied - tongue - white)
    - **mania** (See MIND - Mania - tongue - white)
    - **metrorrhagia** (See FEMALE - Metrorrhagia - accompanied - tongue - white)
    - **morbus** cholera (See RECTUM - Cholera - morbus - accompanied - tongue - white)
    - **nausea** and pain in head (See HEAD - Pain - accompanied - nausea and white)
    - **phthisis** (See CHEST - Phthisis - accompanied - tongue - white)
    - **pneumonia** (See CHEST - Inflammation - lungs - accompanied - tongue - white)
    - **sunstroke** (See HEAD - Sunstroke - accompanied - tongue - white)
    - **syphilis** (See GENERALS - Syphilis - accompanied - tongue - white)
    - **typhoid** fever (See FEVER - Typhoid - accompanied - tongue - white)
    - **typhus** fever (See FEVER - Typhus - accompanied - tongue - white)
    - **vertigo** (See VERTIGO - Accompanied - tongue)
    - **worms** (See RECTUM - Worms - complaints - accompanied - tongue)
  - **Centre**:
    - **brown**: ail$_{a1}$* oci-sa$_{vk1}$
      - **dark**: ail$_{k}$* nat-p$_{k}$*
    - **clean**: diph$_{vk1}$ rham-cal$_{br1}$*
    - **red**: anth$_{vh1}$ sulph$_{vk1}$
      - **stripe** down centre; red: caust$_{k}$* cham$_{k}$* coli$_{jl2}$ *Verat-v*$_{k}$*
  - **Edges**:
    - **clean**: arg-n$_{ptk1}$* **Mag-m**$_{kr1}$*
    - **dark** streaks along edges: petr$_{k}$*
    - **moist** and red: vip$_{k}$*
    - **red**: adam$_{skp7}$•
  - **Glands**; swelling of (See GENERALS - Swelling - glands - accompanied - tongue - white)
  - **Head** and nausea; pain in (See HEAD - Pain - accompanied - nausea and white)
  - **Liver** complaints (See ABDOMEN - Liver - accompanied - tongue; white)
  - **Papillae**; red: *All-s*$_{vh1}$ ant-t$_{hr1}$* ars$_{a1}$ *Bapt*$_{a1}$* bond$_{a1}$ *Med*$_{hr1}$* merc-sul$_{a1}$ mez$_{a1}$ **Nux-m**$_{hr1}$ ptel$_{fr2}$ stram$_{hr1}$ sulph$_{a1}$* tub$_{jl2}$ vac$_{jl2}$ verat$_{hr1}$
  - **Sides** | **dark** streaks along sides: petr$_{k}$*
  - **Stomach**; complaints of (See STOMACH - Complaints - accompanied - tongue - white)
  - **Tip**:
    - **clean** and clean sides: **Mag-m**$_{kr1}$*
    - **red** tip: hipp$_{kr1}$* mangi$_{vk1}$ streptoc$_{jl2}$ sulph$_{vk1}$
    - **red** tip and red sides: rumx$_{kr1}$* *Sulph*$_{kr1}$* *Verat*$_{kr1}$*
  - **apyrexia**; during: *Ip*$_{kr1}$*
  - **bleached**; as if: verat-v$_{ptk1}$
  - **bluish** white: ars$_{ptk1}$* ars-h$_{k}$* gymno$_{k}$*
    - **headache**; during (See HEAD - Pain - accompanied - tongue - white discoloration - bluish)
  - **brownish** white: apoc$_{vh1}$ sarr$_{kr1}$*
  - **catarrh**; after: puls$_{kr1}$*
  - **chalk**; as a layer of: ant-ar$_{mtf11}$ **Ars**$_{kr1}$* bism$_{bg2}$ *Merc*$_{kr1}$* phos$_{bg2}$*
  - **cheesy**: lac-c$_{k}$* merc-i-f$_{k}$* zinc$_{h2}$*

- **white**: ...
  - **chill**; during: *Ant-c* bg2 arn bg2 ars bg2 bell bg2 *Bry* bg2 cham bg2 coloc bg2 graph bg2 ign bg2 ip bg2 lach bg2 lyc bg2 merc bg2 *Nux-m* b7.de* *Nux-v* bg2 op bg2 ph-ac bg2 *Phos* bg2 puls bg2 rhus-t bg2 ruta bg2 sulph bg2
  - **creamy** white: merc-c kr1*
    - **Root** of tongue | **morning**: *Nat-p* kr1*
  - **deeply** coated (See heavily)
  - **diagonally**: rhus-t ptk1
  - **diarrhea** agg.; after: *Kali-m* kr1*
  - **dinner**; after: nit-ac h2*
  - **dirty**: cain k* chin k* dig k* dirc a1* *Gels* hr1 laur a1 myric a1 nat-p k* olnd k* podo k* rhus-t k*
    - **accompanied** by | **scarlatina** (See SKIN - Eruptions - scarlatina - accompanied - tongue - white - dirty)
    - **elevated** papillae; with: olnd k* vac jl2
    - **Centre**: sin-n kr1*
  - **fever**; during: *Acon* kr1* *Ant-c* b7.de* ant-t bg2 apis bg2 arn bg2 **Ars** b4.de* bell bg2 **Bry** b7a.de* *Cham* b7a.de* chin bg2 coloc bg2 *Guare* kr1* ign bg2 ip b7a.de* lach bg2 merc bg2 nux-m b7.de* **Nux-v** b7.de* op b7.de* ph-ac bg2 **Phos** b4.de* *Puls* bg2 rhus-t bg2 ruta b7.de* sabad bg2 sep bg2 sil bg2 sulph bg2 verat bg2
  - **fur**; like: *(↗heavily; Furry - tongue)* acon bro1 aesc bro1 ail tl1 **Ant-c** bro1* *Ant-t* bro1 arg-n bro1 arn bro1 *Bapt* bro1 bell bro1 *Bism* h1* *Bry* bro1 calc bro1 calc-p tl1 carb-v bro1 card-m bro1 *Chel* bro1 chin bro1 cocc b7a.de *Cycl* bro1 ferr bro1 glon bro1 graph ptk1* guaj ptk1 hedeo bro1 *Hydr* bro1 ip bro1 kali-bi bg2 kali-c bro1 kali-chl bro1 kali-m bro1 lac-c bro1 lob bro1 lyc bro1 merc b4.de* merc-c bro1 mez bro1 nat-m bro1 nux-v bro1 ox-ac bro1 par bro1 petr bro1 *Phos* b4a.de* *Puls* b7.de* pyrog tl1 *Rhus-t* b7a.de *Sep* bro1 sulph bro1 tarax bro1 verat-v bro1
    - **morning**: **Merc** kr1*
  - **gray**-whitish: levo vk1 spong fd4.de
    - **Base**: kali-m bro1
  - **heavily** coated: *(↗fur)* **Ant-c** br1* ant-t hr1* asc-t kr1* **Bry** kr1* *Canth* kr1* chlol kr1* cupr-ar kr1* dios kr1* ferr-m kr1* *Gels* kr1* *Guaj* kr1* *Hydr* kr1* iod kr1* joan vk1 lac-ac kr1* lyss kr1* **Merc** kr1* merc-sul kr1* mez kr1* *Nat-c* kr1* nux-v kr1* nyct vk1 *Phos* kr1* **Puls** bg2* **Rhus-t** hr1* still kr1* valer kr1* [heroin sdj2]
    - **accompanied** by:
      - **angina** (See THROAT - Inflammation - accompanied - tongue - white - heavily)
      - **cough** (See COUGH - Accompanied - tongue - white)
      - **diarrhea** (See RECTUM - Diarrhea - accompanied - tongue - white - heavily)
      - **diphtheria** (See THROAT - Diphtheria - accompanied - tongue - white - heavily)
      - **typhus** (See FEVER - Typhus - accompanied - tongue - white - heavily)
      - **Brain** complaints (See HEAD - Complaints - accompanied - tongue - white - heavily)
      - **Centre** and liver disease; black streak down (See ABDOMEN - Liver - accompanied - tongue white)
      - **Centre**; black streak down: *Lept* kr1*
      - **Liver** disease (See ABDOMEN - Liver - accompanied - tongue; white and)
      - **Liver** disease and black streak down tongue (See ABDOMEN - Liver - accompanied - tongue white)
      - **Mouth**; soreness of (See Pain - sore - accompanied - tongue - white - heavily)
      - **Pharynx**; soreness of (See THROAT - Pain - pharynx - accompanied - tongue - white - heavily)
      - **Stomach**; catarrh of (See STOMACH - Catarrh - accompanied - tongue - heavily)
    - **tea** agg.: sel kr1*
    - **Root** of tongue: cupr-ar kr1* *Glon* kr1* *Phyt* kr1*

- **white – heavily** coated – **Root** of tongue: ...
      - **diphtheria**; in (See THROAT - Diphtheria - accompanied - tongue - white - heavily - root)
      - **Brain** complaints; with (See HEAD - Complaints - accompanied - root)
  - **melancholia**; after (See MIND - Sadness - tongue - white)
  - **menses**; during: lyc b4.de
  - **milk**; like curdled: *Borx* b4a.de *Hell* b4a.de *Merc* b4a.de sul-ac b4a.de
  - **milk** white without coating: *Glon* k*
  - **milky**: **Ant-c** k* *Bell* k* *Glon* k* kali-i k* merc-cy k* sul-ac a1
  - **moist**: arg-n k*
    - **accompanied** by | **pneumonia** (See CHEST - Inflammation - lungs - accompanied - tongue - white - moist)
  - **painted**, as if: **Ars** k*
  - **pale**: acon k* aloe k* ambr k* anac k* ang k* ars k* berb k* kreos k* olnd k* phos k*
  - **patches**: *Am-caust* vh1 carc mlr1• cham k* morb jl2 stict c1 syph jl2 **Tarax** k*
    - **left** upper and under side of tongue: hydrc a1*
    - **red**:
      - **dark** red patches, very sensitive to touch: tarax c1
      - **insular** patches; with red: morb jl2 **Nat-m** k*
    - **thick**: syph jl2
  - **perspiration**; during: *Ant-c* bg2 bell bg2 *Bry* bg2 *Cham* bg2 ip bg2 lyc bg2 *Merc* bg2 nux-m bg2 *Nux-v* bg2 op bg2 ph-ac bg2 phos bg2 sulph bg2
  - **quartan** fever; in (See FEVER - Quartan - tongue - white)
  - **sadness**; after (See MIND - Sadness - tongue - white)
  - **silvery**, all over: arg-n k* **Ars** k* carb-ac k* glon k* kali-ar a1 lac-c k*
  - **skin**; as of a white: puls bg2 tarax b7.de*
  - **slightly** coated (See white)
  - **spongy**: *Borx* b4a.de *Hell* b4a.de *Merc* b4a.de *Sul-ac* b4a.de
  - **spots**: hydrog srj2•
    - **clean**: am-m k* choc srj3• manc k* **Tarax** k*
  - **stool** agg.; during: *Ant-c* b7a.de *Ferr* b7a.de *Merc* b4a.de *Puls* b7a.de sulph b4.de*
  - **stripes**: bell k* phel k*
    - **two** white stripes at the margin: phos vk1
  - **strongly** coated (See heavily)
  - **thick**: *Ant-c* br1 iod bg2 kali-n bg2 puls bg2
  - **yellowish** white: aloe kr1* *Arg-n* kr1* *Ars* kr1* ars-s-f kr1* cham mtf33 *Cycl* kr1* *Gels* kr1* glycyr-g cte1• *Hydr* kr1* *Kali-bi* kr1* mand sp1* oci-sa sp1 v-a-b jl2
    - **accompanied** by:
      - **diphtheria** (See THROAT - Diphtheria - accompanied - tongue - white - yellowish)
      - **indigestion** (See STOMACH - Indigestion - accompanied - tongue - white - yellowish)
      - **meningitis** (See HEAD - Inflammation - meninges - accompanied - tongue - white - yellowish)
      - **typhus** fever (See FEVER - Typhus - accompanied - tongue - white - yellowish)
    - **Root**: *Rhus-t* kr1*
  - **Back** (See root)
  - **Border** moist and red (See accompanied - edges - moist)
  - **Centre**: arg-n k* ars a1 bell k* *Bry* k* canth k* card-m k* chin vk1 chinin-s *Croc* kr1* cupr a1 gels k* helon k* *Ip* vk1 *Kali-chl* k* *Kali-m* vk1 kali-p fd1.de• *Merc-cy* hr1 nat-ar k* op a1 *Petr* k* *Phos* k* rhus-v k* sabad k* sin-n k* spong fd4.de stram a1 sulph k* tub xxb verat-v a1*

- **white – Centre**: ...
  - : **accompanied** by:
    - . **broad** tongue (See Broad - sensation - accompanied - tongue - center)
    - . **down** centre | **red** stripe (See accompanied - centre - red - stripe)
    - . **metrorrhagia** (See FEMALE - Metrorrhagia - accompanied - tongue - white - centre)
    - . **pneumonia** (See CHEST - Inflammation - lungs - accompanied - tongue - white - streak - centre)
    - . **Sides**:
      - **dark** streaks along sides (See accompanied - edges - dark)
      - **red**: bell bro1* card-m mrr1 *Gels* kr1* *Ip* kr1* rhus-t bro1* ziz kr1*
    - . **Tip** | **red**: card-m mrr1 ziz kr1*
  - : **dark** brown (See accompanied - centre - brown - dark)
  - : **dark** streaks along sides (See accompanied - edges - dark)
  - : **patch**; yellowish white: ars-i vk1
  - : **red** stripe down centre (See accompanied - centre - red - stripe)
- ⁝ **Edges** (See sides)
- ⁝ **Root**: ange-s vk1 bell bg2* chim kr1* dulc fd4.de *Kali-m* br1* kali-p fd1.de• med k* moni jl2 nat-m ptk1 *Nat-p* hr1 pert-vc vk9 rhus-v a1* sabad a1 sep k* spong fd4.de tub al* ven-m rsj12•
  - : **one** side: nux-v vk1
  - : **morning**: *Calc-p* kr1*
  - : **accompanied** by:
    - . **cardialgia** (See STOMACH - Heartburn - accompanied - tongue - white - root)
    - . **cholera** infantum (See RECTUM - Cholera - infantum - accompanied - tongue - root)
    - . **clean** tongue: *Nux-v* bro1*
    - . **Brain** complaints (See HEAD - Brain; complaints of - accompanied - tongue - root - white)
    - . **Tip**; clean: hyper ptk1
  - : **boys**; in pining: aur kr1*
  - : **fur**; with deep: *Nux-v* kr1*
- ⁝ **Sides**: ange-s jl3* bell bg2 **Caust** k* *Cham* k* hydrc a1 iod k* *Iris* vk1 *Kali-s* k* *Lac-c* hr1 **Mur-ac** hr1* *Nux-v* b7a.de
  - : **one**: calc bg2 *Daph* bg2* irid-met bg2* laur bg2 lob c1* mez h2* **RHUS-T** k ●* sil bg2 thuj bg2
    - . **obliquely**: rhus-t bg2
  - : **right**: *Lob* k*
  - : **accompanied** by:
    - . **neuropathy** (See GENERALS - Neurological - accompanied - tongue - white - sides)
    - . **typhoid** fever (See FEVER - Typhoid - accompanied - tongue - white - sides)
    - . **Centre** of tongue and biliary colic; red streak on (See ABDOMEN - Pain - liver - colic - accompanied - tongue)
    - . **Centre** of tongue and red tip; red streak on: ars kr1* calad ptk1
    - . **Centre**; brown (See brown - centre - accompanied - sides - white)
    - . **Centre**; red streak on: ars vk1 caust ptk1* *Iris* kr1* verat-v ptk1
  - : **patches**: hydrc a1 sang k*
- ⁝ **Tip**: arg-n a1 canth k* chinin-s bg2 verat-v a1
- ⁝ **Triangular** base; at: bell bg2
  - : **Tip**: bell bg2 **Rhus-t** bg2

- **yellow**: **Acon** b7.de* *Adon* bg2* *Aesc* k* agar bg2* aloe k* alum b4.de* ammc vh1* anan hr1* anders bnj1 **Ant-c** k* ant-t k* *Apis* k* arg-n bg2* *Arn* k* ars k* ars-h k* ars-s-f k2 asc-t k* *Aur-m* k* *Bapt* k* bell k* *Bol-la* k* bond a1 bov k* bry k* calc-s tl1 *Camph* k* cann-s k* *Caps* b7a.de *Carb-v* k* carl a1 cassia-s cdd7*• caust b4a.de *Cham* k* **Chel** k* *Chin* k* chinin-ar k* chinin-s k* chion br1 chord-umb rly4• *Cocc* k* *Colch* k* coll k* *Coloc* k* com k* corn k* *Crot-h* k* cupr k* cypra-eg sde6.de• dios k* dioxi rbp6 *Dulc* b4a.de epiph br1 *Eup-per* k* ferr-i k* *Gels* k* guat sp1 *Hell* k* *Hep* k* hydr a1* hyos a1 *Hyper* k* iod b4a.de *Ip* k* jug-c vml3• *Kali-bi* k* *Kali-p* bg2* *Kali-s* k* lac-ac k* lac-c hr1 *Lach* k* lavand-a ctl1• *Lept* k* *Lob* hr1 lyc k* *Mag-c* hr1 *Mag-m* k* **Merc** k* merc-act bg2* *Merc-c* k* *Merc-i-f* k* *Merc-i-r* k* *Mez* k* myric k* *Nat-ar* k* nat-m k* *Nat-p* k* nat-s vk1 *Nit-ac* k* **Nux-m** k* *Nux-v* k* oci-sa sp1* ol-j a1* op a1* ox-ac a1 petr b4.de* *Ph-ac* b4a.de *Phos* k* *Phyt* k* *Plb* k* *Podo* k* *Psor* k* ptel k* *Puls* k* pyrog k* **Rhus-t** k* rumx k* sabad k* sabin k* *Sang* vk1 sanic k* sec k* seneg b4.de* *Sep* k* **Spig** k* *Stann* k* *Sulph* k* thuj k* v-a-b vk1 vac hr1* vario jl2 *Verat* k* *Verat-v* k* verb k* vip k* xan k* yohim c1* zinc b4.de* zinc-m a1 ziz hr1* [heroin sdj2]
- ⁝ **morning**: sang a1
- ⁝ **accompanied** by:
  - : **nausea** (See STOMACH - Nausea - accompanied - tongue - yellow)
  - : **typhoid** fever (See FEVER - Typhoid - accompanied - tongue - yellow)
  - : **Centre**:
    - . **gray**: *Merc* kr1*
    - . **greenish**: merc-sul k*
    - . **red**: aur vk1
  - : **Root** | **pale**: *Merc-c* kr1*
  - : **Sides**:
    - . **gray**: *Merc* kr1*
    - . **indented**: chel ptk1 hydr ptk1
    - . **red**: chel kr1* *Hell* kr1*
  - : **Tip** | **red**: aur vk1
- ⁝ **bright**: merc-i-f k*
  - : **shining**: **Apis** k*
- ⁝ **creamy**: *Nat-p* br1
- ⁝ **dirty**: **Aesc** bro1* *Ars* k* **Bapt** bro1* *Bry* bro1* *Carb-v* bro1* *Cham* bro1* **Chel** bro1* **Chin** bro1* *Chion* bro1* com k* *Ferr* bro1* guat vk1 **Hydr** bro1* *Indol* bro1* **Kali-bi** bro1* *Kali-chl* k* *Kali-s* bro1* *Lach* k* *Lept* bro1* lyc bro1* *Mag-c* k* **Merc** k* **Merc-c** k* **Merc-d** bro1* **Merc-i-f** k* *Myric* k* *Nat-p* bro1* **Nat-s** bro1* *Nux-v* bro1* *Op* k* **Ost** bro1* phos a1 *Podo* bro1* **Puls** bro1* *Sang* bro1* *Sep* k* *Sulph* bro1* vac hr1 vario jl2 verat-v k* **Yuc** bro1*
  - : **accompanied** by:
    - . **ascites** (See ABDOMEN - Dropsy - ascites - accompanied - tongue - yellow - dirty)
    - . **diphtheria** (See THROAT - Diphtheria - accompanied - tongue - yellow - dirty)
    - . **indigestion** (See STOMACH - Indigestion - accompanied - tongue - yellow - dirty)
    - . **stomatitis** (See Stomatitis - accompanied - tongue - yellow - dirty)
- ⁝ **fever**; during: cassia-s ccrh1• polyp-p br1*
- ⁝ **golden** yellow: *Nat-p* k*
  - : **clay**; looks like half dried: calc-s k*
- ⁝ **grayish** yellow: *Ambr* k* ferr a1 phyt k* puls bg2
  - : **Centre**:
    - . **accompanied** by | **Centre** | **red** stripe in the centre: *Tub* vk1
      - **Sides** | **black**: tub vk1
  - : **Root**: kali-m bg2
- ⁝ **greenish** yellow: *Calc-caust* k* chion ptk1 guare k* kali-p k* merc-sul k* mosch vk1
  - : **accompanied** by | **schizophrenia** (See MIND - Schizophrenia - tongue - yellow - greenish)
  - : **Root**: nat-s ptk1
- ⁝ **heavily** coated: *Carb-ac* kr1* *Colch* kr1* ferr-i kr1* nyct vk1 sabad kr1*
- ⁝ **moist**: hydr bg2 merc-i-f ptk1 nat-p ptk1
- ⁝ **patches**: lil-t ptk1 petr h2* sacch-a fd2.de•
- ⁝ **stripes**: *Hydr* hr1 nit-ac a1
  - : **two** yellow stripes: kali-c vk1

- **yellow**: ...
  - **white**: aloe k* alum k* *Arg-n* k* *Ars* k* ars-s-f a1 bell k* *Cham* b7a.de choc srj3• *Cocc* k* *Cupr* k* cycl k* dios k* *Gels* k* *Hydr* k* *Kali-bi* k* lac-c k* lyss k* merc-c k* mez h2* nit-ac h2* paro-i vk1 **Rhus-t** k* sabad a1 sec k* seneg k* zinc k*
    - **thick**: acon k* *Ars* k* ars-s-f k* bac vh bapt k* carbn-s k* gels k*
    - **Base** (See root)
    - **Root**: ferr a1 **Rhus-t** k* zinc h2*
  - **Base**: agar k* arg-n a1 ars k* bol-la calc-s k* chin chinin-s k* cypra-eg sde6.de• kali-bi k* kali-s *Merc* k* merc-c bg2 merc-cy k* **Merc-i-f** k* merc-sul k* **Nat-p** k* **Nat-s** bg2 *Nux-v* k* *Ost* a1 phos bg2* rhus-t bg2 sabin a1 sang bg2 *Sanic* sep bg2 *Sin-n* k* sul-i k2 ter k*
    - **bright**: merc-i-f ptk
    - **golden** yellow: *Nat-p* k*
    - **looks** like half dried clay: calc-s
    - **stripe** running along the center to tip; with a narrow, yellow: stict c1
  - **Centre**: ant-t hr1 **Bapt** a1* bry k* carb-an k* chinin-s k* coll hr1 dulc vk1 fl-ac k* hell k* *Hep* hr1 *Lept* k* merc-cy hr1 *Phyt* bro1* puls k* stram k* verat-v k*
    - **accompanied** by:
      - **Base**:
        - **yellow** | **Tip** and sides white: *Bry* b7a.de *Nux-v* b7a.de
      - **Centre** | **red** stripe: tub vk1
      - **Sides** | **red**: *Chel* a1 hell k* merc-i-f k*
    - **greenish** (See accompanied - centre - greenish)
    - **stripe** in centre; yellow: puls vk1
    - **Edges** red (See accompanied - sides - red)
  - **Root**: ange-s vk1 gink-b vk1 merc-i-f ptk1 *Nat-p* ptk1 nat-s ptk1 phyt ptk1 tamrnd vk1
    - **accompanied** by | **Tongue**; black discoloration of the (See black - accompanied - root - yellow)
  - **Sides**: ange-s vk1 *Mag-m* hr1 plb bg2
    - **left**: tamrnd vk1
    - **accompanied** by gray centre: phos k*
- **yellowish** brown (See brown - yellowish)
- **yellowish** red (See red - yellowish)

DRAWN:

- **backward**:
  - **Tongue**: tarent ptk1
    - **preventing** speech: tarent mtf33
- **down** | **Palate**; soft: stram b7.de*
- **up**:
  - ○ **Palate**; soft: glon bg2
  - **Tongue**: chin ptk1

DRINKING:

- **after** | **amel.**: bry b7.de* carb-an b4.de* *Nit-ac* b4a.de tarax b7.de*
- **agg.**: bell bg2 bry b7.de* canth b7a.de* colch b7.de* ferr b7.de* hyos b7.de* ign bg2 lach b7a.de* *Laur* b7a.de meph bg2 *Merc-c* b4a.de nat-m b4.de* nit-ac bg2 *Phos* b4a.de rhus-t b7.de* sabad b7a.de *Stram* b7.de*
- **amel.**: kali-bi bg2 nux-v b7.de*
- **water** | **agg.**: mez b4a.de

DROPPING:

- **food** | **left** corner: nux-v hr

DRYNESS: abrom-a ks5 **Acon** k* adam skp7• aesc k* aeth agar agn k* all-c allox sp1 aloe *Alum* k* alum-p k2 alum-sil k2 alumn *Am-c* k* ambr k* anac k* androc srj1• ang k* *Ant-c* k* *Ant-t* anthraco aphis *Apis* k* aq-mar skp7• arb-m oss1• *Arg-met* k* arg-n arge-pl rwt5• arizon-l nl2• *Arn* k* **Ars** k* *Ars-h* *Ars-i* *Ars-met* **Ars-s-f** *Arum-t* asaf k* asar b7.de* *Atro* *Aur* b4.de* aur-m bamb-a stb2.de• bapt k* **Bar-c** k* **Bar-m** bar-ox-suc rly4• bar-s k2 **Bell** k* berb k* beryl tpw5* *Bit-ar* wht1• **Borx** k* both-ax tsm2 bov brom bros-gau mrc1 **Bry** k* cadm-m sp1 cadm-met tpw6 cadm-s k2 calad b7a.de *Calc* k* calc-p calc-s calc-sil k2 *Camph* **Cann-i** k* *Cann-s* k* *Canth* k* **Caps** k* carb-an k* **Carb-v** k* *Carbn-s* cartl-s rly4• cassia-s ccrh1• caul *Caust* k* cedr *Cench* **Cham** k* *Chel* k* **Chin** k* chinin-ar chinin-s bg2 chlor chloram vk1 chord-umb rly4• cic h1* cimic cina k* *Cinnb* cist cit-ac rly4• cob-n sp1 coc-c coca-c sk4• *Cocc* k* coff k* colch k* coli rly4• *Coloc* com con k* cop cor-r

Dryness: ...
cortico tpw7* cortiso tpw7 croc b7.de **Crot-c** k* *Crot-h* *Cupr* k* cur cycl b7a.de cypra-eg sde6.de• cystein-l rly4• cyt-l sp1 dios dub c2* dubo-m br1 *Dulc* k* echi euph k* euphr falco-pe nl2• *Ferr* k* *Ferr-ar* ferr-i ferr-p fic-m gya1 flor-p rsj3• fuma-ac rly4• galeoc-c-h gms1• *Gamb* *Gels* ger br1 ger-i rly4• germ-met srj5• glon k* *Graph* k* haliae-lc srj5• ham helia br1* hell helon hipp hippoz hist sp1 *Hydrog* srj2• **Hyos** k* *Hyper* **Ign** k* ind iod ip b7.de* irid-met srj5• iris-t bro1 jab br1 jac-c jatr-c *Kali-ar* **Kali-bi** k* kali-br a1 *Kali-c* k* *Kali-chl* *Kali-i* *Kali-n* k* *Kali-p* k* kali-s kali-sil k2 kola stb3• lac-ac lac-c lac-d lac-h sk4• lac-leo hrn2• lac-lup hrn2• **Lach** k* lact lap-la sde8.de• lat-h bnm5• lat-m bnm6• **Laur** k* lavand-a ctl1• lec led k* *Lil-t* lob loxo-recl knl4• luf-op rsj5• luna kg1• **Lyc** k* lyss m-ambo b7.de m-arct b7.de *Mag-c* k* *Mag-m* k* mag-s k* manc mand rsj7* mang k* med k* melal-alt gya4 menis br1 **Merc** k* merc-c k* merc-i-f merl k* *Mez* k* mill moni jl2 morg-p pte1*• *Morph* bro1 mosch k* mucs-nas rly4• **Mur-ac** k* musa a1 *Myric* **Naja** k* narc-ps br1* (non:nat-act c1) **Nat-ar** **Nat-c** k* **Nat-m** k* nat-p nat-pyru rly4• **Nat-s** k* nat-sil fd3.de• nicc *Nit-ac* k* **Nux-m** k* **Nux-v** k* oena ol-an *Olib-sac* wmh1 olnd k* onos *Op* k* orot-ac rly4• ox-ac oxyt ptk2 ozone sde2• pant-ac rly4• par k* *Petr* k* petr-ra shn4• **Ph-ac** k* phel **Phos** k* *Phyt* pic-ac pieri-b mlk9.de pin-con oss2• pitu-gl skp7• plac rzf5• plac-s rly4• plat *Plb* k* positr nl2• pot-e rly4• *Psor* k* ptel *Puls* k* pyrog jl2 *Rad-br* bro1 ran-b b7.de ran-s k* rat rauw sp1 rheum b7.de *Rhod* k* **Rhus-t** k* ribo rly4• *Ros-d* wla1 rumx ruta k* sabad k* sabin sacch sst1• sacch-a fd2.de• sal-ac k* sal-al blc1• sal-fr sle1• samb k* sang k* sanic sarr *Sars* k* sec k* sel b7.de senec k* *Seneg* k* **Sep** k* ser-a-c jl2 **Sil** k* sin-n sol-ni spig b7.de spong fd4.de *Squil* k* *Stann* b4a.de staph h1* staphycoc rly4• *Stram* k* streptoc rly4• *Stront-c* k* suis-em rly4• suis-hep rly4• suis-pan rly4• sul-ac b4.de* sul-i ptk1 sulfonam ks2 **Sulph** k* tab *Tarent* tax-br oss1• tell k* ter bro1 term-a bnj1 thal-xyz srj8• thea ther thiam rly4• thuj k* *Trios* rsj11• tritic-vg fd5.de tub ptk1 tub-m vn* tung-met bdx1• vac jl2 vanil fd5.de **Verat** k* **Verat-v** k* vero-o rly4*• visc sp1 wye k2 zinc k* zinc-p k2 [bell-p-sp dcm1 cob-p stj2 spect dfg1 tax jsj7]

- **right**: hydrog srj2•
- **morning**●: am-c ambr arg-n arn **Bar-c** bar-i k2 bar-m bar-s k2 berb bros-gau mrc1 bry cann-s caps carb-an carb-v *Carbn-s* cartl-s rly4• *Cham* chin h1* cimic coff cop cortiso tpw7* *Dios* k* *Ferr* *Graph* ham fd3.de• hydrog srj2• jac-c kali-c h2* kali-n h2* kali-p k2 *Lyc* *Mag-c* mag-m h2* manc mang h2* **Mosch** sne mur-ac nat-c h2* nat-s nat-sil fd3.de• *Nit-ac* *Nux-v* ol-an op par petr petr-ra shn4• ph-ac h2* plb podo **Puls** *Rhus-t* *Sabad* sang sars sec gk senec bg1 seneg *Sep* spig spong fd4.de **Sulph** symph fd3.de• thuj tritic-vg fd5.de vanil fd5.de verat zing
  - **early**: alum bg2 am-c bg2 ambr bg2 arn bg2 bar-c bg2 canth bg2 carb-v bg2 coff bg2 *Graph* bg2 hyos bg2 laur bg2 lyc bg2 mag-c bg2 mag-m bg2 mur-ac bg2 nit-ac bg2 nux-v bg2 par bg2 petr bg2 puls bg2 sars bg2 seneg bg2 spig bg2 stront-c bg2 sulph bg2 thuj bg2
  - **waking**; on●: *(↗SLEEP - Waking - dryness)* alum am-c h2* ambr b7.de* ammc apoc bell bg2 bit-ar wht1• calc carb-v cartl-s rly4• clem cob coca graph ina-i mlk9.de iris c1 kali-c kali-p fd1.de• **Lac-c** *Lyc* m-arct b7.de mag-c mang naja ol-an *Par* *Phos* *Podo* *Rhus-t* k* sal-fr sle1• sel b7.de* sep spig stram stront-c symph fd3.de• tarax tritic-vg fd5.de tub xxb tung-met bdx1• vanil fd5.de
    - **thirstless**: ambr a1*
- **forenoon**: allox tpw3 caust hydroph rsj6• sars seneg vanil fd5.de
- **afternoon**: bung-fa mtf kali-s fd4.de laur br1 mag-c h2* olib-sac wmh1 ph-ac h2* spong fd4.de ulm-c jsj8•
- **evening**: aloe alum bg2 am-c k* bar-c bg2 bov k* bry k* cann-s cann-xyz bg2 cench k2 choc srj3• cycl k* kali-c bg2 kali-s fd4.de lac-lup hrn2• lyc merc-c mez h2* naja nux-m k* orot-ac rly4• phos h2* plat h2* *Senec* tritic-vg fd5.de ulm-c jsj8• verat vip fkr4.de
  - **amel.**: pant-ac rly4•
- **night**●: acon am-c k* *Ant-c* arge-pl rwt5• ars-i k2 *Arum-t* bell h1* bry calc *Carbn-s* *Caust* k* *Cench* cina bg2 *Cinnb* *Cocc* k* coff dios bg2 eupi gal-ac a1 glon graph hydrog srj2• jatr-c kali-c h2* kali-p fd1.de• kali-s fd4.de lac-lup hrn2• **Lyc** k ● *Mag-c* k* mag-m k* nat-sil fd3.de• nit-ac bg2 *Nux-m* **Nux-v** k ●* phel **Phos** k ● *Pic-ac* pot-e rly4• ran-s bg2 *Rhus-t* ros-d wla1 rumx ruta fd4.de sel senec **Sep** ●* sil *Sulph* vh symph fd3.de• tarent tub xxb vip fkr4.de
  - **waking**; on: *(↗SLEEP - Waking - dryness)* ambr a1 ars-i *Carbn-s* coca-c sk4• graph k2 nat-sil fd3.de• *Rat* **Rhus-t** k ● ros-d wla1 symph fd3.de•
    - **followed** by | **perspiration**: rein a1
    - **thirstless**: ambr a1

- **accompanied** by:
  - **cough** (See COUGH - Accompanied - mouth - dry)
  - **saliva**; frothy: cocc kr1*
  - **vertigo** (See VERTIGO - Accompanied - mouth)
  - ○ **Nose**; dryness of (See NOSE - Dryness - inside - accompanied - mouth)
  - **Teeth**; pain in (See TEETH - Pain - accompanied - mouth)
  - **Throat**; dryness of (See THROAT - Dryness - accompanied - mouth)
- **alternating** with | **salivation** (See Salivation - alternating - dry)
- **chewing** food agg.: ferr bg1 thuj ptk1
- **chill**; during: acon bg2 apis bg2 *Arn* bg2 ars bg2 bar-c bg2 bell bg2 bry bg2 cham bg2 chin bg2 hyos bg2 ign bg2 kali-c bg2 lach bg2 lyc bg2 m-aust b7.de mag-m bg2 merc bg2 *Mez* b4a.de* mur-ac b4a.de* nit-ac bg2 nux-m bg2 *Nux-v* bg2 petr b4.de* *Ph-ac* b4a.de* *Phos* b4.de* ran-b b7.de* *Rhus-t* b7.de* sabad bg2 *Sep* bg2 staph bg2 stram bg2 *Sulph* bg2 *Thuj* b4a.de* verat bg2
- **coition**; after: nux-v bg2
- **cold** water | **amel**.: abrom-a ks5 cadm-met tpw6 cortico tpw7 ser-a-c jl2 trios rsj11•
- **coryza**; during: alum h2* *Nux-v* b7.de* *Ros-d* wla1
- **cotton** in; as if: hippoc-k szs2
- **diarrhea**; during (See RECTUM - Diarrhea - accompanied - mouth)
- **dinner** | **after** | **agg**.: kali-n h2*
  - **before**: kali-n h2*
- **drinking**; even after: chion ptk1 gard-j vlr2•
- **drinks** | **amel**.: cortico tpw7
- **eating**; after: sulph vanil fd5.de
- **entering** the house amel.: nux-m ptk2
- **exertion** agg.: gins a1
- **fever**; during: aq-mar skp7• *Ars* b4a.de* *Asar* b7.de* *Bell* b4a.de* bry bg2 chin bg2 cocc bg2 coff b7.de* lach bg2 lyc bg2 m-ambo b7.de m-aust b7.de mur-ac b4a.de* *Nit-ac* b4.de* **Nux-m** bg2 *Nux-v* b7.de* op bg2 petr b4.de* *Ph-ac* b4.de* *Phos* b4.de* sabad b7.de* sep b4.de* spig b7.de* stram bg2 sulph b4.de* thuj b4a.de* valer b7.de* verat bg2 zinc h2*
- **menses**; during: *Cedr* **Nux-m**
- **moisten** food, cannot: ars merl
- **perspiration**; during: acon bg2 am-m bg2 apis bg2 bar-c bg2 bry bg2 cham bg2 lach bg2 lyc bg2 *Nit-ac* bg2 *Nux-v* b7.de* petr bg2 *Ph-ac* bg2 **Phos** bg2 rhus-t bg2 sabad bg2 **Sep** bg2 stram b7.de* *Sulph* bg2 *Thuj* bg2 verat bg2
- **rinse**; must: cinnb ptk1
- **rising** agg.: hydrog srj2•
- **saliva** amel.: acon bg
- **salivation**; with: alum ptk1 aral ptk1 colch ptk1 kali-c ptk1 lyc ptk1 mag-m ptk1 *Merc* ptk1 nat-m ptk1 plb ptk1 psil vml3•
- **sand** in it, as if: ars bg2 bov k* cist bg2 gins bg2 rhus-r bg2
- **sensation** of: acon k* aeth a1 aloe bg2 apis b7a.de arg-met h1 ars h2* asaf k* aur h2* bamb-a stb2.de• bell k* *Bry* b7.de* calc-p bg2 *Cann-s* b7.de* caul chin h1* chion br1 cic b7.de* cina cocc b7.de* *Colch* coli rly4• dios dros euph b4.de* glon bg2 iod b4a.de kali-c k* lyc k* m-aust b7.de malar jl2 nat-c hr1 **Nux-m** k* olnd b7.de* ozone sde2• phos bg2 plb b7.de* rheum b7.de* rhus-t b7.de* spig b7.de* stram h1* stront-c k* sul-ac k* tritic-vg fd5.de verat b7.de* viol-o viol-t k*
  - **morning**: asaf stront-c
  - **accompanied** by:
    - **Nose**; dryness of (See NOSE - Dryness - inside - accompanied - mouth - sensation)
    - **Throat**; dryness of (See THROAT - Dryness - accompanied - mouth - sensation)
  - **alternating** with | **Eye**; lachrymation (See EYE - Lachrymation - right - alternating - mouth)
  - **moist** mouth; with: acon coli rly4• hydrog srj2• malar jl2 nux-m k2 sulph viol-t
  - **mucus**; coated with: acon bell dios kali-c merl mtf11
  - **saliva**; with increased: calc bg2 kali-c bg2 malar jl2 *Merc* bg2
  - ▽ **extending** to | **Esophagus**: ozone sde2•
- **shivering**; during: arn b7.de staph b7.de
- **sleep**:
  - **during**: nux-m ptk1
- **sleep**: ...
  - **preventing** sleep: apis bro1 calc bro1 caust bro1 kali-c h2* lach bro1 *Nux-m* bro1 *Par* bro1 puls bro1 tarent bro1
- **swallowing** agg.: bell cortiso sp1 lyc nat-sil fd3.de•
- **talking** agg.: lac-lup hm2•
- **thirst**; with: abrom-a ks5 acon k* allox tpw3 aloe alum h2* am-c h2* aphis c1 arg-n arn k* ars k* *Bar-c* **Bell** bg2 berb bit-ar wht1• **Bry** k* *Camph* cann-i a1 canth k* carb-an bg2 *Carbn-s* cartl-s rly4• cassia-s ccrh1• caust h2* cench k2 cham k* chel k* *Chin* k* chinin-s bg2 cina bg2 cinnb coc-c cocc h1* colch br1 cycl k* dig *Ferr-p* sne gard-j vlr2• graph k2 hydrog srj2• kali-bi *Kali-br* hr1 kali-i kali-s fkr2.de kali-sil k2 kola stb3• kreos k* lac-lup hm2• *Lach* k* lap-la sde8.de• laur k* lavand-a ctl1• *Lec* *Luf-op* rsj5• lyc h2* lyss mag-m h2* *Merc-c* mez h2* mill mim-p rsj8• *Mosch* sne *Nat-c* k* **Nat-m** nat-p fkr6.de nat-s nept-m lsd2.fr nit-ac k* *Nux-m* k* oci-sa sk4• olib-sac wmh1 op k* petr k* petr-ra shn4• *Phos* pitu-gl skp7• plat h2* *Rhus-t* k* ros-d wla1 ruta fd4.de sars sec k* sil mtf33 *Stram* k* sulfonam ks2 sulph k* tab tell rsj10• thiam rly4• thuj h1* tritic-vg fd5.de tub gk verat k*
  - **accompanied** by | **Teeth**; pain in (See TEETH - Pain - accompanied - mouth - dryness - thirst - with)
  - **drinking** | **not** amel.: bit-ar wht1•
- **thirstless**: acon all-c aloe k1 alumn *Ambr* ang k* apis k* arn bg1 ars h2* asaf *Bell* k* **BRY** k* calad b7.de* *Camph* cann-i cann-s k* caps b7.de* carb-an h2* carb-v caust h2* *Cocc* k* coff b7.de* dios k* dulc euph k* euphr gels k2 glon k2 guare hyos b7.de* ign bg1 jatr-c kali-bi bg1 kali-c k* kali-n h2* kali-sil mtf33 lac-c k* lach bro1* lap-la sde8.de• lob mrr1 *Lyc* k* m-arct b7.de m-aust b7.de mag-c h2* *Mag-m* k* mang-p rly4• mez h2* mosch b7.de* nat-m fs* nat-sil fd3.de• nit-ac k* **NUX-M** k* *Nux-v* k* onos op k* *Par* k* ph-ac k* phos h2* positr nl2• **Puls** k* pycnop-sa mrz1 ran-s b7.de* rheum h* ruta b7.de* sabad k* sabin sacch-a fd2.de• samb k* sanic sars k* *Sep* b4a.de* *Sil* spig b7.de* *Stram* k* *Sulfonam* ks2 *Sulph* sne thuj h1* tub xxb ulm-c jsj8• valer b7.de* verat b7.de* vip fkr4.de
  - **accompanied** by | **Teeth**; pain in (See TEETH - Pain - accompanied - mouth - dryness - thirst - without)
  - **water** in mouth to moisten it and then spits it out; desires to hold: nux-m mrr1
- **walking** in open air agg.: sil
- **warm** drinks | **amel**.: cadm-met tpw6 cortiso tpw7*
- ○ **Anterior** part: *Ars* h2* bry bg2* nux-v bg1*
- **Forepart** (See anterior)
- **Gums**: bar-c h2* con bg2 ozone sde2• ther c1
  - **sensation** of: ars b4a.de* bar-c b4.de* bry b7.de* caust b4a.de graph b4a.de merc bg2 phos b4a.de stann b4a.de tab bg2 ther bg2
- **Lips**; inner side of | **Lower**: (↗*FACE - Dryness - lips)* asar h1
- **Mucous** membrane: alum tl1 colum-p sze2• gard-j vlr2•
  - **accompanied** by | **catarrh** (See NOSE - Catarrh - accompanied - mucous)
- **Palate**: acon k* aesc agar *All-c* allox tpw3 ang *Apis* k* arg-met arg-n k* arn k* asar h1* atro *Bell* k* *Bry* k* bufo *Calc* k* *Camph* k* cann-s k* *Carb-an* k* card-m chel chin chlor cina k* *Cist* coc-c cocc k* coloc cop cycl k* *Dros* *Fl-ac* k* glon graph b4.de* grat hell k* *Hyos* lac-ac lach k* led k* mag-c k* mand rsj7• mang meny k* *Merc* k* merc-sul merl mez myric *Nat-m* k* nit-ac b4.de* **Nux-m** k* nux-v b7.de* olnd k* op k* par k* ph-ac k* **Phos** k* phyt plb b7.de* puls rauw tpw8* samb k* *Seneg* k* sep k* staph k* *Stict* k* *Stram* k* stront-c b4.de* suis-em rly4• **Sulph** k* thuj k* **Verat** k* viol-o zing
  - **one-sided**: *Fl-ac*
  - **left** side: fl-ac bg2
  - **morning**: cann-s phyt
    - **waking**; on: mez *Puls* *Sulph*
  - **forenoon**: phos
  - **evening**: chlor *Cycl* fl-ac staph h1*
  - **night**: *Calc* *Nux-m*
  - **air** agg.; in open: mang
  - **eating**; after: bry
  - **nausea**; with: dig
  - **sensation** of: acon b7.de* arn b7.de* bry b7.de* dros b7.de* par b7.de* plb b7.de* ulm-c jsj8• viol-o b7.de*
  - **talking** agg.: graph h2*
  - ○ **Posteriorly**: ars bg2 *Merc* bg2 mez bg2 nux-m bg2
  - **Soft** palate | **leather**; feels like: bell bg2 *Dros* vh nux-m bg2 *Stict* k*

- **Upper** surface: merc-c bg2 thuj bg2
- **Posterior** part only: ars bg2 mez k* mosch bg2 thuj h1* vanil fd5.de
- **Tongue**: *(↗Adheres)* abrom-a vk1* acet-ac k* achy-a vk1 **Acon** k* aeth k* **Agar** k* **Ail** k* aloe k* alumn k* ambr k* anders bnj1 ant-c b7a.de *Ant-t* k* **Apis** k* apoc k* arg-met k* *Arg-n* k* *Arn* k* **Ars** k* *Ars-h* k* *Ars-i* k* *Ars-s-f* k* art-v k* *Arum-t* k* atp rly4• atro k* atro-s kr1* aur k* aur-ar k2 aur-i k2 aur-m k* *Bapt* k* bar-c k* bar-i k2 *Bar-m* k* bar-s k2 **Bell** k* boerh-d bnj1 borx b4a.de* **Bry** k* bufo k* cact k* caesal-b bnj1 cain k* **Calc** k* calc-ar k* calc-i k2 *Calc-p* k* calc-s k* **Camph** k* cann-s b7a.de canth b7.de* carb-ac kr1* *Carb-an* k* *Carb-v* k* *Carbn-s* k* cassia-s ccrh1• **Caust** k* cench k2 cephd-i bnj1 **Cham** k* *Chel* k* **Chin** k* chinin-ar k* chinin-s bg2* chlor k* chlorpr vk1 *Cic* k* *Cist* k* clem b4.de* coc-c k* **Cocc** k* coff b7.de* *Colch* bg2* com k* con k* cory br1 croc k* *Crot-h* bg2* *Crot-t* k* **Cupr** k* cyt-l sp1* daph k* dios k* *Dulc* k* elaps bg2* emb-r vk1 ery-a kr1* eup-per bg2* ferr-m k* *Fl-ac* k* gamb br gels k* glon bg2* glycyr-g cte1• graph k* guare k* **Hell** k* helon k* hippoz kr1* *Hydr* k* **Hyos** k* *Iod* k* *Ip* k* ix bnm8• *Kali-ar* k* *Kali-bi* k* kali-br k* kali-c k* *Kali-i* k* kali-p vk1 *Kalm* k* *Kreos* k* kurch bnj1 *Lac-ac* k* **Lach** k* laur k* *Leon* bro1* lina br1 luf-op vk1 *Lyc* k* lyss kr1* *Mag-m* k* mag-s vk1 manc k* mand rsj7* melal-alt gya4 **Merc** k* *Merc-c* k* merc-i-f k* *Merc-i-r* k* merc-sul k* merl k* mez k* moni jl2 morg-p pte1*• **Morph** bro1* mosch b7a.de **Mur-ac** k* musa a1 mygal kr1* naja bg2* *Nat-ar* k* *Nat-c* k* *Nat-m* k* nat-p k2 nep vk1 *Nit-ac* k* **Nux-m** k* *Nux-v* k* olib-sac wmh1 olnd bg2* op k* ox-ac k* pall kr1* par k* petr b4.de* *Ph-ac* k* *Phos* k* *Phyt* k* *Pic-ac* k* plac-s rly4• plan-mi mfm *Plb* k* *Podo* k* pot-e rly4• psil ft1 **Psor** k* ptel k* **Puls** k* *Pyrog* bg2* rauw tpw8* **Rhus-t** k* rumx k* sacch-a fd2.de• sal-fr sle1• sang mtf11 sarr k* *Sec* k* seneg b4.de* *Sep* k* sin-n k* *Spong* k* staph k* stram k* *Stront-c* k* suis-em rly4• *Sul-ac* k* sul-i k2 **Sulph** k* syc pte1*• tab k* tarax b7.de* tarent k* **Ter** k* thuj b4a.de *Tub* k* vac k* *Verat* k* **Verat-v** k* vib k* *Vip* bg2* visc vk1 zinc b4.de*
  - **morning**: ambr bg2* arg-n k* *Bapt* k* *Bar-c* k* bar-s k2 calc k* canth k* carbn-s k2 *Cist* k* clem k* graph k* hell h1* kali-c k* kali-p k* naja k* *Nit-ac* k* **Op** k* plb bg2* *Puls* k* sep k* *Sulph* k*
    - **waking**; on: arg-n k* atp rly4• bapt a1 *Calc* k* *Clem* k* coc-c k* *Mez* k* *Nux-m* kr1* ol-an k* **Op** k* *Par* k* *Phos* k* *Podo* k* **Puls** k* **Rhus-t** k* sal-fr sle1• sanic k* sep k* **Sulph** k* tarax h1
  - **afternoon**: borx h2*
  - **evening**: aloe k* arg-n k* iod k* **Nux-m** k* petr h2* senec k* tarent k*
  - **night**: all-s k* ang k* ars-i k2 *Calc* k* *Carbn-s* k* mez h2* nat-c h2 **Nux-m** k* nux-v k* *Pic-ac* k* rumx k* tarent k*
  - **accompanied** by:
    - **black** discoloration of the tongue: *Ars* kr1* *Lach* kr1* **Lyc** kr1* merc kr1* merc-sul kr1* *Verat* kr1*
    - **brown** discoloration: **Ail** bro1* **Ant-t** bro1* *Ars* kr1* bapt bro1* bell vk1 *Bry* kr1* cact vk1 cocc vk1 *Hyos* vk1 kali-p bro1* **Lach** bro1* merc mtf33 *Plb* vk1 **Rhus-t** bro1* *Spong* kr1* sulph vk1 *Tart-ac* bro1* *Vip* bro1*
      - **yellowish** brown: *Lachn* kr1*
    - **burning** pain: cyt-l vk1 mand rsj7•
    - **diabetes** (See GENERALS - Diabetes mellitus - accompanied - tongue - dry)
    - **diarrhea** (See RECTUM - Diarrhea - accompanied - tongue - dry)
    - **endocarditis** and white tongue (See CHEST - Inflammation - heart - endocardium - accompanied - tongue)
    - **mucus** (See Mucus - tongue - accompanied - dryness)
    - **nausea** (See STOMACH - Nausea - accompanied - tongue - dry)
    - **peritonitis** (See ABDOMEN - Inflammation - peritoneum - accompanied - tongue - dryness)
    - **pleuritis** (See CHEST - Inflammation - pleura - accompanied - tongue - dryness)
    - **pneumonia** (See CHEST - Inflammation - lungs - accompanied - tongue - dryness)
    - **red** discoloration of the tongue: ant-t kr1* *Merc-c* vk1 sulph mtf33
    - **rheumatism** (See EXTREMITIES - Pain - rheumatic - accompanied - tongue - dryness)
    - **roughness** of tongue: calc kr1* *Laur* kr1*

Dryness – Tongue – accompanied by: ...

- **scarlatina** (See SKIN - Eruptions - scarlatina - accompanied - tongue - dryness)
- **sore** pain: rauw vk1
- **thirst** (See STOMACH - Thirst - accompanied - tongue - dryness)
- **thirstlessness** (See STOMACH - Thirstless - accompanied - tongue)
- **typhoid** fever (See FEVER - Typhoid - accompanied - tongue - dryness)
- **white** tongue and endocarditis (See CHEST - Inflammation - heart - endocardium - accompanied - tongue)
- **Abdominal** tension: ter tl1

- **chill**; during: acon bg2 ars bg2 bell bg2 bry bg2 hyos bg2 lyc bg2 *Nat-m* bg2 ph-ac bg2 *Phos* bg2 rhus-t bg2 sulph bg2
- **fever**; during: ant-t bg2 apis bg2 **Ars** b4a.de* asaf bg2 **Bell** b4a.de* bry bg2 calc bg2 carb-an bg2 carb-v bg2 cham bg2* dulc bg2 hyos bg2 lach bg2 lyc bg2 mez bg2 mur-ac b4a.de* *Nat-m* b4a.de* *Nit-ac* bg2 **Op** b7a.de* par bg2 petr bg2 **Ph-ac** b4a.de* **Phos** b4a.de* rhus-t bg2 stram bg2 sulph bg2 verat bg2
- **menses**; during: *Cedr* k* nux-m bro1 sul-ac k* tarent bro1
- **perspiration**; during: ars bg2 bell bg2 *Calc* bg2 merc bg2 mez bg2 ph-ac bg2 phos bg2 sulph bg2
- **powder**; as if tongue would fall into: **Nux-m** kr1*
- **sensation** of: **Acon** b7.de* arg-met k* arn k* *Ars* k* ars-i k2 bell k* brom *Calc* k* camph b7.de* caps b7.de* chin b7.de* cimic *Cocc* coff b7.de* colch con bg2 mang h2* **Nat-m** k* **Nux-m** k* ph-ac h2* puls k* rhus-t b7.de* ruta b7.de* sang bg2 staph b7.de* valer b7.de*
- **sleep**; during: nux-m bro1 tarent bro1
- **sudden**: ol-an bg2
- **thirst**; without: nat-c h2
- **waking** on (See morning - waking)
- **Anterior** part: *Rumx* bg1*
- **Center**: *Acon* k* ant-c k* ant-t k* arg-met k* *Arum-t* k* *Bapt* k* *Colch* k* *Crot-h* k* hyos k* *Lach* k* **Phos** k* phyt alj rhus-t bro1 seneg k* *Stram* k* sul-ac k* verat k* vip fkr4.de
  - **Sides** moist: *Apis* k*
- **Forepart** (See anterior)
- **Half**: bell ptk1 sang ptk1
- **Root** of: all-c k* camph k*
- **Side**: cocc bg1 lac-ac bg2 sang bg1
- **Tip**: apis bg1 arn k* bell b4a.de* bry bg2* caps b7a.de *Carb-v* k* cod bg1 *Ind* bg1* merc-c bg2* mez h2* *Nux-m* kr1* *Nux-v* k* op b7a.de ox-ac bg2* phos h2* *Phyt* bg1* pot-e rly4• psor k* puls k* *Rhus-t* k* *Rumx* vh *Sec* bg2* term-c vk1 valer b7a.de*
  - **accompanied** by:
    - **throat**; moist: phos b4.de
    - **tongue**; clean (See Clean - accompanied - dryness - tip)
  - **moist**: bry k*
  - **sensation** of: caps h1*

DULLNESS of tongue (= not smooth): *Sep* b4a.de

EATING:

- **after**:
  - **agg.**: agar b4.de* alum b4.de* am-c b4.de* ambr b7.de* ars bg2 bar-c b4.de* bry b7.de calc-p bg2 canth b7.de* *Carb-v* bg2 caust b4.de* cham b7.de* chin b7.de* cina bg2 con b4.de* croc b7.de* dros b7.de* graph b4.de* hep b4.de* ign b7.de* kali-bi bg2 *Lach* bg2 laur bg2 lyc bg2 *Mez* b4a.de nat-m bg2 nat-s bg2 nux-v b7.de* phos b4.de* plat b4.de* plb b7.de* rhod b4.de* rhus-t bg2 sabad b7.de* **Sep** b4.de* sil bg2 spong b7.de* sulph b4.de* verb b7.de* zinc b4.de*
  - **amel.**: am-m b7.de* anac b4.de* bov b4.de* chin b7.de* laur b7.de* nat-c b4.de* sars b4.de*
- **before** | **agg.**: croc b7.de* plb b7.de*

- **while**:
  - **agg.**: alum b4.de* ambr b7.de* ars bg2 borx bg2 bry b7.de* carb-v b4.de* con b4.de* ferr b7.de* ign b7.de* iod b4.de* kali-c b4.de* m-ambo b7.de mag-m b4.de* merc b4.de* nat-m b4.de* ph-ac b4.de* plb b7a.de rhod b4.de* sabad b7a.de sep b4.de* spong b7.de* sulph b4.de* thuj b4.de* zinc b4.de*
  - **amel.**: alum b4.de* benz-ac ptk1 carb-an b4.de* croc b7.de* *Lach* b7a.de lyc b4.de* staph b7.de* zinc b4.de*

ECCHYMOSES:
- **dark** red, bloody: anthraci *Ter*
- **sensation** of: calc b4a.de

○ - **Tongue**: *Phos* k* plb k*

ELONGATION; sensation of:

○ - **Gums**; of: *Nit-ac*
- **Palate**: stry bro1
- **Tongue**; of: mur-ac h2

EMACIATION (See Atrophy)

ENLARGED:
- **sensation** as if: bell k*

○ - **Tongue**: *(↗Clumsy - tongue; Swelling - tongue)* acon k* agath-a nl2• ars k* ars-h k* ars-i k* aza vk1 colch k* crot-h k* cupr k* cupr-n a1 dig k* glon k* graph k* hydr k* iod k* kali-bi k* kali-br k* kali-i k* *Kali-m* kr1* lac-c k* lyss k* merc mtf33 merc-c k* merc-d sne nat-ar k* nat-m k* *Nit-ac* k* nux-v vk1 ox-ac k* par k* petr k* phos k* plb k* positr nl2• sanic mtf33 sep k*
  - **accompanied** by:
    - **indented** tongue: iod mtf33 *Kali-m* kr1*
    - **purple** discoloration of the tongue: *Kali-m* kr1*
  - **sensation** as if: *(↗Broad - sensation)* *Absin* bg1* acon agath-a nl2• alum bg1 ars caj bg1 card-m bg1 caust bg2 colch crot-t cupr dig gels psa glon hydr ina-i mlk9.de kali-bi kali-i lac-ac merc-c nat-ar ox-ac par k* petr phos phys bg1 plb polyg-pe vml2• positr nl2• puls rat bg1 sep spig bg1 xan bg1

○ · **Base**: bapt bg1 calc-chln bg1 spig bg1

EPULIS: calc k* lac-c c1* *Nat-m* k* plb c1* plb-act c1* *Sil* a1 *Thuj* k*
- **soft** and painless: calc

EROSION of tongue (See Mucous membrane - excoriation - tongue)

ERUCTATIONS:
- **agg.**: plat bg2
- **amel.**: lyc b4.de* mag-m b4a.de* phos b4.de*

ERUPTIONS: *Bell-p* sp1 cob-n sp1 hed sp1 merc br1 tritic-vg fd5.de
- **after** | **agg.**: ars bg2 bar-c bg2 bell bg2 carb-v bg2 ign bg2 merc bg2 puls bg2
- **chancre**: *Kreos* b7a.de
- **herpes**: bell-p sp1 cit-ac rly4• gaert pte1*• hed sp1 syc pte1*• [bell-p-sp dcm1]
  - **persistent**: syc fmm1•
  - **sea** bathing; after: zinc ptk1

○ · **Tongue**; on: *Nat-m* k* ros-d wla1 *Zinc* k*
  - **Root**: zinc kr1*
- **miliary** | **Tongue**: par b7.de*
- **pemphigus**: *(↗SKIN - Eruptions - pemphigus)* phos vk1
- **pimples**: caps b7.de* dulc k* ferr-i a1 hydr a1 manc a1 merc a1 ped a1 tritic-vg fd5.de verat a1
  - **sore**: sal-al blc1•

○ · **Cheeks**:
  - **right**:
    - **itching**: ephe-si hsj1•
    - **red**: ephe-si hsj1•
  - **left**: pert-vc vk9
    - **followed** by | **right**: pert-vc vk9
  - **Inner**: caps h1*
    - **And** lips: berb
      - **red** and painful: berb
  - **Gums**: berb dulc fd4.de staph a1
  - **Lips**; inner side of: mag-m h2*
  - **Palate**: bapt k* dulc mur-ac h2 nept-m lsd2.fr nux-v k* psil ft1 rumx thuj bg2 tritic-vg fd5.de

Eruptions – pimples: ...
  - **Tongue**: apis b7a.de bell k* berb k* brom k* *Calc-p* k* caps b7.de* cyclosp sa3• hell b7.de* lyc k* manc k* *Nux-v* k* plb k* propr sa3• tarax k*
    - **painful**: arg-n k* bell k* graph k* mang a1 **Nit-ac** k* nux-v k* sulph k*
      - **bleeding**: graph k*
    - **Below**: nat-c h2 sal-al blc1•
    - **Sides**: apis k* arg-n k* *Brom* b4a.de hura k* nat-c k* nept-m lsd2.fr **Nit-ac** k* osm k* sulph k*
    - **Tip**: *Bell* k* caps k* *Hell* k* *Kali-c* k* lyc bg1 *Nat-c* k* sep h2
      - **painful** when touched: bufo ptk1 caps a1
- **psoriasis**: | **Tongue**: *Castor-eq* br1* graph bro1 kali-bi bro1 *Mur-ac* bro1 *Sep* bro1
- **pustules**: bell-p sp1

○ · **Gums**: carb-an bg2 *Carb-v* bg2 petr bg2
- **ringworm**: ran-s bg3 sanic bg3* tarax bg3

○ · **Tongue**: nat-m ptk1 sanic c2*
  - **right** side: *Nat-m* k* sanic c1
- **scabs** | **Lip**; upper: borx c1
- **tetters**: nat-m b4a.de

○ · **Tongue**: nat-m b4a.de
- **variola**: lyc b4.de phos b4a.de

○ · **Tongue**: mur-ac b4a.de
- **vesicles**: abel agar k* am-c k* am-m k* ambr k* *Anac* k* ant-t **Ars** k* ars-s-f k2 aur k* aur-ar k2 aur-s k2 *Bar-c* k* borx bg1* *Calc* k* calc-s *Canth* k* caps k* *Carb-an* k* *Carb-v* b4a.de cham k* *Chel* k* chim chin cinnb k* crot-t cund sne cupr k* dulc fd4.de fago a1 gamb graph bg2 hell k* iod h* *Kali-ar* kali-bi bg2 kali-c k* kali-m k2 kali-s fd4.de lac-c lac-h htj1• m-ambo b7.de *Mag-c* k* manc med br1* *Merc* k* mez k* moni jl2 nat-ar *Nat-c* k* *Nat-m* k* nat-p nat-s k* nit-ac k* nux-v k* oena olib-sac wmh1 ox-ac ozone sde2• petr-ra shn4• phos k* plac-s rly4• psor al2 rhod k* rhus-t k* ruta fd4.de sep bg2 spig k* spong k* *Staph* k* *Sul-ac* k* sulph k* ter k* *Thuj* k* tritic-vg fd5.de vanil fd5.de
  - **bathing** in the sea; from a: zinc ptk2
  - **biting**: nat-m rhod
  - **blood** vesicles: agar canth b7a.de *Chel* b7a.de dulc fd4.de led k* nat-m positr nl2• ruta fd4.de sec symph fd3.de•
  - **burning**: am-c *Am-m* ambr apis arg-met ars k* bar-c bar-s k2 bry *Caps* *Carb-an* cycl gamb *Kali-c* kali-chl **Kali-i** kali-n *Lyc* lp *Mag-c* mang merl mez mur-ac nat-ar k* nat-c *Nat-m* nat-s orot-ac rly4• phel psor seneg spong sulph symph fd3.de• thuj
  - **cold** things amel.: *Nat-s*
  - **cutting**: mag-s
  - **gangrenous**: sec
  - **herpetic**: cit-ac rly4•
  - **menses**; before: mag-c
  - **painful**: *Anac* apis berb caust cit-ac rly4• dulc fd4.de gink-b sbd1• kali-c *Nat-c* hr1 nux-v orot-ac rly4• petr-ra shn4• phos h2 podo fd3.de• ruta fd4.de symph fd3.de•
  - **red**: petr-ra shn4•
  - **sore**, smarting: apis arg-met lyc petr-ra shn4• sulph
  - **stinging**, stitches: **Apis** cham hell kali-chl nat-m spong
  - **suppurating**: mag-c h2 phos
  - **ulcers**, becoming: calc h2 *Carb-an* clem *Merc*
  - **whitish**: berb canth kali-s fd4.de mez h2 phos symph fd3.de• *Thuj*
  - **yellow**: agar cycl zinc

○ · **Cheeks**; inner side of: calc h2 dulc fd4.de gink-b sbd1• mag-c h2 med hr1* syc fmm1• vanil fd5.de
  - **Gums**: *Ars* b4a.de bell k* berb mtf11 canth k* *Carb-an* b4a.de *Carb-v* b4a.de carc fd2.de• daph *Dulc* b4a.de gink-b sbd1• *Iod* kali-c *Mag-c* k* *Merc* k* mez k* nat-s *Nux-v* b7.de* petr k* podo fd3.de• rhus-v sep k* **Sil** k* staph h1 **Sulph** b4a.de vanil fd5.de zing
    - **black**: petr h2
    - **burning**: bell mag-c mez sep h2
    - **purulent**: aur b4a.de calc b4a.de **Carb-an** b4a.de *Carb-v* b4.de* petr b4a.de
    - **Inner**: staph b7.de*
    - **Upper**: calc b4.de*

- **vesicles**: ...
  - **Lips**:
    - **Inner** side of: cob-n sp1 dulc fd4.de nat-sil fd3.de• plac-s rly4• sep h2* sil h2* tritic-vg fd5.de
    - **Lower** lip | **Inside**: dulc fd4.de nat-sil fd3.de• olib-sac wmh1 phos h2* ruta fd4.de tritic-vg fd5.de
  - **Palate**: carb-v h2 carc fd2.de• dulc fd4.de ham fd3.de• iod *Mag-c* k* manc nat-s k* nit-ac ozone sde2• phos podo fd3.de• rhus-t sulph h2 symph fd3.de•
    - **suppurating**: phos b4a.de
    - **Hard** palate: *Ars* b4a.de calc b4a.de* canth b7.de* *Caps* b7a.de carb-v b4a.de *Dulc* b4a.de iod b4.de* mag-c b4.de* *Merc* b4a.de *Nit-ac* b4.de* nux-v b7.de* phos b4.de* spig b7.de* *Sulph* b4a.de
    - **Soft** palate: canth b7.de* mag-c b4.de* nux-v b7.de* *Sulph* b4a.de
      - **blood**; filled with: canth b7a.de led b7a.de
  - **Tongue**: acon k* **Am-c** k* am-caust vh1 *Am-m* k* ant-c k* **Apis** k* *Arg-met* k* **Ars** k* *Bar-c* k* *Bell* k* berb k* *Borx* k* brom k* bry k* *Calc* k* calc-p bg2* *Canth* k* *Caps* k* *Carb-an* k* carb-v k* *Caust* k* cham k* chim k* chin k* chinin-ar k* chlol k* chlor kr1* clem k* croc b7.de* cund sne cupr k* dulc fd4.de *Graph* k* *Ham* k* *Hell* k* indg k* *Iod* bg2* kali-ar k* *Kali-c* k* kali-chl k* kali-i k* kali-n bg2* kali-s fd4.de* kola stb3• *Lac-ac* k* *Lacer* bro1* *Lach* k* **Lyc** k* *Mag-c* k* mag-m k* manc k* mang k* med k* *Merc* k* merl k* mez k* *Mur-ac* k* *Nat-ar* k* nat-c k* **Nat-m** k* nat-p k* nat-s k* **Nit-ac** k* *Nux-v* k* phel k* phos k* phyt k* plb bg2* psor al2 puls k* ran-s bg2* rhod k* **Rhus-t** k* rhus-v k* ruta fd4.de sabad b7.de* sacch-a fd2.de• sal-ac k* sars k* *Sep* k* spig k* spong k* squil k* *Staph* k* stram k* *Sul-ac* bro1* **Sulph** bro1* symph fd3.de• *Thuj* k* tritic-vg fd5.de tub jl2 vanil fd5.de verat k* vero-o rly3• vip k* zinc k* zinc-p k2 zing k*
    - **bleeding** from slightest touch: *Mag-c* k*
    - **blood**; filled with: canth b7a.de *Led* b7a.de
    - **burning**: *Acon* k* am-c k* **Apis** k* arg-met k* ars k* bar-c k* bar-s k2 bry k* *Calc* k* calc-p k* *Caps* k* *Carb-an* k* *Graph* k* kali-chl k* **Lyc** k* *Mag-c* k* mang k* mez k* *Mur-ac* k* nat-s k* *Nit-ac* k* sal-ac kr1* sep k* **Spig** k* spong k* *Sul-ac* k* *Sulph* k* *Thuj* k*
      - **fire**; like | **right** side: *Phel* k*
    - **eating**; after: phos b4a.de*
    - **painful**: *Ars* k* *Borx* hr1 canth k* **Caust** k* graph k* kali-c k* mag-c k* nat-sil fd3.de• nux-v h1 podo fd3.de• ruta fd4.de sal-ac k* sep h2 symph fd3.de• vanil fd5.de zinc k*
    - **raw**: lyc k*
    - **red**: borx k* ruta fd4.de
    - **scalded**, as if: lyc k* plat tl1 syc bka1•
    - **spices**; after: ignis-alc es2•
    - **stinging**: *Cham* k* kali-chl k* kali-m kr1*
    - **suppurating**: ham fd3.de• mag-c k*
    - **ulcers**, becoming: *Calc* clem *Lach* tub jl2
      - **painful**: tub jl2
      - **small**: tub jl2
    - **Below**: am-c k* bar-c k* bell k* *Cham* k* chin k* dulc fd4.de graph k* *Ham* k* lacer a1* *Lach* k* podo fd3.de• rhod k* rhus-v spong fd4.de *Staph* hr1
      - **burning**: nit-ac h2
    - **Frenum**: plb
    - **Sides**: am-c k* *Apis* bg2* arg-n bg2 berb-a vk1 *Calc* k* canth bg2 *Carb-an* k* carb-v bg2 caust h2* ham bg2 lach bg2* mag-c h2* mang k* merc-cy k* nat-c h2 *Nat-m* bg2* nit-ac h2* phos bg2* *Phyt* k* sep k* *Spong* k* sulph k* *Thuj* k*
      - **ulcers**; become: *Calc*
      - **white**: thuj ptk1
    - **Tip**: agar bg2* am-c k* *Am-m* k* aphis k* *Apis* k* *Bar-c* k* *Bell* k* berb k* *Calc-p* k* caps bg2* carb-an k* **Caust** k* cycl k* **Graph** k* *Hydr* k* indg k* kali-c ptk1 *Kali-i* k* kali-n k* kali-s fd4.de kola stb3• *Lach* k* lap-la sde8.de• **Lyc** k* merc-i-r k* mur-ac bg2* nat-c ptk1 **Nat-m** k* *Nat-p* k* nat-s k* nat-sil fd3.de• phos bg2* podo fd3.de• *Puls* k* ruta fd4.de sal-ac k* sep h2 symph fd3.de• thuj bg2* tritic-vg fd5.de
      - **burning**: am-c kr1* bar-c kr1* *Carb-an* kr1* *Cycl* hr1 kali-n h2 mur-ac h2 phos h2 symph fd3.de•
      - **sensation** as if: bell k* sin-n k*
  - **Velum**: brucel sa3•

Eruptions: ...
- **wheals**: lyc bg2
- ○ - **Palate**: ars bg2 cystein-l rly4• kali-bi bg2 merc bg2
- **Tongue**: galeoc-c-h gms1• nad rly4• nat-m ptk1 orot-ac rly4• sars ptk1 staphycoc rly4• vero-o rly4• zinc ptk1
  - ○ **Side**:
    - **left**:
      - **Middle**: galeoc-c-h gms1•
      - **Tip**; near: galeoc-c-h gms1•
  - **Tip**: galeoc-c-h gms1•

EXCORIATION (See Mucous membrane - excoriation; Scorbutic)

EXCRESCENCES: merc-c bg2 **Staph** b7.de*
- **painful**: staph
- ○ - **Gums**: calc bg2 caust bg2 nat-m ptk1 ph-ac bg2 plb bg2 *Staph* k*
  - **fungus** haematodes: *Sulph* b4a.de
- **Tongue** | **Below**: *Ambr* b7.de* dros bg2* staph b7.de*

EXERTION AGG.; MENTAL (See MIND - Mental exertion - mouth)

EXFOLIATION (See Mucous membrane - excoriation - scaling)

EXOSTOSIS at roof of mouth: asaf *Aur* br1

EXPIRATION agg.: mez b4a.de

EXUDATION (See Mucous membrane - blood)

FALLING off; as if: | **Tongue**: merc bg2 merc-c b4a.de

FASTING agg.: sabad b7.de*

FAT FOOD agg.: cycl b7.de* puls b7.de*

FETID BREATH (See Odor - putrid)

FILTHY Tongue (See Discoloration - tongue - dirty)

FINGERS in the mouth, children put●: *(↗Put everything; MIND - Gestures - fingers - mouth; MIND - Gestures - tics)* *Calc* mtf33 calc-p mtf33 *Cham* mtf33 hell sne **Ip** mtf33 lyc mtf33 med mtf33 nat-m sne nat-s mtf33 nit-ac gk **Phos** gk* sil mtf33 sulph gk* ther sne verat nh*

FISSURED (See Cracked)

FIST in the mouth; children put: ip j*

FISTULA:
- **salivary** fistula: *Nit-ac* b4a.de
- ○ - **Gums**: *(↗Abscess - gums)* *Aur* k* *Aur-m* *Bar-c* *Borx* b4a.de *Calc* k* *Calc-f* bg2* canth k* **Caust** k* coch **Fl-ac** k* gink-b sbd1• hecla mtf11 hep b4a.de* *Kali-chl* *Lyc* k* mag-c *Nat-m* k* nit-ac k* petr k* ph-ac b4a.de phos physala-p bnm7• querc-r svu1• **Sil** k* *Staph* k* *Sulph* k*
  - ○ **Canine**:
    - **Upper**; near (= near eyetooth):
      - **right**: fl-ac
  - **Incisors** | **Upper**: canth ozone sde2•
  - **Lower**: *Hep* b4a.de *Merc* b4a.de
  - **Upper**: calc b4.de* canth b7.de* *Kreos* b7a.de *Phos* b4a.de
- **Palate**:
  - ▽ **extending** to | **Antrum**: merc k2

FLABBY tongue: ant-t bg3 ars bro1 bit-ar wht1• calc-s tl1* **Camph** k* cas-s br1 chel bro1 chinin-s k* cimic k* *Cub* k* dig ptk1 *Hydr* k* ign k* kali-bi bro1 kreos k* *Lycps-v* k* *Lyss* k* *Mag-m* k* med tl1 **Merc** k* merc-c bro1 *Merc-d* bro1 mur-ac bg2* nat-ar k* nat-p bro1 nit-ac bg2* nux-v vk1 *Ph-ac* k* podo bro1* pyrog bro1 rhus-t k* sanic k* *Sep* k* stram k* ter k* term-c vk1 verat bg2* xan k* yuc bro1

- **accompanied** by:
  - **diarrhea** (See RECTUM - Diarrhea - accompanied - tongue - flabby)
  - **dysenteria** (See RECTUM - Dysentery - accompanied - tongue - flabby)
  - **pale** tongue (See Discoloration - tongue - pale - accompanied - flabby)
  - **soft** tongue: ars-h kr1*
  - **stomatitis** (See Stomatitis - accompanied - tongue - flabby)

○ · **Liver**; induration of (See ABDOMEN - Hard - liver - accompanied - tongue - flabby)

FLAT:
○ - **Tongue**: loxo-lae bnm12•
  · **accompanied** by | **Sides**; raised: *Kali-bi* hr1*

FOAM (See Froth)

FOLDED tongue, like little bags on sides: anis k*
- **lead** colic; in: alumn k*

FOOD: | **escapes** from mouth when chewing: *Arg-n* k*

FOREIGN body:
- **sensation** of a:
○ · **Palate**: arg-met bg2
  · **Tongue**; on: cann-xyz bg2 gels bg2

FORMICATION (See Crawling)

FRIGHT; after: *Hyos* b7a.de

FROTH, foam from mouth: (↗*Saliva - soapy*) absin k* acet-ac acon aeth agar k* alet am-m aphis *Ars* ars-s-f k2 art-v asaf atra-r bnm3• *Bell* k* brom k* *Calc* b4.de* *Camph* k* cann-i canth k* *Carb-ac* carb-v *Caust* *Cedr* *Cham* k* *Cic* k* *Cina* k* cocc k* *Colch* k* con cori-m a1 *Crot-c* *Crot-h* **Cupr** k* cupr-act bro1 dulc fd4.de *Glon* hydr-ac k* **Hyos** k* *Ign* k* kreos *Lac-c* *Lac-d* *Lach* k* lact *Laur* k* *Lyc* lyss k* *Mag-m* mosch naja nux-m *Oena* k* olnd *Op* k* par k* ph-ac phos plb k* rhus-t *Sec* k* *Sil* stann k* *Stram* k* stry sul-ac *Tab* tart-ac teucr ther *Verat* k* verat-v ptk1
- **absent** during convulsions: ars bg2 cina bg2 kali-c bg2 nux-v bg2 petr bg2 plat bg2 sil bg2 sulph bg2
- **bloody**: absin bell h1 canth k* *Crot-c* crot-h ptk1 cupr sne *Hyos* b7.de* *Ign* k* lach ptk1 merc-c oena plb a1 sec k* *Stram* k*
  · **morning**: crot-c
- **coma**; with (See MIND - Coma - mouth)
- **convulsions**:
  · **after**: sil h2
  · **during**: (↗*GENERALS - Convulsions - epileptic - during - froth*) aeth hr1* agar ars *Art-v* *Aster* kr1 bell *Bufo* camph canth *Caust* *Cham* chir-fl bnm4• *Cic* bg2* *Cina* k* cocc colch *Cupr* k* dulc fd4.de gels *Glon* hydr-ac bg2 *Hyos* k* ign kr1 *Ind* kr1 *Lach* kr1 laur kr1 lyc h2* lyss med kr1* *Oena* k* *Op* plb kr1 *Sil* kr1 staph k* *Stry* sulph tax vip bg2
- **eggs**; odor of rotten: bell k*
- **full** of: cic bg2 plb bg2
- **greenish**: sec bg2
- **reddish**: bell k* canth hyos *Lach* sec stram
- **shaking** chill, during: ther k*
- **sleep** agg.; during: sil stram
- **talking** agg.: *Lac-d* k* plb
- **waking**; on: musca-d szs1
- **white**-milky: aeth gsy1*
- **yellow**-green: *Sec* k*

○ - **Gums**: camph bg2
- **Tongue**: nat-m bg2 plb b7.de* *Sulph* b4a.de
  · **accompanied** by bubbles on sides of tongue: nat-m bro1
○ · **Edges**: am-c ptk1 apis ptk1 iod ptk1 *Nat-m* ptk1 phos ptk1

FRUIT agg.: *Arg-met* b7a.de

FULLNESS: | **Tongue**: colch bg2

FURROWS; deep:
○ - **Lips** | **Inner**: teucr b7.de*

FURRY: ther ptk1

Furry: ...
○ - **Gums**: sul-ac h2
- **Tongue**: (↗*Discoloration - tongue - white - fur*) allox tpw4 ant-t bro1 ars bg2* *Bapt* bro1 bell bg2 bism a1 both-ax tsm2 canth bro1 *Card-m* bro1 chinin-ar bro1 chinin-s bg2 coca bro1 colch bg2 cycl h1 cypra-eg sde6.de• ferr-pic bro1 gels bro1 guaj bro1 kali-s fd4.de* lyc bro1 merc bg2* myric bro1 nux-m bg2 *Nux-v* bro1 oci-sa vk1 olib-sac wmh1 phos h2 puls bg2* rheum bg2 rumx bro1 ruta fd4.de spong fd4.de syc pte1• tung-met bdx1• vanil fd5.de ven-m rsj12*
○ · **Anterior** part: anh sp1* mand sp1 vanil fd5.de
  · **Root** of: guat sp1*

GAGGING (See STOMACH - Gagging)

GANGRENOUS: ars bg2* bapt bro1 chinin-s bg2 *Crot-h* ferr-ar hydr k* *Kali-chl* bro1 kali-p bro1 *Kreos* bro1 **Lach** k* merc bro1 merc-c k* merc-d *Mur-ac* bro1 sec bro1 sil sul-ac k* sulph
- **accompanied** by | **measles**: ars bro1 kali-chl bro1 lach bro1
- **children**; in: **Ars** k* casc

○ - **Gums**: *Lach* **Merc-c** *Sec*
  · **scabs**: chin sulph
- **Palate**: sec b7a.de
- **Tongue**: *Ars* k* *Bell* b4a.de kali-c k* lach k* merc k* phos b4a.de *Sec* k*

GINGIVAL FISTULA (See Fistula - gums)

GINGIVITIS (See Inflammation - gums)

GLANDULAR SWELLING (See Swelling - glands)

GLAZED:
○ - **Palate**: atro beryl tpw5* *Hyos* lac-c
○ · **Velum**: *Carb-ac*
- **Tongue** (See Smooth)

GLISTENING tongue (See Smooth)

GLOSSITIS (See Inflammation - tongue)

GLOSSY Tongue (See Smooth)

GLUED up sensation: mur-ac k*

GLUTINOUS (See Mucus - ropy; Saliva - gluey)

GRASPING at mouth: (↗*MIND - Gestures - tics*) dulc bg2* sil k*

GREASY sensation: card-m bg2 fl-ac bg2 iris bg2* ol-an k* sabin bg2
○ - **Gums**: iris tril-p c1
- **Palate**: asaf ptk1 card-m bg2* iris bg2 kali-p bg1* ol-an k*
- **Tongue**: *Iris* k* phys ptk1 tril-p c1 yuc a1
  · **accompanied** by | **tongue**; white (See Discoloration - tongue - white - accompanied - greasy)

GROWTHS (See Excrescences)

GUMBOIL (See Boils)

HAIR; sensation of a: pieri-b mlk9.de plut-n srj7• ther k*
○ - **Palate**; on: *Ars* b4a.de *Kali-bi* k*
- **Tongue**: all-c bg2 all-s k* apis bg2 arg-n bg2 ars bg2 carbn-s bg2 coc-c bg2 dulc fd4.de *Kali-bi* k* lyc bg2 *Nat-m* k* nat-p k* nit-ac bg2 *Nux-v* b7a.de puls bg2 ran-b bg2 **Sil** k* sulph bg2 tritic-vg fd5.de
  · **accompanied** by cough (See COUGH - Hair - tongue)
  · **reading** agg.: all-s ptk1
▽ · **extending** to | **Trachea**: sil
○ · **Anterior** part: **Sil**
  · **Root** of: kali-bi ptk2
  · **Tip**: *Ars* b4a.de *Lyc* b4a.de *Nat-m* b4a.de nat-p sil k*

HAIRY tongue: (↗*Roughness - tongue*) chloram vk1

HARD:
- **body** at palate; sensation of a: mang h2
- **spot**: caust
○ - **Palate**: bell bg3* borx c1 calc k* hyos *Nit-ac* bg3* nux-v bg3* *Phos* bg3*
- **Tongue**: aur mtf33 hyos hr1 hyosin a1 *Kali-m* kr1*

- Tongue: ...
○ · **Edges**:
⁝ **accompanied** by:
⁝ **cracked** tongue: | **Edges** (See Cracked - tongue - edges - accompanied - hard - edges)

HAWKING UP MUCUS agg.: ambr bg2 rhus-t b7.de* *Spig* b7a.de

HEAT: *Acon* k* aconin a1 aeth k* agro a1 aloe k2 alum h2* am-c b4.de* anan k* ant-t hr1 *Apis* b7a.de* arg-n bg2* *Ars* k* ars-h k* asaf bg2 asar bg2 aur k* aur-s k2 *Bad* k* **Bell** k* bond a1 **Borx** k* bov k* brach k* brom k* *Calc* k* *Calc-s* *Camph* k* canth b7.de* carb-an b4a.de* *Carb-v* k* cartl-s rly4• caul hr1 **Cham** k* chel k* chin chinin-ar *Cimic* k* cinch a1 cinnb k* clem k* *Colch* k* croc k* crot-c sk4• crot-t k* cupr bg2 cupr-s k* dor k* ferul a1 fl-ac k* gels bg2 hyos a1 *Hyper* k* jab a1 *Jatr-c* kali-bi bg2 *Kali-chl* k* *Kali-i* k* kali-m k2 kali-s k* kali-sula a1* kreos bg2 lac-ac a1 laur b7.de* lyc k* mag-c k* mag-m k* manc k* mand rsj7• merc k* merc-c b4a.de* merl k* mez k* mosch hr1* naja nat-c b4.de* nat-m k* nat-s k* nit-ac bg2 petr bg2 **Phos** b4.de* pieri-b mlk9.de plat bg2 plb b7.de* psor k* puls bg2 rhus-t k* sabad bg2 *Sal-ac* k* *Senec* k* seneg bg2 sep k* sil k* *Spig* b7a.de* spong bg2 squil bg2 stram bg2 *Stront-c* k* *Sulph* k* verat k* zinc bg2 [heroin sdj2]
- **morning**: abrot k* nat-c k*
- **afternoon**, 17 h: hyper
- **night**: am-c k* cinnb k* phos k* *Sulph* k*
- **accompanied** by | **hot** breath: kola stb3•
- **children**; in: | **mother's** nipple; mouth of child feels hot to: borx mtf33
- **coryza**; during: mag-m h2*
- **diarrhea**; during: *Borx* hr1
- **fever**; during: dulc b4a.de petr b4.de
- **streaming** from mouth; as if: nat-c bg2 *Stront-c* bg2

○ - **Gums**: *Acon* k* anan hr1 ars bg2 *Bell* k* *Caps* k* carb-v h2* *Cham* k* con bg2 *Dulc* k* eup-pur k* ferr-p k2 *Kreos* k* lyc b4.de* mag-c bg2 **Merc** bg2 merc-c bg2 mez bg2* mur-ac bg2 nat-s bg2 *Nux-v* bg2 par bg2 petr bg2 ph-ac bg2 phos bg2 puls bg2 rhus-t bg2 sep bg2 sil bg2 stront-c bg2 sulph bg2
  · **cold** sensation in teeth; with: anan
- **Palate**: acon bg2 bol-la *Camph* k* canth k* carb-v bg2 cham bg2 cina bg2 dig bg2 dulc k* ign bg2 lach bg2 led k* mag-c bg2 *Mez* k* ran-b bg2 seneg bg2 squil bg2
  · **fever**; during: dulc b4a.de petr b4a.de
○ · **Hard** palate: dulc bg2 euph bg2 lach bg2 mur-ac bg2 phos bg2
  · **Soft** palate: apis bg2 bell bg2 calc bg2 *Camph* bg2 cann-xyz bg2 canth bg2 caps bg2 *Carb-v* b4.de* caust bg2 cham bg2 cocc bg2 **Dulc** b4a.de* euph bg2 gels bg2 ign bg2 *Kali-bi* bg2 lach bg2 laur bg2 lycps-v bg2 mag-c bg2 *Merc* b4a.de* merc-c b4a.de* mez bg2 mur-ac bg2 nat-s bg2 *Nux-m* bg2 nux-v bg2 par bg2 **Petr** bg2 ph-ac bg2 phos bg2 phyt bg2 ran-b bg2 rhod bg2 sabad bg2 seneg bg2 spig bg2 *Squil* bg2 staph bg2 thuj bg2
- **Tongue**: acon k* alum bg2 am-c k* ang bg2 *Apis* k* am bg2 ars k* asar bg2 aur-ar k2 bar-c bg2 **Bell** k* bry bg2 calc bg2 canth b7.de* caps k* carb-an bg2 carb-v b4.de* caust k* cham bg2 chin bg2 cimic k* coff bg2 *Colch* bg2 con bg2 crot-t k* gels bg2 glon bg2 graph bg2 hep bg2 hyos bg2 ign bg2 kali-c bg2 lach bg2 m-aust b7.de mag-m bg2 manc k* mand rsj7• mang bg2 **Merc** b4a.de* merc-c k* *Mez* k* mur-ac bg2 nat-c bg2 nat-m bg2 *Nat-s* bg2 olnd bg2 op bg2 pana a1 *Ph-ac* bg2 **Phos** bg2 *Phyt* k* plat bg2 plb k* puls k* ran-s bg2 rhod bg2 rhus-t bg2 *Sabad* bg2 sec *Seneg* bg2 spig bg2 stram k* stry k* sulph k* sumb a1 tarax bg2 tax k* tere-ch vk1 thuj bg2 **Verat** bg2
▽ · **extending** to | **Stomach**: aml-ns bg2 apis bg2 arn bg2 ars bg2 aur bg2 brom bg2 calc-p bg2 euph bg2 gels bg2 iod bg2 merc bg2 merc-c bg2 mez bg2 psor bg2 sec bg2
○ · **Base**: calc-p bg2
  · **Root** of: calc-p bg2 cham bg2
  · **Sides** and tip: sin-n k*
  · **Tip**: acon bg2 agar bg2 am-m bg2 arg-n bg2* bapt bg2 bar-c bg2 bell bg2 calad bg2 calc bg2 calc-p bg2 carb-an bg2 carb-v h2* caust bg2 coloc bg2 cycl bg2 gamb bg2 graph bg2 kali-bi bg2 kali-c bg2 kali-i bg2 kali-n bg2 lyc bg2 mez a1 nat-c bg2 nat-m bg2 nat-s bg2 phos bg2 rat bg2 rhus-t bg2 sabad bg2

HEAVINESS:
○ - **Palate**: (↗*Motion - tongue - difficult)* thuj bg2

Heaviness: ...
- **Tongue**: *Anac* k* anh sp1 ars *Bell* k* *Carb-v* k* caust bro1 cimic bg2 *Colch* k* con b4a.de cypra-eg sde6.de• *Gels* bro1* glon ptk1 gua br1* guare k* hyos k* kali-bi ptk1 kali-p fd1.de• lach bg2* *Lyc* k* m-ambo b7.de merl k* *Mur-ac* k* *Nat-c* k* **Nat-m** k* *Nux-m* k* *Nux-v* k* pip-n c2 *Plb* k* podo fd3.de• ruta b7.de* sec k* stram k* *Verat* k*
  · **difficult** to move: (↗*Motion - tongue - difficult)* aesc *Ars* calc *Carb-v* cic con gua br1 **Lach** *Lyc* merc op *Stram*
○ · **Anterior** part: anh sp1

HEMATOMA: *Canth* b7a.de led b7a.de

HEMORRHAGE from (See Bleeding)

HERPES on tongue (See Eruptions - herpes - tongue)

HOLLOW sensation: | **Between** tongue and hard palate: choc srj3• olib-sac wmh1

HUNGRY; while: | **agg.**: canth b7.de*

HYPERTROPHY: | **Tongue** (See Enlarged - tongue)

IMPRINTED on the tongue; teeth are (See Indented - tongue)

INDENTED:
○ - **Gums**: *Carb-v* k*
- **Lips**: sil ptk1
- **Tongue**: ant-t k* **Ars** k* ars-i vk1 ars-met k* atro k* bapt bg2* bit-ar wht1• borx ptk1* brass-n-o srj5• *Calc* bg1* *Carb-v* k* card-m bg2* **Chel** k* cic a1 *Crot-t* bg2* *Dulc* k* get a1 glon k* glycyr-g cte1• guat sp1* *Hydr* k* ign k* *Iod* k* kali-bi bg2* kali-i k* lac-f al* mag-m b2.de* med tl1 **Merc** k* merc-c bro1 **Merc-d** bro1* merc-i-f bg2* **Merc-sul** vk1 morph a1 *Nat-p* bro1* nept-m lsd2.fr ozone sde2• penic vk1 pert-vc vk9 phyt vk1 *Pip-m* bg1* pip-n bg2* plb k* *Podo* k* *Puls* b2.de* pyrog bro1 **RHUS-T** k ●* ruta fd4.de sanic bro1* **Sep** k ●* stram k* sumb k* *Syph* k* tell k* vib k* yuc a1* [tax jsj7]
  · **accompanied** by:
  ⁝ **enlarged** tongue (See Enlarged - tongue - accompanied - indented)
  ⁝ **epithelioma** (See GENERALS - Cancerous - epithelioma - accompanied - tongue - indented)
  ⁝ **stomatitis** (See Stomatitis - accompanied - tongue - indented)
○ · **Sides** indented (See tongue)

INDURATION:
○ - **Cheek**; inside of: *Caust* k*
- **Gums**: brom k*
- **Palate**: calc k* *Mez* k* *Phyt* k*
- **Tongue**: *Alum* vk1 alumn br1* *Arg-n* k* ars k* *Atro* k* *Aur* k* *Aur-m* k* *Bar-c* k* *Bell* b4a.de calc-f br1* carb-an k* *Carb-v* k* con k* cupr k* gamb k* hydr ptk1 **Hyos** k* kali-i k* lyc k* *Merc* k* merc-d ptk1 mez k* mur-ac k* nit-ac b4a.de **Nux-m** k* ph-ac b4a.de *Semp* c2* **Sil** bro1* sul-i k*
  · **accompanied** by | **typhus** fever (See FEVER - Typhus - accompanied - tongue - induration)
  · **certain** places: kali-chl k* *Sulph* k*
  · **glossitis**, after: aur-m hr1* calc-f br1 *Carb-v* kr1*
  · **knotty**: carb-an ptk1
○ · **Center**: bar-c k* bry k*

INFLAMMATION (= stomatitis): *Acon* k* aloe *Alum* k* am-c anh sp1 ant-c bg2 apis k* apoc k2 arg-n bro1 arn ars k* arum-t bro1* aur-m *Bapt* bro1 **Bar-c** b4a.de *Bell* k* bism k* borx bro1* brom bufo calad b7.de* *Calc* calc-s canth k* *Caps* k* *Carb-ac* carb-v k2 *Cinnb* cob-n sp1 *Colch* k* corn bro1 crot-t dig dulc fd4.de guaj ham mtf11 hippoz *Hydr* k* *Ign* k* ip *Iris* kali-chl c2* kali-m bro1 *Kali-p* lac-f c2 lach k* lat-m bnm6• manc mand sp1 mang bg2 med jl2 **Merc** k* *Merc-c* k* *Merc-cy* mez k* *Mur-ac* nat-ar *Nat-c* *Nat-m* c2* *Nit-ac* k* *Nux-v* k* oena ox-ac parathyr jl2 **Petr** k* psor ran-s k* rhus-t k* ruta fd4.de sacch sal-ac sep bro1 sin-a c2 sin-n bro1 spiros-af oss• spong fd4.de *Staph* sul-ac k* sulph k* *Ter* thal-xyz srj8• tritic-vg fd5.de vanil fd5.de verat k* *Vesp* k*

Mouth

- **accompanied** by:
  - ○ · **Kidneys**; inflammation of | **parenchymatous** (See KIDNEYS - Inflammation - parenchymatous - accompanied - stomatitis)
- **follicular**, ulcerative: anac bro1 anan bro1 canth bro1 *Caps* bro1 *Hydrin-m* bro1 **Kali-chl** k* mag-c bro1 *Mur-ac* bro1 myric nat-m bro1 *Rhus-t* bro1 sulph bro1
- **nursing** women: *Bapt* caul *Helon Hydr*
- **sore** spots inside cheek: aloe dulc fd4.de spong fd4.de
- **ulcerative** (See Stomatitis)

○ - **Gums** (= gingivitis): acon k* *Alumn* am-c k* anan a1 arg-n ars k* ars-i aur bg2 aur-m k* bamb-a stb2.de• bell k* borx k* bov b4.de* bufo *Calc-f* bro1 calc-s bro1 calic mld2 *Caps* carb-an bg2 *Cham* k* chinin-s cit-ac mtf11 cob-n sp1 coff k2 com dulc fd4.de eug ferr-p *Hecla* bro1 *Hep* k* *Iod* k* kali-bi bg2 kali-br a1 kali-c k* *Kali-chl* kali-m k2 kali-n k* kali-p k2 kali-s fd4.de **Kreos** k* lach lap-la sde8.de• luf-op rsj5• lyss *M-arct* b7.de mag-c h2* *Merc* k* *Merc-c* k* *Moni* jl2 morg-g pte1• *Mur-ac* naja **Nat-m** k* *Nux-v* k* **Phos** k* *Phyt* pitu-gl skp7• plb *Puls* b7a.de rhus-t bro1 ruta fd4.de sal-ac mtf11 sarr a1 *Sep* bg2 **Sil** k* spiros-af oss• spong fd4.de strept-ent jl2 sulph k* thuj tritic-vg fd5.de tub c1* vanil fd5.de

- · **accompanied** by | **breath**; offensive (See Odor - offensive - accompanied - gums - inflammation)
- · **chronic**: (↗*Pyorrhea)* merc-c mrr1 phos mrr1 sil mrr1
- ○ · **Lower**: am-c b4.de* *Merc* b4a.de petr b4.de* sil bg2 sulph b4.de
  - ⁝ **Incisors**; at: nat-sil fd3.de• petr h2*
- · **Molars**; around: pitu-gl skp7•
- · **Periosteum**: hyos b7.de*
- · **Upper** | **left**: *Kreos* k*

- **Lips**, inside of: *Mur-ac* a1
- **Palate**: *Acon* k* acon-ac rly4• anan a1 *Apis* k* arum-t k2 *Aur* bg2 bar-c bg2 bar-m bg2 *Bell* k* *Calc* k* canth k* cham k* *Chin* bg2 cimic *Coc-c* k* *Colch Gels* kali-c bg2 kali-n bg2 kola stb3• *Lach* k* merc k* nit-ac k2 *Nux-v* k* *Ran-b* k* seneg tritic-vg fd5.de zinc k*
  - · **suppurating** spots: sars
  - ○ · **Arch**: bell berb kali-n
  - · **Hard** palate: ars bg2 borx bg2 *Calc* b4a.de canth bg2 merc bg2 mur-ac bg2 nit-ac bg2 *Phos* b4a.de
  - · **Soft** palate: *Acon* b7a.de *Coff* b7a.de *Par* b7a.de
  - · **Velum**: *Acon* k* ang bg2 apis *Bell* k* *Calc Caps* hr1 carb-v bg2 *Coff* k* kali-c kali-n h2* lac-c *Lach Lyss* **Merc** bg2 nat-m bg2 nux-v bg2 ph-ac bg2 phos bg2 stram bg2 sulph bg2
- **Salivary** glands: anthraci bro1 bry bro1 *Hep* bro1 *Merc* bro1 mur-ac bro1 parathyr jl2 sil tl1
- **Tongue**: *Acon* k* all-s mtf11 am-c k* anan k* ang k* ant-c mrr1 **Apis** k* apoc k2 *Arg-n* k* *Arn* k* *Ars* k* ars-s-f k2 arum-t k* aur-m k* bell k* *Benz-ac* k* borx mrr1 brom k* calc k* *Calc-s* k* *Canth* k* carb-v k* caust k* cham b7.de* chloram vk1 chlorpr vk1 cocc k* con k* **Crot-c** k* **Crot-h** k* *Cupr* k* *Cupr-act* vk1 dulc b4a.de ferr-p k* ham fd3.de• hep k* kali-ar k* kali-chl k* kali-m k2* kreos c2 **Lach** k* lepr mtf11 lyc k* m-arct bg1 *Mag-m* vh mand vk1 mang k2* *Merc* k* *Merc-c* k* merc-d a1* mez k* **Mur-ac** bro1* mygal mtf11 nat-ar k2 *Nat-m* k* *Nit-ac* k* nux-v k* ox-ac k* petr k* petr-ra shn4• *Ph-ac* b4a.de* phos b4a.de *Phyt* k* pitu-gl skp7• *Plb* k* *Prun* bg1* *Ran-b* bg2* ran-s k* sep k* *Sil* k* *Staph* k* streptoc jl2* *Sul-ac* k* *Sulph* k* syph jl2 tarax mrr1 vinc mtf11 **Vip** bro1*
  - · **one** side: nux-v k*
  - · **left** side: ars vk1 ars-s-r k* ruta vk1 sulph vk1
  - · **chronic**: *Cupr* k*
  - · **gouty**: *Benz-ac* k* *Merc* k*
  - · **induration**, with: ars k* *Aur-m* k* carb-v k* con k* *Cupr* k* lyc k* *Merc* k* mez k* sil k*
  - · **mercury**; after abuse of: *Calc* k* *Cupr* vk1 *Hep* k* *Nit-ac* k* phyt k* staph k* *Sulph* k*
  - ○ · **Center**: gels k*
  - · **Papillae**: bell k* *Merc-c* b4a.de neon srj5•
  - · **Root** of: arum-t k2 *Lach* kr1* *Phyt* mrr1
    - ⁝ **right**: *Phyt* mrr1
  - · **Sides** | **scaling** off: syph jl2

INJURIES:
- **agg.**: **Acon** bg2 bell bg2 carb-v bg2 cham bg2 **Cic** bg2 con bg2 ign bg2 lach bg2 **Merc** bg2 nit-ac bg2 puls bg2 sul-ac bg2

○ - **Tongue**: anan kr1* hyper mrr1
  - · **convulsions**; after epileptic (See GENERALS - Convulsions - epileptic - after - injuries)
  - · **insects**; swelling after sting of (See Swelling - tongue - sting)
  - · **laceration**: **Calen** kr1* *Hyper* kr1*
  - · **penetration**: hyper mrr1
  - · **teeth**; by sharp sides of: aloe kr1*

INSENSIBLE:

○ - **Palate**: hipp jl2 verat bg2
- **Tongue**: cocc b7a.de *Colch* b7a.de hell b7.de* nux-m b7.de* *Puls* b7.de* rheum b7.de*

INSPIRATION agg.: hyos b7.de* mez b4.de* ran-b b7.de* rhod b4.de*

ITCHING: *Agath-a* nl2• am-c k* ambr c1 anac k* apis *Arum-t* bg2 arund bro1 aur bg2 aur-m borx bro1 calc bg2 hep k* hist sp1 kali-bi bro1 mag-c bg2 *Merc* k* merc-i-f moni rfm1• phyt ptk1 psor rhus-t ptk1 spong fd4.de sul-ac bg2 tritic-vg fd5.de [heroin sdj2]
- **scarlatina**; during: **Arum-t**

○ - **Cheeks**; inner side of mag-c h2*
- **Gums**: am-c k* bell k* calc k* camph caust k* cimx k* dol vml3• graph k* kali-c b4.de* *Merc* k* *Nit-ac* k* phos k* rhod k* *Rhus-t* b7a.de sulph sne zinc
  - · **bleeding** when scratched: am-c k*
  - · **pain** after scratching; with: cimx
  - · **rubbed**, wants them: dol vml3•
  - ○ · **Between** the teeth: caust k*
  - · **Lower**: am-c b4.de*
- **Lip**; inside upper: thuj h1
- **Palate**: anan a1 antip vh apis k* *Arum-t* bg2* arund k* canth coca bg2 colch bg2 crot-h dioxi rbp6 ferr-ma gels br1* *Glon Kali-c* kali-p ptk1* *Lac-c* lac-loxod-a hrn2• lyss meph bg2 *Merc* k* nux-v bg2* olib-sac wmh1 ozone sde2• *Phos* k* plat bg2 *Polyg-h* ptk1* polyg-pe vml2• polys sk4• puls pyrid rly4• *Ran-b* k* rhus-t bg2 sabad bg2* sil spong fd4.de stry ptk1 sul-ac mrr1 teucr ptk1 tritic-vg fd5.de upa *Wye* k* [heroin sdj2]
  - · **night** | **midnight**:
    - ⁝ **after** | **3-4 h**: dioxi rbp6
    - ⁝ **lying** down agg.: pert c1*
  - · **accompanied** by | **hay** fever (See NOSE - Hay - accompanied - palate)
  - · **burning**: antip vh arund k*
  - · **lying** agg.; after: carbn-s
  - · **rubbing** with tongue amel.: *Wye* mrr1
  - ▽ · **extending** to | **Ear**: teucr ptk1 wye mrr1
  - ○ · **Hard** palate: apis bg2 canth bg2 croc b7.de* kali-c b4.de* par b7.de* phos b4.de* sil bg2
  - · **Soft** palate: carb-v b4.de* crot-h bg2 glon bg2 hep b4a.de phos b4.de* sabad bg2 sil bg2
- **Tongue**: alum k* apis cedr k* cinnb bg2 cist bg2 crot-c k* dulc k* lepi a1 m-arct b7.de mez bg2* nux-v b7.de* ph-ac h2* phos bg2 podo fd3.de• rhus-t bg2 rhus-v a1 spig b7.de* sulph
  - ○ · **Root** of: nux-v h1*
  - · **Tip**: aloe bg2 alum h2* dulc k* ol-an bg2 ph-ac h2* rat bg2* stann bg2* symph fd3.de•

LACERATED Tongue: anan k* art-v k* hyper k*

LAME tongue: calc k* *Dulc* k* euphr k* hydr-ac k*
- **as** if: aesc-g k* *Mur-ac* k*
- **fright**; after: hydr k* hyos k*

LARGE; tongue seems too (See Enlarged - tongue - sensation)

LAUGHING agg.: nat-m bg2

LEATHER:
○ - **Palate** feels like leather; soft (See Dryness - palate - soft - leather)
- **Tongue**:
  - **feels** like leather: acon k* aur ptk1* hyos tl1 sanic tl1
  - **looks** like burnt leather: hyos k*

LEUKOPLAKIA: *(↗Discoloration - white - patches)* borx vk1 ign vk1 nit-ac tl1

LICKS the lips (See FACE - Licking)

LIFTING agg.: *Calc* b4a.de* caust bg2 sil bg2

LIVID tongue (See Discoloration - tongue - blue)

LOLLING of tongue (See Protruding - tongue)

LONG, tongue feels too: acon k* aeth k* lyc b4a.de *Mur-ac* k* sumb

LUMPS (See Nodosities)

LYING:
- **agg.**: am b7.de* *Cham* b7.de* ip b7.de* nux-v b7.de*
- **amel.**: calc bg2 lach bg2
- **bed**; in | **agg.**: nux-v b7.de*
- **side**; on:
  - **left** | **amel.**: m-arct b7.de

LYING DOWN agg.: chin b7.de* mosch b7.de* nux-v b7.de* puls b7.de* sec bg2 sil bg2 staph b7.de*

MAPPED tongue: agar b2.de* alum b2.de* am-m b2.de* ant-c k* ant-t b2.de* *Ars* k* **Bac** bn* borx b2.de* calc b2.de* carb-v b2.de* cham k* colch b2.de* crot-h vk1 cupr b2.de* dulc bg3* *Gins* lp *Graph* b2.de* hydr bg2* *Kali-bi* k* kali-chl bg3 kali-i bg2* kali-m bg3* lac-c bg2* *Lach* k* lil-t bg2* lyc k* manc bg2* med bg2* merc k* *Merc-c* bg2* mur-ac b2.de* *Nat-m* k* nit-ac k* ox-ac bg2* pert-vc vk9 *Phos* b2.de* phyt bg2* pitu-a vml2• ran-b tl1 *Ran-s* k* *Rhus-t* k* sep bg3* sul-ac k* sulph b2.de* syph ptk1* tab bg2* **Tarax** k* *Ter* k* thuj k* tub st*
- **accompanied** by:
  - **amenorrhea** (See FEMALE - Menses - absent - accompanied - tongue - mapped)
  - **diphtheria** (See THROAT - Diphtheria - accompanied - tongue - mapped)
  - **excitement** (See MIND - Excitement - tongue - mapped)

MEASLES; during: *Carb-v* b4a.de

MEMBRANE:
- **false**: ant-t bg2 ars bg2 **Arum-t** bry euph bg2 hippoz *Iod Lac-c Lach Merc-c* bg2 *Merc-cy Mur-ac* k* **Nit-ac** k* phos bg2 *Sul-ac*
- **grayish** white: *Mur-ac* a1
- **loose**; sensation as if: lach bg2
- **offensive**, stringy: cadm-s br1
- **silvery** white all over mouth: *Kali-chl Lac-c* sul-ac
- **white** coating; like: ina-i mlk9.de samb xxb1 sul-ac
- **whitish** yellow: **Nit-ac** *Sul-ac*

○ - **Palate** covered with a false iod ip *Lac-c Lach Merc* k* merc-cy merc-i-f *Mur-ac Nit-ac* k* phos bg2 *Sang* sulph zinc bg2
  - **evening**: **Nat-p**
  - **creamy**: nat-p k*
  - **white**: *Borx* b4a.de *Hell* b4a.de *Merc* b4a.de *Sul-ac* b4a.de tritic-vg fd5.de zinc-m
  - **yellowish** gray: nit-ac

○ - **Velum**: apis *Iod Lach Lyc* merc-cy merc-i-f *Mur-ac Sang* seneg
- **Tongue**: merc-i-f ptk1
  - **heavy** dirty coating: conv br1
  - **thick**: tetox pin2•
    - ⁝ **white**: *Borx* b4a.de *Hell* b4a.de *Merc* b4a.de sul-ac b4a.de
  - **tough** and yellow: *Nit-ac* k*

MENSES:
- **after** | **agg.**: cedr bg2
- **before**:
  - **agg.**: bar-c bg2 cinnb bg2 lac-c bg2 mag-c bg2 nat-m bg2 puls bg2 sep bg2

Menses – before – agg.: ...
- ⁝ **Gums**: *Bar-c* bg2 kali-c bg2 phos bg2
- **during** | **agg.**: agar bg2 bar-c bg2 bry bg2 caul bg2 cedr bg2 cycl bg2 ferr bg2 fl-ac bg2 gels bg2 kali-n bg2 kreos bg2 lac-c bg2 mag-c bg2 mag-m bg2 mang bg2 **Merc** bg2 mosch bg2 nat-c bg2 nat-m bg2 nat-s bg2 *Nux-m* bg2 nux-v bg2 phyt bg2 *Puls* bg2 sep bg2 sul-ac bg2

MERCURIAL affections of gums (See Mercury)

MERCURY; after abuse of: | **agg.**: arg-met b7a.de* **Aur** bg2 bapt bro1 bar-m bg2 bell bg2 calc bg2 *Carb-v* k* chin **Hep** k* hydr k* *Iod* b4a.de **Lach** bg2 *Lyc* b4a.de *Merc* mur-ac bro1 *Nit-ac* k* phyt staph *Sulph* b4a.de* **Thuj** bg2

MILK agg.: cupr bg2

MOIST:
○ - **Tongue**: ars bro1 chel bro1 croc b7.de* *Hydr* bro1 kali-bi bro1 lat-m bnm6• *Merc* bro1 merc-c bro1 *Merc-d* bro1 nat-p bro1 *Podo* bro1 pyrog bro1 *Rhus-t* bro1 sanic bro1 stram bro1 verat b7.de* yuc bro1

○ - **Sides**: ail tl1 merc tl1 nat-m tl1
  - ⁝ **accompanied** by:
    - ⁝ **Centre** | **brown** (See Discoloration - tongue - brown - centre - accompanied - sides - moist)

MOTION:
- **agg.**: chin b7.de* *Spig* b7a.de
- **amel.**: meny b7.de* puls b7.de* rhus-t b7.de*
- **jaw**; of lower:
  - **agg.**: nux-v b7.de*
  - **sideways** agg.: kali-bi bg2
- **sleep**; during: ign b7.de* puls b7.de*
- **talking**; lips move as if (See MIND - Delirium - lips)
- **tongue**; of | **agg.**: apis bg2 borx bg2 cocc b7.de*

○ - **Tongue**: *(↗Protruding - tongue)*
  - **constant**: acon k* aral vh clem k* op k* stram k*
    - ⁝ **accompanied** by | **chorea** (See GENERALS - Chorea - accompanied - tongue - motion)
  - **difficult**: *(↗Heaviness - palate; Heaviness - tongue - difficult; Protruding - tongue - difficulty)* *Aesc* k* anac k* *Ars* k* *Bell* k* bufo k* cadm-s k* calc k* *Carb-an* bg2* carb-v k* *Caust* b4a.de* *Cic* k* *Colch* k* con k* dulc bg2* glon bg2* **Hyos** k* *Kali-br* k* kola stb3• **Lach** k* *Lyc* k* *Merc* k* *Mur-ac* k* *Mygal* k* *Nat-c* k* nat-m b4.de* op k* oxyurn-sc mcp1• **Phos** k* phys k* plb bg2* *Puls* k* sec bg2* spong fd4.de *Stram* k* thal-xyz srj8• verat bg2*
    - ⁝ **crusty** coat; on account of: myric k*
  - **disorderly**: merc k2
  - **hanging** out: acon b7.de* *Apis* b7a.de* **Bell** bg2* crot-h bg2* gels bg2 *Lach* k* merc bg2* plb b7.de* sil k* stram ptk1
  - **lapping**: *Bufo* k* lyc bg2*
    - ⁝ **to** and fro: *Cupr* k* *Hyos* k* *Lach* k* *Sulph* k*
  - **pain**, agg.: aloe k* ant-t k* berb k* chin k* spig k* *Sulph* k*
  - **side** to side: *Hell* k* lach k* *Lyc* k*
  - **spring**; like a: colch vk1
    - ⁝ **withdrawing** the tongue; when: zinc-ar vk1
  - **turning** around in mouth: sul-ac b4a.de
  - **wanting**, immovable: ars-s-f k* *Aur* k* *Carb-v* k* cic k* con k* op k* *Phos* k* *Stram* k*
  - **wavelike** (See Trembling - wavelike)
  - **wire**; like a: colch vk1

MUCOUS MEMBRANE:
- **blood** oozes from: am-caust vh1 aq-mar skp7• ars-h carb-v k2
- **corrugated**: carb-ac
- **detached**: ars b4a.de* carb-ac bg2 caust bg2 cupr bg2 fl-ac bg2 merc b4.de* merc-c b4a.de* sul-ac bg2 sulph b4a.de*
  - **sensation** as if: asaf b7.de* bell bg2 cupr b7a.de mag-c bg2 par b7.de* phos b4.de* phys ptk1 spig b7.de* tarax b7.de*
    - ⁝ **Tongue**: agar bg2
- **excoriation**: agar b4a.de ail k* am-c bg2 am-caust am-m k2 ambr k* ant-c k* apis k2 ars k* ars-s-f k2 **Arum-t** k* arund bamb-a stb2.de• bapt k2 bell k* berb borx bg2 bufo calc k2 *Canth* caps bg2 *Carb-an* k* carb-v bg2* caust bg2 chinin-s bg2 chlor cina coc-c dig k* *Dulc* b4a.de* fl-ac graph bg2 hell hydr k2 ip k*

Mouth

- **excoriation**: ...
kali-ar kali-c k* kola stb3• kreos bg2* lac-ac *Lach* k* mag-m k2 med merc k* merc-c bg2 merc-sul mez mur-ac k* nat-m h2* nit-ac k* nux-v b7.de* op b7.de* ph-ac k* *Phos* k* plb b7a.de rhus-t gk ruta fd4.de sang sep k* spig b7a.de spong staph bg2 stram sul-ac k* sulph symph fd3.de• thuj bg2 *Tub*
  - **menses** agg.: *Kreos* bg1*
  - **places**, in: am-caust bell *Lach* med hr1 phos ros-d wla1
  - **scaling** off: *Hell* b7a.de med hr1 spig bg1
    ⁝ **Palate**: am-c b4.de* ars bg2 borx bg2 euph b4.de* *Merc-c* b4a.de par b7.de*
    ⁝ **Hard** palate: *Par* b7a.de
  - **sour** food; after: bamb-a stb2.de•
  - **whitish**: bism hr1
  - ○ **Gums**: calc b4a.de *Carb-v* b4.de* chinin-s bg2 dig b4.de* kola stb3• *Merc* b4.de* merc-c b4a.de *Nit-ac* b4.de* nux-v b7.de* phos b4a.de *Sep* b4.de* sil b4a.de* staph b7.de*
    ⁝ **Inner**: kali-c b4.de
    ⁝ **Root**: kali-c bg2
  - **Lips**:
    ⁝ **Lower** lip | **Inner** surface: *Ign* b7a.de
  - **Palate**: am-c k* ant-c bg2 apis b7a.de bell bg2 borx bg2 calc bg2 *Canth* caust ptk1 cina bg2 euph graph h2 kola stb3• lach bg2 lycps-v bg2 *Mez* b4.de* mur-ac bg2 nat-ox rly4• nit-ac b4.de* nux-v bg2 par k* ph-ac b4.de* phos bg2 phyt plb b7a.de podo fd3.de• staph bg2
    ⁝ **sensation** as if: agar bg2 alum b4.de* apis b7a.de bell b4.de* calc-caust c1 carb-v bg2 *Caust* b4.de* dig bg2 fl-ac bg2 graph b4.de* ign b7.de* kola stb3• lach k* mag-c b4.de* mang b4.de* merc b4.de* merl mtf11 mez bg2 mur-ac bg2 nit-ac bg2 nux-m b7.de* *Nux-v* b7.de* par k* phos b4.de* plat b4.de* puls b7.de* rumx bg2 ruta b7.de* seneg b4.de* staph b7.de* thuj b4.de* viol-o b7.de*
    ⁝ **Palate**; hard: *Lach* b7a.de
    ⁝ **shrivelled**, as if burnt: borx k*
    ⁝ **spot**: mur-ac h2
    ⁝ **Soft** palate: ph-ac bg2 ruta bg2
  - **Tongue**: agar b4.de* apis b7a.de* ars k* ars-s-f k2 arum-t k2 *Aur* aur-m k2 bac bn bapt k2 *Calc Canth* k* *Carb-ac* carb-v b4a.de* cic b7.de* *Cist* dig b4.de* *Hell* b7a.de kali-ar kali-c b4.de* *Lach* bg2* laur bg2 lyc b4.de* **Merc** k* *Merc-c* mez bg2 moni rfm1• *Mur-ac* k* nat-c b4.de* nat-m b4.de* *Nit-ac* k* *Nux-v* b7.de* op b7.de* ox-ac ph-ac bg2 *Phos* bg2* *Ran-s* k* rhus-t k2 sabad bg2 **Sep** k* *Sil* b4.de* spig b7.de* sul-ac k* sulph syph k2 tarax k* thuj b4a.de
    ⁝ **accompanied** by | **dysentery** (See RECTUM - Dysentery - accompanied - tongue - excoriation)
    ⁝ **sensation** of: agar b4a.de
    ⁝ **spots**; in: nat-m gk
    ⁝ **Center**: am-c k*
    ⁝ **Frenum**: kali-c h2
    ⁝ **Sides**: raja-s jl3*
    ⁝ **Tip**: kali-c h2
- **glossy**: apis bro1 nit-ac bro1 ter bro1
- **inflamed**: canth colch *Dulc* k* ign merc-i-r
  - **burns**; from: apis bro1 canth bro1
- **irritation**: fuli br1
- **milky**: kali-i k* lac-c k2
- **pale**: acet-ac chinin-s *Eup-per Ferr* k* mang *Merc* morph bro1 *Nat-m*
- **purple**: *Lach*
- **red** | **dark**: *Bapt* bro1 lach bro1 morph bro1 *Phyt* bro1
- **scalded**, as if: *(↗Pain - burnt)* ham
- **shredded**: aur-m-n bg2
- **spongy**: camph
- **swollen**: *Dulc* b4a.de
  - **red**:
    ⁝ **accompanied** by | **gray** based ulcers: kali-chl bro1
- **thickened**: sul-ac symph fd3.de•
- **yellowish**:
  - **gray**: **Nit-ac**
  - **white**: aq-mar skp7•

MUCOUS PATCHES (See Patches)

MUCUS: *(↗Odor; Pasty; Saliva; Sticky; Taste)* aloe alum k* alum-sil k2 am-c ang k* ant-c br1 ant-t k2 aphis apoc arg-n k* arn ars ars-i asar k* aur aur-ar k2 *Bar-c Bar-m* bar-s k2 *Bell* k* borx h2 brom bry *Calc* k* calc-s calc-sil k2 caps k* *Caust* k* cedr **Chel** k* *Chin* k* chinin-s bg2 chlor cist k2 colch bro1* *Crot-h* cupr k* cycl h1 dulc bro1* echi euph *Fl-ac* graph k* hep k* hydr hyos h1 *Ign* k* iod *Ip Kali-ar Kali-c* kali-chl k* kali-p kali-s kali-sil k2 kreos k* *Lac-c Lach* k* laur lyc k* mag-c mag-m k* manc *Merc* k* *Merc-c* mur-ac bg2 nat-c h2* **Nat-m** k* nat-s k2 nit-ac bg2* **Nux-m** k* *Nux-v* k* oena op ox-ac *Petr* k* *Ph-ac* k* phos k* plat h2 plb k* positr nl2• *Psor Puls* k* *Rheum* c2 *Rhus-t* k* sel sep *Sil* k* spig k* squil k* staph stram k* suis-pan rly4• sul-ac sul-i k2 *Sulph* k* tab bg1 teucr k* ther k* verat
- **morning**: agar alum h2* arg-n a1 ars-i **Bell** calc calc-s carb-an h2* chin h1* cupr dios *Fl-ac Graph* ign *Iod* kali-n h2* lyc mag-c mag-m manc merc mur-ac **Nat-m** sne nicc *Nux-v* ph-ac plat h2* plb *Podo* **Puls** rheum sars *Sep* sil spig *Stront-c Sulph* thuj til zinc h2* zing
- **evening**: alum am-c ang calc
- **night**: sulph h2*
- **acid**: *(↗Taste - sour)* benz-ac
- **adhesive**: alum b4a.de mag-c b4a.de myric ptk1
- **agg.**: kali-bi bg2
- **balls** of: mag-p bg1 *Nit-ac* b4a.de
- **blackish**: bell b4a.de
- **bloody**: bism h1*
- **brown**: gels bg2 nat-p bg2 sul-ac bg2
- **burning**: graph h2*
- **clay**; tasting like: *Puls* b7a.de
- **cotton**, like: **Puls**
- **detached** by hawking; easily: *Carb-v* b4a.de
- **dirty**: con bg2
- **eating**; after: hyper *Lac-c* plat verat
- **exertion** agg.: chin h1*
- **fever**; before: chin b7a.de rhus-t b7a.de spig b7a.de
- **flies** from mouth when coughing: *(↗EXPECTORATION - Flies)* bad k* *Chel*
- **frothy** (See Froth)
- **greenish** expelled while sneezing: colch k*
- **lumps**; in: *Agar* b4a.de seneg b4a.de
- **offensive**: bar-i k2 bry myric ptk1 rheum ptk1 zinc h2
- **plastic**, malleable: *Brom* b4a.de *Hep* b4a.de
- **putrid**: bar-i k2
- **red**: mez bg2 thuj b4a.de
- **ropy**: *(↗Saliva - ropy; Saliva - viscid)* aesc ail ant-t k2 chel ferr-m hydr k2 **Kali-bi** kali-br *Lyc* med *Phyt* sul-ac
  - **epileptic** convulsions; during: kali-bi
- **salty**: graph h2*
- **sensation** of: *Cycl* b7a.de
- **sleep**; after: rheum ptk1
- **slimy**: calc bg2 kali-i bg2 puls bg2
- **soft**: *Dros* b7a.de
- **thick**: *Aesc* aloe alum b4a.de ant-t k2 apis arg-n br1 atro bar-c bell bufo ery-a ip *Mag-c* b4a.de myric nat-s k2 *Nux-m* k* pyrog jl2 suis-pan rly4• verat verat-v
- **viscid**: **Aesc** agn ail ang apis arg-n *Arum-t Bar-c Bar-m* bell *Bry* **Caps** carb-ac *Carb-v* chel cinnb cop *Crot-h* cycl ery-a ferr-m hell *Hydr* **Kali-bi** kali-br *Lach* bg1 lyc lyss mag-c manc med *Mur-ac* myric *Nat-s* k* nit-ac pall ph-ac *Phyt* plat podo c1 psor puls **Rhus-t** rhus-v ruta sel squil stann stram suis-pan rly4• sul-ac sumb tab verat
- **white** | **milky**: kali-m k2
- **yellowish**: *Aesc* aq-mar vk1 hydr k2 hyos oci-sa sp1 plb pyrog jl2 spig tab
- ○ **Gums**: nux-v b7.de*
- **Palate** | **tough**: puls h1
- **Tongue**; collection of mucus on: *(↗Sticky - tongue)* *Acon* b7.de* agar b4.de* all-c k* alum k* *Alumn* k* arg-n k* arn vk1 ars-h k* ars-met k* arum-d k* arum-t sne *Bar-c* k* bar-m k* *Bell* k* berb k* bov kr1* calc k* canth k* caps b7a.de carb-ac k* carb-an k* *Cham* b7.de* chel k* **Chin** b7.de* chinin-ar k* chinin-s bg2 *Cina* b7.de* *Cocc* k* colch k* cupr k* cupr-act kr1* cupr-n a1 cycl vk1 *Dig* b4a.de* dulc k* eucal ptk1 fl-ac k* grat k* *Hydr* k* *Ign* b7.de* jug-r k* kali-bi bg2* kali-n k* kali-p k* kali-s k* kreos k* *Lach* k* lact k* m-arct b7.de mag-c h2 mag-m h2 *Merc* k* merc-c k* morg-p pte1*• nat-c bg2 **Nat-m** k* *Nat-s* k* nux-m k* *Nux-v* b7.de* *Petr* k* ph-ac k* *Phos* k* phyt k* plb b7.de* positr nl2•

- **Tongue**; collection of mucus on: ...
  Puls k* rhus-t k* sec k* seneg bg2 **Sep** k* sil b4.de* stann b4.de* stront-c b4.de* *Sulph* k* thuj b4a.de *Verb* k* viol-t k* zinc k*
  - **morning**: agar k* mag-m h2 sang k* sulph h2 verb k*
  - **evening**: ars-h kr1* arum-d kr1*
  - **accompanied** by:
    - **dryness** of tongue: *Calc* kr1*
    - **dysmenorrhea** (See FEMALE - Menses - painful - accompanied - tongue - mucus)
    - **hemorrhoids** (See RECTUM - Hemorrhoids - accompanied - tongue - mucus)
    - **Head**; complaints of (See HEAD - Complaints - accompanied - tongue - mucus)
    - **Throat**; sore (See THROAT - Inflammation - accompanied - tongue - mucus)
    - **Uterus**; induration of (See FEMALE - Induration - uterus - accompanied - tongue - mucus)
  - **brown**: **Rhus-t** kr1* *Sil* kr1*
    - **accompanied** by:
      - **typhoid** fever (See FEVER - Typhoid - accompanied - tongue - mucus - brown)
      - **Intestines**; complaints of (See ABDOMEN - Complaints - intestines - accompanied - tongue)
    - **mustard**; like stale liquid: kali-p kr1* podo ptk1
    - **Sides**:
      - **except** on sides:
        - **morning** | **rising** agg.: *Rhus-t* a1*
  - **eating**; after: sep h2 verb k*
  - **salty**: sulph h2
  - **sensation** of mucus: chin h1
  - **shiny**: agar bg2 arn bg2 chel bg2 cycl bg2 grat bg2 kali-bi bg2 puls bg2 rhus-t bg2 sep bg2
  - **slimy** | **Sides**: *Nat-m* bg2 phos bg2
  - **sticky**: bell bg2 ph-ac bg2
  - **streak**: phos bg2
  - **string**; can be pulled off in a: bell k*
  - **thick**: bar-c bg2 bell bg2 bry bg2 *Cham* bg2 chin bg2 **Kali-bi** bg2 *Lach* bg2 **Merc** bg2 nux-v bg2 phos bg2 puls bg2 **Sabad** bg2 sabin bg2 sel bg2 sulph bg2
  - **tough**: ant-t bg2 bell k* cupr k* dulc k* lach k* merc k* nux-v k* ph-ac k* puls k* sulph k* verb h
  - **white**: aq-mar vk1 cain kr1* viol-t kr1* zinc kr1*
    - **morning**: benz-ac kr1*
    - **accompanied** by:
      - **angina** (See THROAT - Inflammation - accompanied - tongue - mucus - collection - white)
      - **cholera** (See RECTUM - Cholera - accompanied - tongue - mucus)
      - **gastritis** (See STOMACH - Inflammation - accompanied - tongue - mucus - white)
      - **jaundice** (See SKIN - Discoloration - yellow - accompanied - tongue - mucus)
      - **nausea** (See STOMACH - Nausea - accompanied - tongue - white mucus)
      - **ovaritis** (See FEMALE - Inflammation - ovaries - accompanied - tongue - mucus)
      - **taste**; loss of (See Taste - wanting, loss - accompanied - tongue)
      - **thirst** (See STOMACH - Thirst - accompanied - tongue - mucus)
      - **typhoid** fever (See FEVER - Typhoid - accompanied - tongue - mucus)
      - **Stomach**; inflammation of (See STOMACH - Inflammation - accompanied - tongue - mucus - white)
    - **yellowish** white: *Bell* kr1*

Mucus – **Tongue**; collection of mucus on: ...
  - **yellow**: chinin-ar kr1*
    - **accompanied** by red sides of tongue: oci-sa vk1
  - ○ **Root**:
    - **accompanied** by | **clean** tongue: alum kr1*
  - **Tip**: scroph-n bg2

NECROSIS: | **Palate**; hard: **Aur** bg2* bar-c bg2 calc bg2 *Lach* bg2 *Merc* bg2 sil bg2

NERVOUS persons; complaints of: ign bg2

NODOSITIES: antip vh1 ars-h bro1 *Aur* bro1 aur-m-n bro1 castm bro1 *Gali* bro1 iod k* lyss bg1 mag-c k* merc-i-r mur-ac bro1 nit-ac bro1 phos k* ruta fd4.de stront-c k* sulph k2 syph k2 *Thuj* bro1
- **bleeding** and burning when touched: mag-c h2*
- ○ **Gums**: berb *Calc* bg2 caust k* *Kreos* b7a.de nat-c bg2 nat-s ph-ac k* plb k* *Staph* k* thuj bg2
- **Lips**; inner surface of | **Lower**: *Ign* b7a.de
- **Palate**: *Asaf* k* carc tpw2* mang k* mang-act br1
- **Tongue**: ambr k* *Ars-h* vk1 aur k* *Aur-m-n* vk1 **Carb-an** k* *Castor-eq* vk1 dros b7.de* eupi k* (non:gal-ac br1) gali hl9* graph bg2* helo-s bnm14• iod k* kali-i k* lyc k* mag-c b4.de* mang k* mur-ac k* *Nit-ac* vk1 phos b4.de* *Sil* k* sulph k2 **Thuj** vk1
  - **right** side:
    - **coming** to a point: ars-h k*
    - **Under**: ambr k*
  - ○ **Below**: ambr k* sulph k2
  - **Edges**; along: helo-s bnm14• nat-m mtf33
  - **Tip** of tongue; a hard forming vesicle on | **unclean** ulcer with hard sides; resulting in an: ph-ac k*

NOMA (See Stomatitis - gangrenous)

NUMBNESS: *Acon* k* aids nl2• ambr k* bapt bg2* bar-c k* bell ptk1 *Bov* k* carbn-s colch con bg2 *Gels* bg2 hyos mtf11 indg jatr-c *Kali-br* k* kali-c k* kali-i k* ketogl-ac rly4• lap-la rsp1 lat-m bnm6• lyc k* mag-c k* mag-m b4.de* mag-s mand sp1 nat-p nat-s k* nit-ac k* orot-ac rly4• pieri-b mlk9.de sinus rly4• stram bg1 stront-c b4.de* suis-em rly4• ther k* vero-o rly4*•
- **one** side: nat-m
  - **accompanied** by:
    - **Tongue** | **paralysis** of tongue (See Paralysis - tongue - accompanied - numbness)
- **morning**: (non:ambr k*) bar-c bov kali-c a1 kali-i k* mag-m h2* stront-c
  - **waking**; on: ambr bg1* kali-i mag-c
- **headache**; during: nit-ac h2*
- **menses**; during: mag-m k*
- ○ **Cheek**; spot inside: mag-c h2
- **Gums**: *Acon* *Apis* am b7.de* ign k* *Kali-br* hr1 m-arct b7.de*
- **Lip**; inside upper: bar-c h2
- **Palate**: bapt k* bar-c h2* ketogl-ac rly4• lap-la rsp1 mag-c bg2 verat k*
  - **morning** | **waking**; on: mag-c
- **Tongue**: *Acon* k* agar k* agath-a nl2• am-c b4.de* ambr k* *Apis* k* *Ars* k* atra-r bnm3• bapt k* bell k* borx k* bov k* brach *Calc-p* camph carbn-s k* *Colch* k* con bro1 crot-h crot-t bg2 echi bro1* *Eos* br1 eup-pur falco-pe nl2• ferr k* ferr-ar *Fl-ac* **Gels** k* *Glon* k* *Hell* k* *Hyos* k* ictod *Ign* k* jatr-c kali-ar lath br1* *Laur* k* lith-m c2 lyc k* mag-c b4.de* mand sp1* mang meph merc k* merc-c k* merl k* nat-ar nat-c **Nat-m** k ●* nat-p **Nux-m** k* nux-v bro1 olnd ptk1 ozone sde2• plat bro1 puls k* rad-br bro1 *Rheum* k* sabad bg2 sec bro1 sep k* sil k* suis-em rly4• sul-ac tab bg2 ther *Thuj* b4a.de vip zinc
  - **one** side: gels c1 **Nat-m** k ●* nux-v puls gk
    - **night**: gels kr1
    - **accompanied** by | **vertigo**: agar ptk1
  - **morning** | **waking**; on: am-c bov kali-c h2* mag-c
  - **accompanied** by | **Head**; pain in (See HEAD - Pain - accompanied - tongue - numbness)
  - **fright**; after a: hyos tl1
  - ○ **Posteriorly** (See root)
  - **Root** of: **Bov** bg1*
  - **Tip**: agath-a nl2• bell bg2 hydrog srj2• phos bg2
    - **Half** of: nat-m bg2

Mouth

ODOR: *(↗Mucus)*
- **acrid**: agar
- **alkaline**: *Kali-c*
- **bad**: *Arn* bg3 ars bg3 aur bg3 bacls-10 pte1• bapt bg3 *Carb-v* bg3 cham bg3 dros gk elaps br lach bg3 *Merc* bg3 morg-p pte1• nit-ac bg3 *Nux-v* bg3 puls bg3 sep b4.de* ser-a-c jl2 sulph bg3 verat-v bg3
  - **morning**: ser-a-c jl2
  - **sense** of: ant-c b7.de* bar-c bg2 bell b4.de* chin b7.de* cocc b7.de* laur b7.de* nat-m bg2 ol-an bg2 plan bg2 spig bg2
- **burnt**: dros b7.de*
  - **cough** agg.; during: dros h1
- **cadaverous**: **Ars** k* caps *Carb-v* b4a.de *Dulc* b4a.de *Hyos* *Lach* b7a.de **Nit-ac** k* phos pyrog k2
  - **morning** | **evening**; and: *Hyos*
- **cheesy**: *Aur* k* *Hep* *Kali-c* k* kali-p mez k*
- **chloroform** of ether; like: verat-v hr1*
- **cress**; like: par k*
- **earthy**: mang b4a.de* stront-c b4.de*
  - **morning**: mang
- **eating**; after: arn aur carb-v cham k* merc nux-v k* sil *Sulph* k* zinc
- **eggs**; like rotten: arn mrr1* querc-r-g-s mtf11
- **fecal**: bell bg2
- **fetid** (See putrid)
- **fever**; during: arn bg2
- **fish** brine: anac bg2 bell bg2 bufo bg2 calc bg2 *Graph* bg2 hep bg2 med bg2 *Ol-an* bg2 sanic bg2 *Tell* bg2 thuj bg2 uran-n bg2
  - **asthma** attack: | **before**: **Sanic** vh
- **garlicky**: *Ars* b4a.de kalag br1 petr k* sin-n *Tell* k*
- **herring**; like spoiled: *Chel* b7a.de
- **horse**-radish: agar k*
- **menses**; during: ovi-p bg1
- **mercury**: ant-c bar-m k* merc k2 sil
- **metallic**: berb *Merc-i-f* mez
- **milk**; like: spong b7.de*
  - **fresh** milk; like: *Dros* b7a.de
- **musty**: *Alum* *Crot-h* k* eup-per nat-c pot-e rly4• rhus-t
- **nausea**: diph mtf11
- **offensive**: *(↗TEETH - Odor)* abies-n br1* acet-ac acon k* *Agar* k* ail bg2* *All-c* aloe alum k* alum-p k2 alum-sil k2 am-c k* *Ambr* k* *Anac* k* anan ang b2.de* ant-c b2.de* ant-t b2.de* *Anthraci* apis k* aq-mar skp7• arg-met *Arg-n* k* arge-pl rwt5• **Arn** k* **Ars** k* **Ars-i** ars-s-f k2 *Arum-t* bg2* asar b2.de* *Aur* k* aur-ar k2 aur-s k2 bacls-10 fmm1• bamb-a stb2.de• *Bapt* k* *Bar-c* k* bar-m k* bar-s k2 *Bell* k* berb bism b2.de* borx b2.de* bov k* brom bg2 *Bry* k* bufo cact calag bro1 *Calc* k* calc-i k2 calc-s calc-sil k2 camph b2.de* canth b2.de* *Caps* k* **Carb-ac** k* carb-an k* **Carb-v** k* *Carbn-s* carc fd2.de• *Carl* cas-s br1 castm *Caust* **Cham** k* **Chel** k* *Chin* k* chinin-ar chinin-m c1 *Cimic* cina cist k* *Clem* coc-c cocc b2.de* coch coff b2.de* cop *Croc* k* crot-h bg2* cupr b2.de* cupr-ar cypra-eg sde6.de• daph k* dig b2.de* diosm br1 *Diph* br1* dros k* *Dulc* k* elaps br ferr b2.de* *Fl-ac* *Gels* gink-b sbd1• glycyr-g cte1• *Graph* k* hell b2.de* *Hep* k* hir skp7• *Hyos* k* ign b2.de* indol bro1 *Iod* k* ip k* irid-met srj5• kali-ar *Kali-bi* k* kali-br bg2* *Kali-c* k* kali-chl bg2* *Kali-i* k* kali-m k2 kali-n k* **Kali-p** k* kali-perm bro1 kali-s kali-sil k2 *Kali-tel* bro1 **Kreos** k* *Lac-c* *Lac-d* lach-h sk4• **Lach** k* laur b2.de* led k* *Lyc* k* m-ambo b2.de* m-arct b2.de* m-aust b2.de* *Manc* mang med k2 meph ptk1 **Merc** k* **Merc-c** k* merc-cy bg2* *Merc-d* bro1 *Merc-i-f* k* mez k* mim-p rsj8• *Mur-ac* k* nat-c bg2 **Nat-m** k* *Nat-s* nat-sil fd3.de• *Nat-tel* bro1 nicc **Nit-ac** k* *Nux-m* k* *Nux-v* k* olib-sac wmh1 olnd b2.de* *Petr* k* *Ph-ac* k* phos k* *Phyt* k* plan **Plb** k* podo k* psor bro1* *Puls* k* *Pyrog* bg2* *Querc* bro1 querc-r c1 rheum b2.de* rhus-t k* ruta b2.de* sabin k* sal-ac sanic sars k* sec bg2 seneg k* *Sep* k* sil k* sin-n bro1* spig k* *Stann* k* staph k* stram b2.de* stront-c k* suis-em rly4• suis-pan rly4• *Sul-ac* k* sul-i k2 **Sulph** k* syph xxb ter bro1 teucr thal-xyz srj8• thea thuj b2.de* **Tub** k* valer b2.de* verat-v ptk1 verb k* zinc k* [tax jsj7]
  - **morning**: acet-ac agar am-c ambr k* apis *Arg-n* k* arn k* *Aur* bapt bell k* cact *Camph* k* castm chin cimic cop fago grat k* hyos lyc mang nat-sil fd3.de• **Nux-v** k •* phys **Puls** k* rheum h sang sars *Sil* k* sulph k* thea verb h
  - **evening**: aur h2 puls bg2 sulph h2*
    - **or** night: puls bro1 sulph bro1
  - **night**: aur h2 *Podo* puls bg2 sulph bg2

- **offensive**: ...
  - **accompanied** by:
    - **cancer**: cit-ac mtf11 kali-perm mtf11 oxal-a mtf11 sep mtf11
    - **constipation** (See RECTUM - Constipation - accompanied - mouth - odor)
    - **Gums** | **inflammation** of: kreos mrr1
    - **Head**; pain in (See HEAD - Pain - accompanied - breath)
    - **Teeth**; caries of: kreos tl1*
  - **chill**; during: anac bg2 *Apis* bg2 **Arn** bg2 ars bg2 aur bg2 bell bg2 bry bg2 carb-v bg2 cham bg2 dulc bg2 graph bg2 ip bg2 lach bg2 lyc bg2 **Merc** bg2 nit-ac bg2 *Nux-v* bg2 petr bg2 puls bg2 rhus-t bg2 sep bg2 sil bg2 sul-ac bg2 *Sulph* bg2
  - **cough**, during: all-s k* ambr arn **Caps** k* dros k* graph lach m-aust b7a.de mag-c merc mez ph-ac b4a.de sang sep k* stann sulph k*
  - **diphtheria**; during: *Diph* br1 kreos tl1 merc-c tl1
  - **eating**, after: cham b7a.de* *Nux-v* bro1 sulph b4a.de*
  - **fever**; during: *Arn* b7a.de
  - **menses**:
    - **before**: caul *Sep*
    - **during**: bar-m *Cedr* *Merc* ovi-p bg1
  - **oneself**; to: kali-bi bg2 ol-an bg2
  - **perspiration**; during: acon bg2 **Arn** bg2 bry bg2 carb-v bg2 *Cham* bg2 ip bg2 lach bg2 **Merc** bg2 nit-ac bg2 **Nux-v** bg2 puls bg2
  - **stool**; during: *Ars* b4a.de carb-v b4a.de *Merc* b4a.de
  - ○ **Gums**: graph b4a.de*
- **onions**; like: asaf ptk1 kali-i k* lyc bg1 par bg2* petr sin-n k* tell
- **pepper**, like: asc-t c1
- **pitch**: canth k*
- **puberty**, girls: aur bg2*
- **pungent**: agar b4.de*
- **putrid**: acon tl1 act-sp ail k2* alum k* alum-p k2 *Alumn* vh1 ambr *Anac* *Apis* *Arg-met* *Arg-n* **Arn** k* **Ars** k* **Ars-i** *Arum-t* *Aur* k* aur-ar k2 aur-i k2 *Aur-m-n* aur-s k2 bac bn *Bapt* k* bar-c *Bar-m* bar-s k2 *Bell* b4.de* borx br1 bov k* brom bry k* bufo but-ac sp1 cadm-s c1 calc calc-f sp1 calc-sil k2 camph *Caps* **Carb-ac** carb-an *Carb-v* k* carbn-s cedr **Cham** k* chin b7.de* chinin-ar chlol *Chlor* cina cist coca *Crot-h* daph br1 dig *Dulc* elaps br gels gink-b sbd1• *Graph* k* guat sp1 *Hell* hip-ac sp1 *Ign* iod k* *Kali-bi* *Kali-br* k* *Kali-chl* kali-m k2 **Kali-p** **Kreos** k* *Lac-c* *Lach* k* *Lyc* k* *Maland* jl2 *Mang* **Merc** k* *Merc-c* mez b4.de* moni jl2 *Mur-ac* musca-d szs1 **Nat-m** **Nit-ac** k* *Nux-v* k* ol-j petr *Ph-ac* phos k2 **Phyt** plan **Plb** k* **Psor** k2* *Puls* k* pulx br1 pyrog k* *Rhus-t* ruta k* sabin k* sal-ac tl1 sang sec seneg k* sep b4.de* **Spig** k* stann staph stram sul-i k2 sulph k* syph k2* **Tub** k* [helia stj7]
  - **morning**: ambr arg-n camph castm crot-h grat kali-p lyc med puls
    - **and** night: aur puls
  - **night**: syph jl2
  - **accompanied** by:
    - **palpitations** (See CHEST - Palpitation - accompanied - mouth)
    - **salivation** (See Salivation - accompanied - odor)
    - **vomiting** (See STOMACH - Vomiting - accompanied - breath)
  - **anger**; after: arn
  - **cough** agg.; during: *Caps* b7.de* dros b7a.de* m-aust b7a.de sep bg2
  - **eating** | **after** | **agg.**: cham nux-v
    - **while** | **agg.**: chr-ac
  - **menses**; during: *Cedr*
  - **palpitations**; with (See CHEST - Palpitation - accompanied - mouth)
- **sickening**: agar aloe k* *Arn* ars a1 ars-h berb canth carbn-h chlol *Croc* gins kali-br k* merc nat-c *Nit-ac*
- **sour**: agar aloe sne cham k* coc-c crot-h *Eup-per* *Graph* k* mag-c nicc *Nux-v* k* podo bg2 rheum mtf33 sep *Sulph* k* verat
- **stool**; like: bapt sne bell h1 indol sne querc sne
- **sulphurous**: arge-pl rwt5• nux-v b7.de* sulph b4a.de
- **sweetish**: carb-an *Merc* k* nit-ac nux-v bg2 (non:uran-met k) uran-n
- **urine**, like: benz-ac ptk1 canth ptk1 *Coloc* ptk1 *Graph* k* nat-m ptk1 nit-ac ptk1 ol-an ptk1 sec ptk1 urt-u ptk1

- **vinegar**; like: *Borx* b4a.de *Hell* b4a.de sul-ac b4a.de

OPEN: (↗*FACE - Dropping; FACE - Dropping - jaw)* acon b2.de* *Agra* sne ail bg1* *Ang* b2.de* ant-t apis k* arn bg2 ars b2.de* arum-t k* bapt bg2* **Bar-c** bg2* bell k* *Bry* b7a.de bufo k2 *Calad* camph k* *Canth* sne carb-an h2* carb-v b2.de* caust k* cocc bg2 colch k* crot-h bg2 cupr k* dulc bg2* gels k* glon bg2 *Hell* k* hydr-ac *Hyos* k* ign bg2 *Lac-c* sne **Lach** k* *Laur* **Lyc** k* m-ambo b2.de* mag-m br1 merc k* merc-c ptk1 mez k* *Morph* mosch b7a.de *Mur-ac* k* naja k* nat-c bg1* *Nux-v* k* **Op** k* ox-ac ph-ac k* *Phos* k* plb b2.de* podo bg2 puls k* rhus-t bg2* samb k* sil h2* squil k* *Stram* k* stry **Sulph** k* vip bg2 zinc ptk1

- **accompanied** by | **cough**: samb
- **children**; in: bar-m br1
- **convulsions**; epileptic:
  - **before**: *Bufo* k*
  - **during**: cupr ptk1
- **coryza**; during: mag-c h2 mag-m h2 nat-c h2 zinc h2
- **difficult** to: ant-t anthraci ars *Caust* k* chinin-s cocc colch k* dig kali-c h2* **Lach** k* *Merc-c* k* mosch nat-s c1 nicc c1 nit-ac nux-m ptk1 nux-v k* *Phos* k* positr nl2• psor stry sul-ac upa
- **half** open: ars b4a.de bell b4a.de
- **inability** to open: atra-r bnm3•
- **involuntarily**: ix bnm8• ther c1*
- **sleep** agg.; during: am-c tl1 anac b4a.de ars brm brom k* bros-gau mrc1 **Calc** h2* caust cham chim k* dros gk dulc elaps hep h2* ign *Lyc* k* m-ambo b7a.de merc k* nat-c k2* nat-m brm *Nux-v* k* **Op** k* plan puls brm *Rhus-t* k* samb k* *Stram* b7.de* sul-i vario zinc h2*
- **spasmodically**: ign bg2 rhus-t bg2
- **suddenly**; flies open: carb-an bg1 ign bg1 m-arct bg1 *Rhus-t* bg1
- **tension** in anterior throat, from: sil h2*
- **unconsciousness** | **during**: bapt k2
- **yawning**; remains open after: *Ant-t* k*

OSCILLATING tongue (See Protruding - tongue - oscillating)

PAIN: abrot↓ acet-ac↓ acon adon↓ *Aesc*↓ aeth↓ agar↓ ail all-c↓ allox↓ aloe↓ alum k* alum-p↓ alumn *Am-br*↓ am-c b4.de* am-caust↓ am-m↓ ambr↓ anan↓ androc↓ ant-t↓ apis bro1 aq-mar↓ arg-n↓ arizon-l↓ arn↓ **Ars**↓ ars-met↓ ars-s-f↓ **Arum-t** lp* arund↓ asaf↓ asar↓ asim↓ aur↓ aur-m↓ bad↓ bamb-a↓ bar-c↓ *Bar-m*↓ bell bro1 bell-p↓ berb↓ bism↓ borx bro1 bov↓ *Brom*↓ bry↓ bufo↓ but-ac↓ calad↓ *Calc*↓ calc-sil↓ camph↓ canth↓ *Caps*↓ carb-ac↓ carb-an↓ *Carb-v*↓ *Carbn-s*↓ carc↓ cardios-h rly4• cartl-s↓ caust cedr↓ *Cham*↓ chel↓ chin↓ chinin-ar↓ chlol↓ chlor↓ chord-umb↓ *Cimx*↓ cina↓ cinnb↓ clem↓ cob↓ cob-n↓ coc-c↓ coca↓ cocc↓ cocc-s↓ colch↓ coloc con↓ cop corn↓ cortico↓ *Crot-h*↓ crot-t↓ cupr↓ cupr-s↓ cypra-eg↓ cyt-l↓ *Dig*↓ dios↓ dros↓ dulc fd4.de eup-a↓ euph↓ ferr-ar↓ ferr-i ferr-m↓ ferr-p↓ fl-ac galeoc-c-h↓ gels↓ ger-i↓ germ-met↓ glon↓ graph↓ guaj↓ gymno↓ haliae-lc↓ ham↓ hell↓ *Helon*↓ hep bro1 heroin↓ hir↓ hist↓ *Hydr*↓ hydrin-m↓ hydrog↓ hyos↓ hyper↓ *Ign*↓ iod↓ ip **Iris**↓ iris-fl↓ jac-c↓ jatr-c↓ kali-ar↓ kali-bi↓ kali-br↓ kali-c↓ kali-chl↓ kali-i↓ kali-m↓ kali-p kola↓ kreos↓ *Lac-ac*↓ *Lach*↓ lachn↓ *Laur*↓ lyc↓ lyss↓ mag-c↓ *Mag-m*↓ mag-s↓ *Manc*↓ mand↓ mang↓ med↓ merc k* **Merc-c**↓ merc-i-r↓ *Merc-sul*↓ merl↓ mez mucs-nas rly4• mur-ac myric naja↓ *Nat-ar*↓ nat-c↓ nat-f↓ *Nat-m* *Nat-s*↓ *Nit-ac* k* nit-m-ac↓ nit-s-d↓ nux-m↓ nux-v↓ oena↓ op↓ orot-ac rly4• ox-ac↓ ozone↓ par petr↓ *Ph-ac*↓ phasco-ci↓ phos b4.de* pitu-gl↓ plan↓ plat↓ plb↓ podo↓ *Psor*↓ *Puls*↓ rad-br↓ *Ran-b*↓ rauw↓ rhus-t↓ rhus-v↓ rumx↓ ruta fd4.de *Sabad*↓ sal-ac↓ sal-fr↓ samb↓ **Sang**↓ sanic↓ sec↓ seneg↓ *Sep*↓ sin-n↓ spect↓ spig↓ spong fd4.de squil↓ staph↓ staphycoc↓ stict↓ stram↓ suis-em↓ sul-ac sul-i↓ sulfonam↓ *Sulph*↓ symph fd3.de• syph↓ tab↓ tarax↓ *Tarent*↓ tell↓ ter↓ *Thuj*↓ tritic-vg fd5.de upa bro1 vanil fd5.de verat k* *Verat-v*↓ vesp↓ wye↓ xan↓ zinc b4.de* zing↓

- **left** side: pitu-gl↓
  - **sore**: pitu-gl skp7•
- **morning**: *Am-br*↓ **Arum-t**↓ cupr-s↓ dios↓ kali-c↓ mag-m↓ mang↓ mez↓ sulph↓ symph↓
  - **burning**: am-br hr1 **Arum-t** k* cupr-s k* kali-c k* sulph k* symph fd3.de•
  - **burnt**; as if: *Am-br* k* dios k* mag-m h2* mez k*
  - **menses**; during: mag-m↓
    - ⁝ **burnt**; as if: mag-m k*
  - **sore**: arum-t k* dios k* mang symph fd3.de•

Pain – morning: ...

  - **waking**; on: bov↓ nat-c↓
    - ⁝ **burnt**; as if: bov k* nat-c h2*
- **forenoon**: alum b4.de* anac b4.de* ant-c b7.de* carb-v b4.de* caust b4.de* cic b7.de* led b7.de* mag-c b4.de* nat-m b4.de* phos b4.de* plb b7.de* rhod b4.de* rhus-t bg2 sabad b7.de* sars b4.de* seneg b4.de* sil b4.de* verat b7.de* verb b7.de* zinc b4.de*
- **afternoon**: alum b4.de* ant-c b7.de ant-t bg2 arn b7.de* bar-c b4.de* bell bg2 borx b4a.de canth b7.de* cham b7.de* chin b7.de* cic b7.de* croc b7.de* dig b4.de* dros b7.de* dulc b4.de* euph b4.de* graph b4.de* mag-m b4.de* mang b4.de* *Mez* b4a.de nat-c b4.de* nat-m b4.de* nux-v b7.de* phos b4.de* plb b7.de* ran-b b7.de* rhus-t b7.de* rhus-v↓ sabin b7.de* sel b7.de* sul-ac b4.de* sulph b4a.de verb b7a.de zinc b4.de*
  - **burning**: *Mez* k* rhus-v a1
- **evening**: aloe bg2 *Alum* b4.de* am-c bg2 *Ang* b7a.de asaf b7.de* bar-c b4.de* bism b7.de* bov b4.de* bry b7.de* carb-an b4.de* caust b4.de* chin b7.de* cocc b7.de* con bg2 *Croc* b7a.de cycl b7.de* dig b4.de* ferr b7.de* hep b4.de* ign b7.de* kali-bi bg2 kali-c b4.de* kali-n bg2 lach b7.de* lyc b4.de* *M-ambo* b7.de* m-arct b7.de mag-c b4.de* mag-m bg2 mang bg2 merc b4.de* mosch b7.de* nat-c b4.de* nat-m b4.de* nit-ac b4.de* *Nux-m* b7.de* nux-v b7.de* par b7.de* petr b4.de* phos b4.de* plat b4.de* plb b7.de* *Puls* b7.de* *Ran-b* b7.de* rhod b4.de* sel b7a.de seneg b4.de* sep b4.de* sil b4.de* spong b7.de* stann b4.de* staph b7.de* stront-c b4.de* sul-ac bg2 sulph b4.de* thuj b4.de* valer b7.de* verat b7.de* viol-t b7.de* zinc b4.de*
- **night**: alum b4.de* am-c b4.de* am-m bg2 ambr b7.de* ant-c b7.de* calc b4.de* camph b7.de* canth b7a.de* carb-an b4.de* caust b4.de* chinin-s bg2 cocc b7.de* *Graph* b4a.de kali-c b4.de* kali-n b4a.de* kola stb3• lach bg2 lyc b4.de* m-arct b7.de *Mag-c* b4a.de mag-m b4a.de *Merc* b4.de* mez b4.de* *Mur-ac* bg2 nat-c b4.de* nat-m b4.de* nit-ac b4.de* nux-m b7.de* nux-v b7.de* petr bg2 ph-ac b4a.de *Puls* b7.de* ran-s b7.de* rhus-t b7.de* sars b4.de* sep b4.de* sul-ac b4.de* *Sulph* b4.de*
  - **midnight** | **after**: nux-v b7.de puls b7.de rhus-t b7.de
  - **burning**: kola stb3• merc k* nit-ac k* sulph k*
- **accompanied** by:
  - **salivation**; profuse | **children**; in: sacch sst1•
- **alcoholic** drinks: rhus-t bg2
- **biting** pain: ambr b7.de* asar b7a.de carb-v b4.de* colch b7.de* coloc b4.de* dros b7.de* iod b4.de* *Ip* b7a.de merc b4.de* nat-m b4.de* ran-b b7.de* verat-v bg2 zinc b4.de*
- **burning** (= raw and smarting): acet-ac *Acon* k* *Aesc* k* aeth agar ail all-c br1 allox tpw3 aloe k2 alum alum-p k2 alumn k2 am-c am-m k2 ambr h1 ant-t *Apis* k* aq-mar skp7• arn **Ars** k* ars-s-f k2 **Arum-t** k* arund asaf k* asar k* aur aur-m bad bamb-a stb2.de• *Bar-m* **Bell** k* bell-p sp1 berb borx b4a.de* bov k* *Brom* bry bro1 bufo calad calc k* camph k* canth k* *Caps* k* carb-ac k* carb-an k* *Carb-v* k* *Carbn-s* *Caust* k* cedr *Cham* k* chel chlol chord-umb rly4• clem cob coc-c cocc colch k* coloc corn br1 crot-t cupr k* cupr-s cypra-eg sde6.de• cyt-l sp1 *Dig* dios dulc fd4.de euph bg2 ferr-i ferr-p bro1 fl-ac gels glon guaj bg2 gymno hell hir skp7• hist sp1 *Hydr* k* hyper *Ign* *Ip* **Iris** k* iris-fl jatr-c kali-ar kali-bi kali-br a1 kali-c kali-chl kali-i kali-m k2 kali-p kreos k* lach k* laur b7.de lyc *Mag-m* manc k* mand sp1* mang med ptk1* *Merc* k* *Merc-c* k* merc-i-r merc-sul merl **Mez** k* mur-ac *Nat-ar* nat-c nat-f sp1* *Nat-m* *Nat-s* k* *Nit-ac* nux-m nux-v k* oena op ox-ac petr k* ph-ac *Phos* k* plat k* plb k* *Psor* k* *Ran-b* rhus-t rhus-v ruta fd4.de sabad k* sal-ac **Sang** k* sec seneg *Sep* spig k* *Spong* k* squil staph bg2 stict stram *Sul-ac* sul-i ptk1 *Sulph* k* symph fd3.de• tab k* tarax k* ter tritic-vg fd5.de *Verat* k* vesp k* xan zing [heroin sdj2]
  - **accompanied** by:
    - ⁝ **nausea** (See STOMACH - Nausea - accompanied - mouth - pain - burning)
    - ⁝ **sneezing**: verat-v ptk1
    - ⁝ **thirst**: hyper ptk1
    - ⁝ **Tongue**; dryness of (See Dryness - tongue - accompanied - burning)
  - **hot** food in mouth; as from: sang mtf11
  - **pepper**; as from: coca dros k* mez k* *Nat-s* k* rad-br ptk1 ruta fd4.de sulph h2* verat h1*
- **burnt**; as if: (↗*Mucous membrane - scalded)* adon vh1 all-c k* allox tpw4 aloe bg2 alum k* *Am-br* k* ambr b7.de* *Apis* k* arg-n bg1 arizon-l nl2• ars bg1 bad k* bamb-a stb2.de• bar-c b4.de* **Bell** k* berb k* bov k* calad k* camph caust chin k* chinin-ar *Cimx* k* cina a1 coc-c cypra-eg sde6.de• dios k* ferr-m a1 glon k* ham fd3.de• *Hydr* k* hyos **Iris** k* jac-c jatr-c k* kali-c b4.de* *Laur* k* lyc k*

- **burnt**; as if: ...
Mag-m k* mand vk1 med k* merc b4.de* *Merc-c* k* merc-i-r bg2* nat-c b4.de* op b7.de* phasco-ci rbp2 plat k* psor *Puls* bg1* rhus-t bg2 rhus-v k* rumx k* sabad k* sal-ac sal-fr sle1• sang bg1 seneg k* *Sep* k* sin-n bg2 stict k* sulfonam ks2 syph bg1 *Tarent Thuj* k* *Verat-v* k* wye bg2 zinc k*
- **chewing** agg.: nat-c ↓ ph-ac ↓
  - **burning**: ph-ac
  - **sore**: nat-c h2
- **children**; in: merc k2
  - **nursing** infants: borx ↓ eup-a ↓ mur-ac k2 sil ↓ sul-ac ↓ sulph ↓
    - **sore**: borx k2* eup-a br1 mur-ac k2 sil mtf33 sul-ac k2 sulph k2*
- **chill**; during: ars ↓ cham ↓ lach ↓ mez ↓ *Petr* ↓ verat ↓
  - **burning**: ars bg2 cham bg2 lach bg2 mez bg2 *Petr* bg2 verat bg2
- **clawing** pain: mur-ac bg2
- **cold**:
  - **water**:
    - **agg.**: *Ars* ↓ *Bufo* ↓ hir ↓
      - **burning**: *Ars Bufo* hir skp7•
    - **amel.**: acon-f ↓ berb ↓ cham ↓ dros ↓ dulc ↓ merc-c ↓ ruta ↓
      - **burning**: acon-f a1 berb cham k2 dros dulc merc-c k* ruta fd4.de
    - **not** amel.: merc ↓
      - **burning**: merc ptk1
- **contracting**: aesc asar k* nit-ac vanil fd5.de
  - **spasmodic**: calc
- **cramping**: carb-v b4.de
- **cut** off; as if tongue was: anan hydrog srj2•
- **cutting** pain: bov bg2 hell bg2
- **dinner**; after: alum ↓ ham ↓
  - **burnt**; as if: alum k* ham fd3.de•
- **drawing** pain: gymno nux-v k*
- **eating**:
  - **after**:
    - **agg.**: mez ↓
      - **burning**: mez
  - **agg.**: alumn bro1 borx bro1
  - **solid** food agg.: ph-ac ↓
    - **rasping**: ph-ac
  - **warm** food agg.: bros-gau ↓
    - **burning**: bros-gau mrc1
  - **while**:
    - **agg.**: alum ↓ helia ↓ hir ↓ nat-c ↓ ruta ↓
      - **burning**: hir skp7•
        - **taste**; unusually hot: helia c1
      - **sore**: alum nat-c h2 ruta fd4.de
- **eructations**:
  - **after**: kali-c ↓
    - **burning**: kali-c k2
- **excoriated**; as if: aesc ambr asim bism kola stb3• oena ozone sde2•
  - **open** gums; as if: ozone sde2•
- **fever**; during: ars ↓ mez ↓ *Petr* ↓
  - **burning**: ars bg2 mez bg2 *Petr* bg2
- **inspiration** agg.: mez ↓ *Phos* ↓
  - **burning**: mez *Phos* k*
- **menses** | **before**:
    - **agg.**: phos ↓
      - **sore**: phos bro1
  - **during**:
    - **agg.**: but-ac ↓ phos ↓
      - **sore**: but-ac sp1 phos bro1
- **neuralgic**: cocc-s br1
- **nursing** mothers: borx ↓ hydr ↓ merc k2 sin-a ↓ sul-ac ↓ sulph ↓
  - **sore**: borx k2 hydr bro1 sin-a bro1 sul-ac k2 sulph k2
- **opening** mouth; when: ozone sde2•
- **perspiration**; during: apis ↓ ars ↓ *Cham* ↓ mez ↓ *Petr* ↓
  - **burning**: apis bg2 ars bg2 *Cham* bg2 mez bg2 *Petr* bg2
- **pinching** pain: iod b4.de*
- **plate**; from dental: alumn bro1 borx bro1
- **pregnancy** agg.; during: hydr ↓ sin-a ↓
  - **sore**: hydr bro1 sin-a bro1
- **protruding** tongue; when: ozone sde2•
- **rasping**: ambr asar
- **rawness** (See burnt)
- **rheumatic** | **Tongue**: ambr b7.de*
- **salivation**; after | **amel.**: arum-m kr1*
- **scalded**, sensation as if (See burnt)
- **scar**; in old:

  ○ • **Tongue** | **left** side: muru a1
- **scraping** pain: am dig gymno
- **sensation** of: apis ↓ stram ↓
  - **burning**: apis bg2 stram b7.de*
- **shooting** (See stitching)
- **sore**: abrot k* agar k* ail k* allox sp1 aloe alum k* am-c k* am-caust a1 ambr h1* androc srj1• apis *Ars* k* ars-met **Arum-t** k* asaf k* asar bg2 aur-m bg2 bell k* bism k* borx k2 but-ac sp1 *Calc* carb-ac k* carc sp1 cartl-s rly4• caust k* chin chlor k* chord-umb rly4• cinnb k* cob-n sp1 coc-c con k* cortico sp1 *Crot-h* cupr k* dig k* dios k* dulc fd4.de eup-a mtf11 ferr-ar k2 galeoc-c-h gms1• ger-i rly4• germ-met srj5• glon k* graph b4.de* haliae-lc srj5• *Helon Hep* k* hir rsj4• hydr c2 hydrin-m mtf11 hyos *Ign* k* ip kali-ar kali-c k* kali-m k2 kali-p *Lac-ac Lach* k* lachn lyc k* lyss k* mag-c mag-s k* *Manc* bg1 mang med **Merc** k* **Merc-c** k* merc-i-r k* *Merc-sul* k* mez b4.de* naja nat-ar nat-c k* **Nat-m** k* *Nit-ac* k* nit-m-ac c2 nit-s-d c2 nux-v k* ox-ac k* petr ph-ac h2* **Phos** k* pitu-gl skp7• plan a1 plb k* podo psor k2 rauw sp1 rhus-v ruta fd4.de *Sabad* k* samb k* sanic c2 sec k* sin-n spong fd4.de staphycoc rly4• stram k* suis-em rly4• sul-ac k2 tell rsj10• tritic-vg fd5.de vanil fd5.de verat k* [spect dfg1]
  - **accompanied** by:
    - **Tongue**:
      - **white** discoloration of the tongue | **heavily** coated: phos kr1*
- **splinter**; as from a: calc-sil k2 *Nit-ac*
- **stinging**: ambr b7.de* androc srj1• calc-sil k2 *Ph-ac* b4.de*
- **stitching** pain: *Apis* b7a.de aur bg2 calc bg2 phos b4.de* seneg b4a.de spig b7a.de* spong b7.de*
- **swallowing**; when not: ph-ac ↓
  - **burning**: ph-ac
- **tearing** pain: *Bell* k* calc k* carb-v k* colch b7.de* lyc k*
- **touch** agg.: alumn bro1 borx bro1 nat-c ↓
  - **burning**: nat-c k*
- **yawning** agg.: lyc brm

▽ - **extending** to:

  ○ • **Anus**: *Iris* ↓
    - **burning**: *Iris* k*
  - **Bronchi**: ip ↓
    - **burning**: ip k*
  - **Head** and down into neck; through: lyss c1
  - **Stomach**: aesc ↓ am-c ↓ am-caust ↓ brom ↓ chel ↓ gels ↓ gink-b ↓ iris ↓ iris-fl ↓ *Merc-c* ↓ *Mez* ↓ nit-ac ↓ sin-n ↓ sul-ac ↓
    - **burning**: aesc k* am-c am-caust k* brom k* chel k* gels k* gink-b sbd1• iris iris-fl *Merc-c* k* *Mez* k* nit-ac sin-n k* sul-ac k*
  - **Throat**: ozone ↓
    - **excoriated**; as if: ozone sde2•

○ - **Cheeks**: allox ↓
  - **right** side:
    - **Spot**; in a: calc-p ↓
      - **sore**: calc-p a1*
  - **sore**: allox tpw4

  ○ • **Inner** side: bell ↓ calc-p ↓ carb-ac ↓ coloc ↓ corian-s ↓ dros ↓ nat-c ↓ ruta ↓ sal-fr ↓ vanil ↓
    - **biting** pain: coloc h2 dros h1
    - **sore**: bell calc-p hr1 carb-ac k* corian-s knl6• nat-c h2 ruta fd4.de sal-fr sle1• vanil fd5.de
- **Gums**: acon ↓ acon-ac rly4• act-sp ↓ aeth ↓ *Agar* k* aids ↓ allox tpw4* alum k* alum-p k2 alum-sil k2 am-c ↓ am-m ↓ ambr k* anac ↓ androc ↓ ang ↓ antip ↓ apis k* arg-met b7.de* arg-n k* arge-pl ↓ *Arn* **Ars** k* *Ars-i* ars-met ↓

- **Gums**: ...
arum-t k2 arund ↓ asaf ↓ asar ↓ aur aur-m ↓ bamb-a stb2.de• bapt ↓ bar-c ↓ bar-i ↓ bar-m ↓ *Bell* k* bell-p sp1 berb ↓ bism k* borx b4a.de *Bov* k* brom ↓ bry bufo ↓ but-ac sp1 *Calc* k* calc-i k2 calc-s ↓ camph ↓ canth k* *Caps* ↓ *Carb-an* k* *Carb-v* k* carc tl* carl a1 cassia-s ccrh1• castm ↓ *Caust* k* *Cham* chel k* *Chinin-ar* ↓ chinin-s ↓ chord-umb ↓ *Cimx* ↓ clem ↓ cob ↓ cocc ↓ cocc-s ↓ *Colch* ↓ con ↓ cortico sp1 crot-c *Crot-h* cupr-ar ↓ cypra-eg ↓ daph ↓ dig ↓ dios ↓ *Dol* k* dream-p ↓ ephe-si ↓ *Euph* ↓ eupi a1 fuch ↓ gamb ↓ gels ↓ ger-i ↓ germ-met ↓ *Glon* ↓ graph k* *Ham* *Hep* k* *Hir* ↓ hyos k* ign ↓ iod k* kali-ar ↓ *Kali-bi* ↓ kali-br k* kali-c ↓ kali-chl ↓ kali-i k* kali-n b4.de* kiss ↓ kreos tl1* *Lach* k* laur ↓ loxo-recl ↓ luf-op rsj5• lyc k* *Lyss* k* m-ambo b7.de m-arct b7.de mag-c ↓ *Mag-m* b4a.de mang ↓ marb-w ↓ **Merc** k* merc-c k* merc-sul ↓ mez ↓ mucs-nas rly4• mur-ac ↓ musca-d ↓ *Myric* ↓ naja ↓ *Nat-ar* ↓ nat-c ↓ nat-m bg2 nat-ox ↓ *Nat-s* ↓ nat-sil fd3.de• *Nit-ac* ↓ nux-v bg2 orot-ac rly4• oxal-a ↓ par ↓ petr ↓ petr-ra ↓ ph-ac b4.de* phos k* pieri-b ↓ plan ↓ *Plat* ↓ plb k* plect ↓ podo fd3.de• polyg-h ↓ prot ↓ ptel ↓ **Puls** bg2 ran-s a1 raph a1 rauw ↓ rhod ↓ rhus-t ↓ ruta k* sabad ↓ sabin b7.de* sang ↓ **Sars** ↓ sec ↓ sep k* *Sil* k* sin-n ↓ sol-t-ae a1 spig ↓ spong k* stann ↓ **Staph** k* strept-ent jl2 stront-c ↓ sulph b4.de* symph ↓ *Ter* ↓ teucr b7.de* ther ↓ **Thuj** ↓ tritic-vg fd5.de valer ↓ vanil fd5.de wies a1 zinc k* zinc-p k2
  - **right**: androc ↓
    - **aching**: androc srj1•
  - **left**: aids ↓
    - **sore**: aids nl2•
  - **morning**: ars ↓ brom k* caust ↓
    - **aching**: brom
    - **sore**: caust h2*
    - **stitching** pain: ars k*
  - **night**: dol vml3• lyc ↓
    - **drawing** pain: lyc h2*
  - **accompanied** by | **Head**; complaints of (See HEAD - Complaints - accompanied - gums)
  - **aching**: acon-ac rly4• androc srj1• crot-c k* nit-ac k* petr-ra shn4•
  - **biting** pain: asar k* carb-v k* *Zinc*
  - **boring**: *Calc* k* merc bg3*
  - **burning**: act-sp bg1 *Alum* antip bro1 *Ars* k* asar bell k* bufo *Caps* k* castm *Cham* k* con k* fuch br1 *Graph* lyc b4a.de m-arct b7.de mag-c b4.de* **Merc** k* *Merc-c* k* mez k* mur-ac k* *Nat-s* k* nux-v k* petr k* ph-ac k* phos k* *Puls* k* rhus-t k* sang bg2 *Sep* k* sil k* stront-c k* sulph k2 *Ter* k* ther k* **Thuj**
  - **burnt**; as if: ars bg2 ars-met bell b4.de* *Cimx* k* ign k* merc bg2 nat-s hr nux-v bg2 par b7.de* phos bg2 *Sep* k*
  - **chewing**:
    - **agg.**: alum-sil k2 arn bamb-a stb2.de• **Carb-v** ↓ clem ↓ lach *Nit-ac* ↓ petr ↓ sil ↓ spong k* streptoc jl2 teucr ↓ zinc h2*
      - **sore**: **Carb-v** k* clem a1 *Nit-ac* k* petr h2* sil h2* teucr a1
    - **impossible**: zinc h2*
  - **cold**:
    - **agg.**: **Nat-m** ↓
      - **sore**: **Nat-m** k*
    - **air** agg.: alum-sil k2 cob ↓ hyos *Mez* phos rhus-g ↓ *Sil*
      - **sore**: cob rhus-g tmo3•
    - **drinks**:
      - **agg.**: lac-lup ↓ sars staph sulph
        - **sore**: lac-lup hrn2•
      - **amel.**: bov cham k2 laur
    - **water**:
      - **agg.**: **Sil** ↓
        - **sore**: **Sil** k*
  - **contracting**: caust h2* staph h1*
  - **corrosive**: kali-c h2* pieri-b mlk9.de puls b7.de* zinc h2*
  - **cutting** pain: iod h mag-c h2 nit-ac par b7.de*
  - **dentition**; during: berb ↓ bry ↓ dol mtf11 strept-ent jl2
    - **aching**: bry
    - **sore**: berb dol c1
  - **drawing** pain: alum h2* anac h2* ang h1* ars bg2 caps b7.de* carb-an b4a.de* carb-v b4.de* caust h2* con ham fd3.de• iod h* lyss nat-m h2* nux-v b7.de* ruta b7.de* sep h2* staph b7.de*
  - **eating**:
    - **agg.**: cassia-s ccrh1•
    - **while**:
      - **agg.**: aur ↓ caust ↓ *Clem* ↓ mag-c ↓ **Nat-m** ↓ *Phos* ↓ spong ↓ *Staph* ↓ wies ↓ zinc ↓
        - **burning**: mag-c h2* **Nat-m** k*
        - **sore**: aur caust a1 *Clem* k* mag-c h2* *Phos* k* spong wies a1 zinc
        - **tearing** pain: *Staph* a1
  - **extracted**; where tooth has been: graph ↓
    - **corrosive**: graph h2
  - **extraction** of teeth, after: arn bro1* canth fl-ac *Hecla* hyos *Hyper* **Nux-v** podo fd3.de• sep bro1 staph sne
    - **sore**: arn br1*
  - **fever**; during: *Apis* b7a.de* hyos b7.de* rhus-t b7.de* staph bg2
  - **gnawing**: bar-c b4.de* *Euph* k* graph a1 *Puls* raph a1
  - **hacking**: thuj b4.de*
  - **jerking**: ars hep lyc k* thuj h1
  - **neuralgic**: cocc-s br1
  - **pressing** pain: arn ars bg2 aur carc sp1* hep nit-ac h2 rhus-t b7.de* *Sil* staph b7a.de* valer b7.de
    - **outward**: hep b4.de*
  - **pressure** agg.: carc tpw2* phel ↓
    - **ulcerative**: phel
  - **pulsating**: arn bell calc daph rauw sp1 sep thuj h1*
  - **salt** agg.: carb-v h2* germ-met ↓
    - **sore**: germ-met srj5•
  - **scratching** agg.: cimx
  - **sleep**; preventing: dol c1*
  - **smarting**: *Bell* b4a.de
  - **smoking** agg.: sars h2
  - **sore**: agar k* aids nl2• alum k* alum-p k2 alum-sil k2 am-c k* ambr k* apis bg2 arg-met k* *Arg-n* k* arge-pl rwt5• *Arn* **Ars** k* ars-met arund k* asaf k* *Aur* aur-m bapt k* bar-c bar-i k2 bar-m bell k* berb bism k* borx bg2* brom bry k* but-ac sp1 calc k* calc-s *Caps* carb-an k* **Carb-v** k* carc jl2 *Caust* k* *Cham* k* *Chinin-ar* chord-umb rly4• clem k* cob cocc b7.de* cortico sp1 cupr-ar k* cypra-eg sde6.de• dig k* dios k* *Dol* k* dream-p sdj1• gamb k* gels ger-i rly4• germ-met srj5• *Glon* *Graph* k* *Ham* k* *Hep* k* *Hir* rsj4• *Iod* k* kali-ar a1 *Kali-bi* k* kali-chl kali-i k* kiss a1 *Kreos* bro1 lach loxo-recl knl4• m-ambo b7.de m-arct b7.de* mag-c b4.de* mang b4.de* marb-w es1• **Merc** k* *Merc-c* k* merc-sul a1 mur-ac k* *Myric* naja *Nat-ar* *Nat-m* k* nat-ox rly4• *Nit-ac* k* nux-v k* oxal-a rly4• petr k* ph-ac k* *Phos* k* plan a1* *Plat* b4a.de plb k* plect a1 polyg-h prot jl2* ptel k* *Puls* k* raph a1 rhod k* rhus-t k* ruta k* sang a1 sars k* *Sep* k* **Sil** k* sin-n k* spong fd4.de *Staph* k* stront-c b4.de* sulph bro1 symph fd3.de• ter ther a1 thuj k* tritic-vg fd5.de vanil fd5.de wies a1 *Zinc* k* zinc-p k2
  - **spices** agg.: germ-met ↓
    - **sore**: germ-met srj5•
  - **squeezed**; as if: nat-m bg2 rhus-t b7.de*
  - **stitching** pain: aeth k* am-m b7a.de* ang h1* ars k* asar *Bell* b4.de* *Calc* k* camph k* con graph h2* kali-c b4.de* lyc k* merc k2 musca-d szs1 nit-ac petr b4.de* *Puls* k* sabad b7.de* sabin bg2 sars sep b4.de* spig b7a.de stann bg2 staph b7.de* stront-c *Sulph* b4a.de thuj kl
  - **tearing** pain: aeth k* alum k* *Ars* k* bell b4a.de berb calc k* canth k* chinin-s bg2 *Colch* k* gamb k* *Hyos* k* kali-c k* laur k* lyc k* *Merc* k* nux-v bg2 *Ph-ac* b4a.de sabin k* **Sars** k* sec bg2 staph b7a.de* sulph k* *Teucr* k*
  - **touch**:
    - **agg.**: arg-met kl (non:arg-n k*) ars h2* ars-met aur ↓ *Bar-c* bell castm germ-met ↓ graph ↓ **Hell** **Hep** iod kola stb3• **Merc** nat-m h2* nat-sil fd3.de• petr ↓ ph-ac sacch-a ↓ sil *Staph* *Ter*
      - **sore**: aur h2* germ-met srj5• graph h2* ph-ac h2* sacch-a fd2.de•
      - **stitching** pain: petr h2*
    - **tongue** agg.; when touched by the: mag-c ↓
      - **burning**: mag-c h2

- **ulcerative**: acon alum bg2 bapt bg2 bell k* bism bg2 bry bg2 carb-an h2* ephe-si hsj1• graph k* *Hep* mang b4.de* merc bg2 nat-c h2* nux-v b7.de* plan bg2 puls bg2 rhus-t bg2 sars bg2 *Sil* *Staph* bg2 thuj bg2 zinc bg2
- **warm**:
  - **air** agg.: rhus-g ↓
    - **sore**: rhus-g tmo3•
  - **water**:
    - **agg.**: sil ↓
      - **burning**: sil h2*
- **warmth** agg.: **Nat-m** ↓
  - **sore**: **Nat-m**
- ▽ **extending** to:
  - **Temple**:
    - **left**: am-m ↓
      - **stitching** pain: am-m k*
- ○ **Cheeks**; between gums and: hyos ↓ rhod ↓
  - **sore**: hyos h1* rhod k*
- **Inner**: agar bg2 alum bg2 arn ↓ carb-v bg2 chin bg2 colch bg2 graph ↓ ign bg2 kali-c bg2 merc bg2 nat-m bg2 nit-ac ↓ nux-m bg2 phos bg2 puls ↓ rhus-t bg2 ruta ↓ sep bg2 staph ↓ sulph bg2 zinc ↓
  - **burning**: puls b7.de
  - **drawing** pain: ruta b7.de* staph b7.de*
  - **pressing** pain: arn b7.de* rhus-t b7.de*
  - **sore**: graph h2* nit-ac bg2 phos bg2 puls b7.de* ruta b7.de* zinc bg2
- **Lower**: anac ↓ arn ↓ canth ↓ carb-an b4.de* caust ↓ cortico ↓ laur ↓ nat-c ↓ petr ↓ sars b4.de* staph ↓ teucr ↓ thuj ↓
  - **left**: am-m ↓ thuj ↓
    - **sore**: thuj b4.de*
    - **stitching** pain: am-m k*
  - **burning**: petr b4.de
  - **drawing** pain: anac b4.de* caust b4.de*
  - **pressing** pain | **leaden** bullet; like a: arn
  - **sore**: cortico tpw7*
  - **stitching** pain: petr b4.de* sars b4.de* thuj b4.de*
  - **tearing** pain: canth b7.de* laur b7.de* nat-c b4.de* sars b4.de* staph b7.de* teucr b7.de*
  - **ulcerative**: nat-c b4.de*
- **Outer**: rhus-t ↓
  - **pressing** pain: rhus-t b7.de*
- **Skin**; below: arn ↓ hyos ↓
  - **ulcerative**: arn b7.de* hyos b7.de*
- **Spots**; in: aur-m ox-ac
- **Upper**: agar b4.de* ang ↓ ant-c ↓ arg-met ↓ arg-n ↓ aur ↓ bar-c b4.de* calc ↓ canth ↓ carb-an ↓ **Carb-v** ↓ *Cist* ↓ colch ↓ dulc ↓ euph ↓ graph ↓ iod ↓ kali-c ↓ kreos ↓ mag-m b4.de* **Merc** ↓ mez ↓ mur-ac ↓ nat-c ↓ nat-m ↓ nit-ac ↓ *Ph-ac* ↓ phos ↓ ruta ↓ sep ↓ stront-c b4.de* sulph ↓
  - **right**: am-c ↓
    - **stitching** pain: am-c
  - **boring**: calc b4.de* euph bg2
  - **cutting** pain: ant-c bg2 arg-met bg2 arg-n bg2 **Carb-v** bg2 *Cist* bg2 dulc bg2 iod bg2 **Merc** bg2 mez b4a.de nat-c bg2 nit-ac b4.de* *Ph-ac* bg2 phos bg2 sep bg2 sulph bg2
  - **drawing** pain: canth b7.de kreos b7a.de ruta b7.de* sep b4.de*
  - **sore**: aur b4.de* graph b4.de* mur-ac b4.de* ruta b7.de*
  - **stitching** pain: ang b7.de* calc b4.de* stront-c b4.de*
  - **tearing** pain: colch b7.de* kali-c b4.de*
  - **ulcerative**: carb-an b4.de* graph bg2 nat-m bg2 phos bg2
  - **Inner**: am-c ↓ graph ↓ nat-m ↓ ruta ↓
    - **sore**: graph b4.de* nat-m b4.de*
    - **stitching** pain: am-c b4.de* ruta b7.de*

- **Lips**:
  - ○ **Corners**: ant-c ↓ arum-t ↓ graph ↓
    - **burnt**; as if: ant-c ptk1 arum-t ptk1 graph ptk1
  - **Inner** side of: calc-s ↓ sacch-a ↓
    - **burning**: calc-s sacch-a fd2.de•

- **Lips – Inner** side of: ...
  - **Lower**: anis ↓ cartl-s ↓ chin ↓ corian-s ↓ *Ign* ↓ nat-sil ↓ **Nux-v** ↓ vip-l-f ↓
    - **burning**: anis c1
    - **sore**: cartl-s rly4• chin h1* corian-s knl6• *Ign* b7a.de nat-sil fd3.de• **Nux-v** h1 vip-l-f a1
    - **ulcerative**: ign b7a.de
  - **Upper**: bar-c ↓ irid-met ↓ lac-h ↓
    - **burnt**; as if: bar-c h2
    - **sore**: irid-met srj5•
    - **stitching** pain: lac-h sk4•

- **Palate**: *Aesc* ↓ aeth ↓ agar ↓ agro ↓ aids ↓ *All-c* ↓ alum alum-p k2 alum-sil ↓ am-c ↓ ambr ↓ androc ↓ ant-c ↓ aphis ↓ apis ↓ arg-n ↓ arizon-l ↓ arn ↓ arum-t arund ↓ aur bapt ↓ bar-c ↓ *Bell* ↓ benz-ac ↓ *Borx* ↓ brom ↓ bufo *Calc* ↓ calc-s ↓ *Camph* ↓ canth caps ↓ **Carb-v** carc jl2* *Caust* ↓ cham chel chinin-s choc ↓ *Cimx* ↓ cina ↓ cinnb ↓ clem ↓ cob ↓ coc-c coca ↓ *Cocc* ↓ coff coloc ↓ crot-t ↓ cypra-eg ↓ dulc ↓ *Euph* ↓ eupi ferr-m ↓ ferr-s ↓ fl-ac ↓ gamb ↓ glon ↓ graph ↓ *Grat* ↓ gymno ↓ hell ↓ heroin ↓ hura-c ↓ hydr hydrog srj2• ign ↓ iod ↓ iris ↓ *Kali-bi* kali-c kali-p ↓ kola stb3• lac-ac ↓ *Lac-c* ↓ lac-h ↓ lach ↓ laur ↓ lyc ↓ *Mag-c* ↓ mag-m ↓ manc ↓ mand ↓ *Mang* ↓ meny ↓ meph ↓ merc merc-c ↓ mez morph mur-ac ↓ naja ↓ nat-m h2 nat-ox ↓ *Nat-s* ↓ *Nit-ac* nux-m ↓ *Nux-v* ↓ *Par* ↓ petr ↓ ph-ac ↓ *Phos* *Phyt* ↓ plb ↓ plect ↓ podo ↓ polyg-h ↓ positr nl2• psil ft1 pycnop-sa ↓ ran-b k2 ran-s rauw ↓ rein ↓ rheum ↓ *Rhus-t* ↓ ruta h1 sabad ↓ sacch-a ↓ sal-fr ↓ *Sang* ↓ sanic ↓ sapin ↓ sars seneg ↓ sep ↓ sil ↓ spig ↓ spong fd4.de *Squil* ↓ *Staph* ↓ *Stram* ↓ streptoc jl2 sul-ac ↓ symph ↓ tarent ↓ tell ↓ ther thuj tritic-vg fd5.de vanil fd5.de verat ↓ viol-o ↓ zinc
  - **right**: clem ↓ plut-n ↓
    - **sore**: plut-n srj7•
    - **stitching** pain: clem a1
  - **left**: aids ↓ aq-mar skp7• vanil ↓
    - **sore**: aids nl2• vanil fd5.de
  - **morning**: aq-mar skp7• **Arum-t** ↓ carc sst• coca ↓ lyc ↓ mang ↓ tritic-vg fd5.de
    - **burning**: **Arum-t** k* coca lyc k*
    - **lasting** 2 hours: aq-mar skp7•
    - **rising** agg.: aq-mar skp7•
    - **sore**: mang h2*
  - **afternoon**:
    - **13** h: interf sa3•
    - **16** h: dendr-pol sk4•
  - **evening**: carc sst•
  - **evening** and night: mur-ac ↓
    - **burning**: mur-ac h2*
  - **night**: *Aur* br1 *Calc* ↓
    - **burnt**; as if: *Calc*
  - **aching**: alum bufo chel chinin-s eupi hydr *Kali-bi* merc morph *Nit-ac* *Phos* sars ther
  - **biting** pain: canth carb-v *Kali-c* mez ran-s sep h2 *Zinc*
  - **boring**: *Aur* k*
  - **bread**:
    - **amel.**: mang ↓
      - **sore**: mang h2*
  - **burning**: *Aesc* k* agro a1 *All-c* ambr k* ant-c k* arizon-l nl2• arn k* *Arum-t* k* arund k* bapt tl1 *Bell* k* benz-ac k* *Borx* calc *Camph* k* *Canth* k* carb-v k* *Caust* k* *Cimx* k* cina cinnb k* coc-c k* *Cocc* k* coloc k* crot-t cypra-eg sde6.de• dulc *Euph* k* glon k* *Grat* k* gymno hura-c a1 hydrog srj2• ign iris kola stb3• lac-h sk4• lach k* laur k* *Mag-c* k* manc k* merc merc-c *Mez* k* mur-ac k* naja *Nat-s* k* *Nit-ac* k* nux-m k* *Nux-v* *Par* k* ph-ac k* *Phos* k* plect a1 podo k* polyg-h ptk1 *Ran-b* k* rein a1 rheum sabad k* sacch-a fd2.de• *Sang* k* sanic k* seneg k* sep k* spig k* *Squil* k* staph k* *Stram* tl1 sul-ac mrr1 ther k* thuj k* tritic-vg fd5.de zinc
    - **excoriated**; as if: mag-c h2*
    - **pepper**; as from: coca crot-t *Mez* k*
  - **burnt**; as if: arizon-l nl2• arum-t ptk1 bar-c h2* bell ptk1 *Borx* hr1 *Calc* caust ptk1 cimx k* cina a1 ferr-m a1 hydrog srj2• iris ptk1 lac-ac lach ptk1 merc ptk1 mez a1 **Nit-ac** ptk1 nux-v ptk1 petr a1 *Phos* ptk1 phyt ptk1 podo hr1 pycnop-sa mrz1 sal-fr sle1• sang bg3* sanic ptk1 sep tarent verat b7.de

- **chewing** agg.: aloe ↓ borx h2* vanil fd5.de zinc
  - **aching**: aloe
- **cold**:
  - **air** agg.: hydrog srj2•
  - **drinks**:
    - **agg.**: carc sst•
    - **amel.**: aq-mar skp7• carc xxb
- **contracting**: arn cinnb glon
- **cough** agg.; during: calc ↓ dig ↓
  - **burning**: dig
  - **stitching** pain: calc b4a.de
- **cramping**: cham b7.de*
- **cutting** pain: grat bg2 hell b7.de* rhus-t b7.de*
- **dinner**; after: phos ↓
  - **stitching** pain: phos h2*
- **drawing** pain: hydr sars ther
- **excoriated**; as if: nat-ox rly4• par b7.de*
- **menses** | **before**:
  - **agg.**: germ-met ↓
    - **sore**: germ-met srj5•
  - **during**:
    - **agg.**: *Nat-s* ↓
      - **burning**: *Nat-s* k*
      - **sore**: nat-s
- **nursing** the child agg.; when: borx bro1
- **pinching** pain: ant-c k* caps h1*
- **pressing** pain: arum-t aur caps h1* **Carb-v** k* cham iod h meny h1 ruta h1 sars staph h1 thuj
  - **ball** of cloth; as from a: psil ft1
- **pricking**: arg-n calc caust cob
- **rasping**: aphis carb-v mez mur-ac ran-s
- **scraping** pain: camph k* hell k* meph a1 sep h2
- **scratching**: ambr ant-c aphis hell mez
- **smarting**: fl-ac bg2 mur-ac b4a.de ran-s bg2 sep bg2 staph b7.de* viol-o b7.de*
- **sneezing** agg.: ictod
- **sore**: agar k* aids nl2• all-c alum k* alum-p k2 alum-sil k2 androc srj1• apis *Arum-t* k* bell bg3* benz-ac k* brom k* calc-s caps k* carc mg1.de* *Caust* k* choc srj3• cinnb eupi k* ferr-s gamb k* glon graph k* ign k* iris k* kali-bi kali-p fd1.de• *Lac-c* bg1* lach k* laur bg1 mand rsj7• *Mang* k* merc h1* *Mez* k* mur-ac k* nat-m k* nat-s **Nit-ac** k* *Nux-v* k* par phos k* *Phyt* k* plb bg1 rauw tpw8* rhus-t a1 ruta fd4.de sacch-a fd2.de• sang k* sapin a1 sil k* spong fd4.de streptoc rly4• symph fd3.de• tell rsj10• thuj k* tritic-vg fd5.de vanil fd5.de [heroin sdj2]
- **stitching** pain: *Aesc* k* aeth a1 bar-c k* *Calc* k* *Camph* k* caust k* clem a1 cob coc-c k* ign kali-c lach k* mag-m k* merc a1 nit-ac ph-ac k* ran-s k* sabad k* spong fd4.de *Staph* k* stram k* zinc
- **suppurating**: caust bg2
- **swallowing**:
  - **agg.**: ant-c ↓ caps coc-c hell ↓ interf sa3• meny ↓ positr nl2•
    - **cutting** pain: hell
    - **pinching**: ant-c k* caps h1
    - **pressing** pain: caps k*
    - **stitching** pain: meny k*
  - **amel.**: ruta ↓ staph ↓
    - **aching**: ruta
    - **sore**: staph h1
  - **empty** | **agg.**: aq-mar skp7•
  - **saliva**:
    - **agg.**: thuj ↓
      - **sore**: thuj h1*
- **talking** agg.: coc-c spong fd4.de
- **tearing** pain: ambr k* lach k* zinc bg2
- **tobacco**: chin ↓
  - **biting** pain: chin h1
- **touch** agg.: choc ↓ iris ↓ merc ↓ nat-s ↓
  - **sore**: choc srj3• iris merc k* nat-s
- **ulcerative**: agar bg2 alum bg2 am-c k* apis bg2 caps bg2 caust k* iris bg2 lach b7a.de lyc bg2 mang bg2 merc bg2 mez bg2 mur-ac bg2 nat-m bg2 nit-ac bg2 nux-v bg2 phos bg2 *Rhus-t* k* ruta bg2 sil bg2 thuj bg2
- **walking** agg.: kali-bi ↓
  - **sore**: kali-bi
- **warm** drinks agg.: carc jl2 sanic ↓
  - **burning**: sanic
  - **sore**: carc mlr1•
- **yawning** agg.: zinc h2
  - **aching**: zinc

▽
- **extending** to:
  - **Brain**: staph ↓
    - **stitching** pain: staph k*
  - **Chin**: bov ↓
    - **stitching** pain: bov k*
  - **Ear**: agar ↓ cob ↓ *Ign* ↓ thuj ↓
    - **left**: ambr ↓
      - **tearing** pain: ambr k*
    - **sore**: thuj h1
    - **stitching** pain: agar a1 cob *Ign* k*
  - **Eyes**: phos bg1
  - **Fauces**: cham ↓ merc ↓
    - **drawing** pain | **convulsive**: cham k* merc k*
  - **Nose**; root of: phos bg1
  - **Parotid** gland; to right: agar ↓
    - **stitching** pain: agar
  - **Posterior**: dig ↓
    - **stitching** pain: dig h2

○
- **Arches**:
  - **swallowing** agg.: coc-c ↓
    - **drawing** pain: coc-c k*
- **Hard** palate: agar ↓ ant-c ↓ apis ↓ arn ↓ bar-c ↓ borx b4a.de bov ↓ bufo bg2 *Camph* ↓ cann-s ↓ canth ↓ caps ↓ *Carb-v* ↓ caust ↓ cham ↓ cimic ↓ cocc ↓ coloc ↓ dulc ↓ euph ↓ ferr ↓ ign ↓ iod ↓ kali-bi bg2 kali-c ↓ lach ↓ laur ↓ m-ambo b7.de mag-c ↓ mag-m ↓ meny ↓ merc ↓ merc-c ↓ mez ↓ mur-ac ↓ nit-ac ↓ nux-m ↓ *Nux-v* ↓ *Par* b7a.de *Ph-ac* ↓ phos b4.de* ran-s ↓ rhod ↓ rhus-t ↓ ruta ↓ sabad ↓ *Seneg* ↓ sep ↓ spig ↓ *Squil* ↓ staph ↓ stram ↓ thuj ↓ verat ↓ zinc b4.de*
  - **biting** pain: canth b7.de* carb-v b4.de* cham b7.de* coloc b4.de* kali-c b4.de* merc b4.de* mez b4a.de ran-s b7.de* seneg b4.de* zinc b4.de*
  - **burning**: apis b7a.de *Camph* b7.de* cann-s b7.de canth b7.de *Carb-v* b4.de* caust b4.de cocc b7.de dulc b4a.de euph b4.de ign b7a.de laur b7.de mag-c b4.de* merc b4a.de merc-c b4a.de mez b4.de mur-ac b4.de nux-m b7.de par b7.de *Ph-ac* b4.de* phos b4.de rhod b4.de sabad b7.de *Seneg* b4.de* spig b7.de *Squil* b7.de* staph b7.de thuj b4.de
  - **burnt**; as if: bar-c b4.de* cimic bg2 sep b4.de* verat bg2
  - **pinching** pain: ant-c b7.de* caps b7.de*
  - **pressing** pain: arn b7.de* caps b7.de* iod bg2 meny b7.de* *Nux-v* b7.de* ruta b7.de*
  - **stitching** pain: agar bg2 bar-c b4.de* bov b4.de* camph b7.de* caust b4.de* coloc b4.de* ferr bg2 ign b7.de* kali-c b4.de* lach b7a.de* mag-m b4.de* meny b7.de* mez bg2 nit-ac bg2 ph-ac bg2 phos b4.de* rhus-t b7.de* sabad b7.de* staph b7.de* stram bg2 zinc b4.de*
  - **tearing** pain: kali-c b4a.de zinc b4.de
- **Sides**: nat-m ↓
  - **sore**: nat-m bg2
- **Soft** palate: ap-g ↓ aur ↓ *Bell* ↓ bufo bg2 calc ↓ canth ↓ carb-v ↓ caust ↓ *Cham* ↓ chin ↓ coff b7.de* dig ↓ ham ↓ iod ↓ kali-c ↓ lyc ↓ merc ↓ nux-m ↓ phos b4.de* ran-b ↓ ran-s ↓ rhod ↓ ruta ↓ sars ↓ staph ↓ thuj ↓ valer ↓ zinc b4.de*
  - **left**: aq-mar skp7•
  - **evening** | **20 h**: aq-mar skp7•
  - **biting** pain: carb-v b4.de* chin b7.de* kali-c b4.de* ran-s b7.de*
  - **burning**: *Bell* bg2 canth bg2 *Cham* b7a.de nux-m b7.de ran-b b7.de*
  - **cold** drinks | **amel.**: aq-mar skp7•

- **Soft** palate: ...
  - ⁝ **drawing** pain: cham b7.de* ran-s b7.de* sars b4.de*
  - ⁝ **pressing** pain: aur b4.de* carb-v b4.de* caust b4.de* iod b4.de* ruta b7.de* sars b4.de* staph b7.de* thuj b4.de*
  - ⁝ **sore**: ap-g vh1
  - ⁝ **stitching** pain: bell bg2 calc b4.de* *Cham* b7a.de dig b4.de* ham bg2 kali-c b4.de* merc b4.de* ran-s b7.de* rhod b4.de* valer b7.de*
  - ⁝ **swallowing** agg.; empty: aq-mar skp7•
  - ⁝ **tearing** pain: lyc b4.de*
- **Spots**; in: *Caust* ↓ mur-ac ↓
  - ⁝ **burning**: mur-ac k*
  - ⁝ **sore**: *Caust* mur-ac k*
- **Velum**: *Ambr* ↓ arg-n ↓ *Calc* ↓ coloc ↓ *Crot-c* ↓ *Lach* ↓ nux-m ↓ ph-ac ↓ ran-b ↓ rhus-t ↓ ruta ↓ sil ↓ thuj ↓ zinc h2
  - ⁝ **burning**: *Ambr* k* arg-n k* *Calc Crot-c Lach* nux-m k* ph-ac ran-b k*
  - ⁝ **pressing** pain: (non:ruta kl) thuj h1
  - ⁝ **sore**: ph-ac rhus-t ruta h1
  - ⁝ **stitching** pain: coloc sil h2*

- **Salivary** glands: acon ↓ bell ↓ merc bg2
  - **sore**: acon bg2 bell bg2 merc bg2
- **Spots**; in: phos ↓
  - **sore**: phos
- **Sublingual** glands: arund c1 calc k2 fic-m ↓ iod ↓ maias-l ↓
  - **pressing** pain: fic-m gya1 iod h
  - **pricking**: maias-l hrn2•
  - **stitching** pain: iod h
  - ○ **Lower**: maias-l ↓
    - ⁝ **pricking**: maias-l hrn2•
- **Tongue**: abrom-a bnj1 abrot ↓ absin ↓ acet-ac ↓ achy-a ↓ acon bro1 adam ↓ adon ↓ aesc ↓ agar bg2 all-c allox sp1 aloe ↓ alum ↓ alum-sil ↓ alumn k* am-br ↓ am-c ↓ am-caust k* *Am-m* ↓ ambr androc ↓ ang ↓ ant-c ↓ ant-t ↓ *Apis* aran ↓ arg-met arg-n a1 arizon-l ↓ arn ↓ ars k* *Ars-i* ↓ ars-s-f ↓ *Arum-m* ↓ *Arum-t* k* asar ↓ aspar ↓ astac k* aster ↓ atra-r ↓ *Aur* ↓ aur-ar ↓ aur-i ↓ aur-m ↓ bad ↓ bamb-a ↓ *Bapt* ↓ *Bar-c* ↓ bar-i ↓ bar-s ↓ bell k* bell-p sp1 benz-ac ↓ berb ↓ bit-ar ↓ borx b4a.de *Bov* ↓ brach brass-n-o ↓ brom ↓ bry ↓ bung-fa ↓ cact ↓ *Calc* k* calc-i ↓ calc-p ↓ *Calc-s* ↓ calc-sil ↓ camph ↓ cann-i ↓ cann-xyz ↓ *Canth* ↓ caps bg2 carb-ac ↓ carb-an k* *Carb-v* ↓ *Carbn-s* ↓ castm ↓ caust bg2 cedr ↓ cerv c2 *Cham* ↓ chel ↓ chim ↓ **Chin** ↓ chin-b ↓ chinin-ar ↓ chir-fl ↓ chlor ↓ chord-umb ↓ cic ↓ *Cimx* ↓ *Cist* ↓ clem ↓ coc-c ↓ cocc b7.de* coch ↓ coff ↓ *Colch* ↓ *Coloc* ↓ colum-p ↓ *Con* k* conv ↓ cop ↓ cortico sp1 croc ↓ crot-c crot-h bg2 crot-t ↓ cund cupr ↓ cupr-ar ↓ cupr-s ↓ cycl ↓ *Cyclosp* sa3• daph ↓ der a1 *Dig* ↓ dios ↓ *Dros* ↓ dulc fd4.de dys ↓ *Echi* ↓ elaps ↓ eos ↓ euon ↓ eup-pur ↓ eupi k* ferr b7.de* ferr-ar ↓ ferr-i ↓ ferr-p ↓ fl-ac ↓ fum rly4• galeoc-c-h gms1• gamb ↓ gels ↓ gink-b sbd1• *Glon* ↓ graph b4.de* guare ↓ *Ham* hell ↓ hep ↓ heroin ↓ hura *Hydr* ↓ hydrog srj2• hyos ↓ ictod ↓ ign b7.de* indg ↓ iod k* ip bg2 irid-met ↓ **Iris** ↓ jac-c ↓ jal ↓ jatr-c kali-ar bro1 kali-bi k* kali-br a1 *Kali-c* kali-chl ↓ kali-i bro1 kali-m ↓ kali-p ↓ kali-s ↓ kali-sil ↓ *Kalm* ↓ kola ↓ kreos ↓ lac-ac ↓ lac-f ↓ **Lach** ↓ lap-la ↓ *Laur* ↓ lavand-a ↓ led ↓ lob-c ↓ lyc k* m-ambo b7.de m-arct ↓ m-aust ↓ mag-c bg2 *Mag-m* ↓ malar ↓ manc ↓ mand ↓ *Mang* ↓ meny ↓ *Merc* k* *Merc-c* ↓ merc-i-r ↓ merc-sul ↓ *Merl* ↓ *Mez* ↓ morg-g ↓ morg-p ↓ mur-ac k* murx ↓ naja ↓ nat-c ↓ nat-m ↓ nat-p k2 nat-s ↓ nat-sil ↓ nit-ac k* nit-s-d ↓ *Nux-v* ↓ oena ↓ ol-an ↓ olnd ↓ op ↓ orot-ac ↓ osm ↓ ox-ac k* ozone ↓ pall ↓ ped a1 petr ↓ ph-ac ↓ phel ↓ phos k* *Phys* ↓ *Phyt* bro1 *Plat* ↓ plb k* *Podo* ↓ positr nl2• prun ↓ *Psor* ↓ ptel ↓ *Puls* ↓ rad-br sze8• ran-s k* raph ↓ rat ↓ rauw sp1 rhod ↓ rhus-t ↓ *Rhus-v* ↓ *Rumx* ↓ ruta bro1* sabad sabin ↓ sacch-a fd2.de• sang sanic ↓ sars ↓ sec ↓ sel b7.de* semp bro1 seneg ↓ sep b4.de* sil ↓ sin-n ↓ sinus ↓ spig bg2 spong fd4.de stann ↓ *Staph* ↓ staphycoc ↓ stram ↓ stront-c ↓ stry ↓ suis-em ↓ *Sul-ac* ↓ sul-i ↓ sulph syc ↓ symph fd3.de• syph jl2 tarax ↓ tell ↓ *Ter* ↓ term-c ↓ teucr ↓ ther ↓ thuj b4.de* tritic-vg fd5.de *Tub* ↓ ulm-c ↓ ust vanil fd5.de verat ↓ **Verat-v** ↓ *Vesp* k* *Vip* k* visc ↓ xan ↓ xanth ↓ zinc ↓ zinc-p ↓ zinc-s a1
  - **one** side: *Calc* ↓
    - ⁝ **burning**: *Calc* bg1*
  - **right** side: ars ↓ dros ↓ dulc fd4.de rosm lgb1 sep h2* spig ↓ [heroin sdj2]
    - ⁝ **boring**: ars
    - ⁝ **stitching** pain: dros spig
  - **left** side: chir-fl ↓ iris ↓ jac-c ↓ positr nl2• tarax ↓
    - ⁝ **burning**: chir-fl gya2 iris c1 jac-c k* tarax h1*

- **Tongue**: ...
  - **daytime**: olib-sac ↓
    - ⁝ **burning**: olib-sac wmh1
  - **morning**: am-br ↓ bamb-a ↓ cedr ↓ ham ↓ *Mag-m* ↓ mez ↓ nat-c ↓ nat-sil ↓ ozone ↓ stann ↓ sulph ↓ tritic-vg ↓
    - ⁝ **burning**: am-br hr1 ham fd3.de• *Mag-m* k* nat-sil fd3.de• ozone sde2• stann k* sulph k* tritic-vg fd5.de
    - ⁝ **burnt**; as if: bamb-a stb2.de• mez k* nat-c a1
    - ⁝ **stitching** pain: cedr k*
  - **afternoon**: mag-m ↓ mag-s ↓
    - ⁝ **16**-22 h: bung-fa mtf
    - ⁝ **burning**: mag-m h2* mag-s a1
  - **evening**: alum ↓ cycl ↓ dios ↓ dulc ↓ kali-n ↓ sulph ↓ tritic-vg ↓
    - ⁝ **aching**: sulph
    - ⁝ **burning**: alum k* cycl dulc fd4.de kali-n h2*
    - ⁝ **sore**: dios a1 kali-n h2* tritic-vg fd5.de
  - **night**: con ↓ galeoc-c-h ↓ nat-m ↓ ph-ac ↓ *Phos* ↓
    - ⁝ **boring**: con
    - ⁝ **burning**: nat-m k* ph-ac hr1 *Phos* k*
    - ⁝ **sore**: galeoc-c-h gms1•
    - ⁝ **stitching** pain: ph-ac
  - **aching**: all-c astac a1 *Sang* sulph vesp
  - **asthma**, before: borx ↓
    - ⁝ **cutting** pain: borx ptk1
  - **biting** pain: absin acon b7.de* arn k* ars b4.de* asar k* bell b4.de* carb-ac *Cham* k* chin b7.de* coch coloc b4.de* croc b7.de* dios dros b7.de* ign k* ip b7.de* jal *M-ambo* b7.de* mez k* nat-c b4.de* nat-m b4.de* ol-an k* op b7.de* ran-s b7.de* sep b4.de* sulph b4.de* teucr k* zinc b4.de*
  - **bitten**, as if: caust k* chin-b plb k*
  - **boring**: ars bg2 clem k* con bg2 nat-s bg2 spig b7.de* stann bg2
  - **burning**: acet-ac achy-a vk1 **Acon** k* adon ptk1 aesc k* all-c k* alum k* alumn am-c b4.de am-caust k* *Am-m* k* ang k* *Apis* k* arg-met b7.de arg-n a1 arizon-l nl2• arn k* **Ars** k* *Ars-i* ars-s-f k2 *Arum-m* hr1 **Arum-t** k* asar k* *Aur* k* aur-ar k2 aur-i k2 bad k* *Bapt* k* *Bar-c* k* bar-i k2 bar-s k2 *Bell* k* bell-p sp1* benz-ac k* berb k* *Bov* k* bry b7.de *Calc* k* calc-i k2 calc-p ptk1 *Calc-s Canth* k* caps bro1* carb-ac k* *Carb-an* k* *Carb-v* k* *Carbn-s* castm *Caust* k* cedr k* *Cham* k* chel k* chim **Chin** k* chinin-ar chir-fl gya2 chlor k* chord-umb rly4• *Cimx* k* coc-c a1 cocc coch k* coff k* *Colch* k* *Coloc* k* colum-p sze2• con k* croc b7.de crot-t k* cupr k* dios hr1 *Dros* dulc fd4.de dys pte1*• *Echi* eos br1 ferr k* ferr-ar ferr-i k* ferr-p gamb k* gels k* glon k* graph k* ham k* hep b4a.de *Hydr* k* hyos k* ign b7.de* indg k* iod k* *Ip* k* irid-met srj5• **Iris** k* jac-c k* jatr-c *Kali-ar* kali-bi kali-c k* kali-chl k* kali-i ptk1 kali-m k2 kali-p kali-s kola stb3• lac-ac k* lac-f c1 *Lach* k* lap-la sde8.de• *Laur* k* led k* *Lyc* k* m-ambo b7.de mag-c bg2 *Mag-m* k* manc k* mand sp1* *Mang* k* *Merc* k* *Merc-c* k* merc-sul *Merl* k* *Mez* k* morg-g pte1*• morg-p fmm1• mur-ac k* naja nat-c b4.de nat-m b4.de* nat-s k* nat-sil fd3.de• nit-s-d hr1 ol-an olnd b7.de op k* *Ox-ac* k* pall petr k* ph-ac k* phel *Phos* k* *Phys* a1* *Phyt* k* *Plat* k* plb k* *Podo* k* prun k* *Psor* ptel a1* puls b7a.de* *Ran-s* k* raph k* rat rhod k* rhus-t k* rhus-v a1 rumx ruta fd4.de *Sabad* b7.de* *Sang* k* sanic k* sars sec k* seneg k* *Sep* k* sin-n k* spig k* spong b7.de* stram b7a.de *Sul-ac* k* sul-i k2 *Sulph* k* syph jl2 tarax k* *Ter* hr1* ther hr1 thuj k* tritic-vg fd5.de verat k* **Verat-v** k* vesp k* vip fkr4.de xan k* zinc zinc-p k2 [heroin sdj2]
    - ⁝ **accompanied** by | **Tongue**; cracked: *Mag-m* kr1*
    - ⁝ **pepper**; as from: agar bg2 ang h1* cann-i a1 cann-xyz bg2 chin bg2* con bg2 hell bg2 lach k* malar jl2 manc bg2 merl k* *Mez* k* nat-s bg2 op k* sanic sep k* teucr k* xanth bg2
  - **burnt**; as if: adon bg2* aesc k* agar bg2 all-c k* alum am-br hr1 am-m b7a.de apis k* *Arg-n* k* arizon-l nl2• arn bg2 **Ars** k* arum-t bg2 asar bg2 bad k* bamb-a stb2.de• bapt k* bar-c bg2 *Bell* hr1 bit-ar wht1• bov bg2 cact br1 calc bg2 caps bg2 carb-v k* *Caust* k* chin k* chlor k* *Cimx* k* colch bg2 *Coloc* k* conv br1 cund sne cupr-s daph dios k* dys fmm1• ferr k* glon k* *Ham* k* hep bg2 hydr k* hyos k* ign k* *Iris* k* kali-c bg2 kreos k* lac-ac lach bg2 *Laur* k* lavand-a ctl1• *Lyc* k* *Mag-m* k* *Merc* k* merc-i-r a1 *Mez* k* morg-p fmm1• nat-m b4a.de* *Nux-v* ptk1 ol-an ptk1 petr a1 ph-ac bg2 *Phos* k* phys a1* *Phyt* k* *Plat* k* plb bg2 podo k* positr nl2• prun k* psor k* ptel c1 *Puls* k* ran-s bg2 rhod bg2 rhus-t bg2 *Rhus-v Rumx* sabad k* *Sang* k* seneg bg2 sep k* sil ptk1 sin-n k* sul-ac k* symph fd3.de• term-c vk1 ther k* tub xxb verat bg2 **Verat-v** k* [heroin sdj2]

- **chewing** agg.: bung-fa mtf calc h2* lyc a1 ruta fd4.de sep h2* spig a1
- **cold** drinks agg.: osm bg1*
- **contracting**: arum-t borx vanil fd5.de
- **corrosive**: teucr b7.de*
- **cramping**: carb-v b4.de*
- **cutting** pain: *Bov* k* *Colch* b7a.de euon guare hydrog srj2• orot-ac rly4• thuj k*
- **drawing** pain: *(↗jerking)* aster k* castm k* m-arct b7.de *Staph* b7a.de
  - **string** to the hyoid bone; as if by a: castm k*
- **eating**:
  - **after**:
    - **agg.**: chir-fl ↓ graph ↓ laur ↓
      - **burning**: chir-fl gya2 graph k* laur a1
  - **agg.**: bell-p ↓
    - **burning**: bell-p vk1
  - **amel.**: staph ↓
    - **stitching** pain: staph h1*
  - **not** eating or drinking agg.; when: ferr ↓
    - **burnt**; as if: ferr k*
  - **while**:
    - **agg.**: *Ign* ↓ *Nat-m* ↓
      - **burning**: *Ign* k* *Nat-m* k*
      - **burnt**; as if: ign
- **excoriated**; as if: apis b7a.de arum-m k* aur-m k* ozone sde2• tarax b7.de
- **fissures** in: mag-m ↓
  - **burning**: mag-m
- **jerking**: *(↗drawing)* aster castm cham ptk1 m-arct b7.de
- **lacerated** wounds, from: hyper ↓
  - **sore**: hyper
- **menses**; during: cedr bg2 lyc bg2 merc bg2 nux-m bg2 sul-ac bg2 verat-v bg2
- **motion**:
  - **agg.**: aloe ant-t berb chin hydrog srj2• kalm lap-la sde8.de• ruta fd4.de spig sulph vanil fd5.de
    - **stitching** pain: *Sulph*
  - **amel.**: meny ↓
    - **stitching** pain: meny h1
- **neuralgic**: agar bg2 apis ptk1 crot-h bg2 crot-t ptk1 kali-ar c2* kali-i c2 mag-c bg2 mang ptk1 ulm-c jsj8•
- **peppery**: indg ↓ sep ↓ teucr ↓
  - **biting** pain: indg sep h2 teucr
- **pinching** pain: ang b7.de* morg-g fmm1• nux-v sabad b7.de* syc fmm1•
- **pressing** pain: astac chin h1 *Ham Merc* ruta fd4.de ust
  - **upward**: mag-m b4.de
- **pressure** with teeth; from: arum-m croc
- **pricking**:
  - **accompanied** by | **abscess** on tongue (See Abscess - tongue - accompanied - pricking)
- **protrudes** it to cool it: irid-met ↓ sanic ↓
  - **burning**: irid-met srj5• sanic k*
- **salt** agg.: *Nat-m* ↓ petr ↓ spong ↓
  - **burning**: *Nat-m* hr1 petr h2* spong fd4.de
  - **sore**: petr h2*
- **scraping** pain: bapt k* camph k* caust k* graph k*
- **sensation** of: acon ↓
  - **stitching** pain: acon tl1
- **smarting**: acon bg2 arg-n bg2 asar bg2 bapt bg2 bar-c bg2 calc bg2 ign b7.de* mag-m bg2 nat-m bg2 nat-s bg2 petr bg2 ptel bg2 rhus-t bg2
- **smoking** agg.: sep ↓
  - **burnt**; as if: sep h2*
- **sore**: abrot k* acet-ac adam skp7• *Agar* k* allox sp1 aloe alum k* alum-sil k2 am-c bg2 androc srj1• ant-c k* *Apis* k* arg-met b7.de* arn k* ars ars-i *Arum-t* k* asar bg2 aur-ar k2 *Bapt* k* bar-c bell k* benz-ac k* berb brach k* bung-fa mtf *Calc* k* calc-sil k2 canth caps ptk1 *Carb-v* k* caust k* chel chim chin b7.de* chinin-ar cic *Cist* k* cocc b7.de* conv br1 cop cortico sp1 *Crot-h* k* cupr-ar k* *Dig* k* dulc fd4.de eupi a1 fl-ac k* galeoc-c-h gms1• gamb gels *Glon* graph k* hep b4a.de ictod *Ign* b7.de* ip kali-c k* kali-m k2 kali-p kali-s kali-sil k2 lac-ac a1 *Lach* k* laur k* lob-c a1 *Lyc* k* mag-c b4.de* merc *Merc-c* k* *Mur-ac* k* nat-m k* **Nit-ac** k* nux-v k* oena a1 osm k* ox-ac k* phel c2* phys a1* positr nl2• puls ptk1 *Ran-s* bro1 rauw tpw8* rhus-t k* rumx ruta fd4.de *Sabad* k* sang k* sec bg2 semp bro1 *Sep* k* sil k* sin-n k* sinus rly4• spong b7.de* staph k* staphycoc rly4• stront-c b4.de* stry a1 suis-em rly4• syc bka1*• symph fd3.de• syph k2 tell rsj10• *Ter* bro1 term-c vk1 teucr b7.de* *Thuj* k* tritic-vg fd5.de *Tub* visc c1 zinc k*
- **sour** food, from: petr ↓
  - **burning**: petr h2*
  - **sore**: petr h2*
- **spitting**: calc h2*
- **splinter**; as from a: staph syc bka1•
- **stinging**: alum bg2 apis bg2 kali-bi bg2
- **stitching** pain: *Acon* k* agar b4.de* aloe alum alumn androc srj1• ang b7.de* ant-c k* *Apis* k* aran arg-n a1 ars bg2 *Arum-m* k* *Arum-t* asar aspar aster bell berb k* brach k* brass-n-o srj5• brom k* calc k* canth b7.de* carb-v h2* cham k* *Chin* k* clem k* colch k* cycl k* dros k* elaps eup-pur k* ferr b7.de* gamb *Glon* k* guare hell b7.de* ign b7.de* ip jal *Kali-bi* k* *Kali-c* kali-chl *Kalm* k* **Lach** k* led k* m-aust b7.de mag-m b4.de* mang meny b7.de* merc b4.de* merc-sul k* merl k* mez b4.de* murx k* nit-ac k* nux-v b7.de* olnd b7.de* ph-ac k* phos b4.de* phys prun k* ran-s k* sabad k* sabin b7.de* sars k* sep **Spig** k* spong b7.de* staph k* *Sulph* tarax b7.de* thuj b4.de* zinc b4.de*
  - **burning**: androc srj1• *Chin*
- **swallowing** agg.: abrom-a bnj1 ars ↓ benz-ac ↓ calc *Calc-p* sulph k2
  - **fishbone**; sensation of: ars
  - **sore**: benz-ac k*
- **talking** agg.: acet-ac bell-p ↓ *Fl-ac Kalm* lyc sep h2* sulph k2
  - **burning**: bell-p vk1
- **tearing** pain: ant-t b7.de* bar-c a1 carb-v b4.de* cimx a1 colch k* guare k* ign b7.de* lach b7a.de merc ptk1 puls k* *Rhus-v* sep k*
- **tobacco**; from: anac ↓ cocc-s ↓ nep ↓
  - **biting** pain: anac h2 cocc-s kr1 nep vk1
- **tubercles** under tongue sore: ambr k*
- **twinging**: atra-r bnm3•
- **ulcerative**: arg-n k* arn bg2 *Calc* bg2 caust b4.de* merc-c bg2
- **warm**:
  - **drinks**:
    - **agg.**: osm bg1*
    - **amel.**: ozone sde2•
- **warmth** | **amel.**: *Sil*

▽ • **extending** to:
  - **Abdomen**: crot-c
  - **Frenum**: phos h2*
  - **Mouth**: tub ↓
    - **burning**: tub xxb
  - **Palate**: all-c phos ↓
    - **burning**: phos k*
  - **Stomach**: apis ↓ ars ↓ brom ↓ gels ↓ *Mez* ↓ puls ↓
    - **burning**: apis ars brom k* gels k* *Mez* k* puls k*

○ • **Across**: asar ↓ gink-b ↓
  - **burning**: asar bg1 gink-b sbd1•
- **Anterior** half:
  - **right** side: ars-h ↓
    - **contracting**: ars-h
- **Anterior** part: ars ↓ chir-fl ↓ *Coloc* ↓ gamb ↓ rumx ↓ sep ↓
  - **biting** pain: ars sep h2
  - **burning**: chir-fl gya2 *Coloc* hr1 gamb k*

Mouth

- **Anterior** part: ...
  - **burnt**; as if: rumx bg2
- **Below**: adam ↓ aloe ↓ mag-m ↓ thuj ↓ zinc ↓
  - **biting** pain: zinc h2
  - **pressing** pain: mag-m h2
  - **sore**: adam skp7•
  - **stitching** pain: aloe hr thuj h1
  - **Skin**; below: arn ↓
    - **ulcerative**: arn b7.de
- **Border**:
  - **biting** pain (See sides - biting)
- **Center**: arizon-l ↓ bar-c ↓ bry ↓ chin ↓ ferr ↓ galeoc-c-h ↓ hyos ↓ ozone ↓ plat ↓ psor ↓ *Puls* ↓ sabad ↓ samb ↓ sep ↓ ter ↓
  - **burning**: arizon-l nl2• bar-c h2* bry ferr hr1 ozone sde2• *Puls* hr1 ter hr1
  - **burnt**; as if: arizon-l nl2• chin h1* hyos plat psor puls sabad sep ter
  - **sore**: chin h1* galeoc-c-h gms1• samb
  - **spot** toward tip: kali-ar ↓
    - **burning**: kali-ar
- **Edges**: anan ↓ ant-c ↓ mag-s ↓ puls ↓ rumx ↓
  - **right**: kalm ↓
    - **cutting** pain: kalm a1
  - **left**: ant-c ↓
    - **stitching** pain: ant-c hlb2.de*
  - **burning** (See sides - burning)
  - **burnt**; as if (See sides - burnt)
  - **cutting** pain: anan k* mag-s
    - **cut**; as if: anan
  - **excoriated**; as if: ant-c bg2* puls bg2 rumx bg2
  - **stitching** pain: ant-c bg2
- **Frenum**: all-c ↓ ign ↓ kali-c ↓
  - **sore**: all-c kali-c
  - **stitching** pain: ign
- **Low** down in region of hyoid bone: *All-c* ↓
  - **constricting**: *All-c*
- **Posterior** part: benz-ac ↓ form ↓ lyc ↓ *Nux-v* ↓ phyt ↓ spong ↓ symph ↓
  - **burnt**; as if: phyt bg2
  - **sore**: benz-ac k* form lyc *Nux-v* spong fd4.de symph fd3.de•
- **Root** of: acet-ac br1 acon ↓ am-caust ↓ anan arn ↓ ars ↓ **Arum-t** ↓ bapt ↓ bell ↓ benz-ac ↓ *Calc-p* ↓ carb-v ↓ clem ↓ colch bg2 cortico tpw7 *Crot-c* ferr-i ↓ hydrc ↓ kali-bi bg3* **Kali-i** k* lach bg2* luf-op rsj5• lyss k* manc ↓ med ↓ mez ↓ morg-p pte1*• *Nat-s* ↓ *Nit-ac* ↓ *Phyt* k* ptel a1 rhus-v ruta fd4.de sel spong fd4.de tritic-vg fd5.de ulm-c ↓
  - **right**: phos ↓
    - **burning**: phos h2*
  - **left**: luf-op rsj5• ulm-c jsj8•
  - **night**:
    - **sleep**; going to | **before**: **Kali-i** k*
  - **accompanied** by | **Pharynx**; spasm in: **Kali-i** hr1
  - **biting** pain: mez h2
  - **burning**: am-caust k* **Arum-t** k* bapt k* benz-ac k* *Calc-p* hr1 *Crot-c* manc k* med ptk1 tritic-vg fd5.de
  - **contracting**: acon bell carb-v hydrc lach
  - **motion** of tongue sideways agg.: ulm-c jsj8•
  - **pressing** pain: carb-v h2 ruta fd4.de
  - **putting** out the tongue: cocc kali-bi k2 kali-i mrr1 *Phyt* k*
  - **rheumatic**: ambr h1*
  - **sore**: bell bg2 cortico sp1 ulm-c jsj8•
  - **stitching** pain: arn ars k* clem h2* ferr-i k* *Nat-s* k* *Nit-ac* k*
  - **swallowing** agg.: ars bapt k* *Calc-p* cinnb k* cocc h1* colch k* gels k* kali-bi bg1 ozone sde2• *Phyt* k*
    - **stitching** pain: ars k*
  - **tearing** pain: carb-v h2*
  - **turning** head agg.: ars ↓
    - **stitching** pain: ars h2*
- **Root** of: ...
  - **yawning** agg.: lach
    - **sore**: lach ptk1
  - **extending** to:
    - **Forward**: ulm-c jsj8•
    - **Throat**; sides of: **Kali-i** hr1
  - **Across**: acet-ac br1
  - **Below**: sel c1
- **Sides**: acon ↓ agar ↓ am-br ↓ ant-c ↓ apis ↓ bell ↓ *Calc* h2* *Camph* ↓ canth ↓ carb-v ↓ caust ↓ chir-fl ↓ coloc ↓ cycl ↓ dios ↓ ephe-si ↓ graph ↓ heroin ↓ ictod ↓ ip ↓ kali-i ↓ *Lach* ↓ laur ↓ mag-c ↓ merc ↓ mur-ac ↓ nat-s ↓ phel ↓ plat ↓ positr ↓ *Puls* ↓ rumx ↓ sacch-a fd2.de• sep ↓ spong ↓ sulfonam ↓ symph ↓ tritic-vg fd5.de vip ↓ zinc ↓ [tax jsj7]
  - **right**: carb-v ↓ lac-h ↓ merc ↓ ph-ac ↓ phos ↓ plat ↓ positr ↓ sabad ↓
    - **burning**: phos bg1
    - **sore**: carb-v bg1 lac-h htj1• merc bg1 phos bg1 plat bg1 positr nl2• sabad bg1
    - **stitching** pain: ph-ac h1
  - **left**: chir-fl ↓ galeoc-c-h ↓ graph ↓ *Kalm* ↓ *Lach* ↓ nat-s ↓ ox-ac ↓ phys ↓ sang ↓ symph ↓
    - **burning**: chir-fl gya2 *Lach* bg1* nat-s bg1 ox-ac bg1
    - **putting** out tongue; on: *Graph* ↓
      - **sore**: *Graph*
    - **sore**: galeoc-c-h gms1• graph k* *Kalm* *Lach* k* phys symph fd3.de•
    - **stitching** pain: sang a1
  - **biting** pain: coloc h2 ip h1
  - **burning**: acon k* agar k* apis *Camph* k* caust bg2 chir-fl gya2 cycl k* ephe-si hsj1• kali-i k* mag-c bg2 mur-ac k* nat-s k* phel bg2 plat k* tritic-vg fd5.de vip fkr4.de
  - **burnt**; as if: ant-c bg2 apis k* canth bg2 caust dios a1 puls spong bg2 sulfonam ks2 [heroin sdj2]
  - **pressure** agg.: staph ↓
    - **stitching** pain: staph h1
  - **sore**: agar bg2 am-br a1 ant-c k* apis bg2* bell bg2 calc bg2* carb-v k* coloc bg2 dios k* graph bg2 ictod *Lach* k* laur k* merc bg2 positr nl2• *Puls* k* rumx k* sep symph fd3.de• tritic-vg fd5.de zinc ptk1
  - **Tip**; near: arum-t ↓ *Calc-p* ↓ chin ↓ dios ↓ *Hep* ↓ *Kali-c* ↓ sep ↓
    - **sore**: arum-t *Calc-p* chin dios *Hep* *Kali-c* sep
- **Spots**; in: act-sp ↓ agar ↓ aloe ↓ ant-c ↓ *Ars* ↓ bar-c ↓ cinnb ↓ ind ↓ indg ↓ iod ↓ kali-i ↓ lac-h ↓ nit-ac ↓ nux-v ↓ ph-ac ↓ ran-s ↓ sil ↓ tarax ↓
  - **burning**: act-sp bg1 *Ars* bg1 indg a1 kali-i bg1 ph-ac h2* ran-s
  - **burnt**; as if: aloe *Ars*
  - **sore**: agar bg1* aloe ant-c bg1* bar-c bg1 cinnb bg1 ind bg1 iod bg1 lac-h htj1• nit-ac nux-v ran-s bg1 sil bg1* tarax bg1*
- **Surface** of tongue; under: aur-m-n ↓ brom ↓ bros-gau ↓
  - **burning**: aur-m-n a1 brom k* bros-gau mrc1
- **Tip**: *Acon* ↓ aesc ↓ agar ↓ allox ↓ aloe ↓ alum ↓ alumn ↓ am-br ↓ am-c ↓ am-m ↓ ang ↓ ap-g vh arg-met ↓ **Arg-n** k* *Ars* ↓ arum-t ↓ *Asaf* ↓ aur ↓ bamb-a ↓ bapt ↓ *Bar-c* ↓ bell ↓ bit-ar ↓ borx ↓ bov ↓ brom ↓ *Calc* ↓ calc-ar ↓ **Calc-p** ↓ *Camph* ↓ canth ↓ caps ↓ carb-ac ↓ *Carb-an* ↓ carb-v ↓ carc ↓ castor-eq ↓ caust ↓ chel ↓ **Chin** ↓ chin-b ↓ chir-fl ↓ cinnb ↓ coc-c ↓ coff ↓ *Coloc* ↓ *Con* ↓ croc ↓ crot-c ↓ cycl ↓ dios ↓ *Dros* ↓ dulc fd4.de eup-per ↓ eup-pur ↓ form ↓ fum ↓ galeoc-c-h gms1• galla-q-r ↓ gamb ↓ ger ↓ gink-b sbd1• glon ↓ haliae-lc ↓ ham fd3.de• *Hell* ↓ hep hydr-ac ↓ ictod ↓ ign bg2 indg ↓ iod ↓ ip ↓ *Iris* ↓ kali-bi ↓ *Kali-c* ↓ *Kali-i* ↓ kali-n ↓ kola ↓ lac-h ↓ lac-leo ↓ lact ↓ lath ↓ laur ↓ lavand-a ↓ led ↓ *Merc* ↓ merc-sul ↓ mez ↓ *Nat-c* ↓ *Nat-m* ↓ nat-p ↓ **Nat-s** ↓ nat-sil ↓ nux-v ↓ ox-ac ↓ ozone ↓ ph-ac bg2 phos bg2 *Phys* ↓ *Phyt* ↓ plb ↓ positr nl2• propr ↓ *Psor* k* puls ↓ rad-br ↓ ran-b ↓ rat ↓ rhus-t bg3 ruta fd4.de *Sabad* ↓ sabin ↓ sacch-a ↓ sang ↓ *Sel* ↓ seneg ↓ *Sep* ↓ sil k* sin-n ↓ spong fd4.de staph bg2 stront-c sul-ac ↓ sulfonam ↓ sulph bg3 symph fd3.de• *Ter* ↓ teucr ↓ thuj bg2 tritic-vg fd5.de tub ↓ vanil fd5.de verat ↓ vip ↓ zinc ↓
  - **daytime**: bamb-a ↓
    - **burning**: bamb-a stb2.de•
  - **afternoon**: galeoc-c-h ↓
    - **sore**: galeoc-c-h gms1•
  - **evening**: cycl ↓ galeoc-c-h ↓
    - **burning**: cycl hr1

- **Tip – evening**: ...
  - **sore**: galeoc-c-h gms1•
  - **night**: hep ↓
    - **burning**: hep bg1
  - **biting** pain: ars h2 dros h1 ip h1 nat-c h2* puls
  - **burning**: *Acon* k* agar k* alum b4a.de am-c k* am-m arg-met arg-n k* *Ars* bro1 aur k* bamb-a stb2.de• bapt bg2 *Bar-c* k* bell k* borx b4a.de bov k* *Calc* k* calc-ar k* **Calc-p** k* *Camph* k* caps bg2* carb-ac k* *Carb-an* k* carb-v carc fd2.de• castor-eq caust k* chin-b hr1 chir-fl gya2 coff b7a.de *Coloc* k* croc crot-c k* cycl k* *Dros* galla-q-r nl2• gamb k* ger br1 glon k* haliae-lc srj5• hep k* hydr-ac hr1 indg iod *Iris* bro1 kali-bi bg2 *Kali-c* k* *Kali-i* k* kali-n k* kola stb3• lact hr1 lath br1* laur b7a.de led k* merc merc-sul k* mez k* *Nat-c* k* *Nat-m* k* **Nat-s** k* nat-sil fd3.de• ox-ac ozone sde2• *Phos* k* *Phys* a1* *Phyt* k* plb k* propr sa3• psor k* ran-b b7a.de rat k* rhus-t bg2 ruta fd4.de *Sabad* k* sacch-a fd2.de• sang k* sel k* seneg k* sul-ac sulfonam ks2 sulph k* ter k* *Thuj* k* tritic-vg fd5.de tub xxb vip fkr4.de
    - **pepper**; as from: agar k* ang *Camph* k* caps c1 **Chin** k* coc-c ptk1 con k* mez *Nat-s* k* teucr
  - **burnt**; as if: am-br a1 am-c bg2 bit-ar wht1• calc ptk1 calc-p k* caps ptk1 carb-v bg2 caust chin ptk1 chin-b kr1 chir-fl gya2 coloc ptk1 ham fd3.de• hep bg2 ign bg2* kali-c bg2 kola stb3• lact k* lavand-a ctl1• merc-sul mez k* nat-s ptk1 *Phos* k* phys a1 positr nl2• *Psor* k* sabad bg2 sang k* *Sep* staph bg2 stront-c bg2 ter ptk1 thuj bg2 vip k*
  - **excoriated**; as if: bar-c k* chir-fl gya2
  - **pinching** pain: ang h1*
  - **pricking**: rad-br ptk1 sang hr1
  - **sore**: aesc k* agar k* allox tpw3* am-br a1 am-c ap-g vh1 arg-n bg2 arum-t bell bg2 calc calc-p k* carb-an cinnb a1 dios k* dulc fd4.de fum rly1*• galeoc-c-h gms1• hep k* ictod kali-c k* kali-n h2* lac-h htj1• lac-leo hrn2• lavand-a ctl1• merc-sul k* mez a1 nat-c h2 ox-ac a1 phys k* **Rhus-t** k* sabad k* sang *Sel* *Sep* *Sil* k* sin-n spong fd4.de symph fd3.de• *Ter* **Thuj** k* zinc
  - **stitching** pain: acon bg2* aesc bg2 agar k* aloe bg1 alumn ang k* arg-n bg1 *Asaf* bg2* aur bg2* brom k* canth bg2* chel bg2 chin h1* *Con* bg2* cycl dios bg2* *Dros* k* eup-per bg2 eup-pur k* form glon bg2* *Hell* bg2* ign k* iod bg2 led bg2* *Merc* bg2* merc-sul k* nat-p k* *Nat-s* bg2* nux-v k* ph-ac k* phos k* ran-b sabad k* sabin staph k* verat bg2* zinc h2*
  - **touch** agg.: am-c ↓ bar-c ↓ bell ↓ kola ↓ nat-c ↓ nit-ac ↓ thuj h1*
    - **burning**: am-c k* bar-c bell kola stb3• nit-ac
    - **sore**: nat-c h2*
  - **ulcerative**: aesc calc
  - **waking**; on: bros-gau ↓ nat-m ↓
    - **burning**: bros-gau mrc1 nat-m h2*
- **Transversely** across: agar bg2 cob bg2 lach bg2 merc bg2

PAPILLAE of tongue:
- **absent**: all-s bro1 penic vk1 streptoc jl2 terebe ktp9
  - ○ **Back** part: streptoc jl2
  - **Front** part: streptoc jl2
  - **Sides**: penic jl3*
  - **Tip**; at: carc gk6*
- **enlarged**: *Agar* k* aza vk1 *Bell* k* brass-n-o srj5• cupr k* dulc fd4.de *Ign* k* *Kali-bi* k* lat-m sp1* phos k* ptel c1 tub k*
  - **left**: neon srj5•
  - ○ **Root**, at: dulc fd4.de ham k*
  - **Tip**, at: **Ars** k* sulph k*
- **erect**: agar k* *Ant-t* lp* apis k* **Arg-n** k* *Ars* k* arum-m k* *Arum-t* k* aza vk1 bac bn **Bell** k* bry kr1* caust k* chel k* croc k* cupr k* ham k* *Hydr* k* ictod k* *Ign* kr1* kali-bi k* kali-br a1 *Lach* k* lyc k* *Merc* k* *Merc-c* k* merc-i-f k* *Merc-i-r* lp merc-sul k* mez k* *Nux-m* k* olnd k* *Phos* k* plb k* podo k* psil ft1 ptel k* *Rhus-t* k* *Sabad* b7a.de sapin a1 (non:sapo a1) sep k* stram k* stry k* *Tab* k* *Tarent* k* ter k* tere-ch vk1 zinc k* zinc-p k2
  - **accompanied** by | **roughness** of tongue: *Podo* kr1*
  - **strawberry** tongue: ant-t bg2* arg-n bg2* ars ptk1 arum-t bg2* bac a1* *Bell* bg2* caust ptk1 *Frag* c1* kali-bi k2* lach bg2* merc-c c1 phos bg2* ptel bg2* sapin a1* sapo bro1 ter bg2* *Tub* a1* verat-v c1
  - ○ **Root**: agar k* *Kali-bi* k* nat-ar k*
  - **Tip**: sapin a1

Papillae of tongue: ...
- **hypertrophied** (See enlarged)
- **pronounced** (See erect)
- **reddened**: ant-t k* **Arg-n** vk1 ars k* **Bell** k* ign k* *Kali-bi* vk1 *Lyc* vk1 mez k* *Nux-m* k* *Ptel* k* **Ter** vk1 tub jl2
  - **accompanied** by | **white** discoloration of the tongue (See Discoloration - tongue - white - accompanied - papillae)
  - **elevated**; and:
    - **accompanied** by:
      - **Tip** of tongue | **brown** discoloration: *Merc* kr1*
- **sore**: *Arg-n* k* brass-n-o srj5•

PARALYSIS: oxyurn-sc mcp1•
- ○ **Palate**: diphtox jl2 *Gels* *Lach* *Plb* *Sil*
  - **left** | **sensation** of: meny h1
  - **hardness**; sensation of: anh sp1
- **Tongue**: absin k* *Acon* k* *Acon-c* c2* aesc-g a1 agar bg2* anac k* anh vh1 *Apis* k* *Arn* k* ars k* aster c2 bapt k* *Bar-c* k* bar-m k* *Bell* k* **Both** c2* brom k* bufo k* *Cadm-s* k* **Calc** b4a.de cann-i bro1* canth b7a.de caps k* carb-v b4a.de carbn-s k* **Caust** k* cic a1 *Cocc* k* colch bg2* *Con* k* conin c2 *Crot-c* k* crot-h bg2 *Cupr* k* cupr-s a1 **Cur** bro1* *Dulc* k* **Euph** bg2* *Euphr* b7a.de **Gels** k* glon bg2* graph k* *Gua* c2* guare k* *Hell* k* *Helo-s* rwt2• hep b4a.de hydr bg2* *Hydr-ac* k* *Hyos* k* ip k* ix bnm8• lac-c k* *Lach* k* **Laur** b7.de* linu-u c2* *Lob-p* c2* **Lyc** k* mang-o bro1 meph k* merc-c k* merl c2 **Mez** bg2* *Mur-ac* k* *Naja* k* nat-m b4a.de* *Nux-m* k* nux-v k* olnd bg2* **Op** k* oxyurn-sc mcp1• **Plb** k* plb-xyz c2 pyrus c2 *Rheum* k* *Rhus-t* k* ruta b7.de* sec k* sil bg2* *Stram* k* syph k* tep c2 verat k* vesp k* zinc b4a.de zinc-s c2*
  - **accompanied** by:
    - **aphasia** (See MIND - Aphasia - tongue - paralysis)
    - **meningitis** (See HEAD - Inflammation - meninges - accompanied - tongue - paralysis)
    - **numbness** of one side: *Nat-m* kr1*
    - **scarlatina** (See SKIN - Eruptions - scarlatina - accompanied - tongue - paralysis)
    - **typhoid** fever (See FEVER - Typhoid - accompanied - tongue - paralysis)
    - **Upper** limbs; paralysis of (See EXTREMITIES - Paralysis - upper limbs - accompanied - tongue)
  - **apoplexy**; after: crot-h bg2 lach bg2 olnd bg2
  - **creeping**: kali-p ptk1
  - **drawn** to:
    - **right**: *Cur* k* *Nux-m* k* nux-v hr **Op** k*
    - **left**: *Bell* k* *Glon* k* *Op* k* *Plb* k*
  - **old** people: *Bar-c* k*
  - **sensation** of: *Coc-c* *Cocc* k* germ-met srj5• ip k* kali-p fd1.de• merl phys gt1* syph c1 [tax jsj7]
    - **menses**; during: *Cedr*
  - **weather** agg.; cold wet: *Dulc* k*

PARCHED tongue (See Dryness - tongue)

PASTY: (*↗Mucus; Saliva; Taste - pasty*) bamb-a stb2.de• diaz sa3• nuph petr a1 ser-a-c jl2 v-a-b jl2
- ○ **Tongue**: am-m k* bapt tl1 bufo k* nux-m k* paro-i vk1 *Prot* jl2 ser-a-c jl2
  - ○ **Tip**: lyc bg

PATCHES, syphilitic: arg-n bg3* hydrc *Kali-i* lach bg3* *Merc* k* *Merc-c* merc-i-f bg3* merc-i-r merc-n c2 merc-pr-r c2 *Nit-ac* k* phyt bg3* puls bg3* sang syph k2 *Thuj* c2

PERIODONTOSIS (See Detached)

PHYSICAL EXERTION: | **agg.**: caust b4a.de chin b7.de*

PICKING: | **Lips** (See FACE - Picking - lips)

PIMPLES (See Eruptions - pimples)

PLUMMER-VINSON syndrome: cadm-met mtf11

POINTED Tongue: bond a1 calc k* *Chel* k* cimic k* eup-per k2 ip ptk1* *Lach* k* *Petr* k* plb k* podo k* spig-m k* stram k2
- **abortion**; after: podo kr1*

- **accompanied** by:
  - **diphtheria** (See THROAT - Diphtheria - accompanied - tongue - pointed)
  - **indigestion** (See STOMACH - Indigestion - accompanied - tongue - pointed)
- **stool** agg.; during: **Sec** b7a.de

PRESSING gums together (See GENERALS - Biting - teeth; TEETH - Clenching)

PRESSURE:

- **agg.**: ambr b7.de* bell bg2 lach b7.de* merc-c bg2

○ **amel.** **Cervical** glands; upon
spig b7.de*

PRICKLING: acon bg2 anac antip vh1 cartl-s rly4• cedr colch k* fl-ac k* manc nat-p nit-ac plac-s rly4• positr nl2• psor sec bg2 seneg k* spig suprar rly4• *Zinc*

○ - **Gums**: antip vh1 arn lyc b4.de* puls bg2

- **Palate**: arg-n k* arizon-l nl2• carbn-s k2 caust h2* mez a1 nept-m lsd2.fr plut-n srj7• sang k*
  - **morning**: carc gk6
  - **evening**: carc gk6
  - **accompanied** by | **thirst**: nept-m lsd2.fr
  - **lying** agg.: carbn-s k2
  - ▽ **extending** to | **Vertex**: plut-n srj7•
  - ○ **Hard** palate: phos b4.de* rhus-t bg2
  - **Soft** palate: ol-an bg2 phos b4.de*
- **Tongue**: **Acon** k* acon-c a1 agar k* *Alum* apis k* arizon-l nl2• ars-h arum-m k* arum-t k2 bamb-a stb2.de• bapt bg2 bell borx brach bry cact carb-ac cedr chir-fl gya2 chr-ac dios bg2 dros dulc echi elaps eup-pur k* *Fl-ac* k* ger-i rly4• *Glon* k* hell k* *Kali-bi* k* kali-n lach k* lath br1 lina c2 *Lyss* manc k* *Merc* merl mucs-nas rly4• muru a1 myos-a rly4• nat-m nat-p nux-m petr-ra shn4• phos k* plat k* ptel k* puls rhod k* rhus-t bg2 sang k* sec k* sin-n bg2 spig thuj k* *Ust* k* verat
  - **accompanied** by | **Head**; pain in (See HEAD - Pain - accompanied - tongue - numbness)
  - **menses**; during: *Cedr*
  - **scalded**; as if: chir-fl gya2
  - ○ **Below**: ger-i rly4• *Lyss* k*
  - **Frenum**: phos h2*
  - **Tip**: ars-h cact crot-c k* crot-t dulc k* elaps eup-pur nat-m k* phel bg2 phys rad-br c11 sang k* sec br1
    - **needles**; like a hundred: arum-m carb-ac merc ptk1 nux-v k*

PROTRUDING:

○ - **Gums**: (↗*Detached; Scorbutic)* kreos lach

- **Tongue**: (↗*Motion - tongue)* absin k* acet-ac k* acon k* *Apis* k* bell k* **Bufo** vh1* cina k* cocc k* **Crot-h** k* cupr ptk1* dendr-pol sk4• ferr-m k* *Hell* k* hydr-ac k* hyos k* kara c1 *Lach* k* *Lyc* k* *Merc-c* k* merc-n a1 nux-v k* oena k* op k* oxyurn-sc mcp1• **Phyt** k* plb k* sec k* stram k* stry k* sumb k* syph k* tab k* tep a1 vario ptk1 vip k*
  - **right**: crot-h ptk1 lyc bg2 op ptk1
  - **accompanied** by:
    - **aphasia** (See MIND - Aphasia - tongue - protrusion)
    - **chorea** (See GENERALS - Chorea - accompanied - tongue - protruding)
    - **diphtheria** (See THROAT - Diphtheria - accompanied - tongue - protruding)
    - **meningitis** (See HEAD - Inflammation - meninges - accompanied - tongue - protruding)
  - **agg.**: cist ptk1 cocc b7.de* kali-bi bg2* *Phyt* ptk1 syph ptk1
  - **alternating** with | **withdraw** (See rapidly)
  - **amel.**: med ptk1
  - **brain** affections, in: apis ptk1 hydr-ac ptk1
  - **cannot** be protruded: *Apis* k* *Bapt* vk1 brom k* carb-ac k* colch vk1 dulc k* gels vk1 hyos k* *Lach* vk1 *Lyc* k* *Merc-c* k* mur-ac vk1 *Nux-v* k* *Plb* k* sabad k* vesp k*

Protruding – Tongue – cannot be protruded: ...

- **cough**:
  - **during**: (↗*COUGH - Protruding)*
  - **agg.**: (↗*COUGH - Protruding)* bell dgt
- **difficulty**, with: (↗*Motion - tongue - difficult)* *Anac* bro1* apis bg2* *Ars* bro1* *Bapt* bg2* *Calc* bro1* caust bro1* colch k* *Crot-h* bro1* *Dulc* bro1* gels bg2* *Gua* bro1 **Guaj** vk1 *Hyos* k* **Lach** k* *Lyc* k* *Merc* bro1* *Mur-ac* bg2* mygal bro1* *Nat-m* bro1* oxyurn-sc mcp1• phos ptk1 *Plb* bro1* *Pyrog* bro1* *Stram* bro1* sulfon bro1 *Ter* bro1*
  - **accompanied** by:
    - **chorea** (See GENERALS - Chorea - accompanied - tongue - protruding - difficulty)
    - **jerking**: kali-br ptk1
    - **Throat**; sore: sabad ptk1
  - **catches** on the teeth: *Apis* k* *Hyos* k* **Lach** k* lyc k* sec b7a.de
  - **draw** it in; can hardly: hyos k* vario k*
- **headache**; during: lach hr1*
- **oscillating**: *Hell* k* hyos ptk1 lach k* *Lyc* k*
- **rapidly**, darting in and out like a snake's: absin bro1* crot-h bro1* *Cupr* k* cupr-act br1 elaps pd *Lach* k* lyc bg2* *Merc* bro1* merc-c bg2 sanic bro1* *Vip* bro1*
- **sleep** agg.; during: vario k*
- **spasmodically**: cina k* cocc k* sec k*
- **suffocation**, with: ars h2*
- **trembling** of tongue when protruding (See Trembling - protruding)

PROUD flesh on gums: alumn k* thuj sne

PTYALISM (See Salivation)

PUCKERED sensation: op a1 par a1

○ - **Palate**: arn k*

- **Tongue**: ars k*

PULSATION:

○ - **Gums**: ambr k* *Arn* bell k* bov b4.de* brom bg2 *Calc* k* daph k* kali-n h2 mag-m b4.de* merc k* nit-ac k2 nux-v bg2 petr-ra shn4• phos k* puls k* rauw tpw8 *Sep* k* staph k* *Sulph* k* thuj k*

  - **menses**; during: **Sep**
- **Palate**: glon k* rhus-t k*
- **Tongue**: vesp k*

PURPURA: *Crot-h Lach Phos Psor* ter

PUSTULES: ant-t k* ars-s-f bell-p sp1 berb caps crot-t k* hep k* hydr k* mur-ac bg2 phos bg2

○ - **Gums**: (↗*Abscess - gums)* aur k* calc *Carb-an Carb-v* k* morg-g fmm1• nat-s petr psor jl2 puls

  - ○ **Near** diseased molar: aloe
- **Palate**: ambr ant-t coc-c k* phos k*
  - **left**: psil ft1
- **Tongue**: ant-t k* bell-p sp1 cund k* graph tl1 **Hep** k* lyc tl1 med k* mur-ac k* nat-m tl1 nat-p tl1 nat-s tl1 sep k* vario k*
  - **burning** and stinging: am-c k*
  - ○ **Below**: am-c k* med k* nat-c k*
  - **Sides** | **right**: cund kr1*
  - **Tip**: carc fd2.de• cund k* med k* thuj k*

PUT everything in mouth; children: (↗*Fingers; MIND - Gestures - hands - grasping - mouth - everything)* lyc mtf33 merc bg2* *Sulph* st*

PUTRID gums: (↗*Scorbutic)* am-c k* *Ambr* b7.de* cist *Nat-m* k* nux-v k* *Staph* b7.de*

PYORRHEA ALVEOLARIS: (↗*Discharge - putrid; Inflammation - gums - chronic; Suppuration - gums)* cal-ren mtf11 emetin mtf11 ham mtf11 mag-c mtf11 merc-c mrr1 plan br1 streptoc jl2 symph mtf11 thuj mtf33 tub jl2

QUIVERING of gums: canth b7.de*

RAGGED:

○ - **Gums**: *Merc* b4.de*

- Tongue; edge of: *Merc* b4.de* thuj b4a.de

RAISING HEAD agg.: kali-bi bg2

RANULA: (↗*Swelling - tongue - below*) am-be c2 **Ambr** k* ars-i vk1 bell b4a.de* **Calc** k* *Canth* k* cham k* chr-o c2 ferr-p bro1* fl-ac k* hippoz k* lac-c k* *Lach* k* lyc b4a.de lyss mtf11 *Merc* k* *Mez* k* *Nat-m* k* *Nit-ac* k* *Plb* k* psor k* sacch k* *Staph* k* syph bg1 thlas c2 *Thuj* k* verat k*
- **chewing** agg.: mez ptk1
- **gelatinous**: mez k* nit-ac k* staph k* *Thuj* b4a.de
  - **bluish** red: *Thuj* k*
- **periodical**: chr-ac k* lyss k*
- **talking** agg.: mez ptk1

○ - **Sublingual** gland; in: thuj mtf11

RATTLING: bell vk1 lac-c k*
- **saliva**: petr bg2 tab bg2

RAWNESS (See Mucous membrane - excoriation)

RECEDING gums (See Detached)

RELAXED palate: bell bg2

REST agg.: lyc b4.de*

RESTLESSNESS gums: cimic bg2

RETRACTED gums (See Detached)

RINGWORM: ran-s bg3 sanic bg3* tarax bg3

○ - **Tongue**: nat-m bro1 sanic c2*
  - **right** side: *Nat-m* k* sanic c1

RINSING mouth agg.: rhus-t bg2

RISING: | **after** | **agg.**: croc b7.de* par b7.de* verat b7.de* verb b7.de*
- **bed; from** | **amel.**: arn b7.de* bov b4.de* carb-an b4.de* nux-v b7.de* sars b4.de*

ROOM agg.: bry b7.de* puls b7.de*

ROUGHNESS: am-c k* ang b7.de* berb bov k* calc k* carb-an k* carb-v k* caust k* cina k* clem a1 cocc b7.de* cycl k* dig k* ip b7.de* lyc k* merc bg2 mez bg2 musa a1 nat-c bg2 *Nat-s* k* olib-sac wmh1 op bg2 ph-ac b4.de* phos k* rhus-t bg2 sabad bg2 sep k* spong fd4.de still a1 sulph k*

○ - **Gums**: ammc a1 nat-c h2* sul-ac b4.de*

○ · **Inner** | **left**: nat-c b4.de*
- **Lips**: anac b4.de* apis b7a.de calc b4.de* mag-m b4.de* *Merc* b4a.de* mur-ac b4.de* plat b4.de* sulph b4a.de*

○ · **Lower** lip: merc b4.de* nat-m b4.de*
  - **Upper** lip: calc b4.de* sulph b4.de*
    - **Inside**: mag-m h2
- **Palate**: ang k* ant-c k* apis k* ars h2* *Calc* k* **Card-m** k* cina k* cocc b7.de* dig h2* *Dros* k* guare k* hell b7.de* hyos h1* iris k* kali-bi bg2 mag-c merc bg2 mez k* naja k* nux-m b7.de* nux-v b7.de* phos h2* puls b7.de* sabad bg2 sabin b7a.de sep k* spong fd4.de squil b7.de* staph b7.de* stram k* thuj k*
  - **forenoon**: phos h2*

○ · **Soft** palate: ars b4a.de calc b4.de* dig b4.de* mag-c b4.de* merc b4.de* mez b4.de* ph-ac b4.de* phos b4.de* sep b4.de*
- **Tongue**: (↗*Hairy*) acon b7.de* alum k* alumn k* anac k* ang k* *Apis* bg2* *Arg-n* k* **Ars** bro1* **Arum-t** kr1* *Aur* b4a.de bar-c k* bell k* *Bry* k* caj a1 calc k* cann-s b7a.de **Canth** bro1* carb-v k* casc k* cere-b a1 chel a1 coc-c k* cocc k* coloc k* croc b7a.de* cupr k* cupr-s hr1* dulc k* graph k* *Grat* k* hyos b7.de* *Kali-bi* k* kola stb3• laur k* lina c2* merc b4.de* mez bg2* moni rfm1• musa a1 **Nit-ac** bro1* olnd k* op a1 ox-ac a1 par k* phos k* phys a1 *Phyt* k* *Podo* k* ptel k* **Ran-s** bro1* rhus-v hr1* sars k* sep k* spong fd4.de still a1 stram b7.de* sul-ac k* *Sulph* k* sumb a1 symph fd3.de• tanac a1 *Tarax* bro1* thuj b4.de* tung-met bdx1•
  - **morning**: alum a1 bar-c h2* cocc h1* lyc a1 sars k* sep k*
  - **accompanied** by:
    - **chorea** (See GENERALS - Chorea - accompanied - tongue - roughness)
    - **dryness** of tongue (See Dryness - tongue - accompanied - roughness)
    - **Papillae** | **erected** (See Papillae - erect - accompanied - roughness)
  - **eating**; after: graph kr1* spong fd4.de

Roughness – Tongue: ...
  - **raising** to the palate | **agg.**: rosm lgb1
  - **sand**; as if covered by: coloc b4a.de
  - **streaks**, in: *Calc* k*

○ · **Centre** | **streaks** in: *Calc* kr1*
  - **Lower** part: rosm lgb1
  - **Sides**: osm k*
  - **Tip**: ammc a1* carb-v h2* mez h2* nat-sil fd3.de• phos h2*

SALIVA: (↗*Mucus; Pasty; Sticky*) merc ptk1 sulph ptk1
- **acid** (See sour)
- **acrid**: agar k* am-c k* ars bro1 arum-t k* asaf k* atro hr1 borx bro1 cypra-eg sde6.de• daph bro1 hydr bg1 ign kali-chl bg1* kalm kreos bg2* lac-c *Lach* hr1 lact k* *Merc* k* merc-c b4a.de* *Merc-i-f* k* *Nit-ac* k* ph-ac bg1 plb bg1 *Puls* b7a.de sec bg1 stann bg1 staph b7a.de* sulph bg1* tarax bg1 tax bro1 verat k* zinc bg1
- **albuminous**: am-caust k* calad k* *Stram* k*
- **alkaline**: jab k* plb k* sin-n k*
- **altered**: alum bg2 arg-met bg2 ars bg2 asar bg2 bell bg2 *Borx* bg2 bry bg2 calc bg2 calc-p bg2 camph bg2 cann-xyz bg2 canth bg2 clem bg2 daph bg2 *Dig* bg2 euph bg2 *Hyos* bg2 ign bg2 kreos bg2 mag-c bg2 mag-m bg2 **Merc** bg2 nit-ac bg2 nux-m bg2 nux-v bg2 phos bg2 plb bg2 *Puls* bg2 ran-b bg2 ran-s bg2 rhus-t bg2 sabad bg2 sabin bg2 sep bg2 spig bg2 stann bg2 staph bg2 **Sulph** bg2 thuj bg2 verat bg2 verb bg2
- **aromatic**: coca
- **astringent**: caps bg1 merc-c bg1 par k* sabad bg2*
- **bitter**: arg-n bg2 arn b7.de* *Ars* k* atha bro1 bapt k* borx b4a.de* bry bg2* **Chel** k* coca cupr b7a.de guat vk1 kali-bi k* kali-s bro1 kalm lyc k* mang k* merc b4.de* nux-m b7a.de phos k* plut-n srj7• ptel br *Puls* bro1 *Staph* b7a.de sulph k* tarax b7.de* thuj k* ust k* valer b7a.de
- **bloody**: acon k* alum b4.de* am-c k* am-caust vh1 antip bro1* arg-met k* arn k* ars k* aspar k* bad k* *Bell* k* bism b7.de* borx b4a.de bry k* **Bufo** k* calad k* calc b4a.de camph k* canth k* *Carb-v* k* carbn-s k* chin b7.de* cic k* clem k* **Crot-c** k* *Crot-h* k* cupr b7a.de *Dros* k* eug k* gels k* hep b4a.de *Hyos* k* indg k* iod b4.de* jatr-c k* *Kali-i* k* lyc b4.de* **Mag-c** k* mag-m b4.de* *Merc* k* *Merc-c* k* *Nat-m* k* **Nit-ac** k* *Nux-v* k* op k* **Phos** k* **Plb** a1 *Rhus-t* k* sabin b7.de* *Sec* k* sel b7.de* *Sep* b4a.de staph k* stram k* sul-ac k2 *Sulph* k* thuj k* vip k* zinc k* zinc-p k2
  - **morning**: nit-ac h2
  - **night**: nat-m a1 *Nux-v* hr1*
  - **accompanied** by:
    - **convulsions** (See GENERALS - Convulsions - accompanied - saliva - bloody)
    - **diphtheria** (See THROAT - Diphtheria - accompanied - saliva - bloody)
  - **cough** agg.; during: dros b7.de*
  - **disgusting** taste; with: kali-i ptk1
  - **menses**; before: *Nat-m* k*
  - **sleep**; during: nat-m bg2 rhus-t bg2*
  - **sweetish**: *Kali-i* kr1*
- **bluish**: plb k*
  - **white**: carb-ac k*
- **brassy**: kali-chl k*
- **brownish**: bell k* bism k* bit-ar wht1• crot-c k* plan k* raja-s vk1
- **burning**: manc
- **changed** (See altered)
- **clammy**: arg-met bell berb camph cann-s eug lob k* sacch-a fd2.de•
- **cool**: asar k* bar-c bg2 bor-ac bg2* borx k* *Caust* b4a.de chen-v k* cist k* merc-c k* phos b4.de* phyt k* [heroin sdj2]
- **copious** (See Salivation - profuse)
- **coppery**: merc k* ran-b k*
- **corrosive**: plut-n srj7•
- **cotton**, like: (↗*Velvet*) alet bro1 aq-mar bro1 bell bg2 *Berb* k* bry bro1 canth bro1 lyss bro1 *Nux-m* k* *Nux-v* bro1 ph-ac bro1 **Puls** k* sulph bro1
- **dark**: merc-d ptk1
- **diminished** (See scanty)
- **dries** on palate and lips, becomes tough: lyc k*
- **egg**; like white of: calad ptk1 jab ptk1

- **fetid**: alumn vk1 ang b7.de* ars k* bell b4.de* bov b4.de* bry bg2* calc b4.de* caps bg1* _Carb-v_ b4.de* cham b7.de* chin b7.de* _Dig_ k* _Dulc_ hr1* _Iod_ k* kali-i bg2 _Lach_ hr1* _Manc_ k* **Merc** k* _Merc-c_ vk1 _Merc-cy_ hr1 _Merc-d_ hr1* _Merc-i-f_ k* _Merc-i-r_ vk1 **Nit-ac** k* _Petr_ k* phos b4.de* plb vk1 _Rhus-t_ b7a.de sep b4.de* sulph bg2 valer vk1 zinc b4.de*
  - **morning**: glon vk1 petr vk1
  - **night**: merc vk1
- **foul** water, like: phos h2*
- **frothy**: _(↗soapy)_ acon k* _Alet_ bro1* am-m bg2 ant-c b7.de* _Apis_ k* aq-mar bro1 ars bg2 asaf k2 bac bn bart a1 bell b4.de* berb k* brom k* _Bry_ k* _Bufo_ k* camph b7.de* cann-i k* cann-s b7a.de* canth k* carb-ac bg2* carb-an k* caul bg3* cham k* chlf a1 cic b7.de* cina k* cinnb k* clem bg2 cocc k* colch bg2 _Crot-h_ k* cub a1* _Cupr_ k* _Dig_ k* dulc bg2* eug k* gaul bg1 gels bg2 _Hyos_ k* ign k* iod ptk1 _Ip_ b7.de* irid-met bg2 kali-bi k* kali-m ptk1 _Kreos_ k* lac-c k* lach bg3* lyc h2* lys bg2 lyss k* merc bg2 morph k* naja bg2 nat-c bg2* _Nat-m_ bg2 _Nux-m_ bg2* _Nux-v_ bro1 ol-an bg3* op bg2 ph-ac k* phel k* phos b4.de* phys k* pic-ac k* plb k* puls k* ran-s k* sabin k* sec b7.de* sil b4.de* sin-a a1 spig k* stram k* stry a1 sulph k* sumb a1 ther k2 verat b7.de* [heroin sdj2]
  - **accompanied** by:
    - **cough** (See COUGH - Accompanied - saliva - frothy)
    - **dry** mouth (See Dryness - accompanied - saliva)
    - **typhoid** fever (See FEVER - Typhoid - accompanied - saliva - frothy)
  - **talking**:
    - **agg.**: eug kr1* nat-c k* sabin k*
    - **amel.**: sabin bg2
- **glistening**: stram bg2
- **gluey**: agn b7.de* apis bg2 arg-met bg2 _Arn_ b7a.de ars b4a.de _Aur_ b4a.de bad k* bapt bg2 bell k* boerh-d bnj1 camph bg2 _Cann-s_ b7.de* cimic k* cinnb k* _Kali-bi_ bg2 lach ptk1* mag-p bg2 merc-c bg2 nat-c a1 nux-m k* _Ph-ac_ b4.de* _Phos_ b4.de* plat b4.de* podo bg2 raja-s vk1 ran-b b7.de* samb b7.de* seneg b4.de* _Squil_ b7a.de tab bg2
- **gray**: _Ambr_ b7a.de arg-met b7.de* _Dros_ b7a.de seneg b4a.de
- **green**: carb-v b4.de* cic b7a.de colch b7.de* _Dros_ b7a.de gins k* graph k* nat-c b4.de* nat-m b4.de* par b7.de* plb b7.de* sec k* zinc b4.de*
- **gushing**: carb-v bg2* cop bg2 ign ptk1 musca-d szs1 nat-m bg2*
- **horrible**: chin b7.de*
- **hot**: asar k* daph k* manc k* mosch k* sabad k* tax k*
  - **nausea**; during: sabad tax
- **increased** (See Salivation - profuse)
- **insipid**: asar b7.de* ign b7.de* puls b7.de* rhus-t b7.de* sabad b7a.de spig b7.de* staph b7.de* thuj bg2 _Verat_ b7a.de
- **jellylike**: arg-met b7.de* kali-bi bg2 merc-c bg2 plb b7a.de sabad k*
- **metallic** tasting: _(↗Taste - metallic)_ bism k* cedr k* _Cham_ k* cimic cimx k* _Coc-c_ cocc bro1 _Cupr_ bro1 jatr-c kali-bi k* kali-chl k* lyc k* merc k* _Nit-ac_ bro1 _Phyt_ k* ran-b k* sal-fr sle1• thuj k* zinc k*
- **milky**: _Phos_ b4a.de plb-o bro1
- **musty**: kali-bi k* led k*
- **offensive**: alumn k* ars k* atro bapt bg2* bry _Caps_ k* carb-v k2 chin b7.de* crot-h bg2 cupr b7a.de _Dig_ k* _Diph_ br1 _Dulc_ ign b7.de* _Iod_ k* kali-c bg1 kreos bro1 lac-h sk4• _Lach_ k* _Manc_ k* **Merc** k* _Merc-c_ k* _Merc-cy_ hr1 _Merc-d_ hr1* _Merc-i-r_ **Nit-ac** k* _Petr_ k* phos bg2 plb k* psor bro1 puls b7.de* rheum b7.de* rhus-t bg2 valer k*
  - **morning**: glon k* petr
  - **night**: merc k*
- **oily**: aesc k* cub k*
- **onions**, odor of: kali-i k*
- **pasty** (See gluey)
- **purulent**: kali-c k2
- **putrid**: merc-d ptk1 petr bg2
- **reddish**: sabin k* sec bg2 stram bg2 sul-ac k*
- **repulsive** taste; of: _Merc_ b4.de* sulph bg2
- **ropy**: _(↗viscid; Mucus - ropy)_ am-m bro1 ant-c bro1 arg-n bro1 bell bg2 coc-c bg2* cuc-c vk1 dulc bro1 _Epiph_ bro1 ferr hydr bro1 _Hydrin-m_ bro1 iod bro1 iris k* **Kali-bi** k* kali-chl bro1 lach k* lyss k* _Merc_ bro1 myric bro1 narc-ps c1* nat-m bro1 phyt k* pilo bro1 _Puls_ bro1 sabad ptk1 sanic sulph ptk1 tammd vk1 tarax bro1
- **saltish**: _(↗Taste - saltish)_ alum b4.de* am-c k* ang _Ant-c_ k* ant-t bg2 bov b4.de* _Carb-an_ chin b7a.de colch **Cycl** k* dig k* elaps _Euph_ k* graph b4.de* _Hyos_ k* _Ign_ b7a.de kali-bi k* _Kali-i_ k* kali-p lac-ac k* lac-h sk4• _Lyc_ k* mag-m _Merc_ k* _Merc-c_ k* mez k* nat-c k* _Nat-m_ k* nux-v b7.de* _Phos_ k* rhus-t k* sanic bg1* _Sep_ k* sil b4a.de sin-a stram k* _Sulph_ k* _Tarax_ b7a.de tax ther c1 verat k* verb k*
  - **left**: euph h2
  - **morning**: rhus-t sul-ac k* sulph k*
  - **watery**: carb-an ptk1 verb ptk1
- **scanty**: **Acon** b2.de* agar b2.de* agn b2.de* aloe bg2 alum b2.de* am-c b2.de* am-m b2.de* ambr b2.de* anac b2.de* ang b2.de* ant-c b2.de* ant-t b2.de* arg-met b2.de* arn k* ars k* asaf k* asar b2.de* aspar k* aur b2.de* _Bar-c_ b2.de* bell b2.de* berb k* borx b2.de* bov b2.de* _Bry_ b2.de* calad k* _Calc_ b2.de* camph b2.de* cann-s b2.de* canth b2.de* caps b2.de* carb-an b2.de* carb-v b2.de* caust b2.de* _Cham_ b2.de* chel b2.de* chin b2.de* cina b2.de* clem b2.de* coca k* _Cocc_ b2.de* coff b2.de* colch b2.de* con b2.de* croc b2.de* cupr b2.de* cycl k* dulc b2.de* euph b2.de* ferr b2.de* graph b2.de* hell b2.de* hep b2.de* hyos k* ign b2.de* iod b2.de* ip b2.de* jab k* kali-bi bg2* kali-c b2.de* kali-n b2.de* _Lach_ b2.de* lat-m bnm6• laur b2.de* led b2.de* _Lyc_ b2.de* m-ambo b2.de m-arct b2.de mag-c b2.de* mag-m b2.de* mang b2.de* meny b2.de* _Merc_ b2.de* _Merc-c_ k* merl hr1* mez b2.de* mosch b2.de* mur-ac b2.de* nat-c b2.de* nat-m b2.de* _Nit-ac_ b2.de* _Nux-m_ k* nux-v b2.de* olnd b2.de* op k* _Par_ b2.de* petr k* ph-ac b2.de* phos b2.de* plat b2.de* plb k* _Puls_ b2.de* ran-b b2.de* ran-s b2.de* rheum b2.de* rhod b2.de* **Rhus-t** b2.de* ruta b2.de* sabad b2.de* sabin b2.de* samb b2.de* sars b2.de* sec b2.de* sel b2.de* _Seneg_ b2.de* _Sep_ b2.de* sil b2.de* spig b2.de* spong k* squil b2.de* stann b2.de* staph b2.de* stram b2.de* _Stront-c_ b2.de* sul-ac b2.de* sulph b2.de* tarax b2.de* tax k* thea k* thuj b2.de* verat k* zinc b2.de*
  - **thirst**; with: lyc bg2 sil bg2
- **sharp** taste: ph-ac h2
- **slimy**: bell _Camph_ k* _Caps_ hr1 glon kali-s fd4.de lach _Merc_ nux-m mrr1 petr plb rhus-t sars
- **snow**-white (See white - snow-white)
- **soapy**: _(↗frothy; Froth; Taste - soapy; MIND - Spitting - foamy)_ arg-n bg2 berb k* bry k* _Dulc_ k* iod bg2* _Merc_ k* ph-ac h2* phos k*
  - **morning**: apis k*
- **sour**: _(↗Taste - sour)_ agar alum k* ang atro benz-ac bg2 bry b7a.de _Calc_ k* _Calc-p_ k* carbn-s chin b7.de* con ptk1 crot-t **Ign** k* iris bro1 kali-bi _Kali-chl_ k* lact laur k* lyc mag-m b4.de* manc merc k* nat-c k* nat-m k* _Nit-ac_ bro1 nux-v b7.de* par k* petr ph-ac k* phos k* plb b7.de* podo k* rhod bg2 sec stann k* staph b7.de* _Sulph_ k* tarax k* tax thuj bg2 upa (non:uran-met k) uran-n [heroin sdj2]
  - ○ **Teeth**; between: fl-ac bg2 sulph bg2
- **spoiled** taste: bell h1
- **sticky** (See thick)
- **stringy** (See ropy)
- **suppressed**: bell k* cain cann-s k* merc-c k* op k* phyt k* stram k*
  - **dentition**; during: kali-br
- **swallowing**:
  - **constantly** swallow saliva; obliged to (See THROAT - Swallow, constant - saliva)
  - **impossible** (See THROAT - Swallowing - impossible - saliva)
- **sweet**: _(↗Taste - sweetish)_ acon b7a.de _All-s_ alum k* alumn anac b4.de* asar b7.de* aspar aur k* _Canth_ k* _Carb-an_ **Cham** k* chin k* cop _Cupr_ k* _Dig_ k* hyos k* iris bg2* kali-bi bg2* _Kali-i_ kreos bg2 laur b7.de* lob merc bro1 mez b4a.de* nicc nit-ac k* _Phos_ k* pic-ac _Plb_ k* plb-act bro1 **Puls** k* _Sabad_ k* sep k* stann bro1 sul-ac k* sulph bg2 sumb bg2 syph thuj k*
  - **night**: _All-s_ a1 cham ptk1 _Sulph_
  - **bitter**: bapt bg2
  - **disgustingly**: canth ptk1
  - **eating**; after: all-s ptk1
- **tenacious** (See viscid)
- **thick**: _(↗viscid)_ abel vk1 anan apis b7a.de _Ars_ bapt k2 bell k* bism k* brass-n-o srj5• bros-gau mrc1 cain calad cann-i k* carb-ac cedr cimic cocc crot-c _Dros_ b7a.de formal br1 guat vk1 hoit vk1 iod b4.de* kali-bi bg2* kali-p lach ptk1* lavand-a ctl1• m-arct b7.de _Nux-m_ k* op ozone sde2• paro-i vk1 phyt k* plb ptk1 _Psor_ jl2 rhus-t rhus-v sulph b4.de* tax
  - **morning**: glon k*
- **thin**: _(↗watery)_ jatr-c k* lyss k* manc k*

- **viscid**: *(↗ropy; thick; Mucus - ropy)* acet-ac k* acon k* agn k* alum b4.de* am-br k* am-m b7.de* ambr b7.de* anac b4.de* anag k* anan k* ang b7.de* ant-c b7.de* apis k* arg-met k* arg-n bg2 *Arn* b7a.de *Ars* k* asar b7.de* bapt k* bell k* *Berb* k* bism hr1* bit-ar wht1• *Borx* b4a.de bry b7.de* cain kr1* calad vk1 calc k* camph k* cann-i vk1 cann-s k* caps k* carb-v k* carbn-s k* cedr vk1 cham b7.de* **Chel** k* cimic k* cinnb k* cocc vk1 coff b7.de* con k* *Crot-c* k* cub c1 *Cupr* k* cycl k* der vml3• *Dulc* k* elaps k* eug k* euph b4.de* ferr vk1 fl-ac k* glon ptk1 hippoz hr1 ign k* iod b4.de* iris k* jab br1 jatr-c k* **Kali-bi** k* kali-br a1 kali-c b4.de* kali-chl hr1 kali-i k* kali-p vk1 kali-s fd4.de kola stb3• lac-c k* **Lach** k* lachn k* laur b7.de* lob k* lyc ptk1 **Lyss** k* *Mag-c* b4a.de mag-m b4.de* med k* **Merc** k* **Merc-c** k* merl k* mez b4.de* nat-ar k* nat-c k* *Nat-m* hr1 nat-sil fd3.de• nit-ac k* *Nux-m* k* *Nux-v* b7.de* op b7a.de* ozone sde2• par b7.de* ph-ac k* phos k* phys ptk1 *Phyt* k* pic-ac k* plb b7.de* *Puls* k* *Ran-b* b7.de* rhus-t b7.de* rhus-v vk1 samb b7.de* sanic vk1 sars b4.de* sel b7.de* seneg k* sep h2* spig k* squil b7.de* stann b4.de* *Stram* k* sul-ac k* syph k2 tab bg2 tarax k* tax vk1* thuj b4.de* uran-n kr1* verat k* [lappa stj]
  - **night**: merc k*
  - **accompanied** by:
    - **diphtheria** (See THROAT - Diphtheria - accompanied - saliva - viscid)
    - **indigestion** (See STOMACH - Indigestion - accompanied - saliva - viscid)
    - **scarlatina** (See SKIN - Eruptions - scarlatina - accompanied - saliva - viscid)
  - **dribbles**: stram ptk1
  - **drinking** beer, lemonade, orangeade; after: **Sil** vh
  - **nap**; after: euph h2*
  - **pregnancy** agg.; during: *Kali-i* kr1*
  - **strings**; drawn out in: agn k*
- **watery**: *(↗thin)* acon vh1 am-c b4.de* am-m b7a.de *Ant-t* vh1 asar k* aur-m k* bell bg2 bism bro1 calc k* calc-ar k* camph k* canth b7a.de carb-an k* cob k* *Colch* b7.de* coloc h2* *Cycl* k* dig b4.de* dros k* hell b7.de* iod h* ip b7.de* jab bro1 jatr-c k* kreos k* lach b7.de* laur b7.de* led k* lob k* lyss k* m-aust b7.de mag-m k* manc k* mur-ac b4.de* nat-m k* nux-v b7.de* ox-ac k* par b7.de* phos k* plb b7.de* puls k* seneg b4a.de staph b7.de* *Sul-ac* k* thea k* thymol vk1 trif-r bro1
  - **nausea**; during: thymol sp1*
- **white**: ars k* bell k* borx b4a.de calad k* cann-i k* crot-c a1 ign b7.de* ip b7.de* m-arct b7.de ol-an k* par b7.de* *Puls* b7a.de ran-b k* sabin k* seneg b4.de* spig k* stram b7.de* tab bg2 [tax jsj7]
  - **bluish**: carb-ac k*
  - **snow**-white: ol-an bg3*
- **yellow**: bell bg2 bry b7.de* cycl k* *Dros* b7a.de *Gels* k* kali-bi bg2 lyc k* lyss k* *Manc* k* merc ptk1 *Merc-c* k* op bg2 paro-i vk1 *Phos* b4a.de *Phyt* k* rhus-t k* sec k* *Spig* b7.de*
  - **blood**, as from: *Gels* k*

SALIVATION: abrom-a ks5 acet-ac k* acon k* acon-c c2 act-sp k* adon vk1 aesc k* aeth k* agar k* agath-a nl2• alet k* all-s k* allox sp1* aloe k* *Alum* k* alum-p k2 alum-sil k2 alumn k* **Am-c** k* am-m h2* ambr k* *Anac* k* anag k* anan k* ancis-p tsm2 androc srj1• ang k* anh sp1 ant-c k* ant-t k* anthraci k* aphis k* apis k* apoc k* aran-sc vh arec c1* arg-met k* arg-n k* arn k* ars k* ars-h k* *Ars-i* k* ars-met k* arum-m k* **Arum-t** k* arund k* asaf k* *Asar* k* aspar k* aster k* *Aur* bg2* aur-i k2 *Aur-m* k* bamb-a stb2.de• bapt k* **Bar-c** k* bar-i k2 *Bar-m* k* bar-s k2 *Bell* k* bism k* **Borx** k* both tsm2 both-ax tsm2 bov k* *Brom* k* bry k* bufo k* bung-fa tsm2 but-ac sp1 buth-a sp1 cadm-met sp1 cadm-s k* cain k* calad k* *Calc* k* *Calc-act* vh calc-ar kr1* calc-i k2 *Calc-p* k* calc-s k* *Camph* k* *Canth* k* *Caps* k* carb-ac k* carb-an k* *Carb-v* k* carbn-s k* card-m k* *Caust* k* *Cham* k* *Chel* k* *Chin* k* chinin-ar k* chinin-s bg2* chion vk1 chlor k* choc srj3• *Cic* k* cimic k* cina k* *Cinnb* k* cinnm k* *Clem* k* cob k* *Coc-c* k* cocc b7.de* coch vk1 coff vk1 *Colch* k* coloc h2 colum-p sze2• con k* cop k* croc k* *Crot-c* k* crot-h tsm2* crot-t k* cuc-c vk1 *Cupr* k* cupr-ar k* cycl k* daph k* dendr-pol tsm2 der vml3• dig k* dios bg2 *Dros* k* *Dulc* k* elaps tsm2 epil a1* **Epiph** c2* esin c1* eucal kr1* eug k* eup-pur k* euph k* falco-pe nl2• ferr k* ferr-ar k* ferr-i k* *Ferr-ma* k* *Ferr-p* k* **Fl-ac** k* fuch br1 gaert pte1*• galv c2 *Gamb* k* gard-j vlr2• gins br1 *Glon* k* *Gran* k* *Graph* k* grat k* guaj vk1 guat sp1 *Hell* k* hell-o a1* helon k* hemidsm bnj1 *Hep* k* hipp st* hippoz k* hydr-ac k* hyos k* *Ign* k* **Iod** k* **Ip** k* *Iris* k* jab k* jatr-c k* kali-ar k* kali-bi k* *Kali-br* k* **Kali-c** k* *Kali-chl* k* *Kali-i* k* kali-m k2 kali-n h2* kali-p k* *Kali-perm* hr1* kali-s k* kali-sil k2 kali-tel c2 kalm k* kola stb3• *Kreos* k* lac-ac k* *Lac-c* k* lacer a1* *Lach* k* lachn k* *Lact* k* lat-h bnm5• lat-m sp1 laur k* lavand-a ctl1• led k* lil-t k* lina br1 lob k* *Lyc* k* **Lyss** k* *M-ambo* b7.de* m-arct b7.de* m-aust b7a.de mag-c b4.de* mag-m k* mag-s sp1* *Manc* k* mand sp1 mang k* med k* meny h1* *Merc* b4.de* **Merc-c** k* *Merc-cy* k* *Merc-d* k* **Merc-i-r** k* merc-sul vk1 mez k* morg-p pte1*• mucs-nas rly4• *Mur-ac* k* *Muscin* vk1 *Naja* k* narc-ps a1* nat-ar k* *Nat-c* k* nat-f vk1 **Nat-m** k* nat-p k* *Nat-s* k* nicc k* **Nit-ac** k* **Nit-m-ac** vk1 nit-s-d kr1* *Nux-m* k* **Nux-v** k* oena k* *Ol-an* k* *Olib-sac* wmh1 op k* opun-s a1 *Ox-ac* k* oxyurn-sc mcp1• ozone sde2• pant-ac rly4• par k* parth c2 *Petr* k* ph-ac b4a.de* phel k* *Phos* k* phys st* *Phyt* k* **Pilo** c2* pin-con oss2• pitu-p sp1* plan k* plat b4.de* plat-m-n c1* *Plb* k* plut-n srj7• *Podo* k* polyg-h k* *Positr* nl2• ptel k* *Puls* k* ran-b k* ran-s k* rat k* rauw sp1 rheum b7.de* rhod k* rhus-g tmo3• rhus-t k* ruta k* sabad k* sabin vk1 samb b7.de* sang k* sars b4.de* sec k* sel b7.de* *Seneg* k* *Sep* k* *Sil* k* sin-a c2 sin-n k* sphing kk3.fr spig k* spong k* squil b7.de* stann k* staph k* *Stram* k* stront-c b4.de* suis-em rly4• *Sul-ac* k* sul-i k2 *Sulph* k* syc fmm1• symph fd3.de• **Syph** k2* *Tab* k* tarax k* tell k* ter st teucr k* thal-xyz srj8• thea k* thuj k* thymol sp1 *Trif-p* br1* trif-r c2 tril-p c1* tritic-vg fd5.de tung-met bdx1• (non:uran-met k*) uran-n k* ust kr1* valer k2 vanil fd5.de verat k* verat-v kr1* verb k* vichy-g c2 vinc kr1* viol-t k* wye c2 xan kr1* xanth st *Zinc* k* zinc-p k2 [heroin sdj2]

- **right** side of: hep bg1 mim-p skp7•
- **daytime**: adam skp7• mim-p vml3•
- **morning**: agath-a nl2• alum k* aur k* bapt a1 **Graph** k* iod k* lac-ac k* *Lyc* k* mag-c k* mag-m k* merc-i-f k* ozone sde2• plat h2* rhus-t k* sars k* stann k* *Sulph* k* symph fd3.de• verat k*
  - **bed** agg.; in: agath-a nl2• rhus-t k*
  - **rising** agg.: verat kr1*
  - **sleep** agg.; during: bar-c k* cench k2
  - **stooping** agg.: graph kr1*
  - **waking**; on: coca-c sk4• des-ac rbp6 lac-h sk4• stann k* symph fd3.de•
- **forenoon**: calc h2* ruta fd4.de vanil fd5.de
- **afternoon**: alum k* am-c a1 grat k* mag-c k* mag-m k* phos k* ruta fd4.de
  - **sleep** agg.; during: adam skp7• rhus-t h1
- **evening**: am-c a1 bapt a1 bry k* dulc fd4.de lyc k* neon srj5• ox-ac k* ozone sde2• ruta fd4.de sep h2* sulph k*
  - **bed** agg.; in: alum k* nat-m k*
- **night**: *Arg-n* k* bar-c k* canth k* cench k* cham c1* crot-h k* culx st dig k* gard-j vlr2• gran c1 graph k2* hydrog srj2• ign bg2* lap-la rsp1 menth-pu c2 **Merc** k* *Merc-c* hr1* merc-d sne *Nat-m* k* nit-m-ac br1 nux-v k* phos bg2* ptel k* puls k* rheum br1 *Rhus-t* k* ruta k* sulph k* syph mtf33 vanil fd5.de verat bg1
  - **midnight**:
    - **after** | **1** h: *Merc* k*
  - **amel.**: adam skp7•
  - **bed** agg.; in: **Merc** mrr1 neon srj5• vanil fd5.de
  - **lying**:
    - **agg.**: bell k*
    - **side**; on:
      - **right** | **agg.**: mim-p vk1
- **accompanied** by:
  - **angina** (See THROAT - Inflammation - accompanied - salivation)
  - **aphthae** (See Aphthae - accompanied - salivation)
  - **apoplexy** (See GENERALS - Apoplexy - accompanied - salivation)
  - **appetite**; increased: lob ptk1
  - **asthma** (See RESPIRATION - Asthmatic - accompanied - salivation)
  - **back** | **pain** in back (See BACK - Pain - accompanied - salivation)
  - **breath**; fetid (See odor)
  - **burning** pain: nat-f vk1
  - **cardialgia** (See STOMACH - Heartburn - accompanied - salivation)
  - **colic** (See ABDOMEN - Pain - cramping - accompanied - salivation)

Mouth

- **complaints**; other: lob ptk1
- **coryza** (See NOSE - Coryza - accompanied - salivation)
- **cough** (See COUGH - Accompanied - salivation)
- **dentition** (See TEETH - Dentition - difficult - accompanied - salivation)
- **diarrhea** (See RECTUM - Diarrhea - accompanied - salivation)
- **eructations**: calc-ar kr1*
- **gonorrhea** (See URETHRA - Discharge - gonorrheal - accompanied - salivation)
- **headache** (See HEAD - Pain - accompanied - salivation)
- **hoarseness** (See LARYNX - Voice - hoarseness - accompanied - salivation)
- **hysteria** (See MIND - Hysteria - salivation)
- **indigestion** (See STOMACH - Indigestion - accompanied - salivation)
- **malignant** scarlet fever (See FEVER - Scarlet - malignant - accompanied - salivation)
- **measles** (See SKIN - Eruptions - measles - accompanied - salivation)
- **mumps** (See FACE - Inflammation - parotid - mumps - accompanied - salivation)
- **nausea**: agar bg ant-t bg* **Apom** sne ars h2 asar bg2 bar-c h brom bg bry h calc h2 *Camph* h1* caps h1 carb-v sf1.de carbn-s kr1* *Card-m* vk1 carl bg *Cham* h* *Chin* kr1* cocc h1* crot-t k* cub bg cupr-act bg cycl h1 dig h euph h2* goss vk1 gran al2* hep h2 **Ip** k* kali-bi bg kali-c h kreos bg2 *Lac-ac* mrr1 *Lach* kr1* led bg **Lob** k* lyc h2 mag-c h2 mag-m h2 mang h2 meny h1 merc h mez b4a.de* nat-c h2 nat-pyru rly4• nat-s a1 *Nux-v* ol-an bg op bg ozone sde2• *Petr* k* ph-ac h2 phos h pilo a1 podo fd3.de• puls k* pycnop-sa mrz1 ran-a bg rhus-t h rob bg sabin bg *Sang* k* sep h2 spong h1 squil h staph h1 sul-ac bg *Sulph* h2* symph fd3.de• thea bg thuj bg thymol sp1* tritic-vg fd5.de valer bg2 verat h1* zinc h2* [tax jsj7]
- **odor** from mouth; putrid: hell bg2 iod bg2 *Kali-br* st
- **pain** (See GENERALS - Pain - accompanied - salivation)
- **pain** in mouth (See Pain - accompanied - salivation)
- **paralysis**: mang ptk1
- **prosopalgia** (See FACE - Pain - accompanied - salivation)
- **rheumatic** pain (See EXTREMITIES - Pain - rheumatic - accompanied - salivation)
- **scarlatina** (See SKIN - Eruptions - scarlatina - accompanied - salivation)
- **scarlet** fever (See FEVER - Scarlet - accompanied - salivation)
- **stool**; complaints of (See STOOL - Complaints - accompanied - salivation)
- **syphilis** (See GENERALS - Syphilis - accompanied - salivation)
- **tapeworms** (See RECTUM - Worms - complaints - tapeworm - accompanied - salivation)
- **taste**; nauseous (See Taste - nauseous - accompanied - salivation)
- **typhus** fever (See FEVER - Typhus - accompanied - salivation)
- **vertigo** (See VERTIGO - Accompanied - salivation)
- **whooping** cough (See COUGH - Whooping - accompanied - salivation)

○ • **Face**; pain in (See FACE - Pain - accompanied - salivation)
- **Mouth**; complaints of (See agg.)
- **Stomach**:
  - **complaints** of (See STOMACH - Complaints - accompanied - salivation)
  - **pain** (See STOMACH - Pain - accompanied - salivation)

- **accompanied** by: ...
  - **Throat**:
    - **dryness** (See THROAT - Dryness - accompanied - salivation)
    - **inflammation** of (See THROAT - Inflammation - accompanied - salivation)
    - **pain** (See THROAT - Pain - accompanied - salivation)
    - **swelling** of (See THROAT - Swelling - accompanied - salivation)
  - **Tongue**:
    - **clean**: hell-o a1
    - **cream**-like: mez vk1
    - **green** discoloration of the tongue: *Nit-ac* kr1*
    - **swelling**: bism kr1*
  - **Tonsils**; inflammation of (See THROAT - Inflammation - tonsils - accompanied - salivation)
- **agg.**: *Acon* bg2 *Alum* bg2 ambr bg2 ant-c bg2 arg-met bg2 *Bell* bg2 bry bg2 calc bg2 cham bg2 chin bg2 ign bg2 **Lach** bg2 lyc bg2 **Merc** bg2 nat-m bg2 nit-ac bg2 *Nux-v* bg2 *Phos* bg2 puls bg2 rhus-t bg2 sep bg2 sil bg2 **Sulph** bg2
- **alternating** with | **dry** mouth: calc k* carb-v k* cent a1 con k* gins a1 ign k* *Kali-bi* hr1 phos b4.de* ulm-c jsj8• verat k*
- **angina**; in (See THROAT - Inflammation - accompanied - salivation)
- **apoplexy**, in: *Anac* st1 ant-c hr1 **Nux-v** st1
- **apyrexia**; during: ip kr1*
- **children**; in: *Camph* st1
- **chill**:
  - **before**: ip k* rhus-t k*
  - **during**: acon bg2 *Alum* b4.de* anac bg2 ars bg2 asaf k* bell bg2 brom bg2 calc bg2 *Caps* k* cham b7.de* dros bg2 euph bg2 hep bg2 ip bg2 *Jab* bg2 kreos b7a.de* lach bg2 lyc bg2 *Merc* bg2 **Mez** bg2 nat-m bg2 nit-ac bg2 nux-v bg2 phos bg2 *Rhus-t* b7.de* sep bg2 sil bg2 *Stram* bg2* sulph bg2 verat bg2
- **coffee** agg.: rhus-t a1
- **collecting**; sensation of: phos b4.de*
- **complaints** of salivation: ars bg2 *Caust* bg2 kali-c bg2
- **continuous**: mim-p skp7•
- **convulsions**; with: bar-m k* caust h2* kali-bi k2* *Oena* k*
- **copious** (See profuse)
- **coryza**; during: **Arund** vh *Calc-p* bg2* cupr-ar st1 hep b4a.de* kali-i ptk1 merc b4a.de
- **crawling** in throat, from: am-m h2* carb-v h2*
- **dentition**; during (See TEETH - Dentition - difficult - accompanied - salivation)
- **diphtheria**; in (See THROAT - Diphtheria - accompanied - saliva)
- **dribbling**: mim-p skp7• ruta fd4.de stram tl1*
- **dryness** | **sensation** of, with: abel vh1 agar bg2 alum k* aral bg1 asaf bg1 bell bg2 calad ptk1 calc bg1 chion bg2* colch k* dream-p sdj1• ind bg1 kali-c k* *Kali-m* st1 laur bg1 lyc b2.de* mag-m k* *Merc* b2.de* mez b2.de* nat-m bg2* nux-v b2.de* olib-sac wmh1 plb k* psil ft1* rhod k* sep bg1 spig bg1 uran-n bg2
- **eating**:
  - **after** | **agg.**: *All-s* k* castor-eq k* *Caust* k* cham bg1 chin b7a.de kali-p bg1 lyc h2 mag-c k* *Nat-s* k* *Nux-v* k* petr b4a.de* positr nl2• *Rhus-t* h1* staph h1* sulph k* symph fd3.de•
  - **amel.**: thymol sp1*
  - **while**:
    - **agg.**: spong fd4.de
    - **beginning** to eat: sulph h2
- **excessive** (See profuse)
- **expectoration**; frequent: am-c k* cadm-s k* dig h2* graph k* *Lyss* k* *Puls* k* rhus-t k* sabad k* spig k*
- **fever**; during: dulc fd4.de *Sulph* kr1*
- **headache**:
  - **before**: *Fl-ac* k*

- **during** (See HEAD - Pain - accompanied - salivation)
- **heat**; during: acon bg2 alum b4.de* arund k* bell bg2 brom bg2 carb-v bg2 cic b7.de* *Dros* k* hell k* hep k* hyos b7.de ign bg2 ip bg2 lach k2 lyc bg2 merc bg2 nat-m bg2 *Nit-ac* k* *Nux-v* b7.de* op bg2 *Puls* bg2 *Rhus-t* b7.de* seneg bg2 sep bg2 sil b4.de* *Stram* k* *Sulph* k* verat bg2
- **indigestion**; with: choc srj3•
- **intermittent**: nit-m-ac c2
- **lachrymation**; after: atra-r bnm3•
- **lying**:
  - **agg.**: bell kr1* choc srj3• dulc fd4.de ip k* ptel k* rhus-t k* ruta fd4.de
  - **back**; on | **agg.**: ozone sde2•
  - **side**; on:
    - **right** | **agg.**: mim-p vml3•
- **measles**; in (See SKIN - Eruptions - measles - accompanied - salivation)
- **menopause**; during: jab bro1
- **menses**:
  - **after** | **agg.**: *Cedr* k*
  - **before** | **agg.**: am-c bg2 cinnb al nux-m bg2 *Puls* k* pulx bro1
  - **during** | **agg.**: agar k* cinnb al eupi k* kali-n h2* mag-c k* *Merc* k* *Nux-m* k* phyt bg3* *Puls* k* pulx br1*
- **mental** work, during: merc k* *Merc-c* k* nit-ac k*
- **mercury**; after abuse of: alumn k* anan k* asaf k* bell k* **Chin** k* *Cupr* k* dig k* dulc k* *Hep* k* *Hydr* hr1* **Iod** k* *Iris* bro1 *Kali-chl* bro1* lach k* *Nat-m* k* *Nit-ac* k* op bg2* *Phyt* k* plb hr1 *Sulph* k*
- **mumps**; in (See FACE - Inflammation - parotid - mumps - accompanied - salivation)
- **pain**; during: cocc ptk1 epiph bg2* gran bg3* helo bg3 helon ptk1 kali-bi bg2 kali-c h2 led ptk1 mang ptk1 merc bg3* ozone sde2• *Phos* bg2* plan bg3* rheum ptk1 sulph bg3
- **periodical**: *Culx* vh
- **pregnancy** agg.; during: acet-ac k* ant-t k* ars bro1 *Coff* k* **Goss** c1* **Gran** bro1* *Helon* k* *Iod* bro1* ip st iris tl1 jab c2* *Kali-i* k* **Kreos** k* *Lac-ac* k* lob ptk1 *Merc* bro1* *Muscin* bro1* *Nat-m* hr1* *Nit-ac* bro1* pilo c1* *Sep* bro1* sulph bro1 zinc-s ptk1
- **profuse**: abel vk1 *Acet-ac* bro1 acon b2.de* adam skp7• adon bg2 agar b2.de* all-s bro1 allox tpw4 *Alum* b2.de* am-c b2.de* am-m b2.de* *Ambr* b2.de* anac b2.de* androc bnm2• ang b2.de* *Ant-c* b2.de* ant-t b2.de* apis b7a.de aran-sc vh1 *Arg-met* b2.de* arn b2.de* ars b2.de* ars-s-f k2 arum-t bg2* asaf b2.de* asar b2.de* atra-r bnm3• aur b2.de* bapt bg2* *Bar-c* b2.de* **Bell** b2.de* bism b2.de* borx b2.de* bov b2.de* brom b4a.de* bry b2.de* but-ac vk1 buth-a vk1 cadm-s bg2 *Calc* b2.de* calc-sil k2 camph b2.de* cann-s b2.de* canth b2.de* caps b2.de* carb-ac bg2 carb-an b2.de* carb-v b2.de* carbn-s k2 cardios-h rly4• cassia-s ccrh1• *Caust* b2.de* cench k2 *Cham* b2.de* chel b2.de* *Chin* b2.de* chion bg2* cic b2.de* cina b2.de* cocc b2.de* coff b2.de* *Colch* b2.de* con b2.de croc b2.de* crot-h bg2 cupr b2.de* cycl b2.de* cyn-d vk1 cypra-eg sde6.de• daph bro1 dig b2.de* *Dros* b2.de* *Dulc* b2.de* epiph bg2* euph b2.de* ferr b2.de* ferr-ar k2 fl-ac bg2* formal br1 germ-met srj5• glon bg2 gran bro1 *Graph* b2.de* guaj b2.de* halo vk1 *Hell* b2.de* helo-s bnm14• hep b2.de* hipp jl2 hydr-ac bg2 *Hyos* b2.de* *Ign* b2.de* *Iod* b2.de* *Ip* b2.de* *Iris* bg2* **Jab** br1* *Kali-br* hr1 *Kali-c* b2.de* kali-chl bg2* kali-i bg2* kali-n b2.de* kali-perm bro1 kreos b2.de* lac-ac bg2* lac-c bro1 lac-lup hm2• *Lach* b2.de* lat-m vk1* *Laur* b2.de* led b2.de* *Lob* bro1 lyc b2.de* lyss ptk1* *M-ambo* b2.de* m-arct b2.de* m-aust b2.de* mag-c b2.de* *Mag-m* b2.de* *Manc* ptk1 mand vk1 mang bg2 meny b2.de* merc b2.de* merc-c bro1* merc-cy bro1 merc-d bro1 merc-i-r bro1* mez b2.de* mim-p rsj8*• morg-g fmm1• mur-ac b2.de* muru a1 musca-d szs1 muscin bro1 naja br1 narc-ps br1* *Nat-c* b2.de* *Nat-m* b2.de* nat-ox rly4• neon srj5• nicc-s br1 *Nit-ac* b2.de* *Nit-m-ac* bro1 nux-m b2.de* **Nux-v** b2.de* olnd b2.de* op b2.de* *Par* b2.de* petr b2.de* ph-ac b2.de* phos b2.de* phys bg2 phyt bg2 *Pilo* bro1 pitu-p vk1 plat b2.de* plb b2.de* podo bro1* positr nl2• ptel bro1 **Puls** b2.de* *Ran-b* b2.de* ran-s b2.de* raph br1 rheum b2.de* rhod b2.de* **Rhus-t** b2.de* ruta fd4.de sabad b2.de* sabin b2.de* sacch sst1• sacch-a fd2.de• samb b2.de* *Sang* bg2* sars b2.de* scor a1* sec b2.de sel b2.de* *Seneg* b2.de* *Sep* b2.de* *Sil* b2.de* *Spig* b2.de* spong b2.de* squil b2.de* stann b2.de* *Staph* b2.de* *Stram* b2.de* stront-c b2.de* *Sul-ac* b2.de* *Sulph* b2.de* syc pte1*• symph fd3.de• syph bro1* tab bro1 tarax b2.de* tart-ac br1 teucr b2.de* thuj b2.de* *Trif-p* br1* tritic-vg fd5.de valer b2.de* *Verat* b2.de* verat-v bg2 verb b2.de* viol-t b2.de* xan br1 yohim lp2* *Zinc* b2.de*
  - **night**: merc mtf33 syph jl2*

Salivation – profuse: ...
  - **accompanied** by:
    - **pain** (See Pain - accompanied - salivation)
    - **vomiting**; violent (See STOMACH - Vomiting - violent - accompanied - salivation)
  - **perspiration**; during: bell bg2 chin bg2 *Dros* bg2 dulc bg2 *Merc* bg2 nit-ac bg2 **Rhus-t** bg2 spig bg2
  - **waking** from: cocc-s br1
- **prosopalgia**; with (See FACE - Pain - accompanied - salivation)
- **rage**; during: canth
- **sadness**; during: kola stb3•
- **sensation** of salivation: bamb-a stb2.de•
- **shuddering**; with: arg-met k* arg-n k* euph k*
- **sleep**: (↗*SLEEP - Waking - Salivation)*
  - **during** | **agg.**●: (↗*SLEEP - Waking - salivation)* aeth vh* arg-n bg2 *Arn* vh *Aur* vh bar-c k* carb-an k* cench k2 *Cham* bro1 chin c1 chin-b hr1* cocc-s bro1 *Culx* vh cupr ptk1 des-ac rbp6 dios bg2* dros gk dulc fd4.de gard-j vlr2• glycyr-g cte1• guat sp1* ign bg2* iod bg2 *Ip* hr1* irid-met srj5• kali-c k* lac-ac bro1 *Lac-c* k* lach bg2* **Lyc** ●* lys bg2 m-arct b7.de* **Merc** k* merc-d sne mim-p skp7• nat-m bg2* nit-ac ptk1 nux-v bg2* *Phos* h2* plb c1 ptel a1 **Puls** k ●* rheum bro1 **Rhus-t** k ●* *Staph* gl1.fr• stram a1 sul-ac h2* *Sulph* bg2* *Syph* bro1* tritic-vg fd5.de [tax jsj7]
  - **preventing** sleep: *Ign* st
  - **siesta**: | **after** | **agg.**: zinc h2*
    - **during**: bung-fa mtf
- **smoking** agg.: bry k* kali-bi k* merc k* rhus-t k* sep k*
- **sneezing** agg.: *Fl-ac* kr1*
- **spit**; with constant desire to: abrom-a ks5 am-c bg2 ars bg2 atra-r bnm3• bar-c bg2 cadm-s st1 coc-c ptk1* cocc ptk1 graph st1 grat bg2* hell bg2 ign bg2 kreos bg2 lac-c st1 *Lyss* st1 mag-c bg2 nat-m bg2 nit-ac bg2 puls st1 *Rhus-t* h1* sang bg2 thuj bg2
- **stool**:
  - **after** | **agg.**: mag-m k*
  - **before**: *Fl-ac* k*
  - **during** | **agg.**: colch k* *Rheum* k* vip fe
- **stooping** agg.: **Graph** k* nux-v k*
- **sudden** attacks: carb-v bg1 dig h2* ign k* nat-m bg1* visc c1
- **talking** agg.: bamb-a stb2.de• dulc fd4.de graph k* *Iris* k* *Lach* k* mang bg1* nat-c k* psor al2 ruta fd4.de sabin k* spong fd4.de tritic-vg fd5.de
  - **anxious** matters; of: plut-n srj7•
- **thirst**; with: androc srj1• con bg2 *Hell* bg2 merc mtf33 mez bg2 positr nl2• sec bg2 (non:uran-met) uran-n bg2
- **toothache**; during: bar-c h2 calc h2 caust h2 **Cham** st1 daph st1 graph h2 kali-m st1 mag-c h2 nat-m st1 plan c1 rheum h sep h2
- **vomiting**; before: apom br1
- **walking** agg.: bry sys caust k* petr k*

○ - **Anterior** part: lyc bg1 mez h2* plb bg1

SALTY food agg.: *Ars* b4a.de borx bg2 *Carb-v* b4a.de dros b7a.de*

SCABS: | **Gums**; gangrenous scabs at (See Gangrenous - gums - scabs)

SCORBUTIC Gums: (↗*Bleeding - gums - scurvy; Detached; Protruding - gums; Putrid)* *Agav-a* bro1 all-s alum k* *Alumn* *Am-c* k* *Am-m* bg2 *Anan* *Ant-c* k* ant-t arn bg2* **Ars** k* *Ars-i* ars-s-f k2 **Astac** aur bg2 *Aur-m-n* bapt bro1 *Bov* *Brom* bry bg2 cal-ren bro1 *Calc* k* *Camph* canth k* **Caps** bg2 *Carb-an* k* **Carb-v** k* *Carbn-s* caust b4a.de* chinin-s chr-ac *Cic* b7.de* *Cist* k* coch k* con b4a.de* *Dulc* k* echi bro1 fl-ac ptk1 *Hep* k* *Iod* k* *Kali-c* k* **Kali-chl** k* *Kali-i* *Kali-m* k* kali-n bg2 **Kali-p** k* **Kreos** k* lac-ac lach *Lyc* mag-c bg2 **Merc** k* mez ptk1 **Mur-ac** k* *Nat-m* k* *Nit-ac* k* *Nux-m* *Nux-v* k* olnd bg2 *Ph-ac* *Phos* k* phyt plb bg2 *Psor* sabin bg2 sacch sep k* sil bg2 sil-mar bro1 *Staph* k* sul-ac *Sulph* k* syph ptk1 *Ter* thuj bro1* *Zinc* zinc-p k2
- **salt** eaters; in: coch

SCRAPING: alum a1 am-c a1 *Bell* a1 caust a1 cedr a1 colch a1 croc a1 kali-i a1 lyc h2* phos a1 sal-ac a1

○ - **Gums**: bell h*

○ - **Root**: arn bg2

- **Palate**: aphis c1 cact k* *Camph* k* chin k* coc-c k* coloc k* dig k* *Dros* k* fago k* *Hell* a1 hyos k* lyss k* meph k* *Mez* k* par a1 phos k* ran-b k* sabad a1 staph k*

SCRATCHING: alum h2* bell bg2 caust h2* chel a1 coloc b4.de* croc b7.de* *Dig* b4a.de mez b4.de* nit-ac h2* phos b4.de*

○ - **Gums**: bell h1* cham bg2

- **Palate**: acon bro1 ambr h1* ant-c h2* ars h2* bell h1* camph h1* coloc h2* dig h2* hell h1* squil h1* staph h1*

○ · **Hard** palate: ambr b7.de* apis b7a.de bell b4.de* camph b7.de* carb-v b4a.de* chin b7.de* croc b7.de* dig b4.de* hell b7.de* hyos b7.de* mez b4.de* sabin b7a.de squil b7.de* staph b7.de*

· **Soft** palate: ant-c b7.de* arg-met b7.de* bell bg2 chin bg2 grat bg2 hell b7.de* hyos bg2 lach b7.de* par b7.de* ran-b b7.de* stram b7.de*

- **Tongue**: camph b7.de* caust b4.de* hyos b7.de* seneg b4.de* teucr b7.de* thuj b4.de*

· **fingers**; with: stram bg2*

○ · **Middle**: galeoc-c-h gms1•

SEASONS: | **winter** agg.: mez bg2

SENSITIVE: agar bg2 *Apis* k* bell bg2 bism b7.de* borx br1 *Cic* b7.de* *Coc-c* k* dulc fd4.de graph bg2 iod bg2 ip k* lac-c k2 lyc k* merc bg2 naja k* nat-ox rly4• nit-ac bg2 phos bg2 **Phyt** semp ptk2 sin-n sul-ac k*

- **air**, to: agar k*
- **food** and drink unbearable: sin-n
- **touch**; to: coc-c k2 **Hep** *Nat-s*

○ - **Gums** (See Pain - gums - sore)

- **Palate**: camph bg2 glon bg2 graph b4.de* nat-s bg2 phyt bg2
- **Tongue**: am-caust a1 bell-p sp1 borx b4a.de *Carb-v* k* croc b7.de* *Crot-t* *Fl-ac* gamb graph k* hep b4a.de kali-i k* lavand-a ctl1• *Merc* k* merc-c k* merc-i-r k* *Nat-m* *Nit-ac* k* osm *Ox-ac* k* petr k* *Phyt* k* ran-s bro1 stront-c b4.de* symph fd3.de• **Tarax** k* ter bro1 ziz a1

· **soft** food; even to: *Nit-ac* osm

○ · **Below**: sel b7a.de

· **Tip**: chir-fl gya2 *Crot-t* phyt stront-c sk4•

SEPARATION of gums (See Detached)

SHINY tongue (See Smooth)

SHRIVELLED: (↗*Contraction; Wrinkled)* plb b7a.de

○ - **Gums**: carb-v merc par sul-ac a1

- **Palate**: ant-t bg2 arn h1* borx k* cycl k* phos b4a.de*
- **Tongue**: ars k* carb-v b4a.de mur-ac k* nat-hchls c2 phos a1 sul-ac k* verat bg2* zinc k2

SINGING:

- **after**: agar b4a.de
- **agg.**: bell bg2 *Phos* b4a.de

SITTING: | **agg.**: bar-c b4.de* phos b4.de*

SITTING UP IN BED: | **amel.**: nux-v b7.de*

SKIN; sensation of a new:

○ - **Palate**: stram bg2 verat b7.de

- **Tongue**: rhus-t bg2*

SLEEP: | **after**:

· **agg.**: ambr b7.de* ferr b7.de* kali-i bg2 **Lach** b7a.de* op b7.de* rheum b7.de* sel b7.de*

⁝ **long** sleep: hep b4a.de

- **during** | **agg.**: nux-v b7.de* op b7.de* rhus-t b7.de* sul-ac b4.de*

SLIMY tongue (See Mucus - tongue; Taste - slimy)

SMACKING tongue: bell h1* lyc b4a.de*

SMALL TONGUE: | **from** imperfect development: cupr-s vk1

SMOKING: | **after** | **agg.**: rhus-t b7.de

- **agg.**: chin b7.de ign b7.de *M-ambo* b7a.de m-arct b7.de nat-m b4.de plb b7.de ran-b b7.de seneg b4a.de sep b4.de tarax b7.de

SMOOTH tongue: (↗*Clean; Discoloration - tongue - red - glistening)* *Apis* k* *Arg-n* k* arn k2 *Ars* k* ars-s-f k2 arum-t k2 atro k* bell bg2 carb-ac k* carb-an kr1* cist ptk1 colch bg2* *Crot-h* k* crot-t k* cupr k* dig bg2* eucal k* gamb k* *Glon* k* ip k* jal br1 **Kali-bi** k* kali-br k* **Lach** k* mur-ac k*

Smooth tongue: ...
Nat-m k* *Nux-v* k* *Phos* k* pic-ac kr1* *Plb* k* positr nl2• *Pyrog* k* rhus-t hr1* rob k* *Sec* k* stram k* *Sul-ac* k* sul-i ptk1 sumb k* *Ter* k* terebe ktp9 tub ptk1

- **accompanied** by:

· **clean** tongue: *Nat-m* kr1*

· **facial** erysipelas (See FACE - Erysipelas - accompanied - tongue - smooth)

· **typhoid** fever (See FEVER - Typhoid - accompanied - tongue - smooth)

- **sensation** as if: bell bg2
- **varnished**; tongue looks as if: apis *Canth* vk1 (non:jab) jal vk1 *Nit-ac* vk1 *Pyrog* vk1 rhus-t vk1

○ - **Sides**: bapt k*

· **accompanied** by:

⁝ **brown** | **yellowish** brown discoloration (See Discoloration - tongue - brown - yellowish - accompanied - sides)

- **Tip**: hydrog srj2•

SNEEZING agg.: led b7.de* mag-c b4.de* nux-v b7.de*

SOFT:

○ - **Palate**: merc ptk1 ptel c1

- **Tongue**: ars-h hr1 kali-bi bg2 merc k* moni jl2 rhus-t k* stram k* syph k2

· **accompanied** by | **flabby** tongue (See Flabby - accompanied - soft)

· **sensation** as if: colch bg2 daph falco-pe nl2• mez b4.de*

SOFTENING of gums: arg-met cupr k* iod **Kreos** **Merc** k* ph-ac phos k* plb k* rhus-g mtf11 *Ter*

SORDES: *(↗TEETH - Sordes)*

○ - **Gums**: carb-ac hr1 iris hr1 kali-cy a1 zinc-m a1*

- **Lips**: *(↗FACE - Sordes)* arn k2* ars cda1 atro a1 bapt hr1* carb-ac hr1 kali-cy a1 merc-meth a1 mur-ac cda1* naja a1* plb a1
- **Tongue**: bapt bg3 carb-ac hr1 hyos cda1 naja a1* sulph hr1 ter hr1 zinc-m a1*

SPASMS: acon bg2 bell bg2 carb-v bg2 laur b7.de* mosch bg2 naja gm1 sep b4.de*

- **accompanied** by:

· **froth** (See Froth - convulsions - during)

· **vertigo** (See VERTIGO - Accompanied - mouth - spasms)

- **agg.**: *Dulc* b4a.de

○ - **Palate**: atra-r bnm3•

- **Tongue**: acon bg2* agar k2* *Arg-n* k* atra-r bnm3• bell bg2* borx k* carb-v bg2* carbn c2 cham b7a.de* cic vk1 cina vk1 *Cocc* k* *Con* k* crot-t vk1 glon k* ip vk1 laur vk1 *Lyc* k* *Merc-c* kr1* nux-v vk1 ruta k* sec k* syph k*

SPEECH: *(↗MIND - Speech)*

- **broken**: camph cupr-n a1 irid-met srj5•
- **crying** like a child; hoarse: cupr
- **defective**: nux-m c2
- **difficult**: abel vk1 acet-ac a1 acon k* aesc aeth a1 *Agar* k* alum bg2 am-c k* am-m a1* ambr bg2 *Anac* k* anan k* ant-t k* arg-met b7.de* arg-n k* *Arn* b7.de* ars k* ars-i ars-s-f k2 asim a1 aster k* atro a1* aur k* aur-ar k2 aur-m a1* aur-s k2 *Bapt* k* bar-c k* bar-m bar-s k2 **Bell** k* bism b7.de* *Bry* b7.de* bufo cact cadm-s *Calc* k* calc-s calc-sil k2 *Camph* k* cann-s k* canth b7.de* carb-an k* *Carb-v* k* *Carbn-s* *Caust* k* cedr k* *Cench* chel k* chin chlf a1 chlor k* *Cic* k* cimic *Cocc* k* colch k* *Con* k* cop k* corian-s knl6• **Crot-c** k* *Crot-h* k* crot-t *Cupr* k* cupr-ar a1 cycl cypra-eg sde6.de• *Dig* k* **Dros** a1 *Dulc* k* *Euphr* k* falco-pe nl2• *Ferr* a1 fuma-ac rly4• **Gels** k* germ-met srj5• *Glon* k* *Graph* k* helia a1 helo-s bnm14• hep k* hippoz k* *Hyos* k* ign b7.de* iod bg2 ix bnm8• jab a1 kali-bi bg2 *Kali-br* k* kali-c bg2 kali-s fd4.de kiss a1 kola stb3• lac-c k* **Lach** k* lat-m bnm6• *Laur* k* lol a1* *Lyc* k* lyss k* *M-aust* b7.de* mag-c b4.de* *Mag-p* k* medus a1* *Merc* k* merc-c b4a.de* merl a1 *Mez* k* morph k* mosch k* *Mur-ac* k* narcot a1 *Nat-c* k* **Nat-m** k* nat-p nicc k* nit-ac a1 nitro-o a1 *Nux-m* k* nux-v k* olnd b7.de* **Op** k* ox-ac a1 petr b4.de* ph-ac k* *Phos* k* pip-n c2 *Plb* k* prot pte1*• *Rhus-t* b7a.de ruta k* sec k* sel seneg k* sep k* sil k* spig b7a.de *Spong* k* **Stann** k* **Stram** k* stry k* sul-ac k* sulph k* tab k* tep a1* thal-xyz srj8• tritic-vg fd5.de verat b7.de* vip a1 zinc b4.de*

- **accompanied** by:
  - ⁝ **bulbar** paralysis (See HEAD - Paralysis - medulla - accompanied - speech)
  - ⁝ **Face**; paralysis of (See FACE - Paralysis - accompanied - speech - difficult)
  - ⁝ **Tongue** | **aphthae**: *Nat-m* vk1
- **articulate**, unable to: kali-p fd1.de•
  - ⁝ **waking**, for some time; on: cot br1
- **breath**, from want of: mez h2
- **choking**; from: naja k2
- **chorea**, from: *Agar* k* art-v k* asaf k* *Bufo* **Caust** k* cedr ptk1 cic k* *Cupr* k* *Cupr-act* *Mag-p* k* *Morph* k* mygal sep k* *Stram* k* tarent k*
- **eating**; after: am-c b4a.de*
- **enlarged** tonsils (See THROAT - Swelling - tonsils)
- **fever**; during: ars bg2 **Bell** b4a.de* bry bg2 calc bg2 carb-v bg2 caust bg2 dulc bg2 *Euphr* bg2 hep bg2 *Hyos* bg2 ign bg2 lach bg2 lyc bg2 mez bg2 mur-ac bg2 nat-m bg2 *Nux-v* bg2 op bg2 ph-ac bg2 puls bg2 rhus-t bg2 stram bg2 verat bg2
- **heaviness** of tongue: *Anac* k* *Ars* *Carb-v* k* **Crot-c** **Gels** *Glon* *Lach* *Mag-p* mur-ac h2* *Nat-c* nat-m tl1 nicc k* sol-t a1
- **inarticulate** sounds: (↗*MIND - Speech - inarticulate*) aesc ptk1 anac bell k* *Dulc* hyos mur-ac a1 tab a1 tritic-vg fd5.de vip a1
- **inflammation**; from: **Acon** bg2 alum bg2 ars bg2 **Bell** bg2 bry bg2 calc bg2 *Cann-xyz* bg2 canth bg2 *Dulc* bg2 hep bg2 **Lach** bg2 lyc bg2 **Merc** bg2 nat-m bg2 *Nux-v* bg2 sil bg2 staph bg2 *Sulph* bg2
- **jerking** of head; from: cic b7a.de
- **menses**; during: *Cedr* k* raph a1
- **names**, cannot pronounce: chinin-s
- **pain**; from:
  - ⁝ **Back**; in: cann-s b7a.de
  - ⁝ **Throat**; in: *Hep* b4a.de
- **painful**: am-c k*
- **paralysis**; from: acon bg2 ars bg2 *Bell* bg2 calc b4a.de canth bg2 carb-an bg2 **Caust** b4a.de* chin bg2 *Dulc* bg2 *Euphr* bg2 graph bg2 hyos bg2 *Lach* bg2 laur bg2 *Nat-m* bg2 *Nux-m* bg2 nux-v bg2 op bg2 stann bg2 staph bg2 stram bg2 zinc bg2
- **saliva**:
  - ⁝ **viscid**; from: arg-met k*
  - ⁝ **want** of; from: mez h2
- **spasms**; from: **Bell** bg2 *Canth* bg2 cic bg2 con bg2 cupr bg2 **Hyos** bg2 lach bg2 laur bg2 **Op** bg2 ruta bg2 sec bg2 **Stram** bg2 *Verat* bg2
  - ⁝ **throat**, from: *Arg-n* hr1 cupr k* lyss stry
  - ⁝ **tongue**, from: *Agar* *Arg-n* k* cupr lyc *Ruta* k* sec k* *Stram*
- **stiffness** of the tongue; from: calc-s k2 kali-s fd4.de
- **swallowing** not impeded; but: *Hep* b4a.de
- **swelling** of tongue, from: anan ant-t bapt k* calc-s k2 **Dulc** gels kola stb3• lyc h2* mez h2* morph phos k2
- **tongue** not cooperating; as if: germ-met srj5•
- **typhoid** fever; in: agar *Ars* *Lach*
- **viscid** saliva; from (See saliva - viscid)
- **walking** agg.: petr h2*
- **weakness**; from: (non:am-c kl) cocc ptk1 fuma-ac rly4• lap-la rsp1 manc ulm-c jsj8•
  - ⁝ **chest**; of: *Stann* k*
  - ⁝ **organs** of speech: (↗*LARYNX - Voice - weak*) *Glon* *Nat-m*
  - ⁝ **throat**; of: **Stann** k*
- **whooping** cough; after attacks of: caust b4a.de
- **words**:
  - ⁝ **certain**: *Lach*
  - ⁝ **single** words:
    - ⁝ **can** utter single words with great exertion: art-v cocc *Stram*
    - ⁝ **cannot** utter a single word: androc bnm2•

- **drawling**: carb-an k* spong fd4.de tab
- **faltering** tongue (See stammering)
- **feeble** (See LARYNX - Voice - weak)
- **form** words rightly; cannot (See difficult - inarticulate)
- **high**: lach
- **impeded** (See difficult)
- **inarticulate** sounds (See difficult - inarticulate)
- **indistinct**: agar k2 apis bar-c bry calc caust k* *Cocc* k* *Glon* k* *Lach* k2 *Lyc* k* merc a1 morph a1 nit-ac k* olib-sac wmh1 ozone sde2• phos k2 sec k* spong fd4.de sul-ac hr1 verat k*
  - **morning**: *Lyc*
  - **dryness**:
    - ⁝ **Mouth**; of: lyc h2
    - ⁝ **Throat**; of: bry seneg
  - **excitement** agg.: laur ptk1
- **involuntary** (See MIND - Talking - himself)
- **lisping**: *Acon* k* *Ars* k* carbn-s c1 con *Lach* nat-c k* nit-ac a1 *Nux-v* k* *Verat* k*
- **painful**: bell k2
- **stammering**●: *Acon* k* aesc bg2 agar bg2* agar-ph a1 agav-t jl1 agn bg2 alco a1 amyg a1 anac bg2* anan k* *Arg-n* k* *Arn* b7.de* ars k* ars-i atro a1* aur-m-n wbt2• bar-c bg2 **Bell** k* ben-n both bg2 *Bov* k* *Bufo* k* *Cann-i* k* cann-s k* cann-xyz bg2* canth bg2 carb-an a1 *Carbn-s* carc fb* **Caust** k* cham k* cic bg2* cocc bg2* con cortico tpw7* *Cupr* k* dig k* dulc k* *Euphr* k* gels bg2 *Glon* graph bg2 ham fd3.de* hell k* hyos k* ign bg2 iod k* *Kali-br* k* lac-c k* lac-h sze9• *Lach* k* lat-m bnm6• laur bg2 lyc c2 *Mag-c* k* *Mag-p* k* maias-l hrn2• **Merc** k* morph a1 mygal bg2 nat-ar *Nat-c* k* nat-m b4a.de nat-sal c2 nit-ac j5.de nitro-o a1 nux-m c2 *Nux-v* k* olib-sac wmh1 olnd bg2 op k* ped c2 *Phos* k* phos-h c2 *Plat* k* plb k* puls bg2 ruta c2 *Sec* k* *Sel* k* sep k* sil sne sol-ni c2 sol-t c2 sphing c2 *Spig* k* staph b7a.de **Stram** k* sul-i k2 *Sulph* k* tab a1 thuj bg2* verat k* vip bg2* [*Moly-met* stj2 *Niob-met* stj2 zinc stj]
  - **accompanied** by | **Throat**; constriction of (See THROAT - Constriction - accompanied - stammering)
  - **children**; in: bell bg2* bov br1* bufo mtf33 euphr bg2 lach mtf33 mag-c mtf33 merc bg2* nux-v mtf33 op mtf33 phos mtf33 sulph bg2*
  - **coition**; after: *Cedr* k*
  - **dentition**; during: stram k*
  - **excitement**: *Agar* vh *Caust* k* dig st maias-l hrn2•
  - **exerts** himself a long time before he can utter a word: **Stram** k*
  - **fast**; when talking: maias-l hrn2•
  - **first** syllables: *Spig* b7a.de
  - **last** words of the sentence: lyc k*
  - **letters** S, B, T, W; the: lach sne
  - **loudly**; pronouncing every word: hyos ptk1
  - **quick**, and: maias-l hrn2• *Merc*
  - **singing** agg.: euphr bnt
  - **spasmodic**: lat-m bnm6• mag-p tl1*
  - **strangers**; talking to (See MIND - Excitement - stammers)
  - **suddenly**: mag-c ptk1
  - **talking** rapidly; when: lac-c ptk1
  - **typhoid** fever; in: *Arg-n* k* *Lyc* k* *Verat* k*
  - **vexation** agg.: *Caust*
- **striking** tongue against teeth: nit-ac bg2 sulph bg2
- **subdued** and quick: tab
- **swallowing** his words: *Cic* k* staph k* thuj ptk1*
  - **last** words of sentence: **Thuj** mrr1
- **thick** (= slurred): adam srj5• aesc-g k* agar ptk1 bac bn bapt ptk1* bell k2 both tsm2 both-ax tsm2 botul br1 bung-fa tsm2 caust ptk1 cocc b7.de* coff bg2 con bg2 **Crot-c** crot-h tsm2 dendr-pol tsm2 dulc bg2* elaps tsm2 **Gels** k* *Glon* helo-s bnm14• hyos b7a.de* **Lach** k* lith-br c2 *Mag-p* merc a1 mur-ac a1 naja tsm2 *Nat-c* *Nat-m* **Nux-v** k* op mrr1 phos bg2 *Plat* spong fd4.de stram b7.de* syph k* tub k* *Verat-v* k* vip a1*
  - **drunk**; as if: adam srj5• gels kr1 olib-sac wmh1
- **trembling** (See LARYNX - Voice - tremulous)
- **uncertain**: *Camph* k*

- **unintelligible**: *(↗MIND - Muttering)* acon a1 amyg a1 ars k* art-v k* asaf k* *Bell* k* bufo calc a1 chel k* euph a1 *Fl-ac* *Hyos* k* ix bnm8• lach k2 lyc k* merc k2 naja nux-v a1 *Ph-ac* k* plb a1 rhus-t k* *Sec* a1 sil h2 **Stram** k* tab a1* thuj verat k* zinc k*
- **wanting**: *(↗MIND - Taciturn)* acon a1 agar-ph a1 alum am-caust a1 ant-t k* *Apis* *Arg-n* k* *Arn* a1 *Ars* k* arum-m a1* astac a1 *Bar-c* k* **Bell** k* *Both* a1 *Calc* camph a1 cann-i a1 carb-ac a1 *Caust* k* chin k* chlf a1 chlor a1 *Cic* k* cimic k* cod a1 colch k* *Con* k* *Crot-c* k* *Crot-h* k* cupr k* dulc a1 ferr-m a1 gels a1 *Glon* k* hep k* hydr-ac k* *Hyos* k* ip a1 *Kali-br* k* *Kali-chl* k* kali-cy a1 kali-m k2 kali-n h2* kali-p k* *Lach* k* *Laur* k* linu-c a1 lol a1 lyc a1* *Mag-c* k* manc a1 *Merc* k* merc-c a1 merc-d a1 mosch k* nat-p a1 **Nit-ac** k* *Nux-m* k* *Nux-v* k* oena k* olnd k* op k* past a1 *Phos* a1 *Plb* k* sabad a1 sol-t a1 *Stram* k* stry k* sulph a1 syph hr1* tab a1* tarent a1 tart-ac a1 tep a1 thuj *Verat* k* verat-v a1 vesp a1 vip a1 visc a1 zinc k*
  - **accompanied** by | **convulsions**; one-sided (See GENERALS - Convulsions - one - accompanied - speech)
  - **anxiety**; from: *Ign* kr1
  - **apoplexy**; after: *(↗MIND - Aphasia - apoplexy - after)* *Ars* hr1 *Bar-c* k* crot-c *Crot-h* k* *Ip* k* *Laur* k* **Nux-v** k* oena hr1
  - **cannot** speak a syllable though she makes the effort: calc h2* cimic k*
  - **fright**; after: hyos
  - **heaviness** of whole body, with: thuj a1*
  - **intelligence** unimpaired; but: kali-cy ptk1
  - **paralysis** of organs, from: *Anac* k* *Cadm-s* canth **Caust** k* *Crot-c* crot-h *Gels* k* *Glon* *Mur-ac* staph visc c1
  - **soreness** of lacerated tongue, from: hyper
  - **spasms** in throat, from: cupr k*
  - **typhus** fever; in: agar *Apis* *Ars* *Op* **Stront-c**
  - **uterine** displacement: *Nit-ac* k*
  - **waking**; on: ptel c1

SPITTING (See MIND - Spitting)

SPITTING agg.: bell b4.de*

SPONGY:

○ - **Gums**: alum b4a.de *Alumn* k* **Am-c** bg2 am-m bg2 ant-c bg2 ant-t k* arg-met b7.de* ars k* bacls-10 pte1*• brass a1 bry k* *Canth* k* *Caps* k* carb-an bg2 *Carb-v* k* *Caust* bg2 chin b7a.de chlol k* con bg2 cupr k* *Dulc* k* graph k* *Ham* k* iod b4a.de* kali-br k* kali-c bg2 *Kali-chl* k* kali-n b4a.de* **Kali-p** k* kali-s fd4.de **Kreos** k* **Lach** k* mag-c bg2 **Merc** k* **Merc-c** k* merc-d a1 mez ptk1 mur-ac b4a.de* musca-d szs1 myric k* *Nat-m* b4a.de* **Nit-ac** b4a.de* *Nux-v* b7.de* olnd bg2 plb k* psor k2* rhus-g mtf11 *Rob* k* sabin bg2 *Sang* k* sep bg2* sol-t-ae a1 *Staph* k* **Sulph** bg2 *Ter* thuj ptk1 zinc k* zinc-m a1 [heroin sdj2]
- **Tongue**: benz-ac k* camph a1 hydr k2 stram a1 syph k2

STAMMERING (See Speech - stammering)

STICKS to roof of mouth; tongue (See Adheres)

STICKY, viscid: *(↗Mucus; Saliva)* *Aesc* ptk1 bar-c bg2 bell h1* *Berb* k* calad *Caps* ptk1 carb-v tl1 chel ptk1 hep bg2 **Kali-bi** ptk1 kali-c h2* lach b7a.de* merc ptk1 mur-ac h2 myric ptk1 *Nat-m* ph-ac bg2 phos h2 plat h2* puls ptk1 rhus-t ptk1 ruta k* squil k* sulph bg2 tub ptk1 *Verat* k*
- **morning**: *Berb* *Crot-h* graph h2 olib-sac wmh1 phos h2 plat h2 *Sabad* sulph h2
- **eating** | **amel.**: berb
- **feverish** feeling: *Gels*

○ - **Tongue**: *(↗Adheres; Mucus - tongue)* *Acon* vk1 agar vk1 *Am-m* k* ang vk1 ant-c vk1 ars k* bell k* berb k* *Bry* k* canth vk1 *Carb-v* k* cham vk1 *Chin* vk1 clem vk1 *Colch* vk1 *Con* k* cycl vk1 *Dros* vk1 ferr vk1 hell vk1 hoit vk1 ign vk1 *Lac-ac* k* led vk1 mag-m vk1 meny vk1 merc vk1 merc-i-f kr1* *Merc-i-r* k* mez vk1 nat-m k* *Nit-ac* vk1 **Nux-m** k* nux-v vk1 *Olnd* vk1 *Ph-ac* k* *Phos* b4a.de* *Prun* vk1 puls k* ran-b b7.de* *Ran-s* vk1 *Sabad* vk1 sabin vk1 sin-n k* *Spig* vk1 spong vk1 *Staph* vk1 streptoc rly4• tarax vk1 thuj vk1 *Verat* k* zinc vk1
  - **stool** agg.; during: ph-ac bg2

○ · **Root** of: laur bg1
  - **Tip**: acon vk1 aesc vk1 agar vk1 ang vk1 asaf vk1 aur vk1 brom vk1 canth vk1 chel vk1 chin vk1 con vk1 dios vk1 dros vk1 eup-per vk1 glon vk1 hell vk1 ign vk1 iod vk1 led vk1 merc vk1 nat-s vk1 **Nux-v** vk1 ph-ac vk1 phos vk1 sabad vk1 staph vk1 verat vk1 zinc vk1

STIFF:

○ - **Palate**: crot-h ptk1 grat ptk1 nat-m bg2*
- **Tongue**: aloe k* am-c k* anac b4a.de* ant-t bg2* apis b7a.de* *Ars* k* ars-s-f k* arum-t k* aur-m k* bapt k2 **Bell** k* *Berb* k* borx k* calc b4a.de *Calc-p* k* *Carb-v* k* chim-m c2 chin bg2* cinnb bg2* coc-c k* *Colch* k* *Con* k* *Crot-c* k* *Crot-h* k* cupr-s hr1* dulc k* euphr k* fl-ac k* gels bg2* *Hell* k* hydr-ac k* hyos k* ign b7a.de kali-p k* lac-c bro1* *Lach* k* *Laur* k*. *Lyc* k* med k* *Merc* b4.de* *Merc-c* k* merc-i-r bro1* merl k* *Mez* b4a.de morg-p fmm1• mur-ac k2* *Nat-c* k* *Nat-m* k* nat-s bg2* nicc k* nit-ac k* nux-m k* ox-ac bg2* phys k* **Rhus-t** ptk1 ruta b7.de* sec k* sep k* *Stram* k* vario k* *Zinc* b4a.de
  - **one** side: *Rhus-t* b7a.de
  - **morning**: morg-p pte1*•
    - **waking**; on: nit-ac h2
  - **accompanied** by:
    - **headache** (See HEAD - Pain - accompanied - tongue - stiffness)
    - **hysteria** (See MIND - Hysteria - tongue - stiffness)
  - **spasmodic**: borx c1

STOMATITIS, ulcerative: agav-a c2* allox mtf11 aln bro1 *Alum* k* *Arg-n* bro1 *Ars* k* arum-t bro1* *Arund* k* *Asar* **Astac** *Aur* b4a.de *Bapt* k* berb-a c2 bism c2 borx k* bry mtf11 *Calc* k* *Canth* *Caps* k* carb-ac *Carb-v* k* chin k* *Chlol* chlor bro1 *Cinnb* bro1 corn mtf11 cory bro1 *Crot-h* cund mtf11 dig *Dulc* k* *Ferr* gamb mrr1 hell k* hep k* hydrin-m bro1* hyos b7.de* iod iris-t c2 *Kali-bi* k* kali-c mtf11 *Kali-chl* k* kali-chr mtf11 kali-cy bro1 **Kali-i** kali-p mtf11 kali-perm mtf11 kreos mtf11 lac-ac *Lach* mag-c bro1 manc c2 med jl2 mentho bro1 *Merc* k* *Merc-c* k* mez mtf11 mill moni jl2 mur-ac k* myric nast-o mtf11 nat-hchls vk1 *Nat-m* k* nit-ac k* nit-m-ac bro1 **Nux-v** k* oena c2 ph-ac phos bro1 *Podo* k* psor mtf11 ran-s c2 rhus-g bro1* sal-ac c2* semp mtf11 *Sep* k* *Sil* k* *Staph* k* *Sul-ac* k* *Sulo-ac* c2* **Sulph** k* syph mtf11 tarax bro1 thuj mtf11 tril-p uran-n c2 vinc mtf11
- **accompanied** by:

○ · **Tongue**:
    - **aphthae** on: sulph kr1*
    - **flabby** tongue: *Hydr* kr1*
    - **indented** tongue: *Hydr* kr1*
    - **yellow** discoloration of the tongue | **dirty**: *Kali-m* kr1*
- **cold**; after taking a: dulc
- **gangrenous**: *(↗Aphthae - gangrenous)* alum alumn k* *Ars* k* calc *Carb-v* *Con* k* elat *Guare* kr1 *Kali-chl* c2* *Kali-p* k* merc k* *Merc-c* c2 sil sol-t-ae c1 sul-ac c2 sulph tarent bg3* (non:tarent-c bg2*)
- **nursing** children: mur-ac hr1
- **nursing** mothers: *Bapt* hr1
- **scarlet** fever; after: arum-t bro1 mur-ac bro1
- **syphilitic**: nit-ac bro1

STOOPING agg.: caust bg2 nux-v b7.de* par b7.de*

STRAWBERRY tongue (See Papillae - erect - strawberry)

STRONG JAWS; sensation of (See FACE - Magnetic - between)

SUPPURATION: *(↗Abscess)*

○ - **Gums**: *(↗Abscess - gums; Pyorrhea)* alum bg2 am-c k* arg-n bg2 *Borx* bg2 **Calc** bg2* canth k* carb-an k* carb-v k* caust k* cist ptk1 fl-ac bg2 *Hep* k* kali-bi bg2 kali-c bg2* lach k* lyc bg2 *Merc* k* merc-i-f ptk1 mez nat-m bg2 nat-s petr k* *Phos* k* plan bg2 puls k* **Sil** k* *Staph* bg2* sul-ac bg2 **Sulph** bg2
- **Tongue**: canth k* carb-ac k* lach k* *Merc* k* merc-c k*

SWALLOWING:

- **agg.**: acon b7.de* alum b4.de* *Am-c* b4.de* am-m b7.de* ang b7.de ant-t b7.de *Apis* b7a.de arg-met b7.de* arg-n bg2 ars b4a.de* asaf b7.de* aur b4.de bar-c b4.de* **Bell** b4.de* *Brom* b4a.de *Bry* b7.de* calc b4.de* calc-p bg2 camph b7.de* canth b7.de* caps b7.de* carb-an b4.de carb-v b4.de* caust b4.de* cham b7.de chin b7.de cocc b7.de *Coff* b7.de* croc b7.de dig b4.de *Dros* b7a.de ferr b7.de* graph b4.de* hell b7.de* *Hep* b4.de* ign b7.de ip b7.de* kali-c b4.de* kali-n b4.de kreos b7a.de* **Lach** bg2 laur b7.de* led b7.de* lyc b4.de* m-aust b7.de *Mag-c* b4.de* mag-m b4.de mang b4.de* *Meny* b7.de **Merc** b4.de* mez b4.de* nat-c b4.de nat-m b4.de* *Nit-ac* b4.de* *Nux-v* b7.de* par b7.de petr b4.de* ph-ac b4.de* *Phos* b4.de* plat b4.de plb b7.de **Puls** b7.de* ran-b b7.de rhod b4.de *Rhus-t* b7.de* ruta b7.de* sabad b7.de* sabin b7.de* sars b4.de* seneg b4.de sep b4.de* sil b4.de* spig b7.de stann b4.de *Staph* b7.de* *Stram* b7.de* stront-c b4.de* sul-ac b4.de* *Sulph* b4.de* tarax b7.de *Thuj* b4.de* verat b7.de* zinc b4.de

- **amel.**: cocc b7.de coloc b4.de hep b4a.de *Ign* b7.de mez b4.de puls b7.de rhus-t b7.de spig b7.de tarax b7.de zinc b4.de
- **continued** swallowing | **amel.**: *Ign* b7.de
- **empty** | **agg.**: ambr b7.de arg-met b7.de bar-c b4.de *Bell* b4.de* bov b4.de bry b7a.de caps b7.de cocc b7.de croc b7.de graph b4a.de hep b4a.de **Lach** b7.de* mang b4.de merc b4.de* merc-c b4a.de mez b4.de plat b4.de* *Puls* b7a.de *Rhus-t* b7.de* *Ruta* b7a.de spig b7a.de *Thuj* b4a.de zinc b4a.de
- **food**:
  - **agg.**: *Alum* b4a.de ambr b7a.de *Hep* b4a.de *Nit-ac* b4a.de *Ph-ac* b4a.de sep b4a.de
    - **morsel**; hard: *Bell* b4a.de
    - **solid** food: borx b4a.de hep b4a.de *Iod* b4a.de **Sulph** b4a.de
  - **amel.**: *Ign* b7.de *Lach* b7a.de nux-v b7.de rhus-t b7.de
- **saliva**:
  - **agg.**: borx b4a.de cocc b7.de *Hep* b4a.de **Lach** b7a.de *Merc* b4a.de *Nux-v* b7.de sabad b7a.de sabin b7.de* spig b7a.de **Thuj** b4a.de
  - **amel.**: ip b7.de

SWELLING: *Acon* *Am-c* k* ant-t *Anthraci* apis bg2 asaf k2 bapt tl1 *Bell* k* bism bros-gau mrc1 calad calc calc-s camph canth k* carb-ac carb-an carb-v *Caust* k* cop dulc k* glon *Hydr* hydrog srj2• ign **Kali-chl** k* kali-p lach k* lyc **Merc** k* *Merc-c* k* **Nit-ac** k* nux-v op oxyurn-sc mcp1• par ruta fd4.de sep k* sil suis-hep rly4• sul-ac verat vesp vip zinc b4.de*

- **morning** | **waking**; on: nit-ac h2*
- **edematous**: | **Palate**; soft: apis bg2* bell bg2 hyos bg2 kali-bi bg2 kali-i bg2* lach bg2
- **erysipelatous** after extraction of teeth: sil
- **sensation** of: am-c bell-p sp1 calc-f sp1 *Camph* k* chin h1 cob-n sp1 convo-s sp1 glon bg2 kola stb3• limen-b-c hrn2* limest-b es1• samb [bell-p-sp dcm1]
- ○ **Cheeks**, inside of: am-c k* androc srj1• bism hr1 calc caust k* medul-os-si rly4• nat-hchls vk1 sacch-a fd2.de•
- **Glands**: brom b4a.de falco-pe nl2• iod k*
- **Gums**: **Acon** b7a.de* *Agar* k* agav-a br1 all-s *Alum* k* alum-p k2 alum-sil k2 am-c k* am-m k* ambr k* anac k* anan *Apis* k* arg-met b7.de* *Arg-n* arn **Ars** k* **Ars-i** arund aur k* aur-ar k2 aur-i k2 aur-s c1* *Bar-c* k* bar-i k2 bar-m bar-s k2 bell k* bism k* **Borx** k* bov b4.de* brom bry **Calc** k* calc-i k2 *Calc-s* calc-sil k2 *Camph* canth *Caps* k* *Carb-an* k* *Carb-v* k* **Carbn-s** carc fd2.de• castm **Caust** k* cham k* **Chin** k* *Chinin-ar* *Cist* k* cob cocc b7.de* cocc-s kr1 con k* *Crot-h* crot-t daph *Dol* ferr k* ferr-ar ferr-p fuch br1 *Gels* ger-i rly4• gink-b sbd1• *Glon* **Graph** k* *Ham* *Hep* k* hydr hyos b7.de* *Iod* k* jug-r kali-ar *Kali-bi* k* kali-br *Kali-c* k* *Kali-i* kali-m k2 kali-n k* kali-p k* kali-s fd4.de kali-sil k2 kalm kreos b7a.de* lac-c **Lach** k* *Lyc* k* lyss m-ambo b7.de* *M-arct* b7.de *Mag-c* k* *Mag-m* k* melal-alt gya4 **Merc** k* **Merc-c** k* *Merc-cy* merc-d bro1 *Merc-i-f* *Merc-i-r* k* *Mur-ac* k* naja *Nat-c* b4.de* **Nat-m** k* nat-s bg2 nat-sil fd3.de• nicc **Nit-ac** k* nux-v k* osm ozone sde2• pegan-ha tpi1• *Petr* k* *Ph-ac* k* phel *Phos* k* **Plb** k* puls k* ran-s b7a.de rhod k* rhus-t b7a.de* ruta fd4.de sabad sabin k* sacch-a fd2.de• sal-ac sars k* **Sep** k* *Sil* k* sin-n spig b7.de* spong k* stann b4a.de *Staph* k* *Stront-c* k* suis-hep rly4• *Sul-ac* k* sul-i k2 **Sulph** k* tab bg2 ter bro1 thuj k* tub c1* vanil fd5.de verat b7.de* zinc k* zinc-p k2
  - **right**: aur bell k* castm melal-alt gya4 *Merc*
  - **left**: ruta fd4.de
    - **extending** to | **right**: nat-m k*
  - **morning**: merc a1 mur-ac a1 nat-m h2*
  - **accompanied** by | **indigestion**: kali-p mrr1
  - **bluish** red: con k*
    - **spongy** swelling: nat-m k*
  - **convulsions**; with: kreos stann
  - **extraction** of teeth, after: sil
  - **fever**; during: carb-v bg2 graph bg2 *Staph* bg2
  - **hard**, painful | **Socket** of a tooth that has been out for years; in: med
  - **menses**:
    - **after** | **agg.**: phos b4.de*
    - **before** | **agg.**: ars b4a.de bar-c k* (non:kali-c kl) merc b4a.de phos b4.de*
    - **during** | **agg.**: *Nit-ac* k* phos bro1
    - **instead** of: kali-c h2*
  - **movable**: nat-s bg2

Swelling – Gums: ...

  - **painful**: agar ambr h1* aur h2* bar-c h2* bell borx *Bry* calc k* *Caps* b7a.de carb-an k* crot-t dol st graph k* kali-c kali-chl kali-i kali-s fd4.de lyss *M-arct* b7a.de *Mag-m* k* *Merc* a1 nat-m h2* nat-sil fd3.de• nux-v k* par petr phel phos h2* podo fd3.de• ran-s k* rhod k* sabin k* sars k* sep h2 sil k* staph k* *Sulph* k* thuj k* zinc k*
    - **chewing** agg.: nat-sil fd3.de• ph-ac h2* phos podo fd3.de• spong
    - **swallowing** agg.: staph h1*
    - **touch** agg.: kali-s fd4.de nat-sil fd3.de• ph-ac h2*
  - **painless**: nat-s bg2
  - **pale** red: *Bar-c*
  - **perspiration**; during: calc bg2 carb-v bg2 merc bg2 nat-m bg2 nux-v bg2 phos bg2 rhus-t bg2 *Sep* bg2 staph bg2 *Sulph* bg2
  - **reading** agg.: *All-s* vh1
  - **sensation** of: am-c *Cham* chin b7.de* lyss vh puls k* pyrog vh spong h1* tor vh
  - **stumps**; near: olnd bg2 sabin bg2 **Sulph** bg2
  - **warmth** | **amel.**: *Kali-i*
  - **white**: crot-h nit-ac nux-v k* sabin
    - **dirty**: kali-n
  - ○ **Above** incisors: kali-s fd4.de lyc h2* nat-sil fd3.de• nit-ac h2* vanil fd5.de
  - **Between** gums and:
    - **Cheeks**: rhod k*
    - **Teeth**: nit-ac
  - **Between** the lower incisors: nat-m k*
  - **Decayed** tooth, around: anag bar-c calc h2* calc-s carb-v h2* cocc h1* nat-m h2* phos h2* sabin
  - **Inner**: agar b4.de* ambr k* hep h2 nat-m b4.de* ph-ac b4.de* ruta b7.de* sep b4.de* staph b7.de*
    - **Incisors**: nat-m h2
    - **Upper**: dios melal-alt gya4
  - **Lower**: am-c b4.de* am-m b7.de* anthraq rly4• mag-m b4.de* rhod b4.de* sul-ac b4.de* sulph b4.de*
    - **sensation** of: sabin b7.de* spong b7.de*
  - **Side** | **Lower** left, with stitches up to left temple: am-m k*
  - **Upper**: agar b4.de* anthraq rly4• aur b4.de* bar-c b4.de* bell b4.de* graph b4.de* lyc b4.de* mag-m b4.de* nat-m b4.de* nit-ac b4.de* *Phos* b4a.de ruta b7.de*
- **Lips**:
  - ○ **Inner** side of:
    - **Lower**: dig h2*
      - **sensation** of: vip-l-f a1
- **Palate**: acon bro1 aeth hr1 aloe *Apis* k* arg-met ptk1 *Arg-n* ars arum-t aur bro1 aur-m-n c1 bapt k2 *Bar-c* bar-m bell k* *Calc* *Carb-an* chin cimic coff crot-t fl-ac bro1 *Kali-i* bro1 kali-p k2 **Lach** k* *Merc* merc-c bro1 nat-s *Nux-v* olib-sac wmh1 par petr-ra shn4• *Phyt* podo fd3.de• psor rumx seneg *Sil* staph *Sul-ac* **Sulph** k* syph k2 vanil fd5.de *Zinc*
  - **sensation** of: aloe bg2 androc srj1• arg-n k* *Arum-t* k* *Camph* k* cycl k* glon ign k* limen-b-c hrn2* nux-v k* puls k* sulph h2* til c1
  - **suppuration**, with: *Bar-c* merc nux-v sil sulph
  - **tight**, almost painless, size of pigeon's egg: par
  - ○ **Arch**: bell berb *Caust* chin merc *Nit-ac* seneg
  - **Hard** palate: ant-t bg2 apis b7a.de *Ars* b4.de* aur bg2 *Bar-c* b4a.de bar-m bg2 *Bell* b4.de* *Calc* b4a.de* *Caps* b7.de* chin b7.de* *Dulc* b4a.de *Merc* b4a.de *Nux-v* b7.de* par b7.de* ph-ac b4.de* phyt bg2 *Puls* b7.de* seneg b4.de* zinc b4.de*
    - **sensation** of: glon bg2
  - **Soft** palate: apis bg2 arg-n bg2 bar-c b4a.de* **Bell** b4.de* caust bg2 chin bg2 *Coff* b7.de* *Dulc* b4a.de *Lach* bg2 *Merc* b4.de* nat-m b4.de* nit-ac bg2 nux-v b7.de* phos b4a.de* physala-p bnm7• phyt bg2 seneg b4.de* stram b7.de* zinc bg2
  - **Velum**: acon *Aeth* *Bapt* hr1 bell *Calc* carb-v cimic coff *Merc* **Merc-c** *Spong* *Verat*
- **Salivary** glands: bar-m bg2 *Brom* b4a.de kali-n h2* *Mur-ac* hr1 thuj b4a.de*

- **Tongue**: *(↗Enlarged - tongue; Thick - tongue)* acet-ac k* **Acon** k* agath-a nl2• *Am-m* k* anac k* anan k* ant-t k* antip vh1 **Apis** k* arg-n k* arizon-l nl2• *Ars* k* ars-h kr1* *Ars-i* k* *Ars-s-f* k* arum-m k* arum-t bro1 asaf k* aster k* *Aur* k* aur-ar k2 *Bapt* k* **Bell** k* benz-ac k2 berb k* *Bism* bro1* bit-ar wht1• borx ptk1* **Bry** b7.de* *Caj* c2* calad k* calc k* calc-i k2 *Calc-p* k* calc-s bg2* calc-sil k2 *Camph* k* *Canth* k* castm k* caust ptk1 *Chin* k* *Chinin-ar* k* chlorpr vk1 cic k* *Cimic* k* cob ptm1• coc-c k* cocc k* con k* cory br1 **Crot-h** k* cupr-s kr1* *Dig* k* *Diph* br1* diphtox jl2 dros k* *Dulc* k* elaps k* falco-pe nl2• ferr-m k* ferr-p k* *Fl-ac* k* *Frag* c2* glon k* guare k* *Hell* k* *Helo* k* *Helo-s* bnm14*• *Helon* hippoz k* hoit vk1 *Hydr* k* *Iod* k* kali-ar k* kali-bi bg2* kali-br kr1* kali-c k* kali-chl k* kali-i k* kali-m k2 kali-p k* kali-sil k2 *Kali-tel* c2* *Lach* k* lat-h bnm5• laur k2 limen-b-c hm2• *Lyc* k* *Lyss* k* m-aust b7.de mag-m bg2* *Mag-p* bro1* menis c2 **Merc** k* *Merc-c* k* *Merc-cy* k* merc-sul k* mez k* mill k* moni jl2 morg-p pte1*• **Mur-ac** bg2* *Naja* k* nat-ar kr1* *Nat-hchls* k* *Nat-m* k* nep vk1 nux-m mrr1 oena k* *Op* k* ox-ac k* oxyurn-sc mcp1• ph-ac k* *Phos* k* phyt k* *Plb* k* *Podo* k* polyg-h ptk1 ptel k* puls k* *Ruta* b7.de* sabad b7.de* sec k* sil k* stram k* tell kr1* ter k* thuj k* vac jl2 verat k* vesp k* vesp-xyz c2 **Vip** bg2* vip-t bro1 zinc ptk1 [bell-p-sp dcm1]
  - **one** side: apis k* bism k* calc k* lach bg2* laur bg2* merc bg1 *Sil* k* thuj bg2*
  - **right**: am-be k* apis k* calc bg1 mez k* thuj k*
  - **left**: lach bg1 laur k* zinc k*
  - **night**: merc k2
  - **accompanied** by:
    - **chorea** (See GENERALS - Chorea - accompanied - tongue - swelling)
    - **diphtheria** (See THROAT - Diphtheria - accompanied - tongue - swelling)
    - **epileptic** convulsions (See GENERALS - Convulsions - epileptic - during - tongue - swelling)
    - **meningitis** (See HEAD - Inflammation - meninges - accompanied - tongue - swelling)
    - **salivation** (See Salivation - accompanied - tongue - swelling)
    - **scarlatina** (See SKIN - Eruptions - scarlatina - accompanied - tongue - swelling)
    - **syphilis** (See GENERALS - Syphilis - accompanied - tongue - swelling)
    - **Liver**; induration of (See ABDOMEN - Hard - liver - accompanied - tongue - swelling)
  - **alternating** with contraction (See Contraction - tongue - alternating - swelling)
  - **angioedema**: *(↗SKIN - Eruptions - angioedema)* apis mrr1
  - **fills** whole mouth: apis k2 arum-m k* calad k* cory br1 crot-h k* *Kali-chl* k* merc-c a1 sacch-a fd2.de• sil k2* stram k2 vip a1
    - **sensation** as if: *Caj* hr1* itu a1
  - **glossitis**, after: sul-i c1
  - **menses**; during: *Merc* b4a.de
  - **mercury**; after abuse of: *Kali-i* k*
  - **painful**: bell-p vk1
    - **talking** agg.: *Ph-ac* k*
    - **touch** agg.: con k* ph-ac k* thuj k*
  - **painless**: mez k*
  - **sensation** of: absin bro1 acon bg2 aeth bro1 agath-a nl2• anac k* androc srj1• apis bg2 arizon-l nl2• ars-i vh *Bapt* k* bell bg2 bell-p sp1 calc-f sp1 *Camph* k* *Cimx* cocc colch bg2 convo-s sp1 croc b7.de* crot-h k* crot-t bg2 gels k* glon k* hyos b7a.de kali-ar kola stb3• lach bg2 limen-b-c mlk9.de lyc bg2 m-aust b7.de* merc-c bg2 merl *Mur-ac* *Nux-v* k* par k* petr *Phos* bg2 polyg-h bg2 ptel bro1 puls k* rat bg2 sacch-a fd2.de• sep bg2 spig b7.de* stram bg2 tab bg2 trios rsj11• [bell-p-sp dcm1]
    - **one** side: phos bg2
    - **Edges**: chin bg2
    - **Root**; of tongue: calc bg2 cimic bg2 cocc bg2 spig h1*
  - **spasms** | **before**: plb bg1
  - **sting** of insects, after: *Acon* k* apis mrr1 arn k* bell k* *Carb-ac* k* crot-h k* gent-l sne merc k* nat-m k*
    - **Root**, at: spig h1

Swelling – Tongue: ...

- ○ **Base**, externally and internally: **Ars** k*
- **Below**: *(↗Ranula)* **Ambr** b7.de* bapt bg2* **Calc** b4.de* con b4a.de dulc fd4.de *Hep* b4a.de *Lyc* b4a.de *Merc* bg2* mez b4a.de* mosch bg2* *Nat-m* k* **Nit-ac** b4.de* pitu-gl skp7• *Puls* b7a.de staph b7.de* **Thuj** b4a.de*
  - **left**: pitu-gl skp7•
  - **stinging** pain; with: *Nat-m* k*
- **Center**: *Phos* k*
  - **small**, round swelling: *Dros* k*
- **Root** of: bapt k* caust ptk1 chin b7.de* cimic k* cocc k* ferr-i limest-b es1• merc-c k* phos k* spig bg2*
  - **Sides**: chin h
- **Side** of: chin h1* helo-s bnm14•
- **Tip**: agath-a nl2• *Nat-m* k* phos k* thuj bg2*

TALKING:

- **agg.**: acon b7.de* alum bg2 am-c bg2 arg-met b7.de* *Ars* b4a.de bar-c b4a.de* *Bell* b4.de* bry bg2 calc bg2 carb-v bg2 caust bg2 cic bg2 cocc b7.de* croc b7.de* *Dulc* bg2 fl-ac b4a.de **Hep** b4a.de hyos b7.de* *Ign* b7.de* kali-bi bg2 lach bg2 lyc bg2 mag-c b4.de* mang b4a.de* meph bg2 *Merc* b4.de* *Merc-c* b4a.de *Mur-ac* b4a.de nat-c b4.de* nat-m bg2 nux-v bg2 ph-ac b4.de* phos bg2 plb b7.de* puls b7.de* rhus-t b7.de* stann bg2 staph b7.de* sulph bg2
- **amel.**: *Hep* bg2

TASTE: *(↗Mucus)*

- **acid** (See sour)
- **acrid**: agar bg2 all-c k* alum k* anthraco apoc ars b4a.de asaf k* aur b4a.de* bell b4a.de berb brom k* bry bg2* cact k* calc-s caps choc srj3• crot-t k* fl-ac k* glon bg2* hydr-ac k* iod bg2* kali-chl k* kali-s fkr2.de lac-ac k* laur k* *Lob* k* merc-c b4a.de mur-ac nat-c h2* osm k* pimp a1 plan k* plat plb k* rhus-g tmo3• rhus-t k* sapin a1 seneg k* *Sul-ac* b4a.de thuj bg2* til a1 verat k*
  - **broth** tastes: caps b7a.de
  - **food** in general: asaf b7.de* *Camph* b7a.de *Coff* b7a.de
  - **saliva** tastes: agar
  - **tobacco** tastes: chin b7.de* m-ambo b7.de spong hr1 stann b4a.de* staph b7.de*
  - **wine** tastes: m-aust b7.de
  - ○ **Roots** of teeth; from: fl-ac
- **acute**: *(↗MIND - Senses - acute)* acon b2.de* agar b2.de* anth a1 arn b2.de* ars bg2 aur b2.de* bar-c b2.de* *Bell* k* calc k* *Camph* k* caps k2 **Chin** k* cina k2 cocc b2.de* **Coff** k* colch b2.de* con b2.de* glon k* gran a1 hep b2.de* hippoc-k szs2 kali-bi k* *Lyc* k* lyss k* m-aust b2.de merl a1 mur-ac tl1 nat-c k* nux-v b2.de* olib-sac wmh1 positr nl2• staph k2 thuj b2.de* [bell-p-sp dcm1 heroin sdj2]
  - **excessively**: agar b4a.de *Aur* b4a.de *Bar-c* b4a.de *Bell* b4a.de *Camph* b7a.de chin b7.de* *Coff* b7.de* merc b4a.de phos b4a.de
  - **food**; of | **aftertaste**: hippoc-k szs2
  - **tobacco**; of: coff bg2
- **aftertaste** (See persistent)
- **alkaline**: am-c k* calc-ar k* calc-sil k2* cere-b a1 kali-chl k* *Kalm* k* mez k* rhus-g a1 zinc-m k*
- **almonds**:
  - **bitter**: coff bg2 dig bg2 laur
  - **smoking** agg.; after: dig
  - **sweet**, like: apis bg2 coff k* crot-t dig k*
- **altered**: *Acon* b2.de* *Aesc* c2* agar b2.de* agn b2.de* alum b2.de* am-c b2.de* am-m b2.de* ambr b2.de* anac b2.de* ang b2.de* ant-c b2.de* *Ant-t* b2.de* *Arg-n* c2* *Arn* b2.de* *Ars* b2.de* *Asaf* b2.de* asar b2.de* aur b2.de* bar-c b2.de* *Bell* b2.de* bism b2.de* *Borx* b2.de* bov b2.de* *Bry* b2.de* cadm-s k2 calad b2.de* *Calc* b2.de* *Camph* b2.de* cann-s b2.de* canth b2.de* *Caps* b2.de* carb-an b2.de* carb-v b2.de* caust b2.de* cerv c2 *Cham* b2.de* *Chel* b2.de* *Chin* b2.de* *Cocc* b2.de* coff b2.de* colch b2.de* coloc b2.de* con b2.de* croc b2.de* *Cupr* b2.de* cycl b2.de* dig b2.de* dros b2.de* dulc b2.de* euph b2.de* euphr b2.de* fago c2* ferr b2.de* graph b2.de* guaj b2.de* gymne c1* hell b2.de* hep b2.de* hydr c2* hyos b2.de* *Ign* b2.de* iod b2.de* ip b2.de* *Kali-c* b2.de* kreos b2.de* lach bg2 laur b2.de* led b2.de* *Lyc* b2.de* m-ambo b2.de m-arct b2.de m-aust b2.de *Mag-c* b2.de* *Mag-m* b2.de* mang b2.de* meny b2.de* *Merc* b2.de* *Merc-c* c2* mez b2.de* mosch b2.de* mur-ac b2.de* *Nat-c* b2.de* *Nat-m* b2.de* *Nit-ac* b2.de* nux-m b2.de* *Nux-v* b2.de* olib-sac wmh1 olnd b2.de* op b2.de* par b2.de* *Petr* b2.de* ph-ac b2.de* *Phos* b2.de* plat b2.de* plb b2.de* podo bro1

- **altered**: ...

Puls b2.de* ran-b b2.de* ran-s b2.de* rheum b2.de* rhod b2.de* **Rhus-t** b2.de* ruta b2.de* sabad b2.de* *Sabin* b2.de* *Sars* b2.de* sec b2.de* sel b2.de* seneg b2.de* *Sep* b2.de* sil b2.de* spig b2.de* spong b2.de* *Squil* b2.de* stann b2.de* *Staph* b2.de* stram b2.de* stront-c b2.de* sul-ac b2.de* *Sulph* b2.de* tarax b2.de* teucr b2.de* thal-xyz srj8• thuj b2.de* valer b2.de* *Verat* b2.de* verb b2.de* viol-t b2.de* zinc b2.de* zinc-m bro1 [bell-p-sp dcm1]

- . **daytime**: calc b4.de* carb-v b4.de* lyc b4.de* mang b4.de* phos b4.de* zinc b4.de*
- . **morning**: alum b4.de* am-c b4.de* am-m b7.de* ambr b7.de* arn b7.de* ars b4a.de bar-c b4.de* bism b7.de* *Brom* b4a.de bry b7.de* calc b4.de* canth b7.de* carb-an b4.de* *Carb-v* b4.de* cham b7.de* chin b7.de* coff b7a.de dros b7.de* euphr b7.de* fago bro1 ferr b7.de* graph bro1 hep b4.de* hydr bro1 hyos b7.de* ign b7.de* kali-bi bg2 kali-c b4.de* kreos b7a.de lyc b4.de* m-arct b7.de mag-c b4.de* mang b4.de* merc-c bg2 mosch b7a.de nat-c b4.de* nat-m b4.de* nit-ac b4.de* nux-m b7.de* *Nux-v* b7.de* petr b4.de* ph-ac b4.de* phos b4.de* *Puls* b7.de* ran-b b7.de* rheum b7.de* rhod b4a.de *Rhus-t* b7.de* sars b4.de* seneg b4.de* *Sep* b4.de* sil b4.de* stront-c b4.de* sul-ac b4.de* sulph b4.de* valer b7.de* verb b7.de* zinc b4.de*
- . **forenoon**: con b4.de* dros b7.de* euph b4.de* nit-ac b4.de* nux-v b7.de* petr b4.de* ph-ac b4.de* rhus-t b7.de* sars b4.de* *Sil* b4a.de verb b7.de* zinc b4.de*
- . **afternoon**: alum b4.de* bar-c b4.de* bry b7.de* canth b7.de* ferr b7.de* graph b4.de* ign b7.de* kali-bi bg2 nat-c b4.de* nit-ac b4.de* nux-v b7.de* phos b4.de* *Rhus-t* b7.de* thuj b4.de* valer b7.de*
- . **evening**: arn b7a.de bar-c b4.de* bell b4.de* bry b7.de* *Calc* b4a.de ferr b7.de* ign b7.de* kali-bi bg2 kreos b7a.de m-arct b7.de nit-ac b4.de* nux-m b7.de* olnd b7.de* petr b4.de* phos b4.de* *Puls* b7.de* rhus-t b7.de* thuj b4.de*
- . **night**: cham b7.de* cocc b7.de* dios bg2 fl-ac bg2 lyc b4.de* mag-m b4.de* rhus-t b7.de* thuj bg2
- . **apples**; after: alum b4a.de
- . **beer**; after: coloc b4.de* euph b4.de* puls b7.de* sep b4.de* stann b4.de* staph b7.de*
- . **bread** | **after** bread | **amel**.: phos b4.de*
  - ⁝ **black**: nit-ac bg2
- . **breakfast** agg.; after: con b4a.de euph b4.de* kali-bi bg2 kali-c b4.de*
- . **chewing** agg.: *Puls* b7.de* ran-b b7.de* squil b7.de*
- . **chill**; during: dros b7.de spong b7.de
- . **cigarette**; of his (her) usual: visc sp1* [bell-p-sp dcm1]
- . **coffee**; after: merc b4.de* puls b7.de
- . **cough** agg.; during: bell bg2 caps b7.de* *Carb-v* b4a.de cocc b7.de* lach ptk1 nit-ac bg2 nux-v b7.de* rhus-t b7.de* sang ptk1
  - ⁝ **short** cough; during: nux-v b7.de
- . **drinking** agg.; after: *Ars* b4a.de bell b4.de* bry bg2 chin b7.de* coloc b4.de* **Nux-v** b7.de* **Puls** b7.de* *Sulph* b4a.de
- . **eating**:
  - ⁝ **after**:
    - : **agg.**: alum b4.de* *Am-c* b4.de* ang b7.de* ars b4.de* bell b4.de* bry b7.de* *Carb-v* b4.de* chin b7.de* cocc b7.de* graph b4.de* ign b7.de* kali-bi bg2 **Lyc** b4.de* m-arct b7.de mag-c b4.de* mang b4.de* merc b4.de* mez b4.de* *Nat-m* b4a.de* nit-ac b4.de* nux-v b7.de* petr b4.de* phos b4.de* puls b7.de* ran-b b7.de* rhus-t b7.de* sep b4.de* sil b4.de* squil b7.de* *Sulph* b4.de* teucr b7.de* thuj b4.de* valer b7.de* verb b7.de* zinc bro1
      - . **Throat**; in: hell ptk1
    - : **amel.**: m-aust b7.de merc b4.de* nux-v b7.de* psor bg2 puls b7.de* rhus-t b7.de* sabad b7.de*
  - ⁝ **before** | **agg.**: *Bar-c* b4a.de carb-v b4.de* merc b4.de* nux-v b7.de* ran-b b7.de* sep b4.de* tarax b7.de* valer b7.de*
  - ⁝ **not** eating; when | **agg.**: arn b7.de* bry b7.de* olnd b7.de*
  - ⁝ **while** | **agg.**: chin b7.de* *Dros* b7a.de hell b7.de* m-aust b7.de ran-b b7.de*
- . **eructation**; after: *Am-c* b4a.de cocc b7.de* nux-v b7.de*
- . **expectoration**; during: *Nux-v* b7.de*
- . **fasting** agg.: *Brom* b4a.de bry b7.de* merc b4.de* puls b7.de*
- . **food**; while eating warm: m-aust b7.de

- **altered**: ...
- . **hawking** up mucus: calc-p bg2 nux-v ptk1 teucr ptk1
  - ⁝ **after**: nux-v b7.de* puls b7.de* sabin b7.de* teucr b7.de*
- . **heat**; during: caps b7.de hyos b7.de
- . **heated**; after being: mez b4.de*
- . **licking** lips: valer b7.de*
- . **lying** down agg.; after: bry b7.de*
- . **menses** | **before** | **agg.**: merc bg2 nat-m bg2 sep bg2
  - ⁝ **during**:
    - : **agg.**: *Bry* bg2 calc bg2 chel bg2 *Chin* bg2 cic bg2 *Kali-c* b4.de* lyc b4.de* mag-c b4.de* *Merc* bg2 mosch bg2 nat-m bg2 *Nux-v* bg2 **Puls** bg2 sep bg2 sulph b4.de*
    - : **beginning** of menses | **agg.**: calc-p bg2
- . **milk**; after: ambr b7.de* carb-v b4a.de* ign bg2 lyc b4a.de* *Nux-v* b7.de* phos b4.de* rhus-t b7.de* sabin b7.de* sulph b4.de*
- . **motion** of tongue agg.: *Merc* b4.de*
- . **potatoes**; after: *Alum* b4.de*
- . **rising** | **after** | **agg.**: am-m b7.de* canth b7.de*
  - ⁝ **bed**; from:
    - : **after** | **amel.**: carb-an b4.de* sul-ac b4.de*
- . **sleep**; after: ferr b7.de* rheum b7.de*
- . **smoking** agg.: anac b4.de* ang b7.de* calc b4.de* chin b7a.de dig b4.de* iod b4.de* kali-bi bg2 m-arct b7.de puls b7.de* sabad b7.de* sars b4.de* sel b7.de* stann b4.de* staph b7a.de sulph bg2
- . **sour** food: nat-m bg2
- . **spewing** froth: *Nux-v* bg2
- . **swallowing** food; after: *Nux-v* b7.de* *Puls* b7.de*
  - ⁝ **amel.**: squil b7.de*
- . **vomiting**; after: cham b7.de* cocc b7.de* colch b7.de* *Puls* b7.de*
- . **waking**; on: ambr b7.de* arn b7.de* mang bg2 mosch b7a.de rhus-t b7.de* valer b7.de*
- . **water**: bell bg2

- **aromatic**: bell a1 cham a1 coc-c bg2* glon k* pip-m a1
- **astringent**: acon k* acon-l a1 agar k* *Alum* k* *Alumn* k* am-m vh arg-n k* ars k* *Arum-dru* a1* aur bg2* bar-c k* brom k* calc-i k* caps bg1 card-m bg2* chion bg1* clem bg1 coc-c bg2* coloc bg2* euph bg2 gal-ac a1 gels bg2 gent-c a1 graph h2* hydr-ac ptk1 iod k* kali-bi k* kali-cy bg1* kali-i k* lach k* manc bg2 *Merc-c* k* merc-d bg1 mur-ac k* musa a1 nat-m bg2 ox-ac k* *Phos* k* plb k* psor jl2 sal-p a1 sang bg1
  - . **bitter**: kali-bi bg2
  - . **bread**; of: rhus-t bg2
  - ○ . **Throat**; in: bell bg2
  - . **Tongue** | **Tip**: coloc b4a.de
- **bad**: acon k* agar k* *All-c* k* all-s k* allox tpw3 alumn k* am-m b7.de* anac b4a.de* *Ang* k* ant-t k* anthraci anthraco arn bg3* *Ars* k* ars-i ars-s-f k2 asaf k* atro k* aur-ar k2 aur-m k* bad k* bamb-a stb2.de* *Bapt* k* bar-c k* bar-i k2 bar-m k* bar-s k2 bell bg2* bov k* brom k* *Bry* k* **Calc** k* calc-i k2 *Calc-p* k* *Calc-s* calc-sil k2 camph k* *Cann-s* k* canth b7.de* caps ptk1 carb-ac br1 carbn-s caust k* cedr k* chel k* chin k* chinin-ar chir-fl gya2 cimic k* cinnb k* cob k* *Coc-c* k* con k* corn a1* *Crot-t* k* cycl b7.de* dios a1* dys pte1*• echi erig a1 ferr tl1 ferr-i k* fl-ac k* *Gels* k* gnaph hr1 *Graph* k* ham k* hell-o c1 hippoc-k szs2 *Hydr* k* hyper k* ign k* ind a1 iod k* iris *Kali-ar* *Kali-bi* k* *Kali-c* k* kali-chl k* kali-m k2 kali-n h2* kali-p kali-s fd4.de kali-sil k2 kalm hr1 kola stb3• kreos k* lac-ac lavand-a ctl1• led k* lem-m mrr1 lob-c a1 luf-op rsj5• lyc k* lyss c1 mag-m br1 *Mang* b4a.de med k* **Merc** k* *Merc-i-f* k* *Merc-i-r* k* mez h2* morg-g pte1*• morg-p pte1*• myric k* naja **Nat-c** k* nat-m k* nat-p k* **Nat-s** k* nicotam rly4• nux-m k* **Nux-v** k* op k* **Petr** k* petr-ra shn4• phos k* phys a1 *Phyt* k* pic-ac k* podo k* psor k* **Puls** k* raph k* *Rheum* c2 rhus-t h1* sabad k* sang k* sarr a1 *Sars* k* sel k* seneg k* sep k* sil k* sin-n k* spig b7.de* spong fd4.de squil k* stann k* staph bg3* stry k* *Sul-ac* k* sul-i k2 **Sulph** k* syc pte1*• symph fd3.de• syph ptk1 tab k* tarent k* thuj k* trif-p a1 tub jl2 tung-met bdx1• valer b7.de* vanil fd5.de vario ptk1 vib k* zinc k* zinc-p k2 [bell-p-sp dcm1]
  - . **morning**: am-c k* ars ptk1 arum-d k* *Bar-c* bry k* *Calc* *Calc-p* k* *Camph* k* cann-i k* carb-an h2* cob a1 diaz sa3• echi fago a1 ferr-i k* ham fd3.de• hydr k* jac-c k* jac-g lyc k* mag-m k* med k* *Merc* k* narz a1

Mouth

- **morning**: ...
Nat-c k* *Nat-m* k* **Nat-s** k* nux-m hr1 **Nux-v** k* phos h2* **Puls** k* rhus-t k* sang k* *Sep* k* sulph k* tab k* vanil fd5.de wies a1 zing k*
  - **accompanied** by:
    - **Tongue** | **white** discoloration of the: med kr1*
  - **waking**; on: *Calc-p* guaj ham fd3.de• kola stb3• *Merc* *Merc-i-f* merc-i-r bg1 nat-c nat-p nicc oci-sa sk4• sang sul-ac **Valer** k* vanil fd5.de visc c1
    - **amel.**: ars-s-f k2
- **evening**: bad k* bry a1 vinc a1
- **night**: gal-ac a1
- **accompanied** by:
  - **Tongue**:
    - **clean**: hell-o a1
    - **white** discoloration of the tongue: *All-s* kr1* *Kali-c* kr1* *Podo* kr1*
- **apples**; after: bell bg1
- **blowing** the nose; after: bamb-a stb2.de•
- **bread** tastes bad: bell vh cham b7.de* nux-v bg2 phos b4.de* sil b4.de* stann b4.de*
- **cough** agg.; during: caps b7.de* m-aust b7a.de
- **drinking** | **amel.**: psor jl2
- **eating**:
  - **after** | **agg.**: agar k* ars k* cann-i cann-s k* con k* ign k* *Lyc* k* nicotam rly4• psor jl2 rhus-t k* sil h2* symph fd3.de•
  - **amel.**: lil-t ptk1 sil h2*
  - **overeating** agg.; after: sulph h2
- **epileptic** fit | **before**: syph ptk1*
- **everything**: podo ptk1
- **fever**:
  - **after**: kali-c b4a.de
  - **during** | **agg.**: *Ant-c* b7.de* *Bry* b7a.de *Caps* b7.de* cham b7.de kali-c b4.de* *Staph* b7.de*
- **hawking** up mucus agg.: calc-p bg2
- **meat** agg.: puls zinc
- **menses**; during: kali-c b4.de* lyc b4.de mag-c b4.de
- **milk** agg.: aran
- **mucus** from posterior nares: ars bg2
- **perspiration**; during: ant-c bg2 ars bg2 bry bg2 *Calc* bg2 **Kali-c** bg2 **Nux-v** bg2 puls bg2 sep bg2 stann bg2 *Staph* bg2 valer bg2 zinc bg2
- **smoking**; after: psor jl2
- **teeth**, from hollow: mez h2
- **thirst**; with: choc srj3•
- **tobacco** tastes: *Calc* b4a.de
- **water**, tastes: *Acon* bg1* alum-sil k2 apis bg3* ars bg1* arund aur ptk1 bell ptk1 chinin-ar bg1 colch bg2* *Ferr* k* ichth bg2 *Kali-bi* bg2* *Nat-m* k* puls bg1* samb bg2 *Sil* k* streptoc rly4• sumb bg1 thlas bg3*
- ○ **Throat**; low in: apis bg2 bry bg2 bufo bg2 calad bg2 calc bg2 **Chin** bg2 *Con* bg2 croc bg2 dros bg2 grat bg2 hep bg2 kali-i bg2 kali-n bg2 *Kreos* bg2 lyc bg2 merc bg2 nat-c bg2 nit-ac bg2 nux-v bg2 phos bg2 ptel bg2 rhus-t bg2 sabad bg2 sep bg2 sil bg2 spong bg2 sulph bg2 tarax bg2 thuj bg2 verat bg2 zinc bg2
- **Tongue**: luf-op rsj5•
  - **Base** of: agar

- **banana**; like: mag-p ptk1
- **battery**; like: ozone sde2•
- **bilious**:
  - **fever**; during: cham bro1
  - **food** tastes: acon b7.de* bry b7.de* *Cham* b7.de* colch bg2 lyc bg2 nat-c b4.de* *Puls* b7.de* rhus-t bg2 sulph bg2 verat b7.de*
- **biting**: cimic bg2 nat-c h2 *Rhus-t* b7a.de verat b7.de*
  - **tobacco** tastes: anac b4a.de
- **bitter**: abrom-a ks5 **Acon** k* aesc k* aeth k* agar k* agn k* ail k* alco a1 allox tpw3* aloe k* *Alum* k* alum-p k2 alumn k* *Am-c* k* *Am-m* k* ambr b2.de* ammc vml3• amyg anac k* anan k* anders bnj1* *Ang* k* *Ant-c* k* ant-t k* *Apis* k*

- **bitter**: ...
apoc k* aran *Arg-n* k* arist-m a1 *Arn* k* **Ars** k* ars-h k* ars-i ars-s-f k* asaf k* asar k* *Atha* bro1 atis zzc1• atro a1 *Aur* k* aur-ar k2 aur-m-n aur-s k2 bapt k* *Bar-c* k* bar-i k2 bar-m bar-s k2 *Bell* k* benz-ac k* berb k* bism b2.de* *Bol-la* *Borx* k* *Bov* k* brom k* **Bry** k* bufo cain *Calc* k* calc-p bg2* calc-s k* camph k* cann-s b2.de* *Canth* k* *Carb-an* k* **Carb-v** k* **Carbn-s** *Card-m* k* casc k* cassia-s ccrh1• castm *Caust* k* cench k2 cetr hr1 *Cham* k* **Chel** k* **Chin** k* *Chinin-ar* chinin-s k* cimic bg2* cinnb clem a1 *Coc-c* *Cocc* k* coff b2.de* *Colch* k* coli rly4• coll k* **Coloc** k* *Con* k* convo-s sp1 *Corn* k* croc k* crot-c sk4• *Crot-h* k* crot-t k* cupr k* cupr-ar k* cupr-s k* cur a1 cycl k* *Dig* k* digox a1 dios k* dros k* *Dulc* k* *Elaps* elat k* epiph br1 *Eup-per* k* eup-pur *Euph* k* euphr b2.de* fago a1 ferr k* ferr-ar ferr-i k* gamb k* gast a1 gels k* gent-ch bnj1 gent-l a1 gink-b sbd1• glon k* *Graph* k* *Grat* k* guat sp1 *Hell* k* helon a1* *Hep* k* hipp k* hydr k* hydr-ac a1 hydrog srj2• hygroph-s bnj1 hyos b2.de* *Ign* k* iod k* iodof a1 ip k* iris *Jab* k* jug-r a1 *Kali-ar* kali-bi k* *Kali-c* k* kali-chl a1 kali-i k* kali-m k2 kali-p kali-s fkr2.de kali-sil k2 kalm k* kola stb3• kreos k* *Lach* k* lact k* laur b2.de* led k* *Lept* k* lil-s a1 lob k* *Lyc* k* m-arct b2.de* *Mag-c* k* *Mag-m* k* *Mag-p* *Mag-s* k* malar jl2 *Manc* k* mang k* menis ptk1 meny b2.de* **Merc** k* *Merc-c* k* *Merc-i-r* k* merl k* *Mez* k* morg fmm1• morg-g pte1*• morg-p fmm1• morph a1 mosch k* mucs-nas rly4• *Mur-ac* k* *Myric* k* myris a1 naja k* narcot a1 nat-ar *Nat-c* k* **Nat-m** k* nat-p **Nat-s** k* neon srj5• nicc *Nit-ac* k* *Nux-m* k* **Nux-v** k* olnd b2.de* onos op k* ost a1 ozone sde2• *Par* k* paull a1 *Petr* k* ph-ac b2.de* *Phos* k* phyt k* pic-ac k* pimp a1 pip-m a1 *Plb* k* plut-n srj7• *Podo* k* polyg-h *Prun* k* *Psor* k* *Ptel* k* **Puls** k* ran-b k* *Raph* k* *Rheum* k* rhod b2.de* *Rhus-t* k* ros-d wla1 ruta b2.de* sabad k* *Sabin* k* *Sal-ac* k* sarr al *Sars* k* sec b2.de* *Sep* k* *Sil* k* solid ptk1 sphing a1* *Spong* k* squil b2.de* stann k* staph k* *Stram* k* stront-c b2.de* stry k* suis-em rly4• sul-ac b2.de* sul-i a1* sulfonam ks2 **Sulph** k* suprar rly4• sym-r br1 tab k* *Tarax* k* tarent a1* tep a1 term-a bnj1 tet a1 teucr b2.de* thiam rly4• thuj k* til a1 trios rsj11• tritic-vg fd5.de tub xxb ust v-a-b jl2 valer k* *Verat* k* verat-v a1 verb b2.de* vichy-g a1 viol-o viol-t b2.de* vip a1* vip-l-f a1 zinc k* zinc-p k2 ziz a1 [bell-p-sp dcm1 pop dhh1]
  - **morning**●: alum h2* am-c k* *Am-m* k* anders zzc1• arn k* ars *Bar-c* k* *Bry* k* cadm-met tpw6 calc k* *Calc-p* calc-sil k2 *Carb-an* k* *Carb-v* carbn-s castm **Cham** k* chin k* cinnb dios k* dros k* euphr k* *Hep* k* hyos k* ip k* kali-bi kali-c k* kali-i kali-p kali-sil k2 kreos k* lach *Lyc* k* lyss *Mag-c* k* mag-m mag-s k* mang h2* merc k* mur-ac h2* nat-ar nat-c k* nat-m k* nicc *Nux-v* petr h2* ph-ac h2* *Phos* k* psor al2 **Puls** k* rhus-t k* rumx *Sars* k* sec k* *Sep* *Sil* k* still a1 stront-c *Sulph* k* tab k* thuj k* zinc k*
    - **rising**; after | **amel.**: carb-an nat-c h2
    - **waking**; on●: am-c ambr ars-s-r arund cench k2 chin-b c1 dios helo-s rwt2• *Helon* k* *Kali-i* k* lyss mang h2 merc-i-r bg1 nat-c h2* *Sulph* k* zinc [tax jsj7]
  - **forenoon**: *Bry* a1 coc-c a1 grat a1 kali-bi a1 nit-ac h2* stram a1
  - **noon**: bell h1* coloc a1
  - **afternoon**: iod h* nat-c h2* nit-ac h2* ozone sde2•
  - **evening**: alum k* *Am-c* k* arn k* bell h1* bry k* dios a1 kreos k* lyc petr h2* phos k* **Puls** k* rhus-t k* stann k* tritic-vg fd5.de vichy-g a1
  - **night**●: *Ant-t* *Ars* b4a.de lach **Lyc** k* rhus-t k* solid ptk1
  - **accompanied** by:
    - **anxiety** (See MIND - Anxiety - taste)
    - **headache** (See HEAD - Pain - accompanied - taste - bitter)
    - **sadness** (See MIND - Sadness - taste - bitter)
    - **Tongue** | **clean** | **women**; in old (See Clean - accompanied - bitter - women)
      - **cold** agg.: kali-m ptk1
  - **air** agg.; in open: psor alj
  - **apples** taste: bell h1
    - **eating**; after: alum b4a.de*
  - **apyrexia**, during: *Arn* bol-la
  - **beer**:
    - **after** beer: coloc h2 euph h2 mez *Puls*
    - **tastes** bitter: alum h2 ars b4a.de* chin b7.de* ign b7.de* mez b4.de* puls bg2 stann b4a.de*
  - **bread** tastes: anac b4.de* ars b4a.de* asar k* bell h1* *Calc-p* k* camph k* *Chin* k* *Chinin-s* k* cina k* dig k* dros k* ferr k* *Ign* b7a.de led b7a.de merc k* merl nux-v k* ph-ac k* phos k* puls k* *Rhus-t* k* sars b4a.de* squil k* sul-ac b4a.de* sulph thuj k*

- **breakfast**:
  - **after**:
    - **agg.**: ham fd3.de• kali-chl a1 lyc a1 petr h2* phos a1 sulph a1
    - **amel.**: *Kali-i* lyc a1 mag-m h2* mag-s a1
  - **tastes** bitter: phos h2
- **burning**: ambr bg2 berb bg2 op bg2
- **butter**: chin k* *Led* b7a.de *Lyc* b4a.de puls k* rhus-t ptk1
- **chemical**: positr nl2•
- **chewing** agg.: dros *Puls*
- **chill**:
  - **after**: *Hep* k*
  - **before**: cina *Hep*
  - **during**: acon bg2 alum b4.de* **Ant-c** bg2 arn bg2 ars b4.de* *Bry* bg2 *Cham* bg2 *Chin* bg2 coloc bg2 *Hep* b4a.de* ign bg2 nat-m bg2 nux-v bg2 phos bg2 *Puls* bg2 *Sep* bg2 *Spong* k*
- **coffee**:
  - **after**: *Cham* puls
  - **tastes**: benz-ac bg2 chin k* merc k* podo fd3.de• puls k* sabin k* spong k*
- **diarrhea**, with: allox mgm•
- **drinking**:
  - **after**:
    - **agg.**: acon k* *Arn* b7a.de *Ars* k* *Bry* k* *Chin* k* *Gins* graph b4a.de ign **Kreos** k* mang *Puls* k*
    - **amel.**: **Bry** k* iod ptk1 *Psor* k* tritic-vg fd5.de
- **eating**: *(↗food)*
  - **after**:
    - **agg.**: am-c k* ang k* **Ars** k* berb k* *Bry* k* *Carb-v* dros hell k* hep k* kreos lyc k* mang merc k* *Nat-m* k* nit-ac k* *Phos* **Puls** k* ran-b k* stann k* staph k* *Sulph* k* teucr k* valer k*
    - **amel.**: am-m a1 ammc vml3• nat-c h2* psor a1 rhus-t h1* sep h2* sulph h2*
  - **before** | **agg.**: *Carb-v Tarax*
  - **not** eating; when | **agg.**: *Bry* b7a.de hyos b7a.de mang b4a.de
  - **while** | **agg.**: acon ang ars k* asar *Borx* k* *Bry Camph* cham *Chin* chinin-ar coloc dig dros ferr hell hep *Ign* kreos lyc merc *Nat-m* nit-ac nux-v ph-ac phos **Puls** k* ran-b rheum *Rhus-t Sabin* sars sep h2* stann staph *Stram* sulph teucr valer
- **everything**:
  - **even** saliva: *Borx* k* kreos k*
  - **except**:
    - **saliva**: chin kr1
    - **water**: **Acon** k* **Stann** k*
- **fever**:
  - **before**: ars b4a.de bry b7a.de carb-v b4a.de *Hep* b4a.de nat-m b4a.de sil b4a.de
  - **during** | **agg.**: acon bg2 alum b4.de* *Ant-c* b7.de* arn bg2 *Ars* b4.de* *Bry* b7a.de* carb-v bg2 *Cham* b7.de* chin b7.de* cocc bg2 *Coloc* b4a.de* dros bg2 hep b4a.de* ign bg2 lyc bg2 merc bg2 *Nat-m* b4a.de* nit-ac bg2 *Nux-v* bg2 *Phos* b4.de* *Puls* b7.de* sabad bg2 sars bg2 *Sep* b4.de* sulph bg2 verat bg2
- **fluids**: acon bg2 chin bg2 puls bg2
- **food** tastes: *(↗eating)* acon b7a.de* *Arn* b7a.de ars b4.de* bell bg2 borx b4a.de* **Bry** b7.de* camph k* **Cham** bg2 **Chin** k* **Coloc** b4a.de* con dros bg2 *Ferr* b7.de* graph hell b7.de* hep k* hydrog srj2• ign k* iod ptk1 *Kali-bi* bg2 kreos b7a.de lach led b7a.de lyc h2 mag-m b4.de* merc b4.de* merc-c b4a.de *Nat-c* k* *Nat-m* k* **Nux-v** bg2 ph-ac b4.de* puls k* rheum h* rhus-t k* sabin k* sars k* sep h2* *Sil* k* squil k* stann b4a.de* staph b7.de* stram b7.de* sulph b4.de*
  - **morning**: mang h2*
  - **except** rye bread: anis c1
  - **fever**; during intermittent: *Ant-c Ars Ferr Nat-m*
  - **swallowing** | **after** | **agg.**: ars **Puls** *Sil* sulph
    - **only** when swallowing: chin kreos k* rheum
- **hawking** up mucus:
  - **agg.**: sep h2
  - **amel.**: sulph h2

- **bitter**: ...
  - **meat** tastes: camph k* puls k*
  - **menses**:
    - **during**:
      - **agg.**: sulph b4.de
      - **beginning** of menses | **agg.**: *Calc-p* k* *Caul* k*
  - **milk** tastes: benz-ac bg2 puls bg2 sabin k*
  - **mortification**; from: puls
  - **nausea**; with: allox mgm• bell b4a.de* chinin-s bg2 lyc b4a.de* menis bg2 sep b4a.de*
  - **periodical**:
    - **day** | **alternate**: ars h2
  - **perspiration**; during: acon bg2 alum bg2 *Ant-c* bg2 *Ars* bg2 **Bry** bg2 carb-v bg2 **Cham** bg2 chin bg2 **Hep** bg2 merc bg2 *Nat-m* bg2 nux-v bg2 phos bg2 **Puls** bg2 **Sep** bg2 sil bg2 sulph bg2 verat bg2
  - **plums** taste: iod k*
  - **sadness**; with (See MIND - Sadness - taste - bitter)
  - **sleep** agg.; after: manc
  - **slimy**: hep b4a.de nat-c b4.de* nat-m b4a.de
  - **smoking**:
    - **after**:
      - **agg.**: anac ang cocc k* euphr **Puls** k*
      - **amel.**: aran k*
    - **agg.**: agar a1 asar k* casc k* chin k* **Cocc** k* **Puls** k*
  - **soup**: iod k*
  - **sour** things taste: arg-n ptk1 asar ptk1 bry k2 cupr ptk1 lyc ptk1 merc ptk1 *Nux-v* ptk1 phos ptk1 rhus-t b7.de* sep ptk1 stann ptk1
  - **stool** agg.; during: ant-c b7a.de rheum b7a.de
  - **sugar** tastes: sang
  - **supper** agg.; after: zinc h2*
  - **sweet** things taste: pycnop-sa mrz1 rheum k* sang k*
    - **plums** (See plums)
    - **raisins**: coca-c sk4•
  - **tobacco**:
    - **amel.**: calc-i c1
    - **tastes**: anac asar b7.de* *Camph* k* **Chin** k* *Cocc* k* *Euphr* k* ign b7.de* m-arct b7.de* nat-m *Phos* b4a.de puls bro1 *Spong* k*
  - **vexation**; after: petr
  - **waking**; on: bry b7a.de rhus-t b7a.de
  - **water** tastes: amp rly4• ars k* calc-p k* chin ptk1 chinin-ar k* coff b7a.de sil h2 verat ptk1
    - **except** (See everything - except - water)
  - **wine** tastes: iod k* puls k*
  - **women**; in old:
    - **accompanied** by | **tongue**; clean (See Clean - accompanied - bitter - women)
  - ○ **Fauces**: zinc bg2
  - **Lips**: allox sp1 merc h1*
  - **Palate**; in back of: mag-m bg2
  - **Teeth**; at: euph b4a.de hep b4a.de
  - **Throat**; in: ars b4a.de calc b4a.de chin b7a.de con b4a.de croc b7a.de dros b7a.de hell b7a.de hep b4a.de kali-c b4a.de kreos ptk1 lyc b4a.de nat-c b4a.de nit-ac b4a.de nux-v b7a.de* phos b4a.de sep b4a.de spong b7a.de sulph b4a.de
    - **and** in mouth: con h2 nat-c h2 sep h2 sulph h2
    - **cough** agg.; during: rhus-t b7.de*
    - **not** in mouth: ars h2 calc h2 dros h1 phos h2 podo bg1 ptel bg1 sep h2 sil h2 spong
  - **Tongue**:
    - **Root** of: cocc b7a.de nux-v b7.de* suprar rly4• thuj bg2
      - **accompanied** by | **metallic** taste: arum-dru a1
    - **Tip** of: sabad b7a.de
- **bitterish**-putrid: carb-an h2* euph h2*
- **bitterish**-saltish, bread: chin h1

Mouth

- **bitterish**-sour: aloe asar bg2 bell b4.de* berb bg2 bism h1* carb-an k* caust h2* chin bg1 con b4.de* crot-t bg2 ign bg2 kali-c k* kali-chl k* lyc h2* *Merc* b4.de* petr k* phos b4.de* ran-b k* rhus-t k* sabad k* samb bg2 sep k* sil bg2 stann b4.de* sulph k*
  - **milk**: ambr ptk1 bell h1
- **bitter**-sweet: aesc bg1 arg-n k* aspar chim chinin-s bg1 crot-t dulc bg1 kali-i mag-c k* mag-s meny k* suis-em rly4•
- **bloody**: acon k* alum k* alum-sil k2 *Am-c* k* anan k* *Ars* k* ars-s-f k2 asc-t k* *Bell* k* benz-ac k* berb k* bism k* bov k* bufo k* caes-met wd1 canth k* carb-v k* chel k* chin-b kr1 dios a1 dol elaps k* *Ferr* k* ham k* hyper k* *Ip* k* jatr-c kali-bi bg2 kali-c k* kali-sil k2 kalm *Lil-t* k* linu-c a1 manc k* marb-w es1• naja bg2 *Nat-c* k* nit-ac bg2* osm k* phos *Puls* k* rhus-t k* ruta fd4.de sabin k* sacch-a fd2.de• sil k* spong fd4.de sulph k* symph fd3.de• thuj k* trif-p bro1 vanil fd5.de zinc k*
  - **morning**: berb a1 bism h1* kali-bi a1 *Sil* k* vanil fd5.de
  - **evening**: kali-bi a1 zinc
  - **coition**; during: hura
  - **cough**:
    - **before**: elaps
    - **during** | **agg.**: am-c b4.de* **Bell** k* dol elaps ham ptk1* *Kali-bi* k* nit-ac k* **Rhus-t** k*
  - **expiration** agg.: nat-c h2*
  - **pregnancy** agg.; during: *Zinc* k*
  - **sleep** agg.; after: *Manc*
  - **stool** agg.; after: hyper bg2
  - ○ **Throat**; in: chel bg2 zinc bg2
- **blunted**: squil bg2
- **broth**; like: *Iod* b4a.de
- **burning**: all-c k* allox sp1 am-c a1 crot-t a1 kali-chl k* mez k* morg-p fmm1• osm ox-ac a1 pimp a1 sabad b7.de*
  - **meal**; after every: mez
  - ○ **Throat**; in: morg-p fmm1•
- **burnt**: ars bg2 berb bry k* calad chinin-s k* cycl k* kali-chl laur b2.de* nat-c h2 *Nux-v* k* ph-ac podo fd3.de• **Puls** k* ran-b k* sabad b7a.de sal-ac sars squil k* *Sulph* k* thuj bg2
  - **morning**: berb
  - **bread**; of: benz-ac bg2 *Nux-v* b7.de*
  - **dry** food; after: ran-b
  - **eating**; while: squil
- **cabbage**; like boiled: *Sulph* b4a.de
- **carious** teeth; as from: *Bry* b7a.de
- **carrot** tops, like: nux-v k*
- **cat's** urine; like: psor bg2
- **catarrh**; like old: sep h2*
- **catarrhal**: mez b4.de* puls bg2 sabin b7.de* sulph b4a.de*
- **chalky**: arg-n a1 coli rly4• ign k* *Nux-m* k* suis-em rly4•
  - **quinine**; tastes: gymne c1
- **changeable**: puls gk
- **changed**; the taste of everything has (See altered)
- **cheesy**: aeth k* chin b7.de* kali-c k13 *Lyc* k* par a1* phel k* phos k* sep ptk1 zinc k*
- **chocolate**; like: crot-t bg2
- **cigarette** has changed; the usual taste of his (her) (See altered - cigarette; of his (her) usual)
- **clammy**: bell b4.de* berb *Calad* b7.de* chinin-s chir-fl gya2 corn bg2 crot-t gels k* grat lyc bg2* *Nat-m* k* nux-m *Ph-ac* b4a.de *Phos* k* plan plat b4a.de prun **Puls** k* sil bg2* sulph bg2* sumb bg2* zinc k*
  - **morning**: nicc
  - **perspiration**; during: gels
- **clayish**: acon-l a1 agar k* aloe ammc a1 arg-n a1 *Cann-s* b7.de caps *Carl* a1 *Chin* k* euphr k* *Hep* ign merc a1 phos k* **Puls** stann
  - **food** tastes like: chin sil
- **cold** agg.: kali-bi bg2
- **cool** (See peppermint)
- **coppery**: (↗*metallic)* aesc bro1 agn b7.de* arg-n bg2* ars bro1 bism bro1 brom bg2 cimic tl1 cocc b7.de* conv br1 **Cupr** b7.de* *Cupr-ar* bro1 kali-bi bg2 lac-ac bro1 lach b7a.de *Lob* bro1 med tl1* *Merc-c* bro1 myris br1 nat-m b4a.de* nicc-s br1 nit-m-ac bro1 nux-v bro1 psor bg2 ran-b b7.de* *Rhus-t* b7.de* sulph b4.de* vario jl2 zinc b4a.de
  - **cough** agg.; during: brom bg2
  - **gold** plate tastes: canth k*
  - ○ **Throat**; in: rhus-t bg2
- **cubebs**; of: kreos bg2
- **debauch**; as after a: nux-m b7.de*
- **different**; everything tastes (See altered)
- **diminished**: acon-c a1 alum b2.de* am-m b2.de* anac b2.de* *Ant-c* b2.de* ant-t b2.de* arg-met b2.de* ars b2.de* bar-c b2.de* bell b2.de* bry b2.de* *Calc* b2.de* cann-s b2.de* canth b2.de* caps b2.de* carb-an b2.de* carb-v b2.de* cassia-s ccrh1• caust b2.de* chin b2.de* cic b2.de* cina b2.de* cocc b2.de* colch b2.de* *Coloc* b4a.de cupr b2.de* cycl b2.de* dros b2.de* gink-b sbd1• *Hell* b2.de* hep b2.de* hyos b2.de* ign b2.de* ip b2.de* kali-c b2.de* kali-n b2.de* kreos b2.de* lavand-a ctl1• lyc b2.de m-ambo b2.de m-arct b2.de m-aust b2.de mag-c b2.de* mag-m b2.de* mang b2.de* merc b2.de* morg-p pte1• mosch b2.de* nat-c b2.de* **Nat-m** b2.de* *Nux-v* b2.de* olnd b2.de* op b2.de* *Par* b2.de* *Petr* b4a.de ph-ac b2.de* phos b2.de* plb b2.de* **Puls** b2.de* rheum b2.de* *Rhod* b2.de* rhus-t b2.de* ruta b2.de* sars b2.de* *Sec* b2.de* seneg b2.de* *Sil* b2.de* spong b2.de* *Squil* b2.de* staph b2.de* *Stram* b2.de* stront-c b2.de* sul-ac b2.de* *Sulph* b2.de* tarax b2.de* thuj b2.de* verat b2.de* viol-t b2.de*
- **disordered** stomach, as from: asaf b7.de* asar b7.de* calc b4a.de caust h2* *Ign* b7.de* irid-met srj5• led b7a.de nux-v b7.de* olnd b7.de* petr a1 puls b7.de* rhus-t b7.de*
- **disturbed** (See altered)
- **dough**; bread tastes like: phos h2
- **dry**: ox-ac a1 ptel br
  - **bread** tastes: ferr ph-ac k* puls a1 rhus-t b7a.de* rhus-v thuj k*
  - **food** tastes: ars k* bell b4a.de bry bg2* calad ptk1 chin ptk1 dream-p sdj1• ferr k* hell b7.de* hydrog srj2• ign ptk1 kali-i ptk1 ox-ac ptk1 *Puls* b7a.de raph ptk1 rhus-t h1* ruta k* stront-c thuj b4a.de*
  - **tobacco**: stann h2
- **dung**; like: calc b4a.de verat b7.de*
  - **food** tastes like: cham b7.de*
- **earthy**: aloe arg-n bg2 *Ars* b4a.de cann-s k* caps b2.de* chin k* chinin-ar chinin-s bg2 *Ferr* k* hep k* ign b2.de* *Ip* k* merc b2.de* nat-ox rly4• *Nux-m* k* *Nux-v* b7a.de phos k* pimp a1 puls k* stann bg2 stront-c k* tell k*
  - **food**; of: chin bg2
- **eggs**, like rotten: acon k* ant-t **Arn** k* bar-m bg2 *Bell* bg2 bov bg2 *Bry* bg2 carb-v bg2 caust bg2 cham bg2 con bg2 cupr bg2 *Ferr* k* fl-ac bg2 gast a1 goss graph b4a.de* hep k* kali-bi lyc bg2 **Merc** k* mez b4a.de **Mur-ac** k* *Nat-m* bg2 **Nux-v** bg2 *Petr* bg2 ph-ac b4a.de* phos b4a.de* podo gk psor ptk1 **Puls** bg2 *Rhus-t* bg2 sep bg2 *Sil* k* spig bg2 sul-ac bg2 **Sulph** bg2 thlas ptk1 thuj k* *Verat* bg2 yuc a1
  - **morning**: acon am-c ant-t **Arn** goss **Graph** k* *Hep* ph-ac *Phos* sil k* thuj
  - **cough**; with: *Sep* k*
- **empyreumatic** (See burnt)
- **fasting**; as if: ign b7.de* m-arct b7.de puls b7.de*
  - **long** time; as after: cocc b7.de*
- **fatty**, greasy: (↗*rancid)* aesc agar alum k* ambr b2.de* arn bro1 *Asaf* k* asar b4a.de bar-c b2.de* bry b2.de* bufo bg2 cain carb-v b2.de* *Caust* k* *Cham* k* cycl euon bro1 euph k* fl-ac bg2 glon k* ign b2.de* ip k* iris bg1* kali-bi bg2 *Kali-c* b4a.de *Kali-i* kali-p ptk1 lach bg2 laur b2.de* *Lyc* k* lyss c1 mag-m b2.de* mang k* merc-c b4a.de* *Mur-ac* k* nat-m bg2 ol-an k* petr k* ph-ac b2.de* phos k* phys bg2 *Psor* k* *Puls* k* ran-s b2.de* rhod b2.de* rhus-t k* sabad b2.de* sabin k* sang k* sarr al *Sil* k* sulph h2 thuj k* tril-c bro1 tril-p bg2* tub jl2 valer k* verat
  - **afternoon**: psor jl2
  - **coated** with fat or oil; as if: sabal c1
- **feces**; like: calc bg2 *Merc* b4a.de* plb bg2
- **feverish**: bell bg2
- **fishy**: acon k* astac k* calc ptk1 graph bg1* lach bg2* med ptk1 ol-an ptk1 sanic ptk1 sars bg2* sep ptk1 tell ptk1 thuj ptk1
- **flat** (See insipid)
- **flour**, in morning; like: lach k* nicc
  - **bread**, especially: zing
- **food**; of: agar am-c **Anac** benz-ac camph bg2 tell

- **eaten**: ant-c ptk1 caust ptk1 dios ptk1 nat-m bg2* ph-ac bg2* *Phos* ptk1 puls ptk1 sil ptk1
  - **long** time before: caust h2 nat-m h2 nit-ac h2 ph-ac h2 phos h2 sil h2 sulph h2
  - **several** hours before: am-br
- **foul** (See putrid)
- **fresh** or unsalted; food tastes too: calc bg2
- **fruit**; like | **unripe**: sabad b7a.de
- **game**; like spoiled (See spoiled - game)
- **garlic**, like: asaf calc-ar merl
- **gluey**: marb-w es1• positr nl2•
- **good**:
  - **everything** tastes: cann-xyz ptk1
  - **tobacco**; of: coff b7.de* plb b7.de*
- **greasy**; as if from something: caust b4.de* ichth bg2 *Kali-c* b4a.de mang b4a.de petr b4a.de
- **green** color; from looking at: anh sp1
- **hazelnuts**; like: coff b7.de* *Spong* b7a.de
- **herby**: calad k* cystein-l rly4• nat-m h2* nux-v k* ph-ac k* ptel a1 puls k* rhus-t ptk1 *Sars* k* stann k* verat k*
  - **beer** tastes: nux-v k* stann b4.de*
  - **food** tastes: stram ptk1
  - **milk** tastes: carb-an b4a.de zinc b4a.de
  - ○ **Throat**; in: nux-v bg2 puls bg2
- **herring**; like: nux-m b7.de*
  - **pickle**: anac k*
- **honey**, everything tastes like: apoc-a br1*
- **illusions**: cina k2 podo c2 *Sulph* c2 valer ptk1
- **ink**, like: aloe k* arg-n k* *Calc* k* ferr-i a1 fl-ac k* nat-m bg2 phos bg2
- **insipid**: abrom-a ks5 acon k* aesc a1 aeth a1 agar k* ail *Alum* k* alum-p k2 am-m b2.de* ambr k* ammc **Anac** k* anan k* anders bnj1 ang k* ant-c k* *Ant-t* k* arg-met b2.de* arg-n bg2 arn b2.de* ars k* ars-s-f k2 arund k* asaf k* asar k* aspar k* *Aur* k* aur-m *Bapt* k* bar-c b2.de* bell k* benz-ac berb bol-la *Borx* k* *Bry* k* bufo cain calad calc k* calc-ar calc-p cann-s b2.de* canth a1 *Caps* k* carb-an b2.de* carb-v h2* card-m bg2* carl a1 caust k* cere-b a1 cham b2.de* chel k* *Chin* k* chin-b kr1 chinin-ar chinin-s bg2 clem a1 cob *Cocc* k* *Colch* k* coloc b2.de* con h2* cor-r corn crot-t k* cupr b2.de* cycl k* dig k* dios k* dulc k* elaps ery-a a1 eup-per k* euph k* euph-a bro1 euphr k* *Ferr* k* ferr-ar ferr-i k* ferr-m ferr-p glyc bro1 gnaph gran a1 *Guaj* k* ham k* hell b2.de* hep b2.de* hydr hydrc a1 hyper ign k* ind a1 *Ip* k* iris jac-c k* kali-ar kali-bi k* *Kali-c* k* kali-p kali-s k* kalm kiss a1 kreos k* lac-d k2 lact a1 laur k* lob a1 lyc k* lyss m-ambo b2.de m-arct b2.de* mag-c b2.de* mag-m k* mang k* **Merc** k* merc-sul k* mez b2.de* mosch a1 mur-ac naja k* narcot a1 *Nat-c* k* *Nat-m* k* nat-sil fd3.de• nit-ac k* nux-m k* nux-v b2.de* ol-an k* olnd k* op k* ozone sde2• par k* *Petr* k* ph-ac k* *Phos* k* pitu-p sp1 plat b2.de* *Psor* k* **Puls** k* ran-b k* rat *Rheum* k* rhod b2.de* rhus-g a1 rhus-t k* ruta k* sabad b2.de* sabin k* *Sanic* sapin a1 sars b2.de* sec b2.de* sel k* seneg k* sep k* spig k* *Stann* k* *Staph* k* stram b2.de* stront-c b2.de* sul-ac k* *Sulph* k* sumb a1 tab tanac a1 tep a1 *Thuj* k* tritic-vg fd5.de valer k* verat k* verb k* vinc k* zinc k* zinc-m a1
  - **morning**: aeth a1 alum h2* ammc vml3• cob a1 ign a1 nat-c h2* nat-m h2* ozone sde2• phos h2* puls rat *Sanic* sul-ac h2* **Sulph** k* til a1 valer verat a1 verb k*
    - **rising** | **amel.**: nat-c h2* sul-ac h2*
  - **evening**: *Alum* k* nat-m h2* olnd k* thuj tritic-vg fd5.de
  - **night**: nat-c h2*
  - **beer**:
    - **after**: chin nat-c h2*
    - **tastes**: anac k* ars k* ign a1 ip b7.de* m-ambo b7.de nat-m h2* nux-v stann h2* sumb a1
  - **bitter**: gymne c1
  - **breakfast** agg.; after: euph h2*
  - **butter**, tastes: caps h1
  - **chill**; during: ars bg2 *Aur* bg2 borx bg2 bry bg2 chin bg2 ign bg2 puls bg2 staph bg2
  - **coffee** tastes: *Ign* b7a.de
  - **drinking** agg.; after: chin h1* coloc b4a.de* mang h2*
- **insipid**: ...
  - **eating**:
    - **after**:
      - **agg.**: mang h2 petr h2 thuj verb h
      - **amel.**: nat-c h2 phos h2
    - **not** eating; when | **agg.**: chel b7a.de ign b7a.de olnd b7a.de
  - **everything**: mosch ptk1
  - **food** tastes: alum k* am-c anac k* ars bg2 arund calc k* chin k* colch cupr h2* *Cycl* k* ferr ferr-m jac-c olnd k* ruta k* stram k* stront-c ptk1 thuj bg2 vinc
  - **menses**; during: mag-c h2*
  - **soup** tastes insipid, although it is salted as usual: card-m *Cocc* lyss *Thuj* kl
  - **sugar**: gymne c1
  - **sweet**: ammc vml3• gymne c1
  - **sweets** | **amel.**: ozone sde2•
  - **water**, after drinking: acon ptk1 ail benz-ac vario
- **iron**: calc b4a.de ferr a1 positr nl2• vanil fd5.de
- **jasmine**: querc-r svu1•
- **lead**; like: calc b4a.de
- **lemons**; of: musca-d szs1
- **licorice**; like: spong b7a.de
- **liver**; fried: podo bg2*
- **loss** of (See wanting, loss)
- **manure**, like: *Calc* carb-an hell-f a1 *Merc* *Plb* *Sep* k* verat
- **mealy**: bry a1 grat a1 lach a1 nicc k*
  - **morning**: ozone sde2•
- **meat**; like fresh: bell b4a.de
- **metallic**: (↗*coppery; Saliva - metallic*) *Aesc* k* aeth k* agar k* *Agn* k* aloe k* alum k* alum-p k2 alum-sil k2 *Am-c* k* androc srj1• anh sp1 ant-t a1 *Arg-n* k* arist-cl rbp3• *Ars* k* arum-d a1 *Arum-dru* a* aspar k* aur aur-ar k2 aur-m aur-m-n a1 aur-s k2 bamb-a stb2.de• bell bg2* beryl sp1 bism k* bol-la bufo k* cadm-met sp1 cadm-s *Calc* k* calc-i a1 calc-s calc-sil k2 cann-i k* *Canth* carb-ac carb-an a1 carbn-s card-m k* carl a1 cartl-s rly4• cedr k* cench k2 cere-b a1 cerv a1 chel k* chin a1 chin-b kr1 chinin-ar chr-ac k* cimic k* cimx *Cinnb* k* *Coc-c* k* **Cocc** k* coch coli rly4• *Coloc* k* colocin a1 colum-p sze2• conv *Cupr* k* *Cupr-ar* k* *Cupr-s* k* des-ac rbp6 dream-p sdj1• echi ferr-i fum rly1*• fuma-ac rly4• gard-j vlr2• germ-met srj5• haliae-lc srj5• ham hep k* hippoc-k szs2 hist sp1 hydr-ac ptk1 hydrog srj2• hyos k* indg k* iod ptk1 iodof k* ip b2.de* jatr-c jug-c a1 kali-bi k* kali-chl kali-i k* kali-m k2 kali-n keroso a1 ketogl-ac rly4• kola stb3• lac-ac k* *Lach* k* lap-la rsp1* linu-c a1 *Lyc* k* m-ambo b2.de* m-aust b2.de* manc k* med meph k* **Merc** k* *Merc-c* k* merc-i-r k* merc-n a1 merc-sul mez b4a.de myris a1 naja k* *Nat-ar* **Nat-c** k* nat-hchls nat-m k* nat-n k* nat-p k* nit-m-ac a1* *Nux-v* k* ost a1 ozone sde2• pant-ac rly4• phos k* *Phyt* k* plat-m a1 *Plb* k* positr nl2• pot-e rly4• psil ft1 psor k* puls pulx br1 rad-br ptk1 ran-b k* rauw tpw8* rhus-g tmo3• **Rhus-t** k* ribo rly4• rumx bg2 sal-fr sle1• sars k* sec bg2 **Seneg** k* *Sep* sil k* stram a1 suis-em rly4• suis-pan rly4• *Sulph* k* tell thyr ptk1 tritic-vg fd5.de *Tub* k* tung-met bdx1• ust a1 vario ptk1 ven-m rsj12• vult-gr sze5• yohim c1* *Zinc* k* zinc-chr ptk1 zinc-m a1 zinc-p k2 [bell-p-sp dcm1 heroin sdj2 lith-met stj lith-s stj2]
  - **morning**: alum k* calc h2* ham fd3.de• med c1 sulph k* ust a1
  - **afternoon**: nat-c h2*
  - **accompanied** by:
    - **appetite**; increased (See STOMACH - Appetite - increased - accompanied - metallic)
    - **bitter** taste: gard-j vlr2•
      - **Tongue**; root of (See bitter - tongue - root - accompanied - metallic)
  - **chill**; during: cocc bg2 cupr bg2 ip bg2 nux-v bg2 rhus-t bg2 zinc bg2
  - **cough** agg.: merc alj
  - **dinner**; before: chr-ac
  - **disgusting**: vult-gr sze5•
  - **food** tastes: **Am-c** k* ham fd3.de•
  - **green** color; from looking at: anh sp1
  - **pregnancy** agg.; during: zinc
  - **stool**; before: kali-bi
  - **tobacco** tastes: kali-bi bg2 kali-c bg1

• **water** tastes: amp rly4• hydrog srj2• suis-em rly4•

○ • **Palate**; back of: brom bg2

• **Tongue**:

⁝ **Root** of: bism b7a.de* coc-c bg2 cocc b7a.de kali-bi bg2

⁝ **Tip**: coloc b4a.de thyr ptk1 zinc b4a.de

- **milky**: *Aur* k* phos ptk1

• **burnt**, like: mez bg2 tab

- **muriatic** acid; like: kreos bg2

- **musty**: bry bg2 ham fd3.de• kali-bi k* *Led* k* *Lyc* k* *M-ambo* b7.de* ph-ac bg2* pimp a1 pot-e rly4• rhus-t h1* staph ptk1 tab bg2 teucr bg2*

• **accompanied** by | **Teeth**; pain in (See TEETH - Complaints - accompanied - taste)

• **cough** agg.; during: led ptk1

• **food** tastes: *M-ambo* b7a.de

• **hawking** up mucus; after: *Teucr* k*

• **tobacco**: rhus-t b7.de *Teucr* b7.de* thuj b4.de*

○ • **Throat**, in: borx *Teucr* bg1*

- **natural**, unchanged taste: arn b7.de* *Bar-c* b4a.de chel b7.de* chin b7.de* cocc b7.de* coff b7.de* *Nux-v* b7.de* *Puls* b7.de* ran-b b7.de* rhus-t b7.de* sabad b7a.de sabin b7.de* spig b7.de* squil b7.de* staph b7.de* tarax b7.de* viol-t b7.de*

- **nauseous**: acon k* acon-s a1 agar k* *All-c* k* aloe bg2 anthraco aran k* *Bapt* k* bism k* bol-la bov k* bry k* canth k* *Carb-an* k* carbn-s chel b7.de* chin h1* chir-fl gya2 coc-c cocc crot-t k* cycl a1 gels a1 gins a1 gnaph graph k2 guare a1 hyos k* *Ign* b7.de iod a1 *Ip* k* kali-bi a1 kali-n h2* lach k* linu-c a1 lyc k* merc-br a1 merl k* *Myric* k* nux-v b7.de* pip-m a1 psor bg2* **Puls** k* rheum sabad k* sapin a1 sars h2* sec k* sel seneg k* staph b7.de *Sulph* thuj k* valer b7.de* verb k* wies a1 zinc k*

• **morning**: *Bry* chin h1* cob a1 dios a1 graph k2 kali-bi a1 **Puls** k*

• **accompanied** by | **salivation**: sulph ptk1

• **eating**; after: psor

• **food** and meat taste: chinin-s olnd k* squil

⁝ **flat**, in evening: olnd

• **smoking** agg.: ip h1 **Puls** k*

• **stool** agg.; during: *Crot-t*

• **tobacco** tastes: *Ip* b7a.de

○ • **Throat**-pit; in: scroph-n bg2

- **nuts**; like: coff b7a.de* crot-t bg2 dig bg2 phyt bg2 spong b7a.de

- **offensive**: acet-ac a1 agar k* alco a1 allox sp1 am-c k* am-m b2.de* **Anac** k* ang a1 ant-t b2.de* arg-met b2.de* arge-pl rwt5• **Ars** b2.de* asaf b2.de* asar bamb-a stb2.de• bapt a1 bar-c k* bell k* bism b2.de* brom a1 *Bry* b2.de* *Calc* b2.de* calc-p bg2* cann-s b2.de* canth k* caps b2.de* carb-ac bg2 carb-an b2.de* carb-v a1 caust b2.de* cham k* chel b2.de* chin b2.de* cina b2.de* coc-c k* cocc k* *Coloc* croc b2.de* cupr b2.de* cycl k* dig b2.de* dor a1 dros b2.de* euph b2.de* ferr-i k* form k* guaj b2.de* hydr-ac ign b2.de* *Iod* b2.de* kali-bi a1 kali-c b2.de* lach bg2 laur a1 led b2.de* linu-c a1 lol bg2 m-ambo b2.de m-arct b2.de m-aust b2.de mang b2.de* **Merc** b2.de* merl a1 mez b2.de* myric a1 nat-c b2.de* nat-m b2.de* nux-m a1 nux-v b2.de* par b2.de* petr b2.de* ph-ac b2.de* phos b2.de* plan a1 plb b2.de* puls k* rheum b2.de* rhus-t b2.de* *Sabad* b2.de* sabin b2.de* sars b2.de* sec b2.de* sel b2.de* seneg b2.de* *Sep* k* sil b2.de* spig k* squil b2.de* **Stann** k* staph b2.de* stram b2.de* sul-ac b2.de* sul-i a1 sulph b2.de* tab bg2 teucr b2.de* thuj b2.de* *Valer* k* vario jl2 verat b2.de* verb b2.de* x-ray sp1 *Zinc* b2.de* [helia stj7]

• **morning**: arn a1 *Calc* a1 dios a1 plan a1 sulph a1

⁝ **rising** agg.: marb-w es1• tril-p c1

• **accompanied** by | **pneumonia** (See CHEST - Inflammation - lungs - right - lower - accompanied - mouth)

• **bread** tastes: sep b4a.de

• **breakfast** agg.; after: agar k*

• **drinks** taste offensive: arn ptk1

• **food** and drink: chinin-s bg2 *Coloc* squil b7a.de*

• **milk** agg.: aran nux-v b7.de*

• **tobacco** tastes: camph k* ip bg2 sel b7a.de*

- **oily** (See fatty)

- **onions**; like: aeth k* all-c a1 asaf b7.de* crot-c k* meph merl a1 mosch a1 par a1 ruta fd4.de sin-n a1 spong fd4.de

- **pappy**: abrot st1 acon st1 agar st1 ail st1 aloe st1 *Alum* st1 am-m k* ambr st1 ammc st1 **ANAC** st1 anan st1 ang st1 ant-c br1* *Ant-t* bro1* *Arg-n* k* *Arn* st1 ars bro1* ars-h st arund st asaf st asar st astac atro *Aur* st aur-m st *Bapt* bro1* bell benz-ac st berb st bol-la st borx bro1* bruc *Bry* st bufo st cain st calad st calc calc-ar st calc-p st *Caps* st1 carb-an st carbn-s caust st *Cham* st *Chel* k* chim st *Chin* bro1* chinin-ar st chinin-s st *Cocc* k* *Colch* st cor-r st corn st crot-t st cycl bro1* dig st dios k* dulc st elaps st eup-per st eup-pur euph-a bro1 euphr st *Ferr* bro1* ferr-ar st ferr-i st ferr-m st ferr-p st gels st glyc bro1 *Gnaph* st graph grat st *Guaj* st *Ham* st hell st *Hep* h2* hydr st ign bro1* *Ip* st iris st jac-c st kali-ar st kali-bi st *Kali-c* st kali-p st kali-s k* laur mag-c b4.de* mag-m k* **MERC** st *Nat-m* k* nux-m k* op b7a.de ozone sde2• pall st par st *Petr* k* ph-ac b4a.de* phel st *Phos* st plan st plat st prun st psor st *Puls* k* raph *Sanic* *Sec* b7.de* sul-ac b4.de* **SULPH** k* **VALER** st verat b7.de* verb st visc st zinc st zing st

• **forenoon**: mag-c h2*

- **pasty**: (↗*Pasty*) bry k* clem a1 crot-t a1 *Cycl* k* ephe-si hsj1• ferr a1* hep b4a.de kali-bi bg1 lec mag-m a1 merc nux-m bg1* *Raph* k* *Sulph* verat k*

• **tobacco** tastes: staph

- **peaches**; like: laur bg2

• **pits**: ang b7.de* laur b7.de*

- **peas**, like raw: zinc k*

- **peculiar**: flor-p rsj3•

- **peppermint**; as from: ferr-i k* ignis-alc es2• *Verat* k*

- **peppery**: acon b7.de* *Ars* b4a.de cain bg2 cann-xyz bg2 chin bg1 coca br1* echi ptk1 euph bg1 hydr k* hydrog srj2• iris bg2 kali-br bg2 lach bg2* lyss bg1 manc bg2* mez k* nux-v bg2 ol-an bg1 plat bg1 rad-br ptk1 raph a1 sulph b4a.de* tarax teucr bg2 verat bg2 xan k* xanth bg2

- **perfume**: bell ptk1 cham ptk1 coc-c ptk1 glon ptk1

• **water** tastes: med ptk1

• **wine** tastes like: hist vml3•

- **persiko**; like: laur b7.de*

- **persistent**:

• **beer**: sulph b4a.de*

⁝ **foul**; and: sep b4a.de

• **bitter**: **Puls** b7.de*

• **bread**; of: ph-ac b4a.de*

• **food** eaten: *Am-c* b4a.de bell bg2 caust b4.de* dios bg2 fl-ac bg2 ign bg2 lappa bg2 nat-m b4a.de* nit-ac b4.de* ph-ac b4.de* phos bg2 puls bg2 sil bg2 sulph b4.de*

⁝ **sour**; and: *Nat-m* b4a.de

• **milk**; of: ign b7.de* nux-v bg2

• **sour**: **Nux-v** b7.de*

- **perverted**: fuma-ac rly4• guaj k2 mag-m ptk1 merc k2 nat-c ptk1 podo c2 zinc-m c2

- **pine**-wood: glon bg1

- **pitch**, like: agar bg2 *Cadm-s* k* canth k* coc-c bg2* cocc bg2 glon bg2 kali-bi bg2 sulph bg2 thuj bg2

- **pungent**: acon-c a1 agar a1 am-c a1 asaf bg2 carb-ac a1 chel a1 chim chlor a1 coc-c a1 cocc a1 corn k* cupr-act euph a1 euphr a1 ferr a1 glon a1 hydr laur bg2 lob a1 merc-c a1 nat-c h2* ph-ac h2* pip-m a1 puls rhus-t bg2 sabad a1 stann a1 tarent a1 thuj a1 verat k*

• **food** in general: asaf bg2

• **tobacco**: chin bg2 staph bg2

- **purulent**: bamb-a stb2.de• carl a1 dros k* hydr-ac ptk1 kali-s fd4.de (non:merc b4.de*) (non:nat-c b4.de*) nux-v b7a.de *Puls* k* rhus-t b7a.de tub c1

• **cough** agg.; during: hep alj pyrog alj* tub alj

○ • **Throat**, in: merc h1* *Nat-c* h2*

- **putrid**: *Acon* k* agar k* allox tpw4 am-c **Anac** k* ang k* ant-t k* arizon-l nl2• *Arn* k* *Ars* k* *Ars-i* ars-s-f k2 asar b2.de* asc-t k* *Aur* k* aur-ar k2 aur-i k2 aur-m bro1 aur-s k2 bamb-a stb2.de• bapt k* bar-c b4a.de bar-m bell k* berb k2 borx bro1 bov k* *Bry* k* *Calc* k* calc-p calc-sil k2 **Caps** k* carb-an b2.de* **Carb-v** k* carbn-s carc tpw2* *Caust* k* *Cham* k* chel bro1 chin b2.de* *Cinnb* *Cocc* k* coff b2.de* coloc b2.de* con k* *Crot-c* k* cupr k* cycl k* *Dros* k* ephe-si hsj1• euph k* eupi a1 *Ferr* k* *Ferr-ar* ferr-i ferr-p fl-ac bg2 gels k* glon graph k* ham bg2* *Hep* k* hippoc-k szs2 hydr-ac *Hyos* k* *Ign* k* indol bro1 *Iod* k* iris kali-ar *Kali-bi* k* kali-br hr1 *Kali-c* k* *Kali-i* kali-m k2 kali-p kali-s kola stb3• kreos b2.de* lac-ac *Lac-c* lac-e hrn2• laur led bro1 lem-m bro1 lil-t lob-s a1 lyc b2.de* m-ambo b2.de mag-c b2.de* mag-m b2.de* *Merc* k* merc-c k* mosch k* *Mur-ac* k* *Nat-m* k* nat-s bro1 nux-m b2.de* **Nux-v** k* olib-sac wmh1 olnd b2.de* *Petr* k* *Ph-ac* k* *Phos* k* plac rzf5• plan k* *Podo* k* **Psor** k* **Puls** k* pulx br1

- **putrid**: ...
Pyrog k* rheum b2.de* rhod k* *Rhus-t* k* ruta b2.de* sabin bg2 sars bg2 seneg bg2 *Sep* k* sil k* skat br1 spig k* stann b2.de* *Staph* b2.de* stict *Sul-ac* k* sul-i k2 *Sulph* k* symph fd3.de• teucr b2.de* thuj b2.de* tub xxb valer k* vanil fd5.de vario jl2 *Verat* k* yuc bro1 zinc k*
  - **morning**: **Ars** k* *Chin* fl-ac a1 iod lem-m br1 mag-m h2* *Merc-c* nat-m h2* nux-v rhod a1 *Rhus-t* sil h2* *Sulph* vanil fd5.de
  - **afternoon**: ferr k*
  - **night**: *Cham*
  - **accompanied** by | **nausea** (See STOMACH - Nausea - accompanied - breath)
  - **beer** tastes: fl-ac bg2 *Ign* k*
    - **drinking** agg.; after: euph kl (non:euphr kl) sep h2
  - **bitter**; and: rhod b4a.de
  - **chill**; during: arn bg2 kali-c bg2 merc bg2 nux-v bg2 *Puls* bg2 *Rhus-t* bg2 *Staph* bg2
  - **coition**; after: *Dig* k*
  - **cough**; after: caps k2 nux-v tl1
  - **eating** | **after** | **agg.**: bell h1* rhus-t k* symph fd3.de•
    - **while** | **agg.**: bell con h2*
  - **epileptic** fit, before: syph
  - **fever**; during: acon bg2 arn bg2* ars ptk1 bell bg2 calc bg2 carb-v bg2 cham bg2 con bg2 **Hyos** b7.de* merc bg2 mur-ac bg2 nat-m bg2 nux-v bg2 petr bg2 ph-ac bg2 **Puls** b7a.de* *Rhus-t* b7a.de* sep bg2 *Staph* b7a.de* sulph bg2
    - **intermittent**: **Arn** *Ars* *Puls*
  - **food** tastes: anac bar-m k* cop br1 fl-ac bg2 ign k* mosch k* podo rhus-t
  - **hawking** up mucus agg.: **Nux-v**
  - **meat**:
    - **like**: ars b4a.de *Aur* b4a.de bell b4a.de **Puls** b7.de* rhus-t b7.de*
    - **spoiled**, as from: ars h2 bell h1* bry h1* petr h2 puls h1* rhus-t h1*
    - **tastes**: fl-ac bg2 **Puls** k*
  - **menses** | **before** | **agg.**: *Sep* b4a.de
    - **during** | **agg.**: *Kali-c* k* *Sep* b4a.de
  - **perspiration**; during: arn bg2 carb-v bg2 cham bg2 con bg2 merc bg2 **Puls** bg2 *Rhus-t* bg2 *Sep* bg2 *Staph* bg2 sulph bg2
  - **sleep** agg.; after: rheum h
  - **stool** agg.; during: *Rhus-t* b7a.de
  - **swallowing** agg.: con h2*
  - **sweets** agg.: lac-c br1*
  - **waking**; on: *Rheum* b7a.de rhus-t b7a.de
  - **water** tastes: aur bell caps tl1 chin b7a.de fl-ac bg2 nat-m k* nat-sil fd3.de•
  - ○ **Pharynx**; low down in | **hawking** up mucus agg.: nux-v
  - **Throat**; in: bry b7a.de coloc h2 merc h1* *Nux-v* b7a.de
- **radishes**; like: bufo bg2
- **rancid**: (↗*fatty*) agar k* alum k* ambr k* asaf k* bry k* carb-v ptk1 caust h2* *Cham* k* euph k* hell a1 ip k* kali-bi k* *Kali-i* k* lach k* *Mur-ac* k* petr k* phos b4.de* puls k2 rhod b4.de* syph ptk1 tab a1 thuj ptk1 tub jl2* *Valer* k*
  - **morning**: puls k2
  - **eructation**, also of: alum bg3 carb-v bg3 thuj bg3 *Valer* bg3
  - **food** or drink; after: *Kali-i* k*
  - **swallowing** agg.: ip
  - **sweet** agg.: lac-c ptk1
  - ○ **Throat**, in: alum bg2 ip bg2 *Mur-ac* h2* nat-c a1 petr a1 phos h2* sulph h2*
- **resinous** (See pitch)
- **rough**, bread tastes: rhus-t b7a.de*
- **saltish**: (↗*Saliva - saltish*) agar k* alco a1 allox tpw3 alum k* alum-p k2 am-c k* ambr b2.de* anac b2.de* ant-c k* ant-t k* aral vh1 arge-pl rwt5• arn b2.de* *Ars* k* *Ars-i* ars-s-f k2 atra-r bnm3• atro a1 bar-c k* bell k* benz-ac k* bov b2.de* brom k* bry k* bufo k* cadm-met tpw6 cadm-s br1 caj a1 *Calc* k* cann-s b2.de* *Carb-v* k* *Carbn-s* *Carl* k* caust b2.de* chin k* chin-b kr1 chinin-ar *Cocc* b7a.de coff k* con h2* croc k* crot-c cupr k* *Cycl* k* dig b2.de* dros b2.de* elaps euph b2.de* fl-ac k* *Graph* k* hydr *Hyos* k* iod k* kali-bi k* kali-br kali-c bg2 *Kali-chl* k* kali-i bg2* kali-m k2 kola stb3• lac-ac kr1 lach k* lith-m a1 lyc k* mag-c b2.de mag-m k* mang k* **Merc** k* **Merc-c** k* merl mez b2.de* nat-ar nat-c k* nat-f sp1* **Nat-m** k* nat-p nept-m lsd2.fr nit-ac k* nit-s-d br1 *Nux-m* k* *Nux-v* k* op k* *Ph-ac* k* *Phos* k* positr nl2• prot pte1* *Puls* k* *Rheum* k* rhod k* rhus-t k* rhus-v k* *Sep* k* sphing k* stann b2.de* stram b2.de* sul-ac b2.de* *Sulph* k* *Tarax* k* ther k* tub c1 verat k* verb b2.de* *Zinc* k* zinc-p k2
  - **forenoon**: brom bg1 cupr bg1 fl-ac bg1 *Puls* bg1*
  - **afternoon**: bar-c bg1* kali-bi bg1*
  - **blood** tastes salty: nat-m k*
  - **cough** agg.; during: *Carb-v* b4a.de *Cocc* b7a.de
  - **eating** | **amel.**: sulph h2*
  - **food** tastes: aeth a1 *Ars* k* bell k* benz-ac k* cadm-s *Calc* *Carb-v* k* **Chin** k* cocc cop a1* **Cycl** k* kola stb3• lac-c ptk1 merc k* ozone sde2• positr nl2• puls k* *Sep* k* *Sulph* k* tarax bg2 tarent k* thuj [tax jsj7]
    - **except** rye bread: anis c1
    - **salty**; too: ars b4.de bell b4.de *Carb-v* b4a.de chin b7.de* *Lyc* b4a.de *Mang* b4a.de merc b4.de puls b7.de* *Sep* b4.de* *Sulph* b4.de* tarax b7.de*
  - **water** tastes: ail a1 brom k* bry b7a.de merc nit-ac *Puls* b7a.de sul-ac b4a.de
  - ○ **Gums**: phos bg2
  - **Lips**: allox sp1 merc bg2 nat-m bg2 sulph bg2
  - **Throat**; in: bar-c bg2 cann-xyz bg2 puls bg2
  - **Tongue**; tip of: brom bg2
- **saltish** sour: alum h2* bell h1* cupr k* fl-ac bg2 lach k* mez bg2 sulph h2* tarax b7a.de
  - **butter** tastes: tarax h1*
- **saltish** sweet: croc k* mez h2* phos k* thuj bg2
  - **water**: brom ptk1
- **salty**: ant-c bro1 ars bro1 *Bell* bro1 cadm-s bro1 *Carb-v* bro1 chin bro1 *Cycl* bro1 des-ac rbp6 hippoc-k szs2 *Merc* bro1 merc-c bro1 *Puls* bro1 *Sep* bro1 sulph bro1 zinc bro1
  - **chill**; during: ars bg2 bell bg2 chin bg2 merc bg2 phos bg2 puls bg2 sep bg2
  - **enough**; food does not taste salty: alum b4a.de ars k* *Calc* k* canth card-m cocc k* lyss sulph bg2 *Thuj* b4.de*
  - **fever**; during: bell b4a.de*
  - **only** salty food tastes natural: **Lac-c**
  - **perspiration**; during: ant-t bg2 *Ars* bg2 **Bell** bg2 carb-v bg2 chin bg2 lyc bg2 **Merc** bg2 phos bg2 puls bg2 *Sep* bg2 sulph bg2
  - **things**; as after eating salty: nux-m b7.de*
  - ○ **Lips**: merc bg2* nat-m ptk1 streptoc jl2* sulph ptk1
- **sand**; like: ars bg2 stram bg2
- **sawdust**, food tastes like: cor-r k* hydrog srj2• nux-m
- **scratchy**: ars h2 bar-c b4.de* lyc b4.de* nat-c h2* staph b7.de*
- **semen**; like odor of: verat-v ptk1
- **sleep**, night watching; as if after loss of: *Nat-c* b4.de* nat-m b4a.de
- **slimy**: abrot k* acon aesc a1 aeth a1 allox tpw3 alum b4.de* *Arn* k* ars b4.de* ars-h asaf a1 atp rly4• atro a1 aur-m bro1 bar-c b4.de* bell k* borx bro1 bov b4.de* *Bry* b7a.de cact a1 calc bro1 carb-an k* *Carb-v* bro1 *Carl* a1 cedr a1 *Cham* k* *Chel* k* chim *Chin* k* cob a1 cocc b7.de* cupr br1 dig k* ferr a1* gels a1 graph bro1 hell k* hep k* indol bro1 kali-bi bg3* kali-c laur k* led bro1 lem-m bro1 lyc k* *M-ambo* b7a.de mag-c b4.de* mag-m h2* **Merc** k* *Merc-c* k* merc-i-r k* nat-c k* nat-m bg2* *Nat-s* k* *Nux-m* *Nux-v* k* ost a1 pall par k* *Petr* k* ph-ac b4.de* phel k* *Phos* k* plat k* podo bro1 polyp-p a1 positr nl2• prun k* **Puls** k* *Pyrog* bro1 *Rheum* k* rhus-t k* sabin k* sang k* sars k* seneg k* *Sep* k* sil k* sulph b4.de* tab k* thuj b4.de* til a1 ust k* **Valer** k* yuc bro1 zing k*
  - **morning**: hep h2* jug-r a1 lyc mag-c a1 merc-i-r nat-c a1 puls bg1 sars h2* seneg k* sil bg1 tab a1 **Valer** k* zing k*
    - **waking**; on: bov a1 merc-i-r k* **Valer** zinc k*
  - **beer** tastes: asaf k* sang bg2
  - **drinking** agg.; after: chin
  - **eating**; after: thuj h1*
- **smoky**: bry h1 olib-sac wmh1 ph-ac
  - **bread** tastes: benz-ac k* nux-v k*
  - **food** tastes: *Sep* b4a.de

Mouth

- **soapy**: *(↗Saliva - soapy)* arg-n bg1* benz-ac bg2* cact k* calc-s k* chlor bg1* dulc k* iod k* kali-i bg2 merc b4.de* (non:merl k*) nat-f sp1* *Rhus-t* h1* sil k* symph fd3.de•
  - **drinking** agg.; after: benz-ac k*
- **sodden**: acon bg2 alum bg2 ang bg2 ant-t bg2 *Ars* bg2 bell bg2 *Bry* bg2 caps bg2 chin bg2 euphr bg2 *Ign* bg2 kali-c bg2 mang bg2 olnd bg2 op bg2 petr bg2 ph-ac bg2 phos bg2 ran-b bg2 sabin bg2 seneg bg2 spig bg2 stann bg2 *Staph* bg2 sul-ac bg2 sulph bg2 thuj bg2 valer bg2 *Verb* bg2
- **sooty**: ars k*
- **sour**: *(↗Mucus - acid; Saliva - sour)* abrot k* acet-ac acon b7.de* allox tpw3* aloe k* *Alum* k* alum-sil k2 *Alumn* k* am-c k* am-m k* ambr b2.de* anan a1 *Ant-c* ant-t b2.de* **Arg-n** k* *Ars* k* *Ars-i* ars-s-f k2 asar k* atp rly4• atro a1 aur k* aur-ar k2 aur-i k2 aur-s k2 bamb-a stb2.de• *Bar-c* k* bar-i k2 bar-m bar-s k2 bell k* berb k* bism k* borx b2.de* brom k* bry b2.de* bufo **Calc** k* calc-ar calc-i k2 *Calc-s* calc-sil k2 cann-s b2.de* canth k* *Caps* k* *Carb-an* k* *Carb-v* b2.de* *Carbn-s* card-b a1 *Caust* k* cedr a1 *Cham* k* *Chel* k* *Chin* k* chin-b kr1 *Chinin-ar* cic b7a.de cina b2.de* clem k* cob ptk1 *Cocc* k* con k* cot a1 *Croc* k* *Crot-h* crot-t k* cupr k* cycl b2.de* daph dig b2.de* dirc a1* dros b2.de* euph bro1 ferr k* ferr-i fl-ac k* *Graph* k* hell k* *Hep* k* *Hydr* bro1 **Ign** k* iod k* ip b2.de* irid-met srj5• iris bro1 jac-c k* kali-ar kali-bi k* kali-c k* *Kali-chl* k* kali-i a1 kali-m k2 kali-n k* kali-p kali-s kali-sil k2 *Kalm* k* kola stb3• kreos k* lac-ac k* lac-d k2 *Lach* k* laur b2.de* lec lob bro1 **Lyc** k* m-ambo b2.de m-arct b2.de* m-aust b2.de* **Mag-c** k* *Mag-m* k* *Mang* k* *Merc* k* merc-c a1 merl k* mez k* morg-p fmm1• *Mur-ac* k* naja **Nat-ar** **Nat-c** k* *Nat-m* k* *Nat-p* k* *Nit-ac* k* *Nux-m* k* **Nux-v** k* ol-an k* olnd b2.de* op k* opl a1 *Ox-ac* k* pall k* par b2.de* *Petr* k* *Ph-ac* k* **Phos** k* pic-ac k* plb b2.de* podo k* pot-e rly4• *Puls* k* querc-r svu1• ran-b b2.de* ran-s b2.de* rheum k* rhod k* rhus-t k* rob bg2* sabad b2.de* sabin b2.de* *Sars* k* sec b2.de* sel rsj9• *Sep* k* *Sil* k* sin-a a1 spig b2.de* spira a1 spong b2.de* squil b2.de* *Stann* k* staph b2.de* stram b2.de* suis-em rly4• sul-ac k* sul-i k2 *Sulph* k* tab k* *Tarax* k* tep a1 tetox pin2• thuj k* tritic-vg fd5.de upa a1 verat k* zinc b2.de* zinc-val ptk1 [heroin sdj2]
  - **morning**: alco a1 am-m bamb-a stb2.de• bar-c h2* berb carb-an h2* croc a1 fago a1 ferr k* kali-n h2* *Lyc* k* mag-m a1 mang k* merc bg1* nat-c k* nat-m k* nit-ac h2* **Nux-v** ol-an ox-ac a1 petr a1 phos h2* pot-e rly4• ptel k* *Puls* k* ribo rly4• sars h2* *Sep* k* *Sulph* k* tarent a1 zinc-val bg1
  - **afternoon**: cupr a1 mag-m h2
  - **evening**: alum a1 anac a1 bar-c h2* nat-m a1 nit-ac k* stann a1 sulph h2*
  - **night**: kali-c h2* mag-m h2* staphycoc rly4•
  - **accompanied** by:
    - **Gums**; bleeding (See Bleeding - gums - accompanied - sour)
    - **Head**; complaints of (See HEAD - Complaints - accompanied - sour)
  - **beer** tastes: merc k* puls k* stann h2*
  - **bread** tastes: ang k* *Bell* k* cham k* chin k* cocc k* merl k* nit-ac k* nux-v k* puls k* staph k*
  - **breakfast** | **after** | **agg.**: con h2 sars
    - **amel.**: mang h2
  - **broth** tastes: caps h1
  - **butter** tastes: puls k* tarax k*
  - **chill**; during: bell bg2 calc bg2 chin bg2 ign bg2 nat-m bg2 nux-v bg2 petr bg2 phos bg2 puls bg2 sulph bg2
  - **coffee** tastes: chin k* vac k*
  - **cough** agg.; during: cocc k*
  - **drinking** agg.; after: berb chin k* graph h2* lyc h2* **Nux-v** k* phos sulph
  - **eating**:
    - **after**:
      - **agg.**: am-m bg1 berb k* bry k* *Carb-v* k* chlor cocc k* con bg1* eupi a1 graph k* lyc k* mag-m h2* *Nat-m* nit-ac bg1 *Nux-v* k* *Phos* psor al2 puls k* sabin k* sec *Sep* k* *Sil*
      - **amel.**: phos h2
    - **before** | **agg.**: bar-c *Nat-m*
  - **everything**: podo ptk1
- **sour**: ...
  - **food** tastes: **Am-c** k* arn b7.de* ars k* *Bell* bg2 *Calc* k* *Caps* k* cham b7.de* chin k* iris c1 jac-c kola stb3• lyc k* merc b4a.de mur-ac ptk1 nux-v k* podo puls k* rad-br ptk1 squil b7.de* sulph b4a.de tab *Tarax* b7.de* tarent k*
  - **meat** tastes: caps k* lappa bg1* puls k* tarax k*
  - **menses**; during: lyc b4.de*
  - **milk**:
    - **agg.**: am-c k* ambr k* calad carb-v k* lyc k* *Nux-v* bg2 *Phos* k* puls bg2 rhus-t k* *Sulph* k*
    - **tastes**: bell a1 calad k* calc b4a.de* nux-v k*
  - **pregnancy** agg.; during: *Lac-ac* *Mag-c* ox-ac
  - **putrid**; or: podo ptk1
  - **stool** agg.; during: *Nux-v* b7a.de
  - **sweets**:
    - **after** eating sweets: calc ptk1 *Lach* vh
    - **taste** sour; sweets: aesc vh chin vh dulc vh sulph vh
  - **tobacco**: staph
  - **wine**; of: nat-m bg2
  - ○ **Lips**; on: nat-m bg2 nit-ac bg2
  - **Teeth**; coming from roots of: fl-ac bg2 sulph bg2
  - **Throat**, in: alum b4a.de* cob ptm1• coc-c bg2 kali-bi bg2 kali-n b4a.de mag-c b4a.de mag-m b4a.de* phos b4a.de sars b4a.de*
- **sour-bitter**: **Asar** *Kali-chl* mang h2* samb *Sep*
- **spoiled**: asaf b7.de* *Bar-c* b4.de* bell b4.de* gels bg2 ign bg2 *Kali-c* b4.de* m-ambo b7.de m-arct b7.de nat-c b4.de* nux-v b7.de* petr b4.de* sec b7.de* stram b7.de*
  - **food**: stram h1*
  - **game**: *Aur* k*
  - **meat** (See putrid - meat - spoiled)
- **stale**: bit-ar wht1• bry chinin-s chir-fl gya2 ozone sde2• petr puls staph thuj
- **sticky** aftertaste: agar bg2 ars-h caust bg2 kola stb3• nat-m bg2 op bg2 positr nl2• *Psor* k* **Puls**
- **straw**, like: *Ant-c* bro1 ant-t bro1 arg-n bg2* *Ars* bro1 bapt bro1 borx bro1 chin k* cor-r k* *Cycl* bro1 euph-a bro1 *Ferr* bro1 glyc bro1 ign bro1 kali-i k* kali-s bro1 kreos k* nux-m bro1 *Puls* bro1 rhod k* rhus-t k* *Stram* k* *Sulph* k*
  - **dishes** made of flour: cor-r k*
  - **tobacco** tastes: mez b4a.de*
- **strong**; too: camph b7.de* *Coff* b7.de* hippoc-k szs2
  - **tobacco**: *Coff* b7.de*
- **styptic** (See astringent)
- **sulphur**, like: arge-pl rwt5• *Cocc* k* *Ham* k* nux-v k* plb b7.de*
- **sweetish**: *(↗Saliva - sweet)* *Acon* k* aesc k* aeth k* agar k* *All-c* k* allox tpw3 *Alum* k* alum-p k2 *Alumn* k* am-c k* ammc vml3• anac b2.de* anan k* ant-t a1 *Apoc-a* bro1 aran-sc vh arg-n k* *Ars* k* ars-i ars-s-f k2 arund asar k* aspar k* astac k* atro a1 aur k* aur-ar k2 aur-i k2 aur-m-n a1 aur-s k2 bar-c k* bar-m *Bell* k* bism k* bol-la bov b2.de* brom k* *Bry* k* bufo bg2 caj a1 calad ptk1 calc k* calc-i k2 calc-p k* calc-s canth b2.de* carb-ac bg2 carb-v b2.de* carbn-s chel k* *Chin* k* chinin-ar chlf cob k* *Coc-c* cocc b2.de* *Coff* k* colch k* croc k* crot-t a1 **Cupr** k* cupr-s cypra-eg sde6.de• dig k* dios k* dream-p sdj1• **Dulc** k* falco-pe nl2• ferr k* ferr-ar ferr-i ferr-p fl-ac gamb glon k* glyc bro1 gnaph gran a1 guare a1 hep b2.de* hydr-ac k* hyos b2.de* iod k* ip k* irid-met srj5• iris bg2* kali-ar kali-bi k* *Kali-c* k* *Kali-i* kali-m k2 kali-n a1 kali-s kiss a1 kreos b2.de* lach k* laur k* lil-t ptk1 limest-b es1• linu-c a1 *Lyc* k* m-aust b2.de* mag-c k* **Merc** k* mez k* *Mur-ac* k* nat-ar nat-c k* nept-m lsd2.fr nit-ac k* nuph k* nux-v k* op k* osm phel k* *Phos* k* pip-m a1 plan a1 *Plat* k* *Plb* k* *Podo* k* polyp-p a1 propr sa3• psor al2* **Puls** k* *Pyrog* k* ran-b k* ran-s b2.de* rhus-t k* *Sabad* k* sabin b2.de* samb b2.de* sapin a1 *Sars* k* sel b2.de* seneg k* sep k* spira a1 *Spong* k* *Squil* k* *Stann* k* sul-ac k* **Sulph** k* sumb *Thuj* k* til a1 verat b2.de* verat-v bl1 vip fkr4.de *Zinc* k* zinc-p k2
  - **morning**: aeth k* alum k* *Ars* k* bufo lyc h2* nit-ac k* polyp-p a1 ran-s k* sulph k* til a1
    - **waking**; on: aeth cupr-s kali-c sulph
  - **evening**: thuj k*
  - **night**: fl-ac bg1* sulph a1
  - **beer**:
    - **after**: nat-c h2*

- **beer**: ...
  - **tastes**; beer: cor-r k* *Mur-ac* k* *Puls* k*
- **bread** tastes: **Calc** b4a.de cor-r ptk1 **Merc** k* *Puls* bg2 sang bg2 squil b7.de*
- **breakfast** agg.; after: agar sulph
- **broth** tastes: indg
- **butter** tastes: mur-ac ptk1 *Puls* k* ran-b k* sang k* squil b7.de*
- **chill**; during: acon bg2 alum bg2 dig bg2 phos bg2 plb bg2 puls bg2 sabad bg2 squil bg2
- **cough**; after: aeth k* astac k* chinin-ar phos ptk1
- **drinking** agg.; after: lyc phel vario
- **eating** | **after** | **agg.**: thuj k*
  - **agg.** | **bitter** afterwards; sweetish while eating: phos
- **everything**: mur-ac ptk1 phel ptk1
- **followed** by:
  - **bitter** taste: crot-t bg2
    - **burning** and: cadm-s c1
- **food** tastes: *Calc* b4a.de lyc b4a.de mur-ac k* puls k* squil k* thuj
- **hunger**; with: nit-ac ptk1
- **meat** tastes: *Puls* k* sang bg2 squil k*
- **metallic**: coc-c ptk1
- **milk** tastes: *Puls* k* sang bg2
- **smoking** | **after** | **agg.**: sel
  - **agg.**: agar k* chin h1* kali-bi a1 sars h2*
- **soup** tastes: squil k*
- **sweets** taste too sweet: ars-h pin-con oss2•
- **tobacco** tastes: chin b7.de* dig ptk1 kali-bi bg2 sang bg2 sars b4.de* sel k*
- **water**: coc-c bg2 form ptk1 kali-bi bg2 lyc b4.de* ox-ac bg2 phel bg2
- ○ **Larynx** and trachea: mez bg2
- **Lips**: allox sp1 sel bg2
- **Pharynx**: croc b7a.de
- **Posterior** part: lil-t bg1* thuj bg1
- **Throat**: alum b4a.de* ars bg2 croc bg2 manc bg2 phos b4a.de* seneg bg2 stann b4a.de sulph h2 zinc h2*
- **Tongue**:
  - **Below**: zinc h2*
  - **Edges**: acon-s a1
  - **Forepart**: acon-s a1
  - **Root** of: bar-c b4a.de* bism bg2 kali-bi bg2 phos b4a.de
  - **Tip**: acon-s a1 *Aur* b4a.de iod b4a.de* merc a1 plat b4a.de* ran-b b7a.de* scroph-n bg2 zinc b4a.de*

- **sweetish**-sour: bism chin bg1 crot-t kali-i mag-s meny samb bat1•
- **tallow**; like: nat-m a1 *Valer* k*
  - **bread**; of: ign b7.de* puls b7.de* rhus-t b7.de*
- **tannic**: visc vk1
- **tar**, like: con k*
- **tart**: alum b4.de* apis b7a.de ars b4a.de caps b7.de* euph b4.de* lach b7a.de mur-ac b4.de*
- **tastelessness** (See wanting, tastelessness)
- **tobacco**, juice, as from: gink-b sbd1• nat-c h2 positr nl2•
- **unpleasant** (See bad)
- **unsalted**; food tastes (See salty - enough)
- **urinous**: calc bg2 psor bg2* seneg b4.de*
- **violets**; like odor of: valer b7.de*
- **wanting**, loss of taste: (↗*NOSE - Smell - wanting)* acon b2.de* aeth all-c k* allox tpw3* alum k* alum-p k2 alum-sil k2 am-m k* amyg-p c2* *Anac* k* *Ant-c* k* *Ant-t* k* *Apis* arg-met b2.de* arg-n hr1 ars k* aster a1* atra-r bnm3• atro a1 *Aur* k* aur-ar k2 aur-m k* bar-c b2.de* **Bell** k* berb a1 beryl tpw5 *Borx* k* *Bry* k* cact k* *Calc* k* calc-ar calc-f sp1 calc-sil k2 cann-s k* *Canth* k* carb-an b2.de* carb-v b2.de* card-m k2 caust b2.de* chin k* chlf c2 chlor a1 cina b2.de* cocc k* coff k* *Crot-h* k* cupr k* *Cycl* k* dros k* form bro1 formal br1 gins a1 gymne bro1 hell b2.de* helon a1 *Hep* k* *Hyos* k* hyper hr1 ip k* just bro1 *Kali-bi* kali-br k* kali-c b2.de* kali-chl a1 kali-i a1 kali-n b2.de* kali-s k* kalm hr1 kreos k* lyc k* m-arct b2.de m-aust b2.de* mag-c k* *Mag-m* k* *Merc* k* merl mez a1 morg-p pte1*• myris a1 nat-c b2.de* **Nat-m** k* nat-s k* *Nux-m* k* *Nux-v* k* op k* osteo-a jl2 ox-ac k* ozone sde2• *Par* k* ph-ac b2.de* **Phos** k* plan k*

Taste – wanting, loss of taste: ...
plb b2.de* podo k* positr nl2• *Psor* ptel k* **Puls** k* ran-s a1 rheum k* rhod k* rhus-t b2.de* rhus-v a1 ruta b2.de* sabad k* sang k* sars b2.de* sec k* seneg b2.de* *Sep* k* **Sil** k* spig b2.de* staph b2.de* stram k* stront-c b2.de* *Sul-ac* k* *Sulph* k* syc pte1*• syph *Ther* k* thuj k* tub xxb *Verat* k* zinc h2* [heroin sdj2 spect dfg1]

- **morning**: coca kali-c k* *Nat-s* k*
- **accompanied** by | **Tongue**; white mucus on: ox-ac kr1*
- **chill**; during: am-m bg2 **Ars** b4a.de* aur b4a.de borx b4a.de *Dros* b7.de* puls bg2 sil bg2
- **coryza**:
  - **after**: mag-m ptk1
  - **during**: am-m b7.de* ant-t b7.de* *Cycl* b7a.de mag-m b4a.de* **Nat-m** b4a.de* **Puls** b7.de* rhod b4a.de* sabad b7.de* *Sul-ac* b4a.de

- **wanting**, tastelessness of food: *Alum* k* alum-sil k2 anh sp1 ant-t k* apis arg-n k* ars k* aster aur aur-m bar-c b4.de* bell k* boerh-d bnj1 borx bry k* *Cact* *Calc* k* camph canth b7.de* caps b7.de* carb-v h2 caust b4.de* **Chin** b7.de* cocc b7.de* *Colch* k* *Cor-r* cupr b7.de* cycl k* dros k* eup-per ferr bg2 ferr-m flor-p rsj3• **Hell** k* hir skp7• hydrog srj2• *Ign* k* kali-bi kali-i kola stb3• lap-la rsp1 **Lyc** b4a.de m-ambo b7.de m-arct b7.de m-aust b7.de* *Mang* b4a.de mang-p rly4• merc k* mim-p skp7• mosch b7.de* **Nat-m** k* nat-p fkr6.de nux-v k* olnd b7.de* ph-ac b4.de* pitu-gl skp7• plac-s rly4• plan positr nl2• ptel **Puls** k* rhod k* rhus-t b7.de* ruta k* sal-ac sars k* seneg k* sep h2 sil k* squil k* staph k* stict *Stram* k* stront-c b4.de* *Sulph* b4.de* *Thuj* b4a.de *Verat* k* viol-t k*
  - **beer**: m-ambo b7.de* puls k* rhus-t b7.de* stram b7.de*
  - **bread**: alum puls b7.de* rhus-t b7.de* stram b7.de* tarax b7.de
  - **butter**: puls k* stram bg2 tarax bg2
  - **chocolate** agg.: m-arct b7.de
  - **coffee**: nux-v k*
  - **coryza**; during●: alum *Ant-t* *Calc* *Cycl* k* *Hep* mag-m *Nat-c* **NAT-M** k ● nux-v *Psor* k2 **Puls** *Rhod* *Sep* *Sil* *Sul-ac* *Sulph*
  - **cough**; with: anac gsy1
  - **meat**: alum k* nux-v k* puls k* squil b7.de*
  - **milk**: alum mosch h1 nux-v k* puls
  - **orange** juice: choc srj3•
  - **salt**: *Calc* k* canth k*
  - **solid** foods: ferr bg2
  - **soup**: squil b7.de*
  - **tea**: choc srj3•
  - **things** which formerly had strong taste: acon
  - **tobacco**: anac ant-t chin k* ign b7.de* m-arct b7.de* nux-v b7a.de* puls k* squil b7.de*
- **water**, like putrid: caps h1* phos h2*
- **watery**: bell b4.de* calc b4a.de* caps b7.de* carb-v bg2 chin b7.de* cupr b7.de* form bg2 hyos bg2 ign b7.de* kali-c b4.de* lyc b4a.de mag-m b4.de* nat-m b4.de* ozone sde2• phos bg2 *Rhus-t* b7a.de *Staph* b7.de* verat bg2
  - **food** tastes: cupr b7a.de
- **wine**:
  - **like**: canth b7.de* seneg
  - **water** tastes like: tab
- **wood**; like: ars b4.de* colch b7.de* *Ign* b7a.de ruta b7.de* stram b7.de* sulph bg2 thuj a1*
  - **food** tastes: ruta b7a.de *Stram* b7a.de
  - **foul**, like: sulph h2

○ - **Throat**, not in mouth; in nux-v ptk1 podo vh ptel vh sil ptk1

TENSION: bov b4.de*

○ - **Gums**: *Bry* b7a.de
- **Palate**:
  - ○ **Arches** of: coc-c k*
  - **Soft**: clem a1
- **Tongue**: con b4a.de merc b4.de*
  - ○ **Root** of: kali-i ptk1

THICK; sensation as if: lachn c1 sul-i c2

○ - **Tongue** was: *(↗Swelling - tongue)* absin vh1 ars *Bapt* k* *Bell* k* both tsm2 both-ax tsm2 bung-fa tsm2 calc bg2 *Camph* chord-umb rly4• cocc mrr1 conv br1 cory br1 crot-c mrr1 crot-h bg2* dendr-pol tsm2 elaps tsm2 **Gels** k* *Glon Hyos* kali-bi bg2 kali-p bg2 *Lach* k* laur lyc merc bg2 merc-c merl *Mur-ac* k* naja tsm2 nux-v bg2 *Op* ozone sde2• pert-vc vk9 *Phyt Plat* rhus-t *Stram* syph tere-la rly4• vip tsm2

THINKING of mouth agg.: lach bg2

THREAD (See Hair; sensation)

THRUSH: *(↗Aphthae)* *Aeth* vk1 anan a1 *Ant-t* vk1 arg-n ggd1 *Ars* hr1* asaf ggd1 *Bapt* vk1 **Borx** hr1* *Bry* vk1 but-ac jl3 cand ggd1 carb-ac hr1 *Carb-v* hr1* *Caul* br1 caust vk1 chlorpr jl3 *Eup-a* vk1 hep hr1 *Hydr* vk1 kali-br hr1* **Kali-chl** st* kali-i br1 *Kali-m* hr1* **Merc** hr1* **Merc-c** vk1 **Mur-ac** vk1 nat-c k2* *Nat-m* hr1* nat-p ggd1 *Nit-ac* vk1 nux-v vk1 phos k2 psor k2* *Rhus-g* vk1 **Sars** vk1 **Semp** vk1 sep ggd1 staph hr1 **Sul-ac** hr1* sulo-ac br1 **Sulph** hr1* thuj hr1 urin c1

▽ - **extending** to | **Gastrointestinal** tract: *(↗Aphthae - extending - intestinal)* caul br1

THUMB SUCKING (See MIND - Gestures - fingers - mouth)

TICKLING: nux-v b7.de* phos b4.de*

○ - **Tongue**: acon bg2 alum ptk1 brom bg2 canth b7.de* lach bg2 stann bg2*

○ • **Root** of: rumx bg2 stann ptk1

TINGLING (See Prickling)

TONGUE-TIE: syph vk1

TOUCH agg.: am-c b4.de* bar-c b4.de* **Bell** b4.de* bry b7.de* cic b7.de* croc b7.de* ferr b7.de* hell b7.de* iod b4.de* **Lach** b7.de* merc b4.de* mez bg2 plb b7.de* rhus-t b7.de* staph b7.de* teucr b7.de* thuj b4.de* zinc b4.de*

TREMBLING of tongue: absin k* *Agar* k* **Agarin** vk1 *Agri* bro1 aloe bg2* *Apis* k* arn k* ars k* *Aur* k* bac bn *Bell* k* bry k* calc-hp bg2 **Camph** k* *Canth* k* caps bg2* carb-ac k* caust bro1* cham bro1* cimic k* colch k* *Crot-h* k* cupr k* cupr-ar k* *Gels* k* *Hell* k* hyos k* *Ign* k* **Lach** k* lat-m sp1* *Lyc* k* med k* **Merc** k* mur-ac k* nat-m bg2* oena k* *Op* k* *Ph-ac* k* phos k* pip-n bg2* *Plb* k* rhus-t k* sec k* sil k* stram k* sulph bg2* tab k* *Tarax* k* vip k* zinc k*

- **accompanied** by:
  - • **chorea** (See GENERALS - Chorea - accompanied - tongue - trembling)
  - • **erysipelas** (See SKIN - Erysipelas - accompanied - tongue - trembling)
  - • **typhus** (See FEVER - Typhus - accompanied - tongue - trembling)
  - ○ • **Arm**; abscess on left (See EXTREMITIES - Abscess - upper limbs - left - accompanied - tongue)
  - • **Brain** complaints: cimic kr1*
  - • **Chin**; trembling of: nux-v vk1
- **delivery**; after: *Crot-h* kr1*
- **protruding** it; when: apis k* bapt k2 *Bell* k* crot-h k* ferr k* *Gels* k* *Hell* k* *Hyos* k* ign k* **Lach** k* merc k* *Plb* k* stram k* *Thuj* vh
  - • **beginning** only; in the: sep vk1
  - • **long** time; if protruded for a: ph-ac vk1
- **wavelike**: syph vk1 tub vk1

○ - **Centre** of tongue: sep vk1
- **Tip** of tongue: *Nat-m* bg1* sil vk1

TUBERCLES:

○ - **Gums**, painful: ph-ac **Plb** k*
- **Tongue**: *Graph* k* lyc k* mang k*

○ • **Below**: *Ambr* vh1

TUMORS: *(↗Cancer)* benz-ac calc k* *Lyc* k* *Nit-ac* k* thuj sne
- **left side** | **Last** molar; behind: benz-ac
- **malignant**: calc
- **painless**: calc k* *Nit-ac* k*
- **small**: lyc
- **spongy**: calc thuj sne
- **ulcerated**: benz-ac

Tumors: ...

○ - **Gums**:
  - • **inflamed**: calc-f sne canth merc sne merc-c sne morg-g fmm1• phos sne thuj sne
  - • **painless**, movable, lower Gums: nat-s
  - • **spongy**: *Sulph* b4a.de
  - • **walnut**; size of a: *Nit-ac* staph
    - ⁝ **place** of two bicuspids; in: **Sil**
- **Lip**; inside right side of: calc
- **Palate**:
  - • **hard**: canth hydr
  - • **soft** and tender tumors: tax-br oss1•
- **Tongue**: gali br1 kali-m ptk1 phos sne

○ • **Centre**, size of pea, sensitive to touch; rounded elevation in: castm ptk1
  - ⁝ **drawing** sensation; with | **string** were pulling the centre of tongue toward the hyoid bone; as if a: castm k*
- • **Under** | **cystic**: ambr mrr1

TURNING:
- **head**:
  - • **agg.**: bell b4.de* bry b7.de* cham b7.de* hep b4.de* spig b7a.de
  - • **left** agg.; to: bry bg2 chinin-s bg2 hep bg2 plat bg2

TWITCHING: op ptk1

○ - **Gums**: hep b4.de* lyc b4.de* nux-v h1* sabad b7.de* sec b7.de* thuj b4.de* valer kl
- **Tongue**: agar k2 **Castm** bg2* cham b7a.de* germ-met srj5• glon k* sec k* sulph k* vip bg2*

ULCERS: *(↗Aphthae)* *Agath-a* nl2• *Agn* k* aids nl2• allox tpw4* aln br1 *Alum* k* alumn k2* *Anac* anan ant-t bg2 arg-met b7.de* arg-n bg2 **Ars** k* ars-s-f k2 arum-t k* *Aur* b4a.de *Bapt* k* bar-act bg2 *Bell-p* sp1 beryl sp1* *Borx* k* bry bg2 cadm-s c1 calc k* calc-f br1 calc-i k2 calc-s calc-sil k2 *Canth Caps* k* carb-ac c1 carb-an carb-v b4a.de* carbn-s carc fb* caust k* chlor choc srj3• *Cic* cinnb k2 colch rsj2• cop corn cory br1 *Crot-c* crot-h cupr-s des-ac rbp6 dream-p sdj1• *Dulc* k* *Falco-pe* nl2• *Fl-ac* flor-p rsj3• gamb germ-met srj5• gran *Graph* k* hell hep k* hippoz *Hydr Hydrin-m* c2 hydrog srj2• **Iod** k* irid-met srj5• *Iris* jatr-c k* kali-ar *Kali-bi* k* kali-c bg2* *Kali-chl* **Kali-i** k* kali-m k2 kreos k2 **Lach** k* luf-op rsj5• *Luna* kg1• med k2 *Merc* k* *Merc-c* k* *Merc-cy Merc-d* mez k* mim-p rsj8• morg-p pte1*• **Mur-ac** k* nat-ar *Nat-c* k* *Nat-m* k* nat-pyru rly4• **Nit-ac** k* *Nux-m* nux-v k* op k* ox-ac petr k* *Phos* k* *Phyt* k* pic-ac plb k* positr nl2• prot pte1* *Psor* ran-s bg2 rat bg2 rhus-g c2* rumx k* sanic k* sep b4.de* sil b4.de* sin-a c2 sin-n *Staph* k* *Sul-ac* k* sul-i k2 suprar rly4• syc pte1*• syph c2* tab tarent-c mrr1 tell rsj10• ter tere-la rly4• thuj k* (non:uran-met k) uran-n zinc k* [heroin sdj2 spect dfg1]
- **right**: androc srj1•
- **biting**: nat-m k*
- **bleeding**: borx mrr1 carb-v k2 kreos merc sul-ac syph k2
  - • **eating**; when: borx br1
  - • **menses** | **before** | **agg.**: phos bro1
    - ⁝ **during** | **agg.**: phos bro1
  - • **touching**; when: borx br1
- **bluish**: ars k* aur *Mur-ac*
- **burning**: alum k* alum-p k2 *Ars Caps* k* *Carb-v* k* caust chin cic *Hydr* kali-ar kali-i *Kreos Merc Nat-c* nat-m k* ph-ac sep sin-n k* sulph k2 tarent-c mrr1
- **canker** sore: *(↗between - canker; cheeks - inside - canker; lips - canker; tongue - below - canker; tongue - sides - canker; tongue - tip - canker)* agav-a bro1 ant-c al1* arg-n br1* ars bro1 astac hr1* bapt hr1* *Borx* bro1 canth hr1* caps bro1 carb-v bro1 chinin-ar k2 echi br1* ham a1* hydr bro1 kali-bi bro1 kali-c hr1 *Kali-chl* bro1 kali-m a3* lac-ac hr1* lach bro1 lyc bro1 mag-p c1 med k2* merc bro1 *Merc-c* bro1 mur-ac bro1 nat-hchls bro1 *Nat-m* bro1 *Nit-ac* bro1 oxyg c1 phyt bro1 pic-ac dw1 podo hr1* sal-ac hr1* sin-a cda1 sin-n hr1* staph hr1 *Sul-ac* bro1 sulph bro1
  - • **dentition**; during: calc hr1
- **cold** water | **amel.**: dulc
- **deep**: *Carb-v* gamb kali-bi k2 merc-d *Mur-ac* sul-ac
- **dirty** looking: **Nit-ac** *Plb*
- **fetid**: **Bapt** k* *Merc* nit-ac nux-v plb
- **flat**: *Caps* merc mez *Nat-c* nat-m sul-ac
- **forming** rapidly: *Borx*

- **gangrenous**: *Ars* *Bapt* *Borx* caps tl1 **Lach** *Sul-ac* syph
- **grayish**: carb-v hell merc-c

○ · **Base**:

⁝ **accompanied** by | **Mucous** membrane; red swelling of (See Mucous membrane - swollen - red - accompanied - gray)

- **herpetic**: agath-a nl2• ars-s-f
- **inflamed**: calc-sil k2
- **itching**: chin
- **malignant**: **Ars** *Lach* *Phos*

· **menses**; during: chin al

○ · **Palate**; hard: scol vwe2

- **mercurial**: borx hep *Iod* kali-i *Nit-ac*
- **mothers**: bapt k2
- **painful**: agath-a nl2• *Ars* calc-sil k2 dream-p sdj1• dulc a1 falco-pe nl2• *Fl-ac* hir rsj4• kali-bi *Merc* mur-ac nat-m k* **Nit-ac** petr positr nl2•

· **morning**: zinc h2*

· **biting** teeth together, when: petr

· **sore**, smarting: agath-a nl2• alum bro1 *Arg-n* bro1 *Ars* bro1 ars-met *Arum-t* bro1 *Borx* bro1 bov caps bro1 *Hep* bro1 hydr bro1 *Hydrin-m* bro1 kali-chl bro1 *Merc* bro1 *Merc-c* bro1 *Mur-ac* bro1 nat-ar *Nit-ac* bro1 nux-m bro1 phyt bro1 *Ran-s* bro1 *Rhus-g* bro1 semp bro1 sin-n bro1 sul-ac bro1 tarax bro1

· **splinter**, like a: calc-sil k2 *Nit-ac* k*

· **stinging**, stitches: calc-sil k2 *Nit-ac*

· **touch**; to: calc-sil k2 cic hydrog srj2• *Nat-c* k* *Nat-m* k*

- **painless**: bapt hell phos [heroin sdj2]

· **eruptions** on face; after suppressed brown herpetic: phos

○ · **Lips**; inner side of | **Lower**: phos

- **perforating**: *Kali-chl* merc-cy br1
- **phagedenic**: (↗*spreading*) ars ars-s-f *Caps* k* hydr k2 merc k2 *Merc-c* **Nit-ac** *Sul-ac* sulph k2
- **purple**: carb-v *Plb*
- **small**: *Alum* *Caps* chlor hydrog srj2• *Merc* sel rsj9• zinc zinc-p k2
- **spreading**: (↗*phagedenic*) *Alum* calc-sil k2 *Lach* merc merc-pr-r sul-ac k2
- **syphilitic**: *Aur* aur-ar k2 *Aur-m* *Cinnb* bro1 *Fl-ac* **Hep** hydr **Kali-bi** k* **Kali-i** kali-m k2 *Lach* **Merc** k* *Merc-c* bro1 merc-cy br1 *Merc-i-r* merc-n bro1 merc-pr-r bro1 nit-ac k2* *Phyt* still bro1 **Syph** *Thuj* bro1
- **white**: androc srj1• cic nit-ac k2 *Sul-ac*

· **coated** with milk; as if: *Kali-i*

○ · **Lip**; inside lower | **left**: ars-met

- **yellow**: aloe calc hell *Plb* *Sul-ac* zinc

○ · **Orifice** of salivary glands, at: acon bell **Merc**

▽ - **extending** to | **Gastrointestinal** tract; whole: ars mrr1 tarent-c mrr1 ter ptk1

- **extending** from throat to roof of mouth: ars

○ - **Base**:

· **black**: *Mur-ac* k*

· **lardaceous**: ant-t k* calc-sil k2 caps k* *Hep* **Merc** k* **Nit-ac** phos syph

· **milky**: **Kali-i**

· **spongy**: ars

· **swollen**: hell

- **Between** gums and lips | **canker** sore: (↗*canker*) rham-cal br1
- **Cheeks**:

· **perforating**: merc k2

○ · **Inside**: merc k2 petr a1 sacch-a fd2.de•

⁝ **canker** sore: (↗*canker*) nat-p br1 oxyg c1

⁝ **lichen** planus: borx mtf fl-ac mtf merc mtf nit-ac mtf

- **Edges**:

· **elevated**: hell

· **gray**: hell

· **hard**: *Kali-bi* phos

· **irregular**: ars **Kali-i** merc

· **jagged**: ars merc

- **Gums**: (↗*Abscess - gums*) acon a1 *Agn* b7.de* aids nl2• aloe alum k* alum-sil k2 am-c bg2 anan ang ars k* aur k* aur-ar k2 aur-i k2 aur-m k* aur-s k2 bapt bg2* bell b4a.de* berb k* bond a1 borx bg2* bov b4.de bufo *Calc* k* caps k* *Carb-an* b4a.de *Carb-v* k* caust k* *Cist* bro1 colch rsj2• corn k* *Crot-c* *Cupr* k* dream-p sdj1• emetin bro1 ephe-si hsj1• gink-b sbd1• *Hep* k* hippoz k* hydr k2 hydrog srj2• *Iod* k* *Kali-bi* k* kali-c b4.de* kali-chl k* *Kali-i* k* **Kreos** k* lac-c *Lach* k* *Lyc* k* mag-m b4a.de mand rsj7• **Merc** k* *Merc-c* k* merc-sul a1* mill k* mur-ac k* **Nat-m** k* nat-p nat-s k2 nicc k* nit-ac bg2* *Nux-v* k* ox-ac k* petr b4a.de *Ph-ac* k* **Phos** k* phyt k* plan a1* plb bg2 **Psor** k* raph a1 ruta b7a.de sabin b7a.de* sacch-a fd2.de• sang k* *Sep* k* *Sil* k* stann k* *Staph* k* *Sul-ac* k* sul-i k2 tell rsj10• *Thuj* b4a.de* tub jl2 zinc k* zinc-p k2

· **discharging** blood which tastes salty: alum

· **exuding** blood on pressure: bov k*

· **gray**: kreos bg2

· **scorbutic**: acet-ac mur-ac k*

· **sensation** of | **Root** of tooth; at: am-c k*

· **sloughing**: *Merc* *Merc-c* k* merc-i-r kl (non:merc-pr-r kl) op k* staph k*

· **yellowish**: hell k* sulph k*

○ · **Base** lardaceous: *Hep* k*

· **Inner**: *Staph* b7.de*

· **Lower**: phos b4.de* sabin b7.de* zinc b4.de*

· **Outer**: kali-c b4.de*

- **Lips**; inner side of: beryl tpw5 *Carb-an* b4a.de *Graph* b4a.de mand rsj7• *Mez* b4a.de

· **canker** sore: (↗*canker*) ars vh1 carb-v a1 chinin-ar hr1 med hr1* nat-p br1

· **gangrenous**: ars b4a.de chin b7.de* hell b7.de* kreos b7.de* merc b4a.de *Mur-ac* b4a.de

· **small**: tub jl2

○ · **Lower**: beryl tpw5* borx bg2 *Ign* b7a.de

- **Palate**: allox tpw3* am-c ant-c bro1 *Apis* *Arum-t* bro1 **Aur** *Aur-m* k* calc k2 *Caps* b7a.de chir-fl gya2 *Cinnb* k* *Dros* b7a.de dulc hep k2* hir rsj4*• *Kali-bi* k* kali-i k2 *Kreos* b7a.de *Lach* k* *Lyc* k* **Merc** k* *Merc-c* k* merc-cy dgt *Merl* hr1* *Nat-m* *Nit-ac* k* nux-v k* op a1 *Ph-ac* k* *Phos* k* *Phyt* k* plect a1 rad-br sze8• sacch-a fd2.de• *Sang* k* sanic k* sil k* *Sul-ac* a1* syph k2 tarax bro1

· **perforating**: *Kali-bi* mez *Sil* k*

· **punched** out, looking: *Kali-bi* k*

· **sloughing**: *Kali-bi* k* *Lach* *Merc-c* k* *Nit-ac* *Phos* *Sulph* *Syph*

· **syphilitic**: **Aur** k* **Aur-m** k* *Hep* kali-bi k2 *Kali-i* k* *Lach* hr1 *Merc* hr1 *Nit-ac* hr1 *Syph* k*

○ · **Hard** palate: *Ars* b4a.de *Aur* b4.de* *Carb-v* b4a.de caust bg2 *Dulc* b4a.de kali-bi bg2 *Lach* bg2 merc b4a.de* *Merc-c* b4a.de nat-m b4.de* nux-v bg2 sil b4.de* *Sulph* b4a.de

· **Sides**; ulcers with hard: kali-bi

· **Soft** palate: arg-n bg2 *Aur* b4.de* clem bg2 *Kali-bi* bg2 **Merc** b4.de* merc-cy bg2 nat-m b4.de* *Nit-ac* b4.de* *Ph-ac* b4.de* sil b4.de* sul-ac bg2 *Sulph* b4a.de

· **Velum**, on: dros k* hippoz *Kali-i* *Merc* *Merc-cy* *Nit-ac* *Ph-ac* *Phyt* syph

- **Salivary** glands: *Merc* b4a.de
- **Tongue**: agar k* aloe k* am-c b4.de* ant-c vk1 ant-t k* antip vh1 *Apis* k* *Arg-n* bg2* *Ars* k* ars-h k* ars-s-f k2 arum-d k* arum-t k* *Aur* k* aur-ar k2 aur-m k* aur-s k2 **Bapt** k* *Bar-c* k* *Bar-m* k* bell b4a.de bell-p sp1* benz-ac k* beryl sp1* bov k* *Brom* b4a.de *Calc* k* calc-s k2 canth b7.de* *Caps* k* carb-v b4a.de* *Chin* k* chir-fl gya2 chlol k* cic k* cina vk1 cinnb k* clem k* colch rsj2• corn k* cupr b7a.de *Dig* k* dros k* *Dulc* b4a.de falco-pe nl2• *Fl-ac* k* flor-p rsj3* graph k* hell bg2* hir rsj4* hydr k* *Kali-bi* k* *Kali-chl* k* **Kali-i** k* kali-m k2* *Kreos* k* lac-v c2 *Lach* k* luf-op rsj5• *Lyc* k* med k2 **Merc** k* *Merc-i-r* k* merl k* mez b4a.de* mim-p rsj8• morg-p xyz60 *Mur-ac* k* musca-d szs1 *Nat-m* k* nat-pyru rly4• *Nit-ac* k* **Nit-m-ac** bro1* nux-v b7a.de* oena c2 op k* pert jl2 ph-ac b4a.de *Phyt* k* *Plb* k* positr nl2• **Psor** k* sang bg2* sangin-n bro1* semp bro1* sil k* *Sin-n* k* *Staph* k* sul-ac k* *Sulph* k* syc fmm1• syph bg2* tarent k* thuj b4a.de* tub vk1 verat k*

· **right** side: bov k* chir-fl gya2 cinnb k* sil k* thuj ptk1

· **left** side: apis bg2* chir-fl gya2

⁝ **followed** by | **right** side: chir-fl gya2 *Thuj* k*

Mouth

- **accompanied** by:
  - **amebiasis** (See GENERALS - Amebiasis - accompanied - tongue)
  - **typhus** fever (See FEVER - Typhus - accompanied - tongue - ulcers)
- **black** base, with: mur-ac h2
- **bleeding**: merc k* nat-hchls vk1 raja-s vk1 semp ptk2
- **blue**: *Ars* k* mur-ac k*
- **burning**: hydr k2
- **children**; in: oci-sa vk1
- **deep**: ars-h hr1 bov hr1 kali-bi k2 *Kali-chl* hr1 mur-ac k* *Nit-ac* hr1 phyt hr1 syc pte1*•
- **indurated**: merc k* *Merc-i-r* k* thuj k*
- **lardaceous** base: caps k2
- **painful**: agar k* bov k* *Calc* k* caps k2 falco-pe nl2• *Kali-chl* hr1 nat-pyru rly4• positr nl2• semp ptk2
  - **touch**; to: bov k* *Cic* k* falco-pe nl2• thuj k*
- **phagedenic**: *Agar* k* benz-ac k* *Caps* k* *Fl-ac* k* hydr k2 sil k*
- **symmetrical**: kali-chl a1
- **syphilitic**: aur bro1* cinnb bro1* fl-ac k* *Kali-bi* k* *Kali-i* k* lach bro1* **Merc** k* mez bro1* **Nit-ac** k* *Phyt* k*
- **white**: graph h2*
- **yellow**: aloe k* cupr k* *Hell* k* plb k*
- ○ **Below**: calc b4a.de falco-pe nl2• *Fl-ac* k* *Graph* k* **Lyc** k* *Mag-m* b4a.de nux-m b7.de* plb k* **Sanic** k* thuj k*
  - **canker** sore: *(↗canker)* med c1
- **Center**: cupr-s k* *Fl-ac* k*
  - **accompanied** by | **cracked** tongue in all directions (See Cracked - tongue - directions - accompanied - ulcer)
- **Edges**: ant-t hs1 ars a1 bov hr1* chir-fl gya2 cic hr1 cina he1 des-ac rbp6 kali-bi hr1 merc a1 nit-ac hr1 oena c1
- **Frenum**: agar k* falco-pe nl2• *Kali-c* k* naja k* nat-c bg2* nit-ac bg2* sep k*
- **Margins**, with undermined: mur-ac h2
- **Sides**: agar k* ars k* bov k* *Calc* k* carb-an b4a.de carc mlr1• caust k* *Cic* k* cupr k* *Kali-bi* k* kali-chl k* *Lach* k* *Merc* k* merc-cy k* mez b4a.de **Nit-ac** k* oena a1 sil b4a.de *Thuj* k*
  - **canker** sore: *(↗canker)* maland al2 med c1
- **Tip**: am-c k* beryl tpw5* cinnb k* cupr k* dros k* kali-i mrr1 lyc k* merc k* plb k* raja-s vk1 *Sal-ac* kr1* thuj bg1
  - **left**: thuj bg2*
  - **canker** sore: *(↗canker)* ham a1* med c1

URINATION agg.; after: nit-ac bg2

VARICOSE veins: thuj ptk1
- **ulceration**: ambr bro1 thuj bro1
- ○ **Tongue**: ambr bro1* calc h2* *Dig* k* *Fl-ac* k* *Ham* k* *Puls* k* *Thuj* k*

VARNISHED; tongue looks as if (See Smooth - varnished)

VELVET, sensation as if covered with: *(↗Cotton; Saliva - cotton)* coc-c dig k* nux-m k* vero-o rly3•

VESICLES (See Eruptions - vesicles)

VOMITING; after: | **agg.**: puls b7.de*

WAKING; on: acon b7.de* ambr b7.de* bell b4.de* *Calc* b4a.de clem b4.de* ign b7.de* kali-bi bg2 kali-c bg2 m-ambo b7.de m-arct b7.de mag-c bg2 *Nux-v* b7.de* par b7.de* phos bg2 puls b7.de* spig b7.de* stront-c bg2 tarax b7.de* verat b7.de*

WALKING: | **after** | **agg.**: *Bry* b7.de*
- **agg.**: *Con* b4a.de petr b4.de* stann b4.de*

WARM:
- **applications** | **agg.**: bry b7.de* guaj bg2 nat-m bg2 puls b7.de*
- **drinks**:
  - **agg.**: alum bg2 apis bg2 phyt bg2
  - **amel.**: alum b4.de*

Warm: ...
- **feels** (See Heat)
- **food**:
  - **agg.**: alum bg2 sil bg2 sulph bg2
    - **hot** food: ferr b7a.de
  - **amel.**: alum b4.de*
- **warm** agg.; becoming: ant-c b7.de* *Bell* b4a.de *Bry* b7.de* *Caps* b7.de* *Ign* b7.de*

WARMTH (See Heat)

WARTS: calc-p sne ph-ac thuj sne
- ○ **Palate**: arg-n cupre-l sne positr nl2•
- **Tongue**: aur k* *Aur-m* k* aur-m-n k* cupre-l sne kali-s dh lyc k* mang k* mang-act bro1* morg-p pte1*• phos b4a.de staph k* syc pte1*• thuj b4a.de*
  - **large**, round: chel b7a.de *Lach* b7a.de

WASHING: | **amel.**: asar b7.de*

WATER: | **agg.**: canth b7.de*

WATER BRASH (See STOMACH - Eructations; type - water brash)

WATERY, gums look: **Apis**

WEAKNESS: | **Tongue**: bar-c ptk1 caust ptk1 con ptk1 mur-ac mrr1

WEATHER: | **change** of weather | **agg.**: sulph bg2
- **cold**, wet | **agg.**: *Sulph* b4a.de

WETTING lips constantly: *(↗FACE - Dryness - lips - licks)* *Culx* vh

WHISKEY agg.: rhus-t bg2

WIND agg.: con b4.de*

WITHERED Tongue: kreos k* verat k*

WOOD (See Numbness)

WRINKLED: *(↗Contraction; Shrivelled)* aur bg2 phos bg2
- ○ **Gums**: tung-met bdx1•
  - **sensation** as if wrinkled: par b7.de*
- **Palate**: **Borx** k* phos k*
- **Tongue**: calc-p k* merc-i-r ptk1 nat-ar k* phos k* sul-ac k*
  - **morning**: calc-p k*

YAWNING:
- **agg.**: aloe bg2 am-m b7.de* arg-met b7.de* arg-n ptk1 hep b4.de* mag-c b4.de* meny b7.de* nat-c b4.de* nux-v b7a.de rhus-t b7.de* zinc b4.de*
- **amel.**: manc bg2*

BUCCAL CAVITY (See Complaints)

GUMS; complaints of: agar b2.de* agn b2.de* alum b2.de* am-c b2.de* am-m b2.de* ambr b2.de* anac b2.de* ant-c b2.de* arg-met b2.de* arn b2.de* ars b2.de* aur b2.de* bar-c b2.de* *Bell* b2.de* bism b2.de* **Borx** b2.de* bov b2.de* bry b2.de* *Calc* b2.de* canth b2.de* caps b2.de* *Carb-an* b2.de* *Carb-v* b2.de* *Caust* b2.de* cham b2.de* chin b2.de* chlam-tr bcx2• cic b2.de* colch b2.de* con b2.de* *Graph* b2.de* hep b2.de* hyos b2.de* iod b2.de* kali-c b2.de* kali-n b2.de* kreos b2.de* lach b2.de* lyc b2.de* m-ambo b2.de m-arct b2.de mag-c b2.de* mag-m b2.de* **Merc** b2.de* mur-ac b2.de* nat-c b2.de* *Nat-m* b2.de* nit-ac b2.de* nux-m b2.de* **Nux-v** b2.de* par b2.de* petr b2.de* ph-ac b2.de* *Phos* b2.de* plb b2.de* puls b2.de* ran-s b2.de* rhod b2.de* rhus-t b2.de* *Ruta* b2.de* sabad b2.de* sabin b2.de* sars b2.de* sec b2.de* *Sep* b2.de* sil b2.de* spig b2.de* spong b2.de* stann b2.de* **Staph** b2.de* stront-c b2.de* sul-ac b2.de* sulph b2.de* teucr b2.de* thuj b2.de* zinc b2.de*
- **accompanied** by:
  - ○ **Mouth** | **complaints** (See Complaints - accompanied - gums)
- ○ **Inner**: agar b2.de* am-c b2.de* ambr b2.de* arn b2.de* graph b2.de* kali-c b2.de* nat-c b2.de* nat-m b2.de* ph-ac b2.de* phos ptk1 puls b2.de* rhus-t b2.de* *Ruta* b2.de* sep b2.de* **Staph** b2.de*
- **Lower**: am-c b2.de* am-m b2.de* anac b2.de* canth b2.de* carb-an b2.de* caust b2.de* laur b2.de* mag-m b2.de* *Nat-c* b2.de* *Petr* b2.de* phos b2.de* rhod b2.de* sabin b2.de* **Sars** b2.de* spong b2.de* *Staph* b2.de* sul-ac b2.de* sulph b2.de* teucr b2.de* thuj b2.de* zinc b2.de*

- **Upper**: agar b2.de* am-c b2.de* ang b2.de* aur b2.de* *Bar-c* b2.de* bell b2.de* **Calc** b2.de* canth b2.de* carb-an b2.de* colch b2.de* graph b2.de* kali-c b2.de* *Kreos* b2.de* lyc b2.de* mag-m b2.de* mur-ac b2.de* nat-m b2.de* nit-ac b2.de* **Ruta** b2.de* sep b2.de* stront-c b2.de*

PALATE; complaints of:

▽ - **extending** to | **Upward**: glon bg2 phos bg2

○ - **Hard** palate: acon bg2 am-c b2.de* ambr b2.de* ant-c b2.de* arn b2.de* ars b2.de* *Aur* b2.de* *Bar-c* b2.de* *Bar-m* bg2 **Bell** b2.de* borx b2.de* bov b2.de* *Calc* b2.de* camph b2.de* cann-s b2.de* canth b2.de* *Caps* b2.de* carb-v b2.de* caust b2.de* cham b2.de* chin b2.de* cocc b2.de* coff bg2 coloc b2.de* croc b2.de* dig b2.de* dulc b2.de* euph b2.de* hell b2.de* hyos b2.de* ign b2.de* iod b2.de* kali-c b2.de* *Lach* b2.de* laur b2.de* led b2.de* m-ambo b2.de mag-c b2.de* mag-m b2.de* meny b2.de* **Merc** b2.de* mez b2.de* mur-ac b2.de* nat-m b2.de* nit-ac b2.de* nux-m b2.de* **Nux-v** b2.de* par b2.de* ph-ac b2.de* *Phos* b2.de* puls b2.de* ran-b b2.de* ran-s b2.de* rhod b2.de* rhus-t b2.de* ruta b2.de* sabad b2.de* sep b2.de* sil b2.de* spig b2.de* spong b2.de* *Squil* b2.de* *Staph* b2.de* thuj b2.de* *Zinc* b2.de*

- **Soft** palate: **Acon** b2.de* ant-c b2.de* arg-met b2.de* aur b2.de* *Bell* b2.de* calc b2.de* canth b2.de* caps b2.de* carb-v b2.de* caust b2.de* cham b2.de* chin b2.de* **Coff** b2.de* dig b2.de* dulc b2.de* glon bg2 hell b2.de* hep b2.de* iod b2.de* kali-c b2.de* kali-n b2.de* *Lach* b2.de* led b2.de* mag-c b2.de* meny b2.de* **Merc** b2.de* mez b2.de* *Nat-m* b2.de* nit-ac b2.de* nux-m b2.de* nux-v b2.de* par b2.de* ph-ac b2.de* *Phos* b2.de* ran-b b2.de* *Ran-s* b2.de* rhod b2.de* ruta b2.de* sars b2.de* seneg b2.de* sep b2.de* sil b2.de* staph b2.de* stram b2.de* sulph bg2 thuj b2.de* valer b2.de* zinc b2.de*

TONGUE; complaints of: *Acon* b2.de* agar b2.de* alum b2.de* am-c b2.de* ambr b2.de* anac b2.de* ang b2.de* ant-c b2.de* arg-met b2.de* arn b2.de* **Ars** b2.de* asar b2.de* bar-c b2.de* **Bell** b2.de* bism b2.de* borx b2.de* bov b2.de* *Bry* b2.de* caj br1 calc b2.de* cann-s b2.de* *Canth* b2.de* carb-an b2.de* carb-v b2.de* *Caust* b2.de* *Cham* b2.de* chel b2.de* *Chin* b2.de* cic b2.de* cimic bg2 cina b2.de* clem b2.de* cocc b2.de* coff b2.de* colch b2.de* coloc b2.de* con b2.de* croc b2.de* cupr b2.de* cycl b2.de* dig b2.de* dros b2.de* dulc b2.de* ferr b2.de* *Graph* b2.de* hell b2.de* hep b2.de* *Hyos* b2.de* ign b2.de* iod b2.de* ip b2.de* kali-c b2.de* kali-n b2.de* kreos b2.de* *Lach* b2.de* laur b2.de* led b2.de* lyc b2.de* m-ambo b2.de m-arct b2.de m-aust b2.de mag-c b2.de* mag-m b2.de* mang b2.de* meny b2.de* **Merc** b2.de* mez b2.de* mosch b2.de* *Mur-ac* b2.de* nat-c b2.de* *Nat-m* b2.de* *Nit-ac* b2.de* nux-m b2.de* *Nux-v* b2.de* olnd b2.de* op b2.de* par b2.de* petr b2.de* *Ph-ac* b2.de* *Phos* b2.de* plat b2.de* **Plb** b2.de* **Puls** b2.de* *Ran-s* b2.de* rheum b2.de* rhod b2.de* rhus-t b2.de* ruta b2.de* *Sabad* b2.de* sabin b2.de* sars b2.de* *Sec* b2.de* sel b2.de* seneg b2.de* sep b2.de* sil b2.de* spig b2.de* spong b2.de* *Stann* b2.de* staph b2.de* stram b2.de* stront-c b2.de* sul-ac b2.de* *Sulph* b2.de* tarax b2.de* teucr b2.de* thuj b2.de* *Verat* b2.de* verb b2.de* viol-t b2.de* zinc b2.de* [bell-p-sp dcm1]

- **one** side: bell ptk1 calc bg2* daph bg2 irid-met bg2 laur bg2 lob ptk1 mez ptk1 nat-m ptk1 rhus-t bg2* sang ptk1 sil bg2* thuj bg2*
- **right**: acon bg2 aloe bg2 alum bg2 ars bg2 brom bg2 caps bg2 coca bg2 dros bg2 kali-n bg2 kalm bg2 ph-ac bg2 phel bg2 plat bg2 plb bg2 prun bg2 rumx bg2 sabad bg2 sil bg2 spig bg2 thuj bg2
- **left**: agar bg2 ant-t bg2 apis bg2 arg-n bg2 bar-c bg2 bry bg2 calc bg2 caust bg2 chel bg2 coc-c bg2 colch bg2 con bg2 cycl bg2 glon bg2 graph bg2 hydr bg2 lach bg2 laur bg2 mag-c bg2 nat-s bg2 nux-v bg2 olnd bg2 phos bg2 tarax bg2 zinc bg2
- **diagonally**: rhus-t ptk1

○ - **Across**: acet-ac ptk1 asar ptk1 cob ptk1 kali-p ptk1 **Lach** ptk1 merc ptk1

- **Middle** of: ant-t bg2 arn bg2 bapt bg2 dros bg2 merc bg2 phos bg2 phyt bg2 verat-v bg2
- **Root**: bapt bg2* chinin-s bg2 clem bg2 kali-bi bg2* kali-i ptk1 kali-p bg2 lach ptk1 laur bg2 merc-i-f bg2 nat-s ptk1 par bg2 phyt bg2* rumx bg2 teucr bg2 thuj bg2
- **Sides**: ant-c bg2 *Apis* bg2* bapt bg2 bell bg2 bry bg2 canth bg2 card-m bg2 caust bg2 chin bg2 hydr bg2 kali-bi bg2 kali-i bg2 lach bg2 mag-c bg2 nat-m bg2* nit-ac bg2 phel bg2 phyt ptk1 plb bg2 spong bg2
- **Tip**: kali-c ptk1 *Rhus-t* ptk1 sulph ptk1 thyr ptk1 zinc ptk1
- **Under**: fl-ac ptk1 graph ptk1 *Lyc* ptk1 nat-c ptk1 *Sanic* ptk1

DAY AND NIGHT: ambr b7a.de

DAYTIME: spig b7a.de

MORNING: alum b4.de* am-c b4.de* ant-c bg2 ant-t b7.de* ars b4.de* bar-c b4.de* borx b4a.de bov b4.de* *Bry* b7.de* carb-v bg2 caust b4.de* *Chin* b7.de* dros b7.de* *Hyos* b7.de* **Ign** b7.de* *Iod* b4a.de kali-c b4.de* kali-n b4.de* kreos b7a.de* lach bg2 mag-c b4.de* mag-m b4.de* mang b4.de* **Merc** b4.de* mez b4.de* mur-ac b4.de* nat-c b4.de* nat-m b4.de* **Nux-v** b7.de* par b7.de* petr b4.de* ph-ac b4.de* **Phos** b4.de* plat b4.de* plb b7.de* *Puls* bg2 ran-b b7.de* ran-s b7.de* sabin b7.de* sars b4.de* sep b4.de* sil bg2 *Staph* b7.de* *Sulph* b4.de* thuj b4.de*

- **bed** agg.; in: kali-c bg2 kreos bg2 lach bg2 *Mag-c* bg2 *Nux-v* bg2 ran-b bg2

FORENOON: alum b4.de* am-c b4.de* carb-v b4.de* caust b4.de* kali-n b4.de* mang b4.de* nat-c b4.de* nat-m b4.de* nux-v b7.de* par b7.de* phos b4.de* **Puls** bg2 sars b4.de* sep b4.de* sul-ac b4.de* *Sulph* b4.de*

AFTERNOON: agar b4.de* alum b4.de* am-c b4.de* am-m b7.de* ambr b7.de* calc b4.de* canth b7.de* caust b4.de* kali-c b4.de* lach bg2 lyc b4.de* m-arct b7.de mag-c b4.de* mag-m b4.de **Merc** b4.de* mur-ac b4.de* nat-c b4.de* nat-s bg2 nux-v b7.de* par b7.de* phos b4.de* *Puls* b7.de* ran-s b7.de* sabin b7.de* sars b4.de* sep b4.de* spig b7.de* sulph b4.de* zinc b4.de*

EVENING: agar b4.de* alum b4.de* am-c b4.de* am-m b7.de* ambr b7.de* anac b4.de* ang b7.de* *Ant-c* b7a.de* *Apis* b7a.de bar-c b4.de* **Bell** b4.de* *Borx* b4a.de bov b4.de* *Bry* b7.de* *Calc* b4a.de canth b7.de* carb-an b4.de* cham bg2 chel bg2 *Graph* b4.de* hell b7.de* hep b4.de* hyos b7.de* **Ign** b7.de* kali-c b4.de* laur b7.de* lyc b4.de* m-aust b7.de mag-c b4.de* mag-m b4.de* mang b4.de* **Merc** b4.de* *Mez* b4.de* nat-c b4.de* **Nit-ac** b4.de* nux-m b7.de* *Nux-v* b7.de* olnd b7.de* petr b4.de* phos b4.de* plat bg2 **Puls** b7.de* ran-s b7.de* rhod b4.de* *Rhus-t* b7.de* *Sabin* b7.de* *Sars* b4.de* sel b7a.de sep b4.de* spig b7.de* stront-c b4.de* sul-ac b4a.de* **Sulph** b4.de* tab bg2 thuj b4.de* valer b7.de* zinc b4.de*

- **bed** agg.; in: alum bg2 *Am-c* bg2 **Ant-t** bg2 bar-c bg2 bell bg2 calc bg2 cham bg2 chin bg2 coff bg2 graph bg2 kali-c bg2 mag-c bg2 **Merc** bg2 *Mez* bg2 nit-ac bg2 nux-m bg2 nux-v bg2 phos bg2 **Puls** bg2 rhus-t bg2 *Sabin* bg2 sil bg2 staph bg2 sul-ac bg2 **Sulph** bg2

NIGHT: acon b7.de* alum b4.de* am-c b4.de* am-m bg2 ambr b7.de* anac b4a.de* ant-c b7a.de* ars b4.de* aur-m bg2 bar-c b4a.de* bar-m bg2 **Bell** b4.de* bov b4.de* *Bry* b7.de* calc b4.de* carb-an b4.de* caust b4.de* **Cham** b7.de* *Chin* bg2 clem b4.de* **Coff** b7a.de* cycl b7.de* *Graph* b4.de* grat bg2 hell b7.de* hep b4a.de* *Hyos* b7.de* kali-c b4.de* kali-i bg2 kali-n b4a.de* led b7.de* lyc b4.de* *Mag-c* b4.de* mag-m b4a.de* **Merc** b4.de* merc-c b4a.de* mez b4.de* nat-c b4.de* nat-m b4a.de* nit-ac b4a.de* *Nux-m* b7.de* *Nux-v* bg2 olnd b7.de* par b7.de* petr b4.de* *Ph-ac* b4.de* **Phos** b4.de* **Puls** b7.de* rat bg2* rhod b4.de* *Rhus-t* b7.de* *Sabin* b7.de* sep b4.de* **Sil** b4.de* spig b7.de* **Staph** b7.de* sul-ac b4.de* **Sulph** b4.de* zinc b4.de

- **midnight**:
  - **before**: alum b4.de* am-c b4.de* bov b4.de* *Bry* bg2 *Caust* b4a.de *Cham* b7.de* chin b7.de* graph b4.de* mang b4a.de mez b4a.de nit-ac bg2 petr b4.de* *Phos* b4a.de puls b7.de* rhus-t b7.de* sep b4.de* *Spig* b7a.de sul-ac b4.de* sulph b4.de* thuj b4.de* zinc b4.de*
  - **at**: *Ars* b4a.de sulph bg2
  - **after**: alum b4.de* am-c b4.de* bar-m bg2 bell b4.de* bov bg2 bry b7.de* cham b7.de* hyos bg2 *Merc* b4.de* puls b7.de* rhus-t b7.de* staph b7a.de* sulph b4.de*
- **air** agg.; night: merc bg2 mez bg2
- **amel.**: plan bg2

ABSCESS of roots: am-c aur brm *Bar-c* k* bry gk calc k* calc-s bg2* canth caust euph fl-ac bg2 *Hecla* **Hep** k* iod bg2 jug-r vml3• kali-bi gk kreos ptk1 lach k* *Lyc* k* *Merc* k* merc-i-f bg1 mez myris pkj1 petr phos k* plb puls gk *Pyrog* st querc-r svu1• sec gk **Sil** k* staph ptk1* sulph k* thuj bg2 zinc h2* [spect dfg1]

- **recurrent** (See GENERALS - History - abscesses - teeth)

▽ - **extending** to | **Jaw**: hecla mrr1

ACIDITY:

- **agg.**: arg-n ptk1 castm bg2 mur-ac ptk1
- **amel.**: puls ptk1

ADHERE together (See Stick together)

AIR:

- **blowing** on; sensation of cold air: coc-c k*

Air: ...

- **drawing** in air | **agg.**: alum b4a.de ant-c b7a.de aran bg2 arn bg2 aur bg2 *Bell* b4.de* bry bg2 calc b4.de* caust b4a.de* chin bg2 cic b7a.de* cina b7.de* *Hyos* bg2 kali-n b4.de* m-ambo b7a.de *M-arct* b7.de* *Merc* b4.de* nat-m b4.de* *Nux-m* b7.de* *Nux-v* b7.de* petr b4.de* phos b4.de* sabin b7a.de* sel b7a.de* sep b4.de* *Sil* b4a.de* spig b7.de* *Staph* b7.de* sulph b4.de*
- **forced** into them; sensation of: ambr cocc
- **streaming** from teeth; sensation of air: kali-n a1 nat-c k* (non:nat-s h2) rat ptk2

○ • **Upper** teeth | **right**: kali-n bg2 nat-c b4.de

- **streaming** into teeth; sensation of air: *Bry* b7a.de nux-v b7.de* par bg2 *Rhus-t* b7a.de squil b7.de*
- **wet** air agg.: am-c bg2 borx bg2 nat-c bg2 *Nux-m* bg2 rhod bg2 rhus-t bg2 seneg b4a.de*

AIR AGG.; DRAFT OF: *Bell* bg2 *Calc* b4.de* *Cham* b7a.de **Chin** b7.de* kali-c bg2 *Mag-c* b4a.de merc bg2 *Phos* b4a.de sars b4a.de* *Sep* b4.de* *Sulph* b4.de*

AIR; IN OPEN:

- **agg.**: acon bg2 alum b4.de* am-c b4.de ambr b7.de* anac b4.de* ars b4a.de *Bell* b4.de* bov bg2 calc b4.de* camph bg2 carb-an b4.de* caust b4.de* *Chin* b7.de* cocc b7a.de con b4a.de* graph bg2 *Hyos* b7a.de mag-c bg2 nat-c b4.de* nux-m b7.de* *Nux-v* b7.de* *Petr* b4a.de* *Phos* b4.de* *Rhus-t* b7.de* spig b7a.de* *Staph* b7.de* *Sulph* b4.de*
- **amel.**: *Ant-c* b7a.de* bov b4a.de* **Bry** b7.de* **Hep** b4.de* *M-arct* b7.de mag-m b4.de* *Mez* b4a.de nux-v bg2 **Puls** b7.de* rhus-t bg2 sabad bg2 sel b7a.de sep b4.de* stann bg2

ALCOHOLIC DRINKS agg.: acon bg2 chin bg2 **Ign** bg2 *Nux-v* bg2

ALIVE; sensation of something: syph rb2

BARING teeth: | **amel.**: puls b7.de*

BATHING agg.: ant-c bg2 *Rhus-t* b7a.de

BED:

- **in** bed:
  - **agg.**: *Acon* b7a.de alum b4.de* am-c b4.de* am-m b7.de ambr b7.de* ant-c b7a.de* *Ars* bg2 bar-c b4a.de* bov b4.de bry b7.de* carb-an b4.de* *Caust* b4a.de *Cham* b7.de* clem b4.de* colch bg2 graph b4.de* hell b7.de* kali-c b4.de* *Mag-c* b4.de* mang b4.de* mang-p bg2 **Merc** b4a.de* mez b4.de* nit-ac b4.de* nux-v b7.de* olnd b7.de* petr b4.de* ph-ac b4a.de* phos b4.de* **Puls** b7.de* ran-b b7a.de rhus-t bg2 sabin b7.de* sel b7a.de spig b7.de* *Sul-ac* b4.de*
  - **amel.**: lyc bg2

BEER: | **amel.**: camph ptk1

BENT forward; as if: nit-ac bg2

BITING:

- **agg.**: am-c b4.de* *Bell* b4.de* bry b7.de* carb-an b4.de* caust b4.de* **Coff** b7.de* euph bg2 graph b4.de* hep b4.de* hyos b7.de* ip b7.de* lach b7.de* mag-m bg2 mez ptk1 *Nux-v* bg2 petr b4.de* **Puls** b7.de* rhus-t b7.de* sars b4.de* sep b4.de* staph b7.de* sul-ac b4.de* sulph b4.de* *Thuj* b4a.de
- **amel.**: bell ptk1 caust ptk1 chin ptk1 mur-ac ptk1 ol-an ptk1 *Phyt* ptk1 *Podo* ptk1 prun ptk1
- **elastic**; biting on something | **amel.**: mang b4.de*
- **hands** | **sleep**; during (See MIND - Biting - hands - sleep)
- **hard** which relieves pains; desire to bite on something | **dentition**; during: **Phyt** k*
- **mouth** empty; with: cocc ptk1
- **nails** (See MIND - Biting - nails)
- **teeth** together:
  - **afraid** to bite teeth together (See MIND - Fear - biting)
  - **agg.**: alum b4.de* am-c b4.de* apis b7a.de *Bry* b7.de* **Chin** b7.de* colch b7a.de* graph b4.de* guaj b4.de* hell b7.de* *Hep* b4.de* hyos bg2 lyc bg2 mang b4.de* merc b4.de* mez bg2 nat-m bg2 nit-ac bg2 petr b4a.de ph-ac bg2 phos bg2 puls bg2 rhus-t bg2 sep b4.de* sil bg2 spong bg2 staph bg2 sulph bg2 zinc bg2
    ⁝ **shock** through head, ear and nose; biting sends a: am-c
  - **amel.**: ars b4.de* **Chin** b7.de* cocc b7.de* **Coff** b7.de* *Euph* b4.de* mag-m b4.de* phyt bg2 seneg bg2 *Staph* b7a.de

- **teeth** together: ...
  - **cannot** bite teeth together | **night**: chim
  - **desire** to bite teeth together (See Clenching)
  - **sudden** involuntary: apis k*
- **tumbler** (See MIND - Biting - tumbler)

BLEEDING: am-c bg2 ambr b7.de* ant-c b7a.de* bar-c b4.de* bell bg2 bov b4.de* calc b4a.de carb-v b4a.de* crot-h bg2 lach bg2 ph-ac bg2 phos b4a.de* sep bg2 sulph bg2 *Tarax* b7a.de zinc b4.de*
- **after** | **amel.**: sars b4.de* sel b7.de*
- **sucking** gums; on: rosm lgb1

O - **Gums** (See MOUTH - Bleeding - gums)
- **Hollow** teeth; of: dulc fd4.de graph b4.de* *Merc* b4a.de ph-ac b4.de* tarax h1
  - **right**: tarax b7.de*
- **Molars** | **Lower** molars:
  - **Hollow** | **left**: sulph b4.de*
  - **Upper**: phos b4.de*
    - **right**: am-c b4.de* rosm lgb1
    - **Hollow** | **right**: zinc b4.de*

BLOOD; loss of: | **agg.**: *Chin* b7a.de

BLOOD; rush of:
- **accompanied** by | **pain** (See Pain - accompanied - blood)

BLOW; sensation as from a: (↗*Pain - blow; pain)* calc b4.de* camph b7.de* tarax b7.de*

BLOWING THE NOSE agg.: phos bg2 thuj b4.de*

BLUNT (See Corroded)

BREAD; after: carb-an b4a.de

BREAD CRUMBS agg.: carb-an b4a.de* clem b4.de*

BREAKING off: borx h2 calc mrr1 *Calc-f* mrr1 euph fl-ac k2* lach nat-hchls nat-m b4a.de plb k* sil mrr1* sul-ac [spect dfg1]
- **clenching** jaw; from chronic: syph mrr1

BREATHING through the mouth agg.: *M-arct* b7a.de puls b7.de* sabin b7.de*

BRUSHING, cleaning the teeth:
- **agg.**: bry ptk1 carb-v b4.de* coc-c ptk1 graph bg2 lach bg2* lyc b4.de* ph-ac bg2 ruta b7.de* staph b7.de*
- **amel.**: sep b4.de*

BRUXISM (See Grinding)

BUBBLING sensation, as if bubbles were moving about: nit-ac bg2 spig b7.de*

O - **Hollow** teeth: bell b4.de* *Carb-v* b4a.de lyc b4.de*

CARIES, decayed, hollow: abrot acon k* aloe alum k* alumn k2 *Am-c* k* *Ambr* k* anac k* anan ang k* **Ant-c** k* arg-n bg2 ars asar k* aur k* aur-ar k2 aur-s k2 bac bn* *Bar-c* k* **Bell** k* benz-ac bg2 **Borx** k* *Bov* k* bry k* *Calc* k* calc-f bg2* *Calc-p* k* *Calc-s* calc-sil k2 carb-an k* *Carb-v* k* carbn-s carc gk6* caust k* *Cham* k* *Chin* k* clem k* coca br1 cocc k* coff k* con k* euph k* **Fl-ac** k* *Glon* graph k* guaj bg2 *Hecla* k* *Hep* k* *Hyos* k* ip k* *Kali-bi* *Kali-c* k* *Kali-i* kali-n k* kali-p *Kreos* k* *Lach* k* *Lyc* k* *Mag-c* k* mag-m k* mang k* med meph k* **Merc** k* **Mez** k* **Nat-c** k* nat-m k* nat-p nat-s nat-sil fd3.de• *Nit-ac* k* *Nux-v* k* ox-ac par k* petr k* *Ph-ac* k* *Phos* k* pip-n c2 plan bg2 plat k* **Plb** k* *Puls* k* rheum k* *Rhod* k* *Rhus-t* k* ruta k* sabad k* sabin k* sang sel k* **Sep** k* *Sil* k* spig k* **Staph** k* sul-ac k* *Sulph* k* syph c2* tab *Tarax* k* thuj k* tub mtf33* verat k* zinc k* [kali-f stj1 mag-f stj1]
- **accompanied** by | **breath**; offensive (See MOUTH - Odor - offensive - accompanied - teeth)
- **appear**, as soon as they: *Kreos* k* staph k*
- **children**; premature in: (↗*Crumbling - children)* bac jl2 *Calc* k* *Calc-f* k* *Calc-p* k* carc zzh cocc bro1 coff *Fl-ac* k* hecla bro1 **Kreos** k* merc k2* *Mez* bro1 phos bro1 *Plan* bro1 sil bro1 **Staph** k* tub bro1
  - **syphilitic**: merc mtf33
- **diabetes** mellitus: sul-ac ptk1*
- **painful**: (↗*Pain - hollow)* glycyr-g cte1• kreos tl1 staph mtf33
- **rapid**: ars bar-c *Calc* *Calc-p* *Carb-v* **Fl-ac** k* *Kreos* ptk1 med mez phos plan **Sep** k* staph h1 syph k2
- **sensation** of: agath-a nl2• asar

Caries, decayed, hollow: ...

O - **Crown**: merc bro1 *Staph* bro1
- **Gums**, at edge of: calc gink-b sbd1• nat-sil fd3.de• sil k2 syph k* *Thuj* k*
- **Internal**: sel
- **Molars**:

O - **Upper** | **left**: carb-an b4.de*
- **Roots**, at: agath-a nl2• alum b4a.de am-c k* fl-ac bg2* merc b4a.de* mez k* sil bro1 sulph b4a.de syph bro1 **Thuj** k*
- **Sides** of teeth: mez k* staph k* thuj k*

O - **Outer** side: bac bn

CHATTERING: *Agar* hr1 alum gsy1 am-c bg2 arg-n sne ars bg2 bar-c k* bell bg2 bov b4.de* cact bg2 calc k* calc-caust c1 camph bg2 caps bg2 carb-v h2* chin bg2 cinch a1 cocc coff bg2 colch bg2 gels hr1 hep b4a.de* ign bg2 ip kali-n bg2 kali-p lach bg2* merc bg2 nat-m b4a.de* nat-s bg2* nit-ac bg2 *Nux-v* bg2* phos k* plat b4a.de* plb bg2 rad-br br1* rhus-t bg2 sabad bg2 sars bg2 sphing kk3.fr spig bg2 stann b4.de* sulph bg2 tritic-vg fd5.de visc c1* *Zinc* b4a.de [heroin sdj2]
- **morning** | **waking**; on: phos h2*
- **evening**: plac rzf5•
- **accompanied** by:

O - **Face**; pain in (See FACE - Pain - accompanied - teeth - chattering)
  - **Head**; complaints of (See HEAD - Complaints - accompanied - teeth - chattering)
- **chill**:
  - **with**: am-c h2 ars bg2 bov bg2 bry bg2 calc bg2 camph b7.de* cann-xyz bg2 caps h1* carb-v bg2 chin bg2 cupr b7.de* hep b4.de* ign b7.de* ip h1 kali-n h2 **Lach** b7a.de* merc-c bg2 *Nat-m* b4a.de* nux-v b7.de* phos b4a.de* plac rzf5• plat b4.de* propr sa3• puls b7a.de rad-br ptk1 ran-b b7.de* sabad b7.de* sars h2* stann b4a.de* sulph h2 thuj bg2 zinc bg2
  - **without**: gels hr1
- **cold** drinks agg.; after: elaps a2
- **fear**; from: elaps ptk1
- **fever**; during: ars bg2 *Phos* b4.de* zinc bg2
- **nervous**: gels hr1 kali-p hr1*
- **shivering**; during: caps b7.de
- **sleep** | **during**: puls tl1 tritic-vg fd5.de
- **trembling**; with internal: ant-t k* plac rzf5•

CHEWING:
- **after** chewing agg.: sabin b7.de* *Staph* b7.de*
- **agg.**: alum b4.de* am-c b4a.de* arg-n bg2 arn b7.de *Ars* b4.de* aur b4.de* bov b4.de* **Bry** b7.de* carb-an b4.de* *Carb-v* b4.de* caust b4.de* *Chin* b7.de* cocc b7.de* euph b4.de* graph b4.de* *Hyos* b7.de* kali-c b4.de* lyc bg2 m-ambo b7.de mag-c b4.de* **Merc** b4.de* nat-m b4.de* *Nux-v* b7.de* olnd b7.de* petr b4.de* phos b4.de* puls b7.de* rhus-t b7.de* *Sabin* b7.de* seneg bg2 sil b4.de* spig bg2 spong b7.de* **Staph** b7.de* *Sulph* b4.de* tarax b7.de* teucr b7.de* thuj b4.de* verat b7.de* zinc b4a.de*
- **amel.**: bry b7.de*
- **not** chewing agg.; when: ars b4.de* rhus-t b7.de*

CHILDREN; complaints of teeth in: **Acon** b7.de* arn b7.de* *Bell* bg2 bry b7.de* calc bg2 **Cham** b7.de* cic b7.de* cina b7.de* coff b7.de* cupr b7.de* hyos b7.de* ign b7.de* ip b7.de* *Merc* bg2 nux-v b7.de* op b7.de* puls b7.de* *Rheum* b7a.de rhus-t b7.de* sec b7a.de stram b7.de* sulph bg2

CHILL; during: **Puls** b7.de rhus-t b7.de

CLENCHING teeth together: (↗*MIND - Biting)*
- **agg.** (See GENERALS - Biting - teeth - agg.)
- **amel.** (See GENERALS - Biting - teeth - amel.)
- **desire** to clench teeth together; constant: acet-ac acon k* agar ambr anan bell bg2 bufo calc bg2 camph k* cann-i k* caust k* cob cocc k* cupr *Hyos* k* iod k* lach bg2* laur *Lyc* k* mang merc-i-f k* nux-v k* **Phyt** k* pin-con oss2• *Podo* k* scut c1 spong fd4.de stry tarent [tax jsj7]
  - **clenched** firmly: alum *Bell* k* camph caust bg2 *Cham* b7.de* cic k* cimic bg2 cypra-eg sde6.de• fl-ac bg2 *Hyos* k* merc k* merc-i-f bg2 moni rfm1• phyt bg2 podo k* spong fd4.de *Stann* b4.de* stram sulph h2*
    - **night**: *Hydr-ac* vh moni rfm1• sep k1* *Ther* vh
      - **midnight** | **after**: chinin-s

O - **Molars**: sep h2*
- **sensation** of: plut-n srj7•

- **sleep**; during: bit-ar wht1• cina tl1 marb-w es1• nat-p tl1 tritic-vg fd5.de

CLOSING THE MOUTH agg.: *Mez* b4a.de

COATED (See Mucus; Sordes)

COFFEE agg.: *Bell* b4.de* cann-xyz bg2 canth bg2 carb-v b4a.de *Cham* b7.de* cocc b7a.de *Coff* b7a.de **Ign** b7.de* lach bg2 m-ambo b7.de mang b4.de* *Merc* b4a.de* **Nux-v** b7.de* puls b7a.de* rhus-t b7a.de*

COITION:
- **after**: daph bg2*
- **amel.**: camph b7a.de*

COLD:
- **agg.**: bell bg2 *Calc* bg2 carb-v bg2 *Caust* bg2 *Hell* bg2 *Lach* bg2 merc bg2 **Nat-m** bg2 nit-ac bg2 par bg2 ph-ac bg2 phos bg2 plan bg2 rhus-t bg2 sil bg2 staph bg2 thuj bg2
- **air**:
  - **agg.**: agar bg2 alum b4a.de ant-c bg2 *Arn* b7a.de *Ars* bg2 aur b4a.de **Bell** b4.de* borx b4a.de *Bry* b7.de* *Calc* b4.de* caust b4.de* cham ptk1 chin bg2 chinin-s bg2 *Cina* b7a.de fl-ac bg2 hell bg2 *Hyos* b7.de* kali-c b4.de* kali-n bg2 lyc bg2 *M-ambo* b7.de* m-arct b7.de* mag-c bg2 **Merc** b4.de* mez bg2 *Nat-m* b4a.de nit-ac bg2 nux-m b7.de* nux-v b7.de* par b7.de* petr b4.de* *Ph-ac* bg2 phos b4.de* *Puls* b7a.de rat ptk1 sars b4a.de* sel b7a.de seneg b4.de* sep b4.de* sil b4.de* spig b7.de* **Staph** b7a.de* sul-ac bg2 *Sulph* b4.de* ther bg2 thuj b4.de* tub ptk1
  - **amel.**: ambr bg2 ang bg2 asar bg2 bism bg2 bry bg2 cham bg2 clem bg2* **Coff** bg2 crot-t bg2 ferr bg2 kali-c bg2 laur bg2 mag-c bg2 mag-m bg2 mez ptk1 nat-s bg2* nux-v ptk1 **Puls** b7.de* rhus-t bg2 sel ptk1
  - **drawing** in cold air | **amel.**: mez bg2 nux-v b7.de* puls b7.de*
  - **frosty** air agg.: mez bg2
  - **inspiration** | **amel.**: mez bg2
  - **wet**: *Nux-m* b7a.de
- **applications**:
  - **agg.**: agar b4.de* ant-c ptk1 arg-n bg2* bar-c b4.de* **Calc** b4.de* *Carb-v* bg2 cham bg2 con b4.de *Hell* b7a.de hep ptk1 *Hyos* b7a.de* kali-c bg2* kali-n bg2 lach ptk1 mag-c b4.de* mag-m bg2 *Merc* bg2 merc-i-f ptk1 mez b4a.de *Nat-m* ptk1 nit-ac b4.de* nux-m b7.de* *Nux-v* bg2 par bg2 ph-ac bg2 plb bg2 puls b7.de* rhod ptk1 rhus-t b7.de* sep ptk1 sil bg2 spig b7a.de* *Staph* b7a.de* sul-ac b4a.de sulph bg2 thuj bg2*
  - **amel.**: bism ptk1 *Bry* ptk1 chim ptk1 clem ptk1 *Coff* ptk1 ferr ptk1 nat-s ptk1 *Puls* ptk1
- **bathing** | **agg.**: *Calc* bg2 *Cham* bg2 graph bg2 kali-c bg2 **Merc** bg2 nux-m bg2 nux-v bg2 puls bg2 sep bg2 spig bg2 staph bg2 sulph bg2
- **drinks**:
  - **agg.**: *Acon* b7a.de ant-c b7a.de* bar-c b4.de* borx bg2 bry b7.de* *Calc* b4.de* camph bg2 cann-xyz bg2 carb-an b4a.de* *Cham* b7.de* cina b7.de* colch b7.de* *Graph* b4.de hep b4a.de *M-ambo* b7.de* mang b4.de* **Merc** b4.de* *Mur-ac* b4.de* *Nit-ac* b4a.de nux-m b7.de* **Nux-v** b7.de* *Par* b7a.de plb b7a.de **Puls** b7.de* **Rhus-t** b7.de* *Sars* b4a.de* seneg bg2 sep bg2 sil bg2 *Spig* b7a.de* **Staph** b7.de* *Sulph* b4.de* thuj b4.de*
  - **amel.**: ambr b7.de ang b7.de asar b7.de bry b7.de* cham b7.de clem bg2 laur b7.de puls b7a.de* sel b7a.de
- **food**:
  - **agg.**: agar b4.de* ant-c b7a.de arg-n bg2 *Bell* b4a.de bov b4.de* bry b7.de* *Calc* b4.de* *Carb-v* b4a.de *Caust* b4a.de cham b7.de* con b4.de* hell b7.de* kali-c b4.de* *Kali-n* b4a.de lyc b4.de* **Mag-c** b4a.de mag-m b4.de* *Merc* b4.de* nat-m b4.de* *Nit-ac* b4a.de *Nux-v* b7.de* par b7.de* ph-ac b4.de* *Phos* b4a.de plb b7.de* **Rhus-t** b7.de* sep b4.de* sil b4.de* *Spig* b7a.de sul-ac b4.de* sulph b4.de* thuj b4.de*
  - **amel.**: ambr b7.de* ang b7.de* asar bg2 bism bg2 bry bg2 cham bg2 clem bg2 **Coff** bg2 crot-t bg2 ferr bg2 kali-c bg2 laur bg2 mag-c b4.de* mag-m b4.de* *Mez* b4a.de nat-s bg2 *Phos* b4a.de puls b7a.de* rhus-t bg2 sel b7a.de *Sep* b4a.de
- **hands** | **amel.**: rhus-t b7.de*
- **water**:
  - **agg.**: *Ant-c* b7a.de* arg-n bg2 borx b4a.de* **Bry** bg2 **Calc** bg2 carb-an bg2 *Cham* b7.de* cina bg2 *Graph* b4.de* kali-c b4.de lach bg2 **Merc** bg2 mur-ac bg2 nux-m b7.de* **Nux-v** b7.de* puls b7.de* sang bg2 sars bg2 *Sep* b4.de* **Sil** bg2 spig b7.de* staph b7.de* **Sulph** b4.de*

Cold – water: ...
  - **amel.**: ambr bg2 ang bg2 asar b7.de* bism bg2 *Bry* b7.de* cham b7.de* clem b4.de* **Coff** bg2 crot-t bg2 ferr bg2 hep bg2 kali-c b4.de* laur b7.de* mag-c b4a.de* mag-m bg2 mez b4a.de nat-s bg2 nux-v bg2 *Puls* b7a.de* rhod bg2 rhus-t bg2 sel b7a.de sep b4a.de*
    - **finger**; applied with: *Cham* bg2
    - **followed** by agg.: cham bg2
    - **ice** water: clem ptk1 coff ptk1 ferr ptk1
    - **rinsing**: rumx ptk1

COLD; AFTER TAKING A: **Acon** b7.de* aran bg2 *Bar-c* b4.de* bell b4a.de* *Bry* b7.de* calc b4.de* *Cham* b7.de* chel bg2 chin b7.de* *Dulc* b4a.de* gels bg2 hep b4a.de *Hyos* b7.de* **Ign** b7a.de* *M-arct* b7.de mag-c ptk1 **Merc** b4a.de* nat-c b4.de* nux-m b7.de* **Nux-v** b7.de* phos bg2 **Puls** b7a.de* **Rhus-t** b7.de* sep ptk1 staph b7.de* sulph b4a.de*

COLD AGG.; BECOMING: zinc bg2

COLDNESS: acon alum k* alumn anag anan apis bg2 aran arn bg2 asar k* astac *Carb-v* k* coc-c bg2 cocc cocc-s k* colch k* cop k* dros k* *Gamb* k* grat k* iris-foe kali-chl kola stb3• led *Mez* k* narcot a1 nat-c bg2 *Nit-ac* k* ol-an ox-ac bg1 par petr k* *Ph-ac* k* phos bg2 rat rheum k* sel k* sep k* *Spig* k* spira a1
- **afternoon**: mez k*
- **touch** agg.: spig hr1
- ○ **Edges**: gamb ptk1
- **Incisors**: dros b7.de* m-ambo b7.de petr b4.de*
  - ○ **Lower**: sep b4.de*
    - **right**: aran vh1
  - **Upper**: alum b4.de* asar b7.de* rheum b7.de* spig b7.de*
- **Molars**: ph-ac b4.de* rheum b7.de*
  - ○ **Upper**:
    - **right**: nat-c b4.de*
    - **left**: phos b4.de*
- **Roots**: ph-ac h2
  - **morning**: ph-ac h2
  - **chewing** agg.: ph-ac h2
- **Tips**: ol-an ptk1
- **Upper** teeth: spig b7.de*

COMPLAINTS of teeth: **Acon** ptk1 *Ant-c* ptk1 bell ptk1 bry ptk1 *Calc* ptk1 calc-p ptk1 *Caust* ptk1 **Cham** ptk1 chin ptk1 coff ptk1 kreos ptk1 *Lach* ptk1 **Merc** ptk1 *Mez* br1* nux-v ptk1 plan ptk1 podo ptk1 **Puls** ptk1 *Rhus-t* ptk1 sel br1 **Sep** ptk1 sil ptk1 spig ptk1 staph br1* *Sulph* ptk1 tub-m jl2
- **one** side: calc bg2 **Cham** bg2 chin bg2 coloc bg2 ign bg2 kali-bi bg2 **Merc** bg2 mez bg2 **Nux-v** bg2 ph-ac bg2 plat bg2 **Puls** bg2 *Rhus-t* bg2 spig bg2 sulph bg2
- **alternating** sides: am-m ptk1 ambr ptk1 caps ptk1 chel ptk1 iod ptk1 kali-n ptk1 lyc ptk1 psor ptk1 *Puls* ptk1 stram ptk1 sulph ptk1 *Zinc* ptk1
  - **accompanied** by | **Head**; pain in: kali-p bg2
- **right** side: agar b4a.de* *Agn* b7a.de* alum b4a.de* *Am-c* b4a.de* *Ambr* b7a.de* anac b4a.de* *Ang* b7a.de* apis b7a.de* *Aur* b4a.de* bar-c b4a.de* **Bell** b4a.de* *Bov* b4a.de* brom b4a.de* *Bry* b7a.de* *Calc* b4a.de* *Camph* b7a.de* *Cann-s* b7a.de* canth b7a.de* carb-an b4a.de* carb-v b4a.de* *Caust* b4a.de* chel bg2 *Chin* bg2* *Coff* b7a.de* colch b7a.de* *Coloc* b4a.de* con b4a.de* **Fl-ac** b4a.de* *Graph* b4a.de* *Hell* b7a.de* iod b4a.de* kali-c b4a.de* *Kreos* b7a.de* lach b7a.de* laur b7a.de* *Lyc* b4a.de* *Mag-c* b4a.de* *Mang* b4a.de* *Merc* b4a.de* mez b4a.de* *Nat-c* b4a.de* *Nat-m* b4a.de* *Nit-ac* b4a.de* *Nux-v* b7a.de* olnd b7a.de* *Petr* b4a.de* *Ph-ac* b4a.de* *Plb* b7a.de *Psor* b4a.de* *Puls* b7a.de* *Ran-b* b7a.de* ran-s b7a.de* rhod b4a.de* *Rhus-t* b7a.de* *Ruta* b7a.de* *Sabad* b7a.de* *Sars* b4a.de* *Sep* b4a.de* *Sil* b4a.de* spig b7a.de* spong b7a.de* **Staph** b7a.de* stront-c b4a.de* sulph b4a.de* *Tarax* b7a.de* *Teucr* b7a.de* thuj b4a.de* *Valer* b7a.de* *Verb* b7a.de* zinc b4a.de*
- **left** side: *Acon* b7a.de* *Agar* b4a.de* *Alum* b4a.de* *Am-c* b4a.de* *Am-m* b7a.de* ambr b7a.de* anac b4a.de* *Apis* b7a.de* *Arn* b7a.de* *Asaf* b7a.de* *Asar* b7a.de* *Aur* b4a.de* *Bar-c* b4a.de* bell b4a.de* *Borx* b4a.de* brom b4a.de* *Bry* b7a.de* *Calc* b4a.de* cann-s b7a.de* canth b7a.de* *Carb-an* b4a.de* *Carb-v* b4a.de* **Caust** b4a.de* **Cham** b7a.de* *Chel* b7a.de* *Chin* b7a.de* **Clem** b4a.de* coff b7a.de* *Colch* b7a.de* *Con* b4a.de* *Croc* b7a.de* *Cycl* b7a.de* **Euph** b4a.de* fl-ac b4a.de* graph b4a.de* *Guaj* b4a.de* *Hyos* b7a.de* iod b4a.de* kali-c b4a.de* *Kali-n* b4a.de* *Kreos* b7a.de* *Laur* b7a.de* *Led* b7a.de* lyc b4a.de* *M-arct* b7a.de* *Merc* b4a.de* **Mez** b4a.de* mill b7a.de* nat-c bg2 nat-m b4a.de* *Nux-m* b7a.de* *Nux-v* b7a.de* *Olnd* b7a.de* *Phos* b4a.de* *Puls* b7a.de* ran-s b7a.de* *Rheum* b7a.de* *Rhod* b4a.de* *Rhus-t* b7a.de* sabad b7a.de* *Sabin* b7a.de* *Samb* b7a.de*

- **left** side: ...
Sel b7a.de* *Seneg* b4a.de* **Sep** b4a.de* *Sil* b4a.de* *Spig* b7a.de* spong b7a.de* *Staph* b7a.de* stront-c b4a.de* **Sulph** b4a.de* teucr b7a.de* **Thuj** b4a.de* *Verat* b7a.de* verb b7a.de* *Zinc* b4a.de*
- **accompanied** by:
  - **chill**: euph b4a.de kali-c b4.de* mez b4a.de *Puls* b7.de rhus-t b7.de
  - **fainting**: chin b7.de* *Puls* b7.de* verat bg2
  - **heat**: *Acon* b7a.de ant-c b7a.de hyos b7.de kreos b7a.de rhus-t b7.de
  - **neurological** complaints | **children**; in (See GENERALS - Neurological - children - accompanied - teeth)
  - **palpitation** (See CHEST - Palpitation - accompanied - teeth)
  - **perspiration**: *Merc* b4a.de sep b4a.de
    - **anxious**: clem b4.de*
  - **restlessness** (See MIND - Restlessness - teeth - complaints)
  - **salivation**; profuse: **Bell** bg2 calc b4a.de* caust bg2 cham b7.de* clem b4.de* daph bg2 *Dulc* bg2 kali-bi bg2 **Merc** b4a.de* nux-v b7a.de phos bg2 plan bg2 rheum b7.de* rhod bg2 rhus-t b7.de* stront-c b4a.de*
  - **shivering**: *Puls* b7.de*
  - **sleeplessness**: sil bg2 spig b7.de*
  - **sneezing**: *Cycl* b7a.de
  - **taste**; musty: rhus-t b7.de*
  - **thirst**: *Bell* bg2 *Cham* b7.de* chin bg2 verat bg2
  - **tossing** about in bed: clem b4.de* nat-s bg2
  - **twitching**: **Hyos** b7a.de *Puls* b7a.de
  - **uncover**; aversion to: clem b4a.de
  - **urination**; frequent: olnd b7.de* plan bg2
  - **vexation** (See MIND - Irritability - teeth)
  - **vomit**; inclination to: olnd b7.de*
  - **weariness**: clem b4a.de kreos b7a.de mang b4a.de rhus-t b7.de*
  - **whining** (See MIND - Moaning - teeth)
  - **work**; inability to: clem b4a.de
  - **yawning**: kreos b7a.de
  - ○ **Abdomen**; complaints of lower: carb-v b4.de*
  - **Abdomen**; cramping pain in (See ABDOMEN - Pain - cramping - accompanied - teeth - complaints)
  - **Cheeks**:
    - **coldness** of; sensation of: sel b7a.de
    - **complaints** of: am-c b4.de*
    - **nodosities**: bell b4a.de
    - **pain**: asar b7.de* bism b7.de* borx b4a.de bry b7.de* *Sil* b4a.de staph b7.de* tarax b7.de*
    - **red**: **Acon** bg2 *Bell* bg2 *Cham* b7.de* *M-arct* b7.de nux-m b7.de* nux-v bg2
    - **swelling**: *Am-c* b4a.de *Arn* b7.de* **Ars** b4.de* aur b4.de* bar-c b4a.de* **Bell** b4.de* borx b4a.de* bov b4.de* **Bry** b7.de* calc b4.de* canth b7.de* carb-v bg2 caust b4.de* **Cham** b7.de* chin b7.de* graph b4.de* iod b4a.de* kali-c b4.de* lach b7a.de* lyc b4a.de* *M-arct* b7.de *Mag-c* b4.de* mag-m b4.de* **Merc** b4.de* nat-c b4.de* nat-m b4.de* nit-ac b4.de* **Nux-v** bg2 petr b4.de* ph-ac b4.de* phos b4.de* **Puls** b7.de* samb b7a.de* *Sep* b4.de* *Sil* b4a.de stann b4a.de **Staph** b7.de* *Sulph* b4.de*
      - **sensation** of: samb b7.de*
  - **Chin**; complaints of: cann-s b7.de*
  - **Ears**:
    - **cold**: lach b7.de*
    - **complaints** of: agar b4.de alum b4.de am-c b4.de anac b4.de *Arn* b7a.de ars b4a.de *Bar-c* b4.de bell b4.de borx b4a.de bov b4.de bry b7.de calc b4.de* caust b4.de *Cham* b7.de clem b4.de hell b7.de hep b4a.de iod b4.de kali-c b4.de *Kreos* b7a.de lach b7a.de *Mang* b4.de* *Merc* b4.de *Merc-c* b4a.de *Nat-m* b4.de* nux-m b7.de* nux-v b7.de ph-ac b4a.de phos b4.de plb b7.de *Puls* b7.de ran-s b7a.de *Rhod* b4.de* rhus-t b7a.de sep b4.de *Sil* b4a.de *Spig* b7.de* *Staph* b7a.de sulph b4.de
    - **pain**: cham b7a.de
  - **Eyebrows**; complaints of: *Tarax* b7a.de

- **accompanied** by: ...
  - **Eyes**; complaints of: *Bar-c* b4.de* bov b4.de* *Bry* b7a.de calc b4.de* caust b4.de* cham b7.de* clem b4.de* kali-c b4.de* *Kreos* b7a.de m-arct b7.de *M-aust* b7.de* *Mag-c* b4a.de *Merc-c* b4a.de nat-m b4.de* nux-v b7.de* **Puls** b7a.de samb b7.de* sel b7a.de spig bg2 *Staph* b7.de* sulph b4.de* tarax b7a.de thuj b4.de*
  - **Face**:
    - **complaints** of: am-c b4a.de aur b4a.de *Bell* b4a.de clem b4.de* hyos b7a.de kreos b7a.de led b7.de* *Mag-c* b4a.de mang b4.de* merc b4a.de mez b4a.de *Nit-ac* b4a.de *Nux-v* b7.de*
    - **distorted**: staph b7.de*
    - **heat**: *Acon* b7.de* *Cham* b7.de* graph b4.de* kreos b7a.de olnd b7.de* rhus-t b7.de* sil b4.de* spig b7a.de stann b4a.de staph b7.de*
    - **pain**: ars b4a.de *Bell* b4a.de euph b4a.de *Kali-c* b4a.de *Merc* b4a.de nat-c b4a.de *Puls* b7a.de sil b4a.de
    - **pale**: ars bg2 **Puls** b7.de* *Spig* b7a.de*
    - **red**: **Acon** bg2 *Bell* bg2 cham b7.de* merc bg2 puls bg2 sulph bg2 verat b7a.de*
    - **spots**: nux-v b7.de*
    - **swelling**: borx bg2 cham bg2 verat b7.de*
  - **Fauces**; complaints of: *Nat-m* b4a.de zinc b4.de*
  - **Feet** | **twitching**: mag-c b4a.de
  - **Fingers** | **twitching**: mag-c b4a.de
  - **Forehead**:
    - **complaints** of: *Hyos* b7.de* *Phos* b4a.de sep b4.de*
    - **perspiration**: rhus-t b7.de*
      - **cold**: verat b7.de*
  - **Hands** | **formication**: sep b4a.de
  - **Head**:
    - **coldness**: lach b7a.de
    - **complaints** of: alum b4.de* am-c b4.de* ant-c b7a.de ars b4a.de bar-c b4a.de bell b4.de* borx b4a.de* bov b4.de* bry b7a.de calc b4.de* caust b4.de* clem b4.de* cupr b7a.de euph b4.de* hyos b7.de* kali-c b4.de* kali-n b4a.de *Kreos* b7a.de *Lach* bg2 led b7.de* *Mag-c* b4a.de *Merc* b4.de* mez b4a.de nat-m b4.de* nux-m b7a.de *Nux-v* b7.de* ph-ac b4.de* *Puls* b7a.de rhus-t b7.de* sabad b7.de* sars b4.de* staph b7.de* sulph b4a.de thuj b4.de*
    - **congestion** to: *Acon* b7.de* **Aur** b4a.de *Bell* b4a.de *Caust* b4a.de *Hyos* b7.de* *Puls* b7a.de
    - **heat**: *Aur* b4a.de bell b4a.de
    - **pain**: puls b7a.de verat b7a.de
    - **perspiration**: *Cham* b7.de
  - **Jaw**; lower:
    - **complaints** of: agar b4.de* canth b7.de* cham b7.de* lach b7.de* lyc b4.de* *M-arct* b7.de nux-m b7.de* *Nux-v* b7.de* *Plb* b7.de* sel b7a.de sep b4.de* sil b4.de* staph b7.de* thuj b4.de*
    - **pain**: *M-arct* b7a.de nux-v b7a.de
    - **paralyzed**; as if: nux-m b7a.de
    - **swelling**: camph b7.de* cham b7.de* kali-c b4.de* *Sil* b4a.de* staph b7a.de
  - **Larynx** | **complaints** of: alum b4a.de
  - **Limbs** | **weakness**: clem b4.de*
  - **Lips**; swelling of: bov b4.de* nat-c b4a.de* phos b4a.de
  - **Malar** bones:
    - **complaints** of: clem b4.de* coff b7a.de con b4.de* euph b4a.de kali-c b4.de* kreos b7a.de mag-m b4.de* mang b4.de* mez b4.de* mur-ac b4.de* nux-v b7.de* ph-ac b4a.de phos b4.de* spig b7.de* staph b7.de* sulph b4a.de thuj b4.de*
    - **pain**: *Merc* b4a.de
  - **Maxillary** joints | **spasm**: *Bell* b4a.de **Caust** b4a.de merc b4a.de
  - **Mouth** | **ulcers**: *Merc* b4a.de
  - **Nape** of neck | **pain**: nux-m b7a.de
  - **Nose**:
    - **complaints** of: *Bar-c* b4.de* calc b4.de* caust b4.de*
    - **swelling**: ars b4.de* bov b4.de*
  - **Shoulders**; complaints of: am-c b4.de* rhus-t b7.de*

- **Submaxillary** glands; complaints of: ambr b7.de* camph b7a.de* *Carb-v* bg2 *Cham* b7.de* kali-bi bg2 *Merc* bg2 *Nux-v* bg2 sabad b7.de* *Sep* b4.de* **Staph** b7a.de*
- **Temples**; complaints of: am-m b7.de* ars b4.de* *Bar-c* b4.de* *Bry* b7a.de calc b4.de* caust b4.de* clem b4.de* con b4.de* cupr b7a.de hyos b7.de* *Kreos* b7a.de m-ambo b7.de m-arct b7.de mag-c b4.de* mez b4.de* nux-m b7.de* nux-v b7.de* *Phos* b4a.de rhus-t b7.de* sel b7a.de spig b7a.de sulph b4.de* zinc b4.de*
- **Throat**; complaints of: bry b7.de* lach b7.de* led b7.de* mang b4.de* nat-m b4a.de spig b7a.de zinc b4.de*
- **Upper** limbs; complaints of: mang b4.de* sep b4a.de*

- **alternating** with:

○ • **Ears**; complaints of (See EAR - Complaints - alternating with - teeth)
- **Mammae**:
  - **left**: kali-c ptk1
  - **complaints** of (See CHEST - Mammae - alternating with - teeth)

- **dentition** (See Dentition - difficult)

▽ - **extending** to:

○ • **Cheek**: *Bry* bg2 sep bg2 sil bg2
- **Ears**: alum ptk1 ant-c ptk1 cham ptk1 kali-bi ptk1 lach ptk1 mang ptk1 merc bg2* mez ptk1 plan bg2* puls ptk1 rhod ptk1
- **Eyes**: agar bg2 alum bg2 am-c bg2 ars bg2 bar-c bg2 **Bell** bg2 borx bg2 bov bg2 *Bry* bg2 calc bg2 caust bg2 *Cham* bg2 clem bg2 hell bg2 iod bg2 kali-bi bg2 kali-c bg2 kreos bg2 lach bg2 mang bg2 **Merc** bg2 nat-m bg2 nux-m bg2 nux-v bg2 phos bg2 plb bg2 **Puls** bg2 rhod bg2 rhus-t bg2 *Sep* bg2 **Spig** bg2 **Staph** bg2 *Sulph* bg2
- **Face**: alum ptk1 ant-c ptk1 cham ptk1 *Cupr* bg2 kali-bi ptk1 lach ptk1 mang ptk1 *Merc* ptk1 mez ptk1 plan ptk1 puls ptk1 rhod ptk1 *Staph* bg2
- **Finger** tips: coff ptk1
- **Temples**: merc ptk1 mez ptk1

○ - **Canines** (See Canines)

- **Hollow** teeth (= carious teeth): alum b2.de am-c b2.de ambr b2.de anac b2.de ang b2.de *Ant-c* b2.de asar b2.de *Bar-c* b2.de **Bell** b2.de **Borx** b2.de *Bov* b2.de bry b2.de *Calc* b2.de carb-an b2.de carb-v b2.de caust b2.de *Cham* b2.de chin b2.de clem b2.de cocc b2.de coff b2.de con b2.de graph b2.de hep b2.de *Hyos* b2.de ip b2.de kali-c b2.de kali-n b2.de kreos b2.de *Lach* b2.de *Lyc* b2.de m-ambo b2.de **M-arct** b2.de m-aust b2.de *Mag-c* b2.de mag-m b2.de mang b2.de *Merc* b2.de **Mez** b2.de **Nat-c** b2.de nat-m b2.de nit-ac b2.de *Nux-v* b2.de par b2.de petr b2.de ph-ac b2.de *Phos* b2.de *Plat* b2.de **Plb** b2.de puls b2.de rheum b2.de rhod b2.de *Rhus-t* b2.de ruta b2.de sabad b2.de *Sabin* b2.de sel b2.de **Sep** b2.de sil b2.de *Spig* b2.de **Staph** b2.de sul-ac b2.de sulph b2.de **Tarax** b2.de thuj b2.de verat b2.de zinc b2.de
- **Incisors** (See Incisors)
- **Location**; without precise: acon bg2 aran bg2 arn bg2 clem bg2 kali-c bg2 merc bg2 nit-ac bg2 nux-v bg2 rat bg2 rhus-t bg2 sulph bg2 verat bg2
- **Lower** teeth: *Agar* b2.de* alum b2.de* *Am-c* b2.de* am-m b2.de* ambr b2.de* anac b2.de* ang b2.de* ant-t b2.de* arg-met b2.de* arn b2.de* ars bg2 asar b2.de* *Aur* b2.de* bar-c b2.de* **Bell** b2.de* borx b2.de* bov b2.de* *Bry* b2.de* calc b2.de* **Canth** b2.de* carb-an b2.de* *Carb-v* b2.de* **Caust** b2.de* **Cham** b2.de* *Chin* b2.de* clem b2.de* cocc b2.de* coff b2.de* colch b2.de* coloc b2.de* con b2.de* dros b2.de* euph b2.de* graph b2.de* guaj b2.de* hell b2.de* hep b2.de* hyos b2.de* ign b2.de* kali-c b2.de* kali-n b2.de* kreos b2.de* **Laur** b2.de* lyc b2.de* m-ambo b2.de **M-arct** b2.de* mag-c b2.de* mag-m b2.de* *Mang* b2.de* merc b2.de* mez b2.de* mur-ac b2.de* **Nat-c** b2.de* nat-m b2.de* nit-ac b2.de* nux-m b2.de* nux-v b2.de* olnd b2.de* par b2.de* petr b2.de* ph-ac b2.de* *Phos* b2.de* plat b2.de* **Plb** b2.de* puls b2.de* ran-s b2.de* rheum b2.de* rhod b2.de* *Rhus-t* b2.de* ruta b2.de* sabad b2.de* *Sabin* b2.de* *Sars* b2.de* sel b2.de* seneg b2.de* sep b2.de* *Sil* b2.de* spig b2.de* spong b2.de* squil b2.de* **Staph** b2.de* stront-c b2.de* sul-ac b2.de* sulph b2.de* teucr b2.de* thuj b2.de* *Verat* b2.de* verb b2.de* **Zinc** b2.de*
- **Molars** (See Molars)
- **Roots**: am-c bg2 cann-xyz bg2 caust bg2 cham bg2 coloc bg2 graph bg2 indg bg2 iod bg2 kali-c bg2 lach bg2 lyc bg2 mag-c bg2* mang bg2 meph bg2 merc-i-f bg2* mez bg2 mur-ac bg2 nicc bg2 plan bg2 puls bg2 sep bg2 staph bg2 stram bg2 teucr bg2 zinc bg2
- **Row**; in a whole: ars ptk1 aur ptk1 carb-v ptk1 cham bg2 glon ptk1 lach ptk1 mag-c ptk1 mag-p ptk1 **Merc** bg2* nat-m ptk1 *Nux-v* ptk1 psor ptk1 rhus-t bg2 sep ptk1 spig ptk1 **Staph** bg2* zinc ptk1

Complaints of teeth: ...

- **Sockets**: staph br1
- **Tips**: bar-c bg2 bell bg2 carb-an bg2 chin bg2 cic bg2 dros bg2 gamb bg2 lyc bg2
- **Upper** teeth: acon bg2 *Agar* b2.de* *Alum* b2.de* **Am-c** b2.de* am-m b2.de* ambr b2.de* ang b2.de* aran bg2* arn b2.de* asar b2.de* *Aur* b2.de* *Bell* b2.de* borx b2.de* bov b2.de* bry b2.de* *Calc* b2.de* canth b2.de* carb-an b2.de* **Carb-v** b2.de* caust b2.de* cham b2.de* **Chin** b2.de* clem b2.de* coff b2.de* colch b2.de* con b2.de* cycl b2.de* euph b2.de* graph b2.de* guaj b2.de* hell b2.de* hyos b2.de* *Kali-c* b2.de* kali-n b2.de* **Kreos** b2.de* lyc b2.de* m-ambo b2.de m-arct b2.de m-aust b2.de mag-c b2.de* *Mag-m* b2.de* mang b2.de* merc b2.de* *Mez* b2.de* mur-ac b2.de* *Nat-c* b2.de* *Nat-m* b2.de* *Nit-ac* b2.de* nux-m b2.de* nux-v b2.de* petr bg2 ph-ac b2.de* *Phos* b2.de* plat b2.de* puls b2.de* *Ran-s* b2.de* rheum b2.de* rhod b2.de* rhus-t b2.de* sabad b2.de* sars b2.de* seneg b2.de* sep b2.de* sil b2.de* *Spig* b2.de* *Spong* b2.de* staph b2.de* *Sul-ac* b2.de* sulph b2.de* teucr b2.de* *Thuj* b2.de* verat b2.de* *Verb* b2.de* **Zinc** b2.de*
  - **alternating** with | **Lower** teeth: acon ptk1 laur ptk1 nat-m ptk1 puls ptk1 rat ptk1 rhod ptk1

CONGESTION to teeth; sensation of: *Acon* b7.de* arn b7.de* *Aur* b4a.de* *Bell* bg2 **Calc** b4a.de* cham bg2 *Chin* b7.de* clem b4a.de coff b7.de* ferr bg2 hep b4a.de *Hyos* b7.de* iod bg2 mez bg2 *Nux-v* b7.de* phos bg2 plat bg2 *Puls* b7.de* sep bg2 sulph bg2

CORRODED SENSATION: acon agar h2* **Am-c** k* amph a1 ars k* asaf *Asar* b7a.de atro k13 *Aur* k* bell k* berb k* brom cain calc ptk1 caps k* carbn-s caust cench k2 chin chion ptk1 colch coloc bg2* cop k* cor-r daph dig ptk1 *Dulc* k* ferr bg2 ferr-ma k* fl-ac k* gad a1 grat ptk1 *Iod* k* iris bg3* kali-c h2* kali-chl kali-m k2 **Lach** k* lith-c lyc bg2* lys bg2 lyss k* merc k* merc-c bg2 merc-i-f ptk1 **Mez** k* *Nat-m* k* nit-ac bg2 nux-m b7.de* ox-ac k* parth gm1 petr bg2* ph-ac k* phos k* psor bg2* puls b7.de* ran-s k* *Rob* bg2* ruta ptk1 sedi a1 *Sep* k* sil k* spong k* staph b7.de* stront-c *Sul-ac* k* *Sulph* k* *Tarax* k* tart-ac a1 thuj b4a.de valer ptk1 *Zinc* k* [heroin sdj2]

- **left** side: cor-r
- **night**: mez h2*
- **chewing** agg.: spong h1* tarax h1*
- **covered** with lime; as if: nux-m
- **eructations** agg.: asar bg2 petr bg2 tarax bg2
  - **sour**: asar a3 petr h2 tarax a1
- **menses**; during: *Merc*
- **painful**: lyc h2*
- **vomiting**; from: chion ptk1 rob ptk1
  - **sour**: nat-p bg2 psor bg2 puls bg2 rob bg2 sacch sul-ac bg2

○ - **Incisors**: kali-c b4.de* stront-c b4.de* sul-ac b4.de*

○ • **Lower**: agar b4.de*
- **Upper**: nit-ac b4.de* sil b4a.de

- **Molars**: aur b4.de* spong b7.de*

○ • **Lower** | **Hollow**: nit-ac b4.de*

COUGH agg.: lyc b4.de*

- **diabetes**; in: sec bg2

CRACKING when rubbing: sel k* squil bg2

CRAWLING: (↗*Formication; Itching)* acon b7a.de* arn bg2 bar-c k* borx k* castm k* *Cham* k* dulc fd4.de graph h2* indg bg2 kali-i lach bg2 mag-m k* merc-i-f bg2 mur-ac k* nat-c h2* ol-an rhus-t k* stront-c

- **cold**: nat-c h2*

○ - **Incisors**: borx b4a.de mur-ac b4a.de stront-c b4.de*

- **Lower** teeth: *Mur-ac* b4a.de
- **Molars**:

○ • **Upper** | **right**: *Mur-ac* b4a.de nat-c b4.de* sars b4.de*

- **Root**, at: sars h2*
- **Upper** teeth: cham b7.de*

CRUMBLING: anan ant-c bro1 arg-n bg2* aur bg2 bell bg2 borx k* *Calc* *Calc-f* k* *Calc-p* k* crot-h bg1 epig vh *Euph* k* *Fl-ac* *Kreos* bg1* *Lach* k* med k* merc bro1 phos-h c2* plan ptk1 **Plb** k* ruta fd4.de *Sabad* b7.de* sec bg2 spig bg2* *Staph* k* sul-ac k* syph bro1 *Thuj* k*

- **children**; in: (↗*Caries - children)* staph mrr1* thuj mtf33

CRUSTS, black (See Mucus - black - crusts)

CUPPED: staph bro1 *Syph* bro1 thuj ptk1 vario ptk1

- **children**; in: syph k*

DARK spots (See Discoloration - dark - spots)

DECAYED (See Caries)

DEFORMED: sil gk syph jl2
- **distorted**: sil gk syph k2*

DENTAL FISTULA (See MOUTH - Fistula - gums)

DENTITION: *(↗GENERALS - Children)*
- **difficult**: *(↗GENERALS - Convulsions - dentition; GENERALS - Weakness - dentition; MIND - Shrieking - dentition)* **Acon** b7.de* *Aeth* hr1* agar zr am-c bg2 *Ant-c* hr1* *Ant-t* hr1* *Apis* kr1 *Arn* b7.de* **Ars** b4a.de* arund c1 aster ggd1 bac jl2 *Bell* b4a.de* *Bism* hr1* **Borx** b4a.de* *Bry* b7.de* **Calc** k* calc-f bg2* **Calc-p** k* *Canth* hr1* *Caust* hr1* **Cham** k* cheir bro1 chlol hr1* chlor c1 cic k* cimic c1 *Cina* b7.de* *Coff* b7.de* *Colch* bg2* *Coloc* hr1* cupr k* cypr br1* dol kr1* *Dulc* hr1* *Ferr* bg2* *Ferr-p* hr1* *Gels* hr1* *Graph* hr1* *Hecla* c1* *Hell* hr1* hep k* hyos k* *Ign* k* *Ip* b7.de* *Kali-br* hr1* *Kreos* k* *Lyc* hr1* *Mag-c* b4a.de* **Mag-m** bg2* mag-p kr1* *Meli* hr1* *Merc* b4a.de* *Merc-c* bg2 mill c1 nat-m c1 nit-ac b4a.de* *Nux-m* bg2* **Nux-v** b7.de* op b7.de* passi c1* phos bg2 *Phys* hr1* *Phyt* k* plat c1 plect c1 *Podo* k* *Psor* hr1* puls b7.de* *Rheum* k* *Rhus-t* b7.de* scut c1 sec k* sep k* **Sil** k* sol-ni bro1 stann k* **Staph** j5.de* stram b7.de* sul-ac hr1* **Sulph** b4a.de* syph c1* tarent ggd1 *Ter* c1* thuj bg2 til c1 tub c* tub-k c1 *Verat* hr1* *Zinc* bg2* zinc-br c1* [cupr-act stj2 cupr-f stj2 cupr-m stj2 cupr-p stj2]
  - **accompanied** by:
    - **diarrhea** (See RECTUM - Diarrhea - dentition)
    - **fever** (See FEVER - Dentition)
    - **salivation**: borx bro1 *Hell* kr1* helon ptk1* *Merc* kr1* *Nat-m* kr1* **Sil** kr1*
    - **worms** in children; complaints of: *Cina* bro1 merc bro1 **Sil** vh stann bro1
    - **Brain**; complaints of (See HEAD - Brain; complaints of - dentition)
  - ○ **Incisors** | **Lower**: *Kali-c* b4a.de
  - **Wisdom** teeth: *(↗Wisdom)* *Calc* cheir ferr-pic st *Fl-ac* *Mag-c* k* positr nl2• **Sil** k1*
- **painful** (See difficult)
- **slow**: aster jl* *Bac* bn* **Calc** k* calc-f sf1.de **Calc-p** k* cham pd *Ferr* hr1 *Fl-ac* k* mag-c k* *Mag-m* k* merc sf1.de nep jl phos sf1.de *Phyt* hr1* **Sil** k* sulfa jl sulph sf1.de tarent ggd thuj sf1.de **Tub** bg3* *Zinc* hr1

DINNER: | **before** | **agg.**: sars bg2
- **during** | **amel.**: rumx ptk1

DIRTY looking: *All-c* aur-m-n caps merc bg2 pyrog bg2

DISCHARGE from carious tooth: sulph h2*

DISCOLORATION: *Bac* bn fl-ac mrr1
- **black**: ant-c bro1 *Arg-n* k* calc k2 **Chin** k* *Chlor* *Con* fl-ac ptk1 gaert pte1*• ign k* kreos k* **Merc** k* merc-c b4a.de merl *Nit-ac* phos k* phos-h bro1 plb k* puls sep k* *Squil* k* **Staph** k* syph k* *Thuj* k*
  - **after** aching: sep
  - **in** streaks: staph k*
  - **spots**: kreos ptk1 lyc ser squil ptk1
- **brown**, sooty: chlor suis-em rly4•
- **dark**: *Chin* **Fl-ac** sabin suis-em rly4•
  - **spots**: kreos
- **gray**: **Merc** k* phos k* plb k*
  - **greenish** gray: x-ray sp1
- **green**: bac bn
  - **greenish** yellow: bac bn
- **spotted**: nat-f sp1 syph k2
- **yellow**: *All-c* k* allox tpw3 aloe bg2 ars k* asc-t bell bg2 brom bg2 bry bg2 cadm-met sp1 *Iod* k* kali-c k2 *Lyc* k* med k* *Merc* k* nit-ac k* ph-ac k* plb k* podo fd3.de* psor jl2 *Sil* k* sul-ac bg2 *Thuj* k*
  - **eating**; after: med jl2

DISTENDED; as if: coloc bg2 laur bg2 merc-c bg2 nicc bg2 nux-m bg2 puls bg2 spig bg2
- ○ **Roots**: cham bg2

DRAWN; as if:
- **inward**: coc-c bg2 rhus-t bg2 sel bg2 stann bg2
- **together**: carb-v bg2
- **upward**: coc-c bg2 rhus-t bg2 sel bg2 stann bg2

DRINKING:
- **after** | **agg.**: cham b7.de* spig b7.de
- **agg.**: am-c bg2 caust b4.de* **Cham** b7a.de* dros bg2 lach bg2 rhus-t bg2 sabin b7.de* sil bg2 spig bg2 squil b7.de
- **amel.**: sel b7a.de spig b7.de*

DRY; sensation as if: asaf b7.de* chin b7.de* ign b7.de* merc-i-f bg1* rhus-t b7.de* ulm-c jsj8•

DULL, feel (See Corroded)

DWARFED: bac bn* staph bro1 *Syph* k*

EATING:
- **after**:
  - **agg.**: alum b4.de* ant-c b7a.de* **Bell** b4.de* borx b4a.de* **Bry** b7.de* *Cham* b7.de* *Chin* b7.de* **Coff** b7a.de* euph bg2 euphr b7.de graph b4.de* **Ign** b7.de* kali-c b4.de* lach b7a.de* lyc b4.de* *M-arct* b7.de mag-c b4.de* merc b4.de* nat-c b4.de* nat-m b4a.de* **Nux-v** b7.de* *Ph-ac* b4a.de plan bg2 rhus-t b7.de* sabin b7.de* sep b4.de* sil b4.de* spig b7.de* stann b4a.de **Staph** b7.de* *Sulph* b4.de*
    - **3** hours after: rhod bg2
  - **amel.**: am-c b4.de* ambr b7.de* arn b7.de* calc b4.de* laur b7.de* rhus-t b7.de*
- **before** | **agg.**: ign bg2 nux-v b7.de*
- **not** eating; when | **amel.**: cocc b7.de*
- **while**:
  - **agg.**: alum b4.de* am-c b4.de* ant-c b7a.de* arn b7.de* ars bg2 aur b4.de* **Bell** b4.de* **Bry** b7.de* calc b4.de* canth b7.de* carb-an b4.de* *Carb-v* b4.de* caust b4.de* *Cham* b7.de* chim ptk1 clem b4.de* cocc b7.de* colch bg2 con b4.de* euph b4.de* graph b4.de* *Hep* b4.de* ign bg2 iod b4.de* *Kali-c* b4.de* laur b7.de* lyc b4a.de* m-arct b7.de mag-c b4.de* mag-m b4.de* **Merc** b4.de* *Nat-c* b4.de* nux-m b7.de* petr b4.de* ph-ac b4.de* **Phos** b4.de* *Puls* b7.de* sabin b7.de* sang bg2 sep b4.de* sil b4.de* squil b7.de* *Staph* b7.de* *Sulph* b4.de* thuj b4.de*
  - **amel.**: bell b4.de* bry bg2 cham b7.de* ign ptk1 ip ptk1 m-arct b7.de nit-ac b4a.de* ph-ac bg2 plan ptk1 *Rhod* b4.de* sil b4.de* spig b7.de*
  - **end** of eating: ign b7.de

EDGE; feel as if on (See Corroded)

EDGES feel sharp and hurt gums: aloe k* fl-ac bg2 lyc bg2 mez bg2 spig bg2

ELONGATION; sensation of: agar k* all-c k* *Alum* k* *Am-c* k* amph a1 anac k* **Ant-t** k* arg-n arn k* *Ars* k* ars-i *Aur* k* aur-ar k2 aur-i k2 aur-s k2 bell k* berb k* *Borx* k* brom *Bry* k* bufo calad *Calc* k* calc-sil k2 *Camph* k* caps k* carb-an k* *Carb-v* k* caul **Caust** k* **Cham** k* chel chinin-s chr-ac k* cinnb clem k* cob cocc k* *Colch* k* coloc ptk1 com crot-h daph ferr a1 fic-m gya1 form k* gamb k* *Glon* gran k* hell *Hep* hyos k* iod irid-met srj5• iris kali-c b4.de* *Kali-i* k* kreos k* **Lach** k* lachn laur k* lil-t a1 *Lyc* k* **Mag-c** k* mag-m k* *Merc* k* *Merc-c* *Merc-i-f* k* **Mez** k* mur-ac nat-c b4a.de *Nat-m* k* nat-s k* nicc *Nit-ac* k* nux-m *Nux-v* k* pall parth br1* petr k* *Phyt* k* *Plan* k* ptel k* rat k* rheum b7.de* rhod b4a.de *Rhus-t* k* sanic *Sep* k* *Sil* k* spig spira a1 spong stann k* *Staph* *Sulph* k* symph fd3.de• vip wies a1 *Zinc* k*
- **morning**: ars h2* petr h2* plan a1
- **night** | **bed** agg.; in: anac mag-c h2
- **air** agg.; in open: alum cob
- **bed** agg.; in: lachn c1
- **chewing** agg.: alum brom chel hyos k*
- ○ **Canines**: petr h2*
  - ○ **Lower**: petr b4.de*
- **Decayed** teeth: bov a1 brom a1 carb-an h2* *Clem* hr1 *Cob* a1 cocc a1 *Hep* k* hyos h1* *Plb* rheum h rhus-t h1*
- **Hollow** teeth: borx b4a.de bov b4.de* calc b4a.de clem b4.de* hep b4a.de hyos b7.de* lach b7.de* rheum b7.de* rhus-t b7.de* spig b7a.de
- **Incisors**: agar k* bell k* gamb k* *Lyc* a1 mag-m ozone sde2• pall rat sep b4.de* spig b7a.de sulph h2* tep a1
  - ○ **Upper**: mag-m b4.de* sulph b4.de
- **Lower** teeth: chel a1 coc-c a1 petr a1 sabin b7.de*
- **Molars**: all-c a1 bond a1 *Bry* b7.de* mag-c a1 phos a1 rat a1 sulph a1
  - **left**: mez b4.de*
  - ○ **Hollow**: sep b4.de*
  - **Lower**: hell b7.de* laur b7.de* sil b4.de*

EMOTIONS agg.: acon b7a.de cann-s b7a.de phos b4a.de

ENAMEL deficient: *Calc-f* k* fl-ac ptk1 merc a1 sil k* tab a1

ERUCTATIONS agg.; sour: petr bg2 tarax bg2

ERYSIPELAS; after: am-c b4a.de *Bell* b4a.de *Graph* b4a.de

EXERTION:
- **agg.**: chim ptk1

EXFOLIATION: *(↗Looseness - falling)* arg-n bg2 lach bg2 staph bg2

FALLING out (See Looseness - falling)

FEVER; during: *Rhus-t* b7.de

FILLING teeth agg.; after: mag-p bg2

FISTULA (See MOUTH - Fistula - gums)

FOOD: | **particles** | **agg.**: nux-v b7.de* *Staph* b7.de*
- **remaining** in hollow tooth: mag-m bg2

FOREIGN BODY in teeth; sensation of: calc-p bg2 gels bg2 kali-c bg2 nat-m bg2
O - **Hollow** teeth: kali-c b4a.de

FORMICATION: *(↗Crawling; Itching)* bar-c graph a1 nat-c h2 rhus-t a1 tarent a1
- **evening**: bar-c *Rhus-t* a1
- **painful**: bar-c rhus-t h1

FRUIT agg.: nat-c b4.de* nat-s ptk1 tarax b7.de*

FUZZY; as if: calc-caust bg1* hyper bg1

GINGIVAL FISTULA (See MOUTH - Fistula - gums)

GRINDING: *(↗FACE - Chewing)* *Acon* k* agar bg2 alco a1 aloe sne ant-c k* **Apis** k* arg-n bg2 *Arn* k* *Ars* k* *Art-v* asaf k* atro aur bac bn bar-c k* **Bell** k* borx bg2 bov bg2 *Bry Calc* k* camph k* cann-i bro1 cann-xyz bg2 *Canth* k* *Carb-ac* carc gk cass a1 *Caust* k* *Cham* k* chin mtf11 *Cic* k* cic-m a1 *Cina* k* coca-c sk4• *Cocc* b7a.de coff k* colch k* con k* *Crot-h* k* *Cupr* k* cycl bg2 ferr bg2 *Glon* bg1* *Grat Hell* k* **Hyos** k* ign k* irid-met srj5• kali-br bg2* kali-c b4a.de* *Laur Lyc* k* lyss k* *Merc* k* merc-i-f bg2 morph k* mygal bro1 nux-m bg2 nux-v k* olib-sac wmh1 op phos k* *Phys* bro1 phyt bg2* plan bro1 *Plb* k* *Podo* k* psor bg2 puls sne *Santin* bro1 sec k* *Sep* k* sil gk spig bro1 *Stram* k* suis-em rly4• *Sulph* k* syph tab k* thuj k* *Tub* k2* *Verat* k* vip bg2 *Zinc* k* [spect dfg1]
- **morning** | **awake**; as soon as: ant-c conv
- **night**: *Atis* zzc1•
- **accompanied** by:
  - **cough** (See COUGH - Accompanied - teeth; COUGH - Accompanied - teeth - grinding)

O · **Head**:
  - **complaints** of (See HEAD - Complaints - accompanied - teeth - grinding)
  - **rolling** of head (See HEAD - Motions of - rolling - accompanied - teeth)
- **anger**; after: aloe sne kali-c h2*
- **brain** complaints, in: grat k2
- **chill**; during: acon bg2 ant-c k* apis k* ars k* bell bg2 *Calc* k* cham k* con bg2 hyos bg2 ign bg2 lyc k* phos k* stram k*
- **convulsive**: acon vh1 ars *Bell* bufo ptk1 *Caust Coff* k* (non:ferr slp) ferr-m a1* hyos ptk1 lyc phos *Zinc* k*
- **epilepsy**: *Bufo* hyos mrr1* plb gk sulph tarent
- **fear**; from: plb ptk1
  - **children**; in: kali-br tl1
- **maniacal** rage, during: acon ars *Bell Hyos* k* lyc phos sec *Stram*
- **menses**:
  - **after** | **agg.**: verat b7a.de
  - **close** of; towards: verat k*
  - **during** | **agg.**: coff b7a.de verat b7.de
  - **suppressed** menses; from: hell b7a.de
- **sexual** excitement; during: agn a1
- **shivering**; during: stram b7.de

Grinding: ...
- **sitting** agg.: ant-c k* ars
- **sleep** agg.; during: *Acon* agar k* aloe sne *Ant-c* k* apis bg2 **Ars** k* asaf atis zzc1• aur-ar k2 aur-s k2 **Bac** bn* **Bell** k* *Bry* calc k* *Cann-i* k* cann-xyz bg2* carc mlr1• carl a1* caust cic bro1 **Cina** k* clerod-i bnj1 cocc bg2 *Coff* colch k* con k* *Crot-h* emb-r bnj1 galeoc-c-h gms1• gran a1 *Hell* k* *Hyos* k* *Ign* k* *Kali-br* k* *Kali-c* k* kali-p kola stb3• lac-d **Lyc** b4a.de *Merc* k* *Mygal* nat-p k* nux-v mrr1 phos sne pin-con oss2• plan k* *Plb* k* *Podo* k* psor k* puls sne *Santin* k* sep k* spig bro1 *Stram* k* suis-em rly4• sulph fs* thuj **TUB** k* *Verat* k* *Zinc* k* zinc-m a1 [ant-m stj2 ant-met stj2 ant-t stj2 bism-sn stj2 mag-sil stj2 *Spect* dfg1]
- **stool** agg.; during: podo bg2

HEADACHE; after: | **agg.**: ign b7.de*

HEAT; during: | **agg.**: am bg2 hyos b7.de rhus-t b7.de

HEAT; sensation of: *Arn* bg2 **Bar-c** bg2 caust bg2 chel bg1* chin bg2 fl-ac bg2* graph bg2 *Kali-c* bg2 *Mag-c* bg2 *Merc* bg2 merc-c bg2 mez bg2 nat-m bg2 **Nux-v** bg2 **Ph-ac** bg2 sil bg2 spong bg2 sulph bg2 zinc bg2
O - **Upper** teeth | **left**: *Fl-ac* k*

HEATED; from becoming: acon b7a.de

HEAVINESS: cham bg2 chel bg2 cocc k* fl-ac bg1* sabin k* sep k* verat b7.de*
O - **Incisors**: cocc b7.de*
O · **Upper**: sep b4.de*

HOLLOW; sensation as if: ars b4a.de bell b4a.de mag-c b4a.de merc b4a.de

HOLLOW teeth (See Caries; Complaints - hollow)

HONEY: | **agg.**: nat-c b4.de*

INCRUSTATIONS: plb k*

INFLAMMATION:
O - **Dentin**: **Merc**
- **Pulp**: bell bro1
- **Roots** (See Abscess)

INJURY, dental work; complaints after: *(↗Nerves)* staph bg2

IRREGULAR: bac bn syph jl2
O - **Lower teeth** | **scrofulous** child with mesenteric disease; in a: phos k*

ITCHING in: *(↗Crawling; Formication)* alum anac bamb-a stb2.de• borx h2* carbn-s bg2 castm bg2 caust bg2 cham k* clem k* *Kali-c* k* kali-n k* lach bg2 mag-c bg2 mur-ac k* par b7.de* prun bg2 puls k* rhod b4a.de spong k* zinc bg2
- **air** agg.; in open: anac mag-c h2
- **supper** agg.; after: kali-c k*

O - **Hollow** teeth: calc b4a.de
- **Incisors** | **Lower** | **left**: sulph b4.de*
  - **Upper**: mez b4.de*
- **Molars**:

O · **Lower**:
  - **right**: staph b7.de*
  - **left**: alum b4.de*
- · **Upper**:
  - **right**: alum b4.de*
  - **Hollow** | **left**: kali-n b4.de*

JERKS: acon bg2 anac b4a.de *Ars* b4a.de *Bar-c* b4.de* bell b4.de* calc bg2* castm bg2 caust b4.de* cham b7.de* *Colch* b7a.de cycl bg2 euph b4.de* euphr ptk1 hep bg2 hyper bg2 indg bg2 ip ptk1 lyc b4a.de* m-ambo b7.de* *M-arct* b7.de* mang b4.de* meph bg2 merc b4.de* nat-s bg2 nux-m b7a.de* *Nux-v* b7.de* petr h2* plat b4.de* *Puls* b7.de* rhod bg2* *Rhus-t* b7.de* sep b4.de* sil b4.de* spig bg2 *Sulph* b4.de*
O - **Hollow** teeth (= carious teeth) bell b4.de* kreos bg2 spig b7.de*
- **Incisors**: zinc b4.de*
- **Molars**: nux-m b7.de* sep b4.de*
  - **right**: carb-v b4.de*

O · **Hollow**: carb-v b4.de* *Merc* b4.de*
  - **Lower molars** | **right**: zinc b4.de*

- **Molars**: ...
  - **Upper**: zinc b4.de*
    - **right**: lyc b4.de* ph-ac b4.de*
    - **left**: nux-m b7.de*

LARGE and swollen; sensation as if: berb ptk1 borx calc k* calc-caust c1 caust cinnb fic-m gya1 nux-m k* sil k* spong vip

LOCATION of teeth has changed; as if (See Moved)

LONG; feel too (See Elongation)

LOOSENESS of: acon b7.de* aids nl2• *Alumn* *Am-c* k* *Arg-n* bg2 arn k* *Ars* k* *Aur* k* aur-ar k2 aur-m *Aur-m-n* aur-s k2 bar-c bar-i k2 bar-m k* borx ptk1 *Bry* k* *Bufo* calc k* calc-f ptk1 calc-sil k2 camph k* *Caps* b7a.de **Carb-an** k* **Carb-v** k* *Carbn-s* **Caust** k* cham k* chel k* *Chin* k* chlam-tr bcx2• cist k2 cocc k* colch k2 com *Con* k* cop a1 crot-h dros k* elaps eupi a1 *Flav* jl2 gels gran graph b4.de* *Hep* k* **Hyos** k* ign k* iod *Kali-bi* *Kali-c* k* kali-m k2 kali-n kali-p lac-c lach k* *Lyc* k* m-ambo b7.de *Mag-c* k* mag-s **Merc** k* **Merc-c** k* merc-d a1 merl a1 *Mur-ac* naja nat-ar nat-c k* nat-hchls *Nat-m* k* nat-p nat-s k* **Nit-ac** k* *Nux-m* k* *Nux-v* k* olnd k* op k* *Ph-ac* *Phos* k* phyt plan plat b4.de* *Plb* k* plut-n srj7• *Psor* k* puls k* rat bg2 rheum h* *Rhod* *Rhus-t* k* ruta fd4.de sang k* *Sec* k* *Sep* k* **Sil** k* spong stann k* *Staph* k* *Sulph* k* tep a1 thuj k* tub al ust a1 verat k* **Zinc** k* zinc-p k2 [spect dfg1]

- **morning**: ars k* naja puls k* thuj k*
- **bed** agg.; in: lachn c1
- **falling** out: (↗*Exfoliation*) *Am-c* k* ars k* bry b7.de* bufo cupr *Merc* k* *Merc-c* b4a.de nat-s k2 nux-v k* *Plb* k* *Sec* k* thuj bg2 zinc mrr1
  - **sensation** of: acon caust bg2 *Con* eupi bg2 hyos b7.de* mag-c bg2 *Nit-ac* stram k*
- **painful**: *Ars* k* aur b4.de* bar-c camph **Caust** *Cocc* b7.de* coloc h2* con h2* gels ign b7.de* mag-c h2* merc plat h2* *Puls* thuj b4a.de
  - ○ **Incisors**: aur b4.de* caust b4.de*
  - **Lower** teeth: carb-an b4.de*
- **painless**: nat-c b4.de*
  - ○ **Upper** teeth: carb-an b4.de* carb-v b4.de*
- **sensation**: acon k* aids nl2• *Alum* k* *Am-c* k* arn k* *Ars* k* aur bg2 bar-c bg2 bism bro1 bry k* calc bg2 calc-f bro1 camph bg2 carb-an bg2 *Carb-v* bg2* **Caust** b4a.de* cham bg2 chin bg2 cocc bg2 com *Con* graph b4a.de* hep bg2 *Hyos* k* ign k* iod b4a.de kali-c bg1 lach bg2 lachn lith-c *Lyc* k* m-arct b7.de mag-c b4.de* *Merc* k* *Merc-c* bro1 nat-m k* nat-sil fd3.de• nicc nit-ac bg2* *Nux-m* k* *Nux-v* k* olnd k* op bg2 ozone sde2• ph-ac b4a.de phos bg2 *Plan* bro1 plb bg2 plut-n srj7• **Puls** bg2 *Rhus-t* k* ruta fd4.de sang bg2 sec bg2 sep bg2 sil bg2* spig k* spong k* stann k* *Staph* bg2 *Sulph* k* syph k* tarent bg1 tub c1* verat bg2 zinc bg2*
  - **evening**: sulph h2*
  - **biting** teeth together: calc h2*
  - **chewing** agg.: alum *Con* hyos spong
  - ○ **Hollow** teeth: hyos b7.de* rhus-t b7.de*
  - **Incisors**:
    - **Lower**: mag-c bg2 merc b4.de
    - **Upper**: coff b7a.de nit-ac b4.de*
  - **Lower** teeth: aids nl2• graph b4.de* merc b4.de* sabin b7.de*
  - **Molars**: spong b7.de*
    - **Lower** | **Hollow**: nit-ac b4.de*
    - **Upper** | **left**: kali-c b4.de*
  - **Upper** teeth: m-arct b7.de plat bg2
- **sudden** paroxysm: aur k*
- ○ **Canines**: rhus-t b7.de*
- **Incisors**: caust b4.de* lyc h2* nat-m h2* rhus-t b7.de*
  - ○ **Lower**: *Carb-an* b4a.de graph h2* phos b4.de* *Rhus-t* b7.de* sep b4.de*
  - **Upper**: nit-ac b4.de*
- **Lower** teeth: canth b7.de* carb-an b4.de* *Chel* b7.de* merc b4.de*
- **Molars**: *Bry* b7.de* con h2* kali-n h2* nat-c h2* rhus-t b7.de* ruta fd4.de
  - ○ **Lower**:
    - **left**: zinc b4.de*
    - **Hollow**: nit-ac b4.de*
  - **Upper** | **left**: nat-c b4.de*
- **Sound** teeth: *Am-c* bar-c **Merc** nux-v

LOSS of fluids agg.: *Chin* b7a.de

LYING:

- **agg.**: alum b4.de* aran ptk1 benz-ac ptk1 clem b4.de* graph b4.de* *Ign* bg2 m-arct b7.de *Mez* b4a.de *Nat-m* b4a.de petr b4.de* rat ptk1 rhus-t b7.de* sep b4.de* sul-ac b4.de*
- **amel.**: alum b4.de* am-m b7.de* bry b7.de* lyc b4.de* merc b4.de* nat-c b4.de* nux-v b7.de* spig b7.de*
- **bed**; in:
  - **agg.**: am-m b7.de* ambr b7.de* ant-c b7a.de bry b7.de* *Cham* b7.de* hell b7.de* led b7.de* nux-v b7.de* olnd b7.de* **Puls** b7.de* ran-b b7a.de sabin b7.de* spig b7.de*
  - **amel.**: am-m b7.de*
- **head** on a pillow agg.; with the: nit-ac bg2
- **horizontal** position agg.; in a: clem b4a.de*
- **side**; on:
  - **painful** side:
    - **agg.**: ars b4.de* *Caust* b4a.de nux-v b7.de* plan bg2 spig b7a.de
    - **amel.**: bry b7.de* hyper ptk1 ign b7.de* puls b7.de*
  - **painless** side:
    - **agg.**: *Bry* b7.de* cham b7.de ign b7.de puls b7.de
    - **amel.**: nux-v b7.de*
  - **right** | **agg.**: spig b7.de*

LYING DOWN:

- **after**:
  - **agg.**: *Am-c* b4a.de ang b7.de* arn bg2 ars bg2 bell b4.de* canth b7.de* *Colch* b7a.de hell b7.de* kali-c b4a.de nat-m bg2 puls b7.de* *Sul-ac* b4a.de
  - **amel.**: am-m b7.de* bry b7a.de *Nux-v* b7.de* spig b7.de*

MAIDENS; complaints of young: (↗*Women*) **Acon** bg2 *Bell* bg2 calc bg2

MENSES:

- **after** | **agg.**: calc b4a.de* mag-c b4.de* phos b4.de*
- **before** | **agg.**: ant-c bg2* ars bg2 *Bar-c* b4.de* mag-c bg2 nat-m bg2 phos b4.de* sulph bg2 zinc bg2
- **during** | **agg.**: *Am-c* b4.de* ars b4a.de* bar-c bg2* bov b4.de* **Calc** b4.de* **Carb-v** b4.de* *Cham* bg2* coff bg2* **Graph** b4.de* kali-c b4.de* lach bg2* laur b7.de* *Mag-c* bg2 merc b4a.de nat-m b4.de* nit-ac bg2 phos b4.de* *Sep* b4.de* staph ptk1 sul-ac b4a.de verat b7.de*

MENTAL EXERTION agg.: *Bell* b4.de* ign bg2 **Nux-v** b7.de*

MERCURY agg.; abuse of: bell bg2 **Carb-v** bg2 chin bg2 clem bg2 colch b7.de* hep bg2 kali-i bg2 mez bg2 *Nit-ac* b4a.de* phyt bg2 puls bg2 *Staph* b7.de* sulph bg2 thuj bg2

MOTION:

- **agg.**: **Bry** b7.de* chin bg2 mez bg2 nux-v bg2 *Staph* b7.de*
- **amel.**: m-arct b7.de* mag-c b4.de* ph-ac b4a.de phos b4.de* *Puls* b7.de* rat bg2 *Rhus-t* b7.de*
- **mouth** agg.; of: caust b4.de* cham bg2 merc b4.de* *Nux-v* bg2

MOVED to another location; as if teeth had: bamb-a stb2.de• dulc fd4.de nux-v bg2

MUCUS on teeth: (↗*Sordes*) ail alum k* ant-t arg-met arn k* bell bg2 bov k* *Bry* b7.de* *Caps* b7a.de cham k* chin b7a.de cimic k* *Dulc* b4a.de hydr mrr1 hyos k* iod k* mag-c k* mag-m h2 merc-c bg2 mez k* nat-m bg2 *Nux-v* b7a.de petr bg2 *Ph-ac* bg2 *Phos* b4a.de* plb k* podo bg2* psor pyrog jl2 *Rhus-t* b7a.de* sel k* senec bg1 streptoc rly4• sulph k* *Syph* *Ther* bg1* tub c1

- **morning**: iod mag-c
- **black**: apis *Ars* *Chin* con
  - **crusts**: con
- **brown**: apis ars *Chel* chlol *Colch* *Fl-ac* *Hyos* *Kali-p* nat-p bg1 sulph
- **frothy**: camph b7a.de
- **grayish** green: x-ray sp1
- **offensive**: alum *Dulc* hr1 mez
- **sensation** of: colch ptk1 dios ptk1 *Phos* ptk1
- **slimy**: hydr mrr1 tub jl2
- **sticky**: *Phos* tub jl2 verat
- **stringy**: kali-bi mrr1 tub jl2
- **thick**: alum cain cimic *Dulc* kali-bi mrr1 vario
- **yellow**: *Apis* asc-t hyos iod *Plb* *Sul-ac*

MUSIC agg.: ph-ac ptk1

NOISE: | **agg.**: ars bg2 calc b4.de* coff ptk1 plan ptk1 ther bg2*

NOTCHED (See Serrated)

NUMBNESS: arge-pl rwt5• arn bg2 ars asaf k* aur-s k* bell *Chin* k* *Dulc* k* eupi bg2 graph bg2 ign k* lith-c mez b4a.de nad rly4• nat-m k* petr k* phos k* plat k* *Rhus-t* k* ruta k* thuj

- **morning**:
  - **rising** agg.; after: plat
  - **sexual** excitement; with: plat mrr1
- **sensation** of: caust b4a.de *Chin* b7.de* nat-m bg2 petr bg2 ph-ac bg2 plat bg2 rhus-t bg2

NURSING women; in: *Chin* b7a.de*

ODOR from, offensive: *(↗MOUTH - Odor - offensive)* calc k* carb-v k* *Caust* graph k* iod b4a.de kali-c k* **Kreos** merc mez k* phos b4a.de *Plb* b7.de* *Rhus-t* b7.de*

OIL; sensation as if covered with: aesc k*

OPENING THE MOUTH:

- **agg.**: bry b7.de* caust b4.de* hep b4a.de nux-v b7.de* phos b4.de* puls b7.de* sabad bg2 sabin b7.de
- **amel.**: *Mez* b4a.de

OPERATION; after dental: alumn ptk1 *Arn* ptk1 calen ptk1 ham ptk1 merc-i-f ptk1 *Nux-v* ptk1 staph ptk1 thuj ptk1

PAIN (= toothache in general): abrot↓ *Acet-ac* k* **Acon** k* acon-ac↓ act-sp c2 aesc↓ *Agar* k* agath-a nl2• agn b7.de* aids↓ *Ail* all-c all-s↓ allox tpw3 aloe↓ alum k* alum-p↓ alum-sil↓ am-c k* am-m k* *Ambr* k* amph c2 anac k* anag anan↓ ang k* *Ant-c* k* ant-t k* antip c2* ap-g c2 aphis c2* apis k* *Aran* k* arg-met k* *Arg-n* k* arn k* *Ars* k* ars-h *Ars-i* arum-t↓ **Asaf**↓ asar k* asc-t *Aspar* astac c2 atro bro1 aur k* aur-ar k2 aur-i↓ aur-m aur-s k2 bac jl2 bad↓ bamb-a stb2.de• *Bapt*↓ *Bar-c* k* bar-i↓ bar-m bar-ox-suc↓ bar-s↓ **Bell** k* bell-p-sp↓ *Benz-ac* berb bism k* bit-ar↓ *Borx* k* bov k* brom↓ **Bry** k* *Bufo* caj c2 calad k* *Calc* k* calc-caust c2 calc-f calc-i k2 calc-p calc-sil↓ calo-l gsb1 camph b7.de* cann-i↓ cann-s↓ cann-xyz↓ canth k* caps↓ *Carb-ac* k* carb-an k* *Carb-v* k* *Carbn-s* carc tpw2* card-b↓ carneg-g↓ cassia-s ccrh1• castm↓ caul↓ *Caust* k* cedr c2 **Cham** k* *Chel* chen-a chim c2 chim-m c2 **Chin** k* chinin-ar chinin-s↓ chir-fl gya2 chlam-tr↓ chlol↓ chord-umb↓ chr-o c2 cimic↓ cimx↓ cina b7.de* cinnb↓ cissa-t bta1• cist↓ clem k* coc-c k2 cocc k* cocc-s c2* coch k* **Coff** k* colch k* coli rly4• coloc k* com c2 con k* cor-r croc k* crot-h↓ crot-t↓ cub↓ *Cupr*↓ cupr-ar↓ cycl k* daph c2 der↓ dig c2 dios k* dol↓ dros k* dulc *Echi* elae↓ euon↓ *Euph* k* euphr↓ eupi c2 fago↓ *Ferr* k* ferr-i ferr-p ferr-pic↓ ferr-s c2 *Fl-ac* k* form↓ galla-q-r nl2• galv c2 gamb↓ gels c2* **Glon** k* gran c2 *Graph* k* grat k* guaj k* guare gymno c2 haem↓ ham↓ hecla c2* *Hell* k* **Hep** k* *Hydrog* srj2• *Hyos* k* hyper ign k* ind↓ indg c2 inul c2 *Iod* k* ip k* irid-met↓ *Iris*↓ itu c2 kali-ar↓ kali-bi bg2 *Kali-c* k* kali-chl↓ *Kali-i* kali-m k2 kali-n k* *Kali-p* kali-s *Kalm* ketogl-ac↓ kola↓ *Kreos* k* lac-c↓ **Lach** k* lat-h↓ laur k* lavand-a ctl1• led lil-t↓ limest-b↓ lob *Lyc* k* lyss jl2 m-ambo b2.de* m-arct k* m-aust k* *Mag-c* k* *Mag-m* k* mag-p k* *Mag-s* k* mang k* mang-act br1 mang-s c1* marb-w↓ med↓ mela↓ melal-alt↓ meny↓ meph↓ **Merc** k* *Merc-c* k* merc-i-f c2 merc-i-r↓ merl *Mez* k* mosch↓ mucs-nas rly4• mur-ac k* muru a1 musca-d szs1 naja↓ *Nat-ar* **Nat-c** k* nat-hchls c2 *Nat-m* k* *Nat-p* *Nat-s* nat-sil↓ nicc k* *Nit-ac* k* *Nux-m* k* *Nux-v* k* ol-an↓ olib-sac wmh1 olnd k* onis c2 op b7.de* ox-ac bro1 ozone sde2• par k* parth c2 *Petr* k* petr-ra shn4• ph-ac k* phel↓ *Phos* k* *Phyt* k* pieri-b mlk9.de pip-m c2 pip-n c2 *Plan* k* plat k* plb k* plect c2 podo↓ positr nl2• pot-e rly4• prun k* psor jl2 ptel c1 *Puls* k* ran-b b7.de* ran-s k* raph k* rat rheum k* **Rhod** k* rhodi↓ *Rhus-t* k* ribo rly4• rob↓ rumx↓ ruta k* sabad k* sabin b2.de* sacch-a↓ sal-fr↓ *Samb*↓ sang hr1 sanic c2 saroth sp1 *Sars* k* sass mfm sec↓ sel k* seneg k* **Sep** k* sil k* sinus↓ sol-cp bta1• sphing kk3.fr spig k* spong k* squil k* stann↓ **Staph** k* stram b7.de* streptoc rly4• stront-c k* stry succ-ac↓ suis-pan rly4• sul-ac k* sul-i↓ *Sulph* k* suprar rly4• symph↓ syph↓ tab k* tarax k* *Tarent* tep c2 ter↓ teucr k* ther k* thiam rly4• thuj k* til c2 tong c2 tritic-vg fd5.de trom c2 tub-m jl2 urt-u↓ *Valer* k* vanil fd5.de verat k* verb k* vero-o rly3• vinc viol-o↓ wies↓ xan c1* **Zinc** k* zinc-act c2 zinc-p k2 [hypt-p dbx1.fr]

- **one** side: acon bg1 *Bell* b4a.de *Caust* b4a.de
- **alternating** sides: ambr c1 chel k* clem coloc *Dulc* lac-c lycps-v bg2 psor bg2 zinc bg2
- **right**: aesc↓ alum↓ aphis c1 astac bamb-a stb2.de• bar-c↓ **Bell** brach *Bry* *Calc* cann-s k* *Carb-ac* carb-an↓ *Caust* chr-ac cinnb coff com *Cycl* dios dol dulc fd4.de echi↓ **Fl-ac** gamb↓ germ-met srj5• iod↓ kola↓ lach lyss *Mag-c*

Pain – right: ...
mag-m↓ nat-m nit-ac *Nux-v* oci-sa sp1 *Petr* petr-ra shn4• phos plut-n srj7• *Psor* ruta fd4.de sacch-a fd2.de• sal-fr sle1• sars b4.de* spig **Staph** symph fd3.de• teucr↓ tritic-vg fd5.de verb zinc↓

  - **cutting** pain: nat-m bg2
  - **drawing** pain: alum b4.de* caust b4.de* iod b4.de* nat-m b4.de* staph b7.de*
  - **pulsating** pain: carb-an b4.de*
  - **stitching**, stinging: aesc bar-c *Caust* cycl dulc fd4.de echi gamb kola stb3• teucr zinc
  - **twitching**: mag-m b4.de* spig
  - ▽ **extending** to | **left**: **Acon** carneg-g rwt1• lyc
  - ○ **One** lower molar, with sensation as if headache came from that side: aeth↓
    - **grumbling** pain: aeth k*
  - **Upper**: arn↓
    - **stitching**, stinging: arn
- **left**: *Acon* agar *Aids* nl2• ail↓ am-m↓ anac↓ *Apis* apoc-a vh arg-n *Arn* arum-t *Aur* bar-c bell↓ brom bry↓ calc↓ carb-an↓ carb-v castm **Caust** **Cham** chel *Chin* **Clem** con↓ dulc fd4.de *Form* *Guaj* hyos iod↓ kali-bi↓ *Kali-c* k* kali-i↓ kola stb3• laur melal-alt gya4 merc **Mez** neon srj5• *Nux-m* *Olnd* *Phos* pieri-b mlk9.de positr nl2• rhus-t ruta fd4.de sacch-a fd2.de• samb↓ **Sep** *Sil* sul-ac↓ **Sulph** syph **Thuj** *Zinc*
  - **boring** pain: con b4.de*
  - **clawing** pain: carb-an b4.de*
  - **cutting** pain: agar bg2
  - **lying** down agg.: ail↓
    - **stitching**, stinging: ail
  - **pressing** pain: phos b4.de*
  - **pressure** amel.; external: ail↓
    - **stitching**, stinging: ail
  - **stitching**, stinging: ail anac bell con b4.de* iod phos samb sul-ac *Sulph* zinc h2
  - **tearing** pain: agar a1 am-m a1 arum-t a1 bry a1 kali-bi a1 kali-i a1 samb h1* sul-ac b4.de*
  - **twitching**: calc k* dulc fd4.de kola stb3• zinc a1
  - **walk**; compelled to: ail↓
    - **stitching**, stinging: ail
  - ▽ **extending** to | **right**: all-c gamb
- **daytime**: bar-c bell calc carb-an caust h2* clem a1 *Cocc-s* k* graph a1 mag-c h2* mez h2* nux-v tarent a1 ust
- **morning**: ant-t k* arg-n ars bar-c bry calad k* camph k* carb-v caust k* cham a1 chel↓ chin clem k* *Dros*↓ dulc fd4.de *Ferr* *Hyos* k* hyper↓ kali-n↓ kali-s fd4.de kreos lach mag-c h2* mang↓ merc mez a1 nat-m nux-v k* ph-ac phos plat *Puls* *Ran-s*↓ rhod *Rhus-t* spong fd4.de staph↓ sulph k* tarent a1
  - **bed** | **in** bed:
    - **agg.**: kali-c k* kreos lach mang mez nux-v phos↓ ran-b *Staph*
      - **gnawing** pain: phos k*
      - **waking** him or her from sleep: *(↗wakes)* calad k* coc-c a1 nat-c h2*
    - **waking**; in bed on: bell carb-v cham a1 coc-c k* hydrog srj2• *Ign* kali-c k* *Lach* mag-c h2* *Nux-v* k* sacch-a fd2.de• sil k*
  - **carious** tooth, in; and in corresponding tooth of opposite side: *Staph*↓
    - **drawing** pain: *Staph* h1*
  - **drawing** pain: chel a1 chin a1 mang h2* phos h2* *Ran-s* k* staph k* sulph k*
  - **jerking** pain: *Ran-s* a1 sulph h2*
  - **lying** agg.: phos↓
    - **boring** pain: phos h2
  - **rising**:
    - **after**:
      - **agg.**: bar-c h2* gran a1 mag-c k* plat sep k*
        - **jerking** pain: mag-c h2*
        - **washing**; when: arg-n
      - **amel.**: sil h2*

• **stitching**, stinging: *Camph* *Dros* sulph h2
• **tearing** pain: arg-n k* caust k* hyos h1* hyper kali-n h2* mang k*
• **waking**; on: bell ↓ kali-c ↓
  ⁝ **stitching**, stinging: bell kali-c h2
• **walking** agg.; after: mag-c ↓ *Mez* ↓
  ⁝ **tearing** pain: mag-c h2 *Mez*
• **washing**; after: arg-n ↓
  ⁝ **tearing** pain: arg-n

- **forenoon**: all-s carb-v caust k* cham k* coc-c a1 dulc fd4.de hyper a1 kali-c h2* kali-n ↓ kali-p mag-s a1 mang h2* nat-c h2* nat-m nux-v puls spong fd4.de staph sulph k*
  • **9** h: carbn-s ↓
    ⁝ **jerking** pain: carbn-s
  • **10** h: anac ↓
    ⁝ **drawing** pain: anac
  • **stitching**, stinging: nat-m h2
  • **tearing** pain: kali-n h2*
- **noon**: cocc dulc fd4.de kali-c a1 kali-n ↓ rhus-t spong fd4.de
  • **boring** pain: kali-n h2*
- **noon**, toward: aphis ↓ zinc ↓
  • **drawing** pain: aphis zinc h2
- **afternoon**: agar amph a1 anan calc canth ↓ carb-an ↓ carbn-s ↓ caust k* cham a1 cocc ↓ coloc ↓ dulc fd4.de *Form* hyper a1 ip mag-c merc merc-i-r a1 mez a1 nat-c h2* *Nux-v* phos ruta fd4.de sep ↓ spong fd4.de sulph k* ther thuj tritic-vg fd5.de vanil fd5.de zinc ↓
  • **14-19** h: adam skp7•
  • **16** h: lyc tl1
  • **17** h: zing ↓
    ⁝ **drawing** pain: zing
  • **dinner**; after: berb lach *Nux-v* puls
  • **drawing** pain: canth k* carb-an k* cocc k* coloc k* ruta fd4.de vanil fd5.de
  • **jerking** pain: sep h2*
  • **tearing** pain: agar h2* carbn-s caust h2* sep h2* thuj a1 zinc h2*
- **evening**: ail *Alum* alum-p k2 **Am-c** am-m ↓ ambr amph a1 anac *Ant-c* apis arum-t bamb-a ↓ bar-c *Bell* k* borx ↓ bov bry bufo cain ↓ calad k* *Calc* ↓ calc-s a1 canth ↓ carb-an ↓ *Carbn-s* caust cham k* chel k* clem a1 dulc fd4.de ferr k* graph k* hep *Hyos* ign kali-c k* *Kali-i* kali-n h2* kali-p kali-s *Kalm* *Lyc* k* mag-c h2 mag-m ↓ *Mag-s* k* mang meph k* *Merc* mez k* nat-c h2* nat-m sne nicc nit-ac nux-m *Nux-v* k* petr ↓ *Phos* ptel a1 **Puls** *Rat* *Rhus-t* ruta fd4.de sabin k* sacch-a fd2.de• sars h2* sep ↓ spong fd4.de *Staph* stry a1 *Sul-ac* *Sulph* k* tab tarent a1 ther thuj k* tritic-vg fd5.de zinc ↓
  • **18** h, lasting till 1 or 2 h: sep
  • **21** h: alum ↓ **Merc**
    ⁝ **gnawing** pain: alum
  • **bed**:
    ⁝ **in** bed:
      : **agg.**: alum **Am-c** ambr h1 ang h1 **Ant-c** aran bar-c bell bov *Bry* *Calc* carb-an *Cham* chr-ac graph *Ign* *Kali-c* kali-n h2 led **Mag-c** mag-m *Merc* nat-c nit-ac phos *Puls* sel *Sul-ac* **Sulph** zinc
        . **drawing** pain: *Kali-c*
        . **jerking** pain: ant-c c1 *Bry* k* zinc
      : **amel.**: alum am-m ↓ mag-s c1
        . **tearing** pain: am-m h2
  • **boring** pain: alum h2* borx a1 clem a1 nat-c h2*
    ⁝ **tearing** and digging; with: alum
  • **digging** pain: alum k* clem a1 ign a1 nat-c h2*
  • **drawing** pain: alum k* bov k* bry k* canth a1 dulc fd4.de hep k* *Kali-c* h2* puls k* ruta fd4.de sulph a1
  • **gnawing** pain: *Calc* k* phos k* **Puls** k*
  • **jerking** pain: mag-m h2* petr a1 sep h2*
  • **lying**:
    ⁝ **agg.**: phos ↓
      : **boring** pain: phos k*

- **evening – lying**: ...
    ⁝ **bed**; in:
      : **agg.**: alum ↓
        . **cutting** pain: alum k*
  • **lying** down on right side; going off after: alum ↓
    ⁝ **drawing** pain: alum
  • **pulsating** pain: carbn-s k2
  • **sleep**; preventing: lyc ↓
    ⁝ **drawing** pain: lyc h2
    ⁝ **stitching**, stinging: lyc h2
  • **smoking** amel.: spig
  • **stitching**, stinging: bell borx h2 bufo dulc fd4.de kali-c h2 zinc
  • **tearing** pain: ail k* alum am-m k* bamb-a stb2.de• bell cain carb-an h2* kali-n h2* mag-c h2* mag-s k* nat-c h2* petr a1 sep k* tab zinc k*
  • **walking** agg.: nat-c ↓
    ⁝ **digging** pain: nat-c h2*
○ • **Upper** molars, now in lower molars; now in:
    ⁝ **pressing** with tip of finger; when: *Bry* ↓
      : **jerking** pain: *Bry*
- **night**: alum h2* *Am-c* k* ambr anac k* *Ant-c* k* aran k* *Ars* *Aur* aur-ar k2 bamb-a stb2.de• bar-c *Bell* k* berb bov bry bufo calc calc-p calc-sil k2 carb-an *Carb-v* **Carbn-s** caust h2* *Cedr* **Cham** k* *Chel* k* chin chinin-ar *Clem* k* coff *Colch* crot-c *Cycl* der a1* dulc ↓ *Glon* **Graph** k* grat hell *Hep* hydrog srj2• hyper k* ina-i mlk9.de ip kali-c h2* kali-i kali-n *Kali-p* kola stb3• **Lyc** k* **Mag-c** k* mag-m mag-p bro1 **Merc** k* *Merc-c* k* *Mez* k* naja nat-ar nat-c k* nat-hchls *Nat-m* k* nat-p *Nat-s* nat-sil fd3.de• nicc *Nit-ac* nux-m *Nux-v* k* *Olnd* par petr *Ph-ac* *Phos* k* *Psor* *Puls* k* *Rhod* *Rhus-t* rob sabad sabin k* *Sep* k* *Sil* k* *Spig* k* spira a1 *Staph* stry a1 sul-ac h2* **Sulph** k* syph xxb tarent a1 thiam rly4• tritic-vg fd5.de vanil fd5.de
  • **midnight**:
    ⁝ **before**: alum am-c bov bry *Cham* chin graph merc ↓ *Nat-m* petr puls rhus-t sep stry sul-ac sulph thuj zinc
      : **22** h: ozone sde2• rhus-t
      : **22-0** h: mang h2
      : **tearing** pain: am-c merc petr h2 sul-ac h2
    ⁝ **at**: kali-bi a1 stry a1
    ⁝ **after**: alum am-c *Ars* k* bar-m bell bry carb-v cham k* chin hyper a1 kola stb3• *Merc* nat-m k* puls k* rhus-t *Staph* sulph k*
      : **2** h: calc-caust c1
      : **3** h: bry k* cham kali-n h2
      : **jerking** pain: alum sulph h2
      : **rising**; after:
        . **amel.**: alum ↓
          stitching, stinging: alum
      : **stitching**, stinging: alum bar-m sulph h2
      : **tearing** pain: alum h2 *Bell* *Sulph*
  • **boring** pain: phos h2*
  • **chilliness** when toothache disappears: merc
  • **cold** | **drinks**:
      : **agg.**: kali-n ↓
        . **pulsating** pain: kali-n c1
    ⁝ **food**:
      : **agg.**: kali-n ↓
        . **pulsating** pain: kali-n c1
  • **drawing** pain: am-c k* ambr k* bell k* calc h2* carb-an k* *Cham* a1 clem k2 dulc fd4.de *Hep* hr1 mag-c k* nat-c k* nat-m k* nit-ac k* sep h2* sulph h2* tritic-vg fd5.de vanil fd5.de
  • **gnawing** pain: *Cham* coff mag-c h2*
  • **jerking** pain: *Cycl* k* mag-c h2* **Merc** rhus-t sep h2*
  • **lying**:
    ⁝ **agg.**: *Aran* ars bg1 graph phos
    ⁝ **side**; on:
      : **painful** side:
        . **agg.**: ars ↓
          tearing pain: ars
  • **lying** down agg.: canth ↓ olnd ↓

- **lying** down agg.: ...
  - **drawing** pain: canth olnd
- **pulsating** pain: carb-n-s k2 dulc fd4.de tritic-vg fd5.de
- **stitching**, stinging: bufo clem hell h1 kali-c h2 nit-ac h2 petr h2 phos h2 *Sil*
- **tearing** pain: alum k* *Ars* k* *Calc* calc-p carb-an hell h1* mag-c k* *Merc* k* nat-c k* nat-m nicc k* nux-m sep sil sul-ac h2* sulph h2*
- **waking** him or her from sleep: calc ↓
  - **pricking** pain: calc
- **waking**; on: sulph ↓
  - **stitching**, stinging: sulph h2

- **accompanied** by:
  - **beside** himself; being (See MIND - Beside - teeth)
  - **blood**; rushes of: mez bg2 sep bg2
  - **chill**: euph bg2 *Kali-c* bg2 mez bg2 **Puls** bg2 rhus-t bg2
  - **coldness** of teeth: kola stb3• verat bg2
  - **complaining** and wailing (See MIND - Complaining - pain - teeth)
  - **complaint**; any other (See GENERALS - Complaints - accompanied - teeth)
  - **constipation**: bry bg2 **Merc** bg2 nux-v bg2 *Staph* bg2
  - **cough**: lyc ptk1 *Sep* bg2*
  - **diarrhea**: **Cham** bg2 *Dulc* bg2 rhus-t bg2
  - **erections**: daph bg2
  - **exhaustion** (See weakness)
  - **faintness**: cham bro1
  - **heat** of body: cham bro1 lach bg2 sil bg2 verat bg2
  - **hysteria** (See MIND - Hysteria - teeth)
  - **indigestion**: tarent tl1
  - **irritability** (See MIND - Irritability - teeth)
  - **nausea**: verat bg2
  - **palpitation** (See CHEST - Palpitation - accompanied - teeth)
  - **perspiration**; anxious: clem bg2
  - **pulsation**; general: sep bg2
  - **respiration**; affected: **Puls** bg2 sep bg2
  - **restlessness** (See MIND - Restlessness - teeth - pain)
  - **sleepiness**: sulph bg2
  - **sleeplessness**: *Aur* kr1 bar-c b4a.de canth b7.de* *Cham* kr1 *Cocc-s* kr1 hell a1 *Mag-c* b4a.de mag-m b4a.de* merc-c a1 rat a1 **Sep** a1* *Sil* kr1 spig h1* staph kr1 trom kr1
  - **thirst**: cham bro1
  - **weakness**: clem bg2* verat bg2
  - ○ **Cheeks**:
    - **heat**: ferr-p ptk1
    - **swelling**: am-c h2 arn ars aur h2 **Bell** k* borx h2* **Bry** *Calc* caps h1 caust h2 cham bro1 *Hecla* bro1 hep bro1 **Lach** *Lyc* k* mag-c h2 **Merc** k* nat-c h2 *Nat-m* nit-ac h2 nux-v petr ph-ac phos *Puls* sep h2 *Sil* bro1 staph sulph
  - **Ears**:
    - **complaints** of: bry b7.de* *Cham* b7.de* hell b7.de* lach b7.de* nux-m b7.de* nux-v b7.de* plb b7.de* *Puls* b7.de* ran-s b7a.de rhus-t b7a.de *Spig* b7.de*
    - **pain**; aching: **Bell** bg2 borx bg2 plan bg2 **Puls** bg2 rhod bg2
  - **Eyes**; pain in | **burning**: *Bell* bg2
  - **Face**:
    - **heat**: all-c hr1 ferr-p sla* graph h2* nat-m h2* phos h2* sil h2* spig hr1 stann h2* staph h1*
    - **pain**:
      - **aching**: ars bg2 clem bg2 euph bg2 *Hyos* bg2 kali-c bg2 kreos bg2 mag-c bg2 sil bg2 **Spig** bg2
      - **Bones**: clem bg2 *Hyos* bg2 mag-c bg2 **Merc** bg2 **Nux-v** bg2 *Rhus-t* bg2 *Spig* bg2 sulph bg2
    - **swelling**: spig bg2
  - **Feet**; jerking: mag-c bg2

- **accompanied** by: ...
  - **Fingers**:
    - **cold** tips: **Ars** bg2
    - **pain**: mag-c ↓ sep bg2
      - **twitching**: mag-c k*
  - **Forehead** | **cold**: *Verat* bg2
  - **Head**:
    - **complaints** (See HEAD - Complaints - accompanied - teeth)
    - **congestion**: **Acon** bg2 *Aur* bg2 calc bg2 *Chin* bg2 hyos bg2* lyss c1 m e z bg2 **Puls** bg2 sulph bg2
    - **heat** of: **Acon** bg2 *Aur* bg2 hyos bg2 puls bg2
    - **pain**: antip vh1 neon srj5• sang bro1
      - **aching** (See HEAD - Pain - aching - accompanied - teeth)
  - **Jaw**; lower | **complaints**: sil ptk1
  - **Legs**; heaviness: lach bg2
  - **Limbs**; weakness of: clem h1*
  - **Mouth**:
    - **dryness**: *Chin* bg2 *Puls* bg2
      - **thirst**:
        - **with**: *Chin* bg2
        - **without**: *Puls* bg2
    - **heat**: mag-c hr1
  - **Neck**; nape of:
    - **pain**: nux-m bg2
    - **stiffness**: lyc bg2
  - **Nose**:
    - **bleeding** (See epistaxis)
    - **epistaxis**: nat-s bg2
  - **Stomach**; complaints of (See STOMACH - Complaints - accompanied - teeth)
  - **Submaxillary** glands; swelling of: clem h2
  - **Throat** | **dryness**: *Bell* bg2
- **aching**: aids nl2• allox sp1 bar-ox-suc rly4• carc mg1.de* carneg-g rwt1• cham bro1 chlam-tr bcx2• chord-umb rly4• kreos bro1 limest-b es1• marb-w es1• melal-alt gya4 merc bro1 mez bro1 staph bro1 succ-ac rly4• suis-pan rly4•
- **air**:
  - **drawing** in air:
    - **agg.**: acon alum *Am-c* ant-c arn *Aur* *Bell* berb *Bry* **Calc** *Calc-p* **Caust** chin cic cina clem ↓ cob fl-ac grat kali-c h2 kali-n **Merc** *Mez* *Nat-m* nat-sil fd3.de• nux-m *Nux-v* *Petr* *Rhod* rhus-t sabin sel *Sil* spig **Staph** k* *Sulph* thuj
      - **sore**: bell
      - **stitching**, stinging: am-c ant-c clem h2
    - **amel.**: *Clem* mez k* nat-s nux-v *Puls* sars sel
- **air** agg.; draft of: *Bell* **Calc** calc-p *Cham* *Chin* dulc fd4.de echi ptk2 gymno *Mag-c* nat-m bg1 sars sep **Sulph** k*
- **air**; in open:
  - **agg.**: *Acon* alum alum-p k2 *Am-c* ambr anac ant-c bac al2 bell carb-an carb-v castm caust k* *Cham* k* *Chin* con hyos kali-n h2* mez nat-c k* nat-m nux-m *Nux-v* k* petr *Phos* rhus-t sabin ↓ sep spig **Staph** k* **Sulph** k*
    - **cutting** pain: alum
    - **drawing** pain: chin k* *Nux-v* k* sabin c1 sep k* *Sulph* k*
    - **tearing** pain: caust h2 kali-n h2 phos h2
  - **amel.**: all-c ant-c k* bov k* bry chin ↓ hep mag-m *Puls* sep stann *Sulph* thuj
    - **boring** pain: mag-m h2
    - **drawing** pain: chin hep h2* puls k*
    - **tearing** pain: mag-m h2
- **alternating** with:
  - **catarrh**: all-c

- **dizziness** (See VERTIGO - Alternating - teeth)
- **vertigo** (See VERTIGO - Alternating - teeth)
- O **Cervical** region; stiffness in (See BACK - Stiffness - cervical - alternating)
- **Ear**; itching in: agar
- **Head**; pain in (See HEAD - Pain - alternating - teeth)
- **Heart**; pain in (See CHEST - Pain - heart - alternating - teeth)
- **Limbs**; tearing in: merc
- **Mamma** | **pain** in left; stitching: *Kali-c*

- **anger**; after: ant-t vh cham k* nux-v
- **anxiety**; with: *(↗MIND - Anxiety)* acon *Coff* *Merc-c*
- **appearing**:
  - **suddenly** and disappearing gradually: bac bn
  - **suddenly** and disappearing suddenly: *Bell* melal-alt gya4 sanic
- **autumn** agg.: aur bry chin colch merc nux-m nux-v rhod rhus-t verat
- **beating** (See pulsating)
- **bed**:
  - **driving** out of bed: mag-c h2 petr h2 spig h1
  - **going** to bed:
    - **after**: **Acon** ↓
      - **tearing** pain: **Acon**
    - **when**: carb-an kali-c
  - **in** bed:
    - **agg.**: **Ant-c** *Aphis* *Bar-c* bell *Bov* bry *Carb-an* *Cham* *Clem* com *Graph* *Kali-c* lachn a1 **Mag-c** k* *Mag-p* **Merc** nux-v olnd *Petr* ph-ac *Phos* *Puls* rhus-t sabin *Sul-ac* **Sulph**
      - **drawing** pain: aphis *Kali-c*
    - **amel.**: am-m a1 lyc a1*
- **beer**: nux-v rhus-t sulph zinc
  - **amel.**: camph k*
- **bending**:
  - **backward** | **agg.**: calc k*
  - **forward**:
    - **forehead** on table; with:
      - **agg.**: nit-ac
      - **amel.**: mang k*
  - **side**; to | **agg.**: calc
- **binding** tightly amel.: kali-c b4.de* sep b4.de*
- **biting**:
  - **agg.**: am-c ↓ calc k* caust ↓ cocc mang ↓ phel rhod k* sulph ↓ zinc h2*
    - **stitching**, stinging: am-c caust mang a1 sulph h2
  - **amel.**:
    - **elastic** substance; on an: mang
    - **something**; on: marb-w es1•
  - **only** when biting: am-c ↓ ruta ↓
    - **drawing** pain: am-c k* ruta fd4.de
- **biting** pain: calc k* *Carb-v* bg2 *Cham* bg2 cocc con bg2 kali-c bg2 phel phos bg2 *Puls* bg2 rhod *Staph* bg2 sul-ac bg2 *Thuj* bg2 zinc h2
- **biting** teeth together: aesc *Alum* alum-sil k2 **Am-c** amph a1 ars *Aur* bell borx *Bry* calc carb-an caust chin chinin-ar coc-c colch k2 fl-ac graph *Guaj* hell *Hep* hyos *Ip* lach lith-c lyc mag-c k2 mag-m mang *Merc* **Mez** nux-v petr ph-ac phos podo fd3.de• *Puls* *Rhus-t* **Sep** *Sil* spong *Staph* *Sul-ac* *Sulph* tab ulm-c jsj8• *Verb* zinc-o
  - **afraid** to bite, for fear they would fall out: nit-ac
  - **agg.**: aesc *Alum* alum-sil k2 **Am-c** amph a1 ars *Aur* bell borx *Bry* calc carb-an caust chin chinin-ar cinnb ↓ coc-c colch k* fl-ac graph *Guaj* hell *Hep* hyos *Ip* lach lith-c lyc mag-c k2 mag-m mang *Merc* **Mez** nux-v petr ph-ac phos podo fd3.de• *Puls* *Rhus-t* **Sep** *Sil* spong *Staph* *Sul-ac* *Sulph* tab ulm-c jsj8• *Verb* zinc-o
    - **fly** to pieces; as if they would: cinnb
    - **tearing** pain: **Am-c** hell h1
  - **amel.**: ars bell brom bry cocc coff euph galla-q-r nl2• gink-b sbd1• ign mag-m mur-ac bg1 nat-m ol-an bg1 phos **Phyt** puls rhus-t sanic syph c1
    - **tearing** pain: mag-m
  - **desire** to | **menses**; during: merc-i-f
- **biting** teeth together: ...
  - **menses**; during: am-c
- **bleeding** of gums amel.: *(↗picking teeth - amel. - bleed)* bell caust sanic sars sel
- **blow**; pain as from a: *(↗Blow; sensation)* calc chin h1 m-ambo b7.de nux-v k* ruta b7.de* tarax
- **blowing** the nose:
  - **agg.**: culx bro1 phos thuj k*
  - **amel.**: acon bg1
- **boring** pain: alum k* alum-p k2 *Ant-c* bg2 arg-n bg2 *Bar-c* bar-s k2 *Bell* k* borx k* *Bov* k* bufo calad k* calc k* *Calc-p* calc-sil k2 camph k* cann-i castm *Caust* k* cham bg2* chel k* chin clem a1 con k* *Cycl* k* daph euph grat *Ign* k* indg kali-bi k* *Kali-c* k* kali-i bg2 kali-n k* kola stb3• *Lach* k* *Laur* b7.de* lyc k* mag-c k* mag-m merc bg2 *Mez* k* mur-ac bg1 *Nat-c* k* *Nat-m* k* *Nat-p* nicc bg1 *Nit-ac* *Nux-v* k* petr k* ph-ac k* *Phos* k* plan k* *Plat* bg2 *Puls* bg2 rhod k* ruta bg2 sang bg2 sel k* *Sil* k* spig b7.de* sul-ac bg2 *Sulph* k* verat
- **bread** agg.: carb-an
- **break** off; as if they would: bell k* ign bg2 kali-i j5.de* nat-m bg2* sulph h2*
- **breakfast** agg.; after: borx a1 petr h2
  - **tingling** pain: borx c1
- **breathing**:
  - **agg.**: carb-v vanil fd5.de
  - **deep** | **agg.**: *Nux-v*
- **bruised**, as if (See sore)
- **brushing** teeth | **agg.**: *Bry* carb-v **Lach** lyc pieri-b mlk9.de *Staph*
- **bubbling**: berb k* carb-v lyc k* nit-ac k* spig
- **burning**: ars bg2* bar-c k* bell bro1 carbn-s bg2 *Caust* k* cham chel bg2 chinin-s bg2 clem bg2 coc-c bg2 *Coloc* k* dig bg2 dulc fl-ac bg2 gels bg2 graph k* kali-c k* kali-i bg2 m-ambo b7.de *Mag-c* k* merc k* *Merc-c* b4a.de mez k* *Nat-m* nit-ac k* *Nux-v* k* *Ph-ac* k* phel phos k* puls raph a1 rhus-t rob sil k* spig spong *Staph* hr1 sulph k* ther k* urt-u zinc k* zinc-p k2
- **burnt**; as if: cimx bg2
- **burrowing**: alum b4.de *Ant-c* b7a.de *Bell* b4a.de borx b4a.de bov b4.de *Calc* b4a.de caust b4a.de *Cham* b7a.de *Ign* b7a.de kali-c b4a.de nat-c b4.de *Nux-v* b7.de plat b4a.de *Puls* b7.de rheum b7.de* *Rhus-t* b7a.de *Ruta* b7a.de seneg b4a.de *Sil* b4a.de sulph b4.de
- **bursting** pain: bar-c bg2* chin bg1 *Hyos* b7a.de ph-ac bg2* sabin k* thuj k*
- **butter** agg; cold: lavand-a ctl1•
- **buzzing**: hyos k* m-arct b7.de meny b7.de* nux-v b7.de* sep h2* sulph h2* teucr b7.de*
- **catarrh** is better toothache is worse and vice versa; when: all-c
- **chamomile**:
  - **agg.**: alum k* *Puls*
  - **amel.**: carl c1 gink-b sbd1•
- **chewing** (See chewing - agg.)
  - **after** chewing agg.: nat-m sabin staph
  - **agg.**: *Alum* alum-p k2 *Am-c* anan ant-c arg-met arg-n *Arn* ars aur aur-ar k2 bamb-a stb2.de• bell *Bry* calc *Calc-p* calc-sil ↓ carb-an *Carb-v* *Carbn-s* *Caust* **Cham** chel *Chin* chinin-m c1 *Cocc* *Coff* con crot-t dulc fd4.de *Euph* ferr-ma *Graph* hura *Hyos* *Ign* kali-ar *Kali-c* kali-p *Lach* *Lyc* mag-c *Mag-m* med k2 *Merc* **Nat-m** **Nit-ac** *Nux-m* *Nux-v* olnd ozone sde2• *Ph-ac* *Phos* *Puls* rhus-t sabin *Sang* *Sil* spig spong *Staph* *Sul-ac* sulph syph *Thuj* tritic-vg fd5.de vanil fd5.de verat zinc zinc-p k2
    - **food**, not from empty chewing; only when: cocc
    - **only** when: calc lyc olnd sabin c1
    - **pricking** pain: am-c
    - **sore**: ars *Aur* calc-sil k2
  - **amel.**: bry rhod seneg
- **children**; in: acon *Ant-c* *Bell* *Calc* **Cham** **Coff** ign *Merc* nux-m nux-v *Puls* rheum
- **chill**:
  - **after**: nux-m c1
  - **before**: **Merc** bg2
  - **during**: agar k* apis b7a.de* bar-c bg2 calc bg2 *Carb-v* k* *Graph* k* hell k* kali-c k* led bg2 mag-c bg2* merc b4.de* mez bg2 nat-m b4a.de* nit-ac bg2 puls bg2 **Rhus-t** k* sep k* staph k*
    - **stitching**, stinging: graph h2

- **chilliness**; with: daph k* euph k* hell lach k* *Merc* bg2 puls k* rhod rhus-t
- **chocolate** agg.: musca-d szs1
- **chronic**: *Caust*
- **clawing** pain: am-c b4.de* ign bg2 stront-c k*
- **clenching** teeth | **desire** to clench teeth: cassia-s ccrh1• chin bro1 lyc h2 *Ol-an* bro1 **Phyt** mrr1 staph bro1
- **coffee** agg.: anan *Bell* k* *Camph* k* carb-v **Cham** k* cocc *Ign* k* lachn k* merc *Nux-v* *Puls* rhus-t sacch-a fd2.de• sil
- **coition**:
  - **agg.**: daph k*
  - **amel.**: camph
- **cold**:
  - **agg.**: chin ↓ coc-c ↓ *Nux-v* ↓ **Sep** ↓
    - **drawing** pain: chin hr1 coc-c k2 *Nux-v* k* **Sep** k*
  - **air**:
    - **agg.**: *Acon* bro1 *Agar* all-c *Alum* alum-sil k2 *Anan* androc srj1• ant-c bac bn* *Bell* k* borx bry k* bufo **Calc** k* calc-sil k2 camph carbn-s k2 **Caust** **Cham** k* chin cina dulc fd4.de fl-ac *Hep* hyos *Mag-c* *Mag-p* **Merc** k* nat-m *Nux-m* *Nux-v* *Phos* plan plat *Puls* k* *Rhod* bro1 *Rhus-t* sabad *Sars* sel c1 seneg *Sep* *Sil* k* *Spig* *Staph* streptoc rly4• *Sul-ac* **Sulph** *Ther* thuj trom tub c
      - **tearing** pain: bufo carbn-s
    - **amel.**: bry k2 chel *Clem* k* kali-s k* mag-m mez *Nat-s* k* *Nux-v* **Puls** k* sars *Sel* thuj
    - **drawing** in cold air:
      - **agg.**: camph ↓ *Rhus-t* ↓
        - **gnawing** pain: *Rhus-t*
        - **stitching**, stinging: camph h1
      - **amel.**: *Nux-v* ↓
        - **gnawing** pain: *Nux-v*
  - **amel.**: ambr ↓ mag-m ↓
    - **boring** pain: mag-m h2*
    - **drawing** pain: ambr k*
    - **tearing** pain: mag-m h2*
  - **anything** cold in mouth; from:
    - **agg.**: agar anan androc srj1• ant-c k* arg-n *Ars* *Bar-c* bar-s k2 bov *Calc* k* calc-p calc-sil k2 *Carb-v* carbn-s castm coc-c *Colch* k* *Con* dulc fd4.de grat ham fd3.de• hell hyos bro1 irid-met srj5• **Kali-c** k* kali-i kali-n kali-p kola stb3• *Lyc* k* *Mag-c* k* mag-m *Mag-p* k* mag-s c1 mang mang-act br1 *Merc* k* **Nat-m** *Nit-ac* nux-m *Nux-v* bro1 par ph-ac *Phos* pieri-b mlk9.de *Plan* k* plb psor puls **Rhus-t** rob ruta fd4.de **Sep** sil k* *Spig* k* spong fd4.de *Staph* k* *Sul-ac* sulph k* syph ther tl1 thuj tritic-vg fd5.de
      - **stitching**, stinging: *Nit-ac* *Sulph*
      - **warm** agg.; or: carb-v bg1 carl c1 dulc fd4.de lach bg1
    - **amel.**: *Ambr* bell bism bg1 bry calc caust bg1 cham chin *Coff* *Ferr-p* k* *Glon* mag-c h2* mag-m h2* merc nat-s bg1 nux-v phos *Puls* k* sacch-a fd2.de• sep bg1 staph sulph
  - **applications**:
    - **agg.**: borx ↓
      - **drawing** pain: borx c1
  - **bathing** | **agg.**: ant-c br1*
  - **drinks**:
    - **agg.**: agar anan androc srj1• **Ant-c** arg-n *Ars* bar-c bar-s k2 borx h2 bry *Calc* carb-an *Carb-v* carbn-s castm caust cench *Cham* chinin-ar cina coc-c *Fl-ac* germ-met srj5• graph gymno **Hep** kali-ar **Kali-c** kali-p **Lach** mag-p *Mang* *Merc* *Mur-ac* **Nat-m** *Nux-m* *Nux-v* *Phos* *Plan* puls rhod **Rhus-t** rumx sabad sang a1 *Sars* sel sil spig **Staph** *Sulph* *Ther* thiam rly4• thuj til
      - **pinching** pain: carb-an
      - **sore**: *Ars* bry
    - **amel.**: *Bism* bro1 *Bry* bro1 cham mrr1 chim bro1 *Coff* bro1 ferr bro1 ferr-p bro1 nat-s bro1 *Puls* bro1
  - **finger**:
    - **amel.**: ang ↓
      - **drawing** pain: ang
- **cold**: ...
  - **food**:
    - **agg.**: agar androc srj1• bov bry *Calc* k* carb-v *Con* dulc fd4.de *Glon* hell lach bro1 mag-p bro1 merc k* nux-v k* par plb rhus-t rob sabad staph bro1 sulph k* tritic-vg fd5.de vanil fd5.de
      - **tearing** pain: carb-v k2
  - **food** and drinks:
    - **amel.**: mag-m ↓
      - **boring** pain: mag-m h2
  - **hands** | **amel.**: ang k* kali-p k2 rhus-t
  - **washing**:
    - **after**:
      - **agg.**: calc cham graph kali-c merc nux-m nux-v puls sep *Spig* staph **Sulph** k*
      - **amel.**: *All-c* asar bell bry cham clem kali-c laur *Puls*
  - **water**:
    - **agg.**: agar ↓ arg-n ↓ borx ↓ chlam-tr bcx2• mag-c h2* nat-sil fd3.de• *Nux-m* ↓ ozone sde2• phos ↓ *Sars* ↓ staph ↓ sulph ↓ vanil fd5.de
      - **tearing** pain: agar arg-n borx h2 mag-c h2* *Nux-m* phos *Sars* staph k* sulph h2*
    - **amel.**: *Aesc* *All-c* *Ambr* ap-g bell *Bism* **Bry** camph k* *Caust* *Cham* k* chel k* *Chim* c1 *Chin* chinin-m c1 *Clem* k* **Coff** *Ferr* *Ferr-p* fl-ac hydrog srj2• kali-c h2* *Lac-c* laur *Mag-c* mag-m merc *Nat-s* nux-v phos **Puls** rhus-t sel sep sulph thuj
      - **held** in the mouth: cham k2 clem k2* coff mrr1
      - **icy** cold: ferr br1
      - **momentarily**: bry ↓
        - **screwing** pain: bry
      - **neuralgic**: coff tl1
      - **pulled** out; as if being: chim ptk1
- **cold**; after taking a: *Acon* *Bar-c* bell camph carb-v *Caust* *Cham* chin colch dulc *Gels* glon grat *Hyos* ign kali-c kali-p *Merc* mez nat-c h2 nit-ac nux-m *Nux-v* phos h2 *Puls* rhus-t staph sul-ac zinc
  - **spring** agg.: puls
- **cold** agg.; becoming:
  - **head**: kali-c h2
  - **overheating**; after: *Cham* *Glon* kali-c *Rhus-t*
- **cold** air; sensation as from: cedr coc-c par
  - **forced** into teeth; were: ambr cocc-s
  - **rushed** out of teeth: nat-c
    - **and** in teeth: kali-n h2
- **coldness** agg.: kola ↓
  - **pressing** pain: kola stb3•
- **compressed**; as if: cann-s b7.de* nux-m bg2
- **concussion**; from (See jar)
- **constricting** pain: kali-c bg2 petr bg2
- **contracting**: borx k* cann-s carb-an carb-v k* nit-ac petr b4.de* stann h2* staph b7.de* stront-c b4.de* symph fd3.de•
- **corrosive**: bar-c b4a.de calc k* carb-v cham k* con kali-c k* *Lyc* b4a.de mag-c b4a.de merc bg1 nicc *Nux-v* b7a.de op b7.de* phos puls *Rhus-t* b7a.de spig b7.de* staph k* sul-ac thuj k*
- **coryza**; during: am-m b7a.de* chin b7.de* lach b7.de* ozone sde2• sep a1 tub jl2
- **cough** agg.; during: bry lyc k* sep k*
- **cramping** (See jerking)
- **crawling**: syph k2
- **crumbs** of bread, from: clem nux-v *Staph*
- **crushed**; as if: *Ign* b7.de* lyc k* m-arct b7.de
- **cutting** pain: acon k2 alum k* am *Aur* aur-s a1 bell k* benz-ac k* calc k* *Camph* k* daph graph ham hydrog srj2• iod bg2 kali-c *Lach* *Mez* k* olnd k* petr k* plan bg2* ran-b k* *Rhod* k* rhus-t b7.de* rob sep k* *Staph* hr1 sulph h2* zinc bg2
  - **air**; as from a cold draft of: sulph h2
- **damp** places; from working in: *Ars* **Calc** *Dulc* **Rhus-t**
- **darting** (See stitching)
- **decreasing** suddenly | **two** or three hours; after: rhod ptk1
- **dental** work, after: acon bg1 am bg1* dulc fd4.de hecla bg1 hep bg1 hyper mrr1 merc-i-f vh nat-sil fd3.de• staph bg1

- **dentition**; as from: kola stb3•
- **digging** pain: ambr k* anan ant-c k* arg-n k* bell k* berb borx *Bov* bry bufo calc calc-sil k2 castm *Caust* k* *Cham* k* chin k* clem a1 fl-ac *Glon* ign k* kali-c kali-i a1 kola stb3• lyc h2* mag-m mela a1 *Nat-c* k* nux-v plan k* plat k* *Puls* k* rat rheum rhus-t b7.de* ruta seneg sep h2* sil spig sul-ac sulph h2*
- **dinner**; after: ambr ↓ calc ↓ *Kali-c* ↓ mag-c ↓ nat-c ↓
  - **boring** pain: kali-c
  - **pressing** pain: *Kali-c*
  - **stitching**, stinging: ambr calc nat-c h2*
  - **tearing** pain: mag-c h2 nat-c h2
- **dislocated**; as if: arn b7a.de* merc b4.de* nux-v b7.de* prun bg2
- **diverted** amel.; when: bar-c dulc fd4.de pip-m thuj
- **dragging**: merc-i-r bg2 *Puls* b7.de* staph b7.de*
- **drawing** in air (See air - drawing - agg.)
- **drawing** pain: abrot k* agar k* all-c all-s alum k* alum-p k2 *Am-c* k* *Ambr* k* *Anac* k* anan k* ang k* ant-c arg-n ars h2* asaf astac k* aur aur-i k2 aur-s k* bad bar-c k* bar-i k2 bar-s k2 *Bell* k* berb bism k* borx k* *Bov* k* *Bry* k* calad *Calc* k* calc-p k* calc-sil k2 camph cann-s k* canth k* caps k* carb-an k* **Carb-v** k* *Carbn-s* card-b a1 *Caust* k* **Cham** k* *Chel* k* chim k* chin k* chir-fl gya2 *Clem* k* *Coc-c* k* *Cocc* k* cocc-s a1* *Coff* b7.de* colch k* *Coloc* a1* *Con* k* crot-t *Cupr* b7.de* cycl k* daph dulc fd4.de fl-ac *Glon* k* **Graph** k* guaj k* hep k* hyos k* hyper iod k* irid-met srj5• kali-bi k* kali-c k* kali-i a1 kali-n k* kali-p fd1.de• kalm k* kreos k* *Lach* k* led lyc k* lyss m-ambo b7.de *Mag-c* k* mag-m k* mang b4.de* melal-alt gya4 meph k* **Merc** k* *Merc-c* k* merc-i-f mez k* mosch b7.de* naja nat-c h2* *Nat-m* k* nat-s k* nit-ac k* nux-m k* *Nux-v* k* ol-an olnd k* par k* petr k* ph-ac k* phos k* *Plat* k* podo fd3.de• *Prun* bro1 *Puls* k* ran-b *Ran-s* k* *Rhod* k* rhus-t k* ruta fd4.de sabad k* sabin k* sars k* *Sep* k* sil k* spig b7a.de* spong fd4.de *Staph* k* *Sulph* k* tab tarax k* ter thuj k* tritic-vg fd5.de valer b7.de* vanil fd5.de verat k* zinc k* zinc-p k2
  - **biting** pain: carb-v h2
  - **bubbling**: berb
  - **intermittent**: calc h2* sil h2*
  - **jerking** pain: puls h1* zinc h2*
  - **lancinating** | **current** of air rushed into; as if a: ambr
  - **paroxysmal**: cocc-s a1 kali-c h2* podo fd3.de•
  - **pressing** pain: ars
  - **pulsating** pain: cocc-s a1* hyos k* sep sulph h2* zinc h2*
  - **stretched**; as if nerves were: anac coloc k* **Puls**
  - **tearing** pain: abrot am-c h2
  - **twitching**: plat h2*
  - **wandering** pain: ambr k* hyos k*
- **drinking**:
  - **agg.**: bar-c *Caust* *Cham* k* chir-fl gya2 con *Mag-p* sabin k* sil suis-pan rly4• *Sulph* ↓ vanil fd5.de
    - **stitching**, stinging: con *Sulph*
  - **amel.**: chlam-tr bcx2• sel spig
  - **cold** water:
    - **agg.**: agar ↓
      - **jerking** pain: agar k*
  - **tea**: chin coff dulc fd4.de ferr ign lach *Sel* *Sep* thuj k*
- **dull** pain: *(↗grumbling)* aur k* borx bg2 bov b4.de* caust b4.de* chel b7.de* chin k* clem k* cocc-s k* cycl b7.de* daph dol k* euph b4.de* hyos k* kali-i kali-p fd1.de• kalm k* lob k* lyc k* lyss nat-m b4.de* *Nux-v* b7.de* ox-ac a1 sep b4.de* sil h2* thuj b4.de* tritic-vg fd5.de vanil fd5.de zinc
  - **griping** pain: *Borx* k*
  - **soft** and would bend on chewing; as if: coch
- **eating**:
  - **after**:
    - **agg.**: *Alum* alum-sil k2 am-c **Ant-c** k* arg-n tl1 ars-i bar-c k* bar-s k2 *Bell* k* borx *Bry* k* *Carb-v* carbn-s carl a1 *Cham* k* chel k* *Chim* chin coff k* euphr a1 ferr-p *Graph* k* *Hep* k* *Ign* indg a1 iod k* *Kali-c* k* kola ↓ *Lach* k* *Lyc* k* *Mag-c* k* mag-s k* *Merc* k* merc-i-r a1 *Nat-c* k* *Nat-m* k* *Nux-m* k* *Nux-v* k* phos k2 plan a1 puls k* rhus-t k* ruta fd4.de *Sabin* k* sal-fr ↓ sep a1 *Sil* spig k* stann k* **Staph** k* sul-i k2 *Sulph* zinc
      - **drawing** pain: bry k* *Cham* k* *Hep* k* kali-c h2* nat-m h2* rhus-t h1 staph h1*
- **eating** – **after** – **agg.**: ...
      - **gnawing** pain: **Ant-c** staph h1
      - **grumbling** pain: lyc h2*
      - **jerking** pain: ant-c c1 *Bry* a1 kali-c h2* nat-c a1 sal-fr sle1• stann sulph h2*
      - **stitching**, stinging: kola stb3• mag-c h2
      - **tearing** pain: sep h2*
    - **amel.**: am-c ambr arn calc carb-v ign bro1 ip ph-ac plan bro1 **Rhod** rhus-t sil *Spig* bro1
  - **agg.**: bry ↓ carb-an ↓ con ↓ psor ↓ sil ↓
    - **stitching**, stinging: bry k2 carb-an h2 con psor sil h2
  - **amel.**: am-c ↓ ambr ↓ calc ↓ *Cham* ↓ *Ign* ↓
    - **drawing** pain: am-c k* ambr k* *Cham* k*
    - **sore**: *Ign*
    - **stitching**, stinging: calc
  - **before** | **agg.**: nux-v sulph
  - **cold** food agg.: *Con* ↓
    - **drawing** pain: *Con* k*
  - **while**:
    - **agg.**: *Am-c* anan ant-c k* aur bar-c h2* bell bro1 *Bry* k* *Calc* k* calc-sil k2 canth carb-an carb-v k* carbn-s cassia-s ccrh1• *Castm* *Caust* k* cench k2 *Cham* a1* chim bro1 cocc k* cocc-s ↓ *Con* crot-h crot-t dulc fd4.de euph germ-met srj5• graph hep hydrog srj2• ign **Kali-c** k* kola stb3• *Lyc* m-arct b7a.de *Mag-c* *Mag-m* mag-p bro1 mag-s **Merc** mez bro1 *Nat-c* k* nux-m nux-v bro1 petr-ra shn4• phos psor puls k* sabin sal-fr sle1• sep k* *Sil* k* *Spig* bro1 *Staph* k* sulph k* thuj trom vanil fd5.de verat zinc bro1
      - **drawing** pain: am-c k* bry k* carb-an h2* cocc-s a1* con k* hep c1 sabin c1 sep verat
      - **tearing** pain: aur h2 bry carb-an euph h2 kali-c h2 sal-fr sle1• *Sep* sil *Staph*
    - **agg.**; only while eating: calc kali-c
    - **amel.**: am-c bell *Cham* chin coff ign sne ip ph-ac sel sil *Spig*
    - **beginning** to eat: euph ↓
      - **gnawing** pain: euph h2
- **eructations** agg.: sulph h2*
- **excitement**; emotional:
  - **agg.**: *Acon* bell *Cham* *Coff* k* *Gels* hyos
  - **amel.**: thuj
- **exertion** agg.: chim k* nux-v bro1
- **extraction** of teeth; after: arn br1* staph br1*
  - **long** after extraction: gink-b sbd1•
- **fever**:
  - **before**: *Carb-v* b4a.de graph b4a.de kali-c b4a.de
  - **during** | **agg.**: *Apis* b7a.de* carb-v bg2 graph b4.de* hyos bg2 *Kali-c* b4.de* lach bg2 nat-c bg2 puls bg2 *Rhus-t* b7.de* **Sep** b4a.de* staph bg2
- **filling**, after●: **Arn** *Cham* sne *Hyper* sne merc *Merc-i-f* nat-sil fd3.de• **Nux-v** k* sep k* *Staph* sne
- **fine**: indg bg2 led bg2 mag-m bg2
- **flatus**; passing | **amel.**: kola stb3•
- **forced** out (See pressing - outward)
- **foreign** body between; as from a (See pressing - wedged)
- **fruit** agg.: nat-c nat-s
- **gnawing** pain: agar k* **Ant-c** bar-c k* berb k* **Calc** k* camph k* canth carb-v k* castm k* *Cham* k* *Con* k* daph k* euph k* indg k* kali-bi k* kali-c b4a.de *Kali-i* k* lac-c k* laur a1 mag-c b4a.de* mez bro1 naja nicc k* *Nux-v* k* op k* ph-ac b4a.de phos k* plan bro1 **Puls** k* raph a1 rhus-t k* sec sil bro1 **Staph** k* sul-ac k* *Thuj* k*
- **gout**; after suppressed: sabin c1
- **grasping** pain: ign b7.de nux-m bg2 stront-c b4a.de
- **griping** pain: am-c bg2 ant-c bg2 *Borx* bg2* carb-an h2* carb-v bg2 ign bg2 kali-c h2* kali-i bg2*
- **grumbling** pain: *(↗dull)* alum h2 aur k* bar-c cann-s carb-an cham kali-i kali-n lil-t mag-s meny nit-ac nux-m bg1 ph-ac **Rhod** sep teucr bg1
- **hacking** pain: aur b4a.de* cocc-s a1

- **heat**:
  - • **stove**; of:
    - ⋮ **agg.**: graph
    - ⋮ **amel.**: **Ars**
- **heated**; when: phos$_{k*}$ zinc$_{h2*}$
- **increasing** gradually:
  - • **decreasing**:
    - ⋮ **gradually**: bell$_{k*}$ stann
    - ⋮ **suddenly**: sul-ac$_{k*}$
- **inspiration** agg.: carb-v$_{h2*}$ *Nux-v* ribo$_{rly4•}$
- **intermittent**: **Ant-t** ars-i astac *Bell Borx* bry calc *Cham Chin Coff* dulc$_{fd4.de}$ melal-alt$_{gya4}$ merc nux-v *Puls* rhod rhus-t sabad sil *Staph Sulph*
- **jar** agg.: acon$_{dx}$ **Arn** *Nux-m*$_{k*}$ ozone$_{sde2•}$
- **jerking** pain: all-c all-s alum *Am-c* anac *Ant-c* apis ars aur-m *Bar-c* bar-m *Bell*$_{k*}$ benz-ac berb borx$_{c1}$ bov *Bry* **Calc**$_{k*}$ calc-sil$_{k2}$ cann-xyz$_{bg2}$ *Carb-an* carb-v carbn-s *Caust*$_{k*}$ **Cham** *Chin* chinin-ar *Clem Coc-c* cocc-s$_{k*}$ *Coff Con*$_{k*}$ cycl$_{k*}$ **Euph** hep *Hyos* hyper indg kali-c$_{k*}$ kali-i$_{k*}$ kali-n kali-p kreos *Lach* laur$_{k*}$ *Lyc*$_{k*}$ mag-c mag-m$_{k*}$ mag-s mang$_{bg1}$ meph *Merc* mez mur-ac$_{a1}$ nat-ar$_{k2}$ nat-c$_{k*}$ nat-s$_{bg1}$ nat-sil$_{fd3.de•}$ nit-ac nux-m$_{k*}$ *Nux-v*$_{k*}$ ox-ac par *Phos*$_{k*}$ plat plb prun *Puls Ran-s*$_{k*}$ rat *Rhus-t*$_{k*}$ ribc$_{rly4•}$ *Sep*$_{k*}$ sil spig$_{k*}$ stann stront-c *Sulph*$_{k*}$ syph tarax$_{h1*}$ zinc$_{k*}$ zinc-p$_{k2}$
  - • **stretch** and let loose; as if nerves were put on: **Puls**$_{k*}$
  - • **torn** out; as if:
    - ⋮ **nerves** in teeth would be torn out; as if: ant-c$_{rb2}$ coloc$_{rb2}$
    - ⋮ **teeth** would be torn out; as if: astac$_{kr1}$ berb bov$_{rb2}$ calc$_{rb2}$ cocc cocc-s$_{rb2}$ cycl$_{rb2}$ *Euph*$_{rb2}$ ind ip prun$_{rb2}$ rhus-t$_{rb2}$
- **joy**; from excessive: coff$_{k2}$
- **knocking** pain: ars carb-an kali-c
- **lachrymation** (See MIND - Weeping - pains - with - teeth)
- **lancinating** (See tearing)
- **laying** forehead on table amel.: mang$_{h2}$
- **leaning** against pillow: nit-ac$_{h2*}$
- **lying**:
  - • **after**:
    - ⋮ **agg.** | **immediately** after lying: *Aran* bell canth hell ign puls rat sanic
  - • **agg.**: alum↓ aran$_{k*}$ ars bell bry$_{k*}$ *Cham Clem Graph Hyos* ign kola$_{stb3•}$ mag-c$_{bro1}$ merc nat-s$_{bro1}$ nux-v olnd *Petr Phos* puls *Rat*$_{bro1}$ *Rhus-t* sep$_{k*}$ staph *Sul-ac* sulph trom
    - ⋮ **cutting** pain: alum$_{k*}$
  - • **amel.**: alum am-m *Bry* lyc nat-c *Nux-v* spig$_{k*}$
  - • **head** high; with the | **agg.**: spig
  - • **head** low; with the | **agg.**: puls
  - • **side**; on:
    - ⋮ **painful** side:
      - : **agg.**: ars guare ign nux-v puls tritic-vg$_{fd5.de}$
        - . **tearing** pain: **Ars**
      - : **amel.**: **Bry**$_{k*}$ chinin-s hyper ign kali-n$_{h2*}$ mag-c puls
    - ⋮ **painless** side:
      - : **agg.**: **Bry** *Cham* ign puls
        - . **tearing** pain: puls
      - : **amel.**: nux-v
    - ⋮ **right** | **agg.**: spig
- **meals**, between: ign↓
  - • **sore**: ign$_{k*}$
- **menses**:
  - • **after** | **agg.**: am-c bry$_{bg2}$ *Calc*$_{k*}$ cham$_{k*}$ mag-c$_{k*}$ mag-p phos$_{k*}$ rhod$_{bg2}$ sabin$_{bg2}$ thuj$_{k*}$
  - • **before**:
    - ⋮ **agg.**: agar$_{k*}$ am-c$_{k*}$ *Ant-c*$_{k*}$ ars$_{k*}$ bar-c$_{k*}$ calc$_{bro1}$ cham$_{b7a.de*}$ mag-c$_{k2*}$ *Nat-m*$_{k*}$ phos *Puls*$_{k*}$ sep$_{bg2*}$ *Sulph*$_{k*}$ thuj$_{k*}$ zinc$_{h2*}$
      - : **stitching**, stinging: sulph$_{h2}$
      - : **tearing** pain: *Ars*
- **menses**: ...
  - • **during**:
    - ⋮ **agg.**: agar$_{bg2*}$ *Am-c*$_{k*}$ *Ars*$_{k*}$ bar-c$_{k*}$ bell$_{bg2}$ *Bov*$_{k*}$ *Calc*$_{k*}$ carb-v$_{k*}$ castm *Cedr Cham*$_{k*}$ chim$_{al}$ cic$_{bg2}$ *Coff*$_{k*}$ cycl$_{bg2}$ glon$_{bg2}$ *Graph*$_{k*}$ hyos$_{bg2}$ kali-ar *Kali-c*$_{k*}$ kiss$_{a1}$ *Lach*$_{k*}$ laur$_{k*}$ mag-c$_{k*}$ mang$_{bg2}$ **Merc**$_{b4a.de*}$ nat-c$_{bg2}$ *Nat-m*$_{k*}$ *Nit-ac*$_{k*}$ phos$_{k*}$ *Puls*$_{k*}$ rhus-t$_{bg2}$ **Sep**$_{k*}$ sil$_{hr1}$ **Staph**$_{k*}$ sul-ac$_{k*}$ *Verat*$_{bg2}$
      - : **drawing** pain: **Am-c**$_{k*}$ sep$_{k*}$
      - : **jerking** pain: graph$_{h2*}$
      - : **menorrhagia**: *Ferr-s*
      - : **stitching**, stinging: graph$_{h2}$
      - : **tearing** pain: ars$_{k*}$ mag-c$_{k*}$ nat-m$_{k*}$ sul-ac$_{h2*}$
    - ⋮ **beginning** and end of menses agg.: *Puls*
    - ⋮ **beginning** of menses | **agg.**: agar$_{bg2}$ *Ars*$_{b4a.de}$ *Nat-m Puls*$_{k*}$ *Sep*$_{b4a.de}$
    - ⋮ **decreases**; when flow: **Lach**
  - • **suppressed**; from: **Puls**↓
    - ⋮ **stitching**, stinging: **Puls**
- **mental** exertion agg.: bell *Ign Nux-v*$_{k*}$
  - • **drawing** pain: *Nux-v*
- **mercury**; after abuse of: carb-v$_{k2}$ colch *Hep Nit-ac Staph*
- **motion**:
  - • **agg.**: *Bry* chel$_{k*}$ *Chin* clem coff$_{k2}$ daph hyper kali-c$_{h2*}$ merc *Mez*$_{k*}$ *Nux-v* sabin spig staph$_{k*}$
  - • **amel.**: am-c↓ *Mag-c*$_{k*}$ phos *Puls Rhus-t*
    - ⋮ **tearing** pain: am-c
- **music** agg.: ph-ac
  - • **drawing** pain: ph-ac
- **nerve**; from injury of: *Hyper*$_{mrr1}$
- **nerve** was exposed; as if: *Kalm*$_{bg1*}$
- **nerve** were rubbed; as if bare, exposed: bov$_{b4.de*}$
- **nerve** were touched; as if: bry$_{b7.de*}$
- **nervous** patients: *Acon Ars Bell* **Cham Coff** *Gels Mag-p Puls* staph
- **neuralgic**: **Acon**$_{bg2*}$ agar$_{bg2}$ ant-c$_{bg2}$ apis$_{bg2}$ aran$_{bg2*}$ ars$_{bg2*}$ asar$_{bg2}$ **Bell**$_{k*}$ borx bry$_{bg2}$ calc$_{bg2}$ *Carbn-s* caust$_{bg2}$ cedr$_{bg2*}$ *Cham*$_{k*}$ *Chel*$_{k*}$ chin$_{bg2}$ chlol cimic clem$_{bg2}$ cocc-s$_{br1}$ **Coff**$_{k*}$ *Coloc*$_{k*}$ dol$_{bro1}$ ferr-pic$_{bro1}$ gels$_{k*}$ guaj$_{bg2}$ **Hyos**$_{bg2}$ *Ign*$_{bg2*}$ *Iris Kali-p* kalm$_{a1}$ kreos$_{bg2*}$ lach$_{bg2}$ mag-c$_{bg2*}$ **Mag-p**$_{k*}$ merc$_{bro1}$ mez$_{bg2*}$ *Nux-m* **Nux-v**$_{bg2}$ phos$_{bg2}$ *Phyt*$_{k*}$ *Plan*$_{k*}$ plat$_{bg2}$ puls$_{bg2}$ rat$_{bg2}$ rhod rhodi$_{br1}$ sep$_{bg2}$ *Sil* **Spig**$_{bg2*}$ staph$_{bg2*}$ sulph$_{bg2}$ tab$_{bg2}$ thuj$_{bg2}$ verat$_{bg2}$ verb$_{bro1}$
- **noise** agg.●: asar$_{mtf11}$ calc *Coff* tarent *Ther*$_{k*}$
  - • **shrill**; from: ther$_{bro1}$
- **nursing** mothers; in: acon ars bell *Calc* dulc merc nux-v phos staph sulph
  - • **nurses**, while the infant: *Chin*$_{k*}$
- **opening** the mouth agg.: bry caust hep indg↓ kola$_{stb3•}$ nux-v petr$_{h2}$ phos puls sabin
  - • **tearing** pain: caust indg
- **operation**; after dental (See dental; filling)
- **paroxysmal**: all-s anac borx calc *Cham* dulc$_{fd4.de}$ gels glon hyper ip lac-c lyc melal-alt$_{gya4}$ merc *Nux-m* petr *Plat* rumx sep spig$_{bg2}$ sulph$_{h2*}$
- **pears** agg.: nat-c
- **periodical**: aran ars$_{k*}$ bry$_{a1}$ cham chel$_{a1}$ chinin-ar$_{k*}$ chinin-s$_{bro1}$ cocc-s$_{hr1}$ coff$_{bro1}$ coloc$_{k*}$ lach$_{bg1}$
  - • **day**:
    - ⋮ **alternate**: *Cham* nat-m
    - ⋮ **seven** days; every: ars calc-ar phos sulph
- **perspiration**:
  - • **amel.**: all-c aphis$_{k*}$ carb-ac carb-an cham$_{bro1}$ *Chen-g*$_{bro1}$
    - ⋮ **drawing** pain: aphis
  - • **during**: bry$_{bg2}$ **Carb-v**$_{bg2}$ *Cham*$_{bg2}$ **Chin**$_{k*}$ graph$_{bg2}$ hyos$_{k*}$ kali-c$_{bg2}$ *Merc*$_{bg2}$ nux-v$_{bg2}$ puls$_{bg2}$ **Rhus-t**$_{bg2}$ *Sep*$_{bg2}$ staph$_{bg2}$ verat$_{bg2}$ zinc$_{bg2}$
    - ⋮ **Head**: *Cham*$_{bg2}$
  - • **feet**; after suppressed perspiration of: **Sil**
  - • **suppressed** perspiration; from: cham
  - • **tendency** to perspire: daph
- **picking** pain: chin$_{b7.de*}$ cimic$_{bg2}$ kali-c$_{h2*}$ zinc$_{h2*}$

- **picking** teeth:
  - **amel.** by picking teeth: *All-c* am-c h2* bell ph-ac sanic
    - **bleed**; until the gums: *(↗bleeding)* *Bell* hr1
  - **excited** by: kali-c *Puls* *Sang* k*
- **piercing** pain: acon ant-c bell *Bry* calc calc-sil k2 caust *Cham* chin *Lach* *Merc* nux-m nux-v ph-ac *Puls* rhus-t sil staph
- **pinching** pain: am-c ambr bg2 anac bg2 *Aran* carb-v h2* cham bg2 iod h* kali-c h2* lyc h2* mag-c h2* nux-m bg2 plat bg2 spig bg2 thiam rly4•
- **pregnancy** agg.; during: *Acon* k* alum k* apis *Bell* k* bry *Calc* k* *Calc-f* bro1 *Cham* k* chin k2 coff bro1 *Hyos* *Kreos* bro1 **Lyss** k* *Mag-c* k* *Merc* *Nux-m* k* nux-v k* *Puls* k* raph c2 *Rat* k* rhus-t **Sep** k* *Staph* k* *Tab* k*
  - **tearing** pain: nux-m sep h2*
- **pressing** pain: acon *All-c* k* allox tpw4 am-c k* anac k* aran *Arn* k* ars h2* asaf b7.de* bism k* borx k* bov bry k* *Calc* k* calc-sil k2 carb-v k* caust k* cham k* chel k* chin k* clem b4a.de *Coloc* k* con h2* cor-r dulc fd4.de euph k* *Graph* k* guaj k* guare hydrog srj2• hyos ign iod k* *Kali-c* k* kali-p *Kalm* k* ketogl-ac rly4• kola stb3• led lob m-ambo b7.de **Merc** merc-c b4a.de mez h2* *Nat-c* k* *Nat-m* k* nat-p nux-m k* nux-v k* olnd k* petr k* ph-ac b4a.de phos k* *Puls* a1 *Rhod* k* *Rhus-t* k* sabin b7.de* sep b4.de* *Sil* k* spig k* *Staph* k* *Sulph* k* tarax k* thuj b4.de* tritic-vg fd5.de *Valer* b7.de* verat k*
  - **asunder**: anan kalm mur-ac k* nat-m h2* ph-ac ran-b k* sabin spig spong thuj
  - **blood** were forced into them; as if: arn calc h2 chin
  - **close** together; as if: acon arn bell calc cham chin *Coff* hep hyos nat-sil fd3.de• *Nux-v* puls symph fd3.de•
  - **held** in a grip; as if: nux-m *Sil*
  - **inward**: rhus-t staph sul-ac a1
  - **meat** were between the teeth; as if a shred of: *Caust* *Cor-r* *Lach* ptel bg1
  - **outward**: arn k* bell berb caust bg2 coc-c rb2 kola stb3• *Phos* *Puls* spig k* zinc
  - **pressed**; as if:
    - **apart**: am-c bg2 ambr bg2 graph bg2 mur-ac b4a.de* nux-v bg2 ph-ac bg2 puls bg2 ran-b b7a.de ran-s bg2 rhod bg2 sabin b7a.de* spig b7a.de* spong bg2 thuj bg2
    - **gums**; into: staph b7.de*
    - **sockets**; into: alum am-c
  - **wedged** in between; as if something were: anan *Caust* *Cor-r* *Lach* k* nat-sil fd3.de• ptel bg1 ran-b b7.de* *Rhus-t* b7.de* spong k* symph fd3.de•
- **pressure**:
  - **agg.**: adam skp7• calc-p k2 carb-an **Cham** ham fd3.de• hyos kali-bi kola stb3• mag-m nat-c nat-m phos sal-fr sle1• sep spig sul-ac sulph suprar rly4• tritic-vg fd5.de zinc zinc-p k2
  - **amel.**: ail *Alum* am-c am-m ars bell *Brom* k* bry k* cann-i a1 chin k* clem cocc coloc com dulc fd4.de euph grat hist sp1 ign indg *Kali-c* kali-n h2* laur *Mag-m* *Mag-p* merc-i-f mur-ac nat-c nat-m k* nat-p oci-sa sp1 ol-an *Phos* puls rhus-t ruta fd4.de sep *Staph* tab
    - **sore**: alum
    - **tearing** pain: mag-m h2*
  - **cold** hand amel.; of: rhus-t
- **pricking** pain: am-c k* ant-c bar-m calc caust hell mag-s melal-alt gya4 nux-m phos prun
- **pulled** into their sockets; as if: rhus-t b7.de
- **pulled** out; as if being: anan arn astac bell berb bov b4.de* bry b7.de* bufo *Calc* b4.de* caust k* chim br1* coc-c cocc bg2 cocc-s com k* con bg1 cycl bg2 der vml3• euph b4.de* indg bg2 ip k* kola stb3• laur bg2 lyc bg2 m-arct b7.de* *Mag-c* bg1* mang k* *Mez* k* mur-ac h2* nat-c k* nat-m bg2 nux-m k* nux-v ph-ac k* pieri-b mlk9.de prun k* psor bg2 puls *Rhus-t* k* sabin c1 sel k* *Spig* b7a.de stront-c k* sulph k* zinc k*
  - **and** left in their sockets: sanic
- **pulsating** pain: *Acon* k* agar agn *All-c* aloe alum b4a.de am-c k* ang k* apis k* arg-n bg2 arn k* *Ars* k* aur b4.de* bar-c k* bar-m **Bell** k* bit-ar wht1• brom *Bry* b7a.de *Calc* k* canni-i cann-s b7.de* carb-an k* *Carb-v* k* *Carbn-s* k* **Caust** k* **Cham** k* **Chin** k* *Chinin-ar* k* coc-c cocc-s k* *Coff* k* colch bg2 *Coloc* k* daph k* dulc fd4.de elae a1 *Euph* euphr b7.de* eupi bg2 form bg2 *Glon* k* hep *Hyos* k* hyper tl1 kali-ar *Kali-c* k* kali-i bg2 kali-n k* kali-p **Lach** *Lyc* k* m-ambo b7.de m-arct b7.de *Mag-c* k* mag-m b4.de* mag-s *Merc* k* merc-c b4a.de mur-ac k* nat-ar k* nat-c k* *Nat-m* k* nat-p k* *Nat-s* k* nat-sil fd3.de• *Nit-ac* k* nux-m k* par k* phos k* pip-n bg2 plat k* pot-e rly4• psor k* *Puls* k* rat *Rhus-t* k* ribo rly4• sabad k* sabin k* sacch-a fd2.de• sel b7a.de **Sep** k* *Sil* k* *Spig* k* *Staph* k* stram k* **Sulph** k* tab bg2 *Tarent* k* thuj k* tritic-vg fd5.de *Verat* k* zinc zinc-p k2
  - **synchronous** with pulse: clem h2*
- **pushed** out; as if: *Puls* b7.de*
- **quinine**, from abuse of: *Hep* *Nit-ac* **Puls**
- **radiating**: ant-c bg2 arn bg2 ars bg2 cham bg2 coff bg2 ferr bg2 hyos bg2 kali-bi ptk1 mang bg2 *Merc* bg2* mez bg2* nux-v ptk1 plat bg2 puls bg2 rhus-t bg2 spig bg2 staph bg2*
  - **accompanied** by | **Glands**; swelling of: kali-bi ptk1
- **raging**: nat-s bg2
- **rapidly**: **Bry** ↓ *Caust* ↓ mang ↓ *Puls* ↓
  - **wandering** pain: **Bry** b7a.de *Caust* b4a.de mang b4a.de* *Puls* b7a.de
- **reading** agg.: all-s ↓ calc ign *Nux-v* thuj
  - **drawing** pain: all-s k*
- **reflex** neuralgia of lids; with: plan br1*
- **rheumatic**: acon k* ant-c bg2 **Ant-t** k* aran bg2 arn bg2 bell k* bry bg2* calc-p k* *Caust* bg2 *Cham* k* chel bg2 **Chin** bg2 chinin-s bro1 *Cimic* clem bg2 coch coff bg2 *Colch* k* cycl bg2 guaj bg2* indg lach a1 lyc bg2 *M-arct* b7.de *Mag-c* k* *Mag-p* mang bg2 *Merc* k* mez bg2 mill nat-m bg2 nux-v k* phos bg2 *Phyt* k* **Puls** bg2* rhod k* rhus-t b7.de* sabin bg2 sep h2* sil spig bg2 staph k* **Sulph** bg2 verat bg2 wies a1
- **riding** in a carriage agg.: calc k* *Mag-c* k*
- **rising**:
  - **bed**; from:
    - **after**:
      - **agg.**: ign a1* plat a3 sep h1*
      - **amel.**: alum ↓
        - **jerking** pain: alum
    - **amel.**: alum ↓ clem mag-c h2* olnd *Phos* k* sabin
      - **tearing** pain: alum
- **rubbing** cheek | **amel.**: **Merc** k* *Phos*
- **saliva**, with involuntary flow of: bell *Cham* k* daph k* *Dulc* k* hydrog srj2• **Merc** k* merc-i-r hr1 nat-m k* plan hr1 *Staph* sne
- **salt**:
  - **agg.**: carb-v
    - **tearing** pain: carb-v k2
  - **amel.**: *Carb-an* mag-c
- **scraping** pain: arn b7.de* *Bell* b4a.de berb cham k* kola stb3• *Rhus-t* b7a.de
- **screwing** pain: *Bry* k* **Euph** k* mag-c h2* *Stront-c* b4a.de*
- **shivering**; during: graph b4a.de led b7.de
- **shocks** (See jerking)
- **shooting** (See stitching)
- **shooting** through gums to roots of incisors and canines: camph ↓
  - **cutting** pain: camph k*
- **sitting**:
  - **agg.**: am-c am-m ant-c cocc-s k* graph merc *Puls* rhus-t
  - **erect** | **agg.**: mang k*
  - **still** | **amel.**: spig
- **sitting** up in bed:
  - **amel.**: acon b7a.de alum k* *Ars* k* bar-m merc k* *Nat-m* b4a.de petr k* rhus-t k*
    - **gnawing** pain: alum k*
    - **jerking** pain: *Ars* k*
- **sleep**:
  - **after**:
    - **agg.**: bar-m bell bry calc calc-sil k2 carb-v *Caust* con graph *Kali-c* kali-p *Lach* nux-v *Phos* sabin sil spig sulph zinc
    - **amel.**: merc nux-v puls sanic
  - **going** to sleep; on | **agg.**: ant-t ars kola stb3• melal-alt gya4 *Merc* sulph zinc-p k2
- **smoking**:
  - **agg.**: *Bry* *Caust* *Cham* chin clem k* *Ign* k* *Merc* *Nux-v* plan bro1 sabin sars **Spig** k* thuj
    - **jerking** pain: bry k*
  - **amel.**: aran borx camph h1* *Merc* *Nat-c* k* *Nat-s* sel spig

- • **amel.**: ...
  - ⁝ **jerking** pain: spig
  - ⁝ **tingling** pain: borx c1
- **sneezing** agg.: androc srj1• thuj
- **sore** (= bruised): acon-ac rly4• alum k* apis *Arn* ars k* aur *Bapt* k* bar-c bell k* *Bry* k* *Calc* k* carb-an carb-v k* caul caust k* cham chir-fl gya2 cina k* cinnb clem b4a.de colch k* coli rly4• crot-h crot-t euph b4.de* fago bg2 graph k* *Ign* k* iod b4a.de kali-ar kali-c kali-p lach bg2 *Lyc* k* *M-ambo* b7.de* mang med **Merc** k* mez b4a.de* *Nat-m* k* *Nux-v* k* *Phos* phyt *Plan* k* psor ptel c1 *Puls* k* rhod k* *Rhus-t* k* sep k* sil bg2 *Staph* k* tab thuj k* *Zinc* k* zinc-p k2
- **soup**; warm: eupi c1
  - • **amel.**: lavand-a ctl1•
- **sour** things, from: arg-n cimic bg1 cupr bg1 dulc bg1 kola stb3•
  - • **amel.**: puls
- **splintered**; as if: sabin
- **sprained**; as if: *Arn* k*
- **spring**, in the: acon aur *Bell Bry Calc* carb-v *Dulc* **Lach** lyc *Nat-m* nux-v *Puls* rhod *Rhus-t* sep sil sulph verat
- **squeezed**; as if: am-c bg2 anac b4a.de *Calc* b4a.de guaj bg2 lach bg2 lyc b4.de* merc bg2 merc-i-f bg2 plat b4.de* spong bg2 ter bg2
- **standing** up:
  - • **after**: ign plat sep
  - • **amel.**: alum nux-v olnd phos sabin spig
- **sticking** inside; as from something: nat-m h2*
- **stimulants** agg.: acon
- **stitching**, stinging: acon k* aesc *Agar* all-c alum alum-p k2 alum-sil k2 *Am-c* k* am-m ambr k* ant-c k* *Apis Asaf* aur k* aur-s *Bar-c* k* bar-m bar-s k2 bell k* benz-ac berb borx k* *Bov* k* **Bry** k* bufo *Calc* k* calc-p calc-sil k2 canth b7.de* *Carb-an* k* carb-v k* *Carbn-s* **Caust** k* *Cham* k* chin k* cist *Clem* k* coff k* colch k* con k* crot-h cub *Cycl* k* daph *Dros* k* dulc fd4.de echi *Euph* k* euphr k* gels **Graph** k* grat guaj k* haem hell k* hep k* iod h *Iris* kali-bi k* *Kali-c* k* kali-chl kali-m k2 kali-n k* kali-p kali-s fd4.de kalm kola stb3• **Lach** laur k* led b7.de* **Lyc** k* lyss *M-aust* b7a.de mag-c k* *Mag-p* mang *Merc* k* merc-c b4a.de *Mez* k* nat-c k* *Nat-m* k* *Nit-ac* k* nux-m k* *Nux-v* k* ol-an *Petr* k* ph-ac b4.de* phel *Phos* k* prun psor *Puls* k* ran-s k* raph rat rhod k* *Rhus-t* k* *Sabad* k* sabin k* *Samb* k* sars **Sep** k* *Sil* k* spig b7a.de* spong k* squil k* *Staph Stront-c* k* *Stry Sulph* k* tab valer k* vero-o rly4• zinc k* zinc-p k2
  - • **accompanied** by | **Head**; pain in: borx c1
  - • **intermittent**: *Asaf* borx h2
  - • **needles**; as from: con bg2 hyper bg2 nux-v bg2 [bell-p-sp dcm1]
  - • **outward**: **Asaf**
  - • **rasping**: sang
  - • **tickling**: carb-v h2 staph h1
- **stooping**:
  - • **agg.**: sep spig
  - • **amel.**: arn
- **stroking** head amel.: *Ars* ↓
  - • **jerking** pain: *Ars* k*
- **sucking**:
  - • **teeth**:
    - ⁝ **agg.**: bell *Bov Carb-v* castm dulc fd4.de kali-c mang *Nux-m* nux-v sil zinc
    - ⁝ **amel.**: all-c bov caust *Clem* mang sep
- **sudden**: carb-an ↓ coc-c ↓
  - • **drawing** pain: carb-an h2* coc-c k*
- **summer** agg.: ant-c bell bry calc carb-v cham lach lyc nat-c *Nat-m* nux-v puls sel
- **supper** agg.; after: borx ↓
  - • **tingling** pain: borx c1
- **swallowing** agg.: alum chinin-s phos k* staph
  - • **pressing** pain: alum
- **sweets** agg.: am-c bamb-a stb2.de• dulc fd4.de ham fd3.de• irid-met srj5• kali-p fd1.de• kola stb3• menth c1 *Nat-c* k* phos k* podo fd3.de• ruta fd4.de **Sep** k● spong fd4.de symph fd3.de• tritic-vg fd5.de
- **swelling**; with:
  - ○ • **Cheeks**; of (See accompanied - cheeks - swelling)
  - • **Submaxillary** glands; of (See accompanied - submaxillary)
- **swollen** submaxillary gland, seems to originate in: camph ↓
  - • **cutting** pain: camph k*
- **talk** of others agg.: ars bry
- **talking** agg.: am-c bg1 ars bry *Cham* k* chel nux-m bg1 *Nux-v* phos k2 sep trom
- **tearing** pain: abrot k* **Acon** act-sp aesc *Agar* k* agn ail k* alum k* alum-p k2 alum-sil k2 **Am-c** k* am-m k* ambr k* anac k* anag anan ang ant-c b7a.de ant-t k* aphis apis arg-n k* arn k* *Ars* k* ars-i arum-t k* *Aur* aur-ar k2 aur-i k2 aur-s a1* bamb-a stb2.de• bar-c bar-i k2 bar-m bar-s k2 *Bell* k* benz-ac berb k* borx k* *Bry* k* bufo calc k* calc-p calc-sil k2 camph canth k* *Carb-an* k* **Carb-v** k* *Carbn-s* castm **Caust** k* *Cham* k* chel k* *Chin* k* chinin-ar clem *Coc-c* cocc-s a1* *Coff* k* *Colch* k* *Coloc* k* con k* *Cupr* k* cupr-ar *Cycl* k* daph k* euon a1 euph b4.de* gamb gels *Graph* k* grat k* *Guaj* k* haem a1 hell k* *Hyos* k* hyper k* indg k* iod ip k* kali-ar kali-bi k* *Kali-c* k* kali-i k* kali-n b4.de* *Kali-p* kola stb3• kreos k* *Lach* k* laur k* *Lyc* k* *M-aust* b7.de* *Mag-c* k* *Mag-m* k* mang k* meph k* **Merc** k* *Merc-c* b4a.de merl k* *Mez* k* mur-ac bg2 nat-ar *Nat-c* k* *Nat-m* k* nat-s k* nat-sil fd3.de• *Nicc* k* *Nit-ac* k* *Nux-m* k* *Nux-v* k* ol-an olnd k* petr k* *Ph-ac* k* phel k* *Phos* k* plb k* prun *Psor* k* *Puls* k* ran-b *Rat* k* *Rhod* k* *Rhus-t* k* sabin k* sal-fr sle1• *Samb* k* **Sars** k* **Sep** k* *Sil* k* sinus rly4• *Spig* k* **Staph** k* stront-c k* sul-ac k* sul-i k2 *Sulph* k* tab k* tarent k* tep a1 teucr k* *Thuj* k* til a1 verb k* vinc k* viol-o k* wies a1 zinc k* zinc-p k2
  - • **air**; as from a draft of: ambr
  - • **glowing**: sulph h2
  - • **jerking** pain: nat-c h2 ph-ac h2 zinc h2
  - • **paroxysmal**: anac calc h2*
  - • **pulsating** pain: agar h2* agn bell
  - • **wandering** pain: mag-c
- **temperature**; from change of: kola stb3•
- **thinking** | **other** things (See diverted)
- **thinking** of it agg.: bar-c *Nux-v Spig* thuj
- **thunderstorm**:
  - • **before**: **Rhod**
    - ⁝ **cutting** pain: *Rhod*
    - ⁝ **drawing** pain: rhod k*
  - • **during**: rhod bro1
- **tingling** pain: alum borx calc carb-v castm hyos bg2 ign bg2 indg lach lat-h bnm5• merc-c b4a.de mur-ac *Rhus-t* sulph k* zinc b4.de*
- **tobacco**; from chewing: *Bry*
- **torn** out; as if being (See jerking - torn - teeth)
- **touch**:
  - • **agg.**: alum alum-p k2 am-c anac anag ant-c *Arn* ars aur aur-ar k2 aur-s k2 bar-c *Bell* k* borx *Bry Calc* calc-f bro1 calc-p k2 camph carb-an *Carb-v* carbn-s castm caust k* chel k* **Chin** k* chinin-ar clem coc-c coff daph *Euph Graph Hep* ign kali-c bro1 kali-n kali-s fd4.de *Lyc* mag-c mag-m k* mag-s *Mang* merc *Merc-c Mez* k* *Nat-m Nux-m Nux-v Ph-ac Phos* plan k* psor *Puls* rat rhod rhus-t sabin **Sep** k* *Staph* k* *Sulph* thuj tritic-vg fd5.de
    - ⁝ **drawing** pain: coc-c k2 tritic-vg fd5.de
    - ⁝ **tearing** pain: aur h2* borx h2
  - • **amel.**: bry nat-m k* nux-v sep
  - • **cheek** agg.; of: mag-m bg1 nat-c h2
  - • **food**; of: bell camph kali-c kali-s fd4.de *Mag-m* k* mag-s nit-ac rob sang
  - • **slight** touch agg.: *Chin* c1
  - • **tongue** agg.; when touched by the: am-c anac **Ant-c** borx h2 bry calc h2 carb-v castm chin ign mag-c bg1 *Merc Mez* nat-c nat-m h2 phos rhus-t sep thuj
    - ⁝ **drawing** pain: borx c1
- **touching** decayed teeth: am-c ↓
  - • **pricking** pain: am-c k*
- **travelling**, while●: ars *Bry Cham* puls rhus-t staph sulph
- **twitching**: all-c am-c b4a.de* anac b4a.de* ant-c k* apis ars k* aur h2* aur-m bell k* bov b4.de* bry k* calc k* caust k* *Cham* b7.de* chel chin b7.de* cist *Clem* k* coff k* coloc k* con b4.de* cupr-ar dulc fd4.de graph b4.de* hep k* hyos kali-c b4.de* kola stb3• kreos bg2 *Lach* laur b7.de* m-ambo b7.de* *M-aust* b7.de* mag-c b4.de* *Merc* k* merc-c b4a.de *Mez* k* mur-ac b4.de* nat-c b4.de*

- **twitching**: ...
nit-ac b4a.de* *Nux-v* k* *Phos* k* plb b7.de* *Puls* k* ran-s b7.de* *Rhus-t* b7.de* sep b4.de* **Sil** b4a.de* **Spig** b7.de* stann b4a.de* stront-c b4a.de* sulph h2* thuj b4.de* zinc b4.de*
- **ulcerative** pain: alum b4.de* am-c k* am-m bg2 arn bg2 bell k* carb-v b4.de* caust k* coc-c eupi bg2 graph bg2 hep b4a.de kali-i k* kali-n lyc h2* mag-c k* mang k* nat-c bg2 nux-v bg2 petr h2* phos k* *Sil* k*
- **uncovering** body | **amel.**: puls
- **vexation**; after: *Acon Cham* rhus-t *Staph*
- **vibrating**: hyos b7.de* ign b7.de* sep b4a.de sulph b4.de
- **vinegar** amel.: puls h1* tong bg1
  - **stitching**, stinging: puls h1
- **wakes** from pain: (↗*morning - bed - in - agg. - waking)* ars bell h1 calc h2 *Carb-an* chel lach mag-c mez h2 spig h1 sulph h2 zinc h2
- **walking**:
  - **about** | **must** walk about: cham bg2 mag-c bg2 rat bg2 spig bg2
  - **agg.**: camph guare nat-c h2* nux-v k* *Phos* k*
    - **drawing** pain: camph
  - **air**; in open:
    - **agg.**: agn cham con dros graph kali-c kali-n mag-s *Nat-c* nux-v phos sabad sabin staph
      - **drawing** pain: *Con*
    - **amel.**: **Ant-c** k* bov bry calc tl1 clem hep *Kali-s* lyc m-arct mag-m *Nux-v* par **Puls** rhus-t sep
  - **amel.**: *Mag-c* k* *Puls* rat k* *Rhus-t* spig
  - **wind**; in the | **agg.**: graph
- **wandering** pain: ambr k* bell bg2 graph h2* hep bg2 hyos iod bg2 kola stb3• mag-c bg2 mag-p mang nit-ac bg2 nux-v ozone sde2• puls k* thuj til
- **warm**:
  - **applications**:
    - **agg.**: ambr ↓
      - **drawing** pain: ambr
    - **amel.**: **Ars** ↓ rhus-t ↓
      - **tearing** pain: **Ars** rhus-t a1
  - **bed**:
    - **agg.**: ant-c bell bry **Cham** chel clem graph jug-r led *Mag-c* **Merc** *Ph-ac* phos **Puls** rhod sabin sulph
      - **tearing** pain: graph *Ph-ac*
    - **amel.**: *Lyc* mag-s *Nux-v Sil* spig vinc
      - **stitching**, stinging: *Lyc*
      - **twitching**: spig
  - **drinks**:
    - **agg.**: aesc agn *All-c* am-c am-m bism *Bry Carb-v* carbn-s k2 cench k2 **Cham** k* chlam-tr bcx2• clem mrr1 **Coff** *Dros* dulc fd4.de *Ferr-p* fl-ac **Lach** *Merc* mill *Nat-s Nit-ac* nux-v ↓ ph-ac **Puls** rhus-t sabad **Sep** sil syph trom
      - **drawing** pain: am-c nux-v k* **Sep** k*
    - **amel.**: *Ars* bry castm germ-met srj5• *Lyc Mag-p* k* nux-m *Nux-v* puls *Rhus-t* sang sil staph sul-ac sulph trom
  - **food**:
    - **agg.**: agn *Ambr Bar-c* bell *Bism* bro1 *Bry* k* *Calc* k* carb-v *Carbn-s Caust* bro1 **Cham** *Clem* bro1 *Coff* k2* *Graph* guare *Hell* **Kali-c** m-arct m-aust mag-s merc bro1 *Nat-m* nit-ac ↓ *Nux-v* par ph-ac *Phos* **Puls** k* rhod sabad sep *Sil* k* vanil fd5.de
      - **hot** food: *Carb-v* **Coff** dulc fd4.de **Kali-c** ph-ac sabad sep
      - **stitching**, stinging: bar-c nit-ac
      - **tearing** pain: carb-v k2
  - **room**:
    - **agg.**: *All-c* ant-c apis bry *Cham* ham *Hep Iris Kali-s Mag-c* merc nicc nux-v ph-ac **Puls** rhod sep spig sulph thuj
      - **drawing** pain: hep h2* **Puls** k*
      - **gnawing** pain: *Nux-v* k*
    - **amel.**: *Ars* nux-v phel *Phos* sulph
    - **entering** a warm room; when: all-c ↓
      - **pressing** pain: all-c k*
- **warm**: ...
  - **things**: agn am-c *Ambr* anac *Bar-c* bar-s k2 *Bry* **Calc** calc-p *Carb-v* carbn-s **Cham** k* chel k* clem **Coff** colch dulc fd4.de *Ferr-p* glon *Graph* ham fd3.de• hell **Kali-c** kali-p fd1.de• lach lachn mag-m mag-s *Merc* k* mill k2 nat-m nat-s c1* *Nit-ac* par ph-ac *Phos Plan* prun k* **Puls** k* ruta fd4.de *Sep* k* *Sil* spig h1* staph *Sulph* vanil fd5.de
    - **amel.**: bov calc calc-sil k2 *Com* kali-i *Lyc Mag-p* mur-ac nit-ac h2* *Nux-m Nux-v* psor *Rhod Rhus-t Sil* sul-ac
  - **water** | **amel.**: ozone sde2•
  - **wrapping** up head | **amel.**: bac bn **Nux-v** phos **Sil**
- **warmth**:
  - **external**:
    - **agg.**: all-c *Ambr* arn *Bry* carb-v bg1 carbn-s cham k2 chel **Coff** *Cor-r* dulc fd4.de *Ferr Ferr-p* graph hell helon c1 hep lach bg1 mag-c mag-s nux-m ph-ac *Phos* **Puls** k* sabin *Sulph* syph xxb
    - **amel.**: am-c androc srj1• arg-n *Ars* k* *Ars-h* bov *Calc* calc-sil k2 *Castm Chin* k* *Com* der vml3• hir skp7• *Kali-ar Kali-c* lach *Lyc* k* mag-m **Mag-p** k* **Merc** k* *Mur-ac* nat-ar *Nat-c* nat-p **Nux-m Nux-v** k* phos *Psor Puls* **Rhod Rhus-t** sabad *Sil* staph *Sul-ac*
- **washerwomen**, in: *Phos* k*
- **washing**; after: ant-c bry *Calc* cham *Merc Nux-m* nux-v phos *Rhus-t* sil staph **Sulph**
- **water**:
  - **feet** in; from: nat-n bg1
  - **hands** in warm or cold water; from having: *Phos*
  - **held** in mouth agg.: camph kali-c h2
- **weather**:
  - **change** of weather: am-c k2 anan aran bro1 mag-c merc bro1 *Rhod* k*
  - **cold** agg.: ars coff k2 kali-c k2 nux-m *Phos*
  - **dry** | **agg.**: *Caust*
  - **stormy** (See windy)
  - **wet** | **agg.**: acon all-c am-c aran *Borx Calc Dulc* **Merc** nat-c *Nat-s Nux-m Phos Rhod* **Rhus-t** seneg *Sil*
  - **windy**: rhod bro1*
- **wedged**; as if (See pressing - wedged)
- **wet**:
  - **finger** amel.: cham bro1
  - **getting**; from: bell *Calc* **Lach** rhus-t
- **wind**:
  - **agg.**: camph ↓ mag-p mrr1 sil ↓
    - **stitching**, stinging: camph h1 sil h2
  - **amel.**: calc
  - **cold**:
    - **agg.**: *Germ-met* srj5•
    - **dry** | **agg.**: **Acon** *Caust*
  - **raw** wind; in: **Acon** all-c *Graph* kali-c k2 phos k2 *Puls Rhod* rhus-t sil
- **wine** agg.: *Acon* anan *Camph* ign nux-v
- **winter**: *Acon* **Ars** bell bry calc carb-v caust cham dulc **Hep** hyos ign **Merc** *Nux-m* **Nux-v** *Ph-ac Phos* puls **Rhus-t** **Sil** sulph
- **wrapping** (See warm - wrapping - amel.; warmth - external - agg.)
- **wrenching**: nux-v prun

▽ - **extending** to:
  - **right** side; other teeth at: aphis ↓
    - **drawing** pain: aphis
  - ○ **Another**; from one tooth to: bry *Mang* melal-alt gya4 nux-m prun puls bg1 rhod til bg1
  - **Arms**: mang sep
    - **left**: coloc
  - **Back**: lycps-v bg2
  - **Cheek**: am-c ↓ sep ↓
    - **drawing** pain: am-c sep
  - **Cheeks**: bry cham
  - **Chest**: kali-c

- **Downward**: ant-c calad carb-v bg1 caust coff bg1 crot-h bg1 dulc fd4.de nat-sil fd3.de•
- **Ear**: alum am-c *Ammc* anac aphis *Arn* ars bar-c bell borx brach bry *Calc* calc-ar *Caust* *Cham* chel chin *Chr-ac* clem cocc-s coloc con dulc ↓ gels ↓ gink-b sbd1• hep indg iod ↓ kali-ar kali-c kola stb3• **Kreos** *Lach* lil-t ↓ lyss mag-c **Mang** k* meph **Merc** mez *Nat-m* nicc nux-m nux-v ol-an petr *Plan* k* puls ran-s rat **Rhod** rhus-t sabad sang **Sep** **Staph** **Sulph** symph fd3.de• thuj tritic-vg fd5.de tub c1 viol-o
  - **right**: glon hydrog srj2• *Mang* hr1 nicc spig
  - **left**: kola stb3•
  - **drawing** pain: alum am-c *Ammc* anac aphis bar-c cocc-s iod h kali-c h2 **Kreos** *Nat-m* sep h2
  - **jerking** pain: anac c1
  - **stitching**, stinging: borx bry calc dulc fd4.de gels lil-t mang *Nat-m* rhod **Sep** *Sulph* **Thuj**
  - **twitching**: hep h2*
  - **And** eye: clem ↓
    - **twitching**: clem h2*
- **Ears**: am-c ↓ anac ↓ aphis ↓ lach ↓ nat-m ↓ nicc ↓ nux-m ↓ sep ↓ sil ↓
  - **left** ear; out through: sep ↓
    - **tearing** pain: sep
  - **tearing** pain: am-c anac aphis lach nat-m nicc c1 nux-m c1 sep h2 sil h2
- **Esophagus**: nat-m
- **Eyes**: aids nl2• bar-c bell bov ↓ calc k* *Calc-p* camph ↓ **Caust** k* cham chel chim clem h2 con hydrog srj2• hyos kali-c kreos lach *Mag-c* merc nat-m nicc nux-v puls rob ruta fd4.de samb ↓ sel spig bg1 staph sulph tarax
  - **cold** air; on going into: camph
  - **drawing** pain: chel kali-c h2 nat-m
  - **stitching**, stinging: bov calc camph h1 nat-m samb h1* sulph
  - **tearing** pain: caust h2 samb h1*
  - **Eyebrows**: tarax c1
- **Face**: alum k* am-c k* *Bry* caust cham cocc ferr-p k2 gels glon *Hyos* k* kali-c kali-p k2 kreos lyss mag-c **Merc** k* mez bg2 nux-v k* phos puls k* rhus-t k* ruta fd4.de sabad *Sil* staph sulph k* tarax
  - **right** side: clem ↓ kali-p k2
    - **stitching**, stinging: clem h2
  - **left** side: clem a1 plan
  - **menses**; during: sep
- **Fingers**: coff bg1 sep
- **Forehead**: aids nl2• chr-ac cocc-s kr1 *Hyos* kali-c phos rhus-t sil zinc
- **Head**: alum alum-sil k2 **Ant-c** k* apis *Ars* k* aur bg2 bar-c k* **Bell** bg2 borx k* *Bry* calc k* caust k* *Cham* k* chinin-m c1 clem k* cupr glon grat *Hyos* k* kali-ar kali-bi bg2 kali-c *Kreos* *Mag-c* k* merc k* mez k* nux-m nux-v k* *Ph-ac* phos psor puls k* rhus-t k* *Sang* staph k* sulph k* tritic-vg fd5.de
  - **side**: alum ↓ apis ↓ borx ↓
    - **right**: *Agar* ↓ germ-met ↓
      - **stitching**, stinging: *Agar* germ-met srj5•
    - **drawing** pain: alum apis
    - **tearing** pain: borx h2
  - **drawing** pain: borx c1
  - **jerking** pain: rhus-t
  - **tearing** pain: caust h2 ph-ac h2
- **Larynx**: *Alum* com *Mang* nit-ac
  - **drawing** pain: alum nit-ac
- **Lower** limbs: kali-c bg1
- **Malar** bone: alum ↓ aphis ↓ con ↓
  - **and** temple; from lower incisors to malar bone: alum ↓
    - **drawing** pain: alum
  - **drawing** pain: alum aphis con h2
  - **tearing** pain: alum
- **Malar** bones: alum aphis k* caust con ham hydrog srj2• hyos kali-c mag-c mag-m *Mang* mez nux-v phos rob ruta fd4.de *Sil*
- **Maxillary** bones: calc cupr-ar gels ruta fd4.de sel tritic-vg fd5.de
  - **Lower**: hyos tritic-vg fd5.de

- **extending** to: ...
  - **Neck**: *Alum* *Bry* chinin-m c1 *Mang* spig thuj zinc
    - **drawing** pain: *Alum*
  - **Nose**: aids nl2• bar-c calc **Caust** cham hyos rhus-t
    - **stitching**, stinging: calc h2
  - **Occiput**: cocc-s dulc fd4.de
  - **Orbital** arch: tarax ↓
    - **drawing** pain: tarax h1
  - **Other** parts: **Mang**
  - **Outward**: chin bg1 kola stb3•
  - **Parts**, to other: alum ↓
    - **drawing** pain: alum
  - **Shoulders**: *Alum* rhus-t
    - **drawing** pain: alum
  - **Side**, entire left: aids nl2• sep
  - **Temple**: alum ↓ calc ↓ con ↓ cupr ↓ indg ↓ mag-c ↓ mez ↓ nux-m ↓ zinc ↓
    - **right**: bar-c ↓ kreos ↓
      - **drawing** pain: bar-c kreos
    - **drawing** pain: alum h2 con h2
    - **tearing** pain: alum calc cupr h2 indg mag-c h2 mez nux-m c1 zinc h2
  - **Temples**: act-sp alum aphis c1 ars bar-c calc cham chel clem h2 con cupr daph gels glon hyos ↓ iod kali-ar kali-c **Kreos** mag-c mez nat-m k* nux-m phos puls rhus-t rob ruta fd4.de sel sil spig zinc
    - **jerking** pain: ars hyos h1*
  - **Throat**: **Mang** *Nat-m* k*
    - **drawing** pain: nat-m
  - **Tongue**: (non:cic slp) cit-v slp dulc fd4.de
  - **Upward**: caps bg1 caust clem bg1 nat-c bg1 nit-ac bg1 ol-an bg1 syph bg1 thuj bg1
  - **Vertex**: clem h2
  - **Zygoma**: **Caust** chinin-s gels ↓ mag-m ↓ mang a1 phos
    - **stitching**, stinging: gels
    - **tearing** pain: caust mag-m phos
- ○ **Bicuspids**: bamb-a stb2.de• carbn-dox knl3• kola stb3• ulm-c jsj8•
  - **right**: bamb-a stb2.de•
    - **tearing** pain: bamb-a stb2.de•
  - **left**: kola stb3•
  - **tearing** pain: bamb-a stb2.de•
  - ○ **Lower**:
    - **First** bicuspid: ars
    - **Second** bicuspid:
      - **left**:
        - **accompanied** by | **Head**; pain in left side of: adam skp7•
  - **Upper**: bamb-a ↓
    - **right**: cinnb
    - **tearing** pain: bamb-a stb2.de•
- **Canines**: am-c anac calc calc-p k* *Carb-an* choc srj3• dulc fd4.de laur mag-m mur-ac nat-c petr *Rhus-t* k* sep sphing kk3.fr squil ↓ staph stront-c succ-ac rly4• sul-ac tritic-vg fd5.de zinc
  - **right**: stront-c ↓
    - **twitching**: stront-c b4.de*
  - **left**: am-c ↓ nat-c ↓
    - **twitching**: am-c b4.de* nat-c b4.de*
  - **drawing** pain: staph b7.de*
  - **pulsating** pain: calc b4.de*
  - **stitching**, stinging: rhus-t b7.de* sep b4.de* squil b7.de*
  - **twitching**: rhus-t b7.de*
  - ○ **Hollow**: ser-a-c jl2
  - **Lower**: crot-t ↓
    - **left**: anac b4.de*
    - **drawing** pain: crot-t
  - **Upper** (= eyeteeth): carb-an ↓ fl-ac ↓ med ' sep ↓ ther bro1 zinc ↓
    - **right**: choc srj3• mag-m ↓ vanil fd5.de

• **Upper – right**: ...
: **tearing** pain: mag-m b4.de*
: **left**: laur↓ mur-ac↓ nat-c↓ sul-ac↓ zinc↓
: **pressing** pain: mur-ac b4.de*
: **stitching**, stinging: zinc b4.de*
: **tearing** pain: laur b7.de* nat-c b4.de* sul-ac b4.de*
: **burning**: fl-ac bg2
: **jerking** pain: carb-an
: **sore**: med hr1*
: **stitching**, stinging: sep h2 zinc h2
- **Decayed** teeth; in: (↗_hollow_) _Ant-c_ bro1 _Cham_ bro1 dulc fd4.de _Kreos_ bro1 mag-c bro1 _Merc_ bro1 _Mez_ bro1 nux-v bro1 spig kr1 staph bro1* thuj bro1
- **Filled** tooth; in a: chlol↓ cic dios merc-i-f podo fd3.de•
• **pressing** pain: chlol
- **Gums** until blood comes amel.; pricking | **pricking** pain (See picking teeth - amel. - bleed)
- **Here** and there: graph↓
• **stitching**, stinging: graph b4.de*
- **Hollow** teeth: (↗_decayed; Caries - painful_) alum b4a.de ambr b7.de* ang b7a.de ant-c b7.de* _Bar-c_ b4.de* bell b4a.de _Borx_↓ bov↓ _Bry_↓ calc b4a.de carb-v↓ caust↓ _Cham_ b7.de* _Chin_ b7.de* _Cocc_ b7.de* coff↓ con b4a.de glycyr-g cte1• graph↓ hep b4a.de hyos↓ _Ip_↓ kali-c b4.de* kali-n b4a.de _Kreos_↓ _Lach_ b7a.de lyc↓ m-ambo b7.de _M-arct_ b7a.de _M-aust_↓ merc b4a.de _Mez_ b4a.de nat-c↓ nat-m b4a.de nit-ac↓ nux-v b7a.de par b7.de* petr↓ _Ph-ac_↓ phos b4.de* plat↓ _Plb_ b7.de* _Puls_ b7.de* rheum b7a.de _Rhod_↓ _Rhus-t_ b7.de* ruta b7.de* _Sabad_ b7.de* _Sabin_ b7.de* sel↓ sep b4a.de sil b4a.de _Spig_ b7.de* _Staph_ b7.de* sulph b4a.de tarax b7a.de thuj b4a.de _Verat_ b7.de*
• **right**: mag-c↓ phos↓ plat↓ tarax↓
: **drawing** pain: mag-c b4.de* plat b4.de* tarax b7.de*
: **gnawing** pain: mag-c b4.de*
: **tearing** pain: mag-c b4.de*
: **twitching**: phos b4.de*
: **Sound** teeth beside them; and: _Merc_↓
: **tearing** pain: _Merc_ b4a.de
• **boring** pain: bell b4.de* borx b4a.de bov b4.de* cham bg2 lach b7.de* lyc b4.de* _Mez_ b4a.de nat-c b4.de* plat bg2 rheum bg2
• **burning**: _Bar-c_ b4.de* caust b4.de* ph-ac b4.de*
• **burrowing**: bov b4.de _Cham_ b7.de nat-c b4.de plat b4.de _Puls_ b7a.de rheum b7.de sep b4a.de
• **drawing** pain: bell b4.de* bov b4.de* carb-v b4.de* _Cham_ b7.de* coff b7a.de con b4.de* graph b4.de* hep b4.de* kali-c b4.de* kreos b7a.de* m-arct b7.de nat-c b4.de* nux-v b7.de* par b7.de* plat b4.de* sabin b7.de* sep b4.de* spig b7.de* _Staph_ b7.de* _Tarax_ b7a.de
• **dull** pain: borx b4a.de m-aust b7.de nat-c b4.de*
• **food**; only if filled with a particle of: alum h2* ph-ac a1*
• **gnawing** pain: bell b4.de* carb-v b4.de* _Rhus-t_ hr1 _Staph_ b7a.de _Thuj_ b4a.de
• **griping** pain: _Borx_ b4a.de
• **picking** pain: m-arct b7.de
• **pressing** pain: borx b4a.de* hyos b7.de* m-arct b7.de nat-c b4.de* nat-m b4.de* sep b4a.de staph b7.de*
• **pulsating** pain: m-arct b7.de
• **sore**: m-ambo b7.de mez b4.de*
• **squeezed**; as if: _Ip_ b7a.de sel b7a.de
• **stitching**, stinging: ambr b7.de* _Bar-c_ b4.de* _Bell_ b4.de* _Borx_ b4a.de _Bry_ b7.de* kali-c bg2 kali-n b4.de lyc b4.de* _M-aust_ b7.de* _Merc_ b4.de* mez b4a.de nat-c b4.de* nat-m b4.de* **Nux-v** b7.de* petr b4.de* phos b4a.de rhod b4a.de sil b4.de*
• **tearing** pain: ambr b7.de* bell b4.de* borx b4a.de* calc b4.de* ip b7.de* _Kreos_ b7a.de lyc b4.de* nux-v b7.de* _Ph-ac_ b4a.de _Rhod_ b4a.de _Sep_ b4a.de staph b7.de*
• **twitching**: _Ant-c_ b7a.de hyos b7.de* kreos b7a.de mez tl1 nit-ac b4.de* rhus-t b7.de* sabin b7.de* sep b4a.de spig b7.de* thuj b4.de*
○ • **Roots**: thuj bg2
• **Sides** of: mez bg2 staph bg2 thuj c1

- **Incisors**: _Agar_ k* aids nl2• alum k* am-c k* am-m ambr ang arg-met k* asaf asar aur aur-m a1 bac bn bell k* borx bov calc canth carb-an↓ carb-v k* carl a1 caust cham k* chel chin k* cocc coff _Colch_ k* dig b4.de* dios a1 dros dulc fd4.de fl-ac↓ gran a1 hydrog srj2• ign k* iod kali-ar k2 _Kali-c_ kali-s fd4.de kalm a1 kreos k* lach↓ led↓ lyc m-ambo b7.de m-arct mag-c _Mag-m_ _Merc_ k* mez k* mur-ac nat-c _Nat-m_ nit-ac _Nux-m_ k* _Nux-v_ petr ph-ac phos plat podo fd3.de• psor a1 ran-s rat a1 rhod _Rhus-t_ k* ruta fd4.de samb↓ sang a1 sars seneg **Sep** sil k* sphing k* spig k* spong staph _Stront-c_ sul-ac _Sulph_ k* symph fd3.de• tarax k* tarent teucr b7.de* thuj tritic-vg fd5.de tub al vanil fd5.de _Zinc_
• **left**: plut-n↓
: **pressing** pain: plut-n srj7•
• **morning**: carb-v↓
: **tearing** pain: carb-v h2*
• **biting** pain: carb-v b4.de* rhod b4.de*
• **burning**: fl-ac bg2 ph-ac b4.de* spig b7a.de zinc b4.de*
• **burrowing**: ign b7.de* plat b4.de*
• **buzzing**: sep b4.de*
• **drawing** pain: ambr b7.de* calc b4.de* chin b7.de* colch b7.de* iod b4.de* kali-c b4.de* kreos b7a.de m-arct b7.de merc b4.de* nux-v b7.de* petr b4.de* ph-ac b4a.de phos b4.de* plat b4.de* ruta fd4.de _Staph_ b7.de* stront-c b4.de sulph b4.de* tritic-vg fd5.de zinc b4.de*
• **gnawing** pain: ran-s b7.de*
• **pressing** pain: alum b4.de* led b7.de* rhus-t b7.de* staph b7.de* tarax b7.de*
• **pulled** out; as if being: cocc b7.de*
• **pulsating** pain: nat-m b4.de*
• **sore**: iod b4.de*
• **stitching**, stinging: ambr b7.de* chin b7.de* _Kali-c_ k* kali-s fd4.de lach nat-m k* nux-m b7.de* petr h2 ran-s b7.de* rhod k* samb xxb1 sep k* thuj k*
• **tearing** pain: carb-an carb-v colch b7.de* samb xxb1 stront-c k*
• **twitching**: colch b7.de* ran-s b7.de*
○ • **Hollow**: petr↓
: **stitching**, stinging: petr b4.de*
• **Lower**: agar↓ alum↓ arg-n↓ asaf↓ aur-m-n↓ bac bn* carb-v↓ cham↓ chin h1* clem↓ coc-c↓ colch↓ coloc↓ kreos↓ led↓ _Lyc_↓ _M-ambo_↓ mez↓ nat-m h2* nat-s↓ podo fd3.de• positr nl2• sep↓ sil↓ staph↓ sulph↓ _Teucr_↓ thuj↓ tritic-vg fd5.de _Zinc_↓
: **left**: canth↓ lyc↓ sulph↓ zinc↓
: **drawing** pain: zinc b4.de*
: **tearing** pain: canth b7.de* lyc b4.de* sulph b4.de* zinc b4.de*
: **blow**; pain as from a: chin b7.de*
: **boring** pain: chin bg2 lyc bg2
: **drawing** pain: agar k* alum k* arg-n a1 asaf k* aur-m-n a1 carb-v h2* cham b7.de* coc-c a1 colch a1 coloc a1 kreos k* led a1 nat-s a1 sil b4.de* sulph a1 thuj a1 _Zinc_ k*
: **gnawing** pain: staph b7.de*
: **motion** of lower lip agg.: bac al2
: **sore**: _M-ambo_ b7a.de
: **stitching**, stinging: agar b4.de* mez b4.de*
: **tearing** pain: alum k* clem a1 _Lyc_ h2 sep b4.de* sulph a1 _Teucr_ k* zinc k*
: **One**: anac
• **One**: alum↓ ambr↓ kola↓ sul-ac↓
: **drawing** pain: ambr k*
: **pressing** pain: alum kola stb3• sul-ac h2*
• **Roots**: mez↓
: **stitching**, stinging: mez h2
• **Upper**: agar↓ am-m↓ ang↓ bov b4.de* camph↓ canth↓ carb-v↓ _Caust_↓ chel↓ _Chin_↓ form↓ grat↓ kali-n↓ kali-s↓ kreos↓ lavand-a ctl1• m-arct↓ _Mag-m_ b4a.de mez↓ nat-m↓ nit-s-d↓ nux-v↓ petr↓ ph-ac↓ phos↓ sep↓ spig↓ spong↓ sul-ac↓ zinc↓
: **right**: kali-c↓ sul-ac↓
: **pressing** pain: sul-ac b4.de*
: **pulsating** pain: kali-c b4.de*
: **left**: aids nl2• phos b4.de* zinc↓
: **drawing** pain: zinc b4.de*
: **boring** pain: nat-m b4.de*

- **Upper**: ...
  - **burning**: nat-m b4.de*
  - **drawing** pain: agar k* ang k* camph canth b7.de* carb-v b4.de* chel a1 *Chin* b7a.de grat k* kreos k* mez a1 petr h2* ph-ac b4a.de sep h2* spig b7a.de zinc h2*
  - **pressing** pain: m-arct b7.de
  - **pulsating** pain: nat-m b4.de*
  - **stitching**, stinging: am-m k* kali-s fd4.de nux-v b7.de* phos b4a.de* spong b7.de* zinc h2
  - **tearing** pain: am-m b7.de* *Caust* b4a.de *Chin* b7a.de form a1 kali-n h2* mag-m b4.de* nit-s-d a1 phos b4.de* spig b7a.de sul-ac h2*

- **Loose** teeth, in: der
- **Lower** teeth: aesc *Agar* alum am-c am-m ambr anac ang antip bro1 apoc-a vh arg-n ↓ *Arn* arum-t asaf asar asc-t astac *Aur* bar-c bar-ox-suc rly4• **Bell** borx bov *Bry* calc camph cann-i a1 **Canth** carb-an *Carb-v* **Caust** k* **Cham** k* chel *Chin* cic b7.de* clem cocc coff colch k* coloc k* con dros dulc fd4.de euph euphr ↓ fl-ac ↓ graph guaj hell hep hydrog srj2• hyos ign kali-c kali-n kola stb3• kreos k* *Lach* **Laur** lyc m-arct mag-c k* mag-m k* *Mang* melal-alt gya4 meph a1 merc k* mez mur-ac **Nat-c** nat-m nit-ac nux-m nux-v olib-sac ↓ olnd par petr ph-ac *Phos* k* plat *Plb* podo ↓ positr nl2• puls ran-s rheum rhod *Rhus-t* k* ruta sabad *Sabin* *Sars* sel seneg **Sep** *Sil* spig spong k* squil **Staph** k* stront-c sul-ac sulph suprar rly4• symph fd3.de• teucr thuj tritic-vg fd5.de *Verat* verb k* *Viol-o* ↓ **Zinc**
  - **right**: *Agar* ↓ am-c ↓ anac ↓ bov ↓ canth ↓ cham ↓ hydrog srj2• laur ↓ m-arct ↓ mang ↓ musca-d szs1 nat-c ↓ plat ↓ plb ↓ rhod ↓ sars ↓ stront-c ↓ sul-ac ↓ viol-o ↓
    - **boring** pain: laur b7.de*
    - **clawing** pain: am-c b4.de*
    - **drawing** pain: anac b4.de* bov b4.de* cham b7.de* plat b4.de* rhod b4.de* sars b4.de*
    - **gnawing** pain: laur bg2 sul-ac bg2
    - **pulled** out; as if being: mang b4.de*
    - **pulsating** pain: am-c b4.de*
    - **raging**: am-c b4.de*
    - **squeezed**; as if: anac b4.de* m-arct b7.de
    - **stitching**, stinging: *Agar*
    - **tearing** pain: canth b7.de* laur b7.de* plb b7.de* viol-o b7.de*
    - **twitching**: nat-c b4.de* stront-c b4.de*
  - **left**: alum ↓ arg-n ↓ bar-c ↓ cann-s ↓ caust ↓ *Cham* ↓ chel b7.de* colch ↓ hydrog srj2• kali-c ↓ laur ↓ mag-p ↓ mur-ac ↓ *Nat-c* ↓ plat ↓ plb ↓ stront-c ↓ sul-ac b4.de*
    - **boring** pain: kali-c bg2 laur b7.de* mur-ac b4.de* plb b7.de*
    - **burning**: bar-c b4.de*
    - **burrowing**: kali-c b4.de
    - **drawing** pain: caust b4.de* cham b7.de* plat b4.de*
    - **grumbling** pain: arg-n
    - **pulled** out; as if being: mur-ac b4.de*
    - **pulsating** pain: alum b4.de* *Cham* b7.de* mur-ac b4.de*
    - **squeezed**; as if: cann-s b7.de*
    - **tearing** pain: colch b7.de* kali-c b4.de* laur b7.de* mag-p bg2 *Nat-c* b4.de* sul-ac b4.de*
    - **twitching**: laur b7.de* stront-c b4.de*
  - **boring** pain: *Ruta* bg2
  - **burrowing**: *Ruta* b7.de*
  - **buzzing**: mur-ac b4.de*
  - **dragging**: coloc b4.de
  - **drawing** pain: arg-n a1 dulc fd4.de fl-ac olib-sac wmh1 podo fd3.de•
  - **pulsating** pain: bar-c b4.de*
  - **stitching**, stinging: aesc *Carb-an* euph bg2 euphr k* puls b7.de*
  - **tearing** pain: caust b4.de* coloc bg2 laur b7.de* *Merc* b4.de* plb b7.de* *Viol-o* b7a.de
  - **ulcerative** pain: petr b4.de*
  - ○ **Hollow**:
    - **left**: *Sulph* ↓
      - **tearing** pain: *Sulph* b4.de*
      - **twitching**: sulph b4.de*
  - **Premolars** | **left**: nept-m lsd2.fr

- **Molars**: acon ↓ aesc agar k* all-c alum *Am-c* ambr anac anag ↓ ang ant-t antip bro1 apis ↓ aq-mar rbp6 arg-n arge-pl rwt5• arn asar asc-t aur bar-c bell benz-ac ↓ bism borx bov **Bry** k* calad calc camph canth carb-an *Carb-v* castm *Caust* k* cham k* chel **Chin** clem coc-c ↓ cocc coff k* colch k* coli rly4• coloc k* croc crot-h ↓ cycl dios dulc fd4.de euph *Gamb* ↓ graph grat ↓ guaj ham ↓ hell hyos ign indg ↓ iod kali-c kali-n kali-p fd1.de• kali-s fd4.de **Kreos** laur k* lyc m-arct mag-c *Mag-m* mang melal-alt gya4 merc *Merc-c* ↓ mez mur-ac *Nat-c* nat-m ↓ nat-sil fd3.de• *Nit-ac* nux-m k* nux-v olnd par petr k* ph-ac k* *Phos* plat plb podo fd3.de• positr nl2• puls ran-s raph ↓ rheum *Rhod* rhus-t ribo rly4• ruta fd4.de sabad sabin sars k* sel rsj9• seneg **Sep** k* sil spig k* spong *Staph* stront-c sul-ac sulph symph fd3.de• teucr thiam rly4• thuj tritic-vg fd5.de ulm-c jsj8• vanil fd5.de verat verb **Zinc** zing
  - **right**: acon ↓ ambr ↓ ang c1 bell ↓ brass-n-o srj5• cann-i a1 canth ↓ carb-v ↓ castm ↓ caust b4.de* chin ↓ chir-fl ↓ cinnb k* graph b4.de* hell ↓ iod ↓ kreos ↓ mang ↓ nat-sil fd3.de• neon srj5• *Nicc* ↓ petr ↓ positr nl2• sal-fr sle1• sulph ↓ symph fd3.de• teucr ↓ tritic-vg fd5.de
    - **drawing** pain: ambr bell carb-v b4.de* caust b4.de* chir-fl gya2 mang b4.de*
    - **gnawing** pain: castm *Nicc*
    - **picking** pain: chin b7.de*
    - **pressing** pain: chin b7.de* petr b4.de* teucr b7.de*
    - **smarting**: mang b4.de*
    - **squeezed**; as if: iod b4.de*
    - **tearing** pain: acon bg2 canth b7.de* hell h1* kreos b7a.de nat-sil fd3.de• sulph b4.de* teucr b7.de*
  - **left**: arg-n calad ↓ carb-an ↓ carb-v ↓ castm chel coli rly4• con ↓ croc ↓ cycl ↓ dulc fd4.de hydroph rsj6• kali-bi ↓ kali-c ↓ kreos ↓ nat-m h2* olnd ↓ phos ↓ rheum h rhod ↓ ruta fd4.de sel rsj9• vanil fd5.de
    - **boring** pain: con h1 phos b4.de*
    - **drawing** pain: calad carb-an carb-v b4.de* con h2* croc b7.de* kali-bi bg2 kali-c b4.de* kreos olnd b7.de* rhod b4.de*
    - **gnawing** pain: phos h2
    - **pulled** out; as if being: cycl b7.de*
    - **tearing** pain: cycl b7.de* kali-bi bg2 olnd b7.de*
      - **alternating** with:
        - **right** molars; tearing in: am-m
        - **Meatus**; itching in left: agar
  - **night**: sep ↓
    - **grumbling** pain: sep h2*
  - **biting** pain: cocc b7.de*
  - **boring** pain: calc b4.de* mag-m b4.de* melal-alt gya4 sel c1
  - **burrowing**: mag-m b4.de
  - **crushed**; as if: *Ign* k*
  - **cutting** pain: ham bg2
  - **digging** pain: *Mag-m* b4.de* sul-ac b4a.de
  - **dinner**; during: mag-m ↓
    - **tearing** pain: mag-m h2
  - **drawing** pain: acon a1 arg-n a1 asar b7.de* bism b7.de* bry k* calad b7.de* carb-an h2* carb-v b4.de* chel a1 chin b7.de* coc-c a1 coff b7.de* graph b4.de* kali-c a1 nux-v b7.de* olnd k* petr b4a.de* plat b4.de* podo fd3.de• ran-s b7.de* rhod b4.de* sep h2* staph b7.de* sulph b4.de* teucr b7.de* vanil fd5.de zinc b4.de*
  - **dull** pain: rhus-t b7.de* sep b4.de*
  - **gnawing** pain: bar-c b4.de* camph a1 canth b7.de* indg a1 sep b4.de* sul-ac a1
    - **alternating** with:
      - **itching** in ear: agar k*
      - **tearing**; violent:
        - **right** ear; in: nicc
        - **Behind** ear: alum
  - **jerking** pain: crot-h ribo rly4• sil h2* zinc h2*
  - **pressing** pain: bism b7.de* chin b7.de* dulc fd4.de iod b4.de* mez h2* nux-m b7.de* petr h2* rhod b4.de* sabad b7.de* sep b4.de* thuj b4.de* zinc h2*
  - **pricking** pain: am-c k*
  - **pulsating** pain: bar-c b4.de* plat b4.de* rhod b4.de* zinc b4.de*
  - **sore**: coli rly4• ign b7.de*

- **stitching**, stinging: am-c k* borx b4a.de calc k* carb-an h2 *Kali-c* mag-m b4.de* merc-c b4a.de nat-m bg2 par b7.de* puls b7.de* rhod b4.de* zinc h2
- **tearing** pain: alum h2* am-c k* anag apis bar-c k* bell b4.de* benz-ac borx hr1 calc b4a.de *Carb-v* k* cycl h1* *Gamb* k* grat hell b7.de* indg a1 kali-c h2* mag-c h2* mag-m b4.de* mang b4a.de merc b4a.de *Merc-c* b4a.de nat-sil fd3.de• phos h2* raph a1 rhod k* sabin b7.de* stront-c b4.de* zinc k*
- **twitching**: *Bry* b7.de* *Puls* b7.de*
- **wet**; after getting: acon ↓
  - **tearing** pain: acon h1

▽ • **extending** to:

- **Forehead**: sep ↓
  - **drawing** pain: sep h2*
- **Temple**: caust ↓
  - **drawing** pain: caust h2*

○ • **Hollow**: agar ↓ am-c ↓ anac ↓ carb-an ↓ clem b4.de* croc ↓ graph ↓ kali-c ↓ *M-arct* b7.de mag-m ↓ nat-m ↓ olnd ↓ par ↓ sel ↓ sep b4.de* sul-ac ↓

- **right**: mag-c b4.de*
- **left**: mez b4.de*
- **boring** pain: mag-m b4.de*
- **cutting** pain: agar bg2
- **digging** pain: sul-ac b4.de*
- **drawing** pain: anac b4.de* croc b7.de* m-arct b7a.de olnd b7.de* par b7.de* sel b7a.de
- **gnawing** pain: nat-m bg2
- **pressing** pain: kali-c b4.de*
- **sore**: am-c b4.de*
- **stitching**, stinging: sel b7a.de
- **tearing** pain: carb-an b4.de* mag-m b4.de* olnd b7.de*
- **twitching**: am-c b4.de* graph b4.de* par b7.de*

- **Lower**: aesc ↓ agar ↓ alum ↓ anac ↓ bar-c ↓ bell ↓ berb ↓ camph ↓ castm ↓ *Caust* ↓ coloc ↓ hell ↓ *Hyos* b7.de* indg ↓ laur ↓ *M-arct* b7.de mag-c b4.de* mag-m ↓ melal-alt ↓ *Nicc* ↓ phos b4.de* plat ↓ podo ↓ rhus-t ↓ ribo rly4• sabad ↓ sep ↓ spig ↓ staph ↓ stront-c ↓ thiam rly4• vanil fd5.de *Verb* ↓ zinc ↓
  - **right**: am-c ↓ ant-t ↓ canth ↓ carb-v ↓ coloc ↓ hell ↓ kreos ↓ lyc ↓ m-arct ↓ mag-c ↓ nat-c ↓ olnd ↓ phos ↓ plb ↓ ran-s ↓ sabad ↓ sars ↓ spong ↓ staph ↓ verb ↓ zinc ↓
    - **drawing** pain: ant-t b7.de* lyc b4.de* mag-c b4.de* olnd b7.de* phos b4.de* zinc b4.de*
    - **only**; later in right lower molar: aesc ↓
      - **stitching**, stinging: aesc
    - **pressing** pain: zinc b4.de*
    - **pulled** out; as if being: spong b7.de*
    - **pulsating** pain: coloc b4.de*
    - **squeezed**; as if: carb-v b4.de* m-arct b7.de
    - **stitching**, stinging: coloc b4.de* hell b7.de* kreos b7a.de sabad b7.de* sars b4.de* staph b7.de* zinc b4a.de
    - **tearing** pain: am-c b4.de* ant-t b7.de* canth k* hell b7.de* mag-c b4.de* nat-c b4.de* plb b7.de* ran-s b7.de* sars b4.de* verb k* zinc b4.de*
    - **twitching**: plb b7.de* zinc b4.de*
  - **left**: alum ↓ ambr ↓ anac ↓ borx ↓ carb-an ↓ *Cham* ↓ colch ↓ euph ↓ kali-bi ↓ kreos ↓ laur ↓ lyc ↓ mang ↓ mez ↓ nat-c ↓ nat-m ↓ nux-m b7.de* phos ↓ ribo rly4• sabad b7.de* succ-ac rly4• sulph ↓ thuj ↓ vanil fd5.de verb ↓ zinc ↓
    - **boring** pain: ambr bg2 nat-c b4.de
    - **burrowing**: ambr b7.de
    - **digging** pain: laur b7.de*
    - **drawing** pain: anac b4.de* carb-an b4.de* *Cham* b7.de* kreos b7a.de phos b4.de*
    - **gnawing** pain: alum b4.de* phos b4.de*
    - **pressing** pain: ambr b7.de* colch b7.de* euph b4.de*
    - **pulled** out; as if being: mez b4.de*
    - **sore**: zinc b4.de*
    - **stitching**, stinging: borx b4a.de euph b4.de* sabad b7.de* zinc b4.de*
    - **tearing** pain: colch k* kali-bi a1 laur a1 lyc b4.de* mang b4.de* nat-c b4.de* sulph b4.de* thuj b4.de* verb b7.de* zinc b4.de*
    - **twitching**: nat-c b4.de* nat-m bg2 zinc b4.de*
  - **boring** pain: caust b4.de*
  - **burrowing**: caust b4.de
  - **drawing** pain: anac camph mag-c h2* melal-alt gya4 phos h2* plat b4.de* podo fd3.de• sep b4.de* zinc b4.de*
  - **gnawing** pain: alum a1 berb a1 castm indg a1 *Nicc* k*
  - **pressing** pain: rhus-t b7.de*
  - **pulsating** pain: bar-c bg2 hyos b7.de* spig bg2
  - **stitching**, stinging: aesc *Caust* k* coloc h2 hell b7.de* sabad b7.de* staph h1 zinc h2
  - **tearing** pain: aesc agar k* alum bell k* laur b7.de* mag-c h2* mag-m b4.de* staph b7.de* *Verb* b7a.de zinc k*
  - **twitching**: stront-c b4.de*
  - **Hollow**: hyos ↓
    - **right**: am-c ↓ kali-c ↓
      - **clawing** pain: am-c b4.de*
      - **tearing** pain: kali-c b4.de*
    - **left**: bov ↓ *Cham* ↓ zinc ↓
      - **drawing** pain: bov b4.de* *Cham* b7.de*
      - **tearing** pain: zinc b4.de*
    - **tearing** pain: hyos b7.de*
  - **Roots**: sars ↓
    - **stitching**, stinging: sars
  - **Second** molar: aesc
- **Under** left lower molars: ambr ↓
  - **digging** pain: ambr
  - **pressing** pain: ambr
- **Upper**: agar ↓ ambr ↓ anag ↓ ang ↓ apis ↓ *Arn* ↓ bell ↓ *Calc* ↓ canth ↓ caust ↓ chin ↓ cycl ↓ hell ↓ kali-n ↓ kali-p ↓ kreos ↓ lyc ↓ melal-alt ↓ mez ↓ mur-ac ↓ nat-s ↓ nat-sil ↓ nit-ac ↓ plat ↓ pot-e ↓ pyrid ↓ *Ran-s* ↓ rhus-t ↓ ribo ↓ sang ↓ senec ↓ **Sep** ↓ teucr ↓ vanil ↓ zinc ↓
  - **right**: all-s ↓ alum ↓ am-c b4.de* ambr ↓ ang ↓ apis b7a.de aur ↓ bell ↓ calc ↓ canth ↓ chin ↓ chir-fl ↓ dios dulc fd4.de hell ↓ kali-i ↓ kreos ↓ lyc ↓ mez ↓ mur-ac ↓ nat-sil fd3.de• ol-an ↓ ph-ac ↓ phos ↓ ran-s ↓ ribo ↓ sabad ↓ sil ↓ spig ↓ *Staph* ↓ symph fd3.de• taosc iwa1•
    - **drawing** pain: *Am-c* b4a.de ambr b7.de* ang b7.de* bell b4.de* canth b7.de* ran-s b7.de* *Staph* b7.de*
    - **gnawing** pain: calc b4.de*
    - **jerking** pain: all-s lyc h2* ribo rly4•
    - **pressing** pain: spig b7.de*
    - **sore**: alum k* chir-fl gya2
    - **squeezed**; as if: ambr b7.de*
    - **stitching**, stinging: chin b7.de* hell b7.de* kreos b7a.de lyc h2 phos h2 sabad b7.de*
    - **tearing** pain: alum b4.de* aur k* chin b7.de* hell b7.de* kali-i a1 lyc a1 mez h2* mur-ac b4.de* nat-sil fd3.de• ol-an a1 ph-ac k* phos b4.de*
    - **twitching**: phos b4.de* sil b4.de*
    - **extending** to:
      - **Temple**: mez ↓
        - **tearing** pain: mez h2*
  - **left**: agar ↓ alum ↓ am-c ↓ apis ↓ *Arn* ↓ berb ↓ bry ↓ carb-an ↓ carb-v ↓ cassia-s ↓ caust ↓ chin ↓ cupr-ar ↓ euph b4.de* graph ↓ guaj ↓ kali-c ↓ kreos ↓ limest-b ↓ mag-c ↓ mez ↓ nat-c ↓ nux-m b7.de* phos ↓ ran-s ↓ seneg ↓ spong ↓ staph ↓ succ-ac rly4• sul-ac ↓ verat ↓ zinc ↓
    - **burning**: *Arn* b7a.de spong b7.de*
    - **burrowing**: kali-c b4.de* seneg b4.de*
    - **clawing** pain: kali-c b4.de*
    - **digging** pain: kali-c b4.de*
    - **drawing** pain: am-c b4.de* bry b7.de* caust b4.de* chin b7.de* kreos b7a.de nux-m b7.de* ran-s b7.de*
    - **gnawing** pain: sul-ac b4.de*

- **Upper – left**: ...
  - **pressing** pain: carb-v b4.de* caust b4.de* chin b7.de* euph b4.de* guaj b4.de* staph b7.de* verat b7.de*
  - **pulsating** pain: cassia-s ccrh1•
  - **sore**: carb-v b4.de* limest-b es1•
  - **stitching**, stinging: alum euph b4.de* graph b4.de* mez b4.de* zinc b4.de*
  - **tearing** pain: agar b4.de* alum b4.de* am-c k* arn k* berb k* carb-an b4.de* caust h2* chin b7.de* cupr-ar guaj k* kali-c b4.de* kreos b7a.de mag-c b4.de* nat-c b4.de* phos b4.de* staph b7.de* zinc k*
  - **twitching**: alum b4.de* apis b7a.de bry b7.de* chin b7.de* kreos b7a.de zinc b4.de*
- **burrowing**: chin b7.de lyc b4.de
- **drawing** pain: ambr k* ang k* bell k* canth b7.de* kali-n b4.de* kreos b7a.de melal-alt gya4 mez h2* plat b4.de* *Ran-s* b7.de* **Sep** k* teucr b7.de* zinc b4.de*
- **dull** pain: kali-p fd1.de• pyrid rly4• vanil fd5.de
  - **tearing** pain in malar bones; with: anag
- **gnawing** pain: agar k* *Calc* k* sang a1
- **jerking** pain: ribo rly4•
- **mastication**; during: aur ↓
  - **dull** pain: aur
- **picking** pain: chin b7.de*
- **pressing** pain: rhus-t b7.de*
- **pulsating** pain: agar bg2 apis b7a.de *Arn* b7a.de kreos b7a.de* nat-s bg2 pot-e rly4• senec bg2
- **stitching**, stinging: bell caust b4.de* cycl hell b7.de* kali-n b4.de* lyc b4.de* mez h2 nit-ac b4.de*
- **tearing** pain: mur-ac h2* nat-sil fd3.de•
- **trembling** of heart; with: anag ↓
  - **dull** pain: anag
- **First**:
  - **left**: cassia-s ↓
    - **pulsating** pain: cassia-s ccrh1•
- **Hollow**: mez ↓
  - **right**: mez ↓ zinc ↓
    - **tearing** pain: mez b4.de zinc b4.de
    - **twitching**: mez b4.de*
  - **drawing** pain: mez b4.de*
- **Upper** teeth:
  - **Hollow**: borx b4a.de cycl ↓ mang b4.de* mez ↓
    - **burning**: mez b4.de*
    - **stitching**, stinging: cycl b7.de* mez b4.de*

- **Points** of crowns in evening; in: bar-c ↓
  - **tingling** pain: bar-c
- **Roots**: agath-a nl2• alum ↓ am-c k1* am-m ↓ anac ↓ ant-t ↓ arn ↓ bac bn* bell ↓ *Calc* ↓ camph b7a.de cann-xyz ↓ caust ↓ *Cham* ↓ colch ↓ conch ↓ dulc fd4.de graph ↓ iod ↓ *Kali-c* ↓ lach ↓ mag-c ↓ mag-m ↓ mang a1 meph bro1 *Merc* bro1 mez ↓ mur-ac ↓ nat-sil fd3.de• ol-an ↓ pin-con oss2• ruta fd4.de sabin ↓ sep ↓ *Sil* ↓ *Staph* b7a.de* stront-c ↓ *Teucr* b7a.de tong ↓ zinc ↓ zing ↓
  - **left** side posteriorly: ant-t ↓ cycl ↓
    - **tearing** pain: ant-t k* cycl
  - **boring** pain: *Cham* mur-ac h2
  - **chewing** agg.: alum ↓ *Sil* ↓
    - **ulcerative** pain: alum *Sil*
  - **cutting** pain: camph iod h*
  - **dinner** | **after**:
    - **amel**.: arn ↓
      - **tearing** pain: arn
    - **during**:
      - **agg**.: arn ↓
        - **tearing** pain: arn k*
  - **drawing** pain: anac caust h2* iod h* staph k*
  - **eating** | **after**:
    - **agg**.: ant-t ↓ sep ↓
      - **tearing** pain: ant-t k* sep k*

- **Roots – eating**: ...
  - **while**:
    - **agg**.: sep ↓ *Staph* ↓
      - **tearing** pain: sep k* *Staph* a1
  - **jerking** pain: bell lach meph a1
  - **pressing** pain: alum caust *Kali-c* staph zing
  - **pressure** of finger amel.: am-m ↓
    - **tearing** pain: am-m k*
  - **pulsating** pain: alum bg2 cann-xyz bg2 dulc fd4.de mag-m h2* merc k2 mez bg2 sep h2*
  - **scraping** pain | **scraped** with a knife; as if: arn k*
  - **sore**: conch fkr1• iod h
  - **stitching**, stinging: dulc fd4.de mag-c h2 sep h2 zinc h2
  - **tearing** pain: am-m k* ant-t k* camph caust h2* colch k* graph k* lach mag-c h2* meph *Merc* k* ol-an sabin *Staph* k* stront-c *Teucr* k* tong a1 zinc
    - **torn** out; as if being: *Calc*
  - **touch** agg.: mang ↓ sil ↓
    - **ulcerative** pain: mang sil h2
  - **ulcerative** pain: alum am-c merc *Sil*
  - ▽ **extending** to | **Tips**: nat-c bg2
  - ○ **Sound** teeth: ther ↓
    - **drawing** pain: ther a1
- **Sockets**: chinin-s ↓ coc-c ↓
  - **sore**: chinin-s bg2 coc-c bg2
  - ○ **Absent** teeth: cob-n sp1
- **Sound** teeth: **Acon** alum am-c arg-n br1* arn ars bell bry carb-v caust k* *Cham* k* *Coff* con ham hyos kali-c k2 kola stb3• *Mag-c* nux-v plan k* rhod rhus-t spig bro1 staph bro1 sulph zinc
  - **boring** pain: alum plan
- **Stumps**; old: alum ↓
  - **pressing** pain:
    - **pressed**; as if | **sockets**; into: alum
- **Upper** molars and jaws; in right:
  - **forenoon**: all-s ↓
    - **pressing** pain | **jerking**; transitory: all-s k*
- **Upper** teeth: acon ↓ *Agar* *Alum* alum-sil k2 **Am-c** am-m ambr ang aran vh1 arn asar *Aur* bamb-a stb2.de• *Bell* k* borx bov *Calc* cann-i a1 canth carb-ac k* carb-an **Carb-v** *Caust* *Cham* chel k* **Chin** clem cocc coff colch k* con cycl dios dulc fd4.de euph fl-ac bro1 graph guaj ham ↓ hell hydrog srj2• hyos k* *Kali-c* k2 kali-n kola stb3• **Kreos** lyc k* m-arct m-aust mag-c *Mag-m* malar jl2 mang meny ↓ merc *Mez* mur-ac *Nat-c* *Nat-m* nat-sil fd3.de• *Nit-ac* k* nux-m k* nux-v ozone sde2• ph-ac *Phos* k* plat puls ran-s rheum rhod rhus-t sabad sang a1 sars seneg sep sil *Spig* *Spong* staph stry k* *Sul-ac* sulph taosc iwa1• teucr *Thuj* trios rsj11• tritic-vg fd5.de vanil ↓ verat verb **Zinc**
  - **right**: arn ↓ bac bn *Bell* ↓ cench k2 dulc fd4.de kali-i ↓ laur ↓ mur-ac ↓ nat-m ↓ ozone sde2• sul-ac b4.de* taosc iwa1• verb ↓ zinc ↓
    - **night**; all: bell ↓
      - **drawing** pain: bell
    - **drawing** pain: *Bell* b4.de*
    - **gnawing** pain: kali-i bg2 laur b7.de sul-ac b4.de
    - **pressing** pain: nat-m b4.de* sul-ac b4.de*
    - **stitching**, stinging: arn
    - **tearing** pain: mur-ac b4.de* verb b7.de* zinc b4.de*
    - **Premolars**: nept-m lsd2.fr
  - **left**: acon ↓ agar ↓ am-c ↓ am-m ↓ arn chel b7.de* dulc fd4.de rheum h stront-c ↓ stry succ-ac rly4• thuj ↓ ven-m rsj12•
    - **boring** pain: thuj b4.de*
    - **clawing** pain: stront-c b4.de*
    - **gnawing** pain: thuj b4.de*
    - **grumbling** pain: agar
    - **pressing** pain: acon b7.de*
    - **pulsating** pain: agar b4.de*
    - **tearing** pain: agar b4.de* am-c b4.de* am-m b7.de* thuj b4.de*
    - **ulcerative** pain: am-c b4.de*
    - **Second** bicuspid: olnd

- **boring** pain: sep bg2
- **burrowing**: sep b4.de*
- **cold** finger amel.: ang ↓
  - ⋮ **drawing** pain: ang
- **drawing** pain: ang k* bell chin b7.de* ham fd3.de• vanil fd5.de
- **dull** pain: hyos b7.de*
- **pressing** pain: acon aran calc dulc fd4.de kola stb3• nat-m h2*
- **pulsating** pain: cham b7.de* colch b7.de* kreos b7a.de
- **stitching**, stinging: clem b4.de* mang b4.de* meny b7.de* puls b7.de* spig b7.de*
- **tearing** pain: am-m b7.de* *Chin* b7a.de *M-aust* b7a.de meny b7.de*
- **twitching**: aur b4.de* spig b7.de*

○ · **Hollow**: bell ↓
  - ⋮ **stitching**, stinging: bell b4.de*

- **Wisdom** teeth: acon-ac rly4• ph-ac h2* positr nl2• ruta fd4.de
  - **right**: petr-ra shn4•

○ · **Lower**:
  - ⋮ **right**: bit-ar ↓
    - ⋮ **aching**: bit-ar wht1•

PARALYZED; sensation as if: sulph b4.de*

PERFORATED; sensation as if: par b7.de*

PERIODICITY: ars bg2 calc bg2 cham bg2 chel bg2 form bg2 nat-m bg2 nat-p bg2 sulph bg2

PERIODONTOSIS (See MOUTH - Detached)

PERIOSTITIS: agar *Phos Sil*

PERSPIRATION:
- **agg.**: hyos b7.de
- **suppressed** perspiration; from: *Cham* b7a.de

PICKING:
- **Teeth**; picking:
  - **agg.**: kali-c b4.de* **Puls** b7.de* sang bg2*
  - **amel.**: all-c ptk1 am-c bg2 bell ptk1 ph-ac ptk1 sars bg2
  - **bleed**; until they | **amel.**: *Bell* bg2
  - **must** pick teeth: sel b7a.de*

PREGNANCY agg.; during: alum b4.de* am-c bg2 *Bell* b4a.de* *Bry* b7.de* *Calc* b4.de* cham bg2 chin ptk1 *Con* b4a.de *Hyos* b7.de* kali-bi ptk1 *Kreos* ptk1 lyc bg2 lyss ptk1 *Mag-c* b4a.de* *Merc* b4.de* nux-m b7.de* *Nux-v* b7.de* *Puls* b7.de* rat bg2 rhus-t b7.de* **Sep** b4.de* spig b7a.de *Staph* b7.de*

PRESSING together send a shock through head, ears and nose: am-c k*

PRESSURE:
- **agg.**: arg-met b7.de* mag-m b4.de* mag-p bg2 nat-c b4.de* nat-m b4.de* sep b4.de* staph b7.de* sulph b4.de* zinc b4.de*
- **amel.**: alum b4.de* am-c b4.de* am-m b7.de* **Bell** bg2 *Bry* b7.de* chin b7.de* clem b4.de* ign b7.de* kali-c b4.de* laur b7.de* mag-m b4.de* mur-ac b4.de* nat-m b4.de* ol-an bg2 phos b4.de* *Puls* b7.de* rhus-t bg2
- **hard** | **amel.**: staph ptk1

PRICKLING: zinc h2*

○ - **Roots**: merc-c bg2

PROUD flesh, surrounded by: alumn k*

PULSATIONS: rauw tpw8
- **painful** (See Pain - pulsating)
- **painless**: alum ars carc fd2.de• rauw sp1 sanic

READING agg.: ign b7.de* nux-v b7.de*

REFLECTING agg.: *Nux-v* b7.de*

REST:
- **agg.**: bry b7.de* mag-c b4a.de* plat bg2 rhus-t b7.de*
- **amel.**: **Bry** b7.de* clem b4.de* con b4a.de mez b4a.de nux-v b7.de* staph b7.de*

RESTING, supporting: | **forehead** on table | **amel.**: mang b4.de*
- **head** on pillow | **agg.**: nit-ac b4.de*

RETIRING: | **agg.**: aran bg2

RIDING agg.: calc bg2 mag-c b4.de*

RISING:
- **after**:
  - **agg.**: ign b7.de* plat b4.de* sep b4.de*
  - **amel.**: alum b4.de* *Mag-c* b4a.de *Nux-v* b7.de* olnd b7.de* ph-ac b4a.de phos b4.de* sabin b7.de* spig b7.de*

ROOM:
- **agg.**: *Ant-c* b7a.de bov b4a.de cham b7.de* hep b4.de* *M-arct* b7.de mag-c b4.de* *Mez* b4a.de nux-v b7.de* **Puls** b7.de* rhod b4.de* sel b7a.de sep b4.de* spig b7.de* sulph b4.de*
- **amel.**: ars b4a.de cocc b7a.de nux-v b7.de* phos b4.de* staph b7.de* sulph b4a.de

ROUGHNESS, sensation of: chinin-s bg2 dulc fd4.de fl-ac k* nat-sil fd3.de• phys bg2* suis-hep rly4•
- **tartar**, from: *Mez*

RUBBING:
- **agg.**: ph-ac b4.de*
- **amel.**: *Merc* b4.de* phos b4.de*
- **cheek** | **amel.**: *Merc* ptk1 phos ptk1

SALT:
- **agg.**: carb-v b4.de*
- **amel.**: *Carb-an* ptk1 mag-c b4.de*

SEASONS:
- **autumn**: m-arct bg2
- **spring**: m-arct bg2 *Puls* b7a.de

SENSITIVE, tender: agar alum k* alum-sil k2 *Am-c* k* *Ant-c* arg-n aur-m bar-c bell k2 bol-la *Bry* k* calc b4a.de carb-an k* card-m caust k* cham cina b7.de* coc-c k* coff b7a.de *Colch* k* coli rly4• dulc fd4.de ferr *Fl-ac* k* gad a1 gels ptk1 gymno hep b4a.de hippoc-k szs2 *Ign* bg2 kali-bi k* kali-c h2* *Kalm* **Lach** k* lipp a1 *Lyc* a1 lyss k* m-ambo b7.de *Mag-c* k* *Mag-p* manc mang k* *Merc* merc-c k* merc-i-r k* mez k* *Nat-c* k* *Nat-m* k* nat-pyru rly4• olib-sac wmh1 olnd b7.de* opun-s a1 (non:opun-v a1) orot-ac rly4• ox-ac bg1 pall par b7.de* positr nl2• puls b7.de* ran-s b7.de* ribo rly4• ruta fd4.de sabin c1 sars k* sedi a1 senec k* seneg k* *Sep* b4a.de *Sil* staph k* strept-ent jl2 suis-hep rly4• sul-ac k2 *Sulph* k* symph fd3.de• thioc-ac rly4• vanil fd5.de zinc k* [heroin sdj2 *Spect* dfg1]
- **morning**: caust h2* coc-c a1
- **evening**: agar dendr-pol sk4• ruta fd4.de
- **air**, to: *Acon* amp rly4• aran bac jl2 *Bell* berb bry **Calc** calc-p calc-s cina mag-p **Nat-m** ox-ac sin-n sulph h2 tub bg
- **brushing**: chlam-tr bcx2• dream-p sdj1• nat-m k* pant-ac rly4• suis-hep rly4• [heroin sdj2]
- **chewing** agg.: *Acon* bro1 *Agar* arge-pl rwt5• ars bro1 aur h2* bell bro1 *Calc-p* k* *Carb-an* carb-v bro1 cham bro1 clem k* *Coff* bro1 *Fl-ac* bro1 gymno bro1 merc bro1 olnd k* parth bro1 plan bro1 sars h2* sil k* *Staph* bro1 vanil fd5.de
- **chocolate**; to: myos-a rly4•
- **cold** air; to: bac jl2 cina k2

○ · **Filled** teeth; in: sin-n k*

- **cold**; to: *Acon* bro1 amp rly4• arge-pl rwt5• ars bro1 bar-ox-suc rly4• bell bro1 carb-v bro1 cham bro1 *Coff* bro1 coli rly4• dendr-pol sk4• *Fl-ac* bro1 gamb mrr1 gymno bro1 merc bro1 nat-pyru rly4• parth bro1 plan bro1 propr sa3• ribo rly4• *Staph* bro1 suis-hep rly4• thiam rly4• ven-m rsj12•
  - **least**, the: *Carb-an* k* coc-c
- **cold** water; to: acon aids nl2• *Arg-n Ars* brom *Bry* **Calc** calc-s chlam-tr bcx2• cina dendr-pol sk4• gymno hell irid-met srj5• **Lach** merc nat-m *Nux-v* podo fd3.de• positr nl2• sep *Sil Staph* sulph symph fd3.de• *Ther*
- **dental** operation; cannot bear●: **Ant-c** k* *Fl-ac Ign* kl *Mag-c Staph*
- **pressure**, to: agar ars *Hecla Kali-bi* nat-pyru rly4• ozone sde2• sal-fr sle1• sulph h2*
- **sounds** reverberate painfully in●: *Ther* k*
- **touch**; to: *Acon* bro1 agar aloe ars bro1 bell bro1 berb carb-an h2* carb-v bro1 cham bro1 coc-c *Coff* bro1 *Fl-ac* bro1 gymno bro1 **Lach** *Lyc* mag-c merc bro1 **Nat-m** parth bro1 plan bro1 staph k*
- **warm** drinks | **agg.** | **Filled**; teeth in: sin-n a1*
  - **amel.**: chlam-tr bcx2•
- **warmth**, to: bar-ox-suc rly4• dulc fd4.de **Lach** *Nat-m* nat-pyru rly4• podo fd3.de• positr nl2• ruta fd4.de symph fd3.de• ven-m rsj12•

○ - **Crown**: nat-c bg2 *Sulph* bg2

- **Hollow** teeth (= carious teeth): aloe caps carb-an b4.de* card-m *Cham* spig b7a.de *Staph* k* symph fd3.de•
- **Incisors**: agar k* aur h2* aur-m coff b7a.de coloc a1 dendr-pol sk4• kola stb3• *M-arct* b7.de *Mag-m* nux-m b7a.de* pall sars *Spig* b7a.de thuj a1
  - ○ **Lower**: *Nat-c* b4a.de seneg b4.de*
  - **Upper**: am-c b4.de* aur b4.de* mag-m b4.de* *Sars* b4a.de sulph b4.de*
- **Lower** teeth: bar-c b4.de* nat-c b4.de*
  - **left** | **Hollow**: sulph b4.de*
- **Molars**: nux-m bg2 ribo rly4• symph fd3.de• thiam rly4•
  - **eating** agg.: aloe
  - ○ **Decayed**: aeth aloe
  - **Lower**: aeth
  - **Upper**: manc zinc h2*
    - **left**: zinc b4.de*
- **Points** of: carb-an b4a.de sulph k* *Thuj* b4a.de
- **Upper** teeth:
  - **right**: sars b4.de*
  - **left**: sulph b4.de*

SERRATED: bac bn lach med k* plb staph bro1 syph k* tub k*

SHARP and hurt tongue; sides seem: aloe symph fd3.de•

SHIVERING agg.: led b7.de* *Puls* b7.de* stram b7.de*

SHOCKS, electric: aeth am-c bro1 aran bro1 nux-v bro1 sal-fr sle1• tab a1 thuj k*

SITTING: | **agg.**: am-m b7.de* graph b4.de* m-arct b7.de **Puls** bg2 *Rhus-t* bg2

SLEEP:
- **after** | **agg.**: bar-m bg2
- **amel.**: nux-v b7.de* puls b7.de*
- **during** | **agg.**: mez b4.de*
- **falling** asleep; when:
  - **agg.**: ant-c b7.de* *Ars* b4.de* *Merc* b4.de*
  - **amel.**: *Merc* b4a.de*

SLIME on teeth (See Mucus)

SMOKING:
- **agg.**: *Bry* b7.de* *Chin* b7.de* clem b4.de* *Ign* b7.de* sabin b7.de* sars b4.de* spig b7.de* thuj bg2
- **amel.**: borx b4a.de* camph b7a.de *Merc* b4.de* nat-c b4.de* sel b7a.de spig b7.de*

SMOOTH feeling: aesc ptk1 carb-v bg1 colch bg2* dios bg2* phos b4.de* sel b7.de* sul-ac b4a.de* sul-i ptk1

SOFT, feel: alum bg2 calc-p ptk1 *Caust* k* cinnb coch eupi bg2 ign bg2 lepi k* lyc bg2 med k* merc k* nat-sil fd3.de• *Nit-ac* k* nux-m k* sul-i a1* zinc k*

SORDES: (↗*Mucus; MOUTH - Sordes*) **Ail** k* alum k* *Apis* arn k2 **Ars** k* asc-t bg2* bac br1* **Bapt** k* *Bry* k* *Cact* cadm-s cal-ren c2* calen ptk1 *Camph* *Carb-ac* k* *Carb-v* carbn-s bg2* caust tl1 **Chin** k* chinin-s bg2 cub sne *Dig* *Echi* bro1 epiph bg2* frag br1* *Gels* hippoz sne **Hyos** k* iod bg2* *Iris* kali-cy sne *Kali-p* k* lac-c k2 lach k2 *Merc* k* *Merc-c* k* merc-i-f sne merc-k-i sne merc-meth sne *Mur-ac* k* nit-ac bg2 ox-ac *Petr* **Ph-ac** k* **Phos** k* plan bro1 *Plb* k* *Pyrog* k* **Rhus-t** k* sec sil-mar c2 *Stram* *Sul-ac* sulph tab thuj bg2* tub al* zinc-m sne
- **accompanied** by:
  - **typhoid**:
    - **fever**; and:
      - **painful**: bapt bg2 bry bg2 hyos bg2 rhus-t bg2
      - **painless**: ph-ac bg2 phos bg2
- **black**: **Chin** k* *Con* k* *Fl-ac* ptk1 lach k2
- **bloody**: plan k* sec k*
- **brown**: ail sne *Apis* am sne bapt ptk1* *Cact* carb-ac sne *Colch* cub sne dig sne *Kali-p* mur-ac sne *Vario* zinc-m sne
- **dark**: *Chin* **Fl-ac** tab k*
- **sensation** of: agar bg2 ars bg2 asaf bg2 bell bg2 carb-v bg2 caust bg2 chin bg2 coc-c bg2 dig bg2 merc bg2 nux-m bg2 phos bg2 puls bg2 rhod bg2 rhus-t bg2 ther bg2
- **slimy**: rhus-t ptk1

SOUR food agg.: arg-n bg2 mur-ac bg2

SPONGY, feel: caust bg2 nit-ac k*

STICK together, as if glued: arg-met eupi bg2* *Psor* k* syph bg3 zinc k* zinc-o zinc-ox

STICKY: arg-met k* crot-h ptk1 eupi bg2 iod lach ptk1 psor bg2* rhus-t b7a.de sang k* syph bg2* zinc bg2

STIFFNESS; sensation of: rhus-t bg2

STOOL; after: | **amel.**: alum bg2 sang b7a.de

STOOPING agg.: m-ambo b7.de sep b4.de* *Spig* b7a.de

STRENGTH; sensation of loss of: am-c b4.de* merc bg2

STRETCHED: coloc bg2

SUCKING:
- **air** | **amel.**: clem b4.de* *Mez* b4a.de*
- **blood** | **amel.**: bov b4.de* nit-ac b4a.de
- **gums**:
  - **agg.**: bov b4.de* carb-v b4.de* chin ptk1 kali-c b4.de* mang ptk1 nux-m b7.de* nux-v b7.de* *Sil* b4a.de zinc b4.de*
  - **amel.**: all-c ptk1 clem ptk1
- **tongue**; with:
  - **agg.**: am-c bg2 bell bg2 carb-v bg2 kali-c bg2 nit-ac bg2 nux-m bg2 nux-v bg2 zinc bg2
  - **amel.**: mang b4.de* *Mez* b4a.de

SUPPURATING; as if: lyc bg2

SWALLOWING agg.: apis b7a.de staph b7.de*

SWEETS agg.: am-c b4.de* *Cham* b7a.de merc-i-f ptk1 mur-ac bg2* nat-c b4.de* *Spig* b7a.de

SWELLING: | **Periosteum**: sil bg2

SWOLLEN sensation: kola stb3• olib-sac wmh1 spong h1*

TALK of others agg.: ars bg2 *Bry* bg2

TALKING agg.: am-c bg2 nux-m b7.de* sep b4a.de*

TARTAR (See Sordes)

TEA agg.: ferr bg2 *Ign* bg2 sel bg2* thuj b4.de*

TEETHING (See Dentition)

TEMPERATURE agg.; changes of: ozone sde2•

TENSION in: anac coloc k* ham fd3.de• hyper k* kali-s fd4.de merc-i-f bg1 nat-m nat-sil fd3.de• phos a1 **Puls** k* sil h2* symph fd3.de• ther k*
- **right** side: bar-c k*
- ○ **Lower** teeth: coloc b4.de*
- **Molars** | **Hollow**: *Am-m* bg2 anac b4.de* coloc bg2 kali-n bg2 merc-i-f bg2 puls bg2
- **Nerves**: coloc b4a.de* **Puls** b7a.de*

THINKING agg.: bar-c bg2 bell bg2 nux-v bg2

TOOTHACHE (See Pain)

TORPOR, sensation of: chin petr

TOUCH:
- **agg.**: anac b4.de* ant-c b7a.de arg-met b7.de* *Arn* b7.de* ars b4.de* aur b4.de* **Bell** b4.de* borx b4a.de* bov b4.de* *Bry* b7.de* calc b4.de* carb-v b4.de* caust b4.de* chel b7.de* *Chin* b7a.de* clem b4.de* coff b7a.de euph b4.de* graph b4.de* *Hep* b4.de* iod b4.de* kali-c b4.de* kali-n b4.de* lyc b4.de* m-ambo b7.de *M-arct* b7.de *Mag-c* b4a.de mag-m b4a.de* mag-p bg2 mang b4.de* **Merc** b4.de* mez b4a.de* nat-c b4.de* *Nat-m* b4.de* nux-m b7.de* *Nux-v* b7.de* petr b4.de* **Ph-ac** b4.de* phos b4.de* plan bg2 *Puls* b7.de* rhod b4.de* rhus-t b7.de* ruta b7.de* sabin b7.de* sep b4.de* sil bg2 *Staph* b7.de* stront-c b4a.de sul-ac b4.de*
- **amel.**: bry b7.de* m-arct b7.de nat-m b4.de* sep b4.de*
- **food**; of: mag-m ptk1
- **slight** touch agg.: chin bg2
- **tongue** agg.; when touched by the: *Ant-c* ptk1 carb-v bg2 chin bg2 **Ign** bg2 mag-p bg2 *Merc* bg2* mez ptk1 phos bg2 rhus-t bg2

TRANSPARENT: calc gk

TREMBLING: phys ptk1

TWISTED; sensation as if: kali-i ptk1 lact k*

TWITCHING in teeth: kali-c h2* kali-n h2* mur-ac h2* nat-c h2* phys bg2
○ - **Carious** teeth; in: rhus-t h1
- **Molars** | **Upper**: am-m bg1 *Glon* bg1* phos bg1
- **Tips**, in: sulph h2

ULCERATION of roots: alum k* fl-ac k2 mez

UNDRESSING agg.: plat bg2 rhus-t bg2

UNEASINESS in teeth: cimic bg2

VINEGAR: | **amel.**: puls b7.de*

VOMITING:
- **during** | **agg.**: *Puls* b7.de* verat bg2

WAKING agg.: **Bell** bg2 bry b7.de* calc b4.de* carb-v b4.de* con b4.de* graph b4.de* kali-c b4.de* *Kreos* b7a.de nat-s bg2 nit-ac bg2 *Nux-v* b7.de* phos b4.de* ran-b b7.de* sabin b7.de* spig b7.de* zinc b4.de*

WALKING:
- **about** | **must** walk about: *Mag-c* b4a.de
- **air**; in open:
  - **agg.**: *Con* b4.de* graph b4.de* kali-c b4.de* nat-c b4.de* *Nux-v* b7.de* phos b4.de* sabad b7.de* sabin b7.de* *Staph* b7.de*
  - **amel.**: bov b4.de* bry b7.de* *M-arct* b7.de *Puls* b7.de*
- **amel.**: *M-arct* b7.de mag-c bg2 par b7.de* *Puls* b7.de* rat bg2 *Rhus-t* b7.de*
- **wind**; in the | **agg.**: *Puls* b7a.de

WARM:
- **agg.**: bell bg2 *Calc* bg2 carb-v bg2 *Caust* bg2 *Hell* bg2 *Lach* bg2 merc bg2 **Nat-m** bg2 nit-ac bg2 par bg2 ph-ac bg2 phos bg2 plan bg2 rhus-t bg2 sil bg2 staph bg2 thuj bg2
- **applications**:
  - **agg.**: *Arn* b7a.de bry b7a.de* calc ptk1 cham bg2 *Coloc* b4a.de crot-t bg2 dros ptk1 graph b4.de* hell b7.de* hep b4a.de* *M-arct* b7.de mag-c b4.de* nux-m b7a.de* nux-v bg2 ph-ac b4.de* phos b4.de* *Puls* b7.de* rhod bg2 sabin b7.de*
  - **amel.**: am-c b4.de* *Ars* b4.de* bov b4.de* *Chin* b7a.de cycl bg2 kali-c b4.de* lach b7a.de* lyc b4.de* mag-m b4.de* **Merc** b4.de* *Mur-ac* b4a.de nat-c b4.de* *Nux-m* b7.de* *Nux-v* b7.de* *Rhus-t* b7.de* sabad b7.de* sil bg2 *Spig* b7a.de *Staph* b7.de* sul-ac b4a.de* *Sulph* b4a.de*
- **bed**:
  - **agg.**: **Bell** bg2 *Bry* bg2 *Cham* b7.de* graph bg2 *Led* b7.de* mag-c bg2 **Merc** b4a.de* *Ph-ac* b4a.de* phos b4a.de* **Puls** b7.de* sabin b7.de* sep bg2 spig bg2 sul-ac bg2
  - **amel.**: am-c bg2 bry bg2 lyc b4a.de* nux-v bg2
- **drinks**:
  - **agg.**: agn b7.de* am-c bg2 *Ambr* b7a.de **Bry** b7a.de *Cham* b7.de* dros b7.de* lach b7a.de* m-arct b7.de *M-aust* b7a.de **Merc** b4.de* merc-c b4a.de *Mez* b4a.de nux-m b7.de* *Nux-v* b7.de* *Par* b7a.de *Puls* b7a.de* rhus-t b7.de* sel b7a.de sil b4.de*
  - **amel.**: lyc b4.de* *Nux-m* b7.de* *Nux-v* b7.de* rhus-t b7.de* spig b7a.de *Sulph* b4.de*
- **food**:
  - **agg.**: *Acon* b7a.de agn b7.de* am-c b4a.de ambr b7.de* anac b4a.de* *Bar-c* b4.de* **Bell** b4a.de* **Bry** b7.de* **Calc** b4.de* *Carb-v* b4a.de* *Caust* b4a.de *Cham* b7.de* *Coff* bg2 *Hell* b7.de* kali-c b4.de* lach b7a.de* m-arct b7.de *M-aust* b7.de* mag-m b4.de* mag-p bg2 *Merc* b4.de* *Mez* b4a.de nat-m b4.de* nux-v b7.de* par b7.de* ph-ac b4a.de* *Phos* b4.de* **Puls** b7.de* rhod b4.de* sep b4.de* *Sil* b4.de* *Spig* b7a.de *Sulph* b4.de*
    - **hot** food: ph-ac b4.de* sep b4.de*
  - **amel.**: *Ars* b4a.de con b4a.de kali-c b4a.de *Lyc* b4a.de mag-m b4.de* mag-p bg2 *Mur-ac* b4a.de nit-ac b4.de* *Nux-m* b7.de* nux-v b7.de* phos b4a.de* rhus-t b7.de* sil bg2 spig b7a.de sul-ac b4.de* sulph b4.de*
- **room** | **agg.**: *Cham* bg2 *Hep* bg2 mag-c bg2 nux-v bg2 *Phos* bg2 **Puls** bg2 rhod bg2 *Sulph* bg2
- **sensation** as if teeth were (See Heat; during; Heat; sensation)
- **stove** agg.: puls b7.de*
- **water** | **amel.**: nux-m b7.de* *Nux-v* b7a.de *Puls* b7a.de
- **wraps** on cheeks | **amel.**: *Mur-ac* b4a.de nux-v b7.de* *Ph-ac* b4a.de phos b4.de* *Spig* b7a.de

WARM AGG.; BECOMING: cham bg2 zinc bg2

WARMTH; sensation of (See Heat; sensation)

WASHING:
- **agg.**: *Phos* b4a.de
- **face** | **agg.**: plan bg2

WATER: | **agg.**: acon b7a.de *Nux-v* b7a.de

WATER coming from; sour, fetid: nicc

WEAKNESS in teeth: am-c h2* merc h1* sulph bg2

WEATHER:
- **cold**:
  - **wet** | **agg.**: am-c b4.de* borx b4a.de* nat-c b4.de* *Nux-m* b7.de* *Rhod* b4.de*
- **rainy** | **agg.**: nat-c bg2
- **thunderstorm**; during | **agg.**: *Rhod* b4.de*

WEDGE-SHAPED: *Kreos* k*

WET agg.; getting: calc-p bg2

WIND agg.: *Acon* bg2 cocc b7a.de graph b4.de* *Puls* b7.de* *Rhus-t* bg2 sil bg2

WINE agg.: **Ign** bg2 *Nux-v* bg2

WISDOM teeth, ailments from eruption of: *(↗Dentition - difficult - wisdom)* *Calc* k* **Cham** ●* chap c1 cheir c1* ferr-pic st *Fl-ac* k* *Mag-c* k* ozone sde2• petr-ra shn4• positr nl2• *Sil* k*

WOMEN; complaints in: *(↗Maidens)* *Acon* bg2 **Bell** bg2 calc bg2 *Cham* bg2 chin bg2 *Coff* bg2 *Hyos* bg2 ign bg2 plat bg2 **Puls** bg2 sabin bg2 **Sep** bg2 *Spig* bg2

WORM; sensation of a: kali-i bg2 mag-m bg2 syph c1*

YAWNING agg.: apis b7a.de

YELLOW (See Discoloration - yellow)

CANINES; complaints of: am-c b2.de* anac b2.de* calc b2.de* laur b2.de* mag-m b2.de* mur-ac b2.de* nat-c b2.de* nux-v bg2* petr b2.de* *Rhus-t* b2.de* sep b2.de* squil bg2 staph b2.de* stront-c b2.de* sul-ac b2.de* zinc b2.de*

INCISORS; complaints of: *Agar* b2.de* alum b2.de* am-c b2.de* am-m b2.de* ambr b2.de* ang b2.de* arg-met b2.de* asar b2.de* aur b2.de* bell b2.de* borx b2.de* bov b2.de* calc b2.de* canth b2.de* carb-v b2.de* caust b2.de* cham b2.de* chin b2.de* cocc b2.de* coff b2.de* **Colch** b2.de* dros b2.de* ign b2.de* iod b2.de* *Kali-c* b2.de* kreos b2.de* lyc b2.de* m-ambo b2.de m-arct b2.de mag-c b2.de* *Mag-m* b2.de* merc b2.de* mez b2.de* mur-ac b2.de* nat-c b2.de* *Nat-m* b2.de* nit-ac b2.de* *Nux-m* b2.de* nux-v b2.de* petr b2.de* ph-ac b2.de* phos b2.de* plat b2.de* ran-s b2.de* rhod b2.de* *Rhus-t* b2.de* sars b2.de* seneg b2.de* *Sep* b2.de* sil b2.de* spig b2.de* spong b2.de* staph b2.de* *Stront-c* b2.de* sul-ac b2.de* *Sulph* b2.de* tarax b2.de* teucr b2.de* thuj b2.de* *Zinc* b2.de*
○ - **Behind**: *Phos* ptk1

MOLARS; complaints of: agar b2.de* alum b2.de* *Am-c* b2.de* ambr b2.de* anac b2.de* ang b2.de* ant-t b2.de* arn b2.de* ars bg2 asar b2.de* aur b2.de* bar-c b2.de* bell b2.de* bism b2.de* borx b2.de* bov b2.de* **Bry** b2.de* calad b2.de* calc b2.de* canth b2.de* carb-an b2.de* *Carb-v* b2.de* caust b2.de* cham b2.de* **Chin** b2.de* clem b2.de* cocc b2.de* coff b2.de* colch b2.de* coloc b2.de* con bg2 croc b2.de* cycl b2.de* euph b2.de* graph b2.de* guaj b2.de* hell b2.de* hyos b2.de* ign b2.de* iod b2.de* kali-c b2.de* kali-n b2.de* **Kreos** b2.de* laur b2.de* lyc b2.de* m-arct b2.de mag-c b2.de* *Mag-m* b2.de* mang b2.de* meph bg2 merc b2.de* mez b2.de* mur-ac b2.de* *Nat-c* b2.de* nit-ac b2.de* nux-m b2.de* nux-v b2.de* olnd b2.de* par b2.de* petr b2.de* ph-ac b2.de* *Phos* b2.de* plat b2.de* plb b2.de* puls b2.de* *Ran-s* b2.de* rheum b2.de* *Rhod* b2.de* rhus-t b2.de* sabad b2.de* sabin b2.de* sars b2.de* seneg b2.de* sep b2.de* sil b2.de* spig b2.de* spong b2.de* *Staph* b2.de* stront-c b2.de* sul-ac b2.de* sulph b2.de* teucr b2.de* thuj b2.de* verat b2.de* verb b2.de* **Zinc** b2.de*

NERVES, injuries to dental: *(↗Injury)* hyper

NIGHT: flav jl2

ABSCESS (See Suppuration)

ADENOIDS (See NOSE - Adenoids)

ADHESION:
O - **Uvula**:
· **Tonsil**; to: lach bg2 nat-m bg2
⁝ **right**: nat-m bg2
⁝ **left**: lac-c bg2

ADHESIVE, sticky; as if: aesc ptk1 *Aur* b4a.de bapt ptk1 caust bg2* chel ptk1 galla-q-r nl2• **Kali-bi** ptk1 kali-n bg1 *Lach* ptk1 myric ptk1 ph-ac ptk1 puls ptk1 sec ptk1 *Sep* b4a.de sul-ac ptk1

ALIVE in; sensation of something: anan c1 raph bg2 verat b7.de*

ANESTHESIA: *(↗Numbness)* *Acon* *All-c* arg-met *Gels* hyos mtf11 *Kali-br* k* kali-c mag-s olnd verat-v
- **alcohol**; from: hyos mtf11 kali-br mtf11
O - **Fauces**: arg-met ptk1 kali-br bro1
- **Pharynx**: gels bro1 *Kali-br* bro1

ANGINA (See Inflammation)

ANXIETY and apprehension in throat: *(↗MIND - Fear - throat)* cann-s a1* plut-n srj7• stram bg2 urol-h rwt•
- **oppression**; with | **Tonsils**; in: am-m vh

APHTHAE: *(↗GENERALS - Aphthae)* *Aeth* k* ars k* arum-t *Bell* k* borx k2 *Bry* k* *Canth* k* carb-v k2 *Dros* b7a.de *Gels* **Ign** *Kali-chl* kali-i mrr1 lach k2 med c1 plb k* *Spong* b7.de* staph b7.de* sul-ac a1* sulph
O - **Pharynx**: *Canth* bro1 eucal bro1 *Hydrin-m* bro1 nit-ac bro1
- **Tonsils**, on: *Bell* calc *Gels* *Myric* hr1

APPLE core had lodged, sensation as if (See Foreign - apple)

ASCENDING sensation:
- **drinks**; of: aur bg2 **Bell** bg2 *Lach* bg2 *Merc* bg2 petr bg2 **Phos** bg2
- **food**; of: *Sil* bg2

ASTRINGENT sensation: ail k* arg-n bg2 brom bg2 kali-cy a1 lach bg2 naja phyt k* podo bg2

ATROPHY: lach bg2

BALL; sensation of a (See Lump)

BITING sensation in back part of fauces between acts of swallowing: ambr a1*

BLACK (See Discoloration - black)

BLISTERED: canth k*

BLOOD:
- **hawks** up dark clotted blood: zinc h2
- **oozing**: **Acon** k* *Adren* br1 am-c k2 *Arn* k* ars bapt k2 *Bell* calc-sil k2 *Canth* k* *Carb-v* *Chin* k* *Crot-h* cur dros k2 *Ferr* k* *Ferr-p* k* *Ham* k* *Ip* k* kali-bi bg2 kreos k2 *Lach* merc-c k* merc-cy *Mill* k* *Phos* k* *Sang* k* *Sec* sep k* sul-ac k2 ter hr1
· **sensation** of: zinc h2*
O · **Tonsils**: *Crot-h* *Lach* *Phos* sec ter
· **Uvula**: lac-c k*

BLOTCHES (See Mucous)

BONE in; sensation of a: *(↗Foreign; Pain - splinter)* bapt dx1 *Calc* calc-caust c1 **Hep** ign irid-met srj5• lach *Nit-ac* phys

BREAD crumbs, sensation of: *(↗Foreign; COUGH - Crumb; LARYNX - Crumb)* *Coc-c* k* dros k* kola stb3• **Lach** k* **Nit-ac** pall k* *Sabad* sanic santa wd tritic-vg fd5.de
- **hawking** up mucus | **amel.**: **Lach** k*

BREAK:
- **sensation** as if going to | **Uvula**: ham bg2

BUBBLING in esophagus: chel k*

CALCAREOUS deposit: *Calc* k*

CANCER: aur mrr1 bar-i rmk1• *Carb-an* *Lach* rmk1• led *Phos* rmk1• tarent

Cancer: ...
O - **Esophagus**: carb-v mtf *Con* rmk1• hydr rmk1• lyc mtf phos gm1 plat-m gm1 rumx-ab mtf
- **Nasopharynx**: cist mtf11

CASEOUS deposits in tonsils: *Chen-a* k* *Kali-chl* *Kali-m* mag-c vs morg ptj• morg-p xyz60 phos mtf33 psor ez syc ptj• vip

CATARRH: acon bg2 alum h2* alumn k* am-m k2 androc srj1• *Anemps* br1 arg-n k2* ars k2 aur-m *Bad* k* bar-c k2 *Bar-m* k* **Bell** bg2 brom *Calc* caps bg2 carb-v bg2* carbn-s *Cham* bg2 cist tl1 cub br1 diphtox jl2 dulc bg2 euph mtf11 falco-pe nl2• *Fl-ac* formal br1 *Graph* k* hep bg2* *Hippoz* k* *Hydr* k* kali-bi k* *Kali-chl* k* kali-i lac-f c2 lach bg2 lem-m mtf11 linu-c a1 mand sp1 med k2 melal-alt gya4 *Merc* k* *Merc-i-r* hr1 myric hr1 **Nat-m** *Nux-v* k* petr a1 *Phyt* k* positr nl2• *Puls* k* rhus-t bg2 *Rumx* sabad k2 sal-al blc1• sal-fr sle1• *Sang* seneg bg2 sil k2 *Sulph* k* sumb c2 syc fmm1• visc sp1 [spect dfg1]
- **accompanied** by | **fullness** (See Fullness - accompanied - catarrh)
- **adherent**: ambr mtf11 lac-h mtf11 vip mtf11
- **dry**: sal-ac mtf11
- **smokers**, of: arg-n br1
- **waking**; on: hydrog srj2•
O - **Esophagus**: seneg c2
- **Pharynx**: anemps br1 hepat br1 kali-bi br1 solid br1 toxo-g jl2
· **chronic**: am-br br1 *Coll* br1
· **portal** congestion; from: coll br1

CHEESY:
- **lumps**; hawks up cheesy (See Hawks)
- **spots**; cheesy looking: *Bell* k* bry *Kali-bi* *Psor* syc ptj•
- **tubercles**; hawks out cheesy (See Hawks)

CHOKING: *(↗Narrow; Narrow - sensation; LARYNX - Constriction)* abies-n br1 absin *Acon* k* *Aesc* aeth agar k* agath-a nl2• ail bg2* aloe *Alum* k* alum-p k2 am-c k* am-m ambr k* aml-ns bg2 anan ant-t bg2 *Apis* k* arb-m oss1• arg-met ptk1 *Arg-n* k* arn b7.de* *Ars* ars-h ars-i ars-s-f k2 arum-t k* asaf asar asc-t atra-r bnm3• *Aur* b4a.de *Bapt* k* *Bar-c* k* **Bell** k* benz-ac *Brom* bry k* *Bufo* buth-a sp1 **Cact** k* cadm-met sp1 *Calc* k* calc-p bg2 *Calc-s* cann-s b7a.de* *Canth* k* *Caps* k* carb-ac carb-an k* *Carb-v* k* *Carbn-s* castm **Caust** k* cedr **Cham** k* chel k* chin k* chin-b c1 chinin-ar chinin-s chir-fl bnm4• chlor cic cimic *Cimx* *Cina* bg2 cinnb *Coc-c* *Cocc* k* colch con k* cop cot br1 croc b7.de* *Crot-c* *Crot-h* *Crot-t* k* *Cupr* cur cycl cystein-l rly4• dig dios dros dulc b4a.de elaps eup-per *Ferr* k* ferr-ar ferr-p *Fl-ac* fum rly1*• gamb k* *Gels* k* gent-c ger-i rly4• *Glon* k* *Graph* k* *Hell* *Hep* k* hura hydrog srj2• **Hyos** k* **Ign** k* indg *Iod* k* *Ip* k* iris c1 jac-c kali-ar kali-bi k* *Kali-c* k* kali-chl kali-i k* kali-m k2 *Kali-n* k* kali-p *Kali-s* *Kola* stb3• kreos k* lac-ac **Lac-c** k* lac-h sk4• **Lach** k* **Laur** k* lil-t bg2 **Lyc** k* lycps-v ptk1 lyss m-arct b7.de mag-c b4.de* *Mag-p* maias-l hrn2• *Manc* *Meph* bg2* merc k* merc-c k* merc-i-r ptk1 merc-sul c1 merl *Mez* k* morg-p fmm1• *Mosch* k* myric **Naja** k* nat-ar nat-c b4.de* *Nat-m* k* nat-s nicc nit-ac k2 nux-m bg2 *Nux-v* k* oena ol-an bg2 op k* ox-ac petr ph-ac k* phos k* phys *Phyt* k* plac-s rly4• *Plat* k* **Plb** k* polys sk4• prot jl2 ptel *Puls* k* ran-s k* raph rat k* rheum h* *Rhod* k* rhus-t k* rumx ptk1 sabad k* sabin k* sarcol-ac sp1 sars k* sec bg2 seneg k* *Sep* k* *Sil* h2* **Spong** k* still *Stram* k* strept-ent mtf11 streptoc mtf11 stroph-h ptk1 *Stry* k* suis-pan rly4• sul-ac k* **Sulph** k* sumb k* syc bka1*• syph bg1* *Tab* k* tarent bg2* ter bg1* thioc-ac rly4• *Thuj* k* thyr ptk1* tritic-vg fd5.de tub c1* valer b7.de* vario jl2 *Verat* k* vip vip-l-f a1 visc c1 *Zinc* k* zinc-p k2 [heroin sdj2]
- **daytime**: nat-s k*
- **morning**: agar k* aster k* cham k* *Fl-ac* gels sne naja ol-an k* spong fd4.de stry k*
· **waking**; on: agar k* aster a1 gels sne irid-met srj5•
- **forenoon**: fl-ac k*
- **afternoon**: nat-ar nicc k* sang k* spong fd4.de stry k*
· **13 h** | **night**; until: abrom-a ks5
· **15 h**: lyss
- **evening**: alum k* chinin-s **Ign** mag-c h2* ol-an bg1 phys k* tritic-vg fd5.de
- **night**: arg-n k* arum-t k* cop *Gad* bg1* glon k* hir rsj4• kali-n h2* kola stb3• nit-ac phos h2* ran-s k* spig sul-ac h2* *Tab*
· **midnight**:
⁝ **after**:
⁝ **4 h**: sumb
⁝ **5 h**: raph

- **accompanied** by:
  - **croup** (See LARYNX - Croup - accompanied - choking)
  - **goitre**; exophthalmic (See EXTERNAL - Goitre - exophthalmic - accompanied - choking)
  - **respiration**; asthmatic (See RESPIRATION - Asthmatic - accompanied - throat - choking)
  - **vertigo**: iber ptk1
- **alternating** with | **Fingers** and toes; contraction of: asaf ptk1
- **angina** pectoris: tab hr1
- **bending**:
  - **head**:
    - ⁝ **agg.**: ph-ac k*
    - ⁝ **backward** | **amel.**: hep ptk1 lach ptk1
- **bowing** the head: con k*
  - **amel.**: cench k2
- **breathing** agg.: chel ptk1
- **cardiac** pain, with: arg-n hr1 *Cact* hr1
- **clearing** the throat; when: (↗*STOMACH - Retching*) *Ambr* *Anac* **Arg-n** borx *Bry* *Calc-p* cench k2 *Coc-c* *Ip* *Kali-c* **Nux-v** osm *Stann*
- **clothing** agg.: agar ambr *Apis* *Bell* *Cact* cench k2 chel elaps glon k2 kali-bi kali-c k* **Lach** k* *Sep* vip-l-f a1
- **convulsive**: acon k* ars k* *Bell* k* *Calc* *Caps* k* *Carb-v* k* *Cic* *Con* **Hyos** ign gk *Mag-p* sars k*
- **cough**:
  - **during**:
    - ⁝ **agg.**: ars coc-c cocc k* kali-c mtf33 lach pitu-gl skp7• tarent ptk1
    - ⁝ **amel.**: hir rsj4•
- **dinner** | **after** | **agg.**: bar-c h2* *Carl* a1
  - **during** | **agg.**: *Bar-c* k*
- **distended**, as if throat were: mag-c h2*
- **drinking** agg.●: abies-n bro1 acon h1 *Anac* bro1 caj bro1 *Cann-s* bro1 cimx glon bro1 **Hyos** k* ign gk iod kali-n h2 manc meph k* *Merc-c* bro1 mur-ac bro1 **NAT-M** k ● nicc bro1 nit-ac bro1 phos bg1 *Phyt* bro1 *Pip-m* bro1 rhus-t santin bro1 sumb bro1
  - **looked** at; if: *Ph-ac*
- **dryness** in larynx; from: ars-s-f k2
- **easily**: hyos mtf33 kali-c mtf33 morg-p mtf11 syc mtf11
- **eating**:
  - **after** | **agg.**: agar h2* sil h2* stram a1* sulph h2* zinc-val ptk1
  - **agg.**●: (↗*swallowing - agg.*) abies-n bro1 acon h1 anac br1* caj bro1* *Cann-s* bro1 glon bro1 hydrog srj2• kali-bi *Kali-c* kali-n h2 **Lach** k ● *Meph* *Merc-c* k* mur-ac bro1 nicc bro1 nit-ac k* *Phyt* bro1 *Pip-m* bro1 santin bro1 sumb bro1
  - **attempting** to eat; on: zinc-val ptk1
  - **bread** agg.: ran-s
- **expectoration**; with: ambr br1 pitu-gl skp7•
- **froth**; from: lyss c1
- **grasped**, as if: agath-a nl2• lach tl1
- **hawking** up mucus agg.: ambr ptk1 *Arg-n* ptk1 nux-v ptk1
  - **morning**: ambr a1
- **headache**; during: *Glon*
- **hysterical**: cact k2
- **lying** down agg.: apis *Kali-bi* lach mtf33 ol-j
- **lying** on back | **amel.**: *Spong*
- **menses**; before: puls
- **mucus**; from: hippoc-k szs2
  - **mouth**; in: sul-ac h2
  - **posterior** nares; in: spig h1 spong fd4.de
- **nervous**: mosch ptk1
- **palpitations**; from: iber a* lach a* lec naja a*
- **paroxysmal**: cocc a1 verat k*
- **raising** arm agg.: plb
- **restlessness**; with: kola stb3•
- **rising** sensation: bell h1 carb-an h2
- **sensation** of: aesc vh1 arg-n br1 botul br1 cit-v c2 oxal-a rly4• physala-p bnm7• pitu-gl skp7• stry mrr1 vario jl2 vip-l-f a1
- **sitting** up in bed | **amel.**: hir rsj4•

Choking: ...

- **sleep**: (↗*LARYNX - Constriction - Larynx - sleep - falling; LARYNX - Constriction - Larynx - sleep - falling - when*)
  - **agg.**: *Lach* ptk1 spong ptk1 valer ptk1
  - **during**: lach ptk1 spong ptk1 valer ptk1
  - **going** to sleep; on: (↗*LARYNX - Constriction - Larynx - sleep - falling - when*)
    - ⁝ **agg.**: (↗*LARYNX - Constriction - larynx - sleep - falling*) **Bell** *Cench* *Crot-h* kali-c *Lac-c* **Lach** k* *Naja* **Nux-v** sep teucr valer k*
- **smoking** agg.: sep k*
- **spasms** in epiglottis; from: med mtf11
- **speaking**, when: acon a1 dros h1* *Manc* k* meph k* spong fd4.de
- **stooping** agg.: caps fkm1•
- **sudden**: samb ptk1
- **swallowing**: (↗*STOMACH - Retching; STOMACH - Retching - Swallowing - agg.*)
  - **agg.**: (↗*eating - agg.; STOMACH - Retching; STOMACH - Retching - Swallowing*) acon ambr c1 ant-t ptk1 ars *Bar-c* bell k* *Bry* calc kr1 cann-s br1 chen-a c1 *Cic* *Cupr* k* dig ptk1 galeoc-c-h gms1• gent-c *Graph* k* *Hyos* k* kali-c lach k2* *Laur* **Lyc** k* mag-p manc meph *Merc* mur-ac k* nat-c h2 *Nat-m* nat-s hr nit-ac k2 onos ozone sde2• par *Plb* **Puls** k* rhus-t *Stram* ptk1 stry syc fmm1• tarent verat zinc
  - **food** | **agg.**: *Carb-v* k* lach **Puls** k*
  - **liquids** | **agg.**: **Hyos** k* lyss k* *Mag-p* merc-c ptk1 nat-s rhus-t
  - **must** swallow: borx cact *Lach* *Sep*
  - **pills** agg.: lyss mrr1
- **thyroid** gland; from enlargement of the: graph ptk1 merc-i-f ptk1 spong bg2*
- **walking**:
  - **agg.**: nat-s k*
  - **amel.**: dros k*
  - **wind**; as from walking in: plat h2
- **warm**:
  - **drinks**:
    - ⁝ **agg.**: lach k2
    - ⁝ **amel.**: calc-f ptk1
  - **room** | **agg.**: lach k2
- **water**:
  - **drinking** agg.: bapt ptk1 bell ptk1 canth ptk1 hyos ptk1 lyss mrr1 nat-m ptk1 stram k2* sumb ptk1
  - **sight** or thought of: anan *Lyss*
- **writing** agg.: *Bar-c* k*

O - **Esophagus**: acon *Aesc* agar *Alum* k* *Alumn* am-caust vh1 anac *Arg-met* *Ars* ars-s-f k2 bar-c k2 *Bell* **Cact** cadm-s *Calc* canth *Carb-ac* cham chel chin *Cic* *Cimx* coc-c k* *Colch* crot-c *Cupr* dig dros graph k2 *Hyos* **Ign** iod **Kali-c** kali-chl lob lyc lyss **Merc-c** naja *Nat-ar* *Nat-m* nit-ac ox-ac *Phos* *Plb* *Sabad* spirae br1 stram sul-ac sul-i k2 zinc zinc-p k2
  - **morning** | **waking**; on: alum
  - **night**: alum
  - **below** upwards: *Lob* *Plb*
  - **inspiration** agg.: zinc
  - **pressure** in larynx, from: chel h1
  - **swallowing**:
    - ⁝ **agg.**: *Alum* bar-c k2 zinc
    - ⁝ **food** | **agg.**: caj
    - ⁝ **liquids** | **agg.**: hyos *Manc*
- **Hyoid** bone; region of: *All-c*

CLEARING throat (See Hawk; disposition)

CLOSED by a growth; as if grown together and: nit-ac b4a.de

CLUCKING sound, esophagus: *Cina* k*

COATED: (↗*Membrane*) apis bg2 ars k* bapt bg2 bell bg2 canth bg2 chin bg2 chord-umb rly4• hydrog srj2• kali-m bg2 lach bg2 lil-t k* lipp a1 luf-op rsj5• merc bg2 merc-cy bg2 petr k* phyt bg2 plb bg2 podo fd3.de• puls bg2 sep k* [heroin sdj2]

O - **Tonsils**: merc-c k*

- **Tonsils**: ...
  - **chalk**-like: brucel sa3•

COLD:
- **air**:
  - **agg.**: *Fl-ac* irid-met srj5•
  - **amel.**: diph ptk1
- **applications** | **agg.**: alum ptk1 *Ars* ptk1 hep ptk1 lac-c ptk1 lob ptk1 **Lyc** ptk1 manc ptk1 merc-i-r ptk1 nux-v ptk1 rhus-t ptk1 sabad ptk1 sil ptk1 syph ptk1
- **sensitive** to (See air - agg.)

COLD; AFTER TAKING A: bell ptk1 cist ptk1 *Dulc* ptk1 lach ptk1 *Merc* ptk1 *Nux-v* ptk1

COLDNESS, sensation of: acon bg2 agar *All-c* k* all-s *Arg-met* b7a.de* bamb-a stb2.de• bism bg2 caj k* carb-v k* caust k* chel bg1 *Cist* k* cor-r cur form a1 kali-bi k* kali-chl k* kali-n b4.de* kola stb3• lach bg2 lact k* laur b7a.de* lyc k* lyss meny b7.de* mez b4.de* ol-an bg2* ozone sde2• phos b4.de* plan k* raph k* *Rhus-t* bg2* sanic sep k* spira bg2 spirae a1 sulph b4.de* symph fd3.de• tell hr1 ter k* vac jl2 ven-m rsj12• verat k* [heroin sdj2]
- **right**: bamb-a stb2.de•
- **left** | **sensation** of cold wind: olnd
- **forenoon**: ozone sde2•
- **evening**: sep k* spirae a1 symph fd3.de•
- **air** agg.; in open: bamb-a stb2.de• cadm-met tpw6
- **chilliness** beginning in throat: sep
- **cold**:
  - **air**; as from cold: *Aesc* coca cor-r ol-an k* ozone sde2• symph fd3.de•
  - **water** were dropping down, as if: tarent
- **expiration** agg.; during: rhus-t k*
- **icy** coldness: **Cist** mrr1 coc-c cur
- **inspiration** agg.: chlf a1 *Cist* k* sulph k* symph fd3.de•
- **peppermint**; as from: agar bg1 form k* mez k* ozone sde2• pycnop-sa mrz1 sanic ptk1 tell k* *Verat* k* [heroin sdj2]
- **swallowing** agg.: nat-m k*
- **warm** drinks seem cold: *(↗GENERALS - Food and - warm drinks - aversion - hot - cold)* nat-m k*
- **wind** agg.; cold: lyc mez c1

○ - **Esophagus**: acon agar all-s vh1 anan cain lact lyss *Meny* k* [heroin sdj2]
  - **icy**: anan k*
- **Pharynx**: **Cist** bro1*
  - **cold air** | **inspiration** agg.: **Cist** mrr1
  - **inspiration** agg.: **Cist** mrr1

COMPLAINTS of throat: agra br1 *Apis* ptk1 arg-n ptk1 arum-t ptk1 *Bar-c* ptk1 **Bell** ptk1 caust ptk1 elaps br1 gels ptk1 helodr-cal knl2• *Hep* ptk1 *Kali-bi* ptk1 lac-c ptk1 **Lach** ptk1 *Lyc* ptk1 **Merc** ptk1 *Merc-c* ptk1 merc-cy ptk1 merc-i-f br1* *Merc-i-r* ptk1 nat-sal br1 *Nit-ac* ptk1 nux-v ptk1 *Phos* ptk1 phyt ptk1 puls ptk1 *Rhus-t* ptk1 stram br1 sulph ptk1 wye br1
- **alternating** sides: *Alum* ptk1 am ptk1 cocc ptk1 coloc ptk1 *Lac-c* bg2* podo ptk1 puls ptk1 sulph ptk1
- **right**: agar bg2* aloe bg2 am-c bg2* apis bg2* ars bg2 bar-c bg2 *Bell* bg2* bry ptk1 carb-ac bg2* carb-v bg2 caust bg2 dios bg2 ign bg2* iod bg2 iris bg2 kali-m bg2* kali-p bg2 kreos ptk1 lac-c bg2 lach bg2 **Lyc** bg2* meph bg2 merc bg2* merc-d bg2* merc-i-f bg2* nux-v bg2 phyt bg2* plat bg2 sang bg2* stann bg2* stict bg2 sulph bg2* syph ptk1 tarent bg2*

▽ · **extending** to | **left**: apis bg2* ars bg2 *Bell* bg2* calc ptk1 caust bg2* kali-m bg2 **Lyc** bg2* *Merc-i-f* bg2* phos bg2* sabad bg2* sang bg2* sul-ac bg2* syph ptk1
- **left**: brom bg2 calc bg2* caust bg2* crot-h bg2* diph ptk1 elaps bg2 ferr bg2* hep bg2* iod bg2 kali-c bg2* lac-c bg2* **Lach** bg2* manc bg2 merc-c ptk1 *Merc-i-r* bg2* naja bg2* nit-ac bg2 petr bg2* ph-ac bg2* rhus-t bg2* *Sabad* bg2* sep bg2* sil bg2* teucr ptk1 til ptk1 verat bg2
  - **forenoon**: cimic ptk1 rhus-t ptk1

▽ · **extending** to | **right**: calc bg2* **Lach** bg2* merc-i-r bg2* *Rhus-t* bg2* sabad bg2* stann bg2*
- **night**: flav jl2

Complaints of throat: ...
- **accompanied** by:

○ · **Eyes**; complaints of (See EYE - Complaints - accompanied - throat - complaints)
  - **Teeth**; complaints of (See TEETH - Complaints - accompanied - throat)
- **acute**: mangi br1
- **alternating** with | **Nose**; obstruction of: lach bg2
- **spot**; in a: acon bg2 arg-met bg2 arg-n bg2 bry bg2 chin bg2 cimic bg2 cist bg2 *Con* bg2 crot-h bg2 gels bg2 graph bg2 hep bg2 lach bg2 lith-c bg2 lyc bg2 mur-ac bg2 nat-m bg2 phos bg2 phyt bg2 sil bg2 stann-i bg2
- **streak**; in a: ol-an bg2

▽ - **extending** to:

○ · **Back**: acon ptk1 cocc ptk1 kali-c ptk1 laur bg2 *Merc* ptk1 nit-ac ptk1 rhus-t ptk1
  - **Downward** and then upward: calc bg2 coc-c bg2 lach bg2
  - **Ears**: ail bg2 **Bell** bg2 bry bg2 calad bg2 calc bg2 caust bg2 dios bg2 gels bg2* guaj ptk1 **Hep** bg2* ign bg2 kali-bi bg2* kali-m ptk1 kali-n bg2 **Lach** bg2* lith-c bg2 mag-p bg2 **Merc** bg2* merc-c ptk1 merc-d ptk1 nux-v bg2 petr bg2 phys ptk1 *Phyt* bg2* podo bg2 sang ptk1 staph bg2* sulph bg2
    - **yawning** agg.: hep ptk1
  - **Neck** and Shoulders: kali-bi ptk1
  - **Scapulae** | **right**: spig bg2
  - **Upper** limbs: gran bg2

○ - **Nasopharynx**: acon bg2 *Aesc* bg2 agar bg2 ail bg2 all-c bg2 alum bg2 am-c bg2 am-m bg2 arg-n bg2 bar-c bg2 bry bg2 caps bg2 chin bg2 chr-ac mtf11 cimic bg2 cinnb bg2* *Cist* bg2* coc-c bg2 colch bg2 cor-r bg2* dulc bg2 elaps ptk1 euph bg2 fl-ac bg2 *Hep* bg2 hip-ac br1* **Hydr** bg2* **Kali-bi** bg2 kali-c bg2 kali-i bg2 lach bg2 *Lyc* bg2* mag-c bg2 mag-m bg2 mentho br1 **Merc** bg2* *Merc-c* ptk1 merc-d bg2 *Merc-i-r* bg2* mez bg2 nat-c bg2* *Nat-m* bg2* nat-p bg2 nit-ac bg2 osm bg2 petr bg2 phos bg2* *Phyt* bg2 psor bg2 rumx bg2* sang bg2 sep bg2* *Sil* bg2 **Spig** bg2* staph bg2* sulph ptk1 tell bg2 teucr bg2 ther ptk1 thuj ptk1 verat bg2 zinc bg2 zinc-i ptk1
- **Pharynx** (See Pharynx)
- **Throat**-pit: anac bg2 apis ptk1 arg-met ptk1 *Cham* ptk1 chinin-s bg2 chlor ptk1 hep ptk1 kali-bi ptk1 lach bg2 phos bg2* rumx bg2* sang ptk1 *Sep* ptk1 zinc bg2 zinc-chr ptk1
- **Tonsils** (See Tonsils)

CONCRETIONS in tonsils (See Hawks)

CONDYLOMATA: *Arg-n* cupre-l sne *Merc-c* nat-s bg2 *Nit-ac* *Thuj*

CONGESTION: arg-n bg2 arge-pl rwt5• phyt bg2

○ - **Pharynx**: helia br1

CONSTRICTION: *(↗Spasms; Tension)* abrom-a ks5 acon tl1 agar bg2 *Alum* b4.de* aml-ns vh1 ant-t bg2 antip vh1 apis b7a.de* aran-ix sp1 ars b4.de* asaf bg2* *Bapt* bg2* bar-c b4.de* **Bell** b4.de* bit-ar wht1• brom bg2 bufo bg2 *Cact* bg2* cadm-s bg2 calc b4.de* calc-f sp1 cann-s b7a.de canth bg2 caps bg2 carb-v b4a.de* carc fd2.de• caust bg2 *Chel* b7.de* chir-fl gya2 *Cic* bg2* coc-c bg2 cocc b7.de* colch b7.de* coloc bg2 con b4a.de* corv-cor bdg• croc bg2 crot-h bg2 cupr bg2 cyt-l br1 dig b4.de* dros mrr1 dulc b4a.de elaps bg2 ferr b7.de* fl-ac bg2 gent-l c2 glon bg2 graph b4.de* hed sp1 helodr-cal knl2• hep b4a.de hydr-ac bg2 *Hyos* b7.de* **Ign** b7.de* iod b4.de* ip b7.de* kali-sula a1* lac-ac c2 **Lach** bg2 laur bg2 lina br1 lob bg2 lyc b4a.de* maias-l hrn2• manc bg2 med al2 merc-c b4a.de* *Mez* b4.de* naja bg2 nat-m b4.de* nat-s bg2 *Nux-v* b7a.de* ol-an bg2 petr a1 petr-ra shn4• phos b4.de* physala-p bnm7• plat b4.de* *Plb* b7.de* rhod b4.de* *Sabad* b7.de* sal-fr sle1• sars b4.de* seneg bg2 sep b4.de* sil bg2 sinus rly4• smilcin hs1 spig bg2 spong bg2* **Stram** b7.de* stry mrr1 *Sulph* b4.de* sumb bg2 tab br1 tarax b7.de* *Trios* rsj11• tritic-vg fd5.de *Verat* b7.de* vip bg2 visc sp1 zinc b4a.de* [bell-p-sp dcm1 heroin sdj2]
- **afternoon**:
  - **13** h | **night**; until: abrom-a ks5
- **night**: calc-f sp1

- **accompanied** by:
  - **bulbar** paralysis (See HEAD - Paralysis - medulla - accompanied - throat)
  - **eructations** (See STOMACH - Eructations - accompanied - throat - constriction)
  - **gagging**: verat bg2
  - **respiration**:
    - **difficult** (See RESPIRATION - Difficult - accompanied - throat)
    - **impeded** (See RESPIRATION - Difficult - accompanied - throat)
  - **stammering**: mag-p tl1
- **band**; as from a: bry bg2 dios bg2 op bg2
- **cold** drinks agg.: calc-f sp1
- **cough** agg.; during: asaf b7a.de asar b7.de* *Verat* b7a.de
- **drinking**; on attempting to: canth bg2 stram bg2
- **forced** through a small opening; as if: tab bg2
- **nervous**: ol-an bg2 sabad bg2
- **painful**: cycl hr1
- **spasmodic** | **Pharynx**: cham tl1
- **swallowing**; difficult: bit-ar wht1•
- **talking** agg.: dros mrr1
- **walking** | **amel.**: dros mrr1

○ - **Esophagus**: abies-n bro1 alum bro1* am-m bro1 *Ars* bg2 *Asaf* bro1 bapt bro1* *Bell* bro1 cact br1* cadm-met tpw6 *Caj* bro1 caps bro1 chinin-s bg2 cic bro1* cob ptm1• cortico tpw7 cund bro1 gels bro1 hyos bro1 ign bro1 *Lyss* bro1 merc-c bro1 naja bro1 nat-ar c2 *Phos* bro1 plat bro1 plb bro1 rheum c2 rhus-t bro1 stram bro1 stront-c br1 sulph c2 verat-v bro1
  - **intestinal** irritation, from: cic hr1
- **Pharynx**: *Acon* bro1 aesc bro1 agar bro1 alum bro1 apis bro1 *Arg-n* bro1 ars bro1 arum-t bro1 asaf bro1 *Bapt* bro1 *Bell* bro1 both bro1 cact bro1 caj bro1 calc bro1 *Canth* bro1 *Caps* bro1 *Cic* bro1 cocain bro1 cupr bro1 elaps br1 *Hyos* bro1 *Ign* bro1 lach bro1 *Merc-c* bro1 mez bro1 morph bro1 nux-v bro1 *Phyt* bro1 plb bro1 puls bro1 rat bro1 sang bro1 *Sangin-n* bro1 sarcol-ac bro1 *Stram* bro1 *Stry* bro1 sumb bro1 valer bro1
- **Sides**:
  - **right**: nat-m h2 plut-n srj7•
  - **left**: plut-n srj7•
- **Throat**-pit | **accompanied** by cough (See COUGH - Constriction - throat-pit)
- **Uvula**: acon bro1 seneg b4a.de

CONTRACTION (See Choking)

CONVULSIONS: | **epilepsy**; during: bell tl1

COTTON; sensation of: phos bg2*

COUGH agg.; during: arg-met ptk1 arum-t ptk1 caps ptk1 cist ptk1 ol-an ptk1

○ - **Uvula**: ham ptk1

CRACKING in throat: caust h2* ign bg2 lyc bg2 merc bg2 thuj bg2

CRAMP: acon k* aeth bg2 ars k* bar-c k2 bell bg2 canth bg2 carb-v bg2 chel k* *Gels* k* *Graph* k* hyos bg2 kali-c h2* kali-i k* lach bg2 nat-m h2* phos *Sars* k* sep k* sul-ac k* zinc bg2
- **night**: sars h2*
- **eructations** agg.: coloc h2*
- **swallowing** food, compelled to retch; on: graph

○ - **Esophagus**: arg-n a1 zinc h2
  - **accompanied** by | **palpitation**: coloc ptk1
  - **eructations** agg.: coloc ptk1
  - **swallowing** agg.: op k*

CRAWLING: *(↗Tingling)* acon k* aesc k* am-m bry k* *Carb-v* k* cedr cist hr1 colch k* croc b7.de* *Crot-c* k* dros k* glon grat k* hyper k* ign k* **Kali-c** *Lach* k* lob lyc h2* merc k* mez k* nux-v b7.de* pall paull a1 petr k* phos plb k* prun k* puls k* sabad k* sabin samb k* sec k* seneg bg2 sep k* spong k* stann k* sul-i k* sulph bg2 tab k* thuj
- **morning**: lach k*

Crawling – morning: ...
  - **bed** agg.; in: iod lach
- **evening**: nux-v k*
- **coryza**; during: kali-c b4.de* merc b4a.de
- **cough** | **causing**: am-m h2 bry *Carb-v* euph *Kali-c Lach* mag-m a1 prun stann
- **eating** agg.: hepat c1
- **menses**; during: nux-v k*
- **nausea**; during: lyc k*
- **swallowing** agg.: tab k*
- **worm** were squirming in; as if a: hyper merc *Puls*

○ - **Esophagus**: anan ign tl1 kali-c h2 plb zinc
- **Pharynx** | **menses**; during: nux-v b7.de

CRUMBS (See Bread)

CUTICLE (See Membrane)

DENUDED (See Erosion)

DIPHTHERIA: *(↗Membrane)* ail br1* alum bg2 am-c bg2 apis bg2* arg-n bg2 *Ars* bg2* ars-i bro1* arum-t bro1 *Bapt* bro1 *Bell* bro1 borx bg2 brom bg2* calc-chln bro1 *Canth* bro1 carb-ac bro1 chin bg2 chr-ac br1 *Crot-h* bro1 diph br1* diphtox jl2 echi bro1 euph bg2 guaj bro1 hep bg2 hippoz mtf11 iod bg2* kali-bi bg2* kali-chl bro1 *Kali-m* bro1 kali-perm br1* kalm mtf11 kreos bg2 lac-c br1* lach bg2* lachn bro1 led bro1 lob br1* *Lyc* bg2* *Merc-c* bro1 *Merc-cy* bg2* merc-i-f bro1 merc-i-r br1* mur-ac bro1* naja bro1 nat-s hr *Nit-ac* bg2* *Nux-v* bg2 ozone sde2• phos bg2 phyt bg2* pyrog br1 rhus-t bro1 sang bro1 spong bg2 **Sui-ac** bg2 *Sulph* bg2* *Tarent-c* br1* vario mtf11 vinc br1* zinc bro1
- **right** side first: lyc tl1

▽ • **extending** to | **left**: lyc bro1
- **left** side first: lach tl1

▽ • **extending** to | **right**: lac-c bro1 *Lach* bro1 sabad bro1
- **accompanied** by:
  - **ataxia**; locomotor (See GENERALS - Locomotor - accompanied - diphtheria)
  - **coryza** (See Membrane - accompanied - coryza)
  - **croup**: acet-ac bro1 *Brom* bro1 hep bro1 iod bro1* *Kali-bi* bro1 kali-m bro1 *Lach* bro1* merc-cy bro1 phos bro1 samb bro1 spong bro1*
  - **fetor** (See MOUTH - Odor - offensive - diphtheria)
  - **fever**: ail tl1
    - **intense**: tarent-c ptk1
  - **measles**: lach bro1 merc-cy bro1
  - **restlessness**: rhus-t tl1
  - **saliva**: lac-c bro1* merc-cy bro1
    - **bloody**: *Merc-c* kr1*
    - **viscid**: *Kali-bi* kr1* kali-m kr1*
  - **sleep**; deep: diph bro1
  - **stringy** discharge: kali-bi tl1
  - **torticollis**: lachn gsy1*
  - **urine**; scanty: apis bro1 ars bro1 canth bro1 lac-c bro1 merc-cy bro1 naja bro1
  - **weakness** (See GENERALS - Weakness - diphtheria)

○ • **Glottis**; spasm of: mosch bro1 samb bro1
  - **Tongue**:
    - **aphthae**: merc-cy vk1
    - **black** discoloration: merc-cy kr1*
    - **brown** discoloration: *Chinin-ar* kr1*
      - **yellowish** brown: bapt kr1*
    - **gray** discoloration: *Merc* kr1*
    - **mapped** tongue: *Nat-m* kr1*
    - **pointed** tongue: *Lach* kr1*
    - **protruding**: **Phyt** kr1*
    - **purple** discoloration of the tongue: *Lach* kr1*
    - **red** discoloration of the tongue: *Merc-cy* kr1*
      - **Tip**: *Merc-cy* kr1*
    - **swelling**: *Merc-i-r* kr1*
    - **white** discoloration of the tongue: *Bapt* kr1* **Phyt** kr1*
      - **heavily** coated: *Chinin-ar* kr1* lac-c kr1* *Merc-i-r* kr1*

- **accompanied** by – **Tongue** – **white** discoloration of the tongue
  - – **heavily** coated: ...
    - . **Root** of tongue: *Merc-i-f* kr1*
    - : **yellowish** white: lac-c kr1*
  - : **yellow** discoloration of the tongue | **dirty** yellow: *Lach* kr1*
- **beginning** of; at the: ferr-p tl1
- **children**; in: | **fair** skin; with: brom tl1
- **followed** by | **voice**; complaints of: bell bg2 carb-v bg2 dros bg2 **Hep** bg2 *Phos* bg2
- **malignant**: *Ail* bro1 apis bro1 ars bro1 *Carb-ac* bro1 chinin-ar bro1 crot-h bro1* diph br1* diphtox jl2 *Echi* bro1 kali-p bro1 lac-c bro1 *Lach* bro1 merc-cy br1* mur-ac bro1 pyrog bro1 tarent tl1
- **painless**: apis ptk1 carb-ac ptk1 *Diph* bro1*
- **passive**: diph bro1
- **prolonged**: chinin-ar br1
- **prophylactic**: apis bro1* diph bro1* *Lac-c* tl1 merc-cy ptk1
- **sleep**; after: am-c tl1 lach tl1

▽ - **extending** to:

○ • **Downward**: iod bro1 *Kali-bi* bro1 lac-c bro1 merc-cy bro1

• **Upward**: brom bro1

○ - **Lips** | **accompanied** by a pale tongue: rhus-t hr1*

DISCHARGE:

- **watery**:
  - • **dripping** | **Uvula**; from: all-c bg2* aral ptk1 hydr bg2* kali-bi ptk1 merc-c bg2* spig bg2*

DISCOLORATION:

- **black**: (↗*Gangrene)* merc-sul
  - • **spots**: carb-v k2 psor a1
- **bluish**: cupr bg2 merc bg2 tab bg2

○ • **Tonsils**: am-c gsy1
  - : **diphtheria**; during: phyt tl1
  - : **purple**: *Am-c* vh1

- **brownish** red: kali-sula a1*

○ • **Fauces**: kali-sula a1

- **copper**-colored: *Kali-bi* k* **Merc** k*
- **dark**: *Aesc* k* ail ptk1 arag br1 arg-n ptk1 *Bapt* k* carb-ac bg2 crot-h ptk1 lach bg2* merc-cy bg2 **Phyt** k*

○ • **Blood** vessels: thymu br1

- **gray**:
  - • **dirty**: kali-m bg2 merc-cy bg2 phyt bg2* sang bg2
  - • **spots**: *Iod* b4a.de

○ • **Tonsils**: kali-m ptk1 merc-cy ptk1

- **livid**: ail br1* alum h2* caps tl1

○ • **Fauces**: *Gymno* br1

- **mottled**: ail bg1 am-br vh1 bapt caps k2 kali-perm bg1 *Lach*
- **pale**: bar-c lac-d k2 *Nat-m* hr1 phyt hr1
- **pink**: mag-p bg2
- **purple**: aesc k2 **Ail** k* am-c apis ptk1 *Bapt* bell k2 caps k2 dros k2 fl-ac *Kali-bi* kali-chl lac-c hr1 **Lach** k* *Merc* *Nat-ar* nit-ac *Nux-v* k* ox-ac *Puls* k* *Sanic* vh sulph tarent vario hr1
  - • **spots**: ail tl1 sars k2

○ • **Pharynx**: pen br1

  - • **Tonsils**: hep k2 *Kali-br* hr1 *Lach* k* *Phyt* k*
- **redness**: absin **Acon** k* *Aesc* k* aeth k* *Ail* k* alco a1 *Alum* k* am-br k* *Am-c* bg2 am-caust a1 ant-t k* *Apis* k* **Arg-n** k* *Ars* k* ars-s-f k2 asim hr1 atra-r skp7*• atro k* aur-m k* bamb-a stb2.de* bapt k* bar-c bg2 *Bar-m* hr1 **Bell** k* berb k* beryl sp1 brom k* bry k* calc k* calc-f sp1 *Calc-p* k* *Calc-s* k* calc-sil k2 canth k* **Caps** k* **Carb-ac** k* carb-an k* carb-v k* carbn-s k2 caust k* *Cham* bg2* chel hr1 chlol k* *Cist* clem k* coc-c k* coff bg2 colch k* cop k* cortiso sp1 crot-t cupr cycl dirc c1 *Dros* b7a.de dulc k2 ery-a a1 falco-pe nl2• ferr-i a1* ferr-p k* *Fl-ac* flav jl2 *Gels* gent-c k* gink-b sbd1• gins k* *Graph* hr1 *Guaj* ham fd3.de• hep bg2 hippoz k* hir rsj4• *Hyos* ign k* ind k* iod b4a.de* iris *Kali-bi* k* *Kali-chl* k* kali-i k* kali-m k2 kali-n k* lac-ac lac-c k2* lac-h sk4• *Lach* k* lat-m sp1 **Lyc** k* lyss c1 mag-c bg2 mang k2 *Merc* k* *Merc-c* k* *Merc-i-f* k* merc-i-r ptk1 mez k2 mill k2 *Morb* jl2 *Mur-ac* k* *Nat-ar* *Nat-c* k* nat-m k2 *Nit-ac* k* nux-m *Nux-v* k* op ox-ac k* *Petr* phos k* **Phyt** k* pic-ac k* psil ft1 puls b7a.de* ran-b k2 rhus-t k* rhus-v sal-ac a1* sang hr1 sec k* sep k* ser-a-c jl2 sil spong b7.de* staph bg2 **Stram** k* streptoc jl2 stry a1 suis-hep rly4• sul-ac k* *Sulph* k* tab tarent k* thuj hr1 trios rsj11• tritic-vg fd5.de verat

Discoloration – redness: ...

- • **right**: cench k2
- • **left**: naja bg2
- • **accompanied** by | **coryza**: caps mrr1
- • **bluish**: mur-ac hr1
- • **bright**: acon bg2 am-c bg2 apis bg2 bell bg2 merc-c bg2 phyt bg2 sulph bg2
  - : **Tonsils**: acon ptk1 *Bell* ptk1 phyt ptk1
- • **dark** red: acon k* *Aesc* k* *Ail* am-br hr1 **Arg-n** k* **Bapt** k* bell mrr1 brom hr1 caps k* carb-v bg2 **Cham** k* choc srj3• *Crot-h* k* dros k2 ham bg2* *Kali-bi* k* *Kali-br* hr1 *Kali-i* k* kali-p k2 kali-s *Lach* k* merc bg1 merc-c bg2* *Merc-cy* k* merc-i-f hr1 *Merc-i-r* k* *Mez* k* mur-ac k2 *Naja* k* nat-ar ozone sde2• phos h2* *Phyt* k* *Puls* k* *Rhus-t* k* sal-ac hr1 sang hr1 tarent hr1 vac jl2
  - : **accompanied** by | **scarlatina**; malignant: am-c br1
  - : **Fauces**: bapt tl1 *Gymno* br1
  - : **Tonsils**: aesc ptk1 bapt ptk1 carb-ac ptk1 *Lach* ptk1
- • **network**: brom k* ham fd3.de•
- • **patches**: calc k2
- • **spots**, in: kali-chl merc k2 ros-d wla1

○ • **Fauces**: asim br1 *Bell* bro1 carb-ac bro1 ferr-p bro1 gymno bro1 mentho bro1 *Merc-cy* bro1 *Merc-i-r* bro1 mez bro1 naja bro1 puls bro1 stram tl1

- • **Pharynx**: *Acon* k* aesc bro1 alumn ant-t k* **Apis** ars k* bamb-a stb2.de• bell k* beryl tpw5 bry k* calc-p k* calc-s k* chlor a1 coc-c k* cop dulc fd4.de ferr-p bro1 gent-c gins bro1 *Ham* hr1 iod k* kali-n k* lyss hr1 *Merc* k* *Merc-c* k* *Merc-i-f* k* merc-i-r bro1 merc-n bro1 merl k* *Mez* hr1 nat-ar *Nat-m* k* ox-ac k* phos k* sal-ac bro1 scarl jl2 stram k* strept-ent jl2 suis-hep rly4• sul-ac k* *Sulph* bro1 ust k* verat k* yuc a1
  - : **cough** agg.; during: beryl tpw5
  - : **dark** red: *Ail* bro1 alum bro1 *Am-c* bro1 am-caust bro1 amyg bro1 *Apis* bro1 arag bro1 *Arg-n* bro1 ars bro1 *Bapt* bro1 bell bro1 canth bro1 caps bro1 crot-h bro1 diph bro1 *Gymno* bro1 ip hr1 *Lach* bro1 lyss hr1 merc-c bro1 mur-ac bro1 *Naja* bro1 nat-ar bro1 *Nat-m* hr1 pen bro1 phyt hr1* puls bro1 sep hr1 vario hr1 wye bro1 zinc-c bro1
  - : **Back** part: am-caust a1 dulc fd4.de gins a1 *Hep* k* *Kali-bi* k* *Merc-i-f* k* nit-ac k* plect a1
- • **Tonsils**: *Acon* k* aegle-f bnj1 *Apis* *Aur* k* **Bapt** k* **Bell** k* *Cham* bg2 cop *Ferr-p* k* fl-ac gels bg2* gymno iris a1 *Kali-bi* k* lac-c tl1 *Lach* *Merc* *Merc-i-f* *Nit-ac* bg2* *Phyt* positr nl2• *Puls* k* staph bg2 *Sulph*
  - : **left**: *Brucel* sa3•
  - : **dark** red: ail bro1 amyg bro1 *Bapt* bro1 brom bro1 caps bro1 **Carb-ac** vh diph bro1 gymno bro1 *Lach* bro1 merc bro1 *Phyt* bro1
- • **Uvula**: **Acon** k* *Apis* **Arg-n** k* ars k* **Bapt** **Bar-m** **Bell** k* calc k* *Calc-p* k* caust cimic k* colch k* cortiso sp1* *Crot-t* k* cupr der a1 *Fl-ac* gent-c k* gins a1 iris a1 *Kali-bi* k* kali-br *Lach* merc *Merc-i-f* k* nat-m k* ozone sde2• petr *Puls* bg2 streptoc jl2 sulph k*
  - : **dark** red: *Arg-n* k* **Bapt** *Calc* k* caust k* cupr-act *Lach* yuc a1
- **white**: ars a1 carb-an a1 kreos bg2* sul-ac a1
  - • **spots**: bry k2 iod k2 kali-p k2 *Mur-ac* k* nit-ac k*
    - : **diphtheria**; during: phyt tl1
    - : **red** halo, with: *Caps* hr1
  - • **stripe**: sal-fr sle1•

○ • **Tonsils**: cycl a1

  - • **Uvula**: carb-ac c1 cycl a1
- **yellow**: arist-cl jl3
  - • **spots**: lac-c lach lyc *Nit-ac* k*
    - : **diphtheria**; during: phyt tl1

○ • **Tonsils**: arist-cl sp1

DISTENSION; sensation of: anac b4a.de* aur b4.de* caust bg2 mag-c h2* par b7.de* phyt hr1 sulph h2* upa bg1 verat b7.de*

○ - **Esophagus**: aur h2 hyper k* op k* phyt hr1 upa bg1* verat k*

DRAWN out sensation: mag-c h2

DRINKING:

- **amel.**: tell ptk1
- **sips**; in | **amel**: cist ptk1

DRYNESS: abrom-a ks5 acet-ac a1 *Acon* k* adox a1 **Aesc** k* aeth k* *Agar* k* agath-a nl2• agav-t jl1 *Aids* nl2• ail k* *All-c* k* allox tpw3* aloe *Alum* k* alum-p k2 alum-sil k2 alumn k* am-c k* am-m k* ambr k* *Ammc* *Anac* k* **Anag** k* *Androc* srj1• ang b7.de* ant-c k* ant-t a1* anthraq rly4• *Apis* k* *Arg-n* k* arge-pl rwt5• arist-cl sp1 arizon-l nl2• arn a1 *Ars* k* ars-i ars-s-f a1* arum-d ptk2 *Asaf* k* asar k* atra-r skp7*• *Atro* k* *Aur* b4a.de aur-m k2 aur-m-n k* bac bn bamb-a stb2.de• bapt k* *Bar-c* k* bar-m bar-s k2 bart a1 **Bell** k* berb k* beryl tpw5 bit-ar wht1• bol-s a1 bond a1 borx b4a.de* both *Bov* k* brach a1 brom k* **Bry** k* *Bufo* cadm-met tpw6* cadm-s k* cain **Calad** k* **Calc** k* calc-f sp1 calc-i k2 calc-p k* calc-s calc-sil k2 **Cann-i** k* cann-s k* **Canth** k* caps bro1* carb-ac k* carb-an b4.de* *Carb-v* k* *Carbn-s* cardios-h rly4• cartl-s rly4• cassia-s cdd7*• **Caust** k* cent a1 cephd-i bnj1 cham k* *Chel* k* chen-a vml3• chin k* chinin-ar chinin-s k* chir-fl gya2 chlf br1 chlol a1 chlor k* chord-umb rly4• *Cic* cimic k* *Cimx* *Cinnb* k* **Cist** k* clem cob k* cob-n sp1 **Coc-c** k* coca cocain bro1 *Cocc* k* *Colch* k* *Coloc* *Con* k* convo-s sp1 cop *Cor-r* k* cortico tpw7* cortiso tpw7* *Crot-h* k* crot-t k* cub c1 cupr k* cycl k* cyclosp sa3• cystein-l rly4• cyt-l sp1 der c1 dig k* dios k* dream-p sdj1• *Dros* k* dub a1* dubo-m br1 dulc k* dys pte1*• erig hr1 erio a1 ery-m a1 eug k* eup-per k* euph bg2 eupi k* eys sp1 fago k* falco-pe nl2• ferr a1 ferr-i k2 ferr-p bro1 fic-m gya1 flor-p rsj3• franz a1 gala br1 gamb br gast a1 *Gels* k* gent-l a1 ger-i rly4• gins a1 glon k* graph k* guaj bg2* ham k* helia ptk2 hell k* *Helon* hr1 *Hep* k* hip-ac sp1 hist sp1 hydr k* hydr-ac bg2 hydrobr-ac br1 *Hydrog* srj2• *Hydroph* rsj6• *Hyos* k* iber a1 *Ign* k* *Iod* k* *Ip* k* irid-met srj5• *Iris* jac-c k* jatr-c jug-c a1* just bro1 *Kali-ar* **Kali-bi** k* *Kali-br* k* *Kali-c* k* *Kali-chl* k* *Kali-i* k* kali-m k2 kali-n bg2 kali-p kali-perm kali-pic a1 *Kali-s* kali-sil k2 kali-sula a1* *Kalm* k* ketogl-ac rly4• kola stb3• kreos k* lac-ac k* **Lac-c** k* lac-del hrn2• lac-h htj1*• *Lach* k* *Lachn* k* lat-m sp1 laur k* lavand-a ctl1• lem-m br1* lil-s a1 limen-b-c hrn2* limest-b es1• lob k* lob-c k* lobin a1 luf-op rsj5• *Luna* kg1• **Lyc** k* **Mag-c** k* *Mag-m* k* mag-p bg2 mag-s k* *Manc* k* mand sp1* mang k* med k* medul-os-si rly4• menis br1 meny k* **Merc** k* *Merc-c* k* merc-i-f k* merc-n a1 merc-sul k* merl bro1 **Mez** k* mill a1 *Moni* rfm1• morg-p pte1*• morph k* mosch k* *Mur-ac* k* myric k* *Naja* k* narc-ps a1* narcot a1 narz a1 *Nat-ar* *Nat-c* k* **Nat-m** k* nat-n bg2 *Nat-p* *Nat-s* k* nat-sil fd3.de• neon srj5• nicot a1 nicotam rly4• *Nit-ac* k* nit-s-d a1 **Nux-m** k* *Nux-v* k* ol-an k* *Olib-sac* wmh1 olnd k* onos c2* *Op* k* orot-ac rly4• ox-ac k* ozone sde2• pall a1* pant-ac rly4• par k* petr k* petr-ra shn4• ph-ac k* phel k* **Phos** k* *Phyt* k* plac rzf5• plac-s rly4• plan k* *Plat* k* plb k* *Podo* k* polyp-p a1 pot-e rly4• propl ub1• psil ft1 *Psor* k* ptel **Puls** k* pyrid rly4• quill br1* rad-br sze8• raph k* rauw tpw8* rhod kgp5• rhus-g tmo3• **Rhus-t** k* rhus-v k* ribo rly4• rumx **Sabad** k* *Sabin* k* sacch sst1• sacch-a gmj3 sal-ac a1* sal-al blc1• samb k* **Sang** k* sangin-n bro1 sanic sarcol-ac bro1* *Sars* k* sec k* sel k* *Senec* k* **Seneg** k* **Sep** k* **Sil** k* *Sin-n* bg2 sinus rly4• sol-ni *Spong* k* squil k* *Stann* k* staph k* **Stict** k* still k* **Stram** k* stront-c b4.de* stry k* succ-ac rly4• suis-em rly4• suis-pan rly4• sul-ac k* sul-i k2* **Sulph** k* sumb k* syc pte1*• symph fd3.de• tab k* tarax k* tell k* tere-la rly4• tetox pin2• thiam rly4• thres-a sze7• *Thuj* k* thyr ptk1 tub c* *Tung-met* bdx1• ulm-c jsj8• upa a1 uran-n bg2 ust k* valer k* vanil fd5.de ven-m rsj12• **Verat** k* **Verat-v** k* verb k* vip fkr4.de visc c1* voes a1 wye k* xan c1 *Zinc* k* zinc-p k2 zing k* [bell-p-sp dcm1 heroin sdj2 **Spect** dfg1]

- **right**: stann h2*
- **left**: atra-r bnm3• colch rsj2• sel rsj9•
- **daytime**: cartl-s rly4• mez k*
- **morning**: agath-a nl2• *Ail* k* all-c k* alum am-c k* ambr *Ammc* ant-c k* ant-t a1 arg-n k* berb k* bufo calc k* cann-s k* caust k* cortiso tpw7* dulc fd4.de fago a1 hep h2* hyos k* lac-del hrn2• lach lyc k* mag-c k* mag-m k* mag-s k* mang meny a1 mez k* nat-ar nat-sil fd3.de• ol-an k* petr k* petr-ra shn4• phyt k* plan k* plb k* polyp-p a1 **Puls** k* ran-s k* sacch-a fd2.de• sars k* spong fd4.de stann k* stram k* stront-c sulph k* tell k* ust k* zinc k*
  - **waking**; on: *Alum* k1* alum-sil k2 am-c k1 *Ambr* kr1* borx vh *Bov* k1 cadm-met sp1 carb-ac choc srj3• coc-c kali-i mag-c ol-an phos podo fd3.de• **Puls** rauw sp1 sacch-a fd2.de• sars *Seneg* sep zinc
  - **walking** agg.: zinc k*
- **forenoon**: anac k* genist a1 jab a1
- **noon**: mag-m k*
- **afternoon**: am-c k* bart a1 canth k* *Cist* mang h2* phyt k* sang sep k* sulph k*
  - **17** h: phyt sulph tell
  - **waking**; on: sel k*
- **evening**: **Alum** k* alum-p k2 am-c *Bar-c* k* brom k* chlor a1 cist dirc a1 dulc k* fago a1 kali-p lyc k* nat-sil fd3.de• olib-sac wmh1 ox-ac k* phos k* podo fd3.de• polyp-p a1 sel senec k* sep k* stram k* tell k* thiam rly4• *Zinc* k*
- **evening**: ...
  - **18** h: mang
  - **sleep**; before: sep k* staph k*
- **night**: abrom-a ks5 acon k* alumn k* arg-n k* ars k* *Calc* calc-p k* caust k* cimic a1 *Cinnb* k* *Cist* k* coc-c k* flav jl2* gal-ac a1* glon k* graph k* hydrog srj2• kali-c ketogl-ac rly4• **Lach** k* lyc h2* mag-m k* menis a1 nat-c h2* nat-sil fd3.de• nit-ac h2* phel phos h2* plat h2* pot-e rly4• *Puls* k* rhus-t *Senec* k* *Seneg* sep k* sil spong fd4.de *Sulph* k* *Ust*
  - **midnight**: *Arum-t* *Kali-bi* lat-m bnm6• puls sul-ac
    - **after**: puls sul-ac h2
      - **2-3** h: kali-c k2
      - **3** h: cyclosp sa3•
  - **waking**; on: lachn c1 spong fd4.de
- **accompanied** by:
  - **mouth**; dryness of: ulm-c jsj8•
    - **sensation** of: ulm-c jsj8•
  - **salivation**: agar bg2 *Colch* kr1* rhod kr1*
    - **Mouth**; in anterior part of: lyc bg2 *Merc* b4.de* *Merc-c* b4a.de mez b4.de* *Nux-v* bg2
  - **thirst** (See STOMACH - Thirst - accompanied - throat)
  - ○ **Nose**; dryness of (See NOSE - Dryness - inside - accompanied - throat)
  - **Teeth**; pain in (See TEETH - Pain - accompanied - throat - dryness)
- **air**; in open:
  - **agg.**: ammc gins mang
  - **amel.**: ozone sde2•
- **bed** agg.; in: phyt k* rhus-t k*
- **burnt**; as if: syc fmm1•
- **chill**; during: phos h2* thuj k* ven-m rsj12•
- **cold**; after taking a: nat-ar k2 quill br1
- **cold** water | **amel.**: (↗*thirst - with - water - cold*) abrom-a ks5 cadm-met tpw6 cassia-s ccrh1• cortico tpw7 rauw tpw8
- **coryza**; during: cham b7a.de nux-v b7a.de
- **cough**:
  - **agg.**: bell bg2 cadm-met tpw6 calc-p bg2 *Cham* b7a.de eug a1 mang-p rly4• petr-ra shn4• **Puls** b7.de* rhus-t b7.de* squil b7.de* *Sulph* a1 thuj bg2* [tax jsj7]
  - **during** | **agg.**:
    - **honey** | **amel.**: cortiso tpw7
    - **amel.**: stann h2*
- **dinner**; after: zinc k*
- **diphtheria**; during: phyt tl1
- **drinking** | **not** amel.: acon-ac sne* atra-r skp7*• cladon sne colch sne eug sne hydrog srj2• lipp sne lob sne psil ft1 sang k* sarr c1* sep h2* sinus rly4• stram k2* sulph sne verat h1*
- **eating** | **after** | **agg.**: aesc k* mag-c b4a.de nat-m k*
  - **amel.**: anac h2* cadm-met tpw6* *Cist* k* phos h2* tell a1
- **expectoration**; after: agath-a nl2•
- **hawking** agg.: *Spong*
- **heat**; during: acon bg2 asar k* bell bg2 ign bg2 nit-ac b4a.de* *Nux-m* bg2 nux-v bg2 olnd k* op k* phos bg2 puls bg2 rhus-t bg2 sep h2* stram bg2 sulph k*
- **honey**; warm | **amel.**: cortiso tpw7*
- **inspiration** agg.: eupi a1 ham k* ind a1 nat-ar plac-s rly4•
- **itching**: mang h2*
- **lying** agg.: caust lyc
- **menses**; during: nux-m bro1 tarent bro1
- **painful**: aids nl2• anac h2* atra-r bnm3• dream-p sdj1• dulc fd4.de hydrog srj2• lac-del hrn2• lac-lup hrn2• *Lach* rad-br sze8• tell c1
- **perspiration**; during: **Bell** bg2 *Cham* bg2 cocc bg2 hyos bg2 lach bg2 *Nit-ac* bg2 nux-v bg2 **Phos** bg2 puls bg2 sabad bg2 sel bg2 staph bg2 stram bg2 verat bg2
- **rest** agg.: con k*
- **rising** agg.: cob k* ham k*
- **roughness**: ang vh **Dros** vh
- **sensation** of: am-m b7.de* apis b7a.de ars bg2 asaf b7.de* bell bg2 *Bry* b7.de* carb-v bg2 chin b7.de* dros b7.de* kreos b7a.de *Lach* b7a.de lyc bg2 *Mang* b4a.de meny b7.de* mosch b7.de* nat-s bg2 *Nux-m* b7.de* puls b7.de* rhus-t b7.de*

- **sensation** of: ... sabad b7.de* sang bg2 sel b7a.de squil b7.de* stann b4a.de* stram b7.de* tarax b7.de*
- **singing** agg.: cortico sp1 sang ptk1
- **sleep**; during: nux-m bro1 seneg k2 tarent bro1
- **spots**: cist ptk1 con bg2 lach bg2 phyt bg2
- **swallowing**:
  - **agg.**: atra-r bnm3• carb-v h2 caust h2 lac-del hrn2• lyc mag-c h2 podo fd3.de• rauw tpw8 vanil fd5.de
  - **amel.**: cist mrr1 cortico tpw7 stann h2
  - **empty** | **agg.**: cortiso tpw7
  - **saliva** | **amel.**: *Cist* cub ptk1
- **talking** agg.: alumn cadm-met tpw6 dulc fd4.de graph merc-act bg1 sil h2 vanil fd5.de
  - **difficult**; very: bry merc seneg xan c1
- **tea** | **amel.**: cadm-met tpw6
- **thirst**:
  - **with**: *Bry* sne cimic sne stram ptk1
    - **water**; for:
      - **cold**: (↗*cold water - amel.)* abrom-a ks5 allox tpw4
      - **warm**: abrom-a ks5
  - **without**: androc srj1• ang b7.de* *Apis* k* asaf k* *Calad* k* calc h2* canth b7.de* caps tl1 carb-an h2* caust k* *Cocc* b7.de* dream-p sdj1• eupi c1 hyos b7.de* kali-c bg1 kola stb3• *Lach* lyc h2* mag-m h2* mang h2* meny k* nat-c nux-m k* op b7.de* pall par ph-ac psor puls bg2 sacch-a fd2.de* samb sep bg1 stram b7.de* suis-pan rly4•
- **urination** agg.; after: nit-ac h2*
- **waking**; on: aids nl2• *Alum* alum-p k2 alum-sil k2 *Ambr* atp rly4• bov cadm-met tpw6 chir-fl gya2 *Cinnb* *Cist* coc-c cyclosp sa3• flor-p rsj3• *Lac-c* **Lach** *Lachn* lyc mag-c *Manc* medul-os-si rly4• morph naja nat-ar nat-sil fd3.de• **Nux-m** ol-an par phos rauw tpw8 rhus-g tmo3• sars sel k* sep sil sul-ac b4.de* sulph trios rsj11• zing
- **walking** in open air agg.: dulc fd4.de nat-c h2 tell
- **warm** drinks | **amel.**: cortiso tpw7
- **water** | **amel.**: chir-fl gya2
- **weather**:
  - **cold** agg.: sacch-a gmj3
  - **wet** | **agg.**: sacch-a gmj3

○ - **Esophagus**: acon k* adox a1* alum vh1 ars bell k* bufo *Cocc* k* fic-m gya1 kali-br *Lach* k* merc-i-f *Mez* k* naja bro1* nat-m op petr-ra shn4• ptel schin c2 sec a1 *Sep* k* *Sulph* k* sumb
- **Fauces**: acon bro1 *Aesc* bro1 bell bro1* canth bro1 caps bro1 cist tl1 gels bro1 jug-c bro1 kali-sula a1 *Nux-m* bro1 *Phos* bro1 *Phyt* bro1 *Sabad* bro1 sal-ac tl1 senec bro1 stram tl1 xan c1
  - **stool** agg.; during: ferr bg2
- **Lower** part: nit-ac bg2
- **Nasopharynx**: adox a1* beryl tpw5 colch rsj2• hydroph rsj6• lem-m br1 phyt tl1 rhus-g tmo3•
  - **morning**: cortiso tpw7
- **Pharynx**: bell ptk1 cimic hr1 cortiso tpw7 helia br1 nux-m ptk1 sin-n br1
  - **honey** | **amel.**: cortiso tpw7
  - **swallowing** empty | **agg.**: cortiso tpw7
  - **warm** drinks | **amel.**: cortiso tpw7
- **Posterior** part: caust bg1 cimic **Dros** vh *Hydrog* srj2• kali-c merc bg1 mez plut-n srj7• rhus-t bg1
- **Soft** palate (See MOUTH - Dryness - palate - soft)
- **Tonsils**: phyt bg2
- **Uvula**: cortiso tpw7 nat-m bg2 sil bg2
  - **honey** | **amel.**: cortiso tpw7
  - **swallowing** empty | **agg.**: cortiso tpw7
  - **warm** drinks | **amel.**: cortiso tpw7

DUST in; as if: am-c bg2* bell bg2* calc hr1 chel bg2* coc-c bg2* crot-c k* flav jl2 verat bg2*

ELONGATED:

○ - **Tonsils**: *Aur* b4a.de
- **Uvula**: acon k* alum bg2* *Alumn* k* *Apis* aur k* aur-s k2 *Bapt* k* bar-c bro1 **Bar-m** k* bell b4a.de* brom k* calc k* calc-f bro1 *Cann-s* b7a.de canth bro1

Elongated – Uvula: ... *Caps* k* carl a1 chel b7.de* clem a1 *Coc-c* bro1 cocc-s bro1 *Coff* k* *Croc* k* **Crot-t** k* dulc bg2 fago a1* get a1 *Hep* k* hydr k* **Hyos** k* ind k* *Iod* k* kali-bi bg2* *Kali-c* k* **Kali-i** k* lac-ac k* *Lac-c* k* **Lach** k* lyc k* lyss k* *Manc* k* med hr1 *Merc* k* merc-c k* merc-i-f k* merc-i-r k* mill k* nat-ar *Nat-m* k* nux-v k* ph-ac b4a.de **Phos** k* phys a1 phyt c2* plat b4.de* psor *Puls* b7a.de rumx-act c2* sabad b7.de* sil k* sul-i br1 **Sulph** k* thuj wye bro1 zinc b4a.de
  - **sensation** as if: acon rb2* alum vh1 calc b4a.de* *Cann-s* b7a.de cham bg2 chel bg2 coc-c rb2* cocc-s br1* croc b7.de* crot-h rb2 crot-t xyz61 dulc b4a.de* iod b4a.de kali-bi bg2 plat b4a.de* spig b7a.de sulph h2 thuj bg2 wye xyz61
    - **hawking**; from constant: coc-c ptk1
    - **pressing** on something hard: caps ptk1

EMPTINESS: calc-p k* chin b7.de* cimic bg2 elat bg1 fl-ac bg1* iris bg1* lach ptk1 lob bg1* lyc k* mur-ac bg2 nat-ar phyt ptk1 ptel bg1* rumx ptk1 sanic bg1* x-ray sp1 xan bg1*
- **swallowing** agg.: aq-mar skp7• lyc k*

○ - **Pharynx** had disappeared; hollow feeling as if lach bro1 phyt bro1 x-ray rb2

ENLARGEMENT:
- **sensation** of: sanic ptk1

○ - **Esophagus**:

○ - **Upper** part | **sensation** of enlargement of: elat c1
- **Tonsils** (See Swelling - tonsils)

EPISTAXIS: | **amel.**: tarent bg2

EROSION: *Aesc* *Apis* ars k* brom mez k2 sumb k*
- **spots**: brom k*

ERUCTATIONS agg.: phys ptk1

ERUPTIONS: merc br1 phyt bg2 suis-hep rly4•
- **angioneurotic** edema: *(↗Swelling - edematous)* **Apis** mrr2*
- **erythema**: kali-bi bg2
- **tetters** | **white**: zinc b4a.de
- **vesicles**: ant-t k* apis ars k* aur-m-n hr1 canth b7.de* ph-ac bg2 *Rhus-t* rhus-v hr1 sep

○ - **Pharynx**: ant-t k* brucel sa3• canth k*
  - **Tonsils**: aur-m-n iris nit-ac
  - **Uvula**: calc b4a.de* carb-an bg2 *Sulph* b4a.de
    - **Tip**: psor jl2

ESOPHAGITIS (See Inflammation - esophagus)

EXCORIATION: *(↗Pain - raw)* acon bg2 *Aesc* **Alum** bg2 am-m bg2 *Ambr* bg2 anac bg2 ant-c *Apis* b7a.de* *Arg-met* b7.de* arg-n bg2 ars asaf bg2 bapt bg2 *Bar-c* bg2 bell bg2 borx bg2 bov bg2 brom bg2 bros-gau mrc1 bry b7.de* calc b4a.de* canth carb-v bg2* *Caust* bg2 chin bg2 dig b4a.de* dros bg2 fago ferr bg2 ferr-p bg2 *Graph* bg2 grat bg2 ham bg2 hell hep bg2 ign bg2 irid-met bg2 kali-bi bg2 kali-c bg2 kali-n bg2 kreos b7a.de lach b7a.de* laur bg2 lyc bg2 lycps-v bg2 mag-c bg2 mag-m bg2 mag-p bg2 manc bg2 mang bg2 *Merc* bg2 merc-c b4a.de* mez b4a.de* mur-ac k* nat-c bg2 nat-m bg2 *Nit-ac* k* *Nux-v* b7.de* ol-an bg2 ph-ac bg2 phos bg2* phyt k* puls b7.de* sabad bg2 sang k2 sep bg2 sil bg2 spong bg2 stann bg2 stront-c bg2 sul-ac sulph bg2 tab bg2 thuj bg2 zinc bg2
- **yellow**: plb b7a.de

EXUDATION (See Membrane)

FEATHER; sensation of a: flav jl2 *Pneu* jl2

FISHBONE (See Pain - splinter)

FISSURED: arum-t ptk1 bell ptk1 elaps ptk1 kali-bi bg2*

○ - **Pharynx**: bar-c elaps k* kali-bi bg1* ph-ac phos
  - **left** side: kali-bi c1

FOOD:
- **lodges** in throat: acet-ac all-c bg2 arg-n bg2* arge-pl rwt5• am bg2 ars bg2* bar-c bg2* *Bell* b4a.de bry k* calc bg2 *Caust* k* chin k* croc crot-h ferr-i k2 germ-met srj5• graph ptk1 ign k* iris k* kali-bi bg2 kali-c k* lac-ac bg2 **Lach** k* lyc k* nat-m bg2* **Nit-ac** k* op bg2 petr puls bg2* sabad bg2 sep k* sil sulph k* thuj bg2 *Zinc* k*
  - **bread** crumb: graph h2
  - **children**; in: | **nurslings**: kali-c mtf33
  - **eating** fast; when: lach hr1

- **lodges** in throat: ...
  - · **sensation** as if: pall ptk1
- **passes** into posterior nares: *(↗Liquids; Paralysis)* *Bell* bro1* caust mtf33 diph bro1* kali-perm bro1* *Lach* bro1* lyc k* merc bro1* *Merc-c* bro1* nit-ac petr phyt tl1 *Sil*
- **sensation** of: ambr h1 arg-n arn *Calc* ferr-i zinc h2

○ · **Epiglottis**, about: hepat c1*

○ - **Esophagus**:

- · **felt** until it enters the stomach; food is: alum k* ambr k* bry phos
- · **sensation** as if food lodged in: abies-c rb2 allox tpw3 am-m gsy1 *Ars* k* *Bar-c* k* *Calc* k* *Caust* k* cham h1 *Chin* k* dig *Gels* k* *Kali-c* k* lac-ac c1 m-arct b7.de *Puls* k* rhus-t hr1
  - ⁝ **length**; whole: alum ptk1
- · **turns** like a corkscrew on swallowing: elaps k*
  - ⁝ **passes** over raw places: bar-c

○ · **Cardia**: ign h1

FOREIGN body; sensation of a: *(↗Bone; Bread; Lump)* *Abies-n* vh acon bg2 aesc agar k* agath-a nl2• ail am-c k* ambr k* *Ant-c* k* *Apis* k* aral br1* *Arg-met* b7a.de arg-n arn k* aur b4a.de bar-c b4.de* **Bell** b4.de* brom bry bufo cadm-met tpw6 calc k* carb-v chel chinin-s cic k* coc-c mgm• coloc *Con* k* cop bg2 croc b7.de* **Crot-c** *Crot-t* cyclosp sa3• *Dros* b7a.de falco-pe nl2• gels bg2* graph k* ham bg2 hep b4a.de* ign b7a.de* kali-bi bg2 kreos k* lac-leo sk4• **Lach** k* led mag-c *Merc* k* mez mur-ac b4.de* myric nat-s k* *Nit-ac* b4a.de *Nux-m* ol-an k* phos phyt bg2 plan plb k* psil ft1 *Ruta* b7a.de sabad k* sabin k* samb bat1• *Sep* sol-t-ae stront-c sk4• suis-hep rly4• sulph tritic-vg fd5.de zinc k*

- **morning**: am-c cob
- **afternoon**: phos
- **evening**: am-c
- **apple** core: aral ptk1 hep c1 meny bg2 merc bg2* morg-p pte1*• nit-ac bg2* pall ptk1 phyt k* plan ptk1 verat ptk1
- **bone** (See Bone)
- **bread** crumbs (See Bread)
- **cough** | **not** amel.: samb bat1•
- **flesh**; piece of: phos bg2 plat bg2
  - · **cough** agg.; during: *Phos* b4a.de
- **lodged** in throat: *Lach* b7a.de *Spong* b7a.de
- **moving** up and down: calc bg2 lach b7a.de* lyc bg2 plb b7.de* rumx bg2
- **skin** hanging loose in throat, and he must swallow over it: acon agn *Alum* k2* ant-c ant-t wd bar-c rb2 berb ptk1 ferr rb2 iod ptk1 iris bg2 kreos k* *Lach* k* mang rb2 merc ptk1 ol-an phos k* plat k* *Sabad* k* spong rb2 sulph ptk1 valer ptk1

○ · **Hyoid** bone; near: pall ptk1

- **smoking** agg.: plb sep
- **sneezing** agg.: bar-c h2 plb bg2
- **stone**: bufo stram bg2
- **string**, as if a: sabad valer
- **swallowing**:
  - · **agg.**: graph ust
  - · **amel.** | **while**; for a: falco-pe nl2•
  - · **must** swallow: ant-c ptk1
  - · **not** amel.: agar ant-c cadm-met tpw6 *Crot-c* *Kali-bi* **Lach** *Sep*
- **walking** rapidly agg.: nat-c h2

○ - **Esophagus**: agath-a nl2• anac bell *Gels* k* *Lyc* k* nit-ac phos verat-v

FORMICATION (See Crawling)

FULLNESS: aesc k* ail k* aloe am-m k* ammc a1* anan *Apis* k* arag br1 arg-n bg2 arn ptk1 arum-d a1 atro a1 bapt k* *Bell* k* brom k* carb-an k* carb-v k* carbn-s caul hr1 caust cench k2 chinin-s chir-fl gya2 cimic k* *Cinnb* coca-c sk4• *Con* k* cot br1 *Eucal* bg1* eup-pur k* ferr-p sne gels bg2 glon k* helodr-cal knl2• *Iber* bg1* iod k* kali-p lac-ac k* lac-c lac-h sk4• *Lach* mag-c b4.de* phos b4.de* phys k* *Phyt* k* puls k* raph *Sang* *Sil* sulph k* syph *Thuj* zinc h2*

- **afternoon**: bapt k*
- **accompanied** by | **catarrh**: anemps br1
- **eructations**; with (See STOMACH - Eructations - accompanied - throat - fullness)
- **lying** down agg.: apis

Fullness: ...

- **swallowing**:
  - · **agg.**: eucal a1 *Sang*
  - · **amel.**: cench k2
- **turning** head | **left** agg.; to: phyt k*
- **writing** agg.: phyt k*

FUR; as of soft: phos bg2

GANGRENE: *(↗Discoloration - black)* **Ail** k* *Am-c* k* *Anth* arn **Ars** k* **Arum-t** k* bapt k* bell canth carb-ac k* *Carb-v* k* *Carbn-s* *Chin* k* chinin-ar con k* **Crot-h** k* echi bro1 euph k* kali-chl bro1 kali-n bro1 *Kali-p* k* kali-perm bro1 *Kreos* k* *Lach* k* merc k* *Merc-c* k* merc-cy k* *Mur-ac* k* *Nit-ac* k* *Phyt* k* *Sang* *Sec* *Sil* k* sul-ac k* *Sulph* k* tarent vario mtf11

○ - **Uvula**: chinin-ar lac-c k* *Lach* k*

GLAZED appearance: **Apis** k* arag br1 bell bg2* beryl sp1 *Carb-ac* k* cist *Hydr* bg2* *Hyos* hr1 *Kali-bi* k* **Lac-c** k* *Nat-ar* *Nat-m* k* petr k* *Phos* k* phyt k* stram bg2*

○ - **Pharynx**: alum bro1 apis bro1* arag bro1 bell bro1 beryl tpw5 cist bro1 hydr bro1 kali-bi bro1 *Lac-c* bro1 phos bro1

- **Tonsils**: apis ptk1 lac-c ptk1

GLOBUS hystericus (See Lump)

GLUEY: sep h2*

GOUTY metastasis: colch bro1 merc bro1

GRANULATED: alum bg2* bar-c calc-f k2 calc-p sne hom-xyz c2 *Hydr* *Kali-bi* k* *Kali-m* sne *Merc-d* sne mez k2 morg-p pte1*• *Phyt* k* yuc c2

GULPING UP (See STOMACH - Eructations; type - food)

GURGLING; esophagus is: euphr b7a.de*

- **convulsions**; during: **Cina** *Oena*
- **cough**; after: **Cina** k* cupr mtf33 mur-ac h2
- **drinking** agg.: arn k* **Ars** k* *Cina* *Cupr* k* *Cupr-act* bro1 *Elaps* *Hell* **Hydr-ac** k* **Laur** b7.de* phos b7a.de sil thuj k*
- **sleep** agg.; during: lyc
- **swallowing** agg.: cina mrr1 cupr tl1 thuj mtf33

HAIR; sensation of a: *(↗Hanging in - thread)* aesc-g bro1 all-s bro1 ambr bro1 aq-mar c1 *Arg-n* bg1* ars k* carbn-s caust bro1 coc-c k* dros bro1 hepat bro1 hydrog srj2* iod sne *Kali-bi* k* kali-s fkr2.de kola stb3• lach bro1 nat-m bro1 nit-ac bro1 nux-v bro1 pieri-b mlk9.de polys sk4• positr nl2• pulx bro1 sabad bro1* sang bro1 scor bg1 *Sil* k* *Sulph* k* thuj k* uran-n bg1 valer k* yuc bro1

- **right**:

▽ · **extending** to | **Eye**; through facial bones to: hydrog srj2•

- **afternoon**: *Sulph* k*

○ - **Posterior** part: coc-c ptk1

HANGING in throat; sensation as if something were: acon bg2 agn bg2 alum bg2 ant-c bg2 kreos bg2 **Lach** bg2 ol-an bg2 *Phos* bg2 plat bg2 sabad bg2 thuj bg2 **Yuc** a1*

- **cloth**; a piece of: agn a1*
- **mucus**: *(↗Mucus - hanging)* agn vh *Carb-an* vh lach vh *Merc-c* vh phos vh thuj vh **Yuc** a1*
- **skin** hanging loose in throat (See Foreign - skin)
- **thread**: *(↗Hair)* ars bg2 coc-c k* cocc bg2 *Kali-bi* bg2 nat-m bg2 pulx br1* sabad bg2* *Sil* bg2 sulph bg2 urt-u bg2 *Valer* k*
  - · **accompanied** by:
    - ⁝ **salivation**: valer ptk1
    - ⁝ **vomiting**: valer ptk1

HANGING to one side:

○ - **Uvula**: lach ptk1

- · **right** side: apis ptk1 nat-m ptk1

HARD, as if: *Cupr* bg1*

HAWK; disposition to: *(↗LARYNX - Scraping)* aesc k* aeth k* aids nl2• *Ail* all-c *Alum* k* alum-p k2 alum-sil k2 am-c b4.de* am-m k* ambr k* anac ang b7.de* ant-c b7.de* apis b7a.de* *Arg-met* k* **Arg-n** k* *Arum-t* k* asar b7.de* aur b4.de* *Bar-c* bar-s k2 *Bell* k* berb beryl tpw5 bism b7.de* bit-ar wht1• borx k* *Brom* b4a.de *Bry* k* bufo cain calad calc b4.de* calc-ar calc-f calc-p k* camph b7.de* cann-s b7.de* canth b7.de* carb-ac k* *Carb-an* k*

Hawk; disposition to: ...
Carb-v k* *Carbn-s* *Caust* k* cench k2 cham b7.de* chel chin b7.de* chinin-ar cimic *Cimx* *Cina* b7.de* *Cist* k* cob-n sp1 *Coc-c* k* cocc b7.de* colch k* con h2* **Cor-r** k* croc b7.de* *Crot-t* k* cycl cypra-eg sde6.de• dig b4.de* *Dros* b7a.de *Dulc* k* eucal bro1 eug ferr-i ferr-ma *Fl-ac* flor-p rsj3• *Gels* gent-c gink-b sbd1• *Graph* k* grat *Guaj* k* gymno k* **Hep** k* hepat br1* *Hydr* k* hyos b7.de* iber bro1 iod b4.de* just bro1 *Kali-bi* k* **Kali-c** k* *Kali-chl* *Kali-m* bro1 kali-n b4.de* kali-p kali-perm kali-s kreos bg2 lac-ac **Lach** k* laur k* *Lil-t* lob **Lyc** k* m-ambo b7.de mag-c k* *Mag-m* k* *Manc* mang h2* **Med** mrr1 meph a1 merc k* *Merc-i-f* k* *Merc-i-r* k* *Mez* k* naja k* *Nat-ar* **Nat-c** k* **Nat-m** k* nat-p *Nat-s* k* *Nit-ac* k* nux-m b7.de* **Nux-v** k* olib-sac wmh1 olnd b7.de* onos ox-ac k2 paeon pall par k* petr k* petr-ra shn4• ph-ac k* **Phos** k* *Phyt* k* pieri-b mlk9.de plat k* plb k* positr nl2• *Psor* k* ptel k* puls ptk1 ran-b b7.de* rhod b4.de* rhus-t k* *Rumx* k* ruta fd4.de *Sabad* k* sabin b7.de* samb b7.de* sang k2 sars k* *Sel* k* senec *Seneg* k* **Sep** k* *Sil* k* silphu bro1 spig k* spong bro1* *Stann* k* *Staph* b7.de* *Stram* *Sulph* k* *Tab* bro1 tarax b7.de* teucr k* *Thuj* k* thymol sp1 trif-p bro1 tritic-vg fd5.de tub bg* valer b7.de* vanil fd5.de vinc bro1 viol-t k* wye k* xan *Zinc* k* zinc-p k2

- **morning**: *Ail* am-m ambr k* arg-n a1 borx *Calc* **Caust** k* cench k2 *Cist* cob fl-ac grat **Kali-bi** kali-n h2* mag-m h2* nat-c h2* *Nat-m* k* *Petr* k* *Phos* phyt rhus-t k* sars *Sep* k* spong fd4.de
  - **mucus**; from thick, postnasal: **Caps** vh spong fd4.de
- **forenoon**: arg-n
  - **11** h: *Viol-t*
- **evening**: *Alum* caust h2* hep h2* kali-n h2* nat-sil fd3.de• stann
- **night**: aur sulph h2*
- **air** agg.; in open: *Carb-ac* nat-ar
- **breakfast** agg.; after: calc-p
- **breathing** deep agg.: sulph h2
- **constant**: **Caust** mrr1 **Med** mrr1 wye mrr1
- **dryness**, from: aids nl2• alum h2* fic-m gya1 podo fd3.de• spong fd4.de
- **eating**; after: hep bg1 kali-bi bg2 ol-an bg1 sabad bg2
- **ineffectual**: **Caust** cench k2 mag-c h2* *Mez* phos thuj
- **mucus** in throat and mouth; from thick: arg-n br1 hepat br1 kali-bi mrr1 kali-s fd4.de positr nl2• ruta fd4.de spong fd4.de tritic-vg fd5.de vanil fd5.de
- **roughness**, from: *Alum* petr-ra shn4•
- **sitting** up in bed | **must** sit up: nat-p k2
- **sleep** | **after** | **agg.**: *Lach*
  - **during**: calc-p k*
- **talking**:
  - **agg.**: arg-met ptk1 calc-p k* petr-ra shn4• podo fd3.de•
  - **before** being able to talk: bamb-a stb2.de• carc tpw2*
    - **chronic**: carc mlr1•
    - **infection**; from: carc mlr1•
- **tickling**; from: olib-sac wmh1 sulph h2* vanil fd5.de
- **walking** in open air agg.: ant-c carb-ac

HAWKS up cheesy lumps: *Agar* k* arg-n bg1 bry bg2* *Chen-a* k* coc-c bg2* *Hep* ptk1 ign bg1 *Kali-bi* k* **Kali-chl** **Kali-m** k* kali-p k* lyc bg2* *Mag-c* k* merc ptk1 merc-c bg2 merc-i-f ptk1 merc-i-r bg1* mez k2 nat-s bg2 nit-ac bg1 **Phos** k •* *Psor* k* sanic ptk1 sec k* sep ptk1 sil k* tub bg1

HEAT: *Acon* k* aesc k* aeth agar-ph a1 alco a1 aloe k2 alum bg2 alumn k* am-c bg2 am-caust a1 ant-c h2* *Apis* bg2 apoc hr1 arg-met bg2 arg-n k* arn bg2 *Ars* k* ars-s-f k2 *Arum-t* ptk1 *Asaf* bg2 aster k* aur bg2 bapt bg2 bar-c bg2 *Bell* k* benz-ac k* bism bg2 bol-la borx bg2 bov bg2 brom k* *Bry* bg2 bufo bg2 cain calc bg2 camph k* cann-xyz bg2 canth k* *Caps* k* carb-an k* carb-v k* carc fd2.de• carl a1 cassia-s cdd7*• **Caust** bg2* cerv a1 *Cham* k* chel bg2 chin k* chinin-ar cinch a1 cinnb bg2 *Cist* k* clem cob k* coca cocc k* coff bg2 colch k* con bg2 cop crot-t k* cub ptk1 cupr bg2 *Cycl* bg2 dros bg2 dulc k* *Euph* k* euphr ptk1 *Ferr* k* ferr-ar ferr-p k* fl-ac k* *Gels* *Glon* k* graph bg2 guaj bg2 hell k* hep k* hura hydr-ac k* hyos k* hyper k* iber a1 ign bg2 iod b4.de* iris k* iris-fl jatr-c kali-ar kali-bi bg2 kali-c k* kali-chl k* kali-m k2 kali-n k* kali-s k* kali-sula a1* kreos bg2 lac-c ptk1 *Lach* bg2* laur k* led lyc k* lyss k* manc k* mang bg2 *Merc* k* merc-c k* merc-i-f bg2 merc-sul k* merl a1 **Mez** k* morg-p fmm1• mosch k* naja bg2 nat-c b4.de* nat-m k* nat-s *Nit-ac* k* nux-m bg2 **Nux-v** k* oena k* olnd bg2 ox-ac k* paeon k* par bg2 petr bg2* ph-ac bg2 phos k* *Phyt* bg2* pic-ac k* plac-s rly4• plat bg2 plb k* polyg-h bg2 ptel c1 *Puls* bg2 quill br1 ran-b bg2* ran-s bg2 raph *Rhod* b4.de* *Rhus-t* k* **Sabad** bg2 samb k* *Sang* k* *Sec* bg2 sel rsj9• *Senec* k* seneg bg2 sep k* spirae a1 spong bg2 squil k* staph bg2 stram b7.de* streptoc jl2 *Stront-c* b4a.de* stry k* suis-em rly4•

Heat: ...
sul-ac k* *Sulph* k* sumb k* tab k* tarax bg2 tarent k* ter k* teucr k* thuj bg2 ust verat k* verat-v k* vesp k* vip k* zinc k* [heroin sdj2]

- **morning**: fl-ac sulph k*
- **forenoon**: carb-v k*
- **afternoon**: linu-c a1 sep k*
  - **14** h: nat-c
- **evening**: kali-s fd4.de nux-m k* ox-ac k* sumb k*
  - **18**-19 h: sang
  - **21**.30 h: rosm lgb1
- **night**: cinnb nit-ac h2*
- **air** agg.; in open: ant-c c1
- **breathing** agg.: conv br1 mang
- **cold** | **air** | **amel.**: *Sang* k*
  - **drinks** | **amel.**: cassia-s ccrh1•
- **coryza**; during: mag-m h2* quill br1
- **cough**; after: aur-m k* rosm lgb1 [heroin sdj2]
- **sensation** of: am b7.de cocc b7.de coff b7.de
  - **right**: rosm lgb1
- **swallowing** agg.: ars ptk1 *Bar-c* ptk1 ferr hep ptk1 tab k*
- **walking** in open air agg.: led
- ▽ **extending** to:
  - ○ **Body**; whole: cassia-s ccrh1•
  - **Stomach**: all-c crot-t iod bg1 manc merc bg1 naja tab [heroin sdj2]
- ○ **Esophagus**: aesc aeth aml-ns arg-n ars bell benz-ac brom *Camph* canth carb-ac *Colch* crot-t guare hydr-ac iod kali-chl kali-sula a1* merc-c nat-s phos plac-s rly4• plb ptel rhus-t sul-ac wye
  - **rising** up after a fright, or with anxious feelings; heat: hyper c1*
- **Fauces**: *Acon* bro1 aesc bro1 bapt hr1 bell bro1 *Canth* bro1 *Caps* bro1 carb-ac bro1 gels bro1 *Phos* bro1 *Phyt* bro1 sin-n bro1 still bro1
  - ▽ **extending** to | **Ears**: bapt hr1
- **Pharynx**: phyt tl1 sang tl1
- **Throat**-pit: calc-p bg2 chel bg2 kali-bi bg2 lach bg2

HEAVINESS: iod bg2 thuj bg2

HOLLOW feeling (See Emptiness)

HUNGER in; sensation of: mang h2*

INDURATION: mez k2

- ○ **Glands**; of: carc hbh*
- **Tonsils**; of: *Agar* alum ptk1 alumn k2* arg-n hr1 ars-i bro1 aur bro1 bac bro1 **Bar-c** k* **Bar-i** br1* **Bar-m** k* brom bg2* calc bro1 calc-f k2* *Calc-i* bro1 *Calc-p* bro1 *Cham* bg1* con k* cupr bg1* ferr-p bro1 fic-m gya1 *Graph* bg3* hep bro1 *Ign* k* iod bg2* kali-bi bg2* kali-m bro1 merc-i-f bro1 *Merc-i-r* bro1 *Nit-ac* k* petr phyt bro1* *Plb* k* plb-i bro1 sabad sil bro1 *Staph* sul-i bro1 thuj bro1

INFLAMMATION: **Acon** k* aesc k* *Agar* b4.de* agath-a nl2• *Ail* all-c k2 all-s k* aloe *Alum* k* alum-p k2 alum-sil k2 *Am-c* k* *Am-m* k* anan ant-c *Apis* k* *Arg-met* k* **Arg-n** k* *Ars* k* ars-s-f k2 arum-d c2 *Arum-t* *Aur* aur-ar k2 *Aur-m* *Aur-m-n* wbt2• aur-s k2 bac bn bad k* bamb-a stb2.de• *Bapt* k* **Bar-c** k* *Bar-m* k* **Bell** k* benz-ac k2 berb k* bism k* brom k* *Bry* k* *Bufo* cadm-met tpw6 cain calad b7.de* *Calc* k* *Calc-p* k* *Calc-s* k* calc-sil k2 canth k* **Caps** k* carb-v k* carbn c2 carbn-s caust *Cham* k* chim-m c2 *Chin* bg2* chinin-ar chir-fl gya2 chlor c2 cic bg2 cimic *Cinnb* *Cist* k* coc-c k* cocc bg2* *Coff* k* *Colch* k* coloc bg2 com k* con k* cop k* corv-cor bdg• *Crot-c* *Crot-h* k* crot-t k* *Cupr* k* des-ac rbp6 diphtox jl2 dol c2 *Dulc* k* elae c2 elaps euph b4.de* euph-pe c2 fago k* falco-pe nl2• **Ferr-p** k* fl-ac k* flav jl2 *Gels* k* get a1 *Graph* ham hell-v c2 **Hep** k* hippoz k* hura-c c2 hydroph rsj6• ign k* ind c2 *Iod* k* ip k* kali-ar *Kali-bi* k* *Kali-c* k* *Kali-i* k* kali-m k2 kali-n k* kali-p *Kali-perm* kali-s kreos bg2 lac-ac stj5• *Lac-c* k* lac-del hrn2• **Lach** k* lachn c2 lavand-a ctl1• lob-c k* loxo-recl bnm10• luf-op rsj5• **Lyc** k* *Lyss* k* mag-c mag-p bg2 manc c2 mang k* med hr1 **Merc** k* *Merc-c* k* *Merc-cy* **Merc-d** hr1 *Merc-i-f* k* *Merc-i-r* k* *Mez* k* *Mucor* jl2 *Mur-ac* *Naja* k* nat-ar nat-c k* *Nat-m* k* nat-p k* *Nat-s* k* nicc k* **Nit-ac** k* nux-m k* *Nux-v* k* oena k* ol-an k* op b7.de* osteo-a knp1• ox-ac a1 pall *Par* b7a.de paull a1 **Petr** k* ph-ac k* *Phos* k* *Phyt* k* plb plumbg a1 psor k* ptel k* *Puls* k* rad-br sze8• ran-b k* *Rhus-t* k* ruta b7.de* sabad k* sabin b7a.de sal-al blc1• sal-fr sle1• *Sang* k* sec b7a.de seneg k* sep b4.de* *Sil* mrr1 sol-t-ae k* spig bg2 spong fd4.de staph bg2 still strept-ent jl2 stront-c k* suis-hep rly4• sul-ac k* *Sulph* k* syph k2 tarent tell *Thuj* k* trios rsj11•

Inflammation: ...
tritic-vg fd5.de verat bg2* vip xan br1 *Zinc* zinc-m a1 zinc-p k2 zinc-s a1 ziz hr1 [bell-p-sp dcm1 buteo-j sej6 cupr-p stj2 heroin sdj2]

- **alternating** sides: lac-c k2*
- **right**: ars-met aur-m-n wbt2• bamb-a stb2.de• **Bell** k* gels hr1 ham *Lac-c* **Lyc** lyss *Merc* *Merc-i-f* k* phyt k* sars stront-c tarent xan [heroin sdj2]
  - ▽ • **extending** to | **left**: lyc mrr1 merc-i-f xyz61 petr c1
- **left**: *Crot-h* k* *Elaps* form *Lac-ac* **Lach** k* *Merc-i-r* k* *Naja* nicc psil ft1 sec *Sep* thuj
  - ▽ • **extending** to | **right**: lach k2* sabad k2
- **forenoon**: jab k*
- **night**: *Cinnb* kali-s fd4.de **Merc**
- **accompanied** by:
  - • **cough**: *Acon* b7.de* *Cham* b7.de* *Ip* b7.de* nux-v b7.de* puls b7.de*
  - • **influenza**: strept-ent jl2
  - • **salivation**: *Bar-m* st1* merc mrr1
  - ○ • **Ear**; pain in left (See EAR - Pain - left - accompanied - throat)
  - • **Tongue**:
    - **dirty** discoloration: *Kali-m* kr1* merc mrr1
    - **mucus** on tongue:
      - **collection** of mucus: phyt kr1*
        - . **white** mucus: *Ign* kr1*
    - **white** discoloration of the tongue | **heavily** coated: *Merc* kr1*
- **alternating** with | **Eyes**; sore: par
- **burning**, pressing: **Caps** vh
- **children**; in: cham
- **chronic**: *(↗Pain - chronic)* agar k2 *Alum* k* *Arg-n* *Bar-c* k* bar-m bg2 bar-s k2 bell bg2 brom bg2 *Calc* k* *Carb-v* k* *Carbn-s* chin bg2 *Cob* con bg2 dulc bg2 elaps gk *Fl-ac* graph k2 *Ham* *Hep* k* ign bg2 iod bg2 *Jug-c* k* kali-bi bg2 kali-chl *Kali-i* k* kali-m k2 *Lach* k* *Lyc* k* mang k* *Merc* k* mez bg2 *Nat-m* k* *Nit-ac* k* nux-v bg2 ol-j ox-ac k2 *Phos* k* *Phyt* puls bg2 sabad bg2 seneg k* *Sep* k* *Sil* k* staph bg2 sul-i bg2 *Sulph* k* teucr bg2 *Thuj* k* tub bg2
- **cold**; after: *Bar-c* k* *Bell* calc k2 *Cham* *Dulc* kali-c k2 petr h2*
- **cold** drinks | **amel.**: trios rsj11•
- **coryza**; during: bell b4a.de phos b4.de*
- **eating**; after | **amel.**: trios rsj11•
- **erysipelatous**: **Apis** k* bapt *Bell* k* *Canth* bro1 *Crot-c* euph bro1 *Lach* k* lyc *Merc* phyt *Rhus-t* k*
- **fever**; during: acon bg2 am-m bg2 *Apis* bg2 bell bg2 brom bg2 con b4a.de* merc bg2 nit-ac bg2 nux-v bg2 phos bg2 sulph bg2
- **follicular**: aesc *Ail* **Bell** cop dros gk guaj **Hep** *Hydr* k* **Ign** **Iod** *Kali-bi* *Kali-chl* k* *Kali-i* kali-m br *Lac-c* *Merc* *Merc-cy* *Merc-i-r* *Mur-ac* **Nat-m** *Nit-ac* *Phyt* k* *Sec* k* sul-ac k2
  - • **chronic**: sangin-n br1
- **gangrenous**: hip-ac mtf11
- **malignant**: chinin-ar c2 diphtox jl2
- **menses** | **before** | **agg.**: lac-c c1 *Mag-c* senec br1*
  - • **during** | **agg.**: *Lac-c* senec bro1
- **mercury**; after abuse of: *Arg-met* **Hep** *Nit-ac*
- **painful**: diph mtf11 syph mtf11
- **painless**: **Bapt** k*
- **perspiration**; during: **Acon** bg2 am-m bg2 apis bg2 bar-c bg2 **Bell** bg2 bry bg2 cham bg2 *Con* bg2 lach bg2 *Merc* bg2 *Nit-ac* bg2 *Nux-v* bg2 puls bg2 sep bg2 sulph bg2
- **phlegmonous**: *Acon* *Alumn* bar-c *Bell* calc *Hep* *Lach* *Merc* *Nux-v* *Sulph* thuj
- **putrid**: arist-cl sp1 caps b7a.de
- **recurrent** (See GENERALS - History - throat)
- **scarlet** fever: acon bro1 *Ail* bro1 apis bro1 ars bro1 *Asim* bro1 *Bar-c* bro1 *Bell* bro1 brom bro1 chinin-ar k2 kali-perm bro1 lac-c bro1 *Lach* bro1 merc bro1 mur-ac bro1 *Phyt* bro1 rhus-t bro1
- **swallowing** agg.: trios rsj11•
- **tubercular**: bac bn
- **waking**; on: kali-bi *Lach* mand rsj7•
- **warm** bed agg.: apis coc-c
- **weather** agg.; cold wet: kali-bi k2
- **winter**: kali-bi k2
- ▽ - **extending** to:
  - ○ • **Downwards**: merc k2
- **extending** to: ...
  - • **Larynx**: kali-bi k2
  - • **Nose**: kali-bi k2 *Nit-ac* vh
  - • **Upward**: merc k2
    - **And** downward: *Merc* vh
- ○ - **Esophagus** (= esophagitis) acon c1* agath-a nl2• alum bro1 am-caust c2 am k* **Ars** k* asaf k* bell k* bufo *Carb-v* k* cocc k* euph k* *Gels* influ jl2 *Iod* kali-sula c1* laur k* merc k* merc-c bro1 mez k* naja bro1 *Nit-ac* oena k* *Phos* k* plb mrr1 **Rhus-t** k* rob mrr1 rumx-act c2 sabad k* *Sang* mrr1 sec k* streptoc jl2 sul-ac c2* verat bro1 *Verat-v* k* vesp
  - • **reflux** esophagitis: arg-n mrr1 sang mrr1 sulph mrr1
- **Fauces**: ail bro1 apis bro1 *Bell* bro1 cist tl1 ferr-p bro1 *Kali-bi* bro1 mentho bro1 merc bro1 merc-i-f bro1 sal-ac tl1 vario mtf11
  - • **accompanied** by | **Tonsil**; mucus patches on right (See Mucous - tonsils - right - accompanied - fauces)
- **Nasopharynx**:
  - • **acute**: *Acon* bro1 camph bro1 cist bro1 gels bro1 influ jl2* kali-bi bro1 kali-chl c1 mentho bro1 *Merc-c* bro1 nat-ar bro1 sang hr1* wye bro1
  - • **chronic**: am-br br1 aur bro1 calc-f bro1 elaps c2* fago bro1 *Hydr* bro1 influ jl2* *Kali-bi* bro1 *Kali-c* bro1 merc-c bro1 nat-i c1 pen bro1 sep bro1 *Spig* bro1 *Stict* bro1 sulph bro1 thuj bro1
- **Pharynx** (= pharyngitis): acon mrr1 aesc bro1* allox mtf11 *Alum* bro1 am-c mrr1 ant-t mtf11 *Apis* mrr1 arg-met mrr1 arg-n bro1* ars mrr1 ars-i bro1 arum-d br1 arum-m mtf11 bapt mrr1 bar-c mtf11 bar-m mrr1 bell ptk1* brom mrr1 bry mrr1 calc mrr1 canth mrr1 caps mtf11 carb-ac mrr1 cinnm mtf11 cortico mtf11 crot-h mrr1 dros mtf11 dub bro1 dubo-m br1 dys pte1* ferr-p mrr1 guaj mtf11 hed sp1 **Hep** mrr1 hepat mtf11 influ jl2* kali-bi bro1* kali-c mrr1 kali-i mrr1 *Lac-c* mrr1* lach mrr1 luf-op mtf11 lyss mtf11 mangi br1 med mtf11 mentho br1 *Merc* ptk1* merc-c mrr1 morg-p pte1* nat-m mrr1 nit-ac mrr1 nux-v bro1 oxyte-chl mtf11 parat-b mtf11 parathyr jl2 phos mrr1 *Phyt* mrr1* polyg-h mtf11 prot jl2* psor mrr1 rhus-t mrr1 sabad mrr1 sabal bro1 salv mtf11 sangin-n mtf11 *Sil* mrr1 sin-n br1 sulph mrr1 syph mtf11 tub mtf11 *Wye* br1
  - • **right**: bar-c bro1 *Bell* bro1 guaj bro1 lyc bro1* mag-p bro1 merc bro1 merc-i-f bro1* nicc bro1 *Phyt* bro1* podo bro1 *Sang* bro1 *Sulph* bro1
    - **extending** to | **left**: lyc mrr1
  - • **left**: brom mrr1* crot-h mrr1 lach bro1* merc-i-r bro1* sabad bro1*
    - **extending** to | **right**: lac-c bro1 lach bro1* sabad bro1
  - • **afternoon**: lach bro1
  - • **acute**: *Acon* bro1 *Aesc* bro1 apis bro1* arg-n bro1 arum-t mtf11 *Bell* bro1 bry bro1 canth bro1 *Caps* bro1 caust bro1 cist bro1 eucal bro1 ferr-p bro1 *Gels* bro1 glyc bro1 *Guaj* bro1 gymno bro1 *Hep* bro1 iod bro1 *Just* bro1 *Kali-bi* bro1 kali-c bro1 kali-m bro1 lach bro1 lachn bro1 led bro1 mentho bro1 *Merc* bro1* merc-c bro1 merc-i-f bro1 merc-i-r bro1 naja bro1 nat-ar bro1 nat-i bro1 nux-v bro1 *Phyt* bro1 quill bro1 sal-ac bro1 *Sang* bro1 sangin-n br1* *Sil* mrr1 squil bro1 syph xxb wye br1*
  - • **atrophic**: sabal c2
  - • **bed** agg.; in: *Merc* bro1 merc-i-f bro1
  - • **chronic**: aesc bro1 alum k2* am-br bro1 *Am-caust* bro1 arg-i bro1 *Arg-met* bro1 *Arg-n* bro1 ars bro1 arum-t bro1 aur bro1 bar-c bro1 bar-m brom bro1 *Calc* calc-p bro1 calc-sil k2 cann-i bro1 carb-v bro1 caust bro1 cinnb bro1 cist bro1 *Coc-c* bro1 cub bro1 elaps bro1 ferr-p bro1 *Fl-ac* graph bro1 *Hep* bro1 *Hydr* bro1 influ mp4• *Iod* bro1 *Kali-bi* bro1 kali-c bro1 kali-chl bro1 kali-i *Lac-c* lach k* *Lyc* bro1 med bro1 *Merc* bro1* merc-c bro1 merc-i-f bro1 naja *Nat-c* bro1 *Nat-m* k* *Nux-v* bro1 ox-ac bro1 pen br1* *Petr* k* phos bro1 *Phyt* puls bro1 *Rumx* bro1 sabad bro1 sabal bro1 *Sang* bro1 sec bro1 seneg bro1 *Sep* k* **Sil** k* stann bro1 sulph sumb bro1 tab bro1 toxo-g jl2 *Wye* bro1
  - • **cold**:
    - **agg.**: *Cist* bro1 fl-ac bro1 hep bro1 *Lyc* bro1
    - **air**:
      - **agg.**: sabad mrr1
      - **inspiration** | **amel.**: sang bro1
    - **drinks** | **amel.**: apis mrr1
  - • **follicular**: wye br1
    - **acute**: aesc bro1 apis bro1 bell bro1 caps bro1 *Ferr-p* bro1 iod bro1 kali-bi bro1 *Kali-m* bro1 merc bro1 *Phyt* bro1 sangin-n bro1 wye bro1
    - **chronic**: aesc bro1 *Alum* bro1 am-br bro1 *Arg-n* bro1 arn bro1 ars-i bro1 *Arum-t* bro1 calc-f bro1 calc-p bro1 caps bro1 caust bro1 cinnb bro1 cist bro1

- **follicular – chronic**: ... dros bro1 *Hep* bro1 *Hydr* bro1 ign bro1 *Kali-bi* bro1 kali-m bro1 *Lach* bro1 merc-cy bro1 *Merc-i-r* bro1 nat-m bro1 nux-v bro1 phos bro1 *Phyt* bro1 *Sangin-n* bro1 stict bro1 still bro1 sulph bro1 *Wye* bro1
- **gangrenous**: caps tl1
- **herpetic**: *Apis* bro1 ars bro1 borx bro1 hydr bro1 jac-c bro1 *Kali-bi* bro1 kali-chl bro1 lach bro1 merc-i-f bro1 nat-s bro1 *Phyt* bro1 sal-ac bro1
- **influenzal**: parat-b mtf11
- **menses**; during: lac-c bro1
- **nasopharyngitis** (See nasopharynx)
- **perspiration** of feet; after suppressed: *Bar-c* bro1 psor bro1 sil bro1
- **pressure** agg.: lach bro1 merc-c bro1
- **recurrent** (See GENERALS - History - pharynx)
- **rheumatic**: acon bro1 bry bro1 colch bro1 guaj bro1 phyt bro1 rhus-t bro1
- **septic**: am-c bro1 *Hep* bro1 kreos tl1 mur-ac bro1 *Sil* bro1
- **sleep** agg.: *Lach* bro1 lyc bro1
- **swallowing**:
  - **amel.**: gels bro1 *Ign* bro1
  - **empty** | **agg.**: antip bro1 *Bar-c* bro1 crot-h bro1 dol bro1 *Hep* bro1 *Just* bro1 lac-c bro1 *Lach* bro1 *Merc* bro1 merc-i-f bro1 merc-i-r bro1 phyt bro1 sabad bro1
  - **food**:
    - **agg.**: bapt bro1 merc bro1 morph bro1
    - **amel.**: *Ign* bro1 lach bro1
  - **liquids**:
    - **agg.**: bell bro1 bry bro1 ign bro1 *Lach* bro1
    - **amel.**: cist bro1
  - **not** swallowing; when: caps bro1 ign bro1
- **sweets** agg.: spong bro1
- **talking** agg.: kali-i mrr1
- **tubercular**: merc-i-r bro1
- **warm**:
  - **agg.**: coc-c bro1 iod bro1 lach bro1 *Merc* bro1
  - **drinks**:
    - **agg.**: *Lach* bro1 merc-i-f bro1 phyt bro1
    - **amel.**: *Alum* bro1 *Ars* bro1 calc-f bro1 *Lyc* bro1 morph bro1 rhus-t mrr1 sabad bro1*

- **Thyroid** gland (See EXTERNAL - Inflammation - thyroid)
- **Tonsils** (= tonsillitis): *Acon* k* aesc k* *Ail* k* alum bg2* alum-sil k2 **Alumn** k* *Am-c* bg2 aml-ns amyg mtf11 anan ant-t anthraci *Apis* k* arg-n bg2 arist-cl sp1 arn bg2 *Ars* k* ars-s-f k2 arum-t bg2* aur bg2 aur-m-n wbt2* aur-s k2 bac bn bacls-7 pte1* bad bamb-a stb2.de* *Bapt* k* **Bar-c** k* bar-i k2* *Bar-m* k* bar-s k2 **Bell** k* benz-ac berb k* *Brom* bg2* bry a1* bufo calc bg2* calc-f sp1 calc-i sf1.de* calc-p st calc-s c2* calc-sil k2 *Canth* k* *Caps* k* carc gk6* cedr cent a1 *Cham* k* chel *Chen-a* k* cist mrr1 *Colch* k* con sf1.de *Crot-h* k* *Cupr* cupr-ar a1 cur dros gk *Dulc* k* dys fmm1* ferr mtf11 ferr-m c2 ferr-p k* *Fl-ac* fuc sf1.de *Gels* k* gink-b sbd1• graph br **Guaj** k* ham k* hed sp1 *Hep* k* *Ign* k* *Iod* k* *Kali-bi* k* *Kali-chl* *Kali-i* bg2* kali-m k2 kali-p kali-perm mtf11 ketogl-ac rly4• **Lac-c** k* lach k* lat-m sp1 lyc k* mag-f mg1.de* mand sp1 mang bg2 **Merc** k* merc-c bg2 *Merc-cy* **Merc-d** *Merc-i-f* k* merc-i-r k* merc-k-i mtf11 mez bg2 morg-g fmm1• morg-p fmm1* mucor jl2* naja *Nat-m* sf1.de *Nat-s* k* **Nit-ac** k* nux-v bg2* phos bg2* *Phyt* k* phyt-b mtf11 *Plb* k* **Psor** k* puls k* rad-br sze8• ran-s c2 raph c2 *Sabad* *Sang* k* sangin-n c2 sep k* **Sil** k* *Staph* k* still k* streptoc jl2* suis-hep rly4• *Sul-i* sf1.de* sulo-ac br1* *Sulph* k* syc pte1*• syph k2* tarent k* teucr sf1.de *Thuj* bg2* **Tub** sf1.de* ust k* v-a-b jl* vanil fd5.de verat k* vesp k* vesp-xyz c2 zinc zinc-m a1 [bar-p stj1 ferr-s stj1]
  - **alternating** sides: lac-c k2*
  - **right**: bell mrr1 merc-i-f hr1* *Phyt* mrr1
  - **left**: brom mrr1* caps hr1 crot-h mrr1 glycyr-g cte1• merc-i-r mrr1 naja a1 plb hr1 sabad hr1 sep h2 still hr1 ust hr1
  - **accompanied** by:
    - **hoarseness**: arist-cl sp1
    - **salivation**: **Bar-c** kr1*
  - **acute**: *Acon* bro1 *Ail* bro1 am-m bro1 amyg-p bro1 *Apis* bro1 arn br1 *Bapt* bro1 bar-act bro1 *Bar-c* bro1 **Bar-m** bro1* **Bell** bro1* brom bro1 caps bro1 dulc bro1 eucal bro1 ferr-p bro1 gels bro1 gins bro1 *Glycyr-g* cte1•

Inflammation – Tonsils – acute: ... *Guaj* bro1 *Gymno* bro1 hep bro1 *Ign* bro1 iod bro1 kali-bi bro1 *Kali-m* bro1 lac-c bro1 *Lach* bro1 lyc bro1 *Merc* bro1 *Merc-i-f* bro1 *Merc-i-r* bro1 naja bro1 nat-s bro1 *Phyt* bro1 rhus-t bro1 sabad bro1 *Sang* bro1 *Sil* bro1 sulph bro1

- **alternating** with | **Head**; pain in: lac-d kr1*
- **chronic**: **Bar-c** bro1* **Bar-m** mrr1 calc-p bro1 calc-s mtf11 carc fb* fuc bro1 gonotox jl2 hep bro1* ign mtf33 lach bro1 lyc bro1 med jl2 nat-m mtf33 nit-ac mtf33 psor bro1* *Sil* bro1 strept-ent jl2 streptoc mtf11 syph jl2 thuj mtf33 tub mtf11* v-a-b jl2*
- **coryza**; after: sabad kr1
- **follicular**: *Ail* br1 ign br1 kali-m br1 nat-sal br1 penic mtf11
- **followed** by | **rheumatism**: echi ptk1 guaj ptk1 kali-s pd lach ptk1 phyt ptk1 rhod pd
- **menses**; before: bar-c ptk
- **painless**: **Bapt**
- **phlegmonous** | **acute**: acon bro1 apis bro1 *Bar-c* bro1 bar-i bro1 *Bell* bro1 caps bro1 cinnb bro1 guaj bro1 *Hep* bro1 lac-c bro1 lach bro1 lyc bro1 *Merc* bro1 merc-i-f bro1 merc-i-r bro1 *Phyt* bro1 *Psor* bro1 sang bro1 sangin-n bro1 sil bro1 *Tarent-c* bro1 vesp bro1
- **recurrent** (See GENERALS - History - tonsillitis)
- **swelling**: calc-i mtf11 thuj mtf11
- **weather**; at every spell of cold: bar-c k2* *Dulc* hep

- **Uvula** (= uvulitis; staphylitis): *Acon* bro1 aeth a1 agn b7.de* *Alum* alumn k2 amyg-p bro1 **Apis** ars **Bell** b4.de* berb k* bism bg2 borx b4a.de brom k* calc k* cann-s b7a.de canth b7a.de caps bro1 *Carb-v* k* caust bg2 chinin-s cimic k* cist bro1 **Coff** b7a.de* colch cortiso mtf11 cupr-act *Gels* iod bg2* kali-bi k* kali-n k* *Kali-perm* bro1 *Lac-c* lyc bg2 lyss mtf11 **Merc** b4.de* merc-c b4a.de* *Merc-i-f* *Nat-m* bg2 *Nat-s* k* nit-ac k2 nux-v k* *Phyt* plb k* ptel bg2* puls k* ruta b7.de* sabad bg2 *Seneg* k* sil bg2 sul-i bro1 sulph k* thuj b4a.de *Zinc* b4.de*
  - **fever**; during: bell bg2 coff bg2 merc bg2 nux-v bg2 sulph bg2
  - **perspiration**; during: *Acon* bg2 bell bg2 calc bg2 cann-xyz bg2 merc bg2 **Nux-v** bg2 sulph bg2

INJURIES: | **Esophagus**: cic hr1*

IRRITATION: *Ail* k* allox tpw4 am-br a1 arge-pl rwt5• aster k* atro a1 **Bell** k* bov bros-gau mrc1 carb-ac k* *Carb-v* cardios-h rly4• chinin-s chir-fl gya2 cimic k* **Con** *Crot-t* k* cystein-l rly4• dream-p sdj1• dros mrr1 ferr-p a1 gels k* *Glon* k* *Hep* k* hepat br1 hura iod k* ip k* kali-br k* *Kali-i* k* *Kali-perm* br1 lac-h htj1• *Lach* k* *Morb* jl2 morph k* nat-ar nat-p a1 *Nux-v* orot-ac rly4• ozone sde2• petr-ra shn4• polys sk4• puls rham-f a1 rhus-t rhus-v k* sang k* sars k* sec k* sel rsj9• ser-a-c jl2 sil k* stann mrr1 suis-em rly4• sul-ac k* tab k* thev a1 thiam rly4• trif-p a1 ust k* vanad br1 vero-o rly4• wye mrr1

- **right**: choc srj3• cystein-l rly4•
- **morning**: chel k* dios a1 nat-c k* *Sulph* k*
- **afternoon** | **14**.30-15 h: rosm lgb1
- **evening**: chel k* dios a1
- **night**: tab k*
- **agg.**: coc-c ptk1
- **warm** applications | **amel.**: stront-c sk4•
- ▽ **extending** to | **Eustachian** tube: phyt
- ○ **Esophagus**: *Coc-c* k* crot-t phos h2
- **Fauces**; deep in | **causes** cough: **Dros** vh
- **Pharynx**: aesc k* bov k* coch hr1 crot-t a1 cystein-l rly4• *Merc-i-f* a1* olnd k* osm a1 phyt hr1 ran-s a1 trif-p a1 verat k*

ITCHING: aeth agar alum bg2 am-m ambr anac bg1 ant-t a1 *Apis* k* arg-met arge-pl rwt5• arum-t ptk1 bry b7.de* cain calc-s k* canth bg2 cardios-h rly4• caust bg2* chel bg2 *Cist* k* colch con k* cop dulc fd4.de *Glon* k* irid-met srj5• kali-c kali-i lac-h sk4• lac-loxod-a hrn2• nat-ox rly4• nicotam rly4• nux-v b7.de* oci-sa sk4• petr k2 *Plan* bg1* pycnop-sa mrz1 ros-d wla1 sabad bg2 sal-ac bg2 samb k* spig b7.de* *Spong* stront-c bg2 succ-ac rly4• tritic-vg fd5.de *Wye* k* [helia stj7]

- **cough** agg.; during: (*↗COUGH - Itching - throat; COUGH - Itching - Throat; in*) ambr k* zinc-i ptk1
- **laughing**; from: mang k2
- **periodical**: *Cist*
- **swallowing** agg.: nux-v bg1 streptoc rly4•
- **talking** agg.: mang k2
- ▽ **extending** to | **Ear**: wye mrr1
- ○ **Esophagus**: aeth cain
- **Fauces**: cist tl1 phyt bg3* rhus-t bg3*

- **Pharynx**: cain colch hr1 petr tl1 spig k* tritic-vg fd5.de
  - **swallowing** agg.: lachn k* stront-c
- **Posterior** nares (= choanae): ail bg2
- **Tonsils**: caust bg2 dios bg2 nux-v bg2
- **Uvula**: canth bg2 nicotam rly4• sabad ptk1

JERKING: cycl a1 nat-m plat

▽ - **extending** to | **Pit** of stomach: sep

LEAF; sensation of a:

○ - **Pharynx**; in:

- **as** if a leaf lay before posterior nares | **morning** after waking: *Bar-c* k*

LIFTING agg.: caust ptk1 **Sil** ptk1

LIQUIDS taken are forced into nose: *(↗Food - passes; Paralysis; NOSE - Liquids - come)* anan **Arum-t** aur k* *Bar-c* bar-s k2 bell k* bism canth k* *Carb-ac* caust cupr k* *Cur* diph br1 gels k2* hyos k2* ign k* ix bnm8• kali-bi *Kali-perm* **Lac-c** k* **Lach** k* **Lyc** *Lyss* *Merc* k* *Merc-c* k* *Merc-cy* *Nat-m* k* nit-ac bg2 op k2 petr k* phos bg2* *Phyt* k* *Plb* puls sil k* *Sul-ac* k* verat h1

LOOSENING of mucous membrane: kali-bi bg2

LUMP; sensation of a: *(↗Foreign)* acon ptk1 adam srj5• aesc agar *Aids* nl2• ail *All-c* k* allox tpw3* *Alum* k* alum-p k2 alum-sil k2 am-c k* *Ambr* k* *Anac* bg2 anan androc srj1• *Ant-c* k* apis aqui br1* *Arg-n* k* arn k* ars k* ars-s-f k2 arund vh **Asaf** k* atra-r skp7*• aur aur-ar k2 aur-m aur-m-n wbt2• aur-s k2 bamb-a stb2.de• *Bar-c* k* bar-m mrr1 bar-ox-suc rly4• bar-s k2 bell k* benz-ac berb bit-ar wht1• *Brom* k* bry bufo k* cact k2 *Calc* k* calc-s calc-sil k2 carb-v k* *Carbn-s* carc mg1.de* cardios-h rly4• cassia-s ccrh1• *Caust* k* cham k* chel k* chinin-s k* chir-fl gya2 chlorpr pin1• choc srj3• cic *Cina* k* cit-v c2 *Coc-c* k* cocc coloc bg2 colum-p sze2• *Con* k* croc k* *Crot-c* *Crot-h* k* crot-t cur cypra-eg sde6.de• elaps bg2 *Ferr* k* ferr-ar *Ferr-p* k* flav jl2 fuma-ac rly4• *Gels* k* gink-b sbd1• *Graph* k* *Hep* k* hipp c1* hippoc-k szs2 hir rsj4• hist sp1 hydrog srj2• *Hyos* k* **Ign** k* kali-ar *Kali-bi* k* *Kali-c* k* kali-n k* kali-p k* kali-s kali-sil k2 kalm c2 kola stb3• kreos lac-ac k* *Lac-c* k* lac-d k2 lac-leo sk4• lac-v c1 **Lach** k* lact-v c1* laur k* *Led* k* *Lil-t* bg1* *Lob* k* lyc bg2* lycps-v bg2 mag-c k* mag-m b4.de* manc bro1 med merc k* *Merc-i-f* k* *Merc-i-r* k* mez k* *Mosch* bg2* mur-ac b4.de* myric naja bg2* nat-ar nat-c nat-hchls c2 **Nat-m** k* nat-p k* nat-pyru rly4• *Nit-ac* k* *Nux-m* k* *Nux-v* k* ol-an olnd bg2 ozone sde2• par k* petr-ra shn4• ph-ac phos bg2* phys ptk1 *Phyt* k* pieri-b mlk9.de plan plat bro1 *Plb* k* plb-act bro1 podo bg2 polys sk4• positr nl2• *Propr* sa3• psil ft1 **Psor** k* *Puls* b7.de* raph c2* ribo rly4• rumx k* ruta k* *Sabad* k* sabin k* sal-fr sle1• saroth sp1 scut c1 senec ptk1 *Sep* k* *Sil* k* sol-t-ae still stram b7.de* stry succ-xyz c2 suis-pan rly4• sul-ac *Sulph* k* symph fd3.de• tab thiam rly4• *Thuj* tritic-vg fd5.de tub c1* ulm-c jsj8• urol-h rwt• ust bg1* *Valer* bg2* vanil fd5.de vario jl2 verat-v bg2* wye bro1 zinc k* zinc-p k2 [heroin sdj2 tax jsj7]

- **right** side: bit-ar wht1• sil bg1 vario bg2*
- **left** side: bar-c bg1 calc bg1 kali-c h2* lach ptk1 lyc bg2 olib-sac wmh1 positr nl2• sil h2* suis-pan rly4•
- **morning**: am-c bamb-a stb2.de• cob hep h2 lac-h htj1•
- **forenoon**: phos phyt
  - **riding** agg.: phyt
- **afternoon**: *Bar-c*
  - **12-14** h: *Propr* sa3•
- **evening**: am-c *Asaf* kali-p fd1.de• sep
  - **swallowing** agg.: sep
- **night**: carc mrr1 graph mag-m bg1 nat-m tritic-vg fd5.de
- **accompanied** by | **Chest**; constriction in (See CHEST - Constriction - accompanied - throat)
- **bitter** lump: sul-ac h2
- **cold**:
  - **amel.**: carc mrr1
  - **drinks** | **agg.**: cassia-s ccrh1•
- **cough**:
  - **agg.**: lach ptk1
  - **during** | **amel.**: carc fd2.de• irid-met srj5• kali-c k* kola stb3•
- **eating**:
  - **after** | **agg.**: ambr c1 cassia-s ccrh1•
  - **agg.**: sulph h2

Lump; sensation of a – **eating**: ...

  - **amel.**: ozone sde2•
- **eructations** | **amel.**: kali-ar *Mag-m* k*
- **fist** would press on it; as if a: moni rfm1•
- **hard** lump: nux-m ptk1 sul-ac h2
- **lying** on back agg.: atra-r skp7*•
- **menopause**; during: aml-ns bro1 *Lach* bro1 valer bro1 zinc-val bro1
- **painful**: gels hr1* **Lach** nat-m ptk1
- **pea**; like a: phasco-ci rbp2
- **rising** sensation: *(↗STOMACH - Ball - rising)* *Ars* **Asaf** k* aur bg2 **Bell** bg2 cact calc b4.de cann-i caust b4.de cham *Chel* cit-v c2 *Coloc* *Con* k* *Gels* graph b4.de **Ign** k* kali-ar kali-c b4.de kali-p c1 *Kalm* *Lac-d* lach k* *Lec* *Lob* k* **Lyc** k* mag-c *Mag-m* k* merc bg2 **Mosch** k* mur-ac h2 **Nat-m** k* nit-ac h2 *Nux-m* **Nux-v** petr bg2 phys *Plat* *Plb* k* plut-n srj7• *Puls* *Senec* k* *Sep* k* *Sil* b4.de* spong bg1 *Stram* sul-ac h2 *Sulph* k* tarent *Valer* k* verat-v zinc bg1

○ • **Brain**; to: plb a1*
- **sadness**; during: kola stb3• [tax jsj7]
- **sleep** agg.; during: *Crot-c* **Lach** k* **Nux-v** k* *Sep* valer
- **smoking** agg.: plb sep
- **stone**: bufo
- **swallowing**:
  - **left** to right; lump from: xan c1
  - **agg.**: aids nl2• *Bar-c* bros-gau mrc1 calc chir-fl gya2 *Gels* *Graph* kola stb3• *Lach* *Merc* *Nat-m* nat-pyru rly4• nat-s *Nux-v* ozone sde2• petr-ra shn4• pic-ac positr nl2• propl ub1• puls *Sep* sil symph fd3.de• ulm-c jsj8• urol-h rwt• ust xan c1
  - **amel.**: ign bg2
  - **empty**:
    - **agg.**: carc mrr1 cassia-s ccrh1• caust h2 *Ferr* k* graph ptk1 nit-ac h2 *Nux-v* ruta sabad *Sulph* ulm-c jsj8•
    - **painful**: ulm-c jsj8•
  - **impeded**: lob ptk1
  - **impossible**: ign br1
  - **liquids**:
    - **agg.**: ulm-c jsj8•
    - **painful**: ulm-c jsj8•
  - **not** amel.: agar androc srj1• ant-c bamb-a stb2.de• bar-c bg2 bell bg2 crot-c gels c1 hep bg2 *Kali-bi* k* lac-ac c1 **Lach** k* *Nat-m* rumx k2 *Sep*
  - **not** swallowing; when: ferr *Ign* *Nat-m* k* sulph
  - **returns** after: calc bg1 ign *Lac-c* **Lach** k* nat-m gk *Rumx*
  - **sensation**: phys ptk1
  - **solids** | **painful**: ulm-c jsj8•
- **waking**; on: carc mrr1
- **warm**:
  - **agg.**: carc mrr1 valer ptk1
  - **drinks** | **amel.**: cassia-s ccrh1•

○ - **Esophagus**: *All-c* anac arg-met c1 ars bamb-a stb2.de• bar-c bell calc *Caust* chel k* *Chin* k* *Coc-c* *Con* *Croc* der dig fago rb2 *Gels* kola stb3• lac-ac *Lob* lob-s rb2 lyc *Merc-c* naja rb2 nit-ac phos *Plb* podo ptk1 *Puls* raph rb2 rumx sabin sanic tl1 tab verat verat-v
  - **drinking** agg.; after: kola stb3•
  - **eating**; after: elaps kola stb3• *Lac-ac*
  - **hard**: lyc ptk1
  - **hot**: kola stb3•
  - **periodical**: tab
  - **stomach**; rising from: asaf tl1 con tl1
  - **swallowing** | **amel.**: phos

○ • **Cardiac** opening: abies-n br1* (non:tus-fa c1) tus-fr c1
  - **Middle** esophagus: bamb-a stb2.de• (non:chin br1) *Puls* br1*
  - **Upper** esophagus: (non:calc-act br1) coc-c rb2 lob-s rb2 ust rb2
- **Middle**: chin br1 puls br1
- **Pharynx**: calc bg2 kali-c bg2 zinc bg2
- **Posterior** part: flor-p rsj3•
- **Throat**-pit; in (See EXTERNAL - Lumps)
- **Tonsils**: hep bg2 kali-bi bg2 mag-c bg2 merc bg2 merc-i-f bg2
  - **right**: lycpr rb2

- **Upper** throat: lac-ac$_{br1}$

LYING on back: | **amel.**: lach$_{ptk1}$ spong$_{ptk1}$

MAPPED: merc-i-f$_{kr1}$

MEMBRANE: *(↗Coated; Diphtheria)* *Acet-ac* ail *Am-c* ant-t$_{k*}$ **Apis**$_{k*}$ arg-n$_{k*}$ **Ars**$_{k*}$ ars-i *Arum-t* *Bapt*$_{k*}$ bar-c bar-i$_{k2}$ bar-s$_{k2}$ bell$_{k*}$ **Brom** bry$_{k*}$ calc-p canth$_{k*}$ *Caps* *Carb-ac*$_{k*}$ caust$_{bg2}$ chin$_{bg2}$ chinin-ar$_{k2}$ chr-ac$_{br1}$ *Con* *Crot-c* *Crot-h* cupr-act *Echi* *Elaps* ferr-m$_{ptk2}$ hep ign *Iod*$_{k*}$ **Kali-bi**$_{k*}$ **Kali-chl** kali-i$_{bg3*}$ kali-m$_{bg2*}$ kali-p kali-perm *Kreos* **Lac-c**$_{k*}$ **Lach**$_{k*}$ *Lachn* **Lyc** mag-p$_{bg2}$ manc$_{ptk2}$ *Merc*$_{k*}$ *Merc-c*$_{k*}$ *Merc-cy*$_{k*}$ *Merc-i-f*$_{k*}$ *Merc-i-r*$_{k*}$ *Mur-ac*$_{k*}$ naja *Nat-ar* *Nat-m* *Nit-ac*$_{k*}$ ozone$_{sde2•}$ **Phos** **Phyt**$_{k*}$ plb$_{bg2}$ puls$_{bg2}$ **Rhus-t** sabad sal-ac *Sang* *Sec* *Sul-ac*$_{k*}$ sul-i$_{k2}$ *Sulph* tarent$_{k2}$ *Thuj* tub$_{c1}$

- **right**: *Apis* ign lac-c **Lyc** *Merc* *Merc-i-f* phyt rhus-t
▽ • **extending** to | **left**: lac-c **Lyc** *Sulph*
- **left**: bell brom crot-h$_{k*}$ lac-c **Lach** *Manc* *Merc-i-r*
  • **alternating** sides: **Lac-c**
▽ • **extending** to | **right**: lac-c **Lach** naja petr$_{k*}$ xan$_{bg1}$
- **accompanied** by:
  • **coryza**: am-c *Ars* **Arum-t**$_{k*}$ *Carb-ac* chlor crot-h *Ign* **Kali-bi**$_{k*}$ kali-perm *Lac-c* *Lach* *Lyc* *Merc-c* *Merc-cy* *Merc-i-f* *Mur-ac* **Nit-ac**$_{k*}$
○ • **Nose**; obstruction of: am-c hydr *Kali-m*$_{k*}$ *Lyc*$_{k*}$ *Merc-cy*$_{k*}$
- **blood**-streaked: kali-bi
- **bluish**: carb-ac chinin-ar lach merc-cy merc-i-r
- **brownish**: iod
- **curdy**: elaps$_{br}$ lac-c
- **dark**: bapt$_{k*}$ chinin-ar$_{k2}$ diph$_{br1}$ phyt
- **deep**-seated: ail apis kali-bi nit-ac
- **degeneration**: kreos$_{tl1}$
- **dirty**-looking: apis lac-c *Merc-c*$_{hr1}$
- **dry** and shrivelled: *Ars*$_{k*}$
- **elastic**: kali-bi
- **entire** throat: am-c ars kali-perm merc-cy
- **gray**: alumn$_{vh1}$ ant-t$_{hr1}$ apis ars$_{k2}$ carb-ac *Con* *Iod* kali-bi$_{k*}$ kali-m$_{k2}$ lac-c$_{k*}$ lach lyc merc merc-cy merc-i-f *Mur-ac* naja$_{k2}$ nat-ar nit-ac **Phyt**$_{k*}$ sanic sul-ac sul-i$_{k2}$
- **greenish**: elaps *Kali-bi* *Merc-cy*
- **irregular**: lac-c merc-i-f
- **knotty**: kali-i$_{k2}$
- **leathery**: apis$_{bg2}$ kali-n$_{h2*}$ merc-cy
- **loose**: lac-c merc-i-f merc-i-r
- **migratory**: *Lac-c*
- **patches**: canth *Kali-chl*$_{hr1}$ kali-m$_{k2}$ merc-i-r *Mur-ac*$_{hr1}$
  • **isolated**: kali-bi
  • **small** specks: ail apis *Ars*$_{bg1}$ canth iod kali-bi lac-c lach$_{bg1}$ merc-i-r
  • **white**: lach$_{bg1}$ *Mur-ac*$_{hr1}$
- **pearly**: kali-bi **Lac-c** *Sang*
- **profuse**: carb-ac lach lyc merc-c sul-ac
- **putrid**: ail$_{bg2}$ ars$_{bg2}$ ars-i$_{bg2}$ arum-t$_{bg2}$ bapt$_{k*}$ carb-ac$_{k*}$ kali-perm$_{bg2}$ lach$_{bg2}$ lyc$_{bg2}$ merc$_{bg2}$ merc-cy naja$_{bg2}$
- **scanty**: apis$_{k2}$ lach$_{k2}$ merc-i-f merc-i-r
- **sensation** of: bell$_{bg2}$ carb-v$_{ptk1}$ hydrog$_{srj2•}$ *Puls*$_{ptk1}$
- **spreading**: phyt$_{bg2}$
- **thick**: ars ars-i$_{bg2}$ diph$_{br1}$ hip-ac$_{sp1}$ iod ip$_{hr1}$ kali-bi$_{tl1}$ merc-cy$_{k2}$ sul-ac
- **thin**: lac-c merc-cy
- **transparent**: merc-i-f merc-i-r
- **varnished**, shining: *Lac-c*$_{k*}$
- **wash** leather: bapt **Phyt**$_{k*}$
- **white**: am-caust antip$_{vh1}$ *Apis* *Ars* iod ip$_{hr1}$ kali-bi$_{k*}$ **Kali-chl**$_{k*}$ kali-m$_{bg2*}$ kali-p$_{k2}$ kreos **Lac-c** *Lach* lyc *Merc* *Merc-c* *Merc-cy* merc-i-f *Mur-ac*$_{k*}$ nat-ar **Nit-ac** nux-m ox-ac petr$_{hr1}$ **Phyt** stram *Sul-ac* zinc
- **wrinkled**: **Ars**
- **yellow**: apis$_{nh4}$ kali-bi$_{k*}$ kali-s$_{mrr1}$ lac-c$_{k*}$ lach merc *Merc-cy* *Merc-i-f* **Nat-p**$_{k*}$ nit-ac rhus-t *Sul-ac* *Sulph*$_{k*}$ zinc
  • **greenish**-yellow: elaps$_{br}$ merc-i-r$_{bg2}$
▽ - **extending** to:
  • **upward**: brom$_{bg2}$
○ • **Bronchial** tubes: brom$_{k2}$
  • **Larynx**: brom **Kali-bi**

Membrane – extending to: ...
  • **Nose**: kali-bi lyc merc *Merc-c* merc-cy *Nit-ac* sulph
○ - **Fauces**: caps hip-ac$_{sp1}$ merc-cy
- **Larynx**, extending upwards: brom$_{dgt1}$
- **Pharynx**, posterior wall: *Acet-ac*$_{bro1}$ am-caust apis$_{bro1}$ brom$_{bro1}$ canth carb-ac$_{bro1}$ *Kali-bi*$_{hr1*}$ kali-m$_{bro1}$ kali-perm$_{bro1}$ *Lac-c*$_{hr1}$ lach$_{bro1}$ med$_{jl2}$ merc-cy$_{bro1}$ merc-i-f mur-ac$_{k*}$ *Nit-ac*$_{bro1}$ phyt$_{bro1}$ *Sulph*$_{k*}$
- **Tonsils**: ail am-caust *Apis* carb-ac$_{vh}$ cupr-act hip-ac$_{sp1}$ ign iod *Kali-bi* *Kali-br*$_{hr1}$ *Kali-i* kali-p *Lac-c* **Lach** **Lyc** merc merc-i-f **Nit-ac** ozone$_{sde2•}$ **Phyt** strept-ent$_{jl2}$
  • **right**: ign lac-c *Lyc* merc-i-f ozone$_{sde2•}$ rhus-t
  • **left**: lac-c **Lach** merc-i-r
  • **diphtheria**; during: phyt$_{tl1}$
- **Uvula**: *Apis* carb-ac *Kali-bi* *Kali-br*$_{hr1}$ lac-c merc-c merc-i-f *Nit-ac* petr$_{hr1}$ **Phyt**

MENSES; during: bar-c$_{ptk1}$ calc$_{ptk1}$ gels$_{ptk1}$ lac-c$_{ptk1}$ mag-c$_{ptk1}$ sulph$_{ptk1}$
○ - **Tonsils**: lac-c$_{ptk1}$

METASTASIS: | **gout**: benz-ac$_{k2}$ merc$_{k2}$

MUCOUS patches: ars-i *Fl-ac* kali-chl *Merc* *Mur-ac* *Nit-ac* phyt syph
- **gray** | **Tonsils**: kali-m$_{bro1}$
○ - **Forepart** of throat: merc$_{vh}$
- **Tonsils**: lat-m$_{sp1}$
  • **right**:
    ⁝ **accompanied** by | **Fauces**; inflammation of: merc-i-f$_{bro1}$
  • **white** or yellow shining patch: lac-c$_{bro1}$

MUCUS: acon$_{k*}$ aesc$_{k*}$ agar *Agra*$_{br1}$ aids$_{nl2•}$ ail *All-c*$_{k*}$ *Alum*$_{k*}$ alum-sil$_{k2}$ *Alumn*$_{k*}$ am-m$_{k*}$ *Ambr*$_{k*}$ *Anac*$_{k*}$ ang$_{b7.de*}$ ant-c$_{k*}$ *Ant-t*$_{k*}$ aphis apoc$_{hr1*}$ **Arg-met**$_{k*}$ **Arg-n**$_{k*}$ arn$_{k*}$ ars$_{k*}$ *Ars-i* ars-s-f$_{k2}$ arum-d$_{k*}$ *Arum-t*$_{k*}$ asar$_{k*}$ atp$_{rly4•}$ aur$_{k*}$ aur-ar$_{k2}$ aur-i$_{k2}$ aur-s$_{k2}$ *Bamb-a*$_{stb2.de•}$ bapt$_{k*}$ bar-c$_{k*}$ bar-m bell$_{k*}$ benz-ac$_{k*}$ *Berb*$_{k*}$ bism borx$_{k*}$ bov$_{k*}$ bry$_{k*}$ bufo cact$_{k*}$ *Calc*$_{k*}$ calc-ar calc-i$_{k2}$ calc-p$_{k*}$ *Calc-s*$_{k*}$ calo$_{k*}$ camph$_{b7.de*}$ caps$_{b7a.de*}$ carb-ac$_{k*}$ *Carb-an*$_{k*}$ *Carb-v*$_{k*}$ carbn-s **Caust**$_{k*}$ cench$_{k2}$ *Cer-s*$_{k*}$ *Cere-b*$_{k*}$ cham$_{b7.de*}$ chel$_{k*}$ chin$_{b7.de*}$ chir-fl$_{gya2}$ chord-umb$_{rly4•}$ cimic$_{k*}$ cina$_{b7.de*}$ *Cinnb* *Cist* coc-c$_{k2}$ cocc$_{b7.de*}$ coff$_{b7.de*}$ colch$_{k*}$ coli$_{rly4•}$ con$_{k*}$ corian-s$_{knl6•}$ croc$_{k*}$ *Crot-h* crot-t cupr cur cycl cyclosp$_{sa3•}$ cypra-eg$_{sde6.de•}$ cystein-l$_{rly4•}$ diph$_{jl2}$ dros dulc$_{k*}$ echi *Elaps* ery-a$_{k*}$ eucal$_{ptk1}$ eupi$_{k*}$ ferr-i$_{k*}$ ferr-p$_{a1}$ *Fl-ac*$_{k*}$ glon *Graph*$_{k*}$ grat$_{k*}$ guaj gymno helodr-cal$_{knl2•}$ hep$_{k*}$ hippoc-k$_{szs2}$ hydr$_{k*}$ *Hydrog*$_{srj2•}$ hyos$_{b7.de*}$ *Ign*$_{bg2}$ ind$_{k*}$ interf$_{sa3•}$ *Iod*$_{k*}$ irid-met$_{srj5•}$ jug-r$_{k*}$ kali-ar$_{k*}$ **Kali-bi**$_{k*}$ **Kali-c**$_{k*}$ kali-i$_{k*}$ kali-m$_{k2}$ *Kali-p* **Kali-s** kali-sil$_{k2}$ kalm$_{k*}$ ketogl-ac$_{rly4•}$ kiss$_{k*}$ kola$_{stb3•}$ kreos$_{k*}$ lac-ac **Lach**$_{k*}$ lact laur$_{k*}$ lob$_{k*}$ lob-s$_{k*}$ loxo-recl$_{knl4•}$ *Lyc*$_{k*}$ lyss$_{k*}$ m-ambo$_{b7.de}$ mag-c$_{k*}$ mag-m$_{k*}$ mag-s$_{k*}$ mang$_{k2}$ med$_{c1}$ melal-alt$_{gya4}$ *Merc*$_{k*}$ *Merc-c*$_{k*}$ *Merc-i-f*$_{k*}$ *Merc-i-r* *Mez*$_{k*}$ mucor$_{jl2}$ *Mur-ac*$_{k*}$ myric$_{k*}$ **Nat-ar** **Nat-c**$_{k*}$ **Nat-m**$_{k*}$ *Nat-p*$_{k*}$ *Nat-s* nat-sil$_{fd3.de•}$ *Nit-ac*$_{k*}$ nit-s-d$_{a1}$ **Nux-v**$_{k*}$ ol-an olib-sac$_{wmh1}$ op$_{k*}$ osm ox-ac$_{k*}$ oxal-a$_{rly4•}$ par$_{k*}$ petr$_{k*}$ petr-ra$_{shn4•}$ ph-ac$_{k*}$ phel$_{k*}$ *Phos*$_{k*}$ phys$_{k*}$ *Phyt*$_{k*}$ pieri-b$_{mlk9.de}$ plan$_{k*}$ *Plat*$_{k*}$ *Plb*$_{k*}$ podo$_{k*}$ positr$_{nl2•}$ *Psor*$_{k*}$ ptel$_{k*}$ *Puls*$_{k*}$ pyrog$_{jl2}$ *Ran-b*$_{k*}$ raph$_{k*}$ *Rhus-t*$_{k*}$ ribo$_{rly4•}$ *Rumx* sabad samb$_{k*}$ sang$_{k2}$ sars$_{k*}$ *Sel* *Seneg*$_{k*}$ **Sep**$_{k*}$ *Sil*$_{k*}$ sinus$_{rly4•}$ sol-t-ae$_{k*}$ *Spig*$_{k*}$ spong$_{fd4.de}$ stann$_{k*}$ *Staph*$_{bg2}$ stram$_{k*}$ streptoc$_{rly4•}$ suis-hep$_{rly4•}$ sul-ac$_{k*}$ *Sulph*$_{k*}$ sumb$_{k*}$ tab$_{k*}$ tarax$_{k*}$ teucr *Thuj*$_{k*}$ til$_{k*}$ trif-p$_{c2}$ tritic-vg$_{fd5.de}$ *Tung-met*$_{bdx1•}$ vanil$_{fd5.de}$ verat$_{k*}$ viol-t wildb xan$_{br1}$ *Zinc*$_{k*}$ zinc-p$_{k2}$ zing$_{k*}$
- **left** side: aq-mar$_{skp7•}$
- **morning**: all-s$_{k*}$ *Alum* am-m ambr androc$_{srj1•}$ apis apoc$_{vml3•}$ **Arg-met** arg-n$_{a1}$ ars$_{h2*}$ bad *Bar-c* borx bov$_{k*}$ *Calc* carbn-s *Caust* cench$_{k2}$ cer-s$_{a1}$ cimx$_{k*}$ cina$_{h1}$ *Cist* cob$_{k*}$ cupr eupi$_{k*}$ fl-ac gal-ac$_{br1}$ *Graph* hep **Kali-bi** *Kali-c* kali-p$_{k2}$ kali-s kola$_{stb3•}$ kreos lach$_{k2}$ lact laur lyc$_{k*}$ mag-c mag-m$_{k*}$ *Merc-i-f* *Nat-c* *Nat-m*$_{k*}$ nat-s nat-sil$_{fd3.de•}$ nux-v *Petr* phos plac$_{rzf5•}$ plat **Puls** rhus-t$_{k*}$ sabad sars *Sel* seneg *Sep* *Sil* spig stram$_{k*}$ suis-hep$_{rly4•}$ sulph$_{k*}$ sumb syc$_{pte1*•}$ tarax teucr *Thuj* tritic-vg$_{fd5.de}$
  • **waking**; on: *Alum* aq-mar$_{skp7•}$ carb-an cench$_{k2}$ kali-p$_{fd1.de•}$ nat-c$_{h2}$ psil$_{ft1}$ tung-met$_{bdx1•}$
- **forenoon** | **11** h: *Viol-t*
- **afternoon**: aq-mar$_{skp7•}$
  • **16** h: nat-c
- **evening**: *Alum*$_{k*}$ androc$_{srj1•}$ ang aq-mar$_{skp7•}$ bry$_{k*}$ calc-p$_{k*}$ cer-s$_{a1}$ dulc$_{fd4.de}$ hep$_{h2*}$ merl$_{k*}$ stann tritic-vg$_{fd5.de}$ vanil$_{fd5.de}$
  • **18** h: phys

Throat

- **night**: alum cyclosp sa3• duic k2 nat-c h2* nat-p *Nat-s* puls sep k* spig cp
  - **midnight**: arum-t k*
  - **waking**; on: aids nl2• alum
- **acrid**: kola stb3•
- **air** agg.; in open: carb-ac
- **albuminous**: all-c bg1 am-m borx *Caust* cench k2 ketogl-ac rly4• merc-c **Nat-m** *Nat-s* sel spig bg1 sulph
- **bed** agg.; in: iod k*
- **bitter**: am k* ars k* *Cist* cupr h2* ferr-ma k* grat merc nat-m bg2* tarax k*
- **black**: diphtox jl2 dubo-m br1 elaps bg1 sulph bg1
- **bloody**: alco a1 alum am-br k* bad bapt k2 bism k* borx cact k2 carb-v k2 cench k2 chel k* cypra-eg sde6.de• fl-ac k* *Gels* k* hep *Kali-ar* k* *Kali-perm* *Lyc* mag-c k* mag-m k* merc-c bg2 phos bg2 sars k* sel bg2* sep k* *Stann* k* thuj k*
  - **breakfast**; before | **agg.**: sabad
  - **breathing** | **hindering** breathing: aur h2
- **brown**: ol-an bg2
- **cheese**; tasting like old: psor
- **clear**: coc-c bg2 kali-i bg2 nat-m bg2 phos bg2
- **cool**: cist bg2 phos bg2* sin-n bg2
- **copious**: bapt hr1 cor-r br1 hepat br1 mang-act br1 olib-sac wmh1 rumx mrr1 syc fmm1•
  - **fever**; during: *Ant-t* b7a.de
- **coppery**: cimic bg2
- **coryza**; during: nux-v b7.de*
- **cotton**, like: aq-mar vml3•
- **creamy**:

○ • **Tonsils**:
  - ⁝ **extending** to | **Uvula** and soft palate: nat-p bro1
- **crusts** | **adherent**: elaps bro1 kali-bi bro1 kali-m bro1
- **darkish**: abrom-a ks5 bapt bg2
- **difficult** to detach: (↗*tenacious*) *Alum* am-m *Ambr* bamb-a stb2.de• cassia-s ccrh1• cench k2 cer-s a1 lac-lup hrn2• limest-b es1• *Merc-i-f* nat-sil fd3.de• olib-sac wmh1 spong fd4.de
- **dinner**; after: caust h2*
- **dirty**: ars bg2 lach bg2
- **drawn** from posterior nares: *Alum* k* *Alumn* anac ant-c *Arg-n* bamb-a stb2.de• bell k2 bry *Calc* calc-s canth carb-ac *Carb-v* *Caust* k* cench k2 chin cinnb k* **Cor-r** k* cub br1 cypra-eg sde6.de• *Elaps* euph euphr ferr-i k2 gran graph k2 *Hep* k* hydr k* *Hydrog* srj2• kali-bi k* kali-c bg2* *Kali-chl* ketogl-ac rly4• kola stb3• mag-c ptk1 med k2* merc k* merc-c merc-i-f merc-i-r mez *Nat-ar* **Nat-c** k* **Nat-m** k* nat-p nat-s hr* *Nit-ac* k* nux-v ptk1 onos osm paeon petr-ra shn4• ph-ac phyt *Plb* *Psor* k* rhus-t rumx sel ptk1 sep ptk1 sin-n **Spig** k* *Stict* sulph k* tell k* teucr bg2 thuj zinc k* zing
- **easily** discharged: *Arg-met* bamb-a stb2.de• borx h2 *Carb-v* nat-c h2* spong fd4.de
- **eating** | **after** | **agg.**: caust b4a.de tub bg*
  - **while** | **agg.**: caust nux-v k2 thuj verat
- **egg** white; like: nat-m mtf33
- **false** membrane, like: bell *Caust* diphtox jl2 puls

○ • **Tonsils** and fauces; on yellowish-red: merc bro1
  - ⁝ **dark** gangrenous; becoming: merc-cy bro1
- **foul**: alum k2 bry bg2 *Carb-v* nat-c bg2 petr bg2 *Phyt* scroph-n bg2
- **frothy**: am-caust bg1 aphis brom bry kali-bi bg2* lach bg2 plat *Sil* bg1* urt-u bg1
- **gelatinous**: *Arg-met* berb *Caust* cench k2 coc-c k2 **Kali-bi** *Nat-ar* nat-m k2 verat a1
- **gluey** (See sticky)
- **grayish**: *Ambr* k* **Arg-met** ars kali-m bg2 merc bg2 merc-cy bg2 *Nat-ar* nat-s olib-sac wmh1 phos seneg stann sulph bg1
  - **grayish** white:
    - ⁝ **Tonsils** | **cavities**; grayish white mucus in: calc-i ptk1 *Ign* bro1*
  - **grayish** yellow:
    - ⁝ **Tonsils** | **left**: merc-i-r bro1

○ • **Tonsils**:
  - ⁝ **dirty**, thick, with fiery red margins: apis bro1
  - ⁝ **thick** mucus with shred-like borders: merc bro1
  - ⁝ **extending** to:
    - **Posterior** nares and air passages | **purple**-black; and becoming: echi bro1
- **greenish**: ail androc srj1• ars atp rly4• borx cere-b a1 *Colch* k* dros *Lyc* nat-m h2* *Sil* *Stann* k* sumb k* zinc
- **hanging** down: (↗*Hanging in - mucus*) *Carb-an* k* kali-s fd4.de lach med c1 *Merc-c* nat-s hr phos thuj
- **hindering** breathing: aur h2
- **lumps**: *Agar* *Alum* sne androc srj1• merc-i-f bg1 ol-an bg2 olib-sac wmh1 plac rzf5• positr nl2• seneg sin-n br1 teucr bg2 *Zinc* bg1*
  - **eating**; after: merc-i-r bg2
  - **sensation**: ars h2 bamb-a stb2.de• kali-s fd4.de
- **metallic** taste: calc k* kali-bi bg2
- **offensive**: am-c gsy1 aq-mar skp7• bry bg1* *Carb-v* kali-bi bg2 *Lach* bg2 mag-c bg2* mur-ac bg1* psor *Sil* sulph bg2 thuj
- **plugs** of mucus:

○ • **Tonsils** | **cavities**; plugs of mucus in: calc-f bro1
- **putrid**: bapt k2 *Carb-ac* cham bg1 kali-p k2 podo fd3.de•
- **qualmishness**, during: *Graph*
- **rattling**: ambr bg2 *Ign* bg2 *Nux-v* bg2 par bg2 podo bg2* *Puls* bg2 sabad bg2
  - **accompanied** by | **Stomach**; complaints of (See STOMACH - Complaints - accompanied - throat)
- **red** as blood: thuj
- **ropy** (See stringy; tenacious)
- **saltish**: alum k* am-m anac bg1 ars *Calc* *Carbn-s* kali-i bg2 kali-p *Lach* bg2* merc *Nat-m* k* *Nat-s* k* nux-v bg2* phos k* sil sulph k* tell bg2* ther
- **sensation** of: chir-fl gya2 cot c1 dulc fd4.de eupi c1 grat hydrog srj2• mez pen bg1 psil ft1* **Rhod** tub c1 [heroin sdj2]
- **sour**: crot-t laur mag-m h2* mag-s phos plb bg2* tarax bg2* teucr
- **sticky**: aq-mar skp7• bad *Caust* ol-an bg2 pall ptk1 pitu-gl skp7• *Psor* jl2
  - **cough**; with: pitu-gl skp7•
- **stringy**: (↗*tenacious*) dubo-m br1 *Get* br1 *Kali-bi* br1*
- **sudden**: tung-met bdx1•
- **swallow**:
  - **must** be swallowed: **Caust** falco-pe nl2• mag-c h2 mur-ac h2 ruta fd4.de zinc h2
  - **neither** be swallowed nor hawked up; can: am-m h2 bamb-a stb2.de• falco-pe nl2• kali-c h2 mag-s ribo rly4•
- **sweetish**: aesc k* all-c cop kali-bi bg2 lach k* laur bg2 limest-b es1• mag-p bg2 podo fd3.de• sabad k* sumb k*
- **tenacious**: (↗*difficult; stringy*) aesc k* agn k* alco a1 *All-c* k* aloe bro1 *Alum* k* alum-p k2 alum-sil k2 am-br k* am-m k* ambr k* *Anac* k* ant-c k* ant-t a1 *Apis* k* aq-pet a1 **Arg-met** **Arg-n** k* arn arum-t k* asar k* bamb-a stb2.de• bapt bg2* **Bar-c** k* bar-m k2 *Bell* k* berb k* *Borx* bry k* bufo *Calc* calc-ar calc-sil k2 canth k* caps carb-ac *Carb-v* k* carbn-s **Caust** k* cench k2 cer-s a1 chinin-s chr-ac a1 chr-met dx cimic cimx *Cinnb* k* *Cist* k* clem coc-c bg2* coca bro1 cop k* cycl cypra-eg sde6.de• dulc euphr bro1 falco-pe nl2• ferr-i ferr-m graph k* grat hom-xyz br1 hydr bg2* iber bro1 ind k* iod k* irid-met srj5• **Kali-bi** k* *Kali-c* k* kali-m k2 kali-p fd1.de• kola stb3• lac-h htj1• *Lach* k* lact k* laur k* lil-s a1 lith-c lob k* lob-s a1 lyc lyss k* *Mag-c* k* *Mag-m* k* mag-p bg2 *Mag-s* med k2 merc merc-c k* *Merc-i-f* k* merc-i-r k* mez moni rfm1• *Mur-ac* musca-d szs1 *Myric* k* naja nat-ar nat-c k* nat-m bro1 nat-p **Nat-s** k* nat-sil fd3.de• *Nux-v* k* ol-an k* onos ox-ac paeon k* pall petr bro1 *Ph-ac* k* phos k* **Phyt** k* plan k* *Plb* k* podo fd3.de• positr nl2• *Psor* k* *Puls* k* ran-b k* raph *Rhus-t* k* *Rumx* k* *Sabad* sang bro1 sanic tl1 sars k* *Sel* bro1 *Seneg* k* sep k* **Sil** k* silphu bro1 spong fd4.de *Stann* k* sul-ac k* sumb k* tab k* *Thuj* verat k* xan c1 zinc
  - **morning**: *Alum* *Apis* *Arg-met* bar-c k* berb hr1 cupr k* **Kali-bi** k* kali-c h2* lact k* mag-m k* petr hr1 **Puls** k* sars k* seneg sumb k*
  - **evening**: alum k* ran-b k*
  - **night**: dulc k2 **Puls**
  - **swallowing** does not amel.: kola stb3•
  - **thick** yellowish-brown like wash leather, pearly | **extending** to tonsils and soft palate: kali-bi bro1
  - **white** | **Uvula**: am-caust bro1
- **thick**: aesc aloe alum k* am-br a1 *Anac* androc srj1• ant-c apis apoc k2 *Arg-met* **Arg-n** k* bar-s k2 *Bell* k* berb bry calc bg1* calc-s k2 caps carb-ac **Caust** cench k2 chir-fl gya2 cimic *Cist* cur cystein-l rly4• dulc k2 ery-a a1 fago a1 *Glon* k* grat hydr k2 hydrog srj2• ind hr1 **Kali-bi** k* kali-i kali-m k2 ketogl-ac rly4• kola stb3• lac-ac hr1 *Mag-c* mag-m k* merc *Nat-ar* **Nat-c** nat-m k* nat-p nat-s hr nicc k* nux-m olib-sac wmh1 petr h2* *Phyt* k* plb positr nl2• prot jl2 psor ran-s k* sanic tl1 *Sil* sin-n br1 stann suis-hep rly4• sumb k* tung-met bdx1• [heroin sdj2]

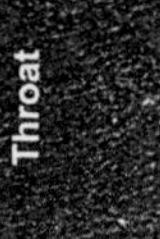

- • **morning**: apoc a1 mag-m k* petr h2* *Sil*
- • **dark** gray or brownish-black | **Tonsils**: diph bro1
- **tough** (See tenacious)
- **viscid** (See tenacious)
- **watery**: aesc k* aids nl2• arist-cl rbp3• chel k* cystein-l rly4• hepat br1 laur k* nat-m mtf33 olib-sac wmh1 thuj
  - • **morning**: spig thuj
- **weather** agg.; wet: mang k2
- **white**: am-br k* am-m *Bell* k* berb *Borx* carb-ac **Caust** k* cob k* hydrog srj2• kali-chl lach k* mag-c merc-c *Merc-i-r* nat-ar **Nat-m** k* nat-p *Nat-s* nux-v raph sel seneg k* spig sul-i k2 sulph
  - • **morning**: chr-ac a1 spig
  - • **milk** white: kali-chl kali-m k2
- **yellow**: aesc alum k2 androc srj1• ant-c apoc k* berb k* bry bg2 *Calc Calc-s* castm cench k2 *Cist* cop dros eug hydr k* ind hr1 **Kali-bi** k* lac-ac hr1 lach k* *Nat-ar* nat-p nat-s hr nat-sil fd3.de• nux-v ol-j olib-sac wmh1 petr-ra shn4• plac rzf5• rumx *Sil* spig stann bg2 staphycoc rly4• suis-hep rly4• sul-i k2 sumb k* verat a1 [heroin sdj2]
  - • **morning**: spig
  - • **forenoon**: lyc
  - O • **Lower** part: alum graph zinc
  - • **Uvula**: sep h2
- O - **Anterior** part: coli rly4• merc bg1
- **Fauces**: psor mtf11
  - • **viscid**: psor mtf11
- **Posterior** nares: am-c bg2

NARROW: (↗*Choking*) acon b7.de* *Alum* b4.de* *Arg-met* b7.de* arg-n bg2 arn bg2 ars b4.de* asaf b7.de* bapt bg2 **Bell** b4.de* bry bg2 *Calc* b4.de* caps b7a.de* carb-v bg2 *Caust* b4.de* chel b7.de* chin b7.de* *Cic* b7.de* cund bg2 *Dros* bg2 hyos b7.de* lach b7a.de* lyc bg2 merc b4.de* mez b4.de* *Nat-m* b4.de* nux-v bg2 phos b4.de* *Puls* bg2 *Rhus-t* b7a.de* rumx bg2 sabad b7.de* sang bg2 stram b7.de* stront-c bg2 **Sulph** b4.de* verat b7.de* zinc b4a.de

- **sensation**: (↗*Choking*) acon k* *Alum* k* alumn arum-m a1 arum-t a1* **Bell** k* bry k* *Calc* k* *Carb-v* b4a.de *Caust* k* chin k* cic b7.de* *Dros* b7a.de elaps fkr8.de ham fd3.de• kali-p fd1.de• merc merc-c b4a.de *Mez* nat-m nicotam rly4• *Nux-v* k* ozone sde2• petr-ra shn4• phos puls b7.de* pyrid rly4• rhus-t k* sabad hr1 sin-a a1 suis-hep rly4• sulph k* tere-la rly4• zinc b4a.de [heroin sdj2]
  - • **night**: ham fd3.de• phos h2*
  - • **cough** agg.; during: calc sne coc-c k*
  - • **swallowing** agg.: **Bell** k* *Calc* k* ham fd3.de• lyc h2* puls h1*

NAUSEA in the throat (See STOMACH - Nausea - throat)

NECROSIS: | **Fauces**: merc-cy bro1

NODOSITIES: lach bg2
O - **Tonsils**: ign bg2

NUMBNESS: (↗*Anesthesia*) acon k* all-c arg-met k* bapt bg2* bar-c bg2 bov bg2* gels *Kali-br* k* kali-c kali-cy gm1 ketogl-ac rly4• mag-s nit-ac bg2* olnd k* sep bg2* tung-met bdx1• verat-v

- **right**: plut-n srj7•
- O - **Tonsil** | **right**: sep h2

OBSTRUCTION: anan androc srj1• atra-r bnm3• calc k* *Con* k* iod h* kali-bi kali-i k* merc-c k* mur-ac ozone sde2• puls k* pyrus stict c1 sumb k* visc c1

- **morning**: mag-c k*
- **chronic**: vip bg2*
- **swallowing** agg.: arund k* *Calc* k* elaps nat-s k*
- **waking**; on: led k*
- O - **Esophagus** | **drinking** agg.: glycyr-g cte1•
- **Tonsils**; from swelling of: **Bar-c** mrr1

PAIN: absin ↓ acal ↓ acon k* acon-f ↓ act-sp ↓ adam ↓ *Aesc* k* *Aeth* ↓ agar agath-a nl2• aids nl2• *Ail* ↓ alco ↓ all-c bg2* allox tpw4 aln ↓ aloe *Alum* k* alum-p ↓ alum-sil ↓ *Alumn Am-br* ↓ am-c am-caust ↓ am-m k* ambr b7.de* ammc ↓ amp ↓ *Anac* ↓ *Anan Androc* ↓ ant-c k* ant-t ↓ anth ↓ (non:anthraci slp) anthraco slp anthraq ↓ antip ↓ *Apis* aq-mar ↓ arag br1 arg-met **Arg-n** k* arge-pl rwt5• arizon-l ↓ *Arn* ↓ ars k* ars-h ↓ ars-i ars-s-f k2 arum-d ptk2 arum-m ↓ **Arum-t** k* asaf *Asar* ↓ asc-c ↓ asc-t ↓ asim ↓ aspar ↓ astac ↓ aster ↓ atp ↓ atra-r ↓ atro ↓ aur ↓ aur-ar ↓ aur-i ↓ aur-m k* aur-s ↓

Pain: ...
Bac ↓ *Bamb-a* stb2.de• **Bapt** k* bar-c b4a.de* bar-i ↓ bar-m k* bar-s ↓ **Bell** k* bell-p ↓ *Benz-ac* berb k* beryl ↓ *Bism* ↓ bit-ar wht1• bol-la ↓ bol-s ↓ bomb-pr ↓ bond ↓ borx ↓ bov k* brach ↓ brass-n-o ↓ brom k* bros-gau ↓ *Brucel* sa3• bry k* *Bufo* ↓ cadm-met tpw6 cadm-s ↓ cain ↓ caj ↓ *Calad* ↓ *Calc* k* calc-f k2 calc-i ↓ calc-p k* *Calc-s* calc-sil ↓ *Camph* ↓ cann-i ↓ cann-s k* canth k* **Caps** k* carb-ac carb-an k* carb-v k* carbn-s carc ↓ cardios-h ↓ carl ↓ cartl-s ↓ cassia-s ↓ castm ↓ caul *Caust* k* cedr ↓ celt ↓ cench k2 ceph ↓ cham k* chel chin b7.de* chin-b ↓ chinin-ar ↓ chinin-s chir-fl gya2 chlf ↓ chlol ↓ chlor ↓ choc ↓ chord-umb ↓ chr-o ↓ cic ↓ *Cimic* ↓ cinch ↓ cinnb *Cist* ↓ clem ↓ cob ↓ coc-c k* coca-c ↓ cocc b7.de* coch ↓ cod ↓ *Coff* colch k* coli ↓ coloc colum-p sze2• *Con* cop corian-s ↓ corn ↓ cortico ↓ cortiso ↓ corv-cor ↓ croc ↓ *Crot-c Crot-h* crot-t cub ↓ cund ↓ *Cupr* k* cupr-act ↓ cupr-ar ↓ cupr-s ↓ cur ↓ cycl k* cypra-eg ↓ cystein-l rly4• cyt-l ↓ delphin ↓ *Dig* ↓ digox ↓ dios ↓ diph-pert-t mp4• dirc ↓ dol c1* dor ↓ dream-p ↓ dros ↓ *Dulc* k* echi ↓ ephe-si hsj1• epil c1 erio ↓ eucal ↓ eug ↓ eup-per ↓ eup-pur ↓ **Euph** ↓ euph-a ↓ fago k* falco-pe ↓ ferr k* ferr-ar ↓ ferr-i ferr-m ↓ ferr-ma ↓ ferr-p ↓ ferul ↓ fic-m ↓ *Fl-ac* ↓ flor-p ↓ form ↓ fum ↓ fuma-ac rly4• gala br1 galla-q-r ↓ gamb ↓ gels bg2 gent-c ↓ gent-l ↓ ger ↓ germ-met ↓ get ↓ gink-b ↓ gins ↓ glon ↓ granit-m ↓ graph k* grat bg2* *Guaj* ↓ gymno ↓ haem ↓ haliae-lc ↓ ham k* helia ↓ helio ↓ hell ↓ hell-o ↓ helodr-cal knl2• *Hep* k* hepat ↓ hera ↓ heroin ↓ hip-ac ↓ hipp ↓ hippoc-k ↓ hir ↓ *Hom-xyz* ↓ *Hura* ↓ hura-c c1 hydr ↓ hydr-ac ↓ hydrc ↓ *Hydrog* srj2• hydroph ↓ hyos b7.de* hyosin ↓ *Ign* k* ignis-alc ↓ ina-i mlk9.de ind ↓ iod k* ip b7.de* irid-met srj5• iris ↓ iris-fl jab ↓ jac-c ↓ jac-g ↓ jal ↓ jatr-c jug-c ↓ kali-ar *Kali-bi* k* *Kali-c Kali-chl* k* *Kali-i* kali-m k2 kali-n k* kali-ox ↓ kali-p kali-perm *Kali-s* kali-sil ↓ kali-sula ↓ kalm ketogl-ac rly4• kola ↓ kreos k* lac-ac *Lac-c* lac-d k2 lac-del hrn2• lac-e ↓ lac-h sk4• lac-loxod-a ↓ lac-v-f ↓ **Lach** k* lachn ↓ lap-la sde8.de• laur k* *Led* ↓ lepi ↓ lil-s ↓ lil-t ↓ limest-b ↓ lipp a1 lob ↓ lob-c ↓ lob-s ↓ lol ↓ loxo-recl bnm10*• luf-op rsj5• *Luna* ↓ *Lyc* k* lycpr ↓ lyss k* m-arct ↓ m-aust ↓ *Mag-c* ↓ *Mag-m* ↓ mag-s k* maias-l ↓ manc ↓ mang ↓ med ↓ melal-alt gya4 menth ↓ meny ↓ *Merc* k* merc-act ↓ merc-br ↓ *Merc-c* k* *Merc-cy* ↓ merc-d ↓ merc-i-f k* merc-i-r k* merc-n ↓ merc-sul a1 merl k* mez k* mill ↓ mim-p rsj8• moni rfm1• morg-p ↓ mosch ↓ mur-ac h2* musca-d ↓ myos-a rly4• myric ↓ myris ↓ nad ↓ naja nat-ar *Nat-c* ↓ *Nat-m* k* nat-ox rly4• nat-p ↓ nat-pyru rly4• nat-s ↓ nat-sil ↓ neon ↓ nicc k* nicotam rly4• *Nit-ac* k* nit-m-ac ↓ *Nux-m* ↓ nux-v k* nymph ↓ oci-sa sk4• oena ↓ ol-an ↓ olib-sac wmh1 olnd ↓ onos ↓ op ↓ orot-ac ↓ ovi-p ↓ ox-ac k* oxal-a ↓ ozone ↓ paeon ↓ pall pant-ac ↓ par paull ↓ pen ↓ peti a1 *Petr* ↓ petr-ra shn4• ph-ac k* phel ↓ *Phos* k* *Phos-pchl* c1 phys ↓ *Phyt* k* pic-ac ↓ plac rzf5• plac-s rly4• plan a1 plat k* plb ↓ plect ↓ plumbg a1 plut-n ↓ podo ↓ polyp-p ↓ polys ↓ pop-cand ↓ positr ↓ pot-e rly4• prin ↓ *Propr* sa3• prun-p ↓ psor k* ptel ↓ puls b7.de* pycnop-sa ↓ quill ↓ rad-br ↓ ran-b k2 ran-s ↓ raph ↓ rat ↓ rauw ↓ rhod b4.de* rhus-g ↓ **Rhus-t** k* rhus-v ribo rly4• ric ↓ rob ↓ rosm lgb1 rumx k* rumx-act ↓ ruta *Sabad* sabal ↓ sabin sacch-a ↓ sal-ac ↓ sal-al ↓ sal-fr ↓ samb ↓ sang hr1 sangin-n br1 sanic ↓ sapin ↓ *Sapo* ↓ sarcol-ac ↓ sars b4.de* scarl jl2 *Sec* ↓ sel ↓ seneg *Sep* k* **Sil** k* sin-a ↓ sinus rly4• sol-ni ↓ sol-t-ae ↓ solid ↓ **Spect** ↓ spig ↓ spira ↓ spirae ↓ spong fd4.de *Squil* ↓ stann h2* *Staph* ↓ stict ↓ **Still** ↓ stram k2 streptoc ↓ stront-c b4.de* stry a1 succ-ac ↓ suis-em rly4• suis-hep rly4• suis-pan rly4• sul-ac k* sul-i ↓ *Sulph* k* sumb ↓ syc ↓ symph ↓ *Syph* ↓ *Tab* ↓ tarax ↓ tarent k* tart-ac ↓ tax ↓ tell tep a1 ter ↓ tere-la ↓ teucr k* ther ↓ thiam rly4• thres-a sze7• thuj b4.de* thymu br1 thyr ↓ til ↓ trif-p ↓ tritic-vg fd5.de tub jl2 *Tung-met* bdx1• tus-p ↓ upa ↓ uran-n ↓ urol-h ↓ urt-u ↓ ust ↓ vanil fd5.de ven-m rsj12• verat k* verat-v bg2 *Vero-o* rly3• vesp ↓ vinc ↓ vip k* visc ↓ wye ↓ xan ↓ *Zinc* k* zinc-i ↓ zinc-m a1 zinc-p ↓ zinc-s ↓ zing ↓ ziz ↓ [bell-p-sp dcm1 buteo-j sej6 ferr-s stj1]

- **alternating** sides: lac-c k2*
  - • **sore**: **Lac-c**
- **right**: aids nl2• am-c *Arg-n* k* ars sne arum-t sne aur-m-n wbt2• *Bar-m Bell* ↓ calc-p sne carb-ac ↓ carb-v k* cassia-s ↓ cench k2 chir-fl gya2 chord-umb ↓ crot-c sk4• dendr-pol sk4• dol br1 dulc fd4.de ferr-ma ↓ ferr-p sne fic-m gya1 galla-q-r nl2• gamb sne guaj sf1.de ham sne helo sne hep sne heroin ↓ hydrog srj2• ina-i mlk9.de ind sne iod k* irid-met srj5• jug-c hr1 kali-p kali-s fd4.de kola stb3• *Lac-c* sne lac-h ↓ *Lach* sne lap-la rsp1 lith-c sne **Lyc** k* lyss sne mag-c sne mag-p ↓ melal-alt gya4 meph k* *Merc* sne *Merc-i-f* myric sne nad ↓ nat-p k2 nicc bg1 ozone sde2• petr-ra ↓ phyt k* plat podo ↓ positr nl2• pot-e ↓ ptel sne ruta fd4.de sal-fr ↓ sang hr1 sars sne sol-ni sne stann ↓ staphycoc rly4• suis-hep ↓ tarent ↓ ter sne tritic-vg fd5.de urol-h rwt• ust sne v-a-b jl vanil fd5.de ven-m ↓ wye sne xan c1 [buteo-j sej6 tax jsj7]

- **sore**: ars *Bell* calc-p carb-ac chir-fl gya2 chord-umb rly4• fic-m gya1 ham ind k* irid-met srj5• *Lac-c* lith-c **Lyc** k* lyss mag-c k* mag-p br1 *Merc* merc-i-f nad rly4• nat-p k* nicc k* petr-ra shn4• phyt plat h2* podo fd3.de• pot-e rly4• ptel sal-fr sle1• sars suis-hep rly4• tarent ter ven-m rsj12• xan k* [heroin sdj2]
- **stitching** pain: am-c k* cassia-s ccrh1• cench k2 ferr-ma a1 *Gamb* k* irid-met srj5• lac-h sk4• sars h2* stann h2* tarent bg1 [tax jsj7]

▽ • **extending** to:
  - **left**: all-c bg1 *Arum-t*↓ bar-c↓ cypra-eg sde6.de• **Lyc**↓ **Merc-i-f** k2 petr c1 *Podo*↓ *Sulph*↓ syph xxb
    - **sore**: *Arum-t* bar-c **Lyc** merc-i-f ptk2 *Podo Sulph*

- **left**: aids nl2• allox sp1 amp↓ antip↓ aq-mar skp7• arum-t sne atra-r↓ bamb-a stb2.de• bell sne brom k* bruc↓ carneg-g rwt1• cench sne choc sne cimic a1 crot-c sk4• *Crot-h* cupr sst3• dios sne dream-p sdj1• dulc↓ echi sne elaps gk falco-pe nl2• form sne fuma-ac↓ germ-met srj5• gink-b sbd1• glon sne grat sne heroin↓ hydrog srj2• hydroph rsj6• kali-bi sne kali-i↓ kali-n sne kali-p sne ketogl-ac↓ kola stb3• *Lac-c* sne lac-del hm2• **Lach** k* limen-b-c mlk9.de mag-c sne mag-m sne manc sne melal-alt gya4 merc-i-r k2* mim-p rsj8• moni rfm1• myos-a rly4• naja k* nat-c sne nat-m sne nicc sne osteo-a knp1• petr-ra shn4• ph-ac h2* plb sne podo↓ positr nl2• *Propr* sa3• psil sne psor sne ptel sne rumx sne ruta fd4.de sabad↓ *Sec* sne sel↓ sep k* sil a1 sinus↓ spong fd4.de staph sne sul-ac h2* sulph sne tax↓ tell↓ teucr k* thioc-ac↓ thyr sne tritic-vg fd5.de tub dp* vanil fd5.de ven-m rsj12• verat h1* zinc sne [arg-met stj1]
  - **burning**: allox tpw3* antip vh1 bruc tpw3
  - **sore**: aids nl2• amp rly4• atra-r skp7*• choc srj3• *Crot-h* echi *Form* fuma-ac rly4• hydrog srj2• kali-bi ketogl-ac rly4• *Lac-c* lac-del hrn2• **Lach** manc melal-alt gya4 merc-i-r k* *Naja* ph-ac k* rumx sabad *Sec* sel rsj9• sinus rly4• *Sul-ac* tell rsj10• thioc-ac rly4• tritic-vg fd5.de ven-m rsj12• [heroin sdj2]
  - **stitching** pain: arum-t k* bell bg1 cupr bg1 dulc fd4.de gink-b sbd1• glon bg1 grat bg1 kali-bi k* kali-i a1 kali-n h2* mag-c k* mag-m h2* melal-alt gya4 nat-c k* nat-m h2* podo fd3.de• psor bg1 sil bg1 staph br sul-ac h2* sulph bg2 tub xxb vanil fd5.de [tax jsj7]
  - **tearing** pain: zinc h2*
  - **waking**; on: galeoc-c-h gms1• melal-alt gya4 samb↓
    - **sore**: galeoc-c-h gms1• samb bat1•

▽ • **extending** to:
  - **right**: acon bg1 hydrog↓ **Lach** k2 lap-la sde8.de• plb↓ ruta fd4.de sabad k2 ven-m↓ xan bg1
    - **sore**: hydrog srj2• **Lach** plb *Sabad* ven-m rsj12•
  - **Ear**: *Sec*↓
    - **sore**: *Sec*
  - **Ears**: germ-met srj5• tub jl2 vanil fd5.de
    - **swallowing** agg.: tub jl2

- **daytime**: dulc↓ **Lach**↓ lyss k* nit-ac↓ pant-ac rly4• ped↓
  - **amel.**: sarcol-ac sp1
  - **burning**: lyss k*
  - **pressing** pain: dulc fd4.de nit-ac k*
  - **sore**: **Lach** k* lyss k* ped a1

- **morning**●: all-c↓ aloe↓ alum alum-p k2 alumn↓ am-c am-m↓ ambr k2 arg-n↓ arum-d↓ *Arum-t*↓ bamb-a stb2.de• berb bov↓ bry↓ cadm-met↓ calc-p *Carb-an*↓ carb-v↓ carc↓ carneg-g rwt1• cartl-s↓ cassia-s↓ caust chel↓ chinin-s cinnb↓ cist cob↓ coc-c↓ colch↓ dios↓ dulc fd4.de fl-ac↓ *Form*↓ gink-b sbd1• graph ham↓ hep↓ kali-bi k* kali-n↓ kali-s↓ kola stb3• *Lach* k* limen-b-c mlk9.de luna↓ lyc k* mez↓ mur-ac↓ myric↓ naja nat-c↓ nat-m h2* nat-sil↓ nicc nicotam rly4• nux-v↓ ox-ac petr-ra shn4• ph-ac↓ phos k* phyt↓ podo↓ polys↓ propl ub1• ptel↓ puls↓ *Rhus-t* k* ruta fd4.de sacch-a fd2.de• sars↓ sil↓ spong fd4.de stann↓ stront-c sk4• sul-i k2 sulph↓ symph fd3.de• taosc iwa1• tong↓ tritic-vg fd5.de urol-h rwt• ust↓ vanil fd5.de zinc↓
  - **7** h: bamb-a↓ sep↓
    - **sore**: bamb-a stb2.de• sep
  - **8-9** h: aloe↓
    - **pressing** pain: aloe
  - **amel.**: crot-c sk4•

- **morning**: ...
  - **burning**: *Arum-t* k* *Carb-an* k* coc-c k* gink-b sbd1• ham fd3.de• *Kali-bi* kali-s fd4.de* lyc k* mur-ac petr-ra shn4• podo fd3.de• sulph k* tritic-vg fd5.de
  - **pressing** pain: aloe am-c k* bamb-a stb2.de• caust k* dulc fd4.de graph k* ham fd3.de• lach naja phos k* vanil fd5.de
  - **raw**; as if: all-c aloe alum am-m k* ambr k2 arum-d a1 bov k* *Carb-an* caust k* fl-ac kola stb3• mez k* mur-ac k* polys sk4• puls k* sars stann k* stront-c tong a1 zinc k*
  - **rising** agg.: graph↓ kali-n↓ ptel↓ symph↓
    - **pressing** pain: graph k*
    - **stitching** pain: graph h2 kali-n ptel symph fd3.de•
  - **sore**: alum k* arg-n k* bov k* bry k* cadm-met sp1 *Calc-p* k* carb-an carb-v carc mg1.de* cartl-s rly4• chel k* cinnb *Cist* k* cob k* colch rsj2• dios k* dulc fd4.de *Form* k* luna kg1• lyc h2* myric nat-m k* nat-sil fd3.de• nux-v sne ph-ac k* phos k* phyt k* polys sk4• puls k* sil k* sul-i k* ust k*
  - **stitching** pain: alum h2 alumn cassia-s ccrh1• gink-b sbd1• hep k* kali-n k* nat-c k* nicc k* ph-ac h2* ptel k* ruta fd4.de sars a1 vanil fd5.de
  - **swallowing**; when not: puls↓
    - **sore**: puls k*
  - **tearing** pain: phos
  - **waking**; on●: aids nl2• androc srj1• arg-n↓ aster↓ bov↓ cadm-met↓ calc-p↓ cartl-s↓ caust celt↓ chel↓ dioxi rbp6 fic-m↓ hydr↓ hydrog srj2• irid-met↓ kali-bi kola stb3• lac-h↓ *Lac-leo*↓ *Lach* k* petr-ra↓ plac rzf5• rauw↓ rhus-t sacch-a fd2.de• sal-fr↓ symph fd3.de• *Trios* rsj1• tritic-vg↓ tung-met bdx1• vanil fd5.de [bell-p-sp dcm1]
    - **burning**: rauw sp1*
    - **pressing** pain: caust k*
    - **sore**: arg-n k* aster k* bov k* cadm-met sp1 calc-p k* cartl-s rly4• celt a1 chel k* fic-m gya1 hydr k* hydrog srj2• irid-met srj5• lac-h htj1• *Lac-leo* hrn2• petr-ra shn4• sal-fr sle1• tritic-vg fd5.de
    - **stitching** pain: lac-h htj1•

- **forenoon**: aesc↓ bol-la↓ cic↓ colch↓ dulc↓ flor-p↓ jug-c↓ led↓ mag-c↓ ozone sde2• rhod↓ ruta↓ spong↓ symph↓ vanil↓
  - **10** h: lyss↓ propr sa3•
    - **sore**: lyss
  - **burning**: cic k* rhod spong k* symph fd3.de•
  - **raw**; as if: bol-la mag-c k*
  - **sore**: aesc k* colch rsj2• dulc fd4.de jug-c k* ruta fd4.de vanil fd5.de
  - **stitching** pain: flor-p rsj3• led h1*

- **noon**: dulc fd4.de phos k* rhus-t↓ sacch-a fd2.de• tritic-vg↓
  - **amel.**: cassia-s↓
    - **stitching** pain: cassia-s ccrh1•
  - **burning**: dulc fd4.de rhus-t k* tritic-vg fd5.de

- **afternoon**: canth kr1 chinin-s dios↓ fago a1 kali-p↓ naja nat-c↓ nux-v↓ op↓ opun-s↓ phys↓ ptel↓ ruta fd4.de spong fd4.de suis-em↓ tritic-vg fd5.de
  - **16** h: *Arum-t*↓
    - **sore**: *Arum-t*
  - **17** h: caust↓ ozone sde2• tritic-vg↓ ulm-c↓
    - **burning**: caust h2 tritic-vg fd5.de ulm-c jsj8•
    - **sore**: caust
  - **sleep**; after: aq-mar skp7•
  - **sore**: canth dios k* op k* opun-s a1 phys k* ptel k* suis-em rly4• tritic-vg fd5.de
  - **stitching** pain: kali-p k2 nat-c k* nux-v a1

- **evening**: adam skp7• *Alum* am-c h2* androc↓ ars k* ars-s-f k2 atra-r↓ bar-c↓ beryl sp1 bol-la↓ bov↓ brach↓ calc-p↓ *Carb-an*↓ *Carb-v*↓ carc mg1.de* cassia-s↓ caust h2* chin sne chlor↓ choc↓ dig↓ dios↓ dulc fd4.de flor-p↓ ham↓ *Hep* hipp a1 hydrog srj2• ina-i mlk9.de ind↓ kali-bi↓ kali-i kali-p↓ kali-s↓ lac-h↓ lac-loxod-a↓ lac-lup hm2• lact lith-c↓ luna↓ mag-c↓ mag-m mang↓ mez↓ mill↓ nat-c↓ nat-m h2* nat-sil fd3.de• nicc k* nit-ac ox-ac↓ ped↓ *Phos*↓ plat sne podo↓ puls raph k* rhus-t↓ ruta fd4.de sabad sne sil↓ sinus↓ stann↓ stront-c sk4• sul-ac sulph sne symph fd3.de• tell↓ tritic-vg fd5.de vanil↓ viol-t zinc↓
  - **18-20** h: aq-mar skp7•
  - **22** h: plut-n↓
    - **burning**: plut-n srj7•

- **amel.**: chinin-s a
- **burning**: alum k* beryl tpw5 carb-an h2* carc fd2.de• dig h2* dulc fd4.de kali-s fd4.de nat-sil fd3.de• ox-ac k* podo fd3.de• rhus-t k* sulph k* tritic-vg fd5.de
- **pressing** pain: alum h2* dulc fd4.de ham fd3.de• *Hep* k* nit-ac k*
- **raw**; as if: alum bol-la bov k* brach k* chlor a1 ham k* kali-bi k* lac-h htj1• mag-m h2* mang k* nat-c k* *Phos* k* sulph k* zinc k*
- **sore**: am-c k* androc srj1• atra-r skp7*• beryl tpw5 bov k* brach k* calc-p k* carb-an h2* *Carb-v* k* carc sp1 choc srj3• dios k* dulc fd4.de flor-p rsj3• ham k* ind k* kali-p lac-h htj1• lac-loxod-a hrn2• lith-c luna kg1• mez k* nat-m k* nat-sil fd3.de• ped a1 podo k* sinus rly4• stann k* *Sul-ac* k* tell k* tritic-vg fd5.de vanil fd5.de viol-t k* zinc
- **stitching** pain: alum bar-c *Carb-an* k* cassia-s ccrh1• chin k* dulc fd4.de mag-c h2* mag-m h2* mill a1 nat-c h2* ruta fd4.de sil k* sul-ac k* sulph
- **ulcerative** pain: cassia-s cdd7•

- **night●**: adam skp7• aids nl2• aloe hr *Alum* am-m *Anac*↓ arg-n k* bac wz bamb-a stb2.de• **Bar-c**↓ bism hr1 calc-f k2 camph canth carb-an↓ carc↓ cassia-s↓ chir-fl gya2 cimic hr1 *Cinnb* crot-c sk4• crot-h↓ cycl k* dream-p sdj1• dulc fd4.de erig↓ gink-b sbd1• graph ham↓ hir↓ ina-i mlk9.de kali-n ketogl-ac↓ lac-c kr1 lac-h↓ lavand-a ctl1• mag-m mag-s manc↓ *Merc* mur-ac↓ nat-c↓ nat-m↓ nux-v↓ phyt podo↓ positr↓ ruta fd4.de sarcol-ac sp1 sars↓ sil sne spira↓ suis-em rly4• sulph sumb↓ symph fd3.de• *Trios* rsj11• tritic-vg fd5.de vanil fd5.de zinc bg
  - **midnight**: *Arum-t*↓ kali-bi↓ nat-sil↓
    - **before**: sal-al blc1•
    - **after**:
      - **2** h: atra-r skp7•
        - **sore**: atra-r skp7*•
      - **5** h: bros-gau mrc1
    - **burning**: *Arum-t* k* kali-bi k* nat-sil fd3.de•
  - **bed** agg.; in: arg-n↓
    - **pressing** pain: arg-n
  - **burning**: bamb-a stb2.de• **Bar-c** calc-f sp1 carb-an h2* gink-b sbd1• ketogl-ac rly4• mur-ac h2* nux-v k* podo fd3.de• spira a1
  - **cold** drinks agg.: calc-f↓
    - **burning**: calc-f
  - **drawing** pain: alum k*
  - **drink** often; which causes him to: cinnb hr1
  - **pressing** pain: arg-n k* kali-n c1 sars h2* sulph k*
  - **raw**; as if: *Anac* k* **Bar-c** k* cassia-s ccrh1• ham fd3.de• mur-ac h2* sumb k*
  - **sore**: bamb-a stb2.de• camph k* canth carb-an h2* carc tpw2* crot-h k* dream-p sdj1• erig k* hir skp7• *Merc* nat-m k* positr nl2• tritic-vg fd5.de zinc h2*
  - **stitching** pain: dulc fd4.de lac-h sk4• mag-m h2* mag-s k* manc nat-c h2* nat-m k*
  - **tearing** pain: cassia-s ccrh1•

- **accompanied** by:
  - **coryza**: (↗*sore - accompanied - coryza*) bamb-a stb2.de• sarcol-ac sp1
  - **dryness**: adam skp7• lavand-a ctl1• luna kg1• mand rsj7•
  - **salivation**; increased: hipp jl2
  - **thirst** for cold water: sulph bl1
  - **voice**; complaints of: *Carb-v* bg2 nit-ac bg2
  - ○ **Ears | tickling**: musca-d szs1
  - **Eyes**; burning in (See EYE - Pain - burning - accompanied - throat)
  - **Head**; pain in (See HEAD - Pain - accompanied - throat)
- **aching**: allox tpw3* lac-h sze9• melal-alt gya4 ozone sde2• [heroin sdj2]
- **acidity**; from: morg-g↓
  - **burning**: morg-g fmm1•

- **air**:
  - **cold | sore** (See cold - air - agg. - sore)
- **air** agg.; draft of: *Ambr* k* bell mrr1 calc k2 chin k* crot-c sk4• dulc fd4.de *Hep* k* kali-bi sne kali-c mrr1* *Lach* sne merc-i-f sne *Nux-v* sne
  - **sore**: *Ambr* k* *Hep*
- **air**; in open:
  - **agg.**: mez↓
    - **sore**: mez
  - **amel.**: kali-bi↓
    - **sore**: kali-bi k*
- **alternating** with:
  - ○ **Anus**; pain in: sin-a bg1
  - **Bones**; boring pain in: kali-bi bg2
  - **Head**; pain in (See HEAD - Pain - alternating - throat)
  - **Sternum**; complaints of (See CHEST - Sternum - alternating - throat)
- **apple** core; as from an: *Merc* k* phyt k*
- **ascending** stairs agg.: nux-v↓
  - **stitching** pain: nux-v
- **asthma**, before: *Bov*↓
  - **stitching** pain: *Bov*
- **awns** of barley in the pharynx; as from: berb kali-p bg2 mag-c k* ph-ac bg2 sars bg2
- **beer**; cold:
  - **amel.**: cassia-s↓
    - **dull** pain: cassia-s ccrh1•
- **bending** head forward agg.: brom k* irid-met srj5• *Lach* a1 phyt propr sa3•
- **biting** pain: ambr b7.de* bar-c bg2 carb-v b4.de* colch a1* dros b7.de* hyos b7.de* merc bg2 mez b4.de* mur-ac bg2 nat-m h2* nux-v b7.de* ph-ac b4.de* phos bg2 plat a1 puls bg2 ran-s b7.de* sep b4.de* tab a1 teucr b7.de* verat b7.de* zinc b4a.de*
- **blowing** the nose agg.: *Carb-v* merc h1*
- **boring** pain: arg-met b7.de*
  - **alternating** with | **Extremities**; pains in bones of: kali-bi a1
- **bread**:
  - **agg.**: rhod↓
    - **burning**: rhod k*
  - **amel.**: phel vml3•
- **breathing**:
  - **agg.**: arg-met↓ arg-n↓
    - **splinter**; as from a: arg-met ptk1 arg-n h1
  - **deep**:
    - **agg.**: hep↓
      - **stitching** pain: hep
- **burning**: absin acal br1 **Acon** k* acon-f a1 *Aesc* k* *Aeth* k* agar k* alco a1 all-c br1 allox tpw3* aloe k2 *Alum* k* alum-p k2 alum-sil k2 alumn k* *Am-c* k* am-m k* ammc k* amp rly4• anan k* ant-c k* ant-t k* anthraq rly4• *Apis* k* arg-met *Arg-n* k* *Arn* k* **Ars** k* ars-h k* ars-i ars-s-f k2 arum-m hr1 *Arum-t* k* *Asaf* k* asc-c a1 aspar hr1 aster k* atp rly4• atro a1 aur k* aur-ar k2 aur-i k2 aur-s k2 bamb-a stb2.de• bapt k* bar-c bar-i k2 bar-m bar-s k2 *Bell* k* berb k* beryl tpw5* bism k* bol-s a1 borx k* *Bov* k* brom k* cain *Calad* k* *Calc* k* calc-f sp1 calc-p k* calc-s calc-sil k2 *Camph* k* cann-i k* cann-s b7.de **Canth** k* **Caps** k* *Carb-ac* k* *Carb-an* k* *Carb-v* k* *Carbn-s* carc fd2.de• cassia-s ccrh1• castm **Caust** k* cedr k* cham k* chel k* chin chin-b c1 chinin-ar chinin-s k* chlf a1 chlol a1 cic b7.de *Cimic* cinch a1 cist k* clem k* *Coc-c* k* coca-c sk4• cocc k* colch k* coloc k* con k* cop corn br1 *Crot-c* *Crot-t* k* cub a1* cupr k* cupr-act cupr-ar cupr-s a1 cur cycl cypra-eg sde6.de• cyt-l sp1 delphin a1 dig k* digox a1 dios k* dros k* dulc b4a.de* echi ephe-si hsj1• erio a1 eucal a1* eup-per k* **Euph** k* ferr k* ferr-ar ferr-i ferr-m ferr-p fl-ac flor-p rsj3• galla-q-r nl2• *Gels* k* gink-b sbd1• glon k* granit-m es1• *Graph* k* *Guaj* k* helio a1 hell k* hell-o a1 *Hep* k* hom-xyz br1 *Hura* hura-c a1* hydr k2 *Hydrog* srj2• hydroph rsj6• *Hyos* k* ign b7a.de* ignis-alc es2• iod k* ip k* irid-met srj5• iris k* jatr-c jug-c k* kali-ar *Kali-bi* k* *Kali-c* kali-chl kali-i k* kali-m k2 kali-n k* kali-ox a1

- **burning**: ...
kali-p kali-perm kali-s k* kali-sil k2 kali-sula a1* ketogl-ac rly4• kola stb3• kreos k* lac-ac k* **Lac-c** lac-del hm2• lac-h sk4• *Lach* k* *Laur* k* lepi a1* lil-s a1 lob k* lob-c a1 lol a1 **Lyc** k* lyss k* m-aust b7.de mag-c k* maias-l hm2• manc k* mang *Merc* k* merc-br a1 **Merc-c** k* *Merc-i-f* k* *Merc-i-r* merl k* **Mez** k* morg-p pte1*• mosch b7a.de *Mur-ac* k* myric myris k* nat-ar nat-c k* **Nat-m** k* nat-p nat-sil fd3.de• *Nit-ac* k* nit-m-ac a1 nux-m b7a.de nux-v k* oci-sa sk4• oena br1 olnd k* op k* *Ox-ac* k* ozone sde2• paeon k* *Par* k* *Petr* k* petr-ra shn4• ph-ac *Phos* k* *Phyt* k* plac rzf5• *Plat* b4a.de plb k* plut-n srj7• podo k* pop-cand c2 *Psor* k* puls k* ran-b k* ran-s k* raph k* rauw tpw8* *Rhod* k* *Rhus-t* k* rhus-v k* ribo rly4• ric a1 *Sabad* k* sal-ac k* **Sang** k* sangin-n br1 *Sec* k* sel rsj9• *Seneg* k* *Sep* k* sil k* solid br1 spira a1 *Spong* k* *Squil* k* still k* *Stram* k* stront-c b4a.de sul-ac k* sul-i k2 **Sulph** k* syc bka1• symph fd3.de• *Syph Tab* k* tarax k* tarent k* tart-ac a1 tep k* ter k* thres-a sze7• thuj k* til a1 tritic-vg fd5.de tub c1* upa k* urt-u k* vanil fd5.de *Verat* k* verat-v k* vesp k* vip k* visc sp1 zinc k* zinc-m a1 zinc-p k2 zinc-s a1
  - **accompanied** by | **coryza**: caps mrr1
  - **ball**; as from a | **hot** ball: phyt mrr1
  - **itching**, smarting pain: bar-c carb-v cist kali-bi merc mez mur-ac ph-ac phos puls teucr zinc
  - **vapor**; as from hot: merc ptk1
- **burnt**; as if: aesc bg2 *Apis* bg2 bov bg2 chin bg2 eup-per bg2 ferr b7a.de iris bg2 mag-m bg2 merc bg2 merc-c bg2 mez bg2 phyt bg2 rhus-t bg2 sang bg2 sec bg2 seneg bg2 syc pte1• ther bg2
- **burrowing**: arg-met b7.de*
- **bursting** pain: pic-ac bg2
- **children**; in:
  - **nursing** infants: bapt ↓
    - **sore**: bapt k2
- **chill**:
  - **before**: eup-pur
  - **during**: bar-c b4a.de* bell bg2 borx b4a.de* bov b4.de* brom bg2 *Bry* b7a.de* con bg2 dros bg2 hipp a1 kali-c bg2 led bg2 mag-c ↓ *Nux-v* b7.de* ph-ac bg2 phos bg2 puls bg2 *Rhus-t* bg2 **Sep** bg2 spig b7.de* thuj ven-m rsj12• zinc bg2
    - **sore**: mag-c ptk1
- **chilliness**; with: cadm-s ↓ ruta ↓
  - **aching**: cadm-s br1 ruta fd4.de
- **chronic**: (↗*Inflammation - chronic*) am-c b4.de* arg-met b7.de* bar-c b4.de* bov b4.de* calc k2 *Caps* hr1 dulc b4.de* granit-m es1• kali-n b4.de* lach b7.de* led b7.de* *Lyc* b4.de* *Mang* b4a.de *Mur-ac* b4a.de nat-m b4a.de puls b7.de* rhus-t b7.de* *Sulph* b4a.de *Zinc* b4.de*
  - **measles**; during: *Carb-v* b4.de*
- **clawing** pain: alum h2* grat a1
- **clearing** throat agg.: alum seneg ↓
  - **raw**; as if: seneg k*
  - **sore**: alum k*
- **cold**:
  - **air**:
    - **agg.**: act-sp ↓ bell bufo ↓ calc k2 cassia-s ↓ chin cist *Coff* ↓ crot-h *Fl-ac Hep* hydrog ↓ lap-la sde8.de• *Merc* mez nux-v pot-e rly4• sabad ↓ stront-c sk4•
      - **burning**: cassia-s ccrh1•
      - **sore**: act-sp c1 **Bell** bufo *Cist* k* *Coff Fl-ac* k* *Hep* hydrog srj2• mez sabad br1
    - **amel.**: all-c *Coff* ign br1 kali-bi sang tritic-vg fd5.de
    - **drawing** in cold air:
      - **agg.**: *Bufo* ↓ **Nux-v** ↓
        - **raw**; as if: *Bufo* k* **Nux-v** k*
    - **inspiration** agg.: act-sp ↓ crot-h ↓
      - **tearing** pain: act-sp k* crot-h
  - **anything** cold; from | **agg.**: *Ars* vh chir-fl gya2 crot-c sk4• **Hep** vh **Lyc** vh sabad vh *Sulph* vh
  - **applications**:
    - **agg.**: cassia-s ↓
      - **burning**: cassia-s ccrh1•
      - **stitching** pain: cassia-s ccrh1•
    - **amel.**: cassia-s ↓

- **cold – applications – amel.**: ...
      - **stitching** pain: cassia-s ccrh1•
  - **drinks**:
    - **after**:
      - **agg.**: *Ars* ↓ calc-f ↓ canth ↓ gink-b ↓ hep ↓ *Merc-c* ↓
        - **burning**: *Ars* calc-f k* canth gink-b sbd1• hep *Merc-c*
      - **amel.**: bamb-a ↓ coc-c ↓
        - **burning**: bamb-a stb2.de• coc-c k2
    - **agg.**●: aq-mar jl arg-n ars atra-r ↓ calc-f k2 canth cassia-s ↓ gink-b sbd1• lac-c lap-la sde8.de• *Lyc* manc ↓ merc-c pycnop-sa mrz1 *Sabad* stront-c sk4• *Sulph* st **Syph** al2* urol-h rwt•
      - **cutting** pain: manc ptk1
      - **raw**; as if: cassia-s ccrh1•
      - **sore**: atra-r skp7*•
      - **tearing** pain: cassia-s ccrh1•
    - **amel.**: *Apis* k* arg-n k2 bar-m mrr1 beryl sp1 carc mg1.de* cassia-s ↓ coc-c ind iris ↓ lac-c k* *Lach* k* *Lyc* k* merc-i-f oci-sa ↓ onos *Phyt* k* plac rzf5• psor jl2 rauw ↓ vesp fkr7.de [arg-met stj1 pop dhh1]
      - **burning**: *Apis* beryl tpw5 iris c1 oci-sa sk4• rauw tpw8
      - **sore**: beryl tpw5
      - **ulcerative** pain: cassia-s cdd7•
  - **food** | **agg.**: *Ars* vh **Hep** vh **Lyc** vh sabad vh *Sulph* vh
  - **ice** | **amel.**: ozone sde2•
  - **water**:
    - **amel.**: hir ↓
      - **sore**: hir skp7•
- **cold**; after taking a: acon all-c a1 alum a1 alumn ↓ bar-c k* bell cham *Dulc* k* lach bg1 ozone sde2•
  - **sore**: alumn br1 lach bg1
- **cold** agg.; becoming●: *Ars Calc Calc-p* calc-sil k2 *Dulc* **Hep** **Kali-c** k* lap-la sde8.de• *Lyc Merc Nit-ac Phos Phyt* podo fd3.de• **Sil**
  - **splinter**; as from a: *Kali-c*
  - **stitching** pain: **Kali-c**
- **compressed**; as if: alum b4.de* coloc bg2
- **corrosive**: apis b7a.de
- **coryza**; during: ant-t b7.de* cham ↓ *Laur* b7a.de led ↓ nit-ac b4a.de nux-v b7.de* ph-ac b4a.de phos b4a.de puls ↓
  - **burning**: cham b7a.de
  - **pressing** pain: led b7.de*
  - **stitching** pain: nit-ac b4.de* puls b7a.de
- **cough**:
  - **after**: atro ↓ beryl ↓ castm ↓ coc-c hep ↓ mag-m ↓ *Mur-ac* ↓ naja ozone ↓ ph-ac ↓ phos ↓ plut-n ↓ podo fd3.de• sulph ↓ tritic-vg fd5.de
    - **burning**: atro a1 beryl tpw5 castm coc-c k* hep mag-m k* *Mur-ac* k* ph-ac phos plut-n srj7• sulph k*
    - **raw**; as if: ozone sde2•
  - **during**:
    - **agg.**: acon k* allox tpw4 ambr k* anac ↓ ant-s-aur ↓ **Arg-met** k* ars b4a.de* *Arum-t* k* bamb-a stb2.de• *Bell* bro1 beryl ↓ borx ↓ bry bg2 cadm-met ↓ calc k* calc-p ↓ calc-sil k2 camph **Caps** k* carb-an k* *Carb-v* k* carbn-s caust bg2 chin k* chinin-s cist cob ↓ coc-c k* cycl ferr-p sne fl-ac germ-met srj5• gink-b sbd1• hep k* hydrog srj2• iod kali-bi *Kali-c* bg2 kali-n h2* kalm lac-c ↓ lac-h ↓ *Lach* k* lachn ↓ lyc k* mag-s **Merc** bg2 merc-i-r bro1 mez ↓ mim-p vml3• mur-ac ↓ nat-m k* nit-ac b4a.de* *Nux-v* k* ozone sde2• petr-ra ↓ *Phos* k* psil ft1 psor puls ↓ pyrid ↓ ran-s rumx ↓ ruta fd4.de sep k* sil k* spong k* stann ↓ stront-c ↓ sul-i k2 sulph k* *Tarent* tung-met bdx1•
      - **burning**: ars b4a.de bell bg2 *Carb-v* b4a.de coc-c bg2 iod b4a.de mez b4a.de mur-ac b4.de* phos b4.de* puls b7a.de
      - **cutting** pain: calc lyc k* sulph k*
      - **dry**: adam ↓
        - **sore**: adam skp7•
      - **pressing** pain: caps b7.de*
      - **raw**; as if: *Ambr* k* anac **Arg-met** carb-v caust chin cob nat-m phos k* rumx sep sil k* **Spong** k* stront-c

• **during** – **agg.**: ...

: **sore**: ambr k* ant-s-aur bg1 **Arg-met** k* bamb-a stb2.de• beryl tpw5 cadm-met tpw6 calc-p bg2 carb-an b4a.de carb-v fl-ac k* lac-h sk4• *Lach* k* lachn c1 lyc k* petr-ra shn4• phos k* pyrid rly4• ran-s k* sep k* spong stann b4a.de tarent k*

: **stitching** pain: borx bry k* cist tl1 hep k* kali-c k* lac-c tl1 lach lyc nit-ac k* nux-v phos k* ruta fd4.de sil

: **tearing** pain: chinin-s *Cist* k*

: **ulcerative** pain: caps b7.de*

: **amel.**: stann ↓

: **stitching** pain: stann h2

• **not** amel.: mim-p skp7•

- **cramping**: zinc h2*

- **cutting** pain: bell bg2 beryl sp1 bufo chinin-s grat bg2 kali-n k* lyc bg2 manc ptk1 mang k* *Merc-c* k* merc-cy bg2* *Nit-ac* b4a.de* plan k* plb k* puls k* rad-br sze8• rob bg1 sep k* stann b4a.de* staph k* sul-ac k* sulph k* thuj bg1 uran-n bg1 ust bg1

- **depressing** the tongue: merc-c

- **digging** pain: arg-met h1 paull a1

- **dinner**; after: dig ↓ dros ↓ lyc ↓ sulph k*

• **burning**: dig h2* dros k* lyc k*

• **drinking** warm drinks:

: **amel.**: bit-ar ↓

: **raw**; as if: bit-ar wht1•

• **raw**; as if: dros k*

- **diphtheria**:

• **after**: phyt ↓

: **sore**: phyt ptk1

• **during**: phyt tl1

- **dragging** down: lil-t k2

- **drawing** pain: alum k* apis arg-met k2 *Arg-n* k* aur k* aur-s a1 bry b7.de* calc-p k* caps k* croc k* cupr cycl b7.de* dulc fd4.de kali-bi k* laur k* lepi a1 merc-c k* mez b4.de* nat-m k* plat k* plb k* sabad k* sabin b7.de* stann k* staph b7.de* *Stram* k* sulph teucr k* verat k* zinc k*

- **drinking**:

• **after**:

: **agg.**: nit-ac ↓

: **sore**: nit-ac h2

: **tearing** pain: nit-ac h2*

: **amel.**: beryl ↓

: **sore**: beryl tpw5

• **agg.**: ambr ↓ **Arum-t** lp brucel ↓ canth cassia-s ↓ dendr-pol sk4• dulc ↓ lyss jl2 par ↓

: **burning**: canth k* dulc fd4.de par k*

: **scratching** pain: brucel sa3•

: **stitching** pain: cassia-s ccrh1•

: **tearing** pain: ambr a1

• **amel.**: adam skp7• allox tpw4* bros-gau ↓ bry k* carb-an ↓ gink-b sbd1• hydrog srj2• ign k* kali-n ↓ kola stb3• plac rzf5• sal-al blc1• suis-em rly4• tell k* *Trios* rsj11•

: **burning**: bros-gau mrc1 carb-an a1 kali-n h2*

• **water**:

: **agg.**: mez ↓

: **burning**: mez bg1

: **amel.**: lavand-a ctl1•

- **dryness**; with: cub ↓ *Hydroph* ↓ lac-del hrn2• mim-p ↓

• **burning**: cub c1 *Hydroph* rsj6• mim-p rsj8•

- **dull** pain: cassia-s ccrh1•

- **eating**:

• **after**:

: **agg.**: am-c ↓ ambr k2 *Anac* ↓ ant-t ↓ aq-mar skp7• ars ↓ *Calc* ↓ con ↓ kali-n ↓ *Lyc* ↓ *Nit-ac* ↓ par ↓ sep ↓ ven-m ↓

: **burning**: am-c h2 ant-t *Calc* con *Lyc* *Nit-ac* par k* sep h2

: **pressing** pain: ars b4a.de

: **raw**; as if: *Anac* k*

: **sore**: anac b4a.de sep b4a.de* ven-m rsj12•

: **stitching** pain: kali-n h2*

- **eating** – **after**: ...

: **amel.**: beryl ↓ carb-an ↓ kali-s ↓ mez ↓

: **burning**: beryl tpw5 carb-an h2 kali-s fd4.de mez

• **agg.**: kali-n ↓ sulph ↓

: **stitching** pain: kali-n h2 sulph

• **amel.**: acon adam skp7• apis benz-ac beryl sp1 carb-an ferr k* gamb ↓ gink-b sbd1• heroin ↓ hydrog srj2• ind vml3• kola stb3• *Lach* k* onos phel ↓ pic-ac spong ↓ tell *Trios* rsj11•

: **raw**; as if: onos

: **sore**: apis beryl tpw5 carb-an k* ferr a1 hydrog srj2• pic-ac k* [heroin sdj2]

: **stitching** pain: gamb a1 phel a1 spong h1*

• **while**:

: **agg.**: aloe gsy1 carb-v dendr-pol sk4• ferr phos psil ↓ spong fd4.de ven-m ↓

: **sore**: carb-v k* ferr k* phos k* psil ft1 ven-m rsj12•

- **eructations**; after: alum ↓ kali-c ↓ lac-ac ↓ sulph h2* urol-h rwt• [tax jsj7]

• **burning**: alum k* kali-c k2 lac-ac c1 *Sulph* [tax jsj7]

- **excoriated**; as if: bros-gau mrc1

- **exertion** agg.: caust bg1 lac-c bg1 manc ↓

• **stitching** pain: manc k*

- **expectoration**:

• **after**: arund ↓

: **sore**: arund c1

• **agg.**: bell k*

• **amel.**: allox tpw4*

- **expiration**:

• **agg.**: crot-t ↓ iris ↓ mez ↓

: **burning**: crot-t k* iris mez k*

• **during**:

: **agg.**: *Arg-met* ign sne ph-ac ↓

: **raw**; as if: *Arg-met* ph-ac k*

: **sore**: *Arg-met*

- **fever**:

• **after**: kali-c b4a.de

• **during**:

: **agg.**: *Euph* ↓ merc ↓

: **burning**: *Euph* b4a.de*

: **stitching** pain: merc b4a.de

- **foreign** body; as from a: mag-c h2*

- **gargling** with warm water:

• **amel.**: cassia-s ↓

: **stitching** pain: cassia-s ccrh1•

- **gnawing** pain: ambr c1 apis bg2 arge-pl rwt5• calc-s bg2 sep bg2

• **worm**; as from a: *Calc* b4a.de

- **hawking**:

• **after**: cob ↓ thuj ↓

: **sore**: cob thuj

- **hawking** up mucus:

• **agg.**: arg-n bg3 *Bell* canth caust bg3 cench k2 choc ↓ cob con bg3 *Kali-bi* bg3 kali-c bg3 **Lach** lyc bg3 *Mang* ↓ *Nat-c* bg3 nat-m bg3 *Phos* bg3 plat ↓ puls bg3 rhus-t bg3 sep thuj

: **burning**: lyc sep

: **cutting** pain: sep k*

: **raw**; as if: choc srj3• cob k* *Mang* k*

: **stitching** pain: plat k*

• **amel.**: androc srj1• gink-b sbd1•

• **must** hawk: gink-b ↓

: **burning**: gink-b sbd1•

- **heat**; during: acon bg2 apis bg2 ars bg2 bell bg2 bov b4.de* dros b7a.de* hist sp1 ign bg2 kali-c b4.de* **Lach** bg2 merc bg2 mosch b7.de nit-ac bg2 nux-v bg2 petr-ra shn4• ph-ac k* phos k* puls bg2 sep k* sulph bg2

- **ice** | **amel.**: ozone sde2•

- **inspiration**:
  - **agg.**: ail ap-g vh apis arg-n arum-t cann-i sne cist↓ hep hura hydrog srj2• mag-m↓ mez nat-n sne plut-n↓ ran-b↓ urol-h rwt•
    - **burning**: cann-i cist mrr1 mez plut-n srj7• ran-b
    - **sore**: mez h2*
    - **stitching** pain: hep k* mag-m h2*
    - **tearing** pain: hura
  - **amel.**: crot-t↓ iris↓ mez↓ *Sang*↓
    - **burning**: crot-t iris mez *Sang*
  - **nose** agg.; through: ap-g vh
- **jerking** pain: nat-m b4.de* plat b4.de* spig b7.de*
- **lancinating**: am-caust k* ars k* aur-s k* bufo ferul a1 manc k* sabin c1 suis-em rly4• ust k*
- **laughing** agg.: nat-m bg1
- **lifting** agg.: (non:calc kl) caust bg1 *Sil* bg3
  - **tearing** pain: caust k*
- **lump**: arg-met↓ calc↓ caust↓ cham↓ ign↓ lac-del↓ laur↓ nux-v↓ petr-ra↓ *Sil*↓
  - **sore**: arg-met c1 calc k* caust k* cham k* ign k* lac-del hrn2• laur k* nux-v petr-ra shn4• *Sil* k*
- **lying**:
  - **agg.**: bell *Lach*
  - **amel.**: calc h2* canth lach bg1
- **lying** down:
  - **agg.**: puls↓
    - **burning**: puls
  - **amel.**: cassia-s↓
    - **quietly**; lying down: cassia-s↓
      - **ulcerative** pain: cassia-s cdd7•
    - **raw**; as if: cassia-s ccrh1•
    - **tearing** pain: cassia-s ccrh1•
- **menses** | **before**:
    - **agg.**: bar-c bg2 calc bg2 canth bg2 con b4a.de* cupr bg2 dig bg2 gels bg2 iod bg2 lac-c k* *Mag-c* k* *Merc* b4a.de nat-s bg1 senec vml3• sep b4a.de sulph b4a.de*
      - **burning**: sulph h2*
      - **sore**: canth bro1 *Lac-c* k* *Mag-c* k*
      - **stinging**: *Mag-c*
  - **during**:
    - **agg.**: am-m bg2 arn bar-c k* cact bg2 *Calc* k* canth↓ *Castm* bg2 *Chel* bg2 cic bg2 con bg2 cupr bg2 gels bg2 *Lac-c* k* laur bg2 mag-c bg2* mez↓ mosch bg2 nat-s bg1 nux-m bg2 nux-v bg2* sul-ac↓ *Sulph* k*
      - **burning**: calc k* nat-s ptk sulph k*
        - **itching**, smarting pain: mez h2
      - **sore**: arn *Calc* k* canth bro1 gels br1 **Lac-c** k* *Mag-c* bro1 sul-ac bg1 *Sulph*
- **mental** excitement; after: *Cist*↓
  - **stitching** pain: *Cist*
- **mental** exertion agg.: caust
  - **tearing** pain: caust
- **milk** agg.: ambr k2
- **motion**:
  - **agg.**: arg-n sne *Bell* merc merl psor
  - **beginning** of:
    - **agg.**: cortico↓
      - **splinter**; as from a: cortico tpw7
  - **head**; of:
    - **agg.**: arg-n↓ cham h1 graph↓ phos h2
      - **splinter**; as from a: arg-n h1*
      - **stitching** pain: graph h2
  - **tongue**; of:
    - **agg.**: alum ambr
      - **drawing** pain: alum
      - **stitching** pain: ambr
- **nervous** angina: mag-p ptk1*
- **onions**; from: alum↓
- **onions**; from: ...
  - **sore**: alum ptk1
- **opening** the mouth:
  - **agg.**: aloe hr bros-gau mrc1 *Kali-c* bg1* melal-alt gya4
  - **difficult**: kali-c↓
    - **pressure** agg.: *Lach*↓
      - **sore**: *Lach*
    - **sore**: kali-c
- **operation**; after: ferr-p↓
  - **sore**: ferr-p ptk1*
- **paroxysmal**: phos k* sep k*
- **peppery**: coloc↓ crot-t↓ euph↓ hydrog↓ *Mez*↓ ol-an↓ plat↓ rad-br↓ sal-ac↓
  - **burning**: coloc bg1 crot-t euph h2* hydrog srj2• *Mez* k* ol-an bg1 plat bg1 rad-br ptk1 sal-ac a1
- **periodical** | **days**; on alternate: lach bg1
- **perspiration**; during: acon bg2 apis bg2 *Ars*↓ **Bell** bg2 bov bg2 *Cham* bg2 con bg2 **Dros** bg2 kali-c bg2 lach bg2 *Merc* bg2 mez↓ nit-ac bg2 nux-v bg2 *Ph-ac* bg2 *Phos* bg2 puls bg2 rhus-t bg2 sabad bg2 **Sep** bg2 sulph bg2 thuj bg2 verat↓
  - **burning**: acon bg2 apis bg2 *Ars* bg2 bell bg2 cham bg2 merc bg2 mez bg2 nit-ac bg2 nux-v bg2 rhus-t bg2 sabad bg2 *Sulph* bg2 verat bg2
- **pinching** pain: colch a1 graph b4.de* iod h* lach a1 nat-m b4.de* nit-ac h2* sep h2*
- **pressing** on larynx, when: kali-n↓
  - **stitching** pain: kali-n h2*
- **pressing** pain: acon k* agar *Alum* k* alum-p k2 alumn am-c k* am-m ambr b7.de* ant-t k* apis b7a.de arn bg2 ars b4.de* asaf k* astac hr1 bamb-a stb2.de• bar-c k* *Bell* k* berb k* brom k* bry k* calc k* calc-i k2 calc-s *Camph* bg2 canth k* **Caps** *Carb-an* k* carb-v k* caust k* cham k* chel b7.de* chin b7.de* cinnb clem coc-c k* colum-p sze2• cop k* croc b7.de* crot-t k* dulc k* ferr k* ferr-i ferr-ma fic-m gya1 gent-c *Graph* b4.de* grat k* ham a1 hell k* hep b4.de* hera a1 hyos k* ign k* iod k* kali-ar kali-bi k* kali-c k* kali-chl k* kali-i k* kali-m k2 kali-n k* kali-p *Kalm* k* kreos k* lac-ac *Lach* k* led b7.de* lob bg2* lyc k* m-arct b7.de mang k* *Merc* k* *Merc-c* k* merc-i-r k* merl k* *Mez* k* naja nat-c b4.de* *Nat-m* nat-sil fd3.de• nit-ac k* *Nux-v* k* par k* ph-ac b4.de* phel k* phos k* plat k* plut-n srj7• *Puls* b7.de* rat rhus-t k* ruta k* sabad k* sabin k* sars b4.de* seneg k* sep k* sin-a a1 spig b7a.de spirae a1 sul-ac b4.de* sul-i k2 sulph k* tab k* tarax k* teucr k* thuj k* tritic-vg fd5.de vanil fd5.de verat k* zinc k* zinc-p k2
  - **asunder**: anac h2* kali-ar
  - **hard**; as from something: arn b7a.de bry b7a.de
- **pressure** agg.: kali-sula a1 **Merc-c**↓ vanil fd5.de
  - **burning**: **Merc-c** k*
- **pulsating** pain: rhus-t a1 tarent
- **putting** out the tongue: cocc *Kali-bi* *Lach* sne **Phyt** sne sabad
- **raising** head from pillow agg.: x-ray↓
  - **cramping**: x-ray sp1
- **raw**; as if: (↗*Excoriation*) acon k* *Aesc* k* aids nl2• all-c k* allox tpw3* aln vva1• aloe *Alum* alum-p k2 alum-sil k2 alumn am-c k* am-m k* *Ambr* *Anac* k* anth a1 apis **Arg-met** k* **Arg-n** k* ars arum-d a1* *Arum-t* k* astac a1 atro a1 bapt k* **Bell** k* bell-p sp1 berb bol-la bov k* brach a1 *Brom* k* *Bry* k* bufo cadm-met sp1 cain *Calc* k* calc-s canth *Carb-an* *Carb-v* k* *Carbn-s* cassia-s ccrh1• **Caust** k* cench k2 chel **Chin** k* chinin-ar chir-fl gya2 chlol hr1 choc srj3• chord-umb rly4• cimic k* cist cob *Coc-c* k* coca-c sk4• cod colch rsj2• coli rly4• *Coloc* crot-h k* dig k* dirc c1 dor k* dros k* dulc k* euph k* ferr k* ferr-ar fic-m gya1 flor-p rsj3• fuma-ac rly4• gamb k* gent-c k* gent-l a1 get a1 granit-m es1• *Graph* k* grat k* ham fd3.de• *Hep* k* hera a1 hippoc-k szs2 hir skp7• *Hom-xyz* br1 hydr k* hydrog srj2• ign k* ina-i mlk9.de ip k* irid-met srj5• iris *Kali-bi* k* kali-c kali-chl k* kali-i k* kali-m k2 kali-n k* kali-p kali-perm kali-s kali-sil k2 kalm k* kola stb3• kreos lac-ac k* *Lac-c* *Lach* k* laur k* **Lyc** k* *Mag-c* k* *Mag-m* k* mang k2 med melal-alt gya4 *Merc* k* merc-br a1 **Merc-c** k* merl k* *Mez* k* morg-p pte1• *Mur-ac* k* *Naja* nat-ar nat-c *Nat-m* k* nicc k* nicotam rly4• **Nit-ac** k* nux-m **Nux-v** k* ol-an k* onos op ox-ac ozone sde2• pen br1 petr k* petr-ra shn4• ph-ac k* phel k* *Phos* k* *Phyt* plac rzf5• plac-s rly4• plan k* *Plat* plb plut-n srj7• prin a1 *Puls* k* pycnop-sa mrz1 rad-br ptk1 samb xxb1 *Sang* sapin a1 sars *Seneg* k* sep k* sil k* sol-ni *Spong* k* *Stann* k* stict c1 **Still** k* stront-c suis-em rly4• suis-hep rly4• suis-pan rly4• *Sul-ac* k* *Sulph* k*

- **raw**; as if: ...
sumb k* syc pte1*• syph hr1 tab k* tarax hr1 thiam rly4• *Thuj* k* til a1 trif-p a1 tung-met bdx1• vero-o rly4*• *Zinc* k* zinc-p k2
- **respiration**: bell ↓ chin ↓
  - **stitching** pain: bell h1* chin h1*
- **rest** agg.: sabin ↓
  - **stitching** pain: sabin
- **rheumatic**: ambr b7.de* *Caust* cham b7a.de gran k* ign b7a.de mez k* *Par* b7a.de
- **rising**:
  - **agg.**: calc k* mang-p rly4•
  - **before**: ptel ↓
    - **burning**: ptel c1
- **salivation** | **after** | **amel.**: arum-m kr1*
  - **agg.**: beryl sp1
    - **burning**: beryl tpw5
    - **sore**: beryl tpw5
- **scratching** pain: calc-f sp1 ina-i mlk9.de lap-la sde8.de• nat-ox rly4• nat-sil fd3.de• olib-sac wmh1 orot-ac rly4• ozone sde2• pant-ac rly4• plac rzf5• ribo rly4• succ-ac rly4• suis-em rly4• suis-pan rly4• tere-la rly4• thiam rly4• tritic-vg fd5.de tub c vanil fd5.de
  - **awn**; like an: berb bg1 kali-bi bg1 mag-c bg1 ph-ac bg1 sars bg1
- **seaside** agg.; at the: iod ↓
  - **burning**: iod
- **sharp**; as from something: flor-p rsj3• galla-q-r nl2• glon k* rhus-t k* tung-met bdx1•
- **shivering**; during: led b7.de rhus-t b7.de sep b4.de
- **shooting** (See stitching)
- **singing** agg.: allox tpw4*
- **sitting** | **amel.**: spong
- **sitting** up in bed:
  - **amel.**: spong ↓
    - **drawing** pain: spong
- **sleep** | **after**:
    - **agg.**: kali-bi lac-c lach merc-i-r
      - **raw**; as if: *Lach*
  - **amel.**: crot-t ↓
    - **burning**: crot-t
- **smarting**: apis bg2 bar-c b4.de* hep b4a.de merc b4a.de ph-ac b4.de* phos b4.de* phyt bg2 plan bg2
- **smokers**: caps ↓
  - **sore**: caps ptk1
- **smoking** | **after** | **agg.**: coc-c k* nat-sil fd3.de• psil ft1
  - **agg.**: bell ↓ coc-c ↓ nat-m ↓ ran-b ↓ tarax ↓
    - **burning**: bell a1 coc-c k* ran-b a1 tarax k*
    - **raw**; as if: nat-m
- **sneezing**:
  - **agg.**: hydrog ↓ hyper ictod led ↓ lyc ↓ mag-c h2* **Phos** k*
    - **pressing** pain: led h1*
    - **sore**: hydrog srj2• hyper k* mag-c a1
    - **stitching** pain: lyc mag-c k*
    - **tearing** pain: phos h2*
  - **amel.**: am-br bg1 petr-ra ↓
    - **sore**: petr-ra shn4•
- **sore**: acon k* adam skp7• *Aesc* k* agath-a nl2• *Ail* k* *All-c* allox sp1 *Alum* k* alum-p k2 alum-sil k2 *Am-br* k* *Am-c* k* am-caust a1 am-m k* ambr b7a.de* anac k* *Androc* srj1• *Ant-c* k* antip c2 *Apis* k* aq-mar a1 arag br1 **Arg-met** k* **Arg-n** k* arizon-l nl2• *Ars* k* ars-s-f k2 arum-d br1 *Arum-t* k* *Asaf* k* asim a1* atp rly4• atra-r skp7• atro a1 aur b4.de* *Bac* bn bamb-a stb2.de• **Bapt** k* *Bar-c* c2 **Bell** k* *Benz-ac* k* beryl tpw5* brach a1 brass-n-o srj5• brom k* bry b7a.de* *Bufo* cadm-met tpw6* cadm-s br1 caj k* **Calc** k* *Calc-p* k* *Calc-s* k* camph b7.de* cann-s k* *Canth* c2 *Caps* k* *Carb-ac* carb-an k* *Carb-v* k* carbn-s carc sp1 cardios-h rly4• carl a1 cartl-s rly4• cassia-s ccrh1• *Caust* k* celt a1 cench k2 ceph a1 *Cham* k* chir-fl gya2 chlor k* choc srj3• chord-umb rly4• chr-o c2 cimic k* *Cist* k* coc-c k* coch br1 coff k* coli rly4• con k* cop k* corian-s knl6• corv-cor bdg• **Crot-c** crot-h k* crot-t k* cund a1 cupr k* cupr-ar k* cycl k*

- **sore**: ...
cystein-l rly4• dig b4.de* dios k* dor k* dream-p sdj1• dulc fd4.de echi ephe-si hsj1• epil c2 eug c2 eup-per k* eup-pur c2 euph-a c2 fago k* falco-pe nl2• ferr k* ferr-ar ferr-p *Fl-ac* k* flor-p rsj3• form k* fum rly1*• fuma-ac rly4• gala br1 gamb c2 *Gels* k* gent-c c2 ger c2 germ-met srj5• glon k* granit-m es1• graph b4.de* *Guaj* gymno c2* haem k* haliae-lc srj5• ham k* helia c2 hell k* helodr-cal knl2• *Hep* c2 hepat c2 hip-ac sp1 hipp a1 hir rsj4*• hom-xyz c2* hydr k* hydr-ac k* *Hydrog* srj2• hydroph rsj6• hyosin c2 **Ign** k* ind k* *Ip* k* iris c1 jab k* jac-c jac-g c2 jatr-c jug-c k* kali-ar k* *Kali-bi* bg2* kali-c k* kali-chl kali-i k* kali-m k2 kali-n br1 kali-p kali-perm k* kali-s kali-sil k2 ketogl-ac rly4• kreos b7a.de* lac-ac k* lac-c c2* lac-d k2 lac-del hrn2• lac-e hrn2• lac-h htj1• lac-loxod-a hrn2• lac-v-f c2 **Lach** k* lachn k* *Led* k* lil-s a1 limest-b es1• lipp a1 lob k* lob-c a1 lob-s c2 *Luna* kg1• **Lyc** k* lycpr c2 *Lyss* k* m-aust b7.de mag-c k* mag-m b4.de* mag-s k* mang b4.de* med hr1 melal-alt gya4 menth c2 **Merc** k* merc-act c2 *Merc-c* k* *Merc-cy* k* merc-d c2 *Merc-i-f* k* *Merc-i-r* k* merc-n a1 *Mez* k* *Mur-ac* b4a.de* musca-d szs1 myric k* nad rly4• naja k* *Nat-ar* nat-c b4.de* nat-m k* nat-p k* nat-pyru rly4• nat-s k* nat-sil fd3.de• neon srj5• nicc k* nicotam rly4• **Nit-ac** k* *Nux-m* *Nux-v* k* nymph c2 oena k* onos c2 orot-ac rly4• ovi-p c2 *Ox-ac* k* oxal-a rly4• petr k* petr-ra shn4• ph-ac k* phel a1 phos k* phys k* *Phyt* k* pic-ac k* plac rzf5• plac-s rly4• plan k* plat b4.de* plect c2 plut-n srj7• podo bg2 polyp-p a1 polys sk4• positr nl2• pot-e rly4• prun-p a1 *Psor* k* ptel k* puls k* pycnop-sa mrz1 quill br1 ran-b b7.de* ran-s k* rhus-g tmo3• *Rhus-t* k* rhus-v k* rumx c2 rumx-act c2 ruta b7a.de* sabad c2 sabal c2 sabin b7.de* sacch-a gmj3 sal-ac c2 sal-fr sle1• samb k* sang k* sangin-n c2 sanic c2 sapin a1 *Sapo* br1 sarcol-ac sp1 seneg k* *Sep* k* *Sil* k* sinus rly4• stann k* *Staph* b7.de* stict c1 still a1 streptoc rly4• stry a1 suis-em rly4• suis-hep rly4• suis-pan rly4• *Sul-ac* k* *Sulph* k* tarent tell c1 tep k* tere-la rly4• ther c1 thuj b4a.de* trif-p a1* tritic-vg fd5.de tus-p a1* upa k* urol-h rwt• urt-u c2 vanil fd5.de verat k* vero-o rly4• vesp k* vinc k* visc c2 wye c2 xan k* zinc k* zinc-m a1 zinc-p k2 zinc-s a1 zing k* ziz a1 [heroin sdj2 **Spect** dfg1]
  - **accompanied** by:
    - **chilliness**: mag-p ptk1
    - **coryza**: *(↗accompanied - coryza)* *Calc-p* *Carb-an* cimic coc-c a1 hydrog srj2• lac-c k2 *Lach* lap-la rsp1 mag-m h2* **Merc** k* **Nit-ac** k* **Nux-v** k* petr-ra shn4• **Phos** k* *Phyt* sep a1
    - **dryness** (See accompanied - dryness)
    - **scarlatina**; malignant: am-c br1
    - **swallowing**; difficult: bit-ar wht1•
    - **Neck** and occiput; aching in: bit-ar wht1•
  - **alternating** with | **Eye**; inflammation of (See EYE - Inflammation - alternating - throat)
- **splinter**; as from a: *(↗Bone)* acon bg2 allox tpw3* *Alum* k* alum-sil k2* *Apis* aq-mar c1 **Arg-n** k* berb *Calc* k* calc-sil k2 caust vh *Chel* cic al cortico tpw7* cortiso sp1 **Dol** k* dream-p sdj1• **Hep** k* hydrog srj2• ign k* irid-met srj5• kali-bi bg2 **Kali-c** k* lac-c *Lach* mag-c merc *Nat-m* k* *Nit-ac* k* phys k* *Phyt* ptk1 podo fd3.de• ruta fd4.de *Sil* k* sol-ni sulph ptk1 thyr ptk1 vanil fd5.de zinc-i rb2
  - **glass**; as from broken: ozone sde2•
- **squeezed**; as if: alum b4.de* lach b7.de* nit-ac bg2 plat b4.de* ran-b bg2 sars bg2 zinc bg2
- **stinging**: *Acon* k* aesc k* **Apis** k* *Arum-t* asar *Bell* caps tl1 carc fd2.de• granit-m es1• *Ip* hr1 jal hr1 led lyss *Mag-c* *Merc* hr1 nat-c h2 *Nit-ac* par plac-s rly4• *Spong* still k* stram bg1* symph fd3.de•
- **stitching** pain: **Acon** k* *Aesc* *Aeth* agar a1* *Alum* k* am-c k* *Am-m* k* ambr b7.de* anan apis k* arg-n bg2* arn k* ars k* ars-s-f k2 arum-m a1 asaf b7.de* *Asar* k* asc-t c1 aur k* aur-ar k2 aur-s k2 bamb-a stb2.de• bapt a1* *Bar-c* k* **Bell** k* berb k* bomb-pr mlk9.de bond a1 *Bov* k* brom k* bros-gau mrc1 *Bry* k* calad a1 *Calc* k* calc-s *Camph* hr1 canth k* caps k* carb-ac carb-an k* *Carb-v* k* carbn-s carc fd2.de• carl k* caust k* cham k* chel k* *Chin* k* chinin-ar chinin-s bg2 cinch a1 *Cist* k* *Coff* b7.de* coloc b4.de* cupr k* cypra-eg sde6.de• *Dig* k* dros b7a.de* dulc fd4.de euph a1 ferr-i a1 ferr-ma k* gamb k* gins a1 glon *Graph* k* gymno hell k* **Hep** k* hydrc a1 *Hyos* k* *Ign* k* iod h* *Ip* k* irid-met srj5• kali-ar kali-bi k* **Kali-c** k* kali-i k* *Kali-n* k* kali-p kali-s ketogl-ac rly4• kola stb3• *Lach* k* lap-la sde8.de• laur *Led* k* lil-s a1 *Lyc* k* mag-c k* mag-m b4.de* mag-s k* manc mang k* melal-alt gya4 meny k* *Merc* k* merc-c k* *Merc-i-r* k* mez k* mill a1 nat-ar *Nat-c* k* *Nat-m* k* nat-p k* nicc k* **Nit-ac** k* nux-m k* *Nux-v* k* par k* *Petr* k* petr-ra shn4• *Ph-ac* k* phel k* phos b4.de* plat b4.de* podo psor **Puls** k* ran-s raph a1 rat k* *Rhus-t* k* ruta fd4.de *Sabad* sabin k* *Sars* k* seneg k* *Sep* k* *Sil* k* spig k* *Spong* k* *Stann* k* staph k* stram k* stront-c b4.de* *Sul-ac* k* *Sulph* k* symph fd3.de• tarax k* tarent teucr k* *Thuj* k* tub xxb urol-h rwt• vanil fd5.de verat k* vesp fkr7.de zinc a1 [tax jsj7]
  - **acorn**; like an: berb bg2 kali-bi bg2 mag-c bg2

Throat

- • **boring** pain: stann h2
- • **needles**; as from | **hot** needles: nat-m bg2
- • **splinters**; as from: sal-al blc1•
- **stooping** | **after**:
  - ⁝ **agg.**: nat-c ↓
    - ⁝ **sore**: nat-c k*
  - • **agg.**: **Caust** k* nat-c
    - ⁝ **rising**; and on: graph ↓
      - ⁝ **stitching** pain: graph h2*
- **stopping** ear with finger | **amel.**: dendr-pol sk4•
- **storm**; during or after north east: lac-c kr1
- **straining** throat, after: **Rhus-t** ↓
  - • **sore**: **Rhus-t**
- **streak**: ol-an ↓
  - • **sore**: ol-an ptk1
- **supper** agg.; after: nit-ac ↓
  - • **burning**: nit-ac k*
- **swallowing**:
  - • **morning** | **amel.**: atra-r skp7•
  - • **after**:
    - ⁝ **agg.**: ambr arum-t mrr1 bry *Calc* *Nux-v* phos puls rhus-t sulph zinc
    - ⁝ **amel.**: allox tpw3* aq-mar jl bapt bell caps cist *Ign* k* kali-bi ketogl-ac rly4• lac-c *Lach* merc olib-sac wmh1 sulph [nicc stj1]
  - • **agg.**: abrom-a ks5 acon k* adren mtf11 aesc aeth ↓ *Agar* bro1 agath-a nl2• aids nl2• *Ail* k* all-c tl1 allox sp1 **Alum** k* alum-p k2 alum-sil k2 *Alumn* ↓ **Am-c** k* am-m k* ambr amyg-p bro1 anac bro1 *Anan* androc srj1• ang b7.de ant-c ant-t k* anth ↓ *Apis* k* aq-mar jl **Arg-met** k* arg-n arn ↓ **Ars** k* ars-s-f k2 **Arum-t** asaf b7.de* atp ↓ atra-r skp7*• atro bro1 **Aur** aur-ar k2 aur-s k2 *Bad* bamb-a stb2.de• *Bapt* bro1 *Bar-c* k* bar-m bar-s ↓ **Bell** k* bell-p sp1 bism bg2 borx b4a.de* both bro1 bov ↓ brom k* bros-gau mrc1 brucel sa3• *Bry* k* bufo *Caj* bro1 *Calc* k* calc-f sp1 calc-i k2 *Calc-p* calc-s calc-sil k2 camph k* *Canth* k* caps k* carb-ac k* *Carb-an* k* *Carb-v* k* carbn-s carneg-g rwt1• cassia-s ccrh1• castm caust k* *Cham* k* chel **Chin** k* *Chinin-ar* chinin-s c1 chir-fl gya2 *Cic* bro1 cimic cinnb clem ↓ coc-c bg2 cocain bro1 cocc b7.de* **Coff** k* colch coli ↓ con k* cor-r croc b7.de* crot-c sk4• cupr-act cur bro1 cycl der ↓ dig dios dirc dol br1 dros dub bro1 dulc fd4.de *Elaps* fago ↓ falco-pe nl2• ferr k* ferr-ar ferr-p fic-m ↓ *Fl-ac* k* foll mtf11 form fuma-ac rly4• gamb ↓ gels k* gins glon *Graph* k* grat k* ham hell k* **Hep** k* hir rsj4• hist sp1 hydr ↓ hydr-ac k* hydrog srj2• hyos bro1* ign k* ina-i mlk9.de ind inul iod bro1 ip k* irid-met srj5• jug-c kali-ar *Kali-bi* k* kali-br bro1 *Kali-c* k* *Kali-chl* k* **Kali-i** kali-m k2* kali-n k* kali-p kali-perm bro1 kali-s kali-sil k2 ketogl-ac rly4• kola stb3• kreos **Lac-c** k* lac-d k* lac-h sk4• lac-lup hrn2• *Lach* k* lat-m sp1 laur k* led k* limen-b-c mlk9.de limest-b es1• lob ↓ loxo-lae bnm12• luf-op rsj5• **Lyc** k* lyss k* m-aust b7.de mag-c k* mag-m b4.de* mag-s mang k* mang-p rly4• melal-alt gya4 *Meny* b7.de* **Merc** k* *Merc-c* k* merc-cy k* *Merc-i-f* k* *Merc-i-r* k* merl *Mez* k* mill mur-ac myos-a rly4• myric nad rly4• naja bg2 *Nat-ar* *Nat-c* k* nat-m k* nat-ox rly4• *Nat-p* k* *Nat-s* nat-sil ↓ nicc nicotam rly4• **Nit-ac** k* *Nux-v* k* oena *Onos* op ox-ac ozone sde2• par k* *Petr* k* petr-ra ↓ *Ph-ac* k* *Phos* k* *Phyt* k* pic-ac plac-s rly4• plb b7.de* plect ↓ podo polys ↓ pop-cand bro1 positr nl2• pot-e rly4• propl ub1• psor bro1* puls k* ran-b b7.de* rauw ↓ *Rhus-t* k* rumx ruta k* *Sabad* k* sabin b7.de* *Sang* k* sangin-n bro1 *Sars* k* scarl jl2 sel rsj9• senec bro1 seneg b4.de* sep k* *Sil* k* sinus rly4• spig b7.de* spong mrr1* **Stann** ↓ *Staph* k* stict k* stram b7.de* streptoc rly4• *Stront-c* k* *Stry* bro1 suis-pan rly4• *Sul-ac* k* sul-i k2* *Sulph* k* sumb ↓ symph fd3.de• tab tarax b7.de* *Tarent* tax ↓ tell c1 *Thuj* k* tritic-vg fd5.de tub mtf11 tung-met bdx1• v-a-b jl* vanil fd5.de vario jl2 ven-m rsj12• verat k* verb c1 x-ray sp1* zinc k* zinc-p k2 [bell-p-sp dcm1 heroin sdj2]
    - ⁝ **right**: mand rsj7•
    - ⁝ **left**: atra-r skp7*• myos-a rly4•
    - ⁝ **morning** | **waking**; on: abrom-a ks5
    - ⁝ **night**: atra-r skp7• bamb-a stb2.de•
    - ⁝ **aching**: allox tpw3
    - ⁝ **burning**: aesc k* allox tpw3 arn k* *Ars* atp rly4• aur k* **Bar-c** calc-sil k2 canth k* carbn-s cassia-s ccrh1• caust h2* coli gmj1 *Hep* kali-bi k* kali-c k* lyc k* mag-c k* merc-c mrr1 mez k* nat-sil fd3.de• ozone sde2• plect a1 rauw tpw8 sil k* sulph h2* symph fd3.de•

- **swallowing – agg.**: ...
    - ⁝ **coryza**; during: *Puls* b7a.de
    - ⁝ **cutting** pain: anth a1 nit-ac gk stann k* sul-ac k*
    - ⁝ **drawing** pain: alum h2
    - ⁝ **dull** pain: cassia-s ccrh1•
    - ⁝ **fever**; during: ph-ac b4.de* phos b4.de sep b4.de
    - ⁝ **lancinating**: ozone sde2•
    - ⁝ **plug**; as from a: cham h1
    - ⁝ **pressing** on swollen glands amel.: spig ↓
      - ⁝ **stitching** pain: spig h1
    - ⁝ **pressing** pain: alum h2* am-m *Bar-c* *Calc* k* *Carb-an* k* dulc fd4.de ferr c1 ham fd3.de• hell h1* **Kali-i** mez h2* **Nit-ac** k* nux-v k* par k* ph-ac h2* puls h1* rhus-t h1* sabad k* sep k* sil h2* sulph h2* thuj h1*
    - ⁝ **raw**; as if: allox tpw3 anth a1 **Arg-met** **Arum-t** lp **Bar-c** k* bry k* der a1 fago k* fic-m gya1 hep k* hydr a1 nat-c k* nicotam rly4• nux-v petr k* polys sk4• **Stann** k* suis-pan rly4• sumb zinc k* [tax jsj7]
    - ⁝ **saliva** (See liquids - agg.)
    - ⁝ **scratching** pain: brucel sa3• mez h2 sep h2 stram h1 tritic-vg fd5.de vanil fd5.de
    - ⁝ **splinter**; as from a: allox tpw3 alum h2 *Apis* *Arg-n* k* calc-sil k2 **Hep** mag-c ptk1 nat-m k2 nit-ac k2 petr h2
    - ⁝ **stinging**: *Alum* am-m *Apis* arum-t *Aur* *Dros* *Kali-c* **Kali-i** *Lyss* *Mag-c* *Merc* *Puls* stram k2 symph fd3.de• thuj
    - ⁝ **stitching** pain: aeth alum alum-p k2 alum-sil k2 *Alumn* am-m **Apis** aur *Bar-c* bar-s k2 *Bell* bov **Bry** **Calc** calc-sil k2 carbn-s cassia-s ccrh1• caust cham chel chin chinin-ar clem a1 coff dulc fd4.de fic-m gya1 gamb graph **Hep** ind iod h kali-bi kali-c kali-n kali-p kali-sil k2 *Lach* led lob lyc mag-c h2 mag-m a1 mag-s mang meny h1 **Merc** mez nat-m **Nit-ac** petr petr-ra shn4• ph-ac rhus-t ruta fd4.de *Sabad* sars h2 *Sep* **Sil** spig staph stram sul-ac **Sulph** symph fd3.de• thuj tub xxb vanil fd5.de
    - ⁝ **Hyoid** bone; behind: **Calc** k*
  - • **amel.**: bit-ar ↓ cassia-s ↓ cortico ↓ hep ↓ *Kali-bi* ↓ rhus-t ↓ stann ↓
    - ⁝ **raw**; as if: bit-ar wht1•
    - ⁝ **splinter**; as from a: cortico sp1 hep ptk1
    - ⁝ **stitching** pain: cassia-s ccrh1• *Kali-bi* rhus-t h1 stann h2
  - • **empty**:
    - ⁝ **agg.**: adam skp7• agar aids nl2• *Ail* allox sp1 alum ambr androc srj1• arg-n *Ars* **Bar-c** k* bar-i k2 *Bell* k* berb k* bry k* calc h2* calc-p carb-ac carbn-s carc mg1.de* *Cench* *Cinnb* k* cob *Cocc* k* con ↓ *Crot-h* dendr-pol sk4• ferr gink-b sbd1• glon graph k* *Grat* ham k* hep k* hydr a1 hydrog srj2• kali-bi **Kali-c** k* ketogl-ac rly4• *Lac-c* **Lach** k* lap-la ↓ lyc h2* mag-c mang mang-p rly4• *Merc* k* merc-c *Merc-i-f* merc-i-r k* nat-ar nux-v k* ozone sde2• petr-ra shn4• phel plat plut-n srj7• psor *Puls* k* rat *Rhus-t* k* ruta sacch-a fd2.de• sep k* sinus rly4• spong fd4.de suis-pan rly4• sulph k* tell k* thuj thymu br1 tritic-vg fd5.de vario k* vesp k* zinc k* [heroin sdj2]
      - ⁝ **burning**: **Bar-c** ham fd3.de• merc-i-f merc-i-r plut-n srj7•
      - ⁝ **stitching** pain: alum con lap-la sde8.de• mag-c mang h2 *Sep* *Sulph*
    - ⁝ **amel.**: bit-ar wht1•
  - • **food**:
    - ⁝ **agg.**: bad k* bar-c k* bry k* cham hr1 dirc c1 dros hep k* *Kali-bi* hr1 *Kali-c* *Lac-c* k* lach nat-s k2 nit-ac k* nux-v ozone sde2• petr ph-ac phos k* rhus-t k* sep k* spong fd4.de stront-c sk4• suis-pan rly4• *Sulph* k*
    - ⁝ **amel.**: *Ign* bg3 lach mrr1
  - • **head** forward and lift up knee; has to bend: bell ptk1
  - • **liquids**:
    - ⁝ **agg.**: **Bell** canth dirc c1 ign kola stb3• **Lach** k* lyc **Merc-c** ozone sde2• sul-ac
    - ⁝ **amel.**: bit-ar wht1• lach tl1
  - • **must** swallow: beryl ↓ gink-b ↓ stroph-h ↓
    - ⁝ **burning**: beryl tpw5 gink-b sbd1• stroph-h ptk1
  - • **neck** to get food or drinks down; has to turn: kali-m ptk1
  - • **not** swallowing; when: aeth alum ambr k2 *Apis* arn **Caps** carc tpw2* cina dig ↓ graph ↓ grat ham fd3.de• **Ign** iod lac-c lac-h htj1• lach laur led lyc sne mag-s mang *Mez* nux-v phel plat puls sabin sulph thuj *Zinc*
    - ⁝ **burning**: ambr h1
    - ⁝ **drawing** pain: *Caps*

- **not** swallowing; when: ...
  - **stinging**: aeth **Apis** arn dig *Ign Led*
  - **stitching** pain: aeth graph **Ign** *Puls Zinc*
- **saliva**:
  - **agg.**: agar↓
    - **tearing** pain: agar k*
- **sore** (See agg.)

- **sweets**:
  - **agg.**: lach bg1 sang **Spong**
    - **burning**: sang k*
    - **sore**: sang **Spong**
  - **amel.**: ars
- **swollen** glands; as from: nat-m h2*
- **syphilitic**: lach k2
- **talking**:
  - **after**: kali-bi↓
    - **stitching** pain: kali-bi
  - **agg.**: acon act-sp↓ allox tpw4* alumn↓ am-c↓ ambr vh androc srj1• arum-t↓ atro↓ bell berb calc k* cassia-s↓ chir-fl gya2 coll↓ dros dulc fd4.de fic-m↓ *Fl-ac* graph↓ hep h2 **Kali-i** k* kali-n↓ luf-op rsj5• mag-c mag-m↓ merc merl nat-s↓ nat-sil fd3.de• nicc k* nit-ac↓ par ph-ac h2 psil ft1 rhus-t sal-fr sle1• spong mrr1 staph suis-em↓ symph↓ tarent
    - **aching**: allox tpw3
    - **burning**: allox tpw3
    - **pressing** pain: fic-m gya1 **Kali-i** nat-sil fd3.de•
    - **raw**; as if: arum-t k2
    - **sore**: act-sp k* alumn kr1 atro a1 coll ptk1 dros bt dulc fd4.de kali-i ptk1 mag-c a1 nat-s hr nicc a1 staph sne suis-em rly4• tarent
    - **stinging**: **Kali-i** mag-c symph fd3.de•
    - **stitching** pain: am-c cassia-s ccrh1• graph h2* kali-n h2* mag-c mag-m h2* nit-ac k*
    - **ulcerative** pain: cassia-s ccrh1•
  - **amel.**: calc h2* lyc sne
  - **not** amel.: mim-p skp7•
- **tea**:
  - **agg.**: phasco-ci↓
    - **burning**: phasco-ci rbp2
  - **amel.**: adam↓ cassia-s↓
    - **raw**; as if: cassia-s ccrh1•
    - **stitching** pain: adam skp7•
    - **tearing** pain: cassia-s ccrh1•
- **tearing** pain: acon k2 act-sp k* *Aeth* agar k* am-c k* ambr k* ars k* bamb-a stb2.de• *Bell* b4a.de *Bism Camph Carb-v* k* cassia-s ccrh1• caust k* cham k* cist k* *Colch* k* crot-h hura iod h* kali-bi bg2 kali-c b4.de* lyc b4.de* med hr1 nat-s k* nit-ac bg2 phyt bg2 sol-t-ae k* staph k* teucr k* *Zinc* k*
  - **jerking** pain: zinc h2*
  - **upward**: lyc h2*
- **thirst**; with: kola stb3•
- **torn** apart; as if: anac b4a.de caust b4.de*
- **torn** off; as if: caust bg2 plb b7.de* rhus-t b7a.de*
- **touch** agg.: agar↓ apis bar-c bg1 bell brom bry chinin-s cic elaps hr1 gamb hep k2 ign k* lac-c **Lach** merc-c mrr1 mez nicc phyt psil ft1* spong k* staph↓ sulph bg teucr zinc
  - **drawing** pain: staph h1*
  - **pressing** pain: merc-c mrr1
  - **stitching** pain: agar k* bell h1*
- **turning** head agg.: *Bell* brom k* bry chinin-s a* hep *Lach* k*
  - **stitching** pain: hep c1
- **twisting** pain: op b7a.de
- **ulcerated**; as if: *Stann* bg2
- **ulcerative** pain: *Arg-n* k* bamb-a stb2.de• *Caps* a1 carb-an k* cassia-s cdd7*• *Cham* b7.de *Graph* k* *Hep* merc b4.de petr a1 ph-ac b4.de* puls b7.de
- **vomiting**:
  - **after**: agar↓ agar-ph↓ arg-met↓ phos↓ puls↓ ric↓ sul-ac↓

- **vomiting** – **after**: ...
    - **burning**: agar agar-ph a1 arg-met bg2 phos k* puls k* ric a1 sul-ac k*
  - **while**: anac↓
    - **pressing** pain: anac h2*
- **waking**; on: amp↓ arg-n↓ arge-pl rwt5• aster↓ atp↓ beryl↓ bit-ar↓ bov↓ calc-p↓ chel↓ cimic hr1 *Crot-h*↓ cyclosp sa3• ephe-si↓ flor-p↓ galeoc-c-h gms1• germ-met↓ hydr↓ *Kali-bi Lach* luna↓ mand rsj7• mang-p rly4• melal-alt gya4 merc-i-r↓ mim-p↓ myric orot-ac↓ oxal-a↓ plac-s↓ plan positr nl2• puls-n↓ raph rauw↓ sacch-a fd2.de• sel↓ spect↓ succ-ac↓ taosc iwa1• *Trios* rsj11•
  - **burning**: flor-p rsj3• puls-n rauw tpw8
  - **raw**; as if: bit-ar wht1• plan k*
  - **sore**: amp rly4• arg-n k* aster k* atp rly4• beryl tpw5 bov k* calc-p k* chel k* *Crot-h* ephe-si hsj1• galeoc-c-h gms1• germ-met srj5• hydr k* kali-bi k* *Lach* luna kg1• mang-p rly4• merc-i-r mim-p skp7• myric k* orot-ac rly4• oxal-a rly4• plac-s rly4• plan k* raph k* sel rsj9• succ-ac rly4• [spect dfg1]
- **walking**:
  - **agg.**: lyc↓
    - **raw**; as if: lyc k*
  - **air** agg.; in open: stann↓
    - **raw**; as if: stann
  - **rapidly**:
    - **agg.**: bry↓
      - **stitching** pain: bry
- **warm**:
  - **applications**:
    - **amel.**: cassia-s↓ polys↓
      - **raw**; as if: cassia-s ccrh1•
      - **sore**: polys sk4•
      - **tearing** pain: cassia-s ccrh1•
  - **bed**:
    - **agg.**: *Coc-c* mag-c *Merc*
      - **burning**: coc-c k2
  - **drinks**:
    - **agg.**: allox tpw4* ambr k2 *Apis* beryl sp1 canth carc mg1.de* cassia-s↓ coc-c k2 dulc fd4.de gels psa guaj k2 **Lach** k* *Lyc* merc-i-f olib-sac wmh1 **Phyt** k* podo fd3.de• psor jl2 spong
      - **burning**: beryl tpw5 coc-c k2 gels psa
      - **dull** pain: cassia-s ccrh1•
      - **raw**; as if: allox tpw3
      - **sore**: beryl tpw5
      - **splinter**; as from a: allox tpw3
      - **ulcerative** pain: cassia-s cdd7•
    - **amel.**: adam skp7• aids nl2• allox sp1 aln vva1• *Alum* androc srj1• arg-n sne arge-pl rwt5• **Ars** bac wz calc-f calc-p cassia-s↓ cench k2 *Cham* crot-c sk4• cupr sst3• dendr-pol sk4• ephe-si hsj1• germ-met srj5• gink-b sbd1• guare **Hep** hydrog srj2• kali-bi c1 lac-c kr1* lac-h↓ lavand-a ctl1• limen-b-c mlk9.de **Lyc** k* mim-p skp7*• nat-m gk nux-v petr-ra shn4• plac rzf5• *Rhus-t* k* sabad stront-c sk4• *Sulph* urol-h rwt• visc sp1 [heroin sdj2]
      - **aching**: allox tpw3
      - **burning**: allox tpw3 alum *Ars* calc-f cassia-s ccrh1• hep lac-h sk4•
      - **sore**: ephe-si hsj1•
  - **food**:
    - **agg.**: kali-c↓
      - **burning**: kali-c h2
  - **room**:
    - **agg.**: *Apis Bry* k* tritic-vg fd5.de
    - **amel.**: mag-c
  - **tea** | **amel.**: mim-p skp7• musca-d szs1
- **warmth**:
  - **agg.**●: carc fb *Coc-c* guaj sf1.de **LACH** k ●* merc phyt
  - **amel.**: alum *Ars* bamb-a stb2.de• *Cham* ham fd3.de• **Hep** k ● *Rhus-t* sabad k2
- **washing** agg.: lach bg1

- **water**:
  - **from**: calc-caust ↓
    - **burning**: calc-caust c1
- **weather**:
  - **change** of weather: **Calc** k*
    - **sore**: **Calc** k*
  - **cold**:
    - **agg.**: sacch-a gmj3
      - **sore**: sacch-a gmj3
    - **wet** | **agg.**: *All-c* br1
  - **wet**:
    - **agg.**●: **Calc** *Dulc Hep* kola stb3• lach bg1 phos ↓ *Rhus-t* sacch-a gmj3
      - **raw**; as if: phos
      - **sore**: *Calc Dulc Hep Rhus-t* sacch-a gmj3
- **winter** agg.: mez ptk1
- **yawning**:
  - **agg.**: aloe gsy am-m bg1 *Arg-met Arg-n* k* bry sys calc-p hep bg1 irid-met srj5• mag-c *Nat-c* k* nat-m bg1 nicc k* phos h2* rhus-t bg1 sil ↓ tarent zinc bg1*
    - **stinging**: am-m nat-c h2
    - **stitching** pain: am-m k* mag-c k* nat-c h2* rhus-t k* sil k*
    - **extending** to:
      - **Ear**: hydrog ↓
        - **sore**: hydrog srj2•
  - **amel.**: manc

▽ - **extending** to:

○ • **Abdomen**: iod ↓ zinc ↓
- **burning**: iod k*
- **pressing** pain: zinc k*

• **Back**: sep ↓
- **pressing** pain: sep h2*

• **Cervical** region: stann ↓
- **stitching** pain: stann h2*

• **Chest**: agar ↓ all-c ↓ lac-c ↓ *Mez* ↓ nat-c ↓ sang ↓ **Stann** ↓ tarent ↓
- **burning**: agar k* *Mez* hr1 sang k* tarent k2
- **raw**; as if: all-c k2
- **sore**: lac-c c1 nat-c k* **Stann** k*

• **Ear**: agar ↓ all-c alum k* *Ambr* androc srj1• apis bg1* bamb-a stb2.de• *Bell* berb ↓ bry *Calc* k* calc-p a1 carb-ac carb-an cham dendr-pol sk4• dulc fd4.de elaps gels c1* gink-b sbd1• *Hep* hydrog srj2• ign ip ↓ irid-met srj5• iris kali-bi bg1 kali-m bg3 kali-n k* kali-p c1 kali-perm kola stb3• *Lac-c* k* lach-h sk4• *Lach* k* *Lith-c Lyc* mag-m bg1 maias-l hrn2• mang k2 merc *Merc-cy* merc-d bg3 nat-m *Nit-ac* nux-v ozone sde2• par phys a1* *Phyt* pieri-b mlk9.de *Podo* ruta fd4.de sars k* sec sol-ni ↓ staph bg1 streptoc rly4• sul-ac sulph bg1 tarent tell thuj ↓ tub c1* vanil fd5.de vesp fkr7.de [nicc stj1]
- **right**: all-c tl1
- **cough** agg.; during: bry sys mag-m ↓
  - **stitching** pain: mag-m h2
- **drawing** pain: all-c alum bry
- **pressing** pain: alum bamb-a stb2.de• bry k* carb-an k* dulc fd4.de nat-m vanil fd5.de
- **stitching** pain: agar br1 ambr berb k* bry k* calc k* dulc fd4.de **Hep** k* hydrog srj2• ign ip k* iris *Kali-bi* k* kali-p mag-m k* mang h2* merc *Merc-cy* nit-ac mrr1 nux-v k* sars k* sol-ni thuj tub c1 vanil fd5.de vesp fkr7.de [nicc stj1]
- **swallowing** agg.●: agar ↓ ail alum ↓ aq-mar c1 *Arg-n* ↓ brom calc ↓ cassia-s ccrh1• con ↓ dol ↓ dulc fd4.de *Elaps* ferr-i ↓ *Gels* guaj ↓ hep ↓ hydrog srj2• *Ign* ↓ irid-met srj5• kali-bi kali-c kali-n k* kali-perm *Lac-c* lach k* limen-b-c hrn2* lyc ↓ mag-m ↓ mag-s sp1* maias-l hrn2• merc **Nit-ac Nux-v** par petr ↓ petr-ra shn4• ph-ac h2* *Phyt* k* psor al2* ruta fd4.de sil ↓ staph ↓ *Sulph* ↓ tarent tub dp• vanil fd5.de
  - **left**: limen-b-c hrn2• staph ↓
    - **stitching** pain: staph br1
  - **stitching** pain●: agar bro1 alum bro1 *Arg-n* bro1 calc h2 con dol bro1 dulc fd4.de ferr-i bro1 *Gels* k* guaj c1* hep br1* *Ign* *Kali-bi* bro1

- **extending** to – **ear** – **swallowing** agg. – **stitching** pain: ... *Kali-c* bro1 *Lac-c* bro1 lyc h2 mag-m h2* *Merc Nit-ac* bro1 **Nux-v** petr k* *Phyt* k* psor bro1 sil bro1 staph c1* *Sulph* vanil fd5.de
  - **talking**; when: calc ↓
    - **stitching** pain: calc h2
  - **turning** head agg.: **Hep** ↓
    - **splinter**; as from a: **Hep**
    - **stitching** pain: hep h2
  - **yawning** agg.: agar ↓ alum ↓ *Arg-n* ↓ dol ↓ ferr-i ↓ gels ↓ guaj ↓ **Hep** ↓ *Kali-bi* ↓ *Kali-c* ↓ *Lac-c* ↓ nat-m ↓ *Nit-ac* ↓ *Phyt* ↓ psor ↓ sil ↓ staph ↓
    - **splinter**; as from a: **Hep**
    - **stitching** pain: agar bro1 alum bro1 *Arg-n* bro1 dol bro1 ferr-i bro1 gels bro1 guaj bro1 hep k* *Kali-bi* bro1 *Kali-c* bro1 *Lac-c* bro1 nat-m h2 *Nit-ac* bro1 *Phyt* bro1 psor bro1 sil bro1 staph bro1

• **Ears**: atp ↓ bell ↓ carbn-o ↓ chir-fl ↓ coca-c ↓ form ↓ hydrog ↓ lith-c ↓ nat-pyru ↓ ozone ↓ ph-ac ↓ *Podo* ↓ pot-e ↓ streptoc ↓ tere-la ↓ ven-m ↓
- **right**: nat-pyru ↓
  - **sore**: nat-pyru rly4•
- **left**: psil ↓
  - **sore**: psil ft1
- **burning**: atp rly4• ozone sde2•
- **raw**; as if: coca-c sk4•
- **sore**: bell k* carbn-o chir-fl gya2 form hydrog srj2• lith-c nat-pyru rly4• ph-ac k* *Podo* k* pot-e rly4• streptoc rly4• tere-la rly4• ven-m rsj12•

• **Esophagus**: acal ↓ *Acon* ↓ agar ↓ *Am-c* ↓ anan ↓ bapt k2 carbn-s ↓ dor ↓ kali-perm ↓ phos k2 vanil fd5.de
- **burning**: acal br1 *Acon* agar *Am-c* anan carbn-s dor kr1 kali-perm

• **Eyes**: merc-c bg1 tarent bg1

• **Head**: hep bg1 merc-c bg1 plat h2* ruta fd4.de

• **Larynx**: arg-met ↓ fl-ac *Lach* k* naja k2 ruta fd4.de
- **raw**; as if: arg-met k2
- **sore**: arg-met k2 fl-ac k* ruta fd4.de

• **Lips**: mez ↓
- **burning**: mez k*

• **Mouth**: ph-ac ↓
- **burning**: ph-ac h2*

• **Nape**: *Lach* ↓
- **sore**: *Lach* k*

• **Neck**; glands of: chir-fl gya2 sep

• **Nose**: choc ↓ falco-pe ↓
- **raw**; as if: choc srj3•
- **sore**: falco-pe nl2•

• **Nostrils**: phos bg1
- **left**: *Gels* ↓
  - **burning**: *Gels*

• **Posterior** nares (= choanae): bapt a1

• **Root** of tongue: *Phyt* ↓
- **stitching** pain: *Phyt*

• **Stomach**: *Acon* ↓ alco ↓ anan ↓ ant-c ↓ *Apis* ↓ *Arn* ↓ ars ↓ calc ↓ carb-ac ↓ *Carb-an* ↓ *Carbn-s* ↓ cic ↓ crot-c cund a1* dor ↓ euph ↓ iris ↓ *Kali-bi* ↓ lach mag-s ↓ mez ↓ *Nux-v* ↓ ol-an ↓ petr ↓ phasco-ci ↓ phos ↓ plb ↓ psor ↓ rhus-t ↓ sec ↓ still ↓ sul-ac k* ulm-c ↓
- **burning**: *Acon* anan ant-c k* *Apis Arn* k* ars k* carb-ac k* *Carbn-s* cic a1 dor k* euph k* iris sne *Kali-bi* k* mag-s k* mez a1 ol-an a1 phasco-ci rbp2 psor k* rhus-t a1 sec k* still k* sul-ac k* ulm-c jsj8•
- **cutting** pain: plb k*
- **pressing** pain: carb-an h2* *Nux-v* phos h2*
- **raw**; as if: calc *Carb-an* petr h2
- **sore**: alco a1 lach k*

• **Submaxillary** glands: *Merc*

• **Temple**: dendr-pol ↓
- **stitching** pain: dendr-pol sk4•

• **Trachea**: adam ↓
- **sore**: adam skp7•

- **Upward**: lyc bg2 sep bg2

○ - **Back** of throat:
- **inspiration** agg.: ap-g↓ conv↓
  - **raw**; as if: ap-g vh1 conv br1

- **Esophagus**: *Acon*↓ aesc↓ aeth↓ agar↓ agath-a nl2• *Alum* alumn *Am-c*↓ *Am-caust* bro1 ammc↓ anac↓ ant-t *Arn*↓ *Ars*↓ arund↓ *Asaf*↓ *Aster*↓ *Bar-c*↓ bell↓ bov↓ brom↓ cain↓ caj *Calc*↓ camph↓ cann-i↓ canth↓ caps↓ *Carb-ac*↓ *Carb-an*↓ carbn-s↓ caust cedr↓ chel↓ chinin-s↓ cimx↓ coc-c↓ coca↓ cocc bro1 colch k* con↓ crot-c crot-h↓ crot-t cupr-ar↓ *Cycl*↓ dig↓ diphtox jl2 *Euph*↓ ferr-ma↓ gels bro1 graph↓ gymno↓ *Hep*↓ heroin↓ hydr-ac hydrc↓ iod↓ *Iris*↓ kali-bi kali-c↓ kali-chl kali-i↓ kali-n↓ kola stb3• kreos↓ lac-ac↓ lach↓ laur↓ lob↓ lyc↓ maias-l hm2• manc↓ merc **Merc-c**↓ *Mez*↓ moni↓ mur-ac nat-c↓ *Nat-m*↓ nit-ac *Nux-v*↓ *Ol-an*↓ ox-ac↓ ozone↓ petr↓ phos k* *Phyt*↓ plac-s↓ *Plb*↓ ran-s↓ raph rhus-t↓ sabad↓ **Sang**↓ sars↓ seneg↓ sin-a↓ spira↓ spirae↓ stry↓ sul-ac sul-i↓ syph↓ tab↓ *Tarent*↓ tritic-vg fd5.de ust↓ vanil↓ verat↓ verat-v↓ vinc↓ xan↓ zinc↓
  - **morning**: cupr-s↓
    - **burning**: cupr-s
  - **forenoon**: carbn-s↓ rhus-t↓
    - **burning**: carbn-s rhus-t a1
  - **noon**: rhus-t↓
    - **burning**: rhus-t
  - **afternoon**: nux-m↓
    - **burning**: nux-m
  - **evening**: maias-l hm2• sin-a↓
    - **burning**: sin-a
  - **accompanied** by | **thirst**: colch mtf11
  - **breath**; taking: ther↓
    - **pressing** pain: ther c1
  - **burning**: *Acon* k* aesc aeth agar *Alumn Am-c* am-caust br1* ammc k* ant-t *Arn Ars* k* arund *Asaf* k* *Aster* bell bov brom cain camph cann-i canth k* caps bro1 *Carb-ac* k* carbn-s cedr chel chinin-s coc-c *Cocc* con *Crot-t* br1* cupr-ar *Cycl* dig *Euph* gels k* gymno *Hep* hydrc iod *Iris* bro1* kali-bi bg2 kali-i kola stb3• kreos lac-ac laur lyc manc merc **Merc-c** k* *Mez* k* moni rfm1• mur-ac nat-m *Nit-ac* nux-v *Ol-an* ox-ac k* ozone sde2• petr *Phos* k* *Phyt Plb* ran-s raph rhus-t a1 sabad **Sang** k* sars seneg sin-a bro1 spira br1 spirae br1 stry k* *Sul-ac* sul-i k2 syph jl2 *Tarent* ust vanil fd5.de verat verat-v k* xan c1 zinc
    - **accompanied** by:
      - **croup**; membranous (See LARYNX - Croup - membranous - accompanied - esophagus - pain - burning)
      - **fatty** taste: colch mtf11
    - **heat**; with great: moni rfm1•
    - **prickling** pain: hydrc
    - **upward**: *Cocc* crot-t mez
  - **cutting** pain: vinc ptk1
  - **drinking** agg.: calc-caust↓ canth↓ glycyr-g cte1• mez↓ ozone↓
    - **burning**: calc-caust canth mez ozone sde2•
    - **water** | **burning** (See swallowing - water - burning)
  - **eating** | **after**:
    - **agg.**: alum↓ am-c↓ ars↓ bar-c↓ con↓ lyc↓ nit-ac↓ phos↓ streptoc jl2 tarent↓ zinc↓
      - **burning**: am-c tl1 con phos ptk1 tarent
      - **pressing** pain: alum h2 ars h2
      - **some** hours after eating: *Plb*↓
        - **burning**: *Plb*
      - **sore**: bar-c b4a.de lyc b4a.de nit-ac b4a.de zinc b4a.de
    - **while**:
      - **agg.**: ars↓ bar-c↓ lyc↓ nit-ac↓
        - **pressing** pain: ars
        - **sore**: bar-c b4a.de lyc b4a.de nit-ac b4a.de
  - **eructations** agg.: aeth↓ calc-ar↓ germ-met↓ lac-ac↓ ol-an↓
    - **burning**: aeth calc-ar germ-met srj5• lac-ac c1 ol-an
  - **mental** exertion agg.: moni↓
    - **burning**: moni rfm1•

- **Esophagus**: ...
  - **motion**:
    - **amel.**: cycl↓
      - **burning**: cycl hr1
  - **nausea**; with: xan↓
    - **stinging**: xan c1
  - **pregnancy** agg.; during: hell↓
    - **burning**: hell ptk1
  - **pressing** pain: alum k* asaf b7.de* bar-c bg1 brom bg1 cain calc bg1 caust bg1 cimx con k2 crot-h tl1 ferr-ma graph bg1 kali-c lach bg1 lob merc nat-c *Nux-v* ol-an phos bg1 spirae br1 tab tritic-vg fd5.de verat
    - **ball**; as from a: anac con k2
    - **upon** the esophagus; as if the larynx was pressed: chel k*
  - **pressure**:
    - **agg.**: **Merc-c**↓
      - **burning**: **Merc-c**
      - **neck**; on: kali-sula a1*
    - **larynx** agg.; on: iod h
  - **raw**; as if: am-c am-caust vh1 *Calc Carb-an* merc **Merc-c**
  - **scratching** pain: ammc br1
  - **sore**: agath-a nl2• alum ars caj calc dig kali-n nit-ac sul-ac [heroin sdj2]
    - **feels** food along whole length of esophagus: *Alum*
    - **swallowing** over a sore spot; as if: *Bar-c* caj *Nat-m*
  - **splinter**; as from a: ars nat-m k2
  - **stinging**: ars plac-s rly4• xan c1
  - **stitching** pain: calc h2 carbn-s kali-c merc-c
    - **bone** had lodged in it; as if a: carbn-s
  - **swallowing**:
    - **agg.**: agath-a nl2• *Alum* **Ars**↓ *Bar-c* carbn-s↓ *Nat-m Nit-ac* ox-ac sang k2 verat
      - **burning**: **Ars** carbn-s ox-ac
      - **pressing** pain: *Alum*
      - **sore**: agath-a nl2•
    - **food** | **agg.**: caj
    - **water** agg.: calc-caust↓ mez↓
      - **burning**: calc-caust mez
  - **tearing** pain: kali-c
    - **flatus**; as if esophagus would be torn apart by force of rising: coca hr1*
  - **typhoid** fever; in: ars↓ bell↓ bry↓ nux-v↓ phos↓ rhus-t↓ sulph↓
    - **burning**: ars ptk1 bell ptk1 bry ptk1 nux-v ptk1 phos ptk1 rhus-t ptk1 sulph ptk1
  - **wine** agg.; red: ozone↓
    - **burning**: ozone sde2•

▽ - **extending** to:
    - **Back**: streptoc jl2
    - **Stomach**: acon↓ ars *Crot-c* euph↓ *Gels*↓ iris↓ kali-bi↓ lyc↓ merc-c mur-ac nit-ac↓ ozone↓ sul-ac
      - **burning**: acon ars euph h2 *Gels* iris kali-bi lyc nit-ac ozone sde2• sul-ac
      - **sneezing** agg.: ictod

○ - **Upper** part: caps h1

- **Fauces** (See Pain) *Arg-met*↓ kali-sula↓
  - **burning**: *Arg-met* vh1 kali-sula a1*
  - **retching**; after: arg-met↓
    - **burning**: arg-met vh1
- **Lymphatic** glands: sarcol-ac↓
  - **sore**: sarcol-ac sp1
- **Pharynx**: acon↓ *Aesc*↓ alumn k* *Am-caust*↓ anth↓ apis ars k* ars-i↓ *Arum-t*↓ astac a1 *Aur*↓ bar-c↓ bell↓ camph↓ canth k* *Caps*↓ carb-ac↓ carb-v↓ *Caust*↓ **Cist**↓ cocain↓ con↓ cop k* cupr-act euph a1 glyc↓ guaj↓ hydr↓ *Iris*↓ kali-bi↓ kali-chl k* kali-n k* *Kali-perm*↓ kali-s fd4.de kreos↓ lac-h↓ lyc↓ melal-alt gya4 merc↓ merc-c k* merc-i-f↓ mez a1 mur-ac k* nat-ar↓ nit-ac↓ ox-ac k* ph-ac *Phos*↓ *Phyt*↓ plut-n srj7• pop-cand↓ quill↓

- **Pharynx**: ...
ran-s k* rosm lgb1 *Sang*↓ sangin-n↓ senec↓ spong fd4.de sulfonam↓ sulph↓ syph↓ thymu↓ tritic-vg fd5.de tub jl2 ven-m rsj12• wye↓
  - **left**: tub jl2
  - **accompanied** by:
    - **Tongue**:
      - **white** discoloration of the tongue | **heavily** coated: phos kr1*
  - **burning**: acon bro1 *Aesc* bro1 *Am-caust* bro1 apis bro1 *Ars* bro1 ars-i bro1 *Arum-t* bro1 *Aur* bro1 bar-c bro1 bell bro1* camph bro1 *Canth* bro1 *Caps* bro1 carb-ac bro1 carb-v ptk1 *Caust* bro1 **Cist** mrr1 cocain bro1 con bro1 glyc bro1 guaj bro1 hydr bro1 *Iris* bro1 kali-bi bro1 *Kali-perm* bro1 kreos bro1 lac-h sze9• lyc bro1 merc bro1 merc-c bro1* merc-i-f bro1 *Mez* bro1 nat-ar bro1 nit-ac bro1 *Phos* bro1 *Phyt* bro1 pop-cand bro1 quill bro1 *Sang* bro1 sangin-n bro1 senec bro1 sulph bro1* syph jl2 thymu br1 wye bro1
  - **burnt**; as if: sulfonam ks2
  - **cold** air:
    - **inspiration** agg.: **Cist**↓
      - **burning**: **Cist** mrr1
  - **cough** agg.; during: *Carb-v*↓ caust↓ mag-m k* ph-ac↓
    - **burning**: *Carb-v* b4a.de caust b4.de* ph-ac b4.de*
    - **sore**: caust b4.de*
  - **hawk**; causing to: acon↓
    - **burning**: acon vh1
  - **inspiration** agg.: **Cist**↓
    - **burning**: **Cist** mrr1
  - **menses**; during: nat-s↓
    - **burning**: nat-s ptk1
  - **raw**; as if: anth vh1
  - **smokers**; of: aesc↓ arg-n↓ caps↓ nat-m↓ nux-v↓
    - **sore**: aesc bro1 arg-n bro1 caps bro1 nat-m bro1 nux-v bro1
  - **sneezing** agg.: ant-t k*
  - **sore**:
    - **alternating** with | **Face**; irritation of: *Prim-o* br1
  - **swallowing** (See swallowing - agg.)
  - **turning** head agg.: *Bell* k*
  - ▽ **extending** to | **Ears**: alum bg2 tub c1*
  - ○ **Lower** part: caj a1 iod kreos mur-ac a1
- **Posterior** part: nat-m↓ v-a-b jl2
  - **pressing** pain: nat-m bg2
- **Sides**: x-ray↓
  - **cramping**: x-ray sp1
  - **turning** head agg.: hydrog srj2•
- **Spot**; in a:
  - **morning** | **waking**; on: conch fkr1•
- **Spot**; in a dry: apis↓ *Cimic*↓ cist↓ con↓ crot-h↓ hep↓ *Hyos*↓ lac-c↓ lach↓ lith-c↓ merc-cy↓ *Nat-m*↓ nit-ac↓ petr-ra↓ *Phos*↓ phyt↓ polys↓ sil↓
  - **sore**: apis bg3 *Cimic* bg1 cist bg1 con bg1 crot-h bg3 hep bg1 *Hyos* bg3 lac-c bg3 lach bg1 lith-c bg3 merc-cy bg3 *Nat-m* bg3* nit-ac bg3 petr-ra shn4• *Phos* bg3 phyt bg1 polys sk4• sil bg1
- **Tonsils**: aesc a1 alum am-c ars bg2 bar-c bg3 bell bg2* *Benz-ac* berb bg2 calc bg2 calc-p cann-i↓ caps↓ *Caust* cham↓ chin-b kr1 cocc a1 con↓ crot-t dios↓ dulc fd4.de graph guaj bg3 gymno↓ *Hep* k* hydroph rsj6• iod bg2 iris c1 kali-bi kali-c k2 kali-p kali-s fd4.de lach k* loxo-recl↓ merc bg3 *Merc-i-f* *Merc-i-r* bg3 merl↓ naja nat-m↓ nit-ac h2* nux-m a1 nux-v↓ ox-ac↓ par↓ phos bg2 phys↓ phyt bg2* psor jl2 *Ran-s*↓ raph rhus-t a1 ruta fd4.de sang↓ sec a1 sep↓ sil k2 staph bg2 sulph↓ symph fd3.de• tarent k* tell↓ ust↓ vac jl2 vanil fd5.de zinc↓
  - **right**: anthraci vh1 aq-mar jl* bapt↓ cadm-met↓ caps hr1 ferr-p sne ham fd3.de• helo-s↓ kali-p k2 kali-s fd4.de lyc↓ *Merc-i-f* *Phyt* mrr1 rosm↓ symph fd3.de• tarent k2
    - **scratching** pain: rosm lgb1
    - **sore**: cadm-met tpw6
    - **stitching** pain: bapt hr1 ham fd3.de• helo-s rwt2• lyc
    - **swallowing** agg.: v-a-b jl2

Pain – Tonsils: ...

  - **left**: aesc a1 alum↓ berb a1* bry a1* calc-p a1 cupr h2* dios a1 gels hr1 grat↓ hipp hr1 hydroph rsj6• ipom-p hr1 kali-bi↓ kali-p↓ lac-c hr1 lac-h↓ lach↓ naja a1 nat-m a1 olib-sac↓ psil ft1 trios rsj11•
    - **cutting** pain: kali-bi bg2
    - **pressing** pain: alum h2* bry hr1 olib-sac wmh1
    - **stitching** pain: cupr h2* grat kali-bi k* kali-p k2 lac-h sze9• lach
    - **extending** to | **Ears**: *Calc* vh cench k2 kali-bi a1*
  - **morning**: bry cadm-met↓ dulc fd4.de ruta fd4.de
    - **8** h: naja
    - **sore**: cadm-met tpw6
    - **waking**; on: bry dulc fd4.de hydroph rsj6•
  - **evening** and night: zinc↓
    - **pressing** pain: zinc h2*
  - **night**: aq-mar skp7• mim-p↓
    - **cutting** pain: mim-p rsj8•
  - **aching**: aesc bg1
  - **air** agg.; in open: kali-c k2
  - **biting** pain: iod h* ox-ac a1
  - **burning**: ars k2 *Bell* caps hr1* dios k* iris merc phys phyt bg2 raph k* sang k2 vanil fd5.de
  - **cold** air:
    - **amel.**: iris↓
      - **burning**: iris
  - **drawing** pain: con k* gymno nat-m k* symph fd3.de•
  - **lancinating**: ust
  - **menses**; before: hydroph rsj6•
  - **pinching** pain: sil ptk1
  - **pressing** pain: alum bell cann-i cham *Cocc* merl nux-v par sep h2* symph fd3.de• tell zinc
  - **pressure** agg.: aq-mar skp7•
  - **raw**; as if: phyt
  - **sore**: loxo-recl bnm10• rhus-t a1 vanil fd5.de
  - **stitching** pain: alum *Bell* k* kali-bi *Merc* k* naja nit-ac h2* *Ran-s* k* raph ruta fd4.de sulph tarent
  - **swallowing** agg.: arist-cl sp1 **Bell**↓ rhus-t↓ rosm↓ zinc↓
    - **pressing** pain: zinc h2*
    - **raw**; as if: rhus-t h1
    - **scratching** pain: rosm lgb1
    - **tearing** pain: **Bell**
  - **talking** agg.: hydroph rsj6•
  - **tearing** pain: **Bell**
  - **warm** room | **amel.**: kali-c k2
  - **yawning** agg.: calc-p zinc↓
    - **pressing** pain: zinc h2*
  - ▽ **extending** to | **Ears**: psor jl2
- **Uvula**: ambr↓ *Apis* k* calc↓ calc-p bg2 canth↓ caps↓ caust↓ colch k* iod↓ *Kali-bi* k* lact↓ merc bg3 *Merc-c* bg2* mez bg2 nat-m↓ nit-ac↓ nux-v↓ phyt bg3 rhod↓ ruta↓ sabad↓ sabin↓ sang hr1* seneg↓ sep↓ streptoc jl2 trif-p c2* tus-p bro1
  - **burning**: *Apis* caust h2* colch k* iod bg2 lact mez k* sabad b7a.de *Sang* tus-p c2
  - **menses**; during: calc b4a.de
  - **raw**; as if: ambr k* calc h2* caps bg2 caust bg2
  - **sore**: calc b4a.de canth b7a.de caust h2* nit-ac b4.de ruta b7.de sabin b7a.de sang hr1
  - **stitching** pain: caust h2* nat-m k* nux-v b7.de* rhod k* seneg k* sep k*
  - ○ **Behind**:
    - **eating**:
      - **amel.**: am-m↓
        - **sore**: am-m bro1

PALENESS: *Ail* *Arum-t* *Bar-c* crot-h ox-ac k* plb k* *Sulph*

PARALYSIS: (↗*Food - passes; Liquids; LARYNX - Paralysis - larynx; NOSE - Liquids - come)* acon b7.de* *Apis* arg-n bg2 **Ars** k* arum-t k2 bapt k* bar-c bg2 bell k* both bro1 cadm-s k2 calc bg2 canth bro1 caps k* carb-v bg2 *Caust* k* cocain bro1 *Cocc* k* con bg2 *Cupr* b7a.de* cur k* *Gels* k* hep bg2 hyos k2* iod bg2 ip b7.de* kali-c bg2 kali-p bg2* *Lac-c* k* **Lach** k* lact *Laur* b7a.de* *Lyc* k* merc k2 nat-f sp1 *Nat-m* *Nux-m* k* *Op* ox-ac bro1 phos bg2* phys bg2 *Phyt* *Plb* k* pop-cand c2 puls bg2 *Rhus-t* k* **Sec** k* sep b4.de* *Sil* k* **Stram** k* sulph bg2

- **post** diphtheritic: *Apis* *Arg-n* bro1 **Ars** *Caust* k* *Cocc* k* con bro1 cur bro1 diph bro1 *Gels* k* kali-p bro1 **Lac-c** **Lach** k* **Naja** *Nat-m* k* olnd bro1 *Phos* bro1 *Plb* k* rhus-t bro1 **Sec** k* sil
- **sensation** of: *Ars* b4a.de* cocc b7a.de* ip b7a.de* kali-c b4a.de* lach bg2 meny b7.de* puls b7.de* sil b4a.de*

○ - **Esophagus**: *Alum* *Alumn* **Ars** arum-t k2 *Bapt* bell calc caps *Caust* k* chlol cocc k2 con k2* crot-c elaps ptk1 *Gels* k* *Hydr-ac* k* hyos k2* *Kali-c* lach *Nux-m* *Op* k* petr *Plb* k* *Stram* tab *Verat*
  - • **sensation** of: **Ars** cocc ip kali-c *Lach* lact puls *Sil*
- **Pharynx**: *Alum* bro1 anac bro1 *Apis* **Ars** k* bar-c bro1 bar-m bro1 *Bell* bro1 caps k* *Caust* k* *Cocc* k* *Con* bro1 cur bro1 gels bro1 hep bro1 hyos k2* *Ign* bro1 **Lach** k* lob bro1 lyc bro1 mang-o bro1 merc bro1 morph k* nat-c k2 nit-ac bro1 nux-m k* nux-v bro1 olnd bro1 *Plb* bro1 *Pop-cand* bro1 *Rhus-t* k* *Sil* k* *Stram* k* sulph bro1
  - • **sensation** of | **cough** agg.; during: meny b7.de*

PARCHED (See Dryness - thirst - with)

PERSPIRATION; after suppressed: | **Feet**; of: *Bar-c* bro1 graph bro1 psor bro1 sanic bro1 sil bro1

PHARYNGITIS (See Inflammation - pharynx)

PIMPLES:

○ - **Pharynx**: hippoz bro1 iod bro1
- **Uvula**: *Bapt* hr1 kali-bi k* rumx

PLUG; sensation of a (See Lump)

POWDER, sensation of a (See Dust)

PRICKLY: acon k* alumn calc-f k* cedr k* kali-bi bg2 lach k* limen-b-c hrn2• manc k* merc bg2 petr-ra shn4• sulph bg1 tell verat k* vero-o rly3• [tax jsj7]

- **left**: naja bg2
- **breathing** deep agg.: hipp jl2
- **swallowing**; only on empty: cench k2

▽ - **extending** down esophagus cedr

○ - **Tonsil** | **left**: psor jl2

PROTRUDING tongue agg.: kali-bi ptk1 sabad ptk1

PUBLIC speakers and singers; in: arge-pl rwt5•

PULSATING: acon bg2 *Am-m* k* aran-ix sp1 arg-n k* *Bell* bufo cham b7.de* chel k* coc-c k* euphr k* *Glon* **Hep** hydrog srj2• ind kali-bi bg2 kalm k* *Lach* nit-ac k* ph-ac k* rauw tpw8 rhus-t k* tarent k* visc sp1 xan [tax jsj7]

- **right**: hydrog srj2•
- **accompanied** by palpitations of heart (See CHEST - Palpitation - accompanied - throat)
- **cough**; after: coc-c
- **lying** on left side agg.: choc srj3•

○ - **Esophagus**: ferr tl1
- **Tonsils**: *Am-m* k* bufo bg2 glon bg2 kalm k* nit-ac k* phyt ptk1
  - • **left**: nat-p k*

PUSTULES: *Aeth* k* ant-t k* ars bg2 psor sep k* vario hr1

○ - **Pharynx**: aeth bro1
- **Tonsils**, on: *Sep* k* streptoc jl2

PUTS finger in throat: bell h1* prot jl2

RANCID; sensation as after eating something: camph b7.de*

REFLUX esophagitis (See Inflammation - esophagus - reflux; STOMACH - Eructations; type - food)

RELAXATION:

- **sensation** of: *Alum* prot pte1*• spong b7.de*

○ • **Pharynx**: pen br1

Relaxation – sensation of: ...

- • **Uvula**: alumn c1* calc-f br1 canth k* ham k* *Kali-bi* k*
  - ⁝ **Larynx**; tickling referred to: calc-f br1

○ - **Fauces**; of: coch br1*
- **Pharynx**: aesc bro1 *Alum* bro1 alumn bro1 am-m bro1 bar-c bro1 *Calc-p* bro1 eucal bro1 pen bro1
- **Uvula**: hyos bg2 nat-m bg2
  - • **baglike**: kali-bi ptk1

REVERSED peristaltic action of esophagus: (↗*ABDOMEN - Peristalsis - reversed)* ambr bro1 *Asaf* k* *Canth* b7a.de ferr-i k2*

RHINOPHARYNGITIS (See Inflammation - nasopharynx)

RIGIDITY: chel lach

ROUGHNESS: **Acon** b7.de* *Aesc* k* agar k* ail k* *Aloe* *Alum* k* *Am-c* k* *Am-caust* bro1 am-m k* *Ambr* k* ammc k* anac k* androc srj1• ang b7.de* ant-c k* anth ptk2 *Apis* **Arg-met** k* *Arg-n* k* ars k* *Arum-t* bro1 aspar k* astac vh aur-m bg2 *Bamb-a* stb2.de• bapt a1 *Bar-c* k* bar-s k2 *Bell* k* borx k* bov b4.de* brom bro1 bry b7.de* cain *Calc* k* calc-ar calc-p k* cann-i k* canth k* caps carb-an b4.de* *Carb-v* k* carbn-s *Caust* k* chel k* chen-a hr1 **Chin** k* cimic k* *Cist* clem cob coc-c k* cocc k* colch b7.de* *Coloc* k* com k* *Con* bg2* *Croc* k* cub br1* dig k* **Dros** k* dulc b4.de* erig a1 eup-per k* euph b4.de* fago bro1 ferr b7.de* gels bro1 glon k* *Graph* k* grat k* hell b7.de* *Hep* k* *Hepat* br1* hom-xyz bro1 hydr bro1 hydrog srj2• hyos k* hyper hr1 ign b7.de* iod bg2* *Ip* k* iris kali-ar k2 kali-bi k* *Kali-c* k* kali-n k* kali-s fd4.de ketogl-ac rly4• kreos k* lac-ac k* lach k* laur k* limen-b-c hrn2* lipp a1 *Lyc* k* lyss k* m-aust b7.de *Mag-c* k* *Mag-m* k* mang k* melal-alt gya4 meny k* *Merc* k* merc-c k* merc-cy bro1 mez k* mosch b7.de* mur-ac b4.de* naja bg2 nat-ar *Nat-c* k* nat-m bg2 *Nat-s* nit-ac bg2* nux-m bg2 **Nux-v** k* onos bro1 ozone sde2• par bg2 pen bro1 petr-ra shn4• ph-ac b4.de* *Phos* k* *Phyt* k* *Plat* k* plb k* podo bg2* *Pop-cand* bro1 propl ub1• ptel hr1* **Puls** b7.de* ran-b k* *Ran-s* b7.de* rat k* *Rhod* k* rhus-t k* rob k* *Rumx* bro1 *Sabad* k* *Sang* bro1 sangin-n bro1 sapin a1 sars k* *Seneg* k* *Sep* k* sil h2* sinus rly4• spong k* squil k* stann k* staph k* stict bro1 stront-c k* *Sul-ac* k* *Sulph* k* sumb k* tab tanac a1 tell k* teucr bg2 *Thuj* k* ust valer bg2 verat k* verb k* zinc k*

- **daytime**: mez k*
- **morning**: agar k* *Ail* k* alum k* ant-c k* ars k* borx caust h2* erig a1 kali-n h2* mang k* rhod k* sars k* seneg k* sep k* sulph thuj k* zinc h2*
  - • **rising** agg.: mang k* sulph k*
  - • **waking**; on: alum k* petr-ra shn4• sars k* seneg k* sulph k*
- **forenoon**: jug-c a1 mag-c h2* seneg a1
- **evening**: *Alum* k* kali-n h2* mang h2* nat-c h2* ozone sde2• *Phos* hr1 podo fd3.de• *Seneg* k* stann sulph h2
- **night**: alum h2* arg-n k* podo fd3.de• sil k*
- **catarrh**; from: nux-v tl1
- **cold**; as from taking: bamb-a stb2.de• ozone sde2•
- **coryza**; during: *Caust* b4a.de graph b4.de* *Hep* b4a.de *Kali-c* b4a.de nit-ac b4.de* *Nux-v* b7.de* phos b4.de* rhod b4.de* *Rhus-t* b7a.de
- **cough** agg.; during: (↗*COUGH - Roughness - throat)* anac h2* ang b7.de* arn k* ars b4a.de bar-c b4a.de calc b4a.de carb-an b4.de* carb-v caust k* cob cop dig **Dros** vh euph b4a.de gels hep k* kali-c k* kali-n k* kali-s fd4.de kreos k* laur k* merc-c nat-s k* nicc ozone sde2• phos k* rhod k* rhus-t a1 sars k* seneg k* sep k* spong k* *Sulph* a1
- **dinner** | **amel.**: am-m a1 mag-c h2*
- **eating** | **after** | **agg.**: anac h2* spong fd4.de
  - • **amel.**: am-m k* nat-c h2*
- **expiration** agg.; during: arg-met h1 ph-ac h2*
- **hawking**, from: sep thuj h1*
- **hiccough** agg.: borx h2
- **sing**; on attempting to: agar ptk1
- **swallowing** agg.: ang hr1 *Arg-met* *Arg-n* calc-p k* cocc k* *Hep* lyc k* petr h2* pic-ac k* *Staph* k* sulph k*
- **talking**:
  - • **agg.**: bamb-a stb2.de• graph h2* seneg ptk1 sil h2* *Staph* k*
  - • **impossible**: ph-ac h2*
- **uncovering** agg.: kali-c h2*
- **weather** agg.; wet: phos h2

○ - **Esophagus**: calc h2 hydrc iod *Nat-c* k* podo c1 sulph
- **Fauces**: aesc bro1 coc-c bro1 dros bro1 *Nux-v* bro1 phos bro1 *Phyt* bro1
- **Pharynx**: phyt tl1
- **Uvula**: sulph k*

Throat

SAND in throat; sensation as if: berb rb2 cist rb2 thuj bg2

SCAB at posterior wall; greenish: elaps

SCRAPING: abrot k* acon k* *Aesc* k* agar b4a.de agn b7.de aloe k* *Alum* k* *Am-c* k* *Am-m* b7a.de *Ambr* k* ammc k* **Anac** k* **Anag** k* ang bg2 ant-c ant-t b7.de aq-pet a1 arg-met k* *Arg-n* k* arn b7a.de* *Ars* k* ars-i ars-s-f k2 arum-d ptk2 asaf b7.de asar k* astac vh aur k* aur-ar k2 aur-m aur-s k2 bamb-a stb2.de• bapt k* bar-c b4.de bar-ox-suc rly4• bart a1 bell k* berb k* beryl sp1 bol-la bol-s a1 bov k* brach k* *Brom* k* bry k* calad a1 *Calc* k* calc-p k* calc-s calc-sil k2 camph k* cann-i a1 canth b7.de* *Carb-an* k* *Carb-v* k* carbn-s k2 carc tpw2 carl a1 *Caust* k* cench k2 cer-s a1 chel k* **Chin** k* chinin-ar k2 chinin-s chord-umb rly4• cic k* cimic k* *Coc-c* k* cocc k* colch k* coli rly4• *Coloc* k* con k* *Croc* k* crot-h k* crot-t a1* cycl k* dig k* dros k* dulc b4.de* elat a1 euph k* ferr-i k2 franz a1 gent-c *Graph* k* guaj b4a.de hell k* *Hep* k* *Hepat* br1 hura hydr-ac k* hyos k* hyper hr1 iod k* kali-ar kali-bi k* *Kali-c* k* kali-chl k* kali-m k2 kali-n k* kali-p *Kalm* k* kola stb3• kreos k* lac-lup hrn2• *Lach* lact k* laur k* lil-s a1 lipp a1 lob a1 lyc k* m-arct b7.de m-aust b7.de mag-c k* mag-p bg2 mang k* med tl1 merc k* merc-br a1 *Merc-c* b4a.de **Mez** k* mosch b7.de* mucs-nas rly4• mur-ac b4.de* naja nat-ar nat-c k* nat-m a1 nat-p nit-ac k* nux-m k* **Nux-v** k* ol-an k* olib-sac wmh1 op ox-ac k* oxal-a rly4• ozone sde2• *Par* k* paull a1 ped a1 petr k* petr-ra shn4• ph-ac k* *Phos* k* phyt k* pic-ac k* plat k* podo *Psor* k* *Puls* k* ran-b k* ran-s k* raph k* rat k* *Rhod* k* rhus-t k* ribo rly4• *Rumx* ruta fd4.de *Sabad* k* sal-ac a1 sapin a1 sars sel mrr1 seneg k* sep k* sil k* sin-n a1 spira a1 spong mrr1 squil k* stann k* staph k* stict c1 stront-c stry a1 succ-ac rly4• sul-ac b4.de sul-i k2 **Sulph** k* sumb k* suprar rly4• *Tab* k* ter a1 *Teucr* k* thuj k* til a1 tub c1 valer k* vanil fd5.de **Verat** k* zinc k* zinc-p k2

- **morning**: *Ail* k* berb k* bov k* calc-sil k2 *Caust* k* cer-s a1 chinin-s dulc fd4.de kali-n h2* kali-p fd1.de• lyc mur-ac k* petr sars stann k* tong a1 vanil fd5.de
- **forenoon**: sep k* sil
- **afternoon**: bol-la gins a1 phos k* tab k*
- **evening**: **Alum** bol-la brom *Carb-an* carb-v a1 caust h2* dig h2 kali-n h2* led a1 mez a1 nat-c k* nat-m a1 phos h2* plan a1 sep a1 sil stann k* sulph h2* zinc
  - **bed** agg.; in: plat h2* sulph h2*
- **night**: bamb-a stb2.de• calc k* *Carb-an* naja nat-m k* phyt k* sil k* vanil fd5.de
  - **lying** on side agg.: sil k*
- **beer**; after: merc-c k* staph k*
- **bread** agg.: *Lach* k* ph-ac k* rhus-t k*
- **clear** throat; desire to (See Hawk; disposition)
- **cough** agg.; during: alum a1 bell h1* bov a1 calc-s a1 croc a1 kreos a1 mag-c a1 nat-c a1 olib-sac wmh1 oxal-a rly4• pneu jl2 syph hr1
- **dryness**, from: **Alum** plac rzf5•
- **ices**, after: thuj k*
- **lying** | **amel.**: nat-c a1
- **reading** aloud, after: nit-ac k*
- **sleep**; after long: hep k*
- **swallowing** | **after** | **agg.**: bar-c *Carb-an* caust h2 fago hep hydr jab lach laur nux-m pic-ac stram
  - **empty** | **after**: *Ars*
- **talk**; before being able to: bamb-a stb2.de• carc tpw2*
- **tobacco**; from: osm k*
- ○ - **Pharynx**: mez ptk1 sang ptk1
- **Posterior** part: v-a-b jl2

SCRATCHING: acon a1 agar k* agn k* alum k* ambr h1* *Arg-met Arg-n* arn k* arum-t k* aur-m k* bamb-a stb2.de• *Bar-c* bell h1* bell-p sp1 benz-ac k* berb bol-s a1 borx bov hr1 calad k* calc-p k* cann-s k* carb-v k* carbn-s chel k* chord-umb rly4• *Cist* cob-n sp1 coli rly4• con h2* cyt-l sp1 ferul a1 fum rly1*• fuma-ac rly4• galla-q-r nl2• graph k* haliae-lc srj5• *Hep* hyos h1* *Kali-bi Kali-c* k* kola stb3• *Kreos Lyc Mag-c* mang h2* *Nit-ac Nux-m* k* **Nux-v** k* olib-sac wmh1 par a1 petr k* *Phos* k* *Plat* podo fd3.de• puls k* pyrid rly4• *Rhod* k* rob k* *Seneg Sep* sil a1 sinus rly4• *Spong Sul-ac Sulph* sumb a1 symph fd3.de• tab k* tell k* ter k* urol-h rwt•

- **morning**: cob k* kola stb3• nux-v hr1 spong fd4.de
- **evening**: dig h2* led k* par a1 sin-a a1 tell a1*
- **night**: con h2*
- **accompanied** by | **Nose**; formication in (See NOSE - Formication - accompanied - throat)
- **coryza**; during: *Hep* b4a.de *Kali-c* b4a.de kreos b7a.de nux-v b7.de*
- **coughing**: *Alum* b4a.de ambr b7.de* anac b4a.de bell b4.de* borx b4a.de *Bry* b7.de* croc b7.de* hep b4.de* kreos b7a.de laur b7.de*

Scratching: ...

- **crumbs** of bread, like: dros *Lach* pall
- **dinner**, after: dig h2*
- **eating**; after: sep b4a.de
- **sand**, as from: *Cist* k* plac rzf5•

SEASONS: | **winter** agg.: mez ptk1

SENSITIVE: alum k2 am-caust k* ant-t k2 *Apis* arum-t bg2 *Coc-c* k* cocc k* cor-r br1 crot-h falco-pe nl2• fl-ac k* hep bg2* kali-i hr1 *Lach* k* merc-c k* naja ser-a-c jl2 sul-ac k* vario jl2 zinc zinc-s a1

- **air**; to: ail cor-r br1 crot-h
- ○ - **Esophagus**: alum k2 ant-t b7.de* cocc b7.de* ferr b7a.de kali-c k* *Lach* b7a.de
- **Pharynx**: *Acon* bro1 *Aesc* bro1 ail bro1 *Apis* bro1 arg-met bro1 *Arg-n* bro1 *Arn* bro1 *Arum-t* bro1 atro bro1 bar-c bro1 *Bell* bro1 brom bro1 bry bro1 calc-p bro1 *Canth* bro1 *Caps* bro1 carb-ac bro1 *Caust* bro1 dol bro1 fago bro1 ferr-p bro1 fl-ac bro1 graph bro1 gymno bro1 *Hep* bro1 hom-xyz bro1 hydr bro1 ign bro1 *Kali-bi* bro1 kali-c bro1 kali-i bro1 *Kali-perm* bro1 *Lac-c* bro1 *Lach* bro1 lachn bro1 led bro1 lyc bro1 mentho bro1 *Merc* bro1 *Merc-c* bro1 *Merc-cy* bro1 *Merc-i-f* bro1 *Merc-i-r* bro1 mur-ac bro1 naja bro1 nit-ac bro1 *Nux-v* bro1 ox-ac bro1 petr bro1 phos bro1 *Phyt* bro1 pop-cand bro1 quill bro1 rhus-t bro1 sabad bro1 *Sang* bro1 sangin-n bro1 spong bro1 sulph bro1 trif-p bro1 verb bro1 wye bro1
- **Tonsils**: phyt bg2
- **Uvula**: clem k* sulph k*

SHOCKS on waking: manc

SHRIVELLED uvula: carb-ac k* cycl a1

SINGING agg.: cortico tpw7 dros h1

SMOKERS; complaints of: arg-n ptk1 caps ptk1 nat-m ptk1

SMOKING agg.: caps ptk1 coc-c ptk1 tarax ptk1

SNEEZING agg.: hyper ptk1 ictod ptk1 *Phos* ptk1

SOFTNESS: cist bg2* sabad bg2

SORE THROAT (See Inflammation; Pain)

SPASMS: (↗*Constriction; Tension)* acon alum b4.de* ammc vml3• *Ant-c* k* *Arg-n* k* ars k* bar-c k2 *Bell* k* brom cact k2 cadm-s k2 *Calc* k* *Canth* b7a.de caps b7.de* carb-v b4.de* **Cham** chel chlol *Cic Cocc* k* coff coloc b4a.de* *Con* k* crot-c mre1.fr crot-h tl1 *Cupr* k* dig b4.de* dros k2 ferr a1 ferr-p k2 *Gels* k* glon tl1 *Graph* k* *Hyos* k* **Ign** k* ip b7.de* *Iris* kali-ar *Kali-i* kali-s k2 *Lach* k* **Laur** k* *Lyss* mag-p tl1 mosch b7a.de naja k* nat-m b4a.de* nicc *Nux-v* k* op ox-ac br1 *Phos* b4.de* plat b4a.de* plb tl1 ran-b b7.de* sabad bg2 samb mrr1 sang hr1* sars k* seneg bg2 sep b4.de* *Spong* b7a.de staph hr1 **Stram** k* **Stry** sul-ac *Sulph* k* sumb c2 tarent k2 verat b7.de* *Zinc* k*

- **afternoon**: sang a1
- **anger**; after: *Cham*
- **cold** applications | **amel.**: lach tl1
- **cough**:
  - **after**: cina hr1
  - **during** | **agg.**: bell k2
- **drinks** | **amel.**: lavand-a ctl1•
- **eating**; after: sulph b4a.de
- **headache**; during: cadm-s c1
- **swallowing** agg.: bell k2 hyos k2 *Iris* lyss jl2 merc-c mrr1 *Mur-ac* nicc **Stram** k* stry k* *Sulph* tarent k2
  - **compelling** him to retch: ammc vml3• **Graph Merc-c**
- **warm** | **applications** | **amel.**: lyc tl1
  - **drinks** | **amel.**: lyc tl1
- **water**, at sight or thought of: anan hyos k2 *Lyss* k* ter tl1
- ○ - **Esophagus**: aconin c2* *Alum* k* *Alumn* arg-cy c2* *Arg-n* k* *Ars* k* *Asaf* k* **Bapt** k* **Bar-c** k* **Bell** k* cact k2 caj mtf11 *Calc* canth bro1 caps h1 *Carb-ac* carb-v carbn-dox knl3• carbn-s cham cic k* *Cimx* coc-c *Cocc* coloc *Con Crot-c Crot-h* k* *Cupr Elaps* k* *Gels* graph hydr-ac *Hyos* k* *Ign* k* iris kali-ar kali-bi kali-c **Lach** k* **Laur** k* *Lyss* k* *Manc* **Merc-c** k* mur-ac k2 *Naja* k* *Nat-c* hr1 nat-m nicc nit-ac *Nux-v* k* ox-ac petr-ra shn4• *Phos Plat Plb* k* ran-b k* rat rhus-t mtf11 sars *Stram* k* stry bro1 *Sulph* verat *Verat-v* k* zinc k*
  - **evening**: *Ars Asaf* cham
  - **night**: *Lach Nux-v*
  - **eating** agg.: cadm-s c1*
  - **eructations** agg.: coloc

- **Esophagus**: ...
  - **old** people can only swallow liquids: *Bar-c*
  - **periodical**: *Lyss*
  - **swallowing**:
    - **agg.**●: **Bapt** **Bar-c** bar-s k4 *Hyos* lyss jl2 **Merc-c** k* *Phos* *Sulph* zinc zinc-p k2
    - **liquids**:
      - **agg.**: *Bell* coc-c elaps *Graph* *Manc* *Merc-c*
      - **can** only swallow liquids: **Bapt** k* *Bar-c* k* *Plb* k*
- **Fauces**: bell tl1
- **Pharynx**: *Bell* bro1 canth bro1 *Sumb* bro1
  - **accompanied** by | **Root** of tongue; pain in (See MOUTH - Pain - tongue - root - accompanied - pharynx)

SPONGY sensation: *Cist* k* elaps ptk1 merc k2

SPOT; sore in a dry (See Pain - spot; in a dry - sore)

SPOTS: apis ptk1 caust ptk1 cimic ptk1 *Cist* ptk1 con ptk1 crot-h ptk1 *Hep* ptk1 *Hyos* ptk1 lac-c ptk1 **Lach** ptk1 lith-c ptk1 merc-cy ptk1 *Nat-m* ptk1 nit-ac ptk1 *Phos* ptk1 phyt ptk1 *Sil* ptk1
- ○ - **Pharynx**; in: *Bufo* *Fl-ac* *Mur-ac* phys bg1

STIFFNESS: aesc *Bell* k* berb brom bg2 calc bg2 *Caust* k* chel ptk1 croc bg2 cupr sst3• ferr-p bg2 gels bg2 *Hydr* lac-c bg1 *Lach* k* *Lyss* mag-c mag-p br1 med hr1 meny merc-i-r ptk1 nit-ac bg1 *Nux-m* k* *Propr* sa3• **Rhus-t** k* sep bg2 *Spong* stry
- ○ - **Pharynx**: aesc bro1 kali-m bro1 mag-p bro1 mez bro1 nux-m bro1 phyt bro1 *Rhus-t* bro1
- **Uvula**: crot-h ptk1

STONE (See Foreign - stone)

STOOPING agg.: caust ptk1

STRANGLE easily (See Choking)

STRANGULATED feeling (See Choking - sensation)

STRICTURE of esophagus: acon k* alumn c2 am-m ptk1 **Ars** k* **Bapt** k* **Bar-c** k* *Bell* k* *Cact* caj c2 *Calc* k* caps c2 card-b c2 cic c2* cund bg3* gels k* indg br1 *Kali-c* k* *Lyss* k* manc c2 *Merc-c* c2 merc-s-cy c2 *Naja* k* **Nat-m** k* *Nux-v* oena c2 *Ox-ac* *Phos* k* plat-m c2 plb-xyz c2 sabad c2 seneg c2 silphu c2 spirae c2 stront-c ptk1 tab c2 verat c2 *Verat-v* k* verin c2 zinc ptk1 zinc-s c2
- **old**: phos ptk1 zinc ptk1

SUFFOCATIVE sensation: act-sp br1 anan *Apis* brom br1 calc-f k* caust k* hydrog srj2• **Lach** k* lact k* lyss k* mangi br1 nux-v k* phyt k* ruta fd4.de sang bg1 spong fd4.de stry k* verat bg1
- **night**: calc-f k* ruta fd4.de
- **close**; as if throat would: calc-f ptk1 carb-v ptk1 mangi br1
- **cold** drinks agg.: calc-f
- **membrane**; from sensation of: hydrog srj2•
- **warm** drinks | **amel.**: calc-f

SULPHUR vapor in throat; sensation of:
- **cough** agg.; during: *Brom* lyc *Puls*
- **inspiration** agg.: croc lyc

SUPPURATION: canth b7.de* ign b7a.de
- **cold**; after taking a: bar-c mtf33
- **warm** drinks | **amel.**: glycyr-g cte1•
- ○ - **Pharynx**: antip bro1 bell bro1 bry bro1 calc bro1 *Calc-i* bro1 ferr-p bro1 *Hep* bro1 *Kali-i* bro1 lach bro1 *Merc* bro1 nit-ac bro1 phos bro1 *Sil* bro1
  - **Tonsils**: aesc *Alumn* am-m *Anac* anan *Apis* k* arg-n bg2 ars bg2 aur k* aur-s k2 bamb-a stb2.de• bapt bg2 *Bar-c* k* **Bar-m** k* bar-s k2 *Bell* k* calc *Calc-s* k* *Canth* k* *Cham* cub cupr cur daph dros gk gink-b sbd1• glycyr-g cte1• *Guaj* k* **Hep** k* hydr bg2 ign k* iod bg2 *Kali-bi* k* *Lac-c* k* *Lach* k* *Lyc* k* *Manc* **Merc** k* merc-c *Merc-i-f* *Merc-i-r* myris mtf11 nat-m ptk1* nit-ac bg2* phyt k* *Plb* psor al2* *Sabad* *Sang* *Sep* k* **Sil** k* streptoc mtf11 *Sulph* k* *Tarent* ptk1 tub c1
    - **right**: bar-c bell mrr1 *Lyc*
    - **left**: crot-h mrr1 *Lach* sep h2*
    - **acute**: **Bell** mrr1
    - **chronic**: *Bar-c* ptk1

SWALLOW, constant disposition to: acon bg2* aesc bro1 aeth agar a1 alum bg2 **Am-m** b7a.de androc srj1• anth vh1 apis ars bg2 arum-t k* *Asaf* k* bamb-a stb2.de• bapt k* *Bell* k* beryl sp1 borx b4a.de *Bry* k* cact k* *Calc* k* caps bg2* carb-ac k* carbn-s **Caust** k* *Cedr* k* cench k2 cham bg2* chin bg2* chlorpr pin1• cimic k* *Cina* k* *Cinnb* cist cob k* *Coc-c* *Con* k* convo-s sp1 cop crot-h cub c1* culx cur cypra-eg sde6.de• dios hr1 elaps fkr8.de euph ferr fl-ac flor-p rsj3• *Gels* k* glon **Graph** k* grat haem hell *Hep* hydrog srj2• **Ign** bg2* ip k* kali-bi bg2 kali-c bg2 lac-ac k* lac-c bg2* *Lach* k* lil-s a1 *Lyc* k* *Lyss* k* *Merc* k* **Merc-c** k* merc-i-f k* mur-ac k2 myric bro1 *Nat-m* nat-s *Nux-m* k* **Nux-v** bg2 ped a1 *Phos* bg2 phyt k* plb k* *Puls* bg2 rosm lgb1 *Sabad* k* sang bg2 senec ptk1 seneg k* **Sep** k* *Spong* b7a.de *Staph* k* stram sul-i sulph k* sumb k* thuj k* til verat *Verat-v* k* wye k2* zinc h2* [heroin sdj2]
- **evening**: *Asaf*
- **night**: cimic glon naja ozone sde2•
- **anger**; after: anac ptk1
- **bitter** taste, from: caul ptk1 chin h1*
- **choking**, from●: cina **Graph** k* *Lyc* k* merc ptk1 **Merc-c** k* *Sep* k*
- **cold** water | **amel.**: ozone sde2•
- **contraction** in larynx, from: coloc k* **Graph** plat
- **deep** in the throat: calc bg1
- **drink**; must: bar-c ptk1 *Bell* ptk1 *Cact* ptk1 calad ptk1 guaj ptk1 kali-c ptk1 nat-c ptk1 nat-m ptk1
- **eating** | **amel.**: *Caust* k* **Merc-c** k*
- **excitement** agg.: androc srj1• *Staph* k*
- **fear** of suffocation; with (See MIND - Fear - suffocation - swallow)
- **fullness** in throat, from: *Cinnb* lac-ac **Lach**
- **lump** in throat, from●: aesc agar all-c ptk1 androc srj1• *Asaf* calc h2* calc-f chir-fl gya2 *Coc-c* coff k* *Con* cypra-eg sde6.de• ign lac-ac **Lac-c** hr1 **Lach** k* *Lyss* k* *Nat-m* *Phyt* sne psil ft1* *Sabad* k* *Sep* sulph k*
- **lying**:
  - **side**; on:
    - **left** | **amel.**: ozone sde2•
- **mucus**, from thick●: *Alum* **Caust** k* chir-fl gya2 choc srj3• ozone sde2• sep [heroin sdj2]
- **pain** in larynx, from: all-c mrr1 fl-ac
- **saliva**; from: arg-met bg2 cina bg2 crot-h bg2 *Ip* bg2* lac-ac bg2 merc ptk1 seneg st1
- **spasm** in throat, from●: **Graph** **Merc-c**
- **talking** agg.●: *Cic* ptk1 *Staph* k* thuj ptk1
- **vertigo**; with: caul ptk1
- **walking** in wind; while: *Con* k*

SWALLOWING:
- **constantly** swallowing (See Swallow, constant)
- **difficult**: acet-ac *Acon* k* aegle-f bnj1 *Aesc* k* aeth agar k* aids nl2• *Alum* k* alum-p k2 alum-sil k2 *Alumn* **Am-c** k* am-caust a1* **Am-m** b7a.de ambr k* amph a1 ant-c k* ant-t k* anthraci *Apis* k* *Arg-met* k* *Arg-n* k* arn b7.de* *Ars* k* ars-i ars-s-f k2 arum-m a1 arum-t k* asar k* aspar hr1 *Aur* k* aur-ar k2 aur-i k2 aur-m bg2* aur-s k* bamb-a stb2.de• *Bapt* **Bar-c** k* bar-i k2 bar-m k* bar-s k2 *Bell* k* benz-ac k* beryl tpw5 bism k* bit-ar wht1• both-ax tsm2 botul br1* brass-n-o srj5• *Brom* k* brucel sa3• bry k* bufo bung-fa tsm2 buth-a sp1 *Cact* cadm-s c1* caj a1* calad a1 *Calc* k* calc-p k* calc-s calc-sil k2 camph k* cann-s k* *Canth* k* *Caps* k* carb-an b4.de* *Carb-v* k* carbn-s card-b a1 card-m k* cardios-h rly4• *Caust* k* cedr k* cham k* *Chel* k* **Chin** k* chinin-ar chinin-s bg2 chlol k* chlor k* choc srj3• *Cic* k* cimic k* cimx cina k* cob-n sp1 *Coc-c* k* *Cocc* k* coch hr1 *Colch* k* coloc k* con k* conin a1 convo-s sp1 cop cot a1 *Crot-c* k* crot-h bg2 crot-t *Cupr* k* cur k* dendr-pol tsm2 dig dios k* diphtox jl2 dros k* *Dulc* k* *Elaps* epil a1* fago k* falco-pe nl2• ferr k* ferr-ar fl-ac k* flav jl2 form k* galeoc-c-h gms1• gamb hr1 *Gels* k* gent-c glon k* graph k* grat k* guaj bg2 guare a1 haem a1 *Hell* k* helo c1 helo-s c1* *Hep* k* hip-ac sp1 hydroph rsj6• **Hyos** k* *Ign* k* ind k* inul hr1 *Iod* k* *Ip* k* irid-met srj5• iris ix bnm8• jac-c k* kali-ar kali-bi k* kali-br a1 **Kali-c** k* kali-chl k* kali-m k2 *Kali-n* k* kali-perm kali-s kali-sil k2 *Kalm* k* kreos bg2 *Lac-ac* **Lac-c** hr1* lacer c1 **Lach** k* lact k* lat-h bnm5• lat-m bnm6• laur b7.de* loxo-lae bnm12• loxo-recl bnm10• *Lyc* k* **Lyss** k* manc k* med ptk meli meny k* *Merc* k* *Merc-c* k* merc-cy k* merc-d hr1 merc-i-f k* *Merc-i-r* k* merl a1 mez k* mim-p rsj8• mit a1 morph a1 mur-ac k* myric k* *Naja* k* nat-ar nat-c k* nat-m k* nat-s bg2* nicc k* **Nit-ac** k* nitro-o a1 nux-m k* **Nux-v** k* ol-an bg2* *Op* k* ox-ac k* ozone sde2• paeon k* peti a1 ph-ac b4.de* phasco-ci rbp2 phos k* phys tl1 physala-p bnm7• *Phyt* k* pic-ac k* *Plb* k* polys sk4• *Psor* k* puls k* pycnop-sa mrz1 raph k* **Rhus-t** k* rhus-v k* rumx *Sabad* k* sal-ac a1* sang bg2 sapin a1 sarcol-ac sp1 scarl jl2 sec b7a.de

Throat

- **difficult**: ...
Sep k* Sil k* spong b7.de* stann hr1 stict bg2 **Stram** k* streptoc jl2* **Stry** k* Sul-ac k* sul-i bg2 sulfonam ks2 sulph k* sumb k* syc pte1*• Tab k* tarax k* tarent tep a1 teucr b7a.de* thal-xyz srj8• ther hr1* thiam rly4• thuj k* trif-p a1 trios rsj11• tub c* ust k* vario jl2 verat-v bg2 vesp k* vinc a1* vip k* visc c1 Wye k* x-ray sp1 zinc k* zinc-m a1 zinc-p k2
  - **morning**: am-c k* arum-t k* canth k* cham k* mit a1
  - **forenoon**: fl-ac k*
  - **noon**: ferr-i k* phos k*
  - **evening**: am-c coc-c k* fl-ac k* lyc k*
  - **night**: Alum naja
  - **accompanied** by:
    - **chilliness**: ozone sde2•
    - **Face**; paralysis of (See FACE - Paralysis - accompanied - swallowing)
    - **Lips**; difficult motion of: abel vh1
  - **acrid** foods: **Lach** k*
  - **bending** forward | **amel.**: nit-ac bg1
  - **breakfast**: merc-c
  - **children**; in: androc bnm2• kali-br ptk1 kali-c mtf33 loxo-lae bnm12•
    - **newborns**: kali-c mtf33
    - **nurslings**: kali-c mtf33
  - **choking**; with: (↗*impossible - choking*) galeoc-c-h gms1• streptoc mtf11
  - **chorea**, from: Agar k* Art-v hr1* Verat-v hr1
  - **cold** things; from (See drinks - cold; food - cold)
  - **drink** in order to swallow; must: bar-c bg1 Bell k* Cact k* calad bg3* cur k* elaps Guaj bg2 kali-c Nat-c nat-m
  - **drinks** | **cold** drinks; from: kali-c bg2 sabad k2
  - **fluids**• only, but solid food gags; can swallow: Bapt k* bar-c k* calad vh cench k2 cham bro1 Crot-c Crot-h nat-m bro1 Plb k* Sil k*
  - **food**:
    - **cold** food; from: sabad k2
    - **small** pieces at a time; can only swallow: alum ptk1
  - **inertia** of esophagus; from: kali-c mtf33
  - **liquids**: alumn k* anan anth k* bar-c mrr1 bell k* bism both bro1 Brom b4a.de bry bro1 cact bro1 Canth k* caust c1 Cic cina coc-c k* con convo-s sp1 Crot-c crot-h bg1* Cupr k* gels bro1 grat br1 Hydr hr1 Hyos k* Ign k* Iod k* Kali-br **Lach** k* Lyc k* **Lyss** k* mag-p Merc k* merc-c k* mez k* Mur-ac hr1 nat-m k* Nit-ac nux-v k* Phos k* podo fd3.de* psil ft1 pycnop-sa mrz1 sil hr1* **Stram** k* sul-ac k* sul-i k2 Upa k* zinc k* zinc-p k2
    - **amel.**: alum bg2 arn bg2 bapt bg2 kali-c bg1 nit-ac bg2 nux-v bg2
    - **more** difficult than solids: brom coc-c cocc h1* hyos ign k* Lach sanic c1 stram bg1
    - **regurgitate** through the nose (See Liquids)
  - **menses**; during: calc
  - **nervous**, when: gels bg1 nux-v bg1 phys bg1
  - **painless**; but: apis ptk1 ars b4.de* bell b4.de* carb-ac ptk1 carb-v b4.de* op b7.de* stram b7.de
  - **paralysis**, from (See Liquids; Paralysis)
  - **pills**; big: **Lyss** vh*
  - **saliva**: bar-c mrr1 haem k* **Lach** k* meny k* myris k* olib-sac wmh1 spig k*
  - **solids**: Alum k* Alumn ambr b7a.de* Apis Arg-n k* atro k* **Bapt** **Bar-c** k* bar-s k2 Bell k* bry k* Carb-v k* Cham k* chin b7a.de Crot-c Crot-h Dros hep k* ign b7a.de Kali-c kola stb3• lac-ac k* Lac-c Lach k* lyc k* med ptk merc bg2 Nat-m k* nat-p nit-ac bg2* Nux-v k* phos bg2 Plb Rhus-t k* sep bg2 Sil k* stram k* sulph bg2 tub jl2 zinc-p k2
    - **morning**: stram k*
    - **amel.**: ign bg2
    - **dry** morsels: kali-bi bg2
  - **sour** | **agg.**: apis ptk1
  - **sweets**:
    - **agg.**: bad ptk1 **Lach** k* sang ptk1 Spong ptk1
    - **amel.**: ars ptk1

- **difficult**: ...
  - **waking**; on: Alum sul-ac a1 sulph zing k*
  - **warm** food agg.: gels br1
- **eating**; after: bry bg2 ferr bg2 merc bg2 staph bg2 sulph bg2
- **fast** agg.: anac ptk1
- **hindering** swallowing: Acon bg2 alum k* **Am-c** k* ambr k* ang k* ant-c k* apis b7a.de Arn k* Ars k* Bapt bell k* bufo cact cadm-s caj vh Calc b4.de* cann-s b7a.de Canth k* Carb-v k* Caust b4a.de Cham bg2 Chel k* chlor k* cic k* Cina k* cocc b7.de* con k* crot-h k* cupr k* elaps hep k* **Hyos** k* ina-i mlk9.de iod k* kali-bi k* kali-c k* kali-n k* lach k* lat-h bnm5• Laur k* lob lyc k* meny k* **Merc** b4.de* merc-c b4a.de naja Nat-s k* Nux-v k* Op k* ozone sde2• Plb k* Sabad sil b4a.de staph b7.de* Stram k* sulph k* teucr b7.de* vesp k* zinc b4a.de
  - **night**: alum k*
  - **arrested**; food and drinks suddenly | **fall** heavily into stomach; then: elaps br1
  - **children**; in: | **nurslings**: kali-c mtf33
  - **drink** at every mouthful to wash down the food; must: Bell Cact cur elaps kali-c Nat-c nat-m
  - **food** (See solids)
  - **liquids** only, least food gags; can swallow: **Bapt** k* bar-c Crot-c Crot-h Plb Sil
    - **solids** reach a certain point and are violently ejected: **Nat-m** k*
  - **lying** agg.: cham k*
  - **pressure** on larynx, from: Chel
  - **solids**: Alum Apis Bry con ptk1 cur dros Graph Ign Lyc lyss c1 mur-ac a1 nit-ac rhus-t zinc
  - ○ **Esophagus** | **Cardiac** orifice: con k2
- **impossible**: acet-ac k* acon k* aeth k* ail vh1 Alum Alumn Am-caust vh1 aml-ns vh1 amph a1 amyg hr1 ant-c c1 Ant-t k* Apis Arum-m a1 Arum-t k* atra-r bnm3• atro hr1 Bapt k* bar-c k* Bell k* bism k* calc ptk1 Camph k* cann-i k* carb-ac k* Carb-v cham chlor k* Cic k* Cina cocc bg2* Crot-c Crot-h k* cupr k* cur k* dulc Gels k* Graph k* hydr-ac k* **Hyos** k* Ign k* ip k* iris kali-bi k* kali-br a1 kreos k* **Lac-c** k* Lach k* laur k* linu-c a1 Lyc k* lyss k* manc k* med ptk merc-c k* morph a1 mur-ac k* naja k* **Nit-ac** k* Nux-v k* oena k* Op k* oxyum-sc mcp1• ph-ac bg2 Phos phys k* phyt bg2 Plb psor k* rad-br sze8• Sabad sabin hr1 sep ptk1 spong k* stict bg2 **Stram** k* stry a1 sul-ac a1* Sulph Tab k* tanac a1 ter a1 thuj Verat k* vip bg2 visc a1 zinc-m a1
  - **noon**: epil a1*
  - **accompanied** by | **bulbar** paralysis (See HEAD - Paralysis - medulla - accompanied - swallow)
  - **choking**, from: (↗*difficult - choking*) Hyos k* Iod Kali-c manc k* mur-ac visc c1
  - **cold** things: kali-c lach k2
  - **constriction** of esophagus: Alum Alumn Bapt **Bar-c** cact Cic k* dros k2 gels tl1 Hyos Kali-c **Phos**
    - **night**: alum h2
    - **Esophagus** | **Cardiac** orifice: **Phos**
  - **food**: Bar-c b4a.de cham b7a.de* **Hep** b4a.de Iod b4a.de Merc b4a.de merc-c b4a.de Nit-ac b4a.de Petr b4a.de Phos b4a.de Plb b7a.de Sep b4a.de **Sulph** b4a.de tub dp•
  - **liquids**, anything but: bapt bar-c Canth b7a.de Cina k* crot-c Crot-h cupr b7a.de hyos b7a.de ign b7a.de Kali-c lach b7a.de
    - **teaspoonful** of; even a: acet-ac ptk2 Lyc k* **Nit-ac** k*
      - **nausea**; as from: arn ptk1
  - **lying** agg.: cham k* sec k*
  - **menses**; during: petr
  - **mucus** is hawked out, until: Thuj
  - **paralysis**; from: Alum Alumn Apis ars arum-t k2 bapt k* caps ptk1 caust Cocc k* cur k* Gels k* lac-ac lac-c lach k* lact lyc Nat-m Nux-m k* Nux-v k* op k* phos k2 phyt plb k2 sec hr1 **Stram** Tab visc c1
  - **saliva**: amph a1 spig h1*
  - **swelling** of the tongue: apis
  - **typhus** fever; in: bapt Camph
  - **warm** soup: lyc h2*
  - **water**: epil a1

- **incomplete**: bell b4a.de benz-ac k* calc b4.de* cham b7.de* merc b4a.de petr b4.de* *Sil* b4a.de
- **involuntary**: *Cina* k* con k* m-aust b7.de merc k* mur-ac ptk1 **Sep** k* *Staph* k*
  - **walking** in the wind, when: con k*
- **must** swallow | **cough**; after: cina bg2
- **noisy**: am b7.de* *Ars* bg2* caust ptk1 cic bg2 cina ptk1 cocc ptk1 *Cupr* b7a.de* elaps bg2 gels ptk1 hell bg2* hydr-ac bg2* lach ptk1 *Laur* b7a.de* *Phos* ptk1 sil bg2 thuj bg2*
  - **laughing** agg.: cina bg2
- **sleep**, in: aml-ns bg2 bry bg2 *Calc* k* cina bg2* dulc fd4.de ign bg2

SWEETS:
- **agg.**: bad ptk1 lach ptk1 sang ptk1 spong ptk1
- **amel.**: ars ptk1

SWELLING: acon k* aesc k* agath-a nl2• **Ail** k* alum k2 am-c am-caust a1 am-m k* anan ant-t k* ap-g br1 *Apis* k* arag br1 arg-met b7.de* arizon-l nl2• arn k* *Ars* k* ars-i arum-m a1 asim hr1 atro a1 aur k* aur-ar k2 aur-i k2 aur-s k2 bapt k2 bar-c b4a.de* **Bell** k* benz-ac k* berb a1* *Brom* k* *Bry* b7.de* bufo *Calc* k* calc-p k* *Calc-s* k* *Canth* k* caps k2* carb-ac hr1 carb-an b4.de* carb-v k* carbn-s carl a1 caust k* cham b7.de* *Chin* b7.de* chinin-ar chlor k* cic k* coc-c k* corv-cor bdg• crot-h k* crot-t k* cupr-act cypra-eg sde6.de• dios k* dros hr1 ery-a a1 falco-pe nl2• ferr a1 gamb k* gink-b sbd1• glon k* *Graph* k* hell a1 helodr-cal knl2• **Hep** k* hippoz hr1 hyos b7.de* *Ign* b7.de* iod k* jug-c k* kali-ar *Kali-bi* hr1 kali-c k* kali-i ptk1 kali-m k2 kali-n kali-p kali-perm kali-s kali-sil k2 kalm k* **Lach** k* lachn a1 led k* *Lyc* k* **Merc** k* **Merc-c** k* *Merc-cy* k* merc-d a1 merc-sul hr1 *Mur-ac* k* nat-ar nat-c b4.de* *Nat-m* nicotam rly4• *Nit-ac* k* *Nux-v* k* op k* ox-ac k* petr k* *Phos* k* **Phyt** k* pin-con oss2• plan a1 *Plb* k* psor k* puls k* rhod b4.de* *Rhus-t* k* rhus-v k* rumx sabad k* samb k* sars k* sec k* *Seneg* k* *Sep* k* sil k* spig k* **Spong** k* *Stann* k* stram stry k* sul-ac k* sul-i k* *Sulph* k* *Thuj* k* verat k* vesp k* vip a1 *Wye* k* xan k* zinc k* zinc-m a1 zinc-p k2 zinc-s a1
- **right**: bell mtf33 cench k2
- **left**: antip vh1 spig h1* symph fd3.de•
  - **pressure** agg.: choc srj3•
- **morning**: bry k* epil a1* myric a1
- **evening**: aesc k* mez k* stry a1
- **night**: inul a1 merc **Spong** hr1
- **accompanied** by:
  - **diphtheria**: apis tl1
  - **salivation**: *Anthraci* st1
- **angioedema**: **Apis** mrr1
- **cough** agg.; during: ars bg2* lach bg2
- **edematous**: (↗*Eruptions - angioneurotic)* *Ail* k* anthraci *Apis* k* arg-n ptk1 ars bro1 bapt k2 crot-t hyos bg2 kali-bi k* kali-i bg2 kali-perm bro1 lac-ac ptk1 *Lac-c* lach bro1 loxo-recl bnm10• mag-p bro1 mur-ac bro1 *Nat-ar* k* *Nit-ac* phos k* phyt bro1* rhus-t k* sul-ac
- **scarlet** fever: am-c tl1
- **sensation** of: acon k* agath-a nl2• aloe am-c b4.de* ambr b7.de* ant-c b7a.de apis bg2 arg-met b7.de* *Arg-n* k* am b7a.de ars k* ars-s-f k2 bamb-a stb2.de• bapt k* bar-c b4.de* bell k* benz-ac *Bry* k* calc k* carb-v k* casc *Caust* k* chin k* chir-fl gya2 coca-c sk4• coff colch k* com bg2 dig b4.de* dulc fd4.de falco-pe nl2• fic-m gya1 fl-ac bg2 fuma-ac rly4• *Glon* k* graph b4.de* *Hep* k* hydrog srj2• hyos b7.de* ign k* iod bg2* ip k* iris bg2 jug-c hr1 kali-s fkr2.de kalm lac-c **Lach** k* lachn c1 led limen-b-c hrn2* lob bg2 lyc h2* *Mang* b4a.de merc k* merc-c b4a.de merc-i-f bg2 mez bg2 nit-ac k* nux-v k* op b7.de* petr b4.de* phos b4.de* *Plb* k* psor al2 puls k* *Rhus-t* k* sabad k* *Sabin* k* *Sang* k* sep b4.de* sil b4.de* *Spig* b7a.de stann k* stram b7.de* *Sulph* k* tarax k* thuj b4a.de* tritic-vg fd5.de tub al urol-h rwt• verat k* *Wye* xan rb2 xanth bg2 zinc b4.de*
  - **right** side: tub rb2
  - **cough** agg.; during: caps b7.de* *Puls* b7.de*
  - **waking**; on: cadm-met tpw6*
  - ○ **Tonsils**: cortico sp1* gels bg2 iod bg2 *Rhus-t* bg2
  - **Uvula** (See uvula - sensation)
- **warm** applications agg.: apis tl1
- ○ **Adenoids** (See NOSE - Adenoids)
- **Blood** vessels; of: aloe bg2 aran bg2 am bg2 *Ars* bg2 *Bell* bg2 calc bg2 canth bg2 con bg2 graph bg2 hep bg2 hydr-ac bg2 *Lach* bg2 lyc bg2 nux-v bg2 olnd bg2 *Op* bg2 puls b7a.de rhus-t bg2 spong bg2 *Thuj* bg2 thymu br1

Swelling: ...
- **Esophagus** | **Glands**: asaf bg2 *Merc* bg2 nat-c bg2
- **Fauces**: ap-g vh1 asim br1 sal-al blc1•
- **Palate**; soft: ap-g vh1 am br1
- **Pharynx**: *Acon* bro1 aesc bro1 ail bro1 *Apis* bro1 arg-n bro1 arum-t bro1 bapt bro1 *Bar-c* bro1 *Bell* bro1 canth bro1 *Caps* bro1 crot-h bro1 gymno bro1 *Hep* bro1 kali-bi bro1 *Kali-m* bro1 *Kali-perm* bro1 lac-c bro1 *Lach* bro1 *Merc* bro1 merc-c bro1 *Merc-cy* bro1 *Merc-i-f* bro1 *Merc-i-r* bro1 naja bro1 nat-ar bro1 *Phyt* bro1 sabad bro1 sang bro1 tub jl2 vesp bro1 wye bro1
- **Tonsils**: acon k* aegle-f bnj1 *Agra* br1 ail k2 alum k* alum-p k2 alum-sil k2 *Alumn* k* *Am-c* k* am-m b7a.de* amph a1 ant-t k* *Apis* k* arg-n bg2 ars-i bro1 arum-t asim br1 *Aur* k* aur-m-n wbt2• aur-s k2 *Bac* bn* **Bapt** k* bar-act bro1 **Bar-c** k* bar-i k* **Bar-m** k* bar-s k2 **Bell** k* benz-ac c2* berb brom k* bufo k* **Calc** k* calc-f k2* *Calc-i* k* *Calc-p* k* *Calc-s* calc-sil k2 canth k* caps k2* *Carb-ac* carbn-s carc gk6* *Cedr* **Cham** k* *Chel* *Chen-a* chin cinnb bro1 cist br* coc-c cocc bg2 *Colch* con bg2* cop *Crot-t* diph bro1 diphtox jl2 dros gk *Dulc* k* elaps hr1 fago *Ferr* ferr-p k* fic-m gya1 *Fl-ac* *Gels* k* *Graph* k* *Guaj* k* guare k* ham **Hep** k* hippoz ign k* *Iod* k* irid-met srj5• *Kali-bi* k* *Kali-c* k* *Kali-chl* *Kali-i* k* kali-m k2* kali-p kali-s kali-sil k2 ketogl-ac rly4• kola stb3• **Lac-c** k* **Lach** k* led **Lyc** k* *Manc* med br1 *Merc* k* *Merc-c* k* *Merc-cy* *Merc-i-f* k* *Merc-i-r* k* *Mez* b4a.de *Mucor* jl2 *Mur-ac* k* nat-ar nat-c b4a.de* *Nat-m* k* nat-s k* nicc **Nit-ac** k* nux-v k* op wbt• petr **Phos** k* **Phyt** k* plat k* *Plb* k* plb-i c2* polyp-p c2 psor k2* puls *Ran-s* k* raph *Sabad* sang hr1 *Sangin-n* bro1 scarl jl2 *Sep* k* **Sil** k* sol-ni spong k2 stann k* *Staph* k* streptoc jl2 sul-ac k2 sul-i k2* **Sulph** k* syc pte1*• symph fd3.de• *Syph* k* tarent tep thuj k* **Tub** bg2* tub-m ih v-a-b jl2 vac jl2 verat k* vesp zinc k* zinc-p k2 [*Bar-br* stj2 bar-p stj1]
  - **right**: am-c bg1 apis bg1* ars-s-f k2 bar-c bg1 bar-m mrr1 *Bell* gels bg1 ham bg1 helodr-cal knl2• hep bg1 lac-c *Lyc* merc bg1 merc-d bg1 *Merc-i-f* naja bg1 nat-c h2* nicc bg1 phos bg1 phyt plat sabad spong sulph gk tarent thuj bg1
  - **left**: aesc bg1* antip vh1 apis bar-c *Brucel* sa3• calc-f sp1 cist vh dream-p sdj1• helodr-cal knl2• ind hr1 iod kali-c h2* kali-p bg1 kola stb3• lac-c k* **Lach** lat-m sp1 lycpr c1 maland al2 merc-i-r k* nux-m bg1 olib-sac wmh1 phos h2* sep h2* sulph ust bg1 x-ray sp1
  - **accompanied** by:
    - **cough**: bar-c ptk1 lach ptk1
    - **hearing**; impaired: *Staph* b7a.de
    - **swelling** | **Blood** vessels on tonsils; of: brom mtf33
    - **Ear**; complaints of (See EAR - Complaints - accompanied - tonsils)
  - **children**; in: *Bar-c* br1 bufo mtf33 calc-i mtf11 calc-p mtf33 graph mtf33 lac-c mtf33 phos mtf33 sil mtf33 syc fmm1• syph mtf33
    - **pale**, scrofulous children: chen-a hr1
  - **chronic**: bar-m br1 syph mtf33
  - **coryza**; after: sabad ptk1
  - **cough**; before: bar-c bro1 lach bro1
  - **diarrhea**, with: asim br1
  - **diphtheria**; during: phyt tl1
  - **opening** the mouth agg.: calc-p ptk1
  - **painless**: *Brucel* sa3•
  - **sensation** of swelling: cortico tpw7 nicotam rly4•
  - ○ **Pharyngeal** tonsils (See NOSE - Adenoids)
- **Uvula**: acon k* aeth a1 *Alumn* amyg a1 **Apis** k* arg-n h1* am br1 ars bg2 bar-m bell k* berb bg2* borx b4a.de brom bg2 calad k* *Calc* k* *Calc-p* k* calc-sil k2 canth b7a.de *Carb-v* k* *Caust* bg2* chel chin k* *Coff* k* cop a1 crot-t k* der a1 dulc b4.de* *Fl-ac* *Hep* hydr a1 ind k* *Iod* k* *Kali-bi* k* kali-br a1 **Kali-i** k* kali-m k2 kali-perm c2 lac-c *Lach* lyc k* *Merc* k* **Merc-c** k* merc-d sne *Mur-ac* k* nat-ar k* nat-s k* *Nit-ac* k* *Nux-v* k* par **Phos** k* physala-p bnm7• *Phyt* puls b7.de* raph a1 rhus-t rumx sabad k* sal-al blc1• seneg b4.de* **Sil** k* spong sul-ac k* sul-i a1* *Sulph* k* tab bg2* tep a1 zinc k* zinc-p k2
  - **baglike**: kali-bi bg2
  - **edematous**: **Apis** k* ars bro1 caps bro1 crot-t **Kali-bi** k* *Kali-br* k* *Kali-i* k* kali-m k2 kali-perm k* lach merc-c bg3* morg-g pte1*• *Mur-ac* k* nat-ar k2* *Nit-ac* nux-v bg2 phos k* phyt bg3* rhus-t bg3* *Sul-ac* tab k*
  - **sensation** of swelling: arg-n a1 puls h1*

SYPHILITIC affections: *Ars-i* *Asaf* *Aur* k* **Aur-m** bell bro1 borx bro1 calc-f bro1 carb-v bg2 *Cinnb* bro1 *Fl-ac* k* **Hep** hydr bro1 *Kali-bi* k* **Kali-i** k* *Kalm* lac-c tl1 *Lach* k* *Lyc* k* **Merc** k* *Merc-c* bro1 merc-d bro1 *Merc-i-f* bro1 *Merc-i-r* bro1 merc-n bro1 **Mez** k* **Nit-ac** k* ph-ac bg2 phos bg2 *Phyt* k* still bro1 sulph bro1 syph *Thuj* bg2

TALKING:
- **agg.**: acon ptk1 alum ptk1 bar-c ptk1 bry ptk1 dulc ptk1 ign ptk1 *Kali-i* ptk1 mang ptk1 merc ptk1 phos ptk1 rhus-t ptk1 sulph ptk1
- **amel.**: kali-bi ptk1

TENSION: *(↗Constriction; Spasms)* acon k* alum b4.de* *Arg-met* k* asaf k* bell b4.de* bov k* brom k* *Caust* k* *Cham* b7.de* chel k* chin k* cimx a1 cycl b7.de* dig k* *Glon* k* hydrog srj2• *Ign* b7.de* iod h* kali-n k* lyc meph a1 **Merc** k* merc-c k* merc-i-f ptk1 mez k* naja nat-m k* nux-m k* nux-v k* ph-ac k* phos k* puls k* rhus-g tmo3• rhus-t ptk1 rosm lgb1 sabad k* sec k* senec ptk1 seneg b4.de* sep k* stann k* suis-em rly4• tab k* *Verb* k*
- **right** side: alum h2* **Arg-met** meph a1
- **left** side: lac-loxod-a hm2•
- **afternoon**: tab
- **cough** agg.; during: *Nux-v* b7a.de
- **menses**; before: *Iod* k*
- **swallowing** agg.: *Asaf* coc-c a1 *Lyc* mez h2* nat-m k* *Puls*
- **yawning** agg.: *Arg-met* k*
- ○ - **Esophagus**: cham cortico tpw7 cycl
- **Throat**-pit (See EXTERNAL - Tension - throat-pit)
- **Thyroid** (See EXTERNAL - Tension - thyroid)

THICK sensation: agath-a nl2• ail k* both tsm2 both-ax tsm2 bung-fa tsm2 crot-c tsm2 crot-h tsm2 dendr-pol tsm2 elaps tsm2 naja tsm2 sep k* vip tsm2

THREAD hanging in, sensation of (See Hanging in - thread)

TICKLING: *(↗LARYNX - Tickling; LARYNX - Tickling - larynx)* aids nl2• *Am-br* vh1 arg-n bg2 bell bg2 calc-f sp1 *Caps* hr1 cassia-s ccrh1• caust bg2 cham tl1 chinin-s bg2 cist tl1 crot-h bg2 dros bg2 dulc fd4.de granit-m es1• grat bg2 hepat br1 hist sp1 hydroph rsj6• *Iod* tl1 kali-bi bg2 kali-br a1 kali-n bg2 lac-h sk4• *Lach* b7a.de* lobin a1 luna kg1• mag-c b4.de* mez b4.de* mim-p skp7• nat-c b4.de* nit-ac b4.de* olib-sac wmh1 petr b4.de* pitu-gl skp7• sel rsj9• seneg b4.de* sep b4a.de spig b7.de* *Spong* mrr1 stict bg2* tritic-vg fd5.de
- **right**: taosc iwa1•
- **morning**: pitu-gl skp7•
- **evening** | **20** h: aq-mar skp7•
- **night**: tritic-vg fd5.de
  - **midnight**: neon srj5•
- **accompanied** by:
  - **hawk**; tendency to: aq-mar skp7•
  - **lachrymation**: chel ptk1 cocc ptk1
  - **vision**; complaints of (See VISION - Complaints - accompanied - throat)
  - ○ • **Eyes**; complaints in (See EYE - Complaints - accompanied - throat - tickling)
- **cold** air; from: *Rumx* mrr1
- **cough**; causing (See COUGH - Tickling - throat; in)
- **followed** by:
  - **cough**; dry irritating: cassia-s ccrh1•
  - **discharge**; watery: cassia-s ccrh1•
  - **thirstlessness**: cassia-s ccrh1•
  - ○ • **Head**; heaviness in: cassia-s ccrh1•
- **hair** in throat; as from a (See Hair)
- **sleep**; during: hep b4a.de
- **talking** agg.: pitu-gl skp7•
- ▽ - **extending** to | **Ear** | **swallowing** agg.: petr h2
  - **Lungs**: verat ptk1
- ○ - **Pharynx**: stict ptk1

TINGLING: *(↗Crawling)* acon amp rly4• antip vh1 arum-t k2 carb-ac choc srj3• coli rly4• echi glon bg2 kola stb3• lac-h htj1• limen-b-c mlk9.de spig bg2 vero-o rly4*•
- ○ - **Esophagus**: *Acon*
- **Fauces**: acon bro1 echi bro1 phyt bro1

TONSILLITIS (See Inflammation - tonsils)

TURNING about in: lach k* suis-pan rly4•

TWITCHING: *Arg-n* k* chel k* crot-t k* cycl k* sep k*
- ▽ - **extending** to | **Pit** of stomach: sep k*

ULCERS: acet-ac k* aesc k2 ail tl1 all-s aln br1 alum k* alum-sil k2 *Alumn* am-c k2 anac b4a.de anan **Apis** k* arg-met b7.de arg-n k* **Ars** k* ars-i *Arum-t* k* asaf k2 *Aur* k* aur-i k2 *Aur-m* aur-s k2 *Bapt* k* bell k* borx k* cain *Calc* k* calc-f k2* *Calc-s* calc-sil k2 *Caps* k* carb-v carbn-s chel chlor k* *Cinnb* clem k* dros k* *Elaps* k* ery-a a1 ferr tl1 *Fl-ac* graph k2 **Hep** k* *Hippoz* k* *Hydr* ign k* ind c2 *Iod* k* kali-ar *Kali-bi* k* *Kali-chl* *Kali-i* k* kali-m k2 kali-perm kreos k* *Lac-c* k* *Lach* k* *Lyc* k* *Manc* **Merc** k* **Merc-c** k* *Merc-cy* k* *Merc-d* k* *Merc-i-f* k* *Merc-i-r* k* mez k* mill *Mur-ac* k* *Nat-c* bg2 nat-m k* **Nit-ac** k* nux-v k* petr k* phos tl1 *Phyt* k* *Psor* k* ptel k* rhus-t bg3* rumx c2 sal-ac k* *Sang* k* sanic sars *Sil* k* stann a1 *Staph* bg2 sul-ac bg3* *Sulph* k* syph c2* thuj k* vinc k* viol-t k* zinc k*
- **right**: lyc *Psor* a1 ptel
- **left**: elaps *Lach*
- **accompanied** by:
  - **scarlet** fever: *Am-c* bro1 apis bro1 *Ars* bro1 arum-t bro1 bar-c bro1 crot-h bro1 hep bro1 *Lach* bro1 *Merc-cy* bro1 merc-i-r bro1 *Mur-ac* bro1 nit-ac bro1
  - ○ • **Tongue** | **brown** discoloration: lyc kr1*
- **bleeding**: bell k2 carb-v k2
- **bluish**: carb-v k2
- **burning**: ars mrr1 *Caps* carb-v k2 *Manc* merc-c k2
  - **eating**; preventing: ars mrr1
- **cold** agg.: anan
- **corroding**: merc k2
- **deep**: *Apis* ars mrr1 *Kali-bi* *Kali-i* lach
- **dirty**: nit-ac k2
- **eruptions**; after suppressed: mez
- **flat**: merc k2
- **menses**; before: *Mag-c*
- **mercury**; after abuse of: aur hep bro1 hydr bro1 *Iod* *Kali-i* lyc k* *Nit-ac* k*
- **offensive**: alum
- **painless**: bapt k2*
- **perforating**: kali-i k2
- **phagedenic**: ars-s-f k2 kali-i k2
- **scarlet** fever does not come out, when: apis cham bro1
- **spreading**: apis *Ars* bapt k2 *Kali-bi* lach merc k2 **Merc-c** nit-ac k2 sul-ac k2
- **stinging** in: kali-bi *Lac-c* *Merc* *Nit-ac*
- **syphilitic**: ars-s-f k2 aur bro1 calc-f bro1 *Fl-ac* bro1 hippoz bro1 jac-g bro1 *Kali-bi* bro1 kali-i bro1 lach k2* lyc bro1 merc bro1 *Merc-c* bro1 merc-i-f bro1 merc-i-r bro1 *Nit-ac* bro1 phyt bro1 still bro1
- **white**: nit-ac k2
- ○ - **Esophagus**: *Iod*
- **Fauces**: *Ail* k* alum k2 arum-t k* **Bapt** k* *Borx* *Canth* k* caps k* *Carb-v* chlor k* cory br1* *Fl-ac* hippoz hr1 **Kali-bi** k* kali-br tl1 **Kali-i** k* lac-c hr1 **Lach** k* **Merc** k* **Merc-c** k* *Merc-i-r* k* *Myric* hr1 *Nat-s* k* **Nit-ac** k* *Phyt* k* psor hr1 sal-ac tl1 sang bro1 sars k* sol-t-ae k*
  - **burning**; with: *Caps*
  - **chronic**: alum bg
- **Mucous** membranes | **Margins**: lach k2
- **Pharynx**: ail bro1 am-c bro1 *Apis* bro1 aral bro1 ars-s-f k2 bapt bro1 *Cinnb* bro1 hydr bro1 *Hydrin-m* bro1 *Kali-bi* k* kali-m bro1 lach bro1 merc bro1* *Merc-c* k* merc-cy k2* merc-i-f bro1 *Merc-i-r* hr1* *Merl* hr1 *Mez* k* mur-ac bro1 *Nit-ac* k* *Phyt* bro1 sang bro1 *Sulph* k* vinc bro1 zinc k*
- **Tonsils**: **Ail** k* *Am-c* *Apis* k* ars bg2* *Aur* *Aur-m* aur-m-n vml3• aur-s k2 bar-c k* bell *Calc* k* eberth jl2 echi bro1 *Fl-ac* *Hep* k* hippoz ign k* *Kali-bi* k* kali-i k2 *Lac-c* *Lach* bg2* *Lyc* k* *Manc* *Merc* k* *Merc-c* k* *Merc-i-f* k* *Merc-i-r* k* merl bro1 *Mur-ac* hr1 nat-s k* **Nit-ac** k* *Phyt* k* sep *Sil* bro1 thuj bg2 zinc k*
  - **deep**: ail tl1
  - **gangrenous**: am-c bro1 ars bro1 bapt bro1 crot-h bro1 *Lach* bro1 *Merc-cy* bro1 mur-ac bro1
  - **small**: nit-ac tl1
  - **yellow**: calc k* zinc k*
  - ○ • **Behind**: ars ptk1 merc ptk1

- **Uvula**: ars bg2 *Aur* aur-s k2 bism *Fl-ac* hep k2 ind k* *Kali-bi* k* kali-i k2 *Merc* *Merc-c* k* *Nit-ac* k* phos phyt sulph
    - **spreading**: bism *Kali-bi* **Merc-c**
    - **syphilitic**: *Aur* aur-s k2 *Fl-ac* *Kali-bi* *Merc* *Merc-c* *Nit-ac* phyt

UNEASINESS; sensation of: stram bg2

VALVE, flap; sensation of a: ant-t bg2 bar-c bg2 ferr bg2 hydr bg2 ign bg2 iod b2.de* phyt bg2 *Spong* b2.de*

VAPOR, fumes, etc. rising in throat; sensation of: apis bg2* ars bg1 asaf bg1 brom bg1 bry bg1 carb-v bg1 chin bg1 colch bg2* ferr bg2* hep bg2* ign bg1 ip bg2* kali-chl bg1 lach bg1 lyc bg2* merc bg2* mosch bg1 nux-v bg2* ol-an bg2* op bg1 par bg1 puls bg2* rhus-t bg2* sabad bg2* sars bg2* sulph ptk1 thuj bg2* zinc bg2*

- **bad**: ferr bg2
- **coughing**; while: ol-an ptk1
- **hot** vapor: hydrog srj2•

VARICOSE: aesc bg2* *Alumn* *Bar-m* k* brom *Carb-v* bg2 cench k2 *Fl-ac* guaj bg2 **Ham** k* kali-bi bg2 nat-c bg2 *Puls* k* thuj

O - **Esophagus**: **Ham** hr1*
    - **portal** congestion; from: card-m mrr1
- **Pharynx**: **Aesc** k* aloe br1* *Bar-m* bro1 *Carb-v* cench k2 *Fl-ac* **Ham** k* *Kali-bi* *Lach* *Lyc* k* *Mang* nat-ar bg1 phyt bg1* *Puls* k* vesp
- **Tonsils**: *Bar-c* k* *Bar-m* brom dgt1 cench k2 *Ham* *Lach*

WARMTH; sensation of (See Heat - sensation)

WART like excrescences (See Condylomata)

WATER:

- **full** of: hep bg1
- **seems** to run outside, not going down esophagus: *Hep* hr1 verat tl1*

WEAKNESS: calc-p bg2 iod bg2 lac-c ptk1 stann ptk1

- **exertion** agg.: lac-c bg1
- **talking** agg.: *Stann* br1

WHEEZING: bell bg2

WORM; sensation of a: bry bg2 calc b4a.de* hyper ptk1 merc bg2 puls bg2*

ESOPHAGUS; complaints of: am-c bg2 arg-n bg2 *Ars* bg2 asaf bg2 canth bg2 carb-v bg2 **Cocc** bg2 lach bg2 nat-c bg2

PHARYNX; complaints of: *Acon* b2.de* agar b2.de* agn b2.de* *Alum* b2.de* am-c b2.de* am-m b2.de* ambr b2.de* anac b2.de* ang b2.de* ant-c b2.de* ant-t b2.de* *Apis* bg2 *Arg-met* b2.de* arn b2.de* ars b2.de* asaf b2.de* asar b2.de* aur b2.de* bar-c b2.de* **Bell** b2.de* bism b2.de* borx b2.de* bov b2.de* brom bg2 bry b2.de* calad b2.de* *Calc* b2.de* camph b2.de* cann-s b2.de* *Canth* b2.de* caps b2.de* carb-an b2.de* *Carb-v* b2.de* caust b2.de* *Cham* b2.de* chel b2.de* chin b2.de* cic b2.de* cina b2.de* cocc b2.de* coff b2.de* colch b2.de* coloc b2.de* con b2.de* croc b2.de* cupr b2.de* cycl b2.de* dig b2.de* *Dros* b2.de* dulc b2.de* euph b2.de* ferr b2.de* flav jl2 graph b2.de* guaj b2.de* hell b2.de* hep b2.de* *Hyos* b2.de* *Ign* b2.de* *Iod* b2.de* ip b2.de* kali-c b2.de* kali-n b2.de* kreos b2.de* *Lach* b2.de* laur b2.de* led b2.de* lyc b2.de* m-ambo b2.de m-arct b2.de m-aust b2.de mag-c b2.de* mag-m b2.de* mang b2.de* meny b2.de* *Merc* b2.de* mez b2.de* mosch b2.de* mur-ac b2.de* nat-c b2.de* nat-m b2.de* *Nit-ac* b2.de* nux-m b2.de* **Nux-v** b2.de* olnd b2.de* op b2.de* par b2.de* pen br1 petr b2.de* ph-ac b2.de* **Phos** b2.de* plat b2.de* plb b2.de* **Puls** b2.de* ran-b b2.de* ran-s b2.de* rhod b2.de* rhus-t b2.de* ruta b2.de* *Sabad* b2.de* sabin b2.de* samb b2.de* sars b2.de* sec b2.de* sel b2.de* *Seneg* b2.de* *Sep* b2.de* sil b2.de* spig b2.de* *Spong* b2.de* squil b2.de* stann b2.de* staph b2.de* *Stram* b2.de* stront-c b2.de* sul-ac b2.de* *Sulph* b2.de* tarax b2.de* teucr b2.de* thuj b2.de* valer b2.de* *Verat* b2.de* verb b2.de* zinc b2.de*

- **chronic**: aesc ptk1 cinnb ptk1 rumx ptk1 sep ptk1
- **nervous**: bapt mtf11 cist mtf11

TONSILS; complaints of: alum bg2 *Am-c* bg2 arg-n bg2 bapt ptk1 bar-c bg2* **Bell** bg2* calc bg2* *Calc-p* ptk1 *Canth* bg2 *Cham* bg2 guaj ptk1 *Hep* bg2* *Ign* bg2 lac-c ptk1 **Lach** bg2* *Lyc* bg2* **Merc** bg2* merc-d ptk1 **Merc-i-f** ptk1 **Merc-i-r** ptk1 *Nit-ac* bg2* *Nux-v* bg2 *Phos* bg2* *Phyt* ptk1 *Puls* bg2 sep bg2 sil ptk1 *Staph* bg2 sulph bg2* thuj bg2 tub ptk1

- **left** | **chronic**: calc mtf33

UVULA; complaints of: alum bg2 apis bg2* bell bg2 brom bg2 calc bg2 caps bg2 carb-v bg2 caust bg2 coff bg2 crot-t bg2 hyos bg2 iod bg2 kali-bi bg2* kali-c bg2 kali-i bg2 lach bg2 lyc bg2 merc ptk1 merc-c bg2* mur-ac bg2 nat-m bg2 nux-v bg2 phyt ptk1 plat bg2 puls bg2 sil bg2

ALTERNATING sides: am-m ptk1 calc-p ptk1

ABSCESS: *Cham* **Hep** kali-c *Kali-i* k* *Lach* k* *Lyc* **Merc** *Nit-ac* phos psor k* sep *Sil* sul-ac sulph
- O - **Cervical** glands: *Ars* b4a.de *Bell* b4.de* *Canth* b7a.de *Hep* b4a.de hyos b7.de* kreos b7a.de *Lach* b7a.de psor jl2 sars b4.de* *Sil* b4.de* streptoc jl2 *Toxo-g* jl2
  - **Throat**-pit: *Ip* b7a.de

AIR:
- **agg.**: ail *Caust* crot-h k* crot-t *Fl-ac* *Hep* k* *Merc* k* *Sil* k* tub
- **passing** up and down; sensation as if air were | **Thyroid** and cervical glands; in: spong b7.de*

ALIVE; sensation of something:
- O - **Cervical** glands: spong bg2
  - **Goitre**: spong b7.de*

CLOTHING agg.: *Agar* aids nl2• ambr aml-ns androc srj1• ant-c ptk1 *Apis* arg-n bamb-a stb2.de• **Bell** k ● *Cact* calc gb• calc-caust gb• calc-f dgt1 carb-an b4a.de* carc gk6* caust **Cench** k* chel **Crot-c** **Crot-h** k* *Elaps* glon k* ign fd* irid-met srj5• kali-bi *Kali-c* kreos sne lac-c vh lac-leo hrn2• **LACH** k ●* lact c1 *Mag-c* b4a.de manc mrr1 merc-c ptk1 naja k* nat-m gb• positr nl2• puls gb• sal-fr sle1• sars **Sep** k ●* sulph br *Tarent* k* tub c1
- **tight**; as if clothes too: aml-ns ptk1 sep ptk1

COLD AIR agg.: hydrog srj2•

COLDNESS: alum berb k* germ-met srj5• nat-s k* phos k* *Spong* k* tritic-vg fd5.de
- **evening**: *Spong* k*
- **night**: lyc h2*
- **wind** blowing on; as if: olnd ptk1
- O - **Thyroid** gland; in region of nat-ar

COMPLAINTS of external throat: acon b2.de* agar b2.de* agn b2.de* alum b2.de* am-c b2.de* *Am-m* b2.de* anac b2.de* ang b2.de* ant-c b2.de* ant-t b2.de* arg-met b2.de* arn b2.de* ars b2.de* asaf b2.de* *Asar* b2.de* aur b2.de* bar-c b2.de* *Bell* b2.de* bism b2.de* borx b2.de* bov b2.de* *Bry* b2.de* calc b2.de* camph b2.de* cann-s b2.de* canth b2.de* caps b2.de* carb-an b2.de* carb-v b2.de* caust b2.de* cham b2.de* chel b2.de* chin b2.de* *Cic* b2.de* cina b2.de* clem b2.de* *Cocc* b2.de* coff b2.de* colch b2.de* coloc b2.de* con b2.de* croc b2.de* cupr b2.de* *Cycl* b2.de* dig b2.de* dulc b2.de* euph b2.de* ferr b2.de* graph b2.de* guaj b2.de* hell b2.de* *Hep* b2.de* hyos b2.de* *Ign* b2.de* iod b2.de* ip b2.de* *Kali-c* b2.de* kali-n b2.de* kreos b2.de* *Lach* b2.de* laur b2.de* led b2.de **Lyc** b2.de* *M-ambo* b2.de *M-arct* b2.de mag-c b2.de* mag-m b2.de* mang b2.de* meny b2.de* merc b2.de* mez b2.de* mosch b2.de* mur-ac b2.de* nat-c b2.de* nat-m b2.de* nit-ac b2.de* nux-v b2.de* olnd b2.de* op b2.de* par b2.de* petr b2.de* ph-ac b2.de* phos b2.de* plat b2.de* plb b2.de* *Puls* b2.de* ran-s b2.de* rheum b2.de* rhod b2.de* rhus-t b2.de* ruta b2.de* sabin b2.de* samb b2.de* *Sars* b2.de* sec b2.de* sel b2.de* sep b2.de* sil b2.de* spig b2.de* spong b2.de* *Squil* b2.de* stann b2.de* staph b2.de* stront-c b2.de* sul-ac b2.de* sulph b2.de* *Tarax* b2.de* teucr b2.de* thuj b2.de* verat b2.de* verb b2.de* viol-o b2.de* *Zinc* b2.de* [bar-i stj2 fl-ac stj2 mang-i stj2 merc-i-f stj2 zinc-i stj2]
- **right** side: agn bg2* *Alum* bg2* *Am-c* bg2* anac bg2* ang bg2* ant-c bg2* *Ant-t* bg2* apis bg2 *Arg-met* bg2* asaf bg2* aur bg2* *Bell* bg2* *Bism* bg2* bry bg2* *Calc* bg2* *Camph* bg2* canth bg2* *Caps* bg2* carb-v bg2* **Caust** bg2* *Chel* bg2* *Chin* bg2* *Cina* bg2* cocc bg2* *Colch* bg2* coloc bg2* *Con* bg2* *Cupr* bg2* *Dulc* bg2* **Fl-ac** bg2* guaj bg2* *Hep* bg2* *Iod* bg2* *Kali-c* bg2* *Kali-n* bg2* *Lach* bg2* *Laur* bg2* *Led* bg2* *Lyc* bg2* *M-aust* fse1.de *Meny* bg2* **Merc** bg2* *Mez* bg2* *Nat-c* bg2* *Nat-m* bg2* **Nit-ac** bg2* *Nux-v* bg2* olnd bg2* *Petr* bg2* ph-ac bg2* *Plat* bg2* *Plb* bg2* *Puls* bg2* rhod bg2* sabin bg2* *Sars* bg2* *Seneg* bg2* *Sil* bg2* *Spig* bg2* *Spong* bg2* staph bg2* *Sul-ac* bg2* *Sulph* bg2* *Teucr* bg2* thuj bg2* zinc bg2*
- **left** side: *Acon* bg2* agn bg2* alum bg2* *Am-m* bg2* *Anac* bg2* ang bg2* *Ant-c* bg2* *Apis* bg2 arg-met bg2* *Arn* bg2* ars bg2* **Asaf** bg2* *Asar* bg2* aur bg2* *Bar-c* bg2* bell bg2* *Borx* bg2* *Bov* bg2* brom bg2 *Bry* bg2* **Calc** bg2* *Canth* bg2* *Carb-an* bg2* *Carb-v* bg2* caust bg2* *Cic* bg2* cocc bg2* colch bg2* *Coloc* bg2* con bg2* *Croc* bg2* *Cycl* bg2* fl-ac bg2 *Guaj* bg2* *Hyos* bg2* *Ign* bg2* kali-c bg2* lach bg2* laur bg2* *Lyc* bg2* merc bg2* mez bg2* *Mosch* bg2* nit-ac bg2 *Nux-v* bg2* *Olnd* bg2* *Par* bg2* ph-ac bg2* psor bg2 rhod bg2* *Rhus-t* bg2* *Sabin* bg2* *Sel* bg2* *Sep* bg2* *Sil* bg2* spig bg2* *Spong* bg2* *Squil* bg2* *Staph* bg2* *Stram* bg2* *Sul-ac* bg2* **Sulph** bg2* *Tarax* bg2* teucr bg2* *Thuj* bg2* *Verat* bg2* *Viol-t* bg2* zinc bg2*

Complaints of external throat: ...
- O - **Glands**; of: am-m ptk1 *Bar-c* ptk1 bell ptk1 brom ptk1 calc ptk1 calc-f ptk1 calc-i ptk1 calc-p ptk1 *Cham* ptk1 graph ptk1 hep ptk1 *Ign* ptk1 *Iod* ptk1 lach ptk1 lyc ptk1 nat-m ptk1 rhus-t ptk1 *Spong* ptk1 staph ptk1 sulph ptk1 vip ptk1 zinc-i ptk1
  - • **right**: ars ptk1 kali-c ptk1 *Merc* ptk1 nit-ac ptk1 sil ptk1 zinc-i ptk1
  - • **malignant**: *Cist* br1
    - **Cervical** glands: agn bg2 alum bg2 *Am-c* bg2 *Am-m* bg2 ambr bg2 ang bg2 ant-c bg2 ant-t bg2 arg-met bg2 *Arn* bg2 ars bg2 asaf bg2 asar bg2 *Aur* bg2 *Bar-c* bg2 **Bell** bg2 borx bg2 bov bg2 bry bg2 calad bg2 **Calc** bg2 camph bg2 canth bg2 caps bg2 **Carb-an** bg2 carb-v bg2 caust bg2 *Cham* bg2 chin bg2 cic bg2 cina bg2 *Clem* bg2 cocc bg2 *Con* bg2 cupr bg2 cycl bg2 dulc bg2 euphr bg2 ferr bg2 graph bg2 hell bg2 hep bg2 hyos bg2 ign bg2 iod bg2 *Kali-c* bg2 *Kreos* bg2 **Lach** bg2 **Lyc** bg2 mag-c bg2 mag-m bg2 **Med** bg2 **Merc** bg2 mez bg2 mur-ac bg2 nat-c bg2 nat-m bg2 **Nit-ac** bg2 nux-v bg2 par bg2 petr bg2 ph-ac bg2 *Phos* bg2 plb bg2 puls bg2 ran-s bg2 **Rhus-t** bg2 sabad bg2 sars bg2 sel bg2 seneg bg2 sep bg2 **Sil** bg2 spig bg2 spong bg2 squil bg2 stann bg2 **Staph** bg2 stram bg2 sul-ac bg2 sulph bg2 thuj bg2 verat bg2 viol-t bg2 zinc bg2
- O • **Cervical** glands: agn b2.de alum b2.de am-c b2.de am-m b2.de ambr b2.de ang b2.de ant-c b2.de ant-t b2.de arg-met b2.de arn b2.de ars b2.de asaf b2.de asar b2.de *Aur* b2.de bar-c b2.de **Bell** b2.de borx b2.de bov b2.de bry b2.de calad b2.de *Calc* b2.de camph b2.de canth b2.de caps b2.de *Carb-an* b2.de carb-v b2.de caust b2.de *Cham* b2.de chin b2.de cic b2.de cina b2.de *Clem* b2.de cocc b2.de *Con* b2.de cupr b2.de cycl b2.de dulc b2.de euph b2.de ferr b2.de *Graph* b2.de hell b2.de hep b2.de hyos b2.de *Ign* b2.de iod b2.de *Kali-c* b2.de kreos b2.de lach b2.de lyc b2.de m-ambo b2.de m-arct b2.de m-aust b2.de mag-c b2.de mag-m b2.de **Merc** b2.de mez b2.de mur-ac b2.de nat-c b2.de nat-m b2.de *Nit-ac* b2.de nux-v b2.de par b2.de petr b2.de ph-ac b2.de phos b2.de plb b2.de puls b2.de ran-s b2.de **Rhus-t** b2.de sabad b2.de sars b2.de sel b2.de seneg b2.de sep b2.de *Sil* b2.de *Spig* b2.de *Spong* b2.de squil b2.de stann b2.de **Staph** b2.de stram b2.de sul-ac b2.de sulph b2.de thuj b2.de verat b2.de viol-t b2.de zinc b2.de
  - **Thyroid** gland (See Thyroid)

CONGESTION: am-c h2* bell bg2 *Glon* bg2 kali-c h2* puls bg2*
- **left**: aq-mar skp7•
- **pressing** on heart with the hand; when: am-c h2*

CONSTRICTION: acon k* aids nl2• aloe hr arg-cy st ars k* asar atro a1 coff st coffin st dulc fd4.de fl-ac k* *Glon* iod kali-s fd4.de lac-e hrn2• **Lach** k* musca-d szs1 naja k* olib-sac wmh1 oxal-a rly4• puls rat k* rosm lgb1 *Sep* **Stram** k* *Stry* tab st tritic-vg fd5.de xan bg1 zinc bg2 [tax jsj7]
- **morning**: ignis-alc es2•
- **lying** agg.: bros-gau mrc1 glon
- **sleep** agg.; during: lach
- **waking**; on: ignis-alc es2•
- O - **Beneath** the lower jaw sang bg2*
  - **Cervical** glands: cina bg2
  - **Throat**-pit: apis k* *Brom* ptk1 ign k* olnd b7a.de *Par* b7a.de rhus-t k* staph b7a.de* valer zinc
    - • **eating** | **amel.**: rhus-t k*
    - • **sleep** agg.; on going to: valer
  - **Thyroid** gland: *Calc-s* **Crot-c** k* elaps *Iod* nat-ar spong tritic-vg fd5.de
    - • **finger**; as from a: nat-ar st
- O • **Region** of: nat-ar k2

CONTRACTION: | **Throat**-pit: ph-ac b4a.de*

CRACKING in muscles: limest-b es1• rheum h

CRAMP:
- O - **Sides**: *Agath-a* nl2• bar-c cic h1 graph h2 mang h2 plat h2 sep h2 spong h1
  - **Sternocleidomastoid**:
    - • **left** | **waking**; on: bit-ar wht1•
  - **Throat**-pit: *Zinc* b4a.de

CRAWLING: | **Cervical** glands: con k*

DISCOLORATION: kali-bi kali-s oxal-a rly4• podo k* rhus-v
- **blue**: ars hr1 *Lach* k*
- **brown**: kali-s k*
  - • **nodules**: *Thuj* b4a.de
  - • **spots**; in: kali-bi k* *Sep* k*

- **itching**: kali-n h2
- **lividity**: *Ars* k*
- **purple**: tarent
- **redness**: am-c bg2 am-caust k* apis bg2* bell bg2* graph bg2* iod bg2 *Jab* br1 neon srj5• op bg2 phos bg2 rhus-v k* stann bg2 sulph ptk1 verat bg2*
  - **spots**; in●: am-c h2* **BELL** k ●* carb-v cypra-eg sde6.de• iod k* kali-n h2 kali-s fkr2.de **Sep** k ●* stann k* tarent
    - **swollen**: mang bg2
  - **stripe**; in: mang h2 oxal-a rly4•
- **white** spots: nat-c h2*
- **yellow**: ars bg2* *Calc* kr chel k* hydr bg2*
  - **spots**: *Iod*

○ - **Glands**:
  - **changed** color: bar-c b4a.de *Carb-an* b4a.de clem b4a.de *Con* b4a.de dig b4a.de *Dulc* b4a.de graph b4a.de kali-c b4a.de merc b4a.de
  - **purple**: carb-an k2

DISTENSION:
- **left** side: caust h2*
- **sensation** of:

○ · **Cervical** glands: spong bg2
  · **Goitre**: spong b7.de*

DISTORTED: (↗*Torticollis)* ars h2* conin a1* hyos bg2

EMACIATION: calc-p bg2 iod bg2 kali-i bg2 lyc bg2 nat-m bg2* sars bg2

ENLARGED; sensation as if: hydrog srj2•

○ - **Sides** | **right**: agath-a nl2•

ERUPTIONS: agath-a nl2• *Anac Ars* bamb-a stb2.de• berb bov bry k* calc h2* canth k* caust clem dig h2* *Hep* kali-n kali-s fd4.de kola stb3• lyc k* merc k* moni rfm1• ph-ac raph ribo rly4• ruta fd4.de sars sep spong fd4.de squil h1* thuj tritic-vg fd5.de vanil fd5.de
- **right**: olib-sac wmh1
- **blotches**: graph kali-s fkr2.de nat-m olib-sac wmh1 sars sep spong vanil fd5.de
- **boils**: *Arg-met* bg2 caust bg2 nat-m bg2 sec bg2 sep bg2

○ · **Neck**; side of: caust coloc graph **Kali-i** k* mag-c nat-m nit-ac phyt rhus-v sep ven-m rsj12•
- **burning**: canth a1 kali-n h2*
- **crusts**: anac
- **exfoliating**: kola stb3•
- **herpes**: lac-d k* lyc h2* **Psor** sars k* sep k*
  - **symmetrical**: lac-d hr1
- **itching**: *Agath-a* nl2• bamb-a stb2.de• gink-b sbd1• kali-s fd4.de lyc h2* mag-c h2* merc a1 moni rfm1• spong fd4.de vanil fd5.de
- **moist**: *Caust* merc a1
- **painful**: lac-h sk4• lyc h2* ruta fd4.de spong fd4.de
- **pimples**: agar k* alum h2* ant-c k* am a1 berb k* borx h2 bov k* canth k* *Cinnb* clem corian-s knl6• gels a1 *Hep* k* hydrog srj2• irid-met srj5• *Jug-r* kali-n k* lyc mag-c h2* mez k* mur-ac k* nat-m k* op a1 pall a1 ph-ac propr sa3• *Puls* k* raph k* ruta fd4.de spig h1* spong stann h2* staph h1* sulph k* symph fd3.de• *Thuj* k* tritic-vg fd5.de zinc k*
  - **row**, in a: thuj h1
- **pustules**: aids nl2• ant-c h2* am bg2 aur h2* chel k* grin mtf11 kali-s fd4.de *Psor* sil bg2 sul-i bg2 sulph bg2 zinc-s bg2
- **rash**: am-c k* chin h1* falco-pe nl2•
- **red**: chin h1* lac-h sk4• lyc h2* mez h2* olib-sac wmh1 ph-ac h2* sep h2* spig h1* thuj h1* tritic-vg fd5.de vanil fd5.de vesp a1
  - **spots**: caust a1 hydrc a1 lavand-a ctl1•
- **scratching** agg.; after: mag-c h2*
- **spots**: mur-ac a1
- **stitching**: phos h2*
- **tubercles**: am-c lach lyc mur-ac nicc ph-ac phos sec
- **urticaria**: bamb-a stb2.de• bry k* kali-i
- **vesicles**: canth a1 clem k* grin mtf11 mag-c ph-ac k* sep k* vip

○ · **Sides**: alum k* cob a1
    - **discharge** of ear; from: **Tell**

EXCORIATION: | **rubbing** of clothes; from: olnd h1* squil h1*

FISTULAE: *Phos Sil*

FORMICATION: arund a1 rhus-v k* spong h1*

Formication: ...

○ - **Throat**-pit | **cough**; causing: *Sang* k*
- **Thyroid** gland: ambr bg1

FULLNESS:

○ - **Jugular**; in: *Crot-c*
- **Throat**-pit: cham con *Lach* k*
- **Veins**: crot-c bg2 thuj bg2

GOITRE: (↗*Swelling - thyroid cartilage; Swelling - thyroid gland; Thyroid; GENERALS - Hypothyroidism)* adren st *Ail* aloe am-c k* am-m bg2 *Ambr* k* *Apis* ars-i bg2* *Aur* k* *Aur-i* k* aur-s c1* *Bad* k* bell k* brass-o vs *Brom* k* **Calc** k* *Calc-f* k* *Calc-i* k* *Calc-s* calc-sil k2 *Carb-an* k* *Carbn-s* k* *Caust* k* *Cist* k* con k* crot-c k* dig b2.de* echi br1 *Ferr* c2 *Ferr-i* k* *Fl-ac* k* form k* fuc c1* *Glon* c2 *Graph* bg1* hall c2 ham bg2 *Hep* k* *Hydr* br1 *Ign* ptk1 **Iod** k* iris br1* jab br1 kali-bi gk kali-c k* *Kali-i* k* lac-c sne *Lach* k* lap-a k* *Lyc* k* *Lycps-v* k* mag-c k* mag-p br1 mang bg1 marb-w es1• merc b2.de* *Merc-i-f* k* *Merc-i-r* k* *Nat-c* k* **NAT-M** ●* *Nat-p* k* *Nat-s* k* nux-v st ol-j c2 petr b2.de* *Phos* k* plat k* podo k* sec c2 *Sep* k* *Sil* k* **Spong** k* staph bg2* stram stroph-h ptk1 sul-i bg2* sulph b2.de* syc pte1*• tab *Tarent* k* *Thyr* bg2* *Thyroid* c1* *Tub* k* urt-u k* vip c2* zinc-i ptk1 [calc-br stj1 mag-br stj1]
- **right**: ars bg2 aur-i k2 caust st* hep bg1* iod kali-c bg2 *Lyc* k* mag-c bg1 merc-i-f nat-c nit-ac bg2 *Phos* *Sep* k* sil spong
- **left**: chel bg1* *Iod* sne **Lach** k ●*
- **accompanied** by:
  - **choking**: meph ptk1
  - **obesity**: fuc br1
  - **respiration**; asthmatic (See RESPIRATION - Asthmatic - accompanied - goitre)
- **children**; in: bar-c bg2 nit-ac bg2
- **constriction**: *Calc-s* **Crot-c** k* elaps bg2 *Iod* b4.de* *Lyc* *Spong*
- **cough** agg.: *Psor* vh
- **diffused**: sulfa mtf11
- **exophthalmic** (= Basedow's disease; Graves'disease; oxic goitre): acon mfj adon mtf11 adren br1* **Aml-ns** mfj* anh jl3 antip c2* aq-mar jl3 aran-ix jl3 ars mfj* ars-i bro1* atra-r jl3 *Aur* k* aur-ar vh1 *Aur-i* bad k* bar-c bro1 *Bell* mfj* brom bro1* bry mfj bufo ptk1 *Cact* k* cadm-i gm1 *Calc* k* calc-f mg1.de* calc-i k2* cann-i br1* chin mg1.de chinin-ar mg1.de chr-s bro1 cimic jl3 colch bro1 con k* crot-h k* cupr mg1.de cupr-act mg1.de cyt-l jl3 diphtox jl2 dubo-m br1 echi br1* elaps mg1.de ephe c2* *Ferr* k* *Ferr-i* k* ferr-p bg1* ferr-s br1* *Fl-ac* bro1* flor-p mg1.de fuc br1* *Glon* bro1 graph mrr1 hall c2 hed mg1.de* **Iod** k* *Jab* br1* kali-c bg2* **Kali-i** mrr1 lach mg1.de **Lycps-eu** mfj *Lycps-v* k* mag-c mg1.de mag-f mg1.de meph ptk2 **Nat-m** k ●* nux-v st1 op mg1.de **Phos** k ●* *Pilo* bro1 pineal bro1 *Rauw* jl3 saroth jl3 scut st sec k* sel jl3 sil mfj spartin-s bro1 spig c2 *Spong* k* stram bro1 stroph-h br1* sulph mfj thal jl3* thala jl3 thym-gl bwa3 *Thyr* c1* thyreotr jl3 tub c2* verat c1* verat-v mfj
  - **accompanied** by:
    - **choking**: meph ptk1
    - **trembling**: meph ptk1
    - **Head**; pain in: ephe mtf11
    - **Heart** complaints: adon bg2 ars bg2 aur bg2 bell bg2 cact br1 cadm-i gm1 calc bg2 calc-i bg2 ferr-p bg2 hep bg2 iod bg2 lach bg2 lycps-v bg2 nat-m bg2 phos bg2 spong bg2 stroph-h bg2 thyr bg2
    - **Intestines**; cancer of (See ABDOMEN - Cancer - intestines - accompanied - goitre)
  - **consumptive** state: hippoz jl2
  - **menses**; from suppressed: **Ferr** hr1* ferr-i br1*
  - **tuberculosis** in family; with: dros tl
- **indurated**: brom k2 bufo ptk1 calc-f bg2 *Calc-i* sne fl-ac bg2 iod k* *Mag-c* b4a.de *Nat-c* b4a.de* nat-p tl1 *Spong* k*
- **menses**; before: cimic bg3
- **myxedema** (See GENERALS - Myxedema)
- **nodular**: graph ptk1* phyt ptk1
- **painful**: **Iod** k* *Nat-c* hr1 *Plat* k* spong k*
  - **menses** | **before** | **agg.**: cimic ptk
    - **during** | **agg.**: iod
  - **swallowing** agg.: spong
- **pregnancy** agg.; during: calc-i ptk1 *Hydr* br1*
- **pressure** in goitre; with: nat-c h2* spong a1
- **puberty**: calc-i br1* flor-p a1* *Hydr* br1*

- **pulsating** (See Pulsation - goitre)
- **sensitive**: kali-i k*
- **tickling**: plat h2*
- **toxic** goitre (See exophthalmic)
- **twitching**: lyc h2*
- **vascular**: *Apis* k* *Calc* k*
- **venous**: card-m bg2

GRASPING, sensation of (See Constriction)

HAIR: | **darker**; becomes: arizon-l nl2•

HEAT: carc fd2.de• chord-umb rly4• cycl h1* ign a1 kola stb3• lach hr1 sars h2* sulph h2*
- **flushes**:
  - **left**: lac-d mrr1
  - **excitement** agg.: merc mrr1 nat-m mrr1

HEAVINESS: | **Thyroid** gland: phyt bg2

HYPERTHYROIDISM (See GENERALS - Hyperthyroidism)

HYPOTHYROIDISM (See Goitre; GENERALS - Hypothyroidism)

INDURATION of glands: *Alum* *Alumn* am-c ant-c *Arg-n* hr1 bar-c *Bar-i* **Bar-m** bar-s k2 **Bell** brom k2* **Calc** calc-f **Calc-i** *Calc-p* calc-sil k2 **Carb-an** *Carb-v* carbn-s carc mlr1• chir-fl gya2 *Cist* **Con** *Cupr* k* *Dulc* *Graph* *Hecla* *Hep* hydrog srj2• **Iod** *Kali-i* lap-a br1 *Lyc* *Merc* k* *Nat-c* nat-m *Nit-ac* phyt a1 puls *Rhus-t* *Sars* scir bn* sep **Sil** *Spong* k* staph k* sul-i k2 **Sulph** syph k2 **Tab** **Tub** k* wies a1
- **cords**; like knotted: aeth bg1 bar-c k2 **Bar-i** **Bar-m** berb bg1 *Calc* **Calc-i** *Cist* k* *Dulc* k* hecla hep *Iod* lyc *Merc* nit-ac bg1 *Psor* puls b7a.de rhus-t *Sil* *Sul-i* k2 *Sulph* **Tub** k*

○ - **Cervical**: *Brom* mrr1 *Cham* b7a.de cocc b7.de* *Ferr* b7a.de *Iod* bg2 phyt bg2 plb b7.de* psor jl2 rhus-t b7.de* scarl jl2 spig b7.de* *Spong* bg2 staph b7.de* streptoc jl2 *Toxo-g* jl2 tub jl2

INFLAMMATION:
- **erysipelatous**: rhus-t k2

○ - **Cervical** glands: aur b4a.de **Bar-c** b4.de* *Bell* b4.de* calc b4a.de canth b7.de* *Cham* b7a.de *Kali-c* b4.de* *Lach* b7a.de m-aust b7.de merc b4a.de *Nit-ac* b4.de* petr b4a.de phos b4a.de plb b7.de* psor jl2 rad-br sze8• *Rhus-t* b7a.de sars b4.de* streptoc jl2 sul-ac b4.de* *Sulph* b4a.de thuj b4a.de *Toxo-g* jl2 verat b7.de*
  - **chronic**: v-a-b jl2
- **Thyroid** gland (= thyroiditis): am-c mrr1 lach mrr1 nat-m mrr1
  - **cough** agg.; during: *Alum* b4a.de
  - **dentition**; during: *Mucor* jl2
  - **Riedel's** thyroiditis: hed mtf11

ITCHING: *Agath-a* nl2• **Alum** k* am-m k* ambr anac k* ant-c h2* apis ars h2* aur k* bov k* *Calc* canth k* carb-v k* caust k* chel k* *Cist* k* con k* crot-c sk4• dulc fd4.de fl-ac k* form k* *Glon* k* irid-met srj5• kali-i k* kali-n k* kali-p fd1.de• kali-s fd4.de lac-h sk4• linu-c a1 lyc h2* mag-c k* maias-l hrn2• mez k* moni rfm1• *Nat-c* k* nat-sil fd3.de• nit-ac h2* paull a1 plan k* rhus-v k* samb k* sep k* spong fd4.de stront-c sulph h2* symph fd3.de• tarent k* thuj k* tritic-vg fd5.de vanil fd5.de verat-v a1
- **morning**: mag-c k*
  - **dressing**; while: mag-c k*
- **evening**: mez k* symph fd3.de•
  - **going** to sleep; before: mag-c
- **night**: kalm k*
- **menses**; during: mag-c h2*
- **perspiration** agg.: petr-ra shn4•
- **scratching**:
  - **agg.**: moni rfm1•
  - **amel.**: chel a1 mag-c k* nat-c a1 squil h1*
- **stitching**: carb-v h2* sars h2*
- **swallowing** agg.: aur k* con k*
- **walking** in open air agg.: nit-ac h2*

▽ - **extending** to:

○ • **Chest**: fl-ac k*
  - **Eustachian** tubes: caust k*

Itching – extending to: ...
  - **Larynx**: sil h2* zinc h2*

○ - **Cervical** glands: ant-c b7.de* con b4.de* kali-c b4.de* plat bg2
- **Thyroid** gland: ambr bg2* mag-c bg2
  - **cough** agg.; during: ambr b7.de*

JERKS: | **left**: mez h2*

LUMPS:

○ - **Throat**-pit: agath-a nl2• lach bg2 *Lob* k* [benz-ac xyz62]
- **Thyroid** gland: calc-f bg2

MOTION:
- **larynx** agg.; of: stram ptk1

○ - **Thyroid** gland | **sensation** of: spong b7.de*

NUMBNESS: *Carb-an* k* chel k* dig bg2 hell bg2 olnd petr bg2 plat bg2 sep spig bg2 *Spong* k*

○ - **Cervical** glands: sep b4.de*

PAIN: aeth ↓ agath-a nl2• alum ↓ am-m ↓ ammc ↓ *Anac* ↓ ant-c ↓ apis ↓ arg-met ↓ *Bar-c* k* bar-s k2 *Bell* ↓ bov ↓ *Calc* ↓ caps k* *Carb-v* ↓ chel ↓ chin ↓ *Chinin-s* ↓ clem ↓ cob ↓ colch ↓ corv-cor ↓ crot-h ↓ cupr ↓ cycl ↓ cypra-eg sde6.de• fago k* gels ↓ granit-m ↓ *Hep* ↓ jug-c ↓ kali-bi ↓ kali-chl ↓ kalm ↓ kreos **Lach** ↓ med ↓ *Merc* merc-i-f ↓ mosch ↓ *Nat-m* nat-pyru rly4• *Nicc* ↓ op k* oxal-a ↓ par ↓ petr ↓ ph-ac ↓ phos k* phyt mrr1 *Puls* rham-cal br1 rhus-t ↓ rhus-v ↓ ruta ↓ sabin ↓ sars ↓ sep ↓ spong fd4.de staphycoc ↓ sul-ac k* tarent ↓ tep ↓ *Thuj* ↓ tritic-vg fd5.de vanil fd5.de verat ↓
- **right**: alum ↓ caust ↓ dendr-pol ↓ merc-i-f ↓ phyt mrr1 rosm lgb1 taosc iwa1• vesp ↓
  - **burning**: alum caust merc-i-f vesp
  - **cutting** pain: dendr-pol sk4•
- **left**: ang ↓ berb ↓ coloc ↓ *Con* ↓ form ↓ nat-s ↓ sars ↓ thuj ↓
  - **burning**: berb coloc form nat-s
  - **cutting** pain: thuj
  - **sore**: ang h1
  - **sprained**; as if: *Con* sars h2
- **morning**: calam sa3• phos k* tub jl2
- **forenoon**: iod ↓
  - **sore**: iod k*
- **night**: phyt mrr1
- **burning**: ammc br1
- **cramping**: agath-a nl2•
- **crushed**; as if: sep
- **cutting** pain: ruta h1
- **dinner**; after: grat ↓
  - **burning**: grat
- **drawing** pain: nat-m h2* spong fd4.de tritic-vg fd5.de
  - **cords** were drawing downward; as if: apis b7a.de
- **head** backwards and towards the left; when turning the: agar ↓
  - **sprained**; as if: agar a1*
- **jerking** pain: arg-met h1 caps h1*
- **menses**; during: am-m b7.de
- **motion**:
  - **agg.**: bry ↓ cic ↓ phos h2* stront-c ↓
    - **burning**: stront-c
    - **sore**: bry k* cic h1*
  - **slight** motion | **agg.**: phyt mrr1
- **pinching** pain: ph-ac h2* phos h2*
- **pressing** pain: granit-m es1• ruta fd4.de tritic-vg fd5.de
- **scratching** pain: ammc br1
- **sharp** (See cutting)
- **shooting** (See stitching)
- **sore**: *Bar-c* *Bell* *Calc* chel k* *Chinin-s* clem k* cob k* corv-cor bdg• crot-h bg2 cycl h1* fago a1 gels bg2 granit-m es1• *Hep* jug-c br1 kali-bi k* kali-chl a1 **Lach** med merc bg2 merc-i-f k* *Nicc* oxal-a rly4• sabin bg2 staphycoc rly4• sul-ac k* tarent verat h1*
- **sprained**; as if: petr h2
- **stitching** pain: alum k* am-m h2* *Anac* k* ant-c k* chin k* colch hep h2* kalm nat-m h2* rhus-t rhus-v k* sars h2* tep *Thuj* k* tritic-vg fd5.de vanil fd5.de

External Throat

• **intermittent**: cupr h2*
- **tearing** pain: aeth am-m h2* bov *Carb-v* par tep thuj
• **intermittent**: cupr h2*
- **torn** off; as if: mosch b7a.de
- **touch** agg.: cic a1 oxal-a ↓ phos h2* ruta fd4.de
• **sore**: cic h1 oxal-a rly4•
- **turning** head agg.: calc ↓ hep ↓
• **sore**: calc k*
• **stitching** pain: hep h2*
▽ - **extending** to:
○ • **Ear**: alum ↓ hep ↓ hydrog ↓ phos ↓ tep ↓
⁝ **stitching** pain: alum hep h2* hydrog srj2• phos k* tep
• **Foot**: lyc ↓
⁝ **stitching** pain: lyc h2*
• **Shoulders**: fic-m ↓
⁝ **pressing** pain: fic-m gya1
○ - **Blood** vessels: phos ↓
• **tearing** pain: phos h2*
- **Cervical** glands: acon-ac rly4• aesc ↓ agn ↓ ail ↓ *Alum* b4.de* am-c b4.de* *Am-m* ↓ ambr b7.de* ang ↓ ant-t b7.de* arg-met ↓ arn k* ars ↓ *Aur* b4a.de aur-i k2 **Bell** k* borx h2 bov ↓ bros-gau mrc1 bry b7.de* *Calc* k* calc-s k2 calc-sil k2 canth ↓ *Caps* *Carb-an* b4a.de *Carb-v* k* caust k* chin b7.de* choc ↓ cic b7.de* cina ↓ *Clem* b4a.de cocc ↓ con b4.de* cupr ↓ cycl ↓ *Dulc* hr1 euph ↓ graph b4.de* hell k* *Hep* ↓ hura hydrog srj2• ign b7.de* iod bg2 kali-bi ↓ kali-c k* lach k2 lap-la sde8.de• *Lyc* b4.de* m-ambo ↓ m-arct ↓ mag-c b4.de* *Merc* k* mez ↓ mur-ac ↓ nat-c ↓ *Nat-m* k* nat-pyru rly4• *Nit-ac* b4.de* nux-v b7.de* par ↓ *Ph-ac* b4.de* phos b4.de* *Phyt* ↓ plat bg2 psor k* puls b7.de* ran-s ↓ *Rhus-t* b7.de* ribo ↓ ruta fd4.de sabad ↓ sapin ↓ sel b7.de* seneg ↓ sep b4.de* **Sil** k* spig b7.de* spong b7.de* squil b7.de* stann b4.de* *Staph* b7.de* stram b7a.de stry a1 sul-ac b4.de* sul-i k2 thiam rly4• thuj k* tub c verat b7a.de vesp ↓ wies ↓ [heroin sdj2]
• **right**: nat-pyru rly4•
• **left**: nat-pyru rly4•
• **night**: merc thuj k*
• **air** agg.; in open: kali-c k2
• **boring**: bell b4.de* puls b7.de* sabad b7.de*
• **burning**: bell carb-an k2 **Merc** nit-ac
• **burrowing**: rhus-t b7.de*
• **cough** agg.; during: nat-m k*
• **cutting** pain: arg-met b7.de*
• **drawing** pain: agn b7.de* alum b4a.de* bell b4.de* bov b4.de* cycl b7.de* ign b7.de* puls b7.de* seneg b4.de*
• **fever**; during: *Lach* bg2
• **perspiration**; during: *Bell* bg2 *Calc* bg2 con bg2 lach bg2 lyc bg2 *Nux-v* bg2 phos bg2 sep bg2 sulph bg2 thuj bg2
• **pinching** pain: bry b7.de* m-arct b7.de verat b7.de*
• **pressing** pain: alum b4a.de* ars b4a.de aur b4.de* *Bell* b4.de* chin b7.de* cina b7.de* cocc b7.de* cycl b7.de* ign b7.de* *Merc* b4.de* nat-c bg2 par b7.de* rhus-t b7.de* stram b7.de*
• **smarting**: con b4.de*
• **sore**: aesc k* ail k* **Bell** canth k* choc srj3• clem k* *Hep* kali-bi k* merc k* mur-ac k* nat-m k* *Phyt* *Psor* k* rhus-t k* ribo rly4• sapin a1 sul-i k2 vesp k* wies a1
• **squeezed**; as if: ars b4a.de chin b7.de* ign b7.de* m-arct b7.de sep b4.de* staph b7.de*
• **stitching** pain: alum h2* *Am-m* b7a.de ang b7.de* arg-met b7.de* bell b4.de* borx b4a.de* carb-an b4a.de* chin b7.de* con b4.de* cupr b7.de* euph b4a.de hep k2 ign b7.de* kali-c h2* lyc b4a.de* m-ambo b7.de merc b4.de* mez b4.de* nit-ac b4.de* nux-v b7.de* ph-ac b4.de* ran-s b7.de* rhus-t b7.de* sabad b7.de* sil b4.de* spig b7.de* stann b4.de* sul-ac b4.de*
• **tearing** pain: alum b4a.de bell b4.de* caps b7.de* *Graph* b4a.de sel b7a.de
• **touch** agg.: lach k2 ruta fd4.de streptoc rly4•
• **turning** head agg.: kali-c h2*
• **warm** room | **amel.**: kali-c k2

Pain – **Cervical** glands: ...
▽ • **extending** to:
⁝ **Ear**: nat-pyru rly4•
⁝ **Head**: psor jl2
- **Muscles** of the throat; deep in the: cycl ↓
• **sore**: cycl h1
- **Sides**: abrot k* aeth ↓ alum alumn k* am-m ↓ anac ↓ ant-c ↓ arg-met arg-n ↓ asaf ↓ *Aur* ↓ bamb-a ↓ *Bell* berb ↓ bism ↓ borx ↓ **Bry** ↓ calc ↓ calc-p *Caps* ↓ *Carb-v* ↓ caul ↓ caust ↓ cere-b a1 *Chel* k* chin ↓ chinin-s cic ↓ cinnb clem ↓ cocc ↓ coloc k* crot-c crot-t ↓ cycl ↓ dig ↓ dulc ↓ eup-per ↓ fic-m ↓ form ↓ *Graph* ↓ grat ↓ guaj ↓ hell ↓ hep ↓ hydrog ↓ ign ↓ *Indg* ↓ iod ↓ jac-c k* kali-bi ↓ kali-c k* kali-i kali-n k* kalm k* kola stb3• lach ↓ led ↓ lyc ↓ lyss k* mag-c ↓ manc ↓ mang-p ↓ med ↓ meny ↓ *Merc* ↓ merc-i-f k* nat-c ↓ nat-s k* nat-sil ↓ nit-ac ↓ *Nux-v* ↓ ol-an ↓ *Par* petr ↓ *Ph-ac* ↓ phos ↓ phys k* plat ↓ plumbg a1 podo ↓ psil ↓ psor rat ↓ ruta fd4.de sabin ↓ sars k* sel *Seneg* ↓ sep ↓ sil ↓ spig ↓ spong ↓ squil ↓ staph ↓ stram ↓ stront-c ↓ stry ↓ sul-ac ↓ sulph ↓ symph fd3.de* tab ↓ tarax ↓ tarent teucr ↓ *Thuj* ↓ tritic-vg ↓ vanil fd5.de verat-v k* vesp k* zinc ↓ zinc-p ↓
• **right**: aeth ↓ anac ↓ ang ↓ carb-ac ↓ carb-v ↓ *Caust* ↓ *Chel* ↓ cocc ↓ con ↓ dulc ↓ grat ↓ indg ↓ kali-c ↓ kola stb3• lac-lup hrn2• mag-c ↓ mag-m ↓ nat-c ↓ nux-v ↓ ozone sde2• ph-ac h2* plat ↓ sars h2* sil ↓ spig ↓ spong fd4.de staph ↓ sul-ac ↓ thuj ↓ ulm-c ↓ zinc ↓
⁝ **drawing** pain: *Caust* *Chel* con h2* dulc h2* grat k* indg kali-c k* mag-c h2* mag-m h2* nux-v k* plat k* sars h2* sil h2* spong k* staph k* sul-ac h2* thuj k* ulm-c jsj8• zinc k*
⁝ **pressing** pain: anac h2* carb-v h2* cocc h1* kali-c h2* ozone sde2• thuj h1* zinc h2*
⁝ **stitching** pain: ang h1* carb-ac k* nat-c h2* sars h2* spig h1*
⁝ **tearing** pain: aeth kali-c h2* mag-c h2* nat-c h2*
⁝ **extending** to:
: **Jaw**; lower: indg ↓
. **drawing** pain: indg
• **left**: bros-gau ↓ caul ↓ chel ↓ cic ↓ coloc ↓ cycl ↓ ham fd3.de• hydrog srj2• indg ↓ kali-c ↓ kali-s fd4.de lyc ↓ mez ↓ nat-s ↓ nat-sil ↓ phos ↓ sel sil ↓ spong ↓ sul-ac ↓ sulph ↓ vanil fd5.de verat ↓
⁝ **drawing** pain: caul chel k* cic k* coloc k* cycl h1* lyc h2* nat-s k* nat-sil fd3.de• spong h1 sulph verat h1*
: **jerking** pain: indg
⁝ **pressing** pain: bros-gau mrc1 ham fd3.de• sil h2* sul-ac h2* verat h1*
⁝ **stitching** pain: kali-c h2* phos h2* vanil fd5.de
⁝ **tearing** pain: lyc h2* mez h2* phos h2* *Sel* k* sulph
• **morning**: sars k* tarent k* thuj ↓ zinc k*
⁝ **drawing** pain: thuj k*
⁝ **stitching** pain: thuj k*
⁝ **tearing** pain: zinc k*
⁝ **waking**; on: thuj ↓
: **drawing** pain: thuj
• **forenoon**: fl-ac k*
• **afternoon**: canth ↓ chel k* fl-ac ↓ iris-fl kalm ↓
⁝ **drawing** pain: *Chel* fl-ac k* kalm k*
⁝ **stitching** pain: canth
• **evening**: ant-c ↓ clem ↓ cycl ↓ mag-c ↓ merc-i-r ↓ olnd ↓
⁝ **drawing** pain: ant-c h2* clem a1 cycl h1* mag-c h2*
⁝ **stitching** pain: clem k* merc-i-r a1
⁝ **tearing** pain: mag-c h2* olnd k*
• **night**: kalm ↓ olnd ↓ vesp k*
⁝ **stitching** pain: kalm k*
⁝ **tearing** pain: olnd k*
• **bending**:
⁝ **head**:
: **backward**:
. **agg.**: cycl ↓
drawing pain: cycl k*
: **forward**:
. **agg.**: staph ↓
drawing pain: staph k*
: **right** agg.; to: sulph k*

- **blowing** the nose agg.: merc k*
- **burning**: alumn k* bamb-a stb2.de• berb k* calc h2* caust k* coloc k* eup-per a1 form k* grat k* ign k* mang-p rly4• merc-i-f k* nat-s k* ol-an a1 stram stront-c vh sulph h2* tab k* vesp k*
- **chewing** agg.: zinc ↓
  - **drawing** pain: zinc h2*
- **cutting** pain: thuj k*
- **drawing** pain: alumn ant-c h2* asaf k* bell h1* *Bry* caul chel k* chin h1* cic k* clem k* cocc h1* coloc k* *Crot-c* k* cycl h1* dulc grat k* hell indg k* kali-c k* lyc med nat-s k* nat-sil fd3.de• nit-ac h2* *Nux-v* k* petr h2* ph-ac sars h2* *Seneg* sep k* spong k* squil h1* staph k* sulph k* teucr k* tritic-vg fd5.de zinc k* zinc-p k2
  - **downward**: sil h2* zinc h2*
  - **lancinating**: *Indg* k*
  - **twitching**: plat k*
  - **upward**: lyc thuj k*
- **holding** head erect: zinc ↓
  - **drawing** pain: zinc k*
- **motion**:
  - **agg.**: asaf ↓ *Carb-v* ↓ *Chel* cimic ↓ *Colch* coloc ↓ cycl ↓ ham kali-c h2 nux-v ↓ phys sars ↓ sulph ↓ verat ↓
    - **cramping**: cimic
    - **drawing** pain: asaf k* *Chel* coloc cycl k* nux-v sulph
    - **pressing** pain: sars h2*
    - **tearing** pain: *Carb-v* sulph verat
  - **amel.**: led ↓
    - **pressing** pain: led
  - **head**; of:
    - **agg.**: am-m ↓ com dig ↓ graph ↓ ham fd3.de• sars ↓ tarax h1
      - **stitching** pain: am-m h2 dig h2 graph h2 sars h2
      - **tearing** pain: am-m h2
  - **jaw**; of lower | **agg.**: tarax h1
- **paroxysmal**: *Sel*
- **pinching** pain: hep h2 iod h lyc h2 zinc h2
- **pressing** pain: anac h2* ant-c h2* arg-n asaf k* aur h2* bell h1* bism k* cocc k* *Coloc* k* crot-t k* dig h2* fic-m gya1 form k* kalm k* lach led lyc k* mag-c h2* *Merc* nat-s k* nit-ac h2* *Ph-ac* k* phos psil ft1 sabin k* *Sars* spong h1* squil h1* staph k* tarax h1* zinc k* zinc-p k2
  - **intermittent**: spong k*
  - **upward**: thuj h1*
- **pressure**:
  - **amel.**: zinc ↓
    - **tearing** pain: zinc k*
- **pulsating** pain: manc k* vanil fd5.de
- **rheumatic**: berb ↓ calc-s k* *Chel* cop a1 cycl h1* iod h* phys k* rhus-t staph h1*
  - **tearing** pain: berb k*
- **sitting** agg.: ant-c ↓ *Chel* ↓ nat-sil ↓
  - **drawing** pain: ant-c h2* *Chel* nat-sil fd3.de•
- **sprained**; as if: podo fd3.de•
- **stitching** pain: alum k* aur berb k* borx chin h1* clem k* form k* *Graph* guaj hydrog srj2• kali-bi k* kalm k* meny h1* nat-c h2* phos k* rat k* *Sars* spig k* spong k* staph stront-c vh stry sul-ac tarax h1* *Thuj* k* vanil fd5.de zinc
  - **boring** pain: tarax h1*
- **swallowing**:
  - **amel.**: spong ↓
    - **stitching** pain: spong
  - **hindering** swallowing: anac ↓
    - **pressing** pain: anac h2*
- **talking** agg.: zinc ↓
  - **pressing** pain: zinc
- **tearing** pain: aeth k* am-m h2* anac k* *Aur* berb k* **Bry** calc k* *Caps* *Carb-v* grat k* indg k* iod k* kali-bi k* nat-c k* nat-s k* petr h2* phos k* rat k* sabin k* *Sel* k* staph h1* tarax k* teucr zinc h2*
  - **paroxysmal**: *Sel*

- **Sides**: ...
  - **touch** agg.: bar-c h2* nat-m h2* sars h2* sil h2* sul-ac h2*
    - **pressing** pain: sars h2*
    - **stitching** pain: sars h2*
  - **turning**:
    - **head**:
      - **agg.**: abel arg-met cinnb clem ↓ coc-c ↓ *Coloc* ↓ *Crot-c* ↓ dig ↓ ham fd3.de• hydrog srj2• nat-m h2 nat-sil fd3.de• ph-ac ↓ spong fd4.de *Tarent* tritic-vg ↓ tub c
        - **drawing** pain: clem k* *Crot-c* k* ph-ac h2* tritic-vg fd5.de
        - **pressing** pain: *Coloc* ham fd3.de•
        - **stitching** pain: coc-c dig h2*
      - **painful** side agg.; to: ham fd3.de• vesp
      - **right** agg.; to: arg-met chinin-s psor *Tarent*
  - **waking**; on: phys k*
  - **walking**:
    - **agg.**: canth ↓
      - **tearing** pain: canth
    - **air**; in open:
      - **agg.**: arg-met ↓ camph ↓
        - **drawing** pain: camph
        - **pressing** pain: arg-met
      - **amel.**:
        - **rapidly**; walking: caust ↓
          - **pressing** pain: caust
  - **yawning** agg.: plat h2*
  - ▽ **extending** to:
    - **Arms**: *Berb* ↓
      - **stitching** pain: *Berb*
    - **Axilla**: phos ↓
      - **tearing** pain: phos h2*
    - **Behind**: kola stb3•
    - **Ear**: kola ↓ mez ↓ zinc ↓
      - **tearing** pain: kola stb3• mez k* zinc k*
    - **Ear**; behind: agath-a nl2• nat-s ↓ rhod
      - **drawing** pain: rhod
      - **pressing** pain: nat-s
    - **Elbow**: lyc ↓
      - **drawing** pain: lyc h2
    - **Eye**: ph-ac ↓ sel
      - **drawing** pain: ph-ac h2
    - **Limbs**, into: stram ↓
      - **drawing** pain: stram
    - **Lower** jaw: indg ↓
      - **drawing** pain: indg
    - **Occiput**: berb ↓
      - **tearing** pain: berb k*
    - **Pectoral** muscles: ars
    - **Shoulder**: agath-a nl2• *Chel* con ↓ led ↓ lyc ↓ nat-sil ↓ par rhod ↓ sul-ac ↓ zinc
      - **drawing** pain: *Chel* con h2 led lyc h2 nat-sil fd3.de• rhod
      - **pressing** pain: sul-ac h2
    - **Wrist**: chel
- **Sternocleidomastoid** muscles: *Gels* bro1 petr a1 rhod bro1 tarax bro1 trif-p bro1
  - **left**: elat hr1 kali-s fd4.de
  - **daytime**: adam ↓
    - **dull**: adam skp7•
  - **bending** head forward:
    - **amel.**: adam ↓
      - **dull**: adam skp7•
  - **stretching** the neck: adam ↓
    - **dull**: adam skp7•
  - ○ **Upper** part: gels c1
- **Submaxillary** glands: mez ↓

- **stitching** pain: mez h2

- **Throat**-pit: aesc↓ ambr↓ anac↓ ant-t bg2 ars↓ bell↓ **Brom**↓ calc↓ calc-p↓ *Caust* k* cham↓ chel↓ chin↓ cic↓ elaps↓ graph↓ iod *Lach* k* lob↓ mag-c a1 nit-ac a1 nux-v bg2 olnd↓ *Par*↓ phos↓ ran-s↓ sarr↓ sars↓ spira↓ spong *Staph*↓ thuj↓ *Verat*↓ zinc↓
  - **morning**: elaps↓
    - **burning**: elaps
  - **anger**; after: *Staph*↓
    - **pressing** pain: *Staph*
  - **burning**: ars bg2 calc-p k* chel k* elaps lach k* spira a1 verat b7a.de
  - **cramping**: zinc bg2
  - **drinking** agg.: nit-ac
  - **hawking** of mucus: **Caust** k*
  - **inspiration** agg.: caust↓ thuj↓
    - **pressing** pain: caust
    - **stitching** pain: thuj k*
  - **pressing** pain: aesc k* ambr b7.de* anac k* *Ant-t* b7a.de **Brom** k* calc ptk1 *Caust* k* chin b7.de* cic graph k* **Lach** k* lob olnd b7a.de *Par* b7a.de phos k* sarr k* sars k* *Staph* b7a.de *Verat* b7a.de
    - **foreign** body; as from a: *Caust*
  - **stitching** pain: bell h1* cham bg2 ran-s k* *Spong* k* thuj k*
  - **swallowing** agg.: staph↓
    - **pressing** pain: staph
- **Thyroid** cartilage: atra-r↓
  - **right**: am-c bg2 phyt bg2
  - **pressing** pain | **throat**; sensation as if thyroid cartilage were pressing on outer surface of: atra-r bnm3•
- **Thyroid** gland: ail↓ am-c k* atra-r↓ *Bar-c*↓ *Bell*↓ brom↓ carb-v k* cupr ephe-si↓ flor-p↓ iod tl1 *Kali-i*↓ lyc↓ *Merc*↓ nat-c↓ nat-p↓ nicc↓ podo↓ spig spong fd4.de squil↓ sulph↓ tritic-vg fd5.de zinc-i↓
  - **cough** agg.; during: carb-v↓
    - **ulcerative**: carb-v b4a.de
  - **jerking** pain: lyc bg2
  - **motion** of head agg.: iod
  - **pressing** pain: atra-r skp7• *Bar-c* k* brom bg2 ephe-si hsj1• flor-p rsj3• nat-c bg2 nat-p bg2 *Spong* b7.de*
    - **inward**: bar-c bg2 brom bg2 zinc-i ptk1
    - **outward**: spong b7.de
  - **sore**: ail k* *Kali-i* k* nicc k*
  - **stitching** pain: am-c k* *Bell* b4a.de iod k* *Merc* b4a.de nat-c k* podo fd3.de• *Spong* k* squil bg2 sulph k* tritic-vg fd5.de
  - **swallowing** agg.: spong↓
    - **stitching** pain: spong h1*
  - **ulcerative**: carb-v bg2 iod bg2
- **Thyroid** glands: nat-ar↓
  - **pinching** pain: nat-ar ptk1
- **Upper** side: ruta↓
  - **blow**; as from a: ruta h1

PARALYSIS: gels spig k*
- **diphtheria**; after: *Lac-c*

○ - **Sternocleidomastoid** plb

PERSPIRATION: alum bell k* bros-gau mrc1 cann-s cham k* clem coff crot-c sk4• euph k* ip kali-c lach bg2* **Mang** k* nat-sil fd3.de• nux-v k* par petr k* **RHUS-T** k ● * ruta fd4.de samb spig spong fd4.de **Stann** k* sulph k* vanil fd5.de
- **one**-sided: nit-ac h2*
- **evening**: chel k*
  - **18**-21 h: chel
- **night**: kali-p fd1.de• nit-ac h2* olib-sac wmh1 vanil fd5.de
  - **midnight**: **Rhus-t** k ●
- **amel.**: thuj bg2
- **cold**: stront-c sk4•
- **waking**; on: mang nit-ac ruta fd4.de vanil fd5.de

PRESSES throat with both hands: bell h1*

PROTRUSION:

○ - **Thyroid** cartilage: atra-r bnm3•
  - **sensation** as if thyroid cartilage pressing on outer surface of throat: atra-r bnm3•

PULSATION:

○ - **Carotids**: acon bro1* aml-ns bro1 arg-met k* arg-n k* *Aur* k* aur-m k2 *Bad* **Bell** k* *Bry Cact* k* *Calc* k* calc-p carc fd2.de• cench k2 chin k* cocc colch cupr dirc a1* elaps fago bro1 *Gels Glon* k* *Hep* hyos hyper kali-br hr1 kola stb3• lac-ac k* lil-t bro1 meli k* nat-s a1 olnd b7.de* *Op* k* phos phys podo fd3.de• prun ptk1 pyrog k2 rauw tpw8 rumx sabin bro1 sanguis-s hm2• sec a1 sep sol-ni spig k* spong k* stram *Tarent* k* thuj usn br1 verat-v k*
  - **left**: carc fd2.de• sulph h2*
  - **chill**; during: bell mtf33
  - **epistaxis** | **amel.**: tarent ptk2
  - **excitement** agg.: *Bad*
  - **fever**; during: bell mtf33
  - **headache**; during: gels c1 *Glon* mrr1 sang mrr1
  - **hemorrhage**; after: chin cp
  - **pregnancy**: gels c1
  - **visible**: aur mtf33
  - **walking** rapid after dinner: carb-ac c1
- **Glands**: *Am-m* k* bell bov b4a.de cham b7.de* clem b4.de* iod bg2 lach k* lyc bg2
- **Goitre**: aur bg2 iod h lyc h2*
- **Sides**: cycl *Gent-c* hura lac-ac nat-m sars sulph sumb k* *Tarent*
  - **evening**: cycl sumb a1

SENSITIVE:
- **rope** around neck; sensation of a: aids nl2•
- **touch**; to slightest: aids nl2• ant-t ptk1 apis ptk1 bapt ptk1 bell bg* crot-h ptk1 crot-t ptk1 helo-s rwt2• *Lac-c* k* **Lach** k* merc-c ptk1 nat-pyru rly4• *Nicc* nux-v ptk1 vero-o rly4*•

○ - **Angles** of jaw; at: thyr bg1
- **Cervical** glands: arn b7.de* aur b4.de* con b4a.de spong b7.de* *Squil* b7a.de
  - **fever**; during: *Lach* bg2
  - **perspiration**; during: bell bg2 chin bg2 *Lach* bg2 squil bg2
- **Thyroid** cartilage: lach bg2 spong bg2
- **Thyroid** gland: thuj bg2

SOFTNESS: | **Thyroid** gland: lap-a bg2

SPASMS: | **Sides** of neck: *(↗Torticollis)* *Carb-ac Med* pall hr1

SPOTS: agath-a nl2• ars bell k* bry carb-v k* cinnb cocc k* iod k* lach lyc mur-ac a1 *Sep* k* stann k* vip
- **left**: [bell-p-sp dcm1]

SPRAINED sensation: carb-an h2* lac-h sk4•
- **lying** | **back**; on | **must** lie on the back: lac-h sk4•
  - **side**; on | **agg.**: lac-h sk4•

STIFFNESS of sides: aesc k* agath-a nl2• alum h2* anac k* asc-t k* *Bell* k* benz-ac k* **Bry** k* calc k* camph h1* carb-an a1 *Caust* k* cham h1* *Chel* k* coloc k* *Dig* k* fic-m gya1 granit-m es1• *Guaj* hell a1 hura kali-cy a1 kreos k* *Lachn* k* laur led k* *Lyc* k* *Mang* merc-i-f k* *Mez* k* nat-ar nat-m k* nat-s k* nat-sil fd3.de• *Nux-v* petr k* ph-ac k* phys k* phyt k* pic-ac a1 *Puls* k* rhus-t k2 sec k* sep a1 *Sil* k* *Spong* k* squil k* staph h1* *Stront-c* vh *Stry* k* thuj k* vanil fd5.de zinc k* zing k*
- **right**: agath-a nl2• **Caust** k* *Chel* k* lyss k* mez h2* nat-m k* nit-ac h2* petr k* phyt mrr1 propr sa3• spong fd4.de
- **left**: agath-a nl2• asc-t c1 *Bell* k* carb-an h2* chel k* coloc k* ham fd3.de• hura irid-met srj5• kreos k* laur lyc h2* ph-ac h2* *Puls* k* spong *Stry* thuj k* vanil fd5.de
- **morning**: brom a1 *Chel* phys a1 zinc k*
- **night**: phyt mrr1
- **motion**:
  - **slight** motion | **agg.**: phyt mrr1

STRAINING muscles: sep h2*

STRETCHING OUT: sep h2*

SWALLOWING agg.: zinc ptk1

SWELLING: aesc k* agath-a nl2• *Ail Am-c* am-m k* anan *Apis* ars h2* *Bell* k* calc-i k2 calc-s k2 cann-s k* cartl-s rly4• caust chel k* chord-umb rly4• cic h1* coli rly4• *Crot-c* epil a1* falco-pe nl2• ferr k* glon k2 hyper *Iod* k* kali-i kali-n h2* lac-lup hrn2• **Lyc** k* *Merc* k* op k* pot-e rly4• **Rhus-t** k* rhus-v k* ribo rly4• ruta fd4.de sars h2* *Spong* k* suis-em rly4• sulph k* **Tarent** k* tung-met bdx1• zinc k*

- **cough** agg.; during: ars h2*
- **cramp**, after: graph h2*
- **goitre**; like: vip ptk1
- **menses**; before: iod h*
- **sensation** of: agath-a nl2• mang h2* melal-alt gya4 nat-sil fd3.de• podo fd3.de• xan bg1
- **talking** loudly agg.: iod k*

○ - **Carotid**: *Lyc* b4a.de

- • **left** | **stooping** agg.: ars h2
- **Cervical** Glands: acon vh1 acon-l a1* aesc k* aeth hr1 *Agar* k* agath-a nl2• aids nl2• *Alum* k* alum-sil k2 *Alumn Am-c* k* *Am-m* k* ambr b7.de* ant-c k* ant-t k* *Apis* k* aq-mar mgm• arg-met b7.de* arn k* *Ars* b4a.de ars-br vh **Arum-t** k* *Asaf* b7.de* asar b7.de* astac br1* aur b4.de* bac bro1 bamb-a stb2.de• **Bar-c** k* bar-i k2* **Bar-m** k* bar-s k2 **Bell** k* borx b4a.de* bov k* brom a1* *Bry* b7.de* calad b7.de* **Calc** k* calc-chln bro1 calc-f bro1 calc-i bg2* calc-p k2 calc-s calc-sil k2 camph k* canth k* *Carb-an* k* *Carb-v* k* carbn-s caust b4a.de* *Cham* k* *Chel* b7a.de *Chin* b7.de* chir-fl gya2 chord-umb rly4• *Cic* b7.de* cinnb k* **Cist** k* clem b4.de* cocc b7.de* coli rly4• *Con* k* cupr k* *Dig* b4a.de diph br1 dros tl1 *Dulc* k* ferr k* ferr-i k* glon k2 **Graph** k* hecla bro1 *Hell* k* helodr-cal knl2• *Hep* k* hydrog srj2• ign k* *Iod* k* irid-met srj5• kali-bi k* **Kali-c** k* *Kali-chl* hr1 *Kali-i* k* kali-m bro1 kali-sil k2 ketogl-ac rly4• kiss a1 kola stb3• kreos k* *Lach* k* *Lap-a* k* lap-la sde8.de• led *Lith-c* luna kg1• **Lyc** k* *Mag-m* k* mag-p bro1 marb-w es1• **Merc** k* *Merc-c* k* merc-cy hr1 *Merc-d* hr1 *Merc-i-f* br1* *Merc-i-r* br1* mez b4a.de moni rfm1• *Morb* jl2 mur-ac k* nabal a1 *Nat-c* k* *Nat-m* k* *Nat-s* k* *Nit-ac* k* *Nux-v* b7a.de ozone sde2• *Petr* b4.de* *Ph-ac* b4.de* *Phos* k* *Phyt* k* plb b7.de* polys sk4• pot-e rly4• *Psor* k* *Puls* k* ran-s b7.de* rhus-r bro1 **Rhus-t** k* rhus-v bro1 ruta fd4.de sabad b7.de* sal-fr sle1• sal-mar bro1 sars b4.de* scarl jl2 sel k2 *Sep* k* **Sil** k* *Spig* k* *Spong* k* stann b4.de* **Staph** k* staphycoc rly4• stict c1 *Still* bro1 streptoc jl2* suis-em rly4• sul-ac k* sul-i k2 **Sulph** k* syc bka1*• syph k2 tarent k* tep k* *Thuj* k* *Toxo-g* jl2 *Tub* k* urol-h rwt• v-a-b jl ven-m rsj12• verat b7.de* vesp k* viol-t b7.de* wies a1 zinc k* [heroin sdj2 spect dfg1]
  - • **left**: lac-h htj1• [tax jsj7]
  - • **evening**: *Kali-c* k*
  - • **beads**; around neck like string of (See string)
  - • **chronic**: nat-s hr
  - • **fever**; during: *Bell* b4a.de*
  - • **hard**: am-c hr1 ars-br vh *Bar-m* k* *Calc* k* **Con** k* *Hep* hr1 hydrog srj2• *Iod* lyc k* merc k* phyt mrr1 plut-n srj7• *Sars* sel k2 **Sil** k* *Tub* mrr1
  - • **knocking**: cist st
  - • **menses**; from suppressed: kali-c b4a.de
  - • **one** single gland: *Rhus-t* b7a.de
  - • **painful**: *Ant-c* b7a.de cartl-s rly4• chord-umb rly4• phyt mrr1 sil mrr1 *Spig* b7a.de *Staph* b7a.de
    - ⋮ **touch**; to: cupr h2* granit-m es1• kola stb3• ozone sde2• *Staph* sne
  - • **painless**: *Ign* b7a.de
  - • **perspiration**; during: **Bell** bg2 *Calc* bg2 *Cham* bg2 lyc bg2 *Merc* bg2 *Rhus-t* bg2 spong bg2 staph bg2 thuj bg2
  - • **sensation** of: m-ambo b7.de m-aust b7.de spong b7.de* staph b7.de*
  - • **string** around the neck; glands are like a: aeth c1* cist mrr1
  - • **suppurative**: **Calc** *Cist Hep Lith-c* **Merc** *Nit-ac* **Sil** *Sulph Tub* k* v-a-b jl

▽ • **extending** to | **Shoulder**: *Graph* k*

○ • **Lymphatic** tissue: cypra-eg sde6.de•

- **Larynx**; under: hep bg2
- **Sides**: agath-a nl2• *Ail* alum k* *Am-c Apis* **Bell** calc k* chel k* *Glon* hydrog srj2• hyos h1* kali-perm *Lach Lyc* mang a1 medul-os-si rly4• merc merc-c k* nat-c k* nit-ac k* **Rhus-t** ruta fd4.de *Sars* k* sil spig k* stry thuj tung-met bdx1• vesp k*
  - • **one** side: [pop dhh1]

Swelling – Sides: ...

- • **right**: hydrog srj2• sars h2* sil h2*
- • **sensation**: agath-a nl2• alum h2 mang h2 sep h2
- • **stripe**: mang h2*
- • **suppurative**: hyos h1*

- **Thyroid** cartilage: *(↗Goitre; Thyroid; GENERALS - Hypothyroidism)* sil bg2 sulph bg2
- **Thyroid** gland: *(↗Goitre; Thyroid; GENERALS - Hypothyroidism)* agar bg2 ail k* *Am-c* b4a.de ambr b7.de* ars aur-i k2 aur-s k* bamb-a stb2.de• benz-ac bg2 brom b4a.de* *Calc* b4.de* *Carb-an* k* carbn-s k2 caust k* clem con b4a.de* dig b4a.de dys pte1* gamb bg2 hed sp1 iod b4.de* kali-br a1 kali-c b4.de* *Kali-i* k* lap-la sde8.de• lyc b4.de* mag-c b4.de* marb-w es1• *Merc* b4a.de morg-p pte1* nat-c k* *Nat-m* b4.de* nit-ac ol-j ozone sde2• petr b4a.de phos b4a.de plat b4a.de psor mtf11 sil b4a.de spong b7.de* sulph b4a.de* syc mtf11 thuj k* thyr mtf11 tub mtf11 ven-m rsj12• vip bg2 x-ray sp1
  - • **right**: bamb-a stb2.de• merc
    - ⋮ **sensation** of: mag-c spong rb2
  - • **puberty**; at: calc-i br1
- **Veins**: acon vh1 crot-c mre hyos k* nat-m op k* sil h2* stry k* thuj
  - • **pressure** on left side as if veins were swollen: sil h2

TENDERNESS: | **Thyroid** gland: ail tl1

TENSION: agar vh agath-a nl2• bar-s k2 caust cic h1* des-ac rbp6 ignis-alc es2• ketogl-ac rly4• limest-b es1• mag-c *Nux-m* k* rosm lgb1 sep spong fd4.de tritic-vg fd5.de verb h*

- **menses**; before: iod h*

▽ - **extending** to | **Head**: granit-m es1•

○ - **Cervical** glands: ambr b7.de* ang b7.de* bov b4.de* calc b4.de* clem b4.de* *Graph* b4.de* iod bg2 m-ambo b7.de m-arct b7.de mur-ac b4.de* phos b4.de* puls b7.de* spong b7.de*

- **Sides**: agar agath-a nl2• arg-met bar-c bar-ox-suc rly4• bell berb k* bov *Calc Caust* k* *Chel* k* *Dig* fic-m gya1 ham fd3.de• iod k* kali-bi ketogl-ac rly4• kreos k* laur k* mag-m k* *Med* meph nat-m ph-ac plb *Rhod* sars k* sep h2* *Spong Sulph* k* tung-met bdx1• *Zinc* k*
  - • **right**: agath-a nl2• ang h1* **Caust** k* mag-m h2* rosm lgb1 sars h2* spong
  - • **left**: agath-a nl2• cic h1* des-ac rbp6 ham fd3.de• podo fd3.de• sulph zinc h2*
  - • **morning**: coc-c
  - • **evening**: rat
    - ⋮ **standing** agg.: rat
  - • **night**: staph
  - • **bending** head backward agg.: cic h1*
  - • **convulsive**: agar raph
  - • **lying** on side agg.: thuj
  - • **motion** of head agg.: bov k* graph k* sars k* spong fd4.de verat k*
  - • **painful**: ham fd3.de• sulph
  - • **rheumatic**: iod k*
  - • **swallowing** agg.: colch
  - • **waking**; on: coc-c
  - • **walking** agg.; after: nat-m
- **Throat**-pit: cham bg1 puls bg1 sulph bg1
- **Thyroid** gland: agar bg1* lat-m sp1

TICKLING:

○ - **Gland**: kali-c h2

- **Goitre**: plat h2
- **Thyroid** cartilage: ambr bg2 plat b4.de* puls bg2
  - • **cough** agg.; during: puls b7.de*

TIGHT around neck and waist; cannot bear anything: aids nl2• **Lach** vh *Sep* vh spong fd4.de

TINGLING: acon a1 agath-a nl2• calc h2*

TORTICOLLIS: *(↗Distorted; Spasms - sides)* achy jl *Acon* bro1 aesc-g a1* agar bro1 ang c1* arn bg2 ars k* asar k* atro c1* bar-c ptk bell bg2* bry bg2* bufo a *Calc* k* cann-s mrr1 caul k* *Caust* k* chin b7.de* chin-b hr1* cic b7a.de* cimic bg2* cina cocc bg2 *Colch* k* *Cupr* k* des-ac jl dros bg2 dulc k* elaps a1 eup-per bg2 eup-pur k* ferr-p k2 glon bg2* *Graph* guaj c2* halo jl hist jl hist-m mtf11 hura *Hyos* k* ign bro1* kali-i bg2 kalm bg2 lac-ac lach hr1 **Lachn** k*

Torticollis: ...
Lyc k* mag-c h2* mag-m h2 mag-p bro1 merc k2 mez h2* mygal bro1 nat-m bg nat-p a1* nep jl *Nux-v* k* op bg2 **Phos** k* plan c1 *Ran-b* vh* *Rhus-t* k* rhus-v a1 sang bg2 sil bg2 stry bro1* sulfonam jl sulph k* syc ptj• tere-ch jl thiop jl* thuj bro1 visc sp1

- **accompanied** by:
  - **diphtheria** (See THROAT - Diphtheria - accompanied - torticollis)
  - O **Head**; complaints of (See HEAD - Complaints - accompanied - torticollis)
  - **Joints**; inflammation of: calc bg2 cocc bg2 phos bg2 sil bg2
  - **Throat**; sore: lachn ptk1
- **chronic**: atro c1 bar-c ptk1
- **left**; drawn to the: asar *Bell* ptk1 caul chel c1 coloc bg2 **Lyc** k* *Nux-v* k* **Phos** k*
  - **fright**; from: nux-v hr
- **right**; drawn to the: ang c1 caust *Cupr* k* *Lachn* *Lyc* k* nat-m bg olib-sac wmh1 propr sa3•
  - **followed** by torticollis drawn to the left: ang c1
- **shock**; from: nux-v ptk1
- **shortening**; with: ars bg2 caust bg2
- **spasmodic**: aesc-g a1 ars bg2 *Caust* bg2 cic gsd1 hist jl1 **Hyos** bg2 thiop jl1
- **sternum**; chin drawn to: cann-i c1* *Cann-s* k* med c1* phyt ptk1
- **waking**; on: asc-t a1

TOUCH agg.: apis vh brom vh bry vh lac-c vh lac-e hrn2• **Lach** tl1* **Phyt** vh

TREMBLING: ang hr1 graph h2* merc hr1
O - **Cervical** glands: ang b7.de*

TUMORS: ars sne bar-c ptk1 brom ptk1 **Calc** sne graph sne *Sil* sne
- **one** side: *Brom* k* nat-c h2
- **cystic**: *Brom* k*
  - O **Thyroid** gland: apis bg2
- **fatty**: *Bar-c*
- **fibroid**, recurrent (See GENERALS - History - external)

TWITCHING: *Agar* k* arg-met h1 asaf k* bism k* carb-ac k* crot-c k* gent-c a1 graph h2* mez k* nat-sil fd3.de• phos h2* spong h1* tarax hr1
O - **Cervical** glands: caps b7.de* lyc bg2
- **Sides**: ang h1* kali-c h2* spong fd4.de tarax h1*
  - **right**: lyc h2* nat-sil fd3.de•
  - **left**: mez h2* petr-ra shn4• sars h2* spong fd4.de
    - **Neck** to the left side of the throat; from left side of the: agar k*

ULCERS: ars bros-gau mrc1 lyc *Sil*

UNCOVERING throat:
- **agg.**: alum berb **Hep** k* *Kali-ar* **Kali-c** k* *Merc* st *Nat-m* st *Nat-s* **Nux-v** k* *Phos* **Rhus-t** k* *Rumx* **Sil** k* *Spong* **Squil** k* *Thuj* **Zinc** k*
- **amel.**: lac-e hrn2•

URGING:
- **outward** | **Thyroid** gland: spong bg2

VICE; sensation as in a: xan c1

WARTS: nit-ac k* psil ft1 sil spong fd4.de thuj k*
O - **Sides** | **left**: carc az1.de•

WEAKNESS: | **Throat**-pit: iod bg2

THYROID GLAND; complaints of: *(↗Goitre; Swelling - thyroid cartilage; Swelling - thyroid gland; GENERALS - Hyperthyroidism; GENERALS - Hypothyroidism)* adren bro1 am-c bro1 am-m bro1 apis bro1 aur-s bro1 bad bro1 *Bar-i* bro1* *Bell* bro1 *Brom* bro1 calc br1* calc-f bro1 calc-i bro1 caust bro1 chr-s bro1 cist bro1 cortiso mtf11 *Crot-c* bro1 des-ac mtf11 diph-t-tpt jl2 diphtox jl2 ferr bro1 ferr-s mtf11 *Fl-ac* bro1 flav jl2 *Fuc* bro1 glon bro1 hep bro1 *Hydr* bro1 hydr-ac bro1 influ jl2 **Iod** bro1* *Iris* br1* jab br1 kali-c bro1 kali-i bro1* *Lap-a* bro1 lycps-v mtf11 mag-p bro1 *Merc-i-f* bro1* nat-i mtf11 nat-m bro1* phos bro1 phyt bro1 pineal bro1 psor jl2 puls bro1 sil bro1 spong bro1* strept-ent jl2 sulph bro1 thal-met br1 thyr bro1* *Thyroiod* bro1 v-a-b jl2 [*Lith-i* stj2 *Mang-i* stj2 spect dfg1 *Zinc-i* stj2]
- **right**: ars bg2 kali-s bg2 lyc bg2 merc bg2 merc-i-f bg2

Thyroid Gland: ...
- **accompanied** by:
  - **cardiac** complications (See CHEST - Heart; complaints - accompanied - thyroid)
  - **obesity** (See GENERALS - Obesity - children - thyroid)
  - **respiration**; asthmatic (See RESPIRATION - Asthmatic - accompanied - thyroid)
  - O **Heart**; complaints of the (See CHEST - Heart; complaints - accompanied - thyroid)

ALTERNATING sides: calc-p bg2

MORNING: ang b7.de* apis b7a.de arg-met bg2 hell b7.de* ign b7.de* m-ambo b7.de merc-i-r bg2 nux-v b7.de* ph-ac bg2 spig b7.de* spong b7.de* staph b7.de*

FORENOON: ang b7.de* staph b7.de*

AFTERNOON: canth b7.de* chel b7.de* cic b7.de* laur b7.de*

EVENING: am-m b7.de* ant-c b7.de* ant-t b7.de* cycl b7.de* lach b7.de* laur b7.de* m-ambo b7.de meny b7.de* nux-v b7.de* olnd b7.de* puls b7.de* ran-b b7.de* rhus-t b7.de* spong b7.de* viol-o b7.de*

NIGHT: led b7.de* olnd b7.de* phyt bg2

AIR: | wet air agg.: nux-m b7.de*

AIR AGG.; DRAFT OF: act-sp bg2 calc-p bg2 form bg2

AIR; IN OPEN:
- **agg.**: laur b7.de* m-ambo b7.de nux-v b7.de*
- **amel.**: ang b7.de*

ANGER: | **agg.**: *Staph* b7a.de

ASCENDING STAIRS agg.: ph-ac bg2

BANDAGING: | **agg.**: *Lach* b7a.de

BENDING:
- **head**:
  - **agg.**: cocc b7.de* cupr b7.de* par b7.de* rhus-t bg2
  - **backward** | **agg.**: chel bg2 *Cic* b7a.de cycl b7.de* hep bg2 merc bg2 spong b7.de*

BITING agg.: spong b7.de*

BUBBLING sensation, as if bubbles were moving about: rheum b7.de*

CHEWING agg.: zinc bg2

COLD AIR agg.: ars bg2 bar-c bg2 calc-p bg2 chinin-s bg2 gels bg2

COLDNESS:
- **sensation** of: *Calc* bg2 chel bg2 chin bg2 dulc bg2 meny bg2 phos b4.de* plat bg2 sulph bg2 thuj bg2

▽ - **extending** | **Upwards**: chel bg2

COMPLAINTS of neck:
- **right** side: agn b7a.de alum b4a.de am-c b4a.de anac b4a.de ang b7a.de ant-c b7a.de ant-t b7a.de apis b7a.de arg-met b7a.de asaf b7a.de aur b4a.de *Bell* b4a.de *Bism* b7a.de bry b7a.de calc b4a.de camph b7a.de canth b7a.de caps b7a.de carb-v b4a.de **Caust** b4a.de chel b7a.de chin b7a.de cina b7a.de cocc b7a.de *Colch* b7a.de coloc b4a.de *Con* b4a.de cupr b7a.de dulc b4a.de **Fl-ac** b4a.de guaj b4a.de *Hep* b4a.de *Iod* b4a.de *Kali-c* b4a.de kali-n b4a.de *Lach* b7a.de *Laur* b7a.de led b7a.de lyc b4a.de m-aust b7a.de meny b7a.de **Merc** b4a.de *Mez* b4a.de nat-c b4a.de nat-m b4a.de **Nit-ac** b4a.de *Nux-v* b7a.de olnd b7a.de petr b4a.de ph-ac b4a.de plat b4a.de plb b7a.de puls b7a.de rhod b4a.de sabin b7a.de *Sars* b4a.de *Seneg* b4a.de *Sil* b4a.de spig b7a.de *Spong* b7a.de staph b7a.de *Sul-ac* b4a.de sulph b4a.de teucr b7a.de thuj b4a.de zinc b4a.de
- **left** side: acon b7a.de agn b7a.de alum b4a.de am-m b7a.de anac b4a.de ang b7a.de ant-c b7a.de **Apis** b7a.de arg-met b7a.de arn b7a.de ars b4a.de **Asaf** b7a.de *Asar* b7a.de aur b4a.de bar-c b4a.de bell b4a.de borx b4a.de bov b4a.de brom b4a.de bry b7a.de **Calc** b4a.de canth b7a.de carb-an b4a.de carb-v b4a.de caust b4a.de cic b7a.de cocc b7a.de colch b7a.de *Coloc* b4a.de **Con** b4a.de croc b7a.de cycl b7a.de fl-ac b4a.de *Guaj* b4a.de hyos b7a.de ign b7a.de kali-c b4a.de lach b7a.de laur b7a.de *Lyc* b4a.de merc b4a.de mez b4a.de mosch b7a.de nit-ac b4a.de nux-v b7a.de *Olnd* b7a.de par b7a.de ph-ac b4a.de psor b4a.de rhod b4a.de rhus-t b7a.de *Sabin* b7a.de *Sel* b7a.de sep b4a.de sil b4a.de spig b7a.de spong b7a.de squil b7a.de staph b7a.de *Stram* b7a.de sul-ac b4a.de **Sulph** b4a.de *Tarax* b7a.de teucr b7a.de *Thuj* b4a.de verat b7a.de viol-t b7a.de zinc b4a.de

CONGESTION: bell bg2 bufo bg2 chel bg2 cinnb bg2 crot-c bg2 glon bg2 ham bg2 kali-bi bg2 lycps-v bg2 op bg2 pip-n bg2

CONSTRICTION or band: *Apis* b7a.de arn b7.de* asar b7.de* bell bg2 brom bg2 chel bg2 dulc bg2 ferr b7.de* glon bg2 iod bg2 **Lach** bg2 olnd b7a.de op b7a.de sep bg2

CONTRACTION: am-c b4a.de asar b7.de* cic bg2 coloc b4a.de con b4a.de gels bg2 iod b4.de* laur b7.de* olnd b7.de* sep b4.de* verat b7a.de

COUGH agg.: bell bg2 nat-m bg2

CRACKING noise: *Calc* b4a.de chel bg2 cocc b7.de* *M-ambo* b7.de* *M-arct* b7.de* nat-c b4.de* nit-ac b4.de* nux-v b7.de* petr bg2 psor bg2 puls b7.de* spong bg2 stann b4.de* sulph bg2

CRACKLING noise: *M-arct* b7.de* rheum b7.de*

CREAKING noise: puls b7.de* thuj bg2

DISCOLORATION:
- **red**: *Apis* b7a.de iod b4a.de
  - **spots**: bell b4.de* bry b7.de* carb-v b4.de* cocc b7.de* *Euphr* b7a.de iod b4a.de nux-v b7.de* sep b4.de* stann b4.de*
- **yellow** | **spots**: iod b4.de* lyc b4a.de phos b4a.de *Sep* b4a.de

DISTENSION: con bg2

○ - **Blood** vessels: aran bg2 ars b4a.de* *Bell* b4a.de canth bg2 con b4a.de graph b4a.de hydr-ac bg2 lach b7a.de* nux-v bg2 op b7.de* thuj b4.de*

DISTORTION: | **Muscles**: ars b4.de* asar b7.de*

DRINKING agg.: laur b7.de*

ERUPTIONS: am-c b4a.de am-m b7.de* ant-c b7.de* ant-t bg2 arn bg2 ars b4.de* aur b4.de* borx b4a.de bov bg2 bry b7.de* canth b7.de* carb-v bg2 caust b4a.de* chin b7.de* cinnb bg2 clem bg2 dig b4.de* hep b4.de* kali-n bg2 **Lyc** b4a.de* m-ambo b7.de merc b4.de* mez bg2 nat-c bg2 nat-m bg2 petr bg2 ph-ac b4.de* puls b7.de* sep b4a.de* sil bg2 spig b7.de* spong b7.de* squil b7.de* staph b7.de* sul-i bg2 sulph bg2 thuj b4.de* verat b7.de* verb b7a.de
- **boils**: *Arn* b7.de* carb-an b4a.de caust b4.de* euph b4a.de graph b4a.de *Nat-m* b4a.de sep b4.de*
- **miliaria**: bry bg2
- **pustules**: *Ant-c* b7a.de
- **tetters**: *Calc* b4a.de graph b4a.de sep b4a.de
- **variola**: m-ambo b7.de
- **vesicles**: alum bg2 canth bg2 clem bg2 ph-ac bg2 sep bg2
  - **cracking**: anac bg2 nat-c bg2 nit-ac bg2 nux-v bg2 puls bg2 stann bg2 sulph bg2
  - **cutting**: graph bg2
  - **excoriated**; as if: *Con* bg2 dig bg2 graph bg2 mang bg2 sep bg2
  - **pressing**: acon bg2 arn bg2 carb-v bg2 guaj bg2 ign bg2
  - **pulsating**: kali-n bg2
  - **swelled**: calc bg2
  - **tearing**: lach bg2
  - **tension**: arn bg2

EXCORIATION: bry bg2 *Sulph* b4a.de

EXERTION: | **arms** agg.; of the: ant-c b7.de* cic b7.de*

FORMICATION: spong b7.de*

FULLNESS; sensation of: apis b7a.de gels bg2 glon bg2 ham bg2 sil bg2

HEADACHE; after: ang bg2

HEAT: am-c bg2 ang bg2 *Apis* bg2 arn bg2 *Ars* bg2 asar bg2 **Bar-c** bg2 bell bg2 bry bg2 bufo bg2 *Calc* b4.de* **Carb-v** bg2 caust b4.de* cham b7.de chin bg2 colch bg2 cycl b7.de* graph bg2 **Ign** b7.de* kali-c bg2 *Lach* bg2 *Lyc* b4a.de* mang b4.de *Merc* bg2 mez bg2 **Nat-c** bg2 **Nux-v** bg2 **Par** bg2 *Ph-ac* bg2 phel bg2 *Phos* bg2 plat bg2 **Puls** bg2 rhod bg2 **Rhus-t** bg2 sars b4.de *Sep* b4.de* sil bg2 spig bg2 **Staph** bg2 stront-c b4a.de **Sulph** b4.de* tarax bg2 thuj bg2 zinc bg2
- **sensation** of: samb b7.de*

HEAVINESS: anac bg2 asar b7.de* cann-xyz bg2 carb-an bg2 coloc bg2 kali-c bg2 meny b7.de*

ITCHING: agn b7.de* alum b4.de* am-m b7.de* anac b4.de* ant-c bg2 bov b4.de* bry b7.de* carb-v b4.de* caust b4a.de chel b7.de* ign b7.de* kali-bi bg2 mag-c b4.de* mag-m b4.de* mang b4.de* mez b4.de* mur-ac bg2 nat-c b4.de* nat-m b4.de* nit-ac b4.de* op b7.de* puls b7.de* rhus-t b7.de* sars b4.de* squil b7.de* stann b4.de* stront-c b4.de* sulph bg2 thuj b4.de* zinc-s bg2

LAUGHING; sensation as if from: m-arct b7.de

LEANING head backward: | **amel**: cocc bg2

LIFTING agg.: arg-n bg2 calc bg2 sep bg2

LOOKING: | **backward** | **agg.**: *Cic* b7.de*
- **upward** | **agg.**: *Graph* bg2

Neck

LOOSE; as if flesh were: nux-v b7.de*

LOOSENING neck band: | **amel.**: olnd b7.de*

LUMPS: alum b4.de* carb-an b4.de* caust b4.de* clem b4a.de graph b4a.de* hep b4.de* *Ign* bg2 **Lach** bg2 lyc bg2 mang b4.de* mez b4.de* mur-ac b4.de* nat-c bg2 nat-m b4.de ph-ac b4.de* phos bg2 sec b7.de sil b4.de* verb b7.de* zinc b4.de*

LYING:
- **agg.**: lyc bg2 spong b7.de*
- **bed**; in | **agg.**: ant-c b7.de* ign b7.de*
- **side**; on:
  - **agg.**: graph bg2
  - **painless** side | **agg.**: viol-o b7.de*

MENSES: | **before** | **agg.**: nat-c bg2
- **during** | **agg.**: am-m b7.de*

MOTION:
- **agg.**: acon b7.de* am-m b7a.de ang b7.de* arg-met b7.de* arn b7.de* *Asaf* b7.de* asar b7.de* bry b7.de* camph b7.de* caps b7.de* chin b7.de* cic b7.de* cocc bg2 cycl b7.de* dros b7a.de ferr b7.de* hell b7.de* kali-bi bg2 m-ambo b7.de meny b7.de* nux-v b7.de* petr bg2 plb b7a.de puls b7.de* rhus-t b7.de* spong b7a.de tarax b7.de*
- **amel.**: alum bg2 cina b7.de* spig b7.de* sulph bg2
- **head**; of | **agg.**: alum bg2 cocc bg2

NUMBNESS: carb-an b4.de*

OPENING THE MOUTH agg.: spong b7.de*

PAIN: abrot bg2 acon ↓ aesc ↓ agar ↓ agn ↓ alum ↓ am-c b4.de* am-m ↓ ambr ↓ anac ↓ ang ↓ ant-c ↓ ant-t ↓ apis ↓ arg-met ↓ arg-n ↓ *Arn* ↓ ars ↓ *Asaf* ↓ *Asar* ↓ aur ↓ bar-c ↓ *Bell* b4.de* bism ↓ bov ↓ bry b7.de* calc b4.de* calc-p ↓ camph ↓ cann-s ↓ canth ↓ caps b7.de* carb-an ↓ *Carb-v* ↓ caust b4.de* cham ↓ chin ↓ cic ↓ cina ↓ coc-c ↓ cocc bg2 colch ↓ coloc ↓ croc ↓ cupr ↓ cycl ↓ dig ↓ dulc ↓ ferr b7.de* fl-ac ↓ graph b4.de* grat ↓ guaj ↓ hell b7a.de hep ↓ ign bg2 iod ↓ kali-bi bg2 kali-c b4.de* kali-n ↓ kalm ↓ **Lach** b7.de* led ↓ lyc ↓ m-ambo b7.de m-arct b7.de mag-c ↓ mag-m ↓ mang b4.de* meny ↓ meph bg2 *Merc* ↓ merc-c ↓ mez ↓ mosch bg2 naja ↓ nat-c ↓ nat-m ↓ nat-s ↓ nit-ac ↓ nux-v b7.de* olnd b7.de* par ↓ ph-ac b4.de* phos b4.de* plat ↓ plb ↓ podo ↓ psor ↓ puls ↓ ran-s ↓ *Rhod* ↓ rhus-t ↓ ruta ↓ sabad bg2 sabin b7.de samb ↓ sars ↓ sel ↓ sep ↓ sil b4.de* spig bg2 spong bg2 squil ↓ staph ↓ stront-c ↓ sul-ac bg2 sulph bg2 tarax b7.de* ter ↓ teucr ↓ thuj bg2 verat bg2 verat-v ↓ viol-o ↓ zinc b4.de*
- **right**: sep ↓
  - **drawing** pain: sep bg2
- **left**: zinc ↓
  - **cramping**: zinc ● bg2
- **blow**; pain as from a: lach b7a.de
- **boring** pain: bar-c bg2 cina b7.de* tarax b7.de*
- **burning**: caust bg2 ferr b7.de* grat bg2 ign b7.de* lach b7a.de lyc b4a.de stront-c b4.de*
- **burnt**; as if: calc bg2
- **chill**; during: *Acon* bg2 *Ars* b4a.de* calc bg2 merc bg2 nux-v bg2 puls bg2 *Staph* bg2
- **corrosive**: agn b7.de*
- **cramping**: apis bg2 arg-n bg2 arn b7a.de* *Asar* b7a.de bell bg2 calc-p bg2 camph bg2 cic b7.de* fl-ac bg2 graph bg2 hell bg2 m-ambo b7.de m-arct b7.de meny b7.de* merc bg2 merc-c bg2 par b7.de* sel bg2 sep bg2 squil b7a.de verat-v bg2
- **cutting** pain: graph b4.de* ruta b7.de* samb b7.de*
- **dislocated**; as if: agar bg2 ambr bg2 ars bg2 asar b7.de* calc bg2 carb-an b4.de* merc bg2 sars b4.de*
- **dragging**: caust b4.de*
- **drawing** pain: acon b7.de* alum bg2 ant-c b7.de* arn b7.de* *Asaf* b7.de* bell b4.de* bry b7.de* camph b7.de* canth b7.de* *Carb-v* b4a.de chin b7.de* cic b7.de* cocc b7.de* coloc b4a.de croc b7.de* cycl b7.de* dulc b4.de* graph b4.de* hep b4a.de kali-bi bg2 kali-c b4.de* m-ambo b7.de m-arct b7.de mag-c b4.de* mag-m b4.de* mosch b7a.de nat-m b4.de* nit-ac b4.de* nux-v b7.de* ph-ac b4.de* puls b7.de* *Rhod* b4.de* sabin b7.de* spig b7.de* spong b7.de* squil b7.de* staph b7.de* sul-ac b4.de* teucr b7.de* verat b7.de* viol-o b7.de*
- **jerking** pain: caust bg2 m-arct b7.de mez b4a.de naja bg2 sep b4.de* staph b7.de*
- **lameness**: dig b4.de* lyc b4.de* sulph b4.de*

Pain: ...
- **neuralgic**: acon bg2 bry bg2 cham bg2 coc-c bg2 kalm bg2 merc bg2 nux-v bg2 par bg2 rhus-t bg2 sil bg2 sulph bg2 ter bg2 verat bg2
- **paralyzed**; as if: cocc b7.de* cycl b7a.de
- **pinching** pain: cann-s b7.de* caust b4.de* hep b4a.de lyc bg2 ph-ac b4.de* phos b4.de* thuj b4.de*
- **position**; as from wrong: dulc b4.de thuj b4.de zinc b4.de
- **pressing** pain: acon b7.de* aesc bg2 agar b4.de* alum bg2 anac b4.de* ant-c b7.de* ant-t b7.de* arg-met b7.de* arn b7.de* aur b4.de* bell b4.de* bism b7.de* *Calc* b4.de* cann-s b7.de* carb-v b4.de* caust b4.de* colch b7.de* cycl b7a.de dig bg2 ferr b7a.de guaj b4.de* ign b7.de* kali-c b4.de* lach b7.de* lyc b4.de* m-ambo b7.de m-arct b7.de mag-c b4.de* mag-m b4.de* nit-ac b4.de* olnd b7.de* ph-ac b4.de* sabin b7.de* sars b4.de* sil b4.de* *Spong* b7.de* staph b7.de* sul-ac b4.de* sulph bg2 tarax b7a.de teucr bg2 verat b7.de* zinc b4.de*
  - **outward**: spong b7.de*
- **rheumatic**: acon b7.de* **Bell** bg2 *Bry* b7a.de carb-v b4a.de cycl b7.de* *Dulc* b4a.de iod b4.de* merc b4a.de mez b4.de* **Puls** bg2 *Rhod* b4.de* rhus-t b7a.de squil b7.de* staph b7.de*
- **scratching** pain: ars b4.de*
- **sore**: ang b7.de* arg-met bg2 *Arn* b7.de* bry b7.de* caust bg2 cic b7.de* cycl b7.de* ferr bg2 hep b4.de* naja bg2 nat-m bg2 podo bg2 psor bg2 sabin b7.de* squil b7.de* verat b7.de* zinc bg2
- **squeezed**; as if: bell b4.de* iod b4.de* mang b4.de* meny bg2 plat b4.de* sep b4.de* squil b7.de* thuj b4.de* zinc b4.de*
- **stitching** pain: acon b7.de* alum bg2 am-m b7a.de* anac b4.de* ant-c b7.de* aur b4.de* bell b4.de* bry b7.de* calc bg2 canth b7.de* carb-v b4a.de chin b7.de* cina b7.de* cocc b7.de* cupr b7.de* dig b4.de* graph b4.de* guaj b4.de* hep b4.de* ign bg2 kali-bi bg2 kali-c b4.de* kali-n b4.de* meny b7.de* merc b4a.de mosch b7a.de* nat-c b4.de nat-s bg2 phos b4.de* ran-s b7.de* samb b7.de* sars b4.de* spig b7.de* spong b7.de* squil b7.de* staph b7.de* sul-ac b4.de* tarax b7.de* teucr b7.de* thuj b4.de* verat b7.de* zinc b4.de*
- **tearing** pain: am-m b7.de* arn b7.de* aur b4.de* bov b4.de* bry b7.de* carb-v b4.de* cham b7.de* cupr b7.de* iod b4.de* kali-bi bg2 kali-c b4.de* kali-n b4.de* led b7.de* lyc b4.de* m-arct b7.de mag-c b4.de* *Merc* b4.de* mez b4.de* nat-c b4.de* par b7.de* phos b4.de* plb b7.de* sabin b7.de* sel b7.de* spong b7.de* staph b7.de* sulph b4.de* tarax b7.de* teucr b7.de* zinc b4.de*
  - **downward**: asaf b7a.de camph b7a.de canth b7a.de lyc b4a.de
  - **upward**: bry b7a.de cann-s b7a.de canth b7a.de spig b7a.de thuj b4a.de
- **torn**; as if: puls b7a.de
- **ulcerative** pain: graph b4.de* puls b7.de*

PERSPIRATION: alum bg2 *Bell* b4a.de* cann-s b7.de* cham b7.de* *Clem* b4.de* *Coff* b7.de* euph b4a.de* ip b7.de* kali-c bg2 lach ptk1 **Mang** b4a.de* nux-v b7.de* par bg2 **Rhus-t** b7.de* spig bg2 **Stann** b4a.de* sulph bg2

PRESSURE:
- **agg.**: agar bg2 aml-ns bg2 ant-t bg2 *Apis* bg2 bell bg2 caust bg2 glon bg2 ham bg2 kali-c bg2 **Lach** b7.de* lith-c bg2 *Merc-c* bg2 nux-v bg2 sabin b7.de* sep bg2
- **amel.**: psor bg2 zinc bg2
- **clothes**; of: | **agg.**: agar ptk1 *Apis* ptk1 caust ptk1 chel ptk1 con ptk1 glon ptk1 kali-c ptk1 **Lach** ptk1 merc ptk1 *Sep* ptk1

PULSATION: arg-n bg2 **Bell** bg2 eup-per bg2 *Glon* bg2 hep bg2 ip bg2 kali-n bg2 laur b7.de* *Nux-v* bg2 olnd bg2 op bg2 sars b4.de* sep bg2 spong bg2 stram bg2 sulph b4.de*

○ - **Blood** vessels: bell b4.de* *Calc* b4a.de glon bg2 *Hep* b4.de* lac-ac bg2 lach b7a.de olnd b7.de* op b7.de* phos b4a.de spong b7.de*

RAISING ARMS agg.: ang bg2 graph bg2

REST agg.: ang b7.de* ign b7.de* rhus-t b7.de*

RESTLESSNESS: thuj b4.de*

RISING: | **after** | **amel.**: arg-met bg2 plb b7.de* spig b7.de*
- **stooping**; from:
  - **agg.**: laur b7.de*
  - **amel.**: *Spong* b7a.de

ROOM: | **amel.**: laur b7.de*

RUBBING: | **amel.**: alum bg2 plb b7.de*

RUNNING agg.: laur b7.de*

SENSITIVE: acon bg2 ant-t bg2 apis bg2 bell bg2 coc-c bg2 hep bg2 hyper bg2 **Lach** bg2 sep bg2 spong bg2 squil b7.de*

▽ extensions | ○ localizations | ● Künzli dot | ↓ remedy copied from similar subrubric

SHIVERING: bell b4a.de

SHORTENING of muscles: cic b7.de* nux-v b7.de*

SINGING agg.: spong b7.de*

SITTING:
- **agg.**: ant-c b7.de* chel b7.de*
- **amel.**: tarax b7.de*

SNEEZING agg.: am-m b7a.de arn b7a.de

SPASMS: ant-c b7.de* laur b7.de* spong b7.de*

STANDING agg.: chin b7.de* tarax b7.de*

STIFFNESS: alum b4.de* am-c bg2 *Am-m* b7a.de ang b7.de* arg-met b7.de* ars b4.de* **Bell** b4.de* *Brom* b4a.de **Bry** b7.de* calc b4.de* calc-p bg2 camph b7.de* *Canth* b7a.de carb-an b4.de* caust b4.de* cham b7.de* chel bg2 *Chin* b7.de* cic b7.de* cocc b7.de* coloc b4a.de* croc b7.de* cupr b7.de* cycl bg2 dig b4.de* ferr b7.de* gels bg2 glon bg2 graph b4.de* hell b7.de* *Ign* b7a.de kali-bi bg2 kreos b7a.de laur bg2 lyc b4.de* lycps-v bg2 *M-ambo* b7.de* mang b4.de* merc b4.de* mez b4.de* nat-m b4.de* nit-ac b4.de* nux-v bg2 par b7.de* petr b4.de* ph-ac b4.de* *Phos* b4.de* *Phyt* bg2 plb bg2 rhod bg2 rhus-t b7.de* sel b7a.de sep bg2 sil b4.de* spong b7.de* squil b7.de* staph b7.de* sulph bg2 thuj b4.de* verat b7.de* zinc b4.de*
- **one** side: alum b4a.de *Lyc* b4a.de
- **painful**: berb bg2 calc bg2 caust bg2 chel bg2 cimic bg2 coloc bg2 dulc bg2 ferr bg2 gels bg2 glon bg2 kali-i bg2 kalm bg2 lach bg2 lachn bg2 merc bg2 nux-v bg2 par bg2 petr bg2 rhus-t bg2

STOOPING:
- **agg.**: ant-c b7a.de arn b7.de* camph b7.de* canth b7.de* cycl b7.de* hyos b7.de* nux-v bg2 par b7a.de *Rhus-t* b7.de* spig b7.de* spong b7.de* staph b7.de*
- **amel.**: chin b7.de*

STRETCHING:
- **agg.**: nat-s bg2
- **amel.**: sulph bg2

SWALLOWING:
- **agg.**: *Bry* b7a.de colch b7.de* nicc bg2 *Nux-v* b7a.de spig b7.de* spong b7.de* *Staph* b7a.de stram b7.de*
- **amel.**: spong b7.de*
- **empty** | **agg.**: cocc b7.de*

SWELLING: agar bg2 alum b4.de* am-m b7a.de anac bg2 apis bg2 arn bg2 *Ars* b4.de* bar-c bg2 **Bell** b4.de* bov bg2 calc b4.de* canth b7.de* *Caust* b4.de* cic b7.de* con b4a.de* croc bg2 crot-h bg2 graph bg2 hyos bg2 *Iod* b4.de* *Kali-c* bg2 kali-n b4.de* *Lach* bg2 *Lyc* b4.de* m-ambo b7.de mang b4.de* merc b4.de* *Merc-c* b4a.de nat-c b4.de* nit-ac b4.de* nux-v bg2 op bg2 par bg2 *Phos* b4.de* puls bg2 rhod bg2 *Rhus-t* b7.de* sars bg2 sil b4.de* stram bg2 sul-ac bg2 sulph bg2 thuj bg2 zinc b4.de*
- **one** side: merc bg2
  - **hard**: caust b4.de hyos b7a.de lach b7.de *Lyc* b4.de* merc bg2 *Merc-c* b4a.de nat-c b4.de* nux-v b7.de* *Puls* b7a.de sars b4a.de
- **hard**: caust bg2 lach bg2 **Lyc** bg2 nat-c bg2 nux-v bg2 tarent bg2
- **sensation** of: ang bg2 caust bg2 chel bg2 glon bg2 mang bg2 par b7.de* ptel bg2 spong bg2

○ - **Bones**: calc b4.de*
- **External** neck: alum b4.de am-m b7a.de arn b7.de *Ars* b4.de *Bar-c* b4.de* *Brom* b4a.de canth b7a.de *Caust* b4.de croc b7.de* *Hep* b4a.de hyos b7.de *Iod* b4.de lach b7.de *Lyc* b4.de* *Mag-c* b4a.de *Merc-c* b4a.de mez b4a.de nat-c b4.de *Puls* b7.de* rhod b4.de *Rhus-t* b7a.de

TALKING agg.: arn b7.de* sulph bg2

TENSION: aloe bg2 arg-met b7.de* arn b7.de* *Bar-c* b4.de* bell b4.de* bism b7.de* bov b4.de* **Bry** b7.de* *Calc* b4.de* camph b7.de* caust b4.de* cham b7.de* chel b7.de* chin b7a.de* cic b7.de* colch b7.de* coloc b4a.de crot-h bg2 dig b4.de* graph b4.de* grat bg2 iod b4.de* kali-bi bg2 kali-n b4.de* kreos b7a.de laur bg2 mag-m b4.de* nux-v b7a.de par b7.de* ph-ac b4a.de plb b7.de* puls b7.de* rhod b4.de* *Rhus-t* b7.de* sars b4.de* sep bg2 *Sil* b4a.de spig b7.de* spong b7.de* staph b7.de* sulph b4.de* *Thuj* b4a.de verb b7.de* viol-o b7a.de zinc b4.de*

TOUCH:
- **agg.**: ant-t b7.de* arn b7.de* chin b7.de* colch b7.de* cupr b7.de* *Lach* b7a.de m-arct b7.de nicc bg2 nux-v b7.de* psor bg2 *Puls* b7.de* spong b7.de* teucr b7.de*
- **amel.**: meny b7.de*

TREMBLING: ang bg2 carb-v bg2 graph bg2 m-ambo b7.de merc bg2

TURNING:
- **head**:
  - **agg.**: *Am-m* b7a.de ang b7.de* ant-c b7.de* ant-t b7.de* apis b7a.de arn b7.de* asar b7.de* bell bg2 bry b7.de* camph b7.de* cann-s b7.de* canth b7.de* chin b7.de* *Cic* b7.de* cocc b7.de* coloc bg2 cycl b7.de* hyos b7.de* ign b7.de* ip b7.de* kali-c bg2 laur b7.de* nux-v b7.de* puls b7.de* rhus-t b7.de* sabad b7.de* samb b7.de* *Sel* b7a.de *Spong* b7.de* viol-t b7.de*
  - **right** agg.; to: apis b7a.de *Spong* b7.de*
- **head** around agg.; turning: par b7.de*

TWITCHING: acon bg2 canth b7.de* caps bg2 graph bg2 laur b7.de* lyc bg2 mag-c bg2 sars b4.de* spong b7.de* tarax b7.de* verat b7a.de viol-o b7.de* zinc b4.de*
- **convulsive**: phos b4.de*

○ - **Muscles**: arg-met b7.de* bism b7.de*

ULCERS: *Ars* b4.de* *Hep* b4a.de hyos b7.de* *Kreos* b7a.de *Lyc* b4.de* sec b7.de* *Sil* b4a.de

WAKING: | **after** | **agg.**: arg-met bg2
- **on**: bufo bg2 spong b7.de*

WALKING:
- **agg.**: ruta b7.de*
- **air** agg.; in open: arg-met b7.de* camph b7.de* meny b7.de* nux-v b7.de*
- **beginning** to walk: ph-ac bg2
- **rapidly** | **agg.**: bry b7.de*

WARMTH; sensation of (See Heat - sensation)

WARTS: *Sep* b4a.de

WASHING: | **amel.**: asar b7.de*

WEAKNESS: abrot bg2 aeth bg2 *Ant-t* b7a.de *Arn* b7.de* calc-p bg2 *Cocc* b7.de* colch bg2 cupr bg2 glon bg2 kali-c b4a.de lyc b4a.de nat-c bg2 nux-m bg2 **Nux-v** b7a.de olnd b7a.de par b7a.de* staph b7.de* sul-i bg2 sulph bg2 tarax b7.de* verat b7.de*

WEARINESS: | **sensation** as: ant-t b7.de* m-arct b7.de

WIND: | **sensation** of wind blowing on it: olnd b7.de*

YAWNING agg.: arn b7.de* cocc b7.de* m-arct b7.de nat-s bg2

MORNING: acon bg2 alum b4.de* am-c b4.de* am-m b7.de* *Anac* b4a.de* ant-c b7.de* arg-met b7.de* *Arn* bg2 ars b4a.de* asaf b7.de* *Bar-c* b4.de* *Bar-m* bg2 bov b4.de* bry b7.de* calad b7.de* calc b4.de* cann-s b7a.de canth b7.de* carb-an b4.de* *Carb-v* b4.de* caust b4.de* cham bg2 *Chel* b7a.de chin b7.de* cic bg2 con b4.de* croc bg2 *Dig* bg2 dros bg2 ferr b7.de* *Graph* b4.de* hell b7.de* hep b4a.de* ign b7.de* iod b4.de* kali-bi bg2 kali-c b4.de* kreos bg2 lach bg2 lyc b4.de* mag-m b4.de* mang b4.de* merc-c b4a.de mosch bg2 nat-c b4.de* *Nat-m* b4.de* nit-ac b4.de* **Nux-v** b7.de* par b7.de* petr b4.de* phos b4.de* phyt bg2 plat b4.de* plb b7.de* *Puls* b7.de* ran-b b7.de* ran-s b7.de* rheum b7.de* rhus-t bg2 ruta b7.de* sep b4.de* **Sil** b4.de* spig bg2 squil bg2 staph b7.de* **Sulph** b4.de* valer bg2 *Verat* bg2 zinc b4.de*

FORENOON: alum b4.de* am-m b7.de* borx b4a.de cann-s b7.de* canth b7.de* carb-an b4.de* graph b4.de* kali-n b4.de* lyc b4.de* mag-m b4.de* mosch b7.de* mur-ac b4.de* nat-c b4.de* nat-m bg2 nux-v b7.de* ph-ac b4.de* phos b4.de* puls b7.de* rhod b4.de* sep b4.de* sil b4.de* spong b7.de* stann b4.de* sul-ac b4.de* sulph b4.de* zinc b4.de*
- **11** h: *Sulph* bg2 zinc bg2

NOON: *Arn* b7.de* aur b4.de* bell b4.de* bry b7.de* cham b7.de* ph-ac b4.de* phos b4.de* sep b4.de* zinc b4.de*

AFTERNOON: alum b4.de* am-m b7.de* ambr b7.de* ant-c b7.de* ant-t b7.de* ars b4.de* asaf b7.de* bar-c b4.de* bism b7.de* bry b7.de* calc b4.de* canth b7.de* caps b7.de* carb-an b4.de* carb-v b4.de* caust b4.de* chel b7.de* chin b7.de* cocc b7.de* coloc b4.de* con b4.de* graph b4.de* kali-bi bg2 kali-c b4.de* kreos b7a.de laur b7.de* lyc b4.de* mosch b7.de* nat-c b4.de* *Nux-v* b7.de* par b7.de* petr b4.de* ph-ac b4.de* **Phos** b4.de* rhus-t b7.de* sars b4.de* sil b4.de* spig b7.de* spong b7.de* stront-c b4.de* sulph b4.de* valer b7.de* zinc b4.de*
- **16** h: kali-bi bg2

EVENING: alum b4.de* am-c b4.de* ambr b7.de* anac bg2 ang b7.de* ant-t b7.de* ars b4.de* asar bg2 bell bg2 *Bry* b7.de* calc bg2 caps b7.de* carb-an b4.de* *Carb-v* b4.de* **Caust** b4a.de chel b7.de* chin b7.de* cocc b7.de* con bg2 cycl bg2 dulc b4.de* hyos b7.de* *Ign* b7a.de kali-bi bg2 kali-c b4.de* *Kali-n* b4a.de *Lyc* b4.de* mag-m b4.de* mang b4.de* merc b4.de* mez b4.de* nux-v b7.de* petr b4.de* *Phos* b4.de* *Plb* b7a.de **Puls** b7.de* ran-b bg2 rhod b4.de* *Rhus-t* b7.de* sars b4.de* seneg b4.de* *Sep* b4.de* sil b4.de* sul-ac b4.de* *Sulph* b4.de* thuj b4.de* valer b7.de* zinc b4.de*

NIGHT: alum bg2 *Ambr* b7.de* ant-t b7.de* arg-n bg2 **Ars** b4.de* bell b4.de* *Bry* b7.de* *Calc* b4.de* canth bg2 *Carb-v* b4.de* caust bg2 *Cham* bg2 *Chin* bg2 cina b7.de* cocc b7.de* con bg2 dig bg2 dros bg2 ferr bg2 *Graph* b4.de* ign b7a.de* kali-bi bg2 kali-c b4.de* lach bg2 lob bg2 lol bg2 lyc bg2 merc b4a.de* mur-ac bg2 nit-ac b4.de* *Nux-v* b7.de* *Phos* b4.de* puls b7a.de* ran-s bg2 rhod b4.de* **Rhus-t** b7.de* ruta b7.de* sec b7.de* seneg b4.de* sep b4.de* sil b4.de* **Sulph** b4.de* ther bg2 valer bg2 verat bg2
- **midnight**:
  - **before**: puls b7.de* rhus-t b7.de* valer b7.de*
  - **at**: arg-n bg2 kali-bi bg2
  - **after**: caps b7.de* *Chel* b7a.de nux-v b7.de* ran-s b7.de*

ACETONEMIA (See GENERALS - Acetonemia)

ACIDITY: *(↗Eructations; type - sour; Heartburn; Hyperchlorhydria)* abrot a1 *Aegle-f* zzc1• alum bg2 am-m bg2 ambr bg2 anac bg2 anis a1* *Ant-t* bg2 *Arg-n* bg2* *Ars* bg2 asar bg2 atis zzc1• bar-c bg2 bell bg2 benz-ac bg2 borx bg2 bry bg2* *Calc* bg2* calc-ar c2 caps bg2* carb-an bg2 *Carb-v* bg2* card-m hr1 caust bg2* cham bg2* chen-v hr1* **Chin** bg2* chlf hr1* chlol a1 chlor bg2 cina mtf33 cinnb a1 cob ptk1 cocc hr1 colch rsj2• con b4.de* cortico sp1 cub a1 *Cuph* br1 cycl bg2 daph bg2 dig bg2 elaps hr1* equis-h a1* fago a1* *Ferr* bg2 fl-ac bg2 gels bg2 glycyr-g cte1• *Graph* b4.de* hall a1* helic-p mtf hep h2* hir rsj4• ign bg2* iod bg2 ip bg2 iris bg2 *Kali-c* bg2 kali-fcy c1 lac-f wza1• lach bg2 lappa ptk1 lith-c hr1* lob a2* lob-s c2 luf-op rsj5• luna c2 **Lyc** b4a.de* m-arct b7.de mag-c bg2* mag-m bg2* merc bg2 merc-sul hr1 morg-p pte1*• myric a1 naja a1* nat-ar bg2 nat-c bro1 *Nat-m* bg2* *Nat-p* bg2* *Nit-ac* bg2 nux-m bg2 **Nux-v** bg2* ox-ac a1 par c2 *Petr* bg2* *Ph-ac* b4a.de* **Phos** b4a.de* plat bg2 plat-m a1* plb bg2 podo bg2* positr nl2• pot-e rly4• prot pte1* prun-v c2 psor bg2 **Puls** bg2* ran-s bg2 rob bg2* sabin bg2* sacch a1* sal-ac bwa3 sars bg2 *Sep* bg2* *Sil* b4.de* spig bg2 spira br1 *Stann* bg2 stram bg2 *Sul-ac* b4.de* **Sulph** bg2* syph jl2 tab bg2 thea bg2 thuj a1 uran-n a1 vanil fd5.de verat bg2 vichy-g a1* zinc b4.de* zing a1*
- **accompanied** by:
  - **appetite**; ravenous: graph h2*

Acidty – **accompanied** by: ...
  - **diarrhea** (See RECTUM - Diarrhea - accompanied - stomach)
  - **faint** feeling in stomach (See Emptiness - accompanied - acidity)
  - **indigestion** (See Indigestion - accompanied - acidity)
  - ○ **Head**; pain in (See HEAD - Pain - accompanied - stomach - acidity)
- **children**; in: | **infants**: bell bg2 calc bg2 *Cham* bg2 **Rheum** bg2 sulph bg2
- **eating** | **after** | **agg.**: sabin b7a.de
  - **amel.**: luf-op rsj5• morg-p fmm1•
- **vinegar**; like: iris bg2

ACRIDITY: calc b4.de* carb-v h2 cit-ac rly4• hep h2 lyc bg2 nux-v bg2 rhus-g tmo3• tere-la rly4•

ADHESION sensation: *Puls* b7a.de
- ○ **Diaphragm**: mez h2
- **Epigastrium**: *Hep* b4a.de *Sulph* b4a.de

AEROPHAGIA: med jl2 plat h2 prot jl2

AIR:
- **filled** with air; as if: bell bg2 gard-j vlr2•
- **swallowed** too much air; as if he had | **Epigastrium**: plat b4a.de
- ○ **Sternum**; below: bell h1
- **Through** stomach; as if air was forcing: bar-c k* cob bg1 crot-c bg1* gard-j vlr2•

AIR; IN OPEN:
- **agg.**: acon bg2 anac b4.de *Lyc* b4.de* nit-ac b4.de* nux-v bg2 sil b4.de*
- **amel.**: adon bro1 *Ars* b4a.de *Carb-v* b4a.de *Croc* b7.de* lyc bg2 *Puls* b7.de* tarax bg2

AIRPLANE sickness (See Nausea - airplane)

ALCOHOLIC drinks: | **amel.**: olnd bg2 sul-ac b4.de*

ALIVE in; sensation as if something: anan wd2 chel k* chion a1* coloc **Croc** k* falco-pe nl2• manc rb2 *Nux-v* b7a.de sabad rb2 sabin rb2 sang bg2* sep rb2 tarent k* thuj rb2 urol-h rwt• verat tl1
- ○ **Epigastrium**: chel tl1 croc b7.de* sang bg2

ANGER: hydrog srj2•

ANTS; as if filled with: gink-b sbd1•

ANXIETY: *(↗MIND - Anxiety)* abrot vh* *Acon* k* agar bg2 agar-em a1 am-m anac j5.de androc srj1• ant-t arg-met *Arg-n* **Ars** k* ars-s-f k2 aster vh bar-m bg2 both-ax tsm2 bry *Calc* k* calc-ar *Calc-p* calc-sil k2 *Cann-s* **Canth** bg2* *Carb-v* k* carc gk6* *Caust* *Cham* k* *Chel* k* chin h1* chir-fl gya2 chord-umb rly4• cic k* cocc k* coff k* *Colch* k* coloc ptk1 con j5.de crot-t k* *Cupr* k* *Dig* k* dioxi rbp6 dream-p sdj1• dros h1 ephe-si hsj1• *Ferr* ferr-ar galla-q-r nl2• ger-i rly4• germ-met srj5• gran k* granit-m es1• *Grat* guaj k* haem k* ham fd3.de• hist vml3• hydr hydr-ac bg1 hydrc c1 hydrog srj2• **Ign** j5.de* *Ip* hr1* irid-met srj5• *Jatr-c* k* *Kali-ar* k* kali-bi k* kali-br k* *Kali-c* k* kali-m k2 kali-s kali-sil k2* ketogl-ac rly4• lac-e hrn2• lac-loxod-a hrn2• lact laur k* limest-b es1• *Lyc* merc j5.de* merc-c mez h2* mosch mur-ac nat-m k* nit-ac bro1* *Nux-v* k* *Op* k* osm bg2 oxal-a rly4• *Paeon* petr bg2 phos bro1 plac-s rly4• plb k* positr nl2• *Puls* k* ran-s bg2 rhus-t sabad bg2 sang *Sec* k* sep serp a1 *Sil* *Spig* bg2 squil *Stann* *Stram* k* streptoc rly4• sul-ac sulph k* sumb tab **Tarent** k* ter teucr k* thiam rly4• thuj k* tritic-vg fd5.de tub k2 tung-met bdx1• *Verat* k* vesp [kali-met stj2]
- **morning**:
  - **waking**; on: adam srj5•
    - **alcoholics**; in: **Asar**
- **night** | **rising** up; on: **Ars** kl
- **asthma**, in: *Ferr* k2*
- **convulsions**; after: aster vh
- **diarrhea**, before: mez
- **eating**:
  - **after**:
    - **agg.**: chin lac-del hrn2• osm k* petr k*
    - **small** quantity: osm petr a1
- **excitement**; after: dig vh *Kali-c* vh* mez k2* phos
- **menses**; during: sil

- **people**, on approach of: lyc
- **pressure** | **amel.**: positr nl2•
- **rising** agg.: ars cupr bg2 nat-m bg2
- **sitting** agg.: calc h2 calc-act h1 chin h1
- **standing**:
  - **agg.**: teucr
  - **amel.**: calc h2
- **stool**; before (See MIND - Anxiety - stool - before)
- **vexation**; after: **Lyc**
- **waking**; on: **Asar** k* dioxi rbp6 ferr lac-loxod-a hm2•
- **walking** | **amel.**: calc h2

▽ - **extending** to | **Head**: asar dgt both-ax tsm2 nat-m ptk1 thuj h1

○ - **Epigastrium**: acon bg2 ant-t bg2 arg-n bg2 arn bg2 **Ars** b4.de* *Bry* b7.de* *Calc* b4.de* calc-p bg2 cann-s b7.de* canth b7.de* *Cham* b7.de* chel bg2 chin b7.de* cic b7.de* cocc b7a.de coff b7a.de con b4.de* crot-t bg2 cupr b7a.de dig bg2 ferr b7.de* *Graph* b4a.de guaj b4a.de hydr-ac bg2 ign b7.de* ip bg2 jatr-c bg2 kali-bi bg2 **Kali-c** bg2* laur b7.de* *Lyc* b4a.de* merc b4.de* mez b4.de* nat-m b4.de* **Nux-v** b7.de* *Ph-ac* b4a.de phos bg2 plb b7a.de **Puls** b7.de* sabad b7.de* sabin b7.de* *Sec* b7.de* sep b4a.de* stann b4.de* stram b7.de* sul-ac b4.de* *Sulph* b4.de* teucr b7.de* thuj b4.de* verat b7a.de*
  - **accompanied** by | **respiration**; impeded: cann-s b7.de* ferr b7.de* sabad b7.de* *Stram* b7.de*
  - **excitement** agg.: kali-c mrr1*
  - **stool**; before: caps b7.de* mez b4.de* *Verat* b7.de*

APPETITE:

- **capricious** appetite (= hunger, but knows not for what; refuses things when offered): *(↗GENERALS - Food - many - desire; MIND - Capriciousness; MIND - Mood - changeable)* ail alum-sil k2 ang kr1 arizon-l nl2• arn bt3 ars arum-t vh1 aster bar-c ptk1 bell bit-ar wht1• **Bry** k* bufo calad bg2 calc bg3* *Carb-an* c2 carbn-s carc gk6* cham bg2* **Chin** k* chir-fl gya2 choc srj3• *Cimic* c2 **Cina** k* *Coc-c* bg3* coca coli jl2 croc bg2 fago ferr ptk1 gran bg3 graph ptk1 *Hep* k* **Ign** k* *Iod* bg3* *Ip* k* irid-met srj5• kali-bi kali-s fd4.de kreos k* lac-loxod-a hm2• *Lach* k* limen-b-c hm2* luna c1 mag-c *Mag-m* k* mang-p rly4• merc ptk1 merc-i-f nat-m bg3* nux-m c1 petr k* petr-ra shn4• *Phos* k* **Puls** k* rheum bg2 rhus-g tmo3• rhus-t k2 ruta fd4.de sabal c1 *Sang* k* sil k* spong fd4.de staph bg2 sulph b4a.de* sumb suprar rly4• sym-r br1 symph st syph bg3* tep *Ther* k* tritic-vg fd5.de *Tub* zinc k* zinc-chl ptk1 zinc-p k2
- **changeable**: alum k* am-m bg1* *Anac* *Ars* hr1 bar-s k2 berb k* carc gk6* chir-fl gya2 cimic hr1 **Cina** k* coc-c a1 (non:cocc a1) coloc hr1 *Cur* cycl bg1* falco-pe nl2• fl-ac k2 gels bg1* (non:gran a1) grat a1 ham fd3.de• iod bg1* lach *Mag-m* meph a1 merc bg1* nat-m bg1* *Nit-ac* op bg1* phos podo positr nl2• syph xxb
- **complaints** of: ant-c ptk1 ars ptk1 *Calc* ptk1 **Chin** ptk1 *Cina* ptk1 graph ptk1 iod ptk1 *Lyc* ptk1 merc-cy ptk1 *Nat-m* ptk1 **Nux-v** ptk1 petr ptk1 phos ptk1 **Puls** ptk1 sil ptk1 stroph-h ptk1 **Sulph** ptk1 verat ptk1
- **constant**: bamb-a stb2.de• bov k* calc-p sne cocc bg2 fl-ac k* gran k* *Kali-bi* kali-p *Merc* k* moni rfm1• musca-d szs1 myric k* *Nat-c* k* *Nat-m* plut-n srj7• psil ft1 rat tab
- **desire** for drinks, but refused, when offered: bell h1
- **diminished**: *(↗wanting)* abrom-a ks5 abrot tl1 acet-ac k* acon-ac rly4• agar k* agav-a br1 agn k* aids nl2• alf br1 all-c k* aloe k* **Alum** k* alumn k* androc srj1• anh sp1 ant-c hr1* ant-t k* anthraq rly4• aran *Arg-n* k* arge-pl rwt5• arist-cl sp1 *Arn* hr1 ars k* asc-c a1 *Aur* k* aur-m k* bac bn* bacls-10 fmm1• bad k* bar-c bar-i k* *Bar-m* k* bar-ox-suc rly4• bar-s k2 bell k* berb k* beryl sp1 *Bit-ar* wht1• borx brom k* bros-gau mrc1 bruc a1 but-ac br1 *Cact* calc h2* calen hr1 canth k* carb-v k* carbn-s card-b a1 carneg-g rwt1• cartl-s rly4• cassia-s cdd7*• *Caust* cedr k* cham ptk1 chel k* chin k* chinin-ar chir-fl gya2 choc srj3• chol ptk1 chord-umb rly4• *Cina* clem a1 cob-n sp1 *Coc-c* hr1 coca-c sk4• cocc tl1* *Coff* k* colch tl1 coli rly4• *Coloc* k* *Con* k* cop k* crot-t k* cupr k* *Cycl* k* cystein-l rly4• delphin a1 des-ac rbp6 *Dig* digin a1 dirc k* dream-p sdj1• dulc fd4.de echi ephe-si hsj1• erio br1 ery-a a1 ery-m a1 fago k* falco-pe nl2• *Ferr* k* ferr-i ferr-p ferul a1 fic-m gya1 fl-ac k* fum rly1*• fuma-ac rly4• gal-ac a1* galeoc-c-h gms1• gamb gast a1 *Gels* gent-l a1* ger-i rly4• germ-met srj5• gink-b sbd1• *Glycyr-g* cte1• granit-m es1• grat k* guare a1 haliae-lc srj5• ham fd3.de• hell k* hir skp7• hist sp1 hura *Hydr* k* hydr-ac a1 hydrog srj2• hyos k* iber a1 ign k* iod k* ip tl1 irid-met stj2*• jal mrr1 kali-bi k* kali-c k* kali-chl k* kali-m k2 kali-n k* kali-p fd1.de• kali-s kiss a1 kreos k* lac-ac k* *Lac-d* lac-del hm2• lac-h sk4• lac-leo hm2• *Lac-loxod-a* hm2• lac-lup hm2• *Lach* k* lat-m sp1 laur a1 lavand-a ctl1• linu-c a1 loxo-recl knl4• *Lyc* k* mag-s k* mang-p rly4• med tl1 medul-os-si rly4• merc k* merc-c k* merc-i-f k* mez k* mit a1 *Moni* rfm1• morph a1 muru a1 *Murx* myos-a rly4•

Appetite – diminished appetite: ...

myric k* nabal a1 nad rly4• naja nat-c k* nat-m k* nat-ox rly4• nat-p k* nat-pyru rly4• nat-sil fd3.de• neon srj5• nicotam rly4• nux-v k* ol-an k* onos op k* opun-s a1 (non:opun-v a1) orot-ac rly4• ost a1 oxal-a rly4• pant-ac rly4• petr k* petr-ra shn4• phos k* **Pic-ac** k* pin-con oss2• pin-s k* pip-m k* pitu-gl skp7• plac-s rly4• plan plb k* podo fd3.de• polys sk4• positr nl2• pot-e rly4• psil ft1 *Psor* k* ptel tl1 puls k* *Pycnop-sa* mrz1 querc-r svu1• rham-f a1 rheum *Rhus-g* tmo3• rhus-t k* ribo rly4• ros-d wla1 *Rosm* lgb1 rumx ruta *Sabad* k* sabin sal-fr sle1• sang k* santin sars seneg k* sep k* sil k* sinus rly4• spong stram k* streptoc rly4• succ-ac rly4• suis-em rly4• suis-hep rly4• suis-pan rly4• sulph k* suprar rly4• syc fmm1• tab k* *Tarent* sne tell k* ter k* tere-la rly4• thiam rly4• thuj til k* tritic-vg fd5.de tub k2 tung-met stj2*• ulm-c jsj8• urol-h rwt• ust k* vanil fd5.de verat vero-o rly4*• vichy-g a1 x-ray sp1 yohim c1* zinc k* zinc-p k2 ziz a1 [ant-met stj2 aur-s stj2 bar-br stj2 bar-met stj2 bell-p-sp dcm1 bism-sn stj2 cinnb stj2 hafn-met stj2 heroin sdj2 kali-met stj2 lanth-met stj2 mang-met stj2 merc-d stj2 moly-met stj2 osm-met stj2 plat stj2 plb-m stj2 plb-p stj2 rhen-met stj2 tant-met stj2 tax jsj7 thal-met stj2 titan stj2]

- **daytime**: ars ptk1 granit-m es1•
- **morning**: aloe asc-t k* calc-p k* cinnb k* dream-p sdj1• dulc fd4.de falco-pe nl2• granit-m es1• hydrog srj2• kali-p fd1.de• lyss mag-m h2 mit a1 myric k* narcot k* oxal-a rly4• positr nl2• sel k* suis-hep rly4• suis-pan rly4• sulph tritic-vg fd5.de
- **noon**: ant-t k* calc k* clem k* coloc k* dream-p sdj1• dulc fd4.de indg k* mez k* nat-m k* ox-ac k* sulph k*
- **afternoon**: falco-pe nl2•
  - **17** h: falco-pe nl2•
- **evening**: aq-mar skp7• bit-ar wht1• borx chlor k* dig digin a1 falco-pe nl2• gink-b sbd1• nux-m k* podo fd3.de•
  - **19**-21 h: cassia-s cdd7•
  - **amel.**: ulm-c jsj8•
  - **supper**; at: galeoc-c-h gms1• ignis-alc es2•
- **accompanied** by:
  - **fullness** in stomach; sensation of: bit-ar wht1•
  - **nausea**: bit-ar wht1• melal-alt gya4
  - **obesity** (See GENERALS - Obesity - accompanied - appetite)
  - **Abdomen**; fullness of: cassia-s ccrh1•
- **anxiety**; from: lac-cp sk4•
- **cancer**; in: iod mtf11
- **children**; in: rheum mtf33
  - **accompanied** by | **Umbilicus**; eruption about (See ABDOMEN - Eruptions - umbilicus - around - children - newborns - accompanied - appetite)
- **desire** to eat little; but: mez tl1
- **drunkards**; in: kola br1
- **eating**, when time for: *Chin* k* dulc fd4.de ign k* melal-alt gya4 musca-d szs1
  - **evening**: ignis-alc es2•
- **fatigue**; during: plut-n srj7•
- **menses** | **before** | **agg.**: *Rhus-g* tmo3• suis-pan rly4•
  - **during** | **agg.**: bung-fa mtf irid-met srj5• mag-c k* pitu-a vml2• positr nl2• rhus-g tmo3•
- **perspiration**, after: bell h1
- **pregnancy** agg.; during: sabad ptk1
- **thirst**; with: galeoc-c-h gms1• petr-ra shn4•

- **easy** satiety: acon-l a1 agar k* allox tpw3* *Am-c* k* androc srj1• ant-t k* arg-met k* arg-n arn k* ars k* bar-c k* bar-s k2 borx b4a.de bry k* calad k* calam sa3• carb-an b4.de* carb-v b4.de* *Carbn-s* carc fd2.de• *Caust* k* *Cetr* hr1 cham b7.de* **Chin** k* *Cic* k* cinch a1 *Clem* k* coc-c k* coca gsw1 coff b7.de* *Colch* k* coloc b4.de* con k* croc k* crot-c sk4• *Cycl* k* *Dig* k* dulc k* *Ferr* k* *Ferr-i* fl-ac k* galeoc-c-h gms1• *Gels* k* gink-b sbd1• glycyr-g cte1• guare k* hep b4a.de hydr hyper gsw1 *Ign* k* *Iod* b4a.de kali-bi k* kali-i kali-p fd1.de* kali-s lac-leo sk4• lach b7a.de led k* **Lyc** k* *M-ambo* b7.de* m-arct b7.de mag-c k* mag-m k* mag-s mand sp1 mang marb-w es1• meny h1 merc k* mez k* nat-c b4.de* *Nat-m* k* nit-ac k* *Nux-m* k* *Nux-v* k* oci-sa sk4• olnd k* *Op* k* petr k* petros ph-ac h2 *Phos* k* plan k* **Plat** k* *Podo* polys sk4• prun k* psor k* ptel pycnop-sa mrz1 ran-b b7.de* *Rheum* k* *Rhod* k* rhus-t k* ruta k* sabin b7.de*

- **easy** satiety: ...
Sep k* serp k* *Sil* k* spong k* sul-ac b4.de* *Sulph* k* suprar rly4• symph fd3.de• tarent thea k* *Thuj* k* tub xxb tung-met bdx1• vanil fd5.de vinc *Zinc* b4a.de [tax jsj7]
  - **morning**: cycl k*
  - **evening**: phos k*
  - **bites**; after a few: galeoc-c-h gms1• glycyr-g cte1• suprar rly4•
  - **sadness**; from: plat h2
  - **sudden**: sep mtf33
- **eat**; with inability to (See increased - eating - cannot)
- **eating**; even after: allox tpw3 cic c1 sacch sst1• spong fd4.de tritic-vg fd5.de
  - **fullness**, with: *Rhus-t* a1
- **emptiness**; with (See Emptiness)
- **finicky**: syc fmm1•
- **gnawing**: abies-c br1* abrot k* adon vh1 arg-met k* arn a1 bell bg2 chim k* chim-m hr1 chin colch k* iod h* kreos k* lach bg2 seneg bg2 sep k2* sil k*
  - **prolapsus**; with: *Sep* tl1
  - **satisfied**; seldom: sep tl1
- **hunger**; without: canth b7.de*
- **increased** (= hunger): **Abies-c** k* abrom-a ks5 abrot acal *Acon* k* acon-ac rly4• adam skp7• *Agar* k* agath-a nl2• agn b2.de* *Aids* nl2• ail alf br1 *All-c* all-s br1 allox sp1 aloe *Alum* k* alum-p k2 alum-sil k2 *Alumn* **Am-c** k* am-m b2.de* anac k* anan androc srj1• ang k* anh sp1 ant-c k* ant-t k* *Aq-mar* skp7• ara-maca sej7• **Arg-met** k* arist-cl sp1 arizon-l nl2• arn k* **Ars** k* *Ars-i* asaf asar b2.de* aster sze10• atp rly4• *Aur* k* aur-i k2 bac jl2 *Bapt-c* c1 *Bar-c* k* *Bar-i* *Bar-m* bar-ox-suc rly4• *Bell* k* bell-p sp1 *Berb* beryl sp1* bism bg2 bit-ar wht1• borx b2.de* bov k* brass-n-o srj5• bros-gau mrc1 bry k* bung-fa mtf cadm-met sp1 calad k* **Calc** k* calc-i k2 *Calc-p* k* **Calc-s** k* calc-sil k2 camph **Cann-i** cann-s b7a.de canth k* caps k* carb-ac *Carb-an* k* carb-v k* carbn-s caul *Caust* k* cham b2.de* **Chin** k* *Chinin-s* k* choc srj3• chord-umb rly4• cic b2.de* **Cina** k* **Cinnb** cit-ac rly4• clem a1 cob-n sp1 coc-c coca-c sk4• *Cocc* k* coff k* colch k* coli rly4* coloc k* *Con* cop corian-s knl6• cortiso gse corv-cor bdg• crot-c k* cub cupr k* cycl k* cypra-eg sde6.de• cystein-l rly4• des-ac rbp6 dig k* dios dream-p sdj1• dros dulc k* *Elaps* ephe-si hsj1• equis-h eug euph b2.de* euphr b2.de* falco-pe nl2• *Ferr* k* *Ferr-ar* *Ferr-i* *Fl-ac* k* flor-p rsj3• fum rly1*• galeoc-c-h gms1• galla-q-r nl2• gamb *Gels* gent-c ger-i rly4• germ-met srj5• glycyr-g cte1• gran **Graph** k* grat k* *Guaj* k* *Guare* haliae-lc srj5• hed sp1 hell k* helo-s rwt2• helodr-cal knl2• hep hir rsj4• hura hydr hydr-ac hydrog srj2• hyos k* *Ign* k* ind **Iod** k* jug-c jug-r kali-ar kali-bi kali-br a1 kali-c k* kali-chl kali-i k* kali-m k2 kali-n k* kali-p *Kali-s* kreos *Lac-ac* *Lac-c* *Lac-h* htj1• *Lac-loxod-a* hrn2• lac-lup hrn2• *Lach* k* lact laur k* led lept lil-t limen-b-c hrn2* limest-b es1• luf-op rsj5• **Lyc** k* lyss m-ambo b2.de* m-arct b2.de m-aust b2.de mag-c k* *Mag-m* k* mag-p maias-l hrn2• mand sp1 mang b2.de* mang-p rly4• marb-w es1• med tl1 meny b2.de* *Merc* k* *Merc-c* mez k* mosch b2.de* mucs-nas rly4• *Mur-ac* k* *Myric* nad rly4• *Nat-ar* *Nat-c* k* **Nat-m** k* nat-ox rly4• *Nat-p* nat-pyru rly4• *Nat-s* neon srj5• nicotam rly4• *Nit-ac* k* *Nux-m* k* **Nux-v** k* oci-sa sk4• olib-sac wmh1 **Olnd** k* onos *Op* k* orot-ac rly4• osteo-a knp1• ox-ac oxal-a rly4• ozone sde2• pant-ac rly4• par b2.de* *Pert-vc* vk9 **Petr** k* petr-ra shn4• *Ph-ac* **Phos** k* phys *Pic-ac* pin-con oss2• plac-s rly4• plat k* plb k* plut-n srj7• podo polys sk4• positr nl2• propl ub1• propr sa3• pseuts-m oss1• **Psor** k* ptel c1 **Puls** k* pycnop-sa mrz1 pyrid rly4• ran-b k* raph *Rat* rauw sp1 rein a1 rheum k* rhod b2.de* rhus-g tmo3• rhus-t k* ribo rly4• ros-d wla1 ruta k* **Sabad** k* sal-al blc1• sal-fr sle1• sars k* sec k* sel k* seneg k* *Sep* k* *Sil* k* skat br1 spig k* spong k* squil k* *Stann* k* *Staph* k* stram k* stront-c k* succ-ac rly4• suis-em rly4• suis-hep rly4• suis-pan rly4• sul-ac k* sul-i k2 sulfonam ks2 **Sulph** k* sumb symph fd3.de• tab taosc iwa1• tarent tep ter tetox pin2• *Teucr* k* ther thiam rly4• thuj thymol sp1 tritic-vg fd5.de tung-met bdx1• ust valer k* vanil fd5.de **Verat** k* verb b2.de* vero-o rly4*• vip fkr4.de visc sp1 xan c1 zinc k* zinc-p k2 [ant-m stj2 ant-met stj2 bell-p-sp dcm1 heroin sdj2 mag-i stj1 nat-i stj1 spect dfg1 tax jsj7]
  - **daytime**: cocc b7.de* murx k* nat-m k* *Stann*
  - **morning**: act-sp hr1 agar k* aids nl2• am-c b4.de* ant-c k* *Arg-met* k* asar k* aur k* bar-act bg2 bar-c b4.de* borx k* bry k* calad k* *Calc* k* carb-an k* chel k* chin k* chir-fl gya2 cic b7.de* cycl b7.de* galla-q-r nl2• graph bg2 hyper k* kali-s fd4.de ketogl-ac rly4• lac-del hrn2• lyc lyss k* m-aust b7.de merc b4.de* mur-ac k* murx k* myric k* nat-c k* nat-m k* nit-ac b4.de* nux-v b7.de* olib-sac wmh1 ozone sde2• *Petr* b4a.de petr-ra shn4• phasco-ci rbp2 phos b4.de* plat b4.de* psor k* ran-b k* rhus-g tmo3• rhus-t k* ribo rly4• sabad k* sal-fr sle1• sang *Sel* seneg b4.de* sep k* sil tet a1 teucr k* zinc k* [bell-p-sp dcm1]
    - **7 h**: aloe

- **increased – morning**: ...
    - **8 h**: chin
    - **only**: merc bg2
    - **stool** agg.; after: aloe k*
    - **waking**; on: aeth bg2 aran bg2 gard-j vlr2•
  - **forenoon**: alf br1 aloe arg-met carb-v b4.de* graph b4.de* hell k* hep k* ind k* kali-c bg2 kali-n k* *Nat-c* k* nat-m nux-m k* nux-v b7.de* olib-sac wmh1 phos bg2 rhod b4.de* sulph k* zinc b4.de*
    - **10 h**: calam sa3• iod kali-n lyc nat-c kr1 *Nat-m* thuj
    - **11 h**: euphr hura hydr bg3* ign *Iod* lach *Nat-m* phos bg3* **Sulph** k* visc sp1 *Zinc* k*
      - **eating**; after: aq-mar skp7•
    - **11.30 h**: aq-mar skp7•
  - **noon**: abies-n k* acon am-c chord-umb rly4• clem coc-c colch k* coloc dig falco-pe nl2• ham fd3.de• hyper k* lact lyc mag-c k* *Mez* k* nat-c k* *Nat-m* k* *Nux-m* k* olib-sac wmh1 pip-m a1 pitu-gl skp7• spong fd4.de stront-c sulfonam ks2 sulph k*
  - **afternoon**: arg-met bov a1 calc b4.de* cham b7.de* chin k* coff b7.de* colch k* guaj k* ham fd3.de• lyc nat-c k* nux-m b7a.de nux-v k* psor k* sep b4.de* suis-hep rly4• tritic-vg fd5.de zinc k*
    - **14 h**: chinin-s clem
    - **15 h**: bung-fa mtf
    - **16 h**: calc-p kali-p fd1.de•
    - **17 h**: bros-gau mrc1 myric
    - **drinking** agg.; after: nat-m
  - **evening**: agar k* aids nl2• aloe k* am-m b7.de* arg-n bg2 arn k* aur-m-n wbt2• aur-s wbt2• benz-ac a1 borx b4a.de* bov k* calad k* calc k* camph cann-s carb-an k* cham k* chin k* chinin-s colch k* cop k* croc b7.de* crot-c cycl k* fl-ac k* galeoc-c-h gms1• *Guaj* k* haliae-lc srj5• *Ign* bg2 iod kali-c b4.de *Kali-n* k* lach b7.de* lyc k* *M-ambo* b7.de* *M-arct* b7.de* *M-aust* b7.de* mag-m h2 mez k* nat-c h2 *Nat-m* k* olib-sac wmh1 phos bg1 *Pic-ac* plat b4.de* plb b7.de* psil ft1 *Psor* k* puls k* sabad k* *Sep* k* sil k* spong fd4.de sulfonam ks2 teucr k* thuj k* tritic-vg fd5.de tung-met bdx1• zinc k*
    - **18 h**: sumb
    - **19-19.30 h**: sulfonam ks2
    - **21 h**: cassia-s ccrh1• form
    - **eating**; after: carc zzh rhus-g tmo3•
  - **night**●: abies-n k* anan k* atp rly4• bry k* calc bg2 canth k* **Chin** k* *Chinin-s* k* *Cina* bro1 ham fd3.de• *Ign* k* lac-h sze9• **Lyc** k* nat-c bro1 nat-sil fd3.de• petr b4.de* ph-ac k* **Phos** k* **Psor** k* puls sel k* sil bg2 sulph k* taosc iwa1• tarent tell k* teucr bg2 tub jl2*
    - **midnight**:
      - **before** | **23** h: aids nl2• nat-c k2 ox-ac
      - **at**: *Med* vh
      - **after**:
        - **5** h: nat-c k2*
        - **5.30** h: aids nl2•
  - **accompanied** by:
    - **appetite** wanting (See wanting - hunger)
    - **aversion** to food (See GENERALS - Food - food - aversion - accompanied - hunger)
    - **burning** in stomach: *Graph* b4a.de
    - **fullness** of stomach: beryl sp1
    - **indigestion**: *Merc* b4a.de*
    - **metallic** taste: cocc tl1
    - **nausea**: *(↗ravenous - accompanied - nausea)* arg-met gsy1 bell bg2 *Berb-a* bro1 cadm-met tpw6 caust h2 chin h1 chinin-s bg2 cocc bro1 cycl h1 falco-pe nl2• *Hell* b7a.de ign bro1 irid-met srj5• mag-m b4a.de* nat-c b4a.de* nept-m lsd2.fr olnd b7a.de* petr ptk1 phos b4a.de* rhus-t h1 spig bg2 valer bg2* verat ptk1 [heroin sdj2]
      - **waking**; on: mand rsj7•
    - **pain** (See GENERALS - Pain - accompanied - appetite)
    - **pain** in stomach (See Pain - accompanied - hunger; Pain - eating - not)
    - **sleepiness**: galeoc-c-h gms1•
    - **thirst**: verat b7a.de

Stomach

- **accompanied** by: ...
  - **urination**; copious: verat b7a.de
  - **Abdomen**; rumbling in:
    - **forenoon** | **11** h: mand rsj7•
  - **Head**; complaints of (See HEAD - Fasting)
- **air**; in open | **amel.**: ant-t
- **alternating** with:
  - **loathing** of food (See Loathing - alternating)
  - **loss** of appetite: *Alum* b4a.de am-m k* anac ptk1 ars pd *Berb* k* brucel sa3• calam sa3• *Calc* k* caps hr1* chin pd cina ptk1 cupre-au c1 cycl a1 dros c1 **Ferr** k* *Iod* k* lyc mtf33 nat-m b4a.de* petr-ra shn4• *Phos* k* pin-con oss2• puls pd sep mtf33 sil pd sulph pd *Thuj* [bell-p-sp dcm1]
  - **nausea** (See Nausea - alternating - hunger)
- **aversion** to food; with (See GENERALS - Food - food - aversion - accompanied - hunger)
- **beer**; after: nux-v
- **breakfast** agg.; after: aloe bart a1 tax k*
- **children**; in: cina br1
  - **nurslings**: lap-a br1
  - **sick**; when: cina mtf33
- **chill**: *(↗intermittent)*
  - **after**: *Ars* k*
  - **before**: *Chin* k* **Cina** k* *Eup-per* **Staph**
  - **during**: ail k* ant-c bg2 **Ars** k* calc bg2 cham bg2 *Chin* bg2 *Chinin-s* *Cina* bg2 *Eup-per* *Lec* nux-v k* *Phos* k* puls bg2 **Sil** k* staph verat bg2
- **convulsions**; after: hyos gk2
- **coryza** and cough, with: hep bg2 sul-ac h2
- **coryza**; during: hep b4a.de
- **cough** agg.; during: nux-v ptk1*
- **diarrhea**, with: *(↗ravenous - diarrhea - during)* aloe bro1 ferr bro1 nux-v ptk1 petr tl1* psor vml sec bro1 verat h1
- **dinner**; after: galeoc-c-h gms1•
- **disease**; before the onset of a: bry bg3* calc ptk1 hyos ptk1 nux-v bg3* *Phos* bg3* *Psor* bg3* sep bg3*
- **eating**:
  - **after**: acon k* agar k* *Alf* bro1 all-c bg1 alum alum-p k2 alumn hr1 androc srj1• ang bg2 ant-t bg2 aq-mar skp7• *Arg-met* asc-c k* aur k* bov k* *Calc* k* casc bro1 castor-eq caust bg2 chin b7a.de* chinin-ar ptk1 *Chinin-s* *Cic* k* cina k* coc-c k* colch bg2 conch fkr1• corn dig k* fago k* falco-pe nl2• gran k* grat k* haliae-lc srj5• hura indol bro1 iod bg2* irid-met srj5• kali-chl kali-n bg2 kali-p bg2* lac-c k* lach k* lepi a1 **Lyc** k* marb-w es1• med br1* *Merc* k* murx ptk1 myric nat-m k* nux-v bg2 olib-sac wmh1 olnd bg2 par k* **Phos** k* phyt k* plat k* plb k* *Psor* k* ran-s k* raph k* rheum bg2 ruta bg2 sacch-a fd2.de• sang bg2 sars bg2* sep bg2 sil bg2* spong fd4.de staph k* stront-c k* sulfonam ks2 sulph bro1 syph xxb zinc k* [heroin sdj2 pop dhh1]
    - **evening**: agar bg2 calc bg2 guaj bg2 kali-c bg2 lyc bg2 mez bg2 nat-m bg2 sep bg2 sil bg2
    - **fifteen** minutes: pert-vc vk9
    - **only** while eating; appetite returns: anac bell b4.de* calc carb-an h2 cham b7.de* **Chin** k* mag-c k* meny b7.de* merc b4.de* nat-m b4.de* phos b4.de* sabad bg2 sep b4.de* *Sulph* b4a.de
    - **ten** minutes: rauw tpw8
  - **before** | **agg.**: coff b7.de* ran-b b7.de* rhus-t b7.de*
  - **cannot** eat: allox tpw4 bit-ar wht1• bry gsw1 cartl-s rly4• chin elaps lavand-a ctl1• lyc mtf33 *Sulph* tab
  - **increases** the hunger (See after)
  - **not** amel. by: *(↗insatiable)* cadm-met tpw6 cina mtf33 lac-c mtf33 lavand-a ctl1• staph mtf33 tritic-vg fd5.de
  - **vanishing** (See wanting - eating - attempting)
  - **while** | **agg.**: verat b7a.de*
- **fever**:
  - **after**: *Chin* b7a.de* *Cimx* k* *Cina* dulc k* eup-per ign k* staph k*
  - **before**: chin b7a.de *Staph* b7a.de

- **increased** – **fever**: ...
  - **during** | **agg.**: *Chin* k* *Cina* k* cur eup-pur hell k* **PHOS** k •* podo c1 staph bro1
- **headache**:
  - **after**: iod k*
  - **before**: *Calc* vh dulc h2 epiph ptk1 *Phos* **Psor** k* sep bg1
    - **day** before; the: psor jl2
  - **during**: *(↗HEAD - Pain - accompanied - appetite)* allox tpw4* anac bro1 ars asc-c c1 bry bg3* cact bro1 crot-h elaps *Epiph* bro1 galeoc-c-h gms1• ign bro1 *Kali-c* k* kali-p k* kali-s ptk1 lac-d lyc k* **Phos** k* **Psor** k* ptel sang sel bg3* *Sep* k* sil sulph syph xxb thuj
    - **sleepy**; and: galeoc-c-h gms1•
- **intermittent**, in: *(↗chill)* *Phos* *Staph*
- **knows** not for what; but (See capricious)
- **menses** | **before** | **agg.**: agath-a nl2• cimic gk croc gk mag-c puls gk sep gk spong k*
  - **during** | **agg.**: agath-a nl2• iod al kali-p spong bro1
- **nausea**; with (See accompanied - nausea)
- **pain** in stomach, with (See Pain - accompanied - hunger)
- **pains**; after: *Ars* b4a.de canth b7.de* crot-t bg2 iod bg2
- **perspiration** | **after** | **agg.**: cina ptk1
  - **during**: cimx k* *Cina* ignis-alc es2• sanic k*
- **pregnancy** agg.; during: calc-p ptk1 chel ptk1 *Mag-m* bg2 nat-m bg2 *Nux-v* bg2 *Petr* bg2 psor k2* **Sep** bg2*
- **qualmishness**; after: olnd b7.de*
- **refuses** things when offered (See capricious)
- **sadness**; with (See MIND - Sadness - canine)
- **sitting**; after: rhus-t k*
- **sleep** | **siesta** agg.; after: onos
- **smell** of food; from: olib-sac wmh1 tritic-vg fd5.de
- **stool** | **after** | **agg.**: abrom-a ks5 aloe k* fl-ac kali-p bg3* **Petr** k* verat b7.de*
  - **during** | **agg.**: aloe bg2 olnd b7a.de petr bg2 verat b7.de*
- **sudden**: sec bg2 sep mtf33 sulph ptk1 tung-met bdx1•
- **tormenting**: arg-met bell crot-h *Iod* *Olnd* seneg
- **trembling** (See GENERALS - Trembling - externally - hungry)
- **twilight**; in the: choc srj3•
- **unusual** time: carl a1 chin k* **Cina** coc-c k* gins k* vanil fd5.de
- **vanishing**:
  - **attempting** to eat; on (See wanting - eating - attempting)
  - **sight** of food; at (See wanting - food - sight)
- **vomiting**:
  - **after**: aeth bg2* cina k* *Colch* k* olnd k* podo tab k*
  - **with**: asc-c c1 bell bg2 caust ptk1 chin chinin-s bg2 hell iod bro1 lob bro1 mag-m bg2 nat-c bg2 olnd bg2 phos bg2 sang hr1 spig bg2 valer bg2 verat k*
- **wakefulness**; causing: ign bg2 phos bg2
- **waking**; on: aids nl2• arn bg1 bell h1* cadm-met tpw6 chin choc srj3• dig digin a1 gard-j vlr2• nat-pyru rly4• ptel k* suis-hep rly4• [heroin sdj2]
  - **eating** | **amel.**: cadm-met tpw6 psor jl2
- **walking** agg.: [heroin sdj2]
- **water** | **amel.**: [bell-p-sp dcm1]
- **weakness**; with: arizon-l nl2• gels bg2 ign bg2 ignis-alc es2• lach merc *Phos* sep bg2 spig b7.de* **Sulph**
  - **too** weak to eat: ant-c mtf33
- **wine** agg.: nat-m k*
- **yawning**; with: aloe bg2
- ○ **Spine**; as if coming from: lil-t bg3*

- **indifference** to food and drink: chin b7.de* *M-aust* b7.de* positr nl2• rhus-t b7.de* valer b7.de*
- **indistinct** desire (See capricious)
- **insatiable**: *(↗increased - eating - not; ravenous)* abel vh1 abies-c vh1 aids nl2• allox tpw3* androc srj1• ang bg2* anh sp1 ant-c k* *Arg-met* k* arg-n k* arum-t k* asc-t k* aur k* bamb-a stb2.de• bar-c k* *Bell* bg2 bell-p sp1 bung-fa mtf

- **insatiable**: ...
cadm-met sp1 *Cic* hr1 cina mrr1* cypra-eg sde6.de• dulc fd4.de *Ferr* k* *Ferr-i* hydrog srj2• ign mrr1 **Iod** k* *Kola* stb3• lil-t bg2 limest-b es1• **Lyc** k* marb-w es1• merc bg2 *Moni* rfm1• nat-pyru rly4• nauf-helv-li elm2• ozone sde2• petr k* plat mrr1 propl ub1• puls k* puls-n k* rauw sp1 rhus-g tmo3• *Sec* k* *Sep* *Spong* k* squil k* stann k* staph k* thuj mrr1 tub al ulm-c jsj8• v-a-b jl visc sp1 *Zinc* k*
  - **morning**: arg-n k* bros-gau mrc1 sang a1
  - **noon**: asc-t k* petr h2 zinc k*
  - **evening**: arg-n k* sacch sst1• spong fd4.de zinc
  - **night**: phos h2
- **know** for what; does not (See capricious)
- **lack** of (See wanting)
- **ravenous**: (↗*insatiable; MIND - Bulimia; MIND - Sensual)* abies-c k* abrot k* acet-ac tl1 adon bg2 *Agar* k* agath-a nl2• agn b7.de* *Alf* bro1 *All-c* all-s bro1 allox tpw3* *Alum* k* alum-p k2 alum-sil k2 **Am-c** k* am-m bg2 *Anac* k* anan ang b7a.de ant-t b2.de* aq-mar rbp6 ara-maca sej7• **Arg-met** k* arn k* **Ars** k* ars-br bro1 **Ars-i** ars-s-f k2 asaf k* *Aur* k* aur-ar k2 aur-i k2 aur-s k2 bac bn bamb-a stb2.de• bar-c k* *Bar-i* k* bar-m bar-s k2 bell k* *Berb* bov k* brass bro1 *Bry* k* cact bro1 calad **Calc** k* calc-i k2 **Calc-p** k* **Calc-s** calc-sil k2 calen bro1 camph **Cann-i** k* cann-s b7a.de cann-xyz ptk1 caps k* carb-ac *Carb-an* k* carb-v k* **Carbn-s** carc gk6* card-m cartl-s rly4• cassia-s ccrh1• caul *Caust* k* cham b2.de* chel bro1 **Chin** k* *Chinin-ar* chinin-s bg2 chir-fl gya2 *Cic* b7.de* cimic bro1 **Cina** k* clem a1 clerod-i bnj1 *Coc-c* *Cocc* k* *Coff* k* *Colch* k* *Coloc* *Con* k* conch fkr1.de cop corian-s knl6• *Corv-cor* bdg• crot-c cupr cypra-eg sde6.de• dros k* dulc fd4.de *Elaps* equis-h *Eup-per* falco-pe nl2• **Ferr** k* *Ferr-ar* *Ferr-i* ferr-p *Fl-ac* k* galla-q-r nl2• gamb gels glyc bro1 gran k* **Graph** k* *Guaj* k* guare hell k* hep k* hura hydrog srj2• *Hyos* k* ichth bro1 *Ign* k* ind **Iod** k* irid-met srj5• jug-c kali-ar kali-bi kali-c k* kali-chl kali-m k2 *Kali-n* k* kali-p k* kali-s kali-sil k2 *Kola* stb3• kreos *Lac-ac* k* lac-c k* lach k* lap-a k* lap-la sde8.de• laur k* lil-t k* lob bro1 **Lyc** k* lyss m-ambo b7.de m-arct b7.de m-aust b2.de* mag-c k* mag-m k* mag-p marb-w es1• medul-os-si rly4• melal-alt gya4 meny b2.de* *Merc* k* *Merc-c* *Mez* k* *Moni* rfm1• *Mur-ac* k* myric k* *Nat-ar* *Nat-c* k* **Nat-m** k* nat-ox rly4• *Nat-p* *Nat-s* nat-sil fd3.de• nicotam rly4• *Nit-ac* k* *Nux-m* k* **Nux-v** k* *Ol-j* *Olib-sac* wmh1 **Olnd** k* *Op* k* osteo-a knp1• ox-ac par b7.de* **Petr** k* petr-ra shn4• petros bro1 *Ph-ac* k* **Phos** k* phys pime a1 *Plat* k* plb b7.de* *Podo* k* positr nl2• psil ft1 **Psor** k* ptel **Puls** k* pycnop-sa mrz1 pyrid rly4• *Rat* k* rhus-g tmo3• *Rhus-t* k* ros-d wla1 rumx ptk1 ruta k* **Sabad** k* sanic tl1 *Sec* k* sel b7a.de seneg *Sep* k* **Sil** k* sphing kk3.fr spig k* *Spong* k* squil k* *Stann* k* *Staph* k* stront-c sul-ac k* sul-i k2 **Sulph** k* tab k* tarent tep ter teucr b7.de* ther k2 *Thuj* k* *Thyr* bro1 tritic-vg fd5.de tub tl1 *Uran-n* bro1 ust valer k* vanil fd5.de **Verat** k* visc c1 zinc k* zinc-p k2 [heroin sdj2 lith-i stj2 mang-i stj2 merc-i-f stj2 zinc-i stj2]
  - **morning**: acon-s a1 ant-c *Arg-met* bry k* *Calc* k* hyper k* kola stb3• myric k* nat-c k* plat h2 sabad sacch sst1• sang k* sil k* sulph tl1
  - **forenoon**: aloe kali-n k* *Nat-c* k* spong fd4.de sulph vanil fd5.de
    - **10 h**: iod kali-n *Nat-m*
    - **11 h**: ign *Iod* kola stb3• **Sulph** k* *Zinc* k*
  - **noon**: abies-n k* acon k* coloc k* falco-pe nl2• lyc k* *Mez* k* *Nat-m* k* nat-sil fd3.de• *Nux-m* olib-sac wmh1 pitu-gl skp7• *Zinc*
    - **13 h**: pitu-gl skp7•
  - **afternoon**: *Guaj* lyc k* nat-c k* nux-v k* spong fd4.de vanil fd5.de
    - **14 h**: clem
    - **16 h**: *Calc-p* k*
    - **17 h**: myric
      - **after**: rhus-g tmo3•
  - **evening**: aconin a1 agar k* aloe calc calen a1 cann-s k* carneg-g rwt1• cham chinin-s crot-c k* fl-ac gent-l k* *Guaj* guare iod k* kali-s fd4.de lyc k* mag-c *Mez* *Nat-m* olib-sac wmh1 podo fd3.de• rhus-g tmo3• sabad k* sil k* spong fd4.de teucr vanil fd5.de zinc
    - **18 h**: sumb
    - **20 h**: pip-m
  - **night**●: abies-n k* anan bamb-a stb2.de• bry **Chin** k* *Ign* *Lyc* k* nat-sil fd3.de• petr *Ph-ac* k* **Phos** k* *Psor* k* sacch-a fd2.de• sel sep sil k* sulph tarent k* tub tl visc c1
    - **midnight | before | 23 h**: *Nat-c* k2*
      - **after | 5 h**: *Nat-c* br1*
    - **pregnancy** agg.; during: *Par* vh* psor st*

- **ravenous**: ...
  - **accompanied** by:
    - **acidity** in stomach (See Acidity - accompanied - appetite)
    - **emaciation** (See GENERALS - Emaciation - appetite)
    - **headache** (See HEAD - Pain - accompanied - appetite)
    - **marasmus** (See GENERALS - Emaciation - appetite - children - infants)
    - **nausea**: (↗*increased - accompanied - nausea)* spig b7a.de spong fd4.de valer b7a.de*
    - **thirst**: bry b7a.de hyos b7a.de sulph bg2
    - **thirstlessness**: all-s ptk1 ars ptk1
    - **trembling**: (↗*GENERALS - Trembling - externally - hungry)* olnd bg2
    - **wine**; desire for (See GENERALS - Food - wine - desire - accompanied - appetite)
    - **Epigastrium**:
      - **gnawing** sensation in: cassia-s ccrh1•
      - **weakness**: stann bg2
    - **Head**; complaints of (See HEAD - Complaints - accompanied - appetite - ravenous)
    - **Spine**; pain along: lil-t bg2
  - **ague**, after: eup-per *Staph*
  - **alternating** with:
    - **loathing** of food: *Caps* b7a.de *Lach* b7a.de
    - **loss** of appetite: *Alum* b4a.de calc-hp ll1 *Caps* b7a.de *Iod* b4a.de *Lach* b7a.de nat-m b4a.de
  - **anemic** babies: lap-a br1
  - **appetite**; without: bry b7.de* *Hell* b7a.de olnd b7.de* *Op* b7a.de rhus-t b7.de
  - **apyrexia**, during: **Staph**
  - **beer**; after: *Nux-v* b7.de*
  - **chill**; during: chin bro1 chinin-s bro1 *M-aust* b7.de*
  - **contempt**, during: plat st
  - **convulsions**:
    - **after**: coc-c k*
      - **epileptic**: calc hp
    - **before | epileptic**: *Calc* k* **Hyos** k*
  - **diarrhea**:
    - **during**: (↗*increased - diarrhea)* aloe *Asaf* *Calc* coch *Fl-ac* *Iod* kola stb3• *Lyc* *Olnd* k* ozone sde2• **Petr** k* sec a1 *Stram* sul-i k2 *Sulph* k* *Verat* zinc
    - **preceding**: psor k*
  - **drinking** water amel., then loss of appetite: kali-chl c1
  - **dysentery**; in: **Nux-v**
  - **easy** satiety: am-c bro1 arn bro1 ars bro1 ars-s-f k2 bar-c bro1 carb-v bro1 *Chin* bro1 *Cycl* bro1 ferr bro1 lith-c bro1 *Lyc* bro1 nat-m bro1 nux-v bro1 petros bro1 podo bro1 polys sk4• prun bro1 *Sep* bro1 *Sulph* bro1
  - **eating**:
    - **after** eating:
      - **one** hour after: petr-ra shn4•
      - **soon** after: acon agar allox tpw3 *Arg-met* asc-c bov *Calc* k* **Chinin-s** *Cic* **Cina** k* coc-c corn fago fl-ac k2 grat **Iod** k* kali-m k2 kali-p kali-s fd4.de *Kola* stb3• lac-c mtf33 lach **Lyc** *Med* k* *Merc* k* myric oci-sa sk4• petr-ra shn4• **Phos** k* phyt plb *Psor* ros-d wla1 sacch sst1• sarr spong fd4.de *Staph* stront-c *Sulph* tritic-vg fd5.de zinc zinc-p k2
        - **increases** the hunger: *Kola* stb3• **Lyc** k* petr-ra shn4•
      - **three** hours after: calc-caust c1 **Iod**
      - **two** hours after: allox tpw4 calc-hp ptk1 tax
    - **disappearing** after eating: calc bg2 graph bg2 iod bg2 meny b7.de* rhus-t b7.de* sil bg2
    - **hastily** (See MIND - Hurry - eating)
  - **fever**:
    - **before**: calc b4a.de *Chin* b7a.de *Cina* b7a.de ign b7a.de lyc b4a.de nux-v b7a.de phos b4a.de ruta b7a.de sil b4a.de staph b7a.de verat b7a.de

Stomach

- **fever**: ...
  - ⁝ **during** | **agg.**: agar bg2 ang bg2 arg-met bg2 **Ars** b4a.de* aur bg2 bell bg2 *Bry* b7.de* bufo bg2 calc bg2 *Caps* b7a.de* *Cham* b7.de* **Chin** b7.de* cic bg2 **Cina** b7.de* coff bg2 graph bg2 hell bg2 hyos bg2 ign bg2 lach bg2 lyc bg2 nat-m bg2 nux-m bg2 nux-v bg2 olnd bg2 op bg2 **Phos** b4.de* puls bg2 sabad bg2 sec bg2 sep bg2 spig bg2 stann bg2 staph bg2 sulph bg2 verat bg2
- **followed** by:
  - ⁝ **pain** | **Stomach**; in: mag-c h2*
- **full** of food; while stomach is: asar b7a.de staph b7a.de*
- **gastralgia**, in: *Lyc Sil*
- **headache**; with (See HEAD - Pain - accompanied - appetite)
- **lying** | **amel.**: sil h2
- **menopause**; during: sulph vh
- **menses**; before: mang b4.de
- **nausea**:
  - ⁝ **after**: bry
  - ⁝ **before**: mag-m h2
  - ⁝ **with** (See accompanied - nausea)
- **neuralgia**, with: *Dulc*
- **paroxysmal**: *Kola* stb3• tritic-vg fd5.de
- **perspiration**; with: agar h2 ars bg2 bry bg2 bufo bg2 **Calc** bg2 *Caps* bg2 cham bg2 *Chin* bg2 **Cina** bg2 cocc bg2 ign bg2 iod bg2 *Lyc* bg2 nux-v bg2 phos bg2* puls bg2 rhus-t bg2 ruta bg2 sabad bg2 **Sil** bg2 staph bg2 *Verat* bg2
- **sadness**; with (See MIND - Sadness - canine)
- **satiety**; easy: *Nat-m* b4.de zinc b4a.de
- **sleep**, prevents (See SLEEP - Sleeplessness - hunger)
- **stool** agg.; after: olnd mrr1 petr h2* sulph mrr1
- **walking** agg.: ant-t k* hell k* lyc k* phos
- **worms**; from: bar-c bg2 calc bg2 chin bg2 *Cina* bg2 graph bg2 lyc bg2 nat-m bg2 **Spig** bg2 sulph bg2

- **relish**, without: *Agar* allox tpw3 alum alum-p k2 alum-sil k2 ang st ant-c ars *Bar-c* bar-i bell borx *Bry* calad calc carb-v carbn-s caust cham *Chin* chinin-ar cic clem cocc coff colch cycl dig *Dulc* euphr *Ferr* ferr-ar ferr-i ferr-p hell hep ign iod kali-n *Kali-s* bg1* lac-del hm2• lach limen-b-c hm2* lyc mag-c *Mag-m* merc mez moni rfm1• nat-c **Nat-m** k* nauf-helv-li elm2• nicc nux-v **Olnd** k* **Op** k* phos plat *Puls* **Rheum** k* rhod **Rhus-t** k* ruta sabad *Sil* staph suis-em rly4• *Sul-ac* sul-i k2 sulph sumb thuj valer verat verb [tax jsj7]
  - **until** he begins to eat: chin **Lyc** nat-sil fd3.de• sabad vanil fd5.de
- **thirst**:
  - **with**: **Arg-n** vh galeoc-c-h gms1• graph vh *Kali-bi* a1 tarent tl1 verat tl1
  - **without**: **Arg-n** vh
- **wanting**: (↗*diminished*) *Abies-n* bro1 abrot k* absin acet-ac acetan vh1 *Acon* k* aegle-f bnj1 aesc aeth *Agar* k* agav-t jl1 aids nl2• ail alet bro1* alf bro1 *All-c* k* aloe *Alum* k* alum-p k2 am-c k* am-m k* ambr k* *Anac* k* androc srj1• ang b2.de* anh sp1 anil br1 *Ant-c* k* *Ant-i* c1 ant-t k* *Anthraci* apis k* apoc k2 aran mgm• arg-met k* *Arg-n* k* arist-cl mtf11 arizon-l nl2• *Arn* k* **Ars** k* ars-br vh ars-h ars-i k* arum-t asaf b2.de* **Asar** asc-t c1 aster aur k* aur-m **Bac** bn *Bapt* k* *Bar-c* k* bar-i *Bar-m* bar-s k2 bell k* ben *Berb* beryl tpw5* bism a1* *Bol-la* *Borx* k* *Bov* k* brach *Brom* b4a.de bros-gau mrc1 *Brucel* sa3• *Bry* k* but-ac bro1* *Cact* cadm-met tpw6 calad k* calam sa3• **Calc** k* *Calc-ar* calc-i k2 calc-p k* calc-s calc-sil k2 camph cann-s b2.de* canth k* caps k* *Carb-ac* k* *Carb-an* k* *Carb-v* k* carbn-s carc cd* *Card-m* k* cassia-s ccrh1• *Caust* k* cench k2 cephd-i bnj1 **Cham** k* **Chel** k* **Chin** k* chinin-ar k* chinin-s k* chion br1* chir-fl gya2 *Chlor* *Cic* k* cimic *Cina* k* cinnb clem b2.de* cob-n sp1 coca bro1 **Cocc** k* *Coff* k* *Colch* k* coloc k* *Con* k* convo-s sp1 cop cor-r cortico tpw7* croc b2.de* crot-t cund mtf11 cupr k* cupr-ar cupr-n a1 **Cycl** k* cypra-eg sde6.de• daph dig b2.de* diphtox jl2 dream-p sdj1• dros k* dulc k* echi echit a1 elat enteroc jl2 eup-per euph b2.de* euphr b2.de* falco-pe nl2• **Ferr** k* *Ferr-ar* *Ferr-i* ferr-p k* *Fl-ac* flor-p rsj3• galeg mtf11 gels gent-l bro1* glon glyc bro1 *Glycyr-g* cte1• gran *Granit-m* es1• graph k* *Guaj* k* guat sp1 gymno haliae-lc srj5• ham fd3.de• hed sp1 hell b2.de* hell-o a1* helo-s rwt2• helodr-cal knl2• helon bro1 *Hep* k* hir skp7• *Hydr* k* hydrc *Hydrog* srj2• hyos k* hyper *Ign* k* ind indg *Iod* k* *Ip* k* *Iris* k* ix bnm8• jatr-c jug-c jug-r kali-ar **Kali-bi** k* *Kali-br* kali-c k* kali-chl *Kali-i* kali-m k2 *Kali-n* k* kali-p *Kali-s* kali-sil k2 kola stb3• kreos k* lac-d c1* lac-f c1 lac-leo sk4• lach k* lact lap-la rsp1* lat-h bnm5• laur k* *Lec* k* led k* lil-t limest-b es1• lir-o mtf11 lob **Lyc** k* lyss m-ambo b2.de* m-arct b2.de* m-aust b2.de* *Mag-c* k* mag-m k* mag-s k* malar jl2 manc *Mang* k* med *Meph* *Merc* k* *Merc-c* k* merc-d bro1 *Mez* k* moni rfm1• mosch b2.de* *Mur-ac* k* muru a1 murx musca-d szs1 myric k* naja nat-ar nat-c k* nat-f sp1 **Nat-m** k* nat-ox rly4• nat-p nat-s nat-sil fd3.de• nicc k* nit-ac k* *Nux-m* k* **Nux-v** k* oci-sa sp1 olnd k* op k* osm ox-ac ozone sde2• parathyr jl2 *Petr* k* petr-ra shn4• *Ph-ac* k* **Phos** k* phyt pic-ac pip-m pisc mtf11 plat k* *Plb* k* *Podo* positr nl2• propr sa3• prun bro1 prun-v bro1 *Psor* ptel **Puls** k* ran-b b2.de* ran-s b2.de* raph k* rat rheum b2.de* rhod b2.de* **Rhus-t** k* ros-d wla1 *Ruta* b2.de* sabad k* *Sabin* k* sacch sst1• sal-al blc1• samb b7a.de* *Sang* k* *Sarr* sars b2.de* sec k* sel b2.de* senec *Seneg* k* **Sep** k* **Sil** k* sol-t-ae *Spig* k* spong b2.de* squil k* stann k* staph b2.de* stram k* stront-c k* stry-ar bro1 *Stry-p* bro1 *Sul-ac* k* sul-i k2 sulfa sp1 **Sulph** k* sumb sym-r bro1 symph fd3.de• *Syph* tab tarax bro1 tarent tell rsj10• tep *Ter* term-a bnj1 teucr b2.de* thal-xyz srj8• *Thuj* k* trios rsj11• tritic-vg fd5.de trom *Tub* jl2 tub-a vs* tub-m vn* upa urt-u v-a-b jl vac jl2* valer b2.de* vanad br1 vanil fd5.de verat k* verb b2.de* viol-t b2.de* vip xan yohim c1* zinc k* zing [bell-p-sp dcm1 heroin sdj2 **Spect** dfg1]
  - **morning**: abies-n k* absin a1 agar k* ail k* am-c b4a.de* ant-t k* arg-met h1 arg-n k* asc-t c1 bell k* benz-ac k* bov *Bry* b7a.de calc b4.de* canth b7.de* carb-v k* *Casc* hr1 cass a1 *Caust* k* chin chinin-ar chr-ac a1* cic k* coc-c k* cocc b7.de* con k* cycl k* dig h2 dios k* dor a1 ery-m a1 euph-a a1 euphr k* fago a1 falco-pe nl2• ferr b7a.de* *Ferr-m* galla-q-r nl2• *Guaj* b4a.de gymno ham a1 hydr k* hydrog srj2• ign ind k* kali-bi bg2 kali-p fd1.de• lach k* lec m-aust b7.de meph mez b4.de* myric k* narcot a1 nat-m b4.de* nat-sil fd3.de• nit-ac k* ost a1 petr-ra shn4• phos k* ptel k* rhus-g tmo3• sacch sst1• sang a1 sars k* sel k* *Seneg* k* *Sep* k* sil b4.de* spong fd4.de stram k* sulph k* symph fd3.de• tab k* tritic-vg fd5.de tub vanil fd5.de zinc h2* [heroin sdj2]
    - ⁝ **except** for breakfast: tarent-c br1
  - **noon**: agar k* anac k* ang k* ant-t hr1 arg-n k* borx b4a.de* carb-v h2 chel k* chin k* chlor a1 cic k* cimic hr1 clem k* cycl k* dream-p sdj1• ferr-p a1 grat k* ign sne laur b7.de* m-arct b7.de mang k* merc-sul a1 mosch b7.de* murx k* narcot a1 nat-c k* nit-ac a1 ol-j a1 ost a1 ox-ac k* petr-ra shn4• phos k* pic-ac k* ran-s b7.de* rhus-t k* ruta sabad b7.de* sars h2 spong fd4.de sulph k* sumb k* symph fd3.de• tritic-vg fd5.de vanil fd5.de zinc k* zinc-p k2 [bell-p-sp dcm1]
  - **afternoon**: propr sa3•
  - **evening**: aeth k* am-m k* arn k* ars h2 ars-s-f k2 borx k* bov bg2 brucel sa3• calc-ar hr1 canth b7.de* carb-v h2* cinnb k* clem k* coc-c k* coff b7.de* coloc k* croc b7.de* cupr k* cycl k* dig h2 falco-pe nl2• ferr-p a1 galeoc-c-h gms1• graph k* grat bg2 ham fd3.de• hyper k* lyss c1 mag-m h2 merc k* murx narcot a1 nat-c h2 nat-m k* ox-ac k* pip-m a1 ran-s k* rhus-t b7.de* ruta fd4.de senec k* sil h2 *Stann* b4a.de sulph k* tarent bg2 tritic-vg fd5.de zinc h2
  - **night**:
    - ⁝ **midnight**:
      - ⁝ **before** | **22 h**: brucel sa3•
  - **accompanied** by:
    - ⁝ **emptiness**: tub jl2
    - ⁝ **hemorrhoids** (See RECTUM - Hemorrhoids - accompanied - appetite)
    - ⁝ **nausea**: *Ant-c* b7a.de beryl tpw5 *Con* b4a.de cupr b7a.de dig b4.de* *Hell* b7a.de *Laur* b7a.de pycnop-sa mrz1
    - ⁝ **Abdomen**; pain in: hir skp7•
    - ⁝ **Brain**; complaints of (See HEAD - Brain; complaints of - accompanied - appetite)
    - ⁝ **Head**; complaints of (See HEAD - Complaints - accompanied - appetite - wanting)
    - ⁝ **Mouth**; bad taste in: myric ptk1
    - ⁝ **Throat** | **fullness**: *Phos* b4a.de
  - **alternating** with:
    - ⁝ **appetite**; ravenous (See ravenous - alternating - loss)
    - ⁝ **hunger** (See increased - alternating - loss)
  - **children**; in: lyc mtf33
    - ⁝ **newborns**: lyc mtf33
  - **chill**; during: alum bg2 anac b4.de* *Ant-c* bg2 ant-t bg2 apis bg2 arn bg2 *Ars* bg2 bry b7.de* canth bg2 cham bg2 chin bg2 *Con* bg2 hep b4a.de* ign bg2 *Ip* bg2 kali-c bg2 lach bg2 led bg2 merc-c b4a.de mez bg2 nat-m bg2

- **chill**; during: ...
nux-m b7.de* *Nux-v* bg2 *Phos* b4.de* puls b7a.de* rheum bg2 rhus-t bg2 **Sabad** b7a.de* sep bg2 **Sil** b4.de* staph bg2
- **chronic**: syph ptk1
- **coition**; after: *Agar* k*
- **coryza**; during: phos b4.de* *Puls* b7a.de
- **cough** agg.; during: bell b4a.de con b4a.de dulc b4a.de
- **diseases**:
  - **acute** disease; after: psor al1
  - **severe** disease; after: ant-c ptk1 psor ptk1
- **drinking**:
  - **after**:
    - **agg.**: kali-m ptk1
    - **water** | **agg.**: kali-m br1*
- **dryness** in mouth; after a sensation of: cic c1
- **eating**: (↗*food)*
  - **after** eating the appetite returns: cham h1
    - **mouthful**; eating a: anac *Calc* k* **Chin** k* mag-c *Sabad* k*
  - **attempting** to eat; on: (↗*Loathing - eat on; GENERALS - Food and - food - aversion - eating - attempting)* caust ptk1 cycl ptk1 lyc ptk1 petr-ra shn4• plat ptk1 prun ptk1 rheum ptk1* *Sil* k*
  - **before**: musca-d szs1
  - **suddenly**: bar-c ptk1
- **exertion** agg.; after: *Calc* k*
- **fever**:
  - **before**: ant-c b7a.de chin b7a.de puls b7a.de rhus-t b7a.de
  - **during** | **agg.**: alum b4.de* anac b4.de* **Ant-c** b7.de* ant-t b7.de* *Apis* b7a.de* arn bg2 **Ars** b4a.de* bar-c bg2 bell bg2 bry bg2 calc bg2 *Canth* b7.de* **Chin** b7.de* cic bg2 cocc bg2 *Con* b4.de* cycl bg2 ign bg2 **Ip** b7a.de* *Kali-c* b4.de* lach bg2 merc bg2 mez bg2 nat-m bg2 **Nux-v** b7a.de* op bg2 phos b4.de* plat bg2 **Puls** b7a.de* rheum bg2 rhus-t bg2 ruta bg2 *Sabad* b7a.de* *Sep* b4.de* *Sil* b4.de* staph b7.de* sulph bg2 thuj bg2
- **food**: (↗*eating)*
  - **sight** of; at: alum ars tl1 beryl tpw5 caust k* cocc tl1 *Colch* k* *Crot-c* kali-p k* merc-i-f nux-v h1 *Phos* k* sep tl1 **Sulph** k* tritic-vg fd5.de tub jl2 *Vac* jl2
    - **pregnancy** agg.; during: caust ptk1
  - **smell** of: ars tl1 beryl tpw5 carb-an caust k* cocc tl1 **Colch** k* ip mrr1 nux-v h1 sep tl1 tub jl2 *Vac* jl2
    - **pregnancy** agg.; during: caust ptk1
  - **thought** of: ars tl1 caust tl1 cocc tl1 colch tl1 sep tl1
    - **appetite** returns after thinking of food: calc-p k*
- **fullness**; from sense of: *Chin* lyc k2 petr-ra shn4• phos rhus-t squil h1
- **habitual**: kali-m ptk1
- **headache**; during: *Ant-c* vh1 [bell-p-sp dcm1]
- **hunger**; with: act-sp k* *Agar* k* *Alum* k* ang b2.de* ant-c b2.de* ant-t b2.de* arg-met b2.de* *Ars* k* bamb-a stb2.de• *Bar-c* k* bell b2.de* bit-ar wht1• *Borx* b2.de* bry k* calad b2.de* calc b2.de* canth b2.de* carb-v b2.de* carbn-s hr1 caust b2.de* *Chin* k* *Chinin-s* cic b2.de* clem b2.de* **Cocc** k* coff b2.de* colch b2.de* coloc b2.de* cycl b2.de* dig b2.de* dream-p sdj1• dros b7.de* *Dulc* k* ephe-si hsj1• euphr b2.de* ferr b2.de* granit-m es1• *Hell* k* hep b2.de* hir skp7• hydrog srj2• ign b2.de* iod b2.de* *Kali-n* k* **Lach** st *Lyc* b2.de* m-ambo b2.de* mag-c b2.de* *Mag-m* b2.de* merc b2.de* mez b2.de* nat-c b2.de* **Nat-m** k* nicc **Nux-v** k* olib-sac wmh1 olnd k* op k* *Phos* plat b2.de* positr nl2• psor k* *Puls* b2.de* rheum b2.de* rhod b2.de* *Rhus-t* k* ruta b2.de* sabad k* sang tl1 *Sil* k* staph b2.de* *Sul-ac* k* *Sulph* k* tax thuj b2.de* *Tub* valer b2.de* verat b2.de* verb k*
- **lifting** agg.: sep ptk1
- **menses**:
  - **after** | **agg.**: calc-p bg2 ust bg2
  - **before** | **agg.**: am-c k* ars bg2 bell k* brom b4a.de* calc-p k* ign k* lac-c bg2 mag-c bg2 phos bg2 puls b7a.de

Appetite – wanting – menses: ...
  - **during** | **agg.**: alet bg2 aloe bg2 am-c b4.de* ammc k* bell bg2 brom k* bry bg2 calc bg2 calc-p k* cupr k* cycl k* goss graph bg2 *Ign* k* kali-bi bg2 *Kreos* b7a.de lac-c bg2 lach bg2 lyc k* mag-c k* nat-m bg2 plat bg2 puls k*
  - **suppressed** menses; during: *Cycl* btw1*
- **perspiration**; during: alum bg2 anac bg2 *Ant-c* bg2 ant-t bg2 apis bg2 ars bg2 canth bg2 **Chin** bg2 *Con* bg2 cycl bg2 *Ip* bg2 *Kali-c* bg2 **Nux-v** bg2 phos bg2 puls bg2 rheum bg2 **Rhus-t** bg2 sabad bg2 **Samb** b7a.de* **Sep** bg2 *Sil* bg2 staph bg2 *Stram* b7.de* sulph bg2 thuj bg2 verat bg2
- **returns**:
  - **eating**; after (See eating - after)
  - **thinking** of food; after (See food - thought - appetite)
- **sadness**; from: plat k*
- **satiety**; sensation of: arn b7.de* bar-c b4.de* carb-an b4.de* cham b7.de* **Chin** b7.de* *Cic* b7.de* cina bg2 clem b4.de* *Cycl* b7.de* ferr b7.de* ign b7.de* lyc b4.de* m-aust b7.de mag-c bg2 mang b4.de* nat-m b4.de* nit-ac b4.de* nux-v b7.de* rheum b7.de* rhus-t b7.de* ruta b7a.de* sep b4.de*
- **shivering**; during: alum b4.de led b7.de
- **smoking** agg.: bell h1 sep ptk1
- **stool** agg.; during: nux-m b7a.de*
- **thirst**:
  - **with**: aeth hr1 am-c k* ant-t k* arizon-l nl2• ars k* bism a1 borx *Brucel* sa3• *Calc* k* caust bg2 *Colch* coloc dig ptk1 dream-p sdj1• dulc fd4.de *Ferr* hr1 galeoc-c-h gms1• granit-m es1• *Kali-n* k* kreos k* lyc h2* mag-c h2 *Nit-ac* b4a.de nux-v k* ox-ac petr-ra shn4• *Phos* k* plb btw2* *Psor* k* rhus-t k* seneg k* sep k* sil k* *Spig* k* **SULPH** k •* zinc k* zinc-p k2
  - **without**: apis ptk1 *Arg-n* k2
- **vexation**; after: nat-m petr phos ruta fd4.de sulph dgt
- **weather**; in foggy: **Chin**
- **weeping**; from: cocc a1* hydrog srj2•

○ • **Palate** and throat; felt in: rhus-t b7.de*

- **without** (See wanting)

APPREHENSION in: (↗*MIND - Clairvoyance; MIND - Excitement; MIND - Fear - happen; MIND - Fear - stomach - arising)* asaf *Aur* both-ax tsm2 bry calc *Cann-s* canth chord-umb rly4• *Dig* k* hydrog srj2• kali-bi gk *Kali-c* k* *Lyc* **Mez** k* *Phos* thuj
- **mounting** to head and back again: thuj

APPROACHED agg.; being: lyc bg2

ATONY (See Hanging)

ATROPHY: bell bg2 bism ptk1 calc-ar bg2 kreos ptk1 nux-v bg2 ox-ac ptk1

○ - **Epigastrium**: bell bg2 calc-ar bg2 nux-v bg2

AURA EPILEPTICA felt at solar plexus (See Epileptic)

AVERSION (See GENERALS - Food)

BALANCED up and down, as if stomach were: ph-ac

BALL; sensation of a: abies-n ptk1 androc srj1• arn ptk1 *Bell* k* bov ptk1 coc-c k* con bg2 ham fd3.de• kali-bi bg2 lach k* lob ptk1 marb-w es1• nux-m ptk1 osm ptk1 plb bg2 *Puls* ptk1 sanic ptk1 senec k* tong a1 [heroin sdj2 nicc stj1]
- **night** | **lying** down agg.: marb-w es1•
- **burning**: *Bell* k* kola stb3•
- **rising** up into throat: (↗*THROAT - Lump - rising)* asaf rb2* caust br1 kali-ar rb2 *Lach* lyc c1 lyss rb2 *Mag-m* hr1* *Senec* k*
  - **afternoon**: senec c1
- **rolling** in: arn bg2* grat bg2 lil-t bg2* nat-s bg2 phos ptk1

○ - **Epigastrium**: acon bg2 arn bg2 con bg2 nux-m bg2 plb bg2 ter bg2

BAR: | **over** stomach; bar laid: *Haem* vh *Ric* vh

BEANS and peas: | **agg.**: *Lyc* b4.de*

BEER agg.: acon bg2 *Ars* b4a.de ferr bg2 mez bg2

Stomach

BELCHING (See Eructations)

BENDING:
- **backward**:
  - **agg.**: *Ars* b4a.de *Ign* b7a.de
  - **amel.**: bell b4.de* bism bg2* caust b4a.de chel bg2 *Kali-c* b4a.de
- **forward**:
  - **agg.**: lyc bg2 merc b4.de*
  - **amel.**: bry bg2 mag-m bg2 phos bg2

BENDING DOUBLE:
- **agg.**: bry bg2
- **amel.**: *Carb-v* b4.de* cham bg2 coloc b4.de* merc-c b4a.de

BITTER in stomach; sensation of something: cupr b7a.de*

BLOOD; orgasms of:
O - **Epigastrium** | **extending** to head: calc bg2

BLOW; from a: *Arn* b7a.de *Bry* b7a.de

BLOWING the nose agg.: kali-n b4.de*

BLOWS in pit of stomach, sensation of: *Cic* h1* crot-c nat-c nux-v plat

BRANDY agg.: *Ign* b7a.de **Nux-v** b7a.de

BREAD:
- **agg.**: bell bg2 bry b7a.de* *Caust* b4.de* chin bg2 kali-c b4.de* merc b4.de* nit-ac bg2 plat b4.de* *Puls* b7a.de rhus-t b7a.de* *Ruta* b7a.de sars b4.de* sep b4.de* sul-ac b4a.de zinc b4a.de*
- **amel.**: laur b7.de* nat-c b4.de*

BREAKFAST:
- **after**:
  - **agg.**: am-m b7.de* bell bg2 bov bg2 cham bg2 colch bg2 daph bg2 hyper bg2 kali-n b4.de* nux-m b7.de* plb b7.de* zinc bg2
  - **amel.**: am-m b7.de* mag-m b4.de*
- **before** | **agg.**: iris bg2

BREATHING:
- **agg.**: anac b4.de* caps b7.de* cham b7a.de cocc bg2 euphr b7.de* kali-n b4.de* merc b4.de* rhus-t b7.de* sulph b4a.de
- **deep**:
  - **agg.**: arg-n bg2* *Asaf* b7a.de bar-c b4.de caps b7.de* carb-an b4a.de caust bg2* dros b7.de* puls ptk1 zinc bg2
  - **amel.**: bar-c bg2 rumx ptk1 ter bg2
- **holding** breath | **amel.**: bell b4.de*

BUBBLES were bursting in stomach; sensation as if: phos b4a.de

BUBBLING: cartl-s rly4• caust k* gard-j vlr2• kali-c bg2 lyss k* phos h2 plat bg2 sacch-a fd2.de• tere-la rly4•
O - **Pit** of stomach: rheum h1
O • **Below**: sabin a1*

BUTTER agg.: *Puls* b7a.de

CAKES agg.: cycl bg2

CANCER: *(↗Ulcers - malignant)* *Acet-ac* k* act-sp c2* am-m br1* ant-s-aur gm1 arg-n bg2* **Ars** k* *Ars-i* ars-s-f gm1 ars-s-r gm1 aur ks aur-m-n sne bar-c k* bell k* **Bism** k* bism-sn mtf11 brom sne bry sne bufo sne cadm-act gm1 cadm-ar sne* cadm-br gm1 cadm-chl gm1 cadm-f gm1 cadm-gl gm1 cadm-i gm1 cadm-m gm1 cadm-met gm1 cadm-n gm1 cadm-o gm1 cadm-p gm1 *Cadm-s* k* cadm-sel gm1 calc-f bro1 calen gm1 *Caps* **Carb-ac** k* **Carb-an** k* *Carb-v* k* carc-st mtf carc-st-ad mtf carc-st-sc mtf chel gm1 coloc sne **Con** k* *Crot-h* k* **Cund** k* dulc k2 form-ac bro1 ger sne graph bro1* helic-p mtf *Hydr* k* *Iris* kali-bi k2* kali-c bro1 kali-m mtf11 kali-perm mtf11 kali-s k2 *Kreos* k* *Lach* k* lob-e mtf11 **Lyc** k* mag-p c2* *Merc-c* k* *Mez* k* *Nat-m* b4a.de nep mtf11 nux-v k* orni c* **Phos** k* plat k* plat-m c2 plb bro1 polyg-h mtf11 sec c1* *Sep* *Sil* k* *Staph* k* *Sulph* k* *Thuj* b4a.de* uva mtf11 verat b7a.de*
- **accompanied** by:
  - **hiccough**: *Carb-an* st1
  - **vomiting** blood: calen gm1
  - **vomiting**; persistent: cadm-s br1 carb-ac bro1 kreos bro1

Cancer: ...
- **aluminium** poisoning; from: *(↗GENERALS - Aluminium)* **Cadm-met** gm1

O - **Pylorus**: *(↗Ulcers - pylorus - malignant)* acet-ac ptk1 bry sne *Carb-an* sne graph br1* iris c1 orni tl1 *Sulph* sne

CARDIALGIA (See Heartburn)

CARES; from: *Ign* b7a.de

CARRYING agg.: cadm-s ptk1

CATARRH: abies-c br1* abies-n bro1 alum k2* anis bro1 ant-c bro1* *Ant-t* bro1 *Arg-n* bro1 arn bro1 ars bg2* bals-p bro1 *Bell* bg2 *Bism* bro1 calc bro1 calc-chln bro1 *Caps* bg2* carb-ac bro1 carb-an bg2 carb-v k2* cham bg2 chel tl1 **Chin** bg2* cina bg2 *Colch* bro1 coll bro1 cory br1* dig bro1 dulc bg2 eucal br1 ger bro1 *Graph* bro1 grat k2 hydr br1* hydr-ac bro1 iod bro1 *Ip* bg2* kali-bi k2* kali-c bro1 lyc bro1 mag-c br1 **Merc** bg2 *Merc-c* bro1 nit-ac k2 nit-m-ac br1 *Nux-v* bg2* op bro1 ox-ac bro1 petr bg2* *Phos* bro1 plb k2 podo bro1 **Puls** bg2* rheum bg2 rhus-t bg2 rumx k2* sang k2* sep bro1 sil bro1 spig bg2 **Sulph** bg2* verat bg2* zinc bro1
- **accompanied** by:

O • **Skin**; yellow discoloration of the (See SKIN - Discoloration - yellow - accompanied - catarrh)
  - **Tongue**; white discoloration of the | **heavily** coated: *Dulc* kr1*
- **chilling** stomach with ice water when heated; from: acon tl1 ars tl1
- **chronic**: *Coll* br1 cund br1 euon-a br1
- **drunkards**; in: anis br1 sang mtf11
- **portal** congestion; from: coll br1
- **purulent**: anis br1

CHAMOMILE; after abuse of: bell bg2 ign bg2 *Nux-v* bg2 **Puls** bg2

CHILDREN; complaints of: *Bell* bg2 **Bry** bg2 calc bg2 hyos bg2 **Ip** bg2 lyc bg2 mag-c bg2 **Merc** bg2 *Nux-v* bg2 *Puls* bg2 sulph bg2
- **infants**: bar-c bg2 *Bell* bg2 calc bg2 *Cham* bg2 hyos bg2 **Ip** bg2 lyc bg2 mag-c bg2 *Merc* bg2 **Nux-v** bg2 **Puls** bg2 rheum bg2 sulph bg2

CHILL:
- **during**: am-c b4.de *Ant-c* bro1 arg-n bro1 ars bro1 bol-la bro1 *Bry* b7.de canch bro1 eup-per bro1 *Ip* bro1 lyc bro1 *Nux-v* bro1 puls bro1 sil b4.de sulph b4.de

O - **Epigastrium**: ant-t bg2 arn bg2 ars bg2 bar-c bg2 *Bell* b4.de* camph bg2 caust bg2 *Colch* bg2 ign bg2 *Ip* bg2 laur bg2 nat-m bg2 nux-v bg2 phos bg2 spig bg2 spong bg2

▽ • **extending** to | **Back**: sulph bg2

CHILLINESS; feeling of: arg-n bg2 colch b7.de* *Ip* b7.de* lyc bg2 **Puls** bg2 sul-ac bg2
O - **Epigastrium**: *Alum* b4a.de *Bell* b4a.de caust bg2 spig b7.de

CHOKING sensation: nux-v b7a.de
O - **Epigastrium**: cann-s b7.de* puls b7.de*

CLAWING in (See Pain - clawing)

CLOTHES AGG.; TIGHT: *Am-c* b4a.de am-m bg2 bell bg2 **Bry** bg2 *Calc* bg2 carb-v bg2 *Caust* b4a.de* coff b7.de* con bg2 *Hep* b4a.de* kali-bi bg2 kreos bg2 *Lach* bg2 *Lyc* b4a.de* **Nux-v** b7.de* phos bg2 sars bg2 *Spig* bg2 spong b7.de* *Sulph* bg2
O - **Epigastrium**: *Bry* b7a.de caps b7a.de *Coff* b7a.de *Ign* b7a.de kreos b7a.de **Nux-v** b7a.de *Spong* b7a.de

CLOTHING:
- **disturbs**: am-c k* benz-ac a1 **Bov** *Bry* *Calc* k* carb-v caust k* *Chin* coff *Crot-c* *Crot-h* cupr gins k* *Graph* k* *Hep* k* ignis-alc es2• *Kali-bi* kreos **Lach** k* lith-c **Lyc** k* lyss c1 *Nat-s* **Nux-v** *Petr* *Ph-ac* phos xyz61 *Puls* rumx k2 *Sep* b4a.de* spong sulph thuj a1
- **loosening** | **amel.**: *Bry* b7a.de caps b7.de* coff b7.de* hep b4.de* nux-v b7.de*
- **tight** clothes: | **amel.**: *(↗Pain - tightening)* fl-ac ptk2
- **tightening** amel.: nat-m bg2

CLUCKING: am-c h2 anac h2 carb-an h2 mag-m h2 phos h2 rheum h
- **eating**; after: sacch-a fd2.de• zinc h2

O - **Pit** of stomach: rheum h1

COFFEE:
- **abuse** of | **agg.**: **Cham** bg2 cocc bg2 *Ign* bg2 merc bg2 **Nux-v** bg2 puls bg2 rhus-t bg2 sulph bg2

- **agg.**: canth b7.de* caps bg2 **Cham** b7.de* *Cocc* b7.de* ign b7.de* **Nux-v** b7.de* puls b7.de*
- **amel.**: canth b7.de* *Cham* b7.de* chel bg2 coloc bg2 mag-c bg2 *Puls* b7a.de

COLD:
- **air** | **abdomen** agg.; on: caust bg2
- **drinks**:
  - **agg.**: ars bg2 calc bg2 ferr bg2 iris bg2 kali-c b4.de* kali-i bg2 lept bg2 mag-p bg2 *Nat-c* b4.de* *Nux-v* b7a.de phos bg2 rhod b4.de* sil b4a.de sul-ac b4a.de*
    - **icy** cold: caust ptk1
  - **amel.**: canth b7.de* *Carb-v* b4a.de caust bg2 *Phos* b4a.de*
- **food**:
  - **agg.**: arg-n bg2 **Ars** b4a.de* carb-v bg2 caust b4a.de kali-c b4.de* *Puls* b7a.de*
  - **amel.**: phos bg2
- **fruit** | **agg.**: *Ars* b4a.de *Carb-v* b4a.de
- **sensation** of | **Stomach**; of: cann-s b7.de*

COLD; AFTER TAKING A: acon b7.de* **Ars** b4a.de* bell bg2 bry b7.de* calc b4a.de carb-v bg2 caust b4a.de* cham b7.de* *Cocc* bg2 dulc bg2 *Ip* bg2 lyc b4a.de* *Nux-v* b7.de* **Puls** b7.de* rhus-t b7.de* sep bg2 *Sul-ac* b4a.de* *Verat* b7.de*

COLDNESS: abrot k* absin k* acon agar k* alum k* alum-p k2 *Am-br* k* am-c k* *Ambr* k* amph a1 arg-n k* **Ars** k* ars-s-f k2* arund k* bar-c k* bar-s k2 *Bell* k* berb k* bol-la bov k* cadm-s cain *Calc* k* calc-sil k2* **Camph** k* cann-i a1 cann-s k* **Caps** k* *Carb-an* k* *Carb-v* k* carbn-s *Castm* cham k* chel k* **Chin** k* chinin-ar chinin-s vh *Cist* k* clem k* coc-c k* cocc tl1 *Colch* k* coloc k* con k* crot-c k* crot-h k* elaps k* germ-met srj5• graph k* grat k* helon k* **Hep** xyz61 *Hipp* k* ign k* kali-ar *Kali-bi* k* kali-c k* kali-i k* kali-n k* kali-p kali-s kali-sil k2 *Kreos* k* *Lach* k* *Lact* k* laur k* lepi a1 lyc ptk1 lyss mag-c k* mag-m h2 mag-s k* meny bro1* *Nat-m* k* nit-ac k* nux-m bg2 ol-an k* op k* ox-ac bro1 *Petr* k* ph-ac k* *Phos* k* phyt k* podo fd3.de• pyrus bro1 rhus-t k* sabad k* sec k* sep k* *Sil* spig k* spong k* *Sul-ac* k* sulph k* tab k* *Tarax* tub jl2 verat k* verin a1 vesp k* zinc b4.de*
- **morning** | **bed** agg.; in: bov con k* mag-s k*
- **forenoon**: nat-m k*
  - **eructations**, during and after: alum k*
  - **riding** agg.: (non:puls slp) puls-n slp
- **noon**: zinc k*
- **evening**: alum k* nat-m k*
  - **bed**; in | **amel.**: kali-n h2
- **accompanied** by | **pain**; burning (See Pain - burning - accompanied - coldness)
- **alternating** with | **heat** of stomach (See Heat - alternating - coldness)
- **chilliness** in pit of: **Ars** bell calc cinch rb2 cist hipp
- **cold** drinks agg.; after: *Ars* caps k2 **Chin** k* **Elaps** k* irid-met srj5• *Rhus-t* *Sul-ac*
- **diarrhea**; during: nat-m ptel
- **eating** | **after** | **agg.**: *Carb-an* *Cist* k* *Crot-c* k* graph bg1 nit-ac k*
  - **before** | **agg.**: *Cist* k*
- **fruit** agg.: *Ars* elaps k*
- **heat**; after: grat k*
- **hot** food amel.: germ-met srj5•
- **ice** cream agg.: chinin-s
- **ice**, with pain; like: *Bov* a1 caust bg1 *Colch* ol-an bg1
  - **cold** drinks agg.; after: **Elaps**
- **icy**: acon ptk1 bov bg2 **Caps** k* caust bg2* *Colch* k* elaps bg2 *Hipp* k* kola stb3• kreos br1 lachn bg1 lact ol-an bg2 *Phos* k*
  - **accompanied** by | **perspiration**: zinc-i ptk1
  - **lump**; as from: bov ptk1 kola stb3•
  - **painful**: colch ptk1 kola stb3• lac-h sze9•
  - **rubbing** | **amel.**: carb-an ptk1
  - ▽ **extending** to | **Esophagus**: meny ptk1
- **loosening** clothing amel.: chinin-s
- **menses**; after: kali-c b4.de*

Coldness: ...
- **sensation** of: acon b7.de* alum bg2 am-c bg2 ant-t bg2 **Ars** b4a.de* bar-c bg2 bov b4a.de* camph bg2 *Caps* b7.de* carb-an bg2 chel b7.de* chin b7.de* cist bg2 **Colch** b7.de* *Con* b4a.de* elaps bg2 graph bg2 ign bg2 **Ip** b7a.de* iris bg2 *Kali-n* b4a.de* kreos bg2 *Lach* b7a.de* laur b7.de* mag-c bg2 mag-m bg2 mez b4.de* nat-m bg2 nit-ac bg2 nux-v bg2 petr bg2 ph-ac bg2 *Phos* b4a.de* polyg-h bg2 *Puls* b7a.de* rhus-t b7a.de* sabad b7a.de* sec bg2 spig bg2 spong bg2 sul-ac bg2 *Sulph* bg2 verat b7.de* zinc bg2
  - ○ **Epigastrium**: ant-t b7.de camph b7.de ign b7a.de laur b7a.de nux-v b7a.de spong b7.de*
- **stone**, as of a cold: acon bg1
- **warm** drinks agg.: sec a1
- **water**:
  - **drinking** agg.; after: sul-ac mrr1
  - **sensation** as from cold water: caps ptk1 grat ptk1
- ▽ **extending** to:
  - ○ **Body**: sec
  - **Esophagus**: meny br1 podo fd3.de•
- ○ **Cardiac** opening: kreos bg2
- **Epigastrium**: ant-t bg2 ars b4a.de* *Bell* bg2 berb bg2 bov bg2 camph bg2* caust b4.de* colch bg2 elaps bg2 hep ptk1 ign bg2 kreos ptk1 laur bg2 nat-m b4.de* nux-v bg2 phos b4a.de* sil bg2 spig bg2 spong bg2
- **Pit** of stomach | **burning** pain in stomach; after (See Pain - burning - followed - pit)

COMPLAINTS of the stomach: *Abies-c* br1 abies-n br1 *Acon* b2.de* aeth ptk1 agar b2.de* agn b2.de* alum b2.de* am-c b2.de* am-m b2.de* ambr b2.de* anac b2.de* ang b2.de* anil br1 *Ant-c* b2.de* ant-t b2.de* anth br1 arg-met b2.de* arg-n ptk1 arn b2.de* **Ars** b2.de* asaf b2.de* asar b2.de* ast-a bta1• aur b2.de* *Bar-c* b2.de* **Bell** b2.de* bid-p bta1• bism b2.de* bop-sc bta1• borx b2.de* bov b2.de* **Bry** b2.de* *Cadm-s* br1 calad b2.de* **Calc** b2.de* camph b2.de* cann-s b2.de* canth b2.de* caps b2.de* carb-ac br1 carb-an b2.de* **Carb-v** b2.de* *Caust* b2.de* certhec-t bta1• **Cham** b2.de* cheir c1 chel b2.de* *Chin* b2.de* cic b2.de* cina b2.de* *Cocc* b2.de* coff b2.de* colch b2.de* coloc b2.de* **Con** b2.de* croc b2.de* **Cupr** b2.de* cycl b2.de* dig b2.de* dros b2.de* dulc b2.de* eucl-l bta1• *Eup-per* br1 euph b2.de* ferr b2.de* *Ferr-p* mrr1 gent-l br1 graph b2.de* grat bg2 guaj b2.de* helia br1 *Hell* b2.de* hep b2.de* **Hyos** b2.de* **Ign** b2.de* iod b2.de* ip b2.de* ipom-p bta1• iris br1 kali-bi br1 *Kali-c* b2.de* kali-n b2.de* kreos b2.de* lach b2.de* laur b2.de* led b2.de* lina br1 lob br1 luf-s bta1• *Lyc* b2.de* m-ambo b2.de m-arct b2.de mag-c b2.de* mag-m b2.de* maland jl2 malar jl2 mang b2.de* meny b2.de* **Merc** b2.de* mez b2.de* micr br1 mom-in bta1• mosch b2.de* moscho-r bta1• mur-ac b2.de* *Nat-c* b2.de* *Nat-m* b2.de* nit-ac b2.de* nux-m b2.de* **Nux-v** b2.de* olnd b2.de* op b2.de* osteos-n bta1• othon-n bta1• par b2.de* petr b2.de* ph-ac b2.de* **Phos** b2.de* plat b2.de* plb b2.de* plect-v bta1• *Ptel* br1 **Puls** b2.de* ran-b b2.de* ran-s b2.de* rheum b2.de* rhod b2.de* *Rhus-t* b2.de* roye-v bta1• *Ruta* b2.de* sabad b2.de* sabal br1 sabin b2.de* samb b2.de* sars b2.de* sec b2.de* seneg b2.de* *Sep* b2.de* *Sil* b2.de* skat br1 spig b2.de* spong b2.de* squil b2.de* *Stann* b2.de* staph b2.de* stram b2.de* streptoc jl2 stront-c b2.de* strych-h bta1• *Sul-ac* b2.de* **Sulph** b2.de* sym-r br1 teucr b2.de* thuj b2.de* trichil-e bta1• trimer-a bta1• tur-o bta1• valer b2.de* **Verat** b2.de* verb b2.de* vern-w bta1• wede-n bta1• zanthox-c bta1• zinc b2.de* [*Am-br* stj2 *Ant-m* stj2 *Ant-met* stj2 bell-p-sp dcm1]
- **left**:
  - ▽ **extending** to | **right**: sulph bg2
- **accompanied** by:
  - **appetite**:
    - **increased**: *Aur* b4a.de *Coloc* b4a.de *Graph* b4a.de *Merc* b4a.de *Stann* b4a.de *Verat* b7a.de
    - **ravenous**: *Stann* b4a.de
  - **coldness** of body: m-ambo b7a.de
  - **constipation** (See RECTUM - Constipation - accompanied - stomach)
  - **cough**: kali-bi bg2 nat-m bg2 ph-ac bg2 phos bg2 puls bg2 rumx bg2 sul-ac bg2
  - **eczema**: ant-c br1* iris c1 lyc bro1*
  - **eructations**: *Ars* b4a.de* grat bg2 lach b7a.de* *Mag-c* bg2 nux-v bg2 *Stann* bg2
    - **acrid**: *Ars* b4a.de
    - **bitter**: *Ars* b4a.de *Stann* b4a.de

Stomach

- **eructations**: ...
  - ⁝ **inclination** to: cocc b7.de*
  - ⁝ **ineffectual**: ign b7.de*
  - ⁝ **sour**: *Mag-c* b4a.de
- **flatulence**: *Carb-v* b4a.de* *Lach* bg2
- **gout**: *Ant-c* k* ant-t br1
- **herpes** zoster (See SKIN - Eruptions - herpes - accompanied - stomach)
- **hiccough**: *Kali-bi* st1
- **menses**:
  - ⁝ **disordered** (See FEMALE - Menses - disordered - accompanied - stomach)
  - ⁝ **profuse**: calc bg2 lyc bg2
  - ⁝ **scanty**: cocc bg2 puls bg2
- **mental** symptoms (See MIND - Mental symptoms - accompanied - stomach)
- **nausea**: *Am-c* b4a.de ant-t b7.de* calad b7.de* *Dig* b4a.de *Graph* b4a.de *Ip* b7a.de *Nat-m* b4a.de *Nux-v* b7a.de *Puls* b7a.de *Rhod* b4a.de sec b7.de* *Stann* b4a.de verat b7.de* *Zinc* b4a.de
- **palpitations**: abies-c bro1 *Arg-n* bro1 *Cact* bro1 *Carb-v* bro1 hydr-ac bro1 lyc bro1 *Nat-m* bro1 nux-v bg2* *Puls* bro1 sep bro1 *Spig* bro1 tab bro1
- **portal** congestion (See ABDOMEN - Portal - accompanied - stomach)
- **respiration**; complaints of (See RESPIRATION - Complaints - accompanied - stomach)
- **retching**: lach bg2 nux-v bg2
- **salivation**: caps bg2 *Kali-bi* kr1*
- **sexual** desire; increased: gamb mrr1 *Grat* mrr1 lyc mrr1 nux-v mrr1
- **sleepiness**: aeth bro1 ant-c bro1 bism bro1 *Carb-v* bro1 *Chin* bro1 *Epiph* bro1 *Fel* bro1 graph bro1 grat bro1 kali-c bro1 *Lyc* bro1 *Nat-ch* bro1 *Nat-m* bro1 *Nux-m* bro1 nux-v bro1 *Ph-ac* b4a.de* phos bro1 sarr bro1 staph bro1 sulph bro1
- **suicidal** disposition; with (See MIND - Suicidal - stomach)
- **taste**; bitter: *Lyc* b4a.de
- **thirst**: *Anac* b4a.de *Ant-c* b7a.de
- **typhoid** fever: *Bry* bro1 canth bro1 carb-v bro1 *Hydr* bro1 merc bro1 nux-v bro1 puls bro1
- **vomiting** (See Vomiting - accompanied - stomach - complaints)
- **waking**; frequent: alum bg2 am-c b4.de* bar-c b4.de* calc b4.de* carb-v b4.de* caust b4.de* graph b4.de* kali-c b4.de* mag-c b4.de* merc-c b4a.de nat-c b4.de* nat-m b4.de* nit-ac b4.de* petr b4.de* phos b4.de* seneg bg2 sep b4.de* sil b4.de* sulph b4.de* valer bg2
- **weakness**: *Asaf* b7a.de cadm-s mrr1
  - ⁝ **nervous** (See GENERALS - Weakness - nervous - accompanied - stomach)
- ○ **Abdomen**; cramping pain in (See ABDOMEN - Pain - cramping - accompanied - stomach)
- **Back**:
  - ⁝ **complaints** of: bism bg2 tab bg2
  - ⁝ **pain**: *Arn* b7a.de
- **Chest**:
  - ⁝ **oppression**: **Lyc** b4a.de nux-v b7a.de
  - ⁝ **pain**: *Arn* b7a.de
- **Eyes**; complaints of (See EYE - Complaints - accompanied - stomach)
- **Face**:
  - ⁝ **pale**: *Cann-s* b7a.de* m-ambo b7a.de mag-c bg2 stann bg2
  - ⁝ **perspiration** of: *Cann-s* b7a.de
- **Head**:
  - ⁝ **heat** of: *Caust* b4a.de

- **accompanied** by: ...
  - ⁝ **pain** (See HEAD - Pain - accompanied - stomach - complaints)
  - **Kidneys**; inflammation of the (See KIDNEYS - Inflammation - accompanied - stomach)
  - **Liver** | **pain** (See ABDOMEN - Pain - liver - accompanied - stomach)
  - **Lumbar** region; pain in: *Nux-v* b7a.de
  - **Mammae**; tumors of the (See CHEST - Tumors - mammae - accompanied - stomach)
  - **Teeth**; pain in: cham bro1 kali-c bro1 lyc bro1 nat-c bro1 nit-ac bro1
  - **Throat**; rattling in: cann-xyz bg2
  - **Tongue** | **brown** discoloration | **heavily** coated: verat kr1*
    - ⁝ **white** discoloration of the tongue: *Ang* kr1* *Colch* kr1* *Nat-s* kr1*
- **acute**: thiosin br1
- **allergic**: streptoc jl2
- **alternating** with:
  - **respiration**; asthmatic (See RESPIRATION - Asthmatic - alternating - stomach)
  - **rheumatic** pains (See EXTREMITIES - Pain - rheumatic - alternating - gastric)
  - ○ **Abdomen**; complaints of (See ABDOMEN - Complaints - alternating with - stomach)
  - **Face**; complaints of: bism ptk1
  - **Head**; complaints of (See HEAD - Complaints - alternating - stomach)
  - **Joints**; pain in (See EXTREMITIES - Pain - joints - alternating with - stomach)
  - **Skin**; complaints of: graph ptk1
- **bilious**: aesc bro1 aloe bro1 aq-mar bro1 *Bapt* bro1 berb bro1 *Bry* bro1 card-m bro1 cham bro1 *Chel* bro1 *Chin* bro1 chion bro1 crot-h bro1 dios bro1 *Euon* bro1 eup-per bro1 ferr bro1 gent-l bro1 *Hydr* bro1 *Iris* bro1 kali-c bro1 *Lept* bro1 lyc bro1 mag-m bro1 *Merc* bro1 myric bro1 *Nat-s* bro1 nit-m-ac bro1 *Nux-v* bro1 *Podo* bro1 ptel bro1 *Puls* bro1 sep bro1 *Sulph* bro1 *Tarax* bro1 *Trios* bro1
- **chronic**: petr br1
- **complaining**; with (See MIND - Complaining - stomach)
- **despair**; with (See MIND - Despair - stomach)
- **hypochondriasis**; with (See MIND - Hypochondriasis - stomach)
- **hysteria**; with (See MIND - Hysteria - stomach)
- **increasing** and decreasing gradually: arg-n bg2
- **loathing**; with (See MIND - Loathing - general - stomach)
- **nervous**: *Agar* bro1 bell bro1 coloc bro1 *Mag-p* bro1 *Nux-v* bro1 ol-an br1 sang bro1
- **paroxysmal**: arg-met bg2
- **restlessness**; with (See MIND - Restlessness - stomach)
- **sadness**; with (See MIND - Sadness - stomach)
- **screaming**; with (See MIND - Shrieking - stomach)
- ▽ **extending** to:
  - ○ **Axilla**: am-m ptk1
  - **Backward**: berb ptk1 bism ptk1 con ptk1 kali-c ptk1 sulph ptk1
    - ⁝ **reverse**; or: berb ptk1
  - **Head**: calc ptk1
  - **Limbs**: kali-c ptk1
  - **Shoulder**:
    - ⁝ **right**: sang ptk1
    - ⁝ **Between**: *Bell* ptk1
  - **Spine**: arn ptk1 verat-v ptk1
  - **Upper** arm: am-m ptk1
  - **Upward**: kali-m ptk1 phos ptk1
- ○ **Behind** stomach: arn ptk1 cact ptk1 ham ptk1 kali-c ptk1 stram ptk1
- **Cardiac** opening: ign bg2 kali-bi bg2 phos bg2
- **Epigastrium** (See Epigastrium)
- **Muscles**: merl br1
- **Pylorus**: orni br1 tus-p br1

CONGESTION: nat-m b4.de* verat-v tl1
- **accompanied** by | **respiration**; difficult (See RESPIRATION - Difficult - accompanied - stomach)

○ - **Mucous** membrane: acon hr1* grin br1 *Morg* fmm1•

CONSTRICTION: *Aesc* *Agar* k* alco a1 allox tpw4 *Alum* k* alum-p k2 am-c k* anan *Arg-n* arn b7a.de* *Ars* k* ars-i k2 ars-s-f k2 asaf ptk1 bar-s k2 borx cact k* calc k* calc-s k* camph b7a.de canth b7.de* carbn-s carc tpw2* *Cham* b7a.de **Chel** k* chin b7.de* chinin-s k* clem k* coc-c bg2 *Cocc* k* colch k* *Coloc* k* *Con* b4a.de crot-h crot-t k* dig b4.de* dros k* elat k* *Euph* k* *Ferr* k* *Ferr-ar* fl-ac bg2 gent-l k* germ-met srj5• gins a1 **Graph** k* *Guaj* k* **Guare** k* hyos k* ign (non:iod-h hs1) *Kali-bi* k* kali-c k* kali-m k2 kali-n h2* kali-sil k2 kreos ptk1 lach lact laur lob bg2 *Lyc* k* *Mag-c* k* mag-m *Manc* meny k* merc k* merc-c merc-i-f k* *Mez* k* morph k* mur-ac k* nat-ar *Nat-c* nat-m k* nit-ac bg2 nux-v k* ol-an k* olnd k* *Op* k* petr k* phos k* pip-m k* plat k* plb k* puls bg2 ran-s k* rat ptk1 rheum bg2 rhod k* rob ptk1 sang k* sars k* sec k* sep b4.de* sil b4.de* sphing k* spig k* spong bg2 stront-c *Sul-ac* k* sul-i k2 sulph k* tell k* thea thuj k* tub xxb ven-m rsj12• zinc zinc-p k2
- **morning**: *Kali-bi* kali-n h2 nat-m k*
  - **rising** agg.; after: mang k*
- **forenoon**: nicc k* osm k*
  - **before** eructations: thuj k*
- **afternoon**: bar-c k*
  - **16** h: bry
- **evening**: (non:nat-m kl) rat k* zinc k*
  - **bed** agg.; in: nat-m h2
- **night**: mag-c k* rat k*
  - **midnight** | **before**: nat-m
- **band**; as of a: sep bg2
- **convulsions**; before: *Aesc*
- **convulsive**: acon-c a1 apoc cham k* kali-c k* lact a1 nat-m k* nit-ac k* sec k*
- **dinner**; after: gamb k* nat-c k*
- **eating** | **after** | **agg.**: tab k*
  - **amel.**: germ-met srj5• rat *Sep* *Thuj* ven-m rsj12•
- **eructations** | **amel.**: germ-met srj5• sep h2 [tax jsj7]
- **fasting** agg.: carl k*
- **inspiration**:
  - **agg.**: viol-t k*
  - **deep** | **agg.**: bry k*
- **menses**; before: sulph k*
- **periodical**: *Arg-n* k*
- **pressure**:
  - **amel.**: germ-met srj5•
  - **finger** agg.; of: carb-v h2
- **sitting** agg.: all-c vh1
- **string**; as from a tightly drawn: bac bn sphing kk3.fr

▽ - **extending** to:

○ • **Chest**: alum k* anac b4a.de germ-met srj5• kali-c a1 sep h2
  - ⁝ **left**: germ-met srj5•
  - • **Liver**: dig h2
  - • **Pharynx**: plb k*
  - • **Spine**: borx sec a1
  - • **Throat**: alum k* coc-c a1 jatr-c kr1* kali-c k* *Manc* br1* sep rb2

○ - **Cardiac** opening: alum bro1 *Bar-m* bro1 bry bro1 cortico tpw7 dat-a bro1 euph h2 *Phos* bro1 plb bro1
  - **paroxysmal**: nat-m h2
  - **swallowing** agg.: all-c con tl1 led *Phos*
- **Epigastrium**: agar b4.de* alum b4.de* *Am-c* bg2 asar b7.de* calc b4.de* *Camph* b7a.de *Carb-v* b4.de* dig b4.de* dros b7.de* germ-met srj5• guaj bg2 ign b7a.de kali-bi bg2 kali-c b4.de* merc b4.de* nat-m b4.de* par bg2 plat b4.de* puls bg2 rhod bg2 rhus-t b7.de* sul-ac bg2 sulph b4.de* tarent tl1 zinc b4.de*
  - **accompanied** by | **Abdomen**; cramping pain in: dig bro1
  - **inspiration** agg.: beryl tpw5

▽ • **extending** to | **Chest**: rhus-t bg2
- **Pylorus**, of: *(↗Contraction - pylorus; Hardness - pylorus; Induration - pylorus; Narrow)* abrot bl1* aeth dgt1 bry cann-i br1* chin bro1* crot-h tl1 hep bro1 nux-v bro1* orni bro1 *Phos* k* sil bro1
  - **congenital**: abrot mtf33

CONTRACTION: *(↗Vomiting - spasmodic)* acon b7.de* *Aeth* k* agar alum k* am-c k* anac k* arg-n k* *Arn* k* **Ars** k* *Ars-i* asaf b7a.de* atro k* bar-c b4.de* bell b4.de* borx b4a.de* *Bry* b7.de* calc k* *Carb-an* b4a.de* **Carb-v** k* caust k* *Cham* b7a.de chel k* coca *Cocc* coloc k* con k* **Cupr** k* cupr-act eup-per k* euph k* gamb k* gast a1 gran k* *Graph* b4.de* hydrc k* iod k* irid-met srj5• kali-bi k* kali-c k* kali-i k* *Kali-n* b4a.de *Laur* k* lyc h2* mag-c b4.de* mang b4.de* meny b7.de* merc-c k* mez k* mur-ac b4a.de* nat-ar nat-c k* nat-m b4.de* nit-ac b4.de* *Nux-v* b7.de* ol-an k* op k* orni c osm k* ped a1 petr b4.de* *Phos* k* *Plat* b4a.de *Plb* k* plut-n srj7• podo c1 psor k* ptel k* rheum k* rhod b4a.de sep k* sil b4.de* spong b7a.de stront-c b4.de* *Sul-ac* k* sulph k* thuj tril-p zinc b4.de*
- **morning**: alum h2 carb-v a1 ferr k*
  - **until** noon: borx h2
  - **wakes**: con h2
- **evening**: *Ars* k* hyper k* nat-c h2 rhus-t k* zinc h2
- **night**: con h2 kali-c h2 mag-c h2 merc k* nat-c h2
- **anxious**: sul-ac h2 [aesc-c rcb1]
- **bending** double | **must** bend double: nat-c h2
- **cough**; after: ars
- **dinner**; after: bar-c h2 mag-c k* nat-c h2
- **eating**; after: bell h1 bry k* osm k*
- **raising** arm agg.: anac h2
- **sitting** agg.: castm nat-c k*
- **spasmodic**: ambr h1 *Asaf* br1 *Carb-v* cocc tl1 iris tl1 mag-p tl1
- **stimulants**, after: osm k*
- **stool** agg.; after: mag-m h2
- **stooping**:
  - **agg.**: nat-c k*
  - **amel.**: anac h2
- **stretching** out: am-c h2
- **sudden**: cupr mrr1
- **turning** body agg.: anac h2
- **vomiting**; while: *(↗Vomiting - spasmodic)* crot-t k* dig k* mand rsj7•
- **walking**:
  - **agg.**: castm coloc
  - **amel.**: nat-c k*
- **worm** was climbing upward to throat; as if (See Worm - upwards)

▽ - **extending** to:

○ • **Back**: mag-m h2
  - • **Hypochondria**: nat-c h2
  - • **Spine**: borx h2

○ - **Cardiac** opening: aeth bro1 *Agar* bro1 alum b4a.de am-c bro1 ambr b7a.de *Arg-n* bro1 ars b4.de* *Bar-c* b4a.de *Bell* bro1 bism b7a.de bry b7.de* calc bro1 carb-v b4a.de* caul bro1 cham b7a.de chin b7a.de colch b7a.de *Con* bro1 euph b4.de* hyos bro1 ign b7.de* *Lyc* b4a.de nat-m bro1 nit-ac b4.de* nux-v b7.de* *Petr* b4a.de *Phos* b4.de* puls bro1 ran-b b7.de *Rhus-t* b7a.de* *Sep* b4a.de* sil bro1 *Zinc* b4.de*
- **Epigastrium**: alum b4.de* *Am-c* b4a.de am b7.de* bell b4.de* borx b4a.de* bry b7.de* calc b4.de* carb-v b4.de* con bg2 dros b7.de* ferr b7.de* kali-bi bg2 kali-c b4.de* nat-m b4.de* plat b4.de* rhod b4.de* sul-ac b4.de* sulph b4.de* tell bg2 thuj b4a.de viol-t b7.de*
  - **cough** agg.; during: ars b4.de*
- **Pylorus**: *(↗Constriction - pylorus; Hardness - pylorus; Induration - pylorus; Narrow)* *Bar-m* br1 dys fmm1• mand mtf11
  - **accompanied** by | **Duodenum**; distention of: orni br1
  - **eating**; after | **immediately**: bar-m br1
  - **painful**: *Bar-m* br1 orni br1

COUGH:
- **after** | **agg.**: ip b7.de*
- **before** | **agg.**: *Bell* bg2
- **during** | **agg.**: ambr b7.de* ars b4.de* bell b4a.de *Bry* b7.de* *Calc* b4.de* hell b7.de* ign b7.de* ip b7.de* lach b7a.de lyc b4.de* mang b4.de* phos b4.de* *Puls* b7.de* rhus-t b7.de* ruta b7.de* *Sabad* b7.de* sep b4.de* stann b4.de* teucr bg2 thuj bg2

COVERING agg.: mag-m bg2

Stomach

CRAMP (See Pain - cramping)

CRAWLING: *(↗Worm)* agar k* alum k* apis b7a.de *Ars* *Bry* k* caust b4a.de* *Cocc* colch k* *Graph* b4a.de hyper bg1 kali-c bg1 lact lyc k* nat-c k* nux-m bg1 nux-v k* plat b4a.de *Puls* raph bg1 rhod b4.de* rhus-t b7.de* sep b4a.de **Thuj** b4a.de

▽ - **extending** to throat; from pit of stomach nux-m c1

- • **worm** crawling; as if (See Worm - upwards)

○ - **Epigastrium**: agar bg2 alum b4.de* bry b7.de* caust bg2 lyc bg2 nat-c b4a.de* nux-v b7a.de* plat bg2 puls b7a.de*

CROAKING like frogs: *(↗ABDOMEN - Rumbling - croaking)* coloc h1 nat-m k*

- **turning** in bed; on: nat-m

CURRENT; sensation of a: m-ambo b7.de

DAY; agg. after a whole: apoc bg2 petr bg2 podo bg2

DEATHLIKE sensation: *Ars* k* **Cupr** k* mez vh pic-ac k*

DELICATE (See Disordered)

DESIRES (See GENERALS - Food)

DIARRHEA:

- **agg.**: ant-c bg2 *Ant-t* bg2 **Ars** bg2 asar bg2 *Bell* bg2 calc-p bg2 *Coloc* bg2 cupr bg2 dulc bg2 **Ip** bg2 jatr-c bg2 *Lach* bg2 *Phos* bg2 **Puls** bg2 rheum bg2 seneg bg2 *Stann* b4a.de* stram bg2 **Verat** bg2
- **amel.**: arg-n bg2

DIGESTION:

- **during** | **agg.**: hep b4a.de
- **impeded**: camph b7.de* chin b7.de* *Nux-v* b7a.de op b7.de* par b7.de* plb b7.de* sec b7.de* squil b7a.de
  - • **children**; in: carc jl2
- **rapid**; too | **albuminoid**: rob br1
- **sadness**; with (See MIND - Sadness - digestion)
- **slow** (See Slow)
- **weakness** of digestion (See Indigestion)

DILATATION: | **Cardiac** opening: bism bro1 graph bro1 *Hydrin-m* bro1 kali-bi bro1 *Nux-v* bro1 phos bro1 puls bro1 xan bro1

DINNER; after: kali-bi bg2 lyc b4.de* nat-c b4.de* petr b4.de* phos b4.de* sil b4.de* zinc b4.de*

DISAGREEABLE, sensation: allox tpw3 am-c bg2 bism bg2 coff bg2 croc bg2 kali-bi bg2 kali-p fd1.de• lob bg2 mur-ac bg2 nat-m bg2 phos h2* sabad bg2 zinc bg2

- **stooping** | **amel.**: nat-m h2

○ - **Epigastrium**: nux-v b7.de* sec b7.de*

DISORDERED: *(↗Indigestion; GENERALS - Food)* acon bg2* aesc k2 aeth c2 agath-a nl2• agn b7.de* alet bro1 alum-sil k2 ambr b7.de* amyg-p bro1 **Ant-c** k* **Ant-t** k* **Arg-n** arn b7a.de* **Ars** k* **Asaf** k* astac c2 bar-c b4.de* bell bg2 berb k2 borx b4a.de bov b4.de* bros-gau mrc1 **Bry** k* calc k2 calc-ar k2 calc-p bg2* *Caps* carb-an bro1 **Carb-v** k* *Caust* k* *Cham* k* **Chin** k* *Chinin-ar* cina k2 *Coff* k* corn-f br1 cortico tpw7* crat br1 cycl b7.de* dig bro1 fel br1 ferr k2 gent-l c2 *Graph* k* guat sp1 *Hep* k* hydr k2 ign b7.de* iod b4.de* **Ip** k* kali-ar **Kali-bi** k* *Kali-c* k* kali-i k2 kali-p kali-s lac-c *Lac-e* hrn2• lacer a1* *Lach* bro1 laur b7.de* *Lob* **Lyc** k* m-arct b7.de mag-c b4.de* mag-m c2* mand sp1 **Merc** k* *Mez* mosch k2 mur-ac c2 nat-ar *Nat-c* k* **Nat-m** k* *Nat-p* **Nat-s** **Nux-v** k* op b7.de* *Petr* k* *Phos* k* plb b7.de* podo k2 psil ft1 *Psor* *Ptel* **Puls** k* rauw sp1 rheum c2 rhus-t b7.de* rob ruta b7.de* sabad bg2 sang k2 *Sars* *Sep* k* sil bg2 squil b7a.de stann b4.de* *Staph* bg2 *Sul-ac* k* sul-i k2 sulph b4.de* *Tarax* sp1 *Tarent* k* teucr bg2 *Thuj* k* **Verat** k*

- **evening**: ambr h1*
  - • **18** h: rauw sp1
  - • **21** h: cortico sp1
- **night** | **sensation** of disordered stomach: phos h2*
- **accompanied** by:
  - • **coryza**: carb-v k2 nux-v k2

○ • **Abdomen** | **complaints** (See ABDOMEN - Complaints - accompanied - stomach)

- **acids**, after: *Ant-c* *Caust* ferr *Sep*
- **agg.**: ant-c bg2 *Bry* bg2 carb-v bg2 chin bg2 *Nux-v* bg2 **Puls** bg2
- **beer**; after: aloe k* ferr kali-bi *Sulph*

Disordered: ...

- **bicycle**; riding a: ven-m rsj12•
- **brain** fag; in (See prostration)
- **bread** agg.: bry calc mrr1 **Caust** lyc *Merc* nat-m sars *Sep*
- **cheese**, moldy: *Ars*
- **coition**; after: *Dig*
- **cold**:
  - • **drinks**:
    - ⁝ **agg.**: ars mtf33 calc-p k2
    - ⁝ **amel.**: musca-d szs1
  - • **food** | **after**: calc-ar k2
- **cold**; after taking a: *Ant-c* *Bry*
- **coryza**; during (See accompanied - coryza)
- **dinner**; after: hir rsj4• mag-c h2
- **eating**; after: lyc b4a.de mez b4a.de
  - • **two** hours: mand sp1
- **eggs**: chinin-ar
- **eructations** | **amel.**: cortico tpw7*
- **excitement** agg.: aeth k2 *Bry* *Cham* chin cina k2 coloc *Lac-e* hrn2• *Nux-v* ph-ac staph
- **fat** food; after●: *Caust* *Kali-m* vh *Nat-p* *Ptel* **Puls** *Sep* *Sulph*
- **fish**: chin k2 chinin-ar
- **fresh** meat: *Caust*
- **fruit** agg.: act-sp **Ars** *Bry* calc-p k2 **Chin** *Lyc*
- **heart** failure, with: crat br1
- **ice** cream: *(↗Indigestion - ice; Nausea - ice cream - after)* **Ars** *Calc-p* *Carb-v* **Puls**
- **menses** | **during** | **agg.**: cop br1
  - • **suppressed** menses; from: bry k2
- **mental** exertion agg.: am calc cocc *Lach* *Nux-m* **Nux-v** *Puls* *Sulph* verat
- **milk** agg.: alum ars ars-s-f k2 *Bry* *Calc* calc-ar k2 *Chin* *Iris* kali-c lac-d k2 *Lyc* merc k2 nat-ar *Nat-c* nat-p **Nit-ac** *Sep* sul-ac *Sulph* zinc
- **oysters**●: brom k2 *Bry* **Lyc** k*
- **pastries**; after: puls k2
- **peaches**, after: *Psor*
- **prostration** of mind; during: aeth k2
- **reprimands**; after: *(↗MIND - Sensitive - reprimands)* cina k2
- **sauerkraut**, after: *Bry* petr h2
- **sour** wine; from (See wine - sour)
- **strawberries**: ox-ac vh
- **sweets**: arg-n k2* merc k2*
- **urticaria**; after: cop br1
- **vexation**; after: **Cham** *Ip*
- **warm**:
  - • **drinks**:
    - ⁝ **after**: fl-ac k2
    - ⁝ **amel.**: bry k2
  - • **soup** | **amel.**: nat-c h2
- **weather** agg.; stormy: petr h2
- **wine**; from: chin k2
  - • **sour**: ant-c k2 nat-m k2

○ - **Epigastrium**: adox a1*

DISTENSION: *(↗Flatulence agg.; Flatulence of; ABDOMEN - Distension)* abies-c br1* abies-n mtf11 abrot absin bro1 acet-ac k2 acon k* acon-ac rly4• aesc k* aeth tl1 agar bg2* ail tl1 aloe k* alum k* alumn k* am-c b4.de* *Ambr* bro1 anac bg2* ange mtf11 ant-c k* ant-t k* apis apoc k2* **Arg-n** k* ars k* ars-i *Asaf* k* atra-r bnm3• aur aur-ar k2 aur-i k2 aur-s k2 bacls-7 fmm1• bapt k2 bar-m *Bell* k* berb *Borx* bov b4.de* *Bry* k* bufo but-ac br1* cadm-met tpw6 *Caj* bro1 calad **Calc** k* *Calc-ar* calc-f bro1* *Calc-i* bro1 *Calc-p* bro1 *Calc-s* cann-i br1 caps k* carb-ac br1* carb-an **Carb-v** k* carc br1* carl k* caust bg2 cedr k* *Cham* k* chel k* **Chin** k* *Chinin-s* **Cic** k* cimic k* clem k* coc-c k* *Cocc* k* coff k* *Colch* k* *Con* k* *Croc* k* cupr cycl k* cystein-l rly4• daph *Dig* k* dios k* *Dulc* k* dys pte1*• echi elaps euon bro1 eup-pur falco-pe nl2• fel bro1 ferr k* ferr-ar ferr-i ferr-m ferr-ma bro1 ferr-p gaert pte1*• *Gels* gent-l k* ger-i rly4• gins k* gran k* *Graph* k* grat k* ham mtf11 *Hell* k* *Hep* k* *Hydr* k* hydr-ac k* hydrc hydrinin-m mtf11 hyos k2 *Ign* k* ignis-alc es2• indg br1 indol bro1 iod k* ip bg2 jug-c bro1 kali-ar kali-bi k* **Kali-c** k* kali-p kali-s ketogl-ac rly4• kola stb3• *Lac-d* lac-e hrn2• *Lach* k* laur k* lec k* led lil-t k* lob bro1 **Lyc** k* mag-c k* *Manc* mang h2 **Med** st *Merc* *Merc-c* k*

Distension: ...
merl k* mez mosch k* nat-ar nat-c k* nat-hchls bro1 *Nat-m* k* nat-ox rly4• *Nat-p* k2* nat-pyru rly4• *Nat-s* nit-ac b4.de* **Nux-m** k* *Nux-v* k* ol-an k* op k* orni c* orot-ac rly4• oscilloc jl2 ox-ac bro1 par b7.de* petr k* ph-ac bro1 *Phos* k* phys phyt plat h2 plb pop bro1 pop-c-t bro1 positr nl2• pot-e rly4• propr sa3• prot pte1*• *Prun* k* psor k* *Puls* k* pyrid rly4• raph **Rat** k* rhus-t hr1 rob ruta fd4.de sabad k* sabin k* sang k* sanic vh sars b4.de* sec sep sil bro1 stann b4.de* *Stram* k* sul-ac k* sul-i k2 **Sulph** k* syc pte1• tarent tere-la rly4• thuj k* tung-met bdx1• v-a-b jl2 xanrhi mtf11 zinc b4.de* [bell-p-sp dcm1 *Spect* dfg1]

- **morning**: falco-pe nl2• nat-ox rly4• nux-v *Phos* k* ruta fd4.de
- **forenoon**: myric k* tong a1
  - 9.30-10 h: propr sa3•
- **afternoon**: nat-m petr k* sulph
- **evening**: calc vh dios eupi falco-pe nl2• hydrog srj2• *Kali-bi* osm k* pyrid rly4• sang a1
  - **21** h until midnight: phos
  - **bed** agg.; in: bell h1
  - **eating**; before: hydrog srj2•
- **night**: loxo-recl knl4•
  - **midnight** | **after**: ambr br1
  - **waking**; on: asaf carb-an h2
- **accompanied** by:
  - **eructations** (See Eructations - accompanied - distension)
  - **headache** (See HEAD - Pain - accompanied - stomach - distension)
  - **palpitations** (See CHEST - Palpitation - accompanied - stomach - distension)
- **air**; as if full: lac-h htj1•
- **asthma**; during: lac-d c1
- **chill**; during: *Cocc*
- **contradiction**, after: *Nux-m*
- **convulsions**; during: *Cic* k*
- **dinner** | **after** | **agg.**: alum h2 ant-c k* dig k* ham fd3.de• kalm k* zinc k*
  - **before**: rat k*
- **drinking** agg.; after: apoc k2 calc h2 manc nat-m h2 tab
- **eating**:
  - **after**:
    - **agg.**: agar k* alum k* alum-p k2 *Ambr* *Anac* k* androc srj1• *Apoc* *Arg-n* aur-m bar-c k* **Borx** *Bry* k* calad *Calc* k* calc-s cann-i carb-an **Carb-v** carbn-s carc gk6 *Caust* cham k* **Chin** cimic coc-c k* **Colch** coli jl2 *Cop* dig k* dios dulc k* falco-pe nl2• ferr ferr-p germ-met srj5• graph *Grat* *Hep* ignis-alc es2• kali-c k2 lac-f c1 *Lach* **Lyc** k* mag-c k2 nat-m h2 **Nat-s** *Nux-m* k* **Nux-v** k* op k* *Phos* positr nl2• *Puls* rumx *Sanic* sars k* sin-a k* *Stann* sul-ac k* sulph k* tab
    - **amel.**: cedr ham fd3.de• rat tung-met bdx1•
    - **small** quantity: apoc k2 brass-n-o srj5•
  - **impossible**: puls k2
  - **while** | **agg.**: con k*
- **epilepsy**; during (See GENERALS - Convulsions - epileptic - during - stomach)
- **eructations**: (↗*ABDOMEN - Distension - eructations)*
  - **amel.**●: *Arg-n* k* **CARB-V** k ● carc gk6 mag-c k* *Nat-s*
  - **not** amel.: *Arg-n* mrr1 **CHIN** k ● echi falco-pe nl2• ham fd3.de• **Lyc** k ● phos h2
- **excitement**; after: *Arg-n* nux-m
- **exertion** agg.: arg-n st
- **fish** agg.; pickled: arg-n vh calad
- **flatus**; passing | **amel.**: rat
- **fruit**: verat k2*
- **grief**; from: calc vh
- **lying** on abdomen | **amel.**: con k*
- **menses**:
  - **before** | **agg.**: zinc
  - **during** | **agg.**: lac-e hrn2•
  - **suppressed** menses; from: cham h1
- **mental** exertion agg.: hep

Distension: ...

- **milk** agg.: *Con*
- **motion** | **amel.**: cedr
- **oysters**, after: *Bry* *Lyc*
- **perspiration**; during: carb-v b4a.de
- **rising** agg.; after: coc-c k*
- **sensation** of: (↗*Enlarged - sensation)* ars b4.de* *Bry* b7a.de calc-p bg2 *Carb-v* b4a.de *Con* b4a.de cystein-l rly4• hell b7.de* ign b7.de* kali-c bg2 m-ambo b7.de plat b4.de* sabin b7.de* *Sep* b4a.de *Stann* b4a.de thres-a sze7•
  - **followed** by | **Head**; sensation of distention in: (↗*HEAD - Air - filled)* germ-met srj5•
  - ○ **Epigastrium**: acon b7.de* aur b4a.de bell b4a.de *Bry* b7.de* camph bg2 **Cham** b7a.de dulc b4a.de hell b7a.de mang b4a.de* nat-m b4a.de rhus-t b7.de* zinc bg2
- **stool**:
  - **before**: ars h2
  - **during** | **amel.**: corn falco-pe nl2•
- **supper** | **after** | **agg.**: zinc k*
  - **before**: sang a1
- **walking** | **amel.**: calad cedr k*

○ - **Epigastrium**: acon b7a.de* aloe bg2 alum bg2 ant-t bg2 *Arg-n* bg2 ars b4.de* aur b4.de* *Bell* b4.de* bell-p sp1 **Bry** b7.de* *Calad* b7a.de **Calc** b4.de* *Caps* b7a.de *Carb-v* b4a.de *Cham* b7.de* chin bg2 **Cic** b7.de* coff b7.de* convo-s sp1 *Daph* bg2 ferr b7.de* **Hell** b7.de* *Hep* b4a.de* ign bg2 **Ip** bg2 kali-c b4.de* *Lyc* b4.de* manc ptk1 *Merc-c* b4a.de *Mez* b4a.de nat-c b4.de* *Nat-m* b4.de* **Nux-m** b7a.de* **Nux-v** b7.de* op b7.de* *Petr* b4a.de* phos b4a.de prun bg2 *Puls* b7a.de sabin b7.de* *Sulph* bg2 syc bka1*• verat bg2

  - **night**:
    - **midnight**:
      - **after** | **2**-3 h: dys fmm1•
  - **accompanied** by | **asthmatic** respiration (See RESPIRATION - Asthmatic - accompanied - epigastrium)
  - **menses**; from suppressed: cham b7a.de
- **Pit** of stomach, painful: arg-n br1

DRAWING IN abdomen: | **agg.**: ant-c b7.de* ant-t b7.de* asaf b7.de*

DRAWING UP legs: | **amel.**: *Sil* b4a.de

DRINKING:

- **after** | **angry**; after drinking when | **amel.**: cham b7a.de *Nux-v* b7a.de
  - **much**: nat-c b4.de*
- **agg.**: acon bg2 aloe bg2 ant-t b7.de* apoc ptk1 arg-n bg2 *Arn* b7.de* **Ars** b4a.de* *Bell* b4a.de *Bry* b7.de* cham bg2 *Chin* b7.de* cocc b7.de ferr b7.de* ign bg2 kali-c bg2 lach bg2 merc bg2 *Merc-c* b4a.de mez bg2 mosch b7a.de nat-m bg2 nit-ac bg2 *Nux-v* b7.de* ol-an bg2 ph-ac b4.de* **Puls** b7.de* rhod bg2* rhus-t b7.de* sep bg2 **Sil** b4a.de* tarax bg2 teucr bg2 **Verat** b7.de*
  - **rapidly**: *Sil* b4.de*
- **amel.**: graph b4a.de *Phos* b4a.de
- **aversion** to drink (See GENERALS - Food - drinks - aversion)
- **cold** water | **agg.**: **Ars** b4a.de calc b4a.de nat-c b4a.de podo bg2 rhod b4.de* sul-ac b4a.de*
- **desire** to drink (See Thirst)
- **not** drinking (See Thirstless)

DRINKS:

- **non**-alcoholic | **agg.**: *Sul-ac* b4a.de

DRIVING agg.: ars bg2 bell bg2 borx bg2 **Cocc** bg2 *Colch* bg2 croc bg2 *Ferr* bg2 lyc bg2 nux-m bg2 **Petr** bg2 sec bg2 sep bg2 sil bg2 sulph bg2

DRUNKARDS; complaints in: ant-c bg2 ant-t br1 **Ars** bg2 *Asaf* b7a.de calc bg2 *Carb-v* bg2 coff bg2 ip bg2 kali-bi bg2 *Lach* bg2 led bg2 nat-n bg2 **Nux-v** b7a.de* *Op* bg2 puls bg2 *Sulph* bg2

DRYNESS in stomach; sensation of: calad b7.de* chin bg1 kali-i bg2 moni rfm1• ox-ac bg2* raph bg1 sphing kk3.fr

○ - **Epigastrium**: allox tpw3

  - **eating** | **amel.**: allox tpw3

Stomach

DYSPEPSIA (See Indigestion)

EATING:

- **after**:
  - **agg.**: *Acon* b7.de* agar b4.de* agn bg2 alum b4.de* *Am-c* b4.de* am-m bg2 ambr b7.de* anac b4.de* ang b7.de* *Ant-c* b7.de* ant-t b7.de* arg-met bg2 arg-n bg2 arn b7.de* **Ars** b4.de* asaf b7.de* *Bar-c* b4.de* bell b4.de* bism b7.de* borx b4a.de* bov b4.de* **Bry** b7.de* **Calc** b4.de* calc-p bg2 canth b7.de caps b7.de* carb-an b4.de* *Carb-v* b4.de* caust bg2 *Cham* b7.de* *Chel* b7.de* **Chin** b7.de* chinin-s bg2 *Cic* b7.de* cina b7.de* cist bg2 cocc b7.de* *Coloc* b4.de* *Con* b4.de* croc bg2 **Cycl** b7.de* daph bg2 **Dig** b4.de* dros bg2 dulc b4.de* euph b4.de *Ferr* b7.de* *Ferr-p* bg2 *Graph* b4.de* grat bg2 hell b7.de* hep b4.de* *Hyos* b7.de* ign b7.de* iod b4a.de* ip bg2 kali-bi bg2 *Kali-c* b4.de* *Kreos* b7a.de **Lach** b7.de* laur b7.de* led b7.de* *Lyc* b4.de* m-arct b7.de mag-c bg2 mag-m bg2 **Merc** b4.de* mez b4.de* mosch b7.de* nat-c b4.de* **Nat-m** b4.de* nicc bg2 *Nit-ac* b4.de* *Nux-m* bg2 **Nux-v** b7.de* olnd bg2 op b7.de* par bg2 petr b4.de* ph-ac b4.de* **Phos** b4.de* plat b4.de* plb b7.de* **Puls** b7.de* ran-s bg2 rheum bg2 rhod b4.de* rhus-t b7.de* ruta b7.de* sang bg2 *Sars* b4.de* sec b7.de* seneg b4.de* *Sep* b4.de* *Sil* b4.de* spig bg2 spong bg2 stann b4.de* *Staph* b7.de* stront-c bg2 sul-ac bg2 **Sulph** b4.de* tab bg2 thuj b4.de* valer bg2 **Verat** bg2 zinc b4.de*
  - **amel.**: alum bg2 *Anac* b4.de* ang b7.de* arg-n bg2 asaf bg2 bar-c b4.de* bov bg2 brom bg2 *Calc* b4a.de calc-p bg2 cann-s b7.de* carb-an bg2 cedr bg2 *Chel* b7.de* chin bg2 dios bg2 fago bg2 ferr bg2 gamb bg2 *Graph* b4a.de* grat bg2 hep ptk1 ign b7a.de* iod b4.de* kali-bi bg2 kali-br bg2 kali-p bg2 kreos b7a.de lach b7a.de* laur b7.de* lith-c bg2 lol bg2 mang bg2 mez bg2 nat-c b4.de* nat-s bg2 nicc bg2 nit-ac bg2 nux-v b7.de* op bg2 ox-ac bg2 *Petr* b4.de* phos b4a.de* polyg-h bg2 psor bg2 ptel bg2 puls b7.de* rhus-t b7.de* sabad b7.de* sang bg2 *Sep* bg2 sil b4.de* stront-c b4.de* verat b7.de* zinc bg2
  - **angry**; after eating when: *Cham* b7a.de *Nux-v* b7a.de
  - **several** hours after:
    - **agg.**: anac bg2 kali-bi bg2 lyc bg2 phos bg2 puls bg2 sep bg2
    - **amel.**: kreos bg2
- **aversion** to eat (See Appetite - diminished; Appetite - wanting; GENERALS - Food - food - aversion)
- **before**:
  - **agg.**: cann-s b7.de* sabad b7.de* sabin b7.de*
  - **amel.**: nux-m bg2
- **desire** to eat (See Appetite - increased; Appetite - ravenous)
- **hastily** (See MIND - Hurry - eating)
- **increases** the hunger (See Appetite - increased - eating - after)
- **late** agg.: *Chin* b7a.de
- **overeating** agg.; after: acon bg2 alum bg2 **Ant-c** b7a.de* *Ant-t* b7a.de* *Arg-met* bg2 arn bg2 ars bg2 bell bg2 *Bry* bg2 carb-v bg2 chin bg2 coff bg2 cycl bg2 ferr bg2 hep bg2 **Ip** bg2 mag-c bg2 nat-c bg2 *Nux-v* b7a.de* **Puls** bg2 rheum bg2 rhus-t bg2 staph bg2* sulph bg2
- **small** quantities | **agg.**: calc-p bg2 sulph bg2
- **while**:
  - **agg.**: am-c b4.de* ang b7a.de* ant-t b7a.de* *Arn* b7.de* bar-c b4.de* bell b4.de* borx bg2 bry b7.de* carb-v bg2 caust bg2 cham b7.de* cic b7a.de* cocc b7.de* colch bg2 con b4.de* dig bg2 ferr bg2 graph b4.de* ip bg2 *Kali-c* bg2 kali-n bg2 led b7.de* mag-m bg2 mang b4.de* *Merc* bg2 nat-c bg2 nit-ac b4.de* nux-v bg2 olnd bg2 petr bg2 phos b4.de* phyt bg2 **Puls** b7.de* rhod b4.de* rhus-t b7.de* sars bg2 sep b4a.de* teucr bg2 thuj b4.de* *Verat* b7.de*
  - **amel.**: chin b7.de* kreos bg2 nat-s bg2
  - **beginning** to eat: ang b7.de*

EGG; sensation as of an: | **swallowed** a hard-boiled egg; sensation as if: **Abies-n** a1*

EGGS agg.: colch bg2 ferr bg2

EMOTIONS:

- **agg.**: acon bg2 bry bg2 calc bg2 carb-v bg2 caust bg2 **Cham** bg2 chin bg2 *Colch* bg2 *Coloc* bg2 lyc bg2 nux-v bg2 phos bg2 puls bg2 staph bg2
- **are** felt in: *Ant-c* vh calc bg2* cham bg1 coloc bg1 dig bg1 kali-c bg2* mez bg2* nux-v bg1 phos bg2* tub bg2

EMPTINESS: (↗*Flabbiness; Hanging; Sinking; Weakness*)
abies-c c1* abies-n bg2 abrot acon adon vh1 *Aesc* *Agar* agav-t jl1 ail *All-c* all-s allox tpw4 aloe *Alst-s* br1 alum k* alum-sil k2 alumn am-c k* am-m k* *Ambr* anac k* ang **Ant-c** k* ant-t k* ap-g vh1 apoc k* *Aran* *Arg-met* *Arg-n* arge-pl rwt5• arn *Ars* k* *Ars-i* ars-s-f k2 *Asaf* k* aster atro aur aur-ar k2 aur-i k2 aur-m aur-s k2 bamb-a stb2.de• *Bapt* k* *Bar-c* k* bar-i bar-m k* bar-s k2 bell k* *Brom* bros-gau mrc1 bry k* *Bufo* k* cact *Calad* k* *Calc* k* *Calc-p* k* calc-s calc-sil k2 *Camph* cann-s canth *Caps* k* carb-ac *Carb-an* k* carb-v k* carbn-s card-m *Carl* castm *Caust* k* chel k* *Chin* k* chinin-ar chinin-s chlol choc srj3• *Cimic* k* *Cina* k* cinnb clem k* coc-c coca coca-c sk4• **Cocc** k* coff colch k* *Coloc* k* con cop corn *Croc* *Crot-h* *Crot-t* cupr cupr-ar cypra-eg sde6.de• **Dig** k* dios k* diosm br1 dys fmm1• *Elaps* ery-a euphr fago ferr *Fl-ac* k* *Gamb* gard-j vlr2• *Gels* k* gent-l germ-met srj5• *Glon* k* glycyr-g cte1• *Graph* k* *Grat* ham fd3.de• **Hell** k* hep k* *Hipp* k* hir rsj4• **Hydr** k* *Hydr-ac* k* *Hyos* **Ign** k* ignis-alc es2• ind indg *Iod* k* ip k* jatr-c *Kali-ar* kali-bi k* *Kali-c* k* *Kali-chl* *Kali-fcy* kali-i kali-m k2 kali-n k* *Kali-p* k* *Kali-s* kalm *Kola* stb3• lac-ac **Lac-c** k* lac-loxod-a hrn2• *Lach* k* lap-la rsp1 lat-m bro1* *Laur* k* lil-t *Lob* k* loxo-recl knl4• *Lyc* k* lyss *Mag-c* k* manc marb-w es1• med k2 medul-os-si rly4• meny b7.de* meph k* **Merc** k* merc-i-f merc-i-r merl mez k* moni rfm1• morph bro1 *Mosch* k* *Mur-ac* k* **Murx** k* myric naja narc-ps c1* nat-ar *Nat-c* k* *Nat-m* k* *Nat-p* *Nat-s* k* nicc nit-ac **Nux-v** k* *Olnd* k* *Op* k* orni bro1 ox-ac ozone sde2• pert-vc vk9 *Petr* k* petr-ra shn4• phel **Phos** k* phys phyt plac-s rly4• plan plat b4.de* plb k* **Podo** k* psil ft1 ptel k* **Puls** k* rad-br c11 rad-met bro1 raph rheum h *Rhus-t* k* rumx ruta k* sabad k* sacch sst1• sacch-a fd2.de• *Sang* k* sarr sars k* sec seneg k* **Sep** k* sil spig h1 spong fd4.de squil **Stann** k* staph k* stram succ-ac rly4• suis-hep rly4• sul-ac bg2* *Sul-i* sulfonam ks2 **Sulph** k* sumb **Tab** k* *Tarent* tell k* *Teucr* k* thea k* thuj k* til tril-p k* tritic-vg fd5.de *Tub* k* ust valer **Verat** k* verb k* vib bro1 vinc xan c1 **Zinc** k* zinc-p k2 [bell-p-sp dcm1 beryl-m stj2 heroin sdj2]

- **daytime**: ap-g vml3• nat-p k* stann
- **morning**: *Aesc* k* agar anac ant-c c1 apoc arg-met bufo carb-v h2 castm cimic coloc k* dios k* hell hydr kali-bi k* lac-c lyc k* mag-c k* mag-m mez k* mill k2 nat-m k* nat-p k* nicc k* op orot-ac rly4• petr-ra shn4• phos h2 plat h2 pot-e rly4• ruta fd4.de sang k* sep tarent
  - **2** h (See night - midnight - after - 2)
  - **anxiety** with: lyc nat-m
  - **menses**; during: castm
  - **rising** | **after** | **agg.**: phos h2
    - **agg.**: nat-p k* phos k*
  - **waking**; on: alum h2 ant-c apoc *Lac-c* mill ozone sde2•
- **forenoon**: caust h2 jatr-c mag-c k* *Nat-c* k* nat-m k* nicc puls sulph h2 tritic-vg fd5.de
  - **9-10** h: hep ptk1
  - **10** h | **evening**; until: mur-ac *Nat-c*
  - **11** h: alumn *Asaf* aur-s wbt2• coloc vh hydr ign bg3* ind lach *Nat-c* nat-m nat-p op petr bg3* petr-ra shn4• *Phos* k* sep k* **Sulph** k* visc sp1 *Zinc* k*
    - **dull** pain, with: hydr
- **noon**: fago k* nat-c k* nat-m a1 pitu-gl skp7• ruta fd4.de tritic-vg fd5.de
- **afternoon**: ambr k* borx h2 calc h2 caust h2 fago k* lac-loxod-a hrn2• lach k* puls ruta fd4.de sulph k*
  - **13** h: fago
  - **14** h: *Grat*
  - **15** h: phys
- **evening**: am-br k* ambr calc-p coca-c sk4• ham fd3.de• lac-c olnd
  - **18** h: pitu-gl skp7•
  - **20** h: kali-c kalm
  - **eating**; after | **amel.**: **Sep**
  - **sleep**; before: dig
  - **supper**, before: graph h2
- **night**: dios k* kali-s fd4.de lyc k* petr tarent k*
  - **midnight**: mag-c k* rhus-t
    - **before** | **23** h: nat-c k2
    - **after**: mag-c h2
      - **2** h: podo tell
      - **4** h: raph c1
      - **5** h: nat-c
- **accompanied** by:
  - **acidity** of stomach: elaps br1

- **aversion** to food (See GENERALS - Food - food - aversion - accompanied - stomach)
- **eructations** | **water** brash (See Eructations; type - water brash - accompanied - stomach)
- **hunger**: hep bg2
- **weakness**: *Alst-s* br1
- ○ **Lips**; dryness of: ozone sde2•
- **Teeth**; pain in (See TEETH - Pain - accompanied - faintness)

- **agg.**: *Ign* b7a.de *Phos* b4a.de
- **air**; in open | **amel.**: bapt
- **amel.**: dig ptk1
- **aversion** of food; with (See GENERALS - Food - food - aversion - accompanied - stomach)
- **brandy** | **amel.**: olnd ptk1
- **breakfast**:
  - **after**:
    - **agg.**: am-m coca colch k* *Dig* lyc k* mez h2 puls thuj a1
    - **amel.**: mag-m h2
  - **before** | **agg.**: aesc k* alumn apoc arg-met calc-p carb-v cimic *Kali-bi* lac-c murx sulph
- **breathing** deep | **amel.**: ign ptk1
- **chill**; during: ail *Ars*
- **convulsions**; before epileptic: **Hyos** k*
- **cough**; with: croc ign mur-ac stann
- **diarrhea**, with: *Fl-ac* *Lyc* *Petr* *Stram* *Sulph*
- **dinner**:
  - **after** | **agg.**: ail a1 eucal a1 graph h2 lyc ptel k* thea zinc k*
  - **amel.**: mag-c h2
  - **before**: lyc k* mag-c nux-v k* phos **Sulph**
- **drinking**:
  - **tea**: lac-h sk4•
  - **water** | **amel.**: kali-m pd
- **drowsiness**; during: corn k*
- **eating**:
  - **after**:
    - **agg.**: agar alum arn k* bell bg2 bov calad calc c1 carb-v k* chin c1 chlol k* **Cina** coloc h2 *Dig* *Grat* k* *Hydr* kali-p lach *Laur* *Lyc* k* *Myric* nat-p k* olnd k* op k* petr-ra shn4• phos h2 plan ptel puls raph k* sang k* sars k* sil k* *Stann* sul-ac h2 thuj k* **Verat** k* zinc k*
      - **two** hours after: ulm-c jsj8•
  - **amel.**: *Anac* bro1 ap-g vh1 *Chel* bro1 iod h* mag-c h2 mur-ac bro1 nat-c bro1 petr mrr1 phos bro1 *Sep* bro1 sulph bro1 tritic-vg fd5.de verat h1
  - **before** | **agg.**: alumn bamb-a stb2.de• crot-t k* *Sulph*
  - **must** eat: graph k2 lach k2 petr k2 spong fd4.de
  - **not** amel. by: abel vh1 abies-c vh1 agar alum alum-p k2 alum-sil k2 *Ant-c* *Arg-met* *Ars* asc-t aur calc calc-p calc-sil k2 cann-i *Carb-an* k* castor-eq cic **Cina** k* coc-c coloc h2 dig haliae-lc srj5• ham fd3.de• *Hydr* **Ign** k* kali-bi kali-c k2 kali-i kali-m k2 *Kola* stb3• **Lac-c** k* **Lach** k* **Lyc** k* mag-m med k2 medul-os-si rly4• *Merc* **Mur-ac** k* nat-m *Nux-m* olnd k* op k2 par petr-ra shn4• **Phos** k* phyt plut-n srj7• sang sars **Sep** k* sil *Staph* staphycoc rly4• stront-c *Teucr* **Verat** k*
  - **while** | **agg.**: crot-t verat h1 zinc
- **eructations**:
  - **after**: ambr
  - **amel.**: *Sep*
- **fasting**; sensation as from prolonged: am-m b7.de* anac b4a.de* ars ptk1 bov b4.de* bry ptk1 carb-an b4.de* caust b4.de* chin ptk1 cocc b7.de* ign b7.de* laur b7.de* lyc bg2 mag-m b4.de* mez bg2 nat-c b4.de* phos b4.de* plb b7.de* puls ptk1 sars ptk1 sep b4a.de stann b4a.de teucr b7.de* verat ptk1
- **fever**; during: zinc k*
- **fruit** agg.: nat-c h2
- **headache**, during (See HEAD - Pain - accompanied - stomach - emptiness)
- **heart**; with weak or dilated: chlol ptk1
- **hollow** feeling like a vibrating violin string: coca-c sk4•
- **hunger**:
  - **sensation** as if from: am-m b7.de* ant-c b7.de* arg-met b7.de* **Asar** b7a.de aur b4.de* bell bg2 calad b7.de* *Calc* b4.de* canth b7.de* cocc b7.de* *Coff* b7.de* dig b4.de* euph b4.de* hell b7.de* ign b7.de* kali-bi bg2 *Mag-m* b4a.de mez b4.de* *Nat-c* b4a.de nux-v b7.de* plat b4.de* plb b7.de* puls b7.de* ran-b b7.de* rhod b4.de* rhus-t b7.de* ruta b7.de* seneg b4.de* *Stann* b4a.de staph b7.de* teucr b7.de* verat b7.de*
  - **without**: act-sp *Agar* *Alum* alum-p k2 am-m k* ars *Bar-c* berb bry carb-an h2 chin chinin-s cocc dulc grat k2 hell hydrog srj2• kali-n **Lach** k* *Mur-ac* nat-c a1 *Nat-m* nicc *Olnd* op phos psil ft1 psor raph c1 *Rhus-t* *Sil* *Sul-ac* *Sulph* tax [heroin sdj2]
- **inspiration**:
  - **agg.**: calad petr-ra shn4•
  - **amel.**: petr-ra shn4•
- **intermittent**: mur-ac h2
- **lying** down | **amel.**: ambr k* ign sep bro1
- **meeting** a friend, when: cimic
- **menopause**; during: *Crot-h* *Lach* *Tab*
- **menses** | **before** | **agg.**: *Ign* sep sulph
  - **during** | **agg.**: kali-n h2 kali-p spong tab
- **milk** amel.; sips of: diph ptk1
- **motion** agg.: dig br1
- **music** agg.: coca-c sk4•
- **nausea**; during: (↗ *epigastrium - accompanied - nausea; Nausea - hunger; Nausea - hunger - with)* agar androc srj1• *Arg-met* arg-n asaf bry calc-p caust chel cimic cocc *Cycl* gink-b sbd1• *Hell* hep h2 hydr *Ign* kali-bi kali-c kali-p lac-c pd lach lyc mag-m meph mosch nat-c a1 olnd phel **Phos** k* rheum *Rhus-t* *Sep* *Sil* spig tab thymol sp1 *Valer* verat zinc h2 [heroin sdj2]
- **nursing** the child agg.; after: *Carb-an* k* olnd k*
- **pain**; from: anac tl1 ars h2
- **paroxysmal**: arg-met glon
- **pressure**:
  - **agg.**: **Merc** k*
  - **amel.**: psil ft1
- **rising** agg.; after: coca
- **rumbling** below left ribs amel.: verb c1
- **sighing**: **Ign**
- **sitting** agg.: acon alumn
- **sleep**:
  - **before**: dig k*
  - **during** | **agg.**: lyc ph-ac
  - **siesta**:
    - **after** | **agg.**: ang
- **stool** agg.; after: *Aloe* ambr dios k* fl-ac mur-ac ptk1 **Petr** *Ph-ac* puls *Sep* sul-ac ptk1 sulph
- **sweets** | **amel.**: petr-ra shn4•
- **talking** agg.: *Rumx* k*
- **thinking** of food, when: **Sep** k*
- **throbbing**, with: ant-t *Asaf* calad hydr *Kali-c* mag-c nat-c nat-m sep sulph
- **trembling**: am-c cimic lyc zinc
- **vomiting**; after: ther k*
- **walking**:
  - **about** | **room** agg.; in the: lyc k*
  - **after** | **agg.**: coca ferr bg1
  - **agg.**: chel k* chinin-s rat k* sep bg1
  - **rapidly** | **amel.**: myric ptk1
- **wine** | **amel.**: sep bro1
- ▽ **extending** to | **Heart**: **Lob** k*
- ○ **Epigastrium**: agar bg2 ant-c b7.de* ant-t ptk1 apoc bg2* ars bg2 calc-p bg2 carb-an bg2 cimic bg2 cocc bg2 *Dig* bg2* fl-ac bg2 glon bg2* hydr bg2 hydr-ac ptk1 *Ign* b7.de* ip b7a.de* *Kali-ar* mrr1 kali-bi bg2 kali-c ptk1 lat-m ptk1 lob bg2* mur-ac bg2 nat-m bg2 olnd b7.de* *Op* b7a.de podo bg2 rhus-t b7.de* sep bg2* silphu mp4• stann b4.de* stroph-h ptk1 sulph bg2* tab bg2* verb b7.de* vib bg2 zinc bg2
  - **accompanied** by:
    - **nausea**: (↗ *nausea)* lac-c ptk1
    - **vertigo**: adon pd*

Stomach

- **eating** agg.: myric ptk1
- **fever**; during: polyp-p bro1
- **urination** agg.; after: apoc ptk1
- **walking** fast amel.: myric ptk1

ENLARGED: bar-c ptk1 kali-bi br1 sil ptk1

- **sensation** of enlargement: *(↗Distension - sensation)* falco-pe nl2• rhus-t bg2

EPILEPTIC aura: *(↗GENERALS - Convulsions - epileptic - aura - stomach)* art-v bell bism sf bufo *Calc* k* *Caust* st **Cic** k* cupr **Hyos** h1 *Indg* k* **Nux-v** k* *Sil* k* **Sulph** k*

- **rising** from stomach to head: **Calc** k*

ERUCTATIONS: *(↗Flatulence agg.; Flatulence of)* abies-c k* abies-n c2* abrot a1 absin k* acet-ac k* **Acon** k* acon-a a1 acon-c a1 acon-f a1 *Aesc* k* aeth k* *Agar* k* agar-em a1 agath-a nl2• agn k* *All-c* k* aloe alum k* alumn a1 am-c k* am-caust a1 am-m b2.de* **Ambr** k* ammc a1 anac k* anag vh1 ang b2.de* *Ant-c* k* *Ant-t* k* ap-g a1* apis k* apoc k* apom a1 **Arg-n** k* arist-m br1 **Arn** k* *Ars* k* ars-h k* ars-i arum-d a1 **Asaf** k* **Asar** k* asc-t k* aspar a1* astac a1 atra-r bnm3• aur k* aur-i k2 aur-s a1 bac al2* bacls-7 pte1*• bapt k* *Bar-c* k* bar-i bar-m bar-ox-suc rly4• bar-s k2 bart a1 **Bell** k* benz-ac k* berb k* berbin a1 *Bism* k* bit-ar wht1• bov k* brach k* brom k* **Bry** k* bufo but-ac sp1 cadm-met tpw6 cain *Caj* bro1 calad b2.de* *Calc* k* calc-p k2* calc-s k* *Camph* k* canch a1 cann-i k* cann-s k* *Canth* k* caps k* *Carb-ac* k* *Carb-an* k* **Carb-v** k* **Carbn-s** carc gk6* carl k* carneg-g rwt1• cartl-s rly4• casc a1 *Caust* k* *Cham* k* *Chel* k* chen-a a1 **Chin** k* chin-b hr1 chinin-ar chlf a1 cic b2.de* *Cimic* k* cimx k* cina k* cinch a1 *Cinnb* k* cinnm hr1 cist k* clem k* coc-c k* coca-c sk4• **Cocc** k* cod a1* coff k* *Colch* k* colchin a1 coli rly4• coloc k* com k* **Con** k* cop k* corn a1* cortico tpw7* *Croc* k* crot-c crot-t k* **Cupr** k* cupr-ar k* *Cycl* k* cystein-l rly4• cyt-l a1 del a1 delphin a1 dig k* digin a1 *Dios* k* dream-p sdj1• dros b2.de* *Dulc* k* dys pte1*• elat a1* enteroc jl2 erio a1 eucal a1 *Eup-per* k* eup-pur k* euph b2.de* euphr b2.de* eupi k* fago k* fagu a1 *Ferr* k* ferr-ar *Ferr-i* k* ferr-ma a1 ferr-p k* ferr-s mtf11 *Fl-ac* k* fuma-ac rly4• galeoc-c-h gms1• gard-j vlr2• gast a1 *Gels* k* gent-c k* gent-l a1 ger-i rly4• *Germ-met* srj5• gink-b sbd1• gins k* glon k* glyc bro1 gran k* *Graph* k* grat k* **Guaj** k* gymno ham k* hell k* hell-o a1* hell-v a1 *Helon* k* *Hep* k* hip-ac sp1 hom-xyz br1 *Hydr* k* hydr-ac a1 hydrc k* hydrog srj2• hyos k* hyper k* *Ign* k* ind bro1 indg k* **Iod** k* *Ip* k* irid-met srj5• **Iris** k* jab a1* jatr-c jug-c bro1 *Jug-r* k* kali-ar k* **Kali-bi** k* kali-br a1 **Kali-c** k* kali-chl k* kali-i k* kali-m k2 kali-n k* *Kali-p* k* kali-pic a1* *Kali-s* kali-sil k2 *Kalm* k* kiss a1 kreos k* *Lac-ac* k* *Lac-d* lac-del hrn2• lac-e hrn2• lac-f wza1• lac-loxod-a hrn2• lacer a1 *Lach* k* lact k* lat-m sp1 *Laur* k* *Lec* led k* lepi a1 lil-t k* lina a1* linu-c a1 lipp a1 lith-c lob k* lol a1 loxo-lae bnm12• lup a1 **Lyc** k* lyss k* m-ambo b2.de* m-arct b2.de* m-aust b2.de* **Mag-c** k* *Mag-m* k* mand sp1 mang k* mang-m c2 **Med** k* meny b2.de* meph k* **Merc** k* merc-br a1 merc-c k* merc-i-r k* merc-n a1 merl k* methyl a1 *Mez* k* mill a1 mit a1 morg-g fmm1• morg-p pte1*• morph a1 mosch k* *Mur-ac* k* musca-d szs1 narz a1 **Nat-ar** nat-c b2.de* **Nat-m** k* nat-n a1 nat-ox rly4• *Nat-p* k* nat-pyru rly4• *Nat-s* k* nat-sil fd3.de• nept-m lsd2.fr nicc k* nicot a1 nig-s mp4• *Nit-ac* k* nit-s-d a1* nux-m k* **Nux-v** k* oci-sa sp1 oena a1 ol-an k* olnd k* op b2.de* oreo br1 orni tl1 osm k* *Ox-ac* oxyt ptk2 ozone sde2• pall k* par k* *Petr* k* petr-ra shn4• *Ph-ac* k* **Phos** k* phys k* phyt a1 pic-ac k* picro a1 pimp a1 plac-s rly4• plat k* *Plb* k* plect a1 pneu jl2 podo bro1* positr nl2• pot-e rly4• prot pte1*• psil ft1 **Psor** k* ptel mrr1 **Puls** k* rad-br c11 *Ran-b* k* *Ran-s* k* raph k* rat k* rauw sp1 rham-f a1 rheum rhod k* rhus-r a1 **Rhus-t** k* rhus-v k* rob k* rumx k* *Ruta* k* *Sabad* k* sabin k* sal-ac bro1 sang k* *Sars* k* sec k* sel k* *Seneg* k* **Sep** k* serp a1 *Sil* k* sin-a a1 sin-n a1 *Skat* br1 sol-t-ae k* solin a1 spig k* spira a1* spirae a1 spong k* *Squil* k* *Stann* k* *Staph* k* stram k* stront-c b2.de* stroph-s sp1 suis-hep rly4• suis-pan rly4• *Sul-ac* k* **Sulph** k* sumb k* syc fmm1• symph fd3.de• *Syph* hr1 tab k* *Tarax* k* **Tarent** k* tart-ac a1 tep k* ter k* tere-la rly4• teucr b2.de* *Thuj* k* *Thymol* sp1 til a1 *Trios* rsj11• tritic-vg fd5.de trom a1 tub-r jl2 tus-p a1 upa a1 uran-n bro1 ust a1 *Valer* k* vanil fd5.de **Verat** k* *Verb* k* vesp k* vichy-g a1 vinc a1 viol-t b2.de* visc sp1 wies a1 xan a1 yohim br1* *Zinc* k* zing k* [bell-p-sp dcm1 calc-n stj1 heroin sdj2]

- **daytime**: bry k* carb-v b4.de* graph b4.de* **Iod** k* mag-s a1 petr k* ran-b b7.de* verat b7.de
- **morning**: agar b4.de* all-c alum b4.de* am-m b7.de* anac k* arg-n k* arn k* aster k* bar-c k* bov b4.de* bry k* calc k* calc-s k* calc-sil k2 cina b7.de* cob k* coff b7.de* coloc k* *Con* k* croc k* dulc k* hep k* hyper ign b7.de* *Kali-c* k* kali-s fd4.de *Kalm* k* laur b7.de* lyc mag-c k* mang k* nat-m k* nat-sil fd3.de• nept-m lsd2.fr nit-ac b4.de* nux-v k* **Petr** phos b4.de* plat k* *Puls* k* ran-b b7.de* ran-s b7.de* ruta fd4.de sars k* sep b4.de* sil k* stann k* sul-ac k* *Sulph* k* tab thuj valer k* vanil fd5.de verat k*

Erucations – morning: ...

- **rising | after | agg.**: led h1 mag-c bg2 nat-m bg2 nat-sil fd3.de• ruta bg2 sep bg2 zinc bg2 [pop dhh1]
  - **agg.**: cedr k* nicc k* ruta sep sin-a k* verat k*
- **stool** agg.; after: cob k*
- **waking**; on: bar-c a1* calc a1* ruta fd4.de

- **forenoon**: agar alum b4.de* am-m bry b7.de* calc-p k* carl cocc b7.de* colch k* hep k* ign k* laur b7.de* lyss hr1 mag-c k* mag-m k* mang b4.de* myric k* naja nat-c k* nicc par k* petr b4.de* phos b4.de* plb b7.de* ran-b b7.de* sars k* spong fd4.de sulph k* zinc k* [tax jsj7]
  - **10**-11.30 h: lycps-v c1
- **noon**: dulc fd4.de indg k* ox-ac k* podo fd3.de• ran-b k*
  - **eating**; while: olnd k*
- **afternoon**: aeth agar k* alum b4.de* am-m k* ambr b7.de* ars ars-i k* bar-c k* bry b7.de* calc canth b7.de* caps b7.de* *Carb-v* k* *Caust* chel k* chinin-s *Cic* k* cina b7.de* coff b7.de* con k* crot-t cupr k* dulc fd4.de fago k* fl-ac hydr lach b7.de* laur b7.de* led b7.de* *Lyc* k* mag-c h2 mag-m k* merc k* nat-ar k2 *Nat-c* k* nat-sil fd3.de• nux-v b7.de* op ox-ac k* petr b4.de* ph-ac b4.de* phos b4.de* plat b4.de* puls b7.de* ran-b b7.de* sang k* spong fd4.de squil b7.de* symph fd3.de• thuj k* verat b7.de* zinc b4.de*
  - **16** h: coff nat-m valer
    - **until** night: bar-c h2
  - **eating**; after: nat-ar k2 nept-m lsd2.fr petr
- **evening**: abrot *Alum* k* alum-p k2 am-c *Ambr* k* bell bry b7.de* calc carb-v *Caust* choc srj3• coc-c coff b7.de* con k* crot-h cupr k* cycl k* dream-p sdj1• dros dulc fd4.de eucal a1 eupi k* falco-pe nl2• fl-ac k* gels k* grat k* ham k* hyper ign b7.de* kali-bi k* macro a1 mag-c k* mez k* mim-p rsj8• nat-c hr1 nat-sil fd3.de• nit-ac b4.de* pant-ac rly4• petr b4.de* phos k* pot-e rly4• **Puls** k* *Ran-b* b7.de* ran-s rhus-t k* rumx ruta fd4.de sars k* sep k* sil k* sin-n k* sol-t-ae k* spong fd4.de stram k* sulph k* symph fd3.de• thuj b4.de* ulm-c jsj8• verat k* zinc k* zing k*
  - **until** midnight: phos
  - **eating**; while: cham h1
- **night**: ant-t k* calc k* calc-s canth *Carb-v* chel *Chin* b7.de* *Crot-h* graph b4a.de ham k* kali-bi bg2 *Kali-c* k* kali-p fd1.de• *Lach* bg2 lyc k* mang *Merc* mur-ac k* nat-c b4.de* nat-m b4.de* nit-ac bg2 *Nux-v* k* ox-ac phos k* pip-m k* **Psor** bg2 **Puls** k* ruta fd4.de sil b4.de* *Sul-ac* b4a.de sulph k* symph fd3.de• tanac ther vanil fd5.de
  - **midnight**:
    - **before**:
      - **21** h until midnight: phos
      - **23** h: gels sumb
    - **after | 4** h: lavand-a ctl1•
    - **waking**; on: ferr k*
  - **first** half of: nit-ac k*
  - **lying** agg.: calc k* vanil fd5.de
  - **sleep** agg.; during: sulph h2
  - **waking**; on: calc k* mur-ac k* sil h2
- **accompanied** by:
  - **cough**; barking (See COUGH - Barking - accompanied - eructations)
  - **distension**: gent-l mtf11
  - **dyspnea**: psor al1
  - **flatulence**: ant-c tl1 asaf mtf11 caust bg2 lyc bg2 sang bg2
  - **gallstones**: dios ptk1 lyc ptk1
  - **hawking**: cupr bg2
  - **hiccough** (See Hiccough - accompanied - eructations)
  - **salivation** (See MOUTH - Salivation - accompanied - eructations)
  - ○ **Abdomen**; cramping pain in (See ABDOMEN - Pain - cramping - accompanied - eructations)
  - **Chest**; pain in: *(↗CHEST - Pain - Eructations - agg.)* zinc bg2

- **Head**:
  - **pain** (See HEAD - Pain - accompanied - eructations)
- **Stomach**; pain in: *(↗Pain - eructations - agg.)* calad bg2 cham bg2 cocc bg2 mag-c b4a.de* musca-d szs1 *Phos* b4a.de* spong bg2 *Stann* b4a.de
- **Throat**:
  - **constriction**: caust bg2 nux-v bg2
  - **fullness** of: con bg2

- **acids**, after: ph-ac staph
- **after**:
  - **agg.**: plb b7.de*
  - **amel.**: *Agar* b4a.de alum b4.de* am-m b7.de* ambr b7.de* ant-t b7.de* arg-n bg2 bar-c b4.de* **Bry** b7a.de calc-p bg2 canth b7.de* carb-v bg2 *Caust* b4a.de chel b7.de* *Cocc* b7a.de colch bg2 dig b4a.de* graph b4.de* grat bg2 ign b7.de* iod b4a.de kali-c b4.de* lyc b4.de* mag-c b4.de* mag-m b4.de* mosch b7.de* nat-c b4.de* nicc bg2 par b7.de* phos b4.de* *Rhod* b4a.de sabad b7.de* sabin b7.de* stront-c b4.de* sul-ac b4.de* sulph b4.de* *Verat* b7a.de
- **agg.**: agar ant-c b7.de* bar-c b4.de* bry ptk1 calad b7a.de cann-s carb-an ptk1 carb-v ptk1 **Cham** k* **Chin** k* *Cocc* k* jal ptk1 *Kali-c* bg1* *Lach* k* nux-v bg2* phos k* puls b7.de* *Rhus-t* k* sep k* sil b4.de* spong b7a.de stann k* *Sulph* k* zinc
- **air** agg.; in open: ambr b7.de* kiss a1 nat-m k* sul-ac b4.de*
- **alternating** with:
  - **hiccough** (See Hiccough - alternating - eructations)
  - **yawning** agg.: berb k* lyc k*
- **amel.** (See GENERALS - Eructations - amel.)
- **apyrexia**, during: am-c ant-c sabad hr1
- **asthma**; with: ambr br1
- **bed** agg.; in: alum bg2 verat b7.de*
- **beer**; after: aur h2 ferr sulph b4.de*
- **bread** agg.: bry k* chin crot-h dulc fd4.de merc k* nat-m *Puls* b7a.de symph fd3.de•
  - **butter**; and: chin b7.de*
  - **milk**; and after: zinc
- **breakfast**:
  - **after** | **agg.**: ars k* calc-p k* carb-ac k* carb-v h2 cham k* con k* cycl k* dulc fd4.de grat hell k* hyper k* kali-bi k* kali-br k* kali-p fd1.de• lac-loxod-a hrn2• laur b7.de* mag-c b4.de* mang b4.de* nat-sil fd3.de• phos pic-ac *Plat* plb b7.de* sacch-a fd2.de• sars sep sulph k* tritic-vg fd5.de verat k*
  - **before** | **agg.**: *Bov* k* *Ran-s*
  - **during**: nat-sil fd3.de• ox-ac tritic-vg fd5.de zinc k*
- **butter** agg.: **Carb-v** **Puls**
- **cabbage**; after: **Mag-c**
- **cake**; after: puls b7.de*
- **carrots**; after: kola stb3•
- **chill**:
  - **after**: zinc k*
  - **during**: *Alum* b4.de* am-c bg2 ant-c bg2 arg-n bg2 arn bg2 *Bry* bg2 carb-v bg2 chin bg2 cina bg2 ip bg2 nux-v k* phos bg2 ran-b b7.de* *Rhus-t* b7a.de* *Sabad* bg2 sars bg2 sep bg2 sul-ac bg2
- **chilliness**; with: *Sil* k*
- **choking**, after: caust bg2 chel bg2 op k*
- **chronic**: alum h2
- **coffee** agg.: *Caust* *Coca* cycl k* dulc fd4.de *Puls* k*
- **cold** | **drinks** | **amel.**: germ-met srj5•
  - **water** | **agg.**: mez b4.de* sars b4.de*
- **constant**: ars h2 carb-v k2 *Chel* k* *Con* k* cupr k* euph h2 graph h2 lac-h htj1• **Lach** bg2 mur-ac h2 nat-c h2 nat-sil fd3.de• nit-ac plut-n srj7• pot-e rly4• sars sulph k*
- **convulsions**:
  - **after**: kali-c ptk1
  - **before**: lach ptk1
    - **epileptic**: lach ptk1
- **convulsive**: ars-h k* asaf k2 coc-c k* ham k* kali-bi k* nux-v phos sang k* til k*
- **cough**:
  - **after**: **Ambr** k* ang c1 arn bg3* carb-v bg3* chin bg3* kali-bi ptk1 lob bg3* rumx bg1 **Sang** k* *Sul-ac* k* verat k*
  - **during** | **agg.**: *(↗COUGH - Eructations - excite)* ambr k* caps bro1 kali-bi k* lob bg2 puls bg2 ran-b bg2 *Sang* k* staph b7a.de sul-ac k* verat k*
- **delivery**; during: borx br1*
- **desire** to eructate: ketogl-ac rly4• mang h2
- **difficult**: aeth a1 **Arg-n** k* asaf kr1 calc-p ptk1 cent a1 cocc ptk1 *Con* k* *Graph* k* *Nux-v* k* spira a1
- **dinner**:
  - **after**:
    - **agg.**: agar k* aloe am-c ang k* apis ars bar-c carb-v h2 carl coca cycl dig k* fl-ac ham k* kreos k* lac-e hrn2• lac-loxod-a hrn2• lach k* lyc k* mag-m k* merc k* nat-m nicc nit-ac h2 petr rat sars k* sul-ac *Sulph* k* zinc k*
      - **rising** from stooping agg.: castm
      - **walking** agg.: mag-m
  - **amel.**: mang h2
  - **before**: nat-sil fd3.de• ran-b k*
  - **during** | **agg.**: grat k* mag-m k* ol-an k* sars
- **drinking**:
  - **after**:
    - **agg.**: aeth k* aloe anac k* apis k* arg-n k* ars k* bism calc-p bg2 canth *Carb-v* k* coloc crot-h bg2 crot-t dream-p sdj1• dulc fd4.de ham fd3.de• hyper *Kali-c* lyc merc k* mez k* *Nat-m* nux-v k* rhus-t k* ruta b7.de* *Sep* k* spig b7.de* sulph bg2 tarax k* tritic-vg fd5.de vanil fd5.de zinc
    - **amel.**: *Bry* b7.de* lac-h htj1•
    - **cold** water:
      - **agg.**: mez h2 phos
      - **amel.**: carl
    - **water** | **agg.**: aloe bg2 apis b7a.de* aur-s k2 bar-m k2 bar-s k2 bism bg2 bry b7a.de hyper ptk1 mez bg2 nat-m bg2 positr nl2• tritic-vg fd5.de vanil fd5.de
- **drunkards**; in: *Ran-b* *Sul-ac* k*
- **eating**:
  - **after**:
    - **agg.**: acon aesc k* agar k* all-s k* alum b4.de* alum-sil k2 am-m k* ambr b7.de* *Anac* k* ang b7.de* apis **Arg-n** k* ars k* asaf bamb-a stb2.de• *Bar-c* k* bar-m bar-s k2 bell k* berb k* bit-ar wht1• *Bry* k* bufo calc k* calc-ar k2 calc-s calc-sil k2 *Camph* k* canth b7.de* caps b7.de* carb-an k* **Carb-v** k* **Carbn-s** card-m *Caust* k* cham k* chel b7.de* *Chin* k* chinin-ar chinin-s bg2 cic k* cina k* cob-n sp1 *Colch* coloc k* com k* con k* cop k* cortico sp1 cycl k* daph k* dig k* dream-p sdj1• dulc k* echi **Ferr** k* ferr-ar ferr-i ferr-p grat k* gymno ham k* *Hep* k* hydr kali-ar kali-bi k* *Kali-c* k* kali-m k2 kali-p kali-s kali-sil k2 kola stb3• *Kreos* k* lac-leo hrn2• *Lach* k* lec led b7.de* *Lyc* k* marb-w es1• merc k* mim-p rsj8• mur-ac k* nat-ar *Nat-c* k* **Nat-m** k* nat-p k* *Nat-s* k* nept-m lsd2.fr *Nit-ac* k* *Nux-m* k* *Nux-v* k* onos *Ox-ac* k* petr k* ph-ac k* *Phos* k* *Pic-ac* plat k* *Podo* psil ft1 **Puls** k* ran-b b7.de* *Ran-s* k* rat rhod b4a.de rhus-t k* ruta k* sabin b7.de* sacch-a fd2.de• sang *Sars* k* *Sel* b7a.de *Sep* k* *Sil* k* *Spig* k* spirae a1 *Stann* k* staph sul-ac b4.de* **Sulph** k* symph fd3.de• tarax thuj k* tritic-vg fd5.de vanil fd5.de *Verat* k* *Zinc* k* zinc-p k2 [tax jsj7]
    - **amel.**: am-m b7.de* sulph bg1
  - **before** | **agg.**: carb-v b4.de* croc bg1 nit-ac b4.de* nux-v bg1* plat bg1* ran-b b7.de* ran-s bg1* sel bg1* sulph bg1 valer b7.de*
  - **while** | **agg.**: alum h2 calc b4.de* cycl b7.de* dulc k* grat k* merc k* mur-ac a1 nat-c k* nit-ac k* olnd k* petr bg2 phos k* *Sars* k* thuj b4a.de* tritic-vg fd5.de vanil fd5.de
- **emotions**; after: ozone sde2•
- **excessive**: morg-g fmm1*•
- **excitement**: arg-n
- **faintness**; causing: *Arg-n* k* **Carb-v** hr1* nux-v hr1*
- **farinaceous** food, after: kali-s fd4.de nat-c sulph tritic-vg fd5.de
- **fasting** agg.: acon k* bov cina k* croc k* kali-c b4a.de *Nit-ac* k* *Nux-v* k* plat k* pot-e rly4• ran-b b7.de* ran-s b7.de* valer verat b7.de*
- **fat**; after: *Asaf* b7a.de *Carb-v* b4a.de* *Caust* *Cycl* bg2 *Ferr* k* ferr-m gran a1 nat-m b4.de* **Puls** k* **Sep** k* thuj k*

Stomach

- **fever**:
  - **before**: ars b4a.de phos b4a.de sep b4a.de
  - **during** | **agg.**: alum b4.de* am-c bg2 ant-c b7.de* **Bry** b7.de* *Carb-v* b4.de* chin bg2 cic bg2 con bg2 cub ign bg2 lach k* **Nux-v** b7.de* phos bg2 ran-b k* rhus-t bg2 *Sabad* b7a.de* sep bg2 sulph bg2 thuj bg2
- **forcible**: apis b7a.de *Arg-n* bg2 arn b7a.de bar-c b4.de* bism b7.de* carb-v bg2 caust bg2 ferr b7.de* *Merc* b4.de* mosch b7.de* *Olnd* b7a.de plb b7a.de *Rhus-t* b7.de* *Sep* b4a.de verat b7.de*
- **frequent**: ambr c1 borx hr1 cycl a1 mur-ac h2 rhus-t h1 tritic-vg fd5.de
- **frothy** | **menses**; before: kreos bg2
- **grief**; from: puls-n c1
- **gushing** out: psor jl2
- **headache**: apis k* arg-n bg2* bry bg2 bufo bg2 *Calc* k* camph k* carb-v bg2 *Chel* mrr1 cycl bg2 graph bg2 *Iod* bg2* kola stb3• lyc bg2 **Mag-m** k* nat-c bg2* nit-ac bg2 op bg2 ozone sde2• phos h2* sil h2* spong fd4.de
  - **before**: ozone sde2•
- **heat**; during: alum bg2 am-c bg2 *Ant-c* bg2 **Bry** b7.de* *Carb-v* bg2 chin bg2 cic bg2* con bg2 ign bg2 *Lach* bg2 **Nux-v** bg2 phos bg2 rhus-t bg2 *Sabad* bg2 sep bg2 sulph bg2 thuj bg2
- **hiccough**; after: ars h2*
- **hungry**; when: plat b4.de* psor bg2
- **ineffectual** and incomplete: acon k* agar k* alum k* am-c k* *Am-m* vh1 ambr k* aml-ns bg2 anac h2 ang b7a.de* *Arg-n* k* arn k* *Ars* k* arund k* *Asaf* bro1* asar b7.de* bar-c b4.de* *Bell* k* bry bro1 calad k* calc b4.de* canth k* carb-ac carb-an k* *Carb-v* bro1 carbn-s k* *Carl* k* *Caust* k* chel k* **Chin** k* cic bg2 *Cocc* k* con k* cycl k* ferr k* ferr-ar ferr-m ferr-ma k* **Graph** k* grat k* hyos k* ign b7.de* indg k* iod bg2 kali-bi bg2 kali-c k* kali-m k2 kali-p lac-c bg2 *Lach* k* laur k* *Lyc* k* m-ambo b7.de mag-c b4.de* *Manc* k* **Med** k* mez k* mosch bro1 mur-ac k* **Nat-m** k* *Nux-m* bro1 nux-v k* ol-an bg2* ox-ac bro1 petr k* ph-ac k* phel k* *Phos* k* *Phyt* pic-ac k* plat k* plb k* *Puls* k* rhus-t k* ruta fd4.de sabad k* sars k* seneg bg2 sep b4a.de sin-n bg2 spig k* sul-ac k* sulph k* tab bg2 thymol sp1 verat bg2 zinc k* zinc-p k2 zing k* [spect dfg1]
  - **morning**: ol-an k*
  - **forenoon**: sil k*
  - **evening**: dios k*
  - **night**: caust k* sulph
    - **bed**; when going to: sulph
    - **menses**; before: mang
  - **accompanied** by:
    - **burning** pain (See Pain - burning - accompanied - eructations)
    - **pain** (See GENERALS - Pain - accompanied - eructations)
    - **retching**: *Caust* b4a.de
  - **breakfast** agg.; after: con k*
  - **eating**; after: con b4a.de
  - **menses**; during: carb-an b4.de
- **lean**, dry people; in: alum br1
- **leukorrhea** agg.: sep b4a.de
- **liquid** food; after: anac b4a.de
- **lying**:
  - **agg.**: vanil fd5.de verat bg1
  - **amel.**: aeth k* rhus-t k*
- **lying** down | **after** | **agg.**: aeth bg2 calc bg2 rhus-t bg2 sulph bg2 verat b7.de*
  - **agg.**: lavand-a ctl1•
- **meat** agg.: bamb-a stb2.de• carb-an b4a.de* dulc fd4.de rumx ptk1 ruta k* *Staph* b7a.de
- **menses** | **before** | **agg.**: bry k* chin k* *Kali-c* k* kreos lach k* mag-c k* mang k* *Nat-m* k* *Nux-m* phos *Puls* k*
  - **during** | **agg.**: ant-t ars k* bry b7.de* carb-an b4.de* caul bg2 cham bg2 chin bg2 *Graph* k* kali-c k* kali-i k* kreos bg2 **Lach** k* lyc k* mag-c bg2 mosch bg2 *Nit-ac* k* phos bg2 puls bg2 vib bg3
- **mental** exertion agg.: hep k*
- **milk**; after: alum k* alum-p k2 am-c ant-t k* *Calc* k* carb-ac *Carb-v* k* carbn-s *Chin* k* *Cupr* cycl bg2 dulc fd4.de iris lac-d k2 lyc *Mag-c* *Nat-m* k* nat-s nit-ac bg2 nux-v b7.de petr phos k* spong fd4.de *Sulph* k* trios rsj11• tritic-vg fd5.de *Zinc* k*
- **motion** agg.: cann-i k* cann-xyz bg2 kreos k* tritic-vg fd5.de vanil fd5.de
- **nausea**; after: sabad b7.de*
- **onions** agg.: *Thuj* b4.de*
- **oppressive** gasses pass upward and downward: arn br1
- **oysters**, after: bry
- **paroxysmal**: *Arg-n* bell coff lyss mez a1 *Nat-m* vh petr **Phos** sang sep sulph k*
- **peaches**, after: psor
- **periodical**: aesc k* ip k*
- **perspiration**; during: alum bg2 *Ant-c* bg2 arn bg2 bell bg2 **Bry** bg2 *Carb-v* bg2 cocc bg2 con bg2 merc bg2 nat-m bg2 *Nux-v* bg2 ph-ac bg2 phos bg2 puls bg2 rhus-t bg2 **Sabad** bg2 *Sep* bg2 staph bg2 sul-ac bg2 sulph bg2 thuj bg2 verat bg2
- **pork**, after: ham a1 psor
- **potatoes** agg.: *Alum* k* am-m b7.de* gran k* mag-s bg2
- **pregnancy** agg.; during: carb-ac mrr1
- **pressing**:
  - **painful** parts; when pressing on: *Borx* k*
  - **stomach**; from pressing on: *Sulph* k*
- **pressure** on abdomen agg.: cham bg2 sulph b4a.de*
- **relief**; without: carb-v ptk1 *Chin* ptk1 falco-pe nl2• lyc ptk1
- **respiration**; obstructed: grat bg2 lach bg2
- **rich** food agg.: *Bry* **Carb-v** ferr nat-m *Puls* *Sep* staph thuj tritic-vg fd5.de
- **rising**:
  - **agg.**: arg-n coloc *Rhus-t* h1 verat hr1
  - **lying**; from | **agg.**: *Rhus-t* k*
  - **stooping**; from | **agg.**: *Bry* bg2 *Rhus-t* b7.de*
- **sardines**, after: eupi k*
- **sensation** of: kali-i ptk1
- **shivering**:
  - **after**: sars b4.de
  - **with**: carb-v b4.de dulc ptk1 ip b7.de nux-v b7.de oreo br1 rhus-t b7.de sabad b7.de
    - **shooting** pain, with: bry
- **sitting**:
  - **agg.**: gels phos k*
  - **amel.**: lavand-a ctl1•
  - **bent** forward | **agg.**: rob sabin
- **sleep**:
  - **after**:
    - **agg.**: *Bry* b7.de* hep k*
      - **long** sleep: hep b4a.de
  - **amel.**: chel k* chin k*
  - **during** | **agg.**: *Sulph* b4.de*
- **smoking** | **after** | **agg.**: sel br1
  - **agg.**: agar b4.de* *Lac-ac* sel b7.de* thuj k*
- **sneezing**; with: astac vh ham bg1 lob bg1* mag-c bg1* phos bg1*
- **soup** agg.: alum k* anac carb-v k* dulc fd4.de mag-c phos b4.de* sars b4.de*
- **sour** food; after: *Ars* b4a.de *Ph-ac* b4a.de *Staph* b7a.de
- **stool**:
  - **after** | **agg.**: aesc anac k* *Ars* k* bar-c k* *Calc-s* k* cob *Coloc* k* merc k* nat-m bg2 sil k*
  - **before**: aesc bg2 bism bg2 caps b7.de* petr bg2 sumb k*
  - **during** | **agg.**: *Arg-n* bg2 *Ars* b4a.de cham *Chin* b7a.de con k* dulc k* *Kali-c* k* *Merc* k* *Petr* b4a.de plb bg2 *Puls* k* ruta
  - **urging** to stool; after: hep b4a.de
- **stooping** agg.: cic ip k* manc bg2 merl bg2 phos k* vanil fd5.de
- **stroking** forehead with fingers or behind ears amel.: *Nux-v* b7a.de
- **sudden**: bar-c ptk1 *Carb-an*
- **supper** agg.; after: alum *Carb-v* k* chinin-s cot a1 ferr k* ham k* kali-p fd1.de• lyc sars sep sil k* zinc
- **suppressed**: **Am-c** k* ang a1 *Calc* k* *Con* k* hell a1
  - **followed** by | **Stomach**; pain in: *Con* k*
- **swallowing**:
  - **agg.**: agar
  - **difficult**; with: ox-ac ptk1
  - **empty** | **after**: spig h1
- **sweets** agg.: *Arg-n* *Caust* nat-sil fd3.de• raph symph fd3.de• tritic-vg fd5.de zinc

- **tea**; after: lach b7.de* ruta bg2
- **tobacco**; from: *Sel* thymol sp1
- **transferred** to the right side of the chest, as if settled there; which seemed to be: *Rhus-t* h1
- **turkey**; after: bamb-a stb2.de•
- **urging** to: acon b7.de* *Alum* b4a.de am-c b4.de* arn b7.de* canth b7.de* cic b7.de* cocc b7.de* laur b7.de* phos b4.de* puls b7.de* sars b4.de* seneg b4.de* verat b7.de* zinc b4.de*
- **urination** agg.; during: rhus-t k*
- **vexation**; after: petr h2 podo fd3.de•
- **violent**: ammc vh1 **Arg-n** tl1* bism a1* bit-ar wht1• borx hr1 *Carb-v* tl1 *Kali-pic* a1* lacer a1* lycps-v c1 rhus-t a1
  - **dinner**; after: ambr a1
- **vomiting**:
  - **after**: arg-n bg1 ars bg1 caust bg1* con bg1* mosch b7a.de plac-s rly4• spong fd4.de
    - **sour** vomiting: *Caust* b4a.de
  - **before**: sulph bg1
  - **when**: acon bg2 ars bg2 caust bg2 chinin-s bg2 cimic ptk1 cocc bg2 con a1 diphtox jl2 ip bg2 mosch bg2 mur-ac bg2* nit-ac bg2 petr bg2 phos bg1* phyt sep bg2 spig bg2 sulph bg2
  - **without**: bacls-7 fmm1•
- **waking**; on: bar-c calc con k* ferr mur-ac puls b7.de* rumx sil k* sulph bg2 valer b7.de*
- **walking**:
  - **agg.**: caps carbn-s *Graph* lyc lycps-v *Mag-m* sulph vanil fd5.de
  - **air**; in open | **after** | **agg.**: nux-v b7.de*
    - **agg.**: grat phos stann sul-ac sulph
  - **amel.**: lyc k*
- **warm** drinks; after: lach b7a.de
- **wine** agg.: lyc k*
- **yawning**; with: astac vh

ERUCTATIONS; TYPE OF:

- **acrid**: aloe alum k* *Ambr* *Apis* k* arg-met ars k* ars-s-f k2 asaf k* bell k* bufo cact *Calc* *Calc-s* *Cann-s* caps *Carb-an* carb-v h2* carbn-s cartl-s rly4• *Caust* cham cocc b7.de* con ptk1 cop crot-h crot-t cupr *Dig* dios dor echi fago k* ferr a1 *Fl-ac* *Graph* gymno ptk1 kali-bi ptk1 kali-c k2 *Lac-ac* lac-c ptk1 *Lach* lact lob **Lyc** k* mang *Merc* k* merc-c bg2 mez k* nat-m ptk1 *Nit-ac* *Nuph* nux-m c1 *Nux-v* ol-an ox-ac petr k* *Ph-ac* bg2 phos k* *Phyt* podo ptk1 raph *Rhus-t* **Rob** bg2* *Sang* k* *Sep* k* *Sul-ac* k* ter ther thuj verat zinc zinc-p k2
  - **afternoon**: *Caust* chin
  - **evening**: alum *Ambr* *Caust*
  - **night**: merc
  - **accompanied** by | **respiration**; asthmatic (See RESPIRATION - Asthmatic - accompanied - eructations - acrid)
  - **bitter**; and: *Sul-ac* b4a.de
  - **bread** agg.: crot-h
  - **dinner**; after: aloe petr h2
  - **drunkards**; in: *Sul-ac*
  - **eating**; after: all-s anac carbn-s helic-p mtf nat-m ptk1 nux-m c1 spig
  - **fever**; during: cub
  - **sweets** agg.: raph zinc
- **air**; of (See empty)
- **almonds**, tasting like: *Caust* k* *Laur* k*
- **apples**, tasting like: agar k*
- **audible** (See loud)
- **bad**:
  - **odor**: ars bg2 bism b7.de* *Cocc* b7.de* ferr bg2 kali-bi bg2 *Merc* b4.de* nux-v b7.de* plb bg2 *Sulph* b4.de* thuj b4.de*
  - **tasting**: arg-met h1
- **ball** is moving up and down during; as if a: bar-c ptk1
- **barley** water; tasting like: naja a1*
- **bedbugs**; smelling like: phel a2*
- **bilious**: **Acon** bg2 aloe bg2 ang b7.de* ant-c bg2 ant-t bg2 arn b7.de* ars bg2 asar bg2 berb k2 bism hr1 *Bry* b7.de* calc h2 camph bg2 **Cham** bg2 *Chin* bg2 *Cocc* b7.de* coloc b4.de* daph bg2 dig bg2 dros b7.de* ign bg2 ip bg2 kali-p k2
- **bilious**: ...
  lach bg2 lyc b4.de* **Merc** b4.de* morg-p pte1• nat-c b4.de* nat-m h2 nat-sil fd3.de• nit-ac b4.de* **Nux-v** b7.de* *Puls* b7.de* sec bg2 *Sep* bg2 spong b7.de* staph bg2 sulph bg2 syc pte1*• *Verat* b7.de*
  - **afternoon**: lyc h2
  - **menses**; during: kali-c b4.de* morg-p pte1• prot pte1•
- **bitter**: aesc *Aloe* k* *Alum* k* alum-p k2 alum-sil k2 *Am-c* k* *Am-m* k* *Ambr* k* ang b7.de* ant-c k* ant-t k* *Apis* arg-met **Arn** k* ars k* ars-s-f k2 aur aur-ar k2 aur-s k2 bar-c k* bar-m bar-s k2 bell k* *Berb* bism *Bry* k* but-ac sp1 *Calc* k* *Calc-s* *Cann-s* *Carb-v* k* carbn-s *Carl* caul cham b7.de* *Chel* k* **Chin** k* *Chinin-ar* chinin-s k* *Chion* cic h1 cob *Cocc* k* coloc corn crot-t cupr *Dios* dros k* eup-per ferr k* ferr-ar ferr-i *Ferr-m* ferr-p germ-met srj5• graph *Grat* k* hell hep hyos k* hyper *Ign* k* indg kali-ar kali-c k* kali-i kali-m k2 kali-n kali-p kali-s kali-sil k2 kreos bg2 laur k* led b7.de* *Lyc* k* *Mag-c* b4a.de mag-m mag-s *Merc* k* *Merc-i-r* morg-p pte1• mur-ac k* nat-c k* nat-m b4a.de **Nat-s** k* nat-sil fd3.de• nicc nit-ac b4.de* **Nux-v** k* op petr k* *Ph-ac* k* phos k* phys *Pic-ac* plb **Podo** ptel **Puls** k* raph rhod sabad k* sang k2 *Sars* k* *Sep* k* sil k* spong k* squil k* *Stann* k* staph k* stict c1 stry suis-hep rly4• *Sul-ac* k* sulph k* tarax k* tarent teucr thuj k* upa verat k* verat-v verb k* zinc zinc-p k2
  - **morning**: am-m h2 calc-s hyper lyc sars sil
    - **cough**; after: sul-ac
    - **rising** agg.: cedr sep
  - **forenoon**: am-m ign nat-c nicc
  - **afternoon**: am-m kali-n h2
  - **evening**: bell castm dios kali-n h2 *Puls* sars
    - **milk** soup, after: alum
    - **potatoes** agg.: *Alum*
  - **night**: calc-s castm chel *Merc* *Nux-v* ox-ac **Puls**
  - **and** yellow on stooping: cic c1
  - **anger**; after: arn
  - **bread** and butter agg.: chin
  - **breakfast** agg., after: pic-ac *Sep*
  - **burning**: *Acon* bg2
  - **cough**; after: sul-ac h2
  - **dinner**:
    - **after**:
      - **agg.**: bar-c fl-ac sars h2 sul-ac
      - **amel.**: ferr
    - **before**: sars h2
    - **during** | **agg.**: sars
  - **drinking**:
    - **after**:
      - **agg.**: sars h2
      - **water** | **agg.**: aloe chin bg1
  - **eating** | **after** | **agg.**: ars h2 bell *Bry* k* *Chin* k* cina kali-p kreos lach led h1 **Lyc** *Nat-m* k* *Nat-s* *Sars* k* *Sep* k* *Stann* thuj verat
    - **amel.**: am-m
  - **fasting** agg.: *Nux-v*
  - **fat** food; after: *Ferr* *Ferr-m*
  - **food** comes up: **Lyc** k* *Nat-s* k*
  - **foul**: ant-c bg2
  - **hysteria**; during: tarax ptk1
  - **menses**; during: *Sep* sulph
  - **milk** agg.: chin ptk1 sulph h2
  - **potatoes** agg.: *Alum*
  - **rich** food agg.: ferr *Ferr-m*
  - **soup** agg.: sars h2
  - **sour** food agg.: ph-ac
  - **stool** agg.; during: cham
  - **stooping** agg.: castm cic a1
  - **supper** agg.; after: zinc
  - **walking** in open air agg.: grat
- **bitter**-salty: *Staph* b7a.de

Stomach

- **bitter**-sour: caust$_{b4a.de}$ **Chin**$_{b7.de}$* kali-c$_{h2}$ mag-m$_{b4.de}$* **Nux-v**$_{bg2}$ sars$_{b4.de}$* **Sul-ac**$_{h2}$* *Sulph*$_{b4.de}$*
  - **fluid**: *Sulph*$_{b4a.de}$
- **bitter**-sweetish: plat$_{b4a.de}$*
- **bloody**: merc-c nux-v phos psor$_{jl2}$ raph *Sep*$_{k}$*
- **bread**; like fresh: merc$_{b4.de}$*
- **brown**: psor$_{jl2}$
- **burning**: (*↗sour; Heartburn*) acet-ac$_{bg2}$ *All-s*$_{vh1}$ anac$_{b4.de}$* ars$_{bg2}$ aur$_{bg2}$ bell$_{b4.de}$* *Bry*$_{b7.de}$* calc$_{bg2}$ canth$_{b7.de}$* caps$_{bg2}$ cartl-s$_{rly4}$• *Caust*$_{k}$* chin$_{bg2}$ coff crot-t$_{k}$* cycl$_{bg2}$* ferr$_{k}$* fl-ac$_{bg2}$ ger-i$_{rly4}$• hep$_{b4a.de}$* *Iod*$_{k}$* kali-bi$_{bg2}$ lac-ac$_{bg2}$ lil-t$_{bg2}$ lob$_{bg2}$ *Lyc*$_{k}$* manc$_{bg2}$ mang$_{bg2}$ mez$_{b4.de}$* naja$_{bg2}$ *Nat-m*$_{b4a.de}$ ol-an$_{bg2}$ oxal-a$_{rly4}$• ph-ac$_{b4a.de}$* *Phos*$_{b4.de}$* puls$_{bg2}$ rhod$_{b4a.de}$ rhus-t$_{b7.de}$* sil$_{bg2}$ *Sul-ac*$_{b4a.de}$ sulph$_{b4a.de}$* thymol$_{sp1}$ tub$_{bg2}$ tub-r$_{jl2}$ valer$_{b7a.de}$* zinc$_{bg2}$
  - **horn**: sec$_{a1}$
- **burnt** tasting: bry$_{b7.de}$* cycl$_{h1}$ laur$_{b7.de}$* sabad$_{b7a.de}$
- **cadaverous** odor: bism$_{b7.de}$*
- **cold**:
  - **agg.**: caust$_{ptk1}$ cist$_{bg2}$* mag-c$_{h2}$ *Puls*$_{b7a.de}$ verat$_{ptk1}$
  - **air** agg.: mag-c$_{b4.de}$*
  - **food** | **agg.**: caust$_{b4a.de}$ verat$_{b7.de}$*
- **deep**: rhus-g$_{tmo3}$•
- **disgusting** (See foul)
- **dry**: bry$_{b7.de}$* hell$_{b7.de}$*
- **egg**; tasting like: *Zinc*$_{b4a.de}$
  - **white** of the egg; like: ferr$_{b7a.de}$
  - **yolk** of the egg; like: apis$_{k}$*
- **eggs**; like spoiled: acon$_{k}$* *Agar*$_{k}$* **Ant-c**$_{b7a.de}$* ant-t$_{k}$* apis$_{bg2}$ **Arn**$_{k}$* bell$_{bg2}$ brom$_{k}$* bufo$_{k}$* *Carb-v*$_{b4a.de}$ cham$_{bg2}$* chin$_{b7a.de}$* coff$_{k}$* dios$_{k}$* elaps$_{k}$* ferr$_{bg2}$ **Hep**$_{bg2}$ kali-bi$_{bg2}$ kali-c kola$_{stb3}$• lac-h$_{htj1}$• *Lyc*$_{vh}$ mag-c$_{bg2}$ *Mag-m*$_{k}$* mag-s$_{k}$* med$_{br1}$ petr$_{k}$* phos$_{k}$* plac$_{rzf5}$• plan$_{bg1}$* podo *Psor*$_{k}$* ptel$_{k}$* **Puls**$_{b7a.de}$* rhus-t$_{k}$* ruta$_{fd4.de}$ *Sep*$_{k}$* stann$_{k}$* *Sulph*$_{k}$* *Valer*$_{k}$*
  - **morning**: stann$_{h2}$
    - **rising** agg.: **Arn** graph mag-c *Mag-s* petr sulph valer
    - **waking**; on: valer
  - **evening**: carl ruta$_{fd4.de}$
  - **night**: *Ant-t* mag-c$_{h2}$ phos ruta$_{fd4.de}$
  - **pregnancy** agg.; during: mag-c
  - **smelling** like: arn$_{mrr1}$ *Cham* elaps elat ferr *Podo* psor rhus-t sulph
    - **night**: mag-c
- **empty**: abies-n acon$_{k}$* *Aesc* *Aeth* **Agar**$_{k}$* all-c aloe$_{k}$* alum$_{k}$* alum-p$_{k2}$ alum-sil$_{k2}$ am-br **Am-c**$_{k}$* am-m$_{k}$* *Ambr*$_{k}$* anac$_{k}$* anan androc$_{srj1}$• ang$_{b7a.de}$* **Ant-c**$_{k}$* ant-t$_{k}$* apis$_{b7a.de}$ **Arg-n**$_{k}$* **Arn**$_{k}$* **Ars**$_{k}$* **Ars-i** ars-s-f$_{k2}$ arund *Asaf*$_{k}$* *Asar*$_{k}$* bapt *Bar-c*$_{k}$* *Bar-i* bar-s$_{k2}$ bell$_{k}$* *Berb* **Bism**$_{k}$* bov$_{k}$* brom *Bry*$_{k}$* but-ac$_{sp1}$ cain *Calad*$_{k}$* *Calc*$_{k}$* calc-i$_{k2}$* calc-s calc-sil$_{k2}$ camph$_{k}$* cann-i **Cann-s**$_{k}$* canth$_{k}$* **Carb-ac** *Carb-an*$_{k}$* **Carb-v**$_{k}$* **Carbn-s** card-m carl cartl-s$_{rly4}$• *Casc* castm caul **Caust**$_{k}$* *Cham*$_{k}$* *Chel*$_{k}$* *Chin*$_{k}$* chinin-ar chinin-s$_{k}$* chir-fl$_{gya2}$ chlol cimx cina$_{b7.de}$* cinnb cist clem cob coc-c coca$_{a1}$* *Cocc*$_{k}$* coff$_{k}$* *Colch*$_{k}$* *Coloc*$_{k}$* **Con**$_{k}$* cop corn *Croc*$_{k}$* crot-t$_{k}$* cycl$_{b7.de}$* *Daph* *Dios* dirc$_{c1}$ dulc$_{k}$* elat erig eup-per euph$_{b4.de}$* eupi fago *Ferr* ferr-ar ferr-i ferr-p fl-ac$_{k}$* gamb gent-c gins *Glon* gran **Graph**$_{b4.de}$* grat *Guaj*$_{k}$* gymno ham hell$_{k}$* helon hep$_{k}$* *Hydr* hyos$_{k}$* hyper$_{k}$* ign$_{k}$* indg **Iod**$_{k}$* **Ip**$_{k}$* *Iris* jatr-c *Kali-ar* **Kali-bi**$_{k}$* kali-c$_{k}$* kali-chl **Kali-i** kali-m$_{k2}$ kali-n$_{b4a.de}$ kali-p kali-s kali-sil$_{k2}$ *Kalm* *Kreos*$_{k}$* *Lac-c* lac-d$_{k2}$* *Lach*$_{k}$* lact laur$_{k}$* *Lec* led lob **Lyc**$_{k}$* m-arct$_{b7.de}$ m-aust$_{b7.de}$ mag-c$_{k}$* mag-m$_{k}$* mag-s manc mang med *Meny*$_{k}$* merc$_{k}$* merc-c$_{b4a.de}$ merc-i-f *Mez*$_{k}$* mill mosch$_{k}$* myric *Nat-ar* *Nat-c*$_{k}$* nat-m$_{k}$* nat-p *Nat-s* nicc *Nit-ac*$_{k}$* nux-m **Nux-v**$_{b7.de}$* ol-an olnd$_{k}$* ox-ac pall par$_{b7.de}$* petr$_{k}$* ph-ac$_{k}$* *Phos*$_{k}$* phys phyt **Pic-ac** plan plat$_{b4.de}$* *Plb*$_{k}$* plut-n$_{srj7}$• podo positr$_{nl2}$• ptel **Puls**$_{k}$* ran-b$_{k}$* ran-s$_{k}$* raph rhod$_{k}$* rhus-t$_{k}$* rumx ruta$_{k}$* sabad$_{k}$* sabin$_{k}$* sang$_{k}$* sars$_{k}$* sec senec *Seneg*$_{k}$* sep$_{k}$* sil$_{k}$* sin-a sol-ni spig$_{k}$* spong$_{k}$* squil$_{k}$* stann$_{k}$* staph$_{k}$* stront-c$_{k}$* stry suis-pan$_{rly4}$• sul-ac$_{k}$* sul-i$_{k2}$ **Sulph**$_{k}$* sumb symph$_{fd3.de}$• tab tarax$_{k}$* **Tarent** thuj til tritic-vg$_{fd5.de}$ *Valer*$_{k}$* *Verat*$_{k}$* verat-v verb$_{k}$* vinc viol-t$_{k}$* xan$_{k}$* zinc$_{k}$* zinc-p$_{k2}$ zing
  - **morning**: alum$_{h2}$ anac bar-c bov bry calc cedr cina cob coloc con croc dios kali-c$_{h2}$ mag-c nat-m *Pic-ac* *Plat* stann$_{h2}$ sul-ac *Sulph*
    - **7** h: dios
    - **fasting**, after: bov cina croc nit-ac$_{h2}$ *Plat*
    - **rising** | **after** | **agg.**: nat-m
- **empty – morning – rising**: ...
      - **agg.**: cedr
    - **waking**; on: bar-c calc
  - **forenoon**: castor-eq colch com *Con* hydr ign kali-c$_{h2}$ myric naja par *Pic-ac* sars zinc
    - **9** h: com$_{k}$*
    - **10** h: castor-eq ign
    - **11** h: hydr
  - **noon**: olnd ox-ac
    - **eating**; while: olnd
  - **afternoon**: aeth ambr$_{h1}$ ars bar-c$_{h2}$ *Carb-v* crot-t dios hydr hyper iris lyc mag-m nat-m op ox-ac
    - **17** h: dios hyper ox-ac
    - **coffee** agg.: nat-m
    - **stomach** is empty; while: op
  - **evening**: abrot am-c coc-c dios hyper rumx sars sulph tritic-vg$_{fd5.de}$ verat zinc
    - **18** h: iris
    - **19** h: dios phys
    - **21** h until midnight: phos
      - **walking** in open air agg.: phos
    - **21**.30 h: dirc
    - **hiccough**; during: sulph
    - **lying** agg.: verat
  - **night**: dios dirc kali-c$_{h2}$ mang mur-ac phos phys sumb tanac
    - **23** h: sumb
    - **menses**; before: mang
  - **air** agg.; in open: nat-m
  - **alternating** with | **hiccough**: agar$_{k}$*
  - **beer**; after: vinc
  - **breakfast** | **after** | **agg.**: ars grat hell sulph
    - **before** | **agg.**: *Bov* *Ran-s*
  - **coldness**; during: gamb
  - **cough**; after: **Ambr** ang$_{c1}$ **Sang** sul-ac verat
  - **dinner**; after: alum$_{h2}$ am-c ars cact cycl lyc mag-m *Sulph* zinc$_{h2}$
  - **drinking**:
    - **after**:
      - **agg.**: bism carb-v coloc nat-m rhus-t$_{h1}$ tarax vinc zinc$_{h2}$
      - **cold** water | **agg.**: phos
  - **eating**; after: *Acon* ang$_{b7a.de}$ ars bry calc *Camph* carb-an card-m cench$_{k2}$ coloc cupr$_{sst3}$• cycl grat *Hydr* kali-s$_{fd4.de}$ nat-c *Nat-m*$_{k}$* *Ox-ac* ph-ac *Phos*$_{k}$* *Plat* *Ran-s*$_{k}$* rhus-t$_{k}$* *Sep* spig **Sulph**$_{k}$* tritic-vg$_{fd5.de}$ **Verat**$_{k}$*
  - **fasting** agg.: plat valer
  - **headache**; during: aeth$_{hr1}$ apis *Calc*
  - **hot**: apis$_{vh}$ carb-v$_{vh}$ kali-bi$_{vh}$
  - **hysteria**; during: mang
  - **menses** | **before** | **agg.**: mang
    - **colic**, during menstrual: mang
  - **mental** exertion agg.: *Hep*
  - **nausea**; during: arn coc-c
  - **rising** up: coloc
  - **soup** agg.: carb-v mag-c
  - **stool** agg.; after: bar-c
  - **sugar** agg.: raph
  - **supper** agg.; after: alum lyc sep
  - **waking**; on: bar-c calc rumx
- **explosive**: (*↗loud*) arg-n$_{br1}$ *Asaf*$_{bg2}$ coca$_{ptk1}$
  - **neurotic** persons; in: *Arg-n*$_{br1}$
- **fat**; tasting like: *Carb-v*$_{b4a.de}$
- **feces**: *Bry*$_{b7.de}$* plb$_{ptk1}$
- **fishy**: carb-an$_{h2}$*
  - **spoiled** fish; tasting like: carb-an$_{b4a.de}$

- **fluid**: abies-n agar all-c alum anac ant-c ant-t ars asaf ptk1 aur b4a.de aur-s *Calc* cann-s carbn-s carl caul cham chlol coc-c crot-h cycl dig dream-p sdj1• fago form gent-c gran graph gymno ham hell kali-bi bg2* kali-c k2 *Lac-ac* lyc mag-s c1 mez mosch nicc nux-v *Plat* plb ptel **Puls** k* raph rhod rob sang k2 sul-ac k2* *Sulph* k* ust vanil fd5.de verat verb
  - **morning**: all-c verat verb
  - **forenoon**: *Carl*
  - **afternoon**: valer
    - **16** h: *Valer*
  - **night**: nux-v
    - **bread**; after white: *Crot-h*
  - **breakfast** agg.; after: phos
  - **coffee** agg.: puls
  - **dinner**; after: castm
  - **eating**; after: cina staph
  - **greenish**: ars graph sang k2
  - **milky** (See milk)
  - **preceded** by a quivering in stomach: mag-s c1
  - **yellow**: cic sang k2
- **food** (= regurgitation): acon bg2 *Aesc* aeth k* alum bg2* alum-sil k2 am-m k* ant-c bg2* **Ant-t** bg2* arg-met bg2 *Arg-n* *Arn* bg2* ars k* ars-s-f k2 *Arum-t* asaf k* bar-c bg2 *Bell* k* bros-gau mrc1 *Bry* k* bufo *Calc* k* *Calc-s* k* camph h1* cann-xyz bg2 canth k* carb-an h2 *Carb-v* k* carbn-s *Caust* k* *Cham* k* **Chin** k* chinin-ar chlf br1 cic bg2 cina bg2 coff *Con* k* *Cop* cortico tpw7 cycl k* *Dig* k* diphtox jl2 dros bg2 dulc bg2 echi euph bg2 **Ferr** k* ferr-ar k2 ferr-i k* **Ferr-p** k* ferr-s mtf11 glon graph k* haliae-lc srj5• *Hep* k* hydr k2 ign k* *Ip* bro1 iris kali-ar *Kali-bi* kali-c k* kali-m k2 kali-p kali-s kalm kola stb3• *Lach* k* laur bg2 lob *Lyc* k* mag-c k2 mag-m k* *Mag-p* mang *Merc* k* merc-c bg2 *Mez* k* mosch bg2 *Mur-ac* k* nat-c bg2 *Nat-m* k* nat-p bro1 nit-ac k* *Nux-v* k* olnd bg2 par bg2 petr bg2 **Ph-ac** k* **Phos** k* pic-ac plat k* plb k* *Podo* k* **Puls** k* quas bro1 ran-b k* rauw sp1 rhod bg2 *Rhus-t* k* rob k* ruta fd4.de sabin bg2 sanic bg2* sars k* senec sep bg2 spig k* spong bg2 staph bg2 stront-c bg2 sul-ac k* *Sulph* k* tab k* tell c1 teucr k* thuj k* tritic-vg fd5.de tub-r jl2 ust valer k* vanil fd5.de vario ptk1 verat k* verat-v bg2 verb bg2 zinc bg2
  - **morning**: *Sulph*
  - **noon**: *Ferr*
  - **afternoon**: euphr ferr lyc nat-p ruta fd4.de sulph
  - **evening**: kola stb3• ruta fd4.de sulph
  - **night**: *Canth* kola stb3• *Phos* zinc
    - **midnight**, after: ferr mrr1 sil
    - **food** eaten at noon; from: kali-c h2 *Zinc*
    - **soup** eaten at noon: graph h2
  - **acrid**, sharp tasting: alum bg2 ant-t b7.de* *Apis* b7a.de arg-met b7.de* ars b4a.de* asaf bg2 bell bg2 *Calc* b4a.de camph bg2 carb-v b4.de* caust bg2 dros b7a.de hep bg2 merc b4.de* ph-ac bg2 *Sep* b4a.de *Spig* b7a.de sulph bg2 zinc b4.de*
  - **anxious**: ign b7.de*
  - **bad**; tasting: chel b7.de* puls b7.de* sars b4.de*
  - **bilious**: phos b4.de*
  - **bitter** tasting: am-c bg2 arg-met b7.de* arn b7.de* ars bg2 bar-c b4.de* bry b7.de* *Calc* b4a.de cann-xyz bg2 cic b7.de* dros b7.de* graph b4a.de* grat bg2 ign b7.de* **Lyc** k* merc b4.de* *Nat-c* k* nux-v b7.de* *Petr* b4a.de ph-ac phos b4.de* puls b7.de* rhod b4.de* sabad b7.de* sars b4.de* sul-ac bg2 sulph h2 teucr b7.de* verat bg2
    - **eating**; after: sars b4a.de
    - **rancid**: phos b4.de* rhod b4.de*
    - **sour**: am-m b7.de* *Cann-s* b7.de* cina b7.de* nux-v b7.de* sul-ac b4a.de
  - **bloody**: canth b7.de* chin b7.de* merc b4.de* nux-v b7.de*
  - **burning**: tub-r jl2
  - **burnt**; as if: cycl b7.de*
  - **cough**; after: ferr mtf33 *Raph* k* sul-ac
  - **dinner**; after: lyc nat-p ruta fd4.de sars sulph
    - **walking** agg.: mag-m
- **food**: ...
  - **eating**:
    - **after** | **agg.**: aesc am-c bg2 am-m b7a.de* ant-c b7.de* ant-t b7.de* arn b7.de* asaf bg2 bell b4.de* bry k* calc h* camph b7.de* canth b7.de* *Carb-v* b4.de* *Cham* b7.de* *Con* b4a.de* dulc b4.de* **Ferr** k* graph b4a.de* *Ign* b7.de* *Lach* b7.de* *Lyc* b4.de* mag-m b4.de* mag-p med merc b4.de* mez b4.de* nat-c b4a.de *Nat-m* k* nit-ac b4.de* nux-v b7.de* olnd b7.de* par b7.de* phos k* plb b7.de* podo *Puls* b7.de* sars b4a.de* sep b4.de* sul-ac b4.de* **Sulph** b4.de* teucr b7a.de* thuj b4a.de* tritic-vg fd5.de verat bg2
    - **five** hours after: *Caust* melal-alt gya4
    - **immediately** after: ferr k* *Mag-p* k* *Phos*
    - **nauseous** taste: calc h2
    - **one** hour after: aesc aeth k* sulph h2
    - **two** hours after: ferr lyc ruta fd4.de sulph
    - **while** | **agg.**: cupr-s ferr mrr1 grat mag-p merc k* phos k* sars k*
  - **empyreumatic** (See burnt)
  - **fever**; during: ant-t bg2 arn bg2 *Ars* bg2 bry bg2 calc bg2 cham bg2 **Cina** bg2 coloc bg2 dros bg2 **Ferr** bg2 **Ign** bg2 ip bg2 lyc bg2 merc bg2 mez bg2 *Nat-m* bg2 *Nux-v* bg2 phos bg2 *Puls* bg2 sep bg2 sil bg2 sulph bg2 verat bg2
  - **hot**: anac b4a.de asaf b7.de* canth b7.de* carb-v b4.de* cic b7.de* coff b7.de* croc b7.de* dulc b4.de* hell b7.de* hep b4a.de *Ign* b7a.de kali-bi bg2 m-aust b7.de merc b4.de* nat-m b4a.de nux-m b7.de* nux-v b7.de* *Ph-ac* b4a.de phos b4a.de plat b4.de* verat b7.de*
    - **eating**; after: hep b4a.de
  - **menses** | **after** | **agg.**: verat b7a.de
    - **before** | **agg.**: kreos bg2 nat-m bg2
  - **mouthful**, by the●: aesc arg-n ars *Dig* *Ferr* k* *Hydr* *Hyos* lach lyc morg-p pte1• **Phos** k* sul-ac sulph
  - **painful**: ant-c b7.de*
  - **putrid**: *Con* b4.de*
  - **rancid**: merc bg2 puls valer b7.de*
  - **salty**: ant-t b7.de* arn b7.de* kali-c ptk1 lyc b4.de* *Sep* b4a.de sul-ac bg2 verat b7.de*
  - **scratchy**: ambr b7.de* cann-s b7.de* valer b7.de*
  - **sensation** of: maias-l hrn2•
  - **sitting** agg.: bros-gau mrc1
  - **sour**: alum b4.de* ant-t b7.de* *Apis* b7a.de ars bg2 calc b4.de* cann-s b7.de* *Carb-an* b4a.de carb-v b4a.de* con b4.de* dig b4a.de* dros b7.de* graph b4a.de* hep b4a.de kali-c b4a.de* lyc b4a.de* m-ambo b7.de* mag-c ptk1 mag-m h2 mang b4a.de* mur-ac b4.de* nat-c bg2 nat-m b4a.de* nux-v b7.de* petr b4.de* *Phos* b4a.de* plb b7.de* puls b7.de* rhus-t b7.de* sabin b7.de* sars b4.de* *Sep* b4a.de *Spig* b7a.de spong b7.de* *Sulph* b4a.de* tub-r jl2 zinc b4.de*
    - **eating**; after: con b4a.de dig b4a.de sars b4a.de
  - **spoiled** food; like: *M-ambo* b7.de* *Puls* b7a.de
  - **stool** agg.; during: ant-c b7a.de
  - **stooping** agg.: cic ip *Phos* k* vanil fd5.de
  - **supper** agg.; after: phos
  - **sweetish**: *Acon* b7.de* alum b4.de* bar-c b4.de* chin b7.de* merc b4.de* plat b4.de* plb b7.de* stann b4.de* sul-ac b4.de* verat b7.de* zinc b4.de*
  - **tea**; after: bros-gau mrc1
  - **undigested** food | **eating**; after: sulph b4a.de
  - **vexation**; after: ferr-p k* podo fd3.de•
  - **walking** agg.: *Mag-m* k*
  - **warm**: asaf b7a.de cann-s b7.de* hell b7.de* *Plat* b4a.de rhus-t b7.de* valer b7.de* verat b7.de*
  - **worm**; like a: puls b7.de* *Sulph* b4a.de
  - **yellow**: cic b7.de*
- **food**; tasting like: aesc aeth agar k* aloe alum b4.de* am-c k* am-m k* ambr k* anan **Ant-c** k* *Apis* k* arg-n arn ars aur-s bell k* bism ptk1 bov b4.de* **Bry** k* *Calc* k* calc-sil k2 camph k* canth b7.de* **Carb-an** k* carb-v k* carl castm **Caust** k* cham k* chel k* **Chin** k* cic cina b7.de* cocc k* coff b7.de* colch *Con* k* cop cortico sp1 croc k* crot-h cycl k* echi euphr k* **Ferr** k* *Ferr-ar* *Graph* k* *Grat* ham hep k* ign k* iod b4.de* *Ip* irid-met srj5• kali-bi kali-c k* kali-i lac-ac lach k*

Stomach

- **food**; tasting like: ...
laur k* lyc k* m-ambo b7.de mag-c b4.de* mag-m k* mang k* nat-ar nat-c **Nat-m** k* nux-v k* olnd phel *Phos* k* phyt plb k* psil ft1 **Puls** k* *Ran-s* k* rat r a u w tpw8 rhus-t k* *Rumx* ruta k* sabad b7.de* sabin b7a.de sars k* sep k* *Sil* k* sin-a spig squil b7.de* staph k* still *Sulph* k* sumb tab tell teucr b7.de* *Thuj* k* til trom vanil fd5.de verat k* zinc k* zinc-p k2
  - **morning**: agar mag-c h2
  - **afternoon**: coff euphr petr h2
    - **13** h: chel
    - **dinner**; after: canth cina sars squil
  - **drinking** water agg.: **Apis** k*
  - **eating**; after: bry b7a.de calc b4a.de caust b4a.de ran-s b7a.de sil b4a.de sulph b4a.de thuj b4a.de
  - **smoking** agg.: thuj
- **foul**: acet-ac anan ant-c *Ant-t* k* **Arn** k* ars ars-s-f k2 **Asaf** k* asar aur-m bapt br1 *Berb Bism* k* bufo calc calc-ar calc-s carb-an k* *Carb-v* k* carbn-s caust chir-fl gya2 cina k* *Cocc* k* con cop cortico tpw7* cub *Dig Ferr* ferr-ar ferr-p *Fl-ac Graph* k* *Hep* hydr *Kali-bi* lac-loxod-a hm2• lact merc morg-g fmm1• mosch mur-ac k* naja k* nat-m k* nat-s k* nicc-met sk4• nit-ac nux-v olnd par b7.de* ph-ac b4.de* phos *Plb* k* *Psor* k* *Puls* raph sang sec *Sep* k* squil b7.de* *Sul-ac Sulph* k* thuj thymol sp1 tritic-vg fd5.de valer
  - **morning**: *Nux-v*
  - **forenoon**: cocc
  - **evening**: nat-s phos stram thuj h1
  - **night**: merc
  - **cough** agg.; during: caps bg2
  - **drunkards**; in: sul-ac
  - **eating**; after: carb-v b4a.de coenz-q mtf11
  - **fat** or rich food, after: **Asaf** *Caust* chir-fl gya2 nat-m *Puls*
  - **milk** agg.: nat-m
  - **pastry** or pork, after: *Puls*
  - **peaches**, after: psor
- **frequent**: ambr c1 **Arg-n** mrr1 borx hr1 **Carb-v** mrr1 nat-c h2 nat-sil fd3.de• tritic-vg fd5.de vanil fd5.de
- **frothy**: alet all-c atra-r bnm3• *Canth* cimx bg1 kreos k* *Lach* lyc *Mag-m* k* sep ptk1 verat ptk1
  - **morning**: all-c
  - **white**: mag-m h2
- **garlic**, like: aesc **Asaf** k* *Mag-m* k* mosch nat-sil fd3.de• phos bg2 sul-ac sulph
  - **spasm**, after a: mag-m k*
- **greasy**: aesc alum bg1* ars bg2 asaf b7a.de* carb-v k* caust ptk1 conv mtf11 *Cycl* ferr-i grat bg2 hep bg2 iris ptk1 kali-bi bg2 lyc k* **Mag-c** k* nux-v bg2 *Puls* k* sabad bg2 thuj bg2* valer ptk1 zinc h2*
- **greenish**: ars h2* graph b4a.de*
- **hiccough**, like: agar b4.de* ant-t k* bell b4.de* calc k* canth b7.de* carb-an b4.de* *Cupr* b7a.de *Cycl* k* ham bg2 *Ign* b7.de* lach bg2 meph bg2 merc b4.de* mez k* plat k* ran-b b7.de* sars k* staph b7a.de* sulph k*
  - **dinner**; after: carb-an plat
  - **eating**; after: cycl b7a.de
- **horn**-shavings; like fresh: m-ambo b7.de*
- **hot**: acet-ac apis bg1 ars aur canth k* carb-v bg1 *Caust* cob cop *Hep* k* kali-bi bg1 *Lac-ac* naja *Petr Phos* phys *Podo* puls sang k2 *Sep* b4a.de sil sin-a *Sul-ac* b4a.de valer b7a.de zinc
  - **morning**: tab
  - **bitter**, and: fago pd gymno pd podo pd
  - **eating**; after: hep h2 *Podo*
  - **menses**; during: kali-p bg2
  - **offensive**; and: naja ptk1
  - **smoking** agg.: lac-ac ptk1
- **hysterical**: ruta bg2
- **juniper** berries; tasting like: chel b7.de*
- **large** quantities of wind: **Arg-n** asaf bapt *Carb-v* chir-fl gya2 dios a1 *Hep Lyc Phos*
- **lead**; tasting like: sulph h2
- **lime** water, tasting like: kali-c
- **liquid** (See fluid)
- **long** continued: ger-i rly4• glon k* sul-ac h2
- **loud**: *(↗explosive)* acon ambr k* ant-c k* **Arg-n** k* arn k* **Asaf** k* *Bism* borx *Calc* b4a.de calc-p k* *Carb-v* carbn-s caust k* *Chin* k* *Coca Coloc* com con k* dioxi rbp6 dulc fd4.de ferr-i gamb bg2 gran iris jug-r kali-bi ptk1 kali-c b4.de* kali-n kali-p fd1.de• kreos bg2 lach k* lact mag-c b4.de* manc merc *Merc-i-r* mez b4.de* mosch k* nux-m hr1 *Nux-v* b7a.de par bg2 petr k* *Phos* k* **Plat** k* plb polys sk4• psor al2 *Puls* k* sacch-a fd2.de• *Sil* k* sin-n suis-pan rly4• sulph k* sumb tab k* thuj ptk1* til tritic-vg fd5.de ulm-c jsj8• vanil fd5.de verat verb k* vib ptk1 zinc k*
  - **afternoon**: carbn-s
  - **eating**; after: calc k* kali-p fd1.de• plat h2 sacch-a fd2.de• tab
  - **fasting** agg.: **Plat**
  - **incontrollable**: *Sil* ulm-c jsj8•
  - **involuntary**: asaf
  - **milk** agg.: sulph
  - **stooping** agg.: manc
- **meat**; tasting like: mez k* zinc k*
  - **roasted**: nicc-c c1 (non:nicot c1)
  - **spoiled**: alum-sil k2 **Puls** k*
- **milk**: ant-t b7a.de* lyc bg2
- **milk**; like: ant-t calc carb-ac carb-v cina k2 lyc merc k2 sep k2* sulph k* tritic-vg fd5.de zinc
  - **afternoon**: zinc
  - **walking** agg.: mag-m
- **moldy**: cocc b7.de* crot-h bg2 fl-ac bg2* ign k*
- **mucus**: aesc alum *Arn* k* ars h2 bry k* calc bg1 *Canth* carb-v h2* coca a1 cupr graph bg1* hydr ptk1 hyper bg1* *Kali-c Lach* lyc mag-s nat-s k2 phos puls b7.de* raph sabad k* staph b7.de* stram bg2 sul-ac k* sulph bg2* verat b7.de*
  - **morning**: all-c bry graph hyper
    - **cough**; after: sul-ac
  - **evening**: bry hyper
  - **burning**: thymol sp1
  - **like** mucus: sulph h2*
  - **mouthful**: carb-v h2
  - **tenacious**: sep ptk1
  - ○ **Throat**, from: opun-s a1 staph h1
- **musk**, tasting like: *Caust* k* sumb
- **musk**-like odor: caust b4.de* mosch b7.de*
- **nauseous**: am-m ant-t aq-mar rbp6 arn ptk1 asaf bg3* bapt hr1 bism ptk1 calc *Carb-v* k* carbn-s chin fl-ac *Graph* k* grat helon kali-br nat-m ol-an onos oreo br1 par ptel **Puls** k* *Sep* k* sulph bg3* thymol sp1 verat k* verb k* zinc zing [tax jsj7]
  - **rich** food agg.: nat-m sep
- **nose**; through: atra-r bnm3• diphtox jl2 lyc merc-c phos
- **offensive** (See foul)
- **oil**; olive | **smelling** like: phos b4.de*
- **onions**; like: asaf b7.de* mag-m b4.de* phos b4a.de* sul-ac b4a.de *Sulph* b4a.de
- **oranges**, like: phos b4.de*
- **painful**: acon bg1* anan ant-c bg1 *Ant-t* b7a.de bar-c b4.de* *Bry* k* caps b7.de* *Carb-an* k* caust k* **Cham** k* cocc bg2* coloc b4a.de con k* falco-pe nl2• lach bg2 lob bg1 nat-c k* nicc bg1* nux-v k* ox-ac *Par* k* petr bg2* phos k* plb k* rhus-t b7.de* sabad k* sep b4.de* suis-pan rly4• symph fd3.de•
  - **forcible**, as if esophagus would split: coca ptk1
- **pepper**; tasting like red: caps tl1
- **phosphor**; like: phos b4.de*
- **pine**-oil; like: nux-m b7.de*
- **prussic** acid; like: laur b7.de*
- **pungent**: acet-ac ptk1 arn ptk1 bism ptk1 kreos ptk1 petr ptk1 plb ptk1 psor ptk1 sabad valer ptk1
  - **cough** agg.; during: caps
- **putrid**: *(↗rancid)* *Acet-ac* acon b7.de* *Arn* k* asaf k2 asar k* aur-m bell k* bism bg2 carb-an b4.de* *Caust* b4a.de cocc k* con b4.de* ferr a1 graph hell bg2 h e p bg2 hydr k2 kali-bi bg2 mag-c b4.de* mag-s merc k* mur-ac k* nux-v k* olnd k* oscilloc jl2 petr b4.de* phel bg2 phos b4.de* *Psor* puls k* ruta b7a.de* sang bg2 sep k* *Sul-ac* b4a.de sulph k* tab thuj k* til c1 *Valer* k*
- **radish**, tasting like: osm bg2*

- **rancid**: (*↗putrid; Rancidity*) aeth alum k* *Am* bro1 **Asaf** k* bar-c k* bism bro1 but-ac sp1 cadm-s k* *Calc* k* calc-i bro1 *Carb-v* k* carbn-s *Cham* bro1 *Chin* ptk1 *Croc* *Cycl* k* dios bro1 ferr-i *Graph* k* grat hydr bro1 kali-bi k* *Kali-c* bro1 laur k* lyc ptk1 mag-m bro1 *Mag-s* bro1 merc k* mez k* nux-m orni bro1 phos k* plb bro1 *Psor* k* *Puls* k* ran-s k* raph bro1 rhod sabad k* sang bro1 sanic sep k2* sulph k* tell ptk1 ter thuj k* tritic-vg fd5.de *Valer* k* xero bro1
  - **morning** | **soup**; after: alum
  - **afternoon**: crot-h
    - **16** h: *Valer*
  - **evening**: ran-s
    - **eating**; after: mez
  - **night**: *Merc*
  - **dinner**; during: alum
  - **eating**; after: *Graph* tritic-vg fd5.de
  - **rich** food agg.: thuj
- **repulsive**: cina bg2 nat-m bg2 sep bg2
- **retching**; increasing to: phos bg2
- **rolling**: caust bg2
- **salty**: abrot bg2 agar ant-t am cadm-s *Carb-an* k* caust cham *Kali-c* k* lyc mag-m bg1 nux-v k* sep k* sil bg1 staph k* sul-ac k*
  - **vomiting**; before: sul-ac h2
- **scratchy**: ambr b7.de* ant-c b7a.de* carb-v b4.de* cocc b7.de* lyc b4a.de nat-m b4a.de* nux-m b7.de* petr b4.de* stann bg2 staph b7.de* sulph b4.de* verat b7.de*
  - **eating**; after: nux-m b7a.de
  - **fats**; from: carb-v bg2 ferr bg2
- **short**: am b7.de* squil b7.de* staph b7.de*
- **sobbing**: ant-t bell chin k* coloc cycl manc bg2 meph staph
- **sour**: (*↗burning; water brash; water of; Acidity; Heartburn*) abrot *Acet-ac* k* aesc aeth mtf11 agar ail *All-c* aloe *Alum* k* alum-p k2 alum-sil k2 am-c k* am-m *Ambr* k* ant-c bro1 ant-t k* *Apis* b7a.de aran-sc *Arg-n* k* *Ars* k* ars-i k2 ars-s-f k2 *Asaf* b7a.de asar k* atis zzc1• *Bar-c* k* *Bar-i* k* bar-s k2 bell k* *Bry* k* bufo but-ac sp1 cact *Cadm-s* **Calc** k* calc-i k2* *Calc-p* k* *Calc-s* calc-sil k2 cann-s k* *Canth* caps b7.de* *Carb-ac* k* *Carb-an* k* **Carb-v** k* *Carbn-s* caul *Caust* k* *Cham* k* *Chel* **Chin** k* *Chinin-ar* *Chion* chlol *Cimx* cina k* cob cob-n sp1 *Cocc* coff coloc k* com *Con* k* cop crot-h cub cupr-act *Cycl* k* *Dig* k* *Dios* k* dros k* dulc fd4.de echi elaps *Ferr* k* *Ferr-ar* *Ferr-i* *Ferr-m* *Ferr-p* k* fl-ac k* form k* *Gels* gent-c germ-met srj5• gins *Glycyr-g* cte1• *Graph* k* guare gymno k* *Hep* k* *Hydr* k* hydrc hyos **Ign** k* indg *Iod* k* ip bro1 **Iris** kali-ar **Kali-bi** k* *Kali-c* k* kali-chl kali-m k* kali-p **Kali-s** kali-sil k2 *Kreos* k* lac-ac k* *Lac-d* *Lach* k* lact-v bro1 laur k* lept **Lith-c** *Lob* **Lyc** k* **Mag-c** k* mag-m b4.de* mang merc b4.de* mez morg-p pte1• mur-ac h2* musca-d szs1 **Nat-ar** **Nat-c** k* **Nat-m** k* nat-n bro1 **Nat-p** k* **Nat-s** nicc *Nit-ac* k* nit-m-ac bro1 **Nux-v** k* olib-sac wmh1 *Op* k* ox-ac k* ozone sde2• pall *Petr* k* petr-ra shn4• *Ph-ac* k* **Phos** k* phyt pic-ac pip-m plb *Podo* k* positr nl2• *Psor* k* ptel k* *Puls* k* ran-s k* raph bro1 *Rhus-t* a1 **Rob** k* ruta fd4.de sabad k* sabal bro1 sabin k* sal-ac bro1 sang k2* sanic sars h2* sec *Sel* b7a.de senec k* *Sep* k* *Sil* k* sin-n bro1 sol-t-ae spig k* spong squil k* stann k* staph stict c1 stram k* stroph-s sp1 **Sul-ac** k* sul-i k2 **Sulph** k* syc bka1*• tab thuj tritic-vg fd5.de tub-r jl2 ust vanil fd5.de verat k* verat-v verb bro1 xero bro1 *Zinc* k* zinc-p k2 zing [bell-p-sp dcm1 tax jsj7]
  - **daytime**: *Nux-v* **Sulph**
  - **morning**: calc kali-c h2 *Puls* sil tab tarent
    - **rising** agg.; after: mag-m h2*
    - **walking** agg.; after: nux-v
  - **forenoon**: agar alum nicc
  - **afternoon**: am-m h2 ammc carbn-s fl-ac kali-c h2 lyss *Nat-c* podo sars h2
    - **dinner**; after: nat-m
  - **evening**: calc chinin-s con dios dulc fd4.de nat-m h2 ox-ac phos ran-s ruta fd4.de sars sil h2
    - **air** agg.; in open: carb-v
    - **bed** agg.; in: *Alum*
    - **eating**; after: stann
    - **fluid**: nat-m h2
  - **night**: calc-s *Con* kali-c h2 lyc *Nux-v* positr nl2• tanac tritic-vg fd5.de
  - **bitter**: iris ptk1 nux-v ptk1
  - **bread** agg.: crot-h *Hydr* merc tritic-vg fd5.de zinc
- **sour**: ...
  - **breakfast** | **after** | **agg.**: petr h2 sars
    - **during**: ox-ac
  - **burning**: *Phos* bg2
  - **cabbage**; after: **Mag-c** k*
  - **coffee** agg.: *Cycl* dulc fd4.de *Puls*
  - **cough**; after: raph sul-ac
  - **dinner**; after: ars fl-ac lyc mag-m petr rumx *Sulph* sumb *Zinc*
  - **drinking**:
    - **after**:
      - **agg.**: canth zinc
      - **water** | **agg.**: psor
  - **drunkards**; in: *Sul-ac*
  - **eating** | **after**:
    - **agg.**: bar-c *Bry* k* caps k* carb-v k* cham chin k* cina *Con* k* dig k* dios dulc fd4.de *Ferr* ferr-m *Hydr* iber c1 kali-c k* kali-s kreos lyc *Nat-ar* **Nat-m** k* *Nit-ac* petr ph-ac *Phos* podo puls-n ruta fd4.de sabin sars k* sel b7a.de *Sil* k* spig vml sulph k* zinc k* zinc-p k2
      - **one** to three hours after: *Puls*
      - **two** hours after: com
    - **before**:
      - **agg.** | **one** hour before: pip-m c1
  - **farinaceous** food, after: *Caust* *Nux-v* ozone sde2•
  - **fat** food agg.: *Caust* *Nit-ac* *Rob*
  - **fever**; during intermittent: *Lyc* k*
  - **fruit** agg.: **Chin**
  - **headache**; during: pic-ac bg1
  - **hot**: fago ptk1 gymno ptk1 podo ptk1
  - **lying** on back agg.: carb-v
  - **menses** | **before** | **agg.**: *Kali-c*
    - **during** | **agg.**: *Mag-c*
  - **milk** agg.: am-c *Calc* *Carb-v* *Chin* k* dulc fd4.de iris *Lyc* *Mag-c* merc *Nux-v* phos spong fd4.de *Sulph* k* zinc zinc-p k2
  - **nausea**; during: gamb
  - **pregnancy** agg.; during: nux-v sul-ac k2
  - **rich** food agg.: chin dulc fd4.de sulph zinc
  - **sitting** bent forward agg.: *Rob* sabin
  - **stool** agg.; after: asar bg2 bry bg2 chin bg2 ferr bg2 phos bg2 sul-ac bg2
  - **sugar** agg.: *Caust* k* sulph vh
  - **supper** agg.; after: dulc fd4.de podo fd3.de• sep
  - **vertigo**; during: caul ptk1 sars k*
  - **vomiting**:
    - **after** sour vomiting: caust ptk1
    - **with**: nit-ac ptk1
  - **waking**; on: rumx
  - **walking**:
    - **agg.**: carb-v
    - **air** agg.; in open: stann sul-ac sulph
- **spasmodic**: anac b4a.de ferr b7.de* kali-bi bg2 lyc b4a.de *Nux-v* b7.de* petr b4a.de *Phos* b4.de* *Ran-b* b7a.de ruta b7.de* sang bg2
- **sulfurated** hydrogen (See eggs)
- **sweetish**: acon alum k* bar-c h2 carb-v k* dulc bg1* grat k* ind lachn laur b7.de* merc plat *Plb* k* *Sul-ac* k* sulph k* *Thuj* b4a.de zinc k*
  - **morning**: alum sul-ac sulph
  - **fluid**: *Acon* bar-c h2 *Iris* lachn *Plb*
  - **menses**; before: *Nat-m* k*
  - **pregnancy** agg.; during: nat-m k* *Zinc* k*
  - **water**: ars vh nat-c h2 *Plb*
- **tallow**; tasting like rancid: **Puls** k*
- **tart**: bry b7.de* caust b4.de* kali-bi bg2 kreos bg2
- **tasteless** (See empty)
- **tea**, tasting like: lycps-v ptk1
- **two**: mez h2
- **undigested** food; as of: caust b4.de* *Con* b4a.de *Sil* b4a.de *Thuj* b4a.de

Stomach

- **urine**, like: agn bg1* ol-an a1* phos b4.de*
  - **smells** like old: agn b7.de* ol-an bg2
- **violent**: arg-n bg2 arn bg2 bism bg2 lach bg2 *Merc* bg2 *Mosch* ptk1 plb bg2 verat bg2
- **water** brash: (↗*sour*) *Abies-n* bro1 acet-ac k* acon k* aesc alum k* alum-p k2 alum-sil k2 *Alumn* *Am-c* k* *Am-m* k* ambr k* anac k* ant-c k* *Ant-t* k* *Apis* k* arg-met b2.de* arg-n bg2 arn k* **Ars** k* ars-i **Asaf** b7a.de* asar k* **Bar-c** k* *Bar-i* bar-m bar-s k2 bell k* *Bism* k* bov k* **Bry** k* **Calc** k* calc-ar k2 calc-i k2 *Calc-p* k* *Calc-s* calc-sil k2 camph b2.de* cann-s k* canth k* *Caps* k* *Carb-an* k* **Carb-v** k* carbn-s cartl-s rly4• *Caust* k* cham b2.de chel k* *Chin* k* chinin-ar *Cic* k* *Cina* k* clem b2.de* cob *Cocc* k* coff bg2 colch k* con k* croc k* cupr k* cur cycl k* *Daph* dig k* dios bro1 *Dros* k* dulc k* euph k* fago bro1 ferr k* ferr-ar ferr-i ferr-p *Graph* k* grat hell k* *Hep* k* hydr bro1 *Ign* k* iod k* *Ip* k* kali-ar *Kali-bi* k* *Kali-c* k* kali-m k2 kali-p kali-s kali-sil k2 kreos bg2* *Lac-ac* k* lach k* laur k* *Led* k* lil-t *Lob* lol bg2 **Lyc** k* m-ambo b2.de* m-arct b2.de* m-aust b7a.de mag-c k* *Mag-m* k* mang k* melal-alt gya4 meny k* *Merc* k* **Mez** k* morg-p pte1*• mosch k* mur-ac k* naja ptk1 *Nat-ar* *Nat-c* k* *Nat-m* k* nat-p k* *Nat-s* *Nit-ac* k* nux-m k* **Nux-v** k* olnd k* **Par** k* **Petr** k* petr-ra shn4• ph-ac k* *Phos* k* phys pic-ac plac-s rly4• plat k* plb k* podo k* polys sk4• psil ft1 psor k* **Puls** k* *Ran-b* k* ran-s k* rat *Rhod* k* *Rhus-t* k* *Rob* ptk1* ruta b7.de* **Sabad** k* sabin k* **Sang** k* *Sars* k* sec seneg k* *Sep* k* **Sil** k* spig k* spong k* squil k* stann k* **Staph** k* stram bg2 stront-c b2.de *Sul-ac* k* sul-i k2 **Sulph** k* sym-r br1* tab tarax k* ter *Teucr* b2.de thea thuj k* tub-r jl valer k* **Verat** k* verb k* viol-t b7a.de zinc k* zinc-p k2
  - **morning**: mag-m h2 sulph
    - **rinsing** mouth: sulph h2
  - **noon** | **eating**; after: sulph
  - **afternoon**: sep h2
    - **16** h: ars h2
    - **walking** agg.: nat-s
  - **evening**: anac cartl-s rly4• caust h2 cycl nat-s petr hr1 podo still sulph h2 ter
  - **night**: carb-an h2 *Carb-v* k* genist graph kali-c ptk1
    - **midnight**, after: kali-c h2
    - **menses**; during: *Puls*
  - **accompanied** by:
    - **indigestion**: coll tl1
    - **retching**: lyc b4a.de **Nux-v** bg2
    - **vomiting** (See Vomiting - accompanied - water)
    - **Abdomen**; complaints in (See ABDOMEN - Complaints - accompanied - water)
    - **Stomach**:
      - **emptiness** in: cina bg2
      - **pain** (See Pain - accompanied - water)
    - **Tongue** | **brown** discoloration: sil kr1*
  - **acids** | **after**: phos
  - **acrid**, sharp: *Apis* b7a.de staph b7.de*
  - **agg.**: *Nux-v* b7a.de *Sil* b4a.de
  - **amel.**: *Cocc* b7a.de
  - **bad**; tasting: am-m b7.de canth b7.de *Cocc* b7a.de lol bg2 nat-c b4.de par b7.de sars b4.de
  - **bitter**: am-m bg1 arg-met bg1 ars b4a.de bar-c bg1 calc bg1 *Carb-v* b4a.de *Chel* b7.de* cic bg1 coloc bg1 graph b4.de* grat bg1 ign bg1 lach bg1 lyc b4a.de* mang b4.de* merc bg2* nat-c b4.de* nux-m b7.de* *Nux-v* b7a.de* phos bg1 *Puls* b7a.de rhod b4.de* sul-ac bg1 sulph b4.de* thuj b4a.de valer b7.de* zinc bg1
    - **accompanied** by | **nausea** (See Nausea - accompanied - water)
  - **breakfast** agg.; after: petr h2
  - **burning**: sumb ptk1
  - **convulsions**; before: hydr-ac ptk1
  - **cool** water: calc bg2 caust k* merc bg2
  - **coryza**; during: nit-ac h2
  - **cough**:
    - **after**: abies-n br1*
    - **during** | **agg.**: am-m b7.de* ambr b7.de* ars b4.de* bry b7.de* mez b4.de* spig b7.de* staph b7.de*

- **water** brash: ...
  - **dinner** | **after** | **agg.**: am-m
    - **before**: sulph
  - **drinking**:
    - **after**:
      - **agg.**: nit-ac sep
      - **amel.**: phos bg2
  - **eating**:
    - **after**:
      - **agg.**: alum b4a.de am-c k* am-m k* asaf bg2 *Bry* k* *Calc* k* caps b7.de* chin k* con k* croc k* dig b4a.de* ferr k* graph b4a.de hep b4a.de iod b4a.de* *Kali-c* k* *Lach* bg2 lyc b4.de* *M-arct* b7.de* mag-m b4.de* merc k* nat-c b4a.de* nat-m k* *Nux-v* k* phos k* puls bg2 rhus-t b7.de* sang sars b4a.de* *Sep* k* *Sil* k* *Spig* b7a.de *Sulph* k* thuj b4a.de* *Verat* bg2
      - **amel.**: sep h2 sulph h2
  - **fasting** agg.: grat
  - **fever**; during: bry bg2 calc bg2 carb-v bg2 cocc bg2 lyc bg2 *Nat-m* bg2 nit-ac bg2 **Nux-v** b7a.de* petr bg2 *Rhus-t* bg2 sabad bg2 **Sil** b4.de* sulph bg2
  - **fresh** meat: *Caust*
  - **frothy**: bry b7.de*
  - **green**: graph b4.de*
  - **hawking** up mucus agg.: sulph h2
  - **hot**: aeth bg2 bell bg2 *Nux-v* b7a.de phos bg2
  - **indigestible** food: iod bg2
  - **insipid**: ign b7.de* sabad b7.de*
  - **lying** agg.: caust h2 *Psor* k*
  - **menses** | **before** | **agg.**: am-c b4.de *Nux-m* k* nux-v bg2 *Puls* k* sulph bg2
    - **during** | **agg.**: puls b7.de
  - **milk** agg.: *Calc* *Cupr* k* phos
  - **periodical**:
    - **hour**; at the same: hep bg1
    - **day**; alternate: lyc k*
  - **perspiration**; during: ars bg2 bry bg2 *Calc* bg2 caust bg2 merc bg2 *Nux-v* bg2 *Rhus-t* bg2 sep bg2 **Sil** bg2 *Sulph* bg2 verat bg2
  - **pregnancy** agg.; during: acet-ac dios *Lac-ac* lob *Nat-m* k* *Nux-m* k* *Tab* k*
  - **rancid**: caust b4.de* *Merc* b4.de* rhod b4.de*
  - **riding** in a carriage agg.: *Nux-m*
  - **rising** agg.: lac-d c1
  - **salty**: calc b4a.de carb-an ptk1 caust b4.de* euph b4a.de lyc b4.de* mag-m b4.de* merc b4a.de *Phos* b4a.de rhus-t b7.de* sep b4a.de sul-ac b4.de* verb b7.de*
  - **shivering**; during: ars bg2 bry bg2 cina bg2 ign bg2 lyc bg2 mez b4a.de* nux-v bg2 sabad bg2 *Sil* b4.de* sulph bg2
  - **soapy**: bry b7.de*
  - **sour**: alum b4a.de *Apis* b7a.de bell b4.de* bry b7.de* calc b4.de* carb-an b4.de* con b4.de* kali-bi bg2 manc bg2 nat-c b4.de* nat-s bg2 *Nux-v* b7a.de pyrog bg2 rhus-t b7a.de sars b4.de* stann b4a.de sulph b4.de* tarax b7.de*
    - **food**; after sour: phos h2
  - **stool** | **after** | **agg.**: caust
    - **during** | **agg.**: phos b4a.de
  - **strong** food, after: *Mag-c* psil ft1
  - **supper** agg.; after: am-m
  - **sweetish**: acon b7.de* alum b4.de* ant-c br1* asar b7.de* *Dig* b4a.de kreos bg2 nat-c b4.de* phos b4a.de plb b7.de* sabad b7.de* sul-ac b4.de*
  - **sweets** agg.: calc b4a.de zinc b4.de*
  - **tart**: par b7.de*
  - **tasteless**: apis b7a.de cann-s b7.de canth b7.de *Cocc* b7a.de par b7.de verat b7.de
  - **tobacco**: | **amel.**: ol-an ptk1

- **water**, of: *(↗sour)* acon k* ant-c k* ant-t k* *Apis* b7a.de* arg-met b7.de* arn k* aur-s k2 bar-c k* bar-m k2 bar-s k2 bry k* *Calc* b4a.de cann-i cann-s b7.de* carl castm caust k* cina b7.de* cob *Colch* crot-t cycl b7.de* *Dros* b7a.de *Graph* grat k* hep b4.de* kali-bi bg2 kali-c b4.de* kali-n laur b7.de* *Mag-m* k* mag-s *Merc* k* *Merc-c* *Mez* mosch b7.de* nat-c b4.de* nat-s nux-v b7.de* ol-an par b7.de* petr b4.de* phos k* plat *Plb* k* puls b7.de* sars b4.de* *Sep* b4a.de sil spig b7.de* stann stront-c b4.de* sul-ac k* *Sulph* verat verb b7.de*
  - **morning**: graph
    - **nausea**; during: *Mag-m* mag-s
    - **rising** agg.; after: carb-an mag-m h2
  - **forenoon**: nicc
  - **afternoon**: am-m kali-n h2
  - **evening**: kali-n h2 sars
  - **night**: mang **Merc** vh
    - **menses**; before: mang
  - **badly** tasting: arg-met b7.de* naja bg2
  - **drinking** agg.; after: graph h2
  - **eating**; after: graph h2
  - **green**: graph h2
  - **motion** agg.: mez
  - **nausea**; during: gamb kali-n h2 **Merc** vh
  - **potatoes** agg.: mag-s
  - **sitting** agg.: phos
  - **urine**, like: agn vh

EXPIRATION agg.: ant-t b7.de* olnd b7.de* spig b7.de*

FAINTNESS (See Emptiness; Sinking)

FALLING out; sensation of: hell bg1 mag-c h2*

O - **Epigastrium**: cact bg2

FALSE STEP; at a: *(↗Pain - false)* aloe bg2 bry b7.de* *Puls* b7.de* rhus-t b7a.de*

FASTING:
- **amel.**: *Chin* b7.de*
- **agg.**: *Bar-c* b4.de* bry b7.de* **Calc** b4a.de *Carb-an* b4a.de hell b7.de* kreos b7a.de *Nux-v* b7.de* plat b4.de* staph b7.de* sulph b4a.de
- **sensation** of (See Emptiness)

FAT FOOD agg.: acon bg2 asaf b7a.de* *Carb-an* bg2 carb-v b4a.de* cycl b7.de* dros bg2 merc-c b4a.de nat-c bg2 nat-m bg2 nat-p bg2 nit-ac bg2 nux-v bg2 **Puls** b7.de* sep bg2 tarax bg2 thuj bg2

FEAR:
- **sensation** of: ange-s oss1• carc fb*

O - **Pit** of the stomach: carc jl2 lyc tl1 mez tl1 phos k2*

FERMENTATION: acet-ac k* anac bg2 apoc k* *Caust* *Chin* croc k* graph k* *Plat* k*
- **fruit** agg.: Chin

O - **Epigastrium**; in: croc b7a.de* lyc bg2 plat bg2*

FEVER: | **before** | **agg.**: chin b7a.de cina b7a.de stram b7a.de
- **during** | **agg.**: ars bro1 cocc b7.de* eup-per bro1 ip bro1* nux-v b7.de* puls bro1 rhus-t b7.de* verat-v ptk1

FISH agg.: | **spoiled**: carb-v b4a.de *Chin* b7a.de *Puls* b7a.de

FLABBINESS: *(↗Emptiness; Hanging; Weakness)* ars-h hr1 aster psa1.de calc-p a1* euph k* **Ign** k* ip k* merc petr j5.de spong k* staph b7.de sul-ac h2 tab k* thea

FLATULENCE agg.: *(↗Distension; Eructations)* arn b7.de* nux-v b7a.de

FLATULENCE of stomach: *(↗Distension; Eructations)* arist-m br1 *Asaf* br1 chlf br1 [bell-p-sp dcm1]
- **accompanied** by | **Head**; pain in: asc-t br1
- **sensation** of: ant-t b7.de* arn b7.de* ars b4.de* *Con* b4a.de croc b7.de* laur b7.de* nux-m b7.de* *Nux-v* b7a.de par b7.de* ran-b b7.de*

O • **Epigastrium**: ant-t b7.de*

FLATULENT FOOD agg.: carb-v b4a.de* kali-c b4.de* *Lyc* b4a.de

FLATUS; FROM OBSTRUCTED: coloc b4a.de lyc b4a.de

FLATUS; PASSING: | **amel.**: ant-t b7.de* *Cocc* b7a.de hep b4.de* lach b7a.de *Lyc* b4a.de staph b7.de*

FLOATING in water; as if: abrot ptk1

FLUTTERING (See Trembling)

FOOD:
- **lodges** at cardia: allox tpw3 melal-alt gya4 phos h2*
- **stays** in stomach and will not go down: arn b7.de* ars bg2 bar-c bg2 bry bg2 *Calc* b4.de* cham b7.de* chin b7.de* graph bg2 ign b7.de* lyc bg2 mur-ac b4.de* rheum b7.de rhus-t b7.de* ruta bg2 *Sep* b4.de*

FOOD POISONING (See RECTUM - Diarrhea - food - rancid)

FOREIGN body: cupr k* grat k* hep h2 nat-m k* phos h2 raph k*

O - **Epigastrium**: hep bg2 nat-m bg2 thuj bg2

FORMICATION: aloe ant-t k* apis colch k* hydr-ac a1 kali-c k* laur k* morph a1 plat k* rhus-t k* sulph k* tub jl2 verat k*
- **dust**, as from: plat h2

FRIGHT agg.: *Acon* b7a.de carb-v bg2

FROZEN FOOD agg.: arg-n bg2 *Ars* b4a.de calc-p bg2 carb-v b4a.de ip bg2 *Puls* b7.de* rhus-t bg2

FRUIT agg.: ars b4a.de borx b4a.de* bry b7.de* chin b7.de* merc-c b4a.de nat-c b4.de* *Puls* b7.de* rhod b4.de verat b7.de*

FULLNESS, sensation of: *(↗Heaviness)* acon k* acon-s a1 aesc agar k* aids nl2• allox tpw3* aloe k* alum k* alum-p k2 alumn am-c k* am-m k* anac b4a.de* anan *Ant-c* k* ant-t k* apis k* *Arg-n* k* arge-pl rwt5• arn k* ars ars-i ars-s-f k2 asaf k* asar k* astac vh aur-s k2 bacls-7 fmm1• bamb-a stb2.de• bapt *Bar-c* k* bar-i bar-m *Bell* k* beryl sp1 borx b4a.de* *Bov* k* brach brom bros-gau mrc1 *Bry* k* but-ac br1* *Calc* k* calc-i k2 *Calc-p* calc-s calc-sil k2 camph canth k* carb-ac carb-an k* **Carb-v** k* **Carbn-s** casc *Castor-eq* **Caust** k* cedr cham k* **Chin** k* chinin-ar *Chinin-s* k* chir-fl gya2 choc srj3• chord-umb rly4• cob coc-c *Cocc* k* coff k* *Colch* *Coloc* *Con* corn crot-t *Cycl* k* daph k* dig k* dioxi rbp6 dream-p sdj1• *Dulc* eup-per eup-pur euphr *Ferr* k* ferr-ar ferr-i *Ferr-p* k* *Fl-ac* flor-p rsj3• gent-c ger-i rly4• gink-b sbd1• *Graph* k* *Grat* k* gymno *Hell* k* hep bg2 *Hydr* hyos k* hyper *Ign* k* ind iod k* ip iris jac-c kali-ar kali-bi k* kali-br a1 **Kali-c** k* kali-m k2 *Kali-n* k* *Kali-p* kali-s k* kali-sil k2 *Kola* stb3• *Kreos* k* lach k* lachn lap-la rsp1 laur lec led b7.de* lith-c *Lob* k* **Lyc** k* m-arct b7.de mag-c k* *Manc* mang k* melal-alt gya4 *Merc* k* merl mez k* mill moni rfm1• *Mosch* k* mucs-nas rly4• mur-ac k* myric naja bg2 nat-act k2 *Nat-c* k* *Nat-m* k* nat-p nat-pyru rly4• *Nat-s* k* nat-sil fd3.de• nicc k* nit-ac bg2 **Nux-m** k* *Nux-v* k* *Ol-an* *Op* k* par k* petr k* ph-ac bg2 phel **Phos** k* pitu-gl skp7• plat plb plut-n srj7• positr nl2• pot-e rly4• *Prun* k* *Puls* k* ran-b bg2 ran-s k* raph rat *Rheum* k* *Rhus-t* k* *Rob* rumx k* ruta fd4.de sabad *Sabin* k* sars b4.de* *Sec* sep b4.de* sil k* sphing kk3.fr spong squil *Stann* k* staph k* suis-em rly4• *Sul-ac* k* sul-i k2 **Sulph** k* tarent tell tep tril-p tritic-vg fd5.de valer k* xan c1 zinc k* [heroin sdj2]
- **morning**: aids nl2• am-m asaf cartl-s rly4• dulc fd4.de nat-c h2 phos h2 ran-s rhod sep hr1 sulph
  - **fasting** agg.: bar-c plat
  - **waking**; on: cypra-eg sde6.de• dulc fd4.de sulph
- **noon**: dulc fd4.de ox-ac sep sulph
  - **bread** and milk, after: arg-n
  - **eating**; after: ox-ac
- **afternoon**: am-m calc chinin-s coca ham fd3.de• *Sulph*
- **evening**: ars dios dulc fd4.de eupi ham fd3.de• hyos h1 nat-c phos tritic-vg fd5.de
  - **bed** agg.; in: *Nat-s*
  - **eating** | **after** | **agg.**: kali-bi
    - **agg.**: cham h1
- **night**: ham fd3.de• sphing kk3.fr
  - **midnight**: crot-t
  - **going** to bed; on: rumx

Stomach

- **accompanied** by:
  - **appetite**:
    - **decreased** (See Appetite - diminished - accompanied - fullness)
    - **increased** (See Appetite - increased - accompanied - fullness)
  - **thirst** (See Thirst - accompanied - fullness)
- **air**; of: bell bg2
- **bread** agg.: **Caust** k*
- **breakfast** agg.; after: alum ars-s-f k2 phos ptel sulph tritic-vg fd5.de
  - **hunger**; with sensation of: am-m
- **chill**; during: cocc
- **clothing** agg.: *Gels*
- **coffee** agg.: canth
- **contradiction**, after: *Nux-m*
- **dinner**; after: agar alum h2 ant-c castm *Clem* dig grat kali-s fd4.de kalm nat-m petr ruta fd4.de sacch-a fd2.de• zinc
- **drinking** agg.; after: aloe arg-n sne aspar *Manc* nat-m sin-n tab
- **dry** food; as if filled with: cadm-s ptk1 calad bro1
- **eating**:
  - **after**:
    - **agg.**: aesc agar k* alum alum-sil k2 **Am-c** *Ambr* *Anac* k* ant-c *Apoc* *Arg-n* arn *Ars* ars-s-f k2 aspar aur aur-m bacls-7 fmm1• bamb-a stb2.de• *Bar-c* k* bar-m k2 *Bism* *Borx* k* *Bry* *Calad* *Calc* calc-ar k2 calc-s calc-sil k2 carb-ac carb-an k* **Carb-v** carbn-s cham k* **Chin** k* chinin-ar k2 *Chinin-s* chir-fl gya2 cimic cocc b7a.de **Colch** *Cop* dig k* dulc fd4.de **Ferr** *Ferr-i* ferr-p *Grat* ham fd3.de• *Hep* hippoc-k szs2 *Hydr* irid-met srj5• kali-ar kali-bi *Kali-c* k* kali-s *Lac-ac* *Lach* k* lil-t luf-op rsj5• **Lyc** k* melal-alt gya4 mez k* mosch myric nat-ar nat-c k* *Nat-m* k* nat-p *Nat-s* nauf-helv-li elm2• nicc *Nit-ac* k* *Nux-m* **Nux-v** petr ph-ac k* *Phos* k* *Pic-ac* plb *Ptel* *Puls* rheum *Rhus-t* k* *Rosm* lgb1 ruta fd4.de sanic tl1 sep *Sil* k* *Spong* *Stann* sul-ac *Sulph* tab tritic-vg fd5.de verat zinc k* zinc-p k2 [heroin sdj2]
      - **ever** so little; after: *(↗GENERALS - Food and - food - aversion - eating - little)* adon bg2 agar aids nl2• alet alum alum-sil k2 *Apoc* arg-n dgt bar-c bar-s k2 bit-ar wht1• *Carb-an* carc fd2.de• **Chin** k* croc crot-t cycl *Dig* k* dulc fd4.de elaps **Ferr** *Ferr-i* gink-b sbd1• hippoc-k szs2 *Kali-c* k* kali-p fd1.de• *Kali-s* **Lyc** k* *Manc* mur-ac ptk1 nat-ar *Nat-m* nit-ac bg2 *Nux-v* petr petr-ra shn4• *Ptel* rhod k2 rhus-t senec bg1 sep *Sil* stront-c sk4• *Sulph* thuj tritic-vg fd5.de verat
      - **hunger**; with: luf-op rsj5•
      - **loosening** clothes amel.: lyc tl1 sanic tl1
    - **amel.**: arg-n ferr ham fd3.de• mand mtf11 mang
  - **before** | **agg.**: beryl tpw5*
  - **while** | **agg.**: cham h1 ruta fd4.de
- **eructations** | **amel.**: *Carb-v* euphr iris kola stb3• mag-c melal-alt gya4 *Nux-v* phos sil
- **flatulence**: | **amel.**: chir-fl gya2
- **food**, sight or smell of: dig br1
- **hunger**; during: am-c bg2 am-m arg-met asaf asar h1 chin bg2 cycl bg2 gels bg2 lyc bg2* pot-e rly4•
- **menses** | **before** | **agg.**: am-c b4.de
  - **during** | **agg.**: am-c k* kali-c *Kali-p* zinc b4a.de
- **oppression** of breathing, with: lac-d k2 *Nat-s* nux-m *Nux-v* prun [heroin sdj2]
- **pizza**; after: bamb-a stb2.de•
- **pregnancy** agg.; during: **Nux-m**
- **sleep** | **amel.**: *Phos*
- **slow** digestion; from: puls k2
- **soup** agg.: prun
- **supper** agg.; after: carb-v chinin-s
- **vomiting** | **amel.**: kali-c h2
- **waking**; on: myric sulph
- **walking** agg.; after: colch ferr
- **water**; after: aloe
- **weather** agg.; wet: merc k2
- **wine** agg.: rhus-t

Fullness, sensation of: ...

○ - **Epigastrium**: *Acon* b7.de* arn b7.de* asaf b7.de* bar-c b4a.de bell b4.de* bov b4.de* carb-v b4a.de *Cham* b7.de* con b4.de* cycl b7.de* *Dig* b4a.de *Hell* b7a.de hell-o a1* kali-c b4a.de lyc b4a.de merc b4.de* morg-g fmm1• mosch b7.de* nat-c b4a.de phos b4a.de plat b4.de* *Puls* b7a.de ran-s b7.de* rhus-t b7.de* sabin b7.de* sep b4a.de* spong b7.de* stann b4.de* staph b7.de*
  - **food**; unrelated to: morg-g fmm1•

GAGGING: *(↗Nausea; Retching)* abies-n vml3• acon vh1 agar benz-ac borx k2 bry cadm-s br1 calc-p *Carb-v* *Chin* chinin-s colch k2 cop dulc fd4.de *Kali-c* kali-chl *Lyc* nux-v k2 olib-sac wmh1 par *Podo* k* ruta fd4.de stann k2 tritic-vg fd5.de vanil fd5.de
- **morning**: carb-v a1 *Corn* k* kali-c k* ruta fd4.de
- **night**: *Arg-n* k* ruta fd4.de
- **accompanied** by:
  - **constriction** of throat (See THROAT - Constriction - accompanied - gagging)
  - **vertigo** (See VERTIGO - Accompanied - stomach - gagging)
- **breakfast** agg.; after: calc-p k*
- **children**; in: | **dull** child: agar prf
- **continuous**: ip k2
- **cough** agg.; during: *Agar* ambr k2 ant-t k2 *Arg-n* arn k2 bell k2 bry bufo k2 calc carb-v carc gk caust cench cimx **Cina** k* coc-c cupr dirc bg1 ferr hell hep k2 ip k2 kali-c k* *Lach* *Lyss* mang-p rly4• merc-c nux-v k2 sang k2 sanic sarcol-ac sp1 sep sil k2 squil k2 stann k2 tarent k2
- **drinking** agg.: *Cimic* *Cimx* k*
- **eating**; after: agar k* *Ambr* k* *Kali-c* k* *Lach* k*
- **expectoration**; during: *Arg-n* *Coc-c* par
- **mucus** in fauces, from: anac k* *Arg-n* *Carb-v* k* ip *Lyc* k*
- **touch**:
  - **mouth** inside agg.; touching: coc-c k2
  - **throat** agg.; touching: nux-v k2*
- **x-rays** taken; on having dental:
  - **children**; in: agar prf
  - **women**; in: agar prf

GANGRENE: ars euph kali-bi bg2 phos a1 sec k*

GASTRIC tonic; remedies which act as a (See Slow)

GASTRITIS (See Inflammation)

GASTROINTESTINAL complaints (See ABDOMEN - Gastrointestinal)

GONENESS (See Emptiness)

GOUTY metastasis: **Ant-c** k* benz-ac cinnm hr1 colch tl1 hydr-ac bro1 *Nux-m* k* nux-v bro1 puls bro1 sang

GRIEF agg.: *Ign* b7a.de

GURGLING: agar k* agath-a nl2• **Aloe** ptk1 am-c k* amp rly4• anac k* arizon-l nl2• *Arn* *Ars* berb ptk1 bov k* carb-an k* cartl-s rly4• chel k* chord-umb rly4• cic ptk1 cina k* coca-c sk4• *Colch* coli rly4• croc crot-t k* **Cupr** k* cycl tl1 fl-ac *Gamb* ptk1 ham fd3.de• hydr a1 *Hydr-ac* k* ign tl1 jatr-c ptk1 kali-c k* kali-i k* ketogl-ac rly4• kreos ptk1 lact k* *Laur* k* lec oss• lil-t ptk1 limest-b es1• lob *Lyc* ptk1 lyss hr1 mag-m b4.de* meny k* mucs-nas rly4• nat-pyru rly4• nauf-helv-li elm2• nux-v hr1 orot-ac rly4• phos b4.de* *Podo* ptk1 pot-e rly4• *Puls* ptk1 rhus-g tmo3• ruta fd4.de sacch spong fd4.de squil ptk1 suis-hep rly4• sulph ptk1 tere-la rly4• teucr k* thuj k* tritic-vg fd5.de verb zinc k* [spect dfg1]
- **morning**: bov k* cystein-l rly4• pot-e rly4• ruta fd4.de tritic-vg fd5.de
  - **waking**; on: carb-an k*
  - **walking** agg.: (non:carb-an h2*)
- **drinking** | **after** | **agg.**: **Phos** k* spong fd4.de
  - **agg.**: arn *Ars* cina **Cupr** k* elaps **Hydr-ac** k* laur thuj k*
- **eating**; while: bov k*
- **lying** agg.: lec oss•
- **nausea**; with: aeth k*
- **yawning** agg.: zinc h2

○ - **Epigastrium**: anac b4.de* cina bg2 cocc b7.de* rheum b7.de* sabin b7.de*

HACKING sensation (See Pain - cutting)

HANGING down relaxed; sensation of: *(↗Emptiness; Flabbiness; Weakness)* abrot k* *Acon* b7.de* aesc agar k* alum k* ambr b7.de* anac b4a.de ant-t b7.de* *Apoc* mrr1 arg-met b7.de* arg-n arn b7.de* **Ars** b4.de* bapt bg2 *Bar-c* k* bell b4.de* *Bism* k* bov b4.de bry b7.de* *Calc* k* *Calc-p* k* cann-xyz bg2 canth b7.de* *Caps* b7.de* carb-an b4a.de* *Carb-v* k* **Caust** b4.de* *Cham* b7.de* chel b7.de* chin b7.de* cic b7.de* cina b7.de* coff b7.de* croc b7.de* crot-t k* *Cycl* b7.de* dig b4.de* echi *Euph* k* euphr b7.de* ferr-i k2 graph b4.de *Hep* k* hydr bg2* **Ign** k* **Ip** k* kali-bi bg2 kali-c bg2 kali-n b4a.de lac-lup hrn2• laur b7.de* led b7.de* lob *Lyc* k* m-arct b7.de mag-c k* *Mag-m* b4.de* meny b7.de* merc b4.de* mez k* mosch b7.de* mur-ac b4.de **Nat-c** b4.de* nat-m bg2 nit-ac b4.de* *Nux-v* b7.de* olnd b7.de* par b7.de petr k* phos b4.de* plat b4.de* podoin bro1 *Ptel* br1 puls b7.de* raph rhod b4.de rhus-t k* sabad b7.de* sabin b7.de* seneg b4a.de sil b4.de* spong k* *Staph* k* stront-c b4.de* *Stry-p* bro1 *Sul-ac* k* **Sulph** b4.de* *Tab* k* tarax b7.de* tep psa1.de teucr b7a.de thea a1* thuj b4.de* verat b7.de* zinc b4.de*

- **morning**: *Sulph*
- **eating**; after: cycl b7a.de
- **stool** | **after** | **agg.**: ambr ptk1 bar-c *Sep*
  - **during** | **agg.**: nit-ac b4.de*
- **walking** agg.: hep
- **water**; in: abrot c1

○ - **Epigastrium**: acon b7.de* croc b7.de* glon bg2 **Ign** b7.de* iod b4.de* kali-c b4a.de kali-n b4.de* *Lyc* b4.de* mosch b7.de* nat-c b4.de* phos b4.de* plat b4.de* podo bg2 stront-c b4.de* sulph b4.de* teucr b7.de* verat b7.de* zinc b4.de*
  - **cough** agg.; during: ign b7.de*
  - **menses**; before: ign b7.de
  - **stool** agg.; after: verat b7.de*
  - **urination** agg.; after: ars bg2

HARD upon the stomach; sensation of something: *(↗Pain - pressing) (non:Cupr h2)* mag-m h2

HARDNESS: alco a1 anil a1 ars k* bapt bg2 *Bar-c* k* *Bar-m* carb-v k* chim k* cob k* con b4a.de falco-pe nl2• ferr bg2 ip b7a.de *Kreos* b7a.de lept k* mag-m bg2 merc-i-f k* *Mez* b4a.de mosch bg2 mur-ac a1 nat-m b4a.de *Nux-v* b7a.de phos b4a.de plb b7a.de puls k* rhus-t b7.de* *Thuj* b4a.de

- **drinking** agg.; after: sul-ac b4a.de
- **eructations** | **amel.**: carb-v k*

○ - **Epigastrium**: bar-c b4.de* chin bg2 hep b4.de* *Mez* b4a.de *Phos* bg2
- **Pylorus**: *(↗Constriction - pylorus; Contraction - pylorus; Induration - pylorus)* sep hr1
  - **sensation** of hardness in: kreos k*

HEARTBURN: *(↗Acidity; Eructations; type - burning; Eructations; type - sour)* absin mtf11 acet-ac br1 acon a1 adon bg2 *Aegle-f* zzc1• *Aesc* k* agar k* agav-t jl1 aids nl2• all-s k* allox sp1 *Alum* k* alum-p k2 alum-sil k2 alumn **Am-c** k* **Ambr** k* *Anac* k* ant-c k* ap-g a1* *Apis* apom bro1 arg-met k* arg-n k* arizon-l nl2• arn k* *Ars* k* *Ars-i* ars-s-f k2 asaf k* asar k* atis zzc1• aur bg2 bamb-a stb2.de• bar-c k* bar-i bar-m bar-s k2 bell k* *Berb* k* *Bism* bg2* borx k* bov b2.de* bros-gau mrc1 *Bry* k* cadm-br c2 cadm-s k* caj c2* **Calc** k* calc-i k2 calc-p k* *Calc-s* calc-sil k2 calen bro1 camph bg2 cann-s a1 cann-xyz bg2 *Canth* k* *Caps* k* carb-ac bg2* *Carb-an* k* **Carb-v** k* carbn-s k* card-m bg2 cardios-h rly4• carl a1 carneg-g rwt1• cartl-s rly4• *Caust* k* cham k* *Chel* k* *Chin* k* chinin-ar *Chinin-s* k* choc srj3• **Cic** k* cinch a1* cit-v a1 coc-c k* coca-c sk4• cocc k* coff k* colch k* **Con** k* cop hr1 corn k* corn-f br1 **Croc** k* crot-h k* crot-t k* cupr b7a.de* daph bg2 dat-a bro1 dig k* *Dios* bro1 dream-p sdj1• dulc k* dys pte1*• echi eke-me bta1• emblc mtf11 euph k* euphr a1 fago a1* ferr k* ferr-ar ferr-i k* **Ferr-p** k* *Fl-ac* k* flor-p rsj3• *Gal-ac* br1* galeoc-c-h gms1• gard-j vlr2• *Graph* k* grat bg2 guaj k* ham fd3.de• helic-p mtf hell k* *Hep* k* hir rsj4• hom-xyz mtf11 hydr-ac a1* hyos k* ign k* ignis-alc es2• *Iod* k* irid-met srj5• *Iris* k* kali-ar kali-bi bg2 *Kali-c* k* *Kali-i* k* kali-m k2 kali-n k* kali-p kali-s kali-sil k2 ketogl-ac rly4• kola stb3• lac-ac mrr1* lac-del hrn2• lac-h htj1• *Lach* k* lact-v c2 lap-la sde8.de• lat-m bnm6• lath c1 lith-m a1* *Lob* k* loxo-lae bnm12• **Lyc** k* m-arct b2.de* m-aust b2.de **Mag-c** k* mag-m hr1* mag-s sp1 malar jl2 manc bg2 mang k* *Merc* k* merc-c bg2 merl a1 moni rfm1• morg fmm1• morg-g pte1*• morg-p pte1*• mosch k* mur-ac k* myric a1 narc-ps a1* nat-ar *Nat-c* k* *Nat-m* k* nat-p k* *Nat-s* k* neon srj5• nit-ac k* nit-s-d hr1 nux-m k* **Nux-v** k* op k* orex-tann mtf orot-ac rly4• ox-ac k* oxal-a rly4• ozone sde2• par k* petr k* petr-ra shn4• ph-ac k* *Phos* k* plac-s rly4• plat k* plb b7a.de *Podo* k* positr nl2• pot-e rly4• prot pte1* prun-v c2 **Puls** k* ran-s k* rauw sp1 *Rob* k* ruta fd4.de *Sabad* k* *Sabin* k* sang bg2* schin a1 sec k* sel rsj9• *Sep* k* *Sil* k* sin-a a1* *Sin-n* k* sol-ni c2 squil k* staph k* streptoc rly4• stry-af-cit mtf11 suis-em rly4• *Sul-ac* k* sul-i k2 sulo-ac c2 *Sulph* k* sumb ptk1 syc bka1• symph fd3.de• *Syph* tab k* tarax k* tell k* tep a1 ter k* thiam rly4• thuj k* thymol sp1 tritic-vg fd5.de tub-r jl2 ust a1 *Valer* k* vanil fd5.de *Verat* b2.de* *Verat-v* k* vichy-g a1* visc sp1 *Zinc* k* zinc-s a1* [heroin sdj2 tax jsj7]

- **daytime**: crot-h k*
- **morning**: arg-met h1 canth b7.de* cypra-eg sde6.de• graph b4.de* ign b7.de* nux-v b7.de* par b7.de* petr k* petr-ra shn4• phos k* pot-e rly4• rhus-t b7.de* sep b4.de* sulph k*
  - **rising** agg.: mang h2 mang-p rly4•
  - **smoking** agg.: lyc k*
- **forenoon**: ars b4.de* bry b7.de* carb-v b4.de* cic b7.de* coc-c k* coloc colocin a1 par b7.de* sars b4.de* sep k* sulph b4.de*
- **afternoon**: ant-c b7.de ant-t bg2 ars b4.de* asaf b7.de* atp rly4• bry k* caps b7.de* chel k* chin kr1 choc srj3• cina b7.de* con b4.de* croc b7.de* crot-h k* cupr k* dig h2 hydr k* kali-p fd1.de• ketogl-ac rly4• lach b7.de* lyc b4.de* mag-m b4.de* nat-m b4.de* nept-m lsd2.fr nux-v b7.de* phos k* plac-s rly4• rhus-t b7.de* ruta fd4.de sars b4.de* sep k* sil b4.de* sol-ni staph b7.de* suis-em rly4• sulph k* valer b7.de*
- **evening**: alum b4a.de ambr k* anac b4a.de* bell k* bry b7.de* caust k* choc srj3• con k* conch fkr1* croc b7.de* crot-h cycl b7.de* dig k* dulc fd4.de ferr b7.de* ign b7.de* kali-bi bg2 kali-s fd4.de *M-arct* b7.de* mand rsj7• mang b4.de* merc b4.de* *Nat-m* k* *Ox-ac* k* *Petr* k* positr nl2• sars b4.de* *Sep* b4a.de sin-n a1 sulph k* symph fd3.de• ter k* tritic-vg fd5.de vanil fd5.de
  - **18-0 h**: marb-w es1•
  - **bed**; after going to: cartl-s rly4• *Con* k* sol-ni vanil fd5.de
  - **smoking** agg.; after: lach k* symph fd3.de•
  - **wine** agg.: bry k*
- **night**: *Bry* b7.de* calc b4.de* canth b7a.de* carb-v b4a.de* cardios-h rly4• coc-c k* graph b4a.de* kali-bi k* kali-c b4a.de *Merc* k* nux-v b7.de* phos bg2 plac-s rly4• positr nl2• ptel k* *Rob* k* ruta b7.de* zinc bg2
  - **midnight**: calc nept-m lsd2.fr
    - **before** | **23** h: conch fkr1•
    - **after**:
      - **1-3 h** | **waking**; on: visc sp1
  - **lying** down agg.: *Rob* k*
  - **pregnancy** agg.; during: *Merc* k*
- **accompanied** by:
  - **abdominal** cramp | **evening**: mand rsj7•
  - **asthma** (See RESPIRATION - Asthmatic - accompanied - heartburn)
  - **distension**: nux-v tl1
  - **helicobacter** pylori infection (See Inflammation - helicobacter - accompanied - heartburn)
  - **nausea**: *Lac-ac* mrr1
    - **vomit**; with inclination to: am-c b4a.de
  - **salivation**: alum hr1 puls kr1*
  - ○ **Stomach**; pain in (See Pain - accompanied - heartburn)
  - **Tongue**:
    - **pale**: stram kr1*
    - **red** discoloration of the tongue | **fiery** red: mag-m kr1*
    - **white** discoloration of the | **root**: stram kr1*
- **acids**, after: nux-v
- **air** agg.; in open: ambr c1 cic b7.de*
- **beans**; after: *Chin* b7a.de
- **bed** agg.; in: rhus-t b7.de* *Rob* mrr1 vanil fd5.de
- **beer**; after: bamb-a stb2.de• ferr b7.de* lyc b4a.de phos k*
- **bread**; after: nux-v b7.de*
- **breakfast** | **after** | **agg.**: ign b7.de* nat-m b4.de* par b7.de*
  - **before** | **agg.**: *Nux-v*
- **chill**; during: caps bg2 chin bg2 con bg2 lyc bg2 nux-v bg2 puls bg2
- **coffee** agg.: calc-p k* caps b7.de* ferr-p lac-del hrn2• *Lyc* b4a.de puls b7.de* rhus-t b7.de* tritic-vg fd5.de
- **constant**: corn-f mtf emblc mtf helic-p mtf
- **diet**; errors in: sulph mrr1

Stomach

- **dinner**; after: acon k* calc-p k* crot-t k* ham k* kali-bi k* kali-p fd1.de• lyc k* mag-m h2 merc-i-r k* nat-m h2 sol-ni sulph k*
- **drinking** agg.; after: Alum k* bry bg2 Canth b7a.de graph b4.de* merc b4.de* moni rfm1• Nit-ac b4.de* psor bg2 Sep b4.de*
  - **rapidly**: nit-ac b4a.de
- **drunkards**; in: Nux-v k* Sul-ac
- **eating**:
  - **after**:
    - **agg.**: Aesc k* agar k* allox tpw4* Am-c k* anac k* Calc k* Calc-p k* caps b7a.de carc fd2.de• carl k* caust b4a.de Chin k* coc-c k* con k* croc k* Graph k* Iod k* irid-met srj5• kali-c b4a.de kali-p fd1.de• kola stb3• lac-del hrn2• lyc k* mag-s sp1 marb-w es1• merc moni rfm1• Nat-m k* nat-ox rly4• nept-m lsd2.fr Nit-ac k* Nux-v k* podo fd3.de• positr nl2• sep sil k* symph fd3.de• thiam rly4•
    - **amel.**: lac-h htj1• olib-sac wmh1 rauw sp1 sabad bg2
  - **before** | **agg.**: calc b4a.de
  - **while** | **agg.**: sars b4a.de
- **eggs**; after boiled: sulph
- **eructations**; after: bar-c Calc k* con k* hep b4.de* mang k* phos bg2 valer k* vanil fd5.de
- **excitement**; after: bamb-a stb2.de•
- **fasting** agg.: grat bg2 nux-v b7.de* sep b4.de*
- **fat** food; after: caust k2 nat-c k* nat-m bg2 Nat-p bg2 nit-ac h2 nux-v k* phos k* **Puls** b7a.de* Sulph b4a.de
- **flatulent** food; after: kali-c h2
- **goose** flesh, with: cadm-s ptk1 calen ptk1*
- **hard**, dry food, after: calc h2
- **heavy** food; after: Iod b4a.de
- **hiccough**; during: Nux-v b7.de*
- **hunger**; with: olib-sac wmh1
- **lentils**; after: Chin b7a.de
- **liquid** food; after: anac b4a.de
- **lying** agg.: caust b4.de* psor bg2 rhus-t b7.de*
- **meat** agg.: agar k* Ferr-p
  - **fresh** meat: Chin b7a.de
- **melons**; after: petr-ra shn4•
- **menses** | **before** | **agg.**: nux-m bg2 nux-v bg2 Sulph k*
  - **during** | **agg.**: kali-n bg2 mag-c bg2 puls b7.de*
- **milk** agg.: alum bg2 ambr k* ant-t b7.de* calc b4.de* carb-v b4a.de* Chin k* cupr b7a.de* lyc b4a.de* nux-v bg2 phos bg2
- **motion** agg.: nit-ac b4.de*
- **nausea**; with: am-c bg2 Calc k* iod h irid-met srj5• Puls k* Sang k*
- **pastry** agg.: bamb-a stb2.de•
- **peas**; after: Chin b7a.de
- **pregnancy** agg.; during: acet-ac a1* anac bro1 apis calc bro1 canth bro1 Caps k* carb-ac mrr1 con k* dios c2* lac-ac c1 Merc k* nat-m k* Nux-v bro1 ox-ac k* Puls c2* tab hr1 zinc k*
- **rancid**: con b4.de* graph h2 m-arct b7.de merc b4.de* nux-v b7.de* petr a1 valer b7.de*
  - **vomiting**; after: Puls b7a.de
- **scraping**: carb-an b4a.de staph b7.de*
- **sitting** bent forward agg.: sabin k*
- **sleep**; during: rhus-t b7.de*
- **smoking** | **after** | **agg.**: carbn-s coc-c a1 lach k* lyc k* phos k* rhus-t b7.de* staph b7.de* tarax b7.de*
  - **agg.**: bell k* Calc b4a.de choc srj3• lach lyc puls vh staph
- **soup** agg.: anac k*
- **sour** things, after: ferr b7.de* ferr-p nux-v b7a.de* phos b4a.de*
- **stool** agg.; after: merc k*
- **stooping** agg.: cic b7.de* ip bg2 m-ambo b7.de* phos b4.de* pimp bg2 thuj k*
- **sugar** agg.: Puls b7a.de zinc k*
- **supper** agg.; after: Alum k* caust k* crot-h k* kali-c h2 puls
- **sweets**: ozone sde2• zinc ptk1
  - **thought** of: bamb-a stb2.de•
- **tea**; after: Abies-n vh1 hir rsj4• kali-bi bg2 lach b7.de*
- **tobacco**; from: chel staph tarax thymol sp1
- **violent**: corn-f br1
- **vomiting**; after: Puls b7a.de
- **walking**:
  - **agg.**: mag-m b4.de*

Heartburn – walking: ...

  - **air** agg.; in open: Ambr k* asar b7.de*
- **water**; after: alum b4a.de
- **wine** agg.: bry coc-c k* lyc b4a.de zinc

○ - **Throat**; ascends: con b4a.de* lyc b4a.de* mang b4a.de* nat-m b4a.de*

HEAT:

- **alternating** with | **coldness**: bufo bg2 Lach b7a.de phos h2*
- **during** | **agg.**: bry b7.de cina b7.de sep b4.de
- **fire**; like: nat-m bg2 ol-an bg2
- **sensation** of: abies-c bro1 acet-ac bro1 acon b7.de* Agar bro1 ant-t bg2 apis b7a.de arg-n bro1 ars b4.de* asaf bg2 bism bro1 calo bro1 camph b7.de* canth b7.de* carb-ac bro1 Carb-v bro1 caust bg2* chel bg2 chin bg2 chinin-s bg2 cocc b7.de colch bro1 coloc bro1 con b4.de dig b4.de euph b4.de* ferr bro1 glyc bro1 graph bro1 hell bg2 hep bro1 ign bg2 iod bg2 Iris bro1 Lac-ac bro1 laur b7.de* lob bg2 mag-m b4.de Mang b4.de* Meny b7.de* merc-c bro1 mez b4a.de mur-ac b4.de nat-c bg2 nat-m bro1 nit-ac b4.de nux-m bg2 phos b4.de* plb b7.de sabad bg2 sang bro1 sars b4.de sec bg2 seneg bg2 sep bro1 sul-ac bg2 sulph b4.de* tab bg2 ter bg2*

▽ - **extending** to | **Head**: alum k* mag-m k* tritic-vg fd5.de

○ - **Epigastrium**: acon bg2 apis b7a.de ars b4.de bov bg2 colch bg2 ferr b7.de iod bg2 iris bg2 kali-bi bg2 kreos bg2 laur bg2 mag-c bg2 mang bg2 merc b4.de mur-ac bg2 nat-c bg2 nat-m b4.de op bg2 Phos b4a.de querc-r svu1• rhus-t bg2 sang bg2 sec b7.de verat b7.de zinc bg2
  - **accompanied** by thirst (See Thirst - accompanied - epigastrium)
  - **sensation** of heat: Bry b7.de* chel b7.de* convo-s sp1* sabad b7a.de

HEAT, flushes of:

abrot acet-ac Acon k* aesc aeth agar k* aloe alum Alumn am-c am-m bg2 Anth k* anthraci Apis k* Arg-n k* **Ars** k* ars-h ars-i asaf bg2 aur-s bapt bar-c bar-i bar-m bg2 bar-s k2 bell k* benz-ac bism bg2 brom k* **Bry** k* Calad bg2 Calc k* calc-i k2 Calo br1 Camph k* cann-i cann-xyz bg2 Canth k* Caps bg2 carb-ac carb-an k* Carb-v bg2 carbn-s caust k* cedr cham k* chel k* chin b7.de* chinin-s k* chlf Cic k* cimic cina cinnb coc-c coca cocc cod colch k* coloc con corn-f croc bg2 crot-t cub c1 cupr k* cupre-au c1 dig k* dulc bg2* eup-per euph b4.de* fago ferr k* Ferr-ar ferr-i ferr-p fl-ac k* gels Glon Graph bg2 grat gymno ham fd3.de• hell k* helon hydr-ac Hydrc hyos k* Ign b7.de* iod k* ip k* iris k* jatr-c kali-ar kali-bi k* kali-c kali-chl kali-m k2 kali-n k* kali-s kali-sula a1* kalm kola stb3• Lac-ac Lac-c lach k* laur k* led Lob lyc bg2 mag-m Manc k* mang k* meny k* merc k* mez k* mosch bg2 mur-ac h2 myric nat-ar nat-c k* Nat-m nat-p nat-s nat-sil fd3.de• Nit-ac Nux-m k* **Nux-v** k* ol-an bg2 ol-j olnd op k* ox-ac par k* petr ph-ac bg2 Phos k* phyt plat k* plb k* plut-n srj7• Podo ptel puls k* ran-b bg2 raph rat Rob ruta k* **Sabad** b7.de* sabin k* sang k* Sars k* sec k* seneg k* sep k* Sil bg2 squil stry sul-ac k* sulph h2* sumb tab tarent Ter Thuj tril-p c1 valer k* verat k* verat-v vesp zinc b4a.de zinc-m

- **morning**: am-m apis lith-m mang h2
- **forenoon**: alum h2 dulc fd4.de ham fd3.de•
- **noon**: fago
- **afternoon**: calam sa3• fago
- **evening**: coloc ferr-i hyper
- **night** | **bed** agg.; in: cinnb
- **bread** agg.: sars
- **cold**:
  - **water**:
    - **agg.**: alum
    - **amel.**: alumn hyper
- **dinner**; during: hyper
- **eating**:
  - **after**:
    - **agg.**: con Ferr nat-sil fd3.de• Sep
    - **amel.**: arg-n ferr ozone sde2•
  - **before** | **agg.**: fl-ac
- **empty**, when: naja
- **eructations**:
  - **after**: sumb
  - **amel.**: fago
- **sitting** agg.: phos h2
- **waking**; on: acon-f

▽ - **extending** to:

○ • **Abdomen**: am-c carl chin chinin-s c1 verat

- **extending** to: ...
  - **Arms** and fingers: con h2
  - **Body**, over: ars *Camph* imp c1 op
  - **Chest**, over: bar-m chin chinin-s c1 nat-m ol-an verat
  - **Eyes**: stram
  - **Fauces**: caps
  - **Head**: alum bar-m *Calc* chin cinnb *Glon* hell indg br1 *Lyc* mag-m mang sumb
  - **Nose**: merl c1
  - **Throat**: cinnb nit-ac sumb tarent
    - **Pit** of: plat h2
  - **Upward**: ars asaf bapt hr1 *Calc* carb-ac cinnb *Ferr Glon* iris kali-bi kola stb3• laur *Manc* mang h2 ozone sde2• phos h2 tril-p br1 *Valer*

○ - **Pit** of stomach | **fever**; during: cub c1

HEATED; becoming: | **after** | **agg.**: *Acon* b7.de* **Bry** b7.de* caps b7.de* coff b7.de* ign b7.de* ip b7.de* *Nux-v* b7.de* *Olnd* b7a.de **Sil** bg2 *Thuj* bg2

- **during** | **agg.**: *Thuj* b4.de*

HEAVINESS: (↗*Fullness; Oppression; Stone)* abies-n k* acon k* aesc aeth *Agar* k* *Agath-a* nl2• all-s allox sp1 aloe alum alum-p k2 alum-sil k2 am-c am-m ant-c *Ant-t Apis Apoc Arg-met Arg-n* k* *Arn* k* *Ars* k* asc-t *Aur* b4a.de bapt *Bar-c* k* bar-m bell k* bism b7.de* borx *Brom Bry* k* *Cact* cadm-met tpw6 calad calc bg2* calc-s cann-i carb-ac bg2 *Carb-an Carb-v* k* *Carbn-s Carl* castm cham k* chel **Chin** k* chinin-ar chinin-s cimic cit-v clem coc-c coca cocc k* *Coff* colch k* coli jl2 com *Crot-c Crot-h Cycl* dig k* dirc c1 fago falco-pe nl2• ferr bro1 ferr-i ferr-p bg2 *Fl-ac* form galeoc-c-h gms1• *Gels* gent-c gent-l germ-met srj5• *Graph* bro1 grat hell b7.de* hep b4a.de* hura *Hydr* hyos ign iod *Kali-bi* k* *Kali-c* k* kali-chl kali-i kali-m k2 kali-n k* kali-p *Kali-s* kali-sil k2 kreos lac-ac lac-c lac-h sk4• lacer a1* lach lath c1 led lil-t *Lob* k* **Lyc** k* m-arct b7.de *Mag-m* manc mang-p rly4• merc merc-sul c1 mur-ac nat-ar *Nat-c Nat-m* nat-p *Nat-s* nit-ac **Nux-v** k* *Op* k* osm ox-ac par passi bro1 petr k* *Ph-ac* phel *Phos* k* phys **Pic-ac** k* pilo bro1 *Plat* plat-m-n c1 plb k* plut-n srj7• podo bg2 positr nl2• prun psil ft1 psor *Ptel* puls k* rat rauw tpw8* *Rhus-t* k* *Rob* k* rumx sabad sacch-a fd2.de• *Sang* k* sec seneg sep k* *Sil* k* sol-t-ae spig bg1* spong fd4.de stann stram stront-c sk4• *Stry* suis-pan rly4• sul-ac **Sulph** k* *Tab Tarent* teucr thea upa valer k* visc sp1 wye xan xero bro1 zinc zinc-p k2 zing k*

- **alternating** sides: grat k2
- **morning**: am-c bar-c h2 calc-s k* dios k* ery-a a1 sang sulph
  - **waking**; on: *Carb-an Puls*
- **forenoon**: sulph
- **noon**: alum fago *Lyc* k* mur-ac
  - **eating**; after: *Lyc* k*
- **afternoon**: am-m fago **Lyc** k* *Sang* k* stront-c
  - **eating**; after: *Lyc* k*
- **evening**: alum bell hell k* kali-bi k* rhus-t sulph k*
  - **18 h**: rauw tpw8*
- **night**: *Aesc* cass a1 *Chin* colch crot-t ery-a a1 kali-m k2* petr-ra shn4• tarent k*
  - **waking**; on: sulph
- **accompanied** by | **pressure** (See Pain - pressing - accompanied - heaviness)
- **ascending** stairs agg.: nux-m k*
- **beer**; after: acon k* **Kali-bi**
- **bread** agg.: kali-c merc k* symph fd3.de•
- **breakfast**:
  - **after**:
    - **agg.**: agar k* aids nl2• crot-h k* fago k* gels lyc k* petr ph-ac ptel a1 sang k*
    - **amel.**: bar-c h2
- **breathing** deep | **amel.**: bar-c h2
- **carrying** agg.: bar-c h2
- **chill**; during: sulph h2
- **cold** drinks agg.; after: acet-ac *Ars* podo rhod ptk1
- **digestion**; during: hep h2
- **dinner**; after: grat k* kali-s fd4.de lyc nat-ar ptel k*

Heaviness: ...

- **drinking**:
  - **after**:
    - **water**:
      - **agg.**: chel
      - **amel.**: psil ft1
- **eating**:
  - **after** | **agg.**: *Abies-n* absin k* agar *Agath-a* nl2• aids nl2• allox sp1 alum k* alum-p k2 alum-sil k2 alumn k* *Am-c Ant-c* apis arg-n k* *Ars* k* ars-i ars-s-f k2 bar-c k* *Bar-i* bar-m bar-s k2 bros-gau mrc1 *Bry* k* *Cact* k* calc-ar carb-ac k* cent a1 cham k* **Chin** chin-b hr1* chinin-ar *Chinin-s* cimic cycl *Elaps* falco-pe nl2• ferr ferr-i fl-ac k* germ-met srj5• ham fd3.de• *Hep* k* *Hydr* k* ign ignis-alc es2• *Iod* k* kali-ar k* **Kali-bi** k* *Kali-c* k* *Kali-p* kali-s fd4.de *Lach* k* lob k* **Lyc** k* merc nat-ar nept-m lsd2.fr *Nit-ac* k* **Nux-v** osm petr-ra shn4• *Ph-ac* k* *Phos* phys k* plan k* plb k* podo fd3.de• *Psor Ptel* k* *Puls* k* rhus-t k* *Rumx* sang *Sil* spong fd4.de sul-i k2 **Sulph** k* *Tarent* k* tub-r jl2 vib hr1 zinc-p k2
  - **amel.**: cadm-met tpw6
  - **while** | **agg.**: cann-i
- **empty**, while: *Fl-ac* k*
- **eructations** | **amel.**: aloe bros-gau mrc1 chel fago lac-h htj1• par k* petr-ra shn4•
- **leaning** backward, when: con h2
- **loose**: grat ptk1
- **meat** agg.: ferr c1 *Kali-bi* k* sulph k2
- **menses** | **before** | **agg.**: tarent k*
  - **during** | **agg.**: nat-p zinc
- **motion** | **amel.**: petr-ra shn4•
- **nausea**; during: lyc vesp hr1
- **nuts**; after | **amel.**: germ-met srj5•
- **potatoes** agg.: *Alum*
- **pressure**:
  - **agg.**: gels hr1 ignis-alc es2• phos k* ptel k* sin-a a1
  - **amel.**: cadm-met tpw6
- **sleep** agg.; after: *Lach*
- **spot**; in one: bism ptk1
- **standing** for a long time agg.: hura
- **stones**; as from: par ptk1 puls ptk1
- **stooping** agg.; after: bar-c k*
- **supper** agg.; after: chinin-s plan k*
- **trembling**; with: iod
- **waking**; on: carb-an ptel k* puls sulph
- **walking** in open air | **amel.**: borx petr
- **weather** agg.; wet: kali-c nat-s sil
- **wine** | **amel.**: galeoc-c-h gms1•

○ - **Back** of stomach: ham bg2*

- **Epigastrium**: agar bg2 am bg2 ars bg2 bar-c b4a.de* bell bg2 calad b7.de* dig b4a.de* iod bg2 kali-bi bg2 *Nux-v* b7a.de plb bg2 rumx ptk1 sec bg2 sil bg2 sul-ac bg2 *Sulph* bg2

HEAVY FOOD agg.: iod bg2

HEMATEMESIS (See Vomiting; type - blood)

HEMORRHAGE: (↗*Vomiting; type - blood)*

- **agg.**: tril-p bg2

○ - **Pylorus**, between the mucosa and muscular coat; at the colch mtf11

HERNIA; HIATUS: abies-n mrr1* carb-v gk rob mrr1 sulph mrr1 [heroin sdj2]

HICCOUGH: acet-ac k* acon k* acon-l a1 aegle-f bnj1 aeth k* aether c2 *Agar* k* agar-ph a1 agn k* alco a1 all-c k* *Alum* k* alum-p k2 alum-sil k2 am-c k* **Am-m** k* ambr b2.de* aml-ns bg2* amyg hr1 anac k* androc bnm2• ang k* ant-c k* ant-t k* apom a1 arg-met b2.de* *Arg-n* hr1 arge-pl rwt5• arizon-l nl2• *Arn* k* **Ars** k* ars-h c2* **Ars-i** k* arund k* asaf k2* asar k* aur k* aur-ar k2 aur-i k2 aur-s a1* *Bar-c* k* *Bar-i* bar-m bar-s k2 *Bell* k* benz-ac k* berb k* bism k* bond a1 borx k* bov k* brom k* *Bry* k* bufo caj c2* calad a1 *Calc* k* calc-f k* calc-i calc-sil k2 camph mtf11 cann-s b2.de* canth k* caps bg2* carb-an k* carb-v k* carbn-s card-b a1 carl k* castm caust k* *Cham* k* chel k* *Chin* chinin-ar *Chinin-s* k* *Chlf* k* **Cic** k* cimx k* cina k* cinch a1 cinnm hr1* cob k* cocain bro1 *Cocc* k* *Coff* k* colch k* coloc k* con k* convo-s sp1 crot-h bg2

Hiccough: ...
crot-t k* cupr k* _Cupr-s_ vh cur k* **Cycl** k* der a1 dig k* _Dios_ k* _Dros_ k* dulc k* eug c2 eup-per bg2* _Euph_ k* euphr k* ferr-p k* _Gels_ k* _Gins_ c2* gnaph a1 graph k* grat k* ham k* hell k* hell-o a1* hep k* hydr vh _Hydr-ac_ bg2* **Hyos** k* **Ign** k* indg k* **Iod** k* _Ip_ k* jab k* _Jatr-c_ jug-r k* kali-ar kali-bi k* _Kali-br_ bro1* kali-c k* kali-i kali-m k2 kali-n kali-s k* kali-sil k2 kali-sula a1* _Kreos_ _Lac-e_ hrn2• _Lach_ k* lat-m bnm6• _Laur_ k* led k* lob k* lob-s a1 **Lyc** k* lyss st1 mag-c k* _Mag-m_ k* **Mag-p** k* mand sp1 _Marr-vg_ bg3 _Med_ c1* meny k* **Merc** k* merc-c k* merc-cy a1 merc-n a1 mez k* mill k* mit a1 morph a1* _Mosch_ k* mur-ac k* narc-ps a1* narcot a1 **Nat-ar** **Nat-c** k* **Nat-m** k* nat-s **Nicc** k* nicc-met bro1 nicot bro1 nit-ac k* **Nux-m** k* **Nux-v** k* oci-sa sp1 oena a1 ol-suc bro1 _Op_ k* orig a1 ox-ac k* papin a1 _Par_ k* passi mtf11 petr b2.de* _Phos_ k* phys k* phyt k* plat b2.de* plb k* plect a1 positr nl2• _Psor_ k* _Puls_ k* _Ran-b_ k* ran-s b2.de* rat k* rhus-t b2.de* _Ruta_ k* sabad k* sabin k* sal-fr sle1• samb k* sars k* scut c2* **Sec** k* sel k* _Sep_ k* sil k* sin-n a1* _Spong_ k* _Stann_ k* _Staph_ k* **Stram** k* _Stront-c_ k* succ-xyz c2 _Sul-ac_ k* sul-i k2 sulph k* sumb k* symph fd3.de• tab k* _Tarax_ k* tarent k* **Teucr** k* thiam rly4• thuj b2.de* trif-p a1 tritic-vg fd5.de vanil fd5.de _Verat_ k* _Verat-v_ k* _Verb_ k* wye c2 zinc k* zinc-m a1* zinc-o c2* zinc-val bro1* [spect dfg1 tax jsj7]

- **daytime**: nit-ac k* petr k* phos k*
- **morning**: acon b7.de* all-c k* apoc k* cann-s k* kali-n k* spong fd4.de verat k*
  - **fasting** agg.: kali-n sulph h2
  - **rising** agg.; after: gamb k* graph k* mag-c k*
- **forenoon**: am-c b4.de* ars b4.de* bar-c b4.de* mag-c b4.de* merc b4.de* mur-ac b4.de nux-v b7.de phos b4.de vanil fd5.de zinc b4.de
  - **11** h: ox-ac
  - **eating**; after: bar-c nat-s
- **noon**: kali-c k* sil k* sulph k*
- **afternoon**: agar k* alum b4.de* am-c b4.de* am-m b7.de* ars b4.de* bar-c b4.de* bov b4.de* canth k* carb-v b4.de* graph b4.de* hyos b7.de* _Ign_ k* lyc b4.de* merc b4.de* mur-ac b4.de* nux-v b7.de* phos b4.de* sep b4.de* staph b7.de* sulph b4.de* vanil fd5.de zinc b4.de*
  - **13** h: bov _Verat-v_
  - **14** h: tarent _Verat-v_
  - **15** h: ptel c1
- **evening**: aeth k* alum b4.de* coff b7.de* gels bg2* graph k* ign b7.de* kali-bi k* _Kali-i_ k* lach b7.de* _Lob_ mag-c b4.de* nat-c k* nat-s k* **Nicc** k* petr k* rhus-t k* sars b4.de* sep b4a.de sil k* staph b7.de* sulph b4.de* vanil fd5.de _Zinc_ k*
  - **17**-20 h: phys
  - **18** h: ham nat-c sars
  - **18**.30 h: mag-c
  - **bed** agg.; in: nat-m k* nicc k* sil k* sulph h2
  - **fasting** agg.: sulph k*
  - **followed** by drowsiness: lob hr1
- **night**: apoc k* ars k* bell k* carb-an b4.de* **Hyos** k* merc k* merc-c k* puls k* sul-ac k* vanil fd5.de
  - **midnight**: bell k* hyos h1*
    - **before**: kali-c h2
  - **accompanied** by | **restlessness** (See MIND - Restlessness - night - hiccough)
  - **sleep** agg.; during: puls k*
  - **urination**, with involuntary: hyos st
- **accompanied** by:
  - **biliary** colic in liver (See ABDOMEN - Pain - liver - colic - accompanied - hiccough)
  - **cancer** in stomach (See Cancer - accompanied - hiccough)
  - **cholera** (See RECTUM - Cholera - accompanied - hiccough)
  - **concussion** of brain (See HEAD - Concussion - accompanied - hiccough)
  - **convulsions**: (↗ _EXTREMITIES - Convulsion - hiccough)_ bell **Cic** k* _Cupr_ k* **Hyos** k* _Ran-b_ k* _Stram_ h1*
  - **diarrhea** (See RECTUM - Diarrhea - accompanied - hiccough)
  - **eructations**: ant-c bro1 _Caj_ bro1 chin bro1 cic bro1 cycl ptk1 dios bro1* ign ptk1 nux-v bro1* wye bro1
- **accompanied** by: ...
  - **gastralgia** (See Pain - accompanied - hiccough)
  - **hepatitis** (See ABDOMEN - Inflammation - liver - accompanied - hiccough)
  - **meteorism** (See ABDOMEN - Distension - accompanied - hiccough)
  - **moroseness** (See MIND - Morose - hiccough)
  - **nausea** (See Nausea - accompanied - hiccough)
  - **perspiration**: bell bg2
  - **respiration**; complaints of (See RESPIRATION - Hiccough)
  - **saliva**; profuse: _Lob_ ptk1*
  - **stretch**; impulse to: aml-ns ptk1
  - ○ **Abdomen**; pain in (See ABDOMEN - Pain - accompanied - hiccough)
  - **Back**; complaints of (See BACK - Hiccough)
  - **Brain**; concussion of (See HEAD - Concussion - accompanied - hiccough)
  - **Epigastrium**; blows at: teucr bg2
  - **Eyes**; red discoloration of: apis bg2 arn bg2 asar bg2 bry bg2 chin bg2 lyc bg2 nux-v bg2 puls bg2 sep bg2 sil bg2 verat bg2
  - **Head**; pain in (See HEAD - Pain - accompanied - hiccough)
  - **Meninges**; inflammation of (See HEAD - Inflammation - meninges - accompanied - hiccough)
  - **Mouth**; constriction of (See MOUTH - Constriction - accompanied - hiccough)
  - **Peritoneum**; inflammation of (See ABDOMEN - Inflammation - peritoneum - accompanied - hiccough)
  - **Spine**; complaints of: _Stram_ st1
  - **Stomach**:
    - **complaints** of (See Complaints - accompanied - hiccough)
    - **inflammation** of (See Inflammation - accompanied - hiccough)
    - **pain** in (See Pain - accompanied - hiccough)
  - **Tongue** | **white** discoloration of the tongue: _Nicc_ kr1*
- **alcoholic** drinks; after: **Ran-b** k* sul-ac ptk1
- **alternating** with:
  - **eructations**: agar k* bell b4.de* _Bry_ b7.de* sep k* wye k*
    - **empty** eructations (See Eructations; type - empty - alternating - hiccough)
  - **vomiting** (See Vomiting - alternating - hiccough)
- **back**; with pain in: teucr hr1*
- **bed** agg.; in: lachn k* nat-m k* nicc k* sil k* _Sulph_ k*
- **bread** and butter agg.: nat-s
- **breakfast** agg.; after: carl a1 tarent k* zinc k*
- **carried**; when: _Kreos_ st1
- **children**; in: borx st1 _Ign_ st1 _Ip_ st1 spong fd4.de
- **chill**:
  - **after**: am-c k* ars h2
  - **during**: ars bg2
- **chronic**: stram ptk1 _Zinc-val_ br1
- **coffee**: | **amel.**: hydr-ac bg2
- **cold**; after taking a: phos k*
- **cold** drinks agg.; after: ars h2 lac-h htj1• puls h1
- **concussion** of brain; with (See HEAD - Concussion - accompanied - hiccough)
- **continued**: caust bg2 merc-cy ptk1 verat-v tl1
  - **pregnancy** agg.; during: op ptk
  - **two** years almost uninterrupted, eighteen to twenty times a minute; since: _Nicc_ vk1
- **convulsions**; with (See accompanied - convulsions)
- **convulsive**: aeth k* ars k* bell k* **Gels** _Mag-p_ nux-v _Ran-b_ stram tab k* wies a1
- **cough**:
  - **after**: ang h1* **Tab** k* trif-p ptk1

- • **during** | **agg.**: ang b7.de* lach b7a.de *Puls* b7a.de tab k*
- **dinner**:
  - • **after** | **agg.**: alum k* am-m k* arn k* bov k* carb-ac k* carb-v k* cob k* dulc fd4.de graph k* grat k* hyos k* indg k* *Mag-m* k* *Mur-ac* nat-c h2 *Phos* k* sars k* *Teucr* tong a1
  - • **before**: mag-m *Mur-ac* k* nux-v k*
  - • **during** | **agg.**: cycl grat k* *Mag-m* k* nat-c k*
- **drinking**:
  - • **after**:
    - ⁝ **agg.**: acon b7.de* *Ign* k* lach k* merc-c *Nux-v* *Puls* k* sul-ac thuj bg1
    - ⁝ **cold** water | **agg.**: thuj
    - ⁝ **water** | **agg.**: alum b4.de* ign b7a.de merc-c bg2 thuj b4a.de
- **drunkards**; in: *Hyos* sne *Ran-b* k* sul-ac k2*
- **during** | **agg.**: *Mag-m* b4a.de teucr b7.de*
- **eating**:
  - • **after** | **agg.**: acon k* *Alum* k* alum-p k2 am-m b7.de* arn b7.de* ars k* ars-s-f k2 bar-c b4.de* bell k* borx k* bov k* *Bry* k* *Carb-an* k* carb-v k* carl k* cob *Cocc* b7a.de con b4.de* cop k* *Cycl* k* fil a1* *Graph* k* ham st1 hep k* hura **Hyos** k* *Ign* k* *Lac-e* hrn2• lyc k* mag-m k* merc k* nat-ar nat-c k* nat-m k* nat-s *Nux-v* k* *Par* k* phos k* prot jl2 psor k* rat k* sal-fr sle1• samb k* sars b4.de* *Sep* k* sil k* stann k* staph k* sulph k* symph fd3.de• *Teucr* k* thuj k* verat k* zinc k* zinc-p k2
  - • **before** | **agg.**: bov *Phos* k* sil k*
  - • **overeating** agg.; after: cycl bg2 ign bg2 nux-v bg2 puls bg2
  - • **while** | **agg.**: *Cycl* k* eug k* lac-h htj1• mag-m k* merc k* nat-c b4.de* samb b7.de* teucr k* tritic-vg fd5.de
- **emotions**; after: *Ign* st1
- **eructations**:
  - • **after**: *Agar* b4a.de alum b4.de* bry k* carb-an h2 cycl k* ox-ac hr1 rhus-t b7.de* sep b4.de* til k*
  - • **amel.**: carb-an bg2* ham bg2 zinc bg2
  - • **ineffectual**; after: cocc b7.de*
- **exertion** agg.; after: calc a1 carb-v
- **fever**:
  - • **after**: ars bg2* lach b7a.de*
  - • **before**: calc b4a.de
  - • **during** | **agg.**: ars bg2 crot-h k* *Mag-p* k*
  - • **hour** when the fever ought to come; at the: **Ars** k*
  - • **yellow** fever; during (See yellow)
- **flatulence** agg.: ruta b7.de*
- **followed** by:
  - • **asthma**: cupr ptk1*
  - • **intussusception**: plb st1
  - • **nausea**: cupr b7a.de
  - • **vomiting**: *(↗vomiting - ending)* jab st1
  - ○ • **Extremities**; convulsions of (See EXTREMITIES - Convulsion - hiccough)
  - • **Head**:
    - ⁝ **convulsions** of head: bell a1*
  - • **Limbs**; tension in all (See EXTREMITIES - Tension - hiccough)
  - • **Stomach**; pain in: papin a1
- **food** | **fat**, from: jug-r vml3•
- **frequent**: ars mtf33 cina a1 merc tl1 prot jl2 ran-b tl1 staph tl1
- **fruit**; after cold: ars st1 *Puls* st1
- **greasy**: *Lyc* b4a.de stront-c b4a.de
- **headache**; during (See HEAD - Pain - accompanied - hiccough)
- **hysterical**: gels bro1* *Ign* bro1* mosch k2* nux-m bro1* zinc-val bro1*
- **incomplete**: arn b7.de* caust h2 dig h2 mag-c h2
- **inspiration** agg.: ang h1
- **intermittent**: caust
  - • **after**: *Hyos*
- **lasting** | **seconds**; a few: prot jl2
- **laughing** agg.: calc bg1*
- **loud**: cic k* ign gk ozone sde2•
- **menses**; after: stram b7.de*
- **motion** agg.: carb-v k* merc-c k*
- **nursing** the child agg.; after: borx sne **Hyos** sne stram sne teucr bro1*
- **operation**, after abdominal: *Hyos* fr1*
- **painful**: *Acon* *Am-m* b7a.de borx b4a.de carb-v b4.de* *Cimx* hyos b7.de* mag-m k* mag-p st1 nat-c b4.de* *Nicc* *Phos* *Rat* k* stront-c b4.de* *Sul-ac* sulph b4.de* tab teucr k* *Verat-v* k*
  - • **crying**; with (See MIND - Weeping - hiccough)
- **paroxysmal**: ign mrr1
- **periodical**: ars bg2
  - • **once** a day; at least: prot jl2
- **perspiration**, after: ars h2
- **pork**, after: ham k*
- **pregnancy** agg.; during: *Cycl* k* *Op* k* *Puls* b7a.de
- **quinine**; after: *Nat-m*
- **reading** aloud, while: cycl k*
- **retching**, with: jatr-c bro1 mag-p br1* merc bro1* nux-v bro1*
- **sitting** up in bed agg.: *Kreos* st1
- **sleep** agg.; during: calc b4a.de cina ign ptk1 *Merc-c* k* puls b7.de*
- **smoking** | **after** | **agg.**: ant-c arg-met ptk1 calc k* calen a1* *Ign* k* ip h1 puls ptk1 sel br1*
  - • **agg.**: ambr k* ant-c k* arg-met k* calad *Ign* k* ip b7.de* kali-br bg2 lach k* psor k* *Puls* k* ruta k* *Sang* k* scut st1 sel k* sep k* stann k* *Staph* k* sul-ac k* verat k*
    - ⁝ **eating**; before: sel
- **soup** agg.: alum h2 symph fd3.de•
- **spasmodic**: ars bg2 *Bell* bg2 cic br1 *Nux-v* b7.de* op bg2 *Puls* b7a.de ran-b b7.de* **Sec** b7a.de *Stram* bg2 teucr b7.de* *Verat* b7a.de
- **spasms**:
  - • **before**: bell bg2 cupr k*
  - ○ • **Esophagus**, of: verat-v bro1*
- **suffocative**:
  - • **accompanied** by | **Abdomen**; cramping pain in: verat bro1
- **supper** | **after** | **agg.**: alum cob coca st1 con lyc sep staph
  - • **beginning** of; at: con h2
- **tea**; after: lach b7.de*
- **thinking** about it, on: ox-ac k*
- **typhoid** fever; during: mag-p st1 phos k*
- **unconscious**, when: cupr k*
- **urination** agg.; during: hyos b7.de*
- **vexation**; with: agn bg2
- **violent**: am-c bg2 *Am-m* k* calc-f chinin-s *Cic* k* *Cycl* hyos h1 lob *Lyc* k* mag-m a1 *Mag-p* *Merc-c* mur-ac a1 nat-c h2 **Nat-m** k* **Nicc** k* *Nux-v* k* petr a1 *Puls* b7a.de ran-b k2 rat k* **Stram** k* stront-c k* sul-ac k2 teucr k* vanil fd5.de verat k* verat-v ptk1 zinc h2
- **vomiting**:
  - • **after**: bism b7a.de* bry k* jatr-c ptk1 narcot a1 op bg2 **Verat** verat-v ptk1
  - • **before**: cupr b7.de* jab hr1 jatr-c ptk1 mag-m pd
  - • **ending** in vomiting: *(↗followed - vomiting)* jab st1
  - • **fever**: lach st
  - • **while**: bell j5.de* *Bry* j5.de* cupr jatr-c bro1 lach bg2* mag-p bro1* merc bro1* merc-c k* nux-v bro1* phos bg2 ruta j5.de* **Verat** st1
- **walking** agg.; after: carb-v b4a.de
- **warm**:
  - • **drinks**:
    - ⁝ **agg.**: stram h1 *Verat* k*
    - ⁝ **amel.**: mag-p pd
- **winter**: nit-ac st1
- **yawning**:
  - • **after** | **agg.**: aml-ns bg2 mag-c b4.de*
  - • **agg.**: aml-ns bg2* carl bro1 cocc bro1* cycl ptk1 mag-c b4.de*
  - • **before**: caust h2
- **yellow** fever; during: ars-h st1

HICCUP (See Hiccough)

HOLLOW sensation (See Emptiness)

HORRIBLE sensation, in drunkards:
- **morning** | **waking**; on: **Asar** k*

HUNGER (See Appetite - increased)

HURRIED feeling in: bell bg2

HYPERCHLORHYDRIA: *(↗Acidity)* acet-ac br1* anac bro1* ant-c bro1 *Arg-n* bro1 atis zzc1• *Atro* bro1 bism bro1 calc br1* calc-p bro1 *Carb-v* bro1 cham bro1 chin bro1 chinin-ar br1* coffin bro1 con bro1 grin br1* helic-p mtf hydr bro1 ign bro1 *Iris* bro1 lob bro1 lyc bro1 mag-c bro1 mur-ac bro1 *Nat-c* bro1 nat-p bro1* *Nux-v* bro1 *Orex-tann* bro1 petr bro1 phos bro1 prun-v bro1 *Puls* bro1 rob c1* sul-ac br1* sulo-ac jl3 sulph bro1
- **accompanied** by:
  - **diarrhea**: cham bro1 rheum bro1 rob bro1
  - **respiration**; asthmatic (See RESPIRATION - Asthmatic - accompanied - stomach)
- **alternating** with | **hypochlorhydria**: calc-ar ptk1 chinin-ar ptk1
- **nervous**: grin br1

INACTIVITY: ail k* aloe bell k* *Carb-v* *Hydr* k* manc k* *Op* ran-s k* *Sil* k* visc c1

INDIGESTION: *(↗Disordered; Slow; GENERALS - Food)* abies-c c2* *Abies-n* bro1 abrot k* acet-ac bro1 acon-ac rly4• aesc bro1 aeth bro1* agar bro1 alet c2* alf bro1 all-c k2 all-s br1* aln br1* aloe bro1 alst-s br1 **Alum** k* alum-p k2 am-be c2 am-c bg2 ambr ambro c2 anac k* anemps br1 ang hr1 ant-c bg2* ant-s-aur c2 ant-t k2* apoc bro1 arg-n bg2* arist-cl sp1 arist-m bro1 *Arn* bg2* *Ars* k* *Ars-i* ars-s-f c2 asc-c c2 asc-t br1 atha c2 atis zzc1• atro bro1 aur bg2 bac bn* bapt bro1 **Bar-c** k* *Bar-i* **Bar-m** bell b4a.de* bell-p c2 berb **Bism** k* borx h2* brom bro1 bry b7.de* cact c2 cadm-br c2 cadm-s c2* calad **Calc** k* calc-ar k* calc-chln bro1 *Calc-p* br1* **Calc-s** canth b7.de* caps b7a.de* *Carb-ac* k* *Carb-an* k* **Carb-v** k* carc br1* *Card-m* bro1 cas-s bro1 caust b4.de* cent-cy lsr4.de• *Cham* bro1 **Chel** k* chelo br1 **Chin** k* chloroc-w bta1• cina bro1 cinnmd-c lsr3.de• *Coca* bro1 coch bro1 coenz-q mtf11 *Coff* colch bro1* coli jl2 *Coll* coloc bro1 con b4.de* corn-f br1* cund br1 cupr b7.de* cupr-act bro1 cycl br1* dig b4.de* dios br1* dros bg2 dys pte1*• erio br1 euonin c2 eup-per c2 eup-pur c2 fab br1 fel c2* ferr bg2* *Ferr-p* ferr-s mtf11 flav jl2 frag br1 fuc br1 *Gaert* fmm1• galan lsr4.de• gent-l bro1 ger-i rly4• *Graph* k* haem c2 hell-o c1* **Hep** k* hir rsj4• *Hom-xyz* k* **Hydr** k* hyos b7.de* ign k* iod k* **Ip** k* iris bro1 jal mrr1 kali-bi bg2* kali-c bg2* kali-m bro1 kali-p mrr1 kreos bg2* lac-ac c2 **Lac-d** lac-h sze9• *Lach* k* lepi c2 lept bro1 limen-b-c hrn2* *Lob* bro1 lob-d c2 lob-e c2 luf-op rsj5• **Lyc** k* mag-c b4a.de* *Mag-m* k* mang k2 marb-w es1• *Meny* b7.de* *Merc* k* mez h2 morg-g fmm1• mur-ac b4a.de* nat-ar **Nat-c** k* *Nat-m* k* nat-ox rly4• nat-s bro1 nicc-met br1 nicc-s br1 nit-ac bro1 *Nux-m* k* **Nux-v** k* **Olnd** k* *Op* k* orni tl1 ox-ac c2 par k* paraf c2 peps c1 **Petr** k* petr-ra shn4• *Ph-ac* k* phos b4.de* pic-ac bro1 plac-s rly4• plb b7a.de* pneu jl2 podo bro1 *Pop* br1* prun bro1 prun-v bro1 psil ft1 *Ptel* k* **Puls** k* rhod b4.de* *Rhus-t* bg2 *Rob* bro1 rumx c2* ruta b7.de* sabb bwa3 sal-ac br1* *Sang* k* sanic c2 sars k2 seneg b4.de* *Sep* k* sil h2* spong k* squil k* stann k* staph bg2 stry-af-cit bro1* succ-ac mtf11 suis-pan rly4• sul-ac bro1* sul-i k2 sulfa sp1 **Sulph** k* syc fmm1• tarax mrr1 *Tarent* thiam rly4• tub-m jl2 uran-n bro1 vac br1 valer k* vanad br1 verat b7.de* vesp-xyz c2 vichy-g c2 wies c2 wildb c2 wye c2 xan br1 xero bro1 zinc b4.de* zing [bell-p-sp dcm1 spect dfg1]
- **morning**: bufo
- **evening**: ambr chin ger-i rly4•
- **abuse** of drugs, after●: **Nux-v** k*
- **accompanied** by:
  - **acidity** of stomach: equis-h hr1 *Pop* br1
  - **appetite** | **increased** (See Appetite - increased - accompanied - indigestion)
  - **diabetes** (See GENERALS - Diabetes mellitus - accompanied - indigestion)
  - **eructations**; excessive: orni tl1
  - **flatulence**: *Arg-n* tl1 *Carb-v* tl1 *Pop* br1 *Puls* tl1 vac br1

Indigestion – accompanied by: ...
  - **gout** (See EXTREMITIES - Pain - joints - gouty - accompanied - indigestion)
  - **hemorrhoids** (See RECTUM - Hemorrhoids - accompanied - indigestion)
  - **malaria** (See GENERALS - Malaria - accompanied - indigestion)
  - **nausea** (See Nausea - accompanied - indigestion)
  - **obesity**: all-s br1
  - **saliva**:
    - **saltish**: *Cycl* br1
    - **viscid**: *Nat-m* kr1*
  - **salivation**: *Nat-c* kr1* *Nat-m* kr1*
  - **swelling** | **eating**; after: *Kali-c* tl1
  - **tuberculosis** (See CHEST - Phthisis - accompanied - indigestion)
  - **urticaria**: *Ant-c* bro1 ars bro1 carb-v bro1 cop bro1 dulc bro1 nux-v bro1 *Puls* bro1 rob bro1 trios bro1
  - **water** brash (See Eructations; type - water brash - accompanied - indigestion)
  - ○ **Abdomen** | **heat** in umbilical region (See ABDOMEN - Heat - umbilicus - accompanied - indigestion)
  - **Anus**; prolapsus of (See RECTUM - Prolapsus - accompanied - indigestion)
  - **Gums**:
    - **bleeding** (See MOUTH - Bleeding - gums - accompanied - indigestion)
    - **swelling** (See MOUTH - Swelling - gums - accompanied - indigestion)
  - **Head** pain (See HEAD - Pain - accompanied - indigestion)
  - **Heart**:
    - **complaints** of the (See CHEST - Heart; complaints - accompanied - indigestion)
    - **failure** (See CHEST - Heart failure - accompanied - indigestion)
  - **Kidneys**; complaints of (See KIDNEYS - Complaints - accompanied - indigestion)
  - **Liver** | **inactivity** (See ABDOMEN - Inactivity - liver - accompanied - indigestion)
  - **Tongue**:
    - **gray**: *Kali-c* kr1*
    - **pale**: *Kali-c* kr1*
    - **pointed** tongue: chel kr1*
    - **white** discoloration of tongue: arg-n kr1* *Lyc* vk1
      - **yellowish** white: naja kr1*
    - **yellow** discoloration of the tongue | **dirty** yellow: arn kr1*
    - **Sides** of tongue | **clean**: arg-n hr1*
- **alcoholic** drinks; after: ran-b mrr1 sul-ac mrr1
- **allergies**: gaert fmm1•
- **anxiety**; from: phos k2
- **atonic** (See Slow)
- **bathing**; from cold: ant-c br1*
- **beer**; after: ant-t bro1 bapt bro1 bry bro1 chin mrr1 *Kali-bi* bro1 lyc bro1 *Nux-v* bro1
- **bitter**: morg-p fmm1•
- **brain** fag; from: aeth k2* calc-f ptk1
  - **children**; in: calc-f bro1*
- **bread**; after: ant-c bro1 bry bro1 lyc bro1 nat-m bro1 zinc mrr1
- **butter**; after eating: puls k2
- **catarrh**: syc fmm1•
- **cheese** agg.: ars bro1 carb-v bro1 coloc bro1 nux-v bro1 ptel k*
- **children**; in: amyg-p br1 bar-c bg2 **Calc** bg2 carc jl2 *Ip* bg2 merc bg2 *Nux-v* bg2 *Puls* bg2 **Sulph** bg2 syph mtf33
  - **infants**: *Aeth* bg2 chin bg2 **Ip** bg2 *Nux-v* bg2 *Puls* bg2
    - **artificial** feeding: *Gaert* fmm1•

- **chronic**: cact bro1 carb-v bro1 cas-s br1 chin bro1 hydr-ac bro1 *Nat-m* bro1 ptel tl1 *Sep* bro1 spig bro1 tab bro1
- **coffee** agg.: aeth carb-v bg2 *Cham* k* *Cocc* bg2 cycl *Ign* bg2 kali-c bro1 lyc bro1 merc bg2 **Nux-v** k* puls bg2 rhus-t bg2 sulph bg2
- **coition**; agg.: bar-c ptk1 dig ptk1* phos ptk1
- **cold** | **drinks**:
  - **after**:
    - **agg.** | **ice** water: *Ars* bro1 carb-v bro1 elaps bro1 ip bro1 kali-c bro1 nat-c bro1 *Puls* bro1
  - **food** | **after**: alum *Ph-ac*
- **cold**; after taking a: *Ant-c* *Bry* calc k2 *Camph*
- **contradiction**; after: caps fkm1•
- **debauch**; after: ant-t bro1 *Carb-v* bro1 *Chin* bro1 nat-s bro1 *Nux-v* bro1
- **diet**; from errors in: all-s bro1 *Ant-c* bro1 *Bry* bro1 *Carb-v* bro1 chin bro1 coff bro1 *Ip* bro1 lyc bro1 nat-c bro1 *Nux-v* bro1 *Puls* bro1 xan bro1
- **digestion** stopped: kali-bi k2
- **drinking**:
  - **after**:
    - **much**: xan br1
    - **water** | **agg.**: ars bro1
- **drunkards**; in: caps br1 kola br1
- **eating**:
  - **after**:
    - **agg.**: flav jl2 luf-op rsj5•
      - **fast**; eating and drinking too: anac bro1* coff bro1* *Olnd* bro1*
  - **agg.**:
    - **constant**; from: aeth k2
    - **improper** food: **Ant-c** bg2* ars bg2 *Ip* bg2* *Nux-v* bg2* **Puls** bg2*
  - **overeating** agg.; after: ant-c tl1 carb-v bro1 *Chin* bro1 iod k2 kali-c bro1 *Nux-v* bro1 ruta ptk1 sep ptk1 xan br1
    - **just** a little bit: nux-m c1
  - **small** quantities | **amel.**: lavand-a ctl1•
- **eggs**: chinin-ar colch ferr ferr-m nux-v bro1 oscilloc jl2
- **farinaceous** food, from: ant-c bro1 carb-v bro1 *Caust* ip bro1 kali-m bro1 lyc bro1 *Nat-c* **Nat-m** *Nat-s* *Nux-v* *Puls* bro1 rob br1 *Sulph*
- **fat** food agg.: ant-c bro1 atis zzc1• *Calc* bro1 caps fkm1• carb-v bro1* chel mrr1 chin mrr1 *Cycl* bro1* dys fmm1• *Gaert* fmm1• hir rsj4• ip bro1 kali-m bro1* ptel mrr1 puls bro1* tarax mrr1 thuj bro1
- **fear**; from: **Phos** vh
- **fever**; after | **acute**: chin bro1 quas bro1
- **fish** agg.: *Chinin-ar* irid-met srj5•
  - **spoiled**: ars bro1 carb-v bro1
- **flatulent** food: chin bro1 lyc bro1 puls bro1
- **followed** by:
  - **constipation**: lavand-a ctl1• mag-p bro1
  - **respiration**; asthmatic: sang ptk1
- **food** | **any** kind of food: amyg-p br1
- **fruit** agg.: act-sp ars bro1 *Chin* k* elaps bro1 *Ip* irid-met srj5• *Puls* bro1 verat bro1*
  - **unripe**: chinin-ar c1
- **gastric** juice; from imperfect secretion of: aln br1* *Alum* bro1 lyc bro1
- **grief**; from: (↗*MIND - Ailments - grief*) **Ign** tarent k*
- **heavy** food: ars-s-f k2 iod b4a.de lyc b4a.de puls mrr1
- **ice** cream: (↗*Disordered - ice; Nausea - ice cream - after*) *Ars* *Carb-v* ip **Puls** k*
- **insensibility**; with: cic br1
- **irritability**; with: sang a1
- **lemon** | **amel.**: ptel mrr1
- **long** time; for a: dys fmm1•
  - **sour** food agg.: morg-p fmm1•
  - **sweets**: dys fmm1•
- **meat**: *Caust* bro1 *Ferr* k* *Ferr-p* ip bro1 *Ptel* puls bro1 sil h2*
  - **fat**: ptel mrr1
  - **spoiled**: ars bro1 carb-v bro1
- **melons**; after: ars bro1 zing bro1
- **menses**; during: arg-n bro1 cop bro1 sep bro1 sulph mrr1
- **mental** exertion; after: am k* calc k* cocc k* *Lach* k* **Nux-v** k* *Puls* k* *Sulph* k* verat k*

Indigestion: ...

- **milk**:
  - **agg.**: **Aeth** k* ambr *Ant-c* *Calc* k* carb-v bro1 **Chin** k* *Iris* *Mag-c* k* **Mag-m** k* **Nit-ac** k* *Nux-v* oscilloc jl2 sul-ac bro1 **Sulph** k* zinc mrr1
    - **children**; in: mag-m br1
    - **dentition**; during: aeth bro1 calc bro1 *Mag-m* bro1
  - **amel.**: lavand-a ctl1•
- **nervous**: alf br1 anac br1 cham bro1 nux-m bro1 nux-v bro1 tub-m jl2
  - **eating** | **amel.**: anac br1
- **nursing** mothers; in: *Chin* bro1 sin-a bro1
- **old** people●: *Abies-n* br1* ant-c bg2 ars bro1 *Bar-c* bg2* caps tl1 carb-v bg2* chin bg2* *Chinin-s* *Cic* bg2 fl-ac bro1 *Hydr* bro1 juni-c br1 kali-c bro1 nux-m bg2 nux-v bg2 pop br1
  - **obesity**; inclined to: kali-c tl1
- **onions** agg.: kali-p fd1.de• **Lyc** *Puls* *Thuj*
- **pears** agg.: borx
- **pork**, after: chin bro1 **Cycl** k* *Ip* **Puls** k*
- **potatoes** agg.: **Alum**
- **pregnancy** agg.; during: sabad bro1 *Sin-a* bro1 thea bro1
- **salt**; after | **abuse** of: phos bro1
- **salt** meat, after: act-sp
- **sedentary** life; from: nux-v bro1
- **sleep** | **loss** of sleep; from: nux-v bro1
- **slow** (See Slow)
- **sour** food agg.: aloe k* anac mtf11 anders mtf11 **Ant-c** k* arg-n mtf11 ars bro1 asim mtf11 atro-pur mtf11 caps mtf11 carb-ac mtf11 chin bro1 chinin-ar mtf11 emb-r mtf11 graph mtf11 hom-xyz mtf11 hydr mtf11 hydr-ac mtf11 mag-c mtf11 morg-p fmm1• mucot mtf11 nat-m bro1 nat-p mtf11 nit-ac mtf11 *Nux-v* k* orex-tann mtf11 orni mtf11 phos mtf11 prot fmm1• prun-v mtf11 rob mtf11 stry-af-cit mtf11
- **sprains**; from: ruta ptk1
- **stooping** agg.: merc h1
- **straining**; from: ruta c1
- **sweets**; from: ant-c bro1 *Arg-n* bro1 ip bro1 *Lyc* bro1 zinc bro1
- **tea**; after: abies-n br1* *Chin* bro1 *Dios* bro1 puls bro1 thea bro1 thuj bro1
  - **abuse** of tea; after: thea br1
- **tobacco**; after: abies-n br1* *Nux-v* bro1 sep bro1
- **veal**; after: zinc mrr1
- **vegetables**; from: ars bro1 asc-t bro1 nat-c bro1 nux-v bro1 *Sep* bro1
- **vexation**; after●: **Cham** **Ip** tarent
- **warm** | **drinks** | **after**: ambr k* chin kr1* fl-ac k2
  - **food**:
    - **after**: am-c ign k2
    - **agg.**: ign svg1•
- **water**; after bad●: *All-s* *Ars* *Podo*
- **weather**:
  - **cold** agg.: *Dulc*
  - **warm** | **agg.**: ant-c br1* *Bry* bro1
- **wine**; after: (↗*Wine; Wine - intolerance*) *Ant-c* bro1 caps bro1 carb-v bro1 coff bro1 nat-s bro1 *Nux-v* bro1 sul-ac bro1 sulph bro1 zinc bro1*
- **women**; in: *Mag-m* br1
- **yawning** | **amel.**: *Castm* vh
- **young** people; in | **masturbated** and have seminal emissions together with palpitations; who have: bar-c br1

INDURATION:

- **chronic**: orni br1

○ - **Pylorus**: (↗*Constriction - pylorus; Contraction - pylorus; Hardness - pylorus*) bac bn bar-m br1 bism bro1 *Cund* bro1 graph bro1 *Phos* bro1 sep c2* *Sil* k* *Stry-p* bro1

- **Walls**; of the: *Acet-ac* **Ars** bar-c con *Kreos* *Lyc* *Mez* *Nux-v* phos thuj verat

INERTIA: bell b4.de*

INFLAMMATION (= gastritis): abies-n mrr1 acon k* *Aeth* agar-em c2 agar-ph c2 agro c2 all-c alum alumn anac mrr1 *Ant-c* k* **Ant-t** *Apis* apoc k2* *Arg-n* k* arn mrr1 **Ars** k* ars-i k* ars-s-r c2 asaf b7a.de* asar aur aur-m bar-c k* bar-i *Bar-m* k* **Bell** k* bell-p sp1 benz-ac k2* betu mtf11 *Bism* k* brom k* **Bry** k* *Cact* cadm-s k2* calam lsr4.de• *Camph* k* cann-xyz bg2 *Canth* k* caps mrr1 carb-ac carb-an carb-v mrr1 chel k* *Chin* b7.de* chinin-m c2 chlor c2 cic k* cob-n sp1 *Cocc* colch k* coloc b4a.de* *Con* b4a.de cop c2 cory br1 cund

Inflammation: ...
cupr k* cycl mrr1 cyt-l br1 *Dig* k* elaps mrr1 **Euph** k* euph-c c2 euph-ip c2 ferr mrr1 ferr-p k* ferr-s c2 gaul c2 gels k2 *Graph* k* grat mrr1 guaj mtf11 hell k* *Hydr* hydr-ac **Hyos** k* indg iod k* *Ip* k* kali-ar kali-bi bg2* kali-c mrr1 kali-i kali-m k2 kali-n k* kali-perm c2 kali-s k* kali-sula a1* kreos mrr1 lac-ac mrr1 *Lac-d* k2* lach laur k* levist mtf11 **Lyc** mag-s sp1 mang-s c1* merc-c b4a.de* mez k* nat-c mrr1 nat-m mrr1 nat-s mrr1 **Nux-v** k* orex-tann mtf ox-ac **Phos** k* *Plb* k* puls k* ran-b k* ran-s k* rumx-act c2 sabad k* *Sabin* b7a.de sal-ac c2 *Sang* sanic c2 *Sec* k* sep mrr1 sin-a c2 spig bg2 squil k* stram k* sul-ac mrr1 *Sulph* mrr1 tab mrr1 tarax mrr1 tart-ac c2 *Ter* thal-xyz srj8• tub-d jl2 **Verat** k* *Verat-v* k* zinc mrr1 zinc-act c2 [*Bor-pur* stj2]
- **accompanied** by:
  - **burning** pain: *Ars* mrr1 canth mrr1
  - **hiccough**: hyos mtf33
  - **nausea**: *Phos* mrr1
  - **vomiting**: ip tl1 *Phos* mrr1
  - **weakness**: cadm-s mrr1
  - ○ **Tongue**:
    - **mucus** on tongue; collection of | **white** mucus: *Cocc* kr1*
- **acute**: acon bg2* agar-em bro1 *Ant-t* bro1 *Ars* bro1 bell bro1* bism bro1 bry bg2* canth bro1 ferr-p bro1 hedeo bro1 *Hydr* bro1 hyos bro1 *Ip* bro1 iris bro1 *Kali-bi* bro1 kali-chl bro1 merc-c bro1 nat-ox-act mtf11 nux-v bg2* *Ox-ac* bro1 phos bg2* puls bro1 santin bro1 sin-a bro1 *Verat* bro1 zinc bro1
- **alcoholic**: arg-n ptk1 med jl2
- **chilliness**; with: cadm-s mrr1
- **chronic**: alum bro1 atro bro1 bism bro1 lyc bro1 perh-mal mtf11
- **cold**:
  - **anything** cold; from:
    - **agg.**: **Acon**
    - **overheated**; when: *Acon* bry k2 *Kali-c*
- **cold**; after taking a: bell k2 *Bry* *Coloc*
- **drunkards**; in: anis kr1 arg-n br1* *Ars* bro1 bism bro1 crot-h bro1 *Cupr* bro1 *Gaul* bro1 lach bro1 nux-v bro1* phos bro1
- **gouty**: benz-ac k2
- **helicobacter** pylori infection:
  - **accompanied** by | **heartburn**: helic-p mtf
- **toxic**: *Hyos* kr1*
- ○ **Pylorus**: iod h

INFLUENZA: *Bapt* tl1* oscilloc jl2

INJURIES; after: nux-v ptk1

INSENSIBILITY, sensation: bell b4a.de plat b4.de* sars b4.de*

INSPIRATION:
- **agg.**: *Anac* b4a.de arg-n bg2 asar b7.de* bar-c b4.de* bry bg2 canth b7.de* carb-an b4.de* *Caust* b4a.de chel b7.de* chin b7.de* con b4.de* *Kali-ar* bg2 lyc b4.de* merc b4.de* mez b4.de* mosch b7.de* sep b4.de* stront-c b4.de* sulph b4.de* viol-t b7.de* zinc b4.de*
- **amel.**: olnd b7.de* sep b4a.de

IRRITATION: *Acon* all-c amyg-p c2 ant-t k* *Arg-n* k* *Ars* k* aur-m **Bism** k* bry k2 cadm-s k2* carb-ac k* carb-an mrr1 cob dros br1 eucal br1 *Ip* k* kali-ar kali-br a1 kali-n kali-sula c1 *Merc* merc-c ox-ac *Phos* plb *Podo* sang k2 sec stram vanad br1 verat-v
- **accompanied** by:
  - **dropsy** (See GENERALS - Dropsy - general - accompanied - stomach - irritation)
  - **vomiting**: ant-c bro1 *Ars* bro1 bism bro1 ferr bro1 ip bro1 nux-v bro1 phos bro1 puls bro1 verat bro1
- **children**; in: amyg-p br1
- **diseases**; after long: cadm-s k2
- **meningitis**; after: cadm-s k2
- **spasmodic**: ip br1
- **worms**; from: santin br1

ITCHING in epigastrium: con h2 kali-bi bg2 kali-c h2 lach bg2 nat-m bg2 plat h2 spong b7.de*
○ - **External**: ars bg2 calc bg2 cocc bg2 con bg2 kali-c bg2 puls bg2

JERKING: arn b7.de* calc h2 fago bg1 mez h2 nat-c *Nat-m* k* nux-v k* phos b4.de* plat k* puls b7.de* sang k* *Stry*

Jerking: ...
- **opening** the mouth agg.: stry
- ▽ **extending** to:
  - ○ **Rectum**: ars h2
    - **Epigastrium** to rectum; from: ars h2
  - **Throat**: phos h2
- ○ **Diaphragm**: asaf k2
- **Epigastrium**: ars bg2 calc b4.de* mez b4.de* nat-c b4a.de *Plat* b4a.de sep b4.de*

JUMPING, sensation of: ars bg2 bry b7a.de croc k* elaps bg2 *Kali-bi* kr1 limen-b-c hrn2* sang a1

KNOTTED together; sensation as if: arn b7a.de bry b7.de*

LAYING hand on stomach: | **amel.**: carb-an bg2

LIFTING agg.: arn bg2 bar-c b4a.de* borx b4a.de* *Bry* bg2 calc bg2 *Caust* b4a.de lyc b4a.de* **Rhus-t** bg2 sil b4a.de*

LIGHT FOOD agg.: nux-m bg2

LIVING in, as if something were (See Alive)

LOATHING of food: (↗*Nausea)* absin acon k* act-sp *Alet* aloe bg2 alum k* alum-sil k2 alumn am-c k* anac k* ang b7.de* **Ant-c** k* *Ant-t* k* apis b7a.de arg-met k* *Arg-n* k* *Arn* k* **Ars** k* *Ars-i* ars-s-f k2 asaf k* asar k* bar-c k* bar-i bar-m bar-s k2 **Bell** k* benz-ac k2 bism bg2 borx k* *Bry* k* bufo bg2 calc k* calc-sil k2 *Canth* k* caps fkm1• *Carb-v* k* carbn-s caust k* *Cham* k* chel k* **Chin** k* *Chinin-s* **Cocc** k* **Colch** k* con k* crot-t cupr k* cycl k* dig k* dios *Dros* bg2 *Dulc* k* euph k* *Ferr* k* ferr-i *Gamb* *Grat* k* *Guaj* k* hell k* hep b2.de* *Hydr* hyos k* ign k* iod k* **Ip** k* **Kali-ar** kali-bi k* *Kali-br* **Kali-c** k* kali-i kali-m k2 kali-p kali-s kali-sil k2 *Kreos* lach k* *Laur* k* lyc k* *Mag-c* k* mag-m k* mag-s mang k* meny k* *Merc* k* merc-c b4a.de merc-i-f k* merc-i-r bg2 mosch k* *Mur-ac* k* muru a1 nat-ar nat-c k* nat-m k* *Nux-v* k* *Ol-an* *Olnd* b2.de* op k* petr k* petr-ra shn4• ph-ac bg2 phel *Phos* k* phyt bg2 *Plat* k* plb k* *Prun* k* psor *Puls* k* rat rheum k* rhod k* rhus-t k* ruta k* *Sabad* k* sars k* *Sec* k* seneg k* **Sep** k* *Sil* k* spig k* stann k* stram k* *Sul-ac* k* *Sulph* k* sumb tab bg2 tarent thuj k* tritic-vg fd5.de valer k* zinc bg2
- **morning** | **waking**; on: phyt
- **noon**: pic-ac
- **evening**: alumn *Hep* raph
- **night**: rat
- **accompanied** by | **nausea**: ant-c bg2 bell b4a.de* con b4a.de* cupr bg2 hell bg2 laur bg2 prun bg2
- **alternating** with hunger: berb
- **beer**; after: mur-ac k* nux-v k*
- **chill**; during: am-c bg2 *Ant-c* bg2 *Apis* b7a.de* arn bg2 *Ars* bg2 *Bry* b7a.de* *Cham* bg2 chin bg2 cocc bg2 hell b7a.de* *Ip* bg2 *Kali-c* b4.de* lach bg2 merc bg2 nux-v bg2 petr bg2 puls bg2 *Rheum* bg2
- **cough** agg.; during: *Ip* b7a.de
- **eat**, on attempting to: (↗*Appetite - wanting - eating - attempting)* ant-t k2* cycl bg3 petros a1* rheum hr1 ruta a1 *Sil* sul-ac h2
- **eating** | **after** | **agg.**: alum k* ant-t hr1 cycl k* *Ip* k* kali-c k* nux-v b7a.de ol-an sars k*
  - **while** | **agg.**: ant-t bg2 ars bg2 bell bg2 bry bg2 canth bg2 caust bg2 cham bg2 colch bg2 cycl bg2 sars bg2
- **emotions**; after: *Kali-c*
- **fever**; during: am-c b4.de* *Ant-c* b7a.de *Ars* b4a.de ip b7a.de kali-c b4.de* rheum b7.de*
  - **intermittent**: *Kali-c*
- **food**:
  - **odor** of: *Colch* bg2*
  - **sight** of: interf sa3• *Sep* bg2
- **headache**; during: cench k2 kola stb3•
- **menses**; during: am-c b4.de
- **pain**; during: aloe
- **pregnancy** agg.; during: ant-t hr1 *Laur*
- **repletion**, with: arn br1
- **sudden** while eating: *Bar-c*
- **thought** of food: (↗*Nausea - food - thought)* ant-t vh carb-v bg1

LOSS OF VITAL FLUIDS agg.: bism bg2 calc bg2 *Carb-v* b4a.de* **Chin** b7a.de* cocc bg2 lach bg2 nux-v bg2 *Ph-ac* b4a.de *Ruta* bg2 sulph bg2

LUMP; sensation of a: (↗*Stone*) *Abies-c* vml3• abies-n ptk1 acon pd *Agar* anan *Ant-c* arg-n bg2 arn ptk1 ars b4.de* **Asaf** mrr1 bamb-a stb2.de• bar-c bell ptk1 bov ptk1 *Bry* k* calc h2* chel pd con pd cupr pd dirc gard-j vlr2• *Graph* ham fd3.de• *Hep* hip-ac sp1 *Hydr* hydr-ac *Kali-bi* *Kali-c* *Lach* pd *Lec* lil-t *Lob* k* manc med melal-alt gya4 moni rfm1• naja nat-c nat-m *Nux-m* k* *Nux-v* k* osm ptk1 plb podo fd3.de• positr nl2• *Puls* k* *Rhus-t* k* rumx **Sanic** k* *Sep* k* sil spig k* stroph-s sp1 sulph [nicc stj1]

- **night**:
  - **midnight** | **after**: *Arg-n*
- **cold** drinks agg.; after: acet-ac *Ars*
- **cold** lump: *Ars* b4a.de *Sulph* b4a.de
- **eating**; after: *Abies-n* *Ars* bry mrr1 ham fd3.de• lac-h htj1• med melal-alt gya4 nat-c h2 nat-m *Nux-v* *Ph-ac* podo fd3.de• puls rhus-t a1 rumx
  - **walking** | **amel.**: puls k2
- **eructations** | **amel.**: bar-c melal-alt gya4
- **fallen** to back on rising from seat; as if lump had: laur
- **flatulent** food; after: sil h2
- **hard**: mosch b7a.de nux-m ptk1 nux-v b7a.de puls b7a.de
- **ice** lump: bov bg2*
- **lying** on back agg.: *Sulph*
- **painful**: abies-n vh
- **pulsating**: *Graph*
- **sharp**: hydr ptk1
- **supper** agg.; after: calc h2
- ○ - **Cardia**; in: *Abies-n* vh*
  - **lodges**; as if: *Acon* vh1
- **Epigastrium**: abies-c bg2 **Abies-n** mrr1 acon bg2 *Agar* ptk1 *Arn* b7.de* bry bg2 chel ptk1 con bg2* cupr ptk1 hep bg2 *Kali-c* bg2 *Lach* ptk1 lob bg2 nat-m bg2 *Phos* bg2 plb bg2 puls bg2 *Sep* ptk1 spig b7.de* ter bg2 thuj bg2
  - ○ • **Above**: nat-c ptk1 nat-m ptk1 phos ptk1 puls ptk1

LYING:

- **abdomen**; on | **agg.**: bry bg2 lyc bg2 nux-v bg2
- **agg.**: *Ars* b4.de* bell-p bg2 carb-v b4a.de* con b4.de* mag-m b4.de* rhod b4.de* stann b4.de* sulph b4.de*
- **amel.**: bell bg2 bry b7.de* canth b7.de* caust b4a.de* *Cham* b7a.de chin bg2 graph b4a.de* *Lyc* b4a.de nux-v b7.de* ph-ac bg2 sabad b7.de* spig b7.de* stann bg2 *Sulph* b4.de* ter bg2
- **back**; on:
  - **agg.**: carb-v bg2 caust bg2 lyc bg2 op bg2 sulph bg2 *Verat-v* bg2
  - **amel.**: *Bry* b7.de* chin b7.de* *Ign* b7.de* *Kreos* b7a.de nux-v b7a.de puls b7.de*
- **bed**; in | **agg.**: *Cham* b7.de* chin b7.de* cocc b7.de* ferr b7.de* nux-v b7a.de plb b7.de* *Puls* b7.de* *Rhus-t* b7.de* staph b7.de* valer b7.de*
- **bent**; lying | **amel.**: staph b7a.de
- **legs** drawn up; with | **amel.**: chel ptk1
- **side**; on:
  - **agg.**: *Bry* b7.de* chin b7.de* *Ign* b7.de*
  - **amel.**: bry bg2 lyc ptk1
  - **left**:
    - **agg.**: carb-v bg2 nux-v bg2 ter bg2
    - **amel.**: squil ptk1
  - **right**:
    - **agg.**: castm bg2 rumx bg2
    - **amel.**: nux-v bg2

LYING DOWN: | **agg.**: *Carb-v* b4.de* *Phos* b4a.de

MEAT agg.: colch b7a.de* ferr b7.de* kali-bi bg2 puls b7.de* ruta bg2

- **spoiled**: carb-v b4a.de *Chin* b7a.de *Puls* b7a.de

MENSES:

- **after** | **agg.**: kali-c b4.de*
- **before** | **agg.**: am-c b4.de* arg-n bro1 ars bro1 *Bry* bro1 ign b7.de* kali-c bro1 lach bro1 *Lyc* bro1 mag-c b4.de* nat-m b4.de* nux-m b7.de* *Nux-v* bro1 *Puls* bro1 sep bro1 sulph b4.de*
- **during** | **agg.**: am-c b4.de* arg-n bro1 ars bg2* borx bg2 bry b7.de* caps b7.de* kali-bi bg2 kali-c b4a.de* kali-n bg2 lach bro1 *Lyc* bro1 nux-m bro1 *Nux-v* bro1 puls b7.de* sep bro1 *Sulph* bg2*

MENTAL EXERTION agg.: anac b4a.de *Arn* bg2 ars b4a.de cocc b7.de* colch b7.de* *Ign* b7.de* ip bg2 lach bg2 m-aust b7.de* **Nux-v** b7.de* phos bg2 *Puls* bg2 *Sulph* bg2 verat bg2

MERCURY; after abuse of: *Carb-v* bg2 chin bg2 **Hep** bg2 rumx bg2 sulph bg2

MILK:

- **agg.**: alum b4.de* ant-t bg2 *Calc* b4a.de* carb-an bg2 *Chin* b7a.de con b4a.de* cupr bg2 *Lyc* b4.de* nat-m bg2 nat-p bg2 *Nit-ac* b4.de* phos bg2 samb bg2 spong bg2 *Sulph* bg2 zinc bg2
- **amel.**: ars bg2 graph bg2* merc ptk1 merc-cy ptk1 mez ptk1 ruta bg2* verat bg2
- **cold** agg.: kali-i ptk1

MOTION:

- **agg.**: (↗*Pain - motion - agg.*) ang b7.de* arn b7.de* ars bg2 bar-c b4.de* *Bry* b7.de* bufo bg2 *Calc* b4.de* camph b7.de* carb-v bg2 caust b4a.de* chin b7.de* con b4.de* cupr bg2 dios bg2 ferr b7.de *Kali-bi* bg2 mang b4.de* nit-ac b4.de* nux-v b7.de* ph-ac b4.de* *Plb* b7a.de podo bg2 *Puls* b7a.de rhus-t b7.de* staph b7.de* stram bg2 ther bg2 thuj b4.de* verat bg2 zinc bg2
- **amel.**: *Ars* b4a.de borx b4a.de bov b4.de* carb-an b4.de* cham b7.de* chin b7.de* kali-c b4.de* meny b7.de* nat-c b4.de* *Puls* b7.de* *Rhus-t* b7.de*
- **arms**; of | **agg.**: bry bg2

MOVEMENT in, sensation of: aeth a1 amp rly4• androc srj1• arn chel *Cocc* k* colch coloc **Croc** k* cupr b7.de* iod h* kali-n k* laur *Lyss* k* nat-m k* nicc ol-an ph-ac b4a.de phos sul-ac k* tarent

- **animal** moving; of an: | **Epigastrium**: chel hr1*
- **up** and down: *Ph-ac* b4a.de
  - **eating**; after: *Ph-ac* b4a.de

NARROW, pylorus feels too●: (↗*Constriction - pylorus; Contraction - pylorus; Obstruction*) bry bg2 calc chin ign b7a.de lach bg2 **Lyc** k ● nux-v k* phos k* sulph

NAUSEA: (↗*Gagging; Loathing; Retching; Uneasiness*) absin k* acet-ac k* *Acon* k* acon-ac rly4• acon-l a1 acon-s a1 act-sp adon bg2 adren br1 aegle-f bnj1 *Aesc* k* *Aeth* k* aether c2 *Agar* k* agath-a nl2• agn k* ail k* alco a1 all-c bg2* *All-s* k* *Aloe* vh1 *Alum* k* alum-p k2 alum-sil k2 alumn am-c k* *Am-m* k* am-p a1 ambr k* aml-ns vh1 ammc vml3• *Anac* k* anan ancis-p tsm2 *Androc* srj1*• ang b2.de* *Ango* c1 anh sp1 **Ant-c** k* **Ant-t** k* anth a1 anthraq rly4• apeir-s mlk9.de apis k* apoc k* apoc-a c2 apom k* aq-mar a1* aral a1* *Aran* *Arg-met* k* **Arg-n** k* arge-pl rwt5• arist-cl sp1 arizon-l nl2• arn k* **Ars** k* ars-h k* ars-i arund k* asaf k* *Asar* k* *Asc-c* a1 astac a1 aster k* atis zzc1• atro bro1 aur k* aur-i k2 aur-m-n k* aur-s a1 bacls-10 pte1*• bamb-a stb2.de• *Bapt* k* *Bar-c* k* bar-i bar-m k* bart a1 **Bell** k* bell-p sp1 benz-ac k* *Berb* k* *Bism* k* boerh-d bnj1 *Bol-la* bol-s a1 bomb-pr a1 borx k* both k* both-ax tsm2 *Bov* k* brach k* brom k* brucin a1 *Bry* k* bufo bung-fa tsm2 bux a1 cact k* *Cadm-s* k* cain caj a1 calad b2.de* *Calc* k* *Calc-p* *Calc-s* k* *Camph* k* cann-s k* canth k* *Caps* k* *Carb-ac* k* *Carb-an* k* *Carb-v* k* carbn-dox knl3• **Carbn-s** *Card-m* k* *Cardios-h* rly4• carl k* cartl-s rly4• casc bro1 cassia-s ccrh1• castm catal a1 caul k* *Caust* k* cench tsm2 cent a1 **Cham** k* *Chel* k* chen-a a1 chim-m hr1 **Chin** k* chinin-ar *Chinin-s* k* *Chion* k* chir-fl gya2 chlf hr1 chlorpr pin1• chord-umb rly4• *Chr-ac* chrys-ac a1 *Cic* b2.de* cic-m a1 *Cimic* k* *Cina* k* cinch a1 *Cist* cit-ac rly4• cit-v a1 clem k* cloth tsm2 cob-n sp1 *Coca-c* sk4• **Cocc** k* *Cod* coff k* coff-t a1 **Colch** k* coli rly4• *Coll* k* *Coloc* k* colum-p sze2• com k* *Con* k* convo-s sp1 cop cor-r k* cori-r a1 corian-s knl6• *Corn* croc b2.de* *Crot-c* k* *Crot-h* k* *Crot-t* k* *Cub* k* cund k* **Cupr** k* *Cupr-ar* *Cupr-s* k* *Cycl* k* cystein-l rly4• daph k* delphin a1 dendr-pol tsm2 der a1 des-ac rbp6 **Dig** k* digin a1 digox a1 dios k* diosm br1 diph-t-tpt jl2 dream-p sdj1• dros k* dub a1 **Dulc** k* *Echi* echit a1 elaps k* *Elat* k* emetin a1 enteroc jl2 erech a1 erig a1 erio a1 eryth a1 eug k* euon k* *Eup-per* k* *Euph* k* euphr k* eupi k* fago c2* fagu a1 *Ferr* k* *Ferr-ar* ferr-i ferr-m a1 *Ferr-p* ferr-s a1 *Fl-ac* k* flor-p rsj3• *Form* k* fum rly1*• fuma-ac rly4• gal-ac a1* *Gamb* k* gard-j vlr2• gast a1 *Gels* k* genist a1 gent-c gent-l k* ger-i rly4• germ-met srj5• gins a1 glon k* *Gran* k* *Graph* k* grat k* grin br1 *Guaj* k* haem a1 haliae-lc srj5• ham k* hed bro1 helia br1* **Hell** k* hell-o a1* helo-s bnm14• **Hep** k* hera a1 hippoc-k szs2 home a1 hura hura-c a1 *Hydr* k* hydr-ac a1 hydrc k* *Hydrog* srj2• hydroph rsj6• hyos k* hyper k* iber a1 ichth bro1 *Ign* k* ina-i mlk9.de indg k* inul a1 *Iod* k* **Ip** k* irid-met srj5• **Iris** k* **Iris-fl** ix bnm8• jab a1* jac-c a1 jal br1 jatr-c jug-r k* **Kali-ar** k* *Kali-bi* k* kali-br bg2* **Kali-c** k* kali-chl k* kali-cy a1 kali-i k* kali-m k2 kali-n k* kali-p *Kali-s* k* kali-tel a1 kalm k* ketogl-ac rly4• kiss a1 kou br1 kreos k* *Lac-ac* k* *Lac-c* lac-d k2* lac-del hrn2• lac-e hrn2• lac-f wza1• lac-h sk4*• lac-loxod-a hrn2• lacer a1* *Lach* k* lachn k* lact k* lap-la sde8.de• lat-h bnm5• lat-m bnm6• *Laur* k* lavand-a ctl1• lec led k* lepi a1 lept bg2* lil-t k* limest-b es1• lina br1 linu-c a1 lipp a1 lith-c **Lob** k* lob-c a1 lol a1 loxo-lae bnm12• loxo-recl bnm10*• luf-op a1 **Luna** kg1• lup a1

Nausea: ...
Lyc k* lyss k* m-ambo b2.de m-arct b2.de* m-aust b2.de* mag-c k* *Mag-m* k* *Mag-p* mag-s k* maland vh malar jl2 manc k* mang k* mang-p rly4• med k* medul-os-si rly4• melal-alt gya4 meny k* meph k* *Merc* k* merc-br a1 merc-c k* merc-cy br1 *Merc-i-f* merc-i-r k* merc-n a1 merl k* *Mez* k* micr br1 mim-p rsj8• mit a1 mom-ch br1 morg fmm1• morg-p pte1*• morph a1* *Mosch* k* mucs-nas rly4• *Mur-ac* k* mygal k* myos-a rly4• myric a1 nad rly4• *Naja* k* narc-po a1 narc-ps br1* narcot a1 *Nat-ar* *Nat-c* k* nat-f sp1 **Nat-m** k* nat-ox rly4• *Nat-p* nat-pyru rly4• nat-s k* neon srj5• nept-m lsd2.fr nicc k* nicotam rly4• *Nit-ac* k* nit-s-d a1* nitro-o a1 nux-m k* **Nux-v** k* nyct br1 oci-sa sp1 oena a1* *Ol-an* k* ol-j a1 *Olib-sac* wmh1 olnd k* onis a1 onos op k* opun-f br1* opun-xyz c2 orot-ac rly4• ost a1* *Ox-ac* k* oxal-a rly4• oxyurn-sc mcp1• ozone sde2• paeon k* pall bg2* pana a1 par k* parathyr jl2 paull a1 pegan-ha tpi1• pen a1 **Petr** k* *Ph-ac* k* phel k* *Phos* k* phys k* physala-p bnm7• *Phyt* k* *Pic-ac* k* picro a1 pin-con oss2• pitu-p sp1 plac-s rly4• plan k* *Plat* k* plat-m-n c1 *Plb* k* plb-tae dp2.fr plect a1 plumbg a1 plut-n srj7• *Podo* k* polys sk4• *Positr* nl2• pot-e rly4• prin a1 *Prun* k* psil ft1 *Psor* k* ptel k* **Puls** k* pulx br1 pyrid rly4• quas a1 querc-r svu1• rad-br c11 ran-a a1 *Ran-b* k* *Ran-s* k* *Raph* k* rat k* rauw sp1 rham-f a1 *Rheum* k* *Rhod* k* **Rhus-t** k* *Rhus-v* k* ribo rly4• *Rosm* lgb1 rumx ruta k* *Sabad* k* sabin k* sacch-a fd2.de• sal-fr sle1• *Samb* k* **Sang** k* sangin-t c1 sapin a1 sarcol-ac bro1 *Sars* k* scol a1* *Sec* k* sel k* senec k* *Seneg* k* senn a1 **Sep** k* **Sil** k* sin-n a1 sinus rly4• sol-t-ae a1 sphing a1* spig k* spirae a1 spong k* *Squil* k* stach a1 *Stann* k* staph k* stram k* stront-c k* stry k* succ-ac rly4• suis-em rly4• suis-hep rly4• suis-pan rly4• *Sul-ac* k* sul-h a1 sul-i k2 sulfa sp1 sulo-ac a1 **Sulph** k* sumb k* suprar rly4• syc pte1*• sym-r br1* syph k* **Tab** k* taosc iwa1• *Tarax* k* tarent k* tart-ac a1 tax k* tep a1 *Ter* tere-la rly4• term-a bnj1 teucr b2.de* thal-xyz srj8• *Ther* k* thiam rly4• *Thuj* k* thymol sp1 thyr br1 til a1 trach a1 *Trios* rsj11• tritic-vg fd5.de tub al* *Tung-met* bdx1• tus-p a1 ulm-c jsj8• upa k* (non:uran-met k) uran-n urt-u a1 ust uva br1 v-a-b jl2 **Valer** k* vanil fd5.de *Ven-m* rsj12• **Verat** k* *Verat-v* k* verb b2.de* vero-o rly4*• vesp k* vichy-g a1 vinc k* viol-t k* vip k* wies a1 wye k* x-ray sp1 xan k* yohim br1* **Zinc** k* zinc-fcy a1 zinc-p k2 zing k* ziz a1 [bell-p-sp dcm1 heroin sdj2 spect dfg1]

- **daytime**: alum b4.de* ars k* aur k* cact ptk1 *Carb-v* b4.de* dig b4.de* graph b4.de* hep b4.de* ignis-alc es2• lyc b4.de* mag-m b4a.de merc b4.de* mez k* mosch k* *Nit-ac* k* *Petr* b4.de* phos k* pic-ac k* polys sk4• sep b4.de* **Sil** b4.de* sulph k*
- **morning**: absin acon k* agar k* *Alum* k* alum-p k2 alum-sil k2 alumn k* am-c k* *Am-m* b7a.de ambr b7.de* *Anac* k* androc srj1• ang b7.de* ant-t apoc k* arge-pl rwt5• *Arn* k* *Ars* b4a.de* ars-met atis zzc1• aur-m k2 bac bn bamb-a stb2.de• bar-c k* bar-s k2 benz-ac k* berb bomb-pr mlk9.de borx k* *Bov* k* bry k* bufo *Cact* k* calad k* **Calc** k* calc-sil k2 camph k* canth b7.de caps b7.de* *Carb-ac* carb-an b4.de* **Carb-v** k* carbn-s carc gk6 cardios-h rly4• caust k* *Cham* k* *Chel* b7a.de chlorpr pin1• chord-umb rly4• *Cic* k* cimic ptk1 *Cina* b7a.de cob-n sp1 cocc k* colch bg2 coloc b4.de* *Con* k* convo-s sp1 crot-h cupr b7.de* cupr-act *Cur* cycl b7.de* *Dig* k* digin a1 dios k* **Dros** b7.de* dulc b4.de* elaps euph k* euphr b7.de* fago k* falco-pe nl2• ferr b7.de* form k* gard-j vlr2• gink-b sbd1• granit-m es1• *Graph* k* *Guaj* b4a.de ham fd3.de• helo-s rwt2• hep k* hippoc-k szs2 hir rsj4• hyos h1 hyper k* inul k* iod b4.de* jac-c br1 *Kali-bi* k* kali-c b4.de* kali-s fd4.de *Kalm* kreos k* *Lac-ac* k* *Lac-c* *Lac-d* lac-del hrn2• lac-leo sk4• *Lach* k* laur k* led b7.de* lob k* loxo-recl knl4• luna kg1• lyc k* m-aust b7.de *Mag-c* k* mag-m k* malar jl2 mang *Med* ptk1* meli vml3• merc k* *Mez* mosch k* mucs-nas rly4• nat-c k* *Nat-m* k* nat-p nept-m lsd2.fr nicc k* nicotam rly4• **Nux-v** k* onos ox-ac k* parth vml3• *Petr* k* petr-ra shn4• phos k* pitu-gl skp7• plat k* podo k* positr nl2• *Psor* k* **Puls** k* ran-s k* rhus-t k* rumx ruta fd4.de sabad sabin b7.de* *Sal-ac* sne sang hr1 sars k* senec **Sep** k* *Sil* k* spig k* spong fd4.de squil b7a.de* staph k* suis-pan rly4• sul-ac b4a.de* *Sulph* k* symph fd3.de• tab bg2 ter k* tere-la rly4• teucr b7.de* ther thuj k* tritic-vg fd5.de *Tub* vanil fd5.de verat k* zinc k* zinc-p k2 zing k* [spect dfg1 tax jsj7]
  - **8**-11 h: cadm-met tpw6
  - **bed** agg.; in: alum ambr a1 arg-met graph k* kali-n k* mag-s k* mur-ac a1 **Nux-v** k* positr nl2• sabin k* spong fd4.de tritic-vg fd5.de vanil fd5.de zinc k*
  - **lying** down | **amel.**: rhus-t h1
  - **menses** | **before** | **agg.**: *Am-m* bro1 borx bro1 *Cocc* bro1 *Cycl* bro1 graph bro1 ichth bro1 *Ip* bro1 kreos bro1 meli bro1 nat-m bro1 *Nux-v* bro1 puls bro1 *Sep* bro1 thlas bro1 verat bro1
    - **during** | **agg.**: *Am-m* bro1 borx bro1 *Cocc* bro1 *Cycl* bro1 graph bro1 ichth bro1 *Ip* bro1 kreos bro1 meli bro1 nat-m bro1 nux-v bro1* puls bro1 *Sep* bro1 thlas bro1 verat bro1 vib tl1

- **morning**: ...
  - **rising**:
    - **after** | **agg.**: cina a1 mag-m a1 nux-m gk rhus-t a1 ruta fd4.de
    - **agg.**: asc-t bry calc carb-an dios ferr-p graph hydr iod lac-ac *Lac-d* lyc mag-c mag-m mang nat-m nicc *Nux-v* phos h2 pic-ac podo rhus-t senec *Sep* sil h2 ther v-a-b jl valer verat-v [tax jsj7]
    - **amel.**: sabin k* tritic-vg fd5.de zinc h2*
  - **waking**; on: ail *Alum* k* ambr h1 androc srj1• arg-n a1 ars h2 *Asar* bar-ox-suc rly4• borx bry bg2 card-m vml3• *Con* crot-c sk4• cypra-eg sde6.de• dulc fd4.de euphr h2 hydrog srj2• ignis-alc es2• kola stb3• *Lac-ac* *Lach* bg2 nat-m h2 nept-m lsd2.fr *Petr* k* phyt psil ft1* ruta fd4.de sal-fr sle1• sep h2 sulph h2 symph fd3.de• tere-la rly4• tritic-vg fd5.de tung-met bdx1• v-a-b jl2 vanil fd5.de [tax jsj7]
- **forenoon**: agar k* am-c b4.de* am-m b7.de* androc srj1• arg-n a1 arn k* ars h2 asaf b7.de* bell k* borx h2 bov k* bry k* calc k* canth k* carb-v k* caust b4.de* cham b7.de* chin b7.de* dros b7.de* dulc fd4.de fago k* ferr k* gink-b sbd1• hep k* hippoc-k szs2 ign k* jug-c k* kali-bi bg2 kali-c k* kali-n b4.de* lach k* lyc k* mag-c k* mag-m k* mosch b7a.de naja nat-c b4.de* nat-m k* nat-s k* nicc k* nux-m k* op k* par b7.de* phos b4.de* plat k* puls ran-b b7.de* ruta fd4.de sabad b7.de* sacch-a fd2.de• sars k* sep b4.de* spong fd4.de sulph k* tell rsj10• tong a1 tritic-vg fd5.de vanil fd5.de
  - **10** h: *Borx* corn hir rsj4• sep ven-m rsj12•
    - **10**-12 h: cadm-met tpw6
  - **11** h: **Ars** cadm-met tpw6 calc clem hura ign ind jug-c lac-ac pitu-gl skp7• puls-n
- **noon**: agar k* ant-t bg2 arg-n k* ars-s-f a1 asaf b7.de* bell b4.de* borx bg2* calc b4.de* *Caust* b4a.de chin b7.de* coloc k* dulc fd4.de ery-a a1 euph bg2 graph k* grat k* hyper k* ign k* kali-c h2 kali-s fd4.de ketogl-ac rly4• mang k* phos k* pic-ac plat bg2 puls bg2 spong fd4.de stry k* sul-ac b4.de* sulph k* tritic-vg fd5.de verat b7.de* zinc k* zinc-p k2
- **afternoon**: aesc alum b4.de* am-c b4.de* am-m b7.de* androc srj1• ant-c b7.de* ant-t b7.de* arg-met k* arg-n bg2* arn b7.de* ars b4.de* bism b7.de* borx k* *Bry* b7.de* calc k* calc-sil k2 cann-s b7a.de caps b7.de* carbn-s caust k* *Cham* b7.de* chin k* **Cocc** k* coff b7.de* coli rly4• coloc b4.de* con k* cycl k* dros k* dulc fd4.de fago k* falco-pe nl2• ferr b7.de* ger-i rly4• graph k* grat k* hep b4.de* hippoc-k szs2 hyos b7a.de ignis-alc es2• indg k* *Iod* b4a.de kali-c h2* kali-n k* kali-s fd4.de lach b7.de* lyc k* m-aust b7.de mag-c k* merc b4.de* merl k* mez k* mosch b7.de* nat-ar nit-ac b4.de* *Nux-v* b7.de* *Phos* k* podo k* *Puls* b7a.de *Ran-b* k* ran-s b7.de* *Rhus-t* b7a.de rob k* ruta fd4.de sacch-a fd2.de• sal-fr sle1• sang k* sars k* **Sec** b7a.de seneg b4.de* *Sil* k* spong fd4.de squil b7.de* *Sulph* b4.de* tritic-vg fd5.de tung-met bdx1• vanil fd5.de *Verat* b7a.de
  - **13** h: corn grat hura phys
  - **14** h: cadm-met tpw6 grat hura nux-m phys sulph
    - **14**-18 h: cadm-met tpw6
  - **15** h: **Ars** cadm-met tpw6
    - **15**-22 h: lyc h2
    - **until** evening: borx h2
  - **15**.30 h: nept-m lsd2.fr
  - **16** h: anac calc-p choc srj3• lachn phys
  - **17** h: falco-pe nl2•
    - **17**-19 h: falco-pe nl2•
  - **17**.30 h: falco-pe nl2• lec
  - **sleep** | **siesta** agg.; after: arn h1
- **evening**: *Alum* k* alum-p k2 alum-sil k2 alumn k* anac k* androc srj1• arg-n k* *Ars* bg2 asar k* bapt k* bell b4.de* borx b4a.de* brach k* bry k* *Calc* k* calc-s k* calc-sil k2 canth k* carb-an b4.de* carb-v b4.de* caust b4.de* chel coff b7.de* coli rly4• coloc k* con k* cycl k* dream-p sdj1• dulc fd4.de echi eug k* fl-ac k* gent-l k* ger-i rly4• glon k* grat k* ham fd3.de• hell k* *Hep* k* hippoc-k szs2 hydrog srj2• ind k* kali-bi k* kali-c b4a.de kali-n k* kali-s fd4.de kalm k* kola stb3• kreos *Lach* b7a.de lepi a1 lyc h2 lycps-v mag-c merc k* merc-i-r k* mosch b7.de* naja nat-c nat-m k* nat-p nit-ac h2 nux-m k* nux-v k* *Pall* petr k* ph-ac h2 phos k* plan k* plb k* plut-n srj7• positr nl2• *Puls* k* ran-b k* raph rhus-t b7.de* ruta fd4.de sacch-a fd2.de• sang k* senec k* sep k* sil k* sin-n k* stram b7.de* suis-em rly4• suis-pan rly4• sulph k* tell teucr b7.de* thuj b4a.de trios rsj11• tritic-vg fd5.de vanil fd5.de
  - **20** h: plut-n srj7•
  - **bed** agg.; in: graph h2* phos h2 rhus-t a1 sacch-a fd2.de• tritic-vg fd5.de
  - **drinking** agg.; after: *Nux-v* k*

- **eating** | **after** | **amel.**: tell
  - **while** | **agg.**: caust k* cham h1 phos k*
- **supper**, before: graph h2
- **walking** in open air agg.: lycps-v phos k* *Sep* k*

- **night**: alum k* alum-p k2 alum-sil k2 alumn k* am-c k* ambr b7.de* ant-c b7a.de ant-t b7.de* apis k* arg-met arg-n bg2 arizon-l nl2• arn b7.de* *Ars* b4.de* bar-c b4.de* bell b4.de* bry b7.de* calc k* calc-i k2 calc-sil k2 canth b7.de* *Carb-an* k* carb-v k* carbn-s caust b4a.de* cham k* chel k* *Chin* bg2 cocc b7.de* con k* cycl bg2 dig k* dros b7.de* *Dulc* elaps eupi k* *Ferr* b7.de* form k* glon k* graph k* guaj k* haem a1 hell k* hep k* hippoc-k szs2 ign b7.de* iod k* jug-c k* kali-bi k* kali-c h2* kali-n k* lach bg2 *Lob* k* lyc k* mag-c h2 mag-s k* *Merc* k* *Merc-c* k* mur-ac b4a.de* naja nat-ar nat-m b4a.de nit-ac k* **Nux-v** b7a.de* petr b4.de* phos k* plat h2 plb bg2 puls k* ran-s b7a.de rat rhus-t k* ruta b7.de* sacch-a fd2.de• *Sep* k* sil k* sinus rly4• *Spig* b7a.de spong b7.de* squil b7.de* stram b7.de* sul-i k2 sulph k* tarent k* ther k* thuj b4.de* tritic-vg fd5.de valer b7.de* vanil fd5.de *Verat* b7.de* vib bg2
  - **midnight**: ambr k* bry k* calc k* crot-t k* eupi k* ferr bg2* phel k* ran-s k* sil k*
    - **before**: ferr b7.de* puls b7.de*
    - **after**: ambr h1* ant-t b7.de* bry b7.de* ferr b7.de* ign b7.de* mang h2 mur-ac bg2 ran-s k* squil b7.de*
      - **1** h: lavand-a ctl1•
      - **2** h: arizon-l nl2• indg pyrid rly4• sep
      - **3** h: ars h2 mur-ac
      - **4** h: alum alumn arizon-l nl2•
      - **5** h: dios nat-m
    - **until** morning: dros
    - **rising** agg.: ambr vh nat-m k*
  - **lying** down:
    - **after**:
      - **agg.**: chel con k* dig ind kali-c k* naja nat-m nept-m lsd2.fr nit-ac k* phos pic-ac sang *Tarent*
      - **amel.**: phos h2
  - **rising**:
    - **amel.**: kali-c h2
    - **sleep**; from (See waking)
  - **waking**; on: alum alumn k* ambr h1 dulc fd4.de hyper k* kola stb3• *Lob* lyc k* mez h2 mur-ac h2 op phyt k* ruta h1 *Sep* h2* spong h1 sulph k* tritic-vg fd5.de

- **abdomen**; from pain in (See pain - abdomen)
- **abdomen**; when compressing the (See compressing)
- **accompanied** by:
  - **anorexia** (See MIND - Anorexia nervosa - nausea)
  - **appetite**:
    - **increased** (See Appetite - increased - accompanied - nausea)
    - **ravenous** (See Appetite - ravenous - accompanied - nausea)
    - **wanting** (See Appetite - wanting - accompanied - nausea)
  - **asthma** (See RESPIRATION - Asthmatic - accompanied - nausea)
  - **breath**; foul: cupr bg2 ip bg2
  - **coldness** of body; icy: valer a1*
  - **collapse** and vertigo (See GENERALS - Collapse - accompanied - vertigo)
  - **complaints**; all: *Ip* tl1
  - **confusion** (See MIND - Confusion - nausea)
  - **congestion** (See GENERALS - Congestion - blood - accompanied - nausea)
  - **coryza**: *Graph* bg2
  - **diarrhea** (See RECTUM - Diarrhea - accompanied - nausea)
  - **epistaxis** (See NOSE - Epistaxis - accompanied - nausea)
  - **erections**: kali-bi ptk1
  - **eructations**: (↗*eructations - during)* petr a1

- **accompanied** by: ...
  - **faintness** (See GENERALS - Faintness - accompanied - nausea)
  - **flatus**; passing: ant-t bg2 chinin-s bg2 fic-m gya1 grat bg2 hir rsj4•
    - **noisy** flatus: puls bg2
  - **heat**; general sensation of: ars b4.de* bell bg2 carb-v b4a.de dulc b4.de* ip bg2 merc b4a.de* verat bg2
  - **hemorrhage** (See GENERALS - Hemorrhage - accompanied - nausea)
  - **hiccough**: ars b4a.de bry bg2 sep b4a.de
  - **indigestion**: luf-op rsj5•
  - **inflammation** of stomach (See Inflammation - accompanied - nausea)
  - **irritability** (See MIND - Irritability - nausea)
  - **itching** of skin:
    - **must** scratch until he vomits: ip hr1
    - **urticaria**; before: sang ptk1
  - **loathing** of food (See Loathing - accompanied - nausea)
  - **menses**; painful (See FEMALE - Menses - painful - accompanied - nausea)
  - **metrorrhagia** (See FEMALE - Metrorrhagia - accompanied - nausea)
  - **perspiration**: acon bg2 **Ars** bg2 **Cham** bg2 *Dros* bg2 ip bg2 lob ptk1* nux-v bg2 petr b4.de puls bg2 pyrog jl2 *Rhus-t* bg2 sabad bg2 **Sep** bg2 verat bg2
    - **clammy**: tab mrr1
    - **cold** (See PERSPIRATION - Cold - nausea)
  - **pulse**; slow (See GENERALS - Pulse - slow - accompanied - nausea)
  - **respiration**; complaints of (See RESPIRATION - Complaints - accompanied - nausea; RESPIRATION - Difficult - accompanied - nausea)
  - **retching**: asc-t mtf11
  - **saliva**; watery (See MOUTH - Saliva - watery - nausea)
  - **salivation** (See MOUTH - Salivation - accompanied - nausea)
  - **screaming** (See MIND - Shrieking - nausea)
  - **sepsis** (See GENERALS - Septicemia - accompanied - nausea)
  - **shivering**: mez b4a.de
  - **sleepiness** (See SLEEP - Sleepiness - nausea - with)
  - **stool**; complaints of (See STOOL - Complaints - accompanied - nausea)
  - **taste**; bitter (See MOUTH - Taste - bitter - nausea)
  - **tenesmus** in stomach: hyper bg2
  - **thirst**: *Ars* bg2 bell bg2 canth bg2 ip bg2 luf-op rsj5• phos b4.de* verat bg2
  - **urination**:
    - **complaints** of (See BLADDER - Urination - complaints - accompanied - nausea)
    - **excessive** (See URINE - Copious - accompanied - nausea)
    - **urging** to urinate: cupr bg2
  - **vertigo** (See VERTIGO - Nausea)
  - **vision**; complaints of (See VISION - Complaints - accompanied - nausea)
  - **vomiting** (See Vomiting - nausea - with)
  - **water** brash; bitter: am-m ptk1

- **weakness** (See GENERALS - Weakness - accompanied - nausea)
- **weepy** (See MIND - Weeping - nausea)
- ○ **Abdomen**:
  - **complaints** (See ABDOMEN - Complaints - accompanied - nausea)
  - **distension** (See ABDOMEN - Distension - accompanied - nausea)
  - **emptiness** in: *Kola* stb3•
  - **pain**:
    - **cutting**: agar b4.de* coloc b4.de* stront-c b4.de*
    - **pressing**: haliae-lc srj5• tritic-vg fd5.de
- **Back**:
  - **pain** (See BACK - Pain - accompanied - nausea)
  - **pain**; piercing (See BACK - Pain - piercing - accompanied - nausea)
- **Brain**; congestion to (See HEAD - Congestion - brain - accompanied - nausea)
- **Chest**:
  - **cramp** (See CHEST - Pain - cramping - accompanied - nausea)
  - **pain** (See CHEST - Pain - accompanied - nausea)
  - **restlessness** (See CHEST - Restlessness - accompanied - nausea)
- **Ear**:
  - **complaints** (See EAR - Complaints - accompanied - nausea)
  - **noises** in (See EAR - Noises - accompanied - nausea)
  - **pain** (See EAR - Pain - nausea)
- **Extremities** | **coldness** of: hyos bg2
- **Face**:
  - **heat**: *Stront-c* b4a.de
  - **pale** discoloration of: ant-t tl1 *Hep* b4a.de petr tl1
    - **twitching** of face; and: ip bro1
- **Forehead**:
  - **pain** (See HEAD - Pain - forehead - accompanied - nausea)
  - **pressing** pain: alet ptk1
  - **pulsating**: flor-p rsj3•
- **Hands** | **numbness** of: phos bg2
- **Head** and gray tongue; pain in (See HEAD - Pain - accompanied - nausea and gray)
- **Head** and white tongue; pain in (See HEAD - Pain - accompanied - nausea and white)
- **Head**; pain in (See HEAD - Pain - accompanied - nausea)
- **Heart** failure (See CHEST - Heart failure - accompanied - nausea)
- **Intestines**; downward pressing pain in (See ABDOMEN - Pain - intestines - pressing - downward - accompanied - nausea)
- **Kidneys**:
  - **colic**; stone (See KIDNEYS - Pain - accompanied - nausea; KIDNEYS - Pain - ureters - accompanied - nausea)
  - **inflammation** of (See KIDNEYS - Inflammation - accompanied - nausea)
- **Lips**: valer bg2
- **Liver**; pain in (See ABDOMEN - Pain - liver - accompanied - nausea)
- **Lungs**; congestion to (See CHEST - Congestion - lungs - accompanied - nausea)
- **Mouth**:
  - **pain** | **burning**: kreos bg2
- **Skin**:
  - **cold** agg.: ant-t tl1

- **accompanied** by – **Skin**: ...
  - **moist**: ant-t tl1
  - **relaxed**: ant-t tl1
- **Teeth**; pain in (See TEETH - Pain - accompanied - nausea)
- **Tongue**:
  - **clean**: **Cina** bg2* *Dig* bg2* *Ip* bg2*
  - **dry**: chinin-s bg2 petr bg2
  - **gray** tongue and pain in head (See HEAD - Pain - accompanied - nausea and gray)
  - **white** mucus on tongue: chinin-s bg2 ox-ac kr1* petr bg2
  - **white** tongue and pain in head (See HEAD - Pain - accompanied - nausea and white)
  - **yellow**: chinin-s bg2
- **Upper** part of body | **coldness**: *Ip* b7a.de
- **Vertex**; pain in (See HEAD - Pain - vertex - accompanied - nausea)

- **air** agg.; draft of: ars bg2 hipp k*
- **air**; in open:
  - **agg.**: acon k* ang k* arg-met ars k* bell k* bry b7.de* carbn-s cocc b7.de* coff b7.de* crot-t grat hep b4a.de kali-bi bg2 lyc k* **Nux-v** b7.de* plat b4.de* puls b7.de* seneg k* tab bg2 tarax b7.de* thuj k*
  - **amel.**: am-m b7.de* ant-t anth ars bg2 bor-ac carb-v cit-ac rly4• *Croc* k* dig glon k* goss st grat ham fd3.de• hell b7.de* hippoc-k szs2 kali-bi k* **Lyc** k* naja phos plut-n srj7• *Puls* k* pycnop-sa mrz1 rhus-t b7.de* **Tab** k* tarax b7a.de*
- **airplane**; in an: *(↗riding - carriage - agg.; seasickness; GENERALS - Aviator's)* ars ptk1 bell br1* borx ptk1 carc mlr1• coca ptk1* cocc mtf11 con mtf11 *Petr* ptk1*
- **alcohol**; from: calc-f sp cimic ptk1
- **alcoholics** (See drunkards)
- **alternating** with:
  - **diarrhea** (See RECTUM - Diarrhea - alternating - nausea)
  - **hunger**: berb chir-fl gya2 fic-m gya1 nit-ac h2
  - ○ **Head**; pain in (See HEAD - Pain - alternating - nausea)
- **amorous** caresses, from: ant-c k* sabad k* sabal ptk1
- **anger**; after: granit-m es1• *Kali-c* b4a.de nux-v mrr1
- **anxiety**:
  - **after**: ant-c b7.de* ant-t b7.de* bar-m k2 *Bry* b7.de* cann-s b7.de* caust *Chel* chin b7.de* cupr b7.de* ign b7.de* nux-v k* rhus-t b7.de* tarax b7.de*
  - **with**: *(↗MIND - Anxiety - nausea; increases)* acon bg2 agar bg2 ant-c b7.de* **Ant-t** b7.de* **Ars** b4.de* asar b7a.de* bar-c h2 bar-m bg2 **Bell** b4.de* *Bry* b7.de* *Calc* h2* cann-s b7.de* caust b4.de* chin b7.de* coca-c sk4• cocc ptk1 *Crot-h* ptk1 cupr b7.de* dig b4a.de* dulc b4.de* graph h2 *Ign* b7.de* *Ip* ptk1 irid-met srj5• kali-bi bg2 **Kali-c** b4a.de* lach bg2 limest-b es1• **Lob** ptk1 lyc bg2 merc bg2 *Nit-ac* b4.de* **Nux-v** b7.de* ozone sde2• plat b4.de* plb bg2 positr nl2• puls h1* rhus-t b7.de* sabad bg2 sang bg2 seneg b4.de* **Sep** h2* squil h1 *Tab* bg2* tarax b7.de* tritic-vg fd5.de vanil fd5.de
- **apyrexia**: *Ant-c Chinin-s Puls* k*
- **ascending**, rising from below upwards: ant-t bg2 chel b7.de* puls b7.de*
- **ascending**; when: canth b7.de* glon bg2 nux-v b7.de*
  - **stairs** rapidly: glon k*
- **asthma**; with (See RESPIRATION - Asthmatic - accompanied - nausea)
- **awake**; if kept: phys bg2
- **bacon** | **amel.**: *Ran-b* b7a.de *Ran-s* b7a.de
- **beans**; from: graph b4.de*
- **bed**:
  - **in** bed:
    - **agg.**: con bg2 phos b4.de*
    - **amel.**: nat-c
- **beer**:
  - **after**: brucel sa3• bry k* cadm-s c1 kali-bi k2* lach k* mur-ac k* nux-v
  - **agg.**: ars b4.de* bry bg2 cadm-s c1 ferr b7.de* kali-bi bg2 mez b4.de* mur-ac b4a.de nit-ac bg2 nux-v b7.de* sil b4a.de verat b7.de* zinc bg2

- • **smell** of (See food - smell - beer)
- **bending** double | **amel.**: colch b7.de*
- **bending** forward agg.: hydrog srj2• med jl2
- **blowing** the nose agg.: *Hell* a1 sang bg3* sulph vh
- **brandy** | **amel.**: ars tritic-vg fd5.de
- **bread**; after: **Ant-c** bry b7a.de* nat-m b4a.de nit-ac b4a.de* olnd b7.de* pin-con oss2• puls b7.de* sec b7.de* *Sep* b4a.de teucr b7.de* zinc
  - • **black** bread: ph-ac
- **breakfast**:
  - • **after**:
    - **agg.**: agar k* ambr k* anders zzc1• bell k* borx b4a.de* calc-p k* *Cham* k* coca daph bg2 dig dios ferr bg2 gamb indg k* kali-bi k* mez nat-m b4.de* nat-s k2 nept-m lsd2.fr nux-m b7.de* onos ozone sde2• par k* plb b7.de* ruta fd4.de sabin k* *Sars* k* *Sel* b7a.de *Sil* b4a.de spig sulph b4.de* vanil fd5.de verat b7.de* zinc k*
      - **one** hour after: ozone sde2•
    - **amel.**: alum k* aur-m a1* bar-c h2 lac-ac a1* ozone sde2• sanic c1 symph fd3.de•
  - • **before** | **agg.**: alum alumn anac arg-n k* aur-m bac hr1 bar-c *Berb* k* *Bov* *Calc* k* eupi k* fago k* goss k* *Lyc* k* nept-m lsd2.fr *Nit-ac* k* nux-v bro1 petr k* phos h2 **Sep** k* sin-n k* spig *Tub* visc c1
  - • **during**: agar *Carb-ac* k* carb-an bg2 ind kali-bi bg2 med vh naja plan k* psil ft1 sang k* zinc k*
  - • **first** bite: lac-del hrn2•
- **breath**; at his own: sulph k2
- **breathing**:
  - • **deep**:
    - **agg.**: cadm-s br1 diphtox jl2
    - **amel.**: hydrog srj2•
- **broth**, after: acon st
- **brushing** the teeth; on: all-c mgm• all-s mgm• ars-i k2 crot-c mgm• crot-h mgm• merc mgm•
- **burning** in anus, with: kali-bi ptk1
- **champagne** or aerated water agg.: digox bro1
- **children**; in: calc-p bg2 cham b7.de* cic b7.de* hyos b7a.de *Ip* b7.de* rheum b7.de* ruta b7.de*
- **chill**:
  - • **after**: cocc c1 *Elat* *Eup-per* *Ip* *Kali-c* lyc b4a.de [tax jsj7]
    - **next** chill; lasting until: *Chinin-s*
  - • **before**: *Ars* *Carb-v* *Chin* *Eup-per* *Ip* k* lyc nat-m puls vesp br1
  - • **close** of: *Eup-per*
  - • **during**: acon b7.de* alum b4.de* androc srj1• *Ant-c* bg2 *Apis* b7a.de* arg-n k* arn b7a.de *Ars* k* asar bg2 *Aur* b4a.de* bell k* bov k* bry k* calc k* canth b7.de* caps b7.de* carb-v b4a.de* *Cham* k* chel k* *Chin* b7.de* chinin-s bro1 cina k* cob *Cocc* k* coff b7.de* con k* croc b7.de dros b7.de* dulc b4.de* echi ptk1 **Eup-per** k* euph bg2 *Hep* b4a.de* hyper k* ign k* *Ip* k* *Kali-ar* kali-bi bg2 kali-c k* kali-m ptk1 kali-s kreos k* lach k* laur bg2 *Lyc* k* mag-c h2 merc bg2 mez bg2 mosch b7a.de* nat-c b4.de* *Nat-m* k* nit-ac *Nux-v* bg2 op bg2 petr *Phos* bg2 plat b4a.de* puls k* raph k* rhus-t k* rumx sabad k* sang k* sec k* sep k* sil b4.de* sul-ac k* sulph bg2 thuj b4.de* valer b7.de* verat k* xan c1 zinc k*
    - **death**-like: xan c1
- **chilliness**:
  - • **after**: *Camph* corn *Eup-per* *Kali-bi* *Kreos* *Lach* *Mag-s* *Puls* sabad sal-ac verat-v xan
  - • **with**: alum am-c h2 androc srj1• ant-t bg2 apeir-s mlk9.de *Arg-n* hr1 arist-cl sp bov k* cadm-s bro1 con k* dulc h2 echi bro1 eup-per ptk hep h2* iber c1 *Ip* bro1 kali-m ptk kali-s fd4.de *Kreos* k* nit-ac bg2 puls bg2 sang bg2* sul-ac bg2 tab mrr1 valer bg2 xan c1
- **chocolate**; after: nept-m lsd2.fr
  - • **amel.**: nept-m lsd2.fr
- **chronic**: granit-m es1• parathyr jl2 ruta fd4.de
- **church**; in: ars b4a.de caust b4a.de kali-c b4a.de *Puls* b7a.de
- **closing** the eyes:
  - • **agg.**: *Lach* k* sabad tab k2 *Ther* k* thuj bro1
  - • **amel.**: arn b7.de* con k*
- **Coca** Cola; from: coca-c sk4•
- **coffee**:
  - • **after**: alet bg2 *Ars* b4.de* bry k* *Calc-p* k* cann-xyz bg2 canth b7.de* *Caps* k* *Caust* *Cham* k* cocc b7.de* cycl k* hippoc-k szs2 ign b7.de* ip b7.de* lil-t bg2 mag-c b4.de* nat-m k* nit-ac b4.de* *Nux-v* b7.de* pin-con oss2• podo fd3.de• puls b7.de* rhus-t k* *Sulph* b4.de* symph fd3.de• tritic-vg fd5.de vinc k* [pop dhh1]
  - • **amel.**: alet ptk1 cann-s b7a.de* positr nl2• tritic-vg fd5.de
  - • **smell** of (See food - smell - coffee)
  - • **thinking** of: lil-t kr1
- **coition**:
  - • **after**: kali-c k* kali-i a1 mosch k* sil b4a.de
  - • **during**: sabad bg2* sil k*
  - • **thought** of: sep ptk1
- **cold**:
  - • **drinks** | **after**:
    - **agg.**: agar anac *Ars* k* ars-s-f k2* *Calc* calc-p bg2 camph carb-ac *Cupr* *Dulc* b4a.de ip b7.de* *Kali-ar* *Kali-c* kali-i kali-s lac-d lach *Lyc* *Nat-ar* *Nat-m* nux-v puls **Rhus-t** k* sep bg2 *Sul-ac* teucr ther
      - **heated**; when: *Kali-c*
      - **not** after warm: lyc ther
    - **amel.**: *Bism* calc c1 caust bg2 cortico tpw7 cupr bg2* euphr mg *Phos* k* *Puls* k* verat bg2
      - **sips**: cortico sp
  - • **food** | **amel.**: *Puls* b7a.de
  - • **water** | **agg.** | **icy** cold: lach ptk1 laur ptk1
    - **amel.** | **icy** cold: calc ptk1
- **cold**; after taking a: *Ant-c* b7.de* *Ars* b4a.de *Bell* b4.de* bry b7.de* cham b7.de* cocc b7.de* cupr bg2 *Dulc* b4.de* *Hyos* b7.de* *Ip* b7a.de **Nux-v** b7.de* *Rhus-t* b7.de* verat b7.de*
- **cold** agg.; becoming: cadm-s ptk1 **Cocc** k* crot-t *Hep* k* kali-c ozone sde2• rhus-t b7.de* valer
- **coldness**:
  - • **during**: canth b7.de laur b7.de mosch b7a.de *Valer* b7.de*
  - ○ • **Stomach**; in: kali-n h2
- **compressing** abdomen; when: asar
- **constant**: amyg-p br1 *Ant-c* k* *Ant-t* k* arg-met b7a.de arg-n k* ars asar vh* cadm-s carb-v k* carc mlr1• coloc cupr-ar a1* *Dig* k* digox a1 graph ham fd3.de• hep k* hydrog srj2• *Ip* k* iris bg1* jatr-c *Kola* stb3• *Kreos* *Lac-ac* a1 *Lac-c* lach k2 lil-t *Lyc* mag-m merc-cy a1 nat-ar *Nat-c* k* nat-m k* nat-s k2* **Nux-v** k* petr k* phos plat plut-n srj7• positr nl2• ptel hr1* sars k2 **Sil** k* stront-c taosc iwa1• verat k* vib ptk1
  - • **cold** food or drink amel.; only: phos k2
- **constipation**; during: **Cocc** st* coll tl1 cupr bg2 *Hyper* a1* plb bg2
- **conversation**: | **animated**, after: borx h2
- **coryza**; during: *Ars* b4a.de graph b4.de*
- **cough**:
  - • **after**: coc-c bg2 *Cupr* b7.de* dros b7.de* *Hyos* b7a.de
  - • **during**:
    - **agg.**: acon bg2 ant-t k* arn bg2 ars k* aspar k* bell bg2 bry k* bufo bg2 caj a1 *Calc* k* caps k* carb-v b4.de* cham b7.de* choc srj3• cina bg2 *Coc-c* k* coloc k* con b4.de* cupr k* dig bg2 dros k* elaps ferr b7.de* hep k* hydr k* *Hyos* b7.de* *Ign* k* iod b4.de* **Ip** k* irid-met srj5• kali-ar *Kali-bi* k* *Kali-c* k* kali-p k* kali-s lach k* lap-la rsp1 lyc bg2 meph bg2 *Merc* k* merc-c bg2 mez b4.de* nat-ar nat-c k* nat-m k* nat-p nit-ac k* *Nux-v* k* ozone sde2• petr k* *Ph-ac* k* *Phos* bg2 pic-ac a1 *Pneu* jl2 psil ft1 psor bg2* **Puls** k* *Rhus-t* b7.de* ruta k* sabad b7.de* sabin b7.de* sars *Sep* k* sil bg2 squil k* sul-ac bg2 sulph bg2 syc ptj• thuj k* urol-h rwt• *Verat* k*
      - **lying** on back agg.: *Rhus-t* b7a.de
- **cramps**, with: trios bro1
- **crowd**; in a: sabin k*
- **deathly**: **Aeth** ptk all-c ant-c bg3 arg-n *Ars* *Cadm-s* *Camph* cocc bg3 **Crot-h** cupr dx1 *Dig* k* erio a1 euph a1 ferr-p bg2* hell h1 **Ip** kali-c k2 lac-d k2* linu-c a1 **Lob** *Med* vh morph mg podo k2 ptel a1 puls bg3 sang a1 sep k2 **Tab** k* vib mg
- **delivery**; during: ant-t caul cham *Cocc* **Ip** k* mag-m *Puls*
- **dentition**; during: *Calc* b4a.de
- **descending** agg.: melal-alt gya4 nat-s bg1*
- **diet**; errors in: ant-c mrr1

- **dinner**:
  - **after**:
    - **agg.**: agar k* am-c k* am-m h2 *Ant-t* k* arg-met *Arg-n* k* ars k* berb k* calc k* caps h1 castm cench vh colch k* *Coloc* k* con k* *Cycl* gink-b sbd1• grat k* ham k* kali-ar *Kali-c* kali-n h2 lach k* lepi a1 med c1 nat-m k* nept-m lsd2.fr **Nux-v** k* ol-an k* phos k* ptel k* ruta fd4.de sars k* seneg k* sphing k* squil k* tritic-vg fd5.de verat k* zinc
    - **amel.**: alet ptk1 borx a1 grat a1 mang h1*
  - **before**: ars h2 carb-v k* nux-v k* sabad k* visc c1
  - **delayed**; if it is: sulph k2
  - **during** | **agg.**: am-c h2 ang c1 bry k* calc h2 colch k* gink-b sbd1• grat k* hyper k* lyc k* mag-m k* merc-i-f k* *Nux-v* k* ol-an k* ox-ac k* thuj k*
- **disgusting** ideas, with: sang hr1
- **disordered** stomach; from: *Ant-c* b7.de* ars b4a.de* bell bg2 bry b7.de* ferr bg2 **Ip** b7a.de* **Nux-v** b7.de* **Puls** b7.de* rhus-t bg2 sulph bg2
- **draft** (See air agg.)
- **dreams**; from: arg-met bg2* arg-n k* tritic-vg fd5.de
- **drinking**:
  - **after**:
    - **agg.**: acon b7a.de* agar k* anac k* *Ant-c* bg2* ant-t k* apoc bro1 arge-pl rwt5• arn k* *Ars* k* bell bg2 *Bism* bg2 bry k* calc c1* camph carb-an k* *Cham* b7.de* chin k* cic b7.de* *Cimx* *Cina* bg2 **Cocc** k* croc b7.de* crot-t k* cycl dig digin a1 dros bg2 dulc fd4.de *Eup-per* k* **Ferr** bg2 gamb hydrog srj2• ip b7.de* kali-bi k* *Lach* k* lyc med c1* merc-c b4a.de mez bg2 nat-ar *Nat-m* k* nit-ac k* *Nux-v* k* *Phos* k* **Puls** k* rhus-t k* sec b7.de* sil k* spong fd4.de teucr k* **Verat** b7.de* wies a1
      - **eating**:
        - **after** | **agg.**: *Bry* b7a.de
      - **some time after**: kali-bi bg2 **Phos** bg2
    - **cold** water:
      - **amel.**:
        - **lying** down; then: lach k2
        - **sips** of cold water: cortico sp1*
    - **water**:
      - **agg.**: *Acon* b7a.de anac b4a.de apoc ptk1 ars ptk1 borx b4a.de calc b4a.de* cench xyz63• *Cocc* b7a.de kali-bi bg2 med jl2 merc bg2 *Op* b7a.de **Phos** b4a.de rhod b4a.de* sel b7a.de teucr b7.de* tritic-vg fd5.de verat ptk1
      - **amel.**: anac b4.de* *Bry* bg2 caust b4a.de coloc bg2 cupr b7.de* euph bg2 euphr bg2 lob bg2 phos b4.de*
  - **agg.**: bry
  - **amel.**: **Bry** k* *Cupr* b7a.de cypra-eg sde6.de• digox a1 euphr k* *Lob* k* *Med* vh *Paeon* k* *Phos* k* samb spong fd4.de tritic-vg fd5.de
- **drinks**:
  - **lemonade** | **amel.**: cycl bro1 puls bro1
- **drunkards**: *Apom* br1 *Ars* k* *Asar* cadm-s c1 calc bg2 carbn-s vh graph vh **Kali-bi** k* **Lach** bg2 nux-v k* *Op* b7.de* *Sul-ac* k* sulph bg2 verat b7.de*
- **dryness** in pharynx, from: **Cocc**
- **eating**:
  - **after**:
    - **agg.**: acon k* acon-l a1 adam srj5• aesc *Agar* k* agn all-c k* *Alum* k* alum-p k2 alum-sil k2 **Am-c** k* am-m k* ambr amp rly4• anac k* androc srj1• ant-c b7.de* ant-t k* apis aran *Arg-n* k* arge-pl rwt5• *Arn* bg2 ars k* ars-i ars-s-f k2* asar k* aur-m k* aur-s a1* berb-a bro1 *Bism* k* *Borx* *Bov* k* *Bry* k* bufo *Calc* k* calc-i k2 calc-sil k2 cann-i k* cann-s b7a.de *Canth* b7.de* caps b7.de* carb-an carb-v k* carbn-s cardios-h rly4• carneg-g rwt1• castm *Caust* k* *Cham* k* chin k* chinin-ar *Chinin-s* k* chord-umb rly4• *Cic* clem k* **Cocc** k* coff b7.de* *Colch* coli rly4• coloc k* *Con* k* cuc-p br1* cur cycl k* dig k* dios k* dros k* dulc fd4.de elaps euphr falco-pe nl2• *Ferr* k* *Ferr-ar* *Ferr-i* *Ferr-p* fic-m gya1 flav jl2 fuma-ac rly4• gent-l k* ger-i rly4• glycyr-g cte1• graph k* grat k* gymno ham k* hell k* hep hera a1 hippoc-k szs2 hydrog srj2• *Hyos* b7.de* hyper k* ign k* ind k* iod k* ip k* jatr-c *Kali-ar* k* kali-bi bg2* *Kali-c* k* kali-i kali-p kali-s kali-sil k2 *Kola* stb3• *Kreos* b7a.de* lac-ac *Lach* k* led h1 *Lyc* k* m-aust b7.de mag-c k* mang bg2 mang-p rly4• *Med* c1* merc k* mim-p rsj8• mosch k* nat-ar *Nat-m* k* nat-s k* nat-sil fd3.de• nept-m lsd2.fr *Nit-ac* k* **Nux-v** k* ol-an

- **eating – after – agg.**: ...
  olnd b7.de* *Op* ox-ac k* petr k* ph-ac k* *Phos* k* plac rzf5• plac-s rly4• plb k* pneu jl2 podo polys sk4• positr nl2• prot jl2 psil ft1 *Ptel* **Puls** k* ran-s b7.de* rheum *Rhus-t* k* ribo rly4• ros-d wla1 rumx *Ruta* k* sabin k* sal-fr sle1• sang k* sars k* sec b7.de* sel b7a.de seneg b4.de* **Sep** k* *Sil* k* spira a1 spong fd4.de squil b7.de* *Stann* k* staphycoc rly4• stroph-s sp1 suis-em rly4• sul-ac b4a.de* sul-i k2 *Sulph* k* *Tarent* k* ter thea trios rsj11• tritic-vg fd5.de tung-met bdx1• ven-m rsj12• verat k* *Zinc* zinc-p k2 [bell-p-sp dcm1 spect dfg1 tax jsj7]
      - **fast** eating: *Ip* b7a.de *Nux-v* b7a.de
    - **amel.**: acon k* alum k* androc srj1• arg-n k* arge-pl rwt5• aur-m k* bell bg2 beryl tpw5* brom k* bry cadm-met tpw6 cham k* chel chin b7.de* chinin-m c1 chir-fl gya2 chlor a1 colch rsj2• dig k2 dulc fd4.de fago k* *Ferr* bg2 grat k* hed sp1 hell b7.de* hydrog srj2• ign b7.de* ignis-alc es2• iod k* irid-met srj5• *Kali-bi* k* kali-n bg2 kali-p fd1.de• *Kola* stb3• *Lac-ac* k* lac-h htj1• laur b7.de* *Lob* mag-c k* mag-m bg2 mez k* myos-a rly4• *Nat-c* k* nux-v b7a.de petr bg2 phos k* phyt k* pitu-a vml2• positr nl2• pot-e rly4• psor bg2 rad-br c1 ran-b b7.de* rhus-t b7.de* ruta fd4.de sabad k* sang **Sep** k* sil h2 spig k* spong fd4.de symph fd3.de• tere-la rly4• thymol sp1 tritic-vg fd5.de v-a-b jl valer bg2 vanil fd5.de verat b7.de* verat-v k* [heroin sdj2]
      - **temporarily**: [heroin sdj2]
    - **immediately** after: *Cuc-p* br1
  - **amel.**: arg-n ptk1 fago ptk1 **Lac-ac** bro1* mez bro1* ozone sde2• phyt ptk1 rad-br ptk1 sang ptk1 *Santin* bro1 sep bro1* vib bro1*
  - **before** | **agg.**: acon b7.de* allox tpw3* anac ars k* bell b4.de* berb cadm-met tpw6 carb-v k* *Caust* k* chin choc srj3• cinch a1 ferr k* ferr-ar fuma-ac rly4• graph k* ketogl-ac rly4• lepi a1 lyc med c1 *Nat-s* k* nux-v k* *Ph-ac* polys sk4• puls b7.de* ran-b b7.de* sabad k* suis-em rly4• *Sulph* k* tell k* [heroin sdj2]
  - **overeating** agg.; after: nux-v k2
  - **small** quantities:
    - **agg.**: spong fd4.de xan c1
    - **amel.**: ferr bg2
  - **while**:
    - **agg.**: agar alum-sil k2* am-c ambr bg2 ang b7.de* ant-t b7.de* arg-met bg2 ars bg2 aur *Bar-c* k* bell k* borx k* bov k* brom calc k* calc-sil k2 cann-s b7.de* canth k* carb-v k* *Caust* k* chin b7.de* chinin-s *Cic* k* *Cocc* k* coff k* colch k* *Coloc* b4.de* cycl b7.de* dig k* dream-p sdj1• erio a1 *Ferr* k* graph b4.de* hell k* iod b4a.de *Jac-c* k* kali-bi bg2* kali-c k* kali-n bg2 ketogl-ac rly4• *Lac-c* mag-c k* mag-m bg2 merc-i-r k* morph k* nux-v k* olnd k* phos k* ptel k* *Puls* k* rhus-t b7a.de* ruta k* sabad k* sep bg2 sil k* stann bg2 staph b7.de* thuj k* tritic-vg fd5.de verat k* [tax jsj7]
    - **amel.**: acon a1 anac gsy1 colch rsj2• dig k2 ignis-alc es2• lac-ac stj5• lac-h htj1• limest-b es1• luna kg1• nept-m lsd2.fr rad-br c1 v-a-b jl2 [*Calc-lac* stj2 *Ferr-lac* stj2 *Nat-lac* stj2 tax jsj7]
- **eggs**:
  - **after**: androc srj1• bacls-10 pte1• colch b7a.de* dulc fd4.de *Ferr* b7a.de lyss morg-p pte1• prot pte1• syc pte1*•
    - **morning**: syc fmm1•
  - **smell** of (See food - smell - eggs)
  - **thought** of: syc bka1•
    - **morning**: syc pte1•
- **emotions**; from: acon b7.de* arg-n bg2 ars bg2 bell b4a.de bry b7.de* *Cham* b7.de* coff b7.de* coloc bg2 *Kali-c* b4a.de* nux-v b7.de* *Op* b7.de* rhus-t b7.de* sep bg2 staph b7.de*
- **entering** a room, when: alum h2 carbn-s k2 dulc fd4.de
- **epileptic** convulsions; after (See GENERALS - Convulsions - epileptic - after - nausea)
- **eructations**:
  - **after**: alum h2 bry b7.de* caust bg2 cham b7.de* chel b7.de* *Cocc* b7a.de fl-ac bg2 kali-bi bg2 phos bg2 plb b7.de* puls b7.de* sabin b7.de* squil b7.de* *Verb* b7a.de
  - **amel.**: agar all-c am-m k* ambr b7.de* ant-t k* bapt hr1 calc-sil k2 camph k* cann-xyz bg2 carbn-s *Caust* k* chel k* cinnb fago ferr bg1 glon grat k* kali-p k* lac-c k* laur b7.de* lil-t bg1 lyc k* mag-c bg2 *Mag-m* k* nicc

- **amel.**: ...
  ol-an olnd b7.de* op bg2 osm ozone sde2• par b7.de* phos k* rhod k* rumx k* sabad k* sul-ac k* symph fd3.de• tere-la rly4• verat-v
- **during**: *(↗accompanied - eructations)* am-c b4a.de cadm-met tpw6 chinin-s bg2 cimic ptk1 cob-n sp1 cocc bg2* coloc crot-t goss vh grat *Kali-c* k* lac-h htj1• nept-m lsd2.fr nit-ac ptk1 *Ol-an* a1 ptel verat bg2
- **mucus**, of, amel.: kali-n h2

- **eruptions**; from receding: bry b7a.de *Ip* b7a.de
- **excitement**; after: dys fmm1• **Kali-c** k* kola stb3• mentho bro1 spong fd4.de tritic-vg fd5.de ulm-c jsj8• vanil fd5.de
- **exertion | after | agg.**: androc srj1• aspar bros-gau mrc1 crot-h bg1 *Iris* lob bg1 rhus-t b7.de* *Sil* spong k* tritic-vg fd5.de
  - **agg.**: aloe ars colch spong tab ther
- **exertion** of the eyes agg.: con k* jab br1 phys bg2 sapin a1 *Sars* *Sep* k* *Ther*
- **expectoration**; after: ars h2 diphtox jl2 stann ptk1
- **eye** symptoms; with: calc bg1 *Kalm* bg1* laur bg1 merc bg1 nat-m bg1 nat-s bg1 puls bg1 raph bg1
- **faint-like**: alum k* ang b7.de* apis b7a.de *Arg-n* borx b4a.de* calad vh calc k* carb-an b4a.de* carbn-s caust b4.de* cham k* chel **Cocc** k* coff b7.de* colch b7.de* fago *Glon* graph k* hep b4a.de hyper bg1 *Ip* vh kali-bi bg2 *Kali-c* b4.de* **Lach** k* laur b7.de* mag-m b4a.de* nat-m k* nit-ac b4.de* **Nux-v** k* op petr vh phos b4.de* pic-ac a1 plan vh sil b4.de* stict c1 sul-ac sulph tab bg2 *Tub* vh valer b7.de* verat k* vesp a1
- **fall**; after a: *Arn* b7a.de
- **false** teeth, from: cocc vh
- **fanned**; desires to be: tab k2
- **farinaceous** food; after: nat-s k2
- **fasting** agg.: *Acon* b7.de* alum anac b4a.de aur-m bar-c bry b7.de* *Calc* k* fuma-ac rly4• graph k* *Kola* stb3• kreos bg2 lac-ac stj5• lach b7.de* **Lyc** k* mag-m kr1 meph c1 nux-v b7.de* puls bg1 sep k* sil k* *Spig* b7.de* *Sul-ac* b4a.de teucr b7.de*
- **fat**; after eating: acon b7a.de *Ars* b4a.de bacls-10 pte1• carb-an b4a.de cortiso tpw7* cycl b7.de* *Dros* b7a.de* euph b4a.de falco-pe nl2• ham fd3.de• ip kali-m k2 lyss k* mez bg2 morg-p pte1• nit-ac k* puls k* sep b4a.de* symph fd3.de• tarax b7.de* tritic-vg fd5.de
  - **sensation** as if from fat: acon b7a.de cycl b7a.de *Tarax* b7a.de
- **fever**:
  - **after**: **Ars** dros *Fl-ac*
  - **before**: ant-c b7a.de ars b4a.de calc b4a.de chin b7.de* *Cina* b7.de* *Ip* b7a.de lyc b4a.de nat-m b4a.de nux-v b7a.de puls b7.de* sep b4a.de sil b4a.de sulph b4a.de
    - **intermittent** fever | **night**: *Eup-per* k*
  - **close**, at: *Eup-per* c1
  - **during | agg.**: acon bg2 anac b4a.de* ant-c b7.de* ant-t bg2 arg-met b7.de* arg-n k* *Ars* k* asar bg2 bac bn bell bg2 borx b4a.de* *Bry* k* calc bg2 *Carb-v* k* cham k* *Chel* b7.de* chin b7.de* cic b7.de* *Cimx* cina b7.de* cocc k* con b4.de* cupr bg2 cycl bg2 dig bg2 dros b7.de* *Eup-per* eup-pur ferr b7.de fl-ac bg2 gink-b sbd1• graph bg2 *Guare* k* hell bg2 hep b4.de* ign b7.de* *Ip* k* kali-c k* lyc k* *Merc* b4.de* mosch bg2 nat-c h2 **Nat-m** k* nit-ac k* *Nux-v* k* op par b7.de* phos k* polyp-p br1* ptel k* **Puls** b7.de* rhus-t b7.de* *Sabad* b7a.de *Sang* k* sel k* sep k* sil bg2 squil bg2 stann bg2 sul-ac b4a.de* sulph b4.de* thuj tub lmj valer bg2 *Verat* b7.de* vinc zinc k*
- **fish**:
  - **after**: androc srj1• nat-m k*
  - **smell** of (See food - smell - fish)
- **flatus**; passing:
  - **agg.**: ant-t ptk1
  - **amel.**: ant-t b7.de* bell bg1* mur-ac h2 myos-a rly4• ruta bg2 zinc bg2
- **followed** by:
  - **diarrhea**: narc-ps br1* ven-m rsj12•
  - **hunger**: caust bg2 *Olnd* b7a.de
  - **vomiting**: atra-r bnm3• gard-j vlr2• narc-ps br1* valer a1 ven-m rsj12•
  - ○ **Stomach**; pain in: ven-m rsj12•

- **food**:
  - **looking** at; on: aeth br1* alum-sil k2* ant-t ars bro1* beryl tpw5* calc bg2 cocc bro1* **Colch** k* dig c1 eup-per k2 gamb gk *Hell* bg2 *Kali-bi* k* *Kali-c* lac-h sk4• *Lyc* k* merc-i-f mosch k* nux-v bro1 *Ph-ac* k* polys sk4• puls bro1 sabad k* sep bro1* sil sphing k* squil stann bro1 *Sulph* k* sym-r bro1 tub al xan
  - **relish** for; with: dig
  - **smell** of: aeth bro1 ant-c k2 *Ars* k* beryl tpw5* *Cocc* k* **Colch** k* *Dig* k* eup-per k* gamb gk hydrog srj2• *Ip* k* irid-met srj5• lac-h htj1• merc-i-f ptk1 nux-v bro1* plac-s rly4• podo ptel gk puls bro1 *Sep* k* stann k* syc fmm1• sym-r bro1 *Thuj* tub al tung-met bdx1• vario ptk1
    - **alcoholic** drinks; of: psil ft1
    - **beer**: phos
    - **coffee**: arg-n pin-con oss2• *Thuj* b4a.de
    - **eggs**: **Colch** k*
    - **fish**: **Colch** k*
    - **garlic**: hydrog srj2•
    - **meat**: *Colch* k* eup-per symph fd3.de•
    - **mutton**: ov
    - **oranges**: *Cit-v*
    - **soup**: **Colch**
  - **thought** of: *(↗Loathing - thought)* alum-sil k2* androc srj1• ant-c k2 ant-t k2* *Ars* k* bamb-a stb2.de• borx bry carb-v h2* *Chin* k* **Cocc** k* **Colch** k* dios mrr1 dros b7.de eup-per k2 falco-pe nl2• graph hist vml3• hydrog srj2• mag-c melal-alt gya4 mosch k* petr-ra shn4• sal-fr sle1• *Sars* *Sep* k* sulph thiam rly4• *Thuj* k* tung-met bdx1• zinc
    - **food** eaten: arg-met cann-s h1 graph *Sars* k*
    - **soup**: **Colch**
- **frozen** things agg.: ip bg2 puls bg2 rhus-t bg2
- **fruit** agg.: *Ant-t* k* bry b7.de* dulc fd4.de *Ip* k* nat-c k* puls b7.de* ruta fd4.de verat b7.de*
- **garlic**; smell of (See food - smell - garlic)
- **hawking** up mucus agg.: ambr k* anac bell bg2 calc-p bg2 *Caust* coc-c bg2* *Lac-ac* manc nux-v b7.de* osm k* *Stann* k* tab bg2 tarent k* zinc bg2
- **head**; from pain in (See HEAD - Pain - accompanied - nausea)
- **heat**:
  - **after**: ars b4.de* dros b7.de*
  - **during**: arg-met b7.de ars b4.de* bry b7.de cham b7.de* *Chel* b7a.de chin bg2 *Cic* b7.de cina b7.de* cocc b7.de con b4.de *Dros* b7.de* ip b7.de* lach b7a.de merc b4.de *Nux-v* b7.de* par b7.de phos b4.de puls b7.de* rhus-t bg2 sabad bg2 sep b4.de* *Stram* b7.de* ven-m rsj12• verat bg2
  - **sun**; of the | **agg.**: *Carb-v* k* dulc fd4.de
- **heated** by motion; from becoming: *Sil* b4.de* zinc b4a.de
- **hemorrhage**, with (See GENERALS - Hemorrhage - accompanied - nausea)
- **hiccough**; with: bry b7a.de* cupr bg2 lach bg1* merc-c bg2 ruta b7.de*
- **hunger**: *(↗Emptiness - nausea)*
  - **sensation** as if from hunger: am-m b7a.de hell b7.de* *Puls* b7a.de *Rhus-t* b7a.de spig b7.de* valer b7.de* verat b7.de*
  - **with**: *(↗Emptiness - nausea)* conch fkr1• hell b7.de* ign ptk1 mand rsj7• petr ptk1 *Spig* b7a.de valer ptk1 verat b7.de*
- **hyacinths**, from the odor of: lyc k*
- **ice | amel.**: cench c1*
- **ice** cream | **after**: *(↗Disordered - ice; Indigestion - ice)* *Ars* k* dulc fd4.de *Ip* **Puls** rhus-t k2* vanil fd5.de
- **inability** to vomit: chir-fl gya2 *Nux-v* tub al
- **intense**: ant-t tl1 ip tl1
- **intermittent**: aesc k* *Ant-c* **Ant-t** atro a1 *Cina* *Dros* elat eup-per hep k* iod k* mosch k* plat h2 pycnop-sa mrz1 sabad *Sep* k* **Tab** k*
  - **night** before paroxysm of (See fever - before - intermittent - night)
- **itching** of skin until he vomits; with: *(↗SKIN - Itching - nausea - scratch)* ip hr1*
- **jarring**; from: glon bg2
- **jaundice**; with: bry mrr1 lach k2
- **joy**; after excessive: *Kali-c* b4a.de
- **kneeling** agg.: ther k2

Stomach

- **leaning**:
  - **abdomen** on something agg.: samb h1
  - **head** | **table** amel.; on: plat h2
- **leukorrhea** agg.: *Nat-m* b4a.de
- **light**; from: lach bg1 petr sne
- **liquids** agg.: merc-c k*
- **looking**:
  - **moving** objects, at: *(↗VERTIGO - Nausea - with - looking)* asar bro1* cocc k2* ip bro1* *Jab* k*
  - **steadily**: con *Sars* k* *Sep* *Ther* k*
  - **up**: plat bg2
- **lying**:
  - **abdomen**; on:
    - **agg.**: ruta fd4.de
    - **amel.**: m-aust bg1 neon srj5•
  - **agg.**: androc srj1• arge-pl rwt5• ars k* calc bg2 cham b7.de* coc-c bg2 ephe-si hsj1• ferr b7.de* hep bg2* *Lac-d* k* mag-m b4.de* merc bg2 mill mim-p rsj8• nat-hchls nat-m bg2* olnd b7.de* phos k* phys pot-e rly4• ptel puls k* raph rhus-t k* ruta fd4.de sacch-a fd2.de• sil bg2 sin-a spong fd4.de stram bg2 tritic-vg fd5.de vanil fd5.de
  - **amel.**: acon-f a1 *Alum* alumn k* androc srj1• anh c1 apis b7a.de arn k* beryl tpw5* bry b7.de* *Calc* b4.de* canth b7.de* caust bg1 colch b7.de* echi k* elat a1 ferr bg2 germ-met srj5• granit-m es1• hep b4.de* irid-met srj5• *Kali-c* bro1 ketogl-ac rly4• mill c1 nat-m b4.de* nat-sil fd3.de• *Nux-v* k* olib-sac wmh1 olnd b7.de* ph-ac phos k* phys a1 puls bro1 *Rhus-t* b7.de* sabad b7.de* sep k* sil k* spong fd4.de verat-v bg2
  - **back**; on | **agg.**: hydrog srj2• merc
  - **bed**; in | **agg.**: cham b7.de* puls b7.de* rhus-t b7.de* sabin b7.de*
  - **desire** to lie down; with: **Ars** bg2 asar bg2 cocc bg2 mosch bg2 *Ph-ac* bg2 verat bg2 [bell-p-sp dcm1]
  - **side**; on:
    - **agg.**: bry k* ferr b7.de* ign b7.de* ip
    - **amel.**: ant-t k* nat-m k*
    - **left**:
      - **agg.**: ant-t cann-s bg3 crot-t bg3 ferr bg2* iris bg3 kali-br lach bg2* puls sep k* spong fd4.de sul-ac h2 verat-v
      - **amel.**: cann-s
    - **right**:
      - **agg.**: bry k* cann-s bg3 cann-xyz bg2* crot-h bg2* iris bg2* sang bg2* sul-ac bg2*
      - **amel.**: *Ant-t* bg2 colch b7.de* hydrog srj2• nat-m h2* spong fd4.de
  - **still** | **must** lie still: cadm-s c1
- **lying** down:
  - **after**:
    - **agg.**: petr-ra shn4• *Puls* b7.de* rhus-t b7.de*
    - **amel.**: *Am-m* b7.de* *Nux-v* b7.de*
- **mayonnaise**; after: *(↗GENERALS - Food and - mayonnaise - agg.)* tung-met bdx1•
- **meat**:
  - **after**: *Carb-an* k* *Caust* k* cupr k* dulc fd4.de ferr b7.de* ham fd3.de• lyss merc k* *Puls* b7.de* ruta fd4.de sulph h2 symph fd3.de• ter k* tritic-vg fd5.de
    - **amel.**: verat b7.de*
    - **fresh** meat: caust b4a.de
  - **smell** of (See food - smell - meat)
- **medicine**; after:
  - **allopathic**:
    - **chemotherapy**; after: *(↗GENERALS - Chemotherapy; GENERALS - Weakness - Chemotherapy)* okou mtf sep mrr1 tab mrr1
    - **narcotics**: cham mrr1
- **menopause**:
  - **after**: zinc hr1
  - **during**: *Crot-h* hr1 *Cycl* kr1 *Ferr* vh gels bwa *Glon* vh *Lach* kr1 morg ptj• sang c1 sars vh ther ptk
- **menses**:
  - **after** | **agg.**: canth bg2 chinin-s k* crot-h ptk1 puls bg2 vib bg2
- **menses**: ...
  - **amel.**: eupi c1
  - **before** | **agg.**: am-c k* *Am-m* bro1 ant-t k* arn bg2 aur-s k* bamb-a stb2.de• berb borx bg2* bufo k* caul cimic bg2 cocc k* crot-h k* cupr k* *Cycl* bro1 foll oss• graph bro1 *Hyos* k* ichth bro1 *Ip* k* kreos k* *Lyc* k* mag-c k* mag-p bg2 mag-s sp1 mang b4.de* meli bro1* mosch bg2 *Nat-m* k* *Nicc* nux-v k* phos k* *Puls* k* sep k* sulph b4.de* thlas bro1 verat k* vib vip fkr4.de
  - **during**:
    - **agg.**: am-c k* am-m k* ant-c apoc mrr1 arn ars bell *Borx* k* *Bry* k* *Calc* k* canth k* *Caps* k* carb-v carc gk6 caul k* cham chel cocc k* *Colch* con cop br1 crot-h bro1 cupr *Cycl* bro1 eupi fago k* gels *Graph* k* *Hyos* k* hyper k* ichth bro1 *Ign* b7a.de *Ip* k* kali-ar *Kali-bi* *Kali-c* k* kali-i bg2 kali-p *Kreos* bro1* lach k2 lob *Lyc* k* *Mag-c* k* mang meli bro1 mosch nat-ar nat-c k* nat-m k* **Nux-v** k* phos k* pic-ac *Puls* k* sep k* sym-r br1* tarent k* thlas bro1 thuj verat k* *Vib*
    - **beginning** of menses | **agg.**: carc fb* *Graph* b4a.de hyos b7.de* lac-c bg2 phos b4.de*
  - **suppressed**; from: agn hr1 alum ars caust cimic a1 cocc croc cupr k* cycl *Ip* lob lyc nat-m nit-ac *Nux-v* petr phos **Puls** k* rhus-t sang sulph verat zinc
- **mental** exertion agg.: alco a1 arn b7.de* asar b7.de* *Aur* k* *Borx* cina b7.de* cocc b7.de* cupr-ar ign b7.de* *Lach* nux-v b7.de* puls b7.de*
- **milk**:
  - **agg.**: ant-t k2 **Calc** k* cortiso tpw7* crot-t k* ham fd3.de• lac-d k2 lach k* nat-m h2 **Nit-ac** k* *Puls* k*
  - **amel.**: *Bry* b7a.de chel ptk1 nit-ac bg2 verat b7.de*
- **mortification**; from: *Puls* tritic-vg fd5.de
- **motion**:
  - **after** | **agg.**: stram b7a.de
  - **agg.**: alum h2 ambr vh1 anac b4.de* androc srj1• anh c1 arizon-l nl2• *Arn* **Ars** b4a.de* bar-c b4.de* bov k* *Bry* k* bufo calc-p k* *Camph* b7a.de *Cann-s* b7.de* carb-an b4.de* chin b7.de* **Cocc** k* colch b7.de* crot-h k* dig k* *Eup-per* k* euph k* falco-pe nl2• ger-i rly4• glon k* hep k* *Ip* *Kali-bi* k* **Kali-c** k* kali-s kalm ketogl-ac rly4• *Lac-ac* k* lac-d k2 *Lob* sne mag-c b4.de* med vh nad rly4• narcot a1 nat-s **Nux-v** b7.de* *Op* k* pic-ac k* ptel puls bg2 sep k* sil b4.de sin-a k* spong staph b7.de* stram b7.de* stroph-s sp1 sulph k* suprar rly4• *Sym-r* br1* *Tab* k* ther k* trios bro1 *Verat* k* *Zinc* k*
  - **amel.**: hydrog srj2• irid-met srj5• lac-h htj1• mez b4.de* nit-ac sacch-a fd2.de• tritic-vg fd5.de
  - **eyes**; of | **agg.**: con graph jab puls *Sep*
  - **head**; of | **agg.**: bros-gau mrc1
- **mucus**; from:
  - ○ **Chest**; in: sulph h2
  - **Throat**; in: *Anac* b4a.de *Caust* guaj b4a.de*
- **music** agg.: phys sulph
- **mutton**; smell of (See food - smell - mutton)
- **nervous**: lup br1
- **noise** agg.: *Cocc* *Ther* k*
- **odors**:
  - **agg.**: bamb-a stb2.de• cadm-met gm1 chin k2 cimic gk **Colch** k* *Dig* eup-per k* falco-pe nl2• gard-j vlr2• hippoc-k szs2 kola stb3• nux-m bg2 olib-sac wmh1 ozone sde2• *Ph-ac* psil vml3• ruta fd4.de seneg bg2 *Sep* k* stann bg2 vario bg3*
  - **alcoholic** drinks agg.; of: psil ft1
  - **body** agg.; of his own: **Sulph** k*
  - **fish** agg.; of: lac-lup hrn2•
- **oil**; from: puls b7.de*
- **old** people; in: *Fl-ac* b4a.de
- **opening** the eyes: arn b7.de* nux-v b7.de* *Tab* mrr1
  - **after**: ther a1*
  - **siesta**; after: arn h1
- **operation** on abdomen, after: *(↗Vomiting - operation)* aeth sne *All-c* sne ars sne **Bism** k* bry sne ip sne *Nux-v* sne phos sne staph k* stry sne tab sne
- **oranges**; smell of (See food - smell - oranges)
- **organ**, from sound of: phys k*

- **overheated**, after being: *Ant-c*
- **overloaded** stomach; as from: cocc b7.de*
- **pain**; during: acon bg2 allox sp1 aloe androc srj1• ant-t bg2 ars k* *Asar* b7a.de *Bry* b7a.de cadm-s bro1* calc bg2 carb-v bg2 *Caust* bg2 *Chel* k* chim-m hr1 coloc k2 crot-t k* dulc fd4.de galeoc-c-h gms1• graph bg1 hep bro1 *Ip* k* kali-s fd4.de kalm ptk1 lyc bg2 naja gm1 nat-m k* nux-v bg2 ruta fd4.de sep k* sphing a1 spig k* spong fd4.de ther k2 tritic-vg fd5.de vanil fd5.de [tax jsj7]
  - **increases** with the pain: ap-g br
  - ○ **Abdomen**, in: agar bg2 *Am-c* b4a.de ant-t k* *Arg-n* k* *Arn* k* ars k* arund asar bg2 bell lp* bism bry bg2 calc bg2 canth b7 de* cham bro1 chel k* chin b7.de* cocc b7.de* **Coloc** k* crot-t *Cupr* bg2 cycl b7.de* dulc fd4.de *Gran* graph bg2 grat haem ham fd3.de• hell bg2 hep h2 hyos bg2 *Ip* k* *Kali-c* kali-s fd4.de *Kreos* lat-m sp1 lyc h2 m-arct b7.de merc bg2 mosch bg2 **Nux-v** k* *Ox-ac* petr bg2 *Ph-ac* plb k* polyg-h bro1 *Puls* bg2 rheum b7.de* ruta fd4.de samb bro1* sep k* spong fd4.de staph b7.de* stram bg2 sulph ter tritic-vg fd5.de valer b7.de* vanil fd5.de verat bg2 zinc k*
    - **morning**: mand rsj7•
  - **Back**, in: *Sep*
  - **Cervical** region, in: bamb-a stb2.de• carb-v h2
  - **Chest**, in: croc dulc fd4.de vanil fd5.de
  - **Ear**; in: dulc a1
  - **Eyes**; in: kali-bi bg2 sil bg2
  - **Heart**, in: spig
  - **Sacrum**, in: glon
  - **Stomach**, in: *(↗Pain - nausea - during)* ant-t b7.de* ars b4a.de* calad b7.de* dulc fd4.de kali-n h2 kali-s fd4.de mim-p rsj8• moni rfm1• nat-sil fd3.de• ost bro1 *Puls* b7a.de rhod b4a.de sec b7.de* spong fd4.de
  - **Throat**, in: arag br1 moni rfm1•
- **palpitation** | **sick**; with faint-like nausea causing her to become (See CHEST - Palpitation - nausea - faint-like)
- **palpitations**:
  - **after**: brom nux-v k*
  - **causes**: *Arg-n* k* sil h2
  - **with**: alum gsy1 arg-n gsy1* bar-c h2 bov gt1 brom tl1* bufo gt1 coli rly4• kali-c h2 mygal gt1* nit-ac h2 nux-v gt1 *Sil* hr1* thuj gt1
- **paroxysmal**: androc srj1• dig h2 hep h2 iod h mang h2 nat-m h2 tritic-vg fd5.de
- **pastry** agg.: ant-c k* ham fd3.de• symph fd3.de• tritic-vg fd5.de
- **periodical**: ars bro1 hydrog srj2• ign *Ip* nat-m nux-v phos raph *Sang*
  - **year**; every: hydrog srj2•
- **perspiration**:
  - **amel.**: glon bg2*
  - **during**: acon bg2 *Ant-c* bg2 **Apom** sne **Ars** bg2 *Bry* bg2 camph b7.de **Cham** b7.de* chin bg2 con bg2 *Corn* *Dros* bg2 *Ferr* *Graph* *Hep* bg2 hyos b7.de **Ign** b7a.de* **Ip** b7.de* kali-c bg2 kali-s fd4.de *Led* b7.de* *Lob* *Lyc* bg2 merc k* nit-ac bg2 **Nux-v** k* *Phos* bg2 puls bg2 *Rhus-t* bg2 ruta fd4.de sabad bg2 *Sel* b7a.de* *Sep* k* sil bg2 sul-ac bg2 sulph k* **Thuj** b4.de* ven-m rsj12• *Verat* bg2 zinc
    - **apyrexia**; in: chin bg2
- **pessary**; from: nux-m c1*
- **piano** playing, from: sulph k*
- **plums**, after: mag-c k* ruta fd4.de
- **pork**, after: ham k* *Ip* **Puls**
- **potatoes** agg.: *Alum* k*
- **powder**; after: colch rsj2•
- **pregnancy**:
  - **as** if pregnant: luna kg1•
  - **during**: acet-ac br1* acon k* ail alet k* *Alum* b4a.de *Amyg-p* br1* anac k* *Ant-c* *Ant-t* k* *Apom* bro1 arg-n bro1 arge-pl rwt5• *Ars* k* **Asar** k* *Bell* b4a.de *Bry* k* cadm-s c1 carb-ac k* *Carb-an* carb-v k2 carc mlr1• castm *Cer-ox* bro1 chel tl1 cimic k* *Cocc* bg2* cod *Colch* k* coll tl1 *Con* k* *Cuc-p* bro1 cupr-act bro1 *Cupr-ar* cycl bro1 dig bg2 ferr k* ferr-ar ferr-p gnaph bro1 *Goss* bro1 *Hell* hydrog srj2• ing bro1 *Ip* k* *Iris* k* *Jatr-c* kali-ar kali-bi tl1 kali-br k* *Kali-c* k* kali-m bro1 kali-p **Kreos** k* **Lac-ac** k* *Lac-c* *Lac-d* k* lac-v-c c2* *Lach* k* laur *Lil-t* lob k* *Lyc* *Mag-c* k* *Mag-m* k* **Med** bg2 merc k2* *Merc-i-f* *Nat-m* k* nat-p bro1 *Nux-m* k* **Nux-v** k* *Ox-ac* *Petr* k* ph-ac c2* *Phos* k* pilo c2* plat plb *Podo* *Psor* k* *Puls* k* sang pf sanic tl1 **Sep** k* *Sil* staph k* stry bro1 *Sul-ac* sulph k* *Sym-r* k* **Tab** k* tarent ther bro1 *Thyr* bro1 verat k* [*Calc-lac* stj2]
- **pressure**:
  - **abdomen**; on:
    - **agg.**: asar lac-c samb xxb1 *Tub* k* zinc h2
    - **amel.**: bros-gau mrc1
  - **neck** agg.; on: cimic ptk1
  - **spine** agg.; on: cimic bg3*
  - **spot**; from pressure on a painful: nat-m k*
  - **stomach** agg.; on: ant-t ars bar-c euph gamb grat hell k* hyos k* kali-bi bg2 kali-c h2* merc bg2 nat-m bg2 nept-m lsd2.fr phys ptel (non:sars kl) sulph zinc bg2 [tax jsj7]
  - **throat** agg.; on: *Lach* k*
- **prolonged**: bar-c sang a1
- **protracted** (See chronic)
- **putting** hands in warm water (See warm - water)
- **raising** head from pillow: *Ars* *Bry* colch *Nux-m* *Stram*
- **reading** agg.: *Arg-met* arn k* con glon k* jab lyc k* ph-ac k* plan k* *Sep* k*
- **renal** origin: senec ptk1*
- **resting**, supporting head | **amel.**: plat b4.de*
- **rich** food agg.: ant-c carb-an cycl dros *Ip* *Nit-ac* **Puls** sep *Tarax*
- **riding**:
  - **agg.**:
    - **breakfast**; before | **agg.**: hura
  - **amel.**: *Nit-ac*
  - **bus**; on a | **agg.**: beryl tpw5 cortico tpw7 mim-p rsj8•
  - **carriage**; in a: *(↗GENERALS - Riding - Streetcar; on - agg.; VERTIGO - Riding - Carriage; in a - agg.)*
    - **agg.**: *(↗airplane; seasickness; Vomiting - riding; VERTIGO - Riding - carriage)* allox tpw3* androc srj1• arn bg2* beryl tpw5* borx k* bros-gau mrc1 cadm-m sp1 cadm-met tpw6 *Calc* *Calc-p* carc tpw2* **Cocc** k* colch b7.de* con mtf11 cortico tpw7* croc b7a.de *Cycl* ferr b7.de* *Hep* hydrog srj2• **Hyos** b7a.de ina-i mlk9.de irid-met srj5• *Iris* *Lac-d* br1* *Lyc* k* *Mag-c* mim-p vml3• naja nept-m lsd2.fr *Nux-m* k* *Nux-v* k* **Op** b7a.de ozone sde2• **Petr** k* phos h2 plut-n srj7• podo fd3.de• sacch-a fd2.de• sanic c1* sel k* **Sep** k* *Sil* b4a.de* staph b7a.de sulph k* suprar rly4• symph fd3.de• tab k* *Ther* k* zinc [bell-p-sp dcm1 calc-m stj1 helia stj7 heroin sdj2]
  - **horse**; a: | **after** | **rapidly**; riding: sep b4.de*
    - **agg.**: *Ars* bg2 bell bg2 **Cocc** bg2 *Colch* bg2 croc bg2 *Ferr* bg2 nux-m bg2 **Petr** bg2 phos bg2 sec bg2 sep bg2 sil bg2 spig b7.de* sulph bg2
  - **taxi**; in a | **agg.**: mim-p rsj8•
  - **train**; in a: bros-gau mrc1 carc mlr1•
- **rinsing** the mouth, on: bry k* *Sep* k* sul-ac k*
- **rising**:
  - **after**:
    - **agg.**: am-m b7.de* arg-n a1 bry b7.de* graph k* led b7.de* mag-m h2* olnd b7.de* plut-n srj7• podo bg2 rhus-t b7.de* symph fd3.de• zinc k* [pop dhh1]
    - **amel.**: mur-ac bg2* sabin k* zinc b4.de*
  - **agg.**: acon k* acon-c a1 arg-n k* *Arn* ars bro1 asar bry k* caj a1 caps b7.de* carb-an k* cere-b a1 chel k* cimic bg1 cina b7.de* *Cocc* k* coloc k* cor-r ferr k* glon k* iber a1 ind k* kreos b7a.de led b7.de* mosch b7a.de nat-s k* nit-ac k* *Nux-v* b7.de* olnd k* phos k* plat k* ptel a1 puls bg1 senec sil b4.de* staph b7.de* sym-r bro1 *Tab* bro1 trios bro1 *Verat* k* vib c1 zing k* [bell-p-sp dcm1 pop dhh1]
  - **sitting**; from | **agg.**: ambr b7.de* chin b7.de* ferr b7.de*
  - **stooping**; from | **amel.**: olnd b7.de* puls b7.de* *Spig* b7a.de
- **room**:
  - **amel.**: bry b7.de* cham b7.de* chel b7.de* coff b7.de* lyc b4a.de nux-v b7.de*
  - **closed** room agg.: lyc ptk1* nat-c ptk1* tab ptk1*
- **rumbling** of liquids in abdomen amel.; loud: germ-met srj5•
- **salt**; from: *Ars* b4a.de *Carb-v* b4a.de
  - **thought** of salt: *Nat-m* k*
- **sauerkraut**; from: *Lyc* b4a.de
- **scraping** the larynx; from: calc-p k2
- **scratching** agg.: ip bg2

Stomach

- **seasickness**: (↗*airplane; riding - carriage - agg.; HEAD - Pain - riding - boat - agg.; VERTIGO - Riding - boat; VERTIGO - Riding - Boat - agg.)* aml-ns c2* apom c2* aq-mar c1* arn c1* ars b4a.de* borx c2 caps hr1* *Carb-ac* cer-ox c2* chlf hr1 **Cocc** k* colch **Con** k* croc b7a.de cuc-p c1* des-ac rbp6 **Euph** b4a.de* **Euph-c** c2* ferr b7.de* *Glon* k* hippoc-k szs2 hyos k* *Kali-bi* *Kreos* k* lac-ac *Lac-d* bro1 nat-m nicot c2 nux-m b7.de* **Nux-v** k* **Op** b7a.de **Petr** k* sanic c1* sec b7.de* *Sep* k* sil b4a.de *Staph* k* **Tab** k* ther k*
  - **closing** the eyes:
    - **agg.**: ther st
    - **amel.**: cocc st
- **sewing**; from: lac-d k* sep k*
- **shivering**:
  - **after**: verat b7a.de
  - **during**: asar b7.de bell b4.de* chin b7.de cina b7.de euph b4a.de kali-m ptk1 merc b4.de *Mez* b4a.de phos b4.de rhus-t b7.de *Sabad* b7.de* sul-ac ptk1 sulph b4.de
- **shuddering**; while: am-m h2 ars bg2 asar b7.de* calc h2* chin b7.de cina b7.de dulc h2 euph h2 hyper k* kali-m k2 mag-c h2 mez k* nat-c h2 nat-m phos h2 sabad b7.de* stann verat bg2 zinc
- **sickening** (See Nausea)
- **singing** agg.: ptel bg2*
- **sitting**:
  - **agg.**: acon k* alum ant-t b7.de* ars k* bry k* calc-ar carb-an k* chin b7.de* clem bg2 cor-r euphr bg2 ferr b7.de* hep k* ign bg2 mag-c mag-m b4.de* meny b7.de* phos k* puls b7.de* rhus-t k* rob ruta b7.de* sabad b7.de* tarax k*
  - **amel.**: aloe bg2
  - **bent** forward | **amel.**: zinc
  - **erect**:
    - **agg.**: acon k* colch k* eupi k*
    - **amel.**: hydrog srj2•
- **sitting** down agg.: bry b7a.de calc-ar hydrog srj2• zinc h2
- **sitting** up in bed agg.: *Acon* b7a.de androc srj1• *Arn* b7a.de *Ars* k* asar **Bry** k* chin c1 *Cic* b7a.de **Cocc** k* *Colch* k* cor-r ephe-si hsj1• *Nux-m* olnd b7a.de phos k* pic-ac k2 plat k* rhus-t b7.de* stram b7.de* sulph k* verat b7.de* zinc
- **sleep**:
  - **after** | **agg.**: alum ambr b7.de* androc srj1• apoc k* arund asar borx bry b7.de* cadm-met tpw6 caust chord-umb rly4• *Cocc* b7a.de coli rly4• cupr k* cupr-ar dig k* dream-p sdj1• euphr b7.de* galeoc-c-h gms1• ham k* hydrog srj2• kali-c h2 *Lach* *Lob* loxo-recl knl4• luna kg1• lyc b4a.de* mim-p rsj8• mur-ac myos-a rly4• olnd b7.de* op k* paull a1 positr nl2• rhus-t b7.de* spong k* squil k* sulph k* symph fd3.de• tarent k* thuj tritic-vg fd5.de v-a-b jl2 **Verat** zing k*
  - **amel.**: nat-c h2 rhus-t k* ruta fd4.de
  - **before**: apoc k* bry nat-m k* rhus-t b7.de* sol-ni
    - **going** to sleep; before: lach ptk1
  - **during** | **agg.**: apis bg2 arg-met ferr-p k* nux-m bg1 puls k* seneg k*
  - **inclination** to sleep; with: nux-m c1 tritic-vg fd5.de
  - **siesta**:
    - **after** | **agg.**: zinc h2
- **smell** (See odors - agg.)
- **smoking**:
  - **after** | **agg.**: agar brom k* *Calc* k* *Calc-p* k* *Clem* k* cycl h1 euphr k* ign k* **Ip** k* *Kali-bi* k* lach k* *Lob* **Nux-v** k* op k* *Phos* bro1 *Puls* k* sars sep k* *Tab* k* thuj k*
  - **agg.**: *Brom* b4a.de bry k* caj k* calad k* calc b4.de* camph b7.de* *Carb-an* k* clem k* *Cocc* b7.de* cycl k* euphr k* granit-m es1• *Ign* b7.de* *Ip* b7.de* kali-bi bg2 kali-c lac-c *Lyc* k* merc b4.de* nat-m k* **Nux-v** k* *Op* a1 phos k* psil ft1* puls b7.de* ran-b k* ruta sil k* spong k* *Staph* b7.de* tab thuj b4.de*
  - **amel.**: *Eug* bg1* sanic bg1*
- **sneezing**:
  - **agg.**: agar bg2 hell k* *Lach* bg3* *Petr* b4a.de sang bg3* sulph bg2*
  - **before**: sulph h2
- **solid** food:
  - **agg.**: puls b7.de*
  - **amel.**: kali-bi bg2
- **soup**: acon k* *Carb-v* chel k* stann h2
  - **amel.**: castm kali-bi k* mag-c k* nat-c a1
  - **smell** of (See food - smell - soup)
  - **thought** of (See food - thought - soup)
- **sour** things:
  - **agg.**: *Ars* b4.de* ferr b7.de*
  - **amel.**: arg-n k*
- **spasms**; from | **Stomach**; in: *Puls* b7.de*
- **spitting**, from: *Dig* b4a.de led k*
  - **with**: sang a1
- **standing**:
  - **agg.**: *Agn* k* *Alum* alumn androc srj1• arg-met h1 arn b7.de* colch crot-h bg1* dict bg1 hep b4.de* *Ign* mag-m k* merc bg1 petr ph-ac plut-n srj7• puls b7.de* tarax bg1 v-a-b jl2 vanil fd5.de [bell-p-sp dcm1]
  - **amel.**: dulc fd4.de ruta b7.de* tarax k*
  - **erect** | **agg.**: colch b7.de* olnd b7a.de
- **stitching** in rectum; after: *Ars* b4a.de *Lyc* b4a.de
- **stool**:
  - **after**:
    - **agg.**: acon b7.de* ant-t apoc k* bufo cain *Caust* k* con bg1 crot-t k* ger-i rly4• hyper bg1 *Kali-bi* k* kalm k* lyss bg1 mag-c mag-m k* merc-c bg1 mur-ac *Nat-m* k* nit-ac k* ox-ac petr k* phos b4a.de *Sil* sulph bg2 ter thuj bg1 tung-met bdx1• verat k* zing
      - **loose** stool: acon ptk1
    - **amel.**: amp rly4•
      - **loose** stool: ter ptk1
  - **amel.**: borx bg2 con k* dulc fd4.de ferr k* ip h1 mur-ac bg2* raph k* sang k* thuj b4.de*
  - **before**: acon k* ang bg2 ant-t k* apis b7a.de bry k* calc k* chel chr-ac bro1 cimic k* *Colch* bro1 cycl dulc k* grat hell hydr k* ip k* m-aust b7.de *Merc* k* oena *Podo* puls bg2 *Rhus-t* k* rumx ruta k* *Sep* k* staph k* sulph bg2 *Verat* k*
  - **during** | **agg.**: agar k* ant-t k* apis k* arg-met b7.de* *Ars* k* ars-s-f k2* asar b7.de* bac jl2 *Bell* k* carb-v bg2 cham k* chel k* coll a1 coloc k* crot-h crot-t cupr b7.de* *Dulc* b4a.de ferr k* *Glon* k* gnaph grat guaj k* hell k* hep b4.de* *Ip* k* jatr-c *Kali-ar* kali-bi bg2 *Kali-c* lach bg2 *Merc* k* merc-i-f *Nit-ac* k* nux-v bg2 *Podo* k* prun bg2 *Puls* k* *Rhus-t* sang k* seneg b4a.de *Sil* k* *Sul-ac* b4a.de *Sulph* k* *Verat* k*
  - **urging** to | **during**: androc srj1• bac jl2 *Dulc* k* kola stb3• tritic-vg fd5.de
- **stooping**:
  - **agg.**: bar-c k* calc-p k* carbn-s cina bg2 dig bg2 digin a1 haem a1 *Ip* k* kali-bi bg2 lac-d c1 lach k* m-aust b7.de mill olnd k* petr k* rhod k* rhus-t k* ruta k* sabad bg2 sang k* sapin a1 seneg bg2 zinc h2
  - **amel.**: hyos h1* petr ptk1
- **stretching** backwards | **amel.**: borx b4a.de
- **sudden**: agar ars-h vh bamb-a stb2.de• bol-s a1 chinin-ar chir-fl gya2 coloc k* conch fkr1• cupr k* ferr-p *Hep* bg2 ind k* ip k2 *Kali-bi* k* *Lyc* bg1* mosch musca-d szs1 narcot a1 olib-sac wmh1 petr h2 positr nl2• sul-ac k* sulph tung-met bdx1•
  - **eating**; while: *Bar-c* *Ferr* *Hell* *Ruta* k*
- **sugar** | **amel.**: op bg2
- **supper** agg.; after: alum k* am-m k* castm chr-ac a1 cycl k* ferr-i k* gast a1 graph k* hell-o a1 nat-m k* psor k* ruta fd4.de
- **swallowing**:
  - **agg.**: arn ptk1 *Merc-c* b4a.de plut-n srj7•
    - **empty**; on swallowing: colch ptk1
  - **amel.**: cocc puls b7.de*
  - **saliva** | **agg.**: ant-t *Colch* k* dig k* dios lach lyc rhod k* spig k* sulph
- **sweets**: acon b7a.de* *Arg-n* k* *Bell* b4a.de cycl bg1* dulc fd4.de ferr bg2 **Graph** k* ham fd3.de• *Ip* k* kali-s fd4.de merc b4.de* podo fd3.de• positr nl2• rhodi br1 *Spig* b7a.de spong fd4.de symph fd3.de• tarax bg1 vanil fd5.de
  - **as** from sweets: acon bg2 merc bg2
- **swinging**, from: borx bg2 carb-v bg2 *Cocc* coff *Petr*
- **talking** agg.: alum k* borx k* *Cocc* b7a.de ptel k* *Puls* b7a.de ther c1*
- **taste**; from:
  - **bad**: arg-n bg2

- **sour**: spong bg2
- **sweet**: merc bg2

- **tea**; after: *Aesc* choc srj3• hydrog srj2• lach b7.de* ros-d wla1 symph fd3.de•
- **thinking** of it agg.: arg-met borx bg2* calc dros k* graph lach k* mosch *Puls* bg2 sars *Sep* k*
- **tobacco**:
  - **odor** of: ign mp1• phos k*
  - **thought** of: kali-br k*
- **touch**:
  - **abdomen** agg.; of: rhus-t hr1
  - **lips** agg.; of: *Cadm-s* k* nux-m bg1*
  - **stomach** agg.; of: bar-c b4.de* hyos b7.de* kali-bi bg2 lith-c bg2 merc bg2 nux-m bg2 nux-v b7.de*
- **travelling** (See riding - carriage - agg.; GENERALS - Travelling - ailments)
- **trembling**; with: ars b4.de* borx ptk1 hydrog srj2• nit-ac b4a.de plat b4.de*
- **turning** the eyes: *Sil* b4a.de
- **uncovering**:
  - **amel.**: *Tab* k*
  - **before** | **amel.**: dig c1
- **urination**:
  - **after**:
    - **agg.**: ant-c k* castm k* dig b4.de* merc k* pareir
      - **copious**: dig h2
  - **amel.**: nat-p bg1*
  - **before**: dig b4.de*
  - **during**:
    - **agg.**: **Canth** bg2 dig ptk1 ip bg2 merc b4.de* tab bg2
      - **copious**: verat bg2
- **urine**, if he retains: cur dig bg2
- **using** the eyes: con k* graph jab sep k* *Ther*
- **vaccination**; after: **Sil**
- **vertigo**; during (See VERTIGO - Nausea)
- **vexation**; after: cham ign ip *Kali-c* nat-m petr h2 phos
- **vinegar** | **amel.**: op bg2
- **vomit**; sensation as if about to: acon b7.de* agar b4.de* agn bg2 alum b4.de* am-c b4.de* am-m b7.de* anac b4.de* ant-c b7.de* ant-t b7.de* apis b7a.de arg-met b7.de* arg-n bg2 arn b7.de* ars b4.de* asaf b7.de* asar b7.de* aur b4.de* bar-c b4.de* bell b4.de* bism b7.de* borx b4a.de* bov b4.de* brom bg2 *Bry* b7.de* calc b4.de* camph b7.de* cann-s b7.de* canth b7.de* *Caps* b7.de* carb-an b4.de* carb-v b4.de* caust b4.de* **Cham** b7.de* chel b7.de* chin b7.de* cina b7.de* *Cocc* b7.de* coff b7.de* colch b7.de* con b4.de* *Croc* b7.de* cupr b7.de* cycl b7.de* dig b4.de* *Dros* b7.de* dulc bg2 euph b4.de* euphr bg2 ferr b7.de* fl-ac bg2 glon bg2 graph b4.de* hell b7.de* hep b4.de* hyos b7.de* ign b7.de* iod b4.de* *Ip* b7.de* kali-bi bg2 *Kali-c* b4.de* kali-n b4.de* kreos b7a.de* lach bg2 laur b7.de* led b7.de* lyc b4.de* m-ambo b7.de m-arct b7.de m-aust b7.de mag-c b4.de* mag-m b4.de* mang b4.de* meny b7.de* *Merc* b4.de* merc-c b4a.de mez b4.de* mosch b7.de* mur-ac b4.de* nat-c b4.de* nat-m b4.de* nat-s bg2 nit-ac b4a.de* nux-m b7.de* *Nux-v* b7.de* olnd b7.de* op b7.de* petr b4.de* ph-ac b4.de* phos b4.de* plat b4.de* plb b7.de* podo bg2 psor bg2 **Puls** b7.de* ran-s b7.de* rheum b7.de* rhod b4.de* **Rhus-t** b7.de* ruta b7.de* *Sabad* b7.de* sabin b7.de* sars b4.de* sec b7.de* seneg b4.de* sep b4.de* sil b4.de* spig b7.de* spong b7.de* squil b7.de* stann b4.de* staph b7.de* stram b7.de* stront-c b4.de* sul-ac b4.de* sulph b4.de* tab bg2 teucr bg2 thuj b4.de* valer b7.de* **Verat** b7.de* verb b7.de* zinc b4.de*
  - **anxiety**; with: acon b7.de calc b4.de caust b4.de *Kali-c* b4.de lach b7.de lyc b4.de *Merc* b4a.de *Merc-c* b4a.de nit-ac b4.de *Plat* b4a.de plb b7.de sabad b7.de
  - **cough** agg.; during: bry b7.de *Caps* b7.de* *Dros* b7.de* hep b4a.de iod b4a.de *Ip* b7.de *Merc* b4.de* *Nux-v* b7.de* *Ph-ac* b4a.de *Puls* b7.de* *Ruta* b7.de* squil b7.de
  - **drinking** agg.; after: nux-v b7a.de puls b7a.de rhus-t b7a.de teucr b7a.de
  - **eating** | **after** | **agg.**: agar b4a.de alum b4a.de am-c b4a.de anac b4a.de bism b7a.de bry b7a.de cham b7a.de con b4a.de cycl b7a.de graph b4a.de kali-c b4a.de phos b4a.de puls b7a.de rhus-t b7a.de
    - **while** | **agg.**: cocc b7a.de ferr b7a.de
  - **menses**:
    - **after** | **agg.**: puls b7a.de

- **vomit**; sensation as if about to – **menses**: ...
    - **before** | **agg.**: *Verat* b7.de
    - **during** | **agg.**: calc b4a.de caps b7.de thuj b4a.de verat b7.de*
- **vomiting**:
  - **after**: dig bg2
  - **amel.**: ant-t tl1 ephe-si hsj1• phyt ptk1 pyrog ptk1 visc sp1
  - **before**: apom br1
  - **not** amel.: *Dig* k* **Ip** bg3* sang k* tab mrr1
- **waking**, on (See sleep - after - agg.)
- **walking**:
  - **after** | **agg.**: alum calc-s carb-an h2 chin b7.de* ferr b7.de* graph k* plat h2 *Puls* k* rhus-t b7.de* sep k*
  - **agg.**: acon k* alum bg2 am-c b4.de* ang bg2 ant-t bg2 asar b7.de* bar-c bell k* bry k* calc k* calc-sil k2 carb-an b4.de* chinin-s con euph ferr k* ferr-p galeoc-c-h gms1• gamb kali-bi k* *Kali-c* kali-n h2 lac-del hrn2• led lyc mag-m b4.de* merc mez k* nat-s nux-v b7.de* op petr bg2* ph-ac phos phyt plat ptel rhod seneg b4.de* *Sep* sil sulph thuj k* tritic-vg fd5.de [bell-p-sp dcm1]
    - **hills**; on: galeoc-c-h gms1•
  - **air**; in open:
    - **after** | **agg.**: alum b4.de* graph h2 nit-ac h2 tritic-vg fd5.de
    - **agg.**: acon k* am-m k* ang k* bell h1 bry b7.de* *Gamb* graph lach led b7.de* lycps-v mez b4.de* nat-s nux-v b7.de* petr b4.de* phos plat h2 seneg b4.de* sep k* sil h2
    - **amel.**: ars h2 dulc fd4.de
  - **amel.**: acon k* am-c k* dros b7.de* dulc fd4.de ferr b7.de* grat k* hydrog srj2• nit-ac bg2 ptel tl1 puls k* rhus-t b7.de* tarax b7.de* [tax jsj7]
  - **wind**; against the: plat b4.de*
- **warm**:
  - **drinks**:
    - **agg.**: *Bism* *Lach* **Phos** **Puls** k* ther k2
    - **amel.**: pyrog ptk1* spong fd4.de ther k* [pop dhh1 tax jsj7]
  - **food** agg.: guat sp1* phos k2
    - **hot** food: bry b7a.de ferr b7a.de *Puls* b7.de*
  - **room**:
    - **agg.**: agar alum b4a.de* bell bg2 carb-v croc b7.de* cystein-l rly4• dulc fd4.de euphr ham fd3.de• **Lyc** k* *Mez* **Nat-c** paeon *Phos* *Puls* k* sep k* symph fd3.de• **Tab** k* tarax b7a.de verat vesp zing
    - **entering** a warm room; when | **air**; from open: *Alum* *Am-m* calc-s *Puls* sep
  - **stove**: *Laur* k*
  - **water**; putting hands in warm●: **Phos** k*
- **warmth** agg.: arn b7.de* bry b7.de* cann-s b7.de* croc b7a.de m-arct b7.de puls b7.de*
- **washing** agg.: bry k* ther ptk1 zinc h2*
- **washing** clothes; after: ther c1
- **water**:
  - **drinking**, after (See drinking - after - agg.)
  - **sight** of water, from: phos
  - **thinking** of: ars-h ham a1
- **waves**; in: ant-t ptk1 arge-pl rwt5• bamb-a stb2.de• helo-s bnm14• hippoc-k szs2 pot-e rly4•
- **weakness**; with (See GENERALS - Weakness - accompanied - nausea)
- **weather** agg.; stormy: falco-pe nl2•
- **wine**:
  - **agg.**: *Ant-c* k* bry k* carb-an k* nux-v b7.de* phos k* ran-b b7.de* sel b7.de* **Zinc** k*
  - **amel.**: bry b7a.de coc-c k*
  - **sour**, from: **Ant-c**
- **work**; when thinking at: borx tl1
- **yawning** agg.: arn k* nat-c h2 nat-m k*

▽ - **extending** to chest: plac rzf5•

○ - **Abdomen**; in: agar agn k* ail aloe bg2 androc srj1• ant-t k* apis b7a.de* asar k* aur bg2 bell k* brucel sa3• *Bry* k* cadm-s calc bg2 cic k* cimic bg2* coc-c bg2 cocc k* colch bg2 croc k* crot-t bg2 cupr k* cycl k* cystein-l rly4• des-ac rbp6 fago gels k* graph k* grat bg1 hell k* hep k* ip k* iris lach bg2 lact

Stomach

- **Abdomen**: ...
lact-v bg2 m-arct b2.de* mang k* meny bg2 merc bg2 mur-ac nit-ac k* nux-m k* par k* *Phel* phyt pic-ac plan polyg-h bg2* *Puls* k* rheum k* ruta k* samb k* sep sil b2.de* spig bg2 spong stann k* staph k* sumb tarax bg2 teucr k* thuj valer k* zing k*
  - **stool**; before: cimic bg2
  - ○ **Lower** abdomen: cycl bg2 graph bg2 grat bg2 merc-i-f bg2* puls bg2* rhus-t bg2* sil bg2
  - **Umbilical** region: tarax bg2 ulm-c jsj8• valer b7.de*
    - **starting** from: ant-t bg2 chin bg2 cocc bg2 indg bg2 lach bg2 nit-ac bg2 *Op* b7a.de valer b7.de*
  - **Upper** abdomen: apis b7a.de olib-sac wmh1 puls b7.de* samb b7.de*
- **Chest**, in: acon k* anac k* ant-t bg2* arg-met k* asaf k* bry k* cadm-s calc *Calen* ptk1* *Croc* k* glon lach mang *Merc* k* nux-v k* par k* ph-ac puls bg2 *Rhus-t* k* sec k* spong fd4.de staph k*
- **Ear**; in: dios tl1* dulc tl1
- **Epigastrium**; in: acon b7.de* agn b7.de* ant-t b7.de* arn b7.de* calc b4.de* cann-s b7.de* caps b7.de* cham b7.de* cina b7.de* cocc b7.de* croc b7.de* cupr b7.de* dig b4.de* hell b7.de* merc b4.de* mosch b7.de* nat-m b4.de* nit-ac b4.de* *Nux-v* b7.de* *Phos* b4.de* plat b4.de* *Ruta* b7.de* sabin b7.de* samb b7.de* sil b4.de* squil b7a.de* stann b4.de* sulph b4.de* teucr b7a.de* verat b7.de*
- **Head**, in: ang b7.de* *Cocc* bg2* colch ptk1* sep bg2 sulph bg2 zinc bg2
- **Heart**; about: cham bg2 *Nux-v* bg2
- **High** up: des-ac rbp6
- **Hypochondria**; in: apis b7a.de nit-ac bg2 puls b7.de*
  - **left**: coc-c bg2 graph bg2
- **Mouth**, in: aeth k* agar k* anac b4.de* cadm-s *Cocc* k* ip h1 *Mag-m* k* nit-s-d a1 olnd b7.de* ph-ac b4.de* *Puls* k* rhod k* samb bat1• *Stann* k* staph b7.de* sul-ac k* sulph b4.de*
- **Palate**; in: cupr b7.de* cycl b7.de* merc b4.de* ph-ac b4.de* spig b7.de*
- **Rectum**, felt in: positr nl2• rat bg2 ruta bg1*
- **Stomach**; in (See Nausea)
- **Throat**, in: acon k* alum h2 anac k* ant-c ant-t b2.de* aral ptk1* arg-met k* arn *Ars* k* asar k* aur k* *Bell* k* cann-s k* caps fkm1• carb-ac carb-an caust h2* chin k* chord-umb rly4• coc-c cocc k* *Coff* k* colch coli rly4• *Croc* k* *Cupr* k* **Cycl** k* falco-pe nl2• ferr k* ferr-p hep bg2 hydrog srj2• lyc lycps-v bg2 merc k* *Mez* k* nit-ac k* olnd k* **Ph-ac** k* plut-n srj7• *Puls* k* *Rhus-t* k* ruta tl1 sars k* sil spig k* spong fd4.de *Squil* k* **Stann** k* staph k* sulph k* tarax k* valer k* vanil fd5.de [tax jsj7]
  - **collar**; by tight fitting: hyos bg1 lach
  - **spasm** in throat; from: coli rly4• *Graph*
  - **thread** in throat; as from a: *Valer* b7a.de
  - **worm** in; as if a: puls bg2 spig ptk1
- **Throat-pit**; in: chin b7.de*

NERVOUS feeling: bell bg2

NIBBLING (See MIND - Nibble)

NUMBNESS: acon bg1 bry bg1 *Carb-v* b4a.de castm bg1 plat bg1 sars bg1

NURSING MOTHERS; complaints of: *Carb-v* bg2 chin b7a.de* cocc bg2 nux-v bg2

NURSING THE CHILD agg.; when: *Carb-v* b4.de*

OBSTRUCTION of pylorus; sensation of: (↗*Narrow*) lach k* nux-v k* phos k*

OLD PEOPLE; in: *Nux-m* b7a.de

OPEN; sensation as if stomach were: spong k*
- **air** is passing through: crot-c tl1

OPERATION; after: | **hemorrhoids**; of: croc ptk1

OPPRESSION: (↗*Heaviness*) ant-c b7.de* both-ax tsm2 *Cycl* hr1 lacer a1* *Mosch* b7a.de mur-ac h2 nat-c h2 nat-m h2 phos h2 plat h2 podo bg2 psor bg2 rhus-t b7.de* zinc h2
- **dinner**; after: kali-br a1
- **leaning** backward: con h2
- **menses**; during: plat h2
- ○ **Epigastrium**: ant-c b7.de* *Apoc* vh1 ars b4.de* *Bell* b4.de* bov b4.de* *Bry* b7.de* calc b4a.de chin b7.de* cic b7.de* cina b7.de* *Cocc* b7.de* coff b7a.de* colch b7.de* hyos b7.de* kali-bi bg2 kreos b7a.de* lob br1 mosch b7.de*

Oppression – Epigastrium: ...
nat-m b4.de* plat b4.de* plb b7.de* prun bg2 rhus-t b7.de* sabad b7a.de* sec b7.de* sep b4a.de staph b7.de* sulph bg2 teucr b7.de*
  - **cough**; during (See COUGH - Oppression - epigastrium)

OVERLIFTING agg.: bar-c b4.de* borx b4a.de* bry b7a.de lyc b4.de* rhus-t b7a.de sil b4.de*

OVERLOADED; sensation as if (See Fullness; Heaviness)

PAIN: abies-c ↓ abies-n k* abrom-a ks5 *Abrot* k* acal ↓ *Acet-ac* k* *Acon* k* acon-c ↓ acon-f ↓ act-sp ↓ *Aesc* k* aesc-g ↓ *Aeth* agar k* agar-em ↓ *Agar-ph* ↓ agath-a nl2• agn ↓ aids ↓ ail alco ↓ all-c *All-s* ↓ aloe k* alum k* alum-p ↓ alum-sil k2 alumn am-br ↓ am-c k* am-m bg2 ambr *Aml-ns* amph a1 anac k* anan androc srj1• ang ↓ anis bro1 *Ant-c* k* *Ant-t* k* *Anthraci* ↓ anthraq ↓ *Apis* k* apoc ↓ aran ↓ *Arg-met* **Arg-n** k* arge-pl rwt5• arist-cl sp1 *Arn* k* **Ars** k* ars-h ars-i ars-s-f ↓ arum-m ↓ arum-t ↓ arund *Asaf* asar asc-c a1 asc-t atis zzc1• *Atro* ↓ aur k* aur-ar k2 aur-i k2 *Aur-m* ↓ aur-m-n aur-s k2 bad ↓ bamb-a stb2.de• bapt *Bar-c* k* *Bar-i* *Bar-m* bar-s k2 **Bell** k* bell-p ↓ bell-p-sp ↓ benz-ac k* *Berb* ↓ **Bism** k* bism-sn mtf11 bol-la borx k* botul jl2 *Bov* ↓ brach *Brom* bros-gau ↓ brucel sa3• **Bry** k* bufo ↓ bufo-s ↓ but-ac ↓ *Cact* cadm-br ↓ cadm-met ↓ cadm-s cain ↓ calad k* *Calc* k* calc-ar ↓ calc-f ↓ calc-i bro1 calc-m bro1 *Calc-p* *Calc-s* calc-sil k2 *Camph* k* cann-i ↓ cann-s k* cann-xyz ↓ *Canth* k* *Caps* *Carb-ac* k* *Carb-an* k* **Carb-v** k* carbn-h ↓ **Carbn-s** carc ↓ **Card-m** carl cartl-s rly4• *Casc* ↓ castm ↓ castor-eq ↓ caul **Caust** k* cedr ↓ cench ↓ *Cham* k* **Chel** k* chim-m hr1 **Chin** k* chinin-ar *Chinin-s* chlf br1 chlor ↓ chr-ac ↓ cic cimic *Cina* k* cinnb k2 cit-v a1 clem cob cob-n ↓ coc-c coca-c ↓ cocain ↓ **Cocc** k* cod ↓ coff **Colch** k* coli rly4• coll ↓ **Coloc** k* colum-p sze2• com ↓ *Con* k* cop cor-r *Corn* croc *Crot-c* k* *Crot-h* crot-t cub ↓ cund ↓ **Cupr** k* cupr-act bg2 *Cupr-ar* cupr-m ↓ *Cupr-s* ↓ cupre-l bro1 cur cycl cypra-eg ↓ cystein-l rly4• cyt-l sp1 *Daph* ↓ dat-a ↓ *Dig* k* *Dios* k* *Diosm* br1 *Dros* ↓ dulc k* *Dys* fmm1• echi elaps ↓ elat ↓ *Erig* ↓ eucal br1 eug ↓ euon ↓ eup-a br1 *Eup-per* ↓ eup-pur ↓ *Euph* ↓ euphr ↓ eupi ↓ fago ↓ falco-pe nl2• *Ferr* k* *Ferr-ar* ferr-i ferr-p k* ferul ↓ fic-m gya1 *Fl-ac* ↓ *Form* ↓ gaert pte1*• gal-s ↓ galeoc-c-h gms1• galla-q-r ↓ gamb bro1 gard-j ↓ gast ↓ gaul mtf11 geb-k bta1• *Gels* k* *Gent-c* ↓ *Gent-l* ↓ ger-i rly4• germ-met srj5• gink-b ↓ *Gins* ↓ glon k* *Gran* k* **Graph** k* *Grat* *Guaj* ↓ *Guare* ↓ guat ↓ gymno ↓ haem ↓ ham *Hed* bro1 hell k* hell-o ↓ helo bg2 helo-s rwt2• *Helon* ↓ hep k* heroin ↓ hippoc-k szs2 hir ↓ hom-xyz br1* hura *Hydr* k* *Hydr-ac* hydrc ↓ *Hyos* k* hyper ↓ *Ign* k* ignis-alc es2• ilx-a ↓ ina-i ↓ ind ↓ indg ↓ influ jl2 *Iod* k* *Ip* k* irid-met srj5• *Iris* jab ↓ jac-c ↓ *Jatr-c* ↓ jug-c ↓ jug-r ↓ *Kali-ar* *Kali-bi* k* kali-br ↓ *Kali-c* k* kali-chl kali-i kali-m k2* *Kali-n* k* kali-p kali-pic a1 *Kali-s* kali-sil ↓ kali-sula ↓ *Kalm* kola ↓ *Kreos* k* lac-ac ↓ *Lac-c* ↓ lac-d c1* lac-del hrn2• lac-e ↓ lac-h ↓ lac-loxod-a ↓ lac-lup ↓ lacer ↓ *Lach* k* lachn ↓ *Lact* ↓ lap-a ↓ *Laur* k* lavand-a ctl1• lec ↓ led lepi ↓ *Lept* lil-s ↓ lil-t ↓ limest-b ↓ lina ↓ lith-c ↓ *Lob* lol ↓ loxo-recl ↓ **Lyc** k* lyss ↓ *M-ambo* ↓ m-aust ↓ *Mag-c* k* mag-f ↓ *Mag-m* k* *Mag-p* mag-s malar ↓ manc k* mang k* mang-m ↓ marb-w ↓ *Med* medul-os-si rly4• melal-alt gya4 menth br1 mentho ↓ *Meny* ↓ meph ↓ *Merc* k* *Merc-br* ↓ merc-c b4a.de* merc-i-f merc-sul ↓ merl ↓ mez k* *Mill* ↓ mim-p ↓ *Moni* ↓ morg-p pte1• morph ↓ mosch mur-ac musca-d szs1 *Myric* ↓ naja narcot ↓ narz ↓ **Nat-ar** *Nat-c* k* nat-f sp1 *Nat-m* k* nat-ox rly4• *Nat-p* k* nat-pyru rly4• *Nat-s* nat-sil ↓ nept-m ↓ nicc nicc-met ↓ nicotam rly4• *Nit-ac* k* nit-s-d ↓ *Nux-m* k* **Nux-v** k* nyct ↓ oena ↓ ol-an olnd k* *Op* k* orot-ac ↓ *Osm* ↓ ost ↓ ox-ac ozone ↓ paeon ↓ *Par* ↓ paraf bro1 pegan-ha ↓ *Petr* petr-ra ↓ *Ph-ac* ↓ phel ↓ **Phos** k* phys physala-p ↓ *Phyt* *Pic-ac* ↓ picro ↓ pimp ↓ pin-con oss2• plac ↓ plac-s rly4• plan *Plat* ↓ **Plb** k* plect ↓ pneu ↓ podo polyg-h ↓ polys sk4• positr nl2• pot-e ↓ prot jl2 prun psil ft1 *Psor* ↓ *Ptel* k* **Puls** k* *Pycnop-sa* ↓ quas ↓ rad-br ↓ ran-b k* ran-s k* *Raph* ↓ *Rat* ↓ rham-cal br1 rheum ↓ rhod k* rhus-t k* rob rumx ruta k* *Sabad* b7.de* sabin sacch-a ↓ sal-fr sle1• *Samb* ↓ *Sang* sanguis-s hrn2• *Sarr* ↓ sars ↓ scut bro1 *Sec* k* sel ↓ sem-t ↓ senec seneg k* *Sep* k* **Sil** k* sin-a ↓ sin-n ↓ sinus ↓ sol-ni ↓ sol-t-ae spect ↓ sphing ↓ *Spig* k* spong bg2* squil k* **Stann** k* *Staph* *Stram* streptoc ↓ stront-c k* stroph-s ↓ *Stry* succ-ac ↓ suis-em ↓ suis-pan ↓ *Sul-ac* k* sul-i ↓ **Sulph** k* sumb syc pte1• symph br1 syph ↓ **Tab** k* tarax sp1 *Tarent* tax-br oss1• *Ter* tere-la ↓ teucr thal ↓ thal-met br1* thal-s ↓ thal-xyz ↓ ther k2 thiam ↓ thres-a sze7• thuj k* thymol ↓ til ↓ tril-p ↓ tritic-vg fd5.de tub ↓ tung-met bdx1• (non:uran-met k) *Uran-n* ust valer vanil fd5.de ven-m ↓ **Verat** k* *Verat-v* verb ↓ vichy-g ↓ visc ↓ wies ↓ xan ↓ *Zinc* k* zinc-m ↓ zinc-p k2 zing ziz ↓ [helia stj7]
- **left** side: arg-n ↓ crot-c ↓
  - **gnawing** pain: arg-n
  - **stitching** pain: crot-c sk4•
- **daytime**: nat-m ↓

- **stitching** pain: nat-m
- **morning**: aesc aids nl2• alum↓ am-c↓ anac ant-c asar bamb-a↓ borx↓ calad↓ carb-an carb-v↓ carbn-s carc↓ carneg-g rwt1• *Caust Chin Cina* colch con↓ cupr cupr-s dig digin↓ dios dulc fd4.de fago↓ gran↓ graph ham↓ helo-s↓ hyper iod h *Kali-bi Kali-c* kali-s↓ kiss↓ *Lach* led↓ lyc mag-c mag-s merc↓ merc-c↓ merc-i-f↓ nat-c *Nat-m* nat-ox↓ nat-s nat-sil↓ **Nux-v** petr petr-ra↓ *Phos* plat podo↓ puls ran-s rat↓ ruta fd4.de sang↓ sep spong fd4.de staph *Sulph* taosc iwa1• tarent tritic-vg fd5.de vanil fd5.de zinc zinc-p k2
  - **5 h | gnawing** pain (See night - midnight - after - 5 - gnawing)
  - **8 h**: bad↓
    - **lancinating**: bad c1
  - **13 h**; until: sep
  - **14 h**; until: aids nl2•
  - **bed** agg.; in: carb-an↓ con kali-c↓ kali-n↓ phos phys↓ plb staph tritic-vg fd5.de vanil fd5.de
    - **cramping**: carb-an con phys k*
    - **pressing** pain: kali-c h2 kali-n h2 phos k* staph
    - **sore**: con h2
  - **burning**: *Dios* ham fd3.de• helo-s rwt2• hyper *Kali-bi* merc bg1 nat-s petr-ra shn4• spong fd4.de *Sulph* tritic-vg fd5.de vanil fd5.de zinc
  - **clawing** pain: petr puls
  - **cramping**: bamb-a stb2.de• borx a1 con dig digin a1 dulc fd4.de gran k* hyper k* kali-c h2 kali-s fd4.de nat-c h2 nat-ox rly4• nat-sil fd3.de• *Nux-v* puls rat k* sep h2
  - **cutting** pain: dios k* kali-c k* merc-i-f k*
  - **drawing** pain: carc fd2.de• dig digin a1 kali-c h2 puls k*
  - **eating | after | agg.**: nux-v tarent
    - **amel.**: mag-c h2 nat-s
  - **fasting** agg.: carb-v↓ caust nit-ac↓ petr
    - **gnawing** pain: carb-v nit-ac
  - **gnawing** pain: aesc k* carb-v k* nat-c h2* plat k* ruta h1 vanil fd5.de
  - **pressing** pain: am-c h2 ant-c k* *Carb-an* caust k* *Chin* dulc fd4.de graph k* hyper k* kali-c h2 kali-s fd4.de kiss a1 lach led h1 nat-c k* *Nat-m Nux-v* k* petr h2 podo fd3.de• puls k* ran-s ruta h1 sep sulph zinc k*
  - **rising | after**:
    - **agg.**: caust↓ iod↓ mang↓ nat-s↓ nit-ac↓ vanil↓
      - **cramping**: iod h nat-s k* nit-ac h2
      - **gnawing** pain: nat-s vanil fd5.de
      - **pressing** pain: caust h2 mang h2
    - **agg.**: caust *Cina* crot-h↓ nat-s sacch-a fd2.de• vanil fd5.de zinc
      - **sore**: crot-h
  - **sore**: alum chin dios k* fago k* **Phos** k* sang
  - **standing** agg.: sulph↓
    - **stitching** pain: sulph
  - **stitching** pain: calad carb-an h2 merc-c nat-m ruta fd4.de
  - **stool** agg.; after: con
    - **drawing** pain: con
  - **tearing** pain: con h2 sep h2
  - **turning** in bed agg.: con↓
    - **sore**: con h2
  - **waking**; on: agar aids nl2• anac↓ *Carb-an*↓ caust con h2 cycl dulc fd4.de hep↓ kali-c↓ kali-s↓ kola stb3• *Lach* lyc nat-m nicc nit-ac orot-ac↓ petr↓ phyt psil ft1 sacch-a fd2.de• spong fd4.de staph sulph↓ symph fd3.de• taosc iwa1• til↓
    - **clawing** pain: sulph
    - **cramping**: caust k* dulc fd4.de kola stb3• lyc k* nat-m h2 orot-ac rly4• petr h2 sacch-a fd2.de• til a1
    - **pressing** pain: agar anac h2 *Carb-an* cycl k* hep h2 kali-c h2 kali-s fd4.de nicc k* nit-ac k* phyt k* staph k*
    - **stitching** pain: con h2
  - **walking** agg.: agar carb-an cycl nit-ac phos phyt
- **forenoon**: bamb-a↓ bapt calc↓ carbn-s↓ chel sne dulc fd4.de *Graph* helon indg↓ kali-c↓ lyc mag-m *Nat-c*↓ nat-m nicc podo ruta fd4.de sacch-a↓ sep spong stann sulph↓ thuj ust vanil fd5.de
  - **8-9 h**: cocc
- **forenoon**: ...
  - **burning**: carbn-s kali-c h2 podo fd3.de•
  - **cramping**: graph k* podo thuj k*
  - **cutting** pain: nat-c k*
  - **gnawing** pain: *Nat-c* hr1 nicc k* vanil fd5.de
  - **pressing** pain: bamb-a stb2.de• calc dulc fd4.de *Graph* k* lyc k* mag-m k* *Nat-c* hr1 nat-m k* nicc k* sacch-a fd2.de• sep h2 spong stann k* sulph k* thuj k* vanil fd5.de
  - **stitching** pain: indg nicc vanil fd5.de
  - **stool** agg.; after: calc sulph
- **noon**: agar alum↓ alumn *Aur* dulc fd4.de ham↓ kola stb3• mez nicc↓ podo↓ ruta fd4.de seneg symph↓ zinc
  - **burning**: nicc podo fd3.de•
  - **cramping**: agar k* alumn symph fd3.de•
  - **eating**; after: euphr↓
    - **gnawing** pain: euphr k*
  - **pressing** pain: alum h2 *Aur* ham fd3.de• mez k* ruta fd4.de zinc k*
- **afternoon**: alum alumn am-m arg-n ars bamb-a↓ bar-c↓ bry *Calc* calc-s canth *Chel* sne dig↓ digin↓ dulc fd4.de ferr ham↓ *Iris* kali-bi↓ kali-c↓ kali-n↓ **Lyc** merc-c nat-m↓ nat-sil↓ nicc nux-v par petr ptel↓ *Puls* sang *Sep* spong stront-c↓ sulph tarent tritic-vg fd5.de ust vanil fd5.de
  - **13 h**: rhus-v↓
    - **stitching** pain: rhus-v
    - **yawning** agg.: chel↓
      - **cutting** pain: chel
  - **13-14 h**: con↓
    - **cramping**: con
  - **14 h**: ferr↓
    - **pressing** pain: ferr
  - **15 h**: nicc↓ sulph↓
    - **stitching** pain: nicc sulph
  - **16 h**: alumn↓
    - **cramping**: alumn
    - **cutting** pain: alumn
  - **16-17 h**: bry↓
    - **pressing** pain: bry
  - **17 h**: nat-m↓ puls↓
    - **cramping**: nat-m
    - **cutting** pain: puls
  - **17-19 h**: *Staph* vh
  - **18 h**: lach↓
    - **cramping**: lach
  - **burning**: alum am-m bamb-a stb2.de• bar-c iris kali-bi lyc tritic-vg fd5.de
  - **cramping**: alum k* calc k* calc-s k* par k* puls k* spong fd4.de
  - **cutting** pain: alum h2 ptel spong fd4.de stront-c sulph k*
  - **gnawing** pain: kali-c
  - **lying** down agg.: coc-c↓
    - **stitching** pain: coc-c
  - **pressing** pain: alum h2 am-m k* arg-n k* canth dig digin a1 dulc fd4.de ham fd3.de• kali-c h2 kali-n h2 *Lyc* k* nicc k* petr k* spong tritic-vg fd5.de
  - **sore**: alum
  - **stitching** pain: alum h2 am-m k* dulc fd4.de nat-m h2 nat-sil fd3.de• nicc petr sep k* vanil fd5.de
  - **stool** agg.; after: fago↓
    - **burning**: fago
- **evening**: abrot↓ agar alum alum-p k2 alum-sil k2 alumn ang↓ ars bapt↓ bar-c↓ calad↓ calc calc-s calc-sil k2 carb-an *Carb-v* castor-eq chel cocc↓ coloc con↓ dig dios dulc euphr fago↓ falco-pe nl2• ferr-i↓ form↓ grat↓ ham fd3.de• indg↓ iris↓ kali-bi kali-c↓ kali-n kali-s fd4.de kola stb3• lac-lup hrn2• led↓ lob lyc mag-m mang↓ merc mez↓ nat-c nat-m nux-v↓ petr↓ phos plan propr sa3• **Puls** *Rhus-t* ruta fd4.de sang sars↓ seneg↓ sep sil sin-a↓ spong↓ streptoc rly4• *Sul-ac* sulph↓ symph fd3.de• tarent thuj trios rsj11• tritic-vg fd5.de vanil fd5.de verat↓ zinc zinc-p k2
  - **17-19 h**: *Staph* vh
  - **20 h**: calc-p↓

Stomach

- **20** h: ...
  - **burning**: calc-p
  - **walking** in open air agg.: alumn
- **21** h: galeoc-c-h gms1• lyc ↓
  - **burning**: lyc
  - **until** midnight: phos
- **22** h: phos ↓
  - **stitching** pain: phos h2
- **bed**:
  - **in** bed:
    - **agg.**: alum bell h1 carb-an *Carb-v* kali-c ↓ *Lyc* phos ruta fd4.de ter ↓ thuj ↓
      - **cramping**: alum phos k*
      - **pressing** pain: carb-an h2 carb-v h2 kali-c h2 **Lyc** k* ruta fd4.de ter
      - **stitching** pain: thuj
      - **tearing** pain: thuj
    - **amel.**: kali-n h2
- **burning**: abrot calad dios ferr-i iris ruta fd4.de sang sulph tritic-vg fd5.de verat zinc
- **chill**; during: sulph
- **clawing** pain: petr sul-ac
- **cramping**: agar ang h1 bapt hr1 coloc dulc form k* kola stb3• led merc nat-c k* petr h2 sul-ac h2 thuj k* zinc h2
- **cutting** pain: bar-c indg k* kali-c k* mang nat-m k*
- **eating** fish, on: thuj ↓
  - **burning**: thuj
- **gnawing** pain: nat-m h2 seneg
- **lying** agg.: mag-m ↓
  - **ulcerative** pain: mag-m h2
- **menses**; before: mag-c
- **pressing** pain: alum h2 calc k* calc-sil k2 carb-an k* carb-v chel dig euphr k* kali-bi kali-s fd4.de mez h2 nat-m k* phos k* ruta fd4.de sars sep k* sil k* spong sulph k* tritic-vg fd5.de vanil fd5.de zinc k*
- **singing** agg.: sars
- **sitting** agg.: euphr ↓
  - **stitching** pain: euphr h2
- **sore**: abrot k* alum dig dios k* fago phos sin-a a1 thuj
- **stitching** pain: cocc con dulc fd4.de grat ham fd3.de• nux-v ruta fd4.de sulph h2 vanil fd5.de zinc

- **night**: *Abrot* k* agar alum alum-p k2 alum-sil k2 *Am-c* ambr ↓ anac bro1 *Arg-n* k* ars k* *Ars-s-r* ↓ bapt bar-c ↓ *Bell* borx hr1 but-ac ↓ *Calc* calc-sil k2 camph *Carb-v* *Carbn-s* caust ↓ cham k* cina cocc bro1 *Coloc* com ↓ con galeoc-c-h gms1• *Graph* ham ↓ ign k* kali-ar kali-bi bro1 *Kali-c* kali-s fd4.de kali-sil k2 lach lyc ↓ mag-m ↓ merc-sul nat-m nit-ac nux-v *Orni* c1 ost ↓ ox-ac ↓ paeon ↓ phos plac-s ↓ podo prot jl2 puls rhod rhus-t rob ↓ ruta fd4.de seneg sep sil spong fd4.de *Sulph* symph fd3.de• tarent thuj tritic-vg fd5.de tub ↓ vanil fd5.de ven-m ↓ vip ↓
  - **midnight**: ambr *Chin* lyc
    - **before** | **21** h, until midnight: phos
    - **after**: calad ↓ *Kali-c* ↓ mag-c h2 puls sil ↓ *Sulph*
      - **1** h: mag-m
        - **cutting** pain: mag-m
      - **1-2** h: con ↓
        - **cramping**: con h2
      - **1-3** h:
        - **waking**; on: visc ↓
          - **stitching** pain: visc sp1
      - **2** h: *Ars* kali-bi ↓ *Kali-c* lyc **Med** k* nat-c ↓
        - **cramping**: *Ars* nat-c
        - **cutting** pain: kali-bi vh
        - **pressing** pain: *Kali-c*
      - **3** h: ox-ac vh podo ↓
        - **cramping**: podo
      - **3-5** h: lac-e ↓
        - **burning**: lac-e hm2•
      - **4** h till noon daily: borx ↓

- **night** – **midnight** – **after** – **4** h till noon daily: ...
        - **cramping**: borx
      - **5** h: kali-p ↓ nat-c ↓
        - **gnawing** pain: kali-p nat-c
      - **burning**: sil
      - **cutting** pain: calad k* *Kali-c*
      - **lancinating**: *Kali-c*
      - **pressing** pain: sulph
    - **cramping**: lyc k*
    - **pressing** pain: ambr h1
  - **bed**:
    - **driving** out of bed: calc ↓ lach ↓ lyc ↓
      - **cramping**: calc h2
      - **cutting** pain: lyc
      - **pressing** pain: calc h2 lach
    - **in** bed:
      - **agg.**: cocc mag-c ↓ nat-s ptel
        - **cramping**: ptel
        - **sore**: mag-c k*
  - **burning**: *Abrot* k* *Ars* *Ars-s-r* kali-c h2 kali-s fd4.de* paeon plac-s rly4• podo rob br1 spong fd4.de sulph vip fkr4.de
  - **cramping**: abrot k* but-ac br1 calc k* *Camph* *Carb-v* *Coloc* k* *Graph* kali-c nat-m k* nit-ac k* phos k* ruta fd4.de seneg sil h2 sulph k* tub jl2
  - **cutting** pain: abrot k* bar-c lyc
  - **drawing** pain: sep h2
  - **gnawing** pain: abrot k* ruta h1
  - **lancinating**: ars
  - **lying** on back agg.: lyc
    - **pressing** pain: lyc k*
  - **pressing** pain: *Am-c* k* ambr a1 *Calc* caust h2 *Cina* graph k* ham fd3.de• kali-c k* *Lach* k* nit-ac k* ox-ac phos h2 ruta h1 sep k* sil h2 spong fd4.de *Sulph* tritic-vg fd5.de ven-m rsj12•
  - **sleep** agg.; during: nit-ac
  - **sore**: ost a1 sep spong fd4.de
  - **stitching** pain: abrot hr1 com mag-m h2 spong fd4.de vanil fd5.de
  - **waking**; on: caust hyper podo ↓ sil ↓
    - **amel.**: nit-ac
    - **burning**: hyper podo fd3.de•
    - **cramping**: sil h2

- **accompanied** by:
  - **gout**: colch bro1 urt-u bro1
  - **heartburn**: am-c tl1 ant-c tl1 nux-v tl1
  - **hiccough**: mag-m bg2 *Sil* st1
  - **hunger**: cartl-s rly4• ger-i rly4• hura **Lach** k* lavand-a ctl1• *Lyc* k* meny bg2 nicotam rly4• *Petr* pneu jl2 prot jl2* *Psor* puls sang hr1 *Sil* k* *Stann* bg2 symph fd3.de• *Trios* rsj11• verat bg2
    - **forenoon**: hir rsj4•
      - **11** h: trios rsj11•
  - **liveliness** (See MIND - Vivacious - stomach)
  - **perspiration**: cann-xyz bg2 cham bg2
  - **respiratory** affections (See RESPIRATION - Impeded - accompanied - stomach)
  - **salivation**: gran bg1 lyc hr1
  - **shivering**: caust bg2
  - **sighing** (See MIND - Sighing - pain - stomach)
  - **thirst**: verat bg2
  - **urination**; complaints of (See BLADDER - Urination - complaints - accompanied - stomach)
  - **vertigo** (See VERTIGO - Accompanied - stomach - pain)
  - **voice**; loss of (See LARYNX - Voice - lost - accompanied - stomach)
  - **water** brash: nat-m b4a.de *Sep* b4a.de sil b4a.de

- **weakness** (See GENERALS - Weakness - accompanied - stomach - pain)
- ○ **Abdomen**:
  - **movements** in: kali-n bg2 nat-m bg2
  - **pain** in: cupr bg2
- **Back**; pain in: nit-ac bro1
- **Chest**; pain in (See CHEST - Pain - accompanied - stomach)
- **Face** | **sallow**: nit-ac bro1
- **Fingers**; numb: lyc bg2
- **Head**:
  - **heat**: caust bg2
  - **pain** in (See HEAD - Pain - accompanied - stomach - pain; HEAD - Pain - gastric)
- **Lumbar** region; aching pain in: borx bg2
- **Spine**; pain:
  - **alternating** with | **Throat**; pain in (See BACK - Pain - spine - alternating - throat - accompanied - stomach)
- **Spleen**; congestion of (See ABDOMEN - Congestion - spleen - accompanied - stomach)
- **Tongue** | **clean** tongue: *Mag-p* kr1*
- **Uterus**; complaints of (See FEMALE - Uterus - accompanied - stomach)

- **aching**: aesc bro1 anac bro1 bell-p bg2 gard-j vlr2• *Hydr* bro1 ign bg2 nat-c bg2 nat-f sp1 puls bg2 ruta bro1 [helia stj7]
- **acids**, after: *Ant-c* kreos sulph
- **air**; in open:
  - **agg.**: lyc nux-v ol-an phos
    - **pressing** pain: ol-an
  - **amel.**: hippoc-k szs2 naja
- **alcoholic** drinks agg.: carb-v ↓
  - **burning**: carb-v gm1
- **alcoholics** and gluttons; of: calc ↓ *Carb-v* ↓ lach ↓ **Nux-v** ↓ sulph ↓
  - **cramping**: calc bg2 *Carb-v* bg2 lach bg2 **Nux-v** bg2 sulph bg2
- **alcoholics**; in: *Sul-ac* ↓
  - **burning**: *Sul-ac*
- **alternating** with:
  - ○ **Head**; pain in (See HEAD - Pain - alternating - stomach)
  - **Limbs**; pain in: *Kali-bi* k*
  - **Spine**; pain in (See BACK - Pain - spine - alternating - stomach)
  - **Throat**; pain in: paraf br1
- **anger**; after: **Coloc** *Nux-v* mrr1 staph ulm-c jsj8•
  - **tearing** pain: **Coloc**
- **anxiety**; with: bar-m ↓
  - **pressing** pain: bar-m k2
- **appearing**:
  - **gradually**:
    - **disappearing**; and:
      - **gradually**: *Stann*
      - **suddenly**: *Arg-met*
- **apples** | **agg.** | **sour**: merc-c
  - **amel.**: guaj pd
- **apyrexia**, during: ant-c
- **ascending** stairs agg.: chinin-s ph-ac
  - **cramping**: chinin-s
- **bananas** | **amel.**: galeoc-c-h gms1•
- **bandaging** abdomen amel.: cupr nat-m
  - **pressing** pain: cupr
- **bed**; after going to: dios ↓ laur ↓
  - **cramping**: dios k* laur
- **bedcovers**, from: sulph
- **beer**; after: bamb-a stb2.de• bapt bro1 carb-v ↓ carbn-s *Kali-bi* bro1 lyc k2 *Nux-v*
  - **pressing** pain: carb-v *Nux-v*
- **bending**:
  - **agg.**: carc mlr1• mag-m ↓ [bell-p-sp dcm1]
    - **sore**: mag-m
  - **backward**:
    - **amel.**: *Bell* k* bism bism-sn ↓ caust *Chel* sne *Dios* bro1 kali-c mand sp1 oci-sa sk4•
      - **cramping**: bism-sn mtf11
      - **cutting** pain: *Bell*
      - **pressing** pain: kali-c
    - **must** bend backward: *Bell* ↓
      - **stitching** pain: *Bell*
  - **body**:
    - **right**; to:
      - **agg.**: thuj ↓
        - **tearing** pain: thuj
      - **amel.**: merc-c ↓
        - **tearing** pain: merc-c
  - **forward**:
    - **agg.**: bry ↓ mill ↓ plb ↓ tax ↓
      - **burning**: bry mill c1*
      - **cramping**: [tax jsj7]
      - **gnawing** pain: plb
      - **pressing** pain: bry
    - **amel.**: atro ↓ bamb-a ↓ bell ↓ carb-v ↓ *Chel* ↓ coch ↓ **Coloc** ↓ lac-cp ↓ *Lyc* ↓ verat-v ↓
      - **burning**: lac-cp sk4•
      - **cramping**: (↗*bending double - must - cramping*) atro vh bell k2 carb-v *Chel* coch c1 **Coloc** *Lyc* verat-v k*
      - **pressing** pain: bamb-a stb2.de•
  - **legs** | **agg.**: med k2
  - **must** bend: mag-m h2
  - **right**; to:
    - **agg.**: bry ↓
      - **stitching** pain: bry
- **bending** double:
  - **agg.**: kalm k* lyc
  - **amel.**: alumn antip vh1 bell k2 beryl tpw5 calc-s kr1 carb-v cham *Chel* choc srj3• colch **Coloc** colum-p sze2• lach lyc mang k2 nat-ox rly4• nux-v oci-sa sk4• pin-con oss2• psor ptel *Sil* h2* sol-ni ↓ sulph h2 *Verat-v* [tax jsj7]
    - **cutting** pain: **Coloc** sol-ni
  - **must** bend double: kali-c ↓
    - **cramping**: (↗*bending - forward - amel. - cramping*) kali-c h2
- **biting** pain: am b7.de* hell b7.de* mosch b7a.de stram b7.de* sulph h2
- **blow**; pain as from a: positr nl2•
- **blowing** the nose agg.: **Hep** kali-n
- **blunt** instrument; as from a: lept bg2 mur-ac b4.de*
- **boring** pain: agar bg2 am-c bg2 ars b4.de* carb-an b4.de* kali-bi bg2 kali-n b4.de* nat-s bg2 sep bg2
- **bread**:
  - **agg.**: acon *Ant-c* *Bar-c* **Bry** **Caust** coff ham ↓ kali-c merc *Phos* puls rhus-t ruta sars sep ↓ staph sul-ac zinc zing
    - **burning**: sars
    - **pressing** pain: *Bar-c* *Bry* **Caust** ham fd3.de• *Phos* sep h2 sul-ac k* zinc h2 zing k*
    - **rye** bread: merc-c
      - **cramping**: merc-c
  - **amel.**: nat-c
- **break** inside; as if something would: bism vh
- **breakfast**:
  - **after**:
    - **agg.**: acon-f ↓ agar all-c aloe anac ars bufo ↓ calc-s caps ↓ carbn-s caust crot-h cycl dig ↓ kali-bi kali-c ↓ kali-n ↓ kali-s fd4.de lyc ↓ myric *Nat-c* nat-sil ↓ nux-v ↓ podo ↓ puls sabad ↓ sol-ni ↓ spong fd4.de sulph symph fd3.de• tritic-vg fd5.de verat ↓
      - **burning**: agar caps dig lyc podo sabad sol-ni
      - **cramping**: bufo nat-sil fd3.de• spong fd4.de verat k*

Stomach

- **after** – **agg.**: ...
  - : **cutting** pain: kali-c k* kali-n h2
  - : **pressing** pain: acon-f a1 agar k* aloe anac ars k* carbn-s caust k* cycl k* kali-bi k* myric *Nat-c* nux-v puls sulph tritic-vg fd5.de
  - : **stitching** pain: kali-n h2
  - ⁝ **amel.**: am-m ↓
    - : **gnawing** pain: am-m h2
- **amel.**: *Kali-bi* ↓ *Nat-s* ↓ puls ↓ zinc ↓
  - ⁝ **burning**: *Kali-bi* *Nat-s* zinc
  - ⁝ **clawing** pain: puls
  - ⁝ **cramping**: nat-s k*
- **before** | **agg.**: arg-n bufo *Iris* tritic-vg fd5.de
- **during**: apoc ↓
  - ⁝ **burning**: apoc

- **breath**, taking away: cocc ↓
  - **cramping**: cocc pd
- **breathing**:
  - **agg.**: *Anac* *Ars* bar-c h2 *Bell* ↓ calc ↓ caps coc-c euphr ↓ *Lyc* mang positr nl2• *Puls* rat ↓ spig ↓ *Sulph* ↓
    - ⁝ **cutting** pain: *Bell* rat
    - ⁝ **stitching** pain: **Anac** calc *Caps* euphr h2 lyc h2 spig k* *Sulph*
  - **between** acts of breathing agg.: caps ↓
    - ⁝ **stitching** pain: caps
  - **deep**:
    - ⁝ **after**: nat-m ↓
      - : **pressing** pain: nat-m h2
    - ⁝ **agg.**: bry k2 calad ↓ carb-an ↓ **Caust** kali-n h2 merc h1 zinc ↓
      - : **burning**: calad ptk1
      - : **cramping**: zinc h2
      - : **pressing** pain: carb-an h2
      - : **sore**: *Merc*

- **burning**: *(↗corrosive)* abies-c abies-n bg2 abrot k* acal br1 acet-ac k* acon k* *Aesc* k* aeth agar agar-em bro1 ail k* all-s alum alum-sil k2 alumn am-c k* am-m k* ambr k* anac bg2 ant-c k* ant-t k* *Anthraci* *Apis* k* apoc arg-met k* arg-n k* arn k* **Ars** k* *Ars-h* *Ars-i* ars-s-f k2 asaf k* asc-t aur aur-ar k2 aur-i k2 aur-m aur-s k2 bamb-a stb2.de• bapt bar-c b4.de* bar-m k2 *Bell* k* *Benz-ac* k* *Berb* *Bism* k* bol-la brom k* *Bry* k* bufo cact cadm-br bro1 *Cadm-s* k* *Calad* k* calc k* calc-ar k2 calc-f sp1 calc-i k2 *Calc-p* k* calc-s calc-sil k2 *Camph* k* cann-i cann-s b7a.de **Canth** k* **Caps** k* *Carb-ac* *Carb-an* k* **Carb-v** k* carbn-s *Card-m* cartl-s rly4• casc a1 caul k* caust k* cedr *Cham* k* chel k* chin k* chinin-ar k* chinin-s chlf chr-ac **Cic** k* cimic cob-n sp1 coc-c coca-c sk4• cocc coff **Colch** k* coli rly4• *Coloc* k* colum-p sze2• *Con* k* cop cor-r bg2 *Com* croc k* crot-h *Crot-t* cub cund k* *Cupr* *Cupr-ar* cyt-l bro1* daph bg2* dat-a bro1 *Dig* k* *Dios* k* *Dulc* k* elaps *Erig* *Euph* k* ferr k* ferr-ar ferr-i ferr-p fl-ac k* *Form* k* galla-q-r nl2• gard-j vlr2• gels k* gent-c gink-b sbd1• gran k* *Graph* k* grat guaj guat sp1 gymno ham hell k* hell-o a1* helo-s rwt2• helon *Hep* k* hir rsj4• hura *Hydr* hyos k* *Ign* k* indg iod k* irid-met srj5• *Iris* k* jab *Jatr-c* k* jug-c jug-r *Kali-ar* kali-bi k* kali-br *Kali-c* k* *Kali-i* k* kali-m k2 *Kali-n* k* kali-p kali-s kali-sil k2 kali-sula a1* kola stb3• *Kreos* lac-ac k* *Lac-c* lac-del hrn2• lac-e hrn2• lac-h sk4*• lac-loxod-a hrn2• lach k* lact lap-a br1* *Laur* k* lec *Lept* limest-b es1• *Lob* k* *Lyc* k* mag-c bg2 mag-m b4a.de malar jl2 manc k* mang k* med medul-os-si rly4• melal-alt gya4 *Merc* k* *Merc-c* k* merc-i-f *Mez* k* *Mill* moni rfm1• morg-p pte1*• mosch k* mur-ac k* myric *Nat-ar* nat-c b4.de* *Nat-m* k* nat-p bg2 nat-s k* nicc *Nit-ac* k* *Nux-m* k* *Nux-v* k* nyct c1* oena br1 ol-an olnd b7.de* *Ox-ac* k* paeon par k* petr k* petr-ra shn4• ph-ac k* **Phos** k* phyt plac-s rly4• plat k* plb k* podo c1 polyg-h br1 pot-e rly4• *Ptel* puls k* *Pycnop-sa* mrz1 *Ran-b* k* *Ran-s* k* raph rhus-t k* rob k* rumx ruta k* *Sabad* k* *Sabin* k* sal-fr sle1• *Sang* k* sars k* **Sec** k* seneg k* *Sep* k* *Sil* k* sin-n sol-ni spong fd4.de *Stram* streptoc rly4• *Stry* *Sul-ac* k* sul-i k2 **Sulph** k* syc pte1*• syph jl2 tab *Tarent* k* *Ter* k* tere-la rly4• thiam rly4• thuj thymol sp1 til tril-p br1 tritic-vg fd5.de (non:uran-met vh) *Uran-n* br1* ust valer vanil fd5.de verat k* verat-v visc sp1 *Zinc* k* zinc-p k2 [gal-s stj2 spect dfg1]
  - **accompanied** by:
    - ⁝ **anxiety**: lac-del hrn2•
    - ⁝ **coldness** of stomach: carb-v mtf33
    - ⁝ **eructations**; incomplete: thymol sp1
    - ⁝ **gastritis** (See Inflammation - accompanied - burning)
    - ⁝ **nausea**: hir rsj4•

- **burning**: ...
  - **downward**: nux-v bg1
  - **followed** by | **Pit** of stomach; coldness in: polyg-h br1
  - **paroxysmal**: *Bry* mez h2 *Nat-m* plb
  - **upward**: alum-sil k2 arg-n *Calc* dig hell mang nux-m nux-v ox-ac plac-s rly4• sabad bg1 *Sec* sep sol-ni sulph tril-p verat zinc
- **burnt**; as if: ferr b7a.de
- **burrowing**: am-m b7.de* *Ars* b4a.de chel b7.de* grat bg2 kali-c b4.de* lach bg2 nat-m bg2 nicc bg2 ruta b7.de* *Sil* b4a.de **Stann** b4.de* staph b7.de* stront-c b4.de* sulph bg2
- **bursting** pain: arg-n bg2 bry bg2* kali-c h2
- **cancer** of stomach; in: cund br1
- **cheese**: ptel k* tritic-vg fd5.de
  - **agg.**:
    - ⁝ **spoiled** cheese: *Ars* ↓
      - : **cramping**: *Ars*
- **children**; in: | **school** children; in: *Calc-p* mrr1
- **chill**:
  - **after**: gins ↓
    - ⁝ **drawing** pain: gins k*
  - **before**: aran ↓
    - ⁝ **cutting** pain: aran c1
  - **during**: ant-c bg2 arn bg2 *Ars* k* ars-h ↓ *Bry* k* *Caust* bg2 cham bg2 chin bg2 cina bg2 **Cocc** k* *Eup-per* euph bg2 ferr bg2 ign bg2 ip bg2 lob lyc k* *M-ambo* ↓ merc bg2 merl *Nux-v* k* phos bg2 **Puls** k* rhus-t k* sabad bg2 sang hr1 sep bg2 sil k* sulph k*
    - ⁝ **gnawing** pain: *Ars*
    - ⁝ **pressing** pain: ars ars-h *M-ambo* b7a.de sulph k*
- **chilliness**; during: sang ↓
  - **burning**: sang
- **chilling**: caust ↓
  - **pressing** pain: caust h2
- **circumscribed**: gymno ↓
  - **burning**: gymno
- **clawing** pain: agath-a nl2• ambr b7.de* anan arn k* *Bell* b4a.de calc k* *Carb-an* k* carb-v k* **Caust** k* chin b7.de* *Cocc* k* euph b4.de* *Graph* lyc k* med k2 *Nat-m* nit-ac k* **Nux-v** k* petr k* phos b4.de* puls k* rhod sil *Stann* *Sul-ac* k* sulph k* tab zinc-m
- **clothes**:
  - **agg.**: *Am-c* bell ↓ *Bry* ↓ calc *Coloc* ↓ *Crot-h* ↓ *Hep* ↓ kali-bi **Lach** ↓ lyc nat-m **Nux-v** mrr1 *Ph-ac* ↓ sep spong ↓
    - ⁝ **sore**: bell *Bry* *Calc* *Coloc* *Crot-h* *Hep* **Lach** **Lyc** *Nat-m* **Nux-v** *Ph-ac* spong
  - **tight** clothes agg.: calc ↓ lyc ↓
    - ⁝ **cramping**: calc lyc
- **coffee**:
  - **after**: ambr vh1 canth bro1 **Cham** k* cocc dig ign lyc k2 *Nux-v* k* ox-ac bro1 pin-con oss2• podo fd3.de• vanil fd5.de
  - **agg.**: *Cham* ↓ podo ↓
    - ⁝ **pressing** pain: *Cham* podo fd3.de•
  - **amel.**: brom bg1 coloc bg1 ol-an c1
- **coffee** drinkers, in: *Cham* ↓ *Nux-v* ↓ podo ↓
  - **cramping**: *Cham* *Nux-v* podo fd3.de•
- **coition**; after: graph bg2 *Ph-ac*
  - **pressing** pain: ph-ac
- **cold**:
  - **agg.**: caust ↓
    - ⁝ **pressing** pain: caust h2
  - **air**:
    - ⁝ **blowing** on abdomen: caust
      - : **pressing** pain: caust
    - ⁝ **breathing**: rumx k2
      - : **sore**: rumx k2

- **drinks**:
  - ⁝ **after**:
    - : **agg.**: **Acon** aloe am-br ant-c apoc k2 arg-n **Ars** ars-s-f vh *Ars-s-r*↓ bamb-a stb2.de• bry calad calc k* *Calc-ar Calc-p* calc-sil k2 carb-v bg1 carbn-s *Caust* elaps bg1 ferr *Ferr-ar* form fkr5.de *Graph Iris* kali-ar kali-c lept↓ lyc *Manc* nat-c nit-ac nux-v ol-an orni c1 *Phos* bg1* *Plb*↓ rhod **Rhus-t** sil *Sul-ac* tarent tep tung-met bdx1•
      - . **burning**: *Ars* ars-s-f k2 *Ars-s-r* carb-v k2 lept *Plb Rhus-t*
      - . **cramping**: **Ars** *Calc* ferr *Graph Kali-c Rhus-t*
      - . **cutting** pain: *Calc-p*
  - ⁝ **agg.**: **Phos**↓
    - : **burning**: **Phos** kr1
    - : **overheated**; when: acon **Kali-c** k* nat-c
  - ⁝ **amel.**: alumn apis↓ arg-n bism bro1 *Calc-s Caust* k* **Phos** k* *Puls* pycnop-sa↓ tep
    - : **burning**: alumn c1 apis phos k2 pycnop-sa mrz1
- **food**:
  - ⁝ **after**: **Ars** mrr1 carb-v caust kali-c h2 kreos *Lyc Mang Sul-ac*
    - : **pressing** pain: *Mang*
  - ⁝ **agg.**: kali-c↓
    - : **cramping**: kali-c h2
  - ⁝ **amel.**: *Phos*

- **cold**; after taking a: acon k2 dulc↓ lyc h2 nit-ac↓ phos↓ sep h2
  - **air**; in open: phos↓
    - ⁝ **cutting** pain: phos
  - **burning**: sep h2*
  - **cramping**: dulc nit-ac k* sep h2
  - **stitching** pain: phos k*
- **condiments** | **burning** (See spices - burning)
- **constant**: hydr bg2
- **constipation**; during: bry bro1 graph bro1 nux-v bro1 phys bro1 *Plb* bro1 sacch-a fd2.de•
- **constriction** | **amel.**: bell-p sp1
- **contradiction**, from: carb-v
- **convulsions**:
  - **after**: *Kali-br* hr1
  - **agg.**: agar
- **corrosive**: (↗*burning*) arg-n ars b4.de* calc b4.de* caust b4a.de* *Con* b4a.de cupr b7.de* hep b4a.de iod k* kreos b7a.de *Lyc* b4a.de nux-v k* pycnop-sa mrz1 sabad bg2 **Sep** b4a.de **Thuj** b4a.de
- **cough**:
  - **after**: arund↓
    - ⁝ **burning**: arund c1
  - **before**: ant-t arn bell cham
  - **during**:
    - ⁝ **agg.**: agar↓ agar-em↓ alum↓ am-c ambr↓ apoc *Arn Ars* arum-t↓ arund asc-t bro1 bell k* **Bry** k* cadm-s calc k* calc-sil k2 *Camph* carc tpw2* *Chin* chinin-ar chlor cob↓ cor-r dios↓ *Dros Hell* k* hep↓ hyos *Ip* k* kali-bi k* kreos b7a.de *Lach* lob **Lyc** k* mang nit-ac k* *Nux-v* k* *Phos* k* *Podo*↓ puls k* *Rhus-t* k* rumx k* ruta k* *Sabad* k* *Sep* k* sil k* squil **Stann** sulph bro1 tab hr1 thuj bro1 tub pd verat↓
      - : **burning**: *Ars* b4a.de hep k*
      - : **cutting** pain: verat
      - : **pressing** pain: calc b4a.de* cor-r lyc b4.de* *Phos*
      - : **sore**: agar agar-em a1 alum am-c ambr *Arn Ars* arum-t arund asc-t k* bell **Bry** cob dios **Dros** hell k* hyos ip lach mang **Nux-v** *Phos* sep sil squil **Stann** thuj
      - : **stitching** pain: am-c ars k* *Bry* phos *Podo* sep *Tab* k*
      - : **ulcerative** pain: *Lach*
- **cramping**: (↗*pinching*) *Abies-n* bro1 abrot k* acet-ac bg2 acon k* act-sp k* aesc aesc-g c2 *Aeth* agar k* *Agar-ph* bro1 agn *Alum* alum-p k2 alum-sil k2 alumn am-c k* ambr k* anac k* anan ang c1 *Ant-c* k* ant-t k* apis aran *Arg-n* k* *Arn* k* **Ars** k* ars-i arum-m arum-t asaf k* asar k* asc-t atro bg2 *Aur-m* bamb-a stb2.de• bapt k* *Bar-c* k* bar-i bar-m k* bar-s k2 *Bell* k* **Bism** k* borx botul br1 brom *Bry* k* bufo k* but-ac br1* cact bro1 cadm-met tpw6 *Cadm-s* calad **Calc** k* calc-i k2* *Calc-p* k* calc-s calc-sil k2 camph canni-i cann-s cann-xyz bg2 canth k* *Caps* b7a.de *Carb-an* k* **Carb-v** k* carbn-h **Carbn-s** card-m cartl-s rly4• castm *Caul* k* **Caust** k* cench k2 *Cham* k* **Chel** k* *Chin* k* chinin-ar chinin-s bg2 *Cina*

- **cramping**: ...
coc-c coca-c sk4• cocain bro1 **Cocc** k* coff k* *Colch* coll **Coloc** k* **Con** k* crot-h tl1 crot-t **Cupr** k* cupr-ar cystein-l rly4• daph k* dat-a bro1 dig k* *Dios* k* *Dros* dulc k* eup-pur *Euph* k* falco-pe nl2• *Ferr* k* ferr-ar ferr-i k2 ferr-p fl-ac galecc-c-h gms1• *Gels* gink-b sbd1• gran bro1 **Graph** k* grat k* guaj ham k* hed sp1 hell h1* helo-s rwt2• *Helon* hep bg2 hippoc-k szs2 hydr-ac hydrc *Hyos* k* ign k* ignis-alc es2• ilx-a mtf11 iod k* **Ip** k* *Iris* k* *Jatr-c* k* kali-ar kali-bi k* kali-br *Kali-c* k* *Kali-n* k* kali-p kali-s *Kalm* kola stb3• kreos b7a.de* *Lac-d* lac-h sze9• lac-lup hm2• *Lach* k* lact laur k* lavand-a ctl1• lith-c bg2 *Lob* k* loxo-recl knl4• **Lyc** k* m-ambo b7.de* *Mag-c* k* **Mag-p** k* mang marb-w es1• med k* medul-os-si rly4• melal-alt gya4 meny merc k* merc-c k* merc-i-f mez h2 mill mim-p rsj8• *Moni* rfm1• mur-ac naja *Nat-ar Nat-c* k* nat-f sp1 **Nat-m** k* nat-ox rly4• *Nat-p* nat-s nat-sil fd3.de• nicc nit-ac k* nux-m k* **Nux-v** k* ol-an k* *Op* orot-ac rly4• ox-ac *Par* k* petr k* petr-ra shn4• *Ph-ac Phos* k* physala-p bnm7• phyt k* *Pic-ac* pin-con oss2• plat k* *Plb* k* pneu jl2 **Podo** k* positr nl2• pot-e rly4• psor *Ptel* k* *Puls* k* ran-s *Rat* rhod rhus-t ruta fd4.de sabad b7.de* sacch-a fd2.de• samb xxb1* sang sarr sars k* sec k* sel k* seneg k* *Sep* k* **Sil** k* spong fd4.de **Stann** k* staph k* stront-c bg2 stroph-s sp1 suis-em rly4• *Sul-ac* k* sul-i k2 *Sulph* k* tab tarent ter bg2 teucr k* thal-xyz srj8• thres-a sze7• thuj k* tritic-vg fd5.de tub c1* valer k* **Verat** k* verat-v k* zinc k* zinc-p k2 [bell-p-sp dcm1 heroin sdj2 mag-f stj1]
  - **accompanied** by:
    - ⁝ **indigestion**: mim-p rsj8•
    - ⁝ **uterine** irritation: caul c1
  - **cold**; as from becoming: nit-ac h2 petr h2 sul-ac h2
  - **downward**: sulph h2
  - **intermittent**: kali-c h2 phos h2
  - **paroxysmal**: but-ac sp1 *Carb-v Coloc* k* *Kali-c* h2 nit-ac h2* sil h2
  - **transversely** across: *Arg-met*
  - **worm**; as from a: nat-c h2
- **cramp-like** (See cramping)
- **cutting** pain: *Abrot* k* acon bro1 act-sp bro1 aesc k* aloe k* alum k* alum-p k2 alum-sil k2 alumn am-br k* ambr anac ang b7.de* ant-c k* apis b7a.de *Arg-n* k* *Ars* k* ars-h ars-i ars-s-f k2 asaf b7.de* asar *Atro* bro1 aur k* aur-ar k2 aur-i k2 aur-m k* aur-s k2 bar-c *Bell* k* bism bro1 bol-la bros-gau mrc1 bry k* *Cadm-s* cain calad k* *Calc* k* calc-i k2 *Calc-p* k* calc-s k* calc-sil k2 camph bg2 cann-s k* canth k* carb-v bro1 card-m bro1 caust h2* *Cham* chel k* chim-m hr1 *Chinin-ar* bro1 cimic colch coll k* *Coloc* k* con bro1 crot-t k* cupr k* *Cupr-act* bro1 cupr-ar k* cupr-m bro1 dig k* **Dios** k* ferul a1 gamb glon k* grat helo-s rwt2• *Hydr* k* *Ign* k* iod ip k2 iris bro1 jatr-c *Kali-ar* kali-bi k* *Kali-c* k* kali-chl k* kali-m k2 kali-p kali-s kali-sil k2 laur lepi lil-s a1 *Lyc* mag-m k* *Mag-p* bro1 mang *Merc* musca-d szs1 *Nat-ar Nat-c* k* nicc nit-s-d a1 *Nux-m* nux-v k* *Op* ox-ac bro1 paeon pegan-ha tpi1• petr k* *Phos* k* *Phyt* k* plb k* psor k* ptel puls k* rad-br sze8• raph rat k* rob k* rumx seneg sep k* *Sil* sol-ni spong fd4.de stann k* stront-c k* sul-ac k* sul-i k2 *Sulph* k* sumb k* ter thal bro1 thal-xyz srj8• thres-a sze7• thuj ust k* valer vichy-g a1 zinc zinc-p k2
  - **intermittent**: verb h
  - **paroxysmal**: ant-c *Asaf* kali-c *Phos* sul-ac h2
  - **stool** would come; as if: nat-c h2
- **darting** (See stitching)
- **deathly** feeling:
  - ○ **Sternum**; below: **Cupr**↓
    - ⁝ **cramping**: **Cupr**
- **delivery**; during: borx c1
- **descending**, on: carl↓
  - **stitching** pain: carl
- **descending** stairs agg.: bry bro1
- **diarrhea**:
  - **agg.**: ars h2
  - **suppressed** diarrhea; from: abrot mtf33
- **diet**; indiscretion of: bry mrr1
- **digestion** | **after** | **amel.**: anac tl1 nux-v tl1
  - **during**: kali-i↓
    - ⁝ **burning**: kali-i

Stomach

- **digging** (See gnawing)
- **dinner**:
  - **after**:
    - **agg.**: abrom-a ks5 acon agar alum am-c ang↓ apoc↓ arg-n ars calc↓ **Calc-p** calc-s↓ carbn-s↓ castor-eq chin cinch↓ clem cob coc-c coloc crot-h dig dulc fd4.de elaps graph h2 ham↓ hydr↓ hyper *Kali-bi*↓ kali-br↓ kali-n↓ laur lyc↓ mag-c *Mez* mosch↓ mur-ac↓ myric naja↓ *Nat-c* nat-m↓ *Nux-m* petr phos podo↓ rhod rhus-t↓ sep sil↓ sulph til↓ tritic-vg fd5.de trom verat zinc h2
      - **burning**: lyc podo tritic-vg fd5.de zinc
      - **cramping**: graph h2 ham k* *Nux-m* sil h2 til a1
      - **cutting** pain: ang h1 calc-s k2 hydr k*
      - **drawing** pain: alum k* mur-ac h2 sep k*
      - **gnawing** pain: alum apoc a1 sep h2 *Trom*
      - **pressing** pain: agar am-c k* ars k* carbn-s chin k* cinch a1 *Clem* k* coc-c k* hyper k* kali-br hr1 kali-n h2 mez k* *Nat-c* k* nat-m h2 petr phos rhod rhus-t h1 sulph k* verat k*
      - **sore**: calc-p k* mosch phos
      - **stitching** pain: calc dig dulc fd4.de *Kali-bi* mez k* naja
      - **tearing** pain: ang h1
      - **ulcerative** pain: *Arg-n*
    - **amel.**: kali-c↓
      - **gnawing** pain: kali-c h2
  - **amel.**: aesc↓ caust h2 **Chel** graph mang
    - **burning**: aesc
  - **before**: graph lyc nat-m phos propr sa3• sulph↓
    - **cramping**: sulph k*
    - **gnawing** pain: *Graph* k*
    - **pressing** pain: lyc nat-m k* phos k*
  - **during**:
    - **agg.**: bell↓ corn mag-m↓ thuj tritic-vg fd5.de zinc↓
      - **cramping**: bell h1 thuj zinc h2
      - **sore**: mag-m k*
    - **amel.**: **Anac** vh
- **disappointment**; after: carb-v
- **disposition** to: bell↓ chin↓ **Cupr**↓ stann↓
  - **cramping**: bell chin **Cupr** stann
- **distended** abdomen, with: ant-c tl1 corn br1
- **dragging** down: arg-n bg2 euph bg2 ip bg2 lil-t k2 merc b4.de*
- **drawing** in abdomen, when: zinc↓
  - **pressing** pain: zinc h2
- **drawing** pain: *Abies-n* bro1 acon-f a1 act-sp bro1 agar k* *Agar-ph* bro1 all-c k* *Alum* k* alum-p k2 am-m k* *Anac* apis k* arg-met *Arg-n* k* ars bg2 aur-m k* bapt bro1 bar-c *Bell* bro1 *Bism* bro1 bry bg2 bufo but-ac bro1 cact bro1 calc bro1 calc-i bro1 canth k* *Carb-v* bro1 carc fd2.de• card-m cham k* chel cit-v a1 cocain bro1 *Cocc* bro1 *Coloc* bro1 con k* croc bg2 cupr k* dat-a bro1 dig k* elaps ferr ferul a1 gins k* gran bro1 *Graph* bro1 hell hep ign k* iod k* ip bro1 jatr-c k* kali-c k* kali-i k* lac-loxod-a hrn2• lach lob bro1 lyc k* *Mag-p* bro1 manc mang b4.de* merc k* *Nat-c* k* nit-ac *Nux-v* bro1 petr bro1 ph-ac h2 *Phos* k* plat h2* plb k* ptel bro1 puls k* ran-s rhod ruta fd4.de sem-t sbh sep k* sil h2 *Stram* k* verat verat-v bro1 zinc zing
  - **inward**: dros hell mur-ac h2
  - **lifting**; as from: plat h2
  - **paroxysmal**: aur-m k*
  - **upward**: lac-loxod-a hrn2•
- **drawing** up legs:
  - **amel.**: *Bry* k* chel k* med↓
    - **cramping**: chel med c1
- **drinking**:
  - **after**:
    - **agg.**: acon aloe ant-t↓ *Apis* **Apoc** arn bell canth chel *Chin* *Chinin-s*↓ *Coloc* daph ferr k* hyos↓ iris kali-bi tl1 kali-c kali-s lac-ac *Lac-c* *Lach*↓ *Led*↓ lept↓ *Manc* merc-c nat-c *Nat-m* nit-ac nux-v k* ol-an ph-ac b4a.de plb rhod k* rhus-t sec sil k* sul-ac sulph
      - **burning**: kali-c *Lach* *Led* lept merc-c rhus-t
      - **cramping**: **Apoc** mrr1 bell ferr b7a.de kali-c b4a.de nat-c k* *Nux-v*
      - **pressing** pain: ant-t chel *Chinin-s* hyos ph-ac
- **drinking** – **after** – **agg.**: ...
      - **rapidly**: sil
        - **pressing** pain: sil h2
      - **sore**: nit-ac h2
      - **tearing** pain: nit-ac h2
  - **agg.**: aur-m↓ bell↓ carc↓
    - **drawing** pain: aur-m k* carc fd2.de•
    - **gnawing** pain: bell
  - **amel.**: graph h2
  - **cold** drinks: acet-ac↓ ol-an↓ rhod↓
    - **pressing** pain: acet-ac ol-an rhod
- **drunkards**; in: *Calc* *Carb-v* carbn-s vh graph vh *Lach* *Nux-v* k* sul-ac sulph
- **dull** pain: *Aesc* vh1 fic-m gya1
- **eating**:
  - **after**:
    - **agg.**: *Abies-n* acon k* acon-f↓ aesc *Agar* k* alum alum-p k2 alum-sil↓ *Am-c* k* ambr↓ *Anac* k* ang↓ *Ant-c* ant-t *Apis* **Arg-n** arn **Ars** k* *Ars-i* ars-s-f k2 *Asaf* k* aur-m **Bar-c** k* *Bar-i* bar-m↓ bar-s k2 *Bell* k* berb *Bism* k* borx↓ bov↓ *Bry* k* bufo↓ cact *Calc* k* calc-i k2 **Calc-p** calc-s calc-sil k2 *Canth*↓ *Caps* k* carb-ac carb-an k* *Carb-v* k* carbn-s *Caust* k* *Cham* chel↓ **Chin** k* *Chinin-ar* *Chinin-s* *Cic* k* *Cina* *Cist* *Cob* coc-c *Cocc* k* colch *Coloc* k* con k* *Crot-h*↓ cupr-ar↓ *Cur* cycl daph dig k* dios dulc fd4.de equis-h↓ *Eup-per* euph↓ falco-pe nl2• *Ferr* k* ferr-ar *Ferr-i* ferr-ma ferr-p fic-m gya1 fl-ac fum↓ glon graph k* grat gymno ham helic-p↓ *Hep* k* hippoc-k szs2 hura *Hydr* hyper↓ *Iod* k* iris *Kali-ar* *Kali-bi* k* *Kali-c* k* kali-i↓ kali-n c1 kali-p kali-s kali-sil k2 kreos↓ *Lac-c* lac-cp↓ lac-del↓ lac-lup↓ **Lach** *Led* k* lepi↓ lob **Lyc** k* *Lyss*↓ mag-c k2 mag-m k2 mang marb-w↓ melal-alt gya4 *Merc* k* merc-c mez k* moni↓ morg-g pte1• mosch k* **Nat-ar** *Nat-c* k* *Nat-m* k* nat-p nat-pyru rly4• *Nat-s* nat-sil↓ nit-ac nit-s-d↓ *Nux-m* **Nux-v** k* op↓ orni ktp9 osm ox-ac *Petr* *Ph-ac* k* **Phos** k* phys br1 *Plat* k* *Plb* k* plect↓ positr nl2• *Ptel* **Puls** k* rhod rhus-t k* *Rob* rumx ruta fd4.de *Sang* sanguis-s hrn2• sec↓ **Sep** k* *Sil* k* sinus rly4• spong fd4.de stann b4a.de staph *Stront-c* sul-ac sul-i k2 **Sulph** k* tab *Tarent* ter thiam rly4• thuj til↓ tritic-vg fd5.de tung-met↓ vanil fd5.de verat voes↓ zinc k* zinc-p k2
      - **burning**: arg-n bg1 ars bufo *Calc* calc-s k2 *Caps* k* *Carb-an* *Carb-v* *Daph* dios euph graph k* helic-p mtf kali-ar kali-bi bg1* *Kali-c* k* kali-i kreos lac-cp sk4• lac-del hrn2• *Lach* mez bg1 nit-ac k2 tarent thiam rly4• tung-met bdx1•
      - **clawing** pain: tab
      - **cramping**: bism bry *Calc* k* calc-s k2 chel chin cic *Cina* *Cocc* k* *Coloc* *Crot-h* daph *Ferr* k* ferr-i fum rly4• graph h2 grat ham k* iod *Kali-c* k* lac-lup hrn2• marb-w es1• *Nat-m* **Nux-v** k* phos k* plb positr nl2• puls k* sil b4a.de* spong fd4.de *Sulph* k* tab k*
      - **cutting** pain: ang h1 bry caust chel cic c1 con k* cupr-ar hydr *Kali-c* nit-s-d a1 rhod
      - **drawing** pain: alum b4a.de
      - **first** mouthful: cic↓
        - **aching**: cic c1
      - **gnawing** pain: alum bell h1 calc-s k2 cocc graph h2* *Grat* *Kali-bi*
      - **hours**; some: agar↓ *Nat-m*↓ phos↓ *Plb*↓
        - **burning**: agar *Nat-m* phos *Plb*
      - **little**; eating a: gink-b sbd1• spong fd4.de
      - **one** hour after: *Carb-v* *Mag-m* phos h2 *Puls*
      - **pressing** pain: acon-f a1 agar k* alum h2 alum-sil k2 **Am-c** ambr **Anac** k* ant-t ars ars-s-f k2 *Asaf* bar-c k* bar-m bar-s k2 *Bell* k* berb *Bism* k* borx bov k* *Bry* calc k* calc-s calc-sil k2 *Canth* caps carb-ac carb-an h2* *Carb-v* k* carbn-s *Cham* k* **Chin** k* *Chinin-s* cic *Cina* coc-c k* cocc k* colch k* coloc h2 con k* dig equis-h euph k* *Ferr* k* ferr-ar ferr-i ferr-p fl-ac k* graph h2 grat ham fd3.de• *Hep* k* hura hyper k* iod h kali-ar *Kali-bi* *Kali-c* k* kali-p kali-sil k2 **Lach** k* led *Lob* **Lyc** k* *Lyss* merc k* mez k* moni rfm1• nat-ar k2 *Nat-c* *Nat-m* k* *Nat-p* nat-sil fd3.de• nit-ac k* **Nux-v** k* op k* *Ph-ac* k* **Phos** k* plat plb plect a1 *Ptel* *Puls* rhod *Rhus-t* h1* rumx ruta fd4.de *Sang* sec *Sep* k* *Sil* k* spong fd4.de staph *Stront-c* *Sulph* k* *Tarent* ter thuj k* til k* tritic-vg fd5.de verat k* voes a1 zinc h2
      - **several** hours: eucal br1
      - **soon** after eating: *Abies-n* bro1 arn bro1 ars bro1 calc bro1 *Carb-v* bro1 chin bro1 cocc bro1 *Kali-bi* bro1 *Kali-c* bro1 lach↓ *Lyc* bro1 *Nux-m* bro1 phys bro1 rob k2

- **after – agg.** – **soon** after eating: ...
  - **gnawing** pain: lach ptk1
  - **sore**: bar-c Calc-p k* cocc crot-h k* marb-w es1• nat-m b4a.de* Sang
  - **stitching** pain: calc h2 ham fd3.de• lepi phos
  - **two** or three hours after: aesc bro1 Agar bro1 anac k* bry bro1 calc-hp bro1 Con k* kreos k2 mag-m nat-p nux-v k* ox-ac bro1 phos puls k*
- **amel.**: aesc agar anac k* ang ↓ ap-g vh aur bell-p sp1 Brom k* cadm-met tpw6 Calc-p bro1* cann-i bg1* cham Chel k* chinin-ar Cina con pd dios dulc fd4.de fago galeoc-c-h gms1• gamb Graph k* ham fd3.de• hed ↓ Hep k* hom-xyz br1* hydr-ac bro1 Ign k* Iod k* iris Kali-bi Kalm kreos bro1 Lach k* Lith-c Mag-m mang Med mez Nat-c nat-m bro1 nat-s nicc olib-sac wmh1 ox-ac k* Petr k* Phos pneu jl2 puls bro1 raph k* ruta fd4.de sacch-a fd2.de• sep bro1 symph fd3.de• verat visc ↓
  - **cramping**: Brom Chel Graph k* hed sp1 Ign iod
  - **cutting** pain: ang h1 visc sp1
  - **two** or three hours later: anac tl1 nux-v tl1
- **immediately** after: abies-n vml3•
- **not** amel.: med ↓
  - **cramping**: med jl2
- **agg.**:
  - **little**, after: cham ↓ Chin ↓ Chinin-s ↓ Ferr ↓ Hep ↓ hyper ↓ laur ↓ Lyc ↓
    - **pressing** pain: cham Chin Chinin-s Ferr Hep hyper laur Lyc
- **amel.**: aesc ↓ anac ↓ cadm-met ↓ Chel ↓ chin ↓ dulc ↓ gamb ↓ Graph ↓ hed ↓ Hep ↓ Ign ↓ iod ↓ Kali-bi ↓ kali-c ↓ kali-p ↓ Lach ↓ lec ↓ Lith-c ↓ lyc ↓ Mag-m ↓ Mez ↓ moni ↓ Nat-c ↓ nat-s ↓ nit-ac ↓ nux-v ↓ petr ↓ ptel ↓ pycnop-sa ↓ pyrid ↓ ruta ↓ stront-c ↓ verat ↓ visc ↓
  - **burning**: aesc dulc fd4.de Graph k* Mez nat-s pycnop-sa mrz1 visc sp1
  - **gnawing** pain: anac ptk1 cadm-met tpw6 Chel Graph Hep Ign iod Kali-bi kali-p ptk1 Lach k* Lith-c k* lyc Mag-m k* mez moni rfm1• Nat-c nat-s pyrid rly4•
  - **pressing** pain: anac chin k* dulc fd4.de hed sp1 hep kali-c h2 Nat-c hr1 nit-ac k* petr k* ptel ruta fd4.de stront-c verat
  - **sore**: lec Nat-c hr1 nux-v
  - **ulcerative** pain: gamb moni rfm1•
- **before**:
  - **agg.**: Graph ↓ lyc ↓ Mag-m ↓ nit-ac ↓ ph-ac ↓ rhod ↓ ruta ↓ seneg ↓
    - **cramping**: lyc k*
    - **gnawing** pain: Graph k* Mag-m rhod seneg
    - **pressing** pain: nit-ac h2 ph-ac h2 ruta fd4.de
- **not** amel. by: lavand-a ctl1• petr-ra ↓ prot pte1*
  - **biting** pain: petr-ra shn4•
- **overeating** agg.; after: ant-c ptk1 coff ptk1 ip ptk1 nux-v mrr1 Puls ptk1
- **while**:
  - **agg.**: acon alum-sil k2 ang b7a.de ant-t k* arn Ars aur-m ↓ bar-c b4a.de bry Calc-p carc ↓ cic k* cocc ↓ coff con k* corn crot-c cupr-ar ↓ led lyc b4a.de mang k* merc nat-ox ↓ nit-ac b4a.de op phos plb puls rhod ↓ sep k* thuj verat k* zinc ↓
    - **cramping**: cocc br1 nat-ox rly4•
    - **cutting** pain: cupr-ar k* zinc h2
    - **drawing** pain: aur-m k* carc fd2.de• led merc a1
    - **every** bite: ars ptk1 calc-p ptk1
    - **pressing** pain: acon k* Bry k* coff con led h1 mang rhod sep h2 thuj verat
  - **amel.**: nept-m ↓ pneu jl2
    - **cramping**: nept-m lsd2.fr
  - **beginning** to eat: ang ↓ vero-o ↓
    - **burning**: vero-o rly3•
    - **cutting** pain: ang h1*

- **electric** shocks; as from: (↗Shock) thal-met br1
- **emotions**; after: ozone ↓
  - **pressing** pain: ozone sde2•
- **empty**; when: Anac bro1* cina bro1 hydr-ac bro1 petr bro1*
- **eructations**: lac-del ↓
  - **after**: Calc-p ↓ kali-c ↓ sep ↓ sil ↓ sol-ni ↓
    - **burning**: Calc-p kali-c sep sol-ni
- **erucations – after**: ...
  - **cramping**: sil h2
  - **agg.**: (↗Eructations - accompanied - stomach) ant-c h2 Cham cocc galeoc-c-h gms1• phos sep ↓
    - **sore**: cocc
    - **tearing** pain: phos sep h2
    - **Cardia**: phos ↓
      - **tearing** pain: phos h2
  - **amel.**: aloe alum ↓ alum-sil k2 Ambr ↓ Bar-c Bry Calc Calc-p Carb-v cench ↓ Chel chin chinin-s cimic coloc cycl ↓ dig Dios dulc fd4.de euphr ↓ ferr ↓ galeoc-c-h gms1• gamb ↓ glon Graph helon ↓ hep iod h irid-met srj5• kali-c h2 kali-n ↓ kali-p ↓ lach ↓ limest-b ↓ Lyc mag-c ↓ mag-m ↓ Mang hr1 merl ↓ nat-c ↓ nicc nit-ac h2 ol-an ↓ paeon par phos ↓ pitu-a vml2• plb pycnop-sa ↓ rat ↓ ruta fd4.de sep sul-i k2 sulph ↓ Tarent tritic-vg fd5.de vero-o ↓ zinc ↓
    - **burning**: Ambr carb-v k2 ferr limest-b es1• pycnop-sa mrz1 vero-o rly4*•
    - **cramping**: ambr h1 Bar-c Calc calc-p carb-v k2 cench k2 coloc dulc fd4.de kali-c par rat
    - **cutting** pain: ambr mag-m merl a1 phos vh rat pd
    - **pressing** pain: aloe alum h2 ambr Bar-c bry calc-p Carb-v chel chinin-s cycl euphr gamb Graph helon hep kali-c h2 kali-n kali-p fd1.de• lach mag-c h2 mag-m h2 nat-c h2 nicc ol-an par phos ruta fd4.de sulph tritic-vg fd5.de zinc h2
    - **stitching** pain: phos
  - **before**: staph ↓
    - **pressing** pain: staph h1
  - **burning**: lac-del hrn2•
  - **during**: bry ↓ cocc ↓ rhus-t ↓ sep ↓ staph ↓
    - **stitching** pain: bry k* cocc rhus-t a1 sep staph a1
  - **suppressed**, after: bar-c con
  - **with**: cystein-l ↓ sep ↓
    - **cramping**: cystein-l rly4• sep h2
- **excitement**; after●: Ambr vh1 ant-c mrr1 Cham Coloc kola stb3• mill c1 Nux-v spong fd4.de Staph symph fd3.de• zinc
- **exertion** agg.: ang bry calc bg1 cann-s carl ↓ caust cupr kola stb3•
  - **pressing** pain: carl k* kola stb3•
- **expanding**: calc h2 mang a1
- **expiration**:
  - **agg.**: Aur ↓
    - **pressing** pain: Aur
  - **during**:
    - **agg.**: anac ↓ kali-c ↓ spig ↓
      - **sore**: kali-c h2
      - **stitching** pain: anac h2 spig h1
- **faintness**; with: Ars kr1* Bism cupr bg2 cupr-s kr1 dios kr1 kali-n bg2 laur bg2 Nux-v ran-s sulph kr1
- **false** step; at a: (↗False) aloe bar-c Bry puls rhus-t
  - **stitching** pain: Bry puls
- **farinaceous** food; after: ozone ↓
  - **pressing** pain: ozone sde2•
- **fasting** agg.: Bar-c Calc carb-an ↓ caust Cocc dulc fd4.de fago gran ↓ Graph hura Ign Lach lob nit-ac Petr psor puls k2 rhod seneg sep zinc ↓
  - **burning**: dulc fd4.de graph k* zinc
  - **cramping**: Calc gran k*
  - **pressing** pain: carb-an caust k* nit-ac k* Petr k* sep
- **fat** food:
  - **after**: ars caust Puls tritic-vg fd5.de vanil fd5.de
    - **pressing** pain: Puls vanil fd5.de
  - **amel.**: nit-ac gm1
- **fermentation** amel.: sep ↓
  - **pressing** pain: sep h2
- **fever**; during: (↗FEVER - Pain - from - stomach) acon bg2 am-c bg2 ant-c bg2 Am b7a.de* Ars b4.de* bar-c bg2 bell bg2 Bry bg2 calc bg2 Carb-v bg2 Cham bg2 Chin bg2 Cina bg2 Cocc b7.de* coloc bg2 cupr bg2 Ferr bg2 Ign bg2 Ip b7a.de* kali-c bg2 Lyc b4.de* merc bg2 Nat-m bg2 Nux-v b7.de* ph-ac bg2

Stomach

- **fever**; during: ...
phos bg2 **Puls** b7a.de* *Rhus-t* bg2 sabad b7a.de* **Sep** b4.de* sil b4.de* sul-ac bg2 sulph b4.de* verat bg2 verat-v bg2
  - **pressing** pain: *Am-c* b4.de* ars bg2 bry b7.de carb-v b4.de* *Chin* b7.de* cina b7.de *Ferr* b7.de* nat-m b4a.de nux-v bg2 *Puls* b7a.de sabad bg2 *Sep* b4.de* sil bg2
- **flatulence**; as from: anthraq rly4• ars h2 bros-gau mrc1
- **flatulent** food; after: *Carb-v* dulc fd4.de sil ↓
  - **pressing** pain: sil h2
- **flatus**; passing:
  - **amel.**: agar asar ↓ carb-an h2 carb-v ↓ chel dig dulc fd4.de gels a1 *Hep* kali-c h2 lact *Tarent*
    - **cramping**: carb-v k2 dulc fd4.de
    - **cutting** pain: asar
    - **pressing** pain: carb-v h2 hep h2
- **fluid** is passing through intestines; as if: mill ↓
  - **cramping**: mill ptk1
- **fluids**, after: ars merc
- **fluids**; after loss of: *Carb-v* **Chin**
  - **cramping**: *Chin*
- **followed** by | **nausea**: *Ferr* b7a.de
- **food**: *Arg-n* bro1 bell bro1 *Bry* bro1 ign bro1 kali-bi bro1 morg-p pte1• *Nux-v* bro1
  - **dry** | **agg.**: bry mrr1
  - O **Pylorus**, when food passes: orni c
- **food**, unconnected with taking: dig ↓
  - **neuralgic**: dig br1
- **forced** through; as if something was: bar-c hr1
- **fright**:
  - **after**: *Acon* ↓
    - **burning**: *Acon*
  - **agg.**: carb-v *Ign*
- **fruit** agg.: borx calc-p k2 irid-met srj5• *Lyc*
  - **cramping**: *Lyc*
- **gnawing** pain: abies-c k* abies-n bg2 abrot k* acet-ac k* aesc k* agar k* alum k* alum-p k2 alum-sil k2 am-c **Am-m** k* *Anac* bro1 anan apis k* apoc k* **Arg-met** k* *Arg-n* k* arn *Ars* k* ars-i ars-s-f a1* arum-m bg2 asar bro1 aur-m k* bapt hr1 bar-c k* bar-i bar-s k2 bell b4a.de* bufo bg2 calad k* *Calc* k* calc-ar k2 calc-p k2 calc-s cann-i k* caps carb-an carb-v k* carbn-s *Caust* b4a.de *Chel* k* chin *Cimic* **Cina** k* cocc b7.de* colch coloc tl1* con b4a.de corn a1 *Cupr* k* eup-pur k* galeoc-c-h gms1• *Gamb* k* *Glon* k* graph k* grat k* hep k* ign b7a.de* iod k* *Kali-bi* *Kali-c* k* kali-n k* kali-p k* kalm kola stb3• *Kreos* k* lac-del hm2• lac-h sze9• *Lach* k* lith-c k* *Lyc* k* *Mag-m* *Merc-c* **Mez** b4a.de mill k* nat-ar nat-c nat-ox rly4• nat-p *Nat-s* nicc k* nicotam rly4• *Nit-ac* k* nux-v k* op k* ox-ac k* petr k2 ph-ac h2 phos k* plat b4.de* plb ptel *Puls* k* rhod b4.de* rhus-t k2 *Ruta* k* sabad seneg k* **Sep** k* sil k* spig bg1 **Stann** k* staph succ-ac rly4• sul-ac bg2 sul-i k2 *Sulph* k* thuj b4a.de* (non:uran-met) *Uran-n* bro1 vanil fd5.de verat b7.de* zinc zinc-m a1 zinc-p k2
  - **accompanied** by:
    - **Temples**; complaints of | **left**: lith-c ptk1
  - **paroxysmal**: nat-m h2
  - **worm**; as from a: nat-c h2
- **grief**; from: *Ant-c* vh coloc vh ign vh nat-c vh nux-v vh rob vh staph vh tritic-vg fd5.de
- **grinding** pain: am-m bg2 dios bg2
- **griping** (See cramping)
- **hawking** up mucus:
  - **agg.**: **Caust** k2
  - **amel.**: kali-c ↓
    - **pressing** pain: kali-c h2
- **headache**:
  - **after**: aesc ↓
    - **stitching** pain: aesc vh1
  - **before**: sep ↓
    - **pressing** pain: sep h2
  - **during**: *Sang* ↓
    - **burning**: *Sang*
- **heat**:
  - **after**: grat ↓
    - **pressing** pain: grat k*
  - **during**: abies-n br1 ant-c c1 **Ars** bell **Bry** carb-v *Cham* *Cocc* crot-c sk4• *Eup-per* *Euph* ↓ *Lach* ↓ *Nat-m* **Nux-v** *Puls* *Sep*
    - **burning**: *Ars* k* *Euph* b4a.de *Lach* nux-v k* sep k*
    - **cramping**: bell k* carb-v k* *Cocc* k* nux-v k* puls k*
- **hiccough**, from incomplete: mag-c ↓
  - **cramping**: mag-c h2
- **honey** agg.: nat-c vh **Sulph** vh
- **hot** things (See warm - drinks - agg. - hot; warm - food - agg. - hot)
- **hunger**:
  - **during**: lac-del ↓
    - **burning**: lac-del hm2•
  - **from**: coca-c ↓
    - **cramping**: coca-c sk4•
- **hunger**; during (See accompanied - hunger)
- **hysterical**: asaf bro1 ign bro1 plat bro1
- **ice** cream:
  - **after**: *Arg-n* **Ars** calc-p *Ip* podo fd3.de• rhus-t k2
  - **amel.**: *Phos* k*
- **incarcerated**:
  - **pressing** pain | **flatulence**; as from (See obstructed - pressing - flatulence)
- **increasing** gradually | **ceasing** suddenly: sul-ac k2
- **inflamed**; as if: gard-j vlr2•
- **inspiration**:
  - **agg.**: anac ↓ ars ↓ asar ↓ *Bry* ↓ card-m ↓ *Caust* ↓ chin ↓ coc-c ↓ con ↓ cor-r ↓ dros ↓ ign ↓ kali-c ↓ kali-s ↓ lyc ↓ mag-m ↓ mez ↓ nat-m ↓ nit-s-d ↓ puls ↓ rat ↓ rumx ↓ sep ↓ sulph ↓
    - **burning**: bry kali-s fkr2.de
    - **cramping**: *Caust* dros
    - **cutting** pain: nit-s-d a1 rat k*
    - **pressing** pain: asar con cor-r ign lyc h2 nat-m rumx k2
    - **sore**: ars kali-c
    - **stitching** pain: anac *Bry* k* card-m chin coc-c con mag-m h2 puls sep sulph h2
    - **tearing** pain: mez h2
  - **deep**:
    - **agg.**: **Arg-n** asar bad ↓ bry carb-an *Caust* cor-r dros ign kali-n nat-m op phyt *Puls* zinc
      - **lancinating**: bad
      - **pressing** pain: arg-n a1
- **intermittent** fever: *Aran* ↓
  - **cutting** pain: *Aran*
- **jar** agg.: zinc ↓
  - **stitching** pain: zinc
- **jolting** in a carriage, from: **Bell** lob-s
- **knee** elbow position | **amel.**: con med vh
- **labor**; during: borx c1
- **lactation**; from: *Carb-v* k* chin bro1
- **lancinating**: all-s k* *Ars* aur-s k* bad bol-la cadm-s k* canth k* *Carb-v* *Gins* med k2 nept-m lsd2.fr plac-s rly4• plb k* psil ft1 sinus rly4• sphing a1* suis-pan rly4• tarent thal k* thal-s c1
- **laughing** agg.: lyc bg1 mang hr1
  - **stitching** pain: mang h2
- **lifting**:
  - **after**: *Borx* *Calc* ↓ lyc *Rhus-t*
    - **pressing** pain: *Calc* lyc *Rhus-t*
  - **agg.**: sil ↓
    - **stitching** pain: sil
- **lifting**; as from: plat h2
- **lying**:
  - **abdomen**; on:
    - **agg.**: ambr k*

- **abdomen**; on: ...
  - **amel.**: acet-ac k2 ambr↓ bell gk1 brom dgt *Elaps* m-aust bg1 mag-m gk1
    - **burning**: acet-ac k2*
    - **pressing** pain: ambr h1
- **after**:
  - **agg.**: nux-v↓ sil↓
    - **stitching** pain: nux-v sil
- **agg.**: bell-p bg1 calc-f sp1 *Carb-an Carb-v* k* chel coc-c bg1 cupr↓ lach plac rzf5• puls rhus-t rumx↓ sang hr1 stann sulph tritic-vg↓ vanil fd5.de
  - **cramping**: *Carb-v* chel
  - **cutting** pain: cupr
  - **pressing** pain: carb-an rumx k2 stann h2 sulph tritic-vg fd5.de
- **amel.**: am-c bell *Caust* chin dream-p sdj1• *Graph* kali-i lac-lup hrn2• lach *Lyc* sil spig↓ stann symph fd3.de• tritic-vg fd5.de
  - **cramping**: graph k* *Lyc* sil k*
  - **gnawing** pain: sil k*
  - **stitching** pain: spig k*
- **back**; on:
  - **agg.**: alumn caust↓ *Lyc*
    - **pressing** pain: caust
  - **amel.**: *Calc* chin↓ laur lyc↓ tritic-vg fd5.de
    - **cramping**: laur
    - **pressing** pain: *Calc* chin lyc
- **legs** drawn up; with | **amel.**: carb-ac lac-h sze9• sil h2 tritic-vg fd5.de
- **side**; on:
  - **agg.**: bry carb-ac bg1 chin↓ cupr laur puls bg1 tritic-vg fd5.de
    - **cramping**: laur
    - **pressing** pain: chin tritic-vg fd5.de
    - **stitching** pain: bry
  - **amel.**: *Lyc*
  - **left**:
    - **agg.**: com kali-br plac rzf5• ter↓
      - **pressing** pain: ter
      - **stitching** pain: com
    - **amel.**: *Chel*↓ sang↓
      - **cramping**: *Chel* sang hr1
  - **legs** drawn up; with | **amel.**: *Carb-ac* k13 *Chel*
  - **right**:
    - **agg.**: *Arg-n* merc k2 sang↓ tritic-vg fd5.de
      - **cramping**: sang hr1
    - **amel.**: plac rzf5•

- **lying** down:
  - **agg.**: kali-s↓ puls↓ sang↓ vanil↓
    - **burning**: kali-s fd4.de puls sang bg1* vanil fd5.de
  - **amel.**: coli↓
    - **burning**: coli rly4•
  - **back**; on: lac-del↓
    - **burning**: lac-del hrn2•
- **meat**:
  - **after**: calc ferr *Kali-bi* podo fd3.de• ptel
  - **agg.**: ferr↓
    - **pressing** pain: ferr c1
  - **boiled**, after: *Graph*
- **menses**:
  - **after**:
    - **agg.**: ars b4a.de *Bell* k* borx k* *Ign* b7a.de kali-c k* lach k* nat-p↓ puls bg2 sulph k*
      - **cramping**: *Bell* borx k* kali-c b4.de*
      - **pressing** pain: borx nat-p
  - **before**:
    - **agg.**: am-c bg2 aur-s bamb-a stb2.de• *Bell* k* borx k* *Bry* b7a.de *Calc* b4a.de chin bg2 cupr k* ign bg2 irid-met↓ kali-p bg2 lach k* mag-c k* *Nux-m* k* *Nux-v* b7a.de *Puls* k* sep k* sulph k* tarent vib bg2
      - **cramping**: *Bell* cupr irid-met srj5• lach *Puls Sep* k*
      - **pressing** pain: bamb-a stb2.de• *Nux-m*
- **menses**: ...
  - **during**:
    - **agg.**: am-c k* arg-n bg2* ars k* *Borx* k* bry bg2 calc bg2 caps k* *Carbn-s* cartl-s↓ caul k* *Caust* k* *Cham* chel bg2 cic bg2 *Cocc* k* coloc bg2 croc bg2 *Cupr* k* dios bg2 *Graph* k* hyos bg2 ign bg2* kali-c k* kali-i k* kali-n bg2 kali-p kola stb3• lac-c **Lach** bg2 lyc bg2 mag-br↓ mag-c bg2 mang bg2 mosch bg2 nat-ox↓ nat-p↓ nux-m k* *Nux-v* k* phos k* *Plat*↓ *Puls* k* *Sars* k* sep bg2 streptoc↓ **Sulph** k* tab bg2 tarent↓ thuj k* verat bg2 zinc k* zinc-p k2 [bor-pur stj2]
      - **burning**: tarent
      - **cramping**: ars h2 cartl-s rly4• *Cupr* kali-c kola stb3• nat-ox rly4• phos h2 *Sars* streptoc rly4• [mag-br stj1]
      - **cutting** pain: ars cocc
      - **pressing** pain: am-c k* borx b4a.de *Bry* b7.de* caps k* *Caust Cham* b7a.de *Cocc* b7a.de ign b7a.de nat-p nux-m *Nux-v* b7a.de *Plat* b4a.de puls k* **Sulph** thuj k*
      - **stitching** pain: ars
      - **tearing** pain: graph
    - **beginning** of menses | **agg.**: arg-n br1
  - **instead** of: *Lach*
  - **suppressed**; from: cocc bro1
- **mental** exertion:
  - **after**: anac↓
    - **pressing** pain: anac
  - **agg.**: anac *Arg-n*
- **milk**:
  - **agg.**: alum *Ars Ferr* hyper *Mag-c* **Mag-m** nat-c k* nat-ox rly4• petr samb *Sulph*
    - **pressing** pain: alum *Ferr* hyper k* petr k* samb
  - **amel.**: ars mrr1 asar vh graph k2*
    - **sweet**: ars k* merc bg mez bg3
- **mortification**; from: nux-v
- **motion**:
  - **agg.**: (↗*Motion - agg.*) aloe ang↓ **Bell Bry** k* bufo↓ *Calc* calc-p caps↓ *Caust* cham *Chel Colch* con↓ cycl↓ *Ip* kali-bi kalm mang nat-c nux-v ph-ac ptel↓ *Puls*↓ rhus-t rumx sep↓ spig↓ stann↓ thuj zinc
    - **burning**: *Bry* kali-bi thuj
    - **cramping**: bufo *Ip Nux-v*
    - **cutting** pain: ang h1 bry tl1 ptel tl1
    - **drawing** pain: aloe
    - **pressing** pain: **Bry** *Calc Calc-p* k* caps a1 *Chel* con ph-ac k* ptel rhus-t rumx k2 zinc
    - **sore**: bry k2
    - **stitching** pain: *Bry* k* con *Puls* k* sep h2 spig ptk1
      - **tearing**: cycl h1
    - **tearing** pain: ang h1 kalm
    - **ulcerative** pain: stann h2
  - **amel.**: **Chin** *Cycl* k* dios fago↓ kali-c bg1* nat-c
    - **cramping**: dios
    - **pressing** pain: nat-c
    - **sore**: fago
  - **arms**; of:
    - **agg.**: arg-n bg1 calc-ar↓ nux-v bg1
      - **stitching** pain: calc-ar
- **motion** of fetus agg.: ars↓
  - **burning**: ars
- **nausea**:
  - **before**: tarent↓
    - **cramping**: tarent k*
  - **during**: (↗*Nausea - pain - stomach*) allox tpw3* am-c bg2 ant-t bg2 **Ars** bg2 calad bg2 caps bg2 **Carb-v** bg2 coll tl1 croc bg2 crot-c sk4• *Dig* bg2 dulc fd4.de *Glon* grat bg2 hippoc-k szs2 *Ip* bg2* kali-bi bg2 lac-lup hrn2• mag-m bg2 mang bg2 meph bg2 merc bg2 *Nat-m* bg2 nat-sil fd3.de• **Nux-v** bg2 positr nl2• puls bg2 ruta fd4.de sec bg2 spong fd4.de *Stann* bg2 **Sulph** bg2 tab bg2 tritic-vg fd5.de [tax jsj7]

Stomach

- **neuralgic**: abies-n bro1 acet-ac bro1 aesc bro1 alum bro1 anac bro1 *Arg-n* bro1 *Ars* bro1 *Atro* bro1 *Bell* bro1 *Bism* bro1 *Bry* bro1 *Carb-v* bro1 *Cham* bro1 chel bro1 *Chinin-ar* bro1 cina bro1 *Cocc* bro1 cod bro1 colch bro1 *Coloc* bro1 cund bro1 *Cupr-ar* bro1 dig bro1 *Dios* bro1 ferr bro1 gels bro1 glon bro1 *Graph* bro1 *Hydr-ac* bro1 ign bro1 ip bro1 kali-c bro1 lob bro1 *Mag-p* bro1 mentho bro1 nicc-met bro1 nux-m bro1 *Nux-v* bro1 *Ox-ac* bro1 petr bro1 *Plb* bro1 ptel bro1 puls bro1 quas bro1 rham-cal bro1 ruta bro1 spig bro1 stann bro1 *Stry* bro1 sul-ac bro1 tab bro1 *Verat* bro1 zinc bro1
- **nursing**, from: aeth bro1 carb-v pd
- **nursing** mothers: carb-v ↓
  - **cramping**: carb-v h2
  - **pressing** pain: carb-v h2
- **nuts**; after: **Sil** vh symph fd3.de•
- **obstructed**: nux-m ↓
  - **pressing** pain | **flatulence**; as from: nux-m c1
- **oysters**, after: brom
- **pain** in stomach, during: *Lyc* ↓
  - **gnawing** pain: *Lyc*
- **paroxysmal**: arg-n ars *Bell Carb-v* carl caul k* *Coloc Cupr Guaj Ign* ip mez *Nit-ac Nux-v Phos Pic-ac Plb* ruta
- **pears** agg.: *Borx* k*
  - **pressing** pain: borx
- **pecking**: ars h2 cocc h1
- **periodical**: *Arg-n* ars ↓ bell h1 bism vh calc cupr *Graph* hyos ign *Iod* lyc paeon ↓ phos ↓ rhod ↓ sulph ↓
  - **third** day, every: iod
  - **burning**: graph sulph
  - **cramping**: *Arg-n* ars h2 cupr hyos phos rhod
  - **stitching** pain: paeon
- **perspiration**; during: arn bg2 **Ars** bg2 bry bg2 *Calc* bg2 *Carb-v* bg2 caust bg2 **Cham** bg2 chin bg2 *Cocc* bg2 ferr bg2 *Ip* bg2 lyc bg2 nux-v bg2 *Puls* bg2 **Rhus-t** bg2 sabad bg2 *Sep* bg2 sil bg2 sul-ac bg2 *Sulph* bg2 verat bg2
- **pinching** pain: *(↗cramping)* alum b4.de* am-c b4.de* arg-met b7.de* arn b7.de* asar b7.de* bov b4.de* *Bry* b7.de* calc b4a.de* cann-s b7a.de* canth b7.de* *Carb-v* b4a.de chel b7.de* *Cocc* b7.de* con b4.de* dig b4a.de dulc b4.de* graph b4a.de* hell b7.de* kali-c b4a.de* lac-h sze9• meny b7.de* merc-c bg2 nat-c b4.de* nat-s bg2 nit-ac b4.de* par b7.de* *Phos* b4a.de plat b4a.de* plb b7.de* puls b7a.de* rhus-t b7.de* ruta b7.de* sep b4.de* stann b4.de* stront-c b4.de* sulph b4.de* thuj b4.de*
- **pork**, after: ham ↓
  - **cramping**: ham k*
- **potatoes** agg.: *Alum Coloc*
  - **pressing** pain: alum
- **pregnancy**:
  - **during**: *Con* ↓
    - **agg.**: con dios ip *Petr* bro1* plac rzf5•
    - **cramping**: *Con*
- **pressing** pain: *(↗Hard upon)* *Acon* k* acon-c a1 act-sp *Aesc* k* *Agar* k* alco a1 all-c k* *All-s* aloe *Alum* k* alum-p k2 alum-sil k2 alumn k* *Am-c* k* am-m k* *Ambr* k* *Anac* k* anan ant-c k* *Ant-t* k* apis k* apoc k2 arg-met arg-n k* *Arn* k* **Ars** k* ars-h k* ars-i ars-s-f k2 *Asaf* k* asar k* atro a1 *Aur* k* aur-ar k2 aur-i k2 aur-m aur-m-n aur-s k2 bad bamb-a stb2.de• bapt k* **Bar-c** k* bar-i bar-m k* *Bell* k* bell-p sp1 *Benz-ac* k* berb *Bism* k* borx k* *Bov* k* brom k* *Bry* k* cadm-s bg2 cain calad k* **Calc** k* calc-i k2 *Calc-p* calc-s calc-sil k2 *Camph* k* cann-i k* cann-s k* canth k* caps k* *Carb-an* k* *Carb-v* k* **Carbn-s** carc fd2.de• **Card-m** carl k* *Casc* k* **Caust** k* **Cham** k* *Chel* k* **Chin** k* **Chinin-ar** chinin-s k* chlf a1 chr-ac k* *Cic* k* *Cina* k* clem k* coc-c k* cocc b7.de* coff k* *Colch* k* *Coloc* k* colum-p sze2• *Con* k* cop cor-r crot-h k* crot-t k* cub **Cupr** k* *Cupr-s* cycl b7a.de* cypra-eg sde6.de• cyt-l sp1 daph bg2 *Dig* k* dulc k* elat eucal a1 euph b4.de* euphr k* *Ferr* k* ferr-ar ferr-p *Fl-ac* k* gast a1 *Gent-c* *Gent-l* k* gins k* glon *Graph* k* *Grat* k* guaj h2 guare k* haem ham bg2* hed sp1 hell k* helon k* *Hep* k* hydr-ac k* hyos k* hyper *Ign* k* ina-i mlk9.de ind k* indg a1 *Iod* k* ip k* jab br1 jac-c jatr-c jug-r k* kali-ar k2 kali-bi k* kali-br a1 *Kali-c* k* kali-chl k* kali-i k* kali-m k2 *Kali-n* k* kali-p kali-s kali-sil k2 *Kalm* kola stb3• kreos lac-ac k* lac-del hm2• lacer a1 *Lach* k* *Lact* k* *Laur* k* *Led* k* lina br1 lith-c bg2 lob k* lol a1 **Lyc** k* lyss k* *M-ambo* b7.de* mag-c k* mag-m k* mag-s k* mang k* mang-m a1 *Meny* k* meph bg2* *Merc* k* *Merc-br* a1 merc-c k* merl k* *Mez* k* morph a1 *Mosch* k* mur-ac k* *Myric* k* narz a1 *Nat-ar* *Nat-c* k* **Nat-m** k* *Nat-p* nat-s nat-sil fd3.de• nicc k* *Nit-ac* k* nit-s-d a1 nux-m k* *Nux-v* k* ol-an k*

- **pressing** pain: ...
  olnd b7.de* *Op* k* *Osm* ox-ac k* ozone sde2• paeon par k* *Petr* k* *Ph-ac* k* phel k* **Phos** k* phys k* phyt bg2 *Pic-ac* picro a1 pimp a1 *Plat* k* *Plb* k* plect a1 podo fd3.de• prun *Ptel* k* **Puls** k* ran-b *Ran-s Raph* rheum k* *Rhod* k* *Rhus-t* k* *Rob* ruta b7a.de* sabad b7a.de* sabin k* sacch-a fd2.de• *Samb* k* *Sang* k* *Sarr* k* sars k* *Sec* k* sel b7a.de* *Seneg* k* *Sep* k* **Sil** k* sin-a a1 sol-ni spig k* *Spong* k* *Squil* k* *Stann* k* staph k* stram k* *Stront-c* k* *Sul-ac* k* sul-i k2 *Sulph* k* sumb k* symph fd3.de• tab k* tarent k* ter k* teucr *Thuj* k* til a1 tritic-vg fd5.de *Valer* k* vanil fd5.de ven-m rsj12• *Verat* k* verb k* visc sp1 wies a1 xan zinc k* ziz a1 [heroin sdj2]
  - **accompanied** by:
    - **headache** (See HEAD - Pain - accompanied - stomach - pain - pressing)
    - **heaviness**: gent-l mtf11
    - **sleepiness**: *Ph-ac* b4a.de
    - **taste**; altered: *Lyc* b4a.de
  - **alternating** with | **Head**; pain in (See HEAD - Pain - alternating - stomach - pressing)
  - **band**; as from a: m-ambo b7.de phos bg2
  - **blunt** instrument; as from a: phos b4.de*
  - **crushed**; as if heart were being: ars carb-v cham nux-v
  - **downward**: nat-m h2 plat h2
  - **fist**; as from a: ozone sde2•
  - **flatulence**; as from: mag-m h2 plat h2
  - **hand**; as if pressed by a: arn h1
  - **jerking** pain: dig h2
  - **lifting**; as from: plat h2
  - **lump**; as from a (See Lump; Lump - cold lump)
  - **paroxysmal**: kali-c h2 mez h2 nat-m h2 ph-ac sulph h2
  - **pulsating** pain: caust h2
  - **spot**, food pressing in one: bism pd
  - **stone**, like a (See Stone)
  - **upward**: lac-del hrn2• nat-m bg2
  - **weight**; as from a: abies-n *Acon* arn ars bar-c brom *Bry* cact *Calc* calc-sil k2 *Carb-an Cham* dig h2 elaps fl-ac grat hep kali-bi lob lyc bg1 merc *Nux-v Par Ph-ac* phos h2 *Ptel Puls Rhus-t* sec *Sep* sil *Spig* spong squil staph zinc
- **pressure**:
  - **agg.**: agar alum h2 alum-sil k2 am-c gsy1* ant-c h2 arg-n bro1 arn ars aur ↓ bar-c h2 bism vh borx h2 brom bry cadm-s ↓ *Calc* k* calc-s k2 canth caps carc mlr1• caust ↓ *Chel* chinin-s coch bro1 coloc tl1 dig dulc h1 guaj ign bro1 indg ↓ iod kali-bi kali-c ↓ kali-n h2 led **Lyc** tl1 mag-m mang mang-m ↓ merc-c mez mur-ac a1 nat-m h2 nit-ac *Op* ox-ac *Ph-ac* ↓ phos phys br1 ran-s samb ↓ sep h2 sil h2 sul-ac h2 sulph h2* tarent vip zinc ↓ [tax jsj7]
    - **burning**: kali-c kali-n mez h2 phos zinc
    - **cloths** of: *Am-c* k* *Hep* b4a.de *Lyc* b4a.de *Ph-ac* k*
    - **pressing** pain: agar brom *Calc* caps a1 caust h2 chel dulc h2 indg mang-m mez nit-ac *Ph-ac* ran-s
    - **sore**: cadm-s br1
    - **stitching** pain: aur h2 calc merc-c samb xxb1
    - **tearing** pain: iod
  - **amel.**: alumn *Am-c* ↓ bell-p sp1 bry bro1 carb-an ↓ *Coloc* cupr ↓ dios fl-ac bro1 lac-del ↓ lac-v ↓ mag-p mang nat-m ↓ nat-ox rly4• *Plb* k* podo ↓ puls vh* sol-ni ↓ spig ↓ *Stann* stroph-s ↓ sulph ↓
    - **burning**: lac-del hrn2•
    - **cramping**: *Am-c* k* dios lac-v c1 mag-p k2 stroph-s sp1
    - **cutting** pain: cupr dios sol-ni
    - **hard** pressure amel.: chin gk
    - **pressing** pain: carb-an h2 mang a1 nat-m h2 spig h1 stann h2 sulph h2
    - **stitching** pain: podo
  - **clothes**; of: | **agg.**: dulc fd4.de phos h2
  - **clothes**; of tight:
    - **agg.**: aur ↓
      - **stitching** pain: aur h2
    - **amel.**: cupr ↓ *Nat-m* ↓

- • **clothes**; of tight – **amel.**: ...
  - : **cramping**: cupr k* *Nat-m* k*
- • **spine** agg.; on: *Bell* lach bg1
- • **stomach** agg.; on: cadm-s ↓
  - ⋮ **sore**: cadm-s br1
- **pricking** (See stitching)
- **prickling** pain: *Agath-a* nl2•
- **pulsating** pain: lachn c1
- **radiating**: arg-n bg2* ars bg2 bell bg2 bism bg2 con bg2 dios k* helo bg2 helo-s rwt2• irid-met srj5• *Kali-c* k* *Plb* k* tab bg2 verat bg2 verat-v bg2
- **raising** arm high: anac h2* arg-n
- **raw**; as if: bar-c bg2 calc bg2 camph bg2 carb-v bg2* chin bg2 con bg2 dios bg2 hell bg2 kali-bi bg2 kali-c bg2 lyc bg2 *Nux-v* bg2* puls bg2 ran-b bg2 sulph bg2
- **raw** food | **after**: ruta bg1*
- **reading**:
  - • **agg.**: arg-met ↓ bros-gau ↓
    - ⋮ **burning**: arg-met bros-gau mrc1
  - • **aloud**:
    - ⋮ **agg.**: caust ↓
      - : **pressing** pain: caust
- **recurrent** | **cramping** (See GENERALS - History - stomach - cramping)
- **rich** food **agg.**: ars *Ip* *Ptel* **Puls**
- **riding**:
  - • **agg.**: lyc ↓ puls ↓
    - ⋮ **pressing** pain: lyc k* puls
  - • **air**; in open: rumx ↓
    - ⋮ **cutting** pain: rumx
  - • **amel.**: *Gels* ↓
    - ⋮ **cramping**: *Gels*
  - • **carriage**; in a:
    - ⋮ **after**: phos podo fd3.de•
      - : **drawing** pain: phos
    - ⋮ **agg.**: gels a1 lyc puls
- **rising**:
  - • **after** | **agg.**: caust graph sulph vanil fd5.de zinc
  - • **amel.**: gels kali-s ↓ phys phyt sulph ↓
    - ⋮ **burning**: kali-s fd4.de sulph
  - • **bed**; from:
    - ⋮ **agg.**: caust ↓ *Cina* *Graph* puls ↓ zinc ↓
      - : **clawing** pain: puls
      - : **pressing** pain: caust graph k* zinc
  - • **stooping**; from:
    - ⋮ **agg.**: carb-an ↓ mang ↓ plat ↓
      - : **stitching** pain: carb-an h2 mang h2 plat h2
      - : **tearing** pain: carb-an h2
- **rubbing**:
  - • **amel.**: dulc fd4.de irid-met srj5• *Lyc* k* [nicc stj1]
    - ⋮ **pressing** pain: lyc h2
  - • **back** | **amel.**: **Bism** vh
- **salad**, after: til ↓
  - • **cramping**: til k*
- **sand** passing through; from: thuj bg1
- **sausage**, spoiled: *Ars* ↓
  - • **cramping**: *Ars*
- **scraping** pain: alum bg2 **Ars** k* bell bg2 bry k* bufo bg2 carl k* *Chel* bg1* cic k* croc bg2 crot-t k* hell k* nat-c bg2 nat-m k* *Nux-v* plat k* **Puls** k* ter k*
- **screwing** together: alum b4.de* borx b4a.de kali-c b4.de* sil h2 sulph h2 zinc h2
- **shivering**; during: *Caust* b4a.de *Euph* b4.de*
- **shooting** (See stitching)
- **sickening**: ost bro1
- **singing** agg.: sars ↓
  - • **pressing** pain: sars h2
- **sitting**:
  - • **agg.**: acon *All-c* ↓ alumn ↓ ambr ang ↓ *Ars* asaf borx ↓ bry ↓ calad ↓ calc ↓ caust chin ↓ coll ↓ cyclosp sa3• dig ↓ dios ↓ dros h1 elaps gels a1 hell ↓ hep nat-c nat-s phos puls sang hr1 spig ↓ spong fd4.de sul-ac ↓ sulph
    - ⋮ **burning**: bry k2 calc
    - ⋮ **cramping**: *All-c* ang h1 hell nat-c k*
    - ⋮ **cutting** pain: alumn coll a1 dios k* sul-ac
    - ⋮ **pressing** pain: ambr borx caust chin h1 dig nat-s phos spong fd4.de
    - ⋮ **stitching** pain: calad spig k*
  - • **bent** forward:
    - ⋮ **agg.**: aeth ↓ agn bar-c h2 borx ↓ caps *Kalm* **LYC** k ● sin-n
      - : **cramping**: agn borx h2 caps h1
      - : **gnawing** pain: bar-c h2 caps
      - : **pressing** pain: bar-c h2 borx h2 *Kalm*
      - : **stitching** pain: aeth
    - ⋮ **amel.**: bry *Coloc* kalm vh ox-ac staph sulph
      - : **cramping**: staph
      - : **pressing** pain: bry sulph
  - • **erect**:
    - ⋮ **after**: dig ↓
      - : **pressing** pain: dig k*
    - ⋮ **agg.**: gels nit-ac h2
    - ⋮ **amel.**: dios gels hr1* hell ↓ kalm bg1*
      - : **cramping**: hell
      - : **pressing** pain: *Kalm*
  - • **still**:
    - ⋮ **agg.**: fago ↓
      - : **sore**: fago
- **sitting** up in bed:
  - • **amel.**: coc-c ↓
    - ⋮ **stitching** pain: coc-c k*
- **sleep** | **after**:
  - ⋮ **agg.**: rheum ↓
    - : **pressing** pain: rheum h
    - : **sore**: rheum h
  - • **preventing**: rhus-t ↓
    - ⋮ **pressing** pain: rhus-t h1
- **smarting**: croc b7.de*
- **smoking** amel.: kali-bi ↓
  - • **pressing** pain: kali-bi k*
- **sore** (= bruised, beaten, tenderness): abies-n acet-ac *Acon* aesc *Agar* aids nl2• all-s aloe alum k* alum-p k2 alumn am-br am-c am-m anac ang b7.de* ant-c ant-t *Apis* *Arg-met* b7a.de arg-n **Arn** **Ars** ars-s-f k2 arund asaf k* **Bar-c** k* **Bar-i** bar-m bar-s k2 **Bell** *Bov* brach brom **Bry** k* calad *Calc* calc-i k2 *Calc-p* calc-s calc-sil k2 *Camph* k* cann-s canth *Caps* *Carb-ac* *Carb-an* **Carb-v** k* *Carbn-s* card-m carl *Caust* k* cham *Chel* **Chin** k* *Chinin-ar* *Chinin-s* chlf br1 chlor cina h1 cinnb k* coc-c *Cocc* coff **Colch** k* *Coloc* *Con* k* *Cop* *Crot-c* *Crot-h* *Crot-t* *Cupr* cupr-act daph k* *Dig* k* dios dulc a1 elat *Eup-per* euph k* eupi fago *Ferr* *Ferr-ar* *Ferr-i* *Ferr-p* fl-ac *Gamb* *Glon* grat *Guare* hell b7.de* *Hep* *Hyos* ign ind *Iod* *Ip* **Kali-ar** *Kali-bi* k* **Kali-c** kali-m k2 kali-n *Kali-p* kali-s *Kalm* kreos k* **Lach** **Lyc** k* m-aust b7.de mag-c k* **Mag-m** k* *Manc* mang marb-w es1• *Merc* **Merc-c** merc-sul mosch k* mur-ac myric naja bg2 *Nat-ar* **Nat-c** *Nat-m* k* *Nat-p* *Nat-s* nit-ac k* *Nux-m* **Nux-v** k* ol-an op ox-ac paeon *Petr* *Ph-ac* **Phos** *Phyt* k* plan plb podo ptel *Puls* k* ran-b ran-s b7.de* *Raph* *Ruta* *Sabad* k* sabin b7.de* sal-fr sle1• *Sang* *Sec* *Sep* k* *Sil* *Spig* spong stram stry *Sul-ac* sul-i k2 *Sulph* k* tab tarent ter ther thuj *Verat* *Zinc* k* zinc-p k2 zing
- **soup** agg.: alum ↓ ars dulc fd4.de indg merc-c ↓ stann ↓ zinc ↓
  - • **cramping**: zinc h2
  - • **cutting** pain: indg k*
  - • **pressing** pain: alum h2 ars k* indg k* stann h2
  - • **stitching** pain: merc-c
- **spasmodic**: ant-c b7a.de arn b7.de* ars b4a.de* *Bell* b4a.de *Calc* b4a.de **Carb-an** b4a.de *Carb-v* b4a.de **Caust** b4.de* dulc b4a.de euph b4.de* ign b7.de* iod b4a.de kali-c b4.de* *Kali-n* b4a.de nux-v b7.de* podo bg2 psor bg2 puls b7.de*
- **spices** agg.: guat ↓
  - • **burning**: guat sp1*

Stomach

- **spine**; pressure on (See pressure - agg.)
- **squeezed**; as if: bell$_{b4.de}$* bism$_{b7.de}$* *Calc*$_{b4a.de}$ *Cocc*$_{b7.de}$* dulc$_{b4a.de}$ ferr$_{b7.de}$* kali-n$_{b4a.de}$ lyc$_{h2}$ nux-v$_{b7.de}$* *Puls*$_{b7a.de}$ rob$_{ptk1}$ sabin$_{b7.de}$* sil$_{b4.de}$* *Staph*$_{b7a.de}$ stront-c$_{b4.de}$*
- **standing**:
  - **agg.**: acon agar arg-met ↓ bar-c ↓ beryl$_{tpw5}$ carb-v dig ↓ lac-lup$_{hrn2}$• merc rhod **Sulph**
    - **burning**: arg-met *Sulph*
    - **gnawing** pain: bar-c
    - **pressing** pain: bar-c$_{h2}$ merc
    - **stitching** pain: dig sulph
  - **amel.**: bell$_{bro1}$ dig ↓ dios$_{br1}$* dulc$_{fd4.de}$ kali-s$_{fd4.de}$ kalm$_{bg1}$
    - **pressing** pain: dig
  - **erect**:
    - **amel.**: bry ↓ chinin-s ↓ dulc ↓ phys ↓
      - **cramping**: bry chinin-s dulc$_{fd4.de}$ phys
  - **still** | **amel.**: alumn
- **stepping**:
  - **agg.**: aloe$_{k}$* alumn anac *Bar-c* ↓ **Bell**$_{k}$* bry$_{bro1}$ chel$_{sne}$ hell kali-s mang-m *Puls* ↓ *Sep* zinc ↓
    - **sore**: *Aloe Bar-c Bell* hell$_{k}$* kali-s
    - **stitching** pain: *Bry Puls*$_{k}$* zinc
  - **every** step; at: hell ↓
    - **pressing** pain: hell
  - **hard** | **agg.**: bar-c$_{h2}$ mag-m$_{h2}$
- **stitching** pain: abrot$_{k}$* *Acon* aeth agar$_{k}$* ail$_{k}$* alum$_{k}$* alum-p$_{k2}$ alum-sil$_{k2}$ am-c am-m$_{k}$* ambr$_{k}$* *Anac* anan ant-t$_{k}$* anthraq$_{rly4}$• apis$_{b7a.de}$ arg-n *Arn*$_{k}$* **Ars**$_{k}$* ars-i ars-s-f$_{k2}$ arund asaf$_{k2}$ atro$_{a1}$ aur aur-ar$_{k2}$ aur-i$_{k2}$ aur-m$_{k}$* aur-s$_{k2}$ bar-c$_{k}$* bar-i bar-m bar-s$_{k2}$ *Bell*$_{k}$* *Berb Bism* borx bov *Bry*$_{k}$* bufo-s cain calad calc$_{k}$* calc-ar calc-i$_{k2}$ calc-s calc-sil$_{k2}$ camph cann-i$_{k}$* canth$_{k}$* caps *Carb-an*$_{k}$* *Carb-v* carbn-s card-m *Caust*$_{k}$* *Cham*$_{k}$* *Chel*$_{k}$* chim-m$_{hr1}$ chin$_{k}$* chinin-ar cic cimic cob-n$_{sp1}$ coc-c$_{a1}$ cocc coff$_{k}$* colch coloc com con$_{k}$* croc crot-h crot-t cupr$_{k}$* cur cycl$_{k}$* dig dros dulc eug euon euph *Gamb*$_{k}$* gard-j$_{vlr2}$• gran$_{k}$* graph$_{k}$* grat hydr-ac$_{k}$* hyper *Ign*$_{k}$* iod ip$_{k}$* irid-met$_{srj5}$• jac-c *Kali-ar* kali-bi$_{k}$* *Kali-c*$_{k}$* kali-m$_{k2}$ *Kali-n*$_{k}$* kali-p kali-s kola$_{stb3}$• kreos lac-ac$_{a1}$ lac-h$_{sze9}$• lach lap-a$_{br1}$ laur$_{k}$* lepi lept *Lyc*$_{k}$* m-ambo$_{b7.de}$ *Mag-c*$_{k}$* mag-m$_{k}$* med merc-c$_{k}$* merl$_{a1}$ *Mur-ac* narcot$_{a1}$ *Nat-ar Nat-c*$_{k}$* nat-m$_{k}$* nat-p nat-sil$_{fd3.de}$• nicc *Nit-ac*$_{k}$* *Nux-v*$_{b7.de}$* ol-an *Ph-ac Phos*$_{k}$* phys$_{a1}$ phyt$_{k}$* *Plat*$_{k}$* podo$_{k}$* positr$_{nl2}$• *Psor*$_{k}$* *Puls*$_{k}$* ran-s$_{k}$* raph$_{k}$* rheum rhod$_{k}$* *Rhus-t*$_{k}$* *Rumx* ruta sabin sal-fr$_{sle1}$• samb senec *Sep*$_{k}$* sil$_{k}$* sphing$_{a1}$ spig$_{k}$* spong$_{b7a.de}$* squil$_{h1}$ staph$_{k}$* stram *Stront-c*$_{k}$* stry sul-ac$_{k}$* sul-i$_{k2}$ *Sulph*$_{k}$* symph$_{fd3.de}$• *Tab* thuj tung-met$_{bdx1}$• vanil$_{fd5.de}$ *Zinc*$_{k}$* zinc-p$_{k2}$
  - **downward**: calc nat-m
  - **drawing** pain: mang$_{h2}$
  - **intermittent**: verb$_{h}$
  - **inward**: stram
  - **jerking** pain: chin$_{h1}$
  - **paroxysmal**: arg-met chin$_{k}$* con cop$_{k}$* manc$_{k}$* plb
  - **Transversely**: mag-m$_{h2}$ zinc$_{h2}$
  - **upward**: phys sal-fr$_{sle1}$•
- **stool**:
  - **after**:
    - **agg.**: alum$_{b4a.de}$ calc *Calc-p* ↓ calc-s *Carbn-s* ↓ con crot-t ↓ ferr nat-s ↓ *Pic-ac* ↓ *Puls* samb ↓ sol-ni ↓ sulph
      - **boring** pain: nat-s$_{bg2}$
      - **burning**: *Calc-p Carbn-s* sol-ni
      - **cramping**: ferr
      - **pressing** pain: *Calc* carbn-s crot-t *Pic-ac Puls* samb$_{bg2}$ sulph$_{k}$*
      - **scraping** pain: alum$_{k}$*
      - **stitching** pain: calc
    - **amel.**: alum ↓ carb-an$_{h2}$ *Chel* kali-s$_{fd4.de}$
      - **pressing** pain: alum$_{h2}$
  - **amel.**: crot-h ↓ sulph ↓
    - **burning**: crot-h sulph
  - **before**: aids ↓ alum$_{k}$* ars$_{k}$* calc-s ↓ *Coloc* fl-ac ↓ kali-c ↓ nat-c$_{k}$* nat-ox$_{rly4}$• nat-sil ↓ positr$_{nl2}$• rhus-t
- **stool – before**: ...
    - **burning**: fl-ac
    - **convulsive**: calc-s ↓
      - **cutting** pain: calc-s
    - **cramping**: aids$_{nl2}$• *Coloc* kali-c$_{k}$* nat-sil$_{fd3.de}$• positr$_{nl2}$•
    - **cutting** pain: calc-s
    - **pressing** pain: alum$_{h2}$
  - **causing** urging to: **Nux-v** ↓
    - **cramping**: **Nux-v**
  - **during**:
    - **agg.**: agar$_{b4a.de}$* bell$_{k}$* bry$_{bg2}$ caust$_{bg2}$ con$_{k}$* dios *Ferr*$_{b7.de}$* kali-c$_{k}$* *Lyc* mag-m$_{k}$* *Merc*$_{b4a.de}$ *Nux-v*$_{b7a.de}$ plb$_{b7.de}$* psil$_{ft1}$ puls ran-b rhod$_{k}$* sars
      - **cramping**: bell$_{k}$* *Kali-c*
      - **pressing** pain: sars
  - **urging** to:
    - **during**: nux-v$_{k2}$
    - **with**: petr ↓
      - **cutting** pain: petr$_{h2}$
- **stooping**:
  - **after**:
    - **agg.**: bar-c ↓
      - **tearing** pain: bar-c
  - **agg.**: alum anac ↓ aur-m bar-c dios dros$_{h1}$ glon jatr-c ↓ *Kali-c* kalm meny ↓ nat-c rhod rhus-t ruta$_{fd4.de}$ sep ↓ spong$_{fd4.de}$
    - **cramping**: anac jatr-c nat-c$_{k}$*
    - **cutting** pain: dios$_{k}$*
    - **drawing** pain: aur-m$_{k}$*
    - **pressing** pain: aur-m spong$_{fd4.de}$
    - **sore**: glon meny$_{h1}$
    - **stitching** pain: sep$_{h2}$
  - **amel.**: anac$_{h2}$
- **strain**, from: arn bry rhus-t
- **stretching**:
  - **amel.**: dios mand$_{sp1}$ nat-c
    - **cramping**: nat-c$_{k}$*
- **stretching** out: mang ↓
  - **stitching** pain: mang$_{h2}$
- **sudden**: chinin-s ↓ cic con ↓ *Cupr* dios$_{bg2}$ elaps$_{k}$* kali-p ↓ kali-s$_{fd4.de}$ nit-ac ↓ sul-ac ↓
  - **burning**: nit-ac sul-ac
  - **cutting** pain: chinin-s con$_{a1}$ kali-p$_{fd1.de}$•
  - **gnawing** pain: chinin-s
  - **tearing** pain: cic
- **sugar** agg.: ox-ac
- **supper**:
  - **after**:
    - **agg.**: am-c ↓ asc-t$_{c1}$ bry *Calc Carl* ↓ ham$_{fd3.de}$• lyc nat-c ↓ phos ↓ ptel puls rhod seneg *Sep* zinc ↓
      - **burning**: *Carl*
      - **cramping**: phos$_{h2}$ rhod
      - **pressing** pain: am-c$_{h2}$ *Calc* carl$_{k}$* lyc nat-c$_{h2}$ puls$_{k}$* seneg zinc
    - **amel.**: am-c sep
  - **amel.**: **Sep** ↓
    - **gnawing** pain: **Sep**$_{k}$*
  - **before**: phos ↓
    - **cramping**: phos$_{h2}$
  - **during**: am-c$_{h2}$
- **swallowing**:
  - **agg.**: bar-c$_{k}$* *Calc-p* cor-r nit-ac$_{k}$* sep$_{k}$*
    - **pressing** pain: cor-r
    - **Cardiac** end of stomach; at: alum bry *Nit-ac Phos* sep
  - **food**:
    - **rapidly**: sep ↓
      - **stitching** pain: sep

- **morsel** agg.; after swallowing a: **Bar-c** ↓
  - ⁝ **sore**: **Bar-c**
- **sweets** agg.: guat ↓ ozone ↓ spong ↓ zinc ↓
  - **burning**: guat sp1*
  - **pressing** pain: ozone sde2• spong fd4.de zinc
- **talking** agg.: ars ↓ caps caust ↓ galeoc-c-h gms1• hell kalm mag-m mang hr1 nat-c nat-m ↓ ptel ↓ *Rumx* k*
  - **cramping**: ptel
  - **drawing** pain: kalm
  - **pressing** pain: ars h2 caust
  - **sore**: hell nat-c nat-m rumx k2
  - **stitching** pain: caps
  - **tearing** pain: kalm
- **tea**: abrom-a ks5
  - **agg.**: calad ↓
    - ⁝ **burning**: calad
- **tearing** pain: acon k2 *Aeth* agar aloe alum alumn k* am-c *Anan Ars* k* bar-c chin chinin-ar cic a1 *Cocc Colch* k* *Coloc* con *Cupr Daph* dig dios graph haem a1 iod kali-bi bg2 kalm lyc k* m-ambo b7.de merc merc-c k* nux-v k* petr phos k2 phyt bg2 plac rzf5• plat k* plb rhus-t k* ruta k* sep *Tarent* k* thuj verat *Zinc*
  - **clucking**: lyc h2
  - **intermittent**: lyc h2
  - **paroxysmal**: plb ruta
  - **transverse**: ars h2
- **tenesmus**: lac-h sze9•
  - **accompanied** by | **nausea** (See Nausea - accompanied - tenesmus)
- **throbbing**: arg-n br1 cic br1 ptel c1
- **tightening** clothes amel.: (*↗Clothing - tight clothes - amel.*) fl-ac c1* nat-m hr1*
- **torn** asunder; as if: ars b4.de*
- **torn** loose; as if: alum bg2 ars bg2 calc bg2 petr b4.de* phos b4.de* rhus-t bg2 sep bg2
- **touch**:
  - **agg.**: am-c h2 ant-c c1 apis k2 ars k2 bar-c h2 bell bro1 calc h2* *Caps* ↓ carb-v ↓ chel k2 chin gk cupr ↓ cystein-l rly4• euph h2 hell ↓ hyos h1 ign k* kali-bi bg1 kali-c h2 kali-n h2 lyc h2 mag-c ↓ mang ↓ merc h1 merc-c ↓ **Nat-c** k* nat-m h2 nux-v bro1 *Ox-ac* bro1 petr h2 ph-ac ↓ phos h2* plat ↓ puls k2 ran-b k2 sars ↓ sec a1 sep ↓ *Spig* hr1 sulph h2* thuj h1
    - ⁝ **cramping**: chel h1 merc-c pd
    - ⁝ **pressing** pain: carb-v h2 chel h1 cupr h2 lyc h2 mang h2 ph-ac h2 plat h2 sars h2 sep h2
    - ⁝ **sore**: euph h2 hell h1 mag-c h2 nat-m h2
    - ⁝ **stitching** pain: *Caps* hr1
    - ⁝ **ulcerative** pain: nat-m h2
  - **slightest** touch agg.: ign ↓
    - ⁝ **cramping**: ign c1*
- **turning** | **bed**; in:
  - ⁝ **agg.**: alum bapt
    - ⁝ **sore**: alum
    - ⁝ **ulcerative** pain: alum
  - **body** | **agg.**: anac h2
- **ulcerative** pain: *Acet-ac* k* alum anan *Arg-n* k* *Ars* b4a.de cann-s k* castor-eq gamb hell *Lach Mag-c* k* *Mag-m* k* *Med* mrr1 merc b4.de* merc-c moni rfm1• *Nat-m Puls* b7a.de *Rat Rhus-t* k* spong stann k* verat b7a.de*
  - **pressing** pain: bar-c
- **uncovering**:
  - **agg.**: coc-c ↓
    - ⁝ **stitching** pain: coc-c
  - **must** uncover: mag-m ↓
    - ⁝ **cutting** pain: mag-m h2
- **urination**:
  - **amel.**: carb-an h2 *Phos* ↓
    - ⁝ **cutting** pain: *Phos* vh
  - **during** | **agg.**: *Ip* k* laur k*
- **uterine** complaints; from: borx br1
- **vaccination**; after: **Thuj**
- **veal**; after: kali-n c1
- **vertigo**; during: cic bro1 ptel ↓
  - **cramping**: ptel hr1
- **vexation**:
  - **after**: acon ars cham dulc ↓ ign kali-bi kr1 phos podo fd3.de• **Staph** tritic-vg fd5.de
    - ⁝ **pressing** pain: cham dulc fd4.de ign phos tritic-vg fd5.de
  - **agg.**: lyc ↓
    - ⁝ **stitching** pain: lyc
- **violent**: *Acon* aeth a1 androc srj1• anthraci arg-n *Arn Ars* k* aur k* aur-ar k2 *Bell* **Bism** camph cocc coloc con tl1 *Cupr* k* *Cupr-ar* hell k* hydr-ac hyos *Iod* k* *Ip* k* *Iris* k* kali-s fd4.de kali-sula a1 *Lac-d* lach k* laur br1 **Med** merc k* *Nux-v* k* phos k* *Plb* k* *Podo* ran-b k* ran-s k* rhus-t hr1 sec k* squil h1 stann stram bg2 sul-ac k2 tritic-vg fd5.de *Verat* k*
- **vomiting**: bar-m ↓ jatr-c ↓ sang ↓ sul-ac ↓
  - **after**: gard-j ↓
    - ⁝ **pressing** pain: gard-j vlr2•
  - **agg.**: *Acon* bg2 am-c bg2 ant-t bg2 arg-n bg2 ars h2* asar bg2 bar-m bg2 *Bry* bg2* cadm-s br1 calad bg2 calc bg2 caps bg2 croc bg2 **Cupr** bg2 cystein-l rly4• *Dig* bg2 grat bg2 hyos bg2 **Ip** bg2 kali-bi bg2 kali-c bg2 lach bg2 mag-c bg2 mang bg2 merc bg2 mosch bg2 mur-ac a1 nat-m bg2 **Nux-v** bg2 *Op* bg2 **Phos** bg2 plb bg2 *Puls* bg2 sabin bg2 sec bg2 sep hr1* stann bg2 *Sulph* bg2 ulm-c jsj8• **Verat** bg2
  - **amel.**: ars ↓ hyos bro1 kali-c ↓ lac-h sze9• plb bro1 (non:sep hr1) tarent ↓
    - ⁝ **burning**: ars tarent
    - ⁝ **pressing** pain: kali-c h2
  - **before**: apis ↓ hyos ↓
    - ⁝ **cramping**: apis hyos
  - **burning**: bar-m jatr-c sang k2 sul-ac
  - **during**: podo ↓
    - ⁝ **cramping**: (*↗Vomiting - spasmodic*) podo c1
  - **while**: ampe-qu ↓ ars ↓
    - ⁝ **cutting** pain: ars k*
    - ⁝ **tenesmus**: ampe-qu br1
- **waking** | **after**:
  - ⁝ **agg.**: ham ↓ hyper ↓ lac-loxod-a ↓ pot-e ↓ sabad ↓ sulph ↓
    - ⁝ **burning**: ham fd3.de• hyper lac-loxod-a hrn2• pot-e rly4• sabad sulph
  - **on**: agar aids nl2• alum b4.de* am-c b4.de ambr ant-s-aur ↓ ars b4a.de cadm-met tpw6 calc b4.de* carneg-g rwt1• caust k* con ↓ cycl galeoc-c-h gms1• graph b4.de* hyper kali-c b4.de *Lach* ↓ mag-c b4.de nat-m nat-ox rly4• nicc nit-ac k* phos b4.de phyt plac-s rly4• rumx seneg b4.de* sep b4.de sil k* spong ↓ staph sulph b4.de tritic-vg fd5.de valer b7.de
    - ⁝ **amel.**: nit-ac
    - ⁝ **cramping**: con h2 kali-c h2 nat-ox rly4•
    - ⁝ **gnawing** pain: galeoc-c-h gms1•
    - ⁝ **pressing** pain: agar ambr h1 ant-s-aur caust cycl k* hyper *Lach* nicc k* nit-ac k* phyt k* sil spong fd4.de tritic-vg fd5.de
- **walking**:
  - **agg.**: acon aesc ↓ alumn am-c anac ars bapt hr1 bar-c ↓ **Bell Bry** k* calc carb-v cocc galeoc-c-h gms1• grat ↓ hell hep kali-n kali-s ↓ lac-lup hrn2• mag-m mang ↓ myric nat-c ↓ nux-v *Phos Phyt* puls ↓ rumx k2 sep spig ↓ stront-c ↓ sul-ac ↓ sulph ↓ symph ↓ til ↓ verat
    - ⁝ **burning**: aesc bell sulph
    - ⁝ **cramping**: cocc nat-c h2* til a1 verat
    - ⁝ **cutting** pain: nat-c h2* sul-ac
    - ⁝ **gnawing** pain: bar-c
    - ⁝ **hills**; on: galeoc-c-h gms1•
    - ⁝ **pressing** pain: bar-c h2 bell *Bry* k* mang nat-c k* *Nux-v* stront-c
    - ⁝ **sore**: anac bar-c h2 calc kali-s phos rumx k2 *Sep*
    - ⁝ **stitching** pain: anac bry grat myric puls spig k* symph fd3.de• til
    - ⁝ **tearing** pain: ars
  - **air**; in open:
    - ⁝ **agg.**: anac bell bry calc-sil k2 nit-ac sil

Stomach

- • **air**; in open – **agg.**: ...
  - **20** h: alumn
  - **drawing** pain: anac
  - **pressing** pain: anac bry nit-ac sil
  - **amel.**: ambr
    - **pressing** pain: ambr
- • **amel.**: all-c ambr↓ borx$_{k*}$ bov bry↓ chin$_{gk}$ dios$_{k*}$ dulc↓ elaps fago↓ hell↓ kali-c↓ kali-s↓ lyc nat-c op *Stann*
  - **cramping**: *All-c* dulc$_{fd4.de}$ hell kali-c$_{h2}$ kali-s$_{fd4.de}$ nat-c$_{k*}$
  - **pressing** pain: ambr borx bov bry
  - **sore**: fago
- • **bent** | **amel.**: verat$_{vh}$

- **warm**:
  - • **air** agg.: sec↓
    - **prickling** pain: sec$_{c1}$
  - • **applications**:
    - **agg.**: phos$_{k2*}$
    - **amel.**: bry$_{k2}$ chel irid-met$_{srj5}$• kali-ar$_{k2}$ kola$_{stb3}$• **Mag-p** nux-m *Nux-v*$_{k*}$ *Sil* symph$_{fd3.de}$•
  - • **bathing** | **amel.**: sal-fr$_{sle1}$• tritic-vg$_{fd5.de}$
  - • **bed**:
    - **amel.**: carb-v graph lyc **Nux-v**
      - **cramping**: graph
      - **pressing** pain: graph$_{k*}$
  - • **drinks**:
    - **agg.**: brom$_{k2}$ lach$_{k2}$ nat-ar↓ phos↓
      - **burning**: nat-ar phos$_{k2}$
      - **hot** drinks: brom carc$_{mlr1}$• chel$_{vh}$ *Graph* kali-c
    - **amel.**: alum alum-p$_{k2}$ arg-n$_{hr1}$ *Ars* bry carc$_{mlr1}$• *Graph*$_{k*}$ kali-c$_{bg1}$ lyc$_{k2}$ mang nux-m **Nux-v**$_{k*}$ *Ph-ac* rhus-t *Spong* sulph verat verat-v$_{bro1}$
      - **burning**: *Ars*
      - **hot** drinks: lyc↓
        - **gnawing** pain: lyc$_{pd*}$
  - • **food**:
    - **agg.**: bar-c$_{bro1}$ brom chin *Fl-ac* ign nat-ar↓ **Phos Puls**
      - **burning**: nat-ar phos$_{k2}$
      - **hot** food: chel$_{vh}$
    - **amel.**: chel$_{k2}$ orni$_{c1}$ ph-ac↓
      - **pressing** pain: ph-ac
  - • **milk**:
    - **agg.**: *Ang*↓
      - **cutting** pain: ang
      - **stitching** pain: *Ang*
    - **amel.**: *Chel Graph* lac-h$_{sze9}$•
- **warm** things | **burning** (See warm - drinks - agg. - burning; warm - food - agg. - burning)
- **warmth**:
  - • **amel.**: *Mag-p*↓ *Nux-v*↓
    - **cramping**: *Mag-p Nux-v*
    - **heat** amel.: **Ars** atis$_{zzc1}$• bry$_{k*}$ caust *Cham*$_{bg1*}$ *Chel Lyc* mag-p *Nux-v Sil*
- **water**; desire for:
  - • **sip** water; desire to | **burning** (See Thirst - small)
- **weather** | **warm** | **agg.**: acon$_{k2}$
  - • **wet** | **agg.**: *Kali-c* mang *Sulph*$_{vh}$
- **wine** agg.: bry carb-v↓ lyc↓
  - • **burning**: carb-v$_{gm1}$
  - • **cramping**: lyc
- **worms**; from: *Cina*$_{bro1}$ gran$_{bro1}$
- **wound** inside; as from a: gard-j$_{vlr2}$•
- **yawning**:
  - • **agg.**: **Ars** chel$_{c1}$ phyt↓
    - **cutting** pain: chel$_{c1}$
    - **stitching** pain: phyt
- **yawning**: ...
  - • **amel.**: lyc nat-m

▽ - **extending** to:
- • **left**: ph-ac↓
  - **burning**: ph-ac$_{h2}$
- ○ • **Abdomen**: alum↓ ant-t↓ con↓ *Par*↓ spong↓
  - **burning**: *Par*$_{b7a.de}$
  - **cramping**: con$_{h2}$
  - **sore**: alum$_{h2}$
  - **stitching** pain: ant-t spong$_{fd4.de}$
  - **stretching** agg.: mag-m↓
    - **cutting** pain: mag-m$_{h2}$
  - **tearing** pain: alum$_{h2}$
  - **Over** abdomen: arg-n$_{bg2*}$ **Arn**$_{bg1*}$ borx$_{k2}$ calc caust$_{bg1}$ cocc$_{bg1}$ colch cupr *Mang*$_{hr1}$ nux-v$_{bg1}$ phos$_{h2}$ podo$_{bg2}$ puls ulm-c$_{jsj8}$• [heroin$_{sdj2}$]
  - **Side** of: con↓
    - **left**: colch
    - **tearing** pain: con$_{h2}$
- • **All** directions: arg-n$_{hr1}$
- • **Ankle**: kreos↓
  - **stitching** pain: kreos
- • **Anus**: mill$_{bg2}$ orni$_{bg2}$
- • **Arm**; to right upper: am-m↓
  - **burning**: am-m$_{h2}$
  - **pregnancy** agg.; during: hell↓
    - **burning**: hell$_{pd}$
  - **stitching** pain: am-m$_{h2}$
- • **Arms**: am-m$_{bg2}$ con$_{bg2*}$ indg *Kali-c*$_{bg1*}$ phys$_{bg2}$ plat$_{bg2}$
  - **right**: gels$_{a1}$
- • **Axilla**:
  - **right**: am-m↓
    - **burning**: am-m$_{h2}$
    - **stitching** pain: am-m$_{h2}$
  - **left** axilla and back: kali-c↓
    - **stitching** pain: kali-c
- • **Axillae**: am-m$_{bg2}$
- • **Back**: absin acon$_{bg2}$ agar$_{bg2}$ aloe$_{k*}$ alum$_{bg2}$ am-c$_{h2*}$ anac$_{bg2}$ *Ars*$_{bg2}$ bad$_{kr1*}$ bapt$_{a1}$ bar-c$_{bg2}$ *Bell*$_{bg2}$ bism$_{bg2}$ borx$_{k*}$ calc$_{bg2}$ canth$_{bg2}$ *Carb-v*$_{bg2*}$ carbn-s↓ chel$_{k*}$ *Con*$_{k*}$ cupr$_{bg2*}$ *Cycl*$_{k*}$ dig↓ dulc$_{fd4.de}$ *Ferr* ferr-i↓ grat$_{k2}$ helo$_{bg2}$ helo-s$_{rwt2}$• hep hom-xyz$_{bg2}$ ign$_{k*}$ indg kali-c$_{bg2*}$ laur↓ lept$_{bg2}$ **Lyc**$_{bg2}$ mag-m$_{k*}$ merl$_{bg2}$ mez↓ mosch$_{bg2}$ nat-m$_{k*}$ nicc$_{bg2}$ nux-m$_{bg2}$ *Nux-v*$_{bg2}$ orni$_{c1*}$ ph-ac$_{k*}$ phos$_{k*}$ plat$_{bg2}$ plb$_{bg2}$ puls$_{k*}$ ran-b↓ rob$_{bg2}$ rumx$_{bg2*}$ sabad$_{bg2}$ sabin$_{bg2*}$ *Sep*$_{bg2}$ sul-ac↓ *Sulph*$_{k*}$ tab$_{bg2}$ ter verat$_{bg2}$ verat-v$_{bg2}$
  - **burning**: *Carb-v* dulc$_{fd4.de}$ mez$_{a1}$
  - **cramping**: ferr-i$_{k2}$ nux-v$_{hr}$
  - **cutting** pain: cupr
  - **gnawing** pain: sep$_{h2}$
  - **lancinating**: sabin$_{c1*}$
  - **pressing** pain: mag-m$_{h2*}$ sul-ac sulph
  - **stitching** pain: bar-c **Borx** carbn-s$_{k2}$ **Chel** dig$_{c1}$ kali-c laur *Lyc*$_{b4a.de}$ nicc plb ran-b sabin *Sep*$_{b4a.de}$ sulph$_{b4a.de}$ tab
  - **tearing** pain: sep$_{h2}$
  - **violent**: bad cupr
  - **Around** left side: con↓
    - **stitching** pain: con$_{h2}$
  - **Lumbar** region: am-c$_{bg1}$ *Borx*$_{hr1}$ carb-v$_{bg1}$
  - **Shoulders**; between: **Bell**
  - **Sides** around to; through both: coch↓
    - **cramping**: coch$_{hr1*}$
- • **Bladder** and testes: *Kali-c*
- • **Bowels**; down: arn↓
  - **cramping**: arn$_{pd}$

- **Breasts** | **stitching** pain (See mammae; near - stitching)
- **Chest**: aeth↓ aloe$_{k*}$ alum$_{k*}$ anan↓ arg-met↓ arg-n$_{bg2*}$ aur-m↓ bar-c$_{bg1}$ borx$_{a1}$ *Calc*↓ carb-an↓ cartl-s↓ coloc$_{bg2}$ dulc$_{k*}$ grat$_{k*}$ hyos$_{k*}$ ign$_{bg1}$ *Kali-c*$_{k*}$ lach$_{k*}$ lyc↓ mag-c mag-m$_{bg2}$ mang↓ melal-alt$_{gya4}$ merl mill↓ nat-m$_{k*}$ nux-v$_{bg2}$ ol-an↓ par$_{k*}$ petr$_{bg2*}$ phos$_{k*}$ phys$_{br1}$ plb puls$_{bg2}$ raph rob$_{bg2}$ rumx$_{bg2*}$ sep$_{bg2*}$ spong$_{fd4.de}$ staph↓ streptoc↓ [heroin$_{sdj2}$]
  - **burning**: aeth arg-met cartl-s$_{rly4}$• dulc$_{fd4.de}$ mang$_{k*}$ mill ol-an *Phos* streptoc$_{rly4}$•
  - **cough** agg.; during: raph rhus-t$_{bg1}$
  - **cramping**: kali-c$_{h2}$ lyc$_{h2*}$ phos$_{h2}$
  - **cutting** pain: coloc sep
  - **dinner**; after: nat-m
  - **drawing** pain: aur-m *Phos*
  - **pressing** pain: alum$_{h2}$ dulc$_{a1}$ kali-c$_{h2}$ mag-c$_{h2}$ mag-m$_{h2*}$ nat-m$_{h2}$ spong$_{fd4.de}$ staph$_{h1}$
  - **stitching** pain: alum$_{h2}$ anan *Calc* carb-an$_{h2}$ *Lach*$_{k*}$ mag-c$_{h2}$ nat-m *Rumx*$_{k*}$ sep staph$_{h1}$
  - **tearing** pain: carb-an$_{h2}$
- **Clavicle**; left: agar
  - **drawing** pain: agar
- **Digestive** tract; whole the: *Rob*↓
  - **burning**: *Rob*$_{mrr1}$
- **Downward**: aesc$_{vh1}$ brom$_{bg2}$ calc$_{bg2}$ colch$_{bg2}$ cupr$_{bg2}$ jatr-c$_{bg2}$ nat-m$_{bg2}$ phos$_{bg2*}$ plb$_{bg2}$ puls$_{bg2}$ ruta$_{fd4.de}$ sec↓ *Sep*$_{k*}$ zinc-s$_{bg1}$
  - **burning**: sec$_{a1}$
  - **Upward**; and: cupr$_{bg2}$ phos$_{bg2}$
- **Ear**: mang↓
  - **stitching** pain: mang$_{h2}$
- **Ears**; behind: ozone↓
  - **pressing** pain: ozone$_{sde2}$•
- **Esophagus**: *Aeth*$_{k*}$ bit-ar↓ brom bros-gau↓ cadm-s↓ cimic$_{tl1}$ dig↓ hell↓ hell-o↓ ox-ac↓ plac-s↓ sabad↓ sang↓ tril-p↓ tritic-vg$_{fd5.de}$ zinc↓
  - **burning**: bit-ar$_{wht1}$• bros-gau$_{mrc1}$ cadm-s$_{k2}$ dig$_{k*}$ hell hell-o$_{a1*}$ ox-ac plac-s$_{rly4}$• sabad$_{bg1}$ sang$_{hr1}$ tril-p$_{br1}$ tritic-vg$_{fd5.de}$ zinc
  - **tearing** pain: *Aeth*
- **Flank** | **stitching** pain (See sides - flank - stitching)
- **Groins**: **Plb**
- **Head**: carb-v$_{k*}$ con$_{k*}$ ozone↓ plb$_{bg1}$ tritic-vg$_{fd5.de}$
  - **pressing** pain: ozone$_{sde2}$•
- **Heart**: *Arg-n*$_{vh}$ lach orni$_{c1}$ sol-ni stry
- **Hip** joint: sil↓
  - **stitching** pain: sil
- **Hypochondria**: *Aesc* nat-c$_{a1}$ phos ruta$_{fd4.de}$ spong$_{fd4.de}$ verat
- **Hypogastrium**: ars↓
  - **cramping**: ars$_{h2}$
  - **cutting** pain: ars$_{h2}$
  - **stitching** pain: ars$_{h2}$
- **Kidneys**: grat$_{k2}$
- **Larynx**: kali-c↓
  - **burning**: kali-c
- **Limbs**: dios$_{bg2}$ **Plb**
- **Liver**: arg-n$_{vh}$ asaf$_{bg1}$ hyper$_{bg1}$ mill$_{bg1}$ nat-m$_{bg1}$ rhus-t$_{bg1}$
  - **right** lower lobe: aesc$_{bg2*}$
- **Lumbar** region: am-c$_{bg2}$ borx$_{bg2}$ carb-v$_{bg2}$ nat-c↓ ph-ac↓ sars↓
  - **cramping**: nat-c$_{h2}$ sars$_{h2}$
  - **cutting** pain: nat-c$_{h2}$
  - **drawing** pain: ph-ac
- **Lungs** | **right** lung; base of: guat$_{sp1}$
- **Mammae**: lach$_{bg2}$ puls$_{bg2}$
- **Mammae**; near: lach↓
  - **stitching** pain: lach$_{k*}$
- **Mouth**: *Acon*↓ cadm-s↓ *Caps*↓ cupr-ar↓ *Gels*↓ kali-bi↓ kali-c↓
  - **burning**: *Acon* cadm-s$_{k2}$ *Caps*$_{h1}$ cupr-ar *Gels* kali-bi kali-c
- **Mouth**: ...
  - **sore**: kali-bi
- **Navel** (See umbilicus) nat-c↓ phos↓
  - **cutting** pain: nat-c$_{h2*}$ phos
- **Neck**: arn↓ mag-m↓
  - **pressing** pain: arn mag-m$_{h2}$
- **Nipple**: am-c$_{bg1}$
- **Palate**: mang↓
  - **burning**: mang$_{h2}$
  - **sore**: mang$_{h2}$
- **Pharynx**: alum↓
  - **drawing** pain: alum
- **Ribs**; around: hom-xyz$_{bg2}$
- **Sacrum**: anac↓
  - **stitching** pain: anac$_{h2}$
- **Scapula**:
  - **right**: bad$_{c1}$
  - **left**: *Arg-n*$_{k*}$
- **Shoulders**: cot$_{c1}$ kali-bi$_{bg1}$ kali-c$_{bg1}$ nicc$_{bro1}$ orni$_{c1}$ phos$_{bg1}$ sang$_{pd}$
  - **left**: sol-ni
- **Shoulders**; between: *Nux-v*↓
  - **cramping**: nux-v$_{a}$
  - **pressing** pain: *Nux-v*$_{b7a.de}$
- **Side**:
  - **left**: nat-c↓
    - **cramping**: nat-c$_{h2}$
    - **cutting** pain: nat-c$_{h2}$
- **Sides**: dig↓
  - **stitching** pain: dig$_{c1}$
  - **Flank**: sulph↓
    - **stitching** pain: sulph$_{h2}$
- **Sides**; around: arg-n$_{bg2}$
  - **Back**; then to: colch$_{bro1}$
- **Spine**: bism-sn↓ sep↓ tab↓
  - **cramping**: bism-sn$_{mtf11}$
  - **cutting** pain: sep
  - **stitching** pain: tab
- **Spleen**: borx$_{k2}$
- **Sternum**: aur-m↓ chin↓ nat-m rheum rumx↓ verat↓
  - **drawing** pain: aur-m
  - **pressing** pain: rheum$_{h}$ rumx$_{k2}$ verat
  - **stitching** pain: chin nat-m
- **Throat**: acon↓ aloe alum am-m↓ anac↓ ars↓ berb↓ bov↓ cadm-s↓ calc↓ caps↓ *Carb-v*↓ caust↓ chion$_{bg1}$ cic↓ coc-c$_{bg2}$ con croc↓ cupr↓ cupr-act dig↓ dios↓ grat hell↓ hep↓ *Iris*↓ kali-bi↓ *Kali-c*↓ *Lac-ac*↓ *Lyc*↓ mag-m$_{k*}$ mang↓ nat-m nat-ox↓ nux-v↓ ox-ac↓ phos↓ sabad↓ sang↓ sep↓ sulph↓ tep↓ tub↓
  - **burning**: acon$_{bg2}$ alum$_{bg2}$ am-m$_{k*}$ anac$_{k*}$ ars$_{k*}$ berb$_{k*}$ bov$_{b4.de*}$ cadm-s$_{k2}$ calc$_{b4.de*}$ caps$_{bg2}$ *Carb-v*$_{k*}$ caust$_{bg2}$ cic$_{b7.de*}$ croc$_{b7.de*}$ cupr$_{k*}$ dig$_{bg2}$ dios$_{bg2}$ hell$_{b7.de*}$ hep$_{k*}$ *Iris*$_{bg2}$ kali-bi$_{k*}$ *Kali-c*$_{k*}$ *Lac-ac*$_{k*}$ *Lyc*$_{k*}$ *Nat-m* nat-ox$_{rly4}$• nux-v$_{b7.de*}$ ox-ac$_{bg2}$ phos$_{k*}$ sabad$_{bg2}$ sang$_{k*}$ sep$_{b4.de*}$ tep
  - **cramping**: kali-c sulph$_{h2}$
  - **drawing** pain: con
  - **eating**; after: *Calc*↓ *Kali-c*↓
    - **burning**: *Calc* *Kali-c*
  - **pressing** pain: con$_{h2}$ mag-m$_{h2*}$ tub$_{c1}$
  - **sore**: mang$_{h2}$
  - **Pit** of: sabad↓ sinus↓
    - **burning**: sabad$_{bg1}$ sinus$_{rly4}$•
- **Throat**-pit:
  - **cough**; with: *Caps*↓
    - **drawing** pain: *Caps*$_{hr1}$
- **Transversely**: arn **Chel** *Cina* ip

- **Umbilicus**: brom *Cina* hr1 dulc fd4.de jatr-c bg2 kola stb3• lach bg2* lyc bg1 nit-ac bg1 puls bg2*
- **Upward**: ferr bg1 phos bg1 tritic-vg fd5.de

O - **Abdomen**; in: zinc ↓
- **stitching** pain | **drawing** pain: zinc h2

- **Below** the stomach: euphr ↓
- **stitching** pain: euphr h2

- **Cardia**: ars ↓ *Ign* ↓ lyc ↓ phos ↓ zinc ↓
- **pressing** pain: ars b4.de* *Ign* b7a.de lyc h2 phos b4.de* zinc b4.de*

- **Cardiac** opening: *Agar* bro1 *Arg-n* bro1 asaf bro1 bapt hr1 *Bar-c* b4a.de* bism bro1 bufo ↓ cann-i c1* *Carb-v* bro1 caul bro1 *Cupr* bro1 *Ferr-cy* bro1 ferr-t bro1 form bro1 ign bro1 kali-n c1 mag-m hr1* *Merc-c* b4a.de nat-m bro1 *Nit-ac* b4a.de* *Nux-v* bro1 *Onis* bro1 ran-b ↓ ran-s ↓ ruta fd4.de *Sep* b4a.de stront-c bro1 thea bro1
- **burning**: *Nux-v* b7.de* ran-b b7.de* ran-s b7.de*
- **contracting** | **acute**: *Nux-v* bg2 ran-b bg2
- **eating**; while: bar-c b4a.de nit-ac b4a.de sep b4a.de
- **forced** through; as if something was: bufo bg2*
- **swallowing** agg.: nit-ac h2 sep h2

- **Cardiac** region: bapt hr1
- **stitching** pain: bapt a1

- **Epigastrium**: *Abies-c* bro1 *Abies-n* bro1 abrom-a ks5 *Acon* b7.de* act-sp bro1 aesc bro1 agar ↓ agn ↓ aids ↓ aloe bg2* *Alum* b4a.de am-c ↓ am-m bro1 ambr bg2 aml-ns ↓ anac bro1 androc bnm2• ang ↓ ant-c ↓ *Ant-t* ↓ antip vh1 *Apis* ↓ arg-met ↓ *Arg-n* bro1 arn bro1 *Ars* b4a.de* asaf ↓ asar ↓ *Aur* b4.de* bar-c b4.de* bar-m bro1 bell b4.de* bell-p ↓ berb ↓ bism bro1 borx ↓ bov ↓ *Bry* bro1 cadm-met ↓ calad b7.de* calc bro1 calc-i bro1 camph b7.de* cann-s ↓ canth ↓ *Caps* ↓ carb-ac bro1 carb-an ↓ carb-v b4.de* cassia-s ccrh1• *Caust* ↓ **Cham** ↓ chel ↓ *Chin* ↓ chinin-ar ↓ cic ↓ cina b7.de* coca ↓ *Cocc* b7a.de coff ↓ *Colch* ↓ coloc bro1 con ↓ croc ↓ crot-c ↓ *Cupr* b7.de* cycl ↓ *Dig* ↓ *Dios* bro1 dros ↓ *Dulc* ↓ dys fmm1• euph ↓ euphr ↓ ferr b7.de* gels ↓ glon ↓ graph bro1 grat ↓ guaj ↓ hell b7.de* hell-o ↓ helo-s ↓ hep b4a.de hir rsj4• *Hydr* bro1 *Hyos* b7.de* *Ign* ↓ iod b4.de* ip b7.de* jatr-c bro1 *Kali-ar* ↓ kali-bi bg2* kali-c bro1 *Kali-n* b4.de* kalm bro1 kreos ↓ lach b7.de* lat-m bnm6• laur ↓ led ↓ lob bro1 loxo-lae bnm12• lyc bro1 lycps-v ↓ m-arct ↓ m-aust ↓ mag-c ↓ mang ↓ med ↓ *Merc* b4a.de merc-c bg2 mez ↓ mim-p skp7• morg-g fmm1• morg-p pte1*• mosch b7.de* mur-ac ↓ *Nat-c* b4.de* *Nat-m* b4.de* **Nit-ac** ↓ nux-m ↓ *Nux-v* b7.de* op ↓ ox-ac bro1 paraf bro1 petr ↓ petr-ra ↓ ph-ac b4a.de *Phos* b4.de* phyt ↓ pitu-gl skp7• plat ↓ plb b7.de* prun ↓ psor ↓ *Puls* b7.de* ran-b ↓ ran-s ↓ rheum ↓ rhod ↓ **Rhus-t** ↓ ruta ↓ sabad ↓ sabin ↓ samb ↓ sang bro1 sars ↓ *Sec* b7.de* sel ↓ seneg ↓ *Sep* b4.de* **Sil** b4.de* *Spig* ↓ spong ↓ squil ↓ *Stann* ↓ *Staph* ↓ stram ↓ streptoc ↓ stront-c ↓ sul-ac ↓ sulph b4.de* syc bka1*• tab ↓ tarax ↓ ter ↓ teucr ↓ *Thuj* b4.de* tritic-vg fd5.de vac jl2 valer ↓ *Verat* b7.de* verb ↓ vip ↓ zinc b4.de* [helia stj7]
- **daytime**: cassia-s ccrh1•
- **morning**:
  - **waking**; on: cadm-met ↓
    - **gnawing** pain: cadm-met sp1
- **evening**: cassia-s ↓
  - **cutting** pain: cassia-s ccrh1•
- **night**: dys fmm1•
  - **amel.**: cassia-s ccrh1•
- **accompanied** by:
  - **indigestion**: luf-op rsj5•
  - **mental** symptoms (See MIND - Mental symptoms - accompanied - epigastrium)
  - **respiration**; complaints of: arn bg2 bry bg2 calad bg2 camph bg2 cann-xyz bg2 chin bg2 cic bg2 cina bg2 cocc bg2 ferr bg2 hell bg2 hyos bg2 ign bg2 mosch bg2 nux-m bg2 **Nux-v** bg2 olnd bg2 puls bg2 *Rhus-t* bg2 ruta bg2 sabad bg2 samb bg2 spig bg2 *Stram* bg2
  - **smallpox** (See SKIN - Eruptions - smallpox - accompanied - epigastrium)
  - **vertigo** (See VERTIGO - Accompanied - epigastrium)
- **aching**: ars ptk1 bell-p bg2 graph bg2 kali-bi bg2 nux-v ptk1 sil ptk1 verat ptk1 vip ptk1
- **appearing** suddenly: cassia-s ↓
  - **cramping**: cassia-s ccrh1•

- **Epigastrium** – **appearing** suddenly: ...
  - **disappearing** suddenly; and: cassia-s ↓
    - **cramping**: cassia-s ccrh1•
- **bending** double:
  - **amel.**: sel ↓
    - **cutting** pain: sel rsj9•
- **biting** pain: hell b7.de* mosch b7.de*
- **blow**; as from a: cic b7.de* cocc b7.de* con bg2 crot-c bg2 hell b7.de* ip bg2 kali-c bg2 nat-c b4a.de nat-m bg2 nux-v b7a.de* plat b4.de* puls bg2 tab bg2 teucr b7.de*
- **boring** pain: agar bg2 caps b7.de* nat-m bg2 plb b7.de* thuj bg2
- **breathing** deep agg.: sel ↓
  - **cutting** pain: sel rsj9•
- **burning**: acon b7a.de* am-m b7.de* ambr b7.de* ant-c b7.de* *Apis* b7a.de arg-met b7.de* **Ars** b4.de* bell b4a.de* bov b4.de *Bry* b7.de* calc b4a.de* caps b7.de* carb-v b4.de* cassia-s ccrh1• *Cham* b7.de* cocc bg2 colch b7.de dig b4a.de* *Dulc* bg2 euph b4.de* ferr b7a.de* hell-o a1* iod b4.de *Lach* b7a.de* laur b7.de* mag-c b4.de mang b4.de med bg2* merc b4.de* merc-c b4a.de mez b4.de* mosch b7.de* mur-ac b4.de nat-c b4.de nat-m b4.de* **Nux-v** b7.de* petr-ra shn4• *Phos* b4.de* plat b4a.de* ran-b b7.de* ran-s b7a.de* sec b7.de* **Sep** b4.de* **Sil** b4.de* sulph b4a.de* ter ptk1 thuj b4.de* tritic-vg fd5.de verat b7.de* zinc b4.de
  - **accompanied** by | **vertigo** (See VERTIGO - Accompanied - epigastrium - burning)
  - **coal**; as from hot: verat ptk1
  - **followed** by | **Stomach**; pressure in: hell-o a1*
- **burrowing**: arn b7.de* chin b7.de* cina b7.de* kali-c b4.de* nat-m b4.de* *Phos* b4.de* sabad b7.de* *Sulph* b4.de*
- **bursting** pain: berb bg2
- **chill**; during: ars b4a.de
- **clawing** pain: caust b4.de* m-arct b7.de nux-v b7.de*
- **corrosive**: spong b7.de*
- **cough** agg.; during: *(↗COUGH - Pain - epigastrium)* alum bg2 am-c bg2 ambr b7.de* ars b4a.de* **Bry** b7.de* cham bg2 cina bg2 coff bg2 *Dros* bg2 ip b7.de* lach b7a.de* led bg2 mang b4.de* mim-p skp7• nux-v bg2 phos bg2 puls bg2 sep b4.de* spong bg2 stann b4.de* sulph ↓ thuj b4.de* verat bg2
  - **excoriating**: bry bg2
  - **pressing** pain: phos b4.de* sulph b4a.de
  - **sore**: bry b7.de* stann b4.de*
- **cramping**: agar bg2 alum bg2 aml-ns bg2 ang bg2 ant-c b7a.de arn bg2 bell b4a.de* calc b4.de* cassia-s ccrh1• caust bg2 cocc bg2* gels bg2 hyos b7.de* iod bg2 kali-c b4.de* lach ptk1 laur bg2* lyc b4.de* merc ptk1 mosch b7a.de* *Nat-m* b4.de* nit-ac b4.de* *Nux-v* bg2 op bg2 phos b4.de* puls b7.de* rhod b4.de* rhus-t bg2 **Sil** b4.de* *Stann* b4.de* *Verat* bg2* vip ptk1 zinc bg2
- **cutting** pain: anac b4.de* ang b7.de* ant-c b7a.de* ant-t b7.de* ars bg2 *Bell* b4.de* bry b7.de* calad b7.de* *Calc* b4a.de* cann-s b7.de* canth bg2 cassia-s ccrh1• caust bg2 chel bg2 dig b4.de* hir rsj4• kali-bi bg2 kali-c b4.de* kali-n b4.de* merc b4.de* nux-v bg2 op bg2 phos b4.de* phyt bg2 puls ptk1 sel rsj9• sil bg2 *Sulph* b4.de* valer b7.de* verb b7.de*
- **dragging** down: zinc bg2
- **drawing** pain: agar bg2 alum bg2 anac b4.de* arg-met bg2 ars bg2 aur bg2 bar-c b4.de* chel bg2 con b4.de* croc b7.de* grat bg2 hell bg2 lach bg2 led b7.de* m-arct b7.de nit-ac b4.de* phos bg2 *Puls* b7.de* ran-b bg2 rhod b4.de* sep b4.de* verat b7.de* zinc b4.de*
- **drinking** agg.; after: nux-v b7a.de
- **dull** pain: streptoc jl2
- **eating** | **after**:
  - **agg.**: agar b4a.de am-c b4a.de anac b4a.de bry b7a.de caps b7a.de cassia-s ↓ caust b4a.de cham b7a.de cocc b7a.de hir ↓ hydroph rsj6• nat-c b4a.de nat-m b4a.de nux-v b7a.de pitu-gl skp7• puls b7a.de sil b4a.de thuj b4a.de
    - **cutting** pain: cassia-s ccrh1• hir rsj4•
      - **accompanied** by | **diarrhea**; slight: hir rsj4•
  - **amel.**: luf-op rsj5•

- **empty** stomach; on:
  - **amel.**: cassia-s ↓
    - **cutting** pain: cassia-s ccrh1•
- **fever**; during: ars b4a.de bry b7.de *Rhus-t* b7.de
- **gnawing** pain: agar bg2 arn bg2 ars bg2 bar-c bg2 bell b4.de* cadm-met tpw6 cassia-s ccrh1• *Caust* b4a.de cina bg2 coca bg2 cocc b7.de* kali-bi bg2 kali-c bg2 kali-n bg2 *Lyc* b4a.de nat-m bg2 nit-ac bg2 op bg2 phos bg2 plat b4.de* ruta b7.de* sabad bg2 seneg bg2 sep bg2
  - **accompanied** by:
    - **nausea**:
      - **eating**; after | **rice**; fried: cassia-s ccrh1•
- **inspiration** agg.; deep: act-sp ↓
  - **stitching** pain: act-sp vh1
- **lying** down | **amel.**: cassia-s ccrh1•
- **menses** | **before** | **agg.**: borx bg2 ign bg2 petr bg2
  - **during** | **agg.**: sars b4a.de
- **pecking**: cocc b7.de*
- **perspiration**; during: *Cham* ↓
  - **pressing** pain: *Cham* b7.de
- **pinching** pain: agn b7.de* alum b4.de* ang b7.de* ant-c b7.de* bry b7.de* calc b4.de* cann-s b7.de* caps b7.de* *Caust* bg2 chel b7.de* cocc b7.de* hell b7.de* ign b7.de* ip b7.de* merc b4.de* phos b4.de* plat b4.de* rhod b4.de* rhus-t b7.de* staph b7.de* thuj b4.de* zinc b4.de*
- **pressing** pain: *Acon* b7.de* agar b4.de* alum b4.de* am-c b4.de* ambr b7.de* anac b4.de* ant-c bg2 *Ant-t* b7.de* apis b7a.de arg-met b7.de* arg-n bg2 *Arn* b7.de* **Ars** b4.de* asaf b7.de* asar b7.de* aur b4.de* bar-c b4.de* bell b4.de* borx b4a.de bov b4.de* *Bry* b7.de* *Calc* b4.de* *Camph* b7.de* cann-s b7a.de* canth b7.de* *Caps* b7.de* carb-an b4.de* **Carb-v** b4.de* caust b4.de* **Cham** b7.de* chel b7.de* chin b7.de* chinin-ar br1 cic b7.de* cina b7.de* cocc b7.de* coff b7.de* coloc b4.de* con b4.de* croc b7.de* **Cupr** b7.de* cycl b7.de* *Dig* b4.de* dulc b4.de* euph b4.de* graph b4.de* guaj b4.de* hell b7.de* hep b4.de* hyos b7.de* ign b7.de* *Ip* b7.de* kali-bi bg2 kali-c b4.de* kali-n b4.de* kreos b7a.de led b7.de* lyc b4.de* m-arct b7.de m-aust b7.de* mang b4.de* *Merc* b4.de* mez b4.de* mosch b7.de* nat-c b4.de* **Nat-m** b4.de* nux-m bg2 **Nux-v** b7.de* petr b4.de* ph-ac b4a.de **Phos** b4.de* plat b4.de* plb b7.de* prun bg2 psor jl2 **Puls** b7.de* ran-b b7.de* ran-s b7.de* rheum b7.de* rhod b4.de* **Rhus-t** b7.de* ruta b7.de* sabin b7.de* samb b7.de* sars b4.de* *Sec* b7.de* seneg b4.de* sep b4.de* *Spig* b7.de* spong b7.de* squil b7.de* stann b4.de* *Staph* b7.de* stram b7.de* stront-c b4.de* sul-ac b4.de* *Sulph* b4.de* tarax b7.de* teucr b7.de* thuj b4.de* valer b7.de* **Verat** b7.de* zinc b4.de*
  - **downward**: ars bg2 carb-v bg2 *Cham* bg2 nux-v bg2
  - **inward**: teucr b7.de*
  - **morsel**; as from too large a: rhus-t b7.de*
  - **outward**: acon vh1 nux-v tl1
  - **upward**: arn bg2
- **pressure**:
  - **agg.**: bell-p sp1 hed sp1
  - **amel.**: cassia-s ccrh1•
- **radiating**: arg-n bg2
- **scraping** pain: nux-v b7.de*
- **sitting** agg.: cassia-s ccrh1•
- **sore**: acon bg2 aids nl2• aloe bg2 alum b4a.de* ant-t bg2 *Ars* bg2 bar-c b4.de* *Bar-m* br1 bell bg2 *Bry* b7.de* calc bg2 camph b7.de* carb-an b4.de* *Carb-v* bg2 cham bg2 *Chin* b7.de* cina b7.de* cocc bg2 coloc bg2 con bg2 dig bg2* ferr bg2 glon bg2 hell b7.de* helo-s bnm14• hyos bg2 ign b7.de* *Kali-ar* mrr1 kali-bi bg2 *Kali-c* b4.de* kreos bg2 *Lach* b7a.de* lob bg2 lyc bg2 mang b4.de* morg-p fmm1• mosch b7.de* nat-c bg2 *Nat-m* bg2 *Nux-v* b7.de* ph-ac bg2 phyt bg2 ran-b b7.de* ran-s b7a.de* sabad b7.de* sec bg2 stann b4.de* sul-ac bg2 sulph bg2 tab bg2 thuj bg2 verat bg2 zinc b4a.de*
- **squeezed**; as if: ang b7.de* bry bg2 calc b4.de* canth b7.de* chel b7.de* chin b7.de* cina b7.de* cocc b7.de* coff bg2 dig b4.de* dros b7.de* kreos bg2 lyc b4.de* mosch bg2 petr b4.de* phos b4.de* plat bg2 prun bg2 puls b7.de* rhod b4.de* rhus-t b7.de* sabad bg2 sec bg2 squil b7.de* staph b7.de* sulph bg2 teucr b7.de* *Verat* b7.de* zinc b4.de*

- **Epigastrium**: ...
- **stitching** pain: acon b7.de* am-m b7.de* anac b4.de* ant-t b7.de* *Arn* b7.de* aur b4a.de* bar-c b4.de* bell b4.de* borx b4a.de bov b4.de* **Bry** b7.de* calad b7.de* canth b7.de* caps b7.de* carb-an b4.de* *Caust* b4.de* cham b7a.de chel b7.de* chin b7.de* cic b7.de* cocc b7.de* coff b7.de* *Colch* b7a.de* coloc b4.de* con b4.de* croc b7.de* cupr b7.de* *Dig* b4.de* dros b7.de* dulc b4.de* euphr b7.de* graph b4.de* *Ign* b7.de* iod b4.de* *Ip* b7.de* kali-bi bg2 kali-c b4.de* kali-n b4.de* *Lach* bg2 laur b7.de* lyc bg2 lycps-v bg2 mag-c b4.de* mang b4.de* *Nat-c* b4a.de nat-m b4.de* **Nit-ac** b4a.de* nux-v b7.de* ph-ac b4a.de phos b4.de* plat b4.de* plb b7.de* *Puls* b7.de* ran-s b7.de* rheum b7.de* rhod b4.de* *Rhus-t* b7.de* ruta b7.de* sabad bg2 sabin b7.de* samb b7a.de* *Sep* b4.de* sil b4.de* spig b7.de* squil b7.de* stann b4.de* staph b7.de* stram bg2 *Sulph* b4.de* thuj bg2 *Verat* b7a.de verb b7.de* zinc b4.de*
  - **needles**; as from: ars bg2 sep bg2
- **stool**:
  - **after**:
    - **agg.**: abrom-a ks5 calc ↓ con ↓ ferr ↓ iris bg2 puls b7.de*
      - **cramping**: ferr bg2
      - **drawing** pain: con b4.de*
      - **stitching** pain: calc b4a.de
  - **amel.**: psor ↓
    - **pressing** pain: psor jl2
  - **before**: cassia-s cdd7*•
  - **during** | **agg.**: *Nux-v* b7a.de
- **tearing** pain: act-sp vh1 agar bg2 alum b4.de* ang b7.de* bar-c b4.de* carb-v b4.de* cupr bg2 graph bg2 kali-bi bg2 merc b4.de* merc-c b4a.de ruta b7.de* sep bg2 thuj bg2 zinc b4.de*
- **torn** loose; as if: ars bg2 berb ptk1 lach bg2 petr b4a.de* phos b4a.de* puls b7.de* rhus-t b7a.de*
- **touch**:
  - **agg.**: *Cupr* ↓
    - **pressing** pain | **hard**; as from something: *Cupr* h2
- **ulcerative** pain: ars bg2 *Carb-v* bg2 hell b7a.de* nat-m b4a.de* puls b7a.de rhus-t bg2
- **urging**, pushing: led b7.de*
- **waking**; on: sel ↓
  - **cutting** pain: sel rsj9•
- **walking** agg.: cassia-s ccrh1•
- **warm** drinks:
  - **amel.**: cassia-s ↓
    - **burning**: cassia-s ccrh1•
- ▽ **extending** to:
  - **Back**: *Arn* ↓ dig ↓ *Lyc* ↓ mosch ↓ *Nux-v* ↓ *Plb* ↓ *Sabin* ↓ *Sep* ↓
    - **pressing** pain: arn b7a.de* mosch b7.de* *Nux-v* b7a.de
    - **stitching** pain: *Arn* b7a.de dig b4a.de *Lyc* b4a.de *Plb* b7a.de *Sabin* b7a.de *Sep* b4a.de
  - **Bowels**: arn ↓
    - **cramping**: arn ptk1
  - **Chest**: aloe bg2
  - **Downward**: sulph bg2
  - **Hypochondrium** | **right**: cassia-s ccrh1•
  - **Intestines**: hell-o ↓
    - **burning**: hell-o a1*
  - **Kidneys**: hom-xyz bg2
    - **right**: guat sp1*
  - **Lumbar** region: anac bg2 phos bg2
  - **Rectum**: ars bg2 hell bg2
  - **Shoulders**: sul-ac bg2
  - **Side**: *Dig* ↓
    - **stitching** pain: *Dig* b4a.de
- ○ **Skin**; below the: bry ↓ con ↓ *Nat-m* ↓ stann ↓
  - **ulcerative** pain: bry b7.de* con b4.de* *Nat-m* b4.de* stann b4.de*

- **Pit** of stomach: cimic tl1 cina a1 corn br1 hippoc-k szs2 ulm-c ↓ vac jl2
- **morning**: hippoc-k szs2
- **forenoon**: hippoc-k szs2

Stomach

- **noon**: hippoc-k szs2
- **afternoon**: hippoc-k szs2
- **evening**: hippoc-k szs2
- **night**: hippoc-k szs2
- **accompanied** by | **Abdomen**; distention of: corn br1
- **cramping**:
  - **followed** by | **palpitations**: but-ac sp1*
- **pressure** | **amel.**: aq-mar skp7•
- **stitching** pain: ulm-c jsj8•
- **warm** applications | **amel.**: aq-mar skp7•

- **Posterior** part: am bg2 lob bg2
- **Pylorus**: all-c bro1 ars bg2 canth bro1 dys ↓ equis-h a1 *Hep* bro1 lyc bro1 merc bro1 *Orni* bro1 sep bg2 tus-p bro1 *Uran-n* bro1
  - **cramping**: dys fmm1•
- **Side** under ribs; left: arg-n ↓
  - **ulcerative** pain: arg-n br1
- **Spot**; in a: gymno ↓ phos ↓
  - **burning**: gymno hr1*
  - **sore**: phos pd
- **Spot**; in a small: arg-n kr1 bar-c bg2 bism bg2* *Kali-bi* bg2* kreos pd lach bg2 lyc bg2 ol-an bg2 sabad bg2
- **Spots**; in: phos ↓
  - **pressing** pain: phos h2
- **Umbilicus**; region of:

▽ • **extending** to:
  - **Throat**: acon ↓
    - **gnawing** pain: acon bg2

PARALYSIS: *Apoc* mrr1 lat-m bnm6•

PEPSIN; increased: cortico sp1

PERIODICITY: arg-n bg2 hyos bg2 ign bg2 lyc bg2 nux-v bg2
- **day**:
  - **alternate**: ip bg2
    - **hour**; on the same: ip bg2

PERSPIRATION: carb-v bro1 nat-m bro1 nit-ac bro1 sep bro1

○ - **Pit** of stomach; at: bell k* borx bg2* hyos bg1* kali-n bg2* m-aust b7.de nux-v k* ol-an bg1* sec k*

PLUG; sensation of a: chel ptk1

○ - **Pylorus**: apoc bg2

POLYPI: *Calc* b4a.de merc b4.de* petr b4a.de ph-ac b4a.de

PORK agg.: *Carb-v* b4a.de ip b7.de* **Puls** b7.de* sep b4a.de

POTATOES agg.: alum b4.de*

PREGNANCY agg.; during: acon bg2 ars bg2 bell b4a.de bry b7.de* *Calc* b4.de* canth br1 *Con* bg2 ferr bg2 **Ip** bg2 kreos bg2 lach bg2 mag-m bg2 nat-m bg2 nux-m b7.de* **Nux-v** bg2 *Petr* bg2 phos b4.de* *Puls* b7.de* rhus-t b7.de* *Sep* b4.de* verat bg2

PRESSING against spine; feeling as if: arn br1* plat tl1 plb tl1 verat-v tl1*

PRESSURE:
- **agg.**: acon b7a.de* alum b4.de* *Am-c* b4.de* ant-c b7.de* apis bg2 *Arg-n* bg2 ars b4a.de bar-c b4.de* bell bg2 **Bry** b7a.de* calad b7.de* calc b4a.de* caps b7.de* cina b7.de* coloc b4a.de ign b7.de* kali-bi bg2 lach b7.de* **Lyc** b4.de* mag-c b4.de* merc-c b4a.de* mez b4.de* *Nat-m* b4.de* nit-ac b4.de* **Nux-v** b7.de* olnd b7.de* ox-ac bg2 phos b4.de* *Puls* bg2 ran-s b7.de* ruta b7.de* sabad b7.de* sabin b7.de* samb b7a.de* sep b4.de* **Sil** b4.de* *Spong* b7a.de *Stann* b4.de* staph b7.de* stram b7a.de sulph b4a.de* *Verat* b7.de* zinc b4.de*
- **amel.**: bry b7.de* cupr bg2 *Ign* b7.de* mang bg2 petr bg2 puls b7.de* spig b7.de* stann b4.de
- **clothes** agg.; of: | **Pit** of stomach: lith-c ptk1
- **external** (See Pressure)
- **slight** | **agg.**: *Lach* bg2 merc-c bg2 phos bg2
- **umbilicus**; on | **agg.**: stann b4.de*

PRICKLING: dioxi rbp6 merc-c bg2 nat-m h2

○ - **Epigastrium**: nat-m bg2

PULSATION: **Acon** k* agar alum bg2 alumn k* *Ant-c* **Ant-t** k* *Arg-n* k* ars ars-i ars-s-f k2 *Asaf* k* asar gm1 *Bell* k* bov bry pd *Cact* k* calad k* **Calc** k* calc-i k2 calc-s calc-sil k2 cann-s carb-v carbn-s cench k2 chel k* **Chin** k* chinin-ar **Cic** k* coloc cop *Corn* k* croc crot-h k* cupr k* dendr-pol sk4• *Dig* dros k* eucal bro1 eup-per bg2 **Ferr** k* ferr-ar *Ferr-i* gamb k* gins k* **Glon** k* *Graph* k* *Ham* k* hura *Hydr* k* hydr-ac hyos k* *Iod* k* ip k* jac-c kali-ar **Kali-c** k* kali-i k* kali-n k* kali-s kola stb3• kreos b7a.de* *Lac-c* lach k* lachn laur lyc *Mag-m* k* med *Meny* mez h2 mosch k* mur-ac h2 naja k* nat-ar nat-c k* *Nat-m* k* nat-s k* *Nit-ac* **Nux-v** k* ol-an ptk1 olnd k* op k* ozone sde2• **Phos** k* plat k* plb k* podo bg2 **Puls** k* rheum k* *Rhus-t* k* sel **Sep** k* **Sil** k* spig bg2 *Stann* sul-i k2 *Sulph* k* tab thuj k* urol-h rwt•
- **left**: am bg2
- **morning**: asaf kali-c kali-n *Sep*
- **noon**: sulph
- **evening**: alumn
  - **lying** on the back; while: alumn
- **night**: eup-per *Puls*
- **air**; in open | **amel.**: naja
- **breakfast** agg.; after: nat-s k2
- **cough** | **during** | **agg.**: ip hr1
  - **with**: acon asaf bell cact carb-v cic coloc dros ferr graph iod kali-c lyc nat-m puls sulph
- **dinner**; after: cact
- **eating** | **after** | **agg.**: alumn k* *Asaf* cact cop kali-c kali-sil k2 lyc mez h2 *Nat-m* phos **Sel** k* *Sep*
  - **while** | **agg.**: kola stb3• nat-m *Sep*
- **empty**; when: kali-c k2
- **eructations** | **amel.**: *Sep* k*
- **faintness**; with: sulph h2
- **gastric** and abdominal complaints; during: *Asar*
- **headache**; during: *Kali-c*
- **heart**; as if from: ozone sde2•
- **leaning** against anything: gamb k*
- **lying** on back agg.: alumn *Dios* op k*
- **menses**; after: ferr k*
- **nausea**; with: nat-c
- **reflecting** agg.: raph k*
- **rising** | **amel.**: op k*
- **sitting**:
  - **agg.**: sulph h2
  - **erect** | **agg.**: lycps-v
- **supper** agg.; after: nux-v
- **trembling**: arg-n calc kali-c
- **visible** pulsation in pit of stomach: asaf k1*
- **walking** | **after** | **agg.**: calad
  - **amel.**: op k*

▽ - **extending** to | **Abdomen**; the whole: bruc hr1*

○ - **Back** of stomach: kali-c ptk1
- **Epigastrium**: acon b7.de* agar bg2 ant-t b7a.de* am b7.de* ars b4.de* **Asaf** b7.de* bar-c bg2 bell b4.de* bry bg2* calad b7.de* calc bg2 cann-s b7.de* carb-v b4.de* cham b7.de* chel b7.de* chin b7a.de* *Cic* b7.de* cupr bg2 dros b7.de* eucal bro1 ferr b7.de* graph b4.de* *Hydr* bro1 iod b4.de* ip b7.de* kali-bi bg2 *Kali-c* b4.de* kali-n b4.de* lach ptk1 lyc bg2 m-arct b7.de *Mag-m* b4.de* merc b4.de* nat-m b4.de* nit-ac b4a.de* *Nux-v* b7a.de* olnd b7.de* op b7a.de phos b4.de* plat b4.de* plb bg2 podo bg2 *Puls* b7.de* rheum b7.de* rhus-t b7.de* sel bro1 *Sep* b4.de* sulph b4.de* thuj b4.de* verat-v bg2 zinc b4.de*
  - **accompanied** by | **distention** like a fist: cic pd*
  - **cough** agg.; during: ip b7a.de*
  - **eating**; after: kali-c b4a.de phos b4a.de sep b4a.de
  - **overheating**; as after: *Olnd* b7a.de
  - **perceptible**; clearly: *Asaf* b7a.de nux-v b7a.de puls b7a.de
  - **stool**; before: podo bg2
  - **visible**: *Asaf* b7a.de nux-v b7a.de puls b7a.de sep b4a.de

PYROSIS (See Heartburn)

QUALMISH (See Nausea)

QUIVERING (See Trembling)

RAISING ARMS agg.: anac b4a.de*

RANCIDITY: *(↗Eructations; type - rancid)* bry bg2

RAW FOOD agg.: *Ruta* b7.de*

READING agg.: arg-met b7.de* ign b7.de* nux-v b7.de*

REGURGITATION (See Eructations; type - food)

RELAXATION of pylorus: *Ferr-p* k* *Phos* k*

RELAXED; sensation as if (See Hanging)

REPUGNANCE (See Loathing)

REST:
- **agg.**: caps b7.de* cham b7.de* chin b7.de* ferr b7.de* puls b7.de* rhus-t b7.de* ruta b7.de*
- **amel.**: *Bry* bg2 cham b7a.de*

RESTLESSNESS: allox tpw3 *Canth* b7a.de hep b4a.de* kali-c h2 sil h2 ven-m rsj12•
○ - **Epigastrium**: *Canth* b7a.de

RETCHING: *(↗Gagging; Nausea; Retching - ineffectual; THROAT - Choking - clearing; THROAT - Choking - swallowing; THROAT - Choking - Swallowing - agg.)* absin br1 acet-ac k* *Acon* k* *Aesc* k* aeth bg2 *Agar* k* ail k* alum k* alum-p k2 alum-sil k2 alumn am-c am-caust a1 ambr b2.de* anac k* androc srj1• ant-c k* *Ant-t* k* apom a1 arg-met k* *Arg-n* k* *Arn* k* *Ars* k* ars-h k* *Asar* k* atro k* aur b2.de* aur-m k* *Bapt* k* bar-c bar-i bar-m k* bar-s k2 **Bell** k* bism k* borx bov bg2 brom k* *Bry* k* cact k* *Cadm-s* cain calad k* camph k* cann-i k* cann-s b2.de* canth k* caps k* carb-ac k* *Carb-v* k* carbn-o card-m k* cassia-s ccrh1• **Cham** k* *Chel* *Chin* k* chinin-ar chinin-s k* chion chlor k* chr-ac k* cimic k* cimx coc-c k* *Cocc* k* coch k* coff coff-t a1 **Colch** k* *Coloc* k* con conin a1 crot-h k* crot-t *Cupr* k* *Dig* k* digin a1 digox a1 *Dros* k* dulc k* **Eup-per** k* ferr bg2 fl-ac k* flor-p rsj3• gels k* glon k* *Graph* k* grin br1 *Hell* b2.de* *Hep* k* hydrog srj2• hyos k* hyper k* ign k* indg k* iod k* **Ip** k* iris k* jab k* kali-bi k* kali-br hr1 *Kali-c* b2.de* kali-cy a1 kali-i k* kali-n k* kali-p kali-s k* kalm k* kola stb3• *Kreos* k* lac-ac k* *Lach* k* led k* lil-t *Lob* k* lobin a1 *Lyc* k* mag-c k* mag-m k* med c1 meny k* merc k* merc-c b4a.de* merl k* mez k* morg fmm1• morph k* mosch k* myric k* naja k* *Nat-ar* *Nat-c* k* nat-m k* nat-p k* *Nat-s* k* nit-ac k* nux-m **Nux-v** k* oena k* olnd k* onis a1 *Op* k* ox-ac k* petr k* phos k* phys k* physala-p bnm7• *Phyt* k* plan k* *Plb* k* *Podo* k* psor k* ptel k* *Puls* k* *Raph* k* rhus-t k* ruta fd4.de sabad k* sabin k* sang k2 sars b2.de* *Sec* k* seneg k* *Sep* k* sil k* sin-a k* sol-ni *Spig* b7a.de squil k* *Stann* k* stram k* stront-c k* **Stry** k* sul-ac k* *Sulph* k* *Tab* k* tarent tax k* tell k* ter ther thuj k* tritic-vg fd5.de vanil fd5.de *Verat* k* viol-t k* vip k* zinc k* zinc-m a1 zinc-p k2 zinc-s a1 [*Ant-m* stj2]
- **daytime**: *Stann*
- **morning**: alum k* dig digin a1 graph h2 hep k* kali-c kreos k* lipp a1 morg fmm1• *Nat-c* k* nat-m h2 *Nux-v* phos h2 psil ft1 sulph k*
  - **rinsing** mouth, when: sulph h2
  - **rising** | **after** | **agg.**: led h1
    - **agg.**: mosch
  - **walking** agg.: coc-c
- **noon** | **soup**; after: ant-t k* mag-c k*
- **afternoon**: raph k*
- **evening**: dig k* hyper k* kali-c nat-m phos k* stann k* stram k*
  - **walking** agg.: raph k*
- **night**: arg-n *Arn* k* gamb k* graph *Merc* nat-m k* nux-v *Puls* k* ran-s k* rat k* rhus-t h1 sulph k* ther k*
  - **midnight**: bell h1
    - **after**:
      - **1 h** | **waking**; on: rat
- **accompanied** by:
  - **asthma** (See RESPIRATION - Asthmatic - accompanied - retching)
  - **eructations**:
    - **ineffectual** (See Eructations - ineffectual - accompanied - retching)
    - **water** brash (See Eructations; type - water brash - accompanied - retching)
  - **influenza**: *Sarcol-ac* br1
  - **nausea** (See Nausea - accompanied - retching)
  - **weakness**: ant-t bg2

Retching – accompanied by: ...
- ○ **Forehead**; perspiration on: ant-t bg2
- **Head**; pain in: glon bg2 ip bg2 ozone sde2•
- **Lumbar** region; pain in: lath bro1
- **Stomach**; complaints of (See Complaints - accompanied - retching)

- **agg.**: arn bg2
- **air** agg.; in open: graph k*
- **anxiety**:
  - **from**: chel bg2*
  - **with** (See MIND - Anxiety - retching)
- **bending** forward agg.: hydrog srj2•
- **chill**; before: ip hr1
- **coffee** agg.: caps cham
- **cold** drinks agg.; after: anac ip *Nux-v* puls rhus-t teucr
- **convulsions**; before epileptic: *Cupr* k*
- **convulsive**: bac bn dig k* mag-c k* merc-c k* vip k*
- **cough**; with: agar *Ambr* k* anac bg2 ant-t k* *Apis* *Arg-n* ars ars-i ars-s-f k2 aspar k* bapt bg2 bell k* *Borx* brom k* *Bry* bufo **Carb-v** k* carbn-s carc gk caust cench cham *Chin* k* chinin-ar chlor choc srj3• cimx k* **Cina** k* *Coc-c* k* con h2 crot-h crot-t cupr k* *Daph* **Dros** k* dulc ferr bg2 ferr-m hell **Hep** k* hydrog srj2• *Hyos* ign *Iod* k* *Ip* k* irid-met srj5• *Kali-ar* kali-bi k* *Kali-c* k* kali-i *Kali-s* kali-sil k2 *Kreos* k* *Lach* lob k* lyc k* mag-m mag-p k* mang-p rly4• meph bg2 *Merc* k* mez k* *Nat-m* k* **Nit-ac** k* *Nux-v* k* *Ol-j* ozone sde2• petr bg2* phos ptk1 plan k* psil ft1 **Puls** k* ruta sabad k* sang *Seneg* k* *Sep* k* *Sil* k* spong fd4.de *Squil* k* stann k* *Sul-ac* sul-i k2 sulph k* *Tab* tarent k* thuj k* vanil fd5.de verat k*
  - **amel.**: lach ptk1
- **diarrhea**; during: **Arg-n** k* crot-t *Cupr* k* kola stb3• *Podo* ptk1*
- **dinner**; before: carb-v h2
- **drinking** agg.; after: anac k* ars-h gamb hep k* nat-m h2 plb
- **drunkards**; in: *Ars* asar gm1 *Nux-v* *Op*
- **dyspnea** agg.: am-c k*
- **eating**:
  - **after** | **agg.**: agar am-c bism bry cann-i k* *Cham* chin k* cop k* cycl graph kali-c lac-ac lyc k* mag-c k* nat-s plb puls rhus-t
  - **amel.**: *Ign* k* nat-c k*
  - **while** | **agg.**: verat ptk1
- **emotions** agg.: op ptk1
- **empty**: asar ptk1 sec ptk1
- **eructations** agg.: carb-v ptk1 coloc h2 ruta fd4.de sep h2 sil ptk1 tarent ptk1
- **excitement** agg.: kali-c h2
- **fasting** agg.: berb kali-c k*
- **fat**; after: ozone sde2•
- **foamy**: lyc bg2
- **food**; thought of: merc-cy ptk1
- **happy** surprise: kali-bi k2 kali-c k*
- **hawking** mucus from fauces: *Ambr* k* *Anac* k* **Arg-n** k* borx *Bry* *Calc-p* *Coc-c* ip *Kali-c* *Merc-i-f* nat-ar **Nux-v** k* osm k* *Stann* sulph h2
- **hot** foods; from: mez bg2
- **hysterical**: *Ip* b7a.de
- **incessant**: atra-r bnm3•
- **ineffectual**: *(↗Retching)* ant-c k2 *Ant-t* k* *Arn* k* *Ars* k* *Asar* k* bar-c bg2 bar-m k* *Bell* k* brom k* *Bry* k* chim-m hr1 chin k* crot-t cupr b7.de* cyt-l a1 dig k* dulc a1 grat k* hell b7.de* hyos k* ign b7.de* ip k* kreos mosch b7a.de mur-ac a1 nat-ar nat-c h2 *Nux-v* k* op k* phos bg2 phyt bg2 plb k* *Podo* k* puls rhus-t b7.de* sabad b7a.de sabin sec b7.de* sil k* sul-ac k* sulph ther k* verat k* verat-v k*
  - **anxiety**; with (See MIND - Anxiety - retching - ineffectual)
- **liquids**; after: petr k* sul-ac k* sulph
- **menses**:
  - **before** | **agg.**: *Kali-c* b4a.de
  - **during** | **agg.**: cupr bg2 *Puls* k* thuj k*
  - **suppressed** menses; from: *Cupr* b7a.de
- **milk** agg.: *Calc* k*
- **motion**:
  - **agg.**: ant-t bg3 bry k2 cadm-s
  - **amel.**: nat-c h2
- **mucus**; with accumulation of: morg fmm1•
- **odors** agg.: ozone sde2•

- **painful**: card-m *Merc-c* k* sec tab
- **rising** from bed agg.: morg fmm1•
- **salivation**; with: ant-t k* hep lob ptk1 tritic-vg fd5.de
- **sitting** up in bed | **must** sit up: rhus-t h1*
- **sleep**; during: *Merc-c* b4a.de
- **smoking** agg.; after: *Ip* k* tab
- **soup** agg.: ars
- **spasmodic**: *Merc-c* k* verat k2
- **stool** | **after** | **agg.**: kali-bi bg2 phos h2
  - **during** | **agg.**: ars b4a.de *Cupr Ip Nux-v* podo
- **swallowing**: *(↗THROAT - Choking - swallowing - agg.)*
  - **agg.**: *(↗THROAT - Choking - swallowing)* coc-c k2 *Graph Kali-c* k* *Lach Merc-c* tab
  - **empty** | **agg.**: *Graph* k*
- **touching** inside of throat: *Coc-c*
- **violent**: ant-t k2 *Ars* asar brom cadm-s cham k2 colch mrr1 dig ix bnm8• med c1* phyt ptk1 sang hr1 squil h1 *Verat* br1
- **vomiting**: ant-t bg2 canth bg2 cupr bg2 kali-bi bg2 **Nux-v** bg2 sil bg2 *Verat* bg2*
  - **after**: ant-t *Apis Ars* **Colch** k* *Sep* stram
  - **before**: cham ptk1 *Colch* a1 ruta fd4.de
- **waking** agg.; after: rat sil
- **walking** in open air; during and after: graph h2
- **warm**:
  - **drinks**:
    - **agg.**: *Coc-c* nat-m
    - **amel.**: ther k*

RETRACTION: nat-c h2 verat-v rb2
- **sensation** of: agar bg2 calad dig k* *Dulc* hell *Kali-bi Kali-i* lach lact mosch bg2 mur-ac k* nat-c h2 *Op* plb bg2 spong fd4.de sulph b4a.de
- **stool** agg.; during: mosch b7a.de

○ - **Epigastrium**: apis bg2 calad b7.de* dig bg2 dros b7.de* dulc bg2 hell b7.de* mosch b7a.de mur-ac bg2 staph bg2 thuj bg2

REVERSED ACTION: nux-v k2

RIDING a carriage: | **agg.**: *Cocc* b7.de* lyc bg2 phos b4.de*

RISING:
- **bed**; from | **after** | **amel.**: *Nux-v* b7.de* plb b7.de* ran-b b7.de*
  - **agg.**: bov b4.de* kali-c b4.de* puls b7.de* sil b4.de* staph b7.de verat b7.de
- **sitting**; from | **amel.**: chin b7.de* merc b4.de*

RISING UP into throat; sensation of something: asaf b7.de* asar b7.de* calc b4a.de caust b4a.de con b4a.de hep b4.de* lyc b4a.de m-aust b7a.de mag-m b4a.de merc b4.de* nat-c b4.de nat-m bg2 phos b4.de* plat b4.de* plb b7a.de ran-b b7.de* *Spig* b7.de* sul-ac b4.de* valer b7.de* verat b7.de*
- **cold** agg.: caust b4a.de
- **eating**; after: asaf b7a.de
- **hot**: merc b4a.de *Ph-ac* b4a.de phos b4a.de
- **warm**: *Plat* b4a.de valer ptk1

ROOM agg.: *Croc* b7.de* *Puls* b7.de*

ROUGHNESS, sensation of: hell b7.de* mang h2

RUBBING:
- **amel.**: bry bg2 lyc bg2 phos bg2
- **must** hold and rub stomach: coca-c sk4•

RUMBLING: abrom-a ks5 alum b4.de* am-c b4.de* amp rly4• anac bg2 arn b7.de* carb-an b4.de* cartl-s rly4• coli rly4• cortico tpw7 croc b7.de* falco-pe nl2• fl-ac bg2 gard-j vlr2• ger-i rly4• graph b4.de* hippoc-k szs2 ignis-alc es2• ip b7a.de kali-c b4.de* laur b7.de* mag-c b4.de* malar jl2 mang-p rly4• meny b7.de* musa a1 narc-ps a1* nat-c b4.de* nat-pyru rly4• orot-ac rly4• oxal-a rly4• par b7.de* ph-ac b4.de* phos b4.de* plac-s rly4• positr nl2• pot-e rly4• ran-b b7.de* ribo rly4• ruta fd4.de sep b4.de* spong fd4.de stann b4.de* teucr b7.de* urol-h rwt• verb b7a.de* zinc b4.de*
- **evening**: urol-h rwt•
- **crackling** noise | **Epigastrium**: *M-ambo* b7.de*
- **creaking** noise | **Epigastrium**: m-ambo b7.de
- **eructations**; before: ph-ac h2

RUNNING agg.: *Bry* b7.de* cupr b7.de* *Nux-v* b7.de*

SALT:
- **abuse** of; after: carb-v bg2 spir-n-d bg2
- **agg.**: *Ars* b4a.de *Carb-v* b4a.de

SAND in stomach; as if: ptel bg2*

SATIETY (See Appetite - easy)

SAUSAGES agg.; spoiled: ars b4a.de *Bry* b7a.de ph-ac b4a.de

SENSITIVENESS: acet-ac br1 *Ant-c* b7a.de ant-t b7.de* *Apis* b7a.de cann-s b7.de* canth b7.de* carb-v h2 colch b7.de* hell b7.de* hep b4a.de kali-bi bg2 kali-c h2 kali-n h2* m-arct b7.de mag-m b4a.de myos-a rly4• *Nux-v* b7.de* ol-an bg2 par b7.de* stram b7a.de sul-ac b4a.de* sulph b4a.de *Verat* b7a.de
- **left**: myos-a rly4•
- **bad** news: *(↗MIND - Ailments - bad)* *Dig* mez k2
- **menses**; during: kali-n h2
- **pressure**, to: *All-s* vh1 alum h2 kali-n h2 mag-c h2 nat-c h2
- **stepping**, to hard: bar-c h2
- **talking**; to: caust chel k2 hell kali-c *Nat-c* hr1*
- **tobacco**; to: asc-t c1* ign bro1
- **touch**; to: *Arg-n* bro1 ars bro1 bism bro1 carb-v gt1 chin gk chinin-ar bro1 dig k2 *Nat-c* hr1 spig hr1

○ - **Epigastrium**: alum b4.de* am-c b4a.de* am-m bg2 ant-c b7a.de* *Ant-t* b7a.de *Apis* b7a.de arn b7.de* **Ars** b4a.de bar-c b4a.de brucel sa3• *Bry* b7.de* *Calc* b4a.de* *Camph* b7.de* canth b7.de* carb-v b4.de* caust bg2 chel ptk1 chin ptk1 coff bg2 colch b7.de* coloc b4a.de* crot-t bg2 cupr b7.de* dig b4a.de ferr b7.de* hell b7.de* helo-s bnm14• *Hep* bg2 *Hyos* b7.de* ign bg2 kali-bi bg2 kali-c b4.de* kreos bg2 *Lach* bg2* *Lyc* b4a.de* mag-m b4.de* mag-p mtf11 *Merc* b4a.de *Merc-c* b4a.de nat-c b4.de* nat-m b4a.de* **Nux-v** b7.de* *Petr* b4a.de phos b4a.de* podo bg2 *Sec* b7.de* *Sil* b4a.de spig b7a.de* spong b7.de* stann b4.de* *Sul-ac* b4a.de **Sulph** b4a.de* *Verat* b7.de*
  - **spot**; in a: phos ptk1
  - **touch**; to: ars mtf33 verat mtf33
- **Pit** of stomach: phos k2

SHAKING: anac h2 lyc ptk1 mag-m h2* mez h2
- **laughing**; from: cortico tpw7

○ - **Epigastrium**: anac b4.de* mag-m b4a.de*
  - **eating**; after: anac b4a.de

SHIVERING; during: | **agg.**: *Caust* b4a.de cina b7.de

SHOCK: *(↗Pain - electric)* **Cic** dig pd kali-c h2 nat-c nux-v plat tab
- **convulsions**; before: **Cic**
- **eating** agg.: teucr
- **lying** on side agg.: camph
- **sleep** agg.; during: tab
- **stitching**: plat h2

○ - **Epigastrium**: dig ptk1

SHOOTING in epigastrium (See Pain - stitching)

SICK FEELING in: *Mur-ac* b4a.de

SICK HEADACHE (See HEAD - Pain - accompanied - nausea)

SINGING agg.: sars b4.de*

SINKING: *(↗Emptiness)* abrot *Acon* aesc agar ail alum alum-p k2 alum-sil k2 alumn ant-t apoc arund-d *Bapt* bar-c bg1 brom bufo cact calad calc vh calc-sil k2 cann-i carb-ac chlol *Cimic* k* *Cina* clem *Cocc* colch conv bg1 cop croc *Crot-h Crot-t* cupr **Dig** k* dios elaps flor-p rsj3• *Glon* ham fd3.de* **Hell** hep *Hydr* k* *Hydr-ac* ign jatr-c jug-c kali-ar *Kali-bi* kali-chl *Kali-fcy* kali-i kali-p fd1.de• lach bg1 laur k* **Lec** sne *Lept Lob Lyc* mag-c *Med Merc* merc-i-r mosch **Murx** myric naja narc-ps c1* nat-ar *Nat-m* **Nux-v** k* olib-sac wmh1 olnd op orni c* ozone sde2• *Petr* phos phys pic-ac plan plut-n srj7• podo c1 ptel puls k* rad-br c11 rhod ruta fd4.de sabad sang k2 sec **Sep** k* sil *Stann Staph Sulph* k* symph fd3.de• **Tab** k* tell teucr thea til tril-p c1 tritic-vg fd5.de (non:uran-met k) uran-n vanil fd5.de *Verat* zinc zinc-p k2
- **morning**: apoc k* cimic dios hydr *Kali-bi* lac-c br1 ruta fd4.de symph fd3.de• vanil fd5.de
  - **waking**; on: apoc k* ozone sde2•
- **forenoon**: jatr-c nat-m
  - **11 h**: phos k2 sulph k2*

- **forenoon**: ...
  - **acids**, after: zinc
- **evening**: colch tritic-vg fd5.de vanil fd5.de
- **night**: dios *Lyc* tarent
  - **waking**; on: plut-n srj7•
- **bad** news: *Dig*
- **breakfast** | **after** | **agg.**: colch
  - **before**:
    - **agg.**: *Kali-bi*
    - **amel.**: ozone sde2•
- **breathing** deep | **amel.**: ign br1
- **deathly**: dig k2*
- **eating**:
  - **after** | **agg.**: ars calc cina dig *Iod* lyc ozone sde2• *Petr* plan senn c1 sil staph urt-u
  - **amel.**: alumn k* *Bar-c* tritic-vg fd5.de vanil fd5.de
  - **before** | **agg.**: alumn *Sulph*
- **food**; smell of: dig k2
- **heart** symptoms, in: lepi br1
- **hemorrhages**; from: crot-h bro1 ip k2 tril-p c1*
- **inspiration** agg.: calad
- **meeting** a friend, when: *Cimic* k*
- **menopause**; during: cimic bro1 crot-h bro1 dig bro1 hydr-ac hr1* *Ign* bro1 *Sep* bro1 tril-p bro1
- **motion** agg.: dig br1
- **painful**: orni c
- **paroxysmal**: glon k*
- **pressure** agg.: **Merc**
- **sitting** agg.: acon
- **stool** agg.; after: ambr dios *Ph-ac* **Podo**
- **waking**; on: apoc k*
- **walking** | **amel.**: acon

▽ - **extending** to:
  - ○ **Abdomen**: jug-c vml3•
  - **Heart**: **Lob**

○ - **Epigastrium**: acon bg2 apoc bg2 calad bg2 cham bg2 cimic mrr1 croc bg2 dig bg2 glon bg2 hell bg2 hydr bg2 *Hydr-ac* br1 jatr-c bg2 lob bg2 narc-ps a1 sulph bg2 tab bg2
  - **accompanied** by | **Heart**; complaints of the (See CHEST - Heart; complaints - accompanied - stomach - epigastrium)
  - **fever**; during: polyp-p br1
  - **stool** agg.; after: ph-ac bg2

SITTING:
- **agg.**: acon b7.de* am-m b7.de* ang b7.de* ant-t b7.de* *Ars* b4a.de bov b4.de* calad b7.de* *Carb-v* b4a.de *Caust* b4a.de chin b7.de* dig b4.de* ferr b7.de* hep b4.de* kali-c b4.de* merc b4.de* nat-c b4.de* phos b4.de* puls b7.de* rhus-t b7.de* ruta b7.de* sabad b7.de* *Sep* b4a.de spig b7.de* sulph bg2 tarax b7.de*
- **amel.**: bry b7.de* *Cham* b7a.de dig b4.de* staph b7.de*
- **bent** forward:
  - **agg.**: agn b7.de* *Ars* b4a.de bar-c b4.de* caps b7.de* rhus-t b7.de* sabin b7.de* *Sulph* b4a.de
  - **amel.**: *Cham* b7a.de nux-v b7.de* staph b7.de*
- **erect** | **amel.**: *Ars* b4a.de gels bg2 *Kali-c* b4a.de sabin b7.de* *Sulph* b4a.de
- **long** time agg.; for a: ars b4a.de carb-v b4a.de colch b7.de* *Ign* b7.de* nux-v b7.de* sulph b4a.de

SITTING UP in bed agg.: acon b7.de* *Bry* b7.de* chel b7.de* dig b4.de* mang b4.de* sep b4.de*

SLAKING lime, sensation of: *Caust* k*

SLEEP:
- **after** | **agg.**: ambr b7.de* bry b7.de* *Lach* bg2 petr bg2 rheum b7.de*
- **before** falling asleep agg.: cocc b7.de* rhus-t b7.de* rob bg2
- **long** sleep agg.; after a: *Hep* b4a.de

SLOW digestion: (↗*Indigestion; GENERALS - Food and - diet - agg. - errors)* aesc br1 alet bro1 alf br1* alst bro1 alum h2 *Anac* bro1 ang bro1 *Ant-c* bro1 *Arg-n* bro1 ars bro1 asaf bro1 aur-m k2* aur-s k2 bar-s k2 berb st bism bro1 *Bry* bro1 calc k2* calc-sil k2 caps bro1 carb-ac bro1 *Carb-an* bro1 *Carb-v* bro1 **Chin** bro1* coch bro1 coff bro1 colch bro1 coli jl2 *Corn* st1 corn-f st1 cycl hr1* *Dios* bro1 eucal br1* ferr bro1* ferul c2 flav mtf11 gent-l mtf11 gins mtf11 gran bro1 *Graph* bro1 grin bro1 haliae-lc srj5• hep bro1 *Hydr* bro1 *Ign* bro1 ip bro1 jug-c bro1 kali-bi bro1 *Kali-p* bro1 kreos mrr1 lob bro1 *Lyc* bro1* mag-c bro1* merc bro1 *Nat-c* bro1* nat-m bro1 nat-s ptk nig-s mp4• nit-m-ac c2 *Nuph* st1 *Nux-v* bro1* *Op* st *Par* c2* *Phos* bro1 podo k2 prun-v bro1 *Ptel* bro1 puls k2* quas bro1* rat bro1 rob bro1 *Sabin* st sanic c2 *Sep* st **Sil** st1 sul-ac bro1 sulph bro1 **Tarent** st1 v-a-b jl2 valer bro1 zing bro1
- **accompanied** by:
  - **toothache** (See TEETH - Pain - accompanied - indigestion)
  - ○ **Face**; pain in (See FACE - Pain - accompanied - indigestion)
  - **Head**; pain in (See HEAD - Pain - accompanied - indigestion)
- **alcoholics**; in: ars bg2 bell bg2 *Carb-v* bg2 chin bg2 *Lach* bg2 merc bg2 nat-c bg2 **Nux-v** bg2 puls bg2 *Sulph* bg2
- **emotions**; from: bry bg2 cham bg2 chin bg2 coloc bg2 nux-v bg2 ph-ac bg2 staph bg2
- **fluids**; from loss of vital: *Carb-v* bg2 **Chin** bg2 lach bg2 *Nux-v* bg2 ruta bg2 *Sulph* bg2
- **hypochondriacs**; in: bry bg2 calc bg2 chin bg2 con bg2 lach bg2 *Nat-c* bg2 **Nux-v** bg2 staph bg2 *Sulph* bg2 verat bg2
- **hysteria**; in: bell bg2 bry bg2 calc bg2 con bg2 hyos bg2 **Ign** bg2 lach bg2 nux-m bg2 phos bg2 *Puls* bg2 *Sep* bg2 sulph bg2 verat bg2
- **injuries**; from: am-c bg2 *Arn* bg2 bry bg2 calc bg2 con bg2 puls bg2 rhus-t bg2 ruta bg2
- **mercury**; from abuse of: arn bg2 *Aur* bg2 bell bg2 *Carb-v* bg2 chin bg2 **Hep** bg2 *Lach* bg2 puls bg2 staph bg2 *Sulph* bg2
- **pregnancy** agg.; during: acon bg2 ars bg2 *Con* bg2 ferr bg2 **Ip** bg2 kreos bg2 lach bg2 mag-m bg2 nat-m bg2 nux-m bg2 **Nux-v** bg2 petr bg2 phos bg2 puls bg2 *Sep* bg2
- **quinine**; abuse of: arn bg2 *Ars* bg2 bell bg2 calc bg2 caps bg2 *Carb-v* bg2 cina bg2 *Ferr* bg2 **Ip** bg2 *Lach* bg2 merc bg2 nat-c bg2 nat-m bg2 **Nux-v** bg2 *Puls* bg2 sep bg2 sulph bg2 *Verat* bg2
- **sedentary** living: bry bg2 calc bg2 *Nux-v* bg2 sep bg2 sulph bg2
- **sexual** losses; from: calc bg2 merc bg2 *Nux-v* bg2 ph-ac bg2 staph bg2 *Sulph* bg2
- **sleep**; loss of: arn bg2 carb-v bg2 *Cocc* bg2 nux-v bg2 puls bg2 verat bg2
- **tea**; abuse of: ferr bg2 thuj bg2

SMOKING:
- **agg.**: ambr bg2 ant-c bg2 arg-met bg2 carb-an bg2 clem bg2 cocc bg2 euphr bg2 ign bg2 *Ip* bg2 lach bg2 merc bg2 **Nux-v** bg2 phos bg2 **Puls** bg2 ruta bg2 sang bg2 sel bg2 staph bg2 tarax bg2
- **amel.**: kali-bi bg2

SNEEZING: | **amel.**: *Nux-v* b7a.de

SOFTENING of: ant-c b7a.de* arg-n bg2 ars b4a.de* bar-c bg2 *Bism* b7a.de **Calc** b4a.de* carb-v bg2 *Ign* b7a.de kreos b7a.de* merc-d bro1 nux-v bg2 puls bg2 *Sec* b7a.de* **Sep** b4a.de sulph bg2 *Thuj* b4a.de *Verat* b7a.de*

SOLID FOOD agg.: caust b4a.de plb bg2

SOUP agg.: *Bell* b4a.de

SOUR FOOD agg.: **Acon** bg2 aloe bg2 *Ars* b4a.de* **Carb-v** bg2 *Hep* bg2 *Ign* b7a.de lach bg2 nat-m bg2 nux-v bg2 phos bg2 sulph bg2

SPITTING up food (See Eructations; Vomiting)

SPOT; complaints in a: arg-n ptk1 bar-c ptk1 bism ptk1 kali-bi ptk1 lyc ptk1

STAGNATION:
- **sensation** of stagnation | **Epigastrium**: guaj b4a.de*

STANDING:
- **agg.**: acon b7.de* arg-met b7.de* arn b7.de* bar-c b4.de* dig b4.de* sulph b4.de* teucr b7.de* verat b7.de*
- **amel.**: dig b4.de*

STENOSIS (See Constriction)

STEPPING HARD agg.: aloe bg2 anac b4a.de* bar-c b4.de* **Bry** b7.de* hell b7.de* mag-m b4.de* puls b7a.de* rhus-t b7.de* *Sep* b4a.de

Stomach

STOMACHACHE (See Pain)

STONE; sensation of a: (_↗Heaviness; Lump)_ abies-n k* acon k* _Aesc_ k* agar k* all-s k* alum b4.de* alum-sil k2 anac bro1 ant-t ptk1 arg-n bg2* arn k* **Ars** k* ars-s-f k2 _Aur_ b4a.de bapt a1* **Bar-c** k* bell bg2 bism bg2 bov bg2 _Brom_ k* **Bry** k* cact **Calc** k* calc-s calc-sil k2 caps bg2 carb-an k* carb-v b4.de* cedr k* _Cham_ k* chin bg2* coc-c k* cocc ptk1 colch coloc k* dig b4.de* dios k* elaps eup-per bg1 ferr b7.de* fl-ac gent-c k* graph bro1 _Grat Hep_ b4a.de* ign k* kali-ar _Kali-bi_ k* kali-c k* kali-p kali-s fd4.de kola stb3• _Lac-c_ hr1 lach bg2* lob bg2* lyc bg2* manc ptk1 mang b4.de* melal-alt gya4 _Merc_ k* merl a1 mez mill bg1* mim-p rsj8• mosch b7a.de naja k* nat-ar _Nat-c_ k* nat-m k* nux-m bg2* **Nux-v** k* olnd bg1 op k* osm k* ox-ac bg1* par k* _Ph-ac_ k* phos b4.de* plb bg2 plut-n srj7• positr nl2• _Ptel_ k* puls k* ran-b bg1 rhus-g tmo3• _Rhus-t_ k* rumx bro1 sabad b7.de* sec k* _Seneg_ b4a.de sep k* sil k* _Spig_ b7a.de* spong squil k* staph k* suis-pan rly4• sul-ac k* sulph b4.de* _Tab_ sne tritic-vg fd5.de vanil fd5.de ven-m rsj12• vip fkr4.de visc sp1 zing k*

- **morning**: par k*
  - • **bed** agg.; in: kali-c k*
  - • **waking**; on: puls k*
- **bread** agg.: sep h2
- **cold**: _Acon_ b7a.de _Rhus-t_ b7a.de sil ptk1
  - • **vomiting**; after: _Acon_ sil bg1
- **dinner**; after: ptel k*
- **eating**:
  - • **after**:
    - ⁝ **agg.**: abies-n k2* _Ars Bar-c_ **Bry** kali-s fd4.de melal-alt gya4 naja nat-m **Nux-v** positr nl2• ptel st _Puls_ rhus-t sang a1 sil k* spong fd4.de [tax jsj7]
    - ⁝ **amel.**: ptel k*
- **egg**; as if swallowed an (See Egg; sensation)
- **eructations** | **amel.**: alum h2 _Bar-c_ k* nat-c h2 par k* tritic-vg fd5.de
- **hawking** up mucus | **amel.**: kali-c k*
- **motion** agg.: _Bry Calc Nux-v_
- **pressure**; as from: aesc ptk1 brom ptk1 cham ptk1 squil ptk1
- **rising** sensation: sul-ac h2
- **rubbing** together: cocc ptk1
- **salivation** | **amel.**: sul-ac h2
- **sharp**: hydr ptk1
- **supper** agg.; after: alum h2 _Calc_
- O **Epigastrium**: acon b7.de* aesc bg2 arn b7.de* _Aur_ b4a.de _Bar-c_ b4.de* calc b4.de* **Cham** b7.de* cupr b7.de* dig b4.de* grat bg2 hep bg2 _Ign_ b7a.de* _Lach_ bg2 merc b4.de* nat-m bg2 **Nux-v** bg2 phos b4.de* plb bg2 sep b4.de* spig b7.de* spong b7a.de* _Staph_ bg2

STOOL:

- **after**:
  - • **agg.**: podo bg2
  - • **amel.**: bell bg2
- **during**:
  - • **agg.**: ambr ptk1 puls ptk1 sul-ac ptk1
  - • **amel.**: chel ptk1
- **urging** for stool, felt in stomach: alum h2 kali-sula a1

STOOPING:

- **agg.**: alum b4a.de* **Ars** b4a.de bell b4.de* bry b7.de* cann-s b7.de* canth b7.de* _Ign_ b7a.de merc b4a.de plat b4.de* rhus-t b7a.de* sabin b7.de* staph b7.de* tarax b7.de* valer b7.de*
- **amel.**: anac b4a.de* mosch b7a.de **Nux-v** b7a.de _Staph_ b7a.de

STRETCHING agg.: am-c b4a.de*

STUFFED sensation: | **eating**; after (See Fullness - eating - after - agg.)

SUMMER: _Guaj_ k*

SUPPER:

- **after**:
  - • **agg.**: _Sep_ b4.de*
  - • **amel.**: sep bg2

SWALLOWING; during: | **agg.**: _Bar-c_ b4.de* nit-ac b4.de* phos b4.de* sep b4.de*

SWASHING: abrot bg2 arn k* carb-v bg2 kali-c bg2 lach bg2 lyc bg2 mez k* ol-an bg2 sabad bg2

Swashing: ...

- **morning**: mez

SWEETS agg.: acon bg2 merc bg2 nat-p bg2 sulph bg2 zinc bg2

SWELLING (See Distension)

TALKING agg.: ars b4.de* bry b7.de* caps b7.de* caust ptk1 hell b7.de* ign b7.de* kali-c bg2* mag-m b4.de* nat-c b4a.de* ptel bg2 rhus-t b7.de* rumx bg2*

TEA agg.: ferr bg2

TENSION: acon k* aesc agar allox tpw3* ambr k* anac ant-c c1 _Ant-t_ arg-n k* _Ars_ k* ars-i asaf k* bar-c k* bar-i bar-m bell k* bry k* cain calc calc-sil k2 _Caps_ **Carb-v** k* carbn-s carl k* castm caust k* cham k* _Chel_ k* cic clem cocc k* coff k* coff-t a1 colch coloc cortico tpw7* crot-t cypra-eg sde6.de• dros dulc b4.de* ferr k* ferr-i flor-p rsj3• gent-l k* grat k* guare k* helon k* _Hep_ hura iod k* _Ip_ kali-ar _Kali-c_ k* kali-m k2 kreos k* lac-loxod-a hrn2• _Lact Lob_ **Lyc** k* _Mag-m_ k* merc k* merc-c b4a.de mez k* mosch b7.de* mur-ac nat-ar nat-c h2 nat-m k* nit-ac k* **Nux-v** k* op ph-ac h2 phos k* plat k* _Plb_ k* _Puls_ k* ran-s _Rheum_ b7.de* **Ruta** k* sabad sabin b7.de* sel sep _Sil_ k* **Stann** k* _Staph_ k* _Stram_ sul-ac sulph b4.de* sumb k* tarax _Ter_ tritic-vg fd5.de ven-m rsj12• verat zinc zinc-m a1

- **morning**: arn kali-n k*
  - • **bed** agg.; in: arn staph h1
- **forenoon**: puls
- **noon**: euphr
- **evening**: hura mag-m h2 sulph
- **night**:
  - • **midnight**:
    - ⁝ **after** | **2** h: ars
- **breathing**:
  - • **agg.**: lyc h2
  - • **holding** breath | **agg.**: dros h1
- **clothing** agg.: _Hep Kreos_
- **dinner**; after: nit-ac k* phos sep
- **drinking** amel.: ruta
- **eating** | **after** | **agg.**: anac coff-t hr1 _Iod_ k* phos h2 ruta h1 sul-ac tritic-vg fd5.de
  - • **before** | **agg.**: mez k*
- **erect** position agg.: mag-m h2
- **inspiration** agg.; deep: dros h1 mez h2
- **menses**; during: zinc
- **milk** | **amel.**: **Ruta** k*
- **motion**:
  - • **agg.**: caps sep h2
  - • **amel.**: _Puls_
- **riding** in a carriage agg.: phos k*
- **sitting** agg.: hep h2
- **stool** | **after** | **agg.**: dros h1 sep
  - • **before**: ars h2 dros h1
- **stooping** agg.: sep sf1.de
- **walking** agg.: cocc colch
- ▽ **extending** to | **Back**: sulph h2
- O **Epigastrium**: acon b7.de* anac b4.de* ant-c bg2 ars b4.de* asaf b7a.de **Bell** b4a.de bell-p sp1 _Bry_ b7.de* _Cham_ b7.de* clem bg2 cocc b7.de* dig b4.de* dros b7.de* dulc b4.de* hep b4.de* _Kali-c_ b4.de* _Kreos_ bg2 lyc b4.de* mag-m b4.de* _Merc_ b4.de* mez b4.de* nat-c b4.de* nux-v b7a.de* phos b4.de* plb bg2 puls b7.de* ran-s b7.de* _Rheum_ b7.de* sabin b7.de* samb xxb1 sang ptk1 sep bg2 stann b4.de* staph b7.de* sulph b4.de* tarax b7.de* tarent tl1 _Verat_ b7.de*
  - • **eating**; after: anac b4a.de
  - ▽ • **extending** to | **Shoulders**; between: nux-v b7a.de

THIRST: abrom-a ks5 absin a1 **Acet-ac** k* **Acon** k* acon-l a1 adam srj5• aesc k* aeth k* agar k* agar-ph a1 _Agath-a_ nl2• agn k* _Aids_ nl2• ail k* alco a1 alf bro1 _All-c_ k* all-s allox sp1 aloe alum k* alum-sil k2 _Alumn_ k* am-c k* am-caust c2* _Am-m_ k* _Anac_ k* anan ancis-p tsm2 anders bnj1 _Androc_ srj1*• ang b2.de* _Ant-c_ k* ant-t k* anth a1 anthraci apis k* _Apoc_ k* aq-mar skp7• ara-maca sej7• aran a1 arb-m oss1• **Arg-n** k* arizon-l nl2• _Arn_ k* **Ars** k* ars-h k* _Ars-i_ k* ars-s-f a1 ars-s-r a1 aspar a1 atro a1 aur k* aur-i k2 aur-m k* aur-m-n wbt2• aur-s c1* _Bapt_ k* _Bar-c_ k* bar-i _Bar-m_ k* bar-ox-suc rly4• _Bell_ k*

Thirst: ...
bell-p sp1 benz-ac a1 *Berb* k* bism k* bit-ar wht1• *Bol-la* bol-s a1 *Borx* k* both tsm2 both-ax tsm2 bov k* brass-n-o srj5• brom k* **Bry** k* cact k* cadm-s caesal-b bnj1 cain caj k* calad b2.de* **Calc** k* *Calc-ar* **Calc-s** k* *Camph* k* cann-i k* cann-s b2.de* *Canth* k* **Caps** k* *Carb-ac* carb-an k* *Carb-v* k* carbn-s carl k* cartl-s rly4• cassia-s ccrh1• castm *Castn-v* br1 caul k* **Caust** k* cedr k* cench tsm2 cent a1 **Cham** k* *Chel* k* chen-a vml3• chim hr1 **Chin** k* *Chinin-ar* k* *Chinin-s* k* chir-fl gya2 chlol a1* chord-umb rly4• *Cic* k* *Cimic* k* *Cimx* hr1 *Cina* k* cinnb k* clem k* cloth tsm2 *Coc-c* k* *Cocc* k* cod a1* coff b2.de* *Colch* k* *Coloc* k* *Con* k* conin a1 convo-s sp1 cop k* cor-r k* cortico sp1 *Croc* k* *Crot-c* k* *Crot-h* k* cub a1 *Cupr* k* cupr-ar bro1 cycl k* cystein-l rly4• daph k* **Dig** k* dor k* dream-p sdj1• *Dros* k* *Dulc* k* elaps eucal a1 eug k* **Eup-per** k* euph k* eupi k* fago k* fagu a1 falco-ch sze4• falco-pe nl2• ferr b2.de* ferr-ar ferr-i k* *Ferr-p* ferul a1 fic-m gya1 *Fl-ac* k* flor-p rsj3• form k* fuma-ac rly4• galeoc-c-h gms1• gamb k* gard-j vlr2• gast a1 gent-c k* ger-i rly4• germ-met srj5• get a1 gink-b sbd1• gins k* glon k* granit-m es1• graph k* grat k* guaj k* guat sp1 haliae-lc srj5• ham k* helia a1 **Hell** k* helo-s bnm14*• helodr-cal knl2• helon bro1 *Hep* k* hera a1 hipp a1 hydr-ac k* *Hydrog* srj2• hydroph rsj6• *Hyos* k* ichth bro1 *Ign* b2.de* ind k* indol bro1 **Iod** k* ip k* irid-met srj5• jug-r k* kali-ar k* *Kali-bi* k* kali-br bro1 *Kali-c* k* kali-chl k* *Kali-i* k* kali-n k* kali-ox a1 *Kali-p* k* *Kali-s* k* kali-sula a1* kali-t a1 *Kalm* k* ketogl-ac rly4• kiss a1 kreos k* lac-ac bro1 lac-h htj1*• *Lach* k* lachn k* lact k* lap-la sde8.de• lat-h bnm5• lat-m sp1 *Laur* k* lec br1* *Led* k* lepi a1 lil-t k* limest-b es1• loxo-recl knl4• *Luna* kg1• lyc k* m-aust b2.de *Mag-c* k* mag-m k* mag-p bro1 mag-s k* manc k* mang k* med bro1* medul-os-si rly4• melal-alt gya4 menis a1 **Merc** k* *Merc-c* k* merc-cy a1 merc-d a1 *Merc-i-f* k* merl k* *Mez* k* mill k* morph a1* mosch a1 mur-ac k* myris a1 naja narz a1 *Nat-ar* nat-br a1 *Nat-c* k* nat-f sp1 **Nat-m** k* *Nat-n* bg2 nat-ox rly4• *Nat-p* nat-s k* nat-sil fd3.de• neon srj5• nicc k* nicotam rly4• *Nit-ac* k* nux-m k* *Nux-v* k* oci-sa sk4• oena a1 ol-j k* *Olib-sac* wmh1 olnd k* onis a1 **Op** k* orot-ac rly4• ox-ac k* oxal-a rly4• ozone sde2• paeon k* pant-ac rly4• petr k* petros bro1 ph-ac k* **Phos** k* phys k* phyt a1 pic-ac k* pieri-b mlk9.de pin-con oss2• pin-s a1 plac rzf5• plac-s rly4• plan k* plat k* *Plb* k* plect a1 plut-n srj7• *Podo* k* *Positr* nl2• pot-e rly4• propl ub1• propr sa3• psor k* ptel k* puls k* *Ran-b* k* ran-s b2.de* *Raph* k* *Rat* k* rham-f a1 rheum b2.de* rhod k* rhus-a bro1 rhus-g a1 **Rhus-t** k* ric a1 rob k* ros-d wla1 rosm lgb1 ruta k* sabad k* sal-al blc1• sal-fr sle1• samb k* sang k* santin sapin a1 sars k* **Sec** k* sel k* seneg k* sep k* **Sil** k* sin-a a1 sol-a a1 sol-ni sol-t-ae k* spig k* spira a1 **Spong** b2.de* *Squil* b2.de* stann k* staph k* staphycoc rly4• **Stram** k* stront-c k* stry a1 suis-em rly4• suis-pan rly4• sul-ac k* sul-i a1* **Sulph** k* symph fd3.de• syph k2 tab k* tanac a1 taosc iwa1• *Tarax* bg2 **Tarent** k* tax k* tax-br oss1• tep k* ter k* tere-la rly4• term-a bnj1 thea *Ther* k* *Thuj* k* til a1 tong a1 trach a1 trif-p a1 tritic-vg fd5.de tung-met bdx1• upa k* uran-n bro1 ust k* vac a1 valer b2.de* vanil fd5.de ven-m rsj12• **Verat** k* *Verat-v* k* verb k* vero-o rly3• vinc a1 viol-t b7.de vip a1* voes a1 wies a1 *Zinc* k* zinc-m a1 zinc-s a1 zing k* ziz a1 [*Bar-p* stj1 bell-p-sp dcm1 buteo-j sej6 heroin sdj2]

- **day** and night: bry b7.de* [bell-p-sp dcm1]
- **daytime**: *Bry* b7a.de chin-b hr1 con a1 hep k* kali-n h2 led b7.de* merc b4.de* ol-an a1 petr b4.de* sep b4.de* suis-pan rly4• sulph b4.de* thuj b4.de* zinc b4.de* [bell-p-sp dcm1]
- **morning**: am-c k* am-m h2 ant-c h2 apoc ars k* ars-s-f k2 arund k* bell b4.de* borx k* bry k* calc k* carb-an k* carb-v a1 carbn-s caust b4.de* chin b7.de* chin-b hr1 chinin-s coc-c k* coff b7.de* dros k* eug k* fago k* gaba sa3• glon k* *Graph* k* grat k* hep bg2 hir skp7• hyper k* jab k* kali-c h2 kali-s fd4.de kreos k* mag-m k* mag-s k* nat-ar nat-c k* nat-m k* nat-ox rly4• nat-s k* nat-sil fd3.de• **Nit-ac** k* nux-m k* *Nux-v* k* ox-ac k* ph-ac k* phel a1 phos k* phyt k* plb k* psil ft1 puls k* rhus-t k* ruta fd4.de sabad k* sars k* sep k* spong k* *Stram* k* sulph k* tab k* thuj k* *Verat* k* *Verat-v* vip k*
  - **milk** agg.: nat-m k*
  - **waking** | **after** | **agg.**: sep h2
    - **on**: am-c k* apoc vml3• arund k* bit-ar wht1• chlol a1 der a1 gard-j vlr2• hyper k* jab k* mag-s k* nat-sil fd3.de• nit-ac k* podo fd3.de• sel sep k* thuj k* trios rsj1• tung-met bdx1•
- **forenoon**: agar k* ang h1* apis calc-s k* chin h1 dulc fd4.de elaps hipp a1 ign b7a.de kali-c k* kali-n k* mag-c k* mag-m k* mag-s k* nat-c k* nat-s k* phel a1 phos b4.de* ruta fd4.de *Sep* b4.de* thuj b4.de* zinc k*
  - **10** h: nat-ar *Nat-m*
- **noon**: alum b4.de* am-c b4.de* bell b4.de* **Lyc** mag-c k* mag-m k* nat-c k* nit-ac b4.de* phos k* zinc b4.de*
- **afternoon**: aloe alum b4.de* am-c k* am-m k* anac b4.de* bell b4.de* berb k* borx h2 bov k* brom k* bry b7.de* *Calc* k* calc-sil k2 calen a1 cann-s b7.de* carl k* caust b4.de* chel b7.de* chin k* choc srj3• chord-umb rly4• cic a1 cinch a1 clem k* colch k* con k* croc b7.de* dulc fd4.de ferr b7.de* graph b4.de* ham k* ign k* kali-n k* laur b7.de* mag-c k* mag-m k* mag-s k* *Nat-c* k* nat-m k* nat-s k* nept-m lsd2.fr nicc k* nux-v k* ozone sde2• petr k* ph-ac k* phos k* phys k* plb b7.de* propr sa3• *Ran-b* k* rhus-t k* ruta k* *Samb* b7a.de sars b4a.de* senec k* sep b4.de* sil k* stann b4.de* sulph b4.de* tritic-vg fd5.de verat k* *Zinc* k* zinc-p k2
  - **13**-18 h: *Phos* vh
  - **14** h: **PULS** k ●
  - **14**.30 h: ozone sde2•
  - **15** h: cench k2 ferr lyc nicc staph
  - **16** h: bung-fa mtf chel *Lyc* sulph
    - **chill**; during: sulph
  - **sleep** agg.; after: **Staph** vh ther c1
- **evening**: abrom-a ks5 acon k* *All-c* k* am-c am-m k* amp rly4• anac k* ang b7.de* *Ant-c* k* arg-met k* ars k* ars-i ars-s-f k2 bar-c k* bar-s k2 bell k* benz-ac k* bism k* borx bov k* bry k* calad b7.de* cann-s b7.de* carl k* cench k2 cham k* chin k* chinin-ar chinin-s clem k* coc-c *Croc* k* cur **Cycl** k* dream-p sdj1• dulc fd4.de elaps euphr k* fago k* ferr k* ferr-i galeoc-c-h gms1• *Gamb* k* gran k* graph h2 grat k* ham k* hep bg2 ign b7.de* *Iod* k* jatr-c kali-bi k* kali-c k* kali-n b4.de* kreos lach b7.de* laur k* lavand-a ctl1• lyc k* *Mag-c* k* *Mag-m* k* mag-s merc b4.de* merc-i-f k* mez k* mosch b7.de* nat-ar nat-c k* *Nat-m* k* *Nat-s* k* *Nicc* k* nux-v b7.de* ol-an k* ped a1 phos k* phys k* plat b4.de* plb k* podo k* puls b7.de* ran-b c1 rat k* *Rhus-t* b7.de* rumx ruta fd4.de sabad b7.de* sal-fr sle1• sel k* seneg k* sep k* sin-a k* spig k* spong b7.de* squil k* stann b4.de* sul-i k2 sulph k* tab k* *Thuj* k* verat b7.de* vichy-g a1 vip fkr4.de *Zinc* k* zinc-p k2 zing k*
  - **18** h: bar-c ham tab
  - **20** h: phos bg1
  - **amel.**: ven-m rsj12•
- **night**: *Acon* k* acon-ac rly4• acon-l a1 agath-a nl2• aloe am-c bg2 ambr h1 *Ant-c* k* ant-t k* aphis c1 apis k* aq-mar mgm• am k* *Ars* k* ars-s-f k2 bamb-a stb2.de• bell b4.de* borx b4a.de* bry k* cadm-s calad b7.de* *Calc* k* calc-sil k2 canth k* carb-an k* carb-v h2* caust bg2 cedr k* cham k* chinin-s chir-fl gya2 cina bg2 cinch a1 cinnb *Coff* k* cur *Cycl* k* dros b7.de* dulc fd4.de elaps eug a1* *Eup-per* fago k* fl-ac k* gamb k* gink-b sbd1• glon k* graph h2 *Hep* k* ign b7.de* *Kali-c* b4.de* kali-p fd1.de• kali-s fd4.de lac-h sk4• *Lach* led b7.de* *Lyc* k* *Mag-c* k* mag-m k* mang k* *Merc* k* mez h2 mur-ac k* nat-ar nat-c k* nat-m k* nat-s k* nicc k* nit-ac k* nux-v k* olib-sac wmh1 op k* orig a1 *Phos* k* plan k* plat b4.de* pot-e rly4• psil ft1 psor bg2 puls k* *Ran-s* b7.de* *Rhus-t* k* ruta fd4.de sacch-a fd2.de• sel bg2 sep h2* **Sil** k* *Spong* sul-ac bg2 sulfonam ks2 *Sulph* k* tab k* tere-la rly4• *Thuj* k* tub c1 urol-h rwt• vip fkr4.de wies a1 zing k* [bell-p-sp dcm1]
  - **midnight**: cann-i k* lat-m bnm6• mag-m k* merc k* plat k* puls h1 sul-ac k* sulph k*
    - **after**: bell h1 kali-p fd1.de• mag-m h2 mang h2 puls bg2
      - **3** h: mag-m vip fkr4.de [tax jsj7]
  - **fever**; during: acon bg2 ant-c bg2 bell bg2 bry bg2 cham bg2 rhus-t bg2
  - **waking**; on: agath-a nl2• aloe *Apoc* berb bit-ar wht1• calad carb-an *Coff* kali-s fd4.de kola stb3• *Nat-s* pot-e rly4• ruta fd4.de sacch-a fd2.de• *Stram* k*
- **accompanied** by:
  - **appetite**; ravenous (See Appetite - ravenous - accompanied - thirst)
  - **drinks**; aversion to (See GENERALS - Food and - drinks - aversion - accompanied - thirst)
  - **dropsy** (See GENERALS - Dropsy - general - accompanied - thirst)
  - **fullness**; sensation of: gink-b sbd1•
  - **nausea** (See Nausea - accompanied - tongue)
  - **orgasm** of blood: acon b7.de arg-met b7.de*
  - **pain** in stomach (See Pain - accompanied - thirst)
  - **palpitation** (See CHEST - Palpitation - accompanied - thirst)
  - **respiration**; complaints of: lach bg2

Stomach

- **salivation** (See MOUTH - Salivation - thirst)
- **urinate**; urging to (See BLADDER - Urination - urging - thirst)
- **weakness** (See GENERALS - Weakness - thirst)
- ○ **Abdomen**:
  - **complaints** (See ABDOMEN - Complaints - accompanied - thirst)
  - **heat** (See ABDOMEN - Heat - accompanied - thirst)
  - **pain** (See ABDOMEN - Pain - accompanied - thirst)
- **Epigastrium**; warmth in: bry b7.de*
- **Esophagus**; pain (See THROAT - Pain - esophagus - accompanied - thirst)
- **Heart**; complaints of (See CHEST - Heart; complaints - thirst)
- **Lips**; dryness of: bit-ar wht1• ozone sde2• sulfonam ks2 suprar rly4• tere-la rly4• verat bg2
  - **cold** water; desire for large quantities of: abrom-a ks5
- **Mouth**:
  - **bitter** taste: con ptk1 pic-ac ptk1
  - **heat**: hyper ptk1
- **Palate**; prickling (See MOUTH - Prickling - palate - accompanied - thirst)
- **Teeth**; pain in (See TEETH - Pain - accompanied - thirst)
- **Throat**; dryness of: abrom-a ks5 alum bg2 *Bell* bg2 cann-i tl1 cupr b7a.de guaj bg2 kali-n bg2 kreos b7a.de merc tl1 nat-n bg2 *Phyt* bg2 rhus-t tl1 sel rsj9•
- **Tongue**:
  - **dryness** of tongue: arizon-l nl2• **Bry** kr1* cassia-s cdd7• cham kr1* *Dulc* kr1*
  - **mucus**; white: ox-ac kr1*

- **alternating** with:
  - **aversion** to drink (See GENERALS - Food - drinks - aversion - alternating - thirst)
  - **thirstlessness**: berb br1 colch k2
- **anger**; after: bry nux-v k*
- **anxious**: bell h1 dulc fd4.de
- **apoplexy**; after: xan c1
- **appetite**; with lost (See Appetite - wanting - thirst - with)
- **apyrexia**, during: ars bro1 *Cimx* k* *Ign* b7a.de* *Ip*
- **beer** agg.; after: bry k*
- **breakfast** | **after** | **agg.**: mag-s vh nept-m lsd2.fr
  - **before** | **agg.**: con b4a.de nept-m lsd2.fr
- **burning**, vehement: **Acet-ac** *Acon* aeth *Agar* *Anac* anan apis *Ars* k* ars-s-f k2 *Aur* aur-i k2 aur-s k2 *Bell* k* **Bry** bufo *Calc* calc-sil k2 *Camph* **Cann-i** vh canth k* *Carb-v* carbn-s *Castm* caust cham chin colch *Coloc* *Crot-c* *Crot-h* cub cupr eberth jl2 elaps ferr graph hep hyos iod jatr-c kali-bi *Kali-n* kali-s kola stb3• kreos bg2 *Laur* lyc *Lycps-v* mag-m **Merc** k* merc-c merc-i-f mur-ac nat-ar nat-c nat-p fkr6.de nicc nit-ac nux-v bg3 op ozone sde2• ph-ac **Phos** pieri-b mlk9.de *Plb* puls raph *Rhus-t* ruta fd4.de sabad bg3 *Sec* *Sil* spong squil stann *Stram* sul-ac sul-i k2 *Sulph* **Tarent** thuj tritic-vg fd5.de vanil fd5.de verat verb vip k* zinc [spect dfg1]
  - **water**; only for: *Acet-ac* vh1
  - **without** desire to drink: *Ars*
- **capricious**: am ptk1* des-ac rbp6 lac-leo hrn2•
- **children**; in: androc bnm2•
- **chill**:
  - **after**: all-c k* am-m bg2 **Ars** k* ars-s-f k2* canth k* **Chin** k* *Cimx* k* **Dros** k* ferr k* hell bg2 hep kali-bi kreos k* mag-s k* mang h2 *Nat-m* k* nat-s k* nux-v bg2 psor k* **Puls** k* *Sabad* k* sars k* *Sep* k* sulph k* thuj k*
  - **before**: am-c am-m k* ang b7.de* arn k* **Ars** k* bell b4a.de* borx h2 *Caps* k* carb-v bg2* **Chin** k* chinin-s bro1 *Cimx* hr1 *Cina* bg2 **Eup-per** k* *Eup-pur* gels bro1 *Hep* ign b7a.de* lach k* mag-c h2* meny bro1 nat-m k* *Nux-v* k* nyct br1* ol-an bg2* ol-j k* **Puls** k* rhus-t bg2 sep k* sulph k*
  - **cannot** drink, makes headache unbearable; yet: cimx

- **chill**: ...
  - **during**: *Acon* k* alum k* am-m k* anac b2.de ang bg2 ant-c b2.de* **Apis** k* aran **Arn** k* ars k* asar k* bar-c k* bar-m bell b2.de* borx b2.de* bov k* *Bry* k* calad k* *Calc* k* camph k* cann-s k* canth k* **Caps** k* **Carb-an** b4.de *Carb-v* k* carbn-s cham k* chin b2.de* *Chinin-s* cimx **Cina** k* conv br1* croc k* dros b2.de* *Dulc* b2.de* **Eup-per** k* *Eup-pur* eupi k* *Ferr* k* gamb k* gels hr1 hep b2.de* **Ign** k* *Ip* b2.de* kali-ar *Kali-c* k* kali-i k* kali-m k2 *Kali-n* b2.de* kali-sil k2 kreos b2.de* *Lach* k* laur b2.de* *Lec* *Led* k* m-arct b2.de* m-aust b2.de* mag-m k* mag-s c1 med meny bg2 merc b2.de* mez b2.de* mur-ac k* nat-c k* **Nat-m** k* nat-s k* nux-m bg2 **Nux-v** k* nyct br1* ol-j k* *Op* k* ph-ac b4.de* phos b2.de* *Plb* b2.de* psor k* puls b2.de* **Pyrog** k* ran-b b2.de* ran-s k* *Rhus-t* k* ruta b2.de* sabad k* sanic c1 *Sec* k* **Sep** k* **Sil** k* spong b2.de* squil b2.de* stann b2.de* staph b2.de* *Sulph* k* tarent thuj k* **Tub** k* valer b2.de* **Verat** k* wye bro1
    - **beginning** of: m-arct bg2 m-aust b7.de
- **choking** sensation when drinking, with: squil
- **coition**; after: eug k*
- **cold** | **drinks**:
  - **after** | **agg.**: *Calc* b4a.de
  - **water**: bros-gau mrc1 pyrog jl2
    - **amel.**: allox tpw3* alumn a1* melal-alt gya4 pitu-gl skp7• sec mtf11 *Trios* rsj11• verat tl1
    - **short** intervals: *Acon* bro1 ant-t bro1 *Ars* bro1 hyos bro1 onos bro1 pitu-gl skp7• sanic bro1
- **constant** (See unquenchable)
- **convulsions**:
  - **after**: *Ars* sne bell gt1 ign gt1
  - **during**: cic
- **coryza**; during: ars bg2 *Cham* b7.de* graph b4.de* hep b4a.de* lach bg2 lyc b4.de* mag-m h2 *Merc* b4a.de* nat-c h2 *Nux-v* b7a.de *Samb* b7a.de
- **cough** agg.; during: *Cham* b7a.de samb b7a.de *Verat* b7a.de
- **cramp**; during: cic b7.de*
- **decreased**: anh sp1 bros-gau mrc1 phasco-ci rbp2
- **delivery**; during: *Caul* hr1
- **diarrhea**, with: acet-ac a1 ars bg2 bry bg2 cham bg2 chin bg2 dulc bg2 rheum bg2 sul-ac bg2
- **dinner**; after: aloe anac k* canth k* *Castm* cycl k* ferr k* gamb k* mag-c k* mag-m k* *Nat-c* k* nat-m k* plb k* psor k* thuj k* zinc k*
- **dread** of liquids; with (See MIND - Fear - liquids - thirst)
- **drink**; without desire to (See GENERALS - Food - drinks - aversion - accompanied - thirst)
- **drinking**:
  - **cold** water | **agg.**: adam skp7• aids nl2• *Bism* mrr1 dulc fd4.de kali-s fd4.de pyrog pd ruta fd4.de spong fd4.de tritic-vg fd5.de vanil fd5.de
  - **hurried**: ars bg2 hell bg2 hep bg2 ip bg2 nat-m bg2 nit-ac bg2 nux-v bg2 sil bg2 sulph bg2 verat bg2
  - **little**: hell bg2
  - **water** | **agg.**: abrom-a ks5 convo-s sp1 hir skp7• sal-al blc1• tritic-vg fd5.de
- **drinks**:
  - **cold** (See GENERALS - Food and - cold drink - desire)
  - **warm** (See GENERALS - Food and - warm drinks - desire)
- **dropsy**, with: acet-ac a1* acon bro1 *Apoc* bro1 ars bro1
- **eating** | **after**:
  - **agg.**: aloe k* anac k* ars b4a.de bell k* *Bry* k* calad caust k* cent a1 coc-c cocc k* cycl k* elaps ferr b7.de graph k* guare k* lyc k* nat-c k* nit-ac k* nux-v b7.de phel k* phos k* plb b7a.de podo a1* sil k* sulph b4a.de
    - **evening**: galeoc-c-h gms1•
  - **while** | **agg.**: ail k* aloe k* *Am-c* k* ars-i k2 bufo coc-c k* *Cocc* k* *Lach* *Nat-c* k* nit-ac b4a.de* psor puls vh
- **extreme**: abrom-a bnj1 **Acet-ac** k* achy-a zzc1• **Acon** k* adam skp7• *Aesc* aeth agar k* *Agath-a* nl2• *All-c* all-s alum alum-p k2 alumn k2 *Am-m* k* anac k* anan androc srj1• *Ant-c* k* *Ant-t* k* anthraci vh* anthraco br1 *Apis* k* apoc k2* **Arg-n** *Arn* k* **Ars** k* ars-br vh *Ars-h* ars-i ars-s-f k2* asar aspar aur k* aur-ar k2 aur-i k2 aur-m aur-s k2 **Bapt** c1 bar-c bar-i bar-m *Bell* k* berb k2 bism k* *Borx* botul jl2 *Bov* k* **Bry** k* bufo *Cadm-s* calad **Calc** k* calc-i k2 **Calc-s** calc-sil k2* *Camph* k* cann-s canth k* caps *Carb-ac* carb-an *Carb-v* k* carbn-s cassia-s cdd7*• **Caust** k* *Cedr* cench k2 **Cham** k* *Chel* k* **Chin** k* chir-fl bnm4•

- **extreme**: ...
chlor cic k* cimic sne cina coc-c cocc k* coff k* *Colch* k* *Coloc* k* con k* *Cop* *Croc* k* *Crot-c* *Crot-h* *Crot-t* k* cub *Cupr* k* *Cupr-ar* cur *Cycl* **Dig** dros *Dulc* k* *Elaps* ephe-si hsj1• eucal a1 **Eup-per** *Eup-pur* falco-pe nl2• *Ferr* k* ferr-ar ferr-i ferr-m gamb *Glycyr-g* cte1• *Graph* k* grat guaj k* ham **Hell** k* helo c1 helo-s c1* helon *Hep* k* hydr-ac hydrog srj2• hyos k* hyper ign k* *Iod* k* *Ip* jab k* jatr-c kali-ar kali-bi k* *Kali-br* *Kali-c* kali-chl *Kali-i* kali-m k2 kali-n k* kali-ox a1 *Kali-p* kali-sil k2 *Kalm* *Kreos* *Lac-ac* lac-d lach k* lachn lat-h bnm5• *Laur* k* *Led* lil-t loxo-lae bnm12• *Lyc* k* *Lycps-v* *Lyss* *Mag-c* k* *Mag-m* k* manc k* marb-w es1• *Med* k* **Merc** k* **Merc-c** k* merc-cy a1 merc-d a1 merc-i-f mez k* mill mosch k* mur-ac mygal k* nat-ar *Nat-c* k* **Nat-m** k* *Nat-p* *Nat-s* *Nit-ac* k* nux-m k* *Nux-v* k* *Olnd* *Op* k* ox-ac par *Petr* k* petr-ra shn4• *Ph-ac* k* **Phos** k* *Phyt* k* pieri-b mlk9.de plan plat k* plb k* *Podo* psil ft1 psor bg2 ptel puls k* **Pyrog** k* ran-b ran-s *Raph* rheum k* rhod rhus-g tmo3• *Rhus-t* k* **Rob** rosm lgb1 ruta k* sabad k* samb *Sang* sec k* sel k* seneg *Sep* k* **Sil** k* spig k* *Spong* k* squil k* stann k* staph **Stram** k* stront-c k* stry *Sul-ac* sul-i k2 **Sulph** k* syph syzyg br1 tab bg2 tarax tarent *Tart-ac* a1 tell *Ter* **Ther** k* thuj k* tritic-vg fd5.de tub al* (non:uran-met k) uran-n urol-h rwt• valer **Verat** k* verb k* xan c1 *Zinc* k* zinc-p k2
  - **fever**; with: alumn k1 *Phos* k1
  - **more** than she should; drinks: ars h2
  - **waking**; on: ulm-c jsj8•
- **fear** to drink; with (See MIND - Fear - drinking - thirst)
- **fever**:
  - **after**: ant-c b7a.de ant-t b7.de* ars b4a.de bell b4a.de *Chin* b7.de* ign b7a.de kreos b7a.de *Lyc* b4a.de nat-m b4a.de nux-v b7.de* rhus-t b7a.de
  - **before**: *Arn* b7a.de *Ars* b4a.de bell b4a.de caps b7a.de carb-v b4a.de *Chin* b7.de* cina b7a.de ign b7a.de *Lach* b7.de* mag-c b4a.de nat-m b4a.de *Nux-v* b7a.de *Puls* b7a.de rhus-t b7a.de sep b4a.de *Sulph* b4a.de
  - **during** | **agg.**: **Acon** k* agar bg2 *All-c* k* *Aloe* alumn hr1* am-m k* *Anac* k* *Ang* k* ant-c k* ant-t bg2 anthraci apis bg2 aran c1 arn k* **Ars** k* ars-s-f k2 arum-t asar bg2 **Bell** k* berb borx bg2 bov bg2 **Bry** k* bufo bg2 cact calad k* *Calc* k* *Canth* k* *Caps* k* carb-an h* carb-v h* carbn-s *Cedr* *Cham* k* chel bg2 *Chin* k* chinin-ar *Chinin-s* k* *Cina* k* cist k* clem k* *Cocc* k* *Coff* k* colch k* *Coloc* k* *Con* k* cop k* cor-r *Croc* k* crot-h cur dig bg2 dros h* dulc h* *Elat* **Eup-per** k* ferr k* ferr-p k2 *Gels* graph k* guaj bg2 hell k2 *Hep* k* *Hyos* k* ign k* *Ip* k* *Kali-ar* *Kali-c* k* kali-p kali-sil k2 **Kreos** bg2 *Lach* k* laur bg2 lyc k* mag-c mag-m k* mang-m h med **Merc** bg2 mosch bg2 *Nat-c* bg2 **Nat-m** k* nat-s k2 nit-ac h* nux-m bg2 **Nux-v** k* nyct br1* op k* petr h* ph-ac h* **Phos** k* plat bg2 **Plb** bg2 *Podo* *Psor* k* *Puls* k* *Pyrog* *Ran-s* k* rhod k* *Rhus-t* k* ruta b7.de* sabad bg2 sars h *Sec* k* sep k* *Sil* k* spig h* spong k* stann k* staph k* *Stram* k* *Stront-c* bg2 sul-ac bg2 *Sulph* k* tax k* *Thuj* k* **Tub** k* vac jl2 valer k* verat k* zinc bg2
  - **stages** of fever; during all: acon k1 bry k1 eup-per k1 nat-m k1
- **followed** by | **perspiration**: acon b7.de
- **frequently**; drinking (See Thirst)
- **headache**:
  - **after**: nat-s c1*
  - **during**: aeth agar h2 cadm-s c1 camph chinin-s eug vml3• *Lac-d* **Mag-m** k* *Nat-m* plat h2 pulx bro1* spong fd4.de stram *Ter* *Verat* zing
- **heat**:
  - **after**: agn b7.de* am-m k* anac ant-c b7a.de ant-t b7.de* ars pd bry bg2 cact *Chin* k* coff k* cycl k* dros pd malar nux-v k* op k* puls k* pyrog rhus-t bg2 sep stann k* stram k* tub
  - **before**: *Am-m* b7.de* *Arn* b7a.de ars bg2 bry bg2 canth bg2 caps b7a.de **Chin** b7.de* dros bg2 *Lach* b7.de* nat-c bg2 nux-v b7a.de* nyct br1 **Puls** b7.de* **Sabad** b7.de* *Sep* bg2
  - **during**: **Acon** k* agar b2.de* *All-c* k* *Aloe* alumn hr1 am-m k* *Anac* k* *Ang* k* ant-c k* ant-t b2.de* anthraci apis b7a.de* aran c1 arn k* **Ars** k* ars-s-f k2 arum-t asar b2.de* bar-c b2.de **Bell** k* berb bism b2.de borx b2.de* bov b2.de* **Bry** k* bufo bg2 cact calad k* *Calc* k* *Canth* k* *Caps* k* carb-an b2.de* carb-v b2.de* carbn-s caust b2.de *Cedr* *Cham* k* chel b7a.de* *Chin* k* chinin-ar *Chinin-s* k* cic b2.de *Cina* k* cist k* clem k* *Cocc* k* *Coff* k* colch k* *Coloc* k* *Con* k* cop k* cor-r corh br1 *Croc* k* crot-h cupr b2.de cur dig b2.de* dros b2.de* dulc b2.de* *Elat* **Eup-per** k* ferr k* ferr-p k2 *Gels* graph k* guaj b2.de* hell k2 *Hep* k* *Hyos* k* ign k* iod b2.de *Ip* k* *Kali-ar* *Kali-c* k* kali-p kali-sil k2 **Kreos** b7a.de* *Lach* k* laur b2.de* lyc k* m-aust b2.de* mag-c mag-m k* med **Merc** b2.de* merc-c b4a.de mez b2.de mosch b2.de* *Nat-c* b2.de* **Nat-m** k* nat-s k2 nit-ac b2.de* nux-m b2.de* **Nux-v** k* nyct br1 op k* petr b2.de* petr-ra shn4• ph-ac b2.de*
- **heat – during**: ...
Phos k* plat b2.de* **Plb** b2.de* *Podo* *Psor* k* *Puls* k* *Pyrog* *Ran-s* k* rhod k* *Rhus-t* k* ruta b2.de* sabad b2.de* sars h2 *Sec* k* sep k* *Sil* k* spig b2.de* spong k* stann k* staph k* *Stram* k* *Stront-c* b2.de* sul-ac b2.de* *Sulph* k* tax k* ter bro1 *Thuj* k* **Tub** valer k* verat k* verb b2.de zinc b2.de*
  - **without** heat: *Arn* b7.de bism b7.de bry b7.de coff b7.de laur b7.de m-aust b7.de nux-v b7.de
- **inability** to swallow, with: bell cic k* hyos ign lyss
- **know** for what; but does not (See capricious)
- **large** quantities; for●: abrom-a ks5 acet-ac a1* *Acon* *Agath-a* nl2• allox tpw4 **Ars** k* bac bn* bad bamb-a stb2.de• bell k2 bism vh **Bry** k* bung-fa mtf calen kr1 camph canth b7.de carbn-s carc gk6 cassia-s ccrh1• cephd-i zzc1• *Chin* coc-c k* *Cocc* cop cortiso gse cystein-l rly4• dulc fd4.de *Eup-per* falco-pe nl2• *Ferr-p* ham hir rsj4• irid-met srj5• jatr-c kr1 kali-i k2 kali-s fd4.de lac-c bg1 *Lac-d* lac-leo hrn2• lil-t bg1* lycpr c1 *Lycps-v* melal-alt gya4 merc sne *Merc-c* **Nat-m** k* nept-m lsd2.fr pant-ac rly4• petr-ra shn4• **Phos** k* pic-ac plut-n srj7• *Podo* kr1 positr nl2• ribo rly4• ruta fd4.de sacch sst1• sal-al blc1• sol-ni spong fd4.de *Stram* k* sulfonam ks2 **Sulph** k* taosc iwa1• thiam rly4• *Thyr* vh tritic-vg fd5.de tub c1* tung-met bdx1• vanil fd5.de **Verat** k* vip sf1.de xan c1 [bar-i stj2 iod stj2 merc-i-f stj2 zinc-i stj2]
  - **evening**: abrom-a ks5
  - **fever**; during: **Bry** bg2 canth bg2 stram bg2
  - **long** intervals, at: **Bry** k* cassia-s cdd7*• hell bro1 pitu-gl skp7• podo bro1 sulfonam ks2 *Sulph* bro1 verat bro1
  - **often**; and: abrom-a ks5 *Acon* kr1 arn kr1 ars h2 *Bell* kr1 **Bry** k* cassia-s ccrh1• cop dulc fd4.de *Eup-per* kr1 lac-c *Lac-d* kr1 lac-h sk4• lil-t bg1* melal-alt gya4 *Nat-m* k* ruta h1 samb kr1* stront-c sk4• syph kr1 taosc iwa1• *Tarent* kr1 *Thyr* vh vanil fd5.de
- **menses** | **before** | **agg.**: acon bg2 calc b4.de con bg2 cupr bg2 kali-c k* mag-c k* manc vh* mang k* nat-m puls bg2 sil h2 sulph vh
  - **during**:
    - **agg.**: am-c k* ant-t a1 *Bell* k* bry bg2 castm *Cedr* k* *Cham* k* *Coc-c* cupr bg2 cycl bg2 dig kali-c bg2 kali-n h2* lyc bg2 mag-c bg2 mag-s nat-m vh puls bg2 sep k* sul-ac k* **Sulph** vh verat k* wies a1 *Zinc* k*
    - **beginning** of menses | **agg.**: mag-c bg2
- **often** (See Thirst)
- **pain**:
  - **after**: *Acon* b7a.de apis tl1 ars b4.de* canth b7.de* cham b7a.de
  - **during**: acon k* aran canth b7.de* **Cham** k* kali-n b4.de* *Nat-c* k*
  - ○ **Abdomen**; during pain in: nept-m lsd2.fr
- **periodical** | **day**; alternate: ant-t b7.de*
- **perspiration**:
  - **after** | **agg.**: *Am-m* b7.de* *Ant-c* k* *Ant-t* k* ars bg2 bell k* borx b4a.de* bov k* chin bg2 ign bg2 **Lyc** k* nat-m bg2 *Nux-v* k* pilo a1 rhus-t bg2 sabad
  - **before**: agn bg2 *Am-m* bg2 ant-t bg2 bry b7.de* **Chin** b7a.de* *Coff* b7.de* **Cycl** bg2 **Nux-v** bg2 op bg2 puls bg2 rhus-t bg2 stann bg2 *Stram* bg2
  - **during**: *Acon* k* alum bg2 am-m b2.de anac k* ant-c b2.de* apoc gk **Arn** k* ars b2.de* ars-i bar-c b2.de *Bell* b2.de* bism b2.de borx b2.de bov b2.de *Bry* k* cact calc k* canth b2.de caps b2.de carb-v b2.de caust b2.de cedr **Cham** b2.de* **Chin** k* *Chinin-ar* *Chinin-s* k* cic b2.de cina b2.de cinch a1 *Coff* k* colch b2.de con b2.de croc b2.de cupr b2.de dros b2.de dulc b2.de gels k* *Hep* b2.de* hyos b2.de ign b2.de *Iod* k* *Ip* kali-c b2.de kali-n k* kreos b2.de lach b2.de laur b2.de *Lyc* bg2 mag-m k* merc b2.de* mez b2.de nat-c b2.de* **Nat-m** k* nat-n bg2 nit-ac b2.de nux-v b2.de* op k* *Ph-ac* k* plb b2.de puls k* ran-s b2.de *Rhus-t* k* ruta b2.de sabad b2.de* sec k* *Sep* k* sil b2.de* spong b2.de stann b2.de staph b2.de **Stram** k* stront-c b2.de sul-ac b2.de* *Sulph* b2.de* tarax k* *Thuj* k* valer b2.de **Verat** k* verb b2.de
    - **apyrexia**; in: chin bg2
- **pregnancy** agg.; during: graph dgt *Verat* hr1*
- **salivation**; with (See MOUTH - Salivation - thirst)
- **shivering**:
  - **after**: *Chin* b7.de* hell b7.de*
  - **during**: acon b7.de* ang b7.de* caps b7.de* *Cham* b7.de* led b7.de* nux-v b7.de* rhus-t b7.de* ruta b7.de* staph b7.de*
- **sleep** | **after** | **agg.**: ambr k* apoc bell k* borx ther k*
  - **during** | **agg.**: *Anac* b4a.de *Bry* b7a.de carb-v b4.de* caust b4.de* lyc b4.de* nit-ac b4.de* sil b4.de* sulph b4.de*

Stomach

- **small** quantities, for•: (↗*GENERALS - Food and - cold drink - desire - small)* aids nl2• anac bg1 ant-t apis **Ars** k* arum-t k* bell bry bg1 cact k* calc bg1 caps bg1 carb-v b4a.de* cassia-s ccrh1• cench kr1* *Chin* chinin-ar k2 choc srj3• cimic st cupr cupr-ar k* falco-pe nl2• fum rly1*• galeoc-c-h gms1• gast a1 *Hell* k* hep bg1 hir skp7• hyos lac-c *Lach* k* laur bg1 **Lyc** k* merc-i-r k* mez b4a.de nat-m bg1 nux-v bg1 petr-ra shn4• phos k* *Rhus-t* k* sal-fr sle1• sanic st* *Sil* b4a.de squil *Sulph* tab k* tritic-vg fd5.de tub al* [arg-met stj1 ars-met stj2 kali-ar stj2 nat-ar stj2]
  - **fever**; during: *Ant-t* bg2 **Ars** bg2 *Bell* bg2 borx bg2 *Carb-v* bg2 *Chin* bg2 croc bg2 cupr bg2 hell bg2 *Hyos* bg2 **Lyc** bg2 mez bg2 phos bg2 puls bg2 *Rhus-t* bg2 senec bg2 *Squil* bg2 stram bg2 verat bg2
  - **often**; and: abrom-a ks5 acon k* aids nl2• ant-t k* apis k* **Ars** k* arum-t *Bell* k* bros-gau mrc1 cact *Carb-v* b4a.de cassia-s ccrh1• *Chin* k* *Coloc* *Corn* croc b7.de eup-per hell b7.de hyos k* kali-n sf1.de lac-c lac-lup hrn2• lach lp lyc k* *Nat-ar* puls k* rhus-t k* sanic st *Squil* b7a.de stram b7.de *Sulph* tritic-vg fd5.de verat
- **smoking** agg.; after: spong b7.de*
- **stool**:
  - **after** | **agg.**: acet-ac bro1 alum ant-t arg-n bg2 **Caps** k* chin dulc k* lyc k* mag-c bg2 ox-ac petr bg2 sulph k* trom
  - **before**: *Ars* bry cham chin dulc hell mag-c podo sulph
  - **during** | **agg.**: ars k* bry k* caps bg2 cham k* chin k* dig c1 dulc k* hell k* lil-t mag-c merc-c b4a.de rheum b7a.de* *Sec* b7a.de sul-ac b4a.de* sulph *Verat* bg2
- **supper** agg.; after: aloe carb-an h2 galeoc-c-h gms1• phos k* plat k*
- **symptoms**, before severe: lil-t br1*
- **unquenchable**: abrom-a ks5 *Acet-ac* k* *Acon* k* aeth agar k* aloe am-c k* anac h2 anan androc srj1• *Apis* apoc gk aq-mar rbp6 **Ars** k* ars-i ars-s-f k2 bapt c1 *Bar-c* k* bar-i bar-s k2 *Bell* k* *Bry* k* *Calc* k* calc-i k2 *Camph* *Carbn-s* cartl-s rly4• cent a1 cham k* *Colch* bg2 coloc ptk1 *Crot-h* k* cupr ptk1 cupr-act cycl k* dig k* *Dulc* k* **Eup-per** k* *Ferr* ger-i rly4• germ-met srj5• *Hyos* k* iod k* jatr-c ptk1 kali-n k* *Kali-p* kali-s fkr2.de lac-lup hrn2• *Lach* k* med k2 medul-os-si rly4• *Merc* k* merc-c k* merc-i-r k* *Mur-ac* b4a.de nat-ar nat-c *Nat-m* k* nat-ox rly4• nat-p fkr6.de nept-m lsd2.fr nicc nit-ac bg2 nux-v ptk1 *Op* k* oxal-a rly4• petr k* ph-ac k* **Phos** k* pitu-gl skp7• positr nl2• psil ft1 pyrog ptk1 *Rhus-t* k* ruta sabad ptk1 sec k* sel b7a.de sol-ni *Spig* b7a.de spong bg2* stram k* sul-ac b4a.de sul-i k2 *Sulph* k* tarax bg2 *Tarent* k* tere-la rly4• tritic-vg fd5.de *Verat* k* verb bg2 *Vip* bg2 zing [bell-p-sp dcm1]
  - **night**: germ-met srj5•
  - **cold** water amel.; drinking (See cold - water)
  - **disgust** for drink, with: *Lach*
  - **fever**; during: (↗*FEVER - Burning - thirst - unquenchable)* *Nat-m* bg2
  - **perspiration**; during: ruta bg2
- **vanishing** at sight of water: psil vml3•
- **violent** (See unquenchable)
- **vomiting**:
  - **after**: acon bg2 dros b7.de* olnd k* stram b7.de* *Sul-ac* k*
  - **before**: **Eup-per** k*
  - **with**: acon bro1 ars h2* canth ptk1
- **waking**; on: *Acon* agath-a nl2• apoc k2* arge-pl rwt5• camph k* chord-umb rly4• dros k* ferr k* hyper k* lavand-a ctl1• mag-c k* *Mag-m* nat-m k* nat-sil fd3.de• pot-e rly4• rat k* stram k* [heroin sdj2]
- **walking** agg.; after: *Ferr-m* k* nat-c k* nat-m k* nux-v brm
- **warm** room agg.: hydrog srj2•
- **weather** | **rainy**: carc dgt
- **wine** agg.: sil b4a.de*
- **without** desire to drink (See GENERALS - Food - drinks - aversion - accompanied - thirst)

THIRSTLESS: acet-ac k* acon b7.de* *Aesc* aeth c1* agar k* *Agn* k* aids nl2• all-c am-c k* *Am-m* k* ambr k* ang b2.de* *Ant-c* k* **Ant-t** k* **Apis** k* arg-met b2.de* *Arg-n* arge-pl rwt5• arn b2.de* *Ars* k* *Asaf* k* asar b2.de* asc-t a1 aur b2.de* *Aur-m-n* wbt2• aur-s wbt2• bapt hr1 *Bell* k* berb bro1 bit-ar wht1• *Bov* k* brom brucel sa3• bry k* bufo caj a1 calad k* calc b2.de* *Calen* vh *Camph* k* cann-s b2.de* canth k* caps k* carb-v b2.de* cartl-s rly4• cassia-s cdd7*• caust k* cere-b a1 chel k* chim-m hr1 **Chin** k* chlor hr1 chord-umb rly4• cimic cina b2.de* coca-c sk4• cocc k* coff b2.de* **Colch** k* coli rly4• coloc b2.de* *Con* k* cor-r crot-t *Cycl* k* dig b2.de* digin a1 *Dios* k* dirc c1 dros b2.de* dulc b2.de* ephe-si hsj1• euph k* falco-pe nl2• *Ferr* k* ferr-ar

Thirstless: ... ferr-m galeoc-c-h gms1• gamb k* **Gels** k* germ-met srj5• gins a1 gran a1 *Graph* b4.de* ham k* **Hell** k* hep k* hydr k2 *Hydr-ac* hydrog srj2• hyos b2.de* ign k* ina-i mlk9.de indg k* *Ip* k* irid-met srj5• iris kali-ar *Kali-c* k* kali-n b2.de* kali-p kali-s fd4.de kola stb3• kreos b2.de* lac-h htj1• lac-lup hrn2• lach b2.de* lact a1 lavand-a ctl1• led k* limen-b-c hrn2* *Lyc* k* lyss a1 m-ambo b2.de m-arct b2.de m-aust b2.de* mag-c h2 *Mang* k* marb-w es1• **Meny** k* merc b2.de* merc-c k* mez k* mosch b2.de* mur-ac k* narcot a1 nat-ar nat-c k* nat-m k* nat-s k* nat-sil fd3.de• nauf-helv-li elm2• nit-ac k* **Nux-m** k* nux-v k* *Olnd* k* onos *Op* k* ox-ac k* ozone sde2• petr k* petr-ra shn4• **Ph-ac** k* phos k* pitu-gl skp7• plac-s rly4• plat k* plb a1 plut-n srj7• ptel k* **Puls** k* *Pycnop-sa* mrz1 rheum b2.de* rhod b2.de* rhus-t b2.de* ribo rly4• ros-d wla1 ruta b2.de* **Sabad** k* sabin b2.de* *Samb* k* sars k* sel ptk1 *Sep* k* spig k* spong b2.de* *Squil* b2.de* *Staph* k* *Stram* k* suis-em rly4• suis-hep rly4• sulph k* tab k* tarax b2.de* *Tarent* vh thuj k* tritic-vg fd5.de tub c1 ulm-c jsj8• valer k* vanil fd5.de verat k* vichy-g a1 vip fkr4.de [buteo-j sej6 tax jsj7]
- **daytime**: colch tl1 cycl tl1 ip tl1
- **afternoon** | **15** h: galeoc-c-h gms1•
- **night**: ephe-si hsj1• limen-b-c hrn2•
- **accompanied** by:
  - ○ **Face**; heat of: *Ars* b4a.de bell b4a.de carb-v b4a.de nat-c b4.de* nit-ac b4.de* phos b4a.de sep b4a.de
  - **Hands**; coldness of: *Ars* b4a.de bell b4a.de carb-v b4a.de nat-c b4.de* nit-ac b4.de* phos b4a.de sep b4a.de
  - **Lips**; dryness of: abrom-a ks5 ang b7.de* cadm-met tpw6 canth b7.de* caust bg2 cham b7.de* chin b7.de* cycl b7.de* kreos b7a.de meny b7.de* *Nux-m* b7.de* nux-v b7.de* *Puls* b7.de* rhus-t b7.de*
  - **Mouth**; dryness of: nux-m tl1 puls tl1
  - **Tongue**; dryness of: calc h2 caps k* nat-c h2 *Nat-m* k* pall c1 par k* ph-ac h2 phos h2 **Puls** k*
- **alternating** with thirst (See Thirst - alternating - thirstlessness)
- **chill**; during: *Agar* b2.de* *Agn* b2.de* alum b2.de* am-c b2.de* am-m b2.de* ang bg2 ant-c b2.de* *Ant-t* b2.de* **Ars** b2.de* asar b2.de* *Aur* b2.de* bar-c b4a.de bell b2.de* borx b2.de* bov b2.de* bry b2.de* calad b2.de calc b2.de* camph b2.de *Canth* b2.de* caps b2.de* carb-v b2.de* **Caust** b2.de* chel bg2 **Chin** b2.de* chinin-s bro1 cimx bro1 cina b2.de* cocc b2.de* coff b2.de* coloc b2.de* *Con* b2.de* *Cycl* b2.de* *Dros* b2.de* dulc b2.de* *Eup-pur* bro1 euph b2.de* gels hr1* guaj b2.de* **Hell** b2.de* hep b2.de* *Hyos* b2.de* ip b2.de* kali-c b2.de* kali-n b2.de* *Kreos* b2.de* lach b2.de* led b2.de* *Lyc* bg2 m-aust b2.de* mang b2.de* meny b2.de* merc b4.de* merc-c b4a.de **Mosch** bg2 **Mur-ac** b2.de* nat-c b2.de* nat-m b2.de* nit-ac b2.de* nux-m b2.de* nux-v b2.de* olnd b2.de* op b2.de* petr b2.de* *Ph-ac* b2.de* **Phos** b2.de* puls b2.de* rhod b2.de* *Rhus-t* b2.de* **Sabad** b2.de* sabin b2.de* *Samb* b2.de* sars b2.de* sep b2.de **Spig** b2.de* spong b2.de* squil b2.de* *Staph* b2.de* stram b2.de* *Sulph* b2.de* tarax b2.de* **Thuj** b2.de* verat b2.de zinc b2.de*
- **coryza**; during: ars b4a.de *Nat-c* b4.de* *Puls* b7a.de
- **cough** agg.; during: *Dros* b7a.de
- **days**; for: calad ptk1
- **desire** to drink; with (See GENERALS - Food - drinks - desire - accompanied - thirstlessness)
- **fever**; during: acet-ac a1* acon b7.de aesc kr1 *Aeth* k* agar **Agn** b7.de* all-c bg2 *Alum* alum-p k2 alum-sil k2 am-m b7.de* anac bg2 ang b7.de* *Ant-c* k* *Ant-t* k* **Apis** k* arg-met k* arg-n a1 arn b7.de* *Ars* h* ars-h asaf k* *Bapt* bg2 bar-c bell h* bov brom bg2 bry b7.de* *Calad* kr1 *Calc* k* calc-p bg2 camph k* canth b7.de* *Caps* k* carb-an *Carb-v* k* *Caust* cham h* **Chel** b7.de* chim-m hr1 chin k* chinin-m kr1 *Chinin-s* sf1.de *Cimx* k* **Cina** k* cocc k* *Coff* b7.de* coloc bg2 *Con* h* corh br1 cycl k* dig k* *Dros* k* **Dulc** bg2* euph h* eupi a1 *Ferr* k* **GELS** k•* gran a1 graph bg2 guaj h* hell k* hep h* hydr-ac kr1 hyos kr1 *Ign* k* *Ip* k* *Kali-c* k* kali-n h* kreos b7a.de* *Lach* b7.de* laur b7.de* lec *Led* k* lyc *M-ambo* b7.de* *M-arct* b7.de m-aust b7.de mag-c bg2 mang bg2 med meny k* *Merc* bg2* *Mur-ac* k* nat-c h2* nat-m bg2* *Nit-ac* k* *Nux-m* k* *Nux-v* b7.de *Olnd* b7.de* op k* *Ph-ac* k* *Phos* h* plb b7.de* **Puls** k •* *Rheum* h* *Rhod* b4a.de* rhus-t k* **Ruta** h* **Sabad** k* sabin b7.de* *Samb* k* sanic c1 **SEP** k •* sil h spig k* spong h* squil h* stann h staph h* stram h* *Sulph* k* *Tarax* h* thuj bg2 valer b7.de* vario al2 verat h* *Viol-t* b7.de*
  - **menses**; before: calc b4.de
- **headache**; during: hydrog srj2•
- **heat**; during•: acet-ac a1* acon b2.de* aesc kr1 *Aeth* k* agar **Agn** b2.de* all-c bg2 *Alum* alum-p k2 alum-sil k2 am-m b2.de* ambr b2.de anac b2.de* ang b2.de* *Ant-c* k* *Ant-t* k* **Apis** k* arg-met k* arg-n a1 arn b2.de* *Ars* b2.de* ars-h asaf k* bar-c bell b2.de* borx b2.de bov brom bg2 bry b2.de* *Calad* b2.de*

- **heat**; during: ...
  Calc k* calc-p bg2 camph k* canth b2.de* Caps k* carb-an Carb-v k* Caust cham b2.de* **Chel** b2.de* chim-m hr1 chin k* chinin-m kr1 Chinin-s bro1* Cimx k* **Cina** k* cocc k* Coff b2.de* coloc b2.de* Con b2.de* corh br1 cycl k* dig k* Dros k* **Dulc** b2.de* ephe-si hsj1• euph b2.de* eupi a1 Ferr k* **GELS** k •* gran a1 graph bg2 guaj b2.de* hell k* hep b2.de* hydr-ac kr1 hyos kr1 Ign k* Ip k* Kali-c k* kali-n b2.de* kreos bg2 Lach b2.de* laur b2.de* lec Led k* lyc m-ambo b2.de* M-arct b2.de* m-aust b2.de* mag-c b2.de* mang b2.de* med meny k* Merc b2.de* mosch b2.de Mur-ac k* nat-c b2.de* nat-m b2.de* Nit-ac k* Nux-m k* nux-v b2.de* Olnd b2.de* op k* Ph-ac k* Phos b2.de* plb b2.de* **Puls** k •* pycnop-sa mrz1 Rheum h* Rhod b2.de* rhus-t k* **Ruta** b2.de* **Sabad** k* sabin b2.de* Samb k* sanic c1 sars b2.de **SEP** k •* sil h2 spig k* spong b2.de* squil b2.de* stann h2 staph b2.de* stram b2.de* Sulph k* Tarax b2.de* thuj b2.de* valer b2.de* vario al2 verat b2.de* Viol-t b2.de* wye bro1
- **pain**; during the: Puls b7a.de
- **perspiration**; during: agn b2.de* am-m b2.de* ambr b2.de ang b2.de ant-c b2.de ant-t b2.de* **Apis** bg2 Ars b2.de* asaf b2.de Bell b2.de* bry b2.de* calad b2.de camph b2.de* canth b2.de caps b2.de* carb-v b2.de* caust b2.de* chel b2.de chin b2.de cocc b2.de coff b2.de* con b2.de cycl b2.de* dig b2.de* euph b2.de* gels bg2 **Hell** b2.de* hep b2.de* **Ign** b2.de* ip b2.de* kali-n b2.de led b2.de m-arct b2.de m-aust b2.de* mang b2.de* meny b2.de* merc b2.de* mosch b2.de mur-ac b2.de nit-ac b2.de nux-m b2.de* nux-v b2.de* op b2.de ph-ac b2.de Phos b2.de* **Puls** b2.de* rhod b2.de* **Rhus-t** b2.de* sabad b2.de* Sabin b2.de* **Samb** b2.de* sars b2.de **Sep** b2.de* spig b2.de* squil b2.de Staph b2.de* stram b2.de* sulph b2.de tarax b2.de thuj b2.de* **Verat** b2.de*
- **shivering**; during: ang b7.de Aur b4a.de bry b7.de chel b7.de chin b7.de* cina b7.de Dros b7.de Hell b7a.de hyos b7.de led b7.de Meny b7a.de mosch b7.de Nat-c b4a.de Nux-v b7.de Olnd b7.de puls b7.de rhus-t b7.de Sabad b7.de* spig b7.de spong b7.de Staph b7.de* tarax b7.de
- **urine**; with copious (See URINE - Copious - accompanied - thirstlessness)

THREAD; as if stomach were hanging by a: Ign b7a.de

THRUST or blow: dulc bg2 kali-bi bg2 tab bg2

TICKLING: anac bry crot-t k* nat-m sang k* tarent k* thea

○ - **Epigastrium**: anac bg2 bar-c bg2 bry bg2 cham bg2 crot-t bg2 hep bg2 lach bg2 nat-m bg2 nit-ac bg2 ph-ac bg2 puls ptk1

TIGHT clothing disturbs (See Clothing - disturbs)

TINGLING: ant-t coca-c sk4• colch ham fd3.de• indg nat-c h2 Puls Rhus-t

TOUCH agg.: ant-c b7a.de* ant-t b7.de* apis bg2* arg-n bg2* Arn b7.de* **Ars** b4a.de* Asaf b7a.de aur b4a.de* **Bar-c** b4.de* bell bro1 bov bro1 Bry b7.de* **Calc** b4a.de* calc-i bro1 Camph b7a.de cann-s b7.de* canth b7.de* caps b7.de* Carb-v b4.de* card-m bro1 cham b7.de* chel b7.de* Chin b7.de* cocc b7.de* colch b7a.de* Coloc b4a.de* crot-t bg2 Cupr b7.de* dig b4.de* ferr b7.de* ferr-p bg2 hell b7.de* hyos b7.de* ign b7a.de kali-bi bg2* kali-c bg2* Kreos b7a.de Lach bg2* lec bro1 lyc b4.de* mag-m bg2 manc bg2 mang bg2 Merc b4.de* merc-c b4a.de* Nat-c b4.de* **Nat-m** b4a.de* nux-m bro1 **Nux-v** b7.de* par b7.de* petr b4a.de* ph-ac b4a.de* **Phos** b4.de* puls b7.de* ran-b b7.de* rhod b4.de* Rhus-t b7a.de sabad b7.de* sang bro1 sars b4.de* sec b7a.de* sil bro1 Spig b7a.de* stann b4.de* staph b7.de* **Sulph** b4.de* ter bg2 thuj b4.de* Verat b7.de*

TREMBLING: aesc k* aeth k* agar k* am-c k* arg-met Arg-n k* Ars ars-i k* both-ax tsm2 brach k* bry b7a.de cact calad k* **Calc** k* cann-s b7.de* caps b7a.de* carb-v k* chin bg2 chinin-s cimic k* Crot-h k* Elaps k* falco-pe nl2• ferr graph k2 Ham k* hist sp1 Ign k* **Iod** k* Lyc mag-m mag-s k* med k* nat-c bg2 nat-m k* nat-s k* **Nux-v** k* Phos k* phys k* puls b7a.de* Rhus-t sang ptk1 sul-i pd Sulph k* Tab verat xan [bell-p-sp dcm1]
- **daytime**: calad
- **morning** | **waking**; on: agar k*
- **noon**: Sulph k*
- **breakfast** agg.; after: cimic k*
- **chilly**, when: phos k*
- **conversation**, from: mag-m
- **cough** agg.; during: aesc nux-v
- **eating**; while: elaps
- **heat**; during: caps k* ign k* **Iod** k* lyc k*
- **lying** down agg.: agar k* cocc vh
- **menses**; during: am-c k* arg-n ferr
- **nausea**; with: aeth k* calad
- **noise** agg.: agar

Trembling: ...
- **respiration**; from my neighbor's: gard-j vlr2•
- **urination** agg.; after: ars

▽ - **extending** to:

○ · **Body**; all over: iod h Lyc k*

· **Throat**: [bell-p-sp dcm1]

○ - **Epigastrium**: agar bg2 ars bg2 bell bg2 calc bg2 cimic bg2 crot-h bg2 Iod b4a.de Lyc b4a.de nat-s bg2 nux-v bg2 phos b4.de* sul-i ptk1 sulph bg2

· **fever**; during: Iod b4a.de

TUGGING sensation: | **Epigastrium**: cic b7.de*

TUMOR: | **Epigastrium**: hydr hl1*

TURNING: | **bed**; in | **agg.**: bapt bg2 con b4.de*
- **body** | **agg.**: anac b4a.de

TURNING; as if: aeth k* agn bg2 am-m k* Bell b4a.de hydr k* Ign b7a.de kali-bi bg2 kali-c bg2 kali-n k* lach bg2 nat-c b4.de* nat-m k* Nux-v b7.de* ol-an k* ozone sde2• plb k* puls bg2 ruta bg2 sabad b7.de* sil b4a.de sulph k* tab bg2 tub xyz61
- **morning** | **rising** agg.; after: kali-n k*
- **evening**: ozone sde2•
- **lying** on abdomen agg.: hydr k*
- **motion** agg.: bell
- **over**; seems to be turned: Aeth ptk1
  - · **cough** agg.; during: kali-c rb2 Puls k* ruta k* tab
  - · **turning** in bed; when: orni rb2
- **swallowing** liquids, after: plb k*

TWISTING: agar k* Alum k* am-m b7.de* Arg-n k* ars k* Bar-c k* bry k* calc chin cic Cocc k* crot-c dios gran k* grat k* ign b7a.de iris kali-bi k* kali-c k* kali-chl kali-n bg2 Lyc mez nat-m k* Nux-m Nux-v ol-an k* ox-ac k* ph-ac k* phos k* plat k* Plb sars k* sep h2 sil b4a.de* stry sulph k* tub rb2 zinc-m k*
- **morning**: Cocc hr1 plat k* sil h2
- **forenoon**: nat-c
- **night**: phos k* sulph h2
- **breakfast** agg.; after: agar k* sars h2 sol-t-ae k*
- **dinner**; after: ol-an a1 sars a1 sol-t-ae k*
- **eating** agg.: grat k*
- **lying** on it, while: hydr k*
- **nausea**; before: ph-ac h2
- **paroxysmal**: nit-ac h2 plb
- **sudden**: chin

▽ - **extending** to:

○ · **Abdomen**; into: Arg-n

· **Chest**: alum

· **Throat**: sep ptk1

○ - **Epigastrium**: bry bg2 kali-bi bg2 lyc bg2 nit-ac b4.de* sil b4.de* sulph b4.de* tab bg2

TWITCHING: aesc aloe alumn k* ars k* bry cann-s k* chin b7.de* chinin-s coloc Hydr Ign kali-c h2 lyc mez h2 petros phos k* plat puls k* rat sil stry k* tab
- **convulsive**: ars nux-v bro1
- **eating** | **amel.**: puls k*
- **sitting** agg.: phos k*
- **walking** about | **amel.**: alumn k*

▽ - **extending** to:

○ · **Larynx**: puls k*

· **Rectum** (See Jerking - extending - rectum)

· **Throat**: phos k*

○ - **Epigastrium**: bry bg2 ign b7.de* kali-c b4.de* Nux-v b7a.de puls b7.de*

○ · **Muscles** of: mez b4.de* plat b4.de*

ULCERS: abies-n mrr1 acet-ac k2* acetyls-ac mtf11 acon bg2 aesc k2 agav-a br1 alum k2 alum-p mtf11 alumn k2* anac rs* ant-c mrr1 ant-t bg2* Arg-n k* Ars k* atis-r bnj1 Atro bg2* atro-s mtf11 bapt bg2 bell bg2* berb vh1 bism bg2* brom k2 cadm-met stc cadm-s bg2* calc k* Calc-ar k* calc-p stc canth bg2 carb-ac bg2 carb-an mrr1 carb-v k2* carc fb* caust **Chel** sne chin mrr1 chlorpr mtf11 colch gk con k2 cortico sp1 Crot-h bg2* cund bro1 Cur Dys vh elaps mrr1 emblc mtf11 erig mrr1 euph gm1 ferr bg2 ferr-act bro1 fl-ac mrr1 ger br1* graph bg2* grat vh* grin br1* Ham bg2* hist-m mtf11 **Hydr** k* iod h* Ip bg2* iris mrr1 **Kali-bi** k* Kali-c k* kali-i bg2* kali-p bg2* Kreos k* lach mrr1 lat-m bnm6•

Ulcers: ...
Lyc k* mag-c bg2 med rs* merc bg2* *Merc-c* k* merc-i-f mtf11 *Mez* k* morg-p fmm1• nat-c rs* nat-m bg2* nat-p k* nat-s bg2* *Nit-ac* k* *Nux-v* k* op bro1 orni c2* penic mtf11 petr bg2* ph-ac rs **Phos** k* pin-con oss2• plb bg2 plb-act bro1 prot fmm1* **Psor** k2* ptel sne puls rs ran-b ptk1 rat c2* rob mrr1 ruta stc sal-ac gk **Sep** k1* sil sin-a c2* staph mrr1 sul-ac sulph bg2* symph br1* syph k* tab bg2 thuj rs tub gk (non:uran-met k) *Uran-n* k* vario stc verat stc
- **alcoholics**, in: alum kr1
- **bleeding**: ant-t vh1
- **grief**; after: nat-m mrr1 staph mtf
- **helicobacter** pylori infection: corn-f mtf helic-p mtf
- **hemorrhoids**; from suppressed: nux-v mrr1
- **malignant**: *(↗Cancer)* helic-p mtf hydr mrr1 orni tl1
- **menses**, with scanty: calc-ar dgt1
- **nursing** women, in: lac-c c1
- **painful**: arg-n bro1
  - **burning**: *Ars* mrr1 mez br
  - **intolerable** pains; with: euph stc kali-cy stc
  - **radiating** pain; with: arg-n br1
- **painless**: carb-ac stc
- **quarrels**; from: nat-m mrr1
- **radiation** treatment for acne; after: phos gm1
- **recurrent**: quinhydr mtf11
- **spring**: anac mtf11
- **workaholics**; in: nux-v mrr1

○ - **Duodenal** (See ABDOMEN - Ulcers - duodenum)
- **Gastroduodenal**: prot mtf11
- **Pylorus**; in | **malignant**: *(↗Cancer - pylorus)* carc-st-ad mtf corn-f mtf dys mtf helic-p mtf rad-met mtf

UNDULATION, waving: kali-bi bg2 ph-ac bg2

UNEASINESS: *(↗Nausea)* acon-s a1 aeth k* agar bg2 agn bg2 alumn k* am-c bg2 *Ars* asc-c a1 atro a1 bamb-a stb2.de• bar-c bg2 bell k* bor-ac a1 borx bg2 cadm-met tpw6 *Canth* carb-ac k* **Chinin-s** bg2 cimic k* cina bg2 cinnb k* *Colch* k* cortico tpw7 crot-t cycl dig k* dios k* dirc a1 dulc fd4.de erech a1 fago k* flor-p rsj3• glon k* grat gymno hydr-ac a1 iris kali-bi k* kali-i k* kalm k* lach bg2 limen-b-c hrn2* lith-c lob k* lobin a1 lyc bg2 mur-ac k* naja k* *Nux-m* bg2 **Nux-v** bg2 osm k* petr-ra shn4• ph-ac bg2 phos k* plb b7.de* podo bg2* prin a1 ptel k* rhod bg2 ruta sabad k* sang a1 sec k* sep k* sol-t-ae k* sulph bg2 tarent k* thuj bg2 tub-d jl2 verat-v k* zinc k*
- **accompanied** by:
  - **nausea**; sudden: tub-d jl2
  - **pulse**; weak (See GENERALS - Pulse - weak - accompanied - stomach)
  - **vomiting**; sudden: tub-d jl2
- **alcoholics**, in: alumn k1
- **eating**; after: hir rsj4•
- **flatus**; passing | **amel**.: mur-ac h2
- **nausea**; with: ant-t tl1 tub-d jl2
- **stooping** | **amel**.: nat-m h2
- **urination** agg.; during: hipp jl2

○ - **Epigastrium**: querc-r svu1•

URGING for stool (See Stool)

URINATION: | **after** | **agg.**: ars bg2
- **during** | **agg.**: laur b7.de*

VEAL agg.: *Ip* b7a.de kali-n b4.de*

VEXATION; after:
- **agg.**: *Acon* b7.de* ang bg2 bell bg2 *Bry* b7.de* carb-v bg2 *Cham* b7.de* cocc b7.de* coff b7.de* coloc bg2 ign b7.de* lyc bg2 nux-m b7a.de *Nux-v* b7.de* *Staph* b7.de*
- **anger**; with | **agg.**: **Bry** b7.de* *Cham* b7.de* *Coff* b7.de*
- **anxiety**; with | **agg.**: *Cham* b7a.de op b7a.de ran-s b7a.de sabad b7a.de
- **fright**; with: | **agg.**: **Acon** b7.de* cocc b7.de* ign b7.de* nux-v b7.de* op b7.de* puls b7.de
- **grief**; with silent: | **agg.**: **Ign** b7.de* staph b7.de*
- **indignation**; with | **agg.**: ip b7.de* **Staph** b7.de*
- **rage**; with | **agg.**: *Acon* b7.de* *Bry* b7.de* *Cham* b7.de* *Nux-v* b7.de*
- **respiration**; with complaints of: *Bry* b7a.de *Cham* b7a.de chel b7a.de *Cocc* b7a.de hell b7a.de nux-m b7a.de rhus-t b7a.de spig b7a.de stram b7a.de

VINEGAR agg.: *Ars* b4a.de

VINEGAR, sensation as if she had taken a lot of: acet-ac br1

VOMITING: abrot k2* absin k* acet-ac k* **Acon** k* acon-c a1* acon-f a1 aconin c2 act-sp a1 adren br1 *Aesc* k* **Aeth** k* aether c2 *Agar* k* agar-em a1 agar-ph c2* ail a1* alco a1 alet k* all-c k* alum-sil k2 alumn k* am-c k* am-caust a1* *Am-m* k* ambr k* amyg bro1 amyg-p br1 anac k* ancis-p tsm2 androc srj1• anh sp1 anis br1 **Ant-c** k* **Ant-t** k* anth a1 *Anthraci* **Apis** k* *Apoc* k* apoc-a c2 **Apom** k* apom-m mtf11 aran k* arg-cy arg-met b2.de* **Arg-n** k* arist-cl sp1 *Arn* k* **Ars** k* ars-h k* ars-i ars-s-f a1* ars-s-r a1 arum-m k* *Asar* k* asc-c k* asc-t asim br1 atis zzc1• atra-r bnm3• atro bro1 aur aur-m k* bacls-10 pte1*• bamb-a stb2.de• bapt k* *Bar-c* k* bar-i *Bar-m* k* *Bell* k* bell-p sp1 benz-ac a1 *Bism* k* bol-s a1 bor-ac c2 *Borx* k* *Both* k* both-ax tsm2 bov b2.de* *Brom* b4a.de brucel sa3• **Bry** k* bufo bung-fa tsm2 *Cact* cadm-met sp1 **Cadm-s** k* cain *Calc* k* calc-m c2* *Calc-p* *Calc-s* calth br1 *Camph* k* camph-br mtf11 camph-mbr bro1 cann-i k* cann-s k* *Canth* k* caps b2.de* carb-ac k* carb-an ptk1 *Carb-v* b2.de* carbn-s carc fb* card-m bro1 casc br1* cassia-s ccrh1• caust k* cench tsm2 cer-ox c2* cer-s mtf11 **Cham** k* *Chel* k* **Chin** k* chinin-ar *Chinin-s* chir-fl bnm4• chlf a1 chlol k* chlor a1 chr-ac a1 chrys-ac a1 cic k* cic-m a1 *Cimic* k* *Cina* k* cinnb k2 cit-ac rly4• cit-v a1 cloth tsm2 cob-n sp1 *Coc-c* *Cocc* k* cod a1 coff k* coffin a1 **Colch** k* coll coloc k* *Con* k* conin a1 cop k* cori-r a1* *Crot-c* crot-h k* crot-t k* *Cub* k* cuc-p c2 **Cupr** k* *Cupr-act* bro1 *Cupr-ar* k* cupr-m a1 *Cupr-s* k* *Cycl* k* cystein-l rly4• cyt-l a1* dendr-pol tsm2 der a1 *Dig* k* digin a1 digox c2 *Dor* k* *Dros* k* *Dulc* k* dys fmm1• echi a1 elaps k* elat a1* emetin a1 euon a1 *Eup-per* k* eup-pur c2 *Euph* k* euph-ip a1* euph-l a1 **Ferr** k* *Ferr-ar* *Ferr-i* k* *Ferr-m* c2* ferr-p k* ferr-s a1 *Form* gaert pte1*• **Gamb** k* gaul a1* **gels** k* gent-c a1 ger bro1 germ-met srj5• glon k* *Gran* k* *Graph* k* *Grat* k* guaj b4a.de* helia a1* *Hell* k* hell-f a1 helo-s bnm14• helon a1 *Hep* k* hipp a1* **hist** sp1 home c2 hura-c a1* hydr hydr-ac a1 *Hyos* k* *Ign* k* indg k* influ jl2 *Iod* k* **Ip** k* **Iris** k* iris-t c2 jab a1* jal a1 jatr-c c2* jug-r a1 kali-ar k* *Kali-bi* k* *Kali-br* k* kali-c k* kali-chl a1 kali-chr a1 kali-cy a1 *Kali-i* k* kali-n b2.de* kali-ox a1* kali-p kali-s k* kali-t a1 kalm k* kola stb3• kou br1 **Kreos** k* lac-ac c2* *Lac-d* lac-h sze9• *Lach* k* lact a1 lat-h bnm5• lat-m bnm6• *Laur* k* led b2.de* lept bro1 lim a1 lina a1 **Lob** k* lobin a1 *Lol* a1 lon-x a1 loxo-lae bnm12• loxo-recl bnm10• lup a1 *Lyc* k* lyss jl2 mag-c b2.de* mag-m k2 manc a1 mand sp1 *Mang* k* med c1* *Merc* k* merc-br a1 *Merc-c* k* merc-cy a1 *Merc-d* k* merc-n a1 merc-sul a1 *Mez* k* mill a1 morg fmm1• morg-p pte1*• morph a1* *Morph-s* hr1 mosch k* mucs-nas rly4• mur-ac k* muru a1 naja narc-ps c1* nat-ar k2 nat-c b2.de* nat-f sp1 *Nat-m* k* nat-p k* nicc-c dp2.fr *Nit-ac* k* *Nux-m* k* **Nux-v** k* oena br1 olnd k* op k* *Ox-ac* k* oxyurn-sc mcp1• paeon k* par b7a.de *Parathyr* jl2 pert jl2 *Petr* k* petr-ra shn4• ph-ac k* phal c2 **Phos** k* physala-p bnm7• phyt k* pic-ac k2 pix bro1 **Plb** k* podo k* *Positr* nl2• *Prot* jl2 *Psor* k* ptel k* **Puls** k* pulx br1 rat rham-f c2 rheum b7.de rhod k* rhus-t k* ric br1* ruta k* sabad b2.de* sabin k* sal-ac k* sal-fr sle1• *Samb* k* *Sang* k* santin c2 sarcol-ac bro1 saroth sp1 sars k2 scarl jl2 schin c2 scol a1* *Sec* k* sel k* seneg k* *Sep* k* **Sil** k* sin-a c2 sol-ni spartin bwa3 spig bg2 spong fd4.de squil k* stann b2.de* stram b2.de* stront-c bg2 stroph-h bg3* *Stry* k* stry-af-cit bro1 sul-ac k* sulfa sp1 **Sulph** k* syc fmm1• *Sym-r* bro1 syph k2* **Tab** k* tang c2 *Tarent* k* tart-ac mtf11 tep k* *Ter* k* thal-xyz srj8• *Ther* k* thev c2 thuj k* thymol sp1 tritic-vg fd5.de *Tub* (non:uran-met k) uran-n k* uva br1 *Valer* k* vanil fd5.de vario jl2 **Verat** k* **Verat-v** k* vesp br1 viol-o b7a.de wye k* x-ray sp1 xero bro1 *Zinc* k* zinc-fcy a1 [heroin sdj2 plut-n stj2]
- **morning**: absin ambr ant-t arg-n mrr1 ars bar-c bar-m k* bry k* calc k* calc-sil k2 camph k* **Caps** k* carbn-s carc vh chlorpr pin1• *Cocc* colch k* *Con* cupr ptk1 *Cycl* cypra-eg sde6.de• *Dig* k* *Dros* dulc *Ferr* k* ferr-ar *Ferr-p* form graph k* *Guaj* **Hep** k* *Ign* jac-c br1 kali-ar kali-bi *Kali-br* *Kali-c* k* kali-p kali-s fd4.de kali-sil k2 kreos *Lyc* mag-c h1* merc-c morg fmm1• mosch k* nat-c h2 *Nat-m* nux-v *Petr* petr-ra shn4• phos k* phyt k* plb psor k* ruta fd4.de sec sep *Sil* *Sul-ac* *Sulph* tab *Tarent* thuj *Verat* zinc zinc-p k2
  - **7 h**: elat
  - **alcohol**; after: ant-t bro1 ars k2* caps k2 carb-ac bro1 cupr bro1 *Cupr-ar* bro1 ip bro1 lob bro1 nux-v k2*
  - **alcoholism**: **Caps** hr1
  - **early**: alet bg2 kali-c bg2 *Mag-m* bg2 nux-v bg2 stann ptk1
  - **menses**; during: graph ptk1
  - **rising** agg.: *Cocc* ferr-p k2 mosch k* verat verat-v k*
- **forenoon**: chin colch rsj2• dulc fd4.de elat nat-s nux-v op psor ruta fd4.de sang k*
  - **9 h** | **headache**; during: form
  - **10 h**: cur vh psor

- **11** h: chin cur vh
- **noon**: *Mag-c* k* mag-s phos k* *Verat*
- **afternoon**: bell chinin-s con graph k* hep k* kali-chl mag-s petr-ra shn4• phyt *Sulph* k* tritic-vg fd5.de
  - **13** h: ozone sde2•
  - **14**-15 h: chinin-ar k2 plb
  - **16** h: sulph
- **evening**: agar anac k* bamb-a stb2.de• bell k* bry *Carb-v* k* dig digox a1 elaps eug k* kali-chl k* kali-n a1 merc k* merc-c morph k* nat-s nux-v phos k* phyt positr nl2• psor k* *Puls* k* sec k* stram *Sulph* k* verat
  - **20**.30 h: ozone sde2•
- **night**: agar *Ant-t* k* *Arg-n* k* *Ars* k* ars-s-f k2 bar-c h2 bar-ox-suc rly4• bell bry **Calc** calc-s calc-sil k2 *Chin* chinin-ar *Cocc* *Con* crot-t cupr-act cupr-ar cycl hr1 dig k* dros k* elat k* **Ferr** k* *Ferr-ar* hell hep k* *Ign* kali-ar kali-c k* kali-sil k2 *Lach* k* *Lyc* *Lyss* k* *Merc* k* merc-c k* mucs-nas rly4• mur-ac nat-m nicc nit-ac k* *Nux-v* ox-ac ph-ac k* phos k* *Plb* *Podo* puls k* rat rhus-t k2 ruta fd4.de sec seneg k* sep k* *Sil* k* spong fd4.de *Stram* k* *Sulph* syc pte1*• tab k* thea ther k* tritic-vg fd5.de valer k* *Verat* [heroin sdj2]
  - **midnight**: acet-ac k* agar *Arg-n* choc srj3• ferr bg2* lyc k* phos k*
    - **after**: **Ferr** k* nat-m
      - **1** h | **waking**; on: *Rat*
      - **3** h | **3**-4 h: iris c1
      - **4** h: hir rsj4•
  - **eating**; after: [heroin sdj2]
- **abdomen**; complaints of | **after** (See ABDOMEN - Vomiting - before)
- **accompanied** by:
  - **anemia** (See GENERALS - Anemia - accompanied - vomiting)
  - **appetite**; fickle: ign bro1
  - **blood**; rushes of: verat bg2
  - **breath**; foul: cupr bg2
  - **cholera** (See RECTUM - Cholera - accompanied - vomiting)
  - **coldness** of body; icy: valer ptk1
  - **congestion** (See GENERALS - Congestion - blood - accompanied - vomiting)
  - **constipation**: nux-v bro1 op bro1 plb bro1
  - **cough**: acon b7a.de* alum b4.de* am-c b4.de* anac b4a.de* ang b7.de* **Ant-t** b7a.de* arg-met b7.de* arn b7.de ars b4.de* asaf b7.de* aur b4.de* bell b4.de **Bry** b7.de* calc b4.de* canth bg2 caps b7.de **Carb-an** b4.de* carb-v b4.de* chin bg2 cina b7.de* coc-c bg2 cocc b7.de* coff b7.de* coloc b4a.de con b4.de *Cupr* b7.de dig b4.de* **Dros** b7.de* dulc b4.de* *Ferr* bg2 *Hep* b4.de* *Hyos* b7a.de iod b4.de* *Ip* b7.de* kali-c b4.de* kreos bg2 *Lach* b7a.de* *Lyc* b4a.de m-arct b7.de mez b4.de* nat-m b4a.de* nit-ac b4.de* **Nux-v** b7.de* *Ph-ac* b4.de* phos b4.de* plat b4.de* **Puls** b7.de* **Rhus-t** b7.de* *Sabad* b7.de* *Samb* b7a.de *Sep* b4.de* sil b4a.de* spong b7.de* squil b7a.de stann b4.de* staph b7.de* **Sulph** b4a.de* thuj b4a.de *Verat* b7a.de* zinc b4.de*
  - **hemorrhage** (See GENERALS - Hemorrhage - accompanied - vomiting)
  - **impaction** (See ABDOMEN - Impaction - accompanied - vomiting)
  - **irritation** of stomach (See Irritation - accompanied - vomiting)
  - **jaundice** (See skin)
  - **lachrymation**: cupr h2
  - **loss** of fluids: aeth mrr1
  - **menses**; painful: **Verat** mrr1
  - **metrorrhagia** (See FEMALE - Metrorrhagia - accompanied - vomiting)
  - **neuralgic** pain: aran ptk1
  - **perspiration**: (↗*perspiration - during*) acon bro1 aeth br1* bell bg2 ip bg2 kali-bi bg2 sulph h2* *Tab* bg2
    - **cold**: ars ptk1 *Camph* bg2* *Cupr-ar* bg2* graph ptk *Ip* kr1 spong fd4.de tab ptk1 thea a1 **Verat** bg2* *Verat-v* kr1
    - **Face**: cadm-s c1 camph bg2 sulph bg2
- **accompanied** by: ...
  - **pneumonia** (See CHEST - Inflammation - lungs - accompanied - vomiting)
  - **respiration**; impeded (See RESPIRATION - Impeded - accompanied - vomiting)
  - **sadness**: carc mlr1•
  - **salivation**: ign bro1
  - **scarlatina**: ail bro1 *Bell* bro1 cupr br1
  - **shivering**: dulc ptk1
  - **urine** | **lemon** colored: ign bro1
  - **vertigo** (See VERTIGO - Accompanied - vomiting)
  - **water** brash: anac b4a.de nat-m b4a.de *Sil* b4a.de *Sulph* b4a.de
  - **weakness** (See GENERALS - Weakness - accompanied - vomiting)
  - ○ **Abdomen**:
    - **complaints** of (See ABDOMEN - Complaints - accompanied - vomiting)
    - **rumbling** in: podo bro1
  - **Back**; pain in: puls bg2
  - **Brain**:
    - **complaints** of (See HEAD - Brain; complaints of - accompanied - vomiting)
    - **congestion** to (See HEAD - Congestion - brain - accompanied - vomiting)
  - **Eyes**; red discoloration of: apis bg2 arn bg2 asar bg2 bry bg2 chin bg2 lyc bg2 nux-v bg2 puls bg2 sep bg2 sil bg2 verat bg2
  - **Face**:
    - **grayish**: mag-m bg2
    - **heat**: petr bg2 *Sang* bg2 stront-c bg2
    - **pale**: ant-t bg2 hep bg2 puls bg2
    - **red**: verat bg2
  - **Feet**:
    - **cold**: kreos bg2 phos bg2
    - **cramp**: nux-v bg2
    - **numbness**: phos bg2
    - **pain**: ars bg2
  - **Head**:
    - **congestion**: cic c1
    - **pain** in (See HEAD - Pain - accompanied - vomiting)
  - **Heart**; weakness of (See CHEST - Weakness - heart - accompanied - vomiting)
  - **Ileus** (See ABDOMEN - Ileus - accompanied - vomiting)
  - **Kidney**:
    - **disease** (See KIDNEYS - Complaints - accompanied - vomiting)
    - **inflammation** of (See KIDNEYS - Inflammation - accompanied - vomiting)
    - **stone** colic (See KIDNEYS - Pain - accompanied - vomiting; KIDNEYS - Pain - ureters - accompanied - vomiting)
  - **Lungs**; congestion to (See CHEST - Congestion - lungs - accompanied - vomiting)
  - **Skin**; yellow discoloration of: hip-ac sp1
  - **Stomach**:
    - **complaints**: acon bg2 ant-t bg2 arg-n bg2 **Ars** bg2 asar bg2 bar-m bg2 *Bry* bg2 calc b4a.de* **Cupr** bg2 *Dig* b4a.de* graph bg2 hyos bg2 **Ip** bg2 kali-bi bg2 kali-c bg2 lach b7a.de* mosch bg2 **Nux-v** bg2 *Op* bg2 **Phos** bg2 plb bg2 *Puls* bg2 *Sil* b4a.de *Sulph* bg2 **Verat** bg2
    - **inflammation** (See Inflammation - accompanied - vomiting)
  - **Tongue**; clean: cina bro1 dig bro1 *Ip* bro1
  - **Umbilicus** | **retraction** of: mosch bg2
- **acids**, after: aloe bg2 brom tl1 ferr k* guare bg1

Stomach

- **after**:
  - **agg.**: aeth ptk1 *Ars* b4.de* asar b7.de* calc b4a.de cupr k* *Dig* b4a.de dros k* graph b4a.de *Iod* b4a.de *Ip* ptk1 kali-c b4a.de olnd k* *Phos* b4a.de *Puls* ptk1 ruta b7.de* sil ptk1 *Sulph* b4.de*
  - **amel.**: arg-n bg2 *Ars* b4a.de asar b7.de* hyos b7.de* phos b4a.de *Puls* b7a.de sulph b4a.de tab bg2
- **air** agg.: lach bg2
- **alcohol** | **amel.**: *Olnd* bg2
- **alternating** with:
  - **convulsions**: *Cic* k*
  - **diarrhea**: ars bg2 carc gk6*
  - **gout**: ant-c k2
  - **heat** and coldness: cadm-met gm1
  - **hiccough**: phos bg2
  - **respiration**; asthmatic (See RESPIRATION - Asthmatic - alternating - vomiting)
  - **stupor** (See MIND - Stupor - alternating - vomiting)
- **amel.**: ant-t ptk1 coc-c ptk1 dig ptk1 eup-per ptk1 kali-bi ptk1 nux-v ptk1 *Sang* ptk1 sanic ptk1 sec ptk1 tab ptk1 xan ptk1
- **anger**; after●: ars bg2 carc mlr1• **Cham** k* **Coloc** k* **Nux-v** k* staph bro1 *Valer*
  - **indignation**; with: carc mlr1•
- **anguish**; with (See MIND - Anguish - vomiting)
- **anticipation**; from: carc gk6*
- **apples**; after: bell-p sp1
- **apyrexia**, during: ant-c *Ip* k* verat bro1
- **asthma**; during attacks of: *Ip* vh*
- **bed**:
  - **going** to bed | **after**: **Tarent** k*
- **beer**; after: cupr bro1 ferr k* ip bro1 kali-bi k2* kali-n a1 *Mez* sulph
  - **not** after water; but: mez
- **before** | **agg.**: *Cupr* b7.de* *Puls* b7.de* ran-s b7.de*
- **bend** double in order to vomit; must: plut-n srj7•
- **blood**, at sight of: ph-ac h2
- **brain** tumors; from: (*↗cerebral; HEAD - Tumors - brain)* aml-ns bg2 apis bg2 apom bg2 bell bg2 coc-c ptk1 cocc ptk1* glon bg2 hell bg2 merc bg2 zinc bg2
- **bread** agg.: bry nit-ac
  - **black** bread: nit-ac k* ph-ac
- **breakfast**:
  - **after** | **agg.**: agar k* anders zzc1• *Borx* *Carb-v* colch k* cycl k* daph k* *Ferr* ham fd3.de• kali-c h2 sars k* tritic-vg fd5.de trom k*
  - **amel.**: bov bg2
  - **before** | **agg.**: eupi *Kreos* *Nux-v* psor sel **Tab**
- **bright** light, from: stram
- **brushing** teeth, on: *(↗rinsing)* *Coc-c* k*
- **cancer**; from: carb-ac ptk1 carc mlr1• kreos ptk1
- **carcinoma** of stomach; in (See Cancer - accompanied - vomiting; persistent)
- **cerebral** tumors; from: *(↗brain; HEAD - Tumors - brain)* apom c1* bell bro1 glon bro1 plb bro1
- **chemotherapy**; from: carc mlr1•
- **children**; in: aeth k2* ars tl1 calc-p k2 camph tl1 dulc fd4.de dys fmm1• ing br1* tritic-vg fd5.de
  - **nurslings**: aeth c1 psor jl2 tritic-vg fd5.de
    - **after** nursing; shortly: aeth tl1 ip tl1 sanic tl1 tritic-vg fd5.de
- **chill**:
  - **after**: ant-t *Aran* *Bry* *Carb-v* **Eup-per** k* *Ip* kali-c k* *Lyc* k* **Nat-m** k* rhus-t *Verat* b7a.de
  - **before**: ant-t b7.de* apis arn *Ars* chin *Cina* k* cupr bg2 *Eup-per* *Ferr* lyc nat-m k* puls sec *Verat* b7.de* vesp br1
  - **during**: ail k* alum am-c b4a.de *Ant-c* bg2 arn k* *Ars* bg2 asar borx k* bry bg2 *Caps* k* carb-v b4a.de* *Cham* bg2 *Chin* bg2 *Cina* k* con bg2 *Dros* k* **Eup-per** k* ferr k* gamb hep bg2 *Ign* k* *Ip* k* kali-bi bg2 kali-c b4.de* lach k* laur b7.de* lyc k* nat-c b4.de* *Nat-m* k* nux-v k* nyct bro1 phos bg2 *Puls* k* rhus-t sep stram bg2 sulph bg2 thuj k* valer b7.de* *Verat* k*
- **chloroform**: iod bnt *Phos* k*
- **chronic**: lob bro1
  - **accompanied** by:
    - **Tongue** | **brown** discoloration: *Ip* kr1*
- **closing** the eyes:
  - **agg.**: aml-ns bg2 lach bg2 mosch bg2 nat-m bg2 *Ther* k*
  - **amel.**: tab
- **coffee** agg.: camph k* cann-s k* *Cham* k* glon sulph hs1 trom vml3• verat
- **coition**; after: mosch k* sabad ptk1 sil ptk1
- **cold** food; from: ars mrr1
- **cold**; on becoming: cocc k*
- **coldness** of body; with icy: valer a1*
- **colic**; during: op a
- **coma**; with (See MIND - Coma - vomiting)
- **congestion** of head; with (See headache)
- **constant**: amyg-p br1 ars tl1* carc mlr1• hell ptk1 helo-s bnm14• ip tl1* merc ptk1 plb tl1* pyrog ptk1 syph ptk1
  - **days**; for: oena ptk1
- **convulsions**:
  - **after**: acon k* *Ars* k* *Calc* hr1 colch k* *Cupr* glon k* tanac a1
  - **before**: *(↗GENERALS - Convulsions - epileptic - aura - vomiting)* *Cupr* k* hydr-ac ptk1 op k*
  - **during**: ant-c ptk1 bac bn cic mrr1 *Cupr* bro1 *Hyos* k* op k*
- **convulsive** (See spasmodic)
- **cough**:
  - **after**: *Cupr* b7a.de* dros mtf33 *Kali-br* hr1 kali-c mtf33 mez bg2 pert c1* sul-ac ptk1
  - **during**:
    - **agg.**: *(↗expectoration; hawking)* agar **Alum** k* alum-p k2 alumn bro1 ambr k2 *Anac* k* **Ant-t** k* *Arg-n* *Arn* *Ars* *Ars-i* ars-s-f k2* *Bac* vh bell **BRY** k ●* bufo calc calc-i k2 calc-sil k2 cann-s caps k* *Carb-v* k* carbn-s caust ser *Cham* chin chinin-ar *Cimx* cina tl1 *Coc-c* k* con cor-r ptk1 *Cupr* k* *Cupr-act* bro1 cupr-ar bro1 cur k* *Daph* *Dig* **Dros** k* euph-l bro1 euphr bro1 *Ferr* k* ferr-ar ferr-i ferr-p *Form* gels **Hep** k* *Hyos* indg iod **IP** k ●* irid-met srj5• *Kali-ar* kali-bi **Kali-c** k* *Kali-p* kali-s kali-sil k2 kreos bro1 *Lach* lap-la rsp1 laur k* lob *Meph* k* merc merc-c mez mill myos-a myos-s bro1 nat-ar nat-c *Nat-m* nat-p *Nit-ac* k* *Nux-v* k* pert jl2 *Ph-ac* phos k* plb psor al2 *Puls* k* rhod rhus-t k* *Sabad* sang sarr seneg *Sep* k* *Sil* k* stann k2 sul-ac sul-i k2 *Sulph* syc fmm1• syph *Tarent* thuj verat k* zinc h2
    - **during**:
      - **morning**: kali-c b4a.de limest-b es1• sulph b4a.de
      - **evening**: *Mez* b4a.de
      - **night**: ant-t b7a.de *Mez* b4a.de nux-v b7a.de
    - **eating**; after: anac b4a.de ant-t b7a.de bry b7a.de dig b4a.de
    - **whooping** cough: all-c tl1 ant-t bro1 bell bro1 carb-v bro1* cer-ox br1* *Coc-c* bro1 cupr bro1* *Dros* bro1 ferr tl1 ferr-p st **Ip** bro1* kali-br st lob bro1 verat bro1
- **cyclical** reappearance (See periodical)
- **dentition**; during: *Aeth* hr1* *Ant-c* hr1* *Ant-t* hr1* *Bism* k* *Bry* hr1* calc k* hyos *Ign* st **Ip** hr1 *Kali-br* hr1* phyt hr1 thyr c1 *Verat* hr1*
- **desire** to vomit: des-ac rbp6
- **dialysis**; from: apom mtf ars mtf cupr-ar mtf phos mtf
- **diarrhea**:
  - **before**: anthraci vh1 ars colch crot-t dig h2 lach phos phyt
  - **during**: *Aeth* k* ant-c k* *Ant-t* b7.de* *Apis* arg-met **Arg-n** k* **Ars** k* ars-i k2 asar k* asc-c c1 bapt tl1 bell k* bism k* calc bro1 camph bro1 *Carb-ac* k* cham b7a.de* chin chr-ac bro1 *Colch* k* coloc k* crot-t k* *Cupr* k* cupr-ar k* cycl cypra-eg sde6.de• dios *Dulc* k* elaps fil bro1 **Gamb** k* *Gnaph* gran *Graph* *Grat* *Hell* indg ing br1* *Iod* *Ip* k* *Iris* bro1 *Jatr-c* k* kali-m k2 kali-n kali-p k2 *Kreos* k* lach k* merc k* merc-c k* nit-ac h2 nux-v b7.de opun-xyz bro1 phos k* *Phyt* plb *Podo* k* *Puls* k* pulx bro1 res bro1 rheum bg2 rob samb b7.de sang sec b7a.de seneg k* sep stann stram k* sul-i k2 sulph tab k* trios bro1 tub c1 **Verat** k*
    - **menses**; during: verat zr*
- **difficult**: androc srj1• **Ant-t** k* *Ars* k* asar k* borx h2 bry k* cham tl1 cic k* clem k* (non:coff slp) coff-t a1* cupr k* elat k* gent-c a1 grat k* ix bnm8• kali-n a1 kola stb3• lol a1 plb k* raph k* spong fd4.de stram a1 sul-h a1

- **dinner**:
  - **after** | **agg.**: acon agar anac ant-t graph *Lach* mag-m bg2 nit-ac h2 ol-an k* *Sel* tub c1
  - **amel.**: chinin-m c1
  - **before**: dros k* sulph
  - **during** | **agg.**: mag-c h2
- **disposition** to: diph-t-tpt jl2 hell-o a1* kali-sula a1* malar jl2 nux-v tl1 puls tl1
- **drawing** catarrhal plugs from posterior nares●: *Sep* k*
- **drinking**:
  - **after**:
    - **agg.**: acet-ac bro1 *Acon* k* alum alum-p k2 anac h2 **Ant-c** k* *Ant-t* k* apoc k* *Arn* k* **Ars** k* ars-i ars-s-f k2* bar-c bell k* *Bism* k* *Borx* **Bry** k* bufo *Cadm-s* calc calc-m bro1 calc-sil k2 camph canth k* cham chel chin *Chinin-ar* *Cina* k* cocc colch k* con crot-h bro1 crot-t *Cupr* dig k* dros *Dulc* k* *Eup-per* k* ferr k* ferr-ar ferr-i ferr-p k* hep k* *Hyos* k* iod k* *Ip* k* kali-ar kali-bi ptk1 kali-c *Kreos* *Lyc* k* merc merc-c k* merc-cy k* mez nat-m nit-ac k* *Nux-v* k* olnd *Op* k* petr a1 **Phos** k* plb k* puls k* rhod k* rhus-t sang k2 sanic bro1 sars *Sec* sel *Sil* k* *Sul-ac* k* sul-i k2 sulph k* **Tab** k* vanil fd5.de **Verat** k* *Verat-v* k* xan c1 zinc k* zinc-p k2
    - **cold** water:
      - **agg.**: anac apoc k* apom vh1 arn ars k* ars-i bro1 *Bry* bufo calad bro1 casc bro1 chel k* cina cocc crot-t *Cupr* *Dulc* *Eup-per* ferr gels ip *Jatr-c* kr1* kali-ar *Kali-c* kali-sil k2 lach k2 *Lyc* mez nux-v phos mtf33 podo rhod sanic c1* sarcol-ac sp1 sars ptk1 *Sil* k* *Sul-ac* vanil fd5.de *Verat* k* **Verat-v**
        - **immediately** after: rhus-t hr1
      - **amel.**: *Cupr* k* phos k* puls k*
    - **immediately** after●: *(↗rotavirus)* apoc k* apom vh **Ars** k* **Bism** k* **Bry** k* **Cadm-s** k* cina ptk1 crot-t *Eup-per* jatr-c c1 *Nux-v* phos ptk1 pyrog ptk1 sanic st sep verat ptk1* verat-v ptk1 *Zinc* k*
      - **food** is retained longer; but (See Vomiting; type - water - followed)
  - **amel.**: anac bro1 nit-ac h2* phos bg2 tab bro1
  - **hot** water | **amel.**: ars bro1 *Chel* bro1*
  - **more** than he drinks: kali-bi ptk1
  - **smallest** quantity●: ant-t gsy1 **Apoc** mrr1 **Ars** ars-h **Bism** **Bry** **Cadm-s** ip k2 loxo-lae bnm12• **Phos** plb
    - **not** after eating: sil
  - **warm** in stomach; as soon as water becomes●: *(↗Vomiting; type - liquids - warm)* bism mrr1 *Chlf* kali-bi bg1* **Phos** k* *Pyrog* k*
- **drunkards**; of: *Alumn* **Ars** *Cadm-s* calc *Caps* *Carb-ac* *Crot-h* ichth br1 **Kali-bi** *Kali-br* *Lach* *Nux-v* op *Sang* *Sul-ac* sulph zing
- **during** | **agg.**: cupr b7.de* *Hyos* b7.de* mosch b7a.de *Op* b7a.de *Plb* b7a.de puls b7.de* sabad b7.de* sep ptk1 verat b7.de*
- **easy**: agar k* alum alumn k* ant-t k* *Apoc* bg2* **Ars** k* bapt ptk1 bry bg2 *Calc-p* k* **Cham** k* chel k* colch dig *Ferr* k* graph h2* *Ign* ip ptk1 jatr-c k* *Kali-bi* k* lob bg2 merc-c bg2 mez k* *Nux-v* *Phos* *Phyt* k* *Ran-s* k* sec k* *Tab* k* verat bg2 verat-v bg2 zinc k* zinc-m k* [heroin sdj2]
- **eating**:
  - **after**:
    - **agg.**: acet-ac k* aeth bg2 alum-sil k2 alumn *Am-c* k* anac k* *Ant-c* k* *Ant-t* k* apoc k2 **Ars** k* ars-i k2 ars-s-f k2* aur-s bac bn bell k* bism bro1 brom k2 **Bry** k* bufo *Calc* calc-ar k2 calc-i k2 calc-m bro1 calc-s calc-sil k2 carb-an *Carb-v* *Carbn-s* cham *Chel* **Chin** **Chinin-ar** chinin-s *Cina* k* colch bro1 coloc crot-h k* crot-t cuc-c c1 *Cupr* dig k* *Dros* k* *Ferr* k* *Ferr-ar* ferr-i ferr-m *Ferr-p* k* *Gamb* *Graph* *Hydr* *Hyos* k* *Ign* *Iod* k* **Ip** k* *Iris* kali-ar *Kali-bi* *Kali-br* k* kali-c k* kali-p kali-s kali-sil k2 *Kreos* lach lob *Lyc* k* mag-c **Meph** merc morg-g pte1*• nat-ar *Nat-m* *Nat-s* *Nit-ac* k* *Nux-v* k* olnd k* *Op* k* *Ph-ac* **Phos** k* plb k* prot pte1*• psor k* *Puls* k* ruta *Sanic* sec **Sep** k* **Sil** k* *Stann* k* stram sul-ac k* sul-i k2 **Sulph** k* tab k* **Tarent** k* tritic-vg fd5.de vanil fd5.de **Verat** k* *Verat-v* k* *Zinc* k* zinc-p k2 [heroin sdj2]
      - **hunger**; then: podo bg2
      - **long** time after; a: chel bg2 *Ferr* bg2* kreos bg2 meph bg2 podo bg2 *Puls* bg2 sabin bg2 sulph bg2
      - **only** after: *Ferr* k* sep tl1
    - **amel.**: anac bro1 ant-t ptk1 ferr hed sp1 nux-v ptk1 puls ptk1 tab bro1
    - **immediately** after: *Ars* bg2 sanic mrr1 sec bg2 zinc bg2

- **eating**: ...
  - **agg.** | **sudden** vomiting: am-c *Ars* dig **Ferr** k* iod puls rhus-t sep sil stann verat
  - **overeating** agg.; after: mag-s sp1
- **eggs**:
  - **after**: **Ferr** k* *Ferr-m* morg fmm1• sulph syc pte1*•
  - **smell** of: *Colch* k*
- **eruptions**:
  - **receding**; from: *Cupr* k*
  - **suppressed** eruptions; after: ip k2
- **excessive**: apoc hr1 cupr br1 verat k2*
- **excitement**; after: antip vh1 ferr *Kali-br* k* kali-c *Prot* jl2
- **exertion** agg.: apom vh1 colch crot-h k* ferr *Prot* jl2 stram tab ther verat zinc
- **exertion** of the eyes agg.: apom vh1
- **expectoration**; during: *(↗cough - during - agg.; hawking)* calc-p ptk1 *Coc-c* k* dig k* kali-c lach led bg2 *Sil*
- **fat** food; after: agn bg2 carb-an bg2 cycl bg2 dros bg2 mand sp1 nit-ac bg2 *Puls* k* sep bg2 sin-n spong fd4.de tarax bg2 *Thuj* bg2
- **fetus**, from movements of: *(↗FEMALE - Fetus - motions - nausea)* arn vh psor ptk1
- **fever** | **after**: chin b7a.de cina b7a.de hep b4a.de lach b7a.de sil b4a.de
- **fish**:
  - **fried**; after: kali-c
  - **smell** of: *Colch*
- **followed** by:
  - **diarrhea**: manc ptk1
  - ○ **Head**; pain in (See headache - before)
- **food**; from:
  - **chill**; during: borx h2
  - **colic**; during: op a
  - **sight** of food; from: kola stb3• mosch mrr1
  - **smell** of food; from: colch k2 stann k*
  - **thought** of food; from: colch k2
  - **type** of vomited food (See Vomiting; type - food)
- **food**; type of vomited (See Vomiting; type - food)
- **forcible**: *(↗projectile)* acon ptk1 aeth mtf33 *Ant-t* b7a.de* apoc ptk1* ars h2 *Asar* b7a.de bell bg2 *Colch* b7a.de *Con* k* croc bg2 cupr b7.de* glon k* iod k* ip b7.de* jatr-c kali-bi bg2 lach bg2 manc k* merc-c k* mez k* mosch k* *Nux-v* k* *Petr* k* phos b4a.de *Plb* b7a.de podo bg2 *Sanic* k* stry k* tab bg2 **Verat** k* verat-v ptk1
  - **shortly** after eating: aeth mtf33 *Sanic* k*
- **frequent**: **Ars** k* bar-c bism mtf11 borx hr1 canth **Chin** k* colch *Con* k* cupr h2 hyos lac-h sze9• loxo-recl bnm10• lyc mez ph-ac phos sanic mrr1
- **fright**; from: op ptk1
- **hawking** up mucus agg.●: *(↗cough - during - agg.; expectoration)* *Ambr* *Anac* borx bry k* *Calc-p* k* caust mtf *Coc-c* k* euphr bg1* kali-c lach **Nux-v** k* *Sep* *Sil* *Stann* k*
- **headache**:
  - **before**: iris c1
  - **during** (See HEAD - Pain - accompanied - vomiting)
- **heat**:
  - **after**: apom vh1 calc *Eup-per*
  - **before**: chin b7a.de *Cina* b7a.de* *Ip* b7a.de lyc b4a.de nat-m b4a.de phos b4a.de puls b7a.de sil b4a.de
  - **during**: acon k* aeth all-s k* *Ant-c* k* **Ant-t** aran c1 *Arn* b7a.de* *Ars* k* asar bg2 bac bn bapt pd bell k* borx b4a.de* *Bry* k* cact carb-v bg2 *Cham* k* chin b7.de* cimic bro1 *Cina* k* *Cocc* con k* crot-h cupr bg2 dendr-pol sk4• dor *Elat* **Eup-per** k* eup-pur ferr k* ferr-ar k2 ferr-p gink-b sbd1• hep k* ign k* *Ip* k* kali-c k* lach k* *Lyc* k* nat-c b4.de* **Nat-m** nat-p k2 nux-v k* phos bg2 puls k* sil bg2 squil bg2 *Stram* k* sulph b4.de* ther c1 thuj tub *Verat* k*
- **heated**; becoming: ant-c b7.de* *Bry* b7.de* caps b7.de* ign b7.de* ip b7.de* sil b4a.de*
- **hiccough**; after: cupr bg1* jatr-c ptk1
- **hot** water amel.: ars ptk1 *Chel* k* mag-p pd sul-ac bg1*
- **hysterical**: *Aqui* bro1 ign br1* kali-br ptk1 *Kreos* bro1 plat bro1 valer bro1
- **ice** cream agg.: **Ars** *Calc-p* *Ip* k* *Puls*

- **impossible**: bac bn bell h1 lac-d c1
- **incessant**: acon ant-c ant-t *Arg-n* *Ars* k* ars-h ars-i bar-m borx k2 *Cadm-s* carb-v carc mlr1• cocc bg2 colch k* crot-t cupr k* dig k* eup-per c1 grat *Hell* bg2 *Iod* k* *Ip* k* iris bg2 kali-bi kali-m k2 *Kreos* bg2 lac-d k* lob bg2 mag-p meph *Merc* bg2 *Merc-c* k* mez k* *Nit-ac* nux-v bg2 op petr bg2 *Phos* *Plb* ruta sabin scol ah1 sec squil sym-r k2 verat vip bg2
- **inclination** to: alum b4.de* ant-t bg2 ars bg2 asaf b7.de* asar bg2 bell b4.de* *Brom* b4a.de carc jl2 cham b7.de* cocc b7.de* cupr b7.de* dulc b4.de* kali-bi bg2 kali-sula a1 nat-c b4.de* nat-m b4.de* *Nit-ac* b4a.de **Nux-v** bg2 phos b4.de* plb b7.de* sars b4.de* sel b7a.de sep b4.de* sul-ac b4.de* v-a-b jl2
  - **accompanied** by | **Teeth**; complaints of (See TEETH - Complaints - accompanied - vomit)
- **ineffectual** urging: acon vh1 kali-sula c1*
- **influenza**; during: bapt tl1 sarcol-ac pd
- **injuries**; after: *Arn* bg2 **Bry** bg2 puls bg2 **Rhus-t** bg2 ruta bg2
- **intermittent**, in: **Ant-c** **Ant-t** **Cina** *Elat* *Ferr* loxo-recl bnm10• *Lyc* scol a1*
- **intoxication**; during: crot-h k* **Nux-v**
- **itching** of skin with nausea, must scratch until he vomits: *Ip*
- **larynx**, from irritation: tab k*
- **lemonade** | **amel**.: cycl bg2
- **lifting**; after: sil k*
- **light**; from: sang bg1
- **lying**:
  - **abdomen**; on:
    - **agg.** | **pregnancy** agg.; during: podo c1
  - **after** | **agg.**: olnd puls k*
  - **amel.**: bry bro1 colch bro1 nux-v bro1 sym-r bro1
  - **back**; on:
    - **agg.**: bry bg2 crot-h k* merc bg2 merc-c nux-v rhus-t k*
    - **amel.**: sym-r c1
  - **side**; on:
    - **agg.**: ferr
    - **left** | **agg.**: ant-t sep sul-ac bg3* verat-v
    - **right**:
      - **agg.**: crot-h al1*
        - **liver** complaints; in: bry bg1 crot-h
      - **amel.**: ant-t k* colch
- **measles**; during: **Ant-c** k*
- **meat** agg.: kreos
  - **fresh**: caust
- **medicine**; after:
  - **allopathic** | **narcotics**: *(↗opium)* cham mrr1
- **menopause**; during: aqui bro1
- **menses**:
  - **after** | **agg.**: borx k* canth k* crot-h bg2* gels k* kreos nux-v k* puls k*
  - **before** | **agg.**●: *Am-m* bro1 ant-t bg2 apoc vh1 borx bro1 bry bg2 *Calc* k* caul k* cham k* chin *Cocc* bro1 *Cupr* k* *Cycl* bro1 gels k* graph bro1 ichth bro1 *Ip* bro1 *Kreos* k* meli bro1 nat-m bg2* *Nux-v* k* phos bg2 *Puls* k* *Sep* bro1 sulph h2 thlas bro1 verat k*
  - **during**:
    - **agg.**●: *Am-c* k* *Am-m* k* ant-c k* ant-t bg2 **Apoc** k* arn bg2 ars bg2 bell bg2 borx bg2* bry bg2 *Calc* k* canth bg2 caps bg2 *Carb-v* k* carbn-s carc gk6 caul bg2 cham k* chel bg2 cimic bg2 cocc k* coff k* con k* *Cupr* *Cycl* hr1* gels k* *Graph* k* hyos bg2 ichth bro1 ign k* ip bg2* kali-bi bg2 *Kali-c* k* kali-i k* kali-p kali-s *Kreos* bg2* *Lach* k* lob bg2 *Lyc* k* mag-c bg2 meli bro1 mosch bg2 nat-c bg2 *Nat-m* bg2* nux-v k* *Phos* k* *Puls* k* sars sep k* *Sulph* k* tarent thlas bro1 *Verat* k* *Vib* k* zinc bg2
      - **copious** (See FEMALE - Menses - copious - accompanied - vomiting)
    - **beginning** of menses | **agg.**: am-c bg2 hyos bg2 phos bg2 puls bg2 sec bg2 verat bg2
  - **suppressed** menses; from: ars bell bry cupr k* *Ip* nicc c1 nux-v plb puls verat
- **mental** exertion agg.: ferr nat-m tab
- **milk**; after: **Aeth** k* *Ant-c* k* ant-t k* apom vh1 *Ars* k* ars-i ars-s-f k2 *Atis* zzc1• atro bar-c bell *Calc* k* calc-p bg2 calc-sil k2 carb-v *Cham* b7.de* ferr bro1 *Iod* *Iris* k* kali-bi kreos bro1 lac-d k2 lach k* mag-c k* mag-m bg2* merc bro1 merc-c merc-d k* morph *Ph-ac* phos k* *Podo* k* puls b7.de* samb k*
- **milk**; after: ...
  Sanic k* *Sep* **Sil** k* spong k* sul-i k2 sulph k* tritic-vg fd5.de **Valer** k* vario ptk1 vip zinc bg2
  - **curd**: *Agar* zr
  - **infants**; in: but-ac sp1
  - **mother's**: acet-ac *Ant-c* k* calc calc-p cda1 ip pd *Nat-c* *Ph-ac* *Sanic* **Sil** k* tritic-vg fd5.de *Valer*
    - **anger** of mother; from: coch kr1 valer k2*
- **motion** agg.: *Ant-t* **Ars** **Bry** k* bufo **Cadm-s** cocc bro1* *Colch* k* *Cupr* dig br1* eup-per mrr1 *Ferr* iod k* kali-bi kalm *Lac-d* *Lach* *Lob* *Nux-v* k* *Petr* stram **Tab** k* ther k* *Verat* k* zinc k*
- **moving** from right side: ant-t k*
- **nausea**:
  - **with**: *Aeth* bro1 amyg-p bro1 ant-t bro1 *Apom* br1 bamb-a stb2.de• bry bro1 calc bg2 dulc fd4.de ferr mtf33 **Ip** bg2* iris bro1 kali-bi bg2 *Lob* bro1 merc-c bg2 *Nux-v* bro1 petr bro1 *Puls* bro1 sang bro1 scol ah1 streptoc jl2 sul-ac bg2 sym-r bro1 *Tab* mrr1 verat bro1
  - **without**: ant-c bg3* apoc ptk1 *Apom* bg2* apom-m nh3 arn ptk1 ars ptk1 bry bg2 chel bg3* ferr k2* kali-bi ptk1 kali-p fd1.de• lyc bg1* med k2* merc-c bg2 phyt ptk1 sabin c1 tab bg2 tritic-vg fd5.de verat-v bg2* zinc ptk1
- **nervous**: ambr bg2 ign bg2 lob bg2 ol-an bg2
- **nursing** the child agg.; after: *Sil* bg2
- **nuts**; after: bamb-a stb2.de•
- **odors**:
  - **agg.**: **Colch** mrr1
  - **bad** odor; from: kreos mta1
  - **food** agg.; of (See food; from - smell)
- **operation**; after an: *(↗Nausea - operation)* aeth bro1 all-c c2* bism c2* ferr mrr1 *Nux-v* bro1 *Phos* bro1 staph bro1 *Stry* bro1
  - **abdomen**; on: all-c ptk1 **Bism** hr1* *Nux-v* ptk1 *Phos* ptk1 staph ptk1
- **opium**; after: *(↗medicine - allopathic - narcotics)* **Cham**
- **orange** colored: androc srj1•
- **overheated**, after: *Ant-c*
- **oysters**; from: brom tl1
- **pain**; from: coloc k2 spig k2
- **painful**: anac b4.de* ant-t **Apis** b7a.de arn *Ars* k* asar b7.de* bapt hr1 *Cupr* b7a.de cupr-s dig k* kali-bi bg2 kali-i kali-n k* merc-br a1 ox-ac phos k* phyt bg1* ruta sul-ac verat bg2* verat-v
- **painless**: phyt bg2 sec b7a.de* *Sul-ac* b4a.de [heroin sdj2]
- **palliative** action: *Ip* bg2 *Kreos* bg2
- **palpitations**; with: ars *Crot-h* **Lach** **Nux-v**
- **paroxysmal**: **Ars** bism bro1 bry carc mlr1• helo-s bnm14• kali-bi bg2 **Lob** *Nux-m* osm *Phos* *Plb* (non:uran-met k) *Uran-n*
- **periodical**: ars carc fb* *Chel* k* *Cupr* k* dys fmm1• *Iris* k* *Lept* *Nat-s* nux-v k* plb ptk1 sang sulph
  - **nights**; on alternate: lach bg1
  - **month**; every: crot-h ptk1
  - **alternating** with asthma (See RESPIRATION - Asthmatic - alternating - vomiting)
  - **children**; in: | **infants**: carc mlr1• cupr-ar bro1* ing bro1 iris bro1* kreos bro1* merc-d bro1*
- **persisting**: cadm-s br1 helo-s bnm14• *Ip* br1 ptel hr1
  - **milk**; after: calc-p ptk1 ph-ac ptk1
- **perspiration**:
  - **during**: *(↗accompanied - perspiration)* ant-c bg2 *Arn* b7a.de* **Ars** k* *Bell* b4.de* bry bg2 camph k* **Cham** b7.de* chin k* cina k* *Con* bg2 dros *Eup-per* *Ferr* bg2 *Hep* bg2 *Hyos* b7.de* ign bg2 ip k* kali-c bg2 lach bg2 *Lyc* bg2 merc k* nat-c bg2 nux-v bg2 puls bg2 *Sel* b7a.de* sep bg2 *Sil* bg2 stram bg2 sulph k* *Thuj* b4a.de* *Verat* bg2
  - **fails**; when perspiration: *Cact*
- **pessary** in vagina; from: nux-m ptk1
- **phthisis**; from (See CHEST - Phthisis - accompanied - vomiting)
- **plums**, after: ham k*
- **pregnancy** agg.; during: acet-ac k* acon k* alet k* alst c2 *Amyg* bro1 *Amyg-p* bro1 anac k* *Ant-c* ant-t bro1 *Apis* apom c1* arg-n bro1 *Ars* k* **Asar** k* bism bro1 *Bry* k* *Cadm-s* *Calc* calc-p k2 *Canth* *Caps* *Carb-ac* k* card-m castm k* cer-ox c2* **Chel** k* *Cic* k* *Cimic* c2* cinnm k* cocain bro1 cocc bg1*

- **pregnancy** agg.: ...
cod k* *Colch* k* *Con* k* conv c2 cuc-p c1* *Cupr-act* bro1 cupr-ar cycl c2* dios *Ferr* k* ferr-ar *Ferr-p* gins st gnaph bro1 goss c2* graph bro1 hep c2 ign bro1* ing br1* *Ip* k* *Iris* k* jab ptk1 **Jatr-c** *Kali-bi* k* *Kali-br* k* kali-c kali-m bro1 kali-p **Kreos** k* **Lac-ac** k* lac-c lac-d k2* *Lach* k* *Lil-t* lob k* *Lyc* *Mag-c* bro1 *Mag-m* k* med bg2* merc bro1 merc-i-f k* *Nat-m* k* nat-p k* **Nat-s** k* **Nux-m** k* **Nux-v** k* onos c2 *Op* *Ox-ac* k* *Petr* k* *Ph-ac* *Phos* k* pilo bro1 plat plb *Podo* *Psor* k* *Puls* k* sanic c2* **Sep** k* *Sil* staph bro1 stront-br bro1 stry bro1 *Sul-ac* k* *Sulph* k* sym-r k* symph ptk1 **Tab** k* tarent ther c2* *Thyr* br1* *Verat* k* *Verat-v* zinc zinc-p k2
  - **accompanied** by:
    - **cough**: nux-m mtf11
    - **Tongue**:
      - **brown** discoloration | **yellowish** brown: *Merc-i-f* kr1*
- **pressure**; from:
  - **abdomen**; on: zinc h2
  - **spine** and cervical region; on: cimic bro1*
- **profuse**: canth bg2 eup-per bg2 merc-c bg2 nux-v bg2 *Verat* br1
- **projectile**, like a: (*↗forcible*) acon bg3 am-caust vh1 sanic mrr1 **Verat** mrr1
- **prostration**; with (See GENERALS - Weakness - accompanied - vomiting)
- **purging**; with: aeth ptk1 ant-t ptk1 apis ptk1 arg-n ptk1 *Ars* bg2* asar ptk1 borx ptk1 camph ptk1 cham ptk1 colch ptk1 cupr bg2* euph bg2 *Ip* bg2* iris bg2* jatr-c bg2 merc ptk1 merc-c bg2 olnd bg2 phos ptk1 *Podo* ptk1 sec bg2* seneg ptk1 sul-ac ptk1 sulph ptk1 *Verat* bg2* verat-v ptk1
  - **stool** agg.; after: kali-bi bg2
- **putting** hands in warm water (See Nausea - warm - water)
- **raising** head agg.: acon vh1 apom bro1 *Ars* k* *Bry* k* carb-ac bg2 cocc bg2 colch k* graph bg2 lept bg2 nux-m bg2 *Stram* k* verat hr1 zinc bg2
- **recurrent** (See GENERALS - History - vomiting)
- **reflex** vomiting: apom bro1 cer-ox br1* cocc bro1 *Ip* bro1 kreos bro1 *Valer* bro1
- **relief**; without: ant-c bg2* ars tl1 ip bg2 *Iris* mrr1
- **rice**, after: tell k*
  - **water**: cupr ptk1 kali-bi ptk1 verat ptk1
- **rich** food agg.: aeth *Ip* k* *Puls* samb spong sulph
- **riding** in a carriage agg.•: (*↗Nausea - riding - carriage - agg.*) androc srj1• *Apom* bro1 arn bro1 *Ars* k* bell borx bro1 **Carb-ac** k* cer-ox bro1 **Cocc** k* coff bro1 *Colch* dulc fd4.de *Ferr* ferr-p glon k* *Hyos* ip bro1 *Kreos* bro1 nicot bro1 nux-m *Nux-v* bro1 op bro1 **Petr** k* phos k* sanic bro1 sec sep bro1 *Sil* k* staph k* sulph **Tab** k* ther bro1
- **rinsing** mouth, when: (*↗brushing*) bry bg2 *Coc-c* k* sep bg2*
- **rising** | **after** | **agg.**: ambr k* ars
  - **bed**; from | **agg.**: *Lac-d* sang verat-v
- **rotavirus**; from: (*↗drinking - after - immediately*) aeth mtf *Ant-c* mtf ant-t mtf apoc mtf apom mtf *Ars* mtf ars-h mtf *Bism* mtf *Bry* mtf *Cadm-s* mtf chinin-ar mtf cupr mtf *Cupr-ar* mtf eup-per mtf ip mtf *Jatr-c* mtf *Phos* mtf sec mtf tab mtf *Verat* mtf verat-v mtf
- **sadness**; with (See MIND - Sadness - vomiting)
- **saliva** running down the throat while sitting, from: am-m k*
- **salivation** agg.: anac gsy1
- **scarlet** fever; after: ail bro1 asim bro1 *Bell* bro1 cupr bro1
- **scratching**; when: ip ptk1
- **seasickness**; during: *Apom* bro1 ars bro1 borx bro1 carb-ac bro1 cer-ox bro1 cocc bro1 coff bro1 glon bro1 ip bro1 *Kreos* bro1 nicot bro1 *Nux-v* bro1 op bro1 *Petr* bro1 sep bro1 *Staph* bro1 tab bro1 ther bro1
- **sensation** of: gard-j vlr2• pitu-gl skp7•
  - **empty** stomach; with: gard-j vlr2• pitu-gl skp7*•
  - **eructation**; during: goss ptk1
- **shivering**; during: borx b4a.de
- **sitting** erect agg.: colch k* sil ptk1 zinc h2*
- **sitting** up in bed agg.: *Acon* ail c1* ars *Colch* nat-m h2 *Stram*
- **sleep** agg.; during: apis bg2 merc-c b4a.de positr nl2•
- **sleep**, followed by: aeth bg2* ant-t bg1* bell bg2 cupr ptk1 cycl hr1 ip bg2 nat-m ptk1 sanic ptk1 stram kr1
- **smoking** agg.: agar brom tl1 bufo calad clem k* cocc k* *Ip* k* nat-s tab
- **soup** agg.: ars k* *Mag-c* k*
- **spasmodic**: (*↗Contraction; Contraction - vomiting; Pain - vomiting - during - cramping*) ant-t k2 **Bism** k* *Caps* hr1 caul c1 cer-ox br1 cham b7.de* *Cupr* k* dig h2 hep k* kali-sula a1* lach k* lyss jl2 merc-c k* plb b7.de* podo bg2 scol a1 sul-ac k* tab k* vip k*
  - **accompanied** by | **vertigo** (See VERTIGO - Accompanied - vomiting)
  - **sudden**: cupr mrr1
- **spitting**, after: dig
- **standing** up, on: colch
- **starting** from sleep, after: petr h2
- **stool**:
  - **after** | **agg.**: aeth ptk1 arg-n bro1 colch bg2* cupr bro1 dig bg2 eug bg1 *Ip* bro1 iris bro1 *Nux-v* bro1 phos b4a.de* *Verat* b7.de*
  - **before**: ant-t b7.de* ars k* colch bg2 dig glon k* ip k* ox-ac petr bg2 podo sul-ac b4a.de verat k*
  - **during** | **agg.**: agar b4.de* ant-c b7a.de* ant-t b7.de* apis k* arg-met b7.de* *Arg-n* k* *Ars* k* asar b7.de* bell bg2 bism bg2 borx b4a.de* bry **Camph** bg2 cham b7a.de* *Cocc* colch k* coloc b4.de* crot-t k* *Cupr* k* dulc k* elat euph bg2 hell bg2 *Ip* k* *Iris* bg2 jatr-c bg2 kali-bi bg2 *Merc* k* nit-ac b4.de* nux-v bg2 ox-ac k* *Phos* b4a.de* phyt bg2 podo bg2 rheum bg2 samb bg2 *Sec* bg2 seneg b4a.de* stram sul-ac bg2 *Sulph* b4.de* *Tab* bg2 *Verat* k*
  - **ineffectual** | **after**: bell b4.de* sang k*
  - **straining** at | **after**: ther k*
  - **urging** to | **after**: bell h1 sang hr1
- **stooping** agg.; after: *Cic* k* **Ip** k*
- **stupor**; during (See MIND - Stupor - vomiting - during)
- **sudden**: acon bg2* aeth k* agar am-c bg2 ant-t ptk1 apoc ptk1 *Apom* vh1 *Ars* k* bell bg2* cadm-s ptk1 crot-h k* crot-t k* *Cupr* k* elaps bg2 ferr k* gard-j vlr2• jab a1 kali-bi bg2* kali-chl ptk1 kali-m k2 kali-sula a1 lac-h sze9• *Op* bg2* pic-ac ptk1 podo bg2 rhus-t bg2* sec k* sep bg2 sil bg2 stann bg2 tritic-vg fd5.de vanil fd5.de verat bg2 verat-v bg2 zinc ptk1
  - **fever**; during: bapt ptk1
- **sugar** | **amel.**: op ptk1
- **supper** agg.; after: caul gast a1 gaul k* ip k2 jab k* rob k*
- **swallowing** | **saliva** | **agg.**: colch graph ptk1
  - **trying** to swallow agg.: kali-c mtf33 *Merc-c* k*
- **sweets** | **after**: gaert fmm1•
- **swoon**, after: ars k*
- **sympathetic**: apom c1 kreos tl1
- **talking** loudly agg.: *Coc-c* k* cocc ptk1 vanil fd5.de
- **teething** children, in (See dentition)
- **tenderness** with: cadm-s br1
- **tenesmus**; with (See Pain - vomiting - while - tenesmus)
- **touching** the inside of the mouth: coc-c k2
- **turning** in bed agg.: gard-j vlr2•
- **unconsciousness**, during: ars k* ben-n k*
- **uncovering** abdomen | **amel.**: *Tab* k*
- **urticaria**:
  - **during**: *Apis* cina
  - **suppression** of; from: *Urt-u* k*
- **vertigo**; during (See VERTIGO - Accompanied - vomiting)
- **vexation**; after•: acon *Cham* ign *Ip* k* lyc nat-s *Verat*
- **violent**: acon tl1 aeth k* ail tl1 androc srj1• ant-c tl1 ant-t k* apoc arg-n a1* **Ars** k* ars-i asc-c c1 bell k* bism k* boerh-d bnj1 canth bg3* *Cic* k* *Cina* **Colch** k* con h2* **Crot-t** k* *Cupr* k* cycl a1* cyt-l a1 dig h2 *Elat* br1 *Ferr* ferr-p geo a1 hura-c a1 *Iod* k* *Ip* *Jatr-c* kali-bi bg3* kali-n h2* kali-sula a1 kali-t a1 lac-h sze9• lach k* lob med c1* merc k* merc-sul a1 mez k* mosch k* mur-ac a1 narc-ps br1 nux-v k* petr a1 phal a1* **Phos** k* phyt bg3* *Plb* k* puls bg2 raph sal-fr sle1• sang a1 *Sarcol-ac* br1 scol c1 stann bg3* **Tab** k* **Verat** k* verat-v bg2 vip bg2
  - **accompanied** by:
    - **influenza**: *Sarcol-ac* br1
    - **salivation**; profuse: graph bro1 ign bro1 *Ip* bro1 iris bro1 kreos bro1 lac-ac bro1 *Lob* bro1 phal a1 puls bro1 tab bro1
- **waking**; on: acon k* aeth alum bg2 ambr b7.de* ant-t apis k* apoc k* bell bg2 borx b4a.de* bry k* *Calc* b4a.de cupr bg2 dig bg2 euphr b7.de* form graph lach k* m-aust b7.de nit-ac k* *Nux-v* b7.de* op b7.de* rat rhus-t b7.de* ruta b7.de* sil k* spong bg2 squil b7.de* sulph bg2 thuj k* *Verat* b7.de*

- **walking**:
  - **agg.**: am-c crot-h prin a1
  - **air** agg.; in open: am-m
- **warm**:
  - **drinks**:
    - **after**: bry bro1* *Phos* bro1 *Puls* bro1 pyrog bro1 sanic bro1
    - **agg.**: lat-m bnm6•
  - **room** | **agg.**: phos k2* vesp k2
  - **washing** the hands agg.: phos k2*
- **warm** food; from: brom tl1 guat sp1 phos k2*
- **water**: *(↗Vomiting; type - liquids)* *Acon* k* *Aeth* agar k* all-c k* alum anac ant-t k* *Arn* k* **Ars** k* ars-i asar k* aur-m k* bar-c k* bar-i bar-m k* *Bell* k* *Bism* **Bry** calc *Camph* k* *Cann-s* k* carb-ac k* card-m k* carl k* **Caust** *Chin* clem k* *Coc-c* *Cocc* k* colch k* *Coloc* k* *Con* crot-h k* crot-t k* *Cupr* k* *Cupr-ar* k* cupr-s k* cycl k* cyt-l a1 dig k* dulc k* elat k* euph k* fl-ac k* graph k* *Grat* k* *Guaj* hell k* hep k* hydr-ac k* hyos k* iod k* *Ip* kali-ar *Kali-bi* k* kali-i k* kali-n k* *Kreos* k* lyc mag-c manc k* merc merc-c k* mez mur-ac k* *Nat-m* k* nat-s k* nit-ac k* *Nux-v* olnd k* op k* osm k* ox-ac k* petr k* phos k* phys k* *Phyt* plb k* raph rat k* rhus-t k* **Rob** k* sabad k* sang k* sanic c2 *Sec* k* sel k* seneg k* *Sil* sin-a k* spong fd4.de *Stann* *Stram* k* stry k* *Sul-ac* k* *Sulph* k* *Tab* k* ther k* *Thuj* k* **Verat** verat-v k* vinc k* vip k* zinc k*
  - **sight** of; from: lyss bro1* *Phos* k*
    - **pregnancy** agg.; during: phos tl1
- **whooping** cough (See cough - during - agg. - whooping)
- **wine**: *Ant-c* k*
  - **amel.**: kalm k*
  - **sour**: **Ant-c** k*
- **worms**; from: *Acon* bg2 bell bg2 carb-v bg2 chin bg2 **Cina** bg2 *Ip* bg2 lach bg2 *Merc* bg2 *Nux-v* bg2 *Puls* bg2 **Sulph** bg2

VOMITING; TYPE OF:

- **acrid**: *Apis* b7a.de arg-met k* *Ars* bufo calad chion ptk1 colch coloc con crot-t dor ferr k* gent-c *Hep* ip k* *Iris* k* kali-c ptk1 kali-m ptk1 **Kreos** k* lyc ptk1 med ptk1 merc-c b4a.de phys phyt k* *Rob* bg2* **Sang** k* *Sec* b7a.de sulph k2* ther thuj zinc a1*
  - **morning** | **coughing**; while: thuj
  - **night**: ther
- **albuminous**: ars k* ip k* *Jatr-c* k* kali-bi ptk1 *Merc-c* *Plb* *Verat* k*
- **bile**: *Acon* k* aeth bro1 alum alum-p k2 alum-sil k2 ambr b7.de amyg anan androc srj1• *Ant-c* k* ant-t k* anthraci anthraco br1 *Apis* k* apoc *Arg-n* k* arn k* **Ars** k* ars-h ars-i ars-s-f k2 asar k* asc-t aspar aur aur-ar k2 aur-i k2 aur-s k2 bar-c k* bar-i bar-m bar-s k2 *Bell* k* *Bism* k* boerh-d bnj1 borx b2.de* **Bry** k* bufo cadm-met gm1 *Cadm-s* cain *Calc* k* calc-i k2 calc-s calc-sil k2 camph k* cann-s k* canth k* carb-ac bro1 carb-v k* carbn-s card-m k2* castm **Cham** k* **Chel** k* *Chin* k* *Chinin-ar* *Chion* *Cic* k* cina k* cocc k* coch *Coff* k* **Colch** k* *Coloc* k* con k* *Crot-c* *Crot-h* k* crot-t *Cupr* k* cupr-ar cur cycl cystein-l rly4• *Dig* k* dros k* dulc k* elaps elat c1 eup-a br1* **Eup-per** k* fago *Ferr-p* fl-ac k* gels k2 *Grat* k* hell b2.de* hep k* hyos k* *Ign* k* *Iod* k* **Ip** k* *Iris* k* jab jatr-c *Kali-ar* *Kali-bi* k* kali-c k* kali-i kali-m k2 kali-p kali-s kali-sil k2 *Lac-d* *Lach* k* *Lept* k* *Lyc* k* lyss mag-c k* mang bg2 med k* **Merc** k* **Merc-c** k* **Merc-cy** meth-bchl a1 mez k* morg fmm1• *Morph* mur-ac k* *Nat-ar* *Nat-c* k* *Nat-m* k* nat-p **Nat-s** k* nit-ac k* **Nux-v** k* nyct bro1 olnd k* **Op** k* ox-ac ozone sde2• *Petr* k* **Phos** k* phyt k* *Plb* k* *Podo* k* **Puls** k* *Pyrog* raph rhod b2.de* rhus-t k* rob bro1 sabad k* *Sabin* k* samb b7a.de* **Sang** k* sars *Sec* k* **Sep** k* sil k* stann k* stram k* streptoc jl2 sul-ac sul-i k2 *Sulph* k* sumb tarent tart-ac bro1 tax *Ter* ther c1* thuj k* *Tub* valer k* vanil fd5.de **Verat** k* *Verat-v* zinc k* zinc-m zinc-p k2
  - **morning**: aspar dros hep merc-c **SEP** k ● tarent ther zinc
    - **waking**; on: stann
  - **forenoon** | **10**-11 h: cur vh
  - **afternoon**: phyt
  - **evening**: phos stram
    - **21** h: tax
  - **night**: chin cur dros gk lyc *Merc* op gk phos *Podo*
    - **midnight**:
      - **after** | **3** h: mur-ac h2
    - **alternate** night: dros gk

Vomiting; type of – **bile**: ...

  - **accompanied** by | **Liver**; cirrhosis of (See ABDOMEN - Cirrhosis - accompanied - vomiting)
  - **anger**; after: cham nux-v
  - **chill**:
    - **after**: **Eup-per** kali-c **Nat-m**
    - **before**: cina *Eup-per*
    - **during**: *Ant-c* arn k* *Ars* k* borx b4a.de *Cham* chin k* *Cina* k* *Dros* **Eup-per** ign k* ip lyc *Nux-v* *Puls* k* verat
  - **cold** water, after: *Eup-per* *Rhus-t*
  - **colic**; with: *Chin* coloc *Iod* *Nux-v* op a
  - **cough** agg.; during: anan cadm-s carb-v cham **Chin** *Puls* sabad sars sep stram sulph
  - **cramps**; with: cham ptk1
  - **diet** errors; from: fl-ac ptk1
  - **drunkards**; in: ant-t gm1
  - **eating**; after: ant-c bism ptk1 bry k2 *Crot-h* merc stann
  - **exertion** agg.; after: stram
  - **fever**; during: ant-c b7.de* *Ars* k* bry k* *Cham* k* *Chin* k* *Cina* k* crot-h cupr k* dros k* **Eup-per** gink-b sbd1• ign k* ip k* iris merc k* *Nat-m* *Nux-v* k* op phos k* psor *Puls* k* sec k* sep k* sulph k* thuj verat k*
  - **followed** by:
    - **blood**: agar carb-v verat k*
    - **froth**: verat b7a.de
    - **mucus**: *Verat* b7a.de
      - **blood**; then: verat b7a.de
  - **food**, then: bry
  - **headache**; during: *(↗HEAD - Pain - bilious)* arg-n aur *Bry* cadm-s *Calc* carc zzh card-m k2 **Chel** chion br1 crot-h cur vml eup-per ign gk **Ip** **Iris** kali-c h2 *Lac-d* *Lept* *Lob* nat-m *Nat-s* k* nicc petr *Plb* podo c1 *Puls* rhus-t **Sang** spig streptoc jl2 sulph verat zinc
    - **sweets** agg.: *Iris*
  - **lying** on right side or back: *Crot-h*
  - **mental** exertion; after: nat-m
  - **motion**, on least: *Crot-h* *Stram*
  - **perspiration**; during: ant-c *Ars* bry **Cham** **Chin** ign ip iris merc *Nux-v* puls sep verat
  - **rising** agg.: ars
  - **sitting** up in bed agg.: *Stram*
  - **soup** agg.: stann h2
  - **stooping** agg.: ip ptk1
  - **tea** agg.: sel
  - **trembling** and great nausea, causing prostration: *Eup-per*
  - **vexation**; after: *Nat-s* k*
- **bitter**: *Acon* k* agar ant-c ant-t apis arn *Ars* bar-c b4a.de *Bell* b4a.de benz-ac bol-la borx k* **Bry** k* bufo cadm-s calc k* calc-s calc-sil k2 cann-s k* canth b7.de *Carbn-s* castm *Cham* k* *Chin* b7.de* chion ptk1 clem coc-c *Cocc* k* colch k* *Coloc* k* con *Crot-c* *Crot-h* crot-t cupr k* *Eup-per* k* form gent-c *Grat* hydr *Ip* b7.de iris k* *Kali-bi* k* kali-c h2 lac-d k2 lyc k* mag-c k* manc med *Merc* k* merc-c k* mez k* *Nat-ar* *Nat-c* *Nat-m* k* nat-p *Nat-s* nit-ac k* **Nux-v** k* olnd k* op *Petr* k* **Phos** k* phyt pic-ac ptk1 *Plb* k* ptel *Puls* k* raph rhod k* samb **Sang** k* *Sars* *Sec* b7.de *Sep* k* sil k* *Stann* k* *Sulph* k* tab thuj k* vanil fd5.de *Verat* k* vinc vip zinc k* zinc-p k2
  - **morning**: borx h2 *Bry* cham colch form tab thuj
    - **cough** agg.; during: thuj
    - **waking**; on: form sil thuj
  - **noon** | **soup** agg.: mag-c
  - **afternoon**: sulph
  - **evening**: hell verat
    - **cough** in bed; during: *Sep*
  - **night**: crot-t hell phyt sil h2
  - **breakfast**; before | **agg.**: tab
  - **chill**; during: *Ant-c* bg2 arn bg2 **Ars** bg2 borx bg2 *Cham* k* *Chin* bg2 cina bg2 ign bg2 lyc bg2 *Nux-v* bg2 *Puls* b7a.de* verat bg2

- **chill**; during: ...
  - **close** of; at: ant-t bg2 *Eup-per*
- **coffee** agg.: *Cham* verat
- **cough** agg.; during: cham b7.de *Ip* b7a.de mez b4a.de *Sep* k* verat zinc bg2
- **drinking**:
  - **after**:
    - **agg.**: borx bufo eup-per ptk1
    - **cold** water | **agg.**: podo
- **eating**; after: mag-c k* nat-m b4a.de nit-ac k* stann k*
- **fever**; during: *Cham* b7a.de
- **followed** by:
  - **blood** or mucus: carb-v bg2 kali-bi bg2 verat bg2
  - **food**; eaten: bry bg2
- **headache**; during: form nit-ac *Sang* sulph thuj h1
- **heat**; during: *Ars* b4a.de *Eup-per* thuj
- **menses** | **before** | **agg.**: *Caul*
  - **during** | **agg.**: *Sars*
- **mortification**; from: puls
- **perspiration**; during: ant-c bg2 *Ars* bg2 bry bg2 **Cham** bg2 **Chin** bg2 ign bg2 ip bg2 merc bg2 *Nux-v* bg2 puls bg2 sep bg2 verat bg2
- **soup** agg.: *Mag-c* stann h2
- **standing** agg.: colch
- **waking**; on: sil
- **watery**: lac-d ptk1 mag-c ptk1

- **bitter**-salty: *Sil* b4a.de
- **bitter**-sour: ant-t b7a.de ip b7a.de puls b7a.de
- **black**: acon k* alum ant-t k* *Arg-n* k* arn k2 **Ars** k* ars-s-f k2 bism b2.de* **Cadm-s** k* *Calc* k* camph k* carb-ac card-m *Chin* k* *Chinin-ar* colch bg2 *Con* *Crot-h* k* cur dor hell k* hep b2.de* hydr-ac *Hyos* *Ip* k* kali-i kali-n kali-ox *Kreos* bg2* *Lach* lat-m k* laur k* *Lyc* k* manc k* med merc-c k* *Mez* bg2* *Nat-s* nit-ac k* **Nux-v** k* op k* ox-ac *Petr* k* **Phos** k* phyt pix c2* *Plb* k* puls raph *Sec* k* sil squil b2.de* stram b2.de* sul-ac k* *Sulph* k* **Verat** k* zinc k* zinc-p k2
  - **chill**; during: ars bg2 chin bg2 ip bg2 nux-v bg2 verat bg2
  - **greenish**: dulc bg2 op bg2 *Petr* b4.de* phos b4.de* plb b7.de* sec bg2 stann bg2 stram bg2 verat bg2
  - **menses**, on appearance of: sulph
  - **pain** in stomach, with: *Pix* br1
  - **staining**: arg-n bg2*
- **blood**: (*↗Hemorrhage*) acet-ac k* *Acon* k* *Adren* br1 aeth agar aloe k* alum k* alum-p k2 alumn *Am-c* k* am-caust a1* anan ant-c k* ant-t k* arg-n k* **Arn** k* *Ars* k* ars-h ars-i asar b2.de* aur-m bar-m bell k* borx b2.de* both bro1* brom k* *Bry* k* bufo k* **Cact** k* cadm-s bg2* *Calc* k* calc-i k2 calc-s camph k* cann-s k* *Canth* k* caps b2.de* carb-ac **Carb-v** k* carbn-s card-m k* *Caust* k* cham k* **Chin** k* *Chinin-ar* *Cic* k* clem a1 *Cocain* bro1 colch coloc con k* **Crot-h** k* *Cupr* k* *Cycl* dig dros k* elaps mrr1 *Erig* k* **Ferr** k* *Ferr-ar* ferr-i *Ferr-p* k* fic-r br1* ger br1* guaj **Ham** k* hep k* *Hyos* k* ign iod k* **Ip** k* iris bro1 kali-bi k* kali-chl kali-i kali-m k2 kali-n k* kali-p kali-sula a1* *Kreos* k* *Lach* k* lath c1 led k* lob loxo-lae bnm12• lyc k* *Mangi* br1* merc k* *Merc-c* k* mez k* *Mill* k* morg-p pte1*• mosch k2 mur-ac a1 *Nat-ar* nat-f sp1 nat-m k* nat-s *Nit-ac* k* *Nux-v* k* olnd op k* opun-f bnj1 orni mtf11 ox-ac *Petr* **Phos** k* *Phyt* k* *Plb* k* *Podo* k* prot mtf11 psor k2* *Puls* k* pyrog rat rhus-t k* ruta **Sabin** k* sal-ac tl1 samb *Sang* *Sec* k* *Sep* k* *Sil* k* *Stann* k* stram k* sul-ac k* sul-i k2 *Sulph* k* tab *Ter* thal-xyz srj8• thuj b2.de* tril-p c1* (non:uran-met k) uran-n k* ust k* *Verat* k* *Verat-v* vip *Zinc* k* zinc-m c2
  - **morning**: dros
  - **evening**: guaj merc-c
    - **summer**; in: guaj
  - **night**: *Caust* phyt podo
  - **accompanied** by:
    - **cancer**; stomach (See Cancer - accompanied - vomiting blood)
    - **Spleen**; complaints of: card-m ptk1
  - **black**: acon bg2 alum-sil k2 ars k2* calc-sil k2 canth bg2 card-m chin bg2 elaps mrr1 *Ham* k* nux-v bg2 plb k2 puls bg2 sec bg2 sep bg2 sul-ac bg2
    - **clots**: nux-v bg2

- **blood**: ...
  - **blue**: ars vh kali-c bg2
  - **bright**: arn bg2 bell bg2 carb-v bg2 ferr bg2 hyos bg2 ip bg2 phos bg2* plb bg2 sabin bg2 sulph bg2
  - **brown**: bry bg2 bufo bg2 carb-v bg2 rhus-t bg2
  - **children**; in: | **newborns**; in: acon vh1 lyc ptk1
  - **chill**; during: arn bg2 *Ars* bg2 chin bg2 ferr bg2 ip bg2 nux-v bg2 phos bg2 puls bg2
  - **clotted**: arn k* ars bell bg2 canth bg2 cassia-s ccrh1• caust k* chin bg2 ferr bg2 ham hyos bg2 ip bg2* kali-sula a1* lyc *Merc-c* nux-v k* phyt puls bg2 sabin bg2 sec sulph bg2
  - **cough**; with: anan
  - **dark**: merc-cy vh
  - **drinking** agg.; after: merc-c
  - **drunkards**; in: alumn k* ant-t gm1 *Ars*
  - **eating**; after: stram
  - **exertion** agg.; after: *Phos*
  - **fever**; during: ars b4a.de
  - **foamy**: ars bg2 led bg2 phos bg2 sil bg2
  - **hemorrhoidal** flow; after suppressed: acon *Carb-v* **Nux-v** *Phos* *Sulph*
  - **lying**:
    - **agg.**: *Stann*
    - **back**; on | **agg.**: merc-c
  - **menses**:
    - **during**:
      - **agg.**: sulph
      - **beginning** of menses | **agg.**: sulph b4a.de*
    - **instead** of menses, in girls: *Ham* k*
    - **suppressed** menses; from: bell *Bry* *Ham* nat-m *Phos* puls sulph
  - **motion** agg.: *Erig*
  - **mucus**; then: tab bg2
  - **pregnancy** agg.; during: *Sep*
  - **sharp**: bapt bg2 kali-c bg2 kali-n bg2 sil bg2 sul-ac bg2
  - **stool** agg.; during: *Verat* b7a.de
  - **streaked**: bufo bg2
  - **tenacious**: croc bg2 cupr bg2
  - **thin**: *Erig*
  - **vicarious**: ust bg2
- **blue**: ars bg2* cupr bg2 merc-c bg2
- **bluish**: ars h2 kali-c h2*
- **brownish**: arg-n *Ars* k* bar-c k* bism k* bry ptk1 carb-v ptk1 colch k* cupr k* dig b4a.de kali-bi k* kali-c b4a.de merc-c b4a.de *Mez* b4a.de* mur-ac bg2 *Nat-s* k* nit-ac k* op k* ox-ac k* phos k* phyt k* *Plb* k* rhus-t ptk1 sec k* sul-ac k* sulph k* tab k* verat bg2 zinc k* zinc-p k2
  - **evening**:
    - **coffee** agg.: verat
    - **milk** agg.: mur-ac
- **burning**: mez ptk1 phos bg2 podo bg2* puls bg2 sep bg2 sul-ac bg2
- **cheesy**: aeth mtf33
- **chocolate** colored: bry *Con* kreos bg2 mez h2* sec stann bg2 zinc bg2
- **clear**: colch crot-t elat ferr fl-ac petr phyt sabad sul-ac sulph
- **coffee** grounds, like: *Arg-n* ars k* ars-h brom **Cadm-s** k* colch *Con* k* crot-h a11* cund bwa4 *Cupr* echi gsy1* *Iris* lac-d c1* lach bro1 lyc lyss med c1 *Merc-c* k* mez ptk1* mur-ac *Nat-m* nat-p op mta1 orni bro1 ox-ac cda1 **Phos** k* plb pyrog k* sec a1* stry sul-ac k* uran-n ctj4
  - **gastric** cancer, in: phos k2
- **colorless**: mosch b7a.de
- **copper** acetate; like: plb b7.de*
- **copper**; tasting like: cupr b7.de* plb b7.de*
- **curdled** milk (See milk - curdled)
- **dark**: am-caust ant-t *Ars* cadm-s cassia-s ccrh1• cupr dor merc-c nit-ac op ox-ac *Phos* raph sec stann sul-ac
  - **drinking** agg.; after: mur-ac

Stomach

- **drinks**: *(↗liquids)* acon b7a.de* ant-c b7.de* *Ant-t* bg2 am bg2 **Ars** b4a.de* *Bry* bg2 *Cham* bg2 chin bg2 cic bg2 cocc bg2 con bg2 *Dulc* b4.de* ferr bg2 *Ip* b7.de* merc-c b4a.de nat-m bg2 *Nux-v* b7a.de* puls b7a.de* rhus-t bg2 sec bg2 *Sil* b4a.de* sulph bg2 verat bg2
  - **cough** agg.; during: acon b7a.de ant-c b7a.de *Ip* b7a.de *Nux-v* b7a.de
- **egg** white; like: merc-c b4a.de
- **everything**: acet-ac k2 ant-t k2 apoc st **Ars** ars-h bar-m benz-ac k2 cadm-s k2 *Crot-h Eup-per Ip* merc-c merc-cy bg1 op sarcol-ac sp1 sec sul-ac
  - **drinks** | **warm**; except: chel mrr1
- **fecal**: am bg2 ars atro bg2 *Bell* k* bry k* cain *Colch* k* coloc bg2 cupr k* merc bg2 **Nux-v** k ●* **OP** k ●* **Plb** k ●* pyrog al1* raph k* rhus-t bg2* sulph k* tab ptk1 thuj k* verat bg2
  - **accompanied** by | **intussusception** (See ABDOMEN - Intussusception - accompanied - vomiting - fecal)
- **filamentous**: iod ox-ac *Phos* sul-ac
- **flocculent**: *Cupr* b7a.de phos bg2 *Verat* b7a.de
- **food**: acet-ac br1* acon k* aeth agar agar-ph a1 ail k* alum alum-p k2 alum-sil k2 *Am-c* k* anac k* anan *Ant-c* k* *Ant-t* k* apis k* arg-n k2 *Am* k* **Ars** k* ars-i ars-s-f k2 bac bn *Bell* k* berb bism k* borx k* bov b2.de* brom tl1 **Bry** k* bufo *Cact Cadm-s Calc* k* calc-i k2 calc-p k* calc-s calc-sil k2 canth k* caps k* *Carb-v* k* *Carbn-s* caust k* *Cham* k* *Chel* **Chin** k* chinin-ar *Cic* hr1 *Cina* k* *Cocc* k* coff k* *Colch* k* coloc k* con k* *Crot-h* k* crot-t k* *Cund Cupr* k* *Cycl* k* *Cystein-l* rly4• dig k* *Dros* k* elaps **Eup-per** k* **Ferr** k* **Ferr-ar** *Ferr-i Ferr-p Graph* k* grat k* hep bg2 *Hydr* hydr-ac *Hyos* k* **Ign** k* indg iod k* *Ip* k* *Iris* jatr-c *Jug-r* a1 kali-ar k* *Kali-bi* k* *Kali-c* k* kali-m k2 *Kali-p* kali-s kali-sil k2 **Kreos** k* *Lac-d Lach* k* *Laur* k* led k* lob **Lyc** k* lyss mag-c k* mag-s k* manc k* *Meph* bg2 merc k* merc-c k* merc-cy mtf11 **Mez** b4a.de mill mosch k* mur-ac k* nat-c b2.de* *Nat-m* k* nit-ac k* **Nux-v** k* olnd k* *Op* k* oscilloc jl2 ozone sde2• *Ph-ac* k* (non:phal c1) phel k* **Phos** k* phyt *Plb* k* podo psor k* **Puls** k* raph rat k* rhus-t k* ruta k* sabin k* samb k* **Sang** k* sars k2 *Sec* k* *Sel* b7a.de *Sep* k* *Sil* k* squil *Stann* k* sul-ac k* sul-i k2 *Sulph* k* tab k* tarent k2 tell ter thuj k* tritic-vg fd5.de uran-n bg2 **Verat** k* *Verat-v* k* zinc k* *Zinc-m* a1 zinc-p k2
  - **morning**: crot-h *Plb* **Sep** sil *Sulph*
    - **waking**; on: aspar
  - **afternoon**: calc h2 mag-s ozone sde2•
  - **evening**: carb-v kreos phos *Puls Sulph*
    - **sunset**, after: stram
  - **night**: crot-t kali-c h2* lyc h2 phyt rat sil spong fd4.de
    - **midnight**: agar **Ferr** nat-m
      - **after** | **1** h | **waking**; on: rat
        - **2**.30 h:
          - **waking**; on | **dream** of strangulation; from a: lac-h sk4•
  - **animal** food, all: phos
  - **bile**, then: ant-t ars bg2 bell k* *Bry Colch* k* dig k* lyc b4a.de* *Nat-m* k* phos b4a.de* podo bg2 samb k* zinc b4a.de
    - **water**; then: ip bg2
  - **blood**, then: kali-n bg2 nux-v k* verat bg2
  - **breakfast** agg.; after: *Ferr* sel *Sil*
  - **chill**:
    - **after**: phos
    - **before**: *Ars Cina* eup-per **Ferr**
    - **during**: ail ars bg2 borx h2 *Cina* bg2 ferr bg2 ign k* ip bg2 nux-v bg2 phos k* puls bg2 sulph bg2
  - **cough** agg.●: anac k* anan *Ant-t* k* *Ars* b4a.de **Bry** k* *Coc-c* dig k* *Dros* k* *Ferr* k* **Ip** k* *Kali-c* k* laur *Mez* k* *Nat-m* k* *Nit-ac* **Nux-v** bg2 *Ph-ac* k* *Phos* b4a.de *Puls* k* rhus-t b7.de* sep stann bg2 *Sulph* b4a.de *Verat* hr1
  - **dark**-colored vomiting of food: mag-c h2
  - **dinner**; after: anac calc h2 graph h2 sel
  - **drinks**; not of: *Bry*
  - **eating**:
    - **after**:
      - **agg.**: aeth hr1* am-c b4a.de ant-t b7a.de* **Ars** b4a.de* *Calc* b4a.de* **Ferr** b7a.de* hyos b7a.de* *Lach* bg2 mag-c h2 **Nux-v** bg2 **Phos** b4a.de* *Puls* b7a.de* ruta bg2* sulph b4a.de
        - **days** after food has filled the stomach; some●: **Bism**
        - **five** or six hours after●: atro **Puls** k ●*
        - **hours** after; some: meph **Puls** k ●* spong fd4.de

- **food – eating – after – agg.**: ...
        - **long** after: aeth ptk1 ars-i ptk1 ferr bg2* kreos bg2* plat ptk1 puls bg2* rat bg2 sabin ptk1 sang ptk1
        - **one** day after●: cimx ruta fd4.de sabin
        - **seven** hours after●: sulph h2
        - **undigested** food two or three hours after: aeth bg3 **Kreos** k* sulph
      - **immediately** after●: ant-c ant-t *Apis Ars* ars-h *Bry* carb-an carb-v cupr dig *Ferr* k* *Ferr-p Graph Kali-bi* mosch olnd plb ruta sanic sil sulph verat zinc
    - **while** | **agg.**: am-c ars ferr c1 iod rhus-t sep sil stann verat
  - **empty**; mouthful until stomach is: arg-n k13 bac bn *Ferr* **Phos** k13
  - **feces**; then: plb b7a.de
  - **fever**; during intermittent: *Ferr Ferr-p Nat-m*
  - **heat**; during: cina k* *Eup-per* ferr k* ferr-p k2 ign k* nux-v thuj
  - **hot** food, after: lob
  - **lying**:
    - **agg.**: olnd
    - **back**; on | **agg.**: rhus-t
  - **menses**; during: phos b4a.de
  - **milk**; except: hydr ptk1
  - **mucus**, then: acon bg2 ars bg2 dros k* mag-c nux-v k* psor bg2 puls k* *Sel* b7a.de sil k* verat bg2
    - **bitter**: dig b4a.de sil b4a.de*
  - **only** food: *Ferr* bg2
  - **perspiration**; during: ars bg2 bry bg2 *Cina* bg2 **Ferr** bg2 *Ign* bg2 nux-v bg2 sil bg2
  - **salty** matter; then: *Puls* b7a.de *Sep* b4a.de
  - **smallest** quantity: verat-v ptk1
  - **solid** food; of | **only**: bry k* cupr verat
  - **sour**: calc ferr bg2 ferr-ar k2 hep *Kali-bi* nat-m h2 *Nat-s* podo sars k2 sulph thuj h1
  - **sour** matter; then: psor b4a.de
  - **supper** agg.; after: cupr-s
  - **undigested**: aeth ant-c k* apoc k2* atro bro1 bals-p bro1 bell bism bro1 *Bry* bro1 calc calc-f c1 cench k2 cer-ox br1* *Chin* bro1 colch bro1 cuph br1 cupr bro1 cystein-l rly4• *Ferr* k* *Ferr-m* bro1 ferr-p bro1 gels sys graph bro1 *Ip* k* iris bro1 *Kali-bi* **Kreos** k* lac-c bro1 *Lac-d* **Lyc** k ● merc k2 nat-m nux-v k* petr bro1 phos k* *Puls* k* sabin sang bro1 *Sec* b7a.de sep k2 stann h2 stry-af-cit bro1 ulm-c jsj8• verat bro1
    - **children**; in: calc-f pd
    - **eaten** previous day: sabin spong fd4.de
    - **eating**; hours after (See eating - after - agg. - undigested)
    - **milk**: mag-c pd
  - **vexation**; after: acon cham ign ip lyc verat
  - **waking**; on: jug-r
  - **water**:
    - **except**: hydr ptk1
    - **then** water: ars bg2 ferr b7a.de puls k*
      - **bitter** water: lac-d ptk1
  - **whooping** cough; in: meph ptk1
    - **regaining** consciousness from whooping cough; after: cupr bro1
- **frothy**: acet-ac acon k* *Aeth* k* all-c ant-t *Apis* arg-n bg2* ars k* arund aur bg2 cadm-s *Canth* k* cic bg1 coc-c *Con* crot-t k* cupr bg2 cupr-act ferr k* glon k* *Ip* kali-br kali-s kali-sula a1* **Kreos** k* *Lach* bg2 led ptk1 *Lyc* k* mag-c ptk1 mag-m bg1 med c1 *Merc-c* k* mur-ac k* nat-c h2* nat-m bg2 nat-p *Nux-v* phos bg1* *Podo* k* *Puls* k* sil ptk1 spig bg2 *Tub* urt-u **Verat** k* verat-v zinc k*
  - **mucus**; then: verat b7a.de
- **gelatinous**: ip b7.de*
- **glairy**: alumn *Arg-n* k* *Ars* k* canth k* carbn-s cic bg2 crot-t cupr bg2 cupr-act (non:dig slp) digin slp *Iris Jatr-c Kali-bi* k* kali-n k* med jl2 mur-ac k* phos scol a1* *Sil* sul-ac k* verat bg2 *Verat-v*
- **gray**: acon bg2 colch bg2 op bg2 phos bg2 plb bg2
- **greasy**: ars k* *Iod* k* manc *Mez* k* *Nux-v* k* phos bg2 sabad thuj k*

- **green**: *Acon* k* *Aeth* k* ant-t aqui vh *Arg-n* am k* **Ars** k* asar k* aur-m k2 bell b4a.de* bry k* bufo cadm-s *Cann-s* k* *Canth* k* carb-ac carbn-s *Card-m* *Cham* b7.de* **Chel** k* chin b7a.de cimic k* *Cocc* colch *Coloc* k* *Crot-c* *Crot-h* cupr k* cupr-ar cur cycl cystein-l rly4• dig k* *Dulc* elaps elat *Eup-per* bg2* ferr-p grat k2 guare guat sp1 *Hell* k* *Hep* k* hyos b7.de* *Ign* b7.de* **Ip** k* jatr-c kali-bi k* kali-m k2 *Lach* k* *Lyc* k* manc *Merc* *Merc-c* k* merc-d ptk1 mez k* morph nat-p k2 *Nat-s* k* *Nux-v* k* olnd k* *Op* k* ox-ac *Petr* k* *Phos* k* phyt *Plb* k* podo bg2* *Puls* k* raph rhod k* rhus-t rob br1 sabad *Sabin* sec stann bg2 *Stram* k* sulph b4a.de *Teucr* vanil fd5.de **Verat** k* vip zinc zinc-p k2
  - **morning**: *Aqui* br1
  - **evening**: stram
  - **night**: ars *Cur*
  - **blackish**: (non:cupr slp) cupr-act slp dulc hell h1* osm petr phos plb sol-ni teucr ptk1 verat h1
    - **colic**; with: hell pd
  - **cold** drinks; after: rhod ptk1
  - **curds**: ip k2
  - **dark**: carb-ac br1 *Crot-h* op *Sec* stann verat
  - **fluid**: *Acon* asar *Aur-m* *Card-m* *Coloc* *Cupr* *Cycl* *Hep* *Lach* *Nat-s* olnd *Stram*
  - **grass**, as: ars bg1
  - **headache**; during: carc zzh
  - **menopause**; during: aqui br1
  - **olive** green: carb-ac ptk1
  - **sediment**: op bg2
  - **yellowish**: *Ars* atis zzc1• cadm-s k2 colch convo-s sp1 crot-h (non:cupr slp) *Cupr-act* slp *Iris* nat-p *Nat-s* olnd phos plb sabin vanil fd5.de verat
- **lime** water, like: nat-c h2
- **liquids**: (*↗drinks; water; Vomiting - water)* abrot br1 *Acon* k* ant-c b2.de* ant-t k* aran am k* ars k* *Bism* k* bry k* cham k* chin k* cic b2.de cina bg2 cocc b2.de con b2.de diph br1 dulc k* ferr b2.de *Hyos* bg2 ip k* kreos nat-m b2.de nux-v k* phos psor jl2 puls b2.de* ran-b bg2 rhus-t b2.de sec b2.de sil k* spong k* sul-ac sulph b2.de vanil fd5.de *Verat* b2.de*
  - **drinking** agg. | **followed** by faintness: lyss c1
  - **followed** by food (See water - followed)
  - **warm** in stomach; as soon as they become: (*↗Vomiting - drinking - warm)* chlf **Phos** k* pyrog jl2*
- **loud**: phos b4a.de
- **membranes**: canth k* kali-sula a1* merc-c k* mur-ac bg2 (non:nat-s slp) nat-sula slp nit-ac k* ox-ac phos k* sec k* sul-ac k* zinc bg2
- **metallic** tasting: merc-c b4a.de phos bg2
- **milk**: **Aeth** k* am bg2* *Ars* borx bg1 bry bg1 *Calc* *Calc-p* bg1* carb-v *Cham* b7a.de* *Cina* bg1* *Iod* ip bg1 *Iris* kali-bi lach lyc bg1 merc-c *Merc-d* nux-v bg1 phyt *Podo* rheum bg1 samb k* sanic c2 sep sil k* spong k* sulph tritic-vg fd5.de vario al2
  - **curdled**: **Aeth** k* *Ant-c* k* ant-t **Calc** k* cuph ah1 ip k2* *Mag-c* bro1 mag-m bro1 merc bro1 merc-c merc-d bro1 *Nat-m* nat-p k* podo bro1 sabin sanic bro1* **Sil** k* sul-ac *Sulph* tritic-vg fd5.de **Valer** k*
    - **children**; in: calc mtf33 cuph ah1 sanic mtf33 sil mtf33
      - **nurslings**; in: *Aeth* mrr1* ant-c mtf33 tritic-vg fd5.de
    - **large** curds choking the child: aeth mtf33
    - **sour**: calc ptk1 nat-p ptk1
  - **sour**: ant-c mtf33 cina mtf33
    - **nursed**; soon after child has: ant-c mtf33
  - **swallowing**; immediately after: aeth mtf33
  - **undigested**: mag-c ptk1
- **milky**: aeth k* am k* ars kali-m k2 ox-ac **Sep** k*
  - **pregnancy** agg.; during: **Sep** k ●
  - **water**: sep bg2
- **mucus**: *Acon* k* aeth k* agar alum k* alum-p k2 alum-sil k2 alumn am-caust vh1 am-m b2.de* *Ant-c* k* ant-t k* anthraci *Apis* **Arg-n** k* am k2 *Ars* k* ars-s-f k2 bals-p bro1 bar-c k* bar-m bar-s k2 *Bell* k* borx k* bov k* brom k* bry k* cact cadm-s k* calad calc k* calc-s calc-sil k2 cann-s k* canth k* caps b2.de* *Carb-v* k* carbn-s card-m k2 carl castm cench k2 *Cham* k* *Chel* *Chin* k* chinin-ar *Chinin-s* *Cina* k* cinnb *Coc-c* *Cocc* k* *Coff* colch k* *Con* k* *Cop* cor-r crot-t *Cupr* k* cupr-act a1* cupr-ar k* cupr-s k* *Cycl* *Dig* k* **Dros** k* *Dulc* k* elaps elat ferr b2.de* form glon graph b2.de* grat *Guaj* k* hell hep k* hydr-ac *Hyos* k*

- **mucus**: ...
Ign k* indg iod b2.de* *Ip* k* *Iris* k* *Jatr-c* k* kali-ar **Kali-bi** k* *Kali-c* kali-chl kali-m k2* kali-n k* kali-p kali-s kali-sil k2 kreos k* lac-d k2 lac-h sze9• *Lach* k* lil-t *Lyc* k* *Mag-c* k* mag-s med c1* *Merc* k* *Merc-c* k* *Mez* k* morg fmm1• mosch k* mur-ac nat-ar nat-c k* *Nat-m* nat-p *Nat-s* *Nit-ac* **Nux-v** k* olnd k* *Op* k* osm ox-ac k* petr bro1 **Phos** k* *Phyt* plb *Podo* k* psor **Puls** k* raph rat **Rheum** b7a.de rhus-t ruta fd4.de sabad samb b2.de* sang k2 *Sec* k* sel seneg k* *Sep* b4a.de *Sil* k* sin-a sol-ni spig b2.de* stann staph b7a.de stram k* sul-ac k* *Sulph* k* tab tax *Ter* ther thuj k* tritic-vg fd5.de *Tub* valer k* vanil fd5.de **Verat** k* verat-v vip zinc k* zinc-p k2
  - **morning**: ars camph *Dulc* k* *Guaj* kali-bi kali-s fd4.de sec sulph tab thuj
    - **coffee** agg.: *Cham*
    - **waking**; on: form thuj
  - **forenoon**: nux-v psor ruta fd4.de
    - **10** h: psor
  - **afternoon**: bell con mag-s vanil fd5.de
    - **sleep** | **siesta** agg.; after: lyc h2
  - **evening**: bry elaps nat-s psor stram tritic-vg fd5.de
    - **18** h: nat-s
    - **coffee** agg.: verat
  - **night**: phos sil h2 stram ther vanil fd5.de verat
  - **amel.**: nat-m ptk1
  - **bile**; then: dig bg2 dulc bg2 zinc bg2
  - **blood**: acon k* aeth hr1 ant-t k2 ars h2* brom k* dros hep k* hyos k* ign b7a.de *Kali-bi* k* kali-n k* lach *Merc-c* b4a.de* *Nit-ac* k* phos k* zinc
    - **followed** by | **water**: olnd bg2
  - **chill**:
    - **before**: *Puls* verat h1
    - **during**: ant-c bg2 ars bg2 caps b7.de* cham bg2 cina bg2 dros bg2 ign b7.de* ip bg2 nux-v bg2 *Puls* b7.de* sulph bg2
  - **coffee** agg.: cann-i *Cham* verat
  - **cough** agg.●: ant-t coc-c k2 con k* *Dros* k* hyos b7.de *Ip* k* kali-s fd4.de *Nit-ac* op wbt• *Puls* k* *Sil* k* thuj k* *Verat* k*
  - **diarrhea**; during: **Arg-n**
  - **drinking** agg.; after: aloe
  - **drunkards**; in: ant-t gm1
  - **eating**; after: crot-t ferr sul-ac
  - **fever**; during: *Cham* b7a.de ign b7a.de *Puls* b7a.de
  - **followed** by:
    - **bile**; vomiting of: verat b7a.de
    - **blood**; vomiting of: kali-n bg2 verat bg2
    - **food**; vomiting of: *Ars* b4a.de olnd b7a.de *Zinc* b4a.de
  - **green**: kali-chl ptk1 plb ptk1
  - **headache**; during: con h2 kali-c h2
  - **heat**; during: acon bg2 ars bg2 bell bg2 **Cham** bg2 chin bg2 cina bg2 con bg2 dros bg2 dulc bg2 **Ign** bg2 ip bg2 lyc bg2 merc bg2 *Nux-v* bg2 **Puls** bg2 rheum bg2 sec bg2 sep bg2 sulph bg2 thuj verat bg2
  - **jelly**, like: indg *Ip* jatr-c *Kali-bi*
  - **lumps** of: canth bg1
  - **menses** | **before** | **agg.**: kreos b7a.de
    - **during** | **agg.**: phos b4a.de
  - **perspiration**; during: cham bg2 ign bg2 *Puls* bg2
  - **pregnancy** agg.; during: sul-ac
  - **rinsing** mouth, when: *Coc-c*
  - **ropy**: ant-t k2* iris tl1 kali-bi k2
  - **sour**: kali-bi bg1 kali-c ptk1
  - **stool** | **going** to; on: aloe
  - **stringy**: coc-c bro1 colch vh kali-bi mrr1 vanil fd5.de
  - **sudden**: kali-bi vh
  - **sweetish**: calc k* *Iris* psor k*
  - **tenacious**: ant-t k2
  - **thick**: *Ant-t* vh1 ars h2
  - **waking**; on: sil
  - **water**: guaj ptk1 verat bg2

Stomach

- **white**: *Ant-t* vh1 ars h2 dig h2 ruta fd4.de vanil fd5.de
- **muddy**-like: nat-c bg2
- **musty**: bry bg2
- **offensive** odor: abrot br1 acon bg2* *Ant-t* k* am k* **Ars** k* bar-m bell k* bism k* *Bry* k* calc k* *Canth* k* *Cocc* k* coff k* crot-t *Cupr* k* guaj k* *Ip* k* *Led* k* merc k* nat-c k* **Nux-v** k* *Op* k* ph-ac k* *Phos* *Plb* k* podo pyrog k2* sec k* **Sep** k* *Stann* k* *Sulph* k* thuj k* valer k* verat k*
  - **morning**: bry
  - **fluid**: abrot ptk1
  - **purulent**: kali-bi hr1 kali-c (non:kali-s slp) kali-sula a1* merc-c k* *Nit-ac* k*
- **oil**; tasting like olive: phos b4a.de*
- **pitchy**: *Ip* bg2 lept bg2
- **purulent**: bell b4a.de *Merc* b4a.de merc-c b4a.de
- **putrid**: *Ars* b4a.de bry b7.de* *Cocc* b7a.de nux-v b7a.de *Phos* b4a.de
- **rice** water: colch *Cupr* *Kali-bi* *Verat*
- **ropy** (See stringy)
- **sago**-like matter: phos h2
- **saltpeter**; tasting like: kali-n b4.de*
- **salty**: benz-ac k* *Iod* k* mag-c k* merc-c bg2 *Nat-s* k* puls k* *Sep* b4a.de sil k* sulph k*
  - **eating**; after: mag-c b4a.de
  - **sleep**; then: cycl bg2
- **solids**, only: am bg1* *Ars* b4a.de bry k* cupr k* ferr bg2* *Phos* b4a.de *Puls* b7a.de sep bg1* sulph b4a.de verat k*
  - **cough** agg.; during: *Bry* b7a.de *Cupr* b7a.de
- **soup**: mag-c
- **sour**: abrom-a ks5 acet-ac act-sp aesc am-c k* anac b4a.de ant-c bro1 *Ant-t* k* *Apis* b7a.de arg-n *Ars* k* ars-s-f k2 asar k* bar-c k* bar-s k2 *Bell* k* bol-la *Borx* k* brom k* bry k* cact cadm-met gm1 cadm-s calad k* **Calc** k* calc-s *Camph* caps k* *Carb-v* k* carbn-s *Card-m* k* **Caust** k* *Cham* k* *Chel* **Chin** k* *Chinin-ar* chion ptk1 *Cimic* cimx cina mtf33 cocc k* con k* crot-t cystein-l rly4• *Daph* k* *Ferr* k* *Ferr-ar* *Ferr-p* k* gels gent-c *Graph* k* *Grat* *Hep* k* hydr ign k* iod bro1 *Ip* k* **Iris** k* kali-ar *Kali-bi* k* *Kali-c* k* kali-p kali-s kreos lac-ac k* *Lac-d* k* **Lyc** k* **Mag-c** k* *Manc* med k2* merc-c b4a.de *Merc-d* *Mez* mur-ac k2 *Nat-ar* nat-c k* *Nat-m* k* **Nat-p** k* *Nat-s* k* nit-ac k* **Nux-v** k* olnd k* *Op* k* osm petr k* *Ph-ac* k* **Phos** k* plb podo **Psor** k* **Puls** k* rheum ptk1* **Rob** k* sabin k* sang sars k* sec k* sel sep k* sil k2 spig bg2 stann k* stram k* **Sul-ac** k* sul-i k2 **Sulph** k* **Tab** k* thuj k* *Tub* vanil fd5.de **Verat** k* zinc zinc-p k2
  - **morning**: camph graph kali-bi nux-v tab
    - **stool** agg.; after: phos
  - **forenoon**: nux-v
  - **afternoon**: hep sulph
    - **16** h: sulph
  - **evening**: nux-v phos h2 puls
  - **night**: *Calc* chin crot-t kali-c h2
  - **bitter**; then: grat bg2 nit-ac bg2 phos bg2 plb bg2 zinc bg2
  - **bitterish**: ant-t bism bg1 castm bg1 chelo bg1 cic bg1 cina bg1 dros bg1 grat ip mag-m bg1 nux-v bg1* plat bg1 puls sars bg1* sul-ac bg1* sulph bg1*
  - **breakfast** | **after** | **agg.**: borx sel
    - **before** | **agg.**: psor
  - **chill**:
    - **after**: lyc h2
    - **during**: ars bg2 cham bg2 **Lyc** k* nux-v bg2 phos bg2 *Puls* bg2 rob sulph bg2
  - **coffee** agg.: cann-s
  - **convulsions**; after epileptic: *Calc*
  - **corroding** the teeth (See TEETH - Corroded - vomiting - sour)
  - **cough** agg.; during: cimx nat-c phos k* thuj
  - **drinking** agg.; after: bufo
  - **eating**; after: *Iris* nat-s nit-ac k* sel *Sul-ac*
  - **eructations**; then: *Caust* bg2
  - **fasting**; when | **morning**; in the: borx c1
  - **fever**; during: alum bg2 **Arn** b7a.de* *Ars* bg2 *Bell* bg2 calc bg2 cham bg2 hep ip bg2 **Lyc** k* *Nux-v* bg2 phos bg2 **Puls** b7a.de* rob sep bg2 sulph bg2 verat bg2
- **sour**: ...
  - **fluid**: card-m *Caust* *Ip* nat-c h2 *Nat-m* nat-p k* *Nux-v* k* phos thuj h1
  - **headache**; during: apis kali-c h2 *Nat-p* nux-v op sars
  - **menses** | **before** | **agg.**: *Calc* nux-v *Puls* sulph
    - **during**:
      - **agg.**: am-c k* *Calc* *Carb-v* b4a.de lyc k* nat-m b4a.de *Nux-v* *Phos* *Puls* tarent
      - **beginning** of menses | **agg.**: phos b4.de
  - **motion** agg.: kali-bi
  - **perspiration**; during: calc bg2 chin bg2 **Lyc** bg2 nux-v bg2 phos bg2 *Puls* bg2 sep bg2 sulph bg2
  - **smoking** agg.; after: calad
  - **stool** agg.; after: phos h2
  - **water**: con ptk1
- **sticky**: merc-c bg2 psor jl2
- **stringy**: alum *Arg-n* ars bar-m *Chel* colch bg1• **Cor-r** k* croc ptk1 cupr ptk1 *Dros* dulc hydr mrr1 *Iris* *Kali-bi* k* *Kreos* lac-ac med c1 *Merc-c* k* *Nat-m* *Nit-ac* plb *Sil* verat
- **sweetish**: calc b4.de* cupr *Iris* k* kali-bi **Kreos** k* *Plb* k* psor k* *Tub* k*
  - **cough** agg.; during: calc b4.de
- **tar**; like: anac b4a.de *Ars* b4a.de sul-ac b4a.de
- **tasteless**: *Ant-c* b7.de* kreos b7a.de
- **tenacious**: alumn ant-t arg-n ars borx canth chel colch cupr dulc hep hyos *Kali-bi* kali-c lach *Merc-c* k* nit-ac osm phos rhus-t sec verat
- **thick**: acet-ac ars h2 colch hydr mrr1 merc-c ox-ac podo verat-v
  - **morning**: colch
  - **rinsing** the mouth, on: *Coc-c*
  - **stool** | **going** to; on: aloe
  - **water**, after a glass of: aloe
- **urine**; of: *Op* b7.de*
- **warm** food agg.: lob phos k2
- **water**: *(↗liquids)* abrot bro1 *Acon* k* *Aeth* agar all-c alum k* alum-p k2 alum-sil k2 am-c b2.de* anac ant-c b2.de* ant-t k* apis k* apoc k2 arg-met k* *Arn* k* **Ars** k* ars-i ars-s-f k2 asar k* aur-m bar-c k* bar-i bar-m bar-s k2 *Bell* k* *Bism* k* borx bov b2.de* **Bry** k* calc calc-sil k2 *Camph* *Cann-s* k* carb-ac *Carbn-s* card-m carl **Caust** k* *Chin* k* chinin-ar cina k* clem *Coc-c* *Cocc* colch k* *Coloc* *Con* k* crot-h crot-t *Cupr* k* *Cupr-ar* cupr-s cycl k* dig **Dros** b2.de* dulc elat euph k* euph-c bro1 ferr b2.de* fl-ac gard-j vlr2• graph k* *Grat* *Guaj* k* hell hep k* hydr-ac hyos k* iod k* *Ip* k* *Iris* k* *Jatr-c* k* kali-ar *Kali-bi* k* kali-c b2.de* kali-i kali-n k* kali-sil k2 *Kreos* k* lac-ac bg2 lac-c bro1 laur b2.de* lyc k* mag-c k* mag-m b2.de* manc med c1 merc k* merc-c mez k* mur-ac nat-ar nat-c b2.de* *Nat-m* nat-s nit-ac *Nux-v* k* olnd k* op oscilloc jl2 osm ox-ac par b2.de* petr k* phos k* phys *Phyt* plb k* podo k2 puls b2.de* pyrog tl1 raph rat rhus-t **Rob** k* sabad sal-fr sle1• sang k* sars b2.de* *Sec* k* sel k* seneg sep b2.de* *Sil* k* sin-a sol-ni spig b2.de* *Stann* k* *Stram* k* stront-c b2.de* stry *Sul-ac* k* sul-i k2 *Sulph* k* *Tab* k* ther *Thuj* k* vanil fd5.de **Verat** k* verat-v verb b2.de* vinc vip zinc k* zinc-p k2
  - **morning**: ars bry elaps *Guaj* sil h2 *Sulph* thuj
    - **waking**; on: eupi thuj
  - **forenoon**: nat-s
  - **afternoon**, 16 h: sulph
  - **evening**: merc-c
  - **night**: **Calc** crot-t ox-ac sul-ac ther
    - **midnight**:
      - **before** | **21**-5 h: phyt
  - **breakfast**; before | **agg.**: tab
  - **chill**; during: bry bg2 dros bg2 ip bg2 nux-v bg2
  - **cold** water only: sil
  - **cough** agg.; during: carb-v b4a.de dros k* nat-c *Verat* b7a.de
  - **dinner**; before: sulph
  - **eating** | **after** | **agg.**: crot-t ferr
    - **while** | **agg.**: ferr nat-ar
  - **followed** by food: bism mrr1 colch bg2 *Iod* k* ip k* mag-c b4a.de nux-v k* sep k* sil k* sul-ac k* sulph k* zinc bg2
    - **bitter**: grat bg2 mag-c bg2 sil bg2
  - **greenish**: olnd ptk1

- **heat**; during: hep
- **lying** on back agg.: merc-c
- **menses**; during: am-c sulph
- **pregnancy** agg.; during: sep
- **soup** agg.: *Mag-c* k*
- **standing** agg.: colch
- **sweetish**: iris ptk1
- **walking** in open air agg.: kali-bi

- **water** drunk then food (See water - followed)
- **whey** like: cupr bg2*
- **white**: abrom-a ks5 aeth c1* ars bell carb-ac castm cench k2 colch crot-t cupr bg2 cupr-ar dig fl-ac kali-bi kali-m k2 kali-s k* kali-sula a1* *Merc-c* (*non*: nat-s slp) nat-sula a1 ox-ac ruta fd4.de stram sul-ac tab vanil fd5.de verat verat-v
  - **morning**: ars colch
  - **noon**: *Verat*
  - **night**: verat
- **wine**:
  - **colored**: rhus-t bg2
  - **tastes** of: nat-m bg2
- **worms**: *Acon* k* anac k* ars k* bar-m calc k2 *Cina* k* coff k* *Ferr* k* hyos k* merc k* nat-m k* *Phyt Sabad* k* **Sang** k* sec k* sil k* spig k* sulph b4a.de verat k*
  - **lumbrici**: acon *Cina* sabad sec
  - **sensation** of (See Worm)
- **yeast**-like: nat-c bro1 nat-s bro1
- **yellow**: acet-ac aeth androc srj1• apis arn *Ars* ars-i bry k* bufo k2 cadm-s camph cann-s b7.de* cina *Colch* k* *Coloc Con* crot-t *Dulc* form *Grat* guat sp1 *Iod* ip k* kali-bi k* kali-i lac-h sk4• lil-t merc merc-c merc-sul c1 nat-p k2 olnd k* osm ox-ac oxyurn-sc mcp1• **Phos** k* phyt plb k* ruta fd4.de scol a1* sin-a *Ter* **Verat** k* vip zinc zinc-p k2
  - **daytime**: merc-c
  - **morning**: form
  - **night**: ox-ac
  - **bright**: kali-bi ptk1
  - **headache**; during: form glon verat
  - **walking** in open air agg.: kali-bi
- **yellowish**: *Ars* b4.de* colch b7.de* iod b4.de* kali-bi bg2 olnd bg2 plb bg2 verat bg2
  - **green**: acon b7a.de ars b4.de* atis zzc1• bry b7.de* *Dulc* b4.de* ip b7.de* olnd b7.de* plb b7a.de *Verat* b7.de*

WAKING; on: ambr b7.de* *Anac* b4a.de ant-c b7.de* arg-n bg2 hep b4a.de *Ign* b7.de* *Nux-v* b7.de* puls b7.de* staph b7.de*

WALKING:
- **after** | **agg.**: calad b7.de* puls b7.de* rhus-t b7.de*
- **agg.**: acon b7.de* alum bg2 anac b4.de* ang bg2 arn b7.de* bar-c b4.de* bell b4.de* *Bry* b7.de* calad bg2 *Calc* b4.de* chin b7.de* cocc b7.de* hell b7.de* hep b4a.de* ign b7.de* kali-bi bg2 mag-m b4.de* mang b4.de* nux-v b7.de* *Phos* bg2 *Puls* b7a.de ran-b b7.de* rhod b4.de* sabad b7.de* *Sep* b4.de* sil b4a.de spig b7.de* stann b4.de* staph b7.de* stront-c b4.de* sulph b4.de* verat b7.de*
- **air**; in open:
  - **after** | **agg.**: chin b7.de* ferr b7.de*
  - **agg.**: acon bg2 alum bg2 am-m b7.de* ambr bg2 ang bg2 coff b7.de* nux-v b7.de*
  - **amel.**: am-c bg2 am-m b7.de croc b7.de* *Op* b7a.de puls b7.de*
- **amel.**: hell bg2 op b7.de* puls b7.de* rhus-t b7.de* tarax b7.de*

WARM:
- **applications** | **amel.**: caust b4a.de cocc b7a.de *Nat-c* b4a.de *Nux-v* b7a.de
- **bed** | **amel.**: lyc bg2
- **drinks**:
  - **amel.**: chel bg2 kali-c bg2 mag-p bg2 nux-v b7a.de* petr bg2 sul-ac bg2
    - **hot** drinks: *Ign* b7a.de kreos b7a.de **Nux-v** b7a.de *Sul-ac* b4a.de
- **food**:
  - **amel.**: canth b7.de* kreos bg2 *Nux-v* b7a.de rhus-t b7.de*
    - **hot** food: *Agar* b4a.de *Ars* b4a.de *Ign* b7a.de *Kreos* b7a.de *Lyc* b4a.de **Nux-v** b7a.de *Sep* b4a.de sil b4a.de

WARM IN BED; becoming: | **amel.**: *Graph* b4a.de *Lyc* b4.de

WARMTH; sensation of (See Heat)

WATER:
- **drinking**:
  - **agg.**: aloe bg2
  - **amel.**: caust b4a.de *Phos* b4a.de
- **sensation** as if:
  - **full** of: caps tl1 casc bg2 cic bg2 coc-c bg2* colch bg2 germ-met srj5• grat bg2* **Kali-c** k* laur b7.de* mag-c h2* mill *Ol-an* k* phel rb2 plat bg2 plb bg2 sul-ac bg2
  - **swimming** in: abrot br1*

WATER BRASH (See Eructations; type - water brash)

WEAKNESS: (*↗Emptiness; Flabbiness; Hanging*) abies-c bg2 act-sp bro1 agar bg2 alumn a1* am-c h2 ambr b7.de* anan vh1 ant-c bg2 ant-t bg2* apoc bg2 arg-n bg2 *Ars* bro1 ars-i bg2 bar-c h2* bism bg2 bov bg2 *Calc-p* bg2* *Calc-s* kr1 cann-s bro1 canth b7.de* caps bro1* carb-an bg2* carb-v bg2* caust h2* chel bg2 chin b7.de* choc srj3• cocc bg2 coch br1 coloc bg2 *Crot-t* kr1 cupr bg2 dig h2* eup-per bg2 euph bg2 ferr bg2 fl-ac bg2 gal-ac br1 gamb bg2 gels bg2 gent-l br1 graph bg2* grat bro1 hep bg2 **Hydr** bg2* hydrog srj2• ign b7.de* iod bg2 **Ip** b7a.de* kali-bi bg2 kali-br bg2 kali-c h2* kreos bg2 lach bg2 laur b7.de* lob bg2 lyc h2* mag-c bg2 mag-m h2* merc bg2 mur-ac bg2* nat-c bg2 nat-m bg2 nux-m bg2 nux-v bg2* olnd bg2 op bg2 par bg2 petr h2* phos h2* *Podo* kr1 puls bg2* quas br1 rhod bg2 senec bg2 sep bg2* sil bg2 spong bg2 squil bg2 stann bg2 staph bg2 sul-ac h2* sulph bg2 tab bg2 tell c1 tritic-vg fd5.de valer bg2 verat b7.de* zinc bg2 zing br1
- **accompanied** by | **Back**; weakness in: sep k*
- **diarrhea**; during: nuph vml3•
- **eating**:
  - **after**:
    - **agg.**: sil b4a.de*
    - **not** amel.: carb-an bg2 lyc bg2 olnd bg2 sep bg2 stann bg2
- **pain** in stomach; from: *Nux-v* kr1 *Podo*
- **sensation** of: maias-l hm2•
- **stool** agg.; after: ambr dig br1
- **urination** agg.; after: apoc ptk1 ars h2
- **vertigo**; must lie down with (See VERTIGO - Accompanied - stomach - weakness - lie)

○ - **Epigastrium**: agar bg2 croc b7.de* *Dig* b4a.de *Ign* b7.de* *Ip* b7a.de kali-n b4a.de* *Lyc* b4a.de *Petr* b4a.de psor jl2 rhus-t b7.de*
  - **stool** agg.; after: ambr b7.de*
  - **urination** agg.; after: ars bg2
- **Pit** of stomach: lob mtf11

WEATHER:
- **stormy**:
  - **agg.**: petr bg2
  - **amel.**: ter bg2
- **wet** | **agg.**: *Thuj* b4a.de

WEIGHT (See Heaviness)

WHIRLING: croc b7.de* lyc h2

○ - **Epigastrium**: lyc b4.de*

WHISKEY agg.: ign bg2 olnd bg2

WINE: (*↗Indigestion - wine)*
- **agg.**: ant-c bg2 carb-v bg2 lyc b4a.de* *Nux-v* b7a.de* puls bg2
  - **sour**: *Ant-c* b7a.de
- **amel.**: acon ptk1 *Nux-v* b7a.de
  - **sour**: *Ant-c* b7a.de
  - **sulfurated**: *Puls* b7a.de
- **intolerance** of any; complete: (*↗Indigestion - wine)* ars k*

WORM; sensation of a: (*↗Crawling)* cina hr1 cocc b7.de* lach bg2*

○ - **Upwards** to the throat; climbing from pit of stomach zinc ptk1*
  - **morning**: cocc ptk1

WRITHING in: bar-c bg2 plat bg2

XIPHOID, to back: con bg2

Stomach

YAWNING:
- **agg.**: all-c bg2 arg-n bg2 *Ars* ptk1 *Caust* b4a.de chel b7.de* phyt ptk1 *Rhus-t* b7a.de sul-ac b4a.de
- **amel.**: lyc ptk1 nat-m bg2* *Nux-v* b7a.de

EPIGASTRIUM; complaints of: acon b2.de* agar bg2 alum b2.de* am-c bg2 anac bg2 ant-c b2.de* *Ars* b2.de* aur b2.de* bar-c b2.de* *Bell* b2.de* **Bry** b2.de* *Calc* b2.de* caps b2.de* caust b2.de* cham b2.de* chel ptk1 chin b2.de* *Cic* b2.de* *Cocc* b2.de* coff b2.de* coloc ptk1 con b2.de* croc b2.de* **Cupr** bg2 euph b2.de* ferr b2.de* graph bg2 *Hell* b2.de* hep b2.de* ign b2.de* ip ptk1 *Kali-bi* bg2 kali-c b2.de* kali-n bg2 lach b2.de* lob ptk1 *Lyc* b2.de* m-aust b2.de mang b2.de* mez b2.de* mosch b2.de* nat-c b2.de* **Nat-m** b2.de* nux-v b2.de* op b2.de* petr b2.de* phos b2.de* plat b2.de* plb bg2 *Puls* b2.de* ran-b b2.de* ran-s b2.de* ruta b2.de* sabad b2.de* sabin b2.de* sec b2.de* sep ptk1 sil bg2 spig b2.de* spong b2.de* stann b2.de* **Sulph** bg2* tab bg2* thuj bg2 zinc b2.de*
- **right**: arg-n bg2 phos bg2
- **left**: ars bg2 aur bg2 con bg2 kali-bi bg2 kali-c bg2 kreos bg2 merc bg2 ran-b bg2 sep bg2

▽ • **extending** to | **right**: sulph bg2
- **accompanied** by | **respiration**; complaints of (See RESPIRATION - Complaints - accompanied - epigastrium - complaints)

▽ - **extending** to:

O • **All** directions: arg-n ptk1
- • **Axillae**: kali-n bg3*
- • **Back**: sabin ptk1
- • **Backward**: aloe bg2
- • **Hypochondria**: asaf bg2
- • **Scapulae** or vertebrae: bad ptk1
- • **Throat**: *Acon* ptk1 ars ptk1 calc ptk1 carb-v ptk1 ferr ptk1 kali-bi ptk1 *Kali-c* ptk1 lyc ptk1 nat-m ptk1 nux-v ptk1 phos ptk1

O - **Above**: nat-m ptk1 **Phos** ptk1 puls ptk1

MORNING: acon b7.de* agar bg2 aloe bg2 *Alum* b4.de* am-c b4.de* am-m b7.de* ambr b7.de* ang b7.de* *Apis* b7a.de arg-met b7.de* asaf b7.de* bar-c b4.de* bell b4.de* *Borx* b4a.de bov b4.de* calc b4.de* camph b7.de* canth b7.de* carb-an b4.de* caust b4.de* cham b7.de* chin b7.de* cocc b7.de* coff b7.de* colch b7.de* con b4.de* dig b4.de* dulc b4.de* *Euph* b4a.de ferr b7.de* grat bg2 hep b4.de* hyos b7.de* ign b7.de* iod b4.de* kali-bi bg2 kali-n b4.de* kreos b7a.de laur b7.de* lyc b4.de* m-arct b7.de mag-c b4.de* mag-m b4.de* mang b4.de* meny b7.de* mez b4.de* nat-c b4.de* nat-m b4.de* *Nit-ac* b4.de* nux-m b7.de* **Nux-v** b7.de* petr b4.de* ph-ac b4.de* *Phos* b4.de* plat b4.de* psor bg2 puls b7.de* ran-b b7.de* ran-s b7.de* rheum b7.de* rhod b4.de* rhus-t b7.de* sars b4.de* sep b4.de* spig b7.de* spong b7.de* staph b7.de* stront-c b4.de* sulph b4.de* teucr b7.de* verat b7.de* zinc b4.de*
- **spleen**: am-m bg2
- **sunrise**; at: *Cham* b7a.de*

○ - **Hypochondria**: alum b4a.de am-c b4.de* *Am-m* b7a.de am b7.de* bry b7a.de* carb-v b4.de* con b4.de* dros bg2 ign b7.de* nux-v b7.de* ran-b b7.de* rhod b4.de* *Sel* b7a.de staph b7.de* sulph bg2 teucr b7.de* valer b7.de*
- **Liver**: bry bg2

FORENOON: agar bg2 alum b4.de* am-m b7.de* ant-c b7.de* ant-t b7.de* bry b7.de* cann-s b7.de* carb-an b4.de* chin b7.de* colch b7.de* *Coloc* b4.de* croc b7.de* cupr b7.de* euphr b7.de* kali-bi bg2 kali-n b4.de* laur b7.de* lyc b4.de* mag-c b4.de* mag-m b4.de* mez b4.de* nat-c b4.de* phos b4.de* ran-b b7.de* rhus-t b7.de* sabad b7.de* sars b4.de* seneg b4.de* sep b4.de* sil b4.de* *Spig* b7.de* sul-ac b4.de* sulph bg2

○ - **Hypochondria**: am-c b4.de* am b7.de* mur-ac b4.de* nat-c b4.de* phos b4.de* ran-b b7.de* sul-ac b4.de*

NOON: coloc bg2 mag-c bg2 sang bg2 sulph bg2

AFTERNOON: agar bg2 agn b7.de* alum b4.de* am-c b4.de* *Am-m* b7.de* ambr bg2 *Ant-c* b7.de* ant-t b7.de* ars b4.de* asaf b7.de* bell b4.de* bov b4.de* bry b7.de* calc b4.de* cann-s b7.de* canth b7.de* carb-an b4.de* carb-v b4.de* caust b4.de* cham b7.de* chel b7.de* chin b7.de* cocc b7.de* coloc b4.de* con b4.de* croc b7.de* grat bg2 guaj b4.de* *Ign* b7a.de iod b4.de* kali-bi bg2 kali-n b4.de* lach b7a.de laur b7.de* lyc b4.de* mag-c b4.de* mag-m b4.de* nat-c b4.de* nat-m b4.de* nat-s bg2 *Nux-v* b7.de* op bg2 par b7.de* ph-ac b4.de* phyt bg2 plat b4.de* plb b7.de* *Ran-b* b7.de* *Rheum* b7.de* rhod b4.de* rhus-t b7.de* sabad b7.de* sars b4.de* seneg b4a.de sep b4.de* sil b4.de* spig b7.de* stann b4.de* stront-c b4.de* sulph b4.de* thuj b4.de* valer b7.de* verat b7.de* zinc b4.de*
- **16 h**: *Lyc* bg2
- **18 h**: sulph bg2
- **amel.**: nat-s bg2*

○ - **Hypochondria**: alum b4.de* am-m b7.de* aur b4.de* borx b4a.de canth b7.de* carb-v b4.de* cocc b7.de* kali-bi bg2 laur b7.de* nat-m b4.de* phos b4.de* plb b7.de* rhod b4.de* sabad b7.de* sars b4.de* stront-c b4.de* sul-ac b4.de* valer b7.de* verat b7.de* zinc b4.de*

EVENING: agar b4.de* *Aloe* bg2 alum b4.de* am-c b4.de* *Am-m* b7.de* ambr b7.de* ant-c bg2 ant-t b7.de* *Apis* b7a.de arn b7.de* ars b4.de* bar-c b4.de* bell b4.de* *Borx* b4a.de bov b4.de* *Bry* b7.de* calad b7.de* calc b4.de* cann-s b7.de* canth b7.de* carb-an b4.de* carb-v bg2 caust b4.de* cham b7.de* *Chin* b7.de* cina b7.de* coff b7.de* colch b7.de* *Coloc* b4.de* con b4.de* croc b7.de* cycl bg2 dig b4.de* dros b7.de* graph b4.de* grat bg2 hell b7.de* hep b4.de* hyos b7.de* ign b7.de* ip b7.de* kali-bi bg2 kali-c b4.de* kali-n b4.de* lach bg2 led b7.de* lyc b4.de* *M-arct* b7.de* m-aust b7.de mag-c b4.de* *Mag-m* b4.de* mang b4.de* meny b7.de* merc b4.de* mez b4.de* mosch b7.de* *Nit-ac* b4.de* *Nux-m* b7.de* par b7.de* petr b4.de* ph-ac b4.de* phos b4.de* *Plb* b7.de* **Puls** b7.de* *Ran-b* b7.de* rhod b4.de* sabad b7.de* *Sabin* b7.de* sars b4.de* seneg b4.de* sep b4.de* *Spig* b7.de* spong b7.de* stann bg2 staph b7.de* stram b7.de* stront-c b4.de* sul-ac b4.de* sulph b4.de* teucr b7.de* thuj bg2 *Valer* b7.de* verat b7.de* zinc b4.de*
- **amel.**: kali-n bg2
- **bed** agg.; in: par bg2 sabad bg2 *Valer* bg2 zinc bg2

○ - **External** abdomen: ambr b7.de sabin b7.de* samb b7.de valer b7.de
- **Hypochondria**: alum b4.de* *Am-c* b4a.de ars b4.de* caust b4.de* *Kali-c* b4a.de led b7.de* lyc b4.de* mag-c bg2 mez b4.de* ran-b b7.de* rhod b4.de* seneg b4.de* sep b4.de* sul-ac b4.de* sulph b4.de* teucr b7.de* valer b7.de* zinc b4.de*

NIGHT: acon b7a.de* alum b4a.de am-m b7.de* ambr b7a.de arg-met b7.de* arn b7.de* **Ars** b4a.de* aur b4.de* bar-c b4.de* bell bg2 bov b4.de* bry b7.de* *Calc* b4.de* camph b7.de* canth b7.de* carb-v b4.de* *Cham* b7a.de* chin b7a.de* cina b7.de* *Cocc* b7a.de coff b7a.de *Coloc* b4.de* croc b7.de* cycl bg2 ferr b7a.de* graph b4.de* *Hep* bg2 *Ign* b7a.de kali-c b4.de* kali-n b4.de* kreos b7a.de

Night: ...
laur b7.de* lyc b4.de* m-arct b7.de m-aust b7.de mag-c b4.de* mag-m b4.de* **Merc** b4.de* merc-c bg2 nat-c b4.de* nat-m b4.de* nit-ac b4.de* nux-m b7.de* *Petr* b4.de* ph-ac b4.de* phos b4.de* plb b7.de* *Puls* b7.de* ran-s b7.de* rheum bg2 *Rhus-t* b7.de* ruta b7.de* sec b7.de* sep b4.de* *Sil* b4.de* spong b7.de* stront-c b4.de* sul-ac b4.de* **Sulph** b4.de* thuj b4.de* valer bg2 verat b7a.de* zinc b4.de*
- **midnight**:
  - **at**: alum bg2 bar-c bg2 bov bg2 grat bg2 lyc bg2 merc bg2 nat-m bg2 sep bg2
  - **after**: aloe bg2 ambr b7.de* laur b7.de* m-arct b7.de puls b7.de* rhus-t bg2
- **stretching**; causing endless: plb tl1

○ - **External** abdomen: cic b7.de
- **Hypochondria**: alum b4.de* calc b4.de* cocc b7.de* graph b4.de* ran-b b7.de* ruta b7.de* sulph b4.de*

ABSCESS:

○ - **Diaphragm**; under the (= subphrenic) pyrog jl2*
- **Gallbladder**: eberth jl2
- **Inguinal** region: ars b4.de* aur b4.de* **Hep** *Merc* k* nit-ac b4.de* sil syph tarent-c mrr1

○ · **Glands**: aur bg2 bac jl2 carb-an bg2 carb-v bg2 hep bg2* *Merc* bg2 nit-ac bg2* syph jl2 thuj bg2
  - ⁝ **chronic**: syph jl2
- **Liver**: ars bro1 bell bro1* bold bro1 bry bro1* bufo bg2 chinin-ar bro1 eberth jl2 fl-ac **Hep** k* *Kali-c Lach* k* *Lyc* med c2 *Merc* bro1 **Merc-c** k* *Nux-v* k* phos bro1 puls ptk1 pyrog jl2 raph c2* rhus-t c2* ruta ptk1 sep ptk1 **Sil** k* ther k* vip bro1 yers jl2
  - **accompanied** by | **vertigo** and nausea: ther mtf11
  - **forming**; as if: laur ptk1
- **Pancreas**: eberth jl2
- **Pelvis**: apis bro1 calc bro1 *Hep* bro1 merc-c bro1 pall bro1 *Sil* bro1

○ · **Bones**: aur bg2
- **Spleen**: cean mtf11 *Hippoz* k*
- **Walls**: *Hep* rhus-t *Sil* sulph

ABSENT:

○ - **Anterior** part of abdomen were absent; sensation as if coloc a1
- **Centre**; sensation as if he has no: ignis-alc es2•

ADHESION:
- **sensation** of: dig c1 mez b4.de* **Sep** k ●* verat b7a.de verb k*
  - **back**; as if intestines would adhere to: **Verat** b7a.de
  - **painful** (See Pain - adhesions)

○ · **Hypogastrium** | **cough** agg.; during: *Sep* b4a.de
  - **Liver**; region of: *Nux-v* b7a.de
  - **Umbilicus**: verb bg2

○ - **Intestines**: *Brom* b4a.de
- **Peritoneum**: suis-chord-umb mtf11

AIR: | **evening** | **agg.**: merc b4.de*
- **filled** with; as if | **Hypochondria**: phos bg2

AIR AGG.; DRAFT OF: acon b7.de* chin b7.de* *Ign* b7.de* kali-bi bg2 m-aust b7.de* *Nux-v* b7.de* *Sel* b7.de*

AIR; IN OPEN:
- **agg.**: am-c bg2 borx b4a.de carb-an b4.de* cocc b7.de* coff b7.de* graph b4.de* ign b7.de* kali-c b4.de* mag-c b4.de* merc b4.de* merc-c b4a.de* nit-ac b4.de* nux-v b7.de* ph-ac b4.de* phos b4.de* puls b7.de* sep b4.de* sulph b4.de*
- **amel.**: aloe bg2 con b4.de* nat-c bg2

ALIVE; sensation of something: (↗*Movements*) agath-a nl2• arn xyz61 arund br1 calc-p k* cann-s k* chel bg2 conv **Croc** k* cur *Cycl* k* hyos k* ign k* kali-c b4a.de kali-i lac-d bg1 lyc k* merc k* nux-v k* op bro1* pall sne phos h2* plb b7.de* puls bg1 sabad k* sabin sang sep k* spong b7.de* stram k* stront-c sulph k* tarent xyz61 ther c1 **Thuj** k* verat bro1 viol-t b7.de*
- **animal** were in the abdomen; as if an: thuj b4a.de

○ - **Hypochondria**: phos bg2
- **Iliac** region | **right**: **Thuj**
- **Sides** | **left** especially: croc br1

ANEURYSM: *Bar-m Sec*

ANGER agg.: **Coloc** b4a.de

○ - **Liver**: cocc ptk1

Abdomen

ANXIETY in: *(↗MIND - Anxiety)* acon bg2 acon-f a1 agar k* aloe k* am-m k* ambr tsm1 androc srj1• *Ant-t* bg2 arg-n bg2* **Ars** k* ars-s-f k2 asaf bg2 aur bg2* aur-m-n wbt2• *Bar-c* k* bell bg2 **Bry** bg2* calc k* carb-an bg2 carb-v k* carl a1 cham k* *Chin* b7a.de* colch b7.de* con bg2 *Cupr* b7.de* euph k* germ-met srj5• gran j5.de* *Graph* gl1.fr• ham fd3.de• ign bg2* inul *Kali-c* ptk1 laur bg2 lyc bg2 m-ambo b7a.de merc k* mez bg2* *Mosch* b7.de* mur-ac k* nat-m h2* nat-p bg2* nit-ac k* *Nux-v* b7.de* olnd ozone sde2• phel bg2 phos ptk1 plat k* puls b7a.de rhus-t b7.de* seneg b4.de* sep k* **Staph** gl1.fr• stram k* sul-ac k* *Sulph* k* *Tarent* k* tritic-vg fd5.de tub k2 *Verat* b7a.de* vesp hr1
- **morning**: bry a1 nat-m bg sul-ac k*
  - • **bed** agg.; in: sul-ac
- **forenoon**: castor-eq a1
- **evening**: cham k* ham fd3.de• tarent k*
- **night**: ham fd3.de• nat-m h2* nit-ac k*
- **breakfast** agg.; after: *Ign* k*
- **eating**; after: bar-c h2
- **flatus**; passing | **amel**.: mur-ac k*
- **rising**; from: agar bg2 asaf bg2 bry bg2 dig bg2 dros bg2 ign bg2 laur bg2 phel bg2 stram bg2
- **stool**:
  - • **after**:
    - ⁝ **agg**.: *Apoc* **Ars** ars-s-f k2 carb-v dios **Hydr** lept mur-ac *Nat-p* *Petr* *Ph-ac* **Phos** *Pic-ac* plat **Podo** k* rhod *Sep* *Sul-ac* *Verat*
    - ⁝ **amel**.: mur-ac h2
  - • **before**: aloe vh1 calc k* merc k*
- ○ - **Hypochondria**: acon k* anac anag vh1 *Arn* k* cham k* cupr sst3• dig k* dros k* grat k* *Nux-v* k* ph-ac k* staph k*
  - • **left**: phos h2
- **Liver**: naja bg2
- **Lower** abdomen: nat-m bg2
- ▽ - **extending** to | **Head**; into: laur

APPENDICITIS (See Inflammation - appendix)

APPREHENSION in, sensation of: *(↗MIND - Clairvoyance; MIND - Excitement; MIND - Fear - happen)* androc srj1• arizon-l nl2• *Asaf* kali-bi gk merc-c k* olib-sac wmh1 rhus-t k*
- ○ - **Lower** abdomen: merc-c k*

ASCENDING:
- **agg**.: asc-t bg2
- **stairs** | **agg**.: hell b7.de* merc b4.de* rhus-t b7.de*

ASCITES (See Dropsy - ascites)

ATROPHY:
- ○ - **Liver**: *(↗Cirrhosis)* abies-c bro1 agar-ph mtf11 apoc bro1 arg-n ars k* *Ars-i* bro1 **Aur** k* aur-ar k2 aur-i k2 *Aur-m* bro1 *Aur-m-n* sne aur-s k2 *Bry* **Calc** k* calc-ar bro1 *Carb-v* card-m k* cas-s bro1 *Chel* *Chin* k* *Chion* crot-h mtf11 *Cupr* diosm br1 fel bro1 fl-ac bro1 graph bro1 *Hydr* k* iod k* kali-bi bro1 kali-i bro1 *Lach* laur ptk1 lept *Lyc* k* mag-m *Merc* k* merc-d bro1 *Mur-ac* *Nast* bro1 nat-ch bro1 *Nat-m* nat-s nit-ac k* nit-m-ac bro1 *Nux-v* k* **Phos** k* *Plb* k* podo bro1 puls quas bro1 senec bro1 sep sul-i k2 *Sulph*
  - • **acute** yellow atrophy: dig bro1 *Phos* c2* podo bro1
- **Spleen**: agn bro1 eucal bro1 ign mtf11 iod bro1* phos bro1 plb mtf11

AWARE of the abdomen (See Conscious)

BALL; sensation of a: *(↗Hard body; Lump in)* *Brom* b4a.de *Plat* b4a.de prot fmm1•
- **ascending**: acon b7.de* ign b7.de plb b7.de*
  - ○ • **Throat**; to: *Arg-n* k* raph k*
- **menses**; during: positr nl2•
- **rolling** in: aur-s jatr-c c1 lach *Lyc* k* sabad sep
- ○ - **Hypochondria**: brom ptk1 cupr ptk1
  - • **right**: cycl a1*
  - • **left**: brom calc-caust c1 cupr
- **Hypogastrium**:
  - • **left**: ephe-si hsj1•
  - • **waking**; on: ephe-si hsj1•
- **Inguinal** region: bell bg2
  - • **right**: plan bg2

Ball; sensation of a: ...
- **Liver**:
  - ○ • **Below**: arn ptk1 borx ptk1 echi ptk1 gels ptk1 lach ptk1 *Nat-s* ptk1 thuj ptk1 verat ptk1 zinc ptk1
  - • **In**: aesc ptk1 bar-c k* op bg2
    - ⁝ **hard**: nux-m ptk1
- **Spleen**: brom b4a.de*
- **Upper** abdomen: [bell-p-sp dcm1]

BAND around: *(↗Constriction - band)* caust ptk1 cench k2 *Chel* ptk1 chion ptk1 crot-c k* *Lec* sne lyc ptk1 nux-v ptk1 plb ptk1 *Puls* ptk1 *Sulph* ptk1 symph fd3.de•
- **cold** | **Lower** part of abdomen: lac-f c1
- ○ - **Hypochondria**: acon ptk1 card-m ptk1 *Caust* b4a.de *Con* b4a.de dros ptk1 ign ptk1 *Lec* sne *Lyc* b4a.de nat-m b4a.de nux-v ptk1 *Plat* b4a.de sulph b4a.de *Thuj* b4a.de

BANDAGING: | **amel**.: cupr ptk1 fl-ac ptk1 nat-m ptk1 nit-ac ptk1

BATHING agg.; after: ant-c b7.de* rhus-t b7.de*

BEARING down sensation (See Pain - dragging)

BEER agg.: ferr b7.de* nat-m bg2 nux-v b7.de* *Puls* b7a.de rhus-t b7.de* sep b4a.de sil b4a.de teucr b7.de* verat b7.de*

BELLYACHE (See Pain)

BENDING:
- **backward**:
  - • **agg**.: anac b4a.de thuj b4.de*
  - • **amel**.: alet bg2 ant-t bg2 bell b4a.de* bry bg2 chin b7.de* dios bg2 nux-v b7.de* onos bg2
- **body** | **agg**.: chin b7.de* rhus-t b7.de*
- **forward**:
  - • **agg**.: bell bg2 cocc bg2 verb bg2
    - ⁝ **sitting**; when: ant-t bg2
  - • **amel**.: bell bg2 mag-m bg2 prun bg2
- **side**; to:
  - • **agg**.: bell b4.de* nat-c bg2 plb b7.de*
    - ⁝ **Hypochondria**: lyc b4.de* nat-m b4.de* stann b4.de*
- **side**; to one:
  - • **left** side; to | **Hypochondria**: agar bg2 *Nat-m* b4a.de

BENDING DOUBLE: | **amel**.: ars bg2 bapt bg2 bell b4a.de* brom bg2 bry bg2 calc bg2 castm bg2 chel bg2 chin bg2 colch bg2 **Coloc** b4a.de* cupr bg2 grat bg2 iris bg2 *Kali-c* bg2 lyc bg2 mag-p bg2 merc-c bg2 mosch bg2 phos bg2 podo bg2 puls b7.de* rheum b7a.de* rhus-t b7.de* sabad bg2 sec bg2 sep bg2 staph bg2 stram bg2 tarent bg2

BILIARY COLIC (See Pain - liver - colic)

BLEEDING:
- ○ - **Intestines**: *(↗STOOL - Bloody)* acon bg2 alum bg2 ant-c bg2 arn bg2 ars bg2 bac jl2 bell bg2 carb-v bg2* hydr bg2 ip bg2 nit-ac bg2 parathyr jl2 phos bg2 succ-ac mtf11 yohim mp4*
  - • **accompanied** by:
    - ⁝ **mucus** stool: canth mtf11
    - ⁝ **undigested** stool: acet-ac mtf11
- **Peritoneum**: brom bg2 lach bg2
- **Umbilicus**:
  - • **children**; in: | **infants**: abrot k2* *Calc-p* bro1*

BLOATED (See Distension)

BLOWING the nose agg.: canth b7.de* stront-c b4.de*
- ○ - **Hypochondria**: arn b7.de*

BOILING sensation: lachn vml3•
- **lime**; as from boiling: caust ptk1

BORBORYGMUS (See Rumbling)

BRANDY agg.: *Ign* b7a.de

BREAD agg.: acon bg2 bry bg2 caust bg2 coff b7.de* kali-c bg2 merc bg2 merc-c b4a.de podo bg2 rhus-t bg2 ruta bg2 sars bg2 *Sep* b4a.de sul-ac bg2 teucr b7.de* zinc bg2

BREAKFAST:
- **after**:
  - **agg**.: agar bg2 cic bg2 cycl bg2 graph bg2 kali-c b4.de* kali-n b4.de* laur b7.de* lyc bg2 mag-m bg2 nat-m bg2 nux-m b7.de* nux-v b7a.de* phos b4a.de* plb b7.de* rhod b4.de* sars b4.de* stront-c b4.de* thuj bg2 *Zinc* bg2
    - **Hypochondria**: graph b4a.de nux-v b7.de*
  - **amel**.: mag-m bg2
- **during**: alum bg2

BREATHING:
- **agg**.: anac b4.de* arg-met b7.de* asaf bg2 bov b4.de* bry bg2 calc b4.de* chin b7.de* cina b7.de* clem b4.de* cocc b7.de* coloc b4.de* con b4.de* dig b4.de* euphr b7.de* graph b4.de* hyos b7.de* kali-n b4.de* kreos bg2 lyc b4.de* mag-c b4a.de* mang bg2 mosch bg2 nat-m b4.de* nux-v b7.de* ran-s bg2 sars b4.de* sel bg2 seneg b4a.de* spig b7.de* stann b4.de* sulph b4a.de* thuj b4.de*
  - ○ **Hypochondria**: acon b7.de* agar b4.de* arn b7.de* asaf b7a.de bry b7.de* calc bg2 cocc b7.de* con b4.de* croc b7.de* cupr b7.de* lyc b4.de* merc b4.de* nat-m b4.de* nux-v b7.de* ph-ac b4.de* sars b4.de* sel b7.de* seneg b4.de* *Sil* b4a.de sul-ac b4.de* verat b7.de*
- **amel**.: asaf b7.de* cina b7.de*
- **deep**:
  - **agg**.: *Arg-n* ptk1 arn b7.de* *Caust* ptk1 ign b7.de* kali-bi bg2 kreos b7a.de* mang b4a.de* nux-v b7.de* puls ptk1 ran-s bg2 sulph b4a.de* tab bg2 verb b7.de*
    - **Hypochondria**: aloe bg2 borx b4a.de *Bry* b7.de* calc b4.de* cob bg2 kali-bi bg2 lyc b4.de* *Merc* b4.de* mosch b7.de* nat-c b4.de* nat-s bg2 ran-b bg2 ran-s b7.de sabad b7.de* sil b4a.de
    - **Liver**: *Bell* ptk1 hep ptk1 nat-s ptk1 ptel ptk1 sel ptk1 ther ptk1
    - **Spleen**: card-m ptk1 cob ptk1 sulph ptk1
  - **amel**.: card-m ptk1 fl-ac bg2* thuj bg2*
    - **Liver**: ox-ac ptk1
- **holding** breath:
  - **agg**.: dros b7.de* spig b7.de*
    - **Hypochondria**: led b7.de*
  - **amel**.: *Bell* b4a.de

BUBBLING sensation, as if bubbles were moving about: *(↗Clucking; Gurgling; Rumbling)* agath-a nl2• ant-c h2 cham h1 hell ketogl-ac rly4• **Lyc** k* merc bg2 nat-m ph-ac *Puls* k* rhus-t a1 stann k* *Sul-ac* k* sulph bg2 tarax k* [spect dfg1]
- **bursting**; with sensation as from: cupr b7a.de nat-m bg2 phos bg2 tarax b7a.de
- **flatus**; passing | **amel**.: ulm-c jsj8•
- **lying** on back agg.: *Sul-ac*
- ○ **External** abdomen: rhus-t bg2
- **Inguinal** region: aeth br1 berb k* kali-c h2 lyc
- **Liver**: laur lil-t
- **Muscles**: merc b4.de* rheum b7.de* squil b7.de* tarax b7.de*
- **Sides**: arg-met cham h1 cupr k* dios a1 nux-v k* squil sul-ac k*
  - **left**: carb-v h2 cupr h2* lyc h2 sumb k*
- **Umbilicus**: aeth gsy1* berb bro1 hyper bg3* mez h2
  - ○ **About umbilicus**: plb a1
  - **Below**: coloc a1

BUBO: *(↗Swelling - inguinal region - glands)* acon bro1 alum k* ang bro1 anthraci br1 apis bro1 ars ars-i k* aur k* aur-m k* aur-m-n k* aur-s k2 bad k* bar-m k* bell k* **Bufo** k* calc-s c2 *Calen* c2* *Carb-an* k* carb-v bro1 caust bro1 chel k* **Cinnb** k* clem crot-h dulc a1 **Hep** k* iod k* jac-c bro1 kali-chl k* *Kali-i* k* kali-m c2 lac-c k* lach k* lith-c c2 lyc lyss c2 *Merc* k* merc-i-r bro1* merc-pr-r bro1 *Nit-ac* k* oci c2 pest c1* ph-ac bro1 phyt k* *Sil* k* sulph k* syph c2* tarent-c k* thuj b4a.de zinc k*
- **burning**; with: *Ars* ars-i bell *Carb-an* k* dulc a1 *Tarent-c*
- **chancroidal**: ars-i bro1 *Merc* bro1 merc-c bro1 *Merc-i-r* bro1 sil bro1
- **gonorrhea**; after suppressed: *Aur* aur-m bar-m bufo hep med merc zinc
- **indurated**: alum bro1 bad bro1 *Carb-an* bro1 merc bro1
- **neglected**: carb-an ptk1
- **phagedenic**: *Ars* bro1 graph bro1 hydr bro1 *Kali-i* bro1 lach bro1 *Merc* bro1 *Merc-i-r* bro1 *Nit-ac* bro1 sil bro1 sulph bro1

Bubo
- **suppurating**: anthraci br1 ars k2 *Aur* aur-ar k2 bufo *Carb-an* k* chel k* **Hep** *Iod* kali-chl k* *Kali-i* k* **Lach** k* *Merc* *Merc-i-r* k* nit-ac k* *Sil* *Sulph* tarent-c
  - **chronic**: merc-i-r br1*
  - **refuses** to heal; old bubo: *Carb-an* *Sulph*

BUTTERFLIES; sensation of: olib-sac wmh1

CABBAGE agg.: bry b7.de* cupr b7.de*

CAKE; warm: | **agg**.: kali-c b4.de*

CALCULI, biliary (See Gallstones)

CANCER:
- **aluminium** poisoning; from: *(↗GENERALS - Aluminium)* cadm-met gm1 **Cadm-o** gm1
- ○ **Cecum**: *Orni* br1*
- **Colon**: *(↗Inflammation - colon - cancerous)* **Aloe** mk1• *Lyc* mk1• *Thuj* mk1•
  - ○ **Transverse**: *(↗Inflammation - colon - cancerous; Inflammation - colon - ulcerative; RECTUM - Ulceration)* anthraq mtf11 cadm-i gm1 carc-col-ad mtf11 cund mtf11 germ-met srj5• hydr mtf11 kali-m mtf11 kali-perm mtf11 lob-e mtf11 orni mtf11 polyg-h mtf11 uva mtf11
- **Gall** ducts: card-m mtf mag-p mtf mag-s mtf nat-m mtf nat-s mtf phos mtf
- **Gallbladder**: **Chel** mk1• chion gm1
- **Glands**; inguinal: syph jl2
  - **chronic**: syph jl2
- **Intestines**: cadm-act gm1 cadm-ar gm1 cadm-br gm1 cadm-chl gm1 cadm-f gm1 cadm-gl gm1 cadm-i gm1 cadm-m gm1 *Cadm-met* gm1 cadm-n gm1 cadm-o gm1 cadm-p gm1 cadm-s gm1 cadm-sel gm1 euph-c gm1 graph tl1 **Hydr** mk1• kreos gm1 methyl gm1 naphthoq mtf11 orni br1 phos gm1 ruta ptk1 succ-ac mtf11
  - **accompanied** by:
    - **goitre**; toxic: cadm-met gm1
    - **Heart** complaints: cadm-met gm1
- **Liver**: ars bro1 cadm-act gm1 *Cadm-ar* gm1 cadm-br gm1 cadm-chl gm1 cadm-f gm1 cadm-gl gm1 cadm-i gm1 cadm-m gm1 *Cadm-met* gm1 cadm-n gm1 cadm-o gm1 *Cadm-p* gm1 *Cadm-s* gm1 cadm-sel gm1 *Calc-ar* gm1 carc mlr1• card-m mtf11 **Cean** gm1* **Chel** bro1* chion gm1 chol br1* *Con* bro1* euph gm1 hydr bro1* kali-m mtf11 lach bro1 *Lyc* mk1• myric ptk1 nit-ac bro1 phos bro1* podo mtf11 *Scir* mk1• solid mtf11 ther ptk1*
  - **accompanied** by | **jaundice**: myric ptk1
  - **early**: carc mlr1• senec ptk1
  - **metastasis**: calen gm1
- **Omentum**: lob-e bro1
- **Pancreas**: cadm-i gm1 **Cadm-s** mk1• calc-ar ptk1* **Cean** gm1* **Hydr** mk1•
- **Sigmoid** flexure: spig c2
- **Spleen**: ars mtf11 borx mtf11 cadm-i gm1 cadm-met gm1 **Cean** gm1*

CATARRH: petr k2
- ○ **Duodenum**: anac mtf11
- **Gastrointestinal**: card-m bro1 *Chin* bro1 hydr bro1 sang bro1
- **Intestinal**: bism-n br1 chel tl1 eucal br1 mag-c br1
  - **accompanied** by pale tongue: *Chel* kr1*
  - **chronic**: euon-a br1

CHERRIES agg.: chin b7.de*

CHILDREN; complaints in: acon bg2 bell bg2 borx bg2 calc bg2 caust bg2 *Cham* b7.de* cic b7.de* cina bg2 coff bg2 iod bg2 ip bg2 nux-m b7a.de* nux-v bg2 podo bg2 *Rheum* b7.de* ruta b7.de* sil bg2 staph b7.de* sulph bg2
- **infants**; in: acon bg2 bell bg2 *Borx* bg2 calc bg2 caust bg2 **Cham** bg2 cic bg2 *Cina* bg2 coff bg2 **Ip** bg2 nux-m bg2 **Rheum** bg2 sil bg2 staph bg2

CHILL:
- **during**: *Calad* b7.de chin b7.de cocc b7.de ign b7.de m-aust b7.de nux-m b7.de *Puls* b7a.de ran-b b7.de spig b7.de*
- ○ **External** abdomen: acon bg2 ambr bg2 *Ars* bg2 **Calad** bg2 chin b7.de* colch bg2 kali-c bg2 mag-c bg2 meny bg2 *Merc* bg2 mez bg2 nit-ac bg2 nux-v bg2 op b7.de* *Par* b7.de* ph-ac bg2 *Puls* b7.de* ran-b bg2 sec bg2 *Spig* b7.de* sulph bg2 teucr bg2 zinc bg2
- **Internally**: acon b7.de *Ars* b4a.de colch b7.de puls b7.de
- **Liver**; region of: nux-v b7.de

Abdomen

CHOLECYSTITIS (See Inflammation - gallbladder)

CHOLELITHIASIS (See Gallstones; Pain - liver - colic)

CHOLERA (See RECTUM - Cholera)

CIRRHOSIS of liver: (↗*Atrophy - liver)* abies-c vml3• am-be mtf11 ars mrr1 ars-i vh aur bg2 aur-m mtf11 *Aur-m-n* sne boerh-d bnj1 calc-ar c2* *Card-m* ptk1* cas-s br1 chin c2* chlorpr mtf crot-h mtf11 *Cupr* k* cur br1 diosm br1 dulc k2 euon mtf11 *Hep* k* *Hydr* k* iod bg2 kali-bi br1 kali-i bg2 lact mrr1 lyc bg2* mag-m mrr1 merc mtf11 merc-d br1 *Mur-ac* k* nast-o mtf11 nux-v mtf11 *Phos* k* plb k* quas mtf11 *Sulph* k* urea c2 vip mtf11
- **accompanied** by:
  - **ascites**: apoc mtf mur-ac ptk1
  - **vomiting** bile: cur br1
- **alcoholics**; in: fl-ac br1* perh-mal mtf11
- **chronic**: hed sp1
- **hemorrhoids**; during: card-m vh
- **hypertrophic**: merc-d br1*
- **incipient**: nit-m-ac br1 senec br1
- **inflammation** of liver; from: card-m mtf crot-h mtf phos mtf

CLICKING sound, as if two bones slipped over each other:

O - **Pubic region** | **left**: nat-m bg2

CLOTHES: | **loosening** | **amel.**: *Caps* b7.de* coff b7.de* merc b4.de* *Nux-v* b7.de* sep bg2
- **tight**:
  - **agg.**: caust ptk1
    - ⁝ **Hypochondria**: am-c b4a.de *Calc* b4a.de *Carb-v* b4a.de *Caust* b4a.de hep b4a.de lyc b4a.de
  - **amel.**: fl-ac ptk1 nat-m ptk1 nit-ac ptk1

CLOTHING; sensitive to: amp rly4• *Apis* **Arg-n** k* bamb-a stb2.de• benz-ac k* both-ax tsm2 **Bov** brom pd *Bry* bg2 **Calc** k* caps h1* *Carb-v* k* *Caust* k* cench k2 cham sne *Chin* k* coff k* conv br1 **Crot-c** *Crot-h* cupr bg2 dol c1* dulc fd4.de eup-per ferr lp ferr-p bg2 *Graph* k* helo c1 *Hep* k* hydrog srj2• ign brm kali-s fd4.de kola stb3• *Kreos* k* *Lac-c* k* **Lach** k* lil-t bg2 **Lyc** k* merc-c mim-p rsj8• mosch ptk1 *Nat-s* k* **Nux-v** k* *Onos* vml3• *Orni* sne phos bg2 plb bg2 podo bg2* ptel hr1 puls k* raph k* rhus-t k2 ribo rly4• *Sars* *Sep* sil k2 spig bg2 *Spong* k* *Stann* sulph k* tell c1 thuj a1 [*Spect* dfg1]
- **eating**; after: *Graph* k*
- **nausea**; with: hydrog srj2•
- **wants** to uncover: dol vml3• ferr lp tab k*

O - **Groins**, about: hydr pd*
- **Hypochondria**: am-c b4a.de *Calc* b4a.de caps b7a.de *Carb-v* b4a.de *Caust* b4a.de coff b7a.de hep b4a.de kreos b7a.de lyc b4a.de *Nux-v* b7a.de puls b7a.de spong b7a.de

CLUCKING: (↗*Bubbling; Gurgling; Rumbling)* bar-c calc chin h1 dig h2 graph h2 kali-c h2 mag-c h2 merc h1 plat h2 rheum h sacch-a fd2.de• sars k* sep h2 stann h2 sulph h2 verb h

COBWEB sensation: rhus-t b7.de*

COFFEE:
- **agg.**: *Bell* b4a.de* *Canth* br1 *Cham* b7.de* cocc b7.de* coloc b4a.de* *Ign* b7a.de* merc bg2 nat-m bg2 *Nux-v* b7.de* sulph bg2

O • **Hypochondria**: cham bg2
- **amel.**: **Coloc** bg2 phos bg2

COITION agg.; after: caust ptk1 ph-ac ptk1 ther bg2*

COLD:
- **agg.**: ars bg2 bov bg2 caust h2 kali-c mtf33 meph bg2 op bg2 phos bg2 *Puls* bg2 rhus-t bg2 ruta bg2 sabin bg2 samb bg2 sars bg2 stann bg2 staph bg2 *Verat* bg2
  - **objects**; grasping cold (See Grasping - agg.)
- **air** agg.: alum bg2 caust bg2 kali-bi bg2
- **applications** | **agg.**: alum bg2 mang b4.de* nux-m b7.de* phos b4a.de rhus-t b7.de* sabad b7.de*
- **drinks**:
  - **agg.**: bapt bg2 calc-p bg2 coloc bg2 lyc bg2 mag-p bg2 manc bg2
    - ⁝ **ice-cold**: calc-p ptk1 nux-m ptk1 rhus-t ptk1
    - ⁝ **Hypochondria**: *Nat-c* b4a.de
  - **amel.**: gran bg2
    - ⁝ **ice-cold**: elaps ptk1

Cold: ...
- **food** | **agg.**: mang b4a.de verat bg2
- **water** | **amel.**: calc b4.de* cann-xyz bg2 ferr bg2
- **wet**: am-c bg2

COLD AGG.; BECOMING: alum bg2 cham bg2 chin bg2 coloc bg2 dulc bg2 merc bg2 nit-ac bg2 *Nux-v* bg2 *Puls* bg2 verat bg2
- **feet**: cham b7a.de *Puls* b7a.de

COLD; TAKING A:
- **after**: caust h2
- **agg.**: *Acon* b7.de* alum b4a.de* anac b4.de* bar-c b4a.de* bell b4a.de *Bry* b7.de* camph b7.de* *Cham* b7.de* chin b7.de* cocc b7.de* *Coloc* b4.de* croc b7.de* *Dulc* b4.de* grat bg2 hep b4.de* *Hyos* b7.de* merc b4a.de* nat-c b4.de* *Nit-ac* b4a.de **Nux-v** b7.de* op b7.de phos b4.de *Puls* b7.de rhus-t b7.de ruta b7.de sabin b7.de *Samb* b7.de* sars b4.de stann b4.de staph b7.de verat b7.de*

O • **Hypochondria**: *Nux-v* b7.de*
  - **Intestines**: dulc ptk1

COLDNESS: (↗*Shivering)* acon k* *Aeth* k* agar k* aloe alum k* alum-p k2 **Ambr** k* amyg k* ang b7a.de* anth c1* *Apis* bro1 arg-n k* *Ars* k* asaf k* *Asar* k* aur bro1 bell k* berb k* bov k* cadm-s br1* calad k* *Calc* k* calc-s *Camph* k* cann-s b7.de* caps bro1 caust k* cham k* chel k* chin k* chinin-ar cic k* *Cist* k* coff b7.de* colch k* coloc k* crot-h *Crot-t* k* cupr-s k* dulc k* elaps bro1 eug k* *Grat* k* *Hell* k* hipp a1 hydr-ac k* jatr-c kali-ar *Kali-bi* k* *Kali-br* k* *Kali-c* k* kali-n k* kali-p *Kali-s* kola stb3• *Kreos* k* *Lach* k* *Laur* k* lyc bg2 lyss a1 m-arct b7.de mag-c bg2 mang **Meny** k* meph k* *Merc* k* *Merc-sul* k* merl k* mez k* nat-c bg2 nat-m k* nit-ac k* nux-v b7a.de* ol-j a1 olnd k* op k* *Par* k* *Petr* k* ph-ac k* phel k* *Phos* k* phyt bg2 plan k* plb k* plect a1* podo *Puls* k* rat k* ruta k* sabad k* *Sars* k* *Sec* k* seneg *Sep* k* spig bg2 staph k* sul-ac ptk1 *Sulph* k* *Tab* k* tart-ac a1 *Ter* k* *Teucr* bg2 *Tub* **Verat** k* zinc k* zinc-p k2
- **morning**: meny k* plect k*
- **afternoon**: alum k* chel k* lyc k*
  - **drinking** water; on: chel
- **evening**: ars k* zinc k*
- **night**: cupr-s a1 sulph k* symph fd3.de•
  - **midnight**: calad k*
  - **bed** agg.; in: sulph k*
- **air**; as from a draft of: sulph
- **alternating** with heat in abdomen (See Heat - alternating)
- **burning**; with: phos ptk1
- **chill**; during: *Aeth* apis ars k* ars-s-f k2 **Calc** cham chel chin chinin-ar *Ign* **Meny** k* *Merc* k* *Mez* k* *Ph-ac* k* puls sec sep k* sulph verat zinc
- **cloth** of cold water wrung round his waist; as if he had a: lath c1*
- **cold** drinks agg.; after: *Ars* *Chel* *Rhus-t*
- **cold** water running through; as if: bufo bg1 cann-s *Kali-c* k*
- **dashed** with water, as if: mez k*
- **drinking** agg.; after: asaf k* chel k* *Chin* k*
- **eating**; after: *Chel* chin k* **Puls** k* sulph k*
- **heat**; during: *Meny* b7.de* zinc
- **icy**: colch ptk1 crot-h ptk1 kola stb3•
- **inspiration**, on every: *Chin* k*
- **menses**; during: kali-c k*
- **pain**; with: kali-c k2
- **pressure** agg.: meny h1*
- **sensation** of: *Ambr* b7.de* *Ang* b7a.de asaf b7.de* camph b7.de chin b7.de *Colch* b7a.de *Hell* b7.de* kreos b7a.de *Laur* b7a.de **Meny** b7.de* *Olnd* b7.de* plb b7a.de ruta b7.de *Sabad* b7a.de *Sec* b7.de
  - **fever**; during: ars bg2 calc bg2 *Meny* bg2 petr bg2 sep bg2
- **spirituous** liquors, after: phel
- **stool** | **after** | **agg.**: coloc hr1 graph k* phel k* plect a1
  - **before**: cop a1 graph k*
- **uncovered**, as if: *Lach* ter k*
- **walking** in open air | **amel.**: dulc k* plect a1
- **warm** stove | **amel.**: meph
- **warmth** | **amel.**: kali-ar k2
- **water** running through; as if cold (See cold water)
- **wind** agg.; cold: lyc

O - **External** abdomen: aeth br1* *Ambr* b7.de* apis bg2 calad bg2 camph b7.de* cedr bg2 cham b7.de* chel bg2 chin bg2 cic bg2 coloc b4a.de crot-t bg2 grat bg2 kali-bi bg2 kali-s ptk1 kreos bg2 mag-m bg2 med k* merc k* merc-c b4a.de* nat-m bg2 op bg2 *Par* bg2 puls bg2 *Sep* b4a.de* spig bg2 staph b7.de* **Verat** k*
- . **one** side: *Ambr* b7a.de

- **Hypochondria**: cadm-s nat-c bg2 nit-ac bg2 nux-v k* puls b7.de*
- . **right**: podo bg2

- **Hypogastrium**: plb k*

▽ . **extending** to | **Cheek**: coloc bro1
- **Inguinal** region: plb k*
- . **burning**; becoming: berb

- **Inside** of abdomen: anth vh1
- **Liver**; region of: bar-c k* kali-c bg2 med k* *Nat-c* b4a.de
- **Lower** part | **chill**; during: *Meny* b7a.de teucr b7a.de
- **Sides**: all-c ambr merl olnd sulph symph fd3.de•
- . **one** side only: *Ambr*
- . **left**: *Ambr*

- **Umbilicus**: acon bg2 apis k* coloc k* ran-b k* rat ruta bg2 ter bg2
- . **walking** agg.: coloc k*

O . **Region** of umbilicus: coloc k* kreos k* phos h2 querc-r svu1• rat k* ruta ter k*
- ⁝ **stool** agg.; after: coloc k*

- **Upper** part: ars bg1 camph bg1 kali-c bg1 mang bg1 olnd bg1 ox-ac bg1 sec bg1 sulph bg1

▽ - **extending** to:
O . **Across**: sep
- . **Back**: puls
- . **Chest**: camph
- . **Feet**: calad
- . **Knees**: anth c1
- . **Mouth**; rising up into: *Carb-an*
- . **Stomach**: phel vml3•
- . **Throat**: carb-an ptk1

COLIC (See Pain - cramping)

COLITIS (See Inflammation - colon)

COMPLAINTS of abdomen: acon b2.de* aeth ptk1 agar b2.de* agn b2.de* alum b2.de* am-c b2.de* am-m b2.de* ambr b2.de* anac b2.de* ang b2.de* ant-c b2.de* ant-t b2.de* arg-met b2.de* arg-n ptk1 arn b2.de* *Ars* b2.de* *Asaf* b2.de* asar b2.de* aur b2.de* bar-c b2.de* *Bell* b2.de* bism b2.de* borx b2.de* bov b2.de* *Bry* b2.de* calad b2.de* *Calc* b2.de* camph b2.de* cann-s b2.de* *Canth* b2.de* caps b2.de* carb-an b2.de* *Carb-v* b2.de* catar br1 caust b2.de* cham b2.de* chel b2.de* **Chin** b2.de* cic b2.de* cina b2.de* clem b2.de* *Cocc* b2.de* coff b2.de* colch b2.de* **Coloc** b2.de* con b2.de* croc b2.de* cupr b2.de* cycl b2.de* dig b2.de* *Dios* bg2 dros b2.de* dulc b2.de* euph b2.de* euphr b2.de* ferr b2.de* graph b2.de* guaj b2.de* hell b2.de* hep b2.de* hyos b2.de* *Ign* b2.de* iod b2.de* ip b2.de* *Kali-c* b2.de* kali-n b2.de* kreos b2.de* lach b2.de* laur b2.de* led b2.de* *Lyc* b2.de* m-ambo b2.de m-arct b2.de m-aust b2.de mag-c b2.de* mag-m b2.de* mang b2.de* meny b2.de* *Merc* b2.de* mez b2.de* mosch b2.de* mur-ac b2.de* nat-c b2.de* nat-m b2.de* nit-ac b2.de* nux-m b2.de* **Nux-v** b2.de* olnd b2.de* op b2.de* par b2.de* petr b2.de* ph-ac b2.de* *Phos* b2.de* *Plat* b2.de* **Plb** b2.de* **Puls** b2.de* ran-b b2.de* ran-s b2.de* rheum b2.de* rhod b2.de* **Rhus-t** b2.de* ruta b2.de* sabad b2.de* sabin b2.de* samb b2.de* sars b2.de* sec b2.de* sel b2.de* seneg b2.de* **Sep** b2.de* sil b2.de* spig b2.de* spong b2.de* squil b2.de* stann b2.de* *Staph* b2.de* stram b2.de* stront-c b2.de* *Sul-ac* b2.de* **Sulph** b2.de* tarax b2.de* teucr b2.de* thuj b2.de* valer b2.de* *Verat* b2.de* verb b2.de* viol-t b2.de* *Zinc* b2.de* [bell-p-sp dcm1]

- **alternating** sides: aloe bg2 mang bg2
- **right** side: agar b4a.de* agn b7a.de* alum b4a.de am-c b4a.de am-m b7a.de* *Ambr* b7a.de* anac b4a.de* ang b7a.de* ant-c b7a.de* apis b7a.de* arg-met b7a.de* arn b7a.de* **Ars** b4a.de* asaf b7a.de* aur b4a.de* *Bar-c* b4a.de* bell b4a.de* *Bism* b7a.de* *Bry* b7a.de* calad b7a.de* calc b4a.de* camph b7a.de* cann-s b7a.de* *Canth* b7a.de* *Carb-an* b4a.de* *Carb-v* b4a.de* *Caust* b4a.de* chel b7a.de* chin b7a.de* cic b7a.de* clem b4a.de* cocc b7a.de* colch b7a.de* *Coloc* b4a.de* con b4a.de* croc b7a.de* cupr b7a.de* cycl b7a.de* dig b4a.de* dros b7a.de* dulc b4a.de* fl-ac b4a.de* graph b4a.de* guaj b4a.de* *Ign* b7a.de* iod b4a.de* ip b7a.de* kali-c b4a.de* *Kali-n* b4a.de* kreos b7a.de* *Lach* b7a.de* laur b7a.de* *Lyc* b4a.de* m-aust b7a.de *Mag-m* b4a.de* meny b7a.de* merc b4a.de* **Merc-c** bg2 mez b4a.de* mill b7a.de* mosch b7a.de* nat-c b4a.de* nat-m b4a.de* nit-ac b4a.de* nux-m b7a.de* *Nux-v* b7a.de* olnd b7a.de* petr b4a.de* ph-ac b4a.de* phos b4a.de* plat b4a.de* plb b7a.de* psor b4a.de* puls b7a.de* ran-b b7a.de* ran-s b7a.de* rhod b4a.de* **Rhus-t** b7a.de* sabad b7a.de* sabin b7a.de* samb b7a.de* *Seneg* b4a.de* *Sep* b4a.de* sil b4a.de* spig b7a.de* spong b7a.de* squil b7a.de* *Stann* b4a.de* stront-c b4a.de* sulph b4a.de* tarax b7a.de* teucr b7a.de* *Thuj* b4a.de* verb b7a.de* viol-t b7a.de* zinc b4a.de*
- **left** side: acon b7a.de* agar b4a.de* agn b7a.de* **Alum** b4a.de* *Am-c* b4a.de* *Am-m* b7a.de* ambr b7a.de anac b4a.de* ang b7a.de* ant-c b7a.de* *Ant-t* b7a.de* *Apis* bg2 **Arg-met** b7a.de* arg-n bg2 arn b7a.de* ars b4a.de* **Asaf** b7a.de* asar b7a.de* aur b4a.de* bar-c b4a.de* bell b4a.de* bov b4a.de* **Brom** b4a.de* *Bry* b7a.de* *Calc* b4a.de* camph b7a.de* cann-s b7a.de* canth b7a.de* caps b7a.de* carb-v b4a.de* caust b4a.de* *Cham* b7a.de* chel b7a.de* chin b7a.de* *Cina* b7a.de* cocc b7a.de* colch b7a.de* coloc b4a.de* con b4a.de* croc b7a.de* *Cupr* b7a.de* dig b4a.de* **Dulc** b4a.de* euph b4a.de* **Fl-ac** b4a.de* graph b4a.de* *Guaj* b4a.de* **Hep** b4a.de* ign b7a.de* iod b4a.de* *Kali-c* b4a.de* kreos b7a.de* laur b7a.de* led b7a.de* lyc b4a.de* m-arct b7a.de m-aust b7a.de mag-m b4a.de* mang b4a.de* meny b7a.de* merc b4a.de* mez b4a.de* *Mill* b7a.de* mur-ac b4a.de* nat-c b4a.de* *Nat-m* b4a.de* nit-ac b4a.de* nux-m b7a.de* nux-v b7a.de* olnd b7a.de* op b7a.de* *Par* b7a.de* petr b4a.de* ph-ac b4a.de* plat b4a.de* **Plb** b7a.de* psor b4a.de* *Puls* b7a.de* *Ran-b* b7a.de* **Rheum** b7a.de* rhod b4a.de* rhus-t b7a.de* ruta b7a.de* sabad b7a.de* sabin b7a.de* samb b7a.de* *Sars* b4a.de* sel b7a.de* sep b4a.de* sil b4a.de* *Spig* b7a.de* spong b7a.de* squil b7a.de* stann b4a.de* staph b7a.de* sul-ac b4a.de* **Sulph** b4a.de* **Tarax** b7a.de* teucr b7a.de* thuj b4a.de* *Valer* b7a.de* verat b7a.de verb b7a.de* viol-t b7a.de* zinc b4a.de*
- . **followed** by right side: ip bg2

- **accompanied** by:
- . **bending** double: aur b4.de* bov b4.de* bry bg2 *Coloc* b4.de* grat bg2 sars b4.de* sulph b4.de*
- . **chilliness**: *Ars* bg2 colch bg2 kali-c bg2 mag-c bg2 *Merc* bg2 par bg2 puls bg2
- . **constipation**: *Alum* bg2 bell bg2 bry bg2 calc bg2 carb-v bg2 *Con* bg2 hyos bg2 kali-c bg2 lyc bg2 merc bg2 nat-m bg2 *Nux-v* bg2 op bg2 *Plb* bg2 sep bg2 *Sil* bg2 sulph bg2
- . **convulsions**: ars bg2 bell bg2 *Cham* bg2 *Cic* b7a.de* cocc bg2 *Coloc* bg2 cupr b7a.de* hyos bg2 *Ign* bg2 ip bg2 mag-c bg2 mag-m bg2 *Nux-v* bg2 phos bg2 puls bg2 sec b7a.de* stann b4a.de* sulph bg2
- . **diarrhea**: ambr b7a.de* *Ant-t* bg2 ars bg2 bry b7a.de* *Cham* bg2 chel b7a.de *Coloc* bg2 lach bg2 *Merc* bg2 nat-c bg2 nux-v bg2 phos bg2 *Puls* b7a.de* *Rheum* bg2 sep bg2 spig b7a.de* *Sulph* bg2 verat b7a.de*
- . **eructations**: bell bg2 grat bg2 kali-c b4.de* nux-v bg2 pall bg2 rhod b4a.de* sec bg2
- . **gout**: daph bg2
- . **heat**: ars bg2 carb-v bg2 cocc bg2 coloc bg2 grat bg2 *Nat-c* bg2 nat-m bg2
- ⁝ **other** parts or abdomen; in: nux-v bg2
- . **hemorrhoids**: carb-v bg2 cham bg2 coloc bg2 lach bg2 **Nux-v** bg2 **Puls** bg2 sec bg2 *Sulph* bg2
- . **hiccough**: borx b4a.de
- . **menses**; complaints of: bell bg2 carb-v bg2 cham bg2 cocc bg2 coff bg2 nux-v bg2 *Puls* bg2 sulph bg2 zinc bg2
- . **nausea**: am-c b4a.de ant-c bg2 ant-t b7.de* arn b7.de* *Ars* bg2 bell bg2 canth b7.de* *Cham* b7a.de chel b7.de* chin b7.de* cocc b7.de* con bg2 cycl b7.de* grat bg2 hep b4a.de* *Ign* b7a.de **Ip** bg2 kali-bi bg2 m-arct b7.de mang b4a.de* nat-m bg2 nux-m b7a.de* **Nux-v** b7.de* rheum b7.de* samb b7a.de* stann b4a.de* staph b7.de* sulph bg2 valer b7.de* verat bg2
- . **respiration**; complaints of (See RESPIRATION - Complaints - accompanied - abdomen)
- . **retention** of urine: *Arn* b7a.de
- . **screaming** (See MIND - Shrieking - abdomen)
- . **sighing** (See MIND - Sighing - abdomen)
- . **sleepiness**: ant-t bg2 nux-m bg2 nux-v bg2

Abdomen

- **stool**; urging to (See RECTUM - Urging - accompanied - abdomen)
- **stretching** out: plb ptk1
- **thirst**: chin bg2 verat b7a.de*
- **tossing** about: bell bg2 cham bg2 ip bg2
- **trembling**: bov bg2 cupr bg2 meph bg2
- **urination**; copious: bell bg2 lach bg2 spig bg2 verat bg2
- **vertigo**: calc bg2 coloc b4.de* petr b4.de* spig b7.de* stram b7.de*
- **vexation** (See MIND - Anger - abdomen)
- **vision**; dim: calc bg2
- **vomiting**: *Ant-t* bg2 *Ars* bg2 asar bg2 bell bg2 bry bg2 cupr bg2 hyos bg2 *Ip* bg2 lach bg2 *Nux-v* bg2 puls bg2 sec bg2 verat bg2
- **water** brash: bry bg2 **Sil** bg2 sulph bg2
- **weakness**: nux-v bg2 psor tl1
  - **faint**-like weakness: ran-s bg2

○ • **Anus**; pain at: verb bg2
- **Bladder**; pain in (See BLADDER - Pain - accompanied - abdomen)
- **Calves**; cramp in: camph bg2 coloc bg2 *Cupr* bg2
- **Cheeks**; red discoloration of: merc bg2
- **Chest**; pain in (See CHEST - Pain - accompanied - abdomen)
- **Extremities**:
  - **complaints**: aeth ptk1
  - **lameness**: carb-v bg2
  - **pain** in: coloc bg2 sec bg2
- **Eyes**:
  - **complaints**: arg-n ptk1
  - **dark** circles around: cham bg2 *Cina* bg2 merc bg2 nux-v bg2
- **Face**:
  - **heat** of: hep b4a.de* merc bg2 nux-v bg2
  - **pale** discoloration of: cann-xyz bg2 cham b7a.de phos b4a.de*
  - **shivering**: coloc b4a.de
- **Hands**; yellow discoloration of: sil bg2*
- **Head**; pain in: hyos bg2 phos bg2
- **Heart**; complaints of (See CHEST - Heart; complaints - accompanied - abdomen)
- **Lumbar** region; pain in: alum bg2 am-c bg2 bar-c bg2 calc bg2 caust bg2 cham bg2 kali-c bg2 kreos bg2 mag-m bg2 nat-m bg2 *Nux-v* b7a.de* phos bg2 *Puls* bg2 sec bg2 *Sulph* bg2
- **Nails**; blue discoloration of: sil bg2*
- **Stomach**; disordered: acon bg2 *Ant-c* bg2 ant-t bg2 ars bg2 bell bg2 bry bg2 carb-v bg2 chin bg2 coff bg2 hep bg2 nux-v bg2 *Puls* bg2 sulph bg2

- **alternating** complaints: am ptk1 *Puls* ptk1 sulph ptk1
- **alternating** with:

○ • **Chest**; complaints of: aesc bg2 rad-br ptk1 ran-b b7a.de*
- **Ear**; complaints of (See EAR - Complaints - alternating with - abdomen)
- **Eyes**; complaints of (See EYE - Complaints - alternating with - abdomen - complaints)
- **Feet**; swelling of: *Nux-m* b7a.de
- **Head**:
  - **complaints** of (See HEAD - Complaints - alternating - abdomen)
  - **pain** (See HEAD - Pain - alternating - abdomen - complaints)
- **Nose**; complaints of: calc bg2
- **Organs**; complaints of other: bry ptk1 coloc ptk1 nux-v ptk1 rad-br ptk1 ran-b ptk1
- **Stomach**; complaints of: kali-bi bg2

- **syphilitic**: *Ars* bro1 ars-i bro1 aur bro1 cean bro1 hep bro1 *Kali-bi* bro1 kali-i bro1 merc bro1 merc-aur bro1 *Merc-c* bro1 merc-i-r bro1 merc-tn bro1 *Nux-v* bro1
- **wandering**: coc-c bg2
- **weeping**; with (See MIND - Weeping - abdomen)

○ - **Diagonally**: lach ptk1
- **Duodenum** (See Duodenum)
- **External** abdomen: acon b2.de alum b2.de am-m b2.de *Ambr* b2.de anac b2.de ang b2.de ant-c b2.de apis ptk1 arg-met b2.de arn b2.de ars b2.de asaf b2.de asar b2.de aur b2.de bar-c b2.de *Bell* b2.de bov b2.de **Bry** b2.de* calc b2.de camph b2.de cann-s b2.de *Canth* b2.de caps b2.de carb-v b2.de caust b2.de cham b2.de chel b2.de chin b2.de cic b2.de cocc b2.de colch b2.de *Coloc* b2.de con b2.de croc b2.de cupr b2.de dig b2.de dros b2.de euph b2.de ferr b2.de graph b2.de guaj b2.de *Hyos* b2.de ign b2.de iod b2.de ip b2.de kali-c b2.de lach b2.de led b2.de lyc b2.de m-ambo b2.de m-arct b2.de mag-c b2.de mag-m b2.de mang b2.de meny b2.de **Merc** b2.de* mosch b2.de mur-ac b2.de nat-c b2.de nit-ac b2.de **Nux-v** b2.de* olnd b2.de op b2.de par b2.de petr b2.de ph-ac b2.de phos b2.de plat b2.de plb b2.de* **Puls** b2.de ran-b b2.de ran-s b2.de rheum b2.de rhod b2.de *Rhus-t* b2.de ruta b2.de *Sabad* b2.de sabin b2.de samb b2.de sars b2.de **Sel** b2.de* seneg b2.de *Sep* b2.de sil b2.de spig b2.de spong b2.de squil b2.de stann b2.de staph b2.de stram b2.de stront-c b2.de sul-ac b2.de *Sulph* b2.de* tarax b2.de thuj b2.de valer b2.de verat b2.de viol-t b2.de zinc b2.de
- **Flora**; intestinal (See Flora)
- **Gallbladder** and ducts: am-m ptk1 aran-ix sp1 bapt bg2 bell bg2 berb mtf11 but-ac sp1 *Chel* bg2* chin bg2 dios mtf11 fab mtf11 gels ptk1 guat sp1 *Hed* sp1 hydr ptk1 iris br1 lach bg2 lept bg2 mag-s sp1 merc bg2 merc-d ptk1 nast-o mtf11 nat-p ptk1 *Nux-v* bg2* podo bg2 quas mtf11 rheum ptk1 sulph bg2 tarax mtf11 ter bg2 [*Mag-lac* stj2 *Mag-met* stj2 *Mag-n* stj2 *Mag-sil* stj2]
- **Gallstones** (See Gallstones)
- **Hypochondria** (See Hypochondria; complaints)
- **Ileocecal** region: *Ars* bg2 *Bapt* bg2 *Bell* bg2 *Bry* bg2 *Coloc* bg2 ferr-p bg2 mag-c bg2 merc bg2 nux-v bg2 *Op* bg2 **Rhus-t** bg2 sep bg2 *Sul-i* bg2 *Sulph* bg2
- **Intestines**: *Acal* br1 *Chin* mrr1 coli jl2 cupr mrr1 cupr-ar br1 *Eucal* br1 ferr-ma br1 gard-j vlr2• kali-bi br1 kali-sula c1 lina br1 linu-u br1 micr br1 *Podo* mrr1 skat br1
  - **accompanied** by:
    - **sleepiness**: ant-t tl1
    - **Forehead**; cold perspiration on: ant-t tl1 verat tl1
    - **Tongue**; brown mucus on: colch hr1*
  - **hysteria**; with (See MIND - Hysteria - intestinal)
  - **nervousness**; with | **children**; in (See MIND - Excitement - nervous - children; MIND - Excitement - nervous - children - intestinal)

○ • **Muscles**: merl br1
- **Liver** (See Liver)
- **Lower** abdomen: agar b2.de* agn b2.de* aloe bg2 alum b2.de* am-c b2.de* am-m b2.de* *Ambr* b2.de* anac b2.de* ang b2.de* ant-c b2.de* ant-t b2.de* *Apis* b7a.de arg-met b2.de* *Arn* b2.de* ars b2.de* asaf b2.de* asar b2.de* *Aur* b2.de* *Bar-c* b2.de* **Bell** b2.de* *Bism* b2.de* borx b2.de* bov b2.de* **Bry** b2.de* calad b2.de* *Calc* b2.de* camph b2.de* cann-s b2.de* canth b2.de* *Caps* b2.de* carb-an b2.de* **Carb-v** b2.de* *Caust* b2.de* cham b2.de* chel b2.de* *Chin* b2.de* cic b2.de* cina b2.de* clem b2.de* *Cocc* b2.de* coff b2.de* colch b2.de* *Coloc* b2.de* con b2.de* croc b2.de* cupr b2.de* *Cycl* b2.de* dig b2.de* dros b2.de* dulc b2.de* euph b2.de* euphr b2.de* ferr b2.de* graph b2.de* guaj b2.de* hell b2.de* hep b2.de* hyos b2.de* *Ign* b2.de* iod b2.de* *Kali-c* b2.de* kali-n b2.de* laur b2.de* led b2.de* lil-t bg2 **Lyc** b2.de* m-ambo b2.de* m-arct b2.de* m-aust b2.de* mag-c b2.de* mag-m b2.de* mang b2.de* meny b2.de* *Merc* b2.de* *Merc-c* b4a.de mez b2.de* mosch b2.de* murx bg2 nat-c b2.de* nat-m b2.de* nit-ac b2.de* nux-m b2.de* *Nux-v* b2.de* olnd b2.de* par b2.de* ph-ac b2.de* *Phos* b2.de* plat b2.de* plb b2.de* puls b2.de* **Ran-b** b2.de* rheum b2.de* rhod b2.de* rhus-t b2.de* *Ruta* b2.de* sabad b2.de* sabin b2.de* samb b2.de* sars b2.de* seneg b2.de* **Sep** b2.de* *Sil* b2.de* *Spig* b2.de* spong b2.de* **Squil** b2.de* *Stann* b2.de* staph b2.de* stront-c b2.de* sul-ac b2.de* sulph b2.de* *Tarax* b2.de* tarent bg2 teucr b2.de* *Thuj* b2.de* ust bg2 valer b2.de* *Verat* b2.de* verb b2.de* vib bg2 viol-t b2.de* zinc b2.de*
- **Mesenteric** glands: ars bg2* ars-i bro1 bac bro1 bar-c bg2* bar-m bro1 bell bg2 *Calc* bg2* calc-ar br1 calc-f bro1 *Calc-i* bro1 chim br1 chin bg2 cina bg2 con bro1 frag br1 graph bro1 iod bro1* iodof bro1 lap-a bro1 lyc bg2 *Merc-c* bro1 mez bro1 *Nux-v* bg2 puls bg2 rhus-t bg2 sul-i ptk1 **Sulph** bg2 tub bro1*
  - **accompanied** by | **Extremities**; emaciation of: sil mtf11
- **Muscles** (See Muscles)
- **Pancreas** (See Pancreas)
- **Pelvic** organs: cimic br1 *Lil-t* br1
  - **accompanied** by | **vertigo**: aloe bro1 con bro1
  - **chronic** | **women**; in: med br1
- **Pelvis**: med ptk1

○ • **Around**: sabin ptk1 sep ptk1 vib ptk1
▽ • **extending** to | **Thighs**: thyr ptk1 vib ptk1
- **Peritoneum**: *Acon* bg2 ars bro1 asaf bro1 bell bg2* bov bro1 **Bry** bg2 cann-i bro1 carb-v bro1 cham bg2 *Chim* bro1 coff bg2 coloc bg2 *Cycl* bro1 *Hyos* bg2 kali-bi bro1 lyc bro1 mela bro1 merc bro1 *Nux-v* bg2 *Ol-an* bro1 *Paeon* bro1 rhus-t bg2 *Sanic* bro1 santal bro1 sel bro1 **Sulph** bg2 tell bro1
  • **accompanied** by | **Ovaries**; inflammation of (See FEMALE - Inflammation - ovaries - accompanied - peritoneum)
- **Pubic** region (See Pubic)
- **Sides** (See Sides)
- **Small** intestines: podo br1
- **Spleen** (See Spleen)
- **Transversely** across abdomen: *Chel* ptk1
- **Umbilicus** (See Umbilicus)
- **Upper** abdomen: *Acon* b2.de* agar b2.de* agn b2.de* am-c b2.de* am-m b2.de* ambr b2.de* anac b2.de* ant-c b2.de* ant-t b2.de* *Arn* b2.de* ars b2.de* asaf b2.de* asar b2.de* aur b2.de* bar-c b2.de* bell b2.de* borx b2.de* bov b2.de* bry b2.de* *Calad* b2.de* *Calc* b2.de* camph b2.de* cann-s b2.de* *Canth* b2.de* caps b2.de* *Carb-v* b2.de* **Caust** b2.de* **Cham** b2.de* *Chel* b2.de* **Chin** b2.de* *Cina* b2.de* **Cocc** b2.de* colch b2.de* coloc b2.de* con b2.de* croc b2.de* cupr b2.de* cycl b2.de* dig b2.de* dros b2.de* dulc b2.de* euphr b2.de* ferr b2.de* guaj b2.de* hell b2.de* hep b2.de* hyos b2.de* *Ign* b2.de* *Iod* b2.de* ip b2.de* kali-c b2.de* kali-n b2.de* lach b2.de* laur b2.de* *Lyc* b2.de* m-ambo b2.de* *M-arct* b2.de* m-aust b2.de* mag-m b2.de* meny b2.de* *Merc* b2.de* merc-c b4a.de mez b2.de* mosch b2.de* mur-ac b2.de* nat-c b2.de* *Nat-m* b2.de* nux-m b2.de* **Nux-v** b2.de* olnd b2.de* op b2.de* par b2.de* petr b2.de* ph-ac b2.de* *Phos* b2.de* plat b2.de* plb b2.de* **Puls** b2.de* ran-b b2.de* ran-s b2.de* rhod b2.de* rhus-t b2.de* ruta b2.de* sabad b2.de* sabin b2.de* samb b2.de* seneg b2.de* sep b2.de* sil b2.de* spig b2.de* spong b2.de* stann b2.de* *Staph* b2.de* stram b2.de* stront-c b2.de* sul-ac b2.de* sulph b2.de* tarax b2.de* teucr b2.de* thuj b2.de* valer b2.de* verat b2.de* verb b2.de* viol-t b2.de* zinc b2.de*
  • **mental** exertion agg.: arg-n br1

▽ - **extending** to:
○ • **Axillae**: bell bg2 nat-s bg2
• **Backward**: arn ptk1 **Ars** ptk1 **Bell** ptk1 borx ptk1 carb-v ptk1 chel ptk1 con ptk1 cupr ptk1 ferr ptk1 kali-p ptk1 lyc ptk1 nux-v ptk1 **Phos** ptk1 plb ptk1 puls ptk1 sep ptk1 sulph ptk1 *Tab* ptk1
• **Bladder**: cic bg2
• **Chest**: aeth ptk1 ars bg2 *Cham* ptk1 *Chel* bg2 con bg2 ign bg2 lach ptk1 mag-m bg2 nat-p bg2 plb bg2 spig bg2 tarent bg2
• **Fingers**: caust bg2
• **Forward**: thuj ptk1
• **Genitals**: arg-met bg2 ars bg2 bell bg2 clem bg2 kreos bg2 lyc bg2 nat-c bg2 nat-s bg2 nux-v bg2 phos bg2 plb bg2 puls bg2 ruta bg2 sulph bg2 teucr bg2
• **Groins**: puls ptk1
• **Lower** limbs: lyc bg2
• **Mammae**: plb bg2
• **Penis**: lyc bg2 puls bg2
• **Scapulae** | **right**: nat-m bg2
• **Scrotum**: verat-v ptk1
• **Shoulder**: lach bg2
• **Testes**: bell bg2 gels bg2 plb bg2 *Puls* bg2
• **Thighs**: alum bg2 apis bg2 bry bg2 cact bg2 calc bg2 cham bg2 cimic bg2 coloc bg2 con bg2 gels bg2 lil-t bg2* mag-m bg2 mag-p ptk1 nat-m bg2 nux-v bg2 plb bg2 podo bg2 sabal ptk1 sabin ptk1 sep bg2 spig bg2 staph bg2* thuj bg2 thyr ptk1 vib bg2 xanth bg2
• **Throat**: caust bg2 ign bg2 plb bg2
• **Upper** limbs: lach bg2 phys bg2 plb bg2 ran-b bg2 rhus-t bg2
  ⁝ **Fingers**; and: caust bg2
• **Upward**: acon ptk1 alum bg2 **Ars** ptk1 bry bg2 calc ptk1 *Carb-v* ptk1 gels bg2 kali-bi ptk1 kali-c ptk1 lac-ac ptk1 lach bg2 nux-v bg2 sabad ptk1
  ⁝ **right**: acon ptk1 kali-c ptk1 mag-m ptk1 **Murx** ptk1 seneg ptk1 sep ptk1
  ⁝ **left**: alum ptk1 ign ptk1 *Naja* ptk1 *Nat-s* ptk1 spong ptk1 zinc ptk1
• **Urethra**: nat-m bg2
• **Vagina**: calc-p bg2

COMPRESSION:
○ - **Liver**: ars bg2
- **Upper** abdomen: seneg bg2

CONGESTION: (↗GENERALS - Plethora) *Acon* bg2 aloe bg2* alum bg2 am-c bg2 ant-c bg2 ant-t bg2 *Apis* bg2 aq-mar rbp6 *Arn* bg2 *Ars* bg2 *Asaf* bg2 **Bell** bg2 brom bg2 **Bry** bg2 calad bg2 *Calc* bg2 cann-xyz bg2 canth bg2 caps bg2 carb-an bg2 carb-v bg2 cham bg2 **Chin** bg2 cic bg2 coloc bg2 crot-t bg2 dig bg2 dulc bg2 euph bg2 ferr bg2 *Fl-ac* bg2 graph bg2 hep bg2 hyos bg2 ign bg2 iod bg2 ip bg2 kali-c bg2 kali-n bg2 lach bg2 laur bg2 *Lyc* b4a.de* *Mag-m* b4a.de *Merc* bg2 merc-c bg2 mez bg2 **Nux-v** bg2 op bg2 petr bg2 ph-ac bg2 *Phos* bg2 plat bg2 *Plb* bg2 *Puls* bg2 **Rhus-t** bg2 sabin bg2 sars bg2 sel bg2 **Sep** bg2 *Sil* bg2 spig bg2 spong bg2 squil bg2 stann bg2 stram bg2 sul-ac bg2 **Sulph** bg2 *Thuj* bg2 verat bg2 zinc bg2
- **accompanied** by | **hemorrhoids**: aesc bro1 *Aloe* bro1 coll bro1 ham bro1 neg bro1 nux-v bro1 sep bro1 *Sulph* bro1

○ - **Hypochondria**; of: hep h2
- **Intestines**: canth tl1
- **Liver**; of: abies-c bro1 *Aesc* hr1* aesc-g bro1 agar bg2* aloe bro1* anth vh1 *Apoc* hr1* ars bro1 *Asaf* hr1* *Aur-m-n* sne *Berb* bro1 berb-a bro1 brass bro1 *Bry* bro1 cact bg2 caps bg2 *Card-m* hr1* cham bro1 chel bro1 chelo bro1 chin bro1 chinin-s bro1 *Chol* br1 cimx hr1* coll tl1 croc bro1 dig bro1 diph-t-tpt jl2 euon bro1 euon-a br1 eup-per bro1 ham k2* hep b4a.de* *Hydr* bro1 *Iris* bro1 kali-bi bro1 *Kali-chl* hr1 *Kali-m* kr1* *Lach* bro1 *Led* hr1 lept bro1 *Lyc* bro1 *Mag-m* bro1 merc bro1* merc-c hr1 *Merc-d* bro1 *Morg* fmm1• muc-u bro1 nat-s bro1 nit-ac bro1 nit-m-ac bro1 **Nux-v** hr1* phos bro1* pic-ac bro1 podo bro1* ptel tl1 quas bro1 sel bg2 senn bro1 sep bg2* stel bro1 still bro1 **Sulph** hr1* trom bro1 *Vip* bro1
  • **accompanied** by:
    ⁝ **constipation**: aesc br1
    ⁝ **Kidney**; congestion in (See KIDNEYS - Congestion - accompanied - liver)
    ⁝ **Skin**; yellow discoloration of: ptel tl1
  • **acute**: cact mtf11
  • **chronic**: am-m bro1 cact mtf11 *Chel* bro1 chin bro1 *Chol* bro1 con bro1 *Hep* bro1 hydr bro1 iod bro1 *Kali-c* bro1 lept bro1 *Lyc* bro1 mag-m bro1 merc bro1 merc-d bro1 nat-s bro1 *Podo* bro1 sel bro1 *Sep* bro1 *Sulph* bro1 *Vip* bro1
- **Pelvis**: *Aloe* bro1 *Berb* br1 card-m br1 coll br1* *Sep* bro1 sulph bro1
  • **accompanied** by | **dropsy**: card-m br1
  • **women**; in: *Coll* br1
- **Portal** (See Portal)
- **Spleen**: grin br1
  • **accompanied** by | **Stomach**; pain in: grin br1

CONSCIOUS of the abdomen: limen-b-c hrn2•
○ - **Pelvis**: sanguis-s hrn2•

CONSTIPATION agg.: sil b4a.de

CONSTRICTION: aesc k* *Alum* k* alum-p k2 alum-sil k2 *Alumin* alumn k* ambr c1 apis b7a.de *Arg-n* k* *Arn* k* ars k* ars-s-f k2 aur-m k* bell k* berb k* *Cact* k* *Calc* k* camph carb-an k* carb-v k* carc mg1.de* *Carl* caust bg2 cench chel k* chin k* clem k* coc-c k* cocc k* **Coloc** k* con b4a.de* crot-c cupr dig k* dros k2 euph k* euphr b7.de* ferr-ar ferr-m k* gent-c a1 graph bg2 hydrc k* hydroph rsj6• ign b7.de* kali-bi k* kali-c a1 kali-n h2* kali-sil k2 kola stb3• lach bg2 laur k* *Lim* a1 lipp a1 *Lyc* k* *Mag-c* b4a.de mag-m b4a.de merl k* mez k* mosch k* nat-m k* nat-s k* nit-ac k* nux-m k* *Nux-v* k* olib-sac wmh1 petr k* phos k* *Plat* k* *Plb* k* positr nl2• puls b7.de* ruta b7.de* sabad b7a.de* sabin a1 sars k* *Sec* k* seneg b4a.de *Sep* sil k* suis-em rly4• sul-ac k* sulph k* thuj k* tub c verb b7a.de* zinc h2*
- **morning**: ambr c1 calc k* kola stb3•
- **forenoon**: kali-n h2
- **night**: phos sulph k*
  • **midnight**:
    ⁝ **after** | **4** h: nat-m
- **accompanied** impeded respiration (See RESPIRATION - Impeded - accompanied - abdomen)
- **band** or hoop; as from a: (↗Band around) plat b4a.de

○ • **Umbilicus** | **Region** of umbilicus: bell bg2 puls b7a.de* verb bg2
- **breathing** agg.: caust h2
- **clothes** are too tight; sensation as if: mosch ptk1
- **cough** agg.; during: lach

Abdomen

- **diarrhea**; before: laur
- **eating**; before: hep h2
- **fasting** agg.: carb-an k* hep a1
- **flatus**; passing | **amel.**: sars h2 sil
- **lying** agg.: zinc k*
- **menses**; during: cact cocc croc *Sulph*
- **rhythmical**: caust k*
- **rising** agg.: zinc k*
- **sensation** of: nat-m a1
- **stool**:
  - **after** | **agg.**: *Nux-v* bg2 *Rheum* bg2
  - **amel.**: kola stb3•
  - **during** | **agg.**: sulph k*
  - **urging** to | **during**: ars k* nat-m k* nat-s
- **string**, as by a: caust cench k2 **Chel** k* plat tl1
  - ○ **Intestines**; as if: elaps verat
- **walking**:
  - **agg.**: nat-m k*
  - **air** agg.; in open: nux-v
- **warm** applications | **amel.**: kola stb3•
- ○ **Colon**: con b4a.de
- **Gallbladder**: acon bg2
- **Hypochondria**: *Acon* k* *Arg-n* k* asaf b7.de* asar b7.de* **Cact** k* *Calc* k* *Chel* k* *Con* k* **Crot-c** dig k* *Dros* k* euph bg2 *Ign* b7.de* kreos k* lil-s a1 **Lyc** k* nat-m bg2 nux-m bg2 *Nux-v* k* *Plat* b4a.de puls k* sep staph k* sulph k* tarent k*
  - **right**: *Lach*
  - **left**: cortico tpw7*
  - **daytime**: cortico tpw7*
  - **morning**: ign k*
  - **night** | **amel.**: cortico tpw7*
  - **accompanied** by impeded respiration (See RESPIRATION - Impeded - accompanied - hypochondrium)
  - **bandage**; as if by a: alum ars bg2 *Cact* *Calc* carb-v bg2 chel **Cocc** k ● **CON** k ●* graph k* **Lyc** k ●* *Sec* thuj bg2
    - ⁝ **supper** agg.; after: *Sep*
  - **cough** agg.; during: *Dros* k*
  - **excitement** agg.: cortico tpw7
  - **laced**, as if: *Calc* k*
  - ▽ **extending** to | **Umbilicus**: mag-c k*
- **Hypogastrium**: bar-c *Bell* k* carb-an h2 *Chel* k* clem k* coloc k* euon *Hydr* k* hyos ptk1 kola stb3• sars k* thuj k* verb
  - **forenoon**: sars k*
  - **evening**: sars k*
- **Inguinal** region: bov k* cact k* gamb k* kali-n k* (non:mag-c h2) rat k*
  - **right**: mag-c h2
  - **stretching** | **amel.**: bov k*
  - ▽ **extending** around pelvis: *Cact* k*
- **Liver**; region of: *Con* b4a.de *Dig* b4a.de
- **Lower** abdomen: bell bg2 con b4a.de mag-c b4a.de nat-m bg2 puls bg2 verb b7a.de*
- **Sides**: dros k2
  - **left**: lac-h sk4•
  - ○ **Ribs**; below false:
    - ⁝ **extending** to | **Abdomen**: camph
- **Umbilicus**: bell k* **Coloc** k* mang pd plb k* puls sil k* verb
  - **urination** agg.; during: *Puls* b7a.de
  - ○ **Region** of umbilicus: cench k2 coloc k* lac-h sk4• mag-m k* nat-m k* nit-ac k* petr k* *Plat* k* plb k* suis-em rly4• thuj k* verb k*
- **Upper** abdomen: *Seneg* b4a.de
- ▽ **extending** to:
  - ○ **Bladder**: **Puls**
  - **Chest**: *Calc* k* mang a1 sulph a1
    - ⁝ **stool**; before: nat-s

CONTRACTION: acon k* aeth a1 aids nl2• *Alum* b4a.de am-c k* ant-t apis k* arg-met k* ars k* *Aur* b4.de* *Bell* k* *Brom* b4a.de calc b4.de* carb-an b4.de* carb-v b4.de* caust k* *Cham* k* chel k* *Chin* b7.de* *Cocc* b7.de* colch k* *Coloc* b4.de* con k* *Cupr* k* dig k* dros k* euph b4.de* ferr k* graph b4.de* hep k* hydrc k* ign k* *Ip* b7.de* kali-bi bg2 kali-c b4.de* kali-i k* kali-n b4.de* kreos b7a.de* lach k* lat-m bnm6• laur k* *Lyc* k* mag-c b4.de* *Mag-m* k* mag-p bg2* mang b4a.de* merc k* merc-c k* mez b4.de* mosch bg2 mur-ac k* naja nat-c h2 nat-m b4a.de* nat-s bg2 nit-ac k* *Nux-v* k* *Olnd* k* *Op* bg2 petr b4.de* ph-ac k* phos k* plat b4.de* *Plb* k* rheum b7.de* rhus-t k* sabad k* sabin b7.de* *Sars* k* sec b7.de* sep k* sil k* spig b7.de* squil b7.de* *Staph* b7a.de sul-ac k* sulph k* tab k* tarent thuj b4.de* *Verat* b7a.de

- **morning**: ph-ac k*
  - **bed** agg.; in: nat-m h2
  - **rising** agg.; after: mag-c h2
  - **waking**; on: colch k*
- **forenoon**: am-c k*
  - **walking** in open air agg.: am-c k*
- **evening** | **bed** agg.; in: dros h1
- **night**: sil k*
- **bed**; when going to: naja
- **cough** agg.; during: *Chel* k* dros squil k*
- **diarrhea**, before: mag-c h2
- **expiration** agg.; during: dros h1
- **hourglass**: rhus-t ptk1
- **leukorrhea** agg.: con b4a.de kreos b7a.de *Nat-m* b4a.de sep b4a.de
- **lying** | **abdomen**; on | **amel.**: am-c h2*
  - **amel.**: am-c a1*
- **menses**:
  - **after** | **agg.**: con nat-m
  - **before** | **agg.**: am-c k* eupi k* *Nat-m* k*
  - **during** | **agg.**: *Am-m* b7a.de *Coff* b7a.de con b4a.de *Nux-v* b7a.de
- **pressure** | **amel.**: am-c h2
- **rhythmic**, with palpitation: caust
- **sitting** agg.: dig h2
- **stool** | **after** | **agg.**: arg-met sulph k*
  - **during** | **agg.**: ph-ac k*
- **touch** agg.: colch ptk1
- **twitching**: nat-c h2 nat-m h2
- **walking**:
  - **agg.**: apis arg-met
  - **air**; in open | **must** walk in open air: con
- ○ **External** abdomen: arg-met b7.de* bry bg2 canth b7.de* chin b7.de* cupr ptk1 *Ferr* b7a.de *Hyos* b7.de* m-arct b7.de olnd b7.de* rhus-t b7.de* sabad b7.de* squil b7.de* verat b7a.de
- **Hips**; region of: clem b4.de* *Con* b4a.de dros b7.de* laur b7.de* nit-ac b4.de*
- **Hypochondria**: *Alum* b4a.de am b7.de* bufo bg2 camph b7.de* chin b7.de* *Con* b4.de* *Dig* b4a.de **Dros** b7.de* ign b7.de* ip b7.de* led b7.de* lyc bg2 mag-c b4.de* mang h2 *Nux-v* b7.de* puls b7.de* sep b4.de* sil bg2 *Stann* b4a.de staph b7.de* sul-ac b4.de* sulph b4.de* zinc b4.de*
  - **right**: sulph h2
  - **left**: bar-c h2
  - **cough** agg.; during: **Dros** b7.de*
  - **menses**; during: bufo
- **Hypogastrium**:
  - **night**: phos h2 sil h2
  - **cough** agg.; during: *Dros* b7.de* squil b7.de*
  - **menses**; during: sulph h2
    - ⁝ **extending** to genitalia: nit-ac h2
- **Ileum**: helo-s bnm14•
- **Inguinal** region: aids nl2• arg-n k* carb-an k* laur k* rat rhus-t k*
  - **evening**: kali-n h2
  - **dinner**; after: laur k*
  - **menses**; during: arg-n k*
  - **stool**:
    - ⁝ **amel.**: kali-n h2
    - ⁝ **during** | **agg.**: laur bg2

- **Inguinal** region: ...
  - **stretching** out leg, on: carb-an k*
  - **urination** agg.; during: ars k*
  - **walking** agg.: kali-n k*
  - ○ **Glands**: nit-ac b4.de*
  - ▽ **extending** to | **Downward**: laur k*
- **Intestines**: arec br1 arge br1 bell bro1 chin mtf11 coli jl2 helo-s bnm14•
- **Liver**: bell b4.de* bufo bg2 canth b7a.de* gels bg2 lyc bg2 nat-c b4.de* nux-m bg2 phos b4.de* rhus-t b7.de* sep bg2 sulph bg2
- **Lower** abdomen: apis b7a.de aster sze10• bar-c b4.de* bell b4.de* calc b4.de* caust b4.de* chin b7.de* cina b7.de* clem b4.de* *Cocc* b7a.de *Coloc* b4.de* con b4.de* dros b7.de* graph b4a.de laur b7.de* m-arct b7.de merc b4.de* nat-m bg2 nit-ac b4.de* nux-v b7.de* phos b4.de* *Plat* b4a.de puls b7.de* sabin b7.de* sars b4.de* sep b4.de* *Sulph* b4a.de thuj b4.de*
- **Muscles**: arg-met cocc tl1 **Cupr** k* ferr hyos h1 *Kali-br* *Kreos* lat-m bnm6• mosch h1 nat-m nat-n k* *Plb* sabad squil k* *Tab*
  - **exertion** agg.: ferr c1
  - **hysterical** women; in: *Bry* cocc *Mosch*
  - **stooping** agg.: ferr c1
  - **walking** agg.: arg-met
- **Pubic** region | **urination** agg.; during: ars b4.de*
- **Sides**: am-c b4.de* bar-c b4.de* bov b4.de* cham b7.de* chin b7.de* ign b7.de* laur b7.de* mang b4.de* nit-ac b4.de* nux-m b7.de* petr b4.de* phos b4.de* sep b4.de* spong b7.de* sulph b4.de*
  - **right**: sep h2
  - **left**: aids nl2• dulc h2 phos h2
    - **lying** on right side agg.: spong h1
    - **sitting** agg.: spong h1
- **Spleen**: agar bg2 all-c bg2 bar-c b4.de* dulc b4.de* ferr bg2 *Graph* b4a.de spong b7.de* stann bg2
- **Trunk** | **painful**: *Cocc* br1
- **Umbilicus**: acon b7.de* anac b4.de* asaf b7.de* *Bell* k* *Chel* k* cocc **Coloc** k* gamb k* graph b4.de* kreos k* mag-m b4.de* *Mang* k* merc-c b4a.de mosch b7a.de *Nat-c* k* nat-m bg2 *Ph-ac* k* phos k* *Plat* k* plb k* *Puls* b7a.de ran-s b7.de* rhus-t b7.de* sulph k* thuj k* verb b7.de*
  - **hard** twisted ball; as of a: kreos
  - **inspiration** agg.: anac h2
  - **sleep** agg.; during: *Plat*
  - ○ **Above**: rhus-t a1
  - **Below**: graph h2 phos h2
  - **Region** of umbilicus: coloc mrr1
- **Upper** abdomen: asar b7.de* borx b4a.de *Calc* b4.de* caust b4.de* chel b7.de* chin b7.de* cocc b7.de* ign b7a.de mosch b7.de* nux-m b7.de* plb b7.de* puls b7.de* thuj b4.de*
- ▽ **extending** to | **Chest**: con h2 mang h2

CORD connecting anus and navel; sensation of: | **cutting** pain when straightening up from bending forward; with: *Ferr-i*

CORYZA agg.; after: arg-n bg2

CORYZA; from suppressed: calc b4a.de

COUGH:
- **after** | **agg.**: *Hyos* b7.de*
- **agg.**: anac ptk1 ant-t ptk1 bry ptk1 dros ptk1 lyc ptk1 *Nux-v* ptk1 pall ptk1 phos ptk1
  - ○ **Hypochondria**: dros ptk1 *Eup-per* ptk1 kali-c ptk1 nat-s ptk1
  - **Spleen**: bell ptk1 card-m ptk1 *Chinin-s* ptk1 squil ptk1 sul-ac ptk1 sulph ptk1
- **during**:
  - **agg.**: ambr b7.de* anac b4.de* arn b7a.de *Ars* b4.de* bell b4a.de borx b4a.de canth b7.de* carb-an bg2 caust bg2 chin bg2 clem bg2 *Cocc* b7a.de *Coloc* b4.de* con b4.de* crot-t bg2 *Dros* b7a.de* ferr b7.de* hyos bg2 ip b7.de* kali-bi bg2 kali-n b4.de* kreos bg2 lyc b4.de* *Nux-v* b7.de* ph-ac b4.de* phos b4.de* puls b7.de* sep b4.de* squil b7.de* stann b4.de* staph bg2 sulph bg2 verat b7.de*
    - **Hypochondria**: *Acon* b7.de* am-m b7.de* ambr b7.de* arn b7.de* ars b4.de* *Bry* b7.de* *Cocc* b7.de* **Dros** b7.de* eup-per bg2 hell b7.de* kali-bi bg2 *Merc* b4.de* nat-s bg2 *Nux-v* b7.de* phos b4.de* *Psor* bg2 puls b7.de* sabad b7.de* sep bg2 spong b7.de* sul-ac b4.de* valer b7.de*

Cough – during – agg.: ...
- **Liver**: bry ptk1 chinin-s ptk1 dros ptk1 eup-per ptk1 hep ptk1 kali-c ptk1 nat-s ptk1

COVERING:
- **agg.**: camph lach bg2 lil-t bg2 phos bg2 *Sec* *Tab*
- **amel.** (See Coldness)

CRACKING and crackling: caust h2 coloc h2 kali-bi bg2

CRACKS on surface of abdomen: *Sil* k*

CRAMP (See Pain - cramping)

CRAWLING (See Formication)

CROAKING (See Rumbling - croaking)

CROHN'S Disease (See Inflammation - colon; Inflammation - intestines)

CURRENT; sensation of a: m-ambo b7.de

DANCING:
- **agg.** | **Hypochondria**: borx b4a.de

DELIVERY agg.; during: *Arn* bg2 bell bg2 bry bg2 *Cham* bg2 coloc bg2 hyos bg2 lach bg2 nux-v bg2 puls bg2 sep bg2 verat bg2

DIARRHEA:
- **accompanied** by nausea (See RECTUM - Diarrhea - accompanied - nausea)
- **after**:
  - **amel.**: canth b7.de* nat-c bg2
  - **sensation** as after diarrhea: ant-c h2
- **alternating** with nausea (See RECTUM - Diarrhea - alternating - nausea)
- **eructations** amel. (See RECTUM - Diarrhea - eructations)
- **flatus** passing; after (See RECTUM - Diarrhea - flatus)
- **sensation** as if diarrhea would come on: *(↗RECTUM - Diarrhea - sensation; RECTUM - Diarrhea - sensation as before)* act-sp aeth agar k* ail k* *Aloe* alum-sil k2 am-c am-m ant-c h2 apis apoc k* *Asaf* bamb-a stb2.de• bar-c *Bell* bol-la *Borx* bros-gau mrc1 **Bry** k* calc *Camph* carb-an carb-v h2 carbn-s caust cham chir-fl gya2 cimic cob colch k* coloc k* *Con* *Crot-t* k* cystein-l rly4• dig **Dulc** k* eupi k* ferr form k* graph k* hell helon k* **Hydr** k* hyos h1 irid-met srj5• kali-bi k* *Kali-c* ketogl-ac rly4• kola stb3• *Lach* k* laur led k* lil-t k* lith-c lob mag-m mag-s k* melal-alt gya4 meny meph merc-i-f k* naja *Nat-s* nit-ac h2 **Nux-v** k* olnd onos *Opun-v* a1 ox-ac k* petr h2 *Ph-ac* *Phos* k* phys phyt plac-s rly4• plan k* *Plat* k* positr nl2• prun ptel k* *Puls* k* **Ran-s** k* rhus-t rumx sabin sars h2 *Seneg* *Sep* *Stry* k* sulph k* sumb ter k* thiam rly4• verat zinc [tax jsj7]
  - **drinking** agg.; after: *Caps* a1
  - **menses**; during: bamb-a stb2.de•
- **set** in; as if diarrhea would (See sensation)
- **stool**, after a normal (See RECTUM - Diarrhea - alternating - constipation - diarrhea)
- **tobacco**; after smoking: borx h2

DINNER:
- **after** | **agg.**: agar bg2 alum bg2 anac bg2 calc bg2 *Carb-v* bg2 coloc bg2 crot-t bg2 euphr bg2 grat bg2 kali-bi bg2 lyc bg2 *Mag-c* bg2 mag-m bg2 nat-m bg2 phos bg2 sep bg2 sulph bg2 thuj bg2 zinc bg2
- **amel.** | **Hypochondria**: nat-m bg2
- **before** | **agg.**: *Nux-v* bg2

DISAGREEABLE sensation: ant-t bg2 asaf bg2 aur bg2 cycl bg2 mur-ac bg2 nat-c bg2 nat-m bg2
- **lying** on abdomen agg.: ulm-c jsj8•
- ○ **Hypochondria**: lyc bg2

DISCHARGE from umbilicus: *(↗Inflammation - umbilicus)* *Abrot* k* aids nl2• ambro c2 *Calc* *Calc-p* dulc fd4.de *Kali-c* **Lyc** k● marb-w es1• med alj moni rfm1• *Nat-m* nux-m stann
- **accompanied** by | **emaciation** (See GENERALS - Emaciation - children - newborns - accompanied - umbilicus - discharge)
- **bloody** fluid: abrot vh *Calc* *Calc-p* *Nux-m*
  - **children**; in: | **newborns**: abrot mtf33 calc-p mtf33
- **children**; in: | **newborns**: abrot mrr1*

- **offensive**: aids nl2• moni rfm1•
- **urine**, oozing from: hyos bro1*
- **yellow**: aids nl2• nat-m ptk1

DISCOLORATION:

- **black**: vip
  - **bluish**: aeth c1
  - **spots**; in: vip
- **blotches**: aloe crot-t
- **blue**: ars b4a.de calc b4a.de
  - **spots**; in: *Ars* k* ars-s-f k2 mosch k*
    - ⁝ **Hypochondria**: con b4a.de
  - ○ **Epigastrium**: *Cupr* b7a.de puls b7a.de
- **brown** spots: ars carb-v caul bro1 *Cob* hydr-ac kali-c *Lach* **Lyc** k* nit-ac *Phos* k* sabad **Sep** k* *Thuj* k* wies a1
- **greenish**: rob k*
- **inflamed** spots: ars bell canth *Kali-c* *Lach* led lyc nat-m **Phos** sabad *Sep*
- **redness**: anac k* plb plb-chr a1 *Rhus-t* k* sang ptk1
  - **network**; like a: *Brom* b4a.de
  - **points**: sabad b7a.de
  - **spots**: bell k* caps b7.de* crot-t k* hyos k2* kali-bi k* *Lach* k* led k* manc k* *Merc* nat-m pd rhus-t k* sabad k* sep k*
  - **streak**: par b7.de*
    - ⁝ **Navel**; curved above: par pd
  - ○ **Epigastrium** | **Spots**: lyc h2 nat-m b4.de*
  - **Glands**; inguinal: merc b4.de*
  - **Pubic** region | **Mons** pubis: rhus-t b7.de*
  - **Umbilicus**: morg-p fmm1• phys ptk1 thuj mtf33
    - ⁝ **Below**: rhus-t b7.de*
- **spots**: bell bg2 canth bg2 lach bg2 *Phos* bg2 sabad bg2 sep bg2
- **yellow**: phos k* thuj b4a.de
  - **brown** spots: *Cob* **Lyc**
  - **spots**: ars berb canth k* carb-v cob ptk1 *Kali-c* k* *Lach* *Phos* k* sabad sep k* *Thuj* k*
    - ⁝ **old** spots around navel peeling off: berb hr1*

DISPLACEMENT:

○ - **Pelvis**:
  - **tilted** | **right** side; to: plut-n srj7•

DISTENSION:

(↗Enlarged; Flatulence; STOMACH - Distension) abies-c br1 *Abrot* k* absin br1* acal br1* acet-ac k* **Acon** k* acon-ac rly4• acon-c k* aesc k* *Aeth* **Agar** k* agath-a nl2• aids nl2• *All-c* k* allox sp1 **Aloe** k* *Alum* k* alum-sil k2 alumn am-c k* am-m k* ambr k* *Anac* k* anan androc srj1• anis mtf11 *Ant-c* k* *Ant-t* k* anthraci vh1 anthraq rly4• *Apis* k* *Apoc* aran-ix sp1 *Arg-met* k* **Arg-n** k* arge-pl rwt5• arist-cl sp1 *Arn* k* **Ars** k* ars-i k* ars-s-f k2 *Asaf* k* asar k* aur k* aur-ar k2 aur-m k* *Aur-m-n* wbt2• aur-s k2 bac jl2 *Bapt* k* *Bar-c* k* *Bar-i* *Bar-m* bar-ox-suc rly4• bar-s k2 bell k* *Berb* beryl sp1 bism k* *Bit-ar* wht1• borx k* botul jl2 *Bov* k* *Brom* k* brucel sa3• *Bry* k* bufo k* but-ac sp1 cact k* cadm-met sp1 cain calad k* **Calc** k* calc-ar k2 calc-f sp1 calc-i k2 calc-p k* calc-s cann-i k2 cann-s b7.de* *Canth* k* *Caps* k* *Carb-ac* k* *Carb-an* k* **Carb-v** k* carbn-dox knl3• **Carbn-s** card-m k* carl k* carneg-g rwt1• cartl-s rly4• castm *Caust* k* cedr k* *Cham* k* *Chel* k* **Chin** k* *Chinin-ar* *Chinin-s* chir-fl gya2 chlam-tr bcx2• chord-umb rly4• **Cic** k* cimic *Cina* k* cinnb k* *Cist* cit-ac rly4• clem k* coc-c k* **Cocc** k* coff k* coff-t a1 **Colch** k* coli rly4• coll **Coloc** k* *Con* k* cop *Corn* k* *Croc* k* *Crot-h* k* *Crot-t* k* *Cupr* k* *Cycl* k* cystein-l rly4• *Dig* k* *Dios* c2 dol br1* dream-p sdj1• dulc k* dys pte1*• *Eup-per* euph b4.de* euphr b7.de* fago k* falco-pe nl2• ferr k* ferr-ar ferr-i k* ferr-p fil c2 fum rly1*• fuma-ac rly4• *Gamb* k* gard-j vlr2• ger-i rly4• germ-met srj5• gink-b sbd1• gins k* *Glycyr-g* cte1• gran k* **Graph** k* grat k* guat sp1 haliae-lc srj5• ham fd3.de• *Hell* k* **Hep** k* hydr k2 *Hyos* k* hyper k* ictod k* ign k* *Iod* k* ip k* irid-met srj5• jal br1 *Jatr-c* jug-r k* *Kali-ar* k* *Kali-bi* k* **Kali-c** k* kali-chl k* *Kali-i* k* *Kali-n* k* *Kali-p* *Kali-s* k* ketogl-ac rly4• kola stb3• *Kreos* k* *Lac-c* *Lac-d* k2* lac-e hrn2• lac-h htj1*• lac-leo sk4• lac-loxod-a hrn2• **Lach** k* lact k* lap-la sde8.de• laur k* lavand-a ctl1• led k* lept mtf11 *Lil-t* k* limest-b es1• lob k* luna kg1• **Lyc** k* m-ambo b7.de *M-arct* b7a.de m-aust b7.de* **Mag-c** k* *Mag-m* k* mag-p k2* mag-s k* manc k* mand sp1* mang k* mang-p rly4• med tl1 *Meny* k* **Merc** k* *Merc-c* k* *Merc-d* k* *Mez* k* mill k2 mim-p rsj8• morg-g pte1*• mosch k* mucs-nas rly4• *Mur-ac* k* *Murx* k* myos-a rly4• naja bg2 nat-ar **Nat-c** k* **Nat-m** k* **Nat-p** k* nat-pyru rly4•

Distension: ...
Nat-s nept-m lsd2.fr nicc k* nicotam rly4• *Nit-ac* k* nux-m k* *Nux-v* k* oci-sa sp1 ol-an k* *Olnd* b7a.de onos vml3• *Op* k* opun-s a1 osteo-a knp1• ox-ac k* oxal-a rly4• pall pant-ac rly4• par b7.de paraf c2 *Petr* k* **Ph-ac** k* phasco-ci rbp2 **Phos** k* pin-con oss2• pitu-p sp1 plac-s rly4• plan a1* *Plat* k* plb k* plut-n srj7• podo k* positr nl2• pot-e rly4• prun k* psil ft1 *Psor* k* ptel k* *Puls* k* pulx br1 pyrid rly4• pyrog k* **Raph** k* rauw sp1 rein a1 rheum k* *Rhod* k* *Rhus-t* k* rhus-v k* rob k* *Ruta* b7.de* sabin k* sal-fr sle1• samb k* sang k* sanguis-s hrn2• sanic bro1 saroth sp1 sars k* *Sec* k* *Sep* k* *Sil* k* sphing a1* spig k* spong k* squil k* *Stann* k* *Staph* k* *Stram* k* *Stront-c* k* stroph-s sp1 suis-em rly4• suis-hep rly4• sul-ac k* **Sulph** k* sumb k* suprar rly4• syc pte1*• symph fd3.de• tab k* tarent k* **Ter** k* tetox pin2• thiam rly4• *Thuj* k* *Til* k* *Trios* rsj11• tritic-vg fd5.de tub jl2 (non:uran-met k) uran-n urol-h rwt• vac br1* *Valer* k* vanil fd5.de vario ptk1 *Verat* k* verb k* vero-o rly4*• vip k* visc sp1 yuc mtf11 *Zinc* k* zinc-val mtf11 zing k* [calc-n stj1 heroin sdj2 spect dfg1 tax jsj7]

- **morning**: aloe ars k* asaf k* *Cham* chin k* chinin-ar dulc fd4.de falco-pe nl2• grat k* ketogl-ac rly4• mur-ac a1 nat-c hr1 nat-s nit-ac k* *Nux-v* ol-an k* pant-ac rly4• rhod *Sulph* k* vanil fd5.de
  - **fasting** agg.: dulc k*
  - **waking**; on: anthraq rly4• bry k2 falco-pe nl2• mur-ac k* nat-c nit-ac k* plan k* podo fd3.de• raph k* sulph h2 vanil fd5.de
- **forenoon**: croc k* kali-s fd4.de lil-t k* podo fd3.de• spong fd4.de
- **noon**: sulph k* vanil fd5.de
  - **sleep** agg.; after: con k*
  - **walking** agg.: coloc k*
- **afternoon**: *Calc* k* calc-s k* *Carb-v* k* *Castm* caust k* cham k* chinin-s con k* dulc fd4.de fago k* grat k2 kali-n k* mag-c h2 mag-m h2 nat-c k* osm k* petr k* podo fd3.de• rat k* rein a1 sep k* stann k* stront-c *Sulph* k* tritic-vg fd5.de vanil fd5.de
  - **16** h: lyc sep bg1
    - ⁝ **16**-20 h: **Lyc** vh *Sulph* vh
  - **eating**; after: bry k*
- **evening**: acon k* am-m h2 *Ant-c* k* *Bry* k* calc vh carb-v k* carneg-g rwt1• caust k* cedr k* cham k* choc srj3• con k* crot-t k* dulc fd4.de falco-pe nl2• fuma-ac rly4• grat k2 ham fd3.de• *Hell* k* hyper k* kali-n h2 lyc k* lyss mag-c k* mag-m h2 mag-s k* mur-ac k* nat-c k* nat-m nat-sil fd3.de• nept-m lsd2.fr nux-m k* osm k* petr plat k* podo fd3.de• psil ft1 rhod ruta sang hr1* *Sep* spong fd4.de stram k* *Sulph* tritic-vg fd5.de urol-h rwt• vanil fd5.de zinc k*
  - **18** h: choc srj3• sulph
  - **19** h: caust choc srj3•
  - **lying**:
    - ⁝ **agg.**: hyos k*
    - ⁝ **amel.**: mur-ac h2
- **night**: alum arg-met h1 chlam-tr bcx2• dulc fd4.de haem k* hyper k* kali-s fd4.de *Mag-c* k* merc-c k* nat-c h2 ptel k* *Sulph* k* valer k*
  - **midnight**: bov k* (non:coc-c kl) **Cocc** h1*
    - ⁝ **after**: ambr k* lac-e hrn2• phos
- **accompanied** by:
  - **emaciation** (See GENERALS - Emaciation - accompanied - abdomen - distention)
  - **hiccough**: mag-p bg2
  - **leukorrhea** (See FEMALE - Leukorrhea - accompanied - abdomen - swelling)
  - **nausea**: ulm-c jsj8•
  - **pain** (See Pain - accompanied - distension)
  - **palpitations** (See CHEST - Palpitation - accompanied - abdomen)
  - **respiration**; painful: but-ac sp1
  - **stool**; complaints of (See STOOL - Complaints - accompanied - abdomen - distention)
  - ○ **Head**; pain in (See HEAD - Pain - accompanied - abdomen - distension)
  - **Heart**; pain in (See CHEST - Pain - heart - accompanied - abdomen)
  - **Hypochondrium**; pain in | **right**: aran-ix sp1
  - **Lips**; thick: syph ptk1

- · **Liver**; enlarged (See Enlarged - liver - accompanied - abdomen)
- · **Stomach**; pain in pit of (See STOMACH - Pain - pit - accompanied - abdomen)

- **alternating** with:
- ○ · **Chest**:
  - ⁝ **constriction** (See CHEST - Constriction - alternating - abdomen - distension)
  - ⁝ **pressing** pain (See CHEST - Pain - pressing - alternating)
- **anticipation**; from: lyc vh
- **beer**; after: *Nat-m* k*
- **breakfast** | **after** | **agg.**: agar k* bit-ar wht1• chinin-ar dulc fd4.de nat-m k* podo fd3.de• sin-a a1
  - · **during**: alum k*
- **breathing** | **hindering** breathing: *Caps* a1 con h2 kali-p fd1.de•
- **burst** through the mouth; as if everything would: asaf tl1
- **children**; in●: (*↗emaciation - limbs - children*) **Bar-c** k* bell mtf33 **Calc** k* calc-p mtf33 **Caust** k* cham mtf33 *Cina* k* cupr ferr mtf33 graph mtf33 kali-c mtf33 lyc mtf33 sil k* staph **SULPH** k ●* thuj mtf33
  - · **infants**: lat-m bnm6•
  - · **potbellied** children: (*↗GENERALS - Obesity - children*) sanic c2* staph mtf33
- **chill**; during: ars k* ars-h k* cina *Kali-c* lach k* lyc k* mez k* nux-v b7a.de puls k* rhus-t k* sil b4a.de spig b7.de sulph bg2
- **coffee**: | **amel.**: phos h2
- **constipation**; during: alum h2 am-c h2 bry ery-a graph hyos iod *Lach* mag-m nit-ac ph-ac h2 phos podo fd3.de• sep h2 *Tell* rsj10• ter k*
- **contradiction**; after: nux-m hr1
- **convulsions**; before epileptic: cupr k* *Lach*
- **cough** | **agg.**: rauw sp1
- **diarrhea** agg.; after: mag-c h2
- **diarrhea**, with: acet-ac mtf11 aloe k2 cench k2 mag-c h2 sep h2 sil h2
  - · **amel.**: nat-c h2
- **dinner** | **after** | **agg.**: alum k* anac k* calc k* carb-an **Carb-v** k* euphr k* grat k* hep h2 iod h lyc k* mag-c k* mag-m k* *Nat-m* k* nicc k* *Nux-m* phos k* podo fd3.de• *Sep* k* sulph k* *Thuj* k* til k*
  - · **before**: all-c k* euphr h2 sphing a1*
- **drinking** agg.; after: ambr k* ars k* calc h2 *Carb-v* **Chin** coloc hr1 ferr-i k2 hep k* merc sne mur-ac b4a.de nat-m b4a.de* *Nux-v* k* petr k* rhus-g tmo3•
- **eating**:
  - · **after** | **agg.**: agar *Agn* b7a.de* aloe alum k* alum-sil k2 ambr k* anac k* *Ant-c* k* arg-n mtf33 arn b7a.de ars k* ars-s-f k2 asaf k* *Borx* k* *Brucel* sa3• *Bry* k* calc k* calc-s calc-sil k2 caps k* carb-ac k* *Carb-an* k* **Carb-v** k* carbn-s caust k* *Cham* k* **Chin** k* chinin-ar *Colch* k* coli jl2 con k* cortiso gse dig b4a.de* dream-p sdj1• dulc k* falco-pe nl2• ferr-i k2 *Graph* k* hep b4a.de hippoc-k szs2 ign k* ignis-alc es2• iod b4a.de jug-r k* kali-ar **Kali-c** k* kali-m k2 kali-p kali-s kali-sil k2 *Kreos* lac-h htj1• *Lil-t* **Lyc** k* mag-c k* mag-m h2 mag-s mand sp1 marb-w es1• moni rfm1• mur-ac k* nat-ar *Nat-c* k* *Nat-m* k* nat-p nat-pyru rly4• nat-s mtf33 nat-sil fd3.de• nept-m lsd2.fr *Nux-m* k* **Nux-v** k* par b7a.de petr k* ph-ac b4a.de phos k* plat b4a.de plb k* podo fd3.de• positr nl2• psor k* *Puls* k* raph k* rheum k* rhus-g tmo3• *Rhus-t* k* ruta fd4.de *Sep* k* *Sil* sin-a a1 spong fd4.de **Sulph** tarent ter k* *Thuj* k* tritic-vg fd5.de vanil fd5.de *Zinc* k* zinc-p k2 [helia stj7]
  - · **agg.** | **flatus**; with: ambr k1
  - · **small** quantities | **agg.**: cench k2 dulc fd4.de **Lyc** tl1* rauw sp1 tritic-vg fd5.de
  - · **while** | **agg.**: con b4a.de dulc k* graph k* ign mand sp1 nux-m cka1
- **emaciation**; with:
  - ○ · **Body**; of the: abrot tl1 bar-c tl1* calc tl1* iod tl1 nat-m tl1 sanic mrr1 sil tl1* sulph tl1
  - · **Legs**; of the: abrot mtf33
  - · **Limbs**; of the: calc k2 sil mtf33 sulph k2*
    - ⁝ **children**; in: (*↗children*) sil mtf33 sulph mtf33
- **eructations**: (*↗STOMACH - Distension - eructations*)
  - · **amel.**: calc-f sp1 cann-i k2 *Carb-v* cassia-s ccrh1• hep gk **Lyc** mrr1 sep thuj
  - · **not** amel.: **Chin** mrr1 falco-pe nl2• lyc gk phos h2
- **excessive**: arg-n mtf33 asaf tl1 *Carb-v* mtf33 chin tl1 colch tl1 coloc tl1
- **fat** food; after: bell-p sp1
- **flatulence**:
  - · **from**: aegle-f zzc1• aloe bg2 alum b4.de* ant-c b7.de* cham b7.de* lyc tl1 myos-a rly4• petr h2 phos b4.de*
  - · **sensation** as if distended by flatulence: con h2 graph h2* hep h2
- **flatus**; passing:
  - · **amel.**: aegle-f zzc1• all-c am-m ant-t bism hr1 bov bry calc h2* *Carb-v* cassia-s ccrh1• chir-fl gya2 *Kali-i* **Lyc** k* *Mag-c* mag-m h2 mang mur-ac h2 nat-c nat-m nept-m lsd2.fr *Ph-ac* saroth sp1 *Sulph*
  - · **not** amel.: arg-n mrr1 **Chin** mrr1 phos h2 podo fd3.de• positr nl2•
  - · **with**: aids nl2• ambr k1 *Ango* c1 arg-n tl1 bit-ar wht1• *Carb-v* tl1 cassia-s ccrh1• cham tl1 *Chin* tl1 chir-fl gya2 choc srj3• cocc tl1 colch tl1 dys pte1* *Lyc* tl1 nicotam rly4• podo hr1* pycnop-sa mrz1 suis-hep rly4• *Trios* rsj11*•
- **grief**; from: calc vh coloc vh
- **hard**: *Kali-c* ptk1
- **heat**; during: ars k* *Carb-v* bg2 chin bg2 colch bg2 cupr bg2 ferr bg2 nux-v bg2 rhus-t bg2 sec bg2 sep bg2 sil k* *Stram* b7.de* sulph bg2 ter bg2 verat bg2 vip bg2
- **here** and there: carb-an h2 ign hr mag-m h2* nat-c bg2
- **hot**: merc-d ptk1
- **hysterical**: tarax ptk1
- **labor**:
  - · **after**: *Lyc* k* **Sep** k*
  - · **during**: kali-c
- **leukorrhea** agg.: *Graph* b4.de*
- **localized** swellings; with distinct: canth b7.de* cocc b7.de* m-ambo b7.de plb b7.de*
- **loosening** clothes amel.: ignis-alc es2• lyc tl1 mag-p tl1 onos ptk1
- **lying**:
  - · **agg.**: carb-v ptk1
  - · **amel.**: mur-ac a1
- **menses**:
  - · **after** | **agg.**: cham kreos lil-t mag-c h2 rat
  - · **before** | **agg.**: am-m k* anthraq rly4• apoc bro1 aran bro1 arn berb carb-an carb-v cham bro1 chin k* *Cocc* bro1 con b4a.de cycl granit-m es1• hep k* kali-c bro1 kreos k* *Lach* *Lyc* k* mang k* nux-v bro1 *Puls* sal-al blc1• suis-em rly4• thuj b4a.de tritic-vg fd5.de *Zinc*
  - · **during** | **agg.**: aloe alum k* apoc bro1 aran bro1 arge-pl rwt5• berb brom carb-an k* cham bro1 *Chin* k* chlam-tr bcx2• **Cocc** k* coff croc cycl graph ham hep k* ign *Kali-c* k* kali-p kreos k* lac-c lachn lyc k* mag-c k* *Nat-c* k* *Nicc* k* nicotam rly4• nit-ac k* nux-v k* puls k2 rat sinus rly4• **Sulph** k* zinc k*
  - · **suppressed** menses; from: cham b7a.de* rat k*
- **mental** exertion; from: hep *Nux-m*
- **metrorrhagia**; during: hep b4a.de *Ip* b7a.de
- **milk** agg.: carb-v h2 **Con** k*
- **mortification**; from: *Calc* vh *Coloc*
- **mothers**; in●: iod kali-c hbh nat-c **Sep** k ●
- **motion** | **amel.**: chin hr1 kali-c h2 mand sp1 phos h2
- **operation**; after: carb-an ptk1 hyper ptk1
- **pain** in pit of stomach, with (See STOMACH - Pain - pit - accompanied - abdomen)
- **painful**: (*↗Flatulence - painful*) **Acon** k* *Aeth* hr1 agath-a nl2• alum androc bnm2• ant-t arg-met h1 **Ars** k* *Bar-c* k* bell k* *Brucel* sa3• *Bry* k* calad canth **Caust** k* cham k* chin b7.de* cic hr1 croc b7.de* *Euph* b4a.de falco-pe nl2• germ-met srj5• hedeo br1 hell k* *Hyos* k* ign b7.de* ip b7.de* kali-bi k2 kali-c b4.de* kali-i kali-p k2 kali-s fd4.de **Lach** k* lap-la sde8.de• mag-p k2 melal-alt gya4 **Merc** k* merc-c k* mez h2 nat-c nat-m neon srj5• nit-ac k2 nux-v petr b4.de* raph bro1 rhod b4.de* **Rhus-t** k* sabin b7.de* sep h2* sphing a1* spig b7a.de* spong fd4.de stann h2* stram b7.de* stront-c bg2 sulph tritic-vg fd5.de valer bg2 verat
  - · **accompanied** by | **menses**; absent: castm ptk1
  - · **bending** backward | **amel.**: visc sp1
  - · **flatus**; passing | **amel.**: visc sp1
  - · **menses**; during: coff b7a.de *Ign* b7a.de *Nux-v* b7a.de
  - · **pressure** agg.: *Cina* hr1
  - · **touch** agg.: hyos h1 squil h1

- **painless**: *Ant-c* b7a.de bit-ar wht1• *Hyos* b7a.de
- **pregnancy**:
  - • **as** from pregnancy: vario ptk1
  - • **during** | **agg.**: calc-f sp1
- **radishes**; after: mand sp1
- **riding**, on: sep h2
- **rising** agg.: sep k*
- **rubbing** | **amel.**: chir-fl gya2 choc srj3•
- **sensation** of: agar bg2 allox sp1 apis bg2 ars bg2 bar-c bg2 bell bg2 cann-xyz bg2 caps b7a.de* chel bg2 coch br1 con bg2 dulc bg2 grat bg2 hell bg2 lach bg2 merc-c bg2 morg-g fmm1• nat-m bg2 *Nux-v* bg2 petr bg2 phos bg2 phyt bg2 psor bg2 puls bg2 rhod bg2 rhus-t b7.de* sep bg2 stram bg2 sulfa sp1 sulph bg2 tab bg2 thuj bg2 valer b7.de* visc sp1 [tax jsj7]
- **sitting** agg.: nat-s
- **soup** agg.: mag-c sep k*
- **spots**, in: bell bg2 bov bg2 cocc bg2 coloc bg2 grat bg2 ign bg2 *Mag-m* k* manc k* nat-c bg2 plat h2 plb b7a.de* *Puls* b7a.de ruta bg2 til a1
- **stool**:
  - • **after** | **agg.**: agar k* ars k* asaf k* aur h2 bell bg2 *Carb-v* k* caust b4.de* con b4.de* *Graph* k* hep k* lil-t bg2 **Lyc** k* nat-m k* petr k* phos b4.de* samb bg2 sulph k* vinc a1
  - • **amel.**: alum k* am-m asaf k* calc-p k* chir-fl gya2 corn k* falco-pe nl2• hyper k* nat-c h2 nat-m k* sulph h2
  - • **before**: arn bg2 ars *Corn* fl-ac *Lyc* b4a.de merc b4a.de phyt sulph h2*
  - • **during** | **agg.**: carb-an b4.de* euph b4.de* graph b4.de* lyc b4a.de* *Mag-c* bg2 *Merc* b4a.de sep b4.de* stram k* sulph b4a.de* verat bg2
  - • **urging** to | **with**: bit-ar wht1•
- **stretching** lower limbs impossible: colch ptk1
- **sudden**: kali-i k* *Nat-m* k*
- **supper** agg.; after: alum k* *Arg-n* k* arn k* borx calc h2 *Chin* k* ol-an a1 sep k*
- **tympanitic**: (↗*Flatulence - obstructed)* acet-ac br1 aeth agar ail alum-p k2 ambr c2 anan ant-c *Ant-t* anthraco br1 apis k2 **Arg-n** *Arn* k* **Ars** ars-i ars-s-f k2 asaf c2 aur-m k2 aur-m-n wbt2• bapt k2 bell k* *Brom* k* bros-gau mrc1 *Bry* k* cadm-s br1 *Calc* calc-ar calc-i k2 calc-p calc-sil k2 *Canth* **Carb-v** k* carbn-s **Cham** k* **Chin** k* *Chinin-ar* **Cocc** k* **Colch** k* *Coloc* k* *Con* b4a.de crot-h crot-t *Cupr* dulc fd4.de *Erig* br1 *Eup-per* euph fago falco-pe nl2• ferr a1 *Graph* **Hyos** iod ip k2 kali-ar k2 *Kali-bi* kali-c mtf33 *Kali-p* kali-s kreos **Lach** laur **Lyc** k* mang *Merc* merc-c k* mez *Morph* k* mosch k2 *Mur-ac* *Nat-s* *Nux-v* b7.de* *Op* k* pert-vc vk9 *Ph-ac* **Phos** *Podo* puls b7.de* rham-cath c2 rhus-t k* sabin b7.de* *Sec* sep sil sol-ni c2 spong fd4.de *Stram* sul-i k2 sulph k* *Sumb* **Ter** k* *Thuj* til tub k2 verat b7.de* xan c1*
  - • **accompanied** by:
    - ⁝ **diabetes** (See GENERALS - Diabetes mellitus - accompanied - abdomen - distention)
    - ⁝ **fever**:
      - ⁝ **continued** (See FEVER - Continued - accompanied - tympanites)
      - ⁝ **typhoid** (See FEVER - Typhoid - accompanied - abdomen - distention)
  - • **hysterical**: *Tarax* br1
  - ○ • **Hypochondria** | **right**: pert-vc vk9
- **urination** agg.; before: chinin-s
- **vomiting** | **amel.**: aeth vh1
- **walking**:
  - • **about** | **amel.**: mag-p br1
  - • **air** agg.; in open: calc sep h2
  - • **impossible**: abrot vml3•
- **warm** room | **amel.**: cench k2
- **whooping** cough: kali-s ptk1
- **women**; in: luna kg1•
- ○ - **Cavity**: colch tl1
- **Colon**; transverse: alum mtf11 bell bg1* mit wd morg-g pte1*• sabad wsf syc pte1•
- **Duodenum**:
  - • **accompanied** by | **Pylorus**; contraction of (See STOMACH - Contraction - pylorus - accompanied - duodenum)
- **Hips**; region of: ant-c b7.de* chel b7.de*

Distension – Hips; region of: ...

  - • **urination** agg.; before: borx b4a.de
- **Hypochondria**: aloe k* asaf bg2 aur b4a.de bell k* calc k* *Carb-v* caust h2* cham k* *Chel* k* chin bg2 ferr hr1 hep bg2 ign k* laur k* *Merc* nux-m nux-v k* pert-vc vk9 phos bg2* sil bg2 sulph bg2 ter bg2
  - • **right**: aloe k2 brucel sa3• but-ac sp1 *Chel* k* cycl a1 laur k* lyc h2* *Nat-m* *Phos* k* podo *Sep* sil h2
  - • **left**: caust h2 chinin-ar hep h2 *Merc* mom-b c1 nat-c nit-ac tub k2
  - • **eating**; after: con b4a.de
  - • **sensation** of: m-ambo b7.de
  - • **stool** | **after** | **agg.**: caust h2
    - ⁝ **before**: ars h2
- **Hypogastrium**: aloe alum bell k* brom cann-s *Carb-v* caust chel coli rly4• erig vml3• grat *Hyos* k* *Ign* **Kali-c** k* kali-i lact laur *Lyc* tl1 mur-ac nat-m *Nat-s* nit-ac phos phys ptk1 plb k* ptel *Raph* sep mtf11 sil sul-ac tarent thuj h1
  - • **morning**: aloe
  - • **night**: alum h2
  - • **painful**: alum h2 chin h1
  - • **stool**; before: ars
- **Ileocecal** region: *Colch* fago mag-m
- **Inguinal** and pubic region | **sensation** of: am-m b7.de* m-aust b7.de*
- **Inguinal** region: am-c k* am-m k* cocc b7.de* kali-c k* m-aust b7.de nat-s
  - • **left**: calc h2
  - • **sitting** agg.: am-m k* kali-c k*
  - • **urination** agg.; during: euph b4.de* mez b4.de*
  - ○ • **Hernia**: nit-ac h2
- **Liver**: arn b7.de* *Bry* b7.de* *Calc* b4a.de *Cham* b7a.de chel bg2 *Iod* b4a.de *Kali-c* b4a.de lyc b4.de* *Merc* b4.de* *Merc-c* b4a.de nit-ac bg2 phos bg2 sep b4.de* *Sil* b4a.de* *Sulph* b4a.de *Thuj* b4a.de
- **Lower** abdomen: am-m b7.de* ambr b7.de* *Arn* b7.de* ars b4.de* *Bell* b4.de* canth bg2 chin b7.de* hell b7a.de kali-c b4.de* laur b7.de* nux-m bg2 nux-v b7.de* plb b7.de* *Rhus-t* b7a.de sulph bg2 thuj b4.de*
- **Sides**: am-c b4.de* bry b7.de* calc b4.de* canth bg2 *Caust* k* *Ign* b7.de* laur b7.de* led b7.de* **Nat-m** k* *Rhus-t* b7a.de zinc k*
  - • **right**: act-sp bg2 arn h1 brucel sa3• calc h2 cycl h1 pert-vc vk9 sil h2 spong fd4.de stann h2
  - • **left**: aloe dgt1 chir-fl gya2
- **Spleen**: am-c b4.de* *Brom* b4a.de carb-v b4a.de cham b7a.de hep b4a.de iod b4a.de* *Merc* b4.de* mez b4a.de nat-c b4.de* nat-m b4a.de nit-ac b4.de* *Sulph* b4a.de *Thuj* b4a.de
- **Umbilicus**:
  - ○ • **Below**: anthraq rly4• stroph-s sp1
  - • **Region** of umbilicus: acon bg2 bell bg2 bry b7.de* calc bg2* caust bg2 chel bg2 coloc k* gran bg2 ign k* *Kali-i* k* laur b7.de* lec lyc bg2 merc bg2 *Merc-i-r* k* nat-m bg2 nit-ac k* op k* phys ptk1 plb bg2 prun bg2 puls bg2 rhus-t k* spig b7.de*
    - ⁝ **Above**: sil h2
    - ⁝ **Under**: lyc mtf33
- **Upper** abdomen: acon b7.de* bell b4.de* *Bry* b7a.de *Carb-v* tl1 *Cham* b7.de* *Cocc* b7a.de *Con* b4a.de hell b7.de* hyos b7.de* iod b4.de* nat-c b4.de* nux-m b7.de* nux-v b7.de* puls b7.de* rhod b4a.de* *Sil* b4a.de *Stram* b7.de*
- ▽ - **extending** to:
  - ○ • **Groin** | **left**: sphing kk3.fr

DIVERTICULOSIS: thiop mtf11

DRAGGING: alum h2 caust h2
- ○ - **Waist**; down: visc ptk1*

DRAWING IN abdomen:
- **agg.**: acon b7.de* ambr b7.de* ant-t b7.de* asaf b7.de* asar ptk1 bar-c b4.de* bell b4.de* bov b4.de* ign bg2 lyc b4.de* nux-v ptk1 valer b7.de* zinc b4.de*
  - ○ • **Hypochondria**: ant-t b7.de* asaf b7.de* zinc b4.de*
- **amel.**: ign b7.de* lyc bg2
  - • **distending** abdomen agg.; and: *Ign* ptk1

DRAWN:
- **together**: arg-met bg2 sabad bg2
- **upwards**; as if contents are drawn: antip vh spong hr1*

DRAWN IN (See Retraction)

DRINKING:

- **agg.**: ambr b7.de* *Ant-t* b7.de* **Ars** b4a.de* asaf b7.de* aur b4.de* borx bg2 brom b4a.de* bry b7.de* carb-v bg2 caust bg2 cham bg2 *Chin* b7.de* cocc b7.de* coloc b4a.de* con b4.de* croc b7.de* ferr b7.de* hep b4a.de* ign b7.de* *Meny* b7.de* *Nat-m* b4a.de* nit-ac bg2 **Nux-v** b7.de* petr b4.de* phos bg2 *Plb* b7a.de puls b7.de* *Rhus-t* b7.de* sars bg2 spong b7.de* staph b7.de* **Sulph** b4.de* teucr b7a.de* thuj bg2 verat b7.de*
  - ○ **Hypochondria**: **Nat-c** bg2
- **water** | **agg.**: ars ptk1 bad ptk1 croc bg2 phos ptk1 teucr bg2 zing ptk1

DROPSY: (↗*GENERALS - Dropsy - internal)*

- **ascites**: abrot sne acet-ac k* acon k* adon br1* *Agn* k* alco a1 all-c c2 *Ambr* b7.de* *Ant-c* b7a.de **Apis** k* **Apoc** k* *Arg-n* k* **Ars** k* ars-s-f k2 asaf k* *Aur* k* *Aur-m* aur-m-n k* aur-s k2 bell b4a.de blatta-a br1* *Bry* k* cain br1* *Calc* k* calc-sil k2 camph b7.de* cann-s k* *Canth* k* carb-an sne carbn-s *Card-m* k* caust *Chel* *Chim* *Chin* k* *Chinin-ar* *Chinin-s* cinnm c2 coc-c br1 *Colch* k* coloc **Con** b4a.de cop bro1 crot-h cur *Dig* k* *Digin* bro1 *Dulc* k* euph b4a.de* ferr b7.de* ferr-ar *Fl-ac* k* *Graph* guaj b4a.de *Hell* k* helon hep k* iod h* iris kali-ar *Kali-br* k* *Kali-c* k* *Kali-chl* kali-i mtf11 kali-m k2 kali-p kali-s kalm lach bg lact lact-v c1* *Led* k* lept c2 **Lyc** k* *Mag-m* k* med k* *Merc* k* merc-sul mtf11 mill mur-ac ptk1 myric sne nat-hchls bro1 nat-m k2 nux-v k* oxyd br1* *Ph-ac* b4a.de *Phos* plb bg2* *Prun* k* ptel c1 puls k* querc-r-g-s mtf11 *Rhus-t* b7a.de sabin sacch c2 samb bro1 senec k* seneg b4a.de* sep k* sil k* sol-t-ae a1 spong k* squil k* *Sulph* k* **Ter** k* *Uran-n* br1*
  - **accompanied** by:
    - **diarrhea**; chronic: *Apoc* oena sil ptk1
    - **urine**; scanty: squil ptk1
    - **Heart**; complaints of the (See CHEST - Heart; complaints - accompanied - ascites)
    - **Liver**:
      - **cirrhosis** of (See Cirrhosis - accompanied - ascites)
      - **complaints** of the: lyc br1* querc-r-g-s br1
      - **induration** of: aur lact
    - **Pelvic** region; fold on: colch ptk1
    - **Peritoneum**; inflammation of: bry mtf11 rhus-t mtf11
      - **tubercular**: abrot mtf11
    - **Skin**; dry: cain br1
    - **Spleen**; disease of: agn c2 **Lach** kr1 querc c1 *Querc-r-g-s* br1 squil c1 verat c2
    - **Tongue**:
      - **yellow** | **dirty** yellow: *Ars* kr1*
  - **malignant**: rauw mtf11
  - **menses**; from suppressed: senec ptk1
  - **quinine**, after the abuse of: cann-s
  - **saccular**: cann-s b7a.de* chin b7a.de*
  - **suffocation** lying on left side: *Apis* k*
- **edema**: anan *Apis* *Ars* *Graph* tarent thuj
  - **hepatic** origin: tarax sp1
- **external**: *Colch* b7a.de

DRYNESS: bov bg2 dig bg2 plb bg2

DULLNESS: nit-ac bg2

DYSENTERY: (↗*RECTUM - Dysentery)*

- **after** | **Hypochondria**: aloe bg2

EATING:

- **after**:
  - **agg.**: agar b4.de agn b7.de *Alum* b4.de* am-m b7.de* *Ambr* b7.de* anac b4.de* *Ant-c* b7.de ant-t b7.de arg-met b7.de* arn b7.de ars b4.de asaf b7.de aur b4.de bell b4.de borx b4a.de bov b4.de *Bry* b7.de* *Calc* b4.de* cann-s b7.de canth b7.de caps b7.de carb-an b4.de *Carb-v* b4.de *Caust* b4.de* cham b7.de *Chel* b7.de* **Chin** b7.de* *Cic* b7.de cina b7.de *Cocc* b7.de coff b7.de colch b7.de *Coloc* b4.de* con b4.de croc b7.de dig b4a.de dulc b4.de* *Ferr* b7.de *Graph* b4.de hell b7.de *Ign* b7.de *Iod* b4.de* *Kali-c* b4.de* laur b7.de *Lyc* b4.de* m-ambo b7.de m-arct b7.de m-aust b7.de mag-c b4.de mag-m b4.de *Merc* b4.de mur-ac b4.de nat-c b4.de nat-m b4.de nit-ac b4.de *Nux-m* b7a.de *Nux-v* b7.de* par b7.de *Petr* b4.de* ph-ac b4.de *Phos* b4.de plat b4.de *Puls* b7.de ran-b b7.de* rheum b7.de* rhod b4.de

Eating – after – agg.: ...

Rhus-t b7.de ruta b7.de sars b4.de *Sel* b7a.de *Sep* b4.de* sil b4.de* spong b7.de* stann b4.de staph b7.de* stront-c b4.de sul-ac b4a.de *Sulph* b4.de* teucr b7.de thuj b4.de valer b7a.de verat b7.de verb b7.de zinc b4.de

- **Hypochondria**: anac b4.de* arg-n bg2 bry b7a.de* cann-s b7.de* canth b7.de* cham b7.de* cocc b7.de* graph b4a.de* lyc b4a.de* nux-v b7.de* *Plat* b4a.de plb b7.de* podo bg2 puls b7.de* sars b4.de* *Sel* b7a.de zinc b4.de*

- **amel.**: ambr bg2 ant-c bg2 arg-n bg2 bov b4.de* cocc bg2 graph bg2 laur b7.de* mag-c b4.de* mang b4.de* merc b4.de* mosch bg2 nat-c b4.de* *Plb* b7a.de* psor bg2 rhus-t b7.de* sabad b7.de* sep bg2 stann b4.de* sul-ac bg2 sulph b4a.de*
- **amel.**: anac ptk1 bov ptk1 *Chel* ptk1 *Graph* ptk1 hep ptk1 ign ptk1 kali-p ptk1 lach ptk1 mag-m ptk1 med ptk1 petr ptk1 *Zinc* ptk1
- **before** | **agg.**: colch b7.de euphr b7.de hep b4a.de puls b7.de seneg b4.de
- **overeating** agg.; after: ant-c ptk1 ars bg2 caps bg2 coff bg2* hep bg2 ip ptk1 nux-v bg2* *Puls* bg2*
- **satiety**; to:
  - **agg.** | **Hypochondria**: lyc b4.de*
- **small** quantities | **amel.**: coloc bg2
- **while**:
  - **agg.**: *Ars* b4a.de* *Bell* b4a.de chin b7.de cocc b7.de coff b7.de colch b7.de con b4a.de dig b4.de laur b7.de nux-v b7.de seneg b4.de
  - **amel.** | **Hypochondria**: *Chel* bg2

ECCHYMOSES: lach b7a.de phos bg2

EDEMA (See Dropsy - edema)

EFFUSION: | **Pelvic** cavity; into: *Brom* b4a.de

EMACIATION of muscles of abdomen: calc k2 plb k* sulph k2

- **accompanied** by | **swelling** of mesenteric glands: **Abrot** vh1

EMOTIONS agg.: calc bg2 caust bg2 lyc bg2 *Nux-m* b7a.de

○ - **Hypochondria**: phos bg2

EMPTINESS (= faintness): *Agar* k* ambr k2 ant-c k* **Arg-n** k* arn k* arum-m k* bell bg2 *Calc-p* k* *Carb-v* k* carc gk6 caust k* *Cham* k* *Cina* k* cob **Cocc** k* colch rsj2• *Coloc* k* croc k* *Crot-t* k* *Dig* *Dulc* k* euph k* euphr k* fl-ac k* *Gamb* k* gels k* guaj k* hep k* ip ptk1 jab k* *Kali-c* k* kali-m k2 kali-n b4.de* kali-p *Kola* stb3• lac-loxod-a hrn2• *Lach* k* lil-t k* lyc tl1 mag-c b4.de* *Merc* k* mez k* moni rfm1• *Mur-ac* k* naja *Nat-p* k* nicc k* nux-v b7.de* **Olnd** k* par b7.de* *Petr* k* *Ph-ac* **Phos** k* phys k* phyt bg2 plan k* plut-n srj7• **Podo** k* *Psor* ptel k* **Puls** k* rhod bg2 rhus-t b7.de* ruta k* sabad b7.de* *Sars* k* sec ptk1 seneg **Sep** k* squil k* **Stann** k* staph ptk1 **Sul-ac** k* sulph tl1 **Tab** k* teucr b7.de* tril-p c1 tritic-vg fd5.de tub k2* *Verat* k* zinc k*

- **morning**: euph k* mez k* ruta fd4.de sars k* tritic-vg fd5.de
  - **rising** agg.; after: mag-c k*
  - **stool** agg.; after: mur-ac k*
- **noon**: dios k*
  - **eating**; after: nat-p k* stann k* zinc k*
- **night**: puls
- **accompanied** by:
  - **nausea** (See STOMACH - Nausea - accompanied - abdomen)
  - ○ **Intestines**; knotted sensation in: cham ptk1
- **breakfast** agg.; after: arum-m arum-t c1 phos h2 sars k* tritic-vg fd5.de
- **burning** between shoulders: **Phos** k*
- **dinner**:
  - **after** | **agg.**: nat-p k* zinc k*
  - **amel.**: dios k*
  - **before**: nux-v
- **eating** | **after** | **agg.**: arum-m k* kali-bi k2 nat-p k* ruta fd4.de sars k* *Stann* k* zinc k*
  - **amel.**: ant-c k*
- **eructations** | **amel.**: ambr k2 *Carb-v* nat-s k2 *Sep*
- **fasting**; as if from: coloc bg2 lach b7.de* psor bg2 puls b7.de*
- **flatus**; passing | **after** | **agg.**: phos h2
  - **amel.**: ambr k2 nat-s k2

Abdomen

- **gnawing**: ox-ac ptk1
- **lying** on abdomen | **amel.**: puls
- **menses** | **before** | **agg.**: *Cocc* b7a.de
  - **during** | **agg.**: *Phos* sulph
- **painful**: *Cocc* bro1 hydr bro1 *Kola* stb3•
- **pressure** | **amel.**: caust k* naja **Puls**
- **stool**:
  - **after** | **agg.**: *Agar* ambr k2 apoc k* *Arg-n* *Carb-v* k* caust cob coloc k* con k2 jab k* *Kali-c* *Kali-s* k* *Lach* *Mur-ac* k* *Nat-p* *Olnd* **Petr** k* *Ph-ac* **Phos** k* *Pic-ac* **Podo** k* *Psor* *Puls* rhod k* *Sep* k* *Stann* **Sul-ac** k* sulph verat
  - **amel.**: mur-ac k*
  - **before**: verat h1
- **tightening** clothing amel.: *Fl-ac*
- **walking** agg.: carb-v k* *Phos*
- **wrapping** up the abdomen amel.: puls

O - **Hypochondria**: *Mur-ac* b4a.de
- **Hypogastrium**: kali-s ptk1 sec ptk1
  - **flatus**; passing | **amel.**: kali-s ptk1*
  - **stool** agg.; after: carb-v b4.de* mur-ac b4.de* podo bg2 rhod b4.de* sul-ac b4.de*
- **Lower** abdomen: pic-ac bg2
- **Side** | **left**: sep h2
- **Umbilicus**:

O • **Region** of umbilicus: calc-p bg2 carc gk6 cob bg2* dios bg2 fl-ac k* ptel bg2 scir c1
  ⁝ **hunger** felt in: valer pd*

▽ - **extending** to | **Vulva**: puls

ENLARGED: *(↗Distension; Swelling)* alum ptk1 *Ant-c* b7.de* **Apis** b7a.de arg-n bg2 ars bg2 *Bar-c* k* *Bar-i* bar-s k2 bell bg2 *Calc* k* calc-i k2 calc-p k2 caps bg2 *Carb-v* bg2* caust k* chel chin bg2 chion br1 cina bg2 colch ptk1 *Coloc* k* ferr-i k2 graph b4a.de* hep b4.de* *Iod* k* *Iris* kali-bi gk kali-c b4.de* laur b7.de* *Lyc* k* mag-m b4a.de mang b4a.de* nat-c b4a.de* nux-v bg2 ol-j *Olnd* b7a.de op gk podo *Psor* puls b7a.de* rhus-t bg2 *Sabin* b7a.de **Sanic** k* sec k* **Sep** k* *Sil* b4a.de* staph b7.de* sul-i k2 **Sulph** k* syph ptk1 tab ptk1 *Thuj* k* tril-p c1 vario ptk1 [heroin sdj2]

- **children**; in●: aloe sne alum ptk1 **Bar-c** k* **Calc** k* caust h2* cupr k* mag-m med gk nat-m sne phos mtf33 *Psor* k* *Sanic* k* *Sars* **Sil** k* staph mtf33 *Sulph* k*
  - **marasmus**: abrot tl1 bar-c k2* **Calc** k* iod tl1 nat-m tl1 plb hr1* *Sanic* *Sars* sil tl1* sulph tl1
  - **scrofulous**: ars bg2 bar-c bg2 bell bg2 *Calc* bg2 chin bg2 cina bg2 lyc bg2 *Nux-v* bg2 puls bg2 rhus-t bg2 **Sulph** bg2
- **delivery**; after: *Coloc* bg2 **Sep** bg2
- **fat**: *Am-m* ant-c bg2 ars bg2 bar-c bg2 *Calc* k* caps bg2 lyc bg2 puls bg2 *Sulph* bg2
- **maidens**; in young: calc bro1 *Graph* bro1 lach bg2* sulph bro1
- **mothers**●: coloc bg2 *Iod* k* nat-c k* **SEP** k ●*
- **Peyer's** patches: ars wl1 dros hs2*
- **sensation** as if: sep bg2

O • **Intestines** | **cylindrical** enlargements: tann-ac br1
- **women**; in matrons and old: *Bell* bg2 calc bg2 chin bg2 coloc bg2 nux-v bg2 *Plat* bg2 **Sep** bg2

O - **Glands**; inguinal: ars-i k2 sil mrr1 sul-i k2
- **Liver**: *(↗Swelling - liver)* aconin c2 aesc bro1 agar k* aloe ptk1 anders zzc1• anis c1 ant-t *Ars* k* ars-i aur aur-ar k2 aur-i k2 *Aur-m* aur-s k2 bar-m boerh-d bnj1 brass-n-o srj5• *Bry* bufo caesal-b zzc1• *Calc* *Calc-ar* k* calc-sil k2 *Carb-v* carc fb* card-m k* *Chel* k* **Chin** k* chinin-ar k* *Chion* k* *Cocc* coloc bro1 *Con* k* *Dig* k* eberth jl2 eup-per k2 *Ferr* ferr-ar c2* ferr-i k* ferr-p *Fl-ac* glyc bro1 graph bro1 *Hep* *Hippoz* k* hydr k* *Iod* k* kali-br hr1 *Kali-c* k* kali-s lac-e hm2• lach k* lact lat-m bnm6• *Laur* loxo-lae bnm12• loxo-recl bnm10• luf-b gsb1 **Lyc** k* mag-c mtf33 **Mag-m** k* mang-act bro1 *Merc* k* *Merc-d* bro1 merc-i-r mur-ac k2 *Nat-m* **Nat-s** k* *Nit-ac* *Nux-m* **Nux-v** k* *Phos* k* pin-s c2 plb k* *Podo* k* pop-cand c2 ptel sec k* sel k* senn br1 sep k2* sil stel bro1 sul-i k2 *Sulph* symph fd3.de• tab k* tarax bro1* thuj a1 toxo-g jl2 *Tub* k* urt-u vip c2* *Zinc* k* zinc-p k2
  - **left** lobe: *Mag-c* *Mag-m* k*
  - **accompanied** by:
    ⁝ **apyrexia**: nat-m bro1
    ⁝ **Abdomen**; distention of: mag-m mtf33

Enlarged – Liver – accompanied by: ...
  ⁝ **Skin** | **discoloration**; yellow: dig br1
  ⁝ **Spleen**; enlargement of: iod ptk1
  - **anger**; after: *Cocc*
  - **children**; in: calc-ar k* mag-c mtf33 mag-m mtf33 nat-s mtf33 *Nux-m* k* nux-v mtf33 phos mtf33 sep mtf33 zinc mtf33
    ⁝ **infants**: calc-ar c1
  - **chronic**: chol mtf11 mang ptk1
  - **drunkards**; in: absin bro1 am-m bro1 ars bro1 fl-ac bro1 lach bro1 nux-v hr* sulph bro1
  - **emaciation**; with: iod mrr1
  - **heart** disease; in: aur tl1* mag-m br1*
  - **painful**: nat-s mtf33
- **Lower** abdomen: *Sil* b4a.de
- **Mesenterica**: *Ars* *Ars-i* *Aur* *Bar-c* k* *Bar-i* bar-m bar-s k2 **Calc** calc-i k2 *Carb-an* *Con* *Form* *Hep* *Iod* nat-c k2 nat-s *Ol-j* sul-i k2 sulph
- **Spleen**: aconin c2 agar bro1 agn k* anders zzc1• *Anthraci* *Aran* k* *Ars* k* ars-br vh *Ars-i* k* ars-s-f k2 *Aur-m* k* bell-p bro1 brass-n-o srj5• brom ptk1 *Calc* calc-ar bro1* calc-i k2 *Caps* k* carb-v card-m bro1 **Cean** k* cedr bro1 **Chin** k* chinin-ar *Chinin-s* k* chion br1* cimx mtf11 *Cit-v* *Cocc* *Con* dros tj *Ferr* ferr-act bro1 ferr-ar k* ferr-i k* *Ferr-m* k* ferr-p grin bro1* *Helia* bro1 *Hippoz* hydr *Ign* **Iod** k* kali-br hr1 kali-m k2 *Lach* laur leucas-a mtf11 loxo-lae bnm12• loxo-recl bnm10• luf-b mtf11 mag-m k* malar bro1* merc-i-r k* *Nat-m* k* *Nit-ac* nux-m *Nux-v* *Op* *Ph-ac* k* *Phos* k* plb plb-i c2 polyg-h bro1 *Polym* bro1 **Querc** bro1* *Ran-s* rhus-t hr1 rub-t mtf11 ruta saroth sp1 squil ptk1 staphycoc jl2 succ bro1 *Sul-ac* k* sul-i k2 *Sulph* tab tinas mtf11 toxo-g jl2 tub ptk1* *Urt-u* k* xanrhi br1
  - **accompanied** by:
    ⁝ **apyrexia**: ars bro1 *Cean* bro1 chin bro1 chinin-s bro1 ferr bro1 nat-m bro1
    ⁝ **malaria** (See GENERALS - Malaria - accompanied - spleen)
  - **children**; in: calc-ar br1
  - **emaciation**; with: iod mrr1
  - **sensation** of: gard-j vlr2•

ENTERITIS (See Inflammation - small intestine)

ENTEROPTOSIS (See Hanging - intestines)

EPILEPSY, begins in: bufo

ERUCTATIONS:
- **after** | **amel.**: ambr b7.de* ant-t b7.de* apis b7a.de bapt bg2 bar-c b4a.de* calc-p bg2 cann-xyz bg2 carb-v b4.de* *Cocc* b7a.de colch b7.de* ign b7.de* kali-c b4.de* kalm bg2 lach bg2 mez bg2 nit-ac b4.de* phos b4.de* rhod b4.de* sep b4.de* sil b4.de* sulph b4.de* thuj bg2 *Verat* b7a.de zinc b4.de
- **agg.** | **Hypochondria**: caps b7.de* merc b4.de* zinc bg2
- **amel.**: ambr ptk1 bar-c ptk1 rat ptk1

O • **Hypochondria**: colch b7.de* pall bg2 *Plat* b4a.de sep b4.de* sulph bg2 *Verat* b7a.de
- **not** amel.: *Chin* ptk1 lyc ptk1

ERUPTIONS: agar k* anac k* *Apis* ars k* ars-s-f k2 bar-m k* bell bg2 bry k* calc *Graph* kali-ar kali-bi kali-c *Merc* k* merc-c k* *Nat-c* k* nat-m k* phos rhus-t k* ruta fd4.de spong fd4.de *Sulph* k* symph fd3.de• tritic-vg fd5.de tub c1 vanil fd5.de [heroin sdj2]
- **blotches**: crot-t merc nat-c tritic-vg fd5.de

O • **Umbilicus**; around: marb-w es1• propr sa3•
- **boils**: aln vva1• am-m b7a.de* phos k* rhus-t k* sec k* zinc k*

O • **Epigastrum**: *Euph* b4a.de
  - **Inguinal** region: ars k* merc k* *Nit-ac* k* phos k* rhus-t k* stram k*
    ⁝ **right**: osteo-a jl2
  - **Pubic** region | **Mons** pubis: rhus-t bg2
- **crusts**: anac am k* kali-c
- **desquamating**: merc k* vesp k*
- **eczema**: [heroin sdj2]

O • **Epigastrium**: *Ars* bg2
  - **Inguinal** region: moni jl2
  - **Umbilicus**; round: form fkr5.de merc-pr-r bro1 scroph-n c1 sulph ptk1* symph fd3.de•
- **herpes**: *Sep*

- herpes: ...
  - ringworm (See ringworm)
  - zona●: *Ars* k* *Graph* k* *Merc* k* *Puls* b7a.de *Rhus-t* k* *Sil* b4a.de *Sulph* k* *Thuj* k*
    - warm bed agg.: *Merc*
    - Sides | right: **Iris** k* *Thuj* vh
- ○ · Iliac region: *Tell* k*
  - · Inguinal region: **Graph** sal-al blc1• syc pte1*•
- itching: agar k* calc lac-h sk4• merc k* nat-m h2 petr-ra shn4• rhus-t k* staphycoc rly4• *Sulph* symph fd3.de• vanil fd5.de
- itch-like: merc k* *Nat-c*
- miliaria | Liver; region of: sel bg2
- moist: merc k*
- ○ · Groin; right | menses; before: sars ptk1
- nodules: nat-c h2 ruta fd4.de
- petechia: phos k2
- pimples: agar aloe arn k* ars k* ars-h k* bar-m bry k* cham b7.de* dulc k* fl-ac k* merc k* nat-c k* nat-m k* ozone sde2• petr k* rhus-t k* sel b7.de* spong fd4.de staph k* tritic-vg fd5.de
  - · burning on touch: petr h2
  - · itching: allox tpw3 aloe bry k* dulc k* nat-c k* spong fd4.de *Staph* k*
- pustular: *Ant-c* b7a.de crot-c crot-t k* kali-bi k* merc nat-m h2 puls squil k*
- ○ · Epigastrium: nat-m b4.de*
  - · Inguinal region: puls k* sep k*
  - · Loins: clem h2
  - · Pubic region | Mons pubis: apis bg2
- rash:
  - · fine, over liver region: sel c1*
  - · itching violently: *Calc*
  - · menses; before: *Apis* ars
    - Groins: *Apis* ptk1 ars ptk1
  - · red itching rash over the region of liver: *Sel*
- red: staphycoc rly4•
- ringworm: nat-m k* tell tub c1
- scabies: *Nat-c* b4a.de
- scales: arn kali-c k*
  - · yellow spots: kali-c k*
- ○ · Inguinal region: merc
- tetters | Epigastrium: *Ars* b4a.de
- urticaria: merc k* nat-c k* petr-ra shn4• tub c1
  - · evening: propr sa3•
- vesicles: arn k* caust crot-t kali-bi k* *Merc* k* merc-c k* podo fd3.de• rhus-t k* spong fd4.de vanil fd5.de
- ○ · Inguinal region: nat-c k* sal-al blc1•
  - · Pubic region | Mons pubis: apis bg2 rhus-t b7.de*
  - · Umbilicus; around: marb-w es1• spong fd4.de vanil fd5.de
- ○ - Epigastrium: *Ars* b4a.de
- Hypogastric region: cassia-s ccrh1•
- Inguinal and pubic region: alum b4.de* merc b4.de* phos b4a.de puls b7.de* sars b4.de* sulph b4.de*
- Inguinal region: alum cupr-ar k* *Graph* *Merc* k* morg-p pte1• ozone sde2• sulph vero-o rly3•
  - · right: sal-al blc1•
- Liver: sel b7a.de*
- Mons veneris: sil ptk1
- Pubic region | Mons pubis: sep bg2
- Umbilicus: abrot mrr1 dulc ptk1
- ○ · Around: staphycoc rly4•
  - children; in:
    - newborns; in:
      - accompanied by:
        - appetite; diminished: abrot mrr1
        - emaciation (See GENERALS - Emaciation - children - newborns - accompanied - umbilicus - eruption)

ERYSIPELAS: cop br1 graph k* *Merc* b4a.de
- contusion; from: apis c1
- ○ - Umbilicus | newborns; in: apis bro1

EXCORIATIONS: arn bg2 bry b7.de*
- ○ - Inguinal region: ambr c1 *Ars* arum-t *Bov* bry h1 *Graph* med c1 nux-v b7.de* ph-ac h2
  - · menses:
    - during:
      - agg.: bov sars h2
      - beginning of menses | agg.: sars b4.de
- Pubic region | Mons pubis: rhus-t b7.de*
- Umbilicus: thuj b4a.de

EXCRESCENCE at umbilicus; moist: *Calc* k* morg-p fmm1•

EXERTION agg.: alum b4a.de

EXPIRATION:
- agg.: cocc bg2 coff b7.de dig b4.de* dros b7.de* dulc bg2 rhus-t b7.de* ruta b7.de* spong b7.de* staph b7.de* viol-t b7.de*
- ○ · Hypochondria: chin b7.de* spig b7.de* verat b7.de*
- amel.: am-m b7.de* merc b4.de*

EXTENDING:
- extremities agg. (See Stretching - limbs - agg.)
- lower limbs | amel.: phys ptk1

FAINT feeling in (See Emptiness)

FALLING; sensation of:
- down; intestines falling: abrot br1* acet-ac a1* agn b7.de* laur k* m-arct b7.de *Nux-v* k* plb k* spig b7.de* *Staph* b7a.de
  - · exertion; from: laur hr1*
  - · lying on back agg.: acet-ac a1*
  - · talking agg.: laur hr1
- out of abdomen; intestines falling: *Alum* k* *Bell* b4a.de carb-an bg2 cocc bg2 coloc h2* ferr k* *Kali-br* k* kali-c bg2 *Kreos* b7a.de nat-c bg2 **Nat-m** k ●* *Nux-v* k* plb bg2 ran-b k* **Sep** k ●* staph bg2 tril-p bg2
  - · cough agg.: carb-an h2
  - · dinner; after: ran-b
  - · menses; before: alum b4a.de*
  - · stool agg.; during: kali-br k*
  - · walking:
    - agg.: ferr nat-m h2
    - carefully | must walk carefully: *Nux-v*
- ○ turning in bed; sensation as if intestines were falling down from Side to side: *Bar-c* k* *Merc* k* *Merc-c* k*

FASTING:
- agg.: acon b7.de* asar bg2 *Calc* bg2 croc b7.de* dulc bg2 nux-v b7.de* plat b4.de* sep bg2 staph b7.de* teucr b7.de*
- ○ · Hypochondria: staph b7.de*
- amel.: caust bg2* sil bg2*
- sensation (See STOMACH - Emptiness)

FAT: *Am-m* k* calc **Chel** k*
- accompanied by | emaciation; general: calc tl1

FAT FOOD agg.: carb-v bg2* chin bg2 colch bg2 nat-m bg2 *Puls* bg2*

FATTY DEGENERATION of liver: aur bro1 calc-f sp1 chel k* germ-met srj5• kali-bi bro1 kali-s k2 lac-d k2 *Lyc* lyss mang k2 mang-act br1 *Merc* k* phlor bro1 *Phos* k* pic-ac bro1* vanad bg2*

FERMENTATION: (↗*Flatulence; Rumbling*) acon bg2 agar k* ambr k* ang bg2 aran arg-met bg2 asaf bg2 brom k* *Bry* k* calc k* carb-ac br1 carb-an k* carb-v k* **Chin** k* coff k* croc *Ferr-i* mrr1 *Gran* hell k* *Hep* kali-c bg2 kali-p k2 **Lyc** k* mag-m k* merl mez bg2 mur-ac k* *Nat-m* k* nat-s k* *Phos* k* plb k* *Rhus-t* k* *Sars* k* seneg k* sep h2 stram k* sulph k* vip bg2
- fruit agg.: **Chin** k*
- menses; during: lachn **Lyc** *Phos*
- sensation of: agar bg2 chin ptk1 lyc ptk1 rhus-t bg2*
- stool:
  - · after | agg.: mez bg2
  - · before: sulph bg2
  - · during | agg.: mez bg2 sars bg2

FEVER: | before | agg.: chin b7.de* spong b7.de*

Abdomen

- **during** | **agg.**: ant-t b7.de chin b7.de cina b7.de ferr b7.de ip ptk1 puls b7.de rhus-t b7.de verat ptk1

FIBROSIS: | **Intestines**: penic mtf11

FISTULAE: | **Inguinal** glands; of: hep *Lach Phos Sil* sulph

FLABBY: borx mtf33 calc k2 calc-p mtf33 euph b4.de* ign b7.de* ix bnm8• mag-m bg2 merc b4.de* *Merc-d* br1 phos b4.de* rhus-t b7.de* sanic mrr1 sep b4.de*

- **children**; in: borx mtf33 calc-p tl1
- **feeling**: agar bg2 alum bg2 merc bg2 nat-m bg2 phos bg2 rhus-t bg2 sep bg2 sul-ac bg2
- **stool** agg.; after: mag-m bg2 sep bg2 sul-ac bg2

○ - **Lower** abdomen: nux-m bg2

FLATTENED (See Retraction)

FLATULENCE: (↗*Distension; Fermentation; Gas; Rumbling; RECTUM - Flatus)* *Abies-n* bro1 *Abrot* bro1 absin bro1* acal c2 acet-ac k2* acon b2.de* adon mtf11 aesc aeth *Agar* k* agath-a nl2• *Agn* k* alf bro1 all-c allox tpw3 **Aloe** k* alum k* alum-p k2 alumn am-c k* **Am-m** k* ambr k* ammc amp rly4• anac b2.de* anemps br1 ang b2.de* anis br1* *Ant-c* k* ant-t k* anthraq rly4• *Apis* k* apoc aq-mar skp7• arg-met b2.de* **Arg-n** k* arist-m br1 arn k* **Ars** k* *Ars-i* ars-s-f k2 asaf k* asar k* asc-c hr1 atis zzc1• *Aur* k* aur-ar k2 *Aur-m-n* wbt2• bacls-7 pte1• *Bamb-a* stb2.de• bapt bar-c k* bar-i bar-m bar-s k2 bell k* bism b2.de* bit-ar wht1• borx k* bov k* brom k* *Bry* b2.de* bufo bung-fa mtf cain *Caj* br1* calad b2.de* **Calc** k* calc-f k* calc-i c2* *Calc-p* **Calc-s** calc-sil k2 camph b2.de* cann-i k2 cann-s b2.de* canth b2.de* *Caps* k* *Carb-ac* k* **Carb-an** k* **Carb-v** k* **Carbn-s** carc br1* cartl-s rly4• cassia-s ccrh1• castm c2 *Caust* k* cephd-i bnj1 **Cham** k* *Chel* k* **Chin** k* *Chinin-ar Chinin-s* chir-fl gya2 chlf br1 choc srj3• chord-umb rly4• cic k* cina b2.de* cinnb cinnm br1 clem k* *Coca Coca-c* sk4• *Cocc* k* coff k* **Colch** k* coli jl2* coll k* *Coloc* k* *Con* k* *Cop* croc b2.de* *Crot-c Crot-t* cupr b2.de* cycl k* cygn-ol sze3• dendr-pol sk4• dig k* *Dios* k* dirc k* dream-p sdj1• dros b2.de* dulc b2.de* dys fmm1• *Elaps* enteroc jl2 eup-per euph k* euphr b2.de fago falco-ch sze4• falco-pe nl2• fel mtf11 ferr k* ferr-ar ferr-i ferr-ma c2* ferr-p fl-ac *Form* fuc br1* fum rly1*• fuma-ac rly4• galeoc-c-h gms1• gard-j vlr2• *Gels* gink-b sbd1• gins glon gran **Graph** k* *Guaj* k* hell k* helon hep k* hippoc-k szs2 hir rsj4• hom-xyz c2 **Hydr** k* hyos b2.de* hyper *Ictod* bro1 *Ign* k* indg indol bro1 *Iod* k* ip b2.de* iris bro1 jug-r k* junc-e c2* kali-bi kali-br a1 *Kali-c* k* kali-chl kali-i kali-m k2 *Kali-n* k* kali-p k* kali-s kalm ketogl-ac rly4• kola stb3• kreos b2.de* *Lac-c Lac-d* lac-del hrn2• lac-f wza1• lac-h htj1*• *Lach* k* lachn c1 lact br1 lap-la sde8.de• laur b2.de* led b2.de* lil-t *Lim* bro1 limen-b-c hrn2* limest-b es1• lob-e c1 lob-s c2 **Lyc** k* **M-ambo** b2.de* m-arct b2.de *M-aust* b2.de **Mag-c** k* mag-m k* *Mag-p* k* mand rsj7• mang k* mang-p rly4• marb-w es1• melal-alt gya4 meny k* meph *Merc* k* merc-c bro1 merl c2 mez k* micr br1* mim-p rsj8• mom-b c2* *Moni* rfm1• morg-g pte1*• morg-p pte1*• mosch k* mucs-nas rly4• *Mur-ac* k* myos-a rly4• myric nad rly4• naja k* naphtin bro1 naphtin c2 *Nat-ar Nat-c* k* *Nat-m* k* nat-n c2* nat-ox rly4• nat-p k* **Nat-s** k* nept-m lsd2.fr **Nit-ac** k* nit-s-d br1 **Nux-m** k* *Nux-v* k* oci-sa mtf11 olib-sac wmh1 **Olnd** k* onis bro1 **Op** k* *Opun-f* bro1 orig-d c2 orni c2* orot-ac rly4• osteo-a knp1• ox-ac oxal-a rly4• ozone sde2• pall br1 pant-ac rly4• par b2.de* petr b2.de* petr-ra shn4• *Ph-ac* k* phel *Phos* k* phyt bg2 **Pic-ac** k* pin-con oss2• plac-s rly4• *Plat* k* plat-m-n c1* plb k* *Podo* k* positr nl2• pot-e rly4• propr sa3• prot pte1*• prun *Psor* ptel mrr1 *Puls* k* rad-br bro1* ran-b b2.de* ran-s b2.de* *Raph* k* rham-f c2 rheum k* rhod k* rhus-g bro1* rhus-t k* ribo rly4• rob c2* rumx ruta b2.de* sabad k* sabin b2.de* sacch-a fd2.de• sal-ac c2 sal-fr sle1• samb b2.de* sang sars b2.de* scor a1* scut c2 sec b2.de* *Sel* k* *Seneg* k* senn k* *Sep* k* serp c2 **Sil** k* sin-a c2 slag c2 spig b2.de* spong b2.de* squil k* stann k* staph k* staphycoc rly4• stram b2.de* stront-c k* suis-em rly4• sul-ac b2.de* sul-i k2 **Sulph** k* sumb bro1 suprar rly4• syc bka1• symph fd3.de• *Syph* k* tab taosc iwa1• tarax b2.de* **Tarent** k* tep c2 ter bro1* teucr k* thea bro1 thiam rly4• thioc-ac rly4• *Thuj* k* til tril-p c1 tritic-vg fd5.de tub tl uran-n bro1 vac br1 valer b2.de* vanil fd5.de *Ven-m* rsj12• **Verat** k* verat-v verb b2.de* vesp vib ptk1 vinc viol-t b2.de* xan k* *Zinc* k* *Zing* k* [bell-p-sp dcm1 *Spect* dfg1]

- **daytime**: kali-m k2 kali-s fd4.de ven-m rsj12•
- **morning**: ambr b7.de* *Arg-n* k* ars b4.de* bamb-a stb2.de• calc bg1 camph b7.de* cann-s b7.de* cassia-s cdd7*• cedr k* cist k* con bg1 croc b7.de* (non:euph k*) graph b4.de* hell b7.de* hep k* hir rsj4• hyos b7.de* ign b7.de* kali-c bg1 kalm bg1 *Lach* b7.de* luf-op rsj5• lyc k* m-ambo b7.de m-aust b7.de merc k* nat-c bg2 nat-m b4.de* nat-ox rly4• nat-p fkr6.de nit-ac k* nux-v k* petr bg1 *Plat* b4.de* plb b7.de* *Podo* *Puls* b7.de* rheum b7.de* rhod b4.de* ruta fd4.de

Flatulence – morning: ...

sacch-a fd2.de• senec bg1 spong b7a.de squil b7.de* staph b7.de* stront-c b4.de* suis-em rly4• *Sulph* bg1 tarent k* vanil fd5.de *Verat* b7.de* zinc b4.de*

- • **bed** agg.; in: euph h2 nux-v k* spong bg2
- • **rising** agg.: cann-i c1
- • **waking**; on: *Arg-n* k* cist k* con kali-p fd1.de• oxal-a rly4• rumx
- **forenoon**: cann-s b7.de* carb-an b4.de* chin b7.de* guaj hipp k* mag-c b4.de* nat-m k* phos b4.de* *Puls* sars b4.de* zinc
- **noon**: nat-s k*
- **afternoon**: alum b4.de* am-c b4.de* am-m b7.de* *Ant-c* b7.de* ant-t b7.de* asaf b7.de* aur-m k* *Calc-s* k* canth b7.de* carb-v k* caust b4.de* chin b7.de* cycl b7.de* dulc fd4.de guaj b4.de* hell b7.de* kali-m k2 kali-n k* kola stb3• laur b7.de* *Lyc* b4a.de mag-c b4.de* nat-c b4.de* nux-v b7.de* op k* phos b4.de* sars b4.de* staph b7.de* tritic-vg fd5.de vanil fd5.de zinc b4.de*
  - • **16 h**: *Lyc*
  - • **eating**; after: fago k*
  - • **stool** agg.; during: fago
- **evening**: aegle-f zzc1• aloe k* alum k* *Am-c* k* ambr bg2 apoc k* *Bry* b7.de* calc-f caps b7.de* cassia-s cdd7*• chin b7.de* choc srj3• cist k* cocc b7.de* con b4.de* cycl b7.de* dulc fd4.de fuma-ac rly4• glon k* ham k* hyos b7.de* hyper k* *Ign* b7.de* kali-n b4.de* kali-s fd4.de luf-op rsj5• *Lyc* k* *M-arct* b7a.de m-aust b7.de meny b7.de* merc k* mez bg2 mim-p rsj8• nat-m k* nat-s bg2 nept-m lsd2.fr *Nit-ac* k* nux-m b7.de* *Nux-v* k* *Olib-sac* wmh1 petr b4.de* pic-ac k* plan k* plut-n srj7• *Puls* k* rhod bg2 rhus-t b7.de* sabin b7.de* sacch-a fd2.de• samb bg2 sang k* sars b4.de* *Sep* k* sol-t-ae k* spig bg2 spong b7a.de* stront-c b4.de* sulph b4.de* tritic-vg fd5.de valer b7.de* vanil fd5.de verat k* zinc k*
  - • **bed** agg.; in: bry bg2 carc az1.de• cartl-s rly4•
- **night**: acon b7.de* agar k* alum bg2 am-c b4.de* ambr k* ammc k* arg-met b7.de* arn k* *Aur* k* borx b4a.de bry bg2 calc b4.de* calc-s k* *Carb-v* k* cham b7.de* cic bg2 cist k* cocc k* coff b7.de* com k* ferr k* hep b4.de* hyos b7.de* hyper k* ign k* *Kali-ar* kali-c k* kali-m k2 kali-n b4.de* lyc k* m-arct b7.de m-aust b7.de merc k* mucs-nas rly4• nat-c bg2 nat-m k* *Nat-s* nux-m k* op k* puls k* sec b7.de* sil b4.de* stry k* *Sulph* b4.de* thuj k* *Valer* b7a.de vanil fd5.de zinc k*
  - • **midnight**: aur h2 **Cocc** k*
    - ⁝ **after**: *Ambr* b7.de* caps b7.de* carb-v bg2 cham b7.de* coff b7.de* *Puls* b7.de* ran-s b7.de*
    - ⁝ **before**: led b7.de* nat-s bg2 *Puls* b7.de* rhus-t b7.de* spong b7.de*
- **absence** of: kali-c bg2 nat-c bg2 sil bg2
- **accompanied** by:
  - • **anxiety** (See MIND - Anxiety - flatus - from)
  - • **atrophy** (See GENERALS - Atrophy - accompanied - flatulence)
  - • **distension** (See Distension - flatus - with)
  - • **eructations** (See STOMACH - Eructations - accompanied - flatulence)
  - • **pain** in abdomen; tearing (See Pain - tearing - accompanied - flatulence)
  - ○ • **Skin**; yellow (See SKIN - Discoloration - yellow - accompanied - flatulence)
  - • **Stomach**:
    - ⁝ **complaints** (See STOMACH - Complaints - accompanied - flatulence)
    - ⁝ **pain** (See STOMACH - Pain - flatulence)
  - • **Tongue** | **white** discoloration of the tongue: *Lyc* kr1*
- **acids**, after: ph-ac
- **air** agg.; in open: sep b4.de*
- **apple** pie; after: bamb-a stb2.de•
- **asa** foetida; odor of: dulc bg2
- **back**, felt in: rhod ptk1
- **bathing**; after: calc-s k*
- **beer**:
  - • **after**: teucr b7.de*
  - • **agg.** | **new** beer: *Chin* b7a.de *Puls* b7a.de
- **bending** forward | **amel.**: aloe bg2 bell b4a.de*
- **breakfast** | **after** | **agg.**: caust k* nat-p k* **Nat-s** k* vanil fd5.de
  - • **before** | **agg.**: agar k*

- **breathing** deep agg.: hell b7a.de*
- **children**; in: arg-n kl *Cham* b7a.de chin mtf33 lyc kl staph mtf33 thuj mtf33
- **chill**; during: croc bg2 mez b4a.de* nux-m bg2
- **coition**: graph bg2
- **cold**; after taking a: *Acon* b7a.de *Bry* b7a.de *Nux-v* b7a.de *Samb* b7a.de
- **cold** drinks agg.: nux-v bg2
- **continual**: ven-m rsj12•
- **cough** agg.; during: cocc b7a.de* kali-c b4a.de
- **dinner**:
  • **after** | **agg.**: agar calc-s myric naja nit-ac verat zinc bg2
  • **before**: spig bg2
  • **during** | **agg.**: ant-c h2
- **drinking**:
  • **after**:
    ⁝ **agg.**: aur b4.de* calc-p bg2 carb-an bg2 cham bg2 chin bg2 cocc bg2 ferr bg2 graph bg2 kali-c bg2 meny bg2 merc b4.de* nat-m bg2 *Nux-v* b7.de* rhod bg2 staph bg2 verat bg2
      : **accompanied** by distension: ambr k1 cassia-s ccrh1•
    ⁝ **amel.**: *Sil* b4a.de
  • **tea**: *Chin* dios br1
- **driving**: nux-v bg2
- **eating**:
  • **after**:
    ⁝ **agg.**: aloe bg2 alum b4.de* ambr k2 ant-c b7.de* **Arg-n** k* asc-t br1 aster k* atis zzc1• *Aur* k* bamb-a stb2.de• borx k* bry b7.de* bufo calc k* carb-an k* *Carb-v* k* carc fd2.de• caust k* **Chin** b7.de* chir-fl gya2 coc-c k* cocc b7.de* con b4.de* cortico tpw7 cycl b7.de* *Dios* falco-pe nl2• ferr bg2 ferr-m k* graph k2 hell b7.de* hyos b7.de* *Ign* b7.de* *Kali-c* b4a.de* kali-n k* kali-p fd1.de• lac-del hrn2• lac-e hrn2• lach bg2 **Lyc** k* m-ambo b7.de m-aust b7.de mag-c k2 *Mag-m* mim-p rsj8• moni rfm1• nat-m bg2 nat-p k* nat-s bg2 nept-m lsd2.fr nit-ac b4.de* *Nux-m* bg2 **Nux-v** k* *Phos* b4.de* plat b4.de* puls k* rhod b4a.de rhus-t bg2 rumx sars b4.de* *Sep* b4.de* stann b4.de* staph b7.de* **Sulph** b4.de* suprar rly4• thuj k* verat b7a.de *Zinc* k*
      : **distension** of abdomen; with: ambr k1 moni rfm1• orot-ac rly4• podo fd3.de• tell rsj10•
    ⁝ **amel.**: cassia-s cdd7*• mosch b7.de* squil b7.de*
  • **before** | **agg.**: mag-m b4.de* sel b7.de*
  • **overeating** agg.; after: *Carb-v* bg2 *Chin* bg2 nux-m bg2 nux-v bg2
  • **while** | **agg.**: dulc b4.de* ferr bg2 graph b4.de*
- **emotions**: nux-m bg2
- **empty** stomach; on: cassia-s ccrh1•
- **eructations**:
  • **amel.**: alum b4.de* borx b4a.de lyc b4.de* sars b4.de*
  • **amel.** in general (See GENERALS - Eructations - amel.)
  • **with**: grat bg2 rhod bg2
- **everything** turns to gas: carb-v ptk1 kali-c bg2* nux-m bg2* nux-v ptk1 plb bg2
- **fasting** agg.: mag-m bg2 plat b4.de* rhod b4.de*
- **fever**; during: agar bg2 *Ars* bg2 *Carb-v* bg2 chin bg2 chinin-ar k2 colch bg2 graph bg2 kali-c bg2 nit-ac bg2 **Nux-v** b7.de* ph-ac bg2 phos bg2 rad-br bro1 teucr bg2
- **fish**; after: plb b7.de*
- **flatus**; passing | **amel.**: cassia-s cdd7*•
- **fruit** agg.: **Chin** k* pitu-a vml2• tritic-vg fd5.de
- **headache**; during: asc-t br1* calc-act bro1 calc-p bg2* cann-i bro1 *Carb-v* bro1 xan bro1
- **here** and there: *Carb-v* k* cham h1* chin bg1* cycl bg1 kola stb3• **Lyc** k* nat-m bg1* nat-s bg1 puls ptk1 sil ptk1 spig bg1 verat bg1
- **hysterical**: alet bro1 *Ambr* bro1 arg-n bro1 asaf bro1* caj bro1 cham bro1 cocc bg2* colch b7a.de* ictod bro1 ign b7a.de* kali-p bro1 *Nux-m* b7a.de* plat bro1 puls b7a.de* raph ptk1 *Sumb* bro1 tarax bro1 thea bro1 valer br1*
- **incarcerated** (See obstructed)
- **inspiration** agg.: mag-m bg2 tab bg2
- **lying**:
  • **agg.**: ambr b7.de* bry b7.de* carb-v tl1* cinnb bg2 croc b7.de* ign b7.de* iod bg2 phos b4.de* puls bg2 sep b4.de* spong b7a.de stann b4.de* sul-ac bg2 zinc b4.de*
  • **bed**; in | **agg.**: bry b7a.de ign b7.de* nux-v b7.de* plb b7.de* *Puls* b7.de*
- **lying**: ...
  • **side**; on:
    ⁝ **agg.**: coc-c bg2
    ⁝ **left** | **agg.**: coloc ptk1 glon bg2 nat-s a puls sys
- **lying** down:
  • **after**:
    ⁝ **agg.**: nux-v b7.de* *Puls* b7.de* ran-b b7.de*
    ⁝ **amel.**: nux-v bg2 sul-ac b4.de*
  • **before** | **agg.**: m-aust b7.de
- **malarial**: querc-r-g-s br1
- **meat** agg.: plb bg2
- **menses**:
  • **before** | **agg.**: *Con* b4a.de lac-c bg2 ph-ac b4a.de suis-em rly4• zinc
  • **during**:
    ⁝ **agg.**: aloe bg2 alum b4a.de am-m bg2 *Brom* bg2 carb-v bg2 cham bg2 *Cocc* b7.de* graph b4a.de kali-c k* kali-p bg3* kreos bg2 *Lyc* bg2 mag-c b4.de* mang bg2 nat-c b4.de* nit-ac bg2* nux-m bg3* phos bg2 thuj b4a.de verb bg2 vesp k* vib bg3* *Zinc* b4a.de
    ⁝ **beginning** of menses | **agg.**: mag-c bg2 staph b7.de*
  • **dysmenorrhea**, with: vib ptk1
- **milk** agg.: calc bg2 carb-an b4.de carb-v k* chel b7.de* con b4.de* hell b7.de* merc merc-c a1 *Nat-c* k* *Nat-s* sul-ac k* zinc b4.de
- **motion**:
  • **agg.**: bar-c b4.de* nat-m b4.de* *Sep* b4.de* *Sil* b4.de*
  • **amel.**: carc az1.de•
- **nausea**; during (See STOMACH - Nausea - accompanied - flatus)
- **obstructed**: *(↗Distension - tympanitic)* acon b2.de* agar k* agn hr1 ail tl1 all-c k2 *All-s* vh1 aloe *Alum* alum-sil k2 am-c b2.de* am-m b2.de* *Ambr* k* anac h2 ang b2.de* ant-c k* ant-t k* **Arg-n** k* arn k* *Ars* *Ars-i* *Asaf* bg2* asar k* **Aur** k* aur-i k2 aur-m k2 aur-s k2 bamb-a stb2.de• bar-c b2.de* bell b2.de* borx b2.de* *Calc* k* calc-i k2 calc-p bro1 camph b2.de* cann-s b2.de* canth k* caps b2.de* carb-ac bro1 *Carb-an* k* carb-v k* carbn-s *Caust* k* *Cham* k* **Chin** k* cic b2.de* coca-c sk4• *Cocc* k* coff k* **Colch** k* *Coloc* k* *Con* k* dream-p sdj1• dulc h2 euph b2.de* *Graph* k* guaj k* hell b2.de* hep k* hyos b2.de* ign k* *Iod* k* irid-met srj5• *Kali-ar* *Kali-c* k* *Kali-n* k* *Kali-p* kali-s kali-sil k2 kalm k* ketogl-ac rly4• *Lach* k* lim bro1 *Lyc* k* *M-ambo* b2.de* *M-arct* b2.de* m-aust b2.de* mag-m b2.de* meny b2.de* mez b2.de* *Mom-b* bro1 moni rfm1• mosch k* naja bg2 nat-c k* *Nat-m* k* nat-p *Nat-s* k* **Nit-ac** k* *Nux-m* b2.de* nux-v k* op b2.de* ox-ac ozone sde2• pall bro1 petr b2.de* *Ph-ac* k* phel k* *Phos* k* *Plat* k* plb k* prun k* psil ft1 **Puls** k* **Raph** k* rheum k* rhod k* rhus-g bro1 rhus-t b2.de* rob br1* ruta b2.de* sabad b2.de* sabin b2.de* sars h2 sel b2.de* sep k* **Sil** k* spig b2.de* spong b2.de* squil k* stann k* staph k* stram b2.de* stront-c b2.de* stry sul-ac b2.de* *Sulph* k* taosc iwa1• **Tarent** k* ter tl1 teucr k* *Thuj* b2.de* til trom vml3• valer b2.de* **Verat** k* verb b2.de* *Zinc* k* zinc-p k2
  • **morning**: mang h2 nit-ac h2 sulph h2 zinc h2
  • **afternoon**: kali-n h2
  • **evening**: nit-ac h2
  • **night**: nat-m h2 sil h2 sulph h2
    ⁝ **midnight**: coloc h2
  • **accompanied** by:
    ⁝ **stools** like shreds, watery, bloody: colch tl1
    ⁝ **Back**; pain in (See BACK - Pain - lumbar - accompanied - flatulence)
  • **agg.** | **Hypochondria**: aur b4a.de
  • **descending** colon, with constipation: *Aur* *Iod* luf-op rsj5• **Lyc** k ● rhod **Sulph** k ●
    ⁝ **morning**: luf-op rsj5•
  • **hard** stool; with: caust
  • **sitting** for a long time agg.: lyc h2 ozone sde2•
  • **waking**; on: sil h2
  • **warmth** | **amel.**: bamb-a stb2.de•
○ • **Colon**; in: | **Splenic** flexure: mom-b bro1
  • **Hypochondria**: cham bg2 lyc bg2 nux-v bg2
  • **Hypogastrium**, in: graph h2 spong fd4.de staph h1

Abdomen

- **Lower** abdomen: acon bg2 chin bg2 phos bg2 sul-ac bg2
- **Rectum**: agar bg2 bar-c bg2 calc bg2 carb-an bg2 fl-ac bg2 ign bg2 iris bg2 kreos bg2 lach bg2 mang bg2 nat-c bg2 nux-v bg2 rhod bg2 sil bg2 zinc bg2
- **Sides** | **left**: *Aur* ptk1 carb-v bg2 lyc bg2 sulph bg2

- **old** people: *Carb-ac Phos*
- **operation**; after: (↗*painful - operation)* *Chin* br1* raph ptk1
- **pain**; during: nux-m bg2
- **painful**: *(↗Distension - painful)* acon b2.de* acon-ac rly4• agn bg2 all-c bg2 *All-s* vh1 alum b2.de* am-c b2.de* am-m b2.de* *Ambr* b2.de* *Anac* b2.de* ant-c b2.de* *Ant-t* b2.de* arg-met b2.de* *Arn* b2.de* *Asaf* b2.de* asar b2.de* asc-t c1 *Aur* b2.de* bar-c bg2 *Bell* b2.de* bism b2.de* bry b2.de* cadm-met tpw6 calc b2.de* calc-p bg2 camph b2.de* cann-s b2.de* canth b2.de* caps b2.de* carb-an b2.de* **Carb-v** b2.de* cartl-s rly4• cassia-s ccrh1• caust bg2 *Cham* b2.de* chel b2.de* chin b2.de* chord-umb rly4• cic b2.de* coc-c bg2 *Cocc* b2.de* coff b2.de* colch b2.de* coll ptk1 coloc b2.de* *Con* b2.de* cycl b2.de* dros b2.de* dulc fd4.de euph b2.de* falco-pe nl2• ferr b2.de* fuma-ac rly4• **Graph** b2.de* guaj b2.de* hell b2.de* hep b2.de* *Hyos* b2.de* **Ign** b2.de* iod b2.de* ip b2.de* iris br1 kali-c b2.de* kali-n bg2 *Lach* b2.de* laur b2.de* **Lyc** b2.de* m-ambo b2.de *M-arct* b2.de *M-aust* b2.de mag-c b2.de* mag-p ptk1 meny b2.de* mez b2.de* nad rly4• naja bg2 nat-c b2.de* *Nat-m* b2.de* nat-s ptk1 nit-ac b2.de* *Nux-m* b2.de* **Nux-v** b2.de* op b2.de* ox-ac ptk1 oxal-a rly4• par b2.de* ph-ac bg2 *Phos* b2.de* pip-m br1 plac-s rly4• plat b2.de* *Plb* b2.de* **Puls** b2.de* ran-b b2.de* *Raph* bg2 *Rheum* b2.de* **Rhod** b2.de* rhus-t b2.de* ribo rly4• ruta b2.de* sabin b2.de* samb b2.de* sel b2.de* seneg b2.de* sep b2.de* *Sil* b2.de* spig b2.de* spong b2.de* *Squil* b2.de* stann bg2 staph b2.de* sul-ac b2.de* **Sulph** b2.de* tarax b2.de* *Teucr* b2.de* thiam rly4• thuj b2.de* valer b2.de* **Verat** b2.de* verb b2.de* zinc b2.de* zinc-val ptk1
  - **children**; in: | **nurslings**: *Senn* br1
  - **operation**; after: *(↗operation)* *Raph* br1
  - **stool**; before: caps bg2 castm bg2 gamb bg2 nat-m bg2 sep bg2 thuj bg2
- **painless**: agn b7.de* asar b7.de* bism b7.de* euphr b7.de* hell b7.de* m-ambo b7.de op b7.de* par b7.de* squil b7.de* staph b7.de* stram b7.de*
- **perspiration**; during: am bg2 carb-v bg2 **Cham** bg2 *Chin* bg2 graph bg2 ign bg2 lyc bg2 **Nux-v** bg2 *Ph-ac* bg2 *Phos* bg2 puls bg2 staph bg2 *Verat* bg2
- **potatoes**: alum k2
- **pregnancy** agg.; during: *Calc-f* c1
- **pressure** | **abdomen**; on | **amel.**: bell b4a.de* castm bg2 stann b4.de*
  - **bladder** agg.; pressure on: aloe bg2 carb-v bg2* coloc bg2 gamb bg2 gymno bg2 ign bg2* kali-c bg2* prun bg2 zinc bg2
- **pushing** upward: arg-n ptk1 asaf ptk1 carb-v ptk1 graph ptk1 thuj ptk1
- **retention** of: ambr b7.de* bell b4a.de caps b7.de* *Cham* b7a.de *Chin* b7.de* *Coloc* b4a.de *Hep* b4a.de *Kali-c* b4.de* *Lyc* b4.de* mag-m b4.de* *Mosch* b7a.de *Nat-c* b4.de* nat-m b4.de* nit-ac b4a.de nux-v b7.de* plb b7.de* puls b7.de* rhus-t b7.de* sabad b7.de* *Sil* b4.de* squil b7.de* thuj b4.de* *Verat* b7.de*
- **riding** in a carriage agg.: calc-f ferr k* sep bg2
- **rising**:
  - **bed**; from:
    - **agg.**: hyos b7.de* m-aust b7.de sul-ac b4.de* zinc
    - **amel.**: ambr b7.de* nux-v b7.de*
- **rising** upward: aloe mtf arg-n mtf ars mtf cann-i mtf carb-v mtf carbn-s mtf coca mtf hell mtf nat-n mtf nux-v mtf psor mtf rheum mtf
- **rumbling** (See Rumbling)
- **scratching** | **amel.**: arn bg2 mez bg2 sars bg2
- **sensation** of: agar bg2
- **sitting**:
  - **agg.**: ant-t b7.de* canth b7.de* mur-ac b4.de* phos k*
  - **amel.**: squil b7.de*
  - **long** time agg.; for a: lyc h2
- **sleep**:
  - **during** | **agg.**: agn b7.de* aur b4a.de cupr ptk1 kali-n m-aust b7.de nux-v b7.de*
  - **falling** asleep; when: ign b7.de*
  - **preventing**: *(↗SLEEP - Disturbed - flatulence; SLEEP - Sleeplessness - flatulence)* cartl-s rly4• cocc bg2 coff bg2 kali-m k2 nux-v bg2
  - **siesta**:
    - **after** | **agg.**: cycl k*
- **smoking** agg.: meny b7.de*
- **solid** food; after: *Ph-ac* b4a.de
- **sour** food, from: carb-v bg2 nat-c bg3 *Ph-ac* k*
- **standing** agg.: bism b7.de* ign b7.de* squil b7.de*
- **starch**; after: nat-c k2
- **stool**:
  - **after**:
    - **agg.**: agar b4.de* aloe bg2 apoc vh1 calc-s k* carb-v b4.de* caust b4.de* colch bg2 coloc bg2 con b4.de* dulc fd4.de hep b4.de* **Lyc** k* nux-v b7.de* petr ptk1 phos b4.de* **Pic-ac** k* plb k* puls b7.de* ruta fd4.de sulph b4.de* thuj b4.de*
    - **amel.**: adam skp7•
  - **before**: *Aloe* bg2 *Am-m* b7.de* ant-t b7.de* apis b7a.de apoc k* *Arg-n* bg2 arn b7.de* bell bg2 borx b4a.de brom b4a.de caps b7.de* carb-an b4a.de castm *Cham* b7a.de cocc b7.de* crot-t bg2 dulc b4.de* ferr b7.de* *Fl-ac* gels k* hep k* **Lyc** k* mag-c b4.de* mang b4.de* merc b4.de* mosch b7.de* olnd b7.de* *Op* k* ph-ac b4.de* phel k* phos b4.de* *Puls* b7.de* rhod b4a.de *Sabad* b7a.de seneg b4a.de sep b4.de* spig b7.de* spong b7.de* stront-c b4.de* sumb k* thuj b4.de* valer b7.de* viol-t k*
  - **during** | **agg.**: acon bg1 agar b4a.de* aloe bg2 am-m b7.de* ant-c b7a.de apoc k* arg-n bg2* arn b7.de* arum-d k* asaf b7.de* borx bg2 *Calc-p* bg2 *Cham* b7a.de chin b7a.de cocc b7.de* *Crot-t* k* dig fago k* hep b4a.de hyos b7.de* mang k2 nat-m k* *Nat-s* bg2* olnd b7.de* petr bg1 ph-ac bg2 phel k* podo bg1 rhod b4a.de sabin b7.de* sep bg2 spong b7.de* squil b7.de* staph k* thuj bg1 viol-t bg2
- **stretching** agg.: *Stann* b4.de*
- **supper** agg.; after: coc-c k* hyos k* psor k* zinc k*
- **suspicion**; with: cic bg2
- **sweets**; from: arg-n k2* bamb-a stb2.de•
- **touch** agg.: squil b7.de*
- **undressing**: *Nux-v* bg2
- **urination** agg.; during: hyos b7.de* merc k*
- **vegetables** agg.: caps hr1* pitu-a vml2•
- **waking**; on: ars bg2 ign b7.de* m-ambo b7.de m-aust b7.de nat-c bg2 nux-v b7.de* puls b7.de* valer bg2
- **walking**:
  - **agg.**: ign b7.de* lyc k* mag-c b4.de* sep b4.de* sil b4.de* squil b7.de*
  - **air** agg.; in open: sep
  - **amel.**: phos h2 sil b4.de*
- **warm** drinks agg.: fl-ac k2

○ - **Cecal** region: carbn-s nat-s

- **Hypochondria**●: acon *Aur* **Carb-v** *Cham* k* *Chin* k* cist k* colch b7.de* *Cycl* euph h2 hyos k* ign b7.de* **Lyc** k* m-arct b7.de m-aust b7.de nux-v b7.de* orot-ac rly4• *Phos* k* podo k* puls b7.de* sil sul-ac sulph k* tarent k* verat b7.de* verb bg2
  - **left**: *Aur* sne mez h2 nat-m h2 sulph h2
  - **noisy**: puls b7.de*
- **Hypogastrium**: mag-m h2 pert-vc vk9 phos h2 zinc h2* zinc-val ptk1
- **Inguinal** rings: cham h1
- **Lower** abdomen: acon ptk1 agar bg2 aloe bg2 ambr bg2 apoc bg2 aur bg2 carb-v bg2 cham bg2 chin bg2 cimic bg2 cocc bg2 com bg2 cycl bg2 euph bg2 glon bg2 graph bg2 hyos bg2 iris bg2 jatr-c bg2 kali-c bg2 lyc bg2* mag-m bg2 nat-m ptk1 nux-m ptk1 nux-v bg2 olnd bg2 par bg2 phos bg2 plan bg2 rat bg2 rhus-t bg2 ruta bg2 sil bg2* spig bg2 spong bg2 stann bg2 staph bg2 sul-ac bg2 sulph bg2* tarent bg2 zinc bg2* zinc-val ptk1
  - **right**: bism bg2* **Calc** ptk1 graph ptk1 lil-t ptk1 *Nat-s* ptk1 ox-ac ptk1 *Phos* ptk1 thuj ptk1
  - **left**: hep bg2 nat-m bg2 sep bg2
- **Sides**: phos h2
  - **right**: calc bg2* caps tl1 **Chin** bg2 graph bg2 jatr-c bg2 laur bg2 lil-t bg2 nat-s hr ox-ac bg2 phos bg2 sep bg2 thuj bg2 zinc h2*
  - **left**: aloe bg2 am-m ptk1 arg-n bg2 *Aur* ptk1 carb-v bg2* cedr bg2 con bg2* crot-t bg2* dios bg2* euph bg2* lyc bg2* nat-m bg2* nux-v bg2 ph-ac bg2* seneg bg2* staph bg2* sulph bg2*
- **Spleen**: kali-c bg2
  - **agg.** | **Hypochondria**: meph bg2
- **Upper** abdomen: aeth bg2 bry bg2 carb-v ptk1 chin bg2 croc bg2 crot-t bg2 grat bg2 hydr bg2 kali-c bg2 lach bg2 nat-c bg2 nat-m bg2 nat-s bg2 ol-an bg2 ph-ac bg2 plat bg2 puls tl1* rat bg2 sulph bg2 valer bg2
  - **left**: calc bg2

FLATULENT FOOD agg.: bry bg2 calc bg2 *Chin* bg2 kali-c bg2 *Lyc* bg2 *Petr* bg2 puls bg2 sep bg2 verat bg2

FLATUS; PASSING:
- **after**:
  - **agg.**: camph b7.de* graph b4.de* sul-ac bg2
  - **amel.**: acon bg2 aloe bg2 ambr bg2 anac bg2 ant-t b7.de* arg-met bg2 arg-n bg2 arn b7.de* ars bg2 asaf bg2 asar b7.de* aur bg2 bell bg2 bism bg2 borx bg2 bov bg2 bry bg2 *Calc* bg2 calc-p bg2 canth bg2 caps bg2 carb-an bg2 *Carb-v* bg2 caust bg2 *Cham* b7.de* *Chin* bg2 cic bg2 *Cocc* b7.de* coff b7.de* coloc bg2 con b4.de* crot-t bg2 euphr bg2 *Fl-ac* bg2 gels bg2 graph b4.de* grat bg2 guaj b4.de* hell bg2 hep bg2 hyos bg2 *Ign* b7.de* kali-bi bg2 *Kali-c* bg2 kali-chl bg2 lach bg2 laur bg2 **Lyc** b4.de* m-ambo bg2 m-arct b7.de mang bg2 meny b7.de* *Merc-c* b4a.de* mez bg2 nat-m bg2 nat-n bg2 **Nat-s** bg2 nit-ac bg2 nux-m b7.de* **Nux-v** b7.de* *Ph-ac* bg2 phos bg2 plat b4.de* *Plb* b7.de* psor bg2 **Puls** b7.de* *Rhod* b4.de* rhus-t bg2 ruta bg2 sabin b7.de* sel b7.de* sep bg2 sil b4.de* spig b7.de* spong b7.de* squil b7.de* **Staph** b7.de* stram bg2 **Sulph** bg2 teucr bg2 thuj bg2 *Verat* b7.de* verb bg2 viol-t bg2 zinc bg2
- **agg.**: aur ptk1 canth ptk1 *Con* b4.de* fl-ac ptk1 ox-ac bg2 plat b4.de* *Puls* b7.de* squil ptk1
- **amel.**: carb-an bg2 hep ptk1 kali-c bg2 kali-chl bg2 nat-m ptk1 tarent ptk1

○ • **Hypochondria**: aloe bg2 arn b7.de* asar b7.de* nat-m bg2 sep b4.de*
  - **Umbilicus**: mag-c ptk1
- **before**: chin b7.de* con b4.de* *Graph* b4.de* *Lyc* b4.de* m-ambo b7.de *Nux-v* b7a.de plat b4.de* *Puls* b7.de* ran-b b7.de* rheum b7.de* sil b4.de*

FLORA; intestinal:
- **complaints** of: all-s br1
- **destroyed**:
  - **antibiotics**; from: mucot mtf11
  - **chemotherapeutics**; from: chloram mtf11

FLOWING; sensation as from fluids: | **Spleen**: vib bg2

FLUTTERING (See Trembling)

FOLDS:

○ - **Pelvic** region: *Colch* b7a.de
  - **accompanied** by | **ascites** (See Dropsy - ascites - accompanied - pelvic)

FOREIGN BODY:
- **sensation** of:

○ • **Lower** abdomen | **right**: thuj bg2

FORMICATION: aloe ars k* calad calc calc-p bg2 camph carb-v caust colch k* coloc crot-t cycl k* *Dulc* k* mag-m k* *Nat-c* hr1 nat-sil fd3.de• nux-v b7.de* paeon k* pall k* petr h2 pic-ac k* **Plat** k* puls b7.de* stann tritic-vg fd5.de zinc k*
- **night**: ars h2 tritic-vg fd5.de
- **mouse** creeping; as from a: plb bg2
- **voluptuous**: **Plat** k*

○ - **Hypochondria**: nux-v b7.de*
- **Inguinal** region: camph b7.de*

○ • **Glands**: merc b4.de*
- **Internal** abdomen: aloe bg2 ant-t b7.de* ars bg2 asaf b7.de* calc bg2 camph bg2 carb-v b4.de* caust b4.de* chin b7.de* colch bg2 cycl bg2 dulc b4a.de* grat bg2 ign bg2 *Iod* b4a.de mag-m bg2 merc bg2 *Plat* b4.de* stann b4.de* *Thuj* b4a.de zinc b4.de*
- **Umbilicus** | **Region** of umbilicus: caust bg2
- **Waist**: *Aesc* alj oena ptk1*

▽ - **extending** to | **Urethra**: zinc h2

FOULNESS of: *Petr* bg2

FRIGHT; after:
- **agg.**: plat b4.de
- **amel.**: plat bg2

FROZEN food agg.: calc-p bg2 ip bg2 puls bg2

FRUIT:
- **agg.**: bry b7.de chin b7.de ign b7.de kreos b7a.de lyc ptk1 mag-m b4.de merc-c b4a.de puls b7.de rheum b7.de *Sep* b4a.de verat b7.de

○ • **Hypochondria**: nat-c b4.de*
- **amel.**: bry bg2 chin bg2 ign bg2 mag-m bg2 puls bg2 rheum bg2 verat bg2

FULLNESS, sensation of: (↗*Heaviness*) agar k* agn bg2 all-c **Aloe** k* alum k* alum-p k2 alum-sil k2 alumn k* am-c am-m k* ambr *Anac* k* ant-c k* ant-t k* *Apis* k* aran c1* arg-n bg2* arn k* ars k* ars-s-f k2 arum-t asaf k* asar k* *Aur* k* aur-ar k2 aur-s k2 bamb-a stb2.de• *Bapt* k* bar-c k* bar-m bar-ox-suc rly4• bar-s k2 bell k* bry bg2* cain calad calc k* calc-s calc-sil k2 camph k* cann-s k* canth k* caps carb-ac k* **Carb-v** k* carbn-dox knl3• **Carbn-s** carl k* castm caust k* cham b7.de* chel k* **Chin** k* chinin-ar chord-umb rly4• *Cic* b7.de* cimic k* cinnb clem k* coc-c k* cocc coff k* colch k* coloc k* com k* con k* corn k* croc k* *Crot-t* k* *Cycl* k* **Dig** k* dor k* dream-p sdj1• dulc echi eup-per k* eup-pur a1* fago k* ferr k* ferr-ar ferr-i ferr-p gard-j vlr2• *Gels* k* glon k* **Graph** k* grat k* haem hell k* hep k* hir rsj4• hyos b7.de* hyper ign b7.de* indg k* irid-met srj5• jug-r k* kali-ar kali-bi bg2 **Kali-c** k* kali-i kali-m k2* kali-n k* kali-s kali-sil k2 kola stb3• lac-leo sk4• *Lach* k* lact laur k* lec led k* lil-t k* limen-b-c hrn2* **Lyc** k* m-ambo b7a.de m-aust b7.de mag-c k* mag-m k* mag-s k* mang-p rly4• melal-alt gya4 *Meny* k* merc-c mez k* mim-p rsj8• *Mosch* b7a.de *Mur-ac* k* myric k* naja nat-ar nat-c k* nat-m k* nat-ox rly4• nat-p *Nat-s* k* nux-m k* **Nux-v** k* oci-sa sk4• ol-an k* olib-sac wmh1 olnd k* onos op k* oxal-a rly4• ozone sde2• petr **Ph-ac** k* **Phos** k* phys k* phyt pic-ac k* plac-s rly4• plan k* plat b4.de* plb k* pot-e rly4• puls k* raph rein a1 rheum b7.de* rhod k* rhus-g tmo3• rhus-t k* rumx ruta fd4.de sarr k* sars k* *Sep* k* sil k* spig k* spong b7.de* stann k* stram stront-c k* succ-ac rly4• suis-em rly4• suis-pan rly4• **Sulph** k* sumb k* symph fd3.de• tab ter thioc-ac rly4• thuj b4.de* tritic-vg fd5.de ulm-c jsj8• valer k* verb k* zinc k*
- **daytime**: nux-m k*
- **morning**: dios k* phos k* plat k* sulph
  - **waking**; on: con h2 sulph
- **forenoon**: sulph k*
  - **11 h** | **stool** agg.; after: gels
- **noon**: dig h2 dulc fd4.de
- **afternoon**: clem k* con k* mag-c h2 phyt plb k* spong fd4.de
  - **walking** in open air agg.: plan
- **evening**: bry k* calc k* caust k* dios k* dulc fd4.de graph k* hyper k* kali-s fd4.de mur-ac h2 ruta fd4.de tritic-vg fd5.de
  - **soup**; after: castm
- **night**: graph k* nat-m k* phos k* tritic-vg fd5.de
- **accompanied** by:
  - **hypochondrium**; sensation of fullness in (See RESPIRATION - Painful - accompanied - hypochondrium)
  - **respiration**; impeded (See RESPIRATION - Impeded - fullness - abdomen)
- **anxiety**, as if abdomen would burst; during (See MIND - Anxiety - abdomen; with distension of - burst)
- **breakfast** | **after** | **agg.**: *Carb-v* carbn-s *Sulph*
  - **during**: alum h2
- **coffee**: | **after**: canth
- **constipation**; during: bar-ox-suc rly4• bry dios ery-a graph hyos iod lach mand rsj7• nit-ac nux-v phos suis-pan rly4• ter
- **diarrhea**; during: nat-s
- **dinner** | **after** | **agg.**: alum cob petr h2 petr-ra shn4• thuj
  - **during** | **agg.**: ant-c h2
- **drinking** agg.; after: *Carb-v* caust nux-v ruta fd4.de sars
- **eating**:
  - **after** | **agg.**: agar k* agn b7a.de alum h2 anac b4a.de ant-c b7a.de* arn k* bamb-a stb2.de• calc k* calc-s *Carb-v* carc fd2.de• caust k* cham h1 chin k* *Cob* *Cocc* colch k* con b4a.de croc b7a.de dulc fd4.de graph b4a.de* hep k* ign iod b4a.de kali-bi k* **Kali-c** k* kali-m k2 kali-p kali-s *Kola* stb3• lach k* luf-op rsj5• *Lyc* k* mag-m k* mag-s *Mur-ac* k* myric k* nat-ar nat-hchls nat-m b4a.de *Nit-ac* k* **Nux-v** k* oxal-a rly4• par k* petr-ra shn4• ph-ac k* *Phos* k* *Puls* k* rhod k* rhus-t b7a.de sars k* *Sep* sil k* spig k* spong k* stann k* stront-c sk4• *Sulph* k* tritic-vg fd5.de *Zinc* k* zinc-p k2
  - **amel.**: rhus-t k*
  - **while** | **agg.**: cham h1 *Chin*
- **eructations** | **not** amel.: mim-p rsj8•
- **flatus**; passing | **amel.**: alum h2 graph tl1 grat hell kola stb3• rhod staph tl1 sulph
- **food**; at sight of: **Sulph**
- **hunger**: crot-t bg2 psor bg2
  - **during**: asar luf-op rsj5•

Abdomen

- lying agg.: rumx sphing k*
- sitting | amel.: plan
- smoking agg.: **Meny**
- stones; of (See Stone in - full)
- stool | after | agg.: olib-sac wmh1
  - copious:
    - after: gels bg2 laur bg2
    - amel.: rein a1
    - before: grat bg2 kola stb3•
- supper agg.; after: agar *Arg-n* coff colch coloc tell tritic-vg fd5.de
- urination agg.; after: nat-m bg1
- waking; on: ferr k* myric k* sulph k*
- walking | amel.: mag-c k*

○ - **Hypochondria**: acon k* aesc k* ant-c apoc vh1 aran arg-n ars-s-f k2 aur bell h1 brom k* *Carb-v* card-m k* *Cham* k* chel chin bg2 coc-c k* colch con eup-per k* ferr k* glon grat k* ign k* *Led* b7a.de m-ambo b7.de *Merc* merc-i-f merc-i-r nux-v bg2 phos h2 *Podo* k* ptel bg2 rhus-t b7.de* **Sep** k* sulph k* tell k*
  - right: aesc k* aloe card-m vml3• *Chel* eup-per kali-c nat-m *Podo* k* sang thuj
  - left: grin br1 rhus-t a1 stict k*
  - morning: con k*
  - accompanied by palpitations (See CHEST - Palpitation - accompanied - hypochondrium)
  - eating; after: nat-m
  - stool | amel.: card-m vml3• ferr k*
- **Hypogastrium**: *Aesc* k* bar-c k* *Bell* k* carb-v mag-c bg1 ruta fd4.de sep bg1 sulph k*
  - forenoon:
    - 10 h | evening; until: sulph
  - evening: bell k*
  - eating; after: hep h2
- **Inguinal** region: am-c h2 *Cocc* k* nat-s k* sep k*
- **Liver**: acon bg2 aesc k2 aloe k2 apoc vh1 arg-n bg2* bell k2 berb bg2 bry bg2 cean vml3• chel k2 *Ferr* gels bg2 kali-c k2 kreos k* *Lach* lept bg2 mang k2 myric bg2 nat-m nux-m bg2 *Nux-v* k* phos k2 *Podo* k* ptel bg2 sang k2 *Sep* k* sulph k* thuj

○ - Gallbladder: myric bg2*
  - Region of liver: iber br1
- **Lower** abdomen: aur b4a.de* bell bg2 sil b4a.de ust bg2
- **Sides**: am-c
  - right: bry k2
- **Spleen**: am-c b4.de* apoc vh1 gard-j vlr2• kali-i k* lec
- **Umbilicus** | **moving** around; as if a big bubble was: bamb-a stb2.de•
- **Upper** abdomen: agar bg2 phos bg2 sulph bg2

GALLSTONE COLIC (See Pain - liver - colic)

GALLSTONES: (↗*Pain - liver - colic*) **Ars** b7a.de aur bro1 bapt bro1 bell tl1* berb c2* bold bro1 *Bry* bro1* calc c2* calc-f mrr1 card-m c2* *Cham* b7a.de chel c2* chin bro1* chion br1* chlf c2 chol c2* coloc b7a.de cupr b7a.de* dig b7a.de dios bro1* eberth mtf11 euon c2 euon-a c2* euonin c2 fab c2* fel c2* ferr-s bro1 fuma-ac mtf11 gels bro1 guat sp1 hed sp1 *Hydr* bro1 jug-c br1* lach c2* *Lept* bro1* lith-c c2 lob c2 lyc ptk1 mag-p ptk1 mag-s sp1 mand mtf11 mang c2 **Merc** ptk1 merc-d ptk1 morg-g fmm1• morg-p pte1*• myric bro1* nat-s ptk1 nat-sal br1 nit-s-d c2 nux-v b7a.de* *Phos* ptk1 podo c2* ptel c2* sang ptk1 sulph ptk1 tarax c2* thlas c2 verat b7a.de* vichy-g c2
- **accompanied** by | **constipation**: chion bro1

GANGRENE: **Ars** k* cadm-s k2 *Canth* *Merc-c* b4a.de *Phos* *Plb* *Sec*

○ - **Liver**: *Sec*

GAS: (↗*Flatulence*)
- **trapped** (See Flatulence - obstructed)

GASTROINTESTINAL complaints: *Acal* br1 aeth br1 casc br1 cycl br1 *Dulc* br1 eucal br1 gamb br1 *Grat* br1 *Iris* br1 jatr-c br1 *Lyc* br1 nat-m br1 *Nux-v* br1 plb br1 ric br1 thuj br1 vanad br1

Gastrointestinal: ...
- **accompanied** by:
  - anemia (See GENERALS - Anemia - accompanied - gastrointestinal)
  - convulsions (See GENERALS - Convulsions - accompanied - gastrointestinal)
  - influenza: cupr-ar br1
  - typhoid (See FEVER - Typhoid - accompanied - gastrointestinal)
  - vertigo (See VERTIGO - Accompanied - gastrointestinal)

○ • **Female** genitalia; complaints of: acet-ac bg2
  - **Head**; pain in: agar bro1 aloe bro1 *Ant-c* bro1 arg-n bro1 ars bro1 *Bry* bro1 cann-i bro1 *Carb-v* bro1 *Chin* bro1 ip bro1 *Iris* bro1 nux-m bro1 *Nux-v* bro1 podo bro1 *Puls* bro1 rham-cal bro1 rob bro1
- **alternating** with | **Skin**; complaints of (See SKIN - Complaints - alternating - gastrointestinal)
- **apyrexia**; during: chin bro1 hydr bro1 *Ip* bro1 *Nux-v* bro1 puls bro1
- **catarrh**: bism-n br1
- **convulsions**; before (See GENERALS - Convulsions - gastrointestinal)
- **hypochondriasis**; with (See MIND - Hypochondriasis - gastrointestinal)
- **irritation**: bism-n br1 borx br1
- **weather** agg.; warm: *Acon* br1

GONENESS (See Emptiness)

GOOSE FLESH: sec k* sulph bg2

GOUTY metastasis: ant-c colch tl1

GRASPING a cold object: | **agg.**: *Merc* b4.de*

GRIPING (See Pain - cramping)

GURGLING: (↗*Bubbling; Clucking; Rumbling*) acon k* acon-f a1 *Agar* k* agath-a nl2• **Aloe** k* alum b4.de am-c b4.de* ambr b7.de* amp rly4• ang k* ant-c vh1 ant-t k* apoc bro1 arg-n k* *Ars* k* ars-s-f k2 asaf b7.de asar bg1 bamb-a stb2.de• bapt bro1 bell bro1 bov k* bry k* canth k* carb-an k* carb-v b4.de* carbn-s k* cartl-s rly4• cassia-s ccrh1• cham b7.de* chel k* *Chin* bro1 cina bro1 coc-c k* coca-c sk4• *Cocc* *Colch* bro1 coloc k* con k* conv bro1 croc b7.de **Crot-t** k* cupr-ar bro1 dig k* dios a1* dros eupi k* ferr k* ferr-ar ferr-p franz a1 *Gamb* k* gent-l a1 ger-i rly4• glyc bro1 graph k* grat bro1 haliae-lc srj5• *Hell* k* hell-v a1 helodr-cal knl2• hep bro1 hippoc-k szs2 hir skp7• hyos k* ign k* ip bro1 *Jatr-c* bro1 kali-bi k* kali-c bro1 kali-i k* ketogl-ac rly4• kola stb3• lach k* laur k2 *Lyc* k* *M-arct* b7.de* mag-c k* merc k* mur-ac k* nat-ar nat-c k* *Nat-m* k* nat-ox rly4• nat-p nat-s k2* *Nux-m* a1 *Nux-v* k* olib-sac wmh1 **Olnd** k* op k* par k* petr-ra shn4• *Ph-ac* k* phel a1 *Phos* k* phys k* pimp a1 pitu-gl skp7• plac-s rly4• plat k* plb b7.de **Podo** k* *Psor* k* **Puls** k* *Raph* rhod k* rhus-t k* ric bro1 *Rumx* bro1 ruta sal-fr sle1• sanic bro1 sars b4.de sep b4.de* *Sil* k* sin-a a1 spig k* spong fd4.de squil k* stann b4.de staph k* streptoc rly4• stront-c k* sul-ac k* **Sulph** k* sumb a1 symph fd3.de• tab k* ter k* thea bro1 thiam rly4• thuj k* til a1 valer k* vanil fd5.de verb k* vinc a1 xero bro1 zinc k* zinc-p k2
- **morning**: ferr-i a1 *Nux-v* k* plb k* podo fd3.de• ruta fd4.de spong fd4.de symph fd3.de• ter k* vanil fd5.de
- **forenoon**: ferr k* mag-c k*
- **noon**: ox-ac k*
- **afternoon**: lyc k* ox-ac k* spong fd4.de
  - 15 h: bry
- **evening**: agath-a nl2• ham fd3.de• lyc k* ruta fd4.de spong fd4.de
- **night**: cycl hr1 *Raph* ruta fd4.de *Sulph* k* symph fd3.de• vanil fd5.de
- **breakfast** agg.; after: agar k* symph fd3.de•
- **dinner**; after: grat k* *Laur* podo fd3.de•
- **downward**: cina bg2
- **drinking** agg.; after: laur k2* *Phos* ruta fd4.de
- **eating**:
  - while:
    - agg.: nit-ac
    - amel.: sul-ac
- **inspiration**:
  - agg.: mag-m k* sul-ac tab k*

- **Inspiration**: ...
  - · **deep** | **agg.**: conv br1
- **lying**:
  - · **agg.**: amp rly4• sul-ac h2
  - · **amel.**: cassia-s cdd7•
- **motion**:
  - · **agg.**: bar-c cassia-s cdd7•
  - · **amel.**: nat-m
  - · **breathing** agg.; of: sul-ac h2
- **painful**: pitu-gl skp7•
- **pressure** agg.: plb k*
- **rest** | **amel.**: cassia-s cdd7•
- **stool**:
  - · **after** | **agg.**: bry k* *Crot-t* bg2 ger-i rly4• mag-m bg2
  - · **before**: acon k* **Aloe** k* bry bg2 coloc k* **Crot-t** bg2 ferr bg2 ferr-i a1 *Gamb* bg2* hir skp7• jatr-c pd lach bg1 merc k* nat-s bg2 **Olnd** k* phos bg2 pitu-gl skp7• **Podo** k* puls bg2 rat k* sulph bg2 vanil fd5.de
    - ⁝ **gushing** stool: aloe ptk1 *Crot-t* ptk1 **Gamb** ptk1 iris ptk1 jatr-c ptk1 *Nat-s* ptk1 phos ptk1 podo ptk1 sec ptk1 *Sulph* ptk1 thuj ptk1 verat ptk1
  - · **during** | **agg.**: aloe bg2 calc-act jatr-c c1 nat-s k2 rham-f a1
- **walking**:
  - · **agg.**: cassia-s cdd7• *Lyc* k*
  - · **amel.**: cycl hr1
- **water**, as if from: sul-ac h2
  - · **bowels**; in: cortico tpw7

O - **Hip**, near the: sep
  - · **left**: sep
- **Hypochondria**: cham b7.de* kali-c k* laur bg2 lyc puls k* pyrog bg2 sabin bg2 sul-ac bg2
  - · **left**: *Lyc* mom-b c1 verb c1
- **Inguinal** region: coloc bg2
- **Intestines**: ser-a-c jl2
- **Pubic** region: squil ptk1
- **Sides**: calc k* con k* *Crot-t* k* graph k* kali-c k* *Lyc* k* meny k* nat-m k*
  - · **right**: calc tl1 caps tl1 graph bg2
  - · **left**: con bg2 *Crot-t* k* jatr-c c1 *Lyc* k* nux-v bg2 podo hr1
  - · **pressure** agg.: kali-c k*
- **Spleen**: helo c1 verb k*

O · **Region** of: helo-s rwt2•
- **Upper** abdomen: puls tl1

GUSHING sensation: ars ptk1 bell ptk1 berb ptk1 bry ptk1 **Crot-t** ptk1 elat ptk1 *Gamb* ptk1 grat ptk1 ip ptk1 *Jatr-c* ptk1 kali-bi ptk1 mag-m ptk1 *Nat-c* ptk1 nat-m ptk1 *Nat-s* ptk1 phos ptk1 *Podo* ptk1 rheum bg2 sabin ptk1 squil bg2 stann ptk1 *Thuj* ptk1 tril-p ptk1 *Verat* ptk1

O - **External** abdomen: rheum b7.de* squil b7.de*

HAIR:
- **falling** (See Hair; FEMALE - Hair; MALE GENITALIA/SEX - Hair; SKIN - Hair - falling)
- **pulled**; as if: chin b7.de*
- **standing** on end; sensation as if: sec bg2

HAMMERING (See Pulsation)

HANDS, supports abdomen during urination with: **Lyc** hr1

HANGING down; sensation of: *(↗Sinking)* acet-ac ptk1 laur ptk1 nat-m ptk1 phos ptk1 podo ptk1 *Sep* ptk1
- **walking**:
  - · **agg.**: nat-m ptk1
  - · **bent** | **must** walk bent: carb-v ptk1
  - · **carefully** | **must** walk carefully: nux-v ptk1

O - **Intestines**: *(↗Sinking)* *Agn* k* alum k* carb-v bg2* hep sne **Ign** k* ip sne lach sne *Opun-f* br1 phos k2 *Psor* k* **Staph** k* **Sulph** tab sne
  - · **thread**; by a: *Coloc* b4a.de
- **Sides**: rhus-t bg2

HARD: abrot bro1 acon vh1 alum k* alum-sil k2 *Anac* k* *Apis* b7a.de arn k* *Ars* k* ars-i k* bamb-a stb2.de• **Bar-c** k* **Bar-m** k* bar-s k2 bell k* borx b4a.de calad k* **Calc** k* calc-sil k2 caps k* **Carb-v** bg2* *Carbn-s* caust k* cham k* *Chel* k* chim a1 chin k* *Cina* k* clem k* coff k* colch k* *Coloc* b4.de* con k* cupr k* cupr-ar k* del a1 dig k* dirc k* dulc k* eup-pur k* *Ferr* k* ferr-ar ferr-p flor-p rsj3• gels k* *Graph* k* grat k* guare a1 hep b4.de* hipp a1 hyos b7.de* hyper k* ign iod ptk1 jug-r k* kali-ar *Kali-c* k* kali-p kali-s kali-sil k2 kiss a1 lac-c lach k* lat-m bnm6• laur k* *Lyc* b4.de* *Mag-m* k* mag-s k* marb-w es1• **Merc** k* merc-c k* merc-i-f k* merc-i-r *Mez* k* nat-ar *Nat-c* k* nat-m nat-p k* *Nit-ac* nux-m k* nux-v k* oena a1 *Olnd* b7a.de *Op* k* paeon k* *Petr* bg2 phos k* plb k* *Plb-act* bro1 plb-chr a1 puls k* quas a1 *Raph* k* rat ptk1 *Rhus-t* b7a.de sars sec k* *Sep* k* **Sil** k* sol-t-ae k* spig k* spira a1 spong k* stram k* sulph k* sumb k* tab k* tarax ptk1 *Thuj* b4a.de* valer k* *Verat* b7.de*
- **evening**: caust k* cedr k* cham k* con k* hyper k* *Lac-c* sep h2 spong fd4.de sulph h2
- **night**: graph mez k*
- **children**; in: calc ferr mtf33 kali-c mtf33 plb mtf33 sil k*
- **chronic**: orni br1
- **eating**; after: calc h2 con k* phos k* spira a1
- **flatus**; passing | **amel.**: lact br1
- **menses** | **before** | **agg.**: granit-m es1• mang k*
  - · **during** | **agg.**: ign nat-m puls *Sep*
- **sensation**: cupr bg2 grat bg2 hep bg2 hyos h1 ribo rly4•
- **stool** agg.; after: carb-v h2

O - **Hypochondria**: bar-c bg2 borx bov bg2 brom k* bry k* chinin-s k* ferr hr1 **Iod** k* mag-c phos k*
  - · **right**: *Calc-p*
  - · **left**: *Iod*
  - · **fever**; during intermittent: *Ars Iod*
- **Hypogastrium**: clem graph mang h2 sep
- **Inguinal** region: ant-c k* dulc graph k2 *Lith-c* nat-c k2 sul-i k2

O · **Glands**: carb-an mrr1 clem b4a.de* dulc bg2 hep k2 syph jl2 tub k2*
  - ⁝ **chronic**: syph jl2
- **Liver**: abies-c bro1 am-c bg2 ant-c k2 am b7.de* **Ars** k* ars-s-f k2 aur b4a.de* aur-ar k2 *Aur-m* bar-m k2 bell b4a.de* brom bg2 *Bry* b7.de* *Calc* k* calc-i k2 calc-sil k2 cann-s k* caps bg2 carb-an b4a.de* carb-v b4a.de* *Carbn-s* *Card-m* cham bg2 *Chel* **Chin** k* *Chinin-ar* clem bg2 *Con* k* **Dig** k* ferr b7a.de* *Fl-ac* k* **Graph** k* *Hydr* **Iod** k* kali-c b4a.de* *Kali-i* k* lach bg2* lact *Laur* k* *Lyc* k* *Mag-c* k* **Mag-m** k* *Merc* k* mez bg2 mur-ac bg2* nat-m bg2 *Nit-ac* k* nux-m bg2 *Nux-v* k* **Phos** k* plb bg2 podo puls bg2 **Rat** sep bg2 *Sil* k* sul-i k2 *Sulph* k* tarax b7a.de* zinc k*
  - · **left** lobe: *Card-m*
  - · **accompanied** by:
    - ⁝ **stool**; complaints of: graph bg2
    - ⁝ **Skin** | **discoloration**; yellow: dig br1
    - ⁝ **Tongue**:
      - ⁝ **clean** | **Tip** and sides: *Mag-m* kr1*
      - ⁝ **flabby** tongue: *Mag-m* kr1*
      - ⁝ **swelling**: *Mag-m* kr1*
  - · **sensation**; hard and small: abies-c c1*
- **Lower** abdomen: graph b4a.de* nat-m bg2 sep b4a.de*
- **Mesenteric** glands: *Ars* k* aur *Bar-c* *Bar-m* k2 borx hr1 **Calc** k* con *Lyc* *Nat-s*
- **Muscles**: alum bg2 cupr bg2 eup-per bg2 ferr bg2 ferr-p bg2 lach bg2 mag-m bg2 mang bg2 nat-c b4.de* plb bg2 *Rhus-t* b7a.de sep bg2
- **Pancreas**: bar-m k* *Carb-an* k*
- **Pubic** region | **Mons** pubis: ant-c bg2
- **Sides**: *Mag-m* b4.de*
  - · **right**: mag-m sil h2
  - · **left**: cench k2
- **Spleen**: *Agn* k* *Ars* k* brom k* caps k* carb-v b4a.de **Chin** k* *Ferr* b7a.de *Ign* k* iod k* *Mez* k* nit-ac bg2 nux-m bg2 *Psor* k* *Ran-b* sep b4a.de *Sil* b4a.de *Sul-ac* k* sul-i k2 sulph k*
- **Umbilicus**: bry k* *Merc* b4a.de plb k* puls ptk1 rhus-t k* spig b7.de*
  - · **sensation**: camph h1 dulc fd4.de

O · **Above**: sil h2
- **Upper** abdomen: *Bar-c* b4.de* camph b7.de* **Sil** b4a.de
- **Walls**; abdominal: *Rhus-t* b7a.de

HARD body; sensation of a: *(↗Ball; Lump in)* borx b4a.de*

Abdomen

- **moving** in abdomen: *(↗Movements)* borx k* *Lyc* k*
  - • **rapidly**: sabad ptk1
- **turning** to right side; when: *Lyc*

O - **Inguinal** region; sensation of walnut in left myris c1
- **Umbilicus** | **Region** of umbilicus: kreos bg2

HEAT: abies-c bro1 abrot k* *Acon* k* agar k* aids nl2• all-c k* **Aloe** k* alst bro1 alum bg2 *Am-c* k* ant-c bro1 ant-t k* **Apis** bg2* arg-n bro1 *Ars* k* ars-h ars-i **Asaf** k* aur k* *Bell* k* bov k* brom k* bry k* bufo bg2 cact k* calc b4.de calc-p bg2 *Camph* k* cann-i k* *Canth* k* caps k* carb-an k* *Carb-v* b4.de* caust k* **Cham** bg2* *Chin* k* cic k* cina k* coc-c k* cocc k* coff k* *Colch* bg2* coloc k* crot-h k* crot-t **Cupr** k* cycl k* dig k* dios k* euph k* euphr bg2 ferr k* ferr-ar ferr-i k* fl-ac k* form k* gels bg2 glon bg2 graph k* grat bg2 gymno hell k* hep k* hydr hyos k* iod k* **Ip** b7.de* iris k* jatr-c kali-ar kali-bi k* kali-br a1 **Kali-c** k* kali-i kali-p *Kali-s* k* kali-sil k2 kreos bg2 lac-c lach k* lachn lact k* *Laur* k* *Lim* bro1 lyc k* m-arct b7.de m-aust b7.de mag-m h2 malar jl2 manc k* mang k* meny k* merc-c bg2* *Mez* k* nat-m k* nat-s bro1 nat-sil fd3.de• nux-v b7.de* olib-sac wmh1 ox-ac k* par k* *Ph-ac* bg2* phos k* phys k* phyt bg2 *Plat* bg2 plb k* *Podo* k* ptel k* puls k* ran-b bg2 raph k* rheum *Rhus-t* bg2* ruta k* sabad k* sabin b7.de* sang k* sars k* *Sec* k* seneg b4.de* *Sep* bg2* **Sil** k* spig h1 spong k* squil k* stann b4.de* stram k* stry k* sul-ac b4.de* *Sulph* b4.de* sumb k* *Tab* k* taosc iwa1• tarent k* thuj k* tritic-vg fd5.de vanil fd5.de *Verat* bg2* zinc k* [spect dfg1]

- **morning**: nept-m lsd2.fr nux-v k* phos k*
- **forenoon**: am-c k* kali-c nept-m lsd2.fr phys k*
- **afternoon**: all-c k* tritic-vg fd5.de
- **night**: *Bry* fl-ac k*
- **accompanied** by | **thirst**: nept-m lsd2.fr
- **alternating** with coldness: coff k*
- **ascending** to chest: bell h1 sep bro1
- **children**; in: sil mtf33
- **constipation**; during: plb k*
- **dinner** | **after** | **agg.**: grat k*
  - • **during** | **agg.**: hyper k*
- **during** | **agg.**: caps b7.de cina b7.de mosch b7.de puls b7.de rhus-t b7.de valer b7.de
- **eating**; after: hep b4a.de **Kali-c** *Lyc* b4a.de
- **eruptions**; before: nat-m h2
- **fever**; during: apis cact calad canth chin *Cic* cub c1 ferr lach sel spig stann
- **flushes** of: *Cact* cinnb *Kali-c* ptel sumb yohim c1*
  - • **flowing** in abdomen; as of hot water: *(↗water)* *Sumb* k*
  - • **pouring** from chest into abdomen followed by diarrhea; as if hot water: sang k*
- **menses** | **before** | **agg.**: cycl graph k*
  - • **during** | **agg.**: *Graph* k*
- **sensation**: [bell-p-sp dcm1]

O • **Diaphragm**; around: samb bat1•
  - • **Hypochondria**: sabad bg2
- **smoking** agg.: spong k*
- **soup** agg.: ol-an k*
- **uncovering** | **amel.**: camph *Sec* *Tab*
- **walking** in open air agg.; after: stann h2
- **water** is running down in abdomen; sensation as if hot: *(↗flushes - flowing)* chin h1*

O - **External** abdomen: ars bg2 bell bg2* **Bry** bg2 canth bg2 carb-v bg2 lach b7.de* lyc bg2 mag-m bg2 *Merc* bg2 nat-c bg2 *Nux-v* bg2 polyg-h bg2 puls bg2 **Rhus-t** bg2 *Sabad* bg2 *Sel* bg2 sep bg2 sil bg2* sul-ac bg2 *Sulph* bg2 viol-t bg2
  - • **clothes**; as from hot: nit-ac ptk1
  - • **sensation** of: canth b7.de mag-m b4.de *Rhus-t* b7a.de
  - • **stool** agg.; after: mag-m b4.de*
- **Gallbladder**: myric bg2
- **Hips**; region of: sep b4.de thuj b4.de
- **Hypochondria**: aloe aur k* bapt bell bg2 dios bg2 kali-c k* kreos bg2 nat-m bg2 ox-ac bg2 plb podo k* sabad k* thuj k*
  - • **right**: aur k* bit-ar wht1• cench k2 *Kali-c* k*
  - • **left**: bit-ar wht1• *Glon*
  - • **flushes** rise from: cench k2 glon
- **Hypogastrium**: aur-m k* bry k* camph h1 dream-p sdj1• ferr k* hydrc k* kali-i lil-t k* mang h2 olib-sac wmh1 syph k13

Heat – Hypogastrium: ...

  - • **accompanied** by | **Back**; coldness in (See BACK - Coldness - accompanied - warmth)
  - • **menses**; must have it uncovered during: kali-i
- **Inguinal** region (= groin): alum bg2 *Am-m* bg2 **Ars** bg2 arund k* aur k* calc-p k* canth bg2 graph bg2 *Ign* bg2 kali-c bg2 **Lyc** bg2 *Merc* bg2 mur-ac bg2 **Nux-v** bg2 rhus-t bg2 sep bg2 sil bg2 spig bg2 *Stront-c* bg2 sulph k* thuj bg2 zinc bg2
- **Liver**: *Acon* bg2 **Aloe** bg2* alum bg2 am-c bg2 am-m bg2 apis bg2 arn bg2 *Ars* bg2 **Aur** bg2* bapt bg2 bell bg2 *Bry* bg2 gamb bg2 ign bg2 *Kali-c* bg2 lach bg2* laur bg2 **Lept** bg2* mag-c bg2 mag-m bg2 **Merc** bg2* mill bg2 mur-ac bg2 myric ptk1 ph-ac bg2 phos bg2 plat bg2 plb bg2 podo bg2 *Sabad* b7a.de* sang bg2 *Sec* bg2 sep bg2 *Stann* bg2* sul-ac bg2 sulph bg2 tell bg2 ter bg2 ther ptk1 thuj bg2 zinc bg2
  - • **sensation** of heat in: aloe k* bapt a1 cench k2 kali-c sabad
- **Lower** abdomen: *Apis* b7a.de* **Ars** bg2 bell b4.de* **Bry** b7.de* **Calc** bg2 *Camph* b7.de* caps bg2 coff b7.de* kali-n bg2 lil-t bg2 **Lyc** b4.de* *Ph-ac* b4a.de* phos bg2 ran-b bg2 sabin bg2 *Sep* bg2 *Stann* bg2 sul-ac bg2 sulph b4.de* tarax bg2
  - • **accompanied** by coldness in back (See BACK - Coldness - accompanied - warmth)
  - • **fire**; like: ter bg2
- **Sides**: am-m bg2 chel bg2 graph b4.de nept-m lsd2.fr petr b4.de ruta bg2 sep b4.de sulph b4.de
  - • **left**: nept-m lsd2.fr sulph h2
- **Spleen**: acon bg2 apis bg2 arn bg2 *Ars* bg2 **Asaf** k* bell bg2 borx bg2 bov bg2 *Bry* bg2 cann-xyz bg2 carb-v bg2 caust bg2 chel bg2 *Chin* bg2 coc-c ptk1 graph bg2 grat bg2 *Ign* bg2 kali-i bg2 merc bg2 **Nat-c** bg2 nux-v bg2 plat bg2 podo bg2 puls bg2 *Ran-b* bg2 *Rhus-t* bg2 sars bg2 sec bg2 seneg bg2 spig bg2 sul-ac bg2 *Sulph* bg2 tab bg2 thuj bg2
- **Umbilicus**: *Acon* bg2 aur-m k* bov b4.de* calc bg2 canth k* carb-v b4.de* chin b7.de* crot-h bg2 crot-t bg2 ham bg2 hyos k* kali-c bg2 kali-sula a1* lach bg2 lyc bg2 malar jl2 mang k* mosch bg2 nat-c bg2 nat-m bg2 nux-m bg2 ph-ac bg2 plat bg2 plb k* sabad bg2 sep b4.de* sul-ac h2* sulph b4a.de*
  - • **accompanied** by | **indigestion**: lavand-a ctl1•

O • **Region** of umbilicus: nept-m lsd2.fr sul-ac bg2

▽ • **extending** to | **Chest**: mang k*
- **Upper** abdomen: am-m bg2 *Apis* bg2 **Calad** bg2 *Camph* b7.de* **Canth** bg2 caust bg2 cham bg2 nux-v bg2 *Phos* b4.de* thuj bg2

▽ - **extending** to:

O • **Chest**: alum *Bry* coloc k* ip k* lact k* *Lyc* k* mang h2 spong h1 stram
  - • **Head**: alum carbn-o indg *Kali-c* lyc k* mag-m nat-s plb k* sumb k* tritic-vg fd5.de
  - • **Shoulders**: laur k*

HEAVINESS: *(↗Fullness; Weight)* acon vh1 agar k* *Agath-a* nl2• *Agn* **Aloe** k* alum k* alum-p k2 alum-sil k2 am-c k* am-m k* *Ambr* k* ant-t b7.de* anthraq rly4• apis k* aran c1* arg-n bg2* arge-pl rwt5• arn ptk1 ars k* ars-s-f k2 *Asaf* k* atis zzc1• aur k* aur-s k2 bar-ox-suc rly4• bell k* bov k* *Brucel* sa3• bry k* bufo bg2 *Calc* k* calc-s camph b7.de* carb-an h2 *Carb-v* k* *Carbn-s* carl cartl-s rly4• cassia-s ccrh1• *Cham* k* chel chin k* chinin-ar *Cimic* cop croc k* crot-t cupr ptk1 cupr-s dios dor ferr k* ferr-ar ferr-p gels k* **Graph** k* haliae-lc srj5• *Hell* k* hyos ptk1 ip b7.de* kali-ar kali-bi *Kali-c* k* kali-p kali-s kali-sil k2 lac-cp sk4• lac-d kr1* lac-h sk4• *Lach* k* lact lept bg1 lil-t k* **Lyc** k* *Mag-c* k* *Mag-m* k* mag-s malar jl2 mang k2 melal-alt gya4 meny b7.de* merc b4.de* *Mez* k* *Murx* myric bg1 nat-ar nat-c *Nat-m* k* *Nux-m* b7.de* nux-v k* *Op* k* osteo-a knp1• phos k* pieri-b mlk9.de pitu-gl skp7• plb *Podo* ptel puls b7.de* rein a1 *Rhod* k* rhus-t k* ruta sabin sec b7.de* **Sep** k* sil k* *Spig* ptk1 spong fd4.de **Staph** k* suis-em rly4• suis-pan rly4• *Sulph* k* sumb symph fd3.de• tab k* tep ter k* til trom zinc zinc-p k2 [bell-p-sp dcm1]

- **morning**: ambr k* dios k* **Sep** k*
- **forenoon**: trom k*
- **afternoon**: alum carl k* dios k* spong fd4.de
- **evening**: bry k*
- **night**: mag-m k* nat-m k* petr-ra shn4• zing k*
- **bending** double agg.: verb c1
- **breakfast** agg.; after: agar k* kali-c h2
- **dinner**; after: agar k* alum h2 chinin-ar k2 petr-ra shn4•
- **drinking** agg.; after: *Asaf* k*
- **eating**; after: aegle-f zzc1• atis zzc1• kali-c h2 lyc h2 spong fd4.de symph fd3.de•
- **flatus**; passing | **amel.**: carb-an h2

- **inspiration** agg.: spig k*
- **load**; as from a: nicc-met sk4• stront-c sk4•
- **lying**:
  - **amel.**: cassia-s ccrh1•
  - **side**; on:
    - **left** | **amel.**: *Pall*
- **menses** | **before** | **agg.**: aloe bro1 anthraq rly4• bell bro1 glyc bro1 kali-s bro1 **Puls** k* *Sep* bro1
  - **during** | **agg.**: aloe bro1 apis bell bro1 glyc bro1 graph k* kali-s bro1* nat-m k* *Puls* k* *Sep* bro1
- **motion**:
  - **agg.**: cassia-s ccrh1• *Nat-m* **Sep**
  - **amel.**: rein a1
- **ovulation**; during: granit-m es1•
- **rest** | **amel.**: cassia-s ccrh1•
- **rising** agg.: **Sep** k*
- **rising** up into throat: calc hr1*
- **sitting** agg.: bry k* rhus-t k*
- **stone**, as from a: *(↗Stone in)* aran c1 lac-d c1 op plut-n srj7• *Puls* verb c1
  - **eating**; after: cinch a1
  - **menses**; before: carl a1 puls a1
- **stool**:
  - **after**:
    - **agg.**: agar *Mur-ac Sep* k*
    - **amel.**: cassia-s ccrh1• nicc-met sk4•
- **supper** agg.; after: *Arg-n* k* coloc k*
- **walking**:
  - **agg.**: *Alum* bell cassia-s ccrh1• ferr kali-c k* nat-m k*
  - **bent** | **must** walk bent: carb-v h2
- **warm** drinks | **amel.**: cassia-s ccrh1•

○ - **Hypochondria**: acon k* bell k* *Coc-c* k* kali-c lact k* merc-i-r k* nux-m k* ph-ac podo k* ptel k* sulph *Zinc* k* zinc-p k2
  - **right**: nat-s k2
  - **left**: verb c1
  - **night**: *Kali-c*
  - **walking** agg.: ptel k*
- **Hypogastrium**: agar k* all-s k* aloe am-m *Ammc* k* apis bg1 aran ars k* bar-c k* coloc k* crot-c k* crot-t ferr c1 graph h2 kali-c h2 lil-t k* med ptk1 *Pall* ph-ac ptk1 *Podo* **Sec** k* sep bg1* spong fd4.de sulph k* tarent ptk1
  - **eating**; after: all-s k*
  - **lying** on left side amel.: pall
  - **menses**; during: bar-c k*
  - **standing** agg.: pall
  - **stool** agg.; after: agar k*
  - **walking** agg.: ferr c1 kali-c h2
- **Inguinal** and pubic region: aur bg2 calc b4.de* carb-an b4.de* croc b7.de* kali-bi bg2 lil-t bg2 rhus-t b7.de*
- **Inguinal** region: borx calc k* carb-an *Croc* k* dios k*
- **Intestines**: coli jl2
- **Liver**: aloe bg2 ars bell bg2 berb bg2 *Bol-la Brucel* sa3• bry bg2* camph b7.de* *Carb-v* gels bg2 graph k2 hep bg2 kali-c k* *Lach* lact lept bg2 *Mag-m* k* myric bg2 nat-m bg2 nat-s k2* nux-m b7.de* nux-v k* ph-ac k* plb podo bg2 *Ptel* k* *Sil* b4a.de sulph bg2 tab
  - **lying** on left side agg.: *Ptel* br1
  - **painful**: phyt ptk1
- **Lower** abdomen: agar bg2 all-c bg2 *Aloe* bg2 ant-t bg2 arg-n bg2 *Bell* bg2 bry bg2 coli jl2 graph bg2 hyos bg2 kali-bi bg2 kali-c bg2 nat-m bg2 ph-ac bg2 sabin bg2 sep bg2 spig bg2
- **Pelvic** region: aloe ptk1 gnaph ptk1 *Helon* br1* lil-t ptk1 pall ptk1 tarent ptk1 vib ptk1
- **Pubic** region | **Mons** pubis: aur bg2 kali-bi bg2
- **Sides**: asaf lil-t **Lyc** nat-s nept-m lsd2.fr rhus-t
  - **right**: calc h2 camph h1 tab ptk1
  - **left**: arg-n bg2 **Lyc** k*
- **Spleen**: acon bg2 ferr bg2* kali-i k* merc-i-r bg2* podo bg2 ptel bg2 sulph k*
  - **walking** agg.: mag-m ptk1

Heaviness: ...

- **Umbilicus**: agar bg1* camph h1* canth bg1* carb-v bg1* graph bg1* nit-ac bg1* op bg1* ptel bg1*

○ • **Region** of umbilicus: agar bg2 canth bg2 carb-v bg2 nit-ac bg2 op bg2
- **Upper** abdomen: nux-m bg2 nux-v b7a.de

HEAVY lying on left side of; as if something: **Lyc**

HEMORRHAGE (See Bleeding; STOOL - Bloody)

HEPATITIS (See Inflammation - liver)

HEPATOMEGALY (See Enlarged - liver)

HERNIA; ABDOMINAL: aesc bro1* *Aesc-c* c2 all-c c2 alum c2* am-c bro1 am-m ptk1 amph c2 aur bro1* bry c2 *Calc* c2* calc-p c2* caps c2 carbn-s c2 castm c2 cham c2* cocc c2* coff c2 cot bro1 cub c2 eug c2 gent-c c2 guaj c2 guare c2 hell c2 iris-fa bro1 iris-foe c2 itu c2 ketogl-ac rly4• lach c2 lam c2 lith-c c2 lyc c2* m-arct c2 m-aust c2 mag-c c2* mag-s c2 mez c2 nat-m c2 *Nux-v* c2* osm c2 ox-ac c2* petr bro1 phase-xyz c2 phos bro1 picro bro1 pitu-gl mtf11 prun c2 psor c2 raph c2 rhus-t c2 sars c2 sec gk *Sil* c2* spong c2 sul-ac bro1* sulph ptk1* symph c2 tab c2 ter c2 thuj c2 verat c2* zinc bro1

- **children**; in: *Calc* bro1 lyc bro1 nit-ac bro1 *Nux-v* bro1 sil bro1 sulph bro1
  - **congenital**: mag-m bro1
- **inactivity** of rectum; from: cham tl1
- **inclination** to: cocc tl1 nux-v tl1
  - **rising** from sitting agg.: cocc tl1
- **strangulated**: acon bro1* alum ptk1 aur ptk1 bell bro1* calc ptk1 caps ptk1 cham ptk1 coloc ptk1 lach ptk1 lob bro1 lyc bro1* *Mill* bro1 nit-ac ptk1 nux-v bro1* op bro1* plb bro1* plb-xyz c2 sil ptk1 sul-ac ptk1 sulph ptk1 tab ptk1* ter c2 *Verat* ptk1

○ - **Femoral**: cub c1* *Lyc* k* nux-v k* wies c2
- **Inguinal**: *Acon* bg2 aesc k* *All-c Alum* k* am-c k* *Am-m* b2.de* anac b2.de* ant-c b2.de* *Apis* arg-met b2.de* *Asar* k* *Aur* k* **Bell** b2.de* berb *Bry* bg2 *Calc* k* calc-ar camph b2.de* cann-s b2.de* caps b2.de* *Carb-an* k* *Carb-v* carc mlr1• cham b2.de* chin b2.de* clem b2.de* *Cocc* k* coff b2.de* colch gk coloc b2.de* dig b2.de* euph b2.de* gran c2 graph b2.de* **Guaj** b2.de* hell b2.de* ign b2.de* ip kali-c b2.de* kali-n b2.de* lach k* **Lyc** k* m-ambo b2.de *M-arct* b2.de m-aust b2.de *Mag-c* k* merc b2.de* mez b2.de* *Mur-ac* nat-m b2.de* *Nit-ac* k* **Nux-v** k* *Op* k* petr k* ph-ac b2.de* phos k* plat b2.de* *Plb* b2.de* prun psor puls bg2 rheum b2.de* *Rhus-t* k* sars sec gk sep b2.de* *Sil* k* *Spig* k* spong b2.de* stann b2.de* staph k* stram b2.de* stront-c b2.de* *Sul-ac* k* *Sulph* k* ter teucr b2.de* thuj k* *Verat* k* wies c2 *Zinc* k*
  - **left**: cocc tl1 thuj mtf33
  - **children**; in: **Aur** k* **Bell** b4a.de calc ptk1* carc mlr1• cham bg2* cina gsy1 cocc bg2 lyc k* mag-m ptk1 *Nit-ac* k* nux-v k* psor al2 sil mtf33 sul-ac pd* sulph bg2* thuj mtf33 verat bg2
    - **right**: aur lyc k*
    - **left**: nux-v k* thuj mtf33
    - **congenital**: nux-v gk thuj ptk1
  - **inflammation**: acon k* bar-c h2 iod h nux-v op sulph
    - **vomiting**; with: acon ars bell lach *Tab* verat
  - **old** people: nux-v pd sul-ac pd
  - **overlifting**; from: *Bell* b4a.de *Cocc* b7a.de *Nux-v* b7a.de sul-ac b4a.de sulph b4a.de
  - **painful**: *Acon* b7a.de *Alum* k* amph a1 aur b4.de* **Bell** b4a.de calc b4.de* cham b7.de* chin b7.de* cic k* clem b4a.de* cocc k* coff b7.de* coloc bg2 con b4.de* dig b4.de* guaj b4.de* lyc b4.de* m-ambo b7.de m-arct b7a.de m-aust b7.de* mag-c b4.de* nit-ac b4.de* *Nux-v* b7.de* phos b4.de* plat b4a.de rhus-t b7.de* *Sil* k* spong b7.de* stront-c b4.de* sul-ac b4.de* thuj mtf33 *Verat* b7.de* zinc b4a.de
    - **pressure** | **amel.**: thuj mtf33
  - **protrusion**: *Acon* b7a.de alum b4.de* am-c b4.de* am-m b7a.de ant-c b7.de* arg-met b7.de* ars bg2 *Asaf* b7a.de *Aur* b4.de* **Bell** b4a.de calc b4a.de* cann-s b7.de* caps b7.de* carb-an b4.de* *Cham* b7.de* chin b7a.de clem b4.de* *Cocc* b7.de* coloc b4a.de* graph b4.de* *Guaj* b4a.de hell b7.de* ign b7.de* kali-bi bg2 kali-c b4.de* lyc b4.de* m-ambo b7.de *M-arct* b7.de mag-c b4.de* nat-m b4.de* *Nit-ac* b4a.de **Nux-v** b7.de* op b7.de* petr b4a.de phos b4.de* plb b7.de* rheum b7.de* *Rhus-t* b7.de* sep b4a.de sil b4.de* spig b7.de* stann b4.de* staph b7.de* stram b7.de* stront-c b4.de* sul-ac b4.de* sulph b4a.de **Thuj** b4a.de **Verat** b7.de* zinc b4.de*
    - **cough** agg.; during: *Calc* b4a.de

Abdomen

- **Inguinal – protrusion**: ...
  - ⁝ **menses**; after: lyc b4.de
  - ⁝ **sense** of: kali-bi bg2
- · **pudendal**: camph b7.de*
- · **sensitive**: *Bell* **Lach** *Nux-v Sil*
- · **stitching**: sep h2
- · **strangulated**: acon k* *All-c* alum k* ars aur b4a.de* **Bell** k* calc bg2 caps b7.de* *Carb-v* carbn-s c1 cham b7.de* *Cocc* k* *Coff* coloc bg2 *Dig* ip lach k* lob bg2 lyc bg2 mill k* nit-ac b4a.de* **Nux-v** b7.de* **Op** b7.de* *Plb* k* *Rhus-t* k* sil b4a.de* *Sul-ac* k* *Sulph* k* *Tab* k* verat k*
- · **tendency** to: nux-v tl1 ter tl1
- **Umbilical**: amph a1 *Aur* bg2* bry b7a.de *Calc* k* cham bg2 cocc bg2* gran c2 *Lach* k* lyc b4a.de *Nux-m* k* **Nux-v** k* *Op* k* plb bg2* *Puls* b7a.de rhus-t bg2 sep b4a.de *Sulph* b4a.de* verat b7.de*
  - · **accompanied** by | **constipation**: cocc bro1 nux-v bro1
  - · **children**; in: *Aur* sne nux-v mtf33 plb mtf33 thuj mtf33
    - ⁝ **newborns**: nux-m mrr1

HERRING agg.: nat-m bg2

HOLDING:
- **amel.**: carb-an bg2 carb-v bg2 phos bg2
- **must** hold: agn ptk1 carb-v bg2 lil-t bg1* merc bg1* plb gk rhus-t ptk1 sep bg1* staph bg1*

HOLE; sensation of a: | **Solar** plexus: gard-j vlr2•

HOLLOW (See Emptiness)

HORRIPILATION (See Goose)

HYPOCHONDRIACS; complaints of (See MIND - Hypochondriasis - abdomen)

HYSTERIA agg.: ars bg2 bell bg2 bry bg2 *Cocc* bg2 **Ign** bg2 *Ip* bg2 mag-m bg2 mosch bg2 *Nux-v* bg2 stann bg2 stram bg2 sulph bg2 valer bg2 verat bg2

ILEUS: ars bg2* bell bg2 bry bg2 castm c2 cham bg2 cocc bg2 colch c2 coloc bg2* lyc bg2* nit-ac bg2 nux-v bg2 op bg2* pitu-p sp1 plat bg2 plb bg2* raph mrr1 rhus-t bg2 samb c2 sil bg2 sol-t-ae c2 sulph bg2 tann-ac c2 *Thuj* bg2* verat bg2 zinc bg2
- **accompanied** by | **vomiting**: op mrr1
- **operation**; after: carb-v mrr1 op mrr1 raph mrr1
- **spastic** ileus: kali-chl a1

IMMOBILE (See Rigidity)

IMPACTION: *(↗RECTUM - Impacted)* *Caust* k* gels k* lac-d k* *Lach* k* **Op** k* *Plb* k* pyrog bro1 sel bro1
- **accompanied** by | **vomiting**: op bro1 plb bro1* pyrog bro1

INACTIVITY:
- ○ - **Intestines**; of: *(↗Paralysis)* aeth ptk1 alum b4a.de* am-c bg2 atro bg2 *Bry* bg2 camph b7.de* cann-s b7a.de* caust bg2 cham b7.de* chin b7a.de* *Cocc* b7a.de *Colch* b7a.de* **Con** bg2 hep b4a.de *Kali-c* b4.de* *Lyc* bg2 *Mag-m* bg2 mosch b7a.de **Nat-m** b4a.de *Nux-v* b7.de* **Op** b7.de* phys ptk1 plb bg2 *Rhus-t* b7a.de* *Ruta* b7a.de sars b4a.de* staph b7.de* thuj b4a.de* *Verat* b7a.de
- **Liver**; of: aesc br1 euon-a br1 nit-m-ac br1 podo br1 still br1
  - · **accompanied** by:
    - ⁝ **constipation**: aesc br1 still br1
    - ⁝ **indigestion**: chelo br1
    - ⁝ **Skin**; yellow discoloration of: still br1

INDIGNATION agg.: *Ant-c* bg2 bell bg2 bry bg2 carb-v bg2 coloc bg2 hep bg2 *Nux-v* bg2 **Puls** bg2 sulph bg2

INDURATION (See Hard)

INFANTILE liver: calc-ar mtf11

INFLAMMATION: *Acet-ac* **Acon** k* aloe alumn ant-c b7a.de **Ant-t** k* **Apis** arg-n br1 *Arn* k* **Ars** k* ars-i asc-c hr1 atro *Bapt* **Bell** k* brom b4a.de **Bry** k* bufo k* *Cact Calc* calc-sil k2 *Canth* k* *Carb-v* card-m *Cham* k* chin b7.de* cic b7.de* cocc coff k* **Colch** *Coloc* k* *Crot-c Crot-h* cupr *Echi* euph b4a.de *Ferr* ferr-ar ferr-p gamb *Gels* graph b4a.de guaj b4a.de **Hyos** k* iod k* *Ip* k* kali-ar k2 kali-bi bg2 *Kali-c* k* *Kali-chl* kali-i *Kali-n* k* kali-p **Lach** k* **Laur** k* **Lyc** k* med c1 *Merc* k* *Merc-c* k* *Mez* k* *Nux-v* k* *Op Ox-ac* **Phos** k* plb k* podo bg2 *Puls* k*

Inflammation: ...
Pyrog **Rhus-t** k* sabin k* *Sec Sil* spong k* squil b7.de* *Stram* b7.de* *Sulph* k* **Ter** thuj tub k* (non:uran-met k) *Uran-n* urt-u *Verat* k* *Verat-v* vip bg2
- **after** inflammation; complaints: *Seneg* b4a.de
- **children**, infants: calc gt1
- **chronic**: pyrog st
- **weather** agg.; wet: gels c1
- ○ - **Appendix**: abrot mtf11 ammc c2 **Arn** k2 **Ars** ptk1 bapt c2* *Bell* k* bell-p sp1 **Bry** st* cadm-s calc-ar mtf11 calc-caust c1 *Calc-s* carb-v ptk1 chel *Chin* k* *Cocc* colch c2 **Coloc** ptk1 con *Crot-c* crot-h c2 dios c2 dulc *Echi* k* gins c2* graph *Hep Iris-t* c2* lac-d c2 *Lach* c1* lat-m bnm6• *Lyc* k* *Merc* k* **Merc-c** k* mur-ac ptk1 nat-s k2 *Nit-ac Nux-v* ptk1 *Ph-ac* ptk1* **Phos** k* *Plb* k* plb-xyz c2 puls ptk1 pyrog jl2 rham-cath c2 rham-f c2 rhus-r mtf11 rhus-t c2* sabal c2 scroph-xyz c2 **Sep** ptk1 **Sil** **Sulph** ptk1 ter **Thuj** ptk1 tub c1* tub-d jl2
  - · **acute**: bry mtf11 echi mtf11 lach mtf11 rhus-t mtf11 tub-d jl2
  - · **chronic**: bell-p jl but-ac jl coli jl2 coloc sf1.de iris-t sf1.de kali-c jl merc-d sf1.de periproc mtf11 plb sf1.de pyrog st sil sf1.de streptoc jl2 *Sul-i* sf1.de* *Sulph* sf1.de syc mtf11 tub-k mg1.de
  - · **irregular**: tub-d jl2
  - · **lying** on back | **amel.**: lach ptk1 merc ptk1
- **Cecum** (= typhlitis): acon bro1 **Apis** arn bro1 *Ars* k* bapt bro1 **Bell** k* **Bry** k* *Calad* canth bro1 *Card-m* k* *Chin Colch* k* coll bro1 *Coloc* bro1 *Crot-h* k* *Dios* bro1 *Echi* bro1 ferr-p bro1 gamb c2 gast c2 gins k* hep bro1 iris-t bro1 kali-m bro1 **Lach** k* *Lyc* k* **Merc** k* *Merc-c* bro1 *Nat-s Nux-v* bro1 **Op** k* *Phos Plb* k* plb-xyz c2 pyrog c2 rham-cal bro1 rham-cath c2 **Rhus-t** k* *Samb Sep Sil* k* *Stram* sulph k* **Thuj** tub-r jl2 verat bro1
- ○ · **Region**: tub-r jl2
- **Colon** (= Colitis): abrot mp4• all-s br1 arg-n mrr1 ars mrr1 asaf mrr1 asar ptk1 bism mrr1 cadm-s mrr1 calc-ar mrr1 canth br1* caps mrr1 carc mrr1* cench mtf chin mrr1 colch ptk1 cop ptk1 crot-t mrr1 dys fmm1• eberth jl2 enteroc jl2 *Ferr-i* mrr1 *Gamb* mrr1 guat sp1 hell mrr1 hoit mtf11 influ jl2 kali-bi mrr1 kali-n mrr1 kali-p ptk1 lach mrr1 lil-t mrr1 lyc mrr1 mag-c mrr1 malar jl2 merc mrr1 **Merc-c** mrr1 nat-c mrr1 nat-m mrr1 nat-s mrr1 nit-ac mrr1* nux-v mrr1* olnd mrr1 parathyr jl2 petr mrr1 ph-ac mrr1 phos mrr1* podo mrr1 ptel mrr1 raph gk1 rhus-t ptk1 sulph mrr1 syph jl2* ter tl1 tub jl2* tub-d jl2 uncar-tom mp4• verat mrr1 zinc mrr1 zinc-val ptk1
  - · **accompanied** by:
    - ⁝ **flatulence**: arg-n mtf
    - ⁝ **hemorrhage**: aran mtf11 cyn-d mtf ham mtf merc mtf merc-c mtf streptoc mtf syph jl2
    - ⁝ **respiration**; asthmatic (See RESPIRATION - Asthmatic - accompanied - colon)
    - ⁝ **rheumatic** pains (See EXTREMITIES - Pain - rheumatic - accompanied - colon)
    - ⁝ **sexual** desire; increased: gamb mrr1* *Grat* mrr1 lyc mrr1 nabal mtf
    - ⁝ **weakness**: cadm-s mrr1
  - · **acute**: achy-a mtf11 podo hr1
  - · **amoebic**: ars mtf atis mtf kali-bi mtf kali-c mtf kurch mtf lach mtf merc mtf merc-c mtf nat-s mtf nux-v mtf sulph mtf thuj mtf
  - · **cancerous**: *(↗Cancer - colon; Cancer - colon - transverse)* mag-c mtf mag-m mtf mag-s mtf phos mtf
  - · **chilliness**; with: cadm-s mrr1
  - · **chronic**: gaert mtf lyc mtf oxyte-chl mtf11 podo hr1 sulph mtf tub jl2
  - · **diarrhea** | **amel.**: lach mrr1
  - · **flora**; with pathological intestinal: all-s br1
  - · **grief**; after: *Ign* mtf mag-c mtf mag-m mtf mag-s mtf nat-m mtf nat-s mtf *Staph* mtf
  - · **hemorrhagic**: parathyr jl2
  - · **membranous**: colch tl1
  - · **mucous**: aethi-a mtf11 asar mtf aur-m-n mtf cop mtf coxs mtf11 graph mtf hell mtf hydr mtf merc mtf merc-c mtf pot-e mtf11 x-ray mtf11
  - · **painful**: coloc mtf merc mtf merc-c mtf moni jl2 rhus-t mtf
  - · **radiotherapy**; after: podo mtf11
  - · **recurrent**: enteroc jl2
  - · **spasmodic**: coli jl2 moni jl2
  - · **summer** agg.: ip nh8 kali-bi mrr5 puls mtf vac jl2

- **ulcerative**: *(↗Cancer - colon - transverse; RECTUM - Ulceration)* carc mlr1• *Chloram* mtf11 coloc mtf *Hell* mrr1 lil-t tl1 *Mag-s* mtf merc mrr1 *Nat-s* mrr1 nit-ac mrr1 nux-v mrr1 podo mtf11 *Streptoc* mtf sulph mtf ter tl1 zinc mtf

- **Duodenum**: *Ars* bro1 aur bro1 berb bro1 cham bro1 chel bro1 *Chin* bro1 *Hydr* bro1 *Kali-bi* bro1 lyc bro1 merc bro1 merc-d bro1 nat-s bro1 nux-v bro1 *Podo* bro1 ric bro1 sang bro1 tub-r jl2
  - **accompanied** by | **green** stool: merc-d mtf11
- **Enterocolitis**: cupr-ar br1
  - **acute**: yers jl2
  - **chronic**: nuph hl9 tub jl2
  - **summer**: vac jl2
- **Gallbladder** (= cholecystitis): bell mrr1* berb mrr1* but-ac sp1 calc mrr1 card-m mtf11 chel bg2* chin bg2* coli jl2 coloc mrr1 curc mg1.de eberth jl2 fel mtf11 guat sp1 *Hed* sp1 lach ptk1 lyc bg2* mag-m mrr1 mag-s sp1 malar jl2 mand mtf11 morg fmm1• morg-g fmm1• *Nat-s* mrr1 nux-v mrr1 parathyr jl2 phos ptk1 prot jl2 ptel mrr1 tarax mrr1
  - **acute**: bell mrr1 crot-h mtf11 parathyr jl2 pyrog jl2*
  - **chronic**: beryl mtf11 coli jl2 eberth mtf11 hydroq mtf11 parathyr jl2 quinhydr mtf11
  - **septic**: bry ptk1 bufo ptk1 lach ptk1* *Phos* ptk1
  - **suppurated**: eberth jl2
- **Gastroenteritis**: *(↗RECTUM - Cholera - morbus)* aeth hr1 aloe vh1 alumn bro1 ant-t nh1* anthraci jl2* antip vh1 apis vh1 apom vh1 *Arg-n* bro1 ars bro1* *Bapt* bro1 bism bro1* bry bro1 cadm-s mrr1 canth mrr1 colch mrr1 coloc mrr1 *Cupr* bro1 dios mrr1 *Diosm* br1 gaert fmm1• gamb mrr1 iris mrr1 kali-n br1 kreos mrr1 lac-ac mtf11 lim br1 merc bro1* merc-c bro1 nat-m mtf11 nux-v mtf11 ox-ac br1 podo br1* rhus-t bro1 santin bro1 ser-a-c jl2 syc bka1*• **Verat** mrr1 yers jl2 zinc bro1
  - **accompanied** by:
    - **sexual** desire; increased: *Grat* mrr1
    - **weakness**: kali-n br1
    - **Ileum**; injury of: yers jl2
  - **acute**: acon mtf11 ars mtf11 cupr-ar mtf11 pot-e mtf11 sal-p mtf11 verat mtf11
  - **chronic**: coli jl2 gaert fmm1• syc fmm1•
  - **ice** cream; after: parat mtf11
  - **summer**: parat-b mtf11 yers jl2
- **Glands**; inguinal: bac jl2 bell k* bufo carb-an clem dulc k* graph hep c1 *Merc* k* *Merc-i-r* morb jl2 nit-ac k2 *Puls* *Rhus-t* *Sil* k* syph jl2
  - **chronic**: syph jl2
- **Hypochondria**: *Acon* b7.de* canth b7.de* nux-v b7.de*
- **Ileocecum**: lac-d c1
- **Intestines**: arist-cl sp1 but-ac sp1 canth br1* *Chin* mrr1 coli jl2 cyt-l br1* influ jl2 lyc mrr1 mag-s sp1 malar jl2 merc-c mrr1 nat-m mrr1 nit-ac mtf nux-v mrr1* phos mtf *Podo* mrr1 sulph mrr1 syph mtf tub jl2 tub-d jl2 verat-v ptk1
  - **spasmodic**: moni jl2
  - **Ileum** (= ileitis): but-ac sp1 toxo-g jl2 yers jl2
    - **follicular**: toxo-g jl2
    - **segmentary**: toxo-g jl2
- **Large** intestine (See colon)
- **Liver** (= hepatitis): **Acon** k* act-sp c2* adlu jl aloe mrr1 alum bg2 am-c bg2 ambr bg2 anan androg-p mtf11 ant-c k2 apis arg-n mrr1 *Arn* k* **Ars** k* ars-i astac kr1 *Aur* b4a.de* aur-m k2 bapt k2 **Bell** k* *Brom* b4a.de *Bry* k* cael jl *Calc* k* calc-f mg1.de* *Camph* cann-xyz bg2 canth b7.de* *Caps* bg2 carc gk6* *Card-m* *Cham* k* **Chel** k* *Chin* k* cic bg2 cocc k* coli jl2 cordyc mp4• *Corn* k* crot-h cupr dig bg2* *Diosm* br1 dol mrr1 eup-per k2 flor-p mg1.de graph bg2 guat sp1 *Hep* k* *Hippoz* ign k* iod k* kali-ar k2 kali-bi bg2 *Kali-c* k* kali-chl br1 kali-i bro1 kali-n bg2 kali-p *Lach* k* *Laur* b7a.de* loxo-lae bnm12• loxo-recl bnm10• **Lyc** k* mag-c bg2* *Mag-m* k* malar jl2 mand mg1.de mang mang-s c2 *Merc* k* merc-d bro1 morg awy1• nat-ar nat-c k* *Nat-m* k* **Nat-s** k* *Nit-ac* nit-m-ac br1 nux-m bg2 **Nux-v** k* p-benzq mtf11 petr bg2 ph-ac b4a.de *Phos* k* phyt k* *Podo* k* *Psor* k* *Ptel* k* puls k* ran-b bg2 ran-s sang hr1 scroph-xyz c2 sec k* sel sep b4a.de* *Sil* bg2* stann mg1.de* staph stel c2* sulfa sp1 *Sulph* k* tab toxo-g jl2 vip-a jl
  - **accompanied** by:
    - **hiccough**: *Bell* st1
    - **nausea**: chel tl1
  - **alcohol**; from: med jl2 nux-v mrr1

- **Liver**: ...
  - **chronic**: *Arn* aur hr1 bell kr1 carc fb* *Card-m* k* *Corn* k* crot-h *Lach* k* lact mrr1 **Lyc** k* mag-m nat-c *Nat-m* **Nat-s** k* *Nit-ac* k* *Nux-v* k* *Phos* phyt kr1 podo kr1 *Psor* k* ptel kr1 ran-s sel sil kr1 *Sulph* tub jl2
    - **vesicular** eruption, with: corn c1*
  - **hepatitis** A (= catarrhal jaundice; epidemic catarrhal icterus; pidemic hepatitis): card-m bwa3 chel gtr1 chion cp1 hydr bwa3* ip btw2 lept bwa3 lob vma2 loxo-lae bnm12• merc bwa3* myric bn4 nat-s bl6 sulph bl1 toxo-g jl2
  - **hepatitis** C: mag-m mtf
  - **mortification**; from: *Lyc*
  - **subacute**: phos br1
  - **vexation**; after: *Cham*
- **Mesenteric** glands: *Brom* b4a.de con b4a.de *Merc* b4a.de toxo-g jl2
- **Pancreas** (= pancreatitis): achy mtf11 *Atro* c2 atro-s mtf11 bar-m c2 bell mtf11 bol-la mtf11 carb-an mrr1 *Con* dios mtf11 eberth jl2 fel mtf11 *Iod* k* *Iris* k* *Kali-i* c2 lat-m bnm6• lept mtf11 leptos-ih jl2 *Merc* c2* mom-b mtf11 mucot mtf11 ourl jl2 pancr mtf11 parathyr jl2 phos gk* **Spong** k*
  - **acute**: con tl1 crot-h mtf11
  - **chronic**: parat mtf11
- **Peritoneum**: achil-m mtf11 *Acon* b7a.de* anac mtf11 *Ant-t* ptk1 *Apis* c2* arn bro1 *Ars* c2* atro bro1 *Bell* b4a.de* *Bry* b7a.de* *Calc* c2* *Canth* c2* carb-v bro1* cham c2* *Chin* c2* chinin-s bro1 cimic bro1 colch ptk1 *Coloc* c2* con c2 crot-h c2* eberth jl2 echi mtf11 euph c2 ferr-p bro1* fl-ac c2 gels bro1* *Hep* bro1 hyos bro1* *Ip* bro1* kali-chl bro1 kali-m mtf11 kali-n c2 lach bro1* lat-m bnm6• laur ptk1 led mtf11 *Lyc* c2* merc c2* *Merc-c* c2* merc-d br1* nux-v b7a.de* op bro1* pall bro1* **Phos** ptk1 *Puls* ptk1 pyrog c2* rhus-t bro1* ric c2 sabal c2 sabin bro1 sangin-n bro1 sec bro1 *Sil* bro1 *Sin-n* bro1 sol-ni c2* *Spig* b7a.de *Sulph* c2* ter bro1* til c2* tub verat c2* verat-v bro1 *Wye* bro1
  - **accompanied** by:
    - **hiccough**: *Hyos* bg2* *Lyc* ptk1*
    - **menses**; copious: ars bro1 ham bro1 sabin bro1 thlas bro1
    - **typhoid** fever: ars bro1 *Bell* bro1 carb-v bro1 coloc bro1 *Merc-c* bro1 rhus-t bro1 ter bro1
    - **vomiting**: op a*
    - **Tongue** | **dryness** of tongue: *Atro* kr1*
  - **chronic**: apis bro1 *Lyc* bro1 merc-d bro1 sulph bro1
  - **cold** applications | **amel.**: calc ptk1
  - **delivery**; after: *(↗FEVER - Puerperal)* acon c1* bell bro1* bry bro1 *Merc-c* bro1 pyrog br1* spig hr1 sulph dh1* ter br1* ust al2 verat-v btw2
  - **hysterical**: bell bro1 coloc bro1 verat bro1
  - **infection**; from: merc mtf11
  - **perforation**; before: atro-s mtf11
  - **puerperal**: spig hr1
  - **tubercular**: abrot br1* *Ars* bro1 ars-i bro1* calc bro1 carb-v bro1 *Chin* bro1 iod bro1 psor bro1 sulph bro1 *Tub* bro1 tub-m jl2
- **Perityphlitis**: ars bro1 bell bro1 *Iris-t* bro1 *Lach* bro1 merc-c bro1 rhus-t bro1
- **Small** intestine (= enteritis): acon c2 aloe mrr1 ant-t tl1 *Arg-n* br1 cadm-s mrr1 caps mrr1 eberth jl2 enteroc jl2 lat-m bnm6• levist mtf11 nux-v mtf11 parathyr jl2 pyrog jl2 santin c2 tub jl2*
  - **accompanied** by | **weakness**: cadm-s mrr1
  - **chilliness**; with: cadm-s mrr1
  - **chronic**: tub jl2
  - **infants**: mucor jl2 yers jl2
    - **newborns**: coli jl2
  - **painful**: moni jl2
  - **spasmodic**: moni jl2
  - **summer**: parathyr jl2
- **Small** intestine and stomach (See gastroenteritis)
- **Spleen** (= splenitis): acon k* *Agn* bg2 *Apis* aran bro1 *Arn* k* ars k* ars-i asaf bell *Bry* k* bufo k* calc b4a.de *Caps* bg2 *Cean* k* **Chin** k* chinin-s k* cit-l c2 con cupr daph c2 diosm br1 dros b7.de* ferr b7.de* ferr-p bro1 hell mtf11 hura mtf11 ign k* iod k* nat-ar nat-c *Nat-m* *Nit-ac* *Nux-v* k* plb b7.de* plb-i bro1 *Polym* bro1 querc-r-g-s mtf11 succ bro1 sul-i k2 sulph k* syph jl2 urt-u mtf11 verat-v bro1
- **Typhlitis** (See cecum)
- **Umbilicus**: *(↗Discharge)* dulc fd4.de kali-n moni rfm1• phys c2 sacch-l c2
  - **children**; in: *Arn* b7a.de

· **children**; in: ...
⁝ **newborns**; ulceration of umbilicus in: abrot mtf33 apis pd calc-p mtf33

INFLATING abdomen with air: | **agg.**: ign b7.de*

INJURY: *Arn* bg2 bry bg2* carb-v bg2 lach bg2 rhus-t bg2
- **bleeding** after injury; uncontrolled: crot-h mtf11
- **deep** tissue: (↗*GENERALS - Injuries - operation - ailments - deeper*) bell-p mtf11

○ - **Ileum**:
· **accompanied** by | **gastroenteritis** (See Inflammation - gastroenteritis - accompanied - ileum)
- **Pelvic** organs: bell-p br1*
- **Spleen**: p-benzq mtf11

INSENSIBILITY: *Ars* b4.de*
○ - **Skin**; of: pop-cand br1

INSPIRATION:
- **agg.**: am-m b7.de* anac b4.de bry bg2 camph b7.de caps b7.de chin b7.de cina b7.de croc b7.de guaj b4.de kali-bi bg2 lyc bg2 mag-m bg2 mosch b7.de plat bg2 rheum b7.de rhus-t b7.de* sel bg2 *Seneg* b4.de* spig b7.de stront-c b4.de tab bg2 thuj b4.de verb b7.de viol-t b7.de

○ · **External** abdomen: crot-h bg2
· **Hypochondria**: acon b7.de* agar b4.de* anac b4.de* asaf b7a.de* bry b7a.de* camph b7.de* chin b7.de* cob bg2 con b4.de* croc b7.de* kali-bi bg2 led b7.de* mosch b7a.de plat b4.de* ran-s b7.de* sabad b7.de* sel b7.de* valer b7.de* viol-t b7.de*
· **Liver**: bry bg2 sel bg2
· **Spleen**: agar bg2
- **amel.**: am-c bg2 anac bg2 camph bg2 caps bg2 chin bg2 cina bg2 croc bg2 guaj bg2 kali-bi bg2 mosch bg2 rheum bg2 rhus-t bg2 seneg bg2 spig bg2 stront-c bg2 thuj bg2 verb bg2 viol-t bg2

○ · **Hypochondria**: spig b7.de*

INTERTRIGO: | **Inguinal** region: bov mtf11

INTUSSUSCEPTION: *Acon* k* *Arn* k* **Ars** k* atro bro1 **Bell** k* *Bry* k* *Colch* k* *Coloc* k* *Cupr* k* kali-bi k* kreos k* *Lach* k* *Lob* k* *Lyc* k* *Merc* k* merc-c c2* *Nux-v* k* **Op** k* *Phos* k* **Plb** k* plb-xyz c2 *Rhus-t* k* *Samb* sulph k* tab k* tarent thuj k* **Verat** k*
- **accompanied** by:
· **stool**; complaints of: bry bg2 *Nux-v* bg2 **Op** bg2 plb bg2 *Rhus-t* bg2 sulph bg2 *Thuj* bg2
· **vomiting** | **fecal**: cupr mtf33

○ · **Tongue**; white discoloration of the: plb kr1*
- **hiccough**; after (See STOMACH - Hiccough - followed - intussusception)

IRRITABILITY agg.: cic bg2 kreos bg2 sulph bg2

IRRITABLE BOWEL SYNDROME (See Inflammation - colon)

IRRITATION: iod bg2
- **accompanied** by | **convulsions** (See GENERALS - Convulsions - accompanied - abdomen - irritation)

○ - **Gastrointestinal**:
· **accompanied** by | **vertigo** (See VERTIGO - Accompanied - gastrointestinal - irritation)
- **Intestines**; of: bism-n br1 cina br1 eucal br1 vanad br1
· **chronic**: mangi br1
· **worms**; from: santin br1

ITCHING: agar k* ambr k* anac *Arn* k* *Ars* k* ars-s-f k2 asaf b7.de* aur k* aur-ar k2 bar-c bg2 bell k* *Bov* k* cann-s b7.de* carb-ac carbn-s caust b4a.de chel k* cist k* coc-c k* com k* con k* croc b7.de* crot-t bg2 euph bg2 ferr-ar ferr-ma k* form k* *Graph* ign b7.de* iod b4.de* jug-r k* kali-ar k* kali-bi k* kali-c k* kali-s lac-ac k* lach laur bg2 led b7.de* m-ambo b7.de mag-c b4.de* mag-m b4.de* *Merc* k* merc-c b4a.de merc-i-f k* mez k* nat-c k* nat-m nit-ac k* nux-v b7.de* ol-an petr k* phos k* pin-s bro1 plat b4.de* podo fd3.de• puls k* rhus-t k* rhus-v *Sars* k* *Sep* k* spig bg2 spong fd4.de staphycoc rly4• stront-c b4.de* *Sulph* k* tarax b7.de* *Thuj* k* tritic-vg fd5.de vanil fd5.de viol-t b7.de* zinc k*

Itching: ...
- **daytime**: nat-c k*
- **morning**: petr-ra shn4• rat k* spong fd4.de
· **dressing**; while: nux-v k*
- **evening**: cact k* merc k* spong fd4.de stront-c thuj k*
· **undressing** agg.: cact k* *Nux-v* k*
- **night**: agar k* crot-t k* *Nux-v* k* phos k* **Sulph** k* *Thuj* k* zinc h2
· **going** to bed; on: thuj
- **accompanied** by | **Skin**; yellow discoloration of the (See SKIN - Discoloration - yellow - accompanied - abdomen)
- **burning**: sars h2
- **corrosive**: nat-c h2
- **dinner**; after: *Sulph* k*
- **scratching** | **amel.**: arn k* ferr-ma k* mez k* sars k* spong fd4.de
- **stinging**: alum h2
- **warm** bed agg.: sulph k2

○ - **Hips**; region of: mag-c k* spong fd4.de
- **Hypochondria**: agar k* bov b4.de* iod b4.de* lyc bg2 mag-m b4.de* mosch b7.de* olnd b7.de* sars b4.de* sep b4.de* tab k* tritic-vg fd5.de
· **right**: interf sa3•
· **night**: agar k*
- **Hypogastrium**: agar anac k* *Carb-ac* k* cassia-s ccrh1• dream-p sdj1• elaps indg k* kali-c k* merc k* nat-c k* nat-m k* ph-ac k* rhus-t k* rhus-v k* zinc k*
· **afternoon**: nat-c h2
· **night**: cassia-s ccrh1•
· **air**; in open | **amel.**: cassia-s ccrh1•
· **scratching**:
⁝ **agg.**: cassia-s ccrh1•
⁝ **amel.**: cassia-s ccrh1• ph-ac k*
· **uncovering** agg.: cassia-s ccrh1•
· **walking** agg.: elaps
· **warm** applications agg.: cassia-s ccrh1•
- **Iliac** region: choc srj3• osm k* sulph k* *Tell* k*
· **right**: stront-c
· **evening**: zinc h2
- **Inguinal** region: agar k* agn k* ammc k* bar-c h2* camph b7.de* coc-c bg1 cycl k* form lac-h sk4• laur k* lyc k* mag-c k* mag-m k* merc k* ph-ac b4a.de rhus-t k* rumx sep bg1 spig k* spong ter k* tritic-vg fd5.de
· **right**: ammc k* mag-c k* mag-m k* rhus-t k* ter k*
· **left**: cycl k* pall k* spig k*
· **evening**: pall k* sep k*
· **bed** agg.; in: sep k* verat-v k*
· **rubbing** agg.: sep h2
· **scratching**:
⁝ **amel.**: laur k* mag-c k* mag-s k*
⁝ **not** amel.: mag-m
· **tickling** amel.: sep h2

○ · **Gland**: nit-ac h2 rheum b7.de*

▽ · **extending** to | **Knee**: ars-met
- **Internally**: bell bg2 cann-xyz bg2 kali-c bg2 mag-c bg2 mosch b7.de* nat-c bg2 olnd b7.de* petr bg2* phos bg2 sabad b7a.de sulph bg2 thuj bg2
- **Liver** region: lyc h2 nat-s k2
- **Pubic** region:

○ · **Mons** pubis: acon bg2 lyc bg2 nat-m bg2 nit-ac b4a.de rhus-t b7.de* sep bg2
· **Mons** veneris: eup-per ptk1
- **Sides**: alum k* berb k* coloc k* hura led k* nat-c k* phos k* sars k* tarax h1
· **scratching**:
⁝ **after**: olnd k*
⁝ **amel.**: alum h2 phos k* sars k*

○ · **Flanks**: mag-c h2
- **Umbilicus**: agar bg2 aloe ars bg2 aur-m k* bell h1* cann-xyz bg2 canth bg2 carb-v k* chin bg2 cist k* clem bg2 dros bg2 form fkr6.de ign k* kali-c k* marb-w es1• phos k* podo fd3.de• puls k* ran-b bg2 sars bg2 sep bg2 spong fd4.de staph bg2 *Sulph* vip fkr4.de

- **Umbilicus**: ...
  - • **evening**: aloe
  - • **scratching** agg.; after: puls k*

JARRING agg.: | **Liver**: lach ptk1 nat-s ptk1

JAUNDICE (See SKIN - Discoloration - yellow)

JERKING (See Twitching)

JUMPING:
- **agg.** | **Hypochondria**: spig b7.de

KNEADING abdomen: | **amel.**: nat-s bg2*

KNEADING sensation in: nux-v b7.de*

KNOTTED sensation: bell bg2 bufo bg2 mag-p bg2 nux-m bg2 plb bg2 *Verat* bg2 [bell-p-sp dcm1]
O - **Intestines**: asaf ptk1 elaps ptk1 sabad ptk1 sulph ptk1 ust ptk1 verat ptk1
  - • **accompanied** by | **emptiness** in abdomen (See Emptiness - accompanied - intestines)

LASSITUDE: | **Hypochondria**: puls bg2

LAUGHING agg.: acon b7a.de ars b4.de* coloc b4.de* con b4.de* lyc bg2 nux-v bg2 plb b7.de*
O - **Hypochondria**: acon b7.de* kali-c b4.de* nat-m b4.de* plat b4.de* *Psor* bg2
- **Liver**: psor ptk1

LEAD colic (See Pain - lead poisoning - cramping)

LEAD poisoning. complaints after: alum b4a.de* arg-n bg2 bell b4a.de* cham bg2 *Op* b7a.de* *Plat* b4a.de*

LEANING:
- **backward** against something | **amel.**: ars bg2
- **forward**:
  - • **amel.** | **Hypochondria**: aloe bg2
- **sharp** edge agg.; against a: ran-b bg2 samb b7.de*

LEUKORRHEA:
- **amel.**: aloe bg2 apis bg2 caust bg2 con bg2 mag-c bg2 mag-m bg2 naja bg2 nat-c bg2 nat-m bg2 plat bg2 sil bg2 sulph bg2 zinc bg2

O • **Liver**: phyt ptk1
- **before** | **agg.**: caust b4.de* con b4.de* graph b4.de* ign b7.de* *Kali-c* b4a.de kreos bg2 *Lyc* b4.de* mag-c b4.de* **Mag-m** b4.de* merc b4a.de nat-c b4.de* nat-m b4.de* **Puls** bg2 sep b4a.de *Sil* b4.de* sulph b4.de* zinc b4.de*
- **during** | **agg.**: graph bg2 sep bg2

LIFTING agg.: bry ptk1
O - **Hypochondria**: *Spig* b7a.de

LOOSE; as if intestines were: ail k* cann-s b7.de* coloc k* cycl b7.de* ictod c1 *Lach* vh mag-m k* mang h2* merc b4.de* mez bg1 nat-m k* nat-s c1 nux-v k* rhus-t h1*
- **walking** agg.: mang ptk1

LUMP in abdomen; sensation of a: *(↗Ball; Hard body)* abrot bg2* agar bg2 *Aloe* bg2 anac bg2* ant-t k* ars ptk1 asaf bg2 bamb-a stb2.de• bism ptk1 borx bg1 bry k* bufo bg2 calc bg2 carb-an bg2 carb-v k2 *Cham* b7a.de chin b7.de* coloc bg2 grat bg2 ign ptk1* kali-p fd1.de• kali-s fd4.de kreos b7a.de* lyc bg2 merc bg2 nat-c bg2 nat-s bg2 nit-ac h2 nux-m *Nux-v* ptk1 plb k* puls b7a.de ran-s bg2 rhus-t k* ribo rly4• *Sabad* bg2* *Sec* b7.de* sep h2* **Spig** b7a.de sulph k* *Thuj* k* ust ptk1 verat bg2 verb ptk1 zinc ptk2
- **hard**: abrot br1
- **rising** to throat on coughing: kali-c hr1*
- **rough** substance: nat-m bg2 plb bg2

O - **Inguinal** region: ribo rly4•
- **Liver**: arg-n bg1 arn bg1 bar-c bg1 brom bg1 croc bg1 cupr bg1 cycl bg2* hep bg1 lach bg2* mag-c bg2* nat-c bg1 nat-m bg1 nat-s bg1 nux-m bg2* op bg2* plb bg1 tab k* thuj bg2* verat bg1 zinc ptk2
- **Lower** abdomen: sulph bg2 thuj bg2
- **Spleen**: *Brom* b4a.de sulph verb j5.de
- **Umbilicus**: acon bg1 anac bg1 bell bg1 kali-bi bg1 kreos b7a.de* nat-c bg1 nux-m bg1 nux-v ptk1 ran-s bg1 rhus-t ptk1 sep bg1* *Spig* k* verb bg1* zinc ptk1*

O • **Lumbar** region; extending from above umbilicus to: laur hr1*

LUMPS:

O - **External** abdomen: plb bg2
- **Groins** | **hard,** painful lumps: puls ptk1

LYING:
- **abdomen**; on | **amel.**: am-c b4a.de* *Calc* b4a.de* *Coloc* b4a.de phos b4a.de* plb bg2 rhus-t bg2* sep bg2
- **agg.**: ambr b7.de* aml-ns bg2 ars bg2 asaf b7.de* bell b4.de* cann-s b7.de* carb-an b4.de* caust b4.de* cham b7.de* coloc bg2 con b4.de* dig b4.de* euph b4.de* ferr b7.de* glon bg2 *Lyc* b4a.de mag-c b4.de* nat-c b4a.de ph-ac b4.de* phos b4.de* plb bg2 prun bg2 puls b7.de* rhod b4.de* rhus-t b7.de* sep b4.de* spig b7.de* stann bg2 thuj b4.de* zinc b4.de*

O • **Hypochondria**: ars b4.de* bell bg2 carb-an b4.de* con b4.de* nat-s bg2 sul-ac b4.de*
- **amel.**: am-c b4.de* apis b7a.de *Bell* b4a.de *Bry* b7.de* calc-p bg2 canth b7.de* carb-an b4.de* cupr b7.de* lyc b4.de* *Merc* b4.de* mur-ac bg2 *Nux-v* b7.de* rhus-t b7.de* *Sabad* b7.de* sil bg2

O • **Hypochondria**: sep bg2
- **back**; on:
  - • **agg.**: lyc bg2 podo bg2
    - : **Hypochondria**: caust b4.de* *Sep* b4a.de
  - • **amel.**: *Bry* b7.de* *Ign* b7.de* mag-p bg2 par b7.de* *Puls* b7.de*
    - : **knees** drawn up; with: bry ptk1 lach ptk1 rhus-t ptk1
    - : **Hypochondria**: *Colch* b7a.de
    - : **Liver**: hydr ptk1 mag-m ptk1 nat-s ptk1
- **bed**; in:
  - • **agg.**: acon b7a.de ambr b7.de* *Cham* b7.de* *Chin* b7.de* cocc b7.de* coff b7.de* dros b7.de* ign b7.de* m-arct b7.de mosch b7.de* nux-m b7.de* nux-v b7.de* *Par* b7a.de *Puls* b7.de* *Rhus-t* b7.de* sabin b7.de* spig b7.de* staph b7.de* teucr b7.de* valer b7.de* verat b7.de*
    - : **Hypochondria**: cocc b7.de* staph b7.de*
- **hypochondria**; on | **amel.**: *Puls* b7a.de
- **knees** and elbows; on | **amel.**: euph bg2
- **must** lie down: ant-t bg2 nux-v bg2
- **side**; on:
  - • **agg.**: aloe bg2 bry b7.de* ign b7.de* par b7a.de
  - • **amel.**: podo bg2
  - • **left**:
    - : **agg.**: carb-v bg2 glon bg2 nat-c bg2 par bg2 phos bg2 puls b7.de* rhus-t bg2
      - : **Hypochondria**: arn b7.de* bell b4.de* card-m bg2 colch bg2 dios bg2 *Kali-c* b4a.de nat-c bg2 nat-m b4.de* *Nat-s* bg2 plat b4.de* ptel bg2 seneg b4.de*
      - : **Liver**: arn ptk1 *Bry* ptk1 card-m ptk1 mag-m ptk1 nat-s ptk1 *Ptel* ptk1 sep ptk1
    - : **amel.**: nat-s bg2 squil ptk1
      - : **Hypochondria**: sul-ac bg2
  - • **painful** side:
    - : **agg.**: nux-v b7.de* *Par* b7a.de *Puls* b7a.de spong b7.de*
    - : **amel.**: *Ign* b7.de* puls b7.de* *Rhus-t* b7a.de
      - : **Hypochondria**: *Kali-c* b4a.de
      - : **Liver**: bry ptk1 ptel ptk1 sep ptk1
  - • **painless** side:
    - : **agg.**: bry b7.de* cham b7.de* ign b7.de* *Rhus-t* b7a.de
    - : **amel.**: m-aust b7.de nux-v b7.de*
      - : **Hypochondria**: bell b4.de* sep b4a.de
  - • **right**:
    - : **agg.**: caust b4.de* merc b4.de* spong b7.de*
      - : **Hypochondria**: acon bg2 agar bg2 ars bg2 bell bg2 calc b4.de* calc-f bg2 caust b4.de* dios bg2 *Kali-c* b4a.de *Lach* b7a.de lyc bg2 **Mag-m** b4.de* merc b4a.de* nat-m bg2 phos bg2 phyt bg2 psor bg2 ptel bg2 sil bg2 spong b7.de*
      - : **Liver**: chel ptk1 dios ptk1 hydr ptk1 kali-c ptk1 *Mag-m* ptk1 *Merc* ptk1
  - • **right** side:
    - : **amel.** | **Hypochondria**: ptel bg2 sep bg2

LYING DOWN: | **after** | **agg.**: ars bg2 hyos b7.de* par b7.de* ran-b b7.de*
- **before** | **agg.**: ran-b b7.de*

MALFORMATION: | **Intestines**; congenital malformation of: syph gm1

MEGACOLON: alum mtf11

Abdomen

MENSES:

- **after**:
  - • **agg.**: ars bg2 bell bg2 borx bg2 carb-v bg2 *Cham* bg2 chin bg2 cocc bg2 con b4.de* cycl bg2 graph b4.de* iod bg2 kali-c bg2 **Kreos** bg2 lac-c bg2 lach bg2 lil-t bg2 lyc b4.de* *Nat-m* bg2 nit-ac bg2 nux-v b7.de* *Pall* bg2 phos bg2 **Plat** bg2 *Puls* bg2
    - ⁝ **Hypochondria**: borx bg2
- **appear**; sensation as if menses would (See Pain - menses would)
- **before**:
  - • **agg.**: acon bg2 aesc bg2 aloe bg2 alum b4a.de* am-c b4.de* am-m b7.de* apis b7a.de* arn bg2 ars bg2 aur bg2 *Bar-c* b4.de* **Bell** bg2 borx bg2 bov bg2 brom bg2 bry bg2 bufo bg2 cact bg2 calc bg2 *Calc-p* bg2 canth bg2 carb-an bg2 carb-v b4.de* caul bg2 caust b4.de* **Cham** b7.de* chel bg2 chin bg2 cimic bg2 cina b7.de* cinnb bg2 *Cocc* bg2 coff bg2 **Coloc** bg2 con b4.de* *Croc* b7.de* crot-t bg2 *Cupr* b7.de* cycl bg2 dig bg2 dios bg2 ferr b7.de* gels bg2 graph bg2 ham bg2 hep b4.de* hyos b7.de* hyper bg2 ign b7.de* iod bg2 ip b7.de* **Kali-c** bg2 kali-n b4a.de* lac-c bg2 *Lach* bg2 laur bg2 lil-t bg2 **Lyc** b4.de* mag-c b4.de* mag-m b4.de* mag-p bg2 mang bg2 merc bg2 mosch bg2 mur-ac bg2 murx bg2 nat-c b4.de* **Nat-m** bg2 nit-ac bg2 nux-m bg2 *Nux-v* b7.de* ol-an bg2 petr bg2 ph-ac b4a.de* *Phos* b4a.de* *Plat* bg2 plb bg2 **Puls** b7.de* rhus-t bg2 ruta b7.de* sabad b7.de* sabin bg2 senec bg2 seneg bg2 **Sep** b4.de* sil bg2 spong bg2 staph b7.de* sulph b4.de* tarent bg2 thuj bg2 ust bg2 valer b7.de* verat-v bg2 vesp bg2 vib bg2 zinc b4a.de*
    - ⁝ **External** abdomen: puls bg2
    - ⁝ **Hypochondria**: sulph bg2
      - ⁚ **right**: con bg2 dig bg2 nux-m bg2 nux-v bg2 podo bg2 *Puls* bg2
      - ⁚ **left**: bufo bg2 sulph bg2
    - ⁝ **Inguinal** region: ant-t bg2 arg-n bg2 borx bg2 brom bg2 caps bg2 carb-an bg2 chin bg2 cub bg2 lyc bg2 plat bg2 senec bg2 sul-ac bg2 tab bg2
      - ⁚ **right**: apis bg2 graph bg2 lac-c bg2 podo bg2 sars bg2
      - ⁚ **left**: coloc bg2 *Lach* bg2 thuj bg2 ust bg2 vib bg2 zinc bg2
    - ⁝ **Umbilicus**: kreos bg2
- **during**:
  - • **agg.**: acon bg2 aesc bg2 agar bg2 agn bg2 alet bg2 *Aloe* bg2 alum b4a.de* *Am-c* b4.de* *Am-m* b7.de* ant-c bg2 apis bg2 arg-n bg2 ars b4a.de* asaf bg2 aur bg2 bar-c b4.de* *Bell* bg2 berb bg2 *Borx* bg2 bov b4.de* *Brom* b4a.de* bry b7.de* cact bg2 **Calc** b4.de* calc-p bg2 canth b7.de* carb-an b4.de* carb-v b4.de* castm bg2 caul bg2 *Caust* b4.de* **Cham** b7.de* *Chin* bg2 *Cimic* bg2 cinnb bg2 coc-c bg2 **Cocc** b7.de* *Coff* bg2 *Coloc* bg2 *Con* b4.de* *Croc* b7.de* crot-h bg2 cupr bg2 cycl bg2 dig bg2 dios bg2 elaps bg2 ferr b7.de* ferr-p bg2 gels bg2 **Graph** b4.de* ham bg2 hell bg2 hyos bg2 hyper bg2 ign b7.de* iod bg2 ip bg2 **Kali-c** b4.de* kali-i bg2 kali-n b4a.de* kali-p bg2 *Kreos* bg2 lac-c bg2 **Lach** bg2 laur b7.de lil-t bg2 **Lyc** b4a.de* *Mag-c* b4.de* mag-m b4.de* mang bg2 merc b4a.de* *Mosch* bg2 mur-ac b4.de* murx bg2 **Nat-c** b4.de* nat-m bg2 nat-s bg2 **Nit-ac** b4.de* *Nux-m* b7.de* **Nux-v** b7.de* ol-an bg2 olnd bg2 op bg2 petr bg2 *Phos* b4.de* phyt bg2 **Plat** bg2 plb bg2 podo bg2 **Puls** b7.de* rat bg2 rhus-t bg2 sabin b7.de* sang bg2 sars bg2 *Sec* b7.de* senec bg2 *Sep* b4.de* sil b4.de* stann b4a.de* staph bg2 stram b7.de* stront-c b4.de* sul-ac b4a.de* **Sulph** b4.de* thuj bg2 ust bg2 verat bg2 *Verat-v* bg2 vib bg2 zinc bg2
    - ⁝ **External** abdomen: ham bg2
    - ⁝ **Liver**: ph-ac ptk1
  - • **beginning** of menses | **agg.**: acon bg2 alum bg2 *Am-c* bg2 asar bg2 brom bg2 bufo bg2 calc bg2 caust b4.de* cham bg2 cimic bg2 coff bg2 gels bg2 graph b4.de* lach bg2 lyc b4.de* *Mosch* bg2 nit-ac bg2 nux-v bg2 ol-an bg2 phos b4a.de plat b4a.de* sang bg2 staph b7.de* vib bg2
- **suppressed** menses; from: kali-c b4a.de *Puls* b7a.de

MENTAL EXERTION agg.: hep bg2 ign b7.de* m-ambo b7.de m-arct b7.de nux-v b7.de*

METASTASIS:

- **gouty**:
  - ▽ • **extending** to | **Liver**: benz-ac k2

METEORISM (See Distension)

MILK:

- **agg.**: ang b7.de* bell b4.de* bry b7.de* *Carb-v* b4a.de* con b4a.de* cupr b7a.de* lyc bg2 sul-ac bg2 zinc bg2

Mik: ...

- **amel.**: graph ptk1 merc ptk1 mez ptk1 *Nux-v* ptk1 ruta ptk1 verat ptk1
  - • **warm** milk: bufo bg2 crot-t bg2* op bg2

MOISTURE:

- ○ - **Inguinal** and pubic region thuj bg2
- **Umbilicus** | **Region** of umbilicus: calc-p ptk1

MONONUCLEOSIS (See Inflammation - liver)

MOTION:

- **after** | **agg.**: arn b7.de* *Puls* b7.de* *Ruta* b7a.de *Sep* b4a.de
- **agg.**: aloe bg2 alum b4.de* ang bg2 ant-c b7.de* *Apis* b7a.de arg-n bg2 arn b7.de* asar b7.de* aur b4.de* bar-c b4.de* bell b4.de* **Bry** b7.de* calc b4.de* cann-s b7.de* caps b7.de* carb-v b4a.de *Chin* b7.de* *Cocc* b7.de* colch b7.de* cycl b7.de* dig b4a.de* graph b4.de* ip b7.de* kali-n b4.de* kreos b7a.de* lyc bg2 m-aust b7.de mag-m bg2 *Merc* b4.de* *Merc-c* b4a.de* mez b4.de* mur-ac bg2 nat-c bg2 nat-m b4.de* *Nux-v* b7.de* plb b7a.de* *Puls* bg2 ran-b b7.de* rheum b7.de* rhus-t b7.de* sec b7.de* sep b4.de* sil b4a.de *Staph* b7.de* stram b7.de* sulph b4a.de zinc b4.de*
  - ○ • **External** abdomen: nux-v bg2
  - • **Hypochondria**: ang b7.de* bar-c b4.de* borx b4a.de bry b7.de* bufo bg2 colch b7a.de con b4.de* gels bg2 graph b4.de* hep b4a.de iris bg2 kali-bi bg2 kali-c b4.de* merc b4.de* nat-c b4.de* *Nux-v* b7.de* *Psor* bg2 ran-b b7.de* *Sel* b7a.de sep b4a.de* sil b4a.de sul-ac b4.de* zinc b4.de*
  - • **Liver**: ang bg2 merc bg2 nux-v bg2
  - • **Spleen**: ran-b bg2
- **amel.**: am-c b4.de* ant-t b7.de* aur b4.de* bov b4.de* calc b4.de* canth b7.de* cham b7.de* chin ptk1 coloc b4.de* con b4.de* dulc b4.de* kali-n b4.de* meny b7.de* op b7.de* petr b4.de* phos b4.de* puls b7.de* rhus-t b7.de* sep b4.de* sulph b4.de*
  - ○ • **Hypochondria**: aur bg2 cann-s b7.de* dios bg2 *Lyc* b4a.de *Mag-m* b4a.de xanth bg2
- **arms**; of | **agg.**: con bg2

MOVEMENTS in: (↗*Alive; Hard body - moving*) aesc k* agn b7.de* aloe am-c k* am-m k* anac b4.de* ang b7.de* ant-c b7.de* ant-t b7.de* arn k* ars bg2 arund br1 asaf k* asar b7.de* bell b4.de* berb k* borx b4a.de bov k* *Bry* k* calc k* *Calc-p* k* calc-sil k2 cann-s k* canth k* caps k* *Carb-an* k* *Carb-v* k* *Card-m* castm caust k* cham k* chel k* chin b7.de* chinin-s bg2 cina k* coff k* colch k* *Coloc* k* **Croc** k* crot-t k* cupr b7.de* cur k* *Cycl* k* dig k* dulc k* euph k* ferr bg2 *Gran* k* grat k* hell b7.de* hep b4.de* hir rsj4• hyos h1 ign iod k* jatr-c kali-bi k* kali-c k* kali-chl k* kali-i k* kali-n k* lact laur k* led k* lob k* loxo-recl knl4• *Lyc* k* lyss m-arct b7.de m-aust b7.de *Mag-c* k* mag-m k* mag-s k* mand rsj7• mang k* melal-alt gya4 meny b7.de* meph c1 merc merc-c b4a.de merl a1 *Nat-c* k* nat-m k* nat-s nicc k* nit-ac h2 *Nux-m* k* *Nux-v* b7.de* ol-an k* op osm k* par k* ph-ac bg2 phel k* phos k* plat b4.de* plb k* podo hr1 *Puls* k* *Ran-b* k* rat k* *Rhus-g* tmo3• rhus-t k* ruta b7.de *Sabad* k* sabin sang *Sars* k* seneg k* sep k* sil k* stann b4.de* staph b7.de* stram stront-c k* sul-ac b4.de* sulph k* tarax k* ter k* **Thuj** k* til k* valer b7.de* verat b7.de* *Zinc* k* zinc-p k2

- **morning**: nat-c k* nux-v k* rat k* rumx
  - • **bed** agg.; in: nat-c
  - • **waking**; on: rumx
- **forenoon**: castm castor-eq grat k* mag-m sars k*
  - • **stool**; before: mang
- **afternoon**: camph k* chel k* coloc h2 grat k* laur k* mag-c k*
  - • **13 h**: grat mag-c
- **evening**: plb k* puls ran-b k* *Zinc* k*
  - • **lying** agg.: puls ran-b
- **night**: merc-i-r k*
- **accompanied** by | **Stomach**; pain in (See STOMACH - Pain - accompanied - abdomen - movements)
- **breakfast** agg.; after: cycl k*
- **convulsive** | **convulsions**; after general: bufo ptk1
- **dinner**; after: coloc k*
- **eating** | **after** | **agg.**: nat-m k* sil k*
  - • **while** | **agg.**: ferr-ma k*
- **fetus** (See FEMALE - Fetus - motions)
- **fist** of fetus; like: conv br1* *Nat-c* k* petr-ra shn4• sil zr *Sulph* k* tarent ptk1 **Thuj** k*
- **flatus**; from: agar a1* calc-p k2 calc-sil k2 *Thuj* b4a.de
- **flatus**; passing | **amel.**: mag-m h2

- **herring**; after: nat-m k*
- **jumping**: arund bro1 brach bro1 bran bro1 *Croc* k* cycl k* nux-m bro1 *Op* bro1 sabad bro1 sulph bro1 *Thuj* bro1
- **menses** | **before** | **agg.**: calc-p croc cycl ferr sabin
  - **during** | **agg.**: *Croc* nicc k*
- **rhythmic**, of something: agath-a nl2•
- **sensation** of: cham b7.de* croc b7.de* ign b7a.de nux-v b7.de* phos b4.de* rhus-t b7.de* sulph b4.de* thuj b4.de* zinc b4.de*
- **spasmodic**: cupr bg2 tab bg2
- **stool** | **after** | **agg.**: chel k* colch k* ol-an k*
  - **before**: aeth k* colch k* grat k* kali-i k* mag-c k* mang a1 nat-c k* nat-s k* ol-an k* phos k* plb k* **Puls** k* sil k* thuj k*
- **thread** moving rapidly; as from a: sabad ptk1
- **up** and down, of something: croc tl1 **Lyc** k* sanic tl1 thuj tl1

○ · **Chest**, into: borx hr1
- **walking** agg.: castm
- **water**; as from: hell ph-ac
- **worm**, as from: dulc b4a.de nat-c h2 zinc h2

○ - **Colon** ascendens: | **flatus**; from: podo bro1
- **Hypochondria**: bad k*
  - **left**: nit-ac h2 phos h2
- **Hypogastrium**: coloc k* petr-ra shn4• sabad thuj
  - **dinner**, after stool; after: coloc
- **Inguinal** region: kali-i
- **Sides**: meny h1 rat k*
  - **right**: stann h2
  - **left**: kali-n h2 stann h2
- **Solar** plexus: gard-j vlr2•
- **Umbilicus** | **Region** of umbilicus: aloe cham k* coloc k* crot-t k* hyos k* kali-i a1 plb k* sul-ac k* zinc h2

NAUSEA in abdomen (See STOMACH - Nausea - abdomen; in)

NEURALGIA (See Pain - neuralgic)

NOISES: ant-t bg2 chir-fl gya2 coloc bg2 dig h2 dulc fd4.de hippoc-k szs2 kali-bi bg2 melal-alt gya4 olib-sac wmh1 rhus-g tmo3• spong fd4.de vanil fd5.de
- **croaking** (See Rumbling - croaking)
- **rumbling** (See Rumbling)
- **scream** of an animal; like the: *Thuj* b4a.de
- **squeaking** (See Squeaking)

NUMBNESS: acon ptk1 act-sp bg2 apis b7a.de* arn bg2 ars bg2 bry ptk1 *Calc-p* k* carb-v bg2 dig h2 euph bg2 ferr-i merc nux-v bg2 petr *Plat* ptk1 *Podo* *Puls* ptk1 ruta fd4.de sang bg2 sars ptk1 sulph bg2 tarent bg2 tell tritic-vg fd5.de

○ - **External** abdomen: apis bg2 calc-p bg2 merc b4.de* nux-v b7.de* petr b4.de* plb bg2 pop-cand bg2 sulph bg2 tell bg2
- **Hypochondrium** | **left**: dig h2
- **Hypogastrium**:

▽ · **extending** to:
  ⁝ **Thighs** | **sitting** agg.: petr h2
- **Iliac** fossa:
  - **right** | **lying** on iliac fossa amel.: *Apis*
- **Liver**: chel bg2
- **Sacrum** | **And** lower limb: *Calc-p*
- **Sides** | **left** side: sulph h2
- **Spleen**: apis b7a.de ars b4a.de
- **Wall**; abdominal: calc-p tl1

OBESITY: *(↗GENERALS - Obesity)* pip-n a1

OBSTRUCTION:

○ - **Gall** ducts; of: fel br1

○ · **Duodenum**; of the opening of the gall duct into the: astac a1*
- **Intestines**:
  - **operation**; after: acon bro1 *Arn* bro1 bell bro1 merc-c bro1
  - **sensation** as if: *Op* ptk1
- **Liver**; region of: chin b7a.de nux-v b7a.de
- **Spleen**: chin b7a.de nux-m b7a.de

ODOR:
- **bad** | **Umbilicus**: morg-p fmm1•

OEDEMA (See Dropsy - edema)

OPERATION on abdomen; after: bism ptk1 hep ptk1 *Nux-v* ptk1 op ptk1 raph ptk1 staph ptk1

OPPRESSION (See Constriction)

ORGASM of blood: berb bg2 coloc bg2 laur b7.de* nux-v b7.de* puls bg2 rhus-t bg2 staph bg2

OVERACTIVITY of: | **Liver**: jug-r mtf11

OVERLIFTING agg.: alum b4a.de *Arn* b7.de* carb-v b4a.de* coloc b4.de* lach bg2 nux-v b7.de* *Rhus-t* b7.de* sil b4.de* valer b7a.de

OVERLOADED; sensation as if (See Fullness)

PAIN: *(↗FEMALE - Pain - uterus)* *Abrot*↓ acal↓ acet-ac achy-a zzc1• acon k* acon-ac↓ act-sp↓ *Adren* br1 aegle-f zzc1• *Aesc* *Aeth* k* agar agath-a nl2• agn *Aids* nl2• ail alet↓ *All-c* k* *All-s*↓ allox↓ *Aloe* k* *Alum* alum-p↓ alum-sil k2 alumn *Am-c* k* *Am-m* ambr k* ammc↓ amn-l sp1 amp rly4• anac anan↓ androc srj1• ang↓ *Ango*↓ anis↓ ant-c k* ant-t k* anth↓ anthraci aphis↓ *Apis* k* apoc k2 aq-mar rbp6 aran↓ arg-cy↓ arg-met b7.de* arg-n arge↓ arge-pl↓ arist-cl sp1 arizon-l↓ arn k* **Ars** k* ars-i ars-s-f↓ ars-s-r↓ arum-t↓ arund↓ *Asaf* *Asar* asc-t aster atra-r bnm3• atro↓ aur aur-ar↓ aur-i k2 aur-m aur-s k2 *Bamb-a* stb2.de• bapt bar-c k* bar-i bar-m bar-s↓ *Bell* k* bell-p↓ benz-ac↓ berb bism k* *Bit-ar*↓ *Bol-la* borx bov k* *Brom* *Brucel* sa3• **Bry** k* bufo bung-fa tsm2 but-ac↓ cact cadm-s k2 cain↓ *Caj*↓ calad *Calc* k* calc-i k2 *Calc-p* *Calc-s* calc-sil↓ calen↓ calth br1 camph cann-s **Canth** k* *Caps* k* carb-ac carb-an *Carb-v* k* carbn-dox↓ **Carbn-s**↓ carc mrr1 card-b↓ *Card-m* mrr1 *Cardios-h*↓ *Carl*↓ cartl-s rly4• casc↓ cassia-s↓ castm↓ catar br1 caul↓ caust k* cedr cench↓ cere-b↓ **Cham** k* *Chel* k* chen-v↓ *Chin* k* chinin-ar chinin-s chion↓ chir-fl↓ chlam-tr↓ chlor chlorpr↓ chord-umb rly4• cic k* *Cimic* *Cina* cinch↓ cinnb↓ cit-ac↓ clem cloth tsm2 cob↓ cob-n sp1 coc-c coca↓ coca-c↓ **Cocc** coch↓ *Coff* **Colch** k* coli↓ coll↓ **Coloc** k* colocin↓ com br1 con k* conv↓ *Cop* corian-s↓ corn↓ *Croc*↓ **Crot-c**↓ *Crot-h*↓ crot-t cub **Cupr** k* *Cupr-act*↓ **Cupr-ar** cur↓ cycl k* cypra-eg↓ cystein-l rly4• cyt-l↓ dendr-pol tsm2 dig k* digin↓ *Dios* k* diosm br1 dioxi rbp6 diph-t-tpt jl2 dirc↓ dor dream-p↓ dros k* **Dulc** dys fmm1• echi↓ echit↓ elaps k* *Elat*↓ ephe-si↓ erech↓ erig↓ eryt-j↓ eucal↓ eug euon eup-per k2 eup-pur *Euph* k* euphr k* eupi fago falco-pe↓ *Ferr* k* ferr-ar ferr-i ferr-m ferr-p fic-m↓ fil↓ fl-ac↓ flor-p rsj3• form↓ fum↓ gaba sa3• gal-ac↓ gamb mrr1 gard-j↓ gels gent-c↓ ger-i↓ gink-b↓ gins glon↓ gnaph↓ *Gran* granit-m es1• **Graph** k* grat guaj↓ guat↓ gymno haliae-lc↓ *Ham*↓ *Hedeo*↓ hedy↓ hell k* helon↓ hep heroin↓ hippoc-k szs2 hir rsj4• hist↓ hom-xyz br1 hura↓ *Hydr* hydr-ac↓ hydrc↓ hydrog↓ *Hydroph*↓ hyos k* hyper↓ ign k* ind indg inul↓ iod k* **Ip** k* irid-met srj5• *Iris* *Iris-t*↓ jab↓ jac-c *Jal*↓ jatr-c jug-r **Kali-ar** kali-bi kali-br **Kali-c** k* kali-chl kali-i kali-m k2 *Kali-n* k* kali-p *Kali-pic*↓ kali-s kali-sil↓ kalm↓ ketogl-ac↓ kola↓ kreos lac-ac↓ lac-c k2 lac-d k2 lac-f↓ lac-h sk4• lac-loxod-a↓ lac-lup↓ lach lact↓ lang↓ lap-la sde8.de• lat-h↓ lat-m bnm6• *Laur* *Lec*↓ *Led* lept liat↓ lil-t *Lim*↓ limen-b-c↓ limest-b↓ lith-c lob loxo-lae bnm12• luf-op↓ luna kg1• lyc k* lycps-v lyss *M-ambo*↓ *M-arct*↓ m-aust↓ mag-br↓ mag-c b4.de* mag-f↓ *Mag-m* k* mag-p k2* mag-s maias-l↓ malar↓ manc mand↓ mang marb-w↓ *Med*↓ melal-alt gya4 mentho↓ meny↓ *Meph* merc k* *Merc-c* k* merc-i-f merc-i-r merc-pr-r↓ merc-sul↓ merl *Mez* k* micr↓ mim-p rsj8• moni rfm1• morb jl2 morg-g fmm1• morph mosch mucs-nas rly4• mur-ac murx musca-d↓ myos-a rly4• myric nad rly4• naja k* nat-ar *Nat-c* k* nat-f↓ **Nat-hchls**↓ *Nat-m* *Nat-n*↓ nat-ox rly4• nat-p nat-pyru rly4• **Nat-s** nat-sil↓ neon↓ nicc nicotam↓ nig-s↓ nit-ac k* *Nux-m* *Nux-v* k* oci-sa↓ oena↓ *Ol-an*↓ ol-j↓ olnd onis↓ onos↓ **Op** k* oreo↓ orot-ac rly4• oscilloc↓ ourl jl2 ovi-p↓ *Ox-ac* oxal-a↓ ozone↓ paeon pall pant-ac rly4• par paraf↓ parathyr jl2 pegan-ha↓ *Petr* k* petr-ra shn4• ph-ac k* phel↓ **Phos** k* *Phys*↓ phyt pic-ac pieri-b↓ pitu-gl skp7• plac-s rly4• plan plat k* plb k* *Plb-act*↓ plb-chr↓ plect-b jsx1.fr plut-n↓ **Podo** k* polyg-h↓ polys↓ positr↓ pot-e rly4• propr sa3• prun pseuts-m oss1• psil ft1 *Psor* ptel **Puls** k* *Pycnop-sa*↓ pyrog k2* rad-br sze8• *Ran-b* k* ran-s *Raph* rat rauw↓ *Rheum* k* rhod↓ rhus-g↓ *Rhus-t* k* rhus-v ribo rly4• rob ros-d↓ *Rumx* ruta k* sabad k* sabal↓ *Sabin* sacch-a↓ sal-fr↓ samb b7.de* sang sanguis-s↓ saroth↓ sars scarl jl2 scop↓ **Sec** k* sel rsj9• senec *Seneg* *Senn* **Sep** k* *Sil* k* *Sin-n*↓ sinus rly4• sol-t-ae↓ *Spect*↓ spig k* spira↓ spong squil *Stann* k* *Staph* stram streptoc↓ stront-c sk4• stroph-s↓ *Stry* suis-em rly4• suis-hep rly4• suis-pan rly4• sul-ac sulfa↓ *Sulph* k* sumb suprar rly4• syc fmm1• symph↓ tab tann-ac br1 taosc iwa1• tarax *Tarent* tax↓ tell↓ *Ter* tere-la↓ tetox↓ *Teucr*↓ thal-met↓ thal-xyz↓ *Thuj* til toxo-g↓ *Tril-p*↓ tritic-vg fd5.de trom↓ tub↓ tung-met bdx1• ulm-c↓ urol-h↓ urotrop bwa3 urt-u ust v-a-b↓ valer k* vanil fd5.de ven-m↓ **Verat** k* verat-v *Verb*↓ vero-o↓

Abdomen

Pain: ...
vesp↓ vib↓ *Viol-t*↓ vip↓ visc↓ vit vs1.fr xan↓ zinc k* zinc-fcy↓ zinc-p k2 zing [calli-al dbx1.fr niob-met stj2]

- **one** or both sides: ign↓
  - · **cramping**: ign br1
- **alternating** sides: am bg2 cimic bg2 ign bg2 lyc bg2
- **right**: *Gins*↓
  - · **lancinating**: *Gins* k*
  - ▽ · **extending** to:
    - ⁝ **left**: **Lyc**↓ nux-m↓
      - : **cutting** pain: **Lyc**
      - : **stitching** pain: nux-m
- **left**: aids↓ sal-fr↓
  - · **lancinating**: aids nl2• sal-fr sle1•
  - ▽ · **extending** to:
    - ⁝ **right**: *lp*↓ lyss↓
      - : **cutting** pain: *lp*
      - : **tearing** pain: lyss
- **daytime**: brucel sa3• nat-m↓ plan k* sulph k*
  - · **cutting** pain: nat-m k*
- **morning**: agar aids↓ all-c k* aloe alum alum-p k2 am-c↓ ambr androc srj1• apis *Asaf*↓ bar-c bar-m bar-s k2 *Bell*↓ bell-p-sp↓ berb k* borx bov k* *Calc* calc-s k* calc-sil k2 camph↓ canth↓ carbn-s *Caust* k* cedr k* cham k* cob coc-c↓ colch rsj2• coloc con k* crot-t k* cupr↓ dig↓ *Dios* k* dor k* dulc fd4.de euphr↓ ferr k* ferr-p gels k* glon k* graph k* ham k* hell k* *Hep* k* hydrog srj2• hydroph rsj6• hyos interf sa3• kali-bi↓ kali-c↓ kali-i kali-n k* kali-s fd4.de kola stb3• kreos lac-h sk4• lact↓ lil-t↓ lob↓ *Lyc* k* mag-c *Mag-m* mang↓ mur-ac k* naja nat-c k* nat-m *Nat-s* k* nat-sil↓ nicc↓ nit-ac nux-m **Nux-v** op k* ox-ac k* oxal-a↓ petr *Phos* k* plan↓ *Plat* k* plb k* *Podo* psor↓ *Ptel* k* *Puls* k* ran-b k* ran-s raph↓ rat↓ rhus-t↓ ruta↓ sabin↓ sal-fr↓ *Sars* k* **Sep** k* sil spong k* stann *Staph*↓ stry↓ *Sulph* k* suprar↓ symph fd3.de• tab k* taosc iwa1• tarent k* tere-la rly4• tritic-vg fd5.de trom↓ vanil fd5.de *Verat* k* xan↓ zinc k* zinc-p k2
  - · **6** h: choc↓ *Coloc* dirc a1 ox-ac
    - ⁝ **cramping**: choc srj3• *Coloc*
  - · **7** h: am-c gnaph
  - · **8** h: dirc
  - · **9**-18 h: **Sep**↓
    - ⁝ **dragging**, bearing down: **Sep**
  - · **bed** agg.; in: acon k* agar ambr k* berb k* cham k* chin↓ con bg2 dios k* dulc fd4.de euph↓ ign↓ kali-c↓ lact↓ lyc mag-c↓ mang mez h2 mur-ac k* nat-c nat-m↓ nit-ac bg2 **Nux-v** k* pall phos k* plat podo↓ psor ptel k* *Puls*↓ sabin↓ sep k* spig↓ spong↓ sulph↓ tritic-vg fd5.de vanil↓
    - ⁝ **cramping**: agar euph h2 kali-c h2 lact k* mag-c h2 mang a1 mur-ac a1 nat-m k* **Nux-v** k* podo fd3.de• psor k* *Puls* sabin k*
    - ⁝ **cutting** pain: nat-m h2 **Nit-ac** k* spig h1 sulph h2
    - ⁝ **pressing** pain: chin h1 vanil fd5.de
    - ⁝ **sore**: ign nat-m h2 **Nux-v**
    - ⁝ **stitching** pain: chin h1 spong fd4.de
  - · **burning**: canth k* rat k*
  - · **contracting**: spong fd4.de
  - · **cramping**: agar am-c calc k* carbn-s **Caust** coc-c k* colch k* coloc k* con cupr k* **Dios** k* dulc k* euphr graph ham fd3.de• hep k* kali-bi k* kali-c kali-n h2 lact k* lob k* *Lyc* k* mag-m k* mang k* nat-c k* nat-m k* nat-s k2 nit-ac k* **Nux-v** k* phos k* plan k* psor k* *Puls* rat k* rhus-t a1 ruta sabin k* sal-fr sle1• sars h2 sep k* *Staph* k* sulph k* suprar rly4• tarent k* xan k* zinc k* zinc-p k2
  - · **cutting** pain: alum h2 ambr k* bov calc k* caust k* con k* *Dios* k* dulc k* graph k* kali-n k* lyc mag-m nat-c k* nat-m k* nicc k* **Nit-ac** k* nux-v ox-ac k* *Petr* k* puls k* sep k* spong k* stry k* vanil fd5.de zinc h2
  - · **dragging**, bearing down: *Bell* hyos h1 mag-c
  - · **drawing** pain: calc k* nat-sil fd3.de• spong fd4.de tritic-vg fd5.de vanil fd5.de
  - · **eating**; after: con k* grat nux-m
  - · **fasting** agg.: dulc gran k* hell k* spong fd4.de
    - ⁝ **cramping**: dulc k*
- **morning**: ...
  - · **menses** would appear; as if: ferr plat h2
  - · **pressing** pain: ambr k2 bell h1 camph h1 caust h2 mag-c nat-m sil k* spong fd4.de tritic-vg fd5.de vanil fd5.de
  - · **rising**:
    - ⁝ **after**:
      - : **agg.**: am-m↓ ars↓ crot-t k* dulc fd4.de ferr k* kali-p fd1.de• lyc h2 mag-c h2 mag-m mang nat-m nat-sil fd3.de• nit-ac ox-ac k*
        - . **cramping**: am-m h2 ars h2 mag-m h2* nit-ac h2
        - . **cutting** pain: ars h2 nat-m k*
      - : **amel.**: nat-m↓
        - . **cramping**: nat-m h2
    - ⁝ **agg.**: calc-s k* caust k* kali-s fd4.de lyc sne nat-m *Nat-s* phos k* plat h2 ruta *Sep* k*
      - : **cramping**: nat-m ruta
  - · **sore**: apis *Asaf* dios k* *Hep* lil-t k* lyc k* **Nux-v** raph k* **Sep** spong fd4.de trom k*
  - · **stitching** pain: agar aids nl2• dig k* kali-n h2 kola stb3• oxal-a rly4• plat k* *Ran-b* k* spong fd4.de sulph k* [bell-p-sp dcm1]
  - · **stool** | **after**:
    - : **agg.**: arg-met↓
      - . **contracting**: arg-met h1
    - ⁝ **during**:
      - : **agg.**: ambr↓ suprar↓
        - . **cramping**: suprar rly4•
        - . **cutting** pain: ambr k*
  - · **sunrise**: *Cham*
  - · **tearing** pain: alum k* con h2 dig k* kola stb3• naja
  - · **uncovering** agg.: rheum↓
    - ⁝ **cramping**: rheum h
  - · **waking** | **after** | **agg.**: tritic-vg fd5.de verat h1
    - ⁝ **on**: agar bros-gau mrc1 bry *Calc* castor-eq cob↓ coc-c↓ colch coloc k* corn a1 dios k* dirc a1 hep k* kali-i kola stb3• lyc k* mang↓ nat-c h2 nat-m nux-m k* petr↓ pic-ac k* podo fd3.de• *Puls* rheum↓ sal-fr↓ symph fd3.de• tere-la rly4• ulm-c jsj8• vanil fd5.de xan
      - : **cramping**: agar cob coc-c a1 colch k* lyc k* mang h2 nat-m k* petr hr1 rheum h sal-fr sle1• xan k*
      - : **cutting** pain: calc k* petr h2
  - · **walking** agg.: ran-b↓
    - ⁝ **stitching** pain: ran-b k*
- **forenoon**: agar k* am-c am-m asc-t k* bamb-a↓ bapt bros-gau↓ bry k* carb-an↓ colch rsj2• coloc cupr↓ dios k* ham↓ kali-bi kali-n↓ kola stb3• lach k* lith-c lyc mag-c k* mag-m mag-s↓ *Nat-c* nat-m nat-s paeon↓ phos pic-ac k* ptel k* *Rhus-t*↓ ruta fd4.de sars *Sep* spong fd4.de sulph tell↓ thuj k* tritic-vg fd5.de vanil↓ xan↓
  - · **9** h: dios mag-c↓ pip-m **Sep**
    - ⁝ **cramping**: mag-c
    - ⁝ **pressing** pain: **Sep**
  - · **10** h: carbn-s↓ hir↓ ptel
    - ⁝ **cramping**: carbn-s hir rsj4•
  - · **11** h: corn↓ gaba sa3• pert-vc vk9
    - ⁝ **11**-12 h: crot-h bg1
    - ⁝ **cramping**: corn
  - · **chill**; during: bov
  - · **cramping**: agar k* am-c k* am-m coloc k* **Dios** kali-bi k* kali-n h2 lyc k* mag-c k* *Nat-c* paeon k* sars k* sulph k* tell xan
  - · **cutting** pain: agar carb-an k* ham fd3.de• lyc nat-c h2 nat-m k* *Rhus-t* k*
  - · **dragging**, bearing down: sep
  - · **menses**; during: mag-c k* nicc
  - · **pressing** pain: bamb-a stb2.de• bros-gau mrc1 cupr h2 kola stb3• lyc k* phos ruta fd4.de tritic-vg fd5.de vanil fd5.de
  - · **sore**: nat-m k* spong fd4.de sulph
  - · **stepping**:
    - ⁝ **every** step; at: *Sulph*↓
      - : **sore**: *Sulph*

  - **stitching** pain: mag-s k* ruta fd4.de
  - **tearing** pain: mag-m k*
  - **walking** in open air agg.: am-c sulph thuj k*
- **noon**: alumn ↓ ars ↓ calc-s k* carb-v ↓ chin k* coloc k* kali-c kali-s fd4.de lyc k* mag-c ↓ nat-s phos ↓ ran-b rhus-t ↓ ruta fd4.de sang ↓ stront-c sk4• sulph thuj k* tritic-vg fd5.de vanil fd5.de
  - **burning**: ars k*
  - **cramping**: alumn carb-v h2 kali-c mag-c h2 sulph k*
  - **cutting** pain: mag-c k* sang k*
  - **eating** | **after** | **agg.**: coloc k* lyc k*
    - **before** | **agg.**: chin k*
  - **soup** agg.: ambr ↓ mag-c ↓
    - **cutting** pain: ambr mag-c k*
  - **standing** agg.: verat
  - **stitching** pain: kali-s fd4.de lyc k* phos k* rhus-t
  - **walking** agg.: *Coloc* k* nat-s ran-b verat
- **afternoon**: agar all-c k* *Alum* alum-p k2 am-c k* am-m ammc k* *Ars* k* atp ↓ bamb-a ↓ berb ↓ bism bov k* bry ↓ calc-s ↓ canth k* carb-v carbn-s castm caust cham k* chel chinin-s *Coloc* k* corn ↓ dios k* dirc k* dulc fd4.de fago k* gels k* grat hura *Iris* *Kali-n* k* laur limen-b-c mlk9.de **Lyc** k* mag-c mag-m k* myric k* nat-c k* nat-m ↓ nat-p nat-s nicc ↓ nux-v k* op ↓ osm ↓ pall ↓ par ↓ petr h2 phos k* phyt ↓ plb rat ruta fd4.de sang k* sanguis-s hrn2• sars ↓ senec ↓ sep sil spig ↓ spong fd4.de streptoc rly4• stront-c ↓ sulph k* tell k* tritic-vg fd5.de vanil fd5.de verat
  - **13** h: dios grat ↓ mag-m nux-v
    - **cramping**: mag-m
    - **cutting** pain: grat
    - **sore**: nux-v
  - **13.30** h: dirc
  - **14** h: aq-mar rbp6 chinin-s dirc
  - **14-16** h: laur ↓
    - **cutting** pain: laur
  - **15** h: hura sanguis-s hrn2• tell
    - **15-22** h: lyc ↓
      - **cramping**: lyc h2
  - **16** h: caust coloc hell **Lyc** mag-m phys puls ↓
    - **16-17** h: coloc ↓ kali-br ↓ *Lyc* ↓
      - **cramping**: coloc bro1 kali-br bro1 *Lyc* bro1
    - **16-18** h: carc tpw2*
    - **16-20** h: carc tpw2 nat-s k2
    - **16-21** h: *Coloc* ↓
      - **cramping**: *Coloc*
    - **cramping**: caust coloc hell **Lyc** k* puls sys
  - **16-23** h: alum ↓
    - **cutting** pain: alum h2
  - **17** h: aran ↓ elaps fago hura *Kali-br* ↓ limen-b-c hrn2• nat-m sars ↓ spig sulph tell ↓
    - **cramping**: aran *Kali-br* hr1 tell
    - **cutting** pain: sars
    - **pressing** pain: sulph
  - **burning**: alum k* ars k*
  - **cramping**: agar k* alum h2 atp rly4• bamb-a stb2.de• bism bry k* carb-v k* carbn-s coloc k* corn grat k* kali-n k* laur lyc k* mag-c k* nat-c k* nat-m k* nat-s k* nicc op k* pall c1 par k* phyt k* senec k* sil k* spig h1 sulph k* *Verat*
  - **cutting** pain: agar berb k* calc-s k* chel k* coloc k* grat kali-n h2 laur k* mag-m nat-c k* nat-m k* sars h2 sep spong fd4.de stront-c vanil fd5.de
  - **dragging**, bearing down: mag-m **Sep**
  - **drawing** pain: dulc fd4.de grat k* ruta fd4.de tritic-vg fd5.de vanil fd5.de
  - **eating**; after: puls-n
  - **pressing** pain: caust k* chel k* ruta fd4.de spig h1 spong fd4.de vanil fd5.de
  - **short** sleep amel.: borx h2
  - **sore**: coloc k* fago k* lyc k* osm k* spong fd4.de tritic-vg fd5.de
  - **stitching** pain: sep k* vanil fd5.de

- **afternoon**: ...
  - **tearing** pain: nux-v k* sep h2
  - **walking** agg.: lyc k*
- **evening**: acon k* agar agath-a ↓ aids ↓ aloe alum alumn am-c ambr ant-c ant-t ↓ aran bamb-a stb2.de• bar-c *Bell* bell-p-sp ↓ bism ↓ bit-ar wht1• *Borx* bry calad ↓ *Calc* k* calc-p k* carb-v carbn-s cardios-h ↓ carneg-g ↓ castm ↓ *Caust* ↓ *Chin* k* cob coloc k* com k* con cop crot-t cycl ↓ dig k* dios k* dirc k* dream-p ↓ *Dulc* fago ↓ ferr ferr-p fl-ac gels k* grat ↓ ham k* hep hir skp7• hura hyper k* ign *Iris* kali-c ↓ kali-n ↓ kali-p ↓ kali-s ↓ kalm lach led *Lyc* k* mag-c *Mag-m* mag-s ↓ mang k* meph k* merc k* merc-i-r k* *Mez* murx myric k* naja nat-m ↓ nat-s nicc nit-ac nux-m k* nux-v ox-ac par *Petr* ph-ac *Phos* k* phys k* phyt k* plan k* plat plb k* propr sa3• psor k* ptel **Puls** k* rat ↓ *Rhus-t* k* rumx ruta fd4.de sabin ↓ sacch-a fd2.de• sars ↓ sel ↓ senec k* *Seneg* *Sep* k* spong fd4.de stann k* staph ↓ stram k* *Stront-c* stry sul-ac *Sulph* k* taosc iwa1• tarent k* ter k* thuj k* trios rsj11• tritic-vg fd5.de *Valer* k* vanil fd5.de verat k* *Zinc* k* zinc-p k2
  - **17** h:
    - **night**; lasting all: canth ↓
      - **cutting** pain: canth
  - **18** h: mag-s ↓
    - **stitching** pain: mag-s
  - **19** h: elaps ↓ stry sulph ↓
    - **cutting** pain: elaps sulph
  - **21.30** h: ven-m ↓
    - **menses** would appear; as if: ven-m rsj12•
  - **19.30-19.45** h: hir skp7•
  - **air**, in: *Merc* k*
  - **bed**:
    - **in** bed:
      - **agg.**: alum ars ↓ hyos ↓ ign nat-m ↓ par *Valer* k* zinc
        - **21** h: *Sep* ↓
          - **dragging**, bearing down: *Sep*
        - **cramping**: alum k* ars h2 hyos h1 *Valer*
        - **cutting** pain: ars h2
        - **pressing** pain: nat-m h2
      - **amel.**: plat ↓
        - **menses** would appear; as if: plat h2
  - **burning**: dirc k* rhus-t
  - **coffee** agg.: hyper k*
  - **contracting**: nat-m h2 spong fd4.de
  - **cramping**: alum k* am-c ambr a1 bism k* calad **Calc** carb-v k* cardios-h rly4• carneg-g rwt1• castm chin k* cycl dream-p sdj1• dulc a1 grat k* *Iris* kali-n h2 led lyc pd mag-c h2 mag-m mag-s k* meph a1 merc k* nat-m h2 petr k* ph-ac k* plan k* plb k* *Puls* sars senec k* stann h2 sul-ac h2 sulph k* tarent thuj k* *Valer* zinc k*
  - **cutting** pain: agar k* aloe ambr k* ant-t k* bar-c k* bell k* calc carb-v k* dig h2 *Dios* k* fago k* hep k* kali-n k* kali-p fd1.de• led k* mag-c k* mang k* merc mez k* nat-m k* nicc k* ox-ac k* *Petr* k* ph-ac h2 phos k* puls k* rat k* rhus-t k* sel k* spong fd4.de staph k* stront-c sulph k* thuj
  - **drawing** pain: ambr c1 borx h2 bry k* kali-n h2 mag-m h2 ruta fd4.de tritic-vg fd5.de vanil fd5.de
  - **drinking** agg.; after: *Puls* k*
  - **eating**; after: alum ant-t k* chin ↓ coloc k* *Gran* k* phos sacch-a fd2.de• tritic-vg fd5.de
    - **pressing** pain: chin h1 phos
  - **ice** cream agg.: calc-p
  - **lying**:
    - **agg.**: *Puls* zinc k*
    - **amel.**: kali-i
  - **lying** down agg.: kali-s ↓ samb ↓
    - **tearing** pain: kali-s fd4.de samb h1*
  - **menses** | **before** | **agg.**: calc k*
    - **during**:
      - **agg.**: castm ↓
        - **sore**: castm
  - **milk** agg.: mag-s

Abdomen

- **pressing** pain: bar-c bell$_{h1}$ caust$_{h2}$ chin$_{h1}$ coloc$_{k*}$ dulc$_{fd4.de}$ ferr$_{k*}$ kali-c$_{h2}$ kali-p$_{fd1.de}$• mez$_{h2}$ phos$_{k*}$ ruta$_{fd4.de}$ tritic-vg$_{fd5.de}$ vanil$_{fd5.de}$ zinc$_{k*}$
- **sitting** still agg.: *Puls* ↓
  - **cutting** pain: *Puls*
- **sore**: castm fago ferr$_{k*}$ ham$_{k*}$ mang$_{h2}$ sabin sep$_{k*}$
- **stitching** pain: agath-a$_{nl2}$• aids$_{nl2}$• *Caust*$_{k*}$ dulc$_{fd4.de}$ kali-n$_{h2}$ kali-p$_{fd1.de}$• *Plb*$_{k*}$ spong$_{fd4.de}$ tarent tritic-vg$_{fd5.de}$ [bell-p-sp$_{dcm1}$]
- **stool**:
  - **before**: mag-c stann$_{k*}$ tab$_{k*}$
  - **during**:
    - **agg.**: borx grat rhus-t$_{k*}$ zinc
      - **pressing** pain: *Zinc*$_{k*}$
- **stooping** agg.: plan$_{k*}$
- **tearing** pain: alum$_{k*}$ bry$_{k*}$ dig$_{h2}$ kali-s$_{fd4.de}$ mag-m$_{k*}$
- **twisting** pain: calad$_{k*}$
- **urination** agg.; after: fago
- **walking** agg.: verat ↓
  - **drawing** pain: verat$_{h1}$
  - **pressing** pain: verat$_{h1}$

- **night**: abrot$_{k*}$ acon alum ↓ am-c$_{k*}$ am-m ambr *Arg-n*$_{k*}$ arizon-l ↓ ars$_{k*}$ ars-s-f$_{k2}$ asc-t$_{k*}$ *Aur* aur-ar$_{k2}$ aur-s$_{k2}$ bar-c$_{h2}$ *Bell* borx bov$_{k*}$ bry but-ac ↓ **Calc**$_{k*}$ calc-s calc-sil$_{k2}$ camph ↓ canth ↓ carb-v carbn-s cardios-h ↓ caust ↓ cedr cench$_{k2}$ cent ↓ cham ↓ *Chin* ↓ cist cob$_{k*}$ *Coc-c* cocc colch$_{k*}$ coloc$_{k*}$ cub$_{c1}$ cupr ↓ *Cycl*$_{k*}$ dig ↓ dream-p$_{sdj1}$• dulc euphr ↓ fago ↓ *Ferr*$_{k*}$ ferr-ar ferr-p gnaph$_{k*}$ *Graph*$_{k*}$ ham ↓ hell$_{k*}$ ign iris kali-ar kali-br ↓ kali-c$_{k*}$ kali-m$_{k2}$ kali-n ↓ kali-p kali-s kali-sil$_{k2}$ ketogl-ac ↓ kola$_{stb3}$• kreos lach$_{k*}$ lyc$_{k*}$ mag-c *Mag-m* mag-s$_{k*}$ mang ↓ **Merc** merc-i-r$_{k*}$ mez moni$_{rfm1}$• mur-ac$_{k*}$ myric ↓ naja nat-ar nat-c$_{k*}$ nat-m nat-p *Nat-s* nicotam ↓ **Nit-ac** *Nux-m* olib-sac$_{wmh1}$ osm ↓ ox-ac *Petr* ph-ac ↓ phos plan$_{k*}$ *Plb*$_{k*}$ *Podo* ↓ prun ptel$_{k*}$ *Puls*$_{k*}$ ran-s ↓ rhus-t$_{k*}$ ruta$_{fd4.de}$ sang$_{k*}$ sars$_{h2}$ senec ↓ senn ↓ *Sep* *Sil* sol-t-ae$_{k*}$ spong$_{fd4.de}$ stront-c$_{sk4}$• *Sul-ac* *Sulph*$_{k*}$ symph$_{fd3.de}$• tab tarent$_{k*}$ thuj$_{k*}$ valer vanil$_{fd5.de}$ verat$_{k*}$ zinc$_{h2}$ zing$_{k*}$
  - **midnight**: alum ↓ ambr ↓ **Arg-n** aur aur-s$_{k2}$ bar-c ↓ canth ↓ *Chin* cit-ac$_{rly4}$• **Cocc** coloc dys$_{fmm1}$• gels lyc lyss nat-m ↓ *Nit-ac* nux-v petr ↓ phos rhus-t sep ↓ sulph *Zinc* ↓
    - **before**: cham ↓
      - **22** h: dirc ferr-i
      - **23** h: aq-mar$_{skp7}$•
      - **stitching** pain: cham$_{h1}$
    - **after**: am-m ↓ ambr ↓ *Ars* ↓ aur ↓ cocc ↓ elaps ↓ sars ↓ sep ↓ sulph ↓ urol-h ↓ zinc ↓
      - **1** h: *Mag-m* ↓ phos ↓
        - **cramping**: *Mag-m*
        - **cutting** pain: phos
        - **uncovered** and crooked; had to lie: *Mag-m*$_{k*}$
      - **2** h: am-m ↓ fl-ac hir$_{rsj4}$• iris$_{c1}$ mag-m ↓ nat-s ↓ nicotam ↓ phos ↓ rhus-v sep
        - **2-3** h: lyc nat-s ↓
          - **cramping**: nat-s$_{tl1}$
        - **cramping**: nat-s nicotam$_{rly4}$• phos$_{h2}$
        - **cutting** pain: am-m mag-m sep$_{h2}$
      - **3** h: am-c amp ↓ carb-v ↓ cyclosp$_{sa3}$• iris$_{c1}$ ox-ac phos ↓ podo$_{c1}$
        - **cramping**: amp$_{rly4}$• carb-v$_{h2}$
        - **cutting** pain: phos
      - **4** h: cob **Petr** ↓ phos *Podo* sulph ↓ verat ↓
        - **cutting** pain: **Petr** sulph verat$_{h1}$
      - **4.30** h: ven-m$_{rsj12}$•
      - **5** h: bov cob nat-m ↓ ox-ac ↓
        - **cramping**: cob
        - **cutting** pain: nat-m ox-ac
        - **until**: nat-s ↓
          - **cramping**: nat-s$_{c1}$
      - **bed** agg.; in: ambr ↓
        - **cramping**: ambr$_{a1}$
      - **contracting**: zinc$_{h2}$
      - **cramping**: am-m$_{gsy1}$ *Ars*$_{bro1}$ aur cocc$_{bro1}$ sulph$_{h2}$ urol-h$_{rwt}$•

- **night – midnight – after**: ...
      - **cutting** pain: ambr elaps sars$_{h2}$ sep$_{h2}$ sulph$_{h2}$
      - **cramping**: alum$_{h2}$ chin$_{k2}$ **Cocc** coloc$_{h2}$ lyc **Nit-ac** petr$_{h2}$ rhus-t *Zinc*
      - **cutting** pain: ambr bar-c lyc nat-m sep sulph
      - **menses** would appear; as if: canth
      - **stitching** pain: sulph$_{k*}$
      - **waking**; on: coloc ↓ sulph ↓
        - **stitching** pain: coloc$_{h2}$ sulph
  - **bed** agg.; in: bry *Con* cub ↓ dig ↓ fago ↓ kali-c$_{k*}$ mag-c ↓ naja ptel$_{k*}$ rhus-t ruta$_{fd4.de}$ sulph$_{k*}$ zinc ↓
    - **cramping**: cub$_{c1}$ dig$_{k*}$ rhus-t
    - **cutting** pain: fago zinc
    - **dragging**, bearing down: mag-c **Sulph**
  - **burning**: arizon-l$_{nl2}$•
  - **cramping**: alum$_{h2}$ arg-n bry$_{k*}$ but-ac$_{sp1}$ **Calc**$_{k*}$ calc-s carbn-s cardios-h$_{rly4}$• caust$_{tl1}$ cent$_{a1}$ cham$_{bro1*}$ *Chin*$_{k*}$ cocc$_{bro1}$ coloc$_{tl1}$ cupr *Cycl*$_{k*}$ dig$_{k*}$ euphr$_{k*}$ ferr$_{c1}$ graph *Ign*$_{st}$ *Iris*$_{k*}$ kali-br$_{a1}$ kali-c$_{k*}$ kali-s ketogl-ac$_{rly4}$• lyc$_{ptk1}$ mez$_{k*}$ moni$_{rfm1}$• mur-ac$_{a1}$ myric$_{k*}$ nat-c$_{h2*}$ *Nat-s* nicotam$_{rly4}$• *Nit-ac*$_{k*}$ osm$_{k*}$ ox-ac$_{k2}$ *Podo*$_{k*}$ *Rhus-t* senec$_{k*}$ senn$_{bro1}$ sep$_{h2}$ stront-c sul-ac$_{k*}$ *Sulph*$_{k*}$ *Valer*$_{k*}$
  - **cutting** pain: ambr$_{k*}$ bar-c$_{k*}$ calc camph$_{k*}$ canth$_{k*}$ fago kali-c$_{h2}$ kali-n$_{h2}$ lyc$_{k*}$ mag-c$_{h2}$ mag-m$_{k*}$ merc$_{k*}$ nat-c$_{k*}$ nat-m$_{k*}$ nit-ac$_{k*}$ ph-ac$_{k*}$ ran-s$_{k*}$ ruta$_{fd4.de}$ sars$_{k*}$ sep$_{k*}$ sil$_{h2}$ sul-ac$_{k*}$ sulph$_{k*}$ zinc$_{k*}$
  - **drawing** pain: graph$_{k*}$ *Mag-m*$_{k*}$ spong$_{fd4.de}$ zing$_{k*}$
  - **menses** would appear; as if: sang$_{hr1}$
  - **pressing** pain: ambr$_{h1}$ ign$_{k*}$ kali-c$_{h2}$ mez$_{k*}$ petr$_{h2}$ phos$_{k*}$ ruta$_{fd4.de}$ sep spong$_{fd4.de}$ sulph
  - **pressing** to urinate, when: graph ↓
    - **cutting** pain: graph$_{k*}$
  - **sore**: mang *Nat-m*$_{k*}$ sep spong$_{fd4.de}$ tab$_{k*}$
  - **stitching** pain: ham$_{fd3.de}$• kali-c$_{h2}$ spong$_{fd4.de}$ *Sulph*$_{k*}$ vanil$_{fd5.de}$
  - **tearing** pain: kola$_{stb3}$• mag-m$_{k*}$ merc$_{k*}$ tab$_{k*}$
  - **uncovering** agg.: bry
    - **cramping**: bry$_{k*}$
  - **violent**: rhus-t$_{h1}$
  - **waking**; on: but-ac ↓ coloc ↓ mag-m nat-c$_{k*}$ sulph ↓ zinc$_{k*}$
    - **cramping**: but-ac$_{sp1}$
    - **cutting** pain: coloc$_{h2}$ sulph$_{h2}$
    - **menses**; during: gink-b$_{sbd1}$•
    - **stitching** pain: coloc$_{h2}$
  - **warm** agg.: cham ↓
    - **cramping**: cham$_{bro1}$

- **accompanied** by:
  - **chill**: buth-a$_{sp1}$
  - **coryza**: acon$_{bg2}$ canth$_{bg2}$
  - **distension**: gent-l$_{mtf11}$
  - **dysentery** (See RECTUM - Dysentery - accompanied - abdomen)
  - **erections** (See accompanied; MALE GENITALIA/SEX - Erections - accompanied - abdomen)
  - **fear** (See MIND - Fear - pain - during - abdomen)
  - **heat**; sensation of: *Cocc*$_{bro1}$ hydr$_{bro1}$ moni$_{rfm1}$•
  - **hiccough**: merc$_{b4a.de}$
  - **nausea** (See STOMACH - Nausea - pain - abdomen)
  - **qualmishness** (See STOMACH - Nausea - pain - abdomen)
  - **respiration**:
    - **asthmatic** (See RESPIRATION - Asthmatic - accompanied - abdomen)
    - **complaints** (See RESPIRATION - Complaints - accompanied - abdomen)

• **restlessness** (See MIND - Restlessness - abdomen)
• **screaming** (See MIND - Shrieking - pain - abdomen)
• **stool**; complaints of (See STOOL - Complaints - accompanied - abdomen - pain)
• **thirst**: bism$_{mrr1}$ chin$_{h1}$
• **urination**:
⁝ **profuse**: acon$_{bg2}$ verat$_{bg2}$
⁝ **urging** to urinate: inul$_{k2}$ lach$_{k*}$ nit-ac nux-v$_{k2}$ puls$_{k*}$ staph$_{sne}$
• **urine**:
⁝ **bloody**: diosm$_{br1}$
⁝ **dark**: diosm$_{br1}$
• **vertigo**: asaf$_{bg2}$ coloc$_{b4.de*}$ hell$_{bg2}$ petr$_{b4.de*}$ spig$_{b7.de*}$ stram$_{b7.de*}$
• **water** brash (See Complaints - accompanied - water)
• **weeping** (See MIND - Weeping - pains - with - abdomen)
○ • **Back**; pain in (See BACK - Pain - accompanied - abdomen - pain)
• **Calves**; cramps in: coloc$_{bro1*}$ *Cupr-act*$_{bro1}$ plb$_{bro1}$ podo$_{bro1}$
• **Face**:
⁝ **bluish**: *Cina*$_{bro1}$ fil$_{bro1}$
⁝ **pale**: phos$_{h2}$
• **Head**:
⁝ **complaints** (See HEAD - Complaints - accompanied - abdomen)
⁝ **pain** in (See HEAD - Pain - accompanied - abdomen - pain)
• **Lumbar** region; pain in: granit-m$_{es1}$• spong$_{fd4.de}$
• **Rectum**; constriction in (See RECTUM - Constriction - anus - pain)
• **Stomach** | **pain** (See STOMACH - Pain - accompanied - abdomen - pain)
• **Thighs**; flexing of (See EXTREMITIES - Flexed - thigh - accompanied - abdomen)
• **Urinary** organs; complaints of: coloc$_{bg2}$ sabal$_{bg2}$ sulph$_{bg2}$
- **aching** (See Pain)
- **acids**, from: aloe$_{bg2}$ dros$_{k*}$ ph-ac
- **adhesions**; with sensation of: allox$_{sp1}$
- **agonizing**: *Coloc*$_{br1}$ lat-m$_{bnm6}$•
- **air** | **sensitive** to air: caust *Sulph*
- **air**; draft of | **every**: kali-bi$_{bg1}$ *Sulph*
- **air**; in open:
• **agg.**: ign mang↓ merc-c↓ *Nux-v* puls$_{h1}$
⁝ **cramping**: ign
⁝ **cutting** pain: mang$_{h2}$ merc-c
⁝ **pressing** pain: mang$_{h2}$
• **amel.**: *Aloe*↓ kali-i nat-c↓
⁝ **cramping**: nat-c
⁝ **cutting** pain: *Aloe* kali-i
- **alternating** with:
○ • **Back**; pain in (See BACK - Pain - alternating with - abdomen)
• **Chest**:
⁝ **constriction** (See CHEST - Constriction - alternating - abdomen - pain)
⁝ **pain** in (See CHEST - Pain - alternating - abdomen)
• **Eyes** | **complaints** of the: *Euphr*
• **Face**; pain in (See FACE - Pain - alternating with - coeliac)
• **Fingers** or toes; pain in: dios$_{hr1*}$
• **Head**; pain in (See HEAD - Pain - alternating - abdomen - pain)
• **Joints**; pain in: plb
• **Limbs**:
⁝ **atrophy**: plb$_{bro1}$
⁝ **pain**: plb$_{bro1}$ vip

- **alternating** with: ...
• **Teeth**; pain in: agar$_{bg1}$
- **anger**; after: aids$_{nl2}$• *Cham*$_{k*}$ cocc *Coloc*$_{k*}$ *Nux-v* spong$_{fd4.de}$ *Staph*$_{k*}$ *Sulph*
- **appears** (See increasing)
- **ascending**:
• **agg.**: merc↓
⁝ **cutting** pain: merc$_{k*}$
• **stairs**:
⁝ **agg.**: asc-t$_{k*}$ hell
: **cramping**: asc-t$_{c1}$ hell
- **babies**, colic: | **cramping** (See children - nurslings - cramping)
- **back**; starting from: mom-b↓
• **cramping**: mom-b$_{a1*}$
- **backache**, with: cham↓ *Coch*↓ *Lyc*↓ melal-alt↓ morph↓ puls↓ samb↓ sars↓
• **cramping**: cham$_{bro1}$ *Coch*$_{c1}$ *Lyc*$_{bro1}$ melal-alt$_{gya4}$ morph$_{bro1}$ puls$_{bro1}$ samb$_{bro1}$ sars$_{ptk1}$
- **bearing** down (See dragging)
- **bed**:
• **driving** out of bed: germ-met$_{srj5}$•
• **going** to bed | **when**: dios$_{k*}$ nat-m$_{k*}$
• **in** bed: alum$_{k*}$ cedr *Chin*$_{bg2}$ dig$_{k*}$ dios kali-c$_{k*}$ lact mag-c nat-m nit-ac$_{bg2}$ **Nux-v**$_{k*}$ psor$_{k*}$ rhus-t$_{k*}$ sulph$_{bg2}$ valer
⁝ **agg.**: aids↓ alum↓ dig↓ dios↓ kali-c↓ lact↓ nat-m↓ **Nux-v**↓ psor↓ rhus-t↓ sabin↓ valer↓
: **cramping**: alum$_{k*}$ dig$_{k*}$ dios kali-c$_{k*}$ lact$_{k*}$ nat-m$_{k*}$ **Nux-v**$_{k*}$ psor rhus-t sabin$_{k*}$ valer
: **stitching** pain: aids$_{nl2}$• nat-m$_{k*}$
- **beer**; after: | **warm**: sil$_{h2}$
- **bending**:
• **amel.**: carc↓
⁝ **constricting** pain: carc$_{mlr1}$•
• **backward**:
⁝ **agg.**$_{●}$: anac atra-r$_{bnm3}$• sulph↓ thuj
: **cutting** pain: sulph
⁝ **amel.**: *Alet*↓ *Bell* *Chel*$_{sne}$ chin$_{sne}$ *Dios*$_{k*}$ kali-c$_{k2}$ *Lac-c* nux-v$_{k*}$ onos plb$_{gk}$
: **cramping**: *Alet*$_{vh1}$ bell dios$_{k*}$ nux-v$_{k*}$ onos plb$_{tl1*}$
⁝ **must** bend backward: kali-c↓
: **cutting** pain: kali-c$_{h2*}$
• **forward**:
⁝ **agg.**: acon↓ ant-t↓ coloc↓ *Dios*↓ sep↓ sin-n↓ verb↓
: **cramping**: acon$_{bro1}$ ant-t$_{bro1}$ *Dios*$_{bro1}$ sin-n$_{bro1}$
: **pressing** pain: coloc$_{h2}$ sep
: **stitching** pain: verb
⁝ **amel.**: *Acon*↓ am-c↓ bell↓ borx↓ carb-v↓ carc↓ *Caust*↓ *Chin*↓ coff↓ *Colch*↓ **Coloc**↓ dios↓ grat↓ *Kali-c*↓ *Lach*↓ *Mag-p*↓ orot-ac↓ phos↓ *Plb*↓ podo↓ prun↓ *Rhus-t*↓ sars↓ senec↓ *Stann*↓ stram↓ urol-h↓ zinc↓
: **burrowing**: grat$_{k*}$
: **cramping**: *(↗bending double - amel. - cramping)* *Acon* am-c bell$_{k2}$ borx$_{a1}$ carb-v$_{pd}$ carc$_{gk6}$ *Caust* *Chin* coff *Colch* **Coloc**$_{k*}$ dios$_{mrr1}$ *Kali-c* *Lach* *Mag-p* orot-ac$_{rly4}$• phos *Plb* podo$_{mrr1}$ prun *Rhus-t* sars$_{h2}$ senec *Stann* stram urol-h$_{rwt}$• zinc
: **knees** drawn up; with: but-ac↓
. **cramping**: but-ac$_{sp1*}$
⁝ **must** bend forward: **Coloc**↓
: **gnawing** pain: **Coloc**$_{k*}$
• **head**:
⁝ **forward** | **agg.**: plb$_{bg2}$
- **bending** double:
• **agg.**$_{●}$: (non:acon-c$_{kl}$) am-c bell cit-ac↓ cocc dios$_{k*}$ dulc$_{h2}$ irid-met$_{srj5}$• *Lac-c* lyc onos sulph
⁝ **cutting** pain: cit-ac$_{rly4}$•
⁝ **lying** on side | **amel.**: podo

Abdomen

• **amel.**●: aloe ars-h ars-i atra-r bnm3• *Bell* *Borx* k* bov↓ carc mg1.de* castm *Caust* *Chin* cimic hr1 *Colch* **Coloc** k* *Cop* cupr dirc c1 dulc fd4.de euph eupi granit-m↓ hydrog srj2• *Iris* **Kali-c** kali-p k2 *Lach* lyc mag-c h2* *Mag-p* k* *Mang* k* merc-c nux-v petr phos podo k* prun ptel c1 **Puls** pycnop-sa↓ *Rheum* rhus-t↓ sars h2 senec sep bg1 *Stann* staph stram stront-c sk4• sulph tarent verat↓ verb zinc [bell-p-sp dcm1]
⁝ **cramping**: (↗*bending - forward - amel. - cramping*) bov bro1 caust tl1 chin bro1* coloc bro1* granit-m es1• kali-c tl1 mag-c lp *Mag-p* bro1 petr hr1* podo bro1 rheum mtf33 sep bro1 *Stann* bro1 sulph bro1 verat bro1
⁝ **cutting** pain: **Coloc** **Kali-c** k* petr pycnop-sa mrz1 rheum h rhus-t h1 staph k*
⁝ **sore**: mag-c

• **must** bend double●: all-c k2 aloe k2 alum h2 apis k2 ars aur-m bar-c h2 bell berb k2 borx bov *Bry* calad calc h2* *Caps* k* *Caust* k* *Cham* k* chel cimic hr1 colch k2 **Coloc** k* crot-t eupi granit-m↓ grat *Iris* kali-c k2 kali-p kola stb3• mag-c↓ *Mag-p* mang a1 marb-w es1• merc nat-m h2 nit-ac nux-v k2 op pd petr h2 plb podo k2 **Puls** *Rheum* *Rhus-t* sabad sec a1 sep spong h1 sulph ter thuj tril-p c1 verat hr1 zinc h2
⁝ **agonizing**: *Coloc* br1
⁝ **cramping**: cham mtf33 granit-m es1• mag-c lp petr a1 podo k2 sec gk

- **biting** pain: alum b4.de* am-c b4.de* bov bg2 merc bg2 nat-c b4.de* phos bg2 zinc bg2
- **blow**; pain as from a: anac b4.de* ant-t bg2 arn b7.de* calc bg2 cann-s b7.de* cic b7.de* cina b7.de* clem b4.de* croc b7.de* m-ambo b7.de m-arct b7.de* manc bg2 nat-m bg2 olnd b7.de* plat b4.de* puls bg2 squil bg2 stann b4.de*
- **blowing** the nose agg.: canth eupi stront-c
  • **burning**: canth
- **boils**; as from: kreos b7a.de
- **boring** pain: aloe bg2 ang b7.de* apis b7a.de arg-met b7.de* ars bg2 asaf b7.de* bry bg2 calen bg2 caust b4a.de cina b7.de* dig b4.de* fl-ac ptk1 m-arct b7a.de manc bg2 ol-an bg2 *Par* b7a.de phyt bg2 *Plb* bg2* polyg-h ptk1 ruta b7.de* sabad b7.de* sars ptk1 sec bg2 seneg b4.de* *Sep* b4.de* stann b4.de* tarax b7.de*
- **brandy**, after: ign
- **breakfast**:
  • **after**:
  ⁝ **agg.**: agar↓ am-c k* borx↓ cain↓ calc-s cycl k* eupi↓ gels grat↓ ham↓ hydr↓ kali-bi↓ kali-c↓ kali-p kali-s↓ lyc↓ mag-m↓ nat-sil↓ nux-m↓ nux-v phos raph spong↓ stront-c↓ thuj k* **Zinc**↓
  : **burning**: agar k* kali-s fd4.de
  : **cramping**: agar eupi grat ham kali-bi lyc h2 nat-sil fd3.de• nux-m stront-c **Zinc**
  : **cutting** pain: borx h2 cain hydr k* mag-m k* spong k* thuj k* **Zinc**
  : **pressing** pain: calc-s k* kali-c h2
  • **before**:
  ⁝ **agg.**: *Nat-s* k* nept-m lsd2.fr
  : **cramping**: nat-s k2
  • **during**: alum h2 apoc k*
- **breathing**:
  • **agg.**: *Anac* arg-met ars *Bell* berb *Bry* cench k2 clem↓ *Coloc* dig hyos kola stb3• kreos lyc mag-c mang mosch pyrog k2 ran-b k2 seneg *Stann* sulph *Thuj*
  ⁝ **lancinating**: clem
  ⁝ **pressing** pain: lyc h2
  • **deep**:
  ⁝ **agg.**: bry k2 calc h2 caust↓ con h2
  : **pressing** pain: caust h2
  • **hindering** breathing: til↓
  ⁝ **stitching** pain: til c1
  • **irregular** breathing agg.: rumx k2
- **bruised** (See sore)
- **burning**: acal br1 acet-ac k* **Acon** k* agar k* ail k* aloe alum k* alum-p k2 alum-sil k2 alumn am-c k* am-m ambr b7.de* anac k* anan ant-t *Apis* k* arg-met b7.de arizon-l nl2• arn k* **Ars** k* *Ars-i* ars-s-f k2 asaf k* asc-t k* bar-m k* *Bell* k* berb k* *Bism* mrr1 *Bov* k* bry k* cact calad k* *Calc* k* calc-i k2 *Calc-p* k* calc-s calc-sil k2 *Camph* k* cann-s k* *Canth* k* **Caps** k* carb-an k* **Carb-v** k* carbn-s card-m k2 *Caust* k* cham k* chel chinin-ar chord-umb rly4• cic b7a.de*

- **burning**: ...
cocc k* colch k* coloc k* *Con* cop crot-h k* crot-t k* cub k* cupr k* *Cupr-ar* k* cur cystein-l rly4• dios k* dirc c1 dor k* dulc *Euph* k* euphr k* gamb k* gels k* glon k* *Graph* k* grat k* guaj k2 ham k2 hydr-ac ign k* iod k* *Ip* b7.de *Iris* k* jatr-c jug-r k* *Kali-ar* kali-bi k* kali-c k* kali-i k* kali-n k* kali-p kali-s kali-sil k2 kola stb3• *Kreos* k* *Lac-c* lach k* *Laur* k* *Lil-t* k* lyc k* lyss k* m-ambo b7.de mag-s maias-l hm2• malar jl2 *Manc* k* mand sp1 merc k* *Merc-c* k* merc-sul merl k* *Mez* k* *Nat-ar* nat-c k* nat-f sp1 *Nat-m* k* nat-p *Nat-s* k* *Nux-v* k* ol-an *Ox-ac* k* *Par* b7.de* ph-ac k* phel k* **Phos** k* phyt k* plat k* plb k* puls b7.de* *Ran-b* k* raph rat k* rhus-t k* rumx ruta *Sabad* k* sabin b7.de sang k2 *Sars* k* **Sec** k* sel seneg k* *Sep* k* sil k* spig k* spong b7.de* *Stann* k* stram k* stront-c k* sul-ac b4.de sulph k* tab k* tarent k* **Ter** k* thuj k* tritic-vg fd5.de **Verat** k* viol-t b7.de* vip k* visc sp1
  • **accompanied** by | **urination**; urging for: lach bg2
  • **coal**; as from hot: verat ptk1
  • **paroxysmal**: plb k*
  • **radiating**: *Graph*
  • **steam** passing through; as from: asc-t ptk1
  • **stones** in abdomen; as from: limest-b es1•
  • **stream** of fire passing through; as from: asc-t ptk1
- **burrowing**: (↗*digging*) agar k* alum b4.de* am-m b7.de* arn b7.de* ars b4.de* asaf b7.de* *Bell* b4.de* calad bg2* calc b4.de* *Cina* b7.de* coloc b4.de* *Con* b4.de* dig k* digin a1 dulc k* graph k* grat bg2 hell k* kali-c b4.de* led b7.de* m-ambo b7.de mag-m k* nat-c b4a.de* nit-ac bg2 olnd a1 *Ph-ac* b4.de* *Phos* b4.de* rheum b7.de* rhod b4.de* *Rhus-t* b7.de* ruta b7a.de* *Sabad* b7.de* sang bg2 seneg b4.de* sep b4.de* spig k* spong b7.de* stann b4.de* staph b7.de* stront-c b4.de* sulph k* valer b7.de*
- **bursting** pain: aloe k2 alum h2 *Am-m* b7a.de anac b4.de* bar-c h2* bell bg2 bry bg2* *Caps* b7.de* *Carb-v* bg2 caust k* coff k* coloc b4a.de* con h2 dulc h2* euph b4.de* hell bg2 hyos k* ign b7.de* kali-c k2 kali-i bg2 kola stb3• lac-c led h1 lyc k* m-arct b7.de mosch b7a.de nit-ac h2* phos k* puls k* sep b4a.de* spig b7.de* sulph k* valer b7.de*
- **cancer**, in: calc-ar↓
  • **burning**: calc-ar pd
- **cheese**; after: coloc↓
  • **cramping**: coloc bro1
- **cherries**, after: mag-m h2 merc-c k*
- **chest**; with pain in: *Clem*↓
  • **dragging**, bearing down: *Clem* hr1
- **childbed**; in (See delivery)
- **children**; in: all-c↓ **Arg-n**↓ bar-c↓ bell↓ bov↓ *Carb-v*↓ *Catar*↓ caust↓ *Cham*↓ chin↓ *Coloc*↓ *Cupr*↓ *Ign*↓ jal↓ lat-h bnm5• lyc↓ *Mag-c*↓ *Mag-m*↓ *Mag-p*↓ nat-p↓ *Nat-s*↓ **Nux-v**↓ rheum↓ **Staph**↓ sulph↓ verat↓
  • **cramping**: all-c lmj **Arg-n** lmj bar-c ptk1* bell mtf33 bov lmj *Carb-v* lmj *Catar* br1* caust lmj *Cham* br1* chin lmj *Coloc* lmj *Cupr* lmj *Ign* lmj jal lmj lyc mtf33 *Mag-c* lmj *Mag-m* lmj *Mag-p* lmj nat-p tl1 *Nat-s* lmj **Nux-v** lmj rheum mtf33 **Staph** lmj sulph lmj verat lmj
  • **emaciated**: bar-c↓
  ⁝ **cramping**: bar-c mtf33
  • **newborns**: coloc ggd1 mag-p ggd1
  • **nurslings**; in: aeth↓ all-c↓ *Anis*↓ **Arg-n**↓ asaf↓ asim↓ bar-c↓ bell↓ *Borx*↓ bov↓ *Calc*↓ calc-p↓ *Carb-v*↓ catar↓ caust↓ **Cham**↓ chin↓ *Cina*↓ *Coloc*↓ *Cupr*↓ dios↓ *Ign*↓ jal↓ kali-br↓ **Lyc**↓ *Mag-c*↓ *Mag-m*↓ *Mag-p*↓ menth↓ *Nat-s*↓ nepet↓ nux-m↓ **Nux-v**↓ rheum↓ senn↓ **Staph**↓ sulph↓ verat↓
  ⁝ **cramping**: aeth bro1 all-c bro1* *Anis* br1* **Arg-n** lmj asaf bro1 asim mtf11 bar-c lmj bell bro1 *Borx* sne bov ggd *Calc* fd2.de• calc-p bro1 *Carb-v* lmj catar bro1 caust ggd **Cham** bro1* chin lmj *Cina* bro1 *Coloc* bro1* *Cupr* lmj dios mrr1 *Ign* hr* jal bro1* kali-br bro1 **Lyc** bro1* *Mag-c* lmj *Mag-m* lmj *Mag-p* bro1* menth bro1* *Nat-s* ggd nepet bro1 nux-m mrr1 **Nux-v** pd* rheum bro1 senn br1* **Staph** bro1* sulph lmj* verat lmj
  ⁝ **lying** on stomach:
  : **amel.**: coloc↓
  . **cramping**: coloc tl1
  • **school** children; in: *Calc-p* mrr1
- **chill**:
  • **after**: ars↓ con↓ tere-la↓
  ⁝ **cutting** pain: ars h2 con h2 tere-la rly4•

- **before**: ars elat eup-per *Spong*
  - **cramping**: ars fla *Spong*
  - **cutting** pain: ars
- **during**: aloe bg2 ant-c bg2 ant-t bg2 apis b7a.de* aran ars k* bar-c bg2 *Borx* b4a.de* *Bov* k* bry k* buth-a sp1 calad k* calc k* carb-v b4a.de* cham bg2 **Chin** k* chinin-ar cic bg2 *Cocc* k* coff k* **Coloc** k* croc b7.de* eup-per ferr bg2 ign k* ip k* kali-c bg2 lach led m-aust b7.de meny bg2 meph merc k* merc-c k* mez b4a.de* nit-ac k* nux-m b7.de* nux-v k* ph-ac bg2 phos k* podo puls k* ran-b b7.de* *Rhus-t* k* rumx *Sep* k* spig b7.de* *Stront-c* b4.de* sulph k*
  - **cramping**: chin mrr1 **Cocc** k* led
  - **cutting** pain: ars h2
  - **drawing** pain: bov k*
- **with**:
  - **menses**; and suppressed: *Puls*
  - **Abdomen**; in: anth c1 cupr-act pd

- **chilled**; as if: agar bg2 aloe bg2 arg-met b7.de* arn b7.de* ars bg2 asaf b7.de* bry b7.de* cann-s b7.de* carb-v b4.de* coloc b4.de* croc b7.de* dig b4.de* hep bg2 ign b7.de* kreos b7a.de meph bg2 merc b4.de* nat-c bg2 nit-ac b4.de* *Nux-v* b7.de* op b7.de* petr bg2 phos bg2 ruta b7.de* sabin b7.de* samb b7.de* valer b7.de*
- **chilliness**; during: cop ↓ nat-c ↓ nux-v ↓ puls ↓ rhus-t ↓ sep ↓
  - **burning**: nat-c k*
  - **cramping**: cop br1 nux-v bro1 puls bro1 rhus-t h1 sep k*
- **chronic**: lyc ↓ staph ↓
  - **cramping**: lyc bro1 staph bro1
- **clawing** pain: acon b7.de* agath-a nl2• alum k* arn b7.de* ars k* *Bell* k* *Calc* b4a.de carb-an k* cham b7.de* coloc k* con b4.de* dros b7.de* hep k* *Ip* k* kreos b7a.de* led b7.de* lyc k* m-aust b7.de mag-c b4.de* mosch k* nux-v b7.de* petr bg2* phos b4.de* puls b7.de* sep k* *Sil* b4.de* stann b4.de* zinc k*
- **clothing** agg.: apis ↓ *Ars* ↓ *Bell* benz-ac ↓ **Calc** ↓ *Caps* hr1 *Carb-v* ↓ coff ↓ diosm br1 gink-b sbd1• *Graph* ↓ *Kreos* ↓ *Lac-c* **Lach** *Lyc* ↓ merc-c ↓ *Nux-v* ↓ puls ↓ raph ↓ rhus-t k2 *Spong* ↓ zinc ↓
  - **sore**: apis *Ars* benz-ac **Calc** *Carb-v* coff *Graph* *Kreos* *Lac-c* **Lach** *Lyc* merc-c *Nux-v* puls raph rhus-t k2 *Spong* zinc
- **clucking**: ruta fd4.de sul-ac h2
- **clutched** with nails of fingers; as if: agath-a nl2• bell k* carb-an bg2* *Coloc* bg2 hep bg2 ip k* mosch bg2 zinc bg2
- **coffee**:
  - **after**: canth k* *Cham* k* ign merc-sul c1 nat-m k* *Nux-v*
  - **agg.**: *Cham* ↓ ign ↓ nat-m ↓ *Nux-v* ↓
    - **cramping**: *Cham* ign nat-m *Nux-v*
  - **amel.**: **Coloc** k*
    - **cramping**: coloc ptk1
- **coition**:
  - **after**: caust
  - **during**: brucel sa3• graph
    - **cramping**: graph
- **cold**:
  - **air**:
    - **agg.**: *Am-c* ↓ lyc ↓
      - **cramping**: *Am-c* lyc
    - **amel.**: lyc k*
  - **drinks**:
    - **after** | **agg.**: apoc k2 calc *Calc-p* calc-s dulc elaps gk manc *Nux-m* *Rhus-t* trom
    - **agg.**: manc ↓
      - **cramping**: manc ptk1
    - **amel.**: elaps symph fd3.de•
  - **food** | **agg.**: mang sep
- **cold**; after taking a: acon lp* all-c aloe k2 alum alumn ↓ bell h1 camph ↓ *Carb-v* **Cham** **Chin** *Coloc* **Dulc** graph h2 *Hep* lyc meli ↓ *Merc* nat-c nit-ac *Nux-v* petr h2 phos ↓ rhus-t ↓ ruta h1 samb h1 **Verat**
  - **cramping**: acon bro1 *All-c* k* alum h2 alumn cham bro1 coloc bro1 *Dulc* k* meli sne nat-c h2 nit-ac h2 nux-v bro1* phos h2 rhus-t h1 samb xxb1
  - **cutting** pain: camph k*
- **cold** agg.; becoming: acon k2 alum h2 **Ars** camph hell merc **Nux-v** *Phos* *Plb*
- **colic** (See cramping)
- **comes** and goes (See increasing)
- **compressed**; as if: acon bg2 ambr b7.de* ant-c b7.de* apis b7a.de* bell bg2 canth b7.de* cham b7.de* con bg2 crot-t bg2 cupr b7.de* euphr bg2 ign bg2 mag-c bg2 mez bg2 mosch bg2 plb bg2 puls bg2 seneg bg2 staph b7.de* thuj bg2 zinc bg2
- **constipation**:
  - **during**: alet ↓ all-s ↓ *Aloe* ↓ *Alum* ↓ am-m ↓ carc ↓ cocc ↓ coll ↓ *Cupr* ↓ glon ↓ grat ↓ lyc ↓ merc ↓ nux-m ↓ *Nux-v* ↓ *Op* ↓ *Plb* ↓ *Plb-act* ↓ *Podo* ↓ senn ↓ sil ↓
    - **cramping**: alet vh1 all-s bro1 *Aloe* bro1 *Alum* bro1 carc gk6 cocc bro1 coll bro1 *Cupr* bro1 glon bro1 grat bro1 lyc bro1 merc k* nux-m mrr1 *Nux-v* bro1 *Op* k* *Plb* k* *Plb-act* bro1 *Podo* senn br1 sil h2*
    - **cutting** pain: am-m h2
  - **from**: ars bell carc tpw2* con cupr kali-c merc op plb sanguis-s hrn2• sil sul-ac tell rsj10• thuj
- **constipation**; as from: cham h1
- **constricting** pain: allox sp1 cact k2 carc sp1 orot-ac rly4• sabin c1* stroph-s sp1
  - **band** or belt; as from a: plb bg2
- **contracted**; as if | **string**; by a: ros-d wla1
- **contracting**: calc h2 dulc fd4.de nat-sil fd3.de• nicotam rly4• plut-n srj7• spong fd4.de symph fd3.de• tritic-vg fd5.de vanil fd5.de zinc h2
- **conversation** agg.: zinc ↓
  - **cramping**: zinc mrr1
- **convulsions**; with: bell ↓ *Cic* ↓ *Cupr* ↓ *Sec* ↓
  - **cramping**: bell bro1 *Cic* k* *Cupr* b7a.de *Sec* b7a.de
- **corrosive**: apis b7a.de *Calc* b4a.de cupr b7.de* dulc b4a.de *Lyc* b4a.de nat-c bg2 *Olnd* b7a.de plat b4a.de *Ruta* b7a.de sulph b4a.de teucr b7a.de
- **coryza**:
  - **after**: calc ↓
    - **cutting** pain: calc h2
  - **during**: acon b7.de* calc bg2 canth b7.de
    - **cutting** pain: calc b4.de
- **coryza**; after suppressed: calc ↓
  - **cramping**: calc ptk1
- **cough** agg.; during: acon ↓ aloe alum b4a.de* am-c am-m ambr k* *Anac* k* apis *Arn* ars k* ars-s-f k2 *Asc-t* k* aur k* aur-ar k2 aur-s k2 **Bell** k* borx b4a.de **Bry** k* calc k* camph canth k* caps k* *Carb-an* caust h1* cench cham *Chel* chin ↓ clem a1 cocc k* *Colch* coloc k* con k* croc crot-t **Dros** k* eupi *Ferr* k* ferr-ar ferr-p hell hep *Hyos* ip k* irid-met srj5• kali-ar kali-bi kali-c k* *Kali-n* k* kali-p kali-sil k2 kreos k* *Lach* lact *Lyc* k* *Nat-m* nit-ac **Nux-v** k* pall ph-ac k* *Phos* k* *Pic-ac* ↓ plb psor *Puls* k* *Ran-b* rhus-t sabad ↓ samb ↓ *Sep* k* sil k* **Squil** k* stann b4.de* staph ↓ sul-ac ↓ *Sulph* k* tarent thuj bro1 valer ↓ verat k*
  - **burning**: canth
  - **bursting** pain: anac k* caust h2 squil h1
  - **cramping**: ars bro1 bell bro1 *Bry* bro1 chel nat-m bro1 pall c1 plb tarent k*
  - **cutting** pain: *Arn* cham chin valer **Verat** k*
  - **sore**: ars *Bry* *Carb-an* *Caust* cench k2 crot-t k* *Ferr* k* hyos *Nux-v* *Pic-ac* plb *Puls* *Stann*
  - **stitching** pain: acon am-m ars *Bell* bry chin lach lyc nit-ac phos sabad samb sep staph sul-ac sulph
- **cramping**: (↗*pinching*) *Abrot* k* acal br1 acet-ac k* *Acon* k* adren bro1 aegle-f zzc1• aesc k* aeth k* **Agar** k* agath-a nl2• aids nl2• ail k* alet bg2* all-c k* **Aloe** k* *Alum* k* alum-p k2 alum-sil k2 *Alumn* *Am-c* k* **Am-m** k* ambr k* ammc a1* amp rly4• *Anac* k* anan ang h1* *Ango* c1 anis bro1 *Ant-c* k* *Ant-t* k* anth vh aphis a1 *Apis* k* apoc bg2 aran arg-cy bro1 arg-met k* *Arg-n* k* arge br1* arge-pl rwt5• arist-cl sp1* arn k* *Ars* k* ars-i ars-s-f a1* ars-s-r a1 *Asaf* k* *Asar* k* atra-r bnm3• *Aur* k* aur-ar k2 aur-i k2 aur-m aur-s k2 bamb-a stb2.de• bapt bg2 bar-c k* bar-i *Bar-m* bar-s k2 **Bell** k* *Berb* k* *Bism* k* *Bit-ar* wht1• *Borx* k* *Bov* k* brom k* *Bry* k* bufo but-ac sp1 cact *Caj* bro1 calad k* **Calc** k* calc-i k2 *Calc-p* k* calc-s calc-sil k2 camph k* cann-s k* canth k* caps k* *Carb-ac* k* *Carb-an* k* **Carb-v** k* carbn-dox knl3• **Carbn-s** carc az1.de• card-b a1 card-m k* *Cardios-h* rly4• carl k* cartl-s rly4• cassia-s cdd7*• castm bg2 catar bro1 caul *Caust* k* cedr cere-b a1 **Cham** k* **Chel** k* chen-v a1 *Chin* k* chinin-ar k* chir-fl gya2 chlorpr pin1• chord-umb rly4• *Cic* k* *Cina* k* cinch a1 cinnb k* cit-ac rly4• clem k* cob coc-c k* coca-c sk4• **Cocc** k* *Coff* k* *Colch* k* coli rly4• coll bro1 **Coloc** k* colocin a1 *Con* k* conv br1 *Cop* k* corn k* croc k* crot-h bg2 *Crot-t* k* cub k* **Cupr** k* *Cupr-act* bro1 *Cupr-ar* k* *Cycl* k* cypra-eg sde6.de•

Abdomen

- **cramping**: ...
cystein-l rly4• cyt-l sp1 *Dig* k* **Dios** k* dros k* **Dulc** k* echi echit a1 elaps *Elat* k* ephe-si hsj1• erech a1 erig eryt-j a1 *Eup-per* k* eup-pur a1 *Euph* k* *Euphr* k* eupi falco-pe nl2• *Ferr* k* ferr-ar ferr-p k* fil bro1 fum rly1*• gamb k* *Gels* k* gent-c gink-b sbd1• glon k* gnaph k* *Gran* k* granit-m es1• **Graph** k* *Grat* k* guaj k* guat sp1 haliae-lc srj5• *Ham* *Hell* k* *Hep* k* hippoc-k szs2 hist sp1 *Hydr* k* hydrc *Hyos* k* hyper k* **Ign** k* iod k* **Ip** k* irid-met srj5• *Iris* k* *Iris-t* bro1 jab k* *Jal* br1* jatr-c k* jug-r k* kali-ar *Kali-bi* k* *Kali-br* *Kali-c* k* kali-i k* kali-m k2 kali-n k* kali-p *Kali-pic* a1* *Kali-s* k* kali-sil k2 ketogl-ac rly4• kola stb3• *Kreos* k* *Lac-c* lac-f wza1• lac-h sk4• lac-lup hm2• *Lach* k* lact k* lap-la rsp1 lat-h bnm5• lat-m sp1 *Laur* k* lec *Led* k* lept bg2* liat br1 *Lil-t* *Lim* bro1 limen-b-c hm2* lob luf-op rsj5• **Lyc** k* lycps-v lyss *M-arct* b7.de m-aust b7.de *Mag-c* k* **Mag-m** k* **Mag-p** k* mag-s k* manc k* mand sp1 mang k* melal-alt gya4 mentho bro1 meny *Merc* k* merc-c k* merl k* *Mez* k* micr br1 *Morph* bro1 *Mosch* k* *Mur-ac* k* musca-d szs1 myos-a rly4• naja *Nat-ar* *Nat-c* k* nat-f sp1 *Nat-m* k* nat-ox rly4• nat-p k* *Nat-s* k* neon srj5• nicc bro1 nicotam rly4• nig-s mp4• *Nit-ac* k* *Nux-m* k* **Nux-v** k* oci-sa sp1 ol-j olnd k* onis bro1 onos **Op** k* oreo br1 orot-ac rly4• oscilloc jl2 ox-ac k* oxal-a rly4• ozone sde2• paeon pall pant-ac rly4• *Par* k* paraf bro1 *Petr* k* **Ph-ac** k* phel k* phos k* *Phyt* k* *Pic-ac* k* plac-s rly4• plan k* *Plat* k* **Plb** k* *Plb-act* bro1 plb-chr bro1 **Podo** k* polyg-h bro1* polys sk4• pot-e rly4• prun k* pseuts-m oss1• psor k* ptel k* **Puls** k* pyrog bg2* rad-br bro1* *Ran-b* k* ran-s k* *Raph* k* rat k* rauw tpw8* *Rheum* k* rhod k* rhus-g tmo3• *Rhus-t* k* rhus-v k* ribo rly4• rob br1 *Rumx* ruta k* sabad k* sabin k* sal-fr sle1• samb k* sang bg2* sanguis-s hm2• saroth sp1 sars k* *Sec* k* senec k* seneg k* **Senn** k* *Sep* k* **Sil** k* *Sin-n* bro1 *Spig* k* spira br1 **Spong** k* squil k* **Stann** k* *Staph* k* *Stram* k* *Stront-c* k* **Stry** k* suis-hep rly4• suis-pan rly4• *Sul-ac* k* sulfa sp1 **Sulph** k* sumb k* suprar rly4• symph fd3.de• tab k* tarax k* *Tarent* k* tell *Ter* k* tetox pin2• teucr k* thal-xyz srj8• *Thuj* k* trom k* tub c1 ulm-c jsj8• urol-h rwt• v-a-b jl2 *Valer* k* **Verat** k* verat-v bg2 verb k* vero-o rly4*• vesp br1* vib k* viol-t k* vip k* *Zinc* k* zinc-fcy a1 zinc-p k2 **Zing** [mag-br stj1 mag-f stj1 spect dfg1]
  - **accompanied** by:
    - **apyrexia**: verat bro1
    - **cholera** (See RECTUM - Cholera - accompanied - cramps)
    - **coldness** of abdomen: calc ptk1 kali-s ptk1
    - **collapse** (See GENERALS - Collapse - accompanied - abdomen)
    - **eructations**: hyos ptk1 oxyt ptk2
    - **fainting**: coll tl1
    - **flatulence**: absin bro1 acon tl1 aesc tl1 agar bro1* alf bro1 all-s mtf11 *Aloe* bro1 *Anis* bro1 *Arg-n* bro1 asaf bro1 *Bell* bro1 but-ac bro1 *Caj* bro1 calc-p bro1 *Carb-v* bro1 carbn-s bro1 *Cham* bro1 *Chin* bro1 cina bro1 cocc bro1* coloc bro1 *Dios* bro1 hydr-ac bro1 ip bro1* iris bro1 *Lyc* bro1 mag-p bro1* mentho bro1 nat-s tl1 *Nux-v* bro1 op bro1 plb bro1 *Polyg-h* bro1 puls bro1* rad-br bro1 *Raph* bro1 rob bro1 sang bro1 *Senn* bro1 tell rsj10• zinc bro1
      - **evening**: luf-op rsj5•
      - **children**; in: senn mtf11
      - **eating**; after: luf-op rsj5•
    - **hemorrhoids**: *Aesc* bro1 all-c bro1 coloc bro1 *Nux-v* bro1 puls bro1 sulph bro1
    - **hiccough**: hyos bro1
      - **suffocative** (See STOMACH - Hiccough - suffocative - accompanied - abdomen)
    - **neuralgic** pain (See GENERALS - Pain - neuralgic - accompanied - colic)
    - **opisthotonos**: dios mrr1 nux-v mrr1
    - **retching**: petr hr1
    - **salivation**: led kr1* rheum kr1*
    - **sleepiness**: spira bro1
    - **symptoms**; other: plb ptk1
    - **urine**:
      - **bloody** (See URINE - Bloody - accompanied - abdomen)
      - **suppressed** (See KIDNEYS - Suppression - accompanied - abdomen)
    - **Aorta**; pulsating in abdominal (See Pulsation - aorta - accompanied - cramping)

- **cramping – accompanied** by: ...
    - **Back**:
      - **complaints** of (See BACK - Complaints - accompanied - abdomen - pain - cramping)
      - **pain** (See BACK - Pain - accompanied - abdomen - pain - cramping)
    - **Bladder**; pain in: lat-m sp1
    - **Cheeks** and hot perspiration; red discoloration of: cham bro1
    - **Chest**; complaints of (See CHEST - Complaints - accompanied - abdomen; cramping)
    - **Epigastrium**; constriction in (See STOMACH - Constriction - epigastrium - accompanied - abdomen)
    - **Face** | **pale**: *Cina* bro1 fil bro1
    - **Hands**; yellow: sil ptk1
    - **Kidneys**; pain in (See KIDNEYS - Pain - accompanied - colic)
    - **Lower** extremities; paralysis of lower: plb tl1
    - **Nails**; blue: sil ptk1
    - **Nose**; itching of: *Cina* bro1 fil bro1
    - **Scapulae**; complaints between: am-c ptk1
    - **Stomach**; complaints of: carb-v bro1 *Chin* bro1 coloc bro1 dios bro1 ip bro1 lyc bro1 *Nux-v* bro1 *Puls* bro1
    - **Teeth**:
      - **complaints** of: plb bg2
    - **Thighs**; pain in: coloc bro1
    - **Tongue**:
      - **black** discoloration: *Alum* kr1*
      - **white** discoloration: *Mag-p* kr1* op kr1*
  - **alternating** with:
    - **delirium** (See MIND - Delirium - alternating - abdomen)
    - **vertigo** (See VERTIGO - Alternating - colic)
    - **Chest**; pain in: *Ran-b*
    - **Joints**; pain in (See EXTREMITIES - Pain - joints - alternating with - colic)
    - **Lumbar** region; pain in (See BACK - Pain - lumbar - alternating - abdomen)
  - **cold**; as from taking a: hep h2 petr h2 stann h2
  - **followed** by:
    - **beer**; desire for (See GENERALS - Food and - beer - desire - colic)
    - **diarrhea**; fetid: oscilloc jl2
    - **nausea**: cassia-s ccrh1•
    - **retching**: cassia-s ccrh1•
    - **Extremities**; painful contraction of: abrot mtf33
  - **jerking** pain: graph h2 mur-ac h2 plat h2
  - **paroxysmal**: coloc tl1 dios mrr1
  - **transversely**: guaj h2 staph h1
  - **upward**: mag-m h2
  - **violent**; very: op tl1
  - **wandering** pain: alum bg2 am-m bg2 bell bg2 colch bg2 cupr bg2 dios bg2 mur-ac h2* nat-s bg2 op bg2 spig h1 staph h1
- **crossing** limbs amel.: **Lil-t**↓ *Murx*↓ **Sep**↓ zinc↓
  - **dragging**, bearing down: **Lil-t** *Murx* **Sep** zinc
- **cucumber**; after: all-c↓
  - **cramping**: all-c bro1
- **cut** off from chest; as if abdomen were: ars b4a.de*
- **cutting pain**: **Acon** k* aeth k* *Agar* k* agn all-c k2 **Aloe** k* *Alum* k* alum-p k2 alum-sil k2 am-c k* am-m k* *Ambr* k* amp rly4• anac k* ang b7.de* *Ant-c* k* *Ant-t* k* *Apis* k* arg-met k* *Arg-n* k* arn k* **Ars** k* *Ars-i* k* ars-s-f k2 arum-t k* asaf k* asar b7.de* asc-t c1 aur k* aur-ar k2 aur-s k2 bapt k* *Bar-c* k* bar-i *Bar-m* bar-s k2 bell k* berb k* *Bol-la* *Borx* *Bov* k* *Bry* k* bufo cact cadm-s c1 cain calad k* *Calc* k* calc-i k2 calc-p k* calc-s calc-sil k2 camph k* cann-s k* **Canth** k* *Caps* k* *Carb-an* k* carb-v k* carbn-s card-m k* *Carl* k* castm caust k* *Cham* k* *Chel* k* **Chin** k* chinin-ar chinin-s chion cic k* cimic *Cina* k* clem k* coc-c k* *Cocc* k* coff b7.de* *Colch* k* **Coloc** k* *Con* k* corian-s knl6• *Croc* b7.de* crot-t k*

- **cutting** pain: ...
cub *Cupr* k* cupr-ar k* cycl k* *Dig* k* **Dios** k* dros k* *Dulc* k* echi elaps *Elat* k* euon k* eupi k* ferr b7a.de gels bg2 glon graph k* grat k* guaj b4.de* hell k* *Hep* k* hydr k* hydrog srj2• hydroph rsj6• **Hyos** k* hyper *Ign* k* indg k* *Iod* k* **Ip** k* *Iris* jatr-c *Kali-ar* *Kali-bi* k* **Kali-c** k* kali-i kali-m k2 *Kali-n* k* kali-p **Kali-s** kali-sil k2 kola stb3• kreos *Lach* k* lact k* *Laur* k* *Led* k* lept k* lil-t k* lob *Lyc* k* m-arct b7.de m-aust b7.de **Mag-c** k* *Mag-m* k* mag-p bg2 *Manc* mang melal-alt gya4 meny b7.de* *Merc* k* *Merc-c* k* merc-i-f k* merc-pr-r mez k* *Mur-ac* k* murx naja k* *Nat-ar* *Nat-c* k* *Nat-m* k* nat-p **Nat-s** nat-sil fd3.de• nicc k* **Nit-ac** k* nux-m k* **Nux-v** k* *Ol-an* k* **Op** k* *Ox-ac* k* paeon k* par k* pegan-ha tpi1• *Petr* k* petr-ra shn4• ph-ac k* phel k* *Phos* k* phyt k* plat k* plb k* podo bg2 polyg-h bg2* pot-e rly4• psor k* ptel **Puls** k* pyrog k2 ran-b b7.de* ran-s k* *Rheum* k* *Rhus-t* k* rob k* rumx ruta *Sabad* k* sabin k* sacch-a fd2.de• sang bg2* sanguis-s hm2• *Sars* k* *Sec* k* *Sel* k* *Seneg* k* *Sep* k* *Sil* k* **Spig** k* spong b7.de* squil stann *Staph* k* *Stront-c* k* **Stry** k* *Sul-ac* k* **Sulph** k* sumb k* ter k* tere-la rly4• *Teucr* b7a.de thuj valer k* vanil fd5.de **Verat** k* verat-v verb k* *Viol-t* k* vip k* zinc k*
  - **accompanied** by | **nausea** (See STOMACH - Nausea - accompanied - abdomen - pain - cutting)
  - **alternating** with | **coryza**: calc c1*
  - **backwards** and upwards during labor: *Gels*
  - **cold**; as from taking a: mur-ac h2 petr h2
  - **electric** shock was darting through the anus; as if an: **Coloc**
  - **flatulence**; as from: caps hr1 hydrog srj2• sep h2
  - **knife**; as with a: chir-fl gya2
  - **labor** pains; as from false: kali-c
  - **menses** would appear; as if: laur
  - **outward**: ang b7a.de
  - **paroxysmal**: calc h2 coloc h2 grat lyc k* ph-ac k* sep k* sil k* stann
  - **pieces**; as if cut into: ant-t b7a.de bov b4a.de *Coloc* b4a.de laur b7a.de *Sabad* b7a.de *Verat* b7a.de
  - **pieces** were in motion; as if hard, sharp: borx h2*
  - **stones** being rubbed together; like sharp: *(↗squeezed - stones; Stone in)* apis **Cocc** k •* **Coloc** k •* staph k*
  - **transversely**: guaj h2 ph-ac h2 sacch-a fd2.de• sep h2 spong fd4.de zinc h2
  - **wandering** pain: bell card-m dulc led stront-c
- **delivery**:
  - **after**: caul k2
  - **during**: phos ↓ puls ↓
    - **cutting** pain: phos puls
- **despair**, driving to: *Coff* coloc k2
- **detached**; as if something became: limest-b es1•
- **diarrhea**:
  - **after**:
    - **agg.**: *Aloe* bro1 *Coloc* bro1 crot-t bro1 dios bro1 dulc fd4.de *Gamb* bro1 grat bro1 mag-c h2 mag-m ↓ merc bro1 *Merc-c* bro1 rheum bro1 stann h2 trom bro1 verat bro1
      - **cutting** pain: mag-c h2 mag-m h2
  - **amel.**: agar ↓ *Alet* ↓ mand ↓
    - **cramping**: *Alet* vh1 mand sp1
    - **cutting** pain: agar h2
  - **before**: aeth ↓ *Aloe* ↓ alst ↓ ambr ↓ ars ↓ *Bell* ↓ borx ↓ bry ↓ camph ↓ casc ↓ *Cham* ↓ *Chin* ↓ cina ↓ coloc mrr1 crot-t ↓ *Cupr-ar* ↓ cycl ↓ *Dios* ↓ dulc ↓ elat ↓ gamb ↓ gard-j ↓ haliae-lc ↓ *Ip* ↓ iris ↓ kali-br ↓ kali-n ↓ lept ↓ mag-c ↓ mag-m ↓ merc ↓ *Merc-c* ↓ merc-d ↓ nux-v ↓ oxal-a ↓ petr ↓ phos ↓ *Rheum* ↓ sal-fr ↓ sars ↓ senn ↓ staphycoc rly4• suis-pan rly4• sulph ↓ suprar ↓ trom ↓ *Verat* ↓
    - **cramping**: aeth bro1 *Aloe* bro1 alst bro1 ambr hr1 ars h2 *Bell* bro1 borx bro1 camph a1 casc bro1 *Cham* bro1 *Chin* bro1 cina bro1 *Coloc* bro1 crot-t bro1 *Cupr-ar* bro1 cycl a1 *Dios* bro1 dulc bro1 elat bro1 gamb bro1 gard-j vlr2• haliae-lc srj5• *Ip* bro1 iris bro1 kali-br a1 kali-n h2 lept bro1 mag-c h2* mag-m h2 merc bro1 *Merc-c* bro1 merc-d bro1 nux-v bro1 oxal-a rly4• phos h2 *Rheum* bro1 sal-fr sle1• senn bro1 staphycoc rly4• sulph h2* suprar rly4• trom bro1 *Verat* bro1
    - **cutting** pain: ars h2 bry tl1 kali-n h2 mag-c hr petr h2 phos h2 sars h2 sulph h2

- **diarrhea**: ...
  - **during**: *Aeth* k* *Agar* k* agath-a nl2• aloe alst ↓ alum k* am-c k* am-m k* ambr ↓ *Anac* k* ang k* ant-t k* anthraq ↓ apoc aran *Arg-n* arge-pl ↓ arn *Ars* k* ars-i asaf k* asar b2.de bamb-a ↓ bapt k* bar-c b2.de *Bell* k* bism mtf11 borx b2.de bov k* bros-gau ↓ *Bry* k* cact calad b2.de calc k* calc-p camph ↓ canth k* caps k* carb-an b2.de carb-v k* carbn-s caust b2.de cean ↓ cench **Cham** k* *Chin* k* chinin-ar cimic cob cob-n sp1 *Cocc* k* *Colch* k* coli gmj1 **Coloc** k* com con b2.de *Cop* croc b2.de *Crot-t* cupr k* cupr-ar cycl dig b2.de **Dios** dros b2.de dulc k* *Elat* ↓ *Emetin* mp4• euph k* ferr ↓ ferr-p fl-ac flor-p rsj3• fuch br1 **Gamb** gard-j ↓ gels *Gran* graph k* guat ↓ ham hell k* hep k* hura ign b2.de iod *Ip* k* iris *Jatr-c* ↓ jug-c ↓ jug-r kali-ar kali-bi *Kali-c* k* kali-i kali-m k2 kali-n k* kali-p kali-s lach k* laur b2.de lept ↓ luf-op ↓ *Lyc* k* lycps-v m-arct b2.de m-aust b2.de *Mag-c* k* mag-m b2.de mag-p ↓ mang b2.de *Med* medul-os-si ↓ meny b2.de *Merc* k* **Merc-c** merc-d ↓ merc-i-r mez k* mur-ac nat-c b2.de nat-m b2.de *Nat-s* nit-ac k* *Nux-v* k* op k* ox-ac oxal-a ↓ ozone sde2• petr k* phos k* phys ↓ plb k* **Podo** polyg-h ↓ puls k* pyrid ↓ *Rheum* k* rhodi ↓ rhus-t k* rhus-v ribo ↓ ric ↓ rumx ruta fd4.de sabad b2.de samb ↓ sanic sars k* sec senec seneg b2.de sep k* sil b2.de* spig b2.de spong b2.de* stann b2.de staph b2.de staphycoc ↓ stram stront-c k* suis-pan ↓ *Sulph* k* suprar ↓ tab ter tere-la ↓ **Thuj** k* *Trios* ↓ tritic-vg fd5.de *Trom* vanil fd5.de *Verat* k* viol-t b2.de zinc b2.de zinc-s zing
    - **cramping**: *Aloe* bro1 alst bro1 anthraq rly4• arge-pl rwt5• ars h2* bamb-a stb2.de• *Borx* hr1 bros-gau mrc1 bry bro1 camph bro1 *Canth* bro1 caps bro1 cean bro1 *Cham* bro1 *Chin* bro1 coli rly4• coloc bro1* crot-t bro1 *Cupr* bro1 *Cupr-ar* bro1 dulc bro1 *Elat* bro1 gamb bro1 gard-j vlr2• guat sp1 *Ip* bro1 iris bro1 *Jatr-c* bro1 lept bro1 luf-op rsj5• mag-c bro1 mag-p tl1 medul-os-si rly4• *Merc* bro1 *Merc-c* bro1 merc-d bro1 oxal-a rly4• petr h2* phos h2 phys ptk1 podo bro1 polyg-h bro1 puls bro1 pyrid rly4• rheum bro1 rhodi ptk2 ribo rly4• ric bro1 samb bro1 sec bro1 sep h2 sil bro1 staphycoc rly4• suis-pan rly4• sulph bro1 suprar rly4• tere-la rly4• *Trios* br1* *Trom* bro1 *Verat* bro1 zinc h2 zing bro1
    - **cutting** pain: ambr c1 ars h2 bov *Crot-t* ferr gamb jug-c kali-c h2 kali-n h2 mag-c h2 mag-m k* *Merc* nit-ac h2 petr h2 sabad br1 sep h2 **Sulph** k*
- **diarrhea**; as from: agar b4.de* agn b7.de* *Aloe* bg2 am-m b7.de* ambr b7.de* ang b7.de* ant-c b7.de* ant-t b7.de* apis b7a.de* arg-met b7.de* asaf b7.de* bar-c b4.de* bell b4.de* *Bism* b7a.de borx b4a.de* *Bry* b7.de* calad b7.de* calc b4.de* canth b7.de* carb-an b4.de* carb-v b4.de* caust bg2 cham b7.de* chin b7.de* coff b7.de* colch b7.de* con bg2 crot-t bg2 cycl b7.de* dig b4.de* *Dulc* bg2 ferr bg2 gels bg2 glon bg2 graph b4.de* hell b7.de* ign b7.de* kali-bi bg2 kali-c b4.de* kali-n bg2 kreos b7a.de* lach bg2 led b7.de* lyc bg2 m-ambo b7.de m-arct b7.de meny b7.de* merc b4.de* mez b4.de* nat-ar bg2 nat-c b4a.de* nat-m bg2 nat-s bg2 nit-ac b4.de* nux-m b7.de* *Nux-v* b7.de* olnd b7.de* op b7.de* petr b4.de* ph-ac bg2 phos b4.de* phyt bg2 plat b4.de* plb bg2 *Puls* b7.de* ran-s b7.de* rhod b4.de* rhus-t b7.de* sabin b7.de* sars bg2 sec b7.de* seneg b4.de* sep b4.de* spig b7.de* *Squil* b7.de* staph b7.de* stront-c b4a.de sulph bg2 tab bg2 teucr b7.de* verat b7.de* zinc b4.de*
- **diarrhea** would come on; as if: act-sp aeth agar ail *Aloe* alum h2 alum-sil k2 am-c am-m ang h1 ant-c h2 apis apoc arg-met h1 ars-s-f k2 *Asaf* *Bar-c* *Bell* bol-la *Borx* **Bry** calc *Camph* carb-an carb-v h2 carbn-s cartl-s rly4• caust cham chin h1 cimic cob colch coloc *Con* crot-t cycl h1 dig **Dulc** eupi ferr form graph hell helon **Hydr** kali-bi *Kali-c* kali-m k2 kali-n h2 ketogl-ac rly4• *Lach* laur led lil-t lith-c lob mag-m mag-s melal-alt gya4 meny meph merc-i-f merc-sul c1 mez h2 naja nat-ar k2 nat-c h2* *Nat-s* **Nux-v** olnd onos ox-ac petr-ra shn4• *Ph-ac* *Phos* *Phys* phyt plan *Plat* podo fd3.de• prun ptel *Puls* **Ran-s** rhus-t rumx sabin *Seneg* squil h1 stann h2 staph h1 *Stry* sulph sumb suprar rly4• ter verat zinc zinc-p k2
- **digestion**; during: chin k* cupr-act
- **digging** pain: *(↗burrowing)* alum h2 am-m b7.de* bell bg2 bry bg2 bufo bg2 calc bg2 carc az1.de• chel bg2 kali-c bg2 kreos b7a.de mag-c b4.de* mag-m h2 nat-c h2 nat-s bg2 *Nux-v* b7.de* rheum bg2 rhod bg2 rhus-t h1* sabad bg2 sep h2* stann h2* sul-ac h2*
- **dinner**:
  - **after**:
    - **agg.**: agar alum k* alumn ↓ asc-t k* bry k* cain ↓ castn-v ↓ cham ↓ cob k* coc-c ↓ cocc k* *Coloc* con crot-t dulc fd4.de gent-c grat hydr ↓ iod ↓ kali-bi kali-c lact ↓ lyc **Mag-c** mag-m ↓ *Naja* nat-c ↓ nat-m k* *Nux-v* phos propr sa3• *Ran-b* rheum ↓ sars ↓ sil ↓ sulph thuj trom valer zinc

Abdomen

• **after – agg.**: ...
: **cramping**: agar k* alum h2 alumn coc-c a1 cocc crot-t k* gent-c kali-c **Mag-c** k* naja nat-c a1 phos k* *Ran-b* thuj k* trom k* valer **Zinc**
: **cutting** pain: cain cham coloc k* grat k* hydr k* lact k* lyc mag-m k* nat-m k* rheum sil sulph k* **Zinc** k*
: **dragging**, bearing down: sulph
: **drawing** pain: con
: **gnawing** pain: *Coloc*
: **pressing** pain: castn-v grat k* iod h sulph k*
: **stitching** pain: sars k*
• **before**: hydr ↓ lyc ↓ propr sa3•
: **cutting** pain: hydr k* lyc k*
: **pressing** pain: lyc k*
• **during**:
: **agg.**: am-c ↓ bry k* cedr k* kali-c ↓ lact ↓ mag-s seneg k* zinc
: **cramping**: am-c h2 kali-c h2 mag-s k* zinc
: **cutting** pain: lact k* zinc k*
- **distension** from flatulence; with: arg-n ↓
• **cramping**: arg-n br1
- **distention**; from (See Distension - painful)
- **doubling** up (See bending double - agg.)
- **dragging**, bearing down: acal br1 aesc agn alet *All-s* vh1 *Aloe* k* am-c b4.de* ant-c *Apis* k* arg-met *Arg-n* k* asaf k* **Bell** k* borx b4a.de *Bry* k* calc k* calc-s *Canth* b7.de* carb-ac carb-an bg2 *Carb-v* k* carbn-s caul caust cham k* chin chinin-ar coc-c *Cocc* b7a.de colch b7.de* coloc b4.de* *Con* k* corn *Croc* b7a.de *Crot-t* k* cycl k* dig k* dirc a1* dulc b4.de* *Ferr* ferr-p *Gels* gran *Graph* k* *Hedeo* hyos ign b7.de* inul br1 iod k* ip irid-met srj5• *Kali-c* k* kali-i kali-p k2 kali-s fd4.de kola stb3• kreos b7a.de* lac-ac *Lac-c* lac-d c1 lac-lup hm2• **Lil-t** lyc k* lyss mag-c k* mag-m k* mag-s mang *Merc* k* merl mosch b7a.de* mur-ac *Murx* *Nat-c* k* **Nat-hchls** *Nat-m* k* nat-s k* *Nicc* *Nit-ac* k* *Nux-m* k* **Nux-v** k* *Op* ovi-p br1 ox-ac *Pall* phos k* *Phyt* *Plat* k* plb k* podo k2 psor **Puls** k* rhus-t sabin k* sars k* *Sec* k* seneg b4.de* **Sep** k* **Stry** **Sulph** tarent teucr k* thuj k* *Tril-p* ust vib visc c1 xan zinc k* zinc-p k2
• **menses** would appear; as if: nat-c h2 plat h2
- **drawing** in abdomen agg.: *Ambr* a1* ant-t a1 *Asaf* a1* bell h1* bov a1 lyc ↓ valer k* zinc k*
• **cutting** pain: valer
• **pressing** pain: lyc h2
- **drawing** in umbilicus agg.: bar-c chel pd plb
- **drawing** pain: abrot acet-ac acon k* agar agn k* aloe bg2 alum k* alumn am-c am-m k* *Anac* k* ang b7.de* ant-t k* apis b7a.de arg-n k* ars k* ars-i asaf k* aur k* aur-i k2 aur-m k* bar-c k* bar-i *Bell* k* berb borx b4a.de* bov bg2 bry b7.de* *Calad* k* *Calc* k* calc-s camph b7.de* cann-s b7.de* **Caps** k* *Carb-v* k* carbn-s *Card-m* caust k* cham k* chel k* chin k* cic b7.de* clem k* cocc k* colch k* *Coloc* k* con k* croc bg2 *Cupr* k* cupr-act dig dros k* dulc fd4.de ferr bg2 gels gink-b sbd1• *Gran* graph b4.de* grat bg2 hell k* *Hep* k* hir rsj4• hyos k* *Ign* k* iod k* irid-met srj5• jug-r k* kali-ar kali-c k* kali-n k* kali-s fd4.de kreos k* lac-h sk4• lach k* *Laur* k* led k* *Lyc* k* lyss k* m-ambo b7.de m-arct b7.de m-aust b7.de mag-c k* *Mag-m* k* mag-s k* mang k* meny b7.de* merc merc-c b4a.de mez k* mosch k* murx nat-ar *Nat-c* k* nat-m k* nat-s nat-sil fd3.de• *Nit-ac* k* *Nux-v* k* op k* orot-ac rly4• par k* petr h2 phos k* *Plat* k* plb b7.de* plut-n srj7• *Podo* ptel k* **Puls** b7.de* ran-b b7.de* rheum b7.de* rhod b4.de* rhus-t k* ruta b7.de* sabin k* sang bg2* sars k* sec k* seneg k* **Sep** k* spig k* spong b7a.de* squil k* stann b4.de* staph k* stram k* stront-c b4.de* sulph k* sumb k* tarax teucr b7.de* thuj k* tritic-vg fd5.de valer k* vanil fd5.de verat k* verat-v k* zing k*
• **cold**; as from taking a: sars h2
• **flatulence**; as from: ars h2 staph h1
• **upward**: lac-loxod-a hrn2• mag-m h2 *Nux-v* b7a.de
- **drawing** up feet amel.: *Coloc* ↓
• **cutting** pain: *Coloc*
- **drinking**:
• **after**:
: **agg.**: ars *Bell* bry b7a.de *Calc-p* ↓ carb-v ↓ caust cham chin b7a.de* **Coloc** k* con croc k* dor k* ferr k* *Manc* nat-m nit-ac *Nux-m* nux-v *Podo* *Puls* k* rhus-t ruta fd4.de spong fd4.de **Staph** k* sulph k* symph ↓ teucr k* tritic-vg fd5.de
: **bursting** pain: carb-v k*

- **drinking – after – agg.**: ...
: **cramping**: coloc bro1 *Rhus-t* a1 sulph bro1
: **cutting** pain: ars k* *Calc-p* k* *Nat-m* k* staph k*
: **drawing** pain: caust k* con k*
: **overheated**; when: ars **Coloc** kali-c
: **pressing** pain: ars k* ferr k* symph fd3.de• tritic-vg fd5.de
: **water**:
: **agg.**: aloe ↓ cham ↓ **Coloc** ↓ *Crot-c* ↓ cupr ↓ irid-met ↓ *Manc* ↓ nat-m ↓ nit-ac ↓ nux-m ↓ *Nux-v* ↓ *Puls* ↓ raph ↓ *Rhus-t* ↓
. **cramping**: aloe k2 cham **Coloc** *Crot-c* cupr bro1 irid-met srj5• *Manc* nat-m nit-ac nux-m c1 *Nux-v* *Puls* raph *Rhus-t*
• **agg.**: kali-p ↓
: **dragging**, bearing down: kali-p k2
• **amel.**: aur-m ↓
: **drawing** pain: aur-m
• **cold** water:
: **agg.**: calc-p ↓
: **cutting** pain: calc-p
: **amel.**: calc ↓ cann-s ↓ symph ↓
: **cutting** pain: calc h2 cann-s symph fd3.de•
- **drinks**: staph ↓
• **cramping**: staph tl1
- **dull** pain: apis b7a.de ars ptk1 coloc ptk1 cupr ptk1 lept ptk1 musca-d szs1 *Nux-v* ptk1 plb ptk1 podo ptk1 puls ptk1 rhus-t ptk1 sep ptk1 verat ptk1 verat-v ptk1
- **dysentery**; as from: arn b7.de* bry b7.de* led b7.de* m-arct b7.de rhus-t b7.de*
- **eating**:
• **after**:
: **agg.**: aesc k2 aeth hr1 agar *All-c* k* aloe ↓ *Alum* k* alum-p k2 alum-sil k2 am-m b7a.de* ambr b7a.de anac b4a.de ant-t k* arg-met b7a.de arn k* *Ars* ars-i ars-s-f k2 asc-t aur aur-ar k2 aur-i k2 aur-s k2 bamb-a stb2.de• bar-c bar-i bar-m bar-s k2 bell bit-ar ↓ borx k* bov b4a.de bry k* bufo cain ↓ calc b4a.de *Calc-p* ↓ caps ↓ carb-an ↓ *Carb-v* k* carbn-s cardios-h ↓ caust k* *Cham* chel b7a.de *Chin* k* chinin-ar cic k* *Cina* ↓ cob k* coc-c *Cocc* *Colch* *Coloc* con k* crot-t k* cupr dig b4a.de dor k* dream-p sdj1• dulc ↓ euon *Ferr* ferr-ar ferr-i k* ferr-p gamb ↓ *Gran* **Graph** k* grat helic-p ↓ hell ↓ hippoc-k szs2 *Hydr-ac* ↓ ign iod k* kali-ar kali-bi *Kali-c* k* kali-m k2 *Kali-p* kali-s kali-sil k2 lach *Lyc* k* *Mag-c* k* marb-w ↓ medul-os-si ↓ merc merc-c bg1 mez ↓ mur-ac k* nat-ar *Nat-c* *Nat-m* k* nat-p nat-sil fd3.de• nit-ac *Nux-m* *Nux-v* k* olnd ↓ par petr k* petr-ra ↓ *Ph-ac* *Phos* k* pitu-a vml2• plb k* podo *Psor* k* *Puls* k* pyrid rly4• raph rheum b7a.de *Rhod* *Rhus-t* k* ruta ↓ sacch-a ↓ *Sang* ↓ *Sars* sec sep sil k* spong k* *Stann* **Staph** k* *Stront-c* k* *Sul-ac* k* sul-i k2 *Sulph* k* symph ↓ tax ↓ *Thuj* tritic-vg fd5.de valer b7a.de vanil fd5.de **Verat** *Zinc* zinc-p k2
: **1** hour after eating: nux-v ↓
. **cramping**: nux-v tl1
: **2** hours after eating: nux-v ↓ sil ↓
. **cramping**: nux-v tl1 sil h2
: **10** minutes after eating: rauw ↓
. **cramping**: rauw sp1
: **boring** pain: carb-an b4a.de
: **burning**: helic-p mtf *Hydr-ac*
: **bursting** pain: carb-v k* dulc k* kali-c k2
: **cramping**: *All-c* aloe k2 *Ant-t* k* aur-i k2 bar-c bro1 bell bit-ar wht1• *Calc-p* bro1 caps h1 carb-v k* cardios-h rly4• caust chin k* cic *Cina* a1 coc-c k* cocc h1 *Colch* *Coloc* k* con cupr gamb k* *Graph* grat k* hell h1 kali-bi bro1 kali-c h2 kali-p lyc k* marb-w es1• medul-os-si rly4• *Nat-c* k* nux-m nux-v bro1* petr-ra shn4• *Psor* bro1 *Puls* pyrid rly4• *Rhus-t* sars k* *Staph* hr1 *Sulph* valer ptk1 *Verat* zinc k*
: **cutting** pain: ant-t k* ars k* cain calc b4a.de calc-p k* *Chel* k* **Coloc** k* ign k* *Kali-bi* lyc b4a.de nat-m k* olnd *Petr* sacch-a fd2.de• sil b4a.de spong *Staph* k* sul-ac h2 vanil fd5.de *Zinc* [tax jsj7]
: **distention**; with: bit-ar ↓
. **cramping**: bit-ar wht1•
: **dragging**, bearing down: carb-v h2 thuj
: **drawing** pain: caust k* con b4a.de
: **half** an hour: atra-r bnm3•

• **after – agg.**: ...
⁝ **pinching** pain: alum b4a.de calc b4a.de carb-v b4a.de kali-c b4a.de nat-c b4a.de nat-m b4a.de sil b4a.de
⁝ **pressing** pain: agar alum ambr k2 ars caps h1 caust h2 coloc dig c1 *Ferr* kali-c h2 kali-p fd1.de• lyc *Mag-c* mez h2 *Nux-v* phos ruta fd4.de sep sil symph fd3.de• thuj tritic-vg fd5.de zinc
⁝ **sore**: *Sang*
⁝ **stitching** pain: alum k* marb-w es1• spong fd4.de thuj k*
⁝ **twinging**: sil h2 tritic-vg fd5.de
⁝ **two** hours after eating: allox sp1 brom bg1 ox-ac sacch-a fd2.de• sil h2
⁝ **amel.**: *Bov*↓ hom-xyz↓ mang↓ nat-s↓ plan↓ psor↓
⁝ **cramping**: *Bov* k* hom-xyz bro1 nat-s ptk plan hr1 psor k*
⁝ **pressing** pain: mang h2
• **agg.**: mang↓ tritic-vg↓
⁝ **drawing** pain: mang h2
⁝ **pressing** pain: mang h2 tritic-vg fd5.de
• **amel.**: aur-m *Bov* calc↓ *Chel* k* graph mrr1 hom-xyz br1* iod kola stb3• mang melal-alt gya4 mez *Nat-c* plan *Psor* k* ruta fd4.de sep↓
⁝ **burning**: kola stb3•
⁝ **cutting** pain: bov calc h2
⁝ **dragging**, bearing down: sep
⁝ **drawing** pain: aur-m mang h2
• **attempting** to eat; on: *Calc-p*
• **cold** agg.; anything: mang↓ sep↓
⁝ **pressing** pain: mang h2 sep
• **cold** food agg.: mang↓
⁝ **cramping**: mang k2
• **while**:
⁝ **agg.**: aloe↓ arg-met c1 ars b4a.de *Calc-p* k* carb-v k* caust b4a.de colch coloc↓ crot-t↓ dulc grat↓ kali-p↓ mur-ac k* nux-v phos↓ plan k* tritic-vg fd5.de zinc↓
⁝ **burning**: phos k*
⁝ **cramping**: carb-v k* caust h2 colch tl1 coloc tl1 dulc k* kali-p *Nux-v*
⁝ **cutting** pain: aloe caust h2 grat zinc
⁝ **tearing** pain: crot-t k*
- **electric** shocks; as from: (↗*Shocks)* thal-met br1
- **erections**; with: zinc↓
• **pressing** pain: zinc h2
- **eructations**:
• **agg.**: mag-p↓ pall↓
⁝ **cramping**: mag-p tl1* pall c1
• **amel.**: ambr↓ *Arg-n* lp *Bar-c* carb-v dios↓ gels psa irid-met↓ jug-r k* kali-c↓ kali-n kola stb3• lach mez↓ nat-s k2 rat↓ sep sil k* *Sulph*↓ taosc iwa1• verat↓ [pop dhh1]
⁝ **cramping**: ambr h1 carb-v dios mrr1 irid-met srj5• kali-c h2 sep *Sulph* verat hr1
⁝ **cutting** pain: rat
⁝ **pressing** pain: mez h2
• **not** amel. by: mag-p↓
⁝ **cramping**: mag-p c1
• **with**: hyos bro1
- **excitement**:
• **after**: acon *Cham* **Coloc** mrr1 **Ign** med gk spong fd4.de *Staph* vanil fd5.de
• **agg.**: coloc↓
⁝ **cramping**: coloc mrr1
- **exertion**:
• **after** | **agg.**: cadm-s br1 *Calc* cupr bg1 pall
• **agg.**: aloe arn berb *Calc*↓ cocc cycl dig ip kali-n kreos nat-m nat-n k* nux-v ol-an *Pall*↓ plb puls sep stram
⁝ **cutting** pain: sep h2
⁝ **pressing** pain: *Calc Pall*
• **amel.**: aq-mar vml3• coloc
- **expiration**:
• **agg.**: dig↓
⁝ **cramping**: dig c1

- **expiration**: ...
• **during**:
⁝ **agg.**: brom coff↓ dig dulc↓ nat-c h2 vanil fd5.de
⁝ **stitching** pain: coff dulc fd4.de vanil fd5.de
- **farinaceous** food, after: coloc st
- **fasting** agg.: dulc↓
• **cutting** pain: dulc k*
- **fat**; after: mag-m mrr1 tritic-vg fd5.de
- **fear**; from (See MIND - Fear - pain - during - abdomen)
- **fever**:
• **after**: ant-t b7a.de bell b4a.de hell b7a.de
• **before**: *Arn* b7a.de ars b4a.de carb-v b4a.de *Chin* b7a.de phos b4a.de rhus-t b7a.de spong b7a.de sulph b4a.de
• **during**:
⁝ **agg.**: ambr↓ caps↓ carb-v↓ cina↓ coloc↓ elat↓ ign↓ ph-ac↓ rhus-t↓ rob↓ verat↓ *Zinc*↓
⁝ **cramping**: caps carb-v cina bro1 elat rhus-t rob verat bro1
⁝ **squeezed**; as if: ambr bg2 coloc bg2 ign bg2 ph-ac bg2 *Zinc* bg2
- **fever**; in asthenic: *Cact*↓
• **dragging**, bearing down (= low fever): *Cact* k*
- **flatulence**; during: *Acon*↓ am-c↓ am-m↓ ambr↓ *Anac*↓ *Anis*↓ ant-t↓ *Arg-met*↓ *Asaf*↓ *Aur*↓ *Bell*↓ *Bism*↓ *Bry*↓ cann-s↓ canth↓ *Caps*↓ *Carb-an*↓ *Carb-v*↓ *Cham*↓ chel↓ *Chin*↓ cic↓ *Cocc*↓ coff↓ **Colch**↓ *Coloc*↓ con↓ *Cycl*↓ dros↓ *Euph*↓ ferr↓ graph↓ guaj↓ hell↓ hep↓ hyos↓ *Ign*↓ *Ip*↓ laur↓ *Lyc*↓ m-ambo↓ *M-arct*↓ m-aust↓ mag-c↓ *Meny*↓ *Mez*↓ nat-c↓ nat-m↓ *Nit-ac*↓ nux-m↓ *Nux-v*↓ *Op*↓ *Par*↓ *Phos*↓ plat↓ *Plb*↓ *Puls*↓ *Rhod*↓ rhus-t↓ ruta↓ samb↓ sel↓ seneg↓ sil↓ spong↓ squil↓ *Staph*↓ *Sul-ac*↓ tarax↓ teucr↓ valer↓ *Verat*↓ verb↓ zinc↓
• **chill**; during: *Mez*↓
⁝ **cramping**: *Mez* b4a.de
• **coition**; during: graph↓
⁝ **cramping**: graph b4a.de
• **cramping**: *Acon* b7.de am-c b4.de ambr b7.de* *Anis* b7a.de *Arg-met* b7a.de *Asaf* b7.de *Aur* b4.de* *Bell* b4a.de *Bry* b7.de cann-s b7.de *Caps* b7.de* *Carb-an* b4a.de *Carb-v* b4a.de *Cham* b7.de *Chin* b7.de* *Cocc* b7.de coff b7.de **Colch** b7a.de *Coloc* b4a.de con b4.de *Cycl* b7.de *Euph* b4a.de ferr b7.de* hell b7.de hep b4a.de hyos b7.de *Ign* b7.de* *Ip* b7.de* laur b7.de* *Lyc* b4a.de m-ambo b7.de* *M-arct* b7.de* m-aust b7.de *Meny* b7.de *Mez* b4a.de nat-m b4.de *Nit-ac* b4.de* nux-m b7.de *Nux-v* b7.de* *Op* b7.de *Par* b7a.de *Phos* b4.de* *Plb* b7.de *Puls* b7.de* *Rhod* b4.de rhus-t b7.de ruta b7.de sel b7.de *Sul-ac* b4a.de teucr b7.de valer b7.de *Verat* b7.de* zinc b4.de
• **drawing** pain: chin b7a.de staph b7.de*
• **menses**; during: *Cocc*↓
⁝ **cramping**: *Cocc* b7.de
• **pinching** pain: am-m b7.de* anac b4a.de ant-t b7.de* *Asaf* b7.de* aur b4a.de *Bism* b7a.de canth b7.de* caps b7.de* *Carb-v* b4.de* chel b7.de* chin b7.de* cic b7.de* dros b7.de* graph b4a.de guaj b4a.de hyos b7.de* ign b7.de* laur b7.de* m-arct b7.de m-aust b7.de mag-c b4.de* mez b4.de* nat-c b4.de* nat-m b4a.de phos b4.de* plat b4.de* puls b7.de* *Rhod* b4.de* rhus-t b7.de* ruta b7.de* samb b7.de* seneg b4.de* sil b4.de* spong b7.de* squil b7.de* *Staph* b7.de* tarax b7.de* teucr b7a.de verat b7.de* verb b7.de* zinc b4.de*
• **sore**: m-aust b7.de verat b7.de*
• **squeezed**; as if: *Anac* b4a.de canth b7.de* carb-v b4.de* teucr b7.de*
- **flatulence**; from (See Distension - painful)
- **flatulence**; with: | **tearing** pain (See tearing - accompanied - flatulence)
- **flatus**; as from passing: kali-n h2 mang h2 nit-ac h2
- **flatus**; from: anac↓ ant-t↓ canth↓ carb-v↓ chin↓ cina↓ coloc↓ con↓ dros↓ iod↓ kali-c↓ laur↓ mag-c↓ *Nat-m*↓ nux-m↓ nux-v↓ plat↓ plb↓ puls↓ *Rheum*↓ ruta↓ sep↓ sil↓ *Squil*↓ staph↓ tere-la↓ thuj↓ valer↓ *Verat*↓ verb↓ zinc↓
• **cutting** pain: anac b4a.de ant-t b7.de* canth b7.de* chin b7.de* coloc h2 con b4a.de dros b7.de* iod b4.de* kali-c h2 laur b7.de* mag-c b4.de* *Nat-m* b4a.de nux-m b7.de* nux-v b7.de* plat b4.de* plb b7.de* puls b7.de* *Rheum* b7a.de ruta b7.de* sep b4.de* sil b4.de* *Squil* b7a.de staph b7.de* tere-la rly4• thuj b4.de* valer b7.de* *Verat* b7.de* verb b7.de* zinc b4.de*

Abdomen

• **stitching** pain: carb-v b4.de* cina a1 coloc h2 laur b7.de* nat-m h2 thuj b4.de* verb b7.de*

- **flatus**; passing:

• **after**:

⁝ **agg.**: puls tl1

⁝ **amel.**: zinc↓

: **dragging**, bearing down: zinc

• **agg.**: absin↓ ambr↓ apis↓ arn↓ asc-t↓ aur bit-ar↓ calc↓ canth cham↓ *Chin*↓ cocc↓ con ptk1 euph↓ ferr↓ ferr-ar↓ fl-ac gink-b↓ graph h2 hep↓ hyos↓ ign↓ kali-c↓ m-ambo↓ m-arct↓ m-aust↓ mag-p↓ mang↓ mill↓ mur-ac↓ nat-ar nat-m↓ nicotam↓ nit-ac↓ nux-m↓ *Nux-v*↓ oxal-a↓ phos↓ plat↓ plb↓ polyg-xyz↓ *Puls*↓ pycnop-sa mrz1 rheum↓ ruta fd4.de *Samb*↓ sanguis-s↓ seneg↓ spig↓ spong↓ squil staph↓ sulph↓ taosc iwa1• thuj↓ *Verat*↓ zinc h2

⁝ **night**: ferr↓

: **cramping**: ferr c1

⁝ **cramping**: absin br1 asc-t c1 aur bit-ar wht1• canth cham c2 *Chin* cocc tl1 euph h2 ferr c1 ferr-ar k2 gink-b sbd1• graph h2 kali-c h2 mag-p c1 mang h2 mill pd mur-ac h2 nicotam rly4• nit-ac h2 oxal-a rly4• phos h2 polyg-xyz c2 *Samb* xxb1 sanguis-s hm2• spig h1 *Squil* staph h1 sulph h2

⁝ **pressing** pain: ambr b7.de* apis b7a.de arn b7.de* aur b4.de* bit-ar wht1• calc b4.de* cham b7.de* chin b7.de* cocc b7.de* hep b4.de* hyos b7.de* ign b7.de* m-ambo b7.de m-arct b7.de* m-aust b7.de* nat-m h2 nux-m b7.de* *Nux-v* b7.de* phos b4.de* plat b4.de* plb b7a.de *Puls* b7.de* rheum b7.de* seneg b4a.de spong b7.de* sulph b4a.de thuj b4.de* *Verat* b7.de* zinc b4.de*

• **amel.**: *Acon*↓ all-c aloe am-c anac↓ arn ars-i↓ asar↓ bapt↓ bov↓ bry↓ but-ac↓ *Calc-p* *Carb-v* caust↓ cham *Chin*↓ *Cimx* cit-ac↓ cocc↓ coloc *Con* corn crot-t dulc *Echi*↓ euph↓ eupi↓ ferr gamb↓ *Graph* grat *Guaj* hep↓ *Hydr*↓ iber↓ irid-met↓ *Iris* jatr-c kali-c↓ kali-n kali-p fd1.de• lap-la↓ laur↓ *Lyc* mag-c mag-m↓ meny↓ merc-c **Nat-ar** nat-c↓ nat-m *Nat-s* nux-m ol-an↓ ox-ac k2 phos↓ phyt plat↓ plb podo↓ *Psor* *Rumx* sel↓ *Sep* sil spig↓ spong squil↓ sulph *Tarent* tax↓ til c1 vanil fd5.de **Verat**↓ viol-t↓ zinc↓

⁝ **cramping**: *Acon* aloe bro1 ~~Am-c~~ but-ac sp1 carb-v h2* caust h2 *Chin* bro1 cimx cit-ac rly4• cocc bro1 *Coloc* k* *Con* dulc a1 *Echi* euph h2 *Graph* grat k2 *Hydr* iber vml3• irid-met srj5• kali-c h2 lyc mag-c mag-m h2 meny h1 merc-c nat-ar nat-c h2 *Nat-m* nat-s bro1 nux-m ol-an plat h2 podo fd3.de• psor rumx sil spig h1 spong squil sulph k* **Verat** hr1

⁝ **cutting** pain: anac ars-i asar h1 bapt bov bry calc-p caust h2 **Con** eupi gamb *Hydr* kali-n h2 lap-la sde8.de• laur mag-m h2 plb psor sel sulph vanil fd5.de viol-t [tax jsj7]

⁝ **pressing** pain: hep h2 meny h1 phos h2 spig h1

⁝ **stitching** pain: zinc h2

• **before**: ars↓ calc-p **Chin** con↓ graph↓ guaj↓ kali-n h2 kali-s↓ lyc↓ mez↓ mur-ac↓ nat-ar k2 *Nit-ac* rheum h sil h2 spig↓ sulph↓ taosc iwa1• tarax↓ zinc↓

⁝ **cramping**: ars h2 graph h2 guaj h2 mez h2 mur-ac h2 rheum h sil h2 spig h1 tarax h1

⁝ **cutting** pain: chin h1 con h2 lyc h2

⁝ **drawing** pain: nit-ac h2

⁝ **stitching** pain: kali-s fd4.de spig h1 sulph h2

⁝ **twinging**: zinc h2

• **not** amel.: *Cham* bro1 chin br1 cina bro1 mag-p bro1 mang↓

⁝ **cramping**: mang a1

• **with**: iod↓ kali-c↓ petr↓ spig↓

⁝ **cutting** pain: iod h kali-c h2 petr h2 spig h1

- **flexing** limbs amel.: (*↗EXTREMITIES - Flexed - thigh - accompanied - abdomen)* ap-g br1 apis k2 *Bell* *Bry* chel **COLOC** k ● grat hydr sne kali-s fd4.de kola stb3• nit-ac ph-ac *Podo* puls rheum rhus-t k2 **Sep** k ● sulph

- **flexing** thighs amel.: ap-g↓ podo↓

• **stitching** pain: ap-g br1 podo k*

- **food**: staph↓

• **cramping**: staph dw1*

• **farinaceous**; from: coloc↓

⁝ **cramping**: coloc k2

- **forced** through; as if something was: bar-c bg1 carb-an bg1* stront-c bg2 ulm-c jsj8•

- **fright** agg.: cham↓ plat

• **stitching** pain: cham h1

- **fright**; as from: plat bg2

- **fruit** agg.: borx↓ *Calc-p* *Chin* **Coloc** mag-m k* *Merc-c* k* petr-ra↓ *Puls* **Verat**

• **acid** fruit: cist↓

⁝ **cramping**: cist tl1

• **cramping**: borx mrr1 calc-p k* *Chin* *Coloc* k* petr-ra shn4• *Puls*

- **gnawing** pain: am-c k* am-m k2 ars k* aur-m *Bell* b4a.de* berb bg2 calc k* canth k* *Carb-v* ptk1 coca bg2 cocc b7.de* colch k* *Coloc* k* cupr k* cycl k* dig dulc k* elat gal-ac a1 *Gels* k* grat bg2 lach bg2 lat-m bnm6• *Lyc* b4a.de* nat-m bg2 olnd k* phos ptk1 plat k* plb k* ruta k* sabad bg2 seneg k* sep ptk1 stry bg2 sulph k* teucr b7a.de thuj b4a.de*

- **grasping** (See clawing)

- **grinding** pain: dios bg2 fl-ac bg1* plb ptk1 polyg-h ptk1 sars ptk1 stann ptk1

- **griping** (See cramping)

- **headache** amel.; pain abdomen amel. when: dirc↓

• **dragging**, bearing down: dirc a1*

- **headache**; during: aloe↓ cocc↓

• **cramping**: aloe bro1 cocc bro1

- **heat**:

• **after**: sil h2

• **during**: acon bg2 **Ant-c** k* ant-t bg2 apis bg2 **Ars** k* bar-c bg2 bell bg2 *Bov* bg2 *Bry* bg2 *Calc* bg2 caps k* **Carb-v** k* *Cham* k* **Chin** bg2 cic bg2 *Cina* k* coff bg2 coloc bg2 dulc fd4.de elat *Ferr* bg2 hep bg2 ign k* *Kali-c* bg2 lyc bg2 merc bg2 *Mosch* b7.de* nat-m bg2 *Nit-ac* bg2 nux-v k* op bro1 phos bg2 *Puls* b7.de* *Ran-b* bg2 **Rhus-t** k* *Sep* bg2 sil bg2 spong bg2 stront-c bg2 sulph k* valer k*

⁝ **cutting** pain: rhus-t

- **hemorrhoidal** flow; suppressed: **NUX-V** k ●

• **cramping**: **Nux-v**

- **hemorrhoids**; from●: *Aesc* caps tl1 carb-v k* coloc k* lach k* *Nux-v* puls k* *Sulph* k* valer

• **cramping**: *Sulph* b4a.de valer b7a.de

- **hiccough**, on: plb↓

• **tearing** pain: plb k*

- **holding** abdomen amel.: mang↓ nux-m gk podo mrr1

• **cramping**: mang h2 podo mrr1

- **honey**, after: calc-p↓

• **cutting** pain: calc-p std

- **hot** milk amel. | **cramping** (See warm - milk - amel. - hot - cramping)

- **hunger**; during: bar-c bro1 irid-met srj5• merc stram

• **tearing** pain: stram k*

- **hysterical**: alet↓ ars↓ asaf↓ bell↓ bry↓ caj↓ *Caust*↓ *Cocc*↓ *Con*↓ *Ign*↓ *Ip*↓ *Mag-m*↓ *Mosch*↓ nux-v↓ *Phos*↓ stann ptk1 *Stram*↓ *Valer*↓

• **cramping**: alet bro1 ars k* asaf bro1 bell k* bry k* caj bro1 *Caust* b4a.de *Cocc* k* *Con* b4a.de *Ign* bro1 *Ip* k* *Mag-m* k* *Mosch* k* nux-v k* *Phos* b4a.de *Stann* k* *Stram* k* *Valer* k*

• **eating**; after: valer↓

⁝ **cramping**: valer b7a.de

- **ice** cream:

• **after**: **Ars** bell-p bg1 calc-p *Puls* ruta fd4.de sep

• **agg.**: **Ars**↓ *Calc-p*↓ *Ip*↓ *Puls*↓

⁝ **burning**: **Ars**

⁝ **cramping**: **Ars** *Calc-p* k* *Ip* *Puls*

- **increasing** | **gradually**:

⁝ **decreasing** | **gradually**: bell h1 carc az1.de• plat *Stann*

• **quickly**: cassia-s cdd7• pitu-gl skp7•

⁝ **decreasing** | **quickly**: **Bell** cycl a1 vib

- **indignation**; after: coloc k2* **Staph**

• **cramping**: **Staph** k*

- **inspiration**:

• **agg.**: aesc agar am-m *Anac* bell-p bg1 brom *Bry* calc calc-p↓ carbn-s caust chin↓ clem↓ cocc↓ dor c1 guaj↓ *Lyc*↓ *Nux-v* rhus-t rumx *Sulph* tab↓ thuj tritic-vg fd5.de

⁝ **cramping**: aesc am-m k* brom k* guaj h2 *Sulph* k*

- agg.: ...
  - **cutting** pain: cocc guaj h2 *Lyc* k*
  - **drawing** pain: rhus-t k*
  - **stitching** pain: agar *Bry* calc k* calc-p k2 chin h1 clem h2 tab tritic-vg fd5.de
  - **tearing** pain: *Calc*
- **deep**:
  - **agg.**: card-m mrr1 conv br1 tritic-vg fd5.de
  - **amel.**: *Card-m* chir-fl gya2
- **intermittent** (See paroxysmal)
- **jar** agg.: acon ↓ aloe ↓ arg-met ↓ **Bell** ↓ *Bell-p* ↓ **Bry** ↓ chel ↓ colch ↓ ferr ↓ kali-s ↓ *Lach* ↓ *Lil-t* ↓ **Nux-v** ↓ ozone ↓ **Phos** ↓ phyt ↓ plb ↓ prun ↓ raph ↓
  - **cramping**: acon bro1 aloe bro1 *Bell* bro1 plb bro1
  - **sore**: arg-met vh1 **Bell** k* *Bell-p* sne **Bry** chel sne colch ferr kali-s *Lach Lil-t* **Nux-v** ozone sde2• **Phos** phyt prun raph k*
- **jar**; as from a: *Am-c* b4a.de
- **jarring** (See jar agg. - sore)
- **jerking** pain: bell h1 carbn-s *Rhus-t* a1 ruta h1
- **kneading** abdomen amel.: *Nat-s* ↓
  - **cramping**: *Nat-s*
- **labor** pain, during: *Sep*
- **labor**-like (See FEMALE - Pain - labor-like)
- **lacerating** (See tearing)
- **laming** (See paralyzed)
- **lancinating**: anan ars k* aur-s bufo cadm-s *Carb-an Carb-v* chord-umb rly4• clem con cur dirc c1 elaps fum rly4• gels k* hippoc-k szs2 kali-i k* ketogl-ac rly4• lat-m bnm6• manc k* murx k* nat-pyru rly4• orot-ac rly4• plac-s rly4• plat plb k* pot-e rly4• raph ribo rly4• sal-fr sle1• streptoc rly4• suis-em rly4• tril-p c1 vanil fd5.de vero-o rly4• *Zinc*
- **laughing** agg.: ars cench k2 con k* jug-r vml3• lac-h sk4• nux-v
- **lead** colic: **Coloc** ↓
  - **cutting** pain: **Coloc**
- **lead** poisoning; from: **Alum Alumn** *Ars* bell ↓ **Coloc** ferr ↓ hyos ↓ nat-s nux-m ↓ nux-v ↓ **Op** *Plat Plb* podo stram ↓ *Sul-ac* sulph ↓ verat ↓ *Zinc*
  - **cramping**: alum b4a.de* alumn bro1 *Ars* b4a.de bell bro1 ferr bro1 hyos b7.de* nat-s bro1 nux-m bro1 nux-v bro1 *Op* b7.de* plat b4a.de* plb mrr1* stram b7.de* sulph bro1 verat bro1
- **leaning**:
  - **abdomen** on something agg.: samb ↓
    - **pressing** pain: samb c1
  - **sharp** edge agg.; against a: ran-b ↓ samb ↓
    - **cramping**: samb h1*
    - **ulcerative** pain: ran-b j5.de*
  - **side**; on the | **agg.**: raph
- **leukorrhea**:
  - **before**: *Am-m* ↓ aral ↓ *Ars* ↓ bell ↓ calc ↓ con h2 graph ↓ haem ↓ ham ↓ ign ↓ lyc ↓ mag-c h2 mag-m ↓ nat-c ↓ nat-m h2 *Sep* ↓ sil ↓ *Sulph* ↓ syph ↓ zinc h2
    - **cramping**: *Am-m* bro1 aral bro1 *Ars* bro1 bell bro1 calc bro1 con h2* graph bro1 haem bro1 ham bro1 ign bro1 lyc bro1 mag-c h2 mag-m h2* nat-c bro1 *Sep* bro1 sil bro1 *Sulph* bro1 syph bro1
    - **cutting** pain: nat-c h2 sulph h2 zinc h2
  - **cramping** | **followed** by: mag-m pd
  - **during**: *Lyc* ↓ nat-c ↓ sil ↓ sulph ↓
    - **cutting** pain: *Lyc* b4.de nat-c b4.de sil b4.de* sulph b4a.de
  - **with**: alum bg2 am-m bg2 aral ↓ *Ars* ↓ bell bg2 calc ↓ caust bg2 con h2* dros bg2 graph ↓ haem ↓ ham ↓ *Ign* bg2 kali-bi bg2 kali-c bg2 *Lyc* bg2 *Mag-c* bg2 *Mag-m* bg2 merc bg2 nat-c bg2 nat-m bg2 puls b7a.de* sec b7a.de sep bg2 sil bg2 sulph bg2 syph ↓ zinc h1*
    - **cramping**: *Am-m* bro1 aral bro1 *Ars* bro1 bell bro1 calc bro1 *Con* bro1 *Dros* b7a.de graph bro1 haem bro1 ham bro1 ign b7a.de* lyc bro1 *Mag-m* bro1 nat-c bro1 *Sep* bro1 sil bro1 *Sulph* bro1 syph bro1 zinc h2*
- **lifting**:
  - **after**: sil ↓
    - **cutting** pain: sil h2
  - **agg.**: arn bry *Calc* coloc h2* kali-n bg1 nat-m sne sil h2* vanil fd5.de
- **long**-lasting: bell tl1
- **lying**:
  - **abdomen**; on | **agg.**:
    - **spasmodic** jerking of pelvis upward; with: cupr ↓
      - **cramping**: cupr mtf33
    - **amel.**: *Acet-ac* ↓ aloe am-c ambr h1* ars-h atra-r bnm3• **Bell** *Bry* **Calc** bg1 chinin-ar chion *Coloc* k* cupr k2 der ↓ elaps mrr1 ind kali-p bg1 *Phos* plb puls bg1 rauw ↓ *Rhus-t* k* *Stann* tritic-vg fd5.de
      - **burning**: *Acet-ac* k2*
      - **cramping**: am-c chion *Coloc* der phos h2 rauw tpw8*
      - **sore**: phos
      - **stitching** pain: phos h2 tritic-vg fd5.de
  - **agg.**: acon ↓ apis bar-c *Bell* k* caust ↓ coloc k* dios k* dulc fd4.de mag-m ↓ nat-m ↓ *Phos Puls* spig tetox ↓ tritic-vg fd5.de
    - **cramping**: acon bro1 *Dios* bro1 mag-m mrr1 nat-m sne *Phos Spig* k* tetox pin2•
    - **cutting** pain: nat-m
    - **dragging**, bearing down: spig bg1
    - **ground** and uncovering; on: jatr-c ↓
      - **burning**: jatr-c kr1*
    - **pressing** pain: bar-c bell h1 tritic-vg fd5.de
    - **stitching** pain: caust dulc fd4.de
  - **amel.**: *All-s* vh1 am-c bar-c ↓ bros-gau ↓ bry canth cupr dios k* ferr ↓ gink-b sbd1• gran k* merc nux-v petr ↓ phos ↓ phys *Podo* ↓ rhus-t ↓
    - **burning**: *Podo*
    - **cramping**: cupr k* ferr nux-v bro1*
    - **drawing** pain: phos
    - **pressing** pain: bar-c h2 bros-gau mrc1 petr hr1 rhus-t
  - **back**; on:
    - **agg.**: ambr bg1 *Ars* dios bg1 lach bg1 mag-p phys plb bg1 podo ptel sulph
      - **cramping**: phys
    - **amel.**: bit-ar ↓ coloc *Kalm* mez onos puls ↓ ulm-c ↓
      - **cramping**: bit-ar wht1• puls sys
      - **knees** drawn up; with: lach ↓ petr-ra shn4• *Rhus-t* ↓
        - **cramping**: lach bro1 *Rhus-t*
      - **pressing** pain: mez
      - **stitching** pain: ulm-c jsj8•
  - **crooked**:
    - **amel.**: brom ↓ dulc ↓
      - **stitching** pain: brom dulc fd4.de
  - **knees** and chest; on:
    - **amel.**: cina ↓
      - **cramping**: cina mrr1
  - **side**; on:
    - **agg.**: *Carb-v* coloc ign ↓ kali-s fd4.de *Kalm* par phos
      - **cramping**: coloc ign
    - **amel.**: bry ↓ cocc ↓ gink-b ↓ nat-s
      - **cramping**: bry bro1 cocc bro1 gink-b sbd1• nat-s
    - **left**:
      - **agg.**: kali-p ↓ *Ptel* mrr1 ven-m rsj12•
        - **dragging**, bearing down: kali-p k2
      - **amel.**: con ↓ nux-v ↓ pall sec
        - **legs** drawn up; with: *Chel* mrr1
        - **pressing** pain: *Pall*
    - **right**:
      - **agg.**: acon caust *Merc* phos bg1 stann tritic-vg fd5.de
        - **sore**: *Merc*
      - **amel.**: nux-v phos phys *Ptel* mrr1
        - **cramping**: phys
- **melons** agg.: **Zing** ↓
  - **cramping**: **Zing**
- **menopause**, with sadness; during: *Psor* vh

- **menses**:
  - **after**:
    - **agg.**: *Am-c* borx cham cocc con *Cycl* ↓ graph iod kali-c *Kreos* *Lach* *Lil-t* ↓ lyc mag-c merl *Nat-m* *Nit-ac* nux-v b7.de *Pall* ↓ plat *Puls* *Sep* ↓ ust
      - **cramping**: *Am-c* cocc kreos merl puls
      - **cutting** pain: con b4.de graph k* kali-c lyc b4.de *Sep* b4a.de
      - **dragging**, bearing down: kreos
      - **drawing** pain: puls
      - **pressing** pain: nat-m
      - **sore**: cham *Cycl* *Lil-t* *Pall* k*
  - **as** for: nat-c ↓
    - **sore**: nat-c h2
  - **before**:
    - **agg.**: aloe *Alum* k* alum-p k2 alum-sil k2 *Am-c* k* am-m b7.de amp ↓ *Apis* b7a.de arist-cl sp1 asar ↓ bar-c k* bar-i *Bell* k* bit-ar ↓ brom k* *Bry* ↓ *Calc* k* **Calc-p** calc-sil k2 carb-v k* carbn-s *Caust* k* *Cham* k* chin chinin-s ↓ cina b7.de cinnb *Cocc* *Coloc* k* *Con* ↓ *Croc* k* *Cupr* k* cycl k* eupi ferr b7.de *Gels* ↓ germ-met ↓ graph k* ham ↓ hep k* hyos b7.de hyper *Ign* k* iod ip b7.de **Kali-c** kali-n b4a.de *Kali-p* kali-s kali-sil k2 kola stb3• kreos b7a.de lac-c ↓ *Lach* k* *Lil-t* ↓ *Lyc* k* *Mag-c* k* mag-m k* *Mag-p* manc mang ↓ mang-p ↓ merc mosch nat-c k* nat-m neon srj5• nux-m *Nux-v* k* ol-an ↓ petr ph-ac *Phos* k* *Plat* k* podo k2 **Puls** k* ruta b7.de sabad b7.de sang sars h2 sec ↓ *Sep* k* *Sil* *Spong* staph b7.de sul-ac sul-i k2 sulph k* tarent k* tep ↓ thioc-ac ↓ thuj k* tritic-vg fd5.de ust valer b7.de *Vib* ↓ zinc k* zinc-p k2
      - **clawing** pain: *Bell*
      - **cramping**: aloe alum *Am-c* k* amp rly4• asar vh bar-c *Bell* bit-ar wht1• brom *Calc-p* k* carb-v k* *Caust* *Cham* chin chinin-s *Cinnb* *Cocc* *Coloc* *Croc* *Cupr* cycl germ-met srj5• hyper k* *Ign* k* **Kali-c** k* *Lach* mag-c *Mag-p* manc k* mang-p rly4• nux-v ph-ac *Plat* podo k2 *Puls* *Sep* spong thioc-ac rly4•
      - **cutting** pain: alum k* *Cham* k* lach *Lil-t* mag-c nat-c nat-m ol-an k* staph h1
      - **dragging**, bearing down: alum *Apis* **Bell** *Chin* *Cina* *Con* eupi *Gels* iod lac-c mag-c h2 mosch *Phos* *Plat* sabad sec *Sep* sulph tarent ust *Vib* zinc
      - **drawing** pain: carb-v *Ign* k* tritic-vg fd5.de
      - **pressing** pain: graph h2 nux-m sep k*
      - **sore**: *Bell* *Bry* ham bro1 lac-c lach mang *Sep* k*
      - **stitching** pain: brom k* con *Kali-c* puls hr1
      - **tearing** pain: *Cinnb* nat-m tep k*
      - **Hip** to hip; from: thuj ↓ ust ↓
        - **cutting** pain: thuj ust
  - **during**:
    - **agg.**: acon agar k* alet aloe alum k* alum-sil k2 *Am-c* k* am-m k* anac ↓ androc srj1• ap-g br1 apis arg-n arge-pl ↓ ars k* *Ars-i* ars-s-f k2 aur aur-ar k2 aur-i k2 aur-s k2 bamb-a stb2.de• bapt *Bar-c* k* *Bar-i* bar-ox-suc ↓ *Bell* k* bit-ar ↓ *Borx* k* bov b4.de *Brom* k* bry bufo cact **Calc** k* calc-i k2 **Calc-p** k* *Canth* k* carb-an b4.de carb-v k* **Carbn-s** carc ↓ castm caul k* *Caust* k* cench k2 *Cham* k* chel *Chin* k* *Chinin-s* ↓ choc ↓ chord-umb rly4• **Cimic** cina cinnb clem *Cocc* k* *Coff* *Coloc* k* *Con* k* croc crot-h k* *Cupr* *Cycl* k* dream-p ↓ eupi k* fago k* ferr ferr-ar ferr-i ferr-p form fum ↓ gink-b sbd1• gran ↓ granit-m es1• **Graph** k* haliae-lc ↓ *Ham* fd3.de• hyos *Ign* k* ignis-alc ↓ inul k* iod ip irid-met ↓ kali-ar *Kali-c* k* kali-i ↓ *Kali-n* k* kali-p kali-s kali-sil k2 kreos k* *Lac-c* lac-d ↓ *Lach* laur b7a.de **Lil-t** ↓ lyc k* *Mag-c* k* mag-m k* *Mag-p* mrr1 mag-s mang med ↓ merc k* *Mill* mom-b ↓ mosch k* mur-ac b4.de *Murx* nat-c k* *Nat-m* *Nat-s* neon ↓ *Nicc* *Nit-ac* k* *Nux-m* **Nux-v** k* ol-an *Op* ↓ pall c1 petr ph-ac ↓ *Phos* k* phyt pic-ac ↓ plac-s rly4• *Plat* k* plb podo k2 **Puls** k* rat k* rhus-t ↓ **Sabin** k* *Sars* k* *Sec* k* *Senec* ↓ **Sep** k* *Sil* k* stann b4a.de* staph *Stram* k* stront-c b4.de sul-ac k* sul-i k2 **Sulph** k* tarent ↓ tep ↓ thuj k* ust ven-m ↓ verat **Vib** xan zinc k* zinc-p k2
      - **night**; waking from sleep at (See night - waking - menses)
      - **burning**: *Ars* bry canth carb-v caust merc nux-v ph-ac phos rhus-t sep sulph tarent k*
      - **bursting** pain: *Coff* b7a.de *Ign* b7a.de *Nux-v* b7a.de
      - **contracting**: am-m h2 cocc tl1
  - **during – agg.**: ...
      - **cramping**: acon alum k* *Am-c* k* anac gsy1 arge-pl rwt5• ars h2 aur-i k2 bar-c k* bar-ox-suc rly4• *Bell* k* *Borx* k* brom calc k* castm bro1 *Caul* *Caust* *Cham* k* chel *Chin* k* choc srj3• *Cimic* *Cinnb* clem **Cocc** k* *Coff* k* *Coloc* k* *Con* k* *Cupr* k* dream-p sdj1• ferr b7a.de form fum rly1• gran k* granit-m es1• *Graph* k* haliae-lc srj5• ign k* ignis-alc es2• irid-met srj5• *Kali-c* kali-n k* kali-s lac-d kr1 *Mag-c* b4a.de mag-m k* *Mag-p* k* mill k2 mom-b br1 mosch nat-c *Nat-m* k* nat-s nicc *Nit-ac* k* *Nux-v* k* *Op* b7a.de *Plat* k* podo k2 *Puls* k* sabin k* sars k* *Sec* b7a.de *Sep* stront-c **Sulph** k* ven-m rsj12• vib k* zinc
      - **cutting** pain: alum h2 am-c ars h2 bar-c k* *Calc* carb-v *Caust* **Cocc** *Eupi* k* ferr k* graph iod ip **Kali-c** k* *Kreos* **Lach** *Lyc* mag-c k* nicc *Ol-an* *Phos* *Senec* *Sulph* zinc k*
      - **double** up; must: coloc ↓ mag-p ↓ op ↓
        - **cramping**: coloc tl1 mag-p tl1 op tl1
      - **dragging**, bearing down: am-c androc srj1• **Bell** bit-ar wht1• borx *Calc-p* carc jl2 *Cham* *Chin* *Con* *Ferr* graph *Kali-c* kali-i **Lil-t** *Mag-c* mag-m med *Murx* *Nat-c* *Nat-m* neon srj5• *Nit-ac* nux-m *Nux-v* **Plat** k* *Podo* **Puls** **Sec** **Sep** *Sulph* *Vib* zinc
      - **drawing** pain: calc k* carb-v croc kreos mosch *Plat* k* plb sep h2 staph *Stram* k* *Sulph* k*
      - **exertion** | **amel.**: *Sulph*
      - **first** day: cassia-s ↓
        - **cramping**: cassia-s ccrh1•
      - **hard**, steady: *Ust*
      - **pressing** pain: alum b4a.de am-m b7a.de* borx b4a.de calc carb-an b4.de cham b7a.de *Coff* b7a.de con b4.de* graph b4a.de* kali-c b4.de mag-c b4a.de mag-m b4.de nit-ac nux-m b7.de* nux-v b7.de plat k* **Puls** k* sec b7.de **Sep** sulph
        - **stone**; as from a: cocc b7.de*
      - **pressure**:
        - **agg.**: lac-h ↓
          - **sore**: lac-h htj1•
        - **amel.**: castm ↓
          - **sore**: castm
      - **rubbing** back amel.: *Mag-m*
      - **sharp**: ap-g br1
      - **sore**: *Bell* brom bry castm *Cocc* *Ham* k* lac-d nat-m k* *Nux-v* pic-ac *Puls* sep bro1 sulph
      - **stitching** pain: ap-g br1 ars h2 borx brom calc k* kali-c mosch **Nux-v** sul-ac k*
      - **tearing** pain: agar k* am-c bov k* *Caust* k* *Chinin-s* cinnb **Graph** **Lach** *Merc* sec tep k*
      - **warmth**:
        - **amel.** | **heat** amel.: **Ars** coloc k* mag-p tl1 *Nux-m* *Nux-v* pall pop-cand c1 puls rhus-t *Sil*
    - **beginning** of menses:
      - **agg.**: **Apis** b7a.de *Calc* *Caust* cham b7a.de eupi ↓ gels ↓ graph *Kali-c* lach b7a.de lap-a lyc mag-c mosch b7a.de phos ↓ **Plat** ↓ *Sep* ↓ staph b7.de vanil fd5.de
        - **cutting** pain: *Caust* k* eupi c1 gels graph k* lyc k* phos b4a.de **Plat** k* *Sep* b4a.de staph h1
        - **drawing** pain: *Mag-c* vanil fd5.de
        - **extending** to:
          - **Chest**: cupr graph
          - **Downward**: bamb-a stb2.de•
          - **Hip** to hip; from: thuj
    - **increases** amel.; when flow: bell kali-c kali-p *Lach* *Lap-a* mag-p pd mosch sep sulph
  - **instead** of: spong ptk1
  - **suppressed** menses; from: acon agn k* *Cham* cocc coloc *Cupr* ↓ graph nux-m sne *Puls* sabad ↓ *Spong*
    - **cramping**: *Cocc* b7a.de *Cupr* b7a.de
    - **pressing** pain: sabad b7a.de
  - ▽ **extending** to:
    - **Hip** to hip; from: thuj ↓
      - **cramping**: thuj

- **menses** would appear; as if: act-sp *Aloe* am-m ambr k* *Apis* *Aur* bit-ar wht1• bry canth bg2 carb-an bg1 chin bg2 chlam-tr bcx2• cina k* cocc k* *Croc* k* falco-pe nl2• ferr k* ferr-p hep h2 inul irid-met srj5• kali-c kali-m k2 kali-p fd1.de• kola stb3• kreos lac-f c1 laur *Lil-t* *Lyc* *Mag-c* mag-m h2 *Med* mez bg2 mosch k* mur-ac k* *Murx* *Nat-c* nat-m onos ozone sde2• phos *Plat* plut-n srj7• *Puls* raph c1 rhus-t rb2 ruta rb2 sabad rb2 sang *Sep* stann k* staph a1 sul-ac sulph rb2 ter rb2 til ven-m rsj12• vib visc c1* [tax jsj7]
- **menstrual** cycle:
  - **before**:
    - **nine** days: chlam-tr ↓
      - **menses** would appear; as if: chlam-tr bcx2•
    - **ten** days: chlam-tr ↓
      - **menses** would appear; as if: chlam-tr bcx2•
  - **thirteenth** day of: ozone ↓
    - **menses** would appear; as if: ozone sde2•
- **metrorrhagia**; during: ferr b7a.de hyos b7a.de sabin b7a.de
- **milk**:
  - **agg.**: ang bell h1 bry bufo carb-v con cupr ↓ lac-d mag-c ↓ *Mag-m* mrr1 mag-s pitu-a vml2• raph ↓ sil ↓ sul-ac sulph gk symph fd3.de• tritic-vg fd5.de zinc ↓
    - **cramping**: bufo c1 cupr *Lac-d* mag-c mrr1 mag-s raph sil mrr1 sulph gk
    - **cutting** pain: ang c1 zinc k*
- **mortification**; from: cham k2 *Coloc* puls ↓
  - **cramping**: cham k2 *Coloc*
  - **cutting** pain: puls
- **motion**:
  - **on**: alum ant-t bar-c bar-s k2 **Bell** brom **Bry** carb-an h2 carbn-s card-m mrr1 caust chin k2 *Cocc* colch con dig dream-p sdj1• eupi ferr mrr1 *Gels* gink-b sbd1• graph hir skp7• hyos k2 **Ip** irid-met srj5• iris jug-r kali-c kali-s *Kalm* kola stb3• kreos mag-m mag-p mang merc nat-m *Nit-ac* **Nux-v** ox-ac puls ran-b raph *Rhus-t* sep stann *Sulph* thuj zinc
  - **agg.**: aids ↓ aloe ↓ alum ↓ arg-n ↓ bar-c ↓ **Bell** ↓ bov ↓ brom ↓ **Bry** ↓ calc-p ↓ caps ↓ cassia-s ↓ **Cocc** ↓ corn-f ↓ cupr ↓ cycl ↓ dig ↓ **Ip** ↓ jug-r ↓ kali-bi ↓ kali-c ↓ kali-n ↓ kola ↓ *Kreos* ↓ mag-m ↓ mag-p ↓ merc-c ↓ *Mur-ac* ↓ *Nit-ac* ↓ *Nux-v* ↓ ox-ac ↓ oxal-a ↓ ph-ac ↓ **Phos** ↓ phys ↓ podo ↓ puls ↓ ran-b ↓ raph ↓ rhus-t ↓ rob ↓ samb ↓ stann ↓ staph ↓ stram ↓ tritic-vg ↓ *Zinc* ↓
    - **burning**: caps h1 kali-n kola stb3•
    - **cramping**: alum h2 brom bry bro1* cassia-s ccrh1• **Cocc** k* corn-f cupr mrr1 dig c1 **Ip** mag-p *Mur-ac* *Nit-ac* *Nux-v* ox-ac k2 phys ran-b raph rhus-t *Zinc*
    - **cutting** pain: aloe *Bry* caps *Cocc* merc-c puls rhus-t stann staph h1
      - **stones** being rubbed together; like sharp: cocc hr1*
    - **dragging**, bearing down: *Kreos* ph-ac
    - **drawing** pain: bry k* jug-r k* mag-m k*
    - **pressing** pain: bar-c kali-c h2 zinc h2
    - **sore**: aids nl2• **Bell** bov **Bry** nux-v oxal-a rly4• **Phos** podo rob k* stram h1
    - **stitching** pain: arg-n a1* bry k2* calc-p k2 caps h1 cycl kali-bi k2 kali-c h2* tritic-vg fd5.de
    - **tearing** pain: *Bry* rhus-t k* samb h1
  - **amel.**: aur-m bov coloc ↓ cub c1 cycl *Gels* ↓ kali-n nicc ↓ *Petr* phos ptel *Puls* ↓ rhus-t sep sne stroph-s sp1 sulph
    - **cramping**: bov coloc tl1 cub c1 *Gels* rhus-t
    - **cutting** pain: nicc *Puls* sep h2
    - **drawing** pain: aur-m
  - **continued** motion | **amel.**: gels
  - **legs**; of:
    - **left** leg agg.; of: kola ↓
      - **burning**: kola stb3•
- **nausea**; after: lat-m ptk1
- **neuralgic**: aran bro1 bell bro1 clem bro1 cocc bg2 *Coloc* bg2* cupr bg2 cupr-ar bg2* dios bg2 ham bro1 iris bg2 mag-p bg2* nux-v bro1 plb bg2 sel bg2 tab bg2 verat bg2
- **noise** agg.: zinc ↓
  - **cramping**: zinc mrr1
- **operation**; after: bism ↓ hep ↓ nux-v ↓ raph ↓ staph ↓
  - **cramping**: bism bro1 hep bro1 nux-v bro1 raph bro1 staph bro1*
- **ovulation**; during: granit-m es1• melal-alt ↓
  - **cutting** pain: granit-m es1• melal-alt gya4
- **owner** is stressed; if the: nux-v ↓
- **paralyzed**; as if: cycl b7.de* grat ptk1
- **paroxysmal**: *Alum* androc srj1• ant-t ars asaf k* *Bell* k* berb calad carb-v *Cham* chel chion br1 *Cocc* coff colch k* **Coloc** k* **Cupr** k* *Cupr-ar* *Cycl* dig k* *Dios* k* dulc fd4.de ferr k* ferr-ar ferr-p *Gels* gent-c graph *Ign* ip kali-ar kali-c k* kali-p kalm kola stb3• lac-c lyc k* mag-c mag-m *Mag-p* merl nat-c nat-p *Nux-v* k* ol-an olnd ox-ac k* ph-ac plat *Plb* k* podo k2 puls pycnop-sa mrz1 ran-s k* *Raph* ribo rly4• sabal c1 samb sang k* sars k* sec k* *Stann* k* staph teucr thuj k* tril-p c1 verb zinc zinc-p k2
- **peaches**, after: psor
  - **pressing** pain: psor
- **pecking**: cocc b7.de* ruta h1
- **periodical**: anis k* aran bro1 *Arg-n* hr1 *Ars* k* cain *Calc* caust ↓ **Cham** k* *Chin* k* *Cimic* k* *Coloc* **Cupr** *Cupr-ar* dios bro1 *Gels* ign *Ip* kali-br bro1 lac-c **Nux-v** samb xxb1 sulph
  - **day**; every: aran k* arn interf sa3• nat-m
  - **hour** | **same** hour: anis br1
  - **cramping** (See periodical)
  - **stitching** pain: caust
- **perspiration** | **during**: ant-c bg2 *Ant-t* bg2 *Ars* bg2 bar-c bg2 **Bell** bg2 bov bg2 *Bry* bg2 *Calc* bg2 **Cham** bg2 *Chin* bg2 cina bg2 coloc bg2 *Ferr* bg2 *Hell* bg2 kali-c bg2 lyc bg2 merc bg2 nit-ac bg2 *Nux-v* bg2 phos bg2 puls bg2 ran-b bg2 **Rhus-t** bg2 **Sep** bg2 **Stram** b7.de* stront-c bg2 *Sulph* bg2 thuj bg2 **Verat** b7.de*
- **piercing** (See stitching)
- **pinching** pain: (↗*cramping*) agar b4.de* alum b4.de* am-c b4.de* am-m b7.de* anac b4.de* ant-c b7.de* ant-t b7.de* ars b4.de* asaf b7.de* aur b4.de* bar-c b4.de* *Bell* b4.de* borx b4a.de* bov b4.de* *Bry* b7.de* *Calc* b4.de* cann-s b7.de* canth b7.de* carb-an b4.de* carb-v b4.de* caust b4.de* cham b7.de* chel b7.de* **Chin** b7.de* *Cic* b7.de* cina b7.de* *Cocc* b7.de* coff b7.de* *Coloc* b4.de* croc b7.de* cupr b7.de* cycl b7a.de dig b4.de* dros b7.de* dulc b4.de* euphr b7.de* graph b4.de* grat bg2 guaj b4.de* hell b7.de* hep b4.de* hyos b7.de* **Ign** b7.de* iod b4a.de *Ip* b7.de* kali-c b4.de* *Laur* b7.de* **Lyc** b4.de* m-ambo b7.de m-aust b7.de mag-c b4.de* mag-m b4.de* mang b4.de* meny b7a.de* **Merc** b4.de* merc-c b4a.de* mez b4.de* mosch b7a.de mur-ac b4.de* nat-c b4.de* nat-m b4.de* nat-s bg2 *Nit-ac* b4.de* **Nux-v** b7.de* *Olnd* b7.de* par b7.de* petr b4.de* ph-ac b4.de* phos b4.de* plat b4.de* plb b7.de* *Puls* b7.de* ran-b b7.de* ran-s b7.de* rheum b7.de* rhod b4a.de **Rhus-t** b7.de* *Ruta* b7.de* sabad b7.de* sabin b7a.de *Samb* b7.de* sars b4.de* seneg b4.de* sep b4.de* sil b4.de* *Spig* b7.de* *Spong* b7.de* squil b7.de* stann b4.de* *Staph* b7.de* stront-c b4.de* sul-ac b4.de* **Sulph** b4.de* tarax b7.de* tell ptk1 teucr b7a.de valer b7.de* *Verat* b7.de* verb b7.de* viol-t b7.de* *Zinc* b4.de*
  - **accompanied** by | **Lower** limbs; complaints of: *Carb-v* b4a.de *Coloc* b4a.de
- **plums**, after: rheum
- **pork**, after: acon ↓ acon-l ↓
  - **cutting** pain: acon acon-l k*
- **potatoes** agg.: alum k* *Coloc* k* mag-s merc-c k*
  - **cramping**: coloc k2
  - **stitching** pain: mag-s
- **pregnancy** agg.; during●: arn k* *Ars* *Bell* k* bell-p sp1 *Bry* k* *Cham* k* *Coloc* *Con* gels ↓ ham ↓ hyos k* *Ip* *Kali-c* lach k* lil-t ↓ nux-m gk **Nux-v** k* plb puls k* sep k* tritic-vg fd5.de *Verat* k* vib ↓
  - **cramping**: gels c1 vib tl1
  - **dragging**, bearing down: *Kali-c* k* lil-t tl1 sep tl1
  - **sore**: arn k2 con k2 ham bro1 *Nux-m* puls bro1 sep tritic-vg fd5.de
- **pressing** feet against support amel.: med ↓
  - **cramping**: med pd
- **pressing** pain: acon k* agar b4.de* *All-s* vh1 aloe alum k* am-c am-m k* *Ambr* k* *Anac* k* ant-c k* *Ant-t* k* apis arg-met k* *Arg-n* k* arn k* ars b4.de* ars-i k2 asaf b7.de* asar k* *Aur* k* aur-s k2 bamb-a stb2.de• bar-c *Bell* k* *Bism* k* bit-ar wht1• bry k* bufo calad b7.de* **Calc** k* calc-i k2 calc-p k* calc-s calc-sil k2 camph b7.de* *Caps* k* carb-an k* carb-v k* carbn-s *Carl* k* casc a1 castm *Caust* k* *Chel* k* chin k* chinin-s bg2 **Cic** hr1 cimic k* cina b7.de* *Cocc* b7.de* coff k* colch k* *Coloc* k* *Con* k* croc k* crot-t *Cupr* k* dig k* dulc fd4.de elaps *Euph* k* euphr k* ferr k* ferr-p flor-p rsj3• graph h2 *Grat* k* haliae-lc srj5• ham fd3.de• hep b4.de* hyper k* ign k* iod h* kali-bi bg2 kali-c k* kali-i k* kali-n

Abdomen

- **pressing** pain: ...
kali-p fd1.de• *Kali-s* kali-sil k2 ketogl-ac rly4• kreos b7a.de lac-c lac-lup hm2• *Lach* k* **Lyc** k* lyss *M-arct* b7.de* m-aust b7.de *Mag-c* k* mang k* meny k* meph k* *Merc* k* *Mez* k* mosch b7.de* mur-ac b4.de* nat-c a1 *Nat-m* k* *Nat-n* nit-ac b4.de* nux-m k* **Nux-v** k* *Op* k* paeon k* *Par* k* *Petr* k* phos b4.de* *Plat* k* plb k* prun *Puls* k* rheum b7.de* rhus-t k* ruta k* sabad b7.de* sabin k* sal-fr sle1• samb k* sars b4.de* sec k* **Sep** k* *Sil* k* *Spig* k* spong fd4.de stann k* staph k* stram h1 **Sulph** k* suprar rly4• symph fd3.de• tab tarax k* tarent k* tell c1 *Ter* k* teucr b7.de* thuj k* tritic-vg fd5.de valer b7.de* vanil fd5.de verat k* *Zinc* k* [heroin sdj2]
  - **accompanied** by | **nausea** (See STOMACH - Nausea - accompanied - abdomen - pain - pressing)
  - **asunder**: *Euph* b4a.de
  - **cold**; as from: petr h2 sars h2
  - **downward**: agn bg2 bell b4a.de chel k2 *Colch* b7a.de *Croc* b7a.de dig bg2 dulc bg2 *Lach* bg2 merc bg2 *Nux-v* b7a.de *Plat* b4a.de *Sabin* b7a.de *Sep* b4a.de *Teucr* b7a.de
  - **flatulence**; as from: ars h2 camph h1 iod h lyc h2 phos h2 positr nl2• sep h2 zinc h2
  - **inward**: anac b4.de* bry b7.de* cycl b7.de* hell b7.de* mez b4.de* rheum b7.de* sars b4.de* sul-ac b4.de* zinc b4.de*
  - **outward**: acon b7.de* all-s vh1 anac b4.de* ang b7.de* asaf b7.de* bell b4.de* cann-s b7.de* carb-an bg2 colch b7.de* *Con* bg2 dulc b4.de* euph bg2 ign bg2 kali-c b4.de* lyc b4.de* m-arct b7.de m-aust b7.de merc b4.de* nit-ac b4.de* nux-v b7.de* ph-ac bg2 rheum b7.de* squil b7.de* sulph bg2 teucr b7.de* thuj b4.de* zinc h2*
  - **plug**; as from a: *Aloe* bro1 alum bro1 anac c1* *Bell* bro1 bry bro1 *Cocc* bro1 hyos bro1 kali-c bro1 mez bro1 *Nux-v* bro1 oena bro1 *Plat* bro1 plb bro1 puls bro1 ran-s bro1 sabin bro1 *Sep* bro1
  - **protrude**; as if something would: nit-ac h2
  - **stone**; as from a: all-c bg2 aloe bg2 *Am-m* b7a.de ant-t b7a.de* ars bg2 bell k* borx a1 calc bg2 chin bg2 cocc b7a.de* *Coloc* bg2 *Cupr* k* hyos b7.de* *M-ambo* b7.de* m-arct b7.de *Merc* k* nat-m bg2 nit-ac bg2 nux-m bg2 **Nux-v** b7.de* op k* *Par* b7a.de **Puls** b7.de* rhus-t b7a.de* sabad b7.de* sep bg2 spig b7a.de* *Sulph* bg2 thuj h1 valer bg2 *Verb* b7.de*
  - **upward**: ars h2 chel k2 con h2 ign b7.de* nat-m bg2 rhus-t b7.de
- **pressure**:
  - **agg.**: acon aids↓ aloe anac androc srj1• ant-t aq-mar skp7• *Arg-met* sne aur↓ bapt a1 bar-s k2 **Bell** bit-ar wht1• bry k2 carb-v *Carbn-s* chinin-s cic cina *Coff* con k* cund sne cycl *Dios*↓ dirc c1 eup-per graph h2 heroin↓ hyos k2 jac-c kali-bi *Lac-c* lac-d c1 *Lach* *Mez* *Nit-ac* *Nux-v* oxal-a↓ plb↓ podo k2 puls *Ran-b* rhus-t k2 samb sars sil k2 sol-t-ae↓ stann h2 stront-c sk4• *Sulph* tann-ac br1 tetox↓ trios rsj11• tritic-vg fd5.de trom vml3• vanil fd5.de xan↓ *Zinc* [spect dfg1 tax jsj7]
    - **cramping**: acon bro1 aloe bro1 *Bell* bro1 bry bro1 *Dios* bro1 plb bro1 tetox pin2•
    - **pulse** beat agg.; every: hep h2
    - **retching**; with: petr↓
      - **cramping**: petr hr1
    - **sore**: aids nl2• oxal-a rly4• podo k2 rhus-t k2 sol-t-ae vml3• xan c1 [heroin sdj2]
    - **stitching** pain: aur nit-ac
    - **tearing** pain: cic k*
  - **amel.**: agar *All-s* vh1 aloe hr alumn am-c aq-mar rbp6 arg-n ars-s-f↓ asaf atra-r bnm3• *Bell* bov brom carc mg1.de* *Card-m*↓ cassia-s↓ castm chinin-ar↓ chir-fl gya2 cina **Coloc** k* dios dros k2 dulc gamb graph k* grat *Hyos* bg1 irid-met↓ kali-c kali-n lac-h↓ mag-m h2 *Mag-p* k* mang meny nat-c nat-m *Nat-s* nit-ac↓ *Plb* k* *Podo* ptel rhus-t↓ sacch-a fd2.de• sec bg1 *Sep* sne **Stann** k ● sul-ac k* tarent k* thuj tritic-vg fd5.de ulm-c↓ vanil fd5.de
    - **constricting** pain: carc sp1
    - **cramping**: am-c brom k* cassia-s cdd7*• chinin-ar c1 cina mrr1 **Coloc** k* irid-met srj5• *Mag-p* k* mang k* nit-ac bro1 plb bro1 *Podo* k* rhus-t bro1 *Stann* k*
    - **cutting** pain: ars-s-f k2 kali-c h2 lac-h sk4•
    - **stitching** pain: *Card-m* ulm-c jsj8•
    - **tearing** pain: plb k*
  - **clothes**; of:
    - **agg.**: flor-p rsj3• *Nux-v* b7.de* puls b7a.de
- **pressure – clothes**; of: ...
    - **amel.**: fl-ac bg1 nat-m bg1
  - **not** amel.: cham↓
    - **cramping**: cham tl1
- **pricking** pain: vanil fd5.de
- **pulsating** pain: *Aeth* bro1 *Aloe* bro1 bar-m bro1 *Bell* bro1 *Berb* bro1 calc bro1 ign bro1 sang bro1 sel bro1 tarax bro1
- **radiating**: *Acon* bro1 arge bro1 *Bell* bro1 *Bry* bro1 calc bro1 *Cham* bro1 *Cocc* bro1 coch bro1 *Coloc* bro1 cupr-act bro1 *Cupr-ar* bro1 dios k* graph bro1 *Ip* k* kali-c bro1 *Lyc* bro1 mag-m bg2 **Mag-p** k* merc bro1 morph bro1 *Nux-v* bro1 ox-ac bro1 paraf bro1 plat bro1 *Plb* k* podo bro1 puls bro1 sulph bro1 toxo-g jl2
- **raising** | **arm** | **agg.**: carb-v
  - **arms**:
    - **agg.**: cupr↓
      - **cramping**: cupr ptk1
- **reaching** high: alum *Rhus-t*
- **rectangular**; as if: melal-alt gya4
- **respiration** (See breathing - agg.)
- **rest**:
  - **amel.**: grat↓
    - **burrowing**: grat k*
- **rheumatic**: carb-v b4.de* caust h2 coloc↓ dios↓ phyt↓ verat↓
  - **cramping**: caust bro1 coloc bro1 dios bro1 phyt bro1 verat bro1
  - ○ **Liver**: meph bg2
- **riding**:
  - **agg.**: caj↓ carb-v↓ cocc↓ psor↓
    - **cramping**: caj a1 carb-v bro1* cocc bro1 psor k*
  - **carriage**; in a:
    - **agg.**: alum-sil k2 *Arg-met*↓ asaf↓ calc-f *Carb-v* *Cocc* lach sne nat-m psor *Sep*
      - **dragging**, bearing down: asaf
      - **sore**: *Arg-met*
  - **horse**; a:
    - **agg.**: nat-c↓
      - **sore**: nat-c
- **rigor**, during: sulph↓
  - **bursting** pain: sulph k*
- **rising**:
  - **after**:
    - **agg.**: chin coloc dig↓ *Lyc* k* nit-ac↓ tritic-vg fd5.de
      - **cutting** pain: dig h2 nit-ac k*
  - **agg.**: bry k* senec k* tritic-vg fd5.de
  - **bed**; from:
    - **agg.**: zinc↓
      - **contracting**: zinc h2
  - **lying**; from | **amel.**: arg-met bar-m
  - **sitting**; from:
    - **agg.**: dig↓ kali-c↓
      - **cramping**: kali-c
      - **tearing** pain: dig k*
    - **amel.**: chin spong
      - **cramping**: chin k* spong
- **rocking**:
  - **amel.**: marb-w↓
    - **cramping**: marb-w es1•
- **rolling** on floor amel.: coloc h2
- **room** agg.: kali-i
- **rubbing**:
  - **agg.**: sulph↓
    - **cramping**: sulph h2*
  - **amel.**: aran vh1 coloc sne mag-p mrr1 mim-p↓ phos mtf33 plb↓ podo bg3* vero-o rly3•
    - **cramping**: mim-p skp7• plb bro1
- **running**:
  - **after**: tub↓ ulm-c↓
    - **stitching** pain: tub ptk1 ulm-c jsj8•

- **agg.**: bit-ar↓
  - **cramping**: bit-ar wht1•
- **scapulae**; with pain between: am-c↓
  - **cramping**: am-c pd
- **scratching** pain: ruta b7.de*
- **screwing** together: nat-m bg2
- **sexual** excitement, during: graph
- **sharp**: fum rly1• hydroph rsj6• neon srj5• pegan-ha tpi1• vero-o rly3•
  - **edge**; as if lying on a sharp: rhus-t bg2
- **shattered**; as if: carb-an k* kreos k* sil bg2 squil k*
- **shattering** pain: kreos bg1*
- **shivering**; during: bar-c b4.de borx b4a.de chin b7.de *Ign* b7.de* merc b4.de nit-ac b4.de
- **shooting** (See stitching)
- **singing** agg.: puls
- **sitting**:
  - **after**: con↓ tritic-vg↓
    - **drawing** pain: con tritic-vg fd5.de
  - **agg.**: all-c alum↓ asaf bar-c k* bit-ar↓ bry↓ *Calc* caust↓ chin chord-umb↓ cina↓ coloc↓ *Con Dig* dios k* dros↓ dulc fd4.de elaps↓ ferr gink-b sbd1• hell↓ iod↓ kali-c k2 kali-p↓ mur-ac↓ nat-c↓ *Nat-m* nat-s↓ nicc↓ **Nux-v**↓ op par↓ *Petr* ph-ac phos↓ puls rhus-t k* ruta *Sep* spig↓ spong staph↓ stront-c sk4• stroph-s sp1 *Sulph* tax↓ *Thuj*↓ tritic-vg fd5.de
    - **burning**: calc sep
    - **cramping**: all-c k2 bit-ar wht1• chin chord-umb rly4• dig elaps ferr gink-b sbd1• par rhus-t h1 spong
    - **cutting** pain: alum asaf k* dros mur-ac k* nat-c h2 nicc *Puls* spig staph h1 [tax jsj7]
    - **drawing** pain: asaf chin h1 con h2 phos tritic-vg fd5.de
    - **pressing** pain: chin h1 coloc h2 hell iod op rhus-t stront-c tritic-vg fd5.de
    - **stitching** pain: bry caust chin h1 cina kali-p fd1.de• nat-s **Nux-v** phos k* ruta *Thuj*
  - **amel.**: alum apis astac↓ bar-c bell bit-ar↓ ferr k* hir skp7• kali-p↓ *Kalm* melal-alt↓ mur-ac↓ nux-v↓ spong fd4.de
    - **cramping**: astac kr1* bell bit-ar wht1• melal-alt gya4 mur-ac h2 nux-v tl1
    - **cutting** pain: melal-alt gya4 mur-ac
    - **dragging**, bearing down: kali-p k2
    - **pressing** pain: bar-c
  - **bent** forward:
    - **agg.**: alum ant-t carb-v dulc gink-b sbd1• kali-n↓ **Lyc** k● sulph
      - **burning**: kali-n
      - **cramping**: carb-v dulc
      - **cutting** pain: alum h2
    - **amel.**: *All-s*↓ *Bell Coloc* merc sars sulph
      - **pressing** pain: *All-s* vh1
    - **must** sit bent forward: kali-c h2
  - **erect**:
    - **agg.**: atra-r bnm3• ptel c1
    - **amel.**: dios↓ *Gels* sin-n↓
      - **cramping**: dios mrr1 sin-n bro1
  - **head** on knees; with:
    - **amel.**: euph↓
      - **cramping**: euph h2
- **sleep**:
  - **amel.**: alum k* am-m mag-m nat-c↓
    - **cramping**: alum h2 mag-m nat-c h2
    - **tearing** pain: mag-m k*
  - **during**:
    - **agg.**: ant-t ptk1 cina kali-n stront-c sk4•
      - **cramping**: kali-n k*
  - **going** to sleep; before: sulph k*
  - **interrupting** sleep: ferr a1 mez k* tab k*
- **smarting**: *Ars* ptk1 bell ptk1 canth ptk1 coloc b4.de* hep b4a.de nux-v ptk1 ph-ac b4.de* ran-b ptk1 sep b4.de* stann b4.de* sulph b4.de*
- **smoking** agg.; after: brom↓ bufo↓ meny↓
  - **cramping**: brom k* bufo c1 meny bro1
- **sneezing** agg.: bell canth carb-v↓ cham eupi ind k* kali-p k2 pall
  - **burning**: canth carb-v
  - **stitching** pain: carb-v h2
- **sore** (= bruised, tenderness, etc): acet-ac **Acon** k* *Aesc* aeth k* agn c1 aids nl2• all-s bro1 aloe k* alum k* *Alumn* am-c am-m k* ambr androc srj1• ang b7.de* ant-t anthraci vh1 **Apis** k* apoc k2* aq-mar skp7• *Arg-met* k* *Arg-n* k* **Arn** k* **Ars** k* ars-i k2 ars-s-f k2 arund asaf k* atro aur k* aur-ar k2 aur-m bamb-a stb2.de• **Bapt** k* bar-c k* **Bell** k* bell-p bg1* bism bol-la bov *Brom* b4a.de **Bry** k* bufo cact cadm-s cain calad *Calc* k* calc-s camph b7.de* cann-s k* *Canth Caps* hr1 *Carb-ac Carb-an* k* carb-v b4.de* carbn-s card-m br1 caust **Cham** *Chel* chin k* *Chinin-ar* cic b7.de* cimic k* *Cina* k* cinnb *Cocc* k* **Colch** k* *Coloc* k* *Con* k* croc b7.de* **Crot-c** *Crot-h* crot-t **Cupr** cupr-ar *Cycl* *Dios* dulc fd4.de eucal bro1 eup-pur euph k* fago *Ferr* k* *Ferr-ar* ferr-p gard-j vlr2• *Gels* ger-i rly4• gnaph gran *Graph* grat gymno *Ham* k* hell k* *Hep* k* *Hydr* *Hyos* k* ign k* *Ip* iris jatr-c *Kali-ar* kali-bi k* kali-c k* *Kali-chl* kali-i kali-m k2 kali-n k* *Kali-p* kali-s ketogl-ac rly4• *Kreos Lac-d* **Lach** lat-m bnm6• *Lec* led k* *Lil-t* k* lob luna kg1• **Lyc** lyss c1 m-ambo b7.de *M-arct* b7.de* m-aust b7.de *Mag-m* *Manc* mang b4a.de marb-w es1• meny k* **Merc** **Merc-c** k* merc-i-r *Mez* mim-p rsj8• murx nat-ar nat-c k* nat-m k* nat-p nat-s k* **Nit-ac** k* *Nux-m* **Nux-v** k* onos *Op* k* ox-ac oxal-a rly4• paeon *Pall* petr k* ph-ac k2 **Phos** k* phys phyt k* plac-s rly4• plb *Podo* ptel *Puls* k* *Pyrog Ran-b* k* *Raph* **Rhus-t** rhus-v ribo rly4• ruta k* sabad sabin samb k* *Sang Sars* sec **Sep** k* sinus rly4• sol-t-ae spong k2 squil *Stann* k* staph k* stram k* stry suis-em rly4• sul-ac **Sulph** k* tab tarent **Ter** til tritic-vg fd5.de *Ust* valer k* *Verat* k* xan zinc k* [heroin sdj2]
- **soup**:
  - **after**: zinc
  - **agg.**: zinc↓
    - **cramping**: zinc
  - **amel.**: nat-c h2
- **sour** food agg.: dros↓
  - **cramping**: dros k2
- **spasmodic**: caust ptk1 kali-bi bg2
- **sprained**; as if: am-m gsy1 ambr b7.de* anac bg2 *Apis* b7a.de arn b7.de* carb-v b4.de* dulc b4.de* hyos h1 ign b7.de* *Nux-v* b7a.de plat b4.de* rhus-t b7.de* thuj b4.de* valer b7.de*
- **squeezed**; as if: *Ambr* b7.de* anac b4.de* ang b7.de* ant-t ptk1 apis b7a.de arn b7a.de* ars b4.de* bufo bg2 carb-v b4.de* cocc b7.de* *Coloc* b4.de* con b4.de* dig b4a.de *Euphr* b7a.de graph b4.de* *Kali-c* b4a.de led b7.de* merc-c b4a.de *Nux-v* b7a.de ph-ac b4.de* phos b4.de* rhus-t b7.de* ruta b7.de* sars b4a.de scop ptk1 staph ptk1 sulph b4.de* teucr b7.de* thuj b4a.de zinc b4a.de
  - **stones**; between two: (↗*cutting - stones*) cassia-s cdd7• cocc pfa1 *Coloc* k* nux-v dh1*
- **standing**:
  - **agg.**: aloe *Bell* bit-ar↓ *Bry*↓ chinin-s coloc k2 *Con*↓ gent-c↓ graph↓ lil-t↓ mur-ac↓ *Murx*↓ nat-m↓ pall↓ ptel k* puls↓ rheum↓ rhus-t↓ **Sep**↓ sulph zinc
    - **burning**: *Sulph* k*
    - **cramping**: bell bit-ar wht1• gent-c mur-ac h2 rheum bro1 zinc
    - **cutting** pain: *Bry* mur-ac k*
    - **dragging**, bearing down: *Con* st graph h2 lil-t k2 *Murx* nat-m pall puls k2 rheum rhus-t **Sep** sulph k2
    - **pressing** pain: graph h2
  - **amel.**: chin↓ spong fd4.de thuj
    - **cramping**: chin h1
    - **pressing** pain: chin h1
  - **bent**:
    - **amel.**: spong↓
      - **cramping**: spong h1
- **stepping**:
  - **agg.**: *All-s*↓ calc↓
    - **dragging**, bearing down: calc h2
    - **pressing** pain: *All-s* vh1
  - **every** step; at: all-s↓ *Arn*↓ chel sne mur-ac h2 *Sil*↓
    - **cutting** pain: *Arn Sil*
    - **stitching** pain: *Mur-ac*

- **every** step; at: ...
  - **tearing** pain: all-s k*
- **stinging**: **Apis** asaf borx hr1 bry *Canth* chel chin ign kali-c *Lyc Phos Puls* sacch-a fd2.de• sep spig verb
- **stitching** pain (= sticking, etc.): *Acon* k* acon-ac rly4• aeth *Agar* k* agn b7.de* aids nl2• all-c k2 aloe *Alum* k* alum-p k2 alum-sil k2 am-c am-m k2 anac k* ang b7.de* ant-t k* apis k* arg-met *Arg-n* k* arge-pl rwt5• *Arn* k* *Ars* k* asaf k* bamb-a stb2.de• bapt *Bell* k* berb *Bov* k* *Brucel* sa3• **Bry** k* *Calc* k* calc-p k2 *Calc-s* calc-sil k2 cann-s b7.de* canth k* caps b7.de* carb-an carb-v k* *Carbn-s Card-m* cardios-h rly4• *Caust* k* cedr *Cham* k* chel chin k* chinin-ar k* cic *Cimic* cina b7.de* clem b4.de* cocc k* *Colch* k* *Coloc* k* con k* *Croc* k* crot-t bg2 cupr k* *Cycl* k* *Dig* k* dulc fd4.de ephe-si hsj1• ferr b7.de* ferr-i fic-m gya1 fl-ac k* graph b4.de* *Grat* k* ham fd3.de• hell k* hep k* hippoc-k szs2 *Hydroph* rsj6• *Ign* b7.de* **Ip** k* irid-met srj5• kali-ar kali-bi k* *Kali-c* k* kali-n k* *Kali-p Kali-s* kali-sil k2 kola stb3• kreos k* lac-c lach k* lang a4 laur led lyc lyss m-arct b7.de m-aust b7.de mag-m *Mag-s* med merc k* merc-c b4a.de* mez k* mosch b7a.de mur-ac bg2 nad rly4• naja nat-ar nat-c k* nat-m nat-n nat-p nat-s bg2 nit-ac k* nux-m b7.de* *Nux-v* k* olnd b7.de* op ox-ac k2 pall *Ph-ac* k* *Phos* k* phys pic-ac pieri-b mlk9.de plat bg2 *Plb* k* podo bg2 positr nl2• psor *Puls* k* *Pycnop-sa* mrz1 ran-b b7.de* rhod k* rhus-t bg2 ribo rly4• ros-d wla1 ruta k* sabad b7.de* sacch-a fd2.de• samb sang bg2 sars b4.de* sel sep k* *Sil Spig* k* spong fd4.de stann k* staph b7.de* stram k* suis-em rly4• **Sulph** k* sumb *Tarax* k* tarent *Ter* thuj k* tritic-vg fd5.de trom vanil fd5.de verat k* *Verb* k* viol-t k* zinc k* zinc-p k2 [*Spect* dfg1]
  - **alternating** with | **Chest**; pain in (See CHEST - Pain - alternating - abdomen - stitching)
  - **burning**: lyc spig h1 zinc k*
  - **downward**: alumn aphis brom cench k2 chin **Ip** kali-c puls ran-s samb til verb
  - **electric** shocks; as from: arg-n
  - **inward**: phos h2
  - **needles**; as from: caust bg2
  - **outward**: asaf b7a.de*
  - **paroxysmal**: *Ip* pycnop-sa mrz1 til c1
  - **stinging**: *Apis Ign Lach Sep Thuj*
  - **upward**: aloe ars st *Bry* naja ph-ac h2 pycnop-sa mrz1 ruta spong
- **stool**:
  - **after**:
    - **agg.**: agar k* *Aloe* alum b4.de* am-c k* am-m k* ambr k* anac b4.de arg-met k* ars b4.de ars-s-f ↓ asc-t a1* aur bamb-a ↓ bar-s k2 borx bg2 bov k* *Canth* b7.de* carb-an k* *Carb-v* k* carbn-s ↓ caust b4.de *Chin* k* colch k* *Coloc* con b4.de cop crot-t k* cupr cupr-ar k* cycl ↓ dig k* dios dros k* dulc b4.de eup-per ↓ fago k* gels ↓ ger-i ↓ glon ↓ graph grat k* hep b4a.de hir skp7• hydrog srj2• iod b4.de ip jug-c ↓ kali-bi k* kali-c k* kali-n ↓ kali-sil k2 lept lil-t ↓ lyc k* m-ambo b7.de mag-m b4.de* mag-p ↓ *Merc* merc-c k* mez k* mur-ac b4.de nat-ar nat-c b4.de *Nat-m* k* nat-sil ↓ **Nit-ac** *Nux-v* b7.de ol-an ↓ op k* osm k* ox-ac k2 pall k* phos k* *Pic-ac* plat b4.de plb k* *Podo Puls* k* *Rheum* k* rhod k* ruta fd4.de sabad ↓ sep b4.de* sil k* spig b7.de spong ↓ stann b4.de staph k* stront-c suis-pan ↓ *Sul-ac* **Sulph** k* tab ↓ trom k* vanil ↓ verat b7.de* xan ↓ *Zinc* k* zinc-p k2
      - **burning**: cupr-ar k* jug-c k* kali-bi k* nat-ar sabad k* sep h2 xan c1
      - **cramping**: agar *Aloe* k* **Am-c** *Ars* k* ars-s-f k2 carb-an k* *Carb-v* k* carbn-s *Coloc* k* con cupr k* cycl hr1 eup-per ger-i rly4• glon k* graph k* grat k* kali-bi k* kali-c lil-t k* lyc mag-m h2* mag-p bg2 nat-c h2 *Nat-m* nat-sil fd3.de• nit-ac k* *Op* k* plb k* podo fd3.de• rheum h rhod k* suis-pan rly4• sul-ac **Sulph** k*
      - **cutting** pain: *Am-c* k* ars k* *Canth* k* carb-v h2 **Coloc** gels kali-bi bg2 kali-n lept *Merc Merc-c* ox-ac *Podo* puls bg2 rheum k* ruta fd4.de staph *Sulph* k*
      - **difficult** and scanty stool, after flatus amel.; after: zinc ↓
        - **dragging**, bearing down: zinc
      - **dragging**, bearing down: *Carb-v Graph*
      - **pressing** pain: ambr c1* dulc h2* grat k* *Iod* kali-c ol-an k* *Pic-ac* xan c1 zinc
      - **sore**: am-m k* crot-t nat-m k* ol-an bg2* puls sul-ac h2 *Sulph* tab k*
      - **stitching** pain: bamb-a stb2.de• spong fd4.de vanil fd5.de zinc k*
      - **tearing** pain: mag-m k*

- **stool – after**: ...
  - **amel.**: achy-a zzc1• aegle-f ↓ agar aloe alum h2 am-c ↓ am-m ↓ apoc k* ars bapt borx h2 bov k* bros-gau ↓ bry k* *Calc-p* k* *Carb-v* carbn-s ↓ caust ↓ chel mrr1 chinin-s chir-fl ↓ cimic hr1 cina ↓ cinnb cit-ac ↓ coc-c **Colch** k* **Coloc** k* dig k* dios k* dirc a1* dulc fd4.de ferr k* **Gamb** k* gels grat hell ↓ helon hir skp7• hydrog srj2• indg ↓ kali-s fd4.de kola stb3• mag-c mag-m ↓ mang ↓ mim-p ↓ mur-ac ↓ naja ↓ nat-ar nat-c k* nat-m ↓ *Nat-s* **Nux-v** plb ↓ podo k2* puls ↓ *Rheum Rhus-t* k* ruta fd4.de sacch-a fd2.de• senec k* seneg ↓ sil k* spong fd4.de sulph k* symph fd3.de• tanac ↓ thuj k* tritic-vg fd5.de trom k* vanil fd5.de verat bg1 zinc h2
    - **burning**: ars h2
    - **cramping**: aegle-f zzc1• agar k* aloe gsy1* bros-gau mrc1 carbn-s chir-fl gya2 cina a1 cinnb k* cit-ac rly4• coc-c k* **Coloc** k* ferr k* *Gamb* k* *Gels* indg k* *Mag-c* mang a1 mim-p skp7• naja nat-ar nat-c a1 **Nat-s** **Nux-v** k* podo mrr1 puls k* rhus-t hr1 seneg k* sulph k* tanac bro1 *Verat* k*
    - **cutting** pain: am-c am-m bry k* *Calc-p* caust k* dig k* hell k* mag-m h2* mur-ac k* nat-c h2 nat-m k* **Nux-v** plb k* *Rhus-t* sil h2 sulph k* vanil fd5.de
    - **sore**: *Podo*
  - **not** amel.: nat-c ↓
    - **cramping**: nat-c a1
- **amel.**: aur-m ↓ dig ↓ meny ↓ ruta ↓ sep ↓ *Spig* ↓ vanil ↓
  - **drawing** pain: aur-m
  - **pressing** pain: dig h2 meny h1 ruta fd4.de sep h2 *Spig* vanil fd5.de
- **before**: achy-a zzc1• acon ↓ aesc aeth ↓ agar k* aids ↓ ail k* **Aloe** alum k* **Am-c** k* *Am-m* k* ang b7.de ant-c ↓ ant-t k* apoc k* **Arg-n** k* arn b7.de ars k* ars-s-f ↓ arum-i ↓ *Asar* b7.de* aur ↓ bamb-a ↓ *Bapt* ↓ *Bar-c* k* *Bar-m* bar-s ↓ bell k* bism ↓ borx b4a.de brom b4a.de *Bry* k* cact k* cain ↓ calc *Calc-p* calc-s ↓ camph k* cann-s k* canth k* caps b7.de* carb-an k* carb-v k* carbn-s ↓ cardios-h ↓ cassia-s cdd7*• caust k* cham k* chel b7.de *Chin* k* chinin-ar chinin-s chlam-tr ↓ cimx k* cina k* cob ↓ coc-c k* *Colch* k* *Coll Coloc* k* con b4.de convo-s sp1 cop croc b7.de *Crot-t* k* cupr k* cupr-s ↓ cycl k* *Dig* k* dros b7.de dulc k* fago k* ferr k* ferr-ar ↓ ferr-i k* ferr-p fl-ac k* form gamb gels ger-i ↓ glon k* gran ↓ graph k* grat guaj k* hell k* hep k* hir skp7• hydr ↓ hyper ↓ ign k* ind k* *Jatr-c* ↓ jug-r k* kali-ar ↓ kali-bi *Kali-c* k* kali-i k* kali-m k2 *Kali-n* k* kali-p kali-s fd4.de kalm ↓ ketogl-ac ↓ kola stb3• lac-h sk4• lach b7.de lact ↓ laur b7.de *Lil-t* ↓ *Lyc* k* lycps-v ↓ m-arct b7a.de *M-aust* b7.de* mag-act ↓ **Mag-c** k* mag-m k* *Mag-p* ↓ *Manc Mang* k* meny b7.de merc k* *Merc-c* b4a.de merc-i-f ↓ merc-i-r k* *Mez* k* mim-p ↓ *Mur-ac* naja nat-ar *Nat-c* k* nat-m k* nat-p k* *Nat-s* nicc *Nit-ac* k* *Nuph* nux-m ↓ *Nux-v* k* *Olnd* k* *Op* k* ox-ac k* petr k* ph-ac b4.de phel ↓ *Phos* k* phys ↓ plan k* plb k* **Podo** k* prun k* *Psor* k* **Puls** k* ran-b k* raph k* rat k* *Rheum* k* rhod k* *Rhus-t* k* rhus-v k* *Rumx* ruta b7.de sabad k* sal-fr ↓ *Sang* k* sars b4.de sec ↓ seneg b4.de *Sep* k* sil b4.de spig b7.de spong fd4.de *Stann* k* staph b7.de* stram k* stront-c b4.de suis-em rly4• suis-pan ↓ **Sulph** k* symph fd3.de• tab ↓ tax k* *Thuj* k* tritic-vg fd5.de *Trom* k* ulm-c ↓ valer b7.de vanil fd5.de verat k* viol-t b7.de* zinc b4.de* zing k*
  - **burning**: aloe sabad bg2
  - **bursting** pain: spig
  - **clawing** pain: petr bg2
  - **cramping**: aesc *Agar* k* aids nl2• **Aloe** alum k* **Am-c** *Am-m* ang h1 **Arg-n** *Ars* k* ars-s-f k2 arum-i k* aur bamb-a stb2.de• *Bapt* hr1 bell k* bism bg2 *Bry* k* calc *Calc-p* camph k* cann-s canth k* *Caps* a1 carb-an k* carbn-s cardios-h rly4• chel bg2 **Chin** *Chinin-s* chlam-tr bcx2• cina coc-c k* *Colch* k* *Coll* **Coloc** k* *Crot-t* k* cupr k* cupr-s k* cycl k* dig dulc h1* ferr k* ferr-ar ferr-i *Gamb* k* gels ger-i rly4• glon k* gran k* grat k* guaj k* hep k* hyper k* ign *Jatr-c* kali-ar kali-bi k* kali-c k* kali-n k* kali-s ketogl-ac rly4• kola stb3• lact k* *Lil-t* lycps-v mag-act bg2 **Mag-c** k* mag-m k* *Mag-p* mang k* meny k* *Merc* k* merc-i-r k* *Mez* mim-p skp7• *Mur-ac* k* nat-ar nat-c k* nat-m nat-p nat-s bg2* nit-ac k* *Nux-v* **Op** k* petr k* phel k* *Phos* k* phys k* **Podo** k* puls k* rat k* rhod k* rhus-t k* rhus-v k* sal-fr sle1• sep k* spig k* stram suis-pan rly4• **Sulph** k* *Thuj Trom* k* *Verat* k* zinc k*
  - **cutting** pain: acon aesc aeth agar k* **Aloe** am-c k* am-m ang c1 ant-c **Ant-t** arn bg2 *Ars* k* ars-s-f k2 *Asar* k* bar-c bar-s k2 borx brom k* *Bry* k* cain *Calc-p* calc-s caps carb-an bg2 carb-v k* carbn-s chel cina cob k* **Coloc** k* con k* crot-t k* dig k* **Dulc** k* gamb k* gels graph grat k*

- **before – cutting** pain: ...
hell k* hep k* hydr k* ign k* kali-c bg2 kali-m k2 kali-n k* kalm k* lact k* laur lyc k* *Mag-c* k* mag-m bg2 manc k* *Merc* *Merc-c* merc-i-f k* nat-ar nat-c k* *Nat-m* k* nicc *Nit-ac* k* nux-m nux-v op bg2 petr k* phos bg2 *Puls* k* rheum k* *Rhus-t* rumx sang k* sec sep k* *Staph* sulph k* *Thuj* valer k* vanil fd5.de verat viol-t k* zinc k*
  - **dragging**, bearing down: mag-m h2 nat-c nit-ac
  - **drawing** pain: cact k* *Nit-ac* k* sang bg2 spong fd4.de zing
  - **mucous** and chilliness: cop ↓
    - **cramping**: cop br1
  - **pressing** pain: dig h2 dulc h2* grat k* kali-c bg2 lach bg2 nat-m bg2 nit-ac bg2 nux-v bg2 thuj bg2 zinc
  - **sore**: nat-m *Sulph* k* tab k*
  - **stitching** pain: aloe calc-s k* kali-n k* mang spong fd4.de suis-em rly4• tritic-vg fd5.de ulm-c jsj8• vanil fd5.de
  - **tearing** pain: dig h2 dulc tl1 hep k* kola stb3• stram k*
  - **twisting** pain: ars h2* caust h2 mez h2
- **during**:
  - **agg.**: achy-a zzc1• acon ↓ aeth *Agar* k* agn b7.de **Aloe** ↓ alum h2 *Am-c* b4.de* am-m b7.de* ambr b7.de anac b4.de ang b7a.de* *Ant-c* b7.de* *Ant-t* b7a.de* anthraq ↓ apis b7a.de *Aran* k* arg-met b7.de *Arg-n* ↓ arn k* *Ars* b4.de* ars-i k2 asaf b7.de* asar b7.de asc-c ↓ asc-t k* aur b4.de bamb-a ↓ bapt ↓ bar-c bg2 bell k* borx k* bov b4.de* brom ↓ **Bry** k* bufo *Calad* b7.de calc-act ↓ calc-s ↓ camph b7.de *Cann-s* b7a.de* *Canth* b7.de* caps b7.de* *Carb-an* k* *Carb-v* k* carl ↓ caust ↓ cham k* chel ↓ chin b7.de* cob k* coc-c ↓ colch ↓ *Coloc* b4a.de* *Con* k* cop ↓ corn ↓ crot-t cupr b7.de cupr-ar ↓ cycl b7.de dig b4.de digin ↓ dios dros b7.de* *Dulc* k* eug ↓ euph b4.de* ferr k* *Graph* k* grat k* guaj b4a.de guare k* hell b7.de* hep b4.de* hir skp7• hydr ↓ hydrog srj2• **Ign** bg2 indg k* iod k* ip k* iris ↓ jug-c k* kali-ar kali-bi k* *Kali-c* k* kali-m k2 *Kali-n* b4.de* kali-p fd1.de• kalm k* kola ↓ lach b7a.de laur k* *Lil-t* *Lyc* k* lyss jl2 m-aust b7a.de *Mag-c* k* **Mag-m** b4.de* mang ↓ meny b7.de merc k* merc-c b4a.de* mez b4.de* mosch b7a.de *Mur-ac* k* naja nat-c bg2 nat-m k* *Nit-ac* b4.de* nux-m b7.de nux-v k* olnd b7a.de op ↓ osm k* par b7.de petr k* petr-ra ↓ ph-ac b4.de phel ↓ phos k* phys k* pitu-gl skp7• plan ↓ plat b4.de plb k* *Podo* k* ptel k* puls k* ran-b b7.de *Rheum* k* rhodi ↓ *Rhus-t* k* *Rhus-v* k* ruta fd4.de sars b4.de* sec sel b7a.de senec senn ↓ *Sep* k* sil k* *Spig* b7.de* spong b7.de *Stann* ↓ staph b7.de* stram k* stront-c b4.de* sul-ac k* sul-i ↓ **Sulph** k* *Tab* tarent k* thuj k* tung-met ↓ vanil fd5.de verat b7.de* *Zinc* k*
    - **burning**: asc-t c1 eug k* sul-ac k*
    - **cramping**: acon vh1 *Agar* k* *Aloe* *Am-c* ambr a1 anac k* *Apis* asc-c k* asc-t c1 aur bamb-a stb2.de• bapt *Borx* canth k* caust h2 coc-c k* colch k* con corn crot-t k* cupr-ar cycl k* dig digin a1 dulc k* ferr k* grat k* hep hydr k* iris kali-bi k* kali-c k* *Lil-t* k* *Mag-c* mang h2 *Merc* k* merc-c bg2 *Mur-ac* hr1 *Nux-v* k* op k* petr hr1 petr-ra shn4• phel k* phos plan k* podo k* puls k* *Rheum* rhodi br1 rhus-t k* sec k* senn k* sep k* sul-ac **Sulph** k* tung-met bdx1• zinc k*
    - **cutting** pain: acon k* agar k* **Aloe** alum k* am-c ambr ant-c k* anthraq rly4• *Arn* k* ars k* *Ars-i* *Asar* k* bov bg2 bry bg2 calc-act bg2 calc-s k* *Canth* k* caps caust cham chel cob k* coloc k* dig h2 dulc k* ferr k* iod iris kali-c h2 kali-n k* kalm k* laur mag-m k* merc k* *Merc-c* nit-ac k* plb k* puls bg2 rheum k* rhus-t sars k* sec staph h1 sul-i k2 **Sulph** k* tab bg2 verat
    - **dragging**, bearing down: arg-n *Bell* iod kola stb3• *Lil-t* *Podo* sars k2 *Stann*
    - **drawing** pain: *Arg-n* k* chin h1
    - **pressing** pain: arn ars brom hep nat-m *Zinc* k*
    - **scanty** stool: cina bro1
    - **slimy** stool: cham bro1 samb bro1
    - **sore**: aloe bg2 *Arn* carl *Sulph*
    - **sour** stool: rheum ↓
      - **cramping**: rheum bro1
    - **tearing** pain: aloe cop k*
    - **twisting** pain: ars bg2
    - **watery** stool: cham bro1 polyg-h bro1 samb bro1
- **hard** stool | **after**:
  - **amel.**: ust ↓
    - **cramping**: ust ptk1

- **stool – hard** stool: ...
  - **before**: meny ↓ *Op* ↓
    - **cramping**: meny h1* *Op*
- **normal** stool:
  - **after**: ambr ↓ *Iod* ↓
    - **pressing** pain: ambr k2 *Iod*
- **straining** at:
  - **agg.**: acon *Aloe* apis k2 bell bry podo ruta fd4.de **Sil** ↓
    - **sore**: **Sil**
- **urging** to: *Aloe* ↓ but-ac ↓ chin ↓ inul k2 lept ↓ nat-s ↓ nux-v k2 op ↓ staph ↓
  - **after**: nit-ac h2
  - **amel.**: alum h2
  - **cramping**: *Aloe* bro1 but-ac sp1 chin bro1 inul k2 lept bro1 nat-s bro1 nux-v k2* op bro1 staph tl1
  - **during**: aloe mrr1 apis bar-c h2 dulc h2 elaps hydr mag-m (non:nit-ac kl) *Nux-v* *Plb* ruta fd4.de spong fd4.de staph bro1 vanil fd5.de verb c1
  - **with**: bit-ar ↓ *Calc-p* ↓ *Con* ↓ *Corn* ↓ dig ↓ *Lept* ↓ **Nux-v** ↓ plat ↓ spig ↓ staph ↓ *Sulph* ↓
    - **cutting** pain: *Calc-p* dig *Lept* *Nux-v* staph h1 *Sulph*
    - **dragging**, bearing down: *Con* *Corn* **Nux-v** plat
    - **pressing** pain: bit-ar wht1•
    - **stitching** pain: *Nux-v* spig h1
    - **tearing** pain: *Nux-v*

- **stool**; as after: alum h2
- **stooping**:
  - **agg.**: alet ↓ am-c bov ↓ calc ↓ caps ↓ cocc ↓ dulc ↓ nux-v ↓ sep spong fd4.de stann stront-c sulph verb
    - **burning**: caps h1
    - **cramping**: alet vh1 am-c dulc nux-v *Sulph* k*
    - **stitching** pain: am-c bov k* calc caps h1 cocc k*
  - **amel.**: carc sst• puls ↓
    - **cutting** pain: puls
- **straightening** up, while sitting: ph-ac ↓
  - **stitching** pain: ph-ac h2
- **stretched**; as if: cann-s b7.de croc b7.de ign b7.de nat-c b4.de phos b4.de
- **stretching**:
  - **agg.**: aloe ↓
    - **cutting** pain: aloe
  - **amel.**: dios mez plb k*
  - **with**: *Cham* mrr1
- **stretching** out: bit-ar wht1• mag-s rhus-t
- **sudden**: bamb-a ↓ sabal ↓
  - **cramping**: bamb-a stb2.de• sabal c1
- **sugar** agg.: ign ox-ac *Sulph*
  - **cramping**: ox-ac k2
- **supper**:
  - **after**:
    - **agg.**: alum bry calc *Chin* k* coff coloc ↓ ferr gels grat ↓ kali-n ol-an ↓ ox-ac ↓ *Puls* sacch-a fd2.de• sep ↓ vanil fd5.de zinc
      - **cramping**: alum calc coff k* gels k* grat k* ol-an k* *Zinc*
      - **cutting** pain: calc h2 coloc k* ox-ac *Puls* sep h2 vanil fd5.de
      - **drawing** pain: kali-n k*
    - **amel.**: *Sep* ↓
      - **dragging**, bearing down: *Sep*
- **surgery**; after: staph mrr1
- **swallowing** agg.: calc-p mrr1
- **sweets**: fil ↓
  - **cramping**: fil bro1
- **swollen**; as if: stram h1
- **tabes** mesenterica; in: santin ↓ thiosin ↓
  - **stitching** pain: santin br1 thiosin br1
- **talking** agg.: bell k2 brom rumx k2
- **tea** agg.: hyper ↓
  - **cramping**: hyper k*

Abdomen

- **tearing** pain: all-c k2 aloe alum k* alum-sil k2 alumn k2 *Am-c* k* am-m k2 anan ant-t k* apis b7a.de arn b7.de* **Ars** k* aur b4.de* bamb-a stb2.de• bar-c k* bar-s k2 bell b4a.de benz-ac k* berb k* bov b4.de* *Bry* k* bufo *Cact* calc k* calc-sil k2 canth k* carb-an k* carb-v b4.de* carbn-s caust b4.de* **Cham** k* chel k2 chin k* chinin-s k* cic k* cocc k* *Colch* k* **Coloc** k* con b4.de* *Cop* k* crot-t k* cupr k* cupr-ar *Cycl* k* *Dig* k* dulc k* *Graph* hedy a1* hell b7.de* ign b7.de* iod b4.de* *Ip* b7.de* kali-bi bg2 *Kali-c* k* kali-i k* kali-n k* kali-s fd4.de kali-sil k2 kola stb3• *Lach* k* laur b7.de* *Lyc* k* lyss m-ambo b7.de m-aust b7.de mag-c b4.de* *Mag-m* k* med *Merc* k* merc-c b4a.de *Mez* k* naja nat-m k* nat-s bg2 nit-ac b4a.de nux-m k* *Nux-v* k* op pall sne *Phos* k* plat b4a.de plb k* *Puls* k* *Rhus-t* k* ruta b7.de* samb b7.de* sec k* *Sep* b4a.de sil k* spig b7.de* squil k* stram k* sulph k* tab k* tarent k* teucr b7.de* thuj b4.de* verat b7.de* verb k* *Zinc* k* zinc-p k2
  - **accompanied** by | **flatulence**: bamb-a stb2.de•
  - **cramping**: samb h1
  - **downward**: kali-i verb
  - **outward**: sep h2
  - **upward**: *Chinin-s* mag-m h2
- **teeth** and with trembling; with chattering of: bov↓ meph↓
  - **cramping**: bov ptk1 meph ptk1
- **tenesmus** (See RECTUM - Pain - tenesmus)
- **thinking** of it agg.: ox-ac k2
- **thrusts** through abdomen; sharp: arn br1
- **tobacco**; after: asc-t vh borx brom bg1 ign spig vh
  - **amel.**: coloc
- **torn** apart; as if: *Alum* b4a.de *Ars* b4a.de caust bg2 dig b4.de* nux-v bg2 *Sulph* b4a.de
- **torn** asunder; as if (See torn apart)
- **torn** out or loose; as if: bell bg2 *Coloc* b4.de* laur b7.de* mag-c bg2 nat-m bg1* nux-v b7.de* plb b7.de* rhus-t b7a.de* ruta b7.de* sep b4.de* *Sulph* b4a.de verb b7.de*
- **tossing** about; with: *Cham* bro1 mag-p bro1
- **touch**:
  - **agg.**: aids↓ aloe sne ars k2 *Bell* mrr1 bry↓ carb-an h2 *Cham* mrr1 cund sne cupr h2 dream-p sdj1• ferr↓ kali-c h2* *Lach* sne lyc↓ mag-m h2 mim-p↓ nat-c h2 nit-ac↓ nux-v↓ petr a1 phos k2 puls k2 ribo rly4• stann h2 sulph h2 trom vml3•
    - **cramping**: bry bro1 nux-v mrr1
    - **pressing** pain: cupr h2 lyc h2
      - **hard**; as from something: *Cupr* h2
    - **sore**: aids nl2• dream-p sdj1• ferr c1 mim-p rsj8• phos h2 stann h2 sulph h2
    - **stitching** pain: nit-ac h2
  - **cold** things agg.; touching: merc
  - **side** agg.; of: stram h1
- **turning**:
  - **amel.**: euph↓ mag-c↓
    - **cramping**: euph h2 mag-c h2
  - **body** | **agg.**: ambr dros h1 tritic-vg fd5.de
- **twinging**: *Bov* k* *Carb-an* castm crot-t k* ger-i rly4• grat k* mag-c *Mag-m* merl mur-ac nat-c h2 nit-ac h2 ruta fd4.de sil spong fd4.de sul-ac tritic-vg fd5.de vanil fd5.de zinc h2
- **twisting** pain: *Agar* k* alum b4.de* anac k* anan ant-t k* ars k* asaf b7.de* aur k* bell bg2 bov k* **Bry** b7.de* cact calad k* calc k* calc-sil k2 *Caps* k* caust k* *Cham* b7a.de chin bg2 chinin-s **Cina** b7.de* *Coloc* bg2 *Con* b4.de* cupr bg2 dig k* *Dios* k* dream-p sdj1• dros k* dulc b4.de* elaps k* eup-pur k* eupi k* falco-pe nl2• grat k* hura ign b7a.de* kali-bi bg2 lyc k* mag-s k* merc k* *Mez* k* nat-c b4.de* nit-ac bg2 nux-m b7.de* *Nux-v* b7a.de olnd b7.de* pall *Plat* k* plb k* prun k* psor bg2 ran-b b7a.de *Ran-s* b7a.de rhus-t k* ruta b7.de* **Sabad** b7.de* sabin b7.de* sang a1 sars bg2 sep h2* sil k* spong b7.de* *Staph* k* stram k* sul-ac k* sumb k* valer b7.de* **Verat** k*
  - **intestines** are twisted; as if:
    - **accompanied** by | **diarrhea** (See RECTUM - Diarrhea - accompanied - intestines - twisted)
- **twitching**: agar b4.de* *Am-m* b7a.de anac b4.de* ars b4a.de* aur b4.de* canth b7.de* caust b4.de* chin b7.de* coff b7.de* con b4.de* dig b4.de* fl-ac bg2 graph b4.de* guaj b4a.de ign b7.de* kali-c b4.de* m-aust b7.de manc bg2 meny b7.de* mez b4.de* nat-c b4.de* olnd b7.de* phos b4.de* psor bg2 ran-b b7.de* rhus-t b7.de* *Sul-ac* b4a.de
- **ulcerative** pain: *Alum* b4a.de arg-n bg2 *Bell* bg2* bov b4.de* cann-s b7.de* carb-an b4a.de* *Carb-v* ptk1 cham bg2 chin b7.de* *Cocc* b7.de* coloc bg2* con b4a.de* *Cupr* b7.de* dig b4.de* ferr bg2 hell b7.de* hep c1 kali-bi bg2 kreos b7a.de* lyc ptk1 mag-c b4.de* mang b4.de* merc b4.de* nat-m bg2 *Nit-ac* b4.de* *Phos* b4a.de* *Puls* b7a.de *Ran-b* b7a.de* rhus-t b7.de* sabad b7.de* sec bg2 sep b4.de* stann b4.de* sulph bg2 valer b7a.de*
- **uncovering**:
  - **agg.**: *Bry* nux-v a1* rheum a1*
    - **cramping**: nux-v bro1 rheum bro1
  - **extremities**:
    - **agg.**: rheum↓
      - **cramping**: rheum bro1
- **urination**:
  - **after**:
    - **agg.**: ars k* chel b7.de* chin k* clem dulc fd4.de eup-per↓ mag-c k* nat-sil fd3.de• *Nux-v* b7a.de ph-ac *Phos* b4a.de spong fd4.de stann↓ staph b7.de* sul-ac b4.de*
      - **cramping**: eup-per bg2
      - **cutting** pain: chin k* stann staph h1
      - **pressing** pain: chin k* ph-ac
  - **amel.**: androc srj1• carb-an dendr-pol sk4• merc bg1
  - **before**: *Arn*↓ cham↓ *Coloc*↓ dendr-pol sk4• *Lyc*↓ mag-c↓ plb↓ *Puls* sul-ac sulph↓
    - **cutting** pain: *Arn* b7a.de cham b7.de* *Coloc* b4a.de *Lyc* b4a.de mag-c plb b7.de* *Puls* b7.de* sul-ac k* sulph k*
  - **close** of; pressing toward genitals at the: ph-ac↓
    - **pressing** pain: ph-ac
  - **during**:
    - **agg.**: bar-c bry k* *Cham* chin k* clem↓ eupi↓ *Ip*↓ irid-met↓ kali-p fd1.de• lach↓ lyc↓ mag-c↓ **Mag-m**↓ *Merc* nat-m nit-ac↓ pall↓ ph-ac↓ plb k* *Rhus-t* b7a.de spig↓ sul-ac↓ til bg1 vanil fd5.de
      - **burning**: lach bg2
      - **cramping**: bar-c *Cham* irid-met srj5• *Merc* pall c1 sul-ac
      - **cutting** pain: chin k* eupi *Ip* b7a.de lyc b4a.de* mag-c merc k* ph-ac b4a.de til bg1
      - **dragging**, bearing down: **Mag-m** bg2
      - **drawing** pain: clem bg2
      - **lancinating**: clem
      - **pinching** pain: bar-c b4.de* spig b7.de* sul-ac b4.de*
      - **pressing** pain: chin k* nat-m k*
      - **stitching** pain: clem k* nit-ac k* ph-ac b4a.de vanil fd5.de
    - **amel.**: tarent↓
      - **cramping**: tarent
  - **impossible**: *Cham*
  - **retention** of urine; from: arn ptk1 graph ptk1
  - **urging** to urinate:
    - **with**: *Clem*↓ nux-v↓ *Pall*↓
      - **dragging**, bearing down: *Clem* hr1 nux-v *Pall*
- **veal**; after: kali-n c1
- **vegetables** agg.: cupr↓
  - **cramping**: cupr h2
- **vexation**; after: **Coloc** scroph-n↓ spong fd4.de *Staph*
  - **cramping**: **Coloc** scroph-n c1 *Staph*
- **vinegar** agg.: aloe↓
  - **cutting** pain: aloe k*
- **violent**: aloe *Ant-c* vh1 ant-t k* *Apis* *Ars* k* bell k* cact canth castm cham k* *Colch* k* *Coloc* k* *Cupr* k* cycl dig euph *Kali-ar* kali-br a1 kali-c kali-n k* *Mag-c* merc-c *Nux-v* petr a1 *Phos* **Plb** k* sang a1 sil **Sul-ac**
- **vomiting**: dys fmm1•
  - **after**: *Ant-t* lach
    - **amel.**: dig h2 nat-c h2 spong fd4.de
  - **before**: aeth↓

- **before**: ...
  - **cramping**: aeth br1
  - **food**; of: manc ↓
    - **cramping**: manc ptk1
- **during**: podo k2
- **with**: *Bell* ↓ bism ↓ cadm-s br1 cic ↓ coloc ↓ *Cupr* ↓ *Cupr-ar* ↓ hyos ↓ op ↓ pix ↓ plb ↓ plb-act ↓ ruta fd4.de sarr ↓ *Verat* ↓
  - **cramping**: *Bell* bro1 bism bro1 cadm-s bro1 cic tl1 coloc tl1 *Cupr* bro1 *Cupr-ar* bro1 hyos bro1* op bro1 pix bro1 plb bro1 plb-act bro1 sarr bro1 *Verat* bro1

- **waking**; on: aeth k* agar ↓ alum k* ambr b7.de* arge-pl ↓ arn b7.de* ars b4.de* bar-c k* calc b4.de* coc-c k* colch colocin ↓ cyclosp sa3• euphr ↓ ferr k* flor-p rsj3• ign b7.de* kali-c b4.de* laur b7.de* lyc k* m-arct b7.de mag-c b4a.de mag-m b4.de* mang b4.de* merc-c b4a.de merc-i-f k* mez morph k* nat-ar nat-c k* nat-m k* nit-ac b4.de* phos b4.de* pic-ac k* podo ↓ ptel k* pyrid rly4• rhus-t b7.de* ribo rly4• sars b4.de* sep b4.de* sil h2 sol-t-ae k* stann k* stront-c sulph b4.de* suprar ↓ tell rsj10• vanil fd5.de xan ↓ zinc k*
  - **cramping**: alum k* arge-pl rwt5• coc-c k* colch colocin a1 euphr ferr k* lyc k* mez nat-m stann k* *Stront-c* suprar rly4• xan *Zinc*
  - **stitching** pain: agar nat-m k* podo k*

- **walking**:
  - **after**:
    - **agg.**: grat ↓
      - **pressing** pain: grat
  - **agg.**: *All-s* ↓ alum k* alum-p k2 alum-sil k2 alumn ang ↓ arg-n ↓ ars-s-f k2 asaf astac ↓ atra-r bnm3• bar-c k* *Bell* brucel sa3• bry cadm-s c1 calc ↓ caps ↓ *Carb-ac* ↓ carb-an h2 caust ↓ cham ↓ chin k* *Coloc* k* con crot-t k* cupr ↓ *Dios* ↓ ferr ferr-p gent-c graph grat hep h2 hyos kali-bi ↓ kali-c ↓ kali-i ↓ kali-s ↓ kola stb3• lac-c lach laur ↓ lob k* lyc melal-alt ↓ *Merc* mez ↓ mur-ac ↓ naja ↓ nat-c k* *Nat-m* nat-p ↓ *Nux-v* olnd ↓ *Ph-ac* phos phyt k* prun ptel k* puls k* *Ran-b* k* rhus-t ↓ sel ↓ *Sep* bg1 *Sil* squil stann stront-c sk4• *Sulph* k* symph ↓ tarent k* *Thuj* **Tril-p** ↓ tritic-vg fd5.de vanil fd5.de verat zinc zinc-p k2
    - **burning**: caps h1 carb-an caust h2 kola stb3• sulph
    - **cramping**: *All-s* vh1 alumn c1 ang h1 astac kr1* bell chin *Coloc* cupr gent-c graph h2 kali-bi melal-alt gya4 mur-ac h2 nat-p ph-ac phos h2 prun *Ran-b* stann h2 *Zinc*
    - **cutting** pain: asaf k* coloc *Dios* k* kali-c h2 laur lyc mur-ac k* naja ph-ac k* phos rhus-t a1
    - **dragging**, bearing down: calc *Chin* *Con* kali-i *Nux-v* puls k2 rhus-t **Sep** **Tril-p**
    - **drawing** pain: con k* squil k* tritic-vg fd5.de vanil fd5.de
    - **eating**; after: zinc ↓
      - **stitching** pain: zinc
    - **pressing** pain: bar-c chin h1 cupr h2 mez h2 ph-ac h2 zinc h2
    - **sore**: *Bell* *Carb-ac* k* coloc *Ferr* hep kali-s phos phyt k* puls ran-b k* sulph
    - **stitching** pain: arg-n caps h1 cham mur-ac olnd ran-b sel symph fd3.de• thuj vanil fd5.de zinc
  - **air** agg.; in open: agar bg2 am-c bg2 ang b7.de* bry b7.de* calc bg2 graph bg2 ign b7.de* jatr-c ↓ m-arct b7.de nux-v b7.de* ph-ac ↓ rhus-t b7.de* sep ↓ sil bg2 staph b7.de* sulph bg2
    - **burning**: agar sep
    - **cramping**: agar am-c bry jatr-c kr1* ph-ac h2 rhus-t sil sulph
    - **cutting** pain: graph
  - **amel.**: all-c ↓ chin k* coloc *Con* cub ↓ *Cycl* dig ↓ dios k* elaps pd fago k* ferr germ-met srj5• lap-la sde8.de• mag-c mag-p ↓ nat-m ↓ op ↓ par ↓ phos ↓ *Puls* *Rhus-t* ↓ *Sep* ↓ spong fd4.de sulph verat ↓
    - **contracting**: nat-m h2
    - **cramping**: all-c bro1 chin h1 cub c1 *Cycl* k* dig dios bro1 elaps ferr mag-p bro1 par puls k* *Rhus-t* bro1 *Sulph* verat bro1
    - **dragging**, bearing down: *Sep*
    - **drawing** pain: phos
    - **pressing** pain: chin h1
  - **bent** | **must** walk bent: aloe bro1 calc h2 *Caust* sne cimic sne *Coloc* k* *Nit-ac* nux-v bro1 *Rhus-t* k* sulph h2
  - **hindering** walking: am-c ↓
    - **stitching** pain: am-c h2
  - **must** walk: mag-p k2

- **walking**: ...
  - **rapidly** | **agg.**: borx h2 *Chin* vanil fd5.de
  - **stone** pavement agg.; on a: con ↓
    - **sore**: con h2*
- **wandering** pain: acon *Aesc* k* alum am-m arn k* ars h2 arund k* bar-c h2 *Bell* bg2 bism hr1 cain calc-s k* cimic k* colch cop dios bg2 dulc k* fl-ac k* ign bg2 irid-met srj5• iris jug-r vml3• kola stb3• *Manc* mur-ac nat-s phyt k* plb k* podo k* *Puls* k* sang staph sne stront-c bg2 symph fd3.de•
  - **shifts** suddenly to distant parts: **Dios** k*
- **warm**:
  - **applications**:
    - **amel.**: cham ↓ mag-p ↓ nux-v ↓
      - **cramping**: cham tl1 mag-p tl1* nux-v mrr1
  - **bathing**:
    - **amel.**: germ-met ↓
      - **cramping**: *(↗warmth - amel. - cramping)* germ-met srj5•
  - **bed**:
    - **amel.**: *Ars* ↓ coloc ↓ staph ↓ symph ↓
      - **cutting** pain: *Ars* coloc staph symph
  - **drinks**:
    - **agg.**: elaps ↓
      - **pressing** pain: elaps
    - **amel.**: *(↗milk - amel. - cramping)* acon carc mg1.de* *Chel* k* crot-t fr kali-c k2 kola stb3• *Mag-p* nux-v ↓ *Spong*
      - **burning**: kola stb3•
      - **constricting** pain: carc sp1
      - **cramping**: *(↗milk - amel. - cramping)* mag-p mrr1 nux-v mrr1
  - **food**:
    - **agg.**: kali-c ol-an
    - **amel.**: acon bro1 mag-c *Ph-ac*
  - **milk**:
    - **agg.**: *Ang* ↓
      - **cutting** pain: *Ang*
      - **stitching** pain: *Ang*
    - **amel.**: ars mrr1 *Chel* k* *Crot-t* k* graph mrr1 op
      - **cramping**: *(↗drinks - amel.; drinks - amel. - cramping)* *Crot-t* k* op k*
      - **hot** milk: *Crot-t* ↓
        - **cramping**: *Crot-t* k*
  - **room**:
    - **amel.**: am-c sul-ac
      - **cramping**: am-c
  - **soup** | **amel.**: acon *Ph-ac*
  - **wraps** amel.: sulph ↓
    - **cutting** pain: sulph h2
- **warmth**:
  - **amel.**: *Aeth* k* alum alum-p k2 alum-sil k2 am-c **Ars** ars-i ars-s-f k2 aur-ar k2 *Bar-c* bry k2 canth *Carb-v* castm caust **Cham** chel mrr1 *Coloc* k* cupr cupr-s ↓ *Ferr* hr1 ferr-ar gink-b sbd1• hydr sne irid-met srj5• kali-ar kali-c k2 kali-sil k2 kola stb3• kreos sne **Mag-p** k* mang meph nat-c h2 **Nux-m** **Nux-v** pall phos h2 plb k* *Podo* k* *Puls* **Rhus-t** *Sabin* *Sep* **Sil** k* *Staph* sne stront-c tritic-vg fd5.de
    - **cramping**: *(↗warm - bathing - amel. - cramping)* alum am-c ars bro1 cham tl1 coloc bro1 cupr-s gink-b sbd1• mag-p k2* nux-v mrr1 podo bro1 puls bro1 sil hr1*
    - **dragging**, bearing down: nat-c h2
    - **drawing** pain: **Mag-p** tritic-vg fd5.de
    - **heat** amel.: alum ↓ chir-fl gya2 *Sulph* ↓
      - **cutting** pain: *Sulph*
      - **tearing** pain: alum k*
    - **sore**: nat-c h2
    - **tearing** pain: alum h2
  - **wet** warmth | **amel.**: aeth c1 *Nux-m*
- **wavelike**: mez h2 spong fd4.de vanil fd5.de
- **weakness** of legs, with: lat-m ↓
  - **cramping**: lat-m br1

Abdomen

- **weather**:
  - · **wet**:
    - : **agg.**: ars *Dulc* **Mang** *Nat-s*
      - : **cramping**: dulc tl1 mang k2
- **weather**; as from cold wet: mez h2
- **wet**, getting feet: *All-c*↓ cham↓ dol↓ dulc↓ meli↓
  - · **cramping**: *All-c* k* cham bro1 dol br1* dulc bro1 meli sne
- **wine** agg.: lyc
  - · **cramping**: lyc k*
- **worms**; from: art-v↓ bism↓ *Cina*↓ fil↓ gran↓ *Indg*↓ merc↓ nat-p br1 sabad↓ spig↓
  - · **cramping**: art-v bro1 bism bro1 *Cina* bro1 fil bro1 gran bro1 *Indg* bro1 merc bro1 nat-p bro1 sabad bro1 spig bro1
- **wound** up into a ball; as if: anac b4.de* ars b4.de* calc b4.de* cham bg2 dig b4.de* *Merc* b4a.de *Thuj* b4a.de
- **wrenched**; as if: kola stb3•
- **yawning** agg.: ruta↓ spira↓ zinc↓
  - · **cramping**: spira bro1 zinc k*
  - · **sore**: ruta h1

▽ - **extending** to:
  - · **right**: fl-ac↓
    - : **stitching** pain: fl-ac
  - · **behind** forward, from: verat h1

○ · **Across**: *Aloe* alum am-c arg-met *Arn* canth carb-v caust cham **Chel** k* chin colch cupr↓ cupr-act euphr guaj hir↓ ip kalm phos phys prun sep spong fd4.de stann staph symph fd3.de• tritic-vg fd5.de zinc
    - : **drawing** pain: hir rsj4•
    - : **stitching** pain: cupr
    - : **Ilium** to ilium; from: asar cimic hydrog srj2• lil-t
  - · **All** parts of body: **Plb**
  - · **Ankles**: kali-n h2
  - · **Anus**: aloe *Coloc* **Crot-t** hydr *Ip* kali-bi gk led mag-m merc bg1 *Nat-m* *Nux-v* ox-ac rhus-t sang *Sulph*
    - : **cutting** pain: *Coloc* nux-v k2
    - : **pressing** pain: crot-t *Sulph*
    - : **stitching** pain: rhus-t sulph
  - · **Anus**; toward: con↓ crot-t↓ lyc↓ mag-m↓ *Sulph*↓
    - : **dragging**, bearing down: con h2 crot-t lyc h2 mag-m a1 *Sulph*
  - · **Arms**: con↓ dios br1
    - : **drawing** pain: con h2
  - · **Around**; all way: acon↓
    - : **cutting** pain: acon b7.de*
  - · **Axilla**: com
  - · **Back**: acon bg2 aesc bg2 alum bg2 bell bg2 cact bg2 calc k* camph bg2 cann-xyz bg2 canth carb-v bg2 caust k* chel bg2* chin bg2 coc-c k* cocc colch bg2 dios br1 elat bg2 germ-met↓ graph bg2 ign bg2 iod bg2 jatr-c bg2 kali-bi k* kali-n bg2 kola stb3• kreos bg2 mag-p bg2 merc-c bg2 nat-s bg1* nux-m bg2 phos bg2 plb bg2 pycnop-sa↓ sep bg2* sil bg2 spong fd4.de sul-ac k2 teucr bg2 tritic-vg fd5.de
    - : **cramping**: germ-met srj5•
    - : **menses** | **before** | **agg.**: *Am-c* bro1 am-m bro1 asar bro1 bell bro1 *Borx* bro1 calc bro1 *Calc-p* bro1 caust bro1 *Cham* bro1 cic bro1 *Cimic* bro1 cupr bro1 cycl bro1 *Gels* bro1 graph bro1 *Helon* bro1 *Kali-c* bro1 kreos bro1 mag-m bro1 nit-ac bro1 *Nux-v* bro1 phos bro1 plat bro1 podo bro1 *Puls* bro1 rad-br bro1 sabin bro1 *Senec* bro1 *Sep* bro1 spong bro1 vib bro1 *Xan* bro1
      - : **during** | **agg.**: *Am-c* bro1 am-m bro1 asar bro1 bell bro1 *Borx* bro1 calc bro1 *Calc-p* bro1 caust bro1 *Cham* bro1 cic bro1 *Cimic* bro1 cupr bro1 cycl bro1 *Gels* bro1 graph bro1 *Helon* bro1 *Kali-c* bro1 kreos bro1 mag-m bro1 nit-ac bro1 *Nux-v* bro1 phos bro1 plat bro1 podo bro1 *Puls* bro1 rad-br bro1 sabin bro1 *Senec* bro1 *Sep* bro1 spong bro1 vib bro1 *Xan* bro1
    - : **stitching** pain: calc canth coc-c cocc kali-bi pycnop-sa mrz1
    - : **tearing** pain: chel k2 kola stb3•
  - · **Back** and sacrum: calc↓
    - : **contracting**: calc h2
  - · **Bladder**: brom carb-v cham cic plb

- **extending** to – **Bladder**: ...
    - : **stitching** pain: brom cic
  - · **Body**; into:
    - : **stepping**:
      - : **every** step; at: mur-ac↓
        - . **stitching** pain: mur-ac
  - · **Calves**: lyc↓
    - : **drawing** pain: lyc h2
  - · **Chest**: *Acon* alum bg1 calc-p↓ *Caps*↓ caust cham chel clem↓ colch rsj2• coloc bg1 con cupr dios bg1* ign kali-c bg1* *Lach* lat-m bnm6• mang mill↓ nat-c h2 nat-m↓ nat-p nat-s bg1 *Nux-v* phos↓ plb positr↓ sep bg1 spig spong tarent thiam rly4• tritic-vg fd5.de
    - : **left**: kali-n↓
      - : **cramping**: kali-n h2
    - : **burning**: calc-p k2 mill k2
    - : **cutting** pain: phos
    - : **menses** | **before** | **agg.**: caul bro1 cham bro1 cimic bro1 *Cupr* bro1
      - : **during** | **agg.**: caul bro1 cham bro1 chinin-s cimic bro1 cupr k* mang
    - : **pressing** pain: *Caps* hr1 nat-m h2
    - : **stitching** pain: *Alum* b4a.de *Cham* clem *Con* ign kali-c bg1 positr nl2•
    - : **stool** agg.; during: **Acon**
  - · **Clavicle**: laur
  - · **Clavicle**, right: laur↓
    - : **stitching** pain: laur
  - · **Distant** parts: *Dios* plb gk
  - · **Downward**: agath-a nl2• aloe alumn am-c bg1 bamb-a stb2.de• bar-c brom calc-p bg2 chel k2 chin coloc sne crot-h **Crot-t** k* elaps ferr-i guaj iod bg2 **Ip** kali-c kali-i nat-m bg2 nux-v phos bg2 plat plb puls k* ran-s ruta bg2 samb sep k* til verb zinc-s bg1 zing
    - : **menses**; at beginning of (See menses - during - beginning - agg. - extending - downward)
  - · **Esophagus**: plb
  - · **Feet**: caul mrr1 plb psil ft1
  - · **Fingers**: dios br1
  - · **Front** to back: cupr↓
    - : **cutting** pain: cupr k2
  - · **Genitals**: alumn calc crot-t dig graph↓ *Lyc* nat-s↓ nux-m k2 plb **Puls** rhus-t *Sep* tep teucr verat zinc bg1
    - : **cramping**: nat-s bg2
    - : **cutting** pain: lyc bg1
    - : **dragging**, bearing down: graph h2
    - : **pressing** pain: graph h2 tep
    - : **tearing** pain: calc
  - · **Groin**: plb mrr1
    - : **menses** | **before** | **agg.**: borx bro1 *Caul* bro1 kali-c bro1 lil-t bro1 plat bro1 tanac bro1 *Ust* bro1
      - : **during** | **agg.**: borx bro1 *Caul* bro1 kali-c bro1 lil-t bro1 plat bro1 tanac bro1 *Ust* bro1
  - · **Groins**: am-m↓ calc↓ cham↓ *Graph*↓ sulph↓
    - : **cutting** pain: am-m
    - : **pressing** pain: calc bg2 cham bg2 *Graph* bg2 sulph bg2
  - · **Head**: ars mang
  - · **Hips**: kali-c lyc sul-ac k2
  - · **Hypochondria**: stann h2
  - · **Hypochondriac** region: coc-c↓
    - : **stitching** pain: coc-c
  - · **Hypogastrium**: con↓
    - : **drawing** pain: con h2
  - · **Inguinal** region: arg-n bar-c borx↓ kali-i plat↓ tarent thuj tung-met bdx1•
    - : **drawing** pain: borx a1 plat h2
  - · **Kidney**: nux-m *Plb*
  - · **Knee**: germ-met↓
    - : **cramping**: germ-met srj5•
  - · **Leg**: **Carb-v** k* lat-m bnm6• **Lil-t**↓ lyc hr1 ter k* thuj k*

- **Leg**: ...
  - **burning**: **Lil-t**
- **Liver**:
  - **menses** | **before** | **agg.**: ph-ac bro1
    - **during** | **agg.**: ph-ac bro1
- **Loins** (See lumbar)
- **Lower** limbs: androc srj1• bar-c **Carb-v** kali-i nux-m k2 nux-v k2 *Plb* k* sang *Sep* ter↓
  - **left**: **Carb-v**
  - **menses** | **before** | **agg.**: *Am-m* bro1 berb bro1 bry bro1 castm bro1 *Caul* bro1 cham bro1 *Cimic* bro1 coff bro1 coloc bro1 con bro1 *Gels* bro1 graph bro1 lil-t bro1 mag-c bro1 mag-m bro1 nit-ac bro1 plat bro1 *Sep* bro1 tril-p bro1 *Vib* bro1 xan bro1
    - **during** | **agg.**: *Am-m* bro1 berb bro1 bry bro1 castm bro1 *Caul* bro1 cham bro1 *Cimic* bro1 coff bro1 coloc bro1 con bro1 *Gels* bro1 graph bro1 lil-t bro1 mag-c bro1 mag-m bro1 nit-ac bro1 plat bro1 *Sep* bro1 tril-p bro1 *Vib* bro1 xan bro1
  - **stitching** pain: sang ter
- **Lumbar** region: *Aesc* agar alum↓ carb-v chel *Coloc* croc fago *Gels* k* guaj↓ iod kali-bi kali-i kali-n↓ laur lyc mag-m bg1 naja nat-m↓ plb ptel sil
  - **burning**: kali-n h2
  - **cramping**: alum h2 guaj h2 kali-n h2 nat-m h2
  - **cutting** pain: mag-m h2*
  - **dragging**, bearing down: mag-m h2
  - **stitching** pain: kali-n h2
  - **tearing** pain: kali-i
- **Mamma**; right: coloc ferr-m
  - **tearing** pain: coloc
- **Ovaries**: sabal c1
  - **right**: podo c1
- **Pelvis**: alumn↓ carb-v bg1 *Cimic*↓ coloc bg1 puls↓ til↓ tritic-vg fd5.de
  - **cramping**: cimic mrr1
  - **stitching** pain: alumn *Cimic* mrr1 puls til c1
  - **Across**:
    - **menses** | **before** | **agg.**: bell bro1
      - **during** | **agg.**: bell bro1
- **Penis**: alumn clem a1 lyc bg1 puls
  - **stitching** pain: alumn
- **Perineum**: phos
  - **stitching** pain: phos
- **Pit** of stomach: nux-m↓
  - **pressing** pain: nux-m
- **Pubic** region: arg-met c1 **Coloc** *Sep*
  - **cough** agg.; during: *Sep*
  - **cramping**: coloc mrr1
  - **menses** | **before** | **agg.**: aln bro1 bov bro1 coloc bro1 cycl bro1 rad-br bro1 *Sabin* bro1 sep bro1 vib bro1
    - **during** | **agg.**: aln bro1 bov bro1 coloc bro1 cycl bro1 rad-br bro1 *Sabin* bro1 sep bro1 vib bro1
- **Rectum**: *Aloe* *Ap-g* vh1 ars bg1 brom crot-t mrr1 dios bg1 eupi guaj bg1 ign bg1 lyc bg1 mag-m meny bg1 nat-m *Nux-v* pot-e rly4• sang spong bg1 tarax bg1
  - **dragging**, bearing down: lyc bg1
  - **menses** | **before** | **agg.**: *Aloe* bro1 xero bro1
    - **during** | **agg.**: *Aloe* bro1 xero bro1
  - **pressing** pain: mag-m nat-m
  - **stitching** pain: brom
- **Ribs**; lower: kola stb3•
  - **stitching** pain: kola stb3•
- **Sacral** region: sec a1
- **Sacrum**: am-m↓ con↓ phos↓
  - **cutting** pain: am-m h2
  - **dragging**, bearing down: con h2
  - **pressing** pain: phos h2
- **Scapulae** | **right**: chel k2*

- **extending** to: ...
  - **Scrotum**: verat
  - **Shoulder**: lach
    - **right**: kali-c k2
  - **Shoulders**: lach↓
    - **stitching** pain: lach
  - **Sides**, to: ars coca *Ip* *Lach* *Lyc* sec a1 spong fd4.de stann h2 tarent
    - **right**: *Ip* *Lach*
    - **left**: anth c1 ars coca *Lyc*
  - **Spermatic** cord: brom verat
    - **cough** agg.; during: verat
      - **stitching** pain: verat
    - **Along**: brom↓
      - **stitching** pain: brom
  - **Spermatic** cords: **Puls**↓
    - **dragging**, bearing down: **Puls**
  - **Spine**: iod lept br1 lyc sil
  - **Stomach**: brucel sa3• *Carb-v* crot-t hep↓ kali-n↓ lyc melal-alt gya4 nux-m ol-an podo k2 stann h2 sulph *Valer*↓ vanil fd5.de
    - **cramping**: kali-n h2
    - **pressing** pain: hep h2 *Valer* b7a.de
  - **Testes**: dig plb positr nl2• **Puls** sec sil teucr
    - **evening** | **eating**; while: sil
    - **cough** agg.; during: sec
    - **dragging**, bearing down: dig h2
  - **Testis**:
    - **cough** agg.; during: sec↓
      - **stitching** pain: sec
  - **Thigh**: *Aloe* alum bg1 apis bg1 bar-c bry bg1 cact bg1 calc bg1 caul mrr1 cham k* cimic bg1 cob bg1 coloc con kali-i kali-s fd4.de lil-t bg1 nat-m nux-m bg1 nux-v plb bg1 podo bg1 sabal bg3 *Sep* spig bg1 staph bg1 stram ter thuj bg1 ust vanil fd5.de verat hr1 vib bg1* xan bg1*
  - **Thighs**: *Cimic*↓ *Coloc*↓ germ-met↓ nit-ac↓ nux-v↓ sabin↓ sul-ac↓ ter↓ vib↓
    - **cramping**: cimic mrr1 germ-met srj5•
    - **cutting** pain: *Coloc* ter
    - **dragging**, bearing down: nit-ac nux-v sabin k2 vib
    - **drawing** pain: sul-ac h2
    - **stitching** pain: *Cimic* mrr1
  - **Throat**: caust kali-bi kali-c↓ kreos merc
    - **pressing** pain: caust kali-c h2
  - **Toe**; first left: ros-d↓
    - **stitching** pain: ros-d wla1
  - **Toes**: dios br1
  - **Transversely**: arn calc↓ cham↓ **Chel** choc srj3• cina colch↓ ip phos↓ sep↓
    - **stitching** pain: *Arn* calc h2 cham colch ip phos sep
  - **Umbilicus**: crot-c
    - **pressing** pain: crot-c
  - **Upward**: aloe anac ars canth chel com ferr-m *Gels* kola stb3• lach bg1 merc naja plb ruta sep h2 spong sulph
  - **Urethra**: glycyr-g cte1• zinc↓
    - **drawing** pain: zinc h2
    - **Forward**: zinc bg1
  - **Uterus**: elaps *Ip*
  - **Vagina**: *Ars* berb calc-p *Kreos* nit-ac
    - **stitching** pain: *Ars* *Kreos*

○ - **Across** abdomen: cham↓
  - **cramping**: cham bg2
- **Anterior** part: ip tl1 pert-vc vk9
- **Appendix**: diph-t-tpt jl2 eberth jl2 morb jl2 oscilloc jl2 streptoc jl2
  - **night**:
    - **midnight**:
      - **before**:
        - **22-23 h**: brucel↓

Abdomen

- **night – midnight – before – 22**-23 h: ... **pulsating** pain: brucel sa3•
- **touch** agg.: glycyr-g ↓
  - ⁝ **sore**: glycyr-g cte1•
- Back and chest, to: *Caust* ↓
  - **radiating**: *Caust*
- **Body**; to all parts of: **Plb** ↓ pyrog ↓
  - **radiating**: **Plb** k* pyrog tl1
- **Colon**: *Bell* ↓ cham ↓ colch ↓ enteroc jl2 gels ↓ merc-c ↓ moni jl2 raph ↓
  - **right**: enteroc jl2
  - **left**: enteroc jl2
  - **cramping** | **transverse**: *Bell* bro1 cham bro1 colch bro1 merc-c bro1 raph bro1
  - **gnawing** pain | **transverse**: gels k*
  - **touch** agg.: coloc mtf merc mtf merc-c mtf rhus-t mtf
  - ○ **Ascendens**: carc ↓ *Iris-t* mtf *Lyc* mtf mag-c mtf rhus-t ↓
    - ⁝ **burning**: carc mrr1
    - ⁝ **cramping**: rhus-t bro1
  - **Descendens**: enteroc jl2 merc mtf naja mtf nat-s mtf spig mrr1
  - **Transverse**: *Bell* mrr1 enteroc jl2 hell-o a1* podo a1*
    - ⁝ **left**: hell-o a1*
  - **Whole** length of the colon: *Ferr-m* k*
- **Diaphragm**: cocc ↓ coli ↓ graph ↓ mez ↓ *Nat-m* ↓ nux-v ↓ stront-c ↓
  - **cramping**: cocc bro1 coli rly4• graph bro1 mez bro1 *Nat-m* bro1 nux-v bro1 stront-c bro1
- **Digestive** tract: *Iris* ↓
  - **burning**: *Iris* ptk1
- **Duodenum**: pert-vc ↓
  - **sore**: pert-vc vk9
- **External** abdomen: acon ↓ alum ↓ ambr ↓ **Apis** ↓ arg-met ↓ *Arn* ↓ ars ↓ asaf ↓ bar-c ↓ *Bell* b4.de* bell-p bg2 bov ↓ brom ↓ bry ↓ calc ↓ canth ↓ carb-v ↓ cham ↓ chel ↓ chin ↓ cocc ↓ colch ↓ *Coloc* b4.de* con ↓ dros ↓ ferr ↓ gels ↓ ham bg2 hell ↓ hyos b7.de* kali-c ↓ *Lach* ↓ led ↓ lyc ↓ mag-m ↓ meny ↓ merc ↓ merc-c ↓ mur-ac ↓ *Nux-v* b7a.de par ↓ ph-ac ↓ phos ↓ plb ↓ puls bg2 ran-b ↓ rhod ↓ *Rhus-t* ↓ ruta ↓ sabad ↓ sabin ↓ samb ↓ sars ↓ sel ↓ seneg ↓ sep b4.de* spong ↓ squil ↓ stann ↓ staph ↓ sulph ↓ tarax ↓ ter ↓ thuj ↓ valer b7.de* viol-t ↓ zinc ↓
  - **boring** pain: dros b7.de*
  - **burning**: arn bg2 carb-v b4.de* merc b4a.de nux-v bg2 phos b4.de* *Rhus-t* b7a.de sabad b7.de* sars bg2 sel b7.de* thuj b4.de*
  - **clawing** pain: thuj b4.de*
  - **compressed**; as if: thuj b4.de*
  - **cramping**: sabin b7a.de samb b7a.de
  - **cutting** pain: dros b7.de*
  - **drawing** pain: alum b4.de* sel b7.de* seneg b4.de* staph b7.de* valer b7.de*
  - **pinching** pain: arg-met b7.de* calc b4.de* cocc b7.de* con b4.de* mur-ac b4.de* samb b7.de* zinc b4.de*
  - **pressing** pain: *Rhus-t* b7a.de squil b7.de* valer b7.de*
  - **sore**: acon ptk1 ambr b7a.de **Apis** bg2* *Arn* bg2 ars ptk1 bar-c b4.de* *Bell* ptk1 bov b4.de* bry ptk1 carb-v b4.de* cham b7.de* chin b7.de* ferr bg2 gels bg2 ham bg2 hell bg2 *Hyos* b7.de* *Lach* ptk1 lyc ptk1 meny b7.de* merc-c ptk1 **Nux-v** b7.de* plb b7.de* puls b7.de* ran-b ptk1 *Rhus-t* b7a.de sabin b7.de* stann ptk1 sulph b4.de* ter ptk1 valer b7.de* zinc b4.de*
  - **squeezed**; as if: apis bg2 arn b7.de* ars bg2 hyos b7.de* led bg2 rhod b4a.de
  - **stitching** pain: arg-met b7.de* arn b7.de* asaf b7.de* bell b4.de* brom bg2 calc b4.de* canth b7.de* chel b7.de* con b4.de* dros b7.de* kali-c bg2 led b7.de* mag-m b4a.de* merc b4.de* mur-ac b4.de* nux-v b7.de* ph-ac b4.de* rhod b4a.de ruta b7.de* samb b7.de* sep b4.de* spong b7.de* squil b7.de* staph b7.de* tarax b7.de* viol-t b7.de*
  - **tearing** pain: arn b7.de* calc b4.de* colch b7.de* par b7.de* samb b7.de*
  - **ulcerative** pain: *Rhus-t* b7a.de
- **Flank** | **jerking** pain (See sides - flanks - jerking)
- **Gallbladder**: bacls-10 fmm1• bamb-a ↓ bapt bg2 brom bg2 chel bg2 coli jl2 *Dios* bg2 dys fmm1• kali-bi bg2 kola stb3• *Lept* bg2 morg-g fmm1• morg-p fmm1• myric ↓ sep bg2 verat bg2 verat-v bg2
  - **cutting** pain: dios bg2 lept bg2 sep bg2
  - **pressing** pain: bamb-a stb2.de•
  - **sore**: *Bapt* ptk1 lept ptk1 morg-g fmm1• morg-p fmm1• myric ptk1
  - **stitching** pain: kola stb3•
  - ○ **Region** of gallbladder: *Lept* ↓ mand ↓ myric ↓
    - ⁝ **burning**: *Lept* ptk1 mand sp1 myric ptk1
    - ⁝ **stitching** pain: mand sp1
- **Gallstones** | **cramping** (See liver - colic)
- **Glands**; lymphatic: calc k2
- **Hips**; above: phos ↓
  - **sore**: phos h2
- **Hips**; region of: acon b7.de* *Agar* ↓ *Agn* ↓ am-m ↓ ambr ↓ anac ↓ ant-c ↓ am ↓ arum-t *Asaf* ↓ aur ↓ bar-c ↓ bell b4.de* berb ↓ borx ↓ bov ↓ bry ↓ calc k* camph ↓ cann-s ↓ canth b7.de* carb-an b4.de* carb-v ↓ caust ↓ chel k* *Chin* ↓ clem ↓ cocc ↓ *Colch* ↓ *Coloc* ↓ con dros ↓ fl-ac hep ↓ hyos b7.de* ign ↓ iod ↓ kali-c ↓ kali-n b4.de* kreos ↓ laur ↓ led ↓ *Lyc* ↓ m-arct ↓ mag-c ↓ mand rsj7• meny ↓ *Mez* ↓ nat-c ↓ nit-ac b4.de* olnd ↓ (non:phos k*) plb b7.de* ran-b b7.de* ran-s ↓ **Rheum** ↓ rhod ↓ ruta ↓ sabad ↓ sabin ↓ samb ↓ sars ↓ sec ↓ sep ↓ spong ↓ staph ↓ stront-c ↓ sulph ↓ tarax ↓ teucr b7.de* thuj ↓ verat b7.de* verb ↓ viol-t ↓ zinc b4.de*
  - **burning**: bar-c ptk1 ran-b b7.de sec b7a.de sep b4a.de
  - **cutting** pain: agn b7.de* arn b7.de* cann-s b7.de* *Canth* b7.de* chel b7.de* clem b4.de* lyc b4.de* mand rsj7• **Rheum** b7.de*
  - **menses**; during: asar b7a.de *Kreos* b7a.de lach b7a.de sec b7.de
  - **pinching** pain: ant-c b7.de* carb-v b4.de* dros b7.de* sulph b4.de* viol-t b7.de*
  - **pressing** pain: ambr b7.de* asaf b7.de* aur b4.de* cocc b7.de* colch b7.de* *Con* b4a.de hep b4a.de ign b7.de* iod b4.de* kali-c b4.de* kali-n b4.de* lyc b4.de* mez b4.de* nit-ac b4.de* olnd b7.de* ran-s b7.de* ruta b7.de* sabin b7.de* tarax b7.de* teucr b7.de* thuj b4.de* *Zinc* b4.de*
  - **squeezed**; as if: aur b4.de* *Colch* b7.de* led b7.de*
  - **stitching** pain: *Agar* k* *Agn* b7.de* am-m b7a.de ambr k* anac b4.de* arn b7.de* *Asaf* b7.de* berb ptk1 borx b4a.de bov b4.de* bry k* calc k* camph b7.de* *Canth* b7.de* carb-an b4.de* caust b4a.de chel b7.de* *Chin* b7.de* *Coloc* b4.de* dros b7.de* hyos b7.de* kali-c k* kali-n b4.de* kreos b7a.de laur b7.de* led b7.de* *Lyc* k* m-arct b7.de mag-c k* meny b7.de* *Mez* k* nat-c k* *Plb* b7.de* *Ran-b* b7.de* rhod b4a.de sabad b7.de* samb k* sars b4.de* sep k* spong b7.de* staph b7.de* stront-c b4a.de sulph k* thuj b4.de* verb b7.de* zinc b4.de*
  - **tearing** pain: kali-c b4a.de kali-n b4a.de
  - **walking** agg.: con
  - ▽ **extending** to | **Hip**; from hip to | **menses**; before: thuj ust
    - ⁝ **Lumbar** region:
      - ⁝ **cough** agg.; during: sulph ↓
        - **stitching** pain: sulph k*
- **Hypochondria**: abrot k* acon act-sp ↓ aesc k* aeth *Agar* k* ail ↓ all-c ↓ *Aloe* k* alum b4a.de* am-c am-caust ↓ am-m ambr ammc ↓ anac ↓ androc ↓ ang ↓ ant-t ↓ **Apis** ↓ arg-met *Arg-n* k* am k* *Ars* k* ars-i asaf k* asar ↓ asc-t k* aur aur-ar ↓ *Aur-m* ↓ aur-s k2 bad ↓ bapt k* bar-c bar-i bar-m *Bell* k* berb bism ↓ borx c1 bov k* brom k* *Bry* k* bufo *Cadm-s* ↓ cain ↓ calc calc-f ↓ calc-i k2 *Calc-p* ↓ *Calc-s* camph cann-s ↓ *Canth* k* caps ↓ carb-ac carb-an k* *Carb-v* k* carbn-s carl ↓ cartl-s ↓ castm ↓ caul caust ↓ cedr ↓ cench k2 *Cham* ↓ *Chel* k* *Chin* k* *Chinin-s* ↓ choc ↓ cimic k* cina ↓ *Cinnb* k* cist k* clem k* coc-c k* cocc bg2 coff coff-t a1 colch ↓ coloc *Con* k* cop k* *Corn* ↓ croc ↓ crot-h ↓ crot-t cupr k* cupr-s ↓ cycl bg2 *Dig* *Dios* k* dros k* dulc fd4.de echi ↓ elaps *Eup-per* ↓ euphr ↓ fago ↓ ferr ferr-ar ferr-i ferr-p form ↓ gamb ↓ gels k* glon k* goss ↓ *Graph* k* grat k* guaj ↓ ham fd3.de• hell ↓ *Hep* *Hydr* bg2 *Hyos* hyper ↓ ign indg k* *Iod* k* *Ip* *Iris* jatr-c jug-c k* *Kali-ar* kali-bi k* *Kali-c* k* kali-chl ↓ kali-i kali-m k2 kali-n ↓ kali-p ↓ kali-s fd4.de kalm k* ketogl-ac ↓ kola stb3• kreos **Lach** ↓ lact k* laur k* led ↓ lept ↓ lil-s a1 lil-t lob-c ↓ **Lyc** k* lycps-v ↓ lyss k* m-ambo ↓ m-arct ↓ m-aust ↓ mag-c mag-m mag-s ↓ manc k* mang bg2 meny ↓ meph k* **Merc** k* merc-c ↓ merc-i-f k* merc-i-r k* morg-g pte1*• morg-p fmm1• mosch ↓ mur-ac k* myrt-c ↓ naja ↓ nat-ar *Nat-c* k* *Nat-m* k* nat-ox ↓ nat-p **Nat-s** nat-sil fd3.de• nicc ↓ nicotam ↓ nit-ac *Nux-m* ↓ nux-v k* ol-an ↓ ol-j ↓ op k* ox-ac k* ozone sde2• par ↓ pert-vc vk9 petr *Ph-ac* ↓

- **Hypochondria**: ...
phos k* phys ↓ phyt plan k* plat ↓ plb k* plut-n ↓ *Podo* ↓ prun psor ↓ *Ptel* k* *Puls* k* pyrus ↓ **Ran-b** k* *Ran-s* ↓ raph ↓ rat ↓ rhod k* *Rhus-t* ribo ↓ *Rumx* ruta b7.de* sabad ↓ samb ↓ sang k* sars ↓ sec b7.de* sel b7.de* senec ↓ seneg sep sil k* spig ↓ spong fd4.de squil ptk1 *Stann* k* *Staph* ↓ stram k* stront-c ↓ stry ↓ sul-ac ↓ *Sulph* k* sumb ↓ suprar ↓ symph ↓ tab ↓ tarax ↓ tarent k* tep ↓ *Ter* ↓ teucr ↓ thuj tritic-vg fd5.de trom k* valer ↓ vanil fd5.de verat k* verb ↓ vip ↓ visc ↓ *Zinc* k* zinc-p k2
· **alternating** sides: aloe bg2 anac bg2 cham bg2 lach bg2 ph-ac bg2 staph bg2 thuj ↓
⁝ **stitching** pain: thuj
· **right**: acon ↓ act-sp ↓ *Aesc* k* aeth ↓ agar all-c ↓ *Aloe* k* *Alum* am-c am-m ↓ ambr anac ↓ ang ↓ ant-c k2 anth vh1 aphis arn k* *Ars* k* aur bro1 aur-ar k2 aur-i k2 *Aur-m* ↓ aur-s ↓ bamb-a ↓ bapt k* bar-c ↓ **Bell** berb bro1* bol-lu bro1 borx ↓ bov k* brom *Bry* k* *Bufo* but-ac ↓ cain calc bro1 calc-f calc-i ↓ *Calc-p* vh calc-sil k2 *Carb-ac* carb-an k* carb-v k* *Card-m* cassia-s cdd7• caul ↓ **Caust** ↓ cedr cench k2 cham ↓ **Chel** k* chen-a k* chim *Chin* bro1 chin-b kr1 *Chinin-s* chion ↓ choc ↓ cinnb k* clem k* *Cob* ↓ coc-c ↓ *Cocc* ↓ *Colch* *Coloc* ↓ *Con* k* *Crot-c* crot-h cycl ↓ **Dig** ↓ *Dios* bro1 dulc h1 echi elaps ↓ elat hr1 erig vml3• eup-per ↓ euphr ↓ fago ferr ↓ *Fl-ac* ↓ form ↓ *Gamb* ↓ gins bro1 hep ↓ hydr hydroph ↓ hyper ↓ *Iod* k* *Iris* jac-c bro1 jal br1 jatr-c bro1 *Kali-bi* k* kali-c k* *Kali-i* ↓ kali-m k2 kali-p ↓ kali-sil k2 kalm k* *Kreos* ↓ *Lac-c* ↓ *Lach* ↓ lact ↓ lap-la ↓ *Laur* ↓ *Lept* vh lil-t ↓ lim bro1 **Lyc** k* lyss k* mag-c ↓ *Mag-m* mag-p mtf11 mang-p ↓ *Med* ↓ meph a1 *Merc* k* *Merc-c* ↓ mez ↓ morg-g fmm1• morg-p pte1*• *Mur-ac* ↓ naja ↓ *Nat-c* *Nat-m* k* **Nat-s** k* nat-sil ↓ neon ↓ nept-m ↓ *Nit-ac* ↓ *Nux-m* ↓ **Nux-v** k* *Ol-j* k* olib-sac ↓ ozone sde2• pegan-ha tpi1• petr ↓ petr-ra shn4• ph-ac ↓ *Phos* k* phyt k* plan plb ↓ **Podo** k* psil ft1 psor ↓ ptel k* pyrog k2 quas bro1 ran-b k2 ran-s bro1 rhus-g tmo3• rhus-t ruta fd4.de samb ↓ *Sang* sars ↓ scroph-n ↓ sec ↓ sel k2 sep sil spect ↓ spig ↓ spong fd4.de stann ↓ staph ↓ stram k* stry k* sul-ac ↓ *Sulph* k* sumb ↓ tab ↓ tarent tep ↓ ter ↓ *Ther* ↓ thuj tritic-vg fd5.de trom k* vanil fd5.de verb ↓ wye bro1 *Zinc* ↓ zinc-p ↓
⁝ **accompanied** by | **distension** of abdomen (See Distension - accompanied - hypochondrium - right)
⁝ **bending** to left agg.: agar
: **stitching** pain: agar
⁝ **boring** pain: nat-m h2
⁝ **breakfast** agg.; after: borx ↓
: **cutting** pain: borx
⁝ **breathing** agg.: guat sp1
⁝ **burning**: am-m *Ars* aur k* *Aur-m* aur-s k2 bamb-a stb2.de• *Bry* k* chel *Crot-c* erig vml3• *Gamb* k* **Kali-c** k* kali-m k2 *Lac-c* *Lach* k* laur k* mag-c h2 mag-m *Med* mur-ac k* *Nit-ac* ph-ac k* phos plb sang k* stann k* sulph k* ter k* *Ther* thuj k* zinc h2
: **ball** of fire; as from a: erig vml3•
⁝ **clawing** pain: **Bell** *Nat-s*
⁝ **cough** agg.; during: borx caps chinin-s cimx cocc kali-bi lach psor sep bg1 sulph h2
⁝ **cramping**: aur-i k2 carb-an h2 cassia-s ccrh1• iod h kali-c h2 mag-c h2 mang-p rly4• nat-m h2 ph-ac h2 phos h2 rhus-t h1 samb h1 staph h1 sulph h2 verb h zinc h2
⁝ **cutting** pain: ang h1 *Aur* k* aur-ar k2 borx hr1 bry *Carb-ac* chel k2 crot-c dulc iod h kali-c k* nat-c h2 nat-sil fd3.de• ptel stann k* stry
⁝ **dragging**, bearing down: calc cham coc-c podo ptel
⁝ **drawing** pain: agar k* alum h2 aur k* bry calc k* carb-v k2 caul hr1 cham k* con h2 mag-m nat-m k* petr a1 ruta fd4.de sep h2 sulph k* tritic-vg fd5.de vanil fd5.de zinc k*
⁝ **eating**:
: **agg.**: lyc mrr1
: **amel.**: *Chel* rhus-t hr1
: **satiety** agg.; after eating to: **Lyc**
⁝ **exertion** agg.; after: *Kali-i* ↓
: **sore**: *Kali-i*
⁝ **gnawing** pain: hydroph rsj6•
⁝ **inspiration**:
: **agg.**: ran-b mrr1
: **deep** | **agg.**: lyc mrr1
⁝ **jerking** pain: con h2
⁝ **lancinating**: aeth aur-s k* bufo calc-f k* calc-i caust

· **right**: ...
⁝ **lying** | **abdomen**; on:
. **amel.** | **can** only lie on abdomen: *Lept* vh *Phyt*
: **side**; on:
. **left**:
agg.: arn ↓ bry ↓ *Card-m* ↓ *Mag-m* ↓ *Nat-s* ↓ *Ptel* ↓
dragging, bearing down: arn k2 bry bro1 *Card-m* *Mag-m* k* *Nat-s* *Ptel* k*
pressure:
amel.: plat ↓
dragging, bearing down: plat
. **painful** side:
agg.: **Bell** *Lyc* *Mag-m* *Nat-m* phyt *Ptel* vh sil tritic-vg fd5.de [dios xyz62 *Phos* xyz62]
pressing pain: *Mag-m* tritic-vg fd5.de
amel.: *Ambr* crot-h ptel mrr1 sep [phos xyz62]
. **painless** side | **amel.**: calc-f
. **right**:
agg.: *Mag-m* ↓ *Merc* ↓ *Sil* ↓
sore: *Mag-m* *Merc* *Sil*
⁝ **motion** agg.: sep h2
⁝ **pressing** pain: acon k* agar k* all-c aloe ambr hr1 anac k* arn k* aur-i k2 bar-c bell h1 brom k* *Calc* k* *Calc-p* carb-v h2 *Card-m* *Chel* k* *Chin* k* *Cocc* *Con* elaps ferr k* hep k* iod k* kali-m k2 kali-p fd1.de• *Laur* lil-t k* **Lyc** k* *Lyss* **Mag-m** merc mez h2 *Nat-m* k* nit-ac k* ph-ac h2 plb k* rhus-t k* ruta fd4.de sars k* sep *Sil* k* spong fd4.de staph h1 sul-ac h2 sulph k* *Tarent* thuj tritic-vg fd5.de zinc h2
⁝ **pressure** agg.: chel k2
⁝ **rubbing**; slight | **amel.**: erig vml3•
⁝ **screwing** together: nat-c h2* sulph h2*
⁝ **sensitive** to touch and pressure: card-m vml3• erig vml3•
⁝ **sitting** for a long time agg.: **Calc-p** vh nept-m lsd2.fr
⁝ **sore**: act-sp k* *Aesc* *Ambr* k* arn ars k* bapt k* **Bry** k* but-ac sp1 *Calc-p* carb-ac carb-v k* *Card-m* *Chel* *Chin* chion *Clem* *Con* **Dig** eup-per fago *Fl-ac* *Iod* k* *Kali-i* kali-m k2 *Kreos* lact k* **Lyc** *Mag-m* *Mur-ac* **Nat-s** k* **Nux-v** *Ol-j* k* *Phos* k* *Phyt* **Ran-b** sang bg1 sec k* *Sep* k* *Sil* sulph k* tarent k*
⁝ **stitching** pain: acon *Aesc* *Agar* k* alum k* am-m anac h2 bamb-a stb2.de• brom *Bry* k* **Calc** k* *Calc-p* carb-an h2 carb-v k* *Card-m* **Caust** cham k* **Chel** chin k* choc srj3• *Cob* *Cocc* *Coloc* k* **Con** k* *Crot-h* cycl a1 dulc h1 euphr k* fago form k* hyper k* iod h *Kali-bi* k* *Kali-c* k* *Kreos* k* lact lap-la sde8.de• *Laur* lyc k* mag-c h2 mag-m h2* *Merc* *Merc-c* k* mez h2 mur-ac h2 naja *Nat-c* k* nat-m k* *Nat-s* neon srj5• nept-m lsd2.fr *Nit-ac* nux-v k* ol-j olib-sac wmh1 ph-ac phos podo k* psil ft1 psor k* *Ptel* k* **Ran-b** *Ran-s* k* rhus-t ruta fd4.de sars h2 scroph-n c1 *Sep* k* spig h1 spong h1 staph h1 sul-ac h2 *Sulph* k* sumb tab k* tarent tep vanil fd5.de verb h *Zinc* k* zinc-p k2 [spect dfg1]
: **accompanied** by | **Head**; pain in: aesc bro1
⁝ **tearing** pain: alum k* chel k2 *Con* k* kali-c h2 mez h2 *Nux-m* zinc k*
⁝ **twinging**: nux-v k*
⁝ **twisting** pain: podo k*
⁝ **extending** to:
: **left**: brom lac-h ↓ *Nux-m* ozone ↓ ruta fd4.de [arn xyz62 lept xyz62 myric xyz62]
. **pressing** pain: ozone sde2•
. **stitching** pain: brom lac-h htj1• ruta fd4.de
: **Back**: *Aesc* bamb-a ↓ **Chel** euphr *Iod* jug-c *Kali-c* **Lyc** **Mag-m** k* *Nat-m* pyrog k2 ruta fd4.de yuc [agar xyz62 bism xyz62 calc xyz62 cham xyz62 dros xyz62 graph xyz62 kali-bi xyz62 laur xyz62 lept xyz62 puls xyz62]
. **sitting** for a long time agg.: calc-p vh
. **stitching** pain: bamb-a stb2.de• **Chel** euphr
: **Chest**: mag-c ↓
. **stitching** pain: mag-c h2
: **Heart**: zinc ↓
. **stitching** pain: zinc h2
: **Inguinal** region and testis: ars h2
: **Scapula**; left: *Lept* vh
: **Scapula**; right: abel vh1 abies-c vh1 bamb-a ↓ mag-m ↓

Abdomen

- **right – extending** to – **Scapula**; right: ...
  - **burning**: bamb-a stb2.de• mag-m
  - **Thigh**: cob ↓
    - **stitching** pain: cob
- **left**: aeth ↓ agar k* *All-s* vh1 allox sp1 *Alum* bro1 alum-sil ↓ am-c ↓ am-caust ↓ am-m bro1 anis mtf11 *Apis* ↓ arg-met ↓ arg-n bro1 arn ↓ *Ars* ↓ *Asaf* ↓ aur bamb-a ↓ *Bapt-c* bro1 bar-c ↓ bell ↓ berb tl1 borx ↓ bov ↓ brom *Cadm-s* ↓ *Calc* *Cann-s* ↓ canth ↓ carb-an ↓ carb-v bro1 carbn-s k2 cassia-s ccrh1• caust cean bro1* cench ↓ chel tl1 chin tl1 chin-b c1 chinin-s tl1 chion mtf11 cic ↓ cimic k* *Coc-c* k* colch ↓ coloc ↓ con bro1* crot-t ↓ **Cupr** ↓ dig br1* dios ↓ dirc ↓ dulc fd4.de ferr ↓ gard-j vlr2• gels k* germ-met srj5• glon k* gran ↓ *Graph* ↓ grat ↓ grin bro1 *Guaj* ↓ haliae-lc srj5• hep ↓ hir ↓ hydrog srj2• iod h ip ↓ irid-met srj5• kali-bi ↓ kali-c bro1 kali-i ↓ kali-n ↓ kali-p ↓ kali-s fd4.de kalm ↓ kola ↓ lac-c ↓ laur ↓ lil-t ↓ lyc bro1 lycps-v ↓ lyss ↓ mag-c *Mag-m* ↓ mag-s ↓ malar jl2 mang ↓ meph merc-i-f k* mez ↓ morg-g fmm1• morg-p pte1*• mur-ac ↓ nat-c bro1 nat-m k* nat-s ↓ nit-ac bro1 ox-ac k2* pall parth bro1 petr ↓ petr-ra shn4• ph-ac ↓ phos phyt ↓ *Plat* ↓ plb ↓ pneu jl2 polym bro1 psil ft1 *Puls* bro1 querc bro1 rat ↓ rheum ↓ rhod rhus-g tmo3• rhus-t ribo ↓ ruta h1 sang *Sars* ↓ sep bro1 sil ↓ spig ↓ spong fd4.de squil bro1* stann ↓ *Sul-ac* ↓ sulph ↓ symph ↓ syph vh tab ↓ tarax ↓ tarent k* tax ↓ ter ↓ thuj ↓ tritic-vg fd5.de urt-u bro1* vanil fd5.de verat hr1 verb c1 *Zinc* ↓
  - **afternoon** | **17**-20 h: cassia-s ccrh1•
  - **evening**: dulc fd4.de mag-c h2 ruta fd4.de vanil fd5.de
  - **blow**; pain as from a: kali-n h2
  - **boring** pain: nat-m h2
  - **breathing** deep agg.: borx ↓
    - **burning**: borx
    - **pressing** pain: borx h2
  - **burning**: am-c am-caust k* borx caust k* chel k* *Coc-c* *Graph* k* grat k* kali-i k* kali-s fd4.de lac-c plat ruta sep sulph h2 tab k* verat
  - **chill**; during: *Chinin-s*
  - **cough** agg.; during: ambr h1* *Caust* chinin-s grat sang sulph til
  - **cramping**: petr-ra shn4• plat h2 rhus-g tmo3• symph fd3.de• zinc h2
  - **cutting** pain: alum-sil k2 arg-met *Arg-n* bar-c h2 borx cench k2 dulc hir rsj4• kali-c h2 mag-m h2 spong fd4.de sul-ac h2 sulph h2 ter
  - **dancing**: borx ↓
    - **continued** amel.: borx ↓
      - **pressing** pain: borx a1
    - **pressing** pain: borx h2*
  - **drawing** pain: *Ars* coc-c k* coloc k* **Cupr** gels k* plat *Rhus-t* a1 ruta fd4.de [tax jsj7]
  - **dull** pain: grin br1
  - **eating** | **amel.**: cassia-s ccrh1• rhod
  - **empty** stomach; on: cassia-s ccrh1•
  - **flatulence**; from: mom-b ↓
    - **cramping**: mom-b mtf11
  - **lancinating**: *Cadm-s* dirc c1 malar jl2 ribo rly4•
  - **lying**:
    - **amel.**: *Sulph* vh *Tarent* vh
    - **side**; on:
      - **left**:
        - **agg.**: coc-c graph k2 mag-c nat-m
        - **amel.**: sang
      - **painful** side:
        - **agg.**: *Coc-c* ↓ *Graph* ↓
          - **burning**: *Coc-c* *Graph*
      - **right** | **agg.**: phos
  - **mortification**; from: ign ↓
    - **sore**: ign
  - **motion** agg.: sulph vh
  - **pressing** pain: aeth k* agar h2 alum-sil k2 arg-n k* *Aur* *Berb* borx bov k* carb-an h2 carb-v h2 con h2 crot-t dig k* dulc fd4.de iod h kali-c h2 nat-c k* nat-m nit-ac h2 petr a1 phyt *Plat* sep h2 spong fd4.de stann h2 sulph h2 tarax h1 thuj h1 tritic-vg fd5.de vanil fd5.de *Zinc* k*
  - **pressure** agg.: germ-met srj5• nat-c h2
  - **pulsating** pain: sul-ac h2
  - **sore**: *Apis* bamb-a stb2.de• *Brom* *Calc* cupr *Iod* lycps-v nat-c k* nat-m sars h2 stann h2 zinc k*
- **left**: ...
  - **stitching** pain: aeth k* alum alum-sil k2 am-c am-m h2 arg-met h1 arn ars *Asaf* aur k* bell h1 *Cann-s* carb-an h2 carb-v h2 caust h2 cench k2 chel k* chin h1 cic h1 colch con h2 dig k* dulc fd4.de ferr gels psa gran *Guaj* k* hep h2 iod h ip k* kali-bi k* kali-c h2 kali-p fd1.de• kali-s fd4.de kalm k* kola stb3• lil-t mag-c k* *Mag-m* mag-s k* mang h2 mez mur-ac h2 *Nat-c* nat-m h2 nat-s k* ph-ac h2 phos h2 puls k* rat k* rheum h ruta fd4.de sang hr1 *Sars* sep k* sil h2 spig h1 spong fd4.de squil br1 stann h2 *Sul-ac* k* sulph tarax h1 vanil fd5.de verb h zinc k* [tax jsj7]
  - **stooping** agg.: phos h2
  - **tearing** pain: ars h2 canth colch kali-c h2 lyss plb sil h2
  - **twinging**: laur k*
  - **twisting** pain: dios k*
  - **walking** rapidly agg.: borx ↓
    - **cutting** pain: borx h2
  - **extending** to:
    - **right**: alum fic-m gya1 ip k2 kali-p k2
      - **stitching** pain: alum
    - **Back**: coc-c nat-m
    - **Chest**:
      - **clearing** throat; when: ars ↓
        - **drawing** pain: ars h2
        - **stitching** pain: ars
    - **Epigastrium**: nat-c ↓
      - **stitching** pain: nat-c h2
    - **Hip**: **Cupr** ↓
      - **drawing** pain: **Cupr**
    - **Inguinal** region: hydrog srj2•
    - **Stomach**: phos ↓
      - **cramping**: phos h2
- **morning**: agar am-m ↓ ammc ↓ androc srj1• asar bov k* castm ↓ cist ↓ con ↓ dios k* dulc fd4.de graph ↓ hep ↓ kali-c ↓ lact k* mag-m ↓ merc-i-r ↓ nat-m ↓ nat-s ↓ nat-sil ↓ ruta fd4.de sang ↓ sars staph stry ↓ sulph ↓ symph ↓ tarent k* teucr vanil fd5.de
  - **8** h: kalm ↓
    - **stitching** pain: kalm
  - **bed** agg.; in: carb-v ↓ con ↓
    - **stitching** pain: carb-v h2 con k*
  - **burning**: dios k* sang k*
  - **cramping**: teucr k*
  - **cutting** pain: castm mag-m h2 nat-sil fd3.de• symph fd3.de•
  - **drawing** pain: merc-i-r k*
  - **pressing** pain: agar sars k* vanil fd5.de
  - **sore**: cist dios k* lact sulph k*
  - **stitching** pain: agar k* am-m h2 ammc con k* graph k* hep k* kali-c h2 nat-m nat-s stry tarent
  - **waking**; on: lac-h ↓
    - **stitching** pain: lac-h htj1•
- **forenoon**: alum bamb-a ↓ calc ↓ fago k* nat-s ↓ nat-sil ↓ ptel k* sars ↓ spong fd4.de *Sulph* tell ↓ thuj ↓
  - **10** h: fago ↓
    - **sore**: fago
  - **burning**: tell k*
  - **drawing** pain: sulph k*
  - **pressing** pain: alum k* spong fd4.de
  - **stitching** pain: bamb-a stb2.de• calc k* nat-s k* nat-sil fd3.de• sars k* thuj k*
  - **tearing** pain: alum k*
- **noon**: plan k*
- **afternoon**: aeth ↓ alum ↓ am-m ↓ aur ↓ borx ↓ bov calc-s k* caust ↓ chinin-s ↓ kali-c ↓ kali-s fd4.de kola ↓ laur ↓ **Lyc** k* mag-c ↓ mag-m ↓ nat-m ↓ phyt ↓ plb ↓ ruta fd4.de sil ↓ spong fd4.de valer ↓
  - **13** h: sars ↓
    - **burning**: sars
  - **14** h: mag-c ↓ ptel valer ↓
    - **stitching** pain: mag-c valer
  - **15** h: dios lyc ↓ tarent
    - **stitching** pain: lyc

- **afternoon**: ...
  - **burning**: alum k* am-m kali-c h2
  - **cutting** pain: chinin-s
  - **pressing** pain: borx kl (non:bov kl) spong fd4.de
  - **sore**: phyt k*
  - **stitching** pain: aeth k* alum k* am-m aur h2 caust k* kali-c h2 kola stb3• laur k* mag-c k* mag-m k* nat-m k* plb k* sil k* spong fd4.de valer k*
- **evening**: all-c↓ alum↓ am-c↓ ars↓ calc↓ calc-s *Carb-v* caust *Chinin-s* coloc dios k* dulc fd4.de kali-bi↓ kali-c↓ lact lyc↓ mag-c k* mag-m↓ mag-s↓ mang mur-ac↓ nat-m↓ phyt plan k* ptel **Ran-b** rat↓ rhod↓ ruta fd4.de sep spig↓ sumb↓ thuj↓ tritic-vg fd5.de vanil fd5.de zinc↓
  - **18** h: *Tarent* vh
  - **bed** agg.; in: ars↓
    - **stitching** pain: ars h2
  - **burning**: mur-ac h2 nat-m k*
  - **cramping**: calc-s k* dios k*
  - **drawing** pain: ars h2 *Carb-v* ruta fd4.de vanil fd5.de
  - **pressing** pain: all-c dulc fd4.de kali-c h2 lact k* mang k* ruta fd4.de sep k*
  - **sore**: **Ran-b**
  - **stitching** pain: alum h2 am-c calc h2 dulc fd4.de kali-bi k* lyc mag-c h2 mag-m mag-s k* mur-ac h2 rat k* rhod k* ruta fd4.de sep k* spig h1 sumb thuj k* zinc
  - **tearing** pain: ars h2 caust
  - **twisting** pain: dios k*
- **night**: aur calc calc-s k* cedr k* coc-c coloc↓ con↓ fago k* kali-c *Mag-c* k* plut-n↓ ruta fd4.de spong fd4.de stry↓ symph↓ vanil fd5.de zing↓
  - **midnight**: brass-n-o↓ phyt k*
    - **after**:
      - **3** h: sulph
        - **pressing** pain: sulph
    - **stitching** pain: brass-n-o srj5•
    - **while** lying on side: phyt k*
  - **bed** agg.; in: calc-s k* cedr k* cham *Coc-c* mag-c k*
  - **cramping**: calc-s k*
  - **cutting** pain: stry k*
  - **drawing** pain: *Coc-c* k* symph fd3.de•
  - **lying** on painful side agg.: fago↓
    - **sore**: fago
  - **pressing** pain: calc
  - **sore**: mag-c h2
  - **stitching** pain: coloc k* con k* *Kali-c* plut-n srj7• spong fd4.de vanil fd5.de zing k*
  - **waking**; on: *Coc-c* ruta h1
- **accompanied** by:
  - **respiration**; complaints of: ars bg2 *Cham* bg2 cocc bg2 dros bg2 hell bg2 ign bg2 led bg2 **Nux-v** bg2 puls bg2 staph bg2
  - **sneezing**: grat bg2
  - **Heart**; complaints of (See CHEST - Heart; complaints - accompanied - hypochondria)
- **air** agg.; in open: ol-an↓ staph↓ sulph↓
  - **stitching** pain: ol-an k* staph h1 sulph k*
- **air**; draft of | **amel**.: pneu jl2
- **alternating** with:
  - **respiration**; difficult (See RESPIRATION - Difficult - alternating - hypochondria)
  - **Chest**; oppression of: zinc
- **band**; as from a: *Sep* vh
- **bed** | **going** to bed:
  - **when**: hir↓
    - **cutting** pain: hir rsj4•
  - **in** bed:
    - **agg**.: cedr k* cham chinin-s coc-c dios k* ox-ac k*
      - **drawing** pain: cham
- **bending**:
  - **body**:
    - **amel**.: *Chin*↓
      - **pressing** pain: *Chin*
    - **forward**:
      - **agg**.: cocc
        - **pressing** pain: *Cocc*
      - **amel**.: *Aloe* chin
    - **left**; to:
      - **agg**.: agar↓
        - **pressing** pain: agar
    - **side**; to: lyc↓
      - **pressing** pain: lyc h2
  - **forward**:
    - **agg**.: agar↓ cassia-s↓ dig↓ *Lyc*↓
      - **cramping**: cassia-s ccrh1• dig h2
      - **stitching** pain: agar h2 *Lyc*
    - **amel**.: cassia-s↓
      - **cramping**: cassia-s ccrh1•
  - **left**; to:
    - **agg**.: agar
      - **stitching** pain: agar
  - **painful** side; to | **amel**.: nat-m
  - **right**; to:
    - **agg**.: sars↓ sul-ac↓
      - **stitching** pain: sars sul-ac h2
- **blow**; pain as from a: cann-s b7.de* nux-v bg2 stann bg2
- **blowing** the nose; when: sulph h2*
- **boring** pain: seneg b4a.de* sep b4.de* stann h2
- **breakfast**: cench↓
  - **after**:
    - **agg**.: borx↓ carb-v↓ graph k* kali-s fd4.de
      - **cutting** pain: borx h2
      - **pressing** pain: carb-v h2
  - **cutting** pain: cench k2
  - **stitching** pain: cench k2
- **breaking**; as if: form bg2 kali-p bg2
- **breathing**:
  - **agg**.: asaf berb bg1 *Bry* ign kali-c **Lyc** *Lyss*↓ pyrog k2 ran-b k2 ran-s staph sulph↓
    - **pressing** pain: **Lyc** *Lyss*
    - **sore**: sulph h2
  - **deep**:
    - **agg**.: croc↓ sel k2
      - **cramping**: croc k*
    - **amel**.: spig↓ vanil↓
      - **stitching** pain: spig h1 vanil fd5.de
- **burning**: acon k* aeth k* aloe bg3 *Am-c* bg2 *Apis* k* asaf b7a.de aur k* aur-m bell k* borx bov k* *Bry* k* bufo cann-s carbn-s caust k* **Chel** k* euphr gamb k* *Graph* k* grat k* ign kali-c k* kali-i k* kali-n kali-s fd4.de *Lach* k* laur k* lept k* merc k* *Mur-ac* k* myrt-c bg3 nat-c h2* nat-m k* ox-ac k* plat seneg spig stann k* *Staph* sul-ac k* sulph b4.de* tab k* *Ter* k* thuj k* zinc k*
- **burrowing**: asaf b7a.de
- **chill**; during: phos↓ podo br ran-b b7.de sep↓
  - **sore**: phos
  - **stitching** pain: sep b4a.de
- **clawing** pain: **Bell** nat-m k* rhod k*
- **clothing**; from: bamb-a↓
  - **stitching** pain: bamb-a stb2.de•
- **cold** drinks agg.; after: *Nat-c*↓
  - **stitching** pain: *Nat-c*

Abdomen

- **cough**:
  - **agg.**: am-c bg2 am-m b7a.de* ambr k* arn b7a.de* ars bg2 *Bell* borx *Bry* k* caps cench k2 chinin-s cimx *Cocc* *Dros* k* *Eup-per* bg2* grat hell b7a.de* hep bg2 kali-bi kali-c bg3 lach k* *Lyc* k* nat-s bg2* nit-ac k* **Nux-v** b7.de* *Phos* bg2 psor sang sep bg2* spong sul-ac sulph k* til valer bg1 zinc
  - **during**:
    - **agg.**: acon ↓ am-m ↓ ambr ↓ ars ↓ aur ↓ *Bell* ↓ *Bry* ↓ cann-s ↓ caps ↓ carb-v ↓ chin ↓ cimx ↓ *Cocc* ↓ lach ↓ lyc ↓ nat-s ↓ nux-v ↓ puls ↓ rhus-t ↓ rumx ↓ sep ↓ spong ↓ valer ↓
      - **cramping**: lyc k*
      - **cutting** pain: bry
      - **exertion**; as if after: puls b7.de*
      - **pressing** pain: *Cocc* k* spong b7.de* valer b7.de*
      - **sore**: *Bry* k* carb-v cimx lach k* nux-v
      - **stitching** pain: acon am-m h2 ars h2 aur h2 *Bell* *Bry* cann-s caps chin nat-s puls rhus-t rumx sep
      - **tearing** pain: ambr
- **cramping**: aesc k* aloe k* am-m k* androc srj1• arg-met k* aur-s k2 bapt hr1 bar-c h2 bell bry k* bufo calc k* *Calc-s* k* camph carb-v bro1 caust h2 *Chin* bro1 choc srj3• croc bg2 cupr dios k* hep bg1 ign k* iod *Ip* k* kali-bi *Kali-c* kali-i k* *Lact* k* *Lyc* k* mag-c h2 *Mur-ac* k* nat-c h2 nat-m k* nat-ox rly4• nicotam rly4• nit-ac h2 nux-v bg2* ph-ac h2* phos k* plan hr1 plat h2 pyrus bro1 rhod bg2 sep k* sil k* stann k* sulph k* symph fd3.de• *Zinc* k*
  - **alternating** with | **Chest**; oppression of: zinc k*
  - **downward**: hell
  - **intermittent**: mag-c h2
  - **paroxysmal**: nit-ac h2 sep h2 sil h2
  - **upward**: mag-c h2
- **cutting** pain: acon bg2 ang b7a.de arg-met arg-n ars k* ars-i asar b7.de* *Aur* k* aur-s k2 bar-c h2 *Bell* k* borx k* brom k* *Bry* calc b4.de* calc-f canth b7.de* cartl-s rly4• caust bg2 chel coc-c k* colch k* coloc k* crot-h dios k* *Dulc* *Graph* hydr k* iod k* kali-ar *Kali-bi* *Kali-c* k* kali-m k2 lyc k* mag-c meny k* merc-i-r k* nat-m nat-p k* nat-sil fd3.de• nicc *Nux-m* bg2 phos k* ptel puls *Ran-b* spong fd4.de stann k* stry k* sulph k* symph fd3.de• trom
  - **downward**: borx cench k2 nat-sil fd3.de•
  - **upward**: bar-c h2
- **dancing**; after: anac aur cham **Lyc** ptel sulph zinc
- **diarrhea**; during: **Arg-n** ↓
  - **sore**: **Arg-n**
- **digging** pain: nat-m bg2
- **dinner**; after: coloc ↓ grat ↓ kali-bi ↓ kali-c ↓ lact ↓ mag-c ↓ nat-m ↓ sars ↓ sulph ↓ suprar ↓ thuj ↓ zinc ↓
  - **pressing** pain: sulph k* suprar rly4•
  - **stitching** pain: coloc k* grat k* kali-bi kali-c h2 lact k* mag-c k* nat-m k* sars h2 thuj k* zinc h2
- **doubling** up amel.: calc-f ↓
  - **lancinating**: calc-f k*
- **drawing** pain: agar k* all-c aur k* bapt k* *Berb* *Calc* k* camph b7.de* *Carb-v* k* caul k* cham k* chin b7.de* *Coc-c* k* coloc k* *Con* gels k* ign b7.de* lact k* mag-m k* merc-i-r k* nat-ar nat-m k* petr k* *Puls* k* rhod b4.de* rhus-t k* ruta fd4.de sil k* squil sulph k* symph fd3.de• teucr k* tritic-vg fd5.de vanil fd5.de zinc k*
  - **downward**: nat-m
  - **upward**: *Rhus-t*
- **drinking** agg.; after: aur nat-c b4a.de tritic-vg fd5.de vanil fd5.de
  - **pressing** pain: aur
- **eating**:
  - **after**:
    - **agg.**: agar h2 anac aur borx b4a.de brom ↓ bry b7a.de cassia-s ↓ cham dulc fd4.de ham fd3.de• hydroph ↓ lact ↓ *Mag-m* ↓ *Nux-v* rhod spong fd4.de stann ↓ sulph b4a.de tritic-vg fd5.de trom vh zinc k*
      - **burning**: stann
      - **cramping**: cassia-s ccrh1•
      - **gnawing** pain: hydroph rsj6•
      - **pressing** pain: anac aur cham *Mag-m* *Nux-v* **Zinc**

- **eating – after – agg.**: ...
      - **sore**: agar
      - **stitching** pain: brom lact spong fd4.de
    - **agg.**: *Podo* ↓ tritic-vg fd5.de
      - **stitching** pain: *Podo*
    - **amel.**: *Chel* nat-m ↓ ruta fd4.de
      - **pressing** pain: nat-m h2 ruta fd4.de
- **eructations**:
  - **agg.**: caps ↓ zinc ↓
    - **stitching** pain: caps h1 zinc h2
  - **amel.**: mez h2 pall c1 sep
    - **cramping**: sep k*
    - **stitching** pain: sep h2
- **exertion**:
  - **agg.**: petr ↓ sep zinc
    - **stitching** pain: petr k*
  - **amel.**: nat-m ↓
    - **pressing** pain: nat-m h2
- **exertion**; as if after: puls b7.de*
- **expiration**:
  - **agg.**: tarax
  - **during**:
    - **agg.**: chin ↓ cic ↓ tarax ↓
      - **pressing** pain: tarax k*
      - **stitching** pain: chin k* cic h1
- **fatty** food: cassia-s ↓
  - **cramping**: cassia-s ccrh1•
- **festering**: carb-an bg2 lach bg2 ol-an bg2
- **fever**; during: ars b4a.de borx b4a.de nux-v b7a.de
- **flatus**; from: sulph ↓
  - **stitching** pain: sulph h2
- **flatus**; passing:
  - **amel.**: kali-m ↓ mur-ac ↓ nat-m ↓ *Sep* vh*
    - **cramping**: mur-ac h2 sep h2
    - **pressing** pain: kali-m k2 nat-m h2
- **gnawing** pain: bufo lach bg2 *Ruta*
  - **worm**; like a: kreos b7a.de puls b7a.de
- **inspiration**:
  - **agg.**: acon ↓ *Aesc* *Agar* *Anac* bar-c *Bell* ↓ calc ↓ calc-p ↓ cann-i ↓ carb-v ↓ cic ↓ cimic cocc ↓ con cupr ↓ cupr-s ↓ kali-bi k* kali-c ↓ **Lyc** mag-m ↓ mang ↓ *Merc* ↓ mosch ↓ nat-m ↓ *Nat-s* ↓ ph-ac ↓ **Ran-b** ↓ ran-s ↓ rhus-t ↓ *Rumx* sul-ac ↓ tab ↓ tarax ↓ zinc ↓
    - **pressing** pain: bar-c h2 cocc h1
    - **stitching** pain: acon agar anac *Bell* calc calc-p cann-i carb-v cic h1 con kali-c h2 lyc h2 mag-m h2 mang *Merc* mosch nat-m h2 *Nat-s* ph-ac h2 **Ran-b** ran-s rhus-t hr1 sul-ac h2 tab tarax h1 zinc h2
    - **tearing** pain: cupr h2 cupr-s k*
  - **deep**:
    - **agg.**: aur ↓ *Bell* ↓ *Calc-p* ↓ form ↓ nat-s ↓ sil ↓
      - **stitching** pain: aur h2 *Bell* *Calc-p* form nat-s sil h2
- **jar** agg.: **Bell** **Bry** ↓ *Calc* colch ↓ hep ↓ *Lach* ↓ **Lyc** *Nat-s* **Nux-v** ↓ sil
  - **sore**: **Bell** **Bry** colch hep *Lach* *Nat-s* **Nux-v** sil
- **jumping**, on: spig ↓
  - **stitching** pain: spig k*
- **lancinating**: aeth bad k* bufo *Cadm-s* calc-f k* chel k2 coloc lach manc k* phys k* ribo rly4• stann sulph tab k* tarent k*
- **laughing** agg.: acon ↓ aesc ↓
  - **stitching** pain: acon aesc
- **leaning** to right: sul-ac ↓
  - **stitching** pain: sul-ac k*
- **lifting**; after: kali-n ↓
  - **stitching** pain: kali-n h2

- **lying**:
  - **amel.**: *Lac-c* ↓ sep ↓
    - **burning**: *Lac-c*
    - **pressing** pain: sep h2
  - **back**; on:
    - **agg.**: caust ruta fd4.de
    - **amel.**: mag-m mag-s ↓
      - **stitching** pain: mag-s
  - **side**; on:
    - **agg.**: ars ↓ *Bell* ↓
      - **stitching** pain: ars h2 *Bell*
    - **left**:
      - **agg.**: arn coc-c colch mag-c **Mag-m** *Nat-s* *Ptel*
        - **sore**: ptel
      - **amel.**: cassia-s ↓ sang
        - **cramping**: cassia-s ccrh1•
    - **painful** side:
      - **agg.**: calc-f ↓ coc-c dios bg1 fago ↓ mag-c phos bg1 phyt sil tritic-vg fd5.de
        - **lancinating**: calc-f
        - **sore**: fago phos
      - **amel.**: bry pyrog k2 sep tarent
    - **painless** side:
      - **amel.**: calc-f ↓
        - **lancinating**: calc-f
    - **right**:
      - **agg.**: calc-f ↓ cassia-s ↓ *Lyc* *Mag-m* *Merc* nat-m sil tritic-vg fd5.de
        - **cramping**: cassia-s ccrh1•
        - **pressing** pain | **outward**: calc-f
- **lying** down; after:
  - **amel.**: mag-s ↓
    - **stitching** pain: mag-s
- **menses**:
  - **after**:
    - **agg.**: borx
      - **pressing** pain: borx
  - **before**:
    - **agg.**: puls ↓ sulph tarent k*
      - **cramping**: sulph k*
      - **stitching** pain: puls
  - **during**:
    - **agg.**: graph ↓ mag-m b4.de* nit-ac sul-ac ↓
      - **pressing** pain: graph hr1 nit-ac k*
      - **stitching** pain: graph b4a.de mag-m k* sul-ac b4.de*
- **motion**:
  - **agg.**: alum ↓ ang ↓ aur bar-c *Bry* ↓ bufo ↓ carb-ac ↓ cassia-s ↓ cimic dios k* graph ↓ *Iris* mang ↓ *Nit-ac* ↓ *Nux-v* ↓ plan ptel pyrog k2 ran-b sep ↓ sil sulph ↓ ter ↓ zinc ↓
    - **cramping**: cassia-s ccrh1• zinc h2
    - **cutting** pain: ang h1 ter
    - **lancinating**: bufo
    - **pressing** pain: aur bar-c mang h2
    - **rapid** motion: ptel k*
    - **sore**: *Bry* carb-ac mang h2 *Ran-b* *Sil* sulph h2
    - **stitching** pain: alum graph k* *Nit-ac* k* *Nux-v* ran-b k2 sep h2
  - **amel.**: *Graph* ↓ phys ↓
    - **burning**: *Graph* k*
    - **rapid** motion: dios bg1
    - **sore**: phys
  - **beginning** of:
    - **agg.**: **Rhus-t** ↓
      - **sore**: **Rhus-t** hr1
- **paralyzed**; as if: mag-c h2
- **paroxysmal**: alum am-m androc srj1• chel *Kali-bi* *Mur-ac* *Ph-ac* rhod *Stann* zinc
- **periodical**: ph-ac ↓
  - **cramping**: ph-ac h2
- **pinching** pain: calc b4.de* ip b7.de* laur b7.de* mosch b7.de* phos b4.de* puls b7.de*
- **position**; as if after wrong: ran-b b7.de*
- **pressing** pain: *Acon* k* aeth k* *Agar* k* *Aloe* alum k* am-c *Ambr* k* anac k* ant-t *Apis* b7a.de arg-n k* arn k* ars asaf b7.de* aur k* *Aur-m* aur-s k2 bar-c *Berb* *Borx* k* bov k* brom k* *Bry* k* cain calc k* calc-p camph k* caps b7.de* carb-v b4.de* carl *Cham* k* *Chel* k* *Chin* k* chinin-s bg2 cocc k* *Con* k* *Crot-t* dig k* dios k* dulc fd4.de elaps ferr k* graph k* ham fd3.de• hep k* ign k* iod k* **Kali-c** bg2 kali-chl k* kali-m k2 ketogl-ac rly4• lil-t k* *Lyc* k* lyss k* m-ambo b7.de m-arct b7.de *Mang* k* meny h1 merc k* *Mur-ac* k* nat-c k* nat-m k* nit-ac k* nux-v b7.de* petr k* ph-ac k* plb k* *Podo* rhod k* rhus-t k* ruta fd4.de sec b7.de* *Sep* *Sil* k* spong k* stann h2 staph b7.de* stront-c b4.de* sulph k* suprar rly4• tab bg2 tarax b7.de* tritic-vg fd5.de vanil fd5.de verat k* *Zinc* k*
  - **flatulence**; as from: kali-c h2 zinc h2
  - **outward**: castm lyc
  - **stone**; as from a: arn bg2 borx bg2 echi bg2 thuj bg2
  - **upward**: agar rhus-t b7.de
- **pressure**:
  - **agg.**: bamb-a ↓ *Berb* ↓ brom k* bry k2 carb-v ↓ clem k* *Crot-h* ↓ mez h2 nat-c a1 *Nux-v* ↓ petr-ra shn4• phos k* ruta h1 zinc k*
    - **stitching** pain: bamb-a stb2.de* *Berb* k* carb-v h2 *Crot-h* *Nux-v*
  - **amel.**: bry ↓ dros k* mag-m h2 mag-s ↓ meny ↓ mur-ac ↓ sang hr1 stann ↓ sul-ac ↓
    - **burning**: mur-ac h2
    - **pressing** pain: stann h2
    - **sore**: bry
    - **stitching** pain: mag-m h2* mag-s k* meny h1 sul-ac k*
  - **clothes**; of: | **agg.**: am-c *Bry* calc carb-v caust *Chin* coff hep lach k2 nat-s nux-v spong sulph
  - **slight**:
    - **amel.**: cassia-s ↓
      - **cramping**: cassia-s ccrh1•
- **pulsating** pain: plut-n srj7•
- **raising** arms agg.: ozone sde2•
- **riding**:
  - **agg.**: borx *Sep* vanil fd5.de
    - **pressing** pain: borx
  - **carriage**; in a:
    - **agg.**: caust ↓
      - **stitching** pain: caust k*
- **rising**:
  - **agg.**: cedr k* hydr ptel k*
  - **stooping**; from:
    - **agg.**: alum ↓ mang ↓
      - **stitching** pain: alum k* mang h2
- **rubbing**:
  - **amel.**: arg-met ↓ phos
    - **burning**: phos h2
    - **cramping**: phos k*
    - **stitching** pain: arg-met h1
- **running**; after: tab k*
- **sitting**:
  - **agg.**: alum ↓ ars ↓ bry ↓ calc ↓ calc-f ↓ carb-an ↓ carbn-s k2 con ↓ dulc ↓ graph ↓ mag-s ↓ meny ↓ mur-ac ↓ nat-c ↓ nept-m ↓ ph-ac ↓ phos ↓ phyt ↓ rhus-t ↓ sul-ac ↓ tell ↓ ter ↓ thuj ↓ viol-t ↓
    - **burning**: graph k* sul-ac k* tell k*
    - **cramping**: carb-an h2 rhus-t h1
    - **cutting** pain: ter viol-t
    - **drawing** pain: alum h2 ars h2
    - **lancinating**: calc-f k*
    - **pressing** pain: calc h2 ph-ac phyt rhus-t
    - **sore**: mur-ac h2
    - **stitching** pain: bry carb-an h2 con dulc h2* mag-s meny h1 nat-c h2 nept-m lsd2.fr phos h2 thuj
    - **tearing** pain: ars h2
  - **amel.**: alum ↓ mag-m ↓

- **sitting – amel.**: ...
  - **stitching** pain: alum k* mag-m
  - **bent** forward:
    - **agg.**: agar bov ↓ brom calc-f mur-ac ph-ac rhus-t stann ↓ *Sulph* ↓
      - **cutting** pain: stann
      - **stitching** pain: agar h2 bov k* *Sulph* k*
- **sleeping** | **agg.**: malar jl2
- **sneezing** agg.: grat ↓
  - **stitching** pain: grat k*
- **sore**: act-sp k* aesc k* *Agar* ail alum k* am-c am-caust a1 *Ambr* k* ant-t **Apis** k* *Arn* k* *Ars* k* ars-i bapt k* **Bell** brom **Bry** k* bufo **Calc** k* *Calc-p* camph b7.de* cann-s k* carb-ac carb-an k* *Carb-v* k* carbn-s *Chel* chin b7.de* clem *Cocc* k* *Corn* cupr k* cupr-s k* dros k* *Eup-per* k* ferr-i hell b7.de* iod k* kali-ar kali-bi k* *Kali-c* k* kali-n kreos *Lach* k* lact k* **Lyc** lycps-v mag-c h2 mang b4.de* **Merc** mur-ac nat-ar nat-m *Nat-s* k* ol-j k* ox-ac k* *Phos* k* phyt k* plb ptel **Ran-b** k* **Rhus-t** ruta bg2 sec k* stann b4.de* stront-c k* *Sulph* k* tab k* tarent k* vip k* visc ptk1 zinc k* zinc-p k2
  - **pulsating** pain: zinc h2
- **spinning**; while: am-m ↓
  - **stitching** pain: am-m k*
- **squeezed**; as if: *Apis* b7a.de colch b7.de* led b7.de* *Mur-ac* b4a.de ph-ac b4.de* puls b7.de* rhod b4.de* *Stann* b4a.de staph b7.de* zinc b4a.de
- **standing**:
  - **agg.**: *Aloe* alum ↓ arn ↓ cham ↓ chin glon ↓ *Lac-c* ↓ ph-ac ↓ phos bg1 ran-b zinc ↓
    - **burning**: *Lac-c*
    - **pressing** pain: *Chin* ph-ac h2
    - **stitching** pain: alum k* arn vh cham glon zinc
  - **amel.**: hydr bg1 prun spong fd4.de
    - **pressing** pain: prun k*
- **stepping**:
  - **agg.**: caust ↓
    - **cramping**: caust h2
  - **every** step; at: *Bell* ↓ *Calc* ↓ *Hep* ↓
    - **pressing** pain: *Calc*
    - **sore**: *Bell Hep*
- **stitching** pain: *Acon* k* aesc k* *Aeth* k* *Agar* k* aloe *Alum* k* am-c am-m k* ammc anac k* androc srj1• apis bg2 arg-met h1 arg-n arn k* ars k* ars-i asaf k* aur k* aur-ar k2 aur-m k* bar-c bar-i bar-m *Berb* k* bism b7.de* brom k* *Bry* k* calc k* calc-p k* cann-s k* canth b7.de* caps k* *Carb-v* k* *Carbn-s* caust cedr cham k* *Chel* k* chin k* *Chinin-s* k* cina a1 cist k* clem k* colch coloc h2 *Con* k* cop k* cupr dig k* dulc h2 euphr k* fago ferr k* ferr-i k2 form k* *Glon* goss k* *Graph* k* guaj k* hep hyos k* hyper k* ign bg3 iod k* ip k* kali-ar *Kali-bi* k* *Kali-c* k* kali-i k* kali-n k* kali-s fd4.de kreos k* *Lach* k* lact k* laur k* lob-c k* *Lyc* k* m-aust b7.de mag-c k* mag-m k* mag-s k* mang k* meny b7.de* merc merc-c k* mosch k* mur-ac naja k* nat-ar *Nat-c* k* *Nat-m* k* nat-s k* nat-sil fd3.de• nicc *Nit-ac* k* nux-v k* ol-an k* ox-ac k* par k* petr k* ph-ac k* phos k* plan k* plb k* podo k* psor k* ptel k* puls k* *Ran-b* k* *Ran-s* k* raph k* rat k* rhod k* rhus-t rumx ruta fd4.de sabad k* samb bg2 sars b4.de* senec k* *Sep* k* **Sil** k* spig b7.de* spong fd4.de sul-ac k* sulph k* sumb tab k* tarent tep thuj k* valer b7.de* vanil fd5.de verb b7.de* zinc
  - **alternating** with | **Head**; pain in (See HEAD - Pain - alternating - hypochondria)
  - **burning**: mag-c h2
  - **flatus**; as from obstructed: iod h
  - **itching**: mag-c h2
  - **needles**; as from | **hot** needles: anac h2
  - **pulsating** pain: dulc h2 spig h1
  - **rhythmical**: kali-n h2
  - **tearing** pain: ars h2
  - **transverse**: sep h2
- **stool**:
  - **after**:
    - **agg.**: caust b4a.de dulc fd4.de mag-m ↓ zinc
      - **cramping**: caust h2
      - **stitching** pain: mag-m h2*
- **stool – after**: ...
    - **amel.**: dulc fd4.de grat k* kali-s fd4.de spong fd4.de zinc ↓
      - **pressing** pain: zinc
  - **before**: anac k* ars k*
  - **during**:
    - **agg.**: anac b4.de* *Calc* ↓ nat-m bg2 sul-ac ↓
      - **cramping**: sul-ac h2
      - **stitching** pain: *Calc*
      - **twisting** pain: nat-m k*
- **stooping** | **after**:
    - **agg.**: **Calc** ↓
      - **stitching** pain: **Calc** k*
  - **agg.**: alum arg-met ↓ clem cocc fago lyc mag-c ↓ mur-ac ↓ petr-ra shn4• rhod k* sep ↓ thuj ↓
    - **cramping**: lyc k*
    - **cutting** pain: arg-met h1
    - **pressing** pain: cocc c1 thuj
    - **sore**: alum
    - **stitching** pain: arg-met h1 mag-c h2 mur-ac sep h2
- **stretching**:
  - **agg.**: lyc ↓ mang ↓
    - **cutting** pain: lyc k*
    - **stitching** pain: mang h2
  - **amel.**: tarent bg1
- **supper** agg.; after: dulc ↓ zinc ↓
  - **stitching** pain: dulc fd4.de zinc k*
- **talking** amel.: nat-m ↓
  - **pressing** pain: nat-m h2
- **tearing** pain: alum k* bism b7.de* canth k* carb-v chin b7.de* colch k* *Con* k* cupr b7.de* cupr-s k* kali-bi k* kali-c k* lyss k* nux-v plb k* teucr k* thuj k* *Zinc* k*
- **torn** out or loose; as if: agar bg2 ambr bg2 berb bg2
- **touch** agg.: ars ↓ bar-c ↓ carb-an h2 carb-v h2 dros h1 iod h mag-c ↓ mang ↓ nat-c ↓ ran-b ↓ ther ↓
  - **burning**: ther
  - **cutting** pain: ars h2
  - **pressing** pain: bar-c h2 mang h2
  - **sore**: mag-c h2 mang h2 ran-b c1
  - **stitching** pain: nat-c h2
- **turning**:
  - **agg.**: **Rhus-t** ↓
    - **sore**: **Rhus-t** hr1
  - **body**:
    - **agg.**: lyc
      - **cramping**: lyc k*
- **twinging**: laur k* nux-v k*
- **twisting** pain: dios k* nat-m k* podo k*
- **twitching**: *Am-m* b7a.de mosch b7a.de puls b7.de*
- **ulcerative** pain: alum bg2 bry bg2 chinin-s bg2 **Lach** b7a.de nat-s bg2 *Nux-m* b7a.de puls b7.de* ruta b7.de* sulph bg2
- **waking**; on: *Cist* coc-c
- **walking**:
  - **after**:
    - **agg.**: ph-ac ↓
      - **cramping**: ph-ac h2
      - **pressing** pain: ph-ac h2
  - **agg.**: *Aesc* alum ↓ am-m ↓ arg-n ↓ ars *Aur* bamb-a ↓ bapt k* *Calc* cassia-s cdd7• cham ↓ hep ↓ iris *Kali-bi* lyss k* *Mag-m* ↓ manc k* nat-c ↓ nat-m k* **Nat-s** ↓ phos ↓ phyt k* ran-b k2 *Rumx* sars sep ↓ *Sil* ↓ spig ↓ stann ↓ staph ↓ sulph sumb ↓ thuj ↓ vanil fd5.de *Zinc*
    - **burning**: am-m nat-c a1
    - **cramping**: cassia-s ccrh1• sulph
    - **cutting** pain: phos h2
    - **drawing** pain: alum h2 bapt k* phos h2
    - **pressing** pain: *Aur Calc Mag-m* nat-m *Zinc*
    - **sore**: **Nat-s** *Sil*

- **walking – agg.**: ...
  - **stitching** pain: am-m arg-n bamb-a stb2.de• cham hep mag-m nat-c h2 nat-m h2 *Nat-s* ran-b k2 sep spig stann h2 staph h1 sulph h2 sumb thuj vanil fd5.de zinc
  - **air** agg.; in open: ars ↓
    - **pressing** pain: ars
  - **amel.**: brom calc-f carb-an ↓ cassia-s ↓ grat ↓ mag-c ↓ malar jl2 plb ↓ sars
    - **burning**: grat
    - **cramping**: cassia-s ccrh1•
    - **lancinating**: calc-f
    - **pressing** pain: sars k*
    - **stitching** pain: carb-an h2 mag-c plb k*
  - **rapidly**:
    - **agg.**: borx ↓
      - **cutting** pain: borx
  - **slowly** | **amel.**: malar jl2
- **writing** agg.: chim
- **yawning** agg.: aur ↓
  - **stitching** pain: aur h2
- ○ **Side** lain on: **Rhus-t** ↓
  - **sore**: **Rhus-t**
- **Spots**; in: kali-c ↓
  - **sore**: kali-c k*
- ▽ **extending** to:
  - **right** side: stann ↓
    - **lancinating**: stann
  - **backward**: acon bg3 *Aesc* k* agar *Berb* *Borx* bg3 calc k* *Calc-caust* bg3 camph carb-v **Chel** k* dios euphr graph *Hydr* bg3 kali-bi bg3 kali-c lact laur **Lyc** mag-m bg3 merc-i-f kr1 naja nat-m plb puls *Ran-b* sep bg2 sil
    - **right**: bry bg2 dios bg2 nat-m bg2
  - **Abdomen**: all-c bg2 carb-v ↓ euphr graph ↓ petr
    - **left** side: con ↓
      - **pressing** pain: con h2
    - **pressing** pain: graph h2 petr
    - **stitching** pain: carb-v h2 euphr
  - **Arms**: phys bg2
  - **Back**: agar ↓ *Berb* ↓ calc ↓ camph ↓ chel ↓ euphr ↓ graph ↓ lact ↓ laur ↓ naja ↓ nat-m ↓ plb ↓ ran-b ↓ **Sil** ↓ sul-ac ↓
    - **clawing** pain: nat-m
    - **cramping**: **Sil** k*
    - **cutting** pain: chel k2 ran-b sul-ac h2
    - **lancinating**: chel k2
    - **stitching** pain: agar *Berb* calc camph chel k2 euphr graph lact laur naja plb ran-b
    - **tearing** pain: chel k2
  - **Back**, across the: sil
  - **Chest**: aloe k* carb-v ↓ cassia-s ↓ chinin-s
    - **cramping**: cassia-s ccrh1•
    - **stitching** pain: aloe carb-v h2 chinin-s
  - **Downward**: ars bapt *Chel* hell lil-t nat-m nux-v
  - **Forward**: laur
  - **Front**: fago ↓
    - **stitching** pain: fago
  - **Genitals**: calc bg2 carl
  - **Hip**: alum cupr **Sil** ↓
    - **drawing** pain: **Cupr Sil** h2
    - **tearing** pain: alum
  - **Hips**: sil ↓
    - **cramping**: sil h2
    - **stitching** pain: sil h2
  - **Ilium**: alum lil-t
    - **lancinating**: lil-t k*
  - **Leg**; left: malar ↓
    - **lancinating**: malar jl2
  - **Legs**: *Carb-v* ↓

- **Hypochondria – extending** to – **Legs**: ...
  - **drawing** pain: *Carb-v*
  - **Lumbar** region: carb-v laur bg2 plb puls bg2
    - **drawing** pain: carb-v plb
  - **Lumbar** vertebrae: camph ↓
    - **cramping**: camph h1
  - **Nipples** | **right**: dios bg2
  - **Outward**: lyc sulph
  - **Sacrum**: thuj
    - **stitching** pain: thuj
  - **Scapula**: *Aesc* borx ↓ bov **Chel** k* hydr k* *Mag-m*
    - **left** scapula: *Lept* vh
    - **pressing** pain: borx h2 bov
  - **Shoulder**: crot-h bg1 cupr k* kali-bi bg1 laur k* nat-s bg2* *Nux-v* rhus-t bg2
    - **sore**: laur *Nux-v*
  - **Shoulder**, right: rhus-t ↓
    - **stitching** pain: rhus-t
  - **Spine**: mag-m bg2 sil
    - **drawing** pain: sil
  - **Spleen**: merl ↓
    - **pressing** pain: merl
  - **Stomach**: cupr nat-c
    - **sore**: nat-c
    - **stitching** pain: cupr nat-c
  - **Symphysis**: calc ↓
    - **drawing** pain: calc h2
  - **Thighs**: nux-v ↓
    - **drawing** pain: nux-v
  - **Umbilicus**: aloe bg2 borx ↓ carl kali-chl ph-ac ↓ rhus-t bg2
    - **cramping**: ph-ac h2 rhus-t a1
    - **cutting** pain: borx
    - **pressing** pain: ph-ac h2
  - **Upward**: agar *Apis* mur-ac *Rhus-t*
- **Hypogastrium**: abrom-a ks5 acon k* aesc k* aeth ↓ *Agar* k* agn ↓ aids nl2• ail k* *All-c* aloe alum ↓ alumn am-c k* am-m ↓ ambr h1* ammc k* *Anac* ↓ androc srj1• ang ↓ ant-t ↓ apis k* aran ↓ arg-met *Arg-n* ↓ arist-cl sp1 *Arn* **Ars** k* ars-i ars-s-f k2 arund k* asaf ↓ asar ↓ asc-t ↓ aur aur-ar ↓ aur-s ↓ bamb-a stb2.de• bapt k* *Bar-c* ↓ bar-i ↓ *Bell* k* bell-p sp1 bism ↓ bros-gau ↓ *Bry* but-ac ↓ *Cact* cadm-met tpw6 calad b7.de* calc k* calc-i ↓ *Calc-p* k* *Camph* ↓ cann-i ↓ canth k* caps ↓ carb-an k* *Carb-v* k* carbn-s *Card-m* cassia-s ↓ caust k* cham ↓ *Chel* k* chin k* chinin-ar cimic k* cina ↓ clem k* coc-c *Cocc* *Colch* ↓ coll k* *Coloc* k* con cop *Croc* crot-h ↓ crot-t k* cupr ↓ cupr-ar k* cycl b7a.de* dendr-pol sk4• dict ↓ dig ↓ *Dios* k* dor k* dream-p ↓ dulc fd4.de elaps ↓ eucal ↓ euon ↓ *Euph* k* fago ↓ ferr k* ferr-ar ferr-i ferr-m ↓ gamb ↓ *Gels* germ-met ↓ *Gins* k* granit-m es1• graph grat ↓ guaj ↓ ham k* hell k* *Helon* ↓ hep ↓ *Hydr* ↓ **Hyos** ↓ ign ↓ iod k* ip ↓ irid-met ↓ iris ↓ jac-c ↓ jug-r ↓ kali-ar kali-bi bg2* *Kali-c* k* kali-i ↓ kali-n b4.de* kali-p kali-s fd4.de kali-sil k2 ketogl-ac ↓ kola stb3• *Kreos* lac-ac ↓ lac-c ↓ lac-d k2 lac-leo sk4• **Lach** ↓ laur ↓ lec lept *Lil-t* lith-c *Lyc* *Lyss* ↓ mag-c ↓ mag-m mag-s ↓ mang ↓ mang-p ↓ *Med* melal-alt ↓ meny ↓ *Merc* merc-c b4a.de merc-i-f ↓ *Mez* ↓ mosch b7.de* mur-ac ↓ murx k* musca-d ↓ nat-ar *Nat-c* k* nat-m k* *Nat-p* k* nat-sil fd3.de• neon ↓ nicc ↓ nit-ac ↓ nux-m ↓ *Nux-v* k* ol-an ↓ olib-sac ↓ onos *Op* ↓ *Pall* ↓ paraf ↓ *Ph-ac* ↓ *Phos* k* phys ↓ physala-p ↓ pic-ac ↓ **Plat** k* plb k* plut-n srj7• podo ↓ prun *Psor* ↓ ptel **Puls** k* pycnop-sa ↓ pyrid ↓ ran-b k* rhus-g ↓ rhus-t k* rhus-v ruta sabad *Sabin* ↓ samb ↓ *Sars* ↓ *Sec* k* sel rsj9• senec ↓ seneg ↓ **Sep** k* *Sil* k* sol-t-ae k* spig ↓ spong fd4.de squil k* stann k* staphycoc ↓ stram ↓ stry succ-ac ↓ sul-ac ↓ sul-i k2 sulfa sp1 **Sulph** k* sumb k* symph fd3.de• *Tab* ↓ tarax ↓ tarent k* tell k* ter k* teucr ↓ thuj k* til ↓ trios ↓ tritic-vg fd5.de trom ↓ valer vanil fd5.de **Verat** k* verat-v ↓ *Verb* b7a.de vib tl1* viol-t ↓ *Zinc* k* zinc-p k2 [*Buteo-j* sej6]
  - **right**: ambr ↓ *Carb-an* *Gins* graph h2 lac-h sk4• lyc ↓ olib-sac ↓ sep ↓ spong fd4.de sulph ↓ *Sumb* ↓ symph fd3.de• vanil ↓ zinc ↓
    - **cramping**: ambr h1
    - **gnawing** pain: *Sumb* k*
    - **pressing** pain: lyc h2 olib-sac wmh1 sep h2 sulph h2 vanil fd5.de zinc h2
    - **sitting**:
      - **amel.**: tax ↓
        - **cramping**: [tax jsj7]

Abdomen

- **right**: ...
  - **sore**: zinc h2
  - **walking** agg.: tax ↓
    - **cramping**: [tax jsj7]
  - **extending** to | **left**: gins kali-p fd1.de•
- **left**: all-c tl1 am-c ↓ cassia-s ↓ dulc ↓ graph ↓ kali-p ↓ ketogl-ac ↓ lac-c ↓ lyc tl1 nat-m ↓ petr-ra shn4• plat ↓ ptel tl1 rhod kgp5• ruta ↓ sel ↓ sep ↓ spong ↓ sulph ↓ vanil ↓ zinc ↓
  - **burning**: am-c graph lac-c plat ruta sep
  - **cramping**: kali-p fd1.de• lyc h2
  - **cutting** pain: spong fd4.de vanil fd5.de zinc h2
  - **pressing** pain: lyc h2 nat-m h2 ruta fd4.de sel rsj9• sulph h2
  - **sore**: ketogl-ac rly4•
  - **stitching** pain: cassia-s ccrh1• dulc fd4.de ruta fd4.de spong fd4.de zinc h2
- **daytime**: stram ↓
  - **cramping**: stram k*
- **morning**: alumn ambr ars ↓ bar-c ↓ *Bell* k* dios k* dulc fd4.de fago ham fd3.de• hyos ↓ kali-p fd1.de• mag-c nat-m ↓ phos ↓ *Plat* ↓ ruta fd4.de sars ↓ sep h2 sol-t-ae k* spong fd4.de tritic-vg ↓ vanil fd5.de
  - **9-18 h**: **Sep** ↓
    - **pressing** pain: **Sep**
  - **bed** agg.; in: mag-c ↓ mag-m ↓ phos ↓
    - **cutting** pain: mag-m h2
    - **pressing** pain: mag-c h2 phos h2
  - **cramping**: ambr k* ars h2 dios k* fago hyos h1
  - **cutting** pain: sars h2
  - **lying**:
    - **agg.**: tritic-vg ↓
      - **pressing** pain: tritic-vg fd5.de
    - **back**; on:
      - **agg.**: bar-c ↓
        - **pressing** pain: bar-c
  - **pressing** pain: bar-c k* *Bell* nat-m h2 *Plat* sep h2 spong fd4.de tritic-vg fd5.de vanil fd5.de
  - **stitching** pain: dulc fd4.de phos k* ruta fd4.de sep k* tritic-vg fd5.de
  - **walking** agg.: phos ↓
    - **pressing** pain: phos h2
- **forenoon**: agar bros-gau ↓ com k* *Phos* ruta fd4.de **Sep** spong fd4.de thuj ↓
  - **cramping**: agar
  - **pressing** pain: *Phos* k*
  - **stitching** pain: ruta fd4.de thuj k*
  - **weight**, as from a: bros-gau mrc1
- **noon**: merc-i-f ↓
  - **pressing** pain: merc-i-f k*
- **afternoon**: dios k* dream-p ↓ dulc ↓ lyc ↓ mag-m h2 plb ↓ rhus-t k* sep ↓ spong fd4.de
  - **14 h**: rhus-t
  - **cutting** pain: sep h2
  - **stitching** pain: dream-p sdj1• dulc fd4.de lyc k* plb k* spong fd4.de
- **evening**: agar ↓ aids ↓ dulc ↓ euphr ↓ kali-c ↓ kali-n ↓ kali-p ↓ lyc ↓ pall phos ↓ pic-ac sabad ↓ sec spig ↓ spong ↓ sumb k* tritic-vg ↓ vanil fd5.de
  - **amel.**: **Sep**
  - **burning**: kali-n
  - **cramping**: aids nl2• dulc h2 kali-p fd1.de• lyc h2
  - **cutting** pain: agar h2 spong h1
  - **pressing** pain: euphr h2 kali-c h2 phos h2 sec k* spig h1 tritic-vg fd5.de
  - **stitching** pain: lyc h2 sabad k*
- **night**: *Aesc* k* bapt ↓ bell carb-an caust h2 chel crot-h ↓ kali-p ↓ lyc mang ph-ac ↓ phos ↓ prun ruta ↓ *Sep* sil h2 *Sulph*
  - **21 h**: **Sep** ↓
    - **pressing** pain: **Sep**
  - **midnight**:
    - **after**:
      - **1 h**: mang ↓
- **night – midnight – after – 1 h**: ...
  - **cramping**: mang h2
  - **5 h**: petr a1
  - **amel.**: cassia-s ↓
    - **cutting** pain: cassia-s ccrh1•
  - **burning**: crot-h k* phos h2
  - **cramping**: chel k* kali-p fd1.de•
  - **cutting** pain: bapt a1 lyc h2
  - **drawing** pain: ph-ac h2
  - **menses**; before: mang ↓
    - **cramping**: mang k*
  - **pressing** pain: phos h2 ruta h1 sep h2 *Sulph* k*
  - **sore**: sep h2
- **accompanied** by | **Portal** congestion (See Portal - accompanied - hypogastrium)
- **bending**:
  - **backward**:
    - **agg.**: sulph ↓
      - **cutting** pain: sulph h2
  - **forward**:
    - **agg.**: calc-caust ↓
      - **stitching** pain: calc-caust c1
  - **left**; to:
    - **agg.**: bell ↓
      - **cramping**: bell h1
- **bending** double:
  - **agg.**: *Prun*
  - **amel.**: puls ↓
    - **cutting** pain: puls h1
  - **must** bend double: astac ↓ *Prun* ↓
    - **cramping**: astac kr1 *Prun*
- **boring** pain: arg-met h1
- **breathing**:
  - **agg.**: asaf **Bell** spong
  - **deep** | **agg.**: nat-c h2
- **burning**: agar all-c alum a1 alumn arund k* bar-c k* *Calad Camph* card-m cassia-s ccrh1• crot-h k* grat k* helon hep h2 irid-met srj5• kali-n *Kreos* lac-c *Lach Lil-t* ph-ac stann stram sulph h2 tarax h1 tarent k*
- **burrowing**: coc-c k* nit-ac h2 rhus-t a1 sep h2 spig h1
- **changing** position, on: ph-ac ↓
  - **stitching** pain: ph-ac k*
- **chill**; during: chin ↓ chinin-s ↓ podo bro1
  - **pressing** pain: chin h1* chinin-s bro1
- **clawing** pain: **Bell** k* lyc puls
- **clothes**; loosening of:
  - **amel.**: onos ↓
    - **cramping**: onos vml3•
- **coition**; after: *All-c* k*
- **cold** | **applications**:
  - **agg.**: cassia-s ↓
    - **stitching** pain: cassia-s ccrh1•
  - **drinks**:
    - **after** | **agg.**: crot-c k* spong fd4.de
- **colic**, during: *Thuj* ↓
  - **pressing** pain: *Thuj* k*
- **coryza**; during: calc h2 carb-v ↓
  - **burning**: carb-v b4.de*
  - **stitching** pain: carb-v b4.de*
- **cough**:
  - **after**: arund ↓
    - **burning**: arund k*
  - **agg.**: ars ↓ bry ↓ carb-an ↓ chin ↓ *Nux-v* ↓ *Puls* ↓ verat ↓
    - **cutting** pain: bry chin verat k*
    - **sore**: ars b4.de* carb-an b4a.de* *Nux-v* b7.de* *Puls* b7.de*

- **cough**: ...
  - : **during**:
    - : **agg.**: ars↓ aur↓ borx↓ caps carb-an carb-v↓ dros k* *Ip* kali-s fd4.de lyc k* *Nat-m*↓ nux-v k* ph-ac k* phos k* sel↓ sep↓ sil k* squil k* verat k*
      - . **blow**; pain as from a: *Nat-m* bg2 squil bg2
      - . **pressing** pain: aur b4a.de sel rsj9•
        - **outward**: carb-an b4a.de
      - . **stitching** pain: ars k* borx b4a.de carb-v b4a.de sep k* verat k*
- **cramping**: *Acon* k* aeth a1 *Agar* aids nl2• all-c bro1 aloe k* am-c am-m h2 ambr h1 *Ars* aur aur-s k2 bapt a1 *Bell* k* bism h1* *Bry* k* but-ac br1* calc k* carb-an h2 *Carb-v* k* carbn-s *Chel* k* chin h1 cimic *Cocc* k* *Coll* k* coloc k* *Con* k* *Cupr-ar* cycl h1 dig h2 *Dios* k* eucal bro1 *Gels* germ-met srj5• granit-m es1• guaj h2 ham bro1 helon kali-c h2* kali-p k2 kreos lil-t k* lyc h2* mag-c h2* mag-m a1 mang-p rly4• melal-alt gya4 meny h1 mez h2 *Nat-c* k* nat-m h2 neon srj5• nit-ac h2 *Nux-v* k* pall bro1 paraf bro1 physala-p bnm7• plat bro1 *Prun* psor k* pyrid rly4• ran-b k* rhus-g tmo3• rhus-t h1 ruta *Sabin* bro1 sel rsj9• sep h2* *Sil* k* spig h1 spong h1 squil h1 stann staphycoc rly4• *Stry* k* sul-ac h2 **Sulph** k* trom bro1 verat-v bro1 vib ptk1 zinc
  - : **accompanied** by:
    - : **Lumbar** region | **pain** in: granit-m es1•
  - : **followed** by | **stool**; watery: tell rsj10•
  - : **paroxysmal**: chin h1 sep h2
  - : **wandering** pain: chin h1
- **cutting** pain: acon tl1 aeth k* agar h2 *All-c* k* am-c k* ang k* *Ars* k* asar h1 aur-s k2 *Bar-c* **Bell** k* bry k* cact calc h2 carb-an h2 carbn-s cassia-s ccrh1• *Cimic* k* coc-c k* *Coll* k* *Coloc* k* *Croc* cycl h1 elaps euon granit-m es1• ham fd3.de• *Hydr* k* **Hyos** k* iris *Kali-bi* kali-c h2 laur *Lept Lil-t Mag-m* k* mag-s mang med *Merc* k* mur-ac h2 nat-ar k2 nat-c k* nicc k* nux-v k* ol-an k* **Puls** k* senec k2 sep k* *Sil* k* spig h1 spong fd4.de squil h1 stann h2 sulph h2 symph fd3.de• ter k* *Thuj* k* trios rsj11• vanil fd5.de *Verat* verat-v a1 zinc h2
  - : **transverse**: stann h2
- **diarrhea**, with: ars↓ cassia-s↓ petr↓ pyrid↓
  - : **cramping**: ars h2 petr hr1 pyrid rly4•
  - : **cutting** pain: ars h2 cassia-s ccrh1•
- **dinner** | **after**:
  - : **agg.**: cham k* kali-n↓ lyc↓ zinc↓
    - . **burning**: kali-n h2
    - . **cutting** pain: lyc h2 zinc h2
    - . **stitching** pain: kali-n
  - : **during**:
    - : **agg.**: am-c↓
      - . **pressing** pain: am-c k*
- **dragging**, bearing down: bell ptk1 dict ptk1 lil-t ptk1 lyc ptk1 nux-v ptk1 plat ptk1 puls ptk1 *Sep* ptk1 *Sulph* ptk1
- **drawing** in abdomen, when: ambr↓ kali-c↓
  - : **stitching** pain: ambr k* kali-c h2
- **drawing** pain: **Agar** aur h2 bell k* canth k* carb-v *Card-m* chin coc-c k* coloc k* con h2 dulc fd4.de kali-p fd1.de• kali-s fd4.de lyc h2 mang a1 meny h1 nat-sil fd3.de• nit-ac h2 plb k* sabad k* spig h1 spong fd4.de stann h2 thuj k* tritic-vg fd5.de valer k* vanil fd5.de
- **drawing** up leg:
  - : **amel.**: aur↓
    - : **sore**: aur h2
- **eating**:
  - : **after**:
    - : **agg.**: alum↓ arn↓ astac↓ cic↓ con↓ kali-p↓ phos↓ ran-b↓ sep↓ spong fd4.de sulph↓ *Verat*↓
      - . **cramping**: astac kr1 con h2 kali-p fd1.de• ran-b k*
      - . **cutting** pain: cic h1 spong h1 *Verat* k*
      - . **pressing** pain: alum h2 arn h1 phos h2 sep h2 sulph h2
      - . **stitching** pain: verat h1
    - : **amel.**: mag-c ran-b ter
  - : **agg.**: arg-met↓ caust bg1
    - : **pressing** pain: arg-met h1
  - : **amel.**: mag-c↓
- **eating – amel.**: ...
  - : **pressing** pain: mag-c h2
- **exertion** agg.: *Calc*
  - : **pressing** pain: *Calc* k*
- **flatulence**; as from: caps h1
- **flatus**; passing:
  - : **after**:
    - : **agg.**: zinc↓
      - . **cutting** pain: zinc h2
      - . **stitching** pain: zinc h2
  - : **amel.**: kali-c↓ kali-p↓ mag-m↓ mez↓ spong↓ squil↓
    - : **cramping**: kali-c h2 kali-p fd1.de• mez h2 squil h1
    - : **cutting** pain: kali-c h2 mag-m h2 spong fd4.de
    - : **pressing** pain: kali-c h2
    - : **stitching** pain: kali-c h2
  - : **before**: nat-m↓
    - : **sore**: nat-m h2
- **gnawing** pain: gamb kali-c h2 seneg sumb k*
- **hemorrhage**; during: sec↓
  - : **pressing** pain: sec hr1
- **inspiration** agg.: bry graph
- **jar** agg.: am-c h2 **Bell** lac-h sk4•
- **jar**; as from a: calc h2
- **lancinating**: aur-s k* elaps plb k*
- **leukorrhea**:
  - : **before**: lyc↓ sulph↓
    - : **cramping**: sulph h2
    - : **cutting** pain: lyc h2
  - : **during**: *Lyc*↓ nat-c↓ *Sil*↓
    - : **cutting** pain: *Lyc* bg2 nat-c bg2 *Sil* bg2
  - : **with**: sep↓
    - : **drawing** pain: sep h2
- **lying**:
  - : **abdomen**; on | **amel.**: chel
  - : **agg.**: *Sep Sulph* tritic-vg fd5.de
    - : **cramping**: sulph h2
    - : **pressing** pain: *Sulph* tritic-vg fd5.de
  - : **amel.**: nux-v↓
    - : **cutting** pain: nux-v
  - : **back**; on:
    - : **agg.**: ambr bar-c kali-s fd4.de spong↓
      - . **cramping**: ambr
      - . **pressing** pain: bar-c spong fd4.de
    - : **amel.**: onos↓
      - . **cramping**: onos vml3•
  - : **must** lie down: lyc↓
    - : **pressing** pain: lyc h2
  - : **side**; on | **left** | **amel.**: sang hr1
    - : **legs** drawn up; with | **amel.**: *Sep*
- **menses**: *Kreos*↓ *Lyc*↓ plat↓ *Puls*↓
  - : **after**:
    - : **agg.**: ars↓ cham iod kali-c↓ kreos mag-c merc nat-m *Plat* puls
      - . **cramping**: kreos
      - . **cutting** pain: kali-c plat puls
      - . **stitching** pain: ars
  - : **before**:
    - : **agg.**: aloe ant-t bg2 carb-v *Caust*↓ cimic *Cocc*↓ com k* crot-h cupr bg2 germ-met↓ **Kali-c**↓ **Lach Lyc** *Mag-p*↓ manc mang *Merc* nat-c↓ **Nat-m** k* neon↓ *Nit-ac Phos* plat raph k* sars senec↓ **Sep Sulph** k* tell↓ tep k* tritic-vg fd5.de *Vib* zinc zinc-p k2
      - . **cramping**: cimic *Cocc* **Kali-c** *Mag-p* manc *Nat-m* neon srj5• *Nit-ac* k* sars **Sulph** k* tell rsj10• *Vib* zinc
      - . **cutting** pain: *Caust* nat-c h2 senec sulph h2
      - . **pressing** pain: *Plat* k* *Sep*
      - . **stitching** pain:
        - **needles**; as from | **hot** needles: germ-met srj5•

Abdomen

- **menses – before – agg.**: ...
  - **extending** to:
    - **Back**: carb-v vib
    - **Umbilicus**: lach lyc phos sep
  - **cutting** pain | **reappear**; as though menses would: *Kreos Lyc* plat *Puls*
  - **during**:
    - **agg.**: abrom-a ks5 *Agar Am-c* arg-n ↓ arist-cl sp1 *Ars Bell* borx ↓ *Bov* bry **Calc** k* *Calc-p Carb-an Carb-v* cassia-s ccrh1• caust *Cimic* **Cocc** ↓ *Con* crot-h granit-m es1• graph kali-bi gk *Kali-c* kali-i ↓ lac-ac lac-d *Lach* lil-t lyc *Mag-c* mag-m *Mag-p* ↓ manc med ↓ merc mom-b br1 mur-ac *Murx* nat-c *Nat-m* nit-ac *Nux-m* petr-ra shn4• *Phos Plat* **Puls** *Sars* **Sec** k* sel gmj2 senec **Sep** sil *Stront-c* sul-ac **Sulph** verat *Xan*
      - **burning**: nat-m
      - **cramping**: *Agar* **Am-c** *Ars* **Cocc** *Con* granit-m es1• **Graph** *Mag-p* med pd nat-m h2 sulph h2
      - **cutting** pain: arg-n calc h2 carb-v h2 *Caust* **Kali-c** k* lil-t ptk1 nat-m *Senec* sulph k*
      - **pressing** feet against support: med ↓
        - **cramping**: med pd
      - **pressing** pain: calc h2 calc-p k* carb-an con *Kali-c* kali-i *Mag-c* mag-m *Murx Nat-c Nat-m Plat* k* **Puls Sec Sep**
      - **stitching** pain: borx nux-m hr1
      - **tearing** pain: *Agar Am-c* lach *Manc*
    - **beginning** of menses | **agg.**: cham bg2 con bg2 nit-ac bg2
  - **scanty**: asc-c ↓
    - **pressing** pain: asc-c c1
- **menses**; as from: lac-ac kr1*
- **metrorrhagia**, with: mag-c h2
  - **cramping**: mag-c h2
- **milk** agg.: ang ↓
  - **cutting** pain: ang h1
- **motion**:
  - **agg.**: **Bell** bry cassia-s ↓ dulc ↓ **Ferr** jug-r ↓ kali-n ↓ lil-t ph-ac ↓ sep ↓ sul-ac ↓
    - **burning**: kali-n h2
    - **pressing** pain: sep h2
    - **stitching** pain: cassia-s ccrh1• dulc fd4.de jug-r k* kali-n ph-ac sul-ac
  - **amel.**: am-c ↓ bar-c ↓ kali-n ↓ nicc ↓
    - **burning**: bar-c kali-n
    - **cutting** pain: nicc k*
    - **pressing** pain: am-c
    - **tearing** pain: kali-n h2
- **overlifting**, from: carb-v h2
- **ovulation**; during: granit-m es1•
- **paroxysmal**: am-c bry but-ac sp1 camph carb-v cham cocc con dig ferr hyos ign iod ip mur-ac nux-v **Puls** stann
- **pressing** pain: agar agn alum h2 am-c k* am-m ambr k* ant-t k* *Apis* aran arg-met ars-i asaf *Aur* aur-s k2 bar-c k* bar-i **Bell** k* bism h1 bry k* *Calc* k* calc-i k2 calc-p k* canth carb-v k* carbn-s caust k* cham chel k* chin k* cina cocc *Colch* coloc k* con k* croc cupr h2 dig h2 elaps gins k* *Helon* ign k* iod k* kali-c k* kali-i k* kali-s kreos **Lil-t** k* **Lyc** *Mag-m* med merc k* merc-i-f k* *Mez Nat-c* k* *Nat-m* k* nat-p nit-ac h2 **Nux-v** k* olib-sac wmh1 pall *Ph-ac* k* *Phos* k* **Plat** k* **Puls** k* ruta *Sec* k* sel rsj9• seneg k* **Sep** k* spig k* spong fd4.de squil *Stann* k* sul-i k2 *Sulph* k* *Tab* tarax tarent *Thuj* k* til tritic-vg fd5.de valer k* vanil fd5.de verb *Zinc* k* zinc-p k2
  - **asunder**: spig h1
  - **cramping**: sulph h2
  - **downward**: aloe gsy1 *Con* cupr h2 lil-t k* merc k* *Pall Psor* k* **Puls** *Sars* **Sep** spong fd4.de sulph
  - **genitals**, toward: **Bell** caust coloc h2 dig **Lil-t** *Nat-c* nit-ac **Nux-v** *Plat* **Puls Sep** sulph
  - **groin**, toward: mag-s c1 *Plat Sars* teucr
  - **inward**: cycl h1*
- **pressing** pain: ...
  - **menses** would appear; as if: am-m ambr *Apis Aur* bry cina cocc *Croc* kali-c kreos *Lil-t Lyc Nat-c* nat-m phos **Plat Puls** ruta h1 **Sep** stann til
  - **outward**: ang h1 **Bell** *Carb-an Kali-c* k* **Lil-t** lyc h2 *Nat-c Nat-m Plat* **Puls** sel rsj9• **Sep**
  - **paroxysmal**: iod h kali-c h2 *Tab* k*
- **pressure**:
  - **agg.**: ambr ↓ stann ↓ sulph ↓
    - **cutting** pain: sulph h2
    - **pressing** pain: stann h2
    - **stitching** pain: ambr k*
  - **amel.**: fago ↓ petr-ra shn4• sang hr1
    - **cramping**: fago k*
- **retraction** of abdomen agg.: bell ↓ kali-c ↓
  - **cramping**: bell h1 kali-c h2
  - **cutting** pain: kali-c h2
- **riding** in a carriage agg.: agar
- **rising** from sitting:
  - **amel.**: aur ↓
    - **sore**: aur h2
- **scratching**; after: cassia-s ↓
  - **burning**: cassia-s ccrh1•
- **sharp**: musca-d szs1 trios rsj11•
- **sitting**:
  - **agg.**: all-c am-c ↓ ang ↓ card-m chin ↓ iod ↓ mur-ac ↓ nicc ↓ nux-m ↓ spig ↓ tritic-vg fd5.de valer viol-t ↓
    - **cramping**: chin h1
    - **cutting** pain: mur-ac h2 nicc k* spig h1
    - **pressing** pain: am-c ang h1 iod h tritic-vg fd5.de
    - **stitching** pain: nux-m hr1 viol-t
  - **bent** forward:
    - **agg.**: *Bell* ↓ coloc ↓
      - **pressing** pain: *Bell*
      - **sore**: coloc h2
    - **must** sit bent forward: kali-c ↓ mag-m ↓
      - **cutting** pain: mag-m h2
      - **pressing** pain: kali-c h2
  - **erect**:
    - **agg.**: glon
    - **amel.**: sulph ↓
      - **cramping**: sulph h2
    - **must** sit erect: sulph ↓
      - **cramping**: sulph h2
- **sore**: *Acon Arg-n Ars* asc-t k* aur k* aur-ar k2 calad **Calc** k* canth k* carb-v h2 caust cycl euph h2 fago k* ferr-ar ferr-m k* *Hyos* k* jac-c kali-n k* ketogl-ac rly4• **Lach** k* *Lyss* mag-m mang k* merc *Nat-m* nit-ac h2 onos *Op* k* *Pall Phos* k* phys k* pic-ac k* prun psor puls *Rhus-t* sabin *Sars* sep spong fd4.de stann succ-ac rly4• *Sulph* **Ter** k* *Valer* **Verat** k* verb
- **standing** agg.: am-c ↓ arn ↓ chin k* dulc fd4.de lil-t ↓ mang ↓ mur-ac ↓ puls sulph ↓
  - **cramping**: chin h1
  - **cutting** pain: mang mur-ac h2
  - **pressing**: arn h1 lil-t br1 sulph h2
  - **stitching** pain: am-c k*
- **stepping**:
  - **agg.**: am-c h2 calc ↓
    - **cramping**: calc h2
  - **every** step; at: nux-v ↓ *Sil* ↓
    - **cutting** pain: nux-v *Sil*
- **stitching** pain: acon k* all-c aloe am-c k* ambr k* ammc k* *Anac* ang h1 ant-t k* arg-met *Ars* arund k* aur k* aur-ar k2 *Bell Bry* calc h2 cann-i k* carb-v h2 carbn-s *Caust* cham k* chel chin cimic k* coloc k* dream-p sdj1• dulc fd4.de elaps graph h2 jug-r k* kali-bi gk *Kali-c* kali-n *Kali-p* kali-s fd4.de lyc k* mang mez mur-ac h2 nat-m k* nit-ac k* nux-m gk *Nux-v* pall c1 *Ph-ac* k* phos k* plb k* plut-n srj7• podo k* ptel

- **stitching** pain: ...
  pycnop-sa mrz1 ran-b k* ruta fd4.de sabad k* samb sep k* spig k* spong fd4.de stann h2 sul-ac sulph h2 tarax k* tarent k* thuj k* tritic-vg fd5.de vanil fd5.de verb k* viol-t zinc h2
  - **cramping**: graph h2
  - **downward**: ptel
  - **followed** by | **nausea**: cassia-s ccrh1•
  - **forward**: laur
  - **needles**; as from | **hot** needles: germ-met srj5•
  - **outward**: calc h2 sulph
  - **transverse**: am-c k*
  - **upward**: cassia-s ccrh1•
- **stool**:
  - **after**:
    - **agg.**: agar ambr arg-met ↓ carb-v ↓ cassia-s ↓ coloc k* iod lyc ↓ pall ↓ *Pic-ac* spong ↓ zinc ↓
      - **cramping**: agar lyc h2
      - **cutting** pain: cassia-s ccrh1•
      - **pressing** pain: ambr k* arg-met h1 iod k* zinc h2
      - **stitching** pain: carb-v h2 pall c1 spong fd4.de
    - **amel.**: pall ↓ zinc ↓
      - **cutting** pain: pall
      - **pressing** pain: zinc h2
  - **before**: *Ars* ↓ *Coll* dulc ↓ gels haem k* mag-m h2 mang ↓ nat-m spig ↓ spong ↓ stram tarent thuj ↓ tritic-vg fd5.de vanil fd5.de
    - **cramping**: *Ars* k* *Coll Gels* stram k*
    - **pressing** pain: nat-m k* spig h1 thuj h1
    - **sore**: nat-m h2
    - **stitching** pain: dulc fd4.de mang h2 spong fd4.de tritic-vg fd5.de
  - **during**:
    - **agg.**: agar ↓ anac ↓ arg-met ↓ *Ars* ↓ calc ↓ kali-p fd1.de• **Lil-t** ↓ meny ↓ *Nat-m* ↓ nux-m ↓ *Podo* ↓ ptel rhus-v k* ruta fd4.de
      - **cramping**: agar h2 anac h2 *Ars* meny h1
      - **pressing** pain: arg-met h1 calc **Lil-t** *Nat-m* nux-m *Podo*
  - **straining** at:
    - **agg.**: sulph ↓
      - **cutting** pain: sulph h2
- **stooping** agg.: am-c kali-c lyc ↓ petr-ra shn4• sep ↓
  - **cramping**: am-c
  - **pressing** pain: kali-c h2 lyc h2 sep h2
- **stretching**:
  - **amel.**: iod ↓
    - **pressing** pain: iod h
- **supper**:
  - **after**:
    - **agg.**: ran-b ↓
      - **cramping**: ran-b k*
    - **amel.**: **Sep**
      - **pressing** pain: *Sep*
- **tearing** pain: anac h2 canth k* carb-v h2 chin k* *Colch* con k* iod k* kali-n h2 kali-s fd4.de lach nat-c h2 spig h1 verb h zinc
- **touch**:
  - **agg.**: cupr ↓ cycl a1 lyc ↓ nat-c ↓ nit-ac ↓ sulph h2 *Thuj* sne
    - **cramping**: cycl h1
    - **pressing** pain: cupr h2 cycl h1 nat-c h2 nit-ac h2 thuj k*
    - **sore**: lyc h2
    - **stitching** pain: lyc h2 nit-ac h2
  - **clothes** agg.; of: lil-t
- **turning** to side in bed: sulph ↓
  - **pressing** pain: sulph h2
- **ulcerative** pain: nit-ac
- **undressing** amel.: onos ↓
  - **cramping**: onos vml3•
- **urination**:
  - **after**:
    - **agg.**: ph-ac ↓ sul-ac ↓

- **urination – after – agg.**: ...
      - **cramping**: sul-ac h2
      - **pressing** pain: ph-ac
  - **amel.**: dios *Sep*
  - **before**: *Chel* ↓ sul-ac ↓ sulph ↓
    - **cramping**: *Chel* sul-ac h2
    - **cutting** pain: sulph h2
  - **delayed**; if desire to urinate is: *Lac-ac* lac-c phos prun puls ruta sep sul-ac
  - **during**:
    - **agg.**: bar-c ↓ *Lil-t* ↓ nit-ac ↓ *Nux-v* ↓ sul-ac ↓ vanil ↓
      - **cramping**: bar-c h2 sul-ac h2
      - **pressing** pain: *Lil-t Nux-v*
      - **stitching** pain: nit-ac k* vanil fd5.de
    - **amel.**: carb-an ↓
      - **stitching** pain: carb-an
  - **impossible**: phos h2
  - **urging** to; during: rhod bg2 spig h1
- **walking**:
  - **agg.**: acon calc coloc ↓ dulc fd4.de graph kali-i ↓ *Lil-t* ↓ mang ↓ merc ↓ mur-ac ↓ nat-c ↓ nat-m h2 *Prun* ↓ *Puls Sil* ↓ sulph ↓ zinc ↓
    - **cramping**: sulph h2 zinc
    - **cutting** pain: coloc h2 mang mur-ac h2 *Sil*
    - **pressing** pain: kali-i *Lil-t* merc nat-c h2
    - **sore**: *Prun*
  - **air**; in open:
    - **agg.**: agar calc kali-c ↓ meny ↓ *Nux-v* ↓
      - **cramping**: agar calc
      - **pressing** pain: kali-c h2 meny h1 *Nux-v*
    - **amel.**: lil-t ↓
      - **pressing** pain: lil-t br1
  - **amel.**: am-c ↓ sep
    - **pressing** pain: am-c
  - **bent**:
    - **must** walk bent: *Lyc* ↓ sulph ↓
      - **pressing** pain: *Lyc* sulph h2
  - **wind**; against the: sulph ↓
    - **pressing** pain: sulph h2
- **wandering** pain: dig h2
- **warmth**:
  - **amel.**: *Ars* nux-m *Nux-v*
    - **cramping**: *Ars*
- **weight**, as from a: bros-gau mrc1 nat-m h2
- **yawning** agg.: nat-c h2

○ • **Across**: **Cimic** ↓ kali-p ↓ *Lil-t* ↓ *Mel-c-s* ↓
  - **burning**: *Lil-t*
  - **sore**: *Mel-c-s* br1
  - **stitching** pain: **Cimic** sne kali-p

▽ • **extending** to:
  - **Back**: bamb-a stb2.de• carb-v *Croc* germ-met ↓ sabin spong fd4.de tritic-vg fd5.de vib
    - **cutting** pain: *Croc*
    - **stitching** pain:
      - **needles**; as from | **hot** needles: germ-met srj5•
  - **Chest**; left: spong ↓
    - **cutting** pain: spong h1*
  - **Epigastrium**: elaps ↓
    - **stitching** pain: elaps
  - **Genitals**: nat-c bg1 nux-m bg1 phos bg1
  - **Groin**: *Gins* mag-s c1 med c1 nat-m nat-sil fd3.de•
    - **stitching** pain: nat-m k*
  - **Hypochondrium**: ran-b ↓
    - **stitching** pain: ran-b k*
  - **Ilium**: mez ↓
    - **stitching** pain: mez k*
  - **Inguinal** region: kali-s ↓ zinc ↓

Abdomen

- **extending** to – **Inguinal** region: ...
  - **tearing** pain: kali-s fd4.de zinc h2
  - **Legs**, down the: con pd
  - **Loins** (See lumbar)
  - **Lower** limbs with painful tingling: *Gins*
  - **Lumbar** region: carb-v
  - **Perineum**: ars bg1 bell bg1 phos bg1
    - **stitching** pain: bell h1 phos h2
  - **Sacrum**: sep
  - **Sacrum** before menses: carb-v ↓
    - **drawing** pain: carb-v h2
  - **Sides**: carb-v
  - **Spermatic** cord: med ↓ verat ↓
    - **right**: med c1
    - **cutting** pain: med
    - **stitching** pain: verat h1
  - **Spine**: iod h
  - **Stomach**: ars elaps
  - **Symphysis**: mang h2
  - **Thighs**: con nat-m ↓ nux-v sep
    - **drawing** pain: nat-m h2
    - **Down** her thighs: granit-m es1•
  - **Umbilicus**: cadm-met tpw6 carb-v ↓ lach lyc phos sep
    - **stitching** pain: carb-v h2
  - **Upward**: [buteo-j sej6]
  - **Urethra**: lyc ↓ nat-c h2
    - **stitching** pain: lyc h2
    - **tearing** pain: nat-c h2
  - **Vagina**: ars dulc ↓
    - **stitching** pain: *Ars* dulc fd4.de

- **Ileocecal** region: agar ↓ aloe ↓ ammc ↓ **Apis** ↓ *Ars* ↓ *Bapt* ↓ bell k2 **Bry** but-ac ↓ *Calad* ↓ camph ↓ *Carb-ac* ↓ *Carbn-s* *Card-m* chel **Chin** *Cocc* coff ↓ colch con cop *Crot-h* dulc *Echi* ferr-p ↓ *Gamb* ↓ gnaph hura ↓ *Hydr* iris-t st *Kali-bi* ↓ kali-c ↓ kali-m ↓ kali-s ↓ kola ↓ *Lach* lim ↓ limen-b-c mlk9.de *Lyc* ↓ mag-c ↓ *Merc* ↓ **Merc-c** morg-g pte1• nat-s k2 neon ↓ *Nit-ac* **Phos** *Plb* pneu mtf11 rad-met ↓ rhus-t ↓ spong fd4.de succ-ac ↓ *Ter* *Thuj* tritic-vg fd5.de verat x-ray ↓
  - **left**: naja mtf11
  - **evening**:
    - **and** night: lyc ↓
      - **stitching** pain: lyc h2
  - **breathing** agg.: lyc ↓
    - **stitching** pain: lyc h2
  - **burning**: *Calad* camph h1 succ-ac rly4•
  - **cramping**: aloe bro1 bell bro1 bry bro1 but-ac sp1* coff bro1 ferr-p bro1 *Gamb* bro1 iris-t bro1 kali-m bro1 lim bro1 mag-c bro1 *Merc* bro1 *Merc-c* bro1 plb bro1 rad-met bro1 rhus-t bro1
  - **drawing** pain: tritic-vg fd5.de x-ray rb2
  - **drawing** up legs: kola stb3•
    - **sore**: kola stb3•
  - **flatus**; from obstructed: verat ↓
    - **pressing** pain: verat h1
  - **gnawing** pain: x-ray rb2
  - **motion** agg.: nit-ac k2
  - **pressure** agg.: but-ac sp1
  - **sharp**: neon srj5•
  - **sore**: **Apis** *Ars* *Bapt* **Bell** **Bry** but-ac sp1 *Calad* *Carb-ac* *Cocc* *Colch* cop *Gamb* *Kali-bi* kali-c kola stb3• *Lach* *Lyc* *Merc* *Merc-c* *Nit-ac* *Phos* plb ter
  - **stitching** pain: agar ammc camph h1 carbn-s *Card-m* hura kali-s fd4.de lyc h2 spong fd4.de succ-ac rly4• tritic-vg fd5.de
  - **stool** agg.; after: carbn-s ↓
    - **stitching** pain: carbn-s
  - **touch** agg.: bell k2
  - **turning** | **body**:
    - **agg.**: lyc ↓
      - **stitching** pain: lyc h2

- **Ileocecal** region – **turning**: ...
    - **side**; to | **right**: ammc
  - **walking** agg.: hura ↓
    - **stitching** pain: hura

- **Iliac** fossa: bacls-10 fmm1• morg-p fmm1• pert-vc ↓ prot fmm1• syc fmm1•
  - **right**: diph-t-tpt jl2 syc bka1•
    - **extending** to:
      - **left**: sang ↓
        - **cutting** pain: sang
  - **left**: syc bka1•
  - **sore**: pert-vc vk9
  - ▽ **extending** to:
    - **Rectum**: sang ↓
      - **cutting** pain: sang

- **Iliac** region: agar k* *Agn* ↓ aids nl2• alum anac ↓ anthraq ↓ aur ↓ berb brom ↓ bros-gau ↓ calc k* *Carb-ac* carb-an ↓ *Carb-v* k* cartl-s rly4• cassia-s ↓ cench k2 cham ↓ cic ↓ cimic k* *Cocc* ↓ crot-t cupr k* dig ↓ dios k* dulc elaps euph ↓ eupi k* gels k* grat hep ↓ heroin ↓ iod ↓ iris kali-chl ↓ kali-n ↓ ketogl-ac ↓ kreos k* laur ↓ led ↓ lil-t k* lith-c lyc ↓ merc ↓ mez ↓ morg-g pte1• nat-ar nat-p ↓ ox-ac k* phos k* plan k* plat plb k* ptel k* sil ↓ spig spong ↓ stann staph ↓ streptoc rly4• suis-em ↓ *Ter* thuj ↓ zinc k* zing k*
  - **right**: bacls-10 pte1• bapt k2 *Cocc* graph ↓ iris-t mtf *Kali-c* lil-t k2 morg-p pte1• phos phys phyt *Pic-ac* plut-n ↓ ptel k* sumb trios ↓ xan ↓ zinc ↓
    - **cramping**: graph h2 xan c1
    - **cutting** pain: trios rsj11•
    - **stitching** pain: plut-n srj7• zinc h2
  - **left**: aids ↓ aln ↓ ap-g br bacls-10 pte1• *Caust* cimic k* *Coloc* *Con* ↓ crot-h cupr k* dios eupi k* fic-m ↓ gels k* morg-p pte1• naja nat-ar ox-ac k* pall ↓ plut-n srj7• puls-n sal-fr sle1• spong ↓ **Thuj** trios ↓
    - **boring** pain: coloc h2
    - **cramping**: trios rsj11•
    - **stitching** pain: aids nl2• aln vva1• *Con* fic-m gya1 pall c1 sal-fr sle1• spong h1
    - **extending** to | **right**: ap-g br
  - **morning**: berb ↓ cench k2 cina ↓ sumb k*
    - **cramping**: cina a1
    - **stitching** pain: berb k*
    - **stool**; before: sumb k*
  - **noon**: thuj
  - **evening**: borx dios lyc ↓ naja rhus-t k* zinc k*
    - **stitching** pain: lyc h2
    - **supper** agg.; after: zinc k*
  - **night**: dios pic-ac k* trios ↓
    - **midnight**:
      - **before** | **23** h: pic-ac
    - **cramping**: trios rsj11•
  - **bending** agg.: puls-n
  - **breakfast** agg.; after: zinc k*
  - **burrowing**: dulc k*
  - **cough** agg.; during: *Caust* eupi k*
  - **cramping**: aur h2 bros-gau mrc1 euph h2
  - **cutting** pain: *Agn* nat-p thuj
  - **diarrhea**; during: bros-gau ↓
    - **cramping**: bros-gau mrc1
  - **dinner**; after: phos k*
  - **drawing** up thigh amel.: aur ↓
    - **sore**: aur k*
  - **eating** | **amel.**: phys
  - **expiration** agg.; during: spong ↓
    - **stitching** pain: spong h1
  - **lancinating**: ketogl-ac rly4• suis-em rly4•
  - **lying** on left side agg.: *Com* k* phys
  - **menses**; during: *Con* ↓

- **menses**; during: ...
  - **stitching** pain: *Con*
- **motion** agg.: cassia-s ↓ ptel$_{k*}$ puls-n
  - **stitching** pain: cassia-s$_{ccrh1}$•
- **paroxysmal**: *Cocc*
- **pressing** pain: hep$_{h2}$ iod$_{h}$ led$_{h1}$ thuj$_{h1}$
- **pressure**:
  - **agg.**: phos ↓
    - **sore**: phos$_{h2}$
  - **amel.**: cassia-s ↓ dulc$_{a1}$ phys
    - **stitching** pain: cassia-s$_{ccrh1}$•
- **raising** arm agg.: eupi$_{k*}$
- **sitting** agg.: agar$_{k*}$ aur ↓ kali-n ↓
  - **sore**: aur$_{k*}$
  - **stitching** pain: kali-n
- **sore**: anthraq$_{rly4}$• aur$_{k*}$ carb-an cic kreos staph$_{h1}$ [heroin$_{sdj2}$]
- **standing**:
  - **amel.**: aur ↓
    - **sore**: aur$_{k*}$
- **stitching** pain: agar alum$_{k*}$ anac *Berb*$_{k*}$ brom cassia-s$_{ccrh1}$• cham$_{k*}$ kali-chl$_{k*}$ kali-n laur$_{k*}$ led$_{k*}$ lyc$_{k*}$ merc$_{k*}$ mez$_{k*}$ sil$_{k*}$ spig$_{k*}$ spong$_{h1}$ thuj$_{k*}$
  - **pulsating** pain: thuj$_{h1}$
- **stool**; before: sumb$_{k*}$
- **stooping** agg.: spong ↓ zinc ↓
  - **stitching** pain: spong$_{h1}$ zinc$_{h2}$
- **supper** agg.; after: zinc
- **tearing** pain: crot-t$_{k*}$ dig$_{h2}$
- **touch** agg.: staph ↓
  - **sore**: staph$_{h1}$
- **waking**; on: trios ↓
  - **cramping**: trios$_{rsj11}$•
- **walking**:
  - **agg.**: cassia-s ↓ con$_{h2}$ eupi
    - **stitching** pain: cassia-s$_{ccrh1}$•
  - **air**; in open | **amel.**: phys
  - **room** agg.; in a: thuj

○ • **Above** | **right**: malar$_{jl2}$
- **Muscles**: *All-s*$_{br1}$
- **Spots**; in small: caps ↓
  - **stitching** pain: caps$_{vh}$

▽ • **extending** to:
  - **Ilium** to ilium; from: asar cimic lil-t sep ↓
    - **stitching** pain: lil-t sep$_{h2}$
  - **Knee**: *Kali-c*
  - **Leg**; down: kreos ↓
    - **stitching** pain: kreos
  - **Testes**: hydr ↓
    - **cutting** pain: hydr
  - **Thighs**, down: *Thuj*

- **Ilium**: alum ↓ chel ↓ cic ↓ nat-c ↓ plat ↓ sulph ↓
  - **left**:
    - **stooping** agg.: stann ↓
      - **sprained**; as if: stann$_{h2}$
  - **morning**: cina ↓
    - **cutting** pain: cina
  - **pressing** pain: alum$_{h2}$ chel$_{k*}$
  - **sore**: cic$_{h1}$ nat-c plat$_{h2}$ sulph$_{k*}$

○ • **Anterior** superior spinous process: sulph ↓
  - **cutting** pain: sulph

- **Ilium**: ...
  - **Crest** of ileum: alum ↓ androc$_{srj1}$• ang ↓ bell berb brom$_{k*}$ calc calc-act ↓ camph carb-an cench$_{k2}$ cham$_{k*}$ cic ↓ eupi$_{k*}$ form$_{k*}$ ip *Iris* *Kali-c* kali-n ↓ kali-s$_{fd4.de}$ kreos ↓ led lyc ↓ manc ↓ merc ↓ naja ↓ nat-m ↓ olnd ↓ plan$_{k*}$ plat ↓ podo ↓ rhus-t ruta ↓ sabad$_{k*}$ sang$_{k*}$ spig ↓ staph stront-c ↓ tell$_{k*}$ *Ter* thuj ↓ zinc
    - **right**: dios$_{kr1}$ kali-s$_{fd4.de}$
    - **left**: berb$_{dgt1}$ eupi$_{k*}$ stann ↓
      - **cramping**: stann$_{h2}$
    - **morning**: staph
    - **night**: sang$_{k*}$
    - **breathing** agg.: calc$_{h2}$
    - **cough** agg.; during: eupi$_{k*}$
    - **cramping**: ang$_{h1}$ calc-act$_{h1}$ plat$_{h2}$
    - **drawing** pain: cic$_{h1}$ lyc$_{k*}$ ruta thuj$_{k*}$
    - **inspiration** agg.: mill ↓
      - **stitching** pain: mill$_{k*}$
    - **motion** agg.: *Ter*
    - **pressing** pain: carb-an$_{h2}$ led$_{h1}$
    - **pressure** | **amel.**: sabad$_{k*}$
    - **raising** arm agg.: eupi$_{k*}$
    - **rising** from sitting agg.: bell
    - **sitting** agg.: sabad$_{k*}$ zinc
      - **tearing** pain: zinc
    - **sore**: carb-an$_{h2}$ podo$_{fd3.de}$•
    - **stitching** pain: ang$_{h1}$ berb$_{k*}$ brom$_{k*}$ eupi kali-n$_{k*}$ kreos$_{k*}$ manc$_{k*}$ merc$_{k*}$ naja nat-m$_{k*}$ olnd$_{k*}$ plan spig$_{k*}$ stront-c thuj$_{k*}$
      - **downward**: zinc
    - **tearing** pain: alum$_{h2}$ *Berb*$_{k*}$ calc$_{h2}$ zinc
      - **upward**: berb
    - **walking**:
      - **agg.**: calc$_{h2}$ eupi$_{k*}$ led
        - **stitching** pain: eupi
      - **amel.**: sabad$_{k*}$ staph
    - **warmth** | **amel.**: staph
    - **Above**: sulph ↓
      - **cramping**: sulph$_{h2}$
    - **extending** to:
      - **Chest**: lach ↓
        - **stitching** pain: lach
      - **Gluteal** muscles: *Berb* ↓
        - **stitching** pain: *Berb*
        - **tearing** pain: *Berb*
      - **Inguinal** region and thigh: sep ↓
        - **stitching** pain: sep$_{h2}$
        - **tearing** pain: sep$_{h2}$
      - **Knee**: **Kali-c**
      - **Lumbar** region: mag-m ↓
        - **stitching** pain: mag-m
      - **Thigh**: berb$_{dgt1}$ ruta ↓ staph thuj ↓ xanth ↓
        - **drawing** pain: ruta thuj xanth$_{c1}$
        - **Front** of thigh, when urinating: berb$_{bg3}$

▽ • **extending** to:
  - **Scapula**: nat-m ↓
    - **cutting** pain: nat-m$_{k*}$
  - **Thigh**: nat-m ↓
    - **cutting** pain: nat-m$_{k*}$

- **Inguinal** and pubic region: agn ↓ alum ↓ am-c ↓ am-m ↓ ant-t$_{b7.de*}$ arg-met ↓ *Ars* ↓ asaf ↓ asar$_{b7.de*}$ aur ↓ bapt ↓ bar-c ↓ *Bell* ↓ bov ↓ bry ↓ calc$_{b4.de*}$ calc-p ↓ cann-s ↓ canth$_{b7.de*}$ carb-an ↓ carb-v ↓ caust ↓ chel ↓ chin ↓ cic ↓ clem ↓ cocc ↓ coff ↓ coloc$_{b4.de*}$ con ↓ croc$_{b7.de*}$ dig ↓ dros ↓ dulc ↓ euph ↓ gamb ↓ gran ↓ *Graph*$_{b4a.de}$ guaj ↓ ham ↓ hell ↓ hydr$_{bg2}$ ign ↓ iod ↓ kali-c ↓ kali-i ↓ kali-n ↓ lach ↓ laur ↓ lyc$_{b4.de*}$ m-ambo ↓ *M-arct* ↓ m-aust ↓ mag-m ↓ merc$_{b4.de*}$ mez ↓ mur-ac ↓ nat-c ↓ nat-m$_{b4.de*}$ nat-s ↓ *Nux-v* ↓ ol-an ↓ phos$_{b4.de*}$ plat ↓ prun ↓ psor ↓ ran-b$_{b7.de*}$ rhod ↓ rhus-t$_{b7.de*}$ sabad ↓ sars ↓ sep ↓ sil$_{b4.de*}$ spig ↓ spong ↓ stann ↓ staph ↓ stront-c ↓ sul-ac ↓ sulph ↓ thuj ↓ valer$_{b7.de*}$ verat$_{b7.de*}$ viol-t ↓ zinc ↓

Abdomen

- **boring** pain: arg-met b7.de* coloc b4.de* *M-arct* b7a.de merc b4.de* spig b7.de* verat bg2
- **burning**: alum b4.de* am-m b7.de* ars b4.de* aur b4a.de bry bg2 canth b7.de* graph b4.de* kali-c b4.de* kali-n bg2 *Lyc* b4.de* mur-ac b4.de* nat-s bg2 sep b4.de* spig b7.de* stront-c b4.de* sulph b4.de*
- **drawing** pain: arg-met b7.de* aur b4.de* bar-c b4.de* bry bg2 calc b4.de* cann-s b7.de* canth b7.de* chin b7.de* clem b4.de* cocc bg2 dig b4.de* dulc b4a.de gran bg2 ham bg2 kali-c b4.de* *Lyc* b4.de* merc b4.de* nat-m b4.de* *Nux-v* b7a.de ol-an bg2 plat b4.de* rhod b4.de* rhus-t b7.de* sabad b7.de* stann b4.de* staph bg2 thuj b4.de* valer b7.de* zinc b4.de*
- **gnawing** pain: lach bg2
- **pinching** pain: alum b4.de* am-c bg2 aur b4.de* bov b4.de* carb-v b4.de* chel b7.de* gamb bg2 kali-c b4.de* kali-i bg2 nat-c b4.de* nat-m bg2 phos b4.de* sars b4.de* stann b4.de* sul-ac bg2
- **pressing** pain: guaj bg2
- **sore**: am-c b4.de* arg-met b7.de* bov b4.de* calc b4.de* caust b4.de* chin b7.de* cocc b7.de* dig b4.de* euph b4.de* m-ambo b7.de m-arct b7.de mag-m b4.de* mez b4.de* *Nux-v* b7a.de sars b4.de* spig b7.de* valer b7.de*
- **stitching** pain: agn b7.de* alum b4.de* am-m b7.de* arg-met b7.de* ars b4.de* asaf b7.de* bapt bg2 *Bell* b4.de* bov b4.de* calc bg2 canth b7.de* carb-an b4.de* caust b4.de* chin b7.de* cocc b7.de* coff b7.de* coloc b4.de* con b4.de* croc b7.de* dig b4.de* dros b7.de* graph b4.de* hell b7.de* ign b7.de* kali-c b4.de* laur b7.de* lyc b4a.de* m-arct b7.de m-aust b7.de mag-m b4.de* merc b4.de* mez b4.de* mur-ac b4.de* nat-c b4.de* nat-m bg2 prun bg2 psor bg2 rhus-t b7.de* sep b4.de* spig b7.de* stann b4.de* staph b7.de* stront-c b4.de* sul-ac b4.de* sulph b4.de* thuj b4.de* verat b7.de* viol-t b7.de* zinc b4.de*
- **tearing** pain: am-m b7a.de ant-t b7.de* *Ars* b4a.de canth b7.de* chin b7.de* euph b4.de* lyc b4a.de* mez b4.de* sil b4.de* spong b7.de* stront-c b4.de* sul-ac b4a.de* thuj b4.de*
- **ulcerative** pain: am-m b7.de* ant-t bg2 arg-met bg2 bell bg2 calc bg2 calc-p bg2 cann-s b7.de* cic b7.de* clem bg2 graph bg2 iod bg2 kali-c bg2 mez bg2 nat-c bg2 ran-b bg2 rhus-t bg2 sars bg2

○ • **Skin**; below the: *Am-m* ↓
  - **ulcerative** pain: *Am-m* b7a.de

- **Inguinal** region (= groin): acon ↓ aesc aeth **Agar** agn ↓ aids ↓ **All-c** aloe alum k* am-c am-m k* ammc ↓ amp ↓ anac ↓ ang ↓ ant-c h2 ant-t ↓ *Apis* *Arg-met* ↓ *Arg-n* ↓ arge-pl rwt5• **Arn** ↓ ars ars-i arund ↓ asaf ↓ asc-c hr1 aspar ↓ aur aur-ar k2 aur-i k2 aur-s k2 bamb-a ↓ bapt bar-c bar-i bar-m ↓ bar-s k2 **Bell** ↓ **Berb** borx *Bov* brach brom **Bry** cact ↓ cadm-met tpw6 calc calc-ar ↓ calc-p calc-s ↓ calc-sil k2 calen ↓ camph ↓ cann-s canth caps hr1 carb-ac ↓ **Carb-an** ↓ carb-v carbn-s carl ↓ castm castor-eq ↓ caul caust *Cham* ↓ *Chel* chin ↓ chinin-s ↓ cic ↓ cimic k* *Clem* cob coc-c *Cocc* coff ↓ *Coloc* *Con* cortico tpw7 croc crot-t cub ↓ cupr ↓ *Cycl* ↓ dig ↓ dios dros ↓ dulc elaps ↓ euph ↓ euphr ↓ eupi c1* ferr ↓ ferr-i fl-ac *Gamb* gent-c ↓ gins *Gran* ↓ graph grat ↓ guaj ↓ ham hell ↓ helon ↓ hep ↓ hura hydr *Ign* ↓ ina-i mlk9.de indg iod jatr-c kali-ar ↓ kali-bi kali-c kali-i kali-m ↓ kali-n kali-s kali-sil k2 kreos *Lac-c* lac-d ↓ lac-h sk4• lac-leo ↓ *Lach* lat-m bnm6• laur ↓ lept *Lil-t* ↓ *Lyc* lycps-v k* lyss *M-arct* ↓ m-aust ↓ *Mag-c* mag-m mag-s manc mang ↓ mang-p ↓ *Med* meny ↓ *Merc* merc-c bro1 merl ↓ mez *Mur-ac* ↓ murx naja nat-ar ↓ *Nat-c* ↓ *Nat-m* nat-ox ↓ nat-s nept-m ↓ nicc ↓ nit-ac nux-m ↓ *Nux-v* pall c1 par ↓ petr ph-ac ↓ phos phys phyt pic-ac *Plat* plut-n ↓ podo bro1 prun ↓ psor *Puls* ↓ ran-b ↓ ran-s ↓ raph rat rheum ↓ *Rhod* ↓ rhus-t ↓ ruta fd4.de sabad ↓ sars ↓ sec senec ↓ *Sep* ↓ sil spig spong stann staph ↓ *Stront-c* ↓ stry ↓ suis-hep ↓ sul-ac sul-i k2 *Sulph* symph ↓ tanac ptk2 tarax ↓ *Tarent* tell ↓ ter ↓ teucr ↓ ther ↓ *Thuj* tritic-vg fd5.de *Valer* ↓ vanil fd5.de verat ↓ verat-v *Vib* ↓ viol-t ↓ zinc zinc-p k2 zing
  - **alternating** sides: ter ↓
    - **dragging**, bearing down: ter
  - **right**: aesc agar ↓ aloe am-m ammc ↓ *Apis* ↓ ars aur ↓ bapt ↓ bar-c *Berb* ↓ bov **Bry** ↓ calc-p ↓ *Carb-an* carb-v card-m ↓ castm cham ↓ clem ↓ cocc ↓ cop dig ↓ dros ↓ dulc fd4.de ferr-i ↓ fl-ac ↓ gamb ↓ gent-c gran ↓ ham fd3.de• hell helon hydrog srj2• indg ↓ iod kali-bi kali-c h2 kali-i ↓ kali-n ↓ kali-s ↓ laur ↓ lyc ↓ lyss mag-c ↓ mang ↓ **Merc** mez **Murx** ↓ nat-c ↓ nat-m ↓ nat-s petr-ra shn4• plut-n ↓ podo br1* prun ↓ psor pycnop-sa ↓ sabad ↓ sars ↓ sep ↓ sil spong fd4.de stront-c ↓ sul-ac *Sulph* ↓ symph fd3.de• tax ↓ ter ↓ thuj ↓ tritic-vg fd5.de vanil fd5.de zinc
    - **then** left: calc-p hydr lyc phys
    - **burning**: am-m h2 *Berb* bry fl-ac kali-c kali-n mang stront-c

- **Inguinal region – right**: ...
    - **cramping**: aloe bov k* carb-v k* dig h2 gamb k* indg k* mag-c k* nat-c h2 plut-n srj7• sul-ac k* zinc k*
    - **cutting** pain: *Bry* hydrog srj2• podo c1 ter
    - **drawing** pain: agar aloe bapt k* bar-c h2 bov card-m gran k* kali-s fd4.de petr-ra shn4• sil thuj k* [tax jsj7]
    - **flexing** the thigh: *Lyc*
    - **pressing** pain: aur carb-v h2 clem h2 hell k* iod k* lyc k* mez nat-s podo fd3.de• sep h2 spong fd4.de symph fd3.de• vanil fd5.de
    - **sore**: *Apis* calc-p iod sars *Sulph*
    - **stitching** pain: am-m ammc *Ars* bapt hr1 bar-c bov **Bry** cham cocc dros ferr-i hell kali-c h2 kali-i kali-n laur lyc mang mez **Murx** nat-c nat-m plut-n srj7• prun pycnop-sa mrz1 sabad sulph thuj tritic-vg fd5.de
    - **tearing** pain: kali-c h2 mez h2 thuj h1
    - **extending** to:
      - **left**: lyc ↓
        - **cutting** pain: lyc
      - **Mamma**; left: **Murx** ↓
        - **stitching** pain: **Murx**
      - **Thigh**: alet vh1 plut-n ↓ podo ↓
        - **stitching** pain: plut-n srj7• podo
  - **left**: aesc ↓ aeth ↓ *All-c* ↓ alum am-m h2 ammc ↓ arg-met ars bapt hr1 bell ↓ berb brach brom brucel sa3• *Bry* calc calc-s ↓ castor-eq ↓ *Chel* cimic ↓ cob coc-c ↓ crot-t *Cycl* ↓ dios ↓ dulc a1 elaps ↓ euphr ↓ gamb ↓ graph ↓ ham fd3.de• hydrog ↓ kali-n ↓ kali-s ↓ *Lac-c* *Lach* ↓ lyc ↓ mag-m ↓ med merc ↓ nat-p ↓ nat-s ↓ nicc ↓ nit-ac pall ↓ petr-ra shn4• phasco-ci rbp2 phos h2 *Pic-ac* plb ↓ plut-n srj7• podo fd3.de• ruta fd4.de sars sep spong fd4.de stann suis-hep ↓ sul-ac ↓ sulph symph ↓ tarent ↓ tell ↓ trios ↓ tritic-vg fd5.de vanil fd5.de visc c1 xan ↓ zinc ↓
    - **then** right: dios lach podo fd3.de•
    - **morning**: *Bry*
    - **burning**: mag-m h2 pall visc c1
    - **cramping**: chel k* kali-n sars k* stann k* suis-hep rly4• symph fd3.de• xan c1
    - **cutting** pain: aesc hydrog srj2• tell trios rsj11•
    - **drawing** pain: aeth k* alum ammc gamb kali-s fd4.de lyc k* stann k* tritic-vg fd5.de vanil fd5.de
    - **micturition**, during: ars ↓
      - **drawing** pain: ars
    - **postoperative**: naja pd
    - **pressing** pain: *All-c* k* berb k* calc podo fd3.de• sulph k* zinc k*
    - **sore**: dios elaps *Lach*
    - **stitching** pain: bell calc-s castor-eq cimic gk coc-c *Cycl* dulc fd4.de euphr graph kali-n h2 mag-m merc nat-p fkr6.de nat-s nicc plb sep bg1 spong fd4.de tarent tell
    - **tearing** pain: sul-ac h2
    - **urinate** be postponed; if desire to: *Lac-ac*
    - **urination** agg.; during: ars
    - **extending** to:
      - **Axilla**: nat-s *Thuj*
        - **stitching** pain: nat-s
      - **Glans**: asar h1
      - **Testes**; into: petr-ra shn4• sep
  - **morning**: rat ↓ sul-ac ↓ symph ↓ tritic-vg ↓ zinc ↓
    - **cramping**: rat k*
    - **pressing** pain: sul-ac k* symph fd3.de• tritic-vg fd5.de
    - **stitching** pain: zinc h2
    - **waking**; on: sul-ac ↓
      - **hernia** would protrude; as if a: sul-ac h2
  - **forenoon**: alum ↓ calc ↓ thuj ↓
    - **11** h: mag-c ↓
      - **cramping**: mag-c
    - **burning**: alum
    - **cutting** pain: alum
    - **stitching** pain: calc thuj
  - **noon**: thuj
    - **drawing** pain: thuj k*

- **afternoon**: all-c ↓ chin ↓ laur ↓ mag-c ↓ mag-m ↓ mag-s ↓ petr-ra shn4• rat ↓
  - **15** h: mag-c ↓
    - **cramping**: mag-c
  - **16** h: nicc ↓ sulph ↓
    - **cramping**: nicc
    - **stitching** pain: sulph
  - **coffee** agg.: all-c ↓
    - **pressing** pain: all-c k*
  - **dragging**, bearing down: mag-c mag-m
  - **pressing** pain: all-c k*
  - **sore**: mag-s
  - **stitching** pain: chin laur rat
  - **walking** in open air agg.: nat-s ↓
    - **stitching** pain: nat-s
- **evening**: alum am-m ↓ borx castm ↓ dios ↓ dulc fd4.de kali-c ↓ kali-n ↓ lyc ↓ mur-ac ↓ sil spong fd4.de teucr ↓ vanil fd5.de
  - **cutting** pain: am-m h2 dios k* lyc k*
  - **dragging**, bearing down: teucr
  - **drawing** pain: borx
  - **pressing** pain: alum k* spong fd4.de
  - **sore**: dios
  - **stitching** pain: am-m h2 castm kali-n h2 mur-ac a1 spong fd4.de
  - **tearing** pain: kali-c h2 sil k*
  - **walking** agg.: hydr vanil fd5.de
- **night**: carb-an ↓ mag-c ↓ zinc ↓
  - **cutting** pain: mag-c
  - **dragging**, bearing down: mag-c
  - **drawing** pain: zinc h2
  - **stitching** pain: carb-an
- **afterpains**: *Cimic*
- **ascending**:
  - **agg.**: alum bg1 pic-ac
  - **stairs**:
    - **agg.**: alum ↓
      - **cramping**: alum k*
      - **stitching** pain: alum
- **bed** agg.; in: dios ↓
  - **sore**: dios
- **bending**:
  - **agg.**: mez ↓
    - **pressing** pain: mez h2
    - **sore**: mez h2
  - **backward**:
    - **amel.**: chin ↓
      - **tearing** pain: chin k*
  - **painful** side; to:
    - **agg.**: ptel ↓
      - **stitching** pain: ptel
- **blow**; pain as from a: camph bg2
- **breathing** deep:
  - **amel.**: carb-an ↓
    - **cutting** pain: carb-an h2
- **burning**: alum *Arn* ars aur bar-c *Berb* bov bry canth clem a1 fl-ac graph grat kali-c kali-i lil-t lyc mag-c mang mur-ac phos ruta h1 sep stront-c sulph
- **burrowing**: am-m b7.de ars b4.de cimic bg1 coc-c k* spig b7.de* spong h1
- **clawing** pain: hep c1 kali-i
- **coffee**; from: *Nux-v* bg2
- **coition**; after: ther k*
- **colic**, during: phos ↓
  - **dragging**, bearing down: phos h2
- **contracting**: rhus-t h1*
- **cough** agg.; during: *Alumn* k* ambr ↓ *Bell* ↓ borx k* brom *Calc* lach ↓ m-aust ↓ *Nat-m* petr petr-ra shn4• tarent thuj ↓ **Verat** ↓
  - **stitching** pain: ambr b7a.de *Bell* b4a.de lach m-aust b7a.de thuj **Verat** b7.de*
  - **tearing** pain: tarent k*
- **cramping**: *Aloe* k* am-c am-m k* ang bg2 arg-met vh1 ars bro1 aur b4.de* aur-i k2 bell bg2 bov k* *Bry* calc k* carb-v k* caust bg2 *Chel* k* chin b7.de* cimic k* coloc bg2 dig b4.de* *Gamb* k* graph bro1 *Ign* b7.de* indg k* kali-c k* kali-i k* *Kreos* k* mag-c k* nat-s k* **Nux-v** bg2 petr k* phos h2 rat k* sep bro1 spong b7.de* stann k* suis-hep rly4• sul-ac k* sulph k* symph fd3.de• thuj bg2 zinc k*
  - **intermittent**: nat-c h2
  - **paroxysmal**: nat-m k*
- **cutting** pain: aesc k* all-c alum k* am-m k* arg-met k* *Arg-n* k* aur k* bamb-a stb2.de• bell bg2 berb borx k2 *Bry* calc calc-p k* *Canth* k* carb-an k* caust k* *Coloc* cycl gamb iod k* kali-bi lyc k* m-arct b7.de mag-c merc k* nat-m par b7.de* ph-ac k* *Puls* bg2 spig k* tell k* ter k* thuj k* valer k*
- **dancing**: alum
  - **while**: alum ↓
    - **drawing** pain: alum
- **delivery**; during: cimic
- **dinner** | **after**:
  - **agg.**: nat-c ↓
    - **cramping**: nat-c h2
  - **during**:
    - **agg.**: mur-ac ↓
      - **stitching** pain: mur-ac
- **dislocated**; as if: agar b4.de* am-m b7.de* euph b4.de* tarax b7.de*
- **dragging**, bearing down: alum b4.de* am-m k* *Apis* aur b4.de* borx bg2 brom bry calc k* calen ptk1 cann-s b7.de* canth carb-an k* caust bg2* *Cham* k* *Chel* k* chin b7.de* clem k* coc-c k* cocc b7.de* *Con* k* cub c1 dulc bg2 ferr gent-c gran graph b4.de* ham helon kali-c k* kali-i kali-n k* lac-d *Lach* *Lil-t* k* lyc b4a.de* m-arct b7.de mag-c k* mag-m k* mag-s med *Merc* b4.de* murx *Nat-c* k* *Nux-v* b7.de* phos k* *Plat* rat rhus-t b7.de* *Sep* stann b4.de* sul-ac b4.de* ter teucr k*
  - **alternating** with | **pressure** in genitals: plat h2
  - **forward**: caust
  - **outward**: con kali-c
- **drawing** in abdomen agg.: kali-c h2*
- **drawing** pain: aeth k* agar k* aloe alum ammc k* aspar aur k* bapt k* bov bry k* cact calc k* calc-p k* *Chel* k* *Clem* k* coc-c k* cocc k* gamb gran k* kali-c k* kali-i k* kali-s fd4.de lil-t k* *Lyc* k* *Lyss* *Merc* k* mez nat-m k* *Plat* k* rat *Rhod* k* ruta fd4.de sil stann k* symph fd3.de• ter k* thuj k* tritic-vg fd5.de valer vanil fd5.de zinc k*
  - **alternating** with | **prickling** pain: zinc k*
  - **convulsive**: chel k*
  - **menses** would appear; as if: cocc k* lyc k* *Plat* k*
  - **spasmodic**: agar *Chel*
- **drawing** up legs:
  - **agg.**: sulph ↓ ther
    - **pressing** pain: sulph h2
  - **amel.**: mez ↓
    - **pressing** pain: mez
  - **must** draw up legs: aur ↓
    - **cutting** pain: aur h2
- **drawing** up the knee; when | **amel.**: *Coloc* mez pall petr-ra shn4•
- **eating**; after: kali-bi ↓
  - **stitching** pain: kali-bi
- **ejaculation**; after: petr ↓
  - **stitching** pain: petr k*
- **exertion**; from: petr-ra shn4•
- **expiration** agg.: mez ↓ nat-c ↓
  - **pressing** pain: mez h2
  - **sore**: mez h2
  - **stitching** pain: nat-c h2
- **face**; causing flushing of: cimic ↓

Abdomen

- **face**; causing flushing of: ...
  - **cramping**: cimic
- **fever**; during: borx$_{b4a.de}$* *Cham*$_{b7a.de}$
- **flatus**; from: graph$_{h2}$
- **flatus**; passing:
  - **amel.**: kali-c ↓
    - **pressing** pain: kali-c$_{h2}$
- **hawking** after rising from seat: nat-c ↓
  - **stitching** pain: nat-c$_{h2}$
- **hernia**; as from a: all-c guaj kali-c$_{h2}$ lycps-v nit-ac spong$_{h1}$ tarent
- **hernia** would protrude; as if a: alum arn ars$_{h2}$ aur aur-s$_{k2}$ bar-c berb *Calc* calc-ar camph$_{h1}$ cann-s *Carb-an* caust cham chin *Clem* **Cocc** *Coloc* *Con* cupr dig gent-c *Gran* graph$_{h2}$ hell$_{h1}$ *Ign* kali-bi *Lyc* nit-ac **Nux-v** petr ph-ac phos *Phyt* prun rhus-t sil spong stann sul-ac *Sulph* ter verat$_{h1}$ zinc$_{h2}$
- **inspiration**:
  - **agg.**: **Bry** ↓ merc ↓ plat sulph ↓
    - **cramping**: sulph$_{h2}$
    - **cutting** pain: *Bry*
    - **drawing** pain: plat$_{h2}$
    - **stitching** pain: **Bry** merc
    - **tearing** pain: plat
  - **deep** | **agg.**: borx$_{hr1}$
- **lancinating**: aids$_{nl2}$• ars$_{h2}$ aur elaps *Mag-c* manc$_{k}$* mang-p$_{rly4}$• spong
- **laughing** agg.: sep ↓
  - **pressing** pain: sep$_{h2}$
- **lying**:
  - **agg.**: **Clem**$_{hr1}$ **Merc** tritic-vg$_{fd5.de}$
    - **back** with legs extended; on: nat-m
  - **amel.**: gent-c ↓ stroph-s$_{sp1}$
    - **dragging**, bearing down: gent-c
- **menses**:
  - **after**:
    - **agg.**: ars ↓ *Borx* brom ↓ kreos ↓ plan ↓ *Plat*
      - **cramping**: borx kreos plan
      - **lancinating**: *Borx*
      - **pressing** pain: plat
      - **stitching** pain: ars borx brom
  - **before**:
    - **agg.**: *Ant-t* *Asar*$_{b7a.de}$ borx ↓ bov calc-p$_{bg1}$ *Carb-an* chin con$_{bg2}$ phos ↓ plat ↓ *Sars* sul-ac tab
      - **cutting** pain: borx$_{k2}$
      - **dragging**, bearing down: phos plat
  - **during**:
    - **agg.**: am-m ant-t apis *Arg-n* arn *Borx* bov brom ↓ bry$_{k2}$ carb-an castm caul$_{hr1}$ goss ↓ iod *Kali-c* kali-i kali-n kreos lyc mag-c ↓ mag-m ↓ mag-s nat-m phos *Plat* sars ↓ senec sep tanac$_{ptk2}$
      - **burning**: kali-n nat-m
      - **cramping**: kali-c
      - **cutting** pain: *Arg-n* borx$_{k2}$ *Nat-m* *Senec*
      - **dislocated**; as if: am-m$_{vh1}$
      - **dragging**, bearing down: borx mag-c mag-m plat$_{h2}$
      - **lancinating**: *Borx*
      - **pressing** pain: *Borx* *Carb-an*$_{k}$* castm kali-c *Plat*$_{k}$* sep
      - **sore**: bov$_{b4.de}$* kali-i sars$_{k}$*
      - **stitching** pain: *Borx*$_{k}$* brom goss
    - **beginning** of menses | **agg.**: *Sars*$_{bg2}$
- **menses** would appear; as if: cocc lyc plat
- **motion**:
  - **agg.**: *Ars* ↓ bapt$_{hr1}$ bar-c ↓ berb caust ↓ kali-c ↓ sep ↓ ther
    - **cutting** pain: caust$_{h2}$
    - **pressing** pain: bar-c$_{h2}$ sep$_{h2}$
    - **stitching** pain: *Ars* kali-c
  - **knees**; of | **agg.**: cortico$_{tpw7}$*
- **paralyzed**; as if: cocc$_{b7.de}$*
- **paroxysmal**: aloe *Bell* caul chel dig ign nat-m
- **periodical**: aloe ↓
  - **drawing** pain: aloe
- **pregnancy** agg.; during: podo ↓
  - **cutting** pain: podo$_{c1}$
- **pressing** pain: agar$_{k}$* *Alum*$_{k}$* am-c$_{k}$* ant-t$_{b7.de}$* arg-n$_{k}$* ars$_{k}$* asaf$_{b7.de}$* *Aur*$_{k}$* bell$_{k}$* berb$_{k}$* borx bry$_{bg2}$ *Calc*$_{k}$* cann-s carb-v$_{b4.de}$* chin$_{b7.de}$* cocc$_{b7.de}$* coloc$_{b4.de}$* croc$_{b7.de}$* dig$_{b4.de}$* euph$_{k}$* graph$_{k}$* hell$_{k}$* iod$_{k}$* kali-bi$_{k}$* kali-c$_{h2}$ *Kali-i* kali-n$_{b4.de}$* lyc$_{k}$* m-aust$_{b7.de}$ meny$_{b7.de}$* merc$_{k}$* mez nat-c$_{b4.de}$* nat-m$_{bg2}$ nat-s *Nux-v*$_{b7a.de}$ petr$_{k}$* *Plat*$_{k}$* ran-s$_{b7.de}$* rhod$_{b4.de}$* ruta$_{h1}$ spong$_{b7.de}$* stann$_{b4.de}$* sul-ac$_{k}$* sul-i$_{k2}$ sulph$_{k}$* symph$_{fd3.de}$• *Thuj*$_{k}$* tritic-vg$_{fd5.de}$ valer$_{b7.de}$* vanil$_{fd5.de}$ zinc$_{k}$*
  - **downward**: *Plat*$_{k}$*
  - **inward**: *Ign*$_{b7.de}$* thuj$_{b4.de}$*
  - **outward**: *Alum* am-m$_{b7a.de}$ anac$_{b4.de}$* aur$_{k}$* bar-c$_{h2}$ **Bell**$_{k}$* *Calc*$_{b4a.de}$ camph$_{k}$* cann-s$_{b7.de}$* caust$_{h2}$ cham$_{b7.de}$* clem$_{b4.de}$* *Cocc*$_{k}$* coff$_{b7.de}$* con$_{h2}$ dig$_{b4.de}$* euph$_{b4.de}$* gran$_{k}$* graph$_{b4.de}$* guaj$_{bg2}$ hell$_{b7.de}$* ign$_{k}$* kali-c lyc$_{k}$* *M-arct*$_{b7.de}$* mez$_{b4.de}$* nux-m$_{k}$* *Nux-v*$_{b7.de}$* petr$_{b4.de}$* ph-ac$_{k}$* phos$_{b4.de}$* rheum$_{b7.de}$* rhus-t$_{k}$* sep$_{b4.de}$* stront-c$_{b4.de}$* sul-ac$_{k}$* sulph$_{b4.de}$* ter teucr$_{k}$* thuj
  - **stone**; as from a: bell$_{bg2}$
  - **wavelike**: sep$_{h2}$
- **pressure**:
  - **agg.**: ant-c$_{h2}$ caust mag-m ph-ac$_{h2}$
    - **pressing** pain: ph-ac$_{h2}$
  - **amel.**: caust ↓ prun ↓
    - **stitching** pain: caust prun
- **pulsating** pain: alum plut-n$_{srj7}$• spong$_{fd4.de}$
- **retract** abdomen; must: aur ↓
  - **cutting** pain: aur$_{h2}$
- **riding** a horse; after: spig ↓
  - **sore**: spig$_{h1}$
- **rising**:
  - **agg.**: con ↓ euphr ↓
    - **stitching** pain: con euphr
  - **amel.**: stann ↓
    - **stitching** pain: stann
  - **sitting**; from:
    - **agg.**: *Cocc* kali-c ↓ lyc nat-m stront-c tritic-vg$_{fd5.de}$ zinc ↓
      - **burning**: kali-c$_{h2}$
      - **cramping**: zinc$_{h2}$
      - **tearing** pain: stront-c
- **rubbing**:
  - **agg.**: *Sulph* ↓
    - **cramping**: *Sulph*
  - **amel.**: mag-c ↓
    - **cramping**: mag-c
- **screwing** together: bov$_{b4.de}$* zinc$_{b4.de}$*
- **sitting**:
  - **agg.**: alum$_{h2}$ am-m$_{h2}$ aur ↓ bar-c ↓ calc ↓ calc-ar carb-an ↓ caust chin ↓ chinin-s ↓ choc$_{srj3}$• dulc$_{fd4.de}$ kali-c ↓ kali-s$_{fd4.de}$ mag-s petr petr-ra$_{shn4}$• rhus-t ↓ ruta$_{fd4.de}$ spong sul-ac thuj tritic-vg$_{fd5.de}$ zinc
    - **burning**: am-m$_{h2}$ bar-c
    - **cramping**: kali-c$_{h2}$ petr$_{k}$* spong$_{k}$*
    - **cutting** pain: carb-an$_{h2}$
    - **dragging**, bearing down: caust
    - **drawing** pain: caust chin$_{h1}$ kali-s$_{fd4.de}$ rhus-t$_{h1}$* thuj$_{k}$* tritic-vg$_{fd5.de}$ zinc$_{k}$*
    - **pressing** pain: aur caust$_{h2}$ chin$_{h1}$ petr$_{h2}$ spong$_{h1}$ tritic-vg$_{fd5.de}$
    - **stitching** pain: am-m chinin-s mag-s
    - **tearing** pain: calc spong$_{h1}$ sul-ac$_{k}$*
  - **amel.**: gent-c ↓
    - **dragging**, bearing down: gent-c
  - **bent** forward:
    - **agg.**: *Ars* ↓ *Bell* ↓ kali-n ↓
      - **burning**: kali-n

- **sitting – bent** forward – **agg.**: ...
    - **pressing** pain: *Bell*
    - **stitching** pain: *Ars*
- **sitting** down agg.: thuj ↓
    - **stitching** pain: thuj$_{h1}$
- **smarting**: sul-ac$_{b4.de*}$
- **sore**: acon$_{vh1}$ alum am-c *Apis Arg-met* **Arn** bar-m calc calc-ar calc-p carl caust chin *Clem* coc-c cocc dig dios elaps ferr-i *Graph* iod kali-c kali-m$_{k2}$ mag-m mag-s mez mur-ac nicc nit-ac$_{h2}$ *Pall* ran-b rhus-t sars spig ther *Valer* zing
- **sprained**; as if: agar$_{h2}$ am-m$_{gsy1*}$ calc euph$_{k*}$ hydr$_{k*}$ nat-m$_{k*}$ tarax$_{h1}$
- **squeezed**; as if | **stones**; between two: nat-m$_{bg2}$
- **standing**:
    - **agg.**: berb$_{kl}$ camph$_{kl}$ euph$_{kl}$ **Lil-t** ↓ mag-s$_{kl}$ mez$_{kl}$ nat-s$_{kl}$ thuj$_{kl}$
        - **dragging**, bearing down: **Lil-t**
        - **drawing** pain: thuj$_{k*}$
        - **pressing** pain: camph nat-s
        - **tearing** pain: euph$_{k*}$
    - **amel.**: aur ↓ thuj ↓
        - **pressing** pain: aur$_{k*}$
        - **stitching** pain: thuj
- **standing**; as from: (non:berb$_{kl}$) (non:camph$_{kl}$) (non:euph$_{kl}$) (non:mag-s$_{kl}$) (non:mez$_{kl}$) (non:nat-s$_{kl}$) (non:thuj$_{kl}$)
- **stepping** agg.: pall
- **stitching** pain: agn *Alum* am-m ammc amp$_{rly4•}$ arg-met$_{h1}$ *Ars* arund bar-c bar-m bar-s$_{k2}$ *Bell Berb Borx Bov Bry* calc calc-s *Canth* carb-ac **Carb-an** carbn-s castor-eq caust cham chinin-s clem$_{a1}$ coc-c cocc con *Cycl* dros dulc$_{fd4.de}$ euphr ferr-i$_{k2}$ gamb graph grat hell indg kali-ar *Kali-c* kali-i kali-n kali-s lac-leo$_{sk4•}$ laur lil-t lyc *Mag-m* mang *Merc* merl *Mez Mur-ac* nat-ar *Nat-c* nat-m nat-ox$_{rly4•}$ *Nat-s* nept-m$_{lsd2.fr}$ nicc pall prun psor rat sabad senec sep spig spong$_{fd4.de}$ *Stann* staph *Stront-c* stry sul-ac *Sulph* tarent tell *Thuj* tritic-vg$_{fd5.de}$ *Vib* viol-t zinc
    - **burning**: mur-ac$_{a1}$ sulph$_{h2}$
    - **downward**: berb caust
    - **outward** through ilium: kali-n
    - **paroxysmal**: berb sabad
    - **pressing** pain: nat-c$_{h2}$
    - **pulsating** pain: berb sabad
    - **upward**: sep$_{h2}$
- **stool**:
    - **after**:
        - **agg.**: gamb ↓ *Lyc*$_{b4a.de}$
            - **stitching** pain: gamb
        - **amel.**: *Lac-c*
    - **before**: agn$_{bg1}$ carb-an ↓ kali-n$_{bg1}$ nat-s phos rat$_{bg2}$ spong$_{fd4.de}$ *Trom*
        - **dragging**, bearing down: carb-an$_{h2}$
        - **pressing** pain: *Trom*
        - **stitching** pain: kali-n
    - **during**:
        - **agg.**: bar-c$_{bg1}$ calc-s ↓ carb-an ↓ kali-c ↓ nicc rat ↓ sep ↓
            - **cramping**: nicc$_{k*}$
            - **dragging**, bearing down: kali-c rat
            - **pressing** pain: bar-c$_{h2}$
            - **stitching** pain: calc-s carb-an$_{h2}$ kali-c nicc sep$_{h2}$
- **stooping**:
    - **agg.**: am-m ↓ ars kali-n laur ↓ meny ↓ petr-ra$_{shn4•}$ plb ↓ sep ↓ stann ↓ sulph ↓
        - **cramping**: sulph$_{h2}$
        - **pressing** pain: meny$_{h1}$ sep$_{h2}$
        - **sprained**; as if: ars$_{h2}$
        - **stitching** pain: am-m$_{h2}$ laur plb stann
    - **amel.**: graph ↓
        - **burning**: graph
        - **pressing** pain: graph$_{h2}$
- **stretched**; as if: clem$_{b4.de*}$
- **stretching**:
    - **agg.**: am-c aur ↓ calen ↓ cocc graph ↓ kali-c ↓ merc-c mez ↓ nat-m
        - **burning**: graph$_{h2}$
        - **cramping**: am-c$_{k*}$
        - **pressing** pain: am-c aur$_{k*}$ graph$_{h2}$ mez
        - **stitching** pain: am-c kali-c
        - **tearing** pain: calen$_{vml3•}$
    - **amel.**: bov ↓ tritic-vg ↓
        - **drawing** pain: bov tritic-vg$_{fd5.de}$
    - **leg**:
        - **agg.** | **sitting**; after: euph$_{h2}$
- **stretching** out: coc-c ↓ merc-c ↓ nat-m ↓
    - **drawing** pain: coc-c merc-c nat-m
- **swollen**; as if: con$_{h2}$ kali-c$_{h2}$
- **talking** agg.: calc ↓
    - **cramping**: calc$_{h2}$
- **tearing** pain: am-m$_{k*}$ *Ars Berb* calc calen$_{vml3•}$ chin$_{k*}$ crot-t$_{k*}$ cycl euph$_{k*}$ *Lach Lyc* mez$_{k*}$ pall$_{c1}$ *Plat*$_{k*}$ sep$_{k*}$ sil$_{k*}$ stront-c sul-ac$_{k*}$ tarent$_{k*}$ thuj$_{k*}$
    - **jerking** pain: thuj$_{h1}$
    - **upward**: thuj$_{h1}$
- **touch** agg.: am-m ↓ arg-n ↓ mang$_{h2}$
    - **pressing** pain: arg-n$_{k*}$
    - **sore**: am-m$_{h2}$
- **twinging**: castm indg$_{k*}$ lyc$_{k*}$
- **ulcerative** pain: am-m cic con
- **urging** to urinate; when: nat-s ↓
    - **stitching** pain: nat-s$_{hr}$
- **urination**:
    - **after**:
        - **agg.**: euph ↓ lyc$_{k*}$ sul-ac ↓
            - **dragging**, bearing down: sul-ac
            - **pressing** pain: euph$_{h2}$ lyc$_{h2}$
    - **during**:
        - **agg.**: agar ars card-m ↓ caust fl-ac$_{bg2}$ merc ↓ mez *Nat-m* ↓ rhod$_{bg2}$
            - **burning**: merc *Nat-m*
            - **cutting** pain: nat-m
            - **drawing** pain: agar$_{k*}$ ars card-m caust
            - **pressing** pain: mez
    - **urging** to urinate: *Bell* carb-an nat-s rhod
- **walking**:
    - **agg.**: agar alum am-m arg-met ↓ bapt$_{hr1}$ berb brom calc ↓ calc-act canth ↓ caust chel chin ↓ *Clem* con ↓ dig ↓ ferr-i helon kali-c ↓ kali-n *Lil-t* ↓ *Lyc* lycps-v mag-c med ↓ *Merc* merl ↓ musca-d$_{szs1}$ nat-m nept-m ↓ par ↓ ph-ac ↓ pic-ac podo$_{fd3.de•}$ sep ↓ spig ↓ sulph thuj tritic-vg$_{fd5.de}$ ust vanil$_{fd5.de}$
        - **cracking**: musca-d$_{szs1}$
        - **cramping**: kali-c$_{h2}$ kali-n mag-c$_{k*}$ *Sulph*$_{k*}$
        - **cutting** pain: canth$_{k*}$ caust$_{h2}$ par$_{k*}$
        - **dragging**, bearing down: *Lil-t* med
        - **drawing** pain: alum chel thuj$_{k*}$ tritic-vg$_{fd5.de}$ vanil$_{fd5.de}$
        - **pressing** pain: dig$_{h2}$ ph-ac$_{h2}$ sep$_{h2}$
        - **sore**: arg-met calc caust ferr-i
        - **stitching** pain: chin$_{h1}$ con dig$_{h2}$ ferr-i$_{k2}$ kali-n merl nept-m$_{lsd2.fr}$ sep$_{h2}$ spig$_{h1}$
        - **tearing** pain: am-m$_{k*}$ calc sep$_{h2}$
    - **air** agg.; in open: *Merc* ↓ nat-s ↓ thuj ↓
        - **stitching** pain: *Merc* nat-s thuj
    - **amel.**: carb-an ↓ mag-s ↓ nit-ac psor thuj ↓
        - **cutting** pain: carb-an$_{h2}$
        - **sore**: nit-ac$_{h2}$
        - **stitching** pain: mag-s thuj
    - **bent**:
        - **must** walk bent: am-m **Arn** ↓ med$_{k2}$
            - **sore**: **Arn**

- **wine**; after: calc-ar$_{k2}$
- **yawning** agg.: *Borx*

○ • **Glands**: am-m ant-c$_{b7.de*}$ *Ars*$_{k*}$ ars-i ↓ bell ↓ berb bov *Brom* *Calc*$_{k*}$ cann-s ↓ caps ↓ *Carb-an* ↓ **Clem** cop dig dulc$_{k*}$ gels ↓ graph$_{k*}$ gymno hell hep$_{b4.de*}$ kreos lat-m$_{bnm6•}$ lyc ↓ lyss m-ambo$_{b7a.de}$ mag-m med$_{k2}$ meny ↓ *Merc*$_{k*}$ merc-c$_{k*}$ mez nit-ac$_{k*}$ plut-n$_{srj7•}$ psor ↓ ran-b rheum ↓ rhus-t *Sil* stann *Staph*$_{hr1}$ sulph$_{b4.de*}$ sumb tarent$_{bg2}$ tarent-c ↓ ter thuj$_{k*}$
  - **night** | **bed** agg.; in: rhus-t$_{h1}$
  - **burning**: *Ars* ars-i bell *Carb-an* tarent-c
  - **contracting**: nit-ac$_{h2}$
  - **drawing** pain: calc$_{b4.de*}$ cann-s$_{b7.de*}$ dulc$_{b4a.de*}$ mez$_{b4.de*}$ sulph$_{b4.de*}$ thuj$_{b4.de*}$
  - **jerking** pain: clem$_{b4.de*}$
  - **pressing** pain: dulc$_{h2}$ meny$_{b7.de*}$ merc$_{b4.de*}$ merc-c$_{b4a.de}$ stann$_{b4.de*}$
  - **sore**: caps *Clem* gels hep lyc$_{h2}$ merc *Sil* sumb thuj
  - **stitching** pain: bell$_{b4.de*}$ dulc$_{h2}$ hep$_{k2}$ nit-ac$_{h2}$ psor rheum$_{h*}$ *Thuj*
  - **tearing** pain: calc$_{h2}$ sulph$_{h2}$
  - **walking** agg.: bapt$_{a1}$
- **Hernia**: *Lyc* ↓ nit-ac ↓ sulph ↓
  - **sore**: sulph$_{h2}$
  - **stitching** pain: *Lyc* nit-ac$_{h2}$
  - **walking**:
    - **agg.**: lycps-v
    - **amel.**: nit-ac
- **Ring**: rhod ↓
  - **cough** agg.; during: am *Bry* *Cocc*$_{k*}$ *Nat-m*$_{k*}$ nux-v$_{k*}$ *Sil*$_{k*}$ sulph$_{k*}$ verat$_{k*}$
    - **extending** to | **Testes**; into: *Nat-m*
  - **drawing** pain: rhod$_{c1}$

▽ • **extending** to:
  - **Abdomen**: bar-c ↓ bry$_{k2}$ lat-m$_{bnm6•}$ ruta$_{fd4.de}$
    - **stitching** pain: bar-c
  - **Axilla**, left: nat-s
    - **stitching** pain: nat-s
  - **Back**: am-m lat-m$_{bnm6•}$ sep *Sulph*
    - **cutting** pain: am-m
  - **Calf**: sec
  - **Chest**: indg ↓
    - **twinging**: indg
  - **Crest** of ilium: lac-c
  - **Down** leg: aloe$_{k*}$ caust dios dulc$_{fd4.de}$ sec symph$_{fd3.de•}$
  - **Genitals**: *Alum* *Lach* *Plat*
    - **pressing** pain: *Alum*$_{k*}$ *Plat*
  - **Hip**: am-m brucel$_{sa3•}$ murx
  - **Hip**, behind: am-m ↓
    - **stitching** pain: am-m
  - **Hypogastrium**, across: *Ferr-i*
  - **Knee**: aloe kali-c podo$_{br1}$ thuj$_{bg1}$ vanil$_{fd5.de}$
    - **cramping**: aloe
    - **drawing** pain: thuj$_{h1}$
  - **Lumbar** region: am-m ↓
    - **stitching** pain: am-m
  - **Mamma**; left: **Murx** ↓
    - **stitching** pain: **Murx**
  - **Nipple**, right: crot-t
    - **tearing** pain: crot-t
  - **Pelvis**; around: *Chel* coloc plat ↓
    - **drawing** pain: coloc plat$_{h2}$
  - **Perineum**: ars ↓
    - **lancinating**: ars$_{h2}$
  - **Pubic** region: elaps ↓
    - **lancinating**: elaps$_{hr1}$
  - **Pubis**: lil-t
    - **drawing** pain: lil-t
  - **Scapulae** | **right**: borx

- **Inguinal** region – **extending** to: ...
  - **Seminal** cord: ars ↓
    - **lancinating**: ars$_{h2}$
  - **Spermatic** cord; along: all-c *Nat-m* visc ↓
    - **twinging**: visc$_{c1}$
  - **Stomach**: phos ↓
    - **cramping**: phos$_{h2}$
  - **Testes**: arg-met calc ↓ *Dios* dulc$_{fd4.de}$ ham$_{k*}$ *Hydr* kreos$_{bg1}$ lept *Nat-m* ol-an$_{bg1}$ phys$_{bg1}$ sep staph ↓ sulph$_{bg1}$ teucr ↓
    - **burning**: staph$_{h1}$
    - **cutting** pain: calc
    - **dragging**, bearing down: hydr teucr
    - **drawing** pain: arg-met ham nat-m staph$_{h1}$
  - **Testis**: euphr ↓ phys ↓ staph ↓
    - **stitching** pain: euphr phys staph$_{h1}$
  - **Thigh**: aloe arg-met ars aur berb bry clem$_{a1}$ coloc laur lil-t lyc plat rhod sec sep thuj vanil$_{fd5.de}$
  - **Thighs**: *Ars* ↓ aur ↓ laur ↓ lyc ↓ nat-p ↓ plat ↓ rhod ↓ sep ↓ thuj ↓ vanil ↓
    - **drawing** pain: aur plat$_{h2}$ rhod
    - **pressing** pain: sep$_{h2}$ vanil$_{fd5.de}$
    - **stitching** pain: *Ars* laur lyc nat-p$_{fkr6.de}$ sep$_{h2}$ thuj
    - **tearing** pain: *Ars* lyc$_{h2}$ plat$_{k*}$ sep
  - **Urethra** to glans penis; through: asar ↓ lyc ↓
    - **cutting** pain: asar lyc
  - **Vagina**: ars ↓
    - **stitching** pain: ars

- **Intestines**: adren ↓ ail ↓ ars ↓ caps ↓ cob ↓ coli ↓ cupr ↓ cupr-ar ↓ *Dios*$_{br1}$ gard-j ↓ ilx-a ↓ influ$_{jl2}$ lacer$_{a1*}$ mag-c ↓ manc ↓ moni$_{jl2}$ parathyr ↓ tab$_{br1}$ thal-met$_{br1}$
  - **accompanied** by | **Lumbar** region; pain in: des-ac$_{rbp6}$
  - **apyrexia**; during: ars$_{bro1}$
  - **boring** pain: ars$_{h2}$
  - **burning**: ail$_{tl1}$ caps$_{tl1}$ manc$_{ptk1}$ parathyr$_{jl2}$
  - **contracting**: adren$_{br1*}$
  - **cramping**: cob$_{ptm1•}$ cupr$_{mtf11}$ *Dios*$_{br1*}$ gard-j$_{vlr2•}$ ilx-a$_{mtf11}$ parathyr$_{jl2}$
    - **followed** by | **perspiration**; cold: gard-j$_{vlr2•}$
  - **drawing** pain: coli$_{jl2}$
  - **neuralgic**: cupr-ar$_{ptk1}$
  - **pressing** pain:
    - **downward**:
      - **accompanied** by | **nausea**: agn$_{bro1}$
  - **sore**: manc$_{ptk1}$
  - **torn** out or loose; as if: mag-c$_{h2}$
  - **vinegar** | **amel.**: lacer$_{a1*}$
  - **water** | **amel.**: lacer$_{a1*}$

  ○ • **Large**: ser-a-c ↓
    - **spasmodic**: ser-a-c$_{jl2}$
  - **Upper** intestines:
    - **eating**; after | **several** hours: eucal$_{br1}$

- **Liver**●: **Acon**$_{k*}$ **Aesc**$_{k*}$ aeth agar$_{k*}$ agn ↓ ail ↓ all-c$_{bg2*}$ allox ↓ *Aloe*$_{k*}$ alum$_{k*}$ alum-p$_{k2}$ alum-sil$_{k2}$ am-c$_{k*}$ am-m$_{b7.de*}$ *Ambr*$_{k*}$ anac ↓ anan androc ↓ ang ↓ ant-c$_{k2}$ ant-t ↓ anth ↓ *Apis* ↓ *Arg-n* arizon-l$_{nl2•}$ am *Ars*$_{k*}$ *Ars-i* ars-s-f$_{k2}$ arund$_{c1}$ *Asaf* ↓ asar astac ↓ aur ↓ aur-i ↓ aur-m ↓ bamb-a$_{stb2.de•}$ *Bapt*$_{k*}$ bar-c$_{b4.de*}$ **Bell**$_{k*}$ bell-p ↓ benz-ac ↓ *Berb*$_{k*}$ bold$_{bro1}$ *Bov* ↓ brom$_{k*}$ bros-gau ↓ *Brucel*$_{sa3•}$ *Bry*$_{k*}$ bufo *Cact* cadm-met$_{gm1}$ cadm-s ↓ cain *Calc*$_{k*}$ calc-f calc-i$_{k2}$ *Calc-p* *Calc-s*$_{k*}$ calc-sil$_{k2}$ camph canth ↓ *Carb-ac* *Carb-an*$_{k*}$ carb-v$_{k*}$ *Carbn-s* *Carc*$_{mrr1}$ *Card-m*$_{k*}$ *Castm*$_{k*}$ caust *Cean*$_{bro1}$ cedr ↓ *Cham* ↓ chap ↓ **Chel**$_{k*}$ chelo$_{bro1}$ **Chin**$_{k*}$ *Chinin-ar* *Chinin-s*$_{k*}$ *Chion* ↓ chlf ↓ choc ↓ chol$_{bro1}$ cimic *Cimx* clem ↓ cob$_{bro1}$ cocc$_{mrr1}$ colch$_{k*}$ *Coloc* ↓ *Con*$_{k*}$ croc$_{b7.de*}$ *Crot-c* *Crot-h*$_{k*}$ *Crot-t*$_{k*}$ cupr ↓ cycl$_{bg2}$ dig$_{b4a.de*}$ dios$_{k*}$ dulc$_{fd4.de}$ eup-per$_{bg2*}$ euphr fago ferr$_{k*}$ ferr-ar ferr-i$_{k2}$ *Ferr-p* fl-ac ↓ *Form* gamb ↓ graph grin$_{c2}$ hell *Hep* ↓ hom-xyz$_{c2}$ hydr ↓ hyos hyper ↓ ign$_{k*}$ *Iod*$_{k*}$ ip ↓ iris jatr-c$_{bro1}$ jug-c ↓ *Kali-ar* *Kali-bi*$_{k*}$ *Kali-br* *Kali-c*$_{k*}$ **Kali-i** ↓ kali-n ↓ kali-p *Kali-s* kali-sil$_{k2}$ kalm kola$_{stb3•}$ kreos lac-e$_{hm2•}$ lac-h$_{sze9•}$ **Lach**$_{k*}$ lact *Laur*$_{k*}$ *Lec* *Led* **Lept**$_{k*}$ *Lith-c* luf-op$_{rsj5•}$

- **Liver**: ...
  Lyc k* m-aust↓ mag-c↓ **Mag-m** k* malar jl2 mang *Med* k* meph a1 **Merc** k* *Merc-c* k* *Merc-d* bro1 *Merc-i-f* merc-i-r↓ merl k* mill mim-p rsj8• morg-p pte1*• mosch↓ mur-ac k2 *Myric* bro1 nat-c b4.de* *Nat-m* k* *Nat-p*↓ **Nat-s** k* nept-m↓ **Nit-ac** nux-m k* **Nux-v** k* nyct↓ ol-an↓ ol-j bro1 olib-sac↓ op b7.de* *Ox-ac*↓ pall k* par↓ parth c2* petr↓ ph-ac↓ *Phos* k* phys↓ phyt plat↓ plb k* plut-n srj7• **Podo** k* prim-o c2* *Prun* psor *Ptel* k* *Puls* b7.de* puls-n c2 quas↓ ran-b c1* ran-s k* raph br1 rhod↓ rhus-t k2 ruta k* sabad sabin c1 sang k2* sanic↓ sars↓ scroph-xyz c2 sec k* sel k* seneg↓ senn↓ **Sep** k* *Sil* *Spig*↓ spong fd4.de *Stann* b4a.de* staph↓ stel↓ stram stront-c↓ *Sul-ac*↓ sul-i k2 *Sulph* k* symph fd3.de• *Tab*↓ *Tarax* k* tarent tell↓ ter↓ teucr↓ *Ther*↓ thres-a↓ thuj↓ thyr↓ tritic-vg fd5.de trom c2 trychs br1 tub c1* ust k* v-a-b↓ vac↓ valer b7.de* vanil fd5.de verat b7.de* verb↓ xanth↓ yuc bro1 *Zinc*↓ zinc-p↓ [spect dfg1]
  - **right**:
    - **extending** to:
      - **left**: card-m↓ kola stb3• *Merc-i-f*
        - **stitching** pain: card-m
  - **morning**: agar brucel sa3• bry kola stb3•
    - **8** h: calc-f↓
      - **stitching** pain: calc-f
  - **afternoon**:
    - **sitting** agg.: nat-m↓
      - **stitching** pain: nat-m h2
  - **evening**: all-c k* caust *Chel* k* *Chinin-s* dulc fd4.de ran-b k2 ruta fd4.de sep↓ tritic-vg fd5.de
    - **sitting** agg.: am-c↓
      - **stitching** pain: am-c h2
    - **stitching** pain: dulc fd4.de ruta fd4.de sep h2
    - **tearing** pain: caust k*
  - **night**: bufo calc k* calc-f k2 ind k* ther k2
    - **midnight**:
      - **after** | **4-9** h: chel
  - **accompanied** by:
    - **hemorrhoids**: dios br1
    - **nausea**: hip-ac sp1* med jl2 petr bg2
    - **respiration**; complaints of (See RESPIRATION - Complaints - accompanied - liver)
    - **urine**; burning: all-c tl1
    - **Scapula**; fixed pain under lower angle of right: *Chel* tl1
    - **Stomach**; complaints of: symph fd3.de•
  - **air** agg.; in open: ars carb-v k*
  - **anger**; after: *Cocc* k* nat-s k2 vanil fd5.de
  - **ascending** stairs agg.: bapt hr1
  - **bending** forward | **amel**.: *Aloe* calc-f nat-m
  - **blow**; pain as from a: acon b7.de* croc b7.de* valer bg2
  - **boring** pain: am-c b4a.de* carb-an bg2 nat-m b4.de* sulph h2* xanth bg2
  - **breakfast** agg.; after: graph h2
  - **breathing** agg.: *Acon*↓ agar↓ allox sp1 aloe↓ **Bell** *Berb*↓ *Bry* calc h2 *Calc-p*↓ con↓ *Crot-h*↓ hed sp1 hep br1 hip-ac sp1 lyc mag-s sp1 *Merc*↓ *Nat-s* ox-ac↓ **Ran-b**↓ *Sel* vanil fd5.de
    - **stitching** pain: *Acon* agar k* aloe *Berb* **Bry** *Calc-p* con *Crot-h* *Merc* *Nat-s* ox-ac k2 **Ran-b**
  - **burning**: *Acon* k* *Agar* aloe k* alum b4.de am-c k* am-m b7.de* anan aur-i k2 aur-m k2 bell k2 berb k2 bry k* carb-v carbn-s card-m k2 crot-c dulc h2 gamb ign b7.de *Kali-c* k* *Lach* bg2 laur b7.de **Lept** k* mag-c b4.de mag-m b4.de* med merc bg2 mur-ac b4.de myric bg1 *Nit-ac* ph-ac b4.de phos b4.de plat b4.de plb *Sabad* b7a.de *Sec* b7.de* stann k* sul-ac b4.de sulph b4.de symph fd3.de• *Ther* thuj b4.de zinc b4.de
  - **burrowing**: carb-an bg1 nat-m bg1 sabad b7.de* sulph bg1
  - **bursting** pain: bry ptk1 calc bg2* chlf bg1 lept ptk1 nat-s bg2*
  - **cheese**; after: ptel ruta fd4.de
  - **chill**:
    - **before**: tarent
    - **during**: acon bg2 all-c bg2 ant-c bg2 *Ars* k* borx bg2 bry k* caps bg2 carb-v bg2 cham bg2 **Chin** k* chinin-s mrr1 cocc bg2 ign bg2 kali-c bg2
  - **chill – during**: ...
    lyc bg2 mag-m bg2 merc bg2 *Nux-v* k* **Podo** puls bg2 ran-b bg2 *Sep* k* sulph bg2 thuj bg2 verat
  - **chopped** up; as if: kola stb3•
  - **clawing** pain: med c1*
  - **cold**:
    - **agg**.: psil ft1
    - **food** (See food - after)
      - **after**: mang
  - **colic**; gallstone●: (↗*Gallstones*) ars k* atro bro1 atro-s bro1 bamb-a stb2.de• *Bapt* **Bell** k* **Berb** k* *Bry* k* cal-bil br1 *Calc* k* **Card-m** k* *Cham* k* *Chel* k* **Chin** k* *Chion* k* *Chlf* k* *Chlol* colch gk *Coloc* bg2* cupr dig k* *Dios* k* *Fab* c1 gels bro1 hep bg2 *Hydr* bro1 *Ip* k* *Iris* k* kali-ar *Kali-bi* k* *Kali-c* k* *Lach* k* lat-m bnm6• laur *Lept* *Lith-c* **Lyc** k* mag-bcit mtf11 *Mag-m* bg2 *Mag-s* sp1* mand mtf11 mang menth bro1 merc *Merc-d* bg2* morph-act bro1 **Nat-s** k* *Nux-v* k* op bro1 ozone sde2• podo k* puls rhus-t ric bro1 *Sep* sil bg2 staph sne sulph bg2* tab hr1 ter bg2* trios br1* **Verat** k*
    - **accompanied** by:
      - **hiccough**: *Chin* st1
      - **Tongue** and white sides; red streak on centre of: *Iris* kr1*
    - **eating** agg.: mag-m pd
    - **tearing** pain: sulph k2
  - **cough** agg.; during: borx b4a.de* brom *Bry* carb-v↓ *Chinin-s* cimx c1 cocc eup-per↓ hep br1 kali-c↓ led↓ merc↓ *Nat-m*↓ psor
    - **stitching** pain: **Bry** k* carb-v eup-per kali-c led b7.de* merc *Nat-m*
  - **cramping**: anth vh1 astac ptk1 bell k2 mag-m ptk1 malar jl2 ph-ac bg2 phos bg2 phys ptk1
  - **cutting** pain: alum-sil k2 ang k* arg-n bg2* ars-i k2 aur *Berb* k* bros-gau mrc1 bufo calc b4.de* calc-f *Carb-an* k* colch k* con bg2 crot-c *Dios* k* dulc b4.de* hydr bg2* iod b4.de* *Iris* kali-ar k2 kali-bi bg2 kali-c b4.de* *Lach* k* merc b4a.de merc-c bg2 merc-i-r nat-c k* nat-m bg2 nux-m bg2* ph-ac bg2 ptel stann b4.de* thyr ptk1
  - **dragging**, bearing down: calc bg2 card-m k2 cham bg2 hyper bg2 podo bg2*
  - **drawing** pain: all-c bg2 alum b4.de* *Bry* b7a.de* camph b7.de* con b4.de* ign b7.de* kali-c b4a.de* mag-m h2* malar jl2 nat-m b4.de* olib-sac wmh1 plat b4.de* *Puls* b7a.de sabad b7.de* sel b7a.de sep b4.de* sulph bg2 teucr b7.de* tritic-vg fd5.de vanil fd5.de
  - **eating**:
    - **after**:
      - **agg**.: allox tpw3 ambr bry b7a.de calc-p k2 graph b4a.de lyc b4a.de mag-m k* *Nat-m* psil ft1 *Ptel*
        - **2** h after eating: podo k2
    - **agg**.: allox sp1
    - **amel**.: allox sp1 *Chel* spong fd4.de
    - **satiety** agg.; after eating to: **Lyc**
  - **eructation**: merc↓
    - **stitching** pain: merc
  - **exertion** agg.: agn ang iris merc nit-ac nux-v
  - **expiration** agg.; during: chin↓ vanil↓
    - **stitching** pain: chin h1 vanil fd5.de
  - **fever**; before: ars b4a.de
  - **gastric** disturbances, with (See accompanied - stomach)
  - **gnawing** pain: bufo k* laur puls b7a.de ruta k* sil
  - **heat**; during: acon bg2 alum bg2 ant-c b7a.de ant-t b7.de *Ars* k* aur bg2 bar-c b4.de *Borx* bg2 bov b4.de* bry b7a.de* calc b4.de* caps bg2 cham b7a.de *Chin* k* cina b7.de elat *Ferr* b7.de* graph bg2 kali-c bg2 lach bg2 lyc bg2 mag-m bg2 merc bg2 nat-c bg2 nit-ac b4.de nux-m bg2 nux-v k* phos b4.de puls b7.de ran-b b7a.de *Rhus-t* b7.de* sep b4.de* stann bg2 stront-c b4.de sulph b4.de*
  - **inspiration**:
    - **agg**.: ran-b mrr1
    - **deep** | **agg**.: card-m mrr1
  - **jar** agg.: **Bell** *Bry* chin *Form* **Lach** *Nat-s* nit-ac ptel gk sel **Sil**
  - **lancinating**: berb k2
  - **laughing** agg.: psor

- **lying**:
  - **amel**.: mag-m nat-s
  - **back**; on:
    - **agg**.: caust
    - **amel**.: *Mag-m*$_{hr1}$ ptel$_{gk}$
  - **liver**; on:
    - **amel**.: card-m ↓ kali-c ↓
      - **stitching** pain: card-m kali-c
  - **side**; on:
    - **left**:
      - **agg**.: arn bry$_{bro1*}$ *Card-m*$_{k*}$ *Mag-m*$_{k*}$ *Nat-s*$_{k*}$ *Ptel*$_{k*}$
        - **stitching** pain: *Card-m*
    - **painful** side:
      - **agg**.: calc-f *Lyc Phyt*
      - **amel**.: bry$_{bro1}$ ptel$_{bro1}$ sep$_{bro1}$ sulph
    - **painless** side | **amel**.: calc-f
    - **right**:
      - **agg**.●: **Bell** calc-f chel$_{bro1}$ dios$_{k*}$ kali-c$_{bro1}$ *Lyc* **Mag-m**$_{k*}$ *Merc*$_{k*}$ nat-s$_{k2}$ phasco-ci$_{rbp2}$ phos$_{h2*}$ *Phyt* psor rhus-t$_{k2}$ sep sil
        - **stitching** pain: merc
      - **amel**.: ambr **Bry Mag-m** *Nat-s*$_{k*}$ *Ptel*
      - **legs** curled up; with | **amel**.: *Nat-s*$_{mrr1}$
- **lying** down:
  - **agg**.: malar$_{jl2}$
  - **amel**.: v-a-b ↓
    - **pricking** pain: v-a-b$_{jl2}$
- **menses** | **before**:
  - **agg**.: con nux-m$_{k*}$ podo puls tarent
    - **stitching** pain: con$_{k*}$
  - **during**:
    - **agg**.: bufo *Nux-m* ph-ac$_{k*}$
      - **cramping**: bufo$_{ptk1}$
      - **sore**: ph-ac$_{ptk1}$
- **mental** labor, after: mang *Merc* **Nat-s** *Nux-v Sulph*
- **mortification**; from: *Lyc*
- **motion**:
  - **agg**.: androc ↓ bamb-a$_{stb2.de•}$ *Bell Bry* bufo calc-p$_{k2}$ card-m$_{k2*}$ chel ↓ clem ↓ iris$_{c1*}$ *Kali-bi* kali-c ↓ phyt rhus-t$_{k2}$ sel$_{k2}$ *Sep*
    - **stitching** pain: androc$_{srj1•}$ bry$_{tl1}$ chel$_{tl1}$ clem kali-c sel
  - **amel**.: calc-f$_{k2}$ vanil$_{fd5.de}$
    - **cutting** pain: calc-f$_{k2}$
- **noise** agg.: ther$_{k2}$
- **paroxysmal**: **Bell** *Berb Chel* ph-ac zinc
- **perspiration**; during: arn$_{bg2}$ *Ars*$_{bg2}$ bry$_{bg2}$ *Calc*$_{bg2}$ cham$_{bg2}$ **Chin**$_{bg2}$ kali-c$_{bg2}$ lach$_{bg2}$ mag-m$_{bg2}$ *Merc*$_{bg2}$ nat-m$_{bg2}$ *Nux-v*$_{bg2}$ sabad$_{bg2}$ **Sep**$_{bg2}$ thuj$_{bg2}$
- **pressing** pain: *Acon*$_{k*}$ aesc agar$_{k*}$ agn$_{b7.de*}$ all-c *Aloe*$_{k*}$ alum-sil$_{k2}$ am-c$_{k*}$ *Ambr*$_{k*}$ anac$_{k*}$ arg-n$_{k*}$ arn$_{k*}$ *Ars*$_{k*}$ ars-i$_{k2}$ *Asaf*$_{k*}$ bar-c$_{b4.de*}$ *Bell*$_{b4a.de}$ berb *Bry* cain *Calc*$_{k*}$ *Calc-p* calc-s camph$_{b7.de*}$ *Carb-an*$_{k*}$ carb-v$_{k*}$ carbn-s *Card-m* cham$_{b7.de*}$ **Chel**$_{k*}$ *Chin*$_{k*}$ *Cocc*$_{k*}$ *Con*$_{k*}$ dig$_{k*}$ *Graph*$_{k*}$ ign$_{b7.de*}$ iod$_{b4.de*}$ kali-ar kali-bi$_{bg2}$ *Kali-c*$_{k*}$ kali-s kali-sil$_{k2}$ kola$_{stb3•}$ kreos$_{k*}$ lact *Laur* lith-c *Lyc*$_{k*}$ **Mag-m**$_{k*}$ *Merc*$_{k*}$ mur-ac$_{k2}$ nat-c$_{h2}$ *Nat-m*$_{k*}$ **Nat-s** nit-ac$_{b4.de*}$ *Nux-m*$_{k*}$ **Nux-v**$_{k*}$ ol-an$_{k*}$ petr$_{k*}$ ph-ac$_{k*}$ *Phos*$_{k*}$ plb$_{k*}$ podo$_{fd3.de•}$ *Prun*$_{k*}$ quas$_{br1}$ ran-b$_{b7.de*}$ ran-s$_{k*}$ raph *Ruta*$_{k*}$ sabad$_{k*}$ sabin$_{k*}$ seneg$_{b4.de*}$ **Sep**$_{k*}$ *Sil*$_{k*}$ *Stann*$_{k*}$ staph$_{b7.de*}$ sul-i$_{k2}$ *Sulph*$_{k*}$ symph$_{fd3.de•}$ tab$_{k*}$ tarax$_{b7.de*}$ ter thuj$_{k*}$ tritic-vg$_{fd5.de}$ vanil$_{fd5.de}$ verat$_{b7.de*}$ *Zinc*$_{k*}$ zinc-p$_{k2}$
  - **accompanied** by | **Spleen**; pressing pain in (See spleen - pressing - accompanied - liver)
- **pressure**:
  - **agg**.: bell berb brom bry$_{k2}$ **Chin** chinin-s$_{c1}$ clem dig$_{k2}$ hip-ac$_{sp1}$ merc-i-f$_{kr1}$ podo$_{k2}$ psor ran-b$_{k2}$ rhus-t$_{k2}$ sabad sel tab
    - **stitching** pain: sel$_{c1*}$
  - **amel**.: malar$_{jl2}$
- **pricking** pain: psor$_{jl2}$ v-a-b$_{jl2}$
- **pulsating** pain: allox$_{tpw3}$ anan bufo$_{c1}$ nux-v$_{h1}$
- **pulse**; with slow: dig$_{k2}$
- **radiating**: arg-n$_{bg2}$ bell$_{bg2}$ berb$_{bg2}$ bry$_{bg2}$ chel$_{bg2}$
- **riding** in a carriage agg.: brom caust ↓ sep
  - **stitching** pain: caust$_{h2}$
- **rising** from stooping agg.: alum ↓
  - **stitching** pain: alum
- **rubbing** | **amel**.: **Podo**$_{k*}$
- **running** agg.: spig ↓
  - **stitching** pain: spig$_{h1}$
- **scraping**: sabad$_{b7.de*}$
- **scratching** pain: nat-m$_{h2}$
- **sitting** agg.: calc-f nat-m ↓ phasco-ci$_{rbp2}$
  - **stitching** pain: calc-f nat-m$_{h2}$
- **sneezing** agg.: *Psor*
- **sore**: acon$_{k*}$ aesc ail$_{tl1}$ *Alum*$_{b4a.de}$ am-c$_{k*}$ ant-t$_{k*}$ anth$_{ptk2}$ *Apis Arg-n* arn$_{k*}$ ars-i$_{k2}$ aur-m$_{ptk1}$ **Bell**$_{k*}$ bry$_{k2*}$ cadm-s$_{br1}$ *Calc Calc-p Calc-s* camph$_{b7.de*}$ carb-an$_{k*}$ **Carb-v**$_{k*}$ *Carbn-s Card-m*$_{k*}$ caust$_{b4.de*}$ chap$_{br1}$ *Chel Chin Chion*$_{k*}$ clem$_{k*}$ cocc$_{bg2}$ *Con* cupr$_{bg2}$ **Dig**$_{k*}$ *Eup-per*$_{k*}$ *Ferr*$_{k*}$ *Ferr-ar* fl-ac graph$_{k2}$ *Iod*$_{k*}$ iris$_{ptk1}$ kali-ar$_{k2}$ kali-c$_{k*}$ **Kali-i**$_{k*}$ *Kali-p* kali-s *Kreos*$_{k*}$ **Lach**$_{k*}$ **Lept**$_{k*}$ **Lyc**$_{k*}$ *Mag-m*$_{k*}$ merc$_{k*}$ morg-p$_{fmm1•}$ mur-ac$_{b4.de*}$ **Nat-s**$_{k*}$ **Nux-v**$_{k*}$ nyct$_{c1*}$ *Ol-j* pall$_{k*}$ *Phos*$_{k*}$ *Podo*$_{k*}$ ptel$_{k*}$ ran-b$_{bg2*}$ raph rhus-t$_{k2}$ ruta$_{tl1}$ sabad$_{b7.de*}$ sanic$_{c2}$ sel senn$_{br1}$ *Sep*$_{k*}$ *Sil*$_{k*}$ *Spig*$_{b7a.de}$ sul-i$_{k2}$ *Sulph* tab *Tarent* zinc
- **sprained**; as if: kali-c$_{b4.de*}$ lyc$_{b4a.de*}$
- **squeezed**; as if: arn$_{b7.de}$ colch$_{b7.de*}$ iod$_{b4.de*}$ kali-c$_{b4.de*}$ mag-c$_{b4.de*}$ ph-ac$_{b4a.de}$ ruta$_{b7.de}$ sel$_{b7a.de}$ sep$_{b4.de*}$ staph$_{b7.de*}$ sul-ac$_{b4.de*}$ zinc$_{b4.de*}$
- **standing** agg.: aloe bros-gau$_{mrc1}$
- **stepping** agg.: calc$_{h2}$ nat-s$_{hr}$ ptel$_{gk}$
- **stitching** pain: *Acon*$_{k*}$ *Aesc* *Agar*$_{k*}$ aloe$_{k*}$ *Alum*$_{k*}$ alum-p$_{k2}$ alum-sil$_{k2}$ am-c$_{b4a.de*}$ am-m$_{k*}$ anac$_{b4.de*}$ androc$_{srj1•}$ arg-n$_{k*}$ arn$_{b7.de*}$ *Asaf*$_{k*}$ asar$_{k*}$ bamb-a$_{stb2.de•}$ bar-c$_{b4.de*}$ *Bell*$_{k*}$ bell-p$_{sp1}$ benz-ac$_{bro1}$ **Berb**$_{k*}$ *Bov*$_{k*}$ **Bry**$_{k*}$ bufo *Cact* **Calc**$_{k*}$ calc-f *Calc-p Calc-s* calc-sil$_{k2}$ camph$_{k*}$ canth$_{k*}$ *Carb-v*$_{k*}$ carbn-s *Card-m Caust*$_{k*}$ cedr$_{k*}$ *Cham*$_{k*}$ **Chel**$_{k*}$ *Chin*$_{k*}$ choc$_{srj3•}$ clem$_{k*}$ *Cocc*$_{k*}$ colch *Coloc*$_{k*}$ **Con**$_{k*}$ *Crot-h* cupr cycl dios$_{bro1}$ dulc$_{b4.de*}$ fago form graph$_{k*}$ *Hep*$_{k*}$ hyos$_{b7.de*}$ *Ign*$_{b7a.de}$ iod$_{b4.de*}$ ip$_{b7.de*}$ jug-c$_{bro1}$ kali-ar$_{k2}$ *Kali-bi*$_{k*}$ *Kali-c*$_{k*}$ kali-i$_{bg2}$ kali-n$_{b4.de*}$ kali-p kali-s kali-sil$_{k2}$ kola$_{stb3•}$ kreos$_{k*}$ *Lach* lact *Laur*$_{k*}$ **Lept**$_{k*}$ lyc$_{k*}$ mag-c$_{k*}$ **Mag-m**$_{k*}$ **Merc**$_{k*}$ merc-c$_{k*}$ merc-i-f mosch$_{k*}$ mur-ac$_{b4.de*}$ *Nat-c*$_{k*}$ *Nat-m*$_{k*}$ *Nat-p* *Nat-s*$_{k*}$ nept-m$_{lsd2.fr}$ *Nit-ac* nux-m **Nux-v**$_{k*}$ nyct$_{c1}$ ol-an *Ox-ac*$_{k*}$ par$_{b7.de*}$ petr$_{a1}$ ph-ac$_{k*}$ phos$_{k*}$ plat$_{b4.de*}$ plb$_{k*}$ *Podo*$_{k*}$ prun$_{bg2}$ psor *Ptel* *Puls*$_{k*}$ quas$_{br1*}$ **Ran-b**$_{k*}$ *Ran-s*$_{k*}$ raph$_{br1}$ rhod$_{b4.de*}$ rhus-t$_{b7.de*}$ ruta$_{fd4.de}$ sabad$_{k*}$ sars$_{b4.de*}$ *Sel*$_{k*}$ **Sep**$_{k*}$ *Sil*$_{k*}$ *Spig*$_{k*}$ spong$_{b7.de*}$ stann stel$_{bro1}$ stront-c$_{b4.de*}$ *Sul-ac*$_{k*}$ sul-i$_{k2}$ *Sulph*$_{k*}$ symph$_{fd3.de•}$ *Tab*$_{k*}$ tarax$_{bg2}$ tell$_{rsj10•}$ thres-a$_{sze7•}$ thuj$_{bg2}$ tub$_{c1}$ v-a-b$_{jl}$ vac$_{jl2}$ valer$_{b7.de*}$ vanil$_{fd5.de}$ verb$_{b7.de*}$ *Zinc*$_{k*}$ zinc-p$_{k2}$
  - **accompanied** by | **Spleen**; stitching pain in (See spleen - stitching - accompanied - liver)
  - **outward**: chin$_{h1}$
  - **upward**: *Ran-b*
- **stool** | **after**:
  - **agg**.: kali-bi ↓ lept ↓ *Lyc* ↓ *Stann* ↓
    - **burning**: lept *Stann*$_{k*}$
    - **cramping**: *Lyc*$_{b4a.de}$
    - **stitching** pain: kali-bi$_{bg2}$
  - **before**: acon$_{b7a.de}$
- **stooping** | **after**:
  - **agg**.: calc ↓
    - **stitching** pain: calc$_{h2*}$
  - **agg**.: aloe alum$_{k*}$ calc clem cocc kali-c lyc petr-ra$_{shn4•}$
    - **sprained**; as if: kali-c$_{h2}$
    - **stitching** pain: calc$_{h2*}$
- **supper** agg.; after: zinc ↓
  - **stitching** pain: zinc
  - **tearing** pain: zinc

- **tearing** pain: acon k2 alum k* berb k2 calc-p bg2 carb-v b4a.de* caust k* clem colch b7.de* *Con* k* *Dios* kali-bi bg2 kali-c b4.de* kola stb3• kreos nat-m k2 sep b4.de* sulph bg2 teucr b7.de* zinc k*
- **torn** apart; as if: arn b7.de*
- **touch** agg.: aeth agar agn hr1 bry calc h2 carb-an carb-v chel k2 **Chin** cimx c1 clem hep br1 iod ↓ kali-c ↓ **Lyc** **Mag-m** k* **Merc** *Nat-m* *Nat-s* *Nux-v* nyct c1 podo k2 ran-b c1* **Sep** k* sulph h2 ther c1* valer
  - **sore**: iod tl1 kali-c h2 nat-s hr
- **turning** in bed agg.: arn
- **twinging**: berb k2 ruta fd4.de
- **twitching**: calc h2 kali-c b4.de* m-aust b7.de nat-c b4.de* **Puls** b7a.de
- **urinate**; on urging to: all-c tl1 *Ferr*
- **urination** agg.; after: malar ↓
  - **cramping**: malar jl2
  - **drawing** pain: malar jl2
- **vexation**; after: bry *Cocc* *Nat-s* vanil fd5.de
- **walking**:
  - **agg.**: androc ↓ *Bapt* con k* hep kali-bi ↓ kali-c k* lec **Mag-m** k* *Nat-s* psor *Puls* ↓ *Sep* thuj
    - **pressing** pain: sep h2
    - **sore**: nat-s k2
    - **stitching** pain: androc srj1• hep kali-bi *Nat-s* *Puls*
  - **amel.**: calc-f ↓
    - **stitching** pain: calc-f
- **warm** | **drinks** | **amel.**: *Graph*
  - **food** | **amel.**: chel k2
- **yawning** agg.: psor
- ▽ **extending** to:
  - **Arms**: dios br1
  - **Back●**: *Aesc* bamb-a stb2.de• **Chel** k* dios pd euphr *Iod* jug-c *Kali-c* **Lyc** **Mag-m** *Nat-m* podo k2 spong fd4.de symph fd3.de• yuc
    - **stitching** pain: **Chel** spong fd4.de symph fd3.de•
    - **Spine**: lept br1 mag-m br1
  - **Chest**: arg-n a1 calc ↓ dios br1* symph fd3.de•
    - **stitching** pain: calc h2
    - **walking** agg.: arg-n ↓
      - **stitching** pain: arg-n hr1
    - **Arm**; and: *Dios* ↓
      - **stitching** pain: *Dios* vh
      - **Nipple**; and: *Dios* ↓
        - **stitching** pain: *Dios* vh
  - **Direction**; every: berb k2
  - **Downward**: *Chel* chelo c1 ptel bg1
  - **Elbow**: med hr1
  - **Epigastrium**: bell berb pd kali-i *Lach* mag-m br1*
  - **Hip**: alum ↓
    - **tearing** pain: alum ptk
  - **Nipple**; right: *Dios* br1*
  - **Renal** region: sel c1
  - **Scapula**, below angle of right: chen-a vml3•
  - **Scapula**; right: aral vh1
  - **Shoulder**; right: bamb-a stb2.de• chel k2 crot-h *Kali-bi* *Med* k* merc-c **Sep** ↓
    - **stitching** pain: **Sep**
  - **Thigh**: cob ↓
    - **stitching** pain: cob
- ○ **Below**: brucel sa3•
  - **walking** agg.: thuj ↓
    - **pressing** pain: thuj h1
- **Lobe**:
  - **right**: chel k2 nept-m lsd2.fr
    - **lying** on it: mag-m k2
  - **left**: carbn-s *Card-m* ↓ chelo br1
    - **sore**: *Card-m* chelo c1
    - **extending** to | **Downward**: chelo br1

- **Liver**: ...
  - **Region** of liver: acon ↓ am-c ↓ am-m ↓ apis ↓ bell ↓ **Bry** ↓ *Calc* ↓ carb-an ↓ chin ↓ chinin-s ↓ *Cocc* ↓ colch ↓ hell ↓ hyos ↓ iber br1 ign ↓ kali-bi ↓ kali-c ↓ **Lach** ↓ *Laur* ↓ lyc ↓ malar ↓ mosch ↓ mur-ac ↓ nat-m ↓ nat-s ↓ *Nux-v* ↓ ol-an ↓ ol-j br1 pall ↓ phos ↓ *Puls* ↓ rhus-t ↓ ruta ↓ sep ↓ *Sil* ↓ spong ↓ sulph ↓ teucr ↓ tub jl2 vac ↓ verb ↓ zinc ↓
    - **accompanied** by | **Skin**; yellow discoloration of: nit-ac tl1
    - **dull** pain: chinin-s bg2 hyos b7a.de malar jl2 spong bg2
    - **pinching** pain: am-c b4.de* am-m b7.de* bell b4.de* *Cocc* b7.de* colch b7.de* hell b7.de* ign b7.de* kali-bi bg2 kali-c b4.de* lyc b4a.de* mosch b7.de* nat-m b4.de* phos b4.de* rhus-t b7.de* teucr b7.de* verb b7.de* zinc b4.de*
    - **pressing** pain | **outward**: *Calc* b4a.de
    - **pulsating** pain: malar jl2
    - **stitching** pain: vac jl2
    - **ulcerative** pain: acon bg2 am-c bg2 apis bg2 bell b4a.de* **Bry** b7a.de calc bg2 carb-an bg2 chin bg2 kali-bi bg2 **Lach** b7a.de *Laur* b7a.de lyc bg2 mur-ac bg2 nat-s bg2 *Nux-v* b7.de* ol-an bg2 pall bg2 *Puls* b7a.de ruta b7.de* sep bg2 *Sil* b4a.de* sulph bg2
    - **Skin**; below the: chin ↓ ran-b ↓
      - **ulcerative** pain: chin b7.de* ran-b b7.de*
- **Loins**:
  - **abortion**; during: cimic bro1
  - **apyrexia**; during: verat bro1
  - **stool**:
    - **before**: *Bar-c* b4a.de
    - **during** | **agg.**: kali-bi bg2
- **Lower** abdomen: *Acon* ↓ agar ↓ agn ↓ aloe ↓ alum ↓ am-c ↓ *Am-m* ↓ ambr ↓ anac ↓ ang ↓ ant-t ↓ *Apis* ↓ arg-met ↓ arn ↓ **Ars** ↓ asaf ↓ asar ↓ aster ↓ aur ↓ bar-c ↓ *Bell* ↓ bism ↓ borx ↓ bov ↓ *Bry* ↓ calc ↓ camph ↓ cann-s ↓ canth ↓ caps ↓ carb-an ↓ *Carb-v* ↓ caust ↓ chel ↓ chin ↓ chlam-tr bcx2• cic ↓ cimic ↓ clem ↓ *Cocc* ↓ colch ↓ *Coloc* ↓ *Con* ↓ cupr ↓ cycl ↓ dig ↓ euphr ↓ guaj ↓ hell ↓ hyos ↓ *Ign* ↓ iod ↓ kali-c ↓ kali-n ↓ *Lach* ↓ laur ↓ *Lyc* ↓ m-arct ↓ m-aust ↓ mag-c ↓ mag-m ↓ mang ↓ *Meny* ↓ merc ↓ mez ↓ *Nat-c* ↓ nat-m ↓ *Nit-ac* ↓ nux-m ↓ *Nux-v* ↓ olnd ↓ par ↓ *Ph-ac* ↓ **Phos** ↓ plat ↓ plb ↓ puls ↓ **Ran-b** ↓ rheum ↓ *Rhus-t* ↓ ruta ↓ sabad ↓ sabin ↓ samb ↓ *Sec* ↓ seneg ↓ *Sep* ↓ sil ↓ spig ↓ spong ↓ squil ↓ *Stann* ↓ staph ↓ stront-c ↓ sul-ac ↓ sulph ↓ *Tarax* ↓ teucr ↓ thuj ↓ valer ↓ **Verat** ↓ verb ↓ viol-t ↓ *Zinc* ↓
  - **right**: bapt ↓
    - **cutting** pain: bapt bg2
  - **left**: sep ↓
    - **burning**: sep bg2
  - **blow**; pain as from a: arn bg2
  - **boring** pain: sabad bg2
  - **burning**: *Acon* bg2 apis b7a.de **Ars** b4a.de* *Bry* b7.de calc b4a.de camph b7a.de* canth bg2 caps b7.de kali-n b4a.de *Lach* bg2 laur bg2 *Nux-v* bg2 ph-ac bg2 **Phos** b4a.de* ran-b b7.de sabad bg2 *Sec* bg2 sep b4a.de sil bg2 *Stann* b4a.de sul-ac b4a.de tarax b7.de **Verat** bg2
  - **burrowing**: sep bg2
  - **chill**; during: *Nux-v* ↓
    - **stitching** pain: *Nux-v* b7a.de
  - **clutched** with nails of fingers; as if: bell bg2 lyc bg2 puls bg2
  - **compressed**; as if: canth b7.de* puls bg2 sil bg2
  - **cramping**: aloe bg2 bell bg2 carb-v bg2 chlam-tr bcx2• con bg2
  - **cutting** pain: agn b7.de* ang b7.de* apis b7a.de ars b4a.de asaf b7.de* asar b7.de* bar-c b4.de* *Bell* b4.de* bov b4.de* calc b4.de* canth b7.de* carb-an b4.de* caust b4.de* chel b7.de* cic b7.de* clem b4.de* cocc b7.de* coloc b4.de* cycl b7.de* dig b4.de* hyos b7.de* kali-c b4.de* laur b7a.de* lyc b4.de* mag-m b4.de* merc b4.de* nat-c b4.de* nat-m bg2 nux-v b7.de* par b7.de* phos b4.de* plat b4.de* sep b4.de* sil b4.de* spig bg2 spong b7.de* squil b7.de* stann b4.de* staph b7.de* stront-c b4.de* teucr b7.de* thuj b4.de* verat b7.de* zinc b4.de*
  - **drawing** pain: chin bg2 valer bg2
  - **gnawing** pain: seneg bg2
  - **lightning**-like: aster sze10•

Abdomen

- **pinching** pain: agar b4.de* alum b4.de* am-m b7.de* asaf b7.de* aur b4a.de* bell b4.de* bism b7.de* bry b7.de* calc b4.de* cann-s b7.de* canth b7.de* *Carb-v* b4.de* chin b7.de* cycl b7.de* guaj b4.de* ign b7.de* laur b7.de* *Lyc* b4a.de m-arct b7.de *Meny* b7.de* nat-c b4.de* nux-m b7.de* plb b7.de* **Ran-b** b7.de* *Rhus-t* b7.de* ruta b7.de* sep b4.de* sil b4a.de* spig b7.de* spong b7.de* squil b7.de* valer b7.de* verat b7.de* zinc b4.de*
- **pressing** pain: am-c b4.de* *Am-m* b7a.de ambr b7.de* anac b4.de* ang b7.de* ant-t b7.de* *Apis* b7a.de arg-met b7.de* arn b7.de* aster sze10• aur b4.de* bar-c b4.de* bell b4.de* bism b7.de* bry b7.de* calc b4.de* camph b7.de* caps b7.de* carb-v b4.de* caust b4.de* chin b7a.de* *Cocc* b7.de* colch bg2 con b4.de* cupr b7.de* cycl b7.de* dig b4.de* euphr b7.de* hell b7.de* ign b7.de* iod b4.de* kali-c b4a.de* lyc b4.de* m-arct b7.de mag-m b4.de* mang b4.de* merc b4.de* mez b4.de* nat-m b4.de* *Nux-v* b7.de* *Ph-ac* b4.de* phos b4.de* plat b4.de* puls b7.de* rheum b7.de* ruta b7.de* *Sep* b4.de* spig b7.de* stann b4.de* staph b7.de* stront-c b4.de* sul-ac b4.de* teucr b7.de* thuj bg2 valer b7.de* verat b7.de* zinc b4.de*
  - **outward**: squil bg2
  - **stone**; as from a: bell bg2 cocc bg2 sep bg2
- **shattered**; as if: squil bg2
- **sore**: bell bg2 cimic bg2 phos bg2 valer bg2
- **squeezed**; as if: ambr b7.de* bell b4.de* carb-v b4.de* *Coloc* b4.de* cycl b7.de* *Ign* b7.de* kali-c b4.de* mag-c b4.de* sil b4.de*
- **stitching** pain: ambr b7.de* anac b4.de* ang b7.de* ant-t b7.de* asaf b7.de* bar-c b4.de* bell b4.de* borx b4a.de bov b4.de* *Bry* b7.de* calc bg2 cann-s b7.de* caps b7.de* carb-v b4.de* caust b4.de* chel b7.de* chin b7.de* cocc b7.de* colch b7.de* hyos b7.de* *Ign* b7.de* kali-c b4.de* lyc b4.de* m-aust b7.de meny b7.de* merc b4.de* mez b4.de* nit-ac b4.de* nux-v bg2 olnd b7.de* ph-ac b4.de* phos b4.de* ran-b b7.de* ruta b7.de* sabin b7.de* samb b7a.de* sep b4.de* spig b7.de* spong b7.de* squil b7.de* stann b4.de* sulph b4.de* *Tarax* b7.de* verat b7.de* verb b7.de* viol-t b7.de* zinc b4.de*
- **stool** agg.; after: sabad ↓
  - **burning**: sabad b7a.de
- **tearing** pain: aur b4a.de bar-c b4a.de carb-v b4a.de *Con* b4a.de lyc b4a.de *Nat-c* b4a.de nit-ac b4a.de stann b4a.de *Zinc* b4a.de
- **touch**:
  - **agg.**: *Cupr* ↓
    - **pressing** pain:
      - **drawing** | **hard**; as from something: *Cupr* h2
- **twitching**: sul-ac bg2
- **ulcerative** pain: *Nit-ac* bg2
- ▽ **extending** to | **Back**; lower: chlam-tr bcx2•

- **Mons veneris**: meny ↓
  - **pressing** pain: meny h1
- **Muscles**: acon ↓ ambr ↓ *Arn* ↓ bapt ↓ bell ↓ *Bell-p* ↓ cimic ↓ cupr ↓ dros ↓ ferr ↓ ham ↓ hyos ↓ lat-m bnm6• lyc ↓ mag-m ↓ nat-m ↓ nat-n ↓ nux-v ↓ par ↓ plb ↓ pyrog ↓ *Rhus-t* ↓ sabin ↓ samb ↓ stram ↓ stry ↓ sulph ↓ tab ↓ valer ↓
  - **night**: cartl-s ↓ lyc ↓
    - **cramping**: cartl-s rly4• lyc h2
  - **cough** agg.; during: *Hyos* b7.de* *Nux-v* b7a.de squil b7.de*
  - **cramping**: acon bro1 *Arn* bro1 bell bro1 *Bell-p* bro1 cupr bg2* dros b7.de* ferr b7a.de* ham bro1 lyc b4a.de* mag-m bro1 nat-m bg2 nat-n bro1 nux-v bg2 par b7.de* plb bg2* *Rhus-t* bro1 sabin bg2 samb bg2 stram b7.de* stry bro1 sulph bro1 tab bg2
  - **sore**: bapt tl1 cimic tl1 pyrog tl1
  - **sprained**; as if: hyos b7.de* valer b7.de*
  - **wound**; as from a: ambr c1
- **Pancreas**: *Iris* ↓
  - **burning**: *Iris* k*
- **Pelvic** region: *Bell-p* ↓ helon ↓ verat-v ↓
  - **sore**: *Bell-p* bro1 helon mrr1 verat-v tl1
  - **walking** erect is impossible: arn ↓
    - **sore**: arn br1
  - ○ **Bones**: *Aesc* ↓ arn ↓ bell-p ↓ lappa ↓ *Tril-p* ↓
    - **sore**: *Aesc* bro1 arn bro1 bell-p bro1 lappa bro1 *Tril-p* bro1
- **Pelvis**: *Helon* ↓ lil-t ↓
- **Pelvis**: ...
  - **alternating** with | **Head**; pain in (See HEAD - Pain - alternating - pelvis)
  - **dragging**, bearing down: *Helon* br1
    - **come** out through vagina; as if everything would: lil-t tl1
  - **menses**; during:
    - **amel.**: vib ↓
      - **cramping**: vib tl1
  - **pressing** pain:
    - **accompanied** by | **menses**; suppressed: ant-c bro1 bell bro1
  - ○ **Organs**; pelvic: vib ↓
    - **cramping**: vib br1
- **Peritoneum**: pert-vc vk9
  - **morning** | **until**: pert-vc vk9
- **Pubic** region: diosm ↓ staph ↓
  - **flatulence**; during: *Calc* ↓
    - **pressing** pain: *Calc* b4a.de
  - **menses**; during: rad-br ptk1
  - **pressing** pain: diosm br1
  - **sprained**; as if: staph h1
  - **stool**:
    - **before**: sabad b7.de*
    - **during** | **agg.**: laur b7a.de*
  - **urination** | **after**:
    - **agg.**: fl-ac bg2 rhod bg2 staph ↓ tarax ↓
      - **sprained**; as if: staph b7.de*
      - **stitching** pain: tarax b7a.de
    - **during**:
      - **agg.**: canth ↓
        - **cutting** pain: canth b7.de*
  - ○ **Mons** pubis: am-m ↓ anac ↓ ant-t b7.de* arg-met ↓ arn ↓ asaf ↓ bell ↓ calc-p bg2 cann-xyz ↓ carb-an ↓ cic ↓ clem ↓ coff ↓ con ↓ dig ↓ hell ↓ hyos ↓ ign ↓ kali-c ↓ laur ↓ lyc ↓ meny ↓ mez ↓ nat-m ↓ nux-v ↓ ph-ac ↓ *Plat* ↓ *Rhus-t* ↓ ruta ↓ sabad ↓ stann ↓ staph ↓ sul-ac bg2 valer ↓ viol-t ↓
    - **blow**; pain as from a: rhus-t b7.de*
    - **burning**: meny b7.de* rhus-t bg2
    - **cramping**: dig bg2 ign bg2 nat-m bg2
    - **cutting** pain: hyos b7.de*
    - **dragging**, bearing down: carb-an bg2
    - **drawing** pain: calc-p bg2 rhus-t b7.de* sabad b7.de* valer b7.de*
    - **jerking** pain: ruta b7.de*
    - **pressing** pain: arg-met b7.de* calc-p bg2 con bg2 hell b7.de* meny b7.de* nux-v b7.de* *Plat* bg2 *Rhus-t* b7.de* valer b7.de*
      - **outward**: bell bg2 cann-xyz bg2 clem bg2 con bg2 ign bg2 kali-c bg2 lyc bg2 mez bg2 ph-ac bg2 rhus-t bg2 sul-ac bg2
    - **smarting**: rhus-t bg2
    - **sore**: coff b7a.de nux-v b7a.de ph-ac bg2 valer b7.de*
    - **sprained**; as if: staph b7.de*
    - **stitching** pain: asaf b7.de* calc-p bg2 laur bg2 meny b7.de* ruta b7.de* stann bg2 viol-t b7.de*
    - **stretched**; as if: rhus-t b7.de*
    - **tearing** pain: anac b4a.de arn bg2 carb-an bg2
    - **ulcerative** pain: am-m bg2 cic bg2
- **Ribs**; below false: arn ↓
  - **stitching** pain: arn br1
  - ▽ **extending** to:
    - **Abdomen**: *Camph* ↓
      - **constricting** pain: *Camph*
- **Sides**: abrot ↓ acon k* acon-ac ↓ agar k* agath-a ↓ all-c k* *Aloe* alum k* alum-p ↓ am-c ↓ am-m ↓ ambr ↓ anac ↓ ang ↓ ant-c ↓ ant-t k* apis ↓ arg-met ↓ arg-n ↓ arn ↓ ars k* *Asaf* ↓ asar b7.de* *Aur* ↓ bad ↓ bar-c ↓ bar-i ↓ bar-s ↓ bell berb ↓ *Borx* bov ↓ brom k* bry cadm-s c1 calc k* calc-p ↓ calc-sil ↓ camph ↓ cann-s ↓ canth b7.de* caps ↓ carb-an k* carb-v k* carbn-s ↓ castm **Caust** ↓ *Cham* chel ↓ chim ↓ chin cina ↓ cinch ↓ clem ↓ cocc ↓ coff ↓ colch ↓ coloc com k* con k* croc ↓ crot-t ↓ cupr cur ↓ cycl ↓ dig ↓ dios ↓ dros ↓ dulc ↓ elaps eup-pur euph ↓ eupi k* ferr k* ferr-ar ferr-i ↓ fic-m gya1 fl-ac k*

- **Sides**: ...
  graph$_{b4.de}$* grat$_{k}$* haem$_{k}$* hep$_{k}$* hyos ↓ ign iod ↓ ip ↓ iris kali-bi ↓ kali-c ↓ kali-n$_{k}$* kali-s ↓ kalm$_{k}$* kreos ↓ lach laur$_{k}$* *Led* ↓ lil-t ↓ lith-c lyc$_{k}$* lyss ↓ m-ambo$_{b7.de}$ m-arct ↓ m-aust ↓ mag-c mag-m ↓ manc$_{k}$* mang ↓ mang-p ↓ med meny ↓ merc ↓ merc-c ↓ mez ↓ mosch ↓ mur-ac murx$_{k}$* naja nat-c$_{k}$* nat-m *Nat-s*$_{k}$* nept-m ↓ *Nit-ac* ↓ nux-m ↓ *Nux-v* olnd ↓ op ↓ par petr ↓ ph-ac ↓ phos$_{k}$* phys ↓ plat ↓ plb$_{k}$* podo ↓ prun$_{k}$* psor ↓ puls ↓ *Ran-b* ↓ ran-s ↓ rat ↓ rheum ↓ rhod ↓ rhus-t rhus-v ruta$_{fd4.de}$ sabad ↓ sabin ↓ samb ↓ sang ↓ sars$_{k}$* sec$_{b7.de}$* *Sel* ↓ seneg sep$_{k}$* sil ↓ sphing$_{a1}$ spig ↓ spong ↓ *Stann* ↓ staph ↓ stram ↓ *Stront-c* ↓ sul-ac sulph$_{k}$* tab ↓ *Tarax* ↓ tarent$_{k}$* teucr ↓ thuj tritic-vg$_{fd5.de}$ valer vanil$_{fd5.de}$ viol-t ↓ zinc zinc-p ↓ *Zinc-s* ↓ zing ↓
  - **right**: acon ↓ agar ↓ aids$_{nl2}$• ambr ↓ ang ↓ ant-c ↓ ars ↓ aur ↓ aur-i ↓ bar-c ↓ bell ↓ berb ↓ bit-ar$_{wht1}$• *Borx* bov ↓ cain ↓ calc ↓ camph ↓ carb-an ↓ carb-v ↓ *Card-m* *Caust* ↓ cham ↓ chel ↓ chin ↓ chol ↓ clem ↓ colch ↓ coloc ↓ con ↓ cupr ↓ cycl ↓ dream-p$_{sdj1}$• dros ↓ fic-m$_{gya1}$ flor-p ↓ glycyr-g$_{cte1}$• ham$_{fd3.de}$• hell ↓ ign ↓ **Kali-c** ↓ kali-n$_{h2}$ kali-p ↓ lac-leo ↓ *Lach* ↓ lap-la ↓ lec lith-c **Lyc**$_{k}$* lyss ↓ mag-c ↓ manc ↓ med$_{c1}$ *Merc* mez ↓ mim-p ↓ nat-c ↓ nat-m nat-s$_{k2}$ nit-ac ↓ nux-m ↓ petr ↓ ph-ac ↓ *Phos*$_{bg1}$ plat ↓ plut-n ↓ positr$_{nl2}$• prun ↓ ptel$_{mrr1}$ pycnop-sa ↓ rhus-t$_{h1}$* sanguis-s ↓ sel sep$_{k}$* sil$_{h2}$ sphing$_{kk3.fr}$ spig$_{kk3.fr}$ spong ↓ stann ↓ staphycoc$_{rly4}$• stront-c ↓ sulph$_{h2}$ symph ↓ tarent$_{k}$* tere-la ↓ thuj ↓ tritic-vg$_{fd5.de}$ ulm-c ↓ zinc$_{bg1}$ zing ↓
    - **boring** pain: carb-an$_{h2}$
    - **burning**: caust$_{h2}$ chol$_{br1}$ petr$_{h2}$ plat$_{h2}$ sep$_{h2}$ stann$_{h2}$
    - **burrowing**: ars$_{h2}$
    - **cramping**: acon$_{k}$* ant-c$_{h2}$ bell$_{k}$* carb-v$_{k}$* caust$_{k}$* hell$_{h1}$ ign$_{bg1}$ lach$_{k}$* **Lyc** mag-c$_{k}$* manc$_{k}$* mez$_{h2}$ nat-m$_{k}$* *Nat-s* phos$_{h2}$ rhus-t$_{h1}$ sep$_{h2}$ zinc$_{k}$*
    - **cutting** pain: aur-i$_{k2}$ clem$_{h2}$ colch$_{bg1}$ con$_{k}$* *Lach* lap-la$_{sde8.de}$• nit-ac$_{h2}$ rhus-t$_{bg1}$ sanguis-s$_{hrn2}$• stront-c tere-la$_{rly4}$• [kali-p$_{xyz62}$]
      - **followed** by | **left**: lac-h$_{sk4}$•
    - **drawing** pain: ang$_{bg2}$ camph$_{h1}$* chin$_{bg2}$ coloc$_{bg2}$ cupr$_{h2}$ lach$_{bg2}$ lap-la$_{sde8.de}$• med$_{k}$* nat-c$_{h2}$ plat$_{h2}$ rhus-t$_{bg2}$ symph$_{fd3.de}$•
    - **flatulence**; from: *Colch* **Nat-s**
    - **lancinating**: cain staphycoc$_{rly4}$•
    - **lying**:
      - **side**; on | **left**:
        - **agg.**: nat-m ↓
          - **cramping**: nat-m
      - **right**:
        - **agg.**: bit-ar$_{wht1}$• prun ↓
          - **pressing** pain: prun
    - **menses**; during: oci-sa$_{sp1}$*
    - **plugged**; as if: sphing$_{a1}$*
    - **pressing** pain: ambr$_{h1}$ ang$_{h1}$ ars$_{k}$* bar-c$_{h2}$ cain calc$_{h2}$ *Card-m* con$_{h2}$ flor-p$_{rsj3}$• lyc$_{k}$* *Merc*$_{k}$* **Nat-s** prun$_{k}$* rhus-t$_{a1}$ sep$_{h2}$ stann$_{h2}$ thuj$_{k}$* zinc$_{k}$*
    - **sore**: ang$_{h1}$* camph$_{k}$* zing$_{k}$*
    - **squeezed**; as if: ambr$_{bg2}$
    - **stitching** pain: agar$_{k}$* bar-c$_{k}$* bell berb$_{k}$* bov$_{k}$* camph$_{h1}$ *Caust* cham$_{k}$* chel$_{bg3}$ cycl$_{h1}$ dream-p$_{sdj1}$• dros$_{h1}$ ham$_{fd3.de}$• **Kali-c**$_{k}$* lac-leo$_{sk4}$• lyss mez$_{h2}$ mim-p$_{rsj8}$• nat-c$_{h2}$ nat-s$_{bg3}$ nux-m$_{k}$* petr$_{k}$* ph-ac$_{h2}$ plat$_{h2}$ plut-n$_{srj7}$• pycnop-sa$_{mrz1}$ rhus-t$_{h1}$ spig$_{k}$* spong$_{k}$* stann$_{k}$* symph$_{fd3.de}$• tritic-vg$_{fd5.de}$ ulm-c$_{jsj8}$• zinc$_{h2}$
      - **alternating** with | **Chest**; stitching in right side of: zinc$_{h2}$
      - **followed** by | **left**: mag-m$_{bg1}$
    - **stool** agg.; after: *Rhus-t*$_{a1}$
    - **tearing** pain: aur$_{k}$* *Lach*$_{k}$* mez$_{h2}$
    - **touch** agg.: bit-ar$_{wht1}$•
    - **Ribs**:
      - **Below**: aq-mar$_{skp7}$• xan$_{c1}$
      - **Edge** of ribs: allox$_{sp1}$ oci-sa$_{sp1}$
    - **extending** to:
      - **left**: dros ↓ med$_{vh}$ nux-m$_{bg1}$ plat ↓ sep ↓
        - **stitching** pain: dros$_{h1}$ plat$_{h2}$ sep$_{h2}$
      - **Back**: phos ↓
        - **cramping**: phos$_{h2}$
  - **left**: agath-a ↓ aids$_{nl2}$• aloe ↓ alum ↓ am-c ↓ am-m ↓ anac ↓ ang ↓ ant-c ↓ ant-t ↓ *Arg-met* ↓ *Arg-n* ↓ arist-cl ↓ ars ↓ *Asaf* ↓ asar ↓ asc-c$_{hr1}$ bar-ox-suc ↓ bell ↓ *Berb* brom$_{k}$* brucel$_{sa3}$• bry ↓ **Calc**$_{bg1}$ calc-p ↓ camph ↓ canth ↓ carb-an ↓ *Carb-v*$_{k}$* *Card-m* castm *Caust* chin ↓ cina ↓ cinch ↓ colch ↓ coloc ↓ con ↓ cupr ↓ dig$_{br1}$ dream-p ↓ dros$_{tl1}$ dulc ↓ elat$_{hr1}$ eup-per ↓ eup-pur$_{k}$* *Eupi*$_{k}$* ferr$_{k}$* *Graph* ↓ grat$_{k}$* ham$_{fd3.de}$• hep ↓ hir$_{skp7}$• hydroph ↓ hyos ↓ iod ↓ **Kali-c** ↓ kali-n ↓ kali-p ↓ kola$_{stb3}$• *Lac-c* ↓ lach ↓ laur ↓ led ↓ luf-op$_{rsj5}$• lyc ↓ mag-c mag-m ↓ mand ↓ *Meny*$_{vh}$ meph$_{a1}$ mez ↓ mim-p$_{rsj8}$• naja *Nat-c* ↓ nat-m ↓ nat-sil$_{fd3.de}$• neon ↓ nicc ↓ *Nit-ac* ↓ nux-v ↓ olib-sac ↓ op ↓ ph-ac ↓ phos ↓ *Plat* ↓ plb ↓ podo$_{fd3.de}$• puls ↓ ran-b ↓ rhus-t ↓ ruta$_{fd4.de}$ sacch-a$_{fd2.de}$• samb ↓ *Sars* ↓ seneg ↓ *Sep* ↓ sil ↓ spong ↓ staph ↓ sul-ac ↓ *Sulph* ↓ *Tarax* ↓ thuj ↓ tritic-vg$_{fd5.de}$ trom$_{vml3}$• vanil$_{fd5.de}$ ven-m$_{rsj12}$• zinc ↓
    - **boring** pain: coloc$_{bg2}$ dig$_{h2}$ mand$_{rsj7}$•
    - **burning**: dream-p$_{sdj1}$• hep$_{h2}$ iod$_{h}$ *Lac-c* *Plat*$_{h2}$
    - **burrowing**: con$_{h2}$ spong$_{h1}$
    - **cough** agg.; during: *Caust*
    - **cramping**: agath-a$_{nl2}$• ant-c$_{h2}$ bry$_{k}$* calc-p$_{k}$* canth$_{k}$* chin cinch$_{a1}$ coloc$_{k}$* cupr$_{k}$* hydroph$_{rsj6}$• naja nat-m$_{h2}$ nux-v$_{k}$* puls$_{h1}$ sars$_{k}$* seneg$_{k}$* staph$_{h1}$ sul-ac$_{k}$* sulph$_{k}$* thuj$_{k}$*
    - **cutting** pain: calc$_{k}$* **Kali-c** mag-c$_{k}$* phos$_{h2}$ sars$_{k}$* thuj$_{k}$*
    - **dragging**, bearing down: dig$_{h2}$
    - **drawing** pain: arg-met$_{bg2}$ ars$_{bg2}$ asaf$_{bg2}$ nat-c$_{bg2}$ olib-sac$_{wmh1}$ rhus-t$_{bg2}$ tritic-vg$_{fd5.de}$ zinc$_{h2}$
    - **festering**: alum$_{bg2}$
    - **pinching** pain: asar$_{bg2}$ carb-v$_{bg2}$
    - **pregnancy** agg.; during: am-m ↓
      - **sore**: am-m$_{bro1}$
    - **pressing** pain: am-c anac$_{k}$* ant-t$_{bg2}$ berb camph carb-an$_{h2}$ carb-v$_{h2}$ kali-c kali-n led$_{h1}$ lyc$_{h2}$ mag-m$_{k}$* *Nat-c* nat-m *Nit-ac*$_{k}$* olib-sac$_{wmh1}$ sars$_{h2}$ sul-ac$_{h2}$* sulph tarax vanil$_{fd5.de}$
    - **sharp**: neon$_{srj5}$•
    - **sore**: *Arg-met* colch$_{k}$* eup-per$_{bg2}$
    - **squeezed**; as if: nat-m$_{bg2}$
    - **stitching** pain: aloe alum$_{h2}$ am-c am-m$_{k}$* ang$_{h1}$ *Arg-n*$_{hr1}$ ars$_{h2}$ *Asaf* bar-ox-suc$_{rly4}$• bell$_{k}$* bry$_{k}$* calc caust$_{k}$* chin cina$_{a1}$ coloc$_{k}$* dulc$_{h1}$ *Graph*$_{k}$* hep$_{k}$* hydroph$_{rsj6}$• hyos$_{k}$* kali-n$_{h2}$ kali-p$_{fd1.de}$• lach laur meny$_{h1}$ mez nicc$_{k}$* olib-sac$_{wmh1}$ op$_{k}$* ph-ac$_{h2}$ plb$_{k}$* ran-b ruta$_{fd4.de}$ samb$_{k}$* *Sars*$_{k}$* *Sep*$_{k}$* sil$_{h2}$ staph sul-ac$_{h2}$ *Sulph*$_{k}$* *Tarax*$_{k}$* thuj$_{k}$* zinc$_{h2}$
    - **stool**; before: tarent ↓
      - **cramping**: tarent$_{bg2}$
    - **tearing** pain: arist-cl$_{rbp3}$• bry$_{k}$* iod$_{h}$ mag-c$_{k}$* samb$_{h1}$* sulph$_{h2}$
    - **yawning** agg.: sphing$_{kk3.fr}$
    - **Ilium**; crest of | **Above**: chel$_{h1}$ *Eupi*
    - **Lower**: meny ↓
      - **stitching** pain: meny$_{h1}$
    - **Ribs**:
      - **Below**: mur-ac ↓
        - **cramping**: mur-ac$_{a1}$
    - **extending** to:
      - **right**: aids$_{nl2}$• asar ↓ carb-v ↓ ip$_{k2}$ kali-p lachn ↓ nicc$_{c1}$ stann ↓ *Ter* ↓
        - **cramping**: asar carb-v
        - **cutting** pain: *Ip* lachn$_{hr1}$
        - **stitching** pain: **Ip**$_{k}$* stann$_{h2}$ *Ter*
      - **Vagina**: borx
  - **daytime**: sulph ↓
    - **stitching** pain: sulph$_{k}$*
  - **morning**: am-c$_{k}$* bar-c ↓ merc merc-c$_{k}$* phos ↓ rhus-t ↓ sars ↓ sulph$_{k}$* vanil$_{fd5.de}$
    - **bed** agg.; in: bell ↓
      - **cutting** pain: bell$_{h1}$
      - **pressing** pain: bell$_{h1}$
    - **cramping**: rhus-t$_{a1}$
    - **drawing** pain: phos$_{k}$*
    - **pressing** pain: bar-c$_{h2}$ merc$_{k}$*
    - **stitching** pain: sars$_{k}$*

Abdomen

- **morning**: ...
  - **waking**; on: sulph k*
- **forenoon**: nat-s ↓ *Ran-b* ↓
  - **stitching** pain: nat-s k* *Ran-b*
- **noon**: ptel k*
- **afternoon**: am-m ↓ ant-c ↓ kola stb3• nit-ac k* ox-ac k*
  - **burning**: am-m k*
  - **cramping**: ant-c h2
- **evening**: agath-a ↓ am-c ↓ ant-c ↓ *Caust* ↓ chinin-s fl-ac kali-c lyc ↓ nicc k* sil ↓ *Sulph* ↓ tritic-vg fd5.de
  - **bed** agg.; in: ars ↓
    - **stitching** pain: ars h2
  - **cramping**: ant-c h2 nicc k*
  - **cutting** pain: lyc h2 nicc k*
  - **lying** agg.: sul-ac ↓
    - **stitching** pain: sul-ac h2
  - **pressing** pain: fl-ac k*
  - **stitching** pain: agath-a nl2• am-c h2 *Caust* sil k* *Sulph* k* tritic-vg fd5.de
  - **tearing** pain: kali-c k*
- **night**: kali-c ↓ lyc ↓ nat-s k* prun k* ruta ↓ sulph ↓ zinc ↓
  - **midnight**: *Sulph* k*
    - **after**: thuj ↓
      - **pressing** pain: thuj h1
  - **cramping**: sulph h2
  - **cutting** pain: sulph
  - **drawing** pain: lyc h2
  - **stitching** pain: kali-c h2 ruta fd4.de zinc h2
- **bending** body:
  - **left** agg.; to: nat-c ↓
    - **stitching** pain: nat-c h2
- **bending** double:
  - **amel.**: kali-n ↓
    - **stitching** pain: kali-n h2
  - **must** bend double: aur ↓
    - **tearing** pain: aur h2
- **bind** abdomen; must: puls ↓
  - **cramping**: puls h1*
- **blowing** the nose agg.: stront-c ↓
  - **stitching** pain: stront-c
- **boring** pain: apis bg2 par bg2
- **breathing** agg.: calc raph k* tritic-vg fd5.de
  - **stitching** pain (See respiration - stitching)
- **burning**: all-c k* am-c k* am-m b7.de apis b7a.de ars k* carb-v k* chel b7.de graph k* grat k* nept-m lsd2.fr olnd k* petr k* plat b4a.de* rat ruta k* sep k* stann b4a.de
- **clawing** pain: hep h2 petr k*
- **coffee** agg.: *Cham*
- **compressed**; as if: canth b7.de* sabin b7.de*
- **contracting**: mang h2
- **cough**:
  - **during**:
    - **agg.**: alum ↓ ambr h1 arn ↓ ars ↓ bell ↓ *Borx* carb-an ↓ caust con k* eupi k* lyc k* sep ↓ spong ↓ squil k* stann ↓ sul-ac ↓ *Sulph* ↓
      - **burning**: sul-ac k*
      - **pressing** pain: spong
      - **stitching** pain: alum h2 arn k* ars k* bell borx carb-an k* sep k* stann k* *Sulph*
    - **amel.**: carb-an h2
- **cramping**: acon k* agath-a nl2• alum k* ant-c h2 bell k* bry k* calc-p k* canth k* carb-v k* caust k* chin cinch a1 coloc k* cupr k* *Ign* k* kali-n lach k* laur k* *Led* *Lyc* mag-c k* manc k* mang-p rly4• mur-ac naja nat-c k* nat-m k* *Nat-s* k* *Nux-v* k* petr h2 *Phos* k* plat h2 puls h1 rat k* rhod k* ruta sars k* seneg k* sul-ac k* sulph k* thuj k* zinc k* zinc-p k2
- **cutting** pain: alum b4.de* ang b7.de* apis b7a.de arn k* ars k* bell b4.de* calc k* canth b7.de* carb-an k* caust clem k* colch b7.de* con k* crot-t dulc k* ign k* ip b7.de* kali-bi k* *Lach* k* laur mag-c k* merc b4.de* mur-ac k* nat-c b4.de* nit-ac b4.de* par k* podo bg2 rheum b7.de* ruta k* sabad b7.de* sars k* *Stront-c* k* thuj k* zinc *Zinc-s* a1
  - **paroxysmal**: kali-bi k*
- **dinner** | **after**:
  - **agg.**: bov ↓ phos ↓ zinc ↓
    - **burning**: bov k*
    - **cutting** pain: phos h2
    - **drawing** pain: zinc h2
  - **during** | **agg.**: am-c k*
- **dragging**, bearing down: dig h2 phos
- **drawing** in abdomen agg.: *Asaf* ↓ laur ↓ nat-m ↓ sulph ↓
  - **pressing** pain: *Asaf* laur k* nat-m sulph k*
- **drawing** pain: am-m k* ant-t k* camph h1 cupr k* cur lyc k* nat-c k* par bg2 phos k* ran-b k* sep k* staph k* tritic-vg fd5.de
  - **menses**, as before: staph h1
  - **together**; drawing: zinc h2
- **eating**; after: alum k* asaf ↓ dream-p ↓ kali-n k* mez ↓ sep ↓
  - **cramping**: mez h2
  - **pressing** pain: sep h2
  - **stitching** pain: asaf dream-p sdj1•
- **exertion** agg.: alum
  - **tearing** pain: alum k*
- **expiration** agg.; during: dig ↓ mur-ac ↓
  - **cramping**: mur-ac h2
  - **stitching** pain: dig h2
- **fever**; during: *Acon* ↓ *Bry* ↓
  - **stitching** pain: *Acon* b7a.de *Bry* b7a.de
- **flatus**; passing:
  - **amel.**: kali-c ↓ laur ↓ plat ↓
    - **cramping**: plat h2
    - **cutting** pain: laur
    - **stitching** pain: kali-c h2
- **hernia** would protrude; as if a: petr h2*
- **hiccough** agg.: bar-c ↓
  - **stitching** pain: bar-c k*
- **holding** hand on side:
  - **must** hold hand on side: chol ↓
    - **burning**: chol br1
- **inspiration**:
  - **agg.**: carb-v ↓ con k* dulc a1 mez ↓ mur-ac ph-ac ↓ phos ↓ **Ran-b** ↓ sel stann ↓ stront-c ↓ sul-ac ↓ sulph ↓ thuj tritic-vg fd5.de
    - **cramping**: mur-ac
    - **cutting** pain: phos h2
    - **stitching** pain: carb-v k* dulc a1 mez ph-ac h2 **Ran-b** stann h2 stront-c sul-ac sulph k* tritic-vg fd5.de
  - **deep**:
    - **agg.**: con ↓ sars ↓ thuj ↓
      - **cramping**: sars h2
      - **pressing** pain: con h2 sars h2 thuj k*
- **kneading** amel.: **Nat-s** ↓
  - **pressing** pain: **Nat-s**
- **lancinating**: acon-ac rly4• ign
- **laughing** agg.: kali-c ↓
  - **stitching** pain: kali-c h2
- **lying**:
  - **agg.**: caust ↓ nat-m ↓
    - **cramping**: nat-m h2
    - **stitching** pain: caust h2
  - **back**; on:
    - **agg.**: sulph ↓
      - **cutting** pain: sulph

- **lying**: ...
  - **side**; on:
    - **agg.**: sul-ac↓
      - **stitching** pain: sul-ac
    - **left**:
      - **agg.**: plat↓
        - **stitching** pain: plat h2
      - **amel.**: nicc↓
        - **stitching** pain: nicc
    - **right**:
      - **agg.**: *Thuj*↓
        - **stitching** pain: *Thuj*
- **menses**; during: ars↓ *Nux-v*
  - **cramping**: ars h2
  - **cutting** pain: ars k*
  - **pressing** pain: *Nux-v* k*
  - **stitching** pain: ars h2
- **motion**:
  - **agg.**: ant-c↓ asar bry↓ eupi k* *Kali-c*↓ nat-s↓ nux-v↓ stront-c sul-ac↓ zinc↓
    - **cramping**: ant-c h2 zinc h2
    - **pressing** pain: asar
    - **stitching** pain: bry *Kali-c* nat-s k* nux-v k* sul-ac h2
  - **amel.**: ars↓
    - **stitching** pain: ars h2
- **periodical**: ph-ac↓
  - **pressing** pain: ph-ac
- **pinching** pain: alum b4a.de am-c b4.de* am-m b7.de* ang b7.de* ant-c b7.de* *Asar* b7a.de bell b4.de* cann-s b7.de* canth b7.de* carb-an b4.de* carb-v b4.de* caust b4.de* cham b7.de* cocc b7.de* coff b7.de* croc b7.de* euph b4.de* ign b7.de* laur b7.de* lyc b4a.de* m-arct b7.de mag-c b4.de* mur-ac b4a.de* nat-c b4.de* nux-v b7.de* phos b4.de* plat b4.de* rhod b4a.de ruta b7.de* sars b4.de* stann b4.de* staph b7.de* teucr b7.de* thuj b4.de* zinc b4.de*
- **pressing** pain: alum k* am-c am-m k* ambr b7.de* anac k* ang b7.de* arn b7.de* ars k* *Asaf* k* asar k* *Aur* k* bar-c b4.de* bell b4.de* berb borx b4a.de calc b4.de* caps b7.de* carb-v k* chin k* coff b7.de* croc b7.de* dios k* hep b4a.de ign k* kali-c k* kalm k* laur b7.de* led b7.de* lyc k* mag-m k* merc k* mur-ac nat-c h2 *Nat-m* k* **Nat-s** nept-m lsd2.fr *Nit-ac* k* *Nux-v* k* par b7.de* ph-ac *Phos* ran-b b7.de* ran-s b7.de* rhus-t b7.de* sabad b7.de* seneg b4.de* *Sep* k* staph k* *Sulph* b4a.de tarax k* *Thuj* k* vanil fd5.de zinc k*
  - **accompanied** by | **heat**: nept-m lsd2.fr
  - **outward**: calc h2 coloc k* lyc h2 *Nux-v* sul-ac
- **pressure**:
  - **agg.**: dulc↓ mez↓ zinc↓
    - **drawing** pain: zinc h2
    - **stitching** pain: dulc h2 mez h2 zinc h2
  - **amel.**: *Asaf*↓ bov mag-c↓ **Nat-s** thuj↓
    - **stitching** pain: *Asaf* mag-c h2 thuj
  - **stomach** agg.; on: bell↓
    - **pressing** pain: bell h1
- **raising** arms agg.: eupi k* ferr-i↓
  - **stitching** pain: ferr-i
- **respiration**: alum↓ bar-c↓ caps↓ carb-v↓ nux-v↓ stann↓ *Sulph*↓ tritic-vg↓ zinc↓
  - **stitching** pain: alum h2 bar-c caps k* carb-v nux-v stann k* *Sulph* tritic-vg fd5.de zinc h2
- **riding** agg.: card-m hep rumx
  - **pressing** pain: *Card-m* hep k*
- **sitting**:
  - **agg.**: aeth↓ am-c↓ am-m↓ asaf↓ calc carb-an carb-v cina↓ dros↓ dulc↓ grat↓ laur↓ meny↓ nat-c↓ nicc↓ phos↓ sabad↓ samb↓ sars↓ sulph tritic-vg fd5.de
    - **burning**: am-m k*
    - **cramping**: carb-an
    - **cutting** pain: carb-an k*

- **sitting – agg.**: ...
    - **pressing** pain: am-c calc k*
    - **stitching** pain: aeth a1 am-m asaf carb-an cina a1 dros dulc h1 grat laur meny h1 nat-c h2 nicc phos sabad samb xxb1 sars
  - **amel.**: cinnb↓ zinc↓
    - **drawing** pain: zinc h2
    - **stitching** pain: cinnb
  - **bent** forward:
    - **agg.**: carb-v↓
      - **cramping**: carb-v
- **sore**: ang bg2 arg-met arn k* bad k* camph caust chim a1 chin colch k* eup-pur k* ferr lil-t k* nux-v ran-b k* stront-c zing k*
- **squeezed**; as if: carb-v b4.de* mag-c b4.de* mez b4.de* nux-v b7.de* zinc b4.de*
- **standing** agg.: alum↓ arg-n kali-n↓ meny↓ nicc↓ samb↓
  - **cramping**: kali-n
  - **drawing** pain: arg-n k*
  - **stitching** pain: alum h2 meny h1 nicc k* samb xxb1
- **stitching** pain: abrot bg3 acon bg3 *Agar* k* agath-a nl2• *All-c* k* aloe alum k* alum-p k2 am-c am-m k* ang b7.de* arg-n k* arn b7.de* *Ars* b4.de* *Asaf* k* asar bar-c k* bar-i bar-s k2 *Bell* berb k* borx b4a.de bov k* bry k* calc k* calc-p k* calc-sil k2 camph b7.de* cann-s b7.de* canth b7.de* carb-an k* carb-v k* carbn-s **Caust** k* cham k* chin b7.de* cina b7.de* cocc k* coff b7.de* coloc k* con k* croc b7.de* crot-t cycl b7.de* dig b4.de* dros b7.de* dulc b4.de* ferr-i graph k* grat k* *Hep* b4a.de hyos k* ign k* iod k* ip k* kali-c k* kali-n k* kali-s kreos b7a.de laur k* led b7.de* lyss m-ambo b7.de m-arct b7.de m-aust b7.de meny b7.de* merc-c b4a.de mez k* mosch b7.de* naja nat-c k* nux-m k* nux-v k* olnd b7.de* op k* petr k* ph-ac k* phos k* phys k* plat k* plb k* psor k* puls k* *Ran-b* k* rhus-t k* ruta fd4.de sabad k* samb b7.de* sang bg3 *Sars* k* *Sel* b7a.de seneg sep k* sil k* spig k* spong k* *Stann* k* staph b7.de* stram stront-c sul-ac k* *Sulph* k* tab k* *Tarax* k* tarent thuj k* tritic-vg fd5.de viol-t b7.de* zinc k* zinc-p k2
  - **boring** pain: dros h1
  - **burning**: sulph h2
  - **downward**: plat
  - **outward**: asaf cann-s lach
  - **tearing** pain: ars h2
  - **upward**: bell
- **stool**:
  - **after** | **agg.**: rhus-t
  - **amel.**: calc↓
    - **cutting** pain: calc k*
  - **before**: mag-c↓ mang↓
    - **cramping**: mag-c k* mang h2
  - **during**:
    - **agg.**: mang↓ nicc k* *Zinc-s*↓
      - **cramping**: mang h2 nicc k*
      - **stitching** pain: nicc k* *Zinc-s* k*
  - **urging** to | **with**: bar-c h2
- **stooping**:
  - **agg.**: alum↓ am-c↓ am-m↓ calc↓ kali-c↓ sep stram↓
    - **cramping**: stram
    - **pressing** pain: kali-c
    - **stitching** pain: alum gsy1 am-c am-m h2 calc k*
  - **amel.**: mag-c↓
    - **stitching** pain: mag-c h2
- **stretching** out: kali-c↓
  - **stitching** pain: kali-c k*
- **supper** agg.; after: *Ran-b*↓ sulph k*
  - **stitching** pain: *Ran-b* k*
- **synchronous** with pulse: ant-c↓
  - **cramping**: ant-c h2
- **tearing** pain: alum k* am-m b4a.de ars b4a.de aur k* bry k* calc k* crot-t k* cupr b4a.de kali-c k* *Lach* k* lyc k* mag-c k* nat-c b4a.de nat-m b4a.de nit-ac b4a.de plat b4a.de plb k* *Sep* b4a.de
  - **jerking** pain: calc h2

Abdomen

- **touch**:
  - **agg.**: ars↓ nat-c↓ sil$_{h2}$
    - **cutting** pain: ars$_{h2}$
    - **pressing** pain: nat-c$_{h2}$
  - **amel.**: meny↓
    - **stitching** pain: meny$_{h1}$
- **turning** | **bed**; in:
  - **amel.**: bell↓
    - **cutting** pain: bell$_{h1}$
    - **pressing** pain: bell$_{h1}$
  - **body**:
    - **agg.**: bar-c↓ calc↓
      - **stitching** pain: bar-c$_{k*}$ calc$_{k*}$
- **ulcer** would form; as if an: alum$_{h2*}$
- **ulcerative** pain: petr$_{h2}$ valer$_{bg2}$
- **walking**:
  - **agg.**: *Asaf*↓ bell↓ calc castm↓ cham↓ chin↓ chol↓ cinnb↓ clem↓ con dros↓ eupi$_{k*}$ ferr-i↓ kali-n↓ led↓ mag-c meny↓ mez↓ nat-c$_{k*}$ nat-m↓ *Nat-s*↓ phos↓ ran-b↓ sep↓ sil↓ spig↓ squil$_{k*}$ sulph zinc↓
    - **burning**: chol$_{br1}$ sep$_{k*}$
    - **cramping**: bell$_{h1}$ nat-m$_{h2}$
    - **cutting** pain: clem$_{h2}$ phos$_{h2}$
    - **drawing** pain: chin$_{k*}$ zinc$_{h2}$
    - **pressing** pain: castm kali-n led$_{h1}$ nat-c$_{h2}$ zinc$_{h2}$
    - **stitching** pain: *Asaf* cham cinnb dros$_{h1}$ ferr-i meny$_{h1}$ mez$_{h2}$ *Nat-s* ran-b sil spig sulph$_{h2}$
    - **tearing** pain: mag-c$_{k*}$
  - **air** agg.; in open: *Nat-s*↓ sulph↓ thuj↓
    - **stitching** pain: *Nat-s* sulph thuj
  - **amel.**: carb-an↓ sars↓
    - **cutting** pain: carb-an
    - **stitching** pain: sars$_{k*}$
- **wine** agg.: borx↓
  - **stitching** pain: borx
- **yawning** agg.: bar-c↓ sphing$_{k*}$
  - **stitching** pain: bar-c$_{k*}$

○ • **Behind**: nat-s$_{bg2}$

- **Flanks**: acon↓ alum↓ ambr↓ ang↓ *Arg-met*↓ ars↓ bar-c↓ bell↓ calc↓ caps↓ carb-v↓ carbn-s↓ card-m↓ caust↓ cham↓ chin↓ coc-c↓ cocc↓ coff↓ colch↓ **Coloc**↓ croc↓ crot-t↓ dulc↓ kali-c↓ mag-c↓ mag-m↓ mez↓ mur-ac↓ nat-c↓ *Nat-s*↓ ph-ac↓ plat↓ puls↓ rhus-t↓ sabad↓ sabin↓ samb↓ sars↓ seneg↓ *Sil*↓ spong↓ squil↓ stann↓ staph↓ stram↓ sulph↓
  - **right**: alum↓
    - **stitching** pain: alum$_{h2}$
  - **burning**: mag-c$_{h2}$ plat seneg stann
  - **cramping**: ambr ang$_{h1}$ bell carb-v carbn-s cocc coff dulc$_{h2}$ mag-c mur-ac ph-ac sars stann
  - **cutting** pain: ang$_{h1}$ sulph
  - **drawing** pain: alum ambr ang$_{h1}$ calc carb-v card-m caust chin cocc coff colch crot-t kali-c plat puls sabad sabin samb sars seneg stann staph sulph
  - **flatus** and during stool; from: spong↓
    - **pressing** pain: spong$_{h1}$
  - **hiccough**; during: borx↓
    - **stitching** pain: borx$_{h2}$
  - **jerking** pain: chin$_{h1}$
  - **pressing** pain: ambr coff colch sabad sars squil$_{h1}$
  - **sneezing**; on: carb-v↓
    - **burning**: carb-v
  - **sore**: ang$_{h1}$ calc caust *Sil* staph$_{h1}$
  - **stitching** pain: acon ambr *Arg-met* ars$_{h2}$ bar-c caps carb-v carbn-s caust$_{h2}$ cham chin coc-c cocc **Coloc** croc mag-m$_{h2}$ mez$_{h2}$ nat-c *Nat-s* rhus-t$_{a1}$ sabad spong$_{h1}$ squil stann stram sulph
  - **stool** agg.; after: mag-m↓
    - **drawing** pain: mag-m$_{h2}$
  - **tearing** pain: crot-t samb

- **Sides – Flanks**: ...
  - **extending** to:
    - **Mamma**; left: alum↓
      - **stitching** pain: alum$_{h2}$
- **Ribs**:
  - **Below**: nept-m$_{lsd2.fr}$
  - **Floating** ribs:
    - **Below**: mang↓ *Sil*↓
      - **sore**: mang$_{h2}$ *Sil*
- **Side** lain on: bell↓
  - **cutting** pain: bell$_{h1}$
  - **pressing** pain: bell$_{h1*}$
- **Side** not lain on: *Graph*
- **Spots**; in: graph↓ hyos↓ ox-ac↓ plat↓
  - **burning**: graph$_{k*}$ hyos$_{k*}$ ox-ac plat$_{k*}$

▽ • **extending** to:

  - **Bladder**: plb
    - **tearing** pain: plb
  - **Chest**: alum↓
    - **stitching** pain: alum$_{gsy1}$
  - **Downward**: med
  - **Groin**: naja↓
    - **stitching** pain: naja
  - **Lumbar** region: calc↓
    - **stitching** pain: calc
  - **Sacrum**: caust↓
    - **stitching** pain: caust
  - **Spermatic** cords: lac-ac↓
    - **stitching** pain: lac-ac
  - **Thighs**: alum$_{h2}$
  - **Umbilicus**: aloe↓
    - **lying** on right side agg.: plat↓
      - **stitching** pain: plat$_{h2}$
    - **pressing** pain: aloe$_{k*}$

- **Sigmoid** flexure: scroph-xyz$_{c2}$
- **Skin**; below the: cocc↓ *Kreos*↓ *Ran-b*↓ rhus-t↓ sec↓ valer↓
  - **ulcerative** pain: cocc$_{b7a.de}$ *Kreos*$_{b7a.de}$ *Ran-b*$_{b7.de}$ rhus-t$_{b7a.de}$ sec$_{b7.de}$ valer$_{b7.de}$
- **Solar** plexus: *Caust*$_{b4a.de}$ chir-fl↓ fum$_{rly1•}$
  - **blow**; pain as from a: chir-fl$_{gya2}$
- **Spleen**: absin$_{vh1}$ acon↓ aesc$_{k*}$ *Agar*$_{k*}$ agn$_{bro1}$ aloe↓ alst↓ alum↓ am-c↓ am-m$_{k*}$ ambr$_{k*}$ anac anan ant-c$_{bg2}$ ant-t$_{b7.de}$ *Apis*$_{b7a.de}$ arg-n↓ arn$_{k*}$ ars$_{k*}$ ars-i ars-met$_{bro1}$ ars-s-f$_{k2}$ arund↓ *Asaf*↓ asar astac↓ aur↓ bapt bapt-c$_{c2}$ bar-c↓ bell↓ bell-p$_{tl1*}$ berb bism↓ borx bov↓ brom$_{k*}$ bry↓ bufo↓ cadm-met$_{tpw6*}$ cadm-s↓ cain$_{c2}$ calad↓ calc↓ calc-p↓ camph↓ cann-s$_{b7.de*}$ canth↓ *Caps*$_{hr1*}$ carb-an↓ *Carb-v*$_{k*}$ *Card-m*↓ caust↓ **Cean**$_{k*}$ cedr↓ *Chel*$_{k*}$ chen-v$_{c2}$ **Chin**$_{k*}$ *Chinin-s*$_{k*}$ cimic$_{bro1}$ clem↓ cob$_{k*}$ *Coc-c* *Cocc* colch$_{k*}$ coloc↓ con cot$_{c1}$ crot-h↓ crot-t↓ cupr dig↓ dios$_{c2*}$ diosm↓ dor$_{c2}$ dulc↓ euphr↓ ferr$_{k*}$ ferr-i$_{k*}$ ferr-m↓ *Fl-ac*$_{k*}$ form$_{k*}$ gels↓ graph↓ grin$_{bg2*}$ guaj↓ gymno$_{c2}$ *Helia*$_{bro1}$ helon$_{k*}$ hep↓ hera$_{c2}$ hom-xyz$_{c2}$ *Hydr* *Ign*$_{k*}$ ilx-a$_{c2*}$ iod$_{k*}$ ip↓ jug-r$_{c2}$ kali-bi kali-c$_{b4a.de}$ *Kali-i*$_{bro1}$ kali-n$_{b4.de*}$ kali-p kreos$_{k*}$ *Lach*$_{k*}$ laur$_{b7.de*}$ lec↓ led↓ lith-c↓ *Lob-c*$_{bro1}$ lyc↓ *Lyss* mag-c$_{c2}$ mag-m↓ *Mag-s*↓ mang↓ med$_{k2*}$ merc↓ *Merc-c*↓ merc-i-r$_{k*}$ *Merl*$_{k*}$ *Mez*$_{k*}$ mosch↓ mur-ac↓ nat-ar↓ nat-c$_{b4.de*}$ *Nat-m*$_{k*}$ nat-s nit-ac *Nux-m*↓ *Nux-v*↓ ol-an↓ olnd↓ opun-s$_{a1}$ pall$_{k*}$ paraf$_{c2}$ parth$_{bro1}$ petr ph-ac↓ phos$_{k*}$ phyt$_{k*}$ plan$_{c2}$ plat↓ plb$_{k*}$ podo$_{fd3.de•}$ polyg-h↓ *Polym*$_{bro1}$ prim-o$_{c2*}$ *Psor*↓ ptel$_{bro1}$ *Puls*$_{b7a.de}$ quas$_{bro1}$ querc$_{bro1}$ ran-b$_{c1*}$ *Ran-s*↓ raph$_{br1}$ rheum↓ rhod$_{k*}$ rhus-t$_{bro1}$ ruta$_{b7.de*}$ sabad↓ sang$_{k*}$ sapin$_{c2}$ sars↓ *Sec*↓ sel↓ seneg↓ sep$_{k*}$ sil↓ spig↓ squil$_{bro1*}$ *Stann* *Stram* *Sul-ac*$_{k*}$ sul-i$_{k2}$ *Sulph*$_{k*}$ symph↓ *Tab*$_{sne}$ tarax↓ tarent$_{k2}$ teucr↓ *Ther*↓ *Thuj*↓ tub$_{c1}$ urt-u$_{bro1}$ vac↓ valer↓ verat↓ verb↓ vib↓ viol-t↓ visc$_{c2}$ *Zinc* zing$_{c2}$
  - **morning**: am-m psor↓ sang
    - **stitching** pain: psor
  - **afternoon** | **14** h: cedr sep
  - **evening**: agar arg-n↓ colch↓ crot-t↓ mag-s *Sulph*↓
    - **stitching** pain: arg-n$_{k*}$ colch$_{k*}$ crot-t$_{k*}$ *Sulph*
  - **night**: agar$_{k*}$ squil$_{vl1.nl}$

- **accompanied** by:
  - **diarrhea**: cean ptk1
  - **dyspnea**: cean ptk1
  - **menses**:
    - **profuse**: cean ptk1
    - **suppressed**: cean ptk1
  - **Head**; complaints in (See HEAD - Complaints - accompanied - spleen)
- **alternating** with | **Heart**; pain in (See CHEST - Pain - heart - alternating - spleen)
- **blow**; pain as from a: dulc b4.de* gels bg2 kali-n b4.de* nat-m b4.de* plat b4.de*
- **boring** pain: kali-bi bg2
- **breathing**:
  - **agg.**: agar am-m
  - **deep**:
    - **agg.**: bry↓ *Card-m*↓ chin↓ cob↓ mosch↓ nat-c↓ *Ran-s*↓ sabad↓ *Sulph*↓
      - **stitching** pain: bry *Card-m* chin cob mosch nat-c *Ran-s* sabad *Sulph*
- **burning**: anan apis b7a.de *Ars* b4a.de bell k* borx b4a.de cann-s b7.de carb-an chel b7.de *Coc-c* graph b4.de ign k* plat b4.de sec k* seneg b4.de spig b7.de symph fd3.de•
- **burrowing**: asaf b7.de*
- **chill**; during: acon bg2 ars bg2 asaf bg2 borx bg2 *Bry* k* caps k* carb-v bg2 cham bg2 chin bg2 **Chinin-s** k* eup-per kali-c bg2 nat-m bg2 nux-v k* **Podo** k* ran-b bg2 rhus-t k* *Sep* k* sul-ac bg2 sulph k* thuj bg2
  - **stitching** pain: *Bry* b7a.de *Rhus-t* b7a.de
- **clawing** pain: med c1*
- **cough** agg.; during: bell↓ carb-v↓ *Chinin-s* con↓ *Puls*↓ sul-ac sulph↓ valer↓ zinc↓
  - **pressing** pain: *Puls* b7a.de valer b7a.de
  - **stitching** pain: bell k* carb-v k* con sulph k* zinc
- **cramping**: agar bg2 aloe bg2 bell bg2 ferr bg2* stann bg2 sulph bg2
- **cutting** pain: ars bg2 bell b4.de* borx bg2 cadm-s bg2 cain calc-p k2 carb-v bg2 *Cean* chin k* coloc bg2 crot-h dulc b4.de* grin bg2 kali-c b4a.de* lyc bg2 nat-m bg2 polyg-h bg2 ptel sulph b4a.de* tarent verb k* viol-t b7.de*
- **drawing** pain: camph b7.de* cupr b7a.de* *Kali-c* b4a.de plat b4.de* rhus-t b7.de* sulph b4a.de* teucr b7.de*
- **drinking** cold water agg.: nat-c↓
  - **stitching** pain: nat-c c1
- **eating**:
  - **after**:
    - **agg.**: verat↓
      - **stitching** pain: verat h1
  - **agg.**: thuj↓
    - **stitching** pain: thuj
  - **amel.**: rhod
  - **while**:
    - **agg.**: am-m↓
      - **stitching** pain: am-m ptk1
- **eructations**; before: sulph↓
  - **pressing** pain: sulph h2
- **exertion** agg.: kali-bi ran-b
- **flatulence**; with sensation of: *Diosm*↓
  - **stinging**: *Diosm* br1
- **gnawing** pain: kreos bg2
- **heat**; during: agn bg2 arn bg2 ars k* asaf bg2 borx k* brom bg2 caps bg2 **Carb-v** k* cham bg2 chin bg2 fl-ac bg2 ign bg2 mez bg2 *Nat-m* k* nit-ac bg2 *Nux-v* k* ran-b bg2 stann bg2 sulph bg2
- **inspiration** agg.: cob mez
- **lancinating**: anan bufo cain nat-m
- **lying**:
  - **agg.**: *Sulph*↓
    - **stitching** pain: *Sulph*
- **lying**: ...
  - **side**; on:
    - **left**:
      - **agg.**: agar cean k* *Cocc* colch
        - **pressing** pain: agar k*
      - **amel.**: phyt squil
- **menses** | **before**:
  - **agg.**: sulph↓
    - **cramping**: sulph b4a.de
  - **during**:
    - **agg.**: apis bufo↓ pall
      - **stitching** pain: bufo
- **motion** agg.: bry↓ *Kali-bi* kali-p nit-ac↓
  - **stitching** pain: bry tl1 kali-bi kali-p nit-ac k*
- **perspiration**; during: arn bg2 asaf bg2 bry bg2 **Carb-v** bg2 chin bg2 ferr bg2 *Ign* bg2 **Nat-m** bg2 rhus-t bg2 sel bg2 sul-ac bg2 thuj bg2
- **pressing** pain: agar k* alum b4.de* am-m b7.de* *Arn* b7.de* *Ars* asaf b7.de* astac vh bell b4.de* berb bg2 borx k* calad b7.de* camph b7.de* cann-s b7.de* carb-an b4a.de *Carb-v* k* chin k* chinin-s colch b7.de* con b4.de* crot-t k* dig bg2 *Fl-ac* graph k* *Ign* k* iod bg2 *Kreos* k* lyc b4.de* lyss *Merl* k* mez b4a.de mur-ac b4.de* nat-c h2* *Nat-m* k* *Nit-ac* k* ol-an k* olnd b7.de* petr b4.de* plat b4.de* polyg-h puls bg2 *Ran-s* b7a.de rheum h* rhod b4.de* rhus-t b7.de* sars b4.de* sep b4.de* stann k* sul-ac b4.de* sulph k* tarax b7.de* teucr b7.de* *Thuj* b4a.de valer b7.de* zinc b4.de*
  - **accompanied** by:
    - **Head**; pain in (See HEAD - Pain - accompanied - spleen)
    - **Liver**; pressing pain in: quas br1
- **pressure**:
  - **agg.**: cean↓ kali-bi↓ zinc↓
    - **pressing** pain: cean tl1 zinc h2
    - **stitching** pain: kali-bi zinc h2
  - **clothes**; of:
    - **agg.**: calad fl-ac kali-bi nat-m puls
    - **amel.**: chinin-s bg1 ruta bg1
- **pricking** pain: arund c1 vac jl2
- **pulsating** pain: *Lyss*
- **respiration**; difficult: squil vl1.nl
- **riding** in a carriage agg.: borx lach k*
- **running** agg.: agar↓ squil vl1.nl tub↓
  - **stitching** pain: agar ptk1 squil vl1.nl tub ptk1
- **sitting** agg.: am-m↓ psor↓
  - **stitching** pain: am-m k* psor al2
- **smarting**: *Asaf* b7a.de
- **sneezing** agg.: hera↓
  - **stitching** pain: hera c1
- **sore**: *Agn* k* alum b4.de* arn *Ars* ars-i k2 asaf b7a.de asar k* bry bg2 calc camph b7.de* *Caps* **Cean** mrr1 **Chin** k* colch b7.de* *Ferr* ferr-m kali-i kreos lec *Phos* k* *Ptel* ran-b b7.de* **Rhus-t** k* sang a1 sars k* stann k* zinc b4.de*
- **squeezed**; as if: colch b7.de* merc b4.de* mosch b7.de* mur-ac b4.de* ph-ac b4.de* stann b4.de* zinc b4.de*
- **standing** agg.: mag-c↓
  - **stitching** pain: mag-c h2
- **stinging**: diosm br1 ther br1
- **stitching** pain: acon k* agar k* aloe alst bro1 alum k* am-c b4.de* am-m k* anac k* arg-n k* arn k* **Ars** k* asaf b7.de* asar b7.de* aur b4.de* bar-c b4.de* bell k* *Bell-p* bro1 berb k* bism b7.de* bov b4.de* bry k* cain calad k* camph cann-s b7.de* canth b7.de* carb-an k* *Carb-v* k* *Card-m* k* caust b4.de* **Cean** k* cedr k* chel k* *Chin* k* clem k* cob *Coc-c* k* *Cocc* k* *Con* k* crot-t bg2 dulc b4.de* euphr k* graph b4.de* grin bg2* guaj b4.de* hep k* ign b7.de* iod b4.de* ip b7.de* *Kali-bi* k* kali-c bg2 kali-n k* kali-p *Lach* k* laur b7.de* lec led k* lith-c lyc k* mag-c b4.de* mag-m b4.de* *Mag-s* mang b4.de* *Merc-c* b4a.de mez b4.de* mosch b7.de* mur-ac b4.de* nat-ar *Nat-c* k* *Nat-m* k* nat-s k* nit-ac k* *Nux-m* k* *Nux-v* b7a.de ol-an k* ph-ac k* phos k* plb b7.de* *Psor* k* puls k* ran-b b7.de* ran-s k* raph br1 rheum b7.de* rhod k* ruta sabad b7.de* sang k* sars k* *Sec* b7a.de sel k* sep k* sil k* spig k* squil k* stann k* *Sul-ac* k* *Sulph* k* tab tarax bg2* *Ther* bro1 thuj bg2 tub c1 valer b7.de* verat k* verb k* vib bg1 viol-t b7.de* *Zinc* k*

Abdomen

- **stitching** pain: ...
  - **accompanied** by:
    - **Head**; pain in: urt-u ptk1
    - **Liver**; stitching pain in: quas br1
- **stool** agg.; during: agar bg2 anac bg2 kali-bi
  - **stitching** pain: anac b4.de
- **stooping** agg.: card-m ↓
  - **stitching** pain: card-m
- **tearing** pain: ambr k* ars b4.de* cann-s b7.de* chin b7.de* con nat-m bg2 plb b7.de* sil b4.de* sul-ac b4.de* *Sulph* b4a.de teucr b7.de*
- **touch** agg.: ran-b c1 sul-ac k2
- **turning** to right side amel.: agar
- **twitching**: ran-b b7.de* sul-ac b4.de*
- **ulcerative** pain: apis bg2 *Asar* bg2 cupr bg2 nat-c bg2 *Puls* b7a.de ran-b bg2 ruta b7.de* zinc bg2
- **walking**:
  - **agg.**: acon ↓ *Arn* chin ↓ hep ign lach *Nat-c* ↓ nat-m ↓ psor ↓ rhod sel verat ↓
    - **stitching** pain: acon arn chin hep k* *Lach* *Nat-c* k* nat-m psor k* rhod sel verat k*
  - **amel.**: agar k*
  - **rapidly**:
    - **agg.**: rhod ↓
      - **stitching** pain: rhod ptk1
  - **slowly**:
    - **agg.**: chin ↓
      - **stitching** pain: chin c1

○ • **Region** of spleen: alum ↓ arg-met ↓ arn ↓ bar-c ↓ chin ↓ laur ↓ mag-c ↓ mur-ac ↓ plat ↓ psor ↓ sars ↓ sul-ac ↓ thuj ↓ vac ↓
  - **paralyzed**; as if: mag-c b4.de*
  - **pinching** pain: alum b4.de* arg-met b7.de* arn bg2 bar-c bg2 chin b7.de* laur b7.de* mur-ac b4.de* plat b4.de* sars b4.de* sul-ac b4.de* thuj b4.de*
  - **pricking** pain: psor jl2 vac jl2

▽ • **extending** to:
  - **Hips**: grin ↓
    - **cutting** pain: grin pd
    - **sore**: grin pd
  - **Lumbar** region: kali-bi ↓
    - **stitching** pain: kali-bi ptk1

- **Spots**; in: ant-t ↓ arg-n ↓ bar-c ↓ bism ↓ bry ↓ coloc ↓ *Kali-bi* ↓ *Ox-ac* ↓ phos ↓ *Rhus-t* ↓ thuj ↓
  - **constipation**; with: *Aur-m-n* ↓
    - **sore**: *Aur-m-n* vh
  - **cramping**: bry bro1 coloc bro1 *Ox-ac* bro1 thuj bg2
  - **sore**: ant-t bg1 arg-n ptk1 bar-c ptk1 bism ptk1 *Kali-bi* ptk1 phos ptk1 *Rhus-t* ptk1
- **Spots**; in small: bism mrr1 irid-met srj5• jug-c vml3• kola stb3• rhus-t bg2 teucr bg2
  - **burning**: kola stb3•
- **Symphysis**: hell ↓ kali-c ↓ stann ↓ symph ↓
  - **cramping**: kali-c h2 symph fd3.de•
  - **eating**; after: lac-e ↓
    - **cramping**: lac-e hrn2•
  - **pressing** pain: hell h1
  - **stitching** pain: stann h2
- **Transversely** | **Hypochondria**: card-m bg2 merc-i-r bg2 sep bg2
- **Umbilicus**: acon ↓ *Aesc* k* aeth ↓ agar k* *All-c* *Aloe* alum ↓ ammc ↓ amph ↓ *Anac* ↓ ant-t ↓ *Apis* k* *Arn* b7a.de *Ars* ars-i arund k* asaf k* bapt k* bar-c bar-i bar-ox-suc rly4• *Bell* ↓ *Benz-ac* ↓ berb ↓ bol-la bov b4.de bry cact ↓ cadm-met tpw6 cain calad ↓ calc *Calc-p* calen ↓ canth b7.de carb-v ↓ carbn-s cassia-s ↓ castm ↓ caul k* *Cham* b7.de **Chel** k* *Chin* k* *Chinin-s* ↓ chion br1 chord-umb ↓ cic ↓ cimic *Cina* k* cinnb ↓ clem ↓ coc-c k* cocc ↓ colch ↓ *Coloc* k* con crot-t k* *Cycl* ↓ *Dig* ↓ *Dios* k* dulc k* echi elaps ↓ eupi ↓ fago ↓ ferr-i k* fl-ac form ↓ fum rly4• *Gamb* ↓ gels gent-c ↓ *Gran* ↓ grat ↓ gymno ↓ ham ↓ hyos ↓ hyper ↓ ign indg iod *Ip* k* iris ↓ kali-bi kali-c b4a.de kali-i ↓

- **Umbilicus**: ...
  kali-n k* kalm k* kola ↓ kreos k* lac-d k2 lac-h sk4• lach ↓ laur lec *Lept* lyc mag-c k* mag-m ↓ mag-s ↓ mang k* merc b4a.de merc-c k* merc-i-f ↓ merl k* mez ↓ mosch b7.de mur-ac nat-c b4.de nat-m nat-pyru ↓ nat-s tl1 nept-m ↓ nit-ac nux-m k* *Nux-v* ↓ oci-sa ↓ *Ox-ac* k* pall ↓ paraf c2 petr-ra shn4• ph-ac k* phos k* phys ↓ phyt pic-ac ↓ plan ↓ *Plat* plb k* *Ptel* k* puls ↓ puls-n ↓ ran-b b7.de raph ↓ rat ↓ *Rheum* ↓ *Rhus-t* ↓ rhus-v k* ruta fd4.de sabad ↓ senec sep k* sil *Spig* ↓ squil stann stram *Stront-c* b4.de* suis-em ↓ sul-ac sul-i ↓ sulph ↓ sumb symph fd3.de• tab ↓ tarax ↓ tax ↓ ter thiam ↓ thuj ↓ tub c1 ust k* valer b7.de verat b7.de* verat-v ↓ verb vip ↓ zinc ↓
  - **left** side of: jac-c ↓
    - **stitching** pain: jac-c
  - **morning**: agar aloe *Apis* con ↓ *Dios* k* mang ↓ nat-c nat-m symph fd3.de• verat-v k*
    - **drawing** pain: con h2 mang h2 nat-c k*
    - **stitching** pain: agar
  - **forenoon**: dulc fd4.de gymno *Rhus-t* ↓ sil ↓
    - **cutting** pain: *Rhus-t* k* sil k*
  - **afternoon**: alum ↓ chel k* cimic ↓ plb ruta fd4.de sil
    - **14** h: laur ↓
      - **tearing** pain: laur
    - **cutting** pain: cimic k*
    - **stitching** pain: alum
  - **evening**: dulc fd4.de nux-m ptel k* ruta fd4.de
    - **cutting** pain: nux-m k*
  - **night**: nux-m ↓
    - **cutting** pain: nux-m k*
  - **alternating** with | **Bladder**; pain in (See BLADDER - Pain - night - alternating - umbilicus)
  - **bending**:
    - **body**:
      - **agg.**: nit-ac ↓ tax ↓
        - **drawing** pain: nit-ac h2 [tax jsj7]
      - **backward** agg.: oci-sa ↓
        - **drawing** pain: oci-sa sk4•
    - **forward**:
      - **amel.**: bov ↓ calad ↓ *Rhus-t* ↓
        - **cutting** pain: bov calad *Rhus-t*
  - **bending** double | **amel.**: aloe **Coloc** echi
  - **boring** pain: sep h2 tarax h1
  - **breakfast** agg.; after: gels k* raph k*
  - **breathing** deep agg.: mang ↓
    - **cutting** pain: mang ptk1
  - **burning**: acon b7.de* aesc ars bro1 bov ptk1 *Canth* b7a.de carb-v k* cassia-s ccrh1• chord-umb rly4• kali-c b4a.de kali-i k* kola stb3• lach k* lyc ptk1 merc-c b4a.de nux-m k* nux-v b7a.de ph-ac b4a.de phyt ptk1 plat b4a.de plb b7.de* sabad b7a.de sep ptk1 sul-ac b4a.de sul-i k2
  - **child** refers to the navel as the most painful part: dulc fd4.de
  - **contracting**: nit-ac h2
  - **cough** agg.; during: ip k* *Lyc* k* sep
  - **cramping**: *Aloe* bro1 *Benz-ac* bro1 berb bro1 *Bov* bro1 *Bry* bro1 calc-p bro1 carb-v bro1 *Cham* bro1 chel bro1 *Cina* bro1 clem a1 *Coloc* bro1 *Dios* bro1 *Dulc* bro1 *Gamb* bro1 *Gran* bro1 hyper bro1 indg bro1 *Ip* bro1 *Kali-bi* bro1 lept bro1 lyc bro1 mag-m a1 *Nux-m* bro1 nux-v bro1 plat bro1 *Plb* bro1 puls bro1 raph bro1 *Rheum* bro1 senec bro1 *Spig* bro1 *Stann* bro1 sulph bro1 *Verat* bro1 verb bro1 vip bro1
  - **cutting** pain: ant-t bol-la bov cact k* calad castm *Chinin-s* cimic k* coc-c k* colch ptk1 *Coloc* ptk1 crot-t k* dios k* dulc ptk1 indg k* *Ip* k* laur *Nux-m* k* *Nux-v* ptk1 plb k* puls-n rhus-t k* rhus-v k* sil k* ter k* **Verat** hr1 verat-v bg1*
  - **diarrhea**:
    - **before**: rhus-v verat hr1
    - **during**: calc-p rhus-v tub c1
  - **dinner**; during: calc

- **drawing** pain: acon aloe anac h2 ars h2* bar-c bell calc-p k* calen bg1 carbn-s *Chel* k* clem k* con k* eupi gamb gent-c grat ign kali-c mang h2 mez k* mosch nat-c k* nit-ac k* nux-m nux-v oci-sa sk4• phos plat tl1* *Plb* k* ran-b bg1 rat k* rhus-t h1 ruta sep k* sulph k* tab zinc k*
  - **paroxysmal**: sep h2 [tax jsj7]
- **eating**; after: calc-p k* cina cob con ↓
  - **drawing** pain: con h2
  - **two hours after eating**: ox-ac
- **fasting** agg.: indg
- **flatus**; passing | **amel.**: cadm-met tpw6 calc-p caul coloc
- **headache**; during: *Lac-d* c1* lept ptk1
- **inspiration** agg.; deep: bapt *Hyos* ↓ indg lyc sil ↓ verb ↓
  - **stitching** pain: *Hyos* sil verb
- **lancinating**: amph a1 elaps nat-pyru rly4• nept-m lsd2.fr plb k* thiam rly4•
- **lying** on back agg.: *Ars* cadm-met tpw6
- **menses** | **before** | **agg.**: chinin-s ip ruta
  - **during**:
    - **agg.**: nux-m
      - **drawing** pain: nux-m
- **motion** agg.: cycl ↓ mag-s ↓ nit-ac ↓ phyt ptel
  - **drawing** pain: nit-ac h2
  - **stitching** pain: cycl h1 mag-s k*
- **paroxysmal**: bell calad ph-ac verb zinc
- **pregnancy** agg.; during: plb k*
- **pressure** | **amel.**: cina coloc k2 dios *Ptel* k*
- **radiating** from: *Dios Plb* senec
- **rising** agg.; after: coloc k* con ↓
  - **drawing** pain: con h2
- **sitting** agg.: *All-c* indg kali-c ↓
  - **drawing** pain: kali-c
- **sleep**:
  - **amel.**: nux-m ↓
    - **burning**: nux-m k*
- **sneezing** agg.: aloe ↓
  - **stitching** pain: aloe
- **sore**: aesc k* aeth *Aloe* anac k* calc k* *Calc-p* chin cina cinnb *Coloc* tl1 con crot-t k* dulc fago k* form iris tl1 kali-c k* nat-m k* nux-m ptk1 ph-ac tl1 phys k* plan *Rhus-t* k* stront-c suis-em rly4• thuj k* verat
- **standing** agg.: alum ↓
  - **stitching** pain: alum
- **stitching** pain: acon **Agar** k* aloe alum ammc k* *Anac* k* ant-t k* asaf k* *Bell* k* cic k* cocc colch coloc *Cycl Dig* k* dulc grat k* gymno ham fd3.de• hyos **Ip** kreos k* laur k* mag-s k* merc-i-f k* nux-v pall pic-ac *Plat* k* **Plb** raph rhus-t ruta fd4.de sep k* sil k* sulph verb
  - **radiating**: *Plb*
- **stool**:
  - **after**:
    - **agg.**: nat-c bg2 puls-n samb bg2
    - **amel.**: oci-sa ↓ senec vml3•
      - **drawing** pain: oci-sa sk4•
  - **before**: aloe bry *Ham* mag-m nat-c plb ust k*
    - **drawing** pain: nat-c k*
  - **during** | **agg.**: bell bg2 caps bg2 cupr bg2 iod bg2 kali-bi k* ox-ac k*
- **stooping** agg.: sep *Verb*
  - **stitching** pain: verb
- **supper** agg.; after: zinc
- **synchronous** with pulse: rhus-t ↓
  - **stitching** pain: rhus-t h1
- **tearing** pain: amph a1 chin k* crot-t cycl laur k* nux-v plb k* stram
- **torn** out or loose; as if: ip h1 stram h1
- **waking**; on: agar ↓
  - **stitching** pain: agar
- **walking**:
  - **agg.**: anac ↓ bry sulph ↓
    - **drawing** pain: anac h2
    - **stitching** pain: sulph h2
  - **amel.**: *All-c* kali-c ↓
    - **drawing** pain: kali-c
  - **rapidly**:
    - **agg.**: chin ↓
      - **stitching** pain: chin h1

○ • **Above**: aur ↓ bell ↓ chel ↓ chord-umb ↓ dig ↓ grat ↓ kali-c ↓ kali-n ↓ mang ↓ nat-m ↓ rhus-t ↓
  - **burning**: chord-umb rly4• kali-n h2
  - **pressing** pain: kali-c h2 mang a1
  - **pressure**:
    - **amel.**: *Cina* ↓
      - **boring** pain: *Cina* hr1
  - **stitching** pain: aur k* bell k* chel k* dig k* grat k* kali-c k* nat-m h2 rhus-t h1
- **Below**: bar-c ↓ calc ↓ chel ↓ chin ↓ coloc ↓ cortico ↓ hyos ↓ kali-bi ↓ kali-c ↓ kali-n ↓ mag-c ↓ mag-m ↓ mez ↓ nat-c ↓ nat-m ↓ olnd ↓ phos ↓ plb ↓ ruta ↓ stroph-s ↓ symph ↓ zinc ↓
  - **morning**: calc ↓
    - **pressing** pain: calc h2
  - **constricting** pain: stroph-s sp1
  - **cramping**: cortico tpw7 kali-c h2 kali-n h2 mag-c h2 mag-m h2 nat-c h2 nat-m h2 phos h2 zinc h2
  - **cutting** pain: mez h2
  - **pressing** pain: symph fd3.de•
  - **stitching** pain: bar-c k* calc h2 chel k* chin coloc hyos h1 kali-bi k* mag-c h2 olnd k* plb k* ruta h1
  - **stool**:
    - **after**:
      - **agg.**: nat-c ↓
        - **cutting** pain: nat-c h2
      - **amel.**: cortico ↓
        - **cramping**: cortico tpw7
    - **before**: cortico ↓
      - **cramping**: cortico tpw7
  - **supper** agg.; after: calc ↓
    - **cramping**: calc h2
  - **extending** to:
    - **Pudendum**: ruta ↓
      - **stitching** pain: ruta h1
- **Region** of | **touch** agg.: kali-br a1 kali-c h2 lyc h2 sep h2 sil h2 til c1
- **Region** of umbilicus: acon mrr1 *Aesc* k* aeth ↓ agar k* *All-c* k* all-s ↓ *Aloe* k* alum ↓ am-c ↓ *Am-m* ambr ↓ aml-ns ↓ ammc ↓ **Anac** ↓ androc ↓ ang ↓ ant-c ant-t apis k* arg-n k* arn ars k* asaf bg2 aspar ↓ astac ↓ atis ↓ atra-r bnm3• bamb-a ↓ bapt k* bar-c *Bell* k* benz-ac ↓ berb bism hr1 bov k* brom ↓ *Bry* k* cact ↓ cadm-met sp1* calad ↓ calc *Calc-p* k* calen ↓ *Camph* ↓ canth bg2 caps ↓ *Carb-an* carb-v k* carbn-s k2 carc ↓ cassia-s ↓ castm ↓ caul bg2 caust bg2 cench k2 *Cham* k* *Chel Chin* k* chinin-ar chinin-s ↓ chion ↓ cimic ↓ cina k* cinnb ↓ cit-ac ↓ clem coc-c *Cocc* ↓ *Colch* coll bg2 **Coloc** k* con ↓ crot-h k* *Crot-t* cub ↓ cupr cycl ↓ dig k* **Dios** k* dirc ↓ dor ↓ dulc erig eucal bg2 euon ↓ euphr ↓ eupi ↓ fl-ac k* form ↓ *Gamb* gels k* gent-c ↓ gent-l ↓ gran br1 graph grat ↓ guaj ↓ gymno *Ham* ↓ hell k* hep bg2 hir skp7• hydr k* hyos ↓ hyper ↓ ign ↓ indg k* *Iod Ip* k* *Iris* k* jatr-c jug-c k* kali-bi k* kali-br ↓ *Kali-c* ↓ kali-i kali-m ↓ kali-n bg2 kali-p ↓ kali-sula a1* kola ↓ kreos k* lac-ac k* lac-c ↓ *Lach* ↓ lact ↓ *Laur* lec ↓ led ↓ *Lept* k* lyc k* mag-c k* mag-m ↓ mag-p ↓ mag-s ↓ malar jl2 mang k* meny ↓ merc merc-c k* merc-i-f k* merc-i-r ↓ merl ↓ mez k* mosch bg2 mur-ac k* myric ↓ naja ↓ nat-ar *Nat-c* k* *Nat-m* **Nat-s** k* nicc ↓ nicotam ↓ nit-ac nux-m k* *Nux-v* k* oci-sa ↓ ol-an ↓ olnd ↓ onos op k* ox-ac k* ozone sde2• paeon ↓ par ↓ paraf ↓ pert-vc vk9 petr *Ph-ac* phel phos k* phys k* *Phyt* k* plan ↓ *Plat* **Plb** k* *Podo* ↓ pot-e ↓ prun ↓ psil ↓ psor ↓ *Ptel* k* *Puls* ↓ ran-b bg2 *Ran-s* ↓ *Raph* rat rauw ↓ *Rheum* ↓ rhod *Rhus-t* k* rhus-v k* ruta fd4.de sabad ↓ sabin k* samb ↓ sang sarr sars *Scir* ↓ senec k* seneg sep bg2 *Sil* ↓ sol-ni ↓ sphing a1 spig k* spong fd4.de squil ↓ stann staph tl1 *Stram* ↓ streptoc ↓ stront-c k* stroph-s sp1 suis-em ↓ suis-hep ↓ *Sul-ac* ↓ sul-i k2 *Sulph* k* sumb k*

Abdomen

- **Region** of umbilicus: ...
tab k* tarax↓ tarent k* tax↓ tep↓ ter↓ teucr k* *Thuj* til↓ toxo-g jl2 tritic-vg fd5.de tub al ust bg2 valer bg2 vanil fd5.de *Verat* k* verat-v k* *Verb*↓ *Zinc* k* zinc-p k2 zing↓ [heroin sdj2]
: **right**: kali-bi↓ kali-c↓ nicotam↓ zinc↓
: **cramping**: nicotam rly4•
: **pressing** pain: kali-bi bg2
: **stitching** pain: kali-c bg2 zinc bg2
: **left**: teucr bg2
: **daytime**: stann↓
: **cutting** pain: stann k*
: **morning**: aeth aloe ant-t k* atra-r bnm3• bar-m borx↓ bov bros-gau↓ bry dig↓ dios k* glycyr-g cte1• hell↓ lach k* lyc mag-c mang k* nat-m↓ *Nat-s* nux-v petr↓ sars↓ spong fd4.de sulph↓
: **6** h: bry
: **7** h: scroph-n↓
. **cutting** pain: scroph-n c1
: **8**.30 h: atra-r↓
. **crawling**: atra-r bnm3•
: **bed** agg.; in: caust↓ lyc↓
. **cramping**: caust h2 lyc
: **cramping**: aeth borx h2 bov lyc mag-c mang a1 nat-m
: **cutting** pain: bros-gau mrc1 hell k* mang petr h2 sars k* sulph k*
: **pressing** pain: mang h2
: **rising** agg.; after: aeth↓
. **cramping**: aeth
: **tearing** pain: dig k*
: **twisting** pain: hell k*
: **waking**; on: bov
. **cramping**: bov
: **forenoon**: agar lyc nat-c sars↓ verat-v k*
: **10** h: verat-v
. **cutting** pain: verat-v
: **cramping**: agar lyc nat-c
: **cutting** pain: nat-c a1 sars k*
: **menses**; during: mag-c↓
. **cutting** pain: mag-c k*
: **noon**: colch k* dios k* mag-m↓ sulph
: **cramping**: mag-m h2 *Sulph*
: **cutting** pain: mag-m h2
: **afternoon**: alum calc↓ euphr lyc↓ naja↓ nat-c ox-ac k* plb↓ ptel↓ ruta fd4.de seneg k* spig a1 **Sulph**
: **14** h: hir skp7• lyc verat-v
: **15** h: pert-vc vk9
. **15**-16 h: chel
: **16** h: lyc↓ *Sulph*
. **cramping**: sulph
. **cutting** pain: lyc
. **pressing** pain: *Sulph*
: **17** h: mag-c ptel sang
. **17**-18 h: spig
. **cramping**: mag-c sang
: **burning**: calc h2
: **cramping**: euphr nat-c plb **Sulph**
: **cutting** pain: lyc k* naja ptel k* spig h1
: **pressing** pain: alum k*
: **standing** agg.: alum↓
. **pressing** pain: alum k*
: **evening**: alum↓ bar-c↓ bry↓ calc-p caust↓ chin↓ coloc con h2 fl-ac↓ nat-m↓ nept-m lsd2.fr *Ox-ac* phos↓ pic-ac plat spig k* staph↓ **Sulph**
: **bed** agg.; in: chin↓ nux-m↓ staph↓ valer↓
. **cramping**: nux-m
. **pressing** pain: chin valer
. **stitching** pain: staph h1
: **burning**: fl-ac k*
: **cramping**: alum h2 caust chin h1 phos h2 plat **Sulph**

- **Region** of umbilicus – **evening**: ...
: **cutting** pain: bar-c k* bry nat-m k* staph k*
: **pressing** pain: nat-m h2
: **stool** agg.; during: inul↓
. **cramping**: inul
: **night**: acon *Aesc* k* arn bar-c bros-gau↓ bry *Calc* carb-v↓ carneg-g rwt1• *Cham* *Chin* coc-c *Coloc* cycl graph hep lyc↓ mag-m merc nux-m *Ox-ac* podo *Puls* *Rhus-t* ruta fd4.de sep sil *Sulph* tritic-vg fd5.de zing
: **midnight**: *Chin* fl-ac sulph↓
. **after**: **Ars**
4 h: tanac c1
. **cutting** pain: sulph
. **stool** agg.; during: fl-ac
: **bed** agg.; in: nux-m↓
. **cramping**: nux-m
: **cramping**: bros-gau mrc1 bry cycl lyc h2 nux-m *Podo*
: **cutting** pain: sil h2
: **pressing** pain: carb-v h2 sep h2 sulph h2
: **twisting** pain: ruta
: **waking**; on: cycl↓
. **cramping**: cycl
: **bed**; when going to: nat-m↓
: **cutting** pain: nat-m k*
: **bending**:
: **backward**:
. **agg.**: atra-r bnm3• hir skp7• lyc k*
crawling: atra-r skp7•
. **amel.**: onos
: **body**:
. **agg.**: nit-ac↓
cramping: nit-ac
. **forward**:
agg.: con↓ dulc↓
cramping: con h2 dulc h1
amel.: *Aloe*↓ **Coloc**↓ rauw↓ senec↓
cramping: *Aloe* **Coloc** rauw tpw8 senec
. **must** bend body: lyc↓
cramping: lyc h2
: **bending** double:
: **amel.**: atra-r↓ hir skp7• stroph-s sp1
. **crawling**: atra-r skp7•
: **biting** pain: petr a1
: **boring** pain: aloe bg2 apis bg2 calen bg2 cina bg2 lac-c bg2 nat-m bg2 plb bg2 seneg bg2 sep bg2 tarax bg2
: **breakfast**:
: **after**:
. **agg.**: agar↓ atra-r bnm3• kali-bi↓
cramping: agar kali-bi
: **before**:
. **agg.**: **Nat-s**↓
tearing pain: **Nat-s** k*
: **during**: alum↓
. **cramping**: alum h2
: **burning**: **Acon** k* ars berb bov calc k* calc-p k* camph canth carb-v k* cassia-s ccrh1• cham chel k* clem k* cocc k* crot-h cub k* dios k* dirc c1 dor k* dulc a1 fl-ac k* gamb mrr1 *Ham* iod k* kali-c k* kali-i kola stb3• lach lyc k* mag-s k* merc k* merc-i-f nat-ar nat-c k* nat-m k* ox-ac ph-ac k* *Phyt* plat k* plb k* raph sabad k* sang k* sep h2* sul-ac til k*
: **burrowing**: con bg2 dulc h2* grat k* nit-ac bg2
: **bursting** pain: dulc bg2 thuj bg2 verb bg2
: **children**; in: sacch sst1•
: **clawing** pain: acon k* *Bell* k* *Hep* kreos k* petr k* stann
: **paroxysmal**: petr k*
: **clutched** with nails of fingers; as if: acon bg2 stann bg2
: **cold**:
: **drinks** | **after**:
agg.: calc-p↓

- **Region** of umbilicus – **cold** – **drinks** – **after** – **agg.**: ...
  - **cutting** pain: calc-p
  - **agg.**: calc-p
- **cold**; after taking a: *Bry* ↓
  - **cramping**: *Bry*
- **compressed**; as if: acon b7a.de
- **contracting**: coloc mrr1
- **cough**:
  - **after**: nit-ac h2
  - **during**:
    - **agg.**: ambr k* ip k* nit-ac h2 *Nux-v* b7a.de *Puls* b7a.de sep stann bg2 verb bg2
      - **pressing** pain: ambr k*
- **cramping**: acon k* aeth a1 agar all-c k2 *Aloe* alum h2 am-m aml-ns bg2 anac h2 ant-c ant-t arg-n bg2* arn aspar astac kr1 atis zzc1• bapt bg2* bar-c *Bell* k* berb *Bry* calad bg2 calc *Camph* caps bg2 *Carb-an* carbn-s caul caust k* cham h1 *Chel* *Chin* chion ptk1 cimic cit-ac rly4• coc-c *Cocc* **Coloc** k* *Crot-t* cupr bg2 cycl **Dios** k* dulc euphr fl-ac *Gamb* k* gent-c gran graph grat guaj h2 ham k* hyos ign *Iod* **Ip** k* jug-c kali-bi k* kali-br a1 kali-i kali-n kreos k* *Laur* lec led lyc mag-c mag-m h2 mag-p mtf11 mang meny h1 merc-c k* *Mez* *Mur-ac* myric naja k* *Nat-c* nat-m k* nat-s tl1* nicc nicotam rly4• nit-ac nux-m k* *Nux-v* k* oci-sa sp1 op bg2 ox-ac k* petr h2 *Ph-ac* k* phos *Phyt* k* *Plat* *Plb* k* *Podo* pot-e rly4• prun bg2 *Ptel* k* *Raph* rauw tpw8 rheum rhod ptk1 rhus-t k* sabad samb sang senec k* sep bg2 sil spig h1 squil stann k* staph h1 streptoc rly4• stront-c k* suis-hep rly4• sul-i k2 *Sulph* k* tab k* tarent thuj k* *Verat* k* verb k* *Zinc* k* zinc-p k2
  - **accompanied** by | **thirst**: nept-m lsd2.fr
  - **cold**; as from taking a: stann h2
  - **downward**: plat
  - **flatulence**; as from: plat h2 zinc h2
- **crawling**: atra-r skp7*•
- **cutting** pain: aesc k* agar k* aloe (non:am-c kl) am-m k* ammc k* ant-t k* arn asaf b7.de* bar-c b4.de* bell bov k* brom k* cact k* calad k* calc-p k* camph k* canth k* caps b7.de* castm k* cham k* chin k* chinin-s bg2 cimic bg2 cocc **Coloc** k* con k* crot-t k* *Cupr* k* **Dios** k* *Dulc* k* graph b4.de* grat k* hell hyos k* hyper ign k* iod k* **Ip** k* kali-bi *Kali-c* k* *Kali-i* k* kali-m k2 *Kali-n* k* kali-p fd1.de• kreos k* laur bg2 led k* lyc *Mag-c* k* mag-m h2 *Mang* k* *Merc-c* k* merl k* mez b4.de* mur-ac k* naja k* nat-c b4.de* *Nat-m* k* nux-m b7.de* **Nux-v** k* ol-an k* *Op* k* paeon petr k* phos b4a.de plan k* plat k* plb b7.de* psor k* ptel k* puls k* raph *Rheum* k* rhus-t b7.de* rhus-v k* *Sars* k* senec k* sep b4.de* *Sil* k* sol-ni spig k* *Stann* k* staph k* *Sul-ac* k* sulph b4.de* tab k* ust k* valer k* verat k* verat-v k* verb k* zinc k* zinc-p k2 zing k*
  - **flatulence**; as from: coloc h2 plat h2
  - **menses** would appear; as if: ip
  - **paroxysmal**: mag-m h2
- **delivery**; during: **Ip** ↓ **Nux-v** ↓
  - **cutting** pain: **Ip** **Nux-v**
- **diarrhea**:
  - **after**:
    - **agg.**: cupr ↓ nat-m ↓
      - **cutting** pain: cupr nat-m
  - **before**: coloc gamb ↓ mag-c ↓ plat
    - **burning**: gamb mrr1
    - **cramping**: coloc mag-c h2 plat
    - **stitching** pain: gamb mrr1
  - **during**: fl-ac ip ↓ iris kali-n ↓ lach
    - **cramping**: ip mtf33 kali-n h2
- **digging** pain: carc gk6 dig h2 mag-c h2 *Scir* c1 stann h2
- **dinner**:
  - **after**:
    - **agg.**: all-c ant-t ↓ bry calc ↓ carbn-s cham ↓ **Coloc** k* crot-t ↓ ham lyc ↓
      - **burning**: lyc
      - **cramping**: ant-t bry calc **Coloc** ham
      - **cutting** pain: cham
      - **tearing** pain: crot-t k*
  - **before**: mang ↓

- **Region** of umbilicus – **dinner** – **before**: ...
  - **cutting** pain: mang h2
  - **during**:
    - **agg.**: kali-c ↓
      - **burning**: kali-c h2
- **distension**, with: astac ↓
  - **cramping**: astac kr1
- **dragging**, bearing down: carb-v bg2
- **drawing** pain: rhus-t a1
- **eating**:
  - **after**:
    - **agg.**: anac ↓ atis ↓ bell ↓ bov ↓ brucel sa3• bry ↓ carb-v ↓ chin ↓ *Coloc* ↓ graph ↓ kali-n ↓ mag-m ↓ *Nux-v* ↓ plat ↓ sulph ↓
      - **cramping**: atis zzc1• bell carb-v graph kali-n mag-m h2 *Nux-v* plat sulph
      - **cutting** pain: *Coloc* k*
      - **half** an hour: atra-r ↓
        - **crawling**: atra-r skp7•
      - **pressing** pain: anac h2 chin h1 *Coloc*
      - **stitching** pain: bov bry vh sulph vh
  - **agg.**: bov bry carb-v cob *Coloc* con h2 dig ↓ graph nux-v ox-ac plat *Sulph*
    - **eructations** | **amel.**: ambr h1
    - **stitching** pain: dig h2
  - **not** amel. by: pert-vc vk9
- **eructations**:
  - **amel.**: ambr ↓
    - **pressing** pain: ambr k*
- **expiration**:
  - **agg.**: coloc ↓
    - **tearing** pain: coloc h2
  - **during**:
    - **agg.**: rhus-t ↓
      - **cutting** pain: rhus-t k*
- **festering**: gran bg2 mag-c bg2 plan bg2 sulph bg2 zinc bg2
- **flatus**; passing:
  - **after**:
    - **amel.**: cassia-s ↓
      - **burning**: cassia-s ccrh1•
  - **amel.**: atis ↓ bar-c ↓ carb-v ↓ *Mag-c* ↓ mag-m ↓ mez ↓ sars ↓ sulph ↓
    - **cramping**: atis zzc1• bar-c h2 carb-v h2 mag-m h2 mez h2 sulph h2
    - **cutting** pain: *Mag-c* sars h2
    - **twisting** pain: mez h2
  - **before**: clem ↓
    - **cramping**: clem a1
- **fruit** agg.: **Coloc** ↓
  - **cramping**: **Coloc**
- **gnawing** pain: ars bg2 berb bg2 cimic bg2 coloc bg2 dulc bg2 gamb bg2 grat bg2 kali-bi bg2 nat-m h2 olnd bg2 ruta k*
- **headache**; after: gels psa
- **hernia** would protrude; as if a: dulc h2
- **ice** cream agg.: calc-p
  - **cutting** pain: calc-p
- **increasing** and decreasing gradually: carc gk6
- **inspiration**:
  - **agg.**: anac ↓ arn ↓ cina ↓ coloc ↓ *Mang* ↓ spig ↓
    - **cramping**: anac h2
    - **cutting** pain: arn k* coloc h2 *Mang* k*
    - **pressing** pain: anac h2 coloc h2
    - **stitching** pain: cina a1 spig h1
  - **deep** | **agg.**: bapt k* ruta fd4.de
- **laughing** aloud agg.: coloc ↓
  - **tearing** pain: coloc h2
- **leukorrhea**: am-m pd
  - **before**: nat-c ↓ sil ↓
    - **cramping**: sil h2

Abdomen

• **Region** of umbilicus – **leukorrhea – before**: ...
. **twisting** pain: nat-c h2
: **with**: am-m ↓ mag-c ↓ sil ↓
. **cramping**: mag-c h2
. **cutting** pain: am-m ptk1 sil h2*
⁝ **lying**:
: **abdomen**; on:
. **amel.**: atra-r ↓ cassia-s ↓
burning: cassia-s ccrh1•
crawling: atra-r skp7•
: **amel.**: hir skp7•
: **back**; on | **agg.**: hir skp7•
: **bent**; lying:
. **amel.**: hell ↓
cutting pain: hell
: **side**; on:
. **amel.**: hir skp7•
. **right** | **amel.**: hir skp7•
⁝ **menses** | **before**:
. **agg.**: *Ip* kreos
clawing pain: kreos k*
cramping: *Kreos*
: **during**:
. **agg.**: *Chinin-s* ↓ clem ↓ mag-c ↓
cramping: *Chinin-s* hr1 clem a1
cutting pain: mag-c k*
⁝ **menses** would appear; as if: sang
⁝ **motion** agg.: bar-c ↓ caps ↓ irid-met ↓ nit-ac ↓ ox-ac k2 phyt k* ptel k* zinc ↓
: **cramping**: bar-c h2 nit-ac
: **cutting** pain: caps k*
: **stitching** pain: irid-met srj5• zinc h2
⁝ **paroxysmal**: nat-m *Plb*
⁝ **periodical**: *Chel* ↓ ph-ac ↓
: **cramping**: ph-ac h2
: **pressing** pain: *Chel* ph-ac h2
⁝ **pinching** pain: acon b7.de* alum b4.de* am-m b7.de* anac b4.de* ant-t b7.de* bar-c b4.de* bell b4.de* bry b7.de* calc b4.de* camph b7.de* carb-an b4.de* *Carb-v* b4.de* caust b4.de* cham b7.de* *Chel* b7.de* chin b7.de* dulc b4.de* graph b4.de* guaj b4.de* *Hell* b7.de* ign b7.de* *Ip* b7a.de kali-bi bg2 *Kreos* b7a.de laur b7.de* mag-c b4.de* mag-m b4.de* meny b7.de* merc-c b4a.de mez b4.de* mur-ac b4.de* nat-c b4.de* nux-m b7.de* nux-v b7.de* par b7.de* ph-ac b4.de* plat b4.de* plb b7.de* ran-b b7.de* rhod b4.de* rhus-t b7.de* sabad b7a.de sabin b7.de* spig b7.de* *Stann* b4.de* stront-c b4.de* verat b7.de* verb b7a.de* zinc b4.de*
⁝ **pressing** pain: acon k* alum k* am-c k* ambr k* **Anac** k* arn asaf b7.de* bell h1 bry k* calc b4.de* camph k* carb-v h2 chel k* *Chin* k* chinin-s k* cina cocc k* colch k* *Coloc* k* crot-h crot-t k* cupr dig b4.de* *Dios* dulc grat hell k* hyos b7.de* ign k* kola stb3• *Lach* k* lact lyc k* mang h2 meny k* merc b4.de* mosch b7a.de *Nat-m* k* nit-ac k* olnd k* petr h2 *Ph-ac* k* *Ran-s* k* raph rheum k* samb k* seneg k* sep k* sil b4.de* *Spig* k* stann h2 staph h1 sul-ac b4.de* *Sulph* k* tab k* teucr k* valer bg2 vanil fd5.de *Verb* k* zinc k*
: **button**; as from a: am-c k* *Anac*
: **flatulence**; as from: coloc h2 zinc h2
: **hernia** would protrude; as if a: dulc
: **paroxysmal**: nat-m k* sep h2
: **plug**; as from a: *Anac* k* *Verb*
: **stone**; as from a: cocc bg2 spig bg2 verb bg2
⁝ **pressure**:
: **agg.**: anac ↓ chel ↓ cina ↓ hir skp7• ip ↓ mag-c h2 mang plb ↓ zinc ↓
. **cutting** pain: chel k* ip h1
. **pressing** pain: anac h2 cina a1 zinc h2
. **tearing** pain: plb k*
: **amel.**: cycl ↓ hir skp7• nat-m ↓ pert-vc vk9 plb *Stann* ↓ vanil fd5.de
. **cramping**: cycl a1
. **cutting** pain: nat-m k* *Stann*

• **Region** of umbilicus – **pressure**: ...
: **hard**:
. **amel.**: atra-r ↓
crawling: atra-r skp7•
⁝ **radiating**: senec bg2
⁝ **respiration**: anac ↓
: **pressing** pain: anac c1
⁝ **retraction** of abdomen agg.: zinc ↓
: **pressing** pain: zinc h2
⁝ **rising**:
: **after**:
. **agg.**: plat sulph ↓
cutting pain: sulph k*
: **agg.**: ham ↓
. **cramping**: ham bg1
: **stooping**; from:
. **agg.**: chin ↓
cramping: chin h1
⁝ **sitting**:
: **agg.**: *All-c* ↓ brucel sa3• chin ↓ nat-c ↓ nat-s k* ph-ac rhus-t ↓ sulph
. **cramping**: *All-c* chin h1 ph-ac sulph h2
. **cutting** pain: nat-c a1 rhus-t
: **bent** forward:
. **agg.**: ant-t ↓ dulc ↓
cramping: ant-t dulc h2
: **erect**:
. **agg.**: atra-r ↓
crawling: atra-r skp7•
⁝ **sore**: aesc bg2* agar *Aloe* bro1 anac bg2* benz-ac bro1 *Bov* bro1 bry bro1 calc bg2 calc-p bg2* *Carb-v* k* caust k* *Cham* bro1 chel bro1 chion bro1 cina k* cinnb k* cocc bro1 *Coloc* k* con h2* crot-t bg2* dig bg2 *Dulc* bro1 euon bro1 form bg2 *Gamb* bro1 gent-c k* gent-l a1 *Gran* bro1 hep h2 *Hydr* hyper bro1 **Ip** k* jatr-c k* kali-bi k* *Kali-c* k* kali-n bg2 lept bro1 lyc k* mag-c *Merc* *Merc-i-f* k* merc-i-r bg2 nat-ar bg2 nat-m bg2 *Nux-m* bro1 *Nux-v* k* olnd bro1 ox-ac k* paraf bro1 *Ph-ac* bro1 plat h2* *Plb* k* psil ft1 *Puls* ran-s bro1 raph bro1 *Rheum* bro1 rhus-t bg2 senec bro1 sil bro1 *Spig* bro1 stann h2* suis-em rly4• sulph bro1 tax bro1 thuj bg2 *Verat* bro1 verb bro1 zinc bro1
⁝ **soup** agg.: kali-n ↓
: **cramping**: kali-n
⁝ **sour** food agg.: asaf
: **cramping**: asaf
⁝ **squeezed**; as if: arn bg2 bell bg2 bry b7.de* calc b4.de* *Coloc* b4a.de mez b4.de* ph-ac b4.de* rhus-t b7.de* stront-c b4.de* sulph b4.de* zinc b4a.de
⁝ **standing** agg.: alum ↓ atra-r bnm3• bry ↓ gent-c ↓
: **cramping**: bry gent-c
: **pressing** pain: alum
⁝ **stepping**:
: **every** step; at: arn ↓
. **cutting** pain: arn
⁝ **stitching** pain: acon b7a.de* aesc k* am-m b7.de* ambr k* anac k* androc srj1• ant-t b7.de* arn k* asaf k* bamb-a stb2.de• bell b4.de* bov k* bry k* canth b7.de* chin b7.de* cina b7.de* cocc b7.de* colch b7.de* *Coloc* k* *Cupr* b7a.de cycl k* dig b4.de* dulc k* eupi k* gamb mrr1 gels k* grat k* hyos b7.de* kali-c b4.de kreos b7a.de lyc k* mag-c b4.de* merc-c k* mosch b7.de* mur-ac k* nat-m k* *Nux-v* k* olnd k* ph-ac k* plat b4.de* plb k* rhus-t b7.de* ruta h1 sep k* sil b4a.de spig b7.de* spong k* staph k* sul-ac b4.de* sulph b4.de* tritic-vg fd5.de vanil fd5.de verb h* zinc k*
: **burning**: sulph h2
: **pulsating** pain: staph h1
: **upward**: con h2
⁝ **stool**:
: **after**:
. **agg.**: aesc *Aloe* ↓ anac ↓ bamb-a ↓ cact ↓ **Coloc** ↓ plat h2
cutting pain: *Aloe* cact **Coloc** k*
pressing pain: anac h2
stitching pain: bamb-a stb2.de•
. **amel.**: cassia-s ↓ glycyr-g cte1•

- **Region** of umbilicus – **stool** – **after** – **amel.**: ...
  burning: cassia-s ccrh1•
  : **amel.**: benz-ac↓ cycl↓ meny↓
  . **cramping**: cycl a1 meny h1
  . **cutting** pain: benz-ac ptk1
  : **before**: aloe **Am-m** ars↓ caps clem↓ *Coloc*↓ crot-t dulc fl-ac k* gamb glycyr-g cte1• graph↓ grat *Ham*↓ kali-n kola stb3• lec↓ mag-m↓ mur-ac↓ nat-c↓ nux-v ox-ac phos↓ plb↓ psor
  . **burning**: ars
  . **cramping**: clem a1 *Coloc* graph h2 *Ham* kali-n lec mag-m mur-ac h2 phos h2 plb psor
  . **cutting** pain: *Gamb* k* graph h2 grat nat-c h2 **Nux-v**
  : **during**:
  . **agg.**: acon mrr1 anac↓ cocc *Corn*↓ *Dulc*↓ fl-ac k* gamb indg↓ iod *Kali-bi* nat-c nat-m phos
  cramping: cocc *Corn* *Dulc* hr1 indg iod phos
  gnawing pain: kali-bi bg2
  pressing pain: anac h2
  : **stooping**:
  : **agg.**: am-m↓ caps↓ phos↓ sulph↓ *Verb*↓
  . **cramping**: am-m phos h2
  . **cutting** pain: caps h1 sulph k*
  . **pressing** pain: *Verb* k*
  : **amel.**: hir skp7•
  : **supper** agg.; after: gels↓
  : **cramping**: gels
  : **tearing** pain: agar k* arn ars b4a.de carbn-s k2 *Cham* k* chin h1 coloc b4a.de* con b4a.de* crot-t k* cupr k* dig k* dios grat k* ip h1 jatr-c mag-c h2 mang b4a.de merc-c b4a.de *Nat-s* k* *Plb* k* psor k* stram k* tep k* ter verb k* zinc b4a.de*
  : **paroxysmal**: *Plb* k*
  : **torn** out or loose; as if: ip bg2 plb bg2 *Stram* b7a.de
  : **touch** agg.: ip↓ zinc↓
  : **cutting** pain: ip h1
  : **stitching** pain: zinc h2
  : **tumor**; as from a: spig h1
  : **turning** body to the left agg.: bamb-a↓
  : **stitching** pain: bamb-a stb2.de•
  : **twisting** pain: all-s k* aloe k* ang bg2 berb k* bry k* calc k* caps k* cimic bg2 *Cina* k* **Coloc** k* con b4a.de* crot-t k* dulc k* hell k* ign bg2 kali-c bg2 mez k* naja k* nat-c k* nat-m bg2 nux-m k* ox-ac k* plat k* *Plb* k* ran-b k* ruta k* sil b4a.de verb ptk1
  : **downward**: nux-m
  : **ulcerative** pain: mag-c h2
  : **urination** | **after**:
  . **agg.**: mag-c↓
  cramping: mag-c h2
  : **during**:
  . **agg.**: til↓
  burning: til k*
  : **vexation**; after slight:
  : **Umbilicus**; below: scroph-n↓
  . **cramping**: scroph-n c1
  : **violent**: aloe *Bell* crot-t *Dios* ip jatr-c *Plb*
  : **waking**; on: sulph↓
  : **cutting** pain: sulph
  : **walking**:
  : **agg.**: all-c anac↓ arn↓ atra-r bnm3• bry caps↓ *Coloc* dios↓ gent-c↓ hir skp7• ph-ac↓ spig↓ sul-ac↓ zinc↓
  . **burning**: ph-ac k*
  . **cramping**: *All-c* gent-c zinc h2
  . **crawling**: atra-r skp7•
  . **cutting** pain: arn caps h1 dios k* sul-ac k*
  . **pressing** pain: anac h2 zinc h2
  . **stitching** pain: spig h1
  : **air** agg.; in open: bry↓
  . **pressing** pain: bry
  : **amel.**: bar-c↓

- **Region** of umbilicus – **walking** – **amel.**: ...
  . **cramping**: bar-c h2
  : **rapidly**:
  . **agg.**: chin↓
  pressing pain: chin h1
  : **warm** soup | **amel.**: mag-c h2
  : **weather**:
  : **cold**:
  . **agg.**: *Dulc*↓
  cutting pain: *Dulc*
  . **wet** | **agg.**: *Dulc*
  : **worms**; from: *Spig* br1*
  : **yawning**:
  : **agg.**: sars↓
  . **cutting** pain: sars k*
  : **with**: cact↓ calc↓
  . **cramping**: calc bg1 [cact xyz62]
  : **Above** umbilicus, comes and goes slowly: carc tpw2*
  : **Spot** beneath navel; in: calc h2 ruta fd4.de
  : **Transversely** across: **Chel** ip lach paeon *Prun*
  : **extending** to:
  : **Abdomen**: calc↓ coloc h2
  . **cramping**: calc
  : **All** directions:
  . **stool**:
  amel.: senec↓
  cramping: senec ptk1
  : **Anus**: nat-m↓ ox-ac↓
  . **cramping**: nat-m
  . **pressing** pain: ox-ac k*
  : **Back**: bapt hr1 plat↓
  . **cramping**: plat h2
  : **Bladder**: carbn-s↓
  . **tearing** pain: carbn-s k2
  : **Chest**: acon mrr1 kali-n↓
  . **cramping**: kali-n h2
  : **Chest, left**: chel↓
  . **pressing** pain: chel
  : **Downward**: nat-m plat thuj
  : **Epigastrium**: crot-t↓
  . **pressing** pain: crot-t k*
  : **Genitals**: sep h2
  : **Groin**: thuj↓
  . **cramping**: thuj
  : **Hip**: mag-c↓
  . **cramping**: mag-c h2
  : **Lumbar** region: bell↓
  . **cutting** pain: bell h1
  : **Mons** veneris: rhus-t↓
  . **drawing** pain: rhus-t a1
  : **Rectum**: aloe k2 brom bg1 nat-m
  . **cutting** pain: aloe k2
  : **Sacrum**: mag-c↓
  . **cramping**: mag-c h2
  : **Sides**; left: hir skp7•
  : **Stomach**: carb-v↓ mag-c↓ sulph↓
  . **cramping**: carb-v mag-c h2 sulph
  : **Testes**: gels psa
  : **Thighs**; into: bar-c
  : **Throat**: kreos↓
  . **cramping**: kreos
  : **Uterus**: *Calc* elaps ind **Ip**
  . **stitching** pain: **Ip**

- **Sides**: crot-t↓ dulc↓ grat↓ kali-c↓ kali-i↓ lyc↓ psil↓ psor↓ raph↓ spig↓
  : **right**: bamb-a↓ dulc↓ grat↓ kali-c↓ lyc↓ nat-m↓ tritic-vg↓ [heroin sdj2]

Abdomen

- **Sides – right**: ...
  - **stitching** pain: bamb-a stb2.de• dulc k* grat k* kali-c k* lyc k* nat-m k* tritic-vg fd5.de [heroin sdj2]
  - **left**: am-m↓ anac↓ cina↓ con↓ crot-t↓ dulc↓ kali-i↓ **Raph** mrr1 sul-ac↓
    - **stitching** pain: am-m k2 anac h2 cina h1 con h2 crot-t k* dulc k* kali-i k* sul-ac h2
  - **stitching** pain: crot-t k* dulc k* grat k* kali-c k* kali-i k* lyc k* psil ft1 psor k* raph k* spig k*

▽ • **extending** to:
  - **Abdomen**: sul-ac↓
    - **stitching** pain: sul-ac h2
  - **Abdomen**; across: **Chel**
  - **Anus**: aloe **Crot-t** ip led nat-m nux-v
    - **drawing** pain: nat-m h2
  - **Back**: lyc oci-sa↓ plat ptel sil
    - **cutting** pain: sil k*
    - **drawing** pain: oci-sa sk4•
    - **stitching** pain: ptel k*
  - **Bladder**: brom bg1 cic
    - **stitching** pain: cic k*
  - **Chest**: *Ang* chinin-s
  - **Downward**: aloe crot-h **Crot-t** ferr-i nux-v plat plb sep
  - **Esophagus**: hydr-ac↓
    - **burning**: hydr-ac ptk1
  - **Heart**: rhus-t↓
    - **stitching** pain: rhus-t h1
  - **Ilium**: coc-c
  - **Inguinal** region: thuj
  - **Legs**: nux-m↓
    - **drawing** pain: nux-m c1
  - **Lumbar** region: plb
  - **Mammae**: *Pall*↓
    - **stitching** pain: *Pall* vh
    - **Region** of: kreos
      - **stitching** pain: kreos
  - **Pelvis**: pall↓
    - **stitching** pain: pall
  - **Pubis**: rhus-t↓
    - **drawing** pain: rhus-t h1
  - **Pudendum**: *Sep*
    - **cough** agg.; during: sep k*
      - **stitching** pain: sep k*
  - **Rectum**: aloe k2 brom bg1 nat-m
  - **Spine**: lyc sil
  - **Sternum**: *Ang*
  - **Stomach**: crot-t↓
    - **cutting** pain: crot-t k*
  - **Stomach**, pit of: carb-v crot-t lyc ol-an sulph
  - **Thighs**: nat-m↓
    - **drawing** pain: nat-m h2
  - **Throat**: kali-bi kreos
  - **Uterus**: elaps *Ip* k*
    - **lancinating**: elaps
    - **stitching** pain: **Ip**
  - **Vagina**: calc-p
    - **drawing** pain: calc-p

- **Umbilicus**; about the:
  - **stool** agg.; after: *Ph-ac*↓
    - **sickening**: *Ph-ac* k*
- **Upper** abdomen: *Acon* b7.de* agar↓ agn↓ am-c↓ am-m↓ ambr↓ anac b4.de* ant-c↓ ant-t b7.de* am↓ *Ars*↓ asaf↓ asar↓ aur↓ bar-c↓ *Bell*↓ borx↓ bov↓ *Bry*↓ calad↓ *Calc*↓ camph↓ cann-s↓ *Canth*↓ caps↓ *Carb-v* b4a.de *Caust* b4a.de cham↓ chel↓ *Chin*↓ cina↓ cocc b7.de* colch↓ coloc↓ con↓ croc↓ cycl↓ dig↓ dulc↓ euphr↓ ferr↓ graph tl1 hep↓ hyos↓ *Ign*↓ iod b4.de* ip↓ *Kali-c*↓ kali-n↓ lach↓ laur↓ *Lyc* b4a.de m-ambo↓ m-arct↓ mag-m↓ *Merc* b4a.de merc-c↓ mez↓ mosch↓ mur-ac↓ nat-c↓

Pain – Upper abdomen: ...
Nat-m↓ nux-m↓ nux-v b7.de* par↓ *Petr*↓ ph-ac↓ *Phos*↓ plat↓ plb↓ puls b7.de* rhod↓ rhus-t↓ sabad↓ sabin↓ samb↓ seneg↓ sep↓ sil↓ spong↓ stann b4a.de staph↓ stram b7.de* stront-c↓ sul-ac↓ sulph↓ tarax↓ teucr↓ thuj↓ valer b7.de* verat↓ verb↓ viol-t↓ zinc↓
- **left**: gard-j vlr2•
- **accompanied** by | **respiration**; impeded (See RESPIRATION - Impeded - pain - abdomen - upper)
- **boring** pain: seneg bg2 thuj bg2
- **burning**: am-m b7.de calad b7.de* camph bg2 canth b7.de* caust b4a.de cham b7.de* nux-v b7.de
- **burrowing**: sep bg2
- **clutched** with nails of fingers; as if: mosch bg2
- **cough** agg.; during: ambr b7.de* *Dros* b7.de* *Nux-v* b7.de* sep↓
  - **stitching** pain: sep b4.de*
- **cutting** pain: agn b7.de* am-c b4.de* ambr b7.de* ant-c b7.de* arn b7.de* asar b7.de* *Calc* b4.de* *Canth* b7.de* cham b7.de* coloc b4.de* *Kali-c* b4.de* kali-n b4.de* laur b7.de* *Lyc* b4.de* mag-m b4.de* merc b4.de* merc-c b4a.de nux-m b7.de* nux-v b7.de* *Petr* b4.de* ph-ac b4.de* *Phos* b4.de* rhod b4.de* seneg b4a.de sil b4.de* spong b7.de* staph b7.de* stront-c b4.de* sulph b4.de* valer b7.de* verb b7.de* zinc b4.de*
- **menses**; during: cocc b7.de graph↓ kreos b7a.de
  - **torn** apart; as if: graph b4a.de
- **must** walk bent: calc↓
  - **contracting**: calc h2
- **pinching** pain: agar b4.de* am-c b4.de* ant-c b7.de* arn b7.de* asaf b7.de* bar-c b4.de* bell b4.de* borx b4a.de calc b4.de* cann-s b7.de* caps b7.de* caust b4.de* *Chin* b7.de* *Cocc* b7.de* con bg2 cycl b7.de* ip b7.de* kali-c b4.de* laur b7.de* m-arct b7.de merc b4.de* merc-c b4a.de mur-ac b4.de* nat-c b4.de* nat-m b4.de* nux-m b7.de* phos b4.de* plb b7.de* puls b7.de* rhod b4.de* rhus-t b7.de* sabad b7.de* stann b4.de* staph b7.de* stront-c b4.de* sul-ac b4.de* verat b7.de* verb b7.de* zinc b4.de*
- **pressing** pain: agn b7.de* ambr b7.de* anac b4.de* ant-t b7.de* *Ars* b4a.de aur b4.de* *Bell* b4a.de *Bry* b7.de* calad b7.de* caps b7.de* *Caust* b4.de* cham b7.de* chel b7.de* chin b7.de* cina b7.de* cocc b7.de* colch b7.de* coloc b4.de* croc b7.de* cycl b7.de* ferr b7.de* hep b4.de* hyos b7.de* ign b7.de* iod b4.de* lach b7a.de lyc b4.de* m-ambo b7.de m-arct b7.de mez b4.de* nat-m b4.de* *Nux-v* b7.de* par b7.de* phos b4.de* plat b4.de* plb b7.de* rhod b4.de* sabad b7.de* sabin b7.de* seneg b4.de* sep b4.de* sulph b4.de* teucr b7.de* verat b7.de* zinc b4.de*
  - **stone**; as from a: nux-v bg2
- **squeezed**; as if: arn b7.de* bar-c b4.de* calad bg2 carb-v b4.de* cina b7.de* *Cocc* b7.de* croc b7.de* dig b4.de* iod b4.de* *Nat-m* b4.de* puls b7.de* staph b7.de* stront-c b4.de*
- **stitching** pain: acon b7.de* anac b4.de* ant-t b7.de* arn b7.de* bov b4.de* *Carb-v* b4.de* *Chin* b7.de* cina b7.de* coloc b4.de* con b4.de* cycl b7.de* dig b4.de* dulc b4.de* euphr b7.de* *Ign* b7.de* kali-c b4.de* kali-n b4.de* laur b7.de* merc-c b4a.de mez b4.de* nat-m b4.de* plb b7.de* puls b7.de* rhus-t b7.de* sabad b7.de* samb b7.de* sep b4.de* stann b4.de* staph b7.de* tarax b7.de* verb b7.de* viol-t b7.de* zinc b4.de*
- **tearing** pain: hep b4a.de phos b4a.de

- **Wall**; abdominal: calc-p tl1

PAINTER'S colic (See Pain - lead poisoning - cramping)

PARALYSIS of intestines●: (↗*Inactivity - intestines)* alum tl1 apoc k2 bry ptk1 con ptk1 esin-sal bro1 lyc ptk1 mag-m ptk1 nux-v ptk1 **Op** k* *Phos* k* **Plb** k* plb-act bro1 pyrog jl2 *Rhus-t* ptk1 samb xxb1 *Sec* k* tab ptk1 thuj ptk1 visc c1
- **operation** on abdomen; after: *Op* ptk1*

PENDULOUS abdomen: bell **Calc-f** sne croc lil-t k2 plat podo **Sep** k ● zinc
- **accompanied** by:

○ • **Glands**; swelling of | **children**; in: mez ptk1
- **children**; in: | **girls** at puberty: calc ptk1 *Graph* ptk1 lach ptk1 sulph ptk1
- **delivery**; after: podo br1
- **mothers**; of: aur bro1 aur-m bro1 bell bro1 frax bro1 *Helon* bro1 iod nat-c phos bro1 *Sep* k*

PERFORATION; sensation of:
O - **Umbilicus** | **Region** of umbilicus: aloe

PERIODICITY: aloe bg2
O - **Hypochondria**: arg-n bg2

PERISTALSIS:
- **increased**: all-s br1 ars bro1 chin h1 fel br1* hyos bro1 *Ign* bro1 lat-m bnm6• *Phos* bro1 phys br1 rhodi br1 tab br1
- **reversed**: (↗*THROAT - Reversed)* adam skp7• *Asaf* k* bism sne cocc vh elaps k* ign c1* lob sne mosch sne nux-v ptk1* op hr* rhus-t ptk1 ter sne verat ptk1*
  - **pressure** agg.: adam skp7•

PERITONITIS (See Inflammation - peritoneum)

PERSPIRATION: **Ambr** k* **Anac** k* **Arg-met** b7.de* *Arg-n* k* asar b7.de* canth bg2 *Caust* k* **Cic** k* **Cocc** k1 *Dros* k* ip b7.de* m-arct b7.de m e r c k* nux-v b7.de* **Phos** k* plb k* rhus-t k* **Sel** k* staph k* sulph k2 thuj
- **forenoon**: arg-met
- **night**: anac k* cic h1 dros h1 kali-p fd1.de• staph h1 sulph k*
- **after**:
  - **agg.**: coloc b4a.de
  - **amel.**: canth b7.de*
- **agg.**: ars bg2 cupr bg2 verat bg2
- **and** chest; on abdomen: (↗*CHEST - Perspiration - abdomen)* **Arg-met** k1 **Cocc** k1 **Phos** k1* **Sel** a1*
- **coition**; after: agar k*
- **cold** agg.: ars bg2 *Dros* verat bg2
- **during** | **agg.**: stram b7.de *Verat* b7.de
- **exertion** agg.: *Ambr*
- **heat**; during: arg-met h1
- **suppressed** perspiration agg.: cham b7a.de chin b7a.de nux-v b7a.de puls b7a.de rhus-t b7a.de
- **walking** agg.; after: caust k*

O - **Groins** | **offensive**: ambr bg2 canth bg2 *Sel* bg2 sep bg2 sulph mrr1 *Thuj* bg2
- **Hypochondria**: caust bg1* conv bg1 ign bg1 iris k* verat bg2*
- **Hypogastrium** | **sitting** agg.: *Sel*
- **Inguinal** region: ambr k* canth k* iris sel k* sep thuj
- **Pubic** region | **Mons** pubis: *Sel* b7.de*
- **Umbilicus**, spreading from: rhus-t k*

PIGMENTARY degeneration: | **Liver**: arg-n bro1

PLETHORA (See Congestion)

PLUG; sensation of a: *Ran-s* b7.de*
O - **Intestines**; pressed in anac k*
- **Liver**: ran-s bg2
- **Pelvis** | **stool**; before: aloe bg2
- **Sides**: sep h2
- **Umbilicus**:
  O · **Behind**: ran-s
  - **Region** of umbilicus: agar bg2 bell bg2 kreos bg2 nat-c bg2 nux-v bg2 rhus-t bg2 sep bg2 spig bg2

PLUMS agg.: rheum b7.de*

PNEUMATOCELE: am-c b4a.de* caps b7.de* *Carb-an* b4a.de

POLYPI:
O - **Intestinal**: brucel sa3•
- **Peritoneum**: med jl2

PORTAL congestion: (↗*Stasis; GENERALS - Stasis - portal)* a e s c br1 **Aloe** br1 card-m br1* coll br1 *Nux-v* br1 podo br1
- **accompanied** by:
  - **constipation**: aesc br1
  - **hemorrhoids** (See RECTUM - Hemorrhoids - congestion; from portal)
  - **menses**; painful: **Coll** vh
  - **venous** stasis: card-m mrr1 podo br1
  O · **Hypogastrium**; pain in: podo br1
  - **Skin**; yellow discoloration of: podo br1
  - **Stomach**; complaints of: carb-v bg2 *Nux-v* bg2
- **women**; in: *Coll* br1

POSITION; change of: | **agg.**: ph-ac b4.de*

POTATOES agg.: alum b4a.de* coloc b4.de* merc-c b4a.de*

POTBELLY (See Distension - children - potbellied)

PREGNANCY:
- **during**:
  - **agg.**: *Apis* b7a.de arn b7a.de* bell b4a.de* bry b7.de* cham b7a.de* hyos b7.de* lach bg2 nux-v b7.de* **Puls** b7.de* sep b4a.de* *Spig* b7a.de verat b7a.de*
    - **External** abdomen: bell-p bg2
    - **Gallbladder**: chel ptk1
    - **Hypochondria**: *Acon* b7.de* *Puls* b7.de*

PREGNANT; sensation of being (See Alive)

PRESSED apart: | **Hypochondria**: calc bg2

PRESSURE:
- **agg.**: acon b7a.de agar bg2 aloe bg2 ambr b7.de* anac b4.de* ant-c b7.de* apis b7a.de* ars bg2* asaf b7a.de *Bell* b4.de* *Bry* b7.de* calc ptk1 chel ptk1 cina b7.de* clem bg2 cupr b7.de* dulc b4.de* graph b4a.de hell b7.de* ign b7a.de ip b7.de* kali-bi bg2 kali-c bg2 led bg2 lyc bg2 meny b7.de* *Merc* b4.de* merc-c b4a.de* mez b4.de* nat-c bg2 nat-m bg2 nit-ac b4.de* nux-v b7a.de* phos b4.de* plat bg2 *Puls* b7a.de ran-b b7.de* ruta b7.de* samb b7.de* sars b4.de* spong b7.de* stann b4.de* staph b7.de* stront-c b4.de* tab bg2 teucr b7.de* valer b7.de* zinc b4.de*
  O · **External** abdomen: kali-c bg2
  - **Hypochondria**: acon b7a.de* ars b4.de* asaf b7.de* borx b4a.de *Bry* b7.de* camph b7.de* cann-s b7.de* carb-v b4.de* chin b7.de* colch b7a.de ign b7.de* iod b4.de* kali-bi bg2 kali-c b4a.de *Merc* b4.de* mez b4.de* nat-c b4.de* plat b4.de* ran-b b7.de* ruta b7.de* sabad b7.de* sel b7.de* sil b4a.de teucr b7.de* valer b7.de* *Verat* b7.de* zinc b4.de*
    - **right**: agar bg2
  - **Liver**: *Aesc* bro1 *Aloe* bro1 bapt bro1 bell bro1* *Berb* bro1 bry bro1* calc bro1 carb-v ptk1 card-m bro1* chap bro1 *Chel* bro1 chelo bro1 chin bro1* *Chion* bro1 *Dig* bro1 *Eup-per* bro1 fl-ac bro1 graph bro1 hep ptk1 hydr bro1 iod bro1 *Iris* bro1 *Kali-c* bro1 lach bro1* lept bro1 lyc bro1* *Mag-m* bro1 *Merc* bro1* *Merc-d* bro1 nat-s bro1 *Nux-v* bro1 nyct bro1 phos bro1* *Podo* bro1 ptel bro1 *Ran-b* bro1 sanic bro1 sel ptk1 senn bro1 *Sep* bro1 stel bro1 sulph bro1 tarax bro1 zinc bro1
- **amel.**: aloe bg2 alum b4a.de* am-c b4.de* arg-n ptk1 asaf b7.de* bell b4a.de* b o r x b4a.de bov b4.de* brom bg2 *Bry* b7.de* castm ptk1 caust b4.de* chin b7.de* cina b7.de* **Coloc** b4.de* cupr ptk1 dros b7.de* graph b4.de* hyos bg2 *Ign* b7.de* kali-bi bg2 kali-c b4a.de* mag-m b4.de *Mag-p* bg2 mang bg2 melal-alt gya4 meny b7.de* mosch b7a.de nux-m b7.de* nux-v b7.de* *Plb* b7.de* podo bg2 *Puls* b7.de* *Rhus-t* b7a.de sec bg2 *Sep* bg2 *Stann* b4.de* sulph b4.de* thuj b4.de* verat b7.de* zinc b4a.de
  O · **Hypochondria**: **Dros** b7.de* dulc b4.de* mag-m b4.de* meny b7.de* mur-ac b4.de* sul-ac b4.de*
- **clothes**; of:
  - **agg.**: arg-n ptk1 bov ptk1 calc ptk1 *Lach* ptk1 *Lyc* ptk1 *Nux-v* ptk1
    - **Groins**: hydr ptk1
    - **Hypochondria**: am-m bg2 **Bry** bg2 **Calc** bg2 *Carb-v* bg2 *Caust* bg2 chel bg2 coff b7.de* graph bg2 hep bg2 kreos bg2 lach bg2 **Lyc** bg2 **Nux-v** b7.de* puls b7.de* sars bg2 *Spig* bg2 spong b7.de* *Sulph* bg2
    - **Waist**: apis ptk1 brom ptk1 carb-v ptk1 graph ptk1 lach ptk1
- **external** (See Pressure)
- **hand**; of:
  - **agg.**: lac-d bg2 nux-v bg2 psor ptk1 zinc-chr ptk1
    - **stomach** and left hand on lumbar region; right hand on | **amel.**: med ptk1
- **liver**; on:
  - **agg.** | **Hypochondria**: ptel bg2 sabad bg2 sel bg2
- **spleen**; on:
  - **agg.** | **Hypochondria**: ign bg2
- **umbilicus**; on:
  - **agg.**: *Graph* b4a.de
    - **Hypochondria**: stann b4.de*
- **umbilicus**; on region of:
  - **agg.**: aloe bg2 ant-t bg2 ars bg2 *Crot-t* bg2 dios bg2 ptel bg2

Abdomen

- **umbilicus**; region of: ...
  - **amel.**: ptel bg2

PRICKLING: kreos bg2 verat bg2 zinc h2
○ - **Hypochondria**: *lp* bg2 ruta bg2
- **Inguinal** region: zinc b4.de*
  - **alternating** with | **drawing** (See Pain - inguinal region - drawing pain - alternating - prickling)

PROLAPSUS: | **Intestines**: *(↗RECTUM - Prolapsus)* bacls-7 fmm1• cupr-ar br1 syc fmm1•

PROTRUSION: calc bg2 sil bg2
- **left** side; sensation of: dig h2
○ - **Here** and there: croc bro1 nux-m bro1 sulph bro1 thuj bro1*
  - **hernia** would form; as if a: carb-an k* ign nat-c h2 *Thuj*
- **Umbilicus**: amph a1 asaf bg2 calc con k* dulc bg2 lyc k* nat-m k* sul-ac k* sulph
  - **children**; in:
    ⁝ **nurslings**:
      : **sycotic**: thuj mtf33
      : **weeping**; when: thuj mtf33
  - **pregnancy**:
    ⁝ **night** | **lying** agg.: sulph h2

PROUD flesh: | **Umbilicus**: **Calc** k* kali-c ptk1 nat-m ptk1

PULSATION (= throbbing): **Acon** k* act-sp bg1 aesc k* aeth k* aloe k* *Alum* k* alum-sil k2 **Ant-t** k* apis b7a.de arn b7.de* ars k* ars-i ars-s-f k2 bar-c bg2 bar-m k2 berb bg1 bruc c2 cact k* cadm-s k* cain calad k* **Calc** k* calc-i k2 calc-s cann-s k* canth b7.de* caps k* card-m caust k* chin b7.de* cina bg1 cinnb bg1 colch k* coloc k* con bg2 cycl bg1* dig br1 dulc b4.de* ferr-i bg1 fl-ac k* gels graph bg1 *Ign* k* *Iod* k* irid-met srj5• kali-ar *Kali-c* k* kali-s ketogl-ac rly4• kola stb3• kreos k* *Lac-c* k* lach k* *Lyc* k* med melal-alt gya4 merc k* naja k* nat-m bg2 nat-s *Nux-v* k* op k* osm bg2 *Ph-ac* phos b4a.de plat b4.de* plb k* ptel k* **Puls** ptk1* ran-b bg1 rauw sp1 rheum bg2 sabin bg2 *Sang* k* sec gk **Sel** k* **Sep** h2* stront-c sul-ac k* sul-i k2 sulph bg2* sumb k* tarent tritic-vg fd5.de visc sp1 zinc b4.de*
- **evening**: ferr-i k* ptel k* tritic-vg fd5.de
- **night**: aloe
  - **midnight**:
    ⁝ **after** | **5** h: kreos
  - **lying** agg.: aloe
- **aneurysm**; from: bar-m ptk1
- **eating**; after: cain kola stb3• **Sel** k*
- **heat**; during: acon bg2 calc bg2 caps bg2 **Kali-c** k* lyc bg2 phos bg2 sep bg2
- **lying** agg.: aloe *Coloc* plb k*
- **menses**; during: aesc kola stb3• kreos k*
- **pregnancy** agg.; during: sel k2*
- **sleep**; preventing: sel br1*
- **stool** agg.; after: agar con k2 *Ph-ac*
- **supper** agg.; after: cain
○ - **Aorta**:
  - **accompanied** by | **cramping** pain in abdomen: dig bro1
- **Arteries**: caps tl1
- **Blood** vessels: *Sel* b7.de*
- **Deep** in abdomen: aesc ptk1
- **Diaphragm**: caps fkm1•
- **External** abdomen: *Coloc* b4.de*
- **Here** and there: cann-xyz ptk1
- **Hypochondria**: acon k* act-sp k* anan asc-t k* bell k* brach k* brom k* calc k* calc-p k* chel cimic cinnb k* graph k* kali-i k* laur lyss k* nux-v k* puls k* ran-b k* sars k* sep k* sil sulph k*
  - **right**: act-sp k* bell k* brach k* brom k* *Calc-p* k* cench k2 *Chel* kali-i k* laur med nat-s nux-v k* petr-ra shn4• ptel sarr sep k* sil sulph k*
  - **left**: agar h2 asc-t k* calc k* cann-s cinnb k* gels ruta h1 sars k*
  - **morning**: stry k*
  - **evening**: apoc k* brom k*
  - **night**: graph h2
  - **eructations** | **amel.**: calc-p
  - **walking** agg.: nat-s

Pulsation: ...
- **Hypogastrium**: aesc k2 ang k* cina petr-ra shn4•
  - **right**: petr-ra shn4•
  - **female**: aesc k* calc-p k*
▽ • **extending** to heart: rauw sp1
- **Ilium**; crest of: cic h1
- **Inguinal** and pubic region: alum bg2 stront-c b4.de* sul-ac b4a.de thuj b4.de*
  - **left**: polyg-h bg2
- **Inguinal** region: alum k* brach k* lyc k* nat-c h2 stann stront-c sul-ac
  - **morning**: brach k*
  - **evening**: lyc k*
  - **deep** in: stann
- **Liver**: act-sp br1 bufo bg2 calc-p k2 chel bg2 coloc bg2 crot-h ptk1 lappa ptk1 *Laur* b7a.de nat-s bg2 *Nux-v* b7.de* phos bg2 sep b4a.de* sil b4a.de*
○ • **Region** of: allox sp1
- **Lower** abdomen: ang bg2 calc-p bg2 cina bg2 [bell-p-sp dcm1]
- **Pelvis**: aesc tl1 dys fmm1• jab ptk1
- **Pubic** region:
○ • **Behind**: aesc ptk1
  - **Mons** pubis: calc-p bg2 lyc bg2 sul-ac bg2
- **Sides**: apis bg2 cadm-s c1 chin h1 graph hura kali-c k* nat-s k* sil bg1
  - **right**: lyc h2
  - **night** | **waking**; on: graph
  - **walking** agg.: cinnb nat-s k*
○ • **Flank**; on inspiration in the: seneg
- **Spleen**: agar bg2 anan asc-t bg2 calc b4.de* crot-t k* gels bg2 grat k* kali-i bg2 lyss nat-s bg2 ran-b k* ruta k* sars b4.de* vib bg2
- **Umbilicus**: acon aloe ars k* cench k2 dulc kali-c ptk1 ketogl-ac rly4• mag-m c1 ptel k* puls gk sec a1 zinc h2
○ • **Region** of umbilicus: acon bg2 aloe bg2 ars bg2 calad bg2 cann-xyz bg2 dulc bg2 glon bg2 kali-c ptk1 nux-m bg2 ptel bg2
- **Upper** abdomen: calad b7a.de* con bg2
▽ - **extending** to:
  - **trunk**; entire: plut-n srj7•
○ • **Head**: rheum h*

PURRING: sul-ac bg2

PUSHING in abdomen; sensation of: thuj ptk1

PUTREFACTION: | **Intestines**: *(↗RECTUM - Flatus - offensive - putrid; STOOL - Odor - eggs; STOOL - Odor - putrid)* indol br1* irid-met br1

QUININE; after abuse of: verat b7a.de
○ - **Hypochondria**: ars bg2 calc bg2 *Caps* bg2 lach bg2 nat-m bg2 **Nux-v** bg2 puls bg2 **Sulph** bg2

QUIVERING:
○ - **Flank**; in | **right**: nat-c h2

RAISING:
- **upper** limbs agg. | **Hypochondria**: carb-v bg2 conv bg2

RATTLING (See Rumbling)

RAWNESS: acon bg2 ambr bg2 *Ang* b7a.de apis bg2 arg-n bg2 *Ars* bg2 asar bg2 *Bell* bg2 calc bg2 canth bg2 con bg2 hep bg2 hyos bg2 ip bg2 meny bg2 *Nux-v* b7.de* petr bg2 *Phos* bg2 ran-b bg2 stann bg2 sul-ac bg2 sulph bg2
○ - **Inguinal** region: sul-ac bg2
- **Liver**: chel bg2 chin bg2 chion bg2 lyc bg2

REACHING UP with the hands agg.: alum bg2 carb-v bg2

READING agg.: m-aust b7.de

REFLECTING agg.: m-arct b7.de

REFLEXES:
- **lost**: lat-m bnm6•
  - **children**; in: lat-m bnm6•

RELAXED feeling: agar k* ail alum k* *Am-m* asar b7.de* bar-c b4.de* borx bg2 calc b4.de* *Carb-v* k* *Castn-v* *Ign* ip b7.de* lob k* lyc h2 m-ambo b7.de mag-m mang *Merc* k* nux-m b7.de* *Op* phos k* plat b4.de* podo bg2 pot-e rly4•

Relaxed feeling: ...
Psor ptel k* rhod b4.de* rhus-t k* rumx *Sep* k* spong b7.de* *Staph* suis-pan rly4• sumb k* verat b7.de*
- **drinking** agg.; after: croc b7a.de
- **lying** on back | **amel.**: castn-v
- **stool** agg.; after: mag-m *Phos* *Sep* k* sulph
- **walking** agg.: alum *Nat-m* rhus-t

○ - **Hypochondria**: nit-ac b4.de
- **Inguinal** region: m-arct b7.de
- **Pelvis** | **Region** of: tril-p br1

REST:
- **agg.**: am-c b4.de* ang b7.de* bov b4.de* ferr b7.de* kali-n b4.de* kreos b7a.de op b7.de* puls b7.de* rhus-t b7.de* ruta b7.de* seneg b4a.de

○ • **Hypochondria**: arn b7.de* lyc b4a.de *Mag-m* b4a.de
- **amel.**: alum b4.de* apis b7a.de arn b7.de* *Bry* b7.de* chin b7.de* *Coloc* b4.de* cupr b7.de* grat bg2 ip b7.de* kreos b7a.de m-arct b7.de m-aust b7.de nux-m b7.de* *Nux-v* b7.de* puls bg2 rhus-t b7.de* staph b7.de* thuj b4.de*

RESTING, supporting:
- **knee**; on | **amel.**: euph b4a.de

RESTLESSNESS, uneasiness, etc.: agar k* agn a1 alum h2 am-c b4a.de* *Ant-t* k* apis k* apoc *Arg-n* k* **Ars** k* *Ars-i* *Asaf* k* asc-t aur k* *Bell* k* bism b7.de* bov bg2 bry k* **Calc** k* carb-an chel bg2 cinnb cist colch k* com corn croc b7.de* crot-t k* cycl k* dirc *Dulc* k* euph k* fago ferr bg2 ferr-ar ferr-ma fl-ac b4a.de* gran grat gymno hell k* iod **Ip** k* jatr-c kali-ar kali-bi bg2 *Kali-c* k* kola stb3• lach b7.de* laur b7.de* mang bg2 merc-c b4a.de merc-i-r mez mim-p rsj8• *Mur-ac* k* nat-ar nat-c k* *Nat-m* k* *Nat-s* *Nit-ac* k* nux-m b7.de* olnd b7.de* par k* petr-ra shn4• **Phos** k* plan plat b4.de* *Podo* k* *Puls* k* rhod bg2 ruta b7.de* sabin b7.de* **Sep** k* spig b7.de* spong b7.de* sul-ac bg2 vesp *Zinc* zinc-p k2 [heroin sdj2]
- **morning**: calc nit-ac sep
  - • **waking**; on: calc
- **forenoon**: cimic
- **afternoon**: grat
- **evening**: am-br
- **night**: bamb-a stb2.de• caust kali-i nit-ac h2 plat h2
- **anxious**: alum h2
- **breakfast** | **after** | **agg.**: grat
  - • **during**: plan
- **cold**; as from: plat h2
- **drinking** agg.; after: caust sul-ac
- **eating**; after: aur h2 caust k* flor-p rsj3• kali-c b4a.de* kali-p fd1.de• petr-ra shn4• sul-ac k*
- **flatulence**; during: calc b4.de* cocc b7.de* nit-ac b4.de*
- **rest** agg.: ars
- **sleep** agg.; after: sulph
- **smoking**, as after: mang h2
- **stool**:
  - • **after** | **agg.**: ars graph
  - • **before**: borx bg2 calc bg2 ind merc b4.de* nux-v bg2
  - • **during** | **agg.**: ars bg2 ind kali-c
- **vomit** or pass stool; cannot tell if he is about to: podo mrr1

○ - **Hypochondria**: aloe chin equis-h manc
  - • **stool**; before: aloe
- **Hypogastrium**: cycl h1
- **Intestines**: cean tl1
- **Liver**: aloe bg2 pneu jl2
- **Lower** abdomen: ars bg2

▽ - **extending** to | **Head**: mang h2

RETCHING; during: | **agg.**: olnd b7.de*

RETRACTION: acon bg2 agar k* *Alum* am-c k* *Apis* k* arn b7.de* ars k* *Bar-c* k* bell k* borx mtf33 *Bry* calc-p bg2* camph k* canth k* *Carb-ac* *Carb-v* b4a.de caust b4a.de *Cocc* colch k* *Con* b4a.de crot-t k* *Cupr* k* dig *Dros* k* elat k* euph k* gamb **Hydr** k* *Iod* iodof bro1 jatr-c kali-bi bro1 kali-br k* kali-c b4.de* laur k* led k* lob k* lyc k* merc k* merc-c k* mez k* mosch bg2 mur-ac k* nat-c b4.de* *Nat-m* k* nat-n *Nux-v* b7a.de op k* paeon k* phos k* plat **Plb** k* *Plb-act* bro1 plb-chr bro1 podo k* ptel bro1 puls k* quas bro1 sec bg2 sil k* staph k* stram k* sul-ac k* *Sulph* b4a.de *Tab* k* ter bg2 thal-s c1 thuj k* valer b7.de* *Verat* k* *Zinc* k*

Retraction: ...
- **accompanied** by:
  - • **cholera**: kali-br ptk1
  - • **constipation**: carb-ac ptk1
  - • **palpitation** (See CHEST - Palpitation - accompanied - abdomen - retraction)
  - • **urine**; scanty: plb bro1
- **agg.**: cupr bg2 puls bg2 valer bg2
- **children**; in: borx mtf33 calc-p tl1
- **drawn** by a string; as if: chel bro1 *Plb* hr1* podo bro1 tab bro1
- **painful**: op hr
  - • **vomiting**; from: verat mtf33
- **pressure** agg.: alumn c1
- **sensation** of: abrot k* alum-p k2 alumn k2 carb-ac k* hydrog srj2• nux-v k2 phos k* plat k2 sabad spong fd4.de sulph k*
- **stool** agg.; during: agar b4a.de* arg-n bg2
- **together**: ars bg2 con bg2 cupr bg2 ferr bg2 lach bg2 laur bg2 plb bg2 rhus-t bg2 sang bg2
- **vomiting**: dros h1 verat ptk1

○ - **Intestines** | **attached** to spine; as if: plat tl1 plb tl1 ter tl1
- **Lower** abdomen: *Acon* b7a.de *Bell* ptk1 *Bry* b7a.de* carb-v ptk1 con bg2 lyc ptk1 *Merc* ptk1 *Nux-v* b7a.de ran-b ptk1 rhus-t bg2 *Sep* ptk1 squil ptk1
- **Spots**: plat h2
- **Umbilicus**: acon k* aloe bg2 *Alum* alumn k2 arn bg2 ars bg2 bar-c k* calc-p k* carbn-s *Chel* k* cina b7.de* crot-t bg2 grat k* kali-bi bg2 kali-c k* mosch k* nat-c k* op hr **Plb** k* podo k* puls ptk1 ran-b k* *Rhus-t* b7.de* ruta b7.de* stann ptk1 tab k* ter k* thuj bg2 verat ptk1 zinc ptk1 zinc-s k*
  - • **morning**: acon
  - • **agg.**: acon bg2 bar-c bg2 chel bg2 nat-c bg2 plb bg2
  - • **attached** to spine; as if: plat tl1 **Plb** a1*
  - • **colic**; during: chel pd nat-c ptk1
  - • **lying** agg.: ter k*
  - • **sitting** agg.: kali-c k*
  - • **stool**; before: crot-t k*
  - • **stooping** agg.: tab
- **Upper** abdomen: thuj ptk1

RIDING:
- **carriage**; in a:
  - • **agg.**: arg-met bg2 **Arn** bg2 calc b4.de* carb-v b4a.de* card-m bg2 cocc b7.de* nat-m bg2 psor bg2 sep b4.de*
    - ⁝ **rough** roads; on | **Hypochondria**: borx bg2 lach bg2 sep bg2
    - ⁝ **Hypochondria**: borx b4a.de lach bg2 sep b4.de*
  - • **amel.**: lyc bg2
- **horse**; a:
  - • **agg.**: borx bg2 carb-v bg2 cocc bg2 hep bg2 nat-c b4.de* nat-m bg2 psor bg2 sep bg2
    - ⁝ **Hypochondria**: *Nat-c* b4a.de

RIGIDITY of muscles: atra-r bnm3• helo-s bnm14• lat-h bnm5• lat-m sp1* loxo-lae bnm12• lyss c1 op bg2 physala-p bnm7•
- **left**: nat-m ptk1*
- **sensation** of rigidity: puls bg2

RISING:
- **after** | **agg.**: am-m bg2 hyos bg2 mag-c bg2 mag-m bg2 mang bg2 meny bg2 nat-m bg2 nit-ac bg2 rhus-t bg2 sep bg2
- **bed**; from:
  - • **after**:
    - ⁝ **agg.**: am-m b7.de hyos b7.de meny b7.de rhus-t b7.de
    - ⁝ **amel.**: ambr b7.de* arg-met b7a.de* bar-c b4.de* cocc b7.de* ign b7.de* mur-ac bg2 *Nux-v* b7.de* ran-b b7.de*
  - • **agg.**: bell b4.de* coloc bg2 hep b4.de*
- **sitting**; from:
  - • **agg.**: bell b4.de* bry bg2 chin b7.de* dig b4.de* ferr bg2 merc-c b4a.de plat b4.de* puls b7.de* rheum b7.de* stront-c b4.de* verat b7.de*
  - • **amel.**: arg-met b7.de* chin b7.de* spig b7.de* spong b7.de* viol-t b7.de*

Abdomen

- **stooping**; from:
  - **agg.**: chin b7.de* *Ferr* b7a.de plb b7.de* rhus-t b7.de*
    - **Hypochondria**: alum b4.de* bell b4.de*
  - **amel.** | **Hypochondria**: bov b4.de* con b4.de* sul-ac b4.de*

RISING; sensation of something: *Caust* b4a.de laur b7.de* nux-v b7.de*

ROCKING agg.: carb-v b4a.de

ROLLING (See Ball - rolling; Rumbling)

ROOM: | **amel.**: sul-ac b4.de*

ROUGHNESS; sensation of: | **Hypochondria**: nat-m bg2

RUBBING:

- **agg.**: (↗*Stroking*) aran ptk1 kali-c ptk1 mag-c ptk1 nat-c ptk1 *Phos* ptk1 plb ptk1
- **amel.**: alum bg2 cham bg2 kali-c bg2 mag-c bg2 nat-m bg2 nat-s bg2* pall ptk1 phos ptk1 *Podo* ptk1 stront-c b4.de*
  - ○ **Hypochondria**: aur bg2 phos b4.de* podo bg2 rhus-t b7.de*
  - **Liver**: *Podo* ptk1
- **gently** with warm hand | **amel.**: lil-t ptk1

RUMBLING: (↗*Bubbling; Clucking; Fermentation; Flatulence; Gurgling*) acal br1* acet-ac k* *Acon* k* aesc k* **Agar** k* agath-a nl2• agn b2.de* ail k* all-c k* allox tpw3* *Aloe* k* *Alum* k* alum-p k2 alum-sil k2 alumn am-c k* am-m k* ambr k* ammc k* amp rly4• ampe-qu br1 **Anac** k* anag hr1* androc srj1• ang b2.de* anis c1* ant-c k* *Ant-t* k* aphis a1 apis k* apoc k* aran vh1 *Arg-met* k* *Arg-n* k* *Arn* k* *Ars* k* ars-i ars-s-f k2 arum-d a1* arund k* asaf k* asar k* asc-t k* asim hr1 aur k* aur-ar k2 aur-i k2 aur-m k* aur-s k2 *Bamb-a* stb2.de• bapt k* bar-c k* bar-i bar-m k* bar-s k2 *Bell* k* bell-p sp1 berb k* *Bism* k* bit-ar wht1• borx k* bov k* brom k* bros-gau mrc1 *Bry* k* bufo cact cain *Calc* k* calc-i k2 calc-p k* calc-s calc-sil k2 cann-s k* *Canth* k* caps k* *Carb-ac* k* *Carb-an* k* *Carb-v* k* carbn-s card-m k* carl k* cartl-s rly4• casc a1* castm *Castn-v* **Caust** k* cedr *Cham* k* *Chel* k* **Chin** k* *Chinin-ar* chinin-s chir-fl gya2 choc srj3• chr-ac hr1 *Cic* k* cimic k* *Cina* b2.de* cinnb clem k* cob k* cob-n sp1 coc-c k* *Cocc* k* coff b2.de *Colch* k* coli rly4• coll k* *Coloc* k* con k* conch fkr1• cop k* *Corn* k* cortico tpw7* croc k* *Crot-c* k* *Crot-t* k* cub c1 cupr b2.de* cupr-ar k* *Cycl* k* cyt-l sp1 dig k* **Dios** k* *Dirc* k* dor k* dream-p sdj1• *Dulc* k* echi elaps elat k* erig k* eug hr1 eup-pur k* euph k* euphr k* eupi k* falco-pe nl2• *Ferr* k* ferr-ar ferr-i k* ferr-ma k* ferr-p fl-ac k* form **Gamb** k* gard-j vlr2• *Gels* k* ger-i rly4• *Glon* k* gnaph k* *Graph* k* grat k* guaj k* haliae-lc srj5• ham fd3.de• **Hell** k* hell-o a1* **Hep** k* hippoc-k szs2 **Hydr** k* hydr-ac k* hydrc k* hyos k* *Ign* k* ind k* indg k* iod k* iodof hr1 ip k* *Iris* jal hr1 **Jatr-c** k* jug-r k* *Kali-bi* k* kali-br k* kali-c k* kali-i k* kali-n k* kali-p kali-s kali-sil k2 ketogl-ac rly4• kola stb3• lach k* lachn k* lact k* lap-la sde8.de• laur k* led k* *Lept* a1* lil-t k* limen-b-c hrn2* lob k* lob-s c2 loxo-lae bnm12• **Lyc** k* **M-ambo** b2.de* m-arct b2.de* m-aust b2.de* *Mag-c* k* *Mag-m* k* mag-s k* malar jl2 *Manc* k* mang mang-m a1* melal-alt gya4 meny b2.de* *Merc* k* merc-c k* merc-i-f k* merc-i-r k* *Mez* k* mom-b mtf11 mosch b2.de* mucs-nas rly4• mur-ac k* musa a1 myric hr1 naja k* nat-ar *Nat-c* k* *Nat-m* k* *Nat-p* **Nat-s** k* nat-sil fd3.de• nept-m lsd2.fr nicc hr1 *Nit-ac* k* nit-s-d a1* *Nux-m* k* **Nux-v** k* oci-sa sp1 ol-an k* *Olnd* k* onos *Op* k* osm k* ox-ac k* paeon k* par k* *Petr* k* petr-ra shn4• **Ph-ac** k* phel k* **Phos** k* *Phyt* k* pic-ac k* pin-con oss2• plac-s rly4• plan k* plat k* plat-m a1 plat-m-n c1 *Plb* k* *Podo* k* positr nl2• *Psor* k* ptel k* **Puls** k* pyrid rly4• pyrog k2 *Ran-b* k* *Ran-s* k* raph k* rheum h* rhod k* rhus-t k* rhus-v k* ribo rly4• rob k* *Rumx* k* ruta k* *Sabad* k* sabin b2.de* sal-fr sle1• samb k* sang k* sangin-n c2 sanic c2* sarr k* *Sars* k* sec k* sel b2.de* *Senec* k* *Seneg* k* *Sep* k* **Sil** k* sin-n a1* sinus rly4• *Spig* k* spong k* *Squil* k* stann k* *Staph* k* stram k* stront-c b2.de* stry k* suis-em rly4• suis-pan rly4• sul-ac k* sul-i k2 **Sulph** k* sumb k* suprar rly4• symph fd3.de• tab k* taosc iwa1• tarax b2.de* *Tarent* k* ter k* teucr b2.de* *Thuj* k* thyr ptk1 trios rsj11• tritic-vg fd5.de tub al tung-met bdx1• urol-h rwt• valer k* vanil fd5.de *Verat* k* verb h* vib hr1 vinc a1* viol-t k* visc sp1 xan k* *Zinc* k* zinc-p k2 [calc-n stj1]

- **daytime**: agath-a nl2• cench k2 nit-ac k* propr sa3• ptel
- **morning**: agar k* all-c k* all-s k* am-m apis arg-n ars bov k* bufo coch hr1* coloc k* dios dulc fd4.de glycyr-g cte1• graph k* kali-s fd4.de limest-b es1• mag-c h2 mag-m h2 myric k* nat-m k* nat-sil fd3.de* *Nux-v* k* plan k* plat h2 plb k* *Podo* hr1 samb stront-c ter k* tritic-vg fd5.de vanil fd5.de *Zinc* k*
  - **coffee** agg.: nat-m k* ox-ac k*
  - **rising** agg.; after: plb k*
    - **followed** by | **stool**; sputtering: nat-s a
  - **stool**; before: ferr-i a1 hell k* nux-v k*

Rumbling – morning: ...

  - **waking**; on: all-s k* am-m arg-n k* ars k* form k* hell-o a1* tritic-vg fd5.de vanil fd5.de
    - **6** h: asc-t mez
    - **7** h: dios nat-m zing
- **forenoon**: agar k* all-s a1 am-c k* ant-c k* bry k* coloc k* fl-ac k* nat-m k* ruta fd4.de stry k* tarent k* ven-m rsj12•
  - **9** h: coloc dirc mag-c
  - **11** h: corn euphr nat-m
- **noon**: graph k* ox-ac k* phos k* ruta fd4.de vanil fd5.de
  - **eating** | **after** | **agg.**: phos k*
    - **agg.**: graph
- **afternoon**: agar k* agath-a nl2• am-c k* am-m k* ammc k* bamb-a stb2.de• carb-v k* dulc fd4.de grat k* ign k* iris kali-p fd1.de• lyc mag-s k* naja *Nat-s* k* nux-v k* ox-ac k* ozone sde2• spong fd4.de suis-pan rly4• *Sulph* k* tab k* vanil fd5.de
  - **13** h: glon mag-c ptel
  - **14** h: ptel
  - **16** h: dirc iris-foe phys
  - **16**-23 h: alum h2
  - **17** h: fago iris-foe
  - **walking** agg.: tab k*
- **evening**: agar h2 agath-a nl2• aran hr1 bamb-a stb2.de• bov k* chin k* dulc fd4.de ferr k* ferr-i k* grat k2 kali-n k* lyc k* mag-c h2 merc k* mez k* nat-c h2 nat-m k* *Nat-s* ox-ac k* petr k* plan k* plb k* **Puls** rumx ruta fd4.de sabin k* sars h2 sep k* spong fd4.de sul-ac sulph *Tarent* k* ter hr1 zinc k*
  - **18** h: agath-a nl2• nat-c
  - **19** h: dirc mag-c nicc stry
  - **21** h: sanic c1
  - **bed** | **going** to bed | **when**: brucel sa3•
    - **in** bed | **agg.**: bry k* grat k*
  - **eating**; after: naja phos k* spong fd4.de
  - **lying** agg.: ran-b k*
  - **stool** agg.; during: zinc k*
- **night**: acon k* ambr k2 arg-met borx cann-i k* coc-c k* euphr k* jatr-c kali-n h2 *Lyc* hr1 merc merc-c a1 *Nuph* hr1 orot-ac rly4• ox-ac hr1 raph ruta fd4.de sinus rly4• **Sulph** k* tarent k* vanil fd5.de
  - **midnight**: alum k*
    - **after**: rhus-t k*
      - **1** h: caul ferr
      - **3** h: asc-t carb-v h2
      - **4** h: ferr
      - **5** h: ferr-i petr k* sulph
  - **stool**; before: **Sulph** k*
- **accompanied** by | **vomiting** (See STOMACH - Vomiting - accompanied - abdomen)
- **anxiety**; with: borx h2*
- **bed** agg.; in: bry k* glon k* grat k* thiam rly4• vanil fd5.de
- **breakfast**:
  - **after**:
    - **agg.**: all-c k* cycl k* grat k* sulph k* thuj k* tritic-vg fd5.de
    - **amel.**: mag-m h2
  - **during**: kali-s fd4.de nat-m k* plan k*
- **colic**; after: ars h2
- **colitis** begins; for several days before: puls sys
- **cries** of an animal; like: thuj b4a.de
- **croaking** like frogs: (↗*STOMACH - Croaking*) arg-met h1* caust h1* coloc a1* epig br1 graph h2* hell a1 lyc ptk1 nux-v h1* sabad c1* spig h1*
- **diarrhea**:
  - **after** | **agg.**: cain nat-c
  - **before**: *Aloe* bro1 ang c1 ant-t ars h2 asaf bro1 bry carb-v bro1 *Colch* bro1 coloc bro1 *Crot-t* cycl gamb bg1* hell-o a1* iris kali-c bro1 kali-n mag-m mag-s nat-m *Nat-s* bro1 olnd bro1 podo k2* puls bro1 *Sulph*
  - **during**: ars h2 crot-t glon hyos iris kali-c podo k2

- **diarrhea** would come on; as if: agath-a nl2• allox tpw3 apis *Cham* cob colch *Dulc* ferr graph **Hydr** kali-bi kali-c h2 mag-s myric naja nat-ar phos ptel sars h2 sinus rly4• stann h2 *Stry*
- **dinner** | **after** | **agg.**: alum ant-c borx coloc grat naja nat-m ox-ac staph *Sulph* ter
  - **before**: kali-c h2
- **drinking** agg.; after: cham graph kali-p bg1 merc rhod
- **eating**:
  - **after** | **agg.**: abies-c k* acon k* aloe k2 alum k* ant-t k* *Arg-n* hr1 *Ars* hr1 bry k* calc h2 *Carb-v* k* caust k* *Chin* k* coc-c k* *Cycl* k* dulc a1 falco-pe nl2• graph b4a.de grat k* ign k* meny k* mez k* mur-ac k* naja nat-m k* nat-s k* nit-ac k* ox-ac hr1 phos k* pitu-a vml2• plan k* *Puls* k* rhod k* ruta fd4.de sars k* sep b4a.de* stann k* *Sulph* k* ter hr1 tung-met bdx1• zinc b4a.de
  - **amel.**: graph k* mag-c h2 mosch k* sanic tl1 squil h1 sul-ac k* sulph tl1 [tax jsj7]
  - **before** | **agg.**: mag-m k* sel k*
  - **while** | **agg.**: calc ferr-ma k* graph ruta fd4.de
- **empty** feeling; with: *Mur-ac* hr1 sars pd
- **eructations** | **amel.**: borx h2 sars h2 taosc iwa1•
- **expiration** agg.; during: calc h2
- **fasting** agg.: tax k*
- **flatus**; passing | **amel.**: acon adam skp7• ant-t ars borx h2 bov **Carb-v** caust coc-c hell *Iris* **Lyc** nat-c h2 **Nat-s** ol-an tritic-vg fd5.de
- **food** enters cardia; when: stann h2
- **frogs** croaking (See croaking)
- **inspiration** agg.: calc h2 mag-c h2 mag-m k* manc k* tab k*
- **loud**: aloe k2 ant-c tl1 aur tl1 *Lyc* tl1* nat-s mrr1 ruta fd4.de tritic-vg fd5.de
- **lying**:
  - **abdomen**; on | **amel.**: am-c
  - **agg.**: cann-i choc srj3• coloc ph-ac plan sep stann
  - **side**; on | **left** | **agg.**: coloc pd glon
    - **right** | **agg.**: coc-c
- **menses**:
  - **after** | **agg.**: am-c b4.de
  - **before** | **agg.**: aloe bell bry calc-p k* ferr kali-c lac-c lyc *Ph-ac* hr1 staph h1 tarent k* *Zinc*
  - **during** | **agg.**: aloe kali-c k* kali-p bg1 *Kreos* k* lyc puls sep k*
- **milk** agg.: ang h1 carb-an h2 pitu-a vml2• trios rsj11•
- **motion** agg.: lyc k* mag-c h2 *Manc* k* phos hr1 sil h2 urol-h rwt•
- **painful**: allox sp1 bit-ar wht1• cardios-h rly4• phos h2 polyg-h bro1
- **pressure** agg.: agar k*
- **rising** agg.: *Bry* crot-t ferr
- **sitting** agg.: canth k* caust k* mur-ac k*
- **sleep** agg.; during: *Agn* k* cupr k* lyc b4.de puls h1
- **standing** agg.: bism h1
- **stool**:
  - **after** | **agg.**: agar k* chel hr1 coloc k* *Crot-t* k* dulc k* ferr-ma k* **Jatr-c** kali-bi k* *Lyc* k* mag-m h2 mez k* nat-c k* nat-m k* ox-ac petr pd plb k* ptel k* sul-ac sulph k* thuj
  - **amel.**: bell-p sp1
  - **before**: aloe bg2 ant-t bg2* ars k* ars-s-f k2 *Asc-t* k* brom k* bry bg2 cact k* carbn-s card-m k* *Castm* k* chel hr1 colch k* *Crot-t* hr1 cycl bg2 dulc k* ferr bg2* ferr-i k* form *Gamb* bg1* glycyr-g cte1• gnaph k* grat k* hell k* hell-o a1* indg k* *Iris Jatr-c* kali-ar kali-c k* kali-m k2 kali-n h2* kali-s kola stb3• **Mag-c** k* mag-m k* merc k* *Mur-ac* k* *Nat-c* hr1 *Nat-m* k* *Nat-s* k* nux-v ol-an bg2 olnd k* ox-ac k* ph-ac bg2 *Phos* k* ptel a1 puls bg2 rat k* rhod k* sabad k* spig k* spong k* stront-c k* sulfonam ks2 *Sulph* bg2* tax k* vanil fd5.de zinc bg2
  - **during** | **agg.**: aq-mar skp7• arn k* ars b4.de* borx b4a.de* calc b4.de* carb-v b4.de* chel coloc ptk1 crot-t bg2 cycl k* elaps form k* gamb k* glon bg2 hep k* hyos bg2 *Iris* kali-bi k* kali-c bg2 lyc b4.de* *Merc* b4a.de merc-c bg2 mez k* olnd b7.de* ph-ac b4.de* phos b4.de* plb bg2 ptel k* rat k* sars b4.de* seneg k* stroph-h ptk1 sul-ac k* thuj k*
- **stretching** agg.: stann k*
- **supper** agg.; after: *Aloe* ham fd3.de• ol-an k* phos k*
- **swallowing** agg.; after: am-c k*
- **urination** agg.; during: verat b7.de*
- **waking**; on: ferr k*

Rumbling: ...
- **walking**:
  - **agg.**: *Lyc*
  - **air** agg.; in open: am-c gamb jab kr1* *Lyc* ptel
- **yawning** agg.: croc k*
- **yeast**; as if full of: stict c1

○ - **Hypochondria**:
  - **right**: asc-t c1 cycl a1
  - **left**: podo fd3.de• verb c1
- **Hypogastrium**: aesc aloe ang h1 ant-c h2* *Bism* h1 carb-v h2 card-m carl k* chin h1 coloc k* con h2 iris mur-ac h2 olib-sac wmh1 rhus-t h1 ruta fd4.de spig h1 squil h1 stann h2 staph h1 sulph h2 tax k*
  - **morning**: ambr k*
  - **night**: com k*
    - **4 h**: iris
  - **coryza**; during: phos b4.de*
  - **eating**; after: *Cycl* h1*
  - **flatus** agg.; after passing: cycl h1*
  - **stool** agg.; after: (non:cycl h1)
- **Ileocecal** region: ketogl-ac rly4• plb
  - **right**: nat-s tl1
- **Iliac** fossa | **right**: eberth jl2
- **Inguinal** region: phos h2
- **Intestines**: cob ptm1• gard-j vlr2•
- **Lower** abdomen: zinc bg2
- **Sides**:
  - **right**: bapt bg2 bism h1 *Nat-s* bg2 podo br zinc h2
  - **left**: arg-met gsy1 bell h1 cench k2 con h2 euph h2 lyc h2 ph-ac h2 sep h2 sulph h2 tarax h1 thuj h1 zinc h2
    - **Upper**: staph h1
- **Spleen**: verb b7a.de*
- **Umbilicus**:

○ - **Below**: mag-c h2 phos h2 symph fd3.de•
  - **Region** of umbilicus: anac bg2 olnd bg2 sul-ac h2 sulph bg2 symph fd3.de• tarax bg2*
    - **vertigo**; during: ptel hr1

RUNNING agg.: | **Hypochondria**: spig bg2

SCAPHOID abdomen (See Retraction)

SEASONS: | **summer** agg.: guaj ptk1

SENSIBILITY (See Sensitive)

SENSITIVE: *Acon* b7.de* **Apis** b7a.de *Arn* b7.de *Bell* b4a.de bism b7.de bov b4a.de *Bry* b7.de *Canth* b7.de* cham b7.de* cic b7.de *Coff* b7.de* *Coloc* b4a.de cupr b7a.de cycl b7.de* *Dulc* b4.de hep b4a.de hyos b7a.de *Lach* b7a.de *M-arct* b7.de* merc b4a.de *Merc-c* b4a.de mosch b7.de *Nux-v* b7a.de olnd b7.de **Puls** b7.de* *Ran-b* b7.de* sars b4.de sec b7.de squil b7.de *Stann* b4a.de *Stram* b7.de* valer b7.de verat b7.de*
- **menses**; before: mang b4.de
- **pressure**; to: verat mtf33

○ - **Hypochondria**: **Bell** bg2 **Chin** bg2 cupr b7a.de *Hyos* bg2 kali-c bg2 *Merc* bg2 nat-c bg2 nat-s bg2 nit-ac bg2 puls bg2 ran-b b7.de* sel b7.de* sulph bg2 verat b7.de*
  - **right**: brucel sa3•
- **Liver**: acon bg2 aeth bg2 agar bg2 ambr bg2 ant-c bg2 ant-t bg2 bapt bg2 bell bg2 berb bg2 bry bg2 carb-v bg2 card-m bg2 *Coli* jl2 dig bg2 ferr-pic br1 graph bg2 hep bg2 hydr bg2 lach bg2 lyc bg2 mag-m bg2 *Merc* bg2 myric bg2 nat-s bg2 **Nux-v** b7a.de* phos bg2 podo bg2 *Puls* b7a.de sel bg2 sulph bg2 tab bg2 tarax bg2
- **Skin**: acet-ac bro1 *Acon* b7.de* aeth c1* aloe bg2* *Apis* b7a.de* *Arg-n* bro1 *Arn* bro1 ars bro1 bapt bro1 bar-c k* bell k* bov k* bry bg2* cain c1 calc bro1 camph bg2 cann-s b7.de canth k* *Carb-v* bro1 card-m bro1 chin bro1 coff k* coloc bro1 con bro1 conv br1 crot-c crot-h bg2 cupr bro1 euon bro1 ferr bro1* gamb bro1 *Graph* bro1 *Ham* bro1 hed bro1 hell bro1 *Hyos* b7.de* kali-bi bg2* kali-n c1 kola stb3• lac-c k2 lach k2* **Lyc** k* m-arct b7.de mag-p bg2 mang bg2 *Merc-c* bro1 mur-ac bro1 nux-v b7.de* pert-vc vk9 plb b7a.de podo bro1 **Puls** b7.de* pyrog jl2 *Ran-b* bro1 ran-s b7.de* *Rhus-t* b7a.de* sars k* *Sep* bro1 sil bro1 stann b4a.de* sulph bro1 *Sumb* bro1 *Ter* bro1 thuj b4a.de *Verat* bro1 vib bro1
  - **coldness**; to: *Aeth* tl1 kreos tl1

Abdomen

- **Skin**: ...
  - ○ • **Hypogastrium**: mang h2
  - • **Iliac** region | **right**: **Bapt** hr1
  - • **Inguinal** region: graph bg2 kali-c h2
  - • **Umbilicus**:
    - ⁝ **Region** of umbilicus: plb bg2
    - ⁝ **Under**: coloc tl1
- **Spleen**: eberth jl2 nat-m bg2

SHAKING: am-c b4a.de* cann-s b7a.de* **Crot-t** mang k* merc k* nux-v bg2 rhus-t b7.de* sil k* staph
- **morning**: mez
- **cough** agg.: *Carb-an* k* hyos hr1 kali-c h2 lact k* *Sil* k* (non:squil h1)
- **walking** agg.: mang h2* merc mez nux-v k* rhus-t k*

SHIVERING: (↗*Coldness*)
- **during** | **agg.**: chin b7.de* ign b7.de* ip b7a.de*
- ○ - **Epigastrium**: *Bell* bg2 caust bg2
- **Hypochondria**: puls bg2
- **Intestines**: arg-n ptk1

SHOCKS: (↗*Pain - electric; Tingling; Tingling - internal)* *Agar* ptk1 ant-t a1 arg-n arn h1 aur h2 bell k* bry ptk1 calc camph caust cic mrr1 clem h2 cur a1 kali-c k* nat-m nux-v ptk1 pert-vc vk9 pip-n plat h2 plut-n srj7• pot-e rly4• puls squil tab k* thal
- **left**:
  - ▽ • **extending** to | **right**: stann h2
- **cough** agg.; during: *Calc* b4a.de
- **electric** shocks:
  - • **passing** through; like an electric shock: coloc bg1
  - ▽ • **extending** to:
    - ⁝ **Fingers**: caust
    - ⁝ **Limb**: camph
- **fetus**, as from: con h2
- **lying** on side agg.: camph
- **motion** agg.: pip-n
- **paralysis** of lower limbs; with: thal
- **pressing** on right side agg.: stann h2
- **tingling**: mag-m petr
- ○ - **External** abdomen: con b4.de* dros b7.de* plat b4.de*
- **Flank** (See sides - flank)
- **Hypogastrium**: am h1 cann-s k*
  - • **cough** agg.; during: *Calc* b4a.de carb-an b4a.de *Kreos* b7a.de nat-m k* *Puls* b7a.de squil k*
- **Inguinal** region: aur b4.de* cann-s b7.de* plat b4a.de stann b4a.de
- **Pelvis**: loxo-recl knl4•
  - ▽ • **extending** to | **Upward**: loxo-recl knl4•
- **Pubic** region: pot-e rly4•
- **Sides**:
  - ○ • **Flank** | **left**: stann
- **Umbilicus**, at left from: anac h2
- **Wall**; abdominal: calc-p tl1

SHORT; as if too:
- ○ - **Intestines**: anac b4a.de
- **Liver**: carb-v bg2
- **Muscles**: *Rhus-t* b7a.de sulph b4a.de*
  - ○ • **Inguinal** region: zinc h2

SHORTENING of intestines; sensation of: anac h2*

SHRIVELLED or wilted appearance: *Borx*

SHUDDERING in: cann-s k* *Coloc* k* tritic-vg fd5.de
- **accompanied** by | **constipation** (See RECTUM - Constipation - accompanied - abdomen - shuddering)
- ▽ - **extending** to | **Body**: *Coloc*

SICK feeling in: abies-c bg2 apis bg2 arg-n bg2 asaf bg2 cic bg2 ferr bg2 graph bg2 phyt bg2 podo bg2 ruta bg2 sul-ac bg2

SINGING:
- **agg.**: puls bg2*
- **amel.** | **Hypochondria**: sep b4.de*

SINKING sensation: (↗*Hanging; Hanging - intestines*) *Alst-s* br1 phos k2
- **accompanied** by | **weakness**: *Alst-s* br1
- **stool** | **after** | **agg.**: **Podo** mrr1
  - • **before**: graph bg2
- ○ - **Epigastrium**; in: plut-n srj7•

SITTING:
- **agg.**: alum b4.de* am-c bg2 am-m b7a.de ambr b7.de* anac b4.de* ang b7.de* ant-t b7.de* arg-met b7.de* asaf b7.de* aur b4.de* calc b4.de* canth b7.de* carb-v b4.de* caust b4.de* *Chin* b7.de* cina b7.de* cocc b7.de* coloc b4.de* con b4.de* crot-t bg2 dig b4.de* dros b7.de* dulc b4.de* grat bg2 hell b7.de* kali-c b4.de* meny b7.de* mur-ac bg2 nat-c b4.de* nat-m b4.de* op b7.de* par b7.de* petr b4.de* ph-ac b4.de* phos b4.de* *Puls* b7.de* **Rhus-t** b7.de* ruta b7.de* sabad b7.de* samb b7.de* sars b4.de* seneg b4.de* sep b4.de* *Spong* b7.de* stront-c b4.de* sulph b4.de* thuj b4.de* valer b7.de* viol-t b7.de*
  - ○ • **Hypochondria**: agar b4.de* am-c b4a.de* calc b4.de* dulc b4.de* mag-c b4.de* meny b7.de* nat-c b4.de* nat-m b4.de* phos b4.de* puls b7a.de rhus-t b7.de* ruta bg2 sabad b7.de* spong b7.de* sul-ac b4.de*
  - • **Liver**: am-c bg2 ruta bg2
  - • **Umbilicus** | **Region** of umbilicus: symph ptk1
- **amel.**: alum b4.de* apis b7a.de* ars bg2 bell b4.de* borx b4a.de bry b7.de* coff b7.de* ign b7.de* m-arct b7.de m-aust b7.de mur-ac bg2 nux-v b7.de*
  - ○ • **Hypochondria**: mag-m b4.de* sul-ac b4.de*
- **bent** forward:
  - • **agg.**: acon b7.de* alum b4.de* ant-t b7.de* *Ars* b4a.de carb-v bg2 dig b4.de* plb b7.de* sabin b7.de* *Sulph* b4a.de
    - ⁝ **Hypochondria**: caust b4.de* rhus-t b7.de* stann b4.de* viol-t b7.de*
  - • **amel.**: aloe bg2 ars b4a.de bell b4.de* borx b4a.de bry b7.de* calad b7.de* carb-v b4a.de cham b7.de* chel b7a.de* chin b7.de* coloc b4.de* *Kali-c* b4a.de kreos b7a.de lyc bg2 *Merc* b4.de* mez b4a.de mosch b7a.de nux-m b7.de* nux-v b7.de* op b7.de* puls b7.de* rheum b7.de* *Rhus-t* b7.de* sabad b7a.de sars b4.de* spong b7.de* staph b7.de* sulph b4a.de*
    - ⁝ **Hypochondria**: nux-m b7.de* spig b7.de*
- **erect**:
  - • **agg.**: kali-c b4a.de
  - • **amel.**: apis b7a.de *Ars* b4a.de sabin b7.de* *Sulph* b4a.de
- **up**:
  - • **amel.** | **Hypochondria**: *Am-m* b7a.de

SITTING DOWN agg.: ruta b7.de*
- ○ - **Hypochondria**: valer b7a.de

SITTING UP in bed agg.: ferr bg2

SLEEP:
- **after**:
  - • **agg.**: ambr b7.de* bry b7.de* ferr bg2 ter bg2
    - ⁝ **Hypochondria**: borx b4a.de
  - • **amel.**: alum b4a.de phos bg2
- **before** | **agg.**: petr bg2 ph-ac bg2 phos bg2
- **during**:
  - • **agg.**: agn bg2 cupr bg2 kali-n bg2 nux-m bg2
  - • **amel.**: am-m b7a.de* mag-m bg2
- **falling** asleep:
  - • **when** | **agg.**: tab bg2

SMALL liver; sensation of: abies-c br1

SMOKING: | **amel.**: coloc b4.de*

SNEEZING agg.: acon bg2 apis b7a.de* bell b4a.de* borx b4a.de canth b7.de* cham bg2 *Nux-v* b7a.de* puls ptk1
- ○ - **Hypochondria**: sil b4a.de
- **Liver**: psor ptk1

SOFT: borx mtf33

SOUP agg.: kali-c b4.de* laur b7.de* mag-c bg2 sep bg2

SOUR food agg.: carb-v bg2 dros b7a.de* kreos b7a.de ph-ac bg2 *Staph* bg2

SPASMS (See Contraction)

SPLENOMEGALY (See Enlarged - spleen)

SPOILED FOOD agg.: ars ptk1

SPONGE; sensation of:
○ - **Hypochondria** | **alternating** sides: lac-c

SPOTS (See Discoloration)

SPRING were unrolled in left hypochondrium; sensation as if a: sol-t-ae k*

SQUEAKING in abdomen: kali-i ptk1

STANDING:
- **agg.**: arn b7.de* asaf b7.de* bell b4.de* bry b7.de* camph b7.de* canth b7.de* dig b4.de* ign b7.de* mur-ac bg2 nat-p ptk1 plb b7.de* rheum b7.de* sulph bg2 thuj b4.de* valer b7.de*
○ • **Hypochondria**: aloe bg2 arn b7.de* chin b7.de* ran-b b7.de* rhod b4.de* sul-ac b4.de* valer b7.de* zinc b4.de*
- **amel.**: ars bg2 chin b7.de* cocc b7.de* ruta b7.de* tarax b7.de* thuj b4.de*
- **bent** | **amel.**: spong b7.de*

STASIS of the portal venous system: (↗*Portal)* aesc br1* bell b4a.de* bry b7a.de* caust b4a.de dig b4a.de* lept br1 nux-v b7a.de* oxyd br1 puls b7a.de* sep br1 sulph b4a.de*
- **accompanied** by | **constipation**: aesc br1

STEAM agg.; exposure to: kali-bi bg2

STEPPING HARD agg.: aloe bg2 am-c b4a.de* arn b7.de* bry b7.de* chin b7.de* cocc b7.de* *Con* b4a.de graph b4.de* nux-v b7.de* rhus-t b7.de* thuj bg2 zinc bg2

STIFFNESS: lat-m bnm6• lil-t bg1* rhus-t bg1* sep bg2 [pop dhh1]
- **painful**: lach mtf33 lat-m bnm6•
○ - **Inguinal** region: aur b4.de*
- **Liver** | **sensation** of: nat-m b4.de* phys bg2
- **Sides**: *Nat-m* bg2
  • **left**: ger-i rly4• nat-m b4.de*
  • **sensation** as is sides of body are stiff: sep h2

STONE in abdomen; sensation of a: (↗*Heaviness - stone; Pain - cutting - stones)* aloe ant-t k* aran a1* ars-h hr1* *Calc* ptk1 chim-m hr1 *Cocc* k* coloc ptk1 cypra-eg sde6.de• hydr ptk1 lac-d hr1* nux-m ptk1 osm ptk1 **Puls** k* scop ptk1 sep ptk1
- **chill**; during: aran ptk1
- **full** of stones; seems: *Ant-t* k* **Calc** k* *Cocc*
  • **sitting** | **bent** forward | **agg.**: ant-t c1
    ⋮ **long** time agg.; for a: ant-t
- **lying** on abdomen agg.: aloe k*
○ - **Hypogastrium**; region of cocc rb2*
- **Liver**; in the: **Nux-m** a1
- **Spleen**: borx b4a.de
- **Umbilicus**:
○ • **About**: *Cocc* k* verb c1*
  • **Below**: nux-v rb2

STONES; pressure of: | **Gallbladder**; in (See Gallstones)

STOOL:
- **after**:
  • **agg.**: agar b4.de alum b4.de am-m b7.de ambr b7.de* anac b4.de arg-met b7.de* ars b4.de bov b4a.de *Canth* b7.de* carb-v b4.de caust b4.de chin b7.de con b4.de dros b7.de dulc b4.de iod b4.de kali-c b4.de lyc b4.de m-ambo b7.de mag-m b4.de mez b4.de mur-ac b4.de nat-c b4.de nat-m b4.de *Nux-v* b7.de op b7.de petr ptk1 *Phos* b4.de* *Plat* b4a.de plb b7.de podo ptk1 puls b7.de *Rheum* b7.de* sep b4.de spig b7.de stann b4.de staph b7.de* sul-ac ptk1 sulph b4.de verat b7.de* zinc b4.de
    ⋮ **Hypochondria**: caust bg2 plat bg2
  • **amel.**: am-m b7.de asaf b7.de bov b4.de bry b7.de canth b7.de cina b7.de colch b7.de gamb bg2 nat-c b4.de nux-v bg2 rheum b7.de rhus-t b7.de senec bg2 seneg b4.de spig b7.de sulph b4.de verat bg2
    ⋮ **Hypochondria**: ferr bg2 zinc bg2
- **amel.**: colch ptk1 *Coloc* ptk1 *Gamb* ptk1 mag-c ptk1 **Nux-v** ptk1 stann ptk1 verat ptk1

Stool – amel.: ...
○ • **Umbilicus** | **Region** of umbilicus: senec ptk1
- **before** | **agg.**: agar b4.de alum b4.de am-c b4.de *Am-m* b7.de* ang b7.de *Ant-t* b7.de arn b7.de *Ars* b4.de *Asar* b7.de* *Bar-c* b4.de* *Bry* b7.de* camph b7.de cann-s b7.de *Canth* b7.de caps b7.de carb-an b4.de carb-v b4.de caust b4.de chel b7.de *Chin* b7.de cina b7.de colch b7.de con b4.de croc b7.de cupr b7.de cycl b7.de dig b4a.de dros b7.de *Dulc* b4.de* ferr b7.de graph b4.de hell b7.de* *Ign* b7.de kali-c b4.de lach b7.de laur b7.de lyc b4.de* m-arct b7a.de *M-aust* b7.de* mag-c b4.de mang b4.de meny b7.de *Merc* b4.de mez b4.de nat-c b4.de nat-m b4.de nit-ac b4.de nux-v b7.de op b7.de *Petr* b4.de ph-ac b4.de phos b4.de *Puls* b7.de* *Rheum* b7.de rhus-t b7.de* ruta b7.de sabad b7.de sars b4.de sep b4.de sil b4.de spig b7.de stann b4.de staph b7.de* stram b7.de stront-c b4.de sulph b4.de valer b7.de *Verat* b7.de* viol-t b7.de* zinc b4.de
- **during**:
  • **agg.**: *Agar* b4.de* agn b7.de am-c b4.de am-m b7.de* ambr b7.de anac b4.de* *Ang* b7a.de *Ant-c* b7.de* ant-t b7a.de arg-met b7.de arn b7.de *Ars* b4.de* *Asaf* b7.de asar b7.de aur b4.de* bar-c bg2 *Bell* b4a.de bism bg2 *Bov* b4.de* *Bry* b7.de* *Calad* b7.de camph b7.de *Cann-s* b7a.de *Canth* b7.de caps b7.de* carb-an b4.de *Cham* b7.de chin b7.de *Coloc* b4a.de *Con* b4a.de cupr b7.de cycl b7.de dros b7.de *Dulc* b4.de* *Euph* b4.de* ferr b7.de* graph b4.de guaj b4a.de hell b7.de* *Ip* b7.de* kali-c b4.de* *Kali-n* b4a.de lach b7a.de laur b7.de lyc b4.de m-aust b7a.de *Mag-c* b4a.de mag-m b4.de meny b7.de *Merc* b4a.de *Mez* b4.de* mosch b7a.de mur-ac b4.de nat-m b4.de* nit-ac b4.de nux-m b7.de *Nux-v* b7.de olnd b7a.de par b7.de petr b4.de* ph-ac b4.de phos b4.de* plat b4.de plb b7.de *Puls* b7.de ran-b b7.de *Rheum* b7.de *Rhus-t* b7.de* sars b4.de sel b7a.de sep b4.de* sil b4.de spig b7.de* spong b7.de staph b7.de* stram b7a.de *Stront-c* b4.de* *Sulph* b4.de* *Verat* b7.de* verb bg2 viol-t bg2 zinc b4.de
    ⋮ **Hypochondria**: anac b4.de*
    ⋮ **Umbilicus** | **Region** of umbilicus: lept ptk1
- **hard** stool | **amel.**: ust ptk1
- **straining** at | **agg.**: aloe bg2
- **urging** for stool; after ineffectual | **agg.**: ambr b7.de* bism b7a.de nux-v b7.de* staph b7a.de verb b7a.de *Viol-t* b7a.de

STOOPING:
- **after**:
  • **agg.** | **Hypochondria**: alum b4.de*
- **agg.**: am-m b7.de* ant-t b7.de* *Apis* b7a.de arn b7.de* *Ars* b4a.de borx b4a.de bov b4.de* caps b7.de* clem bg2 *Cocc* b7.de* coloc b4.de* dros b7.de* ferr bg2 kali-bi bg2 kali-c b4a.de* lyc bg2 mang b4.de* nat-c bg2 nat-m b4.de* nux-v b7.de* plb b7.de* rhod bg2 sep b4.de* spong b7.de* stann b4.de* staph b7.de* *Sulph* b4a.de *Verb* b7.de*
○ • **Diaphragm**: lyc bg2 nat-c bg2
  • **Hypochondria**: alum b4.de* clem b4.de* *Cocc* b7.de* kali-bi bg2 *Kali-c* b4.de* lyc b4a.de* mur-ac b4.de* nat-c b4a.de rhod b4.de* rhus-t b7.de* stront-c b4.de*
  • **Liver**: alum bg2 clem bg2 cocc bg2 lyc bg2
  • **Spleen**: rhod bg2
- **amel.**: ant-t bg2 *Bell* b4a.de ign b7.de* iris bg2 kreos bg2 puls b7.de* rhus-t b7.de* verb b7a.de
○ • **Hypochondria**: chin b7.de* tab bg2

STOPPAGE of spleen: nat-c h2

STOPPED sensation: *Agath-a* nl2• bism bry cham chel *Chin* guaj melal-alt gya4 meny nat-c *Nux-m* **Op** phos puls rhus-t sep spig spong verb

STRETCHING:
- **agg.**: apis b7a.de ars bg2 ran-b b7.de* rhus-t b7.de* stann bg2
- **amel.**: ant-t b7a.de* dios bg2 indg bg2 mez b4.de*
- **limbs** | **agg.**: ars bg2

STRICTURE of intestines: con h2*

STROKING: (↗*Rubbing - agg.)*
- **amel.**: sec bg2

SUGAR agg.: *Arg-n* ptk1 ign ptk1 merc-c b4a.de ox-ac ptk1 **Sulph** ptk1

SUNKEN (See Retraction)

SUPPER agg.; after: aloe bg2 alum bg2 arg-n bg2 arn bg2 borx bg2 chin bg2 coff bg2 colch bg2 coloc bg2 gels bg2 kali-c bg2 kali-n bg2 phos bg2 sep bg2 stront-c bg2

SUPPURATION: acon bg2 bell bg2 camph bg2 cann-xyz bg2 **Canth** bg2 hep bg2 lach bg2 merc bg2 nit-ac bg2 puls bg2 squil bg2 sulph bg2 thuj bg2
○ - **Glands**; inguinal: ars aur k* bar-m bufo *Carb-an* chel crot-h **Hep** k* **Iod** *Kali-i* **Lach** **Merc** k* *Nit-ac* k* phos k* *Sil* k* sul-i k2 sulph k* thuj
- **Liver**: bell bg2 bry bg2 lach bg2 nux-v bg2 puls bg2 ruta bg2 sep bg2 sil bg2
- **Umbilicus** | **Region** of umbilicus: phos ptk1

SWALLOWING agg.: am-c bg2

SWASHING: acon k* *Aloe* arn kr1 bar-c h2* cann-xyz bg2 **Crot-t** k* dulc bg2 hell bg2 kali-c k* mang bg2 merc mez nat-c bg2 *Nat-m* k* nux-v b7.de* **Ph-ac** k* rhus-t bg3 sul-ac bg1 tub al
- **bending** forward and backward: ph-ac h2
- **sensation** of: nux-v bg2 rheum bg2 rhus-t ptk1
- **touch** agg.: ph-ac h2
- **walking** agg.: mang h2

SWEETS agg.: ign b7a.de* sulph bg2 zinc ptk1

SWELLING: (↗*Enlarged)*
○ - **Abdomen**, of (See Distension)
- **External** abdomen: *Puls* b7a.de *Rhus-t* b7a.de
- **Gallbladder**: ser-a-c jl2
- **Hips**:
  - **sensation** of swelling:
    - **Left**; above: chel h1
    - **Right**; above: phos h2
- **Hypochondria**: acon b7a.de bry b7a.de
  - **left**: pneu jl2
  - **painful**: merc bg2
- **Inguinal** and pubic region: am-c b4.de am-m bg2 ars b4.de* gran bg2 *Sil* b4.de* thuj b4.de*
- **Inguinal** region: am-c am-m h2 ant-c *Apis* ars aur-ar k2 *Clem* con k* gran *Graph* hep c1 jac-c kali-c loxo-recl bnm10• *Lyc* psor al2 *Puls* rhus-t sil symph fd3.de• *Ther* thuj [spect dfg1]
  - **right**: *Apis* ars **Clem** con lyss pall c1
  - **left**: am-c sil
  - **afternoon** | **14** h: lyss
  - **evening** | **20** h: phys
  - **elastic**: am-c k*
  - **hard**: clem dulc puls
  - **painful**: clem puls
○ • **Glands**, of: (↗*Bubo)* alum k* am-c anan ant-c k* *Apis* k* ars k* *Asaf* b7a.de *Aur* k* aur-m k2 aur-s k2 bac bro1* **Bad** k* bapt *Bar-c* k* *Bar-m* k* *Bell* k* brom *Bufo* k* **Calc** k* calc-ar *Calc-p* *Carb-an* k* carb-v caust *Chel* *Chin* b7a.de cinnb mrr1 **Clem** k* cocc *Con* b4a.de cop crot-h *Cupr* **Dulc** k* elaps eupi *Ferr* gels *Graph* k* **Hep** k* *Hippoz* *Iod* k* *Kali-c* *Kali-i* k* lac-c **Lach** k* lat-m bnm6• lyc k* *Lyss* med k2 **Merc** k* **Merc-c** k* *Merc-i-f* k* *Merc-i-r* k* nat-ar *Nat-c* k* nat-m **Nit-ac** k* nux-v b7.de* oci br1* ozone sde2• pall bro1 ph-ac k* phos k* *Phyt* pin-s bro1 *Puls* k* *Rhus-t* k* sal-al blc1• sep *Sil* k* sin-n spong k* stann k* *Staph* k* stram k* sul-i k2 **Sulph** k* sumb *Syph* k* tarent tarent-c bg2 tep *Thuj* k* *Tub* k* xero bro1 zinc k*
    - **chronic**: syph jl2
    - **hard**: merc-i-f br1
    - **large**: merc-i-f br1 tub ptk1
- **Liver**: (↗*Enlarged - liver)* absin vh1 acon k* *Aesc* agar bg2 aloe bg2 am-c bg2 ant-c bg2 ant-t anth vh apoc bg2 arg-n bg2 arn b7a.de *Ars* k* asar bg2 aur k* bapt bg2 *Bar-m* k* *Bell* k* bry k* bufo cact bg2 calc k* cann-s k* caps bg2 carb-v bg2 *Card-m* k* cean bg2 *Chel* k* **Chin** k* chinin-s k* chion bg2 cocc tl1* *Coli* jl2 coloc bg2 *Con* k* crot-t bg2 cupr k* cur cycl bg2 dig bg2 dol br1 eup-per bg2 *Ferr* k* ferr-ar fl-ac bg2 graph bg2* guaj bg2 guat sp1 hep bg2 hydr bg2 *Iod* k* iris bg2 kali-c bg2 kali-i bg2 *Lach* k* lact k* *Laur* k* lept bg2 lina br1 loxo-lae bnm12• **Lyc** k* *Mag-m* bg2* **Merc** k* nat-c bg2 nat-m k* **Nat-s** k* nux-m k* **Nux-v** k* parathyr jl2 *Phos* k* *Podo* bg2* *Ptel* k* *Puls* b7a.de rhus-t k2 sel bg2 *Sep* bg2* sil k* *Sulph* k* tarent zinc bg2
  - **left** lobe: *Card-m*
  - **abuse** of quinine, after: nux-v
  - **anger**; after: cocc mrr1
  - **mental** exertion; from: nat-s
- **Mesenteric**: iod bg2

Swelling – Mesenteric: ...
○ • **Glands**: aesc vh1 anthraci vh1 *Ars* *Aur* aur-ar k2 bar-c bar-m borx hr1 *Calc* k* calc-p k2 cist *Con* dros tl1 *Grat* *Hep* *Iod* k* kreos lyc merc nat-s rhus-t k2 sul-i k2 sulph toxo-g mtf11 [mang stj1]
- **Pubic** region | **Mons** pubis: rhus-t bg2
- **Sides**: tub k2
  - **left**: led bg3
  - **running**; after: tub k2
- **Spleen**: absin vh1 agn k* anan aran bg1* ars k* ars-s-f k2 *Asaf* b7a.de brom *Bry* bufo bg2 caps k* *Cean* bg2* *Cham* b7a.de **Chin** k* chinin-s cocc *Ferr* k* *Ferr-ar* grin bg1 ign k* *Iod* k* kali-i c1 lina br1 mag-m mez bg2 morb jl2 nat-m bg1 nit-ac k* *Nux-m* b7.de* nux-v parathyr jl2 phos k* plb k* *Ran-s* ruta k* sec b7a.de sul-ac bg1 *Sulph* bg2 verat hr1*
  - **chill**; during: caps b7a.de chin b7a.de
  - **heat**; during: agn bg2 *Ars* bg2 brom bg2 caps bg2 *Carb-v* k* cham bg2 ign bg2 *Nat-m* k* nit-ac bg2 sil bg2 sulph bg2
  - **painful**: ruta ptk1
  - **quinine**; after: *Aran* *Caps* hr1
- **Umbilicus**: bry k* caust k* plb k* prun ptel k* puls sang c1 sep k*
○ • **Around** | **ring**; like a: puls b7.de*
- **Upper** abdomen | **longitudinal** swelling: *Bell* b4a.de

SWOLLEN sensation: cycl b7.de* laur b7.de* led b7.de* psor bg2 rhus-t b7.de* spig b7.de*
○ - **External** abdomen: hyos bg2 nux-v b7.de puls b7.de valer bg2
- **Glands**; inguinal: aur b4.de* calc b4a.de hep b4.de* merc b4.de* merc-c b4a.de*
- **Hypochondria**: mosch b7a.de nux-v b7.de* rhus-t b7.de*
- **Inguinal** and pubic region: *Am-m* b7a.de ant-c b7.de* con b4.de* rhus-t b7.de* sil b4.de*
- **Intestines**: gard-j vlr2•
- **Liver**: bufo bg2 mag-c bg2
- **Lower** abdomen: bell bg2 hipp jl2
- **Pubic** region | **Mons** pubis: am-m bg2 ant-c bg2
- **Spleen**: gard-j vlr2• laur b7.de*

SYNCHRONOUS with pulse; complaints: hep b4a.de

SYPHILIS: | **Liver**: aur bro1 kali-i bro1 merc-i-r bro1

TABES mesenterica: abrot sne* am-c bg2 arg-met k2 *Ars* k* ars-i *Aur* aur-i k2 aur-m bac jl2 bapt c2* *Bar-c* k* *Bar-i* *Bar-m* bell bg2 **Calc** k* calc-ar bro1 calc-chln bro1 calc-hp bro1 calc-i k2* *Calc-p* k* *Calc-s* *Carb-an* *Carbn-s* k* caust k* chin bg2 cina bg2 cist k2 *Con* k* gaert fmm1• *Hep* k* *Iod* k* kali-c bg2 *Kreos* lach bg2 *Lyc* k* mang k2 merc k* *Merc-c* c2* merc-i-f nat-n br1 *Nat-s* nit-ac bg2 nux-v bg2 ol-j petr c2 phos bg2 plb-act bro1 *Plb-xyz* c2 puls bg2 pyrog c2 rhus-t bg2* sacch c2* santin br1 saroth jl1 sil bg2* sulph k* thiosin br1 *Tub* k*

TALKING agg.: anac b4.de* caust ptk1 hell ptk1 kali-c ptk1 laur ptk1 nat-c bg2 nux-v b7.de*

TENSION: acon k* *Agar* aloe alum k* alum-sil k2 am-c h2 ambr k* anac b4a.de ant-c b7.de* ant-t k* *Apis* bg1* aq-mar rbp6 arg-met *Arg-n* k* arn b7.de* *Ars* k* asaf b7.de* **Bar-c** k* *Bar-i* bar-m bar-s k2 bell k* *Bov* k* *Brucel* sa3• bry k* **Calc** k* calc-s calc-sil k2 canth k* caps k* carb-ac carb-an k* **Carb-v** k* *Carbn-s* cassia-s ccrh1• caust k* *Cham* k* chel k* chin k* *Chinin-ar* chinin-s bg2 clem k* *Cocc* **Colch** k* coloc k* com k* con b4.de* cortico tpw7* crot-h k* crot-t k* **Cupr** k* cycl b7.de* dig k* ferr k* ferr-ar ferr-p *Gamb* k* ger-i rly4• gins *Graph* k* **Hep** k* hyos k* hyper k* *Ictod* br1 ign b7.de* iod k* jatr-c jug-r k* *Kali-ar* kali-bi k* *Kali-c* k* kali-m k2 kali-n k* kali-p kreos k* *Lac-c* lach k* lact laur lil-t ptk1 **Lyc** k* m-ambo b7.de m-arct b7.de mag-c mag-m k* mag-s k* manc k* mang b4.de* medul-os-si rly4• meny k* merc k* merl k* *Mez* k* moni rfm1• mosch k* *Mur-ac* k* naja nat-ar nat-c k* *Nat-m* k* nat-p nat-s nit-ac k* nux-m b7.de* *Nux-v* k* *Op* k* orot-ac rly4• par k* petr k* ph-ac k* *Phos* k* plac-s rly4• *Plat* k* *Plb* k* plut-n srj7• positr nl2• ptel k* puls k* rauw sp1 *Rheum* k* rhod k* *Rhus-t* b7a.de* ruta fd4.de sabin samb k* scop ptk1 sec k* **Sep** k* **Sil** k* spong k* squil k* stann b4.de* *Staph* k* stram k* stront-c k* sul-ac k* **Sulph** k* tep k* *Ter* *Teucr* bg2 *Thuj* k* vanil fd5.de verat k* vip k* zinc k* zinc-p k2 [heroin sdj2]
- **morning**: cinnb k* sep k* *Sulph* k*
- **forenoon**: nat-m k*
- **afternoon**: bry calc k* carb-v h2 mag-c h2 petr k* ruta fd4.de stront-c sulph k*
  - **15** h until evening: mag-c

- **eating**; after: bry k*
- **evening**: arg-n k* hyos k* lac-h sk4• lyc k* mag-c k*
- **night**: chin nat-c k*
- **bending** double | **amel**.: [heroin sdj2]
- **breathing** deep agg.: *Cocc* con
- **children**; in: sil h2
- **diarrhea**, with: mag-c h2 moni rfm1•
- **dinner**; after: cycl k* nit-ac k* plat k* sulph k*
- **drinking** agg.; after: ambr k* *Cocc*
- **eating** | **after** | **agg**.: ambr k* ant-c c1 asaf k* bry k* *Carb-v* ign k* lyc k*
  - **agg**.: phos
- **emissions** agg.; after: sep k*
- **eructations** | **amel**.: nat-m h2
- **exertion** agg.: calc k*
- **fever**; during: ars bg2 bell bg2 calc bg2 carb-v bg2 colch bg2 *Ferr* b7.de* lyc bg2 merc bg2 *Nux-v* b7a.de* puls bg2 sil h2* stront-c bg2 verat bg2
- **flatulence**; during: *Carb-v* b4a.de chin b7.de* *Colch* b7a.de *Graph* b4a.de lyc b4.de* nux-m b7.de* rheum b7a.de *Rhod* b4.de* verat b7.de*
- **flatus**; passing | **amel**.: ant-t calc h2 cassia-s ccrh1• mang h2 mez
- **lamb** agg.; roasted: lyc
- **leukorrhea** agg.: am-m b7a.de
- **menses** | **before** | **agg**.: granit-m es1•
  - **during** | **agg**.: *Cocc* coloc ptk1 *Graph* k* nicc **Nux-m** k*
- **motion** agg.: clem phos
- **pressure** | **amel**.: coloc h2 [heroin sdj2]
- **reaching** high, from: alum
- **sitting**:
  - **agg**.: calc k* crot-t k* kali-c spong
  - **erect** | **agg**.: dig h2
- **stool** | **after** | **amel**.: cassia-s ccrh1• gent-c sulph
  - **during** | **agg**.: apis grat k* plat h2
- **stooping** agg.: nat-c h2 spong h1 stann h2
- **waking**; on: ferr k*
- **walking**:
  - **agg**.: arg-met nat-c h2 spong
  - **amel**.: bry k* ferr k* *Kali-c* *Lyc* k* nat-c

○ - **External** abdomen: alum b4.de* arg-met b7.de* calc b4.de* *Carb-v* bg2 caust bg2 chinin-s bg2 colch b7.de* *Coloc* b4.de* dig b4.de* ferr bg2 *Ip* b7a.de kali-bi bg2 mag-m bg2 *Merc* bg2 nux-m bg2 nux-v b7a.de petr bg2 phos bg2 plat b4.de* plb bg2 puls b7.de* rhod bg2 rhus-t b7.de* sabin b7.de* *Sil* bg2 spong bg2 squil bg2 staph b7.de sulph b4a.de* verat bg2 zinc bg2

- **Hips**; region of: asaf b7.de* zinc b4.de*
- **Hypochondria**: *Acon* k* agar h2 *Aloe* ant-c k* ant-t k* ars k* asaf b7.de* bell k* borx h2 *Bry* k* *Calc* k* *Carb-v* k* caust cham k* chin b7.de* *Chinin-s* k* cimx clem k* coc-c k* coff k* colch k* con k* dig k* eup-per k* *Ferr* b7.de* *Graph* k* hell b7.de* hyper k* ip tl1 *Lach* bg2 lact k* laur b7.de* *Lyc* k* m-ambo b7.de m-arct b7.de mang mang-m mosch k* mur-ac k* murx k* nat-ar nat-c k* *Nat-m* k* *Nat-s* k* nit-ac k* *Nux-v* k* op b7.de* puls k* sep k* staph k* stry k* *Sulph* k* verat k* vip k*
  - **right**: aloe ant-t k* bry k* calc k* *Carb-v* k* card-m chel k2* *Ferr* hyper k* lact k* *Lyc* mag-m h2 mur-ac k* nat-m k* *Nat-s* nit-ac k* sulph k*
    - **lying** on left side agg.: *Card-m* mag-m nat-s ptel
  - **left**: *Ars* k* con h2 cortico tpw7 eup-per k* lyc h2 nat-m h2 nit-ac h2 plat h2 rhod k*
  - **daytime**: cortico tpw7
  - **morning** | **bed** agg.; in: staph h1
  - **forenoon**: nat-m k*
  - **afternoon**: ars nat-m k*
    - **14** h: ars
  - **evening**: murx k*
  - **night** | **amel**.: cortico tpw7
  - **bending** backward agg.: calc h2
  - **breathing** agg.: led k*
  - **chill**; during: borx b4a.de
  - **cough** agg.; during: hell b7.de*
  - **emissions** agg.; after: agar k*
  - **excitement** agg.: cortico tpw7

- **Hypochondria**: ...
  - **flatus**; passing | **amel**.: mur-ac h2
  - **fruit** agg.: nat-c k*
  - **heat**; during: *Ars* k*
  - **lying** | **back**; on | **agg**.: *Caust*
    - **side**; on | **agg**.: ars h2
  - **motion** agg.: sep h2
  - **sitting** agg.: mur-ac k*
  - **stool** | **after** | **agg**.: plat
    - **before**: ars h2
  - **stooping** agg.: nat-c rhod k* sep h2
  - **waking**; on: *Carb-v* k*
  - **walking**:
    - **agg**.: sep h2
    - **air** agg.; in open: nat-c *Nat-s*

  ▽ - **extending** to:
    - **left** side of abdomen: con h2
    - **Back**: nat-m
    - **Upward**: mur-ac
- **Hypogastrium**: agar k* ars k* *Aur* k* *Bell* k* calc h2 caps tl1 chin cimic tl1 coc-c k* gins k* kali-c h2 merc k* nat-c h2 *Nat-m* *Op* k* phos positr nl2• **Sep** k* *Stront-c* sumb k* symph fd3.de• thuj h1
  - **morning**: *Bell* k*
  - **bending** backward agg.: calc h2
  - **coition**; after: sep h2
  - **eating**; after: phel k* symph fd3.de•
  - **inspiration** agg.; deep: sumb thuj
  - **leukorrhea**; with: am-m h2 graph bg2
  - **rising** agg.: dulc k*
  - **sitting** agg.: ruta h1
  - **standing** erect agg.: calc h2
  - **stool**; before: haem k*

  ▽ - **extending** to:
    - **Rectum**: spong h1
    - **Seminal** cord: sep h2
- **Iliac** region: arg-met chel grat k*
  - **left**: arg-met grat k*
- **Inguinal** and pubic region: am-m b7.de* arg-met b7.de* asaf b7.de* *Calc* b4a.de *Carb-an* b4a.de coloc b4.de* crot-h bg2 dig b4.de* dulc b4a.de graph b4.de* kreos b7a.de merc b4.de* merc-c b4a.de rhod b4.de* rhus-t b7.de* spig b7.de* stront-c b4.de*
- **Inguinal** region: **Agar** aids nl2• am-c am-m k* *Apis* *Arg-met* benz-ac k* berb calc canth carb-an k* *Clem* k* coc-c k* *Coloc* k* crot-t k* cycl k* dig *Dulc* gamb k* graph jatr-c kali-i k* kreos *Lac-c* mag-s k* mang h2 merc k* nat-m k* nat-s k* nit-ac *Rhus-t* a1 sars k* spig k* stront-c vanil fd5.de
  - **right**: am-m k* sars k* stront-c
  - **left**: arg-met calc lac-c merc k* merc-c k* nat-m k* vanil fd5.de
  - **morning**: coloc colocin a1
  - **afternoon**: cycl k*
    - **sleep** agg.; after: cycl k*
  - **evening**: nat-m k*
  - **night**:
    - **midnight**:
      - **after** | **5** h: merc-c
  - **ascending** stairs agg.: coloc colocin a1
  - **bending** over: coloc colocin a1
  - **drawing** up limb amel.: agar *Lac-c*
  - **motion** agg.: nat-m k*
  - **pressure** agg.: coloc k*
  - **raising** arms; on: *Apis* k*
  - **rising** from sitting agg.: dulc
  - **sitting** agg.: agar calc rhus-t h1
  - **standing** agg.: gamb lac-c

- **stool** | **amel.**: nat-m k*
- **stretching** out limb: agar k* carb-an k*
- **tendon**, as from a swollen: mang h2
- **touch** agg.: spig k*
- **walking**:
  - **agg.**: am-m *Clem* graph kreos lac-c nat-m
  - **amel.**: agar

O · **Glands**: calc b4.de* dulc b4a.de* nat-m h2 spong b7.de*
- **Liver**: aloe bg2 ars b4.de* aur-m k2 *Bry* b7.de* calc b4.de* carb-v b4.de* caust b4.de* chel ptk1 con b4.de* *Ferr* b7.de* kali-c bg2 *Lyc* b4.de* mag-m b4.de* mur-ac b4.de* nat-m b4a.de* nit-ac b4.de* *Nux-v* b7.de* *Puls* b7a.de sulph b4.de* *Verat* b7.de*
- **Lower** abdomen: ant-t b7.de* arn b7.de* aur b4.de* bell b4.de* calc b4.de* *Carb-v* b4.de* caust b4.de* chin b7a.de* dulc b4.de* kali-bi bg2 kali-c b4.de* *Lyc* b4.de* m-ambo b7.de merc b4.de* phos b4.de* ruta b7.de* stront-c b4.de* thuj b4.de*
  - **fever**; during: sil b4a.de
- **Pubic** region | **Mons** pubis: meny b7.de*
- **Sides**: acon agar *Ars* b4a.de *Aur* k* camph b7.de* caps b7.de* caust k* crot-t cycl k* *Lach* k* merc nat-c b4.de* nat-m k* nit-ac b4.de* rheum b7.de* rhus-t k* spig b7.de* sulph b4a.de tarax b7.de* zinc k*
  - **right**: con h2
  - **left** | **Lower**: phos h2 rheum h
  - **night**: kali-c h2 nit-ac h2
  - **breathing** deep agg.: con h2
  - **eructations** | **amel.**: zinc k*
- **Spleen**: *Ars* hr1 *Asaf* b7a.de camph b7.de* con b4.de* merc b4.de* nat-m b4.de* nit-ac k* rhod k* rhus-t b7.de* sulph k* zinc b4.de*
- **Umbilicus**: anac k* crot-t k* nat-m k* verat

O · **Below**: nat-c h2 plac-s rly4•
  - **Region** of umbilicus: bry bg2 cham k* crot-t k* des-ac rbp6 dulc b4.de* kali-c bg2 mang k* merc-c bg2 nat-c h2* rhus-t bg2 stront-c b4.de* **Sulph** k* thuj k* *Verat* b7.de* zinc k*
    - **midnight**: sulph k*
    - **lying** agg.: crot-t
- **Upper** abdomen: *Ars* b4.de* bell b4.de* bov b4.de* caps b7.de* cham b7.de* chel b7.de* *Chin* b7a.de colch b7.de* dros b7.de* dulc b4.de* lyc b4a.de m-ambo b7.de merc b4.de* nat-c b4.de* nux-m b7.de* ph-ac b4.de* phos b4.de* puls b7.de* ruta b7.de* sep b4.de* spong b7.de* staph b7.de* stront-c b4.de* zinc b4.de*

▽ - **extending** to:

O · **Chest**: caps h1
  - **Sacrum**: stann h2

THRUSTS (See Shocks)

TINGLING: (↗*Shocks)*

O - **Internal**: (↗*Shocks)* loxo-recl knl4• plat btw1
- **Muscles**: calc-p hr1 mag-m hr1 petr hr1

TIRED; sensation as if: bell bg2

TORPOR (See Inactivity)

TOUCH:
- **agg.**: *Acon* b7a.de* agar bg2 aloe bg2 anac b4.de* ant-t bg2 **Apis** b7a.de* arg-n bg2 *Arn* bg2 *Ars* bg2 aur bg2 bar-c b4.de* **Bell** b4.de* bism bg2 bov b4.de* *Bry* b7.de* bufo bg2 calad b7.de* canth b7.de* carb-an bg2 **Carb-v** b4a.de* caust b4a.de* *Cham* b7.de* *Chin* b7.de* cic bg2 clem bg2 *Cocc* b7.de* coff bg2 colch b7.de* *Coloc* b4.de* crot-t bg2 *Cupr* b7.de* cycl b7.de* dros bg2 *Dulc* bg2 ferr b7.de* ferr-p bg2 *Hell* bg2 *Hep* bg2 *Hyos* b7.de* ip b7.de* kali-bi bg2 kali-c b4.de* *Lach* bg2 **Lyc** b4.de* mag-m bg2 *Mag-p* bg2 **Merc** b4a.de* *Merc-c* b4a.de* mosch bg2 nat-c bg2 *Nit-ac* b4.de* **Nux-v** b7.de* olnd bg2 op bg2 *Phos* b4a.de* *Plb* b7.de* podo bg2 *Puls* b7.de* ran-b b7a.de* *Rhus-t* bg2 sabin b7.de* sars bg2 sec b7.de* *Sep* b4.de* sil bg2 spig b7.de* squil bg2 stann b4.de* staph b7.de* stram b7.de* stront-c b4.de* **Sulph** bg2 tab bg2 valer bg2 *Verat* b7.de* zinc b4.de*

O · **External** abdomen: nux-v bg2
  - **Hypochondria**: agar b4a.de* agn b7.de* arn b7.de* aur b4a.de* bar-c b4.de* bell bg2 *Bry* b7.de* calc bg2 carb-an b4.de* carb-v bg2 **Chin** b7.de* clem b4.de* *Colch* b7a.de cupr b7.de* dros b7.de* graph b4.de*

Touch – **agg.** – **Hypochondria**: ...
iod b4.de* kali-c b4.de* laur b7.de* *Lyc* b4.de* *Mag-m* b4.de* merc b4.de* nat-s bg2 *Nux-v* b7.de* op b7.de* phos b4.de* ran-b b7.de* sep b4.de* sil b4a.de stront-c b4.de* sulph b4.de* valer b7a.de* *Verat* b7.de* zinc b4.de*
  - **Liver**: *Aesc* bro1 agar bg2 *Aloe* bro1 bapt bro1 *Bell* bro1 *Berb* bro1 bry bg2* calc bro1 carb-v bg2 *Card-m* bro1 chap bro1 *Chel* bro1 chelo bro1 chin bg2* *Chion* bro1 clem bg2 *Dig* bro1 *Eup-per* bro1 fl-ac bro1 graph bro1 hydr bro1 iod bro1 *Iris* bro1 *Kali-c* bro1 *Lach* bro1 lept bro1 lyc bg2* mag-m bg2* merc bro1 *Merc-d* bro1 nat-s bro1 nux-v bg2* nyct bro1 phos bro1 *Podo* bro1 ptel bro1 *Ran-b* bro1 sanic bro1 senn bro1 *Sep* bro1 stel bro1 sulph bro1 tarax bro1 valer bg2 zinc bro1
  - **Lower** abdomen: lyc bg2 stann bg2 verat bg2
  - **Spleen**: plb bg2
  - **Umbilicus** | **Region** of umbilicus: chin bg2 dulc bg2 phos bg2 stront-c bg2 verat bg2
  - **Upper** abdomen: stann bg2
- **amel.**: calc b4.de* caust b4.de* meny b7.de*

O · **Hypochondria**: calc b4.de*

TREMBLING: ant-t k* arg-n k* both-ax tsm2 bov k* calc ptk1 calc-p bg2 caust bg2 chel k* colch k* *Con* k* *Croc* falco-pe nl2• grat guaj b4.de* *Hydr* k* iod k* kali-c *Kali-s* kali-sil k2 lil-t k* merc bg2 mosch k* **Nux-v** k* phos k* plut-n srj7• podo fd3.de• raph k* sabin ptk1 spong fd4.de staph h1 **Sul-ac** k*
- **morning**: colch k* podo fd3.de•
- **eating**; after: arg-n k*
  - **lying** on back agg.: *Sul-ac*
- **menses**; during: arg-n
- **sensation** of: agath-a nl2• falco-pe nl2•
- **stool** agg.; after: carbn-s
- **talking** of her complaints; when: falco-pe nl2•

O - **Hypochondria**: plut-n srj7•
  - **right**: sulph h2
- **Hypogastrium**: calc-p k* *Lil-t* k* plut-n srj7•
- **Iliac**: plut-n srj7•
- **Inguinal** region: agar *Chel* k* guaj k* merc k* nat-c k*
- **Internal**: calc b4a.de iod b4.de* lil-t bro1 *Nit-ac* b4a.de puls b7a.de staph b7.de*
  - **excitement**; from (See MIND - Excitement - trembling - intestines)
- **Side** | **left**: agar
- **Solar** plexus: gard-j vlr2•

TUBERCULOSIS (See Tabes)

TUMORS: *Abrot* sne *Cadm-s* sne *Calc* sne calc-ar c1 calc-i sne calc-p sne *Con* k* *Merc* sne nat-m sne staph b7.de*

O - **Sides**:
  - **right** | **sensation** as if: med c1

TURNING:
- **backwards**:
  - **agg.** | **Hypochondria**: plb b7.de*
- **bed**; in | **agg.** | **Hypochondria**: *Acon* b7.de*
  - **amel.**: euph b4.de*
- **body**:
  - **agg.**: rhus-t b7.de* stront-c b4.de*
    - **Hypochondria**: alum b4a.de borx b4a.de chin b7a.de lyc bg2 plb b7.de*
  - **amel.**: ambr bg2
- **nates** agg. | **Hypochondria**: plb bg2
- **sensation** of turning: caps k* dig b4a.de ign lact mag-c k* plb b7.de* *Sabad* k* *Sep* b4a.de*

TWITCHING and jerking: acon b7.de* **Agar** agath-a nl2• alum alumn ambr anac h2 ant-t bg2 arn b7.de* ars k* *Bry* cann-s k* caust k* chel k* con k* croc b7.de* cupr dros k* dulc fd4.de falco-pe nl2• graph k* guaj ham fd3.de• hyos kali-ar kali-c k* lyc k* m-arct b7.de manc k* merc k* murx nat-m k* nux-m b7.de* *Nux-v* op phos k* plat k* ran-s k* rheum h rhod b4.de* rhus-t k* ruta b7.de* sec br1 sep bg2 spong fd4.de stann b4.de* sul-ac verat viol-t b7.de*
- **evening** | **bed** agg.; in: agar k*
- **night**: caust k* spong fd4.de
- **flatus**; from: rhus-t b7.de*
- **pulsating**: con h2
- **stool** agg.; during: calc

○ - **External** abdomen: ambr b7.de* ang b7a.de* bry bg2 calc b4.de* caust b4.de* guaj b4a.de* *Merc* b4a.de nux-v b7.de* ran-s b7a.de* rheum b7.de* sec ptk1 sep b4.de* sul-ac b4.de* verat b7.de*
- **Hypochondria**: acon k* berb carbn-s con b4.de* croc falco-pe nl2• lact mag-c k* merc k* nat-c k* nux-v k* puls k* stann k* thuj k* valer k*
  - **right**: acon k* falco-pe nl2• mag-c k* merc k* nat-c k* sep valer k*
    - ⁝ **cough** agg.; during: lyc h2
  - **left**: thuj k*
  - **evening**: nat-c k*
- **Hypogastrium**: arn nat-c h2 phos h2 sul-ac k*
- **Iliac** region: aur h2
- **Ilium** crest: *Cina* guaj h2
- **Inguinal** and pubic region: alum b4.de* aur b4.de* calc b4.de* ign b7.de* ph-ac b4.de* psor bg2
- **Inguinal** region: abrot alum bg1 ammc k* aur bg1 calc k* cann-s clem cycl dulc fd4.de ign bg1 ph-ac k* psor k* spong fd4.de sulph k* zinc k*

○ • **Glands** of: clem h2

▽ • **extending** to:
  - ⁝ **Back**: abrot
  - ⁝ **Penis**: zinc k*
  - ⁝ **Pubis**: rhus-t h1
- **Liver**: acon b7.de* calad b7.de* croc b7a.de *Nat-c* bg2 valer b7.de*
- **Sides**: agath-a nl2• alum chin k* dulc fd4.de fl-ac k* graph k* meny h1 nat-c k* nicc k* sul-ac k*
  - **right**: dulc fd4.de falco-pe nl2• kali-c h2 sep h2
  - **left**: agath-a nl2• aur h2 caust h2 dulc fd4.de stann h2
  - **walking** agg.: sul-ac k*
- **Spleen**; region of: caust b4.de*

TYMPANITES (See Distension - tympanitic)

TYMPANITIC (See Distension - tympanitic)

TYPHLITIS (See Inflammation - cecum)

ULCERS: *Arg-n* k* **Ars** k* bar-m *Calc* calc-p k2 **Carb-v** k* carc gk6* chin k* *Coloc* cupr k* *Hep* kali-ar k2 *Kali-bi* k* lach *Lyc* merc k* **Nit-ac** k* *Phos* k* plb k* ran-b ptk1 *Sil* sulph k* **Ter**
- **spreading**: *Ars* k*

○ - **Duodenum**: acetylch-m mtf11 anac mtf11 chlorpr mtf11 *Dys* fmm1• *Graph* br1* helic-p mtf11 hist-m mtf11 ip mtf11 *Kali-bi* bro1* mand mtf11 med tl1 morg-g fmm1• morg-p fmm1• nat-ox-act mtf11 orni tl1 pin-con oss2• *Prot* jl2* symph br1* uran-n bro1*
  - **perforating**: prot jl2
  - **recurrent**: quinhydr mtf11
- **Hypochondriac**: ars bg1 nat-c bg1 phos bg1
- **Inguinal** region: am-m bg2 anan ars k2 bad bar-m *Carb-an Chel* cic bg2 *Hep* kali-c bg1 *Kali-i Lach* b7a.de lyc bg2 *Merc* k* nat-m bg1
- **Internal**: *Ars* b4a.de bell b4a.de merc b4a.de *Sulph* b4a.de
- **Intestines**: arg-n bro1 cupr bro1 kali-bi bg2* merc-c bro1 podo bg2 sul-ac bro1 sulph bro1 ter bro1 terebe ktp9 *Uran-n* bro1
  - **accompanied** by | **diarrhea**: kali-bi bro1* merc-c bro1*
  - **bleeding**: terebe ktp9
    - ⁝ **dark** blood: terebe ktp9
- **Mesenteric** glands: *Ars* b4a.de *Bell* b4a.de *Calc* b4a.de **Con** b4a.de *Iod* b4a.de *Lyc* b4a.de
- **Pancreas**: eberth jl2
- **Umbilicus**, about: *Aesc* apis *Ars* k* ars-s-f k2 **Calc** calc-p k2 *Caust* b4a.de lach lyc *Nux-m* petr *Rhus-t* sep sil sulph thuj
  - **children**; in: ars mtf33
    - ⁝ **infants**: petr ptk1
    - ⁝ **newborns**: apis ptk1

○ • **Above**: *Ars* b4a.de*

UNCOVERING:
- **agg.**: bry b7.de* coc-c bg2 nux-v b7.de* rheum b7.de*
- **amel.**: bell ptk1 camph ptk1 lac-c ptk1 *Lach* ptk1 lil-t ptk1 med ptk1 phos ptk1 sec ptk1 staph ptk1 tab bg2* vip ptk1
- **extremities** | **agg.**: rheum ptk1

UNEASINESS (See Restlessness)

URGING (See Dragging)

URINATION:
- **after**:
  - **agg.**: ars b4.de* chel b7.de* chin b7.de* clem b4.de* eup-pur ptk1 mag-c b4.de* nat-m bg2 *Nux-v* b7a.de *Phos* b4a.de staph b7.de*
  - **amel.**: bell bg2 calc-p bg2 carb-an bg2 lil-t bg2
- **amel.**: carb-an ptk1 dios ptk1 *Sep* ptk1 tarent ptk1
- **before** | **agg.**: cham b7.de* plb b7.de* *Puls* b7.de*
- **during**:
  - **agg.**: bry b7.de* calc-p bg2 card-m bg2 cham ptk1 chin b7.de* coloc ptk1 hyos b7.de* ip ptk1 merc b4.de* plb bg2 *Puls* b7a.de spig b7.de* til bg2 verat b7.de*
    - ⁝ **Iliac** region: berb ptk1
- **suppressed** urination agg.: arn bg2 graph b4a.de*
- **urging** to urinate agg.: kreos bg2 lach b7.de* meph bg2 *Puls* b7.de* *Staph* b7a.de

VEAL agg.: kali-n b4.de*

VEGETABLES agg.; green: cupr b7.de*

VEINS distended: berb calc bg1 ham bg2 sep k*
- **varicose**: *Ham Sulph*

○ - **Inguinal** region: *Berb*

VEXATION; after: | **Hypochondria**: *Acon* b7.de* bry bg2 *Cham* b7.de* *Cocc* b7.de* *Ign* b7.de* sel b7a.de

VIBRATION and power; sensation of: | **Pelvis**; in: sanguis-s hm2•

VINEGAR agg.: aloe bg2

VOLVULUS: ars b4a.de* bell b4a.de* cham b7a.de* cocc bg2 coloc bg2 lyc bg2 nit-ac bg2 nux-v b7a.de* plat bg2 rhus-t b7a.de* sil bg2 sulph b4a.de* thuj b4a.de* verat b7a.de* zinc bg2

VOMITING:
- **after**:
  - **agg.**: ars bg2 ferr b7a.de
  - **amel.**: dig b4.de* nat-c b4a.de *Verat* b7a.de
- **agg.**: asar b7.de* colch b7.de* cupr b7.de* *Dros* b7a.de graph ptk1 merc ptk1 *Plb* b7a.de staph ptk1 verat b7.de*

○ • **Liver**: podo ptk1
- **amel.**: arg-n ptk1 ars ptk1 asar ptk1 hyos ptk1 plb ptk1 tab ptk1 tarent ptk1
- **before** | **agg.**: ars bg2 coff bg2 colch b7.de*

WAKING; on: alum b4a.de* am-m bg2 ambr b7.de* ant-t b7.de* calc bg2 cham bg2 colch b7.de* ferr bg2 gels bg2 hep b4a.de lyc bg2 m-arct b7.de mag-m bg2 mur-ac bg2 nicc bg2 nit-ac bg2 ox-ac bg2 phos bg2 podo bg2 sars bg2 stann bg2 sulph bg2 verat b7.de*

○ - **Hypochondria**: *Am-m* b7a.de

WALKING:
- **agg.**: acon b7.de* alum b4.de* am-c bg2 ambr bg2 ang b7.de* *Apis* b7a.de arn b7.de* *Asaf* b7.de* asar b7.de* aur b4.de* bell b4.de* borx b4a.de *Bry* b7.de* calc b4.de* caps b7.de* carb-an b4.de* carb-v b4.de* chin b7.de* *Clem* bg2 *Cocc* b7.de* coloc b4.de* con b4.de* cupr b7.de* dig b4.de* ferr b7.de* graph b4.de* hep b4a.de* hyos b7.de* ign b7.de* ip bg2 kali-bi bg2 kali-c b4.de* kali-n b4.de* lach bg2 laur b7.de* led b7.de* lyc bg2 m-aust b7.de mag-m bg2 merc b4.de* *Merc-c* b4a.de mez b4.de* mur-ac bg2 nat-c b4.de* nat-m b4.de* nat-s bg2 nit-ac b4.de* nux-m b7.de* nux-v b7.de* olnd b7.de* par b7.de* ph-ac b4.de* phos b4.de* puls b7.de* ran-b b7.de* rheum b7.de* rhod bg2 rhus-t b7.de* sec b7.de* sel bg2 sep b4.de* sil b4.de* spig b7.de* spong b7.de* squil b7.de* stann b4.de* sul-ac b4.de* *Sulph* b4.de* thuj b4.de* verat b7.de* viol-t b7.de* zinc b4.de*

○ • **Hypochondria**: arn b7.de* chin b7.de* clem b4a.de con b4.de* hep b4a.de* ign b7.de* iod b4a.de kali-c b4.de* lach bg2 *Mag-m* b4.de* mez b4.de* nat-c b4.de* nat-m b4.de* nat-s bg2 phos b4.de* plat b4.de* *Puls* b7a.de rhod b4a.de* *Sel* b7.de* sep b4.de* spig b7.de* *Sulph* b4.de* thuj b4.de* verat b7.de* zinc b4.de*
  - **Inguinal** and pubic region: aloe bg2
  - **Liver**: hep bg2* mag-m bg2 sep bg2
  - **Spleen**: arn bg2 ign bg2 lach bg2 rhod bg2 sel bg2

Abdomen

- **air**; in open:
  - **after** | **agg.**: coff b7.de* ferr b7.de* nux-v b7.de* rhus-t b7.de* *Ruta* b7a.de
  - **agg.** | **Hypochondria**: nat-s bg2
  - **amel.**: am-c b4.de* *Ambr* b7.de* ant-t b7.de* ars bg2 asaf b7.de* bry b7.de* calad bg2 chin b7.de* coloc bg2 cycl bg2 dig b4.de* dros b7.de* ferr b7.de* kali-n b4.de* kreos bg2 lycps-v bg2 mag-c b4.de* par b7.de* *Puls* b7.de* rhus-t b7.de* ruta b7.de* sep bg2 stram bg2 sulph bg2 tarax b7.de* valer b7.de*
- **amel.** | **Hypochondria**: dulc b4.de* sul-ac b4.de* vib bg2
- **bent** | **amel.**: rhus-t b7.de*
- **rapidly**:
  - **agg.**: cupr b7.de* dros b7.de* spig b7.de*
  - ⁝ **Hypochondria**: borx b4a.de rhod b4.de* spig b7.de*
- **stone** pavement agg.; on a: *Con* b4.de*

WALNUT (See Hard body)

WARM:
- **applications** | **amel.**: alum b4.de* am-c b4.de* *Ars* bg2 bar-c b4a.de* canth b7.de* caust b4a.de* cham bg2 *Coloc* b4.de* laur b7.de* *Mag-p* bg2 mang b4.de* meph bg2 *Nux-m* b7.de* nux-v b7.de* podo bg2 rheum bg2 rhus-t b7.de* sabad b7.de* sec bg2 *Sep* b4a.de sil b4.de* staph b7.de* stront-c b4.de*
- **drinks** | **amel.**: lyc ptk1 mag-p bg2* *Nux-v* ptk1 sul-ac ptk1
- **food**:
  - **agg.**: kali-c b4a.de
  - **amel.**: *Coloc* b4a.de lyc ptk1 mag-c b4.de* mag-p ptk1 *Nux-v* ptk1 *Sep* b4a.de sil b4a.de sul-ac ptk1

WARMTH; sensation of (See Heat)

WARTS: | **brown**: thuj k2

WATER:
- **drinking** water agg.: *Ang* b7a.de *Croc* b7a.de nux-m b7.de* teucr b7.de*
- **running** water; sensation as from:
  - **hot** water: chin ptk1 sang ptk1 sumb ptk1
  - ○ **Inguinal** region: lyc bg2

WATER, as if full of: acon bg2 cann-xyz bg2 casc cench k2 crot-t k* hell k* *Kali-c* h2* ol-an vh ph-ac k* sul-ac h2

WATER BRASH: | **amel.**: *Cocc* b7a.de

WAXY liver: calc bro1 *Kali-i* bro1 phos bro1 sil bro1

WEAKNESS, sense of: abrot hr1* acet-ac bro1 acon b7.de* *Aloe* k* alst bro1 alum k* alum-p k2 alumn ambr k2 ant-c bro1 apoc k* **Arg-n** k* *Arn* bro1 ars b4.de* bell bg2 borx k* cadm-s br1 *Calc-p* k* *Carb-an* b4.de* cham bro1 chlor bg2 *Cocc* bro1 colch k* dig k2 euph bro1 ferr b7.de* ferr-p bg2 gels k* glyc bro1 *Hydr* bro1 **Ign** k* *Ip* bg2 kali-c k* led k* lil-t k* mag-m k* *Merc* ptk1 myric a1* *Nat-m* k* olnd k* *Opun-f* bro1 ox-ac k* *Petr* k* **Phos** k* phys bro1 phyt k* *Plat* k* plb-act bro1 *Podo* k* *Psor* k* ptel a1 quas bro1 rhod k* sapin a1 sel rsj9• *Sep* k* spong k* stann b4.de* *Staph* k* **Sul-ac** k* sulfon bro1 *Sulph* bg2 *Verat* k* zinc k* [spect dfg1]
- **left**: calc-p bg2
- **morning**: chel k* dios a1 hell k*
- **evening**: anac k* carb-an h2
- **accompanied** by | **constipation** (See RECTUM - Constipation - accompanied - abdomen)
- **diarrhea** would come on; as if: **Aloe** k* ant-c bro1 ap-g bro1 borx bro1 crot-t bro1 eucal bro1 ferr bro1 form bro1 nux-v bro1 *Opun-f* bro1 ran-s bro1
- **drop**, as if it would: **Staph** k*
- **eructations**:
  - **after**: ambr k2
  - **amel.**: *Kali-m* k*
- **flatus**; passing | **amel.**: ambr k2
- **menses** | **before** | **agg.**: phos k*
  - **would** come on; as if: **Sul-ac**
- **paralytic** weakness | **Intestines**: nux-m br1
- **stool**:
  - **after** | **agg.**: ambr k2 *Arg-n* carbn-s chin dios *Iod* lept k* mag-m h2 *Nat-m* *Nat-p* **Petr** k* *Phos* *Pic-ac* plat k* **Podo** k* *Sep* k* stann bg1 **Sul-ac** sulph **Verat** k*

Weakness, sense of – **stool**: ...
  - **before**: verat-v bg1
  - **during** | **agg.**: form k* ip k* plat bg2 **Podo** bg2
  - **hard** stool: *Plat* *Sep*
- **walking** agg.; after: *Phos*
- ○ **Hypochondria**: carb-an h2 carb-v bg2 *Rhus-t* b7a.de
- **Hypogastrium**: am-c bg1* apoc ptk1 calc ptk1 chion bg1* phos ptk1 plb ptk1 sulph ptk1 verat ptk1
- **Inguinal** region: aloe k* aur k* calc k* m-arct b7.de* m-aust b7.de **Nux-v** k* osm bg2 phys bg2 raph k* tab k* thuj bg2
- **Intestines**: merc ptk1 zing br1
  - **accompanied** by | **diarrhea** (See RECTUM - Diarrhea - accompanied - intestines)
  - **stool** agg.; after: sul-ac b4.de*
- **Lower** abdomen: am-c bg2 apoc bg2 chion bg2 fuc bg2 **Phos** bg2 plb bg2 sep bg2 sulph bg2 verat bg2
  - **stool** agg.; after: *Plat* b4a.de
- **Muscles**: ars h2 carc fd2.de• cocc br1 con h2 sulph h2
- **Pelvis**: *Helon* br1
- **Pubic** region | **Pubic** bones: sep bg2
- **Ring**; abdominal: nux-v tl1
- **Umbilicus** | **Region** of umbilicus: kali-bi bg2 plat bg2
- **Upper** abdomen | **urination** agg.; after: ars b4.de*

WEATHER AGG.; COLD: phos b4a.de

WEIGHT falling; sensation of: *(↗Heaviness)*
- ○ **Hypogastrium** on inspiration spig h1
- **Inguinal** region:
  - **lifting** agg.: cub c1
  - **riding** agg.: cub c1
  - **walking** agg.: cub c1

WET feet agg.; getting: puls bg2

WHIRLING sensation of: hep h2

WHISKEY agg.: ign bg2

WHISTLING: ferr-ma a1* mur-ac h2* sep h2*

WORMS; complaints from: acon b7.de* asar b7.de* bell bg2 *Cic* b7.de* **Cina** b7.de* ferr b7.de* hyos bg2 ign b7.de* lach bg2 *Merc* bg2 nux-m b7a.de* nux-v b7.de* ruta b7.de* *Sabad* b7.de* *Sil* b4a.de **Spig** b7.de* sulph bg2 *Teucr* b7.de* valer b7.de* verat b7.de*

WRAPPING up:
- **tight**:
  - **agg.**: bry b7.de* fl-ac bg2 puls b7.de*
  - **amel.**: *Bry* b7a.de *Puls* b7a.de

WRENCHING; sensation of: | **Liver**: aloe bg2 *Kali-c* bg2 lyc bg2

YAWNING:
- **agg.**: *Ars* ptk1 borx b4a.de croc bg2 nat-c bg2 phyt ptk1 puls b7.de* sars b4.de* zinc bg2
- **amel.**: lyc ptk1 nat-m ptk1

CECUM; complaints of: ars bro1 *Lach* bro1 rhus-v bro1 verat-v bro1

COLON; complaints of: aloe bg2 colch bg2 graph bg2 merc-c bg2 sul-i bg2

DUODENUM; complaints of: ars ptk1 bry bg2 chin bg2* hydr bg2* kali-bi bg2* merc-d bg2* nat-p ptk1 nat-s bg2 nux-v bg2 orni mtf11 petr bg2 phos mtf11 *Podo* bg2* ptel bg2 puls bg2 uran-n bg2*

HIP; complaints of the region of the (= loins): acon b2.de* agar b2.de* agn b2.de* am-m b2.de* ambr b2.de* anac b2.de* ang b7.de ant-c b2.de* arg-met b2.de* *Arn* b2.de* *Asaf* b2.de* *Aur* b2.de* bell b2.de* bov b2.de* calc b2.de* camph b2.de* cann-s b2.de* **Canth** b2.de* carb-an b2.de* carb-v b2.de* caust b2.de* cham b2.de* *Chel* b2.de* chin b2.de* cina b2.de* clem b2.de* cocc b2.de* colch b2.de* *Coloc* b2.de* dig b2.de* dros b2.de* euph b2.de* hep b2.de* hyos b2.de* ign b2.de* iod b2.de* kali-c b2.de* *Kali-n* b2.de* kreos b2.de* *Lach* b2.de* *Laur* b2.de* led b2.de* *Lyc* b2.de* m-arct b2.de mag-c b2.de* meny b2.de* merc b2.de* *Mez* b2.de* nat-c b2.de* nit-ac b2.de* nux-v b2.de* olnd b2.de* *Plb* b2.de* puls b2.de* *Ran-b* b2.de*

Hip; complaints of the region of the: ...
ran-s b2.de* **Rheum** b2.de* rhus-t b2.de* ruta b2.de* sabad b2.de* sabin b2.de* samb b2.de* sars b2.de* sec b2.de* *Sep* b2.de* spig b2.de* spong b2.de* *Staph* b2.de* stront-c b2.de* sulph b2.de* tarax b2.de* teucr b2.de* **Thuj** b2.de* valer b2.de* verat b2.de* verb b2.de* viol-t b2.de* **Zinc** b2.de*

- **alternating** sides: euon bg2

HYPOCHONDRIA; complaints of: **Acon** b2.de* *Alum* b2.de* am-m b2.de* ang b2.de* ant-c b2.de* ant-t b2.de* arg-n bg2 arn b2.de* ars b2.de* *Asaf* b2.de* asar b2.de* aur b2.de* bell b2.de* bism b2.de* bov b2.de* brom tl1 *Bry* b2.de* *Calc* b2.de* *Camph* b2.de* cann-s b2.de* canth b2.de* caps b2.de* carb-an b2.de* *Carb-v* b2.de* caust b2.de* cean tl1 *Cham* b2.de* chel tl1 **Chin** b2.de* cocc b2.de* coff b2.de* colch b2.de* *Con* b2.de* cupr b2.de* dig b2.de* dros b2.de* ferr b2.de* graph b2.de* hell b2.de* hep b2.de* *Ign* b2.de* ip b2.de* kali-c b2.de* kali-n b2.de* lach b2.de* *Laur* b2.de* led b2.de* lyc b2.de* m-ambo b2.de m-arct b2.de m-aust b2.de mag-c b2.de* mag-m b2.de* mang b2.de* meny b2.de* merc b2.de* *Mosch* b2.de* mur-ac b2.de* nat-c b2.de* nat-m b2.de* nat-s ptk1 nit-ac b2.de* *Nux-v* b2.de* op b2.de* ph-ac b2.de* phos b2.de* plat b2.de* plb b2.de* *Puls* b2.de* **Ran-b** b2.de* ran-s b2.de* *Rhod* b2.de* rhus-t b2.de* ruta b2.de* sabad b2.de* sars b2.de* sec b2.de* sel b2.de* seneg b2.de* *Sep* b2.de* sil b2.de* spig b2.de* spong b2.de* *Stann* b2.de* *Staph* b2.de* stront-c b2.de* sul-ac b2.de* *Sulph* b2.de* tarax b2.de* teucr b2.de* thuj b2.de* valer b2.de* verat b2.de* verb b2.de* *Zinc* b2.de*

- **right**: **Acon** b7a.de* aesc bg2 *Agar* b4a.de* *Agn* b7a.de* aloe bg2 *Alum* b4a.de* **Am-c** b4a.de* *Am-m* b7a.de* *Ambr* b7a.de* *Anac* b4a.de* *Ang* b7a.de* *Ant-c* bg2* apis b7a.de* *Arn* b7a.de* *Ars* b4a.de* *Asaf* b7a.de* **Bar-c** b4a.de* **Bell** b4a.de* *Berb* bg2* borx b4a.de* **Bry** b7a.de* calad b7a.de* *Calc* b4a.de* *Canth* b7a.de* *Carb-an* b4a.de* *Carb-v* b4a.de* *Caust* b4a.de* *Chel* b7a.de* *Chin* b7a.de* *Clem* b4a.de* **Cocc** b7a.de* **Colch** b7a.de* *Con* b4a.de* *Dig* b4a.de* dulc b4a.de* euph b4a.de *Ferr* b7a.de* fl-ac b4a.de* *Graph* b4a.de* *Hep* b4a.de* hydr bg2 *Hyos* b7a.de* *Ign* b7a.de* *Iod* b4a.de* iris bg2 **Kali-c** b4a.de* kreos b7a.de* *Lach* b7a.de* *Laur* b7a.de* *Led* b7a.de* **Lyc** b4a.de* *M-arct* b7a.de* *M-aust* b7a.de* **Mag-m** b4a.de* mang b4a.de* *Merc* b4a.de* mill b7a.de* *Mosch* b7a.de* *Nat-c* b4a.de* *Nat-m* b4a.de* nat-s bg2 nit-ac b4a.de* *Nux-m* b7a.de* **Nux-v** b7a.de* par b7a.de* *Petr* b4a.de* *Ph-ac* b4a.de* phos b4a.de* plat b4a.de* *Plb* b7a.de* podo bg2 psor b4a.de* ptel bg2 *Puls* b7a.de* *Ran-b* b7a.de* *Ran-s* b7a.de* rhod b4a.de* *Rhus-t* b7a.de* *Ruta* b7a.de* *Sabad* b7a.de* *Sabin* b7a.de* *Sec* b7a.de* *Sel* b7a.de* *Sep* b4a.de* *Sil* bg2* *Spig* b7a.de* *Stann* b4a.de* staph b7a.de* *Sul-ac* b4a.de* *Sulph* b4a.de* *Teucr* b7a.de* valer b7a.de* *Verat* b7a.de* verb b7a.de* zinc b4a.de*
  - ▽ **extending** to:
    - **left**: carbn-s bg2 ol-an bg2 zinc bg2
    - **Stomach**: bry bg2
- **accompanied** by:
  - **jaundice** (See SKIN - Discoloration - yellow - accompanied - hypochondria)
  - **malaria** (See GENERALS - Malaria - followed - hypochondria)
  - **spasms**: *Stann* b4a.de
  - **tenesmus**: *Acon* b7a.de
  - ○ **Heart**; complaints of (See CHEST - Heart; complaints - accompanied - hypochondria)
  - **Upper** limbs; pain in: nat-m bg2
  - **Uterus**; complaints of: mag-m bg2
- **alternating** with:
  - ○ **Chest**; complaints of: *Zinc* b4a.de
  - **Head**; pain in: plat b4a.de
- **eating**; after: ruta bg2
- **left**: acon b7a.de* agar b4a.de* *Agn* b7a.de* alum b4a.de* am-c b4a.de* *Am-m* b7a.de* anac b4a.de* *Ant-c* b7a.de* *Apis* b7a.de* arg-met b7a.de* *Arn* b7a.de* *Ars* b4a.de* **Asaf** b7a.de* *Asar* b7a.de* aur b4a.de* bar-c bg2 bell b4a.de* *Borx* b4a.de* brom bg2 bry b7a.de* calad b7a.de* calc b4a.de* *Cann-s* b7a.de* carb-an b4a.de* *Carb-v* b4a.de* *Caust* b4a.de* *Cham* b7a.de* chel b7a.de* *Chin* b7a.de* cocc b7a.de* coff b7a.de* coloc b4a.de **Con** b4a.de* *Cupr* b7a.de* dig b4a.de* dulc b4a.de* *Euph* b4a.de* *Ferr* b7a.de* **Fl-ac** b4a.de* graph b4a.de* hep b4a.de* **Ign** b7a.de* *Iod* b4a.de* ip b7a.de* kali-c b4a.de* kali-n b4a.de* kreos b7a.de* laur b7a.de* lyc b4a.de* mang b4a.de* merc b4a.de* *Mez* b4a.de* *Mill* b7a.de* mosch b7a.de* *Mur-ac* b4a.de* nat-c b4a.de* nat-m b4a.de* **Nit-ac** b4a.de* nux-v b7a.de* olnd b7a.de* par b7a.de* petr b4a.de* ph-ac b4a.de* phos b4a.de* plat b4a.de* plb b7a.de* *Psor* b4a.de* puls b7a.de*

Hypochondria; complaints of – **left**: ...
Ran-b b7a.de* ran-s b7a.de* *Rheum* b7a.de* rhod b4a.de* rhus-t b7a.de* ruta b7a.de* sabad b7a.de* sars b4a.de* sec b7a.de* seneg b4a.de* *Sep* b4a.de* sil b4a.de* spig b7a.de* squil b7a.de* stann b4a.de* staph b7a.de* sul-ac b4a.de* **Sulph** b4a.de* teucr b7a.de* valer b7a.de* *Verb* b7a.de* viol-t b7a.de* *Zinc* b4a.de*

▽ - **extending** to:

- ○ **Downward**: aloe bg2 calc bg2 lil-t bg2
  - **right**: ars bg2 bapt bg2 chel bg2
- **Epigastrium**: cupr bg2 sep bg2
  - **left**: mag-m bg2 phos bg2
- **Upward**: cact bg2
  - **right**: mur-ac bg2
  - **left**: kali-bi bg2

ILIAC REGION; complaints of:
▽ - **extending** to | **Thighs**; down: berb ptk1

INGUINAL region; complaints of: acon bg2 aloe ptk1 am-m bg2* aur bg2 bapt bg2 clem bg2 cocc bg2* coloc bg2 gran ptk1 graph bg2 guaj bg2* kali-c bg2 lob bg2 lyc bg2 nux-v bg2 sul-ac bg2 tab bg2 verat bg2 [fl-ac stj2 fl-pur stj2]

- **alternating** sides: arg-n bg2 coloc bg2* dulc bg2 ol-an bg2 phys bg2*
- ○ **External**: alum b2.de* am-c b2.de* am-m b2.de* ambr b2.de* **Ars** b2.de* aur b2.de* bov b2.de* calc b2.de* camph b2.de* cann-s b2.de* canth b2.de* chin b2.de* cic b2.de* cocc b2.de* dig b2.de* euph b2.de* graph b2.de* guaj b2.de* ign bg2 kali-c b2.de* *Lyc* b2.de* m-ambo b2.de m-arct b2.de mag-m b2.de* **Merc** b2.de* mez b2.de* mur-ac b2.de* nat-c b2.de* nit-ac b2.de* nux-v b2.de* ph-ac b2.de* puls b2.de* sars b2.de* *Sel* b2.de* sep b2.de* *Sil* b2.de* spig b2.de* stront-c b2.de* sul-ac b2.de* sulph b2.de* thuj b2.de*
  - **right**: agn b7a.de* alum b4a.de* am-c b4a.de* *Am-m* b7a.de* apis b7a.de* *Ars* b4a.de* *Aur* b4a.de* *Bell* b4a.de* *Borx* b4a.de* **Calc** b4a.de* camph b7a.de* cann-s b7a.de* canth b7a.de* carb-an b4a.de* *Carb-v* b4a.de* cham ptk1 *Cic* b7a.de* **Clem** b4a.de* *Cocc* b7a.de* *Coloc* b4a.de* *Con* b4a.de* dig b4a.de* *Dros* b7a.de* dulc b4a.de* ferr-pic bg2 fl-ac b4a.de* graph b4a.de* *Hell* b7a.de* *Iod* b4a.de* *Ip* b7a.de* **Kali-c** b4a.de* **Lach** b7a.de* *Laur* b7a.de* **Lyc** b4a.de* *Mang* b4a.de* *Merc* b4a.de* *Mez* b4a.de* **Nux-v** b7a.de* *Op* b7a.de* *Petr* b4a.de* *Ph-ac* b4a.de* psor b4a.de* **Puls** b7a.de* *Ran-b* b7a.de* **Rhod** b4a.de* **Rhus-t** b7a.de* *Ruta* b7a.de* *Sabin* b7a.de* sars b4a.de* *Seneg* b4a.de* *Sep* b4a.de* *Sil* b4a.de* spig b7a.de* spong b7a.de* stann b4a.de* *Staph* b7a.de* *Stront-c* b4a.de* **Sul-ac** b4a.de* sulph b4a.de* *Teucr* b7a.de* **Thuj** b4a.de* *Valer* b7a.de* *Verat* b7a.de* zinc b4a.de*
  - **left**: *Agar* b4a.de* agn b7a.de* *Alum* b4a.de* *Am-c* b4a.de* am-m b7a.de* *Ambr* b7a.de* *Ant-c* b7a.de* *Apis* b7a.de* *Arg-met* b7a.de* arn b7a.de* ars b4a.de asar b7a.de* aur b4a.de* bell b4a.de* calc b4a.de* camph b7a.de* cann-s b7a.de* canth b7a.de* *Carb-an* b4a.de* *Chel* b7a.de* cocc b7a.de* *Coloc* b4a.de *Dig* b4a.de* dulc b4a.de* **Euph** b4a.de* fl-ac b4a.de* graph b4a.de* *Ign* b7a.de* kali-c b4a.de* laur b7a.de* lyc b4a.de* *M-arct* b7a.de* *M-aust* b7a.de* **Mag-c** b4a.de* *Mag-m* b4a.de* *Merc* b4a.de* mez b4a.de mur-ac b4a.de naja ptk1 *Nit-ac* b4a.de* nux-m b7a.de* *Nux-v* b7a.de* *Par* b7a.de* *Petr* fse1.de phos b4a.de* rhod b4a.de* rhus-t b7a.de* *Sabad* b7a.de* sabin b7a.de* sars b4a.de* *Sep* b4a.de* sil b4a.de* *Spig* b7a.de* spong b7a.de* *Stann* b4a.de* *Staph* b7a.de* *Sul-ac* b4a.de* *Sulph* b4a.de* *Tarax* b7a.de* *Verat* b7a.de* viol-t b7a.de* **Zinc** b4a.de*
- **Glands**: ant-c b2.de* *Ars* b2.de* asaf b2.de* *Aur* b2.de* bar-c b2.de* *Bell* b2.de* **Calc** b2.de* cann-s b2.de* carb-v bg2 *Clem* b2.de* con b2.de* *Dulc* b2.de* graph b2.de* **Hep** b2.de* iod b2.de* lyc b2.de* m-ambo b2.de meny b2.de* **Merc** b2.de* mez b2.de* nat-c b2.de* *Nit-ac* b2.de* nux-v b2.de* oci ptk1 ph-ac b2.de* phos b2.de* puls b2.de* rheum b2.de* *Sil* b2.de* *Spong* b2.de* stann b2.de* staph b2.de* stram b2.de* *Sulph* b2.de* *Thuj* b2.de*
- **Internal**: agar b2.de* agn b2.de* *Alum* b2.de* am-c b2.de* **Am-m** b2.de* anac b2.de* ant-c b2.de* ant-t b2.de* arg-met b2.de* ars b2.de* asaf b2.de* asar b2.de* **Aur** b2.de* bar-c b2.de* bell b2.de* bov b2.de* *Calc* b2.de* camph b2.de* cann-s b2.de* canth b2.de* caps b2.de* *Carb-an* b2.de* carb-v b2.de* caust b2.de* *Cham* b2.de* chel b2.de* chin b2.de* cic b2.de* *Clem* b2.de* *Cocc* b2.de* coff b2.de* *Coloc* b2.de* con b2.de* croc b2.de* dig b2.de* dros b2.de* dulc b2.de* euph b2.de* graph b2.de* guaj b2.de* hell b2.de* *Ign* b2.de* iod b2.de* kali-c b2.de* kali-n b2.de* kreos b2.de* laur b2.de* **Lyc** b2.de* m-ambo b2.de *M-arct* b2.de m-aust b2.de mag-c b2.de* mag-m b2.de* meny b2.de* *Merc* b2.de* mez b2.de* mur-ac b2.de* nat-c b2.de* nat-m b2.de* nit-ac b2.de* **Nux-v** b2.de* op b2.de* par b2.de* petr b2.de* ph-ac b2.de* phos b2.de* plat b2.de*

Abdomen

- **Internal**: ...
plb b2.de* ran-b b2.de* ran-s b2.de* rheum b2.de* *Rhod* b2.de* *Rhus-t* b2.de* sabad b2.de* sars b2.de* sep b2.de* *Sil* b2.de* *Spig* b2.de* spong b2.de* stann b2.de* staph b2.de* stram b2.de* *Stront-c* b2.de* **Sul-ac** b2.de* *Sulph* b2.de* tarax b2.de* teucr b2.de* *Thuj* b2.de* valer b2.de* *Verat* b2.de* viol-t b2.de* zinc b2.de*

LIVER and region of liver; complaints of: abies-c k* abrot **Acon** k* aegle-f mtf11 *Aesc* k* *Agar* k* agar-ph mtf11 agn b2.de* all-c *Aloe* k* *Alum* k* am-c b2.de* *Am-m* k* ambr b2.de* anac b2.de* anag vh1 anders mtf11 ang b2.de* ant-t *Apoc* *Arg-n* k* *Arn* k* *Ars* k* ars-i k* asaf k* *Astac* bro1 atis zzc1• *Aur* k* aur-ar k2 aur-i k2 aur-m *Aur-m-n* bro1 *Bapt* bar-c k* barbit bro1 **Bell** k* benz-ac k2 **Berb** k* berb-a br1 boerh-d mtf11 bov b2.de* brass bro1 brass-n-o srj5• **Bry** k* **Bufo** cadm-s k2 calad b2.de* **Calc** k* *Calc-f* k* **Calc-p** calc-sil k2 camph k* cann-s b2.de* canth b2.de* *Caps* bg2 *Carb-an* b2.de* *Carb-v* k* **Carbn-s** k* carbn-tm mtf11 **Card-m** k* *Carl* br1 caust b2.de* cean bro1* *Cham* k* **Chel** k* chelo br1* chen-a bro1 *Chin* k* chion br1* chol bro1 chrystl jsx1.fr cic bg2 *Cimx* cinnb clem k* cob bro1 *Cocc* k* coenz-a mtf11 *Colch* k* coli jl2 *Coll* *Coloc* combr-r vs1.fr *Con* k* **Corn** k* *Croc* k* *Crot-c* *Crot-h* k* *Cupr* cyna mtf11 dig k* dios bro1* *Dol* br1* dros dulc k* euon bro1 *Euon-a* br1 *Eup-per* br1* fab br1* ferr k* ferr-ar k2 ferr-p k2 *Ferr-pic* bro1 *Fl-ac* gels k* *Graph* k* grin haru-ma jsx1.fr hed sp1 hell b2.de* *Hep* k* hip-ac br1 *Hydr* k* hyos b2.de* hypoes-t jsx1.fr *Ign* b2.de* **Iod** k* iodof bro1 ip b2.de* *Iris* k* *Kali-bi* k* **Kali-c** k* kali-i k2* kali-n b2.de* kali-s kreos b2.de* lac-d k2 **Lach** k* lachn mtf11 lact mrr1 *Laur* k* **Lept** k* luf-b mtf11 **Lyc** k* m-arct b2.de mag-c k* **Mag-m** k* mang k2 mang-s bro1 marr bro1 **Merc** k* merc-c mez bg2 microg-p jsx1.fr morg fmm1• morg-g fmm1• *Morg-p* fmm1• mosch b2.de* mur-ac k* *Myric* br1* nat-ar nat-c k* *Nat-m* k* nat-p k2 **Nat-s** k* nat-sal br1 **Nit-ac** k* nit-m-ac br1 **Nux-m** k* **Nux-v** k* oci-su jsx1.fr ol-j br1 olib-sac wmh1 op b2.de* orot-ac mtf11 ost br1 par b2.de* petr k* *Ph-ac* k* **Phos** k* plat k* *Plb* k* pneu jl2 **Podo** k* *Prun* *Psor* *Ptel* br1* puls k* querc bro1 ran-b k* ran-s k* raph bro1* rheum ptk1 rhod b2.de* rhus-t k* ruta k* sabad k* sabin b2.de* *Sang* k* sars b2.de* sec b2.de* sel k* seneg b2.de* **Sep** k* ser-ang br1 sil k* spig k* spong b2.de* stann b2.de* staph b2.de* stel bro1 sul-ac k* sul-i k2 **Sulph** k* tab tarax b2.de* teucr b2.de* ther k2 thlas bro1 thuj b2.de* tinas mtf11 trios br1 uran-n bro1 ust ptk1 valer b2.de* vanad bro1 verat k* verb b2.de* visc sp1 yuc br1 *Zinc* k* [*Mag-lac* stj2 *Mag-met* stj2 *Mag-n* stj2 *Mag-sil* stj2]

- **accompanied** by:
  - **anemia**: cean br1
  - **ascites** (See Dropsy - ascites - accompanied - liver - complaints)
  - **cancer** (See GENERALS - Cancerous - accompanied - liver)
  - **constipation** (See RECTUM - Constipation - accompanied - liver)
  - **cough**: am-m br1*
  - **despair** (See MIND - Despair - liver)
  - **diabetes** (See GENERALS - Diabetes mellitus - accompanied - liver)
  - **dropsy** (See GENERALS - Dropsy - general - accompanied - liver)
  - **eczema** (See SKIN - Eruptions - eczema - accompanied - liver)
  - **epistaxis**: chel bro1
  - **hemorrhage**: card-m br1
  - **influenza**: card-m br1*
  - **vesicular** eruption: corn br1
  - ○ **Eyes**; complaints of: con ptk1 *Corn* ptk1
  - **Face**; neuralgic pain in the: **Chel** mrr1
  - **Head**:
    - **complaints** (See HEAD - Complaints - accompanied - liver)
    - **pain** (See HEAD - Pain - accompanied - liver)
    - **Occiput** (See HEAD - Pain - occiput - accompanied - liver)
  - **Heart**; complaints of the (See CHEST - Heart; complaints - accompanied - liver)
  - **Heart**; hypertrophy of (See CHEST - Hypertrophy - heart - accompanied - liver)
  - **Kidneys**; complaints of: berb mtf11

Liver and region of liver; complaints of – **accompanied** by: ...
  - **Lungs**; inflammation of (See CHEST - Inflammation - lungs - accompanied - liver)
  - **Spleen** diseases: chin mtf11 mang-c mtf11 mang-s mtf11
  - **Tongue** white, heavily coated and black streak down centre: *Lept* kr1*
  - **Tongue**; dirty: *Mag-m* kr1*
  - **Tongue**; white: podo kr1*
  - **Tongue**; white and heavily coated: *Lept* vk1
  - **Upper** limbs; complaints of | **right**: bry ptk1 iris ptk1
  - **Uterus**:
    - **atony** of the: nat-chl br1
    - **complaints**: mag-m ptk1
    - **congestion** of the: nat-chl br1
- **alternating** with | **Head**; pain in (See HEAD - Pain - alternating - liver)
- **children**; in: | **puny**, rickety children: mag-m mtf33
- **chronic**: anders mtf11 card-m mrr1 ins mtf11 lact-v mtf11 lina mtf11 mag-m br1
  - **tubercular** patients; in: sep br1
- **coffee** agg.: *Canth* br1
- **coma**; with (See MIND - Coma - liver)
- **degeneration**: uran-n br1 vanad br1
- **eruptions**; after toxically treated skin: dol mtf11
- **functional**: lyc mtf11 marr-vg mtf11
- **menopause**; during: card-m bro1
- **periodical**: aur-m-n mtf11
- **pregnancy** agg.; during: *Chel* br1*

○ - **Deep** in: lach ptk1

▽ - **extending** to:
  - ○ **Back**: arn ptk1 borx ptk1 calc ptk1 echi ptk1 kali-bi ptk1 lept ptk1 rhus-t ptk1 thuj ptk1
  - **Backward**:
    - **right**: acon ptk1 aesc ptk1 aral ptk1 *Borx* ptk1 *Calc* ptk1 **Chel** ptk1 dios ptk1 graph ptk1 *Hydr* ptk1 kali-bi ptk1 *Lyc* ptk1 mag-m ptk1 *Nat-m* ptk1
    - **left**: dios ptk1 dulc ptk1 *Lept* ptk1 myric ptk1
  - **Downward**: chel ptk1
  - **Epigastrium**: lach ptk1 mag-m ptk1
  - **Hip**: vip ptk1
  - **Mammae**:
    - **Nipple** | **right**: dios ptk1
  - **Occiput**: kali-c ptk1 nux-v ptk1 sep ptk1
  - **Scapula**: berb ptk1 *Chel* ptk1 dulc ptk1 lept ptk1 merc ptk1 myric ptk1 sep ptk1
  - **Shoulder**: kali-c ptk1 nux-v ptk1 sep ptk1 vip ptk1
    - **right**: kali-bi ptk1 med ptk1
  - **Spine**: lept ptk1 mag-m ptk1 sil ptk1
  - **Umbilicus**: berb ptk1 dulc ptk1 lept ptk1 myric ptk1 sep ptk1

MONS PUBIS; complaints of (See Pubic)

MONS VENERIS; complaints of: nat-m ptk1 rhus-t ptk1 sil ptk1

MUSCLES of abdomen; complaints of: acon bg2 alum bg2 am-m bg2 *Ambr* bg2 anac bg2 ang bg2 ant-c bg2 **Apis** bg2 arg-met bg2 arn bg2 ars bg2 asaf bg2 asar bg2 aur bg2 bar-c bg2 *Bell* bg2 bell-p bg2 bov bg2 **Bry** bg2 calc bg2 camph bg2 cann-xyz bg2 *Canth* bg2 caps bg2 carb-v bg2 caust bg2 cham bg2 chel bg2 chin bg2 cic bg2 cimic ptk1 cocc bg2 colch bg2 *Coloc* bg2 con bg2 croc bg2 cupr bg2 dig bg2 dros bg2 euph bg2 ferr bg2 gels bg2 graph bg2 guaj bg2 ham bg2 *Hyos* bg2 ign bg2 iod bg2 ip bg2 kali-c bg2 lach bg2 led bg2 lyc bg2 mag-c bg2 mag-m bg2 mang bg2 meny bg2 **Merc** bg2 mosch bg2 mur-ac bg2 nat-c bg2 nit-ac bg2 **Nux-v** bg2 olnd bg2 op bg2 par bg2 petr bg2 ph-ac bg2 phos bg2 plat bg2 plb bg2 **Puls** bg2 ran-b bg2 ran-s bg2 rheum bg2 rhod bg2 *Rhus-t* bg2 ruta bg2 *Sabad* bg2 sabin bg2 samb bg2 sars bg2 **Sel** bg2 seneg bg2 *Sep* bg2 sil bg2 spig bg2 spong bg2 squil bg2 stann bg2 staph bg2 stram bg2 stront-c bg2 sul-ac bg2 *Sulph* bg2 tarax bg2 thuj bg2* valer bg2 verat bg2 viol-t bg2 zinc bg2

○ - **Linea** alba: nat-m bg2

PANCREAS; complaints of: ars bg2* *Atro* bg2* bar-m bg2* bell bg2* calc-ar bro1 carb-an bg2* carb-v bg2* chion bro1* con k* *Iod* k* *Iris* k* jab bg2* kali-i bg2* merc bro1* merc-i-r bg2 nat-s bg2* nux-v bg2* ol-j br1 pancr bro1 *Phos* k •* pilo bro1 puls bro1 *Spong* k* trif-p c2 uran-n bg2
- **accompanied** by:
  - **diabetes** (See GENERALS - Diabetes mellitus - pancreas)
  - **diarrhea**: iod tl1
- **insulin** secretion decreased: cortico sp1*

PUBIC REGION; complaints of: am-c bg2 anac b2.de* ant-t b2.de* arg-met b2.de* asaf b2.de* aur b2.de* bell b2.de* berb bg2 bov bg2 brom bg2 calc bg2 camph bg2 caust bg2 con bg2 dig bg2 ferr bg2 hell b2.de* hyos b2.de* kali-c bg2 *Meny* b2.de* nat-c b2.de* nat-m b2.de* nit-ac b2.de* nux-v b2.de* phos bg2 *Plat* bg2 plb b2.de* **Rhus-t** b2.de* ruta b2.de* sabad b2.de* sel b2.de* sil bg2 staph b2.de* sulph bg2 ter bg2 thuj bg2 *Valer* b2.de* viol-t b2.de*
▽ - **extending** to | **Lumbar** region: calc ptk1 phos ptk1 sabin ptk1

SIDES; complaints of: agar b2.de* agn b2.de* alum b2.de* am-c b2.de* am-m b2.de* ambr b2.de* anac b2.de* ang b2.de* ant-c b2.de* apis b7a.de arn b2.de* ars b2.de* **Asaf** b2.de* asar b2.de* aur b2.de* bar-c b2.de* bell b2.de* bism b2.de* borx b2.de* bov b2.de* bry b2.de* calad b2.de* calc b2.de* camph b2.de* cann-s b2.de* *Canth* b2.de* caps b2.de* carb-an b2.de* **Carb-v** b2.de* caust b2.de* cham b2.de* chel b2.de* **Chin** b2.de* cina b2.de* clem b2.de* *Cocc* b2.de* coff b2.de* colch b2.de* coloc b2.de* croc b2.de* cycl b2.de* dig b2.de* dros b2.de* dulc b2.de* euph b2.de* ferr b2.de* graph b2.de* guaj b2.de* hell b2.de* hep b2.de* hyos b2.de* **Ign** b2.de* iod b2.de* ip b2.de* kali-c b2.de* kali-n b2.de* kreos b2.de* *Laur* b2.de* *Led* b2.de* *Lyc* b2.de* m-ambo b2.de m-arct b2.de* m-aust b2.de* mag-c b2.de* mag-m b2.de* mang b2.de* meny b2.de* merc b2.de* merc-c b4a.de mez b2.de* mosch b2.de* mur-ac b2.de* *Nat-c* b2.de* nat-m b2.de* *Nit-ac* b2.de* nux-m b2.de* *Nux-v* b2.de* olnd b2.de* op b2.de* par b2.de* petr b2.de* phos b2.de* plat b2.de* plb b2.de* puls b2.de* ran-b b2.de* ran-s b2.de* rheum b2.de* rhod b2.de* rhus-t b2.de* ruta b2.de* sabad b2.de* sabin b2.de* samb b2.de* *Sars* b2.de* sec b2.de* seneg b2.de* sep b2.de* sil b2.de* spig b2.de* spong b2.de* stann b2.de* *Staph* b2.de* stront-c b2.de* *Sulph* b2.de* *Tarax* b2.de* teucr b2.de* *Thuj* b2.de* valer b2.de* viol-t b2.de* *Zinc* b2.de*
- **right**: ars ptk1 lach ptk1 *Lyc* ptk1 *Rhus-t* ptk1

▽ • **extending** to | **left**: sep ptk1
- **left**: alum ptk1 arg-met ptk1 asaf ptk1 brom ptk1 dulc ptk1 fl-ac ptk1 hep ptk1 plb ptk1 rheum ptk1 *Sil* ptk1 *Sulph* ptk1 tarax ptk1

▽ • **extending** to | **right**: nux-v ptk1

O - **Across**, from one side to the other side lyc bg2
- **External**:
  - **right**: agar fse1.de *Agn* fse1.de am-m fse1.de *Ambr* fse1.de anac fse1.de *Ang* fse1.de *Ant-c* fse1.de arg-met fse1.de *Arn* fse1.de **Ars** fse1.de asaf fse1.de aur fse1.de *Bar-c* fse1.de bell fse1.de *Bism* fse1.de *Bry* fse1.de *Calad* fse1.de calc fse1.de camph fse1.de cann-s fse1.de *Canth* fse1.de *Carb-an* fse1.de *Carb-v* fse1.de *Caust* fse1.de chel fse1.de chin fse1.de *Cic* fse1.de *Clem* fse1.de cocc fse1.de *Colch* fse1.de *Coloc* fse1.de con fse1.de *Croc* fse1.de cupr fse1.de *Cycl* fse1.de dig fse1.de *Dros* fse1.de dulc fse1.de graph fse1.de guaj fse1.de *Ign* fse1.de iod fse1.de *Ip* fse1.de kali-c fse1.de *Kali-n* fse1.de kreos fse1.de *Lach* fse1.de laur fse1.de *Lyc* fse1.de m-aust fse1.de *Mag-m* fse1.de meny fse1.de *Merc* fse1.de mez fse1.de *Mosch* fse1.de nat-c fse1.de nat-m fse1.de nit-ac fse1.de nux-m fse1.de *Nux-v* fse1.de olnd fse1.de petr fse1.de ph-ac fse1.de *Phos* fse1.de *Plat* fse1.de plb fse1.de *Puls* fse1.de ran-b fse1.de *Ran-s* fse1.de rhod fse1.de *Rhus-t* fse1.de sabad fse1.de *Sabin* fse1.de samb fse1.de *Seneg* fse1.de *Sep* fse1.de sil fse1.de spig fse1.de spong fse1.de squil fse1.de *Stann* fse1.de *Stront-c* fse1.de sulph fse1.de tarax fse1.de *Teucr* fse1.de *Thuj* fse1.de verb fse1.de *Viol-t* fse1.de zinc fse1.de
  - **left**: *Acon* fse1.de agar fse1.de agn fse1.de **Alum** fse1.de *Am-c* fse1.de *Am-m* fse1.de ambr fse1.de anac fse1.de ang fse1.de ant-c fse1.de *Ant-t* fse1.de *Arg-met* fse1.de arn fse1.de ars fse1.de **Asaf** fse1.de *Asar* fse1.de *Aur* fse1.de bar-c fse1.de *Bell* fse1.de *Bov* fse1.de *Bry* fse1.de *Calc* fse1.de camph fse1.de *Cann-s* fse1.de canth fse1.de *Caps* fse1.de carb-an fse1.de carb-v fse1.de caust fse1.de *Cham* fse1.de chel fse1.de *Chin* fse1.de *Cina* fse1.de cocc fse1.de colch fse1.de coloc fse1.de *Con* fse1.de croc fse1.de *Cupr* fse1.de *Dig* fse1.de **Dulc** fse1.de *Euph* fse1.de *Graph* fse1.de *Guaj* fse1.de **Hep** fse1.de *Ign* fse1.de *Iod* fse1.de *Kali-c* fse1.de *Kreos* fse1.de laur fse1.de *Led* fse1.de *Lyc* fse1.de *M-arct* fse1.de m-aust fse1.de mag-m fse1.de *Mang* fse1.de *Meny* fse1.de merc fse1.de *Mez* fse1.de *Mur-ac* fse1.de *Nat-c* fse1.de *Nat-m* fse1.de *Nit-ac* fse1.de nux-m fse1.de *Nux-v* fse1.de *Olnd* fse1.de *Op* fse1.de *Par* fse1.de petr fse1.de *Ph-ac* fse1.de plat fse1.de

Sides; complaints of – **External** – **left**: ...
Plb fse1.de *Puls* fse1.de *Ran-b* fse1.de **Rheum** fse1.de rhod fse1.de rhus-t fse1.de *Ruta* fse1.de *Sabad* fse1.de sabin fse1.de *Samb* fse1.de *Sars* fse1.de *Sel* fse1.de sep fse1.de sil fse1.de *Spig* fse1.de *Spong* fse1.de squil fse1.de stann fse1.de *Staph* fse1.de *Sul-ac* fse1.de **Sulph** fse1.de **Tarax** fse1.de teucr fse1.de thuj fse1.de *Valer* fse1.de *Verb* fse1.de viol-t fse1.de zinc fse1.de

SOLAR PLEXUS; complaints of: *Caust* b4a.de dioxi rbp6 *Ip* b7a.de *Lyc* b4a.de **Thuj** b4a.de

SPLEEN; complaints of: abies-c abrot acon b2.de* aegle-f mtf11 *Agar* k* *Agn* b2.de* aloe bg2 alum k* *Am-c* k* am-m k* anac k* anders mtf11 ant-t b2.de* aran bg2* arg-met b2.de* arg-n bg2 arn k* **Ars** k* *Ars-i* **Asaf** k* asar b2.de* aur b2.de* bar-c b2.de* bell b2.de* bell-p c2 berb bg2* berb-a c2 bism b2.de* boerh-d mtf11 *Borx* k* bov b2.de* *Bry* k* cadm-s k2 calad b2.de* calc-ar br1 calc-caust c2 calc-p camph k* *Cann-s* k* *Canth* k* caps k* carb-an k* carb-v k* card-m bg2* caust k* **Cean** k* cedr k* cham k* chel k* **Chin** k* chinin-s bg2 cimic mtf11 coc-c colch k* con k* cot c2 *Dios* dros b2.de* *Dulc* k* eucal c2 *Euon-a* br1 euph-a c2 *Ferr* k* *Ferr-m* ferr-p mtf11 fl-ac bg2* gran graph b2.de* grin bg2* guaj b2.de* helia c2* hep b2.de* **Ign** k* *Iod* k* ip b2.de* iris ptk1 jug-r kali-bi ptk1 kali-i bg2* kali-n k* kali-p kr1 kiss c2 kreos b2.de* lact-v c2 *Laur* k* lina mtf11 lith-c c2 lob-s c2 luf-b mtf11 lyc b2.de* mag-c k* mag-m k* malar c2 mang k* menth-pu mtf11 merc k* merl c2 mez k* mosch b2.de* *Mur-ac* k* naja ptk1 *Nat-ar* nat-c b2.de* *Nat-m* k* nat-s c2* nit-ac k* nux-m b2.de* *Nux-v* k* olnd b2.de* parth c2 petr b2.de* ph-ac k* phos k* *Plat* k* *Plb* k* plb-xyz c2 polyg-xyz c2 polyp-p c2 psor k* ptel c2* puls b2.de* querc-r c2 querc-r-g-s mtf11 **Ran-b** k* ran-s b2.de* rheum b2.de* rhod k* rhus-t k* rub-t c2* *Ruta* k* sabad b2.de* sacch c2 sars k* sec b2.de* sel b2.de* seneg b2.de* sep b2.de* sil k* slag c2 spig b2.de* spong b2.de* squil k* *Stann* k* succ c2* succ-xyz c2 **Sul-ac** k* sulph k* tarax b2.de* teucr b2.de* ther ptk1 thuj k* tinas mtf11 *Urt-u* k* valer k* verat k* verb k* vib bg2 viol-t b2.de* *Zinc* k* [spect dfg1]
- **accompanied** by:
  - **anemia**: cean br1
  - **dropsy** (See GENERALS - Dropsy - external - spleen; GENERALS - Dropsy - general - accompanied - spleen)
  - **respiration**; complaints of: arn bg2 ruta bg2
  - **stool**; complaints of: anac bg2 asaf bg2 bry bg2 chin bg2 dulc bg2 ign bg2 puls bg2 rhus-t bg2 sul-ac bg2
- **animals**; in domestic: anthraci bro1
- **chronic**: querc-r-g-s br1
- **epidemic**: *Anthraci* br1

▽ - **extending** to | **Chest**: borx ptk1

UMBILICUS; complaints of: *Acon* b2.de* *Aloe* bg2 alum b2.de* am-c b2.de* *Am-m* b2.de* ambr b2.de* *Anac* b2.de* ant-c b2.de* ant-t b2.de* apis b7a.de arg-n bg2 arn b2.de* asaf b2.de* bapt bg2 bar-c b2.de* *Bell* b2.de* berb bg2 *Bov* b2.de* **Bry** b2.de* calad b2.de* calc b2.de* camph b2.de* cann-s b2.de* canth b2.de* caps b2.de* carb-an b2.de* carb-v b2.de* caust b2.de* cham b2.de* *Chel* b2.de* *Chin* b2.de* *Cina* b2.de* cocc b2.de* colch b2.de* *Coloc* b2.de* con b2.de* crot-t bg2 dig b2.de* dios bg2* *Dulc* b2.de* graph b2.de* guaj b2.de* hell b2.de* hep b2.de* hyos b2.de* *Ign* b2.de* iod b2.de* *Ip* b2.de* kali-c b2.de* kali-n b2.de* **Kreos** b2.de* lach b2.de* laur b2.de* lept ptk1 m-ambo b2.de* m-arct b2.de* m-aust b2.de* mag-c b2.de* mag-m b2.de* mang b2.de* meny b2.de* merc b2.de* **Merc-c** b4a.de mez b2.de* *Mosch* b2.de* mur-ac b2.de* *Nat-c* b2.de* *Nux-m* b2.de* **Nux-v** b2.de* *Olnd* b2.de* op b2.de* par b2.de* **Ph-ac** b2.de* phos b2.de* *Plat* b2.de* **Plb** b2.de* ptel bg2 puls b2.de* ran-b b2.de* ran-s b2.de* *Rheum* b2.de* rhod b2.de* **Rhus-t** b2.de* ruta b2.de* sabin b2.de* sars b2.de* seneg b2.de* *Sep* b2.de* sil b2.de* *Spig* b2.de* spong b2.de* stann b2.de* staph b2.de* stram b2.de* *Stront-c* b2.de* *Sul-ac* b2.de* *Sulph* b2.de* tarax b2.de* teucr b2.de* thuj b2.de* valer b2.de* **Verat** b2.de* **Verb** b2.de* viol-t b2.de* zinc b2.de*

O - **Region** of | **alternating** with | **Bladder**; complaints of: ter ptk1

▽ • **extending** to:
- ⁝ **Back**: plat ptk1
- ⁝ **Groin**: verat-v ptk1
- ⁝ **Mammae**: pall ptk1
- ⁝ **Pelvis**: pall ptk1 rumx ptk1 sep ptk1
- ⁝ **Rectum**: aloe bg2* ars ptk1 *Crot-t* bg2* dios bg2* ferr-i ptk1 lyc ptk1 mag-m bg2 nat-m bg2 rhus-t bg2 spong bg2
- ⁝ **Uterus**: ip ptk1

Abdomen

NIGHT: | **Rectum** and anus: ars bg2

ABSCESS: alum-p k2 arg-n bg2 ars bg2 ars-i bg2 bar-m c2 berb bg2 *Calc* k* calc-p k2 *Calc-s* k* carc cd *Hep* k* hydr bg2 *Merc* k* nit-ac bg2* rhus-t bro1* ruta bg2 sang bg2 *Sil* k* sulph mrr1 syph thuj
- **painless**: calc-s k2
- O - **Around**: calc-s c2
- **Below** the coccyx; just: (↗*BACK - Abscess - coccyx)* *Paeon*
- **Glands**; perianal: calc-s mtf11 myric mtf11 tarent-c mtf11
- **Perineum**: ant-c bg2 ant-t bg2 *Caust* bg2 crot-h bg2* *Hep* k* *Merc* k* paeon bg2 *Sil* k*

APHTHOUS condition of anus: (↗*GENERALS - Aphthae)* *Bapt* k* *Borx* k* bry *Kali-chl* *Merc* *Merc-c* *Mur-ac* *Nit-ac* **Sul-ac** k* *Sulph*

BALL in rectum; sensation of a (See Lump)

BATHING:
- **cold**:
  - **amel.** | **Rectum** and anus: aloe bg2 euphr bg2

BEER:
- **amel.** | **Rectum** and anus: aloe bg2

BENDING: | **agg.** | **Rectum** and anus: crot-t bg2
- **amel.** | **Rectum** and anus: chel bg2 petr bg2

BLACK: merc bg2 merc-c

BLEEDING (See Hemorrhage)

BOILS:
- O - **Anus**:
  - O · **In** (See Eruptions - anus - boils)
  - · **Near** (See Eruptions - anus - boils)

BUBBLES:
- **escaping** from anus; as if bubbles are: arg-met bg2 coloc bg2 nat-m bg2
- O - **Anus**; feeling of bubbles in coloc a1* nat-m bg2*

CANCER: **Aloe** sne* *Alum* k* alumn ptk1* ars sne **Ars-i** sne calc-caust sne carb-an sne carb-v vh card-m mtf11 cham sne coll sne germ-met srj5• graph vh grat sne hep sne hura sne hydr sne* iod sne *Kali-c* vh kali-m mtf11 laur c1* lyc vh *Merc* sne merc-c sne mur-ac vh *Nat-s* mrr1* *Nit-ac* k* orni sne paeon sne* phyt c2* polyg-h mtf11 puls sne rat gm1 ruta k* salv sne sang ptk1 *Scir* rmk1• scroph-n sne sed-ac sne sed-t sne sem-t sne sep c2* sil sne sol-t-ae gm1 spig c2* staph sne sulph sne syc sne thiosin gm1 *Thuj* rmk1• toxi gm1 tub al ur-ac sne vario sne
- **accompanied** by | **respiration**; asthmatic: nat-s mrr1
- ▽ - **extending** to | **Sigmoid**: alumn bro1 phyt bro1 spig bro1
- O - **Anus**: *Alum* b4a.de *Ars* b4a.de nux-v b7a.de sulph b4a.de

CATARRH of the rectum: (↗*Moisture)* acon k2 aloe k2 alum k2 *Arg-n* aur kali-ar k2 kali-m k2 *Nit-ac* petr k2

CAULIFLOWER excrescence: *Thuj* k*

CHILLINESS:
- **constipation**; during: lac-d c1
- O - **Anus**; in | **stool** agg.; after: kali-c h2
- **Rectum**; in | **stool**; before: *Lyc* k*

CHOLERA: acon k* agar-ph c2 ampe-qu c2 anil c2 ant-t c2* *Ars* k* aven c1* bism c2 cadm-s br1 calc-ar c2 **Camph** k* caps hr1 carb-ac c2 *Carb-v* k* chinin-s c2 cic k* colch k* crot-h br1 crot-t c2 **Cupr** k* cupr-act mtf11 *Cupr-ar* k* dulc c2 elat c2 euon c2 euonin c2 euph-c c2 euph-l c2 gnaph c2 *Grat* k* gua c2* hell c2 hell-f c2 *Hydr-ac* k* ip c2 iris jatr-c k* *Laur* k* lim c2* mur-ac k* nux-m *Op* k* ph-ac k* *Phos* k* phyt c2 plect c2 *Podo* k* *Psor* k* ric c2 *Salol* c1 *Sec* k* sulph k* *Tab* k* thuj **Verat** k* xan c1 zinc c2
- **accompanied** by:
  - **coldness**: *Camph* tl1 *Verat* tl1
  - **collapse** (See GENERALS - Collapse - accompanied - cholera)
  - **convulsions**: cupr mtf33
  - **cramps**: *Cupr* tl1*
  - **hiccough**: *Aeth* st1 *Arg-n* st1 *Cic* st1 *Cupr* st1 *Mag-p* st1 *Ph-ac* st1 verat st1
  - **perspiration**; copious: verat tl1
  - **vomiting**: ars bro1 camph bro1

Cholera – accompanied by – **vomiting**: ...
  - ⋮ **predominantly**: *Bism* hr1
- O · **Tongue**:
  - ⋮ **blue** discoloration: *Iris* kr1*
  - ⋮ **clean** tongue: *Phos* kr1*
  - ⋮ **mucus**; white: ant-t kr1*
  - ⋮ **pale**: ant-t kr1* *Cupr* kr1* *Verat* kr1*
  - ⋮ **white** discoloration of the: *Iris* kr1* *Ph-ac* kr1*
- **asiatica**; cholera: *Acon* bro1 agar-ph bro1 *Ars* bro1 bell bro1 bry bro1 *Camph* bro1 *Canth* bro1 carb-v bro1* chinin-s bro1 cic bro1 colch bro1 *Cupr* bro1 *Cupr-act* bro1 *Cupr-ar* bro1 dig bro1 euph-c bro1 gua bro1 *Hydr-ac* bro1 *Ip* bro1 jatr-c bro1 kali-bi bro1 lach bro1 merc-c bro1 naja bro1 nux-v bro1 op bro1 *Ph-ac* bro1 phos bro1 quas bro1 rhus-t bro1 *Sec* bro1 sulph bro1* tab bro1 ter bro1 verat bro1* zinc bro1
- **beginning** (= cholerine): ant-c bro1 ars bro1 camph tl1 *Crot-t* bro1 *Cupr-ar* bro1 dios bro1 elat bro1 euph-c bro1 *Grat* bro1 *Ip* bro1 iris bro1 *Jatr-c* bro1 nuph bro1 *Ph-ac* bro1 sec al2* *Verat* bro1
  - · **accompanied** by:
    - ⋮ **coldness**: camph tl1
    - ⋮ **collapse**: camph tl1
    - ⋮ **prostration**; sudden: camph tl1
    - ⋮ **Tongue** | **white** discoloration of the tongue: *Asar* kr1*
- **cholera**-like symptoms: elat br1
  - · **menses** | **before**:
    - ⋮ **agg.**: am-c bro1 bov bro1 verat bro1
      - . **women**; in obese: am-c br1
    - ⋮ **during** | **agg.**: am-c bro1 bov bro1 verat bro1
- **convulsive**: cupr tl1
- **infantum**: acon k* **Aeth** k* ant-c k* ant-t k* *Apis* bro1 arg-n bro1 *Ars* k* *Bac* hr1* *Bell* k* *Bism* k* bism-sn mtf11 bry bro1 cadm-s c1* *Calc* k* calc-act bro1 calc-p c2* camph k* camph-br c2* canth bro1 carb-v k* cham c1* chin bro1 colch k* coloc k* colos corn k* *Crot-t* k* cuph c2* cupr bro1 cupr-act bro1 cupr-ar br1* dros tl1 *Dulc* k* echi mtf11 elat k* euph-c c2* *Ferr* ferr-p bro1 graph bro1 grat k* **Guaj** k* hydr-ac bro1 indol bro1 *Iodof* bro1 *Ip* k* *Iris* k* jatr-c kali-bi kali-br k* *Kreos* k* *Laur* k* *Mag-c* k* manc c2 *Med* k* merc bro1 nat-m k* nux-m tl1 oeno c2 *Op* k* ox-ac c2* passi c2* *Phos* k* phyt bro1* podo k* *Psor* k* *Puls* k* pyrog jl2* raph res bro1 *Rhus-t* k* ric c2 sal-ac tl1 sars *Sec* k* sep bro1 *Sil* k* *Stram* k* sulph k* *Tab* k* thuj k* tub hr *Verat* k* zinc bro1*
  - · **accompanied** by:
    - ⋮ **body**; warm: bism ptk1
    - ⋮ **opisthotonos**: med ptk1*
    - ⋮ **stools**; green watery: aeth tl1 calc tl1 calc-p tl1 sal-ac tl1
    - ⋮ **Tongue**; white discoloration of the | **Root**: verat kr1*
- **morbus** cholera: (↗*ABDOMEN - Inflammation - gastroenteritis; GENERALS - Food poisoning)* ant-c ant-t k* arg-n k2 *Ars* k* bism bro1 camph k* caul c2 chlol bro1 *Colch* k* coloc k* crot-h ptk1 *Crot-t* k* *Cupr* k* *Cupr-ar* k* elat k* euon-a c2 *Ferr* *Grat* k* **Guaj** k* hydr-ac bro1 *Ip* k* *Iris* k* *Jatr-c* kali-bi mag-p k2 op bro1 oper bro1 ph-ac *Phos* **Podo** k* *Psor* raph *Sec* k* *Tab* thuj **Verat** k*
  - · **accompanied** by:
    - ⋮ **Tongue** | **white** discoloration of the tongue: puls kr1*
- **old** people: aeth c1*
- **prophylaxis**: ars bro1* cupr-act bro1 cupr-ar ptk1 verat bro1*
- **spasmodic**: *Cupr* tl1

COFFEE agg.: | **Rectum** and anus: fl-ac bg2

COITION: | **after** | **Rectum** and anus: anac bg2 calc bg2 caust bg2 merc-c bg2 sil bg2
- **during** | **agg.**: caust ptk1 merc-c ptk1 sil ptk1

COLD:
- **agg.** | **Rectum** and Anus: mur-ac bg2

COLD; AFTER TAKING A: | **Rectum** and anus: nat-c bg2

COLDNESS in anus: all-c androc srj1• con tl1 kali-bi k* nat-m k* sil k* sulph k*
- **afternoon**: kali-bi k*
- **drops**, cold: cann-s
- **flatus** and stool, during: *Con* k*
- **waking** agg.; after: nat-m k* sulph k*
- **walking** in open air agg.; after: sil k*

Rectum

COMPLAINTS of rectum: acon b2.de *Aesc* ptk1* aloe bg2* alum b2.de* am-c b2.de am-m b2.de ambr b2.de* anac b2.de* ang b2.de ant-c b2.de ant-t b2.de* arn b2.de ars b2.de* asar b2.de* aur b2.de bell b2.de* borx b2.de* bov b2.de bry b2.de **Calc** b2.de* camph b2.de canth b2.de* carb-an b2.de carb-v b2.de* caust b2.de* cham b2.de chin b2.de* cic b2.de cina b2.de* cocc b2.de* colch b2.de* *Coll* mrr1 con b2.de cupr b2.de dulc b2.de* euph b2.de* ferr b2.de* graph b2.de* hell b2.de* hep b2.de **Ign** b2.de* iod b2.de kali-c b2.de* kreos b2.de* lach b2.de* laur b2.de **Lyc** b2.de* m-ambo b2.de m-arct b2.de m-aust b2.de mag-c b2.de mag-m b2.de* mang b2.de meny b2.de merc b2.de* *Merc-c* ptk1 mez b2.de* mur-ac b2.de nat-c b2.de* **Nat-m** b2.de* nit-ac b2.de* nux-m b2.de **Nux-v** b2.de* op b2.de *Paeon* mrr1 petr b2.de* ph-ac b2.de **Phos** b2.de* plat b2.de plb b2.de* **Podo** bg2* puls b2.de* *Rat* br1* rhod b2.de* rhus-t b2.de* ruta b2.de* sabad b2.de* sars b2.de **Sep** b2.de* sil b2.de* spig b2.de* spong b2.de squil b2.de stann b2.de* staph b2.de stram b2.de stront-c b2.de* sul-ac b2.de **Sulph** b2.de* teucr b2.de* thuj b2.de* valer b2.de verat b2.de zinc b2.de

- **accompanied** by:
  - **menses**; complaints of: erig ptk1
  - O **Bladder**; complaints of: ambr ptk1 *Canth* ptk1 caps ptk1 erig ptk1 lil-t ptk1 *Merc-c* ptk1 pyrog ptk1 sabin ptk1
  - **Nose**; complaints of: calc bg1
- **acute**: thiosin br1
- **alternating** with | **Wrists**; complaints of: sulph ptk1
- ▽ **extending** to:
  - O **Ankles**: alum ptk1
  - **Genitals**: chin ptk1 lil-t ptk1 rhus-t ptk1 sil ptk1 zinc ptk1
  - **Testes**: sil ptk1
  - **Thighs**: alumn ptk1
  - **Upward**: graph ptk1 *Ign* ptk1 lach ptk1 phos ptk1 *Sep* ptk1 sulph ptk1
- O **Anus** (See Anus)
- **Perineum** (See Perineum)
- **Rectum** and anus (See Rectum)

CONDYLOMATA: *Arg-n* aur k* *Aur-m* aur-s k2 benz-ac k* carc gk6 castm sne *Caust* **Cinnb** k* *Euphr* k* jac-c k* kali-br bro1 *Kreos* b7a.de *Lyc* k* med gk merc *Merc-d* *Mill* k* *Nat-s* k* **Nit-ac** k* petr k* phos plut-n srj7• sabin k* sep k* staph k* sulph k* syc bka1*• syph k2 **Thuj** k* vanil fd5.de

- **bleeding**, copious: *Mill*
- **cauliflower**: sabin k2
- **flat**: *Euphr* k* sulph k* **Thuj** k*
- **itching**: euphr h2*
- **moist**: petr hr1
- **sensitive**, extremely: **Staph**
- **sore**: benz-ac *Thuj*
- **stitching**: euphr h2* thuj h1*
  - **touch** agg.: euphr h2

CONGESTION: *Aesc* bro1 *Aloe* bro1 alum bro1 chinin-s br1 *Coll* bro1 hyper bro1 nat-m bro1 neg br1 nit-ac bro1 sabin bro1 sep h2* sul-ac h2* *Sulph* bro1

- **wine** agg.: **Fl-ac** a1
- O **Anus**: bell bg2 carb-v b4.de* podo bg2 sep b4.de* sul-ac b4.de*

CONSTIPATION: (↗*Inactivity*) abies-c a1* abies-n k* abrom-a ks5 *Abrot* acet-ac k2 acon b2.de* **Aesc** k* *Aesc-g* bro1 *Aeth* *Agar* k* agav-a br1 *Agn* k* aids nl2• alet k* allox tpw4* *Aloe* k* **Alum** k* alum-p k2 alum-sil k2 **Alumin** stj2* **Alumn** k* *Am-c* k* *Am-m* k* *Ambr* k* ammc amp rly4• amph a1 *Anac* k* anan anders bnj1 androc srj1*• *Ang* k* ant-c k* ant-t b2.de* anth vh1 anthraq rly4• **Apis** k* aq-mar skp7* *Arg-met* k* *Arg-n* arge-pl rwt5• arist-cl sp1 arn k* **Ars** k* *Ars-i* arund asaf k* asar b2.de* asc-c asc-t aster k* *Aur* k* aur-ar k2 aur-i k2 aur-m *Aur-m-n* wbt2• aur-s k2 bacls-7 pte1*• bad *Bar-c* k* bar-i k2 *Bar-m* bar-ox-suc rly4• bar-s k2 bell b2.de* *Berb* k* bit-ar wht1• bol-la borx k* botul br1* bov k* brach brass-n-o srj5• bros-gau mrc1 brucel sa3• **Bry** k* bung-fa mtf *Cact* cadm-met sp1 *Caesal-b* zzc1• calad k* **Calc** k* calc-f k2* calc-i k2 *Calc-p* k* *Calc-s* calc-sil k2* camph k* cann-s k* canth b2.de* caps b2.de* *Carb-ac* k* *Carb-an* k* *Carb-v* k* carbn-dox knl3• **Carbn-s** carc fb* *Card-m* k* carl br1 carneg-g rwt1• cartl-s rly4• cas-s c1* casc k* cassia-s ccrh1• caul **Caust** k* cham b2.de* *Chel* k* *Chim* *Chin* k* chinin-ar chinin-s chion bro1 chlam-tr bcx2• chord-umb rly4• chr-ac cic b2.de* cimx cina k* **Clem** cob-n sp1 *Coca* k* **Cocc** k* **Coff** k* colch k* coli jl2* **Coll** k* *Coloc* k* **Con** k* *Cop* cor-r cortiso sp1* *Croc* k* *Crot-c* k* *Crot-h* k* crot-t cub cuph br1 cupr k* cycl k* cystein-l rly4• *Daph* k* *Dig* k* *Dios* diphtox jl2 dol br1* dream-p sdj1• dros b2.de* *Dulc* k* dys fmm1• *Elaps* ery-a eug bro1 euon k* eup-per k2 euph b2.de*

Constipation: ...
euphr b2.de* falco-pe nl2• fel bro1 *Ferr* k* *Ferr-ar* *Ferr-i* ferr-p fic-c mtf11 *Fl-ac* flor-p rsj3• *Form* friedr bnh1 fuma-ac rly4• gaert pte1*• gal-ac c1 galeoc-c-h gms1• galla-q-r nl2• *Gamb* gels bro1 ger-i rly4• germ-met srj5• *Glyc* bro1 granit-m es1• **Graph** k* *Grat* bg2* *Guaj* k* guat sp1 haliae-lc srj5• ham k2 hed sp1 hedy a1* *Hell* k* helodr-cal knl2• hep k* hippoz hir rsj4*• *Hydr* k* *Hydrc* hydrog srj2• hydroph rsj6• hyos k* *Hyper* *Ign* k* *Iod* k* irid-met srj5• *Iris* k* ix bnm8• jab jac-c *Jatr-c* *Kali-ar* *Kali-bi* k* *Kali-br* *Kali-c* k* *Kali-chl* *Kali-i* kali-m k2* kali-n b2.de* kali-p *Kali-s* kali-sil k2 ketogl-ac rly4• kola stb3• *Kreos* k* lac-ac bro1 **Lac-d** k* lac-del hrn2• lac-f wza1• lac-h sk4• lac-leo hrn2• **Lach** k* lact-v c1 lat-h bnm5• lat-m bnm6• *Laur* k* led k* *Lept* *Lil-t* limest-b es1• luf-op rsj5• luna kg1• **Lyc** k* lycps-v m-ambo b2.de* m-arct b2.de* *Mag-c* k* **Mag-m** k* mag-s k* malar jl2 *Manc* mand sp1* mang k* marb-w es1• med k* melal-alt gya4 meli *Meny* k* *Merc* k* merc-c k* *Merc-i-f* **Mez** k* mim-p rsj8• mom-f jsx1.fr *Moni* jl2* morg fmm1• morg-g fmm1• *Morg-p* pte1*• morph bro1 *Mosch* k* mucs-nas rly4• *Mur-ac* k* murx musa a1* musca-d szs1 myric nabal bro1 nad rly4• naja *Nat-ar* *Nat-c* k* nat-f sp1 **Nat-m** k* nat-ox rly4• nat-p nat-pyru rly4• nat-s nat-sil fd3.de• neon srj5• nept-m lsd2.fr nicc nicc-met br1* nicc-s br1 nicotam rly4• **Nit-ac** k* nit-m-ac bro1 *Nux-m* k* **Nux-v** k* nyct br1* oci-sa sp1* **Oena** k* olib-sac wmh1 olnd k* **Op** k* oscilloc jl2 osm *Ox-ac* oxal-a rly4• ozone sde2• paeon pall par b2.de* paraf br1* parathyr jl2 pegan-ha tpi1• petr k* petr-ra shn4• ph-ac k* phasco-ci rbp2 **Phos** k* phys bro1 *Phyt* k* pin-con oss2• pitu-gl skp7• plac rzf5• plac-s rly4• **Plat** k* **Plb** k* *Plb-act* bro1 pneu jl2 *Podo* k* polys sk4• positr nl2• pot-e rly4• propr sa3• prot pte1*• *Psor* k* *Ptel* *Puls* k* *Pyrog* k* querc-r c1* ran-b b2.de* *Raph* *Rat* k* rham-cal bro1 rheum b2.de* rhod b2.de* *Rhus-g* tmo3• rhus-t k* rob **Ruta** k* *Sabad* k* *Sabin* k* sal-fr sle1• sang *Sanguis-s* hrn2• **Sanic** k* saroth sp1 *Sars* k* *Sec* k* secret bwa3 *Sel* k* *Seneg* k* senn br1* **Sep** k* **Sil** k* sil-mar bro1 silphu br1 sinus rly4• sol c1 spig b2.de* *Spong* k* squil k* *Stann* k* **Staph** k* **Stram** k* streptoc rly4• stront-c b2.de* **Stry** k* succ-ac rly4• suis-em rly4• suis-hep rly4• suis-pan rly4• *Sul-ac* k* sul-i k2 sulfa sp1 **Sulph** k* sumb suprar rly4• syc fmm1• *Sym-r* br1* syph c1* *Tab* k* tann-ac bro1 *Tarent* k* tax-br oss1• tela zzc1• tell k* *Ter* tetox pin2• thal-s c1 thal-xyz srj8• *Ther* thiam rly4• **Thuj** k* thymul sa3• tril-p *Trios* rsj11• tritic-vg fd5.de *Tub* k2* tub-m vn* urt-u ust v-a-b jl2 vanil fd5.de vario ven-m rsj12• **Verat** k* *Verb* k* vero-o rly4*• vesp *Vib* viol-o k* viol-t b2.de* visc c1* **Zinc** k* zinc-fcy a1 zinc-m bro1 zinc-p k2 [*Alumin-p* stj2 *Alumin-s* stj2 *Ind* stj2 sol-ecl cky1 spect dfg1 tax jsj7]

- **daytime**: pneu jl2
- **morning**: dulc fd4.de luf-op rsj5• xan c1
- **evening**: granit-m es1•
- **accompanied** by:
  - **anemia** (See GENERALS - Anemia - accompanied - constipation)
  - **apyrexia**: nat-m bro1
  - **colic**: | **flatulent**: ambr bg2 cact bg2 carb-an bg2 card-m bg2 dig bg2 graph bg2 iod bg2 mang bg2 plat bg2 senec bg2 uran-n bg2
  - **cough**: nat-c b4.de* *Sep* b4a.de
  - **diabetes** (See GENERALS - Diabetes mellitus - accompanied - constipation)
  - **epilepsy** (See GENERALS - Convulsions - epileptic - during - constipation)
  - **faintness** (See GENERALS - Faintness - accompanied - constipation)
  - **gallstones** (See ABDOMEN - Gallstones - accompanied - constipation)
  - **headache** | **chronic** (See HEAD - Pain - accompanied - constipation)
  - **hemorrhage** from rectum (See Hemorrhage - accompanied - constipation)
  - **hemorrhoids**: aesc bro1* *Aesc-g* bro1 *Aloe* bro1 alumn bro1 am-m bro1 anac bro1 *Calc-f* bro1 caust bro1 coll bro1* euon bro1 glon bro1 graph bro1 hydr bro1 kali-s bro1 lyc bro1 nat-m bro1* nit-ac bro1 *Nux-v* bro1 paraf bro1 podo bro1 *Rat* bro1 sil bro1 *Sulph* bro1 verb bro1 wye bro1
  - **neuralgia** (See GENERALS - Pain - neuralgic - accompanied - constipation)
  - **neurasthenia**: ign ptk1

- **paralysis**; one-sided (See GENERALS - Paralysis - one - accompanied - constipation)
- **straining**: alum ptk1 chin ptk1 coll ptk1 nat-m ptk1 *Nux-v* ptk1 rat ptk1 sep ptk1 sil ptk1
  - **stool**; at soft: hir rsj4•
- **urging**:
  - **Lower** abdomen; felt in: aloe bro1
  - **Upper** abdomen; felt in: anac bro1 *Ign* bro1 verat bro1
- **urination**:
  - **complaints** of (See BLADDER - Urination - complaints - accompanied - constipation)
  - **frequent**: sars ptk1
  - **retention** of urine: canth ptk1
- **urine**:
  - **bloody**: lyc ptk1
  - **hot**: ferr ptk1
- **vomiting** (See STOMACH - Vomiting - accompanied - constipation)
- **well**; feeling unusually: calc bg2 psor bg2
- **worms**; complaints of (See Worms - complaints - accompanied - constipation; Worms - complaints - accompanied - constipation - children)
- ○ **Abdomen**:
  - **complaints** of (See ABDOMEN - Complaints - accompanied - constipation)
  - **shuddering** in: plat bro1
  - **weakness** in: plat bro1
- **Anus**:
  - **itching** of: tub jl2
  - **pain** in; sore: graph bro1 nat-m bro1 nit-ac bro1 sil bro1
  - **spasms** of (See Spasms - anus - accompanied - constipation)
- **Back**; pain in: *Aesc* bro1 euon bro1 *Ferr* bro1 kali-bi bro1 psor al1 sulph bro1
- **Heart**:
  - **complaints** of (See CHEST - Heart; complaints - accompanied - constipation)
  - **weakness** of (See CHEST - Weakness - heart - accompanied - constipation)
- **Liver**; complaints of: asar bg2 bry bg2 card-m bg2 chel bg2 coll bg2 kreos bg2 lyc bg2 *Mag-m* bg2* merc-d bg2 mez bro1 nat-s bg2 nux-v bg2 petr bg2 sulph bg2
  - **congestion** (See ABDOMEN - Congestion - liver - accompanied - constipation)
  - **inactivity** (See ABDOMEN - Inactivity - liver - accompanied - constipation)
- **Lower** limbs; complaints of: ham bg2 lyc bg2 nux-v bg2 ruta bg2 sulph bg2
- **Mouth** | **odor**; offensive: carb-ac ptk1
- **Portal** system; complaints of:
  - **congestion** (See ABDOMEN - Portal - accompanied - constipation)
  - **stasis** (See ABDOMEN - Stasis - accompanied - constipation)
- **Prostate** gland; enlargement of (See PROSTATE - Swelling - accompanied - constipation)
- **Rectum**; burning in: abies-c br1*
- **Skin**:
  - **complaints** of: parth vml3•
  - **eruptions**: parth vml3•
  - **itching** of; intense: dol bwa3*
  - **yellow** discoloration of (See SKIN - Discoloration - yellow - accompanied - constipation)
- **Spine**; complaints in: alum bg2 arg-n bg2 nux-v bg2 phos bg2 plb bg2 sil bg2 sulph bg2

- **accompanied** by: ...
  - **Stomach**; complaints of: *Bry* b7a.de* hydr bro1 *Nux-v* b7a.de* puls bro1
  - **Teeth**; pain in (See TEETH - Pain - accompanied - constipation)
  - **Tongue**:
    - **black**: *Lach* kr1*
    - **clean** tongue: *Nat-m* kr1*
    - **white**: *Kali-s* kr1*
  - **Umbilicus**; hernia of (See ABDOMEN - Hernia - umbilical - accompanied - constipation)
  - **Uterus**:
    - **complaints** of: coll bg2 con bg2 fl-ac bg2 graph bg2 lach bg2 mag-m bg2 mez bro1 plat bg2 sep bg2 sulph bg2
    - **prolapsus** of (See FEMALE - Prolapsus - uterus - accompanied - constipation)
- **alcoholism**; in (See MIND - Alcoholism - constipation)
- **alternating** with:
  - **diarrhea** (See Diarrhea - alternating - constipation)
  - **flatus**: staph bg2
  - **hemorrhoids** (See Hemorrhoids - alternating - constipation)
  - **stool**; mucous (See STOOL - Mucous - alternating)
- **antibiotics**; after: moni jl2
- **anxiety**; with (See MIND - Anxiety - constipation)
- **atonic** (See stool - remains)
- **babies** (See children - infants)
- **bowels**:
  - **action** lost | **sensation** as if: lac-del hrn2•
- **brain** congestion; with: apis k2
- **breath**; with offensive: carb-ac c1* op bro1 psor bro1
- **cancer** of rectum, uterus: alumn pd
- **cathartics**; worse after stool which is induced only with: **Coll** cda1*
- **cheese**; from: coloc bro1
- **childbed**; in (See delivery)
- **children**; in: acon hr1* alum bg2* ambr tsm1 ant-c kr1* bry bg2* **Calc** kr1* *Caust* mtf33 *Cham* kr1* coll br1 dol vml3• *Graph* kr1* *Hep* kr1* *Hydr* kr1* **Lyc** bg2* mag-m kr1* nat-m kr1* nit-ac kr1* **Nux-v** bg2* *Nyct* c1* **Op** bg2* *Plat* kr1* *Plb* kr1* *Podo* kr1* psor kr1* sanic mtf33 *Sep* kr1* *Sil* kr1* staph mtf33 sulph bg2* tarent mtf33 verat bg2* zinc mtf33
  - **infants**: aesc bro1* alum h2* *Apis* bro1* *Bac* bn bell bro1 *Bry* bro1* calc bro1 caust bro1* coll bro1* croc bro1 hydr bro1 lyc bro1* mag-m bro1* *Nux-v* bro1* nyct bro1 **Op** ggd1 *Paraf* bro1 plb ptk1 podo bro1 psor bro1* sanic bro1 sel ptk1 sep bro1* *Sil* bro1 sulph bro1 verat bro1*
    - **bottle** or artificial food; fed with: alum br* nux-v br* op br* *Podo* kr
  - **newborns**: alum tl1* med c1 nux-m mrr1 **Nux-v** vh **Op** vh* *Sulph* vh verat mtf33 *Zinc* hr1*
- **chill**; during: alum bg2 ant-c bg2 bell bg2 *Bry* bg2 calc bg2 cann-xyz bg2 *Cocc* bg2 dulc bg2 *Lyc* bg2 *Nux-v* bg2 op bg2 sep bg2 sil bg2 staph bg2 sulph bg2 *Verat* bg2
- **chronic**: aesc bg2* aeth ptk1 alet bg2 alum bg2 am-m bg2 anac bg2 append-xyz mtf11 asc-t ptk1 bac bn **Bry** bg2* cadm-met gm1 *Calc* bg2 *Carb-v* bg2 caust bg2 chin bg2 chinin-s bg2 cocc bg2 **Coll** tl1* con bg2 cuph br1 cycl bg2 fuc br1 galeoc-c-h gms1• *Graph* bg2* ham bg2 hep bg2 hydr br1* ign bg2 *Kali-bi* bg2 kali-c bg2 kali-n bg2 lac-d ptk1 *Lach* bg2 *Lyc* bg2 *Mag-m* bg2* nat-c bg2 **Nat-m** bg2* nux-m bg2 **Nux-v** bg2* *Op* bg2* pall bg2 petr bg2 phos bg2 plat bg2 **Plb** bg2* psor bg2 ruta bg2 sabad bg2 sars bg2 sel bg2* sep bg2 sil bg2 sul-ac bg2 sul-i bg2* *Sulph* bg2* syph ptk1* tab ptk1 tann-ac br1 thuj bg2* v-a-b jl2 verat bg2* vip bg2 [sol-ecl cky1]
  - **children**; in:
    - **infants**: croc ptk1
    - **nurslings**: verat ptk1
  - **old** people; in: phyt ptk1
- **coffee** agg.: *Mosch* k* **Nux-v** hr1
- **cold**; after taking a: ign hr1*
- **cold** milk | **amel.**: iod ptk1*

Rectum

- **company**, in (See presence)
- **constant** desire: aloe k* anac k* carb-v bg2 caust bg2 coloc *Con* k* ign bg2 kali-c bg2 kali-p fd1.de• lyc bg2 *Mag-c* *Mag-m* mez bg2 nat-m bg2 nat-p nit-ac bg2 **Nux-v** k* op hr* *Plb* *Puls* rhus-t a1 rob bg2 ruta k* sabad bg2 sacch-a fd2.de• sang bg2 *Sil* k* *Sulph* tab bg2 vip bg2
- **constriction** of intestines: nux-v tl1
- **delivery**; after: alum bg2 ambr bg2 ant-c bg2 arn bg2 *Bry* b7a.de* *Coll* bro1 ham bg2 lil-t bro1 lyc bg2* mez h2* **Nux-v** b7a.de* op b7a.de* plat bg2 sep bg2 verat bro1 zinc bro1
- **dentition**; during: *Bry* bg2 dol c1* kreos bro1* *Mag-m* bg2* **Nux-v** bg2* op bro1 sil pfa2
- **diarrhea** agg.; after: asc-t c1 dulc fd4.de moni rfm1•
- **difficult** stool: (*↗stool; Inactivity*) acon b7.de* adam skp7• *Aesc* k* aesc-g bro1 agar k* agn b7.de* alet k2* *All-c* aloe **Alum** k* alum-p k2 alum-sil k2 **Alumn** k* *Am-c* k* **Am-m** k* ambr b7.de* amp rly4• *Anac* k* androc srj1• **Ant-c** k* ant-t b7.de anthraq rly4• *Apis* aral vh1 arn b7.de* ars-s-f k2 asaf b7.de* asar b7.de aster bro1 *Aur* k* aur-i k2 *Aur-m* aur-s k2 bamb-a stb2.de• bapt *Bar-c* k* bar-i k2 **Bar-m** bar-ox-suc rly4• bar-s k2 bell b4.de* *Berb* bit-ar wht1• bov k* brass-n-o srj5• **Bry** k* *Cact* cadm-met tpw6 calad b7.de* *Calc* k* calc-i k2 calc-p *Calc-s* calc-sil k2 *Camph* k* canth k* carb-an b4.de* *Carb-v* k* **Carbn-s** *Card-m* bro1 cassia-s ccrh1• **Caust** k* cham k* chel k* chin k* chinin-s bg2 chir-fl gya2 cimx cina b7.de* *Clem* *Cocc* k* colch k* coli rly4• coll k* coloc k* **Con** k* cop crot-t cycl b7.de cystein-l rly4• dig b4.de* dulc k* euph b4.de *Ferr* ferr-i ferr-p flor-p rsj3• fuma-ac rly4• gels k* germ-met srj5• glyc bro1 **Graph** k* grat k* *Hell* k* **Hep** k* hydrog srj2• hyos b7.de* *Ign* k* *Ind* indol bro1 iod k* *Kali-bi* *Kali-c* k* kali-m k2 kali-n b4.de* *Kali-p* **Kali-s** kali-sil k2 kalm ketogl-ac rly4• kola stb3• kreos k* *Lac-c* **Lac-d** lac-h sk4• **Lach** k* lact laur k* lil-t bg2 *Lyc* k* lyss *M-arct* b7.de m-aust b7.de mag-c k* **Mag-m** k* mag-p bg2 mag-s mang k* med jl2 melal-alt gya4 meli meny b7.de* *Merc* k* merc-c *Mez* k* morph bro1 *Mur-ac* k* naja *Nat-c* k* **Nat-m** k* nat-p nat-s **Nit-ac** k* **Nux-m** k* **Nux-v** k* *Oena* ol-an k* olnd k* **Op** k* ox-ac k2 par b7.de *Petr* b4.de* petr-ra shn4• ph-ac k* *Phos* k* **Plat** k* **Plb** k* plut-n srj7• *Podo* positr nl2• pot-e rly4• prun bg2 psil ft1 *Psor* k* *Puls* k* pycnop-sa mrz1 pyrog bro1 ran-b b7.de* ran-s b7.de* *Rat* rheum b7.de* *Rhod* k* *Rhus-t* b7a.de **Ruta** k* sabad b7.de* *Sabin* k* **Sanic** k* *Sars* k* **Sel** k* senec *Seneg* b4.de* **Sep** k* **Sil** k* spig b7.de* spong b7.de* *Stann* k* staph k* *Stram* k* stront-c k* succ-ac rly4• suis-em rly4• suis-pan rly4• sul-ac b4.de* sul-i bg2 **Sulph** k* sumb suprar rly4• *Tarax* b7.de* *Tarent* **Thuj** k* *Trios* rsj11• tritic-vg fd5.de valer k* vanil fd5.de verat b7.de* *Verb* k* *Vib* xero bro1 **Zinc** k* zinc-p k2
  - **hard** stool (See STOOL - Hard)
  - **natural** stool: graph **Psor** **Sil**
  - **painful** stool: cop br1 nux-v mrr1
    - **children**; in: nux-v mrr1
  - **recedes**; stool: agn k* colch bg2 cortiso tpw7 eug gink-b sbd1• hep bg2 kali-s *Lac-d* k* lac-f c1 *Mag-m* k* med bg1* *Mur-ac* k* *Nat-m* k* nat-sil fd3.de• nit-ac ptk1 nux-v tl1 **Op** k* podo fd3.de• *Sanic* k* **Sil** k* sulph k* *Thuj* k* [sol-ecl cky1]
    - **menses**; during: sil ptk1
    - **sensation** of receding: mur-ac bg2
    - **soft** stool: calc-f sp1
  - **soft** stool: agn k* aloe bg2 **Alum** k* alum-sil k2 *Anac* k* *Arn* b7.de* bamb-a stb2.de• *Bry* bg2 calad k* *Calc-p* *Carb-v* k* chel bro1 *Chin* k* chion bro1 coff b7.de* colch k* cortiso tpw7 dulc k* gels k* graph k* *Hell* **Hep** k* *Ign* k* ind bg1 *Kali-c* *Kali-s* kali-sil k2 kola stb3• *Lac-c* k* lach lob lyc k* mag-c h2 mag-m k* med bg1 mez bg2 *Nat-c* k* *Nat-m* k* *Nat-s* k* nept-m lsd2.fr nicc nit-ac k* **Nux-m** k* oci-sa sk4• olnd b7.de* op gk petr k* petr-ra shn4• ph-ac k* phos *Plat* h2* podo k2 *Psor* k* *Puls* k* rat bro1 *Rhod* k* *Ruta* k* sel bg2 **Sep** k* *Sil* k* sol-t-ae vml3• spig b7.de* *Stann* k* staph k* sul-ac bg2 sulph k* tab bg2 tarax k* ther k2 ulm-c jsj8• vanil fd5.de verat mtf33 verat-v bg2 verb zinc k* [tax jsj7]
  - **urinating**, can pass stool only when: aloe alum
- **drinking** | **amel.**: caps bg1 mosch bg1
- **drugs**, after abuse of: agar k* ant-c k* *Bry* k* chin k* **Coloc** k* *Hydr* k* lach k* **Nux-v** k* *Op* k* ruta sulph k*
- **dryness** of rectum, from: *Aesc* bro1 aeth bro1 alet bro1 *Alum* k* alumn bro1 *Bry* bro1* coffin bro1 *Coll* bro1 ferr bro1 hydr bro1 *Lyc* bro1 meli bro1 mez bro1 *Nat-m* bro1 nux-v bro1 *Op* bro1 phys bro1 *Plat* bro1 *Plb-act* bro1 pyrog bro1 ruta bro1 sanic bro1 sel bro1 *Sulph* bro1 verat bro1
- **dysentery**; before: silphu br1
- **eating** | **overeating** agg.; after: mag-s sp1
- **ejaculation**; after: sep h2 thuj h1*
- **emaciation**; with: kreos vh
- **enemas**; after abuse of: *Op* bro1
- **eruptions**; after suppressed: mez
- **exhaustion**; with complete: ferr-ar mtf11
- **fever**; during: alum bg2 am-c bg2 ambr bg2 anders zzc1• *Ant-c* b7a.de *Ant-t* bg2 *Apis* bg2 arn bg2 *Bell* b4a.de* bry b7.de* calad b7.de* calc bg2 cann-xyz bg2 canth bg2 carb-v bg2 caust bg2 chin bg2 *Cocc* b7.de* con bg2 **Cupr** b7.de* *Dulc* b4.de* fl-ac bg2 graph bg2 guaj bg2 kali-c bg2 kreos bg2 lach bg2 laur bg2 **Lyc** b4.de* mag-m bg2 meny bg2 merc bg2 mez bg2 nat-m bg2 nit-ac bg2 *Nux-v* b7.de* *Op* b7a.de* phos bg2 plat bg2 plb bg2 polyp-p br1* puls bg2 rhus-t bg2 sabad bg2 sars bg2 sel bg2 sep bg2 sil bg2 stann bg2 **Staph** b7.de* sul-ac bg2 sulph bg2 thuj bg2 *Verat* b7.de* verb bg2 zinc bg2
- **fingers**; must assist the evacuation with the (See removed)
- **flatulence**; with: aesc tl1 **Coll** tl1 mag-c a1 mag-p bro1 nat-m tl1 sel rsj9• senn br1 suprar rly4•
  - **hemorrhoids**; and: bac bn **Coll** vh
- **followed** by | **diarrhea**: *Trios* rsj11•
- **fright**; after: op cp
- **fruitless** urging; with (See ineffectual)
- **gestation**; during: coll tl1
- **gouty** subjects: grat bro1
- **hard** stool; from (See STOOL - Hard)
- **headache**; during (See HEAD - Pain - accompanied - constipation)
- **heart** weakness (See CHEST - Weakness - heart - accompanied - constipation)
- **home**, when away from: ambr tsm1 dream-p sdj1• *Lyc* k* nat-m gk
- **inactivity** (See Inactivity)
- **ineffectual** urging and straining: acon k* *Aesc* k* agar k* aids nl2• *All-c* k* allox tpw4 aloe k* *Alum* k* alum-p k2 alum-sil k2 alumn k2 am-c b2.de am-m b2.de* **Ambr** k* **Anac** k* androc srj1• ant-c k* ant-t k* anthraq rly4• aphis ptk2 *Apis* b7a.de arg-met arge-pl rwt5• *Arn* k* *Ars* k* ars-i k* asaf k* aster k* bamb-a stb2.de• *Bar-c* k* bar-s k2 *Bell* k* benz-ac k* berb k* bism k* *Bit-ar* wht1• bov k* brach k* *Bry* k* *Cact* cain *Calc* k* calc-i k2 *Calc-s* calc-sil k2 cann-i k* *Cann-s* k* canth k* *Caps* k* carb-ac k* *Carb-an* k* *Carb-v* k* carbn-s carc ib* *Card-m* hr1 carl k* cartl-s rly4• cass a1 cassia-s cdd7*• **Caust** k* cedr k* cench k2 cere-b a1 chel k* *Chim* k* chin k* chinin-ar chinin-s chord-umb rly4• cic-m a1 cimx k* clem k* coc-c k* *Cocc* k* colch k* **Coll** k* *Coloc* k* **Con** k* corn k* *Crot-h* hr1 crot-t k* cupr k* cycl k* cystein-l rly4• dios k* dirc k* dros k* dulc k* elat k* eucal a1 eup-pur k* euph b2.de* eupi k* fago k* falco-pe nl2• *Ferr* k* ferr-ar ferr-i k* *Ferr-ma* a1 ferr-p fil hr1 fl-ac k* form franz a1 fum rly1*• fuma-ac rly4• ger c2 glon gran k* *Graph* k* grat k* guaj bg2 ham k* hell k* hep k* hir skp7• hura **Hydr** hydrog srj2• hyos b2.de* hyper k* *Ign* k* *Iod* k* ip b2.de* kali-ar *Kali-bi* k* *Kali-c* k* kali-n k* kali-p *Kali-s* kali-sil k2* *Kalm* ketogl-ac rly4• kiss a1 kola stb3• kreos k* *Lac-c* *Lac-d* k* lac-e hm2• **Lach** k* lachn c1 laur k* **Lil-t** k* lipp a1 lob-s k* **Lyc** k* m-ambo b2.de* m-aust b7.de *Mag-c* k* **Mag-m** k* mag-s k* mang b2.de melal-alt gya4 **Merc** k* merc-c k* mez b2.de* mosch k* mucs-nas rly4• mur-ac bg2 murx bg2 myric k* nat-ar *Nat-c* k* **Nat-m** k* *Nat-p* nat-pyru rly4• nicc k* **Nit-ac** k* nux-m b2.de* **Nux-v** k* *Oena* ol-an k* olnd k* *Op* k* ox-ac k* ozone sde2• par k* petr k* petr-ra shn4• ph-ac k* phel k* *Phos* k* phys k* phyt pic-ac hr1 pieri-b mlk9.de plac rzf5• plac-s rly4• **Plat** k* plb k* podo k* positr nl2• pot-e rly4• psor k* ptel k* **Puls** k* pycnop-sa mrz1 ran-b bg2 *Rat* k* rauw tpw8 rheum k* rhod k* rhodi a1 rhus-t k* rob k* *Ruta* k* sabad k* sabin b2.de* *Sang* k* *Sanic* k* **Sars** k* sec k* **Sel** k* seneg b2.de **Sep** k* **Sil** k* sin-n a1 sol-ni spig k* spira a1 spong b2.de* *Stann* k* *Staph* k* stict c1 stram k* stront-c b2.de* suis-em rly4• suis-pan rly4• sul-ac k* sul-i k2 **Sulph** k* sumb k* suprar rly4• tab k* tarax b2.de* **Tarent** k* ter k* thiam rly4• **Thuj** k* til k* *Trios* rsj11• tritic-vg fd5.de valer b2.de vanil fd5.de *Verat* k* vichy-g a1 viol-o k* wies a1 *Zinc* k* zinc-p k2 [heroin sdj2 spect dfg1]
  - **morning**: ulm-c jsj8•
  - **evening**: bism h1* *Sil* k*
  - **fever**; during: acon bg2 arn bg2 *Ars* b4a.de* *Caps* b7.de* *Cocc* bg2 **Lyc** b4a.de* nux-v bg2 rheum bg2 **Rhus-t** bg2 staph bg2 *Sulph* b4a.de* verat bg2
  - **involuntary** stool; then: agar bg1 arg-n bg1
  - **menses**; during: calc falco-pe nl2• kreos b7a.de puls k*
  - **plugged** up; as if: anac br1 ruta fd4.de
  - **pregnancy** agg.; during: *Sep* mrr1
- **infants** (See children - infants)
- **injuries**; after: arn c1* ruta bro1

- **insufficient** (= incomplete, unsatisfactory stools): abrom-a ks5 acon bg2 aegle-f zzc1• allox sp1 **Aloe** k* *Alum* k* alum-sil k2 *Alumn* k* *Anac* k* ang k* anthraq rly4• apis k* aq-mar skp7• arg-met bg2 arg-n bg2 arge-pl rwt5• *Arn* k* ars h2* *Bar-c* k* bar-i k2 bar-s k2 bell k* *Benz-ac* bov b4.de brass-n-o srj5• bros-gau mrc1 *Bry* k* calad bg2 calc k* calc-s canth b7.de* caps bg2* *Carb-ac* carb-an h2* carb-v k* carbn-s **Card-m** k* *Cham* k* **Chin** bg2 colch k* coloc cortiso sp1 *Daph* bg2 dulc fd4.de euphr k* *Gamb* gels glon *Glycyr-g* cte1• graph k* helodr-cal knl2• hep k* hyos k* *Ign* k* *Iod* ip bg2 kali-bi bg2 **Kali-c** k* *Kali-s* kali-sil k2 lac-e hm2• *Lach* b7.de* lact laur bg2 *Lyc* k* mag-c bg2 *Mag-m* k* mand sp1 mang h2 merc bg2 merc-c bg2* mez k* moni rfm1• mur-ac a1 musca-d szs1 mygal zzc1• naja **Nat-c** k* **Nat-m** k* nept-m lsd2.fr **Nit-ac** k* *Nux-m* k* **Nux-v** k* oci-sa sp1 *Oena* **Op** k* osteo-a knp1• par k* petr k* pitu-gl skp7• plat h2* *Plb* plut-n srj7• **Podo** fd3.de• pot-e rly4• psil ft1 *Pyrog* rhod rhus-g tmo3• ruta bg2* sabad k* *Sars* k* **Sel** k* seneg k* *Sep* k* *Sil* k* spong squil k* stann k* *Staph* k* succ-ac rly4• sul-i k2 **Sulph** k* ther bg2 *Thuj* tritic-vg fd5.de ulm-c jsj8• vanil fd5.de visc sp1 *Zinc* k* zinc-p k2 [heroin sdj2]
  - **relief**; but with great: **Nux-v** bg2
  - **second** stool completes: *Rhus-g* tmo3•
- **inveterate** (See chronic)
- **lead** poisoning; from: *(↗painters)* op bro1 plat bro1*
- **lean** far back to pass a stool; must: *Med* k*
- **mechanically**, must remove stool (See removed)
- **menses**:
  - **after** | **agg.**: dirc k* graph k* kali-c ptk1 lac-c
  - **before** | **agg.**: aloe bg2 alum bg2 am-c k* ant-c vld *Apis* b7a.de bry k* coll bro1 *Graph* k* **Kali-c** k* lac-c *Lach* k* mag-c k* nat-m bg2* nat-s nux-v k* petr-ra shn4• plat bro1 *Plb* bro1 sep bro1 **Sil** k* sulph k* thuj bg2 vesp k* [sol-ecl cky1]
  - **during**:
    - **agg.**: alet bg2 *Aloe* bg2 alum k* *Am-c* k* am-m k* ant-c **Apis** k* *Aur* k* aur-s k2 bell bg2 bov k* bry k* calc bg2 chel coll bro1 cycl k* falco-pe nl2• **Graph** k* iod bg2 **Kali-c** k* kali-s kali-sil k2 kreos k* lach bg2 **Nat-m** k* *Nat-s* k* *Nux-v* k* op bg2 phos k* **Plat** k* plb k* plut-n srj7• puls bg2 **Sep** k* **Sil** k* sul-ac bg2 sulph k* thiam rly4• thuj wies a1
      - **delayed**: graph hr1
    - **amel.**: aur ptk1*
  - **instead** of: *Graph* k*
  - **suppressed** menses; from: *Cycl* hr1 *Graph* k* *Ham* k*
- **mental** exertion; after: *Stann* b4a.de
- **mental** shock, after: mag-c br1*
- **mild**: tetox pin2•
- **milk** | **amel.**: iod bg1
- **newborns** (See children - newborns)
- **obstinate** (See chronic)
- **old** people: aloe alum k* alumn ambr bg2* *Ant-c* k* arn bg2 *Bar-c* k* *Bry* k* *Calc-p* k* *Con* k* hydr bro1 hyos mrr1 *Lach* k* lyc bro1 *Nux-v* *Op* k* *Phos* k* *Phyt* k* rhus-t k* ruta *Sel* bro1 *Sulph* k*
  - **alternating** with diarrhea (See Diarrhea - alternating - constipation - old)
- **operation**; after: op sf1.de
- **pain**; from: sil ptk1
- **painful**: *Aesc* bro1 alet k2 *All-s* vh1 aloe bro1 alumn bro1 anthraq rly4• *Ars* bg2 *Asaf* b7.de asar b7.de bry b7.de caps b7.de carb-v bg2 caust bro1 *Cham* b7.de chin b7.de colch b7.de cupr b7.de *Hir* rsj4• hydr bro1 *Ign* bro1 luf-op rsj5• lyc bro1 melal-alt gya4 merc bg2 mur-ac bro1 nat-m k* nat-p k2 **Nit-ac** k* *Nux-v* b7.de oci-sa sp1 petr bg2 plb bg2 puls b7.de rat bro1 *Rheum* b7.de *Rhus-t* b7.de *Sec* bg2 sep bro1 streptoc rly4• sulph bro1 *Tell* rsj10• thuj bro1 *Tub* k* *Verat* b7.de
- **painless**: *Squil* b7a.de
- **painters**; of: *(↗lead)* plb tl1
- **periodical**: anth vh *Kali-bi*
  - **day** agg.; alternate: agar b4.de* alum k* ambr b7a.de* ant-c b7.de* calc b4a.de* carb-v bg2 **Cocc** b7.de* con b4a.de* fl-ac bg2 germ-met srj5• kali-c b4.de* lyc bg2* *Mag-c* bg2 merc bg2 *Nat-m* k* nit-ac bg2 petr-ra shn4• plb bg2 sabad b7.de* sul-ac b4.de* *Sulph* b4a.de* verb b7.de*
  - **weeks**; every three: *Kali-bi*
  - **Monday**: stann hr1*
- **peristaltic** action of intestines; from:
  - **irregular** peristaltic action: anac bro1 nux-v bro1*
- **peristaltic** action of intestines; from: ...
  - **lack** of peristaltic action (See Inactivity)
- **perspiration**; during: *Ant-c* bg2 *Apis* bg2 arn bg2 *Bell* bg2 *Bry* bg2 calc bg2 carb-v bg2 chin bg2 **Cocc** bg2 con bg2 dulc bg2 graph bg2 *Lyc* bg2 merc bg2 mez bg2 nit-ac bg2 **Nux-v** bg2 **Op** bg2 sabad bg2 sel bg2 *Sep* bg2 *Sil* bg2 *Staph* bg2 sul-ac bg2 *Sulph* bg2 thuj bg2 verat bg2
- **portal** stasis, from: **Aesc** *Aloe* card-m vml3• *Croc* hr1 **Nux-v** k* **Sulph** k*
- **pregnancy** agg.; during: *Agar* k* *Alum* k* *Ambr* *Ant-c* k* *Ant-t* hr1 *Apis* *Bry* k* *Coll* k* coloc *Con* **Dol** k* graph bg2 ham bg2 *Hydr* k* lach bg2* *Lyc* k* nat-m bg2 **Nat-s** k* *Nux-m* hr1 **Nux-v** k* *Op* k* **Plat** k* **Plb** k* *Podo* k* *Puls* k* **Sep** k* stann hr1 *Sulph* k*
- **preoccupation** with bowels: *Mag-m* vh
- **presence** of company, such as a nurse; unable to pass stool in the: *(↗MIND - Company - agg.)* **Ambr** k* bry bg3* graph bg1 hydr pd mag-m bg1 nat-m gk op bg1
- **purgatives** or enemas; after: aloe bro1 *Hydr* bro1 *Nux-v* bro1 sulph bro1
  - **amel.**: lac-d ptk1
  - **not** amel.: tarent ptk1
- **recedes**; stool (See difficult - recedes)
- **removed** mechanically; stools have to be: aloe bg1* alum bro1* bry bg1* calc bg1* con bg1 indol bro1 kali-bi bg2 lyc st* med st melal-alt gya4 nat-m bg1* *Nux-m* mrr1 op k2* plat bg3* *Plb* bro1 ruta bro1 sanic bg2* sel bg2* *Sep* bg1* sil bg1* sulph bg1 verat bro1
- **rheumatic** people; in: mag-p bro1
- **riding** in a carriage; from: ign ptk1
- **sadness**; with (See MIND - Sadness - constipation)
- **school**; at: ambr tsm1
- **seaside**; at the:
  - **agg.**: aq-mar bg1* bry bg1* carc mlr1• lyc bro1* mag-m nat-m c1 plat mtf33
  - **amel.**: carc mlr1•
- **seasons** | **summer**; in: bry b7a.de
- **secretion** in intestines; from lack of: bry tl1
- **sedentary** habits agg.: aloe *Ambr* *Bry* k* hydr hr1 *Lyc* k* **Nux-v** k* *Op* k* **Plat** k* *Podo* k* *Sep* *Sulph* k*
- **seminal** emissions; after: thuj b4a.de
- **severe** (See Constipation)
- **shrieking**; with (See MIND - Shrieking - stool - during)
- **spasmodic**: anac bg2 bell bg2 mag-p bg2 *Nux-v* bg2 op bg2 phos bg2 plat bg2 plb bg2 sil bg2 sulph bg2 tub-m jl2 urt-u bg2 zinc bg2
- **standing**; passing stool easier when: *Alum* c1* **CAUST** k •*
- **stool**: *(↗difficult)*
  - **difficult** (See difficult)
  - **hard** (See STOOL - Hard)
  - **intermits**: cench k2
  - **natural** (See difficult - natural)
  - **painful** (See difficult - painful)
  - **recedes** (See difficult - recedes)
  - **remains** long in the rectum with no urging: *(↗Inactivity)* adam skp7• alet ptk1 aloe k2* alum bro1* am-c bry k* *Calc* mrr1 carb-an choc srj3• cocc coll br1 dulc fd4.de **Graph** k* hydr ptk1* *Lach* lyc bro1 mand mtf11 med jl2 melal-alt gya4 nat-m bro1 nux-v k2* **Op** k* petr-ra shn4• pneu jl2 positr nl2• prot jl2 psor jl2 pyrog jl2 ruta fd4.de sep k* ser-a-c jl2 **Sil** bro1* sulph bro1 thiop mtf11 ven-m rsj12•
    - **amel.**; with general: psor
    - **anxiety**; with awful: melal-alt gya4 **Tarent** k*
  - **soft** (See difficult - soft)
  - **straining**; stool passed after great (See difficult)
  - **unsatisfactory** (See insufficient)
  - **urging** to:
    - **constant**; with: aloe anac coloc *Con* *Mag-c* *Mag-m* nat-p **Nux-v** *Plb* *Puls* ruta *Sil* *Sulph*
    - **without** (See remains; Inactivity)
- **strain**; after nervous: mag-c br1* vanil fd5.de
- **stubborn** (See chronic)
- **tobacco**; from: tab mrr1
- **travelling**, while: *Alum* k* ambr tsm1 *Ign* hr1 lyc ptk1 nat-m gk *Nux-v* k* *Op* k* *Plat* k* sep sne tritic-vg fd5.de
- **urticaria**, with: cop br1

Rectum

- **vexation**; after: bry nux-v staph
- **weak**, literary persons: nicc hr1*
- **weather** | **cloudy** weather: | **agg.**: aloe ptk1
  - **cold** agg.: verat ptk1
- **wine** agg.: *Zinc* k*
- **women**; in: *Aesc* bro1 alet bro1 *Alum* bro1 ambr bro1 anac bro1 arn bro1 *Asaf* bro1 bry bro1 calc bro1 coll br1* con bro1 graph hr1* *Hydr* bro1 ign bro1 kali-c hr1 lach bro1 lyc bro1 mez bro1 *Nat-m* bro1 nux-v bro1 op bro1 *Plat* bro1 plb btw2* *Podo* bro1 puls bro1 sep bg1* sil bro1 sulph bro1 tab ah2
- **working**; while: ambr tsm1
- **worries**, cares; from: mag-c br1

CONSTRICTION: *(↗Stricture)* acon *Aesc* k* aesc-g bro1 aeth *Agar* alum alum-p k2 alum-sil k2 am-c am-m bg2 amp rly4• anac bro1 ang h1 arg-n k* ars *Bell* k* benz-ac berb borx k* *Cact* k* *Calc* k* calc-s calc-sil k2 *Camph* k* *Cann-s* carb-an carb-v carc tpw2* **Caust** k* *Chel* k* chin k* cic cimx *Cocc* k* coff *Colch* k* coll bro1 coloc k* cop crot-t der falco-pe nl2• ferr k* ferr-ar ferr-i ferr-p *Fl-ac Form* gal-ac c1* gink-b sbd1• graph grat k* guare hell b7.de* hipp hura hydr bro1 *Hyos* **Ign** k* kali-ar *Kali-bi Kali-br* kali-c kali-sil k2 kreos b7a.de* lac-leo hrn2• **Lach** k* laur k* **Lyc** k* m-ambo b7.de m-aust b7.de* mang *Med* bro1 meli k* merc bro1 merc-c bg2* mez k* nat-c k* *Nat-m* k* nat-p nicotam rly4• **Nit-ac** k* nit-m-ac c2* **Nux-v** k* *Op* k* *Phos* k* **Plb** k* *Plb-act* bro1 pyrus c2 rat k* rhod b4a.de *Rhus-t* ruta fd4.de sanic c2* sars k* sec k* *Sed-ac* bro1 *Sep* k* sil k* sol-t-ae staph k* stront-c k* *Sulph* sumb syph k* *Tab* k* ther thuj k* tritic-vg fd5.de tub c1 vanil fd5.de verb k*

- **morning**: nux-v k* tritic-vg fd5.de
  - **bed** agg.; in: phos h2*
  - **rising** agg.; after: nux-v k* tritic-vg fd5.de
- **forenoon**: *Calc*
- **afternoon**: *Cocc* k* coloc franz a1
- **evening**: chin h1* ign k* vanil fd5.de
  - **walking** agg.: ign k*
- **night**: sec
- **alternating** with:
  - **itching** in rectum: *Chel* k*
  - **pressing** pain in rectum: bell h1*
- **bending**:
  - **agg.**: carc sp1
  - **amel.**: carc mg1.de*
- **breakfast** agg.; after: calc-s k*
- **coition**:
  - **after**: caust h2*
  - **during**: merc-c
- **flatus**; with passing of: fl-ac k*
- **lying** | **amel.**: *Mang* k* vanil fd5.de
- **menses**; during: *Cocc* k* thuj
- **mental** exertion; after: nux-v k*
- **motion**:
  - **agg.**: caust bg1
  - **amel.**: coloc
- **painful**: bell h1* brach *Calc* carc gk6 *Caust Cocc* coloc hydrog srj2• **Ign Lach** *Lyc* k* *Mang Mez* **Nux-v** plac rzf5• **Plb** k* sars h2* *Sep Sil Thuj* tub c1
  - **sitting** agg.: hydrog srj2•
- **pressure** | **amel.**: carc sp1*
- **rising** from sitting agg.: thuj
- **sitting**:
  - **agg.**: chin h1* *Cocc* k* *Mang* k*
  - **amel.**: *Ign*
- **spasmodic**: carl a1 chel k* coff grat k* *Ham* k* *Hipp* k* *Kali-br* hr1 *Lach* k* *Lyc* merc-c nat-m k* **Nit-ac** k* **Nux-v Op** k* *Phos* **Plb** ruta fd4.de **Sil** bg1 ther c1 verb k*
- **standing**:
  - **agg.**: arn ptk1 *Ign* k*
  - **amel.**: sanic vh
- **stool**:
  - **after**:

Constriction – stool – after: ...

- ⁝ **agg.**: aesc k* chel k* colch k* elaps *Ferr* ferr-p bg2 form k* grat k* hell b7.de* hir rsj4• **Ign** k* kali-bi **Lach** k* m-ambo b7.de* mag-art br1 *Mez* k* moni rfm1• **Nit-ac** k* nux-m k* nux-v b7.de* *Phos* k* plac rzf5• plat k* *Sep* spirae a1 stront-c k* *Sulph* k* thuj k*
  - ⁝ **Perineum**: lyc bg2
  - ⁝ **Rectum** and anus: mag-m bg2
- ⁝ **amel.**: nat-ar k2
- ⁝ **hours** after stool; a few: sed-ac br1
  - **before**: *Ham* lach k* *Nat-m* k* *Nux-v* k* phos k* plb sep k*
  - **during** | **agg.**: *Alum* k* alum-p k2 alum-sil k2 *Ars* k* brach a1 *Chel* k* chinin-s coloc k* ferr ferr-i a1 glon k* hell h1* *Kreos* k* mang k* melal-alt gya4 mur-ac h2* **Nat-m** k* **Nit-ac** k* nux-m k* *Nux-v* k* phos k* **Plb** k* rat ptk1 sep k* **Sil** k* *Thuj* k*
  - **hard** stool:
    - ⁝ **after** | **agg.**: ferr ptk1
  - **impossible**: all-c *Berb* k* *Chel Lach* **Lyc** k* *Nat-m Nit-ac Nux-v*
  - **urging** to | **during**: caust k* plb ptk1
- **stooping**:
  - **agg.**: caust h2*
  - **amel.**: carc mlr1•
- **urination**:
  - **during**:
    - ⁝ **agg.**: alum bg2 carbn-s caust bg2* nat-m
    - ⁝ **end** of: *Cann-s*
- **uterine** cancer, from: kreos ptk1
- **walking** agg.: *Caust* k* crot-t k* vanil fd5.de
- **warm** drinks | **amel.**: carc sp1*

▽ - **extending** to:

○ • **Glans**: chin h1
- • **Perineum**: sep h2
- • **Rectum**; into: sil
- • **Testes**: chin sil
- • **Upward**: laur mur-ac h2 sep h2 sil
- • **Vagina**: sep

○ - **Anus**: acon bg2 aloe bg2 alum b4.de* ang b7.de* arn b7.de* ars bg2 *Bell* b4.de* borx bg2 calc b4.de* camph b7.de* cann-s b7.de* caps bg2 carb-an b4.de* caust bg2 cocc b7.de* colch b7.de* coloc bg2 con b4.de* cupr bg2 fl-ac bg2 graph b4.de* grat bg2 ham bg2 hep bg2 *Ign* b7.de* ip bg2 iris bg2 kali-bi bg2 kali-c b4a.de **Lach** b7.de* laur bg2 lil-t bg2 *Lyc* b4.de* *M-ambo* b7.de* m-aust b7.de* mang b4.de* merc-c bg2 mez b4.de* *Nat-m* b4.de* **Nit-ac** b4.de* nit-m-ac br1 *Nux-v* b7.de* op b7.de* phos b4.de* plat b4.de* **Plb** b7.de* prun bg2 rat bg2 rhus-t bg2 sars b4.de* sec b7a.de* sep b4.de* *Sil* b4.de* staph b7.de* *Sulph* b4.de* *Syph* jl2 thuj b4.de* verb b7.de* vip bg2
  - **cough** agg.; during: acon bg2
  - **pain** in abdomen; from: verb h1*
  - **prolapsed** anus: *Lach Mez* k*
    - ⁝ **Around**: bell tl1 coll tl1 ferr tl1 *Lach* hr1 *Mez* hr1* ruta tl1
  - **sensation** of | **stool** agg.; during: ign bg2 lach bg2 mez b4.de* *Nat-m* bg2 *Sil* bg2 staph b7.de* thuj bg2
  - **stool** agg.; during: aloe bg2 alum b4.de* ang b7.de* chel bg2 coloc b4a.de nux-m b7.de* *Nux-v* bg2 plat b4.de* sep bg2 staph b7.de* thuj b4.de*
- **Perineum**: canth bg2 carb-an b4a.de lyc b4.de* *Sep* b4a.de sil h2* sulph k* thuj k* vanil fd5.de

CORD extending from anus to navel: ferr-i k*

COUGH agg.; during: ign ptk1 *Lach* ptk1 nit-ac ptk1 tub ptk1

○ - **Rectum** and anus: ign bg2 *Kali-c* bg2 lach bg2 nit-ac bg2

CRACKS (See Fissure)

CRAMP (See Constriction)

CRAWLING in (See Formication; Itching)

DELIVERY; after: gels ptk1 podo ptk1 ruta ptk1

DIAPER rash (See Eruptions - anus - rash - children - newborns; Eruptions - perineum - children - newborns)

DIARRHEA: acal c2 *Acet-ac* k* *Acon* k* acon-l c2 aegle-f mtf11 *Aesc* k* aeth k* **Agar** k* agar-ph c2 agath-a nl2• agn b2.de* agra c2 aids nl2• *Ail* br1 alet k* all-c c2 all-s k* allox sp1 **Aloe** k* alst c2 alst-s br1 *Alum* k* alum-sil k2 alumn c2 am-c b2.de* am-m k* ambr b2.de* *Ambro* br1 ammc k* amp rly4• anac b2.de* anan anemps br1 ang k* *Ango* c1 *Anis* ant-ar **Ant-c** k* ant-s-aur c2 **Ant-t** k* anthraci k* anthraq rly4• aphis c2 **Apis** k* apoc k* apoc-a c2 aral c2* *Aran* k* arg-met k* *Arg-n* k* arge-pl rwt5• arist-cl sp1 *Arn* k* **Ars** k* ars-i k* ars-met c2 ars-s-f c2* ars-s-r c2 arum-m k* arum-t k2 arund c2 asaf k* *Asar* k* asc-t asim c2* astac k* aster k* atis mtf11 atra-r bnm3• aur k* aur-m k* aur-s k2 aza c2 *Bamb-a* stb2.de• **Bapt** k* **Bar-c** k* bar-i k2 bar-m k* bar-s k2 *Bell* k* bell-p sp1 *Benz-ac* k* berb k* bism k* bol-la c2 *Borx* k* both tsm2 both-ax tsm2 *Bov* k* brach *Brom* k* bros-gau mrc1 **Bry** k* bufo buth-a sp1 cact k* cadm-met sp1 calad b2.de* **Calc** k* *Calc-ar* calc-f k2* calc-i k2 *Calc-p* k* calc-s k* calc-sil k2 calth br1 camph b7.de cann-s b2.de* **Canth** k* *Caps* k* carb-ac k* carb-an b2.de* **Carb-v** k* *Carbn-s* carc jl2* card-b c2 cardios-h bta1• cartl-s rly4• caru a1 *Casc* k* castm castn-v c2* *Caust* k* cean k* cench c2 cent c2 cerev-lg sna1 cetr c2 **Cham** k* chap c2* chel k* chim k* chim-m c2 **Chin** k* *Chinin-ar* k* chinin-s k* choc srj3• chord-umb rly4• chr-met dx chr-o c2 cic k* cimic k2* *Cina* k* cinch c2 cinnm k* *Cist* k* cit-l c2 clem k* cloth tsm2 cob k* cob-n sp1 coca-c sk4• *Cocc* k* *Coff* k* *Colch* k* colchin c2 *Coll* k* *Coloc* k* colocin c2 colos c2 *Con* k* conv c2 convo-a c2 *Cop* k* **Corn** k* cortiso sp1 *Coto* c1* crass-r bta1• croc b2.de* crot-c tsm2* *Crot-h* k* **Crot-t** k* cub k* cucum-m fr1 *Cupr* k* cupr-act c2 cupr-ar k* cupr-s c2 cycl k* cyn-d mtf11 cypra-eg sde6.de• cystein-l rly4• cyt-l br1* der c2 *Dig* k* digin c2 dios k* diosm br1 diph-pert-t mp4• diph-t-tpt jl2 dirc a1* diss-i bta1• dor c2 dream-p sdj1• dros b2.de* **Dulc** k* dys fmm1• eberth jl2 *Echi* k* elae c2 elaeo-v bta1• elaps tsm2 elat c2* eleph-b bta1• emetin mtf11 enteroc jl2 epiph c2 erech c2 ery-a c2 eucal c2* eug c2 euon c2 euonin c2 eup-per c2* euph b2.de* euph-a c2 euph-c c2 euph-hi jsx1.fr euph-l c2* fago c2 fel c2* **Ferr** k* **Ferr-ar** **Ferr-i** k* *Ferr-m* c2 ferr-ma c2 *Ferr-p* k* *Ferr-pern* c1* *Ferr-s* k* ferul c2 **Fl-ac** k* flor-p rsj3• foen-an a1 form c2 franz c2 fuch br1 fum rly1*• gaert fmm1• galeoc-c-h gms1• galla-q-r nl2• galv c2 **Gamb** k* gard-j vlr2• gast c2 gels k* genist c2 gent-c c2 gent-l c2* ger c2 ger-i rly4• germ-met srj5• gnaph c2 *Gran* k* *Granit-m* es1• *Graph* k* *Grat* k* gua c2* guaj k* guar c2 guat sp1 haem c2 haliae-lc srj5• ham k* haru-ma jsx1.fr hed sp1 hedy a1* **Hell** k* hell-o c1* hell-v c2 **Hep** k* heuch bwa3 hip-ac sp1 hir rsj4• hist sp1 hura-c c1* *Hydr* k* hydrog srj2• hymen-ac jsx1.fr *Hyos* k* hyper c2 *Ign* k* ilx-a c2 ind k* indg c2 influ jl2* **Iod** k* **Ip** k* irid-met srj5• **Iris** k* iris-fl c2 iris-g c2 ix bnm8• jab k* jac-g c2 jal c2* *Jatr-c* k* jug-c k* kali-act c2* *Kali-ar* k* **Kali-bi** k* kali-br a1 *Kali-c* k* kali-chl k* *Kali-i* k* kali-m c2* kali-n k* kali-p k* *Kali-pic* a1* *Kali-s* k* ketogl-ac rly4• kiss c2 kola br1* kreos k* lac-ac k* *Lac-c* *Lac-d* lac-del hrn2• lac-f wza1• lac-h sk4• lac-loxod-a hrn2• *Lach* k* lact-v c1* lap-la sde8.de• lat-h bnm5• lat-m sp1 lath c1 laur k* lec led k* *Lept* k* liat c2* *Lil-t* k* lim c2 limest-b es1• lina c2 linu-c c2 lipp c2 lith-c lob c2 luf-am gsb1 luf-op rsj5• luna kg1• **Lyc** k* lycpr c2* lyss k* m-ambo b2.de* m-arct b2.de* m-aust b2.de* *Mag-c* k* *Mag-m* k* *Mag-p* mag-s c2* maland vh malar c2* manc k* mand sp1* mang b2.de* mang-o c2 med mela c2 meli meph a1 **Merc** k* **Merc-c** k* merc-d c2* merc-sul k* mez k* mill c2 mim-p rsj8*• *Moni* rfm1• morph k* morph-s hr1 mosch b7.de* mur-ac k* myos-a rly4• nabal mtf11 naja naphtin c2 narc-ps a1* *Nat-ar* *Nat-c* k* nat-f sp1 **Nat-m** k* nat-ox rly4• *Nat-p* k* **Nat-s** k* nat-sil fd3.de• nat-sulo c2 nicc k* nicc-met sk4• nicotam rly4• **Nit-ac** k* nit-s-d c2 *Nuph* k* *Nux-m* k* *Nux-v* k* nymph c2 oci c2 *Oci-sa* sp1 oeno c2 ol-an k* *Ol-j* k* olib-sac wmh1 *Olnd* k* onos c2 op k* oper br1 opun-f br1 opun-xyz c2 oreo br1 orot-ac rly4• ox-ac k* oxyte-chl mtf11 pall c1 pancr c1* par k* *Parathyr* jl2 paull c2 ped c2 pen c2 *Petr* k* petr-ra shn4• **Ph-ac** k* phel k* **Phos** k* phos-h c2 phys c2 phyt k* pic-ac k* pilios-t jsx1.fr pin-s c2 pitu-p sp1 pix c2 plac rzf5• plac-s rly4• plan k* plat b2.de *Plb* k* plb-chr c2 plect c2 **Podo** k* polyg-xyz c2 positr nl2• pot-e rly4• prin c1* prot jl2 prun k* pseuts-m oss1• psid jsx1.fr *Psor* k* *Ptel* k* *Puls* k* puls-n c2 pyrid rly4• pyrog c2* querc-r c1* rad-br sze8• ran-b b2.de* ran-s b2.de* raph k* rat k* *Rauw* sp1 rham-cath c2 rham-f c2 **Rheum** k* rhod k* rhus-g c2* *Rhus-t* k* rhus-v c2 ribo rly4• ric c2* rubu-r bta1• rumx k* ruta b2.de* sabad k* sabin b2.de* sal-ac c2 sal-fr sle1• sal-n c2 sal-p c2 *Salol* c1* samb k* *Sang* k* sanguis-s hrn2• *Sanic* k* santin c2 sap-o bta1• sapin c2 saroth sp1 sarr c2 sars k* scam c2 schin c2 schot-b bta1• **Sec** k* sel seneg k* *Sep* k* **Sil** k* *Sima* c1 sin-n c2 sinus rly4• slag c2 spartin bwa3 sphing a1 spig b2.de* spong b2.de* squil k* *Stann* k* staph k* staphycoc rly4• stict c2 stram k* streptoc rly4• stront-c b2.de* stry k* suis-em rly4• suis-hep rly4• suis-pan rly4• *Sul-ac* k* sul-ac-ar bwa3 sulfa sp1 **Sulph** k* sumb k* suprar rly4• syc fmm1• symph fd3.de• tab k* tarax k* *Tarent* k* tax-br oss1• tell rsj10• *Ter* k* teucr b2.de* thal-xyz srj8• thev c2 thiam rly4• thom-h jsx1.fr **Thuj** k* thymol sp1 thyr c2 toxo-g jl2 trad a1* trios br1 tritic-vg fd5.de trom k* tub al* tub-d jl2 typh br1 (non:uran-met k) uran-n *Urol-h* rwt• *Vacc-m* c1 *Valer* k* vang-l bta1• vanil fd5.de vario jl2 ven-m rsj12• **Verat** k* verb b2.de* verin c2 vero-o rly4*• viol-t b2.de* vip tsm2 visc sp1 wede-n bta1• wies c2 wye c2 x-ray sp1 xan k* xyma-m jsx1.fr yuc c2 *Zinc* k* zinc-act c2 zinc-fcy a1 zinc-p k2 zinc-val c2 *Zing* k* [ant-met stj2 bell-p-sp dcm1 heroin sdj2 pop dhh1 *Spect* dfg1 titan-s stj2]

- **day** and night: calc-p coloc h2 hyos h1 kali-c merc-c sil
- **daytime**: am-m ang arg-n ars-i vh bapt *Bry* *Calc* b4a.de canth cina *Cocc* k* *Con* k* crot-t *Elaps* fl-ac flor-p rsj3• *Form* *Gamb* glon *Hep* k* jab *Kali-c* k* kali-n mag-c nat-ar **Nat-m** k* nat-s *Nux-v* **Petr** k* phyt ptk1 pilo bro1 squil sul-ac h2 *Thuj* *Trom* vh
- **morning**: acet-ac aeth *Agar* k* all-c k* allox sp1 *Aloe* k* alum alum-p k2 am-c k* am-m k* ang k* ant-c k* ant-t aphis bwa3 *Apis* k* *Arg-n* *Ars* k* *Ars-i* aur aur-ar k2 aur-i k2 aur-s k2 bac jl2 bamb-a stb2.de• *Borx* k* **Bov** k* brom bros-gau mrc1 **Bry** k* *Cact* k* cadm-met tpw6 *Calc* b4a.de calc-p k2 calc-s k* carb-an carbn-s caust h2* chin k* chinin-ar chlor k* cimic k* cist k* cob-n sp1 coca-c sk4• *Coloc* *Cop* k* **Corn** cortiso sp1 crot-t bro1 cystein-l rly4• dendr-pol sk4• *Dig* *Dios* k* *Dulc* dys fmm1• enteroc jl2 eup-per k* *Ferr* k* *Ferr-ar* ferr-i k* ferr-p k* ferr-s bg2 fl-ac k* galeoc-c-h gms1• *Gamb* ger-i rly4• gnaph k* granit-m es1• graph bro1 *Grat* k* *Guaj* haliae-lc srj5• hep hura *Hydr* *Iod* k* iris kali-ar **Kali-bi** k* *Kali-c* kali-i kali-m k2 kali-n k* kali-p kali-s kali-sil k2 kalm k* lac-h sk4• lach k* *Lil-t* k* *Lith-c* luf-op rsj5• *Lyc* k* lyss k* **Mag-c** k* mag-m k* mag-s k* malar jl2 manc *Merc* k* *Merc-c* b4a.de morg-p fmm1• *Mur-ac* k* nat-ar nat-c k* nat-m k* nat-p **Nat-s** k* nat-sil fd3.de• nicc nit-ac nux-m k* *Nux-v* k* ol-j k* olnd onos ptk1 osm k* ox-ac k* parathyr jl2 *Petr* petr-ra shn4• *Ph-ac* k* **Phos** k* phyt plan k* **Podo** k* pot-e rly4• psil ft1 psor k* *Puls* rauw tpw8* rhod rhodi a1 rhus-t k* **Rumx** k* ruta fd4.de sal-fr sle1• sang k* sarr senec k* sil sol-t-ae a1 squil k* staph k* staphycoc rly4• streptoc rly4• suis-em rly4• sul-ac mtf11 sul-i k2 **Sulph** k* sumb k* syc fmm1• *Tab* k* *Thuj* k* trios rsj11• tritic-vg fd5.de trom *Tub* k* urol-h rwt• valer k* vanil fd5.de *Verat* k* *Zinc* zing
  - **6** h: aloe arg-n kali-p lach ox-ac petr *Sulph* k*
    - **6-9** h: allox tpw3*
    - **6-10** h: chinin-ar
    - **6-12** h: *Rumx* vh
  - **7** h: xan
  - **8** h: ars-s-f k2 *Ferr*
    - **8-10** h: plan
  - **afternoon**, until: borx h2 *Nat-m*
  - **accompanied** by | **weakness**: dios ptk1
  - **bed**; driving out of●: allox tpw3 *Aloe* k* alum-sil k2 bell bov bros-gau mrc1 bry cench k2 chin cic dios k* haliae-lc srj5• hep hydr hyper *Kali-bi* kola stb3• *Lil-t* med c1* nat-ar nat-s k* nat-sil fd3.de• nuph petr *Phos* phyt *Podo* psil ft1 *Psor* k* rauw tpw8 rhus-t k2 *Rumx* sal-fr sle1• *Sil* staph gk **Sulph** k* syph k* *Tub* k* *Zinc*
  - **children**; in: cimic ptk1 iod ptk1
  - **early**: acet-ac bro1 *Aloe* bro1 ichth bro1 iris bro1 lil-t bro1 med bro1 merc-sul br1 *Nat-s* bro1 nit-ac bro1 *Nuph* bro1 *Nux-v* bro1 petr bro1 phos bro1 *Podo* bro1 *Psor* bro1 rauw sp1 rhus-v bro1 *Rumx* bro1 stict bro1 *Sulph* bro1 thuj bro1 trom bro1 tub bro1
  - **rising** | **after**:
    - **agg.**: aeth agar aloe ars ars-s-f k2 *Bry* k* cain calc *Cocc* k* fl-ac kali-bi mrr1 lept lil-t ptk1 lyc mag-s nat-c *Nat-m* **Nat-s** k* nat-sil fd3.de• *Nux-v* k* orot-ac rly4• ox-ac k* *Phos* plan podo fd3.de• *Psor* rumx ptk1 staph a1 *Sulph* k* verat
      - **and** moving about: ars-i **Bry** lept *Nat-m* **Nat-s**
      - **immediately**: loxo-recl knl4• syc fmm1•
    - **agg.**: cortiso sp1*
  - **urination** | **urging** to urinate; with: cic br1
  - **waking** with urging●: (↗*Urging - morning - early)* *Cench* k* cic hr1 enteroc jl2 form k* graph k* kali-bi kali-i k* lil-t ptk1* loxo-recl knl4• lyc k* petr k* phos **Sulph** k* trom vml3• tub al* zinc
- **forenoon**: *Aloe* apis *Cact* carb-an flor-p rsj3• *Gamb* kali-c k* lil-t mag-c mur-ac *Nat-m* k* *Nat-s* plan **Podo** k* sabad k* stann *Sulph* *Thuj* k* *Tub*
  - **9** h: *Nat-s* k*
  - **10** h: *Nat-m* vh
    - **10-22** h: aloe
- **noon**: alum ant-c borx carbn-s crot-t ham fd3.de• jab mag-m sulph vanil fd5.de

Rectum

- **afternoon**: agath-a nl2• aids nl2• aloe alum alum-p k2 am-c *Ars* k* ars-s-f k2 *Bell* k* *Borx* calc k* carb-an **Chin** k* *Chinin-ar* corn bro1 dulc k* *Ferr* ferr-ar ferr-p gard-j vlr2• gent-l gink-b sbd1• hell kali-ar kali-c laur k* lec lept k* lyc k* mag-c mag-s *Manc* merc-c mur-ac nat-sil fd3.de• orot-ac rly4• petr h2* petr-ra shn4• phos phyt k* plac-s rly4• *Psor* stann suis-em rly4• sul-ac sulph symph fd3.de• ter k* vanil fd5.de zinc k* zinc-p k2
  - **16** h: puls sys
    - **16**-18 h: agath-a nl2• carb-v rhus-t
    - **16**-20 h: agath-a nl2• hell *Lyc*
  - **17** h:
    - **17**-18 h: dig
    - **17**-19 h: *Benz-ac* vh
  - **periodical**: *Ferr*
- **evening**: agath-a nl2• aids nl2• *Aloe* k* alum k* arge-pl rwt5• atro hr1 borx *Bov* k* bry k* *Calc* k* calc-i k2 calc-p calc-s canth k* carb-an caust k* choc srj3• colch k* cycl k* dig dulc gels ign k* iod k* ip *Kali-c* k* kali-m k2 kali-n k* kali-p kali-s kola stb3• *Lach* k* lept lil-t mag-m k* mang merc k* mez k* mur-ac k* nat-ar nat-m k* nat-s k* nuph k* *Ph-ac* phel *Phos* k* pic-ac podo bro1* puls rhus-t b7a.de* ruta fd4.de *Sang* k* *Sars* senec k* stann sul-i k2 sulph k* ter thuj k* tritic-vg fd5.de valer k* vanil fd5.de ven-m rsj12• verat k* zinc k* zinc-p k2
  - **night**; and: *Ars* bro1 bell-p bro1 bov bro1 calc bro1 chel bro1 *Chin* bro1 dulc bro1 *Ferr* bro1 iris bro1 *Merc* bro1 nat-n bro1 nux-m bro1 podo bro1 psor bro1 *Puls* bro1 *Rhus-t* bro1 *Stront-c* bro1 sulph bro1 wye bro1
  - **cold** air agg.: colch **Merc** k* nat-s
  - **sunset** until sunrise: colch bro1
- **night**: abrot acon k* aeth k* agath-a nl2• aloe anac b4a.de* ang k* ant-c k* ant-t k* **Arg-n** k* *Arn* k* **Ars** k* ars-s-f k2 arum-t asaf k* asc-t k* *Aur* k* aur-ar k2 aur-m k* aur-s k2 bamb-a stb2.de• bar-c k* bar-s k2 borx h2 bov k* brom k* *Bry* k* caj c2 canth k* *Caps* k* carb-v h2* *Carbn-s* *Caust* k* cench k2 *Cham* k* *Chel* k* **Chin** k* **Chinin-ar** *Chinin-s* chlol gm1 *Cinnb* k* cist k* colch k* *Con* k* *Crot-t* k* cub k* diosm br1 **Dulc** k* *Ferr* k* **Ferr-ar** ferr-p fl-ac k* *Gamb* k* *Graph* k* *Grat* k* hep hipp hr1 *Hyos* k* ign k* ip k* **Iris** ix bnm8• jal k* **Kali-ar** k* *Kali-bi* *Kali-c* k* kali-p kali-s kali-sil k2 kola stb3• kreos k* **Lach** k* lith-c lyss *Mag-c* mag-m manc **Merc** k* merc-c k* *Mosch* k* **Nat-ar** *Nat-c* k* nat-m k* *Nat-p* **Nux-m** k* petr b4a.de* ph-ac k* *Phos* k* **Podo** k* **Psor** k* **Puls** k* *Rheum* b7a.de *Rhus-t* k* ruta fd4.de sang hr1 sel senec k* *Sep* b4a.de *Sil* k* spong fd4.de stront-c k* *Stry* k* **Sul-ac** b4a.de **Sulph** k* *Tab* k* ther k* *Tub* verat k* visc sp1 zinc h2*
  - **midnight**:
    - **before**: mag-c k* nux-m k* puls rhus-t symph fd3.de•
    - **after**: all-c hr1 aloe *Arg-n* k* **Ars** k* ars-s-f k2 arum-t k* asc-t k* both-ax tsm2 bry *Chin* *Chinin-ar* cic k* cist dros ferr a1 **Ferr-ar** ferr-p fl-ac k* gamb hipp hr1 iris **Kali-ar** kali-c k* kali-s lyc k* manc k* merc-c nat-ar nat-m *Nux-v* rhus-t b7a.de* sec sinus rly4• squil staph stront-c **Sulph** k* *Verat* b7a.de
      - **1** h:
        - **1**-3 h: asc-t c1
        - **1**-4 h: *Psor*
      - **2** h: aran *Ars* cic kola stb3• phos rhus-v tab
        - **2**-3 h: *Iris* phos
      - **3** h: cimic kola stb3• mag-c nat-c h2 ozone sde2• petr phos podo k2
        - **3**-4 h: aeth *Kali-c* lyc
        - **3**-5 h: coca-c sk4• tub jl2
        - **3**-11 h: nat-m
      - **4** h: bamb-a stb2.de• fl-ac form mang k* *Petr* phos **Podo** k* *Rhus-t* sec urol-h rwt•
        - **4**-6 h: *All-c* phos
        - **4**-7 h: nuph
      - **5** h: *Aloe* mrr1 alum-sil k2 carbn-s k2 cystein-l rly4• *Phos* podo k2 rumx k2 **Sulph** k* syph c1* tub al* urol-h rwt•
        - **5**-6 h: *Nuph*
      - **12** h; until: ars cist
  - **alternating** with asthma (See RESPIRATION - Asthmatic - alternating - diarrhea)
  - **lying** agg.: *Lach*
  - **only**: chin bg1
  - **waking**; on: gink-b sbd1•
- **accompanied** by:
  - **aids** (See GENERALS - Aids - accompanied - diarrhea)
  - **anasarca**: acet-ac bro1* *Apis* ptk1 apoc ptk1* hell ptk1
  - **appetite**; loss of: ars bg2 chin bg2 nux-m bg2 phos bg2 puls bg2
  - **constipation**: **Ant-c** b7a.de ant-t b7a.de bry b7a.de *Caps* b7a.de *Lach* b7a.de *Nux-v* b7a.de olnd b7a.de *Puls* b7a.de *Rhus-t* b7a.de *Ruta* b7a.de *Staph* b7a.de
  - **convulsions**; tonic (See GENERALS - Convulsions - tonic - accompanied - diarrhea)
  - **coryza** (See NOSE - Coryza - accompanied - diarrhea)
  - **diabetes** (See GENERALS - Diabetes mellitus - accompanied - diarrhea)
  - **heat**; lack of vital: chin mtf33 grat ptk1
    - **children**; in: chin ptk1
    - **old** people; in: bov ptk1
  - **hemorrhoids**: caps bro1 coll tl1
  - **hiccough**: cinnm st1 *Verat* bro1*
  - **kidneys**; inflammation of (See KIDNEYS - Inflammation - accompanied - diarrhea)
  - **leukorrhea** (See FEMALE - Leukorrhea - accompanied - diarrhea)
  - **loss** of fluids: aeth mrr1
  - **malaria** (See GENERALS - Malaria - accompanied - diarrhea)
  - **menses**; painful: **Verat** mrr1
  - **nausea**: aeth bro1 *Ant-t* bro1 *Ars* bro1 bac al2* *Bism* bro1 camph bro1 carb-ac bro1 chr-ac bro1 cist ptk1 *Colch* bro1 crot-t bro1 cupr bro1 dulc fd4.de emetin mp4• fil bro1 flor-p rsj3• hir rsj4• *Ip* bro1 *Iris* bro1 *Jatr-c* bro1 luf-op rsj5• luna kg1• merc bro1 opun-f br1 opun-xyz bro1 phos bro1 *Podo* bro1 seneg b4a.de spong fd4.de tab bro1 *Trios* br1* *Verat* bro1
  - **rash**: ant-t ptk1
  - **restlessness** (See MIND - Restlessness - diarrhea - during)
  - **salivation**: *Ant-c* kr1* rheum kr1*
  - **urination**:
    - **copious**: mag-s ptk1
    - **frequent**: gels mrr1
    - **urging**: apis ptk1 ars ptk1 canth ptk1 *Merc-c* ptk1
  - **weakness** (See GENERALS - Weakness - diarrhea - from)
  - ○ **Abdomen**:
    - **complaints** (See ABDOMEN - Complaints - accompanied - diarrhea)
    - **distension** (See ABDOMEN - Distension - diarrhea, with)
  - **Back**:
    - **pain**:
      - **Lumbar** region: bar-c ptk1 *Gua* br1 kali-i ptk1
      - **Sacral** region: *Gua* br1 liat br1
  - **Extremities**:
    - **complaints**: *Cupr* ptk1 jatr-c ptk1 sec ptk1
    - **cramps**: cupr mrr1
  - **Head**:
    - **complaints** (See HEAD - Complaints - accompanied - diarrhea)
    - **heat** of: bell bg2
  - **Hip**; pain in (See EXTREMITIES - Pain - hip - accompanied - diarrhea)
  - **Intestines**:
    - **twisted**; sensation as if intestines are: gard-j vlr2•
    - **ulceration** of (See ABDOMEN - Ulcers - intestines - accompanied - diarrhea)
    - **weakness** of: *Arg-n* bro1 caps bro1 *Chin* bro1 *Ferr* bro1 malar jl2 oena bro1 oreo bro1 *Sec* bro1

- **Legs**; swelling of (See EXTREMITIES - Swelling - leg - accompanied - diarrhea)
- **Liver** complaints: yuc mtf11
- **Lower** limbs; complaints of: camph bg2 jatr-c bg2
- **Lumbar** region, as if menses would come on; pain in: kali-i ptk1*
- **Mouth**; dry: sulph tl1
- **Pupils**; dilated: chin mtf33
- **Stomach**:
  - **acidity** in: zing a1
  - **disordered**: ant-c b7a.de* bry bro1 chin bro1 coff b7a.de coloc bro1 ip bro1 lyc bro1 *Nux-v* bro1 puls b7a.de*
- **Teeth**; pain in (See TEETH - Pain - accompanied - diarrhea)
- **Tongue**:
  - **brown** discoloration: *Bry* kr1* tart-ac br1
  - **dry**: tart-ac br1
  - **flabby** tongue: lyss kr1*
  - **white** discoloration of the: *Apis* kr1*
    - **heavily** coated: *Dulc* kr1*
- **Urinary** organs; complaints of (See URINARY - Complaints - accompanied - diarrhea)

- **acids**, after: *Aloe* k* am-c mrr1 *Ant-c* k* apis ars k* *Brom* k* bry k* cist k* coloc k* lach k* nat-p tl1 nat-s mrr1 nux-v *Ph-ac* k* sars b4a.de *Sulph* k*
  - **amel.**: arg-n k*
- **acrid**: ang b7.de *Ars* b4.de bry b7.de carb-v b4.de cham b7.de* chin b7.de *Ferr* b7a.de ign b7.de lach b7.de *Merc* b4.de* **Merc-c** b4a.de nux-v b7.de **Puls** b7.de* *Sulph* b4a.de verat b7.de*
- **acute**: acal bro1 acet-ac bro1 *Acon* bro1 *Aeth* bro1 agar-ph bro1 *Aloe* bro1 *Alst* bro1 andr bro1 *Ant-c* bro1 ant-t bro1 *Apis* bro1 apoc bro1 *Arg-n* bro1 *Arn* bro1 *Ars* bro1 ars-i bro1 *Asaf* bro1 *Bapt* bro1 *Bell* bro1 benz-ac bro1 *Bism* bro1 bov bro1 *Bry* bro1 cadm-s bro1 *Calc* bro1 calc-act bro1 *Calc-p* bro1 *Camph* bro1 *Canth* bro1 *Caps* bro1 *Carb-ac* bro1 *Carb-v* bro1 *Cham* bro1 *Chel* bro1 *Chin* bro1 *Chinin-ar* bro1 cina bro1 colch bro1 coll bro1 *Coloc* bro1 *Corn* bro1 *Crot-t* bro1 cuph bro1 cupr-act bro1 cupr-ar bro1 *Cycl* bro1 dios mrr1 *Dulc* bro1 echi bro1 *Elat* bro1 epil bro1 *Eucal* bro1 *Euph* bro1 ferr bro1 ferr-p bro1 fl-ac bro1 form bro1 *Gamb* bro1 *Gels* bro1 *Grat* bro1 hell bro1 hep bro1 hyos bro1 iod bro1 *Ip* bro1 *Iris* bro1 jal bro1 *Jatr-c* bro1 *Kali-bi* bro1 kali-chl bro1 kali-p bro1 lept bro1 *Mag-c* bro1 *Merc* bro1 *Merc-d* bro1 morph bro1 mur-ac bro1 nat-m bro1 *Nat-s* bro1 nit-ac bro1 *Nuph* bro1 *Nux-v* bro1 olnd bro1 op bro1 opun-f bro1 oreo bro1 paeon bro1 *Petr* bro1 *Ph-ac* bro1 *Phos* bro1 phys bro1 *Podo* bro1 polyg-h bro1 *Prun* bro1 psor bro1 *Puls* bro1 *Rheum* bro1 *Rhus-t* bro1 rhus-v bro1 ric bro1 *Rumx* bro1 santin bro1 *Sec* bro1 *Sep* bro1 *Sil* bro1 sul-ac bro1 *Sulph* bro1 tab bro1 ter bro1 *Thuj* bro1 valer bro1 *Verat* bro1 zinc bro1 zing bro1
- **acute** diseases, after: *Carb-v* k* *Chin* k* *Psor* k* *Sulph* k*
- **air**:
  - **evening**: **Merc**
  - **night**: nat-s bg2
  - **wet** air agg.: *Lach* bg2 rhod bg2
- **air** agg.; draft of: *Acon* bry bg1 **Caps** **Nux-v** *Sil*
- **air**; in open:
  - **agg.**: agar am-m coff cycl grat merc-c bg2 phos bg2
  - **amel.**: dios iod lyc nat-s **Puls**
- **alcoholic** drinks; after: ant-t k* ars k* lach k* **Nux-v** k* sulph k*
- **aloe**, after abuse of: mur-ac *Sulph*
- **alone** agg.: stram
- **alternate** days; on (See periodical - day - alternate)
- **alternating** with:
  - **bronchitis** (See CHEST - Inflammation - bronchial - alternating - diarrhea)
  - **constipation**: *Abrot* k* acet-ac *Aegle-f* zzc1• agar ail aloe alum bg2 am-m k* **Ant-c** k* ant-t k* anth vh1 *Arg-n* arge-pl rwt5• *Ars* k* ars-i ars-s-f k2 atis zzc1• *Aur* aur-ar k2 aur-i k2 aur-m-n aur-s k2 bac jl2 bell bg2 berb *Bry* k* but-ac br1 calc bg2* calc-chln bro1 *Carb-ac* carbn-s *Card-m* k* *Casc* k* **Chel** k* choc srj3• *Cimic* k* cina k* *Cob* coff colch bg2 *Coll* k* *Con* cop cor-r bg1 crot-h *Cupr* k* *Dig* dios falco-pe nl2• *Ferr* bg2* ferr-cy bro1 *Ferr-i* gamb gink-b sbd1• glycyr-g cte1• gnaph *Graph* bg2 grat k* guat sp1 hell bg2 *Hep* hom-xyz *Hydr* k* *Ign* *Iod* k* kali-ar kali-bi *Kali-c* k*

- **alternating** with – **constipation**: ... *Kali-n* b4a.de kali-s *Lac-d* lac-h sze9• *Lach* k* *Lact* *Lec* lil-t *Lyc* k* mag-s *Manc* *Mang* merc k* mez nat-ar nat-c k* *Nat-m* k* nat-p *Nat-s* k* **Nit-ac** k* *Nux-m* **Nux-v** k* **Op** k* *Phos* k* *Plb* k* **Podo** k* polyg-h prot jl2 psor bg2 *Ptel* k* *Puls* k* rad-br c11* rhus-t k* *Ruta* k* sang saroth sp1 sars sep k* *Staph* b7a.de stram sul-i k2 *Sulph* k* sumb syc bka1• *Tab* k* thymol sp1 *Tub* k* verat bro1 vib bg2 visc sp1 zinc k* zinc-p k2 [bell-p-sp dcm1]
    - **diarrhea** after a normal stool: *Iod* *Kali-s* ph-ac *Sep* *Sulph* k* tritic-vg fd5.de
    - **old** people; in: alum bg1 **Ant-c** k* bry cycl bg1 nux-v op *Phos* k*
  - **cough**; dry (See COUGH - Dry - alternating - diarrhea)
  - **dropsy** in general: apoc k2*
  - **edema**: apoc vh
  - **eruptions**: calc-p crot-t k*
  - **gout** (See EXTREMITIES - Pain - joints - gouty - alternating - diarrhea)
  - **headache** (See HEAD - Pain - alternating - diarrhea)
  - **hemorrhoids**: aloe mrr1 coll tl1
  - **nausea**: squil b7a.de*
  - **other** complaints: podo ptk1 *Rhus-t* b7a.de
  - **physical** complaints: cimic k2
  - **rheumatism** (See EXTREMITIES - Pain - rheumatic - alternating - diarrhea)
  - **sadness** (See MIND - Sadness - alternating - diarrhea)
  - **spasms** (See GENERALS - Convulsions - alternating - diarrhea)
  - **vomiting** (See STOMACH - Vomiting - alternating - diarrhea)
  - ○ **Brain** trouble: mag-p pd
  - **Chest**; catarrh of (See CHEST - Catarrh - alternating)
  - **Head**:
    - **complaints**: aloe ptk1 podo ptk1
    - **heat** (See HEAD - Heat - alternating - diarrhea)
    - **pain** (See HEAD - Pain - alternating - diarrhea)
- **amel.** all symptoms (See GENERALS - Diarrhea)
- **anger**; after: *(↗MIND - Ailments - anticipation; MIND - Anger; MIND - Anger - diarrhea)* acon k* *Aloe* ars k* bar-c k* bry *Calc-p* *Cham* k* **Coloc** k* ip kali-bi gk nit-ac bg2 *Nux-v* k* plac rzf5• *Staph* k*
- **anticipation**, after: *(↗MIND - Ailments - anticipation)* aeth tl1 *Arg-n* k* bit-ar wht1• **Gels** k •* hydrog srj2• med gk *Ph-ac* [lac-mat sst4]
- **anxiety**, after: *(↗MIND - Anxiety)* arg-n vh1* *Ars* k* camph k* phos k2 *Puls* b7a.de raph hr1 sil k* tab k* verat b7a.de*
- **appearing**:
  - **gradually**: chin k2
  - **suddenly**:
    - **disappearing**; and | **suddenly**: bamb-a stb2.de• kola stb3•
- **apyrexia**, during: ars bro1 *Iod* k* puls br1
- **autumn** agg.: *Ars* k* asc-t k* bapt k* bry bg2 carb-v bg2 chin bro1 **Colch** k* dulc bg2 ip k* **Iris** kali-bi tl1 merc k* *Merc-c* k* *Nux-m* k* puls bg2 sulph bg2 *Verat* k*
- **bad** drainage: bapt hr1 *Carb-ac* k* **Carb-v** hr1 *Pyrog*
- **bad** news; after: *(↗MIND - Ailments - bad)* *Gels* k*
- **bathing** | **after**: *Ant-c* bro1 calc k* nux-m bg2 *Podo* k* rhus-t sars k*
- **battle**, on going into: **GELS** k •*
- **beer**:
  - **after**: *Aloe* k* *Chin* k* chinin-m c1 ferr b7.de* *Gamb* ind ip bro1 *Kali-bi* k* **Lyc** k • *Mur-ac* k* puls gk rhus-t b7.de* **SULPH** k •* teucr b7.de*
    - **amel.**: phos hr1
  - **stopping**; after: aloe k2
- **bilious**: *(↗STOOL - Bilious)* *Acon* hr1 agar k* ammc hr1 apis apoc-a vh *Asc-t* k* aspar hr1 *Bry* k* cact k* cham k* colch k* *Con* k* corn hr1 eup-pur k* *Fl-ac* k* gels hr1 *Ip* k* *Iris* jugin br1 lil-t hr1 med k* *Merc* k* *Merc-c* k* *Mur-ac* k* **Nat-s** k* nat-sil fd3.de• *Nit-ac* k* *Ph-ac* k* **Podo** k* *Psor* *Ptel* k* tarax hr1 tarent hr1 ter k*
- **black**:
  - **accompanied** by | **hemorrhoids**: brom tl1

- **blood**; from loss of: colch tl1 eucal mtf11
- **boils** begin to heal, as soon as: rhus-v k*
- **bread** agg.: ant-c mrr1
  - **dark** bread: *Puls* b7a.de
- **breakfast**:
  - **after** | **agg.**: aeth agar aloe k* alum k* alum-p k2 *Arg-n* k* borx k* calc carb-v bg2 carbn-s cortiso sp1 cycl k* helon a1 iris k* kali-p kalm led lyc mag-c bg2 mag-p mez h2* nat-m **Nat-s** k* nit-m-ac a1 nuph k* nux-v ox-ac k* phos podo bg2* psor *Rhod* **Thuj** k* zing a1
  - **amel.**: bov k* nat-s k* trom
  - **before** | **agg.**: bac al2 cycl a1 tab bg2 zing a1
- **burns**; after: ars k* calc hr1*
- **buttermilk** agg.: podo ptk1
- **cabbage**; after: bry k* petr k* podo
- **camping**, from: *Alst* bro1 dulc fd4.de jug-c bro1 podo c2* septi c2
- **cancer** of rectum; due to: card-m ptk1
- **castor** oil, after: bry k*
- **catarrh** or coryza, after: *Sang* k* sel hr1
- **cathartics**, after: carb-v k* *Chin* k* *Hep* k* nit-ac k* **Nux-v** k*
- **cerebral** symptoms; after sudden cessation of (See HEAD - Brain; complaints of - diarrhea)
- **chagrin** (See mortification)
- **chamomile**, after abuse of: *Coff* k* valer k*
- **chest**, after pains in the: sang
- **children**; in: *Acon* aegle-m bnj1 **Aeth** k* *Agar Agn* k* aloe sne ant-c bg2 apis *Arg-n* k* *Ars* k* arund c1 *Bac* hr1* bar-c *Benz-ac Borx* k* **Calc** k* *Calc-p* **Calc-s** k* carb-v b4a.de carc gk6* **Cham** k* chin mtf33 cimic ptk *Cina* coli jl2 *Crot-t* *Dulc* elat c1 *Ferr* k* *Form* gamb gnaph mtf11 hell *Hep* b4a.de hyos bg2 ing br1* iod k2* iodof br1 **Ip** k* *Iris* jal bg1* kreos *Mag-c* k* **Mag-m** mag-s mtf11 med k2* **Merc** k* *Mez* moni rfm1• *Mur-ac* hr1 *Nat-m* nux-m k* *Nux-v* b7a.de olnd ph-ac k2 **Phos** k* **Podo Psor** k* *Puls* k* **Rheum** k* rubu bwa3 sabad k* samb senn bg1 sep k* **Sil** stann *Staph* **Stram** sul-ac k* **Sulph** k* syc bka1• tub br1* *Valer* vanil fd5.de *Verat* b7a.de zinc
  - **night**: bac bn
  - **dentition**; during (See dentition)
  - **emaciated**: acet-ac ptk1 iod mrr1* rheum mtf33 sil mtf33 tub ptk1*
  - **infants**: *Acon* bro1 *Aeth* bro1 apis bro1 *Arg-n* bro1 *Ars* bro1 arund bro1 bapt bro1 *Bell* bro1 benz-ac bro1 bism bro1 *Borx* bro1 *Calc* bro1 calc-act bro1 *Calc-p* bro1 camph bro1 *Cham* bro1 chin bro1 cina bro1 *Coloc* bro1 colos bro1 *Crot-t* bro1 dulc bro1 ferr bro1 grat bro1 *Hell* bro1 hep bro1 *Ip* bro1 jal bro1 kali-br bro1 *Kreos* bro1 laur bro1 lyc bro1 lyss bro1 *Mag-c* bro1 merc bro1 *Merc-c* bro1 *Merc-d* bro1 nit-ac bro1 *Nux-v* bro1 paull bro1 *Ph-ac* bro1 phos bro1 *Podo* bro1 *Psor* bro1 *Rheum* bro1 sabad bro1 sep bro1 *Sil* bro1 sulph bro1* valer bro1 *Verat* bro1
  - **mother's** milk; after drinking (See nursing; after - child)
  - **newborns**: *Aeth* mrr1 coli jl2
  - **nurslings**: arund c1* calc-p br1* calc-s mtf33 cham br1* coli jl2 psor jl2 sep mtf33 *Sulph* mtf33 vanil fd5.de verat mtf33
    - **asthmatic** mothers; with: nat-s mrr1
  - **school** girls: calc-p tl1* ph-ac ptk1
  - **teeth**; during complaints of: *Cham* b7a.de
  - **tubercular**: iod mtf33
- **chill**:
  - **after**: nux-m c1 sec k*
  - **before**: verat vh
  - **during**: aloe bg2 alum bg2 *Ant-c* bg2 apis bg2 arn bg2 ars k* bry bg2 *Calad* b7.de* caps bro1 cham bg2 chin bg2 cina k* coff bg2 coloc bg2 con bg2 elat k* ferr bg2 hyos b7.de* *Ip* bg2* laur b7.de* m-arct b7.de merc bg2 nux-m bg2 nux-v ph-ac bg2 **Phos** k* puls k* rhus-t k* *Spig* b7.de* stront-c b4a.de* sulph b4.de* **Verat** k*
- **chocolate**, after: borx *Lith-c* k*
- **cholera**:
  - **attack** of; after an: sec
  - **epidemic**; during: camph cupr **Ip** k* *Phos* k* podo hr1* psor al2* puls verat k13
- **chronic**: *Abrot* bg2 acet-ac k2* all-s bro1 aloe bro1 anac bg2 ang bro1 ant-c bro1 *Arg-n* bro1 arn bro1 **Ars** b4a.de* ars-i br1* asaf bg2 **Bac** bn* bapt bro1 bry bg2 **Calc** b4.de* calc-p bro1 canth b7.de* carbn-s k2 cetr bro1 chap br1* chin bg2* cist k2 *Coto* c1* crot-t bro1 *Cupr-ar* bro1 dulc b4a.de* elaps br* *Ferr* bg2* gamb bro1 **Graph** bg2* hep bg2* hydr k2 ign bg2 iod bro1* iodof bro1 *Ip* b7.de* kali-bi bro1* kali-c k2 *Kreos* bg2 lac-ac bro1 lac-d k2 lach bg2* *Liat* bro1 lyc bro1 m-ambo b7.de *Mag-m* b4a.de* *Merc* bro1 merc-d bro1 moni rfm1• nabal bro1 nat-m bg2* nat-s k2* *Nit-ac* b4.de* nux-m b7.de* olnd bro1 parat-b gmm1.fr petr b4.de* ph-ac bg2* **Phos** b4.de* *Plb* b7a.de podo br* psor k2* puls bg2* rheum mrr1 rhus-a c2* *Rhus-t* b7.de* rumx bro1 sec b7.de* sep bg2 sil bg2* spong fd4.de *Staph* hr1* stry-ar bro1 sul-ac bg2* *Sulph* b4.de* *Thuj* bro1 thyr mtf11 tril-p br1 *Tub* k2* urt-u bro1 verat tl1
  - **accompanied** by:
    - **food**; aversion to (See GENERALS - Food and - food - aversion - accompanied - diarrhea)
    - **Tongue** | **pale**: *Lyss* kr1*
  - **children**; in: chin mtf33 coll tl1 iodof br1 tub mtf33
- **cider**, after: *Ant-c* k* *Calc-p* k* dulc fd4.de *Podo*
- **Coca** Cola agg.: coca-c sk4•
- **coffee**:
  - **after**: arist-cl rbp3• canth k* caust *Cist* k* coloc corn *Cycl* k* dulc fd4.de fl-ac k* hyper ign k* lyc k2 mosch bg2 nat-m k* osm k* ox-ac k* phos pin-con oss2• podo sne ruta fd4.de *Thuj* k* vanil fd5.de
  - **amel.**: brom k* *Coloc* corn phos k*
  - **smell** of, after: sul-ac
- **cold**:
  - **nights**: acon *Dulc*
  - **agg.**: agra br1 calc ptk1 dulc ptk1 nux-m ptk1 nux-v mrr1 rumx ptk1 tub ptk1
  - **air**:
    - **abdomen** agg.; on: *Caust*
    - **agg.**: ars bg2 caust bg2 merc bg2 nat-s *Sil*
  - **applications** | **amel.**: cycl lyc *Puls*
  - **bathing** | **after**: *Ant-c* k*
  - **drinks**:
    - **after** | **agg.**●: *Acon* bro1 agra bro1 ant-c **Ars** k* bell k* *Bry* k* calc-ar calc-p k2* camph bro1 *Caps Carb-v* k* caust bro1* cham bro1 chin k* chinin-ar cocc k* *Dulc* k* *Ferr Ferr-ar* grat bro1 *Hep* k* kali-ar lept *Lyc* k* manc nat-ar nat-c *Nat-s* k* nit-ac *Nux-m* k* *Ph-ac Puls* k* *Rhus-t* sep k* *Sil Staph* k* *Sul-ac* trom verat k*
    - **agg.** | **summer** agg.: *Bry* b7a.de *Carb-v Nat-s* **Nux-m** k* verat k*
    - **amel.**: *Phos* k*
  - **food**:
    - **agg.**: ant-c k* **Ars** bry bg1 *Carb-v* cocc coloc k* **Dulc** k* hep *Lyc* k* *Nat-s* k* *Nit-ac* nux-m *Nux-v Ph-ac Puls* k* *Rhus-t* sep sul-ac
    - **amel.**: **Phos**
  - **room** | **amel.**: *Puls*
- **cold**; after taking a: acon k* *Aloe* ant-t ars k* bar-c k* bar-s k2 *Bell* k* *Bry* k* *Calc* camph k* *Caust* k* *Cham* k* chin k* chinin-ar coff k* coloc bg2 con cop k* **Dulc** k* elat k* **Ferr** b7a.de gamb k* graph k* guar vml3• *Hyos* b7.de* *Ip* k* *Jatr-c* kali-c h2* kreos bg2 laur bg2 lil-t k2 merc k* *Nat-ar Nat-c* k* nat-m b4a.de nat-s k* nit-ac **Nux-m** k* *Nux-v* k* op k* *Ph-ac* podo k2 puls k* *Rhod* b4a.de *Rhus-t* k* sabin b7.de* samb b7.de* sang sel sep *Sulph* k* verat k* zing k*
  - **summer** agg.: aloe ant-t bry *Dulc* **Ph-ac** k*
- **cold** agg.; after becoming: arg-n *Cocc Dulc* k* nat-ar *Ph-ac*
- **colic**; after: cortiso sp1
- **constipation**: | **after**: mand rsj7•
- **consumption**, of: arn br1 elaps br1
- **coryza**:
  - **after**: *Sang Sel* tub mtf33
  - **during** (See NOSE - Coryza - accompanied - diarrhea)
  - **suppressed** coryza; from: agra pd sang bro1
- **cough**; with: phos bg2 sang k2
- **cucumbers**, after: verat k*
- **dark**, bilious, offensive | **sallow** complexion, with: corn br1
- **darkness** agg.: *Stram*
- **debauch**, after a: ant-c k* *Carb-v* bg2 **Nux-v** k*
- **debilitated**; of the: **Chin** bg2 *Ferr* bg2 nux-m bg2 *Ph-ac* bg2 phos bg2 sec bg2

- **delivery**:
  - **after**: *Ant-c* b7a.de* *Cham* bro1 coll ptk1 dulc b4a.de* hyos b7a.de* psor bro1 puls bro1 **Rheum** b7a.de* *Sec* bro1 stram bro1
  - **during**: ant-c bg2 dulc bg2 hyos bg2 rheum bg2
- **dentition**; during●: acet-ac bro1 *Acon* k* *Aeth* k* ant-c bg2 *Apis* apoc sf1.de* *Arg-n* k* *Ars* k* arund c1* *Bell* k* benz-ac k* *Borx* k* bry bg2 **Calc** k* calc-act bro1 *Calc-p* k* canth carb-v k* **Cham** k* chin *Cina* k* *Coff* k* colch *Coloc* corn cund c1 cupr **Dulc** k* enteroc jl2 **Ferr** k* ferr-ar ferr-p bro1 *Gels* graph hell *Hep* k* ign *Ip* k* jal bro1 *Kali-br* hr1 *Kreos* k* *Mag-c* k* *Mag-p* kr1 med c1 *Merc* k* *Nit-ac* b4a.de nux-m k* nux-v bg2 olnd bro1 ph-ac phos bro1 *Phyt* kr1* *Podo* k* *Psor* k* puls bro1 **Rheum** k* *Sep* k* **Sil** k* sul-ac k* *Sulph* k* zinc k*
- **diet**:
  - **change** of diet; least: all-s nux-v k* ph-ac mrr1
  - **trivial** errors in diet; after (See indiscretion)
- **dinner**; after: alum k* am-m k* ars-s-f hr1 bond a1 borx h2* caps carbn-s chin coloc k* corn a1* ferr-ma a1 **Grat** k* kali-p fd1.de• *Lil-t* k* **Mag-c** k* nat-m k* nat-sil fd3.de• nit-ac k* nux-v k* trom k* verat
- **disorganization**, from: ars bro1
- **domestic** cares; from: *Coff* k*
- **draft**, after (See air agg.)
- **drinking**:
  - **after**:
    - **agg.**: *Arg-n* ptk1 ars b4a.de* caps b7a.de* cina b7a.de* **Crot-t** ptk1 ferr ptk1 nux-v ptk1 phos ptk1 rhus-t ptk1
    - **immediately** after: *Aloe* sne arg-n mtf33 cina mtf33 **Crot-t** mrr1
    - **water** | **immediately** after: **Arg-n** k* cina *Crot-t* *Podo*
  - **agg.**: *Aloe* bro1 *Alst* bro1 *Apis* bro1 apoc bro1 *Arg-n* bro1 *Ars* bro1 bry bro1 canth bro1 *Chin* bro1 *Coloc* bro1 *Crot-t* bro1 *Ferr* bro1 kali-p bro1 lyc bro1 nux-v bro1 *Phos* bro1 podo bro1* puls bro1 rheum bro1 sanic bro1 sulph bro1 tanac bro1 thuj bro1 *Trom* bro1 *Verat* bro1
    - **fluids** go right through him after drinking: **Arg-n** hr1*
- **drugs**; after: *Nux-v* k*
- **drunkards**: | **old** drunkards: ant-t *Apis* *Ars* chin **Lach** nux-v *Phos*
- **dysenteric** (See Dysentery)
- **eating**:
  - **after**:
    - **agg.**: *(↗Urging - eating - after - agg.)* aesc aeth k* *Agar* **Aloe** k* *Alst* bro1 alum k* alum-p k2 am-m k* ant-c *Apis* k* apoc bro1 *Arg-n* k* **Ars** k* ars-i ars-s-f k2 *Asaf* asar k* asim hr1 aur-m k* aur-m-n bamb-a stb2.de• borx k* *Brom* k* *Bry* k* *Calc* k* calc-i k2 calc-p ptk1 calc-s canth bro1 caps k* *Carb-v* k* carbn-s caust k* cedr *Cham* k* **Chin** k* **Chinin-ar** k* *Cina* k* cist k* **Coloc** k* con k* *Corn* k* cortiso tpw7* **Crot-t** k* cub *Dulc* k* *Ferr* k* *Ferr-ar* *Ferr-i* ferr-ma k* ferr-p *Fl-ac* *Form* k* *Gamb* graph ptk1 hep k* hydrog srj2• hyper k* ign *Iod* k* *Kali-ar* kali-n k* *Kali-p* k* kreos ptk1 *Lach* k* laur **Lyc** k* mag-c ptk1 marb-w es1• morg-p fmm1• mur-ac k* **Nat-ar** *Nat-c* k* nat-ox rly4• nat-p *Nat-s* k* nit-ac k* nux-m k* *Nux-v* k* parathyr jl2 *Petr* *Ph-ac* k* *Phos* k* plut-n srj7• **Podo** k* **Puls** k* raph k* *Rheum* k* rhod k* rhus-t ruta fd4.de sanic k* sars k* sec k* spong fd4.de *Staph* k* staphycoc rly4• *Sul-ac* k* sulph k* tab k* tanac bro1* *Thuj* k* **Trom** k* tung-met bdx1• verat k* zinc
    - **immediately** after: apoc vh1 arg-n br1 cina mtf33 **Crot-t** mrr1 dulc fd4.de tanac ptk2
  - **amel.**: arg-n *Brom* *Chel* dios grat *Hep* iod jab *Lith-c* *Lyc* nat-c nicc nit-ac *Petr* plan sang sul-i k2
  - **attempting** to eat; on: ferr mtf33
  - **overeating** agg.; after: petr-ra shn4•
  - **while** | **agg.**: *Aloe* sne ars chin *Crot-t* k* **Ferr** k* *Kali-p* podo k* puls rad-br bg1 trom
- **effluvia**; from noxious: bapt bro1 carb-ac bro1 *Crot-h* k* *Pyrog*
- **eggs**; after: chinin-ar k* *Lyc* b4a.de
- **emaciated** people, in: *Calc* k* *Calc-p* k* iod k* nat-m k* phos k* *Rheum* **Sil** k* *Sul-ac* k* sul-i k2 sulph k*
- **eructations** | **amel.**: *Arg-n* carb-v grat hep lyc sep *Sulph*
- **eruptions**:
  - **during**: ant-t k* ars chin dulc ptk1 squil
  - **suppressed** eruptions; after: ant-t gsy1* apis bro1 *Bry* k* dulc k* graph bg1 *Hep* *Lyc* merc mez petr c1* *Psor* k* **Sulph** k* *Urt-u*
- **exanthema** (See eruptions)
- **excessive**: *Cupr* b7a.de *Verat* b7a.de
- **excitement** agg.: *(↗MIND - Ailments - joy - excessive; MIND - Ailments - surprises - pleasant)* *Acon* bg1* *Aloe* vh ant-c bg1 **Arg-n** k* *Arn* vh bamb-a stb2.de• *Bry* b7a.de* *Calc-p* vh *Cham* b7a.de* chin bg1 cina coch hr1 *Coloc* bg1* dys pte1*• enteroc jl2 *Gels* k* guar vml3• hyos k* ign b7a.de* ip hr1 kali-bi gk *Kali-p* k* lyc hr1 mag-m dgt nux-v b7a.de **Op** bg1* petr ph-ac k* phos bg1 podo k2 puls bg1* sep hr1 sil tl1 *Staph* vh syc fmm1• *Thuj* k* vanil fd5.de verat bg1* zinc bro1
  - **fear**; with: acon k1
  - **theater**; as before: **Arg-n** k*
- **exciting** news, from: *(↗MIND - Ailments - joy; MIND - Ailments - surprises - pleasant)* **Gels**
- **exertion** | **after** | **agg.**: aloe sne ars *Calc* ferr k* nat-s nat-sil fd3.de• podo k2 *Puls* *Rhus-t*
  - **agg.**: *Rheum* vh
- **exhausting**: ambr b7.de *Apis* b7a.de arn b7.de *Bry* b7.de* **Chin** b7.de **Cocc** b7a.de *Colch* b7a.de *Con* b4a.de cupr b7.de *Ferr* b7.de hyos b7.de ip b7.de *Kali-c* b4a.de *Nux-m* b7.de* nux-v b7.de olnd b7.de plb b7a.de puls b7.de **Rheum** b7a.de **Sec** b7.de* *Sep* b4a.de *Sil* b4a.de *Verat* b7.de
- **fat**; after (See food - fat)
- **fat**, flabby people: caps
- **fear**; with (See MIND - Fear - diarrhea - fear)
- **fever**:
  - **after**: phos b4a.de*
  - **before**: ant-c b7a.de chin b7a.de cina b7a.de puls b7a.de rhus-t b7a.de
  - **during** | **agg.**: *Achy-a* zzc1• *Acon* b7a.de* am-c bg2 *Ant-c* b7a.de* ant-t bg2 *Apis* b7a.de* arn b7a.de* ars b4.de* asaf bg2 **Bapt** bg2 borx bg2 brom bg2 *Bry* b7a.de* calad bg2 calc bg2 caps bg2 **Cham** b7a.de* chin bg2* cina b7.de* *Coff* b7a.de* coli jl2 coloc bg2 **Con** b4.de* dig bg2 dulc bg2 ferr bg2 hyos bg2 ip bg2* *Lach* b7a.de* **Merc** b4.de* **Mur-ac** bg2 nat-m bg2 nit-ac bg2 nux-m bg2* nux-v bg2 op bro1 petr bg2 *Ph-ac* bg2 phos b4.de* puls b7.de* rheum bg2 **Rhus-t** b7.de* ruta bg2 sec bg2 sep bg2 **Sil** b4a.de* squil bg2 stann bg2 sul-ac bg2 *Sulph* b4.de* vanil fd5.de **Verat** b7a.de*
  - **hectic**, during: aesc bac bn
  - **intermittent**, during: ant-c c1* ars bapt ptk1 chinin-ar **Cina** k* cocc con gels nux-v ptk1 puls *Rhus-t* k* thuj (non:tub lmj)
  - **paroxysmal**; during: bapt ptk1
  - **pernicious**: camph cupr pyrog
  - **puerperal**: carb-ac *Pyrog* k* sulph
  - **typhoid** fever: *Agar* *Apis* arg-n arn bro1 *Ars* k* *Bapt* k* *Bry* *Calc* crot-h bro1 *Cupr-ar* bro1 echi bro1 *Epil* bro1 eucal bro1 **Hyos** k* *Lach* k* lyss *Merc* bro1 *Mur-ac* k* *Nit-ac* nuph bro1 *Op* k* *Ph-ac* k* **Phos** k* *Rhus-t* k* sec *Stram* k* *Sul-ac* ter verat
- **fish** agg.: chin mrr1 chinin-ar k* kola stb3•
- **flatus**; passing:
  - **after**:
    - **agg.**: granit-m es1• kali-ar ptk1 kali-p fd1.de• nat-m h2* plat h2
    - **amel.**: plat h sep *Sulph*
- **fluids**; after loss of: *Carb-v* *Chin* ph-ac
- **followed** by:
  - **cough**; dry: abrot ptk1
  - **hammering** in anus: lach tl1
  - **perspiration**: tub jl2
  - **respiration**; asthmatic: nat-s bro1
  - **rheumatism**: abrot ptk1 cimic ptk1 dulc ptk1 iod mrr1 *Kali-bi* k*
- **food**:
  - **acid** (See acids)
  - **artificial**, after: alum calc mag-c sulph k*
  - **aversion** to, with: ant-c ptk1 ars bg1* chin bg1* nux-m bg1* phos bg1* puls bg1*
  - **boiled**; after: podo k2
  - **change** of, after: all-s nux-v
  - **crude**, after: cham dh1*
  - **farinaceous**, after: lyc nat-c k* **Nat-m** k* **Nat-s** k*
  - **fat**, after: *(↗rich)* ange-s oss1• ant-c calc-f sp1* carb-v k* cycl k* dys fmm1• *Kali-chl* k* kali-m k2* mag-m mrr1 mag-s sp1 *Puls* k* thuj k*
  - **fried**: mag-s sp1

Rectum

- **rancid**, after: *Ars* carb-v
- **solid**, after: bapt *Olnd* **Ph-ac** *Podo*
- **sour**:
  - **agg.**: lach bg1
  - **amel.**: arg-n
- **fright**; after: acon k* *Arg-n* k* **Gels** k* ign k* *Kali-p* k* *Op* k* ph-ac k* phos k* *Puls* k* verat k*
- **frothy**: *Canth* b7.de* *Chin* b7.de *Coloc* b4.de* iod b4.de *Mag-c* b4.de* merc b4.de* op b7.de *Rhus-t* b7.de *Ruta* b7a.de sulph b4.de
- **fruit**:
  - **agg.**: acon *Aloe* alum-sil k2 ant-t **Ars** k* ars-s-f k2 *Borx* k* **Bry** k* calc *Calc-p* k* *Carb-v* **Chin** k* *Chinin-ar* *Cist* k* **Coloc** k* *Crot-t* k* *Ferr* *Ip* k* *Iris* lach k* lith-c k* *Lyc* k* mag-c mag-m mrr1 *Merc* b4a.de *Merc-c* b4a.de *Mur-ac* **Nat-s** *Olnd* k* *Ph-ac* phos b4a.de *Podo* k* **Puls** k* rheum *Rhod* k* sul-ac k* tritic-vg fd5.de trom **Verat** k* zing bro1
  - **canned**: podo ptk1
  - **juicy**: calc-p tl1
  - **sour**:
    - **after**: *Ant-c* k* *Cist* k* *Ip* *Lach* *Ph-ac* podo br*
    - **with** milk, after: *Podo* k*
  - **stewed**, after: bry k*
  - **unripe** fruit, after: aloe *Ip* ph-ac ptk1 rheum k* *Sul-ac* k*
- **game**; after high: **Ars** *Carb-v* *Crot-h* k* *Lach* pyrog bro1
- **ginger**, after: *Nux-v* k*
- **glistening** objects, looking at: *Stram*
- **goitre**, with: cist ptk1
- **gonorrhea**; after suppressed: **Med**
- **gouty** subjects: benz-ac calc-f k2 iod
- **grief**; from: *(↗MIND - Ailments - grief)* calc-p *Coloc* k* *Gels* k* *Ign* *Kali-br* hr1 merc op *Ph-ac* k*
- **hair** cutting, after: *Bell*
- **headache**:
  - **after**: hydrog srj2•
  - **during**: *(↗HEAD - Pain - diarrhea - during)* *Prot* jl2 vanil fd5.de zinc mrr1
- **heat**:
  - **external** | **amel.**: *Ars* *Hep*
  - **moist** external, amel.: *Nux-m*
  - **sun**; of the | **agg.**: agar k* camph k* carb-v k* petr-ra shn4•
- **hydrocephalus** acutus, during: *Apis* bell *Calc* *Carb-ac* *Hell* k* *Zinc*
- **hyperacidity**; from (See STOMACH - Hyperchlorhydria - accompanied - diarrhea)
- **ice** cream:
  - **after**: arg-n **Ars** k* bry k* calc-p k* *Carb-v* k* dulc k* nat-s k2 *Puls* k*
  - **amel.**: *Phos*
- **imagination**, from exalted: *Arg-n*
- **indignation**; from: *Coloc* *Gels* vh *Ip* *Staph*
- **indiscretion** in eating, after the slightest: *(↗GENERALS - Food - diet - agg. - errors)* aesc *Aloe* *Ant-c* arg-met *Ars* *Asaf* brach *Bry* calc-p k2 *Carb-v* *Chin* cimic *Colch* fl-ac *Gamb* graph h2* guar vml3• *Iod* k* *Ip* kali-chl naja nat-m nuph vml3• *Nux-v* k* *Petr* *Ph-ac* **Phos** k* *Podo* *Psor* ptel **Puls** k* sul-ac k2* *Sulph* zing
- **influenza**; during: bapt tl1 influ jl2
- **injuries**; after: *Arn* nat-s sne
- **interrupted**: cench k2
- **involuntary**: arn k2 ars b4a.de* bapt k2 bell b4a.de bry k2 carb-v k2 colch k2 crot-h k2 gels k2 hell k2 hyos k2 lach k2 laur k2 mur-ac k2 op k2 ph-ac b4a.de* phos k2 rhus-t k2 sec k2 stram tl1* sul-ac k2 sulph b4a.de verat k2 [spect dfg1]
  - **typhoid** fever; during: apis bro1 *Arn* bro1 ars bro1 hyos bro1 mur-ac bro1 *Ph-ac* bro1
  - **urination**; with simultaneous: arn k2 ars k2 carb-v k2 colch k2 hyos k2 laur k2 mur-ac k2 ph-ac k2 phos k2 rhus-t k2 sec k2 stram k2
- **jaundice**; during: *Chion* k* *Dig* k* *Lycps-v* k* *Merc* *Nat-s* k* *Nux-v* k* puls ptk1* rheum ptk1 sep *Sulph*
- **joy**; from sudden: acon kr1 *Coff* gels kr1 **Op**
- **laxatives**; as if after: moni rfm1•
- **lemonade** agg.: ant-c k2 *Cit-ac* *Phyt* k*
- **light**; from bright: *Bell* colch *Stram*
- **lumbar** pain, with: bar-c ptk1 kali-i ptk1
- **lying**:
  - **abdomen**; on | **amel.**: aloe alum calc coloc phos rhus-t
  - **agg.**: *Dios* k* mag-m mrr1 ox-ac k* raph k*
  - **amel.**: anthraq rly4• *Bry* merc podo sabad
  - **back**; on:
    - **agg.**: kali-bi gk phos podo k*
    - **amel.**: *Bry*
  - **side**; on:
    - **agg.**: *Bry* k* nit-ac k*
    - **amel.**: podo k*
    - **left** | **agg.**: *Arg-n* k* arn k* *Phos* k*
    - **right**:
      - **agg.**: ph-ac k*
      - **amel.**: phos k*
- **magnesia**, after: bry k* *Nux-v* k* puls k* rheum
- **measles**:
  - **after**: *Carb-v* chin k* elat hr1 merc k* *Puls* k* squil
  - **during**: ars bro1 chin bro1 *Ip* bro1 merc bro1 *Puls* bro1 squil k* *Sulph* hr1 verat bro1
- **meat**:
  - **calf** (See veal)
  - **from**: *Calc* b4a.de *Caust* ferr lept sep
  - **smoked**, from: calc
  - **spoiled** meat; from: ars bro1 crot-h bro1
- **melons** agg.: *Ars* bro1 *Bry* bro1 petr bro1 *Zing* k*
- **menopause**; during: apis vh **Lach** k* lil-t br1 sulph tab vh
  - **morning**: rumx vh
- **menses**:
  - **after** | **agg.**: am-m ptk1 *Ars* k* borx bg2 bov k* caust ptk1 coloc ptk1 graph k* kreos ptk1 *Lach* k* mag-m nat-m k* nat-s ptk1 ph-ac ptk1 *Phos* ptk1 puls bro1* sec ptk1 sulph ptk1 *Tub* verat ptk1 vib ptk1
  - **before** | **agg.●**: aloe k* alum k* *Am-c* k* *Am-m* bro1 apis ars bro1 **Bov** k* cham bro1 *Cinnb* k* cocc k* elaps gk *Hyos* b7a.de hyper k* kali-bi gk kreos bro1 **Lach** k* mang bg2 merc bg2 *Nat-s* phos bro1 *Puls* bro1 *Sil* k* thuj bg2 tub *Verat* k*
  - **during**:
    - **agg.●**: aloe bg2 alum k* alum-p k2 am-c k* *Am-m* k* ant-c k* ars k* ars-s-f k2 bamb-a stb2.de• **Bov** k* bry k* calc bg2 calc-p k* castm bg2* *Caust* k* cham k* chel k* chord-umb rly4• cinnb k* clem enteroc jl2 ferr bg2 glon graph irid-met srj5• kali-c k* kali-i k* kali-p kali-s kali-sil k2 kola stb3• *Kreos* k* lac-c lach bg1 mag-c k* mag-m bg2 merc bg2 nat-ar nat-c k* nat-m bg2 *Nat-p* nat-s k* nicc k* nux-v ol-an bg2* petr-ra shn4• *Phos* k* plat k* podo *Puls* k* *Sars* sil k* stram bg2 stront-c sul-ac k* sulph bg2 *Tab* k* tub **Verat** k* *Vib* k* zinc
    - **beginning** of menses | **agg.**: **Am-c** vh
  - **suppressed** menses; from: glon ptk1
- **mental** exertion:
  - **after**: *Arg-n* *Nux-v* k* *Pic-ac* k* *Prot* jl2 sabad k*
  - **amel.**: kali-p
- **mercury**; after abuse of: asaf *Hep* k* *Kali-i* lach k* *Nit-ac* k* sars k* staph k* *Sulph* k*
- **milk**:
  - **agg.**: *(↗GENERALS - Food and - milk - agg.)* aeth k* arist-cl sp1 ars k* bry k* **Calc** k* chin bg1* con k* iod bg1 *Kali-ar* *Kali-c* k* lac-d k2* *Lyc* k* *Mag-c* k* **Mag-m** k* med gk **Nat-ar** **Nat-c** k* *Nicc* k* nit-ac *Nux-m* k* pitu-a vml2• podo k* **Sep** k* *Sil* k* *Sulph* k* tritic-vg fd5.de valer bro1
    - **sour**: *Podo* k*
  - **boiled**, after: *Nux-m* k* nux-v ptk1 *Sep* ptk1*
- **mortification**; after: aloe bry cham coloc *Staph*
- **motion**:
  - **agg.**: aloe k* **Apis** k* arn k* ars k* *Bell* k* **Bry** k* cadm-s calc k* chin bro1 *Colch* k* coloc k* *Crot-t* k* **Ferr** k* *Ferr-ar* hura ip k* merc-c k* mur-ac k*

- agg.: ...
  Nat-m k* nat-s k* *Nux-v* ox-ac k* phos *Podo* puls k* rheum k* rumx tab k* *Tub* **Verat** k*
- amel.: coloc cub cycl *Dios* nit-ac plan puls k2 rhod *Rhus-t* zinc
- downward motion agg.: borx k2* cham bro1 sanic bro1

- **nervous**, emotions agg.: acon bg3* **Arg-n** bg2* aur-m-n wbt2• *Cham* bg3* coch c1 *Coff* bg2* ferr ptk1 **Gels** bg2* hyos bg3* ign bg3* *Kali-p* bg2 mag-m bg2* nat-s pd *Op* bg3* phos bg3* podo bg3* *Puls* bg3* *Verat* bg3* zinc c2*
- **noise** agg.: colch *Nit-ac* *Nux-v*
  - **sudden**, from: bell *Borx*
- **noisy**: lem-m br1
- **nursing**; after | **child**; in the: ant-c k* arg-n k2 *Crot-t* k* nat-c k* *Nux-v* k* sil k2
- **nursing** the child agg.; after: *Chin* phos hr1* *Rheum* k*
- **nurslings** (See children - nurslings)
- **old** people: **Ant-c** k* ant-t bg2 **Ars** k* ars-i bapt lp bar-c mtf11 bov bro1* *Bry* bg2 *Carb-v* k* *Chin* bro1 coff con *Fl-ac* **Gamb** k* iod k* kreos lach bg2 nat-m bg2 nat-s **Nit-ac** k* nux-v k* op k* phos k* rhus-t bg2 ruta bg2 sec k* sul-i k2 sulph k*
  - **painful**: carb-v ptk1
  - **prematurely**, with syphilitic mercurial dyscrasia: *Fl-ac*
  - **women**; old: kreos nat-s
- **onions** agg.: lyc nux-v *Puls* *Thuj* k*
- **opium**; after: *Mur-ac* k* *Nat-m* k* nux-v k* **Puls**
- **oranges** agg.: *Olnd* mrr1 *Ph-ac*
- **overheated**, after being: acon aloe **Ant-c** k* *Bry* b7.de caps b7.de *Coff* b7.de elat *Ign* b7.de ip b7.de *Nux-v* b7.de **Puls**
- **oysters**, after: *Aloe* k* *Brom* k* *Lyc* k* *Podo* rosm lgb1 *Sul-ac* k*
- **pain**; from: ars ptk1 bry ptk1 cham ptk1 coloc k2* merc ptk1 merc-c ptk1 rheum ptk1 rhus-t ptk1 sulph ptk1
- **painful**: agar bg2 alum b4.de am-c b4.de* am-m bg2 anac b4.de* *Ang* b7a.de *Apis* b7a.de ars b4a.de* asaf b7.de* asar b7.de* bar-c b4a.de bov b4.de* bry b7.de* canth bg2 caps b7.de* carb-v b4a.de* cham b7.de* chin b7.de* colch b7.de* coloc b4a.de* con b4.de cupr b7.de dig b4.de dulc b4.de* euph bg2 graph b4.de* ign b7a.de* jal bg2 kali-bi bg2 kali-c b4.de kali-n b4.de* lyc b4.de mag-c b4.de mag-m b4.de* merc b4.de* **Merc-c** bg2 nat-c b4.de* nux-v b7.de* petr b4.de* phos b4.de* plb b7a.de puls b7.de* **Rheum** b7.de* **Rhus-t** b7.de* sep b4.de* sil b4.de spig bg2 *Sul-ac* b4a.de sulph b4a.de* verat b7.de* zinc b4.de
  - **chill**; during: bry bg2 cham bg2 coloc bg2 merc bg2 puls bg2 rhus-t bg2 verat bg2
- **painless**: acon b2.de agar bro1 alf bro1 *Aloe* *Alst* bro1 ambr b2.de* anac b2.de ant-t b2.de anthraci *Apis* k* arg-n k* arn k* *Ars* k* ars-i ars-s-f k2 arum-t aur b2.de **Bapt** k* bar-c b2.de* bar-m k* bell k* bell-p bro1 berb bg2 **Bism** k* **Borx** k* both-ax tsm2 bov b2.de* bry k* *Calc* k* calc-s calc-sil k2 *Camph* k* cann-i c1 canth b2.de* carb-an k* carb-v b2.de* carbn-s cench k2 *Cham* k* chap bro1 *Chel* k* *Chin* k* cic b2.de cinnb k* clem k* coca-c sk4• *Cocc* k* coch k* *Coff* k* colch k* coloc k* con k* croc b2.de *Crot-t* k* cupr b2.de dig b2.de *Dulc* k* **Ferr** k* *Ferr-ar* *Ferr-p* gamb k* *Gels* k* graph k* *Grat* k* hell k* **Hep** k* hir skp7• **Hyos** k* *Ign* k* ip k* iris k* jab k* *Jatr-c* *Kali-ar* kali-bi k* kali-br hr1 *Kali-c* k* kali-n k* kali-p k* kali-s *Lach* laur k* lavand-a ctl1• led b2.de *Lyc* k* m-ambo b2.de* m-aust b2.de *Mag-c* k* mag-m b2.de malar jl2 merc k* mur-ac b2.de nat-ar k2 **Nat-m** k* *Nat-p* *Nat-s* k* nat-sil fd3.de• nit-ac k* *Nuph* k* nux-m k* nux-v k* *Olnd* k* op k* pegan-ha tpi1• petr k* *Ph-ac* k* **Phos** k* plat k* **Podo** k* *Psor* k* puls k* *Pyrog* k* ran-b k* rhod k* *Rhus-t* k* ric bro1 rumx k* sabin b2.de* sars b2.de sec k* sep k* *Sil* k* spig b2.de* spong b2.de **Squil** k* stann staph b2.de stram k* stront-c b2.de *Sul-ac* k* **Sulph** k* syph hr1* tab k* thuj k* tril-p c1 **Tub** k* valer b2.de *Verat* k* zinc k* zinc-p k2
  - **night**: ars borx bry canth cham *Chin* dulc merc puls rhus-t sulph verat
    - **only** after eating in daytime: **Chin**
  - **accompanied** by | **urination**; frequent: bism ptk1
  - **chill**; during: ars bg2 chin bg2 ferr bg2 hyos bg2 ph-ac bg2 phos bg2
- **pancakes**; after: mag-s sp1
- **pancreatic** affections; from (See ABDOMEN - Pancreas - accompanied - diarrhea)
- **paroxysmal** (See sudden)
- **passed** ten stools: mim-p skp7•
- **pastry** agg.: arg-n k* dulc fd4.de *Ip* k* *Kali-chl* k* kali-m hr1 *Lyc* *Nat-s* k* *Ph-ac* phos k* **Puls** k*
- **pears** agg.: borx bry *Verat*
- **periodical**: (↗*GENERALS - History - diarrhea)* apis bro1 ars bro1 chin bro1* dulc fd4.de euph-c bro1 gaert pte1• iris bro1 *Kali-bi* bro1 mag-c bro1 pant-ac rly4• podo mrr1 stront-c ptk1 thuj bro1
  - **day**:
    - **alternate**: *Alum* k* *Carb-ac* **Chin** k* dig fl-ac *Iris* k* nit-ac
    - **fourth**; every: sabad k*
    - **every**: petr tl1
    - **ten** to fifteen days interval; at: glycyr-g cte1•
  - **night** | **every** night: iris br1
  - **summer**: *Kali-bi*
  - **hour**:
    - **same**; at the: apis sabad sel thuj
    - **later** every day; an hour: fl-ac
  - **week**:
    - **few** weeks; every: gaert pte1*•
    - **four** to six weeks; every: carbn-s br1
    - **three** weeks; every: mag-c k*
- **perspiration**:
  - **during**: *Acon* b7.de* ant-c bg2 apis bg2 arn bg2 *Ars* bg2 bry bg2 calc bg2 caps bg2 **Cham** bg2 chin bg2 cina bg2 coff bg2 **Con** bg2 crot-t bg2 **Merc** bg2 *Merc-c* bg2 *Ph-ac* bg2 **Phos** bg2 puls bg2 **Rhus-t** bg2 sep bg2 sil bg2 **Stram** b7.de* sulph bg2 verat b7.de*
  - **suppressed** perspiration; from: acon
- **phthisis**, in: acet-ac c1* ars bg2* bry bg2* carb-v bg2* chin bg2* ferr bg2* *Ferr-pem* c1 hep bg2* kali-bi k2 nit-ac bg2* ph-ac bg2* phos bg2* puls bg2* rumx ptk1 sulph bg2*
  - **first** stage: ferr ptk1 kali-i ptk1
- **pizza**; after: bamb-a stb2.de•
- **pneumonia**; in: ant-t gsy1* apis sne ars sne chel sne cupr tl1* *Elaps* sne ferr-p sne *Phos* sne rhus-t sne
- **pork**, after: acon-l a1* ant-c k* bamb-a stb2.de• cycl k* nux-m *Puls* k*
- **potatoes**:
  - **after**: *Alum* coloc sep verat
  - **sweet**, after: *Calc-ar*
- **pregnancy**:
  - **after**: *Phos* a1
  - **during**: alum k* am-m *Ant-c* k* apis *Caps* hr1 cham k* *Chel* k* *Chin* k* dulc k* ferr k* hell k* hyos k* lac-ac hr1 *Lyc* k* merc b4.de* *Nux-m* k* nux-v k* petr k* *Ph-ac* c2* **Phos** k* podo gk *Puls* k* rheum bg2* sec bro1 *Sep* k* *Sulph* k* thuj bg2*
- **quinine**, after abuse of: ferr k* hep k* lach k* nat-m pall k* **Puls** k*
- **recurrent** (See periodical; GENERALS - History - diarrhea)
- **reprimand**; after: staph k2
- **rheumatism** | **during**: dulc ptk1 stront-c ptk1
- **rhubarb** agg.: *Cham* k* *Coloc* k* merc k* nux-v k* puls k*
- **rich** food agg.: (↗*food - fat)* arg-n *lp* kali-chl *Nat-s* phos podo k2 **Puls**
- **riding**:
  - **agg.**: **Cocc** k* nux-m k* *Petr* k* psor
  - **amel.**: *Nit-ac*
  - **train**; in a: med
- **rising**:
  - **after** | **agg.**: nat-s tl1
  - **agg.**: acon beryl tpw5 *Bry* k* cocc colch bg op trom
  - **bed**; from | **amel.**: cub dios mez
- **rubbing** | **amel.**: dios lyc
- **sadness**; with (See MIND - Sadness - diarrhea - during)
- **salmon**, after eating: *Fl-ac*
- **sauerkraut**, after: *Bry* k* nux-v b7a.de *Petr* k* ruta fd4.de
- **school** girls; in (See children - school)
- **scrofulous**: ars bg2 bar-c bg2 **Calc** bg2 chin bg2 dulc bg2 lyc bg2 sep bg2 **Sil** bg2 *Sulph* bg2
- **sea** bathing from: sep
- **seaside** agg.; at the: aq-mar mgm• *Ars* bry syph c1*
- **sensation** as after diarrhea: (↗*ABDOMEN - Diarrhea - sensation)* ant-c h

Rectum

- **sensation** as before diarrhea: *(↗ABDOMEN - Diarrhea - sensation)* agar androc srj1• apoc carl colch crot-t cystein-l rly4• dig dros **Dulc** k* eupi form fum rly4• gels glon grat ind iris kali-n lyc merc-i-f mez nat-m *Nit-ac* *Nux-v* ptk1 phos pip-m plan plb puls ptk1 sinus rly4• sulph
  - **drinking** agg.; after: *Caps* a1
  - **smoking** agg.: borx
  - **walking** agg.: nat-m
- **septic** conditions, from: **Ars** k* *Carb-ac* k* *Carb-v* k* *Crot-h* k* *Lach* k* *Pyrog* *Sulph*
- **shellfish**, from: carb-v
- **shining** objects agg.: *Stram*
- **shivering**; during: *Verat* b7.de
- **sitting**:
  - **agg.**: crot-t dios
  - **amel.**: cocc
  - **erect** | **agg.**: *Bry*
- **sleep**:
  - **after** | **agg.**: bell k* **Lach** k* pic-ac k* plac-s rly4• *Sulph* zing k*
  - **amel.**: alum crot-t *Phos* k*
  - **during** | **agg.**: bry k* *Sulph* k* *Tub* k*
- **smallpox**; during: ant-t *Ars* k* **Chin** k* thuj
- **smoking** agg.: borx k* brom cham
- **soup** agg.: mag-c k*
- **spices**, from: phos k* positr nl2•
- **spirits** (See alcoholic)
- **spring** agg.: *Bry* k* chin b7a.de *Ip* b7a.de iris *Lach* k* sars k*
- **standing**:
  - **agg.**: *Aloe* ars bry *Cocc* k* ign k* lil-t k* rheum **Sulph** k*
  - **amel.**: merc k*
- **strain**, after a: *Rhus-t*
- **sudden**: *(↗STOOL - Forcible)* abrot tl1 aids nl2• anthraq rly4• arist-cl sp1 bac bn* camph al1* **Crot-t** mrr1 dulc fd4.de gink-b sbd1• lavand-a ctl1• morg-g fmm1• morg-p fmm1• nat-ox rly4• nat-s tl1 ozone sde2• phos tl1 psor jl2 syph jl2 thuj mtf33
- **sugar**:
  - **after**: **Arg-n** k* calc crot-t *Merc* ox-ac *Sulph* trom
  - **maple** sugar: calc-s
- **summer**: *(↗weather - warm - agg.)* acon ptk1 *Ambro* br1 *Bry* ptk1 camph ptk1 castm ptk1 *Chin* b7a.de* crot-t ptk1 cyn-d mtf11 ferr ptk1* ferr-p ptk1 gamb ptk1 gnaph mtf11 grat mtf11 iris mtf11 kali-bi ptk1 kreos ptk1 nux-m ptk1 olnd ptk1 *Podo* ptk1 psor mtf33 sil mtf33 *Sul-ac* b4a.de
  - **accompanied** by | **eruptions**: *Hyper* hr1*
  - **alternating** with | **winter** headaches (See HEAD - Pain - winter - alternating - diarrhea)
  - **children**; in: cupr ptk1
- **supper** agg.; after: hyper k* iris kali-p kola stb3• rob a1 ruta fd4.de sacch-a fd2.de• senec a1 trom k* vanil fd5.de
- **suppressed** diarrhea; from: abrot mrr1* mag-p ptk1 zinc ptk1
  - **perspiration**; from suppressed: *Acon* bro1 cham bro1 ferr-p bro1
- **sweets** agg.: *Arg-n* bro1 calc-s bro1 crot-t bro1 dys fmm1• *Gamb* bro1 merc bro1
- **teething** (See dentition)
- **thinking** of it agg.: ox-ac
- **thunderstorm**:
  - **before**: rhod k*
  - **during**: nat-c phos rhod
- **tobacco**; from: borx h2 brom cham k* ign k* puls k* tab bro1
- **travelling**: *Alum* bg2 op bg2 **Plat** bg2
- **tuberculosis**:
  - **during**: acet-ac bro1 arg-n bg1* *Arn* bro1 ars bg1* ars-i br1* *Bapt* bro1 bism bro1 *Calc* bg2 *Chin* bg2* cist bg2 *Coto* c1* *Cupr-ar* bro1 elaps bro1 ferr bg2* iod bg2* iodof bro1 kreos bg2 ph-ac bro1 **Phos** bg2* puls bro1 rumx bro1 tub bg2
  - **family** history of tuberculosis: dros tl1
- **urination** | **after** | **agg.**: dig bg2
  - **agg.**: *Aloe* k* **Alum** k* apis bro1 canth *Hyos* k* squil
- **vaccination**; after: ant-t sil k* *Thuj* k*
- **veal** agg.: *Kali-n* k*
- **vegetables** agg.: ars k* bry k* cist cupr hell lept k* *Lyc* k* nat-ar nat-c k* *Nat-m* *Nat-s* k* petr k* podo verat zing bro1
- **vexation** agg.: aloe *Calc-p* k* cham *Coloc* *Petr* *Staph* sulph
- **vinegar** agg.: *Ant-c* k*
- **vomiting**, with (See STOMACH - Vomiting - diarrhea - during)
- **walking**:
  - **agg.**: *Aloe* alum *Calc* *Gels* merc
  - **must** walk: rheum ptk1
- **warm**:
  - **applications** | **amel.**: alum *Nux-m* podo rhus-t
  - **bathing**:
    - **amel.** | **hot** bath: irid-met srj5• sec ptk1
  - **bed** | **amel.**: coloc *Nux-v* **Sil**
  - **days** and cold nights: acon bg3 dulc bg3 merc-c bg3
  - **drinks** agg.: *Fl-ac* k*
  - **food** agg.: *Phos* k*
  - **milk**:
    - **amel.** | **hot** milk: chel crot-t
  - **room** | **agg.**: apis *Iod* nat-s k* **Puls**
- **warmth**:
  - **agg.**: podo mrr1 *Puls* sec
  - **dry** warmth:
    - **amel.** | **dry** heat amel.: sulph
- **washing** the head agg.; after: podo tarent k*
- **water**:
  - **bad** water; from: *Alst* bro1 camph bro1 *Chin* b7a.de zing bro1
  - **drinking** agg.: *Aloe* ant-c ant-t *Apis* **Arg-n** **Ars** ars-s-f k2 *Asaf* bry calc-ar caps *Cina* coloc *Crot-t* cub *Elat* **Ferr** **Ferr-ar** fl-ac gamb *Grat* kali-ar kali-n lach laur manc nux-m **Nux-v** *Podo* rhod sec sep h2 spong fd4.de staph *Sul-ac* sulph *Trom* verat
  - **hearing** running water agg.: **Lyss**
- **weakness**, without: apis bg2* calc bro1* calc-act bg2 graph bro1* **Ph-ac** k* puls k* rhod b4a.de* *Sulph* k* *Tub* k*
- **weaning**, after: arg-n k* **Chin** k*
- **weather**:
  - **change** of weather: *Acon* bro1 *Bry* bro1 calc calc-s k* *Caps* bro1 colch bro1 *Dulc* k* ip bro1 *Merc* bro1 *Nat-s* bro1 nit-ac k2 *Ph-ac* k* *Psor* k* rhus-t bro1 sil bro1
  - **cold**:
    - **agg.**: asc-t *Calc* **Dulc** ip k2 merc nat-s *Nit-ac* *Nux-v* *Polyg-h* polyg-pe vml2• rhod *Rhus-t*
    - **wet** | **agg.**: asc-t *Calc* k* **Dulc** k* *Merc* nux-m rhod k* rhus-t zing
  - **dry** | **agg.**: alum asar
  - **stormy** | **agg.**: petr h2
  - **warm** | **agg.**: *(↗summer)* *Acon* k* *Aeth* *Aloe* k* ambro bro1 *Ant-c* k* *Ars* k* bapt *Bell* benz-ac k2 *Bism* hr1 *Borx* hr1* **Bry** k* calc **Camph** k* caps bro1 *Carb-v* castm ptk1 *Cham* bro1 **Chin** k* chinin-ar cina k2 coff colch *Crot-h* **Crot-t** k* *Cuph* bro1 *Cupr* *Cupr-ar* *Ferr* k* ferr-p bro1* **Gamb** k* guar vml3• *Hyper* *Iod* k* *Ip* k* iris k* *Jatr-c* *Kali-bi* k* kreos k2* lach mag-c mag-s vh merc k* *Mez* mur-ac *Nat-m* nat-p **Nux-m** k* **Olnd** k* *Ph-ac* *Phos* **Podo** k* *Psor* rheum *Sec* sil bro1* *Sul-ac* verat k* verb c1
  - **wet**:
    - **agg.**: agar aloe ars *Calc* cist colch k2 *Dulc* b4.de* lach *Lept* *Nat-s* puls *Rhod* k* rhus-t sulph
      - **whooping** cough agg. in wet weather; during: nat-s kr1
    - **amel.**: alum asar
- **wet**:
  - **getting**:
    - **after**: *Acon* *Calc* **Dulc** b4a.de **Rhus-t** *Verat* hr1
    - **feet**: acon nux-m **Rhus-t**
  - **ground**; after standing on: **Dulc** elat *Rhus-t*
- **whooping** cough; during: ant-t bro1 castn-v st *Cupr-ar* bro1 euph-l bro1 ip bro1 *Rumx* bro1 verat bro1

- **wind**:
  - **after** exposure to cold: *Acon Dulc*
  - **east**: psor
- **wine**:
  - **agg.**: lach lyc k* *Zinc* k*
  - **amel.**: chel dios
  - **sour**: **Ant-c** k*
- **winter**: asc-t k* nat-s *Nit-ac Ph-ac* b4a.de
- **worms**; from: chin b7a.de cina b7a.de ferr b7a.de sabad b7a.de spig b7a.de teucr b7a.de valer b7a.de
  - **infection**: anth vh1
- **worry**; from: *Dys* fmm1•
- **wrapping** up warmly | **amel.**: **Sil**

DIFFICULT stool (See Constipation - difficult)

DINNER; after: | **Perineum**: nux-v bg2

DISCHARGE (See Moisture)

DISCOLORATION:
- **black**: merc b4a.de
- ○ - **Anus**:
  - **purple**: paeon tl1
  - **red**: aloe ars k* bac bn cham k* *Med* bg3* merc-cy bro1 nat-m ozone sde2• paeon bro1 *Petr* k* **Sulph** k* tritic-vg fd5.de valer *Zing* k*
    - ⁝ **fiery red**: med ptk1
- **Perineum**: | **red**: rhus-t b7.de*

DISTENSION: agar k* linu-c a1 merc bg1 op k* staph bg1 sulph bg1 syc bka1*•
- **sensation** of: bit-ar wht1•

DRAGGING, heaviness, weight: *(↗Fullness; Weight)* acon **Aesc** k* agar **Aloe** k* ambr b7.de ang k* ant-c k* arn bar-c bell berb bry k* *Cact* calc k* cann-s k* *Carb-v* caust k* chel *Cocc* b7a.de coll con *Crot-t* k* cycl k* des-ac rbp6 euphr graph hell b7.de hep hyos inul *Ip* b7.de irid-met srj5• kali-bi kali-c kali-n kali-p kreos k* lach lact laur led lil-t lob lyc mag-m manc merc *Nit-ac* k* nux-m *Nux-v* k* phos plan plat bg1 plb podo bg2 puls rhus-t k* sabin b7.de sacch sep k* spig b7.de staph *Stram* b7.de sulph sumb ther thuj k* verat *Zinc*
- **morning**: lyc
  - **stool** agg.; after: lyc
- **afternoon**: cycl
  - **dinner**; after: cycl
  - **sleep** agg.; after: cycl
- **evening** | **loose** stool; during: op
- **flatus**; passing | **amel.**: zinc h2
- **menses** | **before** | **agg.**: phos
  - **during** | **agg.**: *Aloe*
- **standing** agg.: *Zinc*
- **stool**:
  - **after**:
    - ⁝ **agg.**: am-m b7.de* apis b7a.de bell b4a.de canth b7.de* caps b7.de* cocc b7.de* euph b4.de euphr bg2 hell ip b7a.de kali-bi merc b4a.de nat-m k* *Nux-v* b7.de* ph-ac b4a.de phos b4a.de podo bg2 rheum b7.de* rhod b4.de* rhus-t ruta spong b7.de* stront-c b4.de* sulph b4a.de valer b7.de* zinc
    - ⁝ **amel.**: kreos
  - **before**: aq-mar skp7• hell merc
  - **during** | **agg.**: *Acon* b7.de* agar b4.de* alum b4a.de am-c b4.de* apis b7a.de *Ars* b4a.de bov b4.de* brom b4a.de *Calc* b4.de* canth b7.de* *Caps* b7a.de *Coloc* b4a.de euph b4.de* hell b7a.de hep b4.de* ip b7.de* kali-bi bg2 kali-n b4.de* laur b7.de* merc b4.de* **Merc-c** b4a.de mez nat-c b4a.de *Nit-ac* k* nux-m b7.de* *Nux-v* b7a.de olnd b7a.de op k* phos b4.de* *Rheum* b7a.de rhus-t b7.de* sel b7a.de seneg b4a.de sep b4.de* spong b7.de* stront-c b4.de* sulph b4.de* tab bg2 zinc b4.de*
- ○ - **Anus**: agar b4.de* **Aloe** bg2 *Alum* b4.de* anac b4a.de **Apis** b7a.de *Arn* b7.de ars b4.de bell b4.de bov b4.de bry bg2 calc b4.de* canth b7.de *Caps* b7.de* carb-an b4.de caust b4.de chin bg2 clem bg2 *Cocc* b7.de* con bg2 cupr bg2 dulc b4a.de euph b4.de graph bg2 hell b7a.de* hep bg2 hyos bg2 ign b7.de ip b7a.de*

Dragging, heaviness, weight – **Anus**: ...
kali-bi bg2 kali-c b4.de kali-n b4.de* laur b7.de led bg2 mag-m b4.de mang b4.de merc b4.de* *Merc-c* b4a.de mez b4.de nat-c b4.de nat-m b4.de nit-ac b4.de* nux-v b7.de* op b7.de* phos b4.de *Plat* b4.de* plb bg2 *Rheum* b7.de rhod b4.de *Rhus-t* b7.de ruta b7.de sabin b7.de sars b4.de sep b4.de* *Spong* b7.de* *Staph* b7.de stront-c b4.de sulph b4.de* thuj bg2 valer b7.de *Verat* b7.de zinc b4.de*
- **Perineum**: *(↗Weight - perineum)* aloe bg2 *Ant-t* b7a.de cann-s chim mrr1 con ptk1* graph k* med ptk1 mez b4.de* nat-ar puls sep mrr1 ther k*
  - **stepping** agg.: ther a1

DRAW in anus; desire to: agar k*

DRIPPING from anus; sensation as if cold water was: cann-s b7.de* ferr-i bg1* sulph bg1

DRIVING agg.: | **Rectum** and anus: borx bg2 psor bg2

DRYNESS: *(↗GENERALS - Dropsy - internal)* **Aesc** k* aeth k* agar k* alum h2 *Alumn* bell mrr1 bry k2* calc k* carb-v k* *Graph* hyper a1* *Kali-chl* kiss a1 *Nat-m* k* sulph k* sumb k* vanil fd5.de
- **sensation** of: aesc bg2 agar k* aloe k2 alum b4.de* bry bg2 calc k* carb-v k* coll bg2 nat-m bg2 nat-sil fd3.de• sulph bg2 thuj b4a.de
  - **stool** agg.; during: alum b4.de*
- ○ - **Anus**: *Aesc* ptk1 rat ptk1
- **Intestinal** tract: sel rsj9•

DYSENTERY: *(↗ABDOMEN - Dysentery)* *Acon* k* aegle-f mtf11 *Aeth* k* agar bg2 ail br1* **Aloe** k* alst c2* alst-s br1 alum c2 alumn k* am-m b7a.de ambro br1* anac hr1 ango c1* ant-t k* *Apis* k* *Arg-n* k* *Arn* k* **Ars** k* ars-i k* ars-s-f k2 asc-t c2* atis-r mtf11 *Bapt* k* bar-c b4a.de bar-m k* *Bell* k* ben c2 bol-la c2 bol-s c2 *Bry* k* **Bufo** calc bro1 calc-s c2 calc-sil k2 **Canth** k* **Caps** k* *Carb-ac* k* **Carb-v** k* **Carbn-s** caust cean hr1 *Cham* k* chap c2* *Chin* k* chinin-ar cina b7a.de *Cinnb* k* cist cit-l hr1* clem k* **Colch** k* **Coll** k* **Coloc** k* *Con* k* cop k* *Corn* k* crass-r bta1• croc b7a.de *Crot-c* *Crot-h* k* crot-t cub k* cuph c2* cupr k* cupr-ar br1* cupr-s c2 cyn-d mtf11 der c2 dig b4.de* dios c2 *Dirc* diss-i bta1• dor c2 *Dulc* k* elat k* emetin bro1* enteroc jl2 erig hr1* eucal c2* euonin c2 euph b4.de* euph-a c2 euph-l c2 ferr-m c2 ferr-p c2* gamb k* **Gels** k* ger c2 *Gua* br1 guare hr1 **Ham** k* *Hell* b7a.de *Hep* k* *Hipp* hr1 *Ign* k* *Iod* k* **Ip** k* *Iris* k* *Kali-bi* k* *Kali-chl* k* kali-m c2* kali-n c2 kali-p k* kali-sil k2 kreos bg2 kurch bnj1* *Lach* k* leon c2* lept c2* *Lil-t* k* *Lyc* k* **Lyss** k* **Mag-c** k* mag-m *Mag-p* mag-s c2 manc **Merc** k* **Merc-c** k* *Merc-cy* k* *Merc-d* k* *Mill* k* mons bwa3 mur-ac narc-ps ah1* *Nit-ac* k* *Nux-m* k* **Nux-v** k* *Op* k* *Oper* bro1 *Ox-ac* k* pelarg c1* *Petr* k* ph-ac bro1 **Phos** k* *Phyt* k* plan hr1* plb k* plb-act bro1 podo c2* polyg-xyz c2 prune mtf11 *Psor* k* ptel c2 *Puls* k* pyre-p c2 pyrog c2 ran-b k2 raph k* rat c2 rheum b7a.de* rhod rhus-g c2 **Rhus-t** k* ric c2 *Salol* c1* sec bro1 septi c1* silphu br1* *Sima* c1 staph k* *Sul-ac* k* sul-i k2 **Sulph** k* tab bg2* tanac bro1* *Ter* k* term-c mtf11 thalic-r jsx1.fr thlas c2 tril-p c1* *Trom* k* typh br1 urt-u c2 vac bro1 *Vacc-m* c1* vang-l bta1• vario hr1 verat k* verb b7a.de verin c2 wede-n bta1• xan br1* zinc k* zinc-m c2 zinc-s c2* *Zing* [herna-p dbx1.fr physal-p dbx1.fr]
- **daytime** | **agg.**: petr tl1
- **morning**; early: sulph tl1
- **night**: *Merc* sulph k* trom
- **accompanied** by:
  - **collapse**: camph mrr1
  - **cramps**; violent: mag-p tl1
  - **fever**: bapt tl1* ferr-p ptk1 nux-v bro1*
  - **malaria** (See GENERALS - Malaria - accompanied - dysentery)
  - **rheumatic** pain: asc-t bro1*
  - **stool**:
    - ⁝ **dark**: rhus-t tl1
    - ⁝ **desire** for; no: nux-v tl1
    - ⁝ **small** and unsatisfactory: nux-v tl1
  - **thirstlessness**: ip bro1
  - ○ **Abdomen**; muscular pain in: *Arn* h1*
  - **Back**:
    - ⁝ **pain**:
      - : **Lumbar** region: *Gua* br1
      - : **Sacral** region: *Caps* br1 *Gua* br1 liat br1 *Nux-v*

Rectum

- **accompanied** by: ...
  - **Bladder**:
    - **pain**:
      - **burning**: erig br1
      - **sore**: erig br1
  - **Head** and coldness of limbs; heat of: ip ptk1
  - **Limbs** and heat of head; coldness of (See head)
  - **Thigh**; tearing pain down: rhus-t bro1
    - **stool** agg.; during: rhus-t tl1
  - **Tongue**:
    - **black** discoloration: *Lach* kr1*
    - **bleeding** of tongue: lach kr1*
    - **blue** discoloration: **Ars** kr1*
    - **brown** discoloration: *Ars* kr1* *Ham* kr1*
    - **cracked**: kali-bi ptk1 **Phos** kr1*
    - **excoriation** of tongue: **Canth** vk1
    - **flabby** tongue: cub kr1*
    - **white** discoloration of the tongue: *Merc* kr1* *Trom* kr1*
- **acute**: calo br1
- **alternating** with:
  - **eruptions**: rhus-t k*
  - **herpes**: rhus-t k*
  - **rheumatism**: abrot tl1 kali-bi tl1
- **amoebic**: emetin mp4•
- **autumn**: acon bro1 arn ptk1 asc-t c1 bapt hr1 colch bro1* dulc bro1 *Ip* bro1 *Merc* bro1 *Merc-c* bro1 sulph bro1
- **bacillary**: tub jl2
- **beginning** stage: ferr-p tl1
- **bladder** complaints, with: erig vml3•
- **children**; in:
  - **emaciated**, undersized: *Bar-m* k*
  - **weak**, potbellied: calc ptk1 staph mtf33
- **chronic**: aloe bro1 arg-n bro1 *Ars* bro1 chin bro1 cist tl1 cop bro1 *Dulc* bro1 hep bro1 *Merc-c* bro1 *Nit-ac* bro1 *Nux-v* bro1 ph-ac bro1 podo bro1 rhus-a bro1 *Sulph* bro1
- **cold** feet to knees in dysentery: aloe k1
- **distension** of abdomen; with tympanitic: canth tl1 colch tl1 merc tl1
- **emaciated** undersized children (See children - emaciated)
- **food** or drinks agg.; least: staph ptk1 trom ptk1
- **hemorrhagic**: streptoc mtf11
- **hemorrhoidal**: aloe bro1 coll bro1* ham bro1 sulph bro1
- **high** altitudes; at: coca ptk1
- **menopause**; during: lil-t ptk1
- **old** people; in: bapt br*
- **periodical** | **long** intervals; with: *Arn* bro1 chin bro1
- **seasons** | **spring**; in | **summer**; or early: kali-bi bro1
  - **summer**; in: arn ptk1 kali-bi ptk1
- **septic** origin, of: crot-h st*
- **spring** dysentery: vario jl2
- **stool**; after | **amel.**: nux-v tl1
- **thirst**, with great: acon k1*
- **thunderstorm** agg.: rhod tl1
- **treatment**; from abuse of local: nit-ac bro1
- **weather** agg.; cold wet: dulc tl1 rhod tl1
- **women** during menopause; in plethoric, nervous: lil-t bro1

EASY stool, easy evacuation: borx bg2 *Coff* b7.de* *ign* b7.de* *Ran-b* b7.de*

EATING: | **after** | **Rectum** and anus: aloe bg2 clem bg2 lyc bg2 sel bg2
- **before** | **Rectum** and anus: bry bg2

EMPTINESS:
- **sensation** of: podo c1

Emptiness – sensation of: ...
  - **alternating** with sensation of fullness (See Fullness - alternating)

EMPTY after stool; as if rectum is not (See Constipation - insufficient)

ENCOPRESIS (See MIND - Dirty - urinating and)

EPISTAXIS:
- **amel.** | **Rectum** and anus: am-m bg2

ERECTION; during: | **Perineum**: alum ptk1

ERUPTIONS:

○ - **Anus**; about: *Agar* am-c am-m ant-c ars berb k* *Calc* k* carb-an carb-v k* carbn-s *Caust* chel bg2 cimic gk glycyr-g cte1• *Graph Hep* ign k* ip bg2 kali-c k* *Led* bg2 lyc k* med k* merc k* moni rfm1• **Nat-m** k* *Nat-s* **Nit-ac** k* **Petr** k* polyg-h ptk1 psor k2 *Rhus-t* bg2 sars bg2 sep stann bg2 *Staph* k* *Sulph* k* thuj tub tl
  - **blotches**: carb-v stann *Staph Thuj*
  - **boils**: ant-c c1 calc-p k* carb-an k* caust k* nit-ac k2 petr k* prot jl2 [spect dfg1]
  - **burning**: ars calc petr h2
  - **carbuncle**: nit-ac mtf33
  - **children**; in:
    - **infants**: ars ggd1 benz-ac ggd1 canth ggd1 caust ggd1 *Coli* ggd1 cycl ggd1 *Graph* ggd1 iod ggd1 **Kreos** ggd1 **Med** ggd1 merc ggd1 *Nat-c* ggd1 nit-ac ggd1 rheum ggd1 rhus-t ggd1 sep ggd1 sulph ggd1
    - **newborns**: med c1*
      - **washing** agg.: med c1
  - **crust**: berb k* paeon ptk1 petr a1*
  - **discharging**:
    - **blood**: calc-p k2 glycyr-g cte1•
      - **sticky**: glycyr-g cte1•
    - **pus**: calc-p k2 glycyr-g cte1•
      - **sticky**: glycyr-g cte1•
  - **eczema**: aethi-a mtf11 ars mtf33 bac bn berb bro1* enterob-v mtf11 graph bg2* ign mtf11 *Merc-pr-r* bro1 moni jl2 nat-m bg2 petr bg2
    - **children**; in: med jl2
    - **itching**: nit-ac ptk1
  - **herpetic**: *Berb Graph* lyc *Nat-m* **Petr**
  - **itching**: ars cimic gk cinnb lyc med ptk nit-ac bg **Petr** staph sulph
  - **pimples**: *Agar* brom carb-v *Cinnb* kali-c k* kali-i nit-ac propr sa3• staph
    - **itching**: polyg-h ptk1
  - **pustules**: am-m k* calc caust k*
    - **hard**: caust ptk1*
    - **small**: caust ptk1*
  - **rash**:
    - **children**; in: | **newborns**: **Med** c1*
  - **scurfy**: berb bg2 graph bg2 *Petr* k*
  - **stinging**: kali-c h2 nit-ac
  - **tetters**: *Ars* b4a.de ip b7.de* *Lyc* b4a.de nat-m b4.de* petr bg2 *Verat* b7a.de
  - **ulcerous**: kali-c k*
  - **vesicular**: androc srj1• apis b7a.de brom carb-an b4a.de* carb-v nat-m k2
  - **warm** bed agg.: *Petr*
- **Perineum**: brass-n-o srj5• brom graph med gk morg-p pte1*• *Petr* k* sars *Sulph* k* tell tep
  - **boil**: alum gsy1 ant-c k*
    - **blood**-boils: ant-c b7.de*
  - **children**; in: | **newborns**: med c1*
  - **dry**: *Petr*
  - **eczema**: petr bg2
  - **furuncles** (See boil)
  - **herpes**: kali-c **Petr** k* *Sep* mrr1 tell
  - **pimples**: agar bg2 caust bg2 graph bg2 nat-m bg2 nit-ac k* sars bg2 sep k* sul-ac k* sulph k* thuj bg2
  - **tetters**: *Petr* b4.de*

EVACUATED; as if not fully (See Constipation - insufficient)

EXCORIATION: *Aesc Agar* agn k* all-c aloe k2 alum k* am-c am-m k2 ant-c bg2 *Apis* k* arg-met *Ars* k* ars-s-f k2 asc-c aur-m *Bar-c* k* bell bg2 *Berb* k* *Calc* k* calc-s **Caps** bg2 carb-an k* **Carb-v** k* **Carbn-s** **Caust** k* *Cham* k* coloc k* dirc a1* ferr k* *Gamb* k* gels bg2 **Graph** k* grat hep *Hydr Ign* kali-ar kali-bi bg2 kali-c k* kali-p fd1.de• kali-s k2 lac-ac stj5• lach **Lyc** mag-c b4.de* med c1 *Merc* k* *Merc-c* mur-ac nat-ar *Nat-m* k* *Nat-p* *Nit-ac* k* nux-v k* *Petr* phos k* *Plan Podo* k* psor al2 *Puls* k* rat bg2* rhus-t b7a.de* sacch-a fd2.de• *Sanic Sep* k* **Sulph** k* sumb *Syph Thuj* k* *Tub* urt-u verat b7a.de zinc

- **acrid** moisture, from: carb-v *Merc-c* ozone sde2• *Thuj* zinc
- **riding** | **horse**; a: | **agg.**: carb-an
  - **wagon**; in a: psor
- **rub** anus until raw; must: *Agar* alum am-c *Arg-n Bar-c Calc* **Carb-v** *Carbn-s* **Caust Graph** kali-c **Lyc** *Merc* **Petr** phos *Puls Sep* **Sulph**
- **sensation** of: alum tl1 lyc tl1
- **stools**; from the: allox tpw3 **Aloe** ang b7a.de **Apis** *Ars* arum-t k2 asc-c c1 *Bapt* cham b7a.de coloc dirc c1 ferr b7a.de *Kola* stb3• *Kreos* mag-m h2 melal-alt gya4 *Merc* mur-ac **Nit-ac** nux-m *Nux-v* ozone sde2• rheum sacch-a fd2.de• sang *Sulph Tub*

○ - **Anus**: carb-v ptk1 caust ptk1 graph ptk1 lyc ptk1 sulph ptk1
  - **stool** agg.; after: alum b4.de* *Ars* b4.de* cham bg2 ferr bg2 ign bg2 kali-c b4.de* **Merc** b4.de* nat-c b4.de* nat-m b4.de* nux-v bg2 phos b4.de* puls bg2 sars bg2 sel bg2 stann b4.de* staph bg2 *Sulph* b4a.de
- **Nates**, between: arg-met arum-t *Berb* calc carb-v *Carbn-s Graph* k* *Kreos* nat-m *Nit-ac* puls sacch-a fd2.de• sang k2 *Sep* k* *Sulph*
  - **walking** agg.: arg-met **Caust** graph k2 nat-m *Nit-ac*
- **Perineum**; of: alum k* arum-t aur-m *Calc* carb-an k* *Carb-v* k* *Caust Cham Graph* k* *Hep* ign **Lyc** k* med c1 *Merc* k* petr k* psor al2 puls rhod k* sep k* *Sulph* k* thuj k*
  - **menses**; before: sep b4a.de

FECES remained in, as if●: alum bg2 carb-an h2* dulc fd4.de equis-h a1 *Graph* k* irid-met srj5• **Lyc** k ●* nat-c h2* **NAT-M** k ●* *Nit-ac* k* nux-v bg2* ruta fd4.de **SEP** k ●* stann h2* *Verat* k*

FISSURE: acon-l a1 aesc hr1* *Agn* k* aids nl2• *All-c* k* aloe bg2* alum k* anac gsy1* androc srj1• ant-c k* apis bro1 arg-met arg-n bro1 *Ars* k* ars-s-f k2 arum-t berb k* bry gk calc k* calc-f k* *Calc-p* k* caps hr1 carb-an k* *Carb-v* bro1 carc fb* *Caust* k* **Cham** k* cimx bro1 colch bg2 coll mrr1 *Cund* k* cur *Fl-ac* k* **Graph** k* grat k* ham bro1 *Hydr* k* *Ign* k* iris c2* kali-br hr1 kali-c k* kali-i bro1 lac-ac stj5• *Lach* k* led br1* med *Merc* k* *Merc-d* bro1 merc-i-r mez k* morg-g pte1*• morg-p pte1*• morph bro1 **Mur-ac** k* *Nat-m* k* **Nit-ac** k* nit-m-ac bro1 *Nux-v* k* *Paeon* k* *Petr* k* petr-ra shn4• *Phos* k* *Phyt* k* pip-n c2 plat k* *Plb* k* plut-n srj7• *Podo* hr1 ptel gk **Rat** k* rhus-t k* sangin-n bro1 sanic bro1 sed-ac br1* **Sep** k* *Sil* k* spong fd4.de stront-c mtf11 suis-chord-umb mtf11 sul-ac bg2 *Sulph* k* syph k* **Thuj** k* tritic-vg fd5.de v-a-b jl2 vib bro1 [tax jsj7]

- **bleeding**: graph ptk1 syph jl2
- **children**; in:
  - **infants**; in: kali-i ptk1
  - **tall** children; in: calc-p ptk1*
- **deep**: am ptk1
- **hemorrhoids**; from: caps bro1 caust bg2 cham bg2* *Nit-ac* bro1 rat bro1 *Sed-ac* bro1
  - **bleeding**: nit-ac tl1
- **purulent**: syph jl2
- **sensation** of hammers in: *Lach* vh
- **stool** agg.; after: nat-m bg2
- **ulcerated**: graph ptk1

○ - **Perineum**: am-c bg1 v-a-b jl2

FISTULA: *Aloe Alum* k* alum-p k2 anan mtf ant-c ars mtf11 *Arund-d* mtf aur k* **Aur-m** k* aur-s k2 bar-m bro1 bell benz-ac mtf **Berb** k* bond a1 both mtf bry cact k* **Calc** k* calc-f dgt1* *Calc-hp* mtf **Calc-p** k* calc-s k* calc-sil k2 *Calen* hr1* **Carb-v** k* carbn-s k* carc gk6* **Caust** k* con b4a.de crot-h mtf *Echi* mtf elaps gk euph-l mtf *Fl-ac* k* *Graph* k* *Gunp* mtf *Hep Hippoz* mtf *Hydr* k* ign k* **Kali-c** k* kali-sil k2 *Kreos* k* *Lach* k* lat-m mtf *Lyc Merc* k* myris br1* **Nit-ac** k* nux-v b7a.de* paeon c2* periproc mtf11 *Petr* k* *Phos* k* psor mtf puls k* pyrog jl2* querc bro1 rat bro1 rhus-t mtf11 *Sep* k* **Sil** k* silphu mtf11 *Staph* k* *Staphycoc* mtf *Sulph* k* *Syph* k* *Tarent-c* mtf *Thuj* k* *Vitr-an* mtf *Vitr-cor* mtf

Fistula: ...

- **accompanied** by:
  - **palpitations** (See CHEST - Palpitation - accompanied - anus)

○ - **Chest**; complaints of (See CHEST - Complaints - accompanied - rectum)
- **alternating** with | **Chest**; complaints of (See CHEST - Complaints - alternating - rectum)
- **itching**: berb ptk1
- **pulsating**: *Caust* k* lach k2
- **Glands** | **Anal**: calc-p tl1 kali-c tl1 lach tl1 sil tl1
- **Perineum**: caust bg2 paeon bg2 thuj ptk1
- **Vagina**, and: thuj ptk1

FLATUS: (↗*ABDOMEN - Flatulence*) acon-ac rly4• *Aesc* **Agar** k* agn b7a.de aids nl2• **All-c** k* allox sp1 aln vva1• **Aloe** k* *Alum* k* am-c b4.de* *Am-m* k* amp rly4• ant-c k* *Ant-t* k* *Apoc* arg-met b7.de* **Arg-n** k* arge-pl rwt5• **Arn** k* *Ars* k* *Ars-i Asaf* k* asar b7.de* *Aur* k* aur-i k2 aur-m aur-s k2 *Bamb-a* stb2.de• *Bar-c* k* bar-i k2 bar-m bart a1 *Bell* k* bell-p sp1 *Bism* k* borx k* both-ax tsm2 bov b4.de* brom k* bros-gau mrc1 *Bry* k* *But-ac* sp1 cadm-met sp1 calad calc k* camph k* canth b7.de* carb-ac carb-an k* **Carb-v** k* **Carbn-s** card-m cartl-s rly4• casc k* *Caust* k* **Cham** *Chel* k* **Chin** k* *Chinin-ar* chinin-s bg2 chir-fl gya2 chlor k* cic k* cob-n sp1 *Coc-c* k* **Cocc** k* *Coff* b7.de* *Colch* coli rly4• **Coloc** k* *Con* k* cop **Corn** *Crot-h* *Crot-t* k* cund a1 cycl k* cystein-l rly4• cyt-l sp1 dict a1 dig b4.de* **Dios** k* dioxi rbp6 *Dulc* k* elat k* euph b4.de* fago k* falco-pe nl2• *Ferr* k* *Ferr-ar* ferr-i *Ferr-p* fic-m gya1 fl-ac k* fuma-ac rly4• *Gels* k* gent-l mtf11 ger-i rly4• germ-met srj5• get a1 gins a1 *Glycyr-g* cte1• gnaph **Graph** k* guaj b4.de* haliae-lc srj5• ham k* hell b7.de* *Hep* k* hydrog srj2• hyos k* **Ign** k* *Indg* k* iod k* irid-met srj5• iris bg2 jal br1 *Kali-ar* kali-bi k* *Kali-c* k* kali-i k* kali-n k* *Kali-p Kali-s* ketogl-ac rly4• kreos bg2 lac-del hrn2• lac-e hrn2• lac-leo hrn2• lac-loxod-a hrn2• *Lach* k* lact a1 laur b7.de* led k* *Lil-t* **Lyc** k* m-aust b7.de mag-c k* *Mag-m* k* mand sp1 *Mang* k* mang-p rly4• medul-os-si rly4• melal-alt gya4 meny h1* **Merc** k* *Merc-c* b4a.de merl a1 mez k* mim-p rsj8• moni rfm1• mosch mrr1 mur-ac k* musa a1 musca-d szs1 nad rly4• *Nat-ar Nat-c* k* *Nat-m* k* nat-ox rly4• *Nat-p* nat-pyru rly4• **Nat-s** k* nat-sil fd3.de• nicotam rly4• nit-ac b4.de* nit-m-ac a1 **Nux-v** k* oci-sa sp1 olib-sac wmh1 **Olnd** k* **Op** k* orot-ac rly4• ox-ac k* oxal-a rly4• ozone sde2• pall k* par b7.de* petr b4.de* petr-ra shn4• **Ph-ac** k* **Phos** k* phys k* **Pic-ac** k* pieri-b mlk9.de pimp a1 plac-s rly4• plat k* **Plb** k* plut-n srj7• *Podo* positr nl2• pot-e rly4• psil ft1 *Psor* k* **Puls** k* ran-b b7a.de* **Raph** *Rhod* k* rhodi a1 rhus-t k* ribo rly4• ruta k* sabad k* sacch-a fd2.de• samb b7.de* *Sang* saroth sp1 sars b4.de* *Sec Sel* seneg b4.de* *Sep* k* **Sil** k* sinus rly4• spig k* spong b7.de* squil b7.de* **Staph** k* staphycoc rly4• stram k* stront-c b4.de* suis-em rly4• suis-pan rly4• sul-ac k* **Sulph** k* suprar rly4• symph fd3.de• tarax sp1 tell c1 tep k* ter a1 **Teucr** k* thiam rly4• *Thuj* k* tritic-vg fd5.de urol-h rwt• vanil fd5.de ven-m rsj12• **Verat** k* viol-t b7.de* wies a1 yuc a1 *Zinc* k* zinc-p k2 zinc-val mtf11 [bell-p-sp dcm1 *Spect* dfg1]

- **daytime**: aloe kali-p fd1.de• nat-m k* ox-ac k* plat k* suis-em rly4• **Sulph** k*
- **morning**: **All-c** k* aloe bov bufo caust h2* cedr dulc fd4.de fl-ac fuma-ac rly4• ham fd3.de• hell h1* hep k* lyc mag-m h2* mag-s k* **Nat-s** nat-sil fd3.de• nit-ac k* plb k* pot-e rly4• *Puls* k* ruta fd4.de sacch-a fd2.de• symph fd3.de• vanil fd5.de
  - **stool**, during: chel k* ruta fd4.de
  - **waking**, on: *Carb-v* k* cund a1 dulc fd4.de merc-i-f a1 nat-sil fd3.de• podo fd3.de• rheum h symph fd3.de• vanil fd5.de
- **forenoon**: calc-p k* carb-an dulc fd4.de nat-m k* vanil fd5.de
  - **10 h**: fl-ac
  - **stool**, before: fl-ac k*
- **noon**: nat-ox rly4• ox-ac k* ruta fd4.de spong fd4.de sulph k* vanil fd5.de
- **afternoon**: am-c k* aur-m benz-ac k* carb-v h2* castm cham k* cund sne dig k* fl-ac k* iod lac-e hrn2• mag-c h2* myric k* nat-c nat-s k* nicc k* osm k* phos plb k* stront-c tritic-vg fd5.de vanil fd5.de vichy-g a1 zinc h2*
- **evening**: aesc k* aloe alum h2* am-c h2* anthraq rly4• carb-an k* cartl-s rly4• castm chel k* chinin-s choc srj3• *Colch* crot-t k* cystein-l rly4• dulc fd4.de fago k* *Gamb* k* kali-n h2* kali-p fd1.de• lac-e hrn2• lyc k* nat-m k* nat-p a1 nat-s nept-m lsd2.fr nicc k* *Ph-ac* phos k* podo fd3.de• pot-e rly4• ruta fd4.de sacch-a fd2.de• sarr sol-t-ae k* spong fd4.de stront-c **Sulph** k* symph fd3.de• thiam rly4• thuj k* tritic-vg fd5.de ulm-c jsj8• vanil fd5.de zinc
  - **stool**, during: gels k*

- **night**: all-c k* alum h2* am-c h2* arg-met bry k* carb-v tl1* castm coloc k* hep k* hom-xyz c1* ign k* kali-c kola stb3• lavand-a ctl1• lyc mag-c h2* nat-pyru rly4• orot-ac rly4• ox-ac k* psil ft1 pycnop-sa mrz1 ruta fd4.de sol-t-ae k* suis-pan rly4• **Sulph** k* vanil fd5.de verat k*
  - **menses**, before: mang k*
  - **stool**, during: psor k*
  - **turning** in bed: ammc sys
- **acids**, after: *Ph-ac*
- **agg.** (See GENERALS - Flatus - agg.)
- **alternating** with constipation (See Constipation - alternating - flatus)
- **amel.** (See GENERALS - Flatus - amel.)
- **back**, felt in: rhod ptk1
- **burning**: asc-t a1 cystein-l rly4• mag-m h2
- **cold**: *Con* k*
- **come**, but stool comes; as if flatus would: mag-m h2 plac-s rly4•
- **copious**: *Acon* b7.de* agar bg2* am-c b4.de* *Ant-c* b7a.de ant-t b7.de* *Arg-n* bg2* ars-s-f k2 aur b4a.de *Bar-c* b4.de* bell b4a.de calc-p tl1 camph b7.de* canth bg2 caps b7.de* carb-ac bg2 **Carb-an** b4.de* **Carb-v** b4.de* carbn-s k2 caust b4.de* *Cham* b7a.de **Chin** b7.de* cic b7.de* coff bg2 *Colch* b7a.de fl-ac bg2 flor-p rsj3• glycyr-g cte1• **Graph** b4.de* ign b7.de *Kali-c* bg2 kali-s fd4.de *Lyc* bg2* *M-ambo* b7a.de m-arct b7.de mag-m b4.de* mang bg2 merc bg2 mez b4.de* musca-d szs1 nat-ar k2 *Nat-c* b4.de* nat-m bg2 nicotam rly4• *Nit-ac* b4.de* nux-m b7.de* *Nux-v* b7.de* olnd bg2 op b7.de* ph-ac b4a.de *Phos* bg2 plat b4.de* plb b7.de* rhus-t b7.de* spig b7.de* spong fd4.de squil b7.de* stann b4.de* thuj b4.de* *Trios* rsj11• vanil fd5.de verat bg2 zinc b4a.de zinc-p k2
  - **evening**: *Trios* rsj11•
- **coughing**, on: cocc bg2 graph bg2* *Nux-v* st* sang bg3* *Sulph* hr1
- **diarrhea**, during: *Agar* k* **Aloe** k* alum-sil k2 am-m *Arg-n* k* ars k2 asaf borx h2 both-ax tsm2 bov bros-gau mrc1 *Bry* calc-i k2 *Calc-p* k* **Carb-v** k* *Chin* k* choc srj3• *Colch* *Coloc* cub cupr (non:cupr-m kl) cystein-l rly4• *Dios* dulc fd4.de **Ferr** hr1 ign bro1 jatr-c bro1 *Kali-c* kali-m k2 kali-n h2 kali-p fd1.de• *Lach* *Lyc* mag-m *Manc* *Mur-ac* nat-p **Nat-s** k* *Nicc* nit-ac nux-v **Olnd** orot-ac rly4• petr-ra shn4• ph-ac bro1 *Phos* plan plat podo k2* psil ft1 rhus-t h1 ruta fd4.de sabin samb xxb1 sang k* sars sep sil squil tab thuj bro1 tritic-vg fd5.de urol-h rwt• zing hr1*
  - **flatus**; the first: kali-ar pd
- **difficult**: all-c k* anac h2* calc-p k* camph h1* cartl-s rly4• cocc k* coff k* hep h2* hyos k* ign b7.de* irid-met srj5• kali-c h2* kali-p fd1.de• ketogl-ac rly4• lyc bg2 lyss k* m-arct b7.de m-aust b7.de mez h2* nat-s k* nux-v b7.de* op k* ox-ac k* phos k* plac-s rly4• plat k* plb b7.de* puls b7.de* rhus-t b7.de* sil h2* sul-ac k* tritic-vg fd5.de verat b7.de*
- **dinner**, after: alum h2* ant-c k* *Arg-n* k* *Cycl* k* grat k* hell h1* kali-p fd1.de• lac-del hm2• lac-e hm2• nat-m k* nat-sil fd3.de• nit-ac h2* ruta fd4.de sulph k* urol-h rwt• verat h1*
- **easy**: *Ign* b7.de* laur b7.de* rhus-t b7.de* ruta b7.de*
- **eating**, after: *Aloe* ant-c k* con h2* ferr-m a1 gink-b sbd1• ign k* kali-p fd1.de• lac-e hm2• op k* plat k* podo fd3.de• ran-s a1 ruta fd4.de sep k* spong fd4.de tab k* vanil fd5.de
- **explosive**: falco-pe nl2• germ-met srj5•
- **forcible**: acal sne aesc sne aloe sne ant-c sne ant-t sne arg-n hr1* berb sne calc-p sne choc sne colch sne con sne form sne gran sne graph sne kali-c sne ketogl-ac sne still sne verat bg2
- **hot**: acon k* *Agar* k* **Aloe** k* ant-t k* asc-t a1 bapt *Carb-v* k* cham k* cocc k* dios ferr-p bg2 *M-ambo* b2.de* mag-m b2.de* nux-v b2.de* ol-an bg2 phos k* plb k* *Psor* *Puls* k* *Staph* k* suis-pan rly4• *Sulph* k* sumb k* *Teucr* k* vichy-g a1 *Zinc* k*
- **inspiration**, during: caust k*
- **involuntary**: asaf a1 cystein-l rly4• phos k* pyrog jl2 vanil fd5.de
  - **almost**: graph h2*
- **loud**: acal br1* agn k2 **Aloe** k* alum am-m k* **Arg-n** k* bac bn berb vh calad k* canth b2.de* carb-v h2* **Caust** k* coloc h2* con h2* ferr a1 fl-ac k* hydr vh kali-n k* kali-p k2 kola stb3• *Lach* k* laur b2.de* lipp a1 m-ambo b2.de mag-c h2* marb-w es1• merc b2.de* *Mez* k* moni rfm1• nat-pyru rly4• **Nat-s** k* ox-ac ozone sde2• phos k* plan k* podo fd3.de• positr nl2• pot-e rly4• ruta fd4.de sin-a a1 squil k* *Teucr* k* vanil fd5.de verat h1* *Zinc* k* [pop dhh1]
  - **night**: **Arg-n** vh
  - **pneumonia**; in: sulph hr1
  - **stool**:
    - **after**: cench k2 dios br1 ox-ac k*
- **loud – stool – after**: ...
    - **sputtering** stool, after: aloe ox-ac
    - **during**: *Aloe* alum-sil k2 mur-ac k2 **Nat-s** *Ph-ac* thuj
    - **sputtering** stool, during: **Aloe** choc srj3• eug **Nat-s** *Thuj*
  - **sugar**, after: **Arg-n** k*
- **menses**, during: clem k* kali-c h2* mag-c k* nicc hr1*
- **moist**: *All-c* k* *Ant-c* k* *Carb-v* k* sulph k2 *Zinc*
  - **warm**; and: *Carb-v* b2.de*
- **noiseless**: cina b7.de* sabad b7.de* teucr b7.de*
- **noisy**: am-m b7.de canth b7.de lach b7.de laur b7.de m-ambo b7.de merc b4.de squil b7.de teucr b7.de
  - **breaking** sound: sulph bg2
  - **bursting**: ant-c bg2 coloc bg2 hell b7.de* nat-m bg2 phos bg2 staph b7.de* tarax b7.de*
  - **churning**: ant-c b7.de* calc b4.de* meny b7.de*
  - **cooing**: calc bg2 lyc b4.de*
  - **cracking**: caust b4.de* m-aust b7.de nat-m bg2 puls b7.de
  - **crackling**: caust b4.de*
  - **creaking**: cycl bg2 rhus-t b7.de*
  - **croaking**, quacking: arg-met b7.de* caust b4.de* coloc bg2 graph bg2 lyc bg2 nat-m bg2 *Nux-v* b7.de* sabad bg2 sars b4.de* spig b7.de* zinc b4.de*
  - **crying** of an animal; like: arg-n bg2 thuj bg2
  - **fermenting**: acon b7.de* am-m b7a.de ambr b7.de* ang b7.de* *Arn* b7.de* bry b7.de* calc b4.de* canth b7.de* carb-an b4.de* chin b7.de* *Coff* b7.de* hell bg2 *Hep* b4a.de m-ambo b7.de mag-m b4.de* nux-v b7.de* phos b4.de* plb b7.de* puls b7.de* **Rhus-t** b7.de* sep b4.de* stram b7a.de
  - **growling**: stram bg2
  - **gurgling**: agar b4.de alum b4.de am-c b4.de ambr b7.de* ang b7.de* ant-t b7.de* arg-n bg2 asaf b7.de* bov b4.de carb-v b4.de cham b7.de* chel b7.de* croc b7.de* dig b4.de graph b4.de hell b7.de* lyc b4.de *M-arct* b7.de* mag-c b4.de merc b4.de nux-v b7.de *Ph-ac* b4.de* *Phos* b4a.de plat b4.de plb b7.de* polyg-h bg2 sars b4.de sep b4.de stann b4.de stront-c b4.de sul-ac b4.de valer b7.de* verb b7.de* zinc b4.de
  - **howling**, barking: apis bg2 bry b7.de* m-ambo b7.de
  - **moving** about, changing place; the noise is: agar b4.de* alum b4.de* bov b4.de* carb-v b4.de* caust b4.de* dig b4.de* mez b4.de* **Nat-c** b4a.de nat-m b4.de* *Puls* b7a.de rhus-t b7a.de sars b4.de*
  - **murmuring**, muttering: sabad b7.de* *Spong* b7a.de
  - **rattling**: *Acon* b7.de* agar b4.de* alum b4.de* am-c b4.de* am-m b7.de* ant-c b7a.de apis b7a.de ars b4.de* asaf b7.de* bell b4.de* bism b7.de* bov b4.de* bry b7.de* canth b7.de* carb-v b4.de* *Caust* b4a.de *Chin* b7.de* dig b4.de* dulc b4.de* ferr b7.de* hell b7.de* hep b4.de* *Ign* b7.de* iod b4.de* kali-n b4.de* laur b7.de* lyc b4.de* m-ambo b7.de mag-m b4.de* merc b4a.de mez b4.de* mur-ac b4.de* nit-ac b4.de* nux-m b7.de* nux-v b7.de* olnd b7.de* par b7.de* *Ph-ac* b4.de* *Phos* b4.de* plb b7.de* puls b7.de* rheum b7.de* rhod b4.de* sabin b7.de* sars b4.de* *Sec* b7a.de seneg b4.de* sep b4.de* spig b7.de* squil b7.de* staph b7.de* stront-c b4.de* **Sulph** b4.de* thuj b4a.de valer b7.de* *Verat* b7.de* zinc b4.de*
  - **snapping**: asar b7.de* cina b7.de*
  - **squashing**: arn b7.de* canth b7.de*
  - **thunder**; like distant: agar bg2
  - **whistling**: mur-ac bg2 sep bg2
- **nursing** children: arg-n k2
- **odorless**: **Agar** k* ambr b2.de* arg-n arn b2.de* *Bell* k* cann-s b2.de* carb-v k* carc fd2.de• *Coff* b2.de* coli rly4• dulc fd4.de glycyr-g cte1• ham fd3.de• lyc k* mang h2* merc b2.de* nat-pyru rly4• nicc olib-sac wmh1 op b7a.de *Phos* k* *Plat* k* podo fd3.de• positr nl2• spong fd4.de **Sulph** symph fd3.de• teucr b2.de* *Thuj* vanil fd5.de *Verat* a1 yuc c2 zinc b2.de* [bell-p-sp dcm1]
- **offensive**: acon b2.de acon-ac rly4• *Aesc* k* agar k* *All-c* k* **Aloe** k* alum k* alum-p k2 alum-sil k2 am-m b2.de* ambr tsm1 ammc k* ang b2.de* ant-c k* ant-t b2.de* **Arn** k* **Ars** k* ars-i ars-s-f k2 **Asaf** k* asar b2.de* asc-t a1 *Aur* k* aur-ar k2 aur-s k2 bac bn* bamb-a stb2.de• bapt gk bar-c k* bar-m bar-s k2 bell b2.de bism b2.de *Borx* k* *Bov* k* **Bry** k* calad b2.de* *Calc* k* *Calc-p* k* calc-sil k2 camph k* canth b2.de* carb-ac *Carb-an* k* **Carb-v** k* **Carbn-s** **Caust** k* cedr k* cer-s a1 cham b2.de* *Chin* k* chinin-ar choc srj3• cob-n sp1 *Cocc* k* *Coff* k* *Colch* k* coli jl2 *Coloc* k* con cop k* *Corn* k* crot-t k* cund sne *Dios* k* dirc k* dros b2.de *Dulc* k* ferr-ma k* form k* gent-l a1* germ-met srj5•

- **offensive**: ...
glon k* glycyr-g cte1• *Graph* k* guaj b2.de* haliae-lc srj5• hell k* hep b2.de* hipp k* *Hydr* hydrog srj2• *Ign* k* iod b2.de* ip b2.de* iris c1 kali-c k* kali-m bg2 kali-n k* *Kali-p* kali-s kola stb3• kreos b2.de **Lach** k* lact k* lap-la sde8.de• lec limest-b es1• lipp a1 lith-c luf-op rsj5• lyc k* *M-ambo* b2.de* m-arct b2.de* mag-c k* marb-w es1• med gk medul-os-si rly4• merc k* *Mez* k* mill a1 mur-ac k* musca-d szs1 nat-ar k2 *Nat-c* k* **Nat-m** k* nat-pyru rly4• **Nat-s** k* nat-sil fd3.de• nicc k* nicotam rly4• **Nit-ac** k* nux-m k* *Nux-v* k* *Olnd* k* op k* ozone sde2• par b2.de* petr k* *Ph-ac* k* *Phos* k* phys a1 *Plb* k* *Podo* *Psor* k* **Puls** k* pycnop-sa mrz1 ran-b b2.de* ran-s b2.de rheum b2.de rhod k* *Rhus-g* br1 rhus-t b2.de* rumx a1 ruta k* sabin b2.de sal-al blc1• sang k* *Sanic* k* sarr k* sars b2.de* sec b2.de sep k* **Sil** k* spig b2.de* spong fd4.de squil k* stann k* *Staph* k* *Stram* k* stront-c b2.de* suis-em rly4• sul-ac b2.de* **Sulph** k* sumb suprar rly4• symph fd3.de• tell k* *Teucr* k* til a1 tritic-vg fd5.de *Valer* k* vanil fd5.de verat b2.de visc c1 wies a1 *Zinc* k* zinc-p k2 [bell-p-sp dcm1 pop dhh1 tax jsj7]
  - **morning**: adam skp7•
    - **rising**; after: ferr a1
  - **night**: kali-c a1 lyc a1 op a1 sep h2*
  - **ammoniacal** odor: agn
  - **cabbage**: plut-n srj7•
  - **cheese**-like: *Sanic*
  - **eating**, after: puls h1*
  - **eggs**; spoiled: ant-t k* **Arn** k* bamb-a stb2.de• bros-gau mrc1 *Cham* k* coff k* *Ferr-ma* a1 fl-ac k* fum rly4• gink-b sbd1• *Hep* k* hydrog srj2• iod bg2 kola stb3• kreos b2.de* lac-leo hrn2• lap-la sde8.de• nat-c h2* nat-m k* olnd k* plut-n srj7• *Psor* k* ruta fd4.de sep b2.de* spig h1* stann b2.de* *Staph* k* **Sulph** k* *Tell* k* *Teucr* b2.de* valer b2.de*
  - **garlicky** odor: agar b2.de* agn bg2 asaf bg2* mosch b2.de* ph-ac bg2* phos b2.de*
  - **hepatic**: *Arn* b7a.de teucr b7.de*
  - **meat**; like spoiled: bamb-a stb2.de•
  - **menses** | **during**: kreos b7a.de
  - **musk**-like odor: mosch b7a.de
  - **putrid**: *(↗ABDOMEN - Putrefaction - intestines; STOOL - Odor - eggs; STOOL - Odor - putrid)* bac bn coli jl2
  - **sour** odor: ammc a1 arn b2.de* bell b2.de* **Calc** b2.de* cham b2.de* choc srj3• coloc b2.de* dulc b2.de* *Graph* b2.de* hep b2.de* m-aust b2.de **Mag-c** b2.de* *Merc* b2.de* nat-c b2.de* nat-m h2* petr b2.de* phos b2.de* *Rheum* b2.de* sep b2.de* spong fd4.de *Sulph* b2.de*
  - **spoiled** eggs (See eggs)
  - **stool**; during: suprar rly4•
  - **sulphur** odor: fum rly1•
  - **urine**; like: agn b7.de*
  - **writing**; while: ant-c ptk1
- **only** flatus is passed; during urging for stool (See stool - urging)
- **passing**:
  - **agg.** | **Rectum** and anus: aloe bg2 bar-c bg2 zinc bg2
  - **amel.** | **Rectum** and anus: colch bg2 coloc bg2 kali-c bg2 mag-c bg2 nux-v bg2 plat bg2 zinc bg2
  - **sudden**: graph bg2
- **pressing** against coccyx: zinc h2*
- **putrid**, foul: acon b2.de alum b2.de ant-t b2.de *Arn* b2.de* **Ars** b2.de* asar b2.de aur b2.de bell b2.de bov b2.de bry b2.de calad b2.de* calc b2.de **Carb-v** b2.de* cham b2.de chin b2.de *Cocc* b2.de coff b2.de coloc b2.de *Dulc* b2.de graph b2.de hep b2.de ign b2.de* iod b2.de ip b2.de kreos b2.de lyc b2.de m-ambo b2.de* merc b2.de nat-c b2.de* nat-m b2.de* *Nit-ac* b2.de nux-m b2.de *Nux-v* b2.de *Olnd* b2.de* par b2.de *Puls* b2.de ruta b2.de sabin b2.de sars b2.de* sec b2.de sep b2.de sil b2.de spig b2.de* staph b2.de* stram b2.de *Sulph* b2.de* teucr b2.de *Valer* b2.de zinc b2.de*
- **rarely**: kali-c bg2 lyc bg2 nat-c bg2 sil bg2
- **rumbling** in rectum: hep bg1* nux-v ptk1 sep bg1*
- **short**: calad b7a.de m-ambo b7.de m-aust b7.de mez h2* plat h2* plb b7.de* podo fd3.de• puls b7.de* sabad b7.de* squil b7.de* sul-ac h2*
- **stool**:
  - **after**: aloe am-m gsy1 cench k2 colch k* *Coloc* a1 con bg1 gamb a1 hep h2* ox-ac podo fd3.de•

Flatus – stool: ...
  - **before**: adam skp7* aesc aloe am-m amp rly4• *Apis* k* arg-n asaf bapt bg2 bism bg2* calad camph a1 cocc k* colch *Crot-t* dig digin a1 ferr ferr-m a1 fl-ac k* gels k* hell bg2* hydr a1 kali-p fd1.de• kali-s fd4.de mag-c mang-p rly4• mez k* mosch b7.de* nat-c a1 nat-m k* ol-an bg2 petr h2* phos h2* phys a1 plan plat sabad sang k* sinus rly4• staphycoc rly4• stront-c sk4• suis-em rly4• sulph h2* symph fd3.de• tritic-vg fd5.de vanil fd5.de
  - **during**: *(↗STOOL - Flatulent)* acon-ac rly4• *Agar* k* **Aloe** k* alum-sil k2 am-m gsy1 amp rly4• aq-mar skp7• *Arg-n* k* arn bg2* ars bg2 arum-i a1 asaf k* bamb-a stb2.de• bapt bg2 bell bg2 borx bg2 bov bg2 brom bg2 *Bry* k* but-ac sp1 calc-p bg2 carb-v a1 caust h2* cham bg2 *Chin* coc-c a1 coca-c sk4• cocc k* colch bg2 **Coll** *Coloc* k* *Con* k* *Corn* k* **Crot-t** k* cub dulc bg2* erig a1 eug **Ferr** k* *Ferr-m* a1 fl-ac k* gamb k* gels ger-i rly4• gink-b sbd1• glon a1 glycyr-g cte1• gran bg2 ham fd3.de• hell a1 hipp *Hydr* k* *Ind* vh *Indg* k* *Ip* k* *Iris* jatr-c bg2 kali-bi gk kali-n bg2 kali-p fd1.de• ketogl-ac rly4• kola stb3• kreos bg2 lac-e hrn2• lyc bg2 m-ambo b7a.de mag-c bg2 mag-m a1 mang merc bg2 merc-i-f a1 mur-ac h2* nat-m bg2 nat-n bg2 nat-ox rly4• **Nat-s** k* nat-sil fd3.de• *Nit-ac* k* **Olnd** osm oxal-a rly4• pall a1 petr bg2 petr-ra shn4• *Ph-ac* k* plac-s rly4• plat h2* **Podo** k* *Psor* k* ribo rly4• ruta sabin b7.de* samb bg2 sang k* **Sec** spong b7.de* squil b7a.de* *Staph* k* staphycoc rly4• sul-ac *Sulph* bg2* tab bg2* thiam rly4• **Thuj** k* tritic-vg fd5.de vanil fd5.de vichy-g a1 viol-t b7a.de zinc k* zing
  - **urging** for stool, but only flatus is passed: all-c a1 *Aloe* ant-c but-ac sp1 cain calc-f c1 *Carb-an* *Carb-v* caust h2* chin h1* *Colch* kali-n h2* *Lac-c* lat-h thj1 laur mag-c mag-m k* mez bg1 myric nat-c pd **Nat-s** osm ozone sde2• pall hr1 petr-ra shn4• phos pd plut-n srj7• ruta *Sang* sep
- **sugar**, after: **Arg-n** k*
- **touching** abdomen: squil h1*
- **urination**; during: dulc b4a.de
- **violent**: graph h2*
- **walking**: camph a1 carbn-s k2 coloc a1 com a1 crot-t a1 mag-c h2* podo fd3.de• sep h2* thuj a1 vanil fd5.de

FOOD POISONING (See Diarrhea - food - rancid)

FOREIGN body; sensation of a: *(↗Lump)* der vml3• gran a1 lil-t nat-m ozone sde2• rumx sep sulph
- **hard**, something: caust h2* sin-a a1
- **knife**: ign mrr1
- **poker**: ign mrr1
- **rough** substance: nat-m bg2 rumx bg2

○ - **Anus**: spig b7a.de

FORMICATION:

○ - **Anus**: *Aesc* agar k* ail all-c aloe alum k* alum-p k2 alum-sil k2 ambr k* ant-c ant-t arg-met arg-n k* *Bar-c* bar-s k2 benz-ac *Berb* bov brom bg2 **Calc** k* calc-caust c1 **Calc-s** k* calc-sil k2 canth *Carb-v* k* carbn-s caust k* chel k* chin k* *Cina* b7a.de *Cinnb* coc-c colch k* *Croc* k* elaps k* fago ferr-i ferr-ma gran grat hep *Ign* k* ip b7.de* **Kali-c** k* kali-m k2* kali-p kali-sil k2 kreos k* m-aust b7.de *Mag-c* b4a.de mez mosch k* *Mur-ac* k* *Nat-c* k* nat-m bg2 *Nux-v* k* ol-an phos k* *Plat* k* plb k* rhod k* rhus-t k* *Sabad* k* sabin b7.de* *Sep* k* sil k* spig k* spong k* **Sulph** k* ter k* *Teucr* k* verat-v *Zinc* k*
  - **evening**: euphr kali-c h2 plat spong *Sulph* teucr zinc-p k2
    - **bed** agg.; in: plat *Teucr*
  - **night**: *Nux-v*
  - **bug**; as from a: aesc ptk1 ferr-i ptk1 sulph ptk1
    - **stool** agg.; after: kali-m ptk1
  - **sitting** agg.: **Sulph**
  - **stool**:
    - **after** | **agg.**: aloe k* alum bg2 berb chin b7.de* mez k* phos bg2 teucr k*
    - **before**: kali-c h2 mez bg2* phos
    - **during** | **agg.**: alum b4.de* phos b4.de*
  - **walking** | **after** | **agg.**: phos h2
    - **agg.**: phos h2
  - **worm**; as from: cinnb ptk1
- **Perineum**: acon chel k* petros rhod k*

- **Rectum**: alum b4.de* *Ambr* b7a.de ant-t b7a.de* bell b4.de* *Calc* b4.de* canth b7.de* caust b4.de* chel bg2 chin b7.de* cocc b7.de* hep b4a.de* **Ign** b7.de* laur b7.de* *Mag-c* b4a.de nux-v b7.de* phos b4.de* plb b7.de* rhod b4a.de rhus-t b7.de* *Sabad* b7.de* *Sep* b4.de* sil b4a.de *Spig* b7.de* spong b7.de* sulph b4.de*

FULLNESS: (↗*Dragging; Weight*) acon **Aesc** k* agar allox tpw4 **Aloe** k* alum anac tl1 anthraq rly4• apis k* ars bell berb k* bry carb-v k* caust chion bg2 colch bg2 crot-t bg2 cycl ferr **Ham** k* hydrog srj2• kali-bi *Lach* lil-t k* lyc bg1 mag-p bg2 manc k* med meli k* *Moni* rfm1• **Nit-ac** k* phos plan podo bg2 propr sa3• ruta fd4.de sabin sec a1 sep bg2 stram k* succ-ac rly4• **Sulph** k* suprar rly4• thuj
- **alternating** with sensation of emptiness: thuj
- **constipation**; without: aesc tl1
- **stool** agg.; after: **Aesc** alum alumn k* *Lyc* k* podo bg2 *Sep*
- **urination**; with frequent: ferr-pic ptk1
- **walking** agg.; after: aesc

○ - **Perineum**: alum berb bry *Chin* k* cycl musa a1 nux-v

GRUMBLING: arn bg2 hep b4a.de* mang k*

GURGLING in rectum: aloe mrr1 calc k* carb-an k* hep h2* laur k* stry k* *Sulph* k*

○ - **Perineum**: phyt bg2

HANGING from; sensation of something: | **Rectum** and anus: arg-met bg2 sulph bg2

HEAT: **Aesc** k* agar all-c ptk1* all-s a1 **Aloe** k* apis ars aster a1 bamb-a stb2.de• berb bry calc-p clem k* colch *Con* k* cycl k* *Eup-per* glon iod k* jac-c a1 kali-p fd1.de• kurch bnj1 *Lach* lil-t k* *Merc* *Merc-c* naja nat-m k* nit-ac k* paeon tl1 phyt k* plac-s rly4• podo c1 *Rat* *Rumx* sep sul-i k2 sulph symph fd3.de•
- **morning**: glon
  - **rising** agg.: glon
- **noon**: agar
- **afternoon**: cycl k* symph fd3.de•
- **hemorrhoids**; in: acon vh1
- **stool** | **after** | **agg.**: calc h2* calc-s caps euphr plac-s rly4• sol-t-ae zinc
  - **during** | **agg.**: *Aloe* ant-t *Con* b4a.de form *Glon* kola stb3• nat-m b4a.de **Podo** sulph b4a.de
- **urination** agg.; after: rhus-t k*

○ - **Anus**: acon bg2 **Aesc** bg2 **Aloe** bg2 am-c bg2 ang bg2 ant-t bg2 arg-n bg2 aur bg2 **Berb** bg2 canth b7.de crot-t bg2 ferr bg2 glon bg2 hell bg2 hep bg2 hyos bg2 **Iris** bg2 kali-bi bg2 m-ambo bg2 merc-c bg2 op bg2 plb bg2 psor bg2 ran-b bg2 **Rat** bg2 sars bg2 sil bg2 tab bg2
- **Perineum**: alum ant-c bg2 ant-t bg2 asaf bg2 aur k* **Carb-an** bg2 *Cycl* bg2 irid-met srj5• lyc bg2 mur-ac bg2 *Nux-v* bg2 plb bg2 polyg-h bg2 rhod bg2 sep bg2 sil bg2 spig bg2 **Sulph** bg2 tarax bg2

HEAVINESS (See Dragging)

HEMORRHAGE from anus: (↗*STOOL - Bloody*) acal br1* acet-ac k* **Acon** k* *Adren* br1 *Aesc* k* agar aids nl2• all-c k2 *Aloe* k* alum k* alum-p k2 alum-sil k2 *Alumn* k* *Am-c* k* am-caust vh1 am-m k* ambr k* anac k* *Ant-c* k* *Apis* k* aq-mar skp7• arist-cl sp1 arizon-l nl2• arn k2* **Ars** k* asar k* *Atis* zzc1• aur k* aur-ar k2 aur-m aur-s k2 bac bn* *Bapt* k* **Bar-c** k* bar-m bar-ox-suc rly4• bar-s k2 *Bell* k* berb *Bism* k* blum-o mtf11 *Borx* k* bufo **Cact** k* cadm-met gm1 **Calc** k* calc-f k2* *Calc-p* *Calc-s* calc-sil k2 camph *Canth* k* *Caps* k* carb-an k* *Carb-v* k* *Carbn-s* carc gk6* card-m k* carl **Casc** k* caust h2* *Cham* k* *Chin* k* chinin-ar chinin-s chlor chr-ac bro1 cinnm br1* cob k* cocain bro1 *Cocc* colch k2 **Coll** k* coloc k* con bg2 crat br1 **Crot-h** k* cupr b7.de* *Cycl* cyn-d zzc1• dios dream-p sdj1• dulc fd4.de elaps *Erig* k* *Eug* *Ferr* k* ferr-ar ferr-m ferr-p k* *Fic-r* bro1 *Fl-ac* *Graph* k* **Ham** k* helodr-cal knl2• *Hep* *Hir* c2* hydr k* *Hyos* k* *Hyper* bro1* *Ign* k* *Ip* k* *Kali-ar* *Kali-bi* *Kali-c* k* *Kali-chl* kali-i kali-m k2* kali-n kali-p *Kali-s* kali-sil k2 kola stb3• kreos bg1* lac-ac stj5• **Lach** k* lap-la sde8.de• led k* *Lept* k* lob **Lyc** k* lycps-v bg2* lyss m-ambo b7.de malar jl2 manc k* mand sp1* mangi bro1 med melal-alt gya4 meny bg2 *Merc* k* *Merc-c* k* merc-cy bro1 *Mill* k* morg-g pte1*• morg-p pte1*• *Mur-ac* k* musa a1* **Nat-m** k* *Nat-s* **Nit-ac** k* *Nux-m* **Nux-v** k* oper bro1 paeon parathyr jl2 petr bg2 ph-ac k* **Phos** k* *Phyt* pieri-b mlk9.de plat k* *Podo* *Positr* nl2• pot-e rly4• prot pte1* **Psor** k* *Puls* k* pyrog ran-b b7.de* *Rat* k* rhus-t k* rhus-v *Ruta* sabin k* sars bg2 scroph-n k2* sec bg2* sed-ac bro1 *Sep* k* sil k* stram k* suis-em rly4• sul-ac b4a.de* **Sulph** k* syph k2* ter bro1* thlas bro1 thuj k* tril-p ptk1 tritic-vg fd5.de tub hr valer k* vanil fd5.de verat visc sp1 yohim lp2* zinc k* zinc-p k2

Hemorrhage from anus: ...
- **morning**: acal br1 con h2* melal-alt gya4 mur-ac h2* plan
  - **stool** agg.; after: melal-alt gya4 puls
- **afternoon**: sulph
- **evening**: alum h2* sulph h2*
  - **stool** agg.; during: calc
- **night**: **Nit-ac**
- **accompanied** by:
  - **constipation**: alum bro1 am-m bro1 anac bro1 calc-p bro1 *Coll* bro1 lac-d bro1 lam bro1 morph bro1 nat-m bro1 *Nit-ac* bro1 *Nux-v* bro1 phos bro1 psor bro1 sep bro1 vib bro1

○ • **Abdomen**; congestion of (See ABDOMEN - Congestion - accompanied - hemorrhoids)
- **alternating** with | **rheumatism** (See EXTREMITIES - Pain - rheumatic - alternating - hemorrhoids)
- **amel.**: aesc pd*
- **black**: (↗*dark*) alumn am-c k2 ant-c ars k2 colch crot-h *Ham* merc-c *Rhus-t* hr1* *Sec*
  - **liquid**: elaps
- **bright** (See red)
- **children**; in: lach mtf33
  - **infants**; in: all-c k2
- **clotted**: am-m gsy1 nat-m h2* stram h1*
  - **large** clots: alum ptk1 alumn ptk1
- **congestion** to head, with: calc h2*
- **copious**: bac al2
- **coryza**; during: *Calc* h2*
- **dark**: (↗*black*) aloe bro1 alum h2* *Ham* bro1 hydr bro1 kali-m bro1 *Sulph* bro1
- **dripping** constantly | **stool** amel.; during: cob ptk1 puls ptk1
- **exertion** | **after** | **agg.**: berb mill k2
  - **agg.**: bry sys
- **exhaustion**; from slight: hydr ptk1
- **fetid**: manc bg2
- **flatus** agg.; passing: *Phos* k*
- **heart** complaints; with: cact br1
- **hemorrhoids**; after removal of: nit-ac ptk1
- **injuries**: bac bn mill k2
- **malarial** fevers, in: cact br1
- **meat** scrapings, as if: am-m hr1*
- **menopause**; at: **Lach** vh
- **menses**:
  - **after** | **agg.**: graph h2*
  - **before** | **agg.**: am-c
  - **during** | **agg.**: am-c gsy1* *Am-m* k* ars-met *Graph* k* **Lach** k* lyss
  - **scanty**, during: lach
  - **suppressed** menses; from: abrot mrr1 acet-ac bg1 graph ham zinc
- **old** people; in: | **women**; old: psor ptk1
- **periodical**: bac bn merc k2 *Mur-ac* *Nit-ac*
- **red**; bright: acon vh1 aq-mar skp7• caust h2* dulc fd4.de ozone sde2• suis-em rly4• visc sp1
- **rubbing** agg.: aesc k*
- **standing** agg.: crot-h ptk1
- **stool**:
  - **after** | **agg.**: *Agar* k* aids nl2• *Aloe* k* *Alum* k* **Am-c** k* anthraq rly4• borx b4a.de* cact bg1 calad bg2 calc-f sp1 *Calc-p* k* *Carb-v* k* carbn-s chel k* cycl k* dulc fd4.de echi ptk1 fl-ac grat k* *Ign* *Kali-c* kali-n k* kola stb3• lac-d bro1 *Lach* k* lap-la sde8.de• lob bg1 lyc b4a.de* melal-alt gya4 merc k* *Merc-c* bg2 mez k* nat-m k* nit-ac bg1* *Nux-v* b7a.de *Phos* k* positr nl2• rhus-v sabin b7.de* sel k* sep k* spong sulph k*
  - **difficult** | **from**: aids nl2• dulc fd4.de melal-alt gya4 petr h2
  - **during** | **agg.**: aloe bg2 *Alum* k* alumn k* **Am-c** k* am-m k* *Ambr* k* *Anac* b4a.de* arn bg2 **Ars** bg2 asar bg2* aur aur-m k* bufo *Calc* b4a.de* *Calc-p* k* calc-sil k2 *Carb-an* *Carb-v* k* caust b4a.de* coff bg2 con h2* ferr bg2 gink-b sbd1• graph b4a.de* **Ham** k* *Hep* k* ign k* iod bro1 *Ip* bro1 *Kali-c* k* lyc k* **Merc** b4a.de* **Merc-c** bg2 mez bg2 mur-ac b4a.de* *Nat-c* hr1 **Nat-m** k* *Nit-ac* k* nux-v k* *Petr* bg2 **Phos** k* plan plat b4a.de* positr nl2• prun bg2 psor bro1 *Puls* k* rheum ruta b7.de* sars b4a.de*

- stool – during – agg.: ...
 sel b7.de* sep b4a.de* sul-ac b4a.de* sulph bg2* tarent k2 tela zzc1• **Thuj** b4a.de* tritic-vg fd5.de *Tub* zinc b4a.de*
 - hard stool | agg.: arizon-l nl2• bar-ox-suc rly4• dulc fd4.de *Fl-ac* k* *Kali-c* k* kali-n h2 lam br1 melal-alt gya4 **Nat-m** k* prun sabin c1 *Tub* k*
- tendency to: ferr tl1
- typhoid; during: alumn br1
- urination agg.; during: kali-c b4a.de* merc b4.de*
 - stools; not from the: cob c1
- vicarious: abrot bg2 ham bg2* mill bro1 nux-v bg2 sulph bg2
- walking agg.: alum k* crot-h ptk1 sep k*
- weather:
 - autumnal: colch tl1
 - cold damp: colch tl1

HEMORRHOIDS: abrot k* acet-ac acon k* **Aesc** k* aesc-g c2* aeth **Agar** agn alet c2 all-s mtf11 **Aloe** k* alum k* alum-p k2 alumn am-br k* *Am-c* k* am-m k* ambr k* ambro c2 anac k* anag c2 anan androc srj1• ang k* *Ant-c* k* ant-t k* *Apis* k* apoc aral c2 arg-n *Arist-cl* sp1 arn k* **Ars** k* *Ars-i* ars-met c2 arum-t arund c1 aur k* aur-m aur-m-n c2 *Bac* bn bacls-7 pte1*• bad c2 bapt k* *Bar-c* k* bar-s k2 *Bell* k* berb k* beta mtf11 blum-o mtf11 borx k* bov *Brom* k* brucel sa3• bry *Bufo* *Cact* cadm-met tpw6* *Calc* k* calc-caust c1 calc-f c1* calc-i k2* *Calc-p* *Calc-s* cann-s canth k* *Caps* k* carb-ac **Carb-an** k* **Carb-v** k* carbn-s carc gk6 *Card-m* k* carl cas-s br1 casc **Caust** k* cham k* *Chel* k* chim chin k* chinin-ar chord-umb rly4• chr-ac k* chr-met dx chr-o c2 cic cimic *Cimx* k* clem k* cnic-ar vs1.fr *Coca* k* cocc k* *Coff* colch **Coll** k* *Coloc* k* con cop c2* croc crot-h cupr b2.de* *Cycl* k* *Dios* k* dol br1 dream-p sdj1• dulc c2 echi br1 elaps *Erig* k* ery-a c2 *Eug* euph-a c2 euphr k* *Ferr* k* *Ferr-ar* ferr-m ferr-p k* ferul c2 *Fl-ac* k* galv c2 gast c2 gels *Gran* sne **Graph** k* grat k* **Ham** k* helia c2 *Hell* k* helo-s rwt2• *Hep* k* *Hydr* k* hydroph rsj6• *Hyos* k* hyper c1* *Ign* k* *Iod* k* *Ip* k* kali-act c2 **Kali-ar** *Kali-bi* kali-br c2 **Kali-c** k* kali-chl c2 kali-m c2* kali-n k* kali-p **Kali-s** k* ketogl-ac rly4• kiss c2 kreos lac-del hrn2• **Lach** k* lact lam c2* lap-la sde8.de• laps c1* led b2.de *Lept* lil-t k* lim c2 lina c2 linu-c c2 lipp c2 lob **Lyc** k* lycps-v mrr1 *M-ambo* b2.de m-aust b2.de mag-c b2.de* *Mag-m* k* mag-p k2 manc mand sp1 med *Meli* sne *Merc* k* **Merc-i-r** k* mez mill k* moni rfm1• morg fmm1• morg-g fmm1• morg-p fmm1• mosch muc-u c1* **Mur-ac** k* musa c2 *Nat-m* k* *Nat-s* neg bro1* nig-s mp4• **Nit-ac** k* **Nux-v** k* ozone sde2• **Paeon** k* pen c2 *Petr* k* petros mtf11 ph-ac k* **Phos** k* phys k* *Phyt* k* pin-con oss2• pin-s c2* pip-n c2 plan k* plat k* plb k* plb-xyz c2 *Podo* k* polyg-h br1* polyg-xyz c2 polyp-p c2 prot jl2* *Psor* k* **Puls** k* querc-r-g-s mtf11 rad-br bro1 ran-b b2.de ran-fi c1* ran-s c2 *Rat* k* rauw sp1 rein a1 rhod b2.de rhodi-o-n c2 *Rhus-t* k* rhus-v k* rumx rusc-a vs1.fr *Ruta* *Sabin* k* *Sacch* sne *Sang* *Sanguis-s* hrn2• saroth sp1 sars k2 saxon br1 *Scroph-n* bro1* sec sed-ac bro1* semp br1* **Sep** k* *Sil* k* sin-n c2 slag c2 spig b2.de stann k* *Staph* k* still c2 stram k* streptoc rly4• stront-c k* *Sul-ac* k* sul-i k2 **Sulph** k* sumb symph fd3.de• syph k* tep c2 *Ter* k* ther *Thuj* k* tritic-vg fd5.de *Tub* ulm-c c2 valer b2.de vanil fd5.de verat k* verat-v verb b2.de* visc sp1 wies c2 wye c2* zinc k* zinc-val c2 *Zing* k*

- morning:
 - agg.: aloe **Dios** mur-ac sabin sulph sumb thuj
 - amel.: alum coll
 - bed agg.; in: graph rumx
 - waking him or her from sleep: aloe kali-bi petr sulph
- afternoon: bapt hr1
- evening: coll tl1
- night: aesc aloe alum am-c ant-c ars ars-s-f k2 carb-an carb-v coll k* euphr ferr graph kali-c mrr1 *Merc* phys *Puls* rhus-t **Sulph**
- accompanied by:
 - appetite; loss of: coll tl1
 - constipation (See Constipation - accompanied - hemorrhoids)
 - diarrhea (See Diarrhea - accompanied - hemorrhoids)
 - epistaxis: carb-v bro1 **Ham** mrr1 **Sep** k*
 - indigestion: coll tl1

Hemorrhoids: ...
 - palpitations (See CHEST - Palpitation - accompanied - hemorrhoids)
 - respiration; asthmatic (See RESPIRATION - Asthmatic - accompanied - hemorrhoids)
 - rheumatic complaints (See GENERALS - Pain - rheumatic - accompanied - hemorrhoids)
 - stool; bloody mucous: caps tl1
 - uneasiness: malar jl2
 - weakness: ars bro1 chin bro1 ham bro1 hydr bro1 mur-ac bro1
 - ○ Abdomen:
   - complaints (See ABDOMEN - Complaints - accompanied - hemorrhoids)
   - cramping pain (See ABDOMEN - Pain - cramping - accompanied - hemorrhoids)
   - pain (See ABDOMEN - Pain - hemorrhoids)
 - Back:
   - pain in: *Aesc* br1* aesc-g bro1 *Bell* bro1 calc-f bro1 caps tl1 chr-ac bro1 euon bro1 ham bg2* ign bro1 kali-c bg2 *Nux-v* bro1 sulph bro1
 - Bladder; complaints of (See BLADDER - Complaints of bladder - accompanied - hemorrhoids)
 - Head; complaints of (See HEAD - Hemorrhoids)
 - Head; pain in: coll bro1 nux-v bro1
 - Heart; complaints of (See CHEST - Heart; complaints - accompanied - hemorrhoids)
 - Liver; stitching pains extending to (See Pain - extending - liver - stitching - accompanied - hemorrhoids)
 - Lower limbs; complaints of: ham bg2 lyc bg2 nux-v bg2 ruta bg2 sulph bg2
 - Portal congestion (See congestion; from pelvic; ABDOMEN - Portal - accompanied - hemorrhoids)
 - Prostate gland; enlarged: staph ptk1
 - Sacrum; pain in: abrot vh1
 - Skin; itching: coll br1
 - Sphincter; spasms in: lach bro1 sil bro1
 - Tongue:
   - mucus on tongue; collection of: *Berb* kr1*
   - white discoloration of the tongue: *Aesc* kr1*
 - Veins; relaxation of: calc tl1
- alternating with: abrot ptk1 coll ptk1 sabin ptk1
 - constipation: coll tl1
 - cough (See COUGH - Alternating - hemorrhoids)
 - diarrhea (See Diarrhea - alternating - hemorrhoids)
 - lumbago (See BACK - Pain - lumbar - alternating - hemorrhoids)
 - palpitation (See CHEST - Palpitation - alternating - hemorrhoids; CHEST - Palpitation - alternating - lower)
 - rheumatism (See EXTREMITIES - Pain - rheumatic - alternating - hemorrhoids)
 - ○ Head; pain in (See HEAD - Pain - alternating - hemorrhoids)
 - Heart; complaints of (See CHEST - Heart; complaints - alternating - hemorrhoids)
- appearing suddenly: mur-ac tl1
- bathing | warm agg.: brom ptk1
- beer agg.: *Aloe* bry ferr nux-v rhus-t **Sulph**
- bladder complaints, with: erig vml3•
- bleeding (See Hemorrhage)
- blind: **Aesc** k* anac gsy1 ant-c k* *Arg-n* hr1 am b7.de* ars k* asc-t a1 brom k* calc-f bro1 *Calc-p* caps k* cham k* *Coll* k* coloc b4.de* ferr k* grat *Ign* k* *Kali-br* hr1 m-ambo b7.de* med tl1 muc-u bro1 nit-ac *Nux-v* k* ph-ac b4a.de podo *Puls* k* rhod b4a.de *Rhus-t* k* *Sulph* k* verat k* wye bro1
 - smarting: led ptk1

Rectum

- **stool** agg.; during: brom bg2
- **bluish**: **Aesc** k* *Aesc-g* bro1 aeth *Aloe* bro1 ars k* caps bro1 **Carb-v** k* carbn-s k2 dios fl-ac bg2 *Ham* k* **Lach** k* *Lyc* k* manc k* **Mur-ac** k* *Nit-ac* b4a.de phys *Sulph* tritic-vg fd5.de verat-v
- **bunch**; like a (See grapes)
- **burning**: *(↗Pain - burning)* *Acon* bg2 aesc bro1* aloe bro1 alum b4.de* am-m bro1 ang b7.de* ant-c b7.de* ars b4.de* *Calc* b4.de* caps b7.de* carb-an b4.de* carb-v b4a.de* caust b4.de* euphr b7.de* *Fl-ac* bro1 graph b4.de* *Ign* bro1 kali-c bg2* lach bg2 lil-t tl1 mag-m bro1 med tl1 *Muc-u* bro1 mur-ac b4a.de* neg bro1 nit-ac b4.de* *Nux-v* b7a.de* *Phos* b4.de* psor bro1 *Rat* bro1 sul-ac b4a.de* sulph b4a.de* syph jl2 tritic-vg fd5.de
  - **stool** agg.; during: abrot vh1
  - **touch** agg.: abrot vh1
- **bursting**: ham ptk1
- **children**; in: **Mur-ac** k*
  - **emaciated**: mur-ac hr*
- **chill**; during: caps bro1
- **chronic**: **Aesc** k* *Aloe* am-c calc k* carb-v k* *Carbn-s* caust k* **Coll** k* dios graph k* *Lach* k* *Lyc* **Merc-i-r** k* *Nit-ac* **Nux-v** k* petr k* *Phos* phyt *Podo* **Sulph** k* *Tub*
- **cirrhosis**, with (See ABDOMEN - Cirrhosis - hemorrhoids)
- **cold**:
  - **applications** | **amel.**: *(↗bathing - amel.)* aloe k* brom kali-c tl1 nux-v bro1 rat bro1
  - **bathing**:
    - **agg.**: ant-c k2
    - **amel.**: *(↗applications - amel.)* aloe ptk1 brom ptk1 kali-c ptk1 nux-v ptk1 rat ptk1
  - **water** | **amel.**: aloe a1*
- **congested**: abrot vh1 *Acon* k* aesc br1* agar *Aloe* k* alum androc srj1• ant-c k2 apoc arg-n ars k* *Bell* k* carb-v *Carbn-s* vh *Caust* k* *Cham* k* cop bro1 ferr-p bro1 graph vh ham k2 *Hep* **Kali-c** k* kali-m k2 kali-n kali-p k2 lach mrr1 *Merc* *Mur-ac* k* **Nux-v** k* ozone sde2• **Paeon** k* podo *Puls* k* *Rhus-t* sil *Sulph* k* symph fd3.de• verat-v verb bro1 zing
- **congestion**; from pelvic: *Aloe* bro1 coll br1* ham bro1 hep bro1 muc-u bro1 nux-v bro1 podo br1* sep bro1 *Sulph* bro1
  - **women**; in: *Coll* br1
- **congestion**; from portal: coll br1* podo br1
  - **women**; in: *Coll* br1
- **constipation**:
  - **with** (See Constipation - accompanied - hemorrhoids)
  - **without**: aesc br1
- **cough** agg.: bac bn caust bro1* ign ptk1 *Kali-c* bro1* lach bro1*
- **crawling**: ant-c b7.de* *Kali-c* b4a.de
- **delivery**; after: aloe bro1 apis bro1 kali-c ptk1 lil-t ptk1
- **diarrhea** | **after** | **agg.**: *Aloe* bro1 ham bro1 mur-ac bro1 sulph bro1
  - **suppressed** diarrhea; from: abrot k2*
- **discharging** | **mucus**: *Aloe* bro1 am-m bro1 ant-c bg2* *Borx* bg2 caps bg2* carb-v bg2* caust bro1 ign bg2 lach bg2 merc bg2 puls bg2* sep bro1 sul-ac bro1 sulph bg2*
- **drunkards**; in: aesc-g bro1 *Ars* *Carb-v* *Lach* vh **Nux-v** k* *Sul-ac*
- **excitement**: arg-n gels hyos nat-c nux-v sumb
- **exertion** agg.: bry sys
- **external**: abrot k* **Aesc** all-c **Aloe** alum alum-sil k2 *Am-c* anac *Ang* ant-c apis apoc arn ars ars-i ars-s-f k2 aur aur-ar k2 aur-i k2 aur-s k2 *Bar-c* bar-i k2 *Bar-m* bar-s k2 berb *Brom* bry cact *Calc* *Calc-p* calc-s caps carb-ac carb-an carb-v *Carbn-s* *Caust* *Coll* coloc dios k* *Ferr* *Ferr-ar* ferr-i ferr-p fl-ac *Gran* *Graph* grat **Ham** *Hep* hyper bg1* *Iod* kali-ar kali-c kali-m k2 kali-n kali-p kali-s kali-sil k2 **Lach** *Lyc* med *Merc* **Mur-ac** nat-m *Nit-ac* nux-v *Paeon* ph-ac *Phos* phys *Plat* *Podo* *Puls* **Rat** *Rhus-t* rumx *Sep* *Sil* sul-ac **Sulph** *Ter* thuj tritic-vg fd5.de *Tub* verat zinc zinc-p k2
- **flatulence**; from: caust h2* zinc h2*
- **flatus**, protrude when passing: *Bar-c* k* *Mur-ac* ptk1 *Phos* k*
- **grapes**, like: aesc bro1 aloe bro1* *Am-c* bro1 calc ptk1 caps bro1 *Carb-v* bro1 *Caust* bro1 *Coll* bro1 dios bro1* graph bro1 ham bro1 kali-c bro1 lach bro1 mur-ac bro1* nux-m bro1 *Nux-v* bro1 rat bro1 scroph-n bro1 sep bro1 sulph bro1 thuj bro1
- **hard**: ail alum am-br k* ambr androc srj1• **Caust** k* kali-p fd1.de• *Lach* *Lyc* mur-ac b4a.de phys *Sep* tritic-vg fd5.de
- **heart** complaints relieved; after: coll tl1
- **inflamed** (See congested)
- **internal**: *Aesc* *Alum* ant-c arn **Ars** borx **Brom** *Calc* *Caps* caust **Cham** cimic **Coloc** hep **Ign** kali-ar kali-c kali-p kali-s *Lach* lyc meli sne nit-ac k2 **Nux-v** *Petr* *Ph-ac* *Phos* *Plan* **Podo** polyg-h bro1 **Puls** *Rhus-t* sep stront-c **Sulph** *Ter* tritic-vg fd5.de verat
- **itching** (See Itching - hemorrhoids)
- **large**: **Aesc** agar **Aloe** alum anan vh1 ang arn ars ars-s-f k2 bry *Cact* *Calc* caps **Carb-an** k* *Carb-v* *Carbn-s* **Caust** k* clem *Coloc* cycl *Dios* dulc fd4.de euphr *Ferr* k* ferr-ar gal-ac *Graph* k* **Ham** kali-ar **Kali-c** k* kali-m k2 kali-n kali-p fd1.de• kali-s *Lach* lyc manc *Merc* *Mur-ac* k* nat-m **Nit-ac** **Nux-v** ozone sde2• paeon ptk1 *Podo* *Puls* sep spig b7a.de sul-ac k* **Sulph** thuj *Tub*
- **leukorrhea**; from suppressed: am-m bro1*
- **lifting** agg.: rhus-t ptk1
- **lying** agg.: aesc tl1 puls ptk1
- **lying** down | **amel.**: am-c bro1
- **menopause**; during: aesc bro1* **Lach** bro1*
- **menses**:
  - **after**:
    - **agg.**: cocc k*
      - **painful**: cocc ptk1
  - **before** | **agg.**: cocc phos puls
  - **during**, agg.: *Aloe* am-c k* calc *Carb-v* *Carbn-s* cocc *Coll* k* *Graph* *Ign* *Lach* k* lyss phos podo *Puls* *Sulph*
  - **suppressed** menses; from: phos *Sulph*
- **mental** exertion agg.: *Caust* nat-c
- **mercury**; after abuse of: *Hep* *Sul-ac*
- **milk** agg.: *Sep* k*
- **moisture**; oozing: alum b4a.de* am-c bg2 bar-c b4.de* calc-p ptk1 caust bg2 nat-m bg2 sep b4.de* sul-ac b4a.de* sulph b4.de*
- **motion** agg.: apis carb-an euphr merc *Mur-ac* nat-m puls
- **offensive** (= fetid): carb-v k* manc med k* podo ptk1
- **operation**; after: coll ptk1 croc ptk1
- **painful**: *(↗Pain - hemorrhoids)* aesc br1* aesc-g bro1 *Aloe* bro1 alum bg2 am-c b4.de* anac b4a.de* **Ars** bg2* bac bn *Bar-c* b4.de* bell bro1* *Brom* b4a.de cact bro1 calc b4.de* caps a1* *Carb-v* b4.de* *Caust* b4.de* cham bg2* chin b7.de* *Coll* bro1 coloc b4.de* dios br1 dulc fd4.de ferr-p bro1 **Graph** b4.de* *Ham* bro1 hydroph rsj6• hyper bro1 ign b7.de* iod bg2 *Kali-c* b4.de* kali-n b4.de* kali-p fd1.de• lac-del hrn2• *Lach* bro1 lyc b4.de* m-ambo b7.de mag-c b4.de* mag-m br1* morg-g fmm1• morg-p fmm1• mur-ac k* *Nat-m* b4a.de* nit-ac k* nux-v b7a.de* ozone sde2• paeon k* *Ph-ac* b4a.de phasco-ci rbp2 phos b4.de* plan bro1 podo fd3.de• puls b7.de* rat bg2* ruta bg2 sabin b7.de* *Scroph-n* br1* sed-ac br1* sep b4.de* sil b4.de* staph k* stront-c b4.de* sulph bro1 thuj b4.de* tritic-vg fd5.de verb bro1 zinc b4.de* zing bro1
  - **bleeding**; much pain but little: aesc br1
  - **burning**, smarting: lac-del hrn2•
  - **cough** agg.; during: kali-c b4a.de
  - **cutting**: lach bg2
  - **kneeling**: | **amel.**: aesc tl1
  - **sore**: *Aloe* bg2 am-c bg2 caust tl1 euphr b7.de* graph b4a.de* *Ham* br1 kali-c b4a.de m-ambo b7.de merc b4.de* mur-ac b4a.de* phos b4.de* *Puls* b7.de* rhus-t b7.de* stann b4.de* sulph bg2 zinc bg2
  - **standing** agg.: plan ptk1
  - **stool**:
    - **after** | **agg.**: alumn vh1 am-c bg2 calc b4a.de graph b4a.de* ign b7.de* iod bg2 m-ambo b7.de rhus-t b7.de*
    - **before**: iod bg2
    - **during** | **agg.**: aloe bg2 brom bg2 caps b7.de* coloc bg2 ferr b7.de* ign b7.de* mag-m bg2 puls b7.de* rhus-t b7a.de*
- **parturition** agg.: acon bro1 *Aloe* bro1 bell bro1 ham bro1 *Ign* k* **Kali-c** *Lil-t* *Mur-ac* *Podo* *Puls* k* sep *Sulph*
- **pendulous**: nit-ac k*
- **pneumonia**; with: hyper c1
  - **tendency** to pneumonia; with: hyper c1
- **pregnancy** agg.; during: *Aesc* *Am-m* ant-c k* ars j5.de *Caps* carb-v j5.de *Coll* k* ham k2 *Lach* *Lyc* mur-ac h2* *Nat-m* *Nux-v* podo bro1* puls j5.de sep k* *Sulph* k*
- **pressing**: acon bg2 ferr b7.de* ign b7.de* phos bg2
- **pressure** of nates agg.: kali-c k2 mur-ac k2
- **pricking**: syph jl2

- **protrude**: abrot ptk1 **Aloe** bg2* am-c b4a.de* brom tl1 *Calc* b4.de* *Carb-v* bg2 caust b4a.de* coll tl1 *Ferr* b7.de* *Graph* b4.de* hell bg2 *Hep* b4a.de kali-c b4.de* lil-t tl1 lyc b4a.de* merc b4.de* mur-ac bg2* nit-ac tl1 *Nux-v* bg2 ph-ac b4a.de* phos b4a.de puls b7.de* rhus-t b7.de* *Sep* b4.de* *Sil* b4a.de **Sulph** bg2* tritic-vg fd5.de zinc ptk1
  - **bleeding**: lach ptk1 lept ptk1
  - **lying** agg.: puls ptk1
  - **menses**; during: puls ptk1
  - **sensation** as if hemorrhoids will protrude: | **stool** agg.; after: plut-n srj7•
  - **stool** | **after** | **agg.**: am-c ptk1 dios br1 fl-ac k2 melal-alt gya4 rhus-t a1
    - **during** | **agg.**: abrot vh1 aesc vh agar bg2 aloe bg2 alum bg2 alum-p k2 alumn *Am-c* k* ang b7.de* ars k2 *Bar-c* brom b4a.de* *Calc* k* **Calc-p** k* calc-sil k2 dulc fd4.de fl-ac *Kali-bi* *Kali-c* k* *Lach* lil-t k2 lyc bg2 merc b4.de* *Mur-ac* k* nat-c b4.de* *Nit-ac* k* ph-ac k* phos k* plat k* **Rat** k* *Rhus-t* k* sep h2 *Sil* k*
  - **urination** | **after** | **agg.**: bar-c bro1 merc
    - **during** | **agg.**: aloe **Bar-c** k* *Bar-m* canth *Kali-c* k* merc *Mur-ac* k* nit-ac
  - **walking** agg.: am-c ptk1 sep ptk1
- **pulsating**: caps tl1 ham k2 lach k2* mur-ac tl1
- **purgatives**; after: aloe *Nux-v*
- **purple**: aesc tl1 lach mrr1 med tl1 mur-ac tl1
- **rheumatism** abates; after: abrot k*
- **riding** amel.: *Kali-c* k*
- **sedentary** persons; in: aesc-g bro1 nux-v bro1
- **sensitive**: kali-c bg2 **Mur-ac** bg2
- **sitting**:
  - **agg.**: caust ptk1 graph bro1* ign bro1 ozone sde2• *Thuj* bro1*
  - **amel.**: ars bg1 calc bg1* ign bg1* lach bg1
- **smarting**: m-ambo b7.de *Puls* b7.de*
- **sneezing** agg.: caust bro1 *Kali-c* bro1 lach bro1
- **standing** agg.: *Aesc* k* *Am-c* *Caust* k* *Sulph*
- **stepping** agg.; wide: graph ptk1
- **sticking**: sep ptk1
  - **cough** agg.; during: ign ptk1 *Kali-c* ptk1 lach ptk1 nit-ac ptk1
- **stitching**: alum b4a.de *Apis* b7a.de *Ars* b4.de* bar-c b4a.de* caust b4.de* euphr b7.de* grat bg2 *Kali-c* b4a.de* kali-n b4.de mur-ac b4a.de nat-m b4a.de* *Nux-v* b7a.de phos b4.de* puls b7.de* sil b4.de* sul-ac b4a.de*
- **stool**:
  - **after**:
    - **agg.**: bar-c b4.de* nat-m bg2 sep b4.de*
      - **hours**; for: aesc bro1 am-m bro1 ign bro1 rat bro1 sulph bro1
  - **hard** stool:
    - **after** | **agg.**: coll tl1
  - **impossible**: *Aesc* *Caust* k* *Lach* *Paeon* sul-ac *Thuj*
- **strangulated**: acon c1* *Aesc* **Aloe** k* ars k* bart a1 *Bell* *Canth* bg2 *Caps* bg2 colch bg2 *Coloc* bg2 *Ign* **Lach** k* *Merc* bg2 mez bg2 *Nux-v* k* **Paeon** rat bg2 *Sil* k* *Sulph*
- **suppressed**: (↗*COUGH - Hemorrhoids - disappearance)* abrot vh1* aloe st am-m st apis st ars *Calc* k* *Caps* k* carb-v k* *Coll* hr1* cupr euphr *Ign* hr1* lycps-v c1* *Mill* hr1* **Nat-m** hr1* **Nux-v** k* **Op** hr1* phos puls k* ran-b st rat mrr1 **Sulph** k*
- **suppurating**: anan *Carb-v* *Hep* *Ign* *Merc* **Sil**
- **swollen**: *Aloe* bg2 alum b4.de* ang b7.de* bar-c bg2 *Calc* b4a.de* *Carb-an* b4a.de* **Carb-v** b4.de* caust b4.de* coloc b4.de* ferr bg2 *Graph* bg2 *Kali-c* b4a.de kali-n b4.de* *Mur-ac* b4.de* nit-ac b4a.de* **Nux-v** bg2 *Ph-ac* b4a.de puls b7.de *Sulph* b4a.de
- **tendency** to: caps tl1 dol br1
- **thinking** of them agg.: *Caust* k*
- **thrombotic**: paeon mrr1
- **touch** agg.: abrot k* aloe sne **Bell** k* berb calc calc-sil k2 carb-an *Carbn-s* **Caust** k* graph *Hep* *Kali-c* kali-s fd4.de lil-t lyc merc **Mur-ac** k* nit-ac nux-v paeon k2* phos **Rat** k* sep sil stann h2* sul-ac **Sulph** k* syph **Thuj** k* tritic-vg fd5.de
  - **nates** apart; must hold: bell k2 paeon k2*
- **ulcerating**: aesc k2 alumn k2 carb-v ptk1 *Cham* k* *Hep* **Ign** k* kali-c kali-sil k2 *Lach* nit-ac nux-v bg2 *Paeon* k* ph-ac bg2 phos k* **Puls** bg2 **Sil** k* staph *Sulph* bg2 syph zinc ptk1*

Hemorrhoids: ...

- **urination** agg.: kali-c ptk1
- **voice**; from straining: caust tl1
- **walking**:
  - **agg.**: **Aesc** k* agn alum alum-p k2 androc srj1• ars ars-s-f k2 **Brom** k* calc calc-sil k2 **Carb-an** k* **Caust** k* cycl kali-ar kali-c kali-m k2 **Mur-ac** k* nit-ac phos phys rumx sep k* sil **Sulph** k* sumb ther thuj zinc ptk1
  - **amel.**: **Ign** k*
- **warmth**; external: ars tl1
  - **amel.**: *Ars* k* ign sne lyc ptk1 *Mur-ac* k* nux-v mrr1 petr ptk1 phos ptk1 *Sep* vh zinc ptk1
- **weather**:
  - **warm**:
    - **agg.**: nit-ac
    - **amel.**: *Aesc*
- **white**: carb-v bro1*
- **wine** | **sour** agg.: ant-c k2
- **wiping** after stool agg.: **Aesc** aloe sne **Graph** **Mur-ac** **Paeon** puls *Sulph*

IMPACTED; stool: (↗*ABDOMEN - Impaction)* alum mrr1 calc ptk1 nat-m ptk1 ruta fd4.de sanic ptk1 sel bg2* sep ptk1 sil ptk1

INACTIVITY of rectum: (↗*Constipation; Constipation - difficult; Constipation - stool - remains; Paralysis)* abrom-a ks5 acon b2.de aesc br1 aeth k* agar bg2 agn k* *Aloe* bg3* **Alum** k* alum-sil k2 **Alumn** k* am-c k* am-m k* ambr bg2 **Anac** k* ang b2.de ant-c k* ant-t k* apis bg3 arg-n arist-cl sp1 *Arn* k* asaf k* asim a1 aur k* aur-i k2 aur-s k2 bac bn bamb-a stb2.de• *Bapt* a1 *Bar-c* k* bar-i k2 bar-m bar-s k2 bell k* bov k* **Bry** k* caj a1 *Calc* k* calc-i k2 *Calc-s* calc-sil k2 *Camph* k* canth k* *Carb-an* k* *Carb-v* k* **Carbn-s** carc mg1.de* caust k* **Cham** k* *Chin* k* chinin-s bg2 choc srj3• *Coca* *Cocc* k* coff k* colch k* *Coll* k* con bg2 crot-t dulc k* euphr k* ferr c1 fl-ac fuma-ac rly4• *Gels* **Graph** k* guat dw1* hell helo-s bnm14• **Hep** k* **Hydr** k* hydrog srj2• hyos k* *Ign* k* indol bro1 iod k* kali-bi bg2 *Kali-br* **Kali-c** k* kali-m k2 kali-n k* *Kali-p* kali-s kali-sil k2 kreos k* lac-d *Lach* k* *Lap-a* linu-c a1 lipp a1 *Lyc* k* m-arct b2.de mag-c k* *Mag-m* k* mang k* med k2 meli bg1 merc k* mez k* mosch k* mur-ac k* musca-d szs1 *Nat-c* k* **Nat-m** k* *Nat-p* k* nit-ac k* **Nux-m** k* **Nux-v** k* **Oena** olnd k* **Op** k* ozone sde2• par k* *Petr* k* *Ph-ac* k* **Phos** k* *Phyt* *Plat* k* **Plb** k* plut-n srj7• podo positr nl2• *Psor* k* ptel k* *Puls* k* *Pyrog* k* ran-b bg2 ran-s bg2 *Rat* rheum k* rhod b2.de* rhus-t k* **Ruta** k* sabad k* **Sanic** k* sars k* sec bg3 **Sel** k* seneg k* *Sep* k* **Sil** k* spig k* spong bg2 squil k* stann k* *Staph* k* stram k* stront-c k* sul-ac k* *Sulph* k* sumb *Tab* k* tarax k* **Tarent** k* *Thuj* k* til tub-m vn* ulm-c jsj8• valer k* *Verat* k* verb k* vib k* visc c1 zinc k* zinc-p k2 [heroin sdj2]

- **morning**: staph h1*
- **bending** backward | **amel.**: med jl2
- **chill**; during: alum bg2 cann-xyz bg2 cocc bg2 lyc bg2 nux-v bg2 op bg2 staph bg2 verat bg2

INDURATION:

○ - **Rectum**: alumn br1 *Ars* b4a.de *Sep* b4a.de
  - **sensation** of: caust b4.de*

INEFFECTUAL urging (See Constipation - ineffectual)

INFLAMMATION: *Aesc* bro1 aloe k* alum k* ambr bro1 ant-c k2* bell-p sp1 bop-sc bta1• borx tl1 calc-p bg2 canth k2 carb-an mrr1 colch bro1 coll bro1 cupr bg2 enteroc jl2 ferr-p gamb mrr1 gels k2 *Hep* hydr ip k2 kali-bi bg1 kali-c tl1 kali-i k* lip-as bta1• *Merc* k* merc-c bg2* moni rfm1• nat-s mrr1 *Nit-ac* bro1 ochn-a bta1• *Op* paeon bro1* parathyr jl2 phos bro1* podo bro1* positr nl2• rat mrr1 ric bro1 sabal bro1 sabin k2 sclero-c bta1• sil mrr1 spermc-n bta1• *Sulph* k* syph jl2 thuj mrr1 zing k*

- **chronic**: sil mrr1
- **gangrenous**: lip-as bta1• ochn-a bta1• sclero-c bta1• spermc-n bta1•
- **syphilitic**: bell bro1 merc bro1 *Nit-ac* bro1 sulph bro1

○ - **Anus**: *Coloc* b4a.de *Con* b4a.de
- **Circumanal** glands (See glands)
- **Glands**; perianal: lyc brm
- **Perineum**: plb b7.de*
  - **sensation** as if: alum b4.de*

INSECURITY (See Weakness)

INSENSIBILITY: (↗*Unnoticed)* aloe k* phos k*

Rectum

- **stool**:
  - **during** | **Rectum** and anus: caust bg2

INVOLUNTARY stool: (↗*EXTREMITIES - Paralysis - lower - accompanied - stool)* acon b2.de* agar bg2 agar-ph a1 aids nl2• alco a1 all-s a1 **Aloe** k* alum b4a.de* am-c k* am-caust a1 amyg a1 ant-c b7a.de* ant-t k* *Apis* k* apoc k2* arg-met bg2 arg-n k* **Arn** k* *Ars* k* arum-t k2 atro a1 *Bapt* k* bar-c k* bar-m bar-s k2 **Bell** k* borx h2 *Bry* k* bufo *Calc* k* calc-p bg2 calc-s *Camph* k* *Carb-ac* k* *Carb-v* k* *Caust* k* *Cedr* k* cench k2 *Chel* k* *Chin* k* chinin-ar chinin-s chlf a1* *Cina* k* cocc b2.de* *Colch* k* *Coll* hr1 *Coloc* k* con k* *Cop* k* *Crot-h* k* crot-t k* *Cub* k* *Cupr* k* cupr-ar a1 cycl k* cyt-l a1 *Dig* k* *Dulc* k* euon a1 ferr k* ferr-ar ferr-p gamb k* gels k* glon k* grat k* *Hell* k* hippoc-k szs2 hippoz k* hydr-ac k* **Hyos** k* ign k* ind hr1 iris kali-ar kali-bi k* *Kali-c* k* kali-cy a1 kali-m k2 kali-p k* kali-s lac-c sne lac-e hrn2• *Lach* k* *Laur* k* lyss k* m-aust b2.de manc k* med k* merc k* merc-c k* mosch k* *Mur-ac* k* **Nat-m** k* **Nat-p** k* nat-s k2 *Nux-v* k* oena k* **Olnd** k* **Op** k* *Ox-ac* k* oxyt ptk2 petr k* **Ph-ac** k* **Phos** k* physala-p bnm7• phyt bg2 *Plb* k* *Podo* bg2* positr nl2• *Psor* k* *Puls* k* *Pyrog* k* **Rhus-t** k* rob k* ruta *Sanic* k* sapin a1 **Sec** k* sep k* spong b2.de* squil b2.de* staph k* stram k* stront-c bg2 stry bro1 sul-ac k* **Sulph** k* tab k* tarent k* thal-xyz srj8• thuj ptk1 trom k* *Tub* jl2 **Verat** k* vip bg2* zinc k* zinc-p k2

- **daytime** | **eating**; after: chin
- **morning**: spong hr1 *Zinc* k*
- **night**: arn k* bry k* carb-ac k* carb-an *Chin* k* colch a1 con der a1 hyos mosch nat-m a1 op gk psor k* puls *Rhus-t* k* stram b7a.de
  - **bed** agg.; in: carb-ac k* *Plb* k* *Sulph* k* taosc iwa1• zinc k2
    - **hard** stool: **Aloe Bell** k*
- **bathing** agg.: positr nl2•
- **bending** over, on: *Ruta*
- **bloody** stool: hyos ptk1
- **brain** affections; in: zinc-p k2
- **coition**; after: cedr hr1
- **coma**; with (See MIND - Coma - stool)
- **convulsions**; during: anan vh bufo sne cupr ptk1 lach sne *Oena* k* stry k* tarent a1
- **coughing** or sneezing, on: (↗*sneezing)* bell merc k* ph-ac *Phos* k* rumx spong k* *Squil* k* *Sulph* k* verat
- **delivery**; after: hyos
- **eating** | **after** | **agg.**: *Aloe* chin
  - **while** | **agg.**: ferr
- **excitement** agg.: *Hyos* k* spong fd4.de syc bka1•
- **fever**; with: gels k2 hyos gk
- **flatulence**; as from: ars h2 sulph h2
- **flatus** agg.; passing: acon k* **Aloe** k* *Apoc* ars bg2 bell calc bro1 cann-xyz bg2 *Carb-v* *Caust* k* cench ferr-ma graph bg2 ign k* iod bro1 jatr-c kali-c k* kali-m k2 mur-ac k* *Nat-c* *Nat-m* k* **Nat-p** *Nat-s* k* nux-v k* **Olnd** k* petr-ra shn4• **Ph-ac** k* **Podo** k* pyrog k* *Rhus-t* vh ruta fd4.de sanic k* staph k* sulph k* thuj bg2 *Tub* k* tung-met bdx1• urol-h rwt• **Verat** k*
- **formed** stool: (↗*hard)* *Aloe* k* ars bg2* *Bell* caust bg2* *Coloc* k* hyos bg2*
- **fright**; after: gels k2 **Op** k* *Phos* k* *Verat* k*
- **grief**; from: op
- **hard** stools: (↗*formed)* bell caust k* coloc
- **headache**; during: mosch ptk1
- **laughing** agg.: *Sulph* k*
- **lumps** of: *Aloe* *Coloc*
- **lying** agg.: ox-ac ptk1
- **motion**:
  - **agg.**: apis bry *Ph-ac* *Phos*
    - **children**; in: ph-ac c1*
  - **beginning** of | **agg.**: **Apis** bg2 *Rhus-t* vh
- **mucus** on passing flatus: ruta fd4.de spig h1
- **old** people; in: lac-e hrn2•
- **paralysis**; from: (↗*EXTREMITIES - Paralysis - lower - accompanied - stool)* *Alum* bell *Gels* hr1 hyos k* laur *Nux-v* op **Sec** hr1
- **physical** causes rather than from emotional causes; from: aloe mrr1
- **sleep** agg.; during: aloe sne *Arn* k* *Ars* arum-t k* bell k* *Bry* k* cench chin colch *Con* k* *Hyos* k* lach laur lyss k2 merc mosch k* *Mur-ac* nat-m nat-s k* *Ph-ac* *Phos* **Podo** k* **Psor** k* *Puls* k* *Rhus-t* k* *Sulph* thuj k* *Tub* k* verat zinc
- **sneezing** agg.: (↗*coughing)* *Sulph*

Involuntary: ...

- **solid**, although (See formed)
- **sphincter**; must keep attention on: aloe k2*
- **standing** agg.: aloe ars k* caust b4a.de *Coloc* k* positr nl2•
- **stooping** agg.: *Ruta* k*
- **straining** for stool anymore; when not: agar k2 arg-n k*
- **urination**:
  - **after** | **agg.**: *Aloe* bg2 mur-ac bg2
  - **and** stool: acon ail ptk1 apis *Arg-n* *Arn* *Ars* atro aur bar-c bell bry calc camph carb-v *Chin* k* chinin-ar cina colch con dig *Hyos* *Laur* mosch **Mur-ac** k* nat-m *Olnd* *Ph-ac* *Phos* puls pyrog rhus-t sec stram sulph verat zinc
  - **during** | **agg.**: ail k* *Aloe* k* alum bro1* apis bro1* arg-n k* bell *Carb-ac* carbn-s cic bro1 *Hyos* k* ind k* kali-s fkr2.de *Mur-ac* k* nat-s k* phos positr nl2• squil k* *Sulph* k* verat k* wies a1
- **voluntary** defecation is difficult or impossible; when (See straining)
- **vomiting**; while: amyg a1 arg-n k* ars k* tab hr1
- **walking** agg.: aloe k*
- **yellow**, watery: hyos ptk1

IRRITATION: *Ambr* c2 *Ant-c* c2 arist-m br1 *Brucel* sa3• canth b7.de* *Cina* c2 erig mrr1 med jl2

- **left**: brucel sa3•
- **night**: aral vh1
- **menses** | **before** | **agg.**: sabin bro1
  - **during** | **agg.**: sabin bro1
- **newborns**; in: med jl2

ITCHING: acon k* acon-l a1 **Aesc** k* **Agar** k* agath-a nl2• agn aids nl2• *All-c* **Aloe** k* *Alum* k* alum-p k2 alum-sil k2 alumn k* **Am-c** k* *Am-m* *Ambr* k* anac k* anag a1 anan androc srj1• ang b7.de* *Ant-c* k* ant-t b7.de* anthraq rly4• apis apoc k* arg-met *Arg-n* k* arge-pl rwt5• *Ars* k* *Ars-i* ars-s-f k2 *Asar* b7.de* aur-s k* bapt gk bar-c k* bar-i k2 bar-m bar-s k2 *Bell* k* *Berb* k* borx k* bov k* brom bry k* bufo cact k* cadm-i bro1 cain **Calc** k* calc-act mtf11 *Calc-ar* calc-f k2* *Calc-i* k2 *Calc-p* k* **Calc-s** calc-sil k2 cann-s a1 *Caps* k* carb-ac k* **Carb-v** k* **Carbn-s** carc gk6* card-m *Carl* k* carneg-g rwt1• casc bro1 **Caust** k* cench k2 cham k* *Chel* k* chin k* chinin-ar chinin-s k* *Cic* k* *Cina* k* cinnb cist *Clem* k* coc-c k* cocc k* coff *Colch* k* coli rly4• *Coll* k* coloc k* con k* cop br1* *Croc* crot-t k* cub c1 cupr b7.de* del a1 dict a1 dios k* *Dulc* elaps elat hr1 *Euph* k* eupi a1 ferr k* ferr-ar ferr-i k2* ferr-m k* ferr-ma k* ferr-p ferul a1 **Fl-ac** k* gink-b sbd1• *Gran* k* **Graph** k* grat k* haliae-lc srj5• *Ham* k* hep hir rsj4• hom-xyz bro1 hydrc k* *Ign* k* *Indg* bro1 *Iod* k* *Ip* jac-c k* jug-r k* *Kali-ar* kali-bi k* **Kali-c** k* kali-m k2 kali-n k* kali-p **Kali-s** ketogl-ac rly4• *Lach* k* lap-la sde8.de• laur b7.de* led lil-t lipp a1 lith-c **Lyc** k* mag-c k* *Mag-m* maias-l hrn2• med k* meny b7.de* *Merc* k* merc-c a1 merl a1 *Mez* k* *Mill* morg-g pte1• morph k* *Mur-ac* k* naja *Nat-ar* **Nat-c** k* *Nat-m* k* *Nat-p* k* nat-pyru rly4• nat-s k* **Nit-ac** k* **Nux-v** k* op k* ox-ac k* oxal-a rly4• *Paeon* k* *Petr* k* ph-ac k* phel k* phos k* pin-s a1* *Plat* k* plb k* plut-n srj7• polyg-h bro1 prot jl2 prun k* psor k* **Puls** rad-br bro1 ran-s k* *Rat* k* rhodi a1 rhus-t k* *Rhus-v* k* *Rumx* k* *Ruta* k* *Sabad* k* sabin *Sacch* bro1* sangin-n bro1 sapin a1 *Sars* sec k* sel rsj9• *Sep* k* serp k* *Sil* k* sin-a k* *Spig* k* spira a1 *Spong* k* squil k* *Stann* k* *Staph* k* suis-pan rly4• *Sul-ac* *Sul-i* k* **Sulph** k* symph fd3.de* syph tab k* tell a1* ter bro1 *Teucr* k* *Thuj* k* tritic-vg fd5.de *Tub* uran-n c2* urt-u k* valer b7.de* vanil fd5.de verb c1 visc sp1 wye k* *Zinc* k* zing [spect dfg1]

- **daytime**: pyrid rly4• **Sulph** k*
- **morning**: agar bar-ox-suc rly4• carb-v carbn-s cench dulc fd4.de ham fd3.de• jac-c k* lach k* laur a1 nat-m k* spong fd4.de *Sulph* k* symph fd3.de• tritic-vg fd5.de
  - **bed** agg.; in: carb-v k* sacch-a fd2.de•
- **forenoon**: dios k* dulc fd4.de paeon vanil fd5.de
- **evening**: aids nl2• alumn k* borx *Calc-p* k* cham croc k* dulc fd4.de ham fd3.de• *Iod* kali-bi k* kali-c h2* kali-p fd1.de• lyc k* nux-v k* phos k* *Plat* k* *Puls* ran-s k* sil k* sin-a a1 spong fd4.de *Sulph* k* symph fd3.de• thuj k* tritic-vg fd5.de vanil fd5.de zinc k* zinc-p k2
  - **bed** agg.; in: aln vva1• ant-c cain calc-p k* cinnb *Ign* k* jug-r vml3• kali-p fd1.de• *Lyc* *Nat-m* petr plat sin-a a1 *Sulph* *Teucr*
- **night**: agar k* aloe alum alumn ant-c k* calc-f k* carbn-s con h2* *Ferr* k* fl-ac *Ign* indg c1 irid-met srj5• kali-i a1 kali-p fd1.de• mosch bg1 *Nat-p* petr k* phos pitu-a vml2• rhus-v k* sacch-a fd2.de• sapin a1 spong fd4.de *Sulph* k* tritic-vg fd5.de [spect dfg1]

- **night**: ...
  - **midnight** | **before**: thuj k*
- **accompanied** by | **stool**; complaints of (See STOOL - Complaints - accompanied - rectum - itching)
- **alternating** with:
  - **constriction** of rectum (See Constriction - alternating - itching)
  - ○ **Ear**; itching in (See EAR - Itching - meatus - alternating with - anus)
  - **Nose**; itching in (See NOSE - Itching - alternating - anus)
- **ascarides**, from: anth c1 *Calc* calc-f chin *Ferr* k* graph h2* ign indg c1 irid-met srj5• laur c1 med jl2 mez c1 *Nat-p* nit-ac h2* psor al2 *Sabad* sacch mtf sin-a sulph h2* *Teucr* *Urt-u* k*
- **burning**: *Agar* aloe k2 *Alum* ant-c ars k2 *Berb* bufo calc carbn-s chin k* cocc k* cop a1 *Dulc* hr1 euph h2* gink-b sbd1• gran a1 *Iod* jug-r k* kali-c kali-p fd1.de• limest-b es1• lyc k* merl a1 mur-ac nat-c h2* *Olnd* paeon rhus-v sars k* **Sulph** k* *Thuj*
  - **friction**; after: cic c1
- **coition**; after: anac k*
- **cold** bathing amel.: aloe caust fl-ac petr hr1 **Sulph** mrr1
- **dinner**; after: caust k*
- **discharge** of moisture, after: *Sulph* k*
- **dreadful**: slag c1
- **hemorrhoids**; from: *Acon* bg2 *Aesc* bro1 *Aloe* bg2* ars bg2 caps b7.de* carb-v bg2* caust bro1 cina bg2 cop br1* dulc fd4.de euphr b7.de* *Fl-ac* bg2 glon bro1 **Graph** b4.de* *Ham* bro1 ign b7.de* iod bg2 *Lyc* bg2 *M-ambo* b7.de* m-aust b7.de morg-g pte1*• morg-p pte1*• mur-ac bro1* nit-ac bro1 *Nux-v* bg2* *Petros* br1* phos b4.de* plan mtf11 plb b7.de* polyg-h bg2 prot pte1* puls b7.de* rhus-t b7.de* sep b4.de* sil b4.de* sul-ac b4.de* **Sulph** bg2* tritic-vg fd5.de
  - **menses**; during: phos b4a.de
- **leukorrhea** agg.: cop br1
- **menses** | **before** | **agg.**: graph ptk1
  - **during** | **agg.**: carb-v phos h2
- **pain**, ending in: *Zinc* k*
- **painful**: bell h1*
- **riding** agg.: bov k*
- **rubbing** agg.: *Alum* petr k*
- **scratching** agg.: *Agar* *Alum* k* alum-sil k2 arg-met ars bar-c calc *Caps* carb-v carc gk6 *Caust* chel con merc *Mez* mur-ac nat-c petr k* ph-ac phos **Puls** k* rhus-t rhus-v sep *Sil* stann *Staph* **Sulph**
- **sitting** agg.: ham fd3.de• jac-c k* *Staph* k* sulph h2*
- **sleep**:
  - **after** | **agg.**: carb-v h2* *Lach*
  - **going** to sleep; on | **agg.**: petr
  - **preventing**: merc pd teucr ptk1
- **stool**:
  - **after**:
    - **agg.**: agar k* aloe alum bar-ox-suc rly4• berb bov cain calc carb-v carbn-s clem k* *Euph* eupi k* glech bg1 *Kali-c* kali-m k2 kali-s fd4.de kali-sil k2 kalm ptk1 lyc mag-m k* mang-p rly4• *Merc* *Mur-ac* *Nat-m* k* nicc k* nit-ac k* pic-ac k* plat ptel k* pycnop-sa mrz1 sec k* *Sil* k* sin-a a1 sinus rly4• spira a1 *Staph* sulph tell k* ter *Teucr* thuj k* visc c1 zinc k*
      - **Rectum** and anus: bry bg2 coloc bg2 kali-bi bg2
    - **amel.**: clem
  - **before**: euph k* ozone sde2• sin-a a1 *Spong*
  - **during**:
    - **agg.**: kali-c merc mur-ac nat-m k* phos pic-ac k* sil k* spira a1 spong fd4.de *Sulph* k* teucr zinc ptk2
      - **Rectum** and anus: valer bg2
  - **urging** to: euph h2
- **stooping** agg.: arg-met k*
- **supper** agg.; after: kali-c h2*
- **violent**: aloe k2
- **voluptuous**: *Agar* *Alum* ambr arg-met *Carb-v* cina merc mur-ac petr plat *Puls* sep *Sil* spig **Sulph**
- **walking**:
  - **about** | **must** walk about: jug-r vml3•
  - **agg.**: aesc kali-bi nat-m nit-ac nux-v phos rhus-t a1 spong fd4.de

Itching – walking: ...
  - **air** agg.; in open: arg-met bell h1 nit-ac spong fd4.de
- **warm** bed agg.: *Alum* cain calc-p carb-v *Ign* kali-p fd1.de• lap-la sde8.de• *Lyc* *Nat-p* *Petr* *Sulph* k* *Teucr*
- **worms**; from (See ascarides)
- **worms**; like: arg-met bg2 hir rsj4• sulph bg2

▽ - **extending** to:
  - ○ **Urethra**; into | **stool** agg.; during: thuj k*

○ - **Anus**; around: abrom-a ks5 **Acon** bg2 aesc tl1 agar b4.de* agn **Aloe** bg2 *Alum* b4.de* am-c b4.de* am-m b7a.de *Ambr* b7.de* *Anac* b4a.de ant-c b7.de* *Apis* b7a.de arg-n bg2 *Ars* bg2 aur bg2 bacls-10 pte1*• bamb-a stb2.de• **Bar-c** b4.de* bell b4.de* *Berb* borx b4a.de* *Brucel* sa3• bry k* bufo-s **Calc** b4.de* calc-act c2 caps b7.de* carb-v b4.de* *Caust* b4.de* cham b7.de* chin b7.de* *Cina* b7.de* cocc b7.de* colch b7.de* coll tl1* **coloc** bg2 con b4.de* cop c2 cortiso gse croc b7a.de* cypra-eg sde6.de• des-ac mtf11 **euph** b4.de* *Ferr* bg2 *Fl-ac* k* flor-p rsj3• gaert pte1*• *Graph* b4.de* grat bg2 hir rsj4• hydroph rsj6• *Ign* b7.de* iod b4a.de kali-bi bg2 *Kali-c* b4.de* kola stb3• lyc k* m-ambo b7.de m-aust b7.de *Mag-c* b4a.de med ptk1 meny b7.de* **Merc** b4.de* merc-c b4a.de* *Mez* k* morg fmm1• morg-g fmm1• morg-p pte1*• mur-ac b4.de* nat-c b4.de* nat-m bg2 nat-p tl1 nat-pyru rly4• nat-s **Nit-ac** b4.de* *Nux-v* k* op k* ozone sde2• paeon tl1 pen br1 **Petr** k* ph-ac b4.de* phos b4.de* pin-s c2 plat b4.de* prot pte1* psor bg2* puls b7.de* ran-s b7.de* rham-f c2 rhodi-o-n c2 *Rhus-t* b7.de* *Sabad* b7.de* *Sacch* br1 samb bat1• sars b4.de* seneg b4.de* *Sep* b4.de* serp sil b4a.de* sin-a c2 slag c2 spig b7.de* spong b7a.de* squil b7.de* stann b4.de* staph b7.de* suis-pan rly4• **Sulph** k* symph br1 tab bg2 tarax *Teucr* b7.de* **Thuj** bg2 *Trios* rsj11• tritic-vg fd5.de tub jl2 uran-n c2 *Verb* c2 viol-o ptk1 **Zinc** b4.de*
  - **evening**: sel rsj9•
  - **night**: trios rsj11•
    - **aroused** at: indg br1
  - **bathing**: abrom-a ks5
  - **eating**; after: caust b4a.de
  - **moon**; full: *Sulph* b4a.de
  - **stick**; as from a: rumx ptk1
  - **stool** | **after** | **agg.**: agar bg2 clem bg2 euph b4.de* lyc bg2 *Mag-m* bg2 nat-m bg2 nit-ac b4.de* ozone sde2• sec bg2 sil bg2 teucr b7a.de* thuj bg2 visc bg2 zinc bg2
    - **during** | **agg.**: alum b4.de* ars bg2 cic bg2 euph b4.de* *Merc* b4.de* nat-m bg2 op b7.de* phos bg2 sil b4a.de* sulph b4a.de*
  - **voluptuous**: bamb-a stb2.de•
  - **warm** bed agg.: *Petr*
  - ○ **Vulva**; and (See FEMALE - Itching - vulva - and)
- **Perineum**: agar a1 agn k* *Alum* k* ang ant-c b7.de* ant-t b7.de* ars k* bell k* cann-s k* canth k* carb-v k* *Chel* k* cina con k* falco-pe nl2• *Fl-ac* k* gran k* ign k* kali-c k* mur-ac k* nat-c k* *Nat-s* k* nux-v k* **Petr** k* plb k* prot pte1• *Sars* k* seneg k* **Sulph** k* tarax b7.de* tep k* thuj k* vanil fd5.de
  - **forenoon**: thuj k*
  - **night**: *Carb-v* k* con h2* kali-c k* petr
  - **scratching** agg.: alum k*
    - **after**, pain: alum k* tarax h1*
  - **stool** | **after** | **agg.**: tell bg1*
    - **during** | **agg.**: *Sulph*
  - **touch** agg.: *Carb-v* k*
  - **walking** agg.: ign k*

JERKING: | **Rectum** and anus: bry bg2 nux-v bg2 zinc bg2

LAUGHING agg.: lach ptk1

LIQUID; sensation of: | **Rectum** and anus: aloe bg2

LOOSE; sensation of being: **Aloe** bg2

LUMP; sensation of a: (↗*Foreign; Plug; Weight*) aloe k* anac k* apoc k* bamb-a stb2.de• bry k* cann-i k* cann-xyz bg2 *Caust* k* chin bg2* coll bg2 crot-h bg2* *Crot-t* k* falco-pe nl2• gamb bg2* hell bg2* hydrog srj2• *Kali-bi* k* kali-br tl1 *Lach* k* lil-t k* med nat-c bg2* *Nat-m* k* nicotam rly4• phos bg2* plat bg2* positr nl2• rumx k* ruta fd4.de sacch sang sarr seneg bg2 **Sep** k* *Sil* k* sul-ac bg1 sulph k* ther k* thuj bg2*
- **heavy** | **Rectum** and anus: plat bg2 sep bg2
- **lying** on back agg.: ars-i vh

Rectum

- **menses**; during: _Sil_ k*
- **pregnancy** agg.; during: sep mrr1
- **sitting** agg.: cann-i cann-xyz ptk1 kali-bi lach nat-m
- **standing** agg.: _Lil-t_ k*
- **stool**:
  - **before**: _Lach_ k*
  - **not** amel. by stool: **Sep** k*
- **urging** for urination, with: lil-t ptk1

○ - **Anus**: _Sep_ ptk1
- **Perineum**: arg-n bg1 cann-xyz ptk1 **Chim** hr1* (non:chin ptk2) kali-m ptk1 _Ther_ pd* thuj b4a.de*
  - **sitting** agg.: chim ptk1*
- **Sphincter**; posterior side of: med br1

LYING:
- **agg.** | **Rectum** and anus: graph bg2 ign bg2 sep bg2 sulph bg2

MENSES:
- **after**:
  ○ • **Perineum**: berb bg2 cocc bg2 ferr-p bg2 graph bg2 plat bg2 puls bg2
  • **Rectum** and anus: ars bg2 berb bg2 cocc bg2 ferr-p bg2 graph bg2 plat bg2 puls bg2 zinc bg2
- **before**:
  ○ • **Perineum**: am-c bg2 ars bg2 caul bg2 chin bg2 cocc bg2 ign bg2 _Lach_ bg2 petr bg2 phos bg2 puls bg2 sep bg2 thuj bg2
  • **Rectum** and anus: am-c bg2 ars bg2 caul bg2 chin bg2 cocc bg2 ign bg2 _Lach_ bg2 petr bg2 phos bg2 puls bg2 sep bg2 thuj bg2
- **during**:
  ○ • **Perineum**: aloe bg2 am-c bg2 am-m bg2 ars bg2 asar bg2 aur bg2 _Berb_ bg2 brom bg2 cact bg2 **Carb-v** bg2 caul bg2 cocc bg2 colch bg2 elaps bg2 **Graph** bg2 ham bg2 ign bg2 ip bg2 kreos bg2 **Lach** bg2 nux-v bg2 phos bg2 podo bg2 _Puls_ bg2 sep bg2 sil bg2 ter bg2 thuj bg2 zinc bg2
  • **Rectum** and anus: aloe bg2 am-c bg2 am-m bg2 ars bg2 asar bg2 aur bg2 _Berb_ bg2 _Bov_ bg2 brom bg2 cact bg2 **Carb-v** bg2 caul bg2 cocc bg2 colch bg2 elaps bg2 eupi bg2 **Graph** bg2 ham bg2 ign bg2 ip bg2 kreos bg2 **Lach** bg2 lys bg2 nux-v bg2 phos bg2 podo bg2 _Puls_ bg2 sep bg2 sil bg2 ter bg2 thuj bg2 zinc bg2

MENTAL EXERTION agg.: | **Rectum** and anus: _Nux-v_ bg2 podo bg2

MOISTURE: (↗_Catarrh_) acon _Aesc_ k* agar _Aloe_ k* _Alum_ k* alum-p k2 alum-sil k2 am-c am-m bro1 anac k* **Ant-c** k* apis ars aur aur-ar k2 aur-m k2 aur-s k2 bapt _Bar-c_ k* _Bar-m_ bar-s k2 bell k* _Borx_ bry _Calc_ k* calc-p _Calc-s_ calc-sil k2 _Canth_ _Caps_ k* _Carb-an_ k* **Carb-v** k* **Carbn-s** carl **Caust** k* chel chin chinin-ar clem coc-c coff _Colch_ coloc k* cor-r cypra-eg sde6.de• _Dios_ k* dulc ferr ferr-ar ferr-p gink-b sbd1• **Graph** k* _Hell_ **Hep** k* ign kali-p k2 _Lach_ led lyc med k* meli _Merc_ _Merc-c_ mill _Mur-ac_ _Nat-m_ k* **Nit-ac** k* nit-m-ac bro1 _Nux-v_ _Op_ ptk1 _Paeon_ k* _Petr_ _Phos_ k* _Phyt_ podo _Puls_ ran-s k* _Rat_ k* rhod b4.de rhus-g tmo3• rhus-t **Sep** k* **Sil** k* spig stann sul-ac k* sul-i ptk1 **Sulph** k* syph _Thuj_ k* zinc zinc-p k2
- **evening**: carb-an k* dios
- **night**: _Carb-v_ kali-p fd1.de• nat-m sulph h2*
- **acrid**: ars-s-f k2 _Carb-v_ k* chin b7.de* lach bg1 _Merc-c_ _Nit-ac_ sulph mrr1 _Thuj_ zinc k*
- **black**: merc-i-f ptk1
- **bloody**: alum apis ptk1 _Carl_ op mtf33 puls mtf33 sabad _Sil_ thuj
- **burning**: sulph k2
- **cadaverous** odor: sil h2*
- **colored**:
  - **dark**: med mtf33
  - **orange**: kali-p k2
- **constant**: sep ptk1
- **fetid**: _Calc_ vh kali-p k2 med br1* paeon vh sep vh
- **fishy** odor: hydrog srj2• med mtf33
- **flatus**; from: all-c _Ant-c_ k* _Carb-v_ k* sulph k2 zinc
- **glutinous**: carb-an h2* _Carb-v_ k* **Graph** kali-bi bg1 rhus-g tmo3•
- **herring** brine, smelling like: _Calc_ k* _Med_
- **ichorous**: _Ferr_ vh
- **menses**; during: **Lach** k*
  - **orange**-colored: kali-p pd

Moisture: ...
- **mucus**:
  - **bloody**: op ptk1
  - **offensive**: hep ptk1
  - **urination** agg.; during: carb-ac ptk1
- **musty** odor: _Carb-v_
- **offensive**: _Ant-c_ ptk1 hep ptk1 paeon ptk1 sul-i ptk1

○ • **Glands**; anal: nit-ac tl1 paeon tl1 sil tl1
- **scratching** agg.: _Alum_ **Carb-v** _Caust_ vh dulc **Graph** _Lyc_ _Merc_ _Nat-m_ _Nit-ac_ _Petr_ rhus-t _Sep_ sil sul-ac **Sulph** _Thuj_
- **stool** | **after** | **agg.**: bar-c h2* borx _Graph_ hep h2* _Sep_ k* stann sumb zinc
  - **before**: kali-c
- **warm**: _Acon_ ptk1
- **wine** agg.; sour: ant-c k2
- **yellow**: rhus-g tmo3•
  - **staining**: ant-c ptk1

○ - **Perineum**: carb-an k* _Carb-v_ k* paeon ptk1 thuj ptk1
  - **night**: _Carb-v_

MOTION agg.: | **Rectum** and anus: podo bg2 puls bg2

NO DESIRE FOR STOOL (See Inactivity)

NODULES: | **Perineum**: _Ant-c_ b7a.de

NUMBNESS:
○ - **Anus**: acon k* aloe k2 carb-ac caust ptk1 phos
- **Perineum**: _Coloc_ b4a.de

OBSTRUCTED, closed up; sensation as if: anac bg2 nat-c b4.de* op b7.de* phos b4.de* sep b4.de*
○ - **Rectum** and anus: hell bg2 lach bg2

OPEN anus: (↗_Relaxed_) aesc ail ptk1 **Aloe** ptk1 alum ptk1 apis ptk1 flor-p rsj3• gels tl1 ign ptk1 kali-c ptk1 op ptk1* **Phos** k ●* _Sec_ k* sol-t-ae
- **accompanied** by | **stool**; involuntary: apoc ptk1
- **involuntary** stool; after: apis tl1 chin tl1 phos tl1
- **sensation** of: ail bg1 aloe _Apis_ k* apoc k* **Phos** k ●* puls sec bro1 sol-t bro1 sumb k* trom bro1
  - **stool** agg.; after: apoc ozone sde2• podo fd3.de• sumb
- **standing** agg.: apis bg2 _Phos_ bg2

PAIN: abies-c ↓ acal ↓ acon k* acon-l ↓ **Aesc** k* aeth ↓ agar k* agar-ph ↓ agath-a nl2• agn ↓ agro ↓ aids ↓ alet k2* all-c allox ↓ _Aloe_ k* _Alum_ alum-p k2 alum-sil ↓ _Alumn_ k* am-br ↓ **Am-c** am-m ambr b7.de* anac anan ↓ ancis-p ↓ androc srj1• ang ↓ _Ango_ ↓ ant-c k* ant-s-aur ↓ ant-t ↓ anthraq ↓ aphis ↓ **Apis** ↓ apoc ↓ aq-mar rbp6 _Arg-met_ ↓ **Arg-n** ↓ arge-pl ↓ arist-cl ↓ arist-m ↓ arn k* _Ars_ k* ars-i k* ars-s-f ↓ arum-d ↓ arum-t ↓ arund ↓ asaf ↓ asar ↓ asc-t ↓ aspar ↓ _Atis_ ↓ _Atro_ ↓ aur ↓ aur-ar k2 aur-i ↓ aur-m ↓ aur-s ↓ bac ↓ bamb-a stb2.de• bapt ↓ bar-c bar-i k2 bar-m bar-s ↓ bell ben ↓ _Benz-ac_ ↓ berb k* _Bit-ar_ ↓ bond ↓ borx ↓ bov bg2 **Brom** _Brucel_ ↓ bry k* _Bufo_ cact cadm-met ↓ cain ↓ calad calc k* calc-f k2 calc-p k* calc-s calc-sil ↓ camph k* cann-i ↓ cann-s ↓ canth k* _Caps_ carb-ac ↓ _Carb-an_ _Carb-v_ k* _Carbn-s_ carc ↓ _Card-m_ ↓ carl cartl-s rly4• cassia-s ccrh1• _Castm_ ↓ **Caust** cean ↓ cedr ↓ cench ↓ cham chel k* chin k* chin-b ↓ chinin-ar chinin-s ↓ chlf ↓ choc ↓ chord-umb rly4• chr-ac cic ↓ cimic cina ↓ cinnb ↓ clem ↓ cob ↓ cob-n ↓ coc-c ↓ cocc _Coch_ ↓ coff ↓ colch k* **Coll** k* _Coloc_ k* colocin ↓ con k* convo-s ↓ _Cop_ ↓ _Corn_ ↓ cortiso ↓ _Croc_ _Crot-h_ ↓ **Crot-t** ↓ cub ↓ cuph br1 cupr k* cupr-ar ↓ cycl cystein-l rly4• cyt-l ↓ der ↓ dig ↓ dios k* dirc ↓ dol ↓ dor a1 _Dros_ ↓ dulc elaps ↓ elat ↓ enteroc ↓ erig ↓ ery-a ↓ eucal ↓ eug ↓ euon ↓ _Eup-per_ ↓ eup-pur ↓ _Euph_ ↓ euphr k* eupi a1 fago ↓ falco-pe nl2• ferr ferr-ar ferr-i k2 ferr-m ↓ ferr-ma ↓ ferr-p ferul ↓ form ↓ gal-ac ↓ **Gamb** ↓ gels ↓ gent-l ↓ ger-i rly4• gins ↓ gran ↓ **Graph** k* grat guat ↓ ham hell k* _Hep_ ↓ hist ↓ hydr a1 hydrc ↓ hyos ↓ hyper ↓ **Ign** k* indg ↓ inul c2 iod _Ip_ ↓ irid-met ↓ iris jac-c ↓ jal ↓ jatr-c ↓ _Jug-c_ ↓ jug-r ↓ _Kali-ar_ kali-bi _Kali-br_ ↓ **Kali-c** kali-chl k* _Kali-i_ ↓ kali-m k2 _Kali-n_ k* kali-p kali-s kali-sil k2 kiss ↓ kola ↓ kreos bg2 kurch bnj1 lac-ac k* lac-c ↓ lac-h ↓ lac-leo hrn2• lach k* lachn ↓ lact ↓ laur ↓ led br1 lepi ↓ _Lept_ ↓ liat ↓ lil-s a1 _Lil-t_ k* lim ↓ linu-c ↓ lipp ↓ lith-c ↓ lob ↓ loxo-recl ↓ **Lyc** k* lycps-v ↓ _Lyss_ ↓ m-arct ↓ mag-c k* mag-m b4.de* mag-p k2 mag-s ↓ _Manc_ ↓ mand ↓ mang ↓ med medul-os-si ↓ mela ↓ melal-alt gya4 _Meli_ ↓ menis ↓ _Merc_ k* merc-br ↓ merc-c a1 merc-cy a1 merc-d ↓ merc-i-f ↓ merc-n ↓ merc-sul ↓ merl ↓ mez k* mill mit ↓ morph ↓ morph-s ↓ mosch ↓ _Mur-ac_ _Murx_ ↓ naja ↓ nat-ar k2 nat-c k* nat-hchls ↓ nat-m k* nat-p nat-s ↓ nat-sil ↓ nicc ↓ nicotam rly4• _Nit-ac_ k* nuph ↓ _Nux-m_ ↓ _Nux-v_ k* oena ↓

Pain: ...
ol-an↓ *Olnd*↓ onis↓ onos↓ *Op*↓ ost↓ ox-ac↓ ozone↓ **Paeon** pall↓ pen↓ **Petr**↓ petros↓ ph-ac k* phasco-ci↓ phel k* *Phos* k* phys k* phyt k* pic-ac↓ pin-s↓ pip-m↓ plac-s rly4• plan↓ plat k2 plb plb-chr↓ *Podo* positr↓ pot-e↓ propr↓ *Prun*↓ prun-p c2 *Psor* ptel↓ **Puls** k* pyrog↓ rad-br↓ ran-b↓ ran-s↓ *Rat* k* rauw↓ rham-f↓ rheum↓ rhod↓ rhus-t k* rhus-v k* *Rob*↓ rumx *Ruta* sabad k* sabin↓ sacch-a↓ sang↓ sangin-n↓ sanic↓ saroth↓ sarr↓ sars k* sec k* sel↓ senec↓ seneg senn↓ *Sep* k* sil sin-a↓ sin-n↓ sol-ni↓ sol-t↓ sol-t-ae a1 spect↓ spig↓ spira↓ spirae↓ spong fd4.de squil↓ stann k* staph bg2 stict c2 still a1 stram↓ stront-c k* stry a1 suis-em↓ sul-ac sul-i↓ **Sulph** k* sumb suprar rly4• syc fmm1• symph↓ syph k* tab↓ tarent k* tax↓ tep↓ *Ter*↓ *Teucr*↓ ther k* **Thuj** k* til↓ tong↓ trios rsj11• tritic-vg fd5.de trom↓ tub↓ urt-u↓ valer vanil fd5.de verat↓ verat-v↓ verb↓ vib↓ vichy-g↓ vip a1 visc↓ voes↓ wies↓ xan↓ xero↓ zinc zinc-p k2 zinc-s↓ zing

- **daytime**:
  - • **walking** agg.: nat-m↓
    - ⋮ **burning**: nat-m
- **morning**: aeth↓ agar↓ *Calc*↓ calc-p k* carb-ac↓ colch↓ corn a1 dios k* dor↓ dulc fd4.de glycyr-g↓ graph↓ ham fd3.de• hyper↓ *Kali-bi* kali-p↓ lyc↓ mag-c↓ mag-m↓ mang↓ melal-alt gya4 **Mur-ac**↓ nat-m a1 nat-sil↓ nicc↓ **Nit-ac**↓ ost↓ ph-ac↓ podo ruta fd4.de *Sulph*↓ thuj↓ tritic-vg fd5.de vanil fd5.de vichy-g↓ zinc↓
  - • **7** h: lac-leo hrn2• nat-m
  - • **bed** agg.; in: colch↓ *Graph*↓
    - ⋮ **burning**: colch k*
    - ⋮ **cutting** pain: *Graph* k*
  - • **burning**: *Calc* a1 carb-ac k* colch k* dios a1 dor a1 dulc fd4.de glycyr-g cte1• hyper k* mag-m k* **Mur-ac** k* nat-sil fd3.de• nicc k* **Nit-ac** k* *Sulph* k* thuj k*
  - • **cutting** pain: graph k* lyc h2* mang
  - • **pressing** pain: *Kali-bi* k* ruta fd4.de
  - • **rising** agg.; after: aeth↓ mang↓
    - ⋮ **cutting** pain: mang
    - ⋮ **tenesmus**: aeth k*
  - • **sore**: *Calc-p* podo fd3.de• thuj k* vanil fd5.de
  - • **stitching** pain: kali-p fd1.de• lyc k* mag-c k* thuj a1 vichy-g a1 zinc k*
  - • **stool** | **after** | **agg.**: *Kali-bi* melal-alt gya4
    - ⋮ **during** | **agg.**: but-ac br1 *Podo*
  - • **tearing** pain: melal-alt gya4 ph-ac k*
  - • **tenesmus**: aeth k* agar a1 nicc k* ost a1
  - • **waking** agg.; after: mag-c↓
    - ⋮ **stitching** pain: mag-c k*
- **forenoon**: *Calc*↓ kali-bi lach↓ nat-m ruta fd4.de sep↓ thuj k*
  - • **10** h | **sitting** agg.: **Sep**
  - • **griping** pain: *Calc*
  - • **pressing** pain: kali-bi k* ruta fd4.de
  - • **stitching** pain: calc h2* lach k* sep h2*
  - • **walking** agg.: *Sulph*↓
    - ⋮ **cutting** pain: *Sulph*
- **noon**: agar↓ dios↓ kali-bi↓
  - • **burning**: dios k*
  - • **pressing** pain: agar k* kali-bi k*
- **afternoon**: agar↓ agath-a nl2• bamb-a↓ chel chinin-s↓ *Cocc* coloc↓ cycl dulc fd4.de euphr↓ fago↓ ham↓ lyc↓ nat-m↓ sep↓ *Sulph*↓
  - • **14** h: dios↓
    - ⋮ **burning**: dios
  - • **burning**: coloc k* dulc fd4.de euphr k* fago a1 ham fd3.de• *Sulph* k*
  - • **cutting** pain: sep sulph k*
  - • **griping** pain: *Cocc*
  - • **pressing** pain: chel k* cycl k* sep h2* sulph k*
  - • **sleep** | **after**:
    - ⋮ **agg.**: chin↓
      - . **burning**: chin k*
    - ⋮ **during**:
      - ⋮ **agg.**: cycl↓

- **afternoon** – **sleep** – **during** – **agg.**: ...
      - . **pressing** pain: cycl
  - • **stitching** pain: agar bamb-a stb2.de• chinin-s lyc k* nat-m k* sulph k*
- **evening**: agath-a nl2• bamb-a↓ bar-c↓ benz-ac↓ borx↓ calc↓ calc-p↓ *Carb-an*↓ carb-v k* carbn-s↓ chinin-s↓ choc↓ dios k* dulc fd4.de ferr↓ glycyr-g↓ gran↓ ham fd3.de• *Iod*↓ iris↓ kali-bi↓ kali-c↓ *Lach* k* merc-c↓ mez *Mur-ac*↓ nat-hchls↓ nat-m↓ nit-ac↓ nux-v k* ost↓ ph-ac↓ phos↓ plat↓ ran-s↓ sang↓ spong fd4.de *Sulph* teucr↓ thuj↓ vanil fd5.de visc c1 zinc↓
  - • **19** h: glycyr-g↓
    - ⋮ **burning**: glycyr-g cte1•
  - • **bed** agg.; in: ant-c↓ iod↓ *Nat-m*↓ sin-a↓
    - ⋮ **burning**: ant-c h2* sin-a a1
    - ⋮ **pressing** pain: iod k*
    - ⋮ **stitching** pain: *Nat-m*
  - • **burning**: bar-c k* *Carb-an* k* dulc fd4.de glycyr-g cte1• *Iod* k* kali-c k* *Mur-ac* k* nit-ac k* *Sulph* k* thuj zinc
  - • **cutting** pain: nat-hchls phos sang a1 vanil fd5.de
  - • **griping** pain: mez k*
  - • **lying** agg.: *Ign* k*
  - • **pressing** pain: calc h2* chinin-s ran-s k* spong fd4.de vanil fd5.de
  - • **sore**: bar-c k* *Carb-an* k* choc srj3• kali-bi k* *Sulph* vanil fd5.de zinc k*
  - • **stitching** pain: bamb-a stb2.de• benz-ac k* borx calc-p k* carb-v k* carbn-s gran k* iris kali-c h2* merc-c k* nat-m k* nit-ac **Sulph** k* teucr a1 thuj k* zinc k*
  - • **tearing** pain: ph-ac k*
  - • **tenesmus**: ferr ost a1 plat k*
- **night**: acon-l↓ agath-a nl2• am-c↓ ant-c↓ *Ars*↓ bov↓ coch↓ dulc fd4.de *Iod*↓ irid-met↓ kali-c↓ *Lyc*↓ *Merc*↓ mosch k* nat-m h2* *Nit-ac*↓ ox-ac k* phel↓ ptel↓ *Puls* ruta↓ sars↓ sep↓ spong fd4.de stry↓ **Sulph**↓ thuj↓ vanil fd5.de zinc↓
  - • **22** h: aloe↓
    - ⋮ **cutting** pain: aloe
  - • **midnight**: nux-v k* thuj↓
    - ⋮ **after**:
      - ⋮ **3** h: lac-h↓
        - . **tenesmus**: lac-h sk4•
      - ⋮ **4** h: *Mag-c*
    - ⋮ **before**: thuj↓
      - ⋮ **burning**: thuj
      - ⋮ **stool** agg.; after: op↓
        - . **burning**: op
    - ⋮ **stitching** pain: thuj
  - • **bed** agg.; in: dulc↓ kali-c↓
    - ⋮ **burning**: dulc fd4.de kali-c k2
  - • **burning**: am-c k* ant-c k* *Ars* dulc fd4.de *Iod* kali-c h2* nat-m k* *Nit-ac* k* ox-ac k* puls **Sulph**
  - • **cutting** pain: sep k*
  - • **lying** agg.: **Ars**↓ *Puls*↓
    - ⋮ **stinging**: **Ars** *Puls*
  - • **pressing** pain: *Lyc* k* mosch a1 ptel bg1 spong fd4.de
  - • **sore**: ant-c h2* irid-met srj5• phel k* ruta fd4.de sars k*
  - • **stitching** pain: kali-c mrr1 sep k* stry thuj vanil fd5.de
  - • **tenesmus**: acon-l a1 bov k* coch hr1 *Merc* zinc k*
- **accompanied** by:
  - • **respiration**; complaints of (See RESPIRATION - Complaints - accompanied - rectum)
  - • **vertigo** (See VERTIGO - Accompanied - stool)
  - ○ • **Bladder**: alum↓ **Caps**↓ lil-t↓ *Merc-c*↓ **Nux-v**↓
    - ⋮ **pain**: ambr br1
    - ⋮ **tenesmus**: alum **Caps** k* lil-t *Merc-c* **Nux-v**
- **aching**: *Aesc* ptk1 coll ptk1 graph ptk1 lyc ptk1 *Rat* ptk1
- **bed** agg.; in: chin↓
  - • **tearing** pain: chin k*
- **bending** double | **amel.**: androc srj1• carc sp* ruta fd4.de

Rectum

- **bending** forward:
  - **amel.**: alumn ↓
    - ⁝ **tearing** pain: alumn
- **biting** pain: agar k* all-c a1* alum ambr k* bar-c k* canth caps k* carb-v k* caust chin k* chin-b c1 dulc k* hell kali-c lach led lyc k* merl mez k* mur-ac sne nat-c k* nux-v ph-ac k* phos k* rhod k* sabin sep sin-a a1 spong hr1 *Sulph* k*
  - **worms**, as from: chin-b vh
- **boring** pain: borx h2 bry ptk1 ign sne zinc h2
- **breakfast** agg.; after: kali-p ↓
  - **tenesmus**: kali-p k2
- **burning**: *(↗Hemorrhoids - burning)* abies-c k* **Aesc** k* aeth **Agar** k* agn k2 all-c bro1* allox sp1 **Aloe** k* *Alum* k* alum-sil k2 alumn bro1 am-c k* *Am-m* k* ambr k* anan hr1 androc srj1• ant-c k* ant-t b7.de* aphis a1* *Apis* apoc k* arg-n k* arist-cl mtf11 arist-m br1 arn k* *Ars* k* *Ars-i* arum-d hr1 arum-t k* aspar k* aur k* aur-ar k2 aur-i k2 aur-m k* bamb-a stb2.de• bapt *Bar-c* k* bar-m bell k* **Berb** k* borx k* *Bov* k* brom k2 *Brucel* sa3• *Bry* k* cain **Calc** k* calc-f sp1 calc-p k* calc-s camph b7.de* canth k* **Caps** k* carb-ac hr1 **Carb-an** k* **Carb-v** k* **Carbn-s** *Card-m* k* carl k* *Castm* caust k* cham *Chel* k* chin k* chinin-ar cic b7.de* clem k* coc-c k* cocc k* *Coch* coff colch k* coll k* *Coloc* k* con k* *Cop* corn br1 *Crot-t* k* cub k* cupr k* cycl k* cystein-l rly4• der k* dig k* dol br1 dor k* *Dulc* k* erig k* eucal bro1 euon bro1 *Eup-per* k* *Euph* k* ferr k* ferr-ar ferr-i ferr-p ferul a1 *Gamb* k* gels **Graph** k* grat k* guat sp1 ham k* hell *Hep* k* hydr bro1 hydrc k* hyos k* ign k* *Iod* k* ip k* **Iris** k* jug-c bro1 jug-r k* **Kali-ar** *Kali-bi* k* **Kali-c** k* kali-n k* kali-p **Kali-s** lac-h sk4• *Lach* k* lact k* laur k* *Lil-t* k* lipp a1 loxo-recl knl4• *Lyc* k* lyss k* mag-c h2* *Mag-m* k* mag-p bg2 mag-s k* *Manc* med melal-alt gya4 **Merc** k* *Merc-c* k* merc-d a1 merc-i-f k* merc-sul k* merl k* *Mez* k* *Mur-ac* k* naja **Nat-ar** *Nat-c* k* **Nat-m** k* nat-p nat-s nat-sil fd3.de• nicc **Nit-ac** k* nuph **Nux-v** k* ol-an k* *Olnd* k* onis a1 *Op* ozone sde2• *Paeon* k* pen br1 *Petr* k* petros ph-ac k* *Phos* k* pin-s a1 pip-m a1 plac-s rly4• plat k* plb k* positr nl2• pot-e rly4• *Prun* k* *Psor* k* ptel **Puls** k* *Rat* k* rheum k* rhod b4a.de rhus-t k* rhus-v k* ruta fd4.de sabad k* sabin sang k2 sangin-n bro1 sars senn bro1 **Sep** k* **Sil** k* sin-a k* spira a1 *Spong* stann k* staph *Stront-c* k* *Sul-ac* **Sulph** k* sumb suprar rly4• syph k2 tarent k* tep k* *Ter* k* **Thuj** k* trios rsj11• tritic-vg fd5.de trom bro1 urt-u k* vanil fd5.de verat k* verat-v k* visc sp1 wies a1 *Zinc* k* zinc-p k2
  - **boiling** lead were passing through; as if: thuj tl1
  - **paroxysmal**: colch *Puls*
- **burrowing**: carb-an bg2 carb-v bg2
- **bursting** pain: agar tl1 kali-c h2* staph h1*
- **cancer**, due to: laur c1
- **chill**; during: apis ↓ ars ↓ caps ↓ *Merc* ↓ *Merc-c* ↓ nux-v ↓ rheum ↓ rhus-t ↓ *Sulph* ↓
  - **tenesmus**: apis bg2 ars bg2 caps bg2 *Merc* b4a.de* *Merc-c* b4a.de* nux-v bg2 rheum bg2 rhus-t bg2 *Sulph* bg2
- **clawing** pain (= squeezing, as from a claw in anus): *Ferr* lach nat-c phel *Zinc* bg2*
- **coffee** agg.: *Nat-m* ↓ tax ↓
  - **tenesmus**: *Nat-m* k* [tax jsj7]
- **coition**:
  - **after**: caust
    - ⁝ **drawing** pain: caust k*
  - **during**: calc ↓
    - ⁝ **stitching** pain: calc k*
- **cold | applications**:
  - ⁝ **amel.**: *Aloe* ↓ apis ↓ euphr ↓ *Kali-c* ↓ *Ter* ↓
    - ⁝ **burning**: *Aloe* k* apis euphr *Kali-c* k* *Ter* k*
  - **bathing**:
    - ⁝ **agg.**: mur-ac ↓
      - ⁝ **burning**: mur-ac k2
    - ⁝ **amel.**: sol-ecl ↓
      - ⁝ **burning**: [sol-ecl cky1]
- **colitis**; during: **Merc-c** ↓
  - **tenesmus**: **Merc-c** mrr1
- **constant**: ars ↓ *Kali-c* ↓ lyc ↓ nat-m ↓
  - **burning**: ars *Kali-c* k* lyc ptk1 nat-m
- **constipation**; during: anac ↓ asaf ↓ *Con* ↓ *Nux-v* ↓ petr-ra ↓ plb ↓ vib ↓
  - **tenesmus**: anac tl1 asaf k* *Con* *Nux-v* petr-ra shn4• plb k* vib
- **constricting** (See Constriction)
- **continuous**: am-c am-m calc ferr-p k2 graph ign kali-c kali-chl ptk1 lyc *Nit-ac* k* nux-v phyt ptk1 rosm lgb1 sep stront-c
- **convulsive**: *Lach* k* lyc k* psor k* sang k*
- **cough**:
  - **agg.**: bac bn ign bg1 *Kali-c* *Lach* nit-ac bg1 puls hr1 rosm lgb1 tub al
  - **during**:
    - ⁝ **agg.**: *Ign* ↓ *Kali-c* ↓ **Lach** ↓ nit-ac ↓ tub ↓
      - ⁝ **stitching** pain: *Ign* k* *Kali-c* bro1 **Lach** k* nit-ac k*
      - ⁝ **tearing** pain: lach k* tub bg*
- **cramping** (See Constriction)
- **cutting** pain: aesc k* agar bg2 aloe **Alum** k* alum-sil k2 *Alumn* bro1 am-c b4.de* ant-t bg1 *Ars* asar b7.de* aur-s a1 borx h2 calad calc calc-p canth k* carb-v carbn-s k2 *Caust* k* *Chel* k* coll bg1 con k* *Graph* k* hell b7.de* *Ign* k* indg ip h1* *Kali-ar* kali-bi gk *Kali-c* k* kali-n c1 kali-s kali-sil k2 lach b7a.de laur *Lyc* k* mag-c k* mag-p k2 mang medul-os-si rly4• meli *Merc* mur-ac nat-ar nat-c nat-hchls nat-m bro1 *Nit-ac* k* **Nux-v** k* *Phos* k* plan plat *Rat* k* rhus-t bg1 sabad bg1 sang bg2 sars k* sec sep k* **Sil** k* sin-n a1 spig bg1 spong bg1 stann staph *Sulph* k* sumb k* syph k2 thuj vanil fd5.de zinc k* zinc-p k2
  - **jerking** pain: zinc h2*
- **diarrhea**:
  - **after**:
    - ⁝ **agg.**: bell ↓ bit-ar ↓ *Canth* ↓ caps ↓ carb-an ↓ *Dulc* ↓ ferr ↓ grat ↓ hydr ↓ kali-c ↓ kali-n ↓ kali-p ↓ kola ↓ laur ↓ *Lil-t* ↓ mag-c ↓ mag-m ↓ mez ↓ mur-ac ↓ nat-m ↓ nicc ↓ op ↓ phel ↓ phos ↓ podo ↓ *Rat* ↓ rhus-t ↓ sil ↓ stront-c ↓ **Sulph** ↓ tab ↓ zinc ↓
      - ⁝ **burning**: *Canth* *Dulc* ferr c1 grat kali-c h2 kali-p fd1.de• laur mag-c h2 mag-m h2* mur-ac h2* nicc op phos h2 podo fd3.de• *Rat* sil h2 sulph h2
      - ⁝ **sore**: nat-m phel **Sulph** tab
      - ⁝ **tenesmus**: bell h1 bit-ar wht1• caps h1 carb-an h2 *Dulc* hydr kali-c h2 kali-n h2 kola stb3• laur *Lil-t* mag-c mag-m h2 mez h2 phel phos rhus-t stront-c sulph h2 tab zinc h2
  - **before**: hydr ↓ saroth ↓
    - ⁝ **tenesmus**: hydr saroth sp1
  - **during**: *Acon* ↓ agath-a nl2• **Aloe** ↓ *Alum* ↓ ango ↓ anthraq rly4• arge-pl ↓ *Arn* ↓ ars h2 *Aur* ↓ aur-ar ↓ aur-m ↓ aur-s ↓ bamb-a ↓ *Bell* ↓ bov ↓ bry ↓ calc ↓ *Canth* ↓ **Caps** ↓ carb-ac ↓ carb-an ↓ carb-v ↓ carbn-s ↓ caust ↓ cench ↓ chen-g ↓ chin ↓ chinin-ar ↓ cimic ↓ *Colch* ↓ *Coloc* ↓ con ↓ cop ↓ corn ↓ crot-c ↓ crot-t ↓ cuph ↓ cupr-act ↓ *Cupr-ar* ↓ *Dulc* ↓ form ↓ *Gamb* ↓ glon ↓ graph ↓ grat ↓ *Hell* ↓ hep ↓ hydr ↓ *Ign* ↓ *Ip* ↓ **Iris** ↓ jug-c ↓ *Kali-ar* ↓ *Kali-bi* ↓ *Kali-br* ↓ *Kali-c* ↓ kali-chl ptk1 kali-n ↓ kali-p ↓ kali-s ↓ *Lach* ↓ *Laur* ↓ liat ↓ mag-c ↓ mag-m h2 mag-s ↓ *Manc* ↓ **Merc** ↓ **Merc-c** ↓ *Merc-d* ↓ morph ↓ *Mur-ac* ↓ nat-c ↓ nat-s ↓ *Nit-ac* ↓ *Nuph* ↓ *Nux-v* ↓ op ↓ passi br1 phos ↓ phys ↓ phyt ↓ plb ↓ plb-act ↓ podo fd3.de• prun ↓ ptel ↓ *Rat* ↓ rheum ↓ *Rhus-t* ↓ sarr ↓ sel ↓ *Senec* ↓ sil ↓ *Staph* ↓ sul-ac h2 **Sulph** ↓ tab ↓ ter ↓ tritic-vg ↓ trom ↓ ulm-c jsj8• verat ↓
    - ⁝ **burning**: **Aloe** k* alum anthraq rly4• arge-pl rwt5• *Ars* k* *Aur* aur-ar k2 aur-m aur-s k2 bamb-a stb2.de• bov bry canth k* **Caps** carb-an carb-v bro1 caust chen-g bro1 chin chinin-ar con bro1 crot-c sk4• *Dulc* *Gamb* glon graph grat ip h1 **Iris** k* jug-c k* *Kali-ar* *Kali-c* kali-s *Lach* mag-m h2* *Manc* **Merc** *Merc-d* bro1 *Mur-ac* k* nat-c h2 *Nuph* op podo bro1 prun bro1 *Rat* k* rheum bro1 **Sulph** ter bro1 tritic-vg fd5.de trom bro1 verat bro1
    - ⁝ **cutting** pain: **Ars** k*
    - ⁝ **tenesmus**: *Acon* bro1 *Aloe* bro1 *Alum* ango bro1 *Arn* b7.de* **Ars** k* *Bell* bro1 calc bro1 *Canth* b7.de* *Caps* b7.de* carb-ac bro1 carb-v carbn-s cench k2 cimic *Colch* b7.de* *Coloc* k* cop corn crot-t k* cuph bro1 cupr-act bro1 *Cupr-ar* bro1 *Dulc* hr1 form *Gamb* *Hell* b7a.de hep bro1 hydr *Ign* bro1 *Ip* b7a.de* *Kali-bi* bro1 *Kali-br* hr1 kali-n bro1 kali-p k2 *Laur* b7.de* liat bro1 mag-c bro1 mag-m mag-s *Merc* k* **Merc-c** k* merc-d bro1 morph bro1 mur-ac h2 nat-s bro1 *Nit-ac* k* *Nux-v* b7.de* op k* phos bro1 phys phyt plb plb-act bro1 podo c1* ptel k* rheum bro1 *Rhus-t* b7a.de* sarr sel *Senec* bro1 sil bro1 *Staph* b7.de *Sulph* k* tab k* trom bro1 verat h1*
- **diarrhea** for a long time; as after: rheum h
- **dinner**; after: alum ↓ ant-t ↓ kali-n ↓ mang ↓ nat-m ↓ phos ↓ sep ↓ sulph ↓
  - **burning**: kali-n h2* nat-m a1

- **clawing** pain: phos$_{h2}$
- **pressing** pain: sep$_{h2*}$
- **stitching** pain: kali-n$_{h2*}$ phos$_{k*}$ sulph$_{a1}$
- **tearing** pain: ant-t$_{a1}$ mang$_{k*}$
- **tenesmus**: alum$_{k*}$ nat-m$_{k*}$

- **drawing** in anus agg.: sep ↓ sulph$_{h2*}$
  - **stitching** pain: sep$_{h2}$ sulph$_{h2}$
- **drawing** pain: ambr$_{h1}$ ant-c$_{k*}$ aur-s$_{k*}$ calc$_{k*}$ cann-s carb-v$_{k*}$ chel$_{k*}$ chin$_{k*}$ *Cycl*$_{k*}$ dulc$_{fd4.de}$ eupi$_{k*}$ kreos$_{k*}$ lach$_{k*}$ lact$_{k*}$ mang mez$_{k*}$ phos$_{k*}$ rhod vanil$_{fd5.de}$ zinc
  - **downward**: phos
  - **upward**: mez plb thuj
- **driving**; while: glon ↓
  - **griping** pain: glon$_{k*}$
- **dysentery**:
  - **after** dysenterie: calc ↓
    - **tenesmus**: calc$_{ptk1}$
  - **during** dysentery: acon ↓ aloe ↓ **Apis** ↓ arn ↓ *Ars* ↓ ars-i ↓ ars-s-f ↓ calc ↓ **Caps** ↓ *Carb-ac* ↓ *Carb-v* ↓ **Colch** ↓ **Coll** ↓ *Coloc* ↓ con ↓ cop ↓ dios ↓ erig ↓ ip ↓ *Kali-bi* ↓ *Lach* ↓ *Merc* ↓ **Merc-c** ↓ *Nit-ac* ↓ rheum ↓ sulph ↓ ter ↓ tub ↓ *Urt-u* ↓ xan ↓
    - **burning**: aloe *Ars*$_{k*}$ **Caps**$_{k*}$ *Carb-v*$_{k*}$ *Coloc Lach Urt-u*
    - **cutting** pain: *Merc-c*
    - **tenesmus**: acon **Apis** arn$_{k*}$ ars-i$_{k*}$ ars-s-f$_{k2}$ calc$_{ptk1}$ **Caps**$_{k*}$ *Carb-ac*$_{hr1}$ **Colch**$_{k*}$ **Coll**$_{hr1}$ con$_{k*}$ cop$_{k*}$ dios$_{k*}$ erig$_{hr1}$ ip *Kali-bi*$_{hr1}$ *Merc*$_{k*}$ **Merc-c**$_{k*}$ *Nit-ac*$_{k*}$ rheum sulph$_{k*}$ ter$_{k*}$ tub$_{c1}$ xan$_{k*}$
- **eating**:
  - **after**:
    - **agg.**: aesc$_{k2}$ arist-cl ↓ *Coloc* ↓ crot-t ↓ lyc mang$_{hr1}$ nux-v$_{k*}$
      - **stitching** pain: **Nux-v**$_{k*}$
      - **tenesmus**: arist-cl$_{sp1}$ *Coloc*$_{k*}$ crot-t$_{k*}$
  - **before**:
    - **agg.**: *Caust* ↓
      - **stitching** pain: *Caust*$_{k*}$
  - **while**:
    - **agg.**: coloc ↓ crot-t ↓
      - **tenesmus**: coloc$_{k*}$ crot-t$_{k*}$
- **erect**, when body is: **Petr** ↓
  - **stitching** pain: **Petr**$_{k*}$
- **exertion** agg.; after: coc-c ↓ rosm$_{lgb1}$ sulph ↓
  - **burning**: sulph$_{k*}$
  - **twinging**: coc-c$_{k*}$
- **fever**; during: ferr-p$_{k2}$ nux-v ↓
  - **tenesmus**: nux-v$_{bro1}$
- **fissure**, in: **Graph** ↓
  - **burning**: **Graph**
- **flatus**:
  - **attempting** to suppress flatus; on: acon ↓
    - **tenesmus**: acon
  - **from**: calc ↓ ign ↓ nat-s ↓ zinc ↓
    - **pressing** pain: calc$_{ptk1}$ ign$_{ptk1}$ nat-s$_{ptk1}$ zinc$_{h2*}$
- **flatus**; passing:
  - **after**:
    - **agg.**: *Agar* ↓ **Aloe** ↓ ant-t ↓ bapt ↓ *Carb-v* ↓ cham ↓ cocc ↓ dios ↓ mag-m ↓ phos ↓ plb ↓ psor ↓ *Puls* ↓ *Staph* ↓ *Sulph* ↓ sumb ↓ *Teucr* ↓ *Zinc* ↓
      - **burning**: *Agar* **Aloe** ant-t bapt *Carb-v* cham cocc dios mag-m$_{a1}$ phos plb psor *Puls Staph Sulph* sumb *Teucr Zinc*
  - **agg.**: agar$_{bg2}$ arn$_{bg2}$ bry ↓ calc ↓ camph *Carb-v* con$_{bg2}$ graph$_{bg2}$ ign ↓ kali-c$_{bg2}$ nat-c$_{h2}$ nat-m$_{bg2}$ nat-s ↓ phos ↓ puls$_{bg2}$ sulph ↓ zinc ↓
    - **biting** pain: agar$_{h2}$
    - **burning**: sulph$_{k2}$
    - **pressing** pain: calc$_{ptk1}$ *Carb-v* ign$_{ptk1}$ nat-s$_{ptk1}$ zinc$_{h2*}$
    - **stitching** pain: bry phos
  - **amel.**: ant-c ↓ coloc ↓ kali-bi ↓ *Mag-c* ↓ vichy-g ↓

- **flatus**; passing – **amel.**: ...
    - **pressing** pain: ant-c$_{h2*}$ mag-c$_{a1}$
    - **sticking** pain: coloc$_{ptk1}$ *Mag-c*$_{ptk1}$
    - **stitching** pain: coloc$_{k*}$ *Mag-c*$_{k*}$ vichy-g$_{a1}$
    - **twinging**: kali-bi$_{k*}$
  - **before**: kali-c ↓
    - **pressing** pain: kali-c$_{h2*}$
- **glass**; as from broken: rat$_{mrr1}$
- **gnawing** pain: *Carb-v*$_{k*}$ elaps ferr merc phos stann
- **griping** pain: *Calc* carb-v *Cocc* **Ign** kali-c$_{k*}$ mur-ac$_{k*}$ nat-c$_{a1}$ nat-m$_{k*}$ nit-ac$_{k*}$ ox-ac$_{k*}$ thuj$_{k*}$ verb$_{c1}$
- **hemorrhoids**; from: (↗*Hemorrhoids - painful)* aesc$_{vh1}$ aloe ↓ bac ↓ caust ↓ coll ↓ dulc$_{fd4.de}$ led$_{br1}$ lyc ↓ med ↓ morg-g$_{pte1•}$ morg-p$_{pte1•}$ nux-v ↓ rosm$_{lgb1}$ tritic-vg$_{fd5.de}$
  - **aching**: aesc$_{tl1}$ coll$_{tl1}$ med$_{tl1}$
  - **cutting** pain: nux-v$_{bro1}$
  - **dull**: coll$_{tl1}$ lyc$_{tl1}$
  - **raw**: aesc$_{tl1}$ aloe$_{tl1}$ caust$_{tl1}$
  - **stitching** pain: bac$_{al2*}$
  - ▽ **extending** to | **Back**: *Aesc*$_{vh1}$
- **hot** water amel.: rat ↓
  - **burning**: rat$_{pd}$
- **kneeling**: | **amel.**: *Aesc*
- **knots**; as from hard: nat-c$_{h2*}$
- **lancinating** (See cutting)
- **lying**:
  - **abdomen**; on | **amel.**: nux-v
  - **agg.**: aesc **Ars**$_{sne}$ chel$_{bg1}$ crot-t ign$_{bg1}$ nat-c ↓ nux-v ↓ phos ptel$_{bg1}$ *Puls* sep$_{bg1}$ sulph$_{bg1}$ visc ↓ zinc$_{h2*}$
    - **burning**: *Puls*
    - **pressing** pain: crot-t$_{k*}$ nux-v$_{bg1}$ ptel$_{bg1}$
    - **stitching** pain: nat-c$_{k*}$ **Sulph**$_{k*}$ visc$_{c1}$
  - **amel.**: mang ↓ rat$_{mrr1}$
    - **tenesmus**: mang$_{k2}$
  - **back**; on:
    - **agg.**: chel sulph ↓
      - **sore**: chel sulph$_{h2*}$
    - **amel.**: alumn *Am-c* mang puls$_{h1}$
      - **tearing** pain: alumn
  - **side**; on | **agg.**: puls$_{h1}$
- **menses**:
  - **after**:
    - **agg.**: graph ↓
      - **burning**: graph$_{k*}$
  - **before**:
    - **agg.**: ars ↓ brucel ↓ des-ac ↓ ign *Mur-ac* ↓ petr$_{k*}$ thuj ↓
      - **burning**: brucel$_{sa3•}$
      - **pressing** pain: des-ac$_{rbp6}$ ign$_{k*}$ petr$_{k*}$
      - **sore**: ars$_{bro1}$ *Mur-ac*$_{bro1}$
      - **tenesmus**: thuj$_{k*}$
  - **during**:
    - **agg.**: *Aloe Am-c* ↓ ars berb brucel ↓ *Calc* ↓ carb-v ↓ cocc$_{b7.de}$ kreos ↓ *Mur-ac* ↓ nat-s ↓ phos *Puls*$_{b7a.de}$ spong$_{fd4.de}$ zinc ↓
      - **burning**: berb brucel$_{sa3•}$ carb-v zinc
      - **pressing** pain: *Aloe*
      - **sore**: ars$_{bro1}$ *Berb*$_{st}$ carb-v *Mur-ac*$_{bro1}$
      - **sticking** pain: ars$_{ptk1}$
      - **stinging**: phos
      - **stitching** pain: aloe *Ars*$_{k*}$ *Calc*$_{b4a.de}$ kreos$_{b7a.de}$ phos
      - **tenesmus**: *Am-c*$_{k*}$ nat-s$_{k*}$
- **mental** exertion:
  - **after**: *Caust* nux-v$_{k*}$
    - **stitching** pain: **Nux-v**$_{k*}$
  - **agg.**: caust ↓

Rectum

- **agg.**: ...
  - ⋮ **pressing** pain: caust
- **milk** agg.: nicc↓
  - **tenesmus**: nicc k*
- **motion**:
  - **after**:
    - ⋮ **agg.**: bamb-a↓ crot-t↓ kali-n↓ *Puls*↓
      - : **burning**: crot-t k* kali-n k*
      - : **sore**: bamb-a stb2.de• crot-t k* *Puls* k*
  - **agg.**: bell↓ kali-n↓ *Nux-v* *Thuj* valer↓
    - ⋮ **pressing** pain: *Nux-v*
    - ⋮ **stitching** pain: bell h1* kali-n h2*
    - ⋮ **tearing** pain: valer k*
  - **amel.**: *Puls* k2*
  - **gentle** motion | **amel.**: androc srj1•
- **neuralgic**: *Atro* bro1 bar-m bro1 *Bell* bro1 colch bro1 *Crot-t* bro1 ign bro1 kali-c bro1 lach bro1 lyc bro1 ox-ac bro1 phos bro1 *Plb* bro1* *Stry* bro1 tarent bro1
- **periodical**: agar↓ *Ign*↓
  - **day**; every: *Ign* rosm lgb1
  - **stitching** pain: agar *Ign*
- **pinching** pain: calc h2* eug k* kali-c h2* lyc h2* mag-c h2* merc nat-m *Nit-ac* k* sep h2*
- **pregnancy** agg.; during: *Caps*↓ *Kali-c*↓
  - **burning**: *Caps* k*
  - **stitching** pain: *Kali-c*
- **pressing** pain (= pressure): acon **Aesc** allox tpw3 *Aloe* k* alum k* alum-p k2 alum-sil k2 ambr b7.de* ang ant-c aphis bro1 apoc arg-met arge-pl rwt5• *Arn* k* *Ars* k* asaf *Bar-c* bar-m bar-s k2 *Bell* k* *Berb* bry cact k* cain calc k* *Calc-s* calc-sil k2 carb-an h2 carb-v carbn-s carl **Caust** k* cean bro1 chel *Chin* k* chinin-ar cob coll k* coloc con cop *Crot-t* *Cycl* dulc eug eup-pur euphr bro1 ferr-i form gran *Graph* hell hydr hyper bro1 **Ign** k* iod k* *Iris* kali-ar *Kali-bi* kali-c k* kali-m k2 *Kali-n* kali-p kali-s kali-sil k2 kola stb3• kreos *Lach* k* lact laur **Lil-t** k* *Lyc* k* m-arct b7.de mag-c k* *Mag-m* med bro1 *Merc* merc-i-f merl mez mur-ac *Murx* nat-c k* nat-m **Nit-ac** k* **Nux-v** k* op k* ox-ac **Petr** k* phel *Phos* k* plat prun bro1 ptel *Puls* k* rhus-t ruta fd4.de *Sars* seneg *Sep* k* sil spig k* spong fd4.de *Stann* k* staph k* stry sul-ac bro1 **Sulph** k* tub c1 *Valer* vanil fd5.de verat verb xero bro1 zinc zinc-p k2
  - **alternating** with | **contraction** (See Constriction - alternating - pressing)
  - **diarrhea**; as from: calc nat-m
  - **diarrhea** would come on; as if: anthraq rly4• calc h2 *Crot-t* mag-c
  - **downward**, outward, etc: agar *Aloe* bell h1 berb bry calc-p cann-s *Carb-v* carbn-s k2 cimic cob *Corn* **Crot-t** dios dros inul br1 *Ip* kali-n *Lach* lil-t lyc mag-c *Nit-ac* *Nux-m* nux-v ox-ac pic-ac **Podo** *Puls* sep h2 **Sulph** til c1 verat
    - ⋮ **sharp** instrument; as from a: ign br1
  - **feces** were lodged in rectum; as if: *Caust*
  - **not** for stool; pressing but: *Dros* kali-n a1 **Lach** k* mez k*
- **pressure**:
  - **abdomen**; on:
    - ⋮ **agg.**: carb-v↓
      - : **sore**: carb-v k2
  - **agg.**: sep↓
    - ⋮ **stitching** pain: sep h2*
  - **amel.**: carc mg1.de* kali-c↓ spong fd4.de
    - ⋮ **burning**: kali-c k*
  - **stomach** agg.; on: ferr-p k2
  - **umbilicus** agg. ; on: **Crot-t**
- **prolapsed**, in the: *Apis*↓
  - **burning**: *Apis* k*
- **prolapsus**; from: arist-cl↓
  - **tenesmus**: arist-cl sp1
- **prostate** gland; from enlargement of: phos↓
- **pulsating** pain: aloe bro1 ancis-p tsm2 *Bell* bro1 caps bro1 ham bro1 lach k2* *Meli* bro1 merc bro1 nat-m bro1 phasco-ci rbp2 ruta fd4.de *Sulph*
- **rasping**: ant-c grat nat-m verat
- **rest** | **amel.**: rosm lgb1
- **retention** and pain in bladder, with: cop br1
- **rhagades**: **Graph**↓
  - **burning**: **Graph** k*
- **riding** agg.: hep bg1
- **rising** from sitting agg.: phos↓
  - **pressing** pain: phos h2
  - **stitching** pain: phos h2
- **rubbing**; after: carb-v↓ cic↓ phel↓ *Sabad*↓
  - **burning**: carb-v k* cic h1* phel k* *Sabad* k*
- **scraping** pain: agar a1 am-c h2* ant-c calc-p k* carb-an h2* crot-t k* grat kali-n h2* lob a1 nat-m k* puls sep h2* verat
- **scratching** pain: ars h2 kali-n h2 sep h2
- **sexual** excitement agg.: germ-met srj5•
- **shooting** (See stitching)
- **sitting**:
  - **agg.**: *Aesc* *Aloe* am-m ammc ars bar-c h2* berb calc cann-s caust chel chin↓ cocc coloc h2* crot-t↓ cycl k* dulc fd4.de euphr gran↓ ham fd3.de• heroin↓ hydrog srj2• iod↓ ip↓ kali-c↓ kali-s↓ **Lyc** mag-c↓ *Mang* merc-cy a1 *Mur-ac* nat-c↓ *Ph-ac* phos **Rat** *Ruta* sars k* **Sep** k* sin-a↓ staph k* sulph k* ther k* thuj
    - ⋮ **burning**: ip k* kali-s fd4.de **Sulph** k* thuj k*
    - ⋮ **cutting** pain: **Rat** [heroin sdj2]
    - ⋮ **drawing** pain: chin *Cycl* k*
    - ⋮ **griping** pain: *Calc* *Cocc*
    - ⋮ **pressing** pain: ammc k* calc k* *Cann-s* k* *Cycl* euphr k* staph h1* sulph k* thuj
    - ⋮ **sore**: *Am-m* *Berb* **Caust** chel k* *Cycl* mag-c k* *Mur-ac* **Rat** *Sulph* k*
    - ⋮ **stitching** pain: *Ars* k* *Calc* gran k* iod h* kali-c k* nat-c k* *Ruta* sin-a a1 **Sulph** k* *Thuj* k*
    - ⋮ **tearing** pain: *Ruta* k*
    - ⋮ **tenesmus**: crot-t mang k2 staph h1 *Sulph*
  - **amel.**: ars *Ign* kali-s fd4.de lach
  - **long** time agg.; for a | **after**: calc bg1 nit-ac bg1 ruta bg1
- **sleep** | **during** | **agg.**: kali-c
  - **preventing** sleep: kali-c↓
    - ⋮ **burning**: kali-c h2*
- **smarting** (See burning)
- **sneezing** agg.: bac bn *Lach*↓
  - **stitching** pain: *Lach*
- **sore**: (↗*Sensitive*) **Aesc** k* *Agar* agn aids nl2• **Aloe** alum k* alum-sil k2 am-br k* am-c k* am-m k* ambr ant-c k* ant-s-aur ant-t bg2 **Apis** arn *Ars* k* ars-s-f k2 aspar k* aur aur-ar k2 aur-s k2 bamb-a stb2.de• *Bar-c* **Bar-m** bar-s k2 **Bell** k* **Berb** k* *Bry* k* cadm-met tpw6 *Calc* k* *Calc-p* k* calc-s calc-sil k2 *Caps* *Carb-an* k* *Carb-v* k* *Carbn-s* **Caust** k* cench k2 coloc crot-t *Cycl* dios dirc a1 elaps elat a1 euph b4.de* gal-ac **Gamb** **Graph** k* grat bg2 **Ham** hep k* **Ign** k* **Iris** jal a1 **Kali-ar** kali-bi k* **Kali-c** k* kali-m k2 *Kali-p* **Kali-s** kali-sil k2 lac-ac stj5• **Lach** k* lact lil-t lim a1 **Lyc** k* **Merc** k* *Merc-c* k* merc-cy a1 merc-i-f k* merc-sul k* mez b4.de* **Mur-ac** k* nat-ar nat-c k* *Nat-m* k* nat-p k* nat-s **Nit-ac** k* nux-m k* *Nux-v* k* onos ptk1 **Paeon** petr k* ph-ac k* phos k* phys k* *Podo* positr nl2• prun psor **Puls** k* rad-br c11* **Rat** *Rhus-t* k* ruta fd4.de sacch-a fd2.de• sars *Sep* k* **Sil** sol-t-ae k* spong stann staph sul-ac **Sulph** k* syph tab thuj k* trios rsj11• tritic-vg fd5.de vanil fd5.de verat vib *Zinc* k* zinc-p k2 zing [spect dfg1]
  - **jerking** pain: sep h2*
- **splinter**; as from a: acon bro1 *Aesc* k* agar all-c bro1 *Alum* k* am-m bro1 *Arg-n* *Bar-c* bell bro1 *Carb-v* carc gk6 caust bro1 coll k* hell bg2 *Ign* bro1 irid-met srj5• iris tl1 *Kali-c* bro1 *Lach* bro1 lyc bro1 merc bro1 mez bro1 *Nat-m* bro1 nat-p a1 **Nit-ac** k* plat bro1 **Rat** k* ruta bro1 sanic bg2 *Sep* bro1 *Sil* k* sulph k* syc pte1*• thuj bg2*
- **stabbing** pain: calc-f sp1 visc sp1
- **standing** agg.: *Aesc* arn calc-p k2 crot-h↓ ferr *Ign* kali-s fd4.de *Lach*↓ *Sulph*↓ ter↓ valer↓
  - **burning**: crot-h ptk1 *Lach* k* ter k*
  - **cutting** pain: *Lach* k*
  - **pressing** pain: arn k* *Ferr*
  - **stitching** pain: *Sulph* k* valer k*

- **sticking** pain: acon bg3 **Aesc** k* aloe ant-c *Ars* cact calc *Carb-v* **Caust** k* chel *Coll Coloc* ferr-i **Graph** k* grat hell ptk1 irid-met srj5• **Iris** k* jac-c kali-c kali-n kali-sil k2 lact lyc nat-ar *Nit-ac* k* **Nux-v** k* phos prun-p a1 puls *Rat* k* rumx sanic ptk1 *Sil* sin-a a1 **Sulph** k* sumb *Teucr Thuj* vanil fd5.de
- **sticks**; as if full of: **Aesc** bg2* coll bg2*
- **stinging**: acon k* **Aesc** agath-a nl2• alum bg2 *Am-m* ambr c1 *Apis Ars Caps* k* carb-an *Caust* coch ger-i rly4• grat k2 lyc mag-m melal-alt gya4 *Nat-m* nit-ac bg2* **Nux-v** k* *Phos* pot-e rly4• *Puls* k* sil k* *Staph* sulph k*
- **stitching** pain: *Acon* k* **Aesc** agar k* *All-c* k* *Aloe* alum k* alum-p k2 alum-sil k2 alumn am-m k* ambr h1* ang k* ant-t k* *Apis* arg-n k* arn k* **Ars** k* ars-s-f k2 arund k* asar b7.de* *Atis* zzc1• aur k* aur-ar k2 aur-s bac bn* bamb-a stb2.de• *Bar-c Bar-m* bar-s k2 bell k* *Benz-ac* k* *Berb* k* bond a1 borx k* bov k* brom k* bry k* cact k* cadm-met tpw6 calad k* *Calc* k* *Calc-p* k* calc-s calc-sil k2 cann-i k* cann-s k* canth *Caps* k* **Carb-an** k* *Carb-v* k* *Carbn-s* carl **Caust** k* cham k* chel k* chin k* chinin-ar cina b7.de* coc-c k* colch coloc k* **Con** k* *Cop* k* *Croc* k* crot-t k* cupr h2* cycl k* dirc a1* dulc fd4.de euphr ferr-ar ferr-i ferr-ma k* ferul a1 gins k* *Graph* k* grat k* hell b7.de* **Ign** k* indg k* ip k* jac-c jatr-c jug-r a1 *Kali-ar* kali-bi k* **Kali-c** k* kali-n k* kali-p **Kali-s** kali-sil k2 kiss a1 kreos k* **Lach** k* lachn c1 led k* **Lyc** k* lyss k* m-arct b7.de mag-c k* *Mag-m* k* *Mag-p Med* melal-alt gya4 meli **Merc** k* merc-c k* merc-i-f k* *Mez* k* mosch k* *Mur-ac* k* nat-ar k2 *Nat-c* k* *Nat-m* k* nicc k* **Nit-ac** k* nuph k* nux-m k* nux-v k* ol-an k* paeon gm1 petr k* *Ph-ac* phel k* *Phos* k* *Phyt* k* plat k* plb k* prun-p a1 *Puls* k* ran-b k* ran-s k* *Rat* rhod b4a.de* *Rhus-t Ruta* k* *Sabad* k* **Sep** k* **Sil** k* sin-a a1 sin-n a1 spirae a1 spong stann k* stram stry *Sul-ac* k* **Sulph** k* symph fd3.de• tarent k* teucr k* *Thuj* k* til k* tritic-vg fd5.de valer b7.de* vanil fd5.de vichy-g a1 visc c1 zinc k* zinc-p k2
  - **alternating** with:
    - **Glans** penis; itching in: thuj k*
    - **Prepuce**; burning in: thuj
  - **downwards** and outwards: asar h1 *Carb-v* (non:carbn-s kl) lith-c
  - **inward**: zinc h2
  - **itching**: alum bry k* coloc k* nat-m h2* ph-ac h2* puls vh stann k* sulph k*
  - **outward**: *Carb-v* lith-c
  - **paroxysms**; in (See sudden - stitching)
  - **tearing** pain: graph h2* nat-m h2*
  - **twitching**: zinc h2*
  - **undulating** (See waves)
  - **upward**: aesc androc srj1• *Graph* hell h1 **Ign** k* *Lach* mag-c k* *Mez Rhus-t Sep* thuj
  - **waves**; in: bamb-a stb2.de•
- **stool**:
  - **after**:
    - **agg.**: abrom-a ks5 adam skp7• **Aesc** k* *Aeth* ↓ agar k2 aids ↓ **Aloe** alum tl1 *Alumn Am-c Am-m* ambr ↓ androc srj1• ant-c ↓ ant-t ↓ aphis ↓ **Apis** ↓ apoc aq-mar ↓ arist-cl ↓ *Ars Ars-i* ↓ ars-s-f k2 arund ↓ asaf k* asar bg2 asc-t ↓ aster ↓ aur ↓ aur-ar ↓ *Bac* bn bamb-a ↓ bapt ↓ bar-c bar-i ↓ bar-m ↓ bar-s k2 bell bell-p-sp ↓ *Berb* bit-ar ↓ bov brass-n-o ↓ *Brom* **Bry** ↓ cact calad ↓ calc calc-i ↓ calc-p k* calc-s calc-sil k2 cann-s ↓ canth *Caps* ↓ carb-an ↓ *Carb-v* carbn-s carc ↓ carl casc cassia-s ccrh1• *Castm* ↓ caust cham b7.de chel ↓ chin ↓ cic clem ↓ cob a1 coc-c ↓ cocc *Colch* k* coll ↓ *Coloc* ↓ cop ↓ *Corn* ↓ crot-t *Cub* ↓ cupr ↓ cupr-act ↓ cystein-l rly4• dios dirc ↓ dros ↓ dulc fd4.de elaps erig ↓ euphr ↓ fago ↓ ferr ↓ ferr-ar ↓ ferr-i ↓ ferr-p ↓ fl-ac ↓ franz ↓ **Gamb** ↓ germ-met ↓ gins ↓ glycyr-g ↓ *Graph* k* grat k* guat ↓ hell b7.de hep ↓ hydr hydrog ↓ hydroph rsj6• **Ign** k* ind a1 indg ↓ iod ↓ ip ↓ *Iris* ↓ jug-c ↓ jug-r ↓ *Kali-ar* kali-bi kali-c k* kali-m k2 kali-n ↓ kali-p kali-s kali-sil ↓ *Kalm* kola ↓ lac-h sze9• *Lach* laur ↓ lil-t lim ↓ lipp ↓ lob *Lyc* lyss ↓ *Mag-c* ↓ mag-m h2* mag-s ↓ manc k* mand ↓ mang-p ↓ melal-alt gya4 **Merc** k* merc-c *Merc-d* ↓ merc-i-r mez mill ↓ **Mur-ac** *Nat-ar* ↓ *Nat-c* k* nat-m k* nat-p *Nat-s* ↓ nat-sil ↓ nicc ↓ **Nit-ac** k* nuph ↓ nux-m ↓ nux-v b7.de* ol-an ↓ *Olnd* ↓ osm ↓ ozone ↓ paeon k2* petr b4a.de* ph-ac ↓ phel ↓ phos b4a.de* phys ↓ *Pic-ac* ↓ plac ↓ plac-s ↓ *Plat* ↓ plb ↓ plut-n ↓ *Podo* positr nl2• prun ↓ *Psor* ptel c1 puls k* **Rat** k* *Rheum* ↓ rhod b4a.de rhodi ↓ rhus-t rhus-v *Ruta* sabad k* sabin ↓ sacch-a ↓ sapin ↓ saroth ↓ sars ↓ sec ↓ seneg k* senn ↓ *Sep* sil sin-a ↓ sin-n ↓ sol-ecl ↓ sol-t-ae ↓ spirae ↓ spong fd4.de stann ↓ staph k* stront-c k* *Sul-ac* k* sul-i ↓ **Sulph** k* sumb suprar rly4• symph fd3.de• tab ↓ tarent k* ter ↓ thuj k* trios rsj11• tritic-vg fd5.de *Trom* ↓ urt-u ↓ vanil fd5.de verat-v k* yuc ↓ *Zinc* ↓ zinc-p ↓

- **stool – after – agg.**: ...
  - **biting** pain: agar h2* alum h2* canth a1 caust h2* colch hr1 hell a1 lach a1 mez h2* nat-c h2* nat-m a1 ph-ac h2* phos h2* sep h2* sil h2* sin-a a1
  - **burning**: abrom-a ks5 **Aesc** k* agar k* **Aloe** alum h2* alumn k* am-c k* *Am-m* k* ant-t k* aphis bro1 *Apis* aq-mar skp7• **Ars** k* *Ars-i* ars-s-f k2 arund k* asc-t k* aster k* aur bro1 aur-ar k2 bar-c bar-i k2 bar-m *Berb* k* bov k* **Bry** k* *Calc* k* calc-i k2 calc-s a1 calc-sil k2 cann-s k* *Canth* k* caps k* *Carb-v* k* *Carbn-s Carl* k* *Castm* **Caust** k* cic clem k* cob k* coc-c k* colch bg1 *Coloc* k* cop *Corn* k* crot-t dirc k* dulc euphr k* fago a1 ferr ferr-ar ferr-i ferr-p **Gamb** k* glycyr-g cte1• *Graph* k* grat k* guat sp1 hell k* hep *Hydr* k* hydroph rsj6• ign k* ind k* iod k* *Iris* k* jug-c k* jug-r k* *Kali-ar Kali-bi* k* *Kali-c* k* kali-m k2 kali-n k* kali-p kali-s kali-sil k2 kalm k* *Lach* k* laur k* *Lil-t* k* *Lyc* k* *Mag-c* k* *Mag-m* k* mang-p rly4• *Merc* k* *Merc-c* k* mill a1 *Mur-ac* k* *Nat-ar Nat-c* k* *Nat-m* k* nat-p *Nat-s* k* nat-sil fd3.de• nicc k* **Nit-ac** k* nuph k* nux-m *Nux-v* k* ol-an bro1 *Olnd* osm k* paeon k* *Petr* phel k* *Phos* k* *Pic-ac* k* plac rzf5• plac-s rly4• plut-n srj7• positr nl2• prun bro1 ptel k* *Puls* **Rat** k* rheum rhod k* rhodi a1 rhus-t sabad b7a.de* sapin a1 sars k* sec k* sep k* **Sil** k* sin-a k* sin-n a1 sol-t-ae k* spirae a1 stann k* *Staph Stront-c* k* sul-i k2 **Sulph** k* sumb a1 tab a1 tarent k* ter k* *Thuj* k* tritic-vg fd5.de *Trom* k* urt-u k* vanil fd5.de *Zinc* k* zinc-p k2 [bell-p-sp dcm1 sol-ecl cky1]
  - **cutting** pain: *Aesc* agar *Aloe* calc k* chel k* hell h1* hydroph rsj6• kali-bi gk **Nit-ac Nux-v** k* pic-ac k* *Puls* **Rat** sin-a sin-n a1 staph sumb k*
  - **pressing** pain: alum b4a.de apoc k* bar-c h2* *Calc* k* caust k* germ-met srj5• hell b7.de *Ign* k* jug-r a1 *Kali-bi* k* *Kalm* k* lipp a1 mag-m a1 *Merc* nit-ac nux-v b7a.de ph-ac k* phos k* plat k* *Podo Puls* k* seneg k* sil k* stann b4.de* sul-ac *Sulph* k*
  - **scraping** pain: nit-ac h2 phos h2
  - **sore**: *Aesc* aids nl2• **Aloe** *Alum* k* ant-c **Apis** apoc k* calc-s k* *Carbn-s Cham* chel k* colch k* crot-t k* gamb **Graph** hep hydrog srj2• **Ign** k* iod kali-bi k* kali-c k* kali-m k2 kali-p fd1.de• mag-m k* *Merc* mez k* *Mur-ac Nat-m* **Nit-ac** nux-m nux-v k* phos k* *Podo* puls k* **Rat** ruta fd4.de sacch-a fd2.de• spirae a1 stann k* *Staph* k* *Sulph* k*
  - **splinter**; as from a: carc gk6 saroth sp1
  - **sticking** pain: brass-n-o srj5• **Nux-v Rat**
  - **stinging**: aloe berb *Canth* kali-n **Nit-ac** *Puls Sulph*
  - **stitching** pain: *Aloe* am-m k* *Berb* k* calad k* *Calc* vh canth k* cham k* chin h1* hell h1* kali-n k* kali-s fd4.de laur k* *Lyc* mag-m k* *Mez* nat-m k* nicc **Nit-ac** k* pic-ac k* plac rzf5• *Plat Rat* sep k* stann k* *Thuj* k*
    - **upward**: alumn *Mez* sulph
  - **tearing** pain: aesc k* alumn germ-met srj5• *Kali-c* lyc melal-alt gya4 *Nat-m* **Nit-ac** k*
  - **tenesmus**: *Aeth* k* **Agar** k* aloe bg2* am-m k* ambr k* ant-t k* *Apis* apoc k* arist-cl sp1 ars k* ars-s-f k2 aster k* bamb-a stb2.de• bapt k* *Bell* k* berb hr1 bit-ar wht1• bov k* calc-i k2 calc-p k* calc-s k* *Canth* k* *Caps* k* carb-an b4.de* cob k* *Cocc* k* *Colch* k* coll hr1 corn k* *Cub* hr1 cupr bg2 cupr-act dios dros dulc erig k* fago k* fl-ac k* gamb k* gins k* grat k* guat sp1 hell k* hep bg2 *Ign* k* ind k* indg k* ip k* jug-c k* kali-ar *Kali-bi* k* kali-c k* kali-n k* kali-p *Kali-s* kola stb3• lach k* laur k* lil-t k* lim a1 lyc k* lyss k* *Mag-c* k* *Mag-m* k* mag-s k* manc k* mand sp1 **Merc** k* **Merc-c** k* *Merc-d* bro1 merc-i-r k* *Mez* k* nat-c b4.de* *Nat-m* k* nicc k* nit-ac bro1 nux-v b7a.de* ozone sde2• ph-ac k* phel k* phos h2* phys k* plat k* plb *Podo* k* ptel k* **Puls** *Rheum* k* rhodi br1* *Rhus-t* k* ruta b7.de* sabin b7.de* saroth sp1 sars k* senn bro1 sil bro1 *Staph* b7.de* **Sulph** k* tab k* *Trom* k* yuc a1 zinc k* zinc-p k2
  - **twinging**: canth k* franz a1 grat k*
  - **Perineum**: phos bg2
  - **Rectum** and Anus (*↗RECTUM - Pain - stool; after - agg. - Rectum and anus)*: alum bg2 ant-t bg2 bov bg2 caps bg2 caust bg2 cham bg2 coll bg2 graph bg2 hell bg2 hep bg2 ign bg2 ip bg2 kali-c bg2 lach bg2 lyc bg2 merc bg2 mez bg2 nat-c bg2 nat-m bg2 nux-v bg2 olnd bg2 petr bg2 ph-ac bg2 phos bg2 rheum bg2 sabad bg2 seneg bg2 staph bg2 stront-c bg2 sul-ac bg2 sulph bg2 teucr bg2 thuj bg2
    - **boring** pain: thuj bg2
- **amel.**: acon aesc aloe alum ant-t arn ars asaf bapt bov ↓ bry cain calc-p canth cham clem ↓ colch *Coloc* corn dulc *Gamb* hell lept nat-ar ↓ nat-s nuph **Nux-v** k* pall a1 **Rhus-t** sanic tarent ↓ verat-v ↓

Rectum

- **after – amel.**: ...
  - **burning**: clem verat-v ptk1
  - **cutting** pain: canth ptk1
  - **shortly** after stool: adam skp7•
  - **tenesmus**: acon aesc aloe alum k* ant-t arn k* ars asaf bapt bov bry cain calc-p canth cham colch *Coloc* corn dulc **Gamb** hell lept nat-ar k2 nat-s nuph **Nux-v** k* **Rhus-t** sanic tarent verat-v ptk1
  - **long**-lasting: aesc bro1* agar ptk1 aloe bro1* alumn bro1* am-c ptk1 am-m bro1* calc ptk1 *Colch* ptk1 *Graph* bro1* *Hydr* bro1 *Ign* bro1* merc-cy bro1 mur-ac bro1* *Nat-m* bro1 *Nit-ac* bro1* *Paeon* bro1* **Rat** bro1* *Sed-ac* bro1 sep bro1 sil bro1* stront-c ptk1 sulph bro1* thuj bro1 vib bro1
  - **not** amel.: merc-c tl1
    - **tenesmus**: *Merc-c* br1
  - **one** hour: hir ↓
    - **stitching** pain: hir rsj4•
  - **Rectum** and anus: calc ↓ ol-an ↓
    - **burning** | **fire**; like: ol-an bg2
    - **drawing** pain: calc bg2
- **amel.**: *Nat-ar* ↓ ulm-c ↓
  - **griping** pain: *Nat-ar* ulm-c jsj8•
- **before**: acon ↓ aeth ↓ **Agar** ↓ aloe ↓ alum ↓ am-c am-m ↓ ant-c ↓ anthraq rly4• aq-mar skp7* arn ↓ ars ↓ asar b7.de *Berb* *Caps* ↓ *Carb-an* cartl-s ↓ cench k2 cham ↓ cob ↓ coll ↓ *Coloc* ↓ *Con* ↓ crot-c ↓ dios ↓ dirc ↓ *Dulc* ↓ fago ↓ gamb ↓ glycyr-g ↓ grat ↓ *Hell* ↓ *Hydr* ↓ iod *Iris* ↓ jug-c ↓ kali-bi ↓ *Kali-c* kali-n ↓ kola stb3• lac-h ↓ lach k* lec lil-t *Lyc* mag-c ↓ mag-m ↓ mang-p rly4• medul-os-si ↓ merc **Merc-c** ↓ mez ↓ mur-ac ↓ nat-ar ↓ nat-m nat-s nit-ac *Nux-v* k* ol-an ↓ *Olnd* ↓ *Op* b7.de* ost ↓ pall ↓ *Phos* b4a.de phys ↓ phyt ↓ **Plat** ↓ plb ↓ podo puls bg2 *Rat* ↓ *Rheum* ↓ rhus-t b7.de ruta sabad ↓ sep ↓ spira ↓ spong ↓ *Staph* ↓ sul-ac ↓ sulph tarent ↓ til ↓ valer ↓ verat ↓ verat-v ↓
  - **burning**: aloe bro1 am-m bro1 ars bro1 *Berb* coloc bro1 con bro1 dios glycyr-g cte1• *Hydr* bro1 iod k* *Iris* bro1 jug-c k* merc bro1 *Nat-m* k* ol-an bro1 *Olnd* *Rat* k* rheum bro1 rhus-t h1* sabad k* *Sulph* k* verat k*
  - **cutting** pain: *Asar* grat k2 kali-bi gk mag-c h2* medul-os-si rly4• mur-ac h2* nat-ar k2 nit-ac k2 sep *Staph* hr1 sulph verat-v
  - **drawing** pain: nit-ac k2
  - **pressing** pain: ant-c k* cob k* hell a1 kola stb3• mang-p rly4• *Nat-m* *Nit-ac* *Nux-v* k* phos h2* **Plat** k* sul-ac til k*
  - **stitching** pain: asar k* *Berb* k* *Con* k* gamb k* *Kali-c* kali-n h2* pall c1 phos k* *Plat* spira a1 spong k* sul-ac k*
  - **tenesmus**: acon k* aeth k* **Agar** k* alum k* arn k* berb k* *Caps* b7a.de cartl-s rly4• cham k* coll hr1 *Coloc* k* crot-c k* dirc *Dulc* b4a.de fago k* grat *Hell* b7a.de lac-h sk4• mag-m *Merc* k* **Merc-c** k* mez bg2 *Nux-v* k* ost a1 phys k* phyt bg2 plat k* plb k* *Rheum* b7a.de *Rhus-t* b7a.de sep k* spong b7a.de **Sulph** k* tarent k* valer bg2 verat k*
  - **Rectum** and anus: asar ↓ chin ↓ kali-c ↓ mag-c ↓ nux-v ↓ olnd ↓ sabad ↓ sep ↓ tab ↓
    - **burning**: chin bg2 olnd bg2 sabad bg2
    - **cutting** pain: asar bg2 mag-c bg2 nux-v bg2 sep bg2
    - **pinching** pain: tab bg2
    - **sticking** pain: kali-c bg2 mag-c bg2
- **difficult**:
  - **after**: alum ↓ *Plat* ↓ *Rat* ↓
    - **stitching** pain: alum *Plat* *Rat*
- **during**:
  - **agg.**: abrom-a ks5 **Acon** ↓ aesc tl1 aeth **Agar** ↓ agath-a nl2• aids nl2• all-c ↓ aloe *Alum* k* alum-p ↓ alum-sil k2 alumn k* am-c am-caust ↓ am-m ambr amp rly4• anac androc srj1• ang ↓ *Ant-c* k* ant-t ↓ anthraq rly4• apis ↓ apoc ↓ aq-mar skp7• arg-n ↓ arizon-l nl2• *Arn* ↓ **Ars** k* ars-s-f k2 arum-d ↓ arum-i ↓ arum-t ↓ asaf *Asar* b7.de* asc-t ↓ aster ↓ aur aur-ar k2 aur-s k2 bapt ↓ bar-c bar-m bars-s k2 bell *Berb* *Borx* ↓ bov ↓ brach a1 brom bros-gau ↓ *Bry* cadm-met ↓ **Calc** k* calc-caust ↓ calc-p calc-s calc-sil k2 cann-s ↓ canth k* caps carb-ac ↓ carb-an *Carb-v* *Carbn-s* carl a1 cartl-s ↓ casc castm ↓ *Caust* bg2 *Cedr* ↓ cham *Chel* k* chin chinin-ar chion ↓ chir-fl ↓ chord-umb rly4• cimx clem ↓ cob ↓ coc-c ↓ cocc ↓ coff-t ↓ **Colch** k* colchin ↓ **Coll** coloc k* colocin ↓ con k* cop br1 *Corn* ↓ crot-t cub ↓ cuph br1 *Cupr* cupr-s ↓ cycl ↓ dios ↓ dros dulc ↓ ery-a ↓ fago ↓ falco-pe nl2• ferr k* ferr-ar ferr-i ↓ ferr-m ↓ ferr-p ferul ↓ *Fl-ac* form ↓ franz ↓ gamb ↓

- **during – agg.**: ...
  ger-i ↓ gran ↓ **Graph** grat k* hell b7.de hell-v ↓ hep k* hipp ↓ *Hydr* ↓ hydrog ↓ hyos k* hyper ↓ *Ign* k* **Ip** ↓ irid-met ↓ **Iris** ↓ jug-c ↓ *Kali-ar* *Kali-bi* kali-c kali-chl ↓ kali-i ↓ kali-m k2 kali-n ↓ kali-p kali-s kali-sil k2 kalm ↓ kola stb3• kreos *Lac-c* lac-d mrr1 *Lach* k* lap-la ↓ lat-m sp1 laur ↓ lil-s a1 *Lil-t* lipp ↓ lob-s ↓ **Lyc** k* lyss *Mag-c* ↓ mag-m b4.de* manc k* mang bg2 med k* melal-alt gya4 *Merc* k* **Merc-c** ↓ merc-i-r *Merc-sul* ↓ mez *Morph* ↓ mur-ac k* myric ↓ *Nat-ar* ↓ nat-c h2* nat-m k* nat-p ↓ nat-s k2 nat-sil ↓ nicc ↓ nicc-met ↓ **Nit-ac** k* nux-m b7.de nux-v k* oci-sa sp1 ol-an ↓ **Op** ↓ osm ↓ ost ↓ *Ox-ac* *Paeon* k* petr ↓ ph-ac k* phel ↓ phos phys ↓ phyt ↓ *Pic-ac* ↓ plac ↓ plac-s rly4• plan plat k* *Plb* **Podo** k* positr nl2• pot-e ↓ psil ↓ ptel ↓ puls k* pycnop-sa ↓ pyre-p ↓ **Rat** rheum ↓ rhod ↓ rhus-t rob ↓ *Ruta* bg2 sabad ↓ sabin k* *Sanic* saroth ↓ *Sars* ↓ *Sel* ↓ senec ↓ *Sep* k* **Sil** k* sin-a ↓ spira ↓ spirae ↓ *Spong* ↓ squil ↓ stann k* *Staph* ↓ still ↓ stram ↓ stront-c sk4• suis-em rly4• sul-ac k* **Sulph** k* sumb k* suprar ↓ *Syph* tab ↓ tarent k* tela ↓ tep ↓ ter ↓ tere-la ↓ ther ↓ *Thuj* k* tritic-vg fd5.de *Trom* ↓ *Tub* urt-u ↓ vanil fd5.de verat b7.de vib ↓ vinc ↓ xan ↓ *Zinc* zinc-p k2
  - **biting** pain: agar h2* kali-c a1 phos h2* sumb a1 thuj a1
  - **burning**: agar *Aloe* k* **Alum** k* alum-p k2 alum-sil k2 am-c am-caust a1 am-m k* ang h1* **Ars** k* ars-s-f k2 arum-d a1 arum-i a1 asc-t a1 *Bar-c* k* bar-m *Berb* *Borx* bros-gau mrc1 *Bry* k* *Calc* k* calc-s k* calc-sil k2 cann-s *Canth* caps carb-an k* carb-v k* *Carbn-s* cartl-s rly4• castm caust k* cham chin chinin-ar chion chir-fl gya2 clem k* cob cocc k* coloc k* **Con** k* corn k* crot-t k* cycl k* dios k* dulc fd4.de ferr ferr-ar ferr-p ferul a1 *Fl-ac* gamb k* ger-i rly4• *Graph* k* grat k* hell a1 hep *Hydr* k* **Iris** k* jug-c bro1 kali-ar kali-bi kali-c kali-m k2 kali-p kali-s kali-sil k2 *Lach* k* lil-t lipp a1 *Lyc* k* mag-m k* *Merc* k* *Merc-c* k* *Merc-sul* morph a1 *Mur-ac* k* nat-ar nat-c k* *Nat-m* k* nat-p *Nat-s* k* nat-sil fd3.de• nicc k* nit-ac k2 ol-an bro1 **Op** k* osm k* *Phos* k* phys k* pic-ac k* plac-s rly4• *Plat* k* plb k* positr nl2• pot-e rly4• *Puls* k* pycnop-sa mrz1 *Rat* k* rheum k* rhus-t sabad k* sep k* *Sil* k* sin-a k* spira a1 *Staph* still a1 stram *Stront-c* *Sul-ac* k* **Sulph** k* suprar rly4• tab k* tela zzc1• tep ter k* tritic-vg fd5.de vanil fd5.de *Verat* k* vinc k* *Zinc* k* zinc-p k2
  - **clawing** pain: aeth calc-caust c1 *Thuj* zinc
  - **cutting** pain: agar all-c alum k* alum-p k2 am-c ant-t anthraq rly4• ars ars-s-f k2 asar h1* canth carb-an h2* carb-v k* caust h2* dios hell h1* irid-met srj5• kali-bi gk lap-la sde8.de• mag-c h2* mang h2* *Mur-ac* k* nat-ar nat-c k* *Nat-m* nat-p **Nit-ac** k* *Phos* k* *Pic-ac* k* *Plat* plb k* *Puls* *Rhus-t* hr1 *Sars* sep stann staph h1* **Sulph** sumb k* tere-la rly4• vib
  - **lumps** in rectum; sensation of: nat-c h2*
  - **pressing** pain: alum k* ant-c h2* asaf corn k* dulc a1 *Kali-bi* k* kali-n a1 *Lil-t* k* **Lyc** nat-m ox-ac k* phos h2* *Podo* sin-a k* staph h1* sul-ac h2* **Sulph** k* sumb a1 *Zinc* k*
  - **sore**: *Aesc* *Agar* **Aloe** **Alum** alum-p k2 *Ant-c* k* brach k* cadm-met tpw6* caust k* coloc k* *Graph* *Grat* k* hydrog srj2• lob-s a1 nat-c k* *Nat-m* phos h2* podo fd3.de• spirae a1 spong h1* still a1 *Sulph*
  - **sticking** pain: ferr-i **Nit-ac**
  - **stinging**: agath-a nl2• berb caps k* caust coc-c ger-i rly4• ip *Lyc* mag-m nat-c nat-m nicc **Nit-ac** *Sil* sulph
  - **stitching** pain: am-c k* am-m *Berb* k* calc-s k* carb-an k* *Carb-v* k* carbn-s caust k* chin k* coc-c k* ferr-i k* **Graph** k* *Ign* ip k* laur k* lipp a1 lyc a1 *Mag-m* k* mur-ac h2* *Nat-c* k* nat-m k* **Nit-ac** k* nux-m k* *Nux-v* k* pic-ac k* *Sep* sil b4a.de* sin-a a1 *Staph* sul-ac k* sulph b4a.de* tritic-vg fd5.de
  - **tearing** pain: agar anthraq rly4• arn br1 arum-i a1 *Calc* k* colch ferr k* kola stb3• *Lach* melal-alt gya4 nat-ar **Nat-m** k* *Nit-ac* k* *Sars* *Sel* *Sep* *Sul-ac* k*
    - **asunder**; as if something would be torn: nit-ac tl1 plb tl1
  - **tenesmus**: **Acon** aesc *Aeth* k* **Agar** k* **Aloe** k* alum k* am-c k* am-m ang k* ant-t k* apis k* apoc k* arg-n *Arn* k* *Ars* k* arum-t k* asc-t aster k* bapt k* *Bell* bov bg2 *Calc* k* calc-s canth k* *Caps* k* carb-ac carbn-s *Caust* k* *Cedr* k* cob k* coff-t k* *Colch* k* colchin a1 *Coll* k* *Coloc* k* colocin a1 con k* cop k* *Corn* k* crot-t k* cub hr1 cuph br1 *Cupr* k* cupr-s a1 cycl hr1 dios k* ery-a a1* fago k* ferr k* ferr-ar ferr-m k* fl-ac k* form k* gamb k* gran k* graph k* grat k* hell k*

- **during** – **agg.** – **tenesmus**: ...
hell-v a1 hep k* hipp k* hydr k* hyper k* **Ip** k* iris kali-ar *Kali-bi* k* kali-chl k* kali-i k* kali-n k* kalm k* *Lac-c* lach k* laur k* lil-s a1 *Lil-t* k* lob-s k* lyc k* lyss k* *Mag-c* k* mag-m k* mang k* **Merc** k* **Merc-c** k* *Morph* k* myric k* *Nat-ar* *Nat-c* k* *Nat-m* k* *Nat-s* k* nicc k* nicc-met sk4• *Nit-ac* k* **Nux-v** k* **Op** k* ost a1 ox-ac k* petr k* phel a1 phos a1* phys k* phyt k* pic-ac k* plac rzf5• plan k* plat plb k* *Podo* k* psil ft1 ptel k* pyre-p a1 rhod bg2 *Rhus-t* k* rob k* ruta b7.de* saroth sp1 sars bg2 senec k* sep k* sil bg2 *Spong* k* squil bg2 staph k* still a1 *Sulph* k* tab k* ther k* thuj k* *Trom* k* urt-u hr1 verat k* xan hr1 zinc k*
  - **twinging**: carl a1 franz a1 spong k*
  - **Rectum** and anus: kali-bi ↓ merc ↓ staph ↓
    - **pressing** pain: kali-bi bg2 staph bg2
    - **stitching** pain: merc bg2
  - **amel.**: verat-v ↓
    - **tenesmus**: verat-v ptk1
  - **Rectum** and anus: asc-t ↓ **Iris** ↓ lyc ↓ *Mag-m* ↓ nit-ac ↓
    - **burning** | **fire**; like: asc-t bg2 **Iris** bg2 lyc bg2
    - **pricking**: *Mag-m* bg2 nit-ac bg2
- **hard** stool:
  - **after**:
    - **agg.**: aesc ↓ agar ↓ *Aloe* ↓ alumn ↓ am-m ↓ *Ars* ↓ coc-c ↓ *Kali-bi* ↓ kali-c ↓ kali-sil ↓ lil-t ↓ lyc ↓ mag-c ↓ mag-m ↓ melal-alt ↓ nat-c ↓ *Nat-m* ↓ nit-ac ↓ phos ↓ positr ↓ **Rat** ↓ sabad ↓ sec ↓ **Sil** ↓ *Sulph* ↓ ter ↓ *Thuj* ↓ til ↓
      - **burning**: aesc agar *Aloe* alumn am-m *Ars* coc-c *Kali-bi* kali-c kali-sil k2 lil-t lyc mag-c h2 mag-m nat-c *Nat-m* nit-ac h2 phos positr nl2• **Rat** sabad sec **Sil** *Sulph* ter *Thuj* til
      - **tearing** pain: lyc melal-alt gya4
    - **amel.**: ars ↓
      - **burning**: ars h2
  - **during**: bar-c ↓ bell ↓ ferr-i ↓ hell ↓ *Nat-m* ↓ prun ↓ sul-ac ↓ *Sulph* ↓
    - **sore**: *Nat-m* k* *Sulph* k*
    - **stitching** pain: bar-c bell ferr-i k2 hell h1 prun sul-ac h2 sulph
  - **with**: *Con* ↓
    - **tenesmus**: *Con*
- **loose**:
  - **after**: sel ↓
    - **sore**: sel rsj9•
- **not** at stool; when: carb-v ↓
  - **griping** pain: carb-v
- **straining** at | **after**: *Aesc* ars-s-f k2 bamb-a stb2.de• lach med melal-alt gya4 nux-v phos h2* plb ruta *Sil* *Thuj* trios rsj11•
- **urging** to:
  - **during**: mag-c ↓
    - **stitching** pain: mag-c h2

- **stool**; after:
  - **agg.**:
    - **Rectum** and anus: *(↗RECTUM - Pain - stool; after - agg. - Rectum and anus)*: crot-t ↓ nat-m ↓ nit-ac ↓ phos ↓
      - **scratching** pain: crot-t bg2 nat-m bg2 nit-ac bg2 phos bg2
- **stool**; as from too long retained: pall c1
- **sudden**: bamb-a ↓
  - **stitching** pain: bamb-a stb2.de•
- **tearing** pain: acon-l a1 aesc k2 *All-c* alumn ant-t a1 aur aur-s a1 *Berb* k* calc k* calc-sil k2 carb-v k* carbn-s carl a1 chin k* *Colch* k* erig k* eupi k* ferr k* grat ign *Kali-c* k* kreos k* lach k* laur k* led k* *Lyc* k* mang b4.de* melal-alt gya4 *Mez* k* nat-m k* **Nit-ac** k* **Nux-v** k* ph-ac k* phos k* *Ruta* k* sabad b7.de* sars k* sep k* sul-ac k* sulph k* thuj k* tub ptk1 zinc k* zinc-p k2
  - **jerking** pain: thuj h1
  - **twitching**: carl a1 thuj k*
  - **upward**: *Lach* sep

- **tenesmus**: *(↗Straining; Urging)* acal br1 acon k* **Aesc** aeth a1* agar k* agar-ph a1 agro c2 **Aloe** k* alum k* alum-p k2 alum-sil k2 am-c ambr k* *Anac* k* ang c1 *Ango* c1 ant-c k* aphis c2 **Apis** apoc k* aq-mar rbp6 *Arg-met* **Arg-n** hr1 arist-cl sp1 *Arn* k* *Ars* k* ars-i k* ars-s-f k2 arum-t k* asaf k* asc-t hr1 atro k* aur-m k* bamb-a stb2.de• bar-c bar-i k2 bar-m bar-s k2 *Bell* k* ben berb *Bit-ar* wht1• *Bov* k* brom k* bry k* cact cadm-met sp1 *Calc* k* calc-s k* calc-sil k2 cann-i k* cann-s k* *Canth* k* **Caps** k* carb-ac br1 carb-an *Carb-v* k* carbn-s cartl-s rly4• *Caust* k* cedr hr1 cham chinin-s chlf hr1 choc srj3• cinnb hr1* cob k* cob-n sp1 cocc k* **Colch** k* *Coll* k* *Coloc* k* colocin a1 con k* convo-s sp1 *Corn* k* cortiso gse *Crot-h* hr1 *Crot-t* k* cuph br1 cupr k* cupr-ar k* *Cycl* k* cyt-l a1* der k* dig k* dios k* dirc k* enteroc jl2 erig ptk1 ery-a a1* eug hr1 eup-per k* *Euph* k* eupi k* fago k* ferr k* ferr-ar ferr-i k* ferr-m k* ferr-p gamb k* gels gent-l a1 graph k* grat k* guat sp1 *Ham* hep k* hist sp1 hyos k* ign k* iod *Ip* k* *Iris* *Jug-c* hr1 kali-ar *Kali-bi* k* *Kali-br* a1* kali-c k* *Kali-i* k* kali-m k2 *Kali-n* k* kali-sil k2 kola stb3• kreos lac-ac a1 lac-c lac-h sk4• *Lach* k* lact k* laur k* lepi a1 *Lept* hr1 liat br1 **Lil-t** k* linu-c a1 *Lyc* k* lycps-v *Lyss* k* mag-c br1 mag-s k* manc k* mand sp1 mang hr1 mela a1 menis a1 **Merc** k* merc-br a1 **Merc-c** k* merc-cy k* merc-d a1 merc-n a1 *Mez* k* mill k* mit a1 morph hr1 morph-s hr1 mur-ac k* *Nat-ar* *Nat-c* k* *Nat-m* k* nat-p nicc k* **Nit-ac** k* nux-m k* *Nux-v* k* oena k* ol-an k* onis a1 op k* ost a1 ox-ac k* petr k* ph-ac phel k* phos k* phys k* *Phyt* k* pic-ac k* *Plat* k* plb k* plb-chr c2 podo k* propr sa3• psor k* ptel k* puls pyrog k2* rat rauw sp1 rham-f a1 rheum rhod k* *Rhus-t* k* *Rob* hr1 rumx ruta sang saroth sp1 sarr hr1 sel k* senec k* *Sep* k* *Sil* k* sol-ni sol-t k* sol-t-ae k* spig k* spong k* squil k* stann k* **Staph** k* still a1 *Stront-c* suis-em rly4• sul-i k2 **Sulph** k* sumb tab k* *Tarent* k* tax a1 ter thuj k* til a1 tong a1 trom k* tub al* valer k2 vanil fd5.de verat k* verat-v k* vib hr1 vip k* visc sp1 voes a1 xan hr1* zinc k* zinc-p k2 zinc-s a1
  - **accompanied** by | **menses**; suppressed: podo bro1
  - **jerking** pain: sep h2*
- **thinking** of it agg.: caust ↓
  - **sore**: caust h2*
- **tickling**: petr ↓ *Ran-s* ↓
  - **burning**: petr a1 *Ran-s* k*
- **touch** agg.: ars ↓ calc-p k2 rat mrr1 vanil fd5.de
  - **sore**: ars h2* vanil fd5.de
- **twinging**: caust k* kali-c k* lact k* lyc k* mag-c k* nat-c k* stry a1 zinc k*
- **twisting** pain: calc bg2
- **ulcerative** pain: mag-c h2* mez h2* sulph h2*
- **urination**:
  - **after**:
    - **agg.**: alum ↓ colch ↓ coloc ↓ colocin ↓ mur-ac ↓ *Nit-ac* ↓ phos ↓ *Prun* ↓ rhus-t ↓
      - **burning**: colch bg2 *Nit-ac* k* rhus-t ptk1
      - **tenesmus**: alum bg2 coloc colocin a1 mur-ac k* phos hr1 *Prun* hr1
  - **during**:
    - **agg.**: ars-s-f k2 carb-v ↓ carbn-s ↓ ferr ↓ hipp ↓ med ↓ merc-c ↓ *Prun* ↓ rhus-t k* *Ruta* ↓ sulph ↓
      - **drawing** pain: hipp jl2
      - **stitching** pain: carbn-s sulph k*
      - **tearing** pain: *Ruta*
      - **tenesmus**: carb-v k* carbn-s k2 ferr med k* merc-c k2 *Prun* k*
  - **not** urinating; when: ruta ↓
    - **tearing** pain: ruta tl1
- **vexation** agg.: *Cham* ↓ nat-m ↓
  - **burning**: *Cham* nat-m
- **vomiting**:
  - **after**: kali-c h2*
  - **while**: agar ↓
    - **sticking** pain: agar ptk1
- **walking**:
  - **after**:
    - **agg.**: mag-c ↓ thuj ↓
      - **stitching** pain: mag-c h2* thuj k*
  - **agg.**: aloe sne arg-met ↓ *Ars* ↓ bamb-a ↓ calc-p k2 *Carb-an* ↓ **Caust** coc-c ↓ coloc h2* crot-t ↓ cycl k* *Ign* *Kali-bi* ↓ kali-c h2* kali-s fd4.de mag-c ↓ meli ↓ *Mez* nat-m ↓ nat-p k2 *Nit-ac* ↓ petr ↓ phos ↓ ran-s sep *Sil* ↓ squil ↓ sulph sumb k* *Thuj* ↓ zinc ↓
    - **burning**: *Carb-an* *Mez* k* nat-m sulph k* *Thuj* zinc h2*

- **agg.**: ...
  - **cutting** pain: mag-c meli *Sulph* k*
  - **drawing** pain: *Cycl* k*
  - **pressing** pain: *Cycl* *Ran-s* k* sulph k*
  - **sore**: arg-met **Caust** cycl *Kali-bi* mag-c h2* *Mez* k* *Nit-ac* k*
  - **stinging**: carb-an
  - **stitching** pain: *Ars* coc-c crot-t kali-c h2 meli nat-p petr phos h2 *Sil* squil sulph zinc
  - **tenesmus**: bamb-a stb2.de• *Sulph*
- **air**; in open:
  - **amel.**: thuj ↓
    - **stitching** pain: thuj
- **slowly** | **amel.**: rat mrr1

\- **warm**:
- **applications**:
  - **amel.**: mur-ac ↓
    - **cutting** pain: mur-ac k2
- **bathing**:
  - **agg.**: brom
  - **amel.**: androc srj1• *Ars* calc-p k2 *Ign* sne *Lach* melal-alt gya4 *Mur-ac* phos h2 *Rat* k*
- **drinks** | **amel.**: carc mg1.de*

\- **warm** clothing:
- **amel.**: phos ↓
  - **tearing** pain: phos ptk1

\- **warmth** | **agg.**:
  - **heat** agg.: *Iod* ↓
    - **burning**: *Iod*
- **amel.**: coloc ↓ nux-v mrr1 sulph ↓
  - **heat** amel.: *Ars* ↓
    - **burning**: *Ars*
  - **tenesmus**: coloc sulph

\- **water**, on hearing running: **Lyss** ↓
- **tenesmus**: **Lyss**

\- **weather** agg.; cold: calc-p k2

\- **wiping** anus agg.: aloe pd graph ↓ kali-s fd4.de lach pd mur-ac pd paeon mrr1 vanil fd5.de
- **burning**: graph pd vanil fd5.de
- **sore**: graph pd vanil fd5.de

▽ - **extending** to:
- ○ **Abdomen**: aloe mag-c ↓ mag-m ↓ *Mez* mur-ac ↓ phos h2 plut-n srj7• *Sep* ↓ vanil fd5.de zinc
  - **drawing** pain: aloe zinc
  - **griping** pain: mez mur-ac a1
  - **pressing** pain: zinc h2
  - **stitching** pain: aloe mag-m *Sep* vanil fd5.de
  - **stool** agg.; during: mag-c ↓
    - **tearing** pain: mag-c
  - **tearing** pain: mag-c
- **Back**: *Aesc* ↓ carl ↓ dulc ↓
  - **stitching** pain: *Aesc* mrr1 carl dulc fd4.de
- **Bladder**: canth ↓ *Caps* ↓ *Med* ↓ merc-c ↓ mosch ↓ *Nux-v* ↓ thuj ↓
  - **stitching** pain: mosch thuj
  - **tenesmus**: canth *Caps* *Med* merc-c *Nux-v*
- **Coccyx**; through: carb-an ↓
  - **cutting** pain: carb-an h2
  - **drawing** pain: carb-an h2
- **Genitals**: carb-an chin bg1 germ-met ↓ phyt bg1 rhod *Sep* sil bg1* vanil fd5.de zinc bg1
  - **drawing** pain: carb-an rhod
  - **pressing** pain: germ-met srj5•
  - **stool**; before: carb-an
    - **drawing** pain: carb-an
  - **tearing** pain: germ-met srj5•
  - **walking** agg.: sil ↓
    - **stitching** pain: sil

\- **extending** to: ...
- **Heels**: fago bg1
- **Hips**: **Aesc** mrr1
- **Ilium** and glans penis: petr ↓ *Thuj* ↓
  - **stitching** pain: petr *Thuj*
- **Inguinal** region:
  - **left**: croc ↓ kreos ↓
    - **stitching** pain: croc kreos
- **Legs**; down back of: rhus-t ↓
  - **tearing** pain: rhus-t c1
- **Liver**: *Dios* ↓
  - **stitching** pain: *Dios* br1*
    - **accompanied** by | **hemorrhoids**: dios hr1*
- **Loins** | **stitching** pain (See lumbar - stitching)
- **Lumbar** region: **Aesc** mrr1 aloe ↓
  - **stitching** pain: aloe
- **Ovaries**: [heroin sdj2]
- **Penis**: carl ↓ petr ↓ zinc bg1
  - **stitching** pain: carl petr a1
- **Perineum**: mez ↓
  - **tenesmus**: mez k*
- **Pudendum**:
  - **menses**; during: aloe ↓ ars ↓
    - **stitching** pain: aloe ars h2
  - **stool** agg.; after: castm ↓
    - **stitching** pain: castm
- **Rectum**; up: hell ↓ mur-ac ↓ *Sep* ↓ *Sulph* ↓
  - **cutting** pain: hell mur-ac h2 *Sep* k* *Sulph*
- **Root** of penis: zinc ↓
  - **stitching** pain: zinc
- **Sacroiliac** region: **Aesc** mrr1
- **Testes**: trom vml3•
- **Thigh**: alum bg1 gran bg1 plb bg1 rhus-t bg1 sabin bg1
- **Thigh**; to inner side of: alumn ↓
  - **stitching** pain: alumn
- **Umbilicus**: cadm-met tpw6 ign k2 *Lach*
  - **drawing** pain: *Lach*
- **Upward**: aesc bg2 alum bg2 aral br1 graph bg2 hell bg2 *Ign* bg2 lach bg2 mag-c bg2 merc bg2 mez bg2 nat-m bg2 nat-ox rly4• neon srj5• nux-v k2 phos bg2 sep bg2 sulph bg2 thuj bg2 zinc bg2
- **Urethra**: bry bg1 carbn-s ↓ cocc ↓ hipp mez ↓ *Staph* hr1 thuj bg1
  - **stitching** pain: carbn-s cocc thuj
  - **tearing** pain: mez h2
  - **tenesmus**: mez k*
- **Vulva**: ars

○ - **Anus**: *Acon* ↓ **Aesc** ↓ agar ↓ *Aloe* ↓ alum ↓ am-c b4.de* am-m ↓ ambr ↓ ang ↓ ant-c ↓ ant-t ↓ *Apis* ↓ arg-n ↓ arn ↓ **Ars** ↓ asaf ↓ *Atis* ↓ aur ↓ *Bar-c* ↓ bell ↓ berb ↓ borx ↓ bov ↓ bry ↓ cact ↓ cain ↓ *Calc* ↓ calc-p ↓ cann-s ↓ canth b7.de* caps ↓ carb-an b4.de* *Carb-v* ↓ **Caust** ↓ chel ↓ *Chin* ↓ cocc ↓ colch b7.de* coloc ↓ con ↓ *Croc* ↓ crot-t ↓ cycl ↓ dros ↓ *Dulc* ↓ elaps ↓ euph ↓ euphr ↓ ferr ↓ *Gamb* ↓ glon ↓ graph ↓ grat ↓ hell ↓ *Hep* ↓ ign ↓ iod ↓ *Ip* ↓ *Iris* ↓ kali-ar ↓ kali-bi ↓ kali-c b4.de* kali-m ↓ kali-n ↓ kreos ↓ **Lach** ↓ laur ↓ lil-t ↓ *Lyc* b4.de* m-ambo ↓ m-arct ↓ mag-c ↓ mag-m b4.de* mag-p ↓ mang b4.de* med ↓ merc b4.de* *Merc-c* ↓ mez ↓ mosch ↓ mur-ac ↓ nat-c ↓ nat-m b4.de* nat-p ↓ nat-s ↓ *Nit-ac* ↓ nux-m ↓ *Nux-v* ↓ olnd ↓ op ↓ petr ↓ ph-ac ↓ phos b4.de* plat ↓ plb ↓ podo ↓ psor ↓ *Puls* ↓ pyrog ↓ ran-b ↓ ran-s ↓ rat ↓ rheum b7.de* rhod ↓ rhus-t ↓ sabad ↓ sabin b7.de* sars b4.de* scop ↓ seneg ↓ sep b4.de* sil ↓ spig ↓ spong ↓ squil ↓ stann ↓ staph ↓ stront-c ↓ *Sul-ac* ↓ **Sulph** ↓ tab ↓ teucr ↓ *Thuj* ↓ valer ↓ verat ↓ verb ↓ zinc ↓
- **accompanied** by | **Abdomen**; complaints of (See ABDOMEN - Complaints - accompanied - anus)
- **alternating** with | **Throat**; pain in (See THROAT - Pain - alternating with - anus)

- **biting** pain: alum b4.de* ambr b7.de* ant-c b7.de* *Apis* b7a.de cain bg2 canth b7.de* caps b7.de* carb-v b4.de* caust b4.de* chin b7.de *Dulc* b4.de* graph bg2 hell b7.de* kali-bi bg2 kali-c b4.de* lach b7.de* merc b4.de* mez b4.de* nat-c bg2 nat-m b4.de nux-m b7.de* nux-v b7.de* ph-ac b4.de* phos b4.de* rhod b4.de* sabin b7.de* sars b4.de* sulph b4.de*
- **boring** pain: *Apis* b7a.de borx b4a.de* kali-bi bg2 plb bg2 sil bg2 thuj bg2 valer b7.de* zinc b4.de*
- **burning**: acon bg2 *Aesc* bg2 *Aloe* bg2 alum b4.de* am-c b4.de* am-m b7.de ang b7.de* ant-c b7.de* ant-t b7.de* apis b7a.de* arg-n bg2 **Ars** b4.de* aur b4.de* bar-c b4.de* bell bg2 berb bg2 bov b4.de bry b7.de* calc b4.de* cann-s b7.de* *Canth* b7.de* caps b7.de* carb-an b4.de* *Carb-v* b4.de* caust b4.de* chin b7.de* cocc b7.de* colch b7.de* coloc b4.de* con b4.de* crot-t bg2 dulc bg2 euph bg2 ferr b7.de *Gamb* bg2 glon bg2 graph b4.de* grat bg2 hell b7.de* hep b4.de* ign b7.de* iod b4.de* ip b7.de *Iris* bg2 kali-ar bg2 kali-c b4.de* kreos bg2 lach b7.de* laur b7.de* lil-t bg2 lyc b4.de* m-ambo b7.de mag-c b4.de mag-m b4.de* **Merc** b4.de* merc-c bg2 mez bg2 mur-ac b4.de* nat-c b4.de* nat-m b4.de* nat-s bg2 nit-ac b4.de* *Nux-v* b7.de* olnd b7.de* op b7.de* petr b4.de* ph-ac bg2 **Phos** b4.de* plb b7.de* podo bg2 psor bg2 *Puls* bg2 ran-b bg2 ran-s b7.de rat bg2 rheum bg2 rhus-t bg2 sabad bg2 sars b4.de* scop ptk1 *Sep* b4.de* sil b4.de* spig b7a.de* spong bg2 stann b4.de* staph b7.de* stront-c b4.de* sul-ac b4.de* **Sulph** b4.de* tab bg2 thuj b4.de* verat b7.de* zinc b4.de*
- **bursting** pain: agar bg2 ant-c b7.de* bar-c bg2 *Calc* b4.de* caust bg2 hell bg2 kali-c b4.de* lach bg2 nat-m bg2 nit-ac b4.de* op bg2 phos b4.de* staph bg2 sul-ac b4.de*
- **coition**; after: calc ↓
  - **stitching** pain: calc b4a.de
- **corrosive**: ang bg2 carb-an bg2 carb-v bg2 elaps bg2 ferr bg2 merc b4.de* ph-ac bg2 phos b4.de* spong b7a.de* stann b4.de*
- **cutting** pain: alum b4.de* ars b4.de* bell bg2 carb-v b4.de* *Chin* b7.de* graph b4.de* ip b7.de* kali-c b4.de* lyc b4.de* merc b4.de* mur-ac b4.de* nat-c b4.de* nit-ac b4.de* nux-v b7.de* phos b4.de* plb b7.de* rat bg2 sars b4.de* sep b4.de* stann b4.de* staph b7.de* sulph b4.de* zinc b4.de*
- **drawing** pain: ambr b7.de* ant-c b7.de* calc bg2 carb-an b4.de* caust bg2 chel bg2 chin bg2 cycl b7.de* ign bg2 kali-bi bg2 kreos b7a.de* *Lach* bg2 mang bg2 mez b4.de* rhod b4.de* zinc bg2
- **eating**; after: lyc b4a.de
- **griping** pain: calc bg2 croc b7.de* lyc b4.de* nat-m bg2 nit-ac bg2
- **hammering**: lach ptk1
- **itching**: *Acon* ↓
  - **stitching** pain: *Acon* ptk1
- **leukorrhea** agg.: alum ↓
  - **burning**: alum b4a.de
- **menses**; during: am-m ↓ lach ↓ mur-ac ↓ zinc ↓
  - **burning**: am-m b7.de zinc b4.de
  - **hammering**: lach ptk1
  - **sore**: mur-ac ptk1
- **mental** exertion; after: nux-v tl1
- **paralytic**: sabin b7.de*
- **pinching** pain: kali-c b4a.de m-arct b7.de merc b4.de* mez bg2 nat-m b4.de* sabad b7.de*
- **pressing** pain: *Acon* b7.de* agar b4.de* aloe bg2 alum b4.de* ang b7.de* ant-c b7.de* arn b7.de* ars b4.de* asaf b7.de* *Bar-c* b4.de* bell b4.de* bov b4.de* calc b4.de* cann-s b7.de* carb-an b4.de* carb-v b4.de* caust b4.de* chel bg2 chin b7.de* con b4.de* cycl b7.de* dros b7.de* dulc b4.de* euphr b7.de* graph b4.de* grat bg2 hell b7.de* ign b7.de* kali-bi bg2 kali-n b4.de* lach bg2 laur b7.de* lyc b4.de* m-arct b7.de mag-m b4.de* mag-p bg2 *Merc* b4.de* *Merc-c* b4a.de mez b4.de* nat-c b4.de* nat-m b4.de* nit-ac b4.de* nux-v b7.de* op b7.de* petr b4.de* *Phos* b4.de* plat b4.de* puls b7.de* rhod b4.de* rhus-t b7.de* sars b4.de* seneg b4.de* sep b4.de* spig b7.de* staph b7.de* *Sul-ac* b4.de* *Sulph* b4.de verat b7.de* verb bg2 zinc b4.de*
- **pricking**: cact ptk1 med jl2
- **raw**: am-c bg2 arn bg2 ars bg2 bar-c bg2 calc bg2 *Carb-an* bg2 carb-v bg2 ferr bg2 grat bg2 *Hep* bg2 kali-c bg2 lach bg2 *Merc* bg2 nat-m bg2 nat-p tl1 *Nit-ac* bg2 nux-v bg2 phos bg2 sep bg2 *Sulph* bg2 zinc bg2
- **scraping** pain: acon bg2 kali-n b4.de* nat-m b4.de* nit-ac bg2 phos b4.de* plb b7.de* sep b4.de*
- **sitting** agg.: lach ↓
  - **cutting** pain: lach bg2
- **sleep**; during: kali-c b4.de*
- **sore**: *Aloe* bg2 alum b4.de* *Am-c* bg2 am-m b7a.de ant-c b7a.de* apis b7a.de *Ars* b4.de* bell bg2 berb bg2 calc bg2 calc-p bg2 carb-v b4.de* caust b4.de* crot-t bg2 dulc bg2 graph b4.de* grat bg2 hep bg2 ign b7.de* kali-bi bg2 kali-c b4.de* kali-m ptk1 lyc ptk1 m-ambo b7.de merc b4.de* mez b4.de* mur-ac b4.de* nat-c b4.de* nat-m b4.de* nat-p tl1 nux-v b7.de* petr b4.de* ph-ac bg2 phos b4.de* podo bg2 *Puls* b7.de* pyrog bg2 rhus-t b7.de* sabin b7.de* sars b4.de* sep b4.de* spong b7.de* stann b4.de* staph b7a.de *Sulph* b4.de* *Thuj* bg2 verat bg2 zinc b4a.de*
  - **accompanied** by | **constipation** (See Constipation - accompanied - anus - pain)
- **stitching** pain: acon b7.de* **Aesc** bg2 aloe bg2 alum b4.de* am-m b7.de* ambr b7.de* *Apis* b7a.de *Ars* b4.de* *Atis* zzc1• aur b4.de* borx b4a.de bov bg2 bry b7.de* canth b7.de* caps b7.de* carb-an b4.de* carb-v b4.de* **Caust** b4.de* chin b7.de* colch b7.de* coloc b4.de* con b4.de* *Croc* b7.de* crot-t bg2 graph b4.de* grat bg2 ign b7.de* iod b4.de* *Ip* b7.de* kali-bi bg2 kali-c b4.de* **Lach** bg2 laur b7.de* lyc b4.de* mag-c b4a.de* merc b4.de* merc-c bg2 mosch b7a.de mur-ac b4.de* nat-c b4.de* *Nat-m* b4.de* nit-ac b4.de* nux-v b7.de* ph-ac b4.de* phos b4.de* plat b4.de* ran-b b7.de* sabin b7.de* **Sep** b4.de* sil b4.de* spong b7.de* squil b7.de* stann b4.de* sulph b4.de* teucr b7.de* zinc b4.de*
- **stool**:
  - **after**:
    - **agg.**: aesc ↓ aloe ↓ *Alum* ↓ am-c ↓ am-m ↓ ant-t ↓ apoc ↓ ars ↓ bell ↓ bov ↓ bry ↓ **Calc** ↓ *Canth* ↓ **Caps** ↓ carb-v ↓ caust ↓ cham ↓ chel ↓ *Chin* ↓ *Cocc* ↓ colch ↓ coloc ↓ crot-t ↓ cupr ↓ euph ↓ *Gamb* ↓ *Graph* ↓ grat ↓ hell ↓ *Hep* ↓ *Ign* ↓ iod ↓ *Iris* ↓ kali-bi ↓ kali-c ↓ kali-m ↓ kali-n ↓ lach ↓ laur ↓ lil-t ↓ lyc ↓ m-ambo ↓ mag-c ↓ mag-m ↓ merc ↓ *Merc-c* ↓ merc-d ↓ mez ↓ mur-ac ↓ nat-c ↓ nat-m ↓ nit-ac ↓ *Nux-v* ↓ ol-an ↓ olnd ↓ op ↓ petr ↓ ph-ac ↓ phos ↓ plat ↓ prun ↓ puls ↓ *Rat* ↓ rheum ↓ rhod ↓ rhus-t ↓ ruta ↓ sars ↓ sec ↓ sel ↓ seneg ↓ sep ↓ *Sil* ↓ stann ↓ staph ↓ stront-c ↓ sul-ac ↓ *Sulph* ↓ thuj ↓ trom ↓ verat ↓ zinc ↓
      - **biting** pain: alum b4.de* canth bg2 caust b4.de* colch bg2 hell b7.de* kali-c b4.de* lach b7.de* mez bg2 nat-m bg2 nux-v b7.de* ph-ac bg2 sil b4a.de*
      - **burning**: aesc bg2 aloe bg2* alum b4.de* am-c b4.de* am-m b7.de* ant-t b7.de* apoc bro1 ars b4.de* bell b4a.de bov b4.de* bry b7.de* **Calc** b4.de* *Canth* b7.de* **Caps** bg2* carb-v b4.de* caust b4.de* chel bg2 *Chin* bg2 *Cocc* b7.de* colch bg2 coloc bg2* crot-t bg2 cupr bg2 euph b4.de* *Gamb* bro1 grat bg2* hell b7.de* *Hep* b4a.de *Ign* bg2 iod b4.de* *Iris* bro1 kali-bi bg2 kali-c b4.de* kali-n bg2 lach b7.de* laur b7.de* lil-t bg2 lyc b4.de* m-ambo b7.de* mag-c b4.de* mag-m b4.de* merc b4a.de* *Merc-c* bg2* mez bg2 mur-ac b4.de* nat-c b4.de* nat-m b4.de* nit-ac b4.de* nux-v b7.de* ol-an bg2 olnd b7.de* op bg2 petr b4.de* phos b4.de* prun bro1 puls bg2 *Rat* bro1 rheum bg2 rhod bg2 rhus-t bg2 ruta b7.de* sars b4.de* sec bg2 sep bg2 *Sil* b4a.de* stann b4.de* staph b7.de* stront-c b4.de* sul-ac bg2 *Sulph* b4a.de* thuj b4a.de* trom bg2* verat bro1 zinc b4.de*
      - **cutting** pain: aloe bg2 alum b4a.de calc b4a.de* chel bg2 hell b7.de* ign bg2 nat-c b4a.de *Nux-v* bg2 sulph bg2
      - **pressing** pain: aloe bg2 *Alum* bg2 calc bg2 caust bg2 hell bg2 ign b7.de* *Nux-v* b7.de* phos b4a.de puls b7.de* seneg b4.de* stann bg2 sul-ac bg2 sulph bg2
      - **sore**: alum b4a.de *Graph* b4a.de *Ign* b7.de* kali-m ptk1 m-ambo b7.de merc-d br1 nux-v b7.de puls b7.de sel b7.de staph b7.de
      - **stitching** pain: aloe bg2 alum b4a.de* am-c b4.de* canth b7.de* cham b7.de* chin b7.de* hell b7.de* kali-c b4a.de kali-n bg2 lyc bg2 nat-m bg2 nit-ac bg2 plat b4.de* sep bg2 stann bg2 sulph b4.de* thuj bg2
      - **tearing** pain: kali-c b4a.de mez b4.de*
  - **before**: apis b7a.de asar bg2 bell bg2 carb-an b4.de* carb-v b4a.de* colch b7.de* euph b4.de* ferr b7.de* kali-c b4.de* lach b7.de* mang b4.de* merc bg2 mur-ac bg2 *Nux-v* bg2 olnd b7.de* op bg2 *Phos* b4.de* plat b4.de* rhus-t bg2 sabad ↓ spong b7.de* sul-ac b4.de* valer b7.de
    - **burning**: sabad b7a.de

Rectum

- **stool**: ...
  - **during**:
    - **agg.**: acon bg2 agar↓ *Aloe*↓ *Alum*↓ am-c b4.de* am-m↓ ang bg2 ant-c b7.de* ant-t↓ apis↓ **Ars** bg2 asaf↓ asar bg2 aur↓ bapt↓ bar-c bg2 borx↓ bov↓ *Brom* b4a.de bry bg2 calc bg2 calc-p↓ cann-s↓ canth b7.de* **Caps** bg2 carb-an↓ carb-v bg2 caust bg2 *Cham* bg2 chel bg2 *Chin*↓ cic↓ *Cocc* bg2 colch b7.de* *Coloc*↓ con↓ crot-t bg2 cycl↓ dulc bg2 euph bg2 ferr b7.de* **Gamb**↓ graph↓ grat↓ hell bg2 hep bg2 hyos b7.de* ign b7.de* iod↓ ip bg2 **Iris**↓ kali-bi↓ kali-c↓ kali-n bg2 lach bg2 laur bg2 lyc↓ mag-c↓ *Mag-m* b4.de* **Merc** b4.de* *Merc-c* bg2 mez↓ mur-ac↓ nat-c↓ *Nat-m* bg2 nit-ac bg2 nux-m bg2 *Nux-v* bg2 *Olnd*↓ op bg2 petr↓ ph-ac↓ *Phos*↓ plat↓ plb↓ podo bg2 *Puls* bg2 rat↓ rhod↓ rhus-t bg2 sabad↓ sabin bg2 sars b4.de* sel bg2 sep b4.de* sil bg2 spig bg2 spong bg2 squil↓ stann↓ *Staph*↓ stront-c b4a.de* *Sul-ac*↓ **Sulph** bg2 tab↓ tarax↓ ter↓ thuj b4.de *Verat*↓ verb↓ zinc↓
      - **biting** pain: *Ant-c* b7.de* canth b7.de* caps b7.de* *Chin* b7.de* *Dulc* b4.de* kali-c b4.de* lyc bg2 merc b4.de* nat-m b4a.de* nux-m b7.de* ph-ac b4.de* phos b4a.de *Puls* b7.de* sabin b7.de* sulph b4a.de
      - **burning**: agar bg2 *Aloe* bg2 alum b4.de* am-m b7.de* ang b7.de* ant-c bg2 ant-t bg2 **Ars** b4.de* aur b4.de* bapt bg2 bar-c b4.de* borx bg2 bov b4.de* **Bry** b7.de* *Calc* b4a.de* calc-p bg2 cann-s b7.de* canth b7.de* *Caps* b7.de* carb-an b4.de* carb-v b4.de* caust bg2 **Cham** bg2 chel bg2 chin b7.de* cic bg2 *Cocc* b7.de* *Coloc* b4.de* con b4.de* crot-t bg2 cycl bg2 euph b4.de* *Ferr* b7a.de **Gamb** bg2 graph b4.de* grat bg2 hell bg2 *Ign* b7a.de iod b4a.de ip b7.de* **Iris** bg2 kali-bi bg2 kali-c b4.de* lach b7.de* *Laur* b7.de* lyc b4.de* mag-m b4.de* *Merc* b4.de* merc-c b4a.de* mur-ac b4a.de* nat-c b4.de* *Nat-m* b4.de* nit-ac b4.de* *Nux-v* bg2 *Olnd* b7a.de op b7.de* petr bg2 *Phos* b4.de* plb b7.de* *Podo* bg2 *Puls* b7.de* rat bg2 rhus-t bg2 sep b4.de* sil b4.de* squil bg2 *Staph* b7.de* stront-c b4.de* sul-ac b4.de* *Sulph* b4.de* tab bg2 ter bg2 *Thuj* b4.de *Verat* b7.de* zinc b4.de*
      - **cutting** pain: aloe bg2 alum b4.de* ars b4.de* canth b7.de* carb-v b4.de* *Caust* b4.de* chel bg2 *Chin* b7.de* hell b7.de* laur b7a.de merc b4.de* mur-ac b4.de* nat-c b4.de* nit-ac bg2 phos b4.de* plb b7.de* sars b4.de* sep b4.de* stann b4.de* *Staph* b7.de* *Sulph* b4.de*
      - **pressing** pain: acon b7.de* agar b4.de* alum bg2 ang b7.de* ant-c b7.de* asaf b7.de* *Bar-c* b4.de* chel b7a.de hell b7.de* hep b4.de* kali-bi bg2 kali-n b4.de* lach b7a.de laur b7.de* *Merc* b4.de* mez b4.de* *Puls* b7.de* rhod b4.de* sars b4.de* sep bg2 spig b7.de* staph b7.de* *Sul-ac* b4.de* *Sulph* b4.de* tarax b7.de* verb b7a.de zinc b4a.de
      - **scraping** pain: crot-t bg2 nat-m b4.de* plb b7.de* sep b4.de*
      - **soft** stool: nit-ac↓
        - **tearing** pain: nit-ac ptk1
      - **sore**: apis b7a.de *Ars* b4.de* ign b7.de* merc b4.de* *Merc-c* b4a.de petr b4.de* phos b4.de* sabad bg2 sabin b7.de sep bg2 spong b7.de* staph b7a.de
      - **stitching** pain: am-m b7.de* bry bg2 caps b7.de* carb-an b4.de* carb-v b4.de* caust b4.de* chin b7.de* coloc bg2 graph b4.de* hell b7.de* ip b7.de* kali-c bg2 laur bg2 lyc b4.de* mag-m bg2 nat-c b4.de* *Nat-m* b4.de* nit-ac b4.de* nux-m b7.de* nux-v bg2 phos b4.de* plat b4.de* sabin b7.de* sil b4.de* sul-ac b4.de* sulph b4a.de* zinc b4.de*
      - **tearing** pain: mez ptk1 nat-m ptk1
      - **torn** asunder; as if: *Alum* b4a.de ant-c b7.de* bov bg2 *Calc* b4.de* colch bg2 ferr bg2 lyc bg2 mag-c bg2 nat-m bg2 nit-ac b4.de* sars bg2 staph b7.de* sul-ac b4.de*
- **tearing** pain: acon bg2 *Colch* b7.de* kali-c b4.de* mez b4.de* nat-m bg2 nux-v b7.de* ph-ac b4.de* puls b7.de* sep b4.de* thuj b4.de* valer b7.de* zinc b4.de*
- **ulcerative** pain: ant-c b7a.de cycl b7a.de
- **urination** agg.; during: colch↓
  - **burning**: colch b7.de*
- **walking** agg.: kali-m↓
  - **sore**: kali-m ptk1
- **writhing**: *Croc* k*

- **Anus**: ...
  - ▽ **extending** to:
    - **Urethra**; through: hipp↓ mez↓
      - **drawing** pain: hipp k* mez h2*
  - ○ **Skin**; below the: agn↓ cycl↓ sulph↓
    - **ulcerative** pain: agn b7.de* cycl b7.de* sulph bg2
- **Perineum**: agn bg3 aloe↓ alum k* am-m↓ ant-c k* ant-t↓ *Asaf*↓ aur k* bell↓ *Berb* k* bov bry↓ calc-p *Canth* k* carb-an carb-v bg3 *Carl* a1 **Caust** k* chel k* chin↓ cupr-ar k* *Cycl* k* echi↓ germ-met↓ kali-bi laur↓ *Lyc* k* mag-m↓ mela a1* merc↓ mez↓ mur-ac↓ nat-c↓ nit-ac↓ nux-v k* ol-an↓ ozone↓ phos k* plb k* podo↓ *Puls* *Rhod*↓ sanic↓ sel sep↓ sil↓ spig↓ spong fd4.de sulph thuj tritic-vg fd5.de vanil fd5.de
  - **morning**: lyc↓
    - **cutting** pain: lyc k*
  - **evening**: am-m↓ sep↓
    - **cutting** pain: am-m
    - **stitching** pain: am-m sep k*
  - **biting** pain: agn bg2 carb-an a1
  - **blowing** the nose agg.: alum↓
    - **pressing** pain: alum a1
  - **boring** pain: merc bg2 spig b7.de*
  - **burning**: alum bg2 ant-c k* ant-t b7.de* aur k2 cycl bg2 mur-ac k* nit-ac k* nux-v bg2 plb k* *Rhod* k* sil k* thuj k* vanil fd5.de
  - **burrowing**: carb-an b4a.de*
  - **bursting** pain: sanic ptk1
  - **coition**:
    - **after**: alum bro1* sil↓
      - **burning**: sil k*
    - **during**: alum bg2*
  - **corrosive**: agn b7.de*
  - **cutting** pain: am-m aur bov lyc k* nux-v k* thuj k*
  - **drawing** pain: berb *Cycl* k* *Kali-bi* k* mez k* sulph k*
  - **erection**; during: alum ptk1
  - **jerking**: bell b4.de* nux-v bg2
  - **menses**; during: luna kg1•
  - **pinching** pain: carb-an h2 lyc h2 *Puls* k*
  - **pressing** pain: *Alum* k* *Asaf* berb ptk1 bry b7.de* cycl b7.de* laur bg2 *Lyc* k* mez h2 nux-v b7.de* ol-an ptk1 sulph thuj
    - **outward**: asaf b7.de*
  - **rising** from sitting agg.: alum h2
  - **sitting** agg.: alum h2* *Cycl*↓ lyc h2*
    - **drawing** pain: *Cycl* k*
  - **sore**: aloe bg2 alum k* carb-v bg2 echi ozone sde2• podo fd3.de• rhod bg2 sep bg2 spig b7.de* spong fd4.de sulph bg2 thuj bg2 tritic-vg fd5.de vanil fd5.de
  - **squeezing**: alum b4.de*
  - **standing** agg.: alum h2*
  - **sticking** pain: alum bell bov carb-v mag-m merc sep thuj
  - **stinging**: aur k2
  - **stitching** pain: agn bg2 alum k* am-m k* aur bell b4.de* berb k* bov k* bry bg2 *Calc-p* carb-an bg2 carb-v k* chel k* chin k* mag-m k* merc k* nat-c h2* nit-ac k* nux-v b7.de* sep k* spig k* sulph thuj k*
  - **stool** | **after**:
    - **agg.**: lyc h2* nit-ac↓ sanic↓
      - **burning**: nit-ac tl1 sanic tl1
      - **bursting** pain: sanic ptk1
      - **sore**: nit-ac tl1 sanic tl1
    - **during** | **agg.**: sanic tl1
  - **suppurative**: cycl bg2
  - **tearing** pain: am-m k* germ-met srj5• mez k*
  - **ulcerative** pain: cycl b7a.de*
  - **urination**:
    - **after**:
      - **agg.**: am-m↓ lyc↓

- urination – after – agg.: ...
  - pressing pain: am-m bro1 lyc bro1
  - during:
    - agg.: lyc ↓ phos h2*
      - pressing pain: lyc bg2
      - squeezing: lyc b4.de*
    - urging to urinate: ant-t k* aran cop lyc bro1 sep bro1
- walking agg.: am-m c1 cycl ↓
  - drawing pain: cycl k*
- walking or sitting; when: cycl ↓
  - ulcerative pain: cycl bro1

▽ • extending to:
  - Anus: mela ↓ nit-ac ↓
    - drawing pain: mela c1
    - stitching pain: nit-ac k*
  - Penis: *Calc-p* ↓
    - stitching pain: *Calc-p* k*
  - Urethra: kali-bi ↓
    - drawing pain: kali-bi
  - Uterus: berb ↓
    - stitching pain: berb k*

○ • Skin; below the: cycl ↓
  - ulcerative pain: cycl b7.de*

- **Rectum** and anus: acon bg2 arn ↓ bell ↓ caust bg2 con bg2 iris ↓ nux-v bg2 seneg bg2 thuj ↓
  - clawing pain: arn bg2 bell bg2 thuj bg2
  - stitching pain | needles; as from: iris bg2

PARALYSIS: (↗*Inactivity*) acon aeth agar aloe k* *Alum* k* alum-p k2 alum-sil k2 alumn k2 arn ars ars-i ars-s-f k2 atro *Bar-m* *Bell* bry *Calc* caust k* chin chinin-ar cocc k2 coll coloc con k2 cupr *Erig* bro1 ferr ferr-ar k2 *Gels* k* *Graph* k* hydr k2 *Hyos* k* kali-ar kali-c kali-m k2 kali-p lac-d k2 *Laur* mag-c k2 manc **Mur-ac** k* nat-c k2 nat-m nux-v k2 op bro1* oxyt bro1 ph-ac k* **Phos** k* **Plb** k* puls rhus-t **Sec** sel **Sil** k* stann k2 sulfon bro1 sulph syph k2* *Tab* k* tarent thuj k* verat

- **hemorrhoids**, after removal of: kali-p ptk1
- **sensation** of: **Aloe** alum tl1 calc-sil k2 coll tl1 graph kali-c petr ph-ac rhod bg1 sabad k*

○ - **Sphincter** ani: acon b7.de* agar bg2 **Aloe** bg2* *Alum* b4a.de* anac bg2 *Apis* bg2 apoc bg2* bell b4.de* carb-v bg2 *Caust* bg2* chin bg2 *Coloc* b4.de* *Dulc* b4a.de *Erig* bro1 ferr bro1 gels bg2* graph b4a.de* *Hep* bg2 *Hyos* b7.de* ix bnm8• kali-c bg2 laur b7a.de* merc bg2 **Mur-ac** bg2* *Nat-m* b4a.de nux-m bg2 *Nux-v* bro1 *Olnd* bg2 op bro1* oxyt bro1 petr bg2 ph-ac bro1 **Phos** b4a.de* plb bro1 sanic bro1 **Sec** bg2* sel bg2 sep bg2 sil bg2* stann bg2 stram b7.de* sulfon bro1 sumb bg2 tab bg2*
  - stool | after | agg.: *Coloc* b4.de*
    - during | agg.: *Hyos* b7a.de

PARASITES: | **worms** (See Worms)

PERIODICITY: | **Rectum** and anus: plat bg2

PERSPIRATION about the anus and perineum: agar k* *Alum* k* *Aur* bg2 bell k* bond a1 brass-n-o srj5• calc b4a.de* carb-an k* carb-v bg2 chin-b c1 coloc bg2* con k* *Hep* k* kali-c k* nux-v bg2 psor k* rhus-t k* *Sep* bg2* thuj k*

- **morning**: *Thuj* k*
- **night**: kali-c k*
- **acrid**: arum-t k2
- **stool**, before and during: sep h2*

PLUG; sensation of a: (↗*Lump*) *Aloe* bro1 *Anac* br1* apoc bg2 cann-i bro1 cann-xyz ptk1 crot-t ptk1 kali-bi bg2* *Lach* ptk1 lil-t ptk1 med bro1 nat-m ptk1 *Plat* bro1* plb bro1 **Sep** bro1* sul-ac bro1*

- **pressing** out: bry *Crot-t* k* kali-bi *Lach* lil-t *Sep* *Sil*
- **wedged** between pubis and coccyx: aloe

POLYPI: am-m calc *Calc-p* k* form mtf11 hydr mtf11 *Kali-br* k* *Nat-s* mrr1 *Nit-ac* k* nux-v **Phos** k* psor al2 ruta sang teucr k*

- **accompanied by** | **respiration**; asthmatic (See RESPIRATION - Asthmatic - accompanied - rectum - polypi)

PREGNANCY; during: | **Rectum** and anus: caps bg2 hydr bg2 mur-ac bg2 podo bg2

PRESSURE:

- **abdomen**; on:
  - **amel.** | **Rectum** and anus: alum bg2
- **hard** pressure:
  - **amel.** | **Rectum** and anus: camph bg2 kali-c bg2
- **umbilicus**; on:
  - **agg.**: *Crot-t* ptk1
  - **amel.**: kali-c ptk1

PRICKLING: agar k* ars bg2 bapt bg2 bry k* cact k* calc-p bg2 colch k* grat k* lact k* lith-m a1 *Mag-m* bg2 **Nit-ac** k* rhus-g tmo3• spirae a1 *Ter*

- **stool** | **after** | **agg.**: grat k* sin-a a1 spira a1 spirae a1
  - **during** | **agg.**: cact k*

PROCTITIS (See Inflammation)

PROLAPSUS: (↗*ABDOMEN - Prolapsus - intestines*) *Aesc* k* *Aesc-g* bro1 all-c all-s hr1* **Aloe** bg2* alum b4a.de alumn k* *Am-m* b7a.de anac b4a.de ant-c k* **Apis** k* apoc k* aral c2* arg-n bg1 arist-cl sp1 arn k* *Ars* k* ars-s-f k2 arum-m hr1* arund c1 *Asar* k* aur k* aur-ar k2 aur-s k2 *Bell* k* bry b7.de* bufo k* **Calc** k* calc-f mtf11 calc-p mtf11 *Calc-s* k* canth k* carb-v b4a.de* *Carbn-s* carc mg1.de* card-m mtf11 caust k* chinin-s c2 cic k* cocc *Colch* k* *Coll* k* *Crot-c* crot-t k* *Dig* dios *Dulc* k* elaps ery-a hr1* euph-a c2 euphr c2 *Ferr* k* ferr-ar *Ferr-i* ferr-p k* fl-ac k* *Gamb* k* *Gels* k* gran *Graph* k* ham hr1* *Hep* k* *Hydr* k* hyper mtf11 **Ign** k* indg c2* *Iris* k* *Kali-bi* k* kali-c bro1 kali-n k* *Lach* k* lept br1 *Lyc* k* m-ambo b7.de* *Mag-m* k* mag-p c2* *Mang* med k* **Merc** k* *Merc-c* k* mez k* morg-g pte1• **Mur-ac** k* *Nat-m* k* *Nat-s* *Nit-ac* k* nux-m k* **Nux-v** k* *Phos* k* phyt k* pip-m c2 *Plb* k* plb-xyz c2 **Podo** k* polyp-p a1* psor rad-br c11* rat mtf11 rhus-t k* *Ruta* k* sec bg2 **Sep** k* *Sil* k* sol-t bro1 sol-t-ae k* stram b7a.de *Sulph* k* sumb syc pte1*• syph k* tab k* ther k* thuj k* trom c2* valer k* zinc zinc-p k2

- **morning**: podo k*
- **forenoon**: rhus-t k*
- **evening**: **Ign**
- **night**: *Aesc*
- **accompanied** by:
  - **indigestion**: arn tl1
  - **stool**; complaints of: rat bg2
  - **urging**: ruta ptk1
- **acute**: ars ptk1 bell ptk1
- **alternating** with:
  - **retraction**: sol-t-ae vml3•

○ • **Head**; pain in (See HEAD - Pain - alternating - prolapsus)

- **burning**; with: *Alum* vh
- **children**; in: bell bro1 carc fb* chinin-s c1 *Ferr* k* *Ferr-p* bro1 *Hydr* ign h1* ind hr1 med jl2 merc b4a.de* mur-ac bro1 *Nux-v* k* plb mtf33 **Podo** k*
  - **infants**: podo c1
- **convulsive**: *Ars*
- **cough** agg.; during: caust h2*
- **delivery**; after: gels ptk1 *Podo* k* *Ruta* k*
- **diarrhea**; during: aesc bro1 *Aloe* bro1 *Calc* carb-v bro1 colch bro1 crot-t bro1 **Dulc** k* fl-ac bro1 gamb k* ham bro1 *Ign* bro1 kali-c bro1 mang-m **Merc** k* *Mur-ac* k* nux-v ptk1 phos bro1 **Podo** k* *Ruta* bro1 *Sulph* bro1
- **drunkards** leading sedentary life; in: aesc-g bro1
- **flatus**, when passing: *Mur-ac* ptk1 valer k*
- **hemorrhage** of rectum; after: *Ars* k*
- **hemorrhoids**; during: aesc tl1* aesc-g bro1 lept br1 podo bro1
- **kneeling** agg.: ail
- **menses**; during: aur k* podo
- **mental** excitement; from: podo k*
- **painful**: *Ars* *Nit-ac* hr1 ther
- **paralysis**; with: plb ptk1
- **pregnancy** agg.; during: podo br1*
- **replacing** difficult: mez ptk1
- **sensation** of: *Aesc* k* asc-t hr1 chel dios k* germ-met srj5• iris til c1
- **sitting** agg.: ther k*
- **smoking** agg.: *Sep* k*
- **sneezing**; after: podo k*
- **squatting**: ruta h1
- **standing** agg.: *Ferr-i*

- **stool**:
  - **after** | **agg.**: Aesc k* Aloe bro1 alum bro1 ant-c apoc ars asar calc-act bro1 canth k* carb-v k* Cocc k* crot-t euph k* ham bro1 Hep Ign k* Indg k* iris kali-bi k* Lach k* Merc k* mez k* mur-ac Nat-m k* Nit-ac k* Phos k* pip-m a1 plat **Podo** k* rat hr1 ruta bg2 Sep k* sol-t-ae stann bg2 Sulph k* taosc iwa1• Trom k*
  - **before**: Podo k* Ruta k*
  - **during** | **agg.**: aesc k2 ail aloe bg2 Ant-c k* ars b4.de* asar k* bell k* bry k* Calc k* calc-p bg2 Canth b7.de* cic bg2 Cinnb k* colch crot-t k* dulc k* ferr ferr-ar ferr-p Fl-ac k* Gamb k* **Ign** k* kali-bi bg2 kali-n k* kali-p fd1.de* lach b7a.de* **Lyc** k* M-ambo b7.de* mag-m k* Merc b4.de* mez k* mur-ac k* nat-c bg2 nat-m bg2 nit-ac bg2 Nux-v k* plan k* **Podo** k* Rhus-t k* Ruta k* **Sep** k* sol-t-ae vml3• Sulph k* Trom k*
  - **straining** at:
    - **agg.**: Aesc bro1 alum bro1 cench k2 ferr bro1 Ign bro1 lyc bro1 med bro1 nit-ac bro1 Podo bro1* ruta bro1 sep bro1 sulph bro1
    - **without**: Graph
  - **urging** to | **with**: ruta ptk1
- **stooping** agg.: ruta
- **urination**:
  - **difficult**: mur-ac bro1 Sep
  - **during** | **agg.**: ant-c bg2 graph bg2 kali-bi bg2 **Mur-ac** k* nat-s bg2 phos bg2 Valer
- **vomiting**; while: Mur-ac k* Podo k*
- **walking** agg.; after: am ptk1
- **washing** | **amel.**: arn ptk1
- **weakness**; from: podo bro1

PROTRUSION:
- **sensation** of:
  - **stool**; before | **Rectum** and anus: ang bg2

PULSATION: aloe k* alum k* alumn k* am-m k* apis ben berb k* calc-p k* caps carc gk6* caust cench k2 crot-t k* cycl dulc fd4.de dys pte1• grat k* Ham **Lach** k* lyss k* manc k* meli Nat-m k* rhod k* seneg k* sil bg1 Sulph k*
- **evening**: am-m k* dulc fd4.de Lach hr1
  - **sitting** up in bed | **amel.**: am-m k*
- **eating**; after: aloe gsy1
- **menses**; during: lach Lyss k*
- **sitting** agg.: Aloe am-m k*
  - **hammers**; like little: **Lach**
- **stool** | **after**:
  - **agg.**: aloe alumn k* apis berb k* caps Lach k* manc k* sang seneg k* Sulph k*
    - **Rectum** and anus: lach bg2 manc bg2 seneg bg2 sulph bg2
  - **during** | **agg.**: nat-m k*
- ○ **Anus**: aloe bg2 alum b4a.de* am-m bg2 apis b7a.de* berb bg2 bry bg2 calc-p bg2 crot-t bg2 grat bg2 ham bg2 lach b7.de* manc bg2 meli bg2 Nat-m b4.de* rhod b4.de* sel bg2 seneg b4.de* sulph b4.de*
  - **stool** agg.; after: lach b7.de* seneg b4.de sulph b4.de
  - **walking** agg.: cench vh
- **Perineum**: bov Caust k* dys pte1*• polyg-h

RAWNESS: alum bg2 ant-c bg2 grat bg2 ign bg2 lyc bg2 merc bg2 phos bg2 sep bg2 sulph bg2
- ○ **Perineum**: carb-v bg2 rhod bg2

RECEDES, stool (See Constipation - difficult - recedes)

REDNESS of anus (See Discoloration - anus - red)

RELAXED anus: (↗Open) **Aloe Apis** apoc ars k2 ars-h vh Carb-v chin hydr k2 kali-c kali-p mur-ac k2 narc-ps a1* oxyt ptk2 Petr **Phos** k* puls rhod Sec zing
- **sensation** of, after stool: lept podo

RETENTION OF STOOL (See Constipation)

RETRACTION: agar bapt bry k* Kali-bi k* lach b7a.de nat-p bg2* Op k* phos bg2 plb k* tell thuj bg2
- **painful**: Kali-bi
- **stool** agg.; after: Kali-bi k* thuj bg2

REVERSED ACTION: nux-v k2

RIDING: | **agg.** | **Rectum** and anus: bov bg2
- **amel.** | **Rectum** and anus: Kali-c bg2

RUBBING: | **Perineum**: Cina hr1

RUMBLING (See Grumbling)

SALMONELLOSIS (See FEVER - Typhoid)

SCRATCHING: | **agg.** | **Rectum** and anus: alum bg2 borx bg2
- **amel.** | **Rectum** and anus: sars bg2

SENSITIVE: (↗Pain - sore) Aloe Bell berb k* calc Caust k* cupr bg2 Graph k* Hep Lach lil-t Lyc **Mag-m** k* **Mur-ac** k* **Nit-ac** k* nux-v Podo k* rat k* Sep sil sul-ac syph thuj k*
- **stool** agg.; after: Alum b4a.de mag-m b4.de* phos h2*
- ○ **Anus**: **Mur-ac** bg2

SHOCK, electric-like: apis k* stry
- **stool**; before: apis k*

SITTING:
- **agg.**:
  - ○ **Perineum**: cycl bg2*
  - **Rectum** and anus: calc bg2 chel bg2 chin bg2 cocc bg2 graph bg2 mag-c bg2 mur-ac bg2 nat-m bg2 nux-v bg2 puls bg2 staph bg2 sulph bg2
- **amel.** | **Rectum** and anus: cann-xyz bg2 ign bg2

SLIP back; stools (See Constipation - difficult - recedes)

SLOW action of rectum (See Inactivity)

SNEEZING agg.: lach ptk1
- ○ **Rectum** and anus: podo bg2

SPASMS in: Caust k* Colch k* euph-a c2 Ferr k* ign bro1* nux-v k2 paeon mrr1 petr-ra shn4• Tab k*
- **morning**: petr-ra shn4•
- **coition**:
  - **after**: merc-c bg2
  - **during**: merc-c nux-v mrr1
- **stool**; before | **Rectum** and anus: colch bg2
- **urination** | **urging** to urinate; with: Caust k*
- **walking** agg.: caust k*
- ○ **Anus**:
  - **accompanied** by | **constipation**: caust bro1 Lach bro1 Lyc bro1 Nat-m bro1 nit-ac bro1 plb bro1 plb-act bro1 sil bro1

STANDING:
- **agg.**: Petr ptk1
  - ○ **Rectum** and anus: aloe bg2 caust bg2 ign bg2 nit-ac bg2 sulph bg2 valer bg2
- **amel.** | **Rectum** and anus: sulph bg2
- **stool** passes better when (See Constipation - standing)

STOOL:
- **after**:
  - **agg.**:
    - **long** after:
      - **Anus**: nit-ac ptk1 paeon ptk1
      - **Rectum** and anus: nit-ac bg2
    - **Rectum** and anus: aloe bg2 ant-c bg2 kali-bi bg2 phos bg2
  - **not** amel.: dios bg2 merc bg2 **Merc-c** bg2
- **during** | **agg.** | **Perineum**: sanic ptk1
  - **amel.** | **Rectum** and anus: calc bg2 sep bg2

STOOPING:
- **agg.**: caust ptk1 ruta ptk1
  - ○ **Rectum** and anus: Ruta bg2
- **amel.**: chel ptk1
  - ○ **Rectum** and anus: chel bg2

STRAINING: (↗Pain - tenesmus) cystein-l rly4• musca-d szs1
- **impossible**: bell h1*
- **ordinary** stool; to pass: alum tl1
- **stool** agg.; after: agar tl1 merc-c tl1

○ - **Perineum**: mez bg2

STRICTURE: *(↗Constriction)* aesc agar k* *Aloe* alum alum-p k2 ang bapt hr1 *Bar-m* bell k* *Borx* calc *Calc-sil* *Camph* *Cann-s* hr1 coff bro1 colch con crot-t elaps fl-ac hep hydr bro1 ign k* *Kali-br* hr1 kreos *Lach* k* *Lyc* k* m-ambo b7a.de med mez *Nat-m* nit-ac k* op b7.de* phos k* plb k* *Ruta* k* sec *Sil* bro1 syph ptk1* tab c2* *Thiosin* c1* thuj
- **hemorrhoids**; from: bapt ptk1

SWELLING of anus: *Aesc* *Apis* k* ars b4a.de aur k* bell borx k* bufo calc bg2 camph b7.de* cham ptk1 *Coll* con b4a.de crot-t cur *Graph* k* *Hep* k* ign k* kali-i kali-p k2 lach med *Merc* b4a.de mur-ac nat-m bg2 nit-ac b4a.de nux-v k* *Paeon* k* phys *Podo* k* sarr sep *Sulph* k* teucr k* tritic-vg fd5.de
- **black**: *Carb-v* *Mur-ac*
- **hemorrhoids**; from: caps tl1 mur-ac tl1
- **menses**; during: sep
- **sensation** of: *Aesc* k* *Brucel* sa3• cact k* camph bg2 crot-t bg2 graph k* hep k* kali-p fd1.de• nat-m k* nux-m k* sacch-a fd2.de• sulph k* teucr bg2
  - **constipation**; without: aesc tl1
- **stool** agg.; during: ant-c tl1 ign tl1

○ - **Perineum**: ant-c b7a.de plb b7.de*

○ · **Raphe**: thuj k*

TENESMUS (See Pain - tenesmus)

TENSION: *Calc* chin k* euphr graph *Ign* k* *Lyc* k* *Nux-v* k* rhus-t k* *Sep* k* **Sil** k* symph fd3.de•
- **convulsive**: ign k*
- **stool** agg.; after: adam skp7• berb k* sep k*

○ - **Anus**: ign b7.de* lyc b4a.de* rhus-t b7.de* sep b4.de* sil b4.de* spong b7.de*
- **Perineum**: ant-t b7.de* echi
  - **urination** agg.; before: ant-t b7.de*

THICKENING of skin: *Nat-m* b4a.de

THINKING: | **Rectum** and anus agg.; of: caust bg2

TICKLING (See Itching)

TINGLING: ambr c1 *Carb-v* k* *Colch* k* ferr-ma plat podo fd3.de• rhus-t c1 ruta fd4.de sabin c1 ter tritic-vg fd5.de
- **evening**: plat
- **night**: acon vh1
- **stool** agg.; during: *Carb-v*

TOUCH agg.: | **Rectum** and anus: ars bg2 merc bg2 nat-m bg2 op bg2

TREMBLING in anus: agn b7.de* con k*

TRICKLING: | **Rectum** and anus: con bg2

TUBERCLE on Perineum: bac vh *Thuj* k*

TWITCHING: agn ars k* bry k* calc k* carb-ac k* colch k* *Coloc* k* iod k* meny h1* *Merc* nat-m k* *Sil* k* *Staph*
- **afternoon**: coloc k* franz a1
- **bed** agg.; in: chin k*
- **stool**:
  - **during** | **Rectum** and anus: bry bg2

○ - **Anus**: calc b4.de* colch b7.de* coloc bg2 iod b4.de* lach bg2 nat-m bg2 nux-v b7.de* sil b4.de*

ULCERATION: *(↗ABDOMEN - Cancer - colon - transverse; ABDOMEN - Inflammation - colon - ulcerative)* alum k2 **Alumn** k* aur-m k2 bapt hr1* *Calc* caust **Cham** k* cub ham k2 *Hep* *Hydr* kali-c *Kali-i* *Nat-s* nit-ac ptk *Paeon* k* *Petr* phos *Phyt* puls ruta k2 sars k* **Sil** k* staph sulph mrr1 syph k*

○ - **Anus**: *Aesc* bg2 aloe bg2 *Ars* b4a.de bell b4a.de bry b7a.de canth bg2 carb-an b4a.de *Carb-v* ptk1 caust b4.de* cham b7a.de* cycl b7a.de *Hep* b4a.de kali-bi bg2* kali-c b4a.de mag-c b4.de* **Merc** b4a.de merc-c bg2 *Nit-ac* ptk1 paeon bg2 petr b4a.de phos b4a.de puls b7a.de sars bg2 *Sil* bg2 *Sulph* b4a.de*
- **Perineum**; on: | **Anus**; near: paeon tl1 syph jl2

UNNOTICED stool: *(↗Insensibility)* acon k* *Aloe* *Arg-n* hr1 **Arn** b7a.de ars k* carl k* *Caust* mtf33 colch k* coloc con b4a.de cur *Cycl* hr1 ferr-ma grat k* *Hyos* lach bg2 m-aust b7a.de *Mur-ac* k* op gk* ph-ac k* *Plb* k* *Staph* k* sulph bg2 tab k* verat k*
- **hard** stool: **Aloe** *Caust* mtf33 *Coloc*
- **physical** causes rather than from emotional causes; from: aloe mrr1

Unnoticed stool: ...
- **thin** watery, passes while urinating: *Mur-ac*

URGING: *(↗Pain - tenesmus)* abrot acon k* **Aesc** aeth **Agar** k* aids nl2• all-c allox sp1 *Aloe* k* *Alum* k* alum-sil k2 alumn am-c b2.de* ambr b2.de* *Anac* k* androc srj1• ang b2.de* ant-c b2.de* ant-t b2.de* *Apis* k* apoc bg2 arg-met k* *Arg-n* *Arn* k* *Ars* k* ars-h ars-i k* arum-t asaf b2.de* *Asar* k* asc-t atro aur aur-ar k2 aur-m aur-s k2 *Bamb-a* stb2.de• bar-c k* *Bell* k* bell-p sp1 benz-ac *Berb* k* *Bism* k* borx b2.de* bov k* *Bry* k* bufo but-ac sp1 cadm-s cain calad calc k* calc-p calc-sil k2 camph k* cann-s cann-xyz bg2 canth k* caps k* carb-an k* carb-v k* carbn-s castm castn-v castor-eq caust k* cench k2 cham *Chel* k* chin k* chinin-s k* chir-fl gya2 chord-umb rly4• cic k* cimic *Cimx* cist clem cob k* cob-n sp1 coc-c cocc k* coff k* *Colch* k* coli rly4• *Coloc* k* com *Con* k* convo-s sp1 cop br1 *Corn* croc k* crot-c crot-t k* cupr cycl cystein-l rly4• dig k* dios k* *Dulc* k* elaps ephe-si hsj1• eug euph b2.de* fago ferr k* ferr-ar ferr-i ferr-ma ferr-p k2 gamb gent-l glon gran *Graph* k* grat ham *Hell* b2.de* *Hep* k* hydr hyos k* hyper **Ign** k* indg iod ip b7.de* iris kali-ar k2 kali-bi k* *Kali-c* k* kali-chl kali-m k2 *Kali-n* k* kali-s k2 kalm ketogl-ac rly4• kola stb3• kreos lach k* lact lept br1 **Lil-t** k* lyc k* m-ambo b2.de* m-arct b2.de m-aust b7.de mag-c k* *Mag-m* k* mag-s malar jl2 manc mand sp1 meny b2.de* **Merc** k* *Merc-c* k* merc-i-f merc-i-r mez k* mosch b2.de* **Mur-ac** b2.de* murx bg2 naja *Nat-ar* *Nat-c* k* nat-m k* nat-ox rly4• nat-p nat-pyru rly4• nat-s k* nicotam rly4• nit-ac b2.de* nux-m k* **Nux-v** k* oena *Op* k* osm ox-ac pall petr k* ph-ac bg2 phel *Phos* k* phys **Pip-m** plac rzf5• plac-s rly4• plan *Plat* k* **Plb** k* *Podo* k* positr nl2• prun psil ft1 ptel *Puls* k* ran-b bg2 *Ran-s* k* rat rauw sp1 *Rheum* k* *Rhod* k* rhus-t k* rob bg2 *Ruta* k* sabad k* sabin k* sal-al blc1• sars k* sec k* sel b2.de* senec seneg b2.de* *Sep* k* serp **Sil** k* sol-t-ae spig b2.de* spong k* squil b2.de* stann k* *Staph* k* stram b2.de* stront-c k* suis-em rly4• suis-hep rly4• sul-ac k* **Sulph** k* sumb suprar rly4• *Tab* k* tarax b2.de tarent tell tere-la rly4• teucr b2.de ther thiam rly4• *Thuj* k* tritic-vg fd5.de trom uran-n bg2 ust vanil fd5.de verat k* verb k* vero-o rly4• vib vinc viol-o b2.de viol-t b2.de* zinc k* [heroin sdj2]
- **morning**: **Apis** b7a.de bac jl2 borx hr1
  - **early**: *(↗Diarrhea - morning - waking)* lil-t br1
- **evening**: aids nl2• bism h1* carb-v h2* lach-h sk4• lyc h2* olib-sac wmh1 sep h2* spong fd4.de stann h2* sulph h2* tritic-vg fd5.de [tax jsj7]
  - **asleep**; when: phyt
  - **sleep** agg.; during: phyt
- **night**: *Aloe* am-c h2* carl k* coloc k* graph k* kali-c h2* kali-s fd4.de kola stb3• lac-lup hm2• lyc k* mag-c h2* merc-i-r k* nat-c h2 nat-m k* nat-pyru rly4• *Olib-sac* wmh1 phys k* ruta fd4.de sil h2* sul-ac h2* **Sulph** thuj k* zinc
  - **midnight**: dios k* lach k*
    - **before**:
      - **22** h: nat-pyru rly4•
      - **23** h: carc az1.de• gels mag-c merc-i-r pip-m
    - **after**:
      - **3** h: olib-sac wmh1
      - **3-5** h: tub jl2
      - **5** h: olib-sac wmh1
  - **awake**; keeping him: kola stb3•
  - **menses**; before: des-ac rbp6 mang k*
  - **waking**; on: *(↗SLEEP - Waking - stool)* (non:aloe a1) (non:ferr-i a1) gink-b sbd1• kola stb3• sil a1
- **abortion**, during: calc st *Nux-v*
- **absent** (See Constipation - presence; Inactivity)
- **accompanied** by:
  - **prolapsus** (See Prolapsus - accompanied - urging)
  - **urination**: *Nux-v* ptk1

○ · **Abdomen**; complaints of: anac b4a.de aur b4a.de bar-c b4a.de phos b4a.de sep b4a.de
  - **Uterus**; labor-like pain in (See FEMALE - Pain - labor-like - accompanied - stool)
- **anxious**: acon coca-c sk4• *Merc* k* *Nux-v* k* ol-an k* sulph h2* tritic-vg fd5.de
- **as if it would never end** (See constant)
- **ball**; from sensation of a (See Lump)
- **breakfast**:
  - **after** | **agg.**: aeth a1 carbn-s grat k* mag-c h2* mag-m h2* podo fd3.de• spong h1* symph fd3.de•
  - **before** | **agg.**: kola stb3•

Rectum

- **during**: dios k* irid-met srj5•
- **chill**; during: caust bg2 hyos bg2 merc bg2 nux-v bg2 puls bg2 sulph bg2 teucr b7.de*
- **chilliness** in hand and thighs; with: **Bar-c** vh
- **clothing**, on tightening: bry k*
- **coffee** agg.: nat-m podo fd3.de•
- **coition**; after: nat-p k*
- **cold**; from getting: dulc k2
- **colic**, during: alum-sil k2 anac c1 coloc k* elaps hr1 ind indg a1 kali-n c1 nat-c a1 nat-p gk2 **Nux-v** op br sec a1
- **constant**: aesc k* anac h2* androc srj1• ant-s-aur arn k* ars k* asaf k* bar-c bar-s k2 bell h1* *Berb* k* bry k* calc k* cob k* cob-n sp1 con k* cop k* **Crot-t** k* ger vh ham k* hyos k* *Ign* ip k2 kali-act kali-ar k* kali-bi gk kali-m k2 kola stb3• lach ptk1 *Lil-t* k* mag-c k* *Mag-m* k* **Merc** k* **Merc-c** k* *Merc-d* k* nat-ar nat-c a1 nat-m k* nat-ox rly4• *Nat-s* k* nicc-met sk4• *Nux-v* k* phyt k* *Pip-m* k* plat h2* podo fd3.de• ptel k* rhus-t h1* ruta sec a1 sep h2* sin-a sin-n *Sulph* k* sumb k* wies a1 yuc a1 zinc-s k*
- **convulsions**; before: calc-ar st
- **diarrhea**:
  - **before**: bit-ar wht1•
  - **during**: arge-pl rwt5• bros-gau mrc1 cartl-s rly4• enteroc jl2 gink-b sbd1• liat br1 mag-c h2 merc mrr1 nat-m mrr1 nit-ac h2 podo mrr1 staphycoc rly4•
- **dinner** | **after** | **agg.**: ant-c k* cann-s k* caps vh caust k* colch k* coloc k* *Ferr-ma* k* kali-bi mag-m k* nat-m k* par phel k* ran-s k* sulph k*
  - **during** | **agg.**: dios k*
- **distress** in stomach and abdomen, with: lept br1
- **drinking** agg.; after: aloe k2 caps hr1*
- **eating** | **after** | **agg.**: *(↗Diarrhea - eating - after - agg.)* **Aloe** alum h2 *Anac* k* ant-c h2 apoc aur h2 bar-c caust b4a.de cham clem **Coloc** ferr-ma fl-ac ham fd3.de• kola stb3• nat-sil fd3.de• phos k* *Rheum* rhus-t ruta fd4.de sep b4a.de spong fd4.de stront-c sk4• sulph tritic-vg fd5.de tung-met bdx1• vanil fd5.de vero-o rly4• zinc
  - **while** | **agg.**: sanic c1*
- **effort**, great desire passes away with: **Anac**
- **erections**; with: ign ptk1 thuj bg2*
- **eructation**, on each: aesc k*
- **exciting** news, after: gels k*
- **fever**; during: am bg2 ars bg2 **Caust** b4.de* hyos bg2 lach bg2 merc bg2 *Nux-v* bg2 podo bg2 puls bg2 *Sulph* b4.de*
- **flatus**; for: alum h2* carb-an h2* caust h2* kali-c h2* mag-c h2* mag-m h2* meny h1* mez h2* osm hr1 phos h2* sep h2*
- **flatus**; passing:
  - **agg.**: **Aloe** k* carb-v ptk1 mag-m ptk1 myric ptk1 nat-c ptk1 nat-s k2* phos ptk1 ruta k* sep ptk1 spig
  - **amel.**: acon bg1 caps carb-v h2 *Colch* kali-c h2 kali-n h2 mag-c mez nat-ar ruta
- **frequent**: abrot k* acon-ac rly4• aids nl2• aloe k2 alumn bro1 *Ambr* k* *Anac* bro1 *Apis* aq-mar rbp6 *Arg-met* k* arn asaf k* aster bro1 bamb-a stb2.de• **Bar-c** k* bar-s k2 bell berb bit-ar wht1• borx brom k* cain calc-p k* carb-an k* carb-v bro1 *Caust* k* *Coloc* **Con** k* **Corn** k* dios k* dulc h1 ferr bro1 glyc bro1 *Gran* bro1 ham k* *Hep* hura *Hyos* k* *Ign* k* iod bro1 kali-p fd1.de• kali-s fd4.de kola stb3• kreos k* lac-c lac-d k* **Lil-t** *Lyc* bro1 marb-w es1• **Merc** k* **Merc-c** k* mim-p rsj8• *Nat-m* k* nat-pyru rly4• nat-s k* nat-sil fd3.de• nicotam rly4• nit-ac k* nit-m-ac bro1 **Nux-v** k* olib-sac wmh1 ox-ac k* ozone sde2• paraf bro1 petr k* *Ph-ac* k* phos k* **Plat** k* podo bro1 *Puls* k* *Ran-s* b7a.de rauw tpw8 *Rheum* k* rhus-t a1 rob bro1 ruta k* sapin a1 sars k* *Sep* bro1 serp a1 **Sil** a1* sinus rly4• spig b7a.de* stann k* staph h1* stram sulph k* symph fd3.de• tab k* tetox pin2• tritic-vg fd5.de vanil fd5.de
- **fright** agg.: *(↗MIND - Ailments - fright)* *Caust*
- **hang** down, letting feet: rhus-t
- **ineffectual** (See Constipation - ineffectual)
- **irresistible**: aloe ptk1 nat-c ptk1
- **labor** pain, with every: nux-v plat
- **lying**:
  - **back**; on | **amel.**: puls sys
  - **double**; bent | **amel.**: staph h1
  - **side**; on:
    - **left** | **agg.**: puls sys
- **lying**: ...
  - **while** (See Diarrhea - lying - agg.)
- **marked**: but-ac sp1
- **menses** | **before** | **agg.**: des-ac rbp6 eupi k* nux-v mrr1
  - **during** | **agg.**: calc k* mang k* nux-v mrr1 puls h1* sep b4a.de*
- **motion** agg.: ars-i k* astac a1 *Bry* *Crot-t* *Mur-ac* *Rheum*
- **mucus**; bloody | **passing**: nat-s mrr1
- **neuralgia**, with: iris pd*
- **painful**: *Aloe* bro1 am bg2 *Ars* bro1 *Bell* bro1 bov bg2 calc bg2 camph bro1 canth bg2 caust bg2 chel bg2 cist bro1 colch mrr1 *Coloc* bro1 con bro1 *Crot-t* bro1 form bro1 gamb bro1 grat bro1 hep bro1 *Ign* bro1 kali-bi bro1 lept bro1 mag-c bg2 merc bro1 merc-c bg2* *Merc-d* bro1 nat-s bro1 *Nux-v* bro1 olnd bro1 phos bro1 podo bro1 rheum bro1 sil bro1 *Stront-c* bro1 sulph bg2* tritic-vg fd5.de *Verat* bro1 [heroin sdj2]
- **paroxysmal**, too painful: kali-c bg1 plb bg1 sulph bg1
- **passes** away before closet can be reached: cench k2
- **perspiration**; during: *Ars* bg2 caps bg2 *Caust* bg2 cocc bg2 *Merc* bg2 nit-ac bg2 *Nux-v* bg2 phos bg2 puls bg2 rheum bg2 *Rhus-t* bg2 staph bg2 **Sulph** b4.de*
- **pregnancy** agg.; during: bell bg2 calc bg2 cocc bg2 con bg2 ip bg2 lyc bg2 merc bg2 nux-v bg2 rhus-t bg2 sep bg2 sulph bg2
- **rising** agg.: *Aloe* dulc fd4.de tung-met bdx1•
  - **sudden**: nat-ox rly4•
    - **morning**: nat-ox rly4•
- **shivering**; during: caust b4.de
- **sitting** agg.: crot-t
- **sleep**; during: phyt bg3*
- **smoking** agg.: calad k* thuj k*
- **standing** agg.: aloe bry cob c1 lil-t k*
- **startled**, when: *Gels*
- **stomach**; urging for stool felt in (See STOMACH - Stool)
- **stool**:
  - **after**:
    - **agg.**: aesc *Aeth* k* agar h2* **Aloe** k* alum b4a.de ambr b7.de* apis b7a.de arg-n bg2 ars k* ars-i *Asar* b7a.de bar-c k* bell b4a.de* berb k* bit-ar wht1• bry k* calc b4a.de calc-p k* camph k* canth b7.de* caps bg2 carb-v b4.de* chin b7.de* cic cocc k* colch coli rly4• crot-t cycl k* dig k* dios k* dros k* ferr k* ferr-ar ferr-i form franz a1 grat k* ign k* iod *Ip* bg2 iris kali-c h2* kali-p *Lach* k* lyc k* m-arct b7.de mag-c h2* *Mag-m* k* **Merc** k* **Merc-c** k* merc-i-r k* mez h2* naja nat-ar nat-c k* nat-m b4.de* *Nat-p* nat-sil fd3.de• nicc *Nit-ac* k* nux-m b7.de* nux-v k* petr k* ph-ac bg2 phos b4.de* plat bg2 podo fd3.de• psor k2 **Rheum** k* ruta k* samb k* sars b4.de* *Sec* b7a.de *Sel* b7a.de sol-t-ae k* spig k* spong fd4.de stann k* staph b7.de* **Sulph** k* suprar rly4• symph fd3.de• tab k* taosc iwa1• tarax b7.de* til k* verat b7.de* zinc bg2
      - **long** time; for a: berb bg2
    - **amel.**: acon aesc aloe alum ant-t ars asaf bapt bry calc-p canth cham colch *Coloc* corn dulc **Gamb** gels hell lept nat-s nuph **Nux-v** **Rhus-t** sanic tarent
      - **small** amount of stool; after a: nux-v k2*
  - **before**: agar k2 all-s k* *Aloe* alum h2* amp rly4• anac tl1 bell h1* berb k* calc-f k* carb-v bg2 cocc b7.de* coli rly4• cystein-l rly4• euphr k* ferr-i k* fl-ac k* gent-c a1 grat k* hell k* kali-n k* lach b7.de* lact k* lyc bg2 mang-p rly4• *Merc* b4.de* **Merc-c** bg2 mez k* nat-c h2* nat-m h2* **Nux-v** bg2 *Op* b7a.de osm k* phos b4a.de* plat bg2 *Podo* psor tl1 *Rheum* k* *Rhod* b4a.de *Rhus-t* k* rumx k2 sec b7a.de *Staph* b7.de* stront-c **Sulph** k* suprar rly4• verat b7.de* viol-o b7a.de
  - **difficult** stool and pain; with: cop br1
  - **during**:
    - **agg.**: abrot k* *Acon* bg2 *Aesc* k* aeth k* agar h2* alum bg2 am-m k* anac k* *Ant-c* k* arg-met **Ars** bg2 ars-i k* astac a1 bar-c h2* bell h1* bov k* brom bg2 bry k* calad k* calc k* calc-s a1 calc-sil k2 *Carb-an* b4a.de *Carb-v* b4a.de carbn-s carl k* chord-umb rly4• coca *Colch* bg2 *Coll* k* con k* cupr bg2 cycl k* dios k* dirc k* dros k* dulc k* euph bg2 eupi k* ferr k* form k* franz a1 gamb k* graph k* grat k* hep k* inul k* ip bg2 irid-met srj5• iris kali-bi bg2 lach bg2 *Laur* bg2 lycps-v mag-m h2* **Merc** b4.de* merc-c bg2 merl k* mez k* muru a1 nat-c k* nat-p k* nicc k* nit-ac k* **Nux-v** bg2 op bg2 ox-ac k* phys k* phyt k* pic-ac k* pip-m k* plan k* plat k* podo bg2 ptel k* ran-s k* rat k*

- **during – agg.**: ... *Rhus-t* k* sars k* sel bg2 sep k* sil k* spong h1* stann k* stram k* sul-ac **Sulph** k* sumb a1 tab k* tarent k* verb k*
  - **yellow**: mag-c h2*
- **flatus** is passed; for stool, but only: **Aloe** bg2 camph bg2 carb-an bg2 carb-v bg2 chin bg2 mag-m bg2 nat-s bg2 osm bg2 pall bg2 phos bg2 sep bg2
- **hard** stool | **during**: mag-c h2*
- **not** for stool; but: **Lach** k*
- **rising** after stool: rheum rumx
- **twice**: *Rhus-g* tmo3•

- **sudden**: aesc k* agar *Aloe* k* ant-c b7a.de ant-s-aur ap-g vml3• bamb-a stb2.de• bar-c k* bit-ar wht1• bry carb-v k* cartl-s rly4• chin bro1 cic k* cist bro1 cocc colch rsj2• **Crot-t** k* cycl dig dirc falco-pe nl2• *Ferr* ferr-ma a1 *Gamb* bro1 gent-l k* gink-b sbd1• graph hippoc-k szs2 hydrog srj2• ign jug-r a1 kali-bi kali-c h2 kali-n kali-s fd4.de ketogl-ac rly4• kola stb3• lac-ac lac-h sk4• *Lach* lil-t k* lyss jl2 mag-m k* manc k* naja *Nat-c* k* nat-m mrr1 nat-ox rly4• *Nat-p* k* *Nat-s* k* nicc-met sk4• onis a1 paeon bro1 plac-s rly4• plat *Podo* k* positr nl2• *Psor* k* ptel k* rhus-g tmo3• rhus-t rob *Rumx* bro1 sacch-a fd2.de• sal-fr sle1• sep k* sinus rly4• spong fd4.de suis-em rly4• **Sulph** k* sumb symph fd3.de• tab k* til c1 trom bro1 tub bro1 tung-met bdx1• vanil fd5.de verat k* viol-t b7a.de zinc
  - **morning**: adam skp7• arg-n hr1 dios a1 gink-b sbd1• hydrog srj2• manc k* positr nl2• sacch-a fd2.de• sal-fr sle1• spong fd4.de **Sulph** k*
  - **afternoon**: gink-b sbd1• ketogl-ac rly4• spong fd4.de
  - **evening**: gent-l k* kali-s fd4.de kola stb3•
  - **night**: nux-v spong fd4.de symph fd3.de•
    - **waking**; on: gink-b sbd1•
  - **eating**; after: bamb-a stb2.de•
  - **painful**: gink-b sbd1•
  - **rising** from bed agg.: syc bka1•
  - **sleep**; while going to: adam skp7•
- **supper** agg.; after: calc-p ox-ac k* podo k*
- **tea**; after: adam skp7•
- **thinking** about it, on: iris *Ox-ac* k* ulm-c jsj8•
- **tormenting**, but not for stool: *Lach* k*
- **urination**:
  - **after** | **agg.**: alum h2* *Cann-s* ham fd3.de•
  - **before**: *Borx* hr1
  - **during**:
    - **agg.**: acon-ac rly4• **Aloe** k* alum aphis cann-s k* *Canth* k* carb-v h2* caust crot-h cycl dig dulc fd4.de kali-s fd4.de merc *Mur-ac* **Nux-v** k* prun *Puls* squil k* staph k* sumb thuj wies a1
    - **amel.**: lil-t pd* nat-m
  - **urging** to urinate | **with**: merc-c k2
- **urine** is discharged, but only: lil-t
- **vertigo**; during: merc-c k2 spig k* zinc h2*
- **voluptuous**: plac rzf5•
  - **followed** by | **pain**: plac rzf5•
- **waking**; on: alum h2* suis-em rly4•
- **walking** agg.: cob k* coloc k* laur k* pall rheum
- **water**; running:
  - **hearing** of: **Lyss** k*
  - **seeing**: lyss jl2

○ - **Upper abdomen**; felt in *Ign* b7a.de

URINATION agg.: *Mur-ac* ptk1 valer ptk1
○ - **Rectum** and anus: alum bg2 arg-n bg2 kali-c bg2 mur-ac bg2 nit-ac bg2 rhus-t bg2

VARICOSE: aesc mrr1
○ - **Perineum**: aloe bg2

VERMINOSIS (See Itching - ascarides; Worms - complaints)

VOMITING agg.: mur-ac ptk1 podo ptk1
○ - **Rectum** and anus: kali-c bg2

WALKING:
- **agg.**:
  ○ - **Perineum**: cycl ptk1
  - **Rectum** and anus: aloe bg2 alum bg2 ars bg2 calc bg2 *Caust* bg2 cic bg2 crot-t bg2 kali-bi bg2 kali-c bg2 mag-c bg2 merc-c bg2 mez bg2 nat-m bg2 nit-ac bg2 nux-v bg2 *Sep* bg2 zinc bg2
- **rapidly**:
  - **agg.** | **Rectum** and anus: sil bg2

WARM APPLICATIONS:
- **amel.**: rat ptk1
  ○ - **Rectum** and anus: phos bg2

WARTS (See Condylomata)

WEAKNESS, weak feeling: *Agar* agn k2 ail ptk1 *Aloe* k* alum alumn k2 anac tl1 apis bg1 apoc bry *Calc* coloc h2 kali-c *Petr* *Phos* *Sep* sulph bg1 tab
- **stool** | **after** | **agg.**: con tl1 lept *Podo* k*
  - **before**: nat-p
    - **Rectum** and anus: kali-c bg2
- **urination** agg.; during: inul

○ - **Anus**: coloc b4.de kali-c b4.de rhod b4.de sep b4.de
  - **stool** agg.; during: rhod b4.de*
- **Perineum**: ozone sde2•
- **Sphincter**; of: influ jl2* ix bnm8• mur-ac mrr1

WEIGHT: *(↗Dragging; Fullness; Lump)*
- **and** a feeling as if a plug were wedged between the pubis and coccyx: *Aloe* k* *Cact* k* caust hep **Sep** k* sil thuj

○ - **Perineum**: *(↗Dragging - perineum)* cact chim mrr1 **Con** k* cop graph k* hydrc puls sep mrr1

WIPING agg.: | **Rectum** and anus: aloe bg2 *Graph* bg2* lach bg2 mur-ac bg2

WORMS:
- **complaints** of worms: abrot bg2 acon k* aesc bg2* ager-c jsx1.fr all-c all-s c2* alum b2.de* am-c st ambr b2.de* ambro c2* anac b2.de* ant-c bg2 ant-t br1 apoc vh apoc-a c2* aq-mar skp7• arec br1 arg-n bg2* *Ars* k* art-v c2* asar b2.de* atis zzc1• *Bapt* c2* bar-c b2.de* bar-m k2 bell b2.de* borx b2.de* calad bg2* **Calc** k* cara-p jsx1.fr carb-an b2.de* carb-v k* carbn-s k2 carc jl2* cassia-o jsx1.fr caust b2.de* celo-t jsx1.fr cham b2.de* chelo c2* chim chin b2.de* *Cic* k* *Cina* k* cinnb bg2 claus-an jsx1.fr coff b2.de* colch b2.de* *Coli* jl2 coloc b2.de* croc b2.de* crot-h bg2 cuc-m jsx1.fr cupr bg2* cupr-act bro1* cupr-o bg2* cupr-ox bro1 dig b2.de* diph-t-tpt jsx1.fr dol dryop-i jsx1.fr dryop-p jsx1.fr dulc b4a.de emb-r mtf11 emb-sc jsx1.fr erlan-c jsx1.fr eucal c2 *Ferr* k* ferr-i k2 *Ferr-m* c2* ferr-s c2* fil k* gaert fmm1• gran bg2* graph k* haru-ma jsx1.fr hed sp1 helm sf1.de hyos b2.de* ichth br1 ign k* indg bg2* iod b2.de* *Ip* bg2* jab c2 jatr-c c2 kali-c b2.de* kali-m bg2* *Kou* br1* lach bg2 laur b2.de* lipp c2 luna c2 *Lyc* b2.de* mag-c b2.de* mag-m b2.de* med vh *Merc* k* merc-c bro1 naphtin c2* nat-c b2.de* *Nat-m* k* *Nat-p* k* nat-s bg2 nit-ac b4a.de *Nux-m* k* nux-v k* oci-sa sk4• passi br1* peti-a lsr3.de• petr k* ph-ac c2 phos b2.de* physal-an jsx1.fr plan kr1* *Plat* b2.de* podo c2* ptel c2 puls b2.de* quas c2* rat bg2* rhus-t b2.de* ruta k* sabad k* sabin b2.de* santin c2* *Scir* c1* sec k* sep b2.de* ser-a-c jl2 *Sil* k* sin-a c2 *Sin-n* **Spig** k* spong k* squil b2.de* *Stann* k* **Sulph** k* sumb c2* tab bg2 tell c2 teph-v jsx1.fr **Ter** k* teucr k* thom-h jsx1.fr thymol sp1 trem-or jsx1.fr urt-u c2 *Valer* b2.de* vanil fd5.de verat k* vern-am jsx1.fr viol-o bg2* *Viol-t* vh zinc b2.de*
  - **accompanied** by:
    - **biting** (See MIND - Biting - worm)
    - **constipation**: fil br1
      - **children**; in: **Dol** vh
    - **convulsions**; during (See GENERALS - Convulsions - worms)
    - **diarrhea** (See Diarrhea - worms)
    - **emaciation**: bar-c bg2 calc bg2 **Cina** bg2 graph bg2 lyc bg2 nat-m bg2 *Spig* bg2 *Sulph* bg2
    - **nausea**: ars b4a.de calc b4a.de *Cina* b7a.de merc b4a.de nit-ac b4a.de *Ruta* b7a.de sil b4a.de sulph b4a.de
    - **scrofula**: sil bg2

Rectum

- **complaints** of worms – **accompanied** by: ...
  - **strabismus** (See EYE - Strabismus - accompanied - worms)
  - **vertigo** (See VERTIGO - Accompanied - worms)
  - **vision**; complaints of (See VISION - Complaints - accompanied - worms)
  - **Eyes**; complaints of (See EYE - Complaints - accompanied - worms)
  - **Nerves**; complaints of (See GENERALS - Neurological - accompanied - worms)
  - **Tongue**; white: fil kr1*
- **children**; in: abrot tl1 calc tl1 carc mlr1• cic vh **Cina** br1* coli jl2 cupr mtf33 *Gaert* vh *Ign* vh* *Nux-m* vh *Ruta* vh sil mtf33 **Spig** vh sulph mtf33 teucr br1 *Viol-o* br1
- **dentition** in children; difficult (See TEETH - Dentition - difficult - accompanied - worms)
- **hookworm** (= necator americanus; ankylostoma americanum; uncinaria americana): carbn-tm br1* card-m ptk1* chen-a br1* thymol br1*
- **itching** (See Itching - ascarides)
- **moon**; full: *Calc* bg2 chin bg2 cina bg2 ferr bg2 *Sulph* bg2
- **pinworms** (= threadworms, oxyuris, enterobius vermicularis; = old rubric "ascarides"): abrot acet-ac acon k* agn alum b2.de* ambr b2.de* ant-t aq-calc br1 arg-n bg2 *Ars* k* asar k* asc-t c1 *Bapt* c2* **Bar-c** k* bar-m bar-s k2 *Calc* k* carb-v h2 carbn-s chelo br1* chin k* cina k* clerod-g bta1• colch b2.de* croc b2.de* crot-t cupr k* dig b2.de* dol st *Ferr* k* ferr-m gaert pte1• graph k* grat hyos b2.de* *Ign* k* indg k* kali-c b2.de* lyc bro1 mag-c k* *Mag-s* med tl1 merc k* *Merc-d* bro1 mill c1 napht ptk1 nat-c b2.de* **Nat-m** *Nat-p* k* nux-m b2.de* nux-v k* petr b2.de* phos k* plat k* prot pte1• *Ptel* vh* *Rat* k* rhus-t b2.de* **Sabad** k* sabin b2.de* santin br1* *Scir* c2* *Sep* k* sil k* sin-a c2 *Sin-n* k* *Spig* k* *Spong* k* squil k* *Sulph* k* tell **Ter** k* *Teucr* k* thuj k* urt-u k* *Valer* k* vanil fd5.de vern-a gsb1* zinc b2.de*
- **roundworm** (= eelworm, ascaris lumbricoides; = old rubric "lumbricoides"): *Abrot* bro1 acon k* aesc bro1 *Agn* hr1 all-s anac k* ant-c bro1 arg-n a1 *Ars* k* asaf mtf11 asar bar-c k* bell k* borx b2.de* calc k* carbn-s caust b2.de* cham k* *Chel* chelo br1* *Chen-a* c2* chen-vg mtf11 chin b2.de* cic k* **Cina** k* clerod-g bta1* coloc b2.de* cupr b7a.de* emb-r mtf11 ferr bro1 *Ferr-s* *Gran* k* graph k* helm bro1 hyos k* ign bro1* indg bro1* iod b2.de* kali-c k* kali-chl bro1 lyc k* mag-c k* mag-m b2.de* merc k* merc-c b4a.de merc-d bro1 napht bro1 nat-m k* nat-p tl1 nux-m b2.de* nux-v k* petr b2.de* phos b2.de* pin-s c2* plect c2 psor al2 rhus-t k* ruta k* *Sabad* k* santin c2* sec k* *Sil* k* **Spig** k* stann k* staph c1 **Sulph** k* ter k* teucr bro1* *Thuj* b4a.de* urt-u bro1 valer b2.de* viol-o mtf11
- **schistosome** (= schistosoma haematobium; bilharzia haematobia): *Ant-t* br1
- **tapeworm** (= taenia; = old rubric "taeniae"): agn bg2 agri bta1• *Ail* alum b2.de* ambr b2.de* anac b2.de* arec c1* *Arg-n* k* arge bro1 ars b2.de* **Calc** k* calc-caust c2 callil-l bta1• *Carb-an* k* *Carb-v* k* carbn-s carli-a lsr4.de* caust b2.de* chin k* cina b2.de* cinnb c2 claus-in bta1• clerod-g bta1• coff b2.de* colch b2.de* croc b2.de* cuc-p c1* cupr k* cupr-act c2* cupr-o mtf11 cupr-ox bro1 emb-k bta1• *Fil* k* *Form* frag k* geb-k bta1• gran c2* *Graph* k* grat ign b2.de* kali-c k* kali-i bro1 kam c2* kou c2* laur b2.de* lyc b2.de* *Mag-m* k* merc k* *Nat-c* k* nat-m b2.de* nat-p bg2 nat-s bg2* nit-ac b4a.de nux-v k* othon-n bta1• pann br1 pellin bro1 petr k* phos k* *Plat* k* psor al2 *Puls* k* rhus-t b2.de* *Sabad* k* sabin b2.de* sal-ac c2 santin bro1 *Sep* k* *Sil* k* spig b2.de* spong b2.de* *Stann* k* stry gm1 strych-h bta1• sulph k* ter k* teucr b2.de* thuj k* thymol sp1 valer b2.de* *Verat* hr1 zinc b2.de*
  - **accompanied** by | **salivation**: sabad kr1*
  - **moon**:
    - **full** moon; during: *Merc* b4a.de
    - **waning** moon; during: *Sulph* b4a.de
  - **Hypochondria**; sensation as if in region of: *Merc* b4a.de
- **trichinae** (= trichinella spiralis): ars bro1 bapt bro1 cupr-ox bro1
- **whipworm** (= trichuriasis): podo mtf11

Worms: ...

- **sensation** of worms (See Formication; Itching)

ANUS; complaints of: acon b2.de* aesc ptk1 agar b2.de agn b2.de alum b2.de* am-c b2.de* am-m b2.de* ambr b2.de* anac b2.de* ang b2.de *Ant-c* b2.de ant-t b2.de* arn b2.de ars b2.de* asar b2.de aur b2.de bar-c b2.de* bell b2.de* borx b2.de bov b2.de bry b2.de calc b2.de* camph b2.de cann-s b2.de canth b2.de* caps b2.de* carb-an b2.de* **Carb-v** b2.de* caust b2.de* cham b2.de chin b2.de* cic b2.de cina b2.de cocc b2.de colch b2.de* coloc b2.de* con b2.de* croc b2.de* cupr b2.de cycl b2.de dulc b2.de euph b2.de euphr b2.de ferr b2.de* **Graph** b2.de* hell b2.de hep b2.de hyos b2.de ign b2.de* iod b2.de ip b2.de **Kali-c** b2.de* kali-n b2.de kreos b2.de lach b2.de* laur b2.de led b2.de lyc b2.de* m-ambo b2.de m-arct b2.de m-aust b2.de mag-c b2.de mag-m b2.de mang b2.de meny b2.de merc b2.de* mez b2.de mosch b2.de *Mur-ac* b2.de* nat-c b2.de* nat-m b2.de* nit-ac b2.de* nux-m b2.de **Nux-v** b2.de* olnd b2.de op b2.de* *Paeon* br1* petr b2.de ph-ac b2.de* **Phos** b2.de* plat b2.de* plb b2.de* puls b2.de* ran-b b2.de ran-s b2.de rheum b2.de rhod b2.de rhus-t b2.de ruta b2.de sabad b2.de* sabin b2.de* sars b2.de seneg b2.de **Sep** b2.de* sil b2.de* spig b2.de spong b2.de* squil b2.de stann b2.de* staph b2.de* stront-c b2.de sul-ac b2.de **Sulph** b2.de* teucr b2.de* thuj b2.de* valer b2.de verat b2.de verb b2.de zinc b2.de*

▽ - **extending** to:

O • **Liver**: *Dios* ptk1 lach ptk1

• **Umbilicus**: coloc ptk1 lach ptk1

O - **Margin**: lyc bg2 nux-v bg2

PERINEUM; complaints of: **Agn** b2.de* **Alum** b2.de* am-m b2.de* *Ant-c* b2.de* *Ant-t* b2.de* ars b2.de* asaf b2.de* bell b2.de* bov b2.de* bry b2.de* calc b2.de* cann-s b2.de* **Carb-an** b2.de* **Carb-v** b2.de* *Caust* b2.de* chim ptk1 chin b2.de* **Cycl** b2.de* graph b2.de* hep b2.de* ign b2.de* *Lyc* b2.de* mag-m b2.de* merc b2.de* mez b2.de* mur-ac b2.de* *Nux-v* b2.de* ol-an ptk1 *Paeon* bg2* *Petr* b2.de* phos b2.de* *Plb* b2.de* *Rhod* b2.de* rhus-t b2.de* sanic ptk1 seneg b2.de* sep b2.de* spig b2.de* **Sulph** b2.de* *Tarax* b2.de* thuj b2.de*

▽ - **extending** to:

O • **Genitals**: bov ptk1

• **Penis**: phyt ptk1

• **Rectum**: bov ptk1

RECTUM and anus; complaints of: | **accompanied** by | **Bladder**; complaints of (See BLADDER - Complaints of bladder - accompanied - rectum)

▽ - **extending** to:

O • **Chest**: lach bg2

• **Genitals**: sep bg2

• **Head**: lach bg2

• **Liver**: dios bg2 lach bg2

• **Thigh**: alum bg2 visc bg2

• **Urethra**: thuj bg2

DAYTIME: aur-m bg2 sulph bg2
- **only**: nat-m bg2 *Petr* bg2

MORNING: agar bg2 *Aloe* bg2 am-m bg2 ang bg2 apis bg2 arg-n bg2 bov bg2 bry bg2 chin bg2 cimic bg2 dios bg2 fl-ac bg2 iod bg2 kali-bi bg2 lach bg2 laur bg2 lept bg2 lol bg2 lyc bg2 *Mag-c* bg2 merc-c bg2 mez bg2 mur-ac bg2 nat-s bg2 nux-v bg2 phos bg2 *Podo* bg2 rhod bg2 rhus-t bg2 rumx bg2 staph bg2 **Sulph** bg2 tab bg2 thuj bg2 valer bg2 zinc bg2
- **evening**; and: kali-c bg2
- **rising** | **agg.** | **on** and after rising: aloe bg2 apis bg2 bry bg2 calc-p bg2 cham bg2 chel bg2 chin bg2 crot-t bg2 fl-ac bg2 kali-bi bg2 **Nat-s** bg2 nux-v bg2 petr bg2 phos bg2 rhod bg2 *Sulph* bg2
  - **bed**; from | **before**: *Aloe* bg2 *Arg-n* bg2 bov bg2 bry bg2 cimic bg2 **Kali-bi** bg2 lyc bg2 *Nat-s* bg2 onos bg2 op bg2 petr bg2 phos bg2 *Podo* bg2 psor bg2 **Rumx** bg2 sil bg2 **Sulph** bg2 verat bg2 zinc bg2

FORENOON: cic bg2 clem bg2 petr bg2 phyt bg2 podo bg2

NOON: rad-br ptk1

AFTERNOON: ars bg2 borx bg2 laur bg2 mag-c bg2 merc-c bg2 phos bg2 phyt bg2

EVENING (= 18-22 h): aloe bg2 bism bg2 bov bg2 bry bg2 caust bg2 coli rly4• *Dig* hr1 galeoc-c-h gms1• kali-bi bg2 kali-c bg2 lach bg2 mag-c bg2 merc bg2 *Nuph* hr1 phos bg2 phyt bg2 puls bg2 rhod bg2 sang bg2 sep h2* sulph h2* thuj bg2 valer bg2 verat bg2 zinc h2*
- **21 h**: galeoc-c-h gms1•

NIGHT: aloe bg2 anac bg2 ant-t bg2 arg-n bg2 arn bg2 *Ars* bg2 aur bg2 aur-m bg2 bapt bg2 bell bg2 borx bg2 bry bg2 canth bg2 *Caps* bg2 caust bg2 **Cham** bg2 chel bg2 **Chin** bg2 cina bg2 colch bg2 coloc bg2 *Dulc* bg2 *Ferr* bg2 fl-ac bg2 graph bg2 hell bg2 hep bg2 jal bg2 kali-c bg2 lach bg2 lyc bg2 **Merc** bg2 merc-c bg2 mosch bg2 nat-m bg2 nux-v bg2 *Phos* bg2 podo bg2 *Psor* bg2 **Puls** bg2 rheum bg2 **Rhus-t** bg2 sil bg2 **Sulph** bg2 tab bg2 thuj bg2 *Verat* bg2 zinc bg2
- **midnight**:
  - **before**: mag-c bg2 nux-m bg2
  - **at**: arg-n bg2 carb-an bg2 lach bg2 op bg2 podo bg2
  - **after**: aloe bg2 *Ars* bg2 cic bg2 cupr bg2 ferr bg2 kali-c bg2 lyc bg2 podo bg2 sulph bg2 tab bg2
- **air**; night: merc bg2
- **amel.**: petr bg2

ACRID (= corrosive, excoriating): acon k* allox tpw3 *Aloe* alum k* am-c k* ang b2.de* *Ant-c* k* *Arn* k* **Ars** k* ars-i ars-s-f k2 arum-t k2 **Bapt** k* bar-c bros-gau mrc1 bry k* calc k* cann-s b2.de* canth k* caps b2.de* carb-an carb-v k* carbn-s caust b2.de* *Cham* k* *Chin* k* choc srj3• colch k* *Coloc* k* colos cuph bro1 *Dulc* k* *Ferr* k* ferr-ar ferr-p *Gamb* k* gard-j vlr2• *Graph* k* hell b2.de* *Hep* *Hydr* k* ign k* **Iris** k* kali-ar kali-c k* kali-m k2 kali-n mrr1 kali-p kali-s kreos k* lac-ac stj5• *Lach* k* lavand-a ctl1• lept lyc tl1 m-ambo b2.de mag-s c1 **Merc** k* *Merc-c* k* *Merc-d* bg2* *Merc-sul* hr1* *Mur-ac* k* nat-c b2.de* **Nat-m** k* *Nit-ac* k* nux-m b2.de* *Nux-v* k* petr b2.de* ph-ac b2.de* *Phos* k* plan k* podo k* psil ft1 **Puls** k* rheum k* ribo rly4• sabin k* sang k2 sars k* scop ptk1 sel b2.de* sep h2* spong b2.de* stann b2.de* *Staph* k* suis-em rly4• sul-ac bg2* *Sulph* k* syc bka1*• syph k* tab bg2 ter bro1 *Tub* **Verat** k* zinc mtf33
- **destroying**:
  - **hair**: coll ptk1
  - **napkin**: sul-ac bg2

AIR AGG.; DRAFT OF: bry bg2

ALBUMINOUS: aloe sne asc-t k* **Borx** carb-an k* crot-t bg2 *Dios* grat bg2 merc merc-c k* *Nat-m* podo bg2
- **coagulated**: carb-an k* merc-c k*
- **yellow**: apis bg2

ASA FOETIDA; like: cic bg2

ASH-COLORED (See Gray)

BALLS, like: (↗*Sheep*) abrom-a ks5 aesc k* aesc-g bro1 **Alum** k* **Alumn** k* am-c gsy1 amp rly4• anthraq rly4• aster bro1 bar-c bro1 bar-ox-suc rly4• brach calc *Calc-p* carb-v sne *Card-m* bro1 cartl-s rly4• caust bro1 *Chel* bro1 chord-umb rly4• cimx sne cob coll bro1 cop cystein-l rly4• dulc fd4.de euphr falco-pe nl2• form glyc bro1 *Graph* bro1 ham fd3.de• hell sne hipp hydr indol bro1 kali-p fd1.de• lac-h htj1• lap-la sde8.de• *Lyc* bro1 **Mag-m** k* mag-p sne marb-w es1• *Med* **Merc** *Mez* morph bro1 **Nat-m** nat-sil fd3.de• **Nit-ac** k* *Nux-v* k* **Op** k* oxal-a rly4• ozone sde2• petr bro1 phos plac-s rly4•

Balls, like: ...
Plat bro1 **Plb** k* podo fd3.de• positr nl2• pot-e rly4• psor ptel pyrog bro1 ribo rly4• ruta fd4.de sanic bro1 *Sep* bro1 *Sil* vh* spong fd4.de streptoc rly4• suis-em rly4• suis-pan rly4• sul-ac k2 **Sulph** k* thlas sne thuj k* tritic-vg fd5.de vanil fd5.de verat k* verb bro1 vib vip fkr4.de xero bro1 zinc bro1
- **black**: **Alumn** **Op** k* *Plat* k* **Plb** k* *Pyrog* *Verat* k* vib hr1
- **brown**: *Nux-v* podo fd3.de• thuj h1*
- **light** colored: coll k*
- **sheep** (See Sheep)
- **small**: alum sne carb-v sne cimx sne hell sne mag-p sne mand sne nad rly4• op sne plb mrr1 pot-e rly4• psor sne pyrog sne sanic mtf33 sil sne suis-pan rly4• thlas sne
  - **dry**: sanic mtf33

BENDING BACKWARD: | **amel.**: med bg2

BILIOUS: (↗*RECTUM - Diarrhea - bilious*) acon aeth k* *Agar* agar-ph a1 alco a1 *Aloe* k* ant-t k* apoc k* apoc-a a1* *Ars* k* ars-h k* ars-s-f k2 ars-s-r a1* arum-d a1* aspar a1* bism k* *Bry* k* cact k* calc-p k* carb-ac k* card-m bro1 carl a1 *Cham* k* *Chin* k* chinin-ar cina k* *Colch* k* coll k* *Coloc* k* *Corn* k* cot a1 **Crot-h** k* crot-t k* cub k* cupr bg2 cupr-ar a1 dig k* dios k* *Dulc* k* elaps elat a1* *Fl-ac* k* gamb bro1 gast a1 gels k* gent-l a1 grat a1 hyper a1* ille c1 *Ip* k* *Iris* k* jug-c a1* kali-i k* kiss a1 lept k* *Lil-t* k* linu-c a1 lyc bro1 med k* **Merc** k* *Merc-c* k* **Merc-d** bg2* mez k* naja narz a1 **Nat-s** k* nat-sil fd3.de• *Nux-v* b2.de* nyct br1* olnd b2.de* op k* osm k* ost a1 *Phos* k* phys a1 phyt k* pin-s a1 **Podo** k* polyp-p a1 pop a1 psor k* **Puls** k* *Sang* k* sangin-t c1* sec k* sel bg2 sep k* serp a1 still a1 *Sulph* k* tarax bro1 **Verat** k* vip a1 wies a1 yohim c1* yuc bro1 zinc k* zinc-s a1
- **daytime** | **warm** drinks agg.: fl-ac k*

BLACK: acet-ac acon k* aesc k* aeth agar agar-ph a1 alco a1 aloe alum k* alum-p k2 *Alumn* k* ant-c tl1 ant-t apis k* *Arg-n* k* arn **Ars** k* *Ars-i* k* ars-s-f k2 asaf bg2 asc-t k* bac jl2 bapt bg2* *Berb* k* bol-la *Brom* k* *Bry* k* cact k* cadm-met tpw6* cadm-s br1 *Calc* k* calc-s k* camph k* canth k* *Caps* k* carb-ac k* carb-v carbn-s carc mlr1• *Card-m* caust k* cench k2 chin k* *Chinin-ar* chinin-s *Chion* k* cic k* *Cina* *Cocc* k* colch k* **Coll** k* coloc b2.de* crot-c sk4• *Crot-h* k* cub k* *Cupr* k* dios k* dulc echi bro1 elae a1 elaps k* elat fago bg2 *Ferr* k* ferr-i a1 ferr-m a1 ferr-p bg2 glon k* graph k* ham k* helia br1* hell b7a.de* *Hep* k* hist sp1 iod k* ip k* iris jac-c kali-ar kali-bi k* kali-br hr1 kali-c b4a.de *Kali-s* k* kiss a1 kola stb3• *Lac-ac* *Lac-c* lac-h sze9• *Lach* k* lat-m **Lept** k* lipp a1 manc k* med k* **Merc** k* **Merc-c** k* merc-cy a1 *Merc-d* k* merc-i-f k* mez bg2 morph bro1 *Nat-m* k* *Nit-ac* k* nux-m k* *Nux-v* k* **Op** k* osm a1 ost a1 ph-ac k* *Phos* k* phys a1 pitu-gl skp7• *Plat* **Plb** k* *Podo* k* psor k* ptel a1 *Pyrog* k* rhod k* rhus-t rhus-v k* rob k* *Rumx* sec k* sep sin-a a1 sol-t-ae a1 squil k* stann *Stram* k* sul-ac k* sul-i k2 sulph k* tab k* tarent mtf33 tell ter k* thuj b4a.de* tritic-vg fd5.de ust k* vanil fd5.de **Verat** k* vip a1 wies a1 yohim c1* zinc k*
- **clots**; in: cadm-s br1
- **fecal**: (↗*Fecal*) ant-t **Brom** k* camph cic tl1 coll tl1 crot-h tl1 cub *Ferr* hipp iris *Lept* med tl1 sulph tab
  - **alternating** with white stool (See White - fecal - alternating)
- **foul**: chion ptk1 crot-h ptk1 lept ptk1
- **hard** followed by white, normal stool; and: aesc ptk1
- **straw**; like burnt: *Lach* bg2

BLOODY: (↗*Reddish; ABDOMEN - Bleeding - intestines; RECTUM - Hemorrhage*) abrot a1* acet-ac a1* *Acon* k* aesc aeth k* agar k* agar-ph a1 ail k* alco a1 all-c a1 allox tpw3* *Aloe* k* **Alum** k* alum-p k2 alum-sil k2 *Alumn* k* am-c b2.de* am-caust a1 *Am-m* k* ambr b2.de* anac k* anan k* ant-c b2.de* ant-t k* anthraci vh1 *Apis* k* apoc a1 **Arg-n** k* *Arn* k* **Ars** k* ars-h a1 ars-i ars-s-f k2 arund k* asar k* atis mtf11 bac bn *Bapt* k* bar-c b2.de* *Bar-m* k* bart a1 *Bell* k* benz-ac k* bol-la bol-s a1 borx b2.de* both bro1 *Bry* k* *Bufo* k* cadm-met tpw6 cadm-s br1* calad k* *Calc* k* calc-i k2 calc-p bg2* calc-s calc-sil k2 **Canth** k* **Caps** k* *Carb-ac* k* carb-an k* carb-v k* carbn-s cartl-s rly4• *Casc* a1 *Caust* k* *Cham* k* chel k* chim hr1 *Chin* k* chinin-ar chlf a1* cina cinnb cinnm a1 clem a1 *Cob* hr1 coff-t a1 **Colch** k* *Coll* k* **Coloc** k* *Con* k* cop k* cortico sp1 croc bg2* *Crot-c* *Crot-h* k* cub k* cupr k* cupr-ar a1* cupr-s a1 cycl a1 cyn-d mtf11 cypra-eg sde6.de* der a1 dios mrr1 diph-t-tpt jl2 dor a1* dros k* *Dulc* k* eberth jl2 elaps k* elat k* enteroc jl2 erig hr1 eucal a1* euon a1 euph-a a1 euph-l a1 eupi a1 ferr k* ferr-ar ferr-i k* ferr-m a1* *Ferr-p* k* fic-v mtf11 gaert fmm1• *Gamb* hr1* gast a1 genist a1 gink-b sbd1• *Graph* k* **Ham** k* hed sp1 hep k* hipp k* *Hir* rsj4• *Hydr* k* hyos b2.de* ign k* ind a1 iod k* *Ip* k* iris jal k* jug-c a1 *Kali-ar* *Kali-bi* k* *Kali-br* k* *Kali-c* k* *Kali-chl* k* kali-chr a1 kali-i k* kali-m k2 kali-n k* *Kali-p* **kali-s** kali-sil k2 kiss a1

Stool

Bloody: ...
Kreos k* *Lac-d* k* lach k* lap-la sde8.de• laur a1 led k* *Lept* lil-t a1* lipp a1 lob a1 lon-x a1 loxo-recl bnm10• *Lyc* k* lyss k* mag-c k* *Mag-m* k* *Manc* k* *Mangi* br1 *Med* k* merc b2.de* **Merc-c** k* merc-cy a1 **Merc-d** a1* *Merc-i-f* merc-i-r k* merc-n a1 merc-sul a1 mez b2.de* mill k* *Moni* rfm1• morg-p fmm1• *Mur-ac* k* *Nat-ar* *Nat-c* k* nat-f sp1 nat-m k* nat-p nat-s k* *Nit-ac* k* *Nux-m* k* **Nux-v** k* olnd a1 osm a1 ox-ac k* petr k* ph-ac b2.de* **Phos** k* *Phyt* k* pic-ac k* plan a1 plat b2.de* *Plb* k* *Podo* k* positr nl2• prot fmm1• psor k* *Puls* k* pyre-p a1 pyrog k2 raph k* rat k* rein a1 *Rhus-t* k* ric a1 *Ruta* k* sabad k* sabin k* sanguis-s hrn2• sarr k* *Sars* k* sec k* sel b2.de* senec k* *Sep* k* *Sil* k* sin-a a1* squil b2.de* stann b2.de* staph k* stram b2.de* suis-em rly4• *Sul-ac* k* *Sulph* k* tab bg2* tarax b2.de* tarent k* tell a1 tep a1 **Ter** k* thal a1 thal-xyz srj8• *Thuj* k* tril-p c1 tritic-vg fd5.de trom k* urt-u k* valer k* vario hr1* *Verat* k* *Verat-v* hr1 vip a1 wies a1 zinc k* zinc-p k2 *Zinc-s* a1

- **bright** red: dros mtf33 sanguis-s hrn2•
- **charred** straw, like: *Lach* k*
- **children**; in:
  - **infants**: calc-s ptk1
  - **newborns**: acon vh1
- **clots**: cadm-s ptk1
  - **black**, offensive: alum nh cadm-s br1 cartl-s rly4•
  - **bright**: alum ptk1
- **covered** with blood: alum b4.de* ambr b7.de* asar b7a.de *Bry* b7.de* coloc b4a.de *Con* b4.de* ferr b7.de* ip b7.de* led b7.de* *Mag-m* b4.de* merc b4.de* merc-c b4a.de *Mur-ac* b4a.de nat-c bg2 nat-m b4.de* nat-s bg2 nux-v b7.de* puls b7.de* *Rhus-t* b7.de* ruta b7.de* sabad b7a.de sabin b7.de* sel b7.de* squil b7.de* sul-ac b4.de* sulph b4a.de* thuj b4.de* *Valer* b7a.de zinc bg2
- **end** of stool; at: alum bg2 sel bg2
- **followed** by | **shivering**: med c1
- **frothy**: zinc h2*
- **grumous** (See lumpy)
- **last** part: daph ptk1*
- **lumpy**: camph bg2 zinc bg2
- **menses** | **after** | **agg.**: graph b4.de
  - **during** | **agg.**: am-m ars-met
- **putrid**: nit-ac mtf33
- **spots**, in: aq-mar skp7• nat-c h2*
- **streaks**, in: agar bro1 aloe bg2* am-c h2* amp rly4• ant-t bg2 apis bg2 arg-n bro1 arn k* arund hr1 bell bro1 bry calc k* canth bg2* *Caps* bro1 carb-an h2* cina colch k* *Coloc* k* con k* cupr bg2 *Cupr-ar* bro1 cycl bg2* *Elat* hr1 erig hr1 euph bro1 *Ip* bro1 *Kali-bi* k* kali-c bg2 kreos bro1 led lil-t bro1 mag-c bro1 mag-m k* **Merc** k* merc-c bg2* merc-d bro1 mez bg2 nat-c bg2 nat-m bg2 *Nat-s* k* **Nit-ac** k* **Nux-v** k* ox-ac bg2 phos bg2* plb bg2 **Podo** k* *Psor* bro1 puls pyrog bg2 rhus-t bg2* sel bg2 squil streptoc rly4• sul-ac h2* *Sulph* k* thuj k* tril-p bro1 *Trom* k*
- **tarry**: ham ptk1
  - **frothy**: elaps ptk1

BLUISH: bapt k* colch k* kali-bi bg2 merc-c bg2 phos k*
- **clayish**: (↗*Clayish)* indg
- **green** on standing; becomes: phos

BREAKFAST agg.: nat-s ptk1 thuj ptk1

BRIGHT COLORED (See Light)

BROTH; like: stram bg2

BROWN: acon adel a1 *Aesc* k* aloe k* ambr b7a.de* ammc a1 anac k* ant-t k* *Apis* k* apoc a1 **Arg-n** k* *Arn* k* *Ars* k* ars-i arum-t a1* asaf k* asc-c a1* asc-t astac a1 aster a1* bapt k* bell k* borx brom b4a.de* *Bry* k* calc k* *Camph* k* canth k* carb-ac a1 carb-v k* carbn-s card-m a1 carl a1 casc a1 *Chel* k* *Chin* k* *Chion* coca-c sk4• coloc k* cop corn bro1 *Crot-h* hr1 *Crot-t* bg2* cupr bg2 cupr-act bro1 cupr-ar bro1 dulc k* ery-a a1 euph-a a1 fago a1 *Ferr* k* *Ferr-ar* ferr-i k* ferr-m bro1 ferr-p k* fl-ac k* franz a1 gamb k* gran a1 *Graph* k* grat k* helon a1 hep b4a.de* hir skp7• hydr k* ind a1 inul a1 iod k* ip ptk1 *Iris* ix bnm8• jab a1 jug-c a1 kali-ar kali-bi k* kali-c k* kali-p kola stb3• kreos k* *Lach* k* *Lept* bg2* *Lil-t* k* lim a1 lipp a1 **Lyc** k* *Mag-c* k* mag-m bg2* **Merc** k* merc-c k* merc-i-f a1* merc-i-r a1* merc-sul k* *Mez* k* *Mur-ac* k* nat-m k* nat-p a1 *Nat-s* nit-ac k* nux-v k* ol-an a1 *Op* k* ox-ac k* petr k* *Phos* k* phys a1 phyt k* *Plan* k* podo hr1* psil ft1 *Psor* k* ptel hr1 *Pyrog* k* ran-b a1 raph bg1* *Rheum* k* *Rhod* k* rhus-t bg2* rhus-v a1 *Rumx* k* *Sabad* k* **Sec** k* *Senec* bro1 sep k* sin-a a1* squil k* stram a1 *Sul-ac* b4a.de sul-i k2 sulph k* sumb a1

Brown: ...
suprar rly4• tarent hr1 ter k* thuj k* tritic-vg fd5.de trom k* tub br1* upa a1 urt-u hr1 vanil fd5.de vario k* **Verat** k* wies a1 xan hr1 yuc a1 zinc k* zinc-p k2 zing k*

- **morning**: granit-m es1•
- **children**; in: | **infants**; in: bry b7.de*
- **chocolate**; like: ars bg2 stram bg2
- **dark** brown: aq-mar skp7• but-ac sp1 squil bg2 tub jl2
- **fecal**: (↗*Fecal)* aesc aloe ant-t k* asaf bapt borx *Bry* k* coloc k* dulc *Ferr* fl-ac k* graph kali-c k* lil-t lyc k* mez k* ox-ac k* petr rheum rhod k* rumx sulph trom k*
- **foamy**: *Arn* bg2 *Kali-bi* bg2 sabad bg2
- **light**: ambr b7.de* cham b7.de* musca-d szs1 suprar rly4• verat bg2 [bell-p-sp dcm1]
- **liver** brown: calc b4a.de carb-v b4a.de lyc bg2 mag-c b4.de*
- **reddish** brown: bit-ar wht1•
- **yellowish**: **Rhus-t** hr1

BURNING: *Ars* b4a.de* bar-c b4a.de carb-v b4a.de *Lach* bg2 mag-m bg2 *Merc* b4a.de* mur-ac b4a.de *Nat-m* b4a.de stront-c b4a.de sulph b4a.de

CALCIUM increased: cortico sp1

CHALKY (See White - chalk)

CHANGEABLE: aesc bg1 am-m k* berb k* cham k* colch k* *Dulc* k* euon bg1* kali-s fd4.de lac-h sze9• merc bro1 mur-ac h2* nat-m bg2 *Podo* k* **Puls** k* ruta fd4.de sanic k* sil bro1* *Sulph* k* tab hr1
- **color**: **Colch** bg2 dulc bg2 podo bg2 *Puls* bg2 *Sanic* bg2

CHOPPED: *Acon* k* arg-n ars k* bar-m k* cadm-met tpw6 **Calc** b4a.de *Cham* k* chin b7.de* dulc fd4.de ferr b7.de* *Ferr-p* hr1 *Ip* hr1 *Kreos* hr1 *Mag-c* b4a.de med hr1 *Merc* b4.de* *Merc-d* hr1 nat-p ptk1 *Nux-m* b7.de* podo fd3.de• *Puls* b7.de* rhus-t k* sul-ac k* *Sulph* b4.de* viol-t k*
- **beets**: *Apis*
- **eggs**: *Cham* k* chinin-s bg2 cur bg2 lach bg2 **Merc** k* *Merc-d* k* *Nux-m* k* **Puls** k* *Rhus-t* bg2 *Sul-ac* bg2 *Sulph* k* viol-t bg2
- **spinach**: **Acon** k* *Arg-n* k* *Cham* k* *Merc*

CLAY COLORED: (↗*Light)* acon bg2* aloe bro1 ars bg2 aur-m-n bell k* benz-ac bro1 *Berb* k* *Calc* b4a.de* carb-v b4a.de **Card-m** k* cartl-s rly4• *Chel* k* chinin-ar *Chion* k* chord-umb rly4• cop *Dig* k* euph bro1 *Gels* k* *Hep* k* hydrog srj2• ign b7.de* *Iod* *Kali-bi* k* kali-c bro1 kali-m k2 kali-p *Lach* k* lept mag-c bg2* mag-m bg2 *Merc* k* merc-c b4a.de *Merc-d* bro1 mez bg2 myric k* **Nat-s** *Nit-ac* ozone sde2• petr-ra shn4• petros k* *Ph-ac* k* phos bg2* plat bg2 *Podo* k* pycnop-sa mrz1 rad-br sze8• sep k* *Sil* bg2 tab tritic-vg fd5.de vanil fd5.de

CLAYISH: (↗*Bluish - clayish; Light; Watery - clay)* arge-pl rwt5• **Calc** k* crot-t bg2 dig k* euph a1 hep bg2 *Lac-c* lach bg2 lob a1 lycps-v mag-c med k* merc-c bg2* phos bg2* *Podo* k* *Sil* k* thuj bg2* zinc bg2 zinc-m a1
- **connected**; tough: plat h2

COFFEE:
- **amel.**: brom bg2 phos bg2
- **grounds**; like coffee: ant-t camph cench *Crot-h* k* *Dig* k* ferr-m kali-t a1 *Lach* bro1 phos k* *Podo* bro1 tart-ac bro1 ter tl1 zinc-m a1

COLD:
- **agg.**: con ptk1 cub bg3* lyc k*
- **milk** | **amel.**: iod bg2

COLD agg.; taking a: calc ptk1 rumx ptk1 tub ptk1

COLORLESS (See White)

COLORS; several: aesc ptk1 colch ptk1 euon ptk1 kali-p ptk1 menis ptk1 sulph ptk1 zinc-cy ptk1

COMPLAINTS of stool:
- **accompanied** by:
  - **erections**; complaints of: thuj bg2
  - **intussusception** (See ABDOMEN - Intussusception - accompanied - stool)
  - **nausea**: rhus-t bg2
  - **salivation**: *Merc* bg2
  - **weakness**: nux-m bg2

- **accompanied** by: ...
○ • **Abdomen**:
  ⁝ **distention** of: bell bg2
  ⁝ **pain** in: ars bg2 bar-c bg2 kali-bi bg2 puls bg2 rhus-t bg2
  • **Bladder**; pain in (See BLADDER - Pain - accompanied - stool)
  • **Face**; red discoloration of: caust bg2
  • **Head**; heat of (See HEAD - Heat - accompanied - stool)
  • **Liver**; hard (See ABDOMEN - Hard - liver - accompanied - stool)
  • **Loins**; pain in (See lumbar)
  • **Lumbar** region; pain in: bar-c bg2
  • **Rectum**:
  ⁝ **itching**: euph bg2
  ⁝ **prolapsus** (See RECTUM - Prolapsus - accompanied - stool)
  • **Spleen**; complaints of (See ABDOMEN - Spleen - accompanied - stool)
- **fear**; with (See MIND - Fear - stool - complaints)

CONSTANT discharge: *Apis* ip k2 ox-ac *Phos* sep *Trom*

COPIOUS: acet-ac k* achy-a zzc1• acon a1 adam skp7• aeth agar a1 agar-ph a1 all-c a1 *Aloe* k* alum-sil k2 alumn k* am-c bg2* am-caust a1 am-m ambr h1* ammc a1 amyg a1 ang k* ant-c k* *Ant-t* k* *Apis* k* *Apoc* k* apoc-a a1 aq-mar skp7• arg-n k* arn k* **Ars** k* ars-h k* ars-i k* arum-d a1* *Asaf* k* asar bg2 asc-c a1* asc-t hr1 aur k* aur-ar k2 aur-i k2 **Bapt** *Benz-ac* k* berb k* bism bro1 bit-ar wht1• bov bg2 bry k* cact k* cain *Calc* k* calc-act bro1 calc-i k2 *Calc-p* k* calc-sil k2 **Camph** k* canth k* **Carb-v** caul c1 *Cench* chel k* **Chin** k* chinin-ar chinin-s bg2 cimic k* cob k* cob-n sp1 coc-c k* coca-c sk4• coch hr1 *Coff* coff-t hr1 *Colch* k* coll k* coloc k* colos con cop k* *Cor-r* hr1 corn k* cortiso tpw7 coto bro1 **Crot-t** k* cub k* cupr k* cupr-s hr1 cycl k* dios k* dor hr1 *Dulc* k* eberth jl2 **Elat** k* *Euon* bro1 eup-per hr1 euph b4.de* euph-c bro1 *Ferr* k* *Ferr-ar* fuch br1 gal-ac br1 **Gamb** k* glon k* gnaph k* *Gran* k* *Grat* k* guar k* hed sp1 hell mrr1 helo-s bnm14• hep hydr k* hyos bg2 *Ign* k* *Iod* k* *Ip* k* **Iris** jal k* *Jatr-c* k* kali-ar kali-bi k* kali-c k* *Kali-chl* k* kali-m k2 *Kali-p* kali-s fd4.de kali-sula a1* *Kreos* k* *Lach* k* *Lept* k* lil-t k* *Lyc* k* lycpr br1 *Lyss* k* mag-c k* *Mag-s* c1 manc hr1 med *Merc* k* merc-c k* *Merc-d* hr1 merc-i-f k* merc-i-r k* *Mez* k* mosch k* *Mur-ac* k* musca-d szs1 narc-ps c1* nat-ar nat-m k* nat-n bro1 **Nat-s** nit-ac bg2 *Nux-m* k* nyct br1 **Olnd** op bg2 oper bro1 *Ox-ac* k* paull bro1 petr k* **Ph-ac** k* **Phos** k* phys a1 phyt k* pic-ac k* pip-m a1 plat b4.de* plb k* **Podo** k* positr nl2• prun a1 *Psor* k* ptel a1 pyrid rly4• pyrog k2 ran-a a1 *Ran-b* k* raph k* rhod bg2 rhus-t k* *Rumx* ruta fd4.de sabad bg2 sal-fr sle1• sapin a1 sarr a1 sars h2* **Sec** k* sel b7a.de senec k* seneg a1 *Sep* *Sil* k* sin-a a1* sol-t-ae a1 spong fd4.de staph h1* stict bro1 still a1 stram bg2* stry k* suis-em rly4• *Sul-ac* *Sulph* k* sumb a1 symph fd3.de• tab k* tarax *Tarent* k* tax a1 tell a1* *Ter* k* teucr b7.de* *Thuj* k* trich bwa3 tritic-vg fd5.de tub-r jl2 vanil fd5.de **Verat** k* *Verat-v* k* verin a1 *Vib* vichy-g a1 vip a1 visc c1 wies a1 yuc a1 zinc k* zinc-p k2
- **evening**: aur h2* lyss jl2
- **night**: chel k* chin **Crot-t** graph *Ign* mosch k2 olib-sac wmh1 ox-ac k* plb k* sol-t-ae a1 stry a1 sulph k* verat-v
- **periodical**, alternate day: chin kr1 glycyr-g cte1•
- **exhaust**; does not: **Ph-ac** k*

CORYZA: | **amel.**: brom bg2

COW-DUNG; like: enteroc jl2

CREAM COLORED: aloe arg-met arg-n calc *Gels* k* *Ph-ac*

CRUMBLING: agar k* aloe k* alum h2* **Am-m** k* apis bg2 astac a1 bapt k* bell bg2 bry k* calc k* cann-s k* cann-xyz bg2 carb-an k* carb-v hr1 caust k* chel bg2 chinin-s coll bg2 crot-t k* cycl k* *Guaj* k* hipp a1 ign br1 kali-c bg2 lach k* lyc k* *Mag-c* k* **Mag-m** k* **Merc** k* nat-c k* **Nat-m** k* nat-p *Nit-ac* nux-v bg2 olnd k* *Op* k* ph-ac k* phos k* *Plat* k* plb bg2 *Podo* k* ruta sanic bro1* sel bg2 sin-a a1* spirae a1 *Sulph* k* syc bka1*• *Tell* k* verb bg2 *Zinc* k* zinc-m a1

CURDLED: ars k* bell k* bufo *Calc* k* calen ptk1 cham gaba sa3• iod ptk1 mag-c med k* merc murx k* nat-m bg2 nat-p *Nit-ac* k* nux-m phos bg2 puls *Rheum* sanic *Stann* k* sul-ac sulph tab ptk1 **Valer** k* viol-t
- **milk**, forcibly expelled; like: aeth *Gamb*

DARK: acon-f a1 *Aesc* k* agar k* aloe k* **Alum** k* alum-sil k2 amp rly4• anis anth a1 arg-n k* *Arn* k* *Ars* k* ars-i a1* arum-i a1 asaf bg2* astac a1 *Bapt* k* bell bg2* *Berb* k* bit-ar wht1• bol-la *Bry* k* but-ac sp1 calc-s a1 carb-v carl a1 cartl-s rly4• caul a1 cench k2 cham bg2* chel bg2* chin ptk1* chinin-s *Chion* k* chord-umb rly4• cimic k* colch coloc a1 convo-s sp1 *Corn* k* crot-h a1 cupr bg2* cyt-l a1 dios a1 dirc a1 dulc fd4.de elat a1 erig a1 fago a1 falco-pe nl2• *Ferr* k* ferr-i a1 ferr-m a1* ger-i rly4• *Glon* hr1 gnaph a1* gran a1 **Graph** k* grat bg2* ham k* hipp hist sp1 ind a1 iod h* jab a1 jug-c a1 kali-ar kali-bi bg2* kali-c k* kali-i a1 kali-n ptk1 kali-p ketogl-ac rly4• lac-del hrn2• lac-h sk4• lac-leo hrn2• *Lach* lil-t k* limen-b-c hrn2* lipp a1 loxo-lae bnm12• lyc bg2* lyss k* mag-p bg2 maland vh mang-p rly4• melal-alt gya4 merc-c bg2* merc-cy a1 mez bg2* mur-ac k* *Nat-ar* nat-c k2 *Nat-s* k* nat-sil fd3.de• nit-ac a1 *Nux-v* k* op k* ost a1 oxal-a rly4• peti a1 phos bg2* phys a1 phyt a1 pip-m a1 plac-s rly4• *Plb* k* plut-n srj7• podo fd3.de• polyp-p a1 **Psor** bg2* ptel k* puls bg2 *Rhus-t* k* rhus-v a1* ruta fd4.de sarr a1* *Sec* k* senec a1 sol-t-ae a1 spong fd4.de squil bg2* staphycoc rly4• stram ptk1* sulph a1 tab a1 tarent k* tub br1 ulm-c jsj8• vanil fd5.de verat *Verat-v* hr1 wies a1 wye a1 zinc bg2 [tax jsj7]
- **fecal**: (↗*Fecal)* *Bapt* k* carb-v k* chin *Ferr* hipp k* mur-ac nux-v k* podo ptel tarent vanil fd5.de

DELIVERY: | **agg.**: con bg2

DENTITION: apoc bg2 arg-n bg2 ars bg2 calc bg2 calc-p bg2 *Cham* bg2 chin bg2 coff bg2 ferr bg2 ip bg2 mag-c bg2 **Merc** bg2 nux-m bg2 podo bg2 rheum bg2 *Sulph* bg2
- **agg.**: *Cham* bg2 podo bg2
- **amel.**: brom bg2

DIFFICULT (See RECTUM - Constipation)

DINNER: | **after** | **agg.**: alum bg2 am-m bg2 ant-c bg2 cann-xyz bg2 caust bg2 cham bg2 colch bg2 coloc bg2 fl-ac bg2 kali-bi bg2 mag-m bg2 nat-c bg2 nat-m bg2 nit-ac bg2 *Nux-v* bg2 par bg2 ran-s bg2 sulph bg2 thuj bg2 verat bg2
- **during** | **agg.**: coloc bg2 glon bg2 *Mag-c* bg2 nat-m bg2

DOG'S, like a: *Cimx* k* kola stb3• **Phos** k* prun a1* staph k*

DRINKING:
- **after** | **agg.**: **Arg-n** bg2 ars bg2 **Caps** bg2 cina bg2 *Coloc* bg2 **Crot-t** bg2 cupr bg2 *Ferr* bg2 iod bg2 lyc bg2 nux-v bg2 podo bg2 puls bg2 rhod bg2 sep bg2
- **agg.**: *Aloe* bg2 ars bg2
- **cold** water | **agg.**: bry bg2 cocc bg2 grat bg2
- **warm** drinks | **agg.**: fl-ac bg2

DRIVING agg.: ign bg2 petr bg2 plat bg2 psor bg2

DRUNKARDS; complaints of: calc bg2 *Lach* bg2 **Nux-v** bg2 op bg2 sulph bg2

DRY: aesc k* aesc-g bro1 aids nl2• alum k* alum-p k2 alum-sil k2 alumn k2* *Am-c* k* am-m bg2 androc srj1• *Ango* c1 *Ant-c* k* aq-mar skp7• *Arg-met* k* *Arg-n* k* ars k* asaf b7.de* asar bg2 aster bro1 aur bg2 bapt k* bar-c bro1 bell a1 bit-ar wht1• brach k **Bry** k* cact k* *Calc* k* calc-s k* calc-sil k2 carb-an bg2 carc sp1* *Card-m* bro1 cartl-s rly4• caust bg2* cham a1 chel bg2* cimic a1 *Cimx* k* cob k* coc-c k* coll bg2* *Coloc* k* *Con* k* cop a1 corn k* cund a1 *Cupr* k* dig a1 dios k* dirc a1 dulc k* ery-a a1 euphr a1 eupi k* falco-pe nl2• ferr a1 glyc bro1 *Graph* bg2* *Guaj* *Ham* k* hell a1* *Hep* k* hyos bg2 hyper a1 indol bro1 irid-met srj5• iris kali-ar *Kali-bi* k* kali-br k* *Kali-c* k* kali-chl k* kali-m k2 kali-n bg2 *Kali-s* kali-sil k2 kreos k* **Lac-d** k* lac-del hrn2• lact k* laur b7.de* linu-c a1 **Lyc** k* lycps-v mag-c bg2* mag-m k* mag-p bg2 mand rsj7• mang k* med c1 melal-alt gya4 merc-c b4a.de* mez tl1 mim-p rsj8• morg-g fmm1• morph bro1 mosch bg2 musca-d szs1 **Nat-m** k* nat-p a1 neon srj5• **Nit-ac** k* **Nux-v** k* oci-sa sp1 ol-an a1 **Op** k* osm k* ost a1 petr bro1 petr-ra shn4• **Phos** k* plac-s rly4• *Plat* k* *Plb* k* *Podo* k* polyp-p a1 *Prun* k* puls k* pyrog k2* rhus-g a1 *Rhus-t* b7a.de rhus-v a1* ruta bg2 sacch sst1• sal-ac hr1 *Sanic* k* sel bg2* seneg k* sep bg2* **Sil** k* sol-t-ae a1 *Stann* k* staph k* stram a1 stront-c sk4• stry a1 sul-i bg2 *Sulph* k* tarent zzc1• ter k* thuj bg2* tril-p trios rsj11• tritic-vg fd5.de tub c1* tub-m vn* ust k* verat k* verb bro1 vib k* vip bg2 xero bro1 **Zinc** k* zinc-m a1 zinc-p k2
- **hard**; and: asc-t ptk1
- **sand**; like: *Arg-met* mang a1

EARLIER, every day: acon bg2 am-c bg2 cartl-s rly4• croc bg2 hyos h1* tarax bg2

EARTHY: med jl2

EATING:
- **after** | **agg.**: **Aloe** bg2 alum bg2 am-m bg2 anac bg2 ant-t bg2 arg-n bg2 **Ars** bg2 asar bg2 bar-c bg2 borx bg2 brom bg2 bry bg2 calc bg2 caps bg2 carb-v bg2 caust bg2 cham bg2 **Chin** bg2 cist bg2 clem bg2 *Coloc* bg2 con bg2 **Crot-t** bg2 **Ferr** bg2 hep bg2 ign bg2 kali-n bg2 *Lach* bg2 laur bg2 lyc bg2 merc-c bg2 mur-ac bg2 nat-c bg2 nat-m bg2 nit-ac bg2 nux-m bg2 *Nux-v* bg2 op bg2 ph-ac bg2 phos bg2 **Podo** bg2 **Rheum** bg2 rhod bg2 rhus-t bg2 sec bg2 sul-ac bg2 sulph bg2 tab bg2 thuj bg2 trom bg2 *Verat* bg2 zinc bg2
- **amel.**: arg-n bg2 brom bg2 dios bg2 grat bg2 hep bg2 iod bg2 lith-c bg2 lyc bg2 nat-c bg2 nicc bg2 sang bg2
- **overeating** agg.; after: coff bg2 *Ip* bg2 nux-v bg2 **Puls** bg2
- **while** | **agg.**: *Ferr* bg2 kali-p bg2

EGGS; like whipped (See Chopped - eggs)

EMISSION; after: aloe bg2 thuj bg2

EMOTIONS agg.: acon bg2 aloe bg2 ant-c bg2 *Arg-n* bg2 calc-p bg2 *Cham* bg2 *Coff* bg2 *Coloc* bg2 con bg2 **Gels** bg2 hyos bg2 ign bg2 kali-p bg2 nux-v bg2 *Op* bg2 puls bg2 sep bg2 staph bg2 *Verat* bg2

ERUPTIONS; after: ars bg2 chin bg2 merc bg2 ph-ac bg2 *Puls* bg2 sulph bg2

EXCITEMENT: | **news** agg.; exciting: gels bg2

EXCORIATING (See Acrid)

EXERTION agg.: phyt bg2

EXPLOSIVE (See Forcible)

FALLING out: *Aloe* hippoc-k szs2

FARINACEOUS food agg.: nat-s bg2

FAT food agg.: thuj bg2

FATTY, greasy: agar bg2 allox tpw4 aloe bg2* alum bg2* ars k* asaf bg2 asar bg2 asc-t bg2* bamb-a stb2.de• bell bg2 brass-n-o srj5• brom bg2 *Bry* bg2 calc ptk1 caps bg2* **Caust** k ●* *Chel* bg2 colch bg2 coloc b4a.de* crot-t bg2 dulc ptk1* fago bg2 ferr bg2 *Glycyr-g* cte1• hell bg2 hep bg2 hyos bg2 *Iod* k* **Iris** bg2* *Kali-bi* bg2 kali-n bg2 kali-s fd4.de kalm bg1 kola stb3• kreos bg2 lac-c bg2 lach bg2 lil-t bg1 lyc bg2 lycps-v bg2 mag-c ptk1* melal-alt gya4 merc-c bg2 merc-i-f bg2 mez bg2* nat-c bg2 nat-m bg2 nat-p fkr6.de nat-s ptk1 nat-sil fd3.de• onos bg1 op bg2* pert-vc vk9 ph-ac bg2 phel bg2 **Phos** k ●* pic-ac k* **Plat** bg2 rad-br sze8• *Rheum* bg2 ruta fd4.de sars bg2 sil bg2 spong fd4.de stann bg2 sul-ac bg2 sulph k* tab bg2 tarax bg2 tarent bg1* thuj k* valer bg2 vanil fd5.de verat bg2 zinc bg2
- **oily**-looking fecal: aloe bg2 ars bg2 asc-t bg2 bol-la caust bg2 colch bg2 fago bg2 *Iod* k* *Iris* bg2 nat-m bg2 **Phos** bg2 pic-ac k* sulph bg2 tarent mtf33 thuj k*
- **particles**: cina ptk1 mez ptk1 phos ptk1

FECAL stool: (↗*Black - fecal; Brown - fecal; Dark - fecal; Green - fecal; Thin - fecal; White - fecal; Yellow - fecal)* am-c b4.de* **Ars** bg2 brom bg2 canth b7.de* *Cham* b7.de* *Cina* bg2 coloc bg2 cupr b7.de* hep bg2 lach b7.de* led b7.de* m-ambo b7.de *Merc* bg2 mosch bg2 *Mur-ac* b4.de* *Ph-ac* b4.de* *Phos* b4.de* plb b7a.de* prun bg2 **Puls** bg2 *Rheum* bg2 *Rhus-t* b7a.de spig b7.de* *Sulph* bg2 verat b7.de* zinc b4.de*

FERMENTED: *Acal* bro1 agar bro1 alf bro1 *Aloe* bro1 ant-t a1* apoc bro1 *Arg-n* bro1 *Arn* k* benz-ac bro1 borx k* *Calc* hr1 *Calc-p* bro1 *Cham* b7a.de* *Chin* bro1 coloc bro1 corn bro1 *Crot-t* bro1 dirc a1 *Elat* bro1 euph h2 gamb bro1 *Gels* hr1 graph bro1 *Grat* bro1 iod bro1 **Ip** k ●* *Jatr-c* bro1 kali-bi bro1 *Mag-c* bro1 *Merc* hr1 mez k* moni rfm1• *Nat-s* bro1 nat-sulo c1* op bro1 *Ph-ac* bro1 phos bro1 plan k* podo bro1* puls bro1 rheum k* rhod k* rhus-t bro1 sabad k* sanic bro1 sec bro1 stict bro1 sul-ac bg2* *Sulph* bro1 *Thuj* bro1 trios bro1 *Verat* bro1 yuc bro1

FILAMENTS like hair in feces: bros-gau mrc1 calc-p bg2 cupr b7.de nux-v b7a.de *Sel* k* squil b7.de* verat b7.de
- **white**: **Ip** bg2 squil bg2 **Verat** bg2

FLAKY: amyg a1 *Arg-n* k* *Ars* b4a.de* asc-t a1* bell bg2* calc-p k* cham b7a.de *Chel* k* cina bg2 colch k* crot-t bg2* cupr k* *Dulc* k* ferr fuma-ac rly4• guaj guar iod bg2* *Ip* k* lac-c bg1 merc-c bg2 merc-cy a1 merc-d hr1 *Nit-ac* k* *Phos* k* sec k* squil b7a.de* sulph k* tritic-vg fd5.de **Verat** k*

FLAT: aesc vh arg-n bg1 arn bg2* asar bg2 carb-ac bg2 chel bg2* dig bg1 lach bg2 mag-p bg2 mang-p rly4• *Merc* k* phos bg2 **PULS** k ●* sep bg2* sulph k* verat k*

FLATULENT: (↗*Noisy; Sputtering; RECTUM - Flatus - stool - during)* agar k* aloe k* apoc ptk1 aq-mar skp7• arg-n br1* *Calc* b4a.de coca-c sk4• coloc ptk1 crot-t k* ferr k* gamb ptk1 *Ign* k* lac-ac stj5• lac-e hrn2• lac-h sk4• nat-c mrr1 *Nat-s* k* nux-m ptk1 olnd tl1 **Podo** mrr1 positr nl2• psor tl1 ruta fd4.de spong fd4.de stroph-h ptk1 thuj ptk1* thyr ptk1 *Trios* rsj11• tub ptk1 vanil fd5.de
- **milk** agg.: trios rsj11•

FLATUS passing; when: *Aloe* bg2* ars-i ptk1 carb-an bg2 caust ptk1 kali-c bg2 lach bg2 mag-c bg2 mag-m bg2 mur-ac ptk1 nat-p ptk1 olnd ptk1 ph-ac ptk1 podo ptk1 sep bg2 sulph bg2 verat ptk1

FLOATING in water: chel br1 lac-h htj1• merc b4.de* nat-p bwa3 sabad b7.de*

FLOCCULI: cop dulc kali-m ptk1 sec

FORCIBLE, sudden, gushing: (↗*Shooting; Thin - pouring; RECTUM - Diarrhea - sudden)* *Acal* vh1 acon bg2 ail k* aloe bg2* am-c h2* androc srj1• ant-c b7a.de* *Apis* k* *Apoc* k* aran k* *Arg-n* k* arizon-l nl2• arn *Ars* k* aster a1* aur-fu a1 bar-c k* bell bg2 bit-ar wht1• bros-gau mrc1 **Bry** bg2* calc-f ptk1 calc-p canth cench cic k* cist k* cob k* cocc bg2 *Colch* k* coloc bg2 *Crot-h* **Crot-t** k* *Cupr* k* cycl k* dig bg2 dios a1 dirc c1 dream-p sdj1• *Dulc* k* **Elat** k* fago a1 falco-pe nl2• *Ferr* k* fuma-ac rly4• *Gamb* k* graph bg2 **Grat** k* haliae-lc srj5• hydrog srj2• *Ign* bg2 *Iod* k* ip bg2 irid-met srj5• *Iris* jal k* **Jatr-c** k* *Kali-bi* k* kali-n bg2 kali-s fkr2.de lac-ac stj5• lac-c lac-h sk4• lach k* lyc k* lycps-v mag-c bg2 *Mag-m* k* mag-p hr1 mang-p rly4• *Merc* k* merc-sul br1 mez bg2 naja **Nat-c** k* **Nat-m** k* nat-ox rly4• *Nat-s* k* nicc k* nux-v bg2 op bg2 orot-ac rly4• *Ox-ac* k* ozone sde2• *Petr* k* *Phos* k* pic-ac bg2 plac rzf5• plat k* **Podo** k* psor bg2* puls pycnop-sa mrz1 *Ran-b* k* *Raph* k* rheum bg2 rhod bg2* *Rhus-g* tmo3• rhus-t k* rhus-v a1 rumx k2 sang bg3* sars bg2 **Sec** k* seneg k* *Sep* k* sil sinus rly4• spong fd4.de staphycoc rly4• streptoc rly4• sulfonam ks2 *Sulph* k* tab k* *Thuj* k* trom k* tub hr1* vanil fd5.de **Verat** k* verb c1 viol-t b7a.de zinc bg2 [pop dhh1]
- **explosion**; like an: falco-pe nl2• fuma-ac rly4• hydrog srj2• kola stb3• **Podo** mrr1 tere-la rly4• thuj mtf33 visc sp1

FREQUENT: abrot tl1 acet-ac k* acon k* agar k* ail k* allox tpw3 aloe k* alum h2* alumn k* *Am-m* k* ambr b7.de* amp rly4• anac b4.de* ang b7a.de* ant-c h2* *Ant-t* k* anthraq rly4• apis arg-n k* *Arn* k* **Ars** k* ars-h hr1 ars-i k* asar k* asc-t hr1* atp rly4• aur b4.de* aur-m hr1* bapt k* bar-c hr1 bar-m k* bar-ox-suc rly4• *Bell* k* bism bg2 bit-ar wht1• *Borx* k* bov k* *Brucel* sa3• *Bry* k* cact k* cadm-s calad b7.de* *Calc* k* calc-act bro1 calc-p k* *Canth* k* **Caps** k* carb-ac k* carb-an b4a.de* *Carb-v* k* carbn-s *Caust* cench k2 **Cham** k* chel k* *Chin* k* *Chinin-ar* chinin-s bg2 chir-fl gya2 choc srj3• cic k* *Cimic* hr1 *Cina* *Clem* b4.de* coc-c k* *Cocc* k* coch hr1 coff k* *Colch* k* coli rly4• *Coll* hr1 *Coloc* k* *Con* k* corn k* croc b7.de* *Crot-t* k* cub hr1 cuph br1* *Cupr* k* *Cupr-ar* bro1 cycl b7.de* cystein-l rly4• dig b4.de* diosm br1 dros k* *Dulc* k* **Elat** k* *Euph* hr1 falco-pe nl2• *Ferr* k* ferr-ar ferr-i k2 ferr-p k* *Fl-ac* hr1 fum rly1*• gaba sa3• *Gamb* k* ger-i rly4• germ-met srj5• granit-m es1• *Graph* k* grat k* *Ham* hr1 hell k* helo-s bnm14• hep k* *Hydr* hr1 hydrog srj2• hyos k* ign k* iod k* *Ip* k* iris jug-r sne kali-ar k* *Kali-bi* k* kali-br k* *Kali-c* k* *Kali-chl* hr1 kali-i ptk1 kali-p k2 kali-s k2 kali-sil k2 ketogl-ac rly4• kola stb3• kreos k* lac-h sk4• *Lach* k* *Lept* hr1 lil-t tl1 limen-b-c hrn2* lob *Lyc* k* *Mag-c* hr1* malar jl2 *Manc* hr1 mang b4a.de* mang-p rly4• medul-os-si rly4• melal-alt gya4 **Merc** k* **Merc-c** k* *Merc-d* hr1 mez k* moni rfm1• mucs-nas rly4• nat-ae-s a1 nat-ar nat-c k* *Nat-m* k* nat-ox rly4• nat-p k* nat-pyru rly4• nat-s k* nat-sil fd3.de• nicotam rly4• *Nit-ac* k* *Nuph* hr1 **Nux-v** k* olnd k* op bg2 opun-f br1 oxal-a rly4• ozone sde2• pall hr1 par b7.de* *Petr* k* *Ph-ac* k* **Phos** k* plan hr1 plat tl1* plb bg2 **Podo** k* positr nl2• pot-e rly4• propr sa3• *Psor* k* puls k* pycnop-sa mrz1 *Ran-b* k* *Ran-s* b7.de* rheum bg2* rhod b4.de* rhus-t k* ribo rly4• rob k* ruta fd4.de sabad bg2 sabin b7.de* samb k* sang bg2 sec k* seneg b4a.de* *Sep* k* *Sil* k* sinus rly4• spig b7.de* stann bg2 staphycoc rly4• suis-em rly4• suis-hep rly4• suis-pan rly4• sul-ac k* sul-i k2 *Sulph* k* suprar rly4• tab bg2* tarax b7.de* tarent hr1 *Ter* k* *Thuj* k* tritic-vg fd5.de trom k* tung-met bdx1• valer b7.de* vanil fd5.de **Verat** k* verb hr1 yohim c1* zinc k* zinc-p k2 zing hr1 [bell-p-sp dcm1 *Spect* dfg1 tax jsj7]
- **morning**: pitu-gl skp7• *Sulph* mrr1
- **night**: diosm br1
  - **midnight**:
    - **after** | 4-9 h: enteroc jl2
- **bloody** water: *Ferr-p* ptk1
- **normal** stool: psor ptk1
- **scanty**; but: ars ptk1 merc ptk1 nux-v ptk1
- **twice** a day: adam skp7• vanil fd5.de

- **unfitness** for work; causing: asc-t ptk1

FROG spawn (See Green - scum)

FROTHY: *Acon* *Aloe* sne ant-t bg2 apoc a1 *Arn* k* ars bg2 arum-i a1 asc-t bg2* bamb-a stb2.de• *Benz-ac* k* bol-la *Borx* *Calc* k* canth k* *Caps* k* carbn-s cedr k* cench cham bg2 chin k* chion cimic colch k* *Coloc* k* crot-t der a1 dulc fd4.de elaps k* elat k* euph bg2 ferr k* fl-ac form bg1* glon bg2* *Graph* *Grat* k* hell k* *Hep* hr1 *Iod* k* ip k* jug-c a1 *Kali-ar* k* **Kali-bi** k* *Lach* k* **Mag-c** k* mag-m **Merc** k* merc-c bg2 merc-i-f k* mez bg2 *Nat-m* k* nat-s k* *Op* k* *Plan* k* **Podo** k* polyp-p a1 ran-b k* *Raph* k* *Rheum* rhod bg2 *Rhus-t* k* ruta k* sabad bg2* saroth sp1* *Sil* k* *Squil* k* stict c1* still k* stram a1 sul-ac k* sul-i k2 **Sulph** k* syc bka1*• tep a1 tub-d jl2 verat k* visc sp1* zinc k*
  - **morning**: stict ptk1
  - **accompanied** by | **coryza** with discharge: calc ptk1 canth ptk1 cham ptk1 chin ptk1 coloc ptk1 iod ptk1 lach ptk1 mag-c ptk1 merc ptk1 op ptk1 rhus-t ptk1 ruta ptk1 sul-ac ptk1 sulph ptk1
  - **bloody**, black: elaps ptk1
  - **gushing**: chin ptk1 crot-t ptk1 elat ptk1
  - **mucous**: dirc c1

FRUIT agg.: **Ars** bg2 calc-p bg2 *Chin* bg2 cist bg2 lach bg2 lith-c bg2 podo bg2 **Puls** bg2 rhod bg2

GELATINOUS (See Mucous)

GRANULAR: apis bg2* arg-met bg2* arg-n bg2 bar-c h2* bell h1* cupr ptk1 eug hr1 hydr ptk1 *Lac-c* bg2* lyc bg2* mang h2* *Mez* bg2* nat-m bg2 *Phos* bg2* plb bg2* **Podo** bg2* sars ptk1 *Zinc* bg2*

GRAY: *Acon* b2.de* alco a1 aloe k* alumn bro1 am-m b2.de* apis bg2 arn b2.de* **Ars** k* asar k* *Aur* k* aur-m k2 aur-s k2 bapt bell b2.de* benz-ac bg2* bros-gau mrc1 *Calc* k* canth ptk1 *Carb-v* k* caust b2.de* cench cham b2.de* *Chel* k* chim chim-m hr1 chin k* chion bro1 cina b2.de* cist k* cocc b2.de* colch b2.de* coll bro1 crot-t k* cupr k* *Dig* k* dol bro1 dros b2.de* dulc b2.de* flor-p rsj3• hep b2.de* *Hydr* k* iber bro1 ign b2.de* indol bro1 iod b2.de* kali-bi bg2 *Kali-c* k* kali-m bro1 kola stb3• kreos k* *Lach* k* lycps-v k* mag-m k* mag-s sp1 malar jl2 mand sp1 **Merc** k* *Merc-d* bro1 merc-sul a1 mez bg2 myric *Nat-m* k* nat-s k* nat-sil fd3.de• nux-m b2.de* nux-v b2.de* **Op** k* **Ph-ac** k* **Phos** k* pic-ac plb k* *Podo* bro1* positr nl2• psor ptel hr1 puls b2.de* rheum k* rhus-t b2.de* sanic bro1 sec k* sep k* spig b2.de* *Spong* b2.de* stel bro1 still bg2* stront-c b2.de* sul-ac b2.de* sulph k* tarax ptk1 thuj hr1 urt-u ptk1 vanil fd5.de verat b2.de* wies a1 [tax jsj7]
  - **whitish**, in part: nat-m **Phos** plb

GREASY (See Fatty)

GREEN: *Acon* k* adam skp7* aesc *Aeth* k* *Agar* k* aloe alum alum-p k2 *Am-m* k* *Ant-c* b7a.de ant-t k* *Apis* k* **Arg-n** k* *Ars* k* ars-s-f hr1 arund k* *Asaf* k* asc-t k* aur k* aur-ar k2 bar-m k* *Bell* k* bond a1 *Borx* k* *Bov* b4a.de brom k* bry k* *Calc* k* calc-act bro1 **Calc-p** k* *Canth* k* *Caps* k* carb-an k* carb-v cass a1 **Cham** k* chel k* *Chin* k* *Chion* chord-umb rly4• cinnb k2 colch k* **Coloc** k* *Con* k* *Cop* k* *Corn* k* **Crot-t** k* cuph bro1 *Cupr* k* cystein-l rly4• cyt-l a1 dig a1 *Dulc* k* *Elat* k* *Eup-per* k* ferr b7a.de* **Gamb** k* gast a1 gels k* glon k* **Grat** k* guar *Hep* k* *Hydr* k* iodof bro1 **Ip** k* *Iris* k* *Kali-ar* kali-bi a1* *Kali-br* k* kali-chl a1 kali-i hr1 kali-m k2 kali-p fd1.de• kali-s fd4.de kola stb3• kreos k* lac-ac lac-c bg1 lac-h sk4• *Laur* k* *Lept* k* *Lyc* k* **Mag-c** k* *Mag-m* k* manc k* melal-alt gya4 **Merc** k* **Merc-c** k* merc-cy a1 *Merc-d* k* merc-i-f k* *Mez* bro1 mucs-nas rly4• *Mur-ac* k* naja **Nat-m** k* *Nat-p* k* **Nat-s** k* *Nit-ac* k* *Nux-v* k* oci-sa sp1 ox-ac a1 *Paull* bro1 petr k* petr-ra shn4• *Ph-ac* k* **Phos** k* phyt a1 **Plb** k* **Podo** k* *Psor* k* **Puls** k* *Raph* hr1 rheum k* *Rhus-t* k* rob k* ruta fd4.de sal-ac hr1* *Sanic* k* **Sec** k* sel b7a.de *Sep* k* sin-a hr1 *Stann* k* succ-ac rly4• *Sul-ac* k* **Sulph** k* suprar rly4• tab k* *Ter* k* thuj b4a.de tritic-vg fd5.de valer k* **Verat** k* wies a1 x-ray sp1 zinc k* zinc-m a1 zinc-p k2
  - **accompanied** by:
    - **cholera** infantum (See RECTUM - Cholera - infantum - accompanied - stools)
    - **small** intestines; inflammation of (See ABDOMEN - Inflammation - duodenum - accompanied - green)
  - **alternating** with | **yellowish**: dulc tl1
  - **blackish**: ars kiss a1 merc op phos sin-a a1 sul-ac suprar rly4• verat
  - **blue**; turning to: calc-p bro1* phos bro1*
  - **bright**: ars bg2
  - **brownish**: ars calc carc fd2.de• crot-t dulc iris c1 kola stb3• mag-c mag-m merc k* sin-a a1 sulph verat
  - **dark**: ars bg2* bac bn coloc bg2 merc-c bg2 [tax jsj7]

Green: ...
  - **fecal**: *(↗Fecal)* ars mag-m podo valer
  - **grass**; like cut: *Acon* bg2* **Ant-t** ptk1 **Arg-n** bg2* calc-p ptk1 **Cham** ptk1* ip ptk1* iris ptk1 *Mag-c* ptk1 merc bg2* merc-d ptk1 thuj ptk1
  - **hard**: *Agar* *Chin* cupr bg1 kreos bg1 *Stann*
  - **mucus** (See Mucous - green)
  - **olive** green: *Apis* ars k* *Elat* k* ruta fd4.de **Sec** k*
  - **paint**, like: ars bg1
  - **scum** on a frog-pond; like: *(↗Mucous - jellylike - frog)* asc-t bg2* *Bry* ptk1 colch ptk1 grat bg2* hell k* *Mag-c* k* merc k* *Phos* bro1 sabad ptk1 sal-ac ptk1 *Sanic* k*
  - **spinach** in flakes; like: **Arg-n** k* cham mrr1
  - **tea**; like: gels bg2*
  - **turns** green: arg-n ptk1 borx ptk1 calc-f ptk1 nat-s ptk1 psor ptk1 rheum ptk1 sanic ptk1
  - **yellowish**: cadm-s br1 cham mtf33 **Grat** a1 lil-s a1 sin-a a1 **Sulph** a1 tab a1 verat a1
    - **turning** yellow: ip ptk1

GRUMOUS (See Lumpy)

GUMMY: asar bg2 colch bg2 sars bg2 zinc bg2

GUSHING (See Forcible)

HAIR (See Filaments)

HARD: *(↗Stone)* abies-n abrom-a ks5 acon b2.de* adam skp7* *Aesc* k* aesc-g a1* aeth k* *Agar* k* *Agn* k* alco a1 alet k2 aloe bg2* **Alum** k* alum-sil k2 **Alumn** k* **Am-c** k* am-caust a1 **Am-m** k* ammc a1 amp rly4• anac a1 anan k* androc srj1• ang k* *Ango* c1 anis **Ant-c** k* ant-t b2.de* anthraq rly4• aphis ptk2 *Apis* aq-mar skp7• arg-met k* *Arg-n* k* arizon-l nl2• arn k* *Ars* k* ars-i ars-s-f k2 arund k* asaf k* asar k* aspar a1 *Aur* k* aur-ar k2 aur-i k2 *Aur-m-n* k* aur-s k2 bamb-a stb2.de• *Bar-c* k* bar-i k2 *Bar-m* bar-s k2 bart a1 *Bell* k* berb k* bond a1 borx h2 *Bov* k* brach a1 brom k* *Brucel* sa3• **Bry** k* bufo bung-fa mtf cact k* **Calc** k* calc-i k2 *Calc-p* k* *Calc-s* k* calc-sil k2 camph b2.de* cann-s b2.de* canth b2.de* caps b2.de *Carb-an* k* *Carb-v* k* carbn-dox knl3• **Carbn-s** carc sp1* **Card-m** k* carl a1 cartl-s rly4• caul a1 *Caust* k* cere-b a1 cham b2.de* *Chel* k* chin k* chinin-ar chinin-s choc srj3• chord-umb rly4• cimic a1 *Cimx* k* *Cina* k* cinnb a1 *Clem* k* cob a1 cob-n sp1 coc-c k* *Cocc* k* coff a1 colch k* coli rly4• **Coll** k* *Coloc* k* *Con* k* cop corn k* cortiso gse crot-h k* crot-t a1 cub bro1 *Cycl* k* daph bg2 digin a1 dios k* dros a1 dulc k* erig a1 ery-a a1 eug k* euph h2* euph-a a1 euph-m a1 euphr k* eupi k* falco-pe nl2• *Ferr* k* ferr-ar *Ferr-i* k* ferr-p fl-ac k* form k* fuma-ac rly4• galeoc-c-h gms1• *Gamb* k* gast a1 gent-l a1 ger-i rly4• gins a1 glon a1* glyc bro1 glycyr-g cte1• granit-m es1• **Graph** k* *Grat* k* *Guaj* k* guat sp1 *Ham* k* hell b2.de* *Hep* k* hipp k* *Hydr* k* hydrog srj2• hyos b2.de* hyper a1 *Ign* k* ind a1 indg a1 indol bro1 inul a1 *Iod* k* irid-met srj5• jab a1 jug-c a1 jug-r a1 *Kali-ar* *Kali-bi* k* **Kali-br** k* *Kali-c* k* kali-chl a1 *Kali-i* k* kali-m k2 *Kali-n* k* kali-p *Kali-s* kali-sil k2 *Kalm* k* kola stb3• kreos k* *Lac-ac* **Lac-d** k* **Lach** k* lact k* lam br1 *Laur* k* led b2.de* lil-t k* lim a1 linu-c a1 *Lipp* a1 **Lyc** k* lycps-v *M-arct* b2.de* *Mag-c* k* **Mag-m** k* mag-p bg2 mag-s k* mand sp1* mang b2.de mang-p rly4• med c1* medul-os-si rly4• melal-alt gya4 meny b2.de* *Merc* k* merc-c k* merc-cy a1 merc-i-f k* merc-sul k* **Mez** k* mill a1 mim-p rsj8• mit a1 moni rfm1• morg-g fmm1• mosch a1 mur-ac k* nabal a1 nad rly4• naja nat-ar nat-c k* **Nat-m** k* nat-p *Nat-s* k* nat-sil fd3.de• nicc k* nicc-met sk4• nicotam rly4• **Nit-ac** k* nux-m b2.de* **Nux-v** k* oci-sa sp1 *Oena* ol-an a1 olnd k* **Op** k* ox-ac k* ozone sde2• pall c1 par b2.de* ped a1 peti a1 *Petr* k* petr-ra shn4• *Ph-ac* k* phasco-ci rbp2 phel a1 **Phos** k* phys a1 phyt k* pic-ac pip-m a1 pitu-gl skp7• plac-s rly4• *Plat* k* **Plb** k* plumbg a1 plut-n srj7• *Podo* k* polyp-p a1 positr nl2• pot-e rly4• prun k* ptel c1 *Puls* k* pycnop-sa mrz1 pyrog ran-b b2.de* raph a1 *Rat* k* rheum b2.de* rhod b2.de* rhus-g a1 rhus-t k* rhus-v k* rumx *Ruta* k* sabad b2.de* *Sabin* k* sal-ac k* sang k* *Sanic* k* sapin a1 sarr k* sars k* **Sel** k* senec bro1 *Seneg* k* **Sep** k* serp a1 **Sil** k* sin-a a1* sinus rly4• sol-ni sol-t-ae a1 spig k* spirae a1 spong k* squil b2.de* *Stann* k* staph k* stram a1 *Stront-c* k* stroph-s sp1 succ-ac rly4• suis-em rly4• suis-pan rly4• sul-ac k* sul-i bg2* **Sulph** k* sumb k* suprar rly4• symph fd3.de• tab k* *Tarent* k* tax a1* tela zzc1• tell rsj10• tep a1 ter k* tere-la rly4• thiam rly4• thuj k* tong a1 tril-p trios rsj11• trom bro1 *Tub* k* tub-m vn* vanil fd5.de **Verat** k* **Verb** k* vib k* viol-t b2.de* visc sp1 wies a1 **Zinc** k* zinc-p k2 zinc-s a1 [sol-ecl cky1]
  - **alternating** hard and soft: ant-c b7.de* ant-t b7a.de* ars k* borx *Bry* b7a.de con bg2 gamb a1 germ-met srj5• ham fd3.de• iod k* *Kali-n* b4a.de lach k* mag-s k* nit-ac k* phos *Puls* b7a.de ruta fd4.de *Staph* b7a.de
  - **blood**, with: arizon-l nl2• ham fd3.de• lam br1
  - **burnt**, as if: alum bg2 **Bry** k* *Plat* k* plb sul-ac b4.de* **Sulph** k*

Stool

- **chill**; during: bry bg2 nux-v bg2 op bg2 sil bg2 sulph bg2
- **followed** by:
  - **fluid** stool: agar k* aloe k* alum bg2 am-c b4.de* am-m b7.de* ang b7a.de arund c1 asaf b7.de* bar-c b4.de* borx h2 **Bov** k* **Calc** k* calc-f calc-p k* canth b7.de* carb-an b4.de* carbn-s chin bg2 coff b7.de* coloc bg2 dulc fd4.de euph bg2 graph bg2 grat bg2 ign b7.de* kali-bi bg2 kali-n bg2 lact **Lyc** k* mag-c b4.de* mag-m b4.de* mosch b7a.de mur-ac b4.de* nat-c k* *Nat-m* k* nat-s nux-m bg2 nux-v b7.de* olnd b7.de* op bg2 ph-ac b4.de* phos bg2 plac rzf5• plat bg2 plb bg2 rheum h* rhus-t b7.de* sars b4.de* sep b4.de* spig b7.de* spong b7.de* stann b4.de* staph b7.de* *Sul-ac* k* sulph b4.de* tarent ulm-c jsj8• zinc b4.de*
  - **pasty** stool: calc bro1 lyc bro1 pall *Ph-ac* stann h2
  - **soft** stool: abrom-a ks5 aeth alumn am-m h2 aq-mar skp7• berb bov bg2 bung-fa mtf calc bg2 carb-an carb-v h2 caust chin-b kr1 chord-umb rly4• dulc fd4.de graph h2 ham fd3.de• kali-c h2 kali-p fd1.de• lac-h htj1• *Lyc* bg2* mag-c h2 mag-m h2* mez h2 mur-ac h2 nat-c h2 ph-ac h2 plac-s rly4• ruta fd4.de sars h2 sep h2 spong h1 staph h1 sul-ac h2 zinc h2
  - **thin** stool: lyc mrr1 nat-m bg2 stann h2
- **menses**, during: *Am-c* k* am-m b7.de **Apis** k* kali-c kreos k* *Nat-m* k* nat-s nux-v b7.de sil k* sul-ac b4.de* sulph
  - **yellow** moisture, with: hep h2
- **tough** and greasy: alum-p k2 *Caust* dulc fd4.de

HAZELNUTS, like: cob c1

HEAVY: nat-m bg2 sanic ptk1

HOT: all-s a1* *Aloe* k* androc srj1• **Ars** bg3* asc-t k* bell bg3* bry ptk1 *Calc-p* k* caps bg3* **Cham** k* cist k* clem a1 dios k* ferr bro1 gamb bg1* **Iris** bg3* kali-p ptk1 lec med k* *Merc* **Merc-c** k* merc-sul k* nux-v k* phos k* pic-ac bg3* podo bg2* puls k* rat bg1 ribo rly4• sabad ptk1 scop ptk1 *Staph* k* stroph-h ptk1 *Sulph* k*

ICHOROUS: *Carb-v* b4a.de *Kreos* b7a.de

INDIGESTION agg.: *Ant-c* bg2 ars bg2 bry bg2 carb-v bg2 chin bg2 coff bg2 **Ip** bg2 lach bg2 lyc bg2 nat-c bg2 **Nux-v** bg2 **Puls** bg2 sep bg2 sulph bg2

INSUFFICIENT (See RECTUM - Constipation - insufficient)

INTESTINES, like: ant-c h2*

JELLYLIKE (See Mucous - jellylike)

KNOTTY, nodular, lumpy: (↗*Lumpy; Sheep)* *Aesc* k* aesc-g bro1 agar k* aloe bg2* **Alum** k* alum-p k2 alum-sil k2 **Alumn** k* am-c k* am-m k* anag anan ang k* *Ant-c* k* aphis br1 apis k* arg-n bg2 arn k* ars k* ars-i asar b7.de* aster bro1 *Aur* k* aur-ar k2 aur-i k2 aur-s k2 bapt k* *Bar-c* k* bar-i k2 bar-s k2 bell b4.de* berb bit-ar wht1• borx b4a.de brach bry bg2* *Calc* k* calc-p *Calc-s* calc-sil k2 carb-an k* carbn-dox knl3• **Carbn-s** card-m k* *Caust* k* **Chel** k* chin k* chinin-ar chlol cic bg2 coc-c *Coll* k* *Con* k* *Cycl* dios dulc fd4.de euph k* euphr falco-pe nl2• fl-ac bg2 genist mcj1• *Glon* k* glyc bro1 **Graph** k* grat guaj b4.de* *Hydr* k* hydrog srj2• indol bro1 *Iod* k* ip kali-ar *Kali-bi* k* *Kali-c* k* kali-p *Kali-s* kali-sil k2 kalm *Lach* k* led b7a.de* *Lept* *Lil-t* **Lyc** k* mag-c b4.de **Mag-m** k* mang k* melal-alt gya4 *Merc* k* merc-c k* mez k* moni rfm1• morph bro1 nat-c b4.de* nat-m *Nat-s* nit-ac b4.de* *Nux-v* k* olnd b7.de* op k* petr k* *Ph-ac* k* phos k* phyt bg2 *Plat* k* **Plb** k* podo fd3.de• polyg-h bg2 prun ptel pyrog bro1 rhus-v ruta b7a.de sacch-a fd2.de• sang k* sanic bg2* senec *Sep* k* **Sil** k* spig k* *Stann* k* staph b7.de* stront-c k* sul-ac k* sul-i k2 **Sulph** k* sumb symph fd3.de• *Thuj* k* ust vanil fd5.de verat k* verb k* viol-o b7a.de* xero bro1 *Zinc* k*
- **black**: calc-f sp1
- **first** knotty, then soft: agar kr dulc fd4.de *Lyc* podo fd3.de• symph fd3.de•
- **green**: *Chin* *Stann*
- **liquid**, and (See Lumpy - liquid)
- **mucus**, covered with: *Alum* caust *Graph* *Mag-m* nux-v *Plb* sep *Spig*
- **united** by threads of mucus: cham h1 **GRAPH** k ●
- **white**: pall bg2 sil bg2

LACTATION agg.: alum bg2 *Ant-c* bg2 **Bry** bg2 lyc bg2 **Nux-v** bg2 *Op* bg2 plat bg2 sep bg2

LARGE: *Aesc* k* *Agn* alet k2* all-c a1 allox tpw3 aloe bro1 *Alum* k* alum-p k2 alum-sil k2 **Alumn** k* ambr hr1 *Ant-c* k* *Apis* apoc a1 *Arg-n* ars k* ars-i k* *Asaf* k* aster a1 *Aur* k* aur-ar k2 aur-s k2 *Bapt* hr1 bart a1 berb k* borx mtf33 **Bry** k* cadm-met tpw6 **Calc** k* calc-s k* calc-sil k2 caust bro1 chel k* cinnb a1 *Cob* k*

Large: ...
coch hr1 *Coloc* cop corn a1 cot a1 crot-t cupr dios a1 dirc a1 *Dulc* k* **Elat** k* euphr k* fago a1 falco-pe nl2• fl-ac k* gamb gels a1* ger-i rly4• glyc bro1 gnaph a1 **Graph** k* grat ham a1* hell bg2* hipp a1 hydr hyos a1 iber a1* *Ign* k* inul a1 *Iod* hr1 jab a1 jal a1 jug-c a1 jug-r a1 kali-ar *Kali-bi* k* **Kali-c** k* kali-m k2 kali-p **Kali-s** k* kali-sil k2 *Kalm* k* kola stb3• lac-c bg2 **Lac-d** k* lach k* **Lept** k* lyc bg3* *M-arct* b2.de* macro a1 mag-c k2 **Mag-m** k* meli bro1 merc k* merc-d a1 merc-i-r a1 **Mez** k* mucs-nas rly4• naja *Nat-m* k* nat-n a1 nat-ox rly4• nat-p a1 nat-s br* *Nux-m* **Nux-v** k* *Oena* op k* orot-ac rly4• ox-ac k* oxal-a rly4• *Petr* phasco-ci rbp2 *Phos* phys a1 pip-m a1 plut-n srj7• *Podo* k* puls k* pyrog bro1* ran-b b2.de* *Raph* rhus-g tmo3• *Rhus-t* k* *Rhus-v* k* ruta k* sabad hr1 *Sanic* k* sarr k* **Sel** k* seneg k* **Sep** k* serp a1 **Sil** sin-n a1* sol-t-ae a1 stann k* staph sne sul-ac k* **Sulph** k* sumb k* symph fd3.de• *Thuj* k* tong a1 tritic-vg fd5.de tub **Verat** k* *Vib* k* *Zinc* k* zinc-p k2 [tax jsj7]
- **burnt**; as if: bry ptk1
- **hard**: bry ptk1 lac-d ptk1
- **small** stool feels large: hydrog srj2•

LATER, every day: carb-v h2* fl-ac bg2* hyos h1* kali-c h2* lach bg2* ruta h1 sul-ac h2*

LAUGHING agg.: aloe bg2 sulph bg2

LEAD; after intoxication by: alum bg2 **Op** bg2 *Plat* bg2

LEAD COLORED: plb b7.de*

LEMONADE agg.: phyt bg2

LIENTERIC (See Undigested)

LIGHT COLORED: (↗*Clay colored; Clayish)* acon bro1 *Aesc* k* *Agar* hr1 aloe bg2 alum k* alumn bro1 ambr c1 anac k* apis k* **Ars** k* ars-i *Aur-m-n* bamb-a stb2.de• *Bar-c* k* bell a1 benz-ac k2 *Berb* **Borx** **Calc** k* calc-s a1 calc-sil k2 carb-an h2* *Carb-v* k* carbn-s **Card-m** k* cass a1 caust b4a.de* cham h1 **Chel** k* **Chin** k* *Chinin-ar* *Chion* k* choc srj3• cocc b7.de* *Coll* k* cypra-eg sde6.de• **Dig** k* dios a1 dol bro1 dulc fd4.de eup-per ferr-i a1 franz a1 fuma-ac rly4• *Gels* gnaph k* *Hep* k* hir rsj4• *Hydr* k* *Hydrog* srj2• iber bro1 indol bro1 *Iod* iris kali-ar *Kali-bi* k* *Kali-c* k* kali-chl hr1 kali-m k2* *Kali-p* *Kali-s* kali-sil k2 linu-c a1 **Lyc** k* lycps-v mag-m k2 **Merc** k* merc-c k* *Merc-d* bro1 merc-i-f a1 merc-sul a1 *Myric* k* naja nat-p *Nat-s* k* *Nit-ac* k* nux-m b7.de* olib-sac wmh1 petr **Ph-ac** *Phos* k* phys a1* pic-ac k* pip-m a1 plb k* *Podo* k* polyp-p a1 psil ft1 pycnop-sa mrz1 rhus-v k* ruta fd4.de **Sanic** k* sep k* **Sil** k* skat br1 spong fd4.de stel bro1 sul-ac bg2 sul-i k2* sulph k* suprar rly4• symph fd3.de• **Tab** k* tritic-vg fd5.de *Tub* ust k* vanil fd5.de verat b7a.de verat-v a1 zinc k* zinc-m a1 zinc-p k2 zing hr1
- **morning**; early: mand sp1

LIQUID (See Thin)

LONG, narrow: (↗*Small; Worm-like)* *Alum* alum-p k2 amp rly4• arn bro1 asar b7.de* bamb-a stb2.de• bell b4.de* *Borx* k* calc-sil k1* *Caust* k* chel bg2 chin bg2 cystein-l rly4• fum rly1*• fuma-ac rly4• *Graph* k* hydrog srj2• hyos k* kali-bi gk kali-p fd1.de• lyc bg2 merc k* merc-c b4a.de* *Mur-ac* k* nat-c k* nat-sil fd3.de• nux-m bg2 nux-v b7a.de* **Phos** k* pot-e rly4• psil ft1 *Psor* bg2 puls k* pycnop-sa mrz1 pyrog k2 sep k* skat br1 stann bg2 staph k* staphycoc rly4• suis-em rly4• suis-pan rly4• sul-ac h2 sulph b4.de* verat b7.de*

LOOSE (See Copious; Curdled; Fatty; Mushy; Pasty; Soft)

LUMPS like chalk: (↗*White)* ars-s-f k2 bell **Calc** dig hep lach med k2 **Podo** k* **Sanic** spong

LUMPY: (↗*Knotty; Sheep)* ars bg2 merc-c bg2 phos bg2
- **liquid**; and: aloe **Ant-c** k* apis *Ars* calc *Con* graph ip kali-bi kali-p fd1.de• lac-h sk4• **Lyc** k* mag-c k2 nat-ar nux-v *Pic-ac* sanic ptk1 sec sil sul-ac sulph thuj mtf33 trom
  - **black** lumps: thuj ptk1
- **small**; and: am-c bg2 guaj bg2 mag-m bg2 merc bg2 ph-ac bg2
- **soft**; and: euph h2 lyc tl1

LYING DOWN agg.: ox-ac bg2 rhus-t bg2

LYING on abdomen agg.: cupr bg2

MEALY sediment, with: bry chinin-ar crot-t bg2 ph-ac **Podo** k* sec bg2 stront-c ptk1

MEMBRANOUS: aloe bg2 *Arg-n* ars bg2 *Brom* k* bry bg2 calc b4a.de* **Canth** k* *Carb-ac* k* **Colch** k* **Coloc** k* cupr bg2 *Ferr* k* ferr-m k* iod kali-bi k2

Membranous: ...
kali-c bg2 kali-n bg2* kola stb3• *Lach Lept* k* merc k* merc-c k* *Nit-ac* k* petr k* phos k* phyt k* sec bg2 sil k* thymol sp1 zinc bg2

MERCURY; after abuse of: carb-v bg2 chin bg2 **Hep** bg2 *Nit-ac* bg2 sulph bg2

MILK:
- **agg.**: *Bry* bg2 **Lyc** bg2 *Mag-c* bg2 nat-c bg2* nicc bg2 nux-m bg2 podo bg2 sep bg2* **Sulph** bg2
- **milk** agg.; boiled: nux-m bg2 sep bg2

MOSS; like: asc-t a1*

MOTION agg.: **Apis** bg2 **Bry** bg2 mur-ac bg2 **Nat-s** bg2 phos bg2 puls bg2 rheum bg2 sep bg2

MUCOUS (= slimy): achy-a zzc1• acon k* aesc *Aeth* k* agar k* agra br1 allox tpw3* aloe k* alum b2.de* am-c b2.de* *Am-m* k* ang k* ant-c b2.de* ant-t k* *Apis* k* **Arg-n** k* arge-pl rwt5• arist-cl sp1 *Arn* k* *Ars* k* ars-i *Asar* k* asc-t a1 aur-m-n mtf bac bn *Bapt* bar-c b2.de* *Bell* k* *Berb Borx* k* *Brom* k* *Bry* k* cact cadm-s c1* calc b2.de* calc-act bro1 *Calc-p* k* *Canth* k* **Caps** k* *Carb-ac* k* carb-an k* *Carb-v* k* carbn-s cassia-s ccrh1• castm mtf11 *Caust* k* *Cham* k* chap br1 *Chel* k* *Chin* b2.de* chord-umb rly4• cic cimic cina k* cinnb k2 *Cocc* k* **Colch** k* **Coll** k* *Coloc* k* con b2.de* *Cop* bro1* *Corn* cortiso gse *Crot-c Crot-t* cupr bg2 cycl a1 cypra-eg sde6.de• dig k* dios dirc a1 dros k* *Dulc* k* dys fmm1• elat enteroc jl2 euph bro1 ferr k* ferr-ar ferr-i ferr-p gaert fmm1• gal-ac br1 **Gamb** k* geo a1 *Glycyr-g* cte1• **Graph** k* grat bg2 guaj b2.de* guat sp1 ham k2 **Hell** k* *Hep* k* hydr k2* hydrog srj2• *Hyos* k* ign k* *Iod* k* *Ip* k* *Kali-bi* k* *Kali-c* k* *Kali-chl* kali-i kali-m bg3* kali-n b2.de* kali-p bg2 **Kali-s** k* kali-sil k2 ketogl-ac rly4• lac-e hrn2• lac-h sk4• lach k* laur b2.de* led b2.de* lil-t k2* lyc b2.de* lycps-v bg2 m-aust b2.de* *Mag-c* k* mag-m b2.de* mag-s sp1 **Merc** k* **Merc-c** k* merc-d bro1 *Moni* rfm1• morg-g fmm1• morg-p fmm1• *Mur-ac* mygal zzc1• naja nat-ar nat-c k* nat-m b2.de* nat-p k2 *Nat-s* nicc nicc-met sk4• nicotam rly4• *Nit-ac* k* nux-m k* **Nux-v** k* ox-ac oxal-a rly4• oxyt bro1 par b2.de* petr k* *Ph-ac* k* **Phos** k* *Phyt* pitu-gl skp7• plac rzf5• *Plb* k* *Podo* k* prun bro1 *Psor* k* **Puls** k* raph *Rheum* k* rhod bg2 *Rhus-t* k* ric bro1 *Ruta* k* sabad k* sabin b2.de* samb xxb1 *Sec* k* sel b2.de* seneg b2.de* sep k* *Sil* k* solid ptk1 spig b2.de* *Squil* k* *Stann* k* *Staph* k* stict suis-em rly4• *Sul-ac* k* **Sulph** k* syc bka1*• tab k* ter k* tritic-vg fd5.de trom tub c1 urt-u k* vanil fd5.de vario **Verat** k* viol-t b2.de*

- **accompanied** by | **Abdomen**; complaints of: viol-t b7a.de
- **acrid**: phos h2*
- **alternating** with constipation: acon vh ruta hr1
- **balls**; like: ip ptk1
- **black**: ars k* cic a1 cocc cortiso gse elat
- **bloody**: *Acon* k* aegle-f zzc1• *Aeth* k* ail *Aloe* alum h2* *Anan* ant-t br1 apis k* arg-n k* am k* *Ars* k* ars-i ars-s-f k2 asar k* bapt k* bar-c k* *Bar-m* bell k* bol-la borx b4a.de *Bry* calad hr1 calc b4.de* *Canth* k* *Caps* k* *Carb-ac Carb-v* k* carbn-s k2 cassia-s ccrh1• caust b4.de* cham chim k* *Cinnb* **Colch** k* coll *Coloc* k* cub k* cupr bg2 daph bg2 dros k* *Dulc* k* elaps k* elat k* erig ferr b7a.de* ferr-p k* gaert pte1• *Gamb* k* graph b4a.de* ham k* hep k* ign k* *Iod* k* *Ip* k* iris kali-bi bg2 *Kali-chl* k* kali-i kali-m k2 kali-p k2 *Lach* k* led k* lept lil-t k* lyss k* mag-c br1 *Mag-m* k* mag-p bg2 malar jl2 **Merc** k* **Merc-c** k* *Merc-d* hr1 mez bg2 morg-p pte1• **Nat-c** k* nit-ac k* **Nux-v** k* ox-ac k* petr k* phyt plb **Podo** k* *Psor* k* *Puls* k* rhus-t k* sabad k* sabin k* sars k* sep b4.de* sil b4.de* sul-ac k* sul-i k2 *Sulph* k* tril-p c1* trom k* *Urt-u* hr1
  - **black**: *Caps* hr1
  - **chronic**: tril-p br1
- **boiled** starch, like: arg-n borx phos mtf33
- **brown**: **Ars** bapt k* borx h2 *Carb-v Dulc* grat k* hir rsj4• *Nux-v* rheum spig zing
- **cheesy**: iod mtf33 phos
- **chopped** eggs and spinach: cham
- **colic** and chilliness; with: cop br1
- **colorless**: (↗*transparent)* **Hell**
- **copious**: ter ptk1
- **covered** with mucus: *Alum* k* *Am-m* k* ars bg2 *Asar* b7a.de bar-m k* bell bg2 calc-p bg2 calen a1 caps b7.de* *Carb-v* k* casc bro1 caust k* cham b7.de* chord-umb rly4• coc-c bg2 coll bro1* con b4.de* cop br1* *Crot-t* hr1 cycl hr1 dig b4.de* **Graph** b4.de* *Ham* k* hep b4a.de *Hydr* bg2* hyos b7.de* ip b7.de* kali-c b4.de* kali-n h2* lac-h sze9• led b7.de* mag-c b4.de* *Mag-m* k* merc b4a.de* *Merc-c* b4a.de merc-i-r hr1 nat-m ptk1 nit-ac b4.de* nux-v k* oxal-a rly4• petr b4.de* phos h2* *Plb* k* podo bg2 ptel c1 *Puls* b7.de* rheum b7.de*

Mucous – covered with mucus: ...
rhus-t b7.de* sarr hr1 sep k* sil b4a.de* *Spig* k* sulph b4.de* tell bg1 thuj bg2 verat b7.de* viol-t b7a.de
  - **threads** of mucous: carb-v bg2 hydr bg2 nux-v bg2 sel bg2
- **cream**-colored: aloe
- **dark**: arg-n k* *Ars* bol-la colch k2 ip k* ketogl-ac rly4• lil-t mur-ac tarent
  - **molasses**, like frothy: ip k*
- **egg** white; like: carb-an b4a.de
- **fetid**: arg-n a1 colch k2 con h2* lach merc-c sul-ac sulph
- **fever**; before: ant-c b7a.de ferr b7a.de puls b7a.de
- **granular**: bell k* *Phos* k*
- **gray**: rheum bg2 thuj bg1 thymol sp1*
- **grayish**: rheum h
- **green**: **Acon** k* aesc *Aeth* k* agar am-m k* *Ant-t Apis* **Arg-n** k* **Ars** k* aur aur-ar k2 aur-s k2 *Bell* k* *Borx Bry Calc-p Canth* k* caps carb-v *Castm* k* **Cham** k* *Chel* k* cina *Cinnb* colch *Coloc* k* corn k* *Dulc* k* elat k* eup-per ferr-p **Gamb** k* guar hep *Ip* k* iris bg2* kreos **Laur** k* lyc **Mag-c** k* med **Merc** k* **Merc-c** k* merc-d bg2 mur-ac naja nit-ac k* *Nux-v* k* petr ph-ac k* *Phos* k* podo psor k* **Puls** k* *Rheum* rhus-t sanic sep k* stann sul-ac *Sulph* k* tab urt-u
  - **red**: bell bg2
  - **staining** skin about anus coppery: cinnb ptk1
- **involuntary**: solid ptk1
- **jellylike**: *Aloe* k* *Apis Am* **Asar** k* asc-t *Bar-m Cadm-s* calc caust *Chel* **Colch** k* *Coloc* dios dulc graph k2 *Hell* k* *Jatr-c Kali-bi* mur-ac nat-p oxyt ptk2 pitu-gl skp7• *Plat* podo k* *Rhus-t* sep k* vanil fd5.de
  - **frog** spawn, like: (↗*Green - scum)* hell
- **liquid**: alum h2* borx h2 carb-v hr1 laur k* malar jl2 ter k*
- **lumpy** mucus: aloe bg2* apis bg2 ars bg2 asar bg2 calc-i bg2 carb-an cop bg2* graph ptk1 hydr bg2 ip ptk1 mag-c ptk1 merc-c phos k* *Rhus-t* hr1 spig bg2*
  - **pea**-like lumps: nat-c h2*
- **offensive**: sep ptk1*
- **only**: ant-c ptk1 asaf ptk1
- **red**: arg-n **Asar** b7a.de bell bg2 borx h2* canth k* *Cina* colch graph k* **Lyc** k* merc k* *Rhus-t* k* sil sulph k*
- **resin**; like: asar b7.de nux-v b7a.de
- **shaggy** masses: arg-n *Asar* k* caps lyc k*
- **shredded** (= shreddy): apis bg2 arg-n bg2* asar bg2 brom bg2 canth bg2* carb-ac ptk1 colch k* coloc bg2* cupr bg2 graph bg2 merc bg2 *Merc-c* b4a.de* petr bg2 phos bg2 phyt bg2 sec bg2 squil bg2 sulph bg2 verat bg2
- **stool**:
  - **after** | **agg.**: asar bg2 borx b4a.de* bry ptk1 calc-p bg2 graph bg2 hep b4a.de* kali-c b4a.de mag-m bg2 *Merc* bg2 *Phos* b4.de* sel bg2 sep b4.de* stann b4.de* thuj bg2*
  - **before**: ars bg2 carb-v bg2 kali-c b4.de* *Puls* bg2 sulph bg2
  - **between**: cham bg2 graph bg2
  - **during** | **agg.**: alum b4a.de* ant-t bg2 *Borx* b4a.de **Colch** bg2 **Kali-c** b4.de* lach b7a.de* lyc b4a.de* mag-m b4a.de* **Merc** bg2 **Merc-c** bg2 **Nux-v** bg2 *Petr* bg2 sel b7a.de* spig b7a.de* **Sulph** bg2
  - **instead** of: arist-cl sp1
- **tenacious**: **Asar** k* borx h2 **Canth** k* *Caps* k* *Crot-t* k* **Hell** k* hydr k2 *Kali-bi* k* spig h1*
- **thick**: mag-m h2* nat-c h2* spig h1*
- **transparent**: (↗*colorless)* aloe am-m h2* apis bg2 asc-t **Borx** k* carb-an **Colch** k* *Crot-t* bg2 cub k* dios **Hell** k* merc merc-c k* *Nat-m* phos bg2 *Podo* hr1 *Rhus-t* k* ulm-c jsj8•
- **watery**: adam skp7• arg-n k* cham hr1 coloc h2* *Ferr* hr1 *Iod* k* lept k* *Merc* hr1 merc-c bg2 puls bg2 ter k*
- **white**: *Aloe* sne *Ars* asc-t bell k* **Borx** k* canth k* carb-an caust k* *Cham* k* cina cocc k* colch dios *Dulc* k* elat k* *Graph* k* *Hell* k* *Iod* k* ip k* kali-c h2* **Kali-chl** k* kali-m k2 mag-m h2* merc merc-c **Nat-m** k* *Ph-ac* k* *Phos* podo k* puls k* rheum silphu br1 *Sulph*
  - **corn**; like little pieces of popped: **Cina**
  - **dysentery**; before: silphu br1
  - **masses**: cop
  - **milk**-white: **Kali-chl** k*
- **worm**, like a: stann h2*

Stool

- **yellow**: aeth hr1 agar k* aloe k2 ant-c c1 *Apis* **Asar** k* bar-ox-suc rly4• bell k* *Borx* k* brom k* *Carb-v* k* *Cham* k* chin k* *Colch* *Cub* k* *Dulc* ign kali-p k2 **Kali-s** k* lac-h sze9• lept bg2 mag-c k* mag-m h2* nicc k* nicotam rly4• osm a1 podo k* puls k* pycnop-sa mrz1 *Rhus-t* k* spig h1* staph *Sul-ac* k* sulph k* ulm-c jsj8• [mag-s stj1]
  - • **yellow**-white: sep mtf33

MUDDY: ars bg2 ferr-p bg2 lept ptk1
- **morning**: lept ptk1

MUSHY: achy-a zzc1• acon bg2 aesc agar k* agath-a nl2• am-m bg2 anac k* ang bg2 ant-t k* anth vh ars bg2 ars-s-f k2 ars-s-r hr1 *Bapt* k* *Berb* k* borx bg2 both-ax tsm2 **Bry** k* cact calad k2 **Calc** bg2 calc-p k* carb-an bg2 carb-v k* chin bg2* chinin-s bg2 cic bg2 cinnb hr1 *Cur* hr1 cycl bg2 dream-p sdj1• dros bg2 *Dulc* bg2 ephe-si hsj1• erig k* glycyr-g cte1• **Graph** bg2 haliae-lc srj5• ham fd3.de• *Hydr* *Hyos* iris kali-s fd4.de *Kalm* k* *Kreos* bg2 lac-ac k* lac-c lept k* mang bg2 melal-alt gya4 mez bg2 *Moni* rfm1• myric k* *Nat-m* bg2 nat-sil fd3.de• *Nit-ac* bg2* olib-sac wmh1 onos ptk1 par bg2 petr bg2 ph-ac bg2 **Phos** bg2* *Pic-ac* podo k* puls ptk1 ran-b bg2 ran-s bg2 rhodi br1 **Rhus-t** k* ruta fd4.de sang bg2 sars k* seneg k* *Sep* k* *Sil* k* *Spig* k* spong fd4.de suis-pan rly4• *Sul-ac* bg2 **Sulph** bg2* ter k* tritic-vg fd5.de vanil fd5.de verat-v hr1
- **black**: cadm-met gm1
- **brown**: aesc
- **gray**: myric bg1
- **white**: *Calc-p* k* podo *Rhus-t* sep spig
- **yellow**: ant-t ars-s-f k2 *Arum-t* *Bapt* *Berb* **Bry** k* carb-v *Hydr* *Hyos* iris lept ph-ac k2 *Pic-ac* *Podo* rhus-t

NARROW (See Long)

NOISY: (↗*Flatulent; Sputtering)* *Acal* vh1 agar ptk1 aloe bg2* apoc ptk1 arg-n br1* coloc ptk1 crot-t ptk1 ferr ptk1 gamb ptk1 *Ign* ptk1 **Nat-s** k* nux-m ptk1 plat h2 stroph-h ptk1 thuj bg3* thyr ptk1 tub ptk1

NURSLINGS; in: alum bg2 *Bry* bg2 lyc bg2 **Nux-v** bg2 *Op* bg2 sulph bg2 verat bg2

OCHRE (See Yellow - ochre)

ODOR:
- **acid** (See sour)
- **ammoniacal**: lach b7.de*
- **blood**; like: colch bg2
- **blotting** paper; like burning: *Coloc* k*
- **brassy**: apis
- **burnt**; as if: coloc bg2
- **cadaverous** (= cadaveric): ail bro1 ant-c bro1 ant-t k* apis arg-n bro1 *Arn* bro1 **Ars** k* *Asaf* bro1 asc-t bro1 bapt k2* bell bg2 *Benz-ac* bro1 *Bism* k* borx k* brom b4a.de* *Bry* bro1 calc bro1 calc-p bro1 carb-ac bro1 **Carb-v** k* *Cham* bro1 *Chin* k* coloc bro1 corn bro1 crot-h bro1 *Dulc* b4a.de fago a1 *Graph* bro1 *Hep* bro1 **Kali-p** k* kreos k* **Lach** k* *Lept* bro1 merc bro1 *Merc-c* bro1 *Merc-d* bro1 mur-ac bro1 nit-ac bro1 nux-m bro1 op bro1 petr bro1 ph-ac bro1 *Phos* bro1 *Podo* bro1 psor bro1* *Ptel* k* pulx bro1 pyrog bro1 *Rheum* bro1 *Rhus-t* k* rumx bro1 sacch-a fd2.de• sanic bro1 *Sec* bro1 *Sil* k* *Squil* bro1 stram k* sul-ac bro1 sulph bro1 *Ter* bro1 tub bro1
- **camphor**, like: petr h2*
- **carrion**; like (See putrid)
- **cheese**; like rotten: **Bry** k* **Hep** k* *Sanic* k* tub pc
- **coppery**: *Iris*
- **currant**; like black: bamb-a stb2.de•
- **eggs**, like rotten: (↗*putrid; ABDOMEN - Putrefaction - intestines; RECTUM - Flatus - offensive - putrid)* arg-n *Arn* mrr1 *Ars* k* asc-t k* bros-gau mrc1 *Calc* k* *Carb-ac* k* carl k* **Cham** k* fago a1 graph bg1 hep k* kali-s fd4.de med k* moni rfm1• nat-c sne olnd bg2 phos bg1 (non:podo hr1) positr nl2• **Psor** k* squil bg2 *Staph* k* sul-ac k* sulph k* suprar rly4• wies a1
- **fish**-brine: med jl2
- **fishy**: amp rly4• hydrog srj2•
- **fleshy**: merc-c bg2
- **fruity**: stroph-s sp1
- **liver**, like cooked: dream-p sdj1•
- **meat**; like burnt: carb-an
- **metallic**: irid-met srj5•
- **musty**: cina bg1 *Coloc* k* op bg2* phos bg2* sarr sulph mtf33
- **offensive**: abrom-a ks5 acet-ac acon k* adam skp7• *Agar* k* agar-ph a1 ail k* *Aloe* alum b2.de alum-sil k2 alumn am-caust a1 am-m b2.de ambr tsm1 anan hr1

Odor – offensive: ...

androc srj1• ang b2.de ant-c k* ant-t k* anthraci jl2 *Apis* k* apoc k* aq-mar skp7• arg-met **Arg-n** k* arizon-l nl2• arn k* **Ars** k* ars-h hr1 *Ars-i* ars-s-f hr1* **Asaf** k* asar b2.de* asc-t k* astac a1 *Aur* k* aur-ar k2 aur-i k2 *Aur-s* wbt2• bac bn* bamb-a stb2.de• **Bapt** k* bar-c b2.de *Bar-m* k* bell b2.de **Benz-ac** k* *Bism* k* borx b2.de* bov b2.de* brom b4a.de* bros-gau mrc1 **Bry** k* bung-fa mtf but-ac sp1 cadm-met tpw6 cadm-s br1 calad b2.de* *Calc* k* *Calc-p* k* calc-sil k2 canth b2.de *Carb-ac* k* carb-an b2.de* **Carb-v** k* **Carbn-s** casc k* caust b2.de cham k* chin k* chinin-ar chinin-s bg2 chir-fl gya2 chlol k* choc srj3• chord-umb rly4• cic k* cimic k* coca coca-c sk4• cocc k* coff k* *Colch* k* coloc k* con k* conch fkr1• cop *Corn* k* **Crot-h** k* crot-t k* cupr k* cupr-ar k* dig k* dios k* dros k* dulc k* eberth jl2 ephe-si hsj1• eug k* euph-a a1 fago k* fl-ac k* gaert fmm1• **Gamb** k* gard-j vlr2• ger-i rly4• gink-b sbd1• *Glycyr-g* cte1• gnaph k* **Graph** k* grat k* *Guaj* k* guat sp1 hell b2.de* hep k* hip-ac sp1 hipp hr1 *Hura* hyos ign b2.de ind k* iod k* *Ip* k* iris **Kali-ar** kali-c k* kali-m k2 kali-n b2.de **Kali-p** k* kali-s k* kali-sil k2 ketogl-ac rly4• kola stb3• kreos k* lac-h htj1*• **Lach** k* lap-la rsp1 lavand-a ctl1• *Lept* k* lil-t k* lith-c lob k* lob-c lyc k* lycps-v *M-ambo* b2.de m-arct b2.de mag-c b2.de manc k* mang-p rly4• med hr1* medul-os-si rly4• *Meph* hr1 merc k* **Merc-c** k* merc-cy k* merc-i-f k* mez k* mim-p skp7• *Moni* rfm1• morg-p fmm1• mur-ac k* myos-a rly4• nat-c b2.de* nat-m k* *Nat-p* **Nat-s** k* nat-sal a1 nat-sil fd3.de• nicotam rly4• *Nit-ac* k* **Nux-m** k* *Nux-v* k* oci-sa sp1 olnd b2.de* **Op** k* orot-ac rly4• oscilloc jl2 ost a1 oxal-a rly4• par k* petr k* *Ph-ac* k* *Phos* k* phys k* picro a1 plac-s rly4• plb k* plut-n srj7• pneu jl2 **Podo** k* positr nl2• psil ft1 **Psor** k* ptel k* *Puls* k* pulx k* *Pyrog* k* ran-b b2.de ran-s k* rat hr1 rheum k* rhod k* rhus-g br1 rhus-t k* rumx ruta b2.de* sabin b2.de sal-ac hr1 sanic mrr1 santin sarr k* sars b2.de* sec k* sep k* serp k* **Sil** k* sin-n k* *Skat* br1 sol-t-ae k* spig b2.de spong fd4.de **Squil** k* stann staph k* stram b2.de* stront-c b2.de* stroph-s sp1 *Sul-ac* k* sul-i k2 **Sulph** k* sumb k* suprar rly4• syc bka1*• tab k* *Tarent* k* *Ter* k* teucr k* thuj k* til k* tril-p tritic-vg fd5.de **Tub** k* valer b2.de* vanil fd5.de vario k* verat k* vero-o rly4*• vip k* visc sp1 zinc k* zinc-m a1 zinc-p k2 [bell-p-sp dcm1 mag-s stj1]
  - • **morning**: graph ptk1
  - • **night** only: *Psor* *Sulph* vh
  - • **permeates** the whole house: psor mtf33
  - • **sticking** to the patient: podo bg1 psor bg1 sulph bg1 zinc-s bg1
    - ⁝ **very** offensive: pyrog tl1
- **onions**; like: jug-c vml3• kola stb3•
- **penetrating**: bapt k2 *Podo* ptk1 *Psor* ptk1 stram ptk1
- **putrid**: (↗*eggs; ABDOMEN - Putrefaction - intestines; RECTUM - Flatus - offensive - putrid)* acet-ac agar aloe sne alum-sil k2 *Alumn* hr1 *Apis* arn br1 **Ars** k* **Asaf** k* bamb-a stb2.de• **Bapt** k* **Benz-ac** k* *Borx* k* *Bry* k* calc k* calc-f ptk1 calc-sil k2 *Carb-ac* **Carb-v** k* cham *Chin* k* cic tl1 cocc k* colch bg2 *Coloc* k* crot-h k2 elat graph k2* ip k* **Kali-p** k* kreos tl1 *Lach* k* lap-la sde8.de• *Mag-c* merc tl1 *Merc-c* k* merc-cy a1 mur-ac k2 *Nat-s* nit-ac k* nux-m k* nux-v ptk1 **Olnd** oxal-a rly4• par k* **Podo** k* **Psor** k* ptel k* puls k* pulx *Pyrog* k* rhus-t rhus-v a1 sanic sep k* **Sil** k* *Stram* k* sul-ac ptk1 *Sulph* pc* tarent k2 **Tub** k*
  - • **old** people; in: bapt gk
- **sour**: aeth k* arg-n k* *Arn* k* bamb-a stb2.de• bell k* **Calc** k* calc-act bro1 calc-sil k2 camph k* carbn-s cham k* chin tl1 colch k* *Coloc* k* *Colos* k* con k* cop k* cuph br1 del a1 *Dulc* k* gard-j vlr2• glycyr-g cte1• *Graph* k* haliae-lc srj5• **Hep** k* iris *Jal* k* kali-bi gk kali-p fd1.de• kali-s fd4.de* kola stb3• lac-ac stj5• lyc k* m-aust b2.de *Mag-c* k* **Merc** k* mez k* moni rfm1• *Nat-c* k* *Nat-p* k* *Nit-ac* k* *Nuph* hr1 olnd k* ozone sde2• petr b2.de* *Phos* k* phys a1 podo k* **Rheum** k* rob k* sal-ac hr1 sep k* sil sin-a a1 spirae a1 spong fd4.de **Sulph** k* ter hr1 *Trios* rsj11• tritic-vg fd5.de ulm-c jsj8• verat [bell-p-sp dcm1]
  - • **children**; in: rheum br1
  - • **milk**:
    - ⁝ **agg.**: trios rsj11•
    - ⁝ **like**: tab ptk1
- **strange**: olib-sac wmh1
- **sulfuretted** hydrogen; of: squil bg2 sulph bg2
- **sulphur**; of: *Cham* b7a.de lac-leo hm2• vero-o rly3•
- **sweetish**: ars hr1 bar-ox-suc rly4• chord-umb rly4• fum rly1*• limest-b es1• mosch b7.de* petr bg2 pic-ac bg2* vanil fd5.de
- **tar**; like: *Brom* b4a.de
- **urine**, like: benz-ac k*
  - • **horse** urine: stroph-s sp1

ODORLESS: aeth k* apis ptk1 *Arn* b7a.de ars bg2* *Asar* k* camph bg2 chin b7a.de coca bg2 *Cur* cycl k* ferr k* ferr-s k* fl-ac bg2* gamb guar k* *Ham* hr1 *Hell Hyos* k* *Ip* b7a.de jatr-c *Kali-bi* k* lac-ac stj5• lyc bg2 merc op bg2 ph-ac k* phos k* plumbg a1 *Rhus-t* k* **Verat** k* xan k* xanth bg2

OVERHEATED agg.; after being: ant-c bg2 *Bry* bg2 caps bg2 *Coff* bg2 ferr-p bg2 *Ign* bg2 ip bg2 kali-bi bg2 *Nux-v* bg2 podo bg2

OYSTERS agg.: aloe bg2 brom bg2 lyc bg2

PAINLESS: **Ars** bg2 bar-m bg2 both-ax tsm2 *Chin* bg2 cina bg2 clem bg2 *Ferr* bg2 *Hyos* bg2 kali-n bg2 *Ph-ac* bg2 **Podo** bg2 **Puls** bg2 *Sulph* bg2 *Verat* bg2

PASTRY agg.: phos bg2

PASTY, papescent: (*↗Soft)* acon k* aesc k* *Agar* k* alf bro1 *Aloe* k* alumn ammc k* anag k* ant-c k* ant-t k* anthraci *Apis* k* apoc k* arg-met arg-n k* *Arn* k* ars k* ars-i k* *Asaf* k* *Asar* b7a.de asim a1* astac a1 *Bapt* k* bar-c bart a1 bell b4.de* *Berb* k* bism k* bor-ac a1 borx k* brom k* bros-gau mrc1 **Bry** k* cact k* calad k* *Calc* k* calc-p k* calc-sil k2 cann-s k* canth k* carb-v b4.de* carbn-s *Card-m* k* *Carl* a1 cedr k* **Chel** k* chin k* chinin-s k* chion br1 cimic k* cina b7a.de* cist k* clem k* coc-c k* colch k* coll k* **Coloc** k* con k* cop k* cor-r k* crot-h k* **Crot-t** k* cund a1 cupr bg2 *Cupr-s* a1 cycl k* dig k* digin a1 dios k* dirc k* dros k* erig a1* eug k* *Euph* k* euphr a1 fago k* ferr a1 fil hr1 fl-ac k* form k* gamb k* gels k* gent-c k* *Graph* k* grat k* hell k* helon a1 *Hep* k* hydr k* hyos k* iber a1 ign k* ind k* inul a1 iod k* ip k* iris jab a1 kali-bi k* *Kali-n* k* kalm k* kiss a1 kreos k* lac-ac a1 *Lach* k* lact k* lap-la rsp1 laur k* led k* *Lept* k* lil-s a1 lim a1 lipp a1 lob k* lyc k* lycps-v macro a1 mag-c k2* *Mag-m* k* mang k* **Merc** k* merc-br a1 **Merc-c** k* merc-cy a1 *Merc-d* bro1 *Mez* k* morg-p pte1*• musca-d szs1 myric k* nat-ar nat-c k* *Nat-m* k* nat-p k* nit-ac k* nit-m-ac a1 nux-m k* nux-v k* ol-an a1 *Op* k* osm k* ost a1 ox-ac k* paeon k* par k* petr k* *Ph-ac* k* phos k* phyt k* *Plan* hr1 *Plat* k* **Podo** k* polyp-p a1 *Psor* k* *Ptel* k* **Puls** bg2 **Rheum** k* rhod k* rhus-t k* rhus-v k* sabad k* sabin b7.de* saroth sp1 sec sel k* seneg k* sep k* sil k* sin-a a1* spig b7.de* squil k* stann k* still a1* stram k* *Sul-ac* k* **Sulph** k* sumb k* tab k* tanac a1 tarax k* tax a1* ter k* tet a1 teucr b7a.de* ther k* thuj k* til k* trom k* ust k* valer k* verat k* verat-v k* vichy-g a1 visc sp1 wies a1 zinc k* zinc-m a1

PEA SOUP; like: mand rsj7•

PERIODICITY: apis bg2 chin bg2 fl-ac bg2 kali-bi bg2 sabad bg2 sel bg2 thuj bg2

- **hour**; at the same: apis bg2 sabad bg2 thuj bg2

PERSPIRATION; during: bell bg2

PITCH-LIKE: asar b7a.de hep b4.de *Ip* bg2* *Lach* bg2 *Lept* bg2 *Merc* b4a.de* *Nux-v* b7a.de* sars b4.de*

PLUMS agg.: hyos bg2

POTATOES agg.: alum bg2 asar bg2 coloc bg2

PREGNANCY:

- **after**: phos bg2
- **during**: alum bg2 *Bry* bg2 coll bg2 lyc bg2 merc bg2 nux-m bg2 **Nux-v** bg2 *Op* bg2 petr bg2 phos bg2 *Plat* bg2 *Plb* bg2 **Sep** bg2 sulph bg2

PRESSURE of clothes agg.: bry bg2

PURGATIVES agg.: ant-c bg2 hydr bg2 lach bg2 *Nux-v* bg2 **Op** bg2 ruta bg2

PURULENT: *Apis* k* **Arn** k* *Ars* k* bac bn bell b2.de* calc k* *Calc-p* k* *Calc-s* k* cann-s b2.de* canth k* carb-v chin k* clem b2.de* cocc k* *Coloc* b4a.de con b2.de* dulc *Hep* k* ign b2.de* *Iod* k* ip k* kali-ar kali-c k* *Kali-p* k* kali-s k* kali-sil k2 *Lach* k* *Lyc* k* **Merc** k* merc-c b4a.de* merc-cy a1 nit-ac bg1 nux-v b2.de* petr b2.de* *Phos* k* **Puls** k* sabin b2.de* *Sec* sep k* *Sil* k* sul-i k2 *Sulph* k* trom k*

- **green**: *Coloc* b4a.de

RECEDING (See RECTUM - Constipation - difficult - recedes)

REDDISH: (*↗Bloody)* androc srj1• apis k2 ars bg2 bell bg2 borx bg2 cadm-met tpw6 *Canth* k* caps b7.de* chel bg2* choc srj3• cina colch k* fuch br1 graph bg2 iod bg2 jal bg2 lyc ptk1 **Merc** k* merc-c bg2 nat-s phos bg2 rhus-t k* *Sil* k* spong fd4.de sulph bg2* tritic-vg fd5.de vanil fd5.de verat b7.de*

- **brick** red: ars bg2 rhus-t bg2
- **tomato** sauce; like: apis ptk1

RHUBARB; after abuse of: **Cham** bg2 coloc bg2 *Merc* bg2 nux-v bg2 *Puls* bg2

RICE grains, like: cub bg3 *Ip* b7a.de

RIDING: | **horse**; a: | **after**: puls bg2

- **streetcar**; on a | **agg.**: med bg2

RISING: | **after** | **agg.**: aloe bg2 calc-p bg2 colch bg2 nat-s bg2 nux-v bg2 ox-ac bg2 phos bg2 rheum bg2 rhod bg2 *Sulph* bg2

- **stooping**; from:
  - **after** | **agg.**: aeth bg2 chin bg2 cimic bg2 coc-c bg2 colch bg2 fl-ac bg2 mag-s bg2 nat-s bg2 puls bg2 rhod bg2 rhus-t bg2 sulph bg2

ROUGH; as if: nat-m bg2

SAND or gravel in: arg-met b7a.de cina bg1 *Dulc* b4a.de hydr bg1 lyc bg1 mang a1 rhus-t bg1 urt-u bg1

SCANTY: abrom-a ks5 acon k* acon-ac rly4• aesc a1• aesc-g bro1 aeth agar k* aloe k* *Alum* k* alum-sil k2 alumn k* **Am-m** k* ambr k* ammc k* anac b2.de* ang b2.de ant-c b2.de apis k* *Apoc* k* aral a1 arg-met k* arg-n k* arn k* *Ars* k* ars-i k* ars-s-f k2 arum-d a1 arum-i a1 *Asar* k* asc-t k* asim a1 aspar a1 astac a1 aster bro1 bar-c k* *Bell* k* benz-ac k* berb k* bit-ar wht1• bor-ac a1 borx bov b2.de *Bry* k* cain *Calad* k* calc k* calc-p k* calc-s k* calc-sil k2 camph k* cann-s k* canth k* caps b2.de* carb-ac k* *Carb-an* k* *Carb-v* k* *Carbn-s* *Card-m* k* carl k* cassia-s ccrh1• caust bro1 cere-b a1 **Cham** b2.de* chel k* chin k* chin-b hr1 chinin-s chord-umb rly4• chr-ac hr1 cimic k* cimx a1 coc-c k* *Cocc* b2.de* *Colch* k* coll bro1 *Coloc* k* con k* cop k* corn k* *Crot-h* hr1 crot-t k* cupr k* cystein-l rly4• dig k* digin a1 dirc k* dros k* *Dulc* k* eug k* euph h2* euph-a a1 euphr k* ferr k* ferr-i *Ferr-p* hr1 fl-ac k* franz a1 *Gamb* k* gels k* genist a1 gent-c a1 *Glon* k* glyc bro1 gran a1 graph b2.de* grat k* hell b2.de* hep k* hura hydr k* hyos k* hyper k* *Ign* k* indg k* indol bro1 inul a1 iod k* *Ip* k* jug-r k* kali-ar *Kali-bi* k* *Kali-c* k* *Kali-i* hr1 kali-n k* kali-s kali-sil k2 kalm k* lach k* lact k* laur b2.de* led k* lim a1 limen-b-c mlk9.de linu-c a1 lipp a1 lyc k* lycps-v mag-c k* *Mag-m* k* mag-s k* mang k* marb-w es1• **Merc** k* *Merc-c* k* merc-cy a1 merc-d a1* merc-i-f k* merc-sul k* mez k* mit a1 morph a1* mygal zzc1• *Nat-ar Nat-c* k* *Nat-m* k* nat-p a1* nat-s k* *Nit-ac* k* nux-m b2.de* **Nux-v** k* ol-an a1 olnd k* *Op* k* ox-ac k* par k* petr k* phos k* pic-ac k* pitu-gl skp7• *Plat* k* **Plb** k* podo k2 pot-e rly4• psil ft1 puls k* pyrog bro1 ran-b k* rat k* rhod k* rhus-t k* rumx ruta k* *Sabad* b2.de* sabin b2.de* sang k* sanic bro1 sapin a1 sars k* seneg k* sep k* serp a1 **Sil** k* sin-n a1* sol-t-ae a1 spirae a1 spong b2.de* squil k* *Stann* k* staph k* stront-c sul-i k2 **Sulph** k* sumb k* tab k* tarent k* tax a1 ter k* tet a1 ther k* thuj k* til k* trom k* tus-p a1 valer b2.de verat k* verb k* wies a1 xero bro1 *Zinc* k*

- **urging** for stool; after: agar b4.de* bar-c b4.de* kali-c bg2 mag-m b4.de nat-c b4.de sars b4.de sep b4.de

SCRAPINGS:

- **intestines**; like scrapings of: asc-t brom *Bry* **Canth** k* *Carb-ac* **Colch** k* **Coloc** k* *Ferr Merc* nux-v petr phos phyt
- **meat**; like scrapings of: am-m

SCRATCHING agg.: nat-m bg2

SEASONS:

- **spring** agg.: ars bg2 bry bg2 carb-v bg2 *Dulc* bg2 merc bg2 nux-m bg2 puls bg2 sulph bg2
- **summer** agg.: *Acon* bg2 ant-c bg2 **Ars** bg2 bell bg2 *Bry* bg2 carb-v bg2 colch bg2 **Dulc** bg2 ferr-p bg2 gels bg2 ip bg2 iris bg2 kali-br bg2 *Merc* bg2 nux-m bg2 *Podo* bg2 puls bg2 rheum bg2 rhus-t bg2

SEDENTARY habits agg.: **Bry** bg2 lyc bg2 **Nux-v** bg2 op bg2 plat bg2 *Sulph* bg2

SEMISOLID (See Soft)

SHEEP dung, like: (*↗Balls; Knotty; Lumpy)* abrom-a ks5 agar b2.de* aloe bg2 **Alum** k* **Alumn** k* am-c b2.de* am-m k* ang b2.de anth arn b2.de *Ars* b4a.de asar b2.de aur b2.de* aur-m-n wbt2• bapt *Bar-c* k* bell b2.de *Berb* k* borx k* brom k* bry b2.de cadm-met tpw6 calc-f sp1 *Carb-an* k* carbn-s *Caust* k* **Chel** k* chin b2.de chinin-s cob cob-n sp1 *Coll* cop *Graph* k* guaj b2.de* ham fd3.de• hydr k* iod b2.de* *Kali-c* k* kali-n k* kali-p fd1.de• *Kali-s* kola stb3• lac-c mtf33 *Lach* k* led b2.de* lyc ptk1 mag-c b2.de* **Mag-m** k* mand sp1 mang b2.de* melal-alt gya4 **Merc** k* nat-c k* **Nat-m** k* *Nat-s* **Nit-ac** k* *Nux-v* k* olib-sac wmh1 olnd b2.de **Op** k* petr b2.de* ph-ac b2.de* plat k* **Plb** k* psor mtf33 pyrog ptk1 ruta k* sanic ptk1 saroth sp1 *Sep* k* *Sil* b2.de* *Spig* k*

Stool

Sheep dung, like: ...
stann b2.de* staph b2.de stront-c k* *Sul-ac* k* **Sulph** k* syph ptk1 tab thuj b2.de* tritic-vg fd5.de *Verat Verb* k* viol-o b2.de*
- **agglutinated** masses: plb bg2
- **green**: chin ptk1 stann ptk1
- **white**: plb bg2

SHEETS; in smooth: *Verat* b7a.de

SHINING (See Fatty)

SHOOTING out: *(↗Forcible)* acon k* aloe k* *Apis* arn ars aster k* *Bamb-a* stb2.de• bell calc-p canth cist k* cob k* **Crot-t** k* cycl k* eug k* **Gamb Grat** iod jab k* **Jatr-c** kali-bi k* kola stb3• lach lept lyc k* mag-m k* merc naja *Nat-c* k* nat-p k* *Nat-s* phys k* **Podo** psor k* puls rhod k* sacch-a fd2.de• sars k* *Sec* seneg sil sulph thuj k*
- **all** at once in a somewhat prolonged effort: **Gamb** k*
- **torrent**, in a: bamb-a stb2.de• kola stb3• melal-alt gya4 *Nat-c* k*

SHREDDED (See Mucous - shredded)

SITTING:
- **agg.**: sulph bg2
- **amel.**: alum bg2 sep bg2

SLATE COLORED: *Bapt* k* ferr-p bg1 kali-bi a1 phos rad-br bg1

SLEEP; during: *Arn* bg2 bry bg2 con bg2 *Hyos* bg2 mosch bg2 *Nux-m* bg2 phos bg2 puls bg2 sulph bg2

SLIMY (See Mucous)

SLIPPERY (See Fatty)

SMALL quantity: *(↗Long)* acon k* adam skp7• agar mtf33 aloe k* **Alum** k* am-c amp rly4• *Ant-c* k* *Arg-met* k* arg-n k* *Arn* k* **Ars** k* asaf asar *Bapt* **Bell** k* bros-gau mrc1 *Brucel* sa3• calad b7.de* calc-p canth **Caps** k* carb-v carbn-s *Cham* k* cocc k* *Colch Coloc Con* corn *Crot-t Dig* dulc erig eug ferr-p fic-m gya1 fl-ac form fuma-ac rly4• gaba sa3• galeoc-c-h gms1• granit-m es1• *Hydrog* srj2• hyos k* ign ind *Ip* b7a.de* kali-ar kali-c kali-p fd1.de• kali-s kola stb3• lac-del hrn2• *Lyc* **Mag-m** k* marb-w es1• **Merc Merc-c** k* merc-i-f mez mur-ac h2 naja nat-c nat-m nat-sil fd3.de• nit-ac **Nux-v** k* olnd op k* osm phos podo positr nl2• puls rhus-g tmo3• rhus-t ribo rly4• *Ruta* b7a.de sal-al blc1• *Sars* sec sil stann staph b7.de* sulph suprar rly4• tab trios rsj1• tritic-vg fd5.de trom urt-u valer b7.de* vanil fd5.de vib zinc k*

SMOKING agg.: calad bg2 lach bg2 thuj bg2

SNEEZING agg.: sulph bg2

SOAPSUDS; like: benz-ac bg2* colch bg2* elat ptk1 glon bg2* iod ptk1 sulph ptk1

SOFT: *(↗Pasty)* abrot a1 acon k* acon-ac rly4• aegle-f zzc1• aesc k* aeth k* agar k* agath-a nl2• *Agn* k* ail k* all-c k* all-s k* allox tpw3 *Aloe* k* **Alum** k* alum-p k2 alum-sil k2 am-c b4.de* **Am-m** k* ambr k* ammc k* amp rly4• *Anac* k* anag hr1 ang k* ant-c b7.de* ant-t k* anth a1 *Apis* k* apoc k* aral a1 *Arg-met* k* arg-n k* arist-m a1 arn k* *Ars* k* ars-i k* arum-i a1 arum-t k* asaf b7.de* asar k* asc-c k* asc-t k* asim a1 astac a1 aster k* atp rly4• aur k* bamb-a stb2.de• *Bapt* k* *Bar-c* k* bar-m bart a1 bell k* ben berb k* bism bit-ar wht1• borx k* both-ax tsm2 bov k* brach a1 brom k* brucel sa3• bry k* bufo cact k* cadm-met tpw6* cain *Calad* k* *Calc* k* *Calc-p* k* calc-s calc-sil k2 camph bg2 canth k* caps k* carb-an k* *Carb-v* k* carl k* cartl-s rly4• cassia-s cdd7*• *Castn-v* caul k* caust k* chel k* chen-v hr1 *Chin* k* *Chinin-ar* chinin-s bg2 chion br1 chir-fl gya2 chlol k* choc srj3• chr-ac hr1 cic k* cimx k* cina bg2 cinch a1 cinnb k* cob k* cob-n sp1 coc-c k* coca coca-c sk4• *Cocc* k* coff k* colch k* *Coloc* k* con k* conch fkr1• cop k* crot-t k* cupr k* cycl k* cypra-eg sde6.de• delphin a1 dema a1 *Dig* k* digin a1 dios k* dros k* dulc k* epiph br1 erig k* *Euph* k* euphr a1 fago k* falco-pe nl2• ferr-i k* ferr-ma k* ferr-p k* fl-ac k* form k* gaba sa3• gad a1 gamb k* gard-j vlr2• gels k* genist a1 gent-l k* ger-i rly4• gink-b sbd1• gins k* glon k* glycyr-g cte1• gran k* *Graph* k* grat k* *Guaj* k* haem a1 ham k* helia a1 hell k* **Hep** k* hipp k* hir skp7• hydr k* hydrog srj2• hyos k* hyper k* iber a1 ictod *Ign* k* indg k* inul a1 iod k* ip k* irid-met srj5• iris ix bnm8• jac-c a1 jatr-c jug-c k* jug-r a1 kali-bi k* kali-br k* kali-c k* kali-chl k* kali-i k* *Kali-n* k* kali-p fd1.de• kali-s kalm k* ketogl-ac rly4• kola stb3• kreos k* lac-ac k* *Lac-c Lac-d* lac-h htj1• *Lach* k* lact lap-la rsp1 laur k* lept k* lim a1 limen-b-c mlk9.de linu-c a1 lipp a1 lith-c lob k* loxo-lae bnm12• loxo-recl knl4• lup a1 lyc k* lyss k* *M-aust* b7.de* mag-c k* mag-m k* mag-s k* malar jl2 mang k* med ser **Merc** k* *Merc-c* k* merc-cy a1

Soft: ...
merc-i-f k* merc-i-r a1 merc-sul k* merl k* *Mez* k* mill k* mim-p rsj8• morph k* mosch k* mucs-nas rly4• mur-ac k* muru a1 musca-d szs1 myric a1 nad rly4• narc-ps a1* nat-ar nat-c k* nat-m k* nat-ox rly4• *Nat-s* k* nat-sil fd3.de• nicc k* **Nit-ac** k* nuph k* *Nux-m* k* nux-v k* oci-sa sk4• ol-an a1 olib-sac wmh1 *Olnd* k* op k* opun-f br1 opun-s a1 (non:opun-v a1) orot-ac rly4• osm k* ost a1 oxal-a rly4• ozone sde2• paeon k* pall k* pant-ac rly4• par k* ped a1 petr k* petr-ra shn4• *Ph-ac* k* phasco-ci rbp2 phel k* **Phos** k* phys k* phyt k* pic-ac k* pip-m a1 pitu-gl skp7• plac-s rly4• *Plat* k* positr nl2• propr sa3• *Psor* k* ptel k* *Puls* k* pycnop-sa mrz1 querc-r svu1• ran-b b7.de* *Ran-s* k* raph k* *Rat* k* *Rheum* k* *Rhod* k* rhus-t b7.de rhus-v k* ribo rly4• ruta k* sabin k* sal-fr sle1• sang k* sapin a1 sars k* sel k* seneg b4a.de* *Sep* k* serp a1 sil k* sin-a a1 spig b7.de spong k* stann k* staph k* stront-c k* succ-ac rly4• suis-em rly4• suis-pan rly4• **Sul-ac** k* sulfonam ks2 **Sulph** k* sumb k* suprar rly4• symph fd3.de• tab k* tanac a1 tarent k* tax a1 tell a1 tet a1 thiam rly4• *Thuj* k* til tong a1 tritic-vg fd5.de trom k* tub-d jl2 tus-p a1 upa k* ust k* vanil fd5.de verat k* verat-v k* verb k* verin a1 vichy-g a1 *Viol-t* k* wye k* zinc k* zing k* [bell-p-sp dcm1]
- **morning**: brucel sa3• gink-b sbd1• hydrog srj2• querc-r svu1• **Sulph** mrr1
- **night**: caust a1 tab a1 zinc h2*
- **breakfast** agg.; after: prot jl2
- **dinner**; after: coloc a1 kali-n a1 nat-m a1 podo fd3.de• zinc h2*
- **motion**; after firm: cortiso tpw7
- **then** hard: alum b4.de* anac b4.de* ant-c h2* dig b4.de* euph b4.de* ham fd3.de• nux-v b7.de* olnd b7.de* plat b4.de* rheum b7.de* sabin b7.de*

SOUP agg.: mag-c bg2

SOUR food agg.: *Ant-c* bg2 brom bg2 *Bry* bg2 lach bg2 *Nux-v* bg2 **Staph** bg2

SPICES agg.: phos bg2

SPONGE; like a: colch bg2

SPUTTERING: *(↗Flatulent; Noisy)* *Acal* vh1 agar ptk1 *Aloe* k* apoc ptk1 arg-n bg3* bros-gau mrc1 cench k2 coca-c sk4• coloc bg3* crot-t ptk1 eug k* ferr bg3* gamb bg3* *Ign* ptk1 kali-s fd4.de* kola stb3• moni rfm1• nat-c mrr1 **Nat-s** k* nux-m ptk1 plat h2* podo k2* ruta fd4.de stroph-h bg3* thuj bg3* thyr bg3* tub bg3* ulm-c jsj8• vanil fd5.de

SQUARE: nat-m ptk1 plb ptk1 sanic bg2* sel ptk1 sep ptk1

STANDING:
- **agg.**: *Aloe* bg2 ars bg2 bapt bg2
- **amel.**: alum ptk1 caust bg2* sul-ac bg2

STARCH; like: colch ptk1 phos ptk1
- **boiled**: arg-n k2* borx k2*

STICKING to toilet (See Fatty)

STONE; like a: *(↗Hard)* coloc bg2

STRINGY: acon-ac rly4• aloe bro1 *Arg-n* bro1 ars bro1 *Asar* k* bol-la bro1 *Canth* bro1 *Carb-ac* bro1 *Carb-v* k* colch bg1* ferr-i hr1 *Graph* bg2* **Grat** k* kali-bi bro1 kali-n bro1 ketogl-ac rly4• lept ptk1 merc bro1 *Merc-c* bro1 mur-ac bro1 *Nit-ac* bro1 ox-ac k* *Phos* ptk1 podo bro1 puls bro1 sel k* **Sul-ac** k* verat bg2 verat-v k* wies a1

SUDDEN (See Forcible; RECTUM - Urging)

SUGAR agg.: *Arg-n* bg2

SUPPER agg.; after: podo bg2 sep bg2

SUPPRESSED: agar bg2 bell h1* bufo bg2 *Carb-v* bg2 dulc bg2 *Stram* bg2* verat bg2
- **perspiration**; during: bell bg2

SWEETS agg.: arg-n bg2

TAILS; with: galeoc-c-h gms1•

TALLOW, like: ars h2* mag-c bg2* *Phos* bg2*

TARRY-LOOKING: asar b7a.de canth k* carc mlr1• *Chion* k* cortico sp1 hist vml3• lac-h sze9• *Lept* k* nit-ac nux-v b7a.de phys bg1* plat bg1 ptel ptk1 verat bg2 vero-o bg2*

TENACIOUS: agar bg2 allox sp1 alum bro1 am-m bg2 arn bg2 ars k* *Asar* b2.de* bamb-a stb2.de• bar-c bg2 bar-ox-suc rly4• bart a1 borx k* brom bg2 calc b2.de* canth bg2 caps bg2* carb-v k* cartl-s rly4• *Caust* b2.de* chel bro1

Tenacious: ...
chion bro1 cit-ac rly4• coloc k* crot-t k* fum rly1*• **Hell** k* hep b2.de* ign k* inul k* *Kali-bi* bro1 kali-c k* kiss a1 kola stb3• *Lac-c* lac-lup hrn2• **Lach** bg2 lipp a1 mag-s k* mang k* med *Merc* k* *Merc-c* k* mez k* nat-c k* nat-m k* nux-v b2.de* op k* ox-ac k* plac-s rly4• **Plat** k* plb k* rhus-g tmo3• sars k* serp a1 sin-a a1 spig k* succ-ac rly4• suis-em rly4• *Sulph* bg2 suprar rly4• tere-la rly4• vanil fd5.de verat k* *Zinc* k*

TENDINOUS parts: ars h2*

THICK: rheum bg2

THIN: (↗*Watery)* abrom-a ks5 acet-ac *Aeth* agar agath-a nl2• agn b7.de* allox tpw3* *Aloe* k* **Alum** k* alum-p k2 alum-sil k2 ammc anan ang k* **Ant-c** k* ant-t k* anthraci jl2 anthraq rly4• **Apoc** *Aran* arg-n bg2* *Arn* k* *Ars* k* ars-s-f k2 arum-t k2 **Asaf** k* asar b2.de asc-t aster aur aur-ar k2 aur-s k2 bamb-a stb2.de• bapt bar-m *Bell* k* **Benz-ac** k* bism k* bit-ar wht1• borx k* *Bov* brom b4a.de* bros-gau mrc1 *Bry* cadm-met tpw6 cain calad **Calc** k* calc-p tl1 calc-sil k2 camph cann-xyz bg2 canth b7.de* *Carb-ac* carb-an b4.de* *Carb-v* k* carbn-o **Carbn-s** cartl-s rly4• cassia-s cdd7*• castor-eq *Caust* k* *Cedr* *Cham* k* *Chel* *Chin* k* *Chinin-ar* *Cic* k* cist *Clem* h2* coca-c sk4• *Cocc* k* *Coff* **Colch** k* coli rly4• *Coloc* k* *Con* k* cop corn cortiso tpw7 **Crot-t** cupr bg2 cycl a1 cystein-l rly4• dig b4.de* dios dros k* dulc *Dys* fmm1• epil a1* euph h2 falco-pe nl2• ferr k* ferr-p k* fum rly1*• fuma-ac rly4• **Gamb** gard-j vlr2• **Graph** k* *Grat* guaj h2 guat sp1 hell bg2 *Hep* k* hip-ac sp1 hir skp7• *Hydr* hydrog srj2• hyos b2.de* ign k* ind ip b7.de* iris tl1 jal br1 **Jatr-c** st *Kali-bi* kali-c b4.de* kali-n k* kali-p fd1.de• kali-s k2 ketogl-ac rly4• kola stb3• *Lac-ac* lac-del hrn2• *Lac-e* hrn2• lac-loxod-a hrn2• *Lach* k* lap-la sde8.de• laur b7.de* lept *Limen-b-c* hrn2• limest-b es1• luf-op rsj5• **Lyc** m-aust b7.de *Mag-c* k* mag-m b4.de* mang-p rly4• mang-s a1 med meph k* *Merc* k* merc-c b4a.de* merc-i-f mez bg2 mim-p rsj8• morg-g fmm1• morg-p fmm1• *Mur-ac* k* narc-ps a1* nat-ar nat-c nat-m bg2 *Nat-p* nat-pyru rly4• **Nat-s** nat-sil fd3.de• nicc nicotam rly4• nit-ac h2 *Nuph* *Nux-m* k* *Nux-v* k* oci-sa sp1 **Olnd** k* *Op* opun-s a1 osm par b7.de* petr a1 **Ph-ac** k* **Phos** k* phyt **Pic-ac** plat h2 plut-n srj7• **Podo** k* *Psor* k* ptel puls b2.de pycnop-sa mrz1 pyrid rly4• pyrog k2 ran-s b7.de* rat rheum b7.de* rhod k* *Rhus-t* k* rhus-v rumx ruta fd4.de sabad k* sabin b7.de* sacch-a fd2.de• sal-fr sle1• samb xxb1 sang saroth sp1 sec k* sel senec *Sep* k* *Sil* sphing kk3.fr *Spig* k* *Spong* *Squil* k* stann h2 staph b2.de* stront-c b4.de* succ-ac rly4• sulfonam ks2 **Sulph** k* suprar rly4• syc bka1*• tab bg2 *Tarent* tell rsj10• tere-la rly4• **Thuj** *Trios* rsj11• tritic-vg fd5.de trom *Tung-met* bdx1• vanil fd5.de vario **Verat** k* vero-o rly4*• visc sp1 yohim c1* zinc b4.de* [bell-p-sp dcm1 *Spect* dfg1]

- **morning**: cortiso tpw7
  - **urgent**: bacls-10 fmm1• morg-p fmm1•
- **accompanied** by | **respiration**; difficult (See RESPIRATION - Difficult - accompanied - stool)
- **black**: acon *Apis* **Ars** asc-t brom *Carb-ac* *Carb-v* *Cocc* *Crot-h* *Kali-s* *Lept* *Squil* *Stram*
- **breakfast** agg.; after: cortiso tpw7
- **brown**: *Apoc* arg-n arn *Ars* asaf aster k* bros-gau mrc1 *Bry* **Graph** k* mag-c mag-m h2* *Nat-s* nux-v *Phos* *Psor* *Raph* ruta fd4.de *Squil* tritic-vg fd5.de
- **dark**: *Ars* *Crot-h* falco-pe nl2• *Nat-s* op psor hr1 squil
- **eating**; after: morg-p fmm1• syc fmm1•
- **fecal**: (↗*Fecal)* *Aloe* alum k* ant-c k* ant-t k* arg-n *Arn* *Ars* *Bapt* k* bar-c k* borx *Bov* *Bry* k* carb-v k* *Caust* *Cedr* k* *Chel* cist k* *Colch* *Coloc* con k* dios k* *Dulc* **Gamb** k* *Hep* k* *Hydr* ign *Iris* kali-n k* *Lept* k* *Lil-t* k* lyc k* **Nat-s** k* nicc k* *Nux-v* k* **Olnd** k* osm phos h2* **Pic-ac** **Podo** psor hr1 ptel *Rheum* rhod k* *Rhus-t* *Rumx* sang k* sars h2* *Sel* **Sulph** k* sumb trom k* *Verat* zinc
- **followed** by:
  - **hard** stool: *Agar* alum am-c bar-c calc carb-an euph k* graph h2 *Lyc* mag-c mag-m mur-ac nat-c ph-ac plat h2 plb bg1 psil ft1 sars sep sul-ac sulph tritic-vg fd5.de vanil fd5.de zinc
  - **watery** stool: rauw tpw8
- **formed** then thin: agar aloe **Bov** **Calc** calc-f lact **Lyc** nat-s *Ph-ac* phos h2* ruta fd4.de *Stann* tritic-vg fd5.de vanil fd5.de
- **frequent**: dys fmm1•
- **green**: aeth agar ant-c *Apis* *Chin* crot-h crot-t **Grat** *Podo* raph
- **liver**-colored: mag-c
- **lumpy** and liquid: aloe **Ant-c** apis *Ars* k* calc *Con* k* graph ip iris bg2 kali-bi **Lyc** *Nat-s* k* *Nux-v* bg2 *Pic-ac* sil sul-ac k* sulph trom
- **milk** agg.: trios rsj11•

Thin: ...
- **pouring** out: (↗*Forcible)* *Apis* *Arn* ars *Benz-ac* bros-gau mrc1 *Calc-p* canth **Crot-t** **Gamb** *Grat* iod lach lyc merc **Nat-s** **Olnd** **Ph-ac** **Podo** puls **Sec** sil **Sulph**
- **red**: kali-i rhus-t
- **rising** agg.; after: cortiso tpw7
- **urging**; with great: morg-g fmm1• morg-p fmm1•
- **urine**; semi fluid with suppression of: cadm-s br1
- **yellow**: aeth agar h2* *Aloe* arg-n hr1 *Bapt* *Bov* *bufo* *Cocc* colch rsj2• coloc cop *Crot-t* **Dulc** **Gamb** *Hydr* iris lyc merc nat-c **Nat-s** nit-ac nux-m **Olnd** **Pic-ac** **Podo** raph rhus-t vanil fd5.de

TOBACCO; from abuse of: cham bg2 **Puls** bg2

TOUGH: agar k* *Am-m* k* arn k* asar k* bar-c k* brom k* *Canth* k* *Caps* k* *Caust* k* dulc fd4.de ham fd3.de• merc-i-f k* phos mtf33 pieri-b mlk9.de podo fd3.de• ruta fd4.de spong fd4.de **Sulph** k* tritic-vg fd5.de vanil fd5.de

TRANSPARENT (See Mucous - transparent)

TRIANGULAR: nat-m bg2 plb bg2 sep bg2

UNDIGESTED: abrot k* acet-ac aesc k* *Aeth* k* aloe k* alum-sil k2 am-m *Ant-c* k* *Apoc* k* aq-mar skp7• arg-met k* *Arg-n* k* arge-pl rwt5• *Arn* k* **Ars** k* ars-s-f k2 asar k* bamb-a stb2.de• bar-c borx k* bros-gau mrc1 **Bry** k* cain **Calc** k* *Calc-p* k* calc-s k* calc-sil k2 *Carbn-s* cham k* **Chin** k* **Chinin-ar** *Chion* hr1* cimic bg2 *Cina* *Coloc* k* *Con* k* cop crot-t k* der a1 dulc k* *Elaps* erig hr1 **Ferr** k* ferr-act bro1 **Ferr-ar** *Ferr-p* k* *Ferr-pern* c1 *Gamb* k* **Graph** k* hell bg2* *Hep* k* ind k* iod k* iodof bro1 ip k* irid-met srj5• *Iris* jab k* kali-c h2* kali-p kreos k* lach k* laur *Lept* k* *Lyc* k* lyss k* *Mag-c* k* **Mag-m** k* mag-p dgt med ser *Meny* b2.de* *Merc* k* merc-c k* mez k* moni rfm1• nat-c k2 nat-s k2 nat-sil fd3.de• *Nit-ac* k* *Nux-m* k* nux-v bg2* ol-j **Olnd** k* ox-ac k* *Petr* k* **Ph-ac** k* **Phos** k* phys k* phyt k* *Plat* k* **Podo** k* *Psor* k* puls hr1* *Raph* k* rheum k* *Rhod* k* *Rhus-t* k* rhus-v k* ribo rly4• *Sang* k* *Sec* k* *Sil* k* sin-a a1* spong fd4.de squil k* stann staph stram sul-ac k* *Sulph* k* thuj k* tritic-vg fd5.de *Tub* valer b2.de* verat k*
- **morning**: *Chin* olnd
- **night**: *Aeth* am-m borx bry **Chin** k* coloc **Ferr** k* verat
- **brown**: kreos ptk1 psor ptk1
- **food** of the previous day: *Olnd* k*
- **fruit** agg.: alum-sil k2 **Chin**
- **hard**: *Calc*
- **milk** agg.: *Mag-c* k* **Mag-m** k*
  - **children**; in: | **nurslings**: mag-c mtf33

URINATION:
- **after** | **agg.**: mur-ac bg2
- **during** | **agg.**: *Aloe* bg2 canth bg2 carb-v bg2 merc bg2 merc-c bg2 nat-m bg2 squil bg2
- **urging** to urinate: sars bg2

VACCINATION; after: apis bg2 thuj bg2

VEAL agg.: kali-n bg2

VEGETABLES agg.: ars bg2

VEXATION agg.: calc-p bg2 coloc bg2

VINEGAR agg.: ant-c bg2

VOLUMINOUS (See Copious)

VOMITING agg.: ars bg2

WAKING agg.: aloe bg2 bry bg2

WALKING agg.: coloc bg2 gels bg2 laur bg2 rheum bg2

WARM:
- **bathing**:
  - **after**: bry bg2
  - **amel.**: sec bg2

WATERY: (↗*Thin)* abrom-a ks5 acet-ac k* achy-a zzc1• *Acon* k* acon-f a1 adel a1 aegle-f zzc1• aesc k* *Aeth* k* **Agar** k* agar-cps a1 agar-ph a1 aids nl2• ail k* *All-s* vh1 *Aloe* k* *Alst* bro1 alum k* alum-sil k2 am-c a1 am-caust a1 am-m k* ammc a1 amp rly4• amyg a1 anac k* anag k* **Ant-c** k* ant-t k* anthraq rly4• **Apis** k* **Apoc** k* *Aran* a1 **Arg-n** k* arizon-l nl2• arn k* *Ars* k* ars-br vh *Ars-i* k* ars-s-f a1* arum-d a1 arum-i a1 *Arum-t* k* **Asaf** k* asar k*

Stool

Watery: ...
asc-c a1 atro a1 aur-m k* bac jl2 *Bamb-a* stb2.de• bapt k* bar-c k* bar-i k2 *Bar-m* k* bar-s k2 bart a1 bell k* **Benz-ac** k* berb k* *Bism* k* bol-s a1 bond a1 *Borx* k* both-ax tsm2 bov b4.de* bros-gau mrc1 *Brucel* sa3• *Bry* bro1 *Bufo* *Cact* k* cain caj a1 calad b7.de* **Calc** k* calc-act bro1 calc-i k2 *Calc-p* k* calc-sil k2 camph cann-i a1 canth k* *Caps* b7.de* carb-ac k* *Carb-v* k* **Carbn-s** carl a1 cassia-s cdd7*• castm castor-eq caul a1* caust k* cench **Cham** k* *Chel* k* *Chin* k* *Chinin-ar* chinin-s chlol a1 *Chr-ac* k* *Cina* k* cist cob k* coc-c a1 *Cocc* k* *Coff* k* **Colch** k* *Coll* k* *Coloc* k* **Con** k* cop k* *Corn* k* cot a1 croc a1 crot-h k* *Crot-t* k* cuph br1* cupr k* cupr-ar a1* cur k* cycl k* cystein-l rly4• cyt-l a1 dendr-pol sk4• *Dig* k* dios k* dirc a1* **Dulc** k* elaps **Elat** k* eup-per a1 euph b4.de* euph-a a1 fago a1 *Ferr* k* ferr-ar ferr-i ferr-m bro1 ferr-ma a1 ferr-p k* ferul a1 fl-ac k* franz a1 **Gamb** k* gent-c a1 ger-i rly4• gnaph k* gran a1 *Graph* k* **Grat** k* guaj k2 haliae-lc srj5• *Hell* k* *Hep* k* hipp k* *Hydr* *Hyos* k* indg a1 *Iod* k* iodof bro1 ip k* irid-met srj5• **Iris** k* jab a1* *Jal* k* **Jatr-c** k* jug-r a1 *Kali-ar* k* **Kali-bi** k* kali-br k* kali-c kali-chl a1 *Kali-i* k* kali-m k2 kali-n k* kali-p k* *Kali-s* k* kali-sil k2 ketogl-ac rly4• kola stb3• kreos k* lac-ac stj5• *Lac-c* lac-h sk4• *Lach* k* laur a1* *Lec* *Led* hr1 *Lept* k* linu-c a1 lipp a1 *Lob* k* lob-s a1 lycpr br1 lyss k* **Mag-c** k* mag-m k* *Mag-p* hr1 mag-s k* manc k* mang-p rly4• med hr1 **Merc** k* merc-br a1 merc-c b4a.de* merc-cy a1 *Merc-d* k* merc-i-r k* *Merc-sul* k* *Mez* k* *Moni* rfm1• morph a1 mosch k* *Mur-ac* k* narc-ps a1* nat-ar *Nat-c* k* **Nat-m** k* nat-ox rly4• *Nat-p* k* **Nat-s** k* *Nit-ac* k* nux-m k* **Nux-v** k* ol-an a1 **Olnd** k* **Op** k* oper bro1 osm k* ox-ac k* oxal-a rly4• ozone sde2• petr k* *Ph-ac* k* phel a1 **Phos** k* phys a1 **Pic-ac** k* plac rzf5• plac-s rly4• plan k* plb k* **Podo** k* polyp-p a1 pot-e rly4• psil ft1 **Psor** k* **Puls** k* pyrid rly4• pyrog k2 ran-a a1 ran-b k* ran-s k* *Raph* k* rat k* *Rheum* bro1 rhus-t k* *Rhus-v* k* ribo rly4• *Ric* a1 rob a1* *Rumx* k* ruta fd4.de sabin a1 sal-ac hr1 samb k* sang k* sapin a1 sars k* **Sec** k* sel k* senec k* seneg k* *Senn* a1 sep k* serp a1 *Sil* k* sol-t-ae a1 spig b7.de* spong fd4.de squil k* staphycoc rly4• stram k* stront-c k* stry k* suis-em rly4• suis-hep rly4• suis-pan rly4• sul-ac k* sul-i k2 **Sulph** k* sumb k* suprar rly4• tab k* tell rsj10• ter k* **Thuj** k* til a1 tril-p c1 trom bro1 tub bro1* tub-d jl2 valer k* vanil fd5.de **Verat** k* **Verat-v** k* vib k* wies a1 zinc k* zinc-m a1 zinc-p k2 zing k* [spect dfg1]

- **morning**: adam skp7• agar ant-c ant-t brucel sa3• cact caust k* coloc ptk1 cop k* der a1 dios k* eucal a1 *Fl-ac* k* glon k* gnaph a1 hep iod kali-bi k* kali-c k* kali-n mag-c k* mur-ac nat-m k* **Nat-s** k* nux-m nux-v k* olnd ox-ac pen a1 petr k* phos k* **Podo** *Rumx* squil k* **Sulph** k* tab k* thuj k2
  • **6.45** h: adam skp7•
- **afternoon**: ferr k*
- **night**: acet-ac agar k* ant-t k* **Arg-n** k* ars castm chel k* *Chin* k* gnaph k* kali-p fd1.de• merc-c merc-cy a1 mosch nat-m k* psor hr1 puls k* senec k* sulph
- **black**: *Apis* am **Ars** k* asc-t bapt camph carb-ac *Chin* chinin-s *Crot-h* *Cupr* *Iod* *Kali-bi* k* *Lept* nat-s *Psor* rumx sec stann *Stram* *Verat* k*
- **bloody**: aloe am-m apis ars h2* *Canth* *Carb-v* ferr-p k* lach merc-c ptk1 petr *Phos* k* **Rhus-t** k* sabad sec k2
  • **meat** washings, like: canth k* merc-d hr1 *Phos* k* *Podo* hr1* **Rhus-t** k*
- **brown**: ant-t apis *Apoc* **Ars** k* arum-t aster ptk1 *Bapt* camph canth k* carb-v cench k2 *Chel* k* chin choc srj3• dulc k* ferr k* ferr-ar *Gamb* k* gels k* **Graph** k* *Kali-bi* k* kreos mag-c k* op gk petr *Phos* plan podo sne *Rumx* staph sne sulph k* *Verat* k*
- **clay** colored: (↗*Clayish)* *Kali-bi* kali-p
- **clear**: alum-sil k2 apis *Benz-ac* coloc *Merc* sec tab
- **dirty**: *Ars* bg2* brom ptk1 bry hr1 *Cact* ferr-p ptk1 jal ptk1 lept ptk1 ox-ac ptk1 ph-ac ptk1 podo k*
- **eating**; after: syc bka1•
- **flakes**; with: cupr k* guar vml3• paull *Verat* k*
- **frothy**: benz-ac *Elat* k* *Graph* *Grat* hr1 *Kali-ar* kali-bi k* *Mag-c* k* ran-b
- **gelatinous** on standing: podo
- **green**: acon aeth am-m ars bell bry **Cham** k* *Chion* colos cupr k* dulc k* *Elat* eup-per ferr-p gamb k* *Gels* hr1 **Grat** k* hep ip k* iris *Kali-br* k* kali-i kreos *Laur* lept *Mag-c* k* med *Merc-d* nat-m nat-s *Nit-ac* *Phos* k* *Podo* k* *Puls* k* rob sanic sec sul-ac k* sulph ter *Verat* k*
  • **accompanied** by | **cholera** infantum (See RECTUM - Cholera - infantum - accompanied - stools)
  • **scum**, with: **Mag-c** k* *Merc*
- **hard**; although: hyos ptk1
- **pale** on standing; becomes: sanic c1
- **perspiration**, after: bell h1*
- **prune** juice, like: ars ter

Watery: ...
- **rice** water, like: ant-t k* apis *Ars* k* **Camph** k* carb-ac cham chel colch k* coloc bg2 **Cupr** cupr-ar ptk1 *Ferr* iris *Jatr-c* bg2* kali-br k* kali-i *Kali-p* k* merc bro1 merc-sul k* *Nat-m* **Ph-ac** k* *Phos* ran-b ric bro1 *Sec* **Verat** k*
- **white**: ang ars-i k2 **Benz-ac** k* *Calc* *Camph* *Castm* *Caust* *Chel* hr1 *Cina* *Cop* dulc k* kali-ar *Kali-bi* kreos merc k* naja bg2 nat-m **Ph-ac** k* *Phos* k* ran-b sec k*
- **yellow**: aesc *Aloe* sne am-m *Apis* *Apoc* ars k* ars-i k2 *Bapt* borx cain *Calc* canth k* cham *Chel* k* *Chin* k* *Cocc* *Colch* colos cop crot-h *Crot-t* k* cycl **Dulc** k* elaps *Eucal* hr1 ferr-p k* **Gamb** k* **Grat** k* *Hydr* *Hyos* k* ip *Iris* jab kali-c kali-i lach *Lec* merc-sul nat-ar *Nat-c* *Nat-s* k* nuph **Olnd** k* *Ph-ac* phos k* pic-ac plb **Podo** k* puls *Rhus-t* sanic sec *Stront-c* k* **Thuj** k* trom
  • **bright**: nux-m bg

WAXY: kali-bi ptk1 lept ptk1

WEATHER:
- **stormy** | **agg.**: rhod bg2
- **warm** | **agg.**: *Lach* bg2 *Podo* bg2
- **wet** | **agg.**: *Dulc* bg2 *Rhod* bg2

WET agg.; getting: acon bg2

WHEY like: cupr bg2* iod bg2* phos bg2

WHITE: (↗*Lumps)* acon k* acon-l a1 aesc k* *Agar-ph* a1 am-m k* anan hr1 ang k* *Ant-c* k* anth a1* anthraci *Apis* k* *Arg-n* k* arn b7.de* ars k* *Ars-i* asar b7.de* asc-t c1 astac a1 aur b4.de* aur-m k* *Aur-m-n* *Bar-c* b4a.de bar-m k* *Bell* k* **Benz-ac** k* berb k2 *Borx* bry tl1 bufo *Calc* k* calc-i k2 calc-p k* calc-s **Canth** k* carbn-s *Castm* k* caul k* *Caust* k* cedr k* *Cham* k* *Chel* k* chin k* *Cimx* hr1 *Cina* k* cocc k* *Colch* k* coloc hr1 *Cop* k* *Crot-h* k* *Cub* hr1* der a1 *Dig* k* dios k* dol br1* dros k* *Dulc* k* elat eup-per k2 *Ferr-i* hr1 *Ferr-p* hr1 *Form* k* gels *Graph* k* *Hell* k* *Hep* k* hydr k* iber k* ign k* *Iod* k* ip hr1* *Kali-ar* k* *Kali-bi* k* *Kali-c* k* *Kali-chl* k* kali-m bro1 kreos k* lac-c k* lach k* lob a1 lyc mag-c h2* mag-m a1* manc mand a1 mang med k* merc k* *Merc-d* bro1 mez bro1 naja nat-m k* nat-p hr1 nat-s nicc a1 **Nux-m** k* *Nux-v* k* op k* pall k* petr k* petros hr1 **Ph-ac** k* *Phos* k* plb k* podo k* **Puls** k* ran-b *Rheum* *Rhus-t* k* rhus-v k* rob k* *Sang* hr1 *Sanic* sapin a1 sec k* *Sep* k* spig k* *Spong* k* still a1* stront-c b4.de* sul-ac b4.de* sul-i k2 sulph k* tab hr1 tarax ptk1 thuj k* trom bro1 urt-u k* verat k* wies a1
- **chalk**, like: acon bro1 alumn bro1 ant-c aur-m-n bell k* **Calc** k* *Chel* k* *Chin* bro1 chion bro1 cimx coll bro1 *Dig* k* dol bro1 granit-m es1• hep k* hydr bro1 iber bro1 indol bro1 kali-m bro1 lach *Merc-d* bro1 mez bg2 **Podo** k* rhus-t **Sanic** k* *Sil* spong stel bro1
  • **curdy**: calen ptk1
- **dentition**; during: *Calc* vh
- **fecal**: (↗*Fecal)* aesc aur-m-n bar-m **Calc** *Calc-p* *Chel* cop *Crot-h* *Dig* k* *Hep* kali-bi *Lyc* k* *Pall* **Podo** k* rhus-t k* sanic *Sil*
  • **alternating** with black stool: aur-m-n k*
- **flakes**; in: ip b7a.de squil b7a.de
- **foamy**: *Benz-ac* bg2 colch bg2 *Elat* bg2 iod bg2 sulph bg2
- **glassy**: ars-i ptk1
- **grains** or particles: *Cina* cub dulc mez h2 *Phos* k*
- **gray**: ars bg3 asar h1* aur-m hr1 aur-m-n *Benz-ac* hr1 calc bg3 chel bg3 dig bg3 kali-c bg3 lach bg3 *Merc* bg3 op bg3 **Ph-ac** *Phos* k*
  • **eggs**; like boiled: urt-u ptk1
  • **streaked** with blood: *Calc*
- **greenish** white: *Ph-ac* k*
- **hard**: bar-m berb *Chel* eup-per *Hydr* iod *Mag-c* *Mag-m* sulph
- **jellylike**: *Hell*
- **milky**, chylous: *Aesc* arg-n am bell berb bufo **Calc** k* carb-ac carb-v *Card-m* **Chel** k* **Chin** k* coloc cop cur bg2 **Dig** k* dulc gels hell *Hep* iod mtf33 *Kali-bi* lept *Mag-c* **Merc** k* myric nux-v petr **Podo** k* rheum **Sanic** k* stront-c sulph tab ptk1 valer
- **parts**; in: phos ptk1
- **putty**; like: dig ptk1 mag-c ptk1 plat ptk1
- **shredded** particles: **Colch** k*
- **streaked**: rhus-t b7a.de*
- **tallow**; masses like: dulc *Mag-c* phos

WINE agg.: lyc bg2 zinc bg2

WORM-like: (↗*Long)* graph bg2 stann bg2

WORMS agg.: acon bg2 *Cina* bg2 *Merc* bg2 spig bg2

YEAST: ant-t bg2 arn b7.de* *Ip* b7a.de
- **brown**, like: am h1*

YELLOW: abrom-a ks5 adam skp7• aegle-f zzc1• aesc k* *Aeth* k* agar k* alf bro1 *Aloe* k* alum b4.de* alum-sil k2 *Alumn* k* am-m k* ambr k* ang k* ant-c k* ant-t k* anth a1 *Apis* k* *Apoc* k* aral a1 *Arg-n* k* arn k* *Ars* k* *Ars-i* ars-s-r hr1 arum-i a1 arum-t k* asaf k* *Asar* k* asc-c a1* asc-t k* asim a1* astac a1 aur bg2 aur-m hr1 bapt bar-c k* bar-i k2 bar-m k* bar-s k2 bell k* *Berb* k* bol-la bond a1 borx k* both-ax tsm2 bov k* brom k* bros-gau mrc1 *Bry* k* bufo but-ac sp1 caj a1 calad a1* *Calc* k* calc-i k2 calc-s cann-i a1* cann-s a1 cann-xyz bg2 canth k* carb-v carbn-s card-m bro1 cassia-s cdd7*• cedr a1 cham k* **Chel** k* *Chin* k* chlol a1 cist k* cob-n sp1 coca-c sk4• cocc k* *Colch* k* coll k* *Coloc* k* colos convo-s sp1 cop crot-c k* crot-h k* *Crot-t* k* cub k* cupr-ar a1 *Cupr-s* a1 cycl k* der a1 dig k* dios k* diosm br1 dirc a1* dream-p sdj1• **Dulc** k* *Echi* elaps erech a1 eucal a1 euph b4.de* ferr a1 ferr-i a1 ferr-p a1* fl-ac k* **Gamb** k* *Gels* k* ger-i rly4• gink-b sbd1• **Grat** k* guat sp1 helon k* *Hep* k* hir skp7• hydr a1* hydrog srj2• hyos k* hyper a1* ign k* ind a1 inul a1 iod ip k* *Iris* k* jab k* jug-c a1 *Kali-ar* *Kali-bi* k* *Kali-c* k* *Kali-i* k* kali-n a1 kali-p kali-s k* kiss a1 kola stb3• lac-h sk4• *Lach* k* laur lept k* lil-s a1 lil-t a1 limest-b es1• linu-c a1 lipp a1 lith-c **Lyc** k* mag-c k* mag-m k* malar jl2 mand sp1 mang k* melal-alt gya4 **Merc** k* **Merc-c** k* merc-cy a1 *Merc-sul* k* myric a1* *Nat-ar* *Nat-c* k* nat-m nat-p *Nat-s* k* nat-sil fd3.de• nicc k* nit-ac b4.de* nit-m-ac a1 nuph k* *Nux-m* k* nux-v k* oci-sa sp1 olnd k* orot-ac rly4• osm a1 ox-ac a1 *Petr* k* petr-ra shn4• **Ph-ac** k* *Phos* k* phys k* phyt a1 **Pic-ac** k* plac rzf5• *Plb* k* **Podo** k* positr nl2• puls k* pyrid rly4• raph k* rat a1* rheum k* rhod b4.de* **Rhus-t** k* rob k* sabad bg2 sal-ac hr1 samb *Sang* k* sanic k* saroth sp1 **Sec** k* senn a1* sep a1* skat br1 spong fd4.de staph k* stront-c k* *Sul-ac* k* sul-i k2 sulph k* tab k* ter k* **Thuj** k* tritic-vg fd5.de trom hr1 urt-u k* vanil fd5.de verat b7.de* yuc a1 zinc bg2 zinc-s a1 [spect dfg1]
- **forenoon**: mag-c h2*
- **alternating** with | **greenish** (See Green - alternating - yellowish)
- **breakfast** agg.; after: prot jl2
- **bright**: aeth bg2* aloe bg3* apis bg2 *Arg-n* hr1 asar bg2 borx bg2 brom bg2* but-ac sp1 *Calc* hr1 **Chel** bg2* colch bg2* coloc bg2 dios bg2 fl-ac k* gels bg3* grat hr1 ham fd3.de• *Hep* hr1 ip bg2* kali-c bg2 *Kali-chl* hr1 kali-p bg3* lach bg2 mand sp1 merc bg2 myric hr1 nat-m bg2 *Nuph* hr1 nux-m bg1* *Nux-v* bg3 *Petr* hr1 **Ph-ac** k* *Phos* bg3* podo bg3* sabad bg2 *Sang* bg2 sul-ac k* sul-i ptk1 thuj hr1 vanil fd5.de
- **brownish**: anan k* *Ant-t* hr1 apis asar coloc h2* cycl a1* cystein-l rly4• ferr a1 fl-ac flor-p rsj3• ind hr1 *Lach* hr1 melal-alt gya4 merc-i-r nat-p petr a1* podo fd3.de• raph hr1 **Rhus-t** hr1 spong fd4.de stann a1 verat a1
- **corn** meal; like: arum-t ptk1
- **eggs**; like yolk of: *Cocc* b7a.de *Ip* b7a.de
- **fecal**: (↗*Fecal*) *Agar* k* *Aloe* *Alumn* am-m k* ant-t k* *Apis* arum-t asaf bapt bol-la borx bov *Calc* k* **Chel** cist k* cocc k* colch coloc k* crot-t cub k* dig k* dios k* fl-ac k* **Gamb** k* gels k* *Hep* k* iris kali-c k* lach k* laur lith-c myric nat-c k* *Nat-p* *Nat-s* **Olnd** k* *Ph-ac* k* **Pic-ac** plb **Podo** **Rhus-t** k* samb *Sulph*
  - **painless**: colch rsj2•
    - **eating**; after | **immediately**: calc
- **foamy**: apoc bg2 coloc bg2 nat-s bg2 podo bg2 rhus-t bg2 sul-ac bg2
- **granular**: bell h1* mang
- **green** on standing, turning: arg-n k* borx mtf33 rheum k*
- **greenish**: aeth ptk1 aloe apis brom bg2 cadm-s coloc k* crot-t k* cupr-s hr1 *Dulc* k* fic-m gya1 *Gamb* hr1 **Grat** k* jug-c k* kali-bi k* kali-p lac-ac k* *Mag-c* hr1 med merc *Merc-c* hr1 nat-p k2 nat-s **Podo** hr1 puls k* sec **Sulph** tab ter k* verat zinc-s a1
- **hard**: agar
- **ochre**: eberth jl2 germ-met srj5• kali-s fd4.de *Sima* c1 spong fd4.de
- **orange**: aeth bg1 apis bamb-a stb2.de• chel bg1 cocc *Colch* k* coli rly4• coloc k* convo-s sp1 dios bg1 gels bg1 ip bg1 kali-bi bg1 kola stb3• *Lach* hr1 loxo-recl knl4• merc k* nat-m k* nuph bg1 osm k* phos bg1 suis-pan rly4• **Sul-ac** syph tritic-vg fd5.de
- **orange**; like pulp of an: apis ptk1 *Nat-c* k*
- **pale**: anth a1 apoc a1 asaf a1 chlol a1 crot-t a1 cycl a1 ferr-i a1 ferul a1 gent-l a1 *Kali-chl* hr1 kali-n a1 lipp a1 luf-op rsj5• mand rsj7• mang h2* samb bat1• syc fmm1• tet a1 zinc h2*
- **red**: petr-ra shn4•
- **saffron**, like: coloc k* croc k* merc merc-c bg2 **Sul-ac** k*
- **salmon**: lac-d k*
- **streaked**: rhus-t b7a.de*

Yellow: ...
- **whitish**: acon k* aur k* cham hr1 *Chel* hr1 cocc k* dig k* ign k* lyc nit-ac h2* **Ph-ac** k* phos k* puls rhus-t k* sul-ac k* *Sulph*

Stool

AGONIZING dysuria: acon bg3

AIR passes (See Gas)

APPREHENSION in region of: *(↗MIND - Clairvoyance; MIND - Excitement; MIND - Fear)* merc-c

ATONY of: ars bro1* **Caust** ptk1 dulc bro1 hep bro1 *M-aust* b7.de mur-ac bg2* *Op* b7a.de* plb bro1* rhus-a br1* rhus-t bro1 squil bro1 stann ptk1 ter bro1
- **laparotomy**; after: op ptk1
- **old** age: ars ptk1 stram ptk1
- **retention**; from long: canth ptk1

BALL in; sensation of a: anac bro1 crot-h kali-br bro1 kreos pd* *Lach* k* naja santa bro1
- **forced** from behind neck of bladder: kali-br phos bg2

BAND (See Constriction)

BED-WETTING (See Urination - involuntary - night)

CALCULI (See Stones)

CANCER: *Anil* sne arg-n sne ars sne blatta-o gm1 chim sne* clem sne con sne congo-r gm1 crot-h hr1* equis-h gm1 gamb gk hydr sne mal-ac mtf11 sabal gm1 sars sne staph gm1 tarax br1 **Ter** rmk1• thuj sne* tor sne
- **painful**; tormenting: naphthoq mtf11

CARTILAGINOUS induration (See Induration - cartilaginous)

CATARRH, mucopus: *(↗URINE - Sediment - purulent)* alum k2 alumn *Ant-c* k* ant-t br1 *Apis* arbin hsa1 arg-met k2 arg-n bg2 aspar baros br1 **Benz-ac** berb k2* *Borx* bg2 *Calc* k* calc-p k2 calc-s calc-sil k2 cann-s *Canth* carb-ac *Carb-v* *Carbn-s* *Caust* *Chim* k* chinin-s coc-c br1 coff coll **Coloc** *Con* k* *Cop* cub k* dam br1 **Dulc** k* *Equis-h* erig eucal *Eup-pur* fab br1 *Ferr* *Gels* ham hep k2 *Hydr* hydrang c2 indg kali-c k* *Kali-chl* kali-p kali-s kali-sil k2 kola stb3• *Lach* **Lyc** med mill nat-m **Nux-v** k* pareir k* *Petr* *Ph-ac* *Phos* k* plb pop k* **Puls** k* rhod rhus-t sabin k2 *Sars* *Senec* *Seneg* k* *Sil* silphu c2* **Sulph** k* *Ter* thuj k2 tril-p c1* **Uva** k* vichy-g c2
- **accompanied** by:
  - ○ • **Tongue**:
    - ⋮ **brown** discoloration | **heavily** coated: uva kr1*
- **acute**: chim br1
- **chronic**: *Chim* br1
- **gonorrhea**; after suppressed: benz-ac cub *Med* *Puls* sil *Thuj*
- **hemorrhoidal** subjects, in: coll
- **old** people; in: *Alumn* *Carb-v* kali-p k2 pop br1 sulph *Ter*

CHILLS spread from the neck of the bladder after urinating: *Sars* k*

CLOSURE of neck; sensation of: op bg2 ruta b7.de* seneg bg2

COITION agg.; after: all-c ptk1

COLD agg.: caust ptk1 dulc ptk1 puls ptk1 sulph ptk1

COLD sensation in: lach bg1 lyss k* sabal ptk1 syzyg bg1
- **alternating** with heat in bladder: coc-c k*
- ▽ - **extending** to | **Genitals**: sabal ptk1

COMPLAINTS of bladder: acon b2.de* alum b2.de am-c b2.de am-m b2.de ambr b2.de ang b2.de ant-c b2.de* ant-t b2.de* apis ptk1 arb br1 arn b2.de* ars b2.de* asaf b2.de* asar b2.de aur b2.de bell b2.de* benz-ac ptk1 *Berb* bg2* *Borx* bg2 brach br1 bry b2.de calad b2.de* *Calc* b2.de* camph b2.de* cann-s b2.de* **Canth** b2.de* caps b2.de* carb-an b2.de carb-v b2.de* caust b2.de* cham b2.de chim br1 chin b2.de* cic b2.de* clem bg2 coff b2.de colch b2.de* coloc b2.de* con b2.de* cyclosp sa3• dig b2.de* *Dulc* b2.de* equis-h br1* *Graph* bg2 guaj b2.de hell b2.de* hep b2.de *Hyos* b2.de* ign b2.de* ip b2.de junc-e br1 kali-c b2.de* lach b2.de* laur b2.de* led b2.de **Lyc** b2.de* m-ambo b2.de *M-aust* b2.de mag-m b2.de mang b2.de meny b2.de *Merc* b2.de* *Merc-c* ptk1 mez b2.de* mosch b2.de* mur-ac b2.de* nat-m b2.de* nit-ac b2.de *Nux-v* b2.de* oci br1 op b2.de* petr b2.de* *Ph-ac* b2.de* phos b2.de* plb b2.de **Puls** b2.de* ran-b b2.de rheum b2.de* rhod b2.de rhus-t b2.de *Ruta* b2.de* sabad b2.de *Sabal* ptk1 sabin b2.de sars b2.de* seneg b2.de sep b2.de* sil b2.de spig b2.de squil b2.de* stann b2.de staph b2.de sul-ac b2.de **Sulph** b2.de* syc fmm1• thuj b2.de uva ptk1 valer b2.de verat b2.de verb br1 zinc b2.de* [*Lith-i* stj2]
- **accompanied** by:
  - • **cough**: caps b7.de*

Complaints of bladder – **accompanied** by: ...
  - • **hemorrhoids**: canth bg2 dig bg2 erig bg2 nux-v bg2
  - • **menses**; complaints of: canth ptk1 erig ptk1 sabal ptk1
  - • **stool**; complaints of: merc-c ptk1
  - ○ • **Rectum**; complaints of: ambr ptk1
    - ⋮ **Anus**; and: apis bg2 canth bg2 erig bg2 merc-c bg2 mur-ac bg2 senec bg2
  - • **Skin**; complaints of: sars mrr1
- **acute**: thiosin br1
- **alternating** with | **Umbilicus**; complaints of: ter ptk1
- **extending** to:
  - ○ • **Back**: sars ptk1
  - • **Pelvis** and thighs | **urination** agg.; after: puls ptk1
  - • **Spermatic** cords: lith-c ptk1
- **operation**; after: pop br1
- ○ - **Muscles**: merl br1
- **Neck** of bladder: bell ptk1 canth ptk1 merc-c ptk1 *Petr* b4a.de

COMPLAINTS of urinary organs (See URINARY - Complaints)

CONSTRICTION: *(↗Contraction)* alum *Berb* k* *Cact* k* caps caust chel k* cocc cub dig hydrc k* lyc petr k* ph-ac k* *Puls* k* *Sars* k* tab br1 thuj k* verat k*
- **afternoon**: *Chel* k*
- **cord**; as of a: thuj bg2
- **urination**:
  - • **after** | **agg.**: cub *Nat-m*
  - • **before**: *Chel* k*
  - • **during** | **agg.**: berb bry k* dig k* petr polyg-pe vml2• thuj k*
- ○ - **Neck** of bladder: ant-c k* *Cact* k* canth k* caps k* colch k* con elaps kali-i k* mag-p *Op* paeon k* petr k* phos plb k* polyg-h bg2 puls bg2 *Ruta* sulph
  - • **morning**: caps k*
  - • **spasmodic**:
    - ⋮ **accompanied** by | **retention** of urine: *Bell* bro1 cact bro1 camph bro1 canth bro1 *Hyos* bro1 lyc bro1 *Nux-v* bro1 op bro1* puls bro1 rhus-t bro1 stram bro1 thlas bro1
  - • **urination** | **after** | **agg.**: bry *Cann-s* cub sulph
    - ⋮ **during** | **agg.**: colch k* kali-i petr polyg-h polyg-pe vml2•

CONTRACTION, sensation of: *(↗Constriction)* ant-c *Berb* bry b7.de* canth b7.de* caps b7.de* carbn-s cic b7.de* coc-c hyos k* kali-i *Lyc* merc-c bg2 *Mez* op petr k* ph-ac b4.de* puls b7.de* pyrog k2 ruta sars b4.de* verat k*
- **urination**:
  - • **during**:
    - ⋮ **agg.**: dig b4.de* petr b4.de* *Puls* b7a.de
    - ⋮ **end** of: bry b7.de*

COUGH agg.; during: caps ptk1 ip ptk1

CRAMP in: *Berb* k* *Caps* k* *Carb-v* k* carbn-s chin-b hr1 coc-c k* mag-p mez ptk1 *Nux-v* k* *Op* a1* ph-ac plb k* prun k* puls ptk1 ruta *Sars* k* sep zinc k*
- **night**: prun k*
- **bending** double | **must** bend double: *Prun* k*
- **operation**; after: coloc ptk1 hyper ptk1
- **urination** | **after** | **agg.**: asaf b7.de* bry bg2 **Cann-s** b7a.de* caust med bg2 *Nat-m* **Puls** bg2
  - • **during** | **agg.**: carbn-s
- ○ - **Neck** of; in | **urination** agg.; after: puls bg2

CRAWLING: sep ptk1
- **urination** agg.; after: *Lyc* k*

DISTENDED feeling: *(↗Swollen)* anth bro1 *Apoc* bro1 ars bro1 berb bro1 bros-gau mrc1 *Con* bro1 conv br1* dig bro1 *Equis-h* bro1 eup-per bro1 fab bro1 gels bro1 *Hyos* bro1 mel-c-s bro1 pareir br1* *Puls* bro1 ruta bro1 santin bro1 *Sars* bro1 sep bro1 staph bro1 stict c1 *Sulph* bro1 uva bro1
- **painful**: pareir br1

DROPS came out of bladder, rest agg.; sensation as if: sep k*

Bladder

DYSURIA (See Urination - dysuria)

EMPTINESS, sensation of: colch dig k* *Stram* k* sumb k*
- **distended**; when: lycps-v ptk1
- **pain**; with: calc-p ptk1
- **urination**; after involuntary: *(↗Urination - involuntary - empty)* helon ptk1

ENURESIS (See Urination - involuntary)

ENURESIS NOCTURNA (See Urination - involuntary - night)

FALLING out; as if: sep bg2

FALLS:
- **forward**, as if: nux-m bg1
- **side** lain on; sensation as if falls to: puls k* *Sep* k*

FULLNESS, sensation of: abrot k* all-c k* allox tpw3 *Apis Arg-n Arn* k* *Ars* ars-s-f k2 bell k* bros-gau mrc1 *Calad* k* chel bg2 *Chim* coc-c k* conv cub **Dig** k* **Equis-h** k* eup-pur k* gels gnaph bg2 guaj k* *Hell* hep hydrog srj2• *Kali-i* lac-ac limest-b es1• lyc lycps-v k* med mel-c-s br1 merc merc-c k* *Nux-v Op* orot-ac rly4• ox-ac k* pall k* petr phys k* plb plect a1 *Puls* k* *Ruta* k* *Sep* k* stann h2* *Staph* k* *Stram Sulph* k* taosc iwa1• tarent a1 ter bg2 thuj k* *Zinc*
- **moving** up and down while walking; sensation of bladder: ruta h1*
- **pregnancy** agg.; during: equis-h mrr1
- **sensation**; without: lac-d ptk1
- **urination** | **after**:
  - **agg.**: *(↗Urination - incomplete; Urination - unsatisfactory)* alumn atra-r bnm3• calc con conv **Dig** k* equis-h mrr1 *Eup-pur* k* gnaph **Hep** bg2 kali-sil k2 lac-c *Lycps-v* merc merc-c b4a.de nat-m k2 *Ruta* k* sars staph sulph
    - **scanty** urination: pall ptk1
  - **urging** to urinate | **without**: **Ars** k* calad **Caust** k* fl-ac hell lac-d k2 *Op* pall *Phos* plb k2 stann *Stram* verat

FUNGOID growths: *Calc* k*

GANGRENE: canth k*

GAS passes from: **Sars** k ● *Thuj* b4a.de
- **urination** agg.; during: canth bg2

HEAT in: **Acon** hr1 *All-c* k* canth k* dig br1 elat hr1 hist vml3• *Puls* k* *Senec* k* sulph k2
- **alternating** with coldness (See Cold sensation in - alternating)

HEAVINESS: *(↗Stones - sensation)* amp rly4• astac hr1 bell bg2* cann-s k* *Canth* k* coc-c k* des-ac rbp6 dig eup-pur mtf11 kali-i k* lepi a1 *Lyc* k* *Nat-m* k* olib-sac wmh1 plect a1 podo fd3.de• puls ptk1 sabal ptk1 *Sep* k*

HEMATURIA (See Hemorrhage; URINE - Bloody)

HEMORRHAGE: *(↗URINE - Bloody)* *Adren* br1 am-c k2 amyg-p br1* arg-n bg2 ars k2 bell k2 cact br1* calc bg2 canth mtf11 carb-v k2* crot-h *Erig* k* *Ferr-p* k* form mtf11 fuma-ac rly4• *Ham* k* **Ip** bg2 loxo-recl bnm10• lyc mill k2* *Nit-ac* bro1 oxyurn-sc mcp1• *Phos* k* rhus-a c2* sabin k2 sars bg2 *Sec* k* senec k2 stigm mtf11 ter ptk1 thlas bro1* thuj bg2
- **menses**; during: nat-m h2

HEMORRHOIDS of: acon k* ant-c borx *Canth* k* carb-v k* euph k* *Ham* k* *Nux-v* k* *Puls* staph bg1 sulph thuj bg1 wies a1
- **bleeding**: *Acon* hr1 ars k* **Calc** k* carb-v k* ferr k* *Ham* k* lyc k* merc k* *Nit-ac* k* nux-v k*

INACTIVITY of: *Ars* **Caust** med k2 *Op* plb k*

INCONTINENCE (See Urination - involuntary)

INDURATION: | **cartilaginous**: pareir k*

INFLAMMATION (= cystitis): *(↗URINE - Sediment - purulent)* **Acon** k* aids nl2• all-c alth vs am-c *Ant-t* k* **Apis** k* arb-m oss1• arbin br1 *Arg-n* arist-cl sp1 *Arn Ars* ars-s-f k2 aspar *Bar-m* **Bell** k* *Berb* k* bism c2 bov mrr1 cact *Calad Calc* k* camph k* *Cann-i* cann-s k* **Canth** k* *Caps* carb-ac *Caust Chim* k* *Chinin-s* cinnb c2 clem mrr1 colch coleus-a mtf11 coli jl2* coloc *Con* k* *Cop* k* corv-cor bdg• *Cub* k* *Dig* k* *Dulc* **Equis-h** k* *Ery-a* *Eup-purk* k* *Fab* c1* ferr gk* ferr-p k* gali br1* *Gels* gonotox jl2 graph bg2 *Hell* k* helon mtf11 *Hydr* k* *Hyos* k* kali-ar kali-bi kali-c k* kali-chl k* kali-m c2 kola stb3• **Lach** k* lil-t k* linu-u br1 lith-c k* **Lyc** k* lyss mrr1 *Med* k* *Merc* k*

Inflammation: ...
Merc-c k* methyl c2 mez bg2 *Moni* rfm1• morg-g pte1*• morg-p pte1*• murx mrr1 musa c1* mut awy1*• myrt-c br1 nat-c mrr1 *Nit-ac* k* *Nux-v* k* oci-sa sp1 parathyr jl2 pareir k* petr k* petros c2* ph-ac phos b4a.de phys mrr1 pip-m c2* plb-xyz c2 polyg-h ptk1 pop k* prot jl2 prun k* psor jl2 **Puls** k* rhus-a br1 *Rhus-t* ruta b7.de* sabal c2* *Sabin* k* santa mp4• **Sars** k* senec seneg **Sep** k* solid ptk1 squil k* staph gk* stigm br1* stram *Sulph* k* syc bka1*• tarent k* tax c2 **Ter** k* thuj k* tritic br1* uva c2* vacc-m mtf11 verat-v vesi c2 xanrhoe br1 [mag-f stj1]
- **accompanied** by:
  - **emission** of prostatic fluid (See PROSTATE - Emission - accompanied - bladder)
  - **fever**: *Acon* bro1 bell bro1 *Canth* bro1 gels bro1 hydrang bro1 stigm bro1
  - **swelling**: calc tl1
  - **urination**:
    - **dribbling**: canth mrr1
    - **involuntary**: canth mrr1
    - **painful**: *Acon* bro1 bell bro1 *Canth* bro1 gels bro1 hydrang bro1 stigm bro1
  - **urine**:
    - **bloody**: *Chim* mrr1 uva br1
    - **burning**: *Canth* tl1
  - ○ **Female** genitalia; inflammation of: canth tl1
  - **Male** genitalia; inflammation of: canth tl1
  - **Prostate** gland; swelling of: sabal ptk1
- **acute**: acon bro1 ant-t bro1 apis bro1 ars bro1 aspar bro1 *Bell* bro1 benz-ac bro1 berb bro1 *Camph* bro1 camph-ac bro1 *Cann-s* bro1 *Canth* bro1 caps bro1 chim bro1 con bro1 *Cop* bro1 *Cub* bro1 dig bro1 *Dulc* bro1 elat bro1 *Equis-h* bro1 erig bro1 *Eucal* bro1 *Eup-pur* bro1 fab bro1 ferr-act bro1 *Ferr-p* bro1 *Gels* bro1 hell bro1 hydrang bro1 hyos bro1 lach bro1 *Merc-c* bro1 methyl bro1 mez mtf11 nit-ac bro1 nux-v bro1 *Ol-sant* bro1 *Pareir* bro1 petros bro1 pip-m bro1 *Pop* bro1 prun bro1 *Puls* bro1 sabal bro1 *Sabin* bro1 sars bro1 *Saur* bro1 sep bro1 *Stigm* bro1 sulph bro1 *Ter* bro1 tritic bro1 uva bro1 vesi bro1
  - **accompanied** by:
    - **urination** | **urging** to urinate: mez mtf11
- **cantharis**; from abuse of: apis bro1 camph bro1
- **catheterization**; after: *(↗Urination - involuntary - catheterization; GENERALS - Catheterism)* arn mrr5 camph-ac mtf pop mtf staph vml2*
- **chronic** cystitis: ars bg1* bals-p bro1 *Baros* bro1 *Benz-ac* bro1 berb bro1 *Cann-s* bro1 *Canth* bro1 carb-v bro1 *Caust* bro1 *Chim* bro1* coc-c bro1 coll hr1 coloc bro1 *Cop* bro1* cub a1* *Dulc* bro1 *Epig* br1* ery-a bro1 eucal bro1 eup-pur bg1* *Fab* c1* grin bro1 *Hydr* bro1 iod bro1 juni-c bro1 *Kali-m* vh lith-c bro1 lyc bro1* *Med* mrr1 *Merc-c* bro1 nat-c mrr1 nit-ac bro1 otit-m-xyz mtf11 *Pareir* bro1 pip-m bro1 *Pop* bro1 prun bro1 *Puls* bro1 rhus-a bro1 *Sabal* c1* santin c2* seneg bro1 *Sep* hr1* silphu bro1 *Stigm* bro1 *Sulph* bg1 *Ter* bro1 thlas bro1* thuj bro1 tritic bro1 *Tub* br1* *Uva* bro1 vesi c1*
  - **accompanied** by:
    - **urination**; dribbling: hyper mtf11
    - **Urethra**; inflammation of: hydr mtf11 med mtf11
- **coition**; after: sabad sne **Staph** mrr1
  - **first** intercourse: **Staph** mrr1
  - **new** sexual relationship; since: *Med* mrr1
- **cold**; after taking a: aur-m-n wbt2• bamb-a stb2.de• **Dulc** k* *Sulph*
- **frequent**: morg-p fmm1•
- **gonorrheal**: bell bro1 benz-ac bro1 *Canth* bro1 *Cop* bro1 cub bro1 merc-c bro1 methyl br1 puls bro1 sabal bro1
- **headache**; during: rhus-t k2
- **hemorrhagic**: **Canth** mrr1
- **hemorrhoids** | **suppression** of; after: *Nux-v*
- **injuries**; after: *Arn Staph*
- **interstitial**: med mrr1
- **married** women; newly (See coition - first)
- **menses**:
  - **before** | **agg.**: senec bro1
  - **during** | **agg.**: senec bro1
  - **suppressed** menses; from: *Nux-v*

- **operation**; after:
  - **abdomen**; on: pop mtf
  - **ovaries**; after removing (= ovariectomy): pop mtf
  - **uterus**; after removing (= hysterectomy): pop mtf
- **operation**; from: pop bro1
- **pain** and almost clear blood; with violent: *Nit-ac*
- **painful**: morg-p fmm1•
- **pregnancy** agg.; during: eup-pur pd pop bro1
- **pus**-like discharge after lithotomy, with: mill
- **recurrent** (See GENERALS - History - cystitis)
- **scarlatina**; after: *Canth*
- **throbbing** all over; with: sabin br1
- **women**; in: mit mtf11

○ - **Neck** of bladder: *Acon* bg2 *Apis* aspar camph bg2 *Cann-xyz* bg2 **Canth** bg2 *Caps* k* cham bg2 *Chim* *Clem* con bg2 *Cop* *Dig* k* elat guaj bg2 hyos ign bg2 lyc bg2 *Merc-c* *Merc-i-r* *Nux-v* k* petr bg2 *Petros* plb bg2 *Puls* k* ruta bg2 *Sars* *Senec* staph bg2 sul-ac bg2 sulph bg2

INJURY, operations after: arn ptk1 calen ptk1 *Staph* ptk1

INSENSIBILITY: ham *Hyos* b7.de* *M-aust* b7.de mag-m k2 plb k2 sars b4a.de stann b4.de*

INVOLUNTARY urination (See Urination - involuntary)

IRRITABLE BLADDER (See Urination - urging - constant)

ITCHING: berb bg2 ign b7.de* nux-v b7.de* petros mrr1 plb b7.de* sep bg2

- **region** of bladder with urging to urinate, agg. night; in: *Sep* k*

○ - **Neck** of bladder: ign bg1* plb a1
  - **morning** | **bed** agg.; in: *Nux-v*

JAR, sensitive to: *Bell* k*

LYING on abdomen: | **amel.**: chel ptk1

MENSES: | **before** | **agg.**: sabin bro1

- **during** | **agg.**: sabin bro1

MOTION in: aln vva1• alum bell lach ruta sep

- **up** and down (See Pain - motion - upward - step)

MOVEMENTS bring up urinary troubles: berb hr1

NERVOUS BLADDER (See Urination - urging - ineffectual)

NUMBNESS (See Fullness; Urination - urging - absent)

OBSTRUCTION of neck, while urinating; sensation of: sulph k*

PAIN: acon k* aeth k* agar↓ agn k* all-c k* aloe↓ alum↓ alum-p↓ alumn k* am-c↓ am-m↓ ambr k* amp↓ androc↓ ang↓ *Ant-c* b7a.de ant-t k* anth↓ aphis *Apis* arge-pl↓ *Arist-cl* sp1 arn k* ars k* ars-s-f k2 asar↓ *Aur*↓ aur-s↓ bamb-a↓ bapt↓ baros↓ **Bell** k* benz-ac k* *Berb* k* borx↓ brach k* brom k* brucel sa3• bry↓ *Cact* k* calad k* calc k* calc-f *Calc-p* k* calc-sil↓ camph bro1 cann-i k* cann-s k* cann-xyz bg2 **Canth** k* *Caps* carb-an *Carb-v* k* *Carbn-s* *Card-m*↓ cartl-s↓ cassia-s↓ caul k* *Caust* k* cham↓ *Chel* k* chen-a↓ *Chim*↓ chin↓ chinin-ar↓ cit-ac↓ *Clem* coc-c k* coff↓ coff-t↓ colch↓ coli rly4• *Coloc*↓ colum-p↓ *Con* k* conv↓ cop k* crot-t↓ cub↓ cycl↓ cyclosp sa3• cypra-eg↓ der k* des-ac↓ dig bro1 dirc k* dulc bro1* elat hr1 **Equis-h** k* erig bro1 *Ery-a* bro1 eup-per↓ *Eup-pur* fab bro1 *Ferr* k* ferr-ar ferr-p k* *Ferr-pic*↓ fil a1 *Fl-ac* k* fuma-ac↓ gal-ac br1 gamb↓ ger-i↓ graph↓ guaj↓ *Hell*↓ hep↓ hist sp1 hydrang↓ hyos↓ ign bro1 indg k* ip k* jal hr1 kali-bi kali-br k* *Kali-c*↓ kali-cy↓ kali-p↓ kali-s↓ kali-sil↓ kola↓ kreos↓ lac-ac↓ lac-d↓ lac-del hrn2• lac-h↓ lach bro1 lachn↓ lact↓ lap-la↓ lat-m sp1 laur↓ *Led*↓ lil-t k* *Lith-c* *Lyc* k* lycps-v↓ lys↓ lyss↓ m-ambo↓ mang↓ mang-p↓ med↓ mel-c-s↓ merc merc-c a1 merc-i-r↓ *Mez*↓ moni↓ morph k* mosch↓ *Musa* c1 napht bro1 nat-ar nat-c↓ *Nat-m*↓ nat-p↓ nat-sil↓ nit-ac bro1 nux-m k* nux-v k* ol-an↓ op bro1 ox-ac k2 oxal-a rly4• pall k* par↓ parathyr jl2 pareir k* petr↓ petros mrr1 ph-ac k* phos k* phyt k* pic-ac k* pilo bro1 pip-n↓ plac-s rly4• *Plb* k* polyg-h *Pop* bro1 prun k* psor↓ ptel k* *Puls* k* pulx bro1 raph↓ rheum↓ rhod *Rhus-a* bro1 rhus-t ribo↓ ruta k* sabad↓ sabin sang k* sanic↓ *Sars* k* *Sec*↓ senec↓ sep sil↓ sinus↓ spig↓ spong fd4.de squil b7.de* stann↓ *Staph* bro1 stict c1 stigm bro1 streptoc↓ stry bro1 suis-em rly4• sul-ac k* sul-i sulph symph↓ taosc iwa1• tarent k* ter k*

Pain: ...
thuj k* til↓ tritic bro1 tritic-vg fd5.de ulm-c jsj8• uran-n bro1 *Uva* bro1 valer↓ vanil fd5.de verat verb↓ *Zinc* k* zinc-ar↓ zinc-p↓

- **right**: germ-met srj5•
- **morning**: alum↓ alumn k* arge-pl rwt5• berb↓ cop morph nat-sil fd3.de• *Nux-v*↓ puls↓ *Sep*↓ sin-n k* sulph↓ symph↓ tritic-vg fd5.de vanil↓
  - **night**; until: abrom-a↓
    ⁝ **burning**: abrom-a ks5
  - **burning**: berb k* *Nux-v* k* symph fd3.de•
  - **cramping**: alum h2*
  - **dragging**: sep sulph k*
  - **pressing** pain: nat-sil fd3.de• puls *Sep* vanil fd5.de
  - **spasmodic**: *Cop* k*
- **forenoon**:
  - **10 h**: all-c↓
    ⁝ **burning**: all-c
    ⁝ **pressing** pain: all-c
- **afternoon**: bamb-a stb2.de• tritic-vg fd5.de
- **evening**: dulc fd4.de ip k* lyss↓ morph k* nux-v↓ pall k* pic-ac k* puls↓ ruta fd4.de *Sep*↓ tritic-vg fd5.de uva
  - **burning**: dulc fd4.de lyss k* nux-v puls k*
  - **pressing** pain: puls *Sep*
  - **urination** agg.; after: sep tritic-vg fd5.de
- **night**: bell carb-an cartl-s↓ des-ac↓ fl-ac↓ kreos↓ lyc phos↓ prun sulph↓
  - **alternating** with | **Umbilicus**; pain in: ter hr1*
  - **burning**: bell k* cartl-s rly4• des-ac rbp6
  - **lying** down; while: *Lyc*↓
    ⁝ **dragging**: *Lyc*
  - **pressing** pain: *Bell* carb-an fl-ac kreos *Lyc* phos h2 sulph
  - **spasmodic**: prun
- **accompanied** by:
  - **stool**; complaints of: sulph bg2
  - ○ **Abdomen**; complaints of: lach bg2 nux-v bg2 prun bg2
  - **Lumbar** region; pain in: des-ac rbp6
- **aching**: *All-c* k* arn bamb-a stb2.de• bell k* *Berb* k* calc-p k* **Caps** k* carb-v *Carbn-s* chel k* conv br1* cop k* crot-t k* *Equis-h* k* erig k* *Eup-pur* k* *Fl-ac* k* *Hell* k* lach lyc k* *Nux-v* k* pall k* phos pop k* *Puls* ribo rly4• sabin *Sep* k* stict bro1 sulph k* ter bro1*
- **alternating** between bladder and rectum: coloc↓
  - **stitching** pain: coloc
- **anxiety**; from: merc-c bg2
- **boring** pain: thuj bg2
- **breathing** agg.: aur↓
  - **stitching** pain: aur
- **burning**: *Acon* k* *All-c* k* androc srj1• ant-c bg2 *Apis* k* arge-pl rwt5• arn b7a.de* *Ars* k* baros bro1 bell k* **Berb** k* calc bg2 camph k* cann-i cann-xyz bg2 **Canth** k* **Caps** k* card-m cartl-s rly4• cassia-s cdd7• caust bg2 cham k* chel chim chin k* cit-ac rly4• clem coff coff-t a1 colch k* coloc cop k* cypra-eg sde6.de• des-ac rbp6 dulc bg2* eup-per bg2 *Eup-pur* k* *Ferr-pic* bro1 fl-ac k* fuma-ac rly4• ger-i rly4• graph bg2 hep k2 hist sp1 hydrang hyos bg2 ign b7.de* indg k* lac-del hrn2• lac-h sze9• lach k* lap-la sde8.de• lyc k* lys bg2 lyss k* m-ambo b7.de merc bg2 merc-c k2* mez bg2 moni rfm1• nit-ac nux-v k* par bg2 petr k* ph-ac b4.de* phos k* pip-n plac-s rly4• plb b7.de *Prun* k* *Puls* k* rheum k* rhus-t ruta bg2 sabin k* sars bg2* senec ptk1 *Sep* k* sil k* squil bg2 staph k* streptoc rly4• suis-em rly4• *Sulph* bg2 symph fd3.de• **Ter** k* thuj k* tritic-vg fd5.de uva k* vanil fd5.de zinc-ar ptk1
  - **accompanied** by | **dysentery** (See RECTUM - Dysentery - accompanied - bladder - pain - burning)
- **bursting** pain: pareir ptk1 *Ruta* b7a.de sanic ptk1 zinc bg1*
- **chronic**: parathyr jl2
- **clawing** pain: led mez valer
- **coition**; after: *All-c* k* sabad sne **Staph** sne
  - **aching**: all-c k*
- **cold**; after taking a: *Dulc* *Eup-pur* *Sars* hr1

Bladder

- **colic**; with (See ABDOMEN - Pain - cramping - accompanied - bladder)
- **constricting** pain: *Berb* k* calad calc-p coc-c con lach *Led* lyc *Mez* nat-sil fd3.de• nit-ac ph-ac k* plb prun *Sars* k* valer zinc
- **convulsive** (See spasmodic)
- **cough** agg.; during: caps k* colch ↓ ip ↓ kreos ↓ *Squil* ↓
  - **pressing** pain: caps colch ip kreos *Squil* b7a.de
  - **stitching** pain: *Caps*
- **cramping**: *Bell* bro1 *Berb* bro1 *Cact* bro1 cann-s bro1 canth bro1 *Caps* bro1 lyc bro1 op bro1 *Polyg-h* bro1 prun bg2* *Sars* bro1 ter bro1 ulm-c jsj8•
  - **accompanied** by | **urine**; bloody: mez ptk1
  - **intermittent**: caul tl1
- **cries** out and twists about (See MIND - Shrieking - pain - bladder)
- **cutting** pain: acon k2* *Aeth* k* am-c k* *Bell* bro1 *Berb* k* calc-p bg2 *Canth* k* caps k* coc-c k* *Coloc* k* con bg2* dig h2* eup-pur k* *Kali-c* k* lach k* *Lyc* k* mang k* mez bg2 nat-c bg2 nux-m bg2* nux-v k* op bg2 pall ptk1 petr b4.de* phos bg2 *Puls* k* ruta fd4.de **Ter** k* thuj k* til ban1• vanil fd5.de
- **cystitis**, in: **Lyc** ↓
  - **pressing** pain: **Lyc** hr1
- **dinner**; after: nux-v ↓
  - **stitching** pain: nux-v
- **distension**; as from: anth
- **dragging**: bamb-a stb2.de• calc bg2 *Canth* *Chel* k* cop k* cycl bg2* dig k* fl-ac k* hyos bg2* lact k* *Lyc* k* mosch k* nat-c h2* psor rheum bg2 ruta bg2 sep sulph bg2*
- **drawing** pain: alum b4.de* aphis *Berb* k* calad k* calc-p bg2* card-m k* coc-c k* dig k* rhod k* sil bg2
  - **upward**: calc-p k* *Phyt*
- **drawn** inward; as if: nux-v b7a.de
- **drinking** agg.: *Canth* k*
- **eating**; after: am ↓ cycl ↓
  - **pressing** pain: am h1 cycl a1
- **flatus**; from: kali-c h2*
- **grasping** pain: led b7.de* valer bg2
- **griping** pain: calc bg2 canth ptk1 coloc bg2
- **jar** agg.: **Bell** k*
- **lancinating** (See stitching)
- **lithotomy**, after: **Staph** k*
- **lying**:
  - **abdomen**; on | **amel**.: chel
  - **agg**.: am-m ↓ fl-ac ↓ *Lyc* ↓ *Nux-v* ↓ ruta ↓
    - **aching**: *Nux-v* k*
    - **burning**: fl-ac k*
    - **pinching** pain | **stitching**; with: am-m
    - **pressing** pain: *Lyc* ruta fd4.de
    - **riding** a horse:
      - **amel**.: *Lyc* ↓
        - **dragging**: *Lyc*
    - **stitching** pain: am-m
  - **back**; on:
    - **agg**.: kreos bg2 thuj bg2
    - **amel**.: uva c1
- **menses**; during: *Nux-v* ↓ **Sep**
  - **aching**: sep k*
  - **burning**: sep k*
  - **cramping**: *Nux-v* b7a.de
- **metrorrhagia**; during: erig vml3•
- **motion**:
  - **agg**.: *Bell* ↓ **Berb** *Canth* ↓ nux-v ↓
    - **pressing** pain: nux-v
    - **sore**: *Bell* berb *Canth*
  - **amel**.: aq-mar mgm•
  - **upward** and downward motion | **step** after urination; at every: ruta k*
- **paroxysmal**: *Caul* chel *Cop* **Puls**
- **piercing** (See stitching)
- **pinching** pain: am-m k* *Berb* lyc k* mez h2* sabad b7a.de sep k*
- **pressing** pain: (↗*Plug; Stones - sensation)* **Acon** k* all-c aloe bro1 alum k* alum-p k2 am-c am-m ang b7.de* ant-t k* aphis **Apis** am k* asar b7.de* *Aur* k* aur-s k2 bell k* berb borx brach k* bry b7.de* *Cact* bro1 *Calc* *Calc-p* calc-sil k2 *Camph* k* cann-s *Canth* k* caps k* carb-an k* *Carb-v* k* carbn-s *Card-m* chel chen-a vml3• *Chim* chin b7.de* chinin-ar coc-c k* coff k* colch k* *Coloc* *Con* k* cop cub cycl dig k* *Dulc* k* *Equis-h* k* *Eup-pur* fl-ac graph hep hyos ign k* *Kali-c* kali-p kali-s kali-sil k2 kreos lach k* lachn lact laur **Lil-t** k* **Lyc** k* mang-p rly4* med mel-c-s bro1 merc-i-r mosch k* nat-c *Nat-m* k* nat-p nat-sil fd3.de• **Nit-ac** bg2 **Nux-v** k* ol-an pall petr *Ph-ac* pop k* *Puls* k* pulx br1* raph rhus-t k* ribo rly4• *Ruta* k* *Sars* k* **Sep** k* sil spig squil k* stann b4.de* *Staph* k* *Sulph* k* symph fd3.de• tarent ter bro1 thuj til tritic-vg fd5.de vanil fd5.de verat k* verb bro1 zinc k* zinc-p k2
  - **cramping**: con h2
- **pressure** agg.: bell k2
- **pulsating** pain: *Dig*
- **rectum**, with pain in: ambr k1*
- **rest**:
  - **agg**.: ter tl1
  - **amel**.: con bro1
- **retention**, with: aur ↓ *Borx* ↓ *Hyos* ↓ ruta ↓ *Sars* ↓
  - **pressing** pain: aur *Borx* *Hyos* ruta fd4.de *Sars*
- **riding** | **carriage**; in a:
  - **agg**.: agar
    - **drawing** pain: agar
  - **horse**; a:
    - **amel**.: lyc ↓
      - **pressing** pain: lyc
- **shooting** (See stitching)
- **short**: caul ↓
  - **cramping**: caul tl1
- **sitting**:
  - **agg**.: card-m con pd mang ↓ tritic-vg fd5.de vanil fd5.de
    - **cutting** pain: mang h2*
    - **drawing** pain: card-m k*
    - **pressing** pain: tritic-vg fd5.de vanil fd5.de
  - **amel**.: bry ↓ con ↓ ign ↓
    - **pressing** pain: bry con ign
    - **stitching** pain: con
  - **crossed** legs; with:
    - **amel**.: sep ↓ zinc ↓
      - **pressing** pain: sep zinc
- **sleep**:
  - **siesta**:
    - **after**:
      - **agg**.: cycl ↓
        - **dragging**: cycl k*
- **smarting**: apis berb k* *Canth* eup-per bg2 eup-pur k* phos k*
- **sore** (= tender): acon *All-c* k* apis ptk1 am *Ars* k* *Bell* k* *Benz-ac* berb brach *Calad* k* *Calc-p* k* cann-s **Canth** k* *Carb-v* *Chim* coff k* coli rly4• dirc **Equis-h** k* eup-pur ger-i rly4• lac-ac lac-d bg1 lac-del hm2• *Lith-c* k* lyc bg2 lycps-v *Merc* nat-ar ox-ac k2 *Puls* k* *Sars* *Sec* k* *Sep* squil sulph k* **Ter** k* thuj k* (non:uran-met k) uran-n
  - **accompanied** by | **dysentery** (See RECTUM - Dysentery - accompanied - bladder - pain - sore)
- **spasmodic**: alum bamb-a stb2.de• *Bell* bro1 *Berb* k* *Canth* k* caps k* *Caul* k* *Chel* coc-c cop k* lith-c bro1 *Lyc* bro1 merc-c bro1 *Pareir* bro1 ph-ac prun puls bro1 *Staph* bro1 ter uva bro1
- **squeezed**; as if: mez b4.de* nat-m bg2 valer b7.de*
- **standing** agg.: am ↓ *Eup-pur* ↓ ferr-p bg1 mang ↓ puls vanil fd5.de
  - **burning**: *Eup-pur* k*
  - **cutting** pain: mang
  - **pressing** pain: am h1
  - **smarting**: *Eup-pur* k*

- **stitching** pain: acon am-m b7a.de amp rly4• ant-t k* aur k* *Berb* calad canth k* caps b7.de* carbn-s cham b7.de* *Chel Clem* coc-c coloc colum-p sze2• *Con* gamb bg2 guaj b4.de* *Kali-c* kali-p kali-s *Lith-c Lyc* k* mosch b7a.de *Nat-m* nux-v b7.de* pall puls b7.de* rhus-t k* sabad k* sinus rly4• spong fd4.de *Sulph* k* thuj
  - **accompanied** by | **respiration**; impeded (See RESPIRATION - Impeded - stitches - bladder)
  - **needles**; as from: bapt bg2
- **stool**:
  - **after**:
    - **agg.**: canth bg2 coloc ↓
      - **pressing** pain: coloc bg2
  - **amel.**: pall ↓
    - **cutting** pain: pall ptk1
  - **before**: alum bg2 carb-v bg2 nat-m bg2 sulph ↓
    - **pressing** pain: *Carb-v Nat-m* sulph h2
  - **during**:
    - **agg.**: apis bg2 arn bg2 *Canth* bg2 erig bg2 ferr bg2 gamb bg2 *Lil-t* bg2 merc-c bg2 senec bg2
      - **stitching** pain: gamb
  - **urging** to:
    - **after**: chin ↓
      - **pressing** pain: chin h1
    - **with** ineffectual urging: aphis ↓ chen-a ↓
      - **pressing** pain: aphis chen-a vml3•
- **straining**; while: phos k2
- **tearing** pain: acon k2 berb k* bry *Kali-c* k* kali-cy a1 kola stb3• nux-v b7.de*
- **tenesmus** (See Tenesmus)
- **touch** agg.: canth bg2 puls bg2
- **turning** over in bed: puls ↓
  - **fall** to side lain on; as if bladder would: puls k*
- **twinging**: lact a1 ter k*
- **twitching**: agar k* lith-c op bg1
- **undulating** (See waves)
- **urination**:
  - **after**:
    - **agg.**: abrom-a ↓ *Acon* ↓ alum ↓ anac ↓ apis bro1 *Arg-n* ↓ arund ↓ asar ↓ atp ↓ bell ↓ berb bro1* bov ↓ *Brach* bry ↓ bufo ↓ *Calc-p* ↓ *Camph* ↓ *Cann-s* ↓ *Canth* bro1 caps mrr1 **Caust** bg2* chim ↓ chin ↓ coch ↓ coli ↓ con ↓ conv ↓ cub ↓ des-ac ↓ *Dig* ↓ dulc ↓ echi bro1 epig bro1 equis-h bro1* fab bro1 *Fl-ac* ↓ guaj ↓ *Kreos* ↓ lac-c ↓ lac-leo ↓ lith-c k* *Lyc* ↓ m-ambo ↓ mag-s ↓ med bro1 merc ↓ merc-act bro1 *Merc-c* ↓ **Nat-c** ↓ *Nat-m* bro1 nat-sil fd3.de• nux-v ↓ oxal-a ↓ petr ↓ petros bro1 ph-ac ↓ phos ↓ plac-s ↓ polyg-h ↓ polyg-pe ↓ prun ↓ puls bro1 rhus-t ↓ ruta bro1 sars bro1 seneg ↓ sep sil ↓ spong fd4.de stann ↓ staph bro1 sulph ↓ *Thuj* bro1 tritic-vg fd5.de uva vh vanil fd5.de zinc ↓
      - **aching**: berb k* calc-p **Canth** k* conv equis-h bro1 *Fl-ac* k* lith-c sulph bro1
      - **burning**: abrom-a ks5 *Acon* bro1 alum anac bro1 apis k* *Arg-n* bro1 atp rly4• bell bg2* *Berb* k* calc-p camph bro1 *Cann-s* bro1 canth k* *Caps* bro1 chim bro1 coch bro1 coli jl2 cub bro1 des-ac rbp6 fab br1* *Fl-ac Kreos* bro1 lac-leo hrn2• *Lyc* k* m-ambo b7.de mag-s bro1 *Merc-c* bro1 **Nat-c** bg2* *Nat-m* bro1 oxal-a rly4• ph-ac bro1 plac-s rly4• puls bro1 rhus-t bro1 seneg bro1 sep sil k* staph bro1 sulph k2* thuj k* tritic-vg fd5.de *Uva* bro1 vanil fd5.de
      - **cutting** pain: *Berb* bro1 bov bro1 calc-p k* camph bro1 *Cann-s* bro1 *Canth* k* *Caps* bro1 coch bro1 cub k* dig bg2 guaj bro1 mag-s bro1 merc-act bro1 nat-c k* *Nat-m* bro1 nux-v bro1 petr petros bro1 phos k* polyg-h polyg-pe vml2• prun bro1 *Sars* bro1 *Thuj* bro1 uva bro1
      - **dragging**: arund bry ruta sulph
      - **empty** bladder; on: calc-p k2 equis-h mrr1
      - **pressing** pain: asar k* berb brach bry bg2 *Calc-p Camph* canth k* chin k* con b4.de* *Dig* k* dulc **Equis-h** lac-c lith-c merc k* nat-m nux-v b7.de* oxal-a rly4• ruta k* sep stann b4.de* sulph k* *Uva* vh zinc b4.de*
        - **deep** in left side: calc-p
      - **stitching** pain: bufo k* guaj b4.de* spong fd4.de
      - **urine**; of slimy: *Uva* ↓

- **urination** – **after** – **agg.** – **urine**; of slimy: ...
  - **burning**: *Uva* br1
    - **amel.**: coc-c bro1 hed bro1 nat-ar ↓ nat-sil ↓ spig ↓
      - **pressing** pain: nat-sil fd3.de• spig h1
      - **sore**: nat-ar
  - **before**: *Acon* bro1 ang ↓ ant-t bg2 *Apis* ↓ arge-pl rwt5• arn ↓ ars ↓ berb k* *Borx* bro1 bry ↓ calc ↓ calc-p ↓ *Camph* ↓ cann-i ↓ cann-s bro1 *Canth* bro1 *Caps* ↓ cartl-s ↓ cham ↓ chel ↓ chim ↓ *Chin* ↓ clem ↓ coch ↓ coff ↓ colch ↓ con ↓ cop ↓ dig ↓ erig bro1 *Fl-ac* fuma-ac rly4• graph ↓ hyos ↓ ignis-alc ↓ kali-c bro1 *Kali-s* ↓ lach ↓ *Lith-c* k* *Lyc* bro1 mag-p ↓ manc mang-p ↓ nat-c ↓ nat-p ↓ *Nux-v* k* pall petr ↓ ph-ac ↓ *Phyt* pilo bro1 prun *Puls* ↓ rheum ↓ *Rhod* ↓ *Rhus-a* bro1 rhus-t ↓ ribo ↓ ruta ↓ sanic bro1 *Sars* bro1 seneg bro1 sep bro1 spig ↓ sulph ↓ thuj ↓ vanil ↓ zinc ↓
    - **aching**: berb *Fl-ac* k* *Nux-v* pall ribo rly4•
    - **burning**: *Apis* ars bro1 *Berb* k* borx bry calc *Camph* bro1 cann-i *Cann-s* bro1 *Canth* k* *Caps* cartl-s rly4• chel clem coch bro1 colch cop bro1 *Fl-ac* fuma-ac rly4• lach nat-c rheum rhod seneg thuj zinc
    - **cutting** pain: bry calc-p k* dig mag-p *Manc* ph-ac phyt sulph k* thuj k* vanil fd5.de
    - **drawing** pain: *Rhod* b4a.de
    - **labor**-like: cham b7.de* chim bg2 coff bg2 graph bg2 puls bg2
    - **pressing** pain: ang k* apis b7a.de arn k* calc-p chim *Chin* k* coff b7.de* con k* graph hyos b7a.de ignis-alc es2• *Kali-s* mang-p rly4• nat-p *Nux-v* k* petr phyt *Puls* k* ribo rly4• ruta *Sep* spig
    - **stitching** pain: apis canth b7.de* *Lith-c* *Manc* puls rhus-a bg2 rhus-t b7.de sep
  - **copious**:
    - **with**: stict ↓
      - **sore**: stict ptk1
  - **delayed**; if desire to urinate is: calc-p ↓ *Lac-ac Lac-c* phos prun *Puls* k* ruta sep *Sul-ac* tub
    - **dragging**: calc-p lac-c
    - **pressing** pain: sep h2
  - **during**:
    - **agg.**: abrom-a ↓ *Acon* bro1 agn hr1 all-c ↓ allox ↓ aloe ↓ alum-sil k2 ambr ↓ amp rly4• anac ↓ anag ↓ androc ↓ ant-c ↓ ant-t k* apis bro1 apoc ↓ *Arg-n* bro1 *Ars* ↓ asar ↓ *Berb* bro1 berb-a bro1 blatta-a bro1 bor-ac bro1 *Borx* ↓ brach *Brucel* ↓ cadm-met tpw6 calc calc-f k2 calc-p camph bro1 cann-i ↓ *Cann-s* bro1 *Canth* b7.de* caps bro1 carb-v carbn-s ↓ cartl-s ↓ caust bg2 cham ↓ *Chim* bro1 *Clem* hr1 coch ↓ *Coloc* bro1 con ↓ *Cop* ↓ cub ↓ cuc-c ↓ cycl ↓ dig k* dor bro1 dulc fd4.de epig ↓ *Equis-h* bro1 erig bro1 ery-a ↓ eup-pur ↓ fl-ac flor-p rsj3• gels ↓ ger-i rly4• glyc ↓ gonotox ↓ graph bro1 hed bro1 hell bg2 helon mtf11 *Hep* ↓ hydrang ↓ hyos ↓ indg ip bg2 kali-bi ↓ kali-c ↓ *Kreos* ↓ lac-leo ↓ *Lach* ↓ lachn ↓ lact ↓ lil-t *Lith-c* bro1 *Lyc* bro1 *Manc* med a1 merc bro1 *Merc-c* ↓ moni ↓ nat-ar ↓ *Nat-c* ↓ *Nat-m* ↓ nit-ac bro1 nux-m ↓ *Nux-v* bro1 oci ↓ *Ol-sant* ↓ olib-sac ↓ op ↓ ox-ac ↓ par ↓ pareir bro1 *Petr* bro1 ph-ac ↓ phos bro1 *Phyt* plac-s ↓ podo ↓ polyg-h ↓ polyg-pe ↓ prun ↓ *Puls* k* rheum ↓ rhod bg2 rhus-a k* ruta bg2 sabal bro1 *Sars* bro1 sec ↓ *Sep* bro1 *Sil* ↓ spig ↓ *Squil* b7a.de staph ↓ streptoc rly4• sul-ac bg2 *Sulph* ↓ syc fmm1• symph fd3.de• *Ter* ↓ thuj ↓ tritic-vg fd5.de uva ↓ verat ↓ verb ↓ *Vesp* ↓ zinc ↓
      - **aching**: carb-v fl-ac
      - **burning**: abrom-a ks5 *Acon* bro1 all-c bro1 allox tpw3 aloe ambr bro1 amp rly4• anac bro1 anag bro1 *Apis* b7a.de* apoc bro1 *Arg-n* bro1 *Ars* bro1 *Berb* bro1 bor-ac bro1 *Borx* bro1 *Brucel* sa3• camph bro1 cann-i bro1 *Cann-s* bro1 *Canth* k* caps k* carb-v bro1 cartl-s rly4• cham k* chim bro1 *Cop* bro1 cub bro1 dig br1* dulc fd4.de epig bro1 *Equis-h* bro1 erig bro1 ery-a bro1 eup-pur k* gels bro1 ger-i rly4• glyc bro1 gonotox jl2 hell bro1 kali-bi kali-c k2 *Kreos* bro1 lac-leo hrn2• lyc k* merc bro1 *Merc-c* bro1 moni rfm1• nit-ac bro1 nux-m c1 nux-v k* oci bro1 *Ol-sant* bro1 olib-sac wmh1 ox-ac bro1 par b7a.de *Pareir* bro1 phos k* plac-s rly4• podo fd3.de• prun puls bro1 rheum k* rhus-a bro1 sars mrr1 *Sep* bro1 staph b7.de* streptoc rly4• *Sulph* bro1 *Ter* k* thuj bro1 tritic-vg fd5.de uva bro1 verb br1* *Vesp* bro1
      - **constricting** pain: cuc-c br1
      - **cutting** pain: *Acon* bro1 androc srj1• ant-c bro1 apis bro1 *Berb* bro1 berb-a bro1 borx bro1 calc camph bro1 *Cann-s* bro1 canth k* coch bro1 coloc bro1 con bro1 dig h2* eup-pur hydrang bro1 kali-c *Nat-c*

Bladder

- **during – agg. – cutting** pain: ... nux-v bro1 *Pareir* bro1 petr b4a.de polyg-h polyg-pe vml2• puls bro1 sec *Ter* thuj k*
  . **accompanied** by | **Lumbar** region; swelling (See BACK - Swelling - lumbar - accompanied - bladder)
  : **dragging**: apis bg2 arg-n cycl op rheum ruta
  : **drawing** pain: calc-p k* dig phyt rhus-a
  : **few** drops pass; after a: berb calc-p **Canth** *Caust* fl-ac lith-c
  : **menses**:
  . **during** | **agg.**: erig zr
  : **pressing** pain: acon b7.de* asar k* berb calc-p *Camph* k* *Chim* con b4.de* cop bro1 dig dulc *Hep* k* hyos *Lach* lachn lact lyc bro1 nat-c *Nat-m* k* **Nux-v** op ph-ac *Sep* bro1 *Sil* spig b7.de* staph b7.de* tritic-vg fd5.de verat k* zinc b4.de*
  : **sore**: ger-i rly4• kali-c k2 nat-ar puls
  : **stitching** pain: carbn-s *Nat-m* k* sep
  : **tearing** pain: kali-c b4.de* nit-ac b4a.de sulph b4a.de
  ⁝ **amel.**: berb mrr1
  ⁝ **beginning** of:
  : **agg.**: acon *Apis* *Ars* cann-s **Canth** *Caust* **Clem** cop manc **Merc** sal-al blc1• symph fd3.de•
  . **stitching** pain: *Manc*
  : **amel.**: prun
  ⁝ **end** of: *Abel* mrr1 apis bro1 bamb-a ↓ *Berb* bro1 cann-s k2* canth bro1 echi bro1 equis-h bro1* *Lith-c* bro1 mag-p ↓ med bro1 merc-act bro1 nat-c mrr1 *Nat-m* bro1 neon srj5• petr ↓ petros bro1 *Puls* bro1* ruta bro1 **Sars** bro1* staph bro1 *Thuj* bro1
  : **cutting** pain: nat-c petr sars thuj
  : **stitching** pain: bamb-a stb2.de•
  . **splinter**; as from a: mag-p bg2
- **not** urinating; when: cit-ac ↓ graph ↓ suis-em ↓
  ⁝ **burning**: cit-ac rly4• graph k2 suis-em rly4•
- **urging**: squil ↓
  ⁝ **pressing** pain: squil bg2
- **urging** to urinate: aids nl2• berb k* calc-p canth ↓ chlam-tr bcx2• eup-pur fl-ac bg2 hell k* *Nux-v* k* pareir mrr1 *Phyt* puls k* pycnop-sa ↓ rhod k* rhus-t ruta k* sul-ac k* vanil fd5.de zinc
  ⁝ **stitching** pain: canth pycnop-sa mrz1 rhus-t
  ⁝ **with** ineffectual urging: *Guaj* ↓
  : **stitching** pain: *Guaj*

\- **urine**; with suppression of: hyos ↓
- **dragging**: hyos

\- **walking**:
- **agg.**: acon k* berb mrr1 bry ↓ con bro1 ign ↓ mang ↓ nat-m ↓ nat-sil ↓ phos a1 prun bro1 *Puls* k* thuj ↓
  ⁝ **cutting** pain: mang thuj k*
  ⁝ **pressing** pain: bry con ign nat-sil fd3.de• phos puls
  ⁝ **smarting**: phos k*
  ⁝ **stitching** pain: con nat-m
- **air**; in open:
  ⁝ **amel.**: ter tl1
  : **burning**: **Ter** k*
  : **rest** agg.: **Ter** ↓
  . **cutting** pain: **Ter**
- **amel.**: ign bro1 ter bro1

\- **warmth** | **amel.**: nux-v mrr1

\- **waves**; in: bamb-a stb2.de•

▽ - **extending** to:

○ • **Back**: caul ↓
  ⁝ **spasmodic**: caul bg1
- **Chest**: alum ↓ caul ↓ murx mrr1
  ⁝ **spasmodic**: alum caul bg1
- **Coccyx**: bamb-a stb2.de• graph bro1 ulm-c jsj8•
- **Kidney**: *Aesc* apis *Canth*
- **Kidneys**: coc-c ↓ oci ↓

\- **extending** to – **Kidneys**: ...
  ⁝ **stitching** pain: coc-c oci
- **Legs**: pareir mrr1
- **Mammae**: murx mrr1
- **Meatus**: *Chim* ↓
  ⁝ **smarting**: *Chim* k*
- **Penis**: bamb-a stb2.de• ruta fd4.de
- **Rectum**: bamb-a stb2.de•
- **Sacral** region: graph bro1
- **Spermatic** cords: anth k* clem bro1 lith-c k* puls bro1 spong bro1
- **Testes**: berb bro1* cain bro1 erig bro1*
- **Thighs**: berb bro1 fl-ac bg1 *Pareir* br1* *Puls* stry a1
- **Upward**: *Murx* mrr1
- **Urethra**: am-m ↓ berb bg1* canth bg1 carbn-s ↓ cycl ↓ dig ↓ eup-pur mtf11 phos ↓ ruta fd4.de thuj ↓
  ⁝ **cutting** pain: *Berb* k*
  ⁝ **stitching** pain: am-m h2 berb carbn-s cycl dig phos thuj
  ⁝ **urination** agg.; during: cycl a1
- **Uterus**: merl tarent k*
- **Vulva**: bamb-a stb2.de•

○ - **Neck** of bladder: acon k* alum k* ant-c ↓ ant-o ant-t ↓ apis arn k* ars bg2 *Atro* ↓ **Bell** *Berb* k* brach k* cact calc-i ↓ *Calc-p* k* *Camph* bg2 *Cann-s* k* **Cann-xyz** bg2 *Canth* k* caps b7a.de* *Carb-v* ↓ *Carbn-s* ↓ carl ↓ cham k* chel ↓ coc-c ↓ con k* *Cop* k* *Dig* k* *Elat* ↓ eup-pur bg2 *Ferr-p* k* graph ↓ guaj k* hyos ign bg2 jatr-c ↓ kali-br ↓ *Kali-c* ↓ lach ↓ lith-c k* lyc k* lyss k* mez mit ↓ *Nux-v* k* op petr bg2 ph-ac ↓ phos ↓ pic-ac k* plb bg2 polyg-h ↓ pop bg2 *Prun* ↓ puls k* ran-b ↓ rhod ↓ ruta k* sabal bg2 sars k* senec bg2 sep k* spong k* stann bg2 *Staph* ↓ *Stry* ↓ suis-em ↓ sul-ac bg2 sulph k* ter *Thuj* ↓ *Zinc* zinc-ar ↓
- **morning**: sulph ↓
  ⁝ **bed** agg.; in: caps ↓
  : **cutting** pain: caps k*
  ⁝ **stitching** pain: sulph
- **forenoon**:
  ⁝ **11** h: sulph ↓
  : **aching**: sulph
- **afternoon**: sulph ↓
  ⁝ **15** h: sulph ↓
  : **aching**: sulph
  ⁝ **stitching** pain: sulph
- **evening**: lyss k* phos ↓
  ⁝ **stitching** pain: phos
- **accompanied** by | **dysuria**: *Agar*
- **aching**: acon calc-p k* con k* cop ign bg1 puls sep k* sulph k*
- **burning**: acon k* *Berb* calc-i k2 **Canth** k* *Cham* k* con k* *Cop* k* *Elat* graph k2 ign mit k* *Nux-v* k* op k* petr k* ph-ac k* plb k* *Prun* k* *Puls* k* ran-b k2 *Staph* k* suis-em rly4• zinc-ar ptk1
- **closure**; at: cann-s ↓ caust ↓ con ↓ dig ↓ med ↓ *Puls* ↓ ruta ↓ *Sars* ↓
  ⁝ **spasmodic**: cann-s k* caust con dig med *Puls* ruta *Sars*
- **coition**:
  ⁝ **amel.**: sul-ac ↓
  : **pressing** pain: sul-ac h2
- **constricting** pain: ant-c carbn-s coc-c *Lyc* *Mez* op petr k*
- **cough** agg.; during: *Caps* ↓
  ⁝ **stitching** pain: *Caps*
- **cutting** pain: berb k* **Canth** k* caps k* *Con* dig br1 *Kali-c* k* lach lyc mez k* nux-v k* op k* petr k* polyg-h k* puls ter
- **drawing** pain: alum berb cop k* jatr-c mez k* rhod
- **ineffectual** effort to urinate, after: *Guaj* ↓
  ⁝ **stitching** pain: *Guaj*
- **lying** | **bent**; lying:
  : **amel.**: staph ↓
  . **burning**: staph k*
  ⁝ **face**; on the:
  : **amel.**: chel ↓

- **lying – face**; on the – **amel.**: ...
  - **stitching** pain: chel
- **neuralgic**: kali-br hr1
- **pressing** during urination, when: *Kali-c* ↓
  - **tearing** pain: *Kali-c* k*
- **pressing** pain: alum apis brach *Canth* carl coc-c jatr-c *Nux-v* sul-ac ter thuj k*
- **rectum**; with pain in: ambr a1
- **sitting**:
  - **agg.**: ter ↓
    - **pressing** pain: ter
  - **amel.**: *Con* ↓
    - **stitching** pain: *Con*
- **smarting**: berb bg2
- **sore**: *Atro* brach *Calc-p* *Carb-v* *Nux-v* *Puls*
- **spasmodic**: jatr-c phos k*
- **stitching** pain: acon ant-t *Bell* berb *Calc-p* *Canth* caps *Carbn-s* *Cham* chel con dig k* *Guaj* jatr-c *Lith-c* *Lyc* k* *Op* *Puls* k* *Stry* sulph k* *Thuj*
- **tearing** pain: canth k* *Kali-c* k* *Nux-v* k*
- **thighs** together, must press: sul-ac ↓
  - **pressing** pain: sul-ac h2
- **twisting**: coc-c k*
- **urination**:
  - **after**:
    - **agg.**: *Apis* apoc calc-p ↓ cann-s canth ↓ con k* dig ↓ fl-ac guaj ↓ merc ↓ nat-m ↓ nux-v petr *Puls* ruta sars k* sep stann sulph ↓ uva ↓
      - **aching**: apoc fl-ac *Sep* k* stann
      - **burning**: *Apis* k* canth merc *Puls* *Sars*
      - **constricting** pain: sulph
      - **last** drops are voided; when: med sars
      - **pressing** pain: con nat-m ruta stann h2 uva vh
      - **sore**: calc-p
      - **stitching** pain: con dig guaj
  - **agg.**: petr ↓
    - **constricting** pain: petr a1
  - **amel.**: ferr-p k2
  - **attempting** to urinate, on: *Cop*
  - **before**: apis ↓ arn ↓ calc-p k2 canth chim ↓ dig ↓ *Lith-c* k* *Nux-v* k* ph-ac ↓ *Phyt* ↓ *Puls* ↓
    - **cutting** pain: *Canth* ph-ac
    - **pressing** pain: apis arn calc-p chim *Nux-v* *Phyt* *Puls*
    - **stitching** pain: apis *Canth* dig
  - **delayed**; if desire to urinate is: lac-ac ↓ prun ↓
    - **pressing** pain: lac-ac
    - **stitching** pain: prun
  - **during**:
    - **agg.**: acon ↓ *Aloe* ↓ *Apis* ↓ berb ↓ *Cann-s* ↓ **Canth** ↓ carbn-s ↓ *Cham* ↓ chin ↓ *Cop* ↓ epig ↓ ign ↓ kali-c ↓ nux-v b7.de* petr ↓ ph-ac ↓ polyg-h ↓ prun ↓ puls ↓ *Ran-b* ↓ rhus-a ↓ stann ↓ staph b7a.de sul-ac ↓ sulph ↓ thuj ↓
      - **burning**: acon k* *Aloe* k* *Apis* k* berb *Cann-s* mrr1 **Canth** *Cham* k* chin bg2 *Cop* epig br1 **Nux-v** k* petr k* ph-ac prun puls *Ran-b* k* staph h1* sul-ac thuj k*
      - **cutting** pain: canth k* kali-c polyg-h
      - **pressing** pain: ign rhus-a stann thuj
      - **stitching** pain: carbn-s sulph
      - **tearing** pain: kali-c k* *Nux-v* k*
    - **beginning** of:
      - **agg.**: *Clem* kali-i ↓ manc ↓ petr ↓
        - **constricting** pain: kali-i
        - **cutting** pain: manc petr
    - **end** of: *Cann-s* caust con dig med **Nat-c** ↓ petr ↓ *Puls* ruta **Sars** st sulph ↓ thuj ↓
      - **cutting** pain: **Nat-c** bg2 petr k* sars sulph thuj c1
  - **not** urinating; when: acon ↓ berb ↓ canth ↓ *Cham* ↓ lith-c mrr1
    - **burning**: acon k* berb canth

Pain – Neck of bladder – **urination – not** urinating; when: ...
  - **stitching** pain: *Cham*
  - **urging** to urinate: anth bell berb *Calc-p* canth dig ferr-p guaj k2 sep spong
- **walking**:
  - **agg.**: con ↓ ign
    - **stitching** pain: con h2
  - **air** agg.; in open: con ↓ ign ↓ mez ↓ nux-v ↓ puls ↓ thuj ↓
    - **cutting** pain: mez k* thuj
    - **pressing** pain: con ign nux-v puls
- **walking** agg., sitting amel.: con ↓ ign ↓
  - **pressing** pain | **stitches**; with: con ign
- ▽ **extending** to:
  - **Penis**; end of: dig ↓ phos ↓ stry ↓
    - **stitching** pain: dig phos h2 stry
  - **Thighs**:
    - **urination** agg.; after: *Puls* ↓
      - **spasmodic**: *Puls* k*
  - **Urethra**; through: **Canth** ↓ suis-em ↓
    - **burning**: **Canth** k* suis-em rly4•
    - **cutting** pain: **Canth** k*
- ○ **And** anus: lyc ↓
  - **stitching** pain: lyc

- **Region** of bladder: *Chel* ↓ thuj ↓
  - **boring** pain: thuj k*
  - **stabbing**: *Chel* k*

PARALYSIS: acon k* agar *Alum* k* alum-p k2 alum-sil k2 *Ant-c* b7a.de apoc bro1 arg-n *Arn* k* **Ars** k* ars-s-f k2 aur k* *Bell* k* *Cact* k* *Camph* k* cann-i bro1 *Cann-s* k* *Canth* k* *Carb-an* carb-v carbn-s **Caust** k* *Cic* k* coloc b4a.de con bro1* *Cupr* dig bro1 **Dulc** k* *Equis-h* bro1 eucal bro1 *Ferr* bro1 *Ferr-p* c2* form **Gels** k* hell k* helon hep k2 *Hyos* k* kali-p *Lach* k* lat-m bnm6• *Laur* k* lyc b4a.de m-aust b7.de* mag-m *Merc* morph bro1 mur-ac k* narcot c2 *Nat-m* b4a.de nat-p **Nux-v** k* **Op** k* **Petr** b4a.de phos *Plb* k* psor k* *Puls* k* *Rheum* b7a.de *Rhus-t* k* *Sec* k* *Sil* staph *Stram* k* *Stry* k* stry-xyz c2 *Sulph* tab k* thuj k* **Zinc** k* zinc-p k2

- **daytime**: thuj
- **delivery**; no desire after●: **Ars** k* canth **CAUST** k ●* ferr *Hyos* kreos nux-v phos zinc
- **forcible** retention seems to paralyze the bladder: *Ars* *Canth* **Caust** k* *Gels* hell hyos *Rhus-t* *Ruta*
- **hysterical** subjects, in: **Zinc** k*
- **laparotomy**, after: op ptk1
- **old** people; in: **Ars** k* bell st camph st *Cann-s* canth st *Caust* st *Cic* con *Equis-h* *Gels* kali-p lach st lyc st mur-ac st nat-m st nux-v ptk op st phos st *Sec* sil st *Sulph* st thuj
- **over-distension**, after: ars *Canth* **Caust** k* hell k* hyos *Nux-v* *Rhus-t* *Ruta* stry *Sulph*
- **sensation** of | **urination** agg.; during: visc sp1
- ○ **Neck** of bladder: acon bg2 **Ars** bg2 bell bg2 cic bg2 *Dulc* bg2 *Hyos* bg2 lach bg2 laur bg2
- **Sphincter**: ars bro1 *Bell* b4a.de* canth b7a.de *Caust* bro1 *Chin* b7a.de cic bro1 *Dig* b4a.de dulc b4a.de* *Hyos* bro1 ign bro1 lach bro1 laur bro1 *Merc* b4a.de nat-m bro1 op bro1* **Petr** b4a.de **Puls** b7a.de *Sec* b7a.de *Seneg* b4a.de *Spig* b7a.de sulph bro1 thuj bro1 *Zinc* bro1

PARALYTIC weakness: (↗*Weakness*) cod k* *Morph* k* op phys mrr1 **Sulph**

- **sensation** of, so that he fears he will wet the bed: | **evening**: alum
- ○ **Neck** of bladder: agar atro bar-c cadm-s canth cub op stram
- **Sphincter**: agar apoc *Bell* canth chlf hr1* *Gels* jug-r *Phos* plan puls *Tab*

PLUG; sensation of a: (↗*Pain - pressing*) anac bg2*

POLYPI: ant-c ars bro1 **Calc** k* con k* graph lyc merc k* phos puls k* sil k* staph bg2 **Teucr** k* thuj k*

PREGNANCY agg.; during: *Bell* bro1 *Canth* bro1 *Caust* bro1 equis-h bro1 ferr bro1 nux-v bro1 pop br1* *Puls* bro1 staph bro1

Bladder

PRESSURE on bladder; feeling of (See Heaviness)

PROLAPSUS: bell-p jl1 chim vml4 hyos a3* puls kkv1 pyrus bro1 ruta hs2 staph al1* [stann stj2]
- **sensation** of: pyrus a1
- ○ - **Vagina**; into (= cystocele) staph bro1

PULSATION: berb canth k* *Dig* k* dulc b4.de* sabin k2
- **urination** agg.; before: *Dig* k*
- ○ - **Neck** of bladder: epig bg1

RELAXATION: ferr mtf33 mur-ac bg2 tub jl2

RETENTION of urine: (↗*Urination - retarded; KIDNEYS - Suppression)* **Acon** k* aesc agar k* agar-ph c2 ail tl1 all-c allox sp1 alum k* alum-p k2 alum-sil k2 **Am-c** amyg-p br1 androc bnm2• anis c1 ant-t k* anthraco c1 ap-g k* **Apis** k* *Apoc* arbin br1 arg-met **Arn** k* **Ars** k* *Ars-i* ars-s-f k2 arum-t tl1 aspar atro aur k* aur-ar k2 aur-i k2 aur-s k2 *Bar-c* bar-i k2 bar-m bar-s k2 **Bell** k* bism k* *Borx* botul jl2 **Bry** b7a.de bufo *Cact* *Calc* k* calc-i k2 calc-s calc-sil k2 *Camph* k* *Cann-i* k* *Cann-s* k* **Canth** k* *Caps* k* carb-v b2.de* carbn-s card-m **Caust** k* chel k* *Chim* k* chin k* chinin-ar *Cic* k* cimic **Cina** b7a.de cinnb *Clem* k* coc-c cocc b7.de coch *Colch* k* coleus-a mtf11 *Coloc* k* **Con** k* cop k* *Crot-h* k* *Cupr* k* cycl bg2 *Dig* k* dios *Dulc* k* elaps ephin-m rwp1 equis-h c2* eup-pur c2* *Euph* k* ferr-m a1* **Gels** graph k* *Hell* k* helon *Hep* k* *Hyos* k* hyper ign k* *Iod* k* *Ip* k* iris ix bnm8• kali-ar kali-bi bg2* *Kali-chl* kali-i kali-m k2 kreos lach b2.de* lat-h bnm5• lat-m bnm6• *Laur* k* led k* loxo-lae bnm12• loxo-recl bnm10• **Lyc** k* m-arct b2.de mag-m k2* *Mag-p* mag-s medus c2 **Meny** bg2 merc k* merc-c k* merc-cy mez k* morph k* mur-ac k* *Nit-ac* k* nux-m **Nux-v** k* olib-sac wmh1 **Op** k* ox-ac **Pareir** k* petr ph-ac k* phos phys mrr1 *Phyt* *Plb* k* *Polyg-h* *Prun* k* *Puls* k* ran-s *Rhus-t* k* ruta k* sabal ptk2 *Sabin* k* *Sars* k* *Sec* k* **Sel** bg2 sep k* sil k* solid c2 squil b2.de* stann k* *Staph* k* stigm c2* *Stram* k* stry bro1 sul-ac sul-i k2 *Sulph* k* **Tarent** **Ter** k* thal-xyz srj8• *Thuj* tritic-vg fd5.de tub urt-u vanil fd5.de *Verat* k* *Zinc* k* zinc-p k2 zing c2 [erech stj]
- **evening**: borx ruta fd4.de
- **night**:
  - **midnight** | **after**, 3-6 h: pareir
- **accompanied** by:
  - **constipation** (See RECTUM - Constipation - accompanied - urination - retention)
  - **paraplegia** (See GENERALS - Paralysis - paraplegia - accompanied - urine)
  - **sleepiness**: ter ptk1
  - **thirst**: mez b4a.de
  - ○ **Prostate** gland; swelling of (See enlarged)
  - **Tongue** | **dirty** discoloration: *Camph* kr1*
- **alcohol**; abuse of: kreos bg2
- **beer**; after: *Nux-v* k*
- **children**; in: *Acon* **Apis** *Art-v* atra-r bnm3• bell *Benz-ac* calc *Caust* *Cop* *Dulc* eup-pur ferr-p *Gels* ip *Lyc* b4a.de *Op* tritic-vg fd5.de
  - **cold**; every time child takes a: **Acon** cop *Dulc* puls sulph
  - **cries** all night from retention; child: acon hr1*
  - **infants**: benz-ac ptk1
  - **newborns**: **Acon** k* *Apis* k* *Ars* benz-ac *Camph* k* *Canth* *Caust* erig hyos *Lyc* nux-v j5.de puls k*
    - **passion** of the nurse; after: *Op* k*
  - **nurslings** | **fright** of the mother; after: op ptk1*
- **chill**; during: apis k* arn k* canth k* hyos k* lyc k* op k* puls k* stram k*
- **cholera**; during: *Camph* k* *Canth* k* carb-v ptk1 lach op **Verat** k*
- **chronic**: *Calc* *Iod*
- **clots**; from:
  - ○ **Bladder**; in the: cact caust
  - **Vagina**; in the: cact k2 coc-c
- **cold**:
  - **air** agg.: acon bro1 *Caust* *Dulc* bro1 gels bro1 rhus-t bro1
  - **pavement** agg.; standing on a cold: *Calc* carb-v ptk1
- **cold**; after taking a: *Acon* *Caust* k* cob bg2 *Cop* *Dulc* ign bg2 olnd bg2 *Puls* sulph
- **colic**: arn *Coloc* **Plb** k* thuj k*

Retention of urine: ...
- **company**; unable to pass urine in presence of: (↗*Urination - retarded - long - others; MIND - Company - aversion - strangers - urination)* acon bg2 aq-mar skp7*• dulc bg2 **Nat-m** k* tarent pd tritic-vg fd5.de
- **concussion**; from: (↗*jar)* arn k2
- **congestion** of brain: bell k2
- **cough** agg.; during: ip b7.de*
- **delivery**:
  - **after**; immediately: **Acon** bg2* *Apis* b7a.de* *Arn* k* **Ars** k* *Bell* k* bry qqh canth **Caust** k* *Equis-h* k* *Hyos* k* ign k* lyc *Nux-v* *Op* k* *Puls* k* rhus-t sec sep stann *Staph* k* stram k*
  - **during**: plb ptk1
- **discharges**; from suppressed | **or** eruptions: camph bro1 caust bg2
- **dribbling**, with (See Urination - dribbling)
- **dysentery**: **Arn** k* merc
- **enlarged** prostate, from: *Apis* bell benz-ac *Cact* canth *Chim* k* *Chin* k* con **Dig** k* ferr hyos kali-i merc-d morph bro1 pareir k* *Puls* *Sabal* ptk2* sep **Staph** k* stram *Tritic* sne zinc bro1*
- **exertion** agg.; after: **Arn** k* **Caps** k* **Rhus-t** k*
- **fever**; during: ferr-p bro1* *Op* b7a.de* puls b7a.de
- **fright**; after: acon k* bell k2 **Op** k*
- **headache**; during: con hr1
- **hysteria**; during: ign bro1* **Zinc** k*
- **illness**; in acute: ferr-p ptk1 lyc ptk1 op ptk1
- **infants**; in newborn (See children - newborns)
- **inflammatory**: *Acon* bg2* bell bg2 cann-i bro1 **Cann-xyz** bg2 **Canth** bg2* cop bg2 dig bg2 dulc bg2 *Merc* bg2 **Nux-v** bg2* *Puls* bg2* sabin bg2 sars bg2 sulph bg2
- **injuries**; after: arn k2
- **jar** agg.: (↗*concussion)* arn k2
- **locomotor** ataxia: *Arg-n* k*
- **menses**; during: ham kali-bi k*
- **music** | **amel.**: tarent ptk1
- **newborns** (See children - newborns)
- **old** people; in: | **men**; old: *Caust* st *Con* st lyc st op st pareir st plb st *Puls* st sars st sep st sil st *Solid* k* staph st sulph st *Ter* st *Zinc* st
- **operation**; after: **Caust** bro1*
- **over**-distension, after (See Paralysis - over-distension)
- **pain**; during: con ptk1
- **painful**: (↗*Tenesmus)* acon k* *Arn* k* ars *Aur* k* bell borx k* calc-p **Canth** k* caps k* **Caust** k* cop crot-h cupr k* *Dulc* k* *Lyc* *Nit-ac* **Nux-v** k* *Op* *Pareir* psor al2 *Puls* k* ruta fd4.de sabin *Sars* sul-ac *Ter* terebe ktp9
  - **abdomen**; when pain in: cham h1
  - **urging**, while lying on the back; with: *Puls*
  - ○ **Rectum** and anus; with pain in: cop a3*
- **painless**: nit-ac ptk1
- **paralytic**: acon bg2 **Ars** bg2 bell bg2 caust bg2* cic bg2 cina bg2 *Dulc* bg2* *Hyos* bg2* lach bg2 laur bg2 nux-v bro1 *Op* bro1 *Plb* bro1 stry bro1
- **perspiration**; from suppressed: acon bg2 *Apis* bg2 arn bg2 ars bg2 camph bg2 *Canth* bg2 colch k2 dulc bg2 hyos bg2 *Lyc* bg2 **Op** bg2 *Puls* bg2 stram bg2 sulph bg2
- **pregnancy** agg.; during: equis-h ptk1 hep b4a.de*
- **sensation** of retention:
  - **contraction** of sphincter; by: sulph
  - **coughing**; with urging on: ip h1
  - **urination** agg.; after: berb ptk1 hep ptk1
- **ship**; on board a: *M-arct* b7a.de
- **sitting** bent backwards amel.: (↗*Urination - retarded - sitting - only; Urination - retarded - sitting - only - backward)* carb-v bg2 kreos bg2 mag-m bg2 *Zinc* k*
- **spasmodic**: bell bg2 *Canth* bg2 caps bg2 caust bg2 cina bg2 coloc bg2 ign bg2 lach bg2 lyc bg2 **Nux-v** bg2 *Op* bg2* *Puls* bg2 rhus-t bg2 ter tl1 verat bg2
- **spastic** (See spasmodic)
- **standing**; cannot pass urine while: zinc mrr1
  - **cold** pavement; on (See cold - pavement)
- **urging**; without: *Ars* ptk1 *Caust* ptk1 phos ptk1 plb ptk1
- **urination** agg.; after: kali-bi ptk1 mag-m ptk1
- **urine** passed by drops (See Urination - dribbling)
- **walking** | **amel.**: mag-m mrr1
- **water**; noise of | **amel.**: hyos ptk1 lyss ptk1 tarent ptk1 zinc ptk1

- **weakness**; from: ter bro1
- **weather** | **cold**, wet: *Acon* ptk1 *Dulc* ptk1 gels ptk1 rhus-t ptk1
- **wet** | **feet**; after getting wet: *All-c Rhus-t*
- **whistling** | **amel.**: cycl ptk1 tarent ptk1

RHEUMATIC affections: clem k* dulc merl k*

SENSATION absent (See Urination - urging - absent)

SENSITIVE: *Acon* bro1 *Bell* bro1 berb bro1 *Calad* b7a.de *Canth* b7a.de* coc-c bro1 con mtf11 *Equis-h* bro1 eup-pur bro1 merc-c bro1 *Puls* b7a.de sars bro1 *Squil* b7a.de stict bro1 *Ter* bro1

SHOCKS; electric:
▽ - **extending** to | **Thigh**; right: fl-ac k*

SITTING:
- **agg.**: card-m ptk1
- **amel.**: con ptk1

SPASM: *Ant-t* k* arn b7a.de asaf k* *Bell* k* berb k* borx br1 calad k* *Calc* k* *Camph* b7.de* *Cann-s* b7a.de *Canth* k* *Caps* k* caul k* caust b4a.de chim chin clem bg2 *Coc-c Colch* b7a.de con bg2 *Cop* dig eup-pur *Gels* k* guar k* hell k* hydr hyos b7a.de* *Ip* k* laur b7a.de merc bg2 *Nux-v* k* op k* petr bg2 *Ph-ac* k* phos bg1 phys bg2 *Prun* k* *Puls* k* *Sars* k* *Sep* k* stry br1 tarent ter uva *Vib* k* zinc k*
- **urination**:
  - **after** | **agg.**: asaf k* *Prun* puls sars bg2 sec bg2
  - **before**: manc uva
  - **during** | **agg.**: *Asaf* k* cann-s k* carbn-s colch op plb bg2

○ - **Neck** of bladder: arg-n **Arn** k* bell bg2* cact cann-s *Colch* k* cop hyos k* kali-br k* mag-p k* polyg-h bg2 *Prun* k* puls ruta
  - **night**: prun k*
  - **anxiety**; from: bell k2
  - **operations** for polypi; after: *Bell* bro1 coloc bro1 *Hyper* bro1
  - **sexual** excesses; after: *Nux-v* k*
  - **shock**; from: bell k2
  - **stricture**, spasmodic: mag-p ruta
  - **urination**; during | **end** of: cann-s k2

SPASMODIC action of: calc-p tarent zinc-p k2

STONES in bladder: all-s hr1 *Ambr* b7.de* ant-c k* ant-t b7.de* apoc hr1 arg-n k* ars hr1 aspar hr1 bell hr1 **Benz-ac** k* **Berb** k* cact k* cal-ren c2 **Calc** k* *Cann-s* b7a.de* **Canth** k* carb-v hr1 card-m k* *Chin* k* *Coc-c* k* *Coch* hr1 coff-t hr1 colch k* coloc hr1 cupr hr1 dig hr1 epig c2 equis-h bwa3 *Eup-per* graph hr1 hydrang c2 kali-c b4a.de *Kalm* hr1 kreos hr1 *Lach* k* lipp c2 *Lith-c* **Lyc** k* *Meny* b7.de* merc b4a.de *Merc-c* b4a.de mez k* *Mill* k* naja nat-m k* nat-s k* *Nit-ac* k* *Nux-m* k* *Nux-v* k* oxyd br1 pall hr1 *Pareir* k* *Petr* k* *Phos* k* *Puls* k* *Raph* rhod b4a.de *Ruta* k* **Sars** k* **Sep** k* *Sil* k* sul-ac b4a.de sulph b4a.de tarent k* thuj k* zinc k* [*Lith-m* stj2 *Lith-p* stj2 *Lith-s* stj2]
- **gravel** (See URINE - Sediment - sand - gravel)
- **operation**; after: *Arn Calen* cham chin cupr mill c1* nux-v **Staph** k* verat
- **sensation** of a stone: (↗*Heaviness; Pain - pressing*) puls k* **Sep** vh

STRESS INCONTINENCE (See Urination - involuntary)

SUPPURATION: (↗*URINE - Sediment - purulent*) *Acon* b7a.de *Canth* k* sars *Staph* b7a.de ter

SWASHING: acon bg2
- **urination** agg.; during: acon b7.de*

SWOLLEN: (↗*Distended*) apoc k* atro k* bell k* chlor k* dig k* gad a1 *Hell* b7a.de kali-bi k* *Kali-i* k* merc-c k* op k* ox-ac k* petr k* plb k* *Puls* b7a.de tarent k*
- **sensation** of | **urination**; without: allox sp1 bufo bg2

○ - **Neck**; region of: *Puls* k*

TENESMUS: (↗*Retention - painful*) *Acon* k* **Agar** k* *Alum* k* alum-p k2 alum-sil k2 am-c k* am-m k* anac *Ang* k* anil a1 *Ant-c* k* *Apis* k* *Arn* k* **Ars** k* aur-m k* *Bell* k* benz-ac bro1 bit-ar wht1• calc k* calc-sil k2 *Camph* k* *Cann-s* k* **Canth** k* *Caps* k* carbn-s caust cham bro1 *Chim* k* *Clem* k* cob-n sp1 *Coc-c* k* colch k* *Coloc* k* *Con* b4a.de cop k* *Croc* b7a.de crot-h k* cub k* *Cupr* cupr-ar hr1 **Dig** k* dulc ptk1 elaps epig bro1 equis-h bro1* ery-a bro1* eug k* *Eup-pur* bro1 fab br1* ferr k* ferr-ar ferr-i k* ferr-p k* fil a1 *Gels* k* hydrang bro1 hyos k* hyper hr1 *Ip* k* *Lach* k* **Lil-t** k* *Lith-c* k* *Lyc* k*

Tenesmus: ...
mand sp1 *Med* k* *Merc* k* **Merc-c** k* *Mez* k* morph k* *Mur-ac* k* nat-c *Nit-ac* k* *Nux-m* k* **Nux-v** k* oci-sa sp1 ol-an *Onis* a1* op k* par b7.de **Pareir** k* phos phys k* plan k* **Plb** k* *Podo* k* polyg-h pop k* **Prun** k* psor k* **Puls** k* pyrog k2* rham-cal br1* rheum *Rhus-t* k* sabad k* *Sabal* bro1 sabin k* sarr a1* *Sars* k* *Senec* k* sep k* *Sil* k* squil k* staph bro1 *Stigm* bro1 sul-ac hr1 sulph ptk1 tarent k* tax k* **Ter** k* teucr hr1 **Thuj** k* *Tub* jl2 ust uva k* verat k* vesi bro1 viol-t k* x-ray sp1
- **morning**: par k* *Senec* k*
- **forenoon**: agar phos
- **evening** | **walking** in open air agg.: *Lith-c*
- **night**: ant-c k* lith-c *Merc* k*
  - **midnight**:
    - ⁝ **after** | **4** h: am-m
  - **lying** down agg.: lyc
- **children**; in: acon b7a.de *Canth* b7a.de cham b7a.de
- **fever**; during: nux-v bro1
- **ice-cold** feet; with: *Elaps*
- **menses**; during: **Tarent** k*
- **painful**: acon b7a.de *Arn* b7a.de *Canth* b7a.de **Puls** b7a.de
- **sitting** agg.: ter k*
- **stool**:
  - **after** | **agg.**: canth k*
  - **during** | **agg.**: *Alum* canth bro1 **Caps** k* lil-t k* *Merc* *Merc-c* bro1* **Nux-v** k* *Rhus-t Staph* k*
  - **urging** to stool; with (See Urination - urging - painful - stool - urging)
- **urination**:
  - **after** | **agg.**: alum h2* ang b7.de* arg-n bro1 *Camph* bro1 *Canth* bro1 chim bro1 colch hr1 cub hr1 epig br1* *Equis-h* bro1 ery-a bro1 fab bro1 ferr guaj b4.de lith-c bro1 mur-ac b4.de* nit-ac bro1 ozone sde2• par b7.de *Pop* bro1 *Puls* bro1 ruta bro1 sabal bro1 sars bro1 squil k* *Staph* bro1 stigm bro1 sulph bro1 trif-p a1
  - **during**:
    - ⁝ **agg.**: ang a1 arn a1 chin-b hr1 *Clem* hr1 coc-c hr1 colch hr1 med br1 op a1 phys a1 *Tub* jl2
    - ⁝ **painful**: arn br1
  - **urging** to urinate | **with**: mur-ac a1
- **vomiting**, purging and micturition: **Crot-h** k*

▽ - **extending** to | **Rectum**: canth ptk1 caps k2* erig ptk1 merc-c ptk1

○ - **Neck** of bladder: acon bg2 arn bg2* **Canth** bg2*

TENSION: **Acon** k* ant-t k* coc-c k* eup-pur k* nux-v k* phos h2*
- **cord**; as of a: thuj bg2

THICKENING of walls of: dulc k* pareir

TUMORS: *Anil* br1 *Calc* k* tarax k13 thuj sne

TWISTING sensation: agar bell k*
- **turning**; and: bell b4.de*

TWITCHING in neck, during urination: op k*

ULCERATION: all-s k* arg-n k2 canth k* *Eup-pur* k* hep k2 *Merc-c* merc-i-r k* petr bg2* puls bg2* ran-b k* sep bg2* *Staph* b7a.de sulph bg2*
- **calculi**, caused by: all-s k*
- **symptoms** of: *Hydr*

UNEASINESS: cedr ptk1 verat-v ptk1

URINARY complaints: asc-c br1 *Cain* br1 *Cann-s* br1 *Canth* br1 chim br1 clem br1 coli jl2 con br1 *Cop* br1 *Cub* br1 cycl br1 dor br1 ery-a br1 eucal br1 gali br1 jac-c br1 lam br1 **Lyc** br1 *Mag-s* br1 naphtin br1 ol-sant br1 pareir br1 *Petros* br1 physal-al br1 pip-m br1 *Prun* br1 pulx br1 rhus-a br1 sabal br1 santin br1 sars br1 *Sel* br1 senec br1 spirae br1 staph br1 stigm br1 *Ter* br1 *Thuj* br1 thymol br1 trib br1 tus-p br1 uva br1

Bladder

- **accompanied** by:
  - **anemia** (See GENERALS - Anemia - accompanied - urinary)
  - **impotency** (See impotency; MALE GENITALIA/SEX - Erections - wanting - accompanied - urinary)
  - O **Heart** complaints and difficult respiration: **Laur** k* *Lycps-v* k*
- **gonorrhea**; after: fab br1
- **pregnancy** agg.; during: kali-chl br1

URINATION:

- **abortion** agg.; after: rheum ptk1
- **complaints** of urination:
  - **accompanied** by:
    - **constipation**: lyc bg2
    - **nausea**: ip bg2
    - **pain** in general: phos bg2
    - **respiration**; complaints of (See RESPIRATION - Complaints - accompanied - urination)
    - **Extremities**; lameness of: lyc bg2
    - **Stomach**; pain in: ip bg2
- **difficult** (See dysuria)
- **dribbling** (= by drops): abel dg acon bg2* aesc bro1 *Agar* k* *All-c* all-s alum k2 am-m anan androc srj1• ang k* ant-c k* ant-t apis k* *Arg-n* *Arn* k* ars k* ars-i ars-s-f k2 atro aur aur-ar k2 aur-i k2 aur-m k2 aur-s k2 *Bell* k* borx bro1 bov k* brom bry *Cact* cadm-met tpw6 calc b2.de* *Camph* k* cann-i c1* *Cann-s* k* **Canth** k* caps k* carb-an b2.de* carbn-s *Caust* k* cham b2.de* chel chim chin b2.de* cic **Clem** k* coff k* colch k* coloc b2.de* *Con* k* *Cop* k* *Dig* k* *Dros* k* *Dulc* k* equis-h k* *Ery-a* euph k* gamb *Gels* graph k* guaj b2.de* ham hell k* hep k2* *Hyos* inul br1* iod kali-ar kali-c k* *Kali-chl* kali-m k2* kali-p kali-s kali-sil k2 kreos b2.de* *Lac-d* lach led b2.de* **Lil-t** k* *Lyc* k* **M-aust** b2.de* *Mag-m* k* mag-s med jl2 **Merc** k* **Merc-c** k* nat-m nit-ac b2.de* *Nux-m* k* **Nux-v** k* olib-sac wmh1 op b2.de* ox-ac *Pareir* k* petr k* ph-ac k* phos pic-ac k* **Plb** k* polyg-h k* prun k* psor k2 **Puls** k* rheum b2.de* *Rhus-t* k* ruta b2.de* *Sabal* bro1 *Sabin* k* samb b2.de* *Sars* k* sec k* sel ptk1* sil k* spig k* spong b2.de* *Staph* k* staphycoc rly4• *Stram* k* sul-i k2 **Sulph** k* tab k* taosc iwa1• tarent **Ter** k* thuj k* tril-p c1 *Verb* vip zinc k* zinc-p k2
  - **morning**: coff
  - **afternoon**:
    - **16** h: **Lyc**
    - **rising** from sitting agg.: spig
  - **evening**: lyc zinc
    - **lying** agg.: lyc
  - **night**: caust lyc ox-ac
    - **staining** shirt red; drops flow from urethra: lachn
  - **accompanied** by | **cystitis** (See Inflammation - accompanied - urination - dribbling)
  - **air** agg.; in open: lycpr br1
  - **angry**; when: puls mtf33
  - **children**; in: ferr mtf33
  - **delivery**; after: *Arn* k* tril-p br1*
    - **forceps** delivery: thlas ptk1
  - **enlarged** prostate, with: *Aloe* arn bar-c bell cop *Dig* mur-ac *Nux-v* k* pareir k* petr *Puls* sabal sel sep *Staph*
  - **involuntary**: *Agar* *All-c* alum k2 apis bg2 *Arg-n* **Arn** k* *Ars* k* ars-i bar-c bg2 *Bell* k* brom bry *Camph* **Canth** k* **Caust** k* chinin-ar **Clem** k* coc-c *Dig* k* *Dulc* *Erig* br1 *Gels* k* *Hyos* iod jug-r *M-aust* b7.de mag-m bg2 mag-p bg2 *Mur-ac* *Nux-v* op bg2 *Petr* k* plat *Puls* k* *Rhus-t* santin *Sel* k* *Spig* k* *Staph* k* *Stram* *Sulph* *Tab* taosc iwa1• thuj k* uran-n bg2 *Verb* zinc k*
    - **day** and night: *Arg-n* ars gels iod *Nux-v* petr *Verb*
    - **angry**; when: puls ptk1
    - **boys**, in: *Rhus-t*
    - **delayed**, if: plan
    - **delivery**; after: *Arn*
    - **drop** flows on making the greatest effort; bladder distended and no pain, but not a: gels
    - **menses**; during: cact *Canth*
    - **stool** agg.; after: chinin-ar

Urination – dribbling: ...

  - **old** persons; in: all-c ptk1 bar-c ptk1 cic ptk1 con ptk1 equis-h ptk1 nux-v ptk1
  - **perpendicularly**, urine drops out: agar bg2 alumn k2* arg-n bg2 bell bg2 caust bg2 gels bg2 **Hep** k* kreos bg2 mur-ac bg2 nat-m bg2 sel bg2 sep bg2
  - **retention**, with: acon alum k2* *Arg-n* k* arn bell canth **Caust** k* chim ery-a *Gels* k* **Nux-v** k* op *Pareir* sabin sep staph sulph
  - **rising** from sitting agg.: spig k*
  - **scalding** water; as if drops of: **Canth** mrr1
  - **season** | **winter**: rhus-t ptk1
  - **sensation** of:
    - **rest** agg.: sep ptk1
    - **urination** agg.; after: sep bg2 thuj b4.de*
  - **sitting**:
    - **agg.**: merc-c ptk1 *Puls* k* *Sars* k*
      - **standing** urine passes freely; when: *Sars*
    - **amel.**: caust bg3
  - **spurts**; then: caps ptk1 thlas ptk1
  - **stitching** in glans penis, with: pareir thuj
  - **stool**:
    - **after** | **agg.**: caust kali-br laur nat-c ptk1 nat-m petr *Sel* k* stram sumb
    - **during** | **agg.**: coloc ptk1 *Kali-br* hr1
    - **pressure** in rectum; with: nat-m k*
  - **urination** | **after** | **agg.**: (↗ *involuntary - urination - after - agg.*) agar k* ammc vh1 ant-c apoc arg-n k* bar-c k* benz-ac bro1 brom k* bry k* calc k* calc-p hr1 camph bro1 **Cann-i** k* cann-s *Cann-xyz* bg2* canth mrr1 *Caust* k* *Chinin-s* **Clem** k* *Con* k* dig *Graph* k* *Helon* **Hep** k* *Kali-c* k* kali-p kola stb3• lac-c bg2 lac-d k2 *Lach* k* lyc k* nat-c k* *Nat-m* k* *Pareir* bro1 *Petr* k* *Petros* phos k* pic-ac psor k* ran-s rhod k* ros-d wla1 *Sel* k* *Sep* sil k* *Staph* k* stram *Thuj* k* verb zing k*
    - **during**:
      - **beginning** of:
        - **agg.**: clem h2 euph h2 kali-n sulph
          - **then** free with stool: all-s am-m
  - **walking**, while (See involuntary - walking)
  - **women**; in: rhus-t ptk1
- **drinking** | **after** | **agg.**: apis ptk1 arg-n ptk1 caps ptk1 *Ferr-p* ptk1 phos bg2 *Samb* ptk1 sars ptk1 seneg bg2
  - **agg.**: apis bg2 phos bg2 seneg bg2
- **dysuria**: **Acon** k* aesc k* aeth k* *Agar* k* alet c2 *All-c* k* all-s aloe *Alum* k* ang ant-c k* ant-t k* anth a1 *Apis* k* *Apoc* k* **Arg-n** k* arge-pl rwt5• *Arn* k* **Ars** k* ars-s-f k2 atro k* aur k* aur-ar k2 aur-m k* bar-c k* bar-m k* bar-s k2 **Bell** k* *Benz-ac* bro1 *Berb* k* cact k* calc k* *Calc-p* calth br1 *Camph* k* *Cann-i* bro1 **Cann-s** k* *Cann-xyz* ptk1 **Canth** k* *Caps* k* carbn-s casc bro1 caul k* *Caust* bro1 *Cham* b7.de* chel k* *Chim* k* cic k* *Clem* k* *Coc-c* k* coff k* colch k* coli jl2 *Coloc* k* *Con* k* **Cop** k* corn k* cub cuc-c bro1 *Cupr* k* **Dig** k* *Dor* k* dros *Dulc* k* epig c2* equis-h k* erig c2* eucal c2 *Eup-pur* k* euph b4a.de* *Fab* c1* ferr-p bro1 fuma-ac rly4• gali br1 *Gamb* gt1 *Gels* k* *Hell* k* *Hep* k* *Hydr* k* hydrang bro1 *Hyos* k* hyper bro1 ind k* jatr-c junc-e br1 *Kali-ar* k* *Kali-c* k* kali-chl kali-n k* kali-p kali-s *Kreos* k* *Lac-c* k* lat-m bnm6• *Laur* k* led b7.de **Lil-t** k* *Lith-c* k* lup c2 **Lyc** k* lyss jl2 mag-m k* malar jl2 med bro1 meph k* *Merc* k* merc-act c2 **Merc-c** k* merc-sul c2 mit k* morph k* mur-ac bro1 nat-ar nat-c k* *Nat-m* k* nat-p k* *Nit-ac* k* nux-m k* **Nux-v** k* oci bro1 *Ol-sant* bro1 **Op** k* oscilloc jl2 **Pareir** k* petr k* **Petros** k* ph-ac k* phos k* pin-s a1* pip-m c2 pip-n c2 plat plat-m a1 **Plb** k* plb-xyz c2 podo k* *Polyg-h* polyg-xyz c2 pop bro1 prun c2* psor k* **Puls** k* rad-br c11 ran-b k* *Rheum* k* *Rhus-a* *Rhus-t* k* ros-ca c1* ruta c2* sabal c2* *Sabin* sang k* santin c2* sars k* sec k* sel k* *Senec* k* *Sep* k* skat br1 solid c2* spig k* stann staph k* stigm bro1 stram k* **Sulph** k* sumb k* syc bka1• syph jl2 tab k* *Tarent* k* tax c2* **Ter** k* terebe ktp9 tetox pin2• thlas c2* *Thuj* k* *Tritic* c1* tritic-vg fd5.de tub jl2 *Uva* k* *Verat* k* verb bro1 verin c2 vib bro1 zinc k* zinc-p k2
  - **morning**: corn k* *Sep* k* tritic-vg fd5.de
    - **old** men, in: *Benz-ac* *Corn* k*
    - **waking**; on: chlam-tr bcx2•
  - **afternoon**:
    - **walking** | **amel.**: lith-c

- **night**: allox tpw3 *Cic* *Merc* spig gt1*
  - **midnight**:
    - **after** | 3-5 h: pareir
  - **accompanied** by | **respiration**; asthmatic (See RESPIRATION - Asthmatic - accompanied - urination - dysuria - night)
- **accompanied** by:
  - **dribbling**: thlas ptk1
  - **stricture**: *Clem* bg2 dulc bg2 merc bg2 **Petr** bg2 puls bg2 rhus-t bg2 *Sulph* bg2
  - **typhoid** fever: apis bro1 ars bro1 *Canth* bro1
  - **Head**; pain in | **children**; in: con ptk1 senec ptk1
  - **Heel**; coldness in the left: *Agar*
  - **Kidneys**; pain in region of (See KIDNEYS - Pain - region - accompanied - dysuria)
  - **Prostate** gland; swelling of: apis ptk1 med ptk1 petros ptk1
  - **Sciatic** nerve; left: *Agar*
    - **coldness** over the course of the nerve: *Agar*
    - **hyperesthesia** of the skin down the course of the left sciatic nerve (See EXTREMITIES - Sensitive - lower - sciatic - left - accompanied - dysuria)
  - **Uterus**; complaints of (See FEMALE - Uterus - accompanied - dysuria)
- **aching** in back, with: vesp
- **alternating** with:
  - **enuresis**: *Gels* k*
  - **involuntary** urination (See enuresis)
- **apyrexia**, during: caps caust dig staph
- **bending** double | **amel.**: prun ptk1
- **children**; in: apis gt1 bell fb *Borx* bro1 lyc bro1 sars bro1
- **chill**; during: canth k* *Cham* k* lyc k* merc k* nux-v k* ph-ac k* puls k* sulph k* thuj k*
- **company**; in: *Ambr* ptk1 hep ptk1 mur-ac ptk1 nat-m ptk1 tarent ptk1
- **delivery**:
  - **after**: apis ptk1 equis-h ptk1 rheum c2
    - **forceps** delivery: thlas ptk1
  - **during**: erig vml3•
- **dentition**; during: erig ptk1*
- **difficult** (See dysuria)
- **dysentery**; in: arn ptk1
- **dysmenorrhea**, during: nux-m ptk1 senec k* verat-v ptk1
- **fever**; during: ant-c k* cann-s cann-xyz bg2 canth k* *Cham* k* colch k* dulc k* nit-ac k* nux-v k* staph k* sulph k*
- **first** portion: chim gt1
- **followed** by | **erections**: rad-br c11*
- **hysterical**: nux-m ptk1
- **irritability**; with nervous (See MIND - Irritability - nervousness - urination)
- **knee**-elbow position; can pass only in: *Med* vh *Par* vh
- **last** portion: arg-n gt1
- **lying** | **amel.**: kreos ptk1
- **married** women, newly: cann-s ery-a **Staph** k*
- **menses**:
  - **before** | **agg.**: sars bg3*
  - **during** | **agg.**: erig vml3•
  - **suppressed** and drawing pains in abdomen; with: *Puls* senec vml3•
- **neuralgic**: prun ptk1
- **painful**: *Acon* bg2* acon-l c2 agav-a br1 ant-t br1* *Apis* bro1 *Apoc* br1* *Arn* bg2 ars bg2* aur bg2 bar-c bg2 bar-m bg2 *Bell* bg2* borx bg2 calc bg2* calc-p bg2 *Camph* bg2* *Cann-s* bro1 **Cann-xyz** bg2 *Canth* bg2* caps bg2* caust bg2 *Cham* bg2 clem bg2 coch c2 colch bg2 coleus-a mtf11 coloc bg2*
- **painful**: ... con bg2* *Cop* bro1 cuc-c br1 dig bg2 **Dulc** bg2* epig c2 ery-a br1* eup-pur c2* *Gels* ptk1 graph bg2 hell bg2 hep bg2 hydrang bro1 hyos bg2 junc-e br1* juni-c bro1 juni-v c2* kali-c bg2 lach bg2* laur bg2 linu-u br1 lyc bg2* **Merc** bg2 **Merc-c** bg2* morph bro1 mur-ac bg2 nat-m bg2 *Nit-ac* bg2 nux-m bg2* **Nux-v** bg2* onis c2 op bg2 *Pareir* bro1 *Petros* bro1 ph-ac bg2 phos bg2 plb bg2 polyg-xyz c2 prun c2* **Puls** bg2* ran-b bg2 rhus-t bg2 ruta bg2 sabal c2 sabin bg2* santin c2 sars bg2* senn bro1 sep bg2 sil c2 stann bg2 *Staph* bg2 stigm bro1 stram bg2 **Sulph** bg2 tax c2 ter br1* terebe ktp9 thlas c2* thuj bg2* trib br1 *Tritic* bro1 *Urt-u* bro1 uva br1 verat bg2 verb bro1 zinc bg2 zing bro1
  - **accompanied** by:
    - **erections**; wanting: trib br1
    - **hemorrhoids**: acon bg2 ars bg2 calc bg2 carb-v bg2 lach bg2 merc bg2 **Nux-v** bg2 *Puls* bg2 *Sulph* bg2
    - **lithiasis**: calc bg2 cann-xyz bg2 **Lyc** bg2 nux-v bg2 petr bg2 phos bg2 **Sars** bg2 sep bg2 sil bg2
    - **metrorrhagia**: erig br1*
    - **Back**; pain in the: cuc-c br1
  - **alcohol**; from: ars bg2 bell bg2 calc bg2 hep bg2 lach bg2 merc bg2 nux-m ptk1 **Nux-v** bg2 *Puls* bg2 *Sulph* bg2
  - **cold**; after taking a: acon bg2 bell bg2 *Dulc* bg2 merc bg2 *Nux-v* bg2 *Puls* bg2
  - **coldness**, numbness and twitching down left leg; with: agar
  - **cry** before urine starts; children: *(↗MIND - Shrieking - urination - before; MIND - Weeping - urination - before)* acon bg2 **Borx** k* canth bg2 crot-h bg2 lach *Lyc* k* *Nux-v* k* plb bg2 sanic bg3 **Sars** k*
  - **dampness**; from: alum bg2 calc bg2 **Puls** bg2 *Sars* bg2 *Sulph* bg2
  - **dances** around the room in agony, so that he: **Apis** k* *Cann-s* cann-xyz ptk1 **Canth** k* *Petros* k*
  - **dinner** and supper, after: nux-m
  - **effort** to urinate agg.: plb
  - **fear**, fright: acon bg2 *Bell* bg2 hyos bg2 *Op* bg2 verat bg2
  - **inflammatory**: *Acon* bg2 bell bg2 **Cann-xyz** bg2 **Canth** bg2 cop bg2 dig bg2 dulc bg2 *Merc* bg2 **Nux-v** bg2 *Puls* bg2 sabin bg2 sars bg2 sulph bg2
  - **injury** or shock; after: arn bg2 *Cic* bg2 con bg2 *Puls* bg2 rhus-t bg2
  - **nervous**: apis bro1 *Bell* bro1 caps bro1 *Ery-a* bro1 morph bro1 petros bro1
  - **paralysis**; from: acon bg2 **Ars** bg2 bell bg2 caust bg2 cic bg2 cina bg2 *Dulc* bg2 *Hyos* bg2 lach bg2 laur bg2
  - **spasm** of the bladder; from: bell bg2 canth bg2 caps bg2 caust bg2 cina bg2 colch coloc bg2 ign bg2 lach bg2 lyc bg2 **Nux-v** bg2 *Op* bg2 *Puls* bg2 rhus-t bg2 verat bg2
  - **spasmodic**: vib ptk1
    - **closure** of the sphincter while finishing: *Cann-s*
  - **thinking** of it agg.: *Hell* nux-v
  - **urination** | **after** | **agg.**: **Equis-h** k*
    - **during** | **end** of: sars
- **perspiration**; during: **Canth** k* **Cham** k* hep k* lyc k* *Merc* k* nit-ac k* puls k* sulph k* *Thuj* k*
- **pregnancy**; in: *Cocc* bg2 con bg2 equis-h bro1* eup-pur ptk1 nux-v bg2 *Ph-ac* b4a.de* plb ptk1 **Puls** bg2 staph ptk1 sulph bg2
- **profuse** urine; with: equis-h ptk1
- **riding** on rough ground; from: eup-pur ptk1
- **sleep** agg.; after: op
- **stool**; with urging to (See urging - painful - stool - urging)
- **tenesmus** of rectum; evening with: ferr
  - **spasm** of urethra; and: *Prun*
- **weather**; wet cold: coli jl2
- **wet** feet; from: all-c ptk1
- **women**; in: apis bro1 caps bro1 *Cop* bro1 dig bro1 *Eup-pur* bro1 lil-t bro1 meny br1 *Sabin* bro1 staph bro1 verat-v bro1 vib bro1
  - **plethoric** women: chim ptk1

○ • **Sphincter** vesicae; with pain in (See Pain - neck - accompanied - dysuria)

- **feeble** stream (= slow): agar k* **Alum** k* alum-p k2 alum-sil k2 alumn am-m *Apis* apoc **Arg-n** k* **Arn** k* atro bacls-7 fmm1• *Bell* k* *Berb* *Calc-p* k* *Camph* k* cann-i canth bg2 carb-v carbn-s *Caust* k* cham k* chim chin k* chinin-s **Clem** k* coc-c *Coloc* b4a.de cop cypra-eg sde6.de• *Dig* dulc h1 *Gels* graph **Hell** k* **Hep** k* hipp hura iris a1* *Kali-bi* *Kali-c* k* kali-m k2 kali-n *Kali-p* kali-sil k2 kreos k* lath mg *Laur* k* lavand-a ctl1• lyc k* *M-aust* b7.de *Med* k* melal-alt gya4 **Merc** k* **Merc-c** k* **Mur-ac** k* nat-m k* *Nit-ac* olnd **Op** k* par bg2 *Petr* k* *Ph-ac* k* phos h2* plat k* plb k* *Prun* psor puls raph rheum b7.de* *Rhus-t* k* **Sars** k* sec sel k* *Sep* k* sil spong staph *Stram* k* sul-ac bg2 **Sulph** k* syph k* thuj k* tritic-vg fd5.de zinc k* zinc-p k2
  - • **morning** | **waking**; on: **Alum** arn hep *Sep*
  - • **night**: kali-c *Sulph* k*
  - • **breathing** and heart symptoms; with difficulty of: **Laur** k*
  - • **copious**; but: plb ptk1
  - • **dribbling** after stool; only slow: sel
  - • **pain** in the bladder, with violent: calc-p k*
  - • **retention**, from long: calc-p *Caust* rhus-t ruta sulph
  - • **rising** agg.; after: merc-act mez sal-ac *Sulph*
  - • **sleep** agg.; after: op
  - • **vertically**; drops: arg-n ptk1 caust ptk1 gels ptk1 *Hep* ptk1
- **fever**; during | **night**: visc c1
- **flatus**; with (See ABDOMEN - Flatulence - urination)
- **forcible** stream: agn k* ant-c *Cann-s* b7a.de carb-an k* chel *Cic* k* coc-c cycl k* *Nux-v* k* op k* prun k* spig staph sulph k* verat-v
- **forked** stream: anag hr1* arg-n k* *Cann-s* k* *Canth* k* *Caust* chim k* chin-b hr1* clem k* kola stb3• *Merc* k* **Merc-c** k* petr k* prun k* *Rhus-t* k* **Thuj** k* vanil fd5.de vero-o rly4*• [tax jsj7]
- **frequent**: *(↗urging - frequent)* abies-c oss4• abies-n abrom-a ks5 acon k* *Aesc* aeth k* agar agath-a nl2• agn b2.de* *All-c* k* allox tpw4* *Alum* k* *Alumn* k* **Am-c** k* am-m k* *Ambr* b7a.de anac k* androc srj1• ang k* anh sp1 *Ant-c* k* ant-t anthraq rly4• aphis a1* **Apis** k* **Arg-met** k* **Arg-n** k* arge-pl rwt5• *Arist-cl* sp1 arn k* ars k* ars-i arum-t k* asc-t k* aspar k* aster hr1 aur k* aur-i k2 aur-m k2 aur-s k2 bacls-10 pte1*• bapt hr1 **Bar-c** k* *Bar-m* k* *Bell* k* benz-ac k* *Bism* k* bit-ar wht1• *Borx* k* bov k* brom k* *Bry* k* bufo *Cact* cadm-met tpw6* cain c2 **Calc** k* **Calc-ar** k* calc-p bg2 calen hr1 *Camph* k* *Cann-i* k* *Cann-s* k* **Canth** k* *Caps* k* *Carb-ac* k* carb-an *Carb-v* k* carbn-s carc mlr1• casc **Castm** **Caust** k* cedr cham b2.de chel k* *Chim* k* chin k* chin-b hr1 chlol k* *Cic* k* cimic k* *Cina* k* cinnb k* *Clem* k* cob k* coc-c k* cocc k* coch hr1 *Coff* k* *Colch* k* coli jl2* *Coloc* k* con k* conv br1 cop k* cortico sp1 cortiso tpw7* crot-c k* crot-h crot-t *Cupr* k* cur k* *Cycl* k* cygn-ol sze3• *Daph* k* *Dig* k* dioxi rbp6 dros k* dulc k* equis-h *Ery-a* k* *Eup-pur* k* euph b2.de **Euphr** k* eys sp1 *Ferr* k* ferr-i k* *Ferr-p* *Fl-ac* k* flor-p rsj3• fum rly1*• **Gels** k* germ-met srj5• glon k* glycyr-g cte1• granit-m es1• **Graph** k* grat k* gua bg3 guaj k* ham k* hed sp1 hell k* hipp hr1* hydr *Hydrog* srj2• *Hyos* k* **Ign** k* ignis-alc es2• indg k* *Iod* k* *Ip* k* irid-met srj5• iris jatr-c *Kali-bi* k* kali-br a1 *Kali-c* k* kali-chl k* kali-i k* kali-m k2 kali-n b2.de* kali-p kali-s *Kalm* k* kreos k* **Lac-ac** k* lac-c k* *Lac-d* k* lac-e hm2• lac-h sk4• **Lach** k* lact k* lappa br1 lath br1 laur k* *Led* k* *Lil-t* k* *Lith-c* k* loxo-lae bnm12• luf-op rsj5• **Lyc** k* lycpr br1 lyss k* m-ambo b2.de* m-arct b2.de m-aust b2.de *Mag-c* k* mag-m k* *Mag-p* k* mand sp1* mang h2* mang-p rly4• med k* meli k* meph k* **Merc** k* **Merc-c** k* *Mez* k* mim-p rsj8• morg-g pte1*• mosch b2.de *Mur-ac* k* *Murx* nat-ar *Nat-c* k* *Nat-m* k* nat-p k* nat-pyru rly4• *Nat-s* k* nicc k* nicotam rly4• nit-ac **Nux-v** k* oci-sa sk4• ol-an c2 olib-sac wmh1 *Olnd* k* *Op* k* ox-ac k* pall k* par k* pareir k* *Petr* k* petr-ra shn4• *Ph-ac* k* phos k* pin-con oss2• pitu-gl skp7• pitu-p sp1 *Plan* k* plat k* plat-m-n c2 plb k* *Podo* k* *Psor* k* **Puls** k* pycnop-sa mrz1 querc-r svu1• rauw sp1 rheum h **Rhus-r** *Rhus-t* k* ros-d wla1 ruta k* sabad hr1 sabal gm1 *Sabin* k* samb b2.de* *Sang* k* santin c2 saroth sp1 *Sars* k* *Sec* k* *Sel* k* *Seneg* k* *Sep* k* ser-a-c jl2 sil k* sin-n hr1 skat br1 *Spig* k* spong k* **Squil** k* *Stann* k* **Staph** k* stict c1 stram b2.de* stroph-s sp1 suis-hep rly4• sul-ac k* sul-i sulfonam ks2 **Sulph** k* syc pte1*• symph fd3.de* syph jl2 tab k* taosc iwa1• tarax b2.de* *Ter* k* *Thuj* k* *Thymol* sp1 til ban1• tritic br1 tritic-vg fd5.de tub c1 *Uva* *Valer* k* vanil fd5.de *Ven-m* rsj12• verat k* verb k* vesp k* vib k* *Viol-t* k* visc c1 zinc k* zinc-p k2 [bell-p-sp dcm1 helia stj7 *Spect* dfg1]
  - • **daytime**: allox tpw3* ham kreos ptk1 *Mag-m* k* nat-m k* *Psor* k* **Rhus-t** k* staph k* (non:uran-met k) uran-n ven-m rsj12•
    - ⁝ **and** night: *Alum* k* apis aur-m k2 cain *Calc* *Canth* *Caust* *Colch* hyos h1* jug-r kali-c h2* lac-ac k* mag-m **Merc** k* nat-ar *Nat-m* phos h2* *Plan* k* *Rhus-t* sars

- **frequent**: ...
  - • **morning**: allox tpw3 am-m k* ambr k* anac h2* bar-act bell k* calc-p caust coca con dulc fd4.de hydrog srj2• kreos *Mez* k* *Phos* k* pic-ac k* sil k* *Sul-i*
    - ⁝ **rising** agg.; after: ambr phos k*
  - • **forenoon**: ant-t k* arg-n k* dulc fd4.de *Kreos* lyc k* *Mez* hr1 nat-m k* sulph
  - • **afternoon**: alum h2* alumn k* bov k* chlol coc-c k* hydrog srj2• ol-an a1 petr k* sars h2* sep spong fd4.de sulph k*
    - ⁝ **17.30-20** h: abrom-a ks5
  - • **evening**: *All-c* hr1 alum am-c h2* calc-p k* cann-i k* cic k* euphr k* ferr-i k* grat k* kreos lyc k* ox-ac sabad sep spong fd4.de sulph vanil fd5.de zinc
  - • **night**: agar b4.de* agn ail allox tpw4 aloe *Alum* k* alum-p k2 alum-sil k2 *Alumn* *Am-c* k* *Am-m* k* ambr k* *Anac* k* androc srj1• ant-c k* ant-t b7a.de* anth anthraq rly4• *Apis* k* *Arg-met* k* arg-n arn k* ars k* ars-i atp rly4• atra-r skp7*• atro k* aur-m k2 bac bn* **Bar-c** k* bar-i k2 *Bar-m* bar-s k2 **Bell** k* **Borx** k* bov b4.de* bry k* bufo k* *Cact* **Calc** k* *Calc-f* k* calc-i k2 calc-p bg2 calc-sil k2 calen hr1 cann-i *Canth* k* *Carb-ac* **Carb-an** k* carb-v k* *Carbn-s* carneg-g rwt1• *Caust* k* chin chlol **Cina** bg2 cinnb clem k* cob coca coff k* coloc k* *Con* k* cop k* croc bg2 *Cupr* k* *Cycl* daph k* dig k* dioxi rbp6 dros k* *Equis-h* *Eug* k* fl-ac galeoc-c-h gms1• gink-b sbd1• *Glon* *Graph* k* hell hep k* *Hyos* k* hyper bg2* iod k* kali-ar *Kali-bi* *Kali-c* k* kali-m k2 **Kali-n** b4a.de kali-p kali-s kali-sil k2 **Kreos** k* *Lac-c* lac-e hrn2• *Lach* k* lil-t k* *Lith-c* k* **Lyc** k* *M-aust* b7.de* mag-c k* mag-m k* mag-p mang-p rly4• **Med** k* *Meph* k* **Merc** k* merc-c b4a.de mur-ac k* **Murx** nat-ar *Nat-c* k* *Nat-m* k* *Nat-p* *Nat-s* k* nicc k* *Nit-ac* k* *Nux-v* k* op k* orot-ac rly4• petr k* *Ph-ac* k* phos k* plan plb *Podo* prun k* psor *Puls* k* ran-b k* *Rhus-t* k* *Rumx* ruta k* sabin b7.de* samb bg2 *Sang* k* saroth sp1 *Sars* k* sel k* *Senec* k* **Sep** k* *Sil* k* spig k* *Squil* k* stann k* staph h1* stict c1 *Stram* k* stront-c b4.de* sul-ac b4.de* sul-i k2 sulfonam ks2 **Sulph** k* tab k* tax-br oss1• **Ter** k* ther k* *Thuj* k* thymol sp1 tub c (non:uran-met k) *Uran-n* k* vinc bg2 zinc k* zinc-p k2 [bell-p-sp dcm1 helia stj7]
    - ⁝ **midnight**:
      - ⁝ **after**: zinc h2*
        - . **4-11** h: abrom-a ks5
    - ⁝ **cries** before urine passes: *Borx*
    - ⁝ **pregnancy** agg.; during: podo
    - ⁝ **seldom** during the day: *Borx* *Ther* k*
  - • **accompanied** by:
    - ⁝ **diarrhea** (See RECTUM - Diarrhea - accompanied - urination)
    - ⁝ **diarrhea**; painless (See RECTUM - Diarrhea - painless - accompanied - urination)
    - ⁝ **urging** (See urging - accompanied - discharge - frequent)
    - ⁝ **urine**:
      - ⁝ **bloody** (See URINE - Bloody - accompanied - urination)
      - ⁝ **milky** (See URINE - Milky - accompanied - urination)
    - ⁝ **Head**; complaints of (See HEAD - Complaints - accompanied - urination)
    - ⁝ **Teeth**; complaints of (See TEETH - Complaints - accompanied - urination)
  - • **anticipation**; from: germ-met srj5• sil vh
  - • **anxiety**; from: hydrog srj2•
  - • **chill**; during: **Ars** k* bell bg2 canth dulc bg2 hyper lec *Lyc* bg2 meph k* **Merc** k* petros ph-ac k* phos k* spig bg2 staph bg2 sulph k*
  - • **coffee** agg.: cain cob k* dulc fd4.de ign olnd
  - • **delivery**; during: cham hr1
  - • **dinner**; after: cycl k* nat-m k*
  - • **drinking** agg.; after: podo c1
  - • **exertion** agg.; after: aeth
  - • **exposure** to cold and wet: alum *Calc* calc-p cop **Puls** **Sars** sulph
  - • **fever**:
    - ⁝ **drinking** agg.; after: cimx eup-pur
    - ⁝ **during** | **agg.**: arg-met k* bell k* *Kreos* k* lyc k* merc k* ph-ac k* pyrog k2 rhus-t k* squil bg2 staph k* stram sulph bg2

- **headache**; during: asc-c$_{bro1}$ *Bell*$_{k*}$ **Gels**$_{k*}$ *Ign*$_{bro1}$ jug-c$_{vml3•}$ *Lac-d*$_{k*}$ meli$_{sne*}$ *Sang*$_{bro1}$ scut$_{bro1}$ sel$_{c1}$ sil$_{bro1}$ spong$_{fd4.de}$ *Verat*$_{k*}$ vib$_{k*}$
- **hour**:
  - **every**: calc-ar$_{ptk1}$
  - **three** hours; every: adam$_{skp7•}$
  - **two** hours; every: allox$_{tpw3}$ aq-mar$_{skp7•}$
- **hysterical**: gels$_{ptk1}$
- **menses** | **before** | **agg**.: *Alum* *Apis* asar canth dig kali-c kali-i$_{k*}$ nux-v phos puls *Sars*$_{k*}$ *Sulph*
  - **during** | **agg**.: alum$_{k*}$ alumn$_{k*}$ apis aur canth caust hyos$_{ptk1}$ *Kali-i* nux-v plat puls *Sars* sulph vib$_{k*}$
- **mental** exertion; after: cench$_{k2}$
- **minutes**; every 10 to 15: borx$_{ptk1}$
- **nervous** origin: cimic$_{ptk1}$ cub$_{br1}$ *Ign*$_{ptk1}$ tritic-vg$_{fd5.de}$ vib$_{ptk1}$
- **occupied**, must run and pass a little urine; when busily: *(↗urging - sudden - occupied)* calc$_{k*}$ calc-i$_{k2}$ kali-c
- **old** people: *Bar-c*
- **pain**; with: aids$_{nl2•}$ rhod$_{c1}$ thuj$_{k13*}$
  - **face**; in: *Calc*
- **periodical** | **day**; alternate: bar-c
- **perspiration**; during: ant-c$_{k*}$ bar-c$_{k*}$ bar-m **Calc**$_{k*}$ *Caust*$_{k*}$ ign$_{k*}$ kali-c$_{k*}$ lach$_{k*}$ **Lyc**$_{k*}$ *Merc*$_{k*}$ mur-ac$_{k*}$ nat-c$_{k*}$ nat-m$_{bg2}$ nat-n nat-p *Ph-ac*$_{k*}$ *Phos*$_{k*}$ **Rhus-t**$_{k*}$ *Sel*$_{k*}$ squil$_{k*}$ staph$_{k*}$ **Sulph**$_{k*}$ thuj$_{k*}$
- **pregnancy** agg.; during: podo$_{ptk1}$
- **riding**:
  - **carriage**; in a:
    - **agg**.: phos$_{h2}$
    - **amel**.: lyc$_{ptk1}$
- **sadness**; after: mand$_{sp1}$
- **scanty**; but: hell$_{ptk1}$
- **sleep**; before going to: nat-m$_{zf}$
- **stool** agg.; during: cic$_{bg2}$ kali-n$_{bg2}$ nat-m$_{bg2}$
- **travelling**: cain$_{c1*}$
- **water**-colored urine in small quantity; emission: *Dig* nat-sil$_{fd3.de•}$
- **weather**:
  - **change** of weather: tub$_{c1}$
  - **cold** agg.: luf-op$_{rsj5•}$

- **gonorrhea**; after: **Cann-xyz**$_{bg2}$ *Canth*$_{bg2}$ puls$_{bg2}$
- **hasty** (See urging - sudden)
- **imperious**: ser-a-c$_{jl2}$
- **impossible** | **stool** agg.; during: *Chin*$_{bg2}$ *Colch*$_{b7a.de}$
- **incomplete**: *(↗unsatisfactory; Fullness - urination - after - agg.)* alumn$_{k2}$ am-m androc$_{srj1•}$ *Berb* bry *Calc* cann-i carl *Caust* **Clem**$_{k*}$ cub *Gels* *Helon* **Hep** hydrog$_{srj2•}$ *Kali-c* kali-chl kali-sil$_{k2}$ lac-c **Lach** *Lyc* **Mag-m** marb-w$_{es1•}$ *Nat-c* *Nat-p* nux-v petr phos podo$_{fd3.de•}$ positr$_{nl2•}$ sal-fr$_{sle1•}$ **Sel** sil *Staph* stram symph$_{fd3.de•}$ *Thuj* tritic-vg$_{fd5.de}$
  - **bladder** full, urging to urinate but scanty urine: abrot$_{k*}$ hydrog$_{srj2•}$
  - **obliged** to urinate five or six times before the bladder is empty: *Thuj*
- **infrequent** (See seldom)
- **injuries**; after: **Arn**$_{bg2}$ con$_{bg2}$ puls$_{bg2}$ *Rhus-t*$_{bg2}$
- **interrupted** (= intermittent): *Agar*$_{k*}$ aloe ammc ant-c$_{k*}$ ant-t apis$_{bg2*}$ arg-n bapt$_{bg2}$ bell$_{k*}$ bov$_{k*}$ cann-i$_{k*}$ cann-s caps$_{k*}$ *Carb-an*$_{k*}$ *Caust*$_{k*}$ chinin-s **Clem**$_{k*}$ **Con**$_{k*}$ *Dulc*$_{k*}$ gamb *Gels*$_{k*}$ *Graph* hep$_{bro1*}$ hydrog$_{srj2•}$ *Iod* *Kali-c*$_{k*}$ kali-p$_{k*}$ *Led*$_{k*}$ *Lyc*$_{k*}$ *M-aust*$_{b2.de*}$ mag-s$_{k*}$ med$_{k*}$ meph nat-sil$_{fd3.de•}$ nux-v$_{bg2}$ *Op*$_{k*}$ pareir *Ph-ac*$_{k*}$ phos *Puls*$_{k*}$ pulx$_{br1*}$ rhus-t sabal$_{bg2*}$ sabin$_{b2.de*}$ sars$_{k*}$ sed-ac$_{bro1}$ *Sulph*$_{k*}$ *Thuj*$_{k*}$ vesp zinc$_{k*}$ zinc-p$_{k2}$
  - **evening**: *Caust*$_{k*}$
  - **burning** in urethra, by: ph-ac$_{h2}$
  - **coition**; after: *Ph-ac*$_{k*}$
  - **contraction** in region of bladder; by violent: petr
  - **erections**; with painful: *Ant-c*$_{k*}$
- **interrupted**: ...
  - **followed** by | **pain**: pulx$_{br1}$
  - **spurts** and with each spurt cutting pain in swollen prostate; in: **Puls**$_{k*}$
  - **standing**; urine flows better when: *Con*
  - **straining**, then flows easily after he relaxes; despite: clem$_{ptk1}$ con$_{mrr1}$
  - **stream**, after which the urine flows out drop by drop: mag-s rheum
  - **sudden**:
    - **followed** by | **pain**: pulx$_{br1*}$
  - **thick**, with cheesy masses like curdled milk; urine so: **Ph-ac**
  - **travelling**; while: cain$_{br1}$
- **involuntary**: *(↗EXTREMITIES - Paralysis - lower - accompanied - urination)* abies-c$_{vml3•}$ acet-ac$_{k*}$ *Acon*$_{k*}$ agar$_{bro1}$ **Ail**$_{k*}$ alco$_{a1}$ allox$_{sp1}$ *Aloe*$_{ptk1*}$ *Alum*$_{k*}$ alum-sil$_{k2}$ alumn$_{k*}$ am-c$_{k*}$ am-m$_{hr1}$ anac$_{k*}$ anan$_{k*}$ androc$_{bnm2•}$ ant-c$_{k*}$ ant-t$_{b2.de*}$ antip$_{c2*}$ **Apis**$_{k*}$ apoc$_{c2*}$ arbin$_{hsa1}$ *Arg-met*$_{b7.de*}$ **Arg-n**$_{k*}$ arist-cl$_{sp1}$ *Arn*$_{k*}$ **Ars**$_{k*}$ **Ars-i**$_{k*}$ asthm-r$_{mtf11}$ atro$_{k*}$ aur-m aur-s$_{c2}$ bamb-a$_{stb2.de•}$ bapt$_{k2}$ *Bar-act* *Bar-c*$_{k*}$ bar-i$_{k2}$ bar-m$_{k*}$ **Bell**$_{k*}$ benz-ac$_{c2*}$ borx$_{b2.de*}$ brach$_{c2}$ *Bry*$_{k*}$ *Bufo* cact$_{k*}$ calam$_{sa3•}$ calc$_{k*}$ calc-i$_{k2}$ *Calc-p*$_{k*}$ calc-sil$_{k2}$ *Camph*$_{k*}$ cann-i cann-s$_{b2.de*}$ *Canth*$_{k*}$ caps$_{b2.de}$ carb-an$_{k*}$ *Carb-v*$_{k*}$ carbn-dox$_{knl3•}$ carbn-s carc$_{zzh}$ casc$_{hr1}$ **Caust**$_{k*}$ *Cedr* cere-s$_{c2}$ cham$_{k*}$ chen-a$_{c1}$ chen-v$_{c2}$ *Chin*$_{k*}$ chinin-ar chlam-tr$_{bcx2•}$ chlol$_{k*}$ *Cic*$_{k*}$ cimic$_{bro1}$ *Cimx*$_{k*}$ *Cina*$_{k*}$ clem$_{b2.de*}$ cob-n$_{sp1}$ cocc$_{b2.de*}$ *Colch*$_{k*}$ coloc$_{b2.de}$ *Con*$_{k*}$ crot-h cub$_{c2}$ cupr$_{k*}$ cycl$_{b2.de}$ dam$_{c2}$ daph$_{a1}$ der$_{a1}$ *Dig*$_{k*}$ dios$_{ptk1}$ dros$_{k*}$ **Dulc**$_{k*}$ *Echi*$_{k*}$ epig$_{br1}$ *Equis-h*$_{k*}$ ery-a$_{c2*}$ eucal$_{hr1}$ eup-per$_{bro1}$ *Eup-pur*$_{k*}$ ferr$_{k*}$ ferr-ar ferr-i *Ferr-p*$_{k*}$ *Fl-ac*$_{k*}$ galla-q-r$_{nl2•}$ *Gels*$_{k*}$ graph$_{k*}$ grat$_{k2}$ guaj$_{b2.de*}$ *Guare*$_{k*}$ ham$_{fd3.de•}$ *Hell*$_{k*}$ *Hep*$_{k*}$ *Hydr*$_{k*}$ *Hydr-ac*$_{k*}$ hydrang$_{c2*}$ *Hyos*$_{k*}$ *Ign*$_{k*}$ *Iod*$_{k*}$ ix$_{bnm8•}$ kali-ar kali-br$_{k*}$ kali-c$_{b2.de}$ kali-cy$_{a1}$ kali-m$_{k2}$ kali-n$_{b4a.de*}$ *Kali-p*$_{k*}$ *Kreos*$_{k*}$ *Lac-c*$_{sne}$ lac-d$_{k*}$ *Lach*$_{k*}$ lat-m$_{bnm6•}$ lath$_{c2}$ *Laur*$_{k*}$ led$_{k*}$ lina$_{c2*}$ *Lup*$_{bro1}$ **Lyc**$_{k*}$ lycpr$_{bro1}$ lyss$_{jl2}$ m-arct$_{b7.de}$ m-aust$_{b2.de*}$ mag-c$_{k*}$ mag-m$_{k*}$ mag-p$_{bro1}$ mag-s$_{c2}$ mand$_{sp1}$ med$_{bro1*}$ meny$_{b2.de}$ *Merc*$_{k*}$ merc-c$_{k*}$ mill$_{k*}$ morg-g$_{pte1*•}$ *Mosch*$_{k*}$ *Mur-ac*$_{k*}$ *Nat-ar* *Nat-c*$_{k*}$ **Nat-m**$_{k*}$ nat-p$_{k*}$ nat-s$_{c2}$ nat-sil$_{fd3.de•}$ *Nit-ac*$_{k*}$ nitro-o$_{c2}$ **Nux-m**$_{k*}$ *Nux-v*$_{k*}$ oena$_{hr1}$ ol-j$_{k*}$ *Olnd*$_{k*}$ *Op*$_{k*}$ ox-ac$_{k*}$ pareir$_{mrr1}$ *Petr*$_{k*}$ *Ph-ac*$_{k*}$ **Phos**$_{k*}$ phys$_{k*}$ physala-p$_{bnm7•}$ pic-ac$_{k*}$ pix$_{c2}$ *Plan*$_{k*}$ plb$_{k*}$ plut-n$_{srj7•}$ *Podo*$_{k*}$ **Psor**$_{k*}$ **Puls**$_{k*}$ pyrog$_{k2}$ rad-br$_{c11}$ rat$_{k*}$ rheum$_{b2.de}$ rhus-a$_{c2*}$ **Rhus-t**$_{k*}$ rumx russ$_{c2}$ *Ruta*$_{k*}$ sabal$_{c2*}$ sang$_{k*}$ *Sanic*$_{k*}$ santin$_{c2*}$ sapin$_{bro1}$ sars$_{c2*}$ scroph-xyz$_{c2}$ *Sec*$_{k*}$ *Sel*$_{k*}$ senec-j$_{c2}$ seneg$_{k*}$ **Sep**$_{k*}$ sil$_{k*}$ *Spig*$_{k*}$ *Spong*$_{k*}$ *Squil*$_{k*}$ **Staph**$_{k*}$ still$_{hr1}$ *Stram*$_{k*}$ stront-c$_{c2}$ stry$_{a1}$ stry-xyz$_{c2}$ sul-ac$_{b2.de*}$ sul-i$_{k2}$ sulfonam$_{ks2}$ *Sulph*$_{k*}$ symph$_{fd3.de•}$ syph$_{jl2}$ tab$_{k*}$ *Tarax*$_{b7.de*}$ tarent *Ter*$_{k*}$ *Thuj*$_{k*}$ thyr$_{c2*}$ til$_{c2}$ tritic$_{c2*}$ tritic-vg$_{fd5.de}$ tub$_{c2*}$ uran-n$_{c2*}$ urt-u$_{br1}$ ust *Uva*$_{bro1}$ *Verat*$_{k*}$ *Verb*$_{k*}$ vesp$_{k*}$ vesp-xyz$_{c2}$ vib$_{k*}$ viol-t$_{b7a.de*}$ visc$_{sp1}$ xero$_{bro1}$ zinc$_{k*}$ zinc-p$_{k2}$
  - **daytime**: apis$_{bg1}$ *Arg-n*$_{k*}$ *Bell*$_{k*}$ caust$_{b4a.de*}$ equis-h$_{bro1}$ *Ferr*$_{k*}$ *Ferr-p*$_{k*}$ **Fl-ac**$_{k*}$ sec$_{bro1}$ ter$_{tl1}$ thuj
    - **and** night: **Arg-n**$_{k*}$ **Ars**$_{k*}$ bell **Caust**$_{k*}$ *Gels* *Hyos* iod *Nux-v* petr *Rhus-a* ruta *Verb*
    - **sleep** agg.; during: *Bell*$_{k*}$
    - **walking** agg.: ferr thuj
  - **morning**: am-c$_{k*}$ carb-v$_{ptk1}$ cina phos$_{k*}$ phys til$_{k*}$
    - **toward**: am-c chlol
  - **forenoon**: bros-gau$_{mrc1}$ phys$_{k*}$
  - **night** (= incontinence in bed): acon$_{k*}$ *Aeth* alet$_{k2}$ *Aloe*$_{sne}$ *Am-c*$_{k*}$ anac anan ant-c$_{b2.de}$ ant-t$_{b2.de}$ **Apis**$_{k*}$ *Apoc* *Arg-met*$_{k*}$ **Arg-n**$_{k*}$ **Arn**$_{k*}$ **Ars**$_{k*}$ ars-s-f$_{k2}$ *Aur* aur-ar$_{k2}$ aur-m aur-s bac$_{wz}$ bac-t$_{c8*}$ bar-c$_{k*}$ bar-m bar-s$_{k2}$ **Bell**$_{k*}$ **Benz-ac**$_{k*}$ borx$_{b2.de}$ bry$_{k*}$ cact *Calc*$_{k*}$ calc-sil$_{k2}$ camph$_{b2.de}$ cann-s$_{b2.de}$ canth$_{k*}$ caps$_{b2.de}$ carb-an$_{b2.de}$ *Carb-v*$_{k*}$ *Carbn-s* carc$_{gk6*}$ **Caust**$_{k*}$ *Cham*$_{k*}$ chin$_{k*}$ chinin-ar$_{k2}$ *Chlol* cic$_{b2.de}$ cimx *Cina*$_{k*}$ clem$_{b2.de}$ coca$_{k*}$ cocc$_{b2.de}$ colch$_{b2.de}$ coloc$_{b2.de}$ con$_{k*}$ *Crot-c* cub cupr cycl$_{b2.de}$ dig$_{b2.de*}$ dulc$_{k*}$ enterob-v$_{mtf11}$ **Equis-h**$_{k*}$ *Eup-pur*$_{k*}$ **Ferr**$_{k*}$ *Ferr-ar* ferr-i$_{k*}$ ferr-p$_{k*}$ *Fl-ac* gels$_{bro1}$ glycyr-g$_{cte1•}$ **Graph**$_{k*}$ guaj$_{b2.de}$ *Hep*$_{k*}$ hyos$_{k*}$ ign$_{k*}$ kali-br$_{hr1*}$ kali-c$_{k*}$ kali-m$_{k2}$ **Kali-n**$_{b4a.de}$ *Kali-p*$_{k*}$ kali-sil$_{k2}$ **Kreos**$_{k*}$ **Lac-c**$_{k*}$ lac-d lach$_{b2.de}$ laur$_{b2.de}$ led$_{b2.de}$ lina$_{br1}$ lyc$_{k*}$ m-aust$_{b2.de*}$ mag-c$_{k*}$ *Mag-m*$_{k*}$ **Mag-p**$_{k*}$ mag-s mand$_{sp1}$ *Med*$_{k*}$ meny$_{b2.de}$ *Merc*$_{k*}$ mur-ac$_{k*}$ *Nat-ar* *Nat-c*$_{k*}$ **Nat-m**$_{k*}$ *Nat-p* **Nit-ac**$_{k*}$ nux-v$_{k*}$ *Op*$_{k*}$ ox-ac *Petr*$_{k*}$ ph-ac$_{k*}$ *Phos*$_{k*}$ phys$_{bro1}$ *Plan*$_{k*}$ plb$_{b2.de}$ *Podo* *Psor*$_{k*}$ **Puls**$_{k*}$ quas$_{bro1}$ rheum$_{b2.de*}$ rhus-a$_{br1*}$ **Rhus-t**$_{k*}$ *Ruta*$_{k*}$ *Sabal*$_{bg2*}$ *Sanic*$_{k*}$ santin$_{bro1}$

Bladder

- **night**: ...
Sars k* sec bro1* sel c1* *Seneg* k* **Sep** k* **Sil** k* spig k* spong b2.de squil k* staph k* *Stram* k* sul-ac b2.de **Sulph** k* *Syc* vh syph ptk1* tab k* ter k* *Thuj* k* *Thyr* br1* tritic br1 *Tub* k* (non:uran-met k) *Uran-n* k* uva bro1 verat k* *Verb* k* *Viol-t* k* zinc k* zinc-p k2 [sil-met stj2]
  - **midnight**:
    - **before**: *Bry* b7a.de **Puls** b7a.de
    - **after**: **Puls** b7a.de *Ruta* b7a.de
      - **5** h: cact
    - **morning**; until: plan
  - **morning**, toward: am-c k* cact *Calc* b4a.de *Caust* b4a.de chlol cina bg1 con b4a.de *Hep* b4a.de petr b4a.de phos b4a.de *Sep* b4a.de *Sil* b4a.de stann b4a.de **Sulph** b4a.de zinc
  - **accompanied** by | **eczema**; history of: psor bro1*
  - **adolescence**: caust mrr1 kali-c ptk1 *Lac-c* vh
  - **catheterization**, after: mag-p ptk1
  - **children**; in: acon vh1 aesc k1* *Carb-v* mtf33 carc mlr1• cina mtf33 lac-c mtf33 mag-m mtf33 med mtf33 nat-p tl1 psor mtf33 puls mtf33 santin tl1 sil mtf33 syph mtf33 thuj mtf33
    - **fright**; after (See fright)
  - **cough** agg.; during: colch ptk1
  - **dreaming** of urinating, while●: equis-h bro1 *Kreos* k* lac-c k* lyc merc-i-f *Ph-ac* *Seneg* **Sep** k ●* **Sulph** k ●
  - **first** sleep●: benz-ac k* *Bry* b7a.de calc b4a.de *Carb-v* b4a.de **CAUST** k●* cina *Graph* b4a.de *Kreos* k* mag-c b4a.de merc b4a.de *Ph-ac* k* phos k2 puls k2 **SEP** k ●* **Sil** b4a.de sulph b4a.de zinc b4a.de
  - **four** times: cob ptm1•
  - **fright**; after: *(↗fright)* op mrr1 stram mrr1
  - **habit**; when there is no tangible cause except: **Equis-h** k*
  - **hysteria**; with (See MIND - Hysteria - enuresis)
  - **injuries** of head; after: sil ptk1
  - **menses**; during: hyos ptk1
  - **moon**; full: cina ptk1 psor ptk1*
  - **old** people: apoc ptk1 benz-ac ptk1 kali-p ptk1 sec ptk1*
  - **pregnancy** agg.; during: podo ptk1
  - **sleep** | **deep**: *Kreos* b7a.de*
  - **spasmodic** enuresis: **Arg-met** bell canth caps castm cina coloc *Gels* hyos ign lach lyc *Nux-v* op puls rhus-t verat
  - **waken** the child; difficult to: *Bell* k* chlol ptk1 **Kreos** k*
  - **weakly** children, in: *Chin* k* kali-p ptk1 thyr ptk1
  - **women**; in: *Sil* vh
  - **worms**; from: cina bro1 *Santin* bro1 sil ptk1* sulph bro1
- **accompanied** by:
  - **cystitis** (See Inflammation - accompanied - urination - involuntary)
  - **erections**; wanting: trib br1
  - **indigestion**: benz-ac bro1 *Nux-v* bro1 puls bro1
  - **locomotor** ataxia: bell bro1 berb bro1 equis-h bro1 ferr-p bro1
  - **sleepiness**: bell ptk1
  - **smelling** urine; strong: med tl1
  - **weakness**; general: calc-p tl1
  - **Prostate** gland; swelling of: iod ptk1 pareir mrr1
  - **Sphincter**; weakness: apoc bro1 *Bell* bro1 *Caust* bro1 coenz-a mtf11 con bro1 ferr-p bro1 *Gels* bro1 nux-v bro1 rhus-a bro1 *Sabal* bro1 sec bro1 *Stry* bro1
- **alternating** with dysuria (See dysuria - alternating - enuresis)
- **blowing** the nose, when: **Caust** k* nat-m k* puls zinc k*
- **boys**, in: *Rhus-t* k* sil k2
- **catheterization**, after: *(↗Inflammation - catheterization; GENERALS - Catheterism)* mag-p bro1
- **children**; in: allox mtf11 aloe sne arg-met k2 dulc fd4.de ferr mtf33 ferr-i br kali-p k2 lac-c sne lyc k2 mag-m mtf33 nat-m mtf33 nux-v mtf33 op mtf33 psor jl2* puls mtf33 sep mtf33
  - **anemia**; in: ferr-i br
  - **nervous**: gels c1
- **children**; in: ...
  - **weakly**: *Chin*
- **chill**:
  - **before**: *Gels*
  - **during**: caust k* dulc k* puls k* rhus-t k* sulph k*
- **coition**; after: cedr hr1 lyc ptk1
- **cold** agg.; becoming: *Alet* k2* bell *Calc* vh **Caust** *Dulc* med hr1 orig vh *Rhus-t*
- **constipation**; with: caust bro1 tarent ptk1
- **convulsions**; during: art-v k* **Bufo** k* *Caust* k* cic sne cocc k* cupr k* **Hyos** k* lach hr1* lyc k2 nat-m hr1* nux-v k* *Oena* k* *Plb* k* stry k* *Zinc* k*
- **coryza**; during: verat b7.de*
- **cough** agg.; during: *Alet* bg2* *Alum* k* alum-p k2 anan *Anemps* bro1 *Ant-c* k* **Apis** k* arge-pl rwt5• ars b4a.de bac bn *Bell* k* *Bry* k* *Calc* bg2* canth bro1* *Caps* k* carb-an **CAUST** k ●* *Cench* *Colch* k* con bg2 dros bg2 dulc ferr k* *Ferr-m* bro1 *Ferr-p* k* gels bg2 gink-b sbd1• glycyr-g cte1• hydrog srj2• hyos ign k* kali-c bg2* *Kreos* k* lach laur *Lyc* mag-c k* mur-ac ptk1 murx **NAT-M** k ●* nat-sil fd3.de• nit-ac **Nux-v** k ●* olib-sac wmh1 *Ph-ac* k* **Phos** k* pin-con oss2• pneu jl2 psor k* **PULS** k ●* rhod rhus-t *Rumx* k* ruta bg2 sel bro1 seneg k* **Sep** k ●* *Spong* k* **Squil** k* staph k* sulph k* tarent k* *Thuj* k* tritic-vg fd5.de *Verat* k* verb bro1* vib k* visc sp1 xero bro1 *Zinc* k* zinc-p k2
  - **pregnancy** agg.; during: cocc ptk1
- **delayed**, if: *Lach* phos k* plan pulx br1 *Sep* squil sulph thuj
- **delivery**; after: *Arn* k* **Ars** k* bell bro1 caust bro1 hyos bro1 tril-p bro1
- **effort**, at least: allox mgm•
- **effort**; no urine flows during: *Gels* k*
- **ejaculation**; with: verb c1
- **empty**; after the bladder feels: *(↗Emptiness - urination)* (non:helo ptk2) helon ptk2
- **epilepsy**; during (See GENERALS - Convulsions - epileptic - during - enuresis)
- **eructations** agg.: hydr bg1
- **excitement** agg.: agar vh1 caust mtf33 *Gels* puls k2
- **exertion** agg.: *Bry* k* caust *Nux-v* ph-ac rhus-t sabal pd tarent k*
- **fever**; during: gels k2
- **flatus**; when expelling: mur-ac ptk1 *Puls* k* sulph k*
- **fright**: *(↗night - fright)* lyc b4a.de* op ptk1 sep ptk1*
- **hurry**; when in a: lac-d ptk1
- **inattention**, from: sep ptk1
- **injuries**; after: arist-cl sp1
- **jar**; by: caust h2
- **laughing** agg.: abies-c vml3• amp rly4• bell bro1 calc bro1 canth bro1 caps bro1 **CAUST** k ●* dulc fd4.de ferr bro1 ferr-m bro1 *Ferr-p* bro1 galla-q-r nl2• ign bro1 kali-c bro1 **Nat-m** k ●* **Nux-v** k ●* psor al2 **Puls** k ●* ruta fd4.de sabal pd sel bro1 **SEP** k ●* *Squil* bro1 sulph bro1 symph fd3.de• tarent k* vib bro1 xero bro1 *Zinc* bro1
- **lying**:
  - **agg.**: bell-p ptk1 ham bg2 kreos k* lach ptk1 lyc ptk1 pic-ac ptk1 *Puls* bg2* uva ptk1
  - **amel.**: ferr-p k2
- **mania**, during: *Cupr*
- **menses**; during: cact calc k* *Canth* hell *Hyos* k*
- **moon**; full: cina bg3 *Psor* c1*
- **motion**:
  - **agg.**: *Bell* *Bry* k* calc ferr k2* *Ph-ac* k* *Phos* ruta staph tarent
    - **sudden** movement, from: ferr k2*
  - **amel.**: *Rhus-t*
- **must** keep her mind on it: puls k2 sep k2
- **noise**, sudden: caust puls k* sep k*
- **old** people; in: *All-c* aloe k* am-be br1* apis arg-n bg2* *Ars* *Aur-m* bar-c bg2 *Benz-ac* bro1 bry bg2 cann-s canth bg2* carb-ac ptk1 chlorpr mtf11 *Cic* k* con bg2 dam br1* equis-h bro1 gels k* *Iod* k* kali-p nit-ac bro1 phos psor jl2 *Rhus-a* bg2* *Sec* k* seneg bro1 *Thuj*

- **old** people; in: ...
  - **men** with enlarged prostate: *All-s* *Aloe* apoc bg3 *Cic* dig *Iod* kali-p nux-v *Pareir* *Sec* *Thuj*
  - **women**: *Caust* mrr1
- **onanists**, in: sep hr1
- **pregnancy** agg.; during: **Ars** k* bell canth caust clem kreos *Nat-m* k* podo **Puls** k* *Sep* k* *Syph* k*
  - **cough** agg.; during: cocc pd
- **prostration**; in nervous: kali-p k2
- **putting** hands in cold water: *Kreos* k*
- **rest** agg.: caust b4a.de puls b7a.de rhus-t b7a.de* *Sep* b4a.de
- **retain**, great pain on attempting to: (non:uran-met k) uran-n
- **riding**:
  - **agg.**: lac-d k2* thuj k*
  - **amel.**: lyc ptk1
- **rising** from sitting agg.: *Mag-c* k* petr bg3* pitu-a vml2• spig k*
- **running** agg.: *Arn* k* *Bry* k* *Lac-d* k*
- **seasons** | **winter**: *Puls* b7a.de *Rhus-t* b7a.de *Sulph* b7a.de
- **sitting**:
  - **agg.**: *Caust* k* *Nat-m* k* **Puls** k* *Rhus-t* k* *Sars* k* sil h2* spig bg1 stram k*
    - **retention** while standing: *Caust*
    - **swing** her foot constantly or the urine will escape; she must: zinc
  - **amel.**: zinc ptk1
- **sneezing** agg.: alet k* allox tpw3* alum bg2 ant-c b7.de* apis bg2 arge-pl rwt5• bamb-a stb2.de* bell bro1 bry b7.de* *Calc* bg2* canth bro1 caps bg2* **Caust** k* colch k* con bg2 dros bg2 *Ferr* b7a.de* ferr-m bro1 ferr-p bro1 gels bg2 glycyr-g cte1• ign bro1* *Kali-c* bg2* kali-p fd1.de• kreos bg2 *Lac-c* mag-c bg2 *Nat-m* k* *Nux-v* k* olib-sac wmh1 orig vh petr *Ph-ac* k* phos k* *Psor* bg2* *Puls* k* ruta bg2 sel bro1 seneg bg2 sep k* spong b7.de* *Squil* b7a.de* staph b7.de* sulph bg2* tarent bg2 thuj bg2 *Verat* b7.de* vib bro1 xero bro1 zinc k*
- **standing** agg.: bell k* caust ferr k* lyc *Nat-m* *Puls* *Rhus-t* sep k*
- **stool**:
  - **after** | **agg.**: acon alum tl1 apis *Arg-n* *Ars* atro aur bar-c bell bry calc camph carb-v caust chin chinin-ar cina colch con dig *Hyos* kali-br *Laur* mosch **Mur-ac** k* nat-m petr *Ph-ac* *Phos* puls rhus-t sec *Sel* stram sulph verat *Zinc* k* zinc-p k2
  - **conscious**, supposing it to be flatus; while fully: *Ars*
  - **during** | **agg.**: *Aloe* bg2 *Alum* bg2 colch bg2 laur bg2 op bg2 tab bg2
  - **dysenteric** | **every**: alum
  - **straining** at | **agg.**: abies-c vml3• *Alum* *Lil-t* k* podo fd3.de• tritic-vg fd5.de
- **surprise**, pleasurable agg.: puls ptk1
- **sycosis**; history of: med bro1
- **thirst** and fear, with: **Acon** k*
- **train**; while catching a: lac-d k2*
- **turpentine**; from drinking: ter tl1
- **typhoid** fever: *Arg-n* arn *Ars* *Colch* *Hell* **Hyos** kali-p k2 *Lach* *Lyc* *Mosch* *Mur-ac* op *Ph-ac* *Phos* psor *Rhus-t* *Stram* sulph *Verat* *Verat-v*
- **unconscious**: apoc bro1 *Arg-n* bro1 *Caust* bro1 sars bro1
- **urination**:
  - **after** | **agg.**: (*↗dribbling - urination - after - agg.*) agar cann-i clem helon sel sil staph
  - **delayed**; if desire to urinate is●: calc dig h2 ham fd3.de• kreos k2 merc nat-m **Puls** k●* **Sep** k● squil **Sulph** k●* *Thuj* k*
  - **stop** the flow; when trying to: *Rhus-t* b7a.de
  - **urging** to urinate | **with**: aloe sne chin h1*
- **vomiting**; while: ars bg1 *Canth* vh crot-h ptk1* merc-sul vh *Par* vh
- **waking**; on: sel mtf11
- **walking**:
  - **agg.**: alet alum-sil anan *Arg-n* arn k* bell k* *Bry* k* *Calc* k* canth bro1 caps bro1 *Caust* k* chlam-tr bcx2• **Ferr** k* ferr-m bro1 ferr-p k* ign bro1 kali-c bro1 kali-s *Lac-d* k* *Mag-c* k* mag-m k* mang-p rly4• **Nat-m** k*

- **involuntary – walking – agg.**: ... olib-sac wmh1 *Ph-ac* phos psor al2 **Puls** k* ruta k* sapin c2 *Sel* k* sep *Squil* bro1 stram sulph bro1 tarent thuj vib bro1* xero bro1 *Zinc* k*
    - **standing** still, nothing passed; yet, on attempting to urinate when: mag-m k*
  - **amel.**: *Rhus-t* k*
  - **rapidly** | **agg.**: alet ptk1
- **water** running from a hydrant, on seeing: *Lyss* k* sulph
- **long**: *Agath-a* nl2•
- **lying**:
  - **agg.**: ham bg2 lyc bg2
  - **back**; on | **agg.**: puls bg2
- **menses** | **before** | **agg.**: kali-i ptk1
  - **during** | **amel.**: sars bg2
- **nervous** (See frequent - nervous)
- **painful** (See dysuria - painful)
- **painless**: led b7.de*
- **paroxysmal**: chel cycl cypra-eg sde6.de• merc-i-f nux-v
- **press** a long time; must (See retarded - press)
- **pressing**, with: arge-pl rwt5• hyos h1* lyc h2*
- **residuary** (See dribbling - urination - after - agg.)
- **retarded**, must wait for urine to start: (*↗Retention*) **Acon** ptk1 agar k* *Alum* k* alum-p k2 alum-sil k2 alumn am-c ptk1 am-m *Apis* k* aran arg-n **Arn** k* *Ars* ptk1 ars-s-f k2 aur-s k2 *Bell* k* *Cact* k* cadm-s c1 calc b4a.de* camph b7.de* *Cann-i* cann-xyz bg2 canth k* *Caps* b7a.de **Caust** k* cham b7.de chel *Clem* coc-c k* *Coloc* b4a.de con b4a.de* **Cop** des-ac rbp6 *Dig* *Dulc* b4a.de erig ptk1 eucal eys sp1 gels ptk1 hed sp1 hell ptk1 **Hep** k* hydr-ac hydrang sne *Hyos* ptk1 ip kali-br *Kali-c* k* kali-m k2 *Kali-n* kali-sil k2 kali-sula gm1 lath mg laur k* **Lyc** k* *M-aust* b7.de mand sp1 med merc-c b4a.de *Mur-ac* k* nat-ar k2 nat-c *Nat-m* k* nat-p *Nit-ac* nux-v k* *Op* k* ozone sde2• par k* *Pareir* k* *Petr* k* *Ph-ac* b4.de* *Phos* b4.de* pitu-p sp1 plan c2 plb b7.de* *Prun* puls k* *Raph* **Rhus-t** *Sars* k* sec *Sel* k* **Sep** k* *Sil* staph *Stram* k* sul-ac b4.de sulfa sp1 sulph symph fd3.de• tarent ptk1 tax ter k* *Thuj* tritic-vg fd5.de ulm-c jsj8• visc sp1 *Zinc* k*
  - **daytime**: sars ptk1
  - **alone**, can only pass urine when: *Ambr* bg3 hep bg3 *Lyc* vh mur-ac bg3 *Nat-m* tarent bg3* tritic-vg fd5.de
  - **cold** | **pavement** agg.; standing on a cold: carb-v ptk1
  - **drops** of urine pass; after great straining a few:
    - **followed** by:
      - **full** stream, with pain; a | **dribbling** urine; after this sometimes: clem
  - **knees** and pressing head against floor; can pass urine only when on the: pareir
  - **last** few drops: caust h2 mand sp1
  - **long** while, and then only a little urine passes: caust
    - **others** are near him; especially if: (*↗Retention - company; MIND - Company - aversion - strangers - urination*) *Nat-m* k*
  - **lying**; can only pass urine while: kreos hr1*
  - **music**; can pass urine only when listening to: *Tarent*
  - **pain** in the fundus of bladder; by: phos
  - **press** a long time before he can begin; must: abies-n *Acon* bro1 agar aloe pd **Alum** k* alum-p k2 anag vh1 *Apis* *Arn* asim bro1 *Bell* *Cact* k* cann-i bro1 cann-xyz bg2 **Caust** k* cench k2 chim bro1* *Coc-c* cycl bg2 equis-h bro1 **Hep** hydrang sne *Hyos* bro1 *Kali-c* k* kali-m k2 *Kreos* bro1 *Laur* lil-t pd lyc bro1 **Mag-m** k* **Mur-ac** nat-c nat-p *Nit-ac* nux-v bg2* **Op** k* pareir bg2* plb *Prun* k* raph rheum *Rhus-t* sabal bg2* sars sec stram syph jl2 tax thuj k* tritic-vg fd5.de tub pd zinc bro1
    - **morning**: **Alum** *Arn* **Hep** **Op** *Sep* syph jl2
    - **abdominal** muscles: *Mag-m* h2* (non:mag-p br1)
    - **continue**; must:
      - **breathe** the urine ceases to flow until he strains again; if he stops to: nat-p *Stram*
      - **last** part; to pass the: rheum
    - **frequent** pressing to urinate with small discharges: thuj
    - **long** pressing, urine passes guttatim; after: bell plb
    - **painful** and frequent urination | **sit** and strain a long time after which a few drops fall; with disposition to: abies-n

Bladder

- **press** a long time before he can begin; must: ...
  - **pressure**, the less it flows; the more: alum bg2 *Kali-c*
  - **protrudes**; so hard to start the urine that anus: **Mur-ac** k*
  - **stand** and press a long time, before urine will start; must: nit-ac
- **sitting** agg.: puls ptk1 sars ptk1
  - **only** pass urine while sitting; can: *(↗Retention - sitting)* caust ptk1* **Zinc** k*
    - **backward**; bent: *(↗Retention - sitting)* alum ptk1 zinc k*
    - **forward**; bent: canth ptk1 pareir prun ptk1 sulph
- **spasm** of sphincter, on account of: **Op** k* sars k2
- **spraying** stream: cann-xyz bg2 kreos bg2
- **standing**:
  - **agg.**:
    - **only** pass urine while standing; can: alum bg1* caust ptk1 con k13* hyper k* **Sars** k* syph ptk1
      - **feet** are wide apart and body inclined forward; while: *Chim* k*
    - **sitting**; flows involuntarily while: *Caust*
    - **walking**; but passes involuntary while: mag-m k*
  - **amel.**: con
- **stool**; can pass urine only while pressing at: aloe k* *Alum* k* am-m caust ptk1 hep ptk1 laur lil-t ptk1 mag-m ptk1 mur-ac tl1* nat-p op ptk1 sel stram tub ptk1
- **stooping** | **amel.**: canth ptk1 pareir ptk1 prun ptk1
- **strange** positions amel.; taking: zinc ptk1
- **urination** | **urging** to urinate:
  - **with**:
    - **pass** no urine; but can: bit-ar wht1•
      - **blood** has passed the vagina; until an enormous clot of black: *Coc-c* k*
  - **urging** to urinate; with: melal-alt gya4
- **urination**; a cutting with ineffectual straining, that stops the flow before: ph-ac
- **water** running; can pass urine only when listening to: lyss k* tarent zinc
- **whistling**; can pass urine only when: cycl tarent

- **rising** agg.: mag-c bg2 spig bg2
- **seldom**: acon k* agar k* aloe alum b2.de* alumn k* am-c b2.de* am-m b2.de* apis ptk1 *Arg-n* k* *Arn* k* ars k* *Aur* k* aur-ar k2 bar-c k* bell k* bism b2.de bry k* calc b2.de camph k* cann-s b2.de **Canth** k* caps b2.de carb-v k* castm caust b2.de chel k* chin b2.de* cic b2.de* clem b2.de coc-c k* *Colch* b2.de* coloc b2.de con b2.de cupr k* *Cycl* k* dig k* dulc b2.de euph b2.de fl-ac bg2 graph b2.de grat k* hell b2.de *Hep* k* hyos k* iod b2.de ip b2.de iris kali-c k* kali-s fd4.de lac-c k* lach b2.de *Laur* k* led b2.de* lob ptk1 *Lyc* k* m-arct b2.de m-aust b2.de mag-m k* **Merc** b2.de* merc-c k* mez k* mur-ac b2.de nad rly4• nat-s nicc k* nit-ac k* *Nux-v* k* *Op* k* par b2.de petr b2.de ph-ac b2.de phos b2.de pitu-p sp1 *Plb* k* prun k* psor k* *Puls* k* pycnop-sa mrz1 *Ruta* k* sabin b2.de sal-fr sle1• sars k* sec k* sep b2.de squil b2.de* stann k* staph k* *Stram* k* stront-c b2.de* sul-ac k* sulfa sp1 sulph b2.de* *Syph* k* thuj k* thymol sp1 vanil fd5.de verat b2.de* x-ray sp1 zinc k*
  - **daytime**: borx ptk1 *Lyc* k* ther ptk1
    - **once**:
      - **profuse**; but: lac-c ptk1 syph ptk1
        - **difficult**: lac-c ptk1
    - **twice**: pyrog ptk1
      - **scanty**; but: pyrog ptk1
  - **chill**; during: arn bg2 canth bg2 hyos bg2 op bg2 stram bg2
  - **fever**; during: *Ars* bg2 chin bg2 colch bg2 hyos bg2 *Op* bg2 *Puls* bg2 stram bg2
  - **perspiration**; during: acon bg2 *Ars* bg2 camph bg2 *Canth* bg2 *Chin* bg2 hep bg2 hyos bg2 *Nux-v* bg2 op bg2 puls bg2 *Sep* bg2 stram bg2
  - **profuse**; but | **children**; in: syph mtf33
- **sitting**:
  - **agg.**: caust bg2 mag-c bg2 puls bg2
  - **amel.**: **Zinc** bg2
- **slow** (See feeble; retarded; thin stream)
- **small** quantities; of (See URINE - Scanty)
- **small** stream (See thin stream)
- **spurting** stream: calc-p k* *Cann-xyz* bg2 canth bg2 cic k* clem ptk1 con ptk1 helon k* kola stb3• kreos bg1* puls k* rhus-t bg2 spig k* thlas ptk1 tub ptk1
  - **cough** agg.; during: caust tl1 colch tl1 kreos k* *Squil* st* staph k*
  - **urination** agg.; after: helo bg2 helon k* *Sil* bg2*
- **standing** | **amel.**: alum bg2 chim bg2 **Sars** bg2
- **stool**:
  - **during** | **agg.** | **only** during stool: aloe ptk1 alum bg2 apis ptk1 mur-ac ptk1
    - **amel.**: alum bg2 mur-ac bg2
- **strangury** (See dysuria - painful)
- **suppressed** (See Retention)
- **thin** stream: agar alum b4a.de apis bell k* *Camph* k* *Canth* k* chim k* chin k* **Clem** k* **Cop** k* eup-pur k* gins k* *Graph* k* gymno hedy a1* hell led b7.de* med jl2 *Merc* k* *Nit-ac* k* ol-an ptk1 *Petr* k* ph-ac bg2 plat b4a.de prun k* *Puls* k* samb k* *Sars* k* *Spong* k* *Staph* k* stram k* *Sulph* k* tax *Thuj* k* trad a1* *Zinc* k*
  - **thread**; like: prun ptk1
- **thinking** of urination agg.: ox-ac bg2
- **twisted** stream: sul-i ptk1
- **unconscious**, urethra insensible: *(↗URETHRA - Sensation - absent)* ail alum pd *Apis* k* apoc k* **Arg-n** k* arn bg2 bell bg2 **Caust** k* cedr chlol *Cupr* grat hell kali-br **Mag-m** k* mag-s merc mur-ac bg2 nux-v op mtf33 *Sars* k* tritic-vg fd5.de
  - **dribbling**: arn b7a.de puls b7a.de spig b7a.de
  - **mania**, in: **Cupr**
    - **urine** and stool: arn bell *Mur-ac* psor *Rhus-t* sulph
- **unsatisfactory**: *(↗incomplete; Fullness - urination - after - agg.)* *Alum* alum-p k2 alum-sil k2 androc srj1• *Arg-n* arn **Ars** k* ars-s-f k2 aspar aur aur-ar k2 aur-s k2 bell *Berb* brach bry cact *Calc* k* calc-sil k2 camph canth **Caust** k* *Cic* *Clem* k* cocc colch con *Cub* dig ptk1 *Gels* gins **Hep** k* hydrog srj2• *Hyos* kali-ar *Kali-c* kali-p lach k* *Laur* lyc *Mag-m* k* merc nat-ar nat-c nat-p *Nux-v* op petr *Ph-ac* phos plb podo fd3.de• positr nl2• psor k2 puls rhod rhus-t ruta *Sars* sec *Sel* k* sil stann *Staph* stram *Sulph* symph fd3.de• *Thuj* verat
  - **emptied**, with dribbling; as if bladder were not: *Staph*
  - **remained** in urethra; as if urine: *(↗URETHRA - Urine - remained)* agar all-c alum ambr *Arg-n* aspar cedr clem dig ery-a hep tl1 *Kali-bi* k* petr rhus-t *Sel* *Sep* *Thuj*
- **urgent** (See imperious)
- **urging** to urinate: *Acon* k* aesc agar k* agath-a nl2• agn b2.de aids nl2• allox sp1 aloe alum k* *Alumn* *Am-c* k* am-m k* ambr b2.de* anac k* androc srj1• ang b2.de* ant-c k* *Ant-t* k* **Apis** k* arg-met k* **Arg-n** k* arge-pl rwt5• *Arist-cl* sp1 *Arn* k* ars k* ars-i ars-s-f k2 asar b2.de* aspar aur b2.de *Aur-m* *Bar-c* k* bar-m bar-s k2 **Bell** k* **Benz-ac** **Berb** k* bism b2.de borx k* both-ax tsm2 bov k* **Bry** k* but-ac sp1 *Cact* *Calc* k* calc-p bg2* calc-sil k2 **Camph** k* **Cann-i** **Cann-s** k* cann-xyz ptk1 **Canth** k* *Caps* k* carb-an k* carb-v k* carbn-s *Card-m* *Carl* c2 cartl-s rly4• castm **Caust** k* *Cham* k* chel k* **Chim** *Chin* k* chinin-ar chinin-s k* chlam-tr bcx2• chlor bg2 cic b2.de* cimic cina k* *Clem* k* cob-n sp1 *Coc-c* *Cocc* b2.de* coch coff k* *Colch* k* *Coloc* k* *Con* k* *Cop* k* cortiso gse croc k* crot-t *Cub* cupr k* cycl k* *Dig* k* *Dros* k* *Dulc* k* equis-h k* erig vml3• ery-a *Eup-pur* euph k* *Ferr* k* ferr-p *Graph* k* *Guaj* k* ham *Hell* k* hep k* hippoc-k szs2 hist sp1 hydr *Hyos* k* *Ign* k* iod k* *Ip* k* kali-ar *Kali-bi* k* **Kali-c** k* *Kali-chl* kali-i kali-m k2 *Kali-n* k* kali-p kali-s kali-sil k2 kola stb3• *Kreos* k* lac-c k2 lach k* laur k* led k* **Lil-t** k* *Lyc* k* *Lyss* m-arct b2.de m-aust b2.de* mag-c k* mag-m k* mang k* meny k* meph k* *Merc* k* **Merc-c** k* mez mit k* moni rfm1• morph mosch b2.de* *Mur-ac* k* nat-c k* **Nat-m** k* nat-ox rly4• nat-p k* nat-s *Nit-ac* k* nux-m b2.de **Nux-v** k* olib-sac wmh1 olnd k* par k* petr k* *Petros* mrr1 **Ph-ac** k* *Phos* k* pin-con oss2• plac-s rly4• *Plan* plb k* *Podo* positr nl2• propl ub1• prun **Puls** k* pulx br1 ran-b b2.de* rhod b2.de* *Rhus-t* k* ribo rly4• ruta k* sabad k* **Sabin** k* sal-al blc1• sal-fr sle1• samb k* sang bg2 sarr **Sars** k* *Sec* k* sel k* *Senec* *Seneg* k* **Sep** k* sil k* *Spig* k* spong k* **Squil** k* stann k* **Staph** k* stram k* stront-c k* suis-hep rly4• **Sulph** k* suprar rly4• taosc iwa1• tarax k* **Thuj** k* thymol sp1 tritic-vg fd5.de valer k* vanil fd5.de verat k* verb k* *Vesp* vib *Viol-t* k* visc sp1 *Zinc* k* zinc-p k2
  - **day** and night: *Apis* arg-met cact *Carb-v* k* castm kali-c k* kali-i mag-c mag-m k* merc k* nat-c k* nat-m k* *Rhus-t* sars k* sil sulph thuj
  - **daytime**: ferr-p k* hippoc-k szs2 kali-bi led mag-m h2* *Mang* phos h2*

- **morning**: *Alum* am-m ambr k* arn b7a.de berb coc-c k* coff graph lil-t ruta senec k* *Sep* **Sulph** taosc iwa1• thuj bg1
  - **8** h: (non:puls slp) puls-n slp
  - **8**-9 h: ferr
  - **early**: ambr bg2 carb-v h2*
  - **rising** agg.: berb mez plan k* **Sulph**
  - **waking**; on: allox sp1 ant-c bg2 ant-t b7.de* apoc k* bamb-a stb2.de• borx b4a.de carb-v bg2 caust b4.de* chinin-s croc b7.de* dig b4a.de hep k* mag-c bg2 merc mez *Sars* sil bg2 tarax b7a.de
- **forenoon**: aloe bros-gau mrc1 mez k*
  - **10** h: am-m *Equis-h*
- **afternoon**: bell k* chinin-s cic k* equis-h ferr k* hyper k* indg k* lil-t merc merc-sul k* *Nux-v* k* petr podo fd3.de• sabad *Sulph*
- **evening**: aloe alum am-c k* *Bell* k* *Coloc* guar guare k* kreos *Lyc* k* nat-m k* nux-m olib-sac wmh1 ozone sde2• pall a1 *Puls* *Sabad* k* *Sep* *Sulph* k* thuj vanil fd5.de *Zinc* k*
  - **21** h | **waking**; on: mag-c h2
  - **lying** agg.: lyc k* zinc h2*
- **night**: agar k* aids nl2• *Alum* k* alum-sil k2 am-c k* am-m bg2 anac k* androc srj1• ant-c h2* ant-t k* apis arg-n bg2* *Arn* k* *Ars* k* *Ars-i* ars-s-f k2 *Aur-m* k* bar-c bg2 *Bell* k* *Borx* k* bov bg2 bry k* *Calc* k* calc-i k2 calc-p bg2 calc-sil k2 *Cann-s* b7a.de carb-an b4a.de* carb-v k* carbn-s cartl-s rly4• caust k* cench k2 chim cina k* clem k* coca-c sk4• coff bg2 *Con* k* croc k* cupr k* daph bg2 **Dig** k* dros bg2 dulc fd4.de equis-h *Ery-a* euphr k* gink-b sbd1• *Graph* k* hep k* hippoc-k szs2 hyper k* iod k* irid-met srj5• kali-ar *Kali-bi* kali-c k* kali-m k2 kali-p kali-s kali-sil k2 kola stb3• *Kreos* k* lac-c bg2 *Lach* k* **Lyc** k* mag-c k* *Mag-m* k* med meph k* *Merc* k* mez mur-ac k* nat-ar nat-c k* *Nat-m* k* nat-p k* nicc k* *Nit-ac* k* nux-m *Nux-v* k* op bg2 pant-ac rly4• petr k* ph-ac k* *Phos* pieri-b mlk9.de podo fd3.de• propl ub1• puls k* *Rhus-t* k* ruta bg2* sabal ptk1 sabin k* sal-fr sle1• *Samb* k* sang bg2 sars bg2 sec k* sep k* **Sil** k* sinus rly4• spig k* spong fd4.de squil k* stram k* stry a1 sul-ac k* sul-i k2 sulfonam ks2 **Sulph** k* suprar rly4• syph tab *Thuj* k* thymol sp1 vanil fd5.de wies a1 zinc zinc-p k2 [bell-p-sp dcm1]
  - **midnight**: aids nl2• ant-t k* hydrog srj2• nat-c k* podo fd3.de• sulph k*
    - **at** | **0**-3 h: acon
    - **after**:
      - **2** h: anth con hyper kola stb3• (non:puls slp) puls-n slp (non:uran-met k) uran-n
      - **3** h: *Dig* kola stb3• sarr
      - **3**.30 h: canth
      - **4** h: mag-c h2 merc
  - **coition**; after: *Nat-p* k*
  - **waking**; on: ant-c h2 ant-t caust dig euph hep luna kg1• mag-m murx sil staph succ-ac rly4•
- **abdomen**, on touching: acon k*
- **absent**: **Ars** bell both-ax tsm2 calad **Caust** ferr hell *Hyos* *Lac-c* lat-m bnm6• mag-m k2 op *Ox-ac* pall *Phos* *Plb* stann verat
  - **distended** bladder, with: **Ars** *Calad* **Caust** fl-ac hell *Hyos* op pall *Phos* *Plb* stann verat
    - **urine** flows without trouble; if desired: phos k*
  - **pregnancy** agg.; during: hyos ptk1
- **accompanied** by:
  - **diarrhea** (See RECTUM - Diarrhea - accompanied - urination - urging)
  - **discharge**:
    - **frequent**: ulm-c jsj8•
    - **profuse**: agar b4.de agn b7.de *Alum* b4.de* ant-t b7.de **Arg-met** b7.de* arn b7.de *Ars* b4.de* *Bar-c* b4a.de* **Bell** b4.de* bism b7.de *Bry* b7a.de calc b4.de **Carb-an** b4a.de* caust b4a.de chel b7.de chin bg2 chinin-s bg2 chlor bg2 *Cic* b7a.de cina b7.de* cocc b7.de colch bg2 coloc b4a.de cycl b7.de* *Guaj* b4a.de *Hell* bg2 hep b4a.de iod b4a.de kali-c b4a.de *Kali-n* b4a.de* **Kreos** b7a.de* lac-c bg2 *Lach* bg2 *Led* b7a.de *Lyc* b4a.de m-arct b7.de mang b4.de *Merc* b4a.de *Mur-ac* b4.de* *Nat-c* b4.de* **Nat-m** b4a.de* *Ph-ac* b4a.de *Rhus-t* b7.de* *Sabin* b7a.de samb b7.de* *Sars* b4a.de spig b7.de* spong bg2 squil b7.de* *Stann* b4.de* *Staph* b7.de* *Sulph* b4.de* tarax b7.de* thuj b4a.de* *Valer* b7.de* verb b7.de* viol-t b7.de* zinc b4.de
- **accompanied** by – **discharge**: ...
    - **scanty**: acon b7a.de* agar b4.de* am-c b4.de* am-m b7.de anac b4a.de* ang b7.de* ant-c b7.de* ant-t b7.de* ars b4a.de aur b4.de* aur-m bg2 bar-c b4.de bell b4.de* brom bg2 bry b7.de* calc b4.de **Cann-xyz** bg2 **Canth** b7.de caps b7.de *Carb-v* bg2 caust b4.de* chel b7.de* chin b7.de* clem b4.de *Cocc* b7.de* coff b7.de colch b7.de* *Coloc* b4.de* con b4.de cupr b7.de* cycl b7.de **Dig** b4.de* dros b7.de* **Dulc** b4a.de euph b4.de* fl-ac bg2 *Graph* b4.de* hell b7.de* hep b4a.de hyos b7.de* iod b4.de* *Ip* b7.de* kali-c b4.de* kali-n b4.de *Kreos* b7a.de lach bg2 laur b7.de led b7.de* *M-aust* b7.de mag-m b4.de* mang b4.de meny b7.de* *Merc* b4.de* mur-ac b4.de nat-c b4.de nat-m b4.de nit-ac b4a.de* nux-m b7.de **Nux-v** b7.de* petr b4.de* ph-ac b4.de* phos b4.de* plb b7.de* **Puls** b7.de* *Rhus-t* bg2 **Ruta** b7.de* sabad b7.de* sabin b7.de* *Samb* b7.de* sars b4.de* sec b7.de *Sep* b4.de* sil b4a.de* **Spong** b7a.de* **Staph** b7.de* stram b7a.de *Sulph* b4.de* *Verat* b7a.de* verb b7.de viol-t b7.de zinc b4.de
  - **pain** (See Pain - urination - urging to)
  - **pain**; pressing (See Pain - urination - urging - pressing)
  - **urine**; bloody (See URINE - Bloody - accompanied - urination - urging)
  - **Abdomen**; pain in (See ABDOMEN - Pain - accompanied - urination - urging)
  - **Face**; pale: ph-ac bg2
  - **Hypogastrium**; pain in (See ABDOMEN - Pain - hypogastrium - urination - urging)
  - **Lumbar** region; pain in (See BACK - Pain - lumbar - urination - urging)
  - **Perineum**; pain in (See RECTUM - Pain - perineum - urination - urging)
- **anxious**: (↗*MIND - Anxiety)* **Acon** k* agn bg2 arn tl1 *Ars* k* canth tl1 **Carb-v** k* caust tl1 *Cham* k* coloc tl1 cur **Dig** k* graph k* ign tl1 ph-ac phyt sanic tl1 sep k* staph tl1 til
  - **urinate**, on beginning to: **Acon**
- **apples**, after: mang h2*
- **apyrexia**: ant-t dros hell hyos lyc ph-ac phos thuj
- **beer**; after: *Puls* b7a.de *Sulph* b4a.de
- **chill**; during: *Ant-t* k* bry k* chin k* dulc k* lyc k* meph nux-v k* ph-ac k* phos k* puls k* sulph k*
- **coffee** agg.: cain cob k* ign k* *Olnd* b7a.de tritic-vg fd5.de
- **coition**; after: *Nat-p* k2* staph bro1
- **constant**: absin a1* *Acon* k* agar k* agath-a nl2• alf br1* all-s aloe bro1 am-c am-m anac k* anan bro1 ant-c **Apis** k* apoc k* aran *Arn* ars ars-i ars-s-f k2 asar k* aur aur-ar k2 *Aur-m* aur-s k2 bar-c bar-i k2 bar-m bar-s k2 baros br1* *Bell* k* *Benz-ac* bro1 *Berb* k* both-ax tsm2 brach k* brom k* *Cact* k* cain calc k* *Camph* bro1 cann-i cann-s k2* **Canth** k* caps bro1 carb-v bro1 carbn-s *Caust* k* cean bro1 chel k* *Chim* cimic hr1 clem k2 coc-c k* *Colch* k* **Con** k* *Cop* k* crot-t cub bro1 *Cycl* **Dig** k* *Dios* k* *Dulc* k* **Equis-h** k* erig bro1* **Ery-a** k* *Eup-per* bro1 eup-pur k* *Ferr* k* ferr-act bro1 ferr-ar *Ferr-m* bro1 ferr-p k* gali c2 gaul br1 gels bro1 graph *Guaj* k* ham k* *Hell* k* hep hyos bro1 ign indg a1* iod k* kali-ar *Kali-bi* k* kali-br bro1 *Kali-c* k* kali-m k2 kali-p k* kali-s kali-sil k2 kreos bro1 **Lac-c** k* **Lil-t** k* *Lyc* k* lyss k* melal-alt gya4 **Merc** k* **Merc-c** k* merc-i-r methyl br1 mill k* mit bro1 morph k* mur-ac *Murx* bro1 nat-ar nat-c k* nat-m k* nat-p nit-m-ac bro1 *Nux-m* *Nux-v* k* onos c2 op bro1 oxyd br1 oxyt c2* **Pareir** k* petr k* *Petros* hr1* ph-ac k* phos k* phys a1* plan mtf11 *Prun* k* *Puls* pyrus c2 rhus-a bro1 rumx ruta k* sabad k* sabal bro1* sabin k2 sang sec *Senec* bro1 *Seneg* c2* *Sep* k* *Sil* k* spirae br1 *Squil* *Staph* k* *Stigm* bro1 **Stry** k* sul-ac k* sulfon bro1 **Sulph** k* sumb k* tab k* tarent k* *Ter* c2* thlas br1 *Thuj* k* tritic c2* tritic-vg fd5.de uva br1 valer k* verat k* verb br1 vesi bro1 viol-t zinc zing bro1
  - **daytime**: kali-bi k*
  - **evening** | **lying** agg.: lyc k*
  - **night**: *Apis* **Dig** k* *Ery-a* *Lil-t* *Merc* k* *Sabal* bro1 thuj
    - **erections**; with: mosch k* *Rhus-t* k*
    - **every** other: bar-c

Bladder

- **constant**: ...
  - **accompanied** by:
    - **Heart**:
      - **inflammation** of | **Pericardium** (See CHEST - Inflammation - heart - pericardium - accompanied - bladder)
    - **Meninges**; inflammation of (See HEAD - Inflammation - meninges - accompanied - bladder)
    - **Ovaries**; inflammation of (See FEMALE - Inflammation - ovaries - accompanied - bladder)
    - **Pleura**; inflammation of (See CHEST - Inflammation - pleura - accompanied - bladder)
  - **cold** agg.; becoming: *Dulc* lyc
  - **delivery**; after: op bro1* *Staph* bro1*
  - **distended** bladder, with passing only a few drops: all-s
  - **pain** in liver, chest and kidneys; with: *Ferr*
  - **prolapsus** of uterus, during: **Lil-t** k* **SEP** k ●* uva
  - **running** water; at sight of: canth bro1 lyss k* sulph bro1
  - **sitting** agg.: caps chim
  - **warmth** | **amel.**: **Nux-v** mrr1
  - **women**; in: berb bro1 cop bro1 cub bro1 *Eup-pur* bro1 gels bro1 hed bro1 kreos bro1 senec bro1 *Sep* bro1 staph bro1
- **cough** agg.; during: *Caps* b7a.de ip b7.de* *Samb* b7a.de
- **delivery**; during: *Kreos* b7a.de nux-v bro1
- **dragging** down in pelvis, with: lac-c *Lil-t* **Sep**
- **drinking** agg.; after: bamb-a stb2.de• podo ruta fd4.de suprar rly4• tritic-vg fd5.de
- **drops** pass until the next stool, when it flows freely; only a few: all-s am-m
- **dyspnea**; during: sul-ac dgt
- **eating** | **after** | **agg.**: bar-c h2* lyc h2* nat-p k2
  - **while** | **agg.**: mang b4a.de*
- **erections**:
  - **before**: pyrog pd
  - **with**: hep kali-p mosch nat-c h2 *Rhus-t* sil
- **fever**; during: acon k* *Ant-t* k* **Apis** k* *Bell* k* bry k* canth k* caust k* dulc k* graph k* hell k* hyos k* kali-c k* lyc k* nux-v k* ph-ac k* *Puls* k* rhus-t k* sabin k* sars k* squil k* staph k* sulph k*
- **frequent**: *(↗frequent)* *Acon* k* act-sp *Aesc* aeth agar k* agath-a nl2• agn bro1 aids nl2• alf bro1 *Aloe* k* *Alum* k* alum-sil k2 alumn am-c am-m amp rly4• anac ang ant-c k* *Ant-t* **Apis** k* aran **Arg-met** *Arg-n* k* **Arn** ars *Ars-i* *Aspar* k* *Aur-m* k* **Bar-c** k* bar-i k2 **Bar-m** bar-s k2 **Bell** k* *Benz-ac* k* *Berb* k* bor-ac br1* *Borx* *Bov* brucel sa3• *Bry* *Cact* *Calc* k* calc-ar bro1 calc-i k2 *Calc-p* k* camph hr1 *Cann-s* k* **Canth** k* *Caps* k* *Carb-an* *Carb-v* carbn-s carl bro1 **Caust** k* cedr *Cham* *Chel* **Chim** k* *Chin* chinin-ar chinin-s *Chlol* cic *Cimic* *Cina* *Clem* k* cob **Coc-c** k* *Cocc* coff *Colch* bro1 **Coloc** k* *Con* conv k* *Cop* corn *Cub* k* *Cupr* cur *Cycl* daph des-ac rbp6 **Dig** k* *Dios* *Dros* dulc echi *Equis-h* k* erig *Ery-a* *Eup-pur* euph euphr ferr-p k* *Ferr-pic* bro1 *Fl-ac* form bro1 *Gels* k* germ-met srj5• glyc bro1 *Guaj* *Guare* ham **Hell** k* *Hep* hippoc-k szs2 hydrang bro1 hydrog srj2• *Hyos* *Ign* k* *Indg* indol bro1 inul br1 iod ip h1 jatr-c bro1 kali-ar kali-bi *Kali-c* k* *Kali-i* kali-m k2 **Kali-n** *Kali-p* kali-s kali-sil k2 kalm k* **Kreos** k* **Lac-ac** k* **Lac-c** lac-d lac-del hrn2• *Lach* lap-la sde8.de• *Led* **Lil-t** k* lith-be bro1 *Lith-c* k* **Lyc** k* *Mag-m* *Mang* mang-p rly4• med br1 *Meny* meph **Merc** k* **Merc-c** k* *Merc-i-r* mez moni rfm1• morph *Mur-ac* murx nat-ar *Nat-c* k* **Nat-m** nat-p neon srj5• *Nit-ac* k* nux-m **Nux-v** k* oci bro1 ol-an *Ol-sant* bro1 *Olnd* ox-ac k* pall par *Pareir* *Petr* *Petros* *Ph-ac* k* *Phos* pilo bro1 pin-con oss2• plb k* plut-n srj7• podo positr nl2• prun k* *Psor* **Puls** k* pulx br1* ran-b c1 raph rat rhod *Rhus-r* **Rhus-t** *Rumx* ruta *Sabad* sabal bro1 *Sabin* k* sacch-a fd2.de• sal-fr sle1• *Samb* k* santin bro1 *Sars* k* sec bro1 *Sel* *Sep* k* sil k* *Spig* *Spong* **Squil** k* *Stann* **Staph** k* stram sul-ac sul-i k2 **Sulph** k* sumb syc pte1• syph tab *Tarax* *Ter* **Thuj** *Tril-p* trios rsj11• tritic bro1 tritic-vg fd5.de tub jl2 *Uva* k* vanil fd5.de verat verb *Vesp* k* viol-t zinc zing k* [bell-p-sp dcm1]
  - **daytime**: allox tpw3
  - **afternoon**: aloe *Chel* a1 equis-h
  - **evening**: guare k* kreos *Lyc* sabad sep *Sulph* k* *Thuj* tritic-vg fd5.de zinc

- **frequent**: ...
  - **night**: alum bro1 *Aur-m* bro1 borx bro1 calc bro1 carb-ac bro1 *Caust* bro1 coc-c bro1 *Con* bro1 elaps fkr8.de ferr bro1 *Ferr-pic* bro1 glyc bro1 *Graph* bro1 *Kali-c* bro1 kali-s fd4.de *Kreos* bro1 lina st lycpr bro1 mag-s a1 murx bro1 nat-c h2* nat-m h2* *Ph-ac* bro1 phys bro1 pic-ac bro1 *Puls* bro1 ruta fd4.de sang bro1 sars bro1 sep bro1 squil bro1 *Sulph* bro1 ter bro1 thuj bro1 wies a1 xero bro1
    - **and** day: aloe apis *Aur-m* carb-v h2* chim *Ery-a* *Lyc* mag-m nit-ac *Rhus-t* k* ruta fd4.de senec k*
  - **accompanied** by:
    - **discharge**:
      - **copious**: *Agn* b7.de *Alum* b4a.de ang b7.de* ant-c b7a.de *Apis* b7a.de *Arg-met* b7.de* ars b4.de *Bar-c* b4a.de *Bell* b4a.de *Bism* b7.de* **Cann-s** b7.de* **Caust** b4a.de chel b7.de* cina b7.de* cocc b7.de* coff b7.de* colch b7a.de cupr b7.de cycl b7.de* *Euphr* b7.de* guaj b4.de *Hell* b7a.de hyos b7a.de ign b7.de* iod ptk1 **Kali-n** b4a.de *Kreos* b7a.de lach b7.de* *Led* b7.de* m-arct b7.de m-aust b7.de *Merc* b4.de* *Mur-ac* b4a.de **Nat-m** b4a.de olnd b7.de *Ph-ac* b4a.de rheum b7.de *Rhus-t* b7.de* ruta b7.de* sabin b7.de **Samb** b7a.de *Sars* b4a.de *Sel* b7.de seneg b4.de *Spig* b7.de* *Squil* b7.de* stann b4.de staph b7.de *Sulph* b4a.de *Tarax* b7.de *Valer* b7a.de *Verb* b7.de* *Viol-t* b7.de*
      - **scanty**: agar b4a.de am-c b4.de* anac b4a.de ang b7a.de ant-c b7a.de *Ant-t* b7a.de bar-c b4.de *Bry* b7.de *Canth* b7a.de caps b7.de *Caust* b4.de* chin b7.de clem b4.de *Cocc* b7.de *Colch* b7.de **Con** b4.de* cupr b7a.de cycl b7.de *Dig* b4.de* dros b7a.de *Dulc* b4a.de euph b4.de* *Graph* b4a.de guaj b4.de *Hell* b7.de hep b4a.de hyos b7a.de **Kali-c** b4.de* kali-n b4.de *Lach* b7a.de *Led* b7a.de mag-m b4a.de meny b7a.de merc b4.de *Merc-c* b4a.de nat-c b4.de* nat-m b4.de* nit-ac b4a.de nux-v b7a.de petr b4.de* *Ph-ac* b4.de* **Phos** b4.de* plb b7.de puls b7.de ruta b7a.de sabad b7a.de sabin b7a.de sars b4.de seneg b4.de sil b4a.de *Stann* b4a.de *Staph* b7.de sulph b4.de *Viol-t* b7a.de
  - **alternating** with suppression of urine (See KIDNEYS - Suppression - alternating)
  - **children**, infants scream before the urine passes: *Borx* lach *Lyc* nux-v *Sars*
  - **cold**; after taking a: *Dulc* *Eup-pur* *Ip* *Lyc* k* puls
    - **air**; in dry cold: acon k1
  - **cutting** pain from umbilical to ovarian region: coloc
  - **desire** increases as the quantity of urine diminishes: *Equis-h* k* scut c1
  - **flatus**:
    - **passing**; when: *Puls*
    - **upward** and downward; with: cycl
  - **immediately**; if he does not urinate | **involuntary**; he feels as if urine passed: bry
  - **menopause**; during: sars vh
  - **menses**:
    - **after** | **agg.**: cham puls sars h2*
    - **before** | **agg.**: *Alum* apis asar kali-c **Kali-i** k* nux-v phos *Puls* *Sars* *Sulph*
    - **during** | **agg.**: calc nux-m
    - **suppressed** menses; from: *Canth* cham *Dig* k* dros *Gels* ign nat-m **Puls** sulph
  - **minutes** | **thirty** minutes; every: allox tpw3 tritic-vg fd5.de
  - **motion** agg.; the slightest: *Berb*
  - **prolapsus**, with: alum aur lac-c **Lil-t** **SEP** k ● uva vh
  - **sitting** | **amel.**: phos h2*
  - **standing** agg.: phos h2*
  - **tone** of sphincter; from loss of: apoc jug-r
  - **urine**; for large amounts of: equis-h mrr1
  - **without** passing any, then while sitting involuntary flow: *Caust*
- **frosty** weather; after: arist-cl sp1
- **heat**; during: ph-ac bg2
- **hysterical**: gels ptk

- **ineffectual**: *Acon* k* agar b2.de* aids nl2• all-c bg2 alum k* alum-sil k2 am-c b2.de* am-m anac b2.de* anan vh1 ang bg2 ant-c b2.de* ant-t bg2 *Apis* **Apoc** k* aran arg-n k* **Arn** k* **Ars** k* ars-s-f k2 atro aur k* aur-ar k2 aur-m bg2 aur-s k2 bar-c b2.de bar-m *Bell* k* bism b2.de *Borx* k* both-ax tsm2 bov b2.de brom bg2 bry b2.de* *Cact* k* *Calc* k* calc-sil k2 *Camph* k* *Cann-i* k* **Cann-s** b2.de* **Canth** k* *Caps* k* carb-ac k* *Carb-an* k* *Carb-v* b2.de* carbn-s **Caust** k* cedr k* *Cham* k* chel k* **Chim** k* *Chin* k* chinin-ar cic b2.de* *Cimx* cit-ac rly4• *Clem* k* coc-c k* coff k* coff-t a1 colch k* *Coloc* k* *Con* k* *Cop* k* croc b2.de crot-h bg2 *Cupr* k* *Cycl* der a1 **Dig** k* dol dros bg2 dulc k* **Eup-pur** euph b2.de* ferr-i k* fl-ac bg2 gels graph k* *Guaj* k* **Hell** k* hep k* **Hyos** k* iod b2.de* *Ip* k* *Kali-ar* *Kali-c* k* kali-chl bg2 kali-m k2 kali-n b2.de *Kali-p* kali-s kali-sil k2 kreos k* *Lach* k* *Laur* k* led b2.de* *Lyc* k* mag-m b2.de* malar jl2 mang b2.de meny bg2 merc k* merc-c k* morph k* mur-ac k* myric nat-c b2.de nat-m k* **Nit-ac** k* nux-m b2.de* **Nux-v** k* **Op** k* par b2.de *Pareir* k* paull a1 petr k* *Petros* **Ph-ac** k* phel **Phos** k* *Plb* k* podo prun k* **Puls** k* rhus-t k* ruta k* sabad b2.de* sabin k* *Samb* **Sars** k* scut c1 sec k* senec *Sep* k* sil k* spong bg2 squil k* stann b2.de* staph k* staphycoc rly4• **Stram** k* stront-c b2.de sulph k* sumb tarent k* ter bg2 thuj k* uran-n bg2 verat k* verb bg2 viol-t b2.de* vip a1 zinc k* zinc-p k2
  - **morning**: alum bg2
  - **night**: alum-p k2 coc-c k* nat-m *Sep*
  - **children**; in: **Acon** *Apis* camph eup-pur *Lyc*
  - **chill**; during: arn k* ars k* canth k* nux-v k* phos k* puls k* sulph k*
  - **cramps** in rectum, with: *Caust*
  - **diarrhea**, with: cupr
  - **fever**; during: ars k* canth k* dig k* hyos k* nux-v k* *Puls* k* rat sars k* sulph k*
  - **headache**; during: **Con**
  - **menses**; during: *Aur*
  - **perspiration**; during: **Ars** k* camph k* *Canth* k* caps bg2 caust k* cocc bg2 dig k* dulc k* hyos k* *Merc* bg2 *Nux-v* k* *Puls* k* rheum bg2 *Rhus-t* bg2 sulph k*
  - **pregnancy** agg.; during: *Lyc* hr1
  - **standing** agg.: *Caust* h2 phos h2*
    - **sitting**, urine flows involuntary; then while: *Caust*
  - **stool** | **urging** to; with: alum *Canth* *Dig* nat-m *Nux-v* sumb
  - **strain**, stool and urine pass involuntarily; but as soon as he ceases to: *Arg-n*
- **intermittent**: sabin b7.de
- **irresistible** (See sudden)
- **lifting**; after: *Bry* k*
- **lying**:
  - **agg.**: androc srj1• calc-sil k2 ham lyc nux-v vanil fd5.de
  - **amel.**: dig b4a.de
  - **back**; on:
    - **agg.**: prun *Puls* k*
    - **amel.**: dig
  - **side**; on:
    - **right** | **agg.**: phos prun
- **married** women, newly: **Staph** k*
- **menses**:
  - **after** | **agg.**: cham puls
  - **before** | **agg.**: alum am-m b7.de apis asar aur bg1 canth kali-c **Kali-i** k* lac-c nux-v phos k* *Puls* k* pulx br1 sars k* *Sulph*
  - **during**:
    - **agg.**: alum ant-t apis calc cham chin kali-i nux-m k* nux-v phos puls rat sabin b7.de* *Sars* k* sep sulph b4a.de
    - **beginning** of menses | **agg.**: sars b4.de
  - **suppressed** menses; from: *Sars* b4a.de
- **mental** exertion agg.: calc kali-c
- **motion** agg.: berb bry calc-sil k2 chlam-tr bcx2•
- **old** people; in: | **women**; old: cop
- **painful**: **Acon** k* *Agar* alumn ant-t k* anth *Apis* k* arn b7.de* *Bell* b4a.de berb borx b4a.de bov *Cann-s* k* **Canth** k* *Carb-an* carbn-s *Chim* cocc b7.de* *Colch* b7a.de *Coloc* b4a.de con *Dig* **Dulc** b4a.de *Eup-pur* graph k* hell k* hep b4a.de ip h1* kali-i k* *Lac-c* laur *Lil-t* *Lyc* k* **Nux-v** k* **Pareir** k* *Phyt* k* plb b7.de* *Prun* k* *Puls* k* raph k* *Rhus-a* rhus-r ribo rly4• ruta b7a.de* sabin b7.de* sec k* spig b7.de* *Staph* b7a.de *Sulph* ter ptk1 thuj *Uva* verat k*
  - **children**; in:
    - **cry**: apis k2 **Borx** lach **Lyc** *Nux-v* **Sars**
      - **urination**; before (See MIND - Weeping - urination - before - children)
    - **grasp** the genitals and cry out: **Acon** merc
    - **jump** up and down with pain, if urging cannot be gratified: *Petros* k*
  - **menstrual** flow starts; disappears when: *Kali-i*
  - **stool** | **urging** to; with: aloe *Alum* *Aphis* canth caps pd cic cub cupr-ar cycl *Dig* erig pd kreos merc-c pd nat-m **Nux-v** *Prun* *Rhus-t* *Staph* sumb tub jl2
- **painless**: cycl b7.de* *Tarax* b7.de*
- **perspiration**; during: *Ant-t* k* apis k* arn k* **Bry** k* canth k* *Caust* k* dulc k* graph k* hell k* hyos k* lyc k* **Merc** k* mur-ac k* *Nux-v* k* *Ph-ac* k* phos k* puls k* rhus-t k* squil k* staph k* sulph k* **Thuj** k*
- **pregnancy** agg.; during: acon bell b4a.de cham b7a.de *Cocc* b7a.de* con bg2 nux-v b7a.de* *Ph-ac* bg2 *Puls* k* sulph k* thuj hr1
- **pressure** in rectum, with: nat-m k* nat-n
- **prolapsus**, with: uva vh
- **riding** a horse: | **amel.**: lyc
- **seminal** emission, after: borx b4a.de* sulph h2
- **shuddering**; with: hyper
- **sitting**:
  - **agg.**: caps caust chim clem bg1 phos
  - **amel.**: bar-c h2* canth k*
- **sleep**; during: dig b4.de
- **standing**:
  - **agg.**: canth k* cop ferr-p bg1* phos k* sars bg2
  - **amel.**: sep bg1
- **stool**:
  - **after**:
    - **agg.**: abrot canth bg2 carb-an k* *Cic* fl-ac dgt lach b7.de* merc-c bg2 phos h2 sel b7.de*
    - **amel.**: alum h2 am-m h2
  - **before**: alum b4a.de *Cham* b7a.de *Colch* b7a.de rheum ptk1 sars b4a.de
  - **urging** to | **with**: *Colch* b7a.de ferr bg1 hippoc-k szs2
- **sudden**: acon bro1 agar k* allox tpw3* *Aloe* k* ambr k* androc srj1• *Apis* bro1 *Arg-n* k* arn ptk1 ars-s-f k2 arum-d ptk2 atp rly4• *Bar-c* k* bar-s k2 bell k2 *Borx* k* bov k* *Bry* k* *Calc* calc-sil k2 *Cann-s* k* canth k* carb-an k* carbn-s carl bro1 caust k* chel k* clem ptk1 coc-c k* cortiso tpw7 cypra-eg sde6.de• dulc fd4.de equis-h bro1 *Ferr* *Ferr-p* graph k* hed bro1 hippoc-k szs2 *Ign* k* ignis-alc es2• kali-br k* ketogl-ac rly4• **Kreos** k* lath bro1 *Lil-t* med bg1 *Merc* k* *Merc-c* bro1 murx bro1 naphtin bro1 nat-c k* *Nat-m* nat-sil fd3.de• *Nit-ac* nux-v ptk1 ol-an bro1 ox-ac pareir bg2* petr **Petros** k* **Ph-ac** k* *Phos* k* *Pop* bro1 positr nl2• *Prun* k* *Puls* k* quas bro1 *Rhus-t* k* ribo rly4• *Rumx* k* *Ruta* k* sabin b7.de* sanic ptk1 santin bro1 scut bro1 **Sep** k* ser-a-c jl2 sinus rly4• spong k* *Squil* k* sulfonam ks2 **Sulph** k* syc bka1• *Thuj* k* zinc-p k2
  - **morning**: phos k*
    - **waking**; on: hep sulph
  - **night**: caust ruta fd4.de *Sulph*
    - **child** wakes but cannot get out of bed soon enough: kreos k*
  - **attended** to; if the desire is not | **escaped**, which is not so; feels as if urine had: *Bry*
  - **hasten** to urinate or urine will escape; must: *Agar* allox tpw3 aloe k* ambr bg2 ant-c ant-t b7.de* apis bg2 *Arg-n* **Arn** ars ars-s-f k2 bar-c k* bar-s k2 bell k* borx k* brom *Bry* k* calc b4.de* *Camph* **Canth** carb-an bg2 *Caust* b4a.de *Chin* b7.de* cic **Clem** *Coc-c* *Colch* vh con bg2 cortiso gse dig bg2 dulc *Ferr-p* *Hyos* **Ign** b7a.de* kali-br kali-c bg1 **Kreos** k* lath bg1 *Lyc* b4a.de *M-aust* b7a.de mag-c bg2 *Merc* k* nat-m bg2 nat-sil fd3.de• **Nit-ac** b4a.de* **Nux-v** petr b4a.de *Petros* k* **Ph-ac** b4a.de* *Phos* k* plan plb prun bg2 **Puls** k* pulx br1 **Rhus-t** b7a.de* *Ruta* bg2 sabin b7.de **Sep** spong b7.de* *Squil* k* staph *Stram* **Sulph** k* *Thuj* k* verat zinc zinc-p k2

Bladder

- **sudden**: ...
  - **menses**; during: borx nat-m
  - **occupied**, she has to run and pass a few drops of urine; when busily: *(↗frequent - occupied)* *Calc* *Kali-c* k*
  - **running** water; at sight of: *Canth* k* kreos **Lyss** k* sulph k*
  - **sticking** forward in urethra, with: nat-c
  - **urine** was passing into glans; as if | **returning** and causing pain in urethra; then: *Prun* k*
  - **women**; in: but-ac sp1
- **thinking** of it, when: hell *Ox-ac* k* oxyt c1* sanic rb2
- **thirst**; with: agath-a nl2• ant-t k* castm caust k* gard-j vlr2• nat-m bg2 ph-ac k* positr nl2• verat k*
- **urination** agg.; after: am-m anac ang k* apis arn bg2 aur bar-c k* bell k2 *Berb* both-ax tsm2 *Bov* k* bry k* cact *Calc* k* *Cann-i* ***Cann-xyz*** bg2 canth bg2* caps bg2 carb-an caust *Chim* colch bg2* *Coli* jl2 con k* cop crot-t dig k* *Equis-h* k* graph *Guaj* k* *Hep* iod kali-c h2* kali-p fd1.de• kali-sil k2 lac-c lach k* laur k* merc k* **Merc-c** bg2* mur-ac h2* nat-c k* *Nux-v* bg2 pareir phos plb bg2 positr nl2• prun bg2 *Puls* k* *Ruta* k* sabad k* sabin sal-fr sle1• sars bg2 *Seneg* sil bg2 squil bg2 *Stann* k* *Staph* k* sulph b4a.de* sumb thuj k* vanil fd5.de verat viol-t k* zinc k* zinc-p k2
  - **immediately** after: *Coli* jl2
- **violent**: *Acon* ant-c arg-n *Arn* bar-m berb borx *Canth* k* **Dig** dulc fd4.de ephe-si hsj1• hist vml3• kali-p fd1.de• kreos led merc merc-c k2 *Nat-m* k* olib-sac wmh1 *Petros* k* phos phyt *Sabin* sep ser-a-c jl2 *Squil* sulph zinc h2*
  - **night**: borx *Sulph*
  - **menses**; during: ant-t chin kali-i nux-v rat sars *Sep*
  - **urination** agg.; after: berb k*
- **walking** agg.: *Alum* apis bg1 bry k* calc k* *Canth* k* caust k* ferr k* lith-c nat-m nat-s olib-sac wmh1 *Phos* puls ruta *Sep* zinc
- **warm** in bed agg.; becoming: *Ph-ac* b4a.de
- **water**:
  - **hearing** running water or putting hands in water: asim canth ham fd3.de• kreos **Lyss** k* **Sulph** k ●
  - **pouring** out medicine or anything liquid; when: ham k*
  - **touch** agg.: glycyr-g cte1•

- **walking** agg.: nat-m bg2

WALKING:
- **agg.**: con ptk1 prun ptk1 puls ptk1
- **air**; in open | **amel.**: *Ter* ptk1
- **amel.**: ign ptk1 ter ptk1

WEAKNESS: *(↗Paralytic)* *All-c* k* aloe bro1 *Alum* k* alum-p k2 alum-sil k2 *Alumn* anan bro1 *Apoc* bro1 *Ars* k* aur aur-m *Bell* c2* *Benz-ac* bro1 brach bro1 cact k2 calc b4a.de calc-p k2 *Camph* k* *Cann-i* bro1 *Canth* k* carl **Caust** k* *Cham* k* clem bro1 con k2* *Equis-h* k* erig bro1 eucal hr1 euphr bro1 gels k* hell k* helon mtf11 **Hep** k* *Hyos* k* ignis-alc es2• ipom-p kali-c kreos k2 laur *Lyc* b4a.de lycpr bro1 *M-aust* b7a.de **Mag-m** k* med jl2 mill **Mur-ac** k* nat-p k* *Nux-v* bro1 **Op** k* pall k* petr bro1 *Ph-ac* k* phyt pic-ac k2* plb pneu jl2* puls bro1 pulx bro1 rheum k* *Rhus-a* bro1 *Rhus-t* k* sabal bro1 santin bro1 *Sars* bro1 sel k* *Sil* *Stann* k* *Staph* bro1 stram suprar rly4• ter k* thuj thymol bro1 trib bro1 uva bro1 *Verb* bro1 vesi bro1 vib xero bro1 zinc zinc-p k2
- **evening**: *Alum* k* con k2
- **delivery**; after: **Ars** k* caust ptk1
- **old** people: *Ars* k* *Gels* k*
- **old** people; in: | **men**; old: alum bro1 *Benz-ac* bro1 carb-ac bro1 clem bro1 con bro1 *Pop* bro1 sel bro1 *Staph* bro1
- **paralytic**: con k2
- **press** to void completely; must: rheum h
- **sensation** of: alum b4a.de
- O - **Sphincter**: agar alumn apoc bell *Caust* k* ferr mtf33 jug-r mur-ac mrr1 pall sil squil zinc
  - **accompanied** by | **involuntary** urination (See Urination - involuntary - accompanied - sphincter)

WORM in; sensation of a: bell k* sep k*

AFTERNOON:
- **14** h: kalm bro1
- **16-20** h: *Morg-g* fmm1•

ABSCESS: arn bro1 *Ars* k* bell bro1 cetr hr1 *Hep* k* hippoz k* *Merc* k* sil k* ter hr1 verat-v bro1
- **perinephrium**: ars ptk1 *Canth* ptk1 chin ptk1 hep ptk1 lyc ptk1 puls ptk1 pyrog mtf11 sil ptk1 sul-i ptk1

ADDISON'S disease: adren c2* ant-c k* apom bro1 arg-n k* *Ars* k* *Ars-i* k* bac c1* *Bell* k* **Calc** k* calc-ar k* calc-i k2 calc-p ptk1 carb-v k* caust k* chin k* coli jl2 cortiso sp1 cupr *Ferr* k* *Ferr-i* k* hydr-ac bro1 **Iod** k* kali-ar *Kali-c* k* kreos k* lyc malar jl2 mang k* med k* **Nat-m** k* nat-s *Nit-ac* k* ol-j k* p-benzq mtf11 petr c2 **Phos** k* pic-ac k* psor sec k* *Sep* k* **Sil** k* *Spig* k* *Sulph* k* *Suprar* bro1 ther thuj bro1 *Tub* bro1 vanad c1*

ANALGESICS; from: (↗*GENERALS - Analgesics*) lyc mtf sulph mtf

ATROPHY: (↗*Renal - chronic*) alum mtf calc-f mtf mag-m mtf mag-s mtf plb mtf

BERGER'S DISEASE (See Inflammation - glomeruli)

BUBBLING sensation in region of: *Berb* k* lyc *Med* k* thuj bg2*

CALCULI (See Stones)

CANCER: calc sne chim sne form sne sars gm1 solid sne

CATARRH: alum k2 canth coll dam br1 dulc k2 kali-c k2 petr k* sars k2 sil sulph

CHILLS; creeping: med tl1

COLD:
- **sensation**: med rb1 spira k*

○ • **Region** of: cham k* coc-c bg2* ozone sde2• [tax jsj7]

COLIC (See Pain; Pain - cramping; Pain - ureters; Pain - ureters - cramping; Stones)

COMPLAINTS of kidneys: (↗*URINARY - Complaints*) acon b2.de* agar bg2 alum b2.de* ambr bg2 ant-c bg2 apis bg2* arg-n bg2 *Ars* ptk1 *Bell* b2.de* **Berb** bg2* borx b2.de* brach br1 calc bg2 camph b2.de* *Cann-s* b2.de* **Canth** b2.de* carb-an bg2 *Chim* br1 chin bg2 clem b2.de* cocc b2.de* colch b2.de* coloc bg2 dig b2.de* germ-met srj5• helon ptk1 *Hep* b2.de* ichth br1 iod bg2 *Kali-bi* bg2* *Kali-c* b2.de* kali-n b2.de* lach bg2 **Lyc** bg2* merc b2.de* **Merc-c** bg2* nat-m bg2* nat-sal br1 nit-ac bg2 nux-m bg2 *Nux-v* b2.de* oci br1 pareir bg2 petr bg2 ph-ac b2.de* phos bg2 plb b2.de* polyg-h ptk1 **Puls** b2.de* ran-s b2.de* rheum bg2 rhus-a br1 rhus-t ptk1 samb ptk1 **Sars** bg2 scop ptk1 sep bg2 *Ser-ang* br1 sil bg2 solid ptk1 squil b2.de* stront-c ptk1 sulph b2.de* ter bg2* terebe ktp9 *Thuj* b2.de* tub br1* vip br1 *Zinc* b2.de* [*Lith-c* stj2 *Lith-i* stj2 *Lith-p* stj2]
- **alternating** sides: cinnb bg2
- **right**: am-be bro1 apis bg2 berb ptk1 cann-i bro1 *Chel* bro1 cimic bg2 clem bg2 coc-c bg2* equis-h bro1 grat bg2 iod bg2 lith-c bro1 lyc bg2* *Nux-v* bg2* oci bro1* phyt bro1 pic-ac bro1 sabin bg2 sars bg2* *Ter* bro1
- **left**: aesc bro1 *Berb* bg2* chin bg2* coloc bg2* dig bg2 *Hed* bro1 hydrang bro1 kali-c bg2 mang bg2 merc bg2* morg-g fmm1• pareir bg2* ran-b bg2 tab bro1 thuj bg2 uva bro1 *Zinc* ptk1
- **accompanied** by:
  - **bone** diseases: calc-act mtf11
  - **diabetes**: saroth mtf11
  - **hypertension**: cupr mtf11 pic-ac mtf11 plb mtf11
  - **hypotension**: cupr mtf11
  - **indigestion**: apoc bro1
  - **rheumatism**: rad-br ptk1 ter ptk1
  - **swelling**; edematous (See GENERALS - Dropsy - external - kidney)
  - **vision**; complaints of (See VISION - Complaints - accompanied - kidneys)
  - **vomiting**: kreos bro1* nux-v bro1 senec ptk1
  - ○ **Back** | **complaints** of: cadm-s ptk1 senec ptk1 solid ptk1
  - **Ears**; complaints of: thuj ptk1 *Viol-o* ptk1
  - **Eyes**; complaints of: ter mtf11 viol-o ptk1

Complaints of kidneys: ...
  - **Head**; complaints of (See HEAD - Complaints - accompanied - kidneys)
  - **Heart**; complaints of the (See CHEST - Heart; complaints - accompanied - kidneys)
  - **Lumbar** region; complaints of: calc-ar ptk1 senec ptk1 solid ptk1 visc ptk1
  - **Lungs**; edema of: cortico sp1
  - **Skin**; complaints of: cub c1 sars mrr1
- **chronic**: meli mtf11
- **toxic**: ars mtf carb-v mtf kali-i mtf op mtf plb mtf

▽ - **extending** to | **Inguinal** region: lycps-v bg2

○ - **Ureters**: apis ptk1 *Bell* ptk1 *Berb* ptk1 canth ptk1 carb-an ptk1 hydrang br1 *Lyc* ptk1 oci ptk1 par ptk1 polyg-h ptk1 **Sars** ptk1 sep ptk1 ter ptk1 verat ptk1
  - **accompanied** by | **vomiting**: **Oci** ptk1

CONGESTION: acon bro1* ant-t hs1 arg-n bro1 arn bro1 ars hs1* atro hr1 aur bro1 bell hs2* benz-ac bro1 berb bro1* bism hs1 bry hs1* cact k2 camph bro1 canth a1* canthin hs1 carb-ac hs1 caust he1 chel hr1 chr-ac hs1 chr-o hs1 cod hs1 colch hs1 con hs1 cub a1 dig bro1 *Dulc* bro1 ery-a br1* eucal bro1 ham hr1* hell hr1* helon a1* hydr-ac bro1 *Juni-c* bro1 kali-bi hs2* lob hs1 merc hs1 merc-c bro1 oena hs1 *Ol-sant* bro1 op bro1 parth c1 phos hs1 pic-ac hr1 rhus-t bro1 sabin hs1 scop ptk1 senec hs2* solid bro1* solin-pur hs1 stront-n c1 sul-ac hs1 tab hs1 tanac hs1 ter hr1* thuj k2 verat-v bro1
- **right** kidney: cic hs1
- **accompanied** by:
  - ○ **Back**; pain in: senec br1
  - **Liver**; congestion in: berb mtf11
- **chronic**: acon bro1 am bro1 bell bro1 *Coffin* bro1 *Conv* bro1 *Dig* bro1 glon bro1 phos bro1 *Stroph-h* bro1 stry bro1 verat-v bro1
- **menses**; instead of: helon br1

CONTRACTED: dig ptk1 nit-ac ptk1 plb tl1*

DEGENERATION: naphthoq mtf11

○ - **Cortex**: fuch br1

EDEMA: scarl jl2 vac jl2

FATTY degeneration: apis bro1 *Ars* bro1 *Aur-m* bro1 bell bro1 cic bro1 *Cupr-act* bro1 ferr-m bro1 hydr-ac bro1 *Kali-i* bro1 lyc bro1 *Nit-ac* bro1 *Ph-ac* bro1 phos k2* rhus-t bro1 ter bro1

FLOATING: bell bro1* cham bro1 coloc bro1 gels bro1 ign bro1* lach bro1 puls bro1 stry-ar bro1* sulph bro1 zinc br1*

FLUTTERING sensation, region of: brach ptk1 chim k* chin bg2

FOREIGN body; sensation of: nux-v bg2

FORMICATION: brach bg1 hydrc k* med bg1
- **right** kidney | **insects**; as from icy cold: med hr1*

○ - **Region** of: coc-c rm dirc k* kiss a1

GLOMERULAR FILTRATION RATE (See GENERALS - Laboratory - creatinine - increased)

HEAT: ars-h hr1 kali-i k* kola stb3• lach k* mit a1 *Nux-v* k* spira a1 zing k*

▽ - **extending** to | **Bladder**: aur k*

○ - **Region** of: **Acon** bg2 aloe bg2 alum bg2 apis bg2 am bg2 ars bg2 arum-t bg2 aur bg2 bapt bg2 *Bell* bg2 benz-ac bg2 berb k* bond a1 **Cann-xyz** bg2 **Canth** bg2 cimic k* hell bg2 *Helo* bg2 *Helon* k* *Hep* bg2 kali-bi bg2 kali-c bg2 kali-i bg2 kola stb3• lach bg2 *Lyc* bg2 merc-c bg2 *Nat-m* k* nit-ac bg2 *Nux-v* bg2 *Phos* phyt k* plb k* puls bg2 rheum bg2 rhus-t bg2 sabad bg2 sang bg2 sep bg2 sul-ac bg2 ter k* thuj bg2 zing bg2
  - **sitting** agg.: nat-m k*
- **Ureters**; in: cedr bg2

HEAVINESS: aeth bg2* androc srj1• *Carl* k* cimic bg2 dirc bg2 equis-h k* helo bg2 *Helo-s* rwt2• helon ptk1 kali-bi ptk1 phos bg2 *Psor* jl2 sang bg2 tell bg2 ter bg2
- **morning**: sang k*
  - **waking**; on: aeth k*
- **sitting** agg.: *Carl* k*

○ - **Region** of: cimic k* dirc k* *Helon* k* phos k* pic-ac a1 sang tell k* *Ter* k* tub jl2

Kidneys

- **Region** of: ...
  - **right**: tub jl2
  - **afternoon**: helon k* sang k*
  - **evening**: helon k*
  - **night**: tell k*
    - **motion** agg.: cimic

HYDRONEPHROSIS: apis bg2 apoc bg2 arg-n bg2 ars bg2 aur bg2 merc mtf11 nit-ac bg2 phos bg2

HYPERTENSION: meli mtf11

INFLAMMATION (= nephritis): *Acon* k* adon br1 *All-c* alum k* alum-p k2 am-c am-caust c2 **Apis** k* apoc br1* *Arg-n* arist-cl sp1 **Arn** k* ars k* ars-br vh ars-s-f k2 arund *Asc-c* *Aur* **Bell** k* **Benz-ac** k* *Berb* k* borx mtf33 *Brach* br1 *Brom* b4a.de *Bry* k* cact calad calc-ar br1* calc-s k* camph k* cann-i k2 *Cann-s* k* *Cann-xyz* ptk1 **Canth** k* *Caps* *Carb-ac* carc sp1* caust *Chel* k* *Chim* k* chinin-fcit hsa1 coc-c k* cocc b7a.de *Colch* k* coli jl2 coll cop cortiso sp1 crot-c crot-h cub dig diph-t-tpt jl2 *Ery-a* *Eup-pur* ferr ptk1* ferr-i br gaul br1 *Gels* *Hell* k* *Helon* *Hep* k* ilx-v br1 indg irid-met vml3• juni-c mtf11 *Kali-ar* kali-bi bg2* *Kali-c* k* **Kali-chl** k* kali-cit c1 *Kali-i* kali-m k2 kali-p kali-s kali-sula hsa1 kalm k2 lach mrr1 lil-t lith-c loxo-lae bnm12• **Lyc** k* lycps-v lyss mrr1 med k2* *Merc* k* *Merc-c* k* merc-cy methyl br1 morg-g pte1• nat-hchls c2 nat-m mrr1 nat-s **Nit-ac** b4a.de* *Nux-v* k* **Oci** k* oci-sa sp1 pareir k* ph-ac *Phos* phys mrr1 *Phyt* pic-ac plb k* plb-xyz c2 *Polyg-h* polyg-xyz c2 prun *Puls* k* pyrog k2* rad-br c11 ren bwa3 *Rhus-t* k* *Sabin* k* samb k* *Sars* k* scarl jl2 sec *Senec* k* sep ser-ang br1 solid br1* spartin-s hsa1* *Squil* b7a.de streptoc jl2 *Stront-c* ptk1* sul-ac **Sulph** k* syc pte1*• tarent **Ter** k* terebe ktp9 *Thuj* k* titan br1 tub c1* (non:uran-met k) uran-n k* vac c2* zinc

- **accompanied** by:
  - **albuminuria**: calc-ar mtf11 fuch br1 mang-act br1 spartin bwa3
  - **diarrhea**: ter bro1
  - **edema**: acon bro1 adon bro1 ant-t bro1 *Apis* bro1 *Apoc* bro1 *Ars* bro1 aur-m bro1 calc-ar mtf11 canth bro1 colch bro1* cop bro1 *Dig* bro1 *Hell* bro1 merc-c bro1 pilo bro1 *Samb* bro1 senec bro1 *Squil* bro1 ter bro1
  - **nausea**: apoc br1
  - **respiration**; difficult: apoc br1
  - **rheumatism**: arge br1 rad-br ptk1 ter ptk1
  - **scarlatina**: ars ptk1 canth ptk1 hell ptk1 hep ptk1 methyl br1 nit-s-d br1 ter ptk1
  - **stones** in kidneys: uva br1
  - **uremia**: aeth bro1 am-c bro1 ars bro1 bell bro1 cann-i bro1 *Carb-ac* bro1 cic bro1 *Cupr-ar* bro1 hell bro1 hyos bro1 *Morph* bro1 *Op* bro1 pilo bro1 stram bro1 urea bro1
  - **vertigo**: apoc br1
  - **vomiting**: apoc br1 hell ptk1
  - **weakness**: ter mrr1
  - ○ **Back**:
    - **sensitiveness** of | **Dorsal** region: *Calc-ar* br1
  - **Brain**; complaints of the: plb br1
  - **Head**; pain in: am-val bro1 zinc-pic bro1
  - **Lungs**; inflammation of the (See CHEST - Inflammation - lungs - accompanied - kidneys)
  - **Optic** nerve; paralysis of: plb br1
  - **Pleura**; inflammation of: ars bro1 *Merc-c* bro1
  - **Stomach**; complaints of the: kali-bi br1
- **acute**: *Acon* bro1 ant-t bro1 *Apis* bro1 apoc bro1 *Ars* bro1 *Aur-m* bro1 *Bell* bro1 *Berb* bro1 *Cann-s* bro1 *Canth* bro1 chel bro1 *Chim* bro1 *Chinin-s* bro1 colch bro1 conv bro1 *Cupr-ar* bro1 dig bro1 dulc bro1 eucal bro1 eup-per bro1 fab bro1 ferr-i br1* fuch bro1 glon bro1 *Hell* bro1 helon bro1 *Hep* bro1 hydrc bro1 irid-met bro1 juni-c bro1 kali-bi bro1 *Kali-chl* bro1 kali-cit bro1 kalm bro1 lach bro1 loxo-lae bnm12• *Merc* bro1 merc-cy br1 *Methyl* bro1 nit-ac bro1 *Ol-sant* bro1 ph-ac bro1 *Phos* bro1 pic-ac bro1 plb br1 plb-act bro1 polyg-h bro1 rhus-t bro1 *Sabin* bro1 *Samb* bro1 sec bro1 senec bro1 *Ser-ang* br1* *Squil* bro1 *Ter* bro1 *Tub-k* bro1 *Verat* bro1 *Verat-v* bro1 zing bro1
- **bloody**: arist-cl sp1 berb br1 phos mtf33
  - **ink**-like, albuminous urine, with: **Colch** terebe ktp9
- **cardiac** and hepatic affections, with: *Aur* k* *Calc-ar* k*
- **catarrhal**: juni-c br1

Inflammation: ...

- **chronic**: ars mtf33 calc mtf33 calc-ar mtf11 calc-p mtf33 chin mtf33 ferr mtf33 form br1 hell mtf11 kali-c mtf33 *Kali-chl* br1 lach mtf33 nat-m mrr1 phos mtf33 pitu-gl br1 plb mtf33 sep mtf33 sulfa mtf11 sulph mtf33
  - **accompanied** by | **urine**; albuminous: ars mtf33 calc-p mtf33 kali-c mtf33 lach mtf33 phos mtf33 plb mtf33 sulph mtf33
- **cold**; from: kali-c ptk1
  - **wet**; or: *Acon* bro1 ant-t bro1 *Apis* bro1 canth bro1 *Dulc* bro1 rhus-t bro1 ter bro1
- **croupous**: kali-chl br1
- **diphtheria**; from: acon bro1 *Apis* bro1 *Ars* bro1 bell bro1 *Canth* bro1 conv bro1 cop bro1 dig bro1 ferr-i bro1 *Hell* bro1 *Hep* bro1 kalm bro1 lach bro1 *Merc-c* bro1 methyl bro1 nat-s bro1 nit-s-d bro1 *Rhus-t* bro1 sec bro1 *Ter* bro1
- **eruptive** disease; after: ferr-i br1 hep ptk1 ter ptk1
- **influenza** agg.: eucal bro1*
- **interstitial**: plb tl1 streptoc jl2 vac jl2
  - **chronic**: apis bro1 *Ars* bro1 *Aur-m* bro1 aur-m-n bro1 cact bro1 *Chinin-s* br1* *Colch* bro1 conv bro1 *Dig* bro1 ferr bro1 *Ferr-m* bro1 *Glon* bro1 *Iod* bro1 kali-c bro1 *Kali-i* bro1 lith-be bro1 lith-c bro1 *Merc-c* bro1 merc-d bro1 *Nat-i* bro1 *Nit-ac* bro1 nux-v bro1 op bro1 ph-ac bro1 phos bro1 *Plb-c* bro1 *Plb-i* bro1 *Plb-m* bro1 sang bro1 tub-k bro1 zinc-pic bro1
- **malaria**; from: *Ars* bro1 eup-per bro1 ter bro1
- **parenchymatous**: *Acon* bro1 ant-t bro1 *Apis* bro1 apoc bro1 *Ars* bro1 *Aur-m* bro1 *Bell* bro1 *Berb* bro1 *Cann-s* bro1 *Canth* bro1 chel bro1 *Chim* bro1 *Chinin-s* bro1 colch bro1 conv bro1 *Cupr-ar* bro1 dig bro1 dulc bro1 eucal bro1 eup-per bro1 fab bro1 ferr-i bro1 fuch bro1 glon bro1 *Hell* bro1 helon bro1 *Hep* bro1 hydrc bro1 irid-met bro1 juni-c bro1 kali-bi bro1 kali-chl br1* kali-cit bro1 kalm bro1 lach bro1 *Merc* bro1 *Methyl* bro1 nit-ac bro1 *Ol-sant* bro1 ph-ac bro1 *Phos* bro1 pic-ac bro1 plb-act bro1 polyg-h bro1 rhus-t bro1 *Sabin* bro1 *Samb* bro1 sec bro1 senec bro1 ser-ang bro1 *Squil* bro1 *Ter* bro1 *Tub-k* bro1 *Verat* bro1 *Verat-v* bro1 zing bro1
  - **accompanied** by:
    - **albuminuria**: phos mtf11
    - **stomatitis**: kali-chl br1
  - **acute**: **Apis** k* *Canth* carb-ac coc-c k2 *Colch* *Con* *Glon* hell mtf11 helon kali-bi br *Kali-chl* kali-s med k2 methyl br1 **Nat-s** *Stram* **Ter** tub c1 (non:uran-met k) uran-n
  - **chronic**: am-be bro1 *Apis* bro1 *Ars* bro1 *Aur-m* bro1 aur-m-n bro1 benz-ac bro1 berb bro1 *Brach* bro1 calc-ar bro1 calc-p bro1 cann-i bro1 *Canth* bro1 chinin-ar bro1 conv bro1 dig bro1 *Euon* bro1 eup-pur bro1 *Ferr-ar* bro1 ferr-cit bro1 *Ferr-m* bro1 ferr-p bro1 form-ac bro1 glon bro1 *Helon* bro1 hydr-ac bro1 juni-c bro1 kali-ar bro1 *Kali-chl* bro1 kali-cit bro1 *Kali-i* bro1 *Kali-m* bro1 kalm bro1 lon-c bro1 *Lyc* bro1 *Merc-c* bro1 nat-hchls bro1 *Nit-ac* bro1 *Pilo* bro1 *Plb* bro1 saroth bro1 senec bro1 solid bro1 *Solin* bro1 *Ter* bro1 tub-k bro1 urea bro1 *Vesi* bro1
  - **incipient**: kali-bi br1
- **pregnancy** agg.; during: apis bro1 apoc bro1 benz-ac dgt1 cupr-ar br1* helon bro1* irid-met br1* kalm bro1 merc-c bro1* sabin bro1
- **scarlet** fever; from: acon bro1 *Apis* bro1 *Ars* bro1 arum-t bro1 bell bro1 *Canth* bro1 conv bro1 cop bro1 dig bro1 ferr-i bro1 *Hell* bro1 *Hep* bro1 kalm bro1 lach bro1 *Merc-c* bro1 methyl bro1 nat-s bro1 nit-s-d bro1 *Rhus-t* bro1 sec bro1 *Ter* bro1
- **subacute**: ser-ang br1
- **suppurative**: *(↗URINE - Sediment - purulent)* acon bro1 apoc bro1 am bro1 *Ars* k* bell bro1 calc-s bro1 camph bro1 *Cann-s* bro1 *Canth* bro1* *Chinin-s* bro1 eucal bro1 hecla bro1 *Hep* k* hippoz kali-n br1* lyc ptk1 *Merc* k* *Merc-c* bro1 naphtin bro1 phos bro1 plb-c bro1 polyg-h ptk1 puls ptk1 *Sil* k* sul-i ptk1 ter bro1 verat-v bro1
- **toxemic**: *Crot-h* k*
- ▽ **extending** to | **Legs**: nux-v bg2
- ○ **Cortex**: fuch br1
- **Glomeruli** (= glomerulonephritis): **Apis** mrr1 eberth jl2 streptoc jl2
  - **acute**: streptoc jl2
  - **membrano**-proliferative: *(↗Nephrotic)* phos mtf
- **Pelvis** (= pyelitis): acon bro1 ars bg2* atro bg2 aur bro1 bell bg2* benz-ac bg2* berb bg2* borx bg2 bry bro1 calc-s ptk1 *Cann-s* bro1 cann-xyz bg2 **Canth** bg2* chin bg2* *Cop* bro1 *Cupr-ar* bro1 epig br1* ferr bg2 *Ferr-m* bro1 hecla bro1 hep bg2* hydr bg2 kali-bi bg2* kali-s ptk1 *Lyc* bg2 *Merc* bg2 merc-c bg2* myrt-c br1 nit-ac bg2* **Puls** bg2* rhus-t bro1* sep bg2 *Sil* bg2 solid bg2 stigm bro1 sul-i ptk1 *Sulph* bg2 ter bg2* thuj bro1 *Tritic* bro1 uran-n bg2 *Uva* br1* *Verat-v* bro1

- **Pelvis**: ...
  - **calculi**; from: hep bro1 *Hydrang* bro1 lyc bro1 *Pipe* bro1 sil bro1 uva bro1
  - **chronic**: ars bro1 *Baros* bro1 *Benz-ac* bro1 berb bro1 *Chim* bro1 chin bro1 chinin-s bro1 *Cop* bro1 hep bro1 hydrin-m bro1 hydrin-s bro1 juni-c br1* *Kali-bi* bro1 lyc mtf33 *Ol-sant* bro1 pareir bro1 puls bro1 sep bro1 sil bro1 stigm bro1 sulph bro1 *Uva* bro1
  - **suppurative** | **chronic**: chin br1
- **Pelvis** and bladder (= pyelocystitis): parathyr jl2
- **Pelvis** and kidneys (= pyelonephritis): apis mrr1 bals-p mtf11 benz-ac mtf11 berb mtf11 bry mtf11 coc-c mtf11 coli jl2 ferr-m ptk2 kali-sula hsa1 lyc mrr1 morg-g fmm1• naphtin br1 nux-v mrr1 podo mtf11 puls mrr1 sars mrr1 syc fmm1• ter mrr1
  - **recurrent**: hep mrr1
- **Region**; renal: acon bro1 bry bro1 chinin-s bro1 hep bro1 merc bro1 sil bro1
- **Ureters**: am *Canth* k* ter

INJURIES: acon bro1 *Arn* bro1 bell bro1 verat-v bro1

INSUFFICIENCY; RENAL (See Renal)

IRRITATION: chel tl1 coff br1 thlas br1

○ - **Ureters**: spirae br1

LAMENESS, region of: agar hr1 berb hr1* cimic k* phys k* *Solid* vh
- **left**, with cramp | **extending** into thighs: agar k*
- **accompanied** by | **Head**; pain in: phys a1*
- **waking**; on: ptel k*

LIFTING agg.: calc-p bro1

LYING:
- **agg.**: berb bro1
- **back**; on:
  - **amel.**: cain bro1
  - **legs** drawn up | **amel.**: colch bro1

LYING DOWN agg.: conv bro1

MOTION agg.: *Berb* bro1* *Canth* bro1* chel bro1* kali-i bro1*

NEPHRITIS (See Inflammation)

NEPHROCALCINOSIS (See Stones)

NEPHROSIS: bar-ox-suc mtf11 calc-ar mtf11 carc mlr1• ferr-ar mtf11 loxo-recl bnm10• morg-g fmm1• phos mtf11 solid mtf11 syc fmm1•
- **accompanied** by:
  - **hypertension**: fuma-ac mtf11
  - ○ **Head**; pain in: zinc-pic mtf11
- **chronic**: kali-ar mtf11

NEPHROTIC SYNDROME: (↗*Inflammation - glomeruli - membrano-proliferative; Sclerosis; GENERALS - Dropsy - external - albuminuria; GENERALS - Dropsy - external - kidney; GENERALS - Hyperlipidemia; URINE - Albuminous)* apis mrr2* apoc mrr2* aran jl3* arg-n mtf *Ars* mtf *Aur* mtf aur-m mtf *Aur-m-n* mtf *Calc-ar* mtf cann-s mtf *Canth* mtf *Carb-ac* mtf carb-v mtf chinin-s mtf cortiso sp1* *Dig* mtf *Ferr* mtf ferr-ar mtf ferr-i mtf ferr-p mtf *Form* mtf gels mtf hell mtf helon mtf kali-bi mtf *Kali-c* mtf *Kali-chl* mtf *Kali-i* mtf kali-m mtf *Lyc* mtf merc gsd1* merc-c mtf merc-i-r mtf *Nat-ar* mtf *Nat-c* mtf nat-m mtf *Nat-s* mtf nit-ac mtf nux-v mtf *Phos* mtf *Plb* mtf rhus-t mtf *Sec* mtf *Sulph* mtf *Syc* mtf tarent mtf *Ter* mtf urea mtf

NUMBNESS, region of: alum bg2 **Berb** k* cann-xyz bg2 cocc bg2 colch bg2 nux-v bg2 plb bg2

OPERATION to kidneys; after: methyl br1

PAIN (= nephralgia): acon act-sp↓ *Aesc* aeth k* agar↓ *Agn* aids↓ *All-c* k* allox sp1 aloe *Alum* k* alum-p k2 am-br c2 ambr anan↓ androc↓ ant-t↓ aphis *Apis* apoc↓ aran↓ *Arg-n* k* arge-pl↓ *Arist-cl* sp1 *Arn* k* ars k* *Ars-h*↓ arund k* *Asaf*↓ asar↓ astac↓ atro bg2 aur↓ aur-m k* bad k* bamb-a↓ bapt↓ *Bell* k* *Benz-ac* k* **Berb** k* borx↓ bov↓ brach↓ *Bry* k* bufo↓ but-ac↓ *Cact*↓ cadm-s↓ cain k* *Calc* k* *Calc-ar*↓ calc-f↓ *Calc-p* k* *Cann-i* k* *Cann-s* k* cann-xyz↓ **Canth** k* *Caps* k* carb-an↓ *Carl*↓ **Caust**↓ cedr k* cere-b a1 *Chel* k* *Chen-a* hr1 *Chim* k* chin↓ chinin-s↓ chlf↓ cimic cina↓ *Cinnb* k* cit-v hr1 *Clem* k* cob-n sp1 coc-c k* *Cocc* b7a.de *Cocc-s*↓ cod hr1 **Colch** k* coloc bg2 con↓ conv↓ cop↓ cortiso sp1 *Crot-c* *Crot-h*↓ crot-t↓ cund↓ cur↓ cycl↓ daph↓ dig↓ *Dios* k* *Dulc* k* ephe-si↓ equis-h c1 erig hr1 ery-a↓ eup-per↓ *Eup-pur* k* *Ferr* k* ferr-ar ferr-i k* ferr-m↓ ferr-p gad a1 gal-ac br1

Pain: ...
galeg↓ galla-q-r nl2• gamb *Gels*↓ gnaph hr1 *Granit-m* es1• **Graph**↓ grat↓ guare a1 guat sp1 ham k* *Hed*↓ hell helo↓ *Helon* k* *Hep* k* hydr *Hydrang*↓ hyper iod↓ *Ip* k* *Ipom-p* irid-met srj5• iris juni-c↓ kali-ar *Kali-bi* k* kali-br *Kali-c* *Kali-chl* k* kali-i k* kali-m k2 kali-n k* kali-p kali-s fkr2.de kola stb3• lac-ac c1 lac-d↓ lac-leo↓ lach lapa c2 lat-m↓ laur↓ lec lept *Lith-c* lob k* lob-s a1* *Lyc* k* lycps-v lyss k* mag-m↓ mag-p bg2 manc mang↓ *Med* k* melal-alt↓ meny↓ meph *Merc*↓ merc-c mez k* *Mill* k* mit c2 *Morg-g* fmm1• nabal a1 nat-ar nat-ch↓ *Nat-m* k* nat-p↓ nat-s nat-sil fd3.de• *Nit-ac* k* nux-m k* *Nux-v* k* oci mrr1 oci-sa sp1 ol-sant↓ orot-ac↓ ox-ac k* oxyt ptk2 ozone sde2• par bg2 *Pareir* pen↓ petr↓ *Ph-ac* k* *Phos* k* phys↓ *Phyt* k* *Pic-ac*↓ pin-con oss2• pin-s c2 *Plb* k* plumbg c2 plut-n↓ podo↓ polyg-h↓ positr nl2• prot fmm1• ptel k* *Puls* k* ran-s raph↓ rat k* rheum↓ *Rhus-t*↓ ruta↓ sabad↓ *Sabin*↓ sal-fr sle1• sang a1 santa mp4• sarcol-ac sp1 saroth sp1 **Sars** k* scroph-n↓ scut↓ *Sel* *Senec* k* *Sep* k* sil a1 solid bg1 spect↓ spira a1* spong fd4.de stann sne *Staph*↓ stel↓ still k* sul-i c2 *Sulph* hr1 syc pte1*• symph↓ tab k* *Tarent* k* tell↓ *Ter* k* thlas↓ *Thuj* thymol sp1 tritic-vg fd5.de tub jl2 upa↓ urt-u bg2 ust↓ *Uva*↓ valer↓ vanil fd5.de vario jl2 verat bg2 vesi↓ *Vesp*↓ vip↓ visc↓ xero↓ *Zinc* k* zinc-p k2 zing
- **right**: *Colch* hr1 dulc fd4.de ephe-si↓ equis-h c1 gink-b↓ guat sp1 ina-i mlk9.de iris c1 kali-n↓ lac-loxod-a hrn2• lac-lup hrn2• luf-op rsj5• lyc bro1* lyss nat-m↓ nux-v bro1 oci bro1* olib-sac wmh1 phyt↓ plut-n srj7• sars bro1 sel hr1 *Senec* k* spong fd4.de symph↓ tritic-vg fd5.de tub jl2 vanil fd5.de ven-m rsj12• [heroin sdj2]
  - **5** h: coc-c↓
    - ⁝ **drawing** pain: coc-c
  - **afternoon** | **14** h: lac-lup hrn2•
  - **cramping**: lyc mrr1 oci br1
  - **pecking**: nat-m bg2
  - **sitting** agg.: germ-met↓
    - ⁝ **stabbing**: germ-met srj5•
  - **sore**: *Helon* *Nux-v* phyt
  - **stitching** pain: dulc fd4.de ephe-si hsj1• gink-b sbd1• kali-n bg2 nat-m bg2 spong fd4.de symph fd3.de• vanil fd5.de [heroin sdj2]
- **left**: all-c hr1 allox mgm• *Benz-ac*↓ berb bro1 canth bro1 chin-b hr1 chlf hr1 dulc fd4.de ephe-si↓ ferr-i k2 grat mrr1 ham fd3.de• kali-c↓ kali-s↓ lac-leo hrn2• lachn↓ *Lyc* hr1 mang↓ ozone sde2• plut-n srj7• podo fd3.de• sal-fr sle1• santa mp4• symph fd3.de• tab bro1 tritic-vg fd5.de vanil fd5.de ven-m rsj12• zinc↓ zing↓ [tax jsj7]
  - **burning**: benz-ac k* lachn k* ozone sde2• zing
  - **cutting** pain: allox sp1
  - **drawing** pain: *Benz-ac* k* kali-c podo fd3.de•
  - **sore**: benz-ac zinc
  - **stitching** pain: ephe-si hsj1• kali-c h2* kali-s fkr2.de lyc h2* mang h2* ozone sde2• symph fd3.de• vanil fd5.de zinc h2*
  - ▽ **extending** to:
    - ⁝ **right**: lachn↓
      - ⁝ **burning**: lachn c1
- **morning**: alum k* bell k* *Cain* chel↓ cocc↓ ham k* kali-c symph↓ tarent k* *Ter*↓ vanil fd5.de
  - **pressing** pain: cocc a1 kali-c k* symph fd3.de• *Ter* a1 vanil fd5.de
  - **rising** agg.; after: *Berb*↓
    - ⁝ **tearing** pain: *Berb*
  - **stitching** pain: chel k* vanil fd5.de
  - **waking**; on: arge-pl rwt5• ox-ac k* plan a1 ven-m rsj12•
- **afternoon**: bad k* chinin-s crot-t↓ kali-c↓ nat-sil fd3.de• sang *Tarent*↓ vanil fd5.de
  - **16** h:
    - ⁝ **16**-20 h: **Lyc**
    - ⁝ **16**-21 h: *Chel*
      - ⁝ **cramping**: *Chel*
  - **17** h: lac-leo hrn2•
    - ⁝ **17**-19 h: lac-leo hrn2•
  - **sore**: kali-c
  - **stitching** pain: crot-t k* *Tarent* vanil fd5.de
- **evening**: canth cot↓ dulc fd4.de ham fd3.de• helon↓ kali-p fd1.de• lac-leo hrn2• meny↓ ox-ac k* positr nl2• sil k* spong fd4.de tarent k* tritic-vg fd5.de upa↓ vanil fd5.de zinc↓

Kidneys

- **aching**: *Canth* cot a1 helon k*
- **bed** agg.; in: coc-c ↓
  - **stitching** pain: coc-c k*
- **sore**: meny
- **stitching** pain: spong fd4.de upa a1 zinc k*

- **night**: arge-pl rwt5• ars-h k* astac ↓ calc cann-i chel k* cinnb k* kali-p fd1.de• podo fd3.de• spira a1 tarent k* upa a1
  - **midnight**:
    - **after**:
      - **4** h: cinnb ↓
        - **stitching** pain: cinnb
      - **5**-8 h: lac-loxod-a hrn2•
  - **aching**: calc *Cann-i* k*
  - **pressing** pain: calc
  - **stitching** pain: astac hr1 *Tarent* k*
  - **undressing** agg.: helon k*
- **accompanied** by:
  - **bloody** urine: ip k2
  - **colic**: *Berb* bro1 calc bro1 dios bro1 ery-a bro1 *Lyc* bro1 *Morph-act* bro1 oci bro1 saroth jl3 sars bro1 *Tab* bro1 *Ter* bro1
  - **cough**: guat sp1
  - **nausea**: *Oci* mrr1
  - **vomiting**: **OCI** k •*
  - ○ **Dorsal** pain: vario jl2
  - **Extremities**; pain in: dios br1
- **aching**: acon bg2* agar bg2 alum bro1 am-br bro1 ambr bg2 apis bro1 apoc *Arg-n* bro1 arge-pl rwt5• bell bg2 benz-ac k* *Berb* bro1 *Calc* k* *Cann-i* k* *Canth* k* caust bg2 chel k* cina bro1 cinnb k* coc-c k* conv bro1 cop bro1 *Crot-h* k* cund a1 equis-h eup-per bg2 *Eup-pur* k* ferr-p bg2 galeg c2 *Hed* bro1 helo bg2 *Helon* k* hydrang bro1 juni-c bro1 kali-bi k* *Lyc* k* med hr1 merc-c bg2 *Nat-ar* nat-ch bro1 *Nux-v* bro1 ol-sant c2* orot-ac rly4• pen a1 phos bg2 phyt bg2* *Pic-ac* bro1 pin-s bro1 plut-n srj7• sabad bg2 *Sabin* bro1 sang bg2 sarcol-ac sp1 scut k* sep bg2* solid bro1* stel bro1 tab bg2 tarent k* *Ter* k* thymol sp1 ust bro1 *Uva* bro1 vesi c2 vesp bro1 zing k* [spect dfg1]
- **alternating** with:
  - **cloudy** and drunken feeling: alum tl1
  - **rheumatism**: benz-ac k2
  - **vertigo**: alum
  - ○ **Penis**; pain in: canth tl1
- **apyrexia**, during: bell chin hep lyc staph
- **ascending** agg.: aesc ↓ apis ↓
  - **stitching** pain: aesc vh apis vh
- **bending**:
  - **body**:
    - **agg.**: chin k* tritic-vg fd5.de
    - **forward** | **amel.**: santa mp4•
- **blowing** the nose agg.: *Calc-p* k*
- **boring** pain: canth bg2 kali-i bg2 lac-d bg2
- **breathing** deep agg.: aeth k* arg-n hr1 astac *Benz-ac* sel tritic-vg fd5.de
- **burning**: *Acon* bro1 apis ars bro1 *Ars-h* k* arund k* aur bro1 *Bell* k* *Benz-ac* k* *Berb* k* bufo but-ac bro1 cann-i k* *Canth* k* hed bro1 *Helon* k* hep k* *Ip* *Kali-bi* *Kali-c* k* *Kali-i* k* kali-n lach bro1 *Lyc* bro1 merc-c bro1 nat-ar k2 nat-m k* *Nux-v* k* ozone sde2• ph-ac ptk1 phos bro1* phyt ptk1 pin-s k* *Puls* rheum sabin bro1* sars mrr1 sep ptk1 spira a1 *Sulph* bro1 **Ter** k* tritic-vg fd5.de zinc
- **burrowing**: apis bg2 thuj bg2
- **chill**; during: ars k* canth k* kali-c k* lyc k* nux-v k* puls k* zinc k*
- **cold** agg.; becoming: *Staph* ↓
  - **stitching** pain: *Staph*
- **constricting** pain: clem bg2 mang h2* nit-ac bg2
- **contracting**: clem k* mang h2* nit-ac bg2
- **cough** agg.; during: *Bell*
- **cramping**: agar hr1 berb ptk1 cadm-s canth ptk1 **Caust** k* *Chel* k* chlf br1 coc-c hr1* colch ptk1 coloc ptk1 cur hr1 cycl kali-i k* lat-m bnm6• lyc bg2* nat-m bg2 *Nit-ac* k* *Nux-m* b7a.de nux-v mrr1 oci k* oci-sa sp1 pareir bg2* polyg-h ptk1 sars bg2* spira a1 sulph bg2 tab ptk1 ter ptk1
  - **accompanied** by | **dysuria**: coc-c ptk1
  - **tenesmus**: berb mrr1
- **cutting** pain: acon aids nl2• apis bg1 arg-n *Arn* k* bad bell bg1 *Berb* k* bufo k* cadm-s cann-i **Canth** k* clem k* coc-c k* *Colch* coloc k* cycl bg2 daph k* eup-per bg2 eup-pur k* granit-m es1• *Graph* k* helon bg1 ip bg1* kali-ar k2 **Kali-bi** *Kali-i* k* *Lyc* bro1 *Merc* k* merc-c bg2 mez *Nux-m* k* plb k* rhus-t bro1 *Staph* k* tab bg1 ter bro1 zinc k*
  - **downward**: **Berb** mrr1
  - **outward**: **Berb** mrr1
  - **paroxysmal**, and burning: **Canth**
- **dancing**; while: alum k*
- **digging** pain: cur k* kali-i k* thuj a1
- **dinner**; after: zinc ↓
  - **stitching** pain: zinc h2*
- **drawing** pain: aloe bg2 berb bg2* *Cann-s* b7a.de* *Canth* bro1 chel bro1 **Clem** k* coc-c k* *Colch* bro1 dulc bro1 iod bg2 kali-n bg2 lach bg2* *Lyc* bro1 meny bg2 nat-sil fd3.de• nit-ac bro1 *Nux-m* k* podo fd3.de• ruta bg2 saroth sp1 solid bro1 **Ter** k* thuj bg2 tritic-vg fd5.de vanil fd5.de zinc k*
- **drinking** water | **amel.**: lac-leo hrn2•
- **dull** pain: sulph bg2 thymol sp1
- **eating**; after: con ↓
  - **stitching** pain: con k*
- **exertion** of muscles; during: apoc ↓
  - **sore**: apoc
- **expiration** agg.: kali-c ↓
  - **stitching** pain: kali-c h2*
- **fever**; with: ferr-p k2
- **gnawing** pain: *Berb* k* *Tarent* k*
- **gonorrhea**; after: benz-ac k2
- **griping** pain: cycl bg2
- **hematuria**; with: ip k2
- **inspiration** agg.; deep: *Ars* ↓ astac ↓ bamb-a ↓ crot-t ↓ cycl ↓ laur ↓ tritic-vg ↓
  - **pressing** pain: bamb-a stb2.de• tritic-vg fd5.de
  - **stitching** pain: *Ars* k* astac k* crot-t k* cycl k* laur k*
- **jar** agg.: aeth alum *Bell* *Berb* calc-p *Cann-i* ↓ cann-s kola stb3•
  - **sore**: aeth alum *Bell* *Berb* calc-p *Cann-i*
- **jerking** pain: mang h2* ran-s b7a.de
- **lancinating** (See cutting)
- **laughing** agg.: *Cann-i* k* cann-s ptk2*
- **lifting** agg.: *Calc-p* k*
- **lying**:
  - **abdomen**; on | **amel.**: chel
  - **agg.**: aeth k* androc srj1• berb colch coloc cortiso tpw7* ham fd3.de• lac-d ↓ nux-v k* ozone ↓ rhus-t k* tritic-vg fd5.de
    - **burning**: lac-d k*
    - **stitching** pain: ozone sde2•
  - **amel.**: santa mp4•
  - **back**; on:
    - **agg.**: chel tritic-vg fd5.de
    - **amel.**: nux-v
  - **backward**; bent | **amel.**: cain br1
  - **face**; on the:
    - **amel.**: chel ↓
      - **stitching** pain: chel
- **menses**:
  - **during**:
    - **agg.**: berb k* cur
    - **beginning** of menses | **agg.**: *Berb* raph *Verat*
- **motion**:
  - **agg.**: aesc alum h2* arg-n k* *Berb* bry k2 cain coc-c k* *Colch* k* dor k* dulc fd4.de *Gels* *Ham* k* kali-bi *Nux-v* ozone ↓
    - **stitching** pain: coc-c hr1* kali-bi ozone sde2•
  - **amel.**: ter k*
    - **pressing** pain: ter
  - **arms**; of:
    - **agg.**: ant-t ↓
      - **stitching** pain: ant-t

- **nail**; as from a: berb bg2
- **nausea**; with: cimic hr1 senec k2
- **oppressed** breathing and faintness, with: bufo ↓
  - **burning**: bufo
- **overlifting** agg.: bry k2
- **paroxysmal**: aran *Bell* *Berb* bro1 *Calc* bro1 *Chel* k* chinin-s bro1 *Coc-c* hydrang bro1 *Lyc* bro1 nux-v bro1 *Sep* bro1 sulph tritic-vg fd5.de urt-u bro1 vanil fd5.de
- **pinching** pain: arge-pl rwt5• lac-leo hm2• zinc bg2*
- **pressing** pain: am-br k* aphis arg-n bro1 *Am* bro1 aur-m bro1 bamb-a stb2.de• *Berb* bro1 borx b4a.de *Calc* k* *Canth* k* *Carl* k* chinin-s bro1 cimic clem k* coc-c k* dulc fd4.de *Gels* hr1 hyper k* *Kali-c* k* lapa a1 *Lyc* bro1 nat-sil fd3.de• *Nit-ac* k* *Nux-v* k* *Oci* bro1 petr bro1 *Ph-ac* bro1 podo fd3.de• ran-s k* *Sep* bro1 symph fd3.de• ter k* *Thuj* k* tritic-vg fd5.de uva bro1 vanil fd5.de xero bro1 zinc k*
  - **outward**: mag-p bg2
- **pressure**:
  - **agg.**: *Berb* k2 canth bg1 dor c1 ferr bg1 helo bg1 helo-s rwt2• ina-i mlk9.de sel k2 *Solid* br1
  - **back**; pressure of clenched fist into | **amel.**: santa mp4•
- **pulsating** pain: berb bufo kola stb3•
- **radiating**: *Arg-n* bro1 arn bro1 *Bell* bro1 *Berb* k* calc bro1 *Canth* bro1 chel bro1 chinin-s bro1 *Coc-c* bro1 *Cocc-s* bro1 *Dios* bro1 ery-a bro1 ferr-m bro1 *Hed* bro1 *Hydrang* bro1 kali-i bro1 lach bro1 *Lyc* bro1 nit-ac bro1 *Nux-v* bro1 *Oci* bro1 oxyt bro1 pareir k* phos bro1 sabin bro1 *Sars* bro1 scroph-n bro1 *Solid* bro1 *Tab* bro1 ter bro1 thlas bro1 vesp bro1
- **raw**; as if: zinc bg2
- **riding**:
  - **agg.**: agar ↓ alum k* berb *Calc* k* orot-ac ↓ vanil fd5.de
    - **aching**: *Calc* k* orot-ac rly4•
    - **drawing** pain | **tensive**: agar
- **rubbing**:
  - **amel.**: kali-c ↓
    - **stitching** pain: kali-c h2*
- **shooting** (See stitching)
- **sitting** agg.: *Berb* carl ↓ chin-b kr1 cortiso tpw7* dig ↓ gink-b ↓ kali-c ↓ meny ↓ *Pall* k* ruta ↓ ter k* thuj ↓ tritic-vg fd5.de valer
  - **pressing** pain: carl a1 pall k* ruta h1 *Ter* k* thuj h1* tritic-vg fd5.de
  - **sore**: kali-c meny
  - **stitching** pain: *Berb* dig k* gink-b sbd1• valer k*
- **sneezing** agg.: *Aeth* k* ars *Bell*
  - **stitching** pain: ars k*
- **sore** (= bruised): acon agar alum k* androc srj1• *Apis* k* apoc bg2 *Arg-n* ars *Asaf* asar benz-ac **Berb** k* brach k* *Cact* cadm-s ptk1 calc *Calc-ar* cann-i k2 *Cann-s* cann-xyz bg2 *Canth* k* *Chel* k* chin bg2 cinnb clem k* *Coc-c* k* cocc bg2 colch equis-h bg2 ferr-i **Graph** k* hell *Helon* *Hep* hydr bg2 kali-c b4a.de* kali-i *Manc* meny k* merc merc-c k* *Nat-s* *Nux-v* ox-ac k2 *Pareir* phos bg2 phys k* phyt k* plb **Puls** k* *Rat* rhus-t sel k* senec ptk1 solid bg1* syc fmm1• tab tarent tell k* *Ter* k* thymol sp1 *Vesp* k* visc ptk1 zinc k*
- **spasmodic**: coc-c br1
- **standing**:
  - **agg.**: zinc ↓
    - **stitching** pain: zinc
  - **amel.**: berb
    - **stitching** pain: berb
    - **tearing** pain: berb
- **stitching** pain (= stinging, sticking): *Acon* k* aesc aeth agar k* alum b4a.de anan ant-t k* apis bg2 *Am* *Ars* k* astac bapt *Bell* k* **Berb** k* borx b4a.de* bov k* calc-f cann-i *Canth* k* carb-an k* *Chel* k* chin k* *Coc-c* colch bro1 *Coloc* con bg2 crot-t cycl k* dig k* dulc fd4.de ephe-si hsj1• erig gamb grat hep k* *Ip* k* kali-ar **Kali-bi** k* *Kali-c* k* kali-i *Kali-n* k* kali-p kali-s *Lach* laur bg2 lob *Lyc* k* mag-m mang k* melal-alt gya4 *Mez* k* *Nat-m* k* nat-p nat-sil fd3.de• *Nux-v* ozone sde2• pareir bro1 ph-ac k* phos k* *Plb* k* podo fd3.de• positr nl2• ran-s k* sep k* spong fd4.de stann h2 *Staph* k* sulph symph fd3.de• *Tarent* *Ter* thuj k2 upa valer k* vanil fd5.de vip zinc k* zinc-p k2
  - **intermittent**: zinc h2*
  - **itching**: staph h1*
  - **pulsating** pain: bufo
- **stitching** pain: ...
  - **radiating**: **Berb**
- **stool** | **during** | **agg.**: *Colch* b7a.de
  - **urging** to: nux-v k2
- **stooping** | **after**:
    - **agg.** | **long** time; stooping for a: sulph k*
  - **agg.**: alum androc srj1• apis *Benz-ac* ↓ *Berb* chin raph ↓ *Sulph* tritic-vg ↓ vanil fd5.de
    - **drawing** pain: *Benz-ac* tritic-vg fd5.de
    - **tearing** pain: berb raph k*
- **straightening** out legs agg.: colch
- **swelling** of right knee, with: benz-ac k*
- **tearing** pain: aesc astac hr1 **Berb** k* **Canth** k* kali-c k* *Lyc* k* *Mez* k* raph k* *Rhus-t* k* zinc k*
  - **calculus**; agonizing in back and hips as from passing a: arn k*
  - **downward**: arg-n bell sars
  - **pulsating** pain: *Berb* k*
  - **radiating**: **Berb** melal-alt gya4
- **throbbing**: act-sp bro1 *Berb* bro1 chim bro1 med bro1 sabin br1*
- **touch** agg.: nux-v mrr1
- **twitching**: *Canth* b7a.de lac-leo hm2•
- **ulcerative** pain: bry bg2 cann-s k* *Canth* b7a.de
- **urination**:
  - **after**:
    - **agg.**: ambr b7.de* bufo bg2 lyc tl1
      - **stitching** pain: bufo
    - **amel.**: **Lyc** *Med* tarent
  - **amel.**: **Lyc** ↓ tarent ↓
    - **aching**: **Lyc** k* tarent k*
  - **before**: colch b7a.de graph *Lyc* k* rheum bg2 thuj ↓
    - **burning**: rheum thuj k*
    - **cutting** pain: graph k*
    - **dragging**, like labor pain: graph b4.de*
    - **pressing** pain: graph
  - **delayed**; if desire to urinate is: con pall rhus-t
  - **during**:
    - **agg.**: *Acon* b7a.de aesc agn hr1 ant-c berb *Brucel* ↓ *Canth* b7.de* *Colch* b7a.de helon mtf11 kali-bi bg2 lach bg2 *Ph-ac* b4a.de phos k* *Puls* k* rheum k* *Senec* *Zinc* b4a.de
      - **aching**: aesc agn ant-c berb
      - **burning**: *Brucel* sa3• rheum
  - **suppression** of: kali-bi k2
  - **urging** to urinate: *Ars-h* *Canth* coc-c *Ferr* gink-b sbd1• graph hep kali-bi k2 kola stb3• *Kreos* merc-c ruta
- **walking** agg.: alum carb-an k* clem ham nit-ac k* *Nux-v* k* santa mp4• sapin a1 zinc
  - **stitching** pain: zinc h2
- **warm**:
  - **amel.**: ozone ↓
    - **stitching** pain: ozone sde2•
  - **bed**:
    - **amel.**: *Staph* ↓
      - **stitching** pain: *Staph*
- **warmth**:
  - **agg.**: canth sne staph sne
  - **amel.**: nux-v mrr1 ozone ↓
    - **burning**: ozone sde2•
- **weather** agg.; wet: *Rhus-t* ↓
  - **tearing** pain: *Rhus-t*

▽ - **extending** to:
- ○ • **Abdomen**: berb canth kali-bi *Nux-v*
  - **Arms**: dios br1
  - **Back**: aids nl2• dios br1 tritic-vg fd5.de

- **Bladder**: arg-n ars aur $_{bg2}$ bell berb canth chel coc-c $_{k*}$ cupr-act ↓ cupre-au $_{c1}$ **Kali-bi** ↓ kali-i *Lach* ↓ *Lyc* nit-ac oci op $_{ptk}$ petr phyt *Sars* tab *Ter* ↓
  - **burning**: bell *Ter*
  - **constricting** pain: nit-ac
  - **cramping**: nit-ac $_{bg}$
  - **stitching** pain: arg-n bell **Berb** coc-c cupr-act **Kali-bi** $_{k*}$ *Lach* oci
- **Buttocks** (See nates)
- **Chest**: dios $_{br1}$ tritic-vg $_{fd5.de}$ zinc ↓
  - **stitching** pain: zinc $_{h2}$
- **Downward**: nat-m $_{bg2}$
- **Epigastrium** | **spreading** over the whole abdomen; then: hydr-ac $_{k*}$
- **Extremities**: dios $_{pd}$
- **Hip**: arn berb lyc *Nux-m* *Nux-v* ox-ac ter
  - **right**: *Ter* ↓
    - **drawing** pain: *Ter*
- **Ilium** to pubis, in women; through left: arund ↓
  - **burning**: arund
- **Ilium**, right: sang
- **Knee**: berb ↓ ip ↓ kali-bi ↓
  - **stitching** pain: berb ip kali-bi
- **Leg**: saroth ↓
  - **drawing** pain: saroth $_{sp1}$
- **Legs**: coc-c $_{k2}$
  - **stitching** pain: coc-c $_{k2}$
- **Nates**: thymol $_{sp1}$
- **Penis**; down ureters to: **Canth** ↓
  - **contracting**: **Canth**
- **Rectum**: nux-v $_{k2}$
- **Testes**: bell $_{sne}$ dios equis-h *Lyc* $_{vh}$ nux-v op $_{ptk}$ puls $_{bg2}$ syph
- **Thigh**: ham $_{fd3.de}$• *Nux-v* podo $_{fd3.de}$• symph $_{fd3.de}$•
- **Thighs**: *Berb* ↓
  - **sore**: *Berb*
- **Thighs**, with stiffness: *Berb* ↓
  - **tearing** pain: *Berb*
- **Ureters** to penis; down:
  - **pressure** on glans amel.:
    - **upwards**; at times pain is extending: canth ↓
      - **constricting** pain: canth
- **Ureters**; down: apis ↓ arg-n ↓ bell ↓ **Berb** ↓ calad ↓ cedr ↓ *Chel* ↓ coc-c ↓ cupr-act ↓ gink-b ↓ **Kali-bi** ↓ *Lach* ↓ **Lyc** ↓ pareir ↓ pin-s ↓ tab ↓ ter ↓
  - **burning**: cedr pin-s
  - **stitching** pain: apis arg-n bell **Berb** calad *Chel* coc-c cupr-act gink-b $_{sbd1}$• **Kali-bi** *Lach* **Lyc** pareir tab ter
- **Urethra**: *Berb* ↓ coc-c ↓
  - **stitching** pain: *Berb* coc-c
- **Uterus**: nat-m
  - **stitching** pain: nat-m

○ - **Region** of: abrot $_{k*}$ acon $_{bg2}$ agar ↓ aids ↓ all-c $_{bg2}$ all-s aloe $_{bg2}$ alum $_{h2*}$ alumn ↓ ambr $_{bg2}$ ant-c ↓ apis $_{bg2}$ apoc $_{bg2}$ arn $_{bg2}$ ars $_{bg2}$ ars-h $_{k*}$ bac $_{al2}$ bamb-a ↓ bell $_{bg2}$ benz-ac ↓ berb $_{bg2*}$ bond ↓ borx ↓ bov $_{k*}$ brach ↓ cadm-s cain *Calc* $_{k*}$ calc-act $_{bg2}$ calc-ar $_{dgt1}$ *Calc-p* $_{k*}$ *Cann-s* ↓ cann-xyz $_{bg2}$ canth $_{bg2*}$ carb-an $_{bg2}$ carl ↓ caust ↓ cean $_{bg2}$ cedr $_{a1}$ cer-s $_{a1}$ chel $_{k*}$ chen-a $_{hr1}$ *Chinin-ar* chlf ↓ cimic ↓ cinnb ↓ clem $_{bg2}$ *Coc-c* ↓ cod $_{a1}$ colch $_{bg2}$ coli $_{jl2}$ *Coloc* ↓ cop cupr $_{bg2*}$ dirc $_{c1}$ dulc ↓ elat ↓ equis-h ↓ erig $_{k*}$ *Ferr* $_{bg2*}$ fl-ac $_{k*}$ granit-m $_{es1}$• ham $_{bg2}$ helo $_{bg2}$ helo-s $_{rwt2}$• helon ↓ hydr $_{k*}$ iod $_{bg2}$ ip $_{bg2}$ kali-bi $_{bg2*}$ kali-br $_{a1}$ kali-c $_{bg2}$ kali-n $_{h2*}$ kola $_{stb3}$• kreos lac-ac $_{hr1}$ *Lac-d* ↓ lac-lup ↓ lach ↓ lachn ↓ lap-la ↓ lob $_{a1}$ lyc $_{bg2*}$ manc $_{a1}$ mand $_{rsj7}$• mang ↓ med $_{k2}$ meny ↓ merc-c ↓ mez $_{bg2}$ mit ↓ myric $_{k*}$ nat-ar ↓ nat-m $_{bg2}$ nat-sil $_{fd3.de}$• nit-ac $_{bg2}$ nux-v $_{k2}$ ox-ac $_{k*}$ ozone ↓ pall ↓ ph-ac $_{bg2}$ phos $_{bg2*}$ phys $_{k*}$ phyt $_{bg2}$ plb $_{bg2*}$ podo $_{bg2}$ prot $_{pte1*}$ **Puls** $_{bg2}$ rhus-t $_{k*}$ ruta ↓ sabad ↓ sabin $_{bg2}$ samb ↓ sang $_{bg2}$ sars $_{bg2}$ *Senec* $_{a1}$ sep $_{bg2}$ sil $_{bg2}$ solid $_{br1}$ *Staph* ↓ still ↓ *Sulph* $_{bg2}$ symph $_{fd3.de}$• syph $_{k2}$ tab $_{bg2*}$ tarent $_{a1}$ tell ↓ *Ter* $_{bg2*}$ thuj ↓ tritic-vg $_{fd5.de}$ uran-n $_{bg2}$ vanil $_{fd5.de}$ wies ↓ zinc $_{bg2*}$ zing $_{bg2}$

- **Region** of: ...
- **right**: cann-i $_{c1*}$ equis-h ↓ gink-b $_{sbd1}$• olib-sac $_{wmh1}$
  - **dull** pain: equis-h $_{hr1}$
- **left**: berb $_{mrr1}$ cench $_{k2}$
- **morning**: cain $_{c1}$
- **afternoon**: *Chinin-s* ↓ sang ↓
  - **aching**: *Chinin-s* sang $_{k*}$
- **evening**: *Canth* ↓
  - **aching**: *Canth* $_{k*}$
  - **sitting** agg.: meny ↓ ruta ↓
    - **drawing** pain: meny ruta
- **night**, 22 h: iris-fl ↓
  - **aching**: iris-fl
- **accompanied** by:
  - **dysuria**: solid $_{br1}$
  - **nausea**: cimic $_{hr1}$
- **aching**: acon $_{k*}$ agar $_{k*}$ all-c $_{k*}$ ambr $_{k*}$ ant-c apoc $_{k*}$ **Berb** $_{k*}$ brach $_{k*}$ calc $_{k*}$ carl $_{k*}$ caust $_{k*}$ chlf $_{a1}$ coc-c $_{k*}$ dirc $_{a1}$ elat $_{k*}$ equis-h ham helon $_{br1}$ *Hydr* $_{k*}$ *Kali-bi* $_{k*}$ lac-lup $_{hrn2}$• lyc $_{k*}$ merc-c $_{k*}$ mit $_{k*}$ nat-ar pall $_{k*}$ phos $_{k*}$ phys $_{k*}$ sabad $_{k*}$ sep $_{k*}$ still $_{k*}$ tab $_{k*}$
- **bands** of clothing, from: chel $_{k*}$
- **burning**: *Berb* $_{k*}$ *Coloc* $_{k*}$ kali-n *Lac-d* $_{k*}$ lachn $_{a1}$ nat-m phyt sabin $_{c1*}$ *Ter* tritic-vg $_{fd5.de}$
- **cutting** pain: aids $_{nl2}$• bond $_{a1}$ dirc $_{a1}$ plb $_{k*}$ *Staph* zinc $_{k*}$
- **digging**, when: calc-p $_{k*}$
- **drawing** pain: aloe alumn $_{k*}$ benz-ac $_{k*}$ berb $_{k*}$ *Cann-s* $_{k*}$ carl $_{k*}$ cinnb $_{k*}$ *Iod* $_{k*}$ kali-n $_{k*}$ lach $_{k*}$ lap-la $_{sde8.de}$• meny ruta **Ter** $_{k*}$ tritic-vg $_{fd5.de}$ vanil $_{fd5.de}$ *Zinc* $_{k*}$
- **drawing** up legs amel.: cench $_{k2}$
- **gnawing** pain: brach $_{k*}$
- **heat** amel., cold agg.: *Staph* ↓
  - **cutting** pain: *Staph*
- **lying** | **back**; on:
  - **amel.** | **can** only lie on the back: colch
  - **side**; on:
    - **left** | **agg.**: cench $_{k2}$
- **pressing** pain: agar ars-h $_{k*}$ bamb-a $_{stb2.de}$• *Berb* $_{k*}$ borx $_{h2}$ calc $_{h2*}$ cimic coc-c $_{a1}$ dulc $_{fd4.de}$ ham hydr iod $_{h*}$ kali-c $_{h2*}$ lyc $_{h2*}$ nat-m $_{a1}$ nit-ac $_{a1}$ pall $_{k*}$ ruta $_{h1}$ samb $_{a1}$ symph $_{fd3.de}$• *Ter* $_{a1}$ thuj $_{h1*}$ vanil $_{fd5.de}$ wies $_{a1}$ zinc $_{h2*}$
- **pressure** agg.: **Berb** ↓
  - **digging** pain: **Berb** $_{k*}$
- **pressure** and friction amel.: plb ↓
  - **cutting** pain: plb $_{k*}$
- **sore**: abrot benz-ac **Berb** brach cann-s *Chel* *Coc-c* equis-h helon $_{br1}$ hydr kali-c $_{h2}$ kola $_{stb3}$• mang merc-c nat-ar *Nux-v* phos phys phyt *Rhus-t* tell ter zinc
- **stabbing**: arn erig $_{k*}$
- **stitching** pain: borx $_{h2}$ vanil $_{fd5.de}$
- **stretching**, after: calc $_{k*}$
- **tearing** pain: kola $_{stb3}$• ozone $_{sde2}$•
- **turning** agg.: borx ↓
  - **stitching** pain: borx $_{h2}$
- **urination**:
  - **after** | **agg.**: ambr $_{a1}$
  - **agg.**: syph $_{k2}$
  - **before**: tab ↓
    - **aching**: tab $_{k*}$
- **waking**; on: still ↓
  - **aching**: still $_{k*}$

▽ - **extending** to:
  - **Bladder**: berb $_{k2}$ petr $_{hr1}$
  - **Calves**: *Berb*
  - **Chest**: benz-ac

- **extending** to: ...
  - **Colon**, ascending: kali-br hr1
  - **Downward**: berb *Sars*
  - **Genitalia**, anus and thighs: kreos
  - **Groin**: kali-bi pareir petr k*
    - **nausea**; with anxious: cann-s k*
  - **Hip**, right: ter ↓
    - **drawing** pain: ter
  - **Inguinal** region; into: cann-s ↓
    - **drawing** pain: cann-s
  - **Lumbar** Region: scut c1
  - **Prostate** gland: graph sel
  - **Thighs**: agar **Berb** hep ip kali-bi nux-v
  - **Ureters**: berb k2 canth chel oci phyt

- **Ureters**: acon bg2 aesc ↓ *Apis* ↓ arg-n bg2 am bg2 *Ars* ↓ aspar ↓ bell bg2 *Benz-ac* ↓ berb bg2 bor-ac bg2* cann-s ↓ canth bg2 **Carb-an** ↓ cedr ↓ cham ↓ chlol ↓ coc-c bg2 colch ↓ *Coloc* ↓ con ↓ *Dios* ↓ equis-h ↓ erig ↓ eup-pur ↓ *Hedeo* br1 helo bg2 indg ↓ kali-ar ↓ *Kali-c* ↓ *Lach* ↓ **Lyc** ↓ *Med* ↓ mel-c-s br1 *Nat-m* ↓ nat-s ↓ nit-ac ↓ *Nux-m* ↓ nux-v bg2* oci mrr1 *Op* ↓ **Pareir** ↓ *Phos* ↓ pin-s ↓ polyg-h ↓ psor ↓ **Sars** ↓ scroph-xyz c2 senec ↓ sep ↓ sil ↓ sulph ↓ tab bg2 ter ↓ thuj ↓ **Verat** ↓ verat-v ↓ zinc ↓ zinc-p ↓
  - **right**: apis astac ↓ **Berb** k ● cann-s canth *Dios* indg **LYC** k ●* *Nux-v* *Oci* k* ozone sde2• *Sars* tab tarent
    - **cramping**: lyc mrr1
    - **drawing** pain: astac k*
  - **left**: aesc agar aloe benz-ac **Berb** k ● calad cann-s canth coc-c ↓ epig grat mrr1 *Ipom-p* kali-c *Lyc* ozone sde2• *Pareir*
    - **drawing** pain: calad coc-c
  - **accompanied** by:
    - **nausea**: *Oci* mrr1
    - **urination**:
      - **urging** to urinate | **frequent**: bor-ac br1
    - **vomiting**: *Berb* sne canth sne nux-v sne *Oci* ●*
  - **burning**: cedr pin-s ter k*
  - **cramping**: *Coloc* mrr1 lyc mrr1 nit-ac ptk1 oci mrr1 polyg-h ptk1 sars mrr1
  - **cutting** pain: aesc *Apis Arg-n Arn Ars* aspar **Bell** k* *Benz-ac* **Berb** k* cann-s *Canth* **Carb-an** k* chlol coc-c k* colch con *Dios* equis-h erig eup-pur indg kali-ar *Kali-c Lach* **Lyc** k* *Med* nat-s *Nux-m Nux-v Oci Op* **Pareir** k* *Phos* polyg-h bg2* psor **Sars** k* senec sep sil sulph bg2 *Tab* **Verat** k* verat-v ptk1 zinc zinc-p k2
    - **alternating** with | **Glans** penis; pain in: canth
  - **drawing** pain: berb cham *Nat-m* k* sulph thuj
  - **radiating** from renal region: **Berb** *Ipom-p* vh pareir
  - **sore**: apis ptk1 berb ptk1 oci ptk1
  - **touch**, motion and inspiration agg.: arg-n ↓ bell ↓
    - **tearing** pain | **downward**: arg-n bell
  - **urination** | **after**:
    - **agg.**: apis ↓
      - **cutting** pain: apis
    - **urging** to urinate:
      - **with**: *Cham* ↓ nat-s ↓
        - **dragging**, like labor pain: *Cham* k*
        - **piercing**: nat-s
  - **vomiting**; with (See accompanied - vomiting) **Oci** ↓
    - **cutting** pain: **Oci** k*
  - ▽ **extending** to:
    - **Bladder**: gal-ac br1
    - **Penis**: cann-i canth con *Dios* k* **Nux-v** k ●
    - **Spermatic** cords: berb k2
    - **Testes**: berb k2* cann-i canth con *Dios* k* **Nux-v** k ●
    - **Thigh**; back of: ozone ↓
      - **tearing** pain: ozone sde2•
    - **Thighs**: **Berb** mrr1
      - **right**: nux-v
      - **And** feet: pareir
    - **Urethra**, into: **Berb** k* canth coc-c

Pain – Ureters – extending to – **Urethra**: ...
  - **Seminal** cords, and: clem dios

POLYCYSTIC kidneys: kres mtf11
- **high**: naphthoq mtf11

PRESSURE agg.: aloe bg2 *Berb* bg2* borx bg2 calc bg2 canth bro1* clem bg2 colch bro1* iod bg2 kali-c bg2 lyc bg2 nat-m bg2 nit-ac bg2 ran-s bg2 *Solid* bro1* thuj bg2 zinc bg2

PULSATION: act-sp k* *Berb* k* bufo k* canth k* chel k* kali-i k* med pic-ac k* sabin k* sulph k*
- **right**: nat-m bg2
- **restless** sensation: puls-n
- **sensitive**, area of: *Solid* vh
- **suprarenal** gland: med tl1
- ▽ **extending** to | **Abdomen**; into: kali-i k*

RENAL FAILURE: am-be mtf11 benz-ac br1* berb mtf11 cupr-ar br1 fuma-ac mtf11 germ-met srj5• helon ptk1 juni-c br1 lat-m bnm6• loxo-recl bnm10• nat-ox-act mtf11 solid ptk1
- **accompanied** by | **pleural** effusion: apoc mrr1
- **acute**: *(↗Suppression)* am-c mtf anthraci mtf *Apis* mtf *Aral-h* mtf bapt mtf canth mtf *Carb-ac* mtf *Crot-h* mtf cupr mtf *Cupr-act* mtf cupr-ar mtf dig mtf germ-met srj5• *Hydr-ac* mtf *Hyos* mtf *Lach* mtf lat-m bnm6• *Laur* mtf *Morph* mtf *Op* mtf pic-ac mtf plb mtf sec mtf *Stram* mtf
- **chronic**: *(↗Atrophy; GENERALS - Dropsy - external - kidney; GENERALS - Kimmelstiel-wilson; GENERALS - Uremia)* aesc-c mtf allox mtf am-c mtf apis mtf apoc mtf arg-n mtf ars mtf arum-t mtf aspidin mtf aur mtf aur-m-n mtf aur-s mtf benz-ac mtf chloram mtf11 creat mtf crot-h mtf juni-v mtf kali-c mtf kres mtf lach mtf lob-e mtf11 *Lyc* mtf mag-c mtf *Mag-m* mtf *Mag-s* mtf merc mtf merc-c mtf nat-c mtf nat-m mtf op mtf ph-ac mtf *Phos* mtf pip-m mtf pitu-p mtf11 plb mtf sep mtf *Ser-ang* mtf solid mtf stram mtf streptom mtf11 *Sulph* mtf ter mtf thuj mtf *Urea* mtf11 urt-u mtf
- **coma**; with (See MIND - Coma - renal)

RESTLESSNESS; sensation of: acon bg2 puls bg2

SCLEROSIS: *(↗Nephrotic)*
- **glomerulosclerosis**: *(↗GENERALS - Kimmelstiel-wilson)*
  - **focal** segmental glomerulosclerosis: syc mtf

SENSITIVENESS: *Acon* bro1 apis bro1 *Berb* bro1 calc-ar bro1 cann-s bro1 *Canth* bro1 equis-h bro1 *Helon* bro1 phyt bro1 *Solid* bro1 *Ter* bro1

SITTING agg.: *Berb* bro1 ferr-m bro1

STANDING: | **amel.**: berb bro1*

STIFFNESS: berb bg2

STONES●: *(↗URINE - Sediment; URINE - Sediment - sand - gravel)* act-sp hr1 alum bg2 am-c bg2 am-m bg2 ambr bg2 *Ant-c* bg2 apoc hr1 *Arg-n* bro1 arn bg2* baros bro1 bell k* bell-p sp1 **Benz-ac** k* *Berb* k* cact mrr1 cal-ren c2* **Calc** k* *Cann-xyz* bg2 *Canth* k* cham bro1 chin bg2 chinin-s bro1 *Chlf* hr1 cimic bg2 coc-c k* coli jl2 coloc k* *Dios* hr1* epig br1* equis-h erig bro1* ery-a bro1 eup-pur hr1* fab br1* frag br1 gali br1* guat sp1 hed sp1 hedeo bro1 hep bro1 hydrang k* ipom-p bro1 kali-bi mrr1 kali-c mrr1 kali-i a1 lach bg2* lipp a1 **Lith-c** k* **Lyc** k* mag-p mtf11 med bro1 mill morg-g pte1*• nat-m bg2 *Nit-ac* bg2* nux-m bg2 nux-v bg2* oci k* onis bro1 op bro1 oxyd bro1 **Pareir** k* *Petr* bg2 *Phos* k* pipe bro1 polyg-h bro1 rub-t mtf11 *Ruta* bg2 saroth sp1 **Sars** k* *Sep* bg2* *Sil* k* solid bro1 *Stigm* bro1 sulfa sp1 sulph bg2 *Tab* hr1* ter hr1* thlas c2* thuj bg2 urt-u bro1 uva bro1 vesi bro1 *Zinc* bg2 [*Lith-f* stj2 *Lith-met* stj2 *Lith-p* stj2]
- **right**: lyc mrr1
- **left**: saxi mtf11
- **accompanied** by | **inflammation** of kidneys (See Inflammation - accompanied - stones)
- **bilious**: ser-a-c jl2
- **phosphate**: cal-ren-p mld2
- **recurrent**: cal-ren mtf11
- **urate** (See GENERALS - Uric - diathesis)

STOOPING agg.: berb bro1

STRETCHING LEGS agg.: colch bro1

SUPPRESSION of urine: *(↗Renal - acute; BLADDER - Retention)* **Acon** k* *Aeth* k* agar-ph bro1 *Ail* k* alf bro1 am-caust *Anthraci* **Apis** k* apoc k* aran k* **Arn** k* **Ars** k* *Ars-h* k* *Ars-i* ars-s-f k2 *Arum-t* k* asc-c hr1* aur k* aur-ar k2 aur-m-n hr1 aur-s k2 *Bell* k* bism k* bry bro1 bufo *Cact* k* calc calc-i k2 calen hr1 *Camph* k* **Canth** k* *Carb-ac* **Carb-v** k* carbn-s caust *Cic* k* coc-c br1 coff bro1 *Colch* k* con k* *Crot-h* k* *Cupr* k* *Cupr-act* bro1 cupr-s k* *Dig* k* dulc k* elaps *Elat* k* *Erig* k* eucal hr1 *Eup-pur* k* form bro1 *Hell* k* hep *Hydr* k* *Hyos* k* *Ign* hr1* iod juni-v bro1 *Kali-bi* k* kali-br hr1 kali-c mrr1 kali-chl k* kali-m k2 *Lac-c* k* **Lach** k* **Laur** k* liat br1 lil-t lob ptk1 **Lyc** k* merc *Merc-c* k* merc-cy k* *Morph* nat-m gk nit-ac k* nux-v *Op* k* osm k* oxyd br1* petr k* *Phos* k* phyt k* pic-ac br1* *Plb* k* plut-n srj7• *Podo* k* puls k* pyrog *Rob* k* **Sec** k* sep bg3 *Ser-ang* br1 *Sil* k* solid bro1* stigm br1* **Stram** k* *Stront-c* vh sul-ac *Sulph* k* tab tarax k* *Tarent* k* *Ter* k* *Urt-u* k* **Verat** k* vip zinc zinc-p k2 zing br1*

- **accompanied** by:
  - **neuralgic** pain of the whole right side: elat hr1
  - O **Abdomen**; cramping pain in: acon bro1 plb-act bro1
- **alternating** with frequent urging: sep h2*
- **children**; in: | **infants**; in: chim ptk1
- **cholera**; during: **Ars** k* camph *Carb-v* k* crot-h hr1 *Cupr* k* kali-br hr1 *Laur* hr1 sec verat
- **concussion** of spinal column, from: *Arn* k* rhus-t *Tarent* k*
- **convulsions**; with: **Cupr** k* dig hyos *Stram* k*
- **dentition**; during: ter ptk1
- **diarrhea**; during: sulph mtf33
- **dropsy**, and: apoc gk aral xyz61 aral-h k1* hell bro1 kali-c mrr1
- **fever**; with: *Arn* k* *Ars* k* *Bell* k* *Cact* k* *Canth* k* colch crot-h *Hyos* k* *Op* k* *Plb* *Sec* *Stram* k*
- **followed** by | **vomiting**: ars-h br1*
- **gonorrhea**; from suppressed: **Camph** **Canth**
- **grief**; from: ign gk
- **menses**; during: kali-bi k*
- **perspiration**; with: acon *Apis* arn ars bell h1* camph *Canth* dulc hyos *Lyc* **Op** puls stram sulph
- **stupor**, with: dig plb
- **typhoid** fever:
  - **after**: zing ptk1
  - **during**: stram mtf33
- **violent**: cic *Cupr* cycl sulph

SUPPURATION (See Inflammation)

SWELLING: **Apis** mtf ars mtf berb mtf hell mtf helon ptk1 kali-c mtf kali-i k* lyc mtf phos mtf plb mtf rhus-t mtf solid ptk1 ter mtf vesp mtf

TENSION: clem bg2* colch bg2 nat-m bg2

TUMORS: | **Ureters**: *Anil* br1

TWITCHING, region of: acon bg2 canth k* mang k*

UREMIA (See GENERALS - Uremia)

URIC ACID increased: chel tl1

URINATION; after: | **amel.**: lyc bro1 med bro1

WALKING: | **amel.**: ferr-m bro1

WARMTH (See Heat)

WEAKNESS: *Psor* jl2

WEARINESS, region of: arg-n benz-ac berb carb-an k* cham k* cimic k* helon k* manc phyt k* tarent k*

WINE agg.: benz-ac bro1

URINARY ORGANS; complaints of (See URINARY - Complaints)

ABSCESS: hep gcj med jl2 merc gcj sil ptk1 staphycoc jl2

BALL; sensation of sitting on a: *(↗Pain - pressing)* cann-i *Chim* k* **Sep** k* sil

CANCER of prostate: bar-ox-suc mtf11 carc mp1*• chim mrr1* **Con** mp1* *Cop* mp1• crot-h ptk1* *Iod* mp1• kali-cy gm1 *Lyc* rmk1• naphthoq mtf11 plb mp1• *Psor* mp1• **Sabal** rmk1• *Scir* rmk1• *Sel* mp1• senec mp1• *Sil* mp1• staph mrr1 sulfonam mtf11 *Sulph* mp1• **Thuj** mp1*• thymol mtf11
- **pain**; with: crot-h mp1•

CATARRHAL discharge: aur mtf11 ign mtf11

COITION agg.: all-c ptk1 alum ptk1 psor ptk1

COMPLAINTS of prostate: aesc bg2* aloe bro1 am-m bg2 apis bg2* aur bg2 bar-c bg2* baros br1* bell bg2 benz-ac bg2 calc bg2 caps bg2 carb-v bg2 caust bg2* chel bg2 chim ptk1 clem bg2 con bg2* crot-h ptk1 dam bro1 dig bg2* fab bro1 ferr-pic bg2* gnaph bg2 hep bg2* *Hydrang* bro1 iod bg2* kali-i bg2* lyc bg2* mag-m bg2 med ptk1 *Mela* bro1 merc bg2* nat-s bg2 nit-ac bg2 nux-v bg2 pareir br1* petr bg2 phos ptk1 phyt bro1 pic-ac bro1 polyg-h ptk1 pop bg2* puls bg2* sabad bg2 sabal br1* sel bg2* senec bg2 sep bg2* solid bro1* spirae br1 staph bg2* sul-i bro1 sulph bg2* thuj bg2* zinc-pic bg2
- **accompanied** by:
  - **dysuria**: con bro1 staph bro1
  - **urination**; frequent: apis ptk1 ferr-pic ptk1 sabal ptk1 staph ptk1
  - ○ **Rectum**; complaints of: podo ptk1
- ▽ **extending** to | **Urethra**: staph ptk1

CONGESTION: *Acon* bro1 *Aloe* bro1 arn bro1 bell bro1 *Canth* bro1 con bro1 cop bro1 cub bro1 ferr-p bro1 gels bro1 gonotox jl2 kali-br bro1 kali-i bro1 lith-c bro1 *Ol-sant* bro1 puls bro1 *Sabal* bro1 thuj bro1

EMISSION of prostatic fluid: *(↗Emission - Accompanied - impotency; MALE GENITALIA/SEX - Pollutions; MALE GENITALIA/SEX - Semen; PROSTATE)* acet-ac bro1 aesc bro1 agar k* *Agn* k* alum k* am-c k* *Anac* k* *Apis* *Arg-n* bro1 ars bg2 *Aur* k* aur-s k2 bell k* *Calc* k* cann-s k* canth k* carb-v b2.de* casc caust b2.de* chim k* *Con* k* cub bro1 *Dam* bro1 daph k* dig k* dulc fd4.de *Elaps* *Ery-a* k* *Euph* k* gels *Hep* k* ign b2.de* iod b2.de* juni-c bro1 kali-bi bro1 kali-c b2.de* *Lyc* k* lyss m-ambo b2.de* *Mag-c* mang k* *Nat-c* k* *Nat-m* k* *Nit-ac* k* nuph bro1 nux-m k* nux-v bro1 *Petr* k* **Ph-ac** k* *Phos* k* pic-ac plat b2.de* plb k* *Psor* *Puls* k* sabal k* **Sel** k* **Sep** k* *Sil* k* *Spig* k* spirae br1 **Staph** k* *Sulph* k* tab k* tarent ter bro1 *Thuj* k* thymol br1* trib br1 *Zinc* k*
- **morning**: ran-b c1
- **accompanied** by:
  - **impotency**: *(↗Emission; MALE GENITALIA/SEX - Pollutions - impotence)* sel mrr1
  - ○ **Bladder**; inflammation of: aspar vh
- **causeless**: zinc ptk1
- **chronic**: dam br1
- **dribbling**: ilx-a c1 *Phos* **Sel**
- **easily** discharged, so that even an emission of flatus causes: mag-c k*
- **emotion**, with every: **Con** k* hep puls sel zinc
- **erections**:
  - **during**: ichth ah1 nit-ac **Ph-ac** *Puls* k*
  - **without**: aur bell cann-s con euph *Lyc* k* lyss k* *Nat-m* k* *Phos* **Sel** thuj
- **flatus** agg.; passing: con *Mag-c* k*
- **fondling** women, while: agn k* **Con** k*
- **involuntary**: sel c1
- **itching** of prepuce; with: con k2
- **lascivious** thoughts, during: **Con** k* *Lyc* *Nat-m* **Nit-ac** k* *Ph-ac* *Phos* pic-ac
- **sitting** agg.: *Sel* k*
- **sleep** | **during**: sel c1*
- **stool**:
  - **after** | **agg.**: agn b7.de* am-c k* anac *Calc* k* *Caust* k* cur *Hep* k* *Iod* k* *Kali-c* lyss *Nat-c* k* *Nit-ac* k* phos k* *Sel* k* *Sep* *Sil* **Sulph** k* zinc
  - **before**: agn b7.de* sel b7.de*
  - **difficult** | **with**: *Agn* alum k* am-c anac arn cann-i *Carb-v* con dulc fd4.de gels *Hep* k* *Nat-c* nat-sil k13 **Nit-ac** k* **Ph-ac** k* *Phos* psor *Sep* **Sil** k* *Staph* **Sulph** k* zinc zinc-p k2

Emission of prostatic fluid – **stool**: ...
  - **soft** stool:
    - **with**: anac ars hr1 *Sel*
    - **diarrheic** stools; during soft: ars k1
  - **with**: acet-ac c1 agar *Agn* k* alum k* alum-p k2 alum-sil k2 am-c k* anac k* ars k* aur-m *Calc* k* calc-sil k2 carb-v k* carl *Caust* k* **Con** k* cor-r k* elaps *Hep* k* *Ign* k* *Iod* *Kali-bi* k* *Nat-c* k* *Nat-m* k* nat-p *Nit-ac* k* nuph vml3• **Nux-v** k* *Petr* **Ph-ac** k* *Phos* k* sabal bg2 **Sel** k* **Sep** k* *Sil* k* staph k* sulph k* thuj b4a.de* zinc k*
- **talking** to a young lady, while: *Nat-m* k* *Phos* k*
- **thinking** of it agg.: nat-m
- **tobacco** agg.: daph c1*
- **urination**:
  - **after** | **agg.**: adam skp7• am-c anac k* calc k* *Caust* cur *Daph* *Hep* k* hipp k* *Kali-c* k* lach bg2 lyc lyss k* *Nat-c* k* nat-m k* nit-ac b4a.de* phos a1 sel *Sep* k* *Sil* **Sulph** k*
  - **before**: psor k* sel a1
  - **during** | **agg.**: agn c1 anac k* calc bg2 hep k* lach bg2 nat-c k* nit-ac ph-ac bg2 sep k* sulph k*
- **walking** agg.: agn **Sel** k* sil

ENLARGEMENT (See Swelling)

FESTERING sensation: cycl

FULLNESS: alum berb bry *Chim* *Cycl* nux-v

GONORRHEA; after: merc bg2 *Thuj* bg2

GURGLING sensation: phyt k*

HARDNESS: *Cadm-p* sne **Con** k* *Cop* k* iod k* med *Phos* sne plb k* senec k* *Sil* k* *Thuj* k*
- **enlargement**, without: cop
- **sensation** of: senec ptk1

HEAT: ptel k* *Puls*

HEAVINESS: cact caust *Con* k* cop graph hydrc k* *Med* bg1* puls sulph
- **lascivious** thoughts, during: graph
- **men**; in: hipp jl2

INDURATION: *(↗Swelling)* am-m b4a.de* bar-c bg2 *Cadm-p* sne *Con* k* *Cop* k* crot-h sne *Iod* k* *Phos* sne plb k* *Psor* *Sel* senec *Sil* k* *Sulph* **Thuj** k*
- **accompanied** by:
  - **cancer** of prostate (See Cancer)
  - ○ **Tongue** | **brown** discoloration: *Iod* vk1
- **chronic**: aur tt1 brach vh1

INFLAMMATION (= prostatitis): acon k* aesc k* agn k* aloe bro1 alum alum-sil k2 anac jl apis k* arg-met jl arist-cl sp1 arn *Aur* bg2* bar-c mrr1 bell k* bov bry bro1 cact cann-i k* cann-s mrr1 cann-xyz bg2 canth k* *Caps* caust k* chim k* cic jl clem mrr1 *Colch* c2* coli jl2 *Con* k* cop k* cub k* cycl k* *Dig* k* *Dulc* vh *Fab* br1* ferr-p bro1 ferr-pic ptk1 *Gels* bro1 gonotox jl2 *Hep* k* hipp k* iod bg2* *Kali-bi* k* kali-br bro1 kali-c jl* kali-i bro1 kali-n bro1 lach lil-t lith-c k* *Lyc* k* med k* *Merc* k* merc-c bro1 merc-d k* naphthoq mtf11 *Nit-ac* bro1* *Nux-v* k* ol-sant bro1 pareir k* petr k* *Ph-ac* pic-ac bro1 pitu-gl br1 podo c2 polyg-h c2 polyg-s bg1 psor jl2 **Puls** k* pyrog st sabad bro1 sabal k* sal-n c2* sars mrr1 sec *Sel* k* senec k* *Sep* k* *Sil* k* solid bro1* spong bg2 *Staph* k* staphycoc jl2 sul-ac *Sulph* k* *Thuj* k* *Trib* br1 tritic bro1 *Verat-v* bro1 vesi c2* zinc k*
- **accompanied** by | **urine**; blood in: *Chim* mrr1
- **chronic**: alum bro1 *Aur* bro1 bar-c bro1 brach bro1 calad bro1 carbn-s bro1 caust kr1* clem bro1 *Con* bro1 *Ferr-pic* bro1 graph bro1 hep bro1 hydrc bro1 iod bro1 *Kali-bi* kr1 *Lyc* bro1 *Merc* bro1 *Merc-c* bro1 *Nit-ac* bro1 *Nux-v* kr1* phyt bro1 *Puls* bro1 pyrog st sabad bro1 *Sabal* bro1 *Sel* bro1 senec kr1 *Sep* bro1 sil bro1 solid bro1 *Staph* kr1* sulph bro1 *Thuj* bro1 *Trib* bro1
- **discharge**; with thick yellow: cub br1
- **gonorrhea**; from suppressed: *(↗URETHRA - Discharge - gonorrheal)* bell caps bro1 *Cop* cub bro1 cupr *Dig* *Med* *Merc* merc-d ptk1 **Nit-ac** k* *Nux-v* pareir bro1 *Petr* *Puls* *Sep* staph *Sulph* **Thuj** k*
- **old** people; in: dig mrr1 *Sel* br1

IRRITATION in: cact k* *Dig* gaul br1 gnaph k*

JERKING in region of: form k*

LUMP; sensation of a (See Ball; Fullness)

MASTURBATION, complaints after: tarent k*

PAIN: acon *All-c* k* *Alum* alum-sil k2 ambr↓ apis asaf *Bell* berb bov brom k* cact calc-p k* calc-sil↓ canth↓ *Caps* k* carb-an↓ *Caust* *Chim* clem a1 *Con* cop k* *Cub* k* cupr-ar k* *Cycl* k* dig gnaph k* graph kali-bi↓ kali-c↓ kali-n↓ laur *Lyc* k* lyss k* med br1 merc mez↓ nat-ar↓ nit-ac↓ ol-an k* pareir ph-ac↓ *Phos* podo polyg-h *Puls* *Rhus-t* sabal↓ sel *Sil* sne *Staph* sul-ac↓ sul-i sulph symph fd3.de• tarent k* thuj visc↓

- **afternoon**: aur↓ kali-bi↓
  - **stitching** pain: aur kali-bi k*
- **aching**: med bg2 sabal bg1 thuj
- **biting** pain: carb-an con
- **bladder**, deep in pelvis, morning and forenoon after coition; and: all-c↓
  - **aching**: all-c
- **blowing** the nose agg.: alum
- **burning**: all-c ambr caps bg2* cop lyss k* ph-ac k* sulph mrr1
- **cancer**, in: cadm-f gm1 carc mlr1• crot-h
- **coition**:
  - **after**: *All-c* k* alum caps *Psor* sel
  - **during**: *Alum*↓
    - **pressing** pain: *Alum*
- **constricting** pain: canth k* *Caust* puls sulph
- **cramping**: visc sp1
- **dragging**: nat-ar sil k*
- **drawing** pain: clem *Cycl* kali-bi mez
- **dull** pain: gnaph bg2
- **ejaculation**; during: agar↓
  - **burning**: agar k2
- **erections**; during: alum
  - **beginning** of erection: *Alum*↓
    - **pressing** pain: *Alum*
- **gonorrhea**; during: *Caps* cub
- **jar** agg.: **Bell**
- **motion** | **amel**.: rhus-t k2
- **nose**, on blowing: alum↓
  - **pressing** pain: alum
- **pressing** pain: (↗*Ball)* all-c k* *Alum* apis asaf berb brom k* cact *Caust* chim *Con* *Cycl* laur *Lyc* merc ol-an k* *Phos* *Puls* *Sel* sil h2* sulph thuj
- **pulsating** pain: caust polyg-h k*
- **riding** agg.: staph
- **shooting** (See stitching)
- **sitting** agg.: *Chim* *Cycl* k* dig rhus-t
- **sitting** or walking: *Cycl*↓
  - **aching**: cycl
  - **drawing** pain: *Cycl*
- **sore**: alum alum-sil k2 calc-sil k2 **Chim** k* *Cycl* *Rhus-t* sul-ac k*
- **standing** agg.: cycl
  - **pressing** pain: cycl
- **sticking** pain: nit-ac
- **stitching** pain: bov calc-p *Con* k* *Cycl* k* *Dig* lp kali-bi k* kali-c k* kali-n k* lyc *Puls*
  - **forward**: sil h2
- **stool** | **after** | **agg.**: phos
  - **urging** to: *Cycl* k* rhus-t
- **urging** for urination or stool; when: cycl↓
  - **stitching** pain: cycl ptk1
- **urination**:
  - **after**:
    - **agg.**: bell↓ lyc polyg-pe vml2• **Puls**
      - **burning**: bell bg2
      - **pressing** pain: lyc **Puls**
  - **during**:
    - **agg.**: *Apis* cact↓ caust↓ cop k* cycl↓ kali-n↓ lyc med br1 merc-d↓ pareir sel↓
      - **pressing** pain: *Lyc*
      - **stitching** pain: cact caust cop cycl kali-n k* merc-d pareir sel
    - **end** of: coca
  - **urging** to urinate: *Cycl* k* *Rhus-t*
- **walking**:
  - **agg.**: all-c brom k* *Cycl* k* *Kali-bi*↓ staph
    - **pressing** pain: all-c brom k* *Cycl*
    - **stitching** pain: *Kali-bi* k*
  - **amel.**: *Rhus-t*
- ▽ **extending** to:
  - ○ **Genitals**: bov↓
    - **stitching** pain: bov
- ○ **Region** of: bov↓
  - **pulsating** pain: bov
  - **urinate**; while straining to: dig↓
    - **pulsating** pain: dig

PROSTATITIS (See Inflammation)

PROSTATORRHEA (See Catarrhal)

QUIVERING, nervous: form k*

SUPPURATION: fab br1 hep **Sil**

SWELLING: (↗*Induration)* alf br1* aloe k* alum alum-p k2 alum-sil k2 *Am-m* k* *Apis* apoc ptk1 *Arg-n* bro1 asar aspar *Aur-m* k* **Bar-c** k* bar-i k2 *Benz-ac* k* *Berb* cact **Calc** k* calc-f bro1 calc-i bro1 calc-sil k2 cann-s k* cann-xyz ptk1 canth k* caust brm chel **Chim** k* chin brm chlam-tr bcx2• chr-s bro1 cic *Cimic* bro1 clem k* **Con** k* cop k* cub k* cuc-p mtf11 dam mtf11 **Dig** k* *Dulc* k* eup-pur br1* *Fab* c1* *Ferr-m* k* ferr-pic bg1* fl-ac mrr1 *Gels* bro1 graph bro1 hed sp1 hep bro1 hipp hydrang bg2* *Hyos* k* *Iod* k* kali-bi bro1 kali-br bro1 kali-c mrr1 *Kali-i* k* kali-p kreos mtf11 lith-c *Lyc* k* mag-s sp1* *Med* k* *Merc* k* merc-d *Nat-c* k* nat-p *Nat-s* k* *Nit-ac* k* nux-v ol-an ptk1 ol-sant bro1 oxyd br1* *Pareir* k* petr sne *Phos* k* pic-ac bro1* pip-m bro1 polytr-c br1 *Pop* bro1 *Psor* **Puls** k* rhus-a bro1 sabal bg2* sars bro1 *Sec* *Sel* k* senec k* sep k* *Sil* k* solid bg1* *Spong* k* *Staph* k* stigm br1 sul-ac sul-i k2 *Sulph* k* symph fd3.de• ther k2* *Thiosin* bro1 *Thuj* k* thymol sp1 thyr bro1 trib bro1 tritic br1* tub jl2 uncar-tom mp4• uva x-ray sp1 *Zinc* mrr1* [*Zinc-i* stj2 *Zinc-m* stj2 *Zinc-n* stj2 *Zinc-p* stj2]

- **accompanied** by:
  - **constipation**: arn bro1 sil bro1
  - **urination**; involuntary (See BLADDER - Urination - involuntary - accompanied - prostate)
  - **urine**; retention of (See BLADDER - Retention - enlarged)
  - ○ **Eyes**; red discoloration of: sabal ptk1 solid ptk1
  - **Perineum**; pressure in: berb ptk1
- **cancerous** (See Cancer)
- **dribbling** urine after stool and after urination: **Sel** k*
- **old** people; in: aloe **Bar-c** k* *Benz-ac* *Con* **Dig** k* ferr-pic br1* *Iod* nux-v prost bwa3 *Sabal* k* **Sel** k* *Staph* sulph
- **sensation** of: alum berb bry chim cycl nux-v senec ptk1 *Ther* k*
- **sexual** excesses; after: thymol sp1

TENSION: clem kali-p fd1.de• lyc k* thuj k*

TWITCHING: form k*

ULCER: apis b7a.de

UNEASINESS: ptel k*

URINATION agg.: lyc ptk1 polyg-h ptk1 *Puls* ptk1

WALKING agg.: cycl ptk1 kali-bi ptk1

WARMTH (See Heat)

ABSCESS: canth bg2* puls bg2* rhus-t bg2*

AGGLUTINATION of meatus: anag k* borx k* bov k* calc-p k* *Camph* k* *Cann-s* k* cann-xyz ptk1 canth k* *Cupr* k* cupr-ar k* gamb k* graph *Med* k* mez b4a.de nat-c k2 *Nat-m* k* *Petros* k* tab k* *Thuj* k*
- **morning**: canth k* *Phos* k* **SEP** k •* *Thuj* k*
- **urination** agg.; during: anag bro1 cann-s bro1

AIR passes from the female urethra: | **urination** agg.; during: sars k*

BALL rolling through; sensation of a: *(↗Drop; sensation - rolling; Stone)* lach k*

BUBBLING sensation, as if bubbles were moving about: chin b7.de* merc b4.de*
- **sitting** agg.: berb merc a1
- **sticking**; like: merc a1*

CARBUNCLE: acon bg2 ars bg2 borx bg2 calc bg2 carb-v bg2 dulc bg2 graph bg2 hep bg2 lach bg2 merc bg2 nit-ac k2 **Nux-v** bg2 **Puls** bg2 *Sulph* bg2

CARTILAGINOUS induration (See Induration - cartilaginous)

CARUNCLE: arg-n ptk1 ars ptk1 bacls-10 pte1• cann-s c2* *Cann-xyz* ptk1 *Eucal* c2* hep ptk1 morg-p pte1*• nit-ac ptk1 sul-i ptk1 sulph ptk1 teucr bro1 *Thuj* bro1
- **vascular** bleeding tumor of: cann-s hr1* *Eucal* hr1* eup-pur hr1 teucr hr1 thuj hr1

CATARRH: ant-t br1 hydr br1 thuj mtf33

CHANCRE (See Ulceration - chancres; GENERALS - Chancre)

CHORDEE: *(↗Chordee - accompanied; MALE GENITALIA/SEX - Erections - continued - painful)* acon hr1* *Agav-a* bro1 **Agn** b7a.de *Anac* bro1 **Arg-n** k* aur-m bell bro1 berb bro1 bry *Camph* k* camph-br c2 *Camph-mbr* bro1 *Cann-i* k* **Cann-s** k* **Canth** k* **Caps** k* chlol k* clem k2* *Colch* k* con cop k* *Cub* k* cur dig k* ery-a k* fl-ac k* gels bro1 hep hyos bro1 jac-c hr1* *Kali-br* k* **Kali-chl** k* kali-i kali-m k2 *Lup* bro1 *Merc* k* merc-c *Mygal* k* nat-c *Nit-ac* k* *Nux-v* oena bro1 ol-sant bro1 *Petros* k* phos k* *Pic-ac* bro1 pip-m bro1 pip-n **Puls** k* sabad sabin b7.de sal-n br1* sep sin-n c2 still hr1 stram c2 **Ter** k* *Thuj* k* tus-p bro1 yohim bro1 zinc-pic bro1 *Zing*
- **accompanied** by: *(↗Chordee)*
  - **burning** in urethra: calc-p
  - **sensitiveness** of urethra; extreme: *Caps*

CLOGGED by pieces of coagulated mucus: cann-s k* graph *Merc* k* *Sep* k* uva

COLDNESS: clem k*
- **painful** shoots, during: *Sulph* k*
- **urination** agg.; during: agar bg2 nit-ac bg2

COMPLAINTS of urethra: acon b2.de* agar b2.de agn b2.de* alum b2.de* am-c b2.de am-m b2.de ambr b2.de* anac b2.de ang b2.de ant-c b2.de ant-t b2.de arg-n bg2* arn b2.de* ars b2.de asar b2.de aur b2.de bar-c b2.de bell b2.de* borx b2.de bov b2.de* bry b2.de* calc b2.de* camph b2.de **Cann-s** b2.de* *Cann-xyz* ptk1 **Canth** b2.de* **Caps** b2.de* carb-an b2.de carb-v b2.de* caust b2.de* cham b2.de chel b2.de* chin b2.de* cic b2.de **Clem** b2.de* cocc b2.de coff b2.de colch b2.de* coloc b2.de con b2.de* cop bg2 croc b2.de cupr b2.de* cycl b2.de dig b2.de* dulc b2.de* euph b2.de ferr b2.de* graph b2.de* guaj b2.de hell b2.de hep b2.de* ign b2.de* iod b2.de ip b2.de* kali-c b2.de* kali-n b2.de lach b2.de* laur b2.de led b2.de* **Lyc** b2.de* m-ambo b2.de m-aust b2.de mag-c b2.de mag-m b2.de mang b2.de **Merc** b2.de* **Merc-c** bg2 mez b2.de* mur-ac b2.de nat-c b2.de* nat-m b2.de* nit-ac b2.de* nux-m b2.de nux-v b2.de* oci br1 op b2.de par b2.de petr b2.de* ph-ac b2.de* **Phos** b2.de* plb b2.de *Puls* b2.de* rhod b2.de rhus-t b2.de* ruta b2.de sabad b2.de sabin b2.de* samb b2.de sars b2.de* sec b2.de sel b2.de* seneg b2.de sep b2.de* sil b2.de spig b2.de squil b2.de stann b2.de staph b2.de* stram b2.de *Sulph* b2.de* syc fmm1• teucr b2.de* **Thuj** b2.de* verat b2.de viol-t b2.de zinc b2.de*
- **accompanied** by | **fever**: *Acon* bro1 ars bro1 *Chinin-ar* bro1 *Gels* bro1 hep bro1 lach bro1 phos bro1 rhus-t bro1 sil bro1
- ▽ **extending** to | **Abdomen**: sars ptk1
- ○ **Prostate**; near: sabal br1

COMPLAINTS of urinary organs (See URINARY - Complaints)

CONSTRICTION: arg-n bg2 arn bg2 bell bg2 bry bg2 calc bg2 camph b7.de* cann-s k* cann-xyz bg2 canth b7.de* carb-v b4a.de* chin bg2 cic bg2 *Clem* k* cocc bg2 con bg2 dig b4.de* dulc b4.de* graph b4a.de* *Iod* b4a.de led b7.de* lob bg2 lyc k* mag-m bg2 merc bg2 nux-v bg2 *Petr* b4.de* phos bg2 puls b7.de* rhus-t b7.de* sabal bg2 sil b4a.de* spong bg2 *Sulph* bg2 thuj b4.de*
- **convulsive**: berb k*
- **sensation** of: arg-n bell bg2 dig *Puls* b7a.de verat b7.de*
  - **behind** glans: verat h1
  - **urination** agg.; during: ang b7.de* arn b7.de* *Cann-xyz* bg2 colch b7.de* rhus-t bg2 sars b4.de*
- **smarting**: berb k*
- **urination** | **after** | **agg.**: cub k*
  - **during** | **agg.**: *Apis* arg-n k* bell bg2 bry k* **Caust** bg2 *Clem* cop dig k* graph nit-ac nux-v op puls stram
- ▽ **extending** to:
  - **backward**, while reflecting: nux-v
  - ○ **Bladder**: cupre-au c1 lyc op phos
    - **urination** agg.; after: lyc a1

CONTRACTION: am-m hr1 asar camph b7.de* *Canth* k* carb-an carb-v k* *Chin* k* *Clem* k* *Coloc* b4a.de *Cop* k* dig indg k* nux-v k* op b7a.de petr k* phos **Puls** k* stram k* verat zinc
- **morning**: carb-v k*
  - **erections**; during: *Canth*
- **gonorrhea**; suppressed: **Puls**
- **stool**; before: *Nat-m* k*
- **urination**:
  - **after** | **agg.**: camph b7.de* chinin-s bg2 *Nux-v* k*
  - **before**: *Nat-m* k*
  - **during** | **agg.**: bry k* *Clem* dig indg k*
  - **urging** to urinate | **with**: *Nat-m*
- ▽ **extending** to | **Backward** after urination: camph h1
- ○ **Internally**: **Canth** k*
- **Meatus**: coc-c thuj

CRACKS in meatus: *Nat-c* k* *Nit-ac* k* ph-ac phos thuj

CRAMP: canth ptk1 chel k* chin ptk1 clem ptk1 nit-ac phos k*

CRAWLING: agar k* ambr h1* berb k* canth b7.de* chin k* colch b7.de* ferr-i k* ign k* junc-e kola stb3• *Lyc* k* merl k* mez k* *Petros* k* *Ph-ac* k* *Puls* b7.de* ran-s k* staph b7.de* tarent thuj k* tus-p k*
- **sticking**: *Mez* k*
- **urination**:
  - **after** | **agg.**: canth k* colch b7.de* *Lyc* **Puls** b7.de*
  - **during** | **agg.**: ign k* petros ph-ac
  - **not** urinating; when: ph-ac k*
- ○ **Fossa** navicularis: **Petros**
- **Meatus**: agar k* puls k* ran-s k* staph k*

DISAGREEABLE sensation: agn b7.de*
- **urination** agg.; after: agn b7.de*

DISCHARGE: *(↗Discharge - Gonorrheal)* agar bg2 agn b7.de* ant-c bg2 arg-n bg2 calc bg2 *Cann-s* b7.de* *Canth* b7.de* *Caps* b7.de* con b4.de dulc bg2 ferr b7.de* hep b4a.de* ign b7a.de ip b7.de* kali-i bg2 med bg2 **Merc** b4.de* merc-c bg2 mez b4.de* nat-m b4.de* nat-s bg2 *Nit-ac* b4.de* nux-v bg2 petr b4.de* **Puls** b7.de* sabin b7.de* sars b4.de* sel b7.de* sep b4.de* *Sulph* bg2* syc fmm1• *Thuj* b4.de*
- **night**: *Merc* b4a.de sep ptk1
- **accompanied** by:
  - **erections**: canth mrr1
    - **painful**: lupin hsa
  - **sexual** desire; increased: canth mrr1
  - ○ **Urinary** organs; complaints of (See URINARY - Complaints - accompanied - urethra)
- **acrid**: **Arg-n** k* aur-m caps cop k* gels bro1 *Hydr* bro1 kreos **Merc-c** k* *Nat-m* *Petros* sars thuj bro1
- **albuminous**: canth nit-ac petros k*

- **bloody**: *Arg-n* k* bell calc ptk1 **Calc-s** cann-s **Canth** k* *Caps* k* cop cub k* cur ferr-p k2 kali-i k* lith-c lyc *Merc* *Merc-c* k* mill k* *Mur-ac* *Nit-ac* k* petr a1 *Psor* *Puls* k* sil ptk1 thuj zinc k*
  - **accompanied** by:
    - **erections**: canth mrr1
    - **sexual** desire; increased: canth mrr1
  - **diarrhea**; in chronic: euph
  - **painful** to touch; urethra: caps
  - **urination** agg.; after: hep bg2 sars bg2 zinc h2*
- **burning**: *Caps* b7a.de
- **cheesy**: hep
- **chronic**: nit-ac mrr1 ter mrr1
- **clear**: brom cann-i *Cann-s* canth cub elaps lyc mez *Nat-m* nit-ac petros ph-ac phos
  - **morning**: phos ptk1
- **colorless**: canth k* *Nat-m* nit-ac petros phos hr1*
- **copious** (See profuse)
- **cream**-like: **Caps** k*
- **egg** white; like: nat-m mtf33
- **fetid**: bar-c *Benz-ac* k* *Carb-v* k* *Hep* k* *Pip-m* bg1 psor puls *Sil* k* sulph thuj
- **filamentous**: merc b4a.de
- **flakes** | **milk** like: ph-ac k2
- **flocculent**, after urination: kali-bi
- **gleety**: *(↗gonorrheal)* abies-c br1* *Agar* **Agn** k* aln c2 aloe c2 **Alum** k* alum-p k2 **Alumn** k* arg-n bro1 aur-m bar-c *Bar-m* k* bar-s k2 **Benz-ac** k* *Bov* k* bry *Calad* k* *Calc* k* *Calc-p* k* calc-s *Cann-i* cann-s k* canth k* *Caps* k* *Carb-v* carbn-s cedr chim k* *Cinnb* k* *Clem* k* *Cob* *Cop* k* *Cub* k* cupr dig b4a.de dor c1* dulc k* equis-h c2 erig k* ery-a k* *Ferr* ferr-p fl-ac k* gamb k* *Graph* k* guaj k2 *Hep* k* *Hydr* k* *Iris* *Kali-bi* k* *Kali-c* **Kali-chl** k* **Kali-i** k* kali-m k2 *Kali-s* k* *Lyc* k* mati hsa1* *Med* k* *Merc* k* merc-c k* merc-i-r bro1 *Mez* k* mill mur-ac *Naphtin* c2* nat-c k2 **Nat-m** k* *Nat-s* k* *Nit-ac* k* nux-v bro1 *Ol-sant* bro1 *Petr* **Petros** k* *Ph-ac* *Phos* k* *Phyt* k* pin-c bro1 pip-m bro1 *Plb* pop bro1 *Psor* k* *Puls* bro1 rhod bro1 sabal c2* sang k* **Sel** k* senec k* **Sep** k* sil b4a.de* spirae br1 stigm bro1 **Sulph** k* tell k* *Ter* k* **Thuj** k* vesi c2 zinc zinc-m bro1
  - **morning**: aur-m ph-ac phos **SEP** k ●
  - **night**: *Fl-ac* *Sep*
  - **children**; in: dor br1
  - **chronic** (See gleety)
  - **impotence**, with: **Agn** k*
  - **painless**: *Agar* *Alum* *Arg-met* bar-c *Cann-s* *Cop* *Ferr* k* *Hep* *Hydr* **Kali-i** *Med* *Merc* k* *Mez* **Nat-m** *Nat-s* petr *Psor* k* *Puls* *Sang* **Sep** *Sulph* *Thuj* k*
  - **protracted** (See gleety)
- **gluey**: agar bg2 *Cann-s* b7a.de *Graph* k* hydr bg2 nat-m bg2 nux-v bg2 petros b7a.de sulph b4a.de thuj bg2
- **gonorrheal**: *(↗gleety; Discharge; EXTREMITIES - Pain - rheumatic - gonorrhea; FEMALE - Inflammation - ovaries - gonorrhea; GENERALS - Gonorrhea; GENERALS - Sycosis; MALE GENITALIA/SEX - Inflammation - testes - gonorrhea; PROSTATE - Inflammation - gonorrhea)* acon b7a.de* agav-a c2 **Agn** k* aloe k* *Alum* k* alum-p k2 alumn k* am-m anag k* *Ant-c* k* apis k* arg-met k2 *Arg-n* k* ars k* ars-s-f k* atro bro1 aur c2 aur-m k* bar-m k* *Baros* bro1 benz-ac c2* *Bism* *Borx* cajan jsx1.fr *Calad* k2* *Calc* k* calc-p c2 calc-s k* camph c2* cann-i k* **Cann-s** k* **Cann-xyz** ptk1 **Canth** k* caps k* caul k* caust bg2 *Cedr* *Cham* *Chel* k* chim k* chin bg2 cinnb k* *Clem* k* cob k* coc-c c2 coch k* con b4a.de cop bg2* *Cor-r* b7a.de crot-h c2 cub k* cupr-ar cupre-au c2 dig k* dor k* dulc b4a.de* echi br1* epiph c2 equis-h c2* erech c2 erig k* ery-a k* eucal k* euph-pi c2* fab c2* ferr b7.de* ferr-i k* ferr-p k* ferr-s c2 fl-ac k* frag c2 gels k* grat br1 hedy c1* hep b4a.de* hib-su bta1• hydr k* hydrc c2 hygroph-aur jsx1.fr ichth c2* jac-c c2* jac-g c2 *Kali-bi* bro1 kali-c k2 **Kali-chl** k* *Kali-i* k* kali-s k* kola stb3• kreos bro1 lac-c k* lach bg2 lachn lact-v c2 lant-t jsx1.fr lappa c2 led k* lup c2 lyc b4.de* **Med** k* **Merc** k* *Merc-c* k* merc-n c2 merc-pr-r c2* methyl c2* *Mez* k* mill mygal c2 *Naphtin* c2* nat-c b4a.de* nat-m k* **Nat-s** k* **Nit-ac** k* nux-v b7.de* oci-car gsb1 oci-g c2* ol-an c2 ol-sant c2* par c2 pareir k* petr k* petros k* ph-ac k* *Phos* *Phyt* k* pin-c bro1 pip-m c2 *Plb* k* polyg-xyz c2 *Psor* k* **Puls** k* rat c2 rhod rhus-t bg2 rumx-ab jsx1.fr sabad sabal c2* sabin k* sal-n c2* salol c2 santa mp4• sars k* sec b7a.de sel b7a.de* senec k* **Sep** k* *Sil* k* sil-mar c2 staph b7.de* stigm bro1 still sul-i c2 *Sulph* k* syc bka1• *Tarent* ter k* thlas c2 **Thuj** k* trad c1* *Tritic* br1* tus-p c2* vesi c2 zing bro1
  - **night**: *Merc* merc-c sep
  - **gonorrheal – night**: ...
    - **only**: sep
  - **accompanied** by:
    - **salivation**: *Merc* kr1*
    - **sensibility** of parts to contact; excessive: caps tl1
    - **tenesmus**; continuous: merc-c br1
  - **acute**: acon bg2 **Cann-xyz** bg2 *Canth* bg2 cinnb bg2 *Merc* bg2 *Merc-c* bg2 sal-n br1 sulph bg2
  - **beginning**: arg-n br1
  - **chronic**: agar k2 *Agn* b7a.de* *Alum* alum-p k2 *Alumn* *Arg-met* bar-m k2 brom **Calc** **Calc-p** **Calc-s** **Cann-xyz** bg2 canth b7a.de caps bg2 chim **Chlor** *Cinnb* **Coch** con bg2 cub *Cupr* dig bg2* dulc bg2 erig br1 *Ferr* k* fl-ac bg2 hep bg2* hydr k* kali-c k2 kali-i ptk1 kali-m k2 *Kali-s* k* lach bg2 lyc bg2 *Med* k* *Merc* bg2 mez bg2 *Mygal* *Myric* **Nat-m** k* **Nat-s** k* nit-ac bg2* nux-v bg2 *Petr* k* *Petros* *Plb* *Psor* k* sabin bg2 sel b7a.de* *Sep* k* *Sil* k* *Sulph* k* **Thuj** k*
  - **increases** after having decreased: bry lil-t *Sep* *Sulph* *Thuj*
  - **later** stage: caps tl1
  - **painful**: *Canth* b7a.de
  - **painless**: *Cann-s* b7a.de
  - **second** stage: merc-c br1
  - **suppressed** (See GENERALS - Gonorrhea)
  - **syphilitics**; in: **Aur-m** cinnb merc *Merc-c*
  - **white**: caps tl1
  - **yellow**: kali-s tl1 puls tl1
- **gray**: *Arg-met* bufo bg1 thuj b4a.de
- **greenish**: arg-met k2 *Bry* calc-sil k2 *Cinnb* *Cob* cop gonotox jl2 *Hydr* *Kali-i* kali-s **Merc** k* *Merc-c* k* *Nat-m* *Nat-s* k* *Nit-ac* puls k2 sulph b4a.de ter *Thuj* k*
  - **night**: **Merc** merc-c
  - **chronic**: *Cinnb* *Cob* kali-i **Nat-s**
  - **thick**: kali-i k* *Merc* **Nat-s**
  - **yellow**: anan *Arg-met* *Cinnb* *Cob* *Cub* cur *Hydr* kali-i kali-s lith-c lyc **Merc** merc-c k2 **Nat-s** k* nux-v phyt **Puls** *Sep* ter *Thuj* k*
    - **thick**, with priapism: *Anan* *Nat-s* **Puls**
- **jellylike**: *Kali-bi*
- **milky**: cann-i bro1 *Cann-s* k* **Cann-xyz** bg2 *Caps* k* *Cop* k* cupr-ar bro1 *Ferr* k* graph bro1 *Hydr* bro1 *Iod* k* *Kali-bi* bro1 *Kali-c* k* *Kali-chl* kali-m k2 *Lach* k* *Merc* k* **Nat-m** k* *Nux-v* k* *Petros* k* puls bro1 **Sep** k* sulph bg2
  - **fat** milk; like: *Caps* b7a.de ferr b7a.de petros b7a.de
  - **pasty**: canth
  - **sticky**: *Nat-m* thuj
    - **urination** agg.; before: mez
  - **stool** agg.; after: *Iod*
  - **urination** agg.; after: cop kali-c lach k* nat-m k* petros rhus-t bg2 sep k*
- **mucous**: agar k* *Agn* k* alum bro1 alum-sil k2 ant-c b7a.de* ant-s-aur arg-met k2 *Arg-n* k* *Baros* br1* bell *Benz-ac* brom bry *Calc* k* *Cann-s* k* *Canth* k* *Caps* k* caust b4a.de cedr *Chim* k* *Clem* *Cob* k* con k* *Cop* k* *Cub* k* dig bro1 dulc k* **Elaps** k* *Ferr* k* ferr-p fl-ac *Graph* k* *Hep* k* hydr k* jac-c bro1 kali-bi k2 kali-i k* kali-s k* lyc k* mag-p k* *Merc* k* *Merc-c* bro1 merc-i-f *Mez* k* nat-c k* *Nat-m* k* *Nat-s* bro1 *Nit-ac* k* *Nux-v* k* ol-sant bro1 *Pareir* k* petr k* petros phos k* **Puls** k* rhod sabin k* sars k* **Sep** k* sil bro1 *Sulph* k* *Thuj* k* tus-p bro1 zing bro1
  - **evening**:
    - **chill**, after a: ferr
    - **urination** agg.; after: nat-m nit-ac nux-v *Ph-ac*
  - **bloody**: canth k* *Merc* b4a.de **Nit-ac** k* puls
  - **gelatinous**, after urination: nat-m
  - **glutinous**: *Agar* k* thuj
  - **lumps**; in: agn b7a.de *Cann-s* b7a.de caps b7a.de merc b4a.de puls b7a.de *Thuj* b4a.de
  - **milky** white: cann-s b7a.de *Kali-chl* puls b7a.de
  - **moving** about, on: mez h2*
  - **purulent**: nux-v b7a.de
  - **relaxation** of genitals, during: *Phos*

- **urinating**: calc bg2 merc bg2 phos h2
- **urination** | **after** | **agg.**: con b4.de* **Merc-c** bg2 nat-m b4.de nit-ac h2
  - **during** | **beginning** of | **agg.**: *Clem* b4a.de *Thuj* b4a.de
    - **end** of: nit-ac h2
- **viscid**, after urination: nit-ac h2
  - **and** purulent: nux-v

- **offensive**: cop bg2 merc b4a.de nit-ac bg2 puls b7a.de sil bg2 *Sulph* b4a.de
- **orgasm**; during: *Ign* zf nat-m zf *Phos* zf
- **painless**: cann-s b7a.de ferr ptk1 kali-i k2 **Merc** b4a.de nat-s ptk1 *Nit-ac* b4a.de **Sulph** b4a.de thuj ptk1
- **pale**: sulph b4a.de
- **persistent**: alum ptk1 arg-met ptk1 kali-bi ptk1 phos ptk1 sulph ptk1
- **profuse**: apis arg-met arg-n k* ars-s-f bufo calc-s k2 *Cann-i* chim k* *Cop Cub* cur *Ferr* k* *Hydr* k* *Kali-bi* lat-h thj1 *Med Petros* sabin c1 *Sep* **Thuj**
  - **morning**: med hr1
- **purulent**: agn k* alum hr1* alum-sil k2 arg-n k* *Arn* k* *Bar-c* k* bar-s k2 *Baros* br1* bov *Calc* **Calc-s** calc-sil k2 *Cann-s* k* *Canth* k* *Caps* k* *Carb-v Chel* chim k* *Clem* k* cob bro1 *Con* k* *Cop* k* *Cub* k* cupr-ar k* dig bro1 graph b4.de* *Hep* bro1 *Hydr* bro1 ip k* jac-c bro1 *Kali-i* k* *Kali-s* k* kola stb3• *Led* k* *Lyc* k* *Med Merc* k* *Merc-c* k* mez b4.de* nat-c b4.de* nat-m k* *Nat-s* bro1 **Nit-ac** k* nux-v k* ol-sant bro1 *Ph-ac* phos psor *Puls* k* sabad *Sabin* k* sars k* sep b4.de* *Sil* k* sulph k* syc fmm1• *Thuj* k* tus-p bro1 zing bro1
  - **bloody**: nit-ac bg2
  - **drop** of pus before urinating: tus-p
  - **urination** agg.; after: nit-ac b4a.de
- **recurrent** (See GENERALS - History - urethra)
- **scanty**: ferr-p k2
  - **accompanied** by | **urging** to urinate (See BLADDER - Urination - urging - accompanied - discharge - scanty)
- **semen**, like: puls k*
- **slimy** (See mucous)
- **staining** linen: canth b7a.de *Nat-m* k*
- **stool** | **after** | **agg.**: sel bg2 sulph bg2
  - **before**: sel bg2
- **stringy**: agar bg2 hydr bg2 kali-bi k* nat-c k2 nat-m bg2 nux-v bg2 sel bg2 thuj bg2
- **suppressed**: agn bg2 **Puls** bg2
- **thick**: *Alum* anan *Arg-met* arg-n k* *Cann-s* k* caps k* *Clem Cub* ferr *Hep Hydr Kali-i* med *Merc* k* *Merc-c* k* nat-c k2 nat-m mtf33 *Nat-s* nux-v *Psor Puls* k* sil k* *Sulph* **Thuj** b4a.de
- **thin**: apis caps cinnb bg2 fl-ac bg1 *Kali-s* lyc k* med merc-c k* mez bg1 *Nat-m* k* nit-ac k* nux-v petr bg1 phos bg1* psor bg1* sabin bg1 sep bg1 sulph bg1* *Thuj* ptk1
  - **gleety**, with formication over body: cedr k*
- **transparent**: cann-s k* mez k* petros phos k*
- **urination** | **after** | **agg.**: anac bg2 calc bg2 con bg2 kali-c bg2 lach bg2 nat-m bg2 nit-ac bg2 nux-v bg2 ph-ac bg2 phos bg2 sars ptk1 sep bg2
  - **before**: berb ptk1
- **viscid**: agar k* agn bov dig graph k2 ham kali-bi k2 kali-s k2 nit-ac *Nux-v* k* ph-ac phos
- **watery**: apoc k* cann-s k* canth k* ferr-p *Fl-ac* k* *Hydr* k* *Kali-s* lyc k* merc k* merc-c k* *Mez* k* mill bro1 *Mur-ac Nat-m* k* ph-ac phos sep bro1 *Sulph* b4a.de* sumb k* **Thuj** k*
  - **glued** up in morning with a watery drop; meatus: *Phos*
  - **moving** about, on: mez k*
  - **nitrate** of silver, after injections of: nat-m
  - **painless**: cann-s
- **white**: ant-o arg-n k* cann-i *Cann-s* k* canth k* *Caps* chim cinnb cob *Cop* cupr-ar k* dulc fd4.de *Ferr Gels* hep k2 *Iod Kali-c Kali-chl* lach med merc *Mez* **Nat-m** k* nit-ac petr *Petros* ph-ac psor k2 sars h2* **Sep** sulph thuj trad a1* zinc
  - **morning** | **prostatic** discharge evening; and: *Ph-ac*
  - **chronic**: caps chim cinnb ferr merc merc-c *Mez* **Nat-m** nit-ac *Sel Sep* sulph thuj zinc
    - **anemic** subjects, in: **Calc-p**
    - **impotence**, with: *Agn Calad* cob
      - **and** fetid urine: calad
    - **nitrate** of silver, after injection of: *Nat-m*
    - **urination** agg.; after: cop lach petros sep

Discharge: ...

- **yellow**: agar **Agn** k* **Alum** k* alum-p k2 alumn k2 anan **Arg-met** arg-n ptk1 ars-s-f *Bar-c* bell *Calc Calc-s* calc-sil k2 cann-i k2 cann-s *Canth* k* *Caps* k* con *Cop* k* *Cub* cur *Fl-ac* k* gonotox jl2 hedy a1* *Hep Hydr* kali-bi *Kali-s* lyc k* *Med* **Merc** k* nat-c k2 *Nat-m* k* **Nit-ac** k* petr petros k* *Psor* k* **Puls** k* sars **Sel Sep** k* sil spong fd4.de sulph k* sumb a1 **Thuj** k* tus-p zing k*
  - **morning**, drop: fl-ac k* *Med* k*
  - **evening**: lyc k*
  - **night**: *Merc* zinc zing k*
  - **chronic**: **Alum** *Alumn* **Arg-met** *Calc-s Fl-ac* hep hydr vh lyc *Med* k* merc *Nat-m Psor* k* **Puls** *Sel Sil*
  - **staining** linen: *Alum* k* *Nat-m* k* *Psor* k*
- **yellow-green**: agn bg2* alum bro1 arg-n bg2* baros bro1 *Cann-s* bro1 **Cann-xyz** bg2 canth bro1 caps bro1 cinnb bg2 cob bro1 cop bg2* *Cub* bro1 dig bro1 *Hep* bro1 *Hydr* bro1 jac-c bro1 kali-bi bg2 kali-i bg2* *Kali-s* bro1 *Merc* bg2* *Merc-c* bg2* nat-m bg2* *Nat-s* bro1 ol-sant bro1 *Puls* bro1 sabin bro1 sep bro1 sil bro1 sulph bro1 thuj bg2* tus-p bro1 zing bro1
  - **obstruction** of urethra; with frequent: cub c1
- **yellowish** white: cann-i sulph k* *Thuj* b4a.de
  - **painless**: cann-i

DISCOLORATION:
- **blue** | **spots** | **Meatus**: borx h2*
- ○ • **Meatus**: borx bg2

DROP; sensation of a: thuj bg2
- **burning** drops run along; after urination: arg-n *Thuj* k*
- **cold** drop of urine passing; as if a: agar k*
- **few** drops passed; as if a: ambr k* aspar bg1 cedr bg1 lact petros bg1 sel bg1 sep bg1 vib bg1
- **remains**; as if a drop (See Urine - remained)
- **rolling** continuously along: *(↗Ball)* lact ptk1 sel ptk1 staph ptk1
- **water** flowing through it; as if a drop of: lam br1

DROPPING from:
- **sensation** of: agar bg2 ambr k* cedr k* lact k* **Sel** k* sep b4.de* thuj b4.de*
- **urination** agg.; after: *Thuj*

DRYNESS, sensation of: alum k* cop k*

ERUPTIONS:
- **vesicles**: stann k*
  - **large** blebs: rhus-t tl1
  - **small** blebs: petr tl1
  - **ulcers**, forming: *Nit-ac*
- ○ • **Meatus**: stann
- ○ - **Meatus**; around: caps bro1*

EVERTED meatus: caps ptk1

EXCORIATION:
- ○ - **Fossa navicularis**: *Cor-r* b7a.de
- **Meatus**; of: stann h2*
  - **urination** agg.; after: ant-t b7a.de laur b7a.de *Par* b7a.de verat b7a.de

EXCRESCENCES: teucr k*

FLATUS: canth bg2
- **passing** agg.: mang ptk1

FOREIGN BODY; sensation of a: cann-xyz bg2 lyc bg2 stram b7.de*
- **urination** agg.; during: stram b7.de*

FUNGOID growth: calc con graph lyc thuj

GLEET (See Discharge - gleety)

GNAWING, when not urinating: bart a1 bov

GONORRHEA:
- **acute** gonorrhea (See Discharge - gonorrheal)
- **chronic** gonorrhea (See Discharge - gleety)
- **suppressed** (See GENERALS - Gonorrhea)

HARD: *(↗Induration)*
- **body**; as if round: cann-i c1
- **node**: alum bov k* lach bg2

Urethra

HARDNESS: *Arg-n* k* *Clem* *Hyper* nit-ac k2
○ - **Meatus**, of: cann-s k* cann-xyz ptk1

HEAT: acon bg2 all-c k* alum k* ambr bg2 ant-c bg2 ant-t bg2 apis bg2 arn bg2 ars bg2 aster vh aur-m k* bar-c bg2 bell bg2 borx bg2 *Bry* bg2 cact k* *Calc* bg2 **Cann-xyz** bg2 canth k* caps bg2 cass a1 *Caust* bg2 *Cham* bg2 chel bg2 *Chin* bg2 clem bg2 **Colch** bg2 coloc bg2 con bg2 cupr bg2 dulc bg2 ferr-p k2 hep bg2 ign bg2 *Ip* bg2 kali-bi k* kali-c bg2 lach bg2 laur bg2 *Lyc* bg2 merc k* **Merc-c** bg2 *Mez* bg2 mur-ac bg2 nat-c bg2 nat-m bg2 nit-ac bg2 **Nux-v** bg2 par bg2 petr bg2 *Ph-ac* b4.de* **Phos** bg2 *Puls* bg2 rheum bg2 rhus-t k* *Ros-ca* c1 sabad bg2 sabin bg2 sars bg2 seneg bg2 *Sep* bg2 sil bg2 spig bg2 **Staph** bg2 sul-ac bg2 sulph k* ter bg2 teucr bg2 **Thuj** bg2 verat bg2 zinc bg2
- **emission** of semen, during: tarent k*
- **hot** wire in urethra; as if a: nit-ac ptk1
- **urination** agg.; during: alum b4.de* ph-ac b4.de*
- **voluptuous**: canth k*

HEAVINESS: eup-per ptk1 sabad ptk1 til ptk1

HEMORRHAGE: aloe alumn k2 am-c k* ambr anan a1 ant-c k* ant-t k* *Arg-n* k* arn *Ars* k* arum-m k* bell bry *Cact* *Calc* k* *Camph* *Cann-s* *Canth* k* *Caps* k* carbn-s *Caust* k* *Chel* k* *Chin* *Chinin-s* *Con* k* *Crot-h* k* cur erig euph b4a.de* *Euphr* *Ferr-m* k* ferr-p k* graph *Ham* hell *Hep* *Ip* k* kali-ar kali-c *Kali-i* k* kali-s lac-c hr1 lach b7a.de *Lyc* k* *Merc* k* **Merc-c** k* mez k* *Mill* mur-ac murx nat-m *Nit-ac* k* *Nux-v* k* *Phos* k* plb k* *Puls* k* sars *Sec* k* senec seneg sep squil *Sul-ac* b4a.de *Sulph* k* ter thuj zinc k* zinc-p k2
- **evening** | **22** h: lac-c hr1
- **burning**; with: ambr chin coch graph kali-c kali-i merc *Nux-v* puls seneg *Sulph* ter
- **coition**; during: *Caust* k*
- **constipation**; during: lyc
- **cut**, from a, hemorrhagic diathesis: ter
- **erections**; during: *Canth*
- **gonorrhea**; after suppressed: **Puls** k*
- **menses**, suppressed: zinc
- **pain**, with:
  - ○ • **Kidneys** and bladder; in: ant-t pd* ip puls
  - • **Stomach** and vomiting; in: ip
- **painful**: merc zinc k*
- **painless**: ars-h k* lyc merc psor sec
- **paralysis** of legs, with: lyc k*
- **pure** blood: bry *Canth* k* caps ham hell mez
  - • **clotted**: cact *Caust* *Chin* *Coc-c* *Nux-v* k*
  - • **urination** | **not** urinating; when: bry k*
- **stool** agg.; during: *Lyc* k* puls k*
- **urination**: alum tl1
  - • **after** | **agg.**: *Caps* b7a.de dulc bg1 **Hep** k* merc-c bg2* mez k* puls k* sars k* sulph k* *Thuj* k* zinc k*
  - • **during**:
    - ⁝ **beginning** of | **agg.**: *Con* k*
- **vicarious**: *Phos* k* zinc k*

INDURATION: (↗*Hard*) arg-n ptk1 arn bg2 calc bg2 camph bg2 canth bg2 carb-v bg2 cic bg2 *Clem* bg2* con bg2 dig bg2 dulc bg2 graph bg2 hyper ptk1 lyc bg2 mag-m bg2 merc bg2 merc-i-r ptk1 **Petr** bg2 phos bg2 puls bg2 rhus-t bg2 sil bg2 spong bg2 sulph bg2
- **cartilaginous**: pareir br1*
- **chronic**: alumn k2 *Arg-n* k* bov k* calc-p k* merc-i-r nit-ac k2*
- **whipcord**; like a: clem ptk1

INFLAMMATION (= urethritis): *Acon* k* agar mrr1 agn mrr1 anemps br1 apis c2* **Arg-n** k* *Ars* k* *Aur* k* aur-ar k2 bell bg2 bov k* *Cact* camph bro1 cann-i mrr1 **Cann-s** k* **Canth** k* caps k* carb-ac mrr1 caust c2* *Chim* k* *Clem* b4.de* *Cop* k* *Cub* k* cycl c2 dig bg2* dor c1* dulc bg2 ferr-p k2 *Gels* bro1 gonotox jl2 gran k* *Hep* k* hydr mrr1 kali-bi c2* *Kali-i* k* kola stb3• lith-c c2 lyc k2* lyss mrr1 med mrr1 *Merc* bg2 *Merc-c* k* napht dx nat-c mrr1 nit-ac k2* *Nux-v* k* oci-sa sp1 pareir k* *Petr* k* *Petros* k* phys mrr1 pip-m c2 psor jl2 puls mrr1 rham-f c2 *Sabin* k* sars bg2* staph mrr1 *Sulph* k* sumb bg2 syc fmm1• tab **Ter** k* teucr k* *Thuj* k* yohim lp2* [calc-f stj1 kali-f stj1 mag-f stj1]
- **accompanied** by:
  - • **urine**; blood in: *Chim* mrr1

Inflammation – **accompanied** by: ...
- ○ • **Bladder**; chronic inflammation of (See BLADDER - Inflammation - chronic - accompanied - urethra)
- **burning**, shooting pain and increased gonorrhea, with: *Arg-n* cann-s
- **cartilaginous**; becomes: pareir vml4
- **children**; in: dor br1
- **chronic**: arg-met mtf11 cann-i mrr1 caps mrr1 gonotox jl2 kali-i mrr1 *Med* jl2*
  - • **new** sexual relationship; since: *Med* mrr1
- **Cowper's** glands: acon bro1 *Cann-s* bro1 fab bro1 gels bro1 *Hep* bro1 merc-c bro1 petros bro1 *Sabal* bro1 sil bro1
- **mucus**, especially in woman; with much: cub br1

○ - **Meatus**: alum bov k* *Calc* calc-p cann-i **Cann-s** canth *Cop* erig eup-pur k* *Hep* k* jac-c k* kali-bi led med nat-m *Nit-ac* k* pareir k* ph-ac rhus-t **Sulph** k* tab thuj
  - • **urination** agg.; during: *Canth* b7a.de

IRRITATION: bell k* *Brucel* sa3• cact k* cann-s mrr1 chim k* *Clem* k* cub k* dor br1 *Ham* hr1 helon k* hydrc k* kali-br hr1 lac-leo sk4• *Lil-t* k* mit a1 nat-c mrr1 onos c2 pop k* pyrus spirae br1 **Staph** k* still hr1 stram k*
- **children**; in: dor br1

○ - **Meatus**: irid-met srj5• kali-bi sulph h2*

ITCHING: acon bro1 *Agar* b4.de* alum k* ambr k* anac k* anag hr1 ang ant-t apis arg-n k* arn k* aur-m k* bell k* *Berb* k* bov k* bry b7.de* calc b4a.de *Cann-s* k* canth k* carb-an bg2 carbn-s caust k* *Chim* chin k* clem k* coc-c k* cocc k* coff bg2 colch hr1 coloc bg2* con k* cop k* cub euph b4.de* *Ferr* k* ferr-i k* fl-ac bg2 gins k* graph k* hydr k* ign k* indg k* kali-bi ptk1 kali-c k* kali-chl k* kali-m k2 kiss a1 kola stb3• laur k* *Led* k* linu-c a1 lith-c *Lyc* k* lyss k* merc k* *Merc-c* k* *Mez* k* *Nat-m* k* *Nit-ac* k* *Nux-v* k* ol-an k* pareir k* *Petr* k* *Petros* k* ptel c1 rheum bg2 rhus-t ptk1 samb b7.de* sars b4.de* sel k* sep k* sil ptk1 staph bro1* *Sul-i* k* **Sulph** k* tab k* *Thuj* k* tus-p bro1 vesp bg1 zinc k*
- **morning**: arg-n k*
- **afternoon**: ferr k*
- **evening**: hydr k* mez h2* sulph k*
- **erections**; during: chlf a1 nux-v *Sel* k*
- **gleet**, with: agar k2 *Nat-m* *Nit-ac* *Nux-v* **Petr**
- **gonorrhea**, with: *Agar* vh **Merc-c** *Nat-m* *Petr* **Petros**
  - • **following**: *Nit-ac*
- **pus**; preceding discharge of: con
- **urination**:
  - • **after** | **agg.**: arg-n arund k* bell bg2 canth k* carb-an h2* clem k* colch k* cop k* lyc k* lyss k* **Merc** bg2 *Nat-m* b4a.de nux-v k* petr sars b4.de* tab k* *Thuj* k* verat a1
  - • **before**: cop k* ferr k* nux-v k* tab k*
  - • **during** | **agg.**: agar *Ambr* k* arg-n k* cop *Ferr* bg2* graph k* *Lyc* k* **Merc** bg2 *Mez* k* nat-m k* *Nux-v* k* ol-an k* pareir k* petr k* rheum sars k* tab thuj k*
  - • **urging** to urinate | **with**: chlf a1 coloc k* petros hr1
- **voluptuous**: alum k* *Ambr* arg-n carb-an h2* colch *Thuj*

▽ - **extending** to | **Bladder**: ferr br1

○ - **Anterior** part: *Arn* k* *Cann-s* k* cocc k* ferr-i k* *Ign* k* *Laur* k* lob merc-c k* nux-v *Thuj* k*
  - • **urination** | **not** urinating; when: arn euph *Sulph*
- **Female** urethra: **Calad** b7a.de canth b7.de* *Coff* b7a.de *Kreos* b7a.de *Nat-m* b4a.de petr k* *Puls* b7a.de *Sep* k* thuj k*
- **Fossa** navicularis: agar k* cic k* *Clem* k* cocc k* colch k* cub k* ferr k* gins k* **Petros** k* *Thuj* vichy-g a1
  - • **shooting** evening; and: sulph
  - • **urination** agg.; after: *Colch* k*
  - • **voluptuous**: *Petros* k* *Thuj*
- **Meatus**: agar k* *Agn* b7a.de alum bg2* alumn k* *Ambr* bro1 arum-t k* brom k* cann-i k* cann-xyz bg2 canth k* **Caust** k* chel k* *Chim* hr1 cic *Clem* k* **Coc-c** k* colch k* coloc k* conv br1 cop k* cupr-act c1 equis-h c1 gins k* hydr k* iod h* kali-c k* kali-m k* kali-n k* kreos bg2 lach led merc-c k* *Nat-m* k* petr *Petros* bro1 plan k* polyg-h bg2 ran-s samb h1* *Sulph* k* syph k* verat bg2 vichy-g a1
  - • **evening**: alumn k* hydr k* nat-m h2*
  - • **coition**; after: nat-p k*
  - • **female**: conv br1

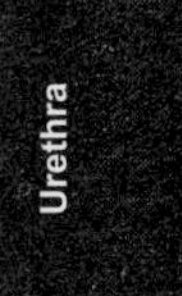

- **Meatus**: ...
  - **scratching** agg.: equis-h$_{a1}$
  - **stool** agg.; after: nat-p$_{k2}$
  - **touch** agg.: jac-c$_{k*}$ jac-g
  - **urination** | **during** | **agg.**: cann-s$_{b7a.de}$
    - **urging** to urinate:
      - **after**: clem *Merc* plan verat
      - **as** if urging to urinate: chel
      - **before**: nat-m$_{h2}$
      - **constant** urging: brom
      - **during**: ambr$_{bro1}$ anthraco cop$_{bro1}$ lyc$_{bro1}$ nux-v$_{bro1}$ petr
  - **voluptuous**: chlf$_{k*}$ chlol gins$_{k*}$ led
  - **walking** agg.: nat-m$_{k*}$ nat-n

JERKING: *Alum*$_{k*}$ ambr cann-i *Cann-s* cann-xyz$_{ptk1}$ *Lyc*$_{k*}$ nat-c$_{k*}$ nat-m nux-v$_{k*}$ *Petr*$_{k*}$ *Phos*$_{k*}$ pic-ac *Sars*$_{k*}$ *Thuj*$_{k*}$
- **standing** agg.: cann-s
- **urination** agg.; after: *Lyc*$_{k*}$
- **voluptuous** formication | **Fossa** navicularis; in: *Thuj*$_{k*}$

KNOTTY sensation: alumn *Arg-n*$_{k*}$ bov cann-s

MOISTURE at meatus: nat-m phos
- **glutinous**: dig
- **remains** a long time: agar$_{k2}$ petr$_{k2}$
- **yellow**, staining: phos

MUCUS; clogged up with coagulated (See Clogged)

NARROW; sensation as if: *(↗Swelling)* anan$_{vh1}$ *Arg-n*$_{k*}$ bry$_{k*}$ coc-c$_{k13}$ dig$_{k*}$ gonotox$_{jl2}$ graph$_{k*}$ stram$_{k*}$ thuj$_{k13}$
- **spasmodic**: bell$_{bg2}$ camph$_{bg2}$ canth$_{bg2}$ cic$_{bg2}$ cocc$_{bg2}$ **Nux-v**$_{bg2}$ puls$_{bg2}$
- **urination** agg.; during: bry$_{b7.de*}$ stram$_{b7.de*}$

NODE, hard (See Hard - node)

NUMBNESS: *(↗Sensation - absent)* apoc arg-n$_{ptk1}$ **Caust**$_{k*}$ *Cedr*$_{k*}$ kali-br$_{k*}$ **Mag-m**$_{k*}$ nux-v sars
- **uneasy** feeling: *Cedr*$_{k*}$

OBSTRUCTED, closed; sensation as if: op$_{b7.de*}$

OPEN; sensation of being: cop$_{bg2*}$

PAIN: acon↓ aesc↓ *Agar* agn aids↓ *All-c*↓ all-s↓ allox$_{sp1}$ aloe↓ alum↓ am-c↓ am-m↓ ambr↓ ammc↓ anac↓ anag↓ ang↓ *Ant-c*↓ *Ant-t*↓ aphis↓ *Apis*↓ aran$_{hr1}$ arg-met↓ *Arg-n*$_{k*}$ arge-pl↓ arist-cl$_{sp1}$ arn↓ **Ars**↓ ars-s-f↓ asaf↓ asar↓ asc-t$_{k*}$ aspar↓ atra-r↓ aur↓ aur-ar↓ aur-m↓ aur-s↓ bamb-a↓ bar-c↓ *Bell*↓ benz-ac↓ berb$_{mrr1}$ bond↓ borx↓ bov↓ brach↓ brom↓ bry$_{k*}$ bufo↓ cact↓ cadm-s↓ cain↓ *Calad*↓ calc$_{b4.de*}$ calc-f↓ calc-p$_{k2}$ calc-s↓ **Camph**↓ cann-i$_{k*}$ cann-s$_{k*}$ cann-xyz↓ *Canth*$_{k*}$ caps$_{k*}$ carb-an↓ carb-v↓ carbn-dox↓ carbn-s↓ *Card-m*$_{k*}$ *Carl*↓ caust$_{b4.de*}$ cedr↓ cham↓ chel$_{k*}$ chim↓ *Chin*↓ chinin-s↓ chlf↓ cic↓ cimic↓ cinnb↓ clem$_{b4.de*}$ cob↓ coc-c↓ cocc↓ coff↓ *Colch*↓ coli$_{jl2}$ coloc↓ con$_{b4.de*}$ convo-s$_{sp1}$ *Cop*↓ crot-t↓ cub↓ cupr↓ cupr-ar↓ cycl↓ cypra-eg↓ der↓ *Dig*↓ *Dulc*↓ *Equis-h*↓ erig↓ *Ery-a*↓ eup-pur↓ euph↓ fago↓ *Ferr*↓ ferr-ar↓ *Ferr-i*$_{k*}$ ferr-pic↓ *Fl-ac*↓ gaert↓ gels↓ gins↓ gran↓ *Graph*↓ guaj↓ hell↓ *Hep*↓ hipp↓ hura↓ *Hydrang*↓ *Hyper*↓ ign↓ indg↓ iod↓ *Ip*↓ iris↓ jab↓ jatr-c↓ kali-ar↓ kali-bi$_{bg2}$ *Kali-c*↓ *Kali-i*↓ kali-n↓ kali-p↓ kali-s↓ kiss↓ kola↓ kreos↓ lac-c↓ lac-h↓ *Lach*↓ lat-m$_{sp1}$ laur↓ led↓ lil-t↓ lith-c lob↓ lup↓ lyc$_{k*}$ lyss↓ m-ambo↓ m-aust↓ mag-c↓ mag-m↓ mag-s$_{sp1}$ manc↓ mang↓ *Med* mela↓ **Merc**↓ **Merc-c**↓ merl↓ *Mez*↓ mosch↓ mur-ac↓ mygal↓ *Nat-c*↓ *Nat-m*↓ nat-ox↓ nat-p↓ nit-ac$_{b4.de*}$ nit-m-ac↓ nux-m↓ **Nux-v**↓ oci-sa$_{sp1}$ ol-sant↓ *Onis*↓ *Op*↓ ox-ac$_{k2}$ pall↓ par↓ *Petr*↓ *Petros*↓ *Ph-ac*↓ phos$_{k*}$ phys↓ pic-ac↓ plan↓ plb$_{b7.de*}$ podo↓ polyg-h↓ polys↓ propl↓ prot↓ *Prun*$_{k*}$ psor↓ ptel↓ *Puls*$_{k*}$ pulx↓ rauw$_{sp1}$ *Rhod*↓ rhus-t↓ *Rhus-v*↓ *Ruta*↓ sabad↓ sabal↓ sabin$_{k*}$ *Sars*↓ sec↓ *Sel*↓ senec↓ seneg *Sep*↓ **Sil**↓ spig↓ spong$_{fd4.de}$ squil↓ stann↓ *Staph*↓ still$_{k*}$ stry↓ sul-ac↓ *Sulph*$_{k*}$ sumb↓ tarent$_{k2}$ tax-br↓ tep↓ *Ter*↓ teucr↓ *Thuj* thymol$_{sp1}$ til↓ tritic-vg$_{fd5.de}$ tus-p↓ uran-n↓ vanil$_{fd5.de}$ verat↓ viol-t↓ zinc↓ zinc-act↓ zinc-p↓ zing↓
- **midnight**: equis-h↓
  - **cutting** pain: equis-h
- **daytime**: still$_{k*}$
- **morning**: alum↓ cimic↓ graph↓ merc↓ rhus-t↓ seneg↓ *Sulph*↓ sumb↓

Pain – morning: ...
  - **biting** pain: rhus-t$_{k*}$
  - **cutting** pain: alum$_{k*}$ graph$_{k*}$ merc$_{k*}$
  - **erections**; after: *Nat-m*↓
    - **burning**: *Nat-m*
  - **stitching** pain: cimic$_{k*}$ seneg$_{k*}$ *Sulph*$_{a1*}$ sumb
  - **urination** | **after**:
    - **agg.**: carb-v↓ con↓ *Fl-ac*↓ thuj↓
      - **burning**: con$_{h2}$ *Fl-ac*$_{a1}$ thuj$_{a1}$
      - **drawing** pain: carb-v$_{k*}$
      - **tearing** pain: carb-v$_{k*}$
    - **during**:
      - **agg.**: adam↓ anag↓ con↓ *Fl-ac*↓ hir↓ ign↓ kola$_{stb3•}$ seneg↓ teucr↓ thuj↓
        - **burning**: adam$_{skp7•}$ anag$_{k*}$ con *Fl-ac*$_{k*}$ hir$_{skp7•}$ ign$_{k*}$ kola$_{stb3•}$ seneg$_{k*}$ teucr$_{k*}$ thuj
  - **waking**; on: alum↓ carb-v↓ sep↓
    - **biting** pain: alum$_{h2*}$ sep$_{h2*}$
    - **drawing** pain: alum$_{k*}$ carb-v sep$_{h2*}$
    - **emissions**; after: carb-an↓
      - **burning**: carb-an
- **forenoon**: caps↓
  - **cutting** pain: caps
  - **stitching** pain: caps
- **afternoon**: sulph↓ thuj↓
  - **seated**; when: ign↓ thuj↓
    - **tearing** pain: ign$_{k*}$ thuj$_{k*}$
  - **stitching** pain: sulph$_{a1}$ thuj$_{k*}$
- **evening**: *Calad*↓ canth↓ caust$_{k*}$ chin↓ lyc↓ mez↓ nat-c↓ nit-ac↓ ox-ac↓ petr↓ phos↓ seneg spong$_{fd4.de}$ sulph↓ thuj↓ tritic-vg$_{fd5.de}$
  - **burning**: chin lyc$_{k*}$ nat-c$_{k*}$ ox-ac petr$_{k*}$ phos$_{k*}$ sulph$_{k*}$ tritic-vg$_{fd5.de}$
    - **acrid** urine would pass; as if a drop of: ox-ac
  - **lying** down agg.; after: fago↓ gran↓
    - **cutting** pain: fago gran
  - **stitching** pain: *Calad*$_{k*}$ canth mez$_{k*}$ nit-ac spong$_{fd4.de}$ sulph thuj$_{k*}$ tritic-vg$_{fd5.de}$
  - **urination** | **after**:
    - **agg.**: am-c↓ tarent↓
      - **drawing** pain: am-c tarent$_{k2}$
    - **during**:
      - **agg.**: seneg↓
        - **pressing** pain: seneg
- **night**: berb↓ canth↓ caust↓ cinnb↓ *Merc*↓
  - **burning**: berb canth$_{k*}$ caust$_{k*}$ cinnb *Merc*
  - **erections**; during: thuj↓
    - **stitching** pain: thuj
- **aching**: bry$_{k*}$ cain canth$_{k*}$ eup-pur$_{k*}$ lob$_{k*}$ sulph
- **all** times, at: ars-s-f↓ calad↓ canth↓
  - **burning**: ars-s-f$_{k2}$ calad canth
- **and** itching, before urination: cop↓ tab↓
  - **biting** pain: cop tab
- **biting** pain: alum$_{k*}$ ambr$_{b7.de*}$ apis$_{c1}$ arn$_{b7.de*}$ ars$_{k*}$ berb$_{k*}$ camph$_{b7.de*}$ cann-s$_{b7.de*}$ canth$_{b7.de*}$ caps$_{k*}$ carb-v$_{b4.de*}$ cham$_{b7.de*}$ chin$_{b7.de*}$ *Clem*$_{k*}$ equis-h$_{bg2}$ *Graph*$_{k*}$ guaj ign$_{b7.de*}$ ip$_{k*}$ kali-c$_{b4.de*}$ kali-n$_{bg2*}$ m-aust$_{b7.de}$ merc$_{b4.de*}$ merc-c$_{b4a.de}$ mur-ac$_{b4.de*}$ nat-m$_{b4.de*}$ prun$_{k*}$ rhus-t$_{k*}$ sabin$_{b7.de*}$ sel$_{b7.de*}$ sep$_{b4.de*}$ staph$_{b7.de*}$ teucr$_{k*}$ thuj$_{k*}$ zinc$_{b4.de*}$ zinc-act
  - **evening** | **burning**: chin$_{k*}$
- **burning**: acon$_{k*}$ aesc$_{k*}$ agar$_{k*}$ agn$_{k*}$ *All-c*$_{k*}$ all-s$_{k*}$ aloe alum$_{k*}$ am-c$_{k*}$ ambr$_{k*}$ ammc$_{k*}$ anac$_{b4a.de}$ ang$_{b7.de}$ *Ant-c*$_{k*}$ *Ant-t*$_{k*}$ *Apis*$_{k*}$ *Arg-n*$_{k*}$ arge-pl$_{rwt5•}$ arist-cl$_{rbp3•}$ arn$_{b7.de}$ **Ars**$_{k*}$ ars-s-f$_{k2}$ asar aspar$_{k*}$ aur$_{k*}$ aur-ar$_{k2}$ aur-m$_{k*}$ bamb-a$_{stb2.de•}$ bar-c$_{b4.de*}$ bell$_{k*}$ benz-ac **Berb**$_{k*}$ borx$_{k*}$ bov$_{k*}$ brom *Bry*$_{k*}$ cact cain$_{bro1}$ calad$_{k*}$ *Calc*$_{k*}$ calc-f$_{k*}$ calc-s **Camph**$_{k*}$ cann-i$_{k*}$ **Cann-s**$_{k*}$ cann-xyz$_{ptk1}$ **Canth**$_{k*}$ *Caps*$_{k*}$ carb-an$_{k*}$ carb-v$_{k*}$ carbn-dox$_{knl3•}$ carbn-s *Card-m*$_{k*}$ *Carl*$_{k*}$ *Caust*$_{k*}$ cedr$_{k*}$ cham$_{k*}$ chel$_{k*}$ chim$_{k*}$ *Chin*$_{k*}$ chinin-s cimic cinnb clem$_{k*}$ cob$_{k*}$ coc-c$_{k*}$ coff$_{b7.de}$ *Colch*$_{k*}$

- **burning**: ...
coloc k* con k* *Cop* k* crot-t cub c1 cupr k* cupr-ar hr1 cypra-eg sde6.de• der k* dig b4a.de* dulc b4.de* *Ery-a* k* eup-pur k* ferr b7.de* ferr-ar ferr-i k* *Fl-ac* k* gaert pte1*• gels bro1 gins k* graph k* hell b7.de hep k* hipp *Hydrang* bro1 *Hyper* hr1 ign k* ip k* jab k* kali-ar kali-bi bg2* kali-c k* *Kali-i* k* kali-n kali-p kola stb3• kreos bg2 lac-c k* laur k* led b7.de lil-t k* *Lith-c* lup br1 *Lyc* k* lyss k* m-ambo b7.de mag-c b4.de* mag-m k* manc k* **Merc** k* **Merc-c** k* merl k* mez b4.de* mosch k* *Nat-c* k* nat-m k* nat-p *Nit-ac* k* nit-m-ac bro1 nux-m b7.de **Nux-v** k* onis bro1 op k* ox-ac k* par k* *Petr* k* *Petros* bro1 *Ph-ac* k* *Phos* k* plb b7.de podo fd3.de• polyg-h polys sk4• prot pte1* **Prun** k* ptel k* *Puls* k* pulx br1 *Rhod* k* rhus-t k* *Rhus-v* k* ruta b7.de sabad b7.de* sabin k* *Sars* k* sec b7.de sel bro1 senec k* seneg b4.de* *Sep* k* **Sil** k* spig b7.de stann k* *Staph* k* still k* stry k* sul-ac b4a.de **Sulph** k* *Tarent* k* tax-br oss1• *Ter* k* teucr k* **Thuj** k* tritic-vg fd5.de (non:uran-met k) uran-n k* vanil fd5.de verat b7.de viol-t b7.de zinc k* zinc-p k2 zing bro1
  - **urine** were passing; as if drops of: ambr k* ox-ac k*
  - **wire**; as a hot: nit-ac bg
- **children**; in: | **dentition**; during: erig hm
- **chill**; during: calen ↓
  - **tearing** pain: calen a1*
- **clots** of blood passing; from: canth ↓
  - **agonizing**: canth k*
- **coition**:
  - **after**: berb ↓ calc ↓ canth b7a.de* coli ↓ merc ↓ merc-c ↓ nat-m ↓ nat-p ↓ *Sep* ↓ sul-ac ↓ **Sulph** ↓
    - **burning**: berb k* *Canth* k* coli jl2 merc b4a.de merc-c bg2 nat-p *Sep* k* sul-ac k* **Sulph** k*
    - **stitching** pain: calc nat-m k*
    - **urination** agg.; during: *Caust* ↓
      - **burning**: *Caust* k*
  - **during**: agar ↓ ant-c ↓ calc ↓ *Canth* ↓ clem ↓ kreos ↓ merc ↓ sep ↓ sulph ↓ thuj ↓
    - **burning**: agar k* ant-c calc *Canth* k* clem ptk1 kreos merc k* sep ptk1 sulph k* thuj
    - **stitching** pain | **stinging**: calc
- **contracting**: *Arg-n* bro1 bry k* *Cann-s* bro1 *Canth* k* caps bro1 *Chin* k* *Clem* k* dig ferr-i bro1 indg k* kola stb3• ol-sant bro1 *Petros* bro1
- **corrosive**: cann-s b7.de* caust b4.de*
- **cough** agg.; during: caps mrr1
- **cutting** pain: aids nl2• alum bg2* anac ant-c k* arg-n k* arn b7.de* asc-t aspar k* *Berb* k* bry k* bufo *Calc* k* **Calc-p** k* cann-s b7.de* **Canth** k* *Caps* k* carb-v b4.de* caust k* *Chel* k* colch k* **Con** k* cupr b7.de* *Dig* k* *Equis-h* eup-pur k* fago k* gran a1 graph b4.de* guaj k* hura iod b4.de* *Ip* k* *Kali-c* k* kali-s lac-h sze9• *Lach* k* *Lyc* k* mang k* *Merc* k* mur-ac k* nat-m k* *Nit-ac* k* nux-m k* nux-v k* *Onis* a1* *Op* k* *Petros* bro1 ph-ac k* *Phos* b4.de* psor puls k* sars k* *Sep* k* staph b7.de* *Sulph* k* ter thuj k* zinc k* zinc-p k2
  - **backward**: arg-n caps
  - **biting**, getting worse towards end of urination, even to last drop; and: atra-r skp7• *Merc*
  - **forward**: apis bg2
  - **outward**: plan
  - **paroxysmal**: eup-pur kali-c
- **darting** (See stitching)
- **discharged**, when semen is | **burning** (See ejaculation - during - burning)
- **dragging**: arg-n k* eup-pur *Lyc* k* ph-ac k* sabad k* sel ter til k*
- **drawing** pain: alum k* arg-n k* asar b7.de* *Berb* bry k* *Cann-s* caps carb-v k* cic k* colch k* con k* cop k* fl-ac ptk1 gran k* hipp k* iod h* *Kali-bi* k* kali-c k* lyc k* *Merc* k* *Mez* k* nat-m b4.de* *Petros* k* ph-ac k* phos k* pic-ac k* puls k* sabad k* sep sulph b4.de* tarent k2 *Thuj* k* zinc k*
- **ejaculation**:
  - **after**: carb-an ↓ carb-v ↓ caust ↓ cob ↓ dig ↓ merc ↓ nat-m ↓ sep ↓ sulph ↓ thuj ↓
    - **burning**: carb-an carb-v k* caust k* cob dig merc k* sep sulph thuj
    - **cutting** pain: nat-m h2
    - **stricture**, during coition; in: *Clem* ↓
      - **burning**: *Clem*
  - **agg.**: cob pip-m sars ser-a-c jl2

- **ejaculation – agg.**: ...
    - **morning** | **waking**; on: carb-an
  - **during**: *Agar* ↓ *Ant-c* ↓ arg-n ↓ *Berb* ↓ borx ↓ *Calc* ↓ *Canth* ↓ clem ↓ con ↓ *Kreos* ↓ merc ↓ nat-m ↓ *Nit-ac* ↓ sars ↓ sep ↓ sul-ac ↓ **Sulph** ↓ tarent ↓ thuj ↓
    - **burning**: *Agar Ant-c* k* arg-n *Berb* borx *Calc Canth* clem *Kreos* merc nat-m *Nit-ac* sars sep sul-ac **Sulph** k* tarent bg1 thuj
    - **cutting** pain: borx con ptk1 nat-m
- **erections**: cann-s ↓ clem ↓ *Nit-ac* ↓ thuj ↓
  - **after**: ambr a1 cann-s k* thymol ↓
    - **burning**: thymol sp1
  - **ceases** during coition: anag ↓
    - **burning**: anag
  - **during**: agar ↓ anag ↓ cain ↓ calc-p ↓ cann-s ↓ *Canth* ↓ carbn-s ↓ ferr-i ↓ mag-m ↓ mosch ↓ mur-ac ↓ nat-m ↓ nit-ac k*
    - **burning**: anag cain calc-p k* *Canth* k* carbn-s ferr-i mag-m mosch nat-m *Nit-ac* k*
    - **sore**: canth k*
    - **tearing** pain: agar cann-s canth mur-ac
  - **stitching** pain: cann-s k* clem *Nit-ac* k* thuj k*
- **exertion** agg.: alum ↓
  - **burning**: alum k*
- **flatus**; passing | **after**:
    - **agg.**: lyc ↓
      - **stitching** pain: lyc h2
  - **agg.**: lyc ↓ *Mang* ↓
    - **burning**: lyc ptk1 mang ptk1
    - **cutting** pain: lyc mang
    - **quietly**; passing flatus: mang ↓
      - **stitching** pain | **dull** pain: mang k*
    - **stitching** pain: *Mang* k*
- **gonorrhea**, with: **Merc** ↓ *Mez* ↓
  - **stitching** pain | **stinging**: **Merc** *Mez*
- **ineffectual** desire to urinate, with: *Calc* ↓
  - **stitching** pain | **cutting** pain: *Calc* k*
- **itching**; with:
  - **urination**:
    - **not** urinating; when: euph ↓
      - **stitching** pain: euph
- **menopause**: berb ↓
  - **burning**: berb hr1*
  - **during**: *Berb* vh
- **menses**:
  - **before** | **agg.**:
      - **urination** agg.; during: canth ↓
        - **cutting** pain: canth
    - **burning** (See URINE - Burning - menses - before)
  - **during**:
    - **agg.**: *Nat-m* ↓
      - **burning**: *Nat-m* k*
- **motion** agg.: alum ↓ bell ↓ chel ↓
  - **burning**: alum h2
  - **cutting** pain: chel k*
  - **stitching** pain: bell chel k*
- **nephritic** colic, with: coc-c ↓
  - **aching**: coc-c
- **paroxysmal**: eup-pur kali-c op prun
- **pinching** pain: am-m b7a.de carb-v k* caust b4.de* cinnb k* coc-c bg2 kali-c k* lyc k* sep bg2 thuj verat b7.de*
- **pressing** pain: agn k* ang b7.de* aphis arn b7.de* bry k* cann-s b7.de* canth b7.de* cocc b7.de* colch k* coloc b4.de* cop *Dulc* k* graph *Lach* k* lyss k* nux-v k* petros k* *Ph-ac* puls k* sabad b7.de* sel b7.de* seneg b4.de* stann b4.de* teucr k* thuj til k* zinc b4.de*
- **pressure**:
  - **agg.**: *Clem* hr1* mez ↓ nat-m ↓

- **agg.**: ...
  - : **sore**: mez h2* nat-m h2*
- **penis**; on glans:
  - : **amel.**: canth ↓
    - . **cutting** pain: canth k*
- **pricking** pain: cann-i c1 iris c1 psor jl2
- **raw**; as if: bar-c bg2 cadm-s br1 cop bg2 lach bg2 merc bg2 mez bg2 nat-c bg2 phos bg2 sep bg2 sulph bg2
- **riding**; after: staph ↓
  - **burning**: staph bg
- **rigors**, with: sulph ↓
  - **stitching** pain: sulph k*
- **rising** agg.; after: thuj ↓
  - **burning**: thuj k*
- **scalding** (See burning)
- **scraping** pain: ign b7.de* sars h2*
- **shooting** (See stitching)
- **shooting** and increased gonorrhea: arg-n ↓ cann-s ↓
  - **burning**: arg-n cann-s
- **sitting** agg.: *Card-m* ↓ par ↓ plan ↓ thuj ↓ tritic-vg ↓
  - **burning**: *Card-m* par k* tritic-vg fd5.de
  - **flatus** agg.; passing: *Mang* ↓
    - : **stitching** pain: *Mang*
  - **stitching** pain: plan k* thuj k*
- **smarting** (See burning)
- **sore**: agn bro1 anag bro1 apis k* *Arg-n* k* *Berb* k* borx bg2 bov b4.de* brach bro1 cadm-s br1 calc b4.de* *Cann-s* k* *Canth* k* *Caps* k* caust bro1 cic b7.de* *Clem* k* colch b7.de* cop k* cub bro1 cupr *Ferr* k* ferr-pic bro1 gels bro1 *Hep* k* *Hyper* k* ign kali-i bro1 *Lach* k* *Med* merc mez k* *Nat-m* k* *Nit-ac* k* nux-v b7.de* ox-ac k2 phys k* *Prun* k* ptel sep k* stann b4.de* staph b7a.de teucr k* thuj til k* tus-p bro1 zinc k*
- **splinter**; as from a: nit-ac k2
- **standing** agg.: aur-m ↓ cann-s ↓ clem ↓ cob k*
  - **stitching** pain: aur-m k* cann-s k*
  - **twinging**: clem k*
- **stinging**: *Apis* bov k* brach hr1 cann-i k* cann-s *Caps* hr1 erig *Merc* hr1 nat-c h2* par hr1 sabal bg3* sars staph sulph k2 thuj
- **stitching** pain: acon k* agar k* alum k* am-m b7a.de ant-t k* *Apis* k* arg-met *Arg-n* k* arn k* asaf k* asar asc-t k* aspar k* aur k* aur-s k2 bamb-a stb2.de• *Bell* k* *Berb* k* bond a1 borx bov k* brach a1 brom k* bry k* *Calad* k* *Calc* k* calc-p bg2 *Cann-i* k* cann-s k* *Canth* k* *Caps* k* carb-v bro1 chel k* *Chin* k* chlf k* cic k* *Clem* k* coc-c k* cocc k* colch k* coloc k* con k* crot-t k* cupr k* cycl k* dulc equis-h euph b4.de* gran a1 graph b4.de* *Hep* k* ign k* indg k* iod b4.de* jatr-c kali-n b4.de* kali-p kiss a1 *Lach* k* led b7.de* *Lyc* k* mag-c b4.de* mang k* mela a1 *Merc* k* *Merc-c* k* mez b4.de* mur-ac b4.de* mygal k* nat-c k* nat-m k* nat-ox rly4• nit-ac k* nux-v k* pall k* par k* petr k* petros bro1 *Ph-ac* k* phos k* plan k* propl ub1• psor rhod b4.de* *Sars* seneg b4.de* *Sep* k* sil spig b7.de* spong fd4.de squil k* stry k* **Sulph** k* sumb tep a1 *Thuj* k* til k* tritic-vg fd5.de verat b7.de* viol-t k* zinc k* zinc-p k2
  - **backward**: berb canth con h2 **Merc-c** *Nux-v* plan psor squil sulph sumb zinc
  - **burning**: agar k* cann-s merc merc-c nit-ac spig k*
  - **cutting** pain: *Calc* k* coc-c *Lach* lyc h2* sars h2*
  - **dull** pain: cic k* merc k*
  - **fine**: agar k* bry k* nat-m k* par k*
  - **forward**: arg-met arg-n aspar bell berb clem h2 dulc jab nat-c nat-m plan sars thuj k* zinc
  - **inward**: psor bg2
  - **jerking** pain: con h2*
  - **needles**; as from: nit-ac tl1
  - **splinter**; as from a: *Arg-n* k* coloc *Nit-ac*
  - **straw** was being thrust back and forth; as if a: dig br1*
  - **tickling**: calc k*
  - **twinging** like lightning, from before backward: *Berb* zinc k*
- **stool**:
  - **after**:
    - : **agg.**: *Nat-c* ↓ staph ↓
      - : **burning**: *Nat-c* k*
      - : **cutting** pain: staph k*
  - **before**: mur-ac ↓ sulph k*
    - : **cutting** pain: mur-ac sulph k*
  - **during**:
    - : **agg.**: carbn-s ↓ *Coloc* ↓ mur-ac ↓ *Nat-c* ↓ ol-j ↓ squil ↓ *Sulph* ↓
      - : **burning**: carbn-s k2 *Coloc* k* ol-j a1
      - : **cutting** pain: mur-ac *Sulph* k*
      - : **stitching** pain: coloc *Nat-c* ol-j squil k*
- **stream** is interrupted, when: clem ↓
  - **burning**: clem k*
- **sudden**, sitting agg.: plan ↓
  - **stitching** pain: plan k*
- **synchronous** with pulse: con ↓ dulc ↓
  - **stitching** pain: con k* dulc
- **tearing** pain: alum k* ant-t b7.de* arg-n ars k* aur k* aur-s k2 *Bry* k* calc k* **Cann-s** k* carb-v b4.de* clem k* coff b7.de* *Colch* k* coloc k* ign k* *Kali-c* k* kali-i k* lyc b4.de* *Mez* *Nat-c* k* **Nux-v** k* phos k2 *Ruta* k* *Sars* k* sep k* *Sulph* k* thuj k* zinc k*
  - **forward**: zinc
- **touch** agg.: berb ↓ borx ↓ caps h1* clem h2* merc ↓ nit-ac h2*
  - **burning**: berb borx merc k*
  - **sore**: borx c1
- **twinging**: arg-n *Cann-s* carb-v k* clem k* lyc k* *Sel* k* zinc
  - **forward**; from behind: sel k*
- **ulcerative** pain (= as from subcutaneous ulceration): arg-n k* cinnb k2 lac-c *Nit-ac* *Rhod*
- **urination**: phos ↓
  - **after**:
    - : **agg.**: agn aids nl2• alum ↓ alumn ↓ anac ↓ ang ↓ ant-t ↓ apis ↓ apoc ↓ aq-pet ↓ *Arg-n* ↓ arn ↓ ars ↓ arum-d ↓ arund ↓ aspar ↓ bamb-a ↓ *Bell* ↓ benz-ac ↓ *Berb* ↓ borx h2* bov brach k* brom ↓ bufo ↓ calc ↓ calc-p ↓ camph ↓ **Cann-i** ↓ **Cann-s** ↓ **Canth** ↓ caps mrr1 *Carb-an* ↓ carb-v ↓ *Card-m* ↓ cassia-s ↓ caust k* cent ↓ *Chel* ↓ chin ↓ *Chinin-s* ↓ cinch ↓ *Clem* ↓ cob ↓ coc-c ↓ colch ↓ coli ↓ coloc ↓ *Con* ↓ convo-s ↓ cop ↓ cub ↓ dig ↓ digin ↓ *Equis-h* ↓ *Fl-ac* ↓ gran ↓ graph ↓ grat ↓ hep ↓ hydrog srj2• iris ↓ *Kali-bi* ↓ *Kali-c* ↓ kali-p ↓ kali-s ↓ kola ↓ kreos ↓ laur ↓ led ↓ *Lil-t* ↓ lob ↓ *Lyc* ↓ lyss ↓ mag-c ↓ *Mag-m* ↓ *Merc* ↓ *Merc-c* ↓ *Mez* ↓ mur-ac ↓ **Nat-c** ↓ nat-s ↓ nat-sil ↓ *Nit-ac* ↓ *Nux-m* nux-v par ↓ *Petros* ↓ *Ph-ac* ↓ phel ↓ *Phos* ↓ pic-ac ↓ plb ↓ ptel ↓ **Puls** k* rauw ↓ rhod ↓ rhus-t ↓ ruta ↓ sabad ↓ **Sars** bg2 sel ↓ seneg ↓ sep ↓ sphing a1 spig ↓ stann *Staph* ↓ sulph symph ↓ tab ↓ tarent ↓ teucr ↓ *Thuj* ↓ thymol ↓ *Uva* ↓ vanil fd5.de verat ↓ zinc ↓
      - : **aching**: apoc k* lob puls k*
      - : **biting** pain: arn b7.de* *Bell* b4a.de borx cann-s b7.de* *Caps* k* *Chinin-s* *Clem* k* con k* cop k* *Equis-h* kali-c b4.de* mur-ac b4.de* petros k* rhus-t k* thuj b4.de* zinc b4.de*
        - . **forcing** its way out; as if a drop was: sel k*
      - : **burning**: alum k* alumn k* ang b7.de* ant-t k* apis k* apoc k* aq-pet a1 arg-n k* arn b7.de* arum-d a1 arund aspar k* bamb-a stb2.de• bell bg2 benz-ac *Berb* k* *Borx* k* bov k* brom k* bufo calc k* calc-p k* **Cann-i** k* *Cann-s* k* **Canth** k* *Caps* k* *Carb-an* k* *Card-m* k* cassia-s ccrh1• *Caust* cent a1 *Chel* k* chin k* cinch a1 *Clem* k* cob coc-c k* colch k* coli jl2 coloc k* *Con* k* convo-s sp1 cop dig k* digin a1 *Fl-ac* k* graph b4.de* grat k* hydrog srj2• iris *Kali-bi* k* *Kali-c* k* kali-p kali-s fkr2.de laur b7.de* led k* *Lil-t* k* *Lyc* k* lyss k* mag-c k* *Mag-m* k* *Merc* k* *Mez* mur-ac **Nat-c** k* **Nat-m** k* nat-s nat-sil fd3.de• *Nit-ac* k* nux-v k* *Ph-ac* b4a.de phel *Phos* pic-ac k* plb k* ptel hr1 *Puls* k* rauw sp1 rhod b4.de* rhus-t ruta b7.de* sars k* seneg k* sep h2* spig b7.de* *Staph* k* sulph b4a.de* symph fd3.de• tab tarent k* teucr b7a.de* *Thuj* k* thymol sp1 vanil fd5.de zinc k* [*Uva* stj]
      - : **coition**, and after: nat-m ↓
        - . **stitching** pain: nat-m
      - : **contracting**: camph h1

- **after – agg.**: ...
  - : **corrosive**: *Caust* b4a.de
  - : **cutting** pain: alum arn b7.de* *Berb* k* calc-p k* **Canth** k* chel k* coc-c k* con k* cub k* dig k* gran a1 *Lyc* k* merc bg2 **Nat-m** k* *Petros* k* rhus-t staph b7.de* *Sulph* k*
  - : **drawing** pain: nat-m b4.de* par b7.de* sabad b7.de*
  - : **liquid**; from discharge of thin: *Nat-m* ↓
    - . **burning**: *Nat-m*
  - : **pressing** pain: brach k* chinin-s bg2 cop bg2 *Puls* k* stann k*
  - : **sore**: *Arg-n* k* borx b4a.de* **Cann-s** b7a.de hep b4a.de kreos b7a.de lil-t k* nux-v k* thuj b4.de*
  - : **stitching** pain: anac bg2 apis arn k* *Berb* k* **Cann-i** k* *Cann-s* b7a.de caps k* con k* kali-bi k* kola stb3• led b7.de* merc k* *Merc-c* b4a.de mur-ac k* nat-c nat-m k* phos b4.de* rhod k* seneg k* *Sulph* a1* *Thuj* b4a.de verat b7.de*
    - . **forward**: sars
  - : **tearing** pain: ars carb-v k* kali-c b4a.de lyc b4.de* sars b4.de* tarent k*
  - : **Root** of penis to glans; from: sars ↓
    - . **tearing** pain: sars
  - : **amel.**: adam skp7•
- **amel.**: berb ↓ bry ↓ coc-c ↓ *Merc* ↓ sep ↓ spig ↓ staph ↓
  - : **burning**: berb k* bry k* coc-c k* *Merc* ptk1 sep h2 spig h1 staph ptk1
- **before**: alum ↓ ant-t ↓ *Apis* ↓ arn ↓ aspar ↓ *Berb* ↓ **Borx** ↓ *Bry* ↓ *Calc* ↓ calc-p ↓ **Cann-i** ↓ **Cann-s** ↓ cann-xyz ↓ **Canth** ↓ caps ↓ cassia-s ↓ chel ↓ coc-c ↓ cocc b7.de* colch ↓ cop ↓ dig ↓ ery-a ↓ fl-ac ↓ fuma-ac rly4• *Merc* ↓ *Merc-c* ↓ *Nat-c* ↓ nat-m ↓ *Nit-ac* ↓ *Nux-v* ↓ ph-ac ↓ phos ↓ *Prun* ↓ *Puls* ↓ rhod ↓ sabad ↓ sel ↓ senec ↓ seneg ↓ *Sulph* ↓ thuj ↓ zinc ↓
  - : **burning**: alum k* ant-t b7.de* *Apis* k* arn b7.de* aspar k* *Berb* k* **Borx** k* *Bry* k* *Calc* k* **Cann-i** k* cann-s b7.de* cann-xyz ptk1 **Canth** k* caps bg2* cassia-s ccrh1• chel k* coc-c colch k* cop k* dig ery-a k* fl-ac *Merc* *Merc-c* k* *Nat-c* k* *Nit-ac* *Nux-v* k* ph-ac phos k* *Prun* *Puls* k* rhod k* sabad b7.de* senec a1* seneg *Sulph* k* zinc k*
  - : **cutting** pain: bry k* calc-p k* **Canth** k* dig k* merc ph-ac k* sel
  - : **pinching** pain: nat-m k*
  - : **pricking** pain: *Nux-v*
  - : **sore**: cop bg2 nux-v b7.de*
  - : **stinging**: cann-i tl1
  - : **stitching** pain: aspar k* calc bg2 *Cann-i* k* **Cann-s** coc-c k* nat-c nux-v k* thuj k*
- **between** acts of urination agg.: *Arg-n* ↓ nux-v ↓ *Prun* ↓
  - : **pressing** pain: nux-v k*
  - : **ulcerative** pain: *Arg-n* *Prun*
- **biting** pain | **backward**: phos
- **during**:
  - : **agg.**: *Acon* ↓ act-sp ↓ adam ↓ *Aesc* *Agar* ↓ **Agn** ↓ allox sp1 aloe ↓ alum ↓ alum-p ↓ alum-sil ↓ am-c ↓ *Ambr* ↓ amp ↓ *Anac* ↓ anag ↓ ang ↓ *Ant-c* ↓ *Ant-t* ↓ anth ↓ aphis ↓ *Apis* ↓ apoc ↓ aq-mar ↓ aran **Arg-n** ↓ arist-cl sp1 *Arn* ↓ ars ↓ ars-s-f ↓ arum-d ↓ asc-c ↓ aur ↓ aur-m ↓ aur-s ↓ bamb-a ↓ *Bapt* ↓ *Bar-c* ↓ bar-m bart ↓ **Bell** ↓ benz-ac ↓ *Berb* blatta-a br1 borx ↓ bov k* brach ↓ *Brucel* ↓ *Bry* ↓ cact ↓ cain br1 *Calad* **Calc** ↓ calc-f ↓ *Calc-p* ↓ calc-s ↓ calc-sil ↓ **Camph** ↓ *Cann-i* k* *Cann-s* **Canth** k* *Caps* ↓ *Carb-an* ↓ *Carb-v* ↓ carbn-s ↓ cassia-s ↓ **Caust** k* cedr ↓ *Cham* ↓ chel *Chim* ↓ chin ↓ chinin-s ↓ *Cinnb* *Cinnm* ↓ **Clem** ↓ cob ↓ coc-c ↓ colch k* coloc ↓ *Con* k* **Cop** ↓ crot-t ↓ **Cub** ↓ cupr ↓ cupr-ar ↓ cur ↓ cycl ↓ daph ↓ dig ↓ *Dor* dulc ↓ *Echi* ↓ elaps *Equis-h* ↓ erig ↓ *Ery-a* ↓ eug ↓ *Eup-pur* ↓ euph ↓ *Ferr* ↓ ferr-ar ↓ ferr-i k* ferr-p ↓ fl-ac ↓ *Gels* ↓ glon ↓ *Graph* ↓ grat ↓ *Guaj* ↓ hell ↓ *Helon* ↓ hep hydr-ac ↓ *Ign* ↓ *Ip* ↓ iris ↓ kali-ar ↓ *Kali-bi* ↓ *Kali-c* ↓ kali-m ↓ *Kali-n* ↓ kali-p ↓ kali-s ↓ kali-sil ↓ kalm ↓ kola stb3• *Kreos* ↓ lach ↓ lact ↓ lat-h bnm5• lat-m sp1 laur ↓ led ↓ **Lil-t** ↓ lipp ↓ lob ↓ lup ↓ lyc m-aust ↓ *Mag-c* ↓ mag-m ↓ mag-s sp1 *Mang* ↓ med k* merc k2 *Mez* ↓ *Mur-ac* ↓ mygal ↓ *Nat-ar* ↓ **Nat-c** ↓ *Nat-m* ↓ nat-p ↓ *Nat-s* ↓ nat-sil ↓ **Nit-ac** b4.de* *Nux-m* ↓ **Nux-v** ↓ oci-sa sp1 ol-an ↓ olib-sac ↓ *Op* ox-ac ↓ par ↓ pen ↓ petr ↓ *Petros* ↓ ph-ac ↓ phos pic-ac ↓ pin-s ↓ pip-m ↓ plat-m k* plb ↓ podo ↓ prun k* *Psor* ↓ ptel ↓ *Puls* ↓ querc-r ↓ ran-b ↓ raph ↓ rat ↓ rham-f ↓ rheum ↓ rhod ↓ rhus-t ↓ *Ruta* ↓ sabad sabin ↓ sapin ↓ *Sars* ↓ sec ↓ *Sel* ↓ senec seneg *Sep* ↓ *Sil* ↓ spig ↓

- **during – agg.**: ...
  stann ↓ *Staph* ↓ still k* *Sul-ac* ↓ **Sulph** ↓ tab ↓ tarent ↓ tep ↓ **Ter** ↓ tere-la ↓ teucr ↓ **Thuj** ↓ thymol sp1 til k* tril-p ↓ tritic-vg fd5.de *Uran-n* ↓ **Uva** ↓ verat ↓ viol-t ↓ yuc ↓ zinc zinc-p ↓ zing k*
  - : **acute**: hep
  - : **biting** pain: act-sp ambr b7.de* ars b4.de* borx b4a.de* camph b7.de* cann-s b7.de* *Canth* k* carb-v k* cham k* chin b7.de* clem k* *Equis-h* *Graph* k* guaj b4.de* *Hep* b4a.de ign k* kali-bi bg2 kali-c b4.de* kali-n k* lyc m-aust b7.de mag-c *Merc* k* **Merc-c** k* nat-m k* nit-ac phos rhus-t k* sabin b7.de* sep k* thuj k*
    - . **salt**; like: caust bg2 hep bg2
  - : **burning**: *Acon* k* adam skp7• *Aesc* k* *Agar* k* **Agn** b7a.de allox sp1 aloe alum k* alum-p k2 alum-sil k2 am-c b4.de *Ambr* k* amp rly4• *Anac* b4a.de anag k* ang b7.de *Ant-c* k* *Ant-t* a1 anth k* aphis apis k* apoc k* aq-mar mgm• **Arg-n** k* ars k* ars-s-f k2 arum-d a1* asc-c k* aur-m k* aur-s k2 bamb-a stb2.de• *Bapt* k* *Bar-c* k* bart a1 **Bell** k* benz-ac k* *Berb* k* bov k* *Brucel* sa3• *Bry* k* cact cain br1 calad k* **Calc** k* calc-f k* *Calc-p* k* calc-s calc-sil k2 **Camph** k* **Cann-i** k* **Cann-s** k* **Canth** k* *Caps* k* *Carb-an* k* *Carb-v* k* carbn-s cassia-s ccrh1• **Caust** k* cedr *Cham* k* *Chel* k* *Chim* k* chin k* chinin-s **Clem** k* cob k* coc-c k* *Colch* k* coloc b4a.de *Con* k* **Cop** k* crot-t k* **Cub** k* cupr k* cupr-ar cur dig k* dulc k* *Echi* *Equis-h* erig br1 *Ery-a* k* eug k* *Eup-pur* k* *Ferr* k* ferr-ar ferr-i ferr-p fl-ac k* *Gels* k* glon k* graph grat k* hell k* helon k* *Hep* k* hydr-ac k* *Ign* k* *Ip* k* kali-ar kali-bi k* *Kali-c* k* kali-m k2 *Kali-n* k* kali-p kali-s kali-sil k2 kalm a1 kola stb3• *Kreos* b7a.de lach k* lact a1 lat-m sp1 laur k* **Lil-t** k* lob k* lup a1 *Lyc* k* *Mag-c* k* mag-m b4.de* mag-s sp1 *Mang* med *Merc* k* **Merc-c** k* mez k* *Mur-ac* k* *Nat-ar* **Nat-c** k* *Nat-m* k* nat-p k* *Nat-s* k* nat-sil fd3.de• **Nit-ac** k* *Nux-m* k* **Nux-v** k* oci-sa sp1 ol-an a1 olib-sac wmh1 op ox-ac k* par k* pareir pen a1 petr k* *Petros* k* ph-ac k* *Phos* k* pic-ac k* pin-s a1 pip-m a1 plb k* podo fd3.de• prun bg2 *Psor* k* ptel k* *Puls* k* ran-b tl1 raph k* rat k* rham-f a1 rheum h* rhod k* rhus-t k* ruta b7.de sabad k* sabin k* sapin a1 *Sars* k* sec k* *Sel* *Seneg* k* *Sep* k* *Sil* k* spig b7.de* stann b4.de *Staph* k* *Sul-ac* k* **Sulph** k* tab k* tarent k* tep a1 **Ter** k* tere-la rly4• teucr b7.de* **Thuj** k* thymol sp1 til ban1• tritic-vg fd5.de (non:uran-met k) *Uran-n* k* **Uva** verat k* viol-t k* yuc a1 zinc k* zinc-p k2
  - : **contracting**: kola stb3•
  - : **corrosive**: *Caust* b4.de* clem b4a.de *Hep* b4.de*
  - : **cutting** pain: alum k* alum-p k2 alum-sil k2 ant-c k* ant-t ptk1 arg-n k* *Arn* b7a.de bell bg2 borx k* bry k* calc k* calc-sil k2 *Cann-s* k* **Canth** k* caps carb-v k* carbn-s caust chel k* colch **Con** k* cub cupr k* graph k* *Guaj* k* hell k* hep k* *Ip* b7a.de iris kali-m k2 kola stb3• led lipp a1 *Lyc* b4a.de *Merc* k* mur-ac k* *Nat-m* k* nat-s k* *Nux-m* k* op k* ph-ac k* *Phos* k* *Psor* k* *Puls* k* rhus-t k* sars k* sil k* *Staph* k* sul-ac *Sulph* k* *Thuj* k* tril-p
  - : **drawing** pain: con h2*
  - : **gravel**; as from: kola stb3•
  - : **menses**:
    - . **during**:
      - **agg.**: zinc b4.de
        - **burning**: zinc h2*
  - : **not** urinating amel.: thuj ↓
    - . **stitching** pain | **forward**: thuj
  - : **pressing** pain: canth b7.de* dig b4.de* seneg b4.de*
  - : **pressure** in rectum, with: ph-ac ↓
    - . **cutting** pain: ph-ac
  - : **pricking** pain: cycl bg2 kali-bi bg2 querc-r svu1•
  - : **rasping**: carb-v lyc mag-c nit-ac phos sep
  - : **scraping** pain: sars bg2
  - : **sore**: *Apis* k* arg-n bg2 bov k* brach k* calc k* canth k* carb-an k* carb-v bg2 cinnb k* *Cinnm* clem bg2 colch k* daph k* *Ferr* k* ferr-i k* hep k* ign k* kali-c k2 *Lyc* k* mag-c bg2 merc-c bg2 *Mez* k* nit-ac k* nux-v k* ox-ac k2 *Phos* bg2 *Sep* bg2 sil k* staph b7a.de thuj b4.de*
  - : **splinter**; as from a: hep k2 nit-ac k2
  - : **sticking**: camph cann-s caps chel clem iris nat-c *Nux-v*
  - : **stinging**: borx bg2

- **during** – **agg.**: ...
  - : **stitching** pain: acon b7a.de bell b4a.de calc-p bg2 **Cann-i** k* **Cann-s** k* caps carbn-s k2 chel b7.de* chin k* *Clem* k* coc-c k* coloc b4a.de cupr k* cycl k* equis-h euph b4.de* *Graph* k* ign b7.de* iris *Kali-bi* hr1 kola stb3• lyc b4a.de mag-c b4.de* merc k* merc-c k* mez b4.de* mygal nat-c b4.de* nat-m b4.de* nux-v k* petr *Puls* seneg k* *Sulph* k* thuj k* tritic-vg fd5.de
    - . **burning**: cop cupr k*
  - : **stool** | **urging** to; with: aloe alum aphis canth cycl dig **Nux-v** prun staph sumb
  - : **stool**, and: mur-ac ↓
    - . **cutting** pain: mur-ac
  - : **tearing** pain: ars b4.de* aur *Carb-v* k* clem b4.de* cur *Helon* hr1 nat-c k* **Nux-v** k* *Ruta* sars b4.de* sulph k*
  - : **ulcerative** pain: arg-n k* nat-c h2
  - : **warm** bath; after: clem ↓
    - . **burning**: clem a1
  - : **extending** to:
    - . **Bladder**: chlam-tr ↓ lyc ↓
      - **burning**: chlam-tr bcx2• lyc k*
    - . **Chest** and shoulders: glyc bro1
  - : **Meatus**:
    - . **Prepuce**; and: calad ↓ calc ↓ *Cann-s* ↓ gels ↓ menth ↓ *Merc-c* ↓ puls ↓
      - **burning**: calad bro1 calc bro1 *Cann-s* bro1 gels bro1 menth bro1 *Merc-c* bro1 puls bro1
- : **beginning** of:
  - : **agg.**: apis ↓ ars ↓ *Cann-s* ↓ canth ↓ caust ↓ *Clem* ↓ iris ↓ **Merc** ↓ nat-ar ↓ petr ↓ plb ↓ *Prun* ↓ sec ↓ teucr ↓
    - . **morning**: ars ↓ hir ↓
      - **burning**: ars h2* hir skp7•
    - . **burning**: apis ars k* *Cann-s* k* canth b7.de* caust b4.de* *Clem* k* **Merc** k* nat-ar plb a1 *Prun* k* teucr
    - . **cutting** pain: iris merc k* petr sec k*
- : **end** of: arg-n ↓ cann-s k2* canth carb-v clem ↓ hydrog srj2• kali-n ↓ kali-s ↓ limen-b-c ↓ lyc med ↓ merc-act ↓ *Mez* ↓ **Nat-c** k* *Nat-m* ↓ nit-ac ↓ petr ↓ petr-ra shn4• ph-ac phys pic-ac **Sars** k* spig k* sul-ac ↓ sulph thuj br1 tritic-vg fd5.de
  - : **burning**: *Cann-s* k* clem ptk1 hydrog srj2• kali-n kali-s fkr2.de limen-b-c hrn2* *Mez* **Nat-c** k* ph-ac tritic-vg fd5.de
  - : **cutting** pain: arg-n canth b7.de* clem med merc-act *Nat-m* nit-ac petr sul-ac *Sulph* k* thuj
  - : **stitching** pain: kali-s fkr2.de ph-ac tritic-vg fd5.de
- : **extending** to:
  - : **Bladder**: chlam-tr ↓ lyc ↓
    - . **constricting**: chlam-tr bcx2• lyc k*
- **impossible**: ph-ac ↓
  - : **burning**: ph-ac h2
- **last** drops cause: arg-n ↓ atra-r ↓ carb-v ↓ *Clem* ↓ colch ↓ coli ↓ coloc ↓ lyc ↓ *Merc* ↓ *Mez* ↓ nux-m ↓ **Sars** ↓ sel ↓ tell ↓
  - : **burning** | **violent** burning: arg-n k* atra-r skp7*• carb-v *Clem* k* colch coli jl2 coloc lyc *Merc* *Mez* nux-m **Sars** bg2 sel tell
- **not** urinating; when: aids ↓ asaf ↓ bell ↓ **Benz-ac** *Berb* bov ↓ bry calad ↓ *Calc-p* ↓ *Cann-s* ↓ *Caps* ↓ cedr *Cham* ↓ *Clem* ↓ cocc coff ↓ cop ↓ euph ↓ *Graph* ↓ *Helon* ↓ ign ↓ kali-c ↓ mag-s ↓ mang ↓ **Merc** ↓ *Merc-c* ↓ *Nat-c* ↓ *Nat-m* ↓ nit-ac ↓ nux-v ph-ac ↓ ruta ↓ sabad ↓ sep ↓ *Staph* ↓ *Sulph* ↓ teucr ↓ thuj ↓ til ↓ verat ↓ viol-t ↓ zinc ↓
  - : **biting** pain: cann-s k* teucr k* zinc k*
  - : **burning**: asaf *Berb* k* bov *Bry* calad cann-s bro1 cedr clem *Graph* **Merc** *Merc-c* *Nat-c* nit-ac sabad *Staph* k* *Sulph* teucr thuj
  - : **cutting** pain: aids nl2• berb k* calc-p caps kali-c mag-s mang k* nux-v k* staph thuj
  - : **pinching** pain: verat k*
  - : **pulsating**: cop
  - : **sore**: teucr k* zinc k*
  - : **stitching** pain: bell bry *Calc-p* k* *Cann-s* k* *Caps* k* *Cham* coff cop euph k* **Merc** k* *Nat-m* *Nux-v* ph-ac k* sep *Sulph* teucr thuj k* til k* viol-t a1
    - : **cutting** pain | **twitching**: thuj k*

- **urination** – **not** urinating; when – **stitching** pain: ...
  - : **drawing**: merc k*
  - : **dull** pain: viol-t k*
  - : **tearing** pain: bry k* *Clem* k* *Helon* ign kali-c nux-v ruta tl1 zinc k*
- **urging** to urinate: *Agar* ant-c ↓ ant-t ↓ **Canth** ↓ cocc con hyper *Nit-ac* ↓ phos ↓ *Prun* ↓ sabad ↓ *Sulph* ↓
  - : **burning**: ant-c ant-t **Canth** con *Nit-ac* phos *Prun* sabad *Sulph*
  - : **during**: nux-v ↓ thuj ↓
    - : **stitching** pain: nux-v bg2 thuj k*
  - : **effort** is made to pass urine; when: calad ↓ prun ↓
    - : **burning**: calad prun
  - : **with**: agar ↓ cain ↓ calc-p ↓ cann-i ↓ *Canth* ↓ *Caps* ↓ cic ↓ *Phos* ↓ spig ↓ sulph ↓
    - : **sore**: cic c1
    - : **stitching** pain: agar cain calc-p cann-i *Canth* *Caps* *Phos* spig sulph
  - : **with** ineffectual urging: puls ↓
    - : **cutting** pain: puls
- **voluptuous**:
- ▽ **extending** to:
  - : **Anus**: sulph ↓
    - : **pressing** pain: sulph k*
- **waking**; on: carb-an *Card-m* sars k*
- **walking**:
  - **agg.**: acon ↓ bell ↓ chel ↓ ign ↓ stry ↓ thuj ↓
    - : **burning**: stry k*
    - : **cutting** pain: thuj k*
    - : **drawing** pain: thuj k*
    - : **stitching** pain: acon bell chel ign
  - **air**; in open:
    - : **agg.**: alum ↓ merc-c ↓ mez ↓
      - : **drawing** pain: mez
      - : **stitching** pain: alum merc-c
      - : **tearing** pain: alum k*
        - . **shooting** and ascending through hypogastrium: alum k*
- **wet**; after getting: calc k*
- **zigzags**: *Cann-s* ↓ *Sars* ↓
  - **tearing** pain: *Cann-s* *Sars*
  - ○ **Hypogastrium**, when walking in open air; toward: alum ↓
    - : **tearing** pain: alum
- ▽ **extending** to:
  - ○ **Abdomen**, evening: merc ↓
    - : **stitching** pain: merc
  - **Anus**: arg-n ↓ canth ↓ nux-v ↓ ph-ac ↓
    - : **morning**:
      - : **urination** agg.; after: thuj ↓
        - . **stitching** pain: thuj
    - : **drawing** pain: ph-ac
    - : **stitching** pain: arg-n canth nux-v
    - : **through** urethra; from anus | **drawing** pain (See RECTUM - Pain - anus - extending - urethra - drawing)
  - **Anus** when passing last drops: arg-n ↓ thuj ↓
    - : **cutting** pain: arg-n thuj
  - **Backward** along: arg-n bg1 berb bg1 canth bg1 caps bg1 fl-ac bg1 merc-c bg1 nux-v bg1 phos bg1 plan bg1 psor bg1 spong fd4.de sumb bg1 thuj bg2* zinc bg1
  - **Bladder**: berb ↓
    - : **stitching** pain: berb
    - : **urination** agg.; after: lyc ↓
      - : **burning**: lyc k*
      - : **dragging**: lyc k*
  - **Body**:
    - : **urination** agg.; during: jac-g ↓
      - : **tearing** pain: jac-g
  - **Down** along: lyc bg1 merc bg1 phos bg1 sulph bg1
  - **Glans**: asar ↓ equis-h ↓ lyc ↓ pall ↓

Urethra

- **Glans**: ...
  - **stitching** pain: asar equis-h lyc pall
- **Hypogastrium**: alum ↓ sulph ↓
  - **stitching** pain: alum sulph
- **Meatus**: bell ↓ brom ↓ con ↓
  - **stitching** pain: bell brom con
  - **Root** of penis after urination; from: sars ↓
    - **stitching** pain: sars
- **Perineum** into urethra; from: | **drawing** pain (See RECTUM - Pain - perineum - extending - urethra - drawing)
- **Tip**; as far as the:
  - **evening**:
    - **urination** agg.; during: sabad ↓
      - **dragging**: sabad

○ - **Anterior** part: alum ↓ ambr ↓ ant-t ↓ bell ↓ bry ↓ cann-s ↓ canth ↓ *Caps* ↓ chel ↓ cic ↓ clem ↓ coc-c ↓ coff ↓ colch ↓ cycl ↓ euph ↓ ign ↓ *Kali-c* ↓ *Lach* ↓ *Lyc* ↓ mag-c ↓ *Merc* ↓ merc-c ↓ *Mez* vh *Nit-ac* ↓ nux-v ↓ pall ↓ *Par* ↓ *Petros* ↓ phos ↓ puls ↓ rhus-t ↓ *Sep* ↓ sil ↓ stann ↓ **Sulph** ↓ tep ↓ thuj ↓ zinc ↓

- **evening**:
  - **urination** agg.; after: am-c ↓
    - **drawing** pain: am-c
- **biting** pain: *Petros* rhus-t k* sep h2* zinc k*
- **burning**: canth k* coff *Nit-ac* k* puls k* *Sep* k* stann k* tep k* thuj k*
- **cutting** pain: alum k* colch k* lach k* lyc k* nux-v k* thuj zinc
- **drawing** pain: bry k* *Kali-c* k* *Lyc* k* par k* zinc k*
- **emission**, after an: carb-v ↓ *Sep* ↓
  - **burning**: carb-v k* *Sep* k*
- **rest** agg., walking amel.: rhus-t ↓
  - **biting** pain: rhus-t k*
- **stitching** pain: bell bry k* cann-s k* *Caps* k* chel cic coc-c k* cycl k* euph k* ign k* *Lach* k* lyc k* mag-c *Merc* k* merc-c k* nit-ac pall *Par* k* phos sil k* **Sulph** k* thuj k*
- **tearing** pain: ambr h1* ant-t k* clem k* coff k* kali-c k* sep k* thuj h1* zinc k*
- **urination**:
  - **after**:
    - **agg.**: alum ↓ cann-s ↓ coc-c ↓ kali-bi ↓ lyc ↓ mez ↓ nit-ac ↓ puls ↓ ran-s k* rhus-t k*
      - **burning**: cann-s kali-bi lyc mez nit-ac puls
      - **cutting** pain: alum k* coc-c k* mez rhus-t a1
        - **lancinating**, and: coc-c
      - **stitching** pain: coc-c
  - **during**:
    - **agg.**: alum ↓ ars ↓ aur ↓ calc ↓ *Cann-s* ↓ caps ↓ carb-v ↓ coch ↓ colch ↓ ery-a ↓ ign ↓ kali-bi ↓ kali-n ↓ *Merc* ↓ nat-c ↓ nat-s ↓ nux-v k* phos k* raph ↓ rhus-t k* seneg ↓ stann ↓ *Sulph* ↓ teucr ↓ verat ↓
      - **burning**: ars k* calc *Cann-s* k* caps carb-v coch ery-a ign k* kali-bi kali-n k* *Merc* nat-c nux-v *Phos* raph k* rhus-t k* seneg stann h2* *Sulph* k* teucr k* verat k*
      - **cutting** pain: alum k* cann-s k* colch nat-s k* rhus-t k*
      - **tearing** pain: aur
  - **not** urinating; when: asaf ↓ berb bry *Cann-s* ↓ *Caps* ↓ euph ↓ kali-bi ↓ *Merc* ↓ nux-v ↓ puls ↓ *Stann* ↓ *Sulph* ↓ teucr ↓ thuj ↓ zinc ↓ zing ↓
    - **burning**: asaf bry *Cann-s* k* caps k* kali-bi nux-v *Stann* *Sulph* k* zinc zing k*
    - **drawing** pain: bry k* puls zinc
    - **stitching** pain: asaf bry a1 cann-s *Caps* k* euph k* *Merc* k* teucr thuj a1
    - **tearing** pain: bry zinc

- **Fossa** navicularis: acon ↓ ammc ↓ cann-s ↓ *Caps* ↓ chel ↓ *Cic* ↓ coc-c ↓ cub ↓ gins ↓ merc ↓ nat-m ↓ nux-v ↓ **Petros** ↓ *Psor* ↓ squil ↓ sulph ↓ thuj ↓
  - **biting** pain: **Petros** k*
  - **burning**: acon k* cann-s cub k* *Petros* k* *Psor* jl2
    - **drops**, burning: thuj
  - **drawing** pain: cic k* *Petros* k*

- **Fossa** navicularis: ...
  - **sore**: nux-v
  - **stitching** pain: acon ammc a1 *Caps* chel *Cic* k* coc-c gins k* merc nat-m k* *Petros* k* squil sulph thuj k*
  - **urination**:
    - **after**:
      - **agg.**: **Petros** ↓ thuj ↓
        - **cutting** pain: **Petros** thuj
    - **before**: bar-c senec ↓
      - **burning**: senec k*
    - **during**:
      - **agg.**: acon ↓ clem ↓ *Kali-bi* ↓ mez ↓ nat-m ↓ petros ↓ thuj ↓
        - **burning**: clem k* *Kali-bi* k* mez h2* nat-m k* petros k* thuj
        - **stitching** pain: acon
      - **beginning** of:
        - **agg.**: psor ↓
          - **burning**: psor jl2
- **Glandular** portion:
  - **urination** agg.; during: apis ↓ cain ↓ camph ↓ dig ↓ kali-bi ↓ nux-v ↓ rhus-t ↓
    - **and** for long time after: apis ↓ dig ↓ *Kali-bi* ↓
      - **burning**: apis dig *Kali-bi* k*
    - **burning**: apis cain br1 camph dig kali-bi k* nux-v rhus-t
- **Lumbar** region:
  - **urination** agg.; during: *Clem* ↓
    - **aching**: *Clem* hr1
- **Meatus**: *Acon* ↓ aesc ↓ agar ↓ am-c ↓ ambr ↓ ammc ↓ aphis ↓ apis ↓ *Arg-n* ↓ arn ↓ arum-d ↓ asc-t ↓ **Aspar** ↓ aur-m-n ↓ bad ↓ berb mrr1 *Borx* brom ↓ bry ↓ *Calc* ↓ calc-f ↓ cann-i ↓ *Cann-s* k* **Cann-xyz** ↓ **Canth** k* *Caps* ↓ carc fd2.de• chel *Chin* ↓ cic ↓ cinnb ↓ clem k* cob ↓ coc-c ↓ coch ↓ coff ↓ coff-t ↓ coloc ↓ con ↓ cop k* cupr ↓ cupr-ar ↓ cycl ↓ *Dulc* ↓ equis-h ↓ franz ↓ gamb ↓ gels ↓ graph ↓ ichth ↓ iod ↓ kali-c ↓ kali-n ↓ *Kali-s* ↓ kreos ↓ lact ↓ led ↓ lyc ↓ mag-s ↓ mang ↓ med ↓ menth ↓ *Merc-c* ↓ mez ↓ mur-ac ↓ *Nat-m* ↓ nat-s ↓ nat-sil ↓ nicc ↓ **Nit-ac** ↓ nit-s-d ↓ nux-v par ↓ pareir ↓ *Petros* ↓ ph-ac ↓ phos ↓ psor ↓ puls ↓ puls-n ran-s ↓ rhod k* *Sars* k* sel ↓ seneg ↓ sep ↓ ser-a-c ↓ *Spig* ↓ squil ↓ stann ↓ staph ↓ **Sulph** ↓ tax ↓ *Thuj* ↓ verat ↓ *Zinc* ↓ zing k*
  - **morning**: kali-c ↓ petros ↓
    - **biting** pain: kali-c k* petros
    - **burning**: kali-c h2*
    - **waking**; on: alum ↓
      - **biting** pain: alum
  - **evening**: canth ↓ coc-c ↓ kali-c ↓ nat-m ↓ nat-sil ↓ petros ↓ rhod ↓
    - **biting** pain: coc-c k* kali-c petros
    - **burning**: nat-m h2* nat-sil fd3.de•
    - **stitching** pain: canth k* rhod k*
    - **urination** | **after**:
      - **agg.**: chinin-s ↓
        - **contracting**: chinin-s c1
    - **during**:
      - **agg.**: seneg ↓
        - **drawing** pain: seneg
  - **night**: *Agar* ↓ calc ↓ canth ↓ ichth ↓
    - **burning**: *Agar* k* calc ichth ah1
    - **stitching** pain: canth k*
  - **aching**: **Cann-xyz** bg2
  - **bath**, during a: bart ↓
    - **twinging**: bart
  - **biting** pain: merc-c bg2* mur-ac bg2* sep h2* staph h1*
  - **burning**: *Acon* bro1 agar k* am-c ambr k* ammc a1 aphis apis arum-d a1* *Berb* k* borx bro1 bry *Calc* k* calc-f k* *Cann-s* k* canth bg2* *Caps* bro1 carc fd2.de• chel k* *Chin* k* cic clem k* cob k* coch coff coff-t a1 cupr cupr-ar k* *Dulc* k* gamb k* gels bro1 graph ichth br1 iod k* kali-c k* *Kali-s* kreos bg2 lact k* lyc mag-s k* med menth bro1 *Merc-c* k* *Nat-m* nat-sil fd3.de• nicc k* nit-ac par k* *Petros* bro1 ph-ac k* phos puls k* ran-s sel bro1 seneg sep k* ser-a-c jl2 *Spig* k* staph **Sulph** k* *Thuj* k* verat k* zing k* [tax jsj7]

- **burning**: ...
  - ⁝ **backward**: cann-s k* phos a1
  - ⁝ **violent**, most: *Berb*
- **coition**; after: *Borx*↓ *Calc*↓ casc↓ nat-p↓
  - ⁝ **burning**: *Calc* k* nat-p k*
  - ⁝ **sore**: *Borx* casc
- **copious** urine, with: agar↓
  - ⁝ **stitching** pain: agar
- **cutting** pain: arn k* bad chel cupr iod k* mez k* nit-ac nit-s-d a1* par *Zinc* k* zing
- **drawing** pain: arg-n k* cop k* phos k*
- **pinching** pain: cinnb thuj
- **pressing** pain: chel k* nux-v puls
- **pricking** pain: coloc cycl k* *Nit-ac* rhod
- **quiet**, when: canth↓ par↓
  - ⁝ **burning**: canth k* par
- **rubbing** of clothes: chin↓
  - ⁝ **burning**: chin kr1*
- **sitting** agg.: par↓ zinc↓
  - ⁝ **burning**: par k*
  - ⁝ **cutting** pain: zinc k*
- **sore**: *Arg-n* arum-d a1 *Borx* bry *Chin* clem k* cop equis-h nux-v k* puls k* stann k*
- **stitching** pain: acon k* aesc agar k* asc-t **Aspar** k* aur-m-n k* bad *Berb* k* brom k* cann-i k* cann-s k* caps k* chel k* cic clem k* coc-c k* con k* cupr h2* franz a1 iod k* kali-n k* led k* mang k* mez k* nat-m k* nat-s k* **Nit-ac** k* nit-s-d a1* pareir k* ph-ac k* psor k* rhod k* squil k* sulph k* thuj k* zinc k*
  - ⁝ **fine**: aspar k*
- **stool** agg.; after: nat-p↓
  - ⁝ **burning**: nat-p k2
- **tearing** pain: kali-c lyc k* pareir zinc
- **twinging**: berb zinc
- **urination**:
  - ⁝ **after**:
    - : **agg.**: arg-n↓ *Borx* *Cann-i*↓ caps↓ card-m↓ casc↓ chin↓ coc-c↓ coloc↓ **Cub** bg2 cupr-ar↓ graph↓ kali-c↓ *Lac-c* **Laur** bg2 lyss↓ mez↓ mur-ac↓ nat-s↓ pareir↓ puls↓ *Sars* tell↓ verat↓ zinc↓
      - . **aching**: puls
      - . **biting** pain: kali-c k* zinc k*
        - **sticking** pain: mur-ac k*
      - . **burning**: *Cann-i* k* caps k* card-m casc k* chin coloc k* cupr-ar k* graph k* kali-c k* lyss k* nat-s k* puls k* tell k*
      - . **cutting** pain: arg-n k* coc-c mez k* nat-s k*
      - . **sore**: borx a1
      - . **stitching** pain: caps h1* mur-ac k* pareir k* verat h1*
      - . **women**; in: cann-s↓
        - **pressing** pain: cann-s k2
  - ⁝ **before**: *Caps*↓
    - : **burning**: *Caps* k*
  - ⁝ **during**:
    - : **agg.**: acon↓ *Agar*↓ aphis↓ arum-d↓ aur-m-n↓ borx↓ *Calc*↓ cann-i↓ **Cann-s**↓ canth↓ caps↓ *Chin*↓ cob↓ con↓ cupr↓ cupr-ar↓ *Dulc*↓ echi↓ erech↓ gamb↓ kali-n↓ merc↓ merc-c↓ merl↓ nat-ar↓ nat-s↓ nicc↓ *Nux-v*↓ ph-ac↓ *Puls*↓ spig↓ spirae↓ *Sulph*↓ thuj↓
      - . **aching**: canth k*
      - . **biting** pain: borx **Cann-s** k* echi merc-c k*
      - . **burning**: acon k* *Agar* k* aphis arum-d hr1 *Calc* k* cann-i k* *Cann-s* k* canth caps k* *Chin* cob hr1 cupr h2* cupr-ar k* *Dulc* k* erech a1 gamb k* kali-n k* merc k* merl nat-s k* nicc k* *Nux-v* k* ph-ac k* *Puls* k* spig h1* spirae a1 *Sulph* k* thuj k*
      - . **cutting** pain: aur-m-n k* con k* cupr k* nat-ar nat-s k*
      - . **stitching** pain: *Cann-s* b7a.de cupr h2*
    - : **end** of: arn↓ nat-s↓ zing↓
      - . **cutting** pain: arn nat-s zing

Pain – Meatus – urination: ...

- ⁝ **not** urinating; when: cann-s↓ *Caps*↓ cocc↓ mang↓ *Nux-v*↓ thuj↓
  - : **aching**: cocc *Nux-v*
  - : **pressing** pain: nux-v
  - : **stitching** pain: cann-s *Caps* k* mang k* thuj k*
- **walking** agg.: nat-m↓
  - ⁝ **burning**: nat-m k*
- **women**; in: *Lac-c* k* *Sars* k*

▽ • **extending** to | **Backward**: **Cann-s** k* thuj bg1

○ • **Female**: berb↓
  - ⁝ **tearing** pain: berb

- **Posterior** part: *Camph*↓ cann-s↓ carb-an↓ kali-bi↓ lyc↓ med↓ mur-ac↓ *Petros*↓ staph↓
  - **biting** pain: *Camph* k* *Petros* k*
  - **burning**: cann-s carb-an kali-bi staph k*
  - **cutting** pain: med hr1 mur-ac h2*
  - **drawing** pain: lyc h2*
  - **ejaculation**; after: carb-an↓
    - ⁝ **burning**: carb-an
  - **sitting** agg.: staph↓
    - ⁝ **burning**: staph h1
  - **urination** agg.; during: *Cann-s*↓
    - ⁝ **burning**: *Cann-s*

▽ • **extending** to:
  - ⁝ **Abdomen**: lyc↓
    - : **cutting** pain: lyc h2*

- **Root** of penis; at: caust↓
  - **burning**: caust h2
  - **urination** agg.; during: rhus-t↓
    - ⁝ **burning**: rhus-t a1
- **Spots**; in: bov↓
  - **sore**: bov bg2

POUTING meatus (See Swelling)

PULSATION: ben brom k* canth k* chin cop k* dulc k* merc k* **Merc-c** k* petr thuj bg2

○ - **Fossa** navicularis | **stitching** and beating: thuj

RAW sensation: ph-ac h2*

REDNESS: *Hep* b4a.de *Thuj* b4a.de

- **spots**: bry

○ - **Meatus**: *Cact* cann-s cinnb k* cub cupr-ar k* *Gels* k* *Hep* k* *Led* k* nit-ac k* nit-s-d a1 petr k* *Sulph* k* thuj k* yuc bg2*

RETRACTION: plb b7.de*

RIDING agg.: staph ptk1

SENSATION:

- **absent**, when urinating: *(↗Numbness; BLADDER - Urination - unconscious)* ail alum b4a.de* *Apis* apoc **Arg-n** k* **Caust** k* cedr chlol *Cupr* grat hell kali-br k* *M-aust* b7.de **Mag-m** k* mag-s merc nux-v *Sars* k*
- **flowing** along; urine (See Urine - flowing)
- **narrow**, as if too (See Narrow)

SENSITIVE: canth b7.de* caps b7.de* chin b7.de* nat-m bg2 nit-ac b4a.de

○ - **Fossa** navicularis: *Nux-v* b7a.de

SPASM: acon bg2 arg-n bg2 camph bg2 canth bg2 carb-an b4.de* chel bg2 chin b7.de* cic bg2 *Clem* b4a.de cocc bg2 nit-ac *Nux-v* bg2* op b7a.de phos bg2 prun *Puls* bg2

- **fissure** of rectum; with: nit-ac
- **seminal** emissions; after: carb-an b4a.de
- **urination** | **end** of; toward: *Arg-n* bro1 bor-ac bro1 puls bro1

STONE in; as of a: *(↗Ball)* coc-c k*

STRICTURE: acon k* agar k* alumn k2 am-m hr1 ant-t k* *Apis* *Arg-n* k* arn bg2* bell *Berb* k* *Calc* k* calc-i bro1 calc-sil k2 camph bg2 *Cann-s* k* **Canth** k* caps bro1 carb-v bg2 *Chim* k* chin k* cic bg2* cinnb **Clem** k* *Con* k* cop bro1 *Dig* k* *Dulc* k* eucal c2* fl-ac bro1* *Graph* k* guaj ptk1 hep k2* *Indg* k*

Stricture: ...
Iod$_{k*}$ *Kali-i*$_{k*}$ kola$_{stb3•}$ lob$_{c2*}$ lyc$_{bg2}$ mag-m$_{bg2}$ med$_{hr1*}$ *Merc*$_{k*}$ merc-pr-r$_{bro1}$ *Nat-m*$_{k*}$ nat-s$_{ptk1}$ **Nit-ac**$_{k*}$ nux-v$_{bro1*}$ ol-sant$_{bro1}$ op$_{k*}$ pareir$_{bro1}$ **Petr**$_{k*}$ *Petros*$_{k*}$ *Phos*$_{bg2*}$ **Puls**$_{k*}$ rhus-t$_{bg2*}$ sep$_{k*}$ *Sil*$_{k*}$ spong$_{bg2}$ sul-i$_{c2*}$ *Sulph*$_{k*}$ tarent$_{k*}$ *Thiosin*$_{bro1}$ thuj$_{k*}$
- **accompanied** by:
  - **urination**; painful (See BLADDER - Urination - dysuria - accompanied - stricture)

O · **Tongue** | **brown** discoloration: *Iod*$_{vk1}$
- **dilatation**, after: con$_{ptk1}$ mag-m$_{ptk1}$
- **drunkards**; in: op$_{ptk1}$
- **gonorrhea**; after: sul-i$_{ptk1}$
- **sensation** of: bry coc-c dig graph sabal$_{c1}$ thuj
- **spasmodic**: *Acon*$_{c2*}$ apis *Bell*$_{k*}$ berb camph$_{k*}$ **Canth**$_{k*}$ carb-v *Cic*$_{k*}$ *Clem* con cop *Dios*$_{k*}$ ery-a$_{bro1}$ eucal$_{k*}$ *Gels*$_{k*}$ hydrang$_{bro1}$ indg **Nit-ac**$_{k*}$ *Nux-v*$_{k*}$ *Op*$_{k*}$ petros$_{bro1}$ ph-ac *Plb*$_{k*}$ *Prun*$_{k*}$ *Sec*$_{k*}$ stram$_{k*}$
  - **morning**: carb-v
- **urination**:
  - **before**: op$_{b7.de*}$
  - **during** | **agg.**: arg-n$_{bg2}$ *Cann-xyz*$_{bg2}$ **Clem**$_{bg2}$ petr$_{bg2}$ rhus-t$_{bg2}$ sulph$_{bg2}$

SUPPURATION (See Discharge - purulent)

SWELLING: *(↗Narrow)* alum$_{k*}$ alum-p$_{k2}$ apis$_{b7a.de}$ *Arg-n*$_{k*}$ cann-s$_{k2*}$ *Canth*$_{k*}$ *Cop*$_{k*}$ gran$_{k*}$ led$_{k*}$ *Merc*$_{k*}$ *Merc-c*$_{k*}$ **Mit**$_{k*}$ nit-ac$_{k*}$ op ph-ac$_{k*}$ *Puls*$_{b7a.de}$ *Rhus-t*$_{k*}$ *Sulph* **Thuj**$_{k*}$
- **sensation** of: *Arg-n*$_{k*}$ cann-s card-m led nit-ac ph-ac$_{bg2}$ rhus-t til$_{k*}$
  - **urination** agg.; during: arg-n$_{bg2}$

O - **Anterior** part: merc
- **Meatus**: acon$_{bro1}$ alum arg-n$_{bro1}$ **Cann-s**$_{k*}$ cann-xyz$_{ptk1}$ canth$_{k*}$ *Cop*$_{k*}$ gels$_{bro1}$ hep$_{k*}$ jac-g led *Merc*$_{bro1}$ *Nit-ac*$_{k*}$ *Ol-sant*$_{bro1}$ ph-ac phos **Sulph**$_{k*}$ **Thuj**$_{k*}$
  - **women**; in: gonotox$_{jl2}$
- **Region** of neck of bladder: puls

TENESMUS: ery-a$_{mtf11}$
- **accompanied** by | **discharge**; gonorrheal (See Discharge - gonorrheal - accompanied - tenesmus)

TENSION: borx$_{h2}$ canth$_{b7.de*}$ croc$_{b7.de*}$ junc-e kola$_{stb3•}$ lyc$_{k*}$ phos$_{b4.de*}$
- **erections**; during: anag$_{a1}$ arg-n$_{a1}$ **Cann-s**$_{k*}$ **Canth** kola$_{stb3•}$
- **urination** agg.; after: borx$_{b4a.de}$

TICKLING (See Itching)

TINGLING: agar$_{k2}$ apis$_{bg2}$ apoc$_{k*}$ cann-s$_{b7.de*}$ *Clem*$_{k*}$ cupr-ar$_{k*}$ equis-h$_{bg2}$ *Petros*$_{k*}$ sep$_{k*}$ staph
- **sitting** agg.: staph
- **urination** | **after** | **Meatus** and urethra: clem$_{bro1}$ thuj$_{bro1}$
  - **during** | **agg.**: petros tere-la$_{rly4•}$

O - **Frenum**; culmination at *Clem*$_{k*}$
- **Meatus**: agar anag cann-i clem coc-c plan$_{k*}$ sep$_{k*}$ staph

TUMOR: *Anil*$_{br1}$ lach$_{k*}$

TWITCHING: *(↗Twitching - Burning)* alum$_{k*}$ ambr$_{k*}$ ant-s-aur *Cann-s*$_{k*}$ cann-xyz$_{ptk1}$ *Canth*$_{k*}$ clem$_{k*}$ coc-c con$_{b4.de*}$ kali-chl nat-c$_{k*}$ nux-v$_{k*}$ petr$_{k*}$ *Phos*$_{k*}$
- **burning** in seminal vesicles to glans penis: *(↗Twitching; MALE GENITALIA/SEX - Twitching - burning)* *Mang*
- **ejaculation** of semen; like: petr
- **urination**:
  - **before**: nux-v$_{b7.de*}$
  - **during** | **agg.**: canth$_{b7.de*}$
  - **not** urinating; when: phos$_{h2*}$ thuj

O - **Anterior** part: coc-c

ULCERATION: alumn$_{k2*}$ arg-n$_{bg2*}$ canth$_{k*}$ hep$_{k2}$ kali-bi$_{bg2}$ merc$_{bg2}$ merc-c$_{ptk1}$ **Nit-ac**$_{k*}$ sulph$_{bg2}$ thuj$_{bg2}$
- **chancres**: *(↗GENERALS - Chancre)* *Arg-n*$_{k*}$ **Nit-ac**$_{k*}$

O - **Meatus**: abrot$_{k*}$ eucal$_{k*}$ lac-c$_{k*}$ **Merc-c** **Nit-ac**$_{k*}$
  - **retained**; with sensation as if urine was: canth

Ulceration – Meatus: ...
  - **sticking**, with: **Nit-ac**$_{k*}$

URETHRITIS (See Inflammation)

URGING: nat-c$_{h2}$ ph-ac$_{h2}$
- **urination** agg.; after: *Mur-ac*$_{hr1}$

URINATION; during: | **amel.**: *Merc*$_{ptk1}$ staph$_{ptk1}$

URINE:
- **cold**; as if urine were: nit-ac
- **flowing**; sensation as if urine was still: aspar kali-bi$_{k2}$ petros$_{k2}$ thuj$_{k2}$ vib
- **remained**, after urinating; as if some: *(↗BLADDER - Urination - unsatisfactory - remained)* agar all-c alum$_{k*}$ ambr *Arg-n* aspar atra-r$_{skp7•}$ *Berb*$_{bro1}$ carbn-s cedr clem dig$_{k*}$ ery-a$_{k*}$ eup-pur$_{bro1}$ gels$_{bro1}$ *Hep*$_{bro1}$ *Kali-bi*$_{k*}$ lact med petr rhus-t ruta$_{bro1}$ sec$_{bro1}$ *Sel* *Sep* sil$_{bro1}$ staph$_{bro1}$ tell *Thuj*$_{k*}$
- **stops** at fossa navicularis: ferr-i$_{k*}$ prun

O - **Fossa** navicularis; as if urine in | **urination** agg.; after: all-c ferr-i *Thuj*

VESICLES (See Eruptions - vesicles)

VOLUPTUOUS sensation: anag lith-c nat-c$_{h2*}$ ox-ac$_{k*}$ thuj$_{k*}$
- **stool** agg.; after: nat-c$_{bg2}$
- **urination** | **after** | **agg.**: fl-ac$_{hr1}$ thuj$_{k*}$
  - **during** | **agg.**: ox-ac$_{k*}$ thuj

WALKING agg.: staph$_{ptk1}$

WARMTH (See Heat)

WEAKNESS: phos$_{b4.de*}$

WEARINESS; sensation of: | **urination** agg.; after: phos$_{b4.de}$

11-OXYSTEROIDS increased: cortiso sp1

17-KETOSTEROIDS:
- **decreased**: cortiso sp1
- **increased**: cortico sp1

ACETONURIA: acet-ac bg2 ars bro1 aur-m bro1 *Calc-m* bro1* carb-ac bro1 carc dgt1 *Caust* bro1* colch bro1 cupr-ar bg2* *Euon* bro1 glyc ah1 *Ins* vh nat-sal bro1 phos bro1 senn br1* sul-ac bg2 sulfa jl1

ACID: acon bro1 arn bg2 benz-ac bg2* canth bro1 chinin-s bro1 euon bro1 hip-ac sp1 lith-c bro1 *Lyc* bro1 merc-c bg2* mur-ac bro1 *Nit-ac* bro1 nit-m-ac bro1 nux-v bro1 oci bro1 puls bro1 *Sars* bro1 sep bro1 *Sulph* bro1 *Uva* bro1
- **amino** acids increased in women: cortico sp1
- **ascorbic** acid increased: cortiso sp1
- **indole** acetic acid increased: rauw sp1
- **uric** acid increased: cortico sp1 cortiso sp1 helo-s bnm14• maland jl2

ACRID: acet-ac hr1 ail k* alum k* alum-p k2 alumn k* ambr b2.de* ant-t k* apoc a1 arg-n a1 **Arn** k* ars b2.de* arund br1 asaf k* astac k* atra-r skp7*• atro k* aur-m k* *Bell* hr1 **Benz-ac** k* *Borx* k* brach k* *Calc* k* calc-i k2 camph b2.de* *Cann-s* k* canth k* caps k* carb-ac a1 carb-v b2.de* carbn-s *Card-m* k* *Caust* k* cham b2.de* *Chel* k* chin b2.de* cimic a1 cinch a1 *Clem* k* *Coc-c* k* colch k* coloc a1 cop a1 *Cupr* k* *Cycl* k* dig k* *Dulc* k* elat hr1 erig a1 ery-a a1 fab br1 fago a1 ferr-m a1 *Fl-ac* k* *Graph* k* guaj b2.de* helon a1 **Hep** k* ign k* *Iod* k* *Kali-bi* k* kali-br a1 *Kali-c* k* kali-chl a1 *Kreos* k* **Laur** k* lept a1 *Lith-c* lyc ptk1 m-aust b2.de* med c1* **Merc** k* **Merc-c** k* merc-sul br1 mit a1* morg-p pte1• *Nat-m* k* *Nat-s* k* *Nit-ac* k* par k* petr k* *Phos* k* *Plan* k* plb hr1 prun k* puls k* rhus-t k* sabin k* sang bg2 *Sars* k* senec k* *Seneg* k* *Sep* k* sin-n hr1 stann k* *Staph* k* sul-ac a1 **Sulph** k* syc pte1*• tell k* *Thuj* k* (non:uran-met k) *Uran-n* urt-u ptk1 vanil fd5.de verat k* zinc mtf33
- **children**; in: *Ign* mtf33 med mtf33 nat-s mtf33 puls mtf33 sulph mtf33 zinc mtf33
  - **newborns**: med c1
- **menses**; during: *Alum* k* apis nat-m k*

ALBUMINOUS: (↗*GENERALS - Dropsy - external - albuminuria; KIDNEYS - Nephrotic)* absin a1 acetan br1* acon k* adon c2* alco a1 all-c k* all-s k* allox sp1 alum alum-p k2 alumn k2 am-be hr1* *Am-c* bg2 am-caust k* ant-c bg2* *Ant-t* k* antip br1* **Apis** k* apoc k* arg-met *Arg-n* k* arist-cl sp1 **Ars** k* *Ars-i* ars-s-f k2 astac hr1 *Aur* k* aur-ar k2 aur-i k2 **Aur-m** k* *Aur-m-n* aur-s k2 bell b4a.de* berb bg2* bism k* borx bg2* *Brach* k* bry bg2* cain br1 *Calc* k* **Calc-ar** k* calc-i k2 calc-p mtf33 *Cann-s* k* cann-xyz bg2 *Canth* k* *Carb-ac* k* *Carb-v Carbn-s* carc fb* caul chel *Chim* k* *Chin* k* *Chinin-ar* chinin-s bro1 chir-fl bnm4• chlol cinnb k* cob hr1 coc-c coch c2 *Colch* k* conv bro1 cop k* cortiso sp1 *Crot-c Crot-h* k* cub c1* *Cupr* cupr-act bro1 cupr-ar bro1 cupr-s k* *Dig* k* diph-t-tpt jl2 *Dulc* k* equis-h bro1 *Euon* bro1 euon-a c2* euonin c2 eup-pur k* faec jl2 *Ferr* k* *Ferr-ar* k* *Ferr-i* k* *Ferr-m* bro1 ferr-p ferr-pic c2* form bg2* fuch br1* *Gels* k* **Glon** k* **Hell** k* helo bg2 *Helon* k* *Hep* k* *Hippoz* k* *Iod* k* kali-ar bg2 *Kali-bi* k* kali-br br1 *Kali-c* k* *Kali-chl* k* *Kali-i* kali-m k* kali-n kali-p kali-s *Kalm* k* kiss c2 kreos bg2 **Lac-d** k* lac-v c2 *Lach* k* lat-h bnm5• lat-m sp1* lec k* *Leptos-ih* jl2 lith-c k* lon-x br1 loxo-lae bnm12• **Lyc** k* lycps-v mag-m k* mang-act br1 med k* mela a1 *Merc* k* **Merc-c** k* *Merc-cy* k* *Merc-i-r* methyl c2* mez morph k* mur-ac k* myric naphtin c2 **Nat-ar Nat-c** k* nat-f sp1 nat-hchls c2 *Nat-m* k* **Nat-p** k* *Nat-s* nat-sal a1 *Nit-ac* k* nux-v hr1 oci c2* oena c2 ol-j ol-sant bro1 op osm k* osm-ac gt2 ourl jl2 *Petr* k* **Ph-ac** k* phase-xyz c2 *Phos* k* *Phyt* k* *Pic-ac* k* pilo c2 pip-m c2 pitu-p sp1 **Plb** k* *Plb-c* bro1 polyg-h puls k* *Pyrog* k* rad-br c11 rad-met bro1 **Rhus-t** k* ric c2 *Sabin* k* sal-ac samb-c c2 sars k* scarl jl2 *Sec* k* *Ser-ang* br1 sil bro1 solid c2* spartin-s br1 squil bro1 stann sne stigm c2 *Stroph-h* bro1 strych-g c2 sul-ac k* sul-i k2 sulfon c2 *Sulph* k* *Syc* pte1*• tab k* *Tarent* tax k* **Ter** k* thal-xyz srj8• thuj bg2* thymol sp1 thyr c2* tub k* tub-m ih (non:uran-met k) *Uran-n* k* urea c2* vac jl2 valer bg2* vanad br1 vesi c2 visc br1* zinc k* zinc-p k2 zing c2
- **accompanied** by:
  - **apyrexia**: ars bro1
  - **gout**: am-be br1
  - **hypertension** (See GENERALS - Hypertension - accompanied - urine)
  - **respiration**; difficult: cain br1

Albuminous – accompanied by: ...
  - ○ **Heart**; complaints of the (See CHEST - Heart; complaints - accompanied - urine - albuminous)
  - **Kidneys**; inflammation of | **chronic** (See KIDNEYS - Inflammation - chronic - accompanied - urine)
  - **Retina**; inflammation of the (See EYE - Inflammation - retina - albuminuria)
  - **Tongue**:
    - **red** discoloration of the tongue | **Tip**: *Apis* kr1*
- **alcohol**, after abuse of: **Ars** k* aur bell *Berb Calc-ar* **Carb-v** k* *Chin Crot-h* cupr ferr *Lach* led merc *Merc-c* hr1 *Nat-c Nux-v* sulph
- **amaurosis**: *Apis Ars* k* cann-i colch k* *Gels* k* *Hep* kalm k* *Merc-c* k* ph-ac phos k* plb k*
- **children**; in: lat-m bnm6•
- **chronic**: *Atro* k* *Cedr* diph-t-tpt jl2 glon k* helon kali-c mtf33 *Petr* k* phos mtf33 *Plb* sep mtf33
- **cold** and dampness, from exposure to: *Calc Colch Dulc* kali-c merc-c nux-v *Rhus-t* sep
- **diphtheria**; after: *Apis Ars Carb-ac* hell hep k* kali-chl k* lach k* lyc *Merc-c* k* merc-cy phyt k*
- **fever**; after intermittent: aur-m k2
- **heart** disease, consecutive to: apis *Ars* ars-i *Aur* k* **Calc-ar** k* coc-c *Colch Crot-h Cupr Dig* glon kali-bi kali-p *Kalm Lach* lyc *Lycps-v* petr ph-ac *Ter* (non:uran-met k) uran-n
- **insanity**, during: phyt
- **menses**; during: helon
- **periodical**: phos ptk1
- **pregnancy**●: *Apis* bro1 *Ars* bro1 aur-m bro1 cupr-ar bro1 gels bro1 glon bro1 *Helon* bro1 ind bro1 *Kali-chl* bro1 kalm bro1 *Merc-c* bro1 *Phos* bro1 sabin bro1 thlas bro1 thyr bro1 *Verat-v* bro1
  - **during**: **Apis** k* apoc k* *Ars* k* ars-i k* *Aur-m* k* benz-ac k* berb k* bry k* cact k* *Calc-ar Canth* k* *Chin* k* cinnb k* *Colch* k* crot-h k* dig k* dulc k* ferr k* *Gels* k* hell k* *Helon* k* *Kali-ar* kali-br k* *Kali-c* k* *Kali-chl* k* kalm k* *Lach* k* led k* *Lyc* k* *Merc* k* **Merc-c** k* *Nat-m* k* *Ph-ac* phos k* rhus-t k* senec k* **Sep** k ● sulph k* *Ter* k* thlas br1* (non:uran-met k) uran-n
    - **beginning** of: merc-c br1
    - **delivery**; and after: *Merc-c* k* ph-ac k* *Pyrog* k*
    - **later** in pregnancy: phos br1
- **scarlet** fever; after: acon bro1 am-c bro1 **Apis** k* apoc bro1 *Ars* k* asc-c br1 asc-t *Aur-m* bar-m k2 bell bry *Canth* k* carb-ac coc-c k2 coch *Colch* k* *Con* cop crot-h dig k* dulc k* *Glon Hell* k* helon *Hep* k* kali-c *Kali-chl* k* *Kali-s Lach* k* **Lyc** *Merc-c* nat-m k2 **Nat-s** k* *Phos* k* phyt k* rhus-t *Sec* senec *Stram Ter* k* (non:uran-met k) uran-n
- **septic**: carb-v ptk1
- **syphilitics**; in: *Aur* aur-i st **Aur-m** *Aur-m-n* kali-bi kali-i *Merc-c* nit-ac k* sars

ALBUMINURIA (See Albuminous)

ALKALINE: am-c k* am-caust k* **Bapt** k* *Benz-ac* k* *Canth* k* **Carb-ac** k* chinin-s chlor k* cina *Ferr* k* *Fl-ac* k* *Hyos Hyosin* a1 *Kali-act* bro1 *Kali-bi* k* *Kali-c* k* kreos k* mag-p bro1 med bro1 morph k* *Nat-m* k* *Ph-ac* bro1 plb k* ser-a-c jl2 stram k* (non:uran-met k) uran-n wies a1 xan k*

ALTERED in general: puls ptk1 sep ptk1 sulph ptk1

ANT; attracting: *Glycyr-g* cte1•

BILE, containing: *Acon* astac a1 *Card-m* k* cean bg2* *Chel* k* **Chion** k* *Con* k* *Crot-h* cupr-s k* kali-chl bro1 kali-i k* lat-m bnm6• lept bg2 *Mag-m* k* *Merc Myric* k* *Nat-s* k* *Nit-ac* k* osm k* phos k* *Sang Sep* k* ser-a-c jl2 sulph k* (non:uran-met k) uran-n valer k*

BITING: sel ptk1

BLOODY: (↗*Sediment - bloody; BLADDER - Hemorrhage)* abrot k2 *Acon* k* alco a1 aloe alumn k* am-c bg2* ambr k* amyg-p br1 ant-c k* *Ant-t* k* antip br1* **Apis** k* **Arg-n** k* **Arn** k* **Ars** k* ars-h a1* ars-s-f k2 asc-t hr1 aspar k* *Aur* k* aur-ar k2 aur-s k2 *Bell* k* bell-p sp1 benz-ac k* *Berb* k* borx br1 **Both** k* bufo bg2 **Cact** k* cadm-met gm1 cadm-s c1* **Calc** k* *Camph* k* **Cann-s** k* **Canth** k* *Caps* k* *Carb-ac* bro1 *Carb-v* k* carbn-s carc jl2* *Caust* k* chel b2.de* *Chim* k* chin k* *Chinin-ar* chinin-s k* chir-fl bnm4• cimic k* cina bro1 **Coc-c** k* coch hr1 *Colch* k* coli jl2 coloc k* *Con* k* *Cop* k* crot-c **Crot-h** k* cub k* cupr k* cupr-s k* cyn-d zzc1• dig b2.de* diosm br1 diph-t-tpt jl2 dulc k* epig bro1 equis-h k* *Erig* k* eucal bro1 euph b2.de* fab bro1 ferr k* *Ferr-ar* ferr-m k* ferr-p k* fic-r br1* fuma-ac rly4• gaert pte1*• gal-ac br1* ger bro1 graph mtf33

Bloody: ...
guat sp1 **Ham** k* *Hell* k* hep k* hydrang br1 *Hyper* k* **Ip** k* jatr-c *Kali-ar* kali-bi k2 *Kali-chl* k* kali-i k* kali-m k2 kali-n k* kalm *Kreos* k* *Lach* k* lat-m sp1* led b7a.de* loxo-lae bnm12• loxo-recl bnm10• *Lyc* k* *Mangi* br1* *Merc* k* **Merc-c** k* *Mez* k* **Mill** k* moni rfm1• murx *Nat-m* k* nat-n br1 *Nit-ac* k* *Nux-v* k* oci bro1 ol-sant bro1 *Op* k* opun-v a1 ox-ac k* oxyurn-sc mcp1• pall k* pareir k* petr k* *Ph-ac* k* **Phos** k* pic-ac c2* *Plb* k* psor **Puls** k* rhod *Rhus-a* k* *Rhus-t* k* sabad k* *Sabin* k* sal-ac br1 santin bro1 *Sars* k* scarl jl2 **Sec** k* *Senec* k* *Sep* k* ser-ang br1 *Solid* bro1 **Squil** k* stigm bro1 *Sul-ac* k* *Sulph* k* tab k* tann-ac br1 tarent k* **Ter** k* terebe ktp9 thal-xyz srj8• *Thlas* bro1 thuj k* tril-p c1 tub c1* uva k* vac jl2 vanad br1 vesp k* vip br1 *Zinc* k* zinc-p k2

- **night**: *Caust* k*
- **accompanied** by:
  - **gonorrhea**: mez ptk1
  - **paraplegia**: lyc ptk1
  - **urination**:
    - **frequent**: ham ptk1
    - **urging** to urinate: sabin ptk1
  - ○ **Abdomen**:
    - **cramping** pain: bov bro1 *Lyc* bro1
    - **cutting** pain: ip ptk1
  - **Back**; pain in (See BACK - Pain - accompanied - urine - bloody)
  - **Bladder**; inflammation of (See BLADDER - Inflammation - accompanied - urine - bloody)
  - **Ovaries**; complaints of (See FEMALE - Ovaries - accompanied - urine)
  - **Spine**; shivering along: nit-ac ptk1
  - **Urethra**; cutting pain in: ip ptk1
- **children**; in: arg-n mtf33 bell mtf33 **Bufo** hr1* carb-v mtf33 graph mtf33 loxo-lae bnm12• sulph mtf33 zinc mtf33
- **chronic**: *Erig* petr hr1
- **clots**: *Alumn* k* apis ars bell k2 *Cact* canth k* *Chim* k* coc-c hr1 colch k* *Ip* k* kreos k2 *Lyc* k* mela a1 *Mill* k* *Ph-ac* k* *Plat* k* puls
  - **large**: canth mrr1
  - **putrid**, decomposed blood, of: colch k*
- **delivery**; during: bufo hr1 loxo-lae bnm12•
- **diarrhea**; from suppressed: abrot k2
- **dysentery**; in: cop k* *Ip* *Merc-c* k*
- **eruptions**; after suppressed: ars bg2 calc bg2 con bg2 *Sulph* bg2
- **excitement**; after: petr k* phos k*
- **fever**; during: caps bg2
- **first** part: con k*
- **hemorrhoidal** flow or menses, after sudden stopping of: *Nux-v* k*
- **last** part: *Ant-t* k* canth k* ferr-p **Hep** k* lyc *Mez* k* *Puls* k* *Sars* k* thuj zinc k*
  - **pain** in the bladder; with violent: ant-t *Sars*
  - **pus**; mixed with blood and: *Sars*
- **menses**; from suppressed: laur lyc mez mill nux-v k* senec
- **pollutions**; after: phos bg2
- **prostate** gland; from enlarged: med brm
- **sexual** excesses; after: *Phos* k*
- **smoky**: **Ter** bg2
- **urination**, blood flows from urethra; after: **Hep** k* mez puls sars sulph *Thuj* k*
- **water**, like: pall

BRICK-DUST (See Sediment - sand - red)

BURNING: *Acon* k* *Aesc* k* agar agn all-c k* **Aloe** k* alum k* alum-p k2 alum-sil k2 alumn am-c am-m k* *Ambr* anan vh1 ang *Ant-c* *Ant-t* **Apis** k* apoc arg-met *Arg-n* arn **Ars** k* ars-s-f k2 *Asaf* asc-c aspar atra-r skp7*• aur aur-ar k2 aur-m aur-s k2 bamb-a stb2.de• bapt bar-c bar-m **Bell** k* *Benz-ac* k* *Berb* boerh-d zzc1• **Borx** k* bov *Bry* k* cact cain br1 calad calc k* calc-ar k2 calc-f k2 *Calc-p* k* calc-sil k2 **Camph** k* **Cann-i** k* **Cann-s** k* *Cann-xyz* ptk1 **Canth** k* *Caps* k* carb-an k* carb-v carbn-s caust k* *Cham* k* *Chel* *Chim* chin k* chinin-ar chinin-s cimic *Clem* cob coc-c k* *Colch* k* coloc *Con* conv k* *Cop* cor-r crot-t **Cub** k* cupr cur *Dig* k* dulc k* equis-h ery-a eug *Eup-pur* eupi c1 fab bro1 *Ferr* k* ferr-ar ferr-p *Fl-ac* glon grat helon **Hep** k* hydr-ac ign k* indg *Ip* k* *Kali-ar* kali-bi k* *Kali-c* k* *Kali-i* kali-m k2 *Kali-n* kali-p kali-s kalm k*

Burning: ...
kreos k* lac-cp sk4• *Lach* lact laur led bg2 *Lil-t* k* *Lyc* k* mag-c med ptk1 **Merc** k* **Merc-c** k* *Mez* k* morg-p fmm1• mur-ac mygal **Nat-ar** **Nat-c** k* nat-m k* nat-p **Nat-s** k* nicc **Nit-ac** k* nux-m **Nux-v** k* olnd k* op ox-ac par k* pareir petr *Petros* k* *Ph-ac* k* phos k* pic-ac plb pop bro1 prun psor ptel c1 *Puls* k* ran-b tl1 ran-s rhod k* *Rhus-r* *Rhus-t* k* sabad k* *Sabin* k* sang *Sars* k* sec k* senec k* seneg k* sep k* sil k* skat br1 spig squil k* *Staph* k* stram k* sul-ac k* **Sulph** k* syc bka1*• tab *Tarent* *Ter* k* **Thuj** k* til ban1• tritic-vg fd5.de **Uva** k* vanil fd5.de verat k* vesp viol-t zinc k* zinc-p k2

- **accompanied** by:
  - **constipation** (See RECTUM - Constipation - accompanied - urine - hot)
  - ○ **Back**; pain in (See BACK - Pain - accompanied - urine - burning)
- **acid**, as from: am tl1 ox-ac
- **children**; in: (↗*urination - after - agg. - children*) borx h2*
- **menses** | **before** | **agg.**: apis *Canth* k* verat zinc
  - **during** | **agg.**: nux-v zinc k*
- **urination** | **after**:
  - **agg.** | **children**; in: (↗*children*) merc mtf33
  - **before** | **after**; and: seneg ptk1

CALCIUM increased: cortico sp1

CASTS, containing: *Apis* k* *Ars* bro1 aur-m bro1 borx br1 brach bro1 calc-ar k2 *Canth* bro1 *Carb-ac* bro1 carc sp1* chel bro1 cortiso sp1 crot-h bro1 fab bro1 guat sp1 kali-chl k* lat-m sp1 loxo-recl bnm10• nat-ar nat-m k2 phos k* pic-ac bro1 plb k* puls-n pyrog k2* rad-br bro1 ser-ang br1 sul-ac k* sulfon bro1 ter bro1 (non:uran-met k) uran-n vanad br1

- **blood**: *Plb* *Ter*
- **children**, infants; in: borx h2
- **cylindroids**: lat-m sp1
- **epithelial**: ant-t *Apis* arg-n k* **Ars** k* bell k* brach k* canth k* carb-ac lycps-v **Merc-c** k* ph-ac hr1 *Phos* k* *Plb* k* *Ptel* a1* sul-ac k* terebe ktp9
- **fat** drops, with: *Merc-c* k* ph-ac k* **Phos** k*
- **fibrous**: cann-s k* cimic *Kalm* k* ph-ac k* phos k* sul-ac
- **granular**: canth carb-ac carc fb* coc-c helo-s bnm14• lat-m bnm6• *Merc-c* k* nat-hchls *Petr* k* phos k* pic-ac *Plb* k* rad-br c11 sul-ac k* tub jl2
- **hyaline**: brach k* carb-ac cortiso sp1 helo-s bnm14• med k2* *Petr* k* *Phos* k* *Plb* k* rad-br c11 tub jl2
- **mucous**: brach k* cann-s cimic
- **pale**: sul-ac k*
- **tubes**, of: ant-c **Apis** bism *Canth* k* *Cimic* k* cortiso sp1 *Hep* k* *Merc-c* k* phos k* pic-ac *Plb* sulph *Ter* k*
- **urate**: benz-ac bg2 berb bg2 chinin-s bg2 coc-c bg2 *Kali-c* vh kali-pic a1 lith-c bg2 *Lyc* bg2 sars bg2 *Senn* vh *Sep* bg2 urt-u bg2
  - **amel.**; discharging them: lith-c bg2 lyc bg2 sep bg2
- **waxy**: brach k* morph k* *Phos* k*
- **yellowish**: sul-ac k*

CHLORIDES:

- **decreased**: bar-m bro1 chel bro1 coloc bro1
- **increased**: chinin-s bro1 guat sp1 pitu-p sp1 rad-br bro1 senn bro1

CLOUDY: acet-ac k* *Acon* k* acon-l a1 *Aesc* k* agar k* agn k* aloe alum k* alum-sil k2 alumn k* am-c k* am-m *Ambr* k* amm-fml br1 *Anac* k* anan vh1 ang c1 *Ant-c* k* *Ant-t* k* **Apis** k* apoc k* arb br1 arg-met k* *Arn* k* *Ars* k* ars-h hr1 ars-i aspar k* atro a1 *Aur* k* aur-i k2 aur-m k* aur-m-n hr1 *Bell* k* benz-ac k* **Berb** k* bond a1 bov k* brom k* **Bry** k* *Cact* k* calad *Calc* k* calc-f k* calc-i k2 calc-sil k2 camph k* *Cann-s* k* **Canth** k* carb-an k* **Carb-v** k* **Carbn-s** *Card-m* k* *Caust* k* **Cham** k* **Chel** k* *Chim* bro1 chim-m hr1 **Chin** k* chin-b hr1 chinin-ar *Chinin-s* k* **Cina** k* cinch a1 cinnb k* clem k* coc-c k* coca *Colch* k* colchin a1 coli jl2 *Coloc* k* com **Con** k* cop k* crot-c sk4• crot-h crot-t k* *Cupr* k* cur cycl k* *Daph* k* *Dig* k* *Dulc* k* elaps ferr k* ferr-ar fic-m gya1 galeoc-c-h gms1• gast a1 *Gels* get a1 **Graph** k* *Grat* k* hell bro1 helon bro1 *Hep* k* hydr-ac hydrc k* hyos k* hyper k* iber a1 ign k* indg k* iod k* *Ip* k* kali-act kali-ar kali-bi *Kali-c* k* kali-chl k* kali-i k* kali-m k2 *Kali-n* k* *Kali-p* kali-s kali-sil k2 ketogl-ac rly4• kreos k* lac-ac a1 *Lac-c* *Lach* k* laur k* lith-c k* *Lyc* k* lyss k* mag-c k* *Mag-m* k* mand rsj7• mang a1 marb-w es1• mela a1 menis a1 meph a1 **Merc** k* *Merc-c* k* mez k* morph a1 mosch b2.de* mur-ac b2.de* **Myric** k* nat-c k* *Nat-m* k* nat-n a1 nat-p *Nit-ac* k* nit-m-ac bro1 *Nux-v* k* oci a1* oena a1 ol-an hr1 olnd *Op* k* pall k* par pen a1 *Petr* k* **Ph-ac** k* **Phos** k* plat k* *Plb* k* *Psor* k* *Puls* k* ran-b c1 raph k* rat k* rhod k* rhus-t k* rob hr1 rumx

Cloudy: ...
ruta b2.de* **Sabad** k* sabin k* *Sang* bg2 sarr k* *Sars* k* sec k* sel b7a.de *Seneg* k* **Sep** k* sil k* sin-a a1 sin-n hr1 sol-t-ae a1 solid bro1 spirae a1 stram k* sul-ac k* sul-i k2 **Sulph** k* sumb a1* **Ter** bg2* *Thuj* k* uva valer k* vario hr1 verat k* *Verat-v* hr1 viol-t k* zinc k* zinc-m a1 zing k*

- **morning**: berb k* cann-s k* chel lyss hr1 meph k* oci-sa sk4• zinc k*
  - **left** standing for a while; when: chel k* chinin-ar dig k*
- **night**: alum k* kali-bi k* ol-an a1 phos k* sulph k* zinc a1
- **brown**: petr h2*
- **chalk** had been stirred into it, as if: alum k* *Ph-ac* k* *Sulph*
- **fever**; with: ars k* bell k* berb bry k* lyc k* ph-ac k* *Phos* k* puls k* rhus-t k* sabad k* sars k* sep k*
- **gray** clouds: lyc k*
- **left** standing for a while; when: acet-ac agar k* aloe alum k* alum-p k2 alumn am-c k* am-m k* ambr k* ang k* ant-t *Apis* arg-n arn k* *Ars* k* ars-s-f k2 arum-m a1 aur k* aur-ar k2 aur-s k2 bar-c **Bell** k* *Berb* bov brom **Bry** k* *Calc* k* *Carbn-s Caust* k* **Cham** k* **Chel Chin** k* chinin-ar k2 *Chinin-s* k* cimic k* *Cina* k* coc-c cocc b2.de* *Coloc* k* colocin a1 *Con* k* crot-t *Cupr Dig* k* *Dulc* k* equis-h ery-a ferr ferr-act ferr-ar ferr-p **Graph** k* *Grat* k* hell b2.de* *Hep* k* iod b2.de* kali-n k* kreos lach *Laur* k* lob **Lyc** mag-m manc k* mang k* *Meph* k* *Merc* k* *Mez* k* nat-c k* *Nit-ac* k* ol-an olnd k* *Par* k* *Petr* k* **Ph-ac** k* phos k* *Plat* k* rat rhod b2.de* *Rhus-t* k* sabad k* sabin b2.de* sang *Sars* k* *Seneg* k* sep k* sil h2* squil k* sul-ac k* *Sulph* k* **Ter** *Thuj* k* *Valer* k* verat verat-v k* visc c1 *Zinc* k* zinc-p k2
- **limewater**: anac b4a.de calc b4a.de canth b7.de* colch bg2 *Ign* b7.de* kali-c b4a.de sabad b7.de* sars b4a.de sep b4a.de* sul-ac b4a.de **Zinc** b4a.de*
- **passing**, soon after: ang k* aspar k* bar-c k* **Berb** k* *Cham* **Chel** k* coloc k* *Lyc* k* nat-c k* rhus-t k* seneg sil k*
- **perspiration**; with: chin k* cina k* con k* dulc k* ign k* **Ip** k* **Merc** k* **Phos** k* puls k* rhus-t k* sabad k* sep k*
- **reddish** clouds: ambr h1* kali-n k*
- **rest**; even after: coli jl2
- **turning** agg.: bell ptk1 berb ptk1 **Bry** ptk1 *Cham* ptk1 chel ptk1 chin ptk1 graph ptk1 lyc ptk1 *Ph-ac* ptk1 ter ptk1
- **urination** agg.; during: *Ambr* anac k* *Ars* k* aspar **Canth** k* carb-an **Chel** k* colch dulc *Hep* hyos *Merc* mur-ac k* nat-ar *Rhus-t* sabin k* santin *Sars* k* *Sep* k* sulph k* **Ter** k* verat k* zinc
- **white** clouds: cann-xyz bg2 chin bg2 cina *Con* bg2 cycl bg2 dulc tl1 gonotox jl2 graph tl1 maland jl2 mur-ac nat-m k* nit-ac h2* oscilloc jl2 ph-ac k* plat k* *Prot* jl2 rhus-t k* *Sars* k* ser-a-c jl2 tub jl2
  - **turbid**, which becomes more so as the emission continues: oscilloc jl2 tub jl2 ven-m rsj12•
    - **flocks**; so that the last drops look like: rhus-t *Sars Sep*

COLD agg.: agar k* *Nit-ac* k*

COLOR:

- **black**: ang k* apis bg2* arn k2 *Ars* k* *Ars-h* k* ben-d c2 *Canth* k* **Carb-ac** k* chion k* cina **Colch** k* *Dig* k* erig k* *Hell* k* hydroph rsj6• kali-ar *Kali-c* k* *Kali-chl* k* kali-m k2 kreos bg2 **Lach** k* merc-c k* *Nat-m* k* *Pareir* k* *Phos* k* sec **Ter** k* verat
  - **dung**; as if mixed with: ars ptk1*
  - **ink**, like: *Apis* bro1 arn k* *Ben-d* bro1 *Benz-ac* bro1 canth bro1 *Carb-ac* bro1 **Colch** k* crot-h tl1 dig bro1 *Hell* bro1 kreos bro1 lach bro1 merc-c bro1 naphtin bro1 nit-ac bro1 pareir bro1 sec k2 *Ter* bro1
  - **left** standing for a while; when: thymol sp1
- **blackish**: kali-c k*
- **bluish**: nit-ac k*
  - **indican**, containing: alf bro1 indol bro1 nit-ac k* nux-m br1* pic-ac k*
- **brown**: *Acon* k* agath-a nl2• aids nl2• alum alumn k* *Ambr* k* ant-c k* ant-t b7.de* apis k* arizon-l nl2• **Arn** k* **Ars** k* ars-h hr1 *Asaf* k* atro a1 *Aur* b4a.de bar-c k* bell k* **Benz-ac** k* brom **Bry** k* bufo cadm-met sp1 calc k* camph k* canth ptk1 *Carb-ac* k* *Card-m* k* carl a1 *Caust* bg2 cere-b a1 **Chel** k* **Chin** bg2 *Cimx* k* cit-ac rly4• coc-c k* *Colch* k* coloc k* *Con* k* cupr *Dig* k* digin a1 dros k* frax a1 graph *Hell* hep k* ip irid-met srj5• kali-bi k* kali-i k* *Kreos* k* lach k* lact k* lil-t lyc k* lyss a1 *Manc* k* med hr1 merc k* **Merc-c** k* *Myric* k* *Nat-c* b4a.de nat-m *Nit-ac* k* olnd k* op k* osm a1 petr k* *Ph-ac* b4a.de *Phos* k* plb k* positr nl2• prun k* *Puls* k* rhod b4.de* sal-ac hr1 *Sec* k* sep k* serp a1 squil k* stann hr1 stram sul-ac k* sulph k* symph fd3.de• tarent k* thuj bg2 valer k* vanil fd5.de zinc k* [tax jsj7]
  - **beer**, like: *Ars* hr1 *Aspar* k* *Benz-ac Bry* k* **Chel** k* *Coloc* k* *Hyper* k* *Myric* hr1 phos k* podo fd3.de• puls k* sacch-a fd2.de• stry k* **Sulph** k*
  - **chestnut**: eupi a1 *Kreos* k*

Color – brown: ...

- **cow**-dung with water, like: **Ars** k*
- **dark**: *Acon* k* aesc k* agath-a nl2• all-c *All-s* k* *Ambr* k* ant-c b7.de* ant-t k* *Apis* b7a.de* apoc bro1 arg-n bro1 *Arn* k* *Ars* k* asaf k* *Bar-c* k* *Bell* bro1 *Benz-ac* bro1 *Bry* bro1 *Calc* k* camph k* *Canth* bro1 *Carb-ac* k* carb-v bro1 *Caust* k* **Chel** k* chinin-s bro1 coc-c bro1 *Colch* k* crot-h bro1 *Dig* k* *Eup-per* k* *Eup-pur* fl-ac bro1 *Graph* k* hell bro1 jatr-c kali-c bro1 kali-chl bro1 *Lach* k* *Lept* k* loxo-lae bnm12• lup a1 *Lyc* k* lyss hr1 *Merc* merc-c bro1 myric bro1 nat-c bro1 nat-hchls bro1 nit-ac k* nux-m b7.de* *Nux-v* bro1 *Op* k* osm k* petr k* ph-ac b4.de* phos k* phyt bro1 pic-ac bro1 *Plb* k* *Podo* k* positr nl2• prun bro1 *Psor* k* puls k* rhod b4.de* rhus-t lp* *Sec* k* **Sep** k* sin-a a1 solid bro1 spirae a1 staph bro1 sul-ac b4a.de sulfon bro1 sulph k* tab k* *Ter* bro1 valer k* *Verat* b7a.de zing k*
  - **prune** juice or prune colored; like: sec
- **fever**; during: *Acon* k* arn k* *Bell* k* bry k* carb-v k* ip k* lyc k* *Nux-v* k* puls k* rhus-t k* **Sep** k* **Verat** k*
- **menses**; during: eupi nat-m k*
- **perspiration**; during: acon k* ant-t k* arn k* **Ars** k* bell k* bry k* *Calc* k* canth k* carb-v k* hep k* ip k* *Merc* k* puls k* *Sel* k* **Sep** k* staph k* *Sulph* k* thuj k* *Verat* k*
- **reddish**: aids nl2• ant-c k* bell k* **Benz-ac** k* *Canth* k* **Chel** k* dig digin a1 iod k* lyc k* nat-ar phos k* plb k* puls hr1 sep k* sul-ac h2* sumb a1 thuj a1 tub jl2 verat k*
- **wash** off; difficult to: cadm-met gm1
- **yellowish**: agath-a nl2• *Ambr* k* card-m hr1 *Dig* k* lyss k* squil h1* [tax jsj7]

- **clay**-colored: agar anac k* berb cor-r laur nat-m sabad k* samb xxb1 sars k* **Sep** sul-ac k* zinc k*
  - **left** standing for a while; when: cham ferr-ma laur
  - **shaking**; while: anac
- **coffee**, like: apis berb cob kali-n k* lac-c k* *Lach* malar jl2 *Nat-m* k* phyt k*
  - **blood**; from admixture with: kali-n
- **dark**: **Acon** k* acon-f a1 *Aesc* k* agar k* agath-a nl2• agn k* all-s k* aloe k* alum k* alum-p k2 am-c b2.de am-caust k* am-m b2.de ambr b2.de anag k* ang k* anil a1 *Ant-c* k* **Ant-t** k* **Apis** k* apoc k* aran hr1 arg-mur a1 *Arg-n* k* *Arn* k* *Ars* k* *Ars-i* k* arum-d a1 asaf k* asc-t k* astac a1 aur b2.de* bad a1 bamb-a stb2.de• *Bapt* k* bar-c b2.de **Bell** k* **Benz-ac** k* berb k* bov k* brach k* brom k* **Bry** k* cadm-met sp1 **Calc** k* calc-f k* calc-i k2 *Calc-p* k* camph b2.de cann-i k* cann-s b2.de* *Canth* k* caps k* *Carb-ac* k* *Carb-v* k* carbn-s k* card-m k* carl a1 caust b2.de* cedr k* cer-s a1 cere-b a1 **Chel** k* chim k* *Chin* k* *Chinin-ar* k* chinin-s k* chlf a1 chlol a1* cic k* cimic k* cinch a1* clem k* cob k* cob-n sp1* coc-c k* coff b2.de **Colch** k* coll a1 coloc b2.de con k* conch a1* conv k* cop k* **Crot-h** k* crot-t k* cub a1* cund a1 cupr k* cur cycl k* *Dig* k* digin a1 diosm br1 dirc a1 dros b2.de* dulc b2.de* eberth jl2 echi *Elat* k* **Equis-h** erig k* ery-a k* eug k* *Eup-per* k* falco-pe nl2• ferr k* ferr-ar ferr-i k* ferr-p form a1 fuc a1 gast a1 gels k* germ-met srj5• get a1* gins a1 glon k* graph k* **Hell** k* *Hep* k* *Hydr* k* hyos k* hyper k* ign b7.de* *Iod* k* *Ip* k* iris *Jab* k* kali-ar k* kali-bi k* kali-br a1 kali-c k* *Kali-i* k* kali-m k2 kali-n k* kali-p kreos b2.de **Lac-ac** k* *Lac-d* k* **Lach** k* lat-m bnm6• led b2.de lepi a1 leptos-ih jl2 *Lil-t* k* lina a1 *Lith-c* loxo-recl bnm10• *Lyc* k* lyss hr1 m-arct b2.de* malar al2 mand rsj7• marb-w es1• med hr1* menis a1 **Merc** k* **Merc-c** k* *Merc-i-f* k* *Merc-i-r* k* merc-n a1 mez k* mill k* mit a1 morph a1 *Mur-ac* k* *Myric* k* *Nat-ar Nat-c* k* *Nat-m* k* nat-p k* nat-s k* nat-sil fd3.de• nit-ac k* *Nux-m* k* *Nux-v* k* oena a1 olnd b2.de op k* oscilloc jl2 osm a1 pall k* par k* petr k* ph-ac k* phasco-ci rbp2 *Phos* k* physala-p bnm7• pic-ac k* plat b2.de **Plb** k* plect a1 *Podo* k* polyp-p a1 *Ptel* k* *Puls* k* pyrog jl2 rheum b2.de* rhod b2.de* rhus-g a1 *Rhus-t* k* ric a1 sabad sabin k* samb k* sang k* sapin a1 sars k* *Sec* k* **Sel** k* senec k* seneg k* **Sep** k* serp a1 sil b2.de sin-a a1 sin-n hr1 sol-t-ae a1 solid ptk1 spig k* squil b2.de* stach a1 stann *Staph* k* still a1 stram k* stront-c k* sul-ac k* sul-i k2 *Sulph* k* tab k* tanac a1 tarax k* tell k* **Ter** k* thuj k* thymol sp1 trif-p a1 tritic-vg fd5.de (non:uran-met k) uran-n ust a1 vac a1 valer k* vanil fd5.de **Verat** k* *Verat-v* k* vip k* wies a1 xan k* zinc k* zinc-p k2 zing
  - **morning**: **Chel** k* mez k* sang k* seneg k*
  - **evening**: digin a1 osm a1 ruta sang k* thuj k*
  - **flecks**; in: hell ptk1
  - **menses**; during: nat-m k* sars k*
- **flesh** colored: coloc bg2
  - **masses**: canth bg2
- **gray**: berb bg2 bufo bg2 chin bg2 hyos bg2 kali-i bg2 merc-c b4a.de* seneg b4.de

Urine

- **greenish**: anac bg2 apis *Ars* k* *Aur* k* bapt k* bell k* berb k* bor-ac bg2 bov k* calc k* **Camph** k* cann-i bro1 *Carb-ac* k* cean bro1* cer-s a1 *Chel* k* *Chim* k* *Chin* k* *Chinin-ar* chinin-s *Cina* k* *Colch* k* *Cop* k* corv-cor bdg• crot-h cupr bg2 cyt-l bro1* dig fic-m gya1 hura bg2 hyos bg2 *Iod* k* iris bg1 kali-ar *Kali-c* k* kali-s fkr2.de *Mag-c* k* mag-s k* mang k* merc **Merc-c** k* methyl br1 nat-m k* *Nit-ac* k* ol-an k* ped a1 phel k* phos k* puls mtf33 *Rheum* k* *Rhod* k* *Ruta* k* sal-ac bg2 sal-fr sle1• *Santin* bro1 saroth sp1 seneg k* *Sep* b4a.de suis-pan rly4• sul-ac sulph k* thymol sp1 (non:uran-met k) uran-n uva bg2* *Verat* k*
  - **afternoon**: mag-c h2*
  - **black**: kali-chl kali-m k2
  - **bright**: sal-fr sle1•
  - **dark**: anac k* *Carb-ac* k* nat-m k* *Santin*
  - **light**: bapt k* cina
  - **red** sediments; with: mag-s ptk1
  - **white**: camph b7.de*
- **high**-colored [=bright] (See greenish - bright; red - bright; yellow - bright)
- **high**-colored [=dark] (See dark)
- **mahogany**: aesc k* *Eup-per* k* phyt bg2 plb k*
- **milky** (See Milky)
- **ochre** (See yellow)
- **olive**-hue, milky: pic-ac k*
- **orange** (See yellow - orange)
- **pale**: acet-ac k* acon k* aeth k* *Agar* k* alco a1 *Alum* k* alum-p k2 *Am-c* k* ambr k* anac k* *Ang* k* ant-c k* ant-t b2.de* anthraci apis k* apoc k* aq-pet a1 *Arg-met* arg-n k* *Arn* k* *Ars* k* ars-h hr1 *Arum-t* k* asaf k* asc-c a1* astac hr1 atro k* aur k* bac jl2 *Bell* k* *Berb* k* bism b2.de* brach k* *Bry* k* bufo cadm-met tpw6 caj a1 calad calc k* *Calc-f* k* calc-i k2 calc-s a1 camph k* *Cann-i* k* **Cann-s** b2.de* cann-xyz ptk1 canth k* caps k* carb-ac k* *Carb-v* k* carbn-s carl a1 *Caul* k* caust b2.de* cedr k* *Cham* k* *Chel* k* *Chin* k* chinin-ar chinin-s k* cimic k* cina cinch a1 *Clem* k* cob k* coc-c k* cocc k* coch a1* cod a1 coff k* coff-t a1 *Colch* k* *Coloc* k* **Con** k* cop k* *Croc* hr1 crot-t k* cund a1 cycl k* dig k* dros b2.de* dulc k* echi elat a1* equis-h k* erig k* eup-per hr1 eup-pur k* euphr k* fago a1 ferr k* ferr-i k* ferr-p k* fl-ac k* gast a1 gels k* glon k* gnaph a1 ham k* hell k* hell-o a1* hell-v a1 helon k* *Hep* k* hydr k* hyos k* *Ign* k* iod k* jac-c a1 kali-ar *Kali-br* a1* kali-c k* kali-i k* kali-m k2 **Kali-n** k* ketogl-ac rly4• *Kreos* k* lac-ac k* *Lac-d* k* lach k* laur k* **Led** lil-t linu-c a1 *Lyc* k* lycps-v bro1 m-aust b2.de* macro a1 *Mag-c* k* mag-m k* mag-s k* med k2 mela a1 merc k* **Merc-c** k* mez k* morph a1 mosch k* *Mur-ac* k* nat-ar nat-c k* **Nat-m** k* nat-n a1 nat-p k* *Nat-s* k* *Nit-ac* k* nit-m-ac a1 nux-m k* *Nux-v* k* oena a1 ol-an k* olnd op k* ox-ac k* par k* ped a1 peti a1 **Ph-ac** k* phel k* *Phos* k* phys a1 phyt k* pic-ac k* *Plan* k* plat k* plb k* podo hr1 positr nl2• *Puls* k* ran-s a1 raph k* rat a1* rheum k* *Rhod* k* *Rhus-t* k* sal-al blc1• samb b2.de* sang bg2* sapin a1 sarr hr1 **Sars** k* sec k* seneg k* sep k* sil h2* sin-n a1 sol-t-ae a1 spig b2.de* spong b2.de* squil k* stann hr1 *Staph* k* *Stram* k* *Stront-c* k* stroph-s sp1 sul-ac k* sulph k* tab k* tanac a1 tarax k* ter k* teucr k* thuj k* til a1 trif-p a1 ust a1 vanil fd5.de verat k* verat-v hr1 vib hr1 vinc k* visc c1 wies a1 zinc k* zing k* [heroin sdj2]
  - **afternoon**: sars h2*
  - **evening**: mag-c h2*
  - **fever**; during: cedr cham
  - **headache** and cardialgia, in: kali-c hr1
  - **perspiration**; during: arn k* *Bell* k* chin k* con k* ign k* **Ph-ac** k* phos k* puls k* rhus-t k* stram k* thuj k*
- **pink**: nat-s k2 sulfon bro1
- **red**: absin a1 *Acon* k* *Aesc* k* aeth k* agar k* agn *All-c* k* aloe *Alum* k* alumn k* am-c b4.de am-caust a1 am-m k* anan vh1 *Ant-c* k* *Ant-t* k* *Apis* k* *Arg-n* k* *Arn* k* ars k* ars-h a1* ars-i art-v hr1 arund a1* asc-t k* aur k* aur-ar k2 aur-m a1 aur-s a1* bad k* *Bapt* k* *Bell* k* **Benz-ac** k* *Berb* k* bond a1 *Bov* k* **Bry** k* bufo *Cact* k* calad calc k* calc-i k2 *Camph* k* cann-i k* cann-s k* **Canth** k* caps k* carb-ac k* *Carb-an* k* *Carb-v* k* carbn-s caust k* cedr k* *Chel* k* chin b7.de* clem k* coc-c k* cocc k* coff k* *Colch* k* coloc b4.de* con k* *Cop* k* corn a1 corv-cor bdg• *Crot-h* k* crot-t k* cupr k* cycl k* daph k* dig k* digin a1 dros bg2 *Dulc* k* elaps epil a1* equis-h ery-m a1 ferr k* ferr-ar ferr-i k2 ferr-ma a1 ferr-p gnaph a1 *Grat* k* haem a1 hell bg2 *Hep* k* hydroph rsj6• *Iod* k* ip k* iris kali-ar *Kali-bi* k* *Kali-c* k* kali-i k* kali-m k2 kali-n k* kali-s kali-sil k2 kola stb3• kreos k* lac-ac a1 lach k* lachn k* laur led k* *Lept* k* lil-t *Lith-c* k* lob k* *Lyc* k* mela a1 *Merc* k* merc-c k* merc-i-f k* merc-i-r k* mez k* mill a1 *Mur-ac* k* nat-m k* nat-p k* *Nux-m* b7a.de *Nux-v* k* **Oci** a1 oena a1 ol-j a1 *Op* k* par k* ped a1 petr k* phos k* phyt k* pic-ac k* *Plat* k* plb k* plumbg a1 podo k* ptel a1 puls k* rheum k* rhod b4.de rhus-r k* *Rhus-t* k* sabin k* sang k* *Sars* k* *Sel* k*
- **red**: ...
  senec k* seneg k* **Sep** k* *Sil* k* sol-t-ae a1 spira a1 squil k* staph k* **Stram** k* sul-ac k* sul-i k2 *Sulph* k* sumb k* tab k* tax k* *Ter* k* thuj k* tong a1 tub k* ust a1 valer b7a.de verat k* verin a1 vesp hr1 voes a1 zinc k*
  - **evening**: **Sel** k* sulph h2*
  - **blood**-red: aesc apis bell k* *Berb* k* *Calc* *Carb-v* *Cham* k* coff k* *Crot-h* k* crot-t k* ferr k* *Hell* k* *Hep* k* *Kali-i* k* merc petr k* pic-ac k* rhus-t k* *Sep* k*
  - **bluish**-red: rhus-t hr1
  - **bright** red: am-m k* bov k* sumb a1 upa a1
  - **brownish** red: *Ant-c* k* *Ant-t* k* apis apoc bell hr1 *Chel* k* coc-c k* *Hep* k* *Kali-pic* a1* *Lac-ac* k* lyc h2* merc k* plb k* puls k* rhod k* sul-ac a1 sulph sumb a1 thuj a1 til a1
  - **children**; in: lyc tl1 sanic tl1
  - **clear**, and: *Acon* chel
  - **cloud**; like a red: ambr bg2* kali-n bg2
  - **dark**-red: *Acon* b7.de* aesc aloe ant-c k* ant-t k* *Apis* b7a.de* *Arg-n* k* *Arn* b7.de* *Ars* b4a.de ars-h a1* asc-t hr1 *Bapt* k* bell b4.de* *Benz-ac* k* *Bry* b7.de* caj a1 *Canth* b7a.de* *Carb-v* k* cedr k* *Chel* b7a.de clem k* cob k* coc-c bro1 *Coloc* b4a.de *Cop* *Crot-h* k* crot-t a1 *Cupr* k* cupr-act bro1 cupr-ar a1 *Cycl* a1* *Dig* bro1 dor a1 *Ferr* k* grat k* *Hep* k* ip k* jug-r a1 *Kali-bi* bro1 *Kali-c* b4a.de *Lob* k* loxo-recl bnm10• *Lyc* k* *Merc* k* merc-c bro1 merc-d bro1 merc-i-f k* merc-i-r nat-p hr1 nat-s k* nux-m b7.de* nux-v bro1 op k* *Pareir* k* petr bro1 phos k* phyt k* pic-ac a1 *Plan* k* plb k* polyg-h puls k* rheum *Rhus-t* b7a.de sec k* sel bro1 **Sep** k* solid bro1 *Squil* k* staph k* sul-ac k* tab k* tarent k* tell k* ter hr1 thuj k* valer k*
    - **night**: crot-t a1 mosch k*
  - **deep**-red: alco a1 ant-c ant-t *Bell* a1 benz-ac a1 carb-v cedr a1 cob a1 cupr fuch br1 hep lob *Merc* phal a1 phyt plb a1 *Rhus-r* sul-ac sumb a1 tell a1
  - **fever**; with: *Nux-v*
  - **fiery** red: *Acon* b7.de* agar a1 all-c bro1 ant-c bro1 ant-t b7a.de *Apis* bro1 apoc bro1 arg-n bro1 ars k* bell k* *Benz-ac* bro1 *Berb* bro1 *Bry* b7.de* camph k* *Cann-s* b7.de* *Canth* bro1 carb-ac bro1 chel bro1 chim bro1 chin colch b7.de* crot-t k* cupr-act bro1 *Equis-h* bro1 euon bro1 glon bro1 *Hell* bro1 *Hep* bro1 kali-bi bro1 *Kali-c* b4a.de* *Lith-c* bro1 *Lyc* bro1 merc k* merc-d bro1 *Myric* bro1 nit-ac bro1 oci bro1 par b7.de* phyt bro1 pic-ac bro1 plb k* puls bro1 rheum bro1 *Rhus-t* bro1 sabin bro1 sars b4a.de* sel k* senec bro1 sul-ac a1 sulph bro1 *Ter* bro1 thuj bro1 uva bro1 verat-v bro1
  - **left** standing for a while; when: dig h2
  - **perspiration**; with: cedr
- **sherry**: apoc k* squil sulph k*
- **smoke**-color: am-be bro1 *Benz-ac* bro1 carb-ac k* crot-h k* hell bro1 nat-hchls **Ter** k*
- **violet**: apis indg k* *Mur-ac* k* nux-m
- **white**: *All-s* k* alum k* alumn k* am-c k* ambr k* ang k* *Apis* b7a.de arn k* aur bg2 bapt k* bell k* berb bry k* cann-s k* canth k* carb-v bg2 *Caust* k* cham *Chel* k* *Chin* k* cina k* *Coloc* k* con k* cycl k* *Dulc* k* elae a1 ferr ferr-i k2 hep bg2 iod bg2 lac-ac k* lepi a1 lyc k* *Manc* a1* marb-w es1• merc k* mur-ac bg2 nat-m k* nit-ac bg2 *Nux-v* hr1 **Ph-ac** bg2* phos k* plan k* *Psor* hr1 *Rhus-t* k* sars b4.de* sec k* *Spong* k* *Sulph* k*
  - **morning**: lac-ac k*
  - **chalk**; as if mixed with: merc *Ph-ac* **Phos**
    - **jellylike**: cina *Coloc*
    - **left** standing for a while; when: nit-ac
  - **close**; at: ph-ac ptk1 sars ptk1
- **yellow**: absin bro1 alum b4.de* am-c bg2 ang bg2 ant-c b7.de* *Arn* b7.de* ars b4.de* aur bg2* *Bell* b4.de* berb bro1* bov b4.de* *Bry* b7.de* canth b7.de* carb-an b4.de* carb-v bg2 card-m bro1* cassia-s ccrh1• cean bro1 *Cham* b7.de* chel tl1 chin bro1 chord-umb rly4• daph bg2* fic-m gya1 hydr bro1 hyos b7.de* ign b7.de* iod b4.de* *Ip* bg2 kalm bro1 lac-ac bro1 *Lach* bg2* laur b7.de* led b7.de* *Lyc* b4a.de mag-m b4.de* mang b4.de* mez b4.de* muru a1 nat-c b4.de* oci bro1 op bro1 petr b4.de* petr-ra shn4• plb bro1 prun bg2 rheum b7.de* sabad b7.de* sabin b7.de samb bg2 *Sars* b4.de* seneg b4.de* *Sep* b4a.de* solid bro1 suis-hep rly4• sulph mtf33 tetox pin2• trad a1* tritic-vg fd5.de uva bro1 verat b7.de* *Zinc* bg2

- **bright**: agar b4.de* alum b4.de* ambr b7.de* anac b4.de* *Ang* b7a.de bell b4.de* carb-v b4.de* card-m bg2 cham b7a.de chel bg2 chin b7.de* colch b7.de* *Coloc* b4.de* *Con* b4a.de dig b4.de* dulc b4.de* hep b4.de* kali-n b4.de* mang bg2 merc b4.de* nat-c b4a.de *Nat-m* b4a.de orot-ac rly4• par b7.de* ph-ac b4.de* plat b4.de* *Rheum* b7.de* rhod b4a.de samb b7a.de sars h2* sec b7.de* *Sep* b4.de* spong b7.de* verat b7a.de *Zinc* b4a.de
- **dark**: absin br1 *Aesc* agar k* agath-a nl2• am-caust a1 am-m b7.de ambr bg2 amp rly4• ang a1 *Arg-n* k* *Ars* astac a1 berb k* bov bro1 bry bro1 bufo bg2 camph bro1 *Cedr* **Chel** k* chen-a bro1 chlf a1 clem a1 *Con* crot-t bro1 ferr a1 ham fd3.de• *Hep* k* *Iod* bro1 *Kali-c* k* kali-p bro1* kali-s fd4.de lac-h htj1• med jl2 myric bro1 *Nat-c* nat-sil fd3.de• ozone sde2• petr h2* *Pic-ac* bro1 plut-n srj7• podo bro1 samb b7.de* *Sang* k* spong b7.de* staph k* suis-hep rly4• symph fd3.de• vanil fd5.de [spect dfg1]
- **golden**: card-m vml3• mang h2 phos h2 podo fd3.de• ruta fd4.de spong fd4.de tritic-vg fd5.de
- **greenish**-yellow: camph b7.de* chin b7.de* iod mtf33
- **lemon**: agar k* ambr k* *Ang* b7a.de bell k* cham b7a.de *Chel* k* coc-c k* eupi k* gins a1 ign k* lac-ac a1 lyc a1 nat-c k* nat-sil fd3.de• op k* plb a1 samb b7a.de santin syph hr1 tab k* tritic-vg fd5.de verat b7a.de zinc k*
- **light**: acon *Agar* *Aloe* *Am-m* ang *Ant-c* k* apis apoc k* arg-n a1 ars k* **Aur** k* bar-m *Bell* k* berb k* bufo cact camph *Cann-s* carb-an carb-v k* *Cham* chel chin colch k* *Crot-t* k* *Daph* k* hydr-ac *Hyos* iod jatr-c kali-bi kali-n kalm **Lach** *Lact* laur k* led mag-m k* *Nat-c* nat-s k2 nit-ac phos a1 plb podo fd3.de• raph samb sarr hr1 **Sep** sin-n hr1 symph fd3.de• thuj a1* verat k* vinc hr1 zinc k*
- **orange**: absin a1 am-m androc srj1• ang k* ars-h hr1 *Canth* b7a.de carb-an k* chord-umb rly4• *Cina* coloc a1 crot-t k* cupr-ar k* cypra-eg sde6.de• ketogl-ac rly4• *Lept* hr1* **Lyc** k● nat-sil fd3.de• nit-ac h2 ol-an a1 phos k* plan k* plb k* santin seneg k* til a1 tritic-vg fd5.de vanil fd5.de zinc k* [tax jsj7]
- **reddish**-yellow: acon berb a1 cycl a1 daph myris a1 nat-m a1 ptel a1 *Staph* a1* sumb a1 tab a1 *Thuj* a1 tong a1
- **saffron**: aloe ars-s-r hr1 *Cina* form a1* kali-p oci a1* santin
- **straw**: agath-a nl2• alum h2 kali-p fd1.de•
- **sulphur**; like: ferr b7a.de
- **thick** and turbid like rotten eggs: con bg2 daph br1 rhus-t bg2
- **wine**: mez h2*

COLORLESS: acon-l a1 *Agar* k* alum k* anac ang apis *Apoc* k* arum-m hr1 atro a1 bar-c bell k* berb calen a1* camph k* **Cann-i** k* carb-ac k* *Caust* *Cham* k* coc-c cod hr1 *Coff* k* coff-t a1 con crot-h k* *Dig* digin a1 *Ferr* k* **Gels** hyos hyosin a1 indg a1 kali-n *Kreos* k* *Lac-d* hr1 laur k* lil-t lith-c *Lyc* lp *Lycps-v* lyss hr1 *Mag-p* med k* mosch k* *Murx* nat-ar **Nat-m** k* *Nux-v* k* ol-an a1 *Ph-ac* k* *Phos* k* *Plan* k* podo fd3.de• *Puls* k* rhus-t rumx *Sang* sarr k* *Sars* k* **Sep** k* *Sil* k* squil k* stram *Sulph* k* ust k* verat k* zing k* [tax jsj7]

- **morning**: kreos hr1
- **menses**; during: *Cham* ph-ac vib
- **pain**; with paroxysms of: phos h2

CONSTITUENTS, where there is diminution of, there is increase of stools: colch k*

COPIOUS (= increased): abrom-a ks5 **Acet-ac** k* *Acon* k* adon br1 aesc *Aeth* k* *Agar* k* *Agath-a* nl2• agn k* aids nl2• all-c k* all-s allox tpw3* **Aloe** k* *Alum* k* alum-p k2 alum-sil k2 alumn am-c k* *Am-m* k* am-n a1 *Ambr* k* anac k* anan vh1 androc srj1• ang k* *Ant-c* k* ant-t k* *Anthraci* *Apis* k* *Apoc* aran-sc vh1 **Arg-met** k* **Arg-n** k* arizon-l nl2• arn k* *Ars* k* ars-br vh ars-i ars-s-f k2 *Arum-t* k* asc-c a1* **Aspar** k* aster atro *Aur* k* aur-ar k2 aur-i k2 *Aur-m* *Aur-m-n* aur-s k2 bac jl2 bamb-a stb2.de• *Bar-c* k* bar-i k2 bar-m *Bell* k* benz-ac berb *Bism* k* bit-ar wht1• bov k* brach brom bry k* bufo *Cact* cadm-met tpw6* *Cain* *Calc* k* calc-f calc-i k2 *Calc-p* k* calc-sil k2 *Camph* **Cann-i** k* cann-s k* cann-xyz ptk1 *Canth* k* caps carb-ac *Carb-an* k* carb-v b2.de* carbn-s card-m k2 caru a1 caust b2.de* cean vml3• cench k2 cham b2.de* *Chel* k* *Chim* *Chin* k* chinin-ar chinin-s k* *Chlol* chlor bg2 cic k* *Cimic* k* *Cina* k* cinnb *Clem* k* cob cob-n sp1 coc-c cocc k* coch br1 *Coff* k* *Colch* k* coli rly4• *Coloc* k* *Con* k* conv cop corv-cor bdg• *Crot-c* *Crot-h* crot-t cub *Cupr* k* cur *Cycl* k* cyt-l sp1 *Daph* k* *Dig* k* dros k* dulc k* *Echi* elaps elat *Equis-h* erig ery-a eucal br1 eup-per *Eup-pur* euph b2.de euphr k* eupi fab br1 fago falco-pe nl2• *Ferr* k* ferr-ar ferr-i ferr-m ptk2 ferr-ma ferr-p k* *Fl-ac* flor-p rsj3• foen-an a1 form gal-ac c1 gali br1 gamb **Gels** k* germ-met srj5• gink-b sbd1• gins glon glycyr-g cte1• gnaph k* graph k* grat guaj k* ham k*

Copious: ... hed sp1 hedy a1* hell k* hell-o a1* helo-s bnm14• *Helon* hep k* hyos k* *Ign* k* ins br1 *Iod* k* ip b7.de *Iris* k* jatr-c junc-e br1 kali-ar *Kali-bi* bg2 kali-br a1 *Kali-c* k* kali-chl *Kali-i* *Kali-n* k* *Kali-p* *Kali-s* kali-sil k2 *Kalm* kola br1 **Kreos** k* lac-ac mrr1 **Lac-c** k* *Lac-d* k2* *Lach* k* lact lappa br1 laur k* *Lec* **Led** k* *Lil-t* k* *Lith-c* lob *Lyc* k* *Lycps-v* k* lyss m-arct b2.de* m-aust b2.de* *Mag-c* k* mag-p *Mag-s* mang k* marb-w es1• med k2 *Meli* **Merc** k* *Merc-c* k* merc-i-f *Merc-i-r* mez morph **Mosch** k* **Mur-ac** k* *Murx* mygal *Nat-ar* **Nat-c** k* nat-m b2.de* *Nat-p* k* **Nat-s** k* nicc nicc-s br1 nit-ac k* nux-m *Nux-v* k* oci-sa sp1 *Ol-an* k* olnd k* op k* opun-s a1 *Ox-ac* oxyt ptk2 ozone sde2• pall par k* petr k* petr-ra shn4• *Petros* **Ph-ac** k* phor-t mie3• *Phos* k* *Phyt* pic-ac pin-s c2 pitu-gl skp7• pitu-p sp1 *Plan* k* *Plb* k* plut-n srj7• *Podo* *Prun* psor ptel c1 **Puls** k* *Raph* rat rauw sp1 rheum h* *Rhod* k* rhodi br1* rhus-g tmo3• **Rhus-r** **Rhus-t** k* *Ros-ca* c1 rumx ruta k* sabad k* *Sabin* k* sacch-a fd2.de• sal-al blc1• samb k* sang sanic tl1 santin c2 saroth sp1 sarr *Sars* k* scop ptk1 sec k* sel k* *Senec* *Seneg* k* sep b2.de* sil k* spartin bwa3 spartin-s br1 **Spig** k* spong k* **Squil** k* stann k* *Staph* k* stict c1 stram k* stront-c k* stroph-s sp1 sul-ac k* sul-i k2 sulfonam ks2 **Sulph** k* suprar rly4• *Syzyg* br1 tab *Tarax* k* *Tarent* k* tax tell c1 *Ter* *Teucr* k* *Ther* k* thiosin c1 *Thuj* k* thymol sp1 *Thyroiod* c1* trad a1* tril-p tritic-vg fd5.de (non:uran-met k) **Uran-n** k* valer k* vanil fd5.de ven-m rsj12• *Verat* k* verat-v **Verb** k* vib tl1* *Viol-t* k* vip visc c1 yohim c1* zinc k* zinc-p k2 zing

- **daytime**: cina ham opun-s a1 (non:opun-v a1) phys a1 pic-ac k* *Sulph* k*
- **morning**: am-m ambr k* asc-c a1 bar-act cain carb-an equis-h laur k* lyc k* mag-s k* merc *Mez* nat-c k* *Nat-p* k* *Op* peti a1 plect a1 *Sars* k* sul-ac k* vanil fd5.de vichy-g a1
  - **6** h: nat-ar
  - **waking** early; on: gink-b sbd1•
- **forenoon**: arg-n k* jug-r a1 lyc k* *Mez* phel a1 phys a1 tritic-vg fd5.de
- **noon**: op k*
- **afternoon**: *All-c* k* aloe alum k* am-c k* borx bov k* dig k* indg a1 laur k* nat-m k* nat-p k* nicc k* ol-an a1 op k* plect a1 rumx thuj k*
  - **sleep** | **siesta** agg.; after: cycl k*
- **evening**: am-c k* ars-h hr1 coloc euphr a1 fl-ac helon k* kali-chl k* laur k* **Lyc** k* lyss k* op k* ox-ac k* pall k* plect a1 sang k* sulph k* thuj k* zinc k*
  - **18**-19 h: bry tl1
  - **19** h: cic pic-ac
  - **20** h: cic
  - **22** h: phos
- **night**: agar k* allox tpw4 aloe alum bg2 am-c *Am-m* k* ambr c1* *Ant-c* k* ant-t *Apis* *Arg-met* arg-n k* ars k* *Bapt* k* bar-c k* bar-s k2 *Bell* k* bov bros-gau mrc1 bry k* *Cact* calc h2* **Calc-f** k* *Carb-ac* k* *Carb-an* k* caust k* chim a1 chin chinin-ar chlol coloc cop cupr cycl k* *Dig* euphr k* *Gels* gink-b sbd1• graph bg2 hep bg2 hyper k* kali-c bg2 kali-chl k* kali-i bro1 kali-m k2 kali-n k* kali-p *Kreos* k* *Lac-c* k* *Led* k* *Lith-c* **Lyc** k* mag-c mag-p *Med* *Merc* k* mez k* *Murx* k* nat-ar nat-c k* *Nat-m* k* nat-p *Nat-s* k* nicc k* nux-v bg2 op k* paeon a1 petr k* *Ph-ac* k* phos a1 phys a1 phyt k* plan k* plect a1 prun k* quas bro1 rhus-r rhus-t bg2 ruta sabad bg2 samb bg2 *Sang* k* *Sars* seneg bg2 *Sil* sin-n hr1 **Spig** k* squil bg2* *Stram* k* **Sulph** k* ther *Thuj* k* tritic-vg fd5.de (non:uran-met k) **Uran-n** vichy-g a1 zinc h2*
  - **midnight**: coff k* op k*
    - **after**: carb-ac ox-ac plb **Sulph** k*
      - **4** h: plb
      - **5** h: carb-ac ox-ac
  - **lying** agg.: bell
  - **menses** | **before** | **agg.**: am-m k* cann-s hyos
    - **during** | **agg.**: ph-ac
  - **stool** agg.; during: am-c sulph k*
- **accompanied** by:
  - **anemia** (See GENERALS - Anemia - accompanied - urine)
  - **cough** (See COUGH - Accompanied - urination - copious)
  - **emaciation**: merc bg2
  - **nausea**: acon bg2 castm bg2 cupr bg2 lach bg2 verat bg2
  - **offensive** urine (See Odor - offensive - accompanied - urination)
  - **thirstlessness**: bamb-a stb2.de•

Urine

- **accompanied** by: ...
  - ○ • **Abdomen**:
    - ⁝ **complaints** (See ABDOMEN - Complaints - accompanied - urination)
    - ⁝ **pain** (See ABDOMEN - Pain - accompanied - urination - profuse)
  - • **Back**; pain in the: gink-b sbd1•
  - • **Lumbar** region; pain in: ph-ac bg2
- **alternating** with:
  - • **scanty** urine: bell bg3* benz-ac k2 *Berb* k* *Dig* k* eup-per ptk1 gels k* nit-ac bg2* petr-ra shn4• sang k* senec bg3*
    - ⁝ **amel.**; copious urine does: benz-ac k2
- **amenorrhea**, with: alum am-c caul *Cham* gels nat-m sulph
- **apyrexia**, during: ars calc chin ferr graph nux-v samb valer
- **bed** agg.; in: crot-c bg2 seneg bg2
- **chill**:
  - • **after**: syph hr1*
  - • **during**: ars b4a.de* gels bg2 lec *Merc* b4a.de spig b7.de sulph b4a.de
- **coffee** agg.: cain olnd k* wies a1
- **convulsions**; after epileptic: caust j5.de *Cupr* k* lach j5.de
- **coryza**; during: *All-c* k* calc k* sep ptk1 verat
- **cough** agg.; during: *Samb* b7a.de
- **delirium**; after: *Stram* k*
- **desire**; with less: petr-ra shn4•
- **diarrhea**, with: acon h1* agar bg1 bell h1* con h2 fl-ac bg1 puls h1* spig h1
- **drunk**, more than is: ambr apis bg1* aur k* aur-m-n *Bell* k* bit-ar wht1• brucel sa3• carb-v h2* caust h2* coc-c bg2 *Coloc* k* ferr a1 irid-met srj5• kali-i kali-n h2* *Lac-ac* bg1* lac-c bg1 lach lyc bg1 *Merc* k* mur-ac h2* nat-c bg1 nat-sil fd3.de• *Nux-v* k* ph-ac k* raph k* sars bg1 sep h2* zinc h2*
- **eating**; after: puls k*
- **exhaustion**, attended with: acet-ac benz-ac *Calc-p* carb-ac chinin-s *Cimic* dig ferr lyc med
  - • **and** much thirst: chinin-s
- **fever**; during: ant-c k* arg-met k* ars *Aur-m-n* k* cedr *Cham* k* *Colch* dulc k* *Eup-pur* *Lyc* k* med k* *Mur-ac* k* ph-ac *Phos* k* pyrog c1 samb ptk1 squil k* **Stram** k*
  - • **scarlatina**; during: arum-t c1
- **headache**:
  - • **after**: asc-c k* gels bg1 ign bg1 *Iris* nux-v bg1 sang bg1
  - • **during**: acon k* *Bell* bov *Canth* *Chinin-s* *Cinnb* k* coloc k* cupr eug ferr-p *Gels* k* *Glon* k* *Ign* k* iris k* kalm k* lac-c **Lac-d** k* *Lil-t* *Mosch* k* *Ol-an* k* sang k* *Sel* sep k* sil k* (non:uran-met k) uran-n *Verat* k* vib k* vip
  - • **followed** by copious limpid urine and vomiting: iris
- **hunger**; with: bell bg2 verat k*
- **hysterical**: ol-an ptk1
- **lying** agg.: bell bg1
- **menses** | **before** | **agg.**: cinnb hyos
  - • **during**:
    - ⁝ **agg.**: canth *Cham* k* *Hyos* k* kali-bi lac-c lac-h htj1• med bg3* **Ph-ac** k* *Phyt* k* rhus-g tmo3• sars h2* sulph vib k*
    - ⁝ **beginning** of menses | **agg.**: bell h1
- **nervous**: acon bg2 bism bg2 ferr ptk1 *Ign* bg2 mosch bg2 sel bg2
  - • **women**: *Ign* valer pd xan hr1
- **pain**:
  - • **during**: arg-met ptk1 coloc bg1 lac-d ptk1 phos bg1 vib bg1
  - • **paroxysms** of: phos h2
- **perspiration**; with: **Acon** k* ant-c k* ant-t bg2 ars bg2 bell k* cham k* **Dulc** k* ign k* lach k* lyc k* mag-c k* *Mur-ac* k* nat-c k* nat-m k* *Ph-ac* k* **Phos** k* **Rhus-t** k* samb k* seneg k* spig k* squil k* stann k* stram k* thuj k*
- **puberty**, in: ferr-m ptk2
- **relief**; without: alum bg2
- **stool** agg.; during: acon bg2 am-m bg2 apis bg2 caust bg2 cic bg2 con bg2 fl-ac bg2 polyg-h bg2 spig b7.de*
- **then** scanty: sul-ac h2*
- **thirst**; with: bell bg2 verat k*

Copious: ...

- **thirstlessness**; with (See accompanied - thirstlessness)
- **travelling**: cain c1
- **vomiting**; with: acon k* ign bro1 lach verat

CREATININE increased (See GENERALS - Laboratory - creatinine)

CUTICLE forming on the surface of the urine: agar k* *All-c* alum k* alum-p k2 *Alumn* **Apis** bg2 arg-n k* aspar bg1 bell bor-ac bg1 calad *Calc* k* calc-i k2 canth k* chin k* chinin-s cob k* *Coloc* b4a.de* com crot-t k* *Dulc* *Graph* k* *Hep* k* iod k* kali-ar kali-bi k* lac-ac laur *Lyc* *Med* k* merc-c k* op **Par** k* *Petr* k* ph-ac k* *Phos* k* pic-ac bg1 plb k* *Psor* k* puls bg1* rumx k* *Sars* k* **Sep** k* sin-a sol-t-ae sul-ac k* *Sulph* k* *Sumb* thuj verat verat-v zinc [adon xyz62 bar-act xyz62]

- **iridescent**●: agar **All-c** k* alumn bapt bell calc b2.de* canth k* chin k* coca coloc bg2 *Cycl* *Graph* *Hep* k* *Iod* k* op k* **Par** k* *Petr* k* **Phos** k* psor bg2 *Puls* k* *Sars* sep k* sin-a *Sulph* k* thuj
  - • **bluish**: alumn
- **oily**: adon ptk1 crot-t ptk1 iod ptk1 med hr1 phos ptk1 sumb ptk1
- **red**: mez ptk1
- **thick**: med hr1
- **whitish**: arg-n kali-bi merc-c plb sep
  - • **morning**: arg-n

CYLINDERS; with (See Casts)

DIABETES (See Sugar)

DIMINISHED (See Scanty)

EXCORIATING; slightly (See Acrid)

FATTY cuticle (See Cuticle)

FLAKY, flocculent (See Sediment - flocculent)

FOAMY (See Frothy)

FREQUENT: | **scanty** (See Scanty - frequent)

FROTHY: acon **All-c** k* allox tpw4* aloe sne aphis ptk2 *Apis* k* arn k* ars aur bg2* bamb-a stb2.de* *Berb* bro1 carb-v cean ptk1* **Chel** k* *Chin* k* chinin-s k* clem k* con k* cop k* crot-t k* cub k* dulc fd4.de glon k* guat sp1 iris jatr-c kali-c k* **Lach** k* laur k* lina a1 lith-c **Lyc** k* mela a1 melal-alt gya4 merc bg2 myric k* nat-m k* *Nat-s* k* nat-sil fd3.de• op k* *Pareir* k* *Phos* k* positr nl2• puls bg2 raph bro1 rhus-t bg1 sars bro1 scop ptk1 **Sel** k* **Seneg** k* sol-t-ae a1 **Spong** k* squil bg2 still a1 succ-ac rly4• syph bg1* thuj k* tritic-vg fd5.de tub jl2 vanil fd5.de ven-m rsj12• verat-v bg2 yohim c1*

- **morning**: ars-h k* crot-t k* hyper k*
- **afternoon**: chel k*
- **night**: allox tpw4 crot-t k* vichy-g a1
- **greenish** yellow: phos k*
- **violet** ring: puls k*

GASSY: sars ptk1

GELATINOUS, lumpy: berb bg2 cina *Coloc* k* crot-h k* ph-ac k* *Puls* bg2

- **left** standing for a while; when: *Ars* b4a.de cina *Coloc* k* crot-h k* dig b4a.de ph-ac

GONADOTROPHIC HORMONE increased: cortico sp1

GRAVITY; specific (See Specific)

HEAVY feeling: coc-c ptk1 thlas bro1*

HEMATURIA (See Bloody)

HOT (See Burning)

INDICAN, containing (See Color - bluish - indican)

INVOLUNTARY (See BLADDER - Urination - involuntary)

IODINE, RADIOACTIVE increased: cortico sp1

IRRITATING (See Acrid)

LIMPID: bell carb-ac chim chin cina coc-c dig dulc elat eup-per **Gels** hydr iris kali-i merc plan podo fd3.de• sarr thuj tritic-vg fd5.de

MILKY: *Agar* k* *Alum* k* ambr h1* ant-t b2.de* **Apis** k* arn **Aur** k* *Aur-m* k* berb bov caj k* *Calc* k* cann-s k* caps *Carb-v* k* card-m caust chel bro1 chin b2.de* chinin-s *Cina* k* clem k* *Coloc* k* con k* cop cycl k* *Dulc* k* eup-pur bro1 *Ferr* *Ferr-i* gels k* **Hep** k* *Iod* k* kali-bi k* kali-p ptk1 lappa ptk1 *Lil-t* k* **Lyc** k* merc k* merc-c k* *Mur-ac* k* nat-m k* *Nit-ac* k* nux-v petros **Ph-ac** k* *Phos* k* plb pot-e rly4• raph bro1* rhus-t k* *Sep* spirae a1 stann k* still k* sul-i k2 *Sulph* k* (non:uran-met k) *Uran-n* uva bro1 viol-o bro1* visc c1*
- **morning**: lil-t nat-m k* oci-sa sk4•
- **afternoon**: **Agar** k*
- **accompanied** by | **urination**; frequent: iod ptk1
- **blood**; with: kali-bi ptk1
- **chalk** had been stirred in it, as if: alum *Ph-ac* k* sulph
  - **emotion**; after every: *Ph-ac*
- **cheesy** milk had been stirred in, as if: alumn k* *Ph-ac* k*
- **curdled**, like: **Ph-ac** k* phos
- **flour**, as if mixed with: *Merc* hr1 *Ph-ac* k* *Sulph* hr1
- **hydrocephalus**; in: *Apis* ptk1
  - **little** but frequent discharges of milky urine; with very | **unconsciousness** and delirium; with: **Apis**
- **left** standing for a while; when: *Cina* k* erech a1 *Ph-ac* k* stann visc c1
- **menses**:
  - **after** | **agg.**: *Nat-m* k*
  - **before** | **agg.**: *Ph-ac* k*
  - **during** | **agg.**: berb nat-m
- **perspiration**; during: phos
- **stool** agg.; after: iod ptk1
- **turbid**, and: bry calc cann-s chin k* *Cina* k* con cycl dulc *Hep* psor rhus-t
- **turns** (See left)
- **urination** | **after** | **agg.**: mur-ac k*
  - **during** | **end** of: *Carb-v* k* coff ph-ac ptk1* rhus-t sars ptk1 *Sep* k*

MUCUS in urine (See Sediment - mucous)

MUDDY: *Aesc* k* alumn a1 guat sp1 hyper k* *Kali-c* k* lyc k* *Nat-m* k* pall *Rhus-t* k* sabad k* uva zinc k*

NEUTRAL: arn k* bapt canth k* dig k* eup-per eup-pur k* helon k* hydr hr1 hyos kali-c k* lept k* phos k* plb k*

NITROGEN increased: allox sp1

ODOR:
- **acrid**, pungent: am-c ant-t b7.de* *Asaf* k* bar-c bg2 bell bg2 benz-ac bg2* **Borx** k* *Calc* k* calc-f camph cann-s caust clem *Cob* cop br1 dig b4.de* *Fl-ac* graph k* hep kreos b7a.de lith-c bg2 *Lyc* merc mosch b7.de* nit-ac k* par pareir bg2 phos b4.de* positr nl2• rhod k* *Rhus-t* sep h2 stram thuj k* trad a1 vanil fd5.de viol-t bg2
- **ammoniacal**: aloe k* am-caust k* am-m k* ant-t b2.de* **Asaf** k* *Aur* k* bell k* benz-ac bg2* borx k* brom k* bufo k* cain k* *Calc* k* carb-ac carb-an b2.de* *Carb-v* k* chel k* chinin-s k* coc-c k* cop bro1 dig k* *Dulc* k* equis-h k* *Ferr* k* ferr-p graph k* **Iod** k* kreos k* *Lach* k* lyc k* malar jl2 med ptk1* *Merc* k* merc-c b4a.de* **Mosch** k* naphtin bro1 *Nit-ac* k* ozone sde2• pareir k* *Petr* k* *Phos* k* pic-ac ptk1 plac-s rly4• puls k* rhod k* sil k* solid bro1 stach a1 stigm bro1 stront-c k* sumb k* tab k* trios rsj11• tritic-vg fd5.de *Tub* viol-t k* *Zinc* b4a.de
  - **children**: med ctj6*
    - **infants**: *Calc* vh *Iod* k*
  - **menses**; during: nit-ac ptk1
- **aromatic**: benz-ac k* bor-ac bg2 carb-ac k* eup-pur k* ferr-i ptk1 germ-met srj5• olib-sac wmh1 onos bg2* positr nl2• ter ptk1
- **asparagus**-like | **eating**; after: but-ac sp1*
- **broth**; like: thuj b4a.de
- **cat's** urine: aspar k* borx h2* caj k* vib *Viol-t* k*
- **chamomile** tea: sulph c1
- **changeable**: *Benz-ac*
- **coffee**: berb k*
- **eggs**; like rotten: bamb-a stb2.de• *Daph* k* kali-s fkr2.de tritic-vg fd5.de
- **fish**-brine: bufo k* ol-an bg2* sanic tl1 uran-n bg2
- **fishy**: astac k* *Nat-c* b4a.de ol-an k* positr nl2• pot-e rly4• sanic ptk1 (non:uran-met k) *Uran-n* k*
- **flowery**: positr nl2•
- **fragrant**: fl-ac bg2
- **fruit**: acet-ac bg2 cupr-ar bg2 senn bg2
  - **putrid** fruit; like: helo-s rwt2•

Odor: ...
- **garlic**, like: bell bg2 cob-n sp1 cupr-ar bg2* kalag br1 phos b4.de* podo fd3.de•
- **haricots**; like cooked: tub jl2
- **horn**; like burnt: arum-m aur-m bg2
- **horrible**: kreos b7a.de
  - **left** standing for a while; when: **Ind** vh
- **horse's** urine, like: absin k* aloe bg2 *Benz-ac* k* *Nat-c* k* **Nit-ac** k* phos plut-n srj7• stroph-s sp1
- **iodine**; like: stront-c b4.de*
- **juniper**; like European: kreos b7a.de
- **leather**; like Russian: clem bg2*
- **manure**; like: *Puls* b7a.de
- **meat**; like raw: bamb-a stb2.de• ph-ac b4a.de*
- **moldy**: am-m camph k* coli rly4• dulc fd4.de kali-s fd4.de olib-sac wmh1 phys spong fd4.de sulph k*
- **mousy**: bry bg1
- **musk**: oci k*
- **nutmeg**: nux-m k*
- **offensive**: agar k* aloe *Am-be* bro1 am-c bro1 ambr k* ant-c mtf33 ant-t k* **Apis** k* *Arg-met* **Arn** k* *Ars* k* ars-i ars-s-f k2 asaf k* *Asar* *Aspar* k* *Aur* aur-ar k2 aur-i k2 aur-m k* aur-s k2 **Bapt** k* *Bar-m* k* **Benz-ac** k* berb bro1 *Borx* k* bufo caj a1 *Calad* k* **Calc** k* calc-i k2 camph k* *Carb-ac* k* *Carb-an* k* **Carb-v** k* *Carbn-s* *Caust* k* cean vml3• chen-v a1* *Chim* k* chin chinin-ar cit-ac rly4• clem k* colch coli jl2 coloc k* conv br1* cupr k* cupr-ar bro1 daph k* der a1 des-ac rbp6 dig k* dros k* **Dulc** k* fl-ac k* glycyr-g cte1• *Graph* k* *Guaj* k* hell hep hydr k* hyper k* *Ind* k* iod k* iris kali-ar kali-bi k* kali-br k* *Kali-c* k* *Kali-i* k* *Kali-p* *Kali-s* *Kreos* k* lac-c bg1 lac-del hm2• lac-h htj1• lach k* *Lyc* k* med *Meph* k* *Merc* k* mosch k2 *Murx* k* musca-d szs1 naphtin bro1 *Nat-ar* *Nat-c* k* nat-m k* nat-p nat-s nat-sil fd3.de• **Nit-ac** k* *Nux-v* k* oci bro1 op k* *Petr* k* *Ph-ac* k* *Phos* k* phys bro1 plb k* positr nl2• *Prot* jl2 *Puls* k* pulx bro1 pyrog *Rhod* k* sal-ac k* sal-al blc1• sec k* seneg bg2 **Sep** k* solid bro1* stann k* stram bg2 stront-br c2* suis-em rly4• sul-i k2 **Sulph** k* syc pte1• tab k* tarent k* *Ter* k* thuj ptk1 tril-p tritic-vg fd5.de trop c2* tub-r vn* (non:uran-met k) uran-n k* urin c1 vanil fd5.de vario k* ven-m rsj12• *Verat-v* k* **Viol-t** k*
  - **accompanied** by | **urination**; profuse: rhod ptk1
  - **alternating** with | **Joints**; pain in (See EXTREMITIES - Pain - joints - alternating with - urine)
  - **fever**, during: arg-met kreos *Lyc* *Merc* *Ph-ac* rhus-t sep b4.de* squil staph sulph
  - **menses**, during: *Nit-ac* k* sep
  - **perspiration**:
    - **during**: ars k* carb-v k* dulc k* nit-ac k* ph-ac k* puls k* *Sep* k* thuj k* viol-t k*
    - **feet**; like perspiration of: sulph
- **onions**: cupr-ar k* gamb k* phos k*
- **pork**; like fresh: bamb-a stb2.de•
- **putrid**: aloe k* ars k* aur k* *Aur-m* bamb-a stb2.de• bapt k2 bar-m *Benz-ac* k* *Calad* **Calc** carb-an carb-v coc-c k* coloc daph des-ac rbp6 hell hydr k* kali-s fd4.de lach sne mur-ac k2 muru a1 nat-c *Ph-ac* pulx br1 pyrog k2* *Sep* k* spirae a1 tarent k2 trop c1 vanil fd5.de
  - **evening**: *Calad*
  - **fever**, during: ars bg2 carb-v bg2 dulc bg2 ph-ac k* puls bg2 *Sep* bg2 viol-t bg2
  - **menopause**, during: **Sep** vh
- **raspberries**: sul-i a1*
- **sickly**: zinc bg1
- **smoked**: plut-n srj7•
- **sourish**: *Ambr* k* benz-ac k* *Calc* k* canth bg2 chel k* coc-c bg2* colch hr1 dulc fd4.de *Graph* k* hep lyc mtf33 m-aust b2.de* *Merc* k* *Nat-c* k* nit-ac bg2 ox-ac bg2 petr k* plb bg2 sars bg2 **Sep** k* solid bro1* streptoc rly4• trad c1 vanil fd5.de
  - **whooping** cough; during: ambr ptk1
- **strong**: absin br1 aesc aloe am-m k* ambr b7.de* amp rly4• *Ant-t* k* arg-n k* arge-pl rwt5• **Asaf** k* *Aspar* k* *Aur* bamb-a stb2.de• bar-m k2 **Benz-ac** k* bit-ar wht1• bond a1 *Borx* c2 bufo calad *Calc* k* calc-f calc-p k* calo a1 carb-ac k* carb-an b4.de* *Carb-v* k* cere-b a1 chel k* **Chin** bg2 chin-b hr1 **Chinin-s** k* chord-umb rly4• cob k* conv cupr-ar hr1 dig k* digin a1 dros k* *Dulc* erig hr1 *Ferr* k* *Fl-ac* k* fuc a1 fum rly1*• germ-met srj5• helodr-cal knl2• hydr k* hydrog srj2• hyper a1 **Iod** iris kali-bi k* kali-s fd4.de kreos k* lac-del hm2• lac-h htj1• *Lach* k* lil-t k* linu-c a1 *Lyc* k* med k* melal-alt gya4 *Merc* k* merc-c k*

- **strong**: ...
mez k* morg-p pte1*• **Mosch** k* nat-m k* neon srj5• **Nit-ac** k* nux-m k* osm a1 ozone sde2• pant-ac rly4• ped a1 *Petr* k* *Phos* k* phys a1 pic-ac k* pin-s a1* plac-s rly4• plan a1 *Plut-n* srj7• positr nl2• ruta fd4.de *Sep* k* stach a1 stram k* streptoc rly4• suis-em rly4• suis-pan rly4• sulph k* *Sumb* suprar rly4• syc bka1*• symph fd3.de• ter hr1 *Thuj* k* til a1 tub tub-r jl2 urol-h rwt• valer k* zinc zing k* [spect dfg1 tax jsj7]
  - **menses**:
    - **before**: merc
    - **during**: *Nit-ac* k*
  - **urinous**, intensely: *Absin* bro1 *Am-be* bro1 arg-n bro1 **Benz-ac** k* *Borx* bro1 *Calc* bro1 carb-v bro1 *Chinin-s* bro1 erig bro1 *Lyc* bro1 pic-ac bro1 pin-s bro1 *Sulph* bro1 viol-o bro1 zing bro1
- **sulphur**, like: bamb-a stb2.de• olib-sac wmh1 phos b4.de* rhus-t a1
- **sweetish**: aeth k* *Arg-met* k* arg-n *Cop* bro1 cub bro1 eucal bro1 eup-pur ptk1 ferr-i k* ham fd3.de• hyper k* ina-i mlk9.de inul bro1 juni-c bro1 kali-act kali-c bg2 kali-s fd4.de *Lact* **Lact-v** bg2 nat-sil fd3.de• *Nux-m* k* olib-sac wmh1 *Phos* b4a.de* prim-o bro1 salol bro1 suis-hep rly4• *Ter* k* thyr bro1
- **tobacco**, like: nit-ac k* tab a1
- **turpentine**; like: *Sep* b4a.de
- **valerian**; like: mosch bg2 murx bg2*
- **violets**, like: camph ptk1 clem k* cop k* cub k* eucal a1* inul k* lact k* lipp a1 nux-m k* osm k* phos k* salol bg1* *Sec* b7a.de sel k* ter k* thyr ptk1 viol-o bg2
  - **evening**: osm k*

ODORLESS: ambr b7.de* bell k* camph k* *Cedr* k* chlol k* coc-c k* dros k* gast a1 gnaph a1 kali-cy k* mela a1 senec k* *Spong* k* til a1 vanil fd5.de

OILY: adon bro1 chinin-s ptk1 *Crot-t* bro1 hep bro1 *Iod* bro1 lyc bro1 *Merc-c* bg2* petr bro1 *Phos* bro1 sumb bro1

PHOSPHOROUS increased: alf ptk1 benz-ac ptk1 calc-p ptk1 cortico sp1 lappa ptk1 nit-ac ptk1 *Ph-ac* ptk1 phos ptk1 pic-ac ptk1 solid ptk1 stann ptk1

POLYPOUS formation in: calc k*

PORPHYRINS increased: beryl sp1 *Sulfon* bro1 trion bro1

POTASSIUM increased: pitu-p sp1

PURULENT (See Sediment - purulent)

RECEDING: prun ptk1

SALTS; deficient in: led ptk1

SCANTY: abrot k* *Acon* k* adon bro1* *Aesc* k* aeth a1 *Agar* k* *Ail* k* *Alf* bro1 all-s k* allox tpw3 *Aloe* alum k* alum-p k2 alum-sil k2 alumn k* am-be hr1 am-c k* am-caust a1 am-m k* ambr k* amyg a1* anac k* anemps br1 ang k* ant-c k* *Ant-t* k* anth a1 anthraci antip vh1 **Apis** k* *Apoc* k* arg-met bg2 *Arg-n* k* *Arn* k* **Ars** k* ars-h a1* *Ars-i* ars-s-f k2 arum-d a1* **Arum-t** k* asaf k* asc-c k* *Aspar* k* *Astac* hr1 atra-r bnm3• atro a1* *Aur* k* aur-ar k2 *Aur-m* k* aur-s k2 bamb-a stb2.de• *Bapt* k* bar-c b2.de* bar-m bg2 *Bell* k* benz-ac k* *Berb* k* bism b2.de boerh-d zzc1• bov k* brach a1 brom k* *Bry* k* bufo cact k* caj a1 calad calc k* calc-ar k* calc-f k* calc-sil k2 *Camph* k* cann-i k* cann-s k* **Canth** k* caps k* *Carb-ac* k* carb-an k* carb-v k* **Carbn-s** *Card-m* k* carl a1 cassia-s ccrh1• castm *Caust* k* cedr k* cent a1 cere-b a1 *Cham* k* chel k* chim k* *Chin* k* *Chinin-ar* *Chinin-s* k* cic k* cimic k* cimx k* cina *Clem* k* *Cob* k* coc-c k* *Cocc* k* coch hr1 coch-o mtf11 cod a1 coff k* coff-t a1 coffin a1 **Colch** k* coloc k* com a1 **Con** k* conv bro1 convo-s sp1 cop k* *Corn* k* *Croc* k* *Crot-h* k* cund a1 *Cupr* k* cupr-ar a1* cupr-s k* cur *Cycl* k* **Dig** k* *Digin* a1 diph-t-tpt jl2 dirc a1 *Dros* k* *Dulc* k* echi elat k* **Equis-h** k* erech br1 erig k* ery-a k* eug k* eup-per k* *Eup-pur* k* euph k* eupi k* eys sp1 falco-pe nl2• *Ferr* k* *Ferr-ar* ferr-i k* ferr-m a1* ferr-p k* ferul a1 *Fl-ac* k* frax a1 fuma-ac mtf11 galeg mtf11 gamb a1 gard-j vlr2• gast a1 gink-b sbd1• gins a1 gnaph a1 **Graph** k* **Grat** k* guaj k* guat sp1 haem a1 *Ham* k* **Hell** k* helon k* *Hep* k* hipp a1 hydr k* *Hyos* k* hyper k* iber a1 ign k* indg k* inul hr1 iod k* *Ip* k* irid-met srj5• iris k* jab a1* jatr-c jug-r a1 *Juni-c* bro1 *Kali-ar* k* *Kali-bi* k* *Kali-br* k* *Kali-c* k* *Kali-chl* k* kali-i k* kali-m k2 **Kali-n** k* kali-p *Kali-s* kali-sil k2 *Kalm* hr1 kola br1 kou a1 *Kreos* k* **Lac-ac** k* **Lac-c** k* *Lac-d* k* *Lach* k* lact k* lat-m sp1* *Laur* k* lec k* *Led* k* lept k* *Leptos-ih* jl2 **Lil-t** k* limest-b es1• lina a1 lipp a1 *Lith-c* k* lob k* lob-s a1 loxo-lae bnm12• lup mtf11 *Lyc* k* lyss k* m-arct b7.de m-aust b2.de mag-c b2.de* *Mag-m* k* mag-s k* manc a1 mang b2.de* marb-w es1• med hr1* menis a1 menth bro1 menth-v bwa3 *Meny* k* **Merc** k* **Merc-c** k* *Merc-cy* hr1* **Merc-d** k* *Merc-i-f* hr1 merc-sul a1* *Mez* k* mill a1 morph k* mosch b7a.de* mur-ac k* myris a1 nabal a1 *Naja* narcot a1 *Nat-ar* *Nat-c* k* nat-f sp1 nat-m k* nat-p k* **Nat-s** k* nicc k* **Nit-ac** k* nit-s-d a1* *Nux-m* k* **Nux-v** k* ol-an a1 olnd k* onis br1 **Op** k* oscilloc jl2 osm k* ox-ac k* ozone sde2• paeon a1 pall k* par k* *Pareir* k* pert-vc vk9 *Petr* k* petr-ra shn4• ph-ac k* phel a1* *Phos* k* *Phys* a1* physal-al br1 physala-p bnm7• *Phyt* k* *Pic-ac* k* pilo a1* pitu-p sp1 **Plb** k* *Podo* k* polyg-h ptk1 polyp-p a1 positr nl2• prun k* *Psor* k* *Ptel* a1* *Puls* k* pulx br1* pyrog k* quas a1 ran-b c1 *Rat* k* rein a1 rhod k* rhus-g a1 rhus-r *Rhus-t* k* ric a1 rob hr1 **Ruta** k* sabad k* sabin k* sacch sal-ac hr1 sal-fr sle1• samb b2.de* sang k* sanic tl1 sarr k* **Sars** k* scut a1* sec k* **Sel** k* senec a1* *Seneg* k* **Sep** k* *Ser-ang* br1* serp a1 sil k* skat br1 sol-t-ae a1 solid c2* spong k* *Squil* k* stach a1 stann k* **Staph** k* stigm br1* *Stram* k* stront-c k* stroph-h br1* stry a1 sul-ac k* sul-i k2* sulfon bro1 **Sulph** k* *Sumb* k* *Syph* k* tab k* tarax k* tell k* tep a1 **Ter** k* ther k* thuj k* til a1* tong a1 tub tub-r vn* upa a1 *Urin* c1 ust a1* *Uva* bro1 vanil fd5.de *Verat* k* verat-v k* *Verb* k* verin a1 vib tl1 vinc a1* viol-t b2.de wies a1 xan k* zinc k* zing bro1 [bell-p-sp dcm1]
- **daytime**: aesc k* *Lyc* k* ther
- **morning**: alum h2* ars-h k* coff k* dig k* dulc fd4.de fl-ac k* graph a1 mez k* oena a1 osm a1 ox-ac k* pip-m a1 sang k* sars h2* sul-ac k* xan c1 zinc k*
- **afternoon**: hell k* plect a1 rumx sumb k* *Thuj* k*
- **evening**: arg-n k* ferr-i k* fl-ac k* mag-c k* nat-m k* phel a1 sel c1 sumb a1 zinc k*
- **night**: ant-c carb-an cic k* coc-c k* lyc k* *Morph* ol-an a1 ulm-c jsj8• xan c1 [bell-p-sp dcm1]
- **accompanied** by:
  - **diphtheria** (See THROAT - Diphtheria - accompanied - urine)
  - ○ **Abdomen**; retraction of (See ABDOMEN - Retraction - accompanied - urine)
  - **Brain**; complaints of the (See HEAD - Brain; complaints of - accompanied - urine)
  - **Heart**; complaints of the (See CHEST - Heart; complaints - accompanied - urine - scanty)
- **alternating** with | **copious** urine (See Copious - alternating - scanty)
- **amenorrhea**, with: acon apis chin cocc ham hell laur lil-t nux-m xan
- **apyrexia**; during: apis c1
- **children**; in: lat-m bnm6•
- **drinks**; less than: kreos ptk1 lith-c ptk1 raph ptk1
- **exertion** agg.; after: bry k2
- **fever**; during: *Apis* k* ars *Arum-t* lp cann-s cann-xyz bg2 canth k* cocc k* colch k* *Eup-per* hr1 eup-pur lyc merc-sul c1 nat-m nit-ac k* nux-v k* op k* *Puls* k* ruta bg2 staph k*
- **frequent**; and: *Acon* b7a.de allox tpw3 *Ant-t* b7a.de *Apis* b7a.de arn b7.de *Bry* b7a.de *Cann-s* b7a.de *Colch* b7a.de *Coli* jl2 *Dig* sne hipp jl2 ignis-alc es2• *Kreos* b7a.de laur b7.de *Led* b7a.de meny ptk1 merc ptk1 nat-m lp ol-an ptk1 phos sne *Squil* b7a.de staph b7.de* *Stram* b7a.de vanil fd5.de *Verat* b7a.de
- **headache**, afterwards copious; during: asc-c iod ptk1 ol-an ptk1 sang
- **menses** | **before** | **agg.**: *Apis* k* sil k*
  - **during** | **agg.**: nat-m k* sabin b7.de
- **nervous** women: *Agar* k*
- **old** people; in: juni-c br1
- **perspiration**; during: ant-t k* apis k* arn k* bell k* bry k* **Calc** k* *Canth* k* carb-v k* caust k* cedr chin k* dig k* dulc k* *Graph* k* **Hell** k* hep k* hyos k* *Merc* k* nit-ac k* *Nux-v* k* **Op** k* puls k* rhus-t k* *Staph* k* **Sulph** k* verat k*
- **thirst**; with: irid-met srj5• lith-c ptk1 sep h2* *Til* lp vanil fd5.de
- **weather** agg.; wet: colch k2

SEDIMENT: (↗KIDNEYS - Stones) *Acon* k* aesc k* agar k* alco a1 alum k* am-c b2.de* am-caust k* am-m k* ambr k* anac b2.de* anan vh1 ant-c k* ant-t k* apis k* arist-cl sp1 arn k* *Ars* k* arund c2 astac a1 aur b2.de bar-c bg2 bell b2.de* *Benz-ac* *Berb* betu lsr3.de• bov b2.de* bry k* but-ac sp1 calad calc k* *Camph* bg2 cann-s b2.de* **Canth** k* caps b2.de* carb-an b2.de* carb-v k* carbn-s card-m a1* caust k* cedr k* cham k* *Chim* chin k* chinin-ar chinin-s k* cimx cina k* cinch a1 clem b2.de cob-n sp1 *Colch* b2.de* **Coloc** k* con k* conch a1 convo-s sp1 *Cop* k* cupr cycl a1 daph bg2 dig k* dulc k* elem br1 euph b2.de* ferr k* ferr-p gast a1 gins a1 graph k* grat a1 guat sp1 hep b2.de hyos b2.de* ign b2.de iod b2.de* ip k* *Kali-ar* *Kali-bi* bg2 kali-c k* kali-i k* kali-n k* *Kali-p* kali-s kreos b2.de* *Lach* b2.de* lat-m bnm6• laur k* led k* lith-c bg2 loxo-lae bnm12• **Lyc** k* mag-m b2.de* *Mang* k* meny b2.de **Merc** k* *Mez* k* *Naja* nat-ar nat-c b2.de* nat-m k* nat-n br1 *Nit-ac* k* nux-m k* nux-v b2.de* ol-an a1 olnd b2.de* op k* par k* pareir bg2 *Petr* k* **Ph-ac** k* phal a1

Sediment: ...
Phos k* plat b2.de plb k* **Puls** k* rheum b2.de rhod b2.de rhus-t k* ruta b2.de* sal-ac **Sars** k* sec b2.de* sel b2.de* **Seneg** b2.de* **Sep** k* *Sil* k* spig b2.de spirae c2 spong k* **Squil** b2.de* *Staph* sul-ac k* *Sulph* k* sumb a1 *Tarent* k* ter thuj k* tong a1 **Valer** k* wies a1 **Zinc** k*

- **accompanied** by | **respiration**; asthmatic (See RESPIRATION - Asthmatic - accompanied - urine - sediment)
- **adherent**: apis bg3* aspar a1* berb sne brom k* canth bg2* chim bg2* chin bg2 *Chinin-s* *Cimx* coc-c coca *Coloc* k* crot-t bg2* *Cupr* k* *Daph* k* *Ferr* k* kali-m bg2* *Lac-c* nat-c nat-m k* nit-ac k* nuph a1 osm a1 *Petr* k* phos k* phyt plat k* polyg-h ptk1 *Puls* k* pyrog k* rad-br bg2* rumx bg1 sapin a1 sec bg2 **Sep** k* stann k* sumb k* thlas bg2 tub ptk1
- **agg.** when discharge of sediment in urine is decreased: **Benz-ac** mrr1
- **albuminous**: adon vh1 apoc k* **Ars** b4a.de **Aur** b4a.de *Bell* b4a.de *Kali-c* b4a.de merc-c oci sul-ac b4a.de
- **alternating** with:
  - **rheumatic** complaints (See EXTREMITIES - Pain - rheumatic - alternating - urine)
  - ○ **Heart**; complaints of (See CHEST - Heart; complaints - alternating - urine)
- **amel.** when discharge of sediment in urine is increased: **Benz-ac** mrr1
- **amorphous**: ang *Hydrang* k* iod k*
- **black**: colch ptk1 **Lach** lp* ter k*
- **bloody**: *(↗Bloody)* *Acon* k* ant-t k* apis **Arn** b2.de* ars bro1 *Ars-h* bro1 *Berb* bro1 **Cact** bg2* cadm-s br1 calc k* cann-s k* **Canth** k* caps b2.de* *Carb-ac* bro1 *Carb-v* cham **Chim** k* chin b2.de* chinin-ar bro1 chinin-s bro1 colch bro1 coloc k* con k* crot-h *Dulc* k* ferr-p bro1 *Ham* bro1 hell hep bro1 ip b2.de* kali-bi bro1 *Kali-chl* bro1 lyc k* merc b2.de* mez k* nat-n bro1 *Nit-ac* bro1 pareir bro1 **Ph-ac** k* phos k* pic-ac bro1 **Puls** k* santin bro1 sec b2.de* **Sep** k* sul-ac k* sulph k* *Ter* k* uva *Zinc* b2.de*
- **bluish**: pic-ac prun k*
- **bran**-like: aloe ambr *Ant-t* bg2* berb cedr k* *Merc* bg2* *Phos* bg2* **Valer** b7.de*
- **bright**: am-c b4.de* *Coloc* b4.de* nat-m b4.de* nit-ac k*
- **brown**: acon bg2* **Ambr** k* *Apis* k* *Arn* k* chinin-s coloc bg2* crot-t k* dig k* epig bg1 *Lach* k* lob k* plb bg2* thuj valer k*
  - **dark**: *Aesc* k* *All-s* k* plb k* spig k*
  - **dirty**: acon k*
  - **light**: *Coloc* k* puls
  - **pinkish**: myric k*
  - **reddish**: lith-c
  - **white**; and: coloc
- **burnt** on; adheres to vessel as if: sep k*
- **cellular**: loxo-lae bnm12•
- **chalk** meal, like: alum anan ant-t bufo calc chel eup-per graph led *Merc* nat-m *Ph-ac* phos phyt ruta sars k2 sulph
- **cheesy**: alumn *Ph-ac* k* **Phos** k* *Sars* k* *Sec* k*
- **chocolate**-colored: chinin-s
- **circles**: chinin-s lac-c sulph
- **clay**-colored: alum alumn k* *Am-c* *Am-m* k* *Anac* k* **Berb** k* canth b2.de* chinin-s k* cor-r eup-per hr1 ign b2.de* kali-c b2.de* mang k* ol-an a1 phos k* *Sars* k* *Sep* k* sul-ac b4.de* *Sulph* k* *Ter* bg2 thuj k* **Zinc** k*
  - **adhesive**: *Sep*
    - ⁝ **menses**, difficult to wash off; during: *Sep*
- **clots**: *Ph-ac* b4a.de
  - **yellow**-red: cob k*
- **cloudy**: alum k* alumn am-m k* ambr k* anac ant-c bg2 *Ars* b4a.de **Berb** k* bov b2.de* bry k* calc-sil k2 carb-v k* caust k* cer-s a1 cham chin k* crot-t k* elaps fagu a1 grat a1 hydr-ac ip tl1 kali-c b2.de* *Kali-n* k* lach k* laur k* **Lyc** bg2 mag-m k* menis a1 merc k* ol-an a1 olnd par k* petr k* *Ph-ac* k* phos k* plat k* ptel a1 rat k* rhod b2.de* sars b2.de* *Seneg* k* sumb ter tl1 *Thuj* k* tong a1 valer k* zinc k* zinc-p k2
- **coffee** grounds, like: *Ambr* k* **Apis** k* dig bro1 **Hell** k* *Lach* k* *Ter* k*
- **copious**: agar k* all-s am-c k* am k* *Ars* k* bell **Berb** k* calc carb-an card-m k2 cham *Chim* k* chin cinch a1 *Coloc* k* con *Cop* k* crot-t k* cycl k* kali-ar kali-bi kali-c laur lyc k* mit a1 nat-n a1 oena a1 op b7.de* *Phos* k* *Puls* sal-ac k* sulph a1 *Tarent* k* thuj k* trad a1*
- **crusty**: agar bg1 calc bg2* caust daph bg2* merc bg2 *Nat-c* *Phos* *Sars* k* *Sep* k* zinc bg1
- **crystals**: ant-c bg2 arg-n k* berb a1* bry k2 chinin-s bg2 coloc k* crot-t k* ferr-m k* ferr-p a1 *Lyc* k* sal-ac a1* sel bg2
- **cylindrical** casts: apis bg2 arg-n bg2 ars bg2 canth bg2 loxo-lae bnm12• merc-c bg2 phos bg2 plb bg2
- **dark**: asc-t a1 carb-ac bg2 *Crot-h* k* **Hell** bg2 iod k* phos k* puls k*
- **dirty**: anac k* chin dor a1
- **earthy**: *Ant-t* a1* berb ptk1 mang k* rhus-t k2 sul-ac k* zinc ptk1
- **filaments**, fibres: cann-s b7.de* seneg bg2
- **fine** deposit: *(↗fine; sand - fine)* sep k*
- **flocculent**: acon k* agar k* *Alum* ambr k* ant-t b2.de* aspar k* *Benz-ac* k* **Berb** k* brom k* calc k* calc-p k* *Cann-s* k* **Canth** k* caust bro1 cent a1 *Cham* k* *Chel* k* chin k* cina cinch a1 *Clem* k* cob k* coc-c k* coca coloc k* crot-t k* cycl k* **Dulc** b4a.de ery-a k* eup-pur gonotox jl2 grat k* hell *Hep* k* iod k* kali-c k* kali-i k* kali-n k* kali-p laur k* lith-c merc k* merc-c k* **Mez** k* mit a1 morph a1 nit-ac k* ol-an a1 par b2.de* pareir bg2 *Petr* k* *Ph-ac* *Phos* k* *Plb* k* prun bg2 *Puls* b7a.de rhus-t k* rumx **Sars** k* seneg k* sin-a a1 spirae a1 squil k* still a1 sumb thuj k* (non:uran-met k) uran-n valer k* zinc k* zinc-p k2
  - **red**: mez tl1 sep tl1
  - **white**: ambr a1 calc h2* kali-bi bg2 merc h1* phos
    - ⁝ **left** standing for a while; when: zinc
  - **yellow**: aloe bg2
- **gelatinous**: ars-h hr1 **Berb** k* calad *Chim* k* *Cina* bro1 coc-c *Coca* **Coloc** k* crot-h *Dulc* k* hydr kali-m bg2 *Oci* bro1 *Pareir* ph-ac k* *Puls* k* spira a1
- **granular**: aloe berb k* chinin-s coloc b4a.de loxo-lae bnm12• lyc hr1
- **gravel** (See sand - gravel)
- **gravity**; specific (See Specific)
- **gray**: agar ant-t k* **Berb** bg2* chin bg2 *Con* k* hyos k* kali-i k* led k* lyc bg2 mang k* merc-c b4a.de* ph-ac *Phos* k* psor bg2 puls k* spong k* trad a1*
  - **brownish** gray: chin k*
  - **whitish** gray: **Berb** k* calc bro1 canth bro1 *Graph* bro1 hyos k* merc-c k* sars bro1 sep bro1 spong k*
- **greasy**: ham bg2
- **hair**-like bodies: *Canth* bg2
- **leukocytes**: carc fb lat-m bnm6•
- **limestone**; like: bufo bg2 calc b4a.de coloc b4a.de graph b4a.de led b7.de* lyc b4a.de nat-m b4a.de *Ph-ac* b4a.de phyt bg2 sabal ptk1
- **loose**: alum k* calc b4a.de carb-an k* *Chin* k*
- **mealy**: *Agar* k* ant-t b2.de* apis bg2* **Berb** k* *Calc* k* *Canth* k* *Cedr* k* *Chin* k* chinin-s cor-r k* gast a1 *Graph* k* *Hyos* k* kali-c k* merc k* *Nat-m* k* ph-ac k* phos bg2* *Sep* sulph k* valer k* zinc k*
- **meat**, like: merc h1*
- **menses**; before: canth b7.de
- **milky**: ant-t k* coloc ferr-i k* lyc merc b4a.de ox-ac *Ph-ac* k* phos k* sec sep mtf33
- **mucous**: aesc k* *Aloe* *Alumn* k* ammc a1 *Ant-c* k* apoc k* *Arg-n* ars k* asc-t k* aspar bro1 *Aur* k* aur-ar k2 aur-s k2 bals-p bro1 bar-c *Baros* bro1 bell k* **Benz-ac** k* **Berb** k* brach k* brom k* bry k* calc k* calc-sil k2 camph k* cann-i k* cann-s b2.de* *Canth* k* *Carb-v* k* carbn-s carl a1 caust k* cent a1 cham b2.de* *Chel* k* **Chim** k* chin b2.de* chinin-s k* *Cimic* cina b2.de* *Clem* *Coc-c* k* *Colch* *Coloc* k* con k* cop k* crot-t k* *Cub* bro1 cupr bg2 dig k* *Dulc* k* *Epig* br1* **Equis-h** k* *Eucal* hr1 eup-pur k* fab bro1 *Ferr* k* ferr-ar ferr-p gaert pte1*• *Glon* k* grat a1 hep b2.de* *Hydr* k* hydrang bro1 hyos k* indg k* ip b2.de* kali-ar *Kali-bi* k* *Kali-c* k* *Kali-chl* k* kali-m k2 kali-n k* kali-p kali-s k2 kali-sil k2 *Lach* k* lith-c lyc k* lycps-v bg2 med c1* menth bro1 *Merc* k* **Merc-c** k* mez b2.de* morph a1 mosch k2 musa a1 naja nat-ar *Nat-c* k* **Nat-m** k* nat-n a1 nat-p *Nat-s* k* *Nit-ac* k* *Nux-v* k* op k* **Pareir** k* *Petr* k* ph-ac k* phos k* phys a1 *Pop* bro1 **Puls** k* rheum b2.de* sal-ac hr1 **Sars** k* *Senec* hr1 seneg k* **Sep** k* sol-t-ae a1 *Solid* bro1 spirae a1 stigm bro1 sul-ac k* sulph k* tab k* *Ter* k* *Thuj* k* *Til* k* tong a1 *Tritic* bro1 tub c1 (non:uran-met k) uran-n *Uva* k* valer k* verat k* wies a1
  - **accompanied** by | **Uterus**; displacement of (See FEMALE - Displacement - accompanied - urine)
  - **left** standing for a while; when: crot-t k*
  - **menses**; before: *Lach* k*
  - **milky** white: *Kali-chl*
  - **tenacious**: caust k* *Coloc* con k* *Dulc* hr1 hydr k2 nat-c *Nux-v* k* *Puls* sil tong a1
  - **thick**: gal-ac br1
    - ⁝ **ropy**, bloody mucous; great quantity of: **Chim** k* *Dulc*

- • **white**: phos h2*
- • **yellow**: nat-c h2*
- **muddy**: ter ptk1
- **offensive**: chinin-s bg2 cupr fl-ac bg2 lyc sep mtf33
- **oily**: calc bg2 chin bg2 hep bg2 iod bg2 par bg2 petr bg2 phos bg2 puls bg2
- **orange**-colored: chinin-s nit-ac h2
- **oxalate** of calcium, lime: berb bg2* brach k* *Caust* k* coca guat sp1 *Kali-s* k* lyc lycps-v lysd bro1 *Nat-p* k* nat-s ptk1 **Nit-ac** k* nit-m-ac c1* ox-ac k* plb rhus-t senn br1* *Ter* k* zinc
- **pasty**: ars **Sep** k*
- **phosphates**: agar k* alf br1* am bg2* aspar aven br1* bell bro1 *Benz-ac* k* brach k* calc bro1 *Calc-p* bg2* cann-s bro1 canth k* chel k* chinin-s k* colch k* *Ferr-m* k* graph bro1 gua bro1 guaj bro1 helon bro1 hydrang bro1 kali-br k* kali-chl bro1 kalm lec k* mag-p k* med k* nat-ar nat-s k2 nit-ac bro1 **Ph-ac** k* *Phos* k* pic-ac k* *Ptel* k* *Raph* k* sang bro1 *Sarr* k* senn bro1 *Solid* bro1 *Stann* k* ter k* thlas bro1 uran-n bro1
  - • **headache**; during: aven br1
- **pink**: apis bg1 *Berb* k* **Bry** *Chin* k* lith-c lob myric bg1 ol-j a1 phyt bg1 rheum rhus-r *Sep* k* *Sumb* k* visc c1
- **protein**: diph-t-tpt jl2
- **purple**: ant-c ant-t k* bov k* *Fl-ac* k* mang k* ptel k*
- **purulent**: *(↗BLADDER - Catarrh; BLADDER - Inflammation; BLADDER - Suppuration; KIDNEYS - Inflammation - suppurative)* acon b2.de* **Apis** b7a.de **Arn** k* *Ars* k* ars-s-f k2 aspar k* bapt ptk1 *Baros* bro1 *Benz-ac* k* berb c2* bry bro1 cadm-s br1 calc k* calc-s tl1 calc-sil k2 *Cann-s* k* **Canth** k* caps b2.de* carb-ac carb-v carbn-s cham chim k* **Clem** k* *Con* k* cop bro1 *Daph* *Dulc* k* *Epig* br1* eucal bg1* eup-pur fab bro1 ham k* *Hell* bg2 hep k* hyos bro1 ip k* kali-ar kali-bi k* kali-c k* *Kali-s* lat-m bnm6• lith-c bro1 *Lyc* k* *Merc* *Merc-c* bro1 *Nat-s* *Nit-ac* k* *Nux-v* k* oci bro1 petr k* phos bg2* polyg-h ptk1 *Pop* bro1 *Puls* k* sabad sabin k* sal-ac *Sars* k* sep k* *Sil* k* staph k* staphycoc jl2 stigm bro1 sul-i ptk1 *Sulph* k* ter bro1 thlas bro1 tritic bro1 (non:uran-met k) uran-n **Uva** k*
  - • **urination** agg.; after: hep ptk1
  - ○ • **Kidney**; after operation to: methyl br1
- **red**: *Acon* k* agar k* *Alum* k* alum-p k2 alum-sil k2 am-c k* am-m b2.de* ambr b2.de* *Ant-c* k* ant-t b2.de* *Apis* *Arg-n* k* *Arn* k* ars ars-h k* arund br1 aspar k* astac k* aur-m hr1* bapt hr1 *Bell* k* *Berb* k* borx br1 bov b2.de* brom k* bry bg1 cact calc b2.de* calc-sil k2 camph k* cann-s b2.de* **Canth** k* carb-v k* cham *Chel* k* chim hr1 *Chin* k* chinin-ar *Chinin-s* k* cimx k* cob k* coc-c coch colch b7a.de *Coloc* k* con a1 *Cop* k* cupr k* cyn-d zzc1• *Daph* k* **Dig** bg2 dirc a1 dulc k* *Elaps* gal-ac c1 gast a1 get a1 gins a1 *Glon* hr1 *Graph* k* hydr-ac iod ip k* kali-ar kali-c k* kali-n b4.de* kali-p kali-s kreos k* lac-ac *Lac-c* k* *Lach* k* *Laur* k* led k* lil-t k* *Lith-c* k* *Lob* k* *Lyc* k* lyss k* mag-s k* mang b2.de* **Merc-c** bg2 *Mez* k* naja **Nat-m** k* nat-s k* *Nit-ac* k* nux-m b2.de* *Nux-v* k* op k* pall k* par k* *Petr* k* ph-ac k* phos k* plat k* plb bg2 *Psor* k* ptel k* **Puls** k* pyrog k2 rhod b2.de* ruta b2.de* sang k* sars b2.de* *Sec* k* sel k* seneg k* **Sep** k* sil k* spira a1 squil k* stann stry a1 sul-ac k* sul-i k2 sulph k* tep a1 *Ter* k* thuj k* **Valer** k* verat-v k* zinc b2.de*
  - • **blood**-color: am-c k* bell bg2 *Calc* bg2 carb-v bg2 coff bg2 hep bg2 merc bg2 petr bg2 rhus-t bg2 sep k* sul-ac bg2
  - • **brick**-color: acon b7.de* am-c bg2 am-m bg2 apis b7a.de* **Arn** b7.de* ars ptk1 bell bg2* bry ptk1 camph bg2 *Canth* bg2* carl a1 **Chin** b7.de* chinin-s bg2 daph bg2 dig br1* graph bg2 ip b7.de* kali-c ptk1 kreos bg2 *Lach* bg2 laur bg2 lob ptk1 **Lyc** bg2* merc-c k* mez bg2 *Nat-m* b4a.de* nat-s k* nux-v bg2 *Oci* lp op b7.de* pall c1 par bg2 pareir ptk1 petr k* phos k* plat bg2 puls k* sars bg2 sel b7a.de* senec ptk1 sep bg2* *Squil* bg2 sulph bg2 tarent ptk1 thuj b4a.de *Valer* bg2* verat hr1
    - ⁝ **dark**: arn br1
  - • **bright**: **Berb** k* ferr-m hr1 *Lyc* k* nit-ac osm k* phos k*
  - • **brownish**: sul-ac k*
  - • **circles**, in: lac-c
  - • **cloudy**: ambr b7a.de
  - • **dark**: carl a1 chin cinch a1 dor k* phyt
  - • **dirty**: *Berb* k* dor
  - • **filaments**, fibres: ant-c h2* ant-t k* *Canth* b7.de*
  - • **flocculent** or powdery: agar ambr bg2 cob kali-n bg2
  - • **grainy**: ant-c bg2 chinin-s bg2 sel k*
  - • **lead**, minium; like red oxide of: valer b7.de*
  - • **mahogany**-colored: chin laur k* phyt
- **red**: ...
  - • **pepper**-like: benz-ac k2 iod bg1* pyrog bg2*
  - • **rosy**: am-p ptk1
  - • **threads** (See filaments)
  - • **wash** off; difficult to: ars-i k1 aspar brom *Cimx* *Cupr* *Daph* *Lac-c* *Phyt* pyrog **Sep**
  - • **white**: ter
- **renal** calculi (See KIDNEYS - Stones)
- **rings**: apis aspar bg1 *Lac-c* pyrog
- **ropy**: *Chim* k* coloc *Hydr* *Kali-bi* *Lyc* *Ph-ac* puls k2
- **rose**: am-p bro1
- **sand**: acon b2.de all-c k* alum b2.de **Am-c** k* ambr k* *Ant-c* k* ant-t b2.de arn k* ars arund k* aspar aur k* aur-ar k2 aur-m k* aur-s a1* bell k* **Benz-ac** k* berb k2 *Calc* k* calc-sil k2 cann-s b2.de canth k* carb-v k* *Chel* k* chim ptk1 chin k* chinin-ar *Chinin-s* coc-c ptk1 eup-pur k* ferr-m gast a1 get a1 graph b2.de ip b2.de kali-c b2.de kali-p kiss a1 *Lach* k* **Led** k* **Lyc** k* mang b2.de meny k* merc *Nat-m* k* *Nat-s* k* *Nit-ac* k* nux-m k* nux-v k* op b2.de petr b2.de ph-ac b2.de **Phos** k* *Puls* k* raph rhod b2.de *Ruta* k* **Sars** k* *Sec* k* **Sel** k* **Sep** b2.de* **Sil** k* sul-ac b2.de sul-i ptk1 sulph b2.de tarent k* thuj k* *Tub* k* valer b2.de **Zinc** k* zinc-p k2
  - • **adherent**: *Puls* k* sep mtf33
  - • **bright** colored in concentric layers: chinin-s
  - • **brown**: *Epig* br1 sul-i ptk1
  - • **fine**: *(↗fine)* epig br1
  - • **gravel**: *(↗KIDNEYS - Stones)* acon bg2 alum bg2 am-c bg2 ambr bg2 *Ant-c* b7a.de* ant-t bg2 arbin hsa1 *Arg-n* k* arn bg2* *Ars* bro1 aspar k* *Bar-m* bro1 baros c2* bell bro1 *Benz-ac* bro1 *Berb* k* borx bg2 brach bro1 cact bro1 cal-ren c2* *Calc* k* cann-s bro1 *Cann-xyz* bg2 canth b7.de* *Carb-ac* bro1 carb-v caust bro1 chel bro1 chin bg2* *Chinin-s* bg2* cimic bg2 coc-c k* cocc-s bro1 coch c2* colch bro1 coloc k* con crot-h bro1 dig bro1 dios bro1 epig c2* equis-h c2 ery-a bro1 eup-a c2* eup-pur c2* fab bro1 ferr-m bro1 gali c2* *Graph* bg2* *Hed* bro1 hep bro1 hydrang c2* ip bg2 kali-bi bro1 kali-c bg2* kali-i k* kreos bro1 lach bg2 led bg2 *Lith-be* bro1 lith-c bg2* lob bg2* **Lyc** k* mang bg2 meny bg2 *Merc-c* bro1 nat-m bg2* nat-s bro1 nit-ac k* *Nit-m-ac* c2* nux-m k* *Nux-v* bg2* oci c2* op bg2 *Ox-ac* c2 pareir bro1 pariet bro1 *Petr* bg2 petros c2 *Ph-ac* b4a.de* phos b4a.de* phys bro1 physal-al br1 pic-ac bro1 pipe bro1 plb-i bro1 podo mtf11 polyg-h ptk1 polyg-xyz c2 puls bg2* rhod bg2 *Ruta* b7.de* sanic bg2 **Sars** k* *Sel* b7a.de* senn bro1 **Sep** k* *Sil* b4a.de* skook bro1 *Solid* bro1 stigm bro1 stront-br c2 sul-ac bg2 sulph bg2* ter bg2* *Thlas* bro1 thuj b4a.de* tritic bro1 urt-u c2* valer b7.de* vesi c2* vichy-g c2 zinc k*
  - • **gray**: phos
  - • **pale**: *Sars*
  - • **red** (= brick-dust): acon act-sp vh1 agar all-c alum k* *Am-c* am-caust ant-c b7.de* ant-t apis arg-n **Arn** **Ars** **Arund** *Aspar* aur-m bapt bell *Benz-ac* *Berb* bry *Cact* *Camph* *Carb-v* *Caust* chel *Chim* chin chinin-ar *Chinin-s* *Cimic* cob coc-c colch b7a.de *Coloc* con *Cop* **Dig** *Elaps* get br1 *Glon* grat hedeo br1 *Hyos* *Ip* *Kali-c* k* kali-n *Lach* *Led* **Lob** **Lyc** k* *Meph* **Merc-c** *Mez* *Nat-m* k* *Nat-s* nit-ac k* nux-m *Nux-v* *Oci* k* *Op* ox-ac pall **Pareir** *Petr* **Phos** k* pic-ac **Plan** *Psor* puls k* pyrog rumx **Sel** k* **Senec** **Sep** k* *Sil* k* sumb **Tarent** ter thuj k* valer zinc zinc-p k2
    - ⁝ **alternating** with | **Head**; pain in (See HEAD - Pain - alternating - red)
    - ⁝ **fever**; during: *Lyc* phos
    - ⁝ **yellowish** red crystals: berb chel chinin-s *Lyc* k*
  - • **sticky**: pyrog ptk1 tub ptk1
  - • **white**: *Am-c* nat-ar nat-hchls c2 phos sars hr1 zinc-p k2
    - ⁝ **precipitated** by heat: nat-ar
  - • **yellow**: canth b7.de* chinin-s cimic k* lach b7a.de santin **Sil** k* thuj
- **straw** colored: *Chinin-s*
- **sugar**, like a conglomerate of candied: chinin-s
- **thick**: aesc k* *Alum* k* alum-p k2 apoc k* *Arn* bg2 ars-s-f k2 asc-t a1 aur-ar k2 aur-s k2 bell k* **Berb** k* *Camph* k* carl a1 *Coloc* *Cop* k* dig k* ferr-i k* hydr-ac iod b4.de* kali-bi bg2 kali-c k2* lach k* laur k* lob merc k* oena a1 ph-ac k* phos k* psor sabad sec k* seneg b4.de sep mtf33 *Spong* k* sulph k* *Sumb* ter k* tong a1 tub bg valer k*
  - • **left** standing over night; when: bry crot-t k*

- **thready**: acon bg2 ant-t bg2 brach a1 cann-s cann-xyz bg2 canth b7.de* coc-c k* merc h1* mez bg2 nit-ac k* prot jl2 seneg bg2
  - **pus**; as if from: cann-s b7.de*
- **translucent**: *Berb* k* *Coloc* k*
- **turbid**: alum b4.de* am-c b4.de* carb-an b4.de* chim ptk1 con b4.de* mang b4.de* rhus-t b7.de* valer b7.de zinc b4.de*
- **urate** cast (See Casts - urate)
- **urobilin**: loxo-lae bnm12•
- **uroxanthine**; increased: cub c1
- **violet** colored: *Ant-t* hr1 bov k* fl-ac *Mang* k* puls k* thuj b4a.de
- **white**: acon acon-l a1 act-sp a1* aesc k* aeth k* agar k* aloe *Alum* k* alum-p k2 alumn am-c k* ant-t b2.de* arist-cl sp1 aspar k* bac jl2 bar-c bg2 bar-m k* bell k* *Benz-ac* k* **Berb** k* brach k* brom k* bry k* *Calc* k* camph k* *Canth* k* caps k* carb-v carbn-s carl a1 *Chin* k* chinin-s cinch a1 cob-n sp1 coc-c colch k* *Coloc* k* con k* conv cot a1 crot-t k* dig k* dirc a1 *Dulc* k* ery-a a1 eup-per eup-pur euph k* ferr k* ferr-i k* fl-ac k* gast a1 **Graph** k* *Hep* k* hyos b2.de* ign k* kali-bi k* **Kreos** k* laur led b2.de* lil-t *Lyc* b4a.de lyss k* mag-c k* mela a1 menis a1 *Merc* hr1 mit a1* murx k* nat-m k* *Nat-s* k* *Nit-ac* k* oci a1 oci-sa sk4• oena a1 *Olnd* k* ox-ac k* *Petr* k* *Ph-ac* k* phos k* phyt k* plan k* prun bg2* ptel a1* **Rhus-t** k* sal-ac a1 **Sars** k* sec k* seneg k* **Sep** k* sol-t-ae a1 spig k* spong k* still bg2* sul-ac k* *Sulph* k* sumb k* tep a1 ter k* tong a1 *Valer* k* zinc k*
  - **adhesive**: brom k* **Sep** k*
  - **cloudy**: aspar benz-ac con k* ph-ac phos plat rhus-t k* sumb *Valer* b7.de*
  - **fever**; during: phos sep
  - **filmy**, very difficult to wash off: **Sep**
  - **floor**; on: glycyr-g cte1•
  - **pearly**: kali-bi k*
  - **snow**-white: rhus-t k*
  - **yellowish** (See yellow - white)
- **yeast**-like: caust k* mag-m k* mosch k* raph k*
- **yellow**: aesc *Aloe* am-c b2.de* am-m b2.de* anac b2.de* aur-s k2 *Bar-c* k* bry b2.de* bufo k* canth b2.de* *Cham* k* *Chin* k* chinin-s k* cimic bg2* cob k* coca *Cupr* k* daph dulc k2 *Kali-chl* k* *Kali-i* k* kali-n k* *Lach* b2.de* *Lyc* k* mang b2.de* *Nat-s* k* ph-ac b2.de* **Phos** k* sars k2 seneg b2.de* **Sep** k* sil k* sol-t-ae a1 spong k* sul-ac k* ter thuj b2.de* zinc k*
  - **adhesive**: *Ferr* k*
  - **dirty**: chin k* *Kali-chl* hr1 *Kali-i* hr1 nux-v k* *Raph*
  - **grayish**: chel k*
  - **pasty**: **Sep** k*
  - **reddish**: all-c k* chel chin chinin-s cinch a1 cob coca *Crot-h* k* *Nat-s* plect a1 *Sep*
  - **sand** (See sand - yellow)
  - **turbid**: con bg2 rhus-t bg2
  - **white**: am-c b4.de* *Carb-an* k* chinin-s coca **Dulc** b4a.de lyss k* nat-s k* phos k* raph sars k2 ter k*

SLIMY (See Sediment - mucous)

SODIUM increased: cortico sp1 pitu-p sp1

SPECIFIC gravity:

- **decreased**: alco a1 apoc k* ars-s-f k2 asc-c a1 brach k* chlf k* cimic k* coff k* colch k* dig digin a1 equis-h ery-a hr1 ferr-i k2 helon k* jab a1 kali-ar merc *Merc-c* k* morph k* murx nat-ar nat-m k* *Phos* k* **Plb** k* quas a1 sapin a1 sulph k* (non:uran-met k) uran-n urea br1 verat-v k* vib hr1
  - **alternating** with increased (See increased - alternating)
- **increased**: apoc k* **Arn** k* ars-s-f k2 asc-c a1* aur-m *Benz-ac* k* brach a1 calc *Calc-p* canth k* chim chion ptk1 coc-c k* **Colch** k* coloc k* dig k* elat k* erech a1 *Eup-pur* k* *Ferr* k* ferr-p guat sp1 *Helon* k* iod k* jab a1 *Kali-act* kali-br a1 *Kali-p* lac-d k2 lat-m bnm6• led k2 loxo-recl bnm10• *Merc* k* merc-n a1 mit a1 morph k* mur-ac k* myric a1 nat-ar nat-n a1 *Nat-s* nit-ac onos ph-ac *Phos* k* *Phyt* k* pic-ac hr1 ptel a1 *Puls* k* sapin a1 sarr k* senec k* sep k* sul-ac k* syzyg br1 tab k* tell k* trif-p a1 tub c1 (non:uran-met k) uran-n yuc a1 zinc zinc-m a1
  - **alternating** with decreased: benz-ac k2

STAINING:

- **chamber** pot, vessel, etc. (See Sediment)
- **linen**, sheets, diapers, etc.: carbn-s a2 chlf a1 dulc gsd1 elat hr1* emb-r bnj1 merc hr1 sel ll1

Staining – linen, sheets, diapers, etc.: ...

  - **brown**: benz-ac ptk1 med al2 nit-ac a1*
    - **yellowish** brown: arn hr1* med al2
  - **dark** stain: benz-ac ll1 ferr hr1
  - **red**: lyc fr3* merc hr1 *Puls* b7a.de sanic c1* sep hr1*
    - **dark** red wine; like stain made by: carb-ac a1
  - **rose** tea color: vario hr1*
  - **yellow**: dulc c1 lac-v c1 lach a1 phyt ptk1 sep hr1
    - **dark** yellow: carl c1 chel a1* sacch-l c1

STONES (See BLADDER - Stones; KIDNEYS - Stones)

SUGAR: (↗*GENERALS - Diabetes mellitus*) *Acet-ac* k* *Adren* bro1 alf st all-s k* alumn k* am-act bro1 am-c k* aml-ns k* ant-c b7a.de ant-t brb* anthraco c1 arg-met b7a.de* arg-n bro1 arist-m bro1 arn bro1 ars k* *Ars-br* bro1* ars-i bro1 aur bg2* aur-m bro1 bar-c bg2* bell bro1 benz-ac berb hr1 *Bor-ac* bro1 bov k* bry b7a.de* calc k* calc-p k* calc-sil k2 camph k* caps bro1 *Carb-ac* k* *Carb-v* k* carc jl2 cean bro1 *Cham* bro1 *Chel* k* *Chim* bro1 *Chin* k* chinin-ar *Chion* bro1 chir-fl bnm4• chlol hr1 *Coca* bro1 *Cod* hr1* coff coff-t hr1 *Colch* k* *Coloc* b4a.de* con bg2* conv cop hr1 crat br1 *Crot-h* bro1 cupr k* cupr-ar bro1 *Cur* k* *Elaps* eup-pur bro1 fel bro1 ferr hr1 ferr-i hr1* *Ferr-m* k* ferr-p hr1 fl-ac bro1 glon bro1 glyc bro1 grin br1* *Hell* bro1 helo bg2 **Helon** k* *Hep* k* *Hydr* hr1 ign rb2 ins br1 iod bro1 *Iris* k* kali-act bro1 kali-bi bg2 kali-br hr1* kali-c bg2 *Kali-chl* k* kali-m k* kali-n k* *Kali-p* k* *Kreos* k* *Lac-ac* k* *Lac-d* k* *Lach* k* lat-m bnm6• *Lec* k* led b7a.de* lith-c **Lyc** k* lycpr c1 *Lycps-v* k* lyss k* mag-c bg2 mag-s k* *Med* k* meph bg2 merc b4a.de* morg-p pte1*• morph k* mosch k* mur-ac bg2* murx bro1 nat-m b4a.de* *Nat-s* k* *Nit-ac* k* *Nux-v* b7a.de* op k* ourl jl2 *Pancr* bro1 petr k* **Ph-ac** k* phase bro1 *Phlor* c1* **Phos** k* *Pic-ac* k* **Plb** k* plb-i bro1 *Podo* k* ran-b b7a.de* *Rat* k* *Rhus-a* bro1 sal-ac k* sec k* sep b4a.de* *Sil* k* squil b7a.de* stry-ar bro1 *Sul-ac* k* *Sulph* k* **Syzyg** c1* tarax bg2* **Tarent** k* **Ter** k* *Thuj* k* (non:uran-met k) **Uran-n** k* urea bro1 vanad bro1* vinc-r vs1.fr vince bro1 zinc k* zinc-p k2 [chr-met stj1]

- **accompanied** by:
  - **paralysis** (See GENERALS - Paralysis - accompanied - urine)
  - **respiration**; asthmatic (See RESPIRATION - Asthmatic - accompanied - diabetes)
- **children**; in: ars mtf33 calc-p mtf33 chin mtf33 crat br1 lach mtf33 lyc mtf33 med mtf33 nat-s mtf33 plb mtf33 thuj mtf33

SUPPRESSED (See KIDNEYS - Suppression)

THICK: acon k* am-be bro1 am-caust k* anan bro1 *Apis* apoc *Arn* k* *Ars* ars-s-f k2 aster k* aur k* aur-ar k2 aur-m k* aur-s c1 bell k* *Benz-ac* k* berb k* bufo k* camph k* canth k* *Carb-v* k* castn-v br1 caust k* *Chim* k* cina k* clem k* coc-c k* coch hr1 coloc b4a.de* *Con* k* *Cop* k* crot-t cur *Daph* k* *Dig* k* dulc k* elaps gast a1 *Hep* k* *Iod* k* *Ip* k* iris kali-m k2 *Lac-d* k* laur lil-t k* *Lyc* b4a.de *Merc* k* **Merc-c** k* *Merc-i-r* k* mosch k* **Nux-v** k* oci a1* oena a1 *Ph-ac* k* *Phos* k* plb k* positr nl2• *Psor* k* raph k* rheum rhus-t k* ric a1 *Sabad* k* seneg k* **Sep** k* sol-t-ae a1 spong hr1 still a1* stram k* sul-ac k* sulph k* urin c1 verat k* vesp k* zing k*

- **left** standing for a while; when: *Alum* k* *Berb* *Bry* k* camph h1* *Cham* k* *Cina* **Coloc** k* ery-m a1 *Hep* k* *Merc* k* seneg b4a.de sulph sumb a1 ter k* thuj k*

TURBID (See Cloudy - white - turbid)

UREA:

- **decreased**: guat sp1 lat-m sp1
- **increased**: eucal br1 senn br1

VISCID: arg-met b2.de* arg-n k* aster k* canth k* **Coloc** k* cop k* *Cot* bro1 cupr k* cur der a1* dulc k* kreos k* *Nat-s* k* pareir bro1 ph-ac k* *Sep* k* tub c1

WATERY, clear as water: *Acet-ac* acon k* acon-s a1 aeth k* agar alum k* alumn am-m b7.de* anac k* ant-ar bg2 ant-c k* ant-t k* anthraci apis b7a.de arb c1* arn k* ars k* arum-m aster aur k* aur-ar k2 bapt bar-c *Bar-m* bell k* benz-ac k2 berb *Bism* k* bry k* calc k* calc-f calc-p cann-s k* canth *Caust* k* cedr cench k2 cham chin chinin-ar chinin-s k* *Cimic* cinnb coc-c *Cocc* k* colch k* *Coloc* k* *Con* b4a.de *Cycl* k* *Dig* k* dros k* dulc bg2 euphr k* *Ferr* hr1 *Fl-ac* **Gels** k* grat hell k* hipp hydr-ac hyos k* **Ign** k* iod k* kali-act kali-ar kali-bi kali-i kali-n b4.de* kali-p *Kali-pic* a1 kalm bg2 *Kreos* b7a.de *Lac-d* k2* lach b7.de* lact laur k* led k2 *Lyc* *Lycps-v* *Mag-c* k* med meph merc **Merc-c** bg2 merc-sul br1 mez k* *Mosch* k* **Mur-ac** k* murx k* nat-ar k2 nat-c h2 *Nat-m* k* *Nat-s* nux-m nux-v k* op k* *Ph-ac* k* *Phos* k* plat k* plb k* *Puls* k*

Urine

Watery, clear as water: ...
rhus-t $_{k*}$ sang $_{k*}$ sars $_{b4.de*}$ *Sec* $_{k*}$ **Sep** $_{k*}$ spig $_{k*}$ **Squil** $_{k*}$ stann *Staph* $_{k*}$ stram $_{k*}$ *Stront-c* $_{b4a.de}$ sul-ac $_{k*}$ sulph $_{k*}$ tab *Ter* $_{k*}$ *Teucr* $_{k*}$ *Thuj* $_{k*}$ tritic-vg $_{fd5.de}$ urea $_{br1}$ vanil $_{fd5.de}$ yohim $_{c1}$ zinc zinc-p $_{k2}$

- **fever**; during: bell $_{pd}$ hyos $_{pd}$ lach $_{pd}$ phos $_{pd}$
- **odorless**, with fetid mucous stool: dros
- **pain**; paroxysms of: phos $_{h2}$
- **scanty**, and: merc-sul $_{c1}$
- **scarlatina**; during: arum-t $_{c1}$
- **typhus** fever; in: **Mur-ac**

WHEY LIKE: agar $_{k*}$ ambr $_{b7.de*}$ *Apis* $_{b7a.de}$ *Arg-met* $_{k*}$ card-m $_{a1*}$ *Cina* $_{b7.de*}$ hyos hyosin $_{a1}$ nat-s $_{k*}$ op *Ph-ac* $_{k*}$ *Puls* $_{b7a.de}$

- **morning**: cann-s
- **left** standing for a while; when: agar
- **menses**; before: ph-ac $_{k*}$

YEAST-LIKE: *Caust* $_{k*}$ mag-m $_{a1}$ mosch $_{b7a.de*}$ *Raph* $_{k*}$

ABORTION; after: rheum ptk1

ACCOMPANIED BY: | **leukorrhea** (See FEMALE - Leukorrhea - accompanied - urinary - complaints)

BEER; after: nux-m bg2

BENDING FORWARD: | **amel**.: thuj bg2

BREATHING agg.: aur bg2

COITION: | **amel**.: sul-ac bg2

COLD AGG.; TAKING: all-c bg2 nux-m bg2 nux-v bg2

COMPLAINTS of urinary organs: *(↗KIDNEYS - Complaints)* acon bg2* apis bg2* arn bg2* ars bg2* bell bg2* *Berb* ptk1 calc bg2* *Camph* bg2* cann-xyz ptk1 *Canth* bg2* *Caust* ptk1 dulc bg2* ferr bg2* hell bg2* hep bg2* hyos bg2* **Lyc** bg2* *Merc* bg2* *Merc-c* ptk1 nat-m ptk1 nit-ac ptk1 **Nux-v** bg2* op bg2* pareir ptk1 ph-ac bg2* phos ptk1 polyg-h ptk1 *Puls* bg2* rhus-t ptk1 sars bg2* sil bg2 squil bg2* staph ptk1 sulph ptk1 *Ter* ptk1 thuj bg2* til ptk1 valer bg2* verat bg2* zinc bg2

- **accompanied** by:
  - **crying** and twisting out (See MIND - Shrieking - urinary)
  - **diarrhea**: apis bg2 arn bg2 canth bg2 lil-t bg2
  - **eczema**: lyc bro1
  - **jaundice**: carb-v ptk1 cham ptk1 chin ptk1 ign ptk1 lyc ptk1 nux-v ptk1 plb ptk1
  - **pain**; labor-like: cham bg2
  - ○ **Abdomen**; pain in (See ABDOMEN - Pain - accompanied - urinary)
  - **Cervix** of uterus; swelling of (See FEMALE - Swollen - uterus - cervix - accompanied - urinary)
  - **Glans**; pain in: pareir bg2
  - **Head**; complaints of: acon bg2 fl-ac bg2 gels bg2 *Ign* bg2 iris bg2 lac-c bg2 lyc bg2 mosch bg2 ol-an bg2 ph-ac bg2 sang bg2 sel bg2 sil bg2
  - **Skin**; complaints of: viol-t ptk1
  - **Urethra**; discharge from: acon bg2 **Cann-xyz** bg2 *Canth* bg2 dig bg2 merc bg2 petr bg2 sulph bg2
  - **Uterus**; irritation of: cycl bg2 erig bg2 pall bg2 senec bg2
- **alternating** with | **rheumatic** complaints: benz-ac ptk1
- **old** people; in: | **men**; old: alf bro1 aloe bro1 cop bro1 hep bro1 phos bro1 *Pop* bro1 staph bro1 sulph bro1

CROSSING limbs: | **amel**.: zinc bg2

EMPTY bladder agg.: ruta bg2

ERUPTIONS; after suppressed: ars bg2 calc bg2 con bg2 *Sulph* bg2

EXERTION agg.; physical: arn bg2 mill bg2

FLATUS; passage of: | **amel**.: coloc bg2

FRUITS agg.; sour: sep bg2

GONORRHEA; after: hep bg2 merc bg2 sabin bg2 sulph bg2 thuj bg2

HANDS AND KNEES; on:

- **agg**.: pareir bg2
- **amel**.: pareir bg2

LYING on back agg.: lyc bg2 puls bg2

MENSES:

- **after** | **agg**.: canth bg2 cham bg2 nat-m bg2
- **before** | **agg**.: alum bg2 am-m bg2 *Apis* bg2 asar bg2 cact bg2 calc-p bro1 cann-xyz bg2 canth bg2* cinnb bg2 coc-c bro1 con bg2 dig bg2 *Gels* bro1 hyos bg2* kali-c bg2 kali-i bg2 lac-c bg2 lach bg2 mag-p bro1 med bro1 merc bg2 *Nux-v* bg2* ph-ac bg2 phos bg2 plat bro1 puls bg2* pulx bro1 *Sars* bg2 *Senec* bro1 sep bro1 sulph bg2 verat-v bg2* vib bro1
- **during**:
  - **agg**.: acon bg2 alum bg2 apis bg2 ars bg2 asar bg2 aur bg2 berb ptk1 cact bg2 calc bg2 calc-p bro1 cann-xyz bg2 **Canth** bg2* caul bg2 *Cham* bg2 chin bg2 coc-c bg2* con bg2 eup-per bg2 *Gels* bro1 graph bg2 ham bg2 helo bg2 hydrc bg2 **Hyos** bg2* ign bg2 kali-bi bg2 kali-i bg2 lac-c bg2 lach bg2 lil-t bg2 mag-c bg2 mag-p bro1 med bro1 nat-m bg2 nit-ac bg2 nux-m bg2 **Nux-v** bg2* ph-ac bg2 phos bg2 phyt bg2 plat bg2* pop bg2 puls bg2*

Menses – during – agg.: ...

pulx bro1 rhus-t bg2 sabal bg2 *Sabin* bg2 **Sars** bg2 senec bg2* *Sep* bg2* verat-v bg2* vib bg2* zinc bg2

- **beginning** of menses | **agg**.: sars bg2 senec bg2

MOTION agg.: berb bg2

PAIN:

- **urination** agg.; after: *Nat-m* ↓ nux-v ↓ puls ↓
  - **spasmodic**: *Nat-m* bro1 nux-v bro1 puls bro1

PREGNANCY agg.; during: podo bg2 pop bg2

PRESSURE agg.: canth bg2

RAWNESS: | **Meatus**: cop bg2 kreos bg2

STANDING agg.: cann-xyz bg2 canth bg2 ferr-p bg2

STEPPING agg.: ruta bg2

TUBERCULOSIS: *Ars-i* bro1 bac bro1 calc bro1 calc-hp bro1 *Calc-i* bro1 *Chinin-ar* bro1 chinin-s bro1 hecla bro1 kali-i bro1 kreos bro1

TUMORS: anil bro1

WAKING agg.: thuj bg2

WALKING agg.: calc bg2 nat-m bg2 *Puls* bg2

WET agg.; getting feet: calc bg2 dulc bg2 ter bg2

WORMS; complaints from: cinnb bg2 sulph bg2

ABSCESS: aur c1
O - **Penis**: bov k* hippoz k* sil k2
- **Testes**: hep bro1* kali-i mrr1 merc bro1* sil k2 still bro1*

ABSENT, sensation as if penis were: *Coca* k* *Cocain*

ADHERE to scrotum, testes: tarent k*

APHRODISIAC (See Sexual desire - diminished)

APHTHAE: (↗*GENERALS - Aphthae)* borx k2

ASLEEP, as if: form k*
- **ascending** stairs agg.: form k*
O - **Penis**: merc a1
O · **Glans**: valer b7.de*

ATROPHY: ant-c bg2 arg-n bg2 bamb-a stb2.de• **Bar-c** mrr1 bufo bg2 carb-an k* cer-s k* cere-s k* iod k* kali-i bg2 lyc bg2 phos staph k*
O - **Penis**: agar k* aloe amyg k* ant-c b7a.de* arg-met k* *Arg-n* k* *Berb* k* caj *Cann-i* k* carbn-s **Ign** k* **Lyc** k* merc k* merc-sul op k* pic-ac k* plb k* staph bro1*
- **Scrotum**: kola stb3•
- **Testes**: agn bro1* ant-c b7a.de* ant-o antho *Arg-n* bro1 *Aur* k* aur-i k2 bar-c k* bufo *Caps* k* *Carb-an* k* carbn-s k* cerc-s bro1 cere-s mp1• chim k* con bg2 *Gels* k* ign mtf33 *Iod* k* kali-br bro1* **Kali-i** k* *Lyss* k* meph k* plb *Rhod* bro1 sabal c1* staph k* testis bwa3 vanil fd5.de x-ray br1* zinc k*
· **children**; in: aur mtf33
· **enlargement**; after: iod mrr1
· **sexual** excesses; after: **Staph** k*

AVERSION to sex (See Sexual desire - wanting)

BALANITIS (See Inflammation - penis - glans)

BEARING down: asaf k* coloc kola stb3•
- **holds** genitals: kola stb3•
O - **Testes** | **sensation** as if: calc bg2 chin bg2 *Nit-ac* bg2 puls bg2 *Sulph* bg2

BENDING:
- **upward** | **Penis**: berb ptk1

BLEEDING, from: | **Penis** | **Prepuce**: ars-h kreos ptk1
- **Scrotum**: petr

BLENNORRHEA of glans: abies-c br1 alum alumn k* *Bry* hr1 calad k* cann-s hr1 caust *Cinnb* k* cor-r dig k* *Jac-c* k* lach *Lyc* *Merc* k* mez k* muru a1 nat-c *Nat-m* k* *Nit-ac* k* *Nux-v* k* petr k* psor k* *Sep* k* spong fd4.de *Sulph* k* *Thuj* k*

BLUENESS (See Discoloration - blue)

BUBBLING sensation, as if bubbles were moving about:
O - **Penis**: graph k* kali-c k*
· **erections**; during: graph k* kali-c k*
O · **Glans**: kali-c b4.de* phyt bg2
- **Scrotum**: staph k*
- **Testes**: valer b7.de*

CANCER: ars k* aur sne bell k* *Carb-an* k* carbn-s sne **Con** k* ox-ac sne phos k* phyt k* plat mrr1 sil k* spong k* sulph hr1 thuj k* zinc-s sne
O - **Penis**: carbn-s sne chion sne ox-ac sne phos sne phyt sne sil sne spong sne stigm sne still sne thuj sne zinc-s sne
O · **Glans**: arg-n bro1* ars bro1* con bro1* thuj bro1*
- **Scrotum** (= epithelioma): ars bro1 aur sne aur-m gm1 carb-an fuli br1* ph-ac spong sne thuj bro1
· **scirrhus**: alum gm1 carb-an k* *Clem* hr1
- **Testes**: arg-met k2 arg-n gm1 ars mrr1 aur mp1* bell sne brom gm1 *Carb-an* mp1* *Clem* mp1* **Con** mp1* med sne ox-ac mp1* phyt mp1• plat mrr1 psor sne puls vh sil mp1• spong k* syph sne thuj mp1•

CELIBACY agg. (See GENERALS - Sexual desire - suppression - agg.)

CHOKING sensation:
O - **Spermatic** cords: am-c b4.de* *Nux-v* b7.de*
- **Testes**: am-c b4.de* **Clem** b4a.de coff b7a.de ign b7.de* m-arct b7.de m-aust b7.de* nux-v b7a.de* plb b7.de* spong b7.de*

CHORDEE (See URETHRA - Chordee)

COITION: (↗*GENERALS - Coition)*
- **agg.**:
O · **Spermatic** cords: mag-m ptk1 nat-p ptk1 sars ptk1 ther ptk1
· **Testes**: mag-m ptk1 ph-ac ptk1
- **aversion** to: aeth a1 aether a1 agar k* agn k* alum h2* am-c b4a.de* *Ant-c* b7a.de am bro1* astac k* borx bufo calad bg2 cann-s k* caust k* chlor k* clem k* coff j5.de cub a1 falco-pe nl2• ferr b7a.de* ferr-ma a1 franz a1 **Graph** k* hell a1 *Ign* b7a.de kali-br sf1.de kali-c k* kali-n a1 kreos sf1.de lach a1 **LYC** k •* m-ambo b7.de* moly-met jl3 nat-m k* nux-m j5.de op a1 petr k* ph-ac k2 phos k* plat hr1 *Psor* k* *Rhod* k* sabad b7.de sabin b7.de* sep k2* spira a1 spirae a1 stann a1 staph sf1.de stram a1 sulph mrr1 tarent a1 teucr b7.de thuj a1
· **dreams**, ending in a pollution; with erotic: *Plat* kr1
· **impotence**, with: *Graph* kr1
· **masturbation**; from: kali-br sf1.de
· **pain**; from: sep sf1.de
- **enjoyment**:
· **absent**: *Agar* k* *Anac* k* anan hr1* arg-n k* bart k* berb k* bufo *Calad* k* calc k* cann-i a1 cann-s k* canna a1 carb-v cur a1 *Dios* hr1* eug k* ferr *Graph* k* ind k* lyc k* lyss k* nat-c j5.de *Nat-m* k* nat-p sf1.de nit-ac nux-m k* onos phos k* *Plat* k* psor k* rhodi a1 sal-ac a1 sanic *Sep* k* sul-ac k* tab sf1.de tarent k* thala jl3
· **burning**; with: cann-i a1
· **diminished**: bart a1 berb j5.de germ-met srj5• plat a1 sep a1 tarent a1
· **extreme**: agn sf1.de ambr sf1.de *Fl-ac* k* lach sf1.de nat-m k* nit-ac stann a1* sulph sf1.de
· **increased**: agn bg2* ambr j5.de* calc-p j5.de falco-pe nl2• lach j5.de* nat-c j5.de *Nat-m* j5.de* spong fd4.de stann a1* sulph bg2* tritic-vg fd5.de
· **insupportable**: stann j5.de*
· **prolonged**: cann-i *Sel* kr1
· **short**: plat a1
- **gentle** and diffuse: falco-pe nl2•
- **interrupted** coition agg. (See GENERALS - Coition - interrupted)
- **involuntary** in a half waking state; almost: kali-fcy a1
- **painful**: arg-n bg2* borx bg2 calc bg2* cupr sst3• ferr bg2 kali-c bg2 kreos bg2* lyss mrr1 merc-c bg2 nat-m bg2* plat bg2 sabal bro1* sep bg2* sulph bg2 thala jl3
- **relief**; without: canth mrr1
- **sensation** as from coition: am-m h2 lach a1
· **morning** | **waking**, before micturition; on: *Kali-c* kr1
· **night**:
⁝ **midnight** | **after**: lyc a1
· **bathing** agg.: nat-c j5.de
· **pollution**, in: lach j5.de
· **sleeping** and waking; between: kreos a1
O · **Inner** parts, in: ambr j5.de

COLDNESS: agar k* **Agn** k* aloe anh sp1 berb k* brom k* calad camph cann-s k* caps k* carb-v k2 carbn-s caust bg2* *Dios* k* *Gels* k* hell ind *Iris* kola stb3• lyc k* merc k* pic-ac k* psor sabad bg2 sabal bg1* *Sulph* k* tritic-vg fd5.de (non:uran-met k) uran-n k*
- **morning**: sulph k*
- **evening**: *Dios* k*
- **touch**; to: sep mtf33
- **urination** agg.; during: iris
O - **Penis**: agar k* **Agn** k* aloe sne bar-c berb k* caps dios k* germ-met srj5• helo c1* helo-s c1* indg k* **Lyc** k* med jl2 merc k* *Onos* k* *Sulph* k*
· **painful**: germ-met srj5•
· **small**; and: agn ptk1 lyc ptk1
O · **Glans**: berb k* *Caust* b4a.de* helo c1 helo-s c1* indg a1 merc k* *Onos* *Sulph* k*
· **Prepuce**: berb k* indg a1 *Sulph* k* zinc k* zing k*
- **Scrotum**: agn bg2* aloe *Berb* k* brom calad bro1* calc bro1* *Caps* k* dios k* gels bro1* iris lyc bg2* *Merc* k* ph-ac bro1* sabad bg2 sep bro1* staph bro1* sulph bg2* tritic-vg fd5.de
· **morning** | **waking**; on: *Caps* k*
· **impotence**; with: caps a1

Male

- **Testes**: **Agn** k* aloe k* berb k* brom k* camph caps k* cer-s k* cere-s *Dios* bro1 gels helo c1* helo-s c1* *Merc* k* sil bro1* zinc
  - **left**: brom k*
  - **evening**: aloe *Merc* k*
  - **night**: *Agn* k* aloe
  - **sensation** of: *Brom* b4a.de* merc b4.de* onos bg2

COMPLAINTS of male genitalia: acon b2.de agar b2.de *Agn* b2.de* alum b2.de* am-c b2.de am-m b2.de ambr b2.de* anac b2.de ang b2.de ant-c b2.de* ant-t b2.de arg-met b2.de arg-n ptk1 **Arn** b2.de* ars b2.de* asaf b2.de asar b2.de aur b2.de* bac jl2 bar-c b2.de bell b2.de* bism b2.de borx b2.de bov b2.de bry b2.de calad b2.de* calc b2.de* camph b2.de *Cann-s* b2.de* cann-xyz ptk1 *Canth* b2.de* caps b2.de* carb-an b2.de carb-v b2.de* caust b2.de* cham b2.de chel b2.de chim br1 chin b2.de* cic b2.de cinnb ptk1 clem b2.de* cob br1 cocc b2.de coff b2.de colch b2.de coloc b2.de con b2.de* croc b2.de cupr b2.de cycl b2.de* dig b2.de dros b2.de dulc b2.de eucal br1 euph b2.de euphr b2.de ferr b2.de* graph b2.de* guaj b2.de hell b2.de hep b2.de* hyos b2.de ign b2.de* iod b2.de* ip b2.de kali-c b2.de* kali-n b2.de kreos b2.de lach b2.de laur b2.de led b2.de lyc b2.de* m-ambo b2.de m-arct b2.de m-aust b2.de mag-c b2.de mag-m b2.de mang b2.de meny b2.de **Merc** b2.de* mez b2.de* mosch b2.de mur-ac b2.de nat-c b2.de* nat-m b2.de* **Nit-ac** b2.de* nux-m b2.de **Nux-v** b2.de* op b2.de par b2.de petr b2.de* ph-ac b2.de* phos b2.de* plat b2.de* plb b2.de* **Puls** b2.de* ran-s b2.de rhod b2.de* rhus-t b2.de* ruta b2.de sabad b2.de sabin b2.de* sal-n br1 samb b2.de sars b2.de sec b2.de *Sel* b2.de* seneg b2.de sep b2.de* sil b2.de* spig b2.de spong b2.de* squil b2.de stann b2.de staph b2.de* stram b2.de sul-ac b2.de **Sulph** b2.de* syc fmm1• tarax b2.de teucr b2.de thuj b2.de* thymol br1 valer b2.de verat b2.de viol-t b2.de zinc b2.de*

- **right** side: *Acon* fse1.de alum fse1.de *Arn* fse1.de *Aur* fse1.de *Bism* fse1.de **Calc** fse1.de *Cann-s* fse1.de *Canth* fse1.de **Caust** fse1.de *Clem* fse1.de *Coff* fse1.de *Coloc* fse1.de *Con* fse1.de *Croc* fse1.de graph fse1.de **Hep** fse1.de *Iod* fse1.de *Lach* fse1.de *Lyc* fse1.de m-arct fse1.de *Meny* fse1.de *Merc* fse1.de mez fse1.de *Mur-ac* fse1.de nit-ac fse1.de **Nux-v** fse1.de petr fse1.de *Puls* fse1.de *Rhod* fse1.de *Sabin* fse1.de *Sec* fse1.de *Sel* fse1.de sil fse1.de *Spig* fse1.de **Spong** fse1.de *Staph* fse1.de **Sul-ac** fse1.de *Sulph* fse1.de tarax fse1.de teucr fse1.de *Valer* fse1.de **Verat** fse1.de *Zinc* fse1.de
- **left** side: *Agar* fse1.de alum fse1.de *Am-m* fse1.de ambr fse1.de *Ang* fse1.de *Ant-c* fse1.de *Arg-met* fse1.de *Aur* fse1.de *Bar-c* fse1.de *Bry* fse1.de calc fse1.de cann-s fse1.de *Chin* fse1.de clem fse1.de *Colch* fse1.de *Con* fse1.de *Euph* fse1.de graph fse1.de *Kali-c* fse1.de lyc fse1.de m-arct fse1.de *Mag-c* fse1.de meny fse1.de *Merc* fse1.de mez fse1.de *Nat-c* fse1.de *Nit-ac* fse1.de petr fse1.de *Ph-ac* fse1.de *Plb* fse1.de *Puls* fse1.de *Rhod* fse1.de *Rhus-t* fse1.de *Sabad* fse1.de sel fse1.de *Sep* fse1.de sil fse1.de spig fse1.de staph fse1.de tarax fse1.de teucr fse1.de **Thuj** fse1.de zinc fse1.de
- **accompanied** by:
  - **anemia** (See GENERALS - Anemia - accompanied - genital)

○ - **Glans** (See Penis - glans)
- **Penis** (See Penis)
- **Prepuce** (See Penis - prepuce)
- **Scrotum** (See Scrotum)
- **Spermatic** cords (See Spermatic)
- **Testes** (See Testes)

CONDYLOMATA: aethi-m bro1 alumn apis *Arg-n* ars b4a.de aur *Aur-m* k* aur-m-n k* aur-s k2 *Calc* k* *Caust* b4a.de *Cinnb* k* cupr b7a.de euphr k* *Fl-ac* **Hep** **Iod** b4a.de kali-i bro1 *Lyc* k* *Med* k* *Merc* k* merc-act bro1 merc-aur bro1 merc-br bro1 merc-c bro1 merc-cy bro1 *Merc-d* k* merc-i-f bro1 merc-i-r bro1 merc-ns bro1 merc-p bro1 merc-pr-r bro1 merc-tn bro1 *Mill* k* **Nat-s** k* **Nit-ac** k* nux-v b7a.de *Ph-ac* k* *Phos* plat-m bro1 psor k* *Sabin* k* sanic mrr1 *Sars* k* sec b7a.de *Sep* k* sil b4a.de *Staph* k* sulph b4a.de* syc bka1• **Thuj** k*

- **bleed** easily: *Calc* *Cinnb* med *Mill* **Nit-ac** k* sulph *Thuj* k*
- **burning**: *Sabin* b7a.de
- **cheese**; smelling like stale: *Calc* *Hep* *Sanic* thuj
- **coxcomb**; like a (= cockscomb): lyc bg2 *Nit-ac* bg2 **Thuj** bg2
- **dry**: cinnb bg2 nux-v bg2 sars bg2 sulph bg2 **Thuj** bg2
- **fetid**, bleeding when touched: *Cinnb* **Nit-ac** k* thuj
- **flat**: merc bg2 **Nit-ac** bg2 sars bg2 **Thuj** bg2
- **hot**: ph-ac k*
- **itching**: euphr bg2 lyc psor *Sabin* k* staph k* thuj k*
- **moist**: *Nit-ac* bg2 *Thuj* b4a.de*
- **offensive**: sanic mrr1

Condylomata: ...

- **sensitive**: euphr bg2 nit-ac k2* ph-ac mp1• sabin bg2 *Staph* k*
- **soft**: calc k2 *Nat-s* hr1 *Sep*
- **sore** pain: sabin b7a.de
- **sticking** pain: nit-ac

○ - **And** around anus: nit-ac
- **Penis**: alumn ant-t ptk1* *Apis* aur vh aur-m k2* bell k* *Calc* k* **Cinnb** euphr *Hep* *Kali-i* vh lac-c *Lyc* k* med ptk1 *Merc* merc-c *Mill* *Nat-s* **Nit-ac** nux-v vh *Ph-ac* **Psor** **Sabin** *Sanic* vh **Sep** k* *Staph* *Sulph* **Thuj** k*
  - **bleeding**: *Cinnb* **Nit-ac** k* sulph *Thuj*
  - **burning**: apis *Cinnb* **Nit-ac** ph-ac *Psor* k* *Sabin* k* *Thuj*
  - **butternut**-shaped hard growth on the dorsum of the Penis: **Sabin**
  - **cauliflower**, like: lac-c **Nit-ac** k*
  - **fan** shaped: **Cinnb** *Thuj* k*
  - **itching**: *Psor* k* *Sabin*
  - **oozing**: aur-m *Cinnb* *Lyc* k* *Nit-ac* k* *Psor* *Thuj* k*
    - **offensive**: *Nit-ac* k*
  - **soreness**: euphr **Nit-ac** ph-ac k* *Sabin* k* thuj
    - **itching**; and: *Psor* *Sabin*

○ • **Glans**: *Ant-t* k* *Aur* k* *Aur-m* k* aur-s k2 *Cinnb* *Kali-chl* *Kali-i* k* *Lac-c* k* lyc k* m-aust b7.de *Med* *Merc* bg2 *Nit-ac* k* *Ph-ac* k* psor *Sabin* k* *Sep* k* *Staph* k* *Sulph* k* **Thuj** k*
  - **Prepuce**: apis bro1 *Aur* *Aur-m* k* aur-m-n k* caust **Cinnb** k* cub hep bro1 kreos bro1 *Lyc* k* *Med* merc merc-c nat-m bro1 *Nit-ac* k* ph-ac k* **Psor** k* *Sabin* k* sep bg* staph bro1 **Thuj** k*
    - **Edge** of, itching and burning: psor k*
    - **Frenum**: **Cinnb**
- **Scrotum**: *Aur* *Aur-m* k* *Med* jl2 sil **Thuj** k*

CONGESTION: yohim br1*

○ - **Scrotum**: (non:coloc k*) colocin a1*
- **Testes**: ham bg2 lycps-v bg2

CONSTRICTION:

○ - **Penis**: kali-bi ptk1

○ • **Glans**, behind: coloc plb puls
  - **coition**; after: calad
  - **Prepuce**: acon bro1 *Apis* bro1 arn bro1 bell bro1 cann-s bro1 *Canth* bro1 caps bro1 *Coloc* b4a.de dig bro1 euphr bro1 ham bro1 merc k* *Merc-c* bro1 nit-ac k* ol-sant bro1 ph-ac bro1 rhus-t k* sabin k* sulph k* *Thuj* bro1
- **Spermatic** cords: nux-v b7a.de
- **Testes**: alum bg2 merc bg2 *Nux-v* b7.de* plb b7.de*

CONSTRINGING sensation: arn asar kali-c mosch

○ - **Penis**: thuj b4a.de
- **Testes**: am-c bg2 ign bg2 plb bg2 spong bg2

CONTRACTION: helo-s bnm14• nit-ac b4a.de phos b4a.de plat b4.de* sulph b4a.de

○ - **Penis**: ign b7.de* puls b7.de*

○ • **Glans**: asar b7.de*
  - **Prepuce**: *Ars* b4a.de *Cann-s* b7a.de* lach b7a.de **Merc** b4.de* merc-c b4a.de *Nit-ac* b4a.de* rhus-t b7a.de* sabin b7a.de* sep bg2 **Sulph** b4a.de* *Thuj* b4a.de*
- **Scrotum**: acon k* arn k* berb k* cann-s k* clem k* ferr bg2 ferr-m op k* petr b4.de* plb k* zinc b4.de*
- **Spermatic** cords: alum b4.de* kali-c b4a.de nux-v bg2
- **Testes**: arg-met c1 *Aur* b4a.de camph b7.de* chin b7.de* phos b4a.de plb b7.de*

CRAB LICE: (↗*HEAD - Lice; SKIN - Lousiness*) cocc c1* sabad k* staph

CRACKS: ars bg2 bacls-10 fmm1• merc bg2 *Sulph* bg2

○ - **Penis**: calc b4a.de

○ • **Glans**: *Ars* k* graph k2 kali-c mosch rhus-t
  - **Prepuce**: hep ptk1 hydrog srj2• merc k* propl ub1• sep k* sul-i ptk1 **Sulph** k •*
- **Scrotum**: petr bg2 thuj b4a.de

CRAWLING (See Formication)

CRYPTORCHISM: *(↗Retraction - testes)* aloe sne aur vh1* iod mrr1 psor mtf33 sil kr syph jl2* *Thyr* br1* tub mtf33

○ - **Abdominal**: aur fry3 bar-c fry3 bar-m fry3 calc klx con fry3 cupr fry3 lyc fry3 pitu-gl fry3 test fry3* thyr fry3 zinc fry3

- **Prepubic**: *(↗Retraction - testes)* aur lmj* aur-m samkn *Bar-c* lmj calc lmj calc-f lmj calc-p lmj* caust lmj *Con* lmj *Fl-ac* lmj *Syph* lmj thyr samkn

DESIRE (See Sexual desire)

DESIRE for ejaculation (See Ejaculation - desire)

DISAGREEABLE sensation: graph b4.de* sil b4.de*

DISCHARGE (See URETHRA - Discharge)

DISCOLORATION:

- **blue**: op b7.de*
  - **spots**; blue: ars k*
  - ○ **Penis**: arn b7.de*
    - **Glans**: apis hr1 ars k*
      - **dark** blue: borx b4a.de
    - **Prepuce**: ars bg2
      - **spots**: *Ars* b4a.de
  - **Scrotum**: amyg *Arn* b7.de* *Ars* k* con b4a.de merc-cy *Mur-ac* k* puls ptk1
    - **eruption**, after: tep
- **dark**:
  - ○ **Penis** | **Prepuce**: rhus-t b7.de*
- **red**:
  - ○ **Penis**: arn b7.de* cann-xyz bg2 hedy a1*
    - **purple**-red: arn tl1
    - **spots**: calc bg2 caust b4.de* sil bg2
    - **Frenum** | **spots**: rhus-t b7a.de
    - **Glans**: alum-sil k2 *Ars* k* calad k* calc-sil k2 cann-s k* *Cor-r* crot-t *Dor* iris c1 m-aust b7.de merc k* nat-m k* rhus-t ruta fd4.de sabad bg2 sabin k* sars k* spong fd4.de tritic-vg fd5.de
      - **spots**; in: arn bg2 carb-v bg2 dulc fd4.de *Lach* bg2 nat-m h2 petr h2 sep h2 sil h2 spong fd4.de tritic-vg fd5.de
      - **Tip**: nat-m h2 *Sel* rsj9•
        - **cold** washing | **amel.**: sel rsj9•
    - **Prepuce**: calc k* cann-s k* caust bg2 **Cinnb** k* *Cor-r* lach lyc *Merc* k* nit-ac bg2 prun rhus-v rumx ruta fd4.de sil k* spong fd4.de *Sulph* k* sumb
      - **spots**: aloe nit-ac bg2 rhus-t b7.de*
  - **Scrotum**: anac ant-s-aur apis arn b7.de* *Chel* cop **Crot-t** *Merc* k* **Petr** k* positr nl2• puls k* rhus-t k* rhus-v sulph trad a1* tritic-vg fd5.de
    - **bluish**: *Mur-ac*
    - **spots**, in: lac-ac tritic-vg fd5.de
    - **Sides**: agar ars petr
  - **Scrotum**; between thighs and: ambr cop **Petr** k* thuj trios rsj11•
    - **warm** applications agg.: trios rsj11•
  - **Testes** | **purple**-red: arn tl1
  - **Thighs**; between: petr
- **spots**; in: arn bg2 carb-v bg2 sil bg2

DRAWING Scrotum: am-c k* clem k* meny h1*

DRAWN up and painful; testes (See Retraction - testes - painful)

DRIBBLING of semen (See Semen)

DRYNESS:

○ - **Penis**:

- ○ **Glans**: bacls-10 fmm1• *Calad* k* lyss k*
- **Prepuce**: alum bg2 calad bg2 ign bg2 mur-ac bg2 nat-c bg2 nux-v bg2 *Sil* bg2 verat bg2

DYSPAREUNIA (See Coition - painful)

ECTOPIA testis (See Cryptorchism)

EJACULATION:

- **night** (See Pollutions - night)
- **absent**: agar k2 *Bar-c* b4a.de calad b7.de* *Calc* bg2 coff b7.de* graph b4a.de* *Kali-c* b4.de* *Lach* bg2 *Lyc* b4.de* *M-aust* b7a.de mill bg2 nat-m bg2 nux-v b7.de* rhus-g tmo3•
- **bloody**: ambr bro1 cann-s k* *Canth* k* *Caust* k* fl-ac bg* led k* **Lyc** ● * **Merc** k* *Petr* k* puls ptk1 *Sars* k* sulph h2* tarent wies st
  - **night**: **Merc** a1*
- **burning**: clem bg2 sulph bg2
  - **coition**; during: *Calc* kr1 cann-i a1
- **cold**, during coition: *Nat-m* k*
- **copious**: agar bell bros-gau mrc1 carb-v carbn-s carl iod kali-c merc-i-f nat-m par petr ph-ac *Pic-ac* sep sil staph sulph ther j5.de zinc
  - **night**: aur carb-an *Dig* hipp ign ol-an a1
    - **midnight**:
      - **after** | **3** h: pip-m a1
  - **coition**; after: bar-c
  - **dreams**, with: kali-c pip-m sars
  - **longer**; and: osm
- **desire** for: ign j5.de* *M-arct* j5.de nux-v j5.de
  - **morning**:
    - **bed** agg.; in: puls a1
    - **rising** agg.; after: nux-v a1
    - **waking** agg.; after: petr a1 rhus-t a1
  - **evening** and after dinner, without sexual desire for: nat-c a1
  - **erection**, without: sulph a1
- **difficult**: anan carbn-s cimic jl lach k* lim a1 lyss kr1 *Zinc* k*
- **early** (See quick)
- **erection**:
  - **feeble** erection; with: sel ptk1
  - **without**: cob ptk1 dios ptk1 gels ptk1 graph ptk1
- **excessive**: carb-v a1 iod a1 sulph a1 zing a1
- **exhausting**: *Carb-an* bg2 *Chin* b7.de* ferr b7.de *Kali-c* b4.de* lach bg2 *Lyc* bg2 *Nux-v* bg2 *Ph-ac* b4a.de* sep b4a.de*
- **failing** during coition: agn bacls-7 fmm1• bar-c k* bufo *Calad* k* calc k* carbn-s carc mlr1• coff bg *Eug* gast a1 **Graph** k* hipp jl2 hydr kali-c kali-i *Lach* j5.de* lim a1 *Lyc* k* *Lyss* k* med tl1* mill nat-m nux-v bg ph-ac *Psor* k* syc bka1*• syph jl2 yohim c1* zinc
  - **occurs** afterwards during sleep: lyss kr1
  - **orgasm** is present; though the: cann-i graph
- **fast** (See quick)
- **frothy**: mur-ac h1*
- **hot**: agar bg* calc bg1* tarent bg*
- **incomplete**: *Agar* agn bg* aloe anan arg-met a1 bar-c berb calad j5.de* calc j5.de* *Camph* bg canth bg carbn-s coff bg *Con* bg dig falco-pe nl2• *Form* hydr a1 ign bg *Kali-c* bg lach sf1.de *Lyc* bg lyss nat-m bg nux-m bg *Phos* j5.de plb k* sel bg sep j5.de* sul-ac bg sulph h2 ther kr1 zinc zing a1*
  - **erections**:
    - **before**: *Sulph* kr1
    - **incomplete** erections; with: calad kr1 *Form* kr1 sel mtf11
- **insensible**: nat-p bg2 plan bg2
- **larger** and continues longer: osm
- **late**, too: *Agar* k* bar-c b4a.de berb k1 borx k* **Calc** k* erig mg1.de eug *Fl-ac* k* hydr lach k* lyc k* *Lyss* merc-c k* *Nat-m* petr k* sel b7a.de *Zinc* k*
  - **orgasm**: *(↗Orgasm - subsides)*
    - **after** orgasm; some time: calc
    - **subsides** (See Orgasm - subsides)
  - **sexual** desire; without: *Nat-m* kr1
- **lemon**-colored: hura a1*
- **lumpy**: alum a1 cere-s a1*
- **milky**: lach a1
- **mortification**, followed by: staph k2
- **odorless**: agn b7.de* *Sel* b7.de* sulph ptk1
- **odors**:
  - **abnormal**: *Sel* kr1

Male

- **odors**: ...
  - **fish** agg.; of: germ-met srj5•
  - **little**: agn a1
  - **strong** odors agg.: *Lach* j5.de* thuj c1
  - **urine**; like stale: *Nat-p* a1*
- **painful**: *Agar* arg-n *Berb Calc Cann-s* bg* cann-xyz ptk1 *Canth* k* clem coli jl2 *Con* k* *Kali-c* k* kali-i *Kreos* merc mosch nat-act nat-c k1* *Nit-ac* ran-s bg sabad bg sabal ptk1 sars *Sep* sul-ac **Sulph** k* thuj
- **pale**: bell a1
- **pleasure**; without: agar vh
- **quick**, too (= premature): adlu jl agar ptk1 agn ptk1 aloe am b7.de* bar-c k* *Berb* k* borx k* brom k* bros-gau mrc1 bufo *Calad* k* *Calc* k* canna a1 canth b7a.de carb-an bg* *Carb-v* k* carbn-s *Chin* b7.de* *Con* k* *Ery-a* bg2* eug *Gels* **Graph** k* ind **Lyc** k* merc mrr1 *Nat-c* k* *Nat-m* k* nux-v bg ol-an bg2 onos petr b4.de* *Ph-ac* k* *Phos* k* pic-ac *Plat* k* *Sel* k* *Sep* k* spong fd4.de staph bg2* sul-ac mrr1 *Sulph* k* thala jl *Titan* k13* ust bg2* vanil fd5.de **Zinc** k*
  - **coition**; during:
    - **followed** by | **Head**; roaring in: carb-v ptk1
  - **dream** of coition; during: sumb a1
  - **enjoyment**; without: bufo kr1 calc h2 canna a1 sul-ac a1
  - **erection**:
    - **after**; shortly: *Ph-ac Sulph*
    - **before** erection is complete: calad kr1 **Graph** kr1 *Sulph* bg*
  - **excitement**; almost without: bufo k1 eug kr1
  - **intromission**, before: *Sulph*
- **reddish** brown: fl-ac st*
- **scanty**: agn b7.de* *Ant-c* b7a.de calad b7.de* *Calc* b4a.de *Camph* b7.de* coff b7.de* graph b4a.de *Kali-c* b4.de* lach b7a.de *Lyc* b4.de* nat-m b4.de* sel b7a.de
- **short**: sep a1
- **sticky**: plat sne *Staph* kr1
- **stream**; running in a: agn a1
- **sudden**: phos a1
- **thick**: alum a1 alumn a1 med kr1 sabal ptk1
  - **threads**; with: med kr1
- **thin**: borx b4a.de sel b7.de*
- **thrill** prolonged: cann-i vh sel ptk1
- **voluptuous** sensation; without: calc h2 vanil fd5.de
- **watery**: agn hr1 bart borx h2* led b7.de* med kr1 mez bg2* mur-ac h2* *Nat-p* bg2* *Sel* b7a.de* *Sep* h2* sulph h2* vanil fd5.de
- **weak**: agn b7.de* bell a1 calc b4a.de* canth b7.de* *Con* b4.de* ign b7.de* merc-c b4a.de nat-m b4a.de* nux-m b7.de* *Ph-ac* b4a.de *Phos* b4.de* rhus-g tmo3• sel b7.de* sep b4a.de* sul-ac b4a.de*

ELEPHANTIASIS scrotum: (↗*Swelling - scrotum - inflammatory)* calo br1 sil k*

EMPYOCELE: (↗*Suppuration) Ars-i Calc* **Calc-sil** *Hep* **Kali-s** k* *Psor Puls* **Sil** k* **Sulph** k*

ENJOYMENT (See Coition - enjoyment)

ENLARGED:

○ - **Spermatic** cords: fl-ac kali-i
- **Testes**: arg-n k* ars k* aur k2 bar-c bro1 bar-m k* *Berb* bro1 brom ptk1 cinnb bro1 *Clem* ptk1 con bro1 dulc ptk1 *Ham* bro1 *Iod* k* *Merc* bro1 merc-i-r bro1 mez ptk1 *Puls* bro1* rhod ptk1 spong ptk1 stigm bro1
  - **right**: arg-n k* **Aur**
  - **left**: *Alum* helo-s rwt2• spong
    - **two** years; for: spong
  - **walking** agg.: *Clem* k*

ERECTIONS: *Canth* ptk1 graph ptk1 merc ptk1 nat-c ptk1 nat-m ptk1 *Nux-v* ptk1 *Phos* ptk1 pic-ac ptk1 plat ptk1 puls ptk1 thuj ptk1
- **day** and night: ferr kr1 *Phos* kr1
- **daytime**: anac cann-i a1 cann-s j5.de *Chel Clem* kali-c j5.de lach lyc j5.de mez h2* nat-c h2* *Phos* puls sabin j5.de sil sin-n kr1 sul-ac h2* valer j5.de
- **morning**: agar *Agn* all-c aloe **Am-c** ambr k* ars ars-h ars-i asc-t aster a1 bar-c bond a1 brom k* calad calc canth caps k* carb-an j5.de caust cham chin-b kr1 *Cimx* coc-c cop dig form a1 *Graph* j5.de* guaj a1 ham fd3.de• kali-ar kali-c kali-n h2 kali-p kali-sil k2 lac-ac *Lach* lact j5.de m-arct j5.de *Mag-m* mur-ac nat-ar nat-c nat-m nat-p nat-s nicc nit-ac *Nux-v* k* ol-an a1 osm pall a1* *Ph-ac*

Erections – morning: ...
phos k* plat j5.de plb psor *Puls* ran-b j5.de *Rhod* j5.de rhus-t *Sel Sil* tab tet a1 ther j5.de* thuj k* valer viol-t
  - **only** morning: *Bar-c* pall
  - **bed** agg.; in: *Caps* j5.de* cham j5.de* kali-n j5.de* *Mag-m* j5.de* mur-ac j5.de* nit-ac j5.de* *Nux-v* j5.de ph-ac j5.de* phos j5.de *Puls* j5.de sabad j5.de
    - **desire**, without: am-c kr1 ambr kr1 calad kr1 chin-b kr1 *Nat-m* kr1 sel kr1
    - **dreaming**; while: colch a1
  - **riding**; after: aur h2 calc h2
  - **rising** agg.: bar-c a1 calc a1 canth a1 caps a1 dig a1 osm a1
  - **standing** agg.: *Ph-ac*
  - **waking**; on: nat-c h2 petr a1
    - **6** h: guaj
    - **and** after: anac h2 arn h1* bamb-a stb2.de• borx h2* *Card-m* kr1 ham fd3.de• nat-c h2* ox-ac a1 petr ph-ac phos h2 pic-ac plat *Sil* sulph thuj
- **forenoon**: caps caust lach nicc ol-an j5.de ox-ac phys a1
  - **lying** down, when: ox-ac a1
  - **riding** in a carriage, when: form a1
- **noon**: kali-n h2* *Nux-v* a1
  - **afternoon**; and: par j5.de
- **afternoon**: alum j5.de caps h1 carbn-s cham eug j5.de lyss *Nux-v* pip-m a1 thuj ust a1
  - **14** h: alumn a1 mag-s a1
  - **15** h: equis-h a1
  - **16** h: ust a1
  - **17** h: equis-h a1
  - **micturition**, after: nat-c a1
  - **sitting** agg.: alum
  - **sleep** | **siesta** agg.; after: eug kr1 kali-s fd4.de *Nux-v* sep h2*
  - **walking** agg.: hyper a1
- **evening**: alum alumn a1 bar-c cact caps h1* cerv a1 cinnb fago lach j5.de laur j5.de *Lyss* kr1 nat-s phos k* sil h2
  - **18** h: equis-h a1
  - **bed** agg.; in: cinnb j5.de con j5.de nit-ac j5.de*
  - **lying** down agg.; after: nit-ac a1
  - **shivering** and great desire; with: bar-c k*
- **night**: agar aloe alum k* alum-p k2 alum-sil k2 ambr h1 **Aur** k* aur-i k2 bamb-a stb2.de• bar-c bell brom a1 bry cain a1 calad calc calc-sil k2 **Canth** k* *Caps* carb-v *Caust* cent a1 con corn kr1 cycl *Dios* euph h2* ferr ferr-i ferr-p k2 **Fl-ac** k* gins j5.de* gymno a1 helon kr1 hep h2 *Kali-br* kali-c kali-p kali-s fd4.de kali-sil k2 *Lach* laur j5.de *Merc* k* merc-c mez *Nat-c* k* nat-m k* nat-p nicc **Nit-ac** k* ol-an *Op* osm ox-ac k2 par petr ph-ac **Phos Pic-ac** pip-m a1 **Plat** k* plb *Puls* j5.de* rhod a1 rhus-t k* sabin j5.de seneg j5.de sep *Sil* sin-n stann staph k* sul-i k2 sumb a1 tell thuj k* yuc a1 zinc k* zinc-p k2
  - **midnight**: ambr j5.de nit-ac a1 osm a1
    - **after**:
      - **2** h: aloe
      - **3-4** h: osm a1
      - **3-8** h: brom a1
      - **4** h: calad a1 pic-ac a1 pip-m a1
    - **waking**; on: ambr a1
  - **bed**, when becoming warm in: ant-c
  - **pollution**, after: nit-ac a1
  - **rising** agg.; after: caj a1
  - **sleep** agg.; during: *Fl-ac* a1 op a1 rhod a1 ther sf1.de
    - **half** asleep, cease when fully awake: calad kr1*
    - **urination** | **urging** to urinate; with: *Rhus-t* kr1
  - **urination**:
    - **after** | **agg.**: aloe lith-c kr1
    - **before**: sin-n a1
    - **during** | **agg.**: staph h1
  - **waking**; on: dig a1 guare a1 *Hep* kr1 nit-ac j5.de* sil kr1 yuc a1

- **accompanied** by:
  - **nausea** (See STOMACH - Nausea - accompanied - erections)
  - **stool**; complaints of (See STOOL - Complaints - accompanied - erections)
  - O **Abdomen**; pain in: zinc ptk1
  - **Teeth**; pain in (See TEETH - Pain - accompanied - erections)
  - **Urethra**:
    - **bleeding** (See URETHRA - Discharge - bloody - accompanied - erections)
    - **discharge** from (See URETHRA - Discharge - accompanied - erections)
- **agg.**: con bg2 lith-c bg2 mur-ac bg2 nit-ac bg2
- **bed** agg.; in: ant-c a1 kali-bi a1 upa a1
- **causeless**: *Am-c* j5.de carl a1 euph a1 ferr h1* nat-m a1 ox-ac a1* sil h2* tarax j5.de
  - **lying** down agg.: ox-ac a1*
- **children**; in: aloe ambr lmj *Calc-p* lmj *Cann-i* lmj canth lmj carc lmj *Fl-ac* lmj **Hyos** lmj lac-c lmj *Lach* k* lyss lmj med lmj *Merc* k* *Mosch* lmj ph-ac gt1* **Phos** lmj staph lmj stram lmj *Tub* k* *Zinc* lmj
- **chordee** (See URETHRA - Chordee)
- **coition**; after: agn k* aur-s k* bry k* calad k* cann-i k* cann-s k* caust k* graph k* grat nat-c k* rhod k* sec *Sep* k* tarent k*
  - **indifference**; with sexual: lyss kr1
- **continued** (= priapism): agar agn a1* *Am-c* j5.de* ambr kr1 androc bnm2• anthraco kr1* apis arg-n k* arn atra-r bnm3• bell *Calc* b4a.de camph k* *Cann-i* *Cann-s* b7a.de* **Canth** k* *Caps* kr1 carb-v carbn-s caust j5.de cinnb c1* clem k* *Coloc* k* cypra-eg sde6.de• dig *Dios* bg2* euph j5.de fl-ac a1* *Gins* bg2* gonotox jl2 *Graph* k* hyos ign bg2 iod *Kali-br* kali-c bg2 kali-chl j5.de kola stb3• lach b7.de* lat-m sp1* *Laur* sf1.de led k* lyss br1* *M-arct* b7.de* *Med* kr1* merc b4a.de* mur-ac h2 mygal kr1 *Nat-c* k* nat-hchls c1* *Nat-m* k* nat-p nit-ac j5.de* nux-v k* oena c1* op b7.de* opun-s a1 (non:opun-v a1) ped a1 *Petros* kr1* ph-ac bg2 *Phos* k* *Pic-ac* k* pip-n c1* *Plat* k* *Puls* k* raph c1* rhod j5.de* *Rhus-t* bg2 sabin sel c1* sep k* sil k* sin-n c1* spirae a1 staph bg2 *Stram* kr1 tarax *Thuj* b4a.de* thymol br1 verat b7.de* visc jl yohim c1* zinc zinc-pic c1* zinc-val c1*
  - **daytime**: clem a1
  - **morning**: asc-t a1 canth a1 dig a1 erech a1 nat-c h2* *Puls* k* yohim c1
    - **waking**; on: diaz sa3• nat-c h2
  - **night**: bamb-a stb2.de• carb-v a1 corn a1* *Dios* sf1.de* *Fl-ac* k* *Kali-br* hr1* *Lach* hr1* nat-m k* nit-ac h2* pic-ac a1* plat k* sep k* sin-n k* staph h1* thuj k*
  - **accompanied** by | **Spine**; disorders of (See BACK - Pain - spine - accompanied - priapism)
  - **coition**; after: agn a1 cann-i a1 germ-met srj5• rhod a1 sep h2*
  - **curvature** of penis, with: canth j5.de
  - **dreaming**; while: *Camph* kr1
  - **eating**; after: hyos a1
  - **falls** asleep; as soon as he: pic-ac kr1
  - **gonorrhea**; in: cann-xyz bg2 **Canth** bg2 thuj bg2
  - **nausea**; with: kali-bi hr1*
  - **old** people; in: | **men**; old: arn kr1
  - **painful**: (↗*URETHRA - Chordee*) acon kr1 **Arg-n** aur-m bry *Camph* *Cann-i* **Cann-s Canth Caps** chlol *Colch* con cop *Cub* cur dig ery-a fl-ac hep jac-c kr1 kali-br **Kali-chl** kali-i *Kali-m* kr1 *Merc* merc-c *Mygal* nat-c *Nit-ac* *Nux-v* *Petros* phos pip-n **Puls** sabad sep still kr1 **Ter** *Thuj* zing
    - **burning** in urethra, with: calc-p
    - **sensitiveness** in urethra; with extreme: *Caps*
  - **pollutions**:
    - **after**: rhod kr1
    - **with**: lyss kr1*
  - **semi**-priapism: oena kr1 *Puls* kr1
  - **spinal** disease, with: *Pic-ac* lp*
  - **trance**-like state, with: *Camph* kr1
  - **urine**, with retention of: coloc kr1
- **convulsive**: nit-ac hr1*
- **convulsive**: ...
  - **child**, in a: *Lach* kr1
- **cough** agg.; during: cann-s k* cann-xyz ptk1 canth k*
- **delayed**: **Bar-c** k* *Calc* k* canth k* carbn-s iod k* kali-i a1 mag-c k* merc-c k* nit-ac k* osm k* par k* pic-ac k* *Sel* k* ser-a-c jl2 sil k*
- **difficult**: acon-ac rly4• aq-mar skp7• canth a1 pers jl3 ser-a-c jl2 tere-ch jl3
- **dinner**; during: alumn a1* nicc a1*
- **disturbing** sleep: alum j5.de ambr j5.de ant-c j5.de* aur j5.de carb-v j5.de* coloc j5.de dig a1 hep h2* kali-c h2* lach j5.de led j5.de lith-c kr1 merc j5.de merc-act j5.de *Nat-c* j5.de* nat-m j5.de* ol-an j5.de* op j5.de par j5.de ph-ac j5.de pic-ac a1* plat j5.de plb j5.de ran-b j5.de sep h2* *Sil* j5.de* *Stann* j5.de thuj j5.de
- **dreams**, with amorous: aur j5.de cact hr1* camph st1 *Cann-i* a1* clem a1 coloc j5.de kreos j5.de lac-ac hr1* led j5.de merc j5.de mur-ac h2* *Nat-c* j5.de nat-m j5.de par j5.de *Ph-ac* h2* pic-ac st1 plat h2* plb j5.de* ran-b j5.de rhod hr1* *Sars* hr1* sep a1 sil h2* sin-n a1* *Spig* a1 stann h2* thuj j5.de
- **easy**, too: (↗*MIND - Ailments - sexual excesses*) *Con* (non:ferr k*) ferr-i a1* kali-c bg2 lyc k* nux-v k* *Phos* k* *Pic-ac* *Plat* *Plb* k* rhod k* sabin k* sumb k* wildb a1
- **eating**; after: alumn c1 nicc j5.de
- **enjoyment**, without: ambr j5.de* canth a1* carb-v h2* mag-m j5.de nat-c j5.de sel a1 tab j5.de*
- **excessive**: (↗*MIND - Ailments - sexual excesses*) *Aur-m* **Canth** k* cop **Fl-ac** k* *Graph* nat-m op *Ph-ac* *Phos* ptk1 *Pic-ac* k* plat ptk1 sabin ptk1 staph
  - **night**: staph h1*
  - **thoughts**, during sexual: cop **Pic-ac** k*
- **exhausting**: aur-m a1*
- **frequent**: (↗*MIND - Ailments - sexual excesses*) acon a1 agar k* *Agn* k* alum k* alum-p k2* alumn am-m k* anth k* anthraco apis arund k* aster hr1* *Aur* sf1.de *Aur-m* aur-s c1 bell k* berb j5.de* cann-i k* cann-s k* *Cann-xyz* bg2 *Canth* j5.de* *Caps* j5.de* carb-v k* caust k* cham a1 *Chel* k* chin k* cic k* cimx k* clem k* *Coc-c* k* cod a1 coloc k* corn k* cyna jl3 cyt-l sp1 *Dig* j5.de* *Dios* a1* erig mg1.de *Ferr* j5.de* fl-ac mrr1 graph j5.de ham k* helon hr1* jug-r a1 kali-c h2* kali-n h2* kalm k* lach sf1.de lat-m sp1 *Laur* sf1.de lyc k* *Mag-m* k* *Med* hr1* merc hr1* merc-c sf1.de mez k* mur-ac j5.de* nat-c k* *Nat-m* k* nat-p nit-ac hr1* nux-v k* onis j5.de* petr h2* ph-ac k* *Phos* k* pic-ac sf1.de plb a1 *Puls* k* ran-b j5.de* rhus-t j5.de sabad k* sabin j5.de* sec a1 sep sf1.de sil k* sin-n a1 *Spig* k* sumb k* *Tab* j5.de ther sf1.de ust k* valer j5.de* visc sp1 zinc sf1.de
  - **daytime**: cann-i a1 cann-s h1* *Chel* hr1* jug-r a1 lyc a1 mez a1 nat-c a1
  - **morning**: *Cimx* hr1* *Mag-m* hr1* ran-b a1* valer a1
  - **night**: *Alum* hr1* calc a1 corn a1* helon hr1* jug-r a1 *Merc* hr1* nat-m a1 *Nit-ac* hr1* op a1 phos h2* sin-n a1
  - **children**; in: ambr lmj *Calc-p* lmj *Cann-i* lmj carc lmj *Fl-ac* lmj **Hyos** lmj **Lach** lmj lyss lmj med lmj **Merc** lmj *Mosch* lmj ph-ac lmj **Phos** lmj staph lmj tub ggd *Zinc* lmj
  - **coition**; after: sec a1
  - **eating**; after: hyos k*
  - **nausea**; with: kali-bi hr1*
  - **old** people; in: | **men**; old: caust
  - **prostatic** fluid, with loss of: *Puls* hr1*
  - **puts** hands to penis: *Stram* kr1
- **fruitless**: aur kr1 con bg2 gins bg2 *Phos* hr1 plat bg2 *Sep* hr1
- **impetuous**: (↗*violent*) kali-c k*
- **incomplete**: achy jl3 acon-ac rly4• *Agar* k* agav-t jl3 **Agn** k* aq-mar jl3 aran-ix jl3 arg-n k* ars k* ars-i *Bar-c* k* berb sf1.de bros-gau mrc1 *Calad* k* *Calc* k* calc-s ptk1 *Camph* k* carb-v sf1.de caust k* chen-v a1* chin ptk1 chinin-ar *Cob* k* coc-c k* **Con** k* cub a1 dig b4.de* ferr-p form k* **Graph** k* *Hep* k* ign ind jl3 iod k* kali-ar kali-br a1 kali-fcy a1 kali-i k* lach k* lact-sa hsa1 linu-c a1 **Lyc** k* lyss k* mang med ptk1 merc k* merc-cy k* moly-met jl3 morph a1 mur-ac k* naja jl nat-ar *Nat-c* k* *Nat-m* *Nat-p* nit-ac j5.de *Nuph* k* *Nux-m* k* *Nux-v* k* oena a1 pall c1 pers jl3 *Petr* k* *Ph-ac* k* *Phos* k* pic-ac sf1.de rhod rhodi a1 sars k* *Sel* k* **Sep** k* stann jl3 sul-i k2* **Sulph** k* tab ptk1 tarent k* ther k* zinc b4.de*
  - **morning**: caust a1 nat-c k*
    - **coition**; after: caust a1
  - **forenoon**: caust k*
  - **night**: calc a1 caust k*
  - **coition**; during: (↗*penis; wanting - coition*) *Arg-n* hr1 *Camph* *Con* k* cyna jl *Form* k* **Graph** k* hep h2* **Lyc** k* lyss hr1* nux-v k2 *Ph-ac* k* *Phos* k* sel k2 *Sep* k* **Sulph** k* ther k*

Male

- **constant**: *Kali-i* hr1*
- **desire**:
  - **strong** desire; with: *Phos* kr1
  - **without**: agn a1
- **ejaculation** too soon: calad kr1
- **excitement**, during sexual: coc-c a1 sel a1
- **vertigo**; with: tarent kr1

○ • **Penis** becomes relaxed: (↗*coition; wanting - coition; wanting - penis - relaxed)* agn mrr1 arg-n k* *Nux-v* k1* ph-ac k* sel k2

- **intolerable**: hura a1
- **involuntary**: am-c h2* anac b4a.de* bell a1 clem a1 tarax a1
- **lying**:
  - **agg.**: alum j5.de ox-ac k*
  - **back**; on | **agg.**: onos
- **old** people; in: | **men**; old: arn h1 fl-ac a1 phos j5.de*
- **painful**: agn k* alum k* alum-p k2 alum-sil k2 ant-c anthraco **Arg-n** k* aur borx j5.de* bry cact *Calad* k* calc-p *Camph Camph-br* br1 *Cann-i* **Cann-s** k* *Cann-xyz* ptk1 **Canth** k* **Caps** k* chin b7.de* clem b4a.de *Colch* coli jl2 con k* cop crot-t *Cub* cur *Dig* k* erig mg1.de ery-a eug ferr-i fl-ac graph b4.de* grat hep k* ign k* jac-c kr1 *Kali-br* kali-c k* *Kali-chl* kali-i kali-p kali-sil k2 kola stb3• lact lupin hsa1 lyc lyss kr1 mag-m b4.de* merc k* merc-c k* mosch bg2 mur-ac h2 mygal nat-c k* nat-m k* nat-p nat-sil k2 *Nit-ac* k* *Nux-v* k* oena ptk1 *Petros Phos* k* pic-ac ptk1 plb b7.de* **Puls** k* sabad k* sabal ptk1 sel c1 seneg k* sep *Sil* staph ptk1 *Stram* kr1 sulph b4.de* sumb tab **Ter** k* *Thuj* k* zinc zing
  - **day** and night: *Dig* hr1* phos k2
  - **morning**: agn k* all-c a1* borx c1 calad k* lact a1* nat-c k* *Nux-v* k* sabad k* sep k* sil k*
    - **coition**; after: bry a1 grat a1
    - **sitting** agg.: sep a1
  - **evening**: calc-p k* cann-s k* con a1
    - **sleep**; before: con h2
  - **night**: alum k* ant-c k* *Cact* k* cann-s a1 *Caps* k* dig h2* ferr-i k2 *Hep* k* *Kali-c* lp *Merc* k* nat-m k* nit-ac k* *Phos* k* *Staph* sne *Thuj* h1* zinc-p k2
    - **coition**:
      - **after**: bry k* calad k* grat
      - **during**: hep k*
    - **dream**; during an erotic: camph ptk1 chin chinin-s a1
  - **accompanied** by | **Urethra**; discharge of (See URETHRA - Discharge - accompanied - erections)
  - **children**; in: *Tub* st1
  - **chordee** (See URETHRA - Chordee)
  - **coition**; during: hep ptk1
  - **desire**, without: all-c hr1* *Calad* hr1*
  - **gonorrhea**; in: agav-a br1
  - **lassitude**, with: sabad kr1
  - **pollutions**, after: grat k* kali-c ptk1
    - **painful** pollutions, after: *Kali-c* kr1
  - **sitting** agg.: gins a1
  - **sleep**:
    - **disturbing** sleep: cact kr1
    - **during** | **agg.**: merc-c ptk1
  - **spasmodic**: *Nit-ac* j5.de*
  - **swelling**; from:
    - **Prepuce**; of: jac-c
    - **Scrotum**; of: jac-c kr1
  - **waking**; on: wildb a1
- **pollutions**:
  - **after**: aloe ars k* grat k* kali-c kali-i a1 mez nit-ac **Ph-ac** k* plb b7.de* rhod k* sabad b7.de* sep
  - **during**: (↗*Pollutions - erections - with)* agar sf1.de anac sf1.de aur sf1.de *Calc* sf1.de cann-i sf1.de cann-s sf1.de *Canth* sf1.de carb-ac sf1.de carb-an sf1.de caust sf1.de chin sf1.de dig sf1.de dios sf1.de ery-a sf1.de form sf1.de *Gins* sf1.de *Iod* sf1.de *Kali-br* kr1 kali-chl j5.de kali-p k2 led sf1.de lyc sf1.de *Merc* sf1.de nat-m sf1.de *Nux-m* sf1.de *Nux-v* bg* par sf1.de

- **pollutions – during**: ...
  phos sf1.de pic-ac a1* pip-m a1 puls sf1.de sil sf1.de staph sf1.de sulph sf1.de ther sf1.de viol-t sf1.de
  - **without**: *Aur* j5.de* *Gins* j5.de* plat j5.de*
- **riding** agg.: *Bar-c* k* *Calc-p* k* *Cann-i* k* form k*
  - **impotence** at all other times, with: bar-c
- **rising** agg.; after: aur a1 caj a1
- **rubbing** scrotum, by: crot-t a1
- **seldom**: achy jl3 ars k* carbn-s kali-br a1 lyc h2* merc-c k* nat-m h2* *Nuph* k* sil a1 sumb a1
  - **enjoyment**, without: sel a1 tab a1
  - **opposite** sex, when with: cere-b a1
- **sexual** desire:
  - **without**: agn *Am-c* ambr anac arn asc-t borx j5.de bry bufo *Calad Calc-p Cann-i* cann-s *Canth* carb-v caust h2 chin-b kr1 cic a1 crot-c sk4• eug euph fl-ac *Graph* ham hyos iod kali-c kali-n h2 kali-p kali-sil k2 kalm *Laur* sf1.de lyss mag-m h2* mag-s nat-c *Nat-m* nat-p *Nit-ac Nux-v* ol-an j5.de* petr h2* *Ph-ac* phos *Pic-ac Plb* sf1.de psor k2 rhus-t a1 sabad j5.de* *Sel* sil *Spig* sul-ac h2* sul-i k2 sulph tab tarent ther c1 thiop jl3
    - **morning**: am-c ambr calad (non:chin k*) chin-b slp *Nat-m* sel
      - **waking**; after: arn h1
- **short**; too: **Agn** b7a.de ambr a1 *Ant-c* b7a.de arg-n berb calad b7.de* calc k* camph carb-v *Con* k* fl-ac a1 *Graph* ign bg2* laur bg2 lyc m-ambo b7.de m-aust b7a.de *Nat-c Nux-m* k* *Nux-v* k* *Ph-ac* k* plb bg2 *Sel* k* sep k* zinc [tax jsj7]
- **sitting** agg.: alum j5.de *Cann-i* a1* cann-s h1* euph a1 gins a1 sep j5.de*
- **sleep**:
  - **after** | **agg.**: *Lach* j5.de*
  - **during**:
    - **agg.**: aster k* clem a1 dig a1 *Fl-ac* k* kali-c a1 kali-s fd4.de merc-c k* mur-ac a1* *Nat-c* k* nat-m a1 nux-v *Op* k* par j5.de pic-ac k2 plat h2* pot-e rly4• rhod k* rhus-t a1 *Ther* sf1.de
      - **impotence** when awake; with: calad k2 op
      - **urinating**; subsiding on: lith-c kr1
  - **falling** asleep | **when**: pic-ac k2
- **sleeplessness**; during: ant-c j5.de *Canth* kr1 m-aust b7a.de *Plat* kr1 sep *Thuj* kr1
- **slow** (See delayed)
- **standing** agg.: sul-ac ptk1
- **stool**:
  - **after** | **agg.**: *Calc* b7a.de nat-m bg2 phos bg2
  - **before**: kali-bi hr1* thuj b4a.de*
  - **during** | **agg.**: calc sne carl k* *Con* b4a.de *Ign* k* sumb k* *Thuj* k*
  - **urging** to | **with** ineffectual urging: *Ign* kr1 thuj h1*
- **strong**: *Agn* j5.de* alum-sil k2 alumn a1 ars-i *Aur* sf1.de bamb-a stb2.de• calad k2 **Canth** cedr cham chinin-m c1 cinnb j5.de clem corn cyt-l sp1* **Fl-ac** *Graph* helon kali-chl j5.de *Lach Laur* sf1.de mag-m merc-c mez *Nat-m* j5.de* nux-v par j5.de **Phos Pic-ac** k* *Puls* sabin sep sil j5.de tarax ther j5.de* yohim lp2* zinc zinc-p k2
  - **morning**: bart a1 cedr a1 lach a1 nux-v a1 ther a1
    - **sitting** agg.: sep a1
    - **waking**; on: all-c a1 borx a1
  - **night**: aur sf1.de bry a1 cedr a1 corn a1* lach a1
  - **pain** in abdomen, with: zinc k*
  - **undressing** in a cold room, while: *Lyss* hr1*
- **sudden**: bar-c a1 nux-v a1
- **supper**; during: nicc
- **thoughts**, without sexual: arn h1 carb-v h2* ol-an j5.de* petr j5.de* ph-ac j5.de phos j5.de sabad j5.de sul-ac j5.de*
- **toothache**; with: daph j5.de*
- **troublesome**: *Agar* b2.de* agn b2.de* aloe j5.de alum k* alum-p k2* alum-sil k2* alumn a1 *Am-c* k* am-m k* ambr b2.de* anac k* ant-c k* anthraco j5.de arn k* ars b2.de *Aur* k* aur-i k2* aur-m k* bar-c b2.de* berb k* borx j5.de bruc a1 caj a1 calad b2.de calc b2.de calc-sil k2* camph j5.de *Cann-i* k* *Cann-s* b2.de* **Canth** k* *Caps* b2.de* carb-an b2.de* carb-v b2.de* *Caust* b2.de* cench k2* cham k* chin k* chinin-s a1 chlor a1 cinch a1 cinnb j5.de* *Clem* b2.de* cocc coff k* coffin a1 *Coloc* b2.de* colocin a1 *Con* b2.de* crot-t j5.de cyt-l a1* daph j5.de* del a1 dig k* dios a1 dream-p sdj1• *Eug* j5.de *Euph* k* ferr k* ferr-i k*

- **troublesome**: ...
ferr-p *Fl-ac* k* gins j5.de* graph k* ham k* hep b2.de* hyos k* ign k* *Iod* k* jug-r a1 kali-bi k* kali-br a1 *Kali-c* k* kali-chl j5.de* *Kali-i* k* kali-m k2 kali-n j5.de kali-sil k2* *Kreos* *Lach* b2.de* lact j5.de lat-m jl3 laur k* led k* lith-c lyc k* m-ambo b2.de m-arct b2.de* mag-c j5.de mag-m k* mag-s k* med ser **Merc** b2.de* mez b2.de* morph k* mosch b2.de* mur-ac k* *Nat-c* k* *Nat-m* k* nat-p k* nat-s j5.de* nat-sil k2* nicc k* nit-ac k* nux-m j5.de **Nux-v** k* ol-an j5.de* onis j5.de* *Op* k* osm c1 ox-ac k* par b2.de* petr k* *Ph-ac* k* **Phos** k* **Pic-ac** k* pip-m a1 **Plat** k* *Plb* k* plect a1 *Puls* k* puls-n a1 ran-b b2.de* rhod k* rhus-t k* sabad b2.de* sabin b2.de* sars b2.de* seneg k* *Sep* k* *Sil* k* spig b2.de* stann k* *Staph* k* *Stram* k* sul-ac k* sul-i k2* sulph b2.de tab k* tarax b2.de* tarent k* teucr j5.de thea a1 ther j5.de* **Thuj** b2.de* tus-p a1 upa a1 ust k* valer b2.de* verat b2.de* viol-t b2.de* voes a1 *Zinc* b2.de* zinc-p k2*
  - **evening | bed** agg.; in: ulm-c jsj8•
  - **night**: kola stb3•
  - **continued** (See continued)
  - **painful** (See painful)
  - **sexual** desire; without: kola stb3• ulm-c jsj8•
  - **violent** (See violent)
- **urination**:
  - **after**:
    - **agg.**: aloe digin a1 form k* lil-t lith-c nat-c rhus-t
      - **morning**: form a1
      - **copious** urination: lith-c ptk1
  - **before**: mosch b7a.de *Rhus-t* b7.de*
  - **during**:
    - **agg.**: cain a1* canth bg2 digin a1 mag-m b4.de* staph b7.de*
      - **involuntary** urination: caust bg2
  - **urging** to urinate | **with**: aspar hr1* canth bg2 dig a1 digin a1 mosch j5.de* rhus-t j5.de*
- **violent**: *(↗impetuous)* agar b4.de* agn k* *Alum* k* alum-p k2 am-c k* am-m b7.de* ambr k* anac k* *Anan* anis a1 ant-c b7.de* arn k* ars b4.de* aur b4.de* bar-c b4.de* bry bg2 calad bg2 calc bg2 calc-p bg2 camph h1* cann-i cann-s b7.de* *Canth* k* caps b7.de* carb-an b4.de* carb-v b4.de* carbn-s caust b4.de* *Cham* k* chin k* cinnb *Clem* k* coloc h2* con k* cop dig b4a.de* eug euph b4.de* ferr b7.de* **Fl-ac** *Gels* *Graph* k* hep bg2 *Hyos* k* ign k* iod a1 *Kali-br* kali-c k* *Kali-chl* *Kali-m* kr1* kali-sil k2 kola stb3• kreos bg2 lach b7.de* led b7.de* lyc bg2 lyss mg1.de m-ambo b7.de m-arct b7.de* mag-m b4.de* med **Merc** b4a.de* merc-c k* *Mez* k* mosch bg2 mur-ac b4.de* mygal k* *Nat-c* k* nat-m k* nat-p nat-sil k2 *Nit-ac* k* **Nux-v** b7.de* *Op* k* osm par b7.de* petr b4.de* ph-ac b4.de* **Phos** k* **Pic-ac** **Plat** k* *Plb* k* psor **Puls** b7.de* ran-b b7.de* rhod b4.de* rhus-t b7.de* sabad bg2 sabin k* sars b4.de* sel seneg b4.de* *Sep* b4.de* *Sil* k* sin-n kr1 spig b7.de* stann b4.de* staph b7.de* *Stram* sul-ac b4.de* sulph bg2 tarax b7.de* **Thuj** b4.de* valer b7.de* verat k* viol-t b7.de* zinc k* zinc-p k2
  - **day** and night: *Canth* b7.de* merc-c bg2 *Nit-ac* bg2 *Phos* bg2 sabin b7.de*
  - **daytime**: cann-s b7.de* canth bg2 caps b7.de* ferr b7.de* hyos b7.de* lach b7.de* m-ambo b7.de phos bg2 puls b7.de* sabin bg2 sil k* *Zinc* bg2
  - **morning**: agn b7.de* am-m b7.de* ambr k* arn b7.de* *Canth* b7a.de caps b7.de* cham b7.de* **Con** b4a.de dig a1 *Graph* bg2 *Kali-p* lach b7.de* *Lyc* b4a.de m-ambo b7.de m-arct b7.de merc-c b4a.de nat-c k* nat-m h2* nit-ac b4a.de **Nux-v** b7.de* phos k* plb b7.de* psor puls b7.de* ran-b b7.de* rhus-t b7.de* sabad b7.de* sel k* *Tab* bg2 tet a1 thuj b4a.de* viol-t b7.de*
    - **rising** agg.: agn a1
    - **waking**; on: nat-c h2* sel a1
  - **evening**: cinnb k* clem b4a.de con b4a.de* led b7.de* mez k* nat-c b4.de* nux-v b7.de* *Phos* b4.de* staph b7.de* tarax b7.de* ulm-c jsj8•
    - **19-22 h**: tetox pin2•
  - **night**: *Fl-ac* a1* kali-c a1 merc-c a1 nat-c a1 nat-m h2* nit-ac h2* *Pic-ac* kr1* *Plat* hr1* sep h2* *Sil* h2* sin-n a1* zinc-p k2
  - **dreams** and pollutions, with: sin-n kr1
  - **frequent**: aur bg2 laur bg2
  - **headache**; during: *Pic-ac* hr1*
  - **itching** of scrotum, with: *Kali-m* kr1
  - **old** people; in: | **men**; old: *Fl-ac* hr1*
  - **sensation** as after a violent erection: chel a1

- **violent**: ...
  - **sleep | during | agg.**: calad hr1* *Dios* hr1* *Fl-ac* hr1* *Merc-c* a1* *Nat-c* a1* *Pic-ac* hr1*
    - **siesta**:
      - **after | agg.**: eug hr1*
  - **thoughts**, without sexual: lyss hr1* sil hr1*
  - **urine**, before the passage of large quantities of: sin-n a1*
- **waking** and after; on: ambr j5.de* anac h2 arn h1* borx j5.de* carb-v j5.de *Card-m* kr1 ferr a1 gnaph kr1 *Hep* kr1 kali-c j5.de kali-s fd4.de lach j5.de nat-c h2* nat-m j5.de op a1 ox-ac a1 petr ph-ac phos h2 pic-ac plat podo fd3.de• pot-e rly4• puls bg1 *Sil* stann j5.de sulph tarent a1 thuj
- **walking** agg.: cann-i kr1*
- **wanting**: aegle-f mtf11 *Agar* k* **Agn** k* aids nl2• alco a1 *Alum* k* alum-p k2 am-c k* ambr hr1 amyg-p c1 anil a1 *Ant-c* k* ant-o a1 arg-met *Arg-n* k* *Arn* c1 ars ars-i arum-d kr1* aur aur-i k2 aur-s aven br1 **Bar-c** k* bar-i k2 bar-s k2 bart a1 bell-p c1 ben-d c1 berb kr1* borx k* *Bufo* k* buth-a jl* **Calad** k* **Calc** k* calc-i k2 **Calc-s** *Camph* k* cann-i kr1 cann-s k* caps k* carb-ac kr1 carb-an b2.de* carb-v b2.de* carbn-s k* carc fb* *Caust* k* cere-s c1 **Chin** k* chinin-s chlf a1 chlol kr1 chlor c1 cinnm kr1 *Cob* k* *Coc-c* coca mrr1 coch cod a1 coff b2.de* coloc k* **Con** k* corn cortico jl cot a1 crot-h a1 crot-t dam c1* dig k* dios dol kr1 dream-p sdj1• *Dulc* k* elaps ery-a c1* ery-m c1 eug eup-pur c1* euph b2.de* *Ferr* k* ferr-i ferr-p bg2* *Fl-ac* k* gast c1 gels k* gins sf1.de *Graph* k* halo jl *Ham* *Hell* k* helon *Hep* b2.de* hipp jl2 hydrc a1 hyos k* *Hyper* c1 ign k* *Iod* k* kali-bi a1 *Kali-br* kali-c k* kali-p kali-s kreos k* *Lach* k* lact sf1.de lact-v br1 lappa c1 lat-m bnm6• lath c1 *Lec* k* **Lyc** k* m-ambo b2.de* m-aust b2.de* *Mag-c* k* **Med** k* meny b2.de* *Merc* k* merc-ns a1 morph a1 *Mosch* k* *Mur-ac* k* musca-d szs1 nat-c k* *Nat-m* k* *Nat-p* *Nit-ac* k* *Nuph* *Nux-m* k* **Nux-v** k* oci-sa jl* *Onos* *Op* k* orch c1 ox-ac k2 oxyt c1 pall c1 perh jl petr b2.de* *Ph-ac* k* phase c1 **Phos** k* *Phyt* *Pic-ac* bg2* plan c1* *Plb* k* polyg-h kr1 *Psor* k* *Puls* k* rhod k* rhodi a1 rhodi-o-n c1 ruta b2.de* sabad k1 *Sabal* c1 sabin b2.de* *Sal-n* c1* saroth jl sec c1 **Sel** k* **Sep** k* sil k* spong k* *Stann* k* *Staph* k* stram k* sul-ac b2.de* sul-i k2 **Sulph** k* sumb *Syph* kr1* tab k* teucr k* thal jl thala jl ther *Thuj* k* tritic-vg fd5.de tus-p *Uran-n* ust *Yohim* c1* zinc b2.de* zinc-p c1*
  - **morning**: *Agn* a1 aids nl2• carb-an h2* crot-t a1 eug a1 graph k* lact [tax jsj7]
  - **afternoon**: lyss hr1*
  - **evening** and night: *Agar* kali-p pall
  - **accompanied** by:
    - **boils** (See SKIN - Eruptions - boils - accompanied - impotence)
    - **diabetes** (See diabetes)
    - **prostatic** dribbling (See PROSTATE - Emission - accompanied - impotency)
    - **sadness** (See MIND - Sadness - impotence)
    - **tobacco**; desire for: **Calad** mrr1
    - **urinary** complaints: trib br1
    - **urination**:
      - **involuntary** (See BLADDER - Urination - involuntary - accompanied - erections)
      - **painful** (See BLADDER - Urination - dysuria - painful - accompanied - erections)
  - **caresses**; even after amorous: calad kr1
  - **celibacy**; from: **Phos** hr1*
  - **chronic**: lyc
  - **coition**; during: *(↗incomplete - coition; incomplete - penis)* aur-s c1 **Graph** mrr1 kreos b7a.de nat-c a1* nux-v b7.de* ph-ac bg2
  - **cold**, from a: mosch k*
  - **constant** erection, after: carbn-s a1
  - **continence**, from: **Con** *Phos* k*
  - **diabetes**, with: *(↗Sexual desire - diminished - diabetes)* acon gk1 cann-s mgb1 coca br1* con mgb1 cupr kr1 eup-pur hl1 *Helon* hr1* kali-c mgb1 mosch hr1* ph-ac ptk1 sulph c1
  - **disappearing | coition**; during: ambr a1 *Camph* kr1 fl-ac a1 m-aust j5.de nux-v j5.de *Ph-ac* kr1
  - **excitement**, from excessive: phos k2*
  - **fancies**; with lascivious: sel br1

Male

- **fright**:
  - **during** coition, from: *Sin-a* kr1 *Sin-n* kr1*
  - **from**: onos vml3•
- **gonorrhea**:
  - **after**: *Agn Calad* k2* cob cub hydr med sulph *Thuj*
  - **suppressed** gonorrhea, from: calad k2 med k2* *Thuj* kr1
- **masturbation**; from: arg-n ptk1 aven vh *Gels* hr1* graph k2* kali-c k2* kali-p sf1.de lyc mtf11 phos k2* sal-n sf1.de stram hr1* trib br1
- **memory**, with loss of: **Kali-br** hr1*
- **old** people; in: **Lyc** hr1*
- **perspiration**, after: **Lyc** hr1* **Phos** hr1* stram hr1*
- **pollutions**, after: *Phos* kr1
- **sadness**, with (See MIND - Sadness - impotence)
- **salt**; excessive use of: phos k2
- **seminal** losses during sleep, stool, urination; with: *Nuph* hr1*
- **sexual** desire:
  - **after**: **Phos** kr1
  - **suppression** of sexual desire; from: *Phos* kr1
  - **with**: acon j5.de* *Agar* b4a.de* *Agn* kr1* *Alum* kr1 *Am-c* b4a.de* *Anan* kr1 aq-mar skp7• *Arg-met* kr1 *Arg-n* kr1 *Aur* kr1 aur-s kr1 bar-c kr1 **Calad** kr1 *Calc* kr1 *Camph* kr1 carb-v b4.de* carbn-s kr1 *Chin* kr1 cob kr1 **Con** b4a.de* corn kr1 crot-h kr1 diaz sa3• *Dig* kr1 euph b4.de* ferr-ma kr1 **Graph** b4a.de* hep kr1 ign kr1 iod b4a.de kali-c kr1* lach kr1 **Lyc** b4a.de* lyss kr1 mag-m kr1 meny kr1 *Mur-ac* b4a.de naja kr1 nat-c b4a.de *Nat-m* b4a.de* *Nat-p* kr1 nuph kr1 *Nux-m* kr1 *Nux-v* kr1 *Onos* mrr1 op kr1 *Ph-ac* b4a.de* *Phos* kr1 *Psor* kr1 puls kr1 sabad kr1 sal-n kr1* *Sel* kr1 *Sep* b4a.de* *Sil* b4.de* stann b4a.de* *Staph* kr1 sulph b4a.de* thuj b4a.de zinc b4a.de
- **sexual** excesses; after: agn k2 alum k2 arn ptk1 aven br1 **Chin** hr1* *Eup-pur* hr1* fl-ac mrr1 graph k2* *Kali-br* hr1* kali-c k2* kali-p sf1.de **Lyc** hr1* **Phos** hr1* *Staph* hr1*
- **stultified** by sudden laxness of penis: arg-n bg1 camph k*
- **suddenly**: chlor hr1* *Fl-ac* hr1*
- **syphilis**; from: merc
- **thinking** about his impotence agg.: (↗*MIND - Thinking - complaints - agg.)* **Arg-n** mrr1
- **tobacco**; from abuse of: calad sf1.de lyc sf1.de
- **waking**; on: *Card-m* hr1* op [tax jsj7]
- **wife**; with his: lyc mrr1
- **work**; with aversion to: onis j5.de
- ○ **Penis**:
  - **relaxed**: (↗*incomplete - penis)* gels k2
    - **excited**, when: aur-s k2 **Calad** k* *Ham* kr1
  - **small** and cold: *Agn* k* *Bar-c* berb caps **Lyc** k* *Sulph*
- **weak**; too: agar b4a.de* *Agn* b7.de *Ant-c* b7a.de *Bar-c* b4.de* calad b7.de* *Calc* bg2 caust b4.de* hep b4a.de* lach b7.de* lyc b4.de* merc b4.de* mur-ac b4.de* nux-m b7.de* **Ph-ac** b4a.de **Sel** b7.de* **Sep** b4a.de sulph b4.de*

ERUPTIONS: agar k* ambr k* anan k* ant-c k* ant-t k* apis arn gsy1 bry bg2 calad k* calc k* calc-sil k2* cann-xyz bg2 carb-v k* caust bg2* chel k* chinin-s cinnb clem crot-h *Crot-t* k* *Dulc* k* *Graph* k* *Hep* k* iod kali-bi kali-c b4a.de *Lach* k* lyc k* *Merc* k* morg-p fmm1• nat-c k* nat-m k* nat-p bg2 *Nit-ac* k* nux-v b7a.de **Petr** k* ph-ac k* phos b4a.de positr nl2• psor k2* rad-br mrr1 **Rhus-t** k* **Rhus-v** k* sabin sars k* *Sep* k* sil k* spong sulph bg2* tell thuj k* urt-u mrr1

- **blotches**: bell bov bry crot-t *Merc* nat-c sep
- **boils** on pubes: apis
- **burning**: ars k2 calc kali-c *Merc* nit-ac petr k2 phos *Rhus-t* k* spong sulph k2
- **copper** colored: calc k*
- **crusts**: caust **Nit-ac** sars thuj
- **dry**: *Dulc* hr1 morg-p fmm1• *Petr* k* *Sep* k*
  - **scaly**: calc merc-i-f sars
- **eczema**: alumn bro1 ant-c bro1 arg-n ars aur bg2 canth bro1 caust bg2 chel k* *Crot-t* k* *Dulc* bg2 *Graph* k* hep k* *Lyc* k* merc bg2 morg-p fmm1• nat-m k* nit-ac k* olnd bro1 petr k* *Ph-ac* bg2* rhus-t k* sanic bro1 sars bg2 sep k* sil bg2 sulph k* thuj k*
  - ○ **Penis | Back**: alumn ptk1 rad-br ptk1
  - **Scrotum | Thighs**; and between: nat-m bg2 *Petr* bg2

Eruptions: ...

- **elevated**: lyc merc k*
- **erosion**:
  - **spots**; in: bar-c
  - ○ **Penis**:
    - **Glans | red**: thuj tl1
- **hard**: bov kreos
- **herpetic**: anan k* ars k2* crot-h *Crot-t Dulc* k* *Graph* k* *Hep Lyc* mrr1 med mrr1 nat-c k2* nat-m k* nit-ac k* **Petr** k* ph-ac plat mrr1 *Rhus-t* mrr1 sars *Sep* k* sil sulph k2* syc bka1• syph k2 *Tell Thuj* mrr1
  - **right**: *Lyc* mrr1
  - ○ **Thighs**; between: lyc mrr1 nat-c mrr1 **Nat-m** k ● **Petr** k ●*
- **itching**: agar ambr k* arn bry calad crot-t graph hep lach nat-m k* *Nit-ac* **Petr Rhus-t** k* sabin *Sep* k* *Sil* k* spong sulph k2 *Til* urt-u mrr1
  - **moist** spots on: *Sil* k*
- **miliary**: bry k* **Rhus-r** *Rhus-t Sars Sil*
- **moist**: *Carb-v* **Graph Hep** merc k* nat-m k* *Petr* ph-ac **Rhus-t** k* *Sars* k* sep k* sil
- **pimples**: agar a1 ambr k* ant-t b7.de* calad k* chel graph k* kali-bi lach k* lyc bg2 *Merc* nat-m *Nit-ac* positr nl2• sil k* thuj til
- **pustules**: *Ant-c* b7a.de ant-o ant-t k* bell-p sp1 cupr-ar k* kali-bi bg2* lyc bg2 *Podo* k*
  - **red**: ant-t k*
- **rash**: bry dulc rhus-t k*
  - **children**:
    - **newborns**: | **extending** through perineum: *Med* vh*
- **red**: bry *Dulc* hr1 merc k* nit-ac *Petr* ph-ac rhus-v k* sep *Thuj* zinc
- **rhus** poisoning (= poison oak poisoning): crot-t mrr1
- **spots**, on: caust bg1 cinnb bg1
- **syphilitic**: *Ars-i* merc **Nit-ac**
  - **mucous** patches: *Asaf* bro1 aur bro1 calc-f bro1 calo bro1 *Cinnb* bro1 *Cund* bro1 fl-ac bro1 *Hep* bro1 iod bro1 *Kali-bi* bro1 kali-i bro1 kali-m bro1 *Merc* bro1 *Merc-c* bro1 merc-d bro1 *Merc-n* bro1 *Merc-pr-r* bro1 *Nit-ac* bro1 phyt bro1 sang bro1 staph bro1 still bro1 *Thuj* bro1
- **tetters**: *Dulc* b4a.de petr b4a.de *Sep* b4a.de sil b4a.de *Thuj* b4a.de
- **urticaria**: clem k* cop k* merc k* nat-c k*
- **vesicular**: ant-t ars k2 carb-v chinin-s **Crot-t** k* cupr-ar k* *Merc* k* morg-p fmm1• *Nat-c* k* nat-m k2 nat-p **Nit-ac** k* petr ph-ac **Rhus-t** *Rhus-v* sep
- ○ **Hairy** parts, on: calad a1 kali-bi bg2* *Lach* k* nat-m a1 sil bg2
- **Penis**: aids nl2• *Ars* b4a.de bufo bg2 *Crot-t* k* graph k* hydrog srj2• petr k* ph-ac k* *Rhus-t* k* sep k* tep k*
  - **copper**-colored: calc
  - **erythematous**: (↗*SKIN - Eruptions - erythema)* petr samb sumb k* tub jl2
  - **herpetic**: *Graph* hr1 phlor c1 sal-al blc1•
  - **nodules**, hard, painful, suppurating: bov k*
  - **pimples**: aids nl2• ambr bg anac anan a1 ant-t bg bell k* graph bg jac-c k* jac-g lach lyc bg *Nit-ac* k* ph-ac k* positr nl2• sil bg sulph k*
    - **itching**: jac-c k*
  - **pustules**: aids nl2• ant-t k* *Ars-h* k* bov k* coc-c k* *Hep* bro1 *Kali-bi* bro1 merc bro1 muru a1 murx k*
  - **red**:
    - **rash**: antip bro1 *Bell* bro1 bry k* calad bro1 cann-s bro1 caust bro1 *Cinnb* bro1 gels bro1 hydrog srj2• lach bro1 *Merc* bro1 nat-m bro1 *Petr* k* *Rhus-t* bro1 samb sep bro1 *Sulph* bro1 thuj bro1
    - **spots**: caust bg2
  - **scabs**: *Kali-bi* k* *Nit-ac* k*
  - **vesicles**: aloe ars-h *Calc* k* carb-v *Caust* **Crot-t** k* *Graph Hep Merc* k* **Nit-ac** k* *Ph-ac Rhus-t* k* *Rhus-v* k* sal-al blc1• *Sep* tep k* thuj k*
    - **burning**: caust *Merc*
    - **itching**: calc k* *Hep* **Nit-ac** ph-ac
    - **ulcers**, becoming: caust **Merc Nit-ac** thuj
      - **meatus**; at: merc-c *Nit-ac*
    - **white**: merc k*
  - ○ **Frenum | vesicles**: ph-ac b4a.de
  - **Glans**: *Ars-h Bry* k* calad k* *Carb-v Cinnb* cor-r hydrog srj2• jac-c k* *Kali-bi Lach* k* *Lyc* k* m-aust b7.de *Merc* k* *Nit-ac* k* *Petr* k* *Ph-ac* propl ub1• *Rhus-t* k* sel b7a.de sep k* stann *Sulph* b4a.de tep a1

- **Penis – Glans**: ...
  - **granular**: *Petr*$_{b4a.de}$
  - **miliary**: bry$_{b7.de*}$
  - **pimples**: cinnb$_{ptk1}$ jac-c$_{k*}$ jac-g lach$_{k*}$ nit-ac$_{k*}$ ph-ac
  - **pustules**: ars-h$_{br1}$
  - **scabby**, red: kali-bi$_{bg2}$
  - **shining** red points: *Cinnb*$_{k*}$
  - **vesicles**: *Ars-h*$_{k*}$ caust$_{k*}$ *Merc*$_{k*}$ nit-ac$_{k2}$ *Ph-ac*$_{k*}$ rhus-t$_{k*}$ stann$_{k*}$ tep$_{a1}$ thuj$_{k*}$
- **Prepuce**: anan *Ars-h*$_{k*}$ aur$_{bg2}$ *Calc*$_{k*}$ calc-sil$_{k2*}$ carb-v$_{bg}$ *Caust*$_{k*}$ cinnb$_{k*}$ dulc$_{k*}$ *Graph*$_{k*}$ hep$_{k*}$ *Merc*$_{k*}$ nat-c **Nit-ac**$_{k*}$ *Petr*$_{k*}$ ph-ac$_{k*}$ *Rhus-t*$_{k*}$ sang$_{k*}$ sars$_{k*}$ sep$_{k*}$ sil$_{k*}$ *Sulph*$_{bg2}$ *Thuj*
  - **blotches**: sep
  - **burning**: caust *Merc* nit-ac$_{h2*}$
  - **eczema**: aur$_{bg2}$ *Caust*$_{bg2}$ dulc$_{bg2}$ graph$_{bg2}$ *Hep*$_{bg2}$ merc$_{bg2}$ nit-ac$_{bg2}$ ph-ac$_{bg2}$ sars$_{bg2}$ *Sep*$_{bg2}$ sil$_{bg2}$ sulph$_{bg2}$
  - **herpetic**: ars$_{k*}$ carb-v$_{bro1}$ caust$_{k*}$ *Crot-t*$_{bro1}$ *Dulc*$_{k*}$ *Graph*$_{k*}$ *Hep*$_{k*}$ jug-r$_{c2*}$ kali-i$_{k*}$ kali-n$_{c2}$ *Merc*$_{k*}$ mez$_{bro1}$ *Nat-c Nit-ac*$_{k*}$ *Petr*$_{k*}$ *Ph-ac*$_{k*}$ phlor$_{c1}$ phys$_{c2}$ *Rhus-t*$_{k*}$ *Sars*$_{k*}$ *Sep*$_{k*}$ sulph$_{k2}$ syph$_{k2}$ *Thuj*$_{k*}$
  - **pimples**: arn$_{k*}$ m-aust$_{b7.de}$ nit-ac$_{k*}$ plan$_{a1}$ sil$_{k*}$
  - **psoriasis**: graph$_{bro1}$ *Sep*$_{bro1}$
  - **pustules**: ars-h$_{br1}$
  - **scabies**: *Thuj*$_{b4a.de}$
  - **scurfy**: caust$_{b4.de*}$ thuj$_{b4.de*}$
  - **tetters**: sars$_{b4a.de}$
  - **vesicles**: ars-h carb-v$_{k*}$ caust$_{k*}$ graph$_{k*}$ med$_{hr1}$ merc$_{k*}$ nit-ac$_{k*}$ rhus-t$_{b7.de*}$ thuj$_{h1*}$
    - **water**; containing: graph$_{b4.de*}$
  - **Under** part: carb-v caust$_{k*}$ *Merc*$_{k*}$ **Nit-ac**$_{k*}$ *Rhus-t*$_{k*}$ sep thuj$_{k*}$
- **Scrotum**: acon$_{bg2}$ anac$_{bg2}$ ant-c$_{b7a.de*}$ ant-t$_{b7a.de}$ ars$_{k*}$ *Ars-i* bufo$_{bg2}$ *Calad*$_{k*}$ calc$_{bg2}$ cann-xyz$_{bg2}$ chel$_{k*}$ *Crot-t*$_{k*}$ cupr-ar$_{k*}$ **Graph**$_{k*}$ **Hep**$_{k*}$ jug-c$_{ptk2}$ kali-c morg-p$_{pte1*•}$ nat-m$_{k*}$ **Petr**$_{k*}$ ph-ac$_{k*}$ pic-ac$_{bg2}$ *Rhus-t*$_{k*}$ *Rhus-v* sars$_{bg2}$ staph$_{bg2}$ syph$_{k2}$ thuj$_{bg2}$
  - **blotches**: arn
  - **crusts**: anac chel
  - **desquamative**: ars crot-t rhus-v
  - **dry**: calad$_{k*}$ chel *Merc-i-f*
  - **eczema**: alumn$_{ptk1}$ calc$_{bg2}$ *Crot-t*$_{k*}$ *Graph*$_{bg2}$ nat-m$_{bg2}$ *Petr*$_{bg2}$ ph-ac$_{ptk1}$
    - **rubrum**: chel$_{k*}$
  - **furuncle**: osteo-a$_{jl2}$
  - **herpetic**: anan$_{k*}$ *Calc* cinnb crot-h *Crot-t*$_{k*}$ **Dulc** *Graph Kali-c* **Petr**$_{k*}$ tell
    - **Thighs**; between scrotum and: eup-per graph$_{h2}$ **Lyc**$_{●*}$ *Nat-c*$_{hr1}$ **Nat-m**$_{k●}$ **Petr**
  - **itching**: ars *Calad*$_{k*}$ *Crot-t*$_{k*}$ **Graph** morg-p$_{pte1•}$ nat-m *Nat-s* **Petr**$_{k*}$ *Rhus-t*
    - **night**: *Calad Crot-t*
    - **moist** spots: *Sil*
  - **miliary**: rhus-t$_{b7.de*}$
  - **moist**: **Graph** hep **NAT-M**$_{k●}$ *Petr Rhus-t* sars$_{k*}$ *Sil Thuj*$_{k*}$
    - **Thighs**; between scrotum and: graph hep **Rhus-t** *Sars*
  - **papular**: anthraco$_{br1}$
  - **pimples**: *Calc-p*$_{k*}$ kali-ar$_{k*}$ ph-ac$_{k*}$ sars$_{k*}$ *Thuj*$_{k*}$ zinc$_{k*}$
    - **Thighs**; between scrotum and: *Petr*
  - **psoriasis**: *Nit-ac Petr* thuj
  - **pustules**: anac$_{k*}$ *Ant-c*$_{b7a.de}$ ant-o ant-s-aur ant-t$_{k*}$ ars$_{k*}$ crot-t$_{k*}$ cupr-ar$_{k*}$ podo$_{k*}$ tep$_{k*}$
  - **rash**: *Petr* puls *Rhus-t*$_{k*}$
  - **red**: chel morg-p$_{pte1•}$ petr$_{k*}$
  - **rhagades**: *Petr*$_{k*}$
  - **scaly**: *Calad*$_{k*}$ calc$_{ptk1}$ *Merc-i-f* morg-p$_{pte1•}$
  - **scurfs**; cracked, dry and red: chel
  - **tetters**: *Ars*$_{b4a.de}$ *Dulc*$_{b4.de*}$ *Hep*$_{b4a.de}$ *Lyc*$_{b4a.de}$ petr$_{b4.de*}$ *Sil*$_{b4a.de}$
  - **tubercles**: bufo

Eruptions – Scrotum: ...

  - **vesicles**: ars bell$_{k*}$ *Chel*$_{k*}$ **Crot-t**$_{k*}$ cupr-ar$_{k*}$ morg-p$_{pte1•}$ *Petr*$_{k*}$ psor$_{k*}$ *Rhus-t*$_{k*}$ *Rhus-v*$_{k*}$ thuj$_{bg2}$
    - **painful**: chel$_{k*}$ psor$_{k*}$
    - **purulent**: psor$_{jl2}$
    - **yellowish**: chel$_{k*}$ *Rhus-t*$_{k*}$
    - **Raphe**, along: *Nit-ac*
  - O **Thighs**; between scrotum and: dulc$_{mrr1}$
- **Thighs**; between: calc$_{bg2}$ *Graph*$_{mrr1}$ hep *Nat-c*$_{hr1}$ nat-m$_{k*}$ *Petr*$_{k*}$ puls *Rhus-t*$_{k*}$

ERYSIPELAS: | **Scrotum**: *Ars*$_{bg2}$ merc$_{bg2}$

EXCITABILITY of genitals: (↗*Sexual desire - increased)*
agar$_{a1}$ aloe$_{a1}$ ang$_{a1}$ ant-t$_{a1}$ ars$_{a1}$ aur$_{b4a.de*}$ aza$_{jl3}$ bufo$_{mtf11}$ cann-i$_{a1}$ canth$_{a1}$ carb-v$_{b4.de*}$ cer-s$_{a1}$ cere-s$_{a1}$ chin$_{a1}$ cocc$_{b7.de*}$ coff$_{b7.de*}$ *Dios*$_{a1}$ erech$_{a1}$ gins$_{a1}$ *Graph*$_{b4.de*}$ hep$_{a1}$ hyos$_{a1}$ ina-i$_{mlk9.de}$ *Lyc*$_{b4.de*}$ lyss$_{mtf11}$ meny$_{b7.de*}$ mygal$_{mtf11}$ naja$_{a1}$ *Nat-m*$_{b4.de*}$ nux-v$_{b7.de*}$ op$_{a1}$ **Phos**$_{b4.de*}$ plat$_{b4.de*}$ *Sil*$_{b4.de*}$ staph$_{bg2}$ stram$_{a1}$ *Sulph*$_{b4.de*}$ thea$_{a1}$ verat$_{mtf11}$ wies$_{a1}$ yohim$_{br1*}$
- **morning** | **sunrise**, at: cedr$_{a1}$
- **noon**: thuj$_{a1}$
- **dreams**, during erotic: hyos$_{a1}$
- **loss** of excitability: *Agn*$_{b7.de*}$

EXCITEMENT (See Sexual desire - increased)

EXCORIATION: alum$_{bg2}$ am-c$_{bg2}$ ambr$_{bg2}$ arn$_{bg2}$ ars$_{bg2}$ aur$_{bg2}$ bar-c$_{bg2}$ calad$_{bg2}$ calc$_{bg2}$ **Carb-v**$_{bg2}$ **Caust**$_{bg2}$ *Cham*$_{k*}$ chin$_{bg2}$ coff$_{bg2}$ **Graph**$_{bg2}$ **Hep**$_{k*}$ hyos$_{bg2}$ ign$_{bg2}$ iod$_{bg2}$ *Lyc*$_{b4a.de*}$ meph$_{bg2}$ **Merc**$_{b4.de*}$ **Nux-v**$_{bg2}$ petr$_{bg2}$ phos$_{bg2}$ plat$_{b4.de*}$ plb$_{bg2}$ *Podo* rhod$_{k*}$ sars$_{mrr1}$ **Sep**$_{bg2}$ sil$_{b4.de*}$ *Sulph*$_{k*}$ thuj$_{mlk1}$ verat$_{bg2}$ zinc$_{bg2}$
- **sensation** of: *Ambr*$_{b7a.de}$ calc$_{b4.de*}$ cann-s$_{b7.de*}$ mez$_{b4a.de}$
- O **Penis**: *Ars*$_{bro1}$ cann-s$_{bro1}$ *Caust*$_{bro1}$ cop$_{k*}$ *Cor-r*$_{bro1}$ crot-t$_{bro1}$ *Hep*$_{bro1}$ kali-i$_{k*}$ *Merc*$_{bro1}$ *Merc-c*$_{bro1}$ mez$_{bro1}$ nat-c$_{bg2}$ **Nit-ac**$_{k*}$ osm$_{bro1}$ sep$_{bro1}$ *Thuj*$_{bro1}$
  - O **Glans**: alum-sil$_{k2}$ anan ars$_{bg2}$ asc-t$_{a1*}$ cor-r graph$_{k2}$ **Merc**$_{k*}$ merc-i-r *Nat-c*$_{k*}$ *Nat-m Nit-ac*$_{k*}$ sep *Sulph* **Thuj** zinc$_{a1*}$
  - **Prepuce**: alum$_{b4a.de*}$ anan *Ars*$_{bro1}$ *Calad*$_{b7.de*}$ cann-s$_{b7.de*}$ carb-v$_{k*}$ *Caust*$_{bro1}$ cham$_{b7.de*}$ chin$_{b7.de*}$ chin-b$_{kr1*}$ cop$_{a1*}$ *Cor-r*$_{bro1}$ hep$_{k*}$ ign$_{k*}$ **Merc**$_{k*}$ *Mez*$_{k*}$ mur-ac$_{k*}$ nat-c$_{b4a.de}$ **Nit-ac**$_{k*}$ nux-v$_{b7.de*}$ ph-ac$_{bro1}$ phyt$_{bro1}$ *Psor* sep$_{k*}$ sil$_{b4a.de*}$ thuj$_{k*}$ verat$_{b7.de*}$
    - **coition**; after: calen$_{ptk1}$
    - **easy**: *Nat-c*$_{k*}$
    - **Margin**, on the: cann-s cham$_{h1*}$ **Ign** *Mur-ac* nit-ac nux-v$_{k*}$ rumx
- **Scrotum**: arn$_{b7a.de*}$ **Ars**$_{k*}$ *Bar-c*$_{b4a.de}$ calc$_{h2*}$ *Calc-p* chel **Hep**$_{k*}$ kali-c$_{b4a.de*}$ lyc$_{bg2}$ nat-c$_{b4a.de*}$ nat-m$_{bg2}$ nit-ac$_{h2*}$ petr$_{b4a.de*}$ ph-ac plb$_{b7.de*}$ polyg-h$_{ptk1}$ sil$_{ptk1}$ **Sulph**$_{k*}$ sumb$_{k*}$ *Thuj* zinc$_{bg2}$
  - O **Sides**: berb$_{k*}$ petr$_{h2*}$ sumb$_{k*}$ *Thuj*
  - **Thighs**; between scrotum and: bar-c caust *Graph* hep **Lyc**$_{k*}$ **Merc**$_{k*}$ **Nat-c**$_{k*}$ *Nat-m Nit-ac* **Petr**$_{k*}$ rhus-t *Sulph Thuj*

EXCRESCENCES: *Bell*$_{b4a.de}$ coloc$_{b4a.de}$ *Kali-c*$_{b4a.de}$ *Plat*$_{b4a.de}$ *Sep*$_{b4a.de}$ *Sulph*$_{b4a.de}$
- O **Penis** | **Glans**: staph$_{b7.de*}$ *Sulph*$_{hr1}$
- **Testes**: bar-c mill$_{c1}$

FIRMNESS: | **increased** testes: brom

FISTULOUS openings at scrotum: *Con*$_{b4a.de}$ *Iod* phyt spong$_{k*}$

FLACCIDITY: acet-ac$_{k2}$ **Agn**$_{k*}$ ant-t$_{k*}$ asc-t bar-c$_{mtf33}$ *Calad*$_{k*}$ camph carb-ac carb-an$_{k*}$ carbn-s cocc$_{b7.de*}$ coff$_{k*}$ crot-h$_{k*}$ cyd$_{br1}$ dig *Dios*$_{k*}$ *Gels*$_{k*}$ graph$_{bg}$ hell$_{k*}$ ign$_{b7.de*}$ lyc m-arct$_{b7.de}$ mag-p$_{bg2}$ merc-c$_{bg2}$ nux-m$_{bg2}$ nux-v$_{bg}$ *Ph-ac*$_{bg2}$ phos$_{k*}$ phyt$_{bg2}$ psor$_{bg2}$ sel$_{mtf11}$ sil staph sulph$_{bg2}$ sumb tab$_{k*}$ ust
- **coition**; during: nux-v$_{ptk1}$ ph-ac$_{ptk1}$ sulph$_{ptk1}$
- **sudden**: graph$_{ptk1}$ lyc$_{ptk1}$ nux-v$_{ptk1}$
- O **Penis**: agar$_{k*}$ **Agn**$_{k*}$ ant-o arum-d$_{hr1}$ aur$_{c1}$ *Bar-c*$_{k*}$ *Calad*$_{k*}$ *Cann-i*$_{k*}$ canth carb-ac$_{k*}$ crot-h$_{hr1}$ eug$_{hr1}$ euph$_{hr1}$ gels$_{hr1}$ hell$_{k*}$ jac-c lach **Lyc**$_{k*}$ mag-m$_{bg*}$ merc$_{k*}$ *Mur-ac*$_{k*}$ musca-d$_{szs1}$ nat-c$_{bg*}$ *Nux-m Nux-v*$_{k*}$ ph-ac pic-ac$_{k*}$ plb prun$_{k*}$ psor$_{k2}$
  - **pollutions**; after: nux-v$_{b7.de*}$
  - O **Glans**: calad$_{bg2*}$

Male

FORCED DOWNWARD; as if (See Bearing - testes - sensation)

FORMICATION: *(↗Tingling)* acon k* alum b4a.de ant-t bg2 berb calc-p bg2 clem euphr bg2 merc bg2 mosch bg2 ph-ac bg2 **Plat** k* **Sec** k* sel b7a.de* spig bg2 *Tarent* k*
- **emissions** agg.; after: ph-ac k*

○ - **Penis**: acon k* alum k* carl k* coloc k* ph-ac h2* puls k* **Sec** k* tab k* valer k*

○ • **Frenum**: *Ph-ac*

• **Glans**: alum k* ant-t b7a.de* chel k* m-aust b7.de merc k* mez b4a.de *Nat-m* k* ph-ac k* puls b7.de* spig b7.de* valer b7.de*

⁝ **urination** agg.; after: *Puls*

• **Prepuce**: croc b7.de* germ-met srj5• merc bg2 merl a1 ph-ac bg2*

- **Scrotum**: acon b7a.de* ang hr1 carb-v k* carl k* *Chel* k* chin k* com k* lachn hr1 merc k* nit-ac k* ph-ac k* plat k* rhus-t rhus-v **Sec** sel b7a.de* sil k* *Staph* thuj k*

• **evening** | **bed** agg.; in: chin k*

• **worms**; as from: staph rb2

- **Spermatic** cords: euphr bg2 merc bg2
- **Testes**: agn k* berb k* carb-v k* euphr k* hipp k* merc k* psil ft1 rhod k* thuj k* zinc k*

FRETTING sensation (= corrosion):

○ - **Testes**: ph-ac plat

FULLNESS; sense of: | **Spermatic** cords: anth ptk2 fl-ac k*

GANGRENE: ars k* *Canth* k* crot-h k* kali-i laur k* plb b7.de* rhus-t bg2

○ - **Penis**: *Ars* k* *Canth* k* *Kali-i* k* *Kreos* **Lach** k* *Laur* k*

• **paraphimosis**, from: ars canth *Lach* k* merc *Merc-i-r* sec tarent

• **threatening**: *Fl-ac* k* *Lach* hr1

○ • **Prepuce**: kreos ptk1

- **Scrotum**: *Chin* b7a.de fl-ac

GLEET (See URETHRA - Discharge - gleety)

GREASY:

○ - **Penis** | **Glans**: *Merc-c* b4a.de *Sel* b4a.de

GURGLING in testes:
- **17** h | **sitting** agg.: valer k*

HAIR falling off: *(↗SKIN - Hair - falling)* alum k2 bell k* hell b2.de* merc bro1 nat-c k* **Nat-m** k* *Nit-ac* k* *Ph-ac* k* rhus-t k* sars k* *Sel* k* thal dx *Zinc* k*
- **offensive** | **perspiration**; from: **Sulph** k*

HANDLING GENITALS: *(↗MIND - Gestures - tics)* *Acon* k* bell k* bufo k* canth k* colch bg2 dream-p sdj1• *Hyos* k* maland c1 med mtf33 *Merc* k* *Puls* hr1* *Stram* k* tab bg2 thuj bg1* vanil fd5.de *Zinc* h2*
- **child**: *Acon* hr1* bell a1 bufo mtf33 hyos mtf33 med mtf33 *Merc* hr1* puls mtf33 *Stram* hr1* tub gk vanil fd5.de *Zinc* hr1*

• **convulsions**; with: *Hyos* vh* sec stram

• **cough** agg.; during: zinc br1

- **cough** agg.; during: *Zinc* hr1*
- **public**; in: *(↗MIND - Naked; MIND - Naked - exhibitionism)* **Hyos** mrr1
- **tearing** at genitals: *(↗MIND - Shrieking - genitals; MIND - Tearing - himself - genitals)* tab a1

HANGING: | **right** | **Testes**: crot-t ptk1
- **down** | **Testes** (See Relaxed - scrotum)

HARDNESS:

○ - **Penis** | **Prepuce**: sulph ptk1

HEAT: ambr bg2 ant-t bg2 *Arn* bg2 *Ars* bg2 calc bg2 cann-s bg cann-xyz bg2 canth k* caps bg2 carb-v bg2 carbn-o caust bg2 con bg2 dulc k* graph bg2 ign bg2 **Kali-c** bg2 *Lyc* bg2 m-aust b7.de meph k* **Merc** bg2 mez bg2 nat-c bg2 nat-m bg2 nit-ac bg2 **Nux-v** bg2 petr bg2 *Ph-ac* bg2 phos bg2 plat bg2 plb bg2 prun k* **Puls** bg2 **Rhus-t** bg2 sabin bg2 sel bg2 sep bg2 sil bro1 spong k* staph bg2 *Sul-ac* k* **Sulph** bg2 sumb k* tarent bg *Thuj* bg2 tub bg
- **night**: meph k*

○ - **Penis**: ant-t bg2 **Arn** bg2 ars k* aur bell calc bg2 *Cann-xyz* bg2 canth k* caps bg2 **Caust** bg2 clem k* coc-c euphr ferr hep k* jac-c *Lyc* bg2 **Merc** bg2 *Mez* k* mosch bg2 mur-ac bg2 nit-ac bg2 *Nux-v* bg2 ph-ac bg2 phos k* plat k* plb bg2

Heat – Penis: ...
puls bg2 rhus-v sabin bg2 sep k* spig bg2 *Spong* k* staph bg2 **Sulph** bg2 *Thuj* bg2

○ • **Glans**: ant-t bg2 arn bg2 *Ars* bg2 calc bg2 *Cann-s* bg *Cann-xyz* bg2 chin bg2 cupr bg2 kola stb3• led bg2 *Lyc* bg2 mang bg2 **Merc** b4.de* **Merc-c** k* *Mez* bg2 **Nit-ac** bg2 *Nux-v* bg2 *Ph-ac* bg2 *Rhus-t* bg2 sabin bg2 sars bg2 sep b4.de* stann bg2 staph bg2 sulph bg2 **Thuj** bg2 ulm-c jsj8• viol-t bg2

• **Prepuce**: calad bg2 calc bg2 cann-s k* *Cann-xyz* bg2 ign bg2 merc k* merc-c bg2 mez bg2 nat-c bg2 *Nit-ac* bg2 *Nux-v* bg2 ph-ac bg2 plat-m k* *Rhus-t* bg2 sep bg2 **Sulph** bg2 **Thuj** bg2

- **Scrotum**: **Arn** bg2 **Ars** bg2 berb bg2 calc ptk1 **Caps** bg2 *Chel* k* chin bg2 clem b4a.de* cocc bg2 crot-t bg2 dulc bg2 euph bg2 graph bg2 hep bg2 nit-ac bg2 *Petr* bg2 ph-ac k* plat bg2 plb bg2 puls k* rhod bg2 **Rhus-t** bg2 sep bg2 sil bg2 *Spong* k* *Staph* bg2 sul-ac **Sulph** bg2 *Thuj* bg2 viol-t bg2

• **spots**, in: coloc

○ • **Sides**, in: sumb k*

- **Spermatic** cords: ambr bg2 ant-c bg2 apis bg2 *Arn* bg2 clem bg2 kali-c k* *Mang* bg2 nit-ac bg2 nux-v bg2 **Puls** bg2 sabal ptk1 *Spong* k* **Staph** bg2 sulph bg2 *Thuj* bg2
- **Testes**: acon **Arn** b7.de* bar-c bg2 caps bg2 chin bg2 clem bg2 coc-c ham iod bg2 kali-c h2* merc bg2 nat-m nit-ac b4.de* *Nux-v* k* oci ph-ac bg2 *Plat* bg2 *Puls* k* sabal c1 sep k* sil spig bg2 spong k* *Staph* bg2 sul-ac b4.de* *Sulph* bg2 sumb tarax bg2 thuj bg2 zinc bg2

• **left**: nat-m bg2

HEAVINESS: agar am-c clem con bg cupr cupre-au c1 elaps hura kola stb3• lob k* *Nat-c* k* nux-v ox-ac ph-ac k* *Psor* k* tarent k* thuj
- **urination** agg.; during: ph-ac k*
- **walking**; during: hura c1

○ - **Penis**:

○ • **Glans**: ph-ac b4.de*

⁝ **urination** agg.; during: ph-ac bg2

- **Scrotum**: am-c bg2

• **weight**; as from a: kola stb3•

- **Spermatic** cords: nat-c b4.de* nux-v bg2
- **Testes**: am-c b4.de* clem bg2 con bg2 nat-c b4.de* nux-v bg2 ox-ac bg2 psor bg2

HEMATOCELE: arn br1* con k* erig c2 *Ham* k* ruta k*

○ - **Scrotum**: acon bro1 *Arn* bro1 con bro1 erig bro1 *Ham* bro1 nux-v bro1 *Puls* bro1 *Sulph* bro1

• **chronic**: iod bro1 *Kali-i* bro1 sulph bro1

HERNIA: ars bro1 *Bar-c* bro1 calc bro1 carb-v bro1 hep bro1 *Merc* bro1 nit-ac bro1 *Sil* bro1 thuj bro1

○ - **Scrotum**: *Bell* b4a.de **Calc** b4a.de mag-c b4a.de* mag-m b4a.de* nux-v b7a.de* *Phos* b4a.de
- **Testes**: lach bg2* *Mag-m* bg2 **Nux-v** bg2

HYDROCELE: abrot k* alting-e mtf11 ambro c2 ammc c2 ampe-qu pfa* ampe-tr bro1 **Apis** k* *Arn* k* ars k* ars-i aur k* aur-i k2 *Bry* bg2* calad bro1 *Calc* k* calc-f bg2* *Calc-p* k* calc-sil k2* canth bg2* *Carbn-s* *Chel* br1* chin b7a.de* cimic mtf11 clem k* con k* *Dig* k* dulc bro1 *Fl-ac* k* gaert pte1*• **Graph** k* *Hell* k* *Hep* k* **Iod** k* *Kali-i* bro1 *Lyc* bg2 *Lyss* k* merc b4a.de* *Merl* *Nat-m* k* *Nux-v* k* phos k* *Psor* k* **Puls** k* ran-b c1* **Rhod** k* rhus-t c1* sam-ox mtf11 samb c2* *Sel* k* **Sil** k* *Spong* k* squil bg2* sul-ac k* sul-i bg2* *Sulph* k* tub jl2
- **left** side: *Dig* k* graph hr1 **Rhod** k*
- **bruise**, caused by a: *Arn* k* samb ptk1
- **children**; of: *Abrot* k* *Ars* *Aur* k* aur-s k2 *Calc* k* *Calc-s* *Graph* k* iod mtf33 *Kali-chl* **Puls** k* **Rhod** k* **Sil** k* sul-i k2* *Sulph*

• **congenital**: rhod k*

- **congenital**: puls c2
- **cysts**; in multilocular: apis ptk1
- **eruptions**; after suppressed: *Abrot* k* *Calc* hell k*
- **gonorrheal** orchitis, after: *Phos* k*
- **herpetic** eruptions, with: **Graph** k*
- **overlifting**, from: rhus-t ptk1
- **scrofulous**: **Sil** bg2

IMPOTENCE (See Erections - wanting; Sexual desire - wanting)

INDURATION:

○ - **Penis**: *Berb* hr1 hep b4a.de sep k*

- **Penis**: ...
  - **erection**, without: mela c1
  - **old** people; in: | **men**; old: *Berb* k*
  - ○ **Glans**: *Cann-xyz* bg2 sulph bg2
  - **Prepuce**: *Lach* k* *Merc* bg2 merc-i-r sep k* *Sulph* k*
- **Scrotum**: calad bro1 **Rhus-t** k* **Sulph** k* syph k2
- **Spermatic** cords: *Con* b4a.de iod b4a.de ph-ac k* *Puls* b7a.de spong b7a.de* *Syph* k*
- **Testes**: acon bg2* agn k* alum k* alum-sil k2 *Arg-met* arg-n k* arn k* ars ars-i *Aur* k* aur-i k2 aur-m bg2* aur-p bg2 aur-s k2 *Bar-c* k* bar-i k2 bar-m k* bar-s k2 bell k* brom bg1* *Calc* k* *Calc-f* k* calc-i k2 calc-p calc-sil k2* *Carb-an* carb-v bro1 *Cinnb* **Clem** k* **Con** k* *Cop* k* *Graph* k* hep b4a.de ign mtf33 *Iod* k* kali-ar kali-c k* kali-chl *Kali-i* kali-m k2 kali-s kali-sil k2 lach k* lyc k* **Med** k* *Merc* k* *Merc-i-r* merl nit-ac *Nux-v* k* ox-ac c2* phos *Phyt* bro1 plb k* psor al2 *Puls* k* **Rhod** k* sel b7.de* **Sil** k* **Spong** k* *Staph* stry sul-i k2 *Sulph* k* syph k2* thuj ust *Viol-t*
  - **right**: arg-met k2 arg-n k* arn ars sne *Aur Clem Con* lach merc *Nit-ac Ox-ac* ph-ac **Rhod** sil thuj sne
  - **left**: *Brom* kali-chl mez oci *Rhod Thuj*
  - **chronic**: *Aur* k* bar-c clem lp psor al2 *Rhod* thuj lp
  - **gonorrhea**, after: *Alum Clem* k* cop *Med* **Rhod** sulph
  - **jarring** agg.; slight: brom ptk1
  - **old** people; in: bar-c br1
  - **painless**: brom ptk1
  - **small**: iod ptk1 puls ptk1 sil ptk1 spong ptk1 tub ptk1
  - **swollen**: *Merc* vh*
  - ○ **Epididymis**: ars *Aur Med* merc nit-ac **Rhod Spong**

INFERTILITY (See Sterility)

INFLAMMATION: *Acon* k* alum-p k2 *Ambr* b7a.de apis *Ars* k* calc k* cann-s k* **Canth** k* carbn-s castm k* con k* *Merc* k* merc-c bg2 mur-ac k* nat-c k* nat-m k* nit-ac k* nux-v k* ph-ac k* plb k* puls k* *Rhus-t* sabin b7.de* sep k* sil k2 *Spong* k* staph k* syc fmm1• thuj k*

- **erysipelatous**: rhus-t k2
- **genitourinary** (See BLADDER - Inflammation - accompanied - male)
- ○ **Hairy** parts | **follicles**: caps bro1 hep bro1 merc bro1 sep bro1 sil bro1
- **Lymphatic** glands: alum-p k2 merc
- **Penis**: *Arn Ars* k* cann-s k* canth k* caps tl1 crot-t k* cub k* hedy a1* iris jac-c k* *Kali-i* k* led k* merc k* nat-c k* plb k* *Psor* k* sabin b7.de* sars k* sep k* spong fd4.de *Sulph* k* syc fmm1• thuj b4a.de
  - **erysipelatous**: hedy a1*
  - **warm** bed agg.: jac-c k*
  - ○ **Frenum**: *Calc Nit-ac* sumb
  - **Glans**: *Acon* bro1 alum *Alumn* antip bro1 *Apis* k* *Arg-n* bro1 arn k* ars k* *Aur* aur-ar k2 aur-s k2 benz-ac mtf11 bry *Calad* k* *Calc Calen* c2 cand mtf11 cann-s k* canth k* carbn-s caust **Cinnb** k* *Cop* bro1 *Cor-r* k* *Cub* bro1 cupr k* *Dig* k* gels bro1 graph ham bro1 hep mrr1 iris c1 *Jac-c* k* **Kali-chl** k* kali-m k2 kali-p *Kali-s* lach led k* *Lyc* lyss m-aust b7.de *Merc* k* *Merc-c* k* mez k* napht dx nat-ar nat-c k* *Nat-m Nit-ac* k* nux-v ozone sde2• petr ph-ac k* prot jl2 *Psor Rhod* rhus-t k* sars k* sep sil spong fd4.de *Sulph* k* syc bka1*• *Thuj* k*
    - **pus**; with | **Prepuce**; under: *Jac-c* mrr1
  - **Lymphatics**: merc bg2
  - **Mucus** membrane: syc fmm1•
  - **Prepuce**: *Acon* j5.de* *Apis* k* *Ars* k* calad bro1 *Calc* k* cann-s k* *Canth* bro1 **Cinnb** k* coc-c bro1 con k* cor-r crot-t bro1 dig bro1 elaps *Gels* bro1 graph bg2 hep *Jac-c* k* lach lyc k* **Merc** k* merc-c bro1 mez k* mur-ac k* nat-ar *Nat-c* k* *Nit-ac* k* ol-sant bro1 positr nl2• *Rhus-t* k* sabin sep sil k* spong fd4.de *Sulph* k* *Sumb* k* syc fmm1• *Thuj* bro1 viol-t bro1
    - **erysipelatous**: *Apis* **Ars Lach** *Puls* **Rhus-t**
    - **Inner** surface: crot-t merc k2 *Nit-ac*
- **Prostate** gland (See PROSTATE - Inflammation)
- **Scrotum**: anac k* *Apis* bro1 *Ars* k* crot-t k* euph-l bro1 *Ham* bro1 jac-c k* mur-ac k* nat-m ph-ac k* plb k* podo k* *Rhus-t* k* *Rhus-v* k* trad a1* verat-v bro1
  - **erysipelatous**: *Ant-c* bro1 *Apis Arn* k* *Ars* k* aur bro1 canth crot-t graph k* merc mur-ac bro1 nat-m nat-s bro1 *Nit-ac* bro1 nux-v bro1 op k* ph-ac plb *Puls* **Rhus-t** k* *Rhus-v* staph bro1

Inflammation: ...

- **Spermatic** cords: *Acon* bro1 aesc bro1 aloe bro1 arn *Bell* bro1 *Berb* k* calc canth bro1 cub bro1 *Ferr-p* bro1 ham hep bro1 kali-br bro1 kali-c *Merc* bro1 nux-v k* phos k2 phyt bro1 plb gk psor **Puls** k* *Rhod* sel bro1 sil bro1 **Spong** k* *Syph* k* verat-v bro1
  - **chronic**: *Agn* bro1 *Arg-n* bro1 aur bro1 bar-c bro1 calad bro1 *Cann-s* bro1 chin bro1 clem bro1 *Con* bro1 *Cub* bro1 ferr-pic bro1 graph bro1 *Hep* bro1 *Iod* bro1 kali-br bro1 *Lyc* bro1 merc bro1 *Nux-v* bro1 *Ox-ac* bro1 *Ph-ac* bro1 phyt bro1 *Puls* bro1 *Sel* bro1 sep bro1 *Sil* bro1 staph bro1 sulph bro1 trib bro1 zinc bro1
- **Testes** (= orchitis): **Acon** k* am-c anan ant-t bro1 arg-met k2* *Arg-n* k* **Arn** k* *Ars Aur* k* aur-ar k2 aur-s k2 **Bapt** k* bar-m *Bell* k* *Berb* botul jl2 brom bro1* bufo bg2 carb-v c2 cham bro1 chel *Chin* k* chinin-s bro1 **Clem** k* clem-vir homp• **Con** k* cub k* der erech c2 fuma-ac mtf11 gels bro1 gonotox jl2 *Ham* bg2* hippoz iod k2 kali-ar kali-c *Kali-i* kali-m k2 kali-s bro1 *Lyc* k* m-ambo c2 med mrr1 *Merc* k* merc-i-r mtf11 mez nat-ar nat-c k* *Nat-m Nit-ac* k* *Nux-v* k* phos *Phyt* k* pip-m c2 *Plb* podo polyg-xyz c2* **Puls** k* **Rhod** k* **Rhus-t** k* sil k2 **Spong** k* *Staph* k* sul-ac teucr-s bro1 trad c2 ust c2 verat-v c2* viol-t c2 visc c2 zinc k*
  - **right**: arg-met mrr1 *Arg-n* chel **Clem** k* *Puls* **Rhod** k*
    - **extending** to | **left**: spong
  - **left**: brom k* mez oci **Puls** k* *Rhod* staph mrr1
  - **night**: **Clem**
  - **accompanied** by | **Skin**; complaints of: clem mrr1
  - **chronic**: agn bro1 arg-met k2 *Aur* hr1* bar-c bro1 *Calc-i* bro1 chin bro1 *Clem* bro1 *Con* bro1 gels bro1 *Hep* bro1 hyper bro1 iod bro1 *Kali-i* bro1 lyc k* merc bro1 nit-ac bro1 phyt bro1 *Puls* bro1 **Rhod** k* *Rhus-t* bro1 *Spong* hr1* sulph bro1 ust k*
  - **cold** agg.; becoming: acon k2 rhod k2
  - **cold**; exposure to: puls k2
  - **cold**; taking a:
    - **after** | **dancing**; while: rhod
  - **contusion**; from: ant-t hr1 **Arn** k* bar-m k* *Con* k* *Ham* k* *Puls* k* zinc k*
  - **gonorrhea** agg.; suppressed: *(↗URETHRA - Discharge - gonorrheal)* *Agn* k* ant-t arg-n aur k* bar-m bell brom canth chel **Clem** k* *Con* k* gels hr1* *Ham* k* kali-chl *Kali-s* **Med** *Merc* k* *Mez* nat-c nat-m *Nit-ac* k* **Puls** k* *Rhod* k* rhus-t sel *Spong* k*
  - **mumps**; from (See FACE - Inflammation - parotid - metastasis - testes)
  - **painful**: phyt mrr1
  - **sitting** on a damp ground: puls k2*
  - **syphilitic**: aur bro1 *Kali-i* bro1 merc-i-r bro1
  - **viral**: ourl jl2
  - **warm** bed agg.: **Clem**
  - ○ **Epididymis** (= epididymitis): *Acon* bro1 aloe sne apis bro1 arg-n bro1 arist-cl sp1 ars k* *Aur* k* aur-s k2 bell bro1* berb k* botul jl2 cann-s bro1 *Chin* k* clem k* *Gels* bro1 gonotox jl2 ham k* kali-n *Med* k* merc k* merc-i-r mtf11 nit-ac k* phyt k* **Puls** k* **Rhod** k* *Sabal* br1* **Spong** k* sulph k* teucr-s bro1 thuj bro1 tub jl2
    - **recurrent**: coli jl2

INJURIES: *Arn* bro1* *Calen* vh con bro1 *Hyper* vh* mill vh *Rhus-t* vh *Staph* pd*

- ○ **Penis**: mill ptk1

IRRITATION: sabal br1 sal-n br1

- **coition**; after: borx b4a.de
- **shivering**; during: plat b4.de
- ○ **Penis**: *Sel* rsj9•
- **Scrotum**: kali-c k2

ITCHING: acon b7.de* agar k* agn k* *Alum* alum-p k2 am-c k* *Ambr* k* anac k* *Ang* k* ars k* benz-ac berb k* borx bg2 calad k2* **Calc** k* cann-s bg cann-xyz bg2 canth k* carb-ac k* carb-an k* *Carb-v* k* carbn-s carl k* **Caust** k* *Chel* k* chinin-s chlam-tr bcx2• clem k* cocc bg2 coff com con k* cortico sp1 crot-t bro1 dulc k* *Eup-per* euphr k* *Fago* bro1 fl-ac bg2 *Graph* k* grat bg2 hep bg2 ictod *Ign* k* *Iris Kali-bi* k* kali-c k* kali-i k* kali-s kola stb3• kreos bg2 lat-m sp1 lyc k* mag-c b4.de* *Mag-m* k* *Merc* k* morg-p fmm1• nat-ar nat-c k* nat-m k* *Nat-s Nit-ac* k* nux-v bg2 ozone sde2• *Petr* k* plan k* **Plat** k* *Podo*

Itching: ...
positr nl2• prot fmm1• puls bg2 rhus-d bro1 *Rhus-t* k* rhus-v k* sal-al blc1• *Sars* scroph-n bg sel *Sep* k* sil k* sphing kk3.fr spong fd4.de *Sulph* k* sumb k* *Tarent-c* br1* thuj bg2 tritic-vg fd5.de urt-u mrr1 vanil fd5.de wies a1

- **morning**:
  - **waking**; on: sulph
    - **red**, raw spot; in a: graph
- **night**: agar k* oci-sa sk4• rhus-v k*
  - **bed** agg.; in: ign *Merc*
- **body**, especially on genitals, after emission; all over: ph-ac
- **burning** and: **Calc** carb-ac k* nat-c h2*
- **hot** applications amel.: rhus-v k*
- **hurriedness**; with (See MIND - Hurry - itching - genital)
- **painful**: ictod
- **scratching**:
  - **agg.**: iris tril-p
  - **amel.**: ign vanil fd5.de
  - **not** amel.: kola stb3•
- **spots**, in: bar-c
- **stitching** as from vermin: nat-c k*
- **urination** agg.; during: am-c bg2 ambr bg2 arg-n carb-v bg2 sil k*
- **voluptuous**: ang c1 berb **Plat** k* spong fd4.de sumb
- **warmth** of bed, agg.: sulph k2

○ - **Hairy** parts: agar bg2 ammc vh1 calc a1 carb-an bg2 carb-v bg2 eup-per hr1 gran a1 kali-bi k* kali-c bg2 lyss nat-m a1 *Rhus-t* b7a.de sep h2* sulph bg2 thuj a1

- **Penis**: *Acon* bro1 agar agn k* alum k* ambr k* ang *Ant-c* k* ant-t b7.de* ars k* ars-i aur-m bell bro1 benz-ac k* berb *Calad* bro1 calc k* calc-sil k2 cann-i k* cann-s b7a.de canth k* caps bro1 carb-ac carl k* **Caust** k* cham k* chin k* cinnb k* coc-c k* com k* con k* cop bro1 cor-r bro1 cortico tpw7* *Crot-t* k* cupr cupr-ar a1 der k* dig k* graph bro1 ham bro1 hedy a1* *Hep* k* *Ign* k* indg k* iod k* kali-ar kali-bi k* kali-c k* kali-n k* kali-p fd1.de• lach lachn k* led k* lyc bro1 mag-m k* merc k* merc-c k2 *Mez* k* nat-c k* nat-m k* *Nat-s* k* nit-ac k* nux-v k* ol-an bg2 petr k* ph-ac k* phos **Plat** k* positr nl2• *Puls* bro1 rhus-v k* sabad k* sel bro1 sep k* spig b7.de* spong k* staph bro1 sul-i k2 *Sulph* k* sumb thuj k* tritic-vg fd5.de viol-t k*
  - **evening** | **bed** agg.; in: chin k* *Ign* mag-m k* nux-v k* phos k* sumb
  - **alternating** with stitching in anus: *Thuj* k*
  - **coition**; during: sep k*
  - **rubbing** agg.: con
  - **voluptuous**: caust k* mang sep spong
    - **increasing** the excitement during coition: sep

○ • **Frenum**: cann-s b7a.de caust k* *Hep* k* merc b4a.de *Ph-ac* k*

  - **Glans**: acon bg2 agn alum k* *Ambr* k* ang b7.de* ant-c k* ant-t b7.de* aphis c1 arn k* *Ars* k* ars-i *Aur-m* bell b4.de* (non:ben a1) *Benz-ac* k* bry hr1 calc k* cann-i k* cann-s k* canth b7a.de caps b7.de* carb-ac *Carb-v* k* caust k* *Chel* k* chin k* **Cinnb** coff b7.de* colch con b4.de* **Crot-t** k* cupre-au c1 dig b4.de* *Dor* hr1 dros euphr k* ferr-ma k* franz a1 gymno hell b7.de* hep k* ictod ign b7.de* ind k* indg k* iod k* ip b7.de* *Kali-bi* k* kali-c h2* kali-n c1 kali-p fd1.de• lach bg led b7.de* *Lyc* k* lyss k* m-aust b7.de mag-m b4.de* mang k* merc k* *Mez* k* moni rfm1• nat-c k* nat-m k* *Nat-s* k* **Nit-ac** k* *Nux-v* k* petr h2* *Ph-ac* k* polyg-h bg2 psor k* puls b7.de* sabin b7.de* senec seneg k* sep b4.de* *Sil* k* spong k* sul-ac b4.de* **Sulph** k* *Thuj* k* tritic-vg fd5.de
    - **alternating** with | **Rectum**; stitching pain in (See RECTUM - Pain - stitching - alternating - glans)
    - **urination** | **after** | **agg.**: calc b4.de calc-p bg2 merc b4.de*
      - **during** | **agg.**: *Dulc* b4a.de seneg b4a.de thuj b4.de*
    - **voluptuous**: acon bg2 aphis br1 euphr a1 merc a1
  - **Hairy** parts: kali-bi lyss
  - **Prepuce**: acon b7.de* agar k* agn a1 aloe ang b7.de* ars bg2* berb k* bond a1 bry b7.de* calad b7.de* calc k* camph b7.de* cann-s k* canth k* *Caps* bro1 carb-v k* **Caust** k* *Cham* k* **Cinnb** k* coc-c a1 colch k* **Con** k* cortico tpw7 euph k* euphr b7.de* graph bro1 gymno *Hep* **Ign** k* jac-c k* *Lyc* k* m-ambo b7.de m-arct b7.de *Merc* k* mez k* nat-ar nat-c h2* nat-m k* nat-p k* **Nit-ac** k* nux-v k* **Petr** k* ph-ac b4a.de phel a1 phos k* plat-m a1 polyg-h bg2 *Puls* k* rhod b4a.de **Rhus-r** **Rhus-t** k* rhus-v a1 seneg b4.de* *Sep* k* *Sil* k* *Sulph* k* sumb k* tarax b7.de* *Thuj* k* *Viol-t* k* zinc k* zing k*
    - **coition**; after: nit-ac bg2

Ithcing – Penis – Prepuce: ...
    - **stool** agg.; after: aloe
    - **urination** agg.; after: mez a1*
    - **Rəphe**: euphr
    - **Tip**: ars h2
    - **Underside**: camph carb-v h2* caust k* com hr1 **Lyc** *Nit-ac* k* *Nux-v* k* *Puls* k* *Rhus-t* k* sil h2* *Thuj* k*
  - **Root**: ars h2* lyss *Rhus-t* tritic-vg fd5.de
  - **Tip**: ant-c h2 nat-m h2 nat-sil fd3.de• *Sel* rsj9• spong fd4.de tritic-vg fd5.de
    - **cold** washing | **amel.**: sel rsj9•
    - **urination** agg.; during: thuj h1
    - **walking** in open air agg.: ang h1*
- **Scrotum**: acon k* agar k* alum k* alum-sil k2 alumn k* am-c k* *Ambr* k* anac k* ang k* ant-c k* ant-s-aur ant-t k* *Apis* arg-met ars-met *Arum-d* **Aur** k* aur-s k2 *Bar-c* k* benzol br1 berb k* calad k* *Calc* k* *Calc-p* calc-sil k2 cann-i k* *Carb-ac* k* carb-v b4a.de* **Carbn-s** carl k* **Caust** k* cham b7.de* *Chel* k* chin b7.de* *Cist* k* coc-c k* *Cocc* k* coff b7a.de com k* con k* **Crot-t** k* euph-l bro1 ferr ferr-ma k* form k* gran a1 **Graph** k* hep b4a.de* hipp k* ign b7.de* indg k* jatr-c **Kali-c** k* *Kali-chl* k* *Kali-s* kali-sil k2 kola stb3• lac-ac k* lachn k* *Lyc* k* m-aust b7.de *Mag-m* k* manc k* *Mang* k* meph k* *Merc* mez a1 *Mur-ac* k* nat-ar nat-c k* **Nat-m** k* nat-p k* nat-s k* **Nit-ac** k* *Nuph* *Nux-v* k* **Petr** k* ph-ac k* pic-ac bg2 plat k* plut-n srj7• positr nl2• prun k* puls k* ran-s bg2 rat k* *Rhod* k* **Rhus-t** k* rhus-v k* *Sars* k* *Sel* k* *Sil* k* spira a1 spong k* *Staph* k* **Sulph** k* thuj k* **Urt-u** k* vichy-g a1 *Viol-t* k* *Zinc* k*
  - **morning**: ant-s-aur a1 coc-c k* puls k* sulph a1
  - **noon**: com k* *Sulph* k*
  - **afternoon**: tell k*
  - **evening**: alum alumn k* sulph k* thuj h1* *Zinc* k*
    - **bed** agg.; in: calc k*
  - **night**: calad k* com k* crot-t kali-c h2* lyc k* *Nat-m* k*
  - **burning**: berb a1 carb-ac cocc k* gran k* plat a1 rhus-r a1 rhus-t a1 rhus-v a1 spong a1
    - **rubbing**; after: thuj h1
    - **scratching**; after: carl a1 *Nat-s* k* rhus-v a1
  - **corrosion**, painful: **Crot-t**
  - **rubbing** | **amel.**: junc-e mag-m rhus-v staph
  - **scratching**:
    - **agg.**: rhus-v k*
    - **amel.**: alum k* carb-ac k* *Crot-t* k* viol-t
    - **not** amel.: *Mur-ac* nat-c k* *Zinc*
  - **spots**, in: franz a1 nicc k* sil ptk1
  - **voluptuous**: *Ambr* *Anac* k* cocc *Crot-t* euphr mur-ac spong *Staph* k*
    - **rubbing** agg.: staph k*
    - **sexual** excesses; after: **Staph** k*
  - **walking** agg.: *Crot-t* k*
  - **warm**, agg.; when: rhus-v

▽ • **extending** to | **Perineum**: rhus-t k* *Sars* k*

○ • **Inside**: caust bg2 cocc b7.de* staph b7.de*

  - **Sides**: agar k* ant-c k* camph a1 coff k* croc k* petr k* thuj k*
- **Spermatic** cords: mang k* ox-ac
- **Testes**: caust b4.de* ign b7.de* iod h* merc b4.de* nux-v bg2 petr b4.de* sel b7.de* spig b7.de*
- **Thighs**, between: carb-v k* nat-m k* oci-sa sk4• *Petr*

○ • **Scrotum**; and: carb-v bg2 *Nat-m* petr bg2 trios rsj11• viol-t
    - **warm** applications agg.: trios rsj11•

JERKING in penis: cinnb k* form k* mez k* nat-m a1 *Thuj* k* zinc k*
- **sleep** agg.; during: cinnb k*

○ - **Glans**: bar-c k*

MASTURBATION; disposition to: agar vh1 agn k* *Alum* bg2* alumn hr1* ambr k* *Anac* c1* **Anan** k* androc srj1• *Apis* c1 arg-met vh *Aur* hr1* *Bar-c* bg2* bell hr1* *Bell-p* c1* **Bufo** k* calad bg2* calc k* *Calc-p* c1 cann-i sf1.de cann-xyz bg2 **Canth** sne **Carb-v** hr1* carc st1* *Caust* st* *Chin* k* *Cina* kr1 cocc *Coff* st *Con* hr1* dendr-pol sk4• *Dig* hr1* dios sf1.de dros bg2 dulc fd4.de falco-pe nl2* *Ferr* hr1* *Gels* hr1* grat c1* hyos k* *Kali-br* c1 kali-p bg2* kola stb3• **Lach** k* *Lyc* bg2* *Med* c1* *Meph* hr1* merc mosch mrr1 nat-m k* *Nux-v* k* *Op* a1* **Orig** k* ozone sde2• petr-ra shn4• *Ph-ac* k* *Phos* k* *Pic-ac*

Masturbation; disposition to: ...
PLAT bg2* *Plb* hr1* podo fd3.de• *Puls* k* sal-n c1* sec sel bg2* **Sep** bg2* sil bg2* *Stann* hr1* **Staph** k* stict bg2* stram k* *Sulph* k* tarent k* thuj k* *Tub* k* *Ust* k* vanil fd5.de zinc c1*
- **morning** | **waking**; on: agar mrr1
- **accompanied** by:
  - **palpitations** | **young** people; in (See CHEST - Palpitation - accompanied - masturbation - young)
- **adolescents**: aven mtf11
- **ailments** from: carc mlr1•
- **childhood**, since: *Hyos* hr1*
- **children**; in: aloe lmj ambr lmj aur mtf33 bell st bell-p st bufo gk3 *Calc-p* lmj *Cann-i* lmj canth lmj *Carc* jl2* dys pte1*• *Fl-ac* lmj **Hyos** lmj* lac-c lmj **Lach** lmj* lyss lmj *Med* st* **Merc** lmj *Mosch* lmj ph-ac lmj **Phos** lmj plat vh* *Scir* st staph c1* stram lmj tub ggd* *Zinc* lmj
- **convulsions**; during epileptic: bufo kr1 **Calc** hr1* *Lach* bg2* *Plat* hr1* *Stram* hr1*
- **depressed**, when: *Ust* sf1.de
- **excessive**: *Alum* hr1* bell hr1* **Calc** hr1* **Carb-v** hr1* *Chin* hr1* *Onos* mrr1 orot-ac rly4• *Stram* hr1* tub mrr1
  - **opportunity**; at every: *Hyos* kr1
- **involuntary**: camph hr1*
- **irresistible** tendency: arg-met vh thuj hr1* *Ust* bg2*
- **itching**; from: *Staph* sf1.de
- **mania**, in: (↗*MIND - Mania - masturbation)* bell hr1*
- **public**; in: (↗*MIND - Naked - exhibitionism)* **Hyos** mrr1
- **relief**; without: canth mrr1
- **sexual** excesses; after: (non:aur-ar k2) carb-v phos sf1.de *Staph* sf1.de
- **sleep** agg.; during: camph carb-v k* *Plat* thuj
- **solitude**, seeks: *Bufo* ust
- **worms**; from: calad sf1.de
- **young** people: bar-c br1 carc jl2

METASTASIS: (↗*Swelling)* *Abrot* *Carb-v* parot mtf11 *Puls*

MOISTURE: **Hep** hr1 *Petr* hr1*
○ - **Penis** | **Glans**: alum bg2 cann-s b7.de* caust bg2 chin bg2 cinnb bg2 kreos bg2 lach bg2 lyc bg2 **Merc** bg2 mez bg2 nat-c bg2 nat-m b4.de* **Nit-ac** bg2 *Nux-v* bg2 *Ph-ac* b4a.de *Sep* bg2 staph b7.de* *Sulph* bg2 tab bg2 **Thuj** bg2
- **Scrotum**: *Ars* b4a.de *Bar-c* b4a.de *Calc-p* k* carb-v b4a.de* chel k* cinnb ptk1 cop k* *Graph* b4a.de* *Hep* b4a.de nat-c **Petr** k* pic-ac bg2 rhod ptk1 *Rhus-t* b7.de* sars bg2 *Sil* k* **Sulph** k* **Thuj** bg2 zinc
  - **acrid**: bar-c cop k*
  - **purulent**: jac-c k* jac-g
  - **serum**; with copious discharge of: bell *Calc-p* hep kali-i rhus-t
  - **spots**; on: sil ptk1
- **Thighs**; between scrotum and: *Bar-c* k* carb-v k* **Hep** k* lyc merc nat-c nat-m petr k* rhod *Sulph* k*

MOTION in testes; sensation as if: sabad thuj valer

NODULES:
○ - **Penis**: bov b4.de* sabin b7.de* *Thuj* b4a.de
  - **blue**: *Ars* b4a.de
○ - **Glans**: bell h*
  - **Prepuce**: *Thuj* b4a.de
- **Scrotum**: arn b7.de* nit-ac bro1
  - **hard** brown: *Nit-ac* k* syph ptk1
- **Spermatic** cords: syph ptk1
- **Testes**: calc-f k2 *Psor* k* syph ptk1

NUMBNESS: ambr k* bar-c k* dig form k* *Graph* k* kali-bi bg2 *Kali-br* hr1 plat mrr1 sulph bg2
○ - **Penis**: bar-c bg2 *Merc* k* plat sil bg2
  - **morning** | **erections**, with violent: ambr
○ - **Glans**: berb bg2* *Caust* b4a.de
    - **Prepuce**; and: berb k*
- **Scrotum**: am-c bro1 *Ambr* bro1 sep bro1
▽ - **extending** to | **Knees**: bar-c ptk1
- **Testes**: caps carbn-s nat-c k*

ODOR (See Perspiration; Perspiration - offensive)

ONANISM (See Masturbation)

ORCHITIS (See Inflammation - testes)

ORGASM:
- **easy**: *Plat* vh
- **subsides**: (↗*Ejaculation - late - orgasm)*
  - **ejaculation**; several times before it leads to: eug
- **wanting**: calad bro1* calc bro1 sel bro1

PAIN: acon↓ agar↓ alum↓ ambr↓ anac↓ ant-s-aur↓ ant-t↓ apis↓ arg-met↓ **Arg-n** k* arn ptk1 ars↓ arum-t↓ asaf↓ aur-i↓ bart↓ *Bell*↓ benz-ac↓ berb↓ borx↓ bov↓ **Calc**↓ cann-s↓ **Canth**↓ carb-ac↓ carb-v↓ castm↓ caust↓ chin cinch↓ cinnb↓ clem↓ cocc↓ colch↓ coloc↓ colocin c2 con↓ croc↓ dig↓ dulc fd4.de euph↓ euphr↓ eupi graph↓ hep↓ ign↓ inul↓ iod↓ jac-c↓ jatr-c kali-bi↓ *Kali-c*↓ kali-n↓ *Kreos*↓ lil-t↓ lyc↓ m-ambo↓ mag-m↓ merc↓ mez↓ mur-ac↓ nat-ar↓ *Nat-c*↓ nat-m↓ *Nit-ac*↓ nux-v↓ petr↓ *Phos*↓ phyt↓ plat plb↓ positr↓ prun↓ psor↓ puls ran-s↓ *Rhod*↓ rhus-t↓ *Sep*↓ sil↓ spong↓ stann↓ staph sul-ac↓ *Sulph*↓ sumb↓ syph al tarent k* thuj tritic-vg fd5.de vanil fd5.de verat↓ viol-t↓ zinc↓
- **morning**:
  - **bed**:
    - **in bed**:
      - **agg.**: nux-v↓ phos↓
        - **pressing** pain:
          - **cramping**: phos
          - **outward**: nux-v
- **night**: agar↓
  - **burning**: agar
- **aching**: **Arn** aur-i k2 chin cinch a1 jatr-c syph bg1
- **biting** pain: ambr b7.de* graph hep plat k* *Puls* ran-s staph thuj
- **burning**: agar ambr k* anac ant-t bg2 arn ars b4a.de* bart a1 bov k* **Calc** k* cann-s **Canth** k* carb-ac carb-v b4.de* caust b4.de* con b4.de* dulc fd4.de graph b4.de* iod b4.de* jac-c *Kali-c* b4.de* *Kreos* k* lyc b4.de* m-ambo b7.de mag-m merc b4a.de* *Nat-c* b4.de* nat-m b4.de* nit-ac b4.de* petr k* *Phos* b4.de* plat bg2 plb b7.de* positr nl2• prun puls rhus-t k* sep b4.de* sil b4.de* stann b4.de* staph bg2 sul-ac ptk1 sulph b4.de* sumb k* viol-t bg2
- **burning** from vesiculae seminales to glans | **dragging** (See dragging - vesiculae - extending - glans - burning)
- **burnt**; as if: apis b7a.de cann-s b7.de*
- **clawing** pain: clem hr1
- **coition**:
  - **after**: carb-v↓ merc↓
    - **burning**: carb-v b4a.de merc b4a.de
  - **during**: *Kreos*↓
    - **burning**: *Kreos* k*
- **constricting** pain: kali-bi bg2 puls
- **cramping**: castm c2 graph b4a.de
- **cutting** pain: borx lyc h2* sil k*
- **darting** (See stitching)
- **dragging**: asaf b7.de* *Bell* b4a.de canth b7.de* cocc b7.de* coloc b4a.de* *Kali-c* b4a.de nux-v b7.de* *Plat* b4a.de *Sep* b4a.de *Sulph* b4a.de
○ - **Vesiculae** seminales:
    - **extending** to:
      - **Glans**: mang↓
        - **burning**: mang
- **drawing** pain: psor bg2 rhod b4.de* vanil fd5.de
- **grinding** pain: phyt bg2
- **lancinating** (See cutting)
- **pressing** pain: alum k* asaf k* benz-ac k* cocc k* graph bg iod b4.de* kali-c k* kali-n k* mag-m k* merc k* *Plat* k* spong bg
  - **alternating** with:
    - **Anus**; contraction of: *Bell* k*
  - **downward**: bell cinnb lil-t *Plat*
- **pricking** pain: *Nit-ac* k*
- **scratching** agg.; after: nat-s↓
  - **burning**: nat-s k2

Male

- **shooting** (See stitching)
- **sit**; must move and cannot: syph↓
  • **aching**: syph$_{kr1*}$
- **sore** (= bruised): acon$_{bg2}$ ant-s-aur arg-met$_{bg2}$ arg-n$_{bg}$ arn$_{k*}$ ars arum-t calc$_{bg2}$ cocc con$_{bg2}$ dig$_{bg2}$ kali-c$_{bg2}$ lil-t nit-ac$_{bg2}$ phos **Plat** *Rhod*$_{bg2}$ *Sulph* syph verat
- **squeezed**; as if: bell$_{b4.de*}$
- **sticking** pain: croc$_{a1}$ lyc merc mur-ac petr phos *Rhod*$_{k*}$ *Sulph* *Thuj* zinc
- **stitching** pain: berb$_{k*}$ borx bov$_{b4.de*}$ *Calc*$_{b4a.de}$ clem$_{k*}$ croc$_{k*}$ dulc$_{fd4.de}$ euphr$_{k*}$ inul$_{k*}$ nat-ar$_{k2}$ positr$_{nl2}$• rhus-t$_{k*}$ sil$_{k*}$ vanil$_{fd5.de}$
  • **lancinating**: croc$_{k*}$
- **stool**:
  • **before**: nat-c↓
    ⋮ **pressing** pain: nat-c$_{k*}$
  • **during**:
    ⋮ **agg.**: *Kali-c*↓
      : **pressing** pain: *Kali-c*
- **tearing** pain: bell$_{bg2}$ calc$_{bg2}$ colch$_{bg2}$ euph$_{bg2}$ kali-c$_{bg2}$ mez$_{bg2}$ puls$_{bg2}$ staph$_{bg2}$
- **ulcerative** pain: ambr$_{bg2}$ ign$_{bg2}$
- **urination**:
  • **after**:
    ⋮ **agg.**: alum↓ arg-n↓ caust↓ kali-c↓ **Kreos**↓ positr↓
      : **burning**: alum arg-n caust kali-c **Kreos**$_{bg2}$ positr$_{nl2}$•
      : **sore** | **smarting**, as from salt: caust
  • **before**: nat-c↓ tarax↓
    ⋮ **burning**: nat-c tarax
  • **during**:
    ⋮ **agg.**: arg-n↓ caps↓ carbn-s↓ clem↓ dulc↓ kali-bi↓ kali-c↓ **Kreos**↓ petr↓ psor↓ sul-ac↓ tarax↓ tarent↓ thuj↓
      : **burning**: arg-n caps carbn-s clem dulc$_{fd4.de}$ kali-bi kali-c **Kreos**$_{bg2}$ petr psor sul-ac tarax tarent thuj
      : **sore**: kreos
    ⋮ **beginning** of:
      : **agg.**: iris↓ *Manc*↓ merc↓ petr↓ sec↓
        . **cutting** pain: iris *Manc* merc petr sec
- **walking** agg.; after: ambr↓
  • **burning**: ambr

○ - **Mons** Veneris: nux-v↓
  • **sore**: nux-v$_{bg1}$
- **Penis**: *Acon*↓ aesc↓ agn↓ aids$_{nl2}$• *All-c*↓ alum↓ alumn↓ ambr↓ ammc↓ anac↓ anan↓ anil$_{a1*}$ ant-c↓ ant-o↓ ant-t↓ apis↓ *Arg-n*↓ *Arn*↓ *Ars*$_{k*}$ asaf↓ asar↓ asc-t↓ asim↓ aspar↓ aur↓ aur-s↓ bell↓ berb↓ borx↓ brach↓ brom↓ calad↓ calc↓ calc-sil↓ *Cann-i*↓ cann-s$_{b7.de*}$ cann-xyz↓ canth$_{k*}$ *Caps*↓ caul$_{k*}$ caust↓ chel$_{k*}$ *Chim*↓ chin↓ cic↓ *Cinnb*↓ clem↓ coc-c$_{k*}$ cocc↓ *Coch*↓ colch↓ coloc↓ con↓ cop↓ cor-r↓ crot-h↓ crot-t↓ cycl dig$_{k*}$ *Dros*↓ dulc$_{fd4.de}$ elaps↓ euon↓ franz↓ *Gels*↓ geum$_{c2}$ graph↓ grat↓ guaj↓ ham↓ hedy↓ *Hep*↓ hera↓ hydrog$_{srj2}$• *Ign*$_{k*}$ **Iod**↓ jac-c$_{k*}$ kali-bi$_{k*}$ kali-c$_{k*}$ kali-i↓ kali-n↓ lac-c lach↓ lact↓ lat-m$_{bnm6}$• lith-c lyc↓ *M-ambo*↓ m-aust↓ mag-s↓ *Merc* *Merc-c*↓ merc-i-f↓ mez$_{k*}$ mosch↓ mur-ac↓ naja naphtin↓ narz↓ nat-ar↓ nat-c nat-m↓ *Nit-ac*↓ nuph↓ nux-m↓ nux-v↓ ol-an↓ osm *Par*$_{bg}$ *Pareir*$_{bg2}$ petr↓ ph-ac↓ phos$_{k*}$ *Phyt*↓ pilo$_{a1}$ plat↓ plb$_{k*}$ plect↓ prun$_{k*}$ psor↓ puls↓ puls-n↓ ran-s↓ rhod$_{bg1}$ rhus-t$_{k*}$ rhus-v$_{k*}$ sabad$_{k*}$ sabin$_{b7.de*}$ sang↓ *Sars*↓ sep↓ sil↓ spig↓ spong↓ stann↓ staph↓ still↓ stry$_{k*}$ *Sulph*↓ sumb$_{k*}$ tab↓ tarax$_{k*}$ tep↓ teucr↓ thuj$_{k*}$ valer↓ *Viol-t*↓ *Zinc*↓
  • **morning**:
    ⋮ **bed** agg.; in: mag-m↓
      : **burning**: mag-m$_{k*}$
  • **afternoon**: asaf↓
    ⋮ **drawing** pain: asaf$_{k*}$
  • **evening**: ol-an↓ puls↓
    ⋮ **coition**; after: lyc↓
      : **burning**: lyc$_{k*}$
    ⋮ **drawing** pain: ol-an$_{a1}$ puls

- **Penis**: ...
  • **alternating** with | **Kidneys**; pain in (See KIDNEYS - Pain - alternating - penis)
  • **biting** pain: cocc$_{k*}$ ign$_{k*}$ narz$_{a1}$ nat-c nat-m$_{k*}$ nux-v$_{k*}$ phos$_{k*}$ viol-t$_{b7.de*}$
  • **burning**: *All-c* anac$_{bro1}$ ant-c$_{k*}$ ant-o ant-t$_{b7.de*}$ *Ars*$_{k*}$ bell$_{bro1}$ calad$_{bg2}$ calc$_{b4a.de}$ *Cann-i*$_{k*}$ cann-s$_{k*}$ canth$_{k*}$ *Caps*$_{bro1}$ caust$_{k*}$ chin$_{k*}$ *Cinnb*$_{bro1}$ clem$_{b4a.de}$ *Coch*$_{k*}$ con$_{bro1}$ cop$_{bro1}$ cor-r$_{bro1}$ crot-t$_{bro1}$ dulc$_{fd4.de}$ *Gels*$_{bro1}$ ign$_{bro1}$ kali-i$_{k*}$ lyc$_{bro1}$ *M-ambo*$_{b7.de*}$ *Merc*$_{k*}$ *Merc-c*$_{bro1}$ *Mez*$_{k*}$ mosch$_{b7a.de}$ mur-ac$_{k*}$ naja *Nit-ac*$_{bro1}$ nuph$_{bro1}$ nux-v$_{bro1}$ plb$_{b7.de*}$ puls$_{bro1}$ rhus-t$_{bg2*}$ rhus-v$_{k*}$ sang$_{k*}$ sep$_{bro1}$ spig$_{b7.de*}$ spong$_{k*}$ stann$_{k*}$ sulph$_{k*}$ thuj$_{k*}$ *Viol-t*$_{k*}$
  • **coition**; during: arg-n$_{ptk1}$ canth$_{k2}$ clem↓ jug-r↓ *Kreos*↓ sep↓
    ⋮ **burning**: clem$_{k*}$ jug-r$_{k*}$ *Kreos*$_{k*}$ sep$_{k*}$
  • **corrosive**: agn$_{b7.de*}$
  • **cough** agg.; during: ign$_{k*}$
    ⋮ **stitching** pain: ign
  • **cramping**: graph$_{b4a.de*}$ hep$_{b4a.de*}$ nux-m$_{b7.de*}$
  • **cutting** pain: *Acon*$_{bro1}$ aids$_{nl2}$• alumn anac apis$_{bro1}$ *Arg-n*$_{bro1}$ asim$_{bro1}$ aur-s$_{c1*}$ calad$_{bro1}$ *Cann-s*$_{bro1}$ *Canth*$_{bro1}$ *Caps*$_{bro1}$ cic con$_{k*}$ crot-h euon *Hep*$_{bro1}$ lyc$_{k*}$ naphtin$_{bro1}$ nat-c$_{k*}$ nat-m$_{bro1}$ *Nit-ac*$_{bro1}$ ol-an *Pareir*$_{bro1}$ petr$_{bro1}$ ph-ac$_{k*}$ *Phyt*$_{bro1}$ prun$_{bro1}$ *Sars*$_{bro1}$ staph$_{bro1}$ still sulph$_{bro1}$ thuj$_{k*}$
    ⋮ **burning** pain: ph-ac
  • **drawing** pain: alum$_{h2*}$ ammc$_{hr1}$ asaf$_{k*}$ asar$_{b7.de*}$ canth$_{k*}$ cic$_{b7.de*}$ coc-c$_{k*}$ franz$_{a1}$ graph$_{k*}$ grat$_{k*}$ hera$_{a1}$ **Iod**$_{k*}$ *Kali-c*$_{k*}$ lact$_{k*}$ lyc$_{k*}$ merc$_{k*}$ mez$_{k*}$ ol-an$_{k*}$ plect$_{a1}$ psor$_{k*}$ puls-n ran-s$_{k*}$ rhod$_{k*}$ sabad$_{k*}$ sil$_{h2}$ teucr$_{k*}$ valer$_{k*}$ *Zinc*$_{k*}$
  • **erections**:
    ⋮ **during**: alum↓ arg-n↓ *Mag-m*↓
      : **burning**: *Mag-m*$_{k*}$
      : **cutting** pain: arg-n$_{ptk1}$
      : **stitching** pain: alum$_{k*}$
  • **jerking**: lach$_{bg2}$ mez$_{b4.de*}$ viol-t$_{b7.de*}$
  • **motion** agg.: berb$_{k*}$
  • **neuralgic**: tab$_{ptk1}$
  • **pinching**: acon alum$_{h2*}$ berb$_{a1}$ brom chel graph$_{k*}$ hep$_{h2*}$ osm
  • **pressing** pain: *Canth*$_{bro1}$ caps$_{bro1}$ graph$_{bro1}$ ign$_{b7.de*}$ iod$_{h*}$ kali-bi$_{bro1}$ *Nit-ac*$_{bro1}$ puls$_{bro1}$ *Rhod*$_{bro1}$ sabin$_{b7.de*}$ viol-t$_{b7.de*}$
  • **pulsating**: coc-c$_{bro1}$ ham$_{bro1}$ lith-c$_{bro1}$ nat-m$_{bro1}$ *Nit-ac*$_{bro1}$
  • **raw**; as if: arn$_{bg2}$ borx$_{bg2}$ cann-xyz$_{bg2}$ cic$_{bg2}$
  • **scratching** agg.; after: carl↓
    ⋮ **burning**: carl$_{k*}$
  • **seminal** emissions; after: dig$_{b4a.de}$
  • **sitting** and walking: mag-s↓
    ⋮ **stitching** pain: mag-s
  • **smarting**: asar$_{k*}$ aur-s$_{k*}$ berb$_{k*}$ *Chim*$_{hr1}$ crot-h$_{k*}$ hedy$_{a1*}$ sulph$_{k*}$
  • **sore**: *Arn*$_{b7.de*}$ asar borx calad *Cann-s* canth cic$_{b7.de*}$ cop hep$_{b4a.de}$ *Ign* lach nat-c rhus-t rhus-v sabad sulph tep *Thuj*
  • **spasmodic**: nux-m
  • **stitching** pain: acon aesc$_{vh1}$ anan arn asaf$_{k*}$ asar asc-t aspar aur berb$_{k*}$ borx brach brom calad calc$_{k*}$ calc-sil$_{k2}$ cann-s caps caul chel cinnb clem$_{b4a.de}$ coc-c coloc$_{h2*}$ con crot-t *Dros*$_{k*}$ dulc$_{fd4.de}$ elaps guaj ham ign kali-n *Lith-c* lyc$_{k*}$ mag-s merc$_{k*}$ merc-i-f *Mez*$_{k*}$ mur-ac$_{k*}$ naja nat-ar$_{k2}$ nat-m osm petr$_{k*}$ ph-ac$_{k*}$ phos$_{k*}$ plat puls$_{k*}$ ran-s sabad$_{k*}$ sabin$_{b7.de*}$ sep sil spig$_{k*}$ stann staph *Sulph*$_{k*}$ sumb *Thuj*$_{k*}$ *Viol-t*$_{k*}$ zinc$_{k*}$
    ⋮ **backward**: aur
    ⋮ **forward**: asar spig
    ⋮ **itching** pain: kali-n$_{h2*}$ ph-ac$_{k*}$ spig$_{h1*}$
    ⋮ **needles**; as if: asaf$_{ptk1}$
  • **stool** agg.; during: hydr$_{k*}$
  • **swelling** of prepuce; from: *Rhus-t*
  • **tearing** pain: ambr aur calc$_{bg2}$ colch coloc con$_{k*}$ ign$_{b7.de*}$ iod$_{k*}$ kali-c$_{k*}$ kali-i m-aust$_{b7.de}$ merc$_{k*}$ mez$_{k*}$ petr ph-ac$_{k*}$ tab thuj$_{k*}$

- **torn** asunder; as if: m-aust b7.de
- **touch** agg.: sumb k*
- **urination**:
  - **after**:
    - **agg.**: aids nl2•
      - **spasms** of urethra and tenesmus of rectum; with: *Prun*↓
        - **stitching** pain: *Prun*
  - **before**: chin↓ cic↓
    - **drawing** pain: cic b7.de*
    - **pressing** pain: chin
  - **during**:
    - **agg.**: aids nl2• aq-mar rbp6 aur↓ *Canth* a1 ferr-i *Merc*↓ nat-m ox-ac a1 petr phos prun↓ sulph
      - **stitching** pain: aur *Merc* nat-m h2* petr h2* prun k* sulph h2*
- **walking** agg.: cann-s ign puls-n thuj
  - **burning**: cann-s

▽ - **extending** to:
  - **Anus**: merc↓ thlas↓
    - **stitching** pain: merc thlas bg1
  - **Glans**: asar↓ brom↓ spong↓
    - **stitching** pain: asar brom spong
  - **Testes**: carbn-s↓ thuj↓
    - **stitching** pain: carbn-s thuj

○ - **Frenum**: hep↓ phos↓ sabin b7.de*
  - **stitching** pain: hep b4a.de phos b4a.de

- **Glans**: acon↓ all-c alum↓ ambr↓ ant-c↓ ant-t↓ arn↓ ars↓ ars-s-f↓ asaf asar aur↓ berb borx↓ brom↓ calc cann-i↓ cann-s↓ **Canth** caps↓ carb-ac↓ card-m↓ *Caul*↓ *Chel* k* chin↓ cic cinnb↓ clem↓ coc-c↓ *Coch*↓ colch coloc↓ con↓ *Cop* k* cor-r↓ crot-t↓ culx↓ cupr↓ cycl *Dor*↓ dros↓ dulc fd4.de *Euph*↓ euphr↓ ferr-ma↓ *Ferr-p* graph↓ hell↓ hep↓ ign↓ iod↓ kali-bi k* kali-c↓ kali-p↓ kola↓ lach↓ lact↓ lyc↓ lyss↓ mang↓ med *Merc* k* merc-c↓ mez narz↓ nat-c nat-m *Nit-ac*↓ nux-v↓ ol-an↓ osm ox-ac **Par Pareir** k* petr↓ ph-ac phos↓ *Prun*↓ puls↓ ran-s↓ rhod↓ rhus-t b7.de* sabin↓ samb↓ sang↓ seneg↓ sep↓ spong↓ squil↓ stann↓ staph↓ *Sulph*↓ sumb↓ tarax↓ **Thuj**↓ valer↓ viol-t zinc↓ zinc-p↓
  - **accompanied** by | **Urinary** organs; complaints of (See URINARY - Complaints - accompanied - glans)
  - **aching**: chel ptk1 osm ptk1
  - **biting** pain: ign b7.de* kali-c h2* narz a1 nat-m b4.de* nux-v k* phos b4.de*
  - **boring**: tarax b7.de*
  - **burning**: *All-c* k* ant-c ant-t k* arn ars k* berb k* calc k* cann-s k* chin b7.de* cinnb clem *Coch* k* crot-t culx vh cupr b7.de* *Dor* k* dulc fd4.de lyc b4.de* lyss k* mang b4.de* merc k* merc-c b4a.de nux-v k* *Par Pareir* ph-ac k* sabin c1* sang a1 sep b4a.de stann k* **Thuj** k* *Viol-t* k*
    - **itching** pain: cinnb
  - **coition**; after: eug↓
    - **sore**: eug bg1
  - **compressing**: alum b4.de* rhus-t b7.de*
  - **corrosive**: nux-v b7.de*
  - **cramping**: ign b7.de* seneg b4.de* sulph bg2
  - **cutting** pain: con euph b4.de* iod h* lyc k* ph-ac k* thuj k*
  - **drawing** pain: alum k* asaf k* cic k* graph k* iod k* kali-c k* lact lyc k* mez h2* ol-an a1 spong b7.de* thuj k* valer b7.de*
  - **ejaculation**, during: clem↓
    - **burning**: clem
  - **groins**, with an out-pressing pain; in both: ph-ac↓
    - **burning**: ph-ac c1
  - **pinching**: acon b7.de* chel a1 kali-bi mez ph-ac rhod b4a.de
  - **pressing** on glans penis agg.: thuj↓
    - **stitching** pain: thuj
  - **pressing** pain: alum caps b7.de* card-m hr1 chin b7.de* lyc k* nit-ac k* puls b7.de* sabin b7.de* seneg viol-t b7.de*
    - **pea** under it; as from a: kola stb3•
  - **pricking** pain: ars hr1 aur a1 carb-ac hr1 ph-ac hr1

- **Glans**: ...
  - **rubbing**; slight: cycl↓ nat-c↓
    - **sore**: cycl ptk1 nat-c ptk1
  - **smarting**: ars b4.de* *Asar* k* berb k* nux-v k*
  - **sore**: asar caps chel cic cor-r b7a.de cycl lach bg2 merc nat-c k* nux-v b7.de* rhus-t sabin b7.de* thuj
  - **stitching** pain: acon k* arn k* ars k* ars-s-f k2 aur b4.de* berb k* borx b4a.de brom k* calc h2* cann-i bg caps b7.de* carb-ac *Caul* chel a1 chin b7.de* cinnb clem coc-c crot-t bg2 cupr b7.de* dros k* dulc fd4.de *Euph* k* euphr k* ferr-ma hell b7.de* hep k* *Kali-bi* kali-c h2* kali-p fd1.de• lyc k* *Merc* k* mez k* nat-c h2* nat-m k* *Nit-ac* bg2 petr b4.de* ph-ac k* phos k* *Prun* ran-s k* rhod k* sabin k* samb spong k* squil b7.de* stann k* staph b7.de* *Sulph* k* sumb bg1 *Thuj* k* zinc k* zinc-p k2
  - **tearing** pain: ambr k* aur b4.de* cinnb *Colch* k* coloc h2* euph k* kali-c k* lyc k* merc k* *Mez* k* *Par Pareir* petr k* thuj k* zinc k*
  - **ulcerative** pain: ambr b7.de*
  - **urination**:
    - **after**:
      - **agg.**: anac k* coc-c↓ coch↓ lyc phos h2* *Prun*↓ *Puls* k* *Sars*↓
        - **aching**: puls
        - **burning**: anac k* coc-c coch k* *Sars* k*
        - **cutting** pain: coc-c hr1 coch k*
        - **stitching** pain: *Prun*
    - **and** dragging in vesiculae seminales to glans: *Mang*↓
      - **burning**: *Mang*
    - **before**: anac↓ asaf↓ aur↓ *Canth* k* chin↓ coch↓ dulc↓ lyc *Stann*↓
      - **burning**: anac k* coch k* dulc b4a.de *Stann*
      - **cutting** pain: coch k*
      - **pressing** pain: chin b7.de*
      - **stitching** pain: aur
      - **tearing** pain: asaf b7.de* aur k*
    - **during**:
      - **agg.**: acon k* act-sp anac k* *Ars*↓ asaf b7.de* casc coch↓ crot-t↓ dig↓ dulc fd4.de euph↓ lyc mez↓ nit-ac↓ ox-ac k* *Par*↓ *Pareir*↓ petr↓ plut-n↓ prun k* *Sars*↓ sulph↓ thuj↓
        - **burning**: anac b4a.de* *Ars* k* coch k* crot-t a1 dig a1 dulc fd4.de *Lyc* mez b4a.de* *Par Pareir* plut-n srj7• thuj b4.de*
        - **cutting** pain: coch k* *Lyc* k*
        - **sore**: *Lyc* nit-ac
        - **stitching** pain: acon euph h2* sulph thuj
        - **tearing** pain: *Par Pareir* petr *Sars*
      - **beginning** of:
        - **agg.**: psor↓
          - **burning**: psor k*
      - **end** of: kali-bi↓ phos↓
        - **biting** pain: phos b4.de*
        - **burning**: kali-bi bg2
    - **urging** to; with: aran aur ferr-p lyc pareir thuj
  - **extending** to:
    - **Root** of penis: sars↓
      - **tearing** pain: sars
  - **Behind**:
    - **urination** agg.; during: ery-a↓
      - **burning**: ery-a k*
- **Prepuce**: *Acon* bro1 ail↓ ang↓ ars↓ bell bro1 benz-ac↓ *Berb* bro1 bry↓ bufo↓ calad k* calc↓ camph↓ **Cann-s** bg* **Cann-xyz** bg2 *Canth* bro1 carb-v↓ cham↓ chin↓ cinnb bro1 coc-c bro1 cocc↓ con bro1 *Cop* bro1 cor-r k* cycl euph↓ euphr↓ germ-met↓ *Hep*↓ ign bro1 jac-c a1 jac-g↓ kali-c↓ lob↓ *Lyc* m-ambo↓ m-arct↓ *Mang*↓ **Merc** b4.de* merc-c bro1 mur-ac↓ *Nit-ac* bg2* nux-v bro1 osm k* plat-m↓ plb↓ polyg-h↓ *Puls*↓ rhus-t k* rhus-v↓ sabin k* sep bg2* sil↓ **Sulph** bg2* sumb↓ thuj bg2* verat k*
  - **evening**: cycl↓
    - **sore**: cycl
  - **biting** pain: bell b4.de* calad b7.de* coc-c a1 ign b7.de* m-ambo b7.de m-arct b7.de merc k* *Nux-v* k* puls k* thuj k*

Male

- **Prepuce**: ...
  - **burning**: ars k* berb k* bry b7.de* bufo calad calc k* camph bg2 cann-s b7.de* kali-c h2* m-ambo b7.de *Merc* k* merc-c k2 *Nit-ac* k* nux-v k* *Puls* rhus-t k* rhus-v k* sep sil k* *Sulph* k* *Thuj* k*
    - **alternating** with | **Rectum**; stitching pain in (See RECTUM - Pain - stitching - alternating - prepuce)
  - **coition**; after: calad b7.de* kreos ↓ lyc ↓ plb b7.de*
    - **burning**: kreos bg2 lyc k*
  - **corrosive**: calad b7.de* plb b7.de*
  - **drawing** pain: coc-c k*
  - **pinching**: jac-c k*
  - **raw**; as if: cham bg2 nux-v bg2 puls bg2 sabin bg2
  - **rubbing**; after slight: cycl ↓
    - **sore**: cycl a1
  - **smarting**: (non:ail k*) bell hr1 benz-ac k1* (non:calad k*) cann-s b7.de* (non:carb-v k*) lob a1* merc b4.de* nux-v k1* puls k1* (non:sep k*) sulph bg2* (non:verat k*)
  - **sore**: ail calad k* cann-s b7.de* carb-v chin b7.de* ign b7.de* nux-v bg1 sep verat [puls xyz62]
  - **stitching** pain: acon a1 ang b7.de* ars k* bry b7.de* camph b7.de* cann-s b7.de* cham k* cocc k* euph bg2 euphr b7a.de germ-met srj5• *Hep* k* jac-c a1 *Mang* k* merc b4.de* *Nit-ac* k* plat-m a1 polyg-h bg2 puls b7.de* rhus-t b7.de* sep k* sumb thuj k*
  - **stool** agg.; after: sil ↓
    - **burning**: sil a1
  - **tearing** pain: chin k* jac-c k* jac-g mur-ac a1
  - **ulcerative** pain: ign b7.de*
  - **urination** | **after**:
    - **agg.**: bell ↓ berb ↓ borx ↓ calad ↓ cann-s ↓ canth ↓ chinin-s ↓ clem ↓ coloc ↓ con ↓ cop ↓ dig ↓ grat ↓ *Hep* ↓ kali-bi ↓ kali-c ↓ led ↓ m-arct ↓ mag-m ↓ *Merc* ↓ *Nat-c* ↓ nat-m ↓ nat-s ↓ seneg ↓ teucr ↓ thuj ↓ zinc ↓
      - **biting** pain: bell b4.de* borx calad k* chinin-s cop *Hep* b4a.de m-arct b7.de
      - **burning**: berb cann-s canth clem coloc con grat kali-bi kali-c led mag-m *Merc* *Nat-c* nat-m nat-s seneg teucr thuj zinc
      - **cutting** pain: berb canth dig nat-m
      - **stitching** pain: berb con kali-bi merc
    - **during**:
      - **agg.**: calad ↓ phos k*
        - **biting** pain: calad b7.de*
  - **walking** agg.: **Merc** ↓
    - **sore**: **Merc**
  - **warm** bath; after: clem ↓
    - **burning**: clem a1
  - **Margin** of prepuce: **Ign** ↓ *Mur-ac* ↓ *Nit-ac* ↓
    - **sore**: **Ign** *Mur-ac* *Nit-ac*
  - **Under** side: carb-v ↓
    - **smarting**: carb-v
- **Root**: ammc ↓ calc-p ↓ chel ↓ equis-h hydr k* hydrog srj2• ign k* lact ↓ ol-an ↓ ozone ↓ *Petros* rat ↓ rhus-t ↓ zinc ↓
  - **morning**:
    - **waking**; on: *Kali-bi* ↓
      - **constricting** pain: *Kali-bi*
  - **afternoon**:
    - **4.30 h**: ozone ↓
      - **stitching** pain: ozone sde2•
  - **burning**: hydrog srj2• ol-an rat rhus-t
  - **dragging**: chel
  - **drawing** pain: lact k* zinc k*
  - **leaning** against lumbar region while standing amel.: ign ↓
    - **tearing** pain: ign k*
  - **stitching** pain: ammc vh1 calc-p ozone sde2• zinc
  - **walking** agg.: ign ↓ zinc ↓
    - **tearing** pain: ign k* zinc
  - **extending** to:
    - **Glans**:
      - **urination** agg.; after: sars ↓

- **Penis – Root – extending** to – **Glans – urination** agg.; afer: ...
  - **tearing** pain: sars
- **Tip**: arum-t ↓ aur ↓ calc ↓ camph k* dulc fd4.de euph ↓ euphr ↓ ferr-m ↓ hell ↓ hipp k* kali-n ↓ kola stb3• mez ↓ nuph k* osm k* ph-ac ↓ phos k* psor k* thuj ↓ zinc ↓
  - **cutting** pain: calc
  - **smarting**: arum-t kali-n c1
  - **stitching** pain: aur h2* dulc fd4.de euph k* euphr k* ferr-m hell a1 mez k* ph-ac thuj k*
  - **tearing** pain: zinc
  - **urination**; during | **beginning** of urination agg.: psor
- **Pubic** bone: calc b4a.de carb-v b4a.de con b4a.de kali-c b4a.de merc b4a.de sulph b4a.de
- **Scrotum**: acon ↓ am-c bro1 *Ambr* ↓ anac ↓ anan ↓ anil br1 *Arn* ↓ ars ↓ ars-s-f ↓ bell ↓ berb bro1 brass-n-o ↓ *Calc* ↓ *Calc-p* ↓ cann-i ↓ *Caps* ↓ carb-an ↓ carbn-s ↓ carl ↓ chin ↓ cic ↓ *Clem* bro1 cocc ↓ coff ↓ con ↓ cop ↓ cupr-ar ↓ euph ↓ hera ↓ ign ↓ iod bro1 kali-c bro1 kali-m ↓ lachn ↓ lyc ↓ meny ↓ *Merc* bro1 mez ↓ narz ↓ nat-ar ↓ nat-c ↓ nux-v bro1 ourl jl2 petr ↓ ph-ac ↓ plat ↓ prun ↓ ran-s ↓ rhod ↓ rhus-v ↓ sil ↓ spig ↓ spong ↓ staph ↓ sulph ↓ teucr ↓ *Thuj* bro1 trad a1* viol-t ↓ zinc ↓
  - **left**: ulm-c ↓
    - **extending** to:
      - **right**: lachn ↓
        - **burning**: lachn c1
    - **stitching** pain: ulm-c jsj8•
  - **biting** pain: hera a1 narz a1 plat k* ran-s k*
  - **burning**: ars k* *Calc* cann-i k* *Caps* b7a.de carl k* *Clem* b4a.de cocc b7.de cop k* euph k* lachn meny h1* mez k* petr plat k* rhod k* rhus-v k* sil spong k* sulph
    - **itching** pain: cocc k*
  - **corrosive**: plat b4.de*
  - **cramping**: clem b4.de*
  - **crushed**: kali-c h*
  - **cutting** pain: bell bg2 con k* meny b7.de*
  - **dragging**: petr b4.de*
  - **drawing** pain: clem b4.de* meny b7.de* petr a1 teucr b7.de*
  - **oozing** fluid: calc-p ↓ cop ↓
    - **sore**: calc-p cop
  - **perspiration** agg.; after: plb ↓
    - **sore**: plb
  - **pinching**: clem euph b4.de* meny h1* mez nux-v b7.de* prun a1
  - **pressing** pain: cic a1 meny h* merc bg2 mez h* thuj b4.de*
  - **raw**; as if: con bg2 ph-ac bg2 ran-s bg2 teucr bg2 zinc bg2
  - **rubbing**; after: rhus-t ↓ rhus-v ↓ thuj ↓
    - **burning**: rhus-t k* rhus-v thuj k*
  - **scratching** agg.; after: carl ↓ *Nat-s* ↓ rhus-v ↓ thuj ↓
    - **burning**: carl a1 *Nat-s* rhus-v a1 thuj h1*
  - **smarting**: berb k* carbn-s ran-s k*
  - **sore**: acon bg2 am-c *Ambr* b7.de* anac *Arn* b7.de* berb *Calc-p* chin coff k* cupr-ar kali-c k* ph-ac k* plat b4.de* staph b7.de* zinc k*
  - **squeezed**; as if: kali-c b4.de*
  - **sticking** pain: brass-n-o srj5•
  - **stitching** pain: anan arn k* ars-s-f k2 berb carb-an b4a.de* chin b7.de* clem ign b7.de* kali-m k2 lyc meny k* merc b4.de* mez k* nat-ar k2 nat-c b4.de* ph-ac k* plat b4.de* rhus-v spig h1* sulph k* **Thuj** k* viol-t k* zinc k*
  - **stretched**; as if: clem b4.de*
  - **tearing** pain: lyc b4.de* sulph b4.de*
  - ○ **Sides**: euph ↓ lach ↓ meny ↓ stry ↓ tarent ↓
    - **aching**: lach meny
    - **burning**: euph k* stry k* tarent k*
  - **Spots**; in: nit-ac ↓
    - **sore**: nit-ac
  - **Thighs**; between: *Caust* ↓ hep ↓ rhod ↓ sulph ↓
    - **sore**: *Caust* hep tl1 rhod sulph tl1

- **Thighs**; between scrotum and: *Bar-c*↓ **Graph**↓ hep↓ **Lyc**↓ *Merc*↓ *Nat-c*↓ *Nat-m*↓ **Petr**↓ rhod↓ *Rhus-t*↓ *Sulph*↓ trios↓
  - **burning**: bar-c
  - **smarting**: hep nat-c
  - **sore**: *Bar-c* **Graph** **Lyc** *Merc* *Nat-c* *Nat-m* **Petr** rhod *Rhus-t* *Sulph* trios rsj11•
  - **warm** applications agg.: trios↓
    - **sore**: trios rsj11•
- **Sides** of: petr↓ thuj↓ zinc↓
  - **sore**: petr thuj zinc
- **Spermatic** cords: *Agar*↓ agn↓ all-c aloe↓ alum↓ am-c k* am-m↓ ambr↓ ammc k* anag↓ ang↓ *Ant-c* b7a.de anth k* apis arg-met k* arg-n k* arn arum-d↓ arum-t↓ arund bro1 aur bro1 aur-m↓ *Bell* bro1 *Berb* k* brach↓ brom↓ *Bry*↓ cain bro1 *Calc* k* calc-ar calc-s↓ camph *Cann-s* bro1 canth↓ caps k* carbn-s↓ cassia-s↓ chel chin b7.de* chinin-ar↓ chinin-s cimic k* *Clem* k* cocc↓ *Colch*↓ coloc con bro1 crot-t↓ *Dios* bro1 echi equis-h↓ goss↓ grat↓ **Ham** k* hydr↓ hydrc↓ ind bro1 *Iod*↓ kali-c bg* kali-n c1 lact↓ lith-c bro1 *M-ambo*↓ m-aust b7.de mang med k2* mentho↓ meny *Merc* *Merc-i-r* bro1 mez↓ morph k* narz a1 nat-c↓ nat-m↓ nat-p k* *Nit-ac* bro1 nux-m↓ nux-v k* *Ol-an* k* osm k* *Ox-ac* k* oxyt c2* petr↓ ph-ac↓ *Phos* k* phyt k* pic-ac bro1 plb k* podo↓ polyg-h polyg-xyz c2 psor↓ puls k* rhod k2 sabad↓ sabin↓ *Sars* k* sec↓ senec k* sil bg2* spira↓ *Spong* k* staph bro1 stry k* sulph bro1 sumb↓ tarent k* tep↓ ter↓ teucr↓ *Thlas* bro1 *Thuj* k* tub c1 tus-p bro1 verat↓ verat-v bro1 *Zinc*↓ zinc-val↓
  - **right**: all-c↓ ammc↓ anag↓ arg-met↓ aur sne cimic k* *Clem* echi ham fd3.de• lact↓ morph k* ox-ac k* ozone sde2• rhod↓ sabin↓ sulph↓ tep↓
    - **afternoon**:
      - **16** h: arg-met↓
        - **tearing** pain: arg-met
    - **burning**: clem
    - **drawing** pain: all-c a1 ammc a1* anag hr1 arg-met lact a1 rhod hr1 sabin k* sulph a1 tep a1
    - **sore**: *Clem*
  - **left**: agar↓ ammc↓ ang↓ ars↓ ars-s-f↓ ars-s-r↓ berb k* calc con↓ crot-t↓ fl-ac↓ ham↓ hydrc↓ kali-br a1 med k2* nat-p k* plb k* stry k* sumb↓ tarent↓ ter↓ tub c1 ulm-c↓
    - **then** right: calc staph↓
      - **stitching** pain: calc staph
    - **burning**: berb
    - **drawing** pain: agar ammc a1 ang a1* ars k* ars-s-f k2 ars-s-r hr1 *Berb* a1 con a1 crot-t a1 fl-ac bg1 ham hr1 hydrc a1 tarent k* ter a1 tub bg1
    - **sitting** and standing: berb
    - **stitching** pain: ulm-c jsj8•
    - **tearing** pain: sumb
    - **urination** agg.; after: lith-c
  - **morning**: calc-s↓ clem k* nat-c↓ phyt↓ sars
    - **aching**: sars k*
    - **drawing** pain: calc-s k* nat-c h2
    - **grinding** pain | **upward**: phyt k*
  - **afternoon**:
    - **16** h: arg-met↓
      - **drawing** pain: arg-met
  - **evening**: ammc↓ bell↓
    - **bed** agg.; in: bell↓
      - **tearing** pain: bell
    - **drawing** pain: ammc k*
    - **stitching** pain: ammc k*
    - **tearing** pain: bell k*
  - **night**: clem k2
  - **aching**: all-c k* chel k* chinin-s *Clem* k* mang nux-v k* *Sars* k* senec k*
  - **boring**: sulph bg2
  - **burning**: ambr k* *Berb* k* carbn-s clem *M-ambo* b7a.de mang k* puls bg* spong ptk1 *Staph* b7.de* thuj k*
  - **coition**; after: arund k* ther
  - **cold**:
    - **amel.**: cassia-s↓

- **Spermatic** cords – **cold** – **amel.**: ...
    - **drawing** pain: cassia-s ccrh1•
  - **constricting** pain: am-c berb k* nux-v
  - **contracting**: alum berb calc **Nux-v**
  - **cough** agg.; during: *Nat-m* verat↓
    - **stitching** pain: verat b7.de*
  - **cramping**: arg-met dios bg2 kali-c **Nux-v** petr h2* plb bg2
  - **cutting** pain: bell berb
  - **dragging**: berb camph bg2 chinin-ar *Iod* sars k* sec k* spong sumb k* teucr b7.de*
  - **drawing** pain: *Agar* k* agn k* *All-c* k* aloe bg2 alum am-c k* ammc k* anag k* ang k* ant-c k* arg-met aur-m k* *Bell* k* *Berb* k* bry cain br1* calc bro1 calc-s bg1* cann-s canth k* caps b7.de* cassia-s ccrh1• *Chel* k* cimic k* *Clem* k* *Con* k* crot-t k* *Ham* k* hydr hydrc k* *Ind* k* lact k* *M-aust* b7.de* *Mang* k* med *Merc* k* mez k* nat-c k* nat-m k* nat-p k* nit-ac k* nux-m b7.de* *Nux-v* k* *Ol-an* k* *Ox-ac* ph-ac *Phos* plb k* psor k* *Puls* k* rhod k* sabad b7.de* sabin b7.de* sec senec bro1 spong k* *Staph* k* sulph k* *Tarent* tep k* ter k* *Zinc* k*
    - **forward**: *Ol-an* br1
    - **paroxysmal**: merc k*
    - **spasmodic**: agar k*
    - **upward**: *Bell* *Ol-an* k*
  - **emissions** agg.; after: *Nat-p*
  - **erections**; after: mag-m nux-m *Sars*
    - **coition**; without: mag-m↓ nux-m↓ *Sars*↓
      - **aching**: mag-m nux-m *Sars*
  - **exertion** agg.; after: calc-ar ox-ac
  - **grinding** pain | **upward**: phyt a1
  - **jar** agg.: ozone sde2•
  - **jerking**: ang mang ox-ac plb
  - **motion**:
    - **agg.**: cassia-s↓ ox-ac
      - **drawing** pain: cassia-s ccrh1•
      - **tearing** pain: ox-ac k2
    - **amel.**: arg-met↓ rhod k2
      - **drawing** pain: arg-met rhod k*
  - **neuralgic**: *Arg-n* bro1 aur bro1 *Bell* bro1 *Berb* bro1 *Clem* bro1 cocc mtf11 coloc bro1 ham bro1 hydr mtf11 mentho bro1 meny mtf11 mez mtf11 nit-ac bro1 nux-v bro1 ol-an br1* ox-ac bro1* petr mtf11 phyt bro1 rhod bro1* *Spong* bro1 zinc-val mtf11
  - **pressing** pain: anth berb brom *Clem* kali-n k* mang h2* meny k* mez b4a.de nat-c h2* nux-m b7.de* *Puls* k* sabin b7.de* sil k* spong k* sulph k* teucr b7.de* thuj k*
    - **downward**: *Iod* nux-m
  - **rest** agg.: arg-met↓
    - **tearing** pain: arg-met
  - **sitting** agg.: berb
    - **drawing** pain: berb
  - **sore**: brach cassia-s ccrh1• **Clem** equis-h phos k2 **Phyt** *Sars*
  - **standing** agg.: ant-c↓ nux-v↓
    - **constricting** pain: nux-v
    - **drawing** pain: ant-c
  - **stitching** pain: all-c k* am-m k* ammc k* *Arn* k* arum-d *Bell* *Berb* k* *Bry* k* calc carbn-s clem goss grat k* *Merc* k* nat-m k* *Nux-v* k* ox-ac petr a1 phos bg2 plb b7.de* podo k* polyg-h *Puls* k* rhod k* spira a1 spong k* *Staph* k* sulph k* sumb *Thuj* k* tub c1 verat b7.de*
    - **downward**: *Berb* calc
    - **upward**: bell thuj
  - **stool** agg.; during: coca phos k*
  - **tearing** pain: anag *Arg-met* arum-t bell k* *Berb* brom bg2 *Calc* *Colch* k* *Iod* m-aust b7.de nat-m bg2 nit-ac k* nux-v ol-an *Ox-ac* k* *Puls* k* *Staph* sumb
    - **downward**: calc staph
    - **upward** in left: bell
  - **touch** agg.: cassia-s↓ chin↓ clem↓ meny↓ merc-i-r↓ sars↓

Male

- **touch** agg.: ...
  - **drawing** pain: cassia-s ccrh1•
  - **sore**: cassia-s ccrh1• chin clem meny merc-i-r sars
- **urination** agg.; during: agar↓ *Apis* bell cain↓ canth caps↓ clem polyg-h polyg-pe vml2• stront-c
  - **aching**: stront-c
  - **after**; and: caps↓
    - **drawing** pain: caps
  - **drawing** pain: agar bell k* cain br1 *Canth* k* caps k* clem k*
  - **pressing** pain: stront-c b4.de*
- **walking** agg.: ammc↓ *Berb*↓ clem k2 crot-t↓ nux-v↓ ox-ac↓
  - **burning**: *Berb*
  - **constricting** pain: nux-v
  - **drawing** pain: *Berb* crot-t k*
  - **stitching** pain: ammc k* ox-ac
  - **tearing** pain: *Berb*
- **warm** | **applications**:
  - **amel.**: rhod k2
    - **drawing** pain: rhod k2
  - **bed** | **agg.**: clem k2
- **warmth** agg.: cassia-a↓
  - **drawing** pain: cassia-a ccrh1•
- **wine** agg.: calc-ar

▽ • **extending** to:
  - **Abdomen**: *Grat*↓ *Staph*↓
    - **stitching** pain: *Grat Staph*
    - **urination** agg.; during: clem↓
      - **drawing** pain: clem
  - **Abdominal** ring; into: *Berb*↓ bry↓
    - **drawing** pain: *Berb* bry
  - **Chest**: grat↓
    - **stitching** pain: grat
  - **Downward**: sars
  - **Epididymis**; into: *Berb* senec
  - **Penis**: puls↓
    - **stitching** pain: puls
  - **Testes**: all-c *Berb* dios **Ham** k* lith-c merc nux-v↓ osm plb puls senec teucr↓ visc c1
    - **aching**: dios a1 senec k*
    - **cramping**: dios
    - **drawing** pain: *Berb* ham fd3.de• nux-v *Puls* teucr
    - **Rectum** to testes; from: sil↓
      - **cramping**: sil
  - **Upward**: clem bg2 osm phyt bg2 visc c1

- **Testes** (= testalgia): abrot k* acon b7.de* aesc↓ agar↓ agn hr1* alum k* alum-p↓ alumn am-c ammc↓ *Ant-c* b7a.de ant-o ant-t↓ *Apis* bro1 **Arg-met** k* *Arg-n* bro1 arist-m↓ *Arn* k* ars↓ arum-t↓ asaf k* asim bro1 **Aur** k* aur-ar↓ aur-i k2 aur-m bg2 aur-s k2 bapt bar-c↓ *Bar-m*↓ *Bell* k* benzol br1 *Berb* k* bism k* *Brom* bro1 *Brucel* sa3• bry↓ bufo↓ cain bro1 *Calc* k* calc-act↓ calc-i k2 calc-s↓ camph bg cann-s k* canth b7.de* caps bg2* carb-v b4a.de* carbn-s card-m↓ carl↓ *Caust* k* cer-s a1 cere-b bro1 cham bro1 chel k* chin b7.de* cimic k* **Clem** k* coc-c↓ cocc coff↓ *Coloc* k* *Con* k* cop bg2 croc b7a.de der k* dig k* dios k* echi↓ equis-h erio bro1 euph↓ euphr↓ ferr-p bg2 *Gels*↓ gins bro1 graph↓ *Ham* k* hep↓ hipp jl2 hydr bro1 hyos↓ ign k* ind k* indg↓ *Iod* k* ip↓ jatr-c bg2 kali-ar k2 kali-bi↓ kali-br k* kali-c bro1 kali-i k* kali-m↓ kali-n k* kali-p↓ kali-s↓ kalm k* lach bg2 *Lith-c* lyc bro1 lycps-v k* lyss m-ambo b7.de* m-arct↓ *M-aust*↓ mag-p↓ mang↓ med jl2 meny↓ *Merc* k* merc-act↓ merc-c↓ merc-i-r bro1 mez↓ mur-ac↓ musca-d szs1 nat-ar↓ nat-c k* *Nat-m* k* nat-p k* nit-ac k* nuph a1 nux-v k* oci↓ ol-an k* op osm k* ox-ac k* oxyt c2* ozone sde2• *Pall*↓ petr↓ ph-ac k* phos k* pic-ac bro1 pip-m k* plat↓ *Plb* k* polyg-h psor↓ **Puls** k* **Rhod** k* rhus-t↓ sabad k* sabin↓ sal-n bro1 sars bg2 sel k* **Sep** k* ser-a-c jl2 sil k* spig↓ **Spong** k* squil bg2 **Staph** k* still↓ sulph bg2* sumb↓ symph fd3.de• tarax k* tarent k* ter↓ teucr↓ thuj k* tub c1 tus-p↓ ust k* vanil fd5.de verat↓ verat-v k* *Zinc* k* zinc-p k2
- **alternating** sides: hist vml3• lycps-v bg2 ol-an bg2 rhod bg2

- **Testes**: ...
- **right**: acon↓ act-sp↓ alum h2* anag↓ **Arg-met** k* arg-n arum-t bg **Aur** bapt↓ bism bry↓ calc↓ cassia-s↓ *Caust* chel k* chinin-s↓ cob coc-c↓ coloc diaz sa3• dig k* germ-met↓ graph↓ ind k* irid-met srj5• jac-c lat-m sp1 mit↓ morph musca-d szs1 nat-ar nat-m nat-p opun-s a1 osm phos↓ **Rhod** k* sabin↓ sel↓ spig↓ *Staph*↓ sulph↓ tax↓ tub jl2 tung-met↓ *Zinc*↓
  - **aching**: *Bism* k* calc k* *Caust* k* chinin-s irid-met srj5• nat-m k*
  - **appearing** suddenly: arum-t bg2
  - **compressing**: (non:arg-met a1*) staph
  - **contracting**: arg-met
  - **cramping**: arg-met phos h2*
  - **crushed**: arg-met bg2
  - **drawing** pain: acon k* anag k* **Aur** bapt hr1 bry cassia-s ccrh1• coc-c a1 mit a1 opun-s a1 **Rhod** k* sulph a1 *Zinc* bg2 [tax jsj7]
  - **pressing** pain: *Aur* bism *Caust* k* *Staph*
  - **sore**: acon **Arg-met** arg-n **Aur** *Caust* dig *Rhod* sabin
  - **stitching** pain: act-sp bg1 bry *Caust* k* coc-c germ-met srj5• graph k* rhod k* sel spig staph bg1 tung-met bdx1•
  - **tearing** pain: arum-t k*
  - **urination** | **after** | **amel.**: cob
    - **before**: equis-h a1
  - **walking** agg.: **Arg-met**↓
    - **crushed**: **Arg-met**
  - **extending** to:
    - **left**: kalm
    - **Abdomen**: arum-t↓
      - **tearing** pain: arum-t
- **left**: aesc↓ agar↓ alum k* ang↓ *Arg-met*↓ aur-m↓ bapt↓ calc↓ calc-s↓ carbn-s↓ chin↓ coloc↓ con der k* dios k* *Fl-ac*↓ jatr-c↓ kali-br k* kali-c↓ kali-p fd1.de• lycps-v med jl2 merc-c↓ nat-ar↓ nat-c k* *Nit-ac*↓ nuph↓ petr-ra shn4• plb a1 polyg-h puls k2 *Rhod*↓ sabad↓ sabin↓ sil↓ *Staph* still↓ sumb tax↓ ter↓ thuj k2 tub c1 verat-v k* zinc↓
  - **then** right: *Zinc*↓
    - **drawing** pain: *Zinc*
  - **aching**: con k* jatr-c nuph k* still k* sumb k*
  - **cramping**: ter bg2
  - **drawing** pain: aesc k* agar hr1 ang k* aur-m a1 calc-s k* chin coloc *Con* fl-ac a1 kali-c petr-ra shn4• *Rhod* ter k* *Thuj* k* zinc
  - **pressing** pain: bapt hr1 *Con* sabad k* sabin a1 sil h2* zinc k*
  - **sore**: *Arg-met* calc nat-ar *Nit-ac* polyg-h bg2 sabad *Thuj*
  - **stitching** pain: carbn-s *Fl-ac* k* merc-c k* puls staph *Thuj* k* zinc k* [tax jsj7]
  - **extending** to:
    - **Spermatic** cord: polyg-h↓
      - **sore**: polyg-h a1*
- **morning**: aur sne calc-s↓ *Clem* k* kalm k* nat-c↓ sars verat-v k*
  - **aching**: sars k*
  - **drawing** pain: calc-s k* nat-c k*
  - **sore**: aur sne sars
- **noon**: *Caust* ust
  - **aching**: *Caust* k* ust k*
  - **pressing** pain: caust k*
- **afternoon**: calc-s↓ caps↓ chin↓ dios k* kalm k*
  - **14 h**: ery-a
  - **cramping**: chin
  - **pinching**: caps k*
  - **sore**: calc-s
  - **extending** to:
    - **Groins**: gels↓
      - **dragging**: gels k*
- **evening**: agar↓ chinin-s con↓ lycps-v ox-ac↓ **Puls**↓ rhod↓ sabad↓ sel k* sulph↓ ust k* verat-v k*
  - **18-23 h**: **Aur**↓
    - **sore**: **Aur**
  - **aching**: chinin-s
  - **bed** agg.; in: *Arg-met*

- **evening – bed** agg.: ...
    - **sore**: *Arg-met*
  - **cramping**: con
  - **drawing** pain: agar k* sulph
  - **sore**: **Puls** sabad
  - **stitching** pain: ox-ac rhod k* *Sel*
  - **urination** agg.; before: equis-h
- **night**: cer-s k* cere-s ham ↓ osm k* sil h2*
  - **bed** agg.; in: coc-c ↓
    - **cutting** pain: coc-c
  - **stitching** pain: ham
- **accompanied** by:
  - **cough** (See COUGH - Accompanied - testes)
  - **respiratory** complaints (See RESPIRATION - Asthmatic - accompanied - testes)
  - **Back**; pain in: abrot
- **aching**: apis bro1 asaf k* **Aur** k* aur-s k2 berb k* bism k* *Calc* k* cann-s bro1 carl k* *Caust* k* chel k* *Clem* bro1 con k* cop k* *Ham* k* *Iod* k* jatr-c lyss k* *Nat-m* k* nit-ac bro1 nuph k* nux-v k* ph-ac bro1 **Puls** k* *Spong* bro1 *Staph* k* still k* sulph bro1 sumb k* thuj k* ust k*
- **alternating** with | **occiput**; with pain in: hist vml3•
- **back**; and (See accompanied - back)
- **boring**: mur-ac h2* plb k* sep bg2 sil
- **burning**: apis arg-met k2 bar-c k* berb k* canth bg2 caps b7a.de coff iod k* nat-m bg2 *Nit-ac* k* ph-ac k* plat k* **Puls** k* spig b7.de* staph k* sumb k* tarax b7.de* ter k*
- **burrowing**: clem a1
- **coition**; during: kali-i ↓
  - **cutting** pain: kali-i
- **cold**:
  - **amel.**: cassia-s ↓
    - **drawing** pain: cassia-s ccrh1•
- **compressing**: am-c petr sil k* squil k* staph thuj k* zinc
- **constricting** pain: **Am-c** berb k* bufo merc-act nux-v ol-an *Plb* sulph
- **contracting**: alum arg-met c1 camph *Chin* merc-act nux-v plb
- **cough** agg.; during: am-c nat-m osm zinc k*
- **cramping**: agn am-c arg-met bapt hr1 caps chin k* con ign lyc *M-aust* b7a.de nux-v petr k* phos k* plb psor ptk1 spong
- **crushed**: acon bg2* **Arg-met** k* *Arg-n* bro1 *Aur* bro1 calc k* carb-v bro1 *Caust* k* cham bro1 clem bg2* con k* dig k* gins bro1 *Ham* bro1 kali-c bro1 kali-p fd1.de• nat-c bg2 nit-ac bg2* *Ol-an* bro1 ox-ac bg2* *Puls* bro1 **Rhod** k* sabad bg2 sabin bg2 sep bro1 spong bg2* staph bro1 teucr bg2 thuj k*
- **cutting** pain: aur bell k* berb cain calc b4a.de* coc-c *Con* k* lyc m-arct b7.de nuph ph-ac rhus-t b7.de* *Sep* k* ter
- **dragging**: cann-s k* *Gels* k* iod k* *Kali-c* lach k* *Med* sumb k*
- **drawing** pain: acon k* aesc k* agar k* am-c k* ammc k* apis **Aur** *Aur-m* bapt k* bell k* berb k* cain br1 calc-act calc-s k* canth carbn-s card-m k* *Chel* k* *Chin* k* *Clem* k* coc-c a1 *Cocc* k* coloc k* *Con* cop k* graph k* *Ham* k* hipp k* hyos ip k* kali-c kali-m k2 kali-n kali-s m-arct b7.de mang k* *Merc* k* mur-ac *Nat-c* k* nat-m k* nat-p k* nit-ac k* *Nux-v* k* ol-an k* op k* ox-ac ph-ac k* phos k* plb k* psor k* *Puls* k* **Rhod** k* rhus-t k* sabad sep k* sil h2* *Staph* k* *Sulph* ter k* *Thuj* k* tus-p k* vanil fd5.de verat k* *Zinc* k* zinc-p k2
  - **paroxysmal**: aur-m k*
- **ejaculation**; after: caps ↓
  - **cramping**: caps k*
- **emissions** | **after**:
    - **agg.**: caps hr1 mag-m ox-ac *Ph-ac*
      - **aching**: *Ph-ac*
      - **dragging**: *Ph-ac*
  - **agg.**: caps
- **erections**; after: con mag-m k* ox-ac
  - **cramping**: con
- **gnawing**: ph-ac k* plat k*
- **gonorrhea**; after suppressed: ant-t pd
- **griping**: merc-c bg2
  - **accompanied** by | **swelling**: dulc ptk1
- **jar**, from a: colch ↓
  - **crushed**: colch
- **jerking**: coloc bg2 m-aust b7.de*
- **lying**:
  - **agg.**: sil k*
  - **back**; on:
    - **amel.**:
      - **knees** drawn up; with: petr-ra ↓
        - **drawing** pain: petr-ra shn4•
- **motion**:
  - **agg.**: asaf berb k* cassia-s ↓ ery-a lat-m sp1* mag-m k* ox-ac vanil fd5.de
    - **drawing** pain: cassia-s ccrh1•
  - **amel.**: arg-met carbn-s *Rhod* k*
    - **drawing** pain: *Rhod* k*
- **nauseating** as from a blow: nat-ar
- **neuralgic**: arg-n bro1 *Aur* bro1 bell bro1 berb bg2* cimic bg2 *Clem* bro1 *Coloc* bro1 con bro1 euphr bro1 ham bro1* ign bro1 mag-p bg2* merc bro1 nux-v bro1 ol-an bro1 *Ox-ac* bro1 oxyt bro1 *Puls* bro1 spong bro1 verat-v bro1 zinc bro1*
  - **accompanied** by | **nausea**: ham ptk1
- **paroxysmal**: spong
- **pinching**: caps k* *Clem* k* con k* kali-c k* musca-d szs1 nat-m k* sep k* **Spong** k*
- **pressing** pain: am-c *Aur* k* aur-s k2 berb k* *Bism* k* calc k* *Cann-s* k* carb-v k* **Caust** k* clem k* *Con* gins k* ign k* kali-n k* kali-p fd1.de• lach k* mang k* merc k* nat-c k* nat-m nat-p ozone sde2• ph-ac k* **Puls** k* *Rhod* sabad k* *Sil* k* spong k* squil k* *Staph* k* *Sulph* k* teucr b7.de* thuj k* **Zinc** k*
- **pressure** of clothes agg.: **Arg-met** k*
- **pulling**: bufo bg2
- **pulsating**: ox-ac ptk1 spong ptk1
- **pushed** up; as if: phos bg2
- **rest** agg.: arg-met ↓ rhod ↓ zinc ↓
  - **cramping**: arg-met
  - **stitching** pain: rhod zinc k*
- **rising** agg.; after: mag-m k*
- **sexual** excitement:
  - **after**: *Iod* kali-n lyss staph
  - **agg.**: *Iod* ↓ *Staph* ↓
    - **aching**: *Iod Staph*
- **sitting** agg.: aur sne bry ↓ petr-ra ↓ **Puls** rhod ter ↓ zinc ↓
  - **drawing** pain: petr-ra shn4• ter k* zinc k*
  - **sore**: **Puls**
  - **stitching** pain: bry h1 rhod k*
- **smarting**: berb a1 calc b4a.de coff b7a.de ph-ac b4.de*
- **sore**: *Acon* k* aesc k* alum k* alum-p k2 am-c apis k* **Arg-met** k* *Arg-n* arn k* ars k* *Aur* k* aur-ar k2 bell bg2* berb bro1 *Brom* b4a.de* *Calc* k* *Caust* chel cimic **Clem** k* *Cocc* k* coff b7a.de coloc con k* cop k* *Dig* k* echi equis-h k* *Ham* k* hep ind bro1 indg kali-bi kali-br kali-c k* kali-n lith-c med *Merc* merc-i-r bro1 mez k* nat-ar nat-c *Nat-m* **Nit-ac** k* oci ol-an k* ox-ac *Pall* ph-ac k* *Phos* polyg-h psor **Puls** k* **Rhod** k* sabad sars bg2 sep bro1 **Spong** k* staph k* tarent teucr b7.de* *Thuj* k* zinc
- **squeezed**; as if: acon b7.de arg-met b7.de calc b4a.de caps b7.de* clem b4a.de con b4.de *Dig* b4.de* meny b7.de* nat-c b4.de* nit-ac b4.de pall c1 petr b4.de* puls k2 *Rhod* b4.de sabad b7.de sabin b7.de *Sil* **Spong** k* squil b7.de* staph b7.de* teucr b7.de* *Thuj* b4.de*
- **standing** agg.: *Cann-s* ↓ puls ↓ rhod
  - **pressing** pain: *Cann-s* k* puls
- **stepping** hard agg.: colch coloc
- **stitching** pain: aesc arist-m a1 arn k* *Bar-m Bell* k* berb k* brom bry k* calc k* carbn-s **Caust** k* clem b4a.de cocc k* graph k* *Ham* hyos b7a.de ip k* lyc k* *Lycps-v* m-arct b7.de merc k* merc-c k* mez b4a.de nat-m *Nux-v* k* op ox-ac polyg-h *Puls Rhod* k* sel spig b7.de* *Spong* k* *Staph* k*

Male

- **stitching** pain: ...
  sulph k* sumb tarax b7.de* *Thuj* k* tub c1 vanil fd5.de verat bg2 zinc k* zinc-p k2
- **stool** | **after** | **agg.**: *Lyc* b4a.de
  - **during** | **agg.**: bell bg2 coca phos k* trom bg2
- **stretched**; as if: nat-c b4.de*
- **swelling**, without: **Puls** ↓
  - **burning**: **Puls**
- **tearing** pain: ant-t k* arum-t k* caust k* *Chin* k* *Con* k* euph k* hyos m-aust b7.de* merc-c bg2 nat-c k* ph-ac k* phos b4a.de **Puls** k* *Rhod* k* sep h2* staph k* ust
- **touch** agg.: aloe sne alum aur pd bism ↓ *Clem* hr1 coca ↓ cocc mag-m k* nit-ac h2* ph-ac h2* rhod tl1 spong staph k* tarent a1 zinc h2*
  - **pressing** pain: aur hr1 bism h1* ph-ac k* *Staph* h1*
  - **sore**: coca
  - **tearing** pain: cocc c1
- **twinging**: coloc
- **urination** | **after** | **agg.**: bell bg2
  - **during**:
    - **agg.**: cain ↓ caps b7.de* polyg-h polyg-pe vml2• thuj ↓
      - **drawing** pain: cain
      - **pinching**: caps
      - **stitching** pain: thuj k*
- **walking**:
  - **agg.**: **Arg-met** k* berb mrr1 clem coloc jac-c k* *Lyc* ox-ac ph-ac ↓ *Staph* sumb thuj zinc
    - **aching**: *Staph* k* sumb k* thuj k*
    - **pressing** pain: ph-ac k* staph
    - **sore**: **Arg-met** *Clem* ox-ac k2 staph thuj
    - **stitching** pain: ox-ac
  - **amel.**: *Rhod* ↓ thuj ↓
    - **drawing** pain: thuj k*
    - **stitching** pain: *Rhod* k*
- **warm** applications agg.: cassia-s ↓
  - **drawing** pain: cassia-s ccrh1•
- **weather**:
  - **change** of weather: rhod mrr1
  - **windy** and stormy | **before**: rhod mrr1
- **wine** agg.: thuj
  - **sore**: thuj

▽ • **extending** to:
  - **left**: polyg-h ↓
    - **sore**: polyg-h
  - **Abdomen**: calc ↓ ham bg2 iod kali-n ↓ rhod mrr1 vanil fd5.de
    - **drawing** pain: calc *Iod* kali-n c1 **Rhod**
    - **Through**: fago
  - **Downward**: berb bg2
  - **Hip**: chel ↓
    - **drawing** pain: chel
  - **Inguinal** ring: aur-m ↓ bry ↓ petr-ra ↓ vanil ↓
    - **drawing** pain: aur-m bry petr-ra shn4• vanil fd5.de
  - **Penis**: mur-ac a1
  - **Spermatic** cord: aesc ↓ arum-t berb ↓ bry bg2 *Clem* ↓ coc-c ↓ equis-h bg2 fl-ac ↓ ox-ac bg2 oxyt ptk2 plb polyg-h puls ↓ **Rhod** ↓ spong bg2 staph *Zinc* ↓
    - **drawing** pain: aesc berb bry *Clem* fl-ac *Zinc*
    - **sore**: *Equis-h* polyg-h puls **Rhod**
    - **stitching** pain: coc-c fl-ac k* ox-ac *Spong* k*
    - **suddenly** shifting to bowels causing nausea: ham
  - **Stomach**: ham k*
    - **stitching** pain: *Ham*
  - **Testes**; from rectum to | **cramping** (See RECTUM - Constriction - extending - testes)
  - **Thighs**: aur ↓ musca-d szs1 oxyt ptk2 rhod ↓ sep bg1
    - **drawing** pain: aur vh rhod sep
  - **Upward**: spong bg2

Pain – Testes: ...
- **extending**:
  - **Lumbar** region; from:
    - **cough** agg.; during: osm ↓
      - **pressing** pain: osm

○ • **Epididymis**: *Clem* b4a.de *Spong* mrr1 vanil fd5.de
  - **touch** agg.: rhod tl1
- **Vesiculae** seminales: ambr ↓
  - **burning**: ambr bg2

PARAPHIMOSIS (See Phimosis - paraphimosis)

PERSPIRATION: acet-ac agn k* alum k* alum-p k2 am-c k* ars k* ars-i ars-s-f k2 asc-t k* **Aur** k* aur-ar k2 aur-i k2 aur-s k2 bar-c k* *Bell* k* *Calad* k* *Calc* k* *Canth* k* carb-an k* *Carb-v* k* carbn-s carl k* con k* *Cor-r* k* dios bg2 **Fl-ac** k* *Gels* k* hep k* *Hydr* k* ign k* iod lachn lyc k* mag-m k* *Merc* k* merc-i-f k* mez k* *Petr* k* ph-ac k* *Puls* k* rhod bg2 **Sel** k* **Sep** k* sil k* spong fd4.de staph k* *Sulph* k* **Thuj** k*
- **morning**: *Aur* k*
- **evening**: carbn-s spong fd4.de
- **night**: bell k* staph h1*
- **briny** odor | **coition**; after: sanic ptk1
- **burnt**; smells as if: thuj k2
- **cold** agg.: *Carb-v* sanic c1
- **exertion** agg.; after: sep bg1
- **fetid**: fl-ac bg2 sulph bg2 thuj bg2
- **offensive**: aloe ars-met aster sze10• calc-sil k2 fago k* *Fl-ac* k* *Hydr* k* *Iod* k* *Nat-m* k* psor k2 *Sars* k* *Sep* **Sulph** k* thuj b4a.de*
- **oily**: *Fl-ac* b4a.de
- **profuse**: thuj mtf33
- **pungent**; smells as if: *Dios* vh *Fl-ac* k*
- **sweetish**; smells as if: spong fd4.de *Thuj* k*

○ - **Penis**: lachn c1 nat-m k* nit-ac k* spong fd4.de thuj k*

○ • **Glans** | **sour**-salt odor: calc bg2 sulph bg2
- **Scrotum**: acon k* agn k* alum-sil k2 am-c k* *Aur* k* aur-s k2 bar-c k* bar-s k2 bell k* calad k* *Calc* k* *Calc-p* k* calc-sil k2 carb-an k* carb-v k* carbn-s cass a1 caust k* *Con* k* cor-r bro1 cupr-act cupr-ar k* daph k* *Dios* k* fago bro1 gels k* *Ham* k* hep k* hydr k* *Ign* k* *Iod* lachn k* *Lyc* k* *Mag-m* k* *Merc* k* mez k* nat-m bro1 *Nat-s* k* *Petr* k* *Psor* k* *Rhod* k* sars bg2 *Sel* k* *Sep* k* *Sil* k* staph k* sul-i k2 **Sulph** k* **Thuj** k* uran-n bro1 ust k*
  - **one** side: thuj k*
  - **morning**: thuj k* ust
  - **evening**: nat-s k* sil k*
  - **night**: ham k* mag-m k*
  - **cold** agg.: plan ptk1
  - **fetid**: dios bg2 sep bg2 thuj bg2
  - **profuse**: gels ptk1
  - **strong** odor: *Dios* k*
  - **sweetish** odor: *Thuj*

○ • **Thighs**, between: cinnb k*

PHIMOSIS: acon apis ptk1 *Arn* k* bufo gk calad *Calc* k* *Cann-s* k* *Canth* k* *Cinnb* k* coloc ptk1 cycl *Dig* k* guaj ptk1 *Ham* k* *Hep* jac-c k* jac-g *Lyc* k* **Merc** k* merc-c k2* narz a1 nat-m **Nit-ac** k* *Rhus-t* k* rumx c2 sabin k* sep k* sil c2 *Sulph* k* sumb k* thuj k*
- **congenital**: am tl1
- **friction**; from: am tl1*
- **gangrene** threatening: *Ars* canth *Cinnb* *Lach* *Merc-i-r*
- **suppuration**, with: *Caps* *Cinnb* k* *Hep* *Merc* *Nit-ac* *Sulph* hr1

○ - **Paraphimosis**: apis ptk1 bell canth ptk1 *Coloc* k* dig c1* guaj ptk1 kali-i k* *Lach* k* m-ambo c2 **Merc** k* *Merc-c* k* nat-m **Nit-ac** k* nux-v c2 *Rhus-t* k* sep *Sulph* hr1 thuj k*
  - **extensive** swelling of glans: *Kali-i* k*

PHTHISIS: *Aur* bro1 bac-t bro1 carbn-s k2 *Merc* bro1 scroph-n bro1 spong bro1 *Teucr-s* bro1

○ - **Testes**: sul-i k2

PLEASANT sensation: (↗*Voluptuous*) ambr bg2 ang bg2 graph bg2 plat bg2

POLLUTIONS: *(↗Pollutions - night; Semen; PROSTATE - Emission)* abrot bg2* acet-ac acon a1 acon-c c1* aesc *Agar* k* *Agn* k* aloe k* *Alum* k* alum-sil k2 alumn kr1 *Am-c* k* ambr b2.de* *Anac* k* anan ang b2.de* anis a1 ant-c k* aphis a1 aq-mar jl *Arg-met* k* *Arg-n* k* arn k* ars k* ars-i ars-s-f kr1* *Art-v* kr1 *Aur* k* *Aur-s* k2 aven br1* **Bar-c** k* bar-i k2 *Bar-m* bar-s k2 *Bell* k* *Berb* *Bism* k* **Borx** k* *Bov* k* brom bry *Bufo* cadm-s kr1* *Calad* b2.de* **Calc** k* calc-act a1 calc-ar calc-caust a1 calc-i k2 *Calc-p* calc-s c1 *Calc-sil* k2 calen a1 camph k* camph-br c1* cann-i c1* cann-s b2.de* canth k* caps k* carb-ac *Carb-an* k* *Carb-v* k* carbn-s *Carl* casc kr1 *Castm* *Caust* k* cere-s a1 *Cham* k* **Chin** k* chinin-ar chinin-s chlol a1 *Cic* k* *Cimx* k* clem k* *Cob* coc-c k1 coca a1* *Cocc* k* cod a1* coff k* coff-t c1* coll kr1 coloc colocin a1 *Con* k* cop *Cor-r* crot-t *Cupr* c1 *Cycl* k* **Cypr** dam c1 **Dig** k* *Digin* c1 **Dios** dros c1 erech a1 erig c1 *Ery-a* *Eug* j5.de euph h2* **Euph-a** a1 *Ferr* k* ferr-ar *Ferr-br* c1* ferr-i ferr-p *Form* gast a1 *Gels* *Gins* sf1.de *Graph* k* grat guaj b2.de* ham k* *Hep* k* hera j5.de* hura a1 *Hydr* kr1 hydr-ac a1 ign b2.de* ind a1* iod iris jac-c a1 kali-ar **Kali-br** k* *Kali-c* k* kali-chl j5.de* kali-i kali-m k2 **Kali-p** *Kali-sil* k2 kiss a1 kola stb3• lac-ac *Lach* k* *Lact* lath c1 led b2.de* lil-t kr1 linu-c a1 lipp a1 *Lup* sf1.de **Lyc** k* m-ambo b2.de* *M-arct* b2.de* m-aust b2.de* mag-c k* *Mag-m* k* mag-p bg2 med *Merc* k* merc-c bg2 merc-i-f k2 merc-i-r kr1 merc-sul a1* *Mill* kr1 *Mosch* k* mur-ac j5.de naja *Nat-ar* **Nat-c** k* **Nat-m** k* **Nat-p** nat-sil k2 *Nit-ac* k* *Nuph* kr1* *Nux-m* k* **Nux-v** k* ol-an *Onos* k* op k* opun-s a1 (non:opun-v a1) *Orig* k* osm c1* ox-ac paeon a1 par k* ped a1 petr k* petros **Ph-ac** k* **Phos** k* phys a1 *Pic-ac* k* pip-m a1 plan c1 *Plat* k* plb k* *Psor* *Puls* k* puls-n a1 ran-b k* ran-s k* rheum a1 rhod k* rhus-t k* ruta k* *Sabad* k* *Sabal* sf1.de sacch a1 *Sal-n* c1* samb b2.de* sang *Sars* k* **Sel** k* **Sep** k* *Sil* k* sin-n a1 *Sol-o* st spirae a1 stann k* **Staph** k* stict c1* *Stram* k* sul-ac j5.de sul-i k2 **Sulph** k* sumb c1 tab tarax k* *Tarent* tax j5.de* *Ter* j5.de* ther *Thuj* k* *Thymol* br1* trib br1 *Tub* k1* uran-n c1* *Ust* vanil fd5.de verb h* vib sf1.de viol-o k* *Viol-t* k* visc jl voes a1* wies a1 zinc k* *Zinc-p* k2 *Zinc-pic* c1* zinc-val c1* zing k* ziz a1*

- **daytime**: arn j5.de* canth k* cyna jl ery-a gels graph k* lach bg2 **Nux-v** ust
  - **sleep** agg.; during: par j5.de staph j5.de thuj j5.de
- **morning**: acon a1 aloe cain carb-v cham chinin-s coc-c st eug a1 fum rly4• grat j5.de lact j5.de* lil-t a1 merc-i-f a1 merc-i-r a1 nat-c h2 nat-m a1 nux-v h1 petr a1 petros a1* phys a1 pip-m plb j5.de* psor puls j5.de ran-b j5.de* rhus-t j5.de sabad j5.de spig a1 thuj vanil fd5.de
  - **early**: adam skp7• aq-mar skp7•
  - **bed**, penis relaxed; in: canth coc-c st
  - **falling** asleep again; on: ol-an a1
  - **sleep** agg.; during: lact a1 vanil fd5.de
  - **stool** | **during** | **agg.**: amyg-p a1 helio a1 nat-m
    - **straining** at | **agg.**: *Ph-ac*
  - **waking**; on: petr j5.de
- **forenoon**: caust j5.de*
  - **sitting** agg.: sulph
- **noon**: cact a1
- **afternoon**: carb-an h2
  - **16** h: carb-an a1
  - **catalepsy**; after: grat a1
  - **relaxed** penis, with: cor-r a1
  - **sleep** | **siesta**; during: aloe kr1* *Alum* h2* carb-an j5.de caust clem cor-r j5.de lach a1 merc par j5.de* phos staph j5.de* stict c1 sulph ther j5.de*
- **evening**: carb-an a1 nat-c j5.de
- **night**: *(↗Pollutions)* adam skp7• bar-c ptk1 borx ptk1 calad mrr1 calc ptk1 camph-br br1 caps h1 *Chin* ptk1 *Cob* b4a.de *Con* ptk1 dig ptk1 dios ptk1 ferr tl1* fum rly1• *Gels* ptk1 iris c2 kali-p ptk1 lyc ptk1 mag-m c2 med jl2 merc b4a.de nat-c ptk1 nat-m ptk1 **Nat-p** ptk1* nit-ac b4a.de nux-v ptk1 onos mrr1 petr b4a.de **Ph-ac** ptk1 **Phos** ptk1 plb ptk1 ruta fd4.de *Sel* ptk1 sep ptk1 stann ptk1 staph ptk1* sulph b4a.de* ther mrr1 thuj b4a.de* *Thymol* sp1 vanil fd5.de visc c1
  - **midnight**:
    - **before**: coloc a1
    - **at**: goss st
    - **after**: *Nux-v* b7a.de ran-s a1 samb b7.de* sil j5.de
      - **1** h: calc-p a1 dig a1 sulfonam jl*
      - **3** h: aloe a1 coff-t kr1
      - **3-5** h | **masturbation**; after: *Sil* kr1
      - **4** h: anth a1 cob a1 pip-m a1
      - **5** h: coc-c a1
- **night – midnight – after**: ...
      - **morning**; towards: erech a1 petros kr1
  - **accompanied** by:
    - **Back**; pain in (See BACK - Pain - accompanied - pollutions)
    - **Sacral** region (See BACK - Pain - sacral - accompanied - pollutions)
  - **followed** by:
    - **impotence**: med jl2
    - **weakness**; great: med jl2
  - **involuntary**: calc tl1
  - **lying** on back agg.: stann a1
  - **recurrent** (= several nights): *Agar* kr1 alum j5.de am-c j5.de ang kr1 aur j5.de bov j5.de *Calc* j5.de calc-p kr1 carb-an j5.de caust j5.de con j5.de *Dig* kr1 *Graph* j5.de ind kr1 kali-c j5.de lac-ac kr1 m-aust j5.de plb j5.de sars j5.de *Staph* j5.de* *Sulph* j5.de ust ptk1 zinc j5.de ziz kr1
- **accompanied** by:
  - **palpitations** | **young** people; in (See CHEST - Palpitation - accompanied - masturbation - young)
  - **relaxation** of genitals: aur bg2 bell bg2
  - **vision**; weak: kali-c bro1
  - ○ **Testes**; wasting: *Iod* bro1 sabal bro1
- **agg.** in general (See GENERALS - Emissions - agg.)
- **amel.** in general: agn calc *Calc-p* elaps *Lach* naja phos sang c1 sil zinc
- **bed** agg.; in: kali-br a1
- **caresses**, during: *Arn* k* canth c1 **Con** k* ery-a bg2 *Gels* k* *Nat-c* k* *Nux-v* petr *Phos* k* *Sars* k* *Sel* k* sulph ptk1 ust
- **coition**:
  - **after**: acon a1* *Agn* k* am-c k* bar-c bry *Calc* *Dig* gels *Graph* kali-c k* lyss c1* **Nat-m** k* *Nat-p* *Ph-ac* k* *Phos* *Rhod* k* sep *Sil* b4a.de
  - **desire** for coition, during: ham a1 sars c1
- **cold** ; after becoming | **extremities**: nux-v bg2
- **colic**, during: plb k*
- **convulsions**:
  - **during**: anan vh art-v kr1
  - **with**: art-v k* grat k* *Nat-p* k*
- **copious**: bell a1 bros-gau mrc1 carbn-s a1 carl a1 ferr-m ptk2 *Kali-c* kr1 merc-i-f a1 nat-m a1 par a1 petr a1 **Ph-ac** a1* *Pic-ac* a1* sil a1 *Staph* kr1 thymol sp1
  - **night**: **Canth** b7a.de *Caps* b7a.de carb-an a1 chin b7a.de *Dig* a1 hipp a1 ign a1 kali-chl a1 ol-an a1 par b7a.de plb b7a.de rhus-t b7a.de sars a1 staph b7a.de
    - **midnight**:
      - **after** | **3** h: pip-m a1
    - **coition**; after: bar-c a1
  - **rising** agg.; after: canth b7a.de
  - **sitting** agg.: *Cann-s* b7a.de
- **desire** for coition, during (See coition - desire)
- **diarrhea**; during: ars k*
- **dinner**; after: agar a1 nat-c j5.de
- **disturbing** sleep: arn j5.de camph j5.de cann-s j5.de carb-an j5.de chel j5.de coloc j5.de con j5.de crot-t j5.de cycl j5.de dig j5.de ferr j5.de kali-chl j5.de lach j5.de lact j5.de nat-c j5.de nat-m j5.de *Nux-v* j5.de par j5.de petr j5.de *Ph-ac* j5.de phos j5.de plat j5.de plb j5.de *Puls* j5.de ran-b j5.de samb j5.de sars j5.de *Sep* j5.de *Sil* j5.de spig j5.de stann j5.de staph j5.de stram j5.de *Sulph* j5.de *Thuj* j5.de
- **dreams**:
  - **with**: *(↗DREAMS - Amorous - pollutions)* *Acon* b7a.de aloe bg *Alum* b4.de* ang j5.de *Ant-c* b7.de* aphis j5.de* aq-mar rbp6 arist-m a1 arn b7.de* ars b4.de* ars-s-f kr1* aur b4.de* bar-c j5.de* bell bg2 bism b7.de* borx j5.de* bov b4.de* cain kr1* *Calc* b4.de* calc-act a1 calc-p a1 *Camph* kr1* cann-i a1* cann-s sf1.de canth sf1.de carb-ac a1* carb-an b4a.de* caust j5.de* chin b7.de* *Cic* kr1 *Cob* a1* coloc j5.de* **Con** b4a.de conch fkr1* cycl j5.de* *Dig* j5.de* dios kr1* euph j5.de ferr j5.de form a1* *Gels* kr1 *Glycyr-g* cte1• *Graph* kr1* grat j5.de* ham bg2* hura a1 hydr a1 ind a1 iod k2 *Iris* a1* *Kali-br* kr1* *Kali-c* b4.de* kali-chl j5.de *Kali-m* kr1* kali-s k2 lac-cp sk4• lach j5.de* lact j5.de led b7a.de* *Lil-t* a1* lipp a1 lyc a1 lyss a1*

Male

- • **with**: ... meli br1 merc bg merc-i-f kr1* merc-sul a1 myric a1 *Nat-c* b4.de* nat-m j5.de nat-p a1* **Nux-v** b7.de* *Olnd* b7.de* op b7.de* paeon a1 par b7.de* *Ph-ac* b4a.de* *Phos* b4.de* *Pic-ac* kr1* plb b7.de* *Puls* b7a.de* ran-b b7.de* ran-s bg rhod b4.de* ruta bg sabad b7.de* samb b7.de* *Sars* j5.de* sel kr1* senec a1* *Sep* b4.de* *Sil* b4.de* sin-n a1* *Spig* b7.de* spira a1 stann j5.de* staph b7.de* stram j5.de sulph b4.de* thuj j5.de* thymol jl* ust kr1* *Viol-t* b7.de* zinc-p k2
  - **morning**: plb a1 spig a1
  - **evening**: cob a1
  - **coition**, of: borx a1 symph fd3.de•
  - **lying** on back agg.: coloc a1
  - **perverted**: thymol sp1
  - **slept**, feels he had not: ham kr1
  - **unpleasant** dreams: lach j5.de sil j5.de
  - **urinate**; after a dream that he must: merc-i-f a1
  - **wakening** up: *Sel* kr1
- • **without** dreams: agar k* aloe bg2 *Anac* k* anan ant-c k* arg-met k* arg-n k* ars k* aur j5.de* bar-c j5.de* bell k* bism k* calad mrr1 calc b4.de* *Camph* carb-v cic k* *Con* k* *Cor-r* dig k* **Dios** k* gels k* *Graph* guaj k* *Ham* hep bro1 ind kali-c jl mag-m hr1 merc b4.de* merc-i-f nat-c k* nat-p k* phos k* *Pic-ac* k* pip-m puls b7.de* ran-s b7.de* ruta b7.de* sep sin-a *Stann* k* staph b7.de* sulfonam ks2 verb k* vib *Zinc* k* *Zinc-p* k2
  - **lascivious**: ph-ac ptk1
  - **vivid**: viol-t ptk1
- **easy**; too: *Con* kr1* *Ery-a* sf1.de nux-v b7a.de *Ph-ac* kr1 *Plb* kr1 sabin b7a.de *Sars* kr1
- **emaciation**; with: *Chin* kr1 *Ph-ac* kr1 *Phos* kr1 *Samb* kr1
- **enjoyment**, without: anac bg2 calad bg2* nat-c j5.de nat-p bg2* plan sf1.de plat bg2 sul-ac h2* tab bg2*
- **erections**:
  - • **with**: (↗*Erections - pollutions - during*) agar sf1.de anac sf1.de aur sf1.de bov bg *Calc* sf1.de cann-i sf1.de cann-s sf1.de *Canth* kr1* carb-ac sf1.de carb-an sf1.de caust sf1.de chin sf1.de dig sf1.de dios sf1.de ery-a sf1.de form sf1.de *Gins* sf1.de goss st *Iod* sf1.de *Kali-br* kr1 kali-chl j5.de kali-p k2 led sf1.de lyc sf1.de *Merc* sf1.de nat-m sf1.de *Nux-v* sf1.de par sf1.de phos sf1.de pic-ac a1* pip-m a1 puls sf1.de sal-n st sil sf1.de staph sf1.de sulph sf1.de ther sf1.de trios k13 viol-t sf1.de
    - **painful**: cann-i bro1 *Canth* bro1 grat ptk1 ign bro1 kali-c ptk1 merc bro1 mosch bro1 *Nit-ac* bro1 nux-v bro1 pic-ac bro1 puls bro1 sabad bro1 thuj bro1
    - **violent**: *Kali-m* kr1
  - • **without**: abrot sf1.de absin agar bg2* *Agn* b7a.de* alum bg2 *Am-c* bg2 anac bg2 arg-met k* *Arg-n* bg2* ars bg2 aur bg2 *Bar-c* bg2* bell k* bism k* bov bg2 brom bg2 calad k* *Calc* bg2* calc-p bg2 canth bg2* carb-an k* **Carb-v** bg2 *Caust* bg2* *Chin* k* cic bg2 **Cob** k* coff bg2* coloc h2 con k* cor-r j5.de dig bg2* **Dios** k* *Ery-a* ferr bg2* fl-ac form bg2 *Gels* k* gins j5.de goss st **Graph** k* ham hep bro1 ign j5.de kali-br bg2* *Kali-c* bg2* kali-p k* led bg2 lup sf1.de *Lyc* bg2* m-arct j5.de mag-c bg2* mag-m bg2 merc bg2 mosch k* *Nat-c* k* nat-m k* *Nat-p* k1 *Nit-ac* bg2* *Nuph* k* *Nux-m* b7.de* nux-v k* op k* par bg2 *Petr* bg2 *Ph-ac* k* phos k* pic-ac bg2* plan sf1.de plat j5.de plb j5.de* puls b7.de* ran-b bg2 ran-s bg2 rhus-t bg2 ruta b7.de* sabad k* sabal bg2 sal-n st sang bg2 *Sars* k* *Sel* k* sep bg2* sil bg2* spig stann h2* staph bg2 sul-ac sf1.de sulph k* thuj bg2 trios a1 verb bg2 vib bg2 viol-o bg2 viol-t bg2 visc sp1 *Zinc* bg2* zinc-pic sf1.de
    - **morning**: coc-c st
    - **sleep** agg.; during: **Dios** kr1 *Nuph* kr1
    - **wine** agg.: *Plb* kr1
- **excitability** of parts, from: *Castm* kr1
- **excitement**; from the least (See easy)
- **exertion**; from: ferr ptk1
- **falls** asleep, as soon as he: *Pic-ac* kr1*
- **fancy**:
  - • **with** excitement of: *Kali-br* kr1
  - • **without**: dios phos sars kr1
- **fast**: bros-gau mrc1
- **frequent**: acon a1 *Alum* alum-sil k2 *Am-c* k* ang b7.de* arg-met k* arg-n bg2 am b7.de* aur k2 bar-m *Borx* bov b4a.de* *Calc* k* calc-act a1 canth b7.de* carb-an k* carb-v k* caust k* **Chin** bg2 cic b7.de* cob *Con* k* cor-r j5.de dig k* ferr k* *Graph* j5.de *Kali-c* k* kali-p lach lact j5.de lyc k* lyss c1* m-aust b7.de* mag-c h2* mag-m *Nat-c* k* nat-m k* *Nat-p* nit-ac k* **Nux-v** k* op k* petr k* **Ph-ac** k* phos k* *Plb* k* *Puls* k* sacch sars k* sel k2 *Sep* k* sil j5.de* stann k* **Staph** k* sulph k* tarax b7.de* zinc j5.de
  - • **following** each other quickly: bar-c j5.de
  - • **old** people; in: | **men**; old: bar-c k* caust k* nat-c k* sulph j5.de
  - • **one** night; in: ind kr1 *Ph-ac* kr1 *Puls* kr1
  - • **sleep** | **during** | **agg.**: *Nuph* kr1
    - **siesta**: | **during**: aloe kr1 alum bg2 carb-an bg2 caust bg2* clem bg2 merc bg2 staph bg2 **Sulph** bg2 ther bg2*
  - • **week**; in a: *Dig* kr1 *Sars* kr1 *Ust* kr1
- **fright** at slight noises, from: aloe kr1
- **frothy**: mur-ac bg2
- **high** living, after: **Nux-v** kr1
- **hot**: sabal c1
- **impotence**, with: (↗*PROSTATE - Emission - accompanied - impotency*) sel mrr1 *Uran-n* kr1
- **indigestion**; from: sang st
- **interrupted** by waking: ox-ac a1 sep a1
- **involuntary**: calc tl1 dios ptk1 ham ptk1 lat-m bnm6• nat-p ptk1 sel ptk1 sep ptk1 sulph tl1
  - • **urination** agg.; after: hipp jl2
- **leaning** the back against anything; as if pollution would come when: ant-c k*
- **linen**; causing no stiffness of: med c1
- **looking** at passing girls; when (See women - looking)
- **lying** on back agg.: cob coloc hyper
- **masturbation**; after: agn sf1.de *Alum* arg-met bar-c bg2* **Chin** k* *Dig* *Ery-a* kr1 *Gels* kr1* *Graph* lup sf1.de **Nux-v** k* *Ph-ac* k* phos *Puls* k* sal-n sf1.de *Sars* **Sep** k* *Sil* kr1 **Staph** *Tarent* ust k*
- **mental** prostration; as from: sil bg2
- **offensive**: thuj h1*
- **painful**: borx b4a.de* calc b4a.de* cann-s b7.de* canth b7.de* clem b4.de* *Con* kr1 *Kali-c* kr1* merc bg2 mosch b7a.de* nat-c b4.de* sabal ptk1 *Sars* b4a.de* *Thuj* b4.de*
- **paralytic** symptoms set in, before: *Kali-br* kr1
- **periodical**:
  - • **night**:
    - **alternate**: nat-p a1 **Nux-v** kr1 *Pic-ac* a1* tarax a1
    - **every**: arg-met vh mag-c h2 *Nat-m* **Nat-p** *Pic-ac* tarax *Ust* kr1
      - **almost**: am-c kr1 *Phos* kr1
    - **third**; every: **Nux-v** kr1
- **perspiration**; with: *Lach* j5.de*
- **premature**: *Agn* bro1 (non:bar-c c1*) *Calad* bro1 *Calc* bro1 carb-v bro1 *Chin* bro1 *Cob* bro1 con bro1 *Graph* bro1 *Lyc* bro1 ol-an bro1 onos bro1 *Ph-ac* bro1 phos bro1 *Sel* bro1 sep bro1 sulph bro1 titan bro1 zinc bro1
- **prostatic** disease, in: *Aesc* kr1
- **puberty**, in: ferr-m ptk2
- **rising** agg.: adam skp7•
- **robust** man; in a: **Nux-v** kr1
- **sadness**; with: agar kr1 *Calad* kr1 *Con* kr1 *Nat-m* kr1 **Ph-ac** kr1 sars kr1 sulph kr1
- **seldom**: *Kali-c* j5.de
- **sensation** of: cere-s a1 *Mez* a1
  - • **before** a pollution; as: dig a1 mur-ac a1
  - • **suppressed**; as if a pollution had been: clem a1
  - • **waking**; on: am-c a1
- **sexual**:
  - • **excesses**; after: *Agn* sf1.de alum k2 *Dig* kr1 *Nat-m* sf1.de **Nux-v** kr1
  - • **excitement** agg.: adam skp7• **Calc** kr1 cod kr1 con kr1 *Gels* kr1 *Nat-m* kr1 petr kr1 **Pic-ac** kr1 stann jl
- **sitting** agg.: sel jl sulph a1
- **sleep** agg.; during: *Agar* kr1 aloe kr1 anac kr1 ang kr1 *Arg-met* kr1 am b7.de* aur kr1 *Camph* kr1 cann-s a1 clem a1 *Cor-r* kr1 crot-t a1 **Cycl** kr1 dig a1 digin a1 **Dios** a1* *Ferr* kr1 *Guaj* kr1 *Ham* kr1 ind kr1 *Lach* kr1 lact a1 lil-t kr1 lyss a1 med kr1 *Meph* kr1 nat-ar a1 nat-c a1 **Nux-v** kr1 ol-an a1 par b7.de* pers jl *Pic-ac* kr1 puls b7.de* ran-b a1 rhod a1 sel b7.de* stann a1 *Stram* b7.de* symph fd3.de• ther kr1 *Thuj* kr1 thymol jl vanil fd5.de verb kr1 vib kr1 *Zinc* kr1
  - • **coition**; after: nat-m a1

- **dinner**; after: agar a1
- **erection**, without: Dios kr1 nat-m a1 Nuph kr1 trios a1
- **waking**:
  - **on**: Thuj kr1
  - **without** waking: tab kr1

- **slow**; too: calc bro1 lyc bro1 nat-m bro1 zinc bro1
- **stool**:
  - **difficult** | **during**: agn alum am-c anac con hep nat-c nit-ac Petr k* ph-ac a1 sep staph
  - **during** | **agg.**: acet-ac k* Alum k2 anac ars carb-v caust cimic con Gels nat-m k* Nuph ol-an bg1 Petr Ph-ac k* plb Sel k* sep sil sulph thymol jl* viol-t k*
  - **straining** at | **agg.**: Alum bro1 canth bro1 Chin bro1 cimic bro1 digin bro1 gels bro1* kali-br bro1 Nuph bro1 ol-an ptk1 ph-ac h2* phos bro1 pic-ac bro1 Sel bro1 trib bro1
- **stupefaction**; after: bov bg2 calc bg2 sil bg2
- **sudden**, during dream of coition: sumb a1
- **talking** about women, from (See women - talking about)
- **tuberculosis**, in: Calc kr1
- **unconscious**: caust Dios Ham ind lach lact j5.de lyss kr1 merc-i-f nat-c j5.de Nat-p plan plb Sel Sep uran-n
- **urination**:
  - **after** | **agg.**: calad bro1 daph k* hep bro1 kali-c k* merc-i-f ptk1 ph-ac bro1
  - **before**: psor jl2
  - **during** | **agg.**: Ery-a st gels bg2 Nuph st Viol-t kr1*
- **vertigo**; with: Sars kr1*
- **voluptuous**: viol-t ptk1
- **waking**; on: acon a1 acon-c a1 aloe bg* am b7.de* ars cain a1 crot-t j5.de cycl j5.de dig j5.de gast a1 naja petr j5.de phos j5.de pic-ac Sel kr1 sil j5.de Thuj j5.de*
- **weak** man; in a: Gels kr1
- **weakness**; from: Agn kr1 dig ptk1 sul-ac sf1.de
- **wine** agg.: plb j5.de
- **women**:
  - **frolicking** with a woman; while (See caresses)
  - **looking** at passing girls; when: calad k2* pic-ac k2 sel k2*
  - **presence** of a woman; when in: Con kr1 Nux-v k* sal-n ptk1 ust k* zinc a1
  - **talking** about women; when: Ust kr1
  - **talking** with women; when: am-c a1 clem a1
  - **touched** | **being** touched by a woman; on: Nux-v a1
  - **touching** a woman; when: borx a1* graph h2* nat-c a1
- **young** people; in: bar-c br1

PRESSURE:
- **clothes** agg.; of: | **Testes**: arg-n ptk1

PRIAPISM (See Erections - continued)

PRICKLING (See Tingling)

PROSTATITIS (See PROSTATE - Inflammation)

PUBERTY: | **never** well since (See GENERALS - Convalescence - puberty)

PULSATION: berb calc-p bg2
- **coition**; after: nat-c k*

○ - **Penis**: berb brach k* Cop k* ham k* ign ptk1 lith-c bg2 nit-ac k* rhod k* sabad b7.de* thuj bg2
  - **left** side: osm

○ - **Glans**: coc-c k* ferr bg2 ham bg2* nat-m bg2* nit-ac k* osm bg2 prun bg1* ptel bg2* rhod k*
    - **urination** agg.; during: ferr
  - **Root**: thuj
- **Scrotum**: hep nat-c k*
  - **coition**; after: kali-i k*
- **Spermatic** cords: Am-m k* sumb k*
  - **walking** agg.: sumb k*

REDNESS (See Discoloration - red)

RELAXED: absin bro1 Agn bro1 ambr bg2 arn bg2 borx bg2 Calad bro1 cann-xyz bg2 caps bro1 cham bg2 Chin bro1 cic bg2 coff bg2 Con bro1 Dios bro1 ferr bg2 Gels bro1 ham bro1 hep bg2 kali-c bg2 kreos bg2 lach bg2 Lyc bro1 nuph bro1 nux-v bg2 ph-ac bg2* phos bro1 psor jl2 puls bg2 ran-s bg2 rhod bg2 rhus-t bg2 sabin bg2 Sel bro1 sep bro1 staph bro1 sulph bro1 uran-n bro1 Zinc bg2
- **accompanied** by | **pollutions** (See Pollutions - accompanied - relaxation)

○ - **Scrotum**: acet-ac vh Agn b7a.de aloe am-c k* arn k* astac k* aur c1 bell k* cain calad Calc k* calc-p camph k* caps carb-ac carb-an k* carb-v k2 carbn-s chin k* chinin-s Clem k* Coff k* Con b4a.de Dios k* Ferr ferr-i Gels Hell k* hep k* hydr k2 hydrc k* iod iris kali-s fd4.de lach k* Lec Lyc k* mag-c Mag-m k* Merc b4a.de Nat-m k* nit-ac k* Nuph k* ol-an k* op Ph-ac phos k2 pic-ac k* Psor k* Puls k* pyrog c1* Rhus-t k* sanic c1 Sel b7a.de Sil k* Staph sul-ac k* sul-i k2 Sulph k* sumb tab tarent k* Tub k* (non:uran-met vh) Uran-n hr1* ust k*
  - **evening** | **bed** agg.; in: Sulph k*

RETRACTION: euphr b7.de* plb b7.de*

○ - **Penis**: berb k* euphr Ign k* mosch Nuph k* plb puls

○ - **Prepuce**: bell k* Calad k* cocc k* coloc k* cycl bg2* ign b7.de* m-ambo b7.de Merc b4.de* nat-c k* Nat-m k* nit-ac bg2 nux-m bg2* nux-v k* prun k* sulph k* Thuj b4a.de
    - **night**: cocc k* coloc a1*
    - **air**, only in open: cycl a1
    - **coition**; after: Calad k*
    - **difficult**: sabin c1*
    - **drawn** back every time after bringing it forwards; was: coloc a1
- **Scrotum**: acon k* lyss bg1 petr plb bro1
- **Testes**: *(↗Cryptorchism; Cryptorchism - prepubic)* agar Agn b7a.de alum h2 alumn arg-n k* aur bro1* Bar-c bell k* Berb k* brom bro1 bufo bg2 Calc k* calc-act slp camph bro1 Cann-s b7a.de Canth chin bro1 cic k* Clem k* coloc k* crot-t euphr k* iod h2* M-aust b7.de* meny k* Merc b4a.de nit-ac bro1 Nux-v k* ol-an k* op (non:par hr1) pareir petr-ra shn4• phos pitu-a mtf11 Plb k* psor mtf33 puls k* Rhod k* sabal ptk1 sec sil k* Stram sulph b4a.de* syph mtf33 thuj k* thyr st1* tub mtf33 Zinc k*
  - **right**: aeth hr1* alum h2 clem k* puls
    - **sensation** as if drawn upwards: antip c1*
  - **left**: calc k* calc-act h1 crot-t k* (non:par hr1) pareir k* thuj k*
  - **painful**: agar k2 antip vh1 arg-n ptk1 berb ptk1 calc h2 calc-act h1* cic ptk1 Clem mrr1 plb a1 sabal c1* Zinc hr1
  - **sensation** as if: ol-an ptk1
  - **walking** agg.: Rhod

○ - **Abdomen**; into the: iod a1
  - **Inguinal** canal; into the: agar a1* cic hs1 gast c1 plb a1 trad a1
  - **Ring**; to external: cic ptk1

RIDING:
- **carriage**; in a:
  - **amel.** | **Spermatic** cords: tarent ptk1

RUBBING:
- **agg.**:

○ - **Penis** | **Prepuce**: cycl ptk1

RUPTURE (See Hernia)

SARCOCELE: Aur k* calc bro1* clem bro1 iod ptk1 Merc-i-r k* Puls k* Rhod bro1* sil bro1 spong bro1* sulph sne tub bro1
- **indolent**: tarent ptk1

SATYRIASIS (See MIND - Satyriasis)

SCIRRHUS (See Cancer - scrotum - scirrhus)

SCURF: | **spots** | **Corona**; red scarfy spots on: cor-r nit-ac

○ - **Prepuce**; inside of: caust k*

SEMEN dribbling: *(↗Pollutions; PROSTATE - Emission)* calad k2* canth gels k2 pic-ac ptk1 Sel a1*
- **sleep** agg.; during: plb j5.de Sel sil tax j5.de
- **stool** agg.; during: Sel mrr1 zinc mrr1
- **unnoticed**: sel a1

Male

SEMINAL discharge:
- **coition**; during (See Ejaculation)
- **coition**; without (See Pollutions)

SEMINAL emission:
- **agg.**: clem bg2 grat bg2 ust bg2
- **amel.**: sulph bg2
- **coition**; during (See Ejaculation)
- **coition**; without (See Pollutions)

SENSITIVENESS: aur br1 *Canth* b7a.de *Cocc* k* coff hr1 franz a1 *Ph-ac* **Plat** k* tarent mtf33 vanil fd5.de verat k*
- **suffering** unbearable; a little: coff
- ○ - **Penis**: cocc corn k* crot-t k* franz a1 tab ptk1 thuj k* verat zinc k* [tax jsj7]
  - ○ • **Glans**: arg-n a1 canth b7.de* *Cor-r* k* galla-q-r nl2• **Merc-c** k* *Prun* bg2 rhus-t b7.de* thuj k*
    - ⁝ **coition**; after: eug k*
  - • **Prepuce**: cann-s k* *Cor-r* k* *Merc* k* sabin bg2 [tax jsj7]
- **Scrotum**: kali-c k* nat-m k* ph-ac k* plat k* **Staph** k* zinc k*
- **Spermatic** cords: *Bell* bro1 chin bg2 clem bg2* equis-h bg2 ham bro1 meny b7.de* merc-i-r bro1 nat-m bg2 *Ox-ac* bro1 *Phyt* bg2* rhod bro1 sars bg2 *Spong* bro1 tus-p bro1
- **Testes**: acon bg2 adel a1 alum bg2 am-c bg2 ant-t bg2 arn bg2* asaf b7.de* aur bg2 cann-s bg cann-xyz bg2 cimic a1 clem b4a.de* cocc bg2* coloc a1 con bg2 cop bg* erio a1 ham bg ign bg2 ind bg kali-bi a1 kali-c k2 kali-n a1* merc-i-r a1 nat-c bg2 nit-ac a1 oci a1 ph-ac bg2* phos bg2 *Rhod* bg2 sabal bg2 sel bg2 **Sep** bg2 sil bg2 *Spong* b7a.de* **Staph** hr1 zinc bg2

SEXUAL AVERSION (See Sexual desire - wanting)

SEXUAL DESIRE:
- **diminished**: acon k* adlu jl aeth a1 agar k* agav-t jl **Agn** k* *Aids* nl2• *Alum* k* am-c k* ambr b2.de amyg-p c2 anac b2.de* ange-s jl *Anh* mg1.de* ant-c b2.de* ant-o a1 anthraci vh1 apis aran-ix mg1.de* arg-met arg-n k* arn b2.de arum-d kr1 *Asar* b7a.de aur aza jl bar-act a1 **Bar-c** k* bar-s k2 bell k* berb k* bit-ar wht1• borx k* *Brom* sf1.de bros-gau mrc1 bry kr1 *Calad* b2.de* calc b2.de* calc-p *Camph* b7.de* cann-s b2.de canth b2.de caps b2.de* carb-ac carb-an k* carb-v b2.de* carbn-s a1 carc jl2 carl a1 **Caust** b2.de* chen-v kr1 chin j5.de chinin-s j5.de* chlorpr jl* clem k* coca mrr1 *Cocc* b7.de *Coff* b7a.de* coloc a1 con b2.de* cortico mg1.de cortiso mg1.de* cund a1 cupr sst3• cycl dam mtf11 des-ac jl *Dios* dream-p sdj1• ephe-si hsj1• erig mg1.de ery-a c2 ery-m c2 euph b2.de falco-pe nl2• *Ferr* k* ferr-m a1 fl-ac a1 franz a1 galeoc-c-h gms1• gast c2 gink-b jl granit-m es1• **Graph** k* halo jl hell k* *Hep* k* hippoc-k szs2 hyos b2.de *Ign* k* ina-i mlk9.de ind indg iod bro1 kali-bi ptk1* kali-br k* *Kali-c* k* kali-chl j5.de* *Kali-i* *Kali-p* kali-s kali-sil k2 *Kreos* kr1 lac-c mrr1 lac-e hm2• *Lach* b7.de* *Lact* j5.de laur b2.de lec bro1 levo jl lil-s a1 limen-b-c hm2* lir-o mtf11 lup a1 **Lyc** k* m-ambo b2.de* m-arct b7.de *Mag-c* k* mag-m b2.de mand mg1.de* mang-p rly4• meny b2.de merc-c a1 moly-met jl morph a1 *Mur-ac* k* *Nat-m* k* nat-p nat-sil fd3.de• nicotam rly4• *Nit-ac* k* *Nuph* k* nux-m b2.de* oci-sa jl* *Onos* br1* op k* orch c2 oxyt bro1 ozone sde2• pall c2 petr k* *Ph-ac* k* phasco-ci rbp2 *Phos* b2.de* pic-ac sf1.de plan a1 plat b2.de *Plb* b7.de* positr nl2• *Psor* k* rauw jl* *Rhod* k* rhodi a1 ribo rly4• rumx a1 sabad k* *Sabal* bro1* sabin b2.de sacch-a fd2.de• sel k* seneg b2.de* *Sep* k* ser-a-c jl2 sieg mg1.de **Sil** k* spig b2.de spong stann b2.de* **Staph** k* sul-ac b2.de sul-i k2 *Sulph* k* teucr k* thala jl ther thiop jl thuj sf1.de upa a1 ust a1 vanil br1 vichy-g a1 visc jl* x-ray bro1 yohim c1* [heroin sdj2 tax jsj7]
  - • **morning**: petr kr1
  - • **evening**: dios a1
  - • **night**: cocc a1
  - • **apathy**, with: falco-pe nl2• kali-chl j5.de
    - ⁝ **chilliness**; and: kali-chl j5.de *Kali-m* kr1
  - • **chilliness**; with: kali-chl j5.de
  - • **diabetes**; in: (↗*Erections - wanting - diabetes*) *Cupr* kr1
  - • **eating**; when: galeoc-c-h gms1•
  - • **erections**:
    - ⁝ **with**: hippoc-k szs2 lyss kr1
    - ⁝ **without**: caust j5.de *Coff* j5.de *Dios* kr1 *Kali-br* kr1
  - • **exertion** agg.: galeoc-c-h gms1•
  - • **gonorrhea**; after dragging: med jl2
  - • **relaxed** genitals; with: acon j5.de* coff j5.de
  - • **sexual** excesses; after: agn mrr1 aven c1 **Staph** kr1 *Sulph* kr1 upa c1

Sexual desire – **diminished**: ...
  - • **spinal** affections, in: *Chin* kr1
  - • **working**; while: galeoc-c-h gms1•
- **excessive**: (↗*MIND - Ailments - sexual excesses; MIND - Satyriasis*) **Agar** k* *Alum* androc srj1• aur-ar vh1 bov kr1 calad mrr1 **Calc** k* *Calc-p* c1 camph sf1.de **Cann-i** k1* **Canth** j5.de* *Carb-v* kr1 caust gl1.fr• chir-fl gya2 colch coloc con sf1.de *Ery-a* kr1 *Fl-ac* kr1* gaul br1 *Gels* c1 *Graph* j5.de* grat kr1 ham *Hyos* k* *Kali-br* k* *Kali-c* kola stb3• *Lach* k* *Lyc* lyss c1* *Med* mrr1 **Merc** kr1* mosch k* *Nat-c* *Nat-m* nit-ac k* **Nux-v** kr1* op h1 *Orig* c1 **Phos** k* phys *Pic-ac* kr1* *Plat* k* *Plb* k* psor *Puls* mrr1 sabin j5.de* sal-n c1* *Sil* **Staph** kr1* **Stram** sulph kr1 *Tarent* k* ther *Tub* k* *Ust* *Verat* kr1* **Zinc** k* zinc-pic c1
  - • **accompanied** by | **nausea**: chir-fl gya2
  - • **ailments** from: chir-fl gya2 **Lyss**
  - • **poor** results, with: agar bg2 am-c bg2 calc bg2 con bg2 graph bg2 lyc bg2 meny bg2 phos bg2 sel bg2
  - • **ungovernable** (See violent)
- **excited**; easy (See increased)
- **incest**: (↗*MIND - Ailments - abused - sexually*) cupr sst3•
- **increased**: (↗*Excitability; MIND - Ailments - sexual excesses; MIND - Sensual*) abrom-a ks5 acon k* *Agar* k* agn k* alco a1 *All-c* aloe alum k* alum-sil k2 *Am-c* k* ambr b2.de* *Anac* k* anag kr1* **Anan** androc srj1• ang vh *Ant-c* k* *Ant-s-aur* a1* ant-t apis k* aran-ix mg1.de* arg-n mrr1 arn k* ars k* arund asaf b2.de* aspar j5.de* aster bg2* *Aur* k* aur-i k2 aur-m aur-s a1* bar-c **Bar-m** bell k* berb a1 bit-ar wht1• borx b2.de* bov k* brass-n-o srj5• brom bry *Bufo* cact a1 cain caj a1 *Calad* bg2* **Calc** k* **Calc-p** k* calc-sil k2 *Camph* k* **Cann-i** k* *Cann-s* k* **Canth** k* caps b2.de* carb-ac carb-v k* carbn-s a1 carc fd2.de* carl a1 *Castm* caust k* cedr cench br1 cent a1 cere-s a1 cham k* chen-v a1* chim-m j5.de* *Chin* k* chinin-s a1* chir-fl gya2 cinch c2 *Cinnb* clem b2.de* *Coc-c* coca a1 *Cocc* k* cod a1 *Coff* k* colch *Coloc* b2.de* colocin a1 **Con** k* cop a1* corv-cor bdg• *Croc* k* crot-h j5.de* *Cub* a1* cypra-eg sde6.de• del a1 dema a1 dendr-pol sk4• der a1 des-ac k2* dig k* *Dios* *Dulc* b2.de* erig mg1.de ery-a a1 eucal a1* *Ferr* k* ferr-i ferr-m a1 ferr-ma j5.de ferr-p ferr-pic sf1.de *Fl-ac* k* form a1* galeoc-c-h gms1• *Gamb* mrr1 *Gels* germ-met srj5• gins k* gnaph kr1 goss a1* gran j5.de* *Graph* k* grat bg2 gymno a1 *Ham* a1* hell bg2 helon *Hep* k* hipp k* hippoc-k szs2 hydr a1 hydr-ac a1 *Hyos* k* hyper a1* *Ign* k* ina-i mlk9.de *Ind* a1* indg a1 *Iod* k* irid-met srj5• *Iris* kr1 *Kali-bi* kali-br k* *Kali-c* k* *Kali-i* *Kali-n* k* kali-p kali-sil k2 kola stb3• kreos b2.de* *Lac-c* k* lac-del hm2• *Lach* k* lact j5.de* lap-la sde8.de• *Laur* k* led k* lil-t k* lim a1 limen-b-c hm2* **Lyc** k* **Lyss** k* m-ambo b2.de* m-arct b2.de* m-aust b2.de* mag-c mg1.de mag-m b2.de* maias-l hm2• manc k* mand sp1 mang k* marb-w es1• **Med** vh* meny k* *Merc* k* merc-i-r a1 merl a1 *Mez* k* mim-p jl* morph a1 *Mosch* k* mur-ac b2.de* murx bg2* musca-d szs1 naja *Nat-c* k* *Nat-hchls* *Nat-m* k* *Nat-p* *Nat-s* nat-sil k2 *Nit-ac* k* nitro-o a1 nuph a1 nux-m k* **Nux-v** k* nymph a1 oci-sa jl* ol-an bro1 onop jl onos bro1 *Op* k* opun-s a1 (non:opun-v a1) *Orig* bg2* osteo-a jl2 ox-ac par k* pegan-ha tpi1• pen a1 pers jl petr b2.de* *Ph-ac* **Phos** k* **Pic-ac** k* pip-m a1 **Plat** k* *Plb* k* plut-n srj7• podo fd3.de• propr sa3• psil ft1 psor ptel a1* **Puls** k* raph bg2* rhod b2.de* rhus-t k* rib-ac jl rob a1 rosm lgb1 ruta k* sabad j5.de* *Sabin* k* sacch *Sal-n* br1* sang saroth mg1.de* sars k* *Sec* b7a.de **Sel** bg2* seneg k* *Sep* k* **Sil** k* sin-n a1* spig b2.de* spira a1 spong bg2 *Stann* k* **Staph** k* stict sf1.de *Stram* k* sul-ac b2.de* sulph k* sumb symph fd3.de• *Tarent* k* tell tep a1 teucr bg2 *Thuj* k* thymol bro1 tritic-vg fd5.de **Tub** k* upa bro1 urol-h rwt• *Ust* vanil br1 verat k* verb b2.de visc jl* yohim bwa3* yuc a1 **Zinc** k* *Zinc-p* k2* *Zinc-pic* sf1.de zing kr1* ziz kr1* [heroin sdj2 zinc-n stj2]
  - • **daytime**: crot-h j5.de* hyos a1 lach a1 sil j5.de
  - • **morning**: agar anac aur h2 bar-c a1 calc a1 calc-p j5.de* carb-v a1 cob a1 coc-c a1 coca a1 form a1 kreos a1 lach j5.de nat-s a1* nat-sil fd3.de• ox-ac a1 petr h2 plat a1 puls h1 rhus-t c1 sil h2 spong fd4.de vanil fd5.de
    - ⁝ **bed** agg.; in: aster a1 kali-cy a1 lach a1 sil a1 spirae a1
    - ⁝ **beer**; after: nat-c h2*
    - ⁝ **erections**; with: nat-s kr1
    - ⁝ **rising** agg.; after: aur j5.de* calc j5.de
    - ⁝ **sleep** agg.; during: cann-s a1
    - ⁝ **waking** | **after** | **agg.**: aloe kr1 anac a1 aur j5.de
      - ⁝ **on**: aeth a1 agar mrr1 carb-ac a1* coc-c a1 gnaph kr1 irid-met srj5• nat-c a1 ptel a1 *Puls* j5.de* thuj a1 vanil fd5.de
  - • **forenoon**: calc a1 hipp a1 phos a1 plumbg a1 symph fd3.de•
    - ⁝ **walking** agg.: calc a1
  - • **afternoon**: agar kr1 hyper a1 lyss a1 nat-sil fd3.de• rhodi a1

- **afternoon**: ...
  - **14**.30 h: cinnb$_{a1}$
  - **17** h: galeoc-c-h$_{gms1}$•
  - **sleep** | **siesta** agg.; after: eug$_{a1}$ lach$_{a1}$ m-aust$_{j5.de}$
  - **sleepiness**; with: agar$_{kr1}$
- **evening**: acon$_{a1}$ *Aloe*$_{a1}$* alum-sil$_{k2}$ bit-ar$_{wht1}$• calc$_{a1}$ cinnb$_{kr1}$ hipp$_{a1}$ nat-s$_{j5.de}$* spong$_{fd4.de}$ thuj$_{a1}$
  - **bed** agg.; in: cic$_{h1}$ nat-m$_{a1}$
  - **lying** agg.: nat-c$_{a1}$
- **night**: alum-sil$_{k2}$ aur$_{j5.de}$* camph$_{a1}$ *Canth*$_{a1}$ cere-b$_{a1}$ cinnb$_{a1}$ gnaph$_{a1}$ guare$_{a1}$ lach$_{a1}$ *Lyc*$_{j5.de}$* mez$_{a1}$ nat-c$_{a1}$ nymph$_{a1}$ ox-ac$_{a1}$ sil$_{j5.de}$ *Sulph*$_{a1}$ thuj$_{a1}$ zinc$_{a1}$
  - **midnight** | **after** | **3** h: calc$_{st}$
    - **waking**; after: ant-s-aur$_{a1}$
  - **erections**; with:
    - **painful**: merc$_{kr1}$
    - **violent**: *Fl-ac*$_{kr1}$
  - **rousing**: *Galeoc-c-h*$_{gms1}$•
- **abdomen**; during distension of: ign$_{a1}$
- **ability** decreased: *Sel*$_{c1}$
- **accompanied** by:
  - **delicacies**; desire for (See GENERALS - Food and - delicacies - desire - sexual)
  - **Colon**; inflammation of the (See ABDOMEN - Inflammation - colon - accompanied - sexual)
  - **Urethra**:
    - **bleeding** (See URETHRA - Discharge - bloody - accompanied - sexual)
    - **discharge** from (See URETHRA - Discharge - accompanied - sexual)
- **agg.** | **Testes**: mag-m$_{ptk1}$
- **alternating** with:
  - **despair** of salvation; religious (See MIND - Despair - religious - alternating - sexual)
  - **moral** obliquity; fear of (See MIND - Fear - moral - alternating - sexual)
  - **religious** affections (See MIND - Religious - too - alternating - sexual)
  - **sadness** (See MIND - Sadness - alternating - sexual)
- **appetite**, with increased: cinnb$_{j5.de}$
- **attacks** of: acon$_{j5.de}$* *Ant-c*$_{bg2}$* apis$_{sf1.de}$ cann-i$_{sf1.de}$ canth$_{sf1.de}$ caps$_{j5.de}$ fl-ac$_{bg2}$ *Hyos*$_{bg2}$* *Ign*$_{sf1.de}$ lach$_{sf1.de}$ *Op*$_{j5.de}$* phos$_{sf1.de}$ *Plat*$_{sf1.de}$ puls$_{sf1.de}$ sel$_{sf1.de}$ sil$_{sf1.de}$ staph$_{sf1.de}$ stram$_{bg2}$* *Verat*$_{bg2}$*
  - **moonlight**, in the: *Ant-c*$_{sf1.de}$
- **attempts** to satisfy it, until it drives him to masturbation and madness: anan
- **bed**:
  - **going** to bed, on: naja$_{a1}$
  - **in** bed | **agg.**: kali-br$_{a1}$
- **children**; in: aloe$_{hr}$* ambr$_{lmj}$ *Bar-c*$_{sf1.de}$* *Calc-p*$_{lmj}$ *Cann-i*$_{lmj}$ carc$_{lmj}$ *Fl-ac*$_{lmj}$ graph$_{mrr1}$ **Hyos**$_{lmj}$ **Lach**$_{lmj}$ lyss$_{lmj}$ med$_{lmj}$ **Merc**$_{lmj}$ *Mosch*$_{lmj}$ ph-ac$_{lmj}$ **Phos**$_{lmj}$ plat$_{mtf33}$ staph$_{lmj}$ tub$_{ggd}$ *Zinc*$_{lmj}$
- **chorea**, in: *Verat-v*$_{kr1}$
- **coition**:
  - **after**: mez$_{j5.de}$ *Ph-ac*$_{kr1}$
  - **desire** for; without: borx$_{j5.de}$
  - **excess** of coition, after: *Ph-ac*$_{kr1}$
- **continued**: galeoc-c-h$_{gms1}$• *Nit-ac*$_{j5.de}$
- **cooking**; while: galeoc-c-h$_{gms1}$•
- **days**, several: sars$_{j5.de}$
- **delirium**; during: **Stann**$_{kr1}$ **Stram**$_{a1}$*
- **driving**, when: apis$_{a1}$
- **drunkenness**; during: calc$_{gl1.fr}$• canth$_{gl1.fr}$• *Caust*$_{gl1.fr}$• chin$_{gl1.fr}$• con$_{gl1.fr}$• nux-v$_{gl1.fr}$• phos$_{gl1.fr}$• sacch-a$_{fd2.de}$•
- **easily** excited: cinnb con *Graph* kali-c *Lyc* nat-c$_{h2}$ *Nux-v* **Phos** *Pic-ac* plat *Plb* **Zinc**
  - **discharge** of prostatic fluid, with: nit-ac
  - **sleep**; when falling asleep: merc-i-r$_{kr1}$
- **eating**; after: aloe colch lyss$_{kr1}$*
- **emotions**; without: polys$_{sk4}$•
- **erections**:
  - **with**: aloe$_{j5.de}$ am-m$_{h2}$* arn$_{j5.de}$ astac$_{kr1}$ aur$_{j5.de}$ calc$_{j5.de}$ **Canth**$_{b7a.de}$* coloc$_{j5.de}$ *Dig*$_{j5.de}$ ferr$_{b7a.de}$ ferr-ma$_{j5.de}$ hyos$_{j5.de}$ lach$_{a1}$ lyss$_{kr1}$ *Nux-v*$_{b7a.de}$ op$_{b7a.de}$* par$_{j5.de}$ *Plb*$_{b7a.de}$ puls$_{b7a.de}$* rhod$_{j5.de}$ sabin$_{b7a.de}$ *Sars*$_{kr1}$ *Sil*$_{j5.de}$ spig$_{b7a.de}$ staph$_{b7a.de}$
    - **incomplete**: aran-ix$_{mg1.de}$ con$_{k2}$
  - **without**: acon$_{j5.de}$ *Agar*$_{k}$* *Agn* *Alum* *Am-c*$_{k}$* *Anan* aq-mar$_{jl}$ aran-ix$_{jl}$ *Arg-met* *Arg-n* *Aur* aur-s bar-c **Calad** *Calc* calc-i$_{k2}$ calc-sil$_{k2}$ *Camph* carbn-s *Chin* chir-fl$_{gya2}$ cob **Con** corn crot-h *Dig* dream-p$_{sdj1}$• ferr-ma$_{k}$* **Graph** hep ign kali-c$_{sf1.de}$ lach **Lyc** lyss$_{kr1}$ mag-m$_{kr1}$ meny naja *Nat-m* *Nat-p* nuph *Nux-m* *Nux-v* op pers$_{jl}$ *Ph-ac* *Phos* pic-ac$_{kr1}$* *Psor* puls sabad sal-n$_{st}$ *Sel* *Sep* *Sil* stann$_{sf1.de}$ *Staph* sulph
- **fancies**:
  - **with**: bit-ar$_{wht1}$• *Ign*$_{j5.de}$ sil$_{j5.de}$
  - **without**: hep$_{j5.de}$ hyos$_{j5.de}$ meny$_{j5.de}$
- **headache**, with throbbing (See HEAD - Pain - accompanied - sexual)
- **indifference**, followed by sexual: tell$_{kr1}$
- **legs** were crossed, while: nat-c$_{a1}$
- **old** people; in:
  - **men**; old: arn$_{h1}$* *Fl-ac*$_{k}$* lyc$_{ptk1}$ mosch$_{h1}$ sel$_{ptk1}$ staph sulph
    - **impotent**; but: lyc$_{bro1}$ sel$_{bro1}$
- **paralytic** disease, in: *Sil*$_{k}$*
- **partner**; only for: galeoc-c-h$_{gms1}$•
- **pollution**:
  - **after** a: aloe$_{k}$* ars con$_{kr1}$ grat kali-c mez$_{k}$* *Nat-m*$_{k}$* nit-ac *Ph-ac*$_{k}$* rhod sep
  - **with**: ferr$_{b7a.de}$ *Nux-v*$_{b7a.de}$ *Op*$_{b7a.de}$ *Plb*$_{b7a.de}$ sars$_{j5.de}$
  - **without**: *Coff*$_{b7a.de}$*
- **priapism**; like: **Cann-s**$_{zzl}$ cann-xyz$_{bg2}$ **Canth**$_{bg2}$ coloc$_{bg2}$ *Graph*$_{bg2}$ ign$_{bg2}$ kali-c$_{bg2}$ *Nat-c*$_{bg2}$ **Nat-m**$_{bg2}$* nit-ac$_{bg2}$ **Nux-v**$_{bg2}$ op$_{bg2}$ ph-ac$_{bg2}$ *Phos*$_{bg2}$ plat$_{bg2}$ *Puls*$_{j5.de}$* *Rhus-t*$_{bg2}$ *Sil*$_{bg2}$* staph$_{bg2}$ thuj$_{bg2}$
- **relaxed** genitals; with: acon$_{j5.de}$ aur-s$_{k2}$ crot-h$_{j5.de}$ dream-p$_{sdj1}$•
- **restlessness**; with: ant-c$_{j5.de}$
- **rising** agg.; after: aur$_{a1}$
- **sadness**; with (See MIND - Sadness - sexual excitement - with)
- **sight** of erotic things, at: tarent$_{a1}$
- **sleep**:
  - **after** | **agg.**: *Agar*
  - **disturbing** sleep: (*↗SLEEP - Restless - sexual)* astac$_{kr1}$ **Canth**$_{kr1}$ *Galeoc-c-h*$_{gms1}$• sars$_{j5.de}$*
  - **during** | **agg.**: *Nat-c*$_{kr1}$ *Stram*$_{kr1}$
  - **falling** asleep | **when**: kali-br$_{a1}$ merc$_{a1}$ merc-i-r$_{a1}$*
- **sleeplessness**; during: ant-c$_{kr1}$
- **stool** agg.; during: nat-c$_{kr1}$ *Nat-s*$_{kr1}$
- **tabes** dorsalis, in: *Fl-ac*$_{kr1}$
- **vibration**; from | **pelvis**; in: plut-n$_{srj7}$•
- **voluptuous** thoughts; without: *Lach*$_{b7.de}$* sulph$_{bg2}$
- **waking**; on: aeth$_{a1}$ carb-ac$_{a1}$ coc-c$_{a1}$ ptel$_{a1}$
- **warm**:
  - **bath**; in a warm: nat-c$_{a1}$
    - **and** on leaving it: nat-c$_{a1}$
  - **bed**; when getting warm in: ant-c$_{a1}$

Male

- **weakness**, with physical: (*↗MIND - Fancies - lascivious - impotence; MIND - Lascivious - impotence; MIND - Thoughts - sexual - impotence)* aq-mar jl aran-ix mg1.de* calad ptk1 calc ptk1 calc-i k2 calc-sil k2 con k2* ferr-ma j5.de graph ptk1 *Kali-c* ptk1 *Lyc* ptk1 nat-m ptk1 *Onos* mrr1 *Phos* ptk1 pic-ac kr1 sel ptk1
- **women**:
  - **company** of women; in: chir-fl gya2 zinc a1
  - **talking** with women; when: am-c a1 chir-fl gya2 clem a1
  - **touching** a woman; when: borx a1 chir-fl gya2 graph a1 nat-c a1

- **insatiable**: galeoc-c-h gms1•
- **suppressed**:
  - **agg.**: (*↗FEMALE - Sexual desire - suppressed - agg.; GENERALS - Sexual desire - suppression - agg.)* *Aeth* vh1 berb kr1* **Camph** kr1 *Carb-v* kr1 **Con** kr1* **Ery-a** kr1 *Hell* kr1 *Kali-br* kr1 *Mosch* kr1 *Ph-ac* kr1 **Puls** kr1
  - **ailments** from (See GENERALS - Sexual desire - suppression - agg.)
  - **amel.**: calad
  - **then** excited: *Ery-a* kr1
- **ungovernable** (See violent)
- **violent**: (*↗MIND - Ailments - sexual excesses; MIND - Impulse - sexual; MIND - Satyriasis)* acon agar b4.de* agn bro1 *Alum* b4a.de* am-c *Anac* k* **Anan** ant-c arn ars b4a.de *Aur* b4a.de *Bar-c* b4a.de bar-m k2 *Bufo* calad k2 camph k2 **Cann-i** **Canth** k* *Caust* gl1.fr• cench k2* chin gl1.fr• chir-fl gya2 *Coloc* b4a.de* con b4.de* cop crot-h j5.de dig bg2 ferr bg2 *Fl-ac* *Graph* k* grat *Hyos* bg2* ign b7.de *Kali-br* k* kali-c b4.de* kola stb3• *Lach* k* *Lyc* b4.de* *Lyss* k* m-arct b7.de *M-aust* b7.de* mag-c gl1.fr• merc k* mosch k* mygal *Nat-c* b4.de* *Nat-hchls* **Nat-m** b4.de* nat-s mrr1 nux-v b7.de* op b7.de* orig br1 ozone sde2• **Phos** k* **Pic-ac** k* **Plat** k* *Plb* b7a.de* *Puls* b7a.de* *Rhus-t* bg2 ruta b7.de sabin b7.de* seneg bg2 sep bg2 **Sil** k* spig bg2 spong fd4.de stann k* staph bg2* *Stram* k* sulph k* *Tarent* k* **Tub** k* verat b7.de* **Zinc** k* zinc-p k2
  - **irresistible**: galeoc-c-h gms1•
  - **sexual** mania, in: apis st chir-fl gya2 **Phos** *Tarent*
  - **suicidal** disposition; with (See MIND - Suicidal - sexual)
  - **trembling**; with: am-c graph **Plat**
  - **yearning** for sex (See violent)
- **wanting**: achy jl aeth a1 **Agn** k* aids nl2• alco a1 aloe kr1 alum am-c k* amyg-p a1 anac k* anan *Anh* mg1.de* ant-c bro1 ant-o a1 anthraci vh1* *Arg-met* a1 *Arg-n* k* arn bro1 ars bro1 arum-d a1 asar j5.de* aven bro1 bar-act a1 bar-c a1* bar-s k2 bart a1 bell k* *Berb* k* bit-ar wht1• borx j5.de* brom kr1 *Bufo* a1* caj a1 calad a1* calc k* calc-f jl* *Camph* k* cann-i kr1 canth a1 *Caps* carb-ac carb-an k* *Carb-v* k* **Carbn-s** k* carc jl2* carl a1 caust a1* cench k2 chen-v a1 *Chin* bro1* chinin-s bro1 chlf a1 chlol kr1 chlor a1 cinnb a1 *Cob* bro1 cob-n jl* coca mrr1 coff a1 con h2* cop cordyc mp4• cortico jl cub a1 dam bro1 dig a1* dios a1* dulc fd4.de elaps a1 equis-h a1 ery-a ery-m a1 falco-pe nl2• ferr ferr-ma ferr-p fl-ac a1 franz a1 gast a1 *Gels* bro1 germ-met srj5• get a1 glyc bro1 *Glycyr-g* cte1• granit-m es1• *Graph* k* *Hell* k* hep k* hipp jl2 hydrc a1 hydrog srj2• hyper bro1 *Ign* k* indg a1 *Iod* k* jac-c a1 **Kali-bi** k* **Kali-br** k1* *Kali-c* k* kali-chl a1 kali-i bro1 kali-p kali-s kali-sil k2 lac-c mrr1 lach k* lec bro1 lil-s a1 *Lyc* k* lyss mag-c a1 med jl2 meph a1 *Merc* kr1 *Merc-c* a1 morph a1 mur-ac myric k* napht a1 *Nat-m* k* nat-p *Nit-ac* k* *Nuph* k* nux-m *Nux-v* bro1 *Onos* k* op h1* osm a1 pen a1 pers jl *Ph-ac* k* phos k* *Pic-ac* bro1 *Plb* k* positr nl2• *Psor* k* ptel a1* rhod a1 rumx a1 ruta fd4.de sabad a1 *Sabal* bro1 sacch-a fd2.de• *Sal-n* bro1 saroth jl sel k* sep k2* sil k* spira a1 spong *Stann* h2* staph j5.de* *Stry* bro1 sul-i k2 *Sulph* k* *Sumb* k* syc bka1• syph jl2 tab k* teucr a1 ther a1 thuj k* trib bro1 tritic-vg fd5.de upa a1 ust a1 v-a-b jl2* vanil fd5.de yohim c1* zinc bro1 zinc-p bro1 [heroin sdj2 lac-mat sst4 moly-met stj2 nat-caust stj2]
  - **morning**: carb-v j5.de*
  - **forenoon**: phys a1
  - **evening**: dios a1
  - **night**: bufo a1
  - **coition**; during: lyss c1
  - **cold** agg.: achy jl
  - **coldness** of scrotum, with: aloe kr1 berb kr1 brom kr1 *Caps* kr1 *Merc* kr1
  - **continued**: lach j5.de
  - **emission**; during: psor ptk1

Sexual desire – **wanting**: ...

- **erections**:
  - **with**: agn b7.de* *Alum* j5.de *Ambr* b7.de* arn b7.de* bry kr1 *Calad* b7.de* cann-xyz bg2 *Caps* b7.de* carb-v b4.de* eug kr1 *Euph* b4a.de ferr-ma j5.de fl-ac bg2* graph b4.de* hyos b7.de* lach bg2 laur b7.de* m-ambo b7.de mag-c kr1 mag-m b4.de* nat-m b4.de* nit-ac kr1 nux-v kr1 petr b4.de* ph-ac b4.de* *Phos* b4.de* plat b4.de* sabad b7.de* sabin b7.de* sel b7a.de **Sep** b4a.de sil b4.de* spig b7.de* staph b7.de* sul-ac b4.de* sulph kr1 tarent kr1
  - **without**: *Camph* kr1 dream-p sdj1• graph j5.de tritic-vg fd5.de
- **fleshy** people, in: **Kali-bi** k*
- **irritation** of genitalia; with: borx b4a.de
- **pollution**; after nocturnal: med jl2
- **waking** agg.; after: *Aloe* kr1 anac j5.de *Puls* j5.de
- **work** | **aversion** to work; with: caust j5.de

SEXUAL EXCESSES (See GENERALS - Sexual excesses)

SEXUAL EXCITEMENT (See Sexual desire)

SEXUAL NEURASTHENIA (See Sexual desire - diminished)

SEXUAL PASSION (See Sexual desire)

SHINING Scrotum: *Graph* k* *Merc* k*

SHIVERING: ang k* coloc k* zinc k*

○ - **Scrotum**: ang b7.de* zinc b4.de*
  - **Testes**: ang bg2 zinc bg2

SHRIVELLED: agar k2 *Agn* b7.de *Arg-n* carbn-s **Ign** k* **Lyc** k* merc

○ - **Penis**: agn bg2 aloe bg2 bell bg2 berb a1
  - **urination** agg.; after: ign b7.de*

○ • **Glans**: calad bg2 merc h*
  - **Scrotum**: arg-n bg2 bell bg2 berb k* caps k* carbn-s *Crot-t* k* rhod k* ther k* zinc k*
  - **Spermatic** cords: *Caps* k*

SMALL:

○ - **Penis**: agn mp1• lyc mp1•
  - **Testes**: ser-a-c jl2

SMEGMA:

- **increased**: alum h2* anan a1 bry bg2* *Canth* k* **Caust** k* cub a1 hep a2 lipp a1 nat-c h2* *Nux-v* k* sang k* sep a1 sulph k* sumb k* symph fd3.de• thuj a1*
- **odors** | **offensive**: sulph ptk1
- **wanting**: canth b7a.de

SODOMY: *Plat* vh

SOFTENING of testes: caps k* *Psor* jl2 ser-a-c jl2 sul-i ptk1

SPOTS: graph bg2 spong bg2

- **yellow** brown: cob ptk1

○ - **Penis**: antip bro1 *Bell* bro1 bry bro1 calad bro1 calc cann-s bro1 caust bro1 *Cinnb* bro1 gels bro1 lach bro1 *Merc* bro1 nat-m bro1 petr bro1 *Rhus-t* bro1 sep bro1 *Sulph* bro1 thuj bro1
  - **granular**: cinnb thuj
  - **red**: arn *Carb-v* caust cinnb con lach nat-m *Nit-ac* petr sep *Sil* ther thuj

○ • **Glans**: arn k* cann-s b7.de* *Carb-v* k* cinnb dulc fd4.de lach nat-m k* *Nit-ac* k* petr k* sep k* *Sil* k* ther thuj
  - **Prepuce**: lach nit-ac rhus-t thuj
  - **Scrotum**: calc *Sil* k*
    - **brown**: con bro1
    - **white**: *Merc* thuj

STERILITY: agn c2 alet c2 apis mrr1 aur-m c2 bar-m c2 bers-l bta1• *Borx* c2 carc sst2• caul c2 chlam-tr bcx2• cissu-c bta1• *Con* c2 dam c2 erios-co bta1• ferr a1* fil c2 form c2 goss c2 grew-oc bta1• gunn-p bta1• helon c2 *Iod* c2 lappa c2 mand sp1 mill c2 nat-c c2 *Nat-m* c2 nat-p c2 phos c2 pyren-sc bta1• roye-l bta1• rub-c bta1• sabal c2 sol-so bta1• sul-ac c2 sulfa jl3 ther c2 trib br1 trium-r bta1• vern-co bta1• wies c2 x-ray br1*

- **self**-reproaching; with (See MIND - Reproaching oneself - sterility)

SUPPURATION: (↗*Empyocele)*

○ - **Penis** | **Glans**: merc b4.de*
- **Prepuce**, under the: caps **Cinnb** k* *Cor-r* dig bg2 *Hep* jac-c k* jac-g jug-r lyc *Merc* k* **Merc-c** *Nit-ac* rhus-t bg2 sep sulph h2*
- **Testes**: aur bg2 calc-s bg2 hep bg2 nit-ac bg2 ph-ac bg2 phyt sil bg2 teucr-s bg2

SWELLING: (↗*Metastasis)* aloe ang k* *Apis* b7a.de **Arn** k* *Ars* k* *Bry* b7a.de calad b7.de* *Canth* k* carbn-o coc-c *Dig* b4a.de graph br1 kali-bi k* kola stb3• *Lach* k* *Lyc* k* *Merc* k* merc-c bg2 plb k* pyrog c1 **Rhus-t** k* ruta b7.de* sacch spong fd4.de urt-u mrr1 wies k*

- **dropsical**: (↗*GENERALS - Dropsy - internal)* *Apis* apoc k2* ars k2 *Dig* **Graph** k* rhus-t
- **edematous**: **Apis** bg2
- **inflammatory**: ars b4.de* *Merc* b4.de*
- **painful**: *Ars* k* *Canth* plb rhus-t

○ - **Penis**: anac k* anil a1* apoc **Arn** k* *Ars* k* aspar k* bufo k* calc-p k* *Cann-s* k* *Canth* k* *Cinnb* k* cop k* cor-r k* cupr k* fl-ac graph hedy a1 iris *Kali-bi* *Kali-i* k* kola stb3• *Kreos* k* *Lac-c* *Led* k* *Merc* k* *Merc-c* k* *Mez* k* *Mill* k* nat-ar nat-c k* nat-p *Nat-s* ph-ac k* phos bg2 plb k* *Rhus-t* k* rhus-v k* sabin k* sel rsj9• *Sil* sol-ni spig bg2 sumb k* tarent k* thuj b4a.de* *Vesp*

- **bluish** red: arn ars con fkr8.de
- **edematous**: *Apis* *Apoc* arn ars k2 *Cann-s* *Canth* *Dig* *Fl-ac* *Graph* *Lyc* *Merc* *Nat-s* *Nit-ac* *Nux-v* puls *Rhod* **Rhus-t** k* sil sulph *Vesp*
- **hard**: arn merc nux-v ph-ac sabin spong
- **hot**: arn form kali-c puls
- **painful**: arn ars calad cann-s canth caps graph hedy a1* lact *Merc* nit-ac nux-v plb puls rhus-t sabin sulph thuj
- **painless**: mez ptk1

○ • **Dorsum**: sabin b7a.de*

- **Glans**: *Acon* bro1 antip bro1 *Apis* bro1 *Arg-n* bro1 arn bro1 *Ars* k* calad bro1 cann-s k* *Canth* k* *Cinnb* *Cop* bro1 *Cor-r* k* *Cub* bro1 dig bro1 dor gels bro1 ham bro1 iris *Kali-i* k* *Led* b7a.de *Merc* k* *Merc-c* bro1 *Nat-c* k* *Nit-ac* bro1 ph-ac bro1 plb **Rhus-t** k* sacch sars bro1 spig h1 sulph sumb thuj k*
  - **one** side: spig k*
  - **inflammatory**: *Sabin* b7a.de
- **Lymphatics**: lact *Merc* k*
- **Prepuce**: *Apis* **Calad** k* cann-s k* canth k* *Caps* carbn-s cham **Cinnb** k* *Cor-r* k* *Dig* *Fl-ac* form k* *Graph* k* *Jac-c* *Jac-g* lac-c *Lach* b7a.de **Merc** k* *Merc-i-f* *Merc-i-r* mez k* mill *Nat-c* k* *Nat-s* **Nit-ac** k* puls k2 **RHUS-T** k ● *Rhus-v* k* sabin k* sep sil k* spong fd4.de *Sulph* k* *Sumb* k* *Thuj* k* **Vesp** k* *Viol-t* k*
  - **coition**; after: calad b7.de*
  - **edematous**: *Apis* bg2 cann-xyz bg2 caps k2 fl-ac bg2 nit-ac bg2* puls bg2
  - **gonorrhea**, from: cann-i k2 fl-ac k2
  - **Frenum**, on: cann-s b7a.de canth b7a.de sabin k*

- **Scrotum**: anac k* anan anil a1* apis k* apoc *Arg-met* b7a.de *Arn* k* *Ars* k* asaf k* bar-m hr1 *Bell* bro1 brom k* calc *Canth* k* *Carb-v* k* carl k* caust *Chel* k* chin k* clem k* colch con bro1 cupr-ar k* glycyr-g cte1• *Graph* k* *Hell* b7a.de *Hep* b4a.de ign b7.de* jac-c k* jac-g kali-c b4a.de *Lach* b7a.de mez k* *Nat-m* k* nit-ac bro1 ourl jl2 ph-ac k* plb k* *Puls* k* rhus-d bro1 **Rhus-t** k* *Rhus-v* k* sacch samb b7a.de* *Sep* k* sol-ni stram k* syph *Vesp* k*
  - **edematous**: abrot bro1 ampe-tr bro1 anan **Apis** k* *Apoc* *Arg-met* **Ars** k* *Aur* bro1 bry bro1 calad k* *Calc* bro1 calc-f bg2* calc-p bro1 *Canth* k* chel bro1 chin bro1 *Colch* k* *Con* bro1 *Dig* k* dulc bro1 ferr hr1 ferr-s fl-ac bg2* **Graph** k* hell bro1 *Iod* bro1 *Kali-c* *Kali-i* bro1 *Lach* *Lyc* merc bro1 *Nat-m* *Nat-s* *Phos* *Puls* bro1 *Rhod* bro1 **Rhus-t** k* samb bro1 *Sel* bro1 sep bg2 *Sil* bro1 *Spong* bro1 squil bro1 sulph bro1 vip bg2 zinc
  - **gonorrhea**; with chronic: brom
  - **inflammatory**: (↗*Elephantiasis)* mim-h a1 ph-ac k* plb k* *Rhus-t*
  - **painless**: bar-m hr1 mez k*

○ • **Sides**: agar k* **Clem** k* mez k* puls k*
  - **left**: glycyr-g cte1•
    - **followed** by | **right**: glycyr-g cte1•
- **Skin**; thickening of: clem bg2 kali-bi bg2 rhus-t b7.de* sil bg2

Swelling: ...

- **Spermatic** cords: anth bro1 arn k* *Berb* k* *Calc* k* *Cann-s* bro1 cann-xyz bg2 cassia-s ccrh1• *Chin* k* coll bg2 coloc k* ham k* iod b4a.de *Kali-c* k* *Kali-i* k* nit-ac b4a.de* ph-ac k* *Phos* k* **Puls** k* *Sars* k* **Spong** k* tarent k* *Thuj* b4a.de
  - **right**: **Clem** puls k*
  - **left**: berb k* kali-br a1
  - **accompanied** by | **Inguinal** glands; complaints of: clem ptk1
  - **sexual** excitement; after: *Sars* k*
  - **walking** agg.: *Berb* k*
- **Testes**: *Acon* k* *Agn* k* alum k* alum-p k2 alum-sil k2 anan k* ant-t apis k* arg-met k2* arg-n k* *Arn* k* *Ars* k* *Ars-i* *Aur* k* aur-ar k2 aur-i k2 aur-m k* aur-m-n br1* aur-s k* *Bapt* k* bar-c k* *Bar-m* k* *Bell* k* borx bg2 *Brom* k* bry calc k* calc-f hr1 calc-i k2 *Calc-p* k* calc-sil k2 cann-xyz bg2 canth k* carb-an k* *Carb-v* hr1* carbn-s *Carl* k* chel *Chin* k* **Clem** k* coloc k* colocin a1 *Con* k* *Cop* k* cub k* *Dig* k* elaps *Graph* k* *Ham* k* **Hep** b4a.de hippoz k* hyos b7a.de ign mtf33 ind k* *Iod* k* jab hr1 jac-c a1 kali-ar kali-br k* *Kali-c* k* *Kali-i* k* *Kali-n* b4a.de kali-s kali-sil k2 *Lach* k* lyc k* m-ambo b7a.de m-aust b7.de* *Med* k* *Merc* k* *Merc-c* k* *Merc-i-r* k* merc-sul k* *Mez* k* mill k* nat-ar nat-c k* *Nat-m* nat-p *Nit-ac* k* *Nux-v* k* oci k* *Ol-an* k* ourl jl2 *Ph-ac* k* phos k2 phyt k* *Plb* k* *Psor* k* **Puls** k* **Rhod** k* rhus-t k* ruta b7.de* sabin hr1 sel b7.de *Sil* k* **Spong** k* stann bg2 staph k* stry k* sul-i k2 sulph k* tarax k* tarent k* tep k* thuj k* tus-p bro1 vario hr1* *Verat-v* bro1 vib k* *Zinc* k* zinc-p k2
  - **right**: apis arg-n k* **Aur** k* aur-s k2 benzol br1 chel k* **Clem** k* colocin a1 graph k* *Ham* hr1 iod *Merc* hr1 nit-ac h2* *Puls* k* **Rhod** k* sul-ac tarent k* tub jl2
  - **left**: alum brom k* *Clem* hr1 cop k* helo-s rwt2• mez nux-v hr1 oci ph-ac podo **Puls** k* *Rhod* k* sel bg2 *Spong* k* staph hr1 stry a1 vario hr1* vib k*
    - **hard**, painless: brom
  - **night**: clem mrr1
  - **gonorrhea**; from suppressed (See Inflammation - testes - gonorrhea)
  - **hard**: clem mrr1
  - **inflammatory**: *Nit-ac* b4a.de
  - **injuries**; after: **Arn** bg2 con bg2 *Puls* bg2 vario al2 zinc bg2
  - **mumps**, from: abrot k* ars *Carb-ac* *Carb-v* k* *Jab* k* *Merc* nat-m nux-v phos **PULS** k ● **Rhus-t** k ● staph
  - **painful**: clem mrr1 ourl jl2 tub jl2
    - **driving**; when: *Brom* vh
  - **shining**: *Merc* b4a.de
  - **thickening** of epididymis, with: carbn-s spong k* sulph k*
  - **unrequited** sexual passion: *Iod* k*

○ • **Epididymis**: m-ambo b7.de
  - **Lower** part: *Aur* b4a.de *Lyc* b4a.de
  - **Vesiculae** seminales: sulph bg2

TENSION: arn bg2 caust bg2 graph k* kali-c bg2 nat-m k* rhus-t k* sulph bg2

- **touched** by clothing, when: graph k*

○ - **Penis**: anac b4a.de ant-s-aur *Arn* b7.de* borx b4a.de calc-p calc-s graph k* kali-c b4.de* kali-i mosch mur-ac k* nat-c k* psor sabin b7.de*

○ • **Frenum**: chin b7a.de sabin b7.de*
  - **Glans**: calc b4a.de kali-c bg2 m-aust b7.de
  - **Prepuce**: *Merc* b4a.de
- **Scrotum**: arn k* *Clem* k* com k*
- **Spermatic** cords: cann-s k* chel k* *Clem* k* kali-n k* m-aust b7.de med ol-an ph-ac k* phos k* *Puls* k* *Sulph* k*
- **Testes**: aur k* aur-m a1 bry a1 bufo bg2 canth a1 chel a1 hipp a1 ip bg2 kali-c b4.de* kali-n k* mur-ac h2* nat-c bg* plb b7.de* *Puls* b7.de* sabin a1 sulph k* valer b7.de

THICKENING:

○ - **Penis** | **Prepuce**: elaps lach bg2* sulph k*
- **Scrotum**: calad a1 *Rhus-t* k* rhus-v a1 *Sulph*

○ • **Skin**: carb-v b4a.de **Clem** b4a.de *Hep* b4a.de *Lyc* b4a.de rhus-t b7a.de zinc b4a.de
- **Spermatic** cords: calad carb-v **Clem** k* rhus-r *Rhus-t* k* *Sulph* k*

▽ • **extending** to | **Abdomen**: kali-n
- **Testes**: sulph bg2

Male

THIN:
○ - **Scrotum**: pyrog ptk1
- **Skin** | **Scrotum**: lach bg2

THRILL:
- **intense**: androc srj1•
- **prolonged**: cann-i k* *Sel* hr1

TICKLING:
- **coition**; during | **withdrawal**; obliging: calc
○ - **Penis**:
○ • **Glans**: asc-c c1 bell h1* benz-ac k* franz a1 iod h* lyss a1 puls a1
• **Tip**: asc-c c1
- **Scrotum**: sel c1

TIED with a cord; sensation as if penis was: plb k*

TINGLING: (↗*Formication*) *Alum* k* ang mosch sel sulph [bell-p-sp dcm1]
○ - **Penis**: ant-t bell berb cop ferr ham iod laur nat-sil fd3.de• puls seneg sumb thuj
○ • **Glans**: acon ant-t bell calc caps b7.de* carb-ac carb-v iod kali-bi k* kali-n c1 lyc lyss merc mez ph-ac puls seneg spig sumb thuj
• **Prepuce**: jac-c jac-g merc ph-ac rhus-t a1 seneg tarax
• **Root**: rhus-t
- **Scrotum**: acon am k* com kali-n lachn k* plat ruta fd4.de sel
- **Testes**: agn carb-v euphr merc rhod sulph k* thuj zinc

TREMBLING: | **Penis** | **Glans**: rhod b4.de*
- **Scrotum**: spig b7.de*

TUBERCLES: *Hydrc* *Staph* hr1 *Thuj* k*
○ - **Penis**: bov thuj k*
○ • **Glans**: hippoz k* thuj a1
- **Scrotum**: con bro1 *Iod* bro1 sil bro1 sulph bro1 teucr bro1
- **Spermatic** cords: ambr *Graph* *Iod* *Kali-c* mang *Merc* *Nit-ac* ph-ac *Phos* plb **Puls** k* sars **Sil** k* **Spong** k* staph sulph thuj zinc
- **Testes**: ambr *Arg-met* bac-t c1* calc carb-v carbn-s caust graph hep hippoz hr1 **Iod** k* kali-c lyc *Merc* nat-m *Nit-ac* *Petr* *Ph-ac* phos plb psor **Puls** k* scroph-n br1 sep **Sil** k* **Spong** k* *Staph* sulph syc bka1• **Tub** k* *Zinc*

TUMOR:
○ - **Testes**: arg-met jl3* tarent mrr1
• **cysts**: *Apis* bro1 con bro1 *Graph* bro1 sep bro1 sulph bro1
• **indolent**: staph mrr1 tarent a1*

TWISTING sensation: | **Testes**: ip b7.de

TWITCHING:
- **burning** in seminal vesicles to glans penis: (↗*URETHRA - Twitching - burning*) *Mang* k*
○ - **Penis**: (↗*MIND - Gestures - tics*) aur k* bar-c *Calc* k* carl caust *Cinnb* graph k* lach lyc mez k* nat-m k* nit-ac k* rhod stann k* **Thuj** k* viol-t zinc k*
○ • **Glans**: chin b7.de* mez k* rhod b4a.de
• **Root**: zinc
- **Scrotum**: graph k*
- **Spermatic** cords: ang b7.de* graph b4a.de* *M-aust* b7.de* *Mang* k* plb b7.de*
- **Testes**: ambr b7.de* coloc b4a.de lyc k* meny k* sil k*

ULCERS: *Ars* k* bell-p sp1 chel b7.de* cupr-ar k* hep kali-bi bg2 *Lach* *Merc* k* *Merc-d* a1 merc-i-r bg2 nit-ac bg2* *Phyt* *Syph* br1 *Thuj* k*
- **burning**: **Ars** k* hep
- **cancer**-like: arg-n br1
- **crural**: arist-cl sp1
- **deep**: *Merc*
- **gangrenous**: *Merc-c*
- **spreading**: **Ars** k* **Merc-c** nit-ac k2
○ - **Groin**, from incised bubos *Carb-an* k* chel k*
- **Penis**: ail anan apis arg-n ars k* ars-h k* *Ars-i* ars-met aur aur-ar k2 aur-m aur-m-n bov b4.de* calc k* cann-s bro1 caust k* *Cinnb* k* cop bro1 *Cor-r* k* crot-t bro1 *Hep* k* *Kali-bi* k* kali-chl kali-m k2 lac-c lyc **Merc** k* **Merc-c** k* *Merc-i-f* mez bro1 nat-c *Nit-ac* k* *Nux-v* osm bro1 *Ph-ac* phyt psor k* sep bro1 **Thuj** k*
• **bleeding**: cor-r hep **Merc** k* *Nit-ac* *Staph* k*

Ulcers – Penis: ...
• **chancres**: (↗*GENERALS - Chancre*) apis arg-n k* ars k* ars-i k2 ars-met *Aur* k* aur-ar k2 **Aur-m** *Aur-m-n* aur-s k2 borx caust k* **Cinnb** k* *Con* *Cor-r* k* dulc bg2 graph bg2 *Hep* k* iod *Jac-c* bro1 *Kali-bi* k* kali-chl kali-i k* kali-m k2 *Lac-c* *Lach* k* lyc k* **Merc** k* **Merc-c** *Merc-i-f* merc-i-r merc-pr-r bro1 mygal **Nit-ac** k* *Ph-ac* k* *Phyt* rhus-t bg2 sars bg2 *Sep* bg2 sil k* *Staph* still *Sulph* k* syph al *Thuj* k* viol-t
⋮ **bleeding**: merc bro1
⋮ **burning**: ars k2 *Ars-met* hep k2
⋮ **elevated** margins: *Ars* *Cinnb* hr1 hep kali-bi **Lyc** *Merc* k* *Nit-ac* *Ph-ac*
⋮ **gangrenous**: ars bro1 lach bro1
⋮ **hard**: carb-an bro1 kali-i bro1 merc bro1 merc-i-f bro1 *Merc-i-r* bro1
⋮ **phagedenic**: **Ars** k* *Aur-m-n* caust k* *Cinnb* bro1 hydr bro1 kali-p *Lach* k* *Merc-c* k* *Nit-ac* k* sil bro1 sulph
⋮ **soft**: cor-r bro1 merc bro1 nit-ac bro1 thuj bro1
• **cheesy** base: hep kali-bi *Merc* h1*
• **deep**: aur-m-n *Kali-bi* *Kali-i* merc k* nit-ac *Sulph* k*
• **discharging** | **yellow** ichor: cor-r br1
• **elevated**: *Cinnb* *Hep* merc
⋮ **lead**-colored, sensitive edges: nit-ac k* *Sil*
• **flat**: aur-m *Cor-r* k* merc k2* *Nit-ac* thuj k*
⋮ **painful**: cor-r k*
• **hard**: aur **Cinnb** *Con* jug-r kali-bi k2 kali-chl **Merc** k* **Merc-c** **Merc-i-f** k* **Merc-i-r** k*
⋮ **Edges**: *Kali-i*
• **indolent**: ars k2 sep k* sil
• **indurated**: cinnb k2
• **inflamed**: cinnb k2
• **itching**: benz-ac lyc merc k* merc-i-f merc-i-r sep *Sulph* k* *Thuj* k*
• **lardaceous** base: arg-n cor-r *Hep* **Merc** k* *Staph* k*
• **mercurio**-syphilitic: aur **Hep** kali-chl *Lach* k* **Nit-ac** *Sil* *Staph* k* still *Sulph* k*
• **offensive**: ars k2 hep merc k* **Nit-ac**
• **painful**: *Cor-r* *Sil*
• **painless**: bapt merc-i-r k* nit-ac op syph al
• **ragged** edges: nit-ac
• **recurrent** (See GENERALS - History - penis)
• **red**: cor-r k* thuj k*
• **serpiginous**: **Ars**
• **sore**: *Merc* k* osm c2
• **splinters**; sticking pains as from: arg-n hep **Nit-ac** *Thuj*
• **swollen**: cinnb k2
○ • **Frenum**: agar bg2 naja bg2 nat-c bg2
⋮ **destroying**: *Nit-ac*
• **Glans**: apis ars k* *Ars-h* ars-i *Aur-m-n* benz-ac *Cinnb* k* cor-r k* kali-i *Lac-c* lyc **Merc** k* **Merc-c** **Nit-ac** k* *Psor* k* sep k* *Sulph* k* syph *Thuj* k*
⋮ **bleeding**: *Thuj* b4a.de
⋮ **superficial** round ulcers: ars-h br1
• **Prepuce**: ail arg-met *Arg-n* k* ars k* *Ars-h* k* ars-s-f k2 **Aur** k* **Aur-m** k* aur-m-n borx cann-s bro1 caust k* *Cinnb* cop bro1 *Cor-r* k* dulc bg2 graph bg2 *Hep* k* ign bro1 kali-bi **Merc** k* **Merc-c** k* merc-i-r *Nit-ac* k* nux-v bro1 ph-ac bg2* *Phos* k* phyt bro1 rhus-t bg2 sars bg2 *Sep* k* *Sil* bro1 staph *Sulph* k* *Thuj* k* viol-t
⋮ **chancres**: arg-n bg2 *Borx* hr1 cor-r bro1 *Hep* b4a.de *Jac-c* bro1 kali-bi bro1 *Merc* b4a.de* merc-pr-r bro1 *Nit-ac* bro1 thuj bro1
⋮ **superficial** round ulcers: ars-h br1
⋮ **Surface** of; under: cor-r br1 lyc nit-ac b4a.de*
• **Tip**: *Merc* k* *Merc-c* *Nit-ac*
- **Scrotum**: am-c aur *Aur-m* cupr-ar k* *Fl-ac* b4a.de *Kali-bi* *Kali-i* nit-ac sep
• **chancres**: (↗*GENERALS - Chancre*) aur-m k2 cor-r bro1 *Jac-c* bro1 kali-bi bro1 *Merc* bro1 merc-pr-r bro1 *Nit-ac* bro1 thuj bro1
○ • **Sides**: crot-t k*

UNDESCENDED testes (See Cryptorchism)

UNDEVELOPED testes in puny boys: aur ptk1

UNEASINESS: | **Spermatic** cords: apis b7a.de

UNREQUITED SEXUAL PASSION agg.: | **Testes**: mag-m ptk1

URINATION:
- **agg.**:
  - ○ · **Spermatic** cords: polyg-h ptk1
  - · **Testes**: polyg-h ptk1
- **amel.** | **Testes**: cob ptk1

VARICOCELE: acon bro1 aesc k* arist-cl mtf11 arn k* *Aur* k* bell k* *Calc* k* carb-v colch *Coll* k* crot-h k* ferr-p bg2* fl-ac k* *Ham* k* *Lach* k* *Lyc* k* *Merc-i-r* k* *Nux-v* k* osm k* pen c2 *Ph-ac* k* plb bro1 *Podo* k* *Puls* k* ruta k* sep k* *Sil* k* *Sulph* k* tab k*
- **accompanied** by | **constipation**; extreme: coll tl1
- **strain**; following a: ruta k*
- ○ - **Penis** | **Prepuce**: ham bro1* lach bro1*

VIBRATION; sensation of: sulph b4.de*
- ○ - **Testes**: plut-n srj7• sabad b7.de* sulph b4.de*

VOLUPTUOUS sensation: *(↗Pleasant)* ambr b7.de* ang b7.de* bov b4.de* euph bg2 euphr b7.de plat b4.de* stann b4.de*
- **scratching**; from: *Crot-t*

WALKING:
- **agg.** | **Testes**: zinc ptk1

WARMTH (See Heat)

WARTS (See Condylomata)

WEAKNESS: absin bro1 agn b7.de* alum bg2* amyg-p c2 *Anac* bro1 *Ant-c* b7a.de apis bg2 aq-mar skp7• arg-met bro1 *Arg-n* bro1 arn bg2* ars bro1 asc-t a1 aur bro1 *Aven* bro1 bar-c b4.de* bell a1 *Calad* bro1 *Calc* bro1 calc-p bg2* camph b7.de* camph-mbr bro1 cann-i bro1 canth bg2* carb-an bg2 carb-v bro1 carbn-s bro1 *Chin* bro1 chlor bro1 cimic bro1 *Cob* bro1 coca bro1 cocc bro1 con br1* cupr bro1 dam br1* dig bg2* *Digin* bro1 *Dios* bro1 ery-a bro1 *Ferr-br* bro1 form bro1 *Gels* bro1 *Gins* bro1 *Graph* bro1 hep b4a.de* hyper bro1 ign b7.de* iod bro1 iris bro1 kali-br a1* *Kali-c* bro1 *Kali-p* bro1 *Lup* bro1 lyc bg2* lyss a1* mang b4.de* *Med* bro1 mosch bro1 mur-ac b4.de* nat-m bg2* nit-ac bro1 *Nuph* bro1 *Nux-v* bro1 *Onos* bro1 op bg2 orch bro1 *Ph-ac* bro1 phos bg2* *Pic-ac* bro1 plb b7.de* plb-p bro1 sabal br1* *Sal-n* bro1 scut bro1 *Sel* br1* sep b4a.de* *Sil* bro1 *Staph* bro1 *Stry* bro1 sul-ac bro1 sulph b4.de* sumb bro1 thuj bro1 thymol br1* titan br1* trib br1* upa bro1 ust bro1 viol-t bro1 *Yohim* bro1 *Zinc-pic* bro1 zing br1
- **coition**; after: *Berb* k* cypra-eg sde6.de•
- **nervous**: dam br1
- **sensation** of: am b7.de canth a1 carb-an k* carb-v b4a.de lyc h2* lyss c1 mang b4a.de* mur-ac h2* *Nat-m* k* staph hr1
  - · **stool** agg.; after: *Calc* *Calc-p* k*
- **urination** agg.; after: calc-p bg2
  - · **emission**; as if he would have an: berb

WHIRLING sensation: | **Testes**: sabad b7.de*

WRINKLED: | **Scrotum**: rhod ptk1

GLANS; complaints of (See Penis - glans)

PENIS; complaints of: acon b2.de agar b2.de agn b2.de* *Alum* b2.de* am-c b2.de am-m b2.de ambr b2.de* anac b2.de ang b2.de ant-c b2.de* ant-t b2.de* **Arn** b2.de* ars b2.de* asaf b2.de asar b2.de aur b2.de bar-c b2.de bell b2.de borx b2.de bov b2.de* bry b2.de* calc b2.de* camph b2.de **Cann-s** b2.de* *Cann-xyz* ptk1 **Canth** b2.de* *Caps* b2.de* carb-an b2.de* *Carb-v* b2.de* caust b2.de* cham b2.de chel b2.de* chin b2.de* cic b2.de **Clem** b2.de* cocc b2.de coff b2.de colch b2.de* coloc b2.de *Con* b2.de* croc b2.de* cupr b2.de* cycl b2.de dig b2.de dros b2.de dulc b2.de* euph b2.de ferr b2.de *Graph* b2.de* guaj b2.de hell b2.de hep b2.de* ign b2.de* iod b2.de* ip b2.de* kali-c b2.de* kali-n b2.de kreos b2.de lach b2.de* laur b2.de led b2.de* *Lyc* b2.de* m-ambo b2.de m-aust b2.de mag-c b2.de mag-m b2.de mang b2.de **Merc** b2.de* mez b2.de* mosch b2.de mur-ac b2.de* nat-c b2.de* nat-m b2.de* *Nit-ac* b2.de* nux-m b2.de **Nux-v** b2.de* op b2.de par b2.de petr b2.de* ph-ac b2.de* *Phos* b2.de* plb b2.de* **Puls** b2.de* ran-s b2.de rhod b2.de rhus-t b2.de* ruta b2.de* sabad b2.de* sabin b2.de* samb b2.de sars b2.de* sec b2.de sel b2.de seneg b2.de **Sep** b2.de* sil b2.de* spig b2.de* spong b2.de squil b2.de stann b2.de *Staph* b2.de* stram b2.de **Sulph** b2.de* teucr b2.de* **Thuj** b2.de* verat b2.de viol-t b2.de* *Zinc* b2.de*

Penis; complaints of: ...
- ○ - **Glans**: acon b2.de alum b2.de* ambr b2.de ang b2.de ant-c b2.de ant-t b2.de am b2.de ars b2.de* asaf b2.de aur b2.de bell b2.de borx b2.de bry b2.de *Calad* b2.de* calc b2.de cann-s b2.de* canth b2.de* caps b2.de carb-v b2.de* caust b2.de* *Chin* b2.de* cinnb bg2 coff b2.de colch b2.de con b2.de cupr b2.de dig b2.de dros b2.de euph b2.de euphr b2.de graph b2.de hell b2.de hep b2.de ign b2.de iod b2.de ip b2.de kali-c b2.de* lach bg2 led b2.de* *Lyc* b2.de* m-aust b2.de mag-m b2.de mang b2.de **Merc** b2.de* *Mez* b2.de* nat-c b2.de* nat-m b2.de* **Nit-ac** b2.de* nux-v b2.de* petr b2.de* ph-ac b2.de* phos b2.de* *Prun* bg2 puls b2.de ran-s b2.de rhod b2.de* rhus-t b2.de* sabin b2.de* sars b2.de sel b2.de seneg b2.de *Sep* b2.de* sil b2.de* spig b2.de spong b2.de squil b2.de stann b2.de staph b2.de* sul-ac b2.de *Sulph* b2.de* tarax b2.de **Thuj** b2.de* valer b2.de viol-t b2.de zinc b2.de
- **Prepuce**: acon b2.de agar b2.de alum b2.de ang b2.de apis bg2* am b2.de ars b2.de* bell b2.de bry b2.de **Calad** b2.de* calc b2.de* camph b2.de *Cann-s* b2.de* canth b2.de carb-v b2.de caust b2.de* cham b2.de chin b2.de* cocc b2.de coloc b2.de con b2.de croc b2.de dig bg2 euph b2.de euphr b2.de fl-ac bg2 graph b2.de* hep b2.de* ign b2.de* kreos bg2 lach b2.de* lyc b2.de* m-ambo b2.de m-arct b2.de m-aust b2.de mang b2.de **Merc** b2.de* *Merc-c* bg2 mez b2.de* mur-ac b2.de nat-c b2.de* nat-m b2.de* *Nit-ac* b2.de* nux-v b2.de* **Ph-ac** b2.de* phos b2.de* plb b2.de puls b2.de* rhod b2.de* rhus-t b2.de* sabin b2.de* sars b2.de sep b2.de* sil b2.de* **Sulph** b2.de* tarax b2.de thuj b2.de* verat b2.de viol-t b2.de*

SCROTUM; complaints of: acon b2.de* agar b2.de* agn b2.de* alum b2.de* am-c b2.de* ambr b2.de* anac b2.de* ang b2.de* ant-c b2.de* ant-t b2.de* **Arn** b2.de* *Ars* b2.de* aur b2.de* bar-c b2.de* bell b2.de* calc b2.de* camph b2.de* cann-s b2.de* canth b2.de* caps b2.de* carb-an b2.de* carb-v b2.de* caust b2.de* cham b2.de* *Chin* b2.de* *Clem* b2.de* cocc b2.de* coff b2.de* con b2.de* *Crot-t* ptk1 dig b2.de* dulc b2.de* euph b2.de* *Graph* b2.de* hell b2.de* *Hep* b2.de* ign b2.de* iod b2.de* kali-c b2.de* lach b2.de* lyc b2.de* m-aust b2.de mag-m b2.de* meny b2.de* merc b2.de* mez b2.de* mur-ac b2.de* nat-c b2.de* *Nat-m* b2.de* nit-ac b2.de* nux-v b2.de* **Petr** b2.de* ph-ac b2.de* plat b2.de* plb b2.de* *Puls* b2.de* ran-s b2.de* rhod b2.de* **Rhus-t** b2.de* samb b2.de* sel b2.de* sep b2.de* *Sil* b2.de* spig b2.de* spong b2.de* staph b2.de* **Sulph** b2.de* teucr b2.de* **Thuj** b2.de* viol-t b2.de* zinc b2.de*
- ▽ - **extending** to | **Anus**: bell bg2

SPERMATIC CORDS; complaints of: agn b2.de alum b2.de am-c b2.de am-m b2.de* ambr b2.de ang b2.de ant-c b2.de* arn b2.de* bell b2.de berb ptk1 cann-s b2.de canth b2.de caps b2.de chin b2.de clem b2.de* colch b2.de graph b2.de ham ptk1 iod b2.de kali-c b2.de* kali-n b2.de m-ambo b2.de *M-aust* b2.de mang b2.de* meny b2.de merc b2.de nat-c b2.de nit-ac b2.de* nux-m b2.de nux-v b2.de* ph-ac b2.de* phos b2.de plb b2.de **Puls** b2.de* rhod b2.de* sabad b2.de sabin b2.de sil b2.de **Spong** b2.de* staph b2.de* sulph b2.de teucr b2.de thuj b2.de* verat b2.de zinc b2.de
- ▽ - **extending** to:
  - ○ · **Abdomen**: rhod ptk1
  - · **Thighs**: rhod ptk1

TESTES; complaints of: acon b2.de agar b2.de *Agn* b2.de* alum b2.de am-c b2.de* ambr b2.de ant-c b2.de ant-t b2.de arg-met b2.de* **Arn** b2.de* ars b2.de* asaf b2.de **Aur** b2.de* bar-c b2.de bell b2.de bism b2.de bry b2.de calc b2.de* camph b2.de cann-s b2.de canth b2.de caps b2.de carb-v b2.de* caust b2.de* chin b2.de* *Clem* b2.de* cocc b2.de* coff b2.de con b2.de* dig b2.de euph b2.de euphr b2.de graph b2.de* hep b2.de hyos b2.de ign b2.de* iod b2.de* ip b2.de kali-c b2.de* kali-n b2.de lyc b2.de* m-ambo b2.de m-arct b2.de m-aust b2.de mang b2.de meny b2.de **Merc** b2.de* mez b2.de nat-c b2.de* nat-m b2.de* **Nit-ac** b2.de* **Nux-v** b2.de* petr b2.de ph-ac b2.de* phos b2.de* plat b2.de plb b2.de* **Puls** b2.de* rhod b2.de* rhus-t b2.de* ruta b2.de sabad b2.de sabin b2.de sel b2.de sep b2.de* sil b2.de* spig b2.de* **Spong** b2.de* squil b2.de staph b2.de* sul-ac b2.de *Sulph* b2.de* tarax b2.de* teucr b2.de* thuj b2.de* valer b2.de verat b2.de zinc b2.de*
- **alternating** sides: berb ptk1 rhod ptk1
- **accompanied** by | **Urethra**; discharge from: agn bg2 **Aur** bg2 clem bg2 merc bg2 nit-ac bg2 **Puls** bg2 rhod bg2
- ▽ - **extending** to | **Anus**: rhod bg2

DAYTIME: borx bro1 cact bro1 carb-an bro1 *Caust* bro1 cycl bro1 *Lil-t* bro1 *Puls* bro1 *Sep* bro1

MORNING: | **daytime**; and: borx bro1 cact bro1 carb-an bro1 *Caust* bro1 cycl bro1 *Lil-t* bro1 *Puls* bro1 *Sep* bro1

ABORTION: *(↗Atony; Fetus - arrest; Metrorrhagia; Metrorrhagia - atony; Metrorrhagia - delivery - inertia; Metrorrhagia - pregnancy)* abrot a1 absin st1 acon k* *Alet* k* aloe a1* ambr k* anac hr1 ant-c k* **Apis** k* arg-n k* arist-cl sp1 *Arn* k* ars a1* art-v hr1* asaf k* *Asar* k* asc-c c1* aur-m hr1* *Bapt* kr1* **Bell** k* borx bg2 *Bry* k* buni-o jl *Calc* k* calc-f bro1 calc-s camph k* *Cann-i* kr1* *Cann-s* k* *Canth* k* caps b2.de* carb-an k* carb-v k* carbn-s a1* *Caul* k* *Caust* kr1* cedr k* **Cham** k* *Chin* k* chinin-s j5.de *Cimic* k* cina bg2 *Cinnm* gt1* *Cocc* k* coff hr1* *Coloc* b4a.de* con k* **Croc** k* crot-h k* cupr k* cycl k* dig hr1* dulc k* **Erig** k* *Eup-per* k2* *Eup-pur* kr1* *Ferr* k* *Ferr-i* ferr-p fil a1* **Gels** k* goss hr1* *Ham* k* *Helon* k* *Hep* hippoz k* **Hyos** k* *Ign* indg c1 iod k* **Ip** k* *Iris* *Kali-c* k* *Kali-m* kr1* kali-p kali-s kou a1* kreos k* lach bg2 lat-m bnm6• lip jl3 *Lyc* k* maesa-l jsx1.fr *Merc* k* merc-c b4a.de* *Mill* k* morb jl2 morph a1* murx c1* nat-c k* nit-ac k* **Nux-m** k* *Nux-v* k* *Op* b2.de* parth c1* *Phos* b2.de* phyt c1* *Pin-l* a1* *Plat* k* *Plb* k* podo **Puls** k* pyrog bro1* rad-br sze8• *Rat* kr1* *Rhus-t* k* rosm a1* rumx c1* ruta k* **Sabin** k* sang kr1 sars st **Sec** k* **Sep** k* *Sil* b2.de* *Stram* b2.de* sul-ac a1 sul-i st1 *Sulph* k* *Syph* kr1* tanac k* tarent k2 *Ter* st* ther c1 thlas bro1* thuj b4a.de* toxo-g jl2* *Tril-p* bg2* *Ust* k* *Verat* k* *Vib* k* vib-p c1* visc c1 wies c1 zinc k*

- **accompanied** by:
  - **anemia** (See GENERALS - Anemia - accompanied - abortion)
  - **chills**: cimic bro1
  - **hemorrhage** (See Metrorrhagia - abortion - during)
  - **joint** pain: caul mrr1
  - **perspiration**: kali-c bro1
  - **septicemia**: pyrog bro1
  - **spasms**: cann-s b7a.de* cham bg2 **Hyos** bg2* *Ip* bg2
  - **varicose** veins in genitalia (See Veins - accompanied - abortion)
  - **weakness**: caul bro1 kali-c bro1
  - ○ **Uterus**; swelling of: sec b7a.de
- **ailments** from (See GENERALS - Convalescence - abortion)
- **anger**; after: acon yl1 cham c1*
- **bad** news; after: *Bapt* gt1* *Gels* kr1
- **cold** agg.; becoming: acon sf1.de
- **cold** wet places; from exposure to: *Dulc*
- **convulsions** or unconsciousness; without tetanic: *Ip* b7a.de
- **cough** agg.: con lp *Kali-br* hr1* *Rumx* gt1*
- **damp**, cold places (See cold wet)
- **diarrhea**, with: erig vml3•
- **excitement** agg.: *Bapt* st cham sf1.de **Gels** k* *Helon* kr1 *Op* sf1.de
- **exertion** agg.: bry k2* **Erig** k* helon k* mill nit-ac *Rhus-t* k*
- **fatty** degeneration of placenta; from: phos bro1
- **fear**:
  - **death**; with fear of (See MIND - Fear - death - abortion)
  - **from**: acon k2 bell mtn *Cimic* kr1 kali-c mtn *Op* kr1 *Sabin* kr1
- **fever**; from asthenic: bapt vh1
- **fright**, from: *Acon* k* cham bro1 cimic hr1* *Gels* k* *Ign* *Op* k*
  - **last** months, in: *Op* st
- **grief**:
  - **from**: ign sf1.de
  - **suppressed** grief; from: ign nat-m
- **incomplete**: helon mrr1 sec mrr1
- **inertia** of uterus, from: alet **Bell** bg2 *Carb-v* *Caul* chin cimic ferr helon nux-v bg2 *Plat* bg2 puls sabin sec senec ust
- **influenza**; during: camph hr1* *Gels* sf1.de
- **injuries**; after: *Arn* k* cinnm bro1 ham bg* *Puls* bg2 *Rhus-t* ruta bg2*
- **labor** pains, from false: nux-m sf1.de
- **lead** poisoning; from: plb hr1*
- **leukorrhea**; with: calc bg2 ferr bg2 *Plb* kr1* *Sep* bg2 **Sulph** bg2
- **month**:
  - **early** months: alco a1* **Apis** k1* caul k2* sep mrr1 tanac a1 vib st*
  - **eighth** month: cann-i c1 *Puls* kr1*
  - **fifth** month: plb a1

Abortion – month – fifth month: ...

  - ⁝ **fifth** or sixth month: ars a1*
  - ⁝ **fifth** to seventh: kali-c vh plb st *Sep* k1*
  - **first** month: alco a1* **Apis** st *Asar* b7a.de *Ferr* b7a.de toxo-g jl2 vib st
  - **fourth** month: **Apis** a1* *Eup-pur* kr1
    - ⁝ **seventh** month; fourth to: sep ptk1
    - ⁝ **threatened**: caul hr1
  - **last** months: op k*
  - **repeating** same period: cedr kr1*
  - **second** month: agar-se a1* apis k* *Cimic* st* **Kali-c** k1* kali-n a1* plb a1* toxo-g jl2 vib ptk1*
    - ⁝ **eighth** week: *Spong* a1*
    - ⁝ **second** or third month: apis kr1 *Cimic* kr1* **Kali-c** kr1* *Sabin* kr1* *Sec* kr1* thuj kr1 tril-p kr1 vib bro1
    - ⁝ **sixth** week: *Ip* kr1* *Sang* vh *Spong* a1*
  - **seventh** month: *Ruta* bg2* sep k2*
    - ⁝ **fetus** dead: *Ruta* st
  - **sixth** month: crot-h j5.de *Lac-c* kr1*
  - **third** month: *Apis* b7a.de* bell k2* cimic *Croc* k1* *Eup-per* vh *Eup-pur* k1* *Kali-c* st* *Kreos* b7a.de* *Merc* *Nux-v* kr1* plb a1* *Sabin* k* *Sec* k* sel st sep k2* thuj k* toxo-g jl2 *Tril-p* kr1* *Ust* k*
    - ⁝ **end** of third month, on the: merc st
- **motion** agg.: sabin bro1
- **overheated**, from becoming: bry k2*
- **overlifting**; from: croc b7a.de
- **placenta** previa; from: *Nux-v* st *Sabin* st *Sep* st *Verat-v* st
- **plethoric** women; in: calc bg2 ferr bg2 lyc bg2 *Sabin* bg2 sulph bg2
- **reaching** up with the hands agg.: aur k2*
- **rectum** agg; tenesmus of: bell ptk1 calc ptk1 cocc ptk1 con ptk1 ip ptk1 lyc ptk1 merc ptk1 nux-v ptk1 rhus-t ptk1 sep ptk1 sulph ptk1
- **repeated**: alet ptk1 apis ptk1 bac ptk1 *Caul* ptk1 ferr ptk1 lyc ptk1 *Plb* ptk1 sil ptk1 *Syph* ptk1 thuj ptk1 toxo-g jl2
- **sequelae** of abortion (See GENERALS - Convalescence - abortion)
- **shock**; after: arn tl1 bapt bro1*
- **syphilis**; from: *Aur* kr1* kali-i bro1* *Merc* kr1* *Merc-c* bro1 *Nit-ac* kr1 phyt kr1 staph kr1 syph kr1 thuj kr1*
- **tendency** to abortion: *Alet* k1* *Apis* k* arg-n asaf k2 asar k* aur k* *Aur-m* kr1* bac bro1 *Bapt* k1* bufo *Calc* k* calc-s k2 cann-xyz bg2 carb-v k* *Caul* k* *Cimic* k* cocc bg2 *Eup-pur* kr1 ferr k* ferr-act sf1.de ferr-m sf1.de *Helon* k* hyos ign sf1.de **Kali-c** k1* kali-chl sf1.de kali-i bro1* kali-n sf1.de kali-perm sf1.de kreos k* *Lyc* bg2* merc bro1* merc-c bro1 mill kr1* nux-m k* nux-v j5.de phyt a1* **Plb** k* puls k* rat ptk1 rhus-t k2 ruta bg2* *Sabin* k* sars kr1* *Sec* j5.de* *Sep* k* sieg mg1.de sil k* sul-i k2 *Sulph* k* syph bro1 thlas mrr1 thuj sf1.de toxo-g mtf11 ust mtf11 vib k* *Vib-p* bro1 *Zinc* bg2*
  - **flabby** women; in: *Caul* kr1* *Sec* kr1 *Ust* kr1
    - ⁝ **feeble**, venous women; in: asaf k2
  - **hemorrhagia**, with tendency to: *Sulph* kr1*
  - **hysterical** women, disposed to faint; chilly: **Nux-m** kr1
  - **leukorrhea**; with: *Plb* kl*
  - **neuralgia**; with: *Sulph* vh
  - **sexual** excesses; after: cann-xyz ptk1
  - **tired** and nervous women, in: kali-p k2
  - **uterine** debility; from: *Caul* vh
  - **women**, who have had children; in: *Plat* kr1
- **threatening** abortion (See Abortion)
- **thunderstorm** agg.: cinnm st1 nat-c rhod
- **unconsciousness**, with: sec a1
  - **stiffness**; and: *Hyos* b7a.de
- **urination**; with constant desire for: canth kr1
- **vexation** agg.: *Acon* hr1* cham sf1.de
- **weakness**; from: *Alet* bro1 caul bro1* chin bro1 chinin-s bro1 *Helon* bro1 kali-c br1 merc ptk1* nit-ac k2 sec bro1 *Sep* sf1.de sil sf1.de*
- **weather** agg.; cold wet: *Dulc*
- ○ - **Ovaries**; from complaints of apis bro1

ABSCESS: *Hep* kali-p *Merc* *Nat-m* nit-ac *Sep* sil k2 *Sulph* tanac ptk2

Female

○ - **Labia**: *Apis* bro1 *Bell* bro1 borx bro1 *Hep* bro1 iod bro1 kreos bro1 lach bro1 *Merc* bro1 puls bro1 rhus-t bro1 sep bg2* *Sil* bro1 sulph bro1 tanac a1
- **Ovaries**: bell k* chin bro1 *Crot-h* k* *Hep* k* *Lach* k* *Merc* k* ph-ac bro1 plat k* psor k* *Pyrog* c2* *Sil* k*
  - **left**: *Lach*
- **Pudendum**: graph bg2 *Nit-ac* bg2 **Sep** bg2 *Thuj* bg2
- **Uterus** | **Os** uteri: ars bg2 bell bg2 chin bg2 cocc bg2 merc bg2 *Nit-ac* bg2 sep bg2 *Thuj* bg2
- **Vulva**: *Apis* bro1 *Bell* bro1 borx bro1 hep bro1* iod bro1 kreos bro1 lach bro1* merc bro1* *Puls* bro1* rhus-t bro1 *Sep* bro1* *Sil* bro1 sulph bro1 tanac ptk2

ADHESIONS: | **Clitoris**: kali-c gm1

AFTERPAINS (See Pain - afterpains)

AIR in vagina (See Flatus)

AMENORRHEA (See Menses - absent)

APHRODISIAC (See Sexual desire - diminished)

APHTHAE: *(↗GENERALS - Aphthae)* agar *Borx* k* *Carb-v* k* *Helon* k* iod *Kreos* k* *Merc* k* *Sul-ac* sulph thuj

○ - **Vagina**: alumn bro1 *Arg-n* bro1 carb-v bro1 caul k* *Graph* bro1 helon hr1* *Hydr* bro1 ign bro1 kreos bro1 lyc bro1 lyss bro1 merc bro1 nat-m bro1 *Nit-ac* bro1 rhus-t bro1 rob bro1 *Sep* bro1 thuj bro1

ASCARIDES (See Worms - pinworms)

ASCENDING agg.: | **Uterus**: plat ptk1

ATONY of uterus: *(↗Abortion; Metrorrhagia - atony; Metrorrhagia - delivery - inertia)* abies-c bro1 alet k* aloe bro1 alst bro1 alum c1* ambr k* bell-p c1* *Carb-v* k* *Caul* k* caust ptk1 *Chin* k* cimic k* *Ferr* ferr-i bro1 gels hr1* goss ptk1 *Helon* k* kali-c ptk1 lapa c1* lappa bro1 *Lil-t* bro1 nat-chl br1 op a1 pitu-gl br1 plb c1* psor **Puls** k* rhus-a c1* *Sabin* k* sec k* *Senec* sep bro1* sulph tril-p k* *Ust* k*
- **accompanied** by | **Liver**; complaints of the (See ABDOMEN - Liver - accompanied - uterus - atony)
- **delivery**; during: indgf-a jsx1.fr lysi-r jsx1.fr op a1* pitu-gl br1 plb c1 sec c1 vero-ab jsx1.fr
- **malaria**; with history of: chin bro1
- **menses** delayed from atony: *Thlas* kr1
- **metrorrhagia**; during: *Carb-v* hr1*
- **parturition**; during (See delivery)
- **pregnancy**; in: bell-p sp1

○ - **Ligaments**: nat-chl br1

ATROPHY: bufo bg2

○ - **Ovaries**: apis bar-c k2* *Bar-m* k* *Carbn-s* *Con* k* helon **Iod** k* orch bro1 ov bro1 plb x-ray br1
  - **enlargement**; after: iod mrr1
- **Uterus**: **Bar-c** mrr1 calen ptk1 caul tl1 iod bg2 plb bg2* ust ptk1
  - **delivery**; during: caul tl1
- **Vagina**: syph jl2

AURA (See GENERALS - Convulsions - epileptic - aura - uterus)

AVERSION to sex (See Coition - aversion; Sexual desire - wanting)

BALL:
- **right** ovary feels like a heavy: carb-an k*
- **sensation** of:
  - **rising** up: lach bg2 plb bg2

○ • **Uterus**: ust ptk1
  - ⁝ **hot** | **rising** up to throat: raph ptk1

BARTHOLIN'S Cysts (See Tumors - vagina - cysts)

BENDING: | **backward**:
- • **amel.** | **Ovaries**: lac-c ptk1
- **double** amel. | **Uterus**: cact ptk1 cimic ptk1 *Nux-v* ptk1

BIRTH (See Delivery)

BLEEDING from uterus:
- **menstrual** period; during (See Menses)
- **non**-menstrual bleeding (See Metrorrhagia)

BLOTCHES: staph

BUBBLING sensation: | **Clitoris**: | **air** in clitoris; as if: bros-gau mrc1
- **Vagina** | **air** or water in vagina; as from: lac-loxod-a hrn2•

CANCER of: carc mlr1•

○ - **Cervix** (See uterus - cervix)
- **Ovaries**: ars k* aur-m sne aur-m-n gm1* bov sne carb-an mrr1 *Con* k* graph k* kreos k* **Lach** k* **Lil-t** rmk1• phos rmk1• plat mrr1 psor k* *Puls* rmk1• *Sep* rmk1• *Thuj* rmk1• vib rmk1•
  - **right**: *Lil-t* rmk1•
  - **left**: *Lach* rmk1•
- **Uterus**: alum alum-sil k* alumn k* amor-r mtf11 anan apis *Arg-met* k* *Arg-n* **Ars** k* **Ars-i** k* asaf k2 aur k* aur-ar k2 aur-m-n k* aur-s k2 bar-c sne bell b4.de* benzq gm1 bomh gm1 bov bro1* brom k* bry b7.de* *Bufo* cadm-i gm1 cadm-met sne* cadm-o gm1 cadm-s gm1 *Calc* k* calc-ar k2* calc-f sne* calc-o-t bro1 calc-sil sne calen c2 calth c1* canth b7.de* *Carb-an* k* *Carb-v* k* carbn-s carc br1* cham b7a.de* chin k* cic cinnb sne clem k* cocc b7.de* **Con** k* *Crot-h* k* cund k* elaps equis-h c1* erod gm1 fuli br1* **Graph** k* helon sne **Hydr** k* *Iod* k* irid-met bro1 kali-ar *Kali-bi* bro1 kali-c c2 kali-p bro1 kali-s bro1 kali-t sne **Kreos** k* **Lach** k* *Lap-a* k* **Lil-t** rmk1• **Lyc** k* mag-c sne mag-m k* mag-p bro1 med bro1 menth-pu sne merc k* merc-c sne *Merc-i-f* k* methyl gm1 **Murx** k* *Nat-c* k* nat-cac bro1 *Nat-m* k* *Nit-ac* k* nux-v b7.de* ol-an gm1 paro-i mtf11 pers sne **Phos** k* *Phyt* k* plat k* plb-i sne psor al2 psoral vs *Puls* b7a.de* rheum b7.de* rhus-t k* sabad hr1 sabin k* sang k* sars ptk1 scir rmk1• scroph-n sne *Sec* k* sed-ac sne **Sep** k* **Sil** k* spig hr1 *Staph* k* sul-i k2 sulph k* syph sne tarent k* thiosin gm1 thlas c2* **Thuj** k* thymol sp1* tril-p bro1 vario sne xan sne *Zinc* k*
  - **accompanied** by:
    - ⁝ **discharge**; offensive: carc br1
    - ⁝ **hemorrhage**: *(↗Metrorrhagia - cancerous)* carc br1 fuli br1 med bro1 phos bro1 thlas bro1 ust bro1
    - ⁝ **pain**: carc br1
  - **epithelioma**: arg-met k2 **Hydr** sne
  - **growing** rapidly: cadm-met gm1
  - **precancerous** stage: moni rfm1•
  - **scirrhus**: *Alumn* k* anan *Arg-met* *Ars* k* aur aur-m-n k* clem hr1 **Con** k* kreos k* lyc mag-m phos *Phyt* rhus-t sep staph

○ • **Cervix**: arg-n sne ars-i sne **Aur-m-n** rmk1• bomh gm1 carb-an bro1 carc mlr1• **Hydr** sne iod bro1 kreos bro1* **Lach** rmk1• **Lil-t** rmk1• *Nat-m* sne phos rmk1• *Puls* rmk1• *Sep* rmk1• tarent ptk1 thuj bro1 thymol sp1*
  - ⁝ **offensive** odor; with: kreos tl1
  - ⁝ **painful**: goss ptk1
- **Vagina**: *Ars* bro1 calen ptk1 con bro1 **Kreos** k* nit-ac sne phos rmk1• plat mrr1 thuj bro1

CATARRH:

○ - **Uterus**: hydr br1
- **Vagina**: grin br1

CAULIFLOWER (See Condylomata - cauliflower; Excrescences - uterus - cervix - cauliflower)

CELIBACY (See GENERALS - Sexual desire - suppression - agg.)

CERVICITIS (See Inflammation - uterus - cervix)

CHEESY deposits: *Helon* k*

CHILDBED (See Delivery - after)

CHILDBIRTH (See Delivery)

CLUTCHING and relaxing sensation of uterus: agath-a nl2• sep k*

COITION:
- **after**:
  - **agg.** | **Ovaries**: apis ptk1 plat ptk1 staph ptk1 syph ptk1

- **agg.**: apis ptk1 *Arg-n* ptk1 ferr ptk1 ferr-p ptk1 hep ptk1 kreos ptk1 lyc ptk1 lyss ptk1 nat-m ptk1 puls ptk1 sep ptk1 sulph ptk1 tarent ptk1 thuj ptk1
- **aversion** to: *(↗Sexual desire - wanting)* aether a1 agar k* *Agn* k* alum alum-p k2 am-c k* *Ant-c* b7a.de arund bar-c b4a.de* bell b4a.de berb j5.de* borx st* bov cann-s k* carb-an carbn-s *Caust* k* chlor bg2 *Clem* k* coff conch fkr1.de cub dam gt1* falco-pe nl2• ferr b7a.de* *Ferr-m* kr1* ferr-ma ferr-p fl-ac franz a1 *Graph* k* hell *Hydr* kr1* ign k* *Kali-br* kali-c k* kali-n kali-p kali-s kreos mrr1 *Lach* *Lyc* b4.de* m-ambo b7.de* mag-c *Med* **Nat-m** k* nep mg1.de onos op ozone sde2• *Petr* k* ph-ac k2 *Phos* k* plat plb pneu jl2 podo k2 polyg-h kr1* positr nl2• *Psor* k* ran-s *Rhod* k* sabad b7.de* sabin b7.de* sal-fr sle1• **Sep** k* spirae a1 stann staph k* stram sul-ac k* sulph k* syph jl2 tarent teucr b7.de* ther thuj tritic-vg fd5.de
  - **anemic** women, in: *Nat-m* kr1
  - **clawing** and biting to avoid: falco-pe nl2•
  - **delivery**; since last: *Lyss* st
  - **grief**; after: nat-m mrr1
  - **leukorrhea**; with: caust kr1
  - **menopause**; during: *Con* st1
  - **menses**; after: arund a1 bart a1 berb *Caust* k* kali-c nat-m *Phos* k* sep sul-ac
  - **pregnancy** agg.; during: sep mrr1
  - **vaginitis**, in: *Cur* kr1*
- **enjoyment**:
  - **absent**: *(↗Insensibility; Vaginismus)* agn k2 alum alum-p k2* anac b4a.de* arg-met jl *Berb* k* *Brom* k* cael jl3 calad calc cann-i a1 cann-s **Caust** k* falco-pe nl2• *Ferr* k* *Ferr-m* k* *Graph* k* *Kali-br* k* *Lyc* st1 lyss *Med* *Nat-m* nep jl3* nit-ac sf1.de onos *Phos* k* plat k* pneu jl3 psor k2* puls rhodi a1 **Sep** k* *Sulph* st1 thala jl3 thiop jl3
  - **diminished**: bart a1 ferr-p k2* plat a1 sep a1 tarent a1
  - **increased**: agn bg2* ambr bg2* cann-s a1 falco-pe nl2• germ-met srj5• lach bg2* nat-m bg2* pycnop-sa mrz1 spong fd4.de stann bg* sulph bg2*
- **frequent**; too: calc tl1
- **interruptus**, ailments from coitus (See GENERALS - Coition - interrupted)
- **orgasm** (See Orgasm)
- **painful**: *(↗Pain - vagina - coition; Pain - vagina - coition - during)* alumn ange-s jl apis kr1* **Arg-n** k* bell k* *Berb* k* borx bg2* calc bg2* *Calc-p* coff cupr sst3• falco-pe nl2• *Ferr* k* *Ferr-m* *Ferr-p* ham *Hep* *Hydr* k1* ign *Kali-bi* *Kali-c* k* *Kreos* k* *Lyc* kr1* **Lyss** k* merc-c bg2 morg-p pte1*• **Nat-m** k* **Plat** bg2* *Rhus-t* *Sabin* k1* **Sep** k* sil *Staph* k* *Sulph* k* *Thuj* k*
  - **dryness**, from: ferr st *Nat-m* st* sep st
- **pleasure**; loss of (See enjoyment - absent)
- **refuses** the conjugal coition: con gl1.fr• lyc gl1.fr• sep gl1.fr•
- **relief**; without: canth mrr1
- **sensation** as from coition:
  - **midnight**, after: lyc a1
  - **coition**; after: lach a1
  - **sleeping** and waking, between: kreos j5.de*
- **voluptuous** sensation, like coition (See Tingling)

COLD: | **drinks** | **amel.**: kreos bro1
- **wet** | **agg.**: phyt bg2

COLD; AFTER TAKING A: **Acon** bg2 agar bg2 alum bg2 am-c bg2 anac bg2 *Ant-c* bg2 arn bg2 *Ars* bg2 aur bg2 bar-c bg2 **Bell** bg2 **Bry** bg2 *Calc* bg2 camph bg2 *Carb-v* bg2 caust bg2 **Cham** bg2 *Chin* bg2 cocc bg2 **Coff** bg2 *Coloc* bg2 *Con* bg2 croc bg2 cupr bg2 *Cycl* bg2 dig bg2 dros bg2 **Dulc** bg2 *Ferr-p* bg2 *Fl-ac* bg2 *Graph* bg2 *Hep* bg2 **Hyos** bg2 ign bg2 **Ip** bg2 *Kali-c* bg2 led bg2 *Lyc* bg2 mag-c bg2 *Mang* bg2 **Merc** bg2 nat-c bg2 *Nat-m* bg2 *Nit-ac* bg2 nux-m bg2 **Nux-v** bg2 op bg2 petr bg2 ph-ac bg2 **Phos** bg2 plat bg2 **Puls** bg2 ran-b bg2 **Rhus-t** bg2 ruta bg2 sabin bg2 *Samb* bg2 sars bg2 sel bg2 *Sep* bg2 **Sil** bg2 **Spig** bg2 stann bg2 staph bg2 stront-c bg2 sul-ac bg2 **Sulph** bg2 valer bg2 *Verat* bg2 *Verat-v* bg2

○ - **Uterus**: hyos ptk1

COLDNESS: anh sp1 carb-v k2 graph bg2 plat k* puls b7a.de sulph k2 *Verat* b7a.de
- **menses**; during: plat verat tl1
- **touch**; to: sep mtf33

Coldness: ...

○ - **Ovaries**:
  - **left** | **sensation** of coldness: ferr-i
- **Uterus**: petr k*
- **Vagina**: bor-ac bro1 *Graph* k* *Nat-m* k* *Sec* k*
  - **icy**: bor-ac ptk1

COMPLAINTS of female genitalia: acon b2.de* agar b2.de* agn b2.de* alum b2.de* am-c b2.de* am-m bg **Ambr** b2.de* ang bg ant-c b2.de* ant-t b2.de* apis ptk1 arn b2.de* ars b2.de* *Asaf* b2.de* *Aur* b2.de* aur-m-n br1 bac jl2 **Bell** b2.de* borx b2.de* bov b2.de* bry b2.de* **Calc** b2.de* camph b2.de* *Cann-s* b2.de* canth b2.de* **Caps** bg *Carb-an* b2.de* *Carb-v* b2.de* castor-eq br1 caul br1 caust b2.de* **Cham** b2.de* chel b2.de* chim br1 *Chin* b2.de* cic bg cimic bg* cina b2.de* clem bg* **Cocc** b2.de* coff b2.de* colch b2.de* coloc b2.de* *Con* b2.de* croc b2.de* cupr b2.de* cycl bg2* dig b2.de* dros b2.de* dulc b2.de* eucal br1 *Eupi* br1 *Ferr* b2.de* fl-ac bg *Graph* b2.de* gua br1 hedeo br1 hell bg hep b2.de* hyos b2.de* *Ign* b2.de* iod b2.de* ip b2.de* *Joan* br1 *Kali-c* b2.de* kali-n b2.de* **Kreos** b2.de* lach b2.de* lam br1 laur b2.de* led bg *Lil-t* ptk1 lyc b2.de* m-aust b2.de mag-c b2.de* mag-m b2.de* mag-s br1 mang bg *Merc* b2.de* merc-c bg mez b2.de* *Mosch* b2.de* mur-ac b2.de* *Murx* br1 nat-c b2.de* nat-m b2.de* *Nit-ac* b2.de* *Nux-m* b2.de* **Nux-v** b2.de* onos ptk1 op b2.de* perh jl3 petr b2.de* ph-ac b2.de* phos b2.de* **Plat** b2.de* plb b2.de* **Puls** b2.de* pulx br1 ran-b b2.de* ran-s b2.de* rheum b2.de* *Rhus-t* b2.de* ruta b2.de* sabad b2.de* **Sabin** b2.de* sal-n br1 sars b2.de* **Sec** b2.de* *Sel* bg senec br1* seneg bg **Sep** b2.de* sil b2.de* spig bg spong bg stann b2.de* staph b2.de* stram bg sul-ac b2.de* **Sulph** b2.de* thuj b2.de* thymol br1 til ptk1 tril-p ptk1 ust ptk1 *Valer* bg verat b2.de* vesp br1 *Vib* br1* viol-o bg vip bg visc ptk1 zinc b2.de* [bell-p-sp dcm1]
- **right** side: *Acon* fse1.de alum fse1.de *Am* fse1.de *Aur* fse1.de *Bism* fse1.de **Calc** fse1.de *Cann-s* fse1.de *Canth* fse1.de **Caust** fse1.de *Clem* fse1.de *Coff* fse1.de *Coloc* fse1.de *Con* fse1.de *Croc* fse1.de graph fse1.de **Hep** fse1.de *Iod* fse1.de *Lach* fse1.de *Lyc* fse1.de m-arct fse1.de *Meny* fse1.de *Merc* fse1.de mez fse1.de *Mur-ac* fse1.de nit-ac fse1.de **Nux-v** fse1.de petr fse1.de *Puls* fse1.de *Rhod* fse1.de *Sabin* fse1.de *Sec* fse1.de *Sel* fse1.de sil fse1.de *Spig* fse1.de **Spong** fse1.de *Staph* fse1.de **Sul-ac** fse1.de *Sulph* fse1.de tarax fse1.de teucr fse1.de *Valer* fse1.de **Verat** fse1.de *Zinc* fse1.de
- **left** side: *Agar* fse1.de alum fse1.de *Am-m* fse1.de ambr fse1.de *Ang* fse1.de *Ant-c* fse1.de *Arg-met* fse1.de *Aur* fse1.de *Bar-c* fse1.de *Bry* fse1.de calc fse1.de cann-s fse1.de *Chin* fse1.de clem fse1.de *Colch* fse1.de *Con* fse1.de *Euph* fse1.de graph fse1.de *Kali-c* fse1.de lyc fse1.de m-arct fse1.de *Mag-c* fse1.de meny fse1.de *Merc* fse1.de mez fse1.de *Nat-c* fse1.de *Nit-ac* fse1.de petr fse1.de *Ph-ac* fse1.de *Plb* fse1.de *Puls* fse1.de *Rhod* fse1.de *Rhus-t* fse1.de *Sabad* fse1.de sel fse1.de *Sep* fse1.de sil fse1.de spig fse1.de staph fse1.de tarax fse1.de teucr fse1.de **Thuj** fse1.de zinc fse1.de
- **accompanied** by:
  - **anemia** (See GENERALS - Anemia - accompanied - genital)
  - **gastrointestinal** complaints (See ABDOMEN - Gastrointestinal - accompanied - female)
  - **palpitations** (See CHEST - Palpitation - accompanied - female)
  - **vertigo**: con bg2 cycl bg2* lach bg2 lil-t bg2 puls bg2 stann bg2
  - ○ **Head**; complaints of (See HEAD - Complaints - accompanied - female)
  - **Lumbar** region; complaints of: kreos bg2 tril-p bg2
- **hormonal** complaints: *Sep* mrr1
- **menses** | **of**: aqui mtf11
- **nervous**: hedeo br1
- **operation**; of: glycyr-g cte1•
- ▽ - **extending** to:
  - ○ **Epigastrium**: iris bg2
  - **Hypochondrium** | **right**: lil-t bg2
  - **Liver**: bell bg2

○ - **External**: acon b2.de* agar b2.de* alum b2.de* am-c b2.de* *Ambr* b2.de* ant-t b2.de* ars b2.de* bell b2.de* borx b2.de* bry b2.de* *Calc* b2.de* canth b2.de* *Carb-v* b2.de* caust b2.de* cham b2.de* chin b2.de* cocc b2.de* coff b2.de* *Con* b2.de* croc b2.de* dulc b2.de* *Ferr* b2.de* graph b2.de* hep b2.de* hyos b2.de* *Kali-c* b2.de* *Kreos* b2.de* lyc b2.de* *Merc* b2.de* nat-c b2.de* nat-m b2.de* *Nit-ac* b2.de* nux-v b2.de* petr b2.de* plat b2.de* puls b2.de* rhus-t b2.de*

Female

- **External**: ...
sars b2.de* sec b2.de* **Sep** b2.de* sil b2.de* *Staph* b2.de* *Sulph* b2.de* thuj b2.de* verat b2.de* zinc b2.de*
- **Ovaries** (See Ovaries)
- **Uterus**: acon bg ant-c bg ant-t bg am bg* asaf bg aur bg **Bell** bg* bov bg bry bg bufo br1 calc bg camph bg *Carb-an* bg carb-v bg castm ptk1 *Caul* ptk1* caust bg **Cham** bg* chin bg *Cimic* br1* *Cocc* bg coff bg **Con** bg *Croc* bg cupr bg cycl br1 dros bg *Ferr* bg *Goss* br1 *Graph* bg *Hyos* bg *Ign* bg iod bg ip bg **Kali-c** bg* *Kreos* bg lach bg **Lil-t** bg* lyc bg mag-c bg* *Mag-m* bg* merc bg mosch bg mur-ac bg nat-c bg *Nat-m* bg nux-m bg **Nux-v** bg op bg pall ptk1* paraf br1 ph-ac bg phos bg **Plat** bg* **Puls** bg* *Rhus-t* bg ruta br1 sabad bg **Sabin** bg* **Sec** bg* **Sep** bg* stann bg stram bg sul-ac bg **Sulph** bg thuj bg ust ptk1 verat bg *Vib* ptk1* *Xan* mrr1 zinc bg
  - **accompanied** by:
    - **arthritis**; chronic: caul bro1 *Cimic* bro1 *Puls* bro1 sabin bro1
    - **congestion** (See GENERALS - Congestion - blood - accompanied - uterus)
    - **constipation** (See RECTUM - Constipation - accompanied - uterus)
    - **convulsions** (See GENERALS - Convulsions - accompanied - ovaries)
    - **epistaxis**: sabin mrr1
    - **urine**; bloody: diosm br1
    - **weakness**: helon mrr1 mag-c br1
    - **Back**; pain in: sabin mrr1
    - **Head**; complaints of (See HEAD - Complaints - accompanied - uterus)
    - **Hypochondria**; complaints of (See ABDOMEN - Hypochondria; complaints - accompanied - uterus)
    - **Lower** limbs; paralysis of (See EXTREMITIES - Paralysis - lower - accompanied - uterus)
    - **Spine**; pain in (See BACK - Pain - spine - accompanied - uterus)
  - **alternating** with | **Head**; pain in (See HEAD - Pain - alternating - abdomen - complaints)
  - **hysteria**; with (See MIND - Hysteria - uterus - complaints)
  - **suppression** of uterine diseases: thlas br1
  - **tubercular** patients; in: sep br1

CONCEPTION:
- **easy**: *Borx* b4a.de* calc b4a.de canth j5.de lyc b4a.de merc b4.de* nat-c bg2 nat-m bro1* *Sulph* b4a.de
- **impossible** (See Sterility)

CONDYLOMATA: *(↗Excrescences)* arg-n k2 *Calc* cinnb k2* euphr *Lyc* med lp* *Merc* **Nat-s** k* neon srj5• **Nit-ac** k* phos k2 *Sabin* k* sanic mrr1 *Sars* *Sep* mrr1 *Staph* k* syc bka1• **Thuj** k*
- **bleeding** easily: nit-ac mrr1
- **cauliflower**, like: graph bg2 kreos bg2 **Nit-ac** phos k2 thuj bg2
- **dry**: *Lyc* k*
- **itching**: euphr k* *Lyc* *Sabin* k*
  - **sore**, burning: sabin hr1
- **offensive**: sanic mrr1
- **pediculated**: *Lyc* k*
- **sensitive**: nit-ac mrr1 staph mrr1
- **soft**, red and fleshy: **Nat-s**
- O - **Uterus**: *Calc* k* *Calen* vh cub k* graph k* *Kreos* k* *Merc* k* *Nit-ac* k* sec k* tarent k* **Thuj** k*
  - O • **Cervix**: calen ptk1 graph mrr1 kali-ar pd med jl2 sec bg2 *Thuj* bg2
- **Vagina**: cypra-eg sde6.de• lyc bg2 *Nit-ac* *Phos* k* sel bg sep bg2 *Staph* tarent k* **Thuj** k*
  - **bleed** easily: *Phos*
- **Vulva**: aur-m bro1 med bro1* thuj bro1

CONFINEMENT (See Delivery - after)

CONGESTION: alet aloe bg2 ambr bamb-a stb2.de• bell k* bry k* *Chin* k* *Croc* k* fl-ac k* gamb k* *Hep* k* kali-c lac-c lach k* *Merc* k* nux-v k* *Phos* k* plat k* sabin k* sec k* sulph k* tarent k* yohim br1

Congestion: ...
- **accompanied** by | **subinvolution** (See Subinvolution - accompanied - congestion)
- O - **Ovaries**: acon k* aesc bro1 alet aloe bro1 am-br bro1 **Apis** k* arg-n bro1 bamb-a stb2.de• *Bell* k* *Bry* k* canth bro1 *Cimic* bro1 coloc bro1 con k* *Gels* bro1 ham k* *Hep* k* *Iod* k* *Kali-i* k* lac-c lach *Lil-t* k* meli *Merc* k* moni jl2 naja k* *Nat-m* bro1 pall plat podo k2 polyg-h puls rhus-t sabin sec k* *Sep* k* staph sulph *Syph* k* tarent bro1 *Thuj* ust k* *Vib* bro1 *Zinc*
  - **continence**, from: apis
  - **menses** | **before** | **agg.**: bamb-a stb2.de• lac-c k*
    - **suppressed** menses; from: *Apis*
  - **motion** agg.: lac-c
  - **painful**: *Morg* fmm1•
- **Uterus**: acon bro1 aloe k* anan arg-n k* arge-pl rwt5• aur bro1 **Bell** k* bell-p c1* borx hr1 cact k2 calc-i k2 caul k* cham k* *Chin* k* cimic bro1 *Coll* bro1 con k2 croc bro1 ferr k* *Frax* bro1 *Gels* k* *Hep* k* iod bro1 *Lac-c* k* **Lach** k* lil-t br1* mag-p bro1 mit bro1 moni jl2 murx k2* *Nat-c* k* nat-chl br1 nat-m k2 *Nux-v* k* **Puls** k* sabal bro1 sabin bro1 *Sec* k* senec k* **Sep** k* stroph-h bro1 sulph k* tarent bro1 ter k* *Verat-v* c2*
  - **accompanied** by:
    - **metrorrhagia**; profuse (See Metrorrhagia - profuse - accompanied - uterus)
    - **neuralgia**: sep bro1
    - **salivation**: sep bro1
    - **Head**; pain in: sep bro1
    - **Heart**; complaints of: cimic bro1 lil-t bro1
    - **Liver**; complaints of the (See ABDOMEN - Liver - accompanied - uterus - congestion)
    - **Teeth**; pain in: sep bro1
  - **chronic**: aesc bro1 *Aur* bro1 calc bro1 cimic bro1 *Coll* bro1 *Helon* bro1 lach bro1 *Polym* bro1 sep bro1 stann bro1 sulph bro1 *Ust* bro1
  - **hemorrhage**; after: *Chin*
  - **irritation** of bladder, with: mit c1*
  - **menses** | **before** | **agg.**: *Chin* **Lach**
    - **during** | **agg.**: acon k* alet **Bell** k* cact k2 caul cham *Chin* cimic bro1 coll bro1 gels bro1 **Lach** nux-v **Puls** k* *Sabin* bro1 sec senec *Sep* k* verat-v bro1
  - **sensation** of: *Caul* vh
  - O • **Cervix**: arg-met k2
  - **Ligaments**: nat-chl br1
- **Vagina** | **Bartholin's** glands: gonotox jl2

CONSCIOUS of the uterus: aesc k2 arge-pl rwt5• fic-m gya1 *Helon* k* lyc bro1 *Lyss* c1* *Med* bro1 *Murx* k* vib br1*
- **move**; feels uterus: **Helon** mrr1

CONSTRICTION of:
- O - **Ovaries**: cact
- **Uterus**: bell cact k* cham *Gels* k* ign kali-i murx mygal nux-v plat sec sep tarent
  - **band**; like a: cact sec
  - O • **Os** uteri: bell b4a.de*
- **Vagina**: **Cact** kreos plat *Puls*
  - **coition**; during: **Cact** vh
  - **introitus**: bell k2
  - **touch** agg.: **Cact**

CONTRACTIONS: *Cocc* b7.de* helo-s bnm14• ign b7.de* kreos bg2 *Lac-c* lob bg2 murx bg2 nux-v b7.de* puls b7.de* sabin b7.de* thuj k*
- **leukorrhea** agg.: chin b7.de
- O - **Uterus**: *Bell* k* cact k* *Calc-p* caul tl1 chinin-s cimic cocc k* hist sp1 ign lac-c murx nat-m nux-v pitu-p sp1 *Puls* k* sabin k* sep staph thuj visc c1
  - **hourglass**: **Bell** k* *Cham* *Cocc* con cupr hyos *Kali-c* nux-v *Plat* puls rhus-t *Sec* k* *Sep* sulph
  - **leukorrhea** agg.: ign b7.de*
  - **menses** | **before** | **agg.**: caul chin b7a.de cimic cocc b7.de* cur
    - **during** | **agg.**: art-v ptk2 *Bell* **Cact** *Puls* *Staph* k*

- **Uterus**: ...
  - O · **Os** uteri | **labor**; spasmodic contraction during: acon aml-ns **Bell** k* cact **Caul** k* *Cham* ptk1 **Cimic** k* con *Gels* ptk1 hyos lach lyc sec sep kr1 verat-v ptk1 vib xan
- **Vagina**: ham bg2* *Kreos* k* *Plb* bg2 *Sep* k*
  - · **accompanied** by | **leukorrhea**: aur-m-n bro1
  - · **rising** from sitting agg.: kreos k*

COTTON in vagina; as if: pulx ptk1*

CRACKS: carb-v graph *Nit-ac* k* urt-u
- O - **Labia**: v-a-b jl2

CRAWLING (See Formication)

CROSSING LEGS:
- **agg.**: iod bg2 nat-c bg2 sars bg2
- **amel.**: lil-t bg2* *Sep* bg2*

CURETTAGE agg.: | **Uterus**: kali-c ptk1 nit-ac ptk1 thlas ptk1

CYSTS: *Apis* bg2 aur bg2 carc mlr1• plac-s rly4• *Sabin* k*
- O - **Ovaries** (See Tumors - ovaries - cysts)
- **Vagina** (See Tumors - vagina - cysts)

DELIVERY:
- **after**; complaints: *(↗during; Lochia; Pain - afterpains; Placenta - retained)* acon b2.de* agn j5.de ant-c k* ant-t k* *Arn* k* asaf k* asar k* aur k* *Bamb-a* stb2.de• **Bell** k* borx b2.de* bov k* *Bry* b2.de* *Calc* b2.de* calc-f sp1 calen bro1 camph k* canth k* *Carb-an* k* carb-v k* caust k* **Cham** b2.de* chin k* cic bg2 cimic k* cina b2.de* cocc k* *Coff* k* colch k* coloc k* con k* *Croc* b2.de* cupr k* cycl bg2 dros k* dulc k* equis-h k1 *Ferr* k* gels k* glon k* graph k* helon k* hep k* *Hyos* k* ign k* iod k* *Ip* b2.de* *Kali-c* b2.de* kreos k* lach k* lyc k* mag-c k* mag-m k* merc k* mosch k* mur-ac k* nat-c k* nat-m k* nit-ac k* nux-m k* *Nux-v* k* op k* ph-ac k* phos k* *Plat* k* puls b2.de* rheum b2.de* rhod bg2 **Rhus-t** b2.de* ruta b2.de* sabad k* **Sabin** k* **Sec** b2.de* **Sep** b2.de* sil k* stann k* stram k* sul-ac k* *Sulph* k* thuj k* verat b2.de* verat-v k* zinc k* [aur-m stj2 aur-s stj2 bell-p-sp dcm1 cinnb stj2 irid-met stj2 merc-d stj2 plb stj2 plb-p stj2 thal-met stj2 tung-met stj2]
  - · **injuries** of parts: arn j5.de
  - · **instrumental** delivery: hyper ptk1 thlas ptk1
  - · **recovery**, slow: *Graph* kr1
  - · **retentio** secundinarum (See Placenta - retained)
  - O · **Ovaries**: lach ptk1
- **during**; complaints: *(↗after; Fetus - arrest; Fetus - position; Lochia; Os; Pain - afterpains; Pain - labor pains; Placenta)* *Acon* kr1* arist-cl c1* *Arn* hr1* *Aur* hr1* *Bell* b4a.de* borx kr1* calc hr1* calc-f c1* *Calen* c1* carb-v c1* **Caul** hr1* **Caust** hr1* **Cham** kr1* *Chin* c1* *Cic* j5.de* *Cimic* hr1* cocc c1 *Coff* b7a.de* *Coff-t* hr1* *Coll* c1* cupr c1 ferr c1 *Gels* hr1* goss hr1* graph c1 hyos j5.de* hyper c1 ign c1 ip bg2* *Kali-c* kr1* *Lyc* hr1* mag-m c1 mill c1* mosch c1 nat-c c1 nat-m c1* *Nux-m* c1 *Nux-v* b7a.de* *Op* c1 plat c1* **Puls** b7a.de* *Pyrog* c1* *Rhod* hr1* rhus-t c1 ruta c1 sabin c1* **Sec** hr1* sep hr1* stann c1 stram c1 sulph kr1* tritic-vg fd5.de verat hr1* vib hr1* visc tl1 [astat stj2 aur-m stj2 aur-s stj2 bar-br stj2 bar-i stj2 bar-met stj2 bism-sn stj2 cinnb stj2 hafn-met stj2 irid-met stj2 lanth-met stj2 merc stj2 merc-d stj2 merc-i-f stj2 osm-met stj2 plb stj2 plb-p stj2 polon-met stj2 rhen-met stj2 tant-met stj2 thal-met stj2 tung-met stj2]
  - · **delayed** delivery: kali-p br1
  - · **grief**; from: *Caust* hr1*
  - · **long**: *(↗Pain - labor pains - prolonged)* *Cupr-act* br1
    - ⁝ **painful**; and: *Arn* kr1
  - · **painless**, almost: goss kr1
  - · **premature**: nux-v a1
    - ⁝ **fear** or fright, from: *Op* kr1
  - · **rapid**, too: cham tl1 *Lyc* kr1
  - · **restlessness**; with: *Acon* kr1 *Camph* kr1 chlf kr1
  - · **rigidity** of muscles, with: *Bell* kr1 coff kr1
  - · **sadness**; with (See MIND - Sadness - delivery - during)
  - · **slow**: *Bell* kr1 *Caul* kr1* chlf kr1 chlol kr1 *Ign* kr1 **Nat-m** hr1* *Sec* kr1 tritic-vg fd5.de visc c1

DESIRE (See Sexual desire)

DEVELOPMENT of genitalia:
- **delayed**: calc-p k2* lyc k2*
  - O · **Uterus**: plb ptk1
- **infantile** (See Infantilism)

DIPHTHERITIC exudations: apis *Kali-bi* k* *Lac-c* merc-cy sep k*

DISCHARGE (See Leukorrhea; Lochia; Metrorrhagia; URETHRA - Discharge)

DISCOLORATION:
- **red**: ars k* aur-m k* *Bell* k* calc k* *Carb-v* k* dulc fd4.de *Helon* k* hydrc k* kali-bi *Lach* hr1 led merc *Sep* k* spong fd4.de *Sulph* k* til
  - O · **Vagina** reddened: rad-br c11
    - ⁝ **accompanied** by | **Uterus** sunken: berb
- O - **Uterus**:
  - O · **Cervix**: hydrc bro1 mit bro1
    - ⁝ **purple**: carb-an k2

DISPLACEMENT of uterus: abies-c c2* aesc k* alet bg2* *Am-m* k* anan hr1 *Aster* hr1 aur bg2 aur-m k* **Bell** k* **Calc** k* *Calc-p* k* carb-ac c2* *Caul* k* *Cimic* eup-pur hr1 eupi c1* ferr k* *Ferr-i* k* frax bro1* graph ptk1 helio c2* helo bg2 helon bro1* ign k2 kali-c k* **Lach** k* lappa bro1* led k* **Lil-t** k* lyss ptk1 *Mag-m* k* mel-c-s br1* *Merc* k* *Murx* k* **Nat-m** k* *Nit-ac* k* *Nux-m* k* *Nux-v* ovi-p c2 pall bro1 phos k2 *Plat* k* *Podo* k* *Puls* bro1 sabal c2* sec bro1 senec bg2* **Sep** k* stann bg2* sulph k* *Tarent* k2* *Thuj* k* tril-p c1 *Ust* vh
- **accompanied** by:
  - · **dysuria**: senec ptk1
  - · **respiration**; difficult: nit-ac ptk1
  - · **urine**; sediment of mucous in: senec ptk1
- **anteposition**: graph vh lil-t vh nux-m hr1 phos vh
- **defective** nutrition, with weakness; from: abies-c br1
- **dysuria**; with: senec c1
- **left**; to: sep ptk1
- **right**; to: murx ptk1 puls ptk1

DISTENDED; sensation as if:
- O - **Clitoris**: borx bg2*
- **Uterus** | **wind**; as if filled with: nux-m c1 ph-ac k*
- **Vagina**: sanic ptk1

DISTORTION:
- O - **Uterus** | **Cervix**: *Nat-c* b4a.de*

DROPSY (See Swollen - ovaries - dropsical; Swollen - uterus - dropsical)

DRYNESS: acon bg2 bacls-10 fmm1• bell b4.de* berb ptk1 chord-umb rly4• ferr-p bg2 lyc ptk1 *Nat-m* k* **Sep** k* suis-em rly4•
- O - **Vagina**: *Acon* k* apis bro1 *Ars* k* atp rly4• *Bell* k* *Berb* bros-gau mrc1 calc bro1 cent a1 cimic gk *Ferr* k* ferr-p bg2* foll oss• ger-i rly4• *Graph* k* helo-s rwt2• iod bg2 **Lyc** k ●* lycps-v lyss bro1 mez bg2 **NAT-M** k ●* nept-m lsd2.fr plut-n srj7• puls k* sacch sst1• sal-fr sle1• **Sep** k ●* spira k* tarent bg* thuj a1 vanil fd5.de vip fkr4.de zinc-chr ptk1
  - · **menses** | **after** | **agg.**: berb *Lyc* nat-m k* *Sep* k*
    - ⁝ **during** | **agg.**: *Graph*
  - · **uneasy** sensation; with: zinc-chr ptk1

DYSMENORRHEA (See Menses - painful)

DYSPAREUNIA (See Coition - enjoyment - absent; Coition - painful; Vaginismus)

ECLAMPSIA (See GENERALS - Convulsions - pregnancy)

EMOTIONS agg.: acon bg2 cimic bg2 gels bg2 hell bg2

ENDOMETRIOSIS: apis mrr1 lach mrr1 malatox mnt1.fr med mrc2 nux-v mrr1 puls mrr1 pyrog mrr1 sec mrr1 sep mrr1 thuj oss• *Xan* zr

ENJOYMENT (See Coition - enjoyment)

ENLARGED:
- O - **Ovaries**: *(↗Swollen - ovaries)* **Apis** arg-met k2 ars-i k2 aur-m-n k* **Bell** k* *Carb-an* k* **Con** k* *Graph* k* hep *Iod* kali-br k* lac-c k* lach k* lil-t *Lyc* k* *Med* k* meli spong k* tarent c2 *Ust* k*
  - · **right**: **Apis** *Bell* *Lach* hr1 **Lyc** *Mag-m* k* *Pall*

Female

- **Ovaries**: ...
  - **left**: *Apis* graph lac-c k* *Lil-t* *Med* k* ust hr1
  - **cold** agg.; every: *Graph*
  - **sensation** as if: arg-met arg-n cur med *Sep* *Sil* tritic-vg fd5.de
    - **right**: arg-n
    - **left**: arg-met tritic-vg fd5.de
    - **menses**; before: *Sil*
- **Uterus**: aesc k* *Am-m* k* apis arg-met k2 *Aur* k* *Aur-m* k* aur-m-n k2 *Bell* k* bell-p sp1 *Calc* hr1 calc-chln lp* calc-i ptk1 calen hr1* *Carb-an* k* **Con** k* frax br1 *Ham* hr1 helo bg2 helo-s rwt2• helon ptk1 *Hep* k* kali-br k* *Kali-i* k* lac-c hr1 *Lach* k* lyc ptk1 lyss k* mag-m bg2* merc-i-r bg1 *Murx* hr1 *Nat-c* k* *Nat-m* hr1 nux-v k* *Phyt* k* plat k* plb bg2* podo k2 sabin k* sec hr1 **Sep** k* sil lp* **Thuj** hr1 tub gk *Ust* k* visc c1
- **Vagina** | **sensation** as if: sanic ptk1
- **Vulva**: | **sensation** as if: sep tl1

EPILEPTIC aura (See GENERALS - Convulsions - epileptic - aura)

ERECT position amel.: bell bg2

EROSION of cervix: aln mtf11 ant-t mtf11 apis ptk2 arg-met ptk1 bell-p sp1 carb-an mtf11 eup-per ptk2 hydr ptk1* hydrc ptk2 kali-bi ptk1 murx mtf11 *Nat-m* sne phyt ptk1 psor sne sul-ac ptk1 thuj ptk1 vesp ptk2

- **bleeding** easily, with leukorrhea: *Aln* bro1 alum bro1 arg-n br1* dict bro1 *Hydr* bro1 hydrc bro1 *Kali-bi* bro1

ERUPTIONS: aeth k* agar alum k* *Anan* k* ang bg2* *Ant-t* k* *Apis* ars aur-ar k2 aur-m k* aur-m-n k* bry k* bufo k* calad *Calc* k* calc-sil k2 canth carb-v k* carbn-s caust k* *Coff* k* con k* cop k* crot-t k* dream-p sdj1• *Dulc* k* ferr k* *Graph* k* ham helon k* kali-c k* *Kali-i* k* kali-sil k2 kreos *Lil-t* k* *Lyc* *Merc* k* moni rfm1• morg-p fmm1• nat-c k2 nat-m k* nat-s k* nit-ac *Nux-v* k* **Petr** k* plac-s rly4• plat psor k2* rad-br mrr1 **Rhus-t** k* *Rhus-v* ribo rly4• rob k* sarr k* sars mrr1 *Sep* k* sil k* spong fd4.de staph suis-hep rly4• sulph k* *Thuj* k* urt-u mrr1 viol-t k* zinc

- **night**: *Merc*
- **burning**: ars k2
- **eczema**: borx br1 caust bg2 *Dulc* bg2 morg-p fmm1• petr bg2* rhus-t k2
- **erysipelatous**: **Rhus-t** k*
- **hard** black pustules (See pustules - black)
- **herpetic**: ars k2* borx mrr1 bufo carb-v caust cench *Dulc* k* *Graph* mrr1 kali-c kreos lyc mrr1* med mrr1 melal-alt gya4 merc musca-d szs1 nat-c k2* nat-m k* nat-sil fd3.de• nit-ac mrr1 nux-v **Petr** k* plac-s rly4• plat mrr1 puls zf *Rhus-t* mrr1 rob kr1* **Sep** k* sulph mrr1 syc bka1• thuj k*
  - **right**: *Lyc* mrr1
  - **cold**; after taking a: *Dulc*
  - **menses**; before: dulc mtf11
  - ○ **Thighs**; between: lyc mrr1 nat-c mrr1 **Petr** mrr1
- **itching**: ambr calc-sil k2 dream-p sdj1• graph k* lach *Nit-ac* nux-v k* petr k2 *Sep* k* sil suis-hep rly4• *Sulph* *Urt-u* [spect dfg1]
  - **warm**; when: aeth k*
- **leukorrhea** agg.: phos k2
- **menses** | **before** | **agg.**: aur-m *Dulc* verat
  - **during** | **agg.**: agar aur-m bry calc k* caust con k* *Dulc* k* *Graph* k* kali-c *Merc* k* nux-v petr *Sep* k* staph
- **moist**: petr k2 sep
- **nodosities**: merc
- **painful**: plac-s rly4• ribo rly4• sil viol-t
- **pimples**: aeth agar alum k* ambr ang bg2* ant-c ant-t bg2 aur-m *Calad* calc k* con k* dream-p sdj1• falco-pe nl2• *Graph* k* kali-c k* lach *Merc* k* nat-m k* nit-ac ozone sde2• ph-ac phos bg2 ribo rly4• *Sep* b4.de* sil spong fd4.de *Sulph* k* *Thuj* verat k* zinc
  - **burning**: alum k* calc kali-c h2*
    - **small**: cub c1
  - **menses** | **before** | **agg.**: aur-m verat
    - **during** | **agg.**: all-s ant-t gt1 caust con gt1 hep kali-c gt1* lyc merc gt1* nat-m gt1 petr
  - **painful**: ribo rly4• sil thuj
  - ○ **Nymphae**, on: graph
- **pustules**: *Anan* k* ant-t k* aur-m k* *Aur-m-n* hr1 bell-p sp1 bry k* carb-ac br1 dream-p sdj1• merc k* nat-s hr1 nit-ac
  - **black**: bry k*
  - **menses**; before: aur-m
  - ○ **Pudendum**: bry bg2
- **rash**: *Anan*
  - **children**:
    - **newborns**: | **extending** through perineum: *Med* vh*
- **scabby**: kali-i k* maland vh sars
- **syphilitic**: *Sil* hr1
- **tetters**: bufo bg2 dulc b4.de* *Petr* b4a.de *Sep* b4a.de *Sil* b4a.de
- **vesicles**: ars k2 crot-t mrr1 dulc fd4.de *Graph* k* lyc morg-p fmm1• nat-m k2 nat-s k* nit-ac br1 petr k2 **Rhus-t** *Sep* k* staph k* sulph k*
- ○ **Labia**: helo bg2 *Lac-c* hr1 sep bg2 [bell-p-sp dcm1]
  - **boils**: musca-d szs1 sal-al blc1• [bell-p-sp dcm1]
  - **eczema**: rhus-t bro1
  - **excoriating**: ambr bg2 sulph bg2
  - **herpetic**: ars bro1 crot-t bro1 dulc bg2* graph bg2 helo bg2 kreos bg2 merc bro1 nat-m bro1 rob bro1 sep bg2* spira bro1 thuj bro1 *Xero* bro1
  - **itching**: helo bg2 kali-bi bg2 kreos bg2 merc bg2 plat bg2 staph bg2
  - **painful**: [bell-p-sp dcm1]
  - **pimples** | **menses**; before: verat b7.de
  - **pustules**: bry bg2 *Carb-ac* bro1 graph bro1 kali-bi bg2 *Sep* bro1 *Sulph* bro1
  - **sensitive**: hep bg2 merc bg2 plat bg2 staph bg2 zinc bg2 [bell-p-sp dcm1]
  - **vesicles**: graph bg2 staph bg2 sulph bg2
- **Pudendum** | **eczema**: am-c bro1 ant-c bro1 ars bro1 canth bro1 *Crot-t* bro1 hep bro1 plb bro1 rhus-t bro1 sanic bro1 sep bro1
- **Thighs**; between: *Graph* mrr1 *Rhus-t* mrr1
  - **menses**; during: *Kali-c* b4.de
- **Vagina**; in:
  - **boils**: prot fmm1•
  - **eczema**; watery: arist-cl sp1
  - **lichen**: moni jl2
  - **oozing**: moni jl2
  - **pustules**: moni jl2
  - **vesicles**: moni jl2
- **Vulva**: morg-p fmm1• sep ptk1
  - **boils**: prot jl2
  - **eczema**: graph ptk1 rhus-t bro1
  - **herpetic**: nat-s ptk1
  - **oozing**: moni jl2

ERYSIPELAS: phos k2

- ○ **Labia**: *Apis* bro1
- **Vulva**: *Apis* bro1

EXCITABILITY of genitals: (*↗Sexual desire - increased*) foll jl3 phos a1 plut-n srj7• yohim br1*

- ○ **Clitoris**; erection of:
  - **menses**; during: kali-br kr1
  - **urination** agg.; after | **sexual** desire, with: calc-p kr1*

EXCITEMENT agg.: *Calc* bro1 *Sulph* bro1 tub bro1

EXCORIATION: agar k2 *Alum* am-c h2* *Ambr* k* ars k2 berb *Bov* *Calc* k* calc-s *Carb-v* k* carbn-s *Caust* k* *Con* bg2 fl-ac k2 *Graph* k* *Hep* k* hyos b7.de* *Kali-c* k* kali-s *Kreos* k* lac-c lil-t lyc k* mag-p bg2 meph k* *Merc* k* *Murx* mrr1 nat-c k* *Nat-m* bg2 *Nit-ac* k* *Petr* k* ph-ac h2* rhus-t b7.de* sabin sars mrr1 *Sep* k* sil k* staph bg2 sulph k* **Thuj** k* til

- **leukorrhea**, from (See Leukorrhea - acrid)
- **menses** | **before** | **agg.**: sep b4a.de
  - **during** | **agg.**: all-c *Am-c* bov carb-v *Caust* *Graph* hep *Kali-c* kreos k2 *Nat-m* b4a.de nat-s rhus-t k2 *Sars* sil k* *Sulph*
- **old** people; in: | **women**; old: merc
- **sensation** of: kreos bg2 nux-v bg2
- ○ **Perineum** (See RECTUM - Excoriation - perineum)
- **Uterus**: alum bg1 arg-n bg1 ferr-i bg2 helo bg2 kali-bi bg1 merc bg1 murx bg2 puls bg2
- **Vagina**: alum hydr k2 hyos bg2 *Kali-bi* k* kali-c mang-p rly4• merc nit-ac k2

- **Vagina**: ...
○ · **Around**: ign br1
- **Vulva**: | **urination** agg.; after: calc b4a.de *Hep* b4a.de

EXCRESCENCES: (*↗Condylomata*) arg-n k2 ars b4a.de calc k2 cinnb k2 crot-h cub falco-pe nl2• graph *Kreos* lac-c merc k* nat-s k2 **Nit-ac** k* phos k2 sabin k2 sec k* *Sep* mrr1 staph sulph b4a.de **Thuj** k*
- **bleeding**: calc k2
○ - **Uterus**:
○ · **Cervix**: cub *Kreos* k* merc **Nit-ac** sec tarent **Thuj** k*
: **bleeding**: merc thuj
: **cauliflower**: crot-h *Graph* kali-ar k* *Kreos* lac-c nat-s k2 *Phos* **Thuj**
: **wart**-shaped: sabin k2 *Thuj*
: **watery**: sec thuj

FETUS:
- **arrest** of development of the: (*↗Abortion; Delivery - during*) sec a1*
- **dead**:
· **expelled**: *Canth* j5.de* *Puls* kr1 ruta st
· **retained**: arist-cl sp1 mand sp1
- **motions**:
· **ceased**: *Caul* kr1
· **decrease** suddenly a lot: caul zr
· **excessive** movements (See violent)
· **fist** of a fetus, like the (See ABDOMEN - Movements - fist)
· **music**; with: carc pc*
· **nausea** and vomiting from the motions: (*↗STOMACH - Vomiting - fetus*) arn k*
· **painful**: arn con k2* croc kr1* op puls *Sep* kr1 **Sil** k*
· **rawness**; produce: sep tritic-vg fd5.de
· **sensation** of: nat-c ptk1 tarent ptk1
· **sleep**; disturbing: arn k2 con k* *Thuj* kr1
· **somersaults**; as if: *Lyc* kr1*
· **tympanitic** abdomen, with: psor
· **urinate**; cutting pain with pain in bladder and desire to: thuj
· **violent**: *Ars* kr1 croc kr1* *Lyc* k* med sys op k* psor k* *Sil* k* *Thuj* kr1* tritic-vg fd5.de
: **vomiting**; with (See STOMACH - Vomiting - fetus)
- **position**, abnormal: (*↗Delivery - during*) *Acon* kr1* cimic sne med sys **Puls** b7a.de* sep sne
· **breech** presentation: *Puls* k4
· **crosswise**, as if lying: *Arn* kr1*
- **room**; as if he had lack of: *Plb* kr1

FISTULA at vagina: *Asar* k* **Calc** k* *Carb-v* k* caust k* *Lach* k* *Lyc* k* *Nit-ac* k* *Puls* k* **Sil** k*

FLATUS from vagina: apis *Bell* k* **Brom** k* bry bro1 *Calc* k* carc vh* chin k* hyos k* *Lac-c* k* luna c2 **Lyc** k* *Mag-c* k* *Nat-c* *Nux-m* k* *Nux-v* k* orig k* **Ph-ac** k* *Phos* vh podo fd3.de• *Sang* k* *Sep* k* sulph k* tarent k*
- **afternoon** | **control**; loss of: sal-al blc1•
- **accompanied** by | **Abdomen**; distension of: sang ptk1
- **menses**; during: brom k* kreos nicc

FLUSHES OF HEAT (See GENERALS - Heat - flushes)

FOETUS (See Fetus)

FOREIGN BODY; sensation of a: plat b4a.de

FORMICATION: (*↗Tingling*) alum-sil k2 *Coff* b7a.de cypra-eg sde6.de• elaps *Plat* k* sec bro1 staph bg2*

FRIGIDITY (See Coition - aversion; Sexual desire - wanting; MIND - Amativeness - want - women)

FULLNESS: calc bg calc-p bg2 chin b7.de* puls b7a.de suis-em rly4•
- **sensation** of fullness during menses: fic-m gya1 *Puls* k*
○ - **Uterus**: aesc k2 alet k* aloe k* apis arge-pl rwt5• atp rly4• *Bell* k* *Caul* hr1 chin bg2 conv bg2 helo bg2 helon ptk1 spig bg2
· **standing** agg.: aloe

Fullness – Uterus: ...
· **walking** agg.: chin k* merc k2
- **Vagina**: ham k* irid-met srj5• lil-t k* suis-em rly4•

GANGRENE: ars *Sec* k*
○ - **Uterus**: apis *Ars* k* bell *Calen* hr1 carb-ac k* carb-an k* carb-v chin cur k* *Kreos* k* **Sec** k*
- **Vagina**: apis ars bell calc chin kreos lach sec k* sul-ac k*
· **accompanied** by | **measles**: ars bro1 kali-chl bro1 lach bro1

GESTATION (See Pregnancy)

GRANULATION: | **Uterus** | **Cervix**: *Arg-n* hr1
- **Vagina**: *Alum* alumn k2 *Nit-ac* staph k* tarent

HAIR falling out: (*↗SKIN - Hair - falling*) alum k2 bell b2.de* hell k* merc bro1 nat-c b2.de* **Nat-m** k* *Nit-ac* k* ph-ac a1* rhus-t k* *Sel* k* sulph thal-xyz srj8• tritic-vg fd5.de vanil fd5.de *Zinc* k*
- **delivery**; after: nat-m k2 ph-ac k2

HANDLING genitals (See Masturbation)

HARDNESS: *Con* k* **Kreos** k* *Merc* k*
○ - **Ovaries**: *Apis* arg-met k2 *Brom* graph lach staph k2 ust
· **right**: **Apis**
· **left**: arg-met k2 *Brom* *Graph* lach *Ust* k*
- **Uterus**: am-m apoc vh1 aur aur-m k2 calc-f sil

HEAT: acon bg2 am-c bg2 ambr bg2 **Apis** b7a.de* ars bg2 asaf bg2 aur k* aur-m k2 aur-s c1 bell bg2* bry bg2 **Calc** bg2 calc-p k* canth b7.de* carb-an bg2 carb-v k* caust bg2 cent a1 cham bg2 chin k* *Cimx* k* con bg2 *Dulc* k* ferr bg2 ham bg2 *Helon* k* hydrc k* hyos bg2 kali-br hr1* *Kali-c* bg2 kali-n bg2 *Kreos* k* lil-t k* **Lyc** bg2 m-aust b7.de merc k* merc-c k* nat-m bg2 nit-ac bg2 nux-v k* petr bg2 podo fd3.de• puls k* rhus-t bg2 ruta bg2 sabin bg2* sarr k* sec sep k* sil bg2 spig bg2 staph bg2 suis-em rly4• sul-ac bg2 **Sulph** bg2 *Thuj* bg2 tub c1 [bell-p-sp dcm1]
- **menses** | **after** | **agg.**: kali-br hr1
· **during** | **agg.**: chin kreos
- **voluptuous** sensation: olib-sac wmh1
○ - **Labia**: *Apis* b7a.de
- **Ovaries**: bufo lac-c med
- **Pudendum**: am-c bg2 ambr bg2 apis bg2 ars bg2 *Bell* bg2 **Calc** bg2 **Canth** bg2 carb-an bg2 carb-v bg2 caust bg2 cham bg2 chin bg2 con bg2 hyos bg2 kali-c bg2 kreos bg2 laur bg2 *Lyc* bg2 *Merc* bg2 mez bg2 nit-ac bg2 *Nux-v* bg2 petr bg2 phos bg2 plat bg2 **Puls** bg2 rhus-t bg2 *Sabin* bg2 sec bg2 **Sep** bg2 staph bg2 sul-ac bg2 **Sulph** bg2 *Thuj* bg2 zinc bg2
· **fire**; like: ter bg2
- **Uterus**: apis ars-met bell k* bufo camph k* cypra-eg sde6.de• lac-c k* *Lach* k* *Nux-v* k* raph k* sarr k* sec k* [bell-p-sp dcm1]
· **flushes**:
: **extending** to | **Head**: raph k*
· **menses**; during: lac-c k*
- **Vagina**: *Acon* k* ars-met aur k* aur-m k* *Bell* k* berb k* bond a1 borx bg2 carb-v bg2* cham bg2 coff k2 coloc k* ferr-p bg2* *Graph* k* ham k* helo bg2 hydr bg2 hydrc k* hyos bg2 iod bg2 kreos bg2 lyc bg2 lycps-v merc bg2 merc-c bg2* mez bg2 nat-m bg2 nit-ac bg2 plut-n srj7• psil ft1 rhus-t bg2 sec k* sep bg2 sulph bg2 tarent bg* thuj bg2
· **menses** | **before** | **agg.**: *Ign*
: **during** | **agg.**: aur

HEAT; FLUSHES OF (See GENERALS - Heat - flushes)

HEAVINESS: aloe bg2 alum k2 carb-v bg2 chin b7.de* lob k* murx k* *Nux-v* b7.de* pall k* *Plat* k*
- **menses**; during: lob murx *Plat* k* plut-n srj7• *Sep* k*
○ - **Ovaries**: **Apis** k* carb-an con k* eup-pur helon kali-c lil-t k* meli onos *Plat* k* *Sep* k*
· **right**: carb-an
· **left**: *Lac-c* *Lac-d* k* lach k*
- **Uterus**: *Alet* k* aloe k* alumn *Apis* atp rly4• aur-m k2 *Bell* k* *Calc* k* calc-p bg1* calc-sil k2 carb-v bg2 *Caul* k* **Chin** k* *Cimic* bg2* con k* elaps *Gels* k* helo bg2 helon ptk1 hydrc k* lac-c **Lil-t** bg2 *Murx* *Nux-v* k* ozone sde2• pall bg* *Pneu* jl2 *Puls* bg2* sabin senec k* **Sep** k* sil tril-p c1 tub k2
· **accompanied** by | **leukorrhea**: cimic ptk1

Female

- **Uterus**: ...
  - **hysteria**; after: elaps ptk1
  - **menses**; during: chin nux-v
  - **standing** agg.: aloe
  - **walking** agg.: *Chin* k*

▽ • **extending** to | **Inguinal** region: ozone sde2•
- **Vagina**: murx bg2* sil hr1
  - **hysteria**; in: elaps ptk1
- **Vulva**: psil ft1

HEMATOCELE: | **Pelvis**: acon bro1 apis bro1 *Arn* bro1 ars bro1 bell bro1 canth bro1 chin bro1 coloc bro1 dig bro1 *Ferr* bro1 *Ham* bro1 ip bro1 *Kali-i* bro1 lach bro1 *Merc* bro1 mill bro1 nit-ac bro1 phos bro1 sabin bro1 *Sec* bro1 *Sulph* bro1 ter bro1 thlas bro1

HEMORRHAGE (See Metrorrhagia)

HYDROMETRA (See Swollen - uterus - dropsical)

HYDROSALPINGITIS (See Inflammation - oviduct)

HYDROSALPINX: *(↗Inflammation - oviduct - hydrosalpingitis)* sil k2

INDURATION: aml-ns ars bg2 *Aur* bg2 **Bell** bg2 **Carb-an** bg2 *Chin* b7.de* clem bg2 cocc bg2 *Con* k* ferr b7a.de* iod bg2 **Kreos** k* lach bg2 *Mag-m* bg2 *Merc* k* phos bg2 plat bg2 puls bg2 rhus-t bg2 sabin bg2 sars bg2 sec bg2 sep k* sil k2 *Staph* bg2 thuj bg2
- **injuries**; after: *Con* k*

○ - **Ovaries**: alum alumn am-br *Apis* k* *Arg-met* ars k* *Ars-i* *Aur* k* aur-i k2 aur-m-n k* *Bar-i* *Bar-m* k* bell k* *Brom* k* carb-an k* **Con** k* **Graph** k* iod k* kreos **Lach** k* *Pall* k* plat k* *Psor* k* sabal bro1 *Sep* k* spong k* staph k2 tarent *Thuj* bro1 ust k* zinc
  - **right**: *Apis* *Carb-an* *Pall* k* *Podo*
  - **left**: arg-met k2 *Brom* *Graph* k* **Lach** k* psor ust
- **Uterus**: aesc tl1 *Alum* k* *Alumn* k* **Aur** k* aur-i k2 *Aur-m* k* aur-m-k c2 aur-m-n hr1* *Bell* k* *Calen* hr1 *Carb-an* k* cham k* *Chin* *Con* k* helon *Iod* k* *Kali-br* k* lyss mag-m a2* pall *Plat* k* sep syph k2 tarent k*
  - **abortions**; after recurrent: aur ptk1
  - **accompanied** by:
    - ⋮ **Tongue** | **mucus** on tongue; collection of: *Carb-an* kr1*

○ • **Cervix**: alumn k* anan arg-met k2 **Aur** k* aur-i k2 *Aur-m* k* *Aur-m-n* k* *Bell* *Carb-ac* k* **Carb-an** k* chin **Con** k* helon bro1 hydr k* *Iod* k* *Kali-cy* bro1 kalm bro1 *Kreos* k* lac-c k* *Mag-m* k* *Nat-c* k* *Plat* k* **Sep** k* *Sil* k* staph syph k2* tarent k* verat k*
    - ⋮ **cancerous**: aur ptk1 carb-an ptk1 con ptk1 nat-c ptk1 sep ptk1
    - ⋮ **pessary**; after use of: hyper
  - **Os**: *Aur* k* *Carb-an* hydr k* *Lil-t* hr1 mag-m hr1 nux-v k* plat k* *Podo* k* *Ust* k*
- **Vagina**: bell calc *Chin* k* clem con *Ferr* k* *Lyc* k* mag-m merc petr *Puls* k* sep *Sil* sulph
  - **painful**: chin ptk1

INERTIA of uterus (See Atony)

INFANTILISM; genital: *(↗Sterility)* bar-c sf1.de* calc-hp sf1.de calc-p sf1.de chim sf1.de con sf1.de ferr sf1.de helon sf1.de iod sf1.de *Ov* sf1.de phos sf1.de senec sf1.de

INFERTILITY (See Sterility)

INFLAMMATION: *Acon* k* ambr anan *Apis* *Arn* b7a.de **Ars** k* *Asaf* k* aur-m k2 *Bell* k* borx c1 bry k* *Calc* k* calc-s k2 cann-s b7.de* canth k2 carb-v *Coc-c* k* coll k* con ferr k* ferr-ar *Ferr-p* k* ign k* *Kali-c* k* **Kreos** k* *Lyc* k* med c1 **Merc** k* *Merc-c* k* *Nat-m* nat-s k* *Nit-ac* k* nux-v *Petr* k* podo bg2 prot fmm1• **Rhus-t** k* *Sec* b7.de* *Sep* k* spong fd4.de staph k* sulph k* syc fmm1• tarent *Thuj*
- **erysipelatous**: *Apis* **Rhus-t**
- **menses**; during: acon bell calc merc nit-ac nux-v sep sulph
- **urine**, from: canth k2

Inflammation: ...

○ - **Cervix** (See uterus - cervix)
- **Genitourinary** (See BLADDER - Inflammation - accompanied - female)
- **Labia**: acon b7a.de *Apis* c2 ars bro1 canth tl1 *Coc-c* c2 crot-t bro1 *Dulc* bro1 merc bro1 nat-m bro1 nux-v b7a.de rob bro1 *Sep* bro1 spira bro1 spong fd4.de sulph h2* thuj bro1 *Xero* bro1
- **Ovaries** (= ovaritis/oophoritis): **Acon** k* aesc am-br k* ambr k* *Ant-c* k* **Apis** k* arg-met arg-n k2 arn ars k* ars-i k* aur k* aur-ar k2 aur-i k2 aur-m k2 **Bell** k* berb mtf11 brom k* *Bry* k* *Cact* k* *Canth* k* caps castm c2 *Chin* k* cimic k* cod hr1* coli mtf11 coloc k* *Con* k* crot-h k* cub k* dulc k* euph k* ferr-p bro1 gels k2 graph k* *Guaj* k* ham k* hep ign k* *Iod* k* *Lac-c* k* *Lach* k* *Lil-t* k* **Lyc** k* mag-p *Med* **Merc** k* *Merc-c* bro1 moni mtf11 nat-ox-act mtf11 nit-ac k* *Nux-v* k* *Pall* k* *Ph-ac* k* **Phos** k* *Phyt* k* *Plat* k* **Podo** k* *Puls* k* pyrog st rhus-t k* sabad k* **Sabin** k* sec k2 staph k* *Syph* k* *Thuj* k* ust k* *Verat-v* k* visc c2* zinc zinc-p k2
  - **alternating** sides: lac-c k2
  - **right**: aesc *Apis* *Arg-met* *Bell* k* *Bry* iod lac-c hr1 **Lyc** k* *Pall* **Podo** k*
  - **left**: arg-met caps graph k* *Ham* hr1 *Lach* k* lil-t k* med mtf11 *Thuj* k* vesp zinc
  - **abortion**; after: sabin c1*
  - **accompanied** by:
    - ⋮ **Bladder** irritation: canth br1
    - ⋮ **Peritoneum**; complaints of: *Acon* bro1 apis bro1 ars bro1 *Bell* bro1 bry bro1 canth bro1 chin bro1 chinin-s bro1 coloc bro1 *Hep* bro1 *Merc-c* bro1 sil bro1
    - ⋮ **Tongue** | **mucus**; white: *Ham* kr1*
  - **chronic**: *Con* bro1 graph bro1 *Iod* bro1 lach bro1 pall br1* plat bro1 sabal bro1 sep bro1 *Thuj* bro1
  - **discharge**; after suppressed: canth mrr1
  - **fear**; from: acon k2
  - **gonorrhea**; after suppressed: *(↗URETHRA - Discharge - gonorrheal)* *Canth* **Med**
  - **hemorrhage**; after: *Chin* *Plat*
  - **menstrual** flow; from a suddenly suppressed: **Acon** k* cimic bro1 *Puls*
  - **sexual** excesses; after: *Chin* *Ham* *Plat* *Staph*
  - **wet** feet; after: *Puls*
- **Oviduct** (= salpingitis): acon bro1 apis bro1* ars bro1* bac jl2 bry bro1 canth bro1 chinin-s bro1 coli jl2* coll ptk1 *Coloc* bro1 eupi bro1 gonotox jl2 hep bro1 lach ptk1 med jl2 merc ptk1 *Merc-c* bro1 prot jl2 *Puls* ptk1 sabal bro1 *Sep* ptk1 sil ptk1 staph ptk1
  - **chronic**: tub-r jl2*
  - **hydrosalpingitis**: *(↗Hydrosalpinx)* gels c2
- **Pelvis** | **cellulitis**: acon bro1 *Apis* bro1 ars bro1 bell bro1 *Bry* bro1 calc bro1 canth bro1 *Cimic* bro1 hep bro1 med bro1 merc bro1 *Merc-i-r* bro1 pyrog bro1 *Rhus-t* bro1 sil bro1 ter bro1 til bro1 *Verat-v* bro1
- **Uterus** (= metritis): *Acon* k* *Agn* k* alum k* ant-c bg2 anti-i bro1 **Apis** k* arg-n k2 *Arn* k* **Ars** k* *Aur* aur-ar k2 aur-i k2* *Aur-m* k* aur-m-n vml3• aur-s k2 **Bell** k* berb mtf11 *Bry* k* bufo *Cact* k* calc k* calen c2 **Canth** k* *Carb-an* k* carbn-s castm c2 caul k* *Cham* k* chin k* *Cimic* bro1 coc-c k2 cocc k* *Coff* k* coli jl2 coloc k* con k* croc k* ferr k* ferr-ar gels k2* gonotox jl2 graph k* *Ham* k* *Hep* k* hydr k* *Hyos* k* hyper k* ign k* inul br1 *Iod* k* ip k* iris kali-c k* kali-i bro1 kali-p kreos k* **Lac-c** k* **Lach** k* lil-t bro1 **Lyc** k* *Lyss* mag-m k* med al* *Mel-c-s* bro1 *Merc* k* *Merc-c* bro1 mosch bg2 murx lp nat-m bg2* *Nux-v* k* op k* ph-ac k* *Phos* k* plat bg2* prot jl2 psor jl2* **Puls** k* pyrog k2 *Rhus-t* k* *Sabad* k* **Sabin** k* **Sec** k* *Sep* k* *Sil* k* *Stram* k* sul-i k2 *Sulph* k* **Ter** k* thuj lp til c2* tub mtf11 *Verat* k* *Verat-v* k* vib ptk1 visc a1* zinc bg2 [calc-br stj1]
  - **abortion**; after: sabin c1*
  - **accompanied** by | **congestion**: aloe bro1 bell bro1 *Coll* bro1 lil-t bro1 mag-m bro1 murx bro1 *Sabin* bro1 *Sep* bro1
  - **anger**; after: *Cham* k*
  - **cellulitis**: acon bro1 *Bell* bro1 canth bro1 coloc bro1 hep bro1 *Merc-c* bro1 sil bro1
  - **chronic**: alet bro1 aloe bro1 *Ars* bro1 *Aur* bro1 aur-m-n bro1* borx bro1 *Calc* bro1 *Carb-ac* bro1 caul bro1 chinin-ar bro1 *Cimic* bro1 *Con* bro1 graph bro1 *Helon* bro1 *Hydr* bro1 hydrc bro1 inul bro1 *Iod* bro1 *Kali-bi* bro1 kali-c bro1 kali-s bro1 kreos bro1 lach bro1 *Mag-m* bro1 mel-c-s br1*

- **Uterus – chronic**: ...
merc bro1 *Murx* bro1 nat-m bro1 nit-ac bro1 *Nux-v* bro1 *Ph-ac* bro1 phos bro1 plb bro1 *Puls* bro1 rhus-t bro1 *Sabin* bro1 *Sec* bro1 *Sep* bro1 sil bro1 stram bro1 *Sulph* bro1 tub jl2 tub-r jl2
  - **delivery**; after: bell bro1 *Canth* bro1 *Cham* hr1 lach bro1 *Nux-v* k* oci-sa sp1 *Sabin* k* *Sec* til c1*
  - **emotional** excitement, from: *Hyos* k* *Ph-ac* hr1
  - **endometritis**: bell mtf11 flav jl2
  - **fear**; from: acon k2
  - **follicular**: *Hydr* bro1 hydrc bro1 iod bro1 merc bro1
  - **hemorrhage**; after: ars bro1 *Chin* ham bro1 led bro1 mill k2 phos bro1 *Sec* bro1 *Thlas* bro1
  - **incipient**: mel-c-s br1
  - **indignation**; from: *Coloc* k*
  - **joy**, excessive: *Coff* k*
  - **menses**; during: phos k2
  - **perimetritis**: acon bro1 *Bell* bro1 canth bro1 coloc bro1 hep bro1 *Merc-c* bro1 sil bro1
  - **pregnancy** agg.; during: phos k2
  - **pyometra**: lach ptk1 merc ptk1 *Puls* ptk1 *Sep* ptk1
  - **sexual** excesses; after: *Chin* k*

○ · **Cervix** (= cervicitis): ant-t bro1 arg-n bro1 *Ars* bro1 *Bell* bro1 calen bro1 carb-an mrr1 con mrr1 gonotox jl2 hydr bro1* kreos mrr1 lyc bro1 mel-c-s br1 merc bro1 *Merc-c* bro1 murx mrr1 nit-ac bro1 prot jl2 sep bro1 syph jl2 tub jl2
  - **endocervicitis**: med jl2
    - **chronic**: hydroph mtf11 tub jl2

- **Vagina** (= colpitis; vaginitis): *Acon* k* alum k* apis bro1 am bro1 ars bro1* aur-m k* bell k* borx mrr1 bov mrr1 calad mrr1 calc bg* cann-s bro1 canth bro1* carb-an mrr1 caul k* caust mrr1 chin mrr1 cimic bro1 *Coc-c* k* coli jl2 con bro1* *Crot-t* bro1 *Cur* k* cycl mrr1 gels bro1 graph mrr1 *Ham* k* helon bro1* hydr bro1* hyper k* kali-c bro1 kali-m bro1 kali-p mrr1 kreos bro1* lyc mrr1 lyss mrr1 *Merc* k* *Merc-c* bro1 moni jl2 murx mrr1 *Nat-act* nat-m mrr1 nit-ac bg* *Nux-v* bg prot pte1* rhus-t bro1* *Sanic* mrr1 sep k* sil mrr1 stann mrr1 sulph bg* syc bka1*• syph jl2 tarent hr1* thuj bro1 [calc-br stj1 calc-f stj1 *Cupr-f* stj2 fl-pur stj2 kali-f stj1 mag-f stj1 plat stj2]
  - **aphthae** (See Aphthae - vagina)
  - **boils**: prot fmm1•
  - **chronic**: ars bro1 borx bro1 *Calc* bro1 grin bro1 hydr bro1 iod bro1 kali-m bro1 *Kreos* bro1 *Med* mrr1 *Merc* bro1 nit-ac bro1 *Puls* bro1 *Sep* bro1 sulph bro1 syph jl2
    - **new** sexual relationship; since: *Med* mrr1
  - **coition**; during: berb kr1 brom kr1 **Cact** vh *Ferr* kr1* ferr-m kr1 ferr-p vh *Ign* vh nit-ac mrr1 phos kr1 *Plat* vh *Thuj* vh
  - **itching**: morg-p fmm1•
  - **lichenoid**: moni jl2
  - **pregnancy** agg.; during: *Sep* mrr1

○ · **Bartholin's** glands: gonotox jl2

- **Vulva** (= vulvitis): acon bg2* ambr bro1 *Apis* bro1 ars bro1 bell bg2* brom bro1 calc bg2* *Canth* bro1 *Carb-v* bro1 chim bro1 coc-c bro1 coll bro1 *Cop* bro1 crot-t bro1 *Dulc* bro1 eupi bro1 goss bro1 *Graph* bro1 ham bro1 *Helon* bro1 *Hydr* bro1 *Kreos* bro1 lyc bro1 mag-p bro1 *Merc* bg2* *Merc-c* bro1 *Moni* jl2 nat-m bro1 nit-ac bg2 *Nux-v* bg2 oci bro1 plat bro1 prot jl2 puls bro1 rhus-d bro1 *Rhus-t* bro1 rob bro1 *Sep* bg2* sil bro1 spira bro1 sulph bg2* syc fmm1• *Thuj* bro1 *Xero* bro1

INJURIES: hyper mrr1
- **operation**; ailments from: glycyr-g cte1•

○ - **Ovaries**: am bro1 *Ham* bro1 psor bro1

INSENSIBILITY of vagina: (↗*Coition - enjoyment - absent; Numbness)* alum *Berb Brom* cann-s *Ferr Ferr-m* kali-br *Phos* k* **Sep** k ●
- **coition**; during: *Berb* hr1* brom hr1* *Cact* st *Ferr* hr1* *Ferr-m* hr1* *Ferr-p* st *Ign* st *Phos* hr1* *Plat* st *Thuj* st*

INVOLUNTARY orgasm (See Orgasm - involuntary)

IRRITATION: *Agar* k* *Am-c* k* bry k* *Calc Canth* k* *Carb-v Con* dulc *Graph* k* hep ign tl1 kali-br k* *Kreos* k* lac-c hr1 lyc merc nat-m k* nit-ac k* nux-v k* *Orig* k* phos k* plat k* puls sabal br1 sal-n br1 *Sep Sil* sulph
- **menses**; before: morg-g fmm1•
- **shivering**; during: plat b4.de

Irritation: ...

○ - **Clitoris**: *Am-c* k*
- **Ovaries**: am-br k* *Apis* ars k* carb-ac cimic k* *Gels* k* ham hep c1 kali-br k* lil-t nux-v k* phyt k* plat k* rhus-t thuj **Ust** k* **Vib** k*
  - **accompanied** by | **rheumatism** (See GENERALS - Pain - rheumatic - accompanied - ovaries)
  - **nervous** persons; in (See MIND - Excitement - nervous - ovaries)
- **Uterus**: ars k* *Bell* k* *Caul* k* *Cimic* bro1 *Hyos* hr1 ign bro1 *Kali-br* hr1 lil-t hr1* *Mag-m* bro1 murx bro1 ph-ac k* *Senec* k* tarent k* *Vib* hr1
  - **accompanied** by | **Urinary** organs; complaints of (See URINARY - Complaints - accompanied - uterus)
- **Vagina**: caul k* *Cocc* hr1 cypr c1 dream-p sdj1• helon k* nit-ac a1

ITCHING: acon bg aeth a1 *Agar* k* alum k* alum-sil k2 alumn **Am-c** k* **Ambr** k* *Anac* anan ang bg ant-c br1 *Ant-t* k* *Apis* arizon-l nl2• ars k* ars-s-f k2 aspar k* aur aur-ar k2 *Aur-m* k* *Aur-s* bell berb k* borx mtf11 bufo k* **Calad** k* **Calc** k* calc-s *Canth* k* *Carb-v* k* *Carbn-s* carneg-g rwt1• *Caust Chin* chinin-ar chir-fl gya2 chlam-tr bcx2• cit-l hr1 *Coff* k* colch bg *Coll* k* *Con* k* *Cop* k* cortico sp1 *Crot-t* k* cub hr1 *Dol* k* *Dulc* k* elaps euph eupi k* fago *Ferr* k* ferr-ar *Ferr-i* k* *Fl-ac* galeoc-c-h gms1• gink-b sbd1• *Graph* k* grin guare ham k* helo bg2 **Helon** k* hydr k* hydrc bg1 hydrog srj2• ign k* kali-ar *Kali-bi* k* *Kali-br* k* *Kali-c* k* kali-i k* *Kali-s* kali-sil k2 **Kreos** k* lac-ac k* *Lac-c* k* lach *Lap-a* lat-m sp1 lil-t k* *Lyc* k* *Mag-c* k* mag-m bg *Med* k* menth vh **Merc** k* morg-p fmm1• mosch bg2 mur-ac murx nat-c bg* *Nat-hchls* **Nat-m** k* nat-s nicc nicotam rly4• **Nit-ac** k* *Nux-v* k* *Onos Orig* k* **Petr** k* ph-ac h2* plac-s rly4• **Plat** k* pot-e rly4• prot fmm1• raph **Rhus-t** k* ribo rly4• ruta fd4.de sabin sacch-a fd2.de• senec pd **Sep** k* **Sil** k* sol-t-ae sphing kk3.fr spong fd4.de *Staph* k* *Sul-ac* k* **Sulph** k* symph fd3.de• syph k* **Tarent** k* *Tarent-c* br1 *Thuj* k* tritic-vg fd5.de *Urt-u* k* vanil fd5.de *Zinc* k* [*Spect* dfg1]
- **morning**: galeoc-c-h gms1• ruta fd4.de syph k* vanil fd5.de
- **afternoon**: sol-t-ae
- **evening**: calc k* dulc fd4.de eupi k* *Nit-ac* ruta fd4.de spong fd4.de vanil fd5.de
- **night**: *Lac-c Nit-ac* ruta fd4.de spong fd4.de tarent
  - **midnight**:
    - **after**:
      - **1 h**:
        - **Labia** majora | **waking** from itching: sabal c1
  - **bed** agg.; in: *Calc* raph ruta fd4.de
- **burning**: **Am-c** k* anan *Aur-m* berb k* calad pd **Calc** k* dulc fd4.de *Kali-i* nit-ac h2* senec pd spong fd4.de sulph pd *Urt-u*
  - **leukorrhea** agg.: *Kreos* b7a.de
  - **menses**; during: kali-br hr1

○ · **Labia**: agar bg2 alum bg2 am-c bg2 ambr bg2 bar-c bg2 bry bg2 **Calc** bg2 canth bg2* carb-v bg2 caust bg2 **Con** bg2 dulc bg2 graph bg2 hep bg2 kali-c bg2 kreos bg2 lyc bg2 mag-c bg2 meph bg2 nat-c bg2 **Nat-m** bg2 nit-ac bg2 *Nux-v* bg2 phos bg2 puls bg2 **Sep** bg2 **Sil** bg2 staph bg2 sulph bg2 *Thuj* bg2
  - **urination** agg.: canth mrr1
  - **Vulva**: calad ptk1 dulc fd4.de *Kali-i* k* senec ptk1 spong fd4.de sulph ptk1 urt-u ptk1
- **cold** agg.; becoming: *Nit-ac*
- **cold** applications | **amel.**: alum-sil k2 calad ptk1
- **hurriedness**; with (See MIND - Hurry - itching - genital)
- **intolerable**: *Agar* k* *Am-c* **Ambr** k* calad k2 *Calc* k*
- **leukorrhea**; from: (↗*Leukorrhea - itching)* agar alum *Anac* ars *Aur-m-n* wbt2• **Calc** calc-s carb-ac br1 *Carb-v* carc sst• *Caust* chin k* *Coll* cub cur *Fago* pd* ferr b7.de *Fl-ac* hydr *Kali-bi* kali-c kali-p **Kreos** med bg1 *Merc* moni rfm1• *Nat-m* **Nit-ac** *Onos* ph-ac puls *Sabin* **Sep** k* *Sulph* symph fd3.de• syph vh zinc
- **lying** | **amel.**: berb k*
- **menses**:
  - **after** | **agg.**: calc calc-s colch *Con* k* cur elaps *Ferr* graph kali-br kali-c kreos k* lyc k* *Mag-c Nat-m* k* **Nit-ac** k* *Ph-ac Sil* sulph **Tarent** k* *Zinc* k*
  - **amel.**: myos-a rly4•
  - **before** | **agg.**: bamb-a stb2.de• bufo *Calc* vh carb-v caust colch **Graph** k* *Kali-c* k* lac-c *Lil-t Merc* sol-t-ae vml3• *Sulph* k* tarent zinc

Female

- menses: ...
  - during | agg.: agar k* Am-c k* Ambr k* amp rly4• bufo bg2 calc calc-s Carb-v k* Caust k* Coff k* Con k* graph bg2 hep k* Kali-bi bg2* Kali-br k* Kali-c k* Kreos k* lac-ac k* lac-c k* lach Lyc k* merc k* nat-m k* nux-v bg2 Petr k* plat sep Sil k* sul-ac sulph bg2* tarent bg* Zinc k*
- **pregnancy** agg.; during: ambr k* Calad k* calc bg1 chlol k* Coll k* Fl-ac k* Helon k* Merc k* sabin bg* **SEP** k •* tab c1* urt-u
- **scratching**:
  - **agg.**: alum-sil k2 am-c aq-mar mgm• onos symph fd3.de•
  - **amel.**: crot-t k* hydrog srj2• sep alj
- **sitting** agg.: berb k* eupi a1
- **urination** | **after** | **agg.**: alum-sil k2 Thuj a1
  - **during** | **agg.**: am-c bg2 ambr k* carb-v k* kreos pd **Merc** k* sil k* Thuj k*
- **voluptuous**: Agar arist-cl sp1 arund br1 bov Bufo Calad k* Calc Canth Coff k* Dulc k* elaps kali-bi pd Kali-br k* kreos lac-f c1 Lach Lil-t **Orig** k* **Plat** k* symph fd3.de• tritic-vg fd5.de Zinc
- **walking** agg.: berb k* colch **Nit-ac** k* Thuj k*
- **warmth** of bed, agg.: Merc sne sulph k2
- **weather** agg.; cold: Dulc k*
- **worms**; from: | **pinworms**: calad pd*

○ - **Labia**; between: falco-pe nl2• kali-bi k2 **Kreos** k* myos-a rly4• ozone sde2• Sulph vanil fd5.de
  - **water** agg.: ozone sde2•
- **Pudendum**: acon bg2 alum bg2 am-c bg2 ambr bg2* ang bg2 arizon-l nl2• bell bg2 **Calad** bg2 **Calc** b4a.de* Canth b7a.de **Carb-v** b4a.de* caust b4.de* coff b7a.de* colch bg2 **Con** b4.de* fago c2 Graph bg2 helo bg2 hydr bg2 **Kali-c** b4a.de* Kreos b7a.de* lach bg2 lyc bg2 mag-m bg2 merc bg2 nat-c bg2 **Nat-m** bg2 nit-ac bg2 petr bg2 plat bg2 sabin vml **Sep** bg2 **Sil** bg2 staph b7.de* **Sulph** b4a.de* tarent c2 thuj bg2 zinc bg2
  - **leukorrhea** agg.: Alum b4.de ars b4a.de Calc b4.de kali-c b4.de Merc b4.de sep b4.de*
  - **menses**:
    - **after** | **agg.**: Con b4.de*
    - **before** | **agg.**: graph b4a.de* Merc b4.de* Sulph b4a.de
    - **during** | **agg.**: caust b4.de hep b4a.de* lyc b4a.de sep b4a.de
  - **urinating**; even when not: ambr
- **Uterus**: bell-p bg1 kreos tl1 plat tl1
- **Vagina**: agar k* agn bg2 alum k* alumn k* androc srj1• antip bro1 apis bg1 arund bro1 atp rly4• aur bg2 Aur-m k* aur-s c1 borx bg2 Brom k* **Calad** k* Calc k* Calc-s Canth k* carb-ac bg2* caust chel bg2 coff bg2* coll bg2 Con k* conch fkr1.de cop k* cub c1 dream-p sdj1• elaps Ferr-i k* ger-i rly4• graph bg2* grat bg2 grin hr1* helo bg2 helon k* hydr bg2* Hydrc k* ign lp irid-met srj5• kali-bi bg2 kali-br bg2 **Kreos** k* Lil-t k* Lyc k* mang-p rly4• Med k* menth mtf11 Merc k* moni jl2* morg-p pte1• nad rly4• **Nit-ac** k* petr lp plac-s rly4• plat bg2* rhus-g tmo3• rhus-t k* sal-fr sle1• sanguis-s hm2• scroph-n br1* **Sep** k* sil bro1 spong fd4.de stann bg2 staph k* streptoc rly4• sul-ac bg2 Sulph k* Tarent k* thlas bg1 thuj bg2* urt-u bg2 zinc k*
  - **evening**: dream-p sdj1• Kreos k*
  - **coition**; after: agar androc srj1• **Nit-ac** k*
  - **menses**:
    - **after** | **agg.**: canth Caust k* con k* elaps Kreos lyc mez k* nit-ac mrr1 sulph tarent mrr1
    - **before** | **agg.**: calc vh conch fkr1* elaps Graph nit-ac mrr1
    - **during** | **agg.**: agar bg2 am-c bg2 ambr bg2 amp rly4• bufo bg2 carb-v bg2 caust bg2 coff bg2 Con k* elaps graph bg2 helon hep bg2 kali-bi bg2 kali-br bg2 Kali-c bg2 kreos k* lac-c bg2 lyc bg2 merc bg2 nat-m bg2 nux-v bg2 **Petr** bg2 sulph bg2 zinc bg2
  - **pregnancy** agg.; during: acon bro1 Ambr bro1 ant-c bro1 borx k* **Calad** k* Coll bro1 ichth bro1 sabin ptk1 Sep bro1* tab bro1
  - **rubbing** agg.: med ptk1
  - **sexual** excitement; with: canth ptk1
  - **urination** agg.; during: kreos ptk1
  - **voluptuous**: Calad **Kreos** k* Lil-t k* neon srj5• nit-ac hr1 sec k2
  - **warm** bathing | **amel.**: med ptk1

○ - **Deep** in: con ptk1
  - **Orifice**: conv br1 podo fd3.de• spong fd4.de

Itching: ...
- **Vulva**: agar bro1 ambr c2* anthraq mtf11 apis bro1 Ars bro1 arund bro1 aur-s c2 bacls-10 pte1*• berb bro1 borx br1 bov bro1 Calad bro1* Calc bro1 Canth bro1 carb-ac bro1 carb-v bro1* cartl-s rly4• caust bro1 chinin-s c2 cod mtf11 coff bro1 coll c2* Con bro1 conv c2* cop br1* corn c2 crot-t bro1 dulc bro1* Fago bro1 falco-pe nl2• ferr-i bro1 ferul c2 fuli br1 gaert pte1*• germ-met srj5• glycyr-g cte1• Graph bro1 grin c2* gua bro1 helon c2* hydr bro1* hydrog srj2• ichth c2 kali-bi c2* kali-br bro1 kali-c bro1 Kreos bro1 lil-t c2* Lyc bro1 med jl2 menth mtf11 mentho br1 Merc bro1 mez bro1 moni jl2 morg-g pte1*• morg-p pte1*• nat-m bro1 nit-ac bro1 Orig bro1 ovi-p c2 petr bro1 pic-ac c2* plat c2* pot-e rly4• prot pte1* rad-br c11* rhus-d bro1 rhus-t bro1* rhus-v bro1 ruta fd4.de sal-fr sle1• scroph-n bro1 senec ptk1 Sep bro1 sil ptk1 sol-t-ae c2 spira bro1 spong fd4.de staph bro1* sulph bro1* syc pte1*• syph jl2 tarent bro1* tarent-c bro1 thuj bro1* tritic-vg fd5.de Urt-u bro1 xero bro1 zinc c1*
  - **accompanied** by | **hemorrhoids**: coll tl1 tarent tl1
  - **and** anus: cop br1 des-ac mtf11 falco-pe nl2• sal-fr sle1•
  - **leukorrhea**; from: agar bro1 alum bro1 Ambr bro1 Anac bro1 calc bro1 cop br1 fago bro1* Helon bro1 hydr bro1* Kreos bro1* merc bro1 Sep bro1 sulph bro1
  - **menses** | **after** | **agg.**: tarent mrr1
    - **during** | **agg.**: agar bg2 am-c bg2 ambr bg2 bufo bg2 carb-v bg2 caust bg2 coff bg2 con bg2 graph bg2 hep bg2 kali-bi bg2 kali-br bg2 Kali-c bg2 Kreos bg2 lac-c bg2 lyc bg2 merc bg2 nat-m bg2 nux-v bg2 **Petr** bg2 sulph bg2 zinc bg2*
  - **urination** agg.; during: ambr ptk1 kreos ptk1

JERKING upwards in vagina: | **morning**: sep k*

KNOTTED; as if: | **Uterus**: ust ptk1

KRAUROSIS VULVAE (= lichen sclerosus et atrophicus): moni jl2

LABOR (See Delivery)

LABOR PAINS (See Pain - labor pains)

LACTATION (See GENERALS - Lactation)

LEUKORRHEA: abrom-a ks5 acon b2.de* acon-l a1 adren a1* Aesc k* agar k* agath-a nl2• agn k* Alet k* allox tpw4* aln c1* aloe kr1 alst c1* **Alum** k* alum-p k2 alumn k* **Am-c** k* Am-m k* ambr k* anac k* ant-c k* Ant-t b2.de* apis k* aq-mar mgm• aral c1* Arg-n k* Arist-cl mg1.de* **Ars** k* **Ars-i** k* Ars-s-f k2* arund a1* asaf k* asc-i bwa3* aur k* aur-ar k2 aur-i k2 Aur-m k* aur-m-n k* aur-s k2 bad k* bamb-a stb2.de* Bar-c k* Bar-m k* Bar-s k2* baros c1* bell b2.de* bell-p sp1 berb k* berb-a c1* bond a1 Borx k* Bov k* brass-n-o srj5• bry k* but-ac sp1 Calad b7a.de **Calc** k* Calc-f sp1 calc-i k2 calc-o-t c1* Calc-p k* **Calc-s** k* cann-s k* canth k* caps k* Carb-ac hr1* **Carb-an** k* Carb-v k* **Carbn-s** card-m k* carl a1 Castm j5.de caul k* **Caust** k* cean hr1* cedr k* cench c1* cham k* chel k* chen-a c1* chim hr1* **Chin** k* chinin-ar chlol c1* Cimic k* Cina c1* Cinnb cinnm hr1* coc-c c1* Cocc k* coch kr1* coff k* colch gk coli rly4• Coll hr1* **Con** b2.de* Cop j5.de* Corn hr1* croc hr1* crot-c k* cub k* cur k* cycl k* cystein-l rly4• cyt-l mg1.de dam c1* der a1 Dict c1* dig k* dros k* dulc k* erig hr1* Ery-a hr1* Eucal hr1* eup-pur a1* euph-pi c1* Eupi k* fago a1 falco-pe nl2• Ferr k* ferr-ar ferr-br c1* Ferr-i hr1* ferr-p Ferr-s hr1* fl-ac mtf11 Frax bro1 fuma-ac rly4• galeoc-c-h gms1• gamb a1* **Gels** k* ger c1* ger-i rly4• germ-met srj5• gink-b jl3* glycyr-g cte1• gran j5.de* **Graph** k* grat k2* gua c1* guaj k* guat sp1 ham k* hed sp1 hedeo c1* helin bro1 helio c1* Hell b7a.de helon k* Hep k* hir mg1.de hura Hydr k* hydrc c1* hydrog srj2• hyper a1* ign b2.de* inul a1* **Iod** k* Ip k* iris c1* jab c1* jac-c bro1 jac-g c1* joan bro1 **Kali-ar** k* Kali-bi k* **Kali-c** k* Kali-chl k* kali-fcy a1* Kali-i k* kali-m c1* kali-n b2.de* Kali-p Kali-s k* kali-sil k2 kalm c1* ketogl-ac rly4• **Kreos** k* Lac-ac hr1* Lac-c k* lac-d c1* lac-v-f c1* Lach k* Lam j5.de* Lap-a hr1* lap-la sde8.de• lapa c1* lappa c1* laur k* lil-t k* lipp a1* Lyc k* lycpr c1* Lyss k* mag-c k* Mag-m k* mag-s k* mand mg1.de* mang k* **Med** k* meli c1 Meli-xyz c2 **Merc** k* Merc-c k* merc-i-f k* merc-i-r k* merc-pr-r bro1 mez k* mill j5.de* mom-b c1* morg-g fmm1• Mucor jl2 **Mur-ac** k* murx k* myric hr1* naja a1* Nat-ar Nat-c k* nat-hchls **Nat-m** k* Nat-p k* nat-pyru rly4• nat-s k* neon srj5• nicc j5.de* **Nit-ac** k* Nux-m k* nux-v k* Oci-sa sp1 ol-an j5.de Ol-j hr1* Op k* Orig k* orig-d c2 ovi-p c1* oxal-a rly4• ozone sde2• Pall k* paraf c1* pareir c1* ped a1 penic jl3* Petr k* petr-ra shn4• Ph-ac k* Phos k* Phys k* Phyt k* pic-ac bro1 pin-con oss2• **Plat** k* plb k* Podo k* pot-e rly4• prot jl2 prun k* Psor k* pulm-a srb2.fr **Puls** k* puls-n a1 pulx bro1 ran-b k* rat k* rhus-g tmo3• rhus-t k* ruta k* Sabin k* sal-fr sle1• sang k* sanic c1* sapin c1* sarr k* Sars k* sec k* senec k* seneg k* **Sep** k* **Sil** k* sol-o c1* solid c1* spira bro1 spong fd4.de

Leukorrhea: ...
squil k* **Stann** k* streptoc rly4• stront-c k* suis-em rly4• suis-pan rly4• *Sul-ac* k* sulfonam jl3 **Sulph** k* suprar rly4• syc fmm1• symph fd3.de• syph k* tab j5.de *Tarent* k* tep c1* thlas c1* *Thuj* k* *Thymol* sp1 til k* *Tong* j5.de tril-p kr1* tritic-vg fd5.de *Tub* c1* urt-u c1* ust k* vanil fd5.de vib hr1* viol-t k* voes a1 wies a1 wye a1 xan hr1* *Zinc* k* *Zinc-p* k2* zing c1 ziz a1* [bell-p-sp dcm1]

- **daytime**: alum bro1 murx plat bro1 *Sep*
  - **agg.**: alum ptk1 calc tl1 murx hr1* *Sep* hr1*
    - **menses**; after: *Kali-fcy* kr1
  - **only**: *Alum* k* irid-met srj5• *Lac-c* k* plat k* sep k*
- **morning**: *Aur* k* *Aur-m* aur-s bamb-a stb2.de• *Bell* k* *Calc-p* *Carb-v* k* *Graph* k* *Kreos* k* *Mag-m* k* murx a1 nat-m k* phos k* plat **Sep** spong fd4.de *Sulph* k* *Zinc* h2*
  - **girls**; in: *Puls* hr1*
  - **rising** agg.: calc-p hr1* carb-v j5.de graph j5.de* kreos j5.de *Sulph* j5.de*
  - **urination** agg.; after: *Mag-m* a1*
  - **walking** agg.: amp rly4• phos a1
- **afternoon**: alum k* calc-p dulc fd4.de iod tl1 lil-t k* mag-c h2* naja ruta fd4.de spong fd4.de
- **evening**: brass-n-o srj5• bufo echi eupi a1 lil-t merc k* phys a1 ruta fd4.de sil a1 tarent a1 *Zinc* h2*
- **night**: alum k* ambr k* *Carb-v* k* *Caust* k* *Con* k* galeoc-c-h gms1• **Merc** k* *Nat-m* k* nit-ac k* ruta st spong fd4.de *Sulph* k* *Syph* k2*
  - **only** at: *Carb-v* kr1 *Caust* kr1 *Nat-m* kr1
- **abortion**, with history of: alet bro1 caul bro1 *Sabin* bro1 sep bro1
- **accompanied** by:
  - **bearing** down pains: caul tl1
  - **complaints**; other: *Alum* b2.de* am-c b2.de* am-m b2.de* ambr b2.de* anac b2.de* ant-c b2.de* ars b2.de* bell b2.de* borx b2.de* bov b2.de* *Calc* b2.de* cann-s b2.de* canth b2.de* carb-an b2.de* carb-v b2.de* caust b2.de* cham b2.de* chin b2.de* cocc b2.de* *Con* b2.de* dros b2.de* ferr b2.de* graph b2.de* hep b2.de* ign b2.de* iod b2.de* *Kali-c* b2.de* kali-n b2.de* **Kreos** b2.de* *Lyc* b2.de* mag-c b2.de* mag-m b2.de* **Merc** b2.de* mez b2.de* nat-c b2.de* **Nat-m** b2.de* nit-ac b2.de* ph-ac b2.de* phos b2.de* plat b2.de* *Puls* b2.de* ran-b b2.de* ruta b2.de* sabin b2.de* sec b2.de* **Sep** b2.de* *Sil* b2.de* sul-ac b2.de* sulph b2.de* thuj b2.de* zinc b2.de*
  - **constipation**: hydr bro1 *Nat-m* b4a.de
  - **diabetes** mellitus (See GENERALS - Diabetes mellitus - accompanied - leukorrhea)
  - **diarrhea**: nat-m bg2 puls bro1
  - **eruptions**: lil-t bg2
  - **fullness**; sensation of:
    - **cold water** | **amel.**: acon bro1
  - **hoarseness** (See LARYNX - Voice - hoarseness - accompanied - leukorrhea)
  - **trembling**: alum bg2
  - ○ **Abdomen**:
    - **pain** (See ABDOMEN - Pain - leukorrhea - with)
    - **swelling**: am-m bg2 graph bg2 sep bg2
  - **Back**; pain in: alet ptk1 cassia-s zzc1•
  - **Cervical** canal; burning in: calc tl1
  - **Face**:
    - **pale** discoloration of: *Ars* bg2 graph bg2 kreos bg2 **Puls** bg2 *Sep* bg2
    - **yellow** discoloration of: chin bg2 ferr bg2 *Lyc* b4a.de *Nat-m* b4a.de* sep bg2
  - **Forehead**; brown spots on: caul c1* sep bro1*
  - **Genitals**:
    - **contraction**: chin bg2
    - **relaxation**: agn bro1 *Caul* bro1 sec bro1 sep bro1
  - **Head** | **pain**: nat-m b4a.de* plat ptk1

- **accompanied** by: ...
  - **Hypogastrium**:
    - **cutting** pain in (See ABDOMEN - Pain - hypogastrium - leukorrhea - during - cutting)
    - **tension** (See ABDOMEN - Tension - hypogastrium - leukorrhea)
  - **Lids**; heaviness of: caul hr1*
  - **Liver**; complaints of: hydr bro1
  - **Lumbar** pain: bar-c bg2 caust bg2 con bg2 gels ptk1 graph bg2 kali-bi bg2 kali-c b4a.de* kali-n b4a.de* kreos bg2 lac-c bg2 *Mag-m* bg2 nat-c b4.de* syph jl2
  - **Sacrum**:
    - **pain**:
      - **contractive**: kreos bg2
      - **violent** (See BACK - Pain - sacral - leukorrhea)
  - **Urinary** organs:
    - **complaints** of: berb ptk1 erig ptk1
    - **irritation** of: berb bro1 *Erig* bro1 kreos bro1 sep bro1
  - **Uterus**:
    - **contraction** of (See Contractions - uterus - leukorrhea)
    - **pain**; stitching (See Pain - uterus - leukorrhea - stitching)
  - **Vagina**:
    - **contractions** (See Contractions - vagina - accompanied - leukorrhea)
    - **pain** in; stinging (See Pain - vagina - stinging - accompanied - leukorrhea)
- **acid** food, after: **Sil** b4a.de*
- **acrid**, excoriating: abrom-a ks5 aesc k* *Agar* k* **Alum** k* *Alum-p* k2 alum-sil k2 alumn a1 *Am-c* k* am-m amor-r jl3 anac k* ange-s jl3 ant-c k* apis aral k* *Arg-met* *Arg-n* **Ars** k* *Ars-i* k* *Ars-s-f* k2 aur k* aur-ar k2 aur-i k2 *Aur-m* k* aur-m-n kr1 aur-s k2 bacls-10 pte1• bapt bar-s k2 *Bell-p* mg1.de* berb **Borx** k* *Bov* k* buni-o jl3 *Calc* k* calc-ar k2 calc-i k2* *Calc-s* calc-sil k2 cann-s b2.de* canth k* carb-ac k* *Carb-an* k* *Carb-v* k* **Carbn-s** **Caul** kr1* *Caust* **Cham** k* *Chel* chin k* chinin-ar *Clem* hr1* *Con* k* cop k* cub *Dig* kr1 eucal bro1 eup-pur sf1.de **Ferr** k* **Ferr-ar** ferr-br bro1 *Ferr-i* *Ferr-p* **Fl-ac** k* **Graph** k* *Gua* bro1 guat sp1* *Hed* mg1.de* *Helin* bro1 helon bg1 *Hep* k* *Hydr* bg* hyper kr1 ign k* *Iod* k* kali-ar kali-bi sf1.de* *Kali-c* k* kali-chl *Kali-i* k* *Kali-m* kr1* *Kali-p* k* kali-s *Kali-sil* k2 kola stb3• **Kreos** k* *Lac-c* kr1 *Lach* k* *Lam* laur *Lil-t* k* lipp a1 *Lob* **Lyc** k* *Mag-c* k* mag-m b2.de* mag-s med br1* **Merc** k* *Merc-c* merc-i-f mez k* morg-g pte1• morg-p pte1• *Murx* bg1* *Myric* kr1 *Nat-m* k* *Nat-p* nat-s **Nit-ac** k* nux-m *Onos* *Petr* ph-ac k* **Phos** k* phyt *Polyg-h* kr1 prun k* psor st* **Puls** k* ran-b k* rhus-t rob kr1 ruta k* *Sabin* k* sang k* sec bg* **Sep** k* **Sil** k* *Sul-ac* k* sul-i k2 *Sulph* k* syc pte1• syph al* thuj k* *Tub* st* urt-u vib kr1* zinc k* zinc-p k2 ziz bro1
  - **night**: *Syph* kr1
  - **afterwards**, at first mild: *Ran-b* kr1
  - **children**; in: cub kr1*
  - **delivery**; after: *Nat-s* kr1
  - **dinner**; after: *Cham* a1
  - **eats** holes in linen: *Iod* k*
  - **first**, not afterwards; at: *Ferr* kr1
  - **food**, after acid: **Sil** kr1
  - **menopause**; during: sang kr1
  - **menorrhagia**, in chronic: *Iod* kr1
  - **menses**:
    - **after** | **agg.**: **Graph** kr1 kola stb3• kreos kr1 *Lach* kr1 mag-c sf1.de mez kr1 *Nit-ac* kr1 ruta kr1 ziz a1*
    - **before** | **agg.**: **Graph** kr1* lach bro1 *Sep* a1* *Sil* kr1 *Ust* kr1
    - **during** | **agg.**: lach bro1 *Phos* kr1 sep bro1
    - **suppressed** menses; from: ruta kr1
- **albuminous**: aesc sf1.de agn k* *Alum* k* am-c **Am-m** k* *Ambr* bro1 arist-cl mg1.de aur bamb-a stb2.de• bell bg2 berb k* **Borx** k* *Bov* k* but-ac sp1 calc k* *Calc-p* k* carb-v a1 coc-c k2 elaps a1 ferr-i bro1 glycyr-g cte1• graph bro1 haem bro1 **Hydr** hr1* inul bro1 iod bro1 kali-m bro1 *Kali-s* bro1 ketogl-ac rly4• kreos bro1 lil-t k* mag-c bro1 med al* *Mez* k* **Nat-m** nat-sil fd3.de* pall k* *Petr* k*

- **albuminous**: ...
  Plat k* *Podo* k* *Puls* bro1 *Senec* kr1 **Sep** *Stann* k* stram *Sul-ac* k* *Thuj* bro1 til bro1 ust k*
  - **hot**: *Borx* k2*
  - **menses** | **agg.**; before: *Ust* kr1
  - **pregnancy** agg.; during: petr sf1.de
  - **walking** agg.: aesc sf1.de
- **alternating** with:
  - **bloody** discharge: ambr st1 oci-sa sp1 tarent a1*
  - **cough**: *Iod* k*
  - **mental** symptoms (See MIND - Mental symptoms - alternating - leukorrhea)
  - **nasal** catarrh: kali-c st1
  - ○ **Back**; pain in (See BACK - Pain - alternating with - leukorrhea)
  - **Head**; pain in | **neuralgic** (See HEAD - Pain - neuralgic - alternating - leukorrhea)
- **amber**-colored: sep a1
- **amel.**: borx hr1
- **amenorrhea**, in: *Graph* kr1
- **anemia**, with: **Calc** kr1 *Cycl* kr1 **Ferr** kr1 *Graph* kr1 *Helon* kr1 *Hep* kr1 *Ph-ac* kr1 *Phos* kr1 senec k2 *Sil* kr1
- **atony**, from: *Alet* hr1* *Caul* hr1* cimic hr1* *Helon* hr1* mill lp puls lp sec hr1* sep lp tril-p kr1 ust hr1*
- **black**: *Chin* hr1* croc k* glycyr-g cte1• kreos ptk1 rhus-g tmo3• *Rhus-t* hr1* *Sec* k* thlas bro1*
- **bladder** complaints, with: erig vml3•
- **bland**: aids nl2• allox tpw4* *Alum* k* *Am-m* k* borx k* *Brom* hr1* calc k* calc-p bro1 carb-v *Caul* k* cycl sf1.de eupi k* fago a1 ferr k* *Frax* bro1* kali-c kali-chl k* kali-fcy kr1 *Kali-m* kr1* *Kali-s* sf1.de ketogl-ac rly4• kreos k* laur lil-t k* *Merc* k* nat-m k* nux-v k* penic jl3* ph-ac k* plat k* *Puls* k* puls-n a1 ran-b k* ruta k* sal-fr sle1• sep k* sil stann bro1 staph k* *Sulph* k* syc pte1• *Thuj* k* ust hr1 ziz a1*
  - **morning**: phyt a1
  - **menses**, before and after: *Puls* hr1*
  - **painless**: *Am-m* hr1* *Nux-v* hr1* **Puls** hr1*
  - **rest** agg.: fago a1
  - **urination** agg.; before: *Kreos* a1*
- **blisters**; causing: am-c ptk1 kreos ptk1 med ptk1 *Phos* b4.de*
- **blond** and phlegmatic women; in: *Cycl* kr1
- **bloody**: acon k* agar aloe *Alum* k* alum-p k2* alum-sil k2* alumn k2 am-m k* amp rly4• *Ant-t* k* *Arg-met* *Arg-n* k* arist-cl mg1.de *Ars* k* *Ars-i* *Ars-s-f* k2* *Bar-c* k* bar-i k2* *Bell* hr1* bufo k* calc k* calc-ar k2* calc-i k2* **Calc-s** k* calc-sil k2* canth k* carb-an k2 *Carb-v* k* carbn-s caust bg2 **Chin** k* chinin-ar chinin-s a1 *Chlor* hr1* chr-ac st1 cimic jl3 cinnb k* **Cocc** k* coff k* coli rly4• *Con* k* cop j5.de* crot-c sk4• crot-h k* dict a1 falco-pe nl2• foll jl3 graph k2 ham k* hep k* *Hydr* hr1* hydroph jl3 *Iod* k* kali-i k* *Kreos* k* *Lac-c* k* *Lach* bg2* *Lyc* k* mag-m b2.de* *Merc* k* *Merc-c* k* murx k* **Nit-ac** k* nux-m k* petr k* ph-ac k* *Phos* k* phys k* podo k* prot jl3 pyrog k2 raph hr1* rob hr1* sabin k* **Sep** k* *Sil* k* *Spira* bro1 streptoc rly4• suis-em rly4• *Sul-ac* k* sul-i k2* tarent hr1* *Ter* k* thlas kr1* thymol sp1* *Tril-p* zinc k* zinc-p k2*
  - **morning**: kreos a1
  - **forenoon**: sep a1
  - **night**: raph a1
  - **menses**:
    - **after** | **agg.**: ars k* canth j5.de* caust *Chin* k* *Lac-c* hr1* pyrog rad-br ptk1 sil h2* *Tarent* hr1* *Zinc* k*
    - **appear**; with sensation as if menses would: *Sul-ac* kr1
    - **before** | **agg.**: aran-ix mg1.de* brucel sa3• prot jl2 streptoc rly4•
    - **instead** of: chin ptk1
  - **old** women, in: arist-cl mg1.de *Phos* hr1*
  - **pregnancy** agg.; during: cocc lp* *Nux-m* hr1* sep a1
  - **stool** agg.; during: murx j5.de* *Vib* hr1*
  - **watery**: *(↗meat; thin)* aids nl2• alum h2 calc ptk1 kreos ptk1 mang ptk1 nit-ac ptk1
  - **weakness**; with: tril-p kr1
- **bluish**: ambr k*
- **bluish**: ...
  - **white**: ambr b7.de*
- **brown**: *Aesc* bro1 aln vva1• *Am-m* k* androc srj1• arg-met arist-cl mg1.de* bamb-a stb2.de• berb buni-o jl3 cocc k* dict a1 dream-p sdj1• dulc fd4.de foll jl3 ger-i rly4• germ-met srj5• hir mg1.de* hydrog srj2• iod ptk1 irid-met srj5• kali-p fd1.de• kali-s fd4.de kreos j5.de* lac-d k2 lap-la sde8.de• **Lil-t** k* mand mg1.de* morg-g pte1*• morg-p pte1*• nat-sil fd3.de• nept-m lsd2.fr **Nit-ac** k* ozone sde2• prot pte1* ruta fd4.de sacch-a fd2.de• *Sec* k* *Sep* bro1 *Sil* k* spig bg2 spong fd4.de streptoc rly4• syc pte1*• thlas sf1.de* *Thymol* sp1* ust bg3* vanil fd5.de
  - **cherry** brown: nit-ac b4.de*
  - **menses**:
    - **after** | **agg.**: bamb-a stb2.de• kali-s fd4.de *Lac-c* hr1* *Nit-ac* hr1*
    - **before** | **agg.**: arist-cl mg1.de bros-gau mrc1 dulc fd4.de hir mg1.de* kali-s fd4.de prot jl2 ruta fd4.de
    - **during** | **agg.**: nept-m lsd2.fr pic-ac a1 spong fd4.de
  - **stains** linen: *Lil-t* k* **Nit-ac** k* petr-ra shn4•
    - **yellow**: lac-d st1
  - **urination** agg.; after: *Am-m* a1*
- **burning**: alum k* alum-p k2* *Am-c* k* ant-c bg2* *Ars* k* ars-i ars-s-f k2* bar-c k* bar-s k2 **Borx** k* **Calc** k* **Calc-s** k* canth k* carb-ac br1* *Carb-an* k* *Carb-v* k* carbn-s castm cham bg2 *Con* k* ferr-i *Fl-ac* k* graph k2 hed st1 hep bg2* hoit jl3 hydr hr1* iod k* kali-ar kali-c k* *Kali-p* kali-s **Kreos** k* *Lach* bg2 lept ptk1 lil-t ptk1 mag-c bg2 mag-s k* mang-p rly4• meph k* *Merc* bg2* *Nit-ac* k* *Phos* k* prot pte1*• **Puls** k* **Sep** k* *Sul-ac* k* *Sul-i* k2* **Sulph** k* tarent k* thuj k* urt-u sf1.de zinc b4a.de
  - **menses**; after: *Phos* hr1*
  - **motion** agg.: *Mag-s* a1*
  - **pain**; after | **Abdomen**; in: calc-p ptk1
- **cachectic** women; in: *Helon* kr1 **Nit-ac** kr1
- **childbed**, in (See delivery)
- **children**; in: bar-c bg2* *Calc* bg2* calc-p bg2* *Cann-s* k* carb-ac br1 carb-v bg2* caul bg2* *Cub* hyper kr1 kali-p k2 *Med* st **Merc** k* *Merc-i-f* k2 mill kr1* *Puls* senec **SEP** k ● *Syph* c1* viol-t kr1
  - **girls**; little: *Asper* bro1 bar-c sf1.de *Calc* k1* calc-p sf1.de *Cann-s* k* cann-xyz ptk1 carb-ac br1* carb-v sf1.de caul c1* *Cina* bro1 *Cub* k* hydr bro1 hyper kr1 kali-p k2 mang ptk1 *Med* st **Merc** k* *Merc-i-f* k2* mill kr1* *Puls* k* senec k* **SEP** k ●* *Syph* c1* viol-t kr1
- **chilliness**; with: *Cycl* hr1* *Puls* hr1*
  - **night**: lach hr1*
- **chilly** women; in: ars kr1 calc kr1 lach kr1
- **chronic** (See constant)
- **clots**; in: ambr b7.de* bov zr galeoc-c-h gms1•
- **coition**; after: cann-s a1 mag-c bg2 nat-c k* *Sep* k*
  - **amel.**: merc ptk1
- **cold**:
  - **agg.**: *Nit-ac* kr1
  - **washing** | **amel.**: *Alum* h2*
- **colic**; after: am-m ptk1 calc-p ptk1 con ptk1 lyc ptk1 mag-c a1* mag-m ptk1 sil ptk1 *Sulph* ptk1
- **colorless**: luf-op rsj5•
- **colors** the clothes, difficult to wash out (See staining - wash)
- **constant**, chronic: *Aesc* kr1* *Alum* j5.de* *Am-m* k* aq-mar mgm• aur sf1.de bell-p sf1.de *Borx* j5.de* calc kr1* cand mtf11 cimic mtf11 **Cinnm** kr1 erig kr1 falco-pe nl2• *Graph* j5.de* hydr mrr1 *Ign* kr1 iod j5.de* *Kali-i* kr1 *Kali-m* kr1 *Kreos* kr1 *Lach* kr1 *Mag-m* j5.de* *Mez* j5.de* *Myric* kr1 nat-c j5.de nat-m mrr1 *Nit-ac* kr1 *Nux-v* bg2* podo sf1.de *Rat* kr1 sec kr1* *Senec* bg2* *Sil* kr1 *Sulph* kr1 thuj bg2* ziz kr1
  - **amenorrhea**, with: *Plat* kr1
  - **menses** | **after** | **agg.**: *Nux-v* kr1
    - **agg.**: **Iod** kr1
  - **sexual** desire; with increased: *Ign* kr1
- **convulsions**; after hysterical: bell b4.de* ign b7a.de mag-c b4a.de *Mag-m* b4.de*
- **copious**: acon k* aesc k2* *Agar* k* agn k2* aloe a1 *Alum* k* alum-p k2* alum-sil k2* alumn k* *Am-c* k* am-m k2 ambr h1* amp rly4• ange-s jl3 *Ant-c* k* apis arg-met k2 *Arg-n* k* *Ars* k* *Ars-i* *Ars-s-f* k2* *Asaf* k* *Aur* k* aur-ar k2 aur-i k2* aur-m k2* *Aur-s* k2* aza jl3 bapt *Bar-c* *Bar-s* k2* bell borx k* bov bry a1 bufo cact

- **copious**: ...
Calc k* calc-f jl3 calc-i k2* calc-p bro1 calc-s *Calc-sil* k2* *Calen* hr1* *Carb-ac* k* carb-an k2 carb-v carbn-s castm j5.de caul k* *Caust* k* *Cean* j5.de* chel a1 chin chinin-ar chlorpr jl3 cinnb coc-c k2 *Cocc* k* coff k* *Con* k* crot-c sk4• cub k* *Cur* cyt-l mg1.de* dict a1 *Dig* hr1* ephe-si hsj1• *Erig* k* eup-pur hr1* *Eupi* k* falco-pe nl2• ferr-i k* *Fl-ac* k* gaert pte1*• glycyr-g cte1• **Graph** k* gua bro1 guaj j5.de *Ham* k* helin bro1 *Helon* k* hep k2 hydr k* *Hydrc* k* iod k* *Kali-fcy* kr1 kali-p *Kreos* k* lac-c k* *Lac-d* k2* *Lach* k* laur a1 *Led* k* *Lil-t* k* *Lob* lup a1 lyc k* lycps-v a1 lyss mg1.de mag-c mag-m k* mag-s k* *Med* al* *Merc* k* *Merc-c* k* *Merc-i-f* hr1* merc-i-r ptk1 morg-g fmm1• *Nat-ar* *Nat-c* k* *Nat-m* k* *Nat-p* *Nat-s* hr1* nat-sil k2* nicc k* nit-ac k* oci-sa sp1 *Onos* *Ovi-p* bro1 *Petr* k* *Ph-ac* k* *Phos* k* *Phys* k* *Phyt* k* *Plat* hr1* prot pte1* puls k* puls-n a1 pulx br1* raja-s jl3 ran-b j5.de *Sabin* k* sal-fr sle1• sars j5.de *Sec* k* **Sep** k* **Sil** k* **Stann** k* *Still* hr1* **Sul-i** k2* *Sulph* k* syc pte1*• *Syph* k* *Thuj* bro1* til a1* tril-p k* *Tub* vh* ust ziz hr1*
  - **daytime**: *Alum* a1* *Alumn* a1 *Lac-c* hr1
  - **morning**: phyt a1
  - **cold** water | **amel.**: *Alum* kr1
  - **menses**:
    - **after** | **agg.**: alum h2* ferr-i hr1 *Lac-c* hr1* mag-s a1* *Merc* hr1 *Nux-v* hr1*
    - **before** | **agg.**: alum h2* *Lach* hr1* *Nux-v* hr1*
    - **between**: *Plat* hr1*
    - **like** the menses: *Alum* k* *Caust* k* *Kreos* k* mag-s k*
  - **ovulation**; during: plut-n srj7• prot jl2
  - **serum**-like discharge from anus and vagina: **Lob** k*
  - **thighs**; down: alum bg2* caust bg2 lept bg2* lyc ptk1 lyss ptk1 onos ptk1 senec bg2* syph ptk1 tub ptk1 zinc bg2
  - **urination** agg.; after: sep a1
  - **vomit**, after efforts to: **Sep** hr1*
  - **walking** agg.: phos k2
  - **washing**, cold (See cold)
- **corrosive**: bacls-10 fmm1• morg-g fmm1• morg-p fmm1• syc fmm1•
- **cough**:
  - **after**: con hr1*
  - **during** | **agg.**: *Nat-m* hr1*
- **cream**-like: alum bufo calc *Calc-p* k* galeoc-c-h gms1• glycyr-g cte1• *Kali-fcy* kr1 lac-h htj1• *Nat-p* k* neon srj5• **Puls** k* sal-fr sle1• *Sec* k* sep *Staph* hr1* streptoc rly4• *Tril-p*
  - **afternoon**: calc-p k*
  - **menses**; before and after: tril-p kr1
  - **painless**: **Puls** hr1*
  - **weakness**; from: *Sec* hr1*
- **curdy**: lac-cp sk4•
- **dark**: *Aesc* k* agar k* croc k* falco-pe nl2• *Helon* hr1 *Kreos* k* nux-m k* sec k* streptoc rly4• *Thlas* kr1* vero-o rly4•
- **delivery**; after: bell-p sf1.de
- **dirty**: arg-met bg2 helo bg2 kreos bg2 nit-ac bg2 *Sec* bg2*
- **dreams**, with amorous (See DREAMS - Amorous - leukorrhea)
- **dropping**: ars j5.de
- **eating**; after: cham j5.de
- **excitement** agg.: calc kr1
- **exertion** agg.: calc tl1 calc-o-t mtf helon kl mag-m mag-s *Sars* kr1 tong bg1
- **flatus**; passing | **after** | **agg.**: caust k*
  - **agg.**: ars a1*
- **flesh**-colored: *Alum* k* bar-c bell a1 bufo canth chin cocc k* kali-i kreos lyc *Nit-ac* k* sabin sep *Tab* j5.de*
  - **afternoon** | **open** air; in: alum h2*
  - **menses**; after: *Nit-ac* hr1*
- **flocculent**: ambr bg2 apis bg2 helo bg2 merc b4.de* sep bg2
- **fluids**; after loss of: *Alet* kr1
- **fright**, before the menarche; from: **Puls** kr1
- **frothy**: but-ac sp1
- **glassy**: stann bg2
- **glue**; like: borx b4a.de
- **gonorrheal**: acon bro1 alumn bro1 apis bro1 arg-n bro1 *Aur-m* *Cann-s* k* *Canth* bro1 cop k* *Cub* bro1 jac-c bro1 kreos bro1 med bro1 *Merc* bro1 merc-c bro1 mez sf1.de **Nit-ac** k* *Ol-sant* bro1 petros bro1 *Plat* **Puls** k* sabin k2* *Sep* k1* sulph bro1 *Thuj* k1*
  - **pregnancy** agg.; during: borx c1
- **gray**: *Arg-met* berb bg3 helon sf1.de kali-s fd4.de kreos bg2* nit-ac sf1.de *Sec* sf1.de
- **greenish**: amor-r jl3 anan apis arg-met jl *Arg-n* *Asaf* k* bacls-10 pte1*• *Bov* k* calc-sil k2 *Carb-ac* k* *Carb-an* hr1* **Carb-v** k* cop cub k* flor-p rsj3* kali-chl *Kali-i* k* *Kali-p* *Kali-s* k* *Lach* k* med jl2* **Merc** k* merc-i-r k* morg-p pte1*• *Murx* k* *Nat-c* **Nat-m** k* **Nat-s** k* **Nit-ac** k* phos kr1* puls k* pulx bro1 rob hr1* sal-fr sle1• *Sec* k* **Sep** k* spong fd4.de stann k2 sulph bro1 syph k2* thuj k* x-ray jl
  - **morning**: murx a1
  - **acrid**: merc-i-r ptk1
  - **menses**; after: *Nit-ac* hr1*
  - **stains** linen: bov k* kali-chl lach k* thuj k*
  - **walking** agg.: *Nat-m* kr1
  - **watery**: *Sep* k*
- **greenish** yellow: arg-met k2 *Bov* j5.de* calc-sil k2* loxo-recl knl4• *Murx* kr1 nat-s br propr sa3• pulx br1 ruta st *Sabin* kr1 *Sep* kr1 **Sulph** kr1 syph k2
- **gushing**: **Calc** k* *Cocc* k* eupi k* fuma-ac rly4• *Gels* k* **Graph** k* kreos ptk1 **Lyc** k* mag-c sf1.de mag-m ptk1 psor ptk1 ruta fd4.de sabin k* **Sep** k* **Sil** k* stann ptk1 thuj k*
  - **cramp**; with: mag-m ptk1
  - **menses**; after: *Nit-ac* hr1*
  - **squatting**; when: cocc ptk1
- **hair** falling off: alum hr1* graph hr1* *Lyc* hr1* *Nat-m* hr1* *Phos* hr1* sulph hr1*
  - ○ **Pubic** bones: *Nat-m* hr1*
- **hemorrhoids**; from suppressed: am-m ptk1
- **hoarseness**; after: con hr1* *Nat-s* hr1*
- **honey**-colored: *Nat-p* hr1* podo fd3.de*
- **hot**: borx b4a.de* ferr-i k2 hep ptk1 *Hydr* kr1 lept ptk1 mang-p rly4•
- **hysteric** women; in: *Am-c* kr1 *Gels* kr1 **Puls** kr1
- **ichorous**: arg-met k2 kreos b7a.de *Sabin* b7.de*
- **insensibility** of vagina from leukorrhea: raja-s jl
- **intermittent**: *Carb-v* kr1 con bro1 spong fd4.de sulph bro1
- **irritating**: *Alum* b4.de* *Bov* b4a.de carb-v b4.de* coli jl2 *Glycyr-g* cte1• *Hep* b4a.de ser-a-c jl2 syph jl2 thuj b4a.de
- **itching**: *(↗Itching - leukorrhea)* agar hr1* agn sf1.de alum b2.de* *Ambr* bro1* *Anac* b2.de* ars b2.de* **Calc** b2.de* *Calc-i* bro1 carb-ac bro1* carc sst* *Caust* hr1* cham bg2 chin b2.de* coff sf1.de *Coll* hr1* con bg2 cub hr1* ferr b2.de* *Fl-ac* hr1* hedeo bro1 helin bro1 helon ptk1 hoit jl3 *Hydr* hr1* irid-met srj5• *Kali-bi* hr1* kali-c b2.de* **Kreos** b2.de* lach bg2 *Merc* b2.de* *Nat-m* b4a.de* *Nit-ac* hr1* ph-ac b2.de* phos bg2 plat sf1.de propr sa3• puls hr1* *Sabin* b2.de* sal-fr sle1• **Sep** b2.de* sil bg2 staph bg2* sulph bg2 syph ptk1 *Zinc* hr1*
  - **menopause**, in: *Murx* kr1
  - **menses**; after: kreos hr1* nit-ac kr1 *Ph-ac* hr1*
- **jellylike**: coc-c *Graph* pall *Sabin* sal-fr sle1• sec sep spong fd4.de
  - **menses**; before and after: *Pall* kr1*
- **lochia**; after cessation of: lyss c1
- **lumpy**: ambr k* *Ant-c* k* ars-met kr1 borx ptk1* *Bov* k* chin k* cur hr1* helon bg3* hep ptk1 hydr bro1 kali-c ptk1 *Merc* k* *Psor* k1* rad-br bg3* *Sep* k* sil bg3* tarent bg3 ust hr1* [rad-met xyz62]
  - **clear**: tarent ptk1
  - **menses**; after: *Chin* hr1*
  - **offensive**: *Chin* hr1* *Psor* hr1*
- **lying** agg.: **Puls** k*
- **masturbation**; from: *Canth* k* orig k* (non:orig-v kr1) *Plat* k* **Puls** k*
- **meat** washings; like: *(↗bloody - watery)* alum bg2* bufo bg2 *Cocc* bg2 kali-i ptk1 kreos bg2 lyc bg2 nit-ac bg2 ozone sde2• phos bg2 sabin bg2 sep bg2 tab a2
- **membranous**: *Borx* sf1.de bov sf1.de hep bg3* hydr sf1.de kali-bi sf1.de nit-ac sf1.de phyt sf1.de vib sf1.de
- **menopause**; during: **Graph** vh* psor al2* *Sabin* kr1* *Sang* hr1* sars vh **Sep** kr1*
  - **continues** after menses cease; leukorrhea: *Sang* kr1*

Female

- **menses**:
  - **after**:
    - **agg.**: aesc k* alet a1 *Alum* k* alum-p k2* alum-sil k2* am-m zr ars k* *Ars-i* ars-s-f k2* bamb-a stb2.de• *Borx* k* **Bov** k* bry b7.de* bufo k* **Calc** k* **Calc-p** k* calc-s calc-sil k2* canth b7.de* carb-ac k* carb-an sf1.de *Carb-v* k* carbn-s carl a1 cassia-s ccrh1• caust k* *Cham* k* chel k* chin k* chinin-ar *Cinnm* hr1* cocc k* *Coloc* bg2* *Con* k* cop k* cub k* *Eupi* k* ferr-i k* *Graph* k* guare k* *Hydr* k* iod k* kali-ar kali-bi kali-c k* *Kali-fcy* kr1 kali-n kali-p kali-sil k2 kalm k* *Kreos* k* lac-c bg2* lac-d k2* lach bg2* lil-t k* luf-op rsj5• *Lyc* k* lyss *Mag-c* k* *Mag-m* bg2* merc k* *Mez* bg2* *Murx* bg2* nat-m k* *Nat-p* nat-s k* *Nicc* k* *Nit-ac* k* nux-v bg2* pall k* *Ph-ac* k* *Phos* k* *Plat* k* psor st1 *Puls* k* *Ruta* k* sabin k* **Sep** bg2* *Sil* k* spig bg2 sul-ac sul-i k2* *Sulph* k* tab k* tarent bg2* tax-br oss1• *Thlas* kr1* thuj k* tril-p bg2* vib *Xan* bro1 zinc k* *Zinc-p* k2*
      - **daytime**, usually in: *Kali-fcy* kr1
      - **some** days, after: *Thlas* kr1
      - **ten** days; after: *Con* kr1 *Hydr* kr1
      - **two** weeks; after: bar-c *Borx* calc-p con *Kali-c* b4a.de mag-m sulph
      - **week**; after a: *Kalm* kr1*
  - **before** | **agg.**: allox jl3 *Alum* k* alum-p k2* alum-sil k2* am-m zr ang bg2* aran-ix jl3 arist-cl mg1.de aur-m k* aur-m-n wbt2• bamb-a stb2.de• *Bar-c* k* bar-i k2* bar-s k2* berb borx bro1* **Bov** k* bufo k1 **Calc** k* *Calc-p* k* *Calc-s* calc-sil k2* *Carb-v* k* carbn-s cassia-s ccrh1• caust bro1 *Cedr* k* chin k* *Cocc* k* con bro1* cub k* ferr k* ferr-act sf1.de ferr-i ferr-p **Graph** k* *Hed* mg1.de* hir mg1.de* iod k* kali-n b4.de* **Kreos** k* lac-c bg2 lac-d k2* *Lach* k* mag-m k* mand mg1.de* mez zr nat-c k* *Nat-m* k* nat-sil k2* *Nux-v* bg2* *Pall* k* *Ph-ac* k* *Phos* k* pic-ac bro1 plat pot-e rly4• prot jl3 psor al2 *Puls* k* ruta k* sabin bg2 **Sep** k* *Sil* k* streptoc rly4• sul-i k2* *Sulph* k* tarent bg2* *Thlas* bg2* thuj b4a.de ust hr1* vib k* *Zinc* k*
  - **between**: aesc bro1 *Alum* bro1 ange-s jl3 **Borx** k* *Bov* bro1 **Calc** k* calc-p kr1 *Cocc* k* *Coloc* con bro1 *Eupi* bro1 ferr b7a.de foll jl3 *Graph* bro1 hydr bro1 hypoth jl3 *Iod* bro1 *Ip* k* kalm bro1 *Kreos* k* *Nit-ac* bro1 ph-ac bro1 plat hr1 prot jl3 *Puls* b7a.de* rob hr1* sabin bro1 **Sep** k* *Sulph* hr1* thlas bro1 thuj kr1 *Xan* bro1
    - **from** one term to another: *Calc-p* kr1 *Thuj* kr1
  - **during**:
    - **agg.**: alum k* am-c bg2 ars k* ars-i st1 bar-c bro1 borx k* bov bg2* calc k2* carb-ac k* carb-an bg2* carb-v k* caust bro1* chin k* chinin-s bg2 *Cocc* k* con k* des-ac jl3 graph k* hura a1 *Iod* k* kali-ar st1 kali-c st1 *Kreos* ptk1* lach j5.de* *Mag-m* k* merc k* mez bg2 mur-ac st1 nat-m bro1* nit-ac st1 phos k* psor st1 puls k* sabin b7.de* sep ptk1* sil st1 spong fd4.de sulph st1 zinc k*
    - **beginning** of menses | **agg.**: *Ruta* b7a.de
  - **instead** of: alum **Ars** k* berb bg3 bov bg1 calc-p *Cedr* k* *Chen-a* k* *Chin* k* *Cocc* k* *Ferr* ger-i rly4• *Graph* k* *Iod* bro1 lac-c mang k2 nat-m bg* *Nux-m* k* *Phos* k* psor st1 puls bro1* rat c1 senec bg1* *Sep* k* *Sil* *Xan* bg* *Zinc*
  - **like** menses: *Alum* *Caust* *Kreos* mag-s zinc
  - **retarded** menses, with: ziz kr1
  - **scanty** menses, with: calc-p k* *Caust* k* *Mez* kr1
  - **smelling** like: *Caust*
  - **suppressed** menses, with: puls b7a.de *Ruta* b7a.de sabin b7.de* ziz kr1
  - **vicarious** menses; before: *Dig* kr1
- **mercury**; after abuse of: **Nit-ac** hr1*
- **mild**: kali-s bg2 *Puls* bg2
- **milky**: *Am-c* k* anan k* ang k* ange-s jl3 aur bro1 bar-c sf1.de bell a1* *Borx* k* **Calc** k* calc-f jl3 *Calc-i* bro1 *Calc-p* k* calc-sil k2* canth bro1 *Carb-v* k* carbn-s chel coff k* *Con* k* cop k* *Euph* hr1* *Ferr* k* ferr-p graph k* haem bro1 *Ign* hr1* iod bro1 *Kali-chl* kali-i k* **Kali-m** k2* kali-p fd1.de• *Kreos* k* *Lach* k* lyc k* naja bro1 nat-m k* *Ovi-p* bro1 paraf bro1 *Phos* k* *Phys* k* podo fd3.de• psor st1 **Puls** k* sabin k* sal-fr sle1• sarr k* **Sep** k* *Sil* k* spong fd4.de *Stann* bro1* *Sul-ac* k* *Sulph* k* *Sumb* *Thuj* b4a.de xan c1
  - **daytime**: **Sep** a1*
  - **morning** | **walking** agg.: *Phos* hr1*
  - **forenoon**: sep a1
  - **coccygodynia**, in: **Kreos** kr1
- **milky**: ...
  - **girls**, in little: hyper kr1
  - **lying** down agg.: **Puls** kr1
  - **menses**; during: phos k* spong fd4.de
  - **urination** agg.; during: *Calc* a1
  - **water** mixed with milk; like: ferr b7.de
- **moon**; full:
  - **at**: **Lyc** vh
  - **before**: *Lyc* j5.de*
- **motion**:
  - **agg.**: *Bov* bro1 **Calc** hr1* carb-an bro1 cassia-s zzc1• euph-pi bro1 graph bro1 helin bro1 mag-c bg2 *Mag-m* b4a.de* mag-s j5.de *Phys* hr1* *Sep* hr1* til bro1
  - **downward** motion agg.: *Borx*
- **mucous**: alum b2.de* am-c bg2 am-m b2.de* ambr b2.de* amp rly4• ant-t bg2 arist-cl sp1 ars b2.de* bell b2.de* **Borx** b2.de* bov b2.de* bry b2.de* but-ac sp1 calc b2.de* canth b2.de* carb-an b2.de* carb-v b2.de* chin bg2 cocc b2.de* con b2.de* ferr b2.de* *Graph* b2.de* guaj b2.de* kali-c h2* kali-n b2.de* kreos b2.de* *Lach* bg2 **Mag-c** b2.de* merc b2.de* mez b2.de* *Nat-c* bg2 nat-m b2.de* nit-ac b2.de* nux-v b2.de* petr b2.de* phos b2.de* plb b2.de* **Puls** b2.de* sabin b2.de* sars b2.de* seneg b2.de* sep b2.de* spong fd4.de **Stann** b2.de* suis-em rly4• suis-pan rly4• sul-ac b2.de* sulfonam ks2 sulph b2.de* thuj b2.de* vero-o rly4• zinc b2.de*
  - **sexual** excitement agg.: senec ptk1
  - **water**; almost the color of: sep b4.de*
  - **white**: calc b4a.de carb-v b4.de* con b4.de* graph b4.de* *Nat-m* b4a.de thuj b4a.de
- **muddy**: nux-m br1
- **odors** | **nauseous**: merc-c bg2
- **offensive**: agath-a nl2• am-m k* amor-r jl3 anan k* aq-mar mgm• *Aral* k* *Arg-met* k* *Ars* k* ars-i ptk1 asaf k* bamb-a stb2.de• bapt k* bufo k* buni-o jl3 calc k* calc-ar k2* calc-p k* calen c2 caps k* **Carb-ac** k* carb-an k* *Carb-v* sf1.de *Chin* k* chinin-ar cimic bg1 *Coloc* k* *Con* hr1* cop sf1.de crot-h k* cub k* cur k* *Eucal* hr1* gaert pte1*• galeoc-c-h gms1• graph k2* gua bro1 *Guare* k* helon k* *Hep* hr1* hist jl3 hydr k* **Kali-ar** k* kali-i **Kali-p** k* ketogl-ac rly4• *Kreos* k* lach lam *Lil-t* lyss hr1* mag-c mg1.de mand mg1.de* med al* *Merc* bro1 merc-c h1 morg-g pte1*• morg-p pte1*• *Myric* hr1* *Nat-ar* *Nat-c* k* **Nit-ac** k* **Nux-v** k* oci-sa sp1 onos *Op* podo fd3.de• pot-e rly4• prot pte1*• **Psor** k* pulx bro1 pycnop-sa mrz1 *Pyrog* k* *Rhus-t* hr1* rob hr1* *Sabin* k* *Sang* k* *Sanic* bro1* sarr k* *Sec* k* **Sep** k* *Sil* k* *Sulph* k* syc pte1*• *Syph* hr1* ter hr1* *Thlas* kr1* *Thymol* sp1* tril-p tub st1 *Ust* k* vanil fd5.de
  - **evening**: sep k*
  - **accompanied** by | **Uterus**; cancer of (See Cancer - uterus - accompanied - discharge)
  - **ammonia**, like: agath-a nl2• am-c k* pycnop-sa mrz1
  - **blackish**, watery: rhus-t
  - **brine** water: *Med* jl2 sanic ptk1
  - **burnt** blood, as: hist mg1.de
  - **carrion**-like: psor tl1
  - **cheese**, like old: agath-a nl2• **Hep** k* ketogl-ac rly4• podo fd3.de• sanic k*
  - **delivery**; after forceps: calen ptk1
  - **fish**-brine, like: bacls-10 fmm1• falco-pe nl2• irid-met srj5• med bg1* ozone sde2• pitu-a vml2• *Sanic* k* thuj bg1
    - **decayed**: *Med* st1
  - **green** corn; odor like: *Kreos* k*
  - **horse's** urine, like: agath-a nl2• but-ac jl3
  - **menopause**, in: *Sabin* kr1
  - **menses**:
    - **after** | **agg.**: ars a1* coloc hr1* *Guare* kreos hr1* nit-ac hr1* tarent hr1*
    - **before** | **agg.**: mand mg1.de*
    - **between**: *Coloc* hr1*
    - **like** menses: caust k*
    - **suppressed** menses; from: sabin c1
  - **pungent**: kreos k*

- **putrid**: arg-met k2 arg-n **Ars** k2 bapt bg2 bufo bg2 cann-xyz bg2 caps bg2 **Carb-ac** k* carb-an k2 *Carb-v* bg2 caust bg2 chin bg2 colch coloc bg2 con bg2 *Cur* hr1* graph k2 helo bg2 *Kali-ar* *Kali-i* k* **Kali-p** k* **Kreos** k* lach k* mur-ac k* *Nat-c* k* nit-ac k* *Nux-v* bg2 ph-ac k* **Psor** k* pulx br1 sabin k* sang bg2 sarr hr1* *Sec* k* *Sep* k* thuj b4a.de *Ust* bg2 vanil fd5.de
  - **night**: galeoc-c-h gms1•
- **sour**: hep k* *Nat-p* k* ozone sde2• pot-e rly4• tung-met bdx1•
- **sweetish**: calc-p k* merc-c k* vanil fd5.de
- **urinous**: ol-an bg1*
- **wood**; like decayed old: bamb-a stb2.de•
- **yeast**-like: agath-a nl2• but-ac sp1 ger-i rly4• sal-fr sle1•

- **oily**: carc dgt thuj b4a.de
- **old** people; in: | **women**; old: ars bro1 *Gels* kr1 *Helon* kr1* nit-ac bro1 *Phos* kr1 sec bro1
- **orange** colored: kali-p ptk1
- **pain**:
  - **abdominal** pain; flowing after: am-m b7.de* bell b4.de* caust b4.de* cham bg2 con b4.de* ferr b7.de* ign bg2 kali-c b4a.de* lyc b4.de* mag-c b4.de* *Mag-m* b4.de* *Merc* b4.de* naja bg2 nat-c b4.de* *Nat-m* b4.de* puls b7a.de sep b4a.de *Sil* b4.de* sulph b4.de* tritic-vg fd5.de *Zinc* b4.de*
  - **backache**; with: abrom-a ks5* lyss c1
    - **right**: abrom-a ks5
  - **with**: mag-m bro1 puls b7a.de sec b7a.de sil bro1 sulph bro1
- **painless**: agn mtf11 *Am-m* hr1* *Ferr* b7a.de *Kreos* b7a.de* nux-v b7.de* *Plat* hr1* **Puls** b7.de* *Ruta* b7a.de
- **paroxysmal**: allox sp1 ant-t lp* eupi a1 lyc b4a.de*
- **periodical**: lyc ptk1
- **pink**: ozone sde2•
- **pregnancy** agg.; during: **Alum** gt1* borx kr1 cimic bg1 *Cocc* k* con h2* kali-c kr1* **Kreos** k* *Murx* k* petr sf1.de plb kr1 *Puls* k* sabin sf1.de* **Sep** k*
  - **abortion**; with tendency to: *Plb* kr1
- **puberty**, at: ferr ptk1 **Sep** hr1*
- **purulent**: aesc bro1* *Agn* bro1 *Alum* k* alum-sil k2* alumn bro1 amor-r jl3 anan k* *Arg-met* k* arg-n bro1 *Ars* bro1 aur-m bro1 *Bov* bg2* bufo k* *Calc* k* calc-s k* calc-sil k2* cann-s bro1 carb-an bro1 cean bro1 cham bro1 *Chin* k* cinnb k* *Cocc* k* con bg2 cop j5.de* cur k* eupi bro1 *Fago* bro1 helin bro1 *Hep* bg2* *Hydr* k* *Ign* k* iod bro1 *Kali-bi* bg1* *Kali-fcy* kr1 kali-p bg* *Kali-s* k* kreos k* lach bro1 lil-t bro1 lyc bro1 *Merc* k* *Merc-c* hr1* *Merc-i-f* k* nat-c k2 *Nat-s* hr1* nit-ac k* *Plat* b4a.de prun bg* **Puls** bg2* pulx bro1 rob hr1* *Sabin* k* sec k* **Sep** k* sil k* *Stann* bro1 *Still* hr1* *Sulph* hr1* *Syph* hr1* thuj b4a.de tril-p bro1 ust bro1
  - **menses** | **after** | **agg.**: *Bov* sf1.de
    - **during** | **agg.**: *Merc* kr1
- **reddish**: alum bg2 calc bg2 chin b7.de* *Cocc* b7.de* kreos b7a.de* lyc b4a.de* nit-ac b4a.de* phos bg2 sabin bg2 sep b4a.de*
  - **blood** red: chin b7.de* lyc b4.de*
- **rest**:
  - **agg.**: fago bro1
  - **amel.**: cassia-s zzc1•
- **rising** from sitting, on: plat h2*
- **ropy**, stringy, tenacious: *Acon* b2.de* acon-l a1* aesc k* alet ptk1* *Alum* bg2* am-m k* androc srj1• ant-t j5.de* aran arg-met jl *Asar* k* bell-p mg1.de* *Borx* k* *Bov* k* *Caust* chel chlam-tr bcx2• *Coc-c* *Croc* dict a1* ferr-br bro1 goss st1 *Graph* k* **Hydr** k* iris bro1 **Kali-bi** k* *Kali-br* kr1 **Kali-m** k2* lac-h htj1• *Mag-m* bg2* *Merc* kr1 mez k* *Nat-c* **Nit-ac** k* *Pall* bro1 ph-ac b2.de* phos b2.de* *Phys* kr1 *Phyt* k* raja-s jl3 rhus-g tmo3• **Sabin** k* *Sil* kr1 spong fd4.de stann k* sulph k2 tarent bg1* tril-p k*
  - **morning**: phyt a1
  - **menses** | **after** | **agg.**: chel a1 phos a1
    - **before** | **agg.**: ferr a1
  - **walking** agg.: *Bov* a1
- **running** down limbs: alum bg2* ant-c bg2 onos bg2 senec bg2
- **scanty**: agn ptk1 but-ac sp1 cassia-s ccrh1• cur hr1* dulc fd4.de galeoc-c-h gms1• graph hr1* mag-c j5.de* murx hr1* phys hr1* puls hr1* *Sars* hr1* *Sulph* hr1* thymol sp1
- **scrofulous** women; in: **Calc** kr1* carb-an kr1 *Iod* kr1
- **sexual** excitement, from (See Sexual desire - increased - accompanied - leukorrhea)
- **sighing** agg.: *Phys* hr1*
- **sitting** agg.: am-c a1 *Ant-t* k* cact bro1 *Cocc* bro1 cycl bro1 *Fago* a1* germ-met srj5• *Mag-c* h2* sumb hr1*
- **sleeplessness**; after: senec kr1
- **slimy** (See mucous)
- **squatting** agg.: cocc ptk1
- **staining** linen: *Abrom-a* zzc1• agn hr1* bov hr1* *Carb-an* j5.de* chel a1* eupi a1 fago a1 graph hr1* *Kreos* j5.de* *Lach* j5.de* *Lil-t* a1* *Nux-v* j5.de* *Prun* j5.de* pulx br1 ruta fd4.de sep hr1* *Thuj* hr1*
  - **wash** out; colors clothes, difficult to: mag-c ptk1 med ptk1 pulx br1* sil ptk1 *Thlas* ptk1 vib ptk1
- **standing**:
  - **agg.**: aesc kr1 *Ars* carb-an kreos lac-c k*
  - **amel.**: fago st
- **starch**, like boiled: **Borx** k* ferr-i k* **Nat-m** k* **Sabin** k* tep a1
- **sticky**: thuj b4a.de
- **stiffening** the linen: *Alum* h2* alumn a1 bell bg2 *Kali-bi* hr1* kali-n b4.de* *Kreos* hr1* *Lach* hr1* *Sabin* bg2
- **stool**:
  - **after** | **agg.**: calc-p kr1 cench k2 *Mag-m* b4a.de* spong fd4.de vib kr1* zinc k*
  - **during** | **agg.**: ferr-i ptk1 mag-c bg1* mag-m bg2 sanic ptk1 spong fd4.de thuj bg1 zinc bg1
  - **every** stool; with: *Mag-m* kr1
- **stooping** agg.: cocc ptk1
- **stringy** (See ropy)
- **stubborn**: mez ptk1
- **students**; in female: *Gels* kr1
- **suddenly** coming and going: *Carb-v* kr1
- **suppressed**: *Am-m* hr1* asaf sf1.de calc-p bg2 carc mlr1• graph sf1.de lac-c bg2 lach sf1.de nat-s bg2 phos bg2 *Sabin* bg2 senec bg2
  - **agg.**: thlas ptk1
- **sycotic**: *Mag-s* st*
- **syphilitic**: *Kali-bi* hr1* *Merc* hr1* *Merc-c* hr1* **Nit-ac** hr1* viol-t hr1*
- **tenacious** (See ropy)
- **thick**: abrom-a ks5 *Acal* hr1* aesc k* alum k* ambr k* amor-r jl3 anac jl anan k* **Ars** k* *Ars-i* ars-s-f k2* *Asar* *Aur* k* aur-ar k2 *Aur-i* k2* aur-s k* bar-c *Borx* k* *Bov* k* bufo **Calc** k* calc-s k* canth a1* carb-ac ptk1 *Carb-v* k* castm *Cean* hr1* *Chlol* hr1* chlorpr pin1• coc-c *Coloc* k* *Con* k* cop j5.de* cur k* goss st helin bro1 **Hydr** k* *Iod* k* **Kali-bi** k* kali-i k2 kali-m bro1 kali-s ketogl-ac rly4• kreos hr1* lach k* lup a1 *Mag-m* k* mag-s k* med st merc a1* mez k* murx k* myric k* *Nat-ar* *Nat-c* k* nat-m k* nit-ac hr1* *Phyt* k* *Podo* k* propr sa3• prot pte1*• *Puls* k* pyrid rly4• rob hr1* *Sabin* k* sarr k* *Sec* hr1* *Senec* ptk1 *Sep* k* spong fd4.de stann k2* staph k* suis-em rly4• *Sul-i* k2* sulph k* symph fd3.de• syph k* thuj bro1 tong j5.de vib k* *Zinc* k*
  - **morning**: aur-s a1 carb-v h2* *Zinc* hr1
  - **night** | **waking**; on: zinc a1
  - **acrid**: bov ptk1 hydr ptk1
  - **creamy**: calc-p ptk1 nat-p ptk1 puls ptk1 sec ptk1
  - **menses**:
    - **after** | **agg.**: ars a1* *Coloc* hr1* *Mag-c* kr1 *Nit-ac* hr1* *Pall* hr1* *Sep* hr1* tab kr1 *Tril-p* kr1 *Vib* kr1 *Zinc* hr1*
    - **before** and after | **agg.**: *Zinc* hr1*
    - **between**: *Coloc* hr1* tril-p kr1
  - **stool** agg.; during: spong fd4.de *Vib* hr1*
  - **urination** agg.; during: **Calc** hr1*
  - **walking** agg.: *Bov* a1
  - **white** paste; as: abrom-a zzc1• *Borx* chlorpr pin1•
- **thin**: (↗*bloody - watery*) abrom-a ks5 abrom-a-r bnj1 *Acal* kr1 agath-a nl2• aids nl2• alum k* alum-p k2 alum-sil k2 am-c k* ambr anan *Ant-c* k* *Ant-t* k* *Arg-met* arist-cl jl *Ars* k* *Ars-i* *Asaf* bapt bg2 bell bro1 bond a1 *Bufo* k* but-ac sp1 *Calc* j5.de* *Calen* kr1 *Carb-an* k* *Carb-v* k* carbn-s cassia-s ccrh1• castm cham k* chin k* chinin-ar *Cocc* cystein-l rly4• *Ferr* k* ferr-ar ferr-i ferr-p fl-ac sf1.de frax bro1* gels sf1.de glycyr-g cte1• **Graph** k* helon *Hydr* kr1 iod irid-met srj5• *Kali-i* k* kali-n k* kali-s k* kola stb3• *Kreos* k* *Lac-c* lept bg2* *Lil-t* k* *Lob* *Lyc* *Mag-c* k* *Mag-m* k* med br1* medul-os-si rly4• merc k* merc-c k* mez k* *Murx* naja bro1 *Nat-m* k* *Nat-p* nicc **Nit-ac** k* *Ol-an* *Ph-ac* *Phos* plat bro1 prun sf1.de* **Puls** k* *Rhus-t* kr1 sabin sarr *Sec* *Sep* k* *Sil* k* stann sul-ac sul-i k2 *Sulph* k* symph fd3.de• syph k* tab kr1* *Tarent* kr1 thuj b4a.de thymol jl* tril-p sne vib

Female

- **morning** | **rising** agg.: *Carb-v* h2* sulph a1
- **forenoon**: mag-c a1
- **afternoon**: *Lil-t* hr1 *Naja* a1*
- **burning**: hydr ptk1
- **dinner**; after: cham h1*
- **menses**:
  - **after** | **agg.**: ars a1* *Mag-c* hr1* *Nit-ac* hr1* tab hr1* *Vib* hr1*
  - **before** | **agg.**: sapin a1
  - **between**: alet
- **pregnancy** agg.; during: *Cocc* hr1*
- **scrofulous** women, in: *Iod* hr1*
- **urination** agg.; after: nicc a1*

- **thin** women; in: abrom-a-r bnj1 phos kr1 *Sec* kr1 *Sep* kr1
- **transparent**: agath-a nl2• *Agn* k* allox sp1 *Alum* k* alumn a1 am-c k* am-m k* anac jl3 *Aur* k* aur-s k2* **Borx** *Bov* k* bufo a1 calc *Calc-p Caust* k* chlorpr jl3 ephe-si hsj1• irid-met srj5• lac-h htj1• *Mez* nabal a1 **Nat-m** k* *Nit-ac* pall k* *Petr Plat* k* *Podo* k* ruta fd4.de **Sep** k* spong fd4.de *Stann* k* stram k* *Sul-ac* k* til st1 ust
  - **menses**; after: *Pall* kr1
  - **rising** from seat, after: plat a1
  - **walking** agg.: *Bov* a1
- **tuberculous** women; in: *Ferr* kr1
- **urination**:
  - **after**:
    - **agg.**: *Am-m* b7.de* carb-v b4.de* con bro1 cur bg2 *Kreos* bro1 mag-m b4.de* *Merc* bro1 *Nat-c* b4.de* nicc j5.de* plat b4a.de* **Sep** b4a.de* **Sil** b4.de* sulph bro1
      - **ceasing** after urination: *Nat-c* kr1
  - **before**: kreos b7a.de*
  - **during**:
    - **agg.**: am-m bg2* calc b4a.de* calc-p bg2* carb-v b4a.de* coff hr1 con bg2* kreos ptk1 merc bg1* nat-c b4.de* plat ptk1 sep ptk1 **Sil** b4.de* *Squil* bg2 streptoc rly4•
      - **fever**:
        - **during** | **agg.**: phos bg2
- **urine**-like: ol-an kl*
- **vaginismus**, in: *Ign* hr1*
- **venereal** disease; from: merc b4a.de mur-ac b4a.de nit-ac b4a.de sul-ac b4a.de sulph b4a.de thuj b4a.de
- **walking**:
  - **agg.**: *Aesc* k* alum k* anan *Aur* k* **Bov** k* calc k* *Carb-an* k* *Graph* kreos k* lac-c k* mag-c h2* mag-m k* *Nat-m* k* onos bg2 *Phos Sars* k* *Sep* k* stront-c k* *Sulph* tong j5.de* *Tub*
  - **amel.**: cact bro1 *Cocc* bro1 cycl bro1 fago st
- **warm**:
  - **bed**, agg.: syph k2
  - **water** flowing down; sensation of warm: *Borx* kr1*
- **washing** | **amel.**: kali-c ptk1
- **watery** (See thin)
- **weak** women; in: **Stann** kr1
- **weakening**: berb sf1.de **Chin** bg2* *Cocc* bg2* coll sf1.de con sf1.de *Frax* sf1.de *Hydr* hr1 *Kali-c* bg2* kreos bg2 nicc sf1.de ph-ac bg2* *Senec* bg2* stann bg2 *Vinc* bg2*
- **weakness**; with: *Aesc* hr1* *Alet* hr1* *Arg-n* hr1* berb hr1* **Calc** hr1* calc-p hr1* *Caul* hr1* *Caust* hr1* con hr1* **Graph** hr1* ham hr1* *Helon* hr1* hydr hr1* *Iod* hr1* **Kreos** hr1* *Lyc* hr1* lyss hr1* **Nat-m** hr1* *Petr* hr1* *Ph-ac* hr1* *Phys* hr1* rob hr1* **Stann** hr1* sul-ac hr1* tarent hr1* thlas mtf11 tril-p kr1 zinc hr1*
- **whey**-like: ferr bg2 kreos bg2
- **white**: abrom-a ks5* alet ptk1* aloe a1 *Alum* alum-sil k2 am-c *Am-m* k* ambr anac jl3 anan *Ant-t Arg-met* arist-cl sp1 *Ars Aur* k* aur-ar k2 *Aur-s* k2* bamb-a stb2.de• bar-c *Bell* h1* berb k* **Borx** k* *Bov* k* bufo *Calc* k* calc-f sp1 *Calc-p* k* calc-sil k2* canth *Carb-v* k* carbn-s cassia-s ccrh1• cench k2 cent a1 chel k* chlam-tr bcx2* coc-c k2 *Con* k* dict a1 elaps a1 falco-pe nl2• *Ferr* k* ferr-ar ferr-p fum rly1*• *Gels* k* goss st1 **Graph** k* guat sp1 haem a1 hydr hr1* kali-c jl3 *Kali-chl* k* *Kali-i* k* *Kali-m* kr1* kali-n k* kola stb3• *Kreos* k* lac-c k* lapa a1 lil-t lyc bg2 *Lyss* k* *Mag-c* b4a.de* mag-s sp1 mand sp1 *Merc* k* merc-c k* *Mez* k* mom-b a1 nabal a1 *Naja* kr1 **Nat-m** k* *Nux-v* hr1* oci-sa sp1 ol-an k*

Leukorrhea – white: ...
olib-sac wmh1 oxal-a rly4• ozone sde2• pall penic srb2.fr *Petr* k* phos k* *Plat* k* *Podo* prun j5.de *Psor* st* *Puls* k* pyrid rly4• rob hr1* sabin k* sal-fr sle1• sarr k* sars k* **Sep** k* sil k* spong fd4.de *Stann* k* stram *Sul-ac* k* sulfonam ks2 sulph k* sumb a1* syc pte1*• symph fd3.de• syph k* *Tarent* hr1* tritic-vg fd5.de ust vib k* *Zinc* k* zinc-p k2*
  - **morning** | **rising** agg.: **Graph** kr1
  - **afternoon**: naja a1
  - **evening**: phos a1
  - **egg** like: borx tl1 nat-m mtf33 petr mtf11
  - **green** afterwards; turns: nat-m ptk1
  - **menses**; after: vib kr1
  - **sitting** agg.: *Sumb* a1
  - **stains** linen yellow: chel k* kreos a1
  - **stool** agg.; during: cench k2* spong fd4.de *Vib* hr1*
- **yellow**: acon k* *Aesc* k* aids nl2• alet sf1.de *Alum* k* alum-p k2* alum-sil k2* *Alumn* anan androc srj1• apis *Arg-met Arg-n* k* **Ars** k* *Ars-i Ars-s-f* k2* *Asar* k* *Aur* k* aur-ar k2 **Aur-i** k2* *Aur-m* k* *Aur-s* bell bg2 bov k* *Bufo* buni-o jl3 **Calc** k* calc-ar k2 calc-f jl3 calc-i k2* *Calc-s* k* calc-sil k2* *Cann-s* hr1 *Carb-an* k* *Carb-v* k* cean sf1.de cench k2* **Cham** k* *Chel* k* chin bg2 *Chlor* hr1* cimic jl3 cinnb k* coli jl2 *Coloc* k* con k* cub k* cycl sf1.de dream-p sdj1• dulc fd4.de *Eupi* fago a1* falco-pe nl2• fl-ac k* foll jl3 gels ptk1 *Gran* k* *Graph* k* **Hydr** k* ign sf1.de *Inul* a1* *Iod* k* *Kali-ar Kali-bi* k* kali-c k* kali-chl k13 *Kali-fcy* kr1 *Kali-i* k* kali-m k2 *Kali-p Kali-s* k* *Kali-sil* k2* *Kalm* k* **Kreos** k* *Lac-ac* lac-c k* *Lac-d* k* lac-f c1 lach *Lil-t* k* *Lyc* k* mag-c mg1.de mand mg1.de* med kr1* *Merc* k* merc-c k* *Merc-i-f* k* merc-i-r k* morg-p pte1*• *Murx* k* myric k* *Nat-ar Nat-c* k* nat-m k* *Nat-p Nat-s* hr1* nat-sil k2* nit-ac *Nux-v* k* oci-sa jl* *Ol-j* k* onos *Pall* k* penic jl3* *Ph-ac* k* phos positr nl2• prun k* psor vh* *Puls* k* rob hr1* ruta fd4.de *Sabin* k* *Sec* kr1 senec ptk1 **Sep** k* ser-a-c jl2 sil spira a1 spong fd4.de *Stann* k* suis-em rly4• sul-ac *Sul-i* k2* **Sulph** k* suprar rly4• syc pte1*• symph fd3.de• *Syph* k* *Thuj* b4a.de* *Tril-p* kr1* tritic-vg fd5.de ust k* vanil fd5.de vib tl1 *Zinc* k* *Zinc-p* k2*
  - **morning**: *Aur-m* a1* kalm a1 **Sep** a1
  - **night**: *Syph*
  - **children**; in: *Merc-i-f* hr1* *Syph* hr1*
  - **menopause**; during: *Sabin* kr1
  - **menses**:
    - **after** | **agg.**: ars a1 lac-d k2 ph-ac a1* *Sep* kr1 **Tarent** kr1
    - **before** | **agg.**: ang a1* ars a1 lac-d k2 *Nat-m* hr1* *Puls* hr1* *Sep* hr1* *Tarent* hr1*
    - **between**: calc k2 *Coloc* hr1* tril-p kr1
    - **during** | **agg.**: calc k2 des-ac jl3 *Puls* hr1*
  - **motion** agg.: *Sep* kr1
  - **scrofulous** women, in: *Iod* hr1*
  - **stains** linen: aeth vh1 *Agn* hr1* *Carb-ac* hr1* *Carb-an* k* chel k* fago c1 **Kreos** k* nit-ac ptk1 *Nux-v* bg2 prun k* ruta fd4.de tritic-vg fd5.de
  - **urination** agg.; before: *Kreos* hr1*
  - **water**; like yellow: nat-c b4.de* *Sep* b4.de* thuj b4a.de
  - **yellow** green (See greenish yellow)

LOCHIA: *(↗Delivery - after; Delivery - during)* hoit jl
- **night**: *Merc* kr1
- **abortion**, after: ruta a1
- **acrid**: *Bapt* k* *Carb-an* k* con **Kreos** k* lil-t k* *Merc Nit-ac* bro1 plat *Pyrog* k* rhus-t *Sep Sil* k*
- **bloody**: acon k* am bg2 bell bg2 bry calc k* caul k* *Cham* k* chin bg2 chr-ac br1* crot-h bg2 erig hr1 ham bg2 ip bg2 rhus-t k* *Sec* j5.de* sep b4a.de sil k* *Tril-p* bg2* ust bg2
  - **again** bloody after growing light; it becomes: *Calc* **Erig** *Kreos Rhus-t* sil
  - **motion**, after least: erig k*
  - **nursing** child, when: *Sil* k*
  - **too**: acon bry calc caul *Cham* rhus-t *Sec* j5.de sil
- **brown**: *Carb-v* k* *Kreos* k* pyrog c1* *Sec* k*
- **cheese**, like: bell bg1
- **clotted**: *Chin* kr1 cimic **Kreos** k* mag-c a1
  - **partly**: **Ust** bg1*

- **complaints** of: bell bg2 bov b4a.de brom bg2 bry bg2 calc bg2 carb-an bg2 chin b7a.de coloc bg2 con bg2 croc bg2 hep b4a.de* hyos bg2 merc b4a.de nux-v bg2 *Plat* bg2 *Puls* bg2 *Rhus-t* bg2 **Sec** bg2 sep b4a.de verat bg2 zinc bg2
- **copious**: abrot a1 acon benz-ac a1 brom bg2 bry k* buni-o jl3 calc k* carb-an *Cham* k* chin *Coff* k* *Con* k* *Croc* k* erig k* hep k* lil-t k* mill k* *Nat-c* nat-m k2* nux-v b7a.de oci-sa sp1 *Plat* k* puls k* *Rhus-t* k* sabin b7.de* *Sec* k* senec sep bg2* **Sil** hr1* sulph tril-p *Ust* k* xan k*
- **dark**: caul bro1 *Cham* k* *Chin* *Croc* **Kreos** k* nit-ac bro1 *Plat* k* pyrog bro1 **Sec** k* ust k*
  - **stringy**; and: *Croc* st
- **excoriating**: kreos tl1
- **green**: lac-c ptk1 sec bg*
- **gushing**: erig bro1 *Plat*
- **hot**: bell k*
- **ichorous**: *Carb-an* rhus-t *Sec*
- **intermittent**: *Calc* con bro1 *Kreos* k* *Plat* pyrog bro1 rhus-t k* sulph bro1
- **milky**: *Calc* k* *Puls* *Sep*
- **motion** agg.: erig bro1
- **nursing** the child agg.; when: **Sil** hr1*
- **offensive**: acon ars sf1.de *Bapt* k* bell k* *Bry* carb-ac k* *Carb-an* k* *Carb-v* k* *Chin* chinin-ar sf1.de **Chr-ac** kr1* *Crot-h* crot-t bro1 *Echi* sf1.de* erig bro1 kali-chl ptk1 **Kali-p** k* **Kreos** k* lach nit-ac bg2* nux-v oci-sa sp1 petr hr1 *Pyrog* k* *Rhus-t* k* *Sal-ac* kr1 **Sec** k* *Sep* k* sil stram k* sulph k*
  - **cadaverous**: stram k*
  - **delivery**, after instrumental: calen vml3•
  - **putrid**: ars bg2 bapt bg2 *Bell* bg2 carb-ac bg2 **Carb-an** bg2 echi bg2 kreos bg2* lach bg2 pyrog bg2 rhus-t bg2 *Sec* bg2
- **periodical** | **weeks**; every two: *Tril-p* c1
- **protracted**: bapt bell bell-p bg2* benz-ac k* buni-o jl3 *Calc* k* **Carb-ac** k* **Carb-an** hr1* caul k* *Chin* k* croc k* helon k* hep *Kreos* k* lil-t k* merc k2 mill bro1 **Nat-m** k* *Plat* *Rhus-t* k* sabin bro1 **Sec** k* **Senec** k* sep k* sulph tril-p k* ust k*
- **purulent**: *Chin* hr1* *Lach* hr1* sulph k2
- **red**: acon bry calc chin psor *Sil* sulph
- **returning**: acon k* *Calc* erig k* helon *Kreos* k* *Psor* *Puls* *Rhus-t* senec sulph
  - **motion**, after least: *Erig* hr1*
- **scanty**: acon *Bell* k* bry k* cham bro1 coloc k* dulc k* guare a1* *Nux-v* k* **Puls** k* *Pyrog* k* rad-br ptk1 **Sec** k* stram k* *Sulph*
- **sexual** desire; with increased: *Verat* kr1
- **suppressed**: acon k* alet aral k* art-v c1 bapt k2 bell k* **Bry** k* *Camph* k* *Carb-ac* hr1* caul k* *Cham* k* *Chin* *Cimic* k* coff b7a.de coloc k* *Dulc* k* echi bro1 *Hep* bg2* *Hyos* k* kali-c bg2* leon bro1 lyss c1 merc k2 mill k* mur-ac a1* *Nux-v* k* op k* par c1* phyt c1 plat k* psor **Puls** k* **Pyrog** k* ruta bg2 *Sec* k* senec c1 sil hr1* *Stram* **Sulph** k* **Ter** bg2* verat k* *Verat-v* hr1 zinc k*
  - **air**; by draft of: *Verat-v* kr1
  - **anger**; after: cham k* coloc k*
  - **cold** agg.; becoming: *Acon* k* *Bry* cham k* *Cimic* k* *Dulc* k* **Pyrog** k* *Sulph*
  - **dampness**, from: *Dulc* hr1*
  - **emotions**, by: *Cimic* hr1* *Ign* hr1*
  - **excitement**, by: cimic k* *Ign* kr1
  - **fever**; with: *Acon* hr1* mill hr1* sec hr1*
  - **fright** agg.: acon ign op k*
  - **grief**; from: ign
  - **vexation** agg.: acon cham sf1.de coloc
- **thin**: bell *Carb-an* k* cimic k* lach k* *Pyrog* *Rhus-t* *Sec* ust
  - **partly** clotted: **Ust** kr1
- **watery**: *Carb-an* bg2
- **white**: *Nat-m* *Puls* *Sep* sulph

LYING:

- **agg.**: *Am-c* bro1 am-m bro1 ambr ptk1 *Bov* bro1 *Cycl* bro1 ferr ptk1 kreos bro1* *Mag-c* bro1 murx ptk1 *Puls* ptk1 *Zinc* bro1

○ • **Uterus**: ambr k*
- **amel.**: bov bro1 cact bro1 caust bro1 lil-t bro1
- **back**; on:
  - **amel.** | **Uterus**: onos ptk1

Lying: ...
- **side**; on:
  - **affected** side:
    - **amel.** | **Ovaries**: apis ptk1 kali-p ptk1 pall ptk1

LYING-IN women (See Delivery - after; Delivery - during)

MASTURBATION, disposition to: agn k2 ambr k* *Anac* c1 anan *Apis* c1 aur-ar k2 bamb-a stb2.de• bell-p c1* bufo k* *Calad* calc c1* *Calc-p* c1 **Canth** sne *Carc* st1* caust st1 *Chin* c1* coff st1 *Gels* *Grat* k* haliae-lc srj5• **Hyos** mrr1* *Kali-br* c1 *Lach* k* lil-t bg2* *Lyc* zf med c1* merc mtf33 mosch mrr1 musca-d szs1 *Nat-m* c1 *Nux-v* hr1* *Onos* mrr1 op a1 **Orig** k* (non:orig-v kr1*) *Ph-ac* c1* phos k2* pic-ac c1 **PLAT** k* puls k* raph ruta fd4.de sal-n c1* sec k2 **Staph** c1* stram mrr1* *Sulph* c1* tarent c1* thuj c1* *Tub* k* ust c1* verat sne **Zinc** j5.de*
- **children**; in: (↗*young*) aloe lmj ambr lmj aur mtf33 bufo mtf33 *Calc-p* lmj *Cann-i* lmj canth lmj carc jl2* dys pte1*• *Fl-ac* lmj grat mrr1 **Hyos** lmj* lac-c lmj **Lach** lmj* lyss lmj med lmj* **Merc** lmj* *Mosch* lmj **Orig** mrr1 ph-ac lmj **Phos** lmj plat mtf33 puls mtf33 staph lmj* stram mtf33 tub ggd* verat sne *Zinc* lmj*
  - **rubbing** thighs together: orig mrr1
- **cough** or spasms; during: *Zinc* sf1.de
- **epileptics**; in: lach bg2
- **itching**, from:

○ • **Clitoris**: agar vh1
  - **Vagina**; in: calad mrr1
    - **children**; in: calad bro1* *Orig* bro1 zinc bro1
  - **Vulva**, in: *Calad* ptk1 *Orig* ptk1 zinc c1*
- **menses**; during: zinc ptk1*
- **public**; in: (↗*MIND - Naked - exhibitionism*) **Hyos** mrr1
- **relief**; without: canth mrr1
- **young** people: (↗*children*) carc jl2

MATURITY (See Development)

MEMBRANE on: | **Labia**: helo bg2 tarent bg2

MENARCHE: | **delayed** (See Menses - delayed)

MENOPAUSE (= climaxis): (↗*GENERALS - Menopause; MIND - Menopause*) acon hr1* *Agar* k* alet bro1* aloe alum k2 *Aml-ns* kr1* ant-c mrr1 *Apis* aq-mar rbp6 aqui br1* *Arg-n* k* arist-cl mg1.de aur bg* bar-c bell bro1* bell-p c1* bor-ac bro1* *Bry* k* *Cact* bro1* calc k* *Calc-ar* hr1* camph k2* caps bg* carb-v bro1* *Carc* st* caul bro1* *Chin* k* *Cimic* k1* *Cocc* k* coff k* *Con* k* *Croc* k* **Crot-c** *Crot-h* k* *Cycl* k* dig c1 ferr bro1* ferr-p bg* *Gels* k* *Glon* k* **Graph** k* ham hr1 *Helon* k* hir sf1.de *Hydr* k* ign k* *Jab* hr1* *Kali-bi* k1* *Kali-br* hr1* *Kali-c* hr1* *Kali-s* st1 *Kreos* c1* **Lach** k* laur c1 lil-t k2 lutin mtf11 lyc bg* mag-c br1* magn-gl st1 *Manc* bro1* **Mang** k* meli ptk1 merc-sul vh* mosch k* **Murx** k* nat-m bg* nicc-s br1 nit-ac k* *Nux-m* c1* *Nux-v* bg* ol-an bg* orch c1 *Ov* c1* ph-ac kr1* *Phos* phys hr1* pilo sf1.de plat bg* plb bg* **Psor** k* *Puls* k* rhus-t bg* *Sabin* bg* sal-ac hr1* *Sang* k* sanguiso sf1.de sars hr1* *Sel* semp c1* **Sep** k* *Stront-c* sf1.de* *Sul-ac* k* **Sulph** k* sumb hr1* *Tab* k* *Ter* k* *Ther* k* tril-p c1 tub mrr1 *Ust* k* valer hr1* *Verat* k* viol-o hr1 vip br1* vip-a vh visc bro1* xan k* zinc bg* *Zinc-val* bro1* [mang-act stj2 mang-i stj2 mang-m stj2 mang-met stj2 mang-n stj2 mang-p stj2 mang-s stj2 mang-sil stj2 stront-m stj2 stront-met stj2]
- **never** well since (See GENERALS - Convalescence - menopause)
- **obese** women; in: calc-ar br1*
- **sadness**; with (See MIND - Sadness - menopause)
- **servants**, in: *Con* st1

MENORRHAGIA (See Menses - copious)

MENSES:
- **daytime** only: *Abies-n* vml3• cact *Caust* k* coff k* cycl k* dulc fd4.de ham k* kali-c bg2 lach zf ozone sde2• **Puls** k* sabin b7a.de [calc-m stj1 chr-m stj2]
  - **walking**; mostly on: **Puls** kr1
- **morning**: am-m *Borx* k* *Bov* k* carb-an ptk1 sep ptk1 sulph k*
  - **evening**; and: *Phel*
  - **day** amel.; during: am-m
  - **only**: *Bov* k* carb-an k* nat-s c1 **Sep** k*
  - **rising** agg.: **Bov** mrr1 mag-c ptk1 plat a1
  - **walking** agg.: glon a1
- **forenoon**, only: lycps-v nat-s

Female

- **noon**: coca a1
- **afternoon**: ferr lyc mag-c a1
  - **ceases** in afternoon: *Mag-c* k*
  - **walking** only, while: nat-s
- **evening**:
  - **lying** agg.: berb a1 bov coc-c
  - **only**: coc-c ptk1 coff k* phel ptk1
- **night**: abrom-a ks5 *Am-c* k* *Am-m* k* *Borx* bro1 *Bov* k* chord-umb rly4• coc-c k* *Coca* ferr sf1.de gink-b sbd1• glon **Mag-c** k* mag-m k* *Nat-m* sep sf1.de sulph *Zinc* k* [mag-lac stj2 mag-met stj2 mag-n stj2 mag-sil stj2]
  - **23 h** | **flow** commences: lac-ac kr1
  - **only**: am-c ptk1 am-m ptk1 borx **Bov** k* coc-c ptk1 coff cycl mag-c k* mag-p ptk1 nat-m k*
  - **sleep**; only during: mag-c
- **absent** (= amenorrhea): *Acon* k* aesc agar agn alet k* all-c kr1 aln c1* *Am-c* am-m ammc kr1 *Anac* kr1 *Ant-c* *Apis* k* *Apoc* k* arg-n *Arist-cl* mg1.de* *Ars* k* *Ars-i* k* asar bg2* asar-c br1 **Aur** k* aur-ar k2 aur-i k2 aur-s k2 aven br1* *Bar-c* *Bell* k* bell-p sp1 benz-ac berb *Borx* brass-n-o srj5• brom bg2* *Bry* k* *Calc* k* calc-i k2 calc-p bg2* calc-s calc-sil k2 cann-s bro1 canth carb-v **Carbn-s** card-m *Caul* k* *Caust* k* *Cham* chel k* *Chin* k* chinin-ar chlorpr jl3 cic cimic k* cina *Coca* kr1 *Cocc* *Coch* kr1 colch *Coll* *Coloc* **Con** k* cortico mg1.de cortiso mg1.de* croc crot-t *Cupr* k* *Cupr-act* kr1 *Cycl* k* *Cypr* kr1* dam c1* dig dream-p sdj1• *Dros* **Dulc** k* euphr k* eupi c1* **Ferr** k* *Ferr-ar* k* **Ferr-i** k* *Ferr-p* *Ferr-r* bro1 gast c1* gels k* *Glon* bg2* goss k* **Graph** k* *Guaj* k* *Ham* hedeo c1* *Hell* k* helo bg2 helon k* hoit jl3 *Hyos* hyper bg2* ictod kr1 *Ign* indg j5.de* *Iod* k* joan br1* *Kali-ar* **Kali-c** k* kali-i *Kali-n* *Kali-p* k* *Kali-perm* bro1 kali-s kreos c1* lac-d sf1.de* lac-f wza1• *Lach* k* lil-t k* linu-c c1* lob k* luf-op mtf11 **Lyc** k* m-arct c1* *Mag-c* k* *Mag-m* mag-s j5.de mand sp1 mang-act bro1 med jl2 *Merc* *Merl* bro1 mill *Mit* kr1 nat-c *Nat-m* k* nat-p nat-s ptk1 nat-sil k2 nep mg1.de* *Nux-m* *Nux-v* k* ol-an bg2* *Ol-j* kr1* op bro1 orot-ac rly4• ovi-p c1* parth c1* ph-ac k* *Phos* k* *Phyt* kr1 pin-l c1* pitu jl3 *Plat* k* plb bg2* podo k* *Polyg-h* bro1 polyg-pe c1 polyg-xyz c2 polytr-c lsr3.de• **Puls** k* puls-n c1* rhod c1* *Rhus-t* k* rub-t sf1.de* *Sabad* sabin sang k* sanic c1* sec k* **Senec** k* *Seneg* bro1 **Sep** k* sieg mg1.de **Sil** k* *Sin-n* kr1* spong kr1* *Staph* k* stram sul-i k2 **Sulph** k* syc pte1*• symph c1 tanac bro1 tep c1* thal-xyz srj8• ther mrr1 thiop jl3 *Thuj* kr1 thyr c1* **Tub** k* urt-u bg2* ust bro1 *Valer* k* verat k* verat-v k* vib kr1 wies c1* wye c1* x-ray sp1 xan k* yohim br1 *Zinc* k* zinc-p k2 [astat stj2 bism-sn stj2 heroin sdj2 lith-c stj2 mang-m stj2 polon-met stj2 thal-met stj2 vanad stj1*]
  - **accompanied** by:
    - **apyrexia**: nat-m bro1
    - **palpitations** (See CHEST - Palpitation - accompanied - menses)
    - **respiration**; difficult (See RESPIRATION - Difficult - accompanied - menses)
    - **Conjunctiva**; inflammation of (See EYE - Inflammation - conjunctiva - accompanied - menses)
    - **Joint** pains: caul mrr1
    - **Mammae**; scirrhus of (See CHEST - Cancer - mammae - scirrhus - accompanied - menses)
    - **Tongue** | **mapped** tongue: *Nat-m* kr1*
  - **bathing**; cold: ant-c bg2
  - **cold**; after taking a: asar-c br1 hell ptk1 senec ptk1
  - **complaints** of menses are present; only: *Ant-c* *Calc* kr1 *Con* *Cur* k* (non:cycl kl) *Senec* kr1
  - **feeble** women; in: *Ars* kr1* **Sep** kr1
  - **girls**; in: apoc vh aqui mtf11 cortico jl3 cortiso jl3 nep jl3 polyg-h br thala jl3 x-ray jl
  - **grief**; from: ign mrr1
  - **hysteric** women; in: *Cypr* kr1 *Sil* kr1
  - **long** period: wies c1*
  - **milk** in mammae, with: phos ptk1 *Rhus-t* kr1*
  - **molimen** only (See complaints)
  - **nervous** women; in: ars k2 ter c1
  - **plethoric** women; in: (↗*GENERALS - Plethora - constitution*) **Calc** kr1 *Petros* kr1
  - **psoric** women; in: *Psor* kr1
- **absent**: ...
  - **scrofulous** women: *Bar-c* kr1 *Sulph* kr1
  - **sexual** desire | **without**: *Helon* kr1
  - **strain**, after psychical and physical: hypoth jl3
- **accompanied** by | **cold** food; desire for (See GENERALS - Food and - cold food - desire - accompanied - menses; GENERALS - Food and - milk - desire - cold)
- **acrid**, excoriating: all-s *Am-c* k* amor-r jl3 ant-t bg2 ars k* ars-s-f k2* aur bg2 aur-m k* bar-c k* bov k* brucel sa3• calc-sil k2* canth k* carb-ac bg2* *Carb-v* k* carbn-s *Caust* k* cham ferr k* *Graph* k* hep k* *Kali-ar* kali-bi k2* **Kali-c** k* kali-chl k13 kali-m k2 *Kali-n* k* kreos k* *Lac-c* **Lach** k* mag-c k* merc k2 nat-c bg2 *Nat-s* k* *Nit-ac* bg2* petr k* phos bg2 prun bg2 puls bg2 raja-s jl3 *Rhus-t* k* sabin bro1 sang bg2* *Sars* k* sep k* **Sil** k* *Stram* bg2* sul-ac k* *Sulph* k* tere-ch jl3 zinc k*
- **after**:
  - **agg.**: agar bg2 ars bg2 berb bg2 bov bg2 brom bg2 canth bg2 chin bg2 coc-c bg2 cocc bg2 *Con* bg2 *Graph* bg2 iod bg2 kali-bi bg2 kali-br bg2 kali-c bg2 **Kreos** bg2 lil-t bg2 lyc bg2 mag-c bg2 merc bg2 mez bg2 *Nat-m* bg2 ph-ac bg2 phos bg2 *Plat* bg2 puls bg2 sep bg2 sulph bg2 tarent bg2 thuj bg2 zinc bg2
    - **Ovaries**: zinc-val ptk1
- **ailments** from menstrual disorders (See GENERALS - Menses; MIND - Menses)
- **albuminous** | **morning**: calc-p a1
- **alternating** with bloody discharge: tarent kr1
- **amelioration** of all complaints during menses (See GENERALS - Menses - during - amel.)
- **ammoniacal**: lac-c ptk1
- **anger** brings on the flow: cham nat-m
- **appear**:
  - **as** if menses would appear: acon-ac rly4• act-sp *Aloe* am-m ambr *Apis* k* aur bit-ar wht1• bry *Calc-p* canth carb-v a1 cina cocc *Croc* k* *Cycl* hr1 dream-p sdj1• ferr hir jl hyos bg2* inul kali-c kreos lat-h thj1 laur lil-t lyc *Mag-c* mag-p bg2 mosch k* mur-ac k* *Murx* *Nat-c* nat-m *Onos* phos phys kr1 phyt a1 *Plat* plumbg a1 *Puls* puls-n a1 sang *Senec* *Sep* stann bg2* staph succ-ac rly4• suis-pan rly4• sul-ac til vib
    - **afternoon**, but evening amel.: pall a1
    - **drawing** pain: calc-p k*
    - **pinching** pain: mur-ac
    - **pressing**: *Mur-ac* plat
  - **cold**; after a: *Puls* j5.de
  - **injuries**; after: **Croc** kr1
  - **proper** age; before the: ambr *Ant-c* k* bell *Calc* bg2* *Calc-p* k* canth k* carb-v bg2* *Caust* *Cham* k* chin k* cina ptk1 coc-c cocc k* ferr goss st hyos ip kali-c kali-p kr1 lyc merc nit-ac *Phos* k* *Puls* k* rhus-t *Sabin* k* sec *Sil* k* sulph verat bg2*
  - **shock**, from a: *Op* k2
  - **suddenly**: bros-gau mrc1 *Nat-m* a1 *Phos* a1
- **before**:
  - **agg.**: bufo bg2 cocc bg2 croc bg2 graph bg2 hyos bg2 kali-c bg2 mag-c bg2 merc bg2 plat bg2 sep bg2 sulph bg2
    - **Ovaries**: ant-t bg2 arg-n bg2 borx bg2 brom bg2 caps bg2 carb-an bg2 chin bg2 cub bg2 lyc bg2 plat bg2 senec bg2 sul-ac bg2 tab bg2 thuj ptk1
      - **right**: apis bg2 graph bg2 lac-c bg2 podo bg2 sars bg2
      - **left**: coloc bg2 *Lach* bg2 thuj bg2 ust bg2 vib bg2 zinc bg2
    - **Pudendum**: ambr bg2 aur-m bg2 bov bg2 bufo bg2 calc bg2 calc-p bg2 carb-v bg2 chin bg2 coc-c bg2 con bg2 croc bg2 dulc bg2 **Graph** bg2 kali-bi bg2 **Kali-c** bg2 lac-c bg2 lil-t bg2 lyc bg2 merc bg2 mosch bg2 murx bg2 *Sep* bg2 sil bg2 sulph bg2 verat bg2 zinc bg2
    - **Uterus**: aesc bg2 alum bg2 am-c bg2 aml-ns bg2 arg-n bg2 asc-t bg2 borx bg2 brom bg2 bry bg2 bufo bg2 cact bg2 carb-an bg2 carb-v bg2 caul bg2 chin bg2 *Cimic* bg2 cocc bg2 con bg2 ferr bg2 gels bg2 graph bg2 hyper bg2 ip bg2 lac-c bg2 lach bg2 lil-t bg2 lyc bg2 mag-c bg2 mosch bg2 *Murx* bg2 nat-c bg2 nat-m bg2 nit-ac bg2 nux-m bg2 ph-ac bg2 phos bg2 sabin bg2 sep bg2 ust bg2 verat-v bg2 vib bg2
    - **Vagina**: bufo bg2 elaps bg2 ferr bg2 graph bg2 mag-c bg2 merc bg2 murx bg2 nat-m bg2 sep bg2 *Sulph* bg2

- **agg.**: ....
  - : **Vulva**: ambr bg2 aur-m bg2 bov bg2 bufo bg2 calc bg2 calc-p bg2 carb-v bg2 chin bg2 coc-c bg2 con bg2 croc bg2 dulc bg2 **Graph** bg2 kali-bi bg2 **Kali-c** bg2 lac-c bg2 lil-t bg2 lyc bg2 merc bg2 mosch bg2 murx bg2 *Sep* bg2 sil bg2 sulph bg2 verat bg2 zinc bg2
- **proper** age; the (See appear - proper)

- **black**: acon b7a.de agath-a nl2• *Am-c* k* *Am-m* k* ant-c k* ant-t a1 apis k* am b7.de* arund asar k* *Bell* k* berb hr1* bism b7.de* bov bro1 *Bry* b7a.de calc-p k* canth k* *Carb-an* k* *Carb-v* k* carbn-s cassia-s ccrh1• caul bro1 *Caust* b4a.de *Cham* b7.de* *Chin* k* cimic bro1 coc-c k* *Cocc* k* coff bro1 *Colch* b7a.de con b4a.de *Croc* k* **Cycl** k* *Elaps* k* *Ferr* k* graph k* ham bro1* helon bro1* hydrog srj2• *Ign* k* jug-r a1 kali-chl hr1 kali-m bg2* **Kali-n** k* kali-p k* kreos b7a.de* lac-h htj1• **Lach** k* *Lil-t* bro1 *Lyc* k* *Mag-c* k* *Mag-m* k* mag-p bro1* *Mag-s* j5.de* mang h2* med bro1 *Nat-hchls* nat-m j5.de nat-s j5.de* *Nit-ac* b4a.de* nux-m b7a.de* *Nux-v* k* *Ol-an* k* *Ph-ac* b4a.de phos b4a.de* *Plat* k* plb bro1 **Puls** k* raja-s jl3 rob k* ruta fd4.de sabin bro1 *Sang* k* *Sec* k* sel b7a.de *Sep* b4a.de* sol-t-ae k* *Stram* k* *Sulph* k* tep a1 ter hr1 thal jl3 *Thlas* bro1 thuj bg1 tril-p bro1 ust k* vanil fd5.de xan k* [astat stj2 bism-sn stj2 polon-met stj2 sol-ecl cky1 thal-met stj2]
  - **forenoon**: carb-an ptk1
  - **clots**, with: alet k2 *Am-c* hr1 arist-cl jl3 *Chin* hr1 hoit jl3 *Lyc* hr1 plat hr1
  - **inky**: agath-a nl2• *Kali-n* j5.de*
  - **pitch**-like: agath-a nl2• bism k* *Cact* *Cocc* k* croc sf1.de *Graph* k* kali-chl hr1 kali-m kr1* kali-n k* *Mag-c* k* *Mag-m* k* mag-p ptk1 nux-v k* *Plat* k* sang k*
  - **sticky**: coc-c ptk1
- **bloody** mucous: alum apis bar-c berb *Cocc* *Croc* kr1 hydrog srj2• lachn nat-s nux-m a1 **Puls** kr1 pycnop-sa mrz1 *Sep* kr1 wies a1
  - **morning**: nat-s a1
  - **last** day: *Apis* kr1
- **bright** red: acon k* aids nl2• aloe alum bg2* am-c k* anan ant-t k* anthraq rly4• aran *Am* k* ars k* atro sf1.de *Bamb-a* stb2.de• bar-c **Bell** k* borx b2.de* bov k* brom k* bry k* bung-fa mtf calc k* *Calc-p* k* calc-sil k2 canth k* carb-an k* carb-v k* *Caust* cench k2 chin k* *Cinnm* k* coloc croc dig k* dros k* **Dulc** k* ergot jl3 **Erig** k* eupi a1 *Ferr* k* ferr-ar ferr-p k* fic-r mg1.de foll jl3 form glyc bro1 graph k* *Ham* k* **Hyos** k* **Ip** k* irid-met srj5• kali-ar *Kali-c* kali-chl kali-m k2 kali-n k* kali-s kali-sil k2 kola stb3• kreos k* *Lac-c* k* lachn c1 laur k* led k* lil-t lyc m-aust b2.de* mag-m k* manc med kr1 meli merc b2.de* merc-c b4a.de **Mill** k* mit zr nat-c k* nit-ac bg2* nux-m k* ozone sde2• pall a1 petr-ra shn4• **Phos** k* plat podo fd3.de• positr nl2• pot-e rly4• puls k* *Rhus-t* k* sabad k* **Sabin** k* sacch-a gmj3 *Sang* k* sapin a1 *Sec* k* sep k* sil k* spig k* stram k* stront-c k* sulph k* syph thioc-ac rly4• thuj k* tril-p k* tritic-vg sna6 *Ust* k* vib bg2* visc sp1* xan c1 zinc k* zinc-p k2
  - **forenoon** | **9h**: sol-t-ae a1
  - **clotted**: *Arn* kr1 *Bell* kr1 caust kr1 kali-s fd4.de lil-t kr1 *Puls* kr1 *Sabin* kr1 tritic-vg fd5.de
    - : **mingled** with dark clots: aids nl2• **Bell** cench k2 kali-s fd4.de *Lyc* *Sabin* k* *Sec* k*
    - : **partly** clotted: tritic-vg fd5.de ust st
  - **dark**; then: *Calc-p* kr1 nat-sil fd3.de•
  - **foul**; and: sang bg1
  - **girls**; in: *Calc-p* kr1
- **brown**: aln vva1• bapt bg2* bar-ox-suc rly4• berb k* **Bry** k* calc k* *Carb-v* k* carneg-g rwt1• choc srj3• coli rly4• *Con* k* goss st1 ham fd3.de• iod ptk1 lac-h htj1• mag-c k* musca-d szs1 *Nit-ac* k* orot-ac rly4• oxal-a rly4• pin-con oss2• plut-n srj7• positr nl2• puls k* rhus-t k* *Sec* k* sep k* thuj bg1* vesp k*
  - **coffee**-ground, as: *Nit-ac* kr1
  - **mauve** brown: (↗*purple*) kola stb3•
- **cease**:
  - **night**: cact bg2 caust bg2 cycl bg2 ham bg2 puls bg2 sulph bg2
  - **headache** comes on; and: lith-c kr1
  - **lying** agg.: caust bg2 lil-t bg2 sil bg2 squil bg2
  - **rest** agg.: squil bg2
  - **sitting** agg.: kreos ptk1
  - **suddenly**: cocc hr1* dream-p sdj1• lavand-a ctl1•
  - **walking** agg.; after: *Kreos* mrr1 *Lil-t* kr1
- **changeable** in appearance: nux-m ptk **Puls** k*
- **childbed**, after (See return - delivery)
- **clotted**: abrom-a zzc1• alet k* aloe k* *Am-c* k* *Am-m* k* ant-c *Apis* apoc k* *Arg-n* k* arist-cl mg1.de* *Arn* k* bamb-a stb2.de• bart a1 **Bell** k* bell-p mg1.de berb bit-ar wht1• borx bov k* bry k* bufo k* buni-o jl3 cact bg2* **Calc** k* **Calc-p** k* canth k* carb-an k* carb-v a1* carl a1 *Caust* k* **Cham** k* **Chin** k* *Cimic* k* cina a1 **Coc-c** k* *Cocc* k* *Coff* k* con k* *Croc* k* **Cycl** k* dream-p sdj1• ephe-si hsj1• *Ferr* k* ferr-p k2* fl-ac k* foll jl3 germ-met srj5• glyc bro1 *Graph* hr1* haliae-lc srj5• ham k2 helon k* hoit jl3 hydrog srj2*• *Hyos* k* hypoth jl3 *Ign* k* inul a1 **Ip** k* irid-met srj5• jug-r a1* kali-bi gk kali-c kali-chl k* *Kali-m* kr1* kali-n k* kali-s fd4.de kreos k* lac-ac stj5• *Lac-c* lac-h htj1• *Lac-loxod-a* hm2• **Lach** k* (non:laur k1) lepi a1 *Lil-t* hr1* *Lyc* k* macro a1 mag-c h2* *Mag-m* k* mag-s sp1 mand mg1.de *Med* k* merc k* mucs-nas rly4• **Murx** k* *Nat-hchls* nat-m k* nat-s k* neon srj5• nit-ac k* nux-m nux-v k* ov st1 ozone sde2• ph-ac k* phos a1* phyt ptk1 pitu-a vml2• **Plat** k* plb bro1* pot-e rly4• prot jl3* psor **Puls** k* raph a1 **Rhus-t** k* rhus-v j5.de* *Sabad* hr1* **Sabin** k* sal-fr sle1• sang k* sanic *Sec* k* sel gmj2 sep k* sol-t-ae k* spig k* staph *Stram* k* stront-c k* *Sulph* k* tep a1 *Thlas* bro1 thuj a1 thymol sp1 til tril-p k* tritic-vg fd5.de *Tub* *Ust* k* vib vip-a jl3 xan xanth bg2 *Zinc* k* zinc-p k2* zing
  - **dark** clots: (↗*dark - clots*) aloe sf1.de am-c k* ambr st1 apis kr1 arund c1 **Bell** k* bit-ar wht1• bov calc-p k2 cench k2 *Cham* k* *Chin* cimic coc-c k* *Cocc* coff sf1.de **Croc** k* culx k2 *Cycl* *Ferr* ham k2 hydrog srj2• ign jug-r vml3• kali-chl kali-m kr1 kali-n kali-s fd4.de *Lyc* mag-m k* med kr1* nux-m sf1.de *Plat* *Puls* **Sabin** k* *Sec* staph k2 *Ust* vip ptk1 vip-a jl3 xan *Zinc* zing [tax jsj7]
    - : **motion** agg.; slightest: **Croc** kr1
    - : **vaginismus**, in: *Ign* kr1
  - **first** day: kali-s fd4.de pitu-a vml2• plb sf1.de
  - **gelatinous** bright blood; with: laur ptk1
  - **large** clots: anthraq rly4• *Apoc* hr1* bros-gau mrc1 coc-c ptk1 dream-p sdj1• *Ip* hr1* murx ptk1 plut-n srj7• *Stram* hr1* zinc ptk1 [ferr stj2 ferr-f stj2 ferr-lac stj2 ferr-n stj2 ferr-sil stj2]
  - **last** days: *Nat-s* hr1* pitu-a vml2• prot jl2
  - **offensive**: *Bell* hr1* berb hr1* cham hr1* *Croc* hr1* helon sf1.de kreos sf1.de plat hr1* sang hr1* *Sec* hr1*
  - **partly** fluid: graph k2* **Sabin** hr1* tritic-vg fd5.de
  - **second** day: erig zr
  - **serum**; clots and: lyc ptk1 ust ptk1
  - **seven** days: prot jl2
  - **slowly**; clotting: sulph b4a.de
  - **urination** agg.; during: coc-c ptk1
- **cold** bathing agg.: ant-c ptk1
- **colors** clothes, difficult to wash out (See staining - wash)
- **complaints** of: (↗*disordered*) acon ptk1 aqui mtf11 **Bell** ptk1 *Calc* ptk1 *Cham* ptk1 cocc ptk1 ferr ptk1 *Graph* ptk1 ip ptk1 *Kali-c* ptk1 kreos ptk1 lach ptk1 mag-c ptk1 nat-m ptk1 **Nux-m** ptk1 nux-v ptk1 phos ptk1 plat ptk1 **Puls** ptk1 *Sabin* ptk1 sec ptk1 sep ptk1 *Sulph* ptk1
  - **accompanied** by:
    - : **vertigo** (See VERTIGO - Accompanied - menses)
    - : **Abdomen**; complaints of (See ABDOMEN - Complaints - accompanied - menses)
    - : **Skin**; complaints of: borx ptk1 carb-v ptk1 *Dulc* ptk1 *Graph* ptk1 kali-c ptk1 mag-m ptk1 *Nat-m* ptk1 sang ptk1 sars ptk1 sep ptk1 stram ptk1 verat ptk1
  - **bathing** | **amel.**: kali-c ptk1
- **copious**: *Abrom-a* zzc1• acal bwa3 acet-ac k2* achil-m bro1 achy-a bnj1 *Acon* k* adon mtf *Agar* k* aids nl2• ail alet k* all-c mtf all-s c1* aloe k* alum b4a.de* alumn a1 *Am-c* k* am-caust j5.de *Am-m* k* *Ambr* k* anac jl3 anan ant-c k* ant-t k* anthraq rly4• *Apis* k* **Apoc** k* aqui mtf aran k* arg-met bg2* *Arg-n* k* arist-cl mg1.de* *Arn* k* **Ars** k* *Ars-i* ars-met kr1 ars-s-f k2 art-v ptk2 arum-m kr1* arund asar bg2* asar-o mtf asc-t kr1 aspar mtf aur aur-ar k2 aur-i k2 aur-m k2 aur-s k2 bac jl2 bacls-7 pte1*• bamb-a stb2.de• bapt k* bar-c k* bar-i k2* bar-m bart a1 **Bell** k* bell-p mg1.de benz-ac bg2* *Bit-ar* wht1• *Borx* k* **Bov** k* brass-o mtf brom *Bry* k* bufo buni-o jl3 cact k* calad b7a.de **Calc** k* calc-act sf1.de calc-ar k2 *Calc-i* k2 **Calc-p** k* *Calc-s* k1 calc-sil k2* *Calc-st-s* mtf *Calen* kr1* camph k* *Cann-i* k* cann-s k* *Canth* k* caps b2.de* *Carb-ac* k* *Carb-an* k* *Carb-v* k* carbn-s *Card-m* cassia-s ccrh1• *Castm* k* *Caul* bg2* *Caust* k* cean bro1 cench k* *Cham* k* *Chel* k* **Chin** k* *Chinin-ar* *Chinin-s* k1* chlam-tr bcx2• choc srj3• *Cimic* k* *Cina* k* *Cinnm* k* cit-ac rly4• cit-l mtf11 *Cit-v* kr1 clem k* clomip mtf coc-c k* **Cocc** k* *Coff* k* coli jl2 *Coll* k* *Coloc* k* *Con* cop cortiso tpw7* *Croc* k*

Female

- **copious**: ...
crot-h k1 culx k2 cupr b2.de* cupr-act j5.de cur **Cycl** k* *Cyn-d* bnj1* des-ac rbp6 *Dig* k* digin a1 diosm br1 dream-p sdj1• dulc k* elaps ephe-si hsj1• erech hl9 ergot jl3 **Erig** k* erod bwa3 eupi c2* fago a1 falco-pe nl2• **Ferr** k* ferr-act he1 *Ferr-ar* *Ferr-i* k* ferr-p k* ferr-r bro1 ferr-s kr1* fic-r c1* *Fl-ac* k* flor-p rsj3* foll mtf* frax sf1.de fum rly1*• galeoc-c-h gms1• *Gamb* kr1 *Gels* bg2* ger bro1 ger-i rly4• germ-met srj5• gink-b sbd1• glon a1 glyc bro1 *Goss* bg2* gran j5.de* graph mtf grat k* guare hall a1 *Ham* k* helo bg2 **Helon** k* *Hep* k* hir mg1.de* hoit jl3 hura *Hydr* k* hydrc sf1.de hydrocort mtf *Hydrog* srj2• hydroph rsj6* *Hyos* k* hyosin mtf hyper *Ign* k* ignis-alc es2• *Iod* k* **Ip** k* iris joan bro1 jug-c mtf jug-r a1* kali-ar k* *Kali-bi* kr1 *Kali-br* *Kali-c* k* *Kali-fcy* k* *Kali-i* *Kali-m* kr1* *Kali-n* k* *Kali-p* k* *Kali-s* kali-sil k2* kiss a1 *Kreos* k* lac-ac a1 *Lac-c* k* lac-h htj1• *Lac-loxod-a* hm2• lac-lup hm2• lac-v-f c1* *Lach* k* lachn kr1 *Laur* b2.de* lavand-a a *Led* k* lil-t bro1 limest-b es1• lipp a1* lob luf-op rsj5• luna kg1• *Lyc* k* *Lyss* m-ambo b2.de* m-arct j5.de m-aust b2.de* *Mag-c* k* *Mag-m* k* mag-s k* *Manc* kr1 mand sp1* *Mang* kr1 *Med* k* menis mtf11 **Merc** b2.de* *Merc-c* k* mez k* **Mill** k* mit kr1* mom-b c1* morg-p pte1*• mosch k* mucs-nas rly4• mur-ac k* **Murx** k* musca-d szs1 *Nat-ar* nat-c k* **Nat-m** k* nat-ox rly4• nat-p k* nat-s nat-sil k2 neon srj5• nep mg1.de* nicc sf1.de *Nit-ac* k* **Nux-m** k* **Nux-v** k* oci-sa jl* *Ol-j* kr1 onos op k* *Ov* st1 ovar bwa3 pall bg2* paraf c1* penic jl3 *Petr* b4a.de* petr-ra shn4• ph-ac k* phel j5.de* **Phos** k* *Phyt* k* **Plat** k* plb k* plut-n srj7• *Polyg-h* kr1 polys sk4• positr nl2• *Prun* k* *Puls* k* pycnop-sa mrz1 pyrog mtf raph k* **Rat** k* rhod k* **Rhus-t** k* rhus-v c1* ribes-n mtf *Ruta* k* sabad b2.de* **Sabin** k* sacch-a gmj3 sal-fr sle1• *Samb* k* sang *Sanguiso* sf1.de **Sec** k* sed-ac bro1 sel k* **Senec** k* *Sep* k* sieg mg1.de *Sil* k* solid bg2* spong k* *Stann* k* staph **Stram** k* stront-c b2.de* suis-hep rly4• suis-pan rly4• *Sul-ac* k* *Sul-i* k2 *Sulph* k* syc pte1*• syph kr1* tab j5.de tanac a1 *Tarent* k* tep a1 ter kr1 tere-ch jl3 thioc-ac rly4• thiop jl3 *Thlas* kr1* *Thuj* k* *Tril-p* k* trios rsj11• tritic-vg sna6 *Tub* k* urol-h rwt• *Urt-u* c2* *Ust* k* *Vac* kr1* vanil fd5.de *Verat* k* vero-o rly4*• *Vib* vib-p c1* vinc k* visc bg2* voes a1 wies a1 x-ray jl* xan k* xanth bg2 yohim lp2* *Zinc* k* zinc-p k2* zing ziz kr1 [alumin-p stj2 ant-m stj2 ant-met stj2 arg-p stj2 astat stj2 bism-sn stj2 bor-pur stj2 cadm-m stj2 cadm-met stj2 cadm-s stj2 calc-lac stj2 calc-m stj1 calc-met stj2 calc-n stj1 chr-m stj2 cob-m stj2 *Ferr-f* stj2 *Ferr-lac* stj2 ferr-m stj1 *Ferr-n* stj2 *Ferr-sil* stj2 heroin sdj2 ind stj2 kali-met stj2 lith-i stj2 lith-p stj2 mag-p stj1 mang-i stj2 mang-p stj2 merc-i-f stj2 moly-met stj2 niob-met stj2 plb-p stj2 polon-met stj2 rhodi stj2 ruth-met stj2 stront-m stj2 stront-met stj2 tax jsj7 techn stj2 tell stj2 thal-met stj2 yttr-met stj2 zinc-i stj2 zirc-met stj2]
- **daytime**: bamb-a stb2.de• *Caust* coff cycl dulc fd4.de ham nat-m puls tritic-vg fd5.de vanil fd5.de
- **morning**: borx *Bov* k* carb-an
- **afternoon**: mag-c a1 nat-s a1 plut-n srj7•
  - **walking** agg.: (non:nat-c k1) nat-s k*
- **evening**: merc a1 murx a1
  - **only**: *Coc-c* kr1
- **night**: aids nl2• ail k1* *Am-c* k* *Am-m* k* bad ptk1 bamb-a stb2.de• bov k* *Coca* k* coff hr1* cycl ferr k* kola stb3• **Mag-c** k* mag-m nat-m h2* plut-n srj7• puls bg2 rhod kgp5• ruta st* sep bg2 *Ust* hr1* *Zinc* k* [mag-met stj2]
- **abortion** or parturition, after: **Apis** kr1* chin bro1 *Cimic* bro1 helon bro1 kali-c bro1 *Nit-ac* bro1 *Plat* kr1 *Sabin* bro1 sep bro1 sulph bro1 thlas bro1 ust bro1* vib bro1
- **accompanied** by:
  - **nausea**: apoc ptk1 caps ptk1 *Ip* ptk1
  - **painful** menses (See painful - accompanied - copious)
  - **urine**; burning: ferr ptk1
  - **vomiting**: apoc vml3• verat ptk1
  - **Peritoneum**; inflammation of (See ABDOMEN - Inflammation - peritoneum - accompanied - menses)
  - **Stomach**; complaints of (See STOMACH - Complaints - accompanied - menses - profuse)
- **alternate** period, every:
  - **absent**: *Lach* kr1
  - **less** copious: *Thlas* kr1*
- **bathing** | **amel**.: kali-c ptk1
- **cachectic** women; in: **Carb-an** kr1
- **chilliness**, after: sulph a1
- **cold** | **air** agg.: am-c k* ip k2
- **coldness**:
  - **Body**; with coldness of: coff kr1
  - **Limbs**; followed by coldness of: *Gels* kr1
- **convulsions**; after: *Op* hr1*
- **dancing**, from: *Croc* k* cycl ptk1 erig sec
- **dysuria**; with: cann-s hr1 *Mit* st*
- **excitement**; after: arg-n k2 **Calc** k*
- **exertion** agg.: **Ambr** bell-p mg1.de *Bov* **Calc** *Calc-p* croc **Erig** *Helon* hr1* mill *Nit-ac* rhus-t *Sec* hr1* tril-p
- **faintness**; with: acon apis chin cocc helon **Ip** k* lach sulph tril-p ptk1
- **forceps** delivery; after: calen ptk1
- **girls**; in young: *(↗women)* buni-o mtf11 mamm bwa3 menis mtf11
- **grief**; from: cocc k2
- **hysteric** women; in: cimic br *Nux-v* kr1
- **infectious** disease, after: ergot jl3
- **intemperate** women; in: crot-h lach *Nux-v*
- **lactation**; during: *Calc* hr1* *Phos* hr1* *Sil* bro1
- **lean** women; in: *Iod* kr1 *Phos* *Sec*
- **leukorrhea**:
  - **after**: *Ferr* kr1
  - **before**: *Thuj* kr1 *Ziz* kr1
- **lying**:
  - **agg**.: coc-c kr1 *Kreos* k*
  - **amel**.: hypoth jl3
- **mania**, with: *Sep* k*
- **menopause**:
  - **after**; long: vinc ptk1
  - **during**: apoc ptk1 aur-m ptk1 bell bg2 bov calc ptk1* cimic croc helon *Kali-br* hr1* **Lach** k* *Laur* k* nat-br mtf11 *Nux-v* paro-i jl3 phos k2 *Plat* bg2* *Plb* k* **Puls** bg2 **Sabin** *Sec* k* **Sep** k* sulph ptk1 tril-p ptk1 *Ust* k* vinc ptk1
- **motion**:
  - **agg**.: *Croc* **Erig** *Ferr* *Helon* k* *Sabin* sapin a1 *Sec*
  - **only** during motion: lil-t
- **nervous** women; in: *Kali-p* kr1
- **nymphomania**; with: *Phos* hr1* plat k* sec stram k*
- **old** people; in: | **women**; old: crot-h kr1 lach mag-m ptk1 *Plat* *Sars* kr1
- **pale** women; in: *Helon* kr1
- **parturition** (See abortion)
- **phthisical** women; in: *Calc* *Kali-c* *Phos* sang *Senec* *Stann* *Tub* hr*
- **plethoric** women; in: *(↗GENERALS - Plethora - constitution)* *Acon* kr1
- **rheumatic** women; in: *Ars*
- **riding**:
  - **agg**.: am-c k*
  - **cold** air; in: *Am-c*
- **sensation** of copious menses: allox sp1
- **shocks**, from: arn ip k2
- **short** duration; and of: am-c ant-c borx h2 falco-pe nl2• hydrog srj2• kali-c *Lach* nat-m phos *Plat* *Sil* *Thuj*
- **sitting** agg.: *Am-c* h2* cycl kreos tl1 mag-m k*
- **sleep**; from loss of: cocc k2
- **sleepiness**; with: **Nux-m** hr1*
- **standing** agg.: *(↗standing)* am-c **Cocc** k* mag-c
  - **tiptoe**: cocc ptk1
- **sterility**, in: *Canth* hr1* *Mill* hr1* *Phos* hr1* *Sulph* hr1*
- **tall** women; in: *Phos*
- **tenesmus** of bladder and rectum, with: erig ptk1
- **thunderstorm** agg.: nat-c phos
- **urine**, with hot: ferr ptk1
- **uterus** congested; with: mit zr
- **vexation**; after: nux-v rhus-t

- **virgins**, in: ergot jl3
- **walking**:
  - **agg.**: *Am-c* **Cocc** k* *Croc* erig *Lil-t* mag-c nat-s pall k* puls *Sabin* ust zinc
  - **amel.**: kreos mag-m sabin hr1
- **withered** women; in: arg-n phos *Sec*
- **women**; in young: (↗*girls)* kali-br ptk1

- **dark**: abrom-a zzc1• acon b2.de* alet k* aloe k* *Am-c* k* *Am-m* k* ambr vh amp rly4• anan k* *Ant-c* k* *Ant-t* bg2 apis arn k* *Ars* k* ars-met kr1 ars-s-f k2* arum-t bg2* arund k* *Asar* k* *Bell* k* berb a1 *Bism* k* bit-ar wht1• borx both-ax tsm2 *Bov* k* *Bry* k* *Cact* k* *Calc* k* **Calc-p** k* calc-s cann-i hr1* canth k* carb-ac k* *Carb-an* k* carb-v k* carbn-s k1 carl a1 **Cham** k* *Chin* k* *Chinin-ar* *Cimic* k* coc-c k* *Cocc* k* coff bg2* *Colch* b7a.de *Coloc* hr1* con b2.de* cop **Croc** k* *Crot-h* k* cupr b2.de* *Cycl* k* dig b2.de* dros b2.de* elaps *Ferr* k* ferr-ar ferr-p *Fl-ac* form a1 galla-q-r nl2• gamb hr1* *Graph* k* **Ham** k* helo bg2 helon k* hypoth jl3 *Ign* k* jug-r sf1.de *Kali-n* k* *Kali-p* k* *Kreos* k* lac-ac stj5• lac-d c1 lac-leo hm2• *Lach* k* *Laur* hr1* led b2.de* *Lil-t* k* lyc k* macro a1 *Mag-c* k* mag-m k* mag-s k* mand mg1.de* *Med* k* merc nat-m k* *Nit-ac* k* *Nux-m* k* **Nux-v** k* ol-an k* *Ph-ac* k* phos b2.de* **Plat** k* plb bg2 plut-n srj7• pot-e rly4• **Puls** k* rhus-g tmo3• ruta fd4.de *Sabin* k* *Sang* k* **Sec** k* sel k* *Sep* k* spig bg2 *Staph* *Stram* k* sul-ac *Sulph* k* *Thlas* kr1 *Thuj* hr1* tril-p tritic-vg fd5.de **Ust** k* vanil fd5.de wies a1 zinc zing [heroin sdj2 hydrog stj2 mag-lac stj2 mag-met stj2 mag-n stj2 mag-sil stj2]
  - **clots**, with: (↗*clotted - dark)* bit-ar wht1• buni-o jl3 cassia-s ccrh1• hypoth jl3 vanil fd5.de
  - **diphtheria**; during: crot-h tl1
  - **motion** agg.: *Croc* kr1
  - **pitch**; like: lac-leo hrn2•
  - **rheumatic** patients, in: **Calc-p** hr1*
  - **wash** out, difficult to: mag-c lp *Med* kr1
  - **watery**, then: thuj
- **decreasing** gradually: abies-n vml3•
- **delayed** in girls, first menses: *Abrom-a* zzc1• acon k* agn k* alet am-c k* ant-c hr1* apis k* *Aur* k* aur-s k2* *Bar-c* bry k* *Calc* k* *Calc-p* k* calc-s *Carbn-s* castm caul **Caust** k* chel k* cic k* cimic cocc k* *Con* k* croc k* cupr k* dam br1* dig k* dros k* dulc k* *Ferr* k* **Graph** k* guaj k* *Ham* helon hyos k* **Kali-c** k* *Kali-p* kali-perm bro1 lac-d ptk1 lach k* *Lyc* k* *Mag-c* k* mag-m k* *Mang* k* merc k* **Nat-m** k* *Petr* k* phos k* polyg-h bro1 **Puls** k* sabad k* *Sabin* k* sang bg2* sars k* **Senec** k* *Sep* k* sil k* spig k* staph k* stram k* stront-c k* *Sulph* k* *Tub* valer k* verat k* vib bg2* *Zinc* k* [bar-m stj1 lith-f stj2 nat-lac stj2]
  - **mammae**, with undeveloped: lyc ptk1
- **delivery**; return too soon after (See return - delivery)
- **discolored**: berb bg2 bry b7.de* lac-c bg2 *Sabin* b7.de*
- **disordered**: (↗*complaints)*
  - **accompanied** by | **Stomach**; complaints of: calc bg2 cham bg2 *Cocc* bg2 lyc bg2 nux-v bg2 **Puls** bg2
- **during**:
  - **agg.**: agar bg2 am-c bg2 ambr bg2 ars bg2 bar-c bg2 *Bell* bg2 *Berb* bg2 bov bg2 brom bg2 bry bg2 calc bg2 cann-xyz bg2 canth bg2 **Carb-v** bg2 caust bg2 coff bg2 *Con* bg2 dulc bg2 elaps bg2 **Graph** bg2 hep bg2 kali-bi bg2 kali-br bg2 **Kali-c** bg2 **Kreos** bg2 lac-c bg2 lil-t bg2 lob bg2 lyc bg2 mag-c bg2 mang bg2 *Merc* bg2 mosch bg2 murx bg2 nat-m bg2 nit-ac bg2 nux-v bg2 petr bg2 *Plat* bg2 rhus-t bg2 sabin bg2 sep bg2 **Sil** bg2 sul-ac bg2 sulph bg2 thuj bg2 zinc bg2
    - **Ovaries**: **Apis** bg2 arg-met bg2 *Bell* bg2 borx bg2 brom bg2 canth bg2 cham bg2 cocc bg2 coll bg2 coloc bg2 con bg2 crot-h bg2 gels bg2 graph bg2 **Iod** bg2 kali-p bg2 lac-c bg2 *Lach* bg2 lil-t bg2 lyc bg2 nat-m bg2 nux-m bg2 nux-v bg2 *Phos* bg2 plat bg2 podo bg2 sabad bg2 sars bg2 thuj bg2 ust bg2 zinc bg2 zinc-val ptk1
    - **Uterus**: acon bg2 aesc bg2 alet bg2 am-c bg2 aml-ns bg2 ant-c bg2 apis bg2 arn bg2 asaf bg2 bar-c bg2 *Bell* bg2 borx bg2 brom bg2 cact bg2 calc-p bg2 cann-xyz bg2 canth bg2 carb-v bg2 caul bg2 *Cham* bg2 chin bg2 *Cimic* bg2 cocc bg2 **Con** bg2 graph bg2 hyos bg2 hyper bg2 **Ign** bg2 iod bg2 kali-c bg2 kali-i bg2 lac-c bg2 *Lach* bg2 lil-t bg2 lyc bg2 mag-c bg2 murx bg2 nat-c bg2 nat-m bg2 nux-m bg2 **Nux-v** bg2 ph-ac bg2 phyt bg2 rhus-t bg2 sabin bg2 sang bg2 sars bg2 senec bg2 staph bg2 ust bg2 verat-v bg2 vib bg2 zinc bg2

- **during – agg.**: ...
    - **Vagina**: agar bg2 am-c bg2 ambr bg2 ars bg2 bar-c bg2 *Bell* bg2 *Berb* bg2 bov bg2 brom bg2 bry bg2 calc bg2 cann-xyz bg2 canth bg2 **Carb-v** bg2 caust bg2 coff bg2 *Con* bg2 dulc bg2 elaps bg2 **Graph** bg2 hep bg2 kali-bi bg2 kali-br bg2 **Kali-c** bg2 **Kreos** bg2 lac-c bg2 lil-t bg2 lob bg2 lyc bg2 mag-c bg2 mang bg2 *Merc* bg2 mosch bg2 murx bg2 nat-m bg2 nit-ac bg2 nux-v bg2 petr bg2 *Plat* bg2 rhus-t bg2 sabin bg2 sep bg2 **Sil** bg2 sul-ac bg2 sulph bg2 thuj bg2 zinc bg2
    - **Vulva**: agar bg2 am-c bg2 ambr bg2 ars bg2 bar-c bg2 *Bell* bg2 *Berb* bg2 bov bg2 brom bg2 bry bg2 calc bg2 cann-xyz bg2 canth bg2 **Carb-v** bg2 caust bg2 coff bg2 *Con* bg2 dulc bg2 elaps bg2 **Graph** bg2 hep bg2 kali-bi bg2 kali-br bg2 **Kali-c** bg2 **Kreos** bg2 lac-c bg2 lil-t bg2 lob bg2 lyc bg2 mag-c bg2 mang bg2 *Merc* bg2 mosch bg2 murx bg2 nat-m bg2 nit-ac bg2 nux-v bg2 petr bg2 *Plat* bg2 rhus-t bg2 sabin bg2 sep bg2 **Sil** bg2 sul-ac bg2 sulph bg2 thuj bg2 zinc bg2
  - **beginning** of:
    - **agg.**:
      - **Ovaries**: mosch bg2
      - **Uterus**: cimic bg2
      - **Vulva**: plat bg2 sars bg2
- **early**; too: acon b2.de* agar bg2 *Agath-a* nl2• aloe bg2 *Alum* b2.de* **Am-c** b2.de* am-m b2.de* **Ambr** b2.de* apis b7a.de aran bg2 aran-ix sp1 arg-n bg2 arn b2.de* ars b2.de* asaf b2.de* asar b2.de* bar-c b2.de* *Bell* b2.de* benz-ac bg2 *Bit-ar* wht1• borx b2.de* *Bov* b2.de* brom bg2 *Bry* b2.de* cact bg2 **Calc** b2.de* calc-p bg2* cann-s b2.de* *Canth* b2.de* carb-an b2.de* **Carb-v** b2.de* carneg-g rwt1• castm bg2 caul bg2* *Caust* b2.de* **Cham** b2.de* chin b2.de* chinin-s bg2 chlam-tr bcx2• cimic bg2 *Cina* b2.de* cit-ac rly4• clem b2.de* coc-c bg2 *Cocc* b2.de* coff b2.de* *Colch* b2.de* coloc b2.de* con b2.de* *Croc* b2.de* cycl tl1* dig b2.de* dulc b2.de* ephe-si hsj1• eupi br1 falco-ch sze4• falco-pe nl2• *Ferr* b2.de* ferr-p ptk1 fl-ac bg2 flor-p rsj3• glycyr-g cte1• granit-m es1• graph b2.de* grat bg2 hell b2.de* hep b2.de* hipp jl2 hydrc mtf11 hyos b2.de* *Ign* b2.de* iod b2.de* **Ip** b2.de* kali-bi bg2 **Kali-c** b2.de* kali-n b2.de* kola stb3• **Kreos** b2.de* lac-c ptk1 lac-e hm2• *Lac-loxod-a* hm2• lach b2.de* lam c2* laur b2.de* led b2.de* luna kg1• lyc b2.de* *M-ambo* b2.de* *M-aust* b2.de* mag-c b2.de* mag-m b2.de* mag-p ptk1 mag-s sp1 *Mang* b2.de* merc bg2 **Merc-c** b4a.de mez b2.de* mim-p rsj8• mosch b2.de* mur-ac b2.de* nat-c b2.de* *Nat-m* b2.de* nat-ox rly4• nicotam rly4• nit-ac b2.de* *Nux-m* b2.de* **Nux-v** b2.de* orot-ac rly4• par b2.de* petr b2.de* ph-ac b2.de* **Phos** b2.de* **Plat** b2.de* plb b2.de* *Positr* nl2• prun bg2 *Puls* b2.de* pycnop-sa mrz1 rat ptk1 rhod b2.de* rhus-g tmo3• **Rhus-t** b2.de* rosm c2 *Ruta* b2.de* **Sabin** b2.de* sal-al blc1• sang bg2 sec b2.de* sel rsj9• **Sep** b2.de* *Sil* b2.de* spig b2.de* spong b2.de* stann b2.de* staph b2.de* stram b2.de* stront-c b2.de* suis-hep rly4• **Sul-ac** b2.de* *Sulph* b2.de* thuj b4a.de* toxo-g jl2 trios rsj11• tritic-vg fd5.de tub c2* tub-ro wl1 ust bg2 vanil fd5.de verat b2.de* visc sp1 zinc b2.de* [alumin stj2 alumin-p stj2 alumin-s stj2 *Buteo-j* sej6 chr-m stj2 mang-act stj2 mang-i stj2 mang-m stj2 mang-met stj2 mang-n stj2 mang-p stj2 mang-s stj2 mang-sil stj2]
  - **delivery**; too soon after (See return - delivery)
  - **diarrhea**; with: verb c1
  - **eleven** days: lam a1
  - **menopause**; during: calc mtf11
  - **menstrual** cycle; in the regular (See frequent)
  - **profuse**; and: alet ptk1 kali-c ptk1 sep ptk1 stann ptk1 verat ptk1 xan ptk1
  - **proper** age; before the (See appear - proper)
  - **scanty**; and (See scanty - early)
  - **seven** to eight days: cassia-s cdd7*•
  - **six** days: bit-ar wht1•
  - **three** days: hir rsj4• til ban1•
  - **two** weeks: ferr-p bg2 hyos mtf11 sang bg2 tril-p bg2
- **excitement** agg. (= mental excitement): **Calc** k* tub k*
- **excoriating** (See acrid)
- **exertion** brings on the flow: abrom-a ks5 **Ambr** ptk1 *Bov* k* *Calc* k* *Erig* ptk1 kreos ptk1 nit-ac ptk1 rhus-t tril-p k*
- **flesh**-colored: apoc sf1.de nat-c j5.de* *Sabin* b7.de* *Stront-c* j5.de*
- **fluid** blood contains clots: alet aloe ant-c apoc k* am **Bell** k* bufo caust *Cham* *Chin* dream-p sdj1• dulc fd4.de *Ferr* k* ham bro1 ign ip lyc nat-s nux-v plat plb bro1 puls **Sabin** k* sang **Sec** k* spong fd4.de stram ust k* vib vip ptk1
- **frequent**; too: adlu jl *Agar* *Agath-a* nl2• *Alet* all-c a1 all-s aloe alum alum-p k2 alum-sil k2 *Am-c* k* am-caust j5.de *Am-m* **Ambr** *Anac* anan androc srj1• ant-c *Ant-t* j5.de* anthraco kr1 apis *Apoc* *Aran* aran-ix jl* *Arg-n*

Female

- **frequent**; too: ...
Arist-cl mg1.de arn **Ars** ars-i **Ars-met** kr1 ars-s-f k2 arund asaf asar j5.de* aur aur-ar k2 aur-m aur-s k2 bamb-a stb2.de• bapt bar-c bar-i k2 bar-m bar-s k2 **Bell** benz-ac *Borx* both-ax tsm2 **Bov** brom **Bry** *Bufo* buth-a mg1.de *Cact* **Calc** k* calc-ar k2 calc-i k2 *Calc-p* *Calc-s* calc-sil k2 *Cann-i* a1* *Canth* **Carb-an** **Carb-v** carbn-s k2 carc sst* castm caul *Caust* k* **Cham** chel *Chin* *Chinin-ar* *Chinin-s* k1 choc srj3• *Cimic* *Cina* *Cinnm* cit-ac rly4• *Clem* coc-c **Cocc** k* *Coff* *Colch* coli rly4• *Coloc* *Con* k* *Cop* *Croc* crot-h cub culx k2 cur **Cycl** k* cyna jl daph dendr-pol sk4• dicha jl dig sf1.de digin a1 dream-p sdj1• dulc a1 elaps *Erig* kr1 eupi fago a1 falco-pe nl2• **Ferr** ferr-ar ferr-i k* *Ferr-p* *Fl-ac* flav jl form fuma-ac rly4• *Gamb* kr1 gent-c germ-met srj5• gink-b jl* goss st granit-m es1• *Graph* h2* grat *Helon* hep a1 hipp hir mg1.de* hist mg1.de* hura hydrc kr1 hydrog srj2• hyos j5.de hyper *Ign* k* ind indg inul a1* iod **Ip** irid-met srj5• **Kali-ar** k* *Kali-bi* **Kali-c** k* *Kali-fcy* kali-i *Kali-m* kr1* kali-n *Kali-p* *Kali-s* *Kali-sil* k2* *Kalm* kola stb3• *Kreos* **Lac-c** lac-h htj1• lac-leo hrn2• lach lachn *Lact* j5.de *Lam* j5.de* *Laur* *Led* lept sf1.de lil-t k* lipp a1 lob lob-e c1 lyc *Lyss* k* *Mag-c* k* **Mag-m** *Mag-p* bro1 *Mag-s* mand mg1.de* **Mang** meph jl merc sf1.de merc-act j5.de *Merc-c* *Mez* *Mosch* *Mur-ac* *Murx* naja jl nat-ar *Nat-c* *Nat-hchls* **Nat-m** k* nat-p nat-sil k2 nep mg1.de* nicc nicotam rly4• *Nit-ac* **Nux-m** **Nux-v** k* ol-an k* *Ol-j* kr1 olib-sac wmh1 onos op orot-ac rly4• *Ov* st ozone sde2• palo jl pant-ac rly4• par *Petr* petr-ra shn4• *Ph-ac* *Phel* **Phos** k* phyt pic-ac a1 **Plat** k* plut-n srj7• pneu jl pot-e rly4• prun puls **Rat** rauw jl *Rhod* **Rhus-t** rhus-v a1 ros-d wla1 rosm a1* *Ruta* **Sabin** k* sang sanguiso sf1.de sars *Sec* k1 sel jl* *Senec* seneg *Sep* k* sieg mg1.de *Sil* k* sin-n kr1* sol-t-ae a1 *Spong* *Stann* staph stram streptoc rly4• stront-c suis-pan rly4• *Sul-ac* sul-i k2 *Sulph* k* *Sumb* a1* tarent tell a1* **Thlas** kr1 *Thuj* thyr jl tong j5.de *Tril-p* *Tub* *Ust* vac k* *Verat* verb kr1 visc jl* voes a1 wies a1 wildb a1 *Xan* k* *Zinc* zinc-p k2 zing [bor-pur stj2 calc-m stj1 heroin sdj2 kali-met stj2]
  - **day**:
    - **eight** days: alet mtf apis mtf *Aran* kr1* bov mtf bry mtf bufo mtf *Cact* mtf *Calc-caust* mtf cassia-s mtf clem mtf *Cocc* kr1 coli rly4• dict mtf form kr1 hura mtf kalm mtf kreos mtf mag-c mtf nit-ac mtf sep mtf sil mtf *Thuj* mtf
    - **fifteen** days; every: glycyr-g cte1•
      - **twenty** days; to: coch kr1
    - **five** days: all-s mtf carb-v mtf carbn-s mtf con mtf kali-c mtf kali-p mtf lac-d mtf lac-lup hrn2• mag-m mtf nat-p mtf nat-sil fd3.de• nep jl* nux-m mtf petr mtf phos mtf tub mtf xan mtf zinc mtf
    - **four** days: act-sp mtf alum mtf am-c kr1 ambr mtf bell mtf bor-ac mtf bov kr1 calc mtf canth mtf carb-an mtf *Cycl* a1 kali-c mtf kreos mtf lac-c mtf lact mtf *Lyc* kr1 merc-act mtf nux-m mtf nux-v mtf phos mtf rosm mtf thlas mtf
    - **seven** days (See week - one)
    - **six** days: aloe mtf *Am-c* kr1 ant-t mtf bufo mtf carb-v mtf caste mtf kali-c mtf lyc mtf mag-c mtf mag-p mtf *Mang* kr1 mosch mtf mur-ac mtf nat-sil fd3.de• paraf mtf petr mtf *Plat* mtf sep mtf sol c1 sul-ac mtf
      - **or** eight days; every six: *Lyc* kr1
    - **ten**:
      - **every**: *Phos* kr1
      - **to** two weeks: *Ign* kr1
    - **three** days: alum mtf ambr mtf asar jl bor-ac mtf both-ax tsm2 bufo mtf calc mtf choc srj3• coc-c mtf cop mtf gent-c mtf granit-m es1• kreos mtf lac-c mtf lipp mtf mag-c mtf mag-s mtf murx mtf nat-c mtf nat-m mtf nat-sil fd3.de• nit-ac mtf nux-v mtf par mtf phos mtf sars mtf sil mtf tanac mtf *Thlas* kr1
    - **twelve** days | **twelve** to sixteen days; every: *Sulph* kr1
    - **two** days too early: *Am-m* mtf bar-c mtf berb mtf calc mtf chel mtf digin mtf dirc c1 gink-b sbd1• graph mtf kali-c mtf kali-p mtf lac-ac kr1 lac-c mtf lac-d mtf lac-leo hrn2• lyc mtf mag-s mtf murx mtf nit-ac mtf phos mtf pilo mtf podo fd3.de• senec mtf sep mtf sil mtf xan mtf
  - **anemic** women; in: *Mang* kr1
  - **chill**; after: sulph a1
  - **driving** in cold air, after: am-c a1
  - **menopause**, in: tell kr1
  - **motion** agg.: *Croc* kr1
  - **overheating**; from: *Croc* kr1
  - **sterility**, in: *Canth* kr1 *Sulph* kr1

- **frequent**; too: ...
  - **week**:
    - **one** week: ambr mtf anthraq rly4• aran-ix jl* aur mtf aur-m mtf bar-ox-suc rly4• berb kr1* calc mtf cassia-s mtf **Cocc** kr1* colch mtf cop mtf cur mtf dream-p sdj1• elaps mtf *Ferr-p* kr1* gink-b sbd1• *Kali-s* kr1* lac-c kr1* lac-leo hrn2• lac-v-f mtf *Lach* kr1* lyc mtf mag-c mtf mag-s mtf *Manc* kr1* nat-c mtf **Nat-m** kr1* nit-ac mtf puls kr1* sec mtf senec kr1* sep mtf sil mtf sol c1 *Stram* kr1* tarent mtf *Thuj* mtf ust kr1* verat kr1* xan kr1*
      - **one** to two weeks: *Elaps* kr1
    - **three** weeks:
      - **every**: berb k* bros-gau mrc1 *Bufo* kr1 elaps hr1 ferr-p ptk1 mag-c mrr1 murx kr1 *Pneu* jl2
        - **intermittent** on the second day: (↗*intermittent)* pneu jl2
      - **too** early: *Murx* kr1
    - **two** weeks; every: *Agath-a* nl2• am-caust vh1 bor-ac mtf borx bro1 bov kr1* brom ptk1* bry mtf calc bg1* calc-p bg1* *Cann-i* kr1* *Cean* kr1* *Cocc* kr1 croc bro1* elaps hr1* ferr-p bro1 *Helon* bro1* ign bro1* ind kr1 *Ip* kr1 *Lac-ac* mtf lac-c kr1 *Lil-t* kr1 lyc ptk1* lyss kr1 mag-c ptk1* mag-s bro1* *Merc* kr1 mez bro1 *Murx* kr1* nit-ac bro1* *Nux-v* kr1* *Ph-ac* kr1* phos bro1* phyt bro1* *Plat* kr1 puls kr1 sabin bro1* sang bg1* sec kr1* sep mtf syph kr1 thlas bro1* thuj kr1 *Tril-p* bro1* tritic-vg sna6 ust bro1* zinc mtf
      - **menopause**; at: *Tril-p* kr1
- **frothy**: arn b7.de* dros b7.de* ferr b7.de* ip b7.de*
- **gray**: berb ptk1 thuj bg1
- **green**: graph bg* *Lac-c* k* manc k* med k* puls bg* pulx bg1* *Sep* k* tub k* x-ray kl*
- **grief** brings on: cocc k2 *Ign* k*
- **gushing**: (↗*sleep - gushing)* bamb-a stb2.de• *Bell* bg2* cham bg2 cinnm sf1.de coca kr1 *Cocc* bg2* erig bg2* *Ip* bg2* lac-c bg2* ozone sde2• puls bg2* *Sabin* bg2* sars sf1.de thuj a1 *Tril-p* bg2* zinc bg2*
  - **rising** agg.: *Cocc* kr1*
  - **waking**; on: coca a1
- **heavy** flow (See copious)
- **hot**: arn k* *Bell* k* bry kali-c bg1* kreos bg* lac-c puls k* sabin bg2* sil bg1* squil ptk1 sulph bg*
  - **fire**; like: lac-c ptk1
- **increased** blood flow (See copious)
- **injuries**; after (See appear - injuries)
- **intermittent**: (↗*frequent - week - three - every - intermittent)* acon b7.de* alum k* alum-sil k2* alumn a1 am-c j5.de ambr ptk1 apis k* apoc k* arg-n ptk1 **Bell** bg2 *Berb* k* borx bov ptk1 bry b7.de* calc k* canth castm *Caust* *Cham* k* chin chlam-tr bcx2• *Cimic* k* clem k* coc-c bro1* cocc k* colch coll tl1 con bg2 cop k* *Cycl* k* des-ac jl3 eupi k* *Ferr* k* ferr-act sf1.de ferr-p glon ham ptk1 hydrog srj2*• iod bg2 irid-met srj5• kali-c kali-i *Kali-s* *Kali-sil* k2* **Kreos** k* lac-ac stj5• *Lac-c* k* *Lach* k* *Lil-t* lyc k* lycps-v k* mag-c k* mag-m b4.de* mag-p bg2 mag-s k* mang ptk1 *Meli* bro1 merc k* mosch bg2* murx k* musca-d szs1 nat-c nat-p a1 nat-s nicc k* *Nit-ac* nux-m bg2 *Nux-v* k* ozone sde2• petr-ra shn4• ph-ac b4.de* *Phel* vh *Phos* k* *Plb* hr1* psor k* **Puls** k* rat k* rhod k* rhus-t b7.de* sabad k* sabin k* sars bg2 *Sec* k* senec k* *Sep* k* sil k* sol-t-ae a1* stram b7.de* suis-pan rly4• *Sulph* k* thuj b4a.de* tril-p k* ust k* verat b7.de* vesp k* *Vib* k* xan hr1* *Zinc* b4.de*
  - **abortion**; after: plat ptk1
  - **alternating** with bronchial trouble: *Phos* hr1*
  - **cease**:
    - **ten** or twelve days; for: *Lyc* kr1
    - **two** days; for: mag-s kr1
    - **two** or three days; for: ferr kr1
  - **every** other day: *Apis* kr1 ovi-p c1 suis-pan rly4• *Xan* hr1*
  - **girls**; in young: polyg-pe vml2•
- **irregular**: abrom-a zzc1• abrom-a-r mtf11 alco a1 alum-p k2* am-c bro1 *Ambr* c1* ammc hr1* *Apis* apoc aran k* **Arg-n** k* *Art-v* k* (non:aur-m-n k*) aur-s a1* *Bell* bro1 *Benz-ac* k* *Brucel* sa3• bry bro1 buni-o jl3 *Calc* k* calc-i k2* calc-p calc-s calc-sil k2* *Carb-ac* k* carbn-s caul k* *Caust* k* chel k* *Chlol* hr1* *Cimic* k* *Cinnm* hr1* *Cocc* k* *Con* k* cortico mg1.de* cortiso mg1.de crot-h hr1* cur k* cycl k* *Dig* k* dys pte1*• ferr ferr-p flav jl3* *Foll* oss• glycyr-g cte1• *Graph* a1* guaj bro1 ham k* hyos k* hypoth jl3 *Ign* k* inul bro1 *Iod* k* *Ip* k* *Iris* joan bro1 *Kali-ar* hr1* kali-bi k* kali-p k* *Kreos* k* *Lac-d* k* *Lach* k* lil-t k* *Lyc* k*

- **irregular**: ...
mag-c mag-m k* mag-s bro1 *Manc* hr1* merc k* mosch a1 *Murx* k* *Nat-c* hr1* nat-m b4a.de* nicc sf1.de *Nit-ac* nit-s-d j5.de **Nux-m** k* *Nux-v* k* oena k* *Ol-j* hr1* op k* ovi-p c1* phos k* *Phys* hr1* pip-n c1* pisc bro1 pitu-a vml2• plb k* puls k* rad-br c11* ruta k* sabad k* sanic c1 **Sec** k* *Senec* k* *Sep* k* *Sil* k* *Staph* k* *Sul-i* k2* *Sulph* k* tab a1 *Ter* hr1* thuj b4a.de* trios jl3 *Tub* k* ust k* verat k* vesp k* xan k* [beryl stj2 beryl-m stj2 chr-m stj2 lith-c stj2 lith-f stj2 sol-ecl cky1 spect dfg1]
  - **accompanied** by | **strabismus** (See EYE - Strabismus - accompanied - menses - irregular)
  - **convulsions**; during epileptic: **Art-v** hr1*
  - **leukorrhea**; before: *Sep* kr1
  - **long** and variable intervals: cimic ptk1 coc-c ptk1 ign ptk1 nux-m ptk1 plat ptk1 *Sulph* kr1 syph jl2
  - **paroxysms**; during: **Sabin** kr1
  - **puberty**, at: *Puls* j5.de
- **itching**; causing: caust bg2 petr b4.de*
- **lactation**; during: borx *Calc* k* *Calc-p* k* chin h1* *Pall* k* *Sil* k*
  - **nursing** the child, while: pall k* *Sil* k*
  - **sexual** excitement with: calc-p br
- **lasting** too long (See protracted)
- **lasting** too short (See short)
- **late**, too: absin a1 *Acon* k* *Agn* k* aids nl2• alet bro1 aln vva1• alum k* alum-p k2 alum-sil k2 am-c k* anan vh1 ang a1* ange-s jl3 *Apis* arg-n arge-pl rwt5• arist-cl sp1* arn b2.de* ars b2.de* ars-i k2 aster *Aur* k* aur-i k2 aur-s k2 bamb-a stb2.de• *Bell* k* benz-ac borx b2.de* bov k* bry b2.de* calc b2.de* *Calc-p* k* calc-s *Camph* sne canth k* *Carb-ac* k* carb-an b2.de* carb-v h2* **Carbn-s** carneg-g rwt1• castm caul k* **Caust** k* cench k2 cham k* *Chel* k* chin k* cic k* *Cimic* k* cinnb cit-ac rly4• coca a1 *Cocc* k* colch b2.de* coloc b2.de* **Con** k* croc b2.de* *Crot-h* cub **Cupr** b2.de* cur *Cycl* k* cyclosp sa3• daph des-ac jl3 dig k* diosm br1 dream-p sdj1• *Dros* k* **Dulc** k* euphr k* *Ferr* k* ferr-i *Ferr-p* flav jl2 flor-p jl3 fum rly1*• gast a1 gels k* gink-b sbd1• glon k* glycyr-g cte1• goss k* **Graph** k* guaj b2.de* ham *Hed* mg1.de* hell b2.de* *Hep* k* hir mg1.de* hist mg1.de* *Hydr* kr1 hydrog srj2*• hyos k* hyper *Ign* k* inul a1 *Iod* k* irid-met srj5• iris a1 joan bro1 **Kali-c** k* kali-chl *Kali-fcy* a1* *Kali-i* kali-m kr1* kali-n *Kali-p* k* *Kali-s* k* *Kali-sil* k2* kalm ketogl-ac rly4• kola stb3• lac-ac stj5• *Lac-c* kr1 lac-d k* *Lach* k* lec k* *Lept* lith-c lol bg2* luna kg1• **Lyc** k* m-arct b2.de* **Mag-c** k* mag-m k* mag-s k* maias-l hrn2• manc kr1 mand mg1.de* mang bg2* *Merc* k* merl kr1* *Mit* kr1 nat-c k* **Nat-m** k* *Nat-p* *Nat-s* nat-sil k2 nicc nit-ac k* **Nux-m** k* nux-v b2.de* *Oci-sa* jl* *Ov* st1 ozone sde2• pant-ac rly4• penic jl3 *Petr* k* petr-ra shn4• *Ph-ac* k* *Phos* k* *Pitu* jl3 plac rzf5• plac-s rly4• *Plat* plut-n srj7• pneu jl3* *Podo* bg2* *Polyg-h* kr1 *Psor* pulm-a srb2.fr **Puls** k* puls-n c2 pulx br1* rad-br c11* rhod b2.de* *Rhus-g* tmo3• rhus-t b2.de* rob kr1 ros-d wla1 ruta b2.de* sabad k* sabal c2 *Sabin* k* sal-fr sle1• sang bg2* sapin a1 saroth mg1.de* **Sars** b2.de* sec b2.de* *Sel* *Senec* k* **Sep** k* **Sil** k* sorb-a mtf11 spig b2.de* *Staph* k* stram b2.de* stront-c k* stry-af-cit bro1 *Sul-ac* k* **SULPH** b2.de* tab tanac ptk2 tarent a1* tell jl3 ter tetox pin2• *Thlas* kr1 thuj a1 til trios rsj11• tritic-vg fd5.de tub uran-n br1 *Valer* k* verat k* verat-v vib bro1* voes a1 xan *Zinc* k* zinc-p k2 ziz bro1 [chr-m stj2 kali-ar stj2 kali-met stj2 mang-act stj2 mang-i stj2 mang-m stj2 mang-met stj2 mang-n stj2 mang-p stj2 mang-s stj2 mang-sil stj2 *Spect* dfg1]
  - **accompanied** by:
    - **pain**:
      - **less** than usual: hir rsj4•
      - **more** than usual: hir rsj4•
  - **alternate** months: syph ptk1 thlas ptk1
  - **alternating** with bronchial trouble: *Phos* kr1
  - **anxiety**; with: *Graph* kr1 *Sulph* kr1
  - **appear** | **sensation** as if menses will appear, but does not do so; with: *Goss* br1
  - **chill**; with: **Nat-m** kr1
  - **eight** days: aster kr1 *Calc* kr1 *Iod* kr1 psor jl2
  - **exertion** agg.; after: bry k2
  - **five** days: am-c mtf ange-s mtf carb-an mtf carb-v mtf flor-p jl phos mtf sars mtf **Sep** kr1 sil mtf
  - **five** months: *Graph* kr1
  - **four** days: plut-n srj7•
  - **fourteen** days: hyper kr1 irid-met srj5• luf-op rsj5• *Mag-m* kr1
- **late**, too: ...
  - **girls**; in: **Nat-m** kr1 tub jl2
  - **leukorrhea**; with: hyper kr1 ziz kr1
  - **profuse**, and: bell h1 *Carb-ac* *Caust* chel cur dulc ferr *Kali-c* *Kali-i* lach luf-op rsj5• nit-ac *Phos* *Sil* staph vib
  - **puberty**, at: *Caust* kr1 *Dros* kr1 *Graph* kr1 *Kali-c* kr1 *Lach* kr1 *Lyc* kr1 *Nat-m* kr1 phos kr1 *Puls* kr1 sep kr1 sil kr1 *Sulph* kr1
  - **scanty**: *Acon* kr1 bov kr1 *Calc* kr1 con kr1 *Graph* kr1 *Merc* kr1
  - **seven** days: calc mtf con mtf graph mtf kreos hr1 *Lac-d* kr1 mag-c mtf *Nit-ac* mtf *Polyg-h* kr1 tell jl*
  - **seventeen** days: *Lac-ac* kr1
  - **several** months: *Kali-c* kr1
  - **six** days: ange-s mtf carb-v mtf phos mtf *Polyg-h* kr1 sal-fr sle1• tell jl
  - **six** to eight weeks: *Crot-h* kr1
  - **six** weeks: *Glon* kr1
  - **sterility**, in: *Phos* kr1
  - **ten** days: hir skp7• vib kr1
  - **thirty**-two days: plut-n srj7•
  - **three** days: cassia-s cdd7*• hir rsj4• [bell-p-sp dcm1]
  - **twenty**-one days: *Puls* kr1
  - **two** days: bov mtf coca mtf dream-p sdj1• kali-cy mtf kali-i mtf *Manc* mtf nat-c mtf nux-m mtf *Sulph* kr1 *Ter* kr1 tub mtf
  - **two** or three months: **Lach** kr1 *Sil* kr1
  - **wet** feet, from getting: *Graph* kr1
- **lifting** agg.: kreos ptk1
- **lochia**-like: amor-r jl3
- **long**; too (See protracted)
- **lying**:
  - **agg.**: kreos ptk1 **Mag-c** st* puls k*
  - **back**; on | **agg.**: cham ptk1
  - **cease** while lying: *Cact* k* *Caust* k* coli gmj1 ham **Lil-t** k* *Puls* kr1 sabin ptk1 sil bg2* squil bg2*
  - **only** when lying: kreos bg2* *Mag-c* bg2* sabin bg2* sep bg2
- **meat**, like putrid: lachn ptk1 syph ptk1
- **meat** water; like (See thin - meat)
- **membranous**: acet-ac k* apoc k* *Ars* bro1 bell bro1 **Borx** k* brom k* *Bry* k* bufo k* *Calc* k* *Calc-act* bg2* *Calc-p* k* *Canth* k* **Cham** k* cimic k* *Coll* k* con c2* *Cycl* k* ferr bro1 gast c2 guaj k* helio c2* *Hep* bg2* *Kali-bi* k* kali-c k* kali-chl k* kali-m kr1 kiss a1 **Lac-c** k* lac-h htj1• lach k* *Mag-p* gt1* merc bro1 nat-c bro1 nat-m k* *Nit-ac* bro1 ph-ac k* *Phos* k* phyt k* *Rhus-t* k* sabin k* sep bg2* sulph bg2* *Tril-p* bg2* tub k* ust k* verat-v hr1 vib k*
- **menopause**:
  - **after**: ulm-c jsj8•
  - **during**: *Lach* vh *Plat* vh *Plb* vh **Sabin** vh *Sec* vh **Sep** vh [mang stj1]
- **milky**: *Puls* hr1*
- **molasses**; like: mag-c ptk1
- **moon**:
  - **full**: *Croc* b7a.de dream-p sdj1• *Nux-v* b7.de* petr h2 ph-ac j5.de puls b7.de rhus-t bg2 sep h2 verat bg2
    - **instead** of at new moon; appeared later, at full moon: pall kr1*
    - **or** new: *Croc* bg2*
  - **new**: *Croc* b7a.de lam j5.de* lyc a1 merc-act j5.de nux-v bg2 puls bg2 rhus-t k* sil j5.de staph h1* verat b7.de*
- **motion**:
  - **agg.**: **Bry** hr1* **Croc** hr1* *Erig* ptk1 *Ferr* hr1* helon ptk1 *Ip* ptk1 sabin ptk1 sec ptk1
  - **amel.**: bov ptk1 *Cycl* hr1* kreos ptk1 mag-c ptk1 sabin hr1*
  - **aversion** to motion | **gush** out; lest it: bit-ar wht1•
  - **downward** motion agg.: *Borx* kr1
  - **only** during motion: cact ptk1 caust ptk1 *Lil-t* kr1* manc ptk1 nat-s ptk1 sec kr1*
- **mucous**: berb hr1 carb-an b4a.de *Cocc* b7.de* *Croc* hr1 puls b7.de* sul-ac b4a.de*
  - **last** day: *Apis* kr1

Female

- **nursing** the child agg.; when: calc k2 pall kr1* phos ptk1 sil ptk1 vip ptk1
- **offensive**: acon a1 acon-l a1* aln vva1• alum alum-sil k2* aral ars k* bapt bg2 bart a1 **Bell** k* **Bry** k* calc-ar k2 calc-p *Carb-an* k* **Carb-v** k* carbn-s carl a1 cassia-s ccrh1• *Caust* k* *Cham* k* chin k* chinin-ar cimic k* *Coloc* hr1* cop bro1 *Croc* k* *Crot-h* hr1* cyna jl3 graph k2 helo bg2 helon k* hist mg1.de* *Ign* k* *Kali-ar* *Kali-c* k* **Kali-p** k* kali-s *Kali-sil* k2* kola stb3• **Kreos** k* lac-c k* lach k* lachn vml3• *Lil-t* k* lyss mag-c bro1 *Manc* hr1* *Med* br1* merc k* nit-ac nux-v k* petr hr1* phos k* *Plat* k* *Polyg-h* kr1 *Psor* k* puls k* pyrog bg2* raja-s jl3 rheum k* **Sabin** k* *Sang* k*. *Sec* k* sep bg2 *Sil* k* sol-t-ae a1 spig k* *Stram* bg2* suis-em rly4• sulph k* suprar rly4• symph fd3.de• syph bg* ust k* vib k* voes a1
  - **acrid**: *Bell* k* *Carb-v* k* kola stb3• raja-s jl3
  - **ammonia**, like: aran jl3 lac-c k*
  - **carrion**-like: *Psor* kr1*
  - **diphtheria**; during: crot-h tl1
  - **extremely**: hist vml3•
  - **fish**, like spoiled: cassia-s ccrh1• sol-t-ae k* syph bg1
  - **lochia**, like: *Lil-t* k*
  - **pungent**: *Kali-c* k* kreos
  - **putrid**: aln vva1• *Alum-sil* **Ars** k2 carb-v k2 hoit jl3 ign k* kali-ar *Kreos* b7a.de lachn bg* *Psor* k* *Sulph* k*
  - **semen**, like: *Stram* hr1* *Sulph*
  - **sour**: carb-v cimic hep mrr1 mag-c mrr1 rheum mrr1 *Sulph* k*
  - **strong**: **Carb-v** cop *Sil* stram bg1 suis-em rly4• suprar rly4•
- **pain**: *(↗painful)*
  - **absence** of pain; flow only in the: *Cocc* mag-c plb
  - **after** the pain; flow only: *Mag-c*
  - **during** the pain; cease: *Cycl* kr1
- **painful**: *(↗pain; Pain - uterus - menses - during - agg.)* abrom-a mtf11* abrom-a-r bnj1* abrot acetan bro1 *Acon* k* acon-ac rly4• aesc kr1 agar k* agav-t jl3 agn j5.de aids nl2• alet k* aln vva1• alum alum-p k2 alum-sil k2 alumn a1 am-act bro1 **Am-c** k1* am-m j5.de* ammc kr1 amor-r jl3 *Anac* kr1* anan ant-c *Ant-t* kr1 antip c2 ap-g br1* *Apiol* bro1 apis k* aqui bro1* aran c2 arg-n arist-cl mg1.de arn sf1.de *Ars* ars-i *Ars-met* kr1 art-v c2 asar k* asc-c kr1* atro bro1* aur kr1 aven br1* bac jl2 bamb-a stb2.de• bar-c bar-i k2 bar-m bar-ox-suc rly4• **Bell** k* bell-p mg1.de* *Berb* k* bit-ar wht1• *Borx* k* bov k* brach c2 brom k* bry k* bufo k2 buni-o jl3 **Cact** k* *Calc* k* calc-act sf1.de calc-i k2 **Calc-p** k* calc-s k2 calc-sil k2 cann-i kr1* canth k* carb-an carb-v carbn-s carc mrr1 castm c2* *Caul* k* *Caust* cer-ox c2* **Cham** k* chin k* chinin-ar chinin-s kr1* chir-fl gya2 *Chlol* kr1* chord-umb rly4• cic k2* **Cimic** k* cinnb *Cit-v* kr1 *Coca* kr1 **Cocc** k1* coch kr1 *Coff* k* coli jl2 coll k* *Coloc* k* *Con* k* *Croc* k* crot-c crot-h c2 cupr k* cur kr1* *Cycl* k* dam c2 der a1 *Dios* k* dream-p sdj1• *Dulc* k* dys pte1*• elaps mrr1 epiph bro1 ergot jl3 **Erig** kr1 eup-pur sf1.de euphr falco-ch sze4• ferr k* ferr-ar ferr-i *Ferr-m* kr1 ferr-p k* flav jl2 flor-p rsj3• fuma-ac rly4• *Gels* k* gink-b sbd1• glon bro1* gnaph c2* goss k* granit-m es1• *Graph* k* grat *Guaj* kr1* haem c2 ham k* hedeo c2 *Helon* k* hir mg1.de* *Hoit* jl3 *Hydr* kr1 hydrog srj2• hyos k* hyper *Ign* k* inul kr1* iod ip k* iris c2 jab c2 juni-c c2 *Kali-ar* kali-bi **Kali-c** k* kali-fcy c2 *Kali-i* kali-m k2 kali-n k* *Kali-p* kali-perm br1* *Kali-s* kali-sil k2 kalm k* ketogl-ac rly4• kola stb3• kreos k* *Lac-c* k* lac-f c2* lac-leo hrn2• lac-lup hrn2• *Lach* k* *Lap-a* k* laur k* led *Lil-t* k* limest-b es1• lob k* *Lyc* k* *Macro* c2* mag-c k* mag-m k* **Mag-p** kr1* mag-s k* mang k* *Med* k* *Meli* k* meli-xyz c2 meph jl3 *Merc* k* *Merl* k* **Mill** kr1* *Mit* kr1* mom-b c2* moni rfm1• morg fmm1• morg-g pte1*• morph a1* mosch mucs-nas rly4• mur-ac murx k* musca-d szs1 naja c2 *Nat-c* k* nat-m nat-ox rly4• nat-p nat-s nicc k* nit-ac nux-m k* *Nux-v* k* ol-an *Ol-j* kr1 onop jl3 op c2* orot-ac rly4• ozone sde2• pall sf1.de palo jl3 passi sf1.de petr k* petr-ra shn4• *Petros* kr1 ph-ac phasco-ci rbp2 *Phos* phyt k* pic-ac a1 pin-con oss2• *Pitu* jl3 *Plat* k* plb plb-xyz c2 plut-n srj7• podo k* polyg-h kr1 polyg-xyz c2 pop-cand c2 pseuts-m oss1• **Psor** k* *Puls* k* raph c2 rauw jl3 *Rham-cal* br1 *Rhod* kr1 *Rhus-t* k* ribo rly4• sabal c2* *Sabin* k* sacch sst1• sal-al blc1• sang k* santin bro1 sapin c2 sars k* *Sec* k* sel rsj9* *Senec* k* *Sep* k* sil sinus rly4• spong staph sf1.de stram k* sul-ac sul-i k2 *Sulph* k* suprar rly4• syc pte1*• *Syph* kr1* *Tanac* a1 *Tarent* kr1* tell rsj10* ter c2 tetox pin2• ther k* thuj k* thyr c2* thyreotr jl3 trios rsj11* *Tub* k* **Ust** kr1* uza sf1.de ven-m jl3 *Verat* k* **Verat-v** kr1* vesp a1* **Vib** c2* vib-p c2* wye a1* **Xan** c2* *Zinc* h2* *Zinc-val* sf1.de* [bell-p-sp dcm1]
  - **abortion**; after: senec ptk1

- **painful**: ...
  - **accompanied** by:
    - **coffee**; desire for (See GENERALS - Food and - coffee - desire - accompanied - dysmenorrhea; GENERALS - Food and - coffee - desire - grounds)
    - **copious** menses: brucel sa3• granit-m es1•
    - **diarrhea** (See RECTUM - Diarrhea - accompanied - menses)
    - **eructation**: vib ptk1
    - **hemorrhoids**: coll tl1
    - **nausea**: *(↗nausea)* ip mrr1
    - **obesity**: cer-ox br1
    - **rheumatic** pains: bry ptk1 caul bro1 caust bro1 **Cimic** bro1* cocc bro1 guaj bro1 lach ptk1 rham-cal bro1 rhus-t ptk1
    - **subinvolution** (See Subinvolution - accompanied - menses)
    - **vomiting** (See STOMACH - Vomiting - accompanied - menses)
    - **weakness** (See GENERALS - Weakness - accompanied - menses) •
    - **Face**; redness of: xan mrr1
    - **Joint** pains: caul mrr1
    - **Nipples**; retracted: sars ptk1
    - **Ovaries**; complaints of: *Apis* bro1 bell bro1 ham bro1 xan bro1
    - **Tongue** | **mucus** on tongue; collection of: lac-c kr1*
    - **Uterus**; complaints of: *Cham* bro1 coff bro1 nit-ac bro1 xan bro1
  - **anger**; after: **Cham** kr1*
  - **beginning**, at: *(↗Pain - uterus - menses - during - beginning - agg.)* cact k2 *Calc* hr1* calc-p k2 cer-ox br1 *Crot-h* hr1* cypra-eg sde6.de• dream-p sdj1• foll jl3 gels sf1.de *Lach* hr1* *Pitu* jl3 sel rsj9* spong fd4.de
  - **bending**:
    - **backward** | **amel.**: lac-c ptk1
  - **bending** double | **amel.**: op ptk1
  - **bones**; preceded by aching: pyrog tl1
  - **chill**; with: *Kali-c* kr1 *Verat* kr1
  - **clothing** agg.: lach mrr1
  - **cold**:
    - **agg.**: coloc tl1 mag-p tl1
    - **exposure** to | **agg.**: nux-m k2
  - **cold** agg.; after becoming: *Acon* sf1.de *Caj* kr1
  - **coldness**; with: **Verat** kr1*
  - **convulsions**; with: aran hr1* caul ptk1 coll tl1 *Nat-m* hr1* *Tarent* hr1*
  - **damp** house, living in: nux-m k2
  - **dinner** or supper, after: *Phyt* hr1*
  - **discharge** of clots: *Cact* mrr1
    - **amel.**: *Vib* kr1
  - **emotions**; from: cham ptk1
  - **end**, at the: buth-a mg1.de
  - **excitement** agg.: arg-n k2 **Calc** hr1*
  - **fever**; with: ferr-p k2
  - **fibroids**; from (See myoma)
  - **first** day: gnaph ptk1 lach ptk1
  - **flow**:
    - **amel.**: cimic tl1 cypra-eg sde6.de• lach tl1* mag-p ptk1 mosch sf1.de sep tl1 zinc k2* *Zinc-val* sf1.de
    - **more** the flow, the greater the pain; the: *(↗Pain - menses - during - agg. - flow)* cann-s k2 cann-xyz ptk1 *Cimic* k2* granit-m es1• phos k2* tarent k2* tub k2*
    - **scanty**: caul ptk1 gnaph ptk1 graph ptk1
    - **smaller** the flow, the greater the pain; the: *Lach* kr1*
  - **fright** agg.: *Acon* sf1.de tub al*
  - **girls**:
    - **first** period; since the: puls k2*
    - **irregular** periods; with: *Mill* kr1

- **girls**: ...
  - **young** girls, in: apis k1 aqui br1 calc-p k1 graph k1
- **horrible** pain, crying and weeping: *Cact* hr1* *Coff* sf1.de *Cupr* sf1.de
- **infantilism**, with: calc-p k2
- **lying**:
  - **amel.**: dream-p sdj1• ven-m jl [chr-m stj2]
  - **back**; on:
    - **amel.** | **legs** stretched; with: sabin ptk1
  - **hard** pillow; on a | **amel.**: mag-m ptk1
- **membranous**: calc-act mtf11
- **menopause**, near the: **Psor** k*
- **motion**:
  - **amel.**: pyrog tl1
  - **downward** motion agg.: borx tl1 guaj tl1 ust tl1 vib tl1
- **myoma** in uterus; from hard and large: aur-m-n mrr1
- **nausea** and vomiting: (↗*accompanied - nausea*) *Verat* jsa*
- **neuralgic**: mag-p tl1 *Xan* br1
- **perspiration**, from checked: *Caj* kr1
- **pressing** feet against something amel.: med ptk1
- **pressure** | **amel.**: mag-c ptk1 *Mag-p* mrr1
- **puberty**:
  - **at**: calc-p mrr1 *Phyt* kr1 *Puls* kr1*
  - **since**: puls k2*
- **riding** in the wind: nux-m k2
- **spasmodic**: acon bro1 agar bro1 *Bell* bro1 *Caul* bro1 cham bro1 *Cimic* bro1 coff bro1 coll bro1 *Gels* bro1 glon bro1 gnaph bro1 mag-m bro1 *Mag-p* bro1 *Nux-v* bro1 *Puls* bro1 sabin bro1 santin bro1 *Sec* bro1 senec bro1 sep bro1 verat-v bro1 vib bro1* *Xan* bro1
- **sterility**, in: cham lp nux-v lp *Phyt* hr1* puls lp
- **supper** (See dinner)
- **vexation**; from: coloc tl1
- **waking**; on: aids nl2• hydrog srj2•
- **walking**:
  - **agg.**: *Sabin* hr1*
  - **amel.**: cortiso sp1
- **warmth** | **amel.**: *Ars* kr1 castm sf1.de caust sf1.de chord-umb rly4• *Coloc* mrr1 *Mag-p* sf1.de* *Nux-m* kr1 ozone sde2• *Sabin* kr1 ven-m jl
- **wet**:
  - **getting**: phyt sf1.de *Zinc* kr1
    - **Feet**: acon dulc merc nat-c nat-m *Phos* **Puls** *Rhus-t* sep sil *Xan* kr1

- **pale**: acon a1 aeth hr1 *Alum* k* alum-p k2* alumn k* am-c k* amp rly4• ant-t apoc am ars k* *Atro* hr1* *Bell* k* *Berb* k* borx k* both-ax tsm2 *Bov* k* bry bufo bg2 calc k* calc-s canth carb-an *Carb-v* k* *Caul* k* cench vh* chin chinin-ar cop a1 cycl hr1* dig b4.de* dros *Dulc* k* eupi **Ferr** k* *Ferr-ar* *Ferr-p* k* form k* goss k* **Graph** k* hyos k* ip irid-met srj5• *Kali-ar* kali-c k* *Kali-i* hr1* kali-n kali-p kali-sil k2* kreos *Lac-ac* a1* *Lac-d* k2* laur led lyc m-aust b7.de* mag-m b4.de* manc k* *Mang* merc k* nat-c b4.de* **Nat-m** k* nat-p k* nit-ac j5.de ozone sde2• *Phos* k* pot-e rly4• prun *Puls* k* *Rhus-t* k* sabad *Sabin* k* sacch a1 *Sec* k* *Sep* k* sil *Staph* stram k* stront-c k* *Sulph* k* *Tarent* a1* thuj b4a.de* til a1* tril-p *Ust* hr1* vib k* zinc k* [alumin stj2 alumin-p stj2 alumin-s stj2]
  - **clots**:
    - **dark**; with: cench st
    - **then** dark and clotted; first pale: *Staph* kr1*
  - **convulsions**; during epileptic: *Atro* hr1*
  - **sexual** desire; with loss of: *Lach* kr1
- **pitch**-like: bism *Cact* k* *Cocc* k* croc bg2* *Graph* kali-m kr1* kali-n *Mag-c* k* mag-m med bro1 nux-v *Plat* k* sang
- **pregnancy** agg.; during: asar ptk1 cham ptk1 cocc k* *Croc* ptk1* ip ptk1 kali-c k* kreos k* lyc ptk1 *Nux-m* k* phos k* plat k* rhus-t k* sabin ptk1 sec k*
  - **first** months, during: *Calc* kr1*
- **premature**:
  - **menstrual** cycle; in the regular (See frequent)
  - **proper** age; before the (See appear - proper)
- **protracted**: *Acon* k* agar b2.de* agn *Aloe* k* am-c k* amor-r jl3 apoc aran *Arg-n* *Ars* k* **Ars-met** kr1 ars-s-f k2 arund k* asar k* aspar j5.de* bac jl2 bar-act a1 *Bar-c* k* bar-s k2 bell k* *Borx* k* bov k* *Bry* k* **Calc** k* calc-ar k2 calc-i bro1 *Calc-s* k* calc-sil k2 cann-i kr1 *Canth* k* **Carb-an** k* **Carb-v** k* carl a1 caust k* chel k* *Chin* k* chinin-ar choc srj3• chord-umb rly4• cina b2.de* cinnm k* coc-c *Cocc* bg2* *Coff* k* *Coloc* b4a.de* *Con* bro1 corian-s knl6• *Croc* k* *Crot-h* k* **Cupr** k* cur cycl daph *Dig* kr1 dulc k* *Erig* **Ferr** k* ferr-act bro1 *Ferr-ar* *Ferr-p* *Fl-ac* k* foll jl3* germ-met srj5• glyc bro1 graph bro1 grat k* ham bg2* hip-ac sp1* hir rsj4• hydrog srj2• hyos k* *Ign* k* ignis-alc es2• ind jl3 *Iod* b4a.de* ip irid-met srj5• jug-r vml3• *Kali-ar* **Kali-c** k* kali-chl kali-m kr1 kali-n k* kali-p kali-s *Kreos* k* lac-h htj1• *Lach* k* laur k* led k* luna kg1• **Lyc** k* *Lyss* *M-ambo* b2.de* m-aust b2.de* mag-c k* *Mag-m* h2* mag-s *Merc* k* merc-c bg2 *Mez* **Mill** k* mucs-nas rly4• *Murx* k* *Nat-ar* *Nat-c* k* **Nat-m** k* *Nat-p* *Nat-s* nat-sil k2 *Nux-m* k* **Nux-v** k* olib-sac wmh1 onos k* *Ph-ac* *Phos* k* pin-con oss2• pitu-a vml2• **Plat** k* prot jl3 psor k2* **Puls** k* rad-br ptk1 raph k* **Rat** k* **Rhus-t** k* ribo rly4• ros-d wla1 ruta *Sabad* b2.de* **Sabin** k* sang a1 sanguiso bro1 saroth mg1.de* **Sec** k* **Senec** k* *Sep* k* *Sil* k* spong fd4.de stann k* *Staph* kr1 staphycoc rly4• *Stram* k* suis-em rly4• sul-ac k* *Sulph* k* tarent thal jl3 *Thlas* kr1* thuj k* thymol sp1* *Tril-p* bro1 trios jl3 tritic-vg fd5.de *Tub* k* *Ust* k* vanil br1 verat-n c1* vinc ptk1 vip ptk1 visc sp1 *Xan* kr1* zinc k* zinc-p k2 [beryl-m stj2]
  - **eight** days: thlas kr1
    - **eight** to fifteen days: *Thlas* kr1
    - **eight** to nine days: *Lach* kr1 **Senec** hr1*
    - **eight** to ten days: plat kr1 **Sep** kr1
    - **longer** than usual; eight days: *Cinnm* kr1
  - **eighteen** days: cann-i kr1 thuj kr1
  - **fifteen** days: thlas kr1
  - **fourteen** days: calc hr1 *Coloc* kr1 *Xan* kr1
    - **interval** of two weeks; with: *Calc* hr1*
  - **grief**; from: cocc k2
  - **menopause**; during: calc mtf11
  - **one** day longer than usual: aspar kr1
  - **seven** days: ruta fd4.de sabin kr1
    - **seven** to fourteen days: thuj kr1
    - **seven** to nine days: *Sec* hr1*
  - **sexual** desire increased, with: kali-br ptk1
  - **sleep**; from loss of: cocc k2
  - **ten** days: thlas kr1
    - **ten** to fourteen days: ust kr1
    - **ten** to twelve days: *Murx* kr1
  - **twelve** days:
    - **twelve** to eighteen days: agn kr1
    - **twelve** to fifteen days: tarent kr1
  - **twenty** days: tub jl2
  - **until** next period:
    - **almost** until next period: carb-v k2 nux-v k2 sabin k2 sec k2
    - **not** ceasing entirely until next period: *Ust* kr1
- **purple**: (↗*brown - mauve*) *Puls* hr1* wye a1
- **red**:
  - **bright** (See bright)
  - **raspberry**: kola stb3•
- **rest** | **agg.**: am-c bg2 *Ferr* bg2 mag-m bg2
- **return**:
  - **ceased**; after the regular menstrual cycle has: (↗*Metrorrhagia - menopause - during*) alum h2* ambr k* arg-n ptk1 *Borx* j5.de bov ptk1 *Calc* carb-v j5.de carl a1 coc-c ptk1 *Cocc* j5.de dream-p sdj1• ferr j5.de* ham ptk1 hydrog srj2• *Kali-c* j5.de kali-i j5.de *Kreos* k* *Lach* k* **Lyc** bg2* lyss a1 mag-c k* mag-m mang k2* mosch j5.de murx nat-m *Nux-v* k* ozone sde2• petr-ra shn4• ph-ac j5.de phos j5.de* plat j5.de puls k* rhod j5.de *Rhus-t* j5.de* sabad ptk1 sabin ptk1 sep sil j5.de* *Staph* j5.de stram j5.de thea a1 thuj tril-p k* ust k* *Verat* j5.de* zinc j5.de
    - **excitement** agg.: *Calc*
    - **old** women, in: *Calc* k* lach mag-c mag-m **Phos**●* *Plat* k* sep staph
    - **overexertion**, after: tril-p
  - **delivery**; too soon after: tub k*
    - **two** weeks after delivery: tub c1

Female

• **menopause**, after: dream-p sdj1•

• **menstrual** cycle; after the bleeding stopped during the (See intermittent)

- **ropy**, tenacious, stringy: arg-n bro1 bamb-a stb2.de• cact k* canth coc-c bro1 *Colch* b7a.de **Croc** k* *Cupr* k* *Ign* hr1* kali-chl kali-m kr1* kreos bro1 *Lac-c* k* lach *Mag-c* k* mag-m k* mag-p bg2* mang k* *Nit-ac* bro1 nux-m bro1 phos k* *Plat* k* *Puls* k* sec k* *Sep* kr1 sulph bro1 *Tril-p* bro1 ust k* *Xan* hr1*

• **last** days: prot jl2

• **motion**; slightest: **Croc** kr1

- **sadness**; with (See MIND - Sadness - menses - during)
- **scanty**: abrom-a zzc1• abrom-a-r mtf11 acet-ac k2* acon k* agav-t jl3 agn b2.de* alet bro1* aln vva1• *Alum* k* alum-p k2* alum-sil k2* alumn k* **Am-c** k* amp rly4• anac ange-s jl3 ant-t a1* anthraq rly4• *Apis* k* aqui br1 **Arg-n** k* *Arist-cl* mg1.de* arn b2.de* *Ars* k* **Ars-met** kr1 *Art-v* k* *Asaf* k* *Atro* hr1* *Aur* k* aur-ar k2 aur-s k2* bamb-a stb2.de• *Bar-c* k* *Bar-s* k2* bell b4.de *Berb* k* *Borx* j5.de* both-ax tsm2 *Bov* k* bros-gau mrc1 bry b2.de* *Bufo* buni-o jl3 *Buth-a* mg1.de *Cact* k* cael jl3 calc k* *Calc-ar* k* calc-f sp1 calc-p ptk1 calc-s calc-sil k2* cann-i k* canth bg2* *Carb-an* k* *Carb-v* k* **Carbn-s** carl a1 *Caul* k* *Caust* k* chel b2.de* chin c1 cic k* *Cimic* k* *Cocc* k* colch b2.de* *Coloc* hr1* **Con** k* croc b2.de* *Crot-h* bg2* crot-t k* cub k* cupr k* cur **Cycl** k* cyclosp sa3• dendr-pol sk4• des-ac jl3 dig k* dros k* **Dulc** k* *Elaps* kr1 erig k* euphr k* eupi a1 *Ferr* k* *Ferr-ar* ferr-i hr1 *Ferr-p* form k* *Gels* bro1 ger-i rly4• gink-b sbd1• glycyr-g cte1• goss k* **Graph** k* guaj b2.de* hed mg1.de* helon k* *Hep* k* hip-ac sp1* hir mg1.de* hist jl3 hura a1 hydrog srj2• hyos b2.de* *Ign* k* iod b2.de* *Ip* b2.de* irid-met srj5• iris a1 *Kali-ar* *Kali-bi* hr1* *Kali-br* k* **Kali-c** k* *Kali-i* j5.de* kali-n a1 *Kali-p* k* *Kali-s* k* kali-sil k2* kalm k* lac-ac a1* lac-c k* lac-d k* lac-lup hrn2• **Lach** k* lam k* laur bg2 lept sf1.de *Lil-t* k* lith-c kr1 lob *Lyc* k* *M-arct* b2.de* *Mag-c* k* mag-m b2.de* mag-s j5.de* **Mang** k* mang-act bro1* *Meli* bro1 *Merc* k* merc-i-f hr1* merl bro1 mez k* mill a1 mosch b2.de* *Murx* hr1 naja *Nat-ar* *Nat-c* k* **Nat-m** k* nat-s k* nat-sil k2 nept-m lsd2.fr nicc k* *Nit-ac* k* nit-s-d j5.de *Nux-m* k* *Nux-v* k* oena k* ol-an k* orot-ac rly4• ozone sde2• *Petr* k* petr-ra shn4• phel j5.de **Phos** k* pieri-b mlk9.de pip-n c1* pitu jl3 plac-s rly4• *Plat* b2.de* *Plb* k* plut-n srj7• pneu jl3* pot-e rly4• pseuts-m oss1• psor k* **Puls** k* rat j5.de rhod b2.de* rhus-t b2.de* ruta k* *Sabad* k* sabin b2.de* sacch a1 sal-fr sle1• sang k* *Sars* k* sel rsj9* **Senec** bg2* **Seneg** k* **Sep** k* *Sil* k* *Stann* hr1* *Staph* k* stram k* stront-c k* stront-n c1* stry-af-cit bro1 suis-em rly4• suis-pan rly4• **Sulph** k* suprar rly4• *Syph* hr1* tarent a1 tell a1 ter k* thuj k* thymol sp1* thyreotr jl3 til c1 tong j5.de* trios rsj11* tritic-vg fd5.de ulm-c jsj8• ust k* valer k* vanad dx* vanil br1* verat k* verat-v k* vero-o rly4*• *Vib* k* vip fkr4.de visc sp1 wye a1 *Xan* k* xanth bg2 *Zinc* k* zinc-p k2* [alumin stj2 alumin-s stj2 bar-m stj1 chr-m stj2 heroin sdj2 mang-i stj2 mang-m stj2 mang-met stj2 mang-n stj2 mang-s stj2 mang-sil stj2 sol-ecl cky1 tax jsj7 zinc-i stj2 zinc-n stj2]

• **daytime**: *Bov* k* **Mag-c** k* pot-e rly4•

• **morning**; only: carb-an plut-n srj7• *Sep*

• **evening**: mag-c a1

• **night**: bros-gau mrc1

• **accompanied** by | **Stomach**; complaints of (See STOMACH - Complaints - accompanied - menses - scanty)

• **acne**, with: sang st1

• **anemic** women; in: mang mrr1

• **chill**; with: **Nat-m** hr1*

• **clotted**: cocc hr1*

• **cold**, from a: **Nux-m** hr1*

• **convulsions** | **during** | **epileptic**: **Art-v** hr1* *Bufo* kr1 *Caust* hr1* *Kali-br* hr1*

⁝ **with**: *Glon* hr1*

• **copious**, then: choc srj3• *Nat-m* hr1* ruta fd4.de tritic-vg fd5.de

• **decreasing** until they disappear: cocc hr1*

• **early**; and too: alum bg2* lept bg2* nat-m bg2*

• **eruption** on face; with: bell-p calc eug psor sang

• **exertion** agg.; physical and mental: *Glon* kr1 **Nux-m** kr1

• **fleshy** women; in: *Kali-br* *Kali-i*

• **fright** agg.: **Nux-m** hr1*

• **hysteric** women; in: **Nux-m** kr1

• **leukorrhea**:

⁝ **after**: *Sep* kr1

- **scanty – leukorrhea**: ...

⁝ **consisting** mostly of leukorrhea: cub c1

⁝ **with**: *Mez* kr1

• **lying** down; cease when: *Cact* kr1

• **motion** agg.: *Sep* kr1

• **plethoric** women; in: (↗*GENERALS - Plethora - constitution*) *Petros* kr1

• **profuse** flow; with sensation of: lac-cp sk4•

• **sexual** desire lost: *Lach* hr1*

• **sleepiness**; with: *Helon* hr1*

• **sterility**, in: *Canth* hr1*

• **three** days; first: mag-m h2 nept-m lsd2.fr

• **weakness**; from: **Nux-m** hr1*

- **short**; too: agath-a nl2• aids nl2• *Alum* k* alum-p k2 **Am-c** k* amp rly4• androc srj1• *Ant-t* a1* apis b7a.de arge-pl rwt5• arist-cl sp1* ars ars-i *Asaf* aur-m bamb-a stb2.de• *Bar-c* k* bar-i k2 bar-ox-suc rly4• *Berb* bit-ar wht1• both-ax tsm2 bov k* carb-an b2.de* carbn-o a1 *Carbn-s* clem *Cocc* colch k* *Con* k* conch fkr1• cystein-l rly4• dirc a1 dream-p sdj1• *Dulc* k* ephe-si hsj1• erig zr euphr k* fl-ac a1 gast a1 gink-b sbd1• glon a1 gran j5.de *Graph* k* hed mg1.de* hir rsj4• hydrog srj2• iod k* *Ip* b2.de* irid-met srj5• kali-c kali-p kali-s fd4.de kali-sil k2 ketogl-ac rly4• *Kreos* lac-leo hrn2• **Lach** k* lith-c a1 luna kg1• lyc k* m-arct b2.de* mag-c k* mag-m k* mag-s *Mang* k* *Merc* k* merl kr1 mosch k* *Nat-m* k* nat-s nicc *Nux-v* oci-sa jl* oena olib-sac wmh1 orot-ac rly4• *Ov* st1 ozone sde2• petr-ra shn4• phel a1 *Phos* k* pieri-b mlk9.de plac-s rly4• *Plat* k* pneu jl3 *Positr* nl2• pot-e rly4• *Psor* **Puls** k* rhod k* ruta k* sabad k* sars k* senec zr *Sep* sil k* stront-c suis-pan rly4• sul-i k2 **Sulph** k* sumb a1 *Thuj* k* til ulm-c jsj8• vib k* vip-a jl3 zinc ziz a1 [alumin stj2 alumin-p stj2 alumin-s stj2 mang-act stj2 mang-i stj2 mang-m stj2 mang-met stj2 mang-s stj2 mang-sil stj2]

• **alternate** days, on: ovi-p bg1

• **few** hours: *Coc-c* kr1 valer ptk1

• **half** to six hours, only a: *Lycps-v* kr1

• **one** day: *Alum* k* *Apis* k* *Arg-n* k* bar-c borx h2 euphr ptk1 lepi mang k2 nux-v psor puls k2 pyrog rad-br ptk1 ruta fd4.de **Sep** k* thuj

• **one** hour: euphr k* psor k*

• **three** or four days: aids nl2• cartl-s rly4• *Lach* kr1 positr nl2•

• **twelve** hours: ziz kr1

• **two** days: agath-a nl2• ant-t kr1 **Apis** kr1 bit-ar wht1• *Mang* kr1* nat-sil fd3.de• pneu jl *Verat* kr1

• **two** or three days: agath-a nl2• dream-p sdj1• *Sep* kr1

- **sitting**:

• **cease** while (See cease - sitting)

• **increase** while (See copious - sitting)

- **sleep**; during:

• **gushing**: (↗*gushing*) *Coca*

• **only**: mag-c

- **sour**: alet bg2 sulph b4.de*
- **staining**: (↗*wash*) mag-c mtf *Mag-m* mtf musca-d szs1 [mag-lac stj2 mag-met stj2 mag-n stj2 mag-sil stj2]

• **black** stain on clothes: *Glycyr-g* cte1•

• **wash** out; colors the clothes, difficult to: *Carb-ac* st croc bg2 culx st *Mag-c* k* *Med* k* merc st puls st pulx br1 *Sil* bg2* vib st

- **standing**, increased while: (↗*copious - standing*) *Am-c* k* cocc ptk1 mag-c h2* psor ptk1
- **stool** | **during** stool; increased: hep k* iod k* lyc ptk1 murx ptk1
- **stooping** | **amel.**: mag-c ptk1
- **stopping** (See cease)
- **stringy** (See ropy)
- **suppressed** menses; from: *Abrot* k* *Acon* k* aeth k* *Agn* k* alet alum k* alum-sil k2* alumn k* *Am-c* k* ambr hr1* *Anan* *Ant-c* k* *Apis* k* apoc k2 *Arg-n* arn k* *Ars* k* ars-h c1* ars-i art-v hr1 arum-t hr1* *Asc-c* hr1* aur k* aur-ar k2 aur-i k2* *Aur-m* k* aur-m-n aur-s *Bar-c* k* bar-i k2* bar-s k2* **Bell** k* berb k* borx k* *Brom* k* *Bry* k* bufo cain kr1 *Calc* k* calc-i k2* *Calc-p* hr1* calc-s calc-sil k2* *Camph* hr1* *Carb-an* k* carb-v k* *Carbn-s* card-m k* caul k* *Caust* k* cean c1* *Cham* k* chel k* *Chen-a* k* chin k* chinin-ar chion bro1 chlol hr1* *Cimic* k* *Coc-c* k* *Cocc* k* coch hr1* cod hr1* coff bg2 *Colch* k* *Coll* hr1* coloc k* **Con** k* *Croc* k* *Cupr* k* **Cycl** k* *Dig* k* dros k* **Dulc** k* euph b2.de euphr bg2 *Ferr* k* *Ferr-ar* **Ferr-i** k* *Ferr-p* galeoc-c-h gms1• gast a1 *Gels* k* glon k* goss

- **suppressed** menses; from: ...
Graph k* guaj k* hedeo a1 *Hell* k* helon k* hep *Hyos* k* ign k* iod k* **Ip** hr1* *Kali-ar* k* **Kali-c** k* *Kali-chl* hr1* kali-i k* *Kali-m* bg2* *Kali-n* k* kali-p *Kali-s* *Kali-sil* k2* *Kalm* *Kreos* bg2* lac-d k* **Lach** k* lap-a c1 leon bro1 *Lept* hr1* lil-t lob k* **Lyc** k* m-arct b2.de* macro a1 *Mag-c* k* *Mag-m* k* mag-s mang k* merc k* **merc-c** bg2 mez k* mill k* morph a1 mosch sf1.de* *Nat-m* k* *Nat-s* hr1* *Nicc* hr1* *Nit-ac* k* *Nux-m* k* nux-v k* op k* ox-ac ozone sde2• *Par* hr1* pegan-ha tpi1• petr b2.de* ph-ac k* *Phos* k* *Phyt* bg2* plat k* plb k* podo k* *Prun* hr1* **Puls** k* *Puls-n* bro1 *Rhod* k* *Rhus-t* k* ruta k* *Sabad* k* sabin k* sang k* sars k* sec k* semp c1* **Senec** k* *Sep* k* **Sil** k* spong k* stann *Staph* k* *Stram* k* stront-c k* sul-i k2* **Sulph** k* symph hr1* *Tanac* bro1 tax bro1 ther k2* thuj k* tub k2* (non:uran-met k) *Uran-n* *Ust* k* *Valer* k* *Verat* k* **Verat-v** c2* visc c1 xan k* *Zinc* k* zinc-p k2* ziz a1* [*Lith-i* stj2 mag-i stj1 mang-i stj2 merc-i-f stj2 nat-i stj1 zinc-i stj2]
 - **accompanied** by:
   - **dropsy** (See GENERALS - Dropsy - external - accompanied - menses)
   - **epistaxis** (See NOSE - Epistaxis - menses - suppressed)
   - **rheumatism**: bry bro1 cimic bro1 rhus-t bro1
   - **Abdomen**; tenesmus in (See RECTUM - Pain - tenesmus - accompanied - menses)
   - **Head**:
     - **congestion** in (See HEAD - Congestion - menses - suppressed)
     - **pain** (See HEAD - Pain - menses - suppressed)
   - **Uterus**; congestion of: sabal bro1
 - **anemic** conditions; from: ars b4a.de* ars-i bro1 caust bro1 ferr-ar bro1 ferr-r bro1 graph bro1 kali-c b4a.de* kali-p bro1 kali-perm bro1 lyc b4a.de mag-act bro1 mag-m b4a.de nat-m b4a.de* ovi-p bro1 petr b4a.de phos b4a.de *Puls* bro1 *Senec* bro1 sep b4a.de sil b4a.de *Stry-af-cit* bro1 sulph b4a.de
 - **anger**; after: cham k* cod *Coloc* k* staph k* sulph k2
   - **indignation**; with: cham bro1 coloc bro1 staph bro1
 - **asthma**, with: **Puls** hr1* spong bro1*
 - **bathing** agg.: *Aeth* k* *Ant-c* k* *Calc-p* hr1* cupr k1* *Nux-m* hr1*
 - **cancer**, from: *Lyc* hr1*
 - **chagrin**; after (See mortification)
 - **chill**, from: bell dulc nux-m puls sep *Sulph*
 - **cold** | **bathing** | **agg.**: *Acon* ant-c bg* kali-m sf1.de lob mrr1 mosch sf1.de
   - **water**:
     - **agg.**: *Acon* bro1 *Ant-c* bro1 bell bro1 calc bro1 cham bro1 cimic bro1 *Con* bro1 *Dulc* bro1 graph bro1 lac-c bro1 *Lac-d* bro1 nux-m sne phos bro1 *Puls* bro1 *Rhus-t* bro1 sulph bro1 verat-v bro1 xan bro1
       - **feet** in; putting: *Nat-m* kr1
       - **hands** in; putting: *Con* *Lac-d* c1*
 - **cold** agg.; becoming: *Acon* c1* *Act-sp* hr1* aral arist-cl sp1 bell bg2 bell-p sp1 bry *Caj* hr1* calc sf1.de *Coc-c* k* *Con* k* *Dulc* k* graph sf1.de lyc sf1.de nux-m k* nux-v *Plat* hr1* podo *Puls* k* *Rhus-t* hr1* senec k* *Sep* k* sulph k*
   - **hands**: lac-d sf1.de
 - **convulsions**; with: *Bufo* kr1 **Calc-p** st1 *Cocc* hr1* *Cupr* hr1* gels hr1* *Glon* hr1* *Mill* hr1* nux-m hr1 **Puls** hr1* **Verat** st1 zinc a2
 - **dampness**, from: calc k* *Dulc* graph k* *Rhus-t*
 - **dancing**, after excessive: cycl k* *Sabin* kr1
 - **diabetes**; in: uran-n ptk1
 - **easily**: bry k2 *Cycl* mrr1
 - **emigrants**, in: bry bro1* *Plat* k*
 - **emotions** agg.: *Cham* sf1.de *Cimic* k* *Ign* sne kali-m sf1.de *Lach* kr1 mosch sf1.de
 - **exertion** agg.: bry k2 *Cycl* k* *Nux-m*
 - **falling**; from: *Coloc* kr1
 - **feeble** women; in: (↗*weakness*) **Sep** kr1
 - **fever**, from: cimic hr1*
 - **fright** agg.: *Acon* k* act-sp hr1* bry calc k* cimic bro1 coff k* *Coloc* b4a.de* gels *Kali-c* k* *Lyc* k* **Nux-m** hr1* nux-v *Op* k* *Rhus-t* kr1 verat bg2*
 - **girls**, in young: alum lp calc-p lp cycl lp podo lp puls lp senec k2* tub lp

- **suppressed** menses; from: ...
 - **grief**; from: cocc k2 **Ign** k* rhus-t kr1
 - **heated**, after being: *Bry* *Cycl* k*
 - **hysteric** women; in: cypr kr1 **Nux-m** kr1 ol-an sf1.de *Sil* kr1
 - **injuries**; after: *Coloc* hr1*
 - **ironing**, by: bry k2
 - **liver** disturbances, in: lept ptk1
 - **love**, from disappointed: (↗*MIND - Ailments - love; MIND - Sadness - love)* hell k* ign nat-m ph-ac
 - **menopause**; during: galeoc-c-h gms1•
 - **mortification**; from: acon *Cham* sf1.de *Chin* **Coloc** k* puls *Staph*
 - **neuralgic** pain in body, with: kalm ptk1
 - **nurse**, after ceasing to: sep st*
 - **overheated**; when: bry k2 *Cycl* hr1
 - **perspiration** of feet; from suppression of: *Cupr* kr1*
 - **plethoric** women; in: (↗*GENERALS - Plethora - constitution)* *Acon* arn *Bell* bry calc k* glon nux-v op plat sulph verat **Verat-v** st*
 - **psoric** women; in: *Psor* kr1
 - **scrofulous** women; in: *Bar-c* kr1 *Sulph* kr1
 - **shock**, from mental: *Nux-v* kr1
   - **suddenly**: *Lac-d* kr1 *Lach* kr1 ziz kr1
 - **sleep**, from loss of: cocc k2
 - **thunderstorm** agg.: nat-c
 - **tuberculosis**, in: *Lob* kr1 *Lyc* kr1 *Senec* kr1 solid ptk1 ust ptk1
 - **walking** agg.: **Kreos** st* mag-c br
 - **warm** bathing agg.: *Aeth* hr1*
 - **weakness**; from: (↗*feeble)* **Nux-m** hr1*
 - **wet**; getting:
   - **agg.**: acon *Calc* *Cycl* mrr1 *Dulc* graph k* *Hell* nux-v *Puls* *Rhus-t* *Senec*
     - **feet**: *Acon* *Graph* *Hell* *Nat-m* nux-m **Puls** k* **Rhus-t** k* senec k2 *Xan* kr1*
 - **working** in water: calc
- **sweet** smelling: ozone sde2•
- **tenacious** (See ropy)
- **thick**: ant-t a1 *Arg-n* k* arn k* *Asar* b7a.de *Bell* k* *Cact* k* *Carb-v* k* coc-c k* *Cocc* k* cortiso jl3 croc k* cupr k* dig b4a.de ferr b7a.de ferul a1 *Fl-ac* k* *Graph* k* kali-n k* *Kali-p* kreos b7a.de lach b7a.de *Lil-t* k* *Mag-c* k* mag-s k* mand mg1.de* mang h2* *Nit-ac* k* *Nux-m* k* nux-v k* *Plat* k* **Puls** k* *Sulph* k* thymol jl3 tril-p *Xan* hr1*
- **thin**: acet-ac k2* aeth k* *Alum* k* alumn k* ant-t j5.de apoc hr1 ars k* ars-met kr1 bamb-a stb2.de• *Bell* k* *Berb* k* *Bov* k* bros-gau mrc1 carb-an b4a.de **Carb-v** b4a.de* cocc h1 *Dulc* k* ephe-si hsj1• erig k* eupi a1* **Ferr** k* *Ferr-p* ferul a1 gast a1 goss hr1* *Graph* k* haem sf1.de ham bg2* irid-met srj5• kali-p k* kreos b7a.de* lac-d k2* lach hr1* *Laur* k* m-aust j5.de *Mag-m* h2* mang merc b4a.de mill bg2* nat-c j5.de* **Nat-m** k* nat-s j5.de* *Nit-ac* k2* nux-m b7.de* ozone sde2• *Phos* *Plat* hr1* pot-e rly4• prun a1 **Puls** k* *Sabin* k* *Sec* k* stram k* stront-c j5.de sul-ac sulph k* tritic-vg fd5.de tub *Ust* k* vib k*
 - **clots**, with: *Cham* k* *Chin* k* *Ferr* k* sec k* *Ust* bg1*
   - **first** thin: mag-m k* pot-e rly4•
     - **then** clotted: stront-c kr1
 - **coagulating**, not: *Kali-p* kr1 ph-ac b4a.de sacch-a gmj3
 - **meat** water, like: apoc bg2 nat-c bg2* ozone sde2• stront-c bg2*
- **traces** of menses between the periods: *Bov* a1 caust a1 eupi a1 lat-h thj1 [heroin sdj2]
- **urinating**, only when: ger-i rly4• m-aust bg1
- **vexation**; after: acon coloc puls staph
- **vicarious**: acon ars bapt bell k* *Brom* hr1* **Bry** k* cact *Calc* chin cimic coll *Crot-h* k* cupr bg2 *Dig* k* dulc erig bro1* eupi c1* ferr k* graph bg* *Ham* k* ip bg2* kali-c bg2* lach bg1* mill k* nat-s bg2* nux-v **Phos** k* puls k* sabad bg2* *Sang* k* sec bg2* *Senec* k* sep sil bro1* sulph k* tril-p bg2* ust k* verat bg2 zinc k*
- **waking**; beginning on: hydrog srj2•
- **walking**:
 - **agg.**: mag-c h2 **Puls** kr1 sabin bg2* squil bg zinc h2*
 - **cease** while walking: coc-c kreos hr1 mag-c c1 sabin sec
 - **less** while walking: cycl sabin

Female

- **only** while walking: *Lil-t* nat-s sec
- **wash** off, difficult to: *(↗staining)* calc-s ptk1 *Carb-ac* st1 culx st1 lach mtf *Mag-c* k* mag-p ptk1* *Med* k* merc st1 puls st1 pulx ptk1* *Sil* st1 thlas ptk1* vib st1
- **watery**: aeth bro1* alumn bro1* am-c b4a.de *Ant-t* b7.de* ars bg2 *Bell* bg2 berb bg2 both-ax tsm2 bov b4.de* *Bry* b7.de* *Calc* bg2 **Carb-v** bg2 cocc bg2 con bg2 *Dulc* b4a.de* eupi bro1 ferr b7.de* ferr-act bro1 *Ferr-m* bro1 goss bro1* **Graph** bg2 hell bg2 kali-c bg2 kali-p bro1 **Lyc** bg2 *M-aust* b7.de* mag-m b4.de* nat-m bg2* nat-p bro1 *Nit-ac* bg2 nux-v bg2 phos b4a.de* *Plat* bg2 plb bg2 prun bg2 **Puls** b7a.de* *Sabin* bro1 sec b7a.de* sep bg2 spig bg2 stram b7.de* stront-c b4.de* **Sulph** bg2 tritic-vg fd5.de ust bg2* vanil fd5.de [mang stj1 mang-act stj2 mang-i stj2 mang-m stj2 mang-met stj2 mang-n stj2 mang-p stj2 mang-s stj2 mang-sil stj2]
- **yellow** | **saffron**: croc b7.de*

METRORRHAGIA: *(↗Abortion)* abrot a1 *Acet-ac* k* achil-m bro1 *Acon* k* *Adren* br1 agar bro1 *Agn* k* alet k* alumn k* am-br k* am-c j5.de* am-m k* ambr k* ant-c b7.de* anthraci kr1 *Apis* k* *Apoc* k* aran k* arg-met *Arg-n* k* arg-o bro1 arge-pl rwt5• *Arn* k* *Ars* k* *Ars-i* art-v hr1 asar b2.de* asc-t k* aur sf1.de aur-m c1 aur-m-k c1* aur-m-n sf1.de aza jl3 bacls-7 pte1• bapt k* **Bell** k* bell-p jl3 borx b4a.de* **Both** *Bov* k* *Brom* b4a.de *Bry* k* bufo k* *Cact* bg2* **Calc** k* calc-act a1 calc-ar k2* calc-f sf1.de* calc-i k2* calc-s *Camph* hr1 cann-i k* *Canth* k* caps bg2 *Carb-an* k* *Carb-v* k* *Carbn-s* *Card-m* k* *Caul* k* *Cean* hr1* *Cham* k* **Chin** k* chinin-ar *Chinin-s* chr-ac hr1 *Cimic* k* cina b7.de* *Cinnm* k* cit-v c1* cob-n jl3 *Coc-c* k* *Cocc* b2.de* *Coff* k* coff-t a1 *Colch* k* coll bro1 *Coloc* k* cop k* **Croc** k* crot-c k* **Crot-h** k* cupr b7.de* cycl k2 dict a1* dig a1 diosm br1 *Elaps* k* epih c1 erech c1* *Erig* k* eupi a1 **Ferr** k* *Ferr-act* bro1 ferr-ar *Ferr-i* *Ferr-m* k* *Ferr-p* k* *Ferr-s* hr1* fl-ac fuli br1* gal-ac c1 gels k* **Glon** hr1* guare a1 **Ham** k* *Helon* k* *Hep* k* hydr bg2* hydrin-m c1 hydrinin-m c1* *Hyos* k* *Ign* k* *Iod* k* **Ip** k* iris joan br1* juni-v a1* kali-ar k2* *Kali-br* k* *Kali-c* k* *Kali-chl* k* **Kali-fcy** *Kali-m* kr1* *Kali-n* bro1 kali-p kali-s k* *Kreos* k* *Lac-c* k* **Lach** k* lap-a c1 laur c1* *Led* lil-t bro1 *Lyc* k* lycpr c2 lycps-v *M-ambo* b7.de *M-aust* b7.de mag-c k* mag-m k* mag-s j5.de mangi bro1 *Med* k* *Meli* hr1* *Merc* k* mez b4.de **Mill** k* mit bro1 morg-p pte1• **Murx** k* nat-ar *Nat-c* k* *Nat-hchls* k* nat-m k* **Nit-ac** k* *Nux-m* k* **Nux-v** k* *Oci-sa* sp1 op k* orig-d c2 petr b2.de* **Phos** k* *Phyt* k* **Plat** k* plb k* plb-xyz c2 polyg-h br1 prun k* **Psor** k* **Puls** k* pyrog k2* raph c1* **RAT** c2* *Rhus-a* c1* rhus-g tmo3• *Rhus-t* k* rob bro1 rosm a1 ruta k* **Sabin** k* samb b7.de* *Sang* a1* **Sec** k* sed-t al* *Senec* k* *Sep* k* *Sil* k* squil k* staph *Stram* k* sul-ac b4a.de* sul-i k2* *Sulph* k* syc pte1• symph fd3.de• *Tarent* k* tep a1* ter bro1 thiop jl3 *Thlas* kr1* thuj b4a.de toxo-g jl2 **Tril-p** k* tritic-vg fd5.de *Tub* urt-u k* **Ust** k* uva br1 vac jl2 vario jl2 verat k* **Vib** bg2* *Vinc* bro1 visc c1* x-ray sp1 xan bro1* zinc k* zinc-s c1*

- **daytime** only: caust sf1.de ham ptk1 symph fd3.de•
- **night**: alet k13 bad c1* *Mag-m* nat-m j5.de *Rhus-t* kr1 sabin c1
  - **midnight**:
    - **after** | **3** h: *Nux-v* kr1
- **abortion**:
  - **after**: alet k2 *Bell* j5.de* *Cham* kr1 *Chin* kr1 croc hr1* *Ferr* kr1 *Ip* kr1 kali-c k2 *Lyc* kr1 *Mill* kr1* *Nit-ac* tl1 *Plat* b4a.de* psor k2 *Sabin* j5.de* *Sec* j5.de sym-r k2 *Thlas* kr1* *Ust* kr1
  - **before**: *Lyc* kr1
  - **during**: anac kr1 *Apis* kr1 arn bg2* bell bg2* bry bg2 caul kr1 cham bg2 *Chin* bg2* **Croc** bg2* *Erig* kr1 ferr bg2 hyos bg2* *Ip* bg2* **Kali-c** kr1 *Lyc* kr1 *Nit-ac* kr1* **Plat** bg2* plb a1 rosm c1 ruta sf1.de **Sabin** bg2* *Sec* sf1.de senec-fu mg1.de *Sil* kr1 *Thlas* kr1* verat-v c1 **Vib** bg2
    - **black** blood: crot-h tl1
    - **coagulated** blood; non: crot-h tl1
  - **excitement**, mental or sexual: *Sil* kr1
  - **motion** agg.; slightest: **Croc** kr1 *Sil* kr1
  - **threatening** abortion, in: *Calc* kr1 cimic sf1.de cinnm kr1 *Croc* kr1* erig sf1.de goss sf1.de *Ham* kr1 **Kreos** kr1 *Lyc* kr1 *Puls* kr1 ruta sf1.de *Sabin* sf1.de senec-fu mg1.de *Tril-p* sf1.de *Ust* sf1.de
- **accident**; after every little: *Ambr* vh1
- **accompanied** by:
  - **chlorosis**: med bro1 phos bro1 thlas bro1 ust bro1
  - **fever**; septic: pyrog bro1
  - **heat**; flushes of: ferr mrr1
  - **nausea**: apoc bro1 caps bro1 **Ip** bro1*
  - **pain**: plat bg2 sabin bg2 vib bg2
    - **sore**: thlas br1
    - **extending** to | **Navel**: ip bro1

Metrorrhagia – accompanied by: ...

  - **palpitations**: apoc bro1
  - **polyps**: erod gm1
  - **pulse**:
    - **accelerated**: apoc bro1
    - **weak**: apoc bro1
  - **respiration**; difficult: fl-ac ptk1 ip bro1
  - **sexual** desire; increased: ambr hr1* coff j5.de plat k* *Sabin* k*
  - **trembling**; internal: caul tl1
  - **urination**; painful (See BLADDER - Urination - dysuria - painful - accompanied - metrorrhagia)
  - **vomiting**: apoc bro1 **Ip** mrr1
  - **weakness**: apoc bro1
  - ○ **Abdomen**; heaviness of: apis bro1
  - **Back**; pain in the: thlas br1
  - **Head**; congestive pain in: bell bro1 glon bro1
  - **Lumbar** pain: kali-c bro1 vario jl2
  - **Tongue**:
    - **dirty** discoloration: *Croc* kr1*
    - **white** discoloration of tongue: *Croc* kr1*
      - **Centre**: *Croc* kr1*
  - **Uterus**:
    - **cancer** of (See Cancer - uterus - accompanied - hemorrhage)
    - **congestion**: sabin bro1
    - **pain** | **cramping**: cham mtf11 chin k2 thlas br1
- **acrid**: sep sne *Sul-ac* sf1.de sulph sf1.de
- **active**: *Acon* k* apis arn **Bell** calc cham chin *Cinnm* *Coff* **Croc** ferr *Ham* k* hyos ign **Ip** mill sf1.de **Phos** plat **Sabin** k* **Sec** thlas sf1.de tril-p *Ust*
- **alternating** with:
  - **dyspnea**: fl-ac
  - **insanity** (See MIND - Insanity - alternating - metrorrhagia)
  - **labor** pains (See Pain - labor pains - alternating - hemorrhage)
  - **laughing** (See MIND - Laughing - alternating - metrorrhagia)
  - **leukorrhea** (See Leukorrhea - alternating - bloody)
  - **mania** (See MIND - Mania - alternating - metrorrhagia)
  - **respiration**; difficult (See RESPIRATION - Difficult - alternating - uterine)
  - ○ **Joints**; pain in (See EXTREMITIES - Pain - joints - alternating with - uterus)
- **anemia**, in: *(↗GENERALS - Anemia - menorrhagia)* calen sf1.de *Chin* sf1.de *Ferr* sf1.de ferr-m sf1.de helon sf1.de *Hydr* kr1 kali-c sf1.de **Puls** kr1 *Thlas* kr1
- **anger**; after: **Cham** k* kali-c k* rhus-t h1* staph
- **appearing** suddenly and ceases suddenly: *Bell*
- **atonic** (See oozing)
- **atony**, from uterine: *(↗Abortion; Atony)* alumin-act br1 *Carb-v* hr1* caul mrr1 *Chin* bro1* *Ham* sf1.de psor k2 visc sf1.de
- **black**: alet k* am-c k* arn k* ars k2 arund a1* asar j5.de bell k* *Carb-v* caul bro1 *Cham* chin k* coch hr1 coff k* *Croc* k* *Elaps* k* *Ferr* k* *Helon* k* ign kali-p c1 *Kreos* k* lach k2* lyc mag-c bro1 nat-m j5.de **Plat** k* *Puls* pyrog jl2 sabin *Sec* k* stram j5.de* *Sul-ac* sulph
  - **liquid**: *Am-c* *Crot-h* k* *Elaps* *Sec* k* *Sul-ac*
- **bright** red: acal kr1* acon aran *Arn* *Bell* k* bov bro1 *Calc* cham k* chin *Cinnm* coff k2 **Erig** k* *Ham* hyos **Ip** k* lac-c k* *Led* lil-t a1 lyc med bro1 *Mill* k* mit bro1* **Phos** k* psor k2 pyrog yl1 rhus-t **Sabin** k* *Sang* sec k* *Tril-p* k* tritic-vg fd5.de ust k* vib visc c1* xan sf1.de
  - **abortion**, after: hyos k2
  - **clots**, with: *Arn* **Bell** *Ip* *Lac-c* kr1 psor k2 pyrog yl1 **Sabin** k* sang hr1 sec mrr1 tritic-vg fd5.de *Ust*
  - **delivery**; during: ip bro1
  - **fluid**: ham **Ip** tl1* mill bro1 *Phos* mrr1 ust

- **cancerous** affections, in: *(↗Cancer - uterus - accompanied - hemorrhage)* bell bro1 crot-h bro1 kreos bro1 lach bro1 phos k2 sabin bro1 *Thlas* bro1 ust bro1
- **chamomile** tea, from: *Chin* k* ign k*
- **changeable** in color and flow: **Puls** hr1*
- **chronic**: *Card-m* hr1* *Cinnm* hr1* *Ust* hr1*
- **coagulated**: acal bro1 *Alet* *Alum* kr1 *Alumn* hr1 *Apoc* k* arg-met *Arn* k* arund a1* **Bell** k* cact **Cham** k* chin k* coc-c k* cocc bro1 coch hr1 *Coff* k* *Croc* k* cycl k* elaps erig bro1 *Ferr* k* ham k2* helon k* *Ip* bro1 kali-c h2* kreos k* lach bro1 laur lyc *Mag-m* hr1 *Merc* *Murx* k* nux-m k2 nux-v phos k2 *Plat* k* plb k* *Puls* k* *Rhus-t* k* *Sabin* k* *Sang* sec k* stram *Thlas* br1* tril-p k* tritic-vg fd5.de **Ust** k* visc c1*
  - **delivery**; after: phos k2
  - **expelled**; clots are:
    - **night**: coch kr1
    - **accompanied** by | **constricting** pain: *Cact* mrr1
    - **paroxysms**; during: *Cham* kr1 *Ferr* *Puls* *Ust*
    - **urination** | **during** | **agg.**: *Coc-c* kr1
      - **urging** for urination; when: chim ptk1
  - **mixed** with:
    - **dark** liquid blood: **Bell** carb-v k2 elaps *Sabin* *Sec*
    - **pale** watery blood: chin
- **coition**:
  - **after**: **Arg-n** k* *Arn* k* *Ars* carc mlr1• *Hydr* k* kola stb3• **Kreos** k* nit-ac bro1* *Sep* k* *Tarent* k*
  - **during**: arg-n sf1.de
- **coitus** interruptus, from: cocc sf1.de
- **coldness** of body, with: *Camph* kr1 **Carb-v** kr1 *Sil* kr1 *Verat* kr1
- **concussions**, from: *Arn* cinnm *Ham* kr1 mill puls *Rhus-t* ruta *Sec* sulph
- **continuous**: apoc k* arn carb-v *Erig* *Ham* k* *Hydr* sf1.de *Hyos* iod j5.de* *Ip* k* kali-c *Kreos* mill *Nit-ac* sf1.de phos *Sec* k* sulph ust vinc sf1.de
  - **slow**; but: carb-v ham psor sec sulph ust
- **convulsions**; with: bell *Chin* *Hyos* k* **Sec**
- **copious** (See profuse)
- **curettage**; after: nit-ac br1* thlas c1
- **dark** blood: am-c k2 ars a1* *Bell* k* *Bry* k* *Cact* sf1.de cadm-met sne* canth carb-v k2 *Cham* k* **Chin** k* coff sf1.de *Croc* k* *Crot-h* k* *Elaps* kr1 *Ferr* gink-b sbd1• ham k* helon k* *Kreos* k* lach sf1.de laur k2* *Lyc* lyss hr1* mang-i bro1 nat-sil fd3.de• *Nit-ac* sf1.de *Nux-m* *Plat* plb *Puls* k* sabin *Sec* k* sep k* sul-ac k* *Sulph* symph fd3.de• tril-p ust k* visc c1
  - **cancer**; in: cadm-met gm1
  - **clots**, with: **Bell** k* *Cham* k* chin coff sf1.de *Croc* k* *Elaps* kr1 *Ferr* jug-r vml3• kreos laur k2 lyc *Puls* *Sabin* *Sec* symph fd3.de• ust k* visc a1*
    - **delivery**; during: sabin bro1 tril-p bro1
  - **fluid**: bry crot-h hr1* (non:crot-t kl) plat sabin sec k*
    - **delivery**; during: sec bro1
    - **thick**; and: nux-m *Plat*
  - **stringy**: croc tl1
- **delivery**:
  - **after**: *Acet-ac* bro1 am-m bro1 aml-ns bro1 *Arn* b7a.de* ars bro1 bell b4a.de* cann-s c2 caul bro1* cham b7a.de* *Chin* bro1 *Cinnm* br1* *Croc* b7a.de* cycl bro1 erig zr ferr bro1 ger bro1 *Ham* bro1 hyos bro1 ign bro1 ip b7a.de* kali-c bro1 mill bro1* nit-ac bro1* nux-v b7a.de *Plat* b4a.de puls bro1 sabin b7a.de* sec c2* thlas bro1 tril-p c1* ust bro1*
    - **eight** days: *Sabin* kr1
    - **one** week: *Kali-c* kr1
    - **some** days: **Cinnm** kr1
    - **two** weeks: *Ust* kr1
  - **before**: tril-p c1
  - **before** and after: erig zr
  - **bright** red: *Hyos* kr1 *Ip* kr1 mill bro1 *Ust* kr1
  - **clotted**: *Croc* kr1 phos k2 *Sabin* kr1 *Ust* kr1
  - **constant**: *Ip* kr1 **Nux-m** kr1 *Sabin* kr1 *Ust* kr1
  - **dark**: caul kr1 chin bro1 *Gels* kr1 *Sabin* kr1 *Ust* kr1
- **delivery**: ...
  - **during** and after: *Acet-ac* kr1 acon adren sf1.de* alet kr1 alum apis *Arn* *Bell* bry *Cann-i* kr1 cann-s carb-v k2 caul k* *Cham* *Chin* *Cinnm* cocc kr1 coff sf1.de *Croc* crot-h sf1.de **Erig** *Ferr* *Gels* kr1 ger kr1 **Ham** *Hydr* kr1 *Hyos* **Ip** kali-c kalm kr1 kreos lach lyc merc mill nit-ac nux-m nux-v op kr1 ph-ac *Phos* *Plat* plb kr1 psor k2 puls kr1 *Rhus-t* kr1 **Sabin** **Sec** senec sep kr1 *Thlas* kr1* thyr c1 tril-p *Ust* k*
  - **gushing**: bell bro1 *Ip* kr1
  - **inertia** uteri, with: *(↗Abortion; Atony)* am-m bro1 caul k2* puls bro1 sec bro1 *Ust* kr1
  - **motion**; slightest: **Croc** kr1
  - **offensive**: *Nit-ac* kr1
  - **prevents** hemorrhagia: *Arn* kr1*
  - **profuse**: **Apis** kr1 *Ip* kr1 *Plat* kr1 *Sabin* kr1
  - **putrid**: *Ust* kr1
- **displacement** of uterus; from: tril-p
- **dysuria**; with: erig st1 mit sf1.de*
- **emotions**, excitement; from: acon bell bry *Calc* *Cham* cocc croc hyos nat-m phos plat puls sep *Sil* stram sulph
- **exertion** agg.; after: **Ambr** *Aur* *Bov* **Calc** cinnm c1 *Croc* **Erig** k* *Helon* hr1* mill k* *Nit-ac* k* rhus-t *Sabin* hr1* *Tril-p*
  - **lumbar** region; exertion of: cinnm br1
- **exhaustion** | **amel.**: *Apoc* vh1
- **faintness**; with: apis bro1 chin j5.de* ferr bro1 *Ip* hr1* *Kreos* hr1* **Tril-p** kr1*
- **false** step; after: cinnm br1
- **fibroids**, from: aur-m-n mrr1 *Calc* k* calc-f st calc-p calc-st-s st foll jl3 *Ham* k* *Hydr* k* *Hydrin-m* c1* *Kali-c* hr1 kali-fcy mrr1 *Kali-i* hr1* lap-a k* led bg* lyc merc nit-ac k* **Phos** k* *Plat* k* *Sabin* k* sec bro1 sil sul-ac k* *Sulph* *Thlas* c1* *Tril-p* c1* ust c1* *Vinc* hr1*
- **fluid**: **Apis** k1 apoc k2 ars *Bell* mrr1 *Both* *Carb-v* chin **Crot-h** *Crot-t* kr1* *Elaps* *Erig* ferr j5.de *Ip* hr1 **Lach** *Mill* k* nat-m **Nit-ac** **Phos** k* prun sf1.de **Sabin** hr1* *Sec* k* *Sul-ac* *Ust* hr1*
  - **alternating** with clots: *Plb* hr1*
  - **clotted**, partly: *Bell* mrr1 puls j5.de sabin bro1 *Ust* hr1*
  - **menses**, between: ham a1
- **fright**; after: *(↗MIND - Ailments - fright)* acon bell *Calc* nux-v
- **girls**; in: *Cina* *Hydr* kr1
- **gushing**: *Bell* *Borx* b4a.de bov bg *Cham* chin *Cinnm* bg1* *Croc* *Erig* sf1.de *Ham* **Ip** k* *Lac-c* hr1* *Mill* **Phos** *Puls* **Sabin** k* *Sec* k* tril-p *Ust*
- **hot**: arn **Bell** k* bry caul tl1 cham sf1.de coff sf1.de *Hydr* kr1 ip tl1 *Lac-c* puls
  - **delivery**; during: ip bro1
- **injuries**; after: *Ambr* bro1 arn bro1* ars sf1.de *Cinnm* bro1* ham bro1 mill sf1.de ruta sf1.de *Sec* kr1
- **intermittent**: ambr st1 apoc *Bell* *Cham* chin erig st1 *Ip* *Kreos* nux-v **Phos** psor k* *Puls* k* rhus-t *Sabin* sec sulph ust
  - **abortion**; during: puls bro1
  - **weakness**; fr·· : apoc vh
- **iron**, after abuse of: puls k*
- **labor** (See delivery)
- **leukorrhea**:
  - **after**: *Mag-m* kr1*
  - **with**: *Calc* kr1 kreos bro1
- **lying**:
  - **agg.**: mag-c al1*
  - **back**; on:
    - **agg.**: ambr k2 *Cham*
    - **amel.**: *Ip* kr1
- **membranous**: apoc k2 brom sf1.de
- **menopause**:
  - **after**: calc k2 ferr k2 mang k2 *Merc* h1* sep bg2 *Vinc* bg2*
  - **before**: arg-met kr1 staph kr1
  - **during**: *(↗Menses - return - ceased)* *Alet* k* *Aloe* k* am-m kl aml-ns bro1 apoc kr1* arg-met k* *Arg-n* hr1* aur-m bro1 *Bell* kr1 bomh gm1 buni-o jl **Calc** k* calc-f mrr1 caps bro1 *Carb-v* chin bro1 *Cimic* bro1 *Croc* crot-c mtf11 **Crot-h** kr1* *Ferr* k* *Gels* kr1 **Graph** st hydrinin-m bro1 *Kali-br* hr1* kali-c **Lach** k* *Laur* k2* lyc *Med* k* *Murx* nit-ac bro1 *Nux-v* paro-i jl phos k2* *Plat* kr1 *Plb* k* **Psor** k* *Puls* rhus-t sf1.de *Sabin* k* **Sang** k*

Female

- **during**: ...
  sanguiso bro1* sarr kr1 *Sec* *Sed-ac* bro1 **Sep** k* sul-ac k2 **Sulph** *Thlas* kr1* thyr c1 *Tril-p* k* tub gk *Ust* k* vinc bro1
- **menses**:
  - **after** | **agg.**: lyc a1 merc a1 rat a1 rhus-t b7.de
  - **before** | **agg.**: bell bg2 calc bg2* chlam-tr bcx2• erig zr lach bg2 mag-m j5.de* merc j5.de* nat-m bg2 nat-s bg2 phos bg2 sil k2 sulph bg2 thuj bg2 verat bg2
  - **between**: **Ambr** k1* arg-n bro1* *Arn* *Bell* k* *Bov* k* bry **Calc** k* calc-sil k2 canth carb-an mrr1 carb-v carc mlr1• caust a1* **Cham** k* chin *Cimic* *Cocc* k* coff k* *Croc* elaps k* eupi a1* ferr flav jl3 foll jl3 galla-q-r nl2• gink-b sbd1• guare st1 *Ham* a1* helon ptk1 hep hydr bg1* iod sf1.de **Ip** k* kali-c kali-sil k2 kreos sf1.de lach lap-a sf1.de lyc k* mag-c mag-s k* mang k* merc murx nat-hchls sf1.de nit-ac nux-v op sf1.de ozone sde2• **Phos** k* pitu-a vml2• puls **Rhus-t** k* rob kr1* **Sabin** k* *Sec* *Sep* **Sil** k* stram sulph ust sf1.de vinc bro1 visc sf1.de zinc
    ⁝ **sexual** excitement, with: ambr ptk1 *Sabin* kr1*
  - **return** of long suppressed menses, after: *Sulph* a1
- **moon**:
  - **full**: *Croc* bg2* kali-bi st
    ⁝ **before**; three days: mag-m a1
  - **new** moon: *Croc* j5.de* kali-bi sf1.de rhus-t h1* sil h2*
- **motion** agg.: ambr sf1.de arg-met k* bell *Bry* cact calc *Coff* *Croc* **Erig** k* ferr a1 *Helon* **Ip** k* lil-t sf1.de psor *Sabin* k* *Sec* k* sulph tril-p ust
- **night** watching; from: *Puls* kr1
- **nursing** the child agg.; when: calc k2* rhus-t bg2 sec a1 *Sil* k*
- **offensive**: *Bell* k* *Cham* k* croc k* crot-h k* *Helon* hr1* kreos k* lach bg2* *Nit-ac* bg2* phos a1 sabin k* sang hr1 *Sec* k* sep sne ust k*
- **oozing**: alet **Carb-v** carbn-s k2 caul k* *Chin* *Chinin-s* cimic cinnm bro1 croc **Erig** *Ferr* k* *Ham* k* *Helon* k* **Kali-fcy** *Kreos* b7a.de* *Lyc* *Mangi* br1 plb *Sec* k* sul-ac thlas sf1.de **Tril-p** kr1 **Ust** k* vinc k*
  - **delivery**; during: sec bro1
- **overlifting**, from: calc k2
- **ovulation**; during: *Flav* jl2 lac-h sze9• ozone sde2•
- **painless**: bov calc croc *Erig* hr1 *Ham* k* **Kali-fcy** k* mag-c *Mill* k* nit-ac bro1 nux-m plat sabin *Sec* k* ust
  - **abortion**; during: mill bro1
  - **delivery**; during: sabin bro1
- **pale**: bell a1 carb-v k* chin *Ferr* hyos k* merc mill prun hr1* sabin sec tarent a1 ust k*
- **paralysis**; from: *Sec* b7a.de
- **paroxysms**; during: apoc kr1* bell *Cham* k* chin k* nux-v **Puls** rhus-t **Sabin** k* ust
- **passive** (See oozing)
- **periodical** | **day** a little dark blood; every: lyss hr1*
- **perspiration**, with cold: **Carb-v** hr1* *Sec* hr1* *Verat* hr1*
- **placenta**:
  - **previa**; from placenta: *Ip* st *Nux-v* st *Sabin* st *Sep* st *Verat-v* st
  - **retained**: *Bell* *Canth* *Carb-v* caul *Ip* kr1 *Kali-c* kr1 mit st1 *Puls* *Sabin* k* sec k* sep stram bro1 verat-v c1
- **polypus**, from: bell *Calc* *Con* k* lyc phos sang k* thuj
- **precancerous** period, in: *Aur* st
- **pregnancy** agg.; during: *(↗Abortion)* *Apis* kr1 *Arn* hr1 asar b7a.de* bell k2 buni-o jl3 *Cann-i* hr1* caul sf1.de *Cham* b7.de* chin bro1 cimic jl3 *Cinnm* hr1* *Cocc* b7a.de* croc b7.de* *Erig* hr1* ham k2* *Ip* b7a.de* kali-c b4.de* kali-p c1 **Kreos** hr1* lyc b4a.de* *Nit-ac* hr1* *Phos* b4.de* phyt c1 *Plat* hr1* *Puls* kr1 *Rhus-t* b7.de* *Sabin* b7.de* sec b7.de* *Sep* kr1* ther c1 *Thlas* mrr1 *Tril-p* kr1*
  - **fifth** and seventh month: **Sep** kr1*
  - **first** part, in: nit-ac kr1
  - **fright**; after: *Ign* hr1*
  - **lying** | **amel.**: *Ign* kr1
  - **overexertion**, from: *Cinnm* kr1 *Erig* kr1 *Nit-ac* kr1
  - **sixth** month: *Cann-i* kr1 erig kr1
  - **third** month: **Kreos** hr1* *Sabin* hr1*
- **profuse**: acon alet k2 am-m k2 ambr k2 apis apoc k2 arg-n *Arn* *Ars* hr1* **Bell** brom sf1.de bry *Cact* sf1.de **Calc** k* caul k* *Cham* *Chin* cinnm k* *Con* hr1* croc erig k* ferr glon ham k* helon k* hyos iod sf1.de **Ip** k* kali-c *Kreos* k* lyc mill k*

Metrorrhagia – profuse: ...
murx nit-ac k* *Nux-v* **Phos** plb sf1.de puls k* *Sabin* k* sanguiso sf1.de *Sec* k* sep sne *Sul-ac* sf1.de thlas sf1.de tril-p vib vinc sf1.de xan sf1.de
  - **accompanied** by | **Uterus**; congested: mit zr
  - **delivery**; during: ip bro1 tril-p bro1
  - **urinating**; as if: tril-p zr
- **puberty**:
  - **at**: helon sf1.de
  - **before**: *Cina* kr1
- **pungent**: kreos
- **putrid**: **Ars** k2 carb-v k2 cham pyrog jl2
- **recurrent**: *Arg-n* *Croc* *Kreos* *Nux-v* *Phos* psor *Sulph*
- **riding** agg.: *Ham* hr1*
- **rising** from bed agg.: psor k2
- **ropy** blood: arg-n **Croc** k* lac-c k* **Ust**
- **scanty**: carb-v k2 caul bro1 coc-c a1 kali-s fd4.de lyss hr1* phos a1 *Puls* hr1
- **seeping** (See oozing)
- **short** duration: arg-n k2
- **sleep** agg., during: *Mag-m* sf1.de
- **standing** agg.: *Mag-m* sf1.de
- **stool**:
  - **after** | **every**: am-m **Ambr** ind iod h* *Lyc*
  - **during** | **agg.**: ambr sf1.de iod b4a.de murx hr1*
  - **hard** stool:
    ⁝ **after** | **agg.**: **Ambr** *Lyc*
- **subinvolution**, from: *Kali-i* kr1 lil-t psor sec sulph ust
- **sudden**: *Ars* k* **Bell** cinnm *Ip* k*
- **thick** blood: carb-v *Nux-m* plat k* puls sec k2* sulph tril-p
- **thin** blood: apoc bry carb-an bro1 *Carb-v* cham bro1 chin k* *Crot-h* *Elaps* *Erig* ferr kreos **Lach** laur lyc *Phos* plat prun j5.de* puls **Sabin** *Sec* k* *Sul-ac* ust
  - **clots**, with: *Chin* *Elaps* *Ferr* kreos *Sabin* *Sec*
    ⁝ **foul** smelling: kreos *Sec*
- **touch** agg.: ust sf1.de
- **urination** agg.; during: coc-c ptk coch hr1*
- **vexation**; after: *Ip* kali-c
- **voluptuous** itching, with: *Coff* hr1*
- **walking**:
  - **after** | **agg.**: ambr a1
  - **agg.**: **Ambr** a1* *Mag-m* sf1.de nat-s a1 sep h2*
  - **amel.**: *Cycl* hr1 *Sabin* k*
- **warm** bath, after: thuj
- **watery**: ant-t berb bov j5.de *Calc* kr1 dulc laur mang k2 phos prun j5.de* puls
  - **instead** of menses: *Sil* hr1*
- **weakness**; from: chin b7a.de *Sabin* b7a.de sec b7a.de
- **widows**, in young: *Arg-n* hr1*
- **women**:
  - **children**; not having: *Arg-n* hr1
  - **old**; in: *Calc* cham hydr *Ign* lach *Mag-m* kr1 *Mang* *Merc* phos sep
  - **pale**, waxy; in: kali-c k2
  - **plethoric**; in: *(↗GENERALS - Plethora - constitution)* **Acon** bg2* arn bg2 *Bell* bg2 bry bg2 calc bg2 **Cham** bg2* coff sf1.de *Croc* bg2 *Erig* sf1.de *Ferr* j5.de* ferr-m sf1.de hyos bg2 ign bg2 *Plat* bg2 *Sabin* bg2* sil bg2 sulph bg2
  - **scrawny**; in: *Sec* k*
  - **sterile**; in: *Arg-n* hr1*
  - **tall**; in: *Phos*
  - **weakly**; in: asaf k2 carb-an bg2 **Chin** j5.de* cocc sf1.de croc bg2 ferr *Ip* bg2 nux-v bg2 phos bg2 psor *Puls* bg2 sec j5.de* sep bg2 sulph k* verat bg2

○ - **Vagina** | **as** if from: plut-n srj7•

MISCARRIAGE (See Abortion)

MOISTURE: *Petr* k*

- **sensation** of: eup-pur k* petr bro1*

○ • **Vagina**: aster ptk1 eup-pur ptk1 petr ptk1
○ - **Thighs**; between: *Petr* mrr1
- **Vagina** | **amel.**: aster ptk1

MOLES: *Ars* hr1 bell kr1 *Calc* hr1 canth bg2* chin k* *Ferr* hr1 *Kali-c* *Lyc* hr1 merc k* *Nat-c* k* *Puls* k* *Sabin* hr1 sec hr1 *Sil* k* sulph k*
- **expulsion** of moles; stimulates: canth bro1 sabin c1*

MOTION:
- **agg.**: bov bro1 bry bro1 canth bro1 caust bro1 erig bro1 *Lil-t* bro1 mag-p bro1 *Sabin* bro1 *Sec* bro1 thlas bro1 *Tril-p* bro1
- **amel.**: am-m bro1 *Cycl* bro1 kreos bro1 *Mag-c* bro1 *Sabin* bro1
- **feet**:
  - **amel.** | **Ovaries**: ars ptk1

MOVEMENTS:
- **like** a fetus (See ABDOMEN - Movements)
- **of** fetus (See Fetus - motions)

○ - **Uterus**; in: tarent ptk1

NARROWING: | **Vagina**: syph jl2

NERVOUS sensation in Uterus: carb-v bg2

NODULES: calc k* kreos b7a.de *Lac-c* merc k* phos k* rhus-t k2 syph k2

○ - **Uterus** | **Os** uteri: kreos bg2
- **Vagina**, in: *Agar* k* syph k2

NUMBNESS: (↗*Insensibility)* eup-pur k* *Kali-br* hr1 mosch *Plat* k* suis-em rly4• vanil fd5.de
- **cold** washing agg.; after: eupi k*

○ - **Ovaries**: apis k* *Podo* k*
  - **beginning** in right ovary:
    - **extending** to hip and ribs and over thigh | **lying** on right ovary amel.: apis
  - **painful**:
    - **extending** to | **Limbs**: podo
- **Uterus**: phys bg2*
- **Vagina**: berb ptk1 brom ptk1 phos k2* sep ptk1
  - **coition**; during: ferr ptk1 kali-br ptk1 phos ptk1

NURSING agg.: | **Uterus**: arn ptk1 *Cham* ptk1 sil ptk1

NYMPHOMANIA (See MIND - Nymphomania)

ODOR:
- **fish**; like | **coition**; during: choc srj3•

ONANISM (See Masturbation)

OOPHORITIS (See Inflammation - ovaries)

OPEN:

○ - **Uterus**:
  - **sensation** as if open: carb-v bg2 lach k* murx bg2 sanic tl1* sep bg2
  - **sensation** as if opening and shutting: nat-hchls k* sec rb2
- **Vagina** | **sensation** as if open: bell bg2
- **Vulva**: | **sensation** as if open: bov ptk1 carb-v bg2 murx bg2 sabal bg* sec ptk1 sep bg2*

ORGASM:
- **night**: arg-n br1* nux-v btw1 urol-h rwt3•
- **delayed**: alum vh1 *Berb* k* brom k* lac-e hm2•
- **dreams**; during amorous (See DREAMS - Amorous - orgasm)
- **easy**: olib-sac wmh1 *Plat* vh positr nl2• *Stann* k1*
- **involuntary**: ang k* *Arg-n* *Ars* *Calc* *Lil-t* k* nat-m *Nux-v* *Op* **Plat** sul-ac
- **painful**: nat-m
- **wanting**: *Brom* calad kola stb3• pneu jl2 tritic-vg fd5.de [heroin sdj2]
- **waves**; in: plac rzf5•

OS UTERI during labor; state of: (↗*Delivery - during)*
- **contracted** spasmodically: *Bell* kr1 *Sep* kr1
- **dilated**: *Gels* kr1 sanic c2
- **half** open: *Sep* kr1
- **rigid**: acon bro1 ant-t arn mrr1 *Bell* k* **Caul** k* **Cham** k* chlf hr1* cimic k* *Con* **Gels** k* ign jab lob k* lyc nux-v sec *Sep* kr1 *Verat-v* k*
- **soft**: *Ust* kr1
- **stenosis**: con k2

OVULATION:
- **during**: cocc dgt2 dream-p sdj1• foll jl3 ham dgt2 hydr dgt2 **Lac-c** dgt2 mag-c dgt2 meli dgt2 merc dgt2 nux-v dgt2 sep dgt2 [vanad stj1*]
- **early**: falco-pe nl2•

PAIN: abrom-a-r bnj1 acon ↓ aesc ↓ aeth ↓ *Agar* ↓ agath-a nl2• aloe alum ↓ alum-sil ↓ *Am-c* ↓ *Ambr* ↓ anac ↓ anan ↓ androc ↓ *Ant-c* ↓ ant-t ↓ apis arg-n k2 *Arn* ↓ *Ars* ↓ *Ars-i* ↓ ars-s-f ↓ asaf asc-c ↓ aur aur-ar ↓ *Aur-m* ↓ aur-s ↓ bar-c bar-m ↓ bar-s ↓ bart ↓ **Bell** ↓ bell-p ↓ berb k* *Borx* ↓ bov ↓ brom *Bry* ↓ bufo ↓ cact ↓ *Calc* ↓ *Calc-p* k* calc-s ↓ calc-sil ↓ camph ↓ *Cann-i* ↓ cann-s ↓ cann-xyz ↓ canth bg caps ↓ *Carb-an* **Carb-v** ↓ *Carbn-s* ↓ castm ↓ caul ↓ caust **Cham** ↓ chel ↓ *Chin* ↓ chinin-s ↓ *Chlol* ↓ *Cimic* ↓ *Cina* ↓ clem ↓ coc-c k* *Cocc* ↓ coff bg colch ↓ coli rly4• *Coloc* ↓ *Con* cop ↓ *Croc* b7a.de cupr ↓ cur ↓ *Cycl* ↓ dream-p sdj1• dros ↓ dulc fd4.de eupi falco-pe ↓ ferr b7.de* ferr-ar ↓ ferr-i ↓ ferr-p ↓ fl-ac ↓ **Gels** ↓ ger-i rly4• germ-met ↓ *Glon* ↓ *Graph* k* ham ↓ *Helon* ↓ *Hep* ↓ heroin ↓ hydr ↓ hydrc ↓ *Hyos* ↓ *Ign* ↓ inul ↓ iod ↓ *Ip* ↓ kali-ar ↓ *Kali-bi* ↓ *Kali-c* *Kali-i* ↓ kali-m ↓ kali-n ↓ kali-p ↓ kali-s ↓ kali-sil ↓ kreos *Lac-c* k* *Lach* bg lil-t lob-e ↓ *Lyc* m-aust ↓ mag-c ↓ mag-m ↓ mag-p ↓ mag-s ↓ mang ↓ med ↓ meli ↓ meph ↓ merc bg2 *Merc-c* k* mez ↓ *Mosch* ↓ mur-ac ↓ *Murx* ↓ naja ↓ **Nat-c** ↓ nat-m ↓ nat-p ↓ nat-s ↓ nicotam rly4• **Nit-ac** ↓ nux-m ↓ nux-v bg2 olib-sac ↓ *Op* ↓ ox-ac ↓ paeon gm1 pall ↓ *Petr* ↓ ph-ac ↓ phasco-ci ↓ *Phos* phyt ↓ plat k* podo ↓ **Puls** ↓ pyrog ↓ *Rhus-t* ↓ ribo rly4• ruta fd4.de sabad ↓ *Sabin* ↓ sacch-a ↓ sal-fr ↓ sec sep k* *Sil* ↓ spig ↓ spong fd4.de stann ↓ *Staph* k* sul-ac ↓ sul-i ↓ sulph bg suprar rly4• symph ↓ tarent ↓ tell ↓ ter ↓ ther ↓ thuj thymol ↓ til ↓ tritic-vg fd5.de tub ↓ *Urt-u* *Ust* ↓ vanil fd5.de vib ↓ visc ↓ xan ↓ xanth ↓ *Zinc* k* zinc-p k2
- **right**:

▽ • **extending** to:
    - **left**: *Lyc* ↓
      - **labor**-like: *Lyc*
- **left**:

▽ • **extending** to:
    - **right**: ip ↓
      - **cutting** pain: ip k*
- **left** sided: puls ↓
  - **labor**-like: puls h1
- **evening**: bar-c ↓
  - **tearing** pain: bar-c k*
- **night**: carb-v ↓ nat-m ↓ olib-sac ↓
  - **bed** agg.; in: anan ↓ coc-c k* olib-sac wmh1
    - **burning**: anan k*
  - **cramping**: olib-sac wmh1
  - **labor**-like: carb-v h2* nat-m h2*
- **abortion**; during: *Cham* ↓ sec ↓
  - **labor**-like: *Cham* b7a.de sec bro1
- **aching**: calc-p k* calc-sil k2 *Lil-t*
- **afterpains**: (↗*Delivery - after; Delivery - during)* acon k* aml-ns bro1 aq-mar rbp6 **Arn** k* asaf k* *Atro* kr1* aur k* **Bell** b2.de* borx k* *Bry* k* *Calc* k* carb-an k* carb-v k* *Caul* bg2* **Cham** k* chin k* cic k* *Cimic* k* cina k* cinnb bg2 cinnm kr1* cocc k* *Coff* k* *Coloc* st *Con* k* croc k* **Cupr** k* cupr-ar bro1 cycl kr1* **Dios** kr1* *Ferr* k* *Gels* k* graph k* hyos k* **Hyper** k* *Ign* k* iod k* ip k* **Kali-c** k* kreos k* *Lac-c* kr1* lach k* lil-t kr1* lyc k* *Mill* kr1* nat-c k* *Nat-m* k* nux-m k* *Nux-v* k* *Op* b2.de* **Par** c2* *Phos* kr1 plat k* *Podo* **Puls** k* pyrog bro1 **Rhus-t** k* *Ruta* k* **Sabin** k* **Sec** k* *Sep* k* sil mrr1 sul-ac k* *Sulph* k* ter st ust kr1* verat ↓ *Vib* k* *Vib-p* bro1 *Xan* k* zinc k*
  - **accompanied** by:
    - **lochia**: xan ptk1
    - **Head**; intolerable pain in: cham ptk1 cimic ptk1
  - **cramping**: arn bg2 bell bg2 *Bry* bg2 **Cham** bg2 *Cimic* mrr1 hyos bg2 lach bg2 nux-v bg2 puls bg2 sep bg2 verat bg2
  - **distant** parts, in: arn tl1 carb-v kr1
  - **distressing**: cham tl1 cimic mrr1 **Cupr** kr1 vib tl1
  - **fear** of death, with: **Coff** kr1*
  - **frequent**: rhus-t ptk1
  - **headache**; during: hyper ptk1*
  - **instrumental** delivery, after: *Arn* kr1 *Hyper* kr1 *Rhus-t* kr1
  - **insupportable**: cham ptk2 cimic ptk2 *Coff* kr1
  - **menses**, with offensive: *Crot-h* st

Female

• **motion** agg.; slightest: *Bry* kr1
• **multipara**, in: cupr st
• **nursing** child, when: *Arn* k* *Cham* k* con puls **Sec** kr1 **Sil** k*
• **prolonged**: *Acon* kr1 arn j5.de calc j5.de *Cham* kr1 *Coff* j5.de* *Gels* kr1 *Puls* j5.de* *Rhus-t* kr1 **Sec** kr1
⁝ **evening**: *Puls* kr1
• **sensitive** women, in: *Gels* kr1 *Nux-v* kr1 *Op* kr1
• **shooting** pain: *Cimic* mrr1
• **stool** | **urging** to; with: nux-v k2
• **violent**: vib ptk1
• **weak**: arn bg2 caul bg2 **Par** kr1 puls bg2
• **women** who had born many children; in: cupr ptk1
▽ • **extending** to:
⁝ **Calves** and soles: cupr bro1
⁝ **Groins**; into: caul k2* *Cimic* kr1*
⁝ **Pelvis**; across: cimic mrr1
⁝ **Thighs**, into: cimic mrr1 *Lac-c* kr1
⁝ **Tibia**, into: carb-v bro1 cocc bro1
○ • **Groin**, felt in: caul bro1 cimic bro1
• **Hip**, in: sil st
- **backache**, with: inul ↓
• **bearing** down: inul br1
- **bearing** down: *(↗uterus - pressing)* aesc k2 *Agar* br1 alum k2 *Ant-c* b7a.de* *Apis* b7a.de asaf b7.de* asc-c c1 aur bg2 **Bell** b4a.de* bell-p sp1 bov cham b7.de* chin k* cina b7a.de cocc b7.de* coloc bg2 con bg2 croc b7.de* ferr bg2 hydr k2 inul br1 *Ip* b7.de* kali-c b4a.de kali-sil k2 *Lil-t* mrr1 lob-e c1 *Lyc* b4a.de med lp mosch k* *Murx* mrr1 nat-c b4a.de nat-m bg2 nit-ac bg2 nux-v b7.de* plat k* podo mrr1 sabin b7a.de* sal-fr sle1• **Sep** b4a.de* thuj b4a.de tritic-vg fd5.de
• **accompanied** by | **coldness**: castm ptk1 sec bg3* sil ptk1
- **bending** double:
• **must** bend double: puls ↓
⁝ **labor**-like: puls h1
- **biting** pain: ambr b7.de* berb k* calc k* carb-v b4.de* *Caust* k* cham b7.de* chin b7.de* eupi *Ferr* b7a.de graph k* kali-bi bg2 kali-c h2* *Kali-i* k* kali-n k* **Kreos** k* *Merc* k* *Rhus-t* k* *Sil* staph k* sulph thuj k* zinc
- **boring** pain: con bg2 ruta fd4.de
- **breathing** agg.: clem ↓
• **lancinating**: clem k*
- **bruised** (See sore)
- **burning**: agar alum k* alum-sil k2 *Am-c* k* *Ambr* k* anan k* *Apis* b7a.de ars k* ars-s-f k2 aur k* aur-ar k2 *Aur-m* k* aur-s k2 bar-c bar-s k2 berb k* bov k* bry k* bufo *Calc* k* calc-p calc-s calc-sil k2 canth k* caps tl1 *Carb-an* k* *Carb-v* k* *Carbn-s* castm *Caust* k* cham k* chel chin b7.de coc-c colch b7.de con cop cur k* dulc k* *Eupi* falco-pe nl2• *Ferr* k* ferr-ar ferr-p *Graph* ham fd3.de• *Helon* k* hep k* hyos b7.de iod b4a.de kali-ar *Kali-bi* k* *Kali-c* k* *Kali-i* k* kali-p kali-s kali-sil k2 *Kreos* k* lac-c lach *Lil-t* k* lyc k* m-aust b7.de mag-s *Merc* k* *Merc-c* **Nit-ac** k* *Nux-v* k* ox-ac k* *Petr* k* *Phos* *Puls* k* *Sabin* k* sec bg* sep k* *Sil* k* spong fd4.de staph *Sulph* k* symph fd3.de• ter tl1 thuj k* til tritic-vg fd5.de tub al vanil fd5.de zinc k*
- **cancer**; in: lap-a ↓
• **burning**: lap-a gm1
• **stinging**: lap-a gm1
• **stitching** pain: lap-a gm1
- **changeable**: cimic mrr1
- **cold**:
• **agg.**: nept-m ↓
⁝ **pressing** pain: nept-m lsd2.fr
• **washing** agg.; after: eupi ↓
⁝ **sore**: eupi k*
- **cold**; after taking a: hyos ↓
• **labor**-like: hyos h1*
- **constricting**, contracting pain: bell b4a.de ign bg2 nit-ac b4a.de *Nux-v* bg2 phos b4a.de pyrog k2 sabin bg2 sep b4.de* sulph b4a.de thuj k*
- **corrosive**: caust b4.de* **Kali-c** b4a.de *Kreos* b7a.de *Lyc* b4a.de nux-v b7.de*
- **cough** agg.: thlas bg1
- **cramping**: agath-a nl2• bell-p sp1 castm c2 *Cocc* b7.de* coli rly4• con k* ign b7.de* *Kreos* b7a.de lil-t bg2 lyc b4.de* mag-m b4.de* mag-p bg2 naja bg2 nux-v b7a.de olib-sac wmh1 phos bg2 plat bg2 ruta fd4.de spong fd4.de staph b7.de* thuj k* thymol sp1 tritic-vg fd5.de visc sp1
- **cry** out, making her: *Bar-c* ↓
• **tearing** pain: *Bar-c* k*
- **cutting** pain: asaf k* cann-s k* carb-v k* caust con k* ip mag-p bg2 med k2 puls b7.de*
- **darting** (See stitching)
- **delivery**; after: arn ↓
• **sore**: arn br1
- **digging** pain: con k*
- **dragging** (See bearing; ABDOMEN - Pain - dragging)
- **drawing** pain: agath-a nl2• *Aur* bar-c dulc fd4.de lyc bg2 mosch k* puls b7.de* rhus-t b7.de* ruta fd4.de sabin b7.de* sacch-a fd2.de• spong fd4.de tritic-vg fd5.de vanil fd5.de
- **dropsy**; during: asc-c ↓
• **labor**-like: asc-c c1
- **fever**; during: mosch ↓ *Puls* ↓
• **bearing** down: mosch b7.de
• **labor**-like: *Puls* b7.de
- **gnawing** pain: bufo bg2 kali-c k* kreos bg2 lil-t bg2 *Lyc*
- **grasping** pain: cact bg2 gels bg2 sep bg2
- **grinding** pain: *Con* k*
- **labor** pains: *(↗Delivery - during)* acon ↓ ambr ↓ **Arn** mrr1 ars ↓ art-v ↓ asaf ↓ *Bell* ↓ borx tl1 *Bry* ↓ calc ↓ carb-an ↓ carb-v ↓ caul k* **Caust** ↓ **Cham** ↓ chin ↓ *Chinin-s* ↓ chlol ↓ cic ↓ cimic k* cinnm ↓ *Cocc* ↓ *Coff* j5.de* coff-t c1 con ↓ conv c1 cupr ↓ cycl ↓ ferr j5.de gels k* **Hyos** ↓ ign ↓ *Ip* ↓ kali-c ptk1 kali-p ptk1 lob ↓ lyc c1 mag-m ↓ mag-p ↓ mit c1 mosch ↓ nat-m ↓ *Nux-m* ↓ *Nux-v* j5.de op j5.de* phos ↓ pituin ↓ plat ↓ puls k* rhus-t j5.de sacch ↓ *Sec* j5.de *Sep* ↓ *Stann* ↓ stram ↓ *Verat* ↓ vib ↓ zinc ↓
• **left**: plat
• **evening**: *Puls* kr1
• **alternating** with:
⁝ **hemorrhage**: puls
⁝ **Eyes**; complaints of: kreos b7a.de
• **ascend** with every pain; fetus seems to: *Gels* kr1
• **bearing** down: caul tl1 cycl bro1
• **ceasing**: acon arn k* asaf b2.de* **Bell** k* *Borx* k* bry b2.de* cact bg* calc b2.de* *Camph* k* carb-an b2.de* *Carb-v* k* *Caul* k* *Caust* k* *Cham* k* chin k* **Cimic** k* cinnm hr1* cocc k* *Coff* k* gels k* *Graph* k* *Guare* a1* hyos b2.de* ign k* **Kali-c** k* kali-p ptk1 kreos b2.de* lach k2 lyc k* mag-c b2.de* mag-m k* merc b2.de* mosch b2.de* nat-c b2.de* *Nat-m* k* nux-m b2.de* *Nux-v* k* **Op** k* phos b2.de* plat k* **Puls** k* rhus-t b2.de* ruta k* **Sec** k* *Sep* k* stann b2.de* sul-ac b2.de* sulph k* *Thuj* k* zinc b2.de*
⁝ **convulsions** come on; and: bell cham cic cupr hyos ign op ptk *Sec*
⁝ **cramps** in hip, from: cimic
⁝ **emotion**, from: cimic k2
⁝ **excitement**, from emotional: cimic k2
⁝ **exhaustion**; from: caul c1
⁝ **hemorrhage**; with: *Chin* cimic puls sec
⁝ **loquacity**, with: *Coff* hr1*
⁝ **wave** from uterus to throat impedes labor: gels k*
• **changeable**: cimic mrr1 puls k2
• **cramping**: *Cimic* mrr1 cycl bro1
• **cutting** | **left**:
⁝ **extending** to | **right**: ip
⁝ **Umbilical** region, in: **Ip**
• **darting** upwards (See extending - upward)
• **deficiency**; with (See weak)
• **desperate**, make her: *Aur* k* *Cham* k* *Coff* kr1
• **distressing**: *(↗painful)* acon k* ambr arn k* aur bell k* *Caul* k* caust k* **Cham** k* cimic k* *Coff* k* con k* **Gels** k* **Kali-c** k* lyc k* nux-v k* phos k* plat k* puls sec k* **Sep** k* verat c1
⁝ **escape**, wants to: bell

- **excessive**: acon k* ambr k* arn art-v hr1 *Bell* k* **Cham** k* chlol hr1 cimic k* *Coff* k* *Coff-t* hr1* con cupr bg2* nux-m b7.de *Nux-v* k* puls k* rhus-t j5.de* sec k* **Sep** k* ust
- **exhausting**: *Caul* hr1* *Stann* hr1* *Verat* hr1*
- **fainting**, causing: *Cimic* k* **Nux-v** k* *Puls* k* sec bro1
- **false**•: *(↗ineffectual)* arn **Bell** k* borx *Bry* b7.de* **Calc** k* **Caul** k* caust bg2 *Cham* k* *Cimic* k* *Cinnb* k* cinnm hr1* coff k* *Con* cupr bg2 *Dios* k* *Gels* k* hyos bg2 ign bg2 ip bg2 *Kali-c* k* kali-p k* *Mit* hr1* *Nux-m* k* *Nux-v* k* *Op* k* **Puls** k* sec k* sep k* stann bg2 vib k*
  - **convulsions**; with: *Kali-c* b4a.de
  - **prophylaxis**: caul ptk1
- **fear** of death, with: *Coff* kr1
- **hip**, leaving the uterus; going to the: cimic k2
- **hourglass** contraction: bell bro1 cham k2 sec bro1
- **ineffectual**: *(↗false)* acon k* arn k* bell calc-f c1 caul ptk1* *Caust* cham c1 chlol c1 cimic k* cinnm hr1* *Coff* k* eup-pur k* gels goss **Kali-c** k* kali-p k* mit hr1* nux-v ptk1 op k* phos plat k* **Puls** k* sec k* sep k* *Ust*
- **insupportable**: *Coff* kr1 *Thuj* kr1
  - **walking** agg.: *Thuj* kr1
- **interrupted**: *Caul* *Mag-m* k* *Plat*
  - **spasms**, by: *Mag-m*
- **irregular**: aeth k* arn *Caul* k* caust cham k2 cimic k2 cocc k* *Coff* k* cupr *Nux-m* k* nux-v **Puls** k* sec k*
- **loquacity**, with: coff kr1
- **metrorrhagia** | **amel.**: cycl bro1
- **noise** agg.: cimic
- **painful**, too: *(↗distressing)* acon b2.de* ant-c b2.de* arn b2.de* aur b2.de* *Bell* b2.de* caul bro1* caust bro1 **Cham** b2.de* chin b2.de* *Cimic* bro1 cocc b2.de* *Coff* b2.de* con b2.de* cupr b2.de* *Gels* bro1 hyos b2.de* ign bro1 lyc b2.de* mag-c b2.de* nat-c b2.de* *Nux-v* b2.de* *Op* b7a.de phos b2.de* pitu jl3 puls bro1 sec b2.de* **Sep** b2.de* sulph b2.de*
- **places**, felt in wrong: cham k2
- **premature**: *Nux-v* b7a.de sabin bro1
- **pressure** in back | **amel.**: caust bro1 *Kali-c* bro1
- **prolonged**: *(↗Delivery - during - long)* *Caul* hr1 chlf hr1 cinnb k* *Cupr-act* br1 kali-c k2 puls **Sec** k* spong hr1 sulph k2
- **restlessness**; with: arn hr1* coff bg2 *Lyc* bg*
  - **between** pains: cupr hr1*
- **running** upward: *Borx* **Calc** **Cham** k* gels lyc
- **shivering**; with: cimic k2
- **shooting** pain: *Cimic* mrr1 kali-c
- **short**: *Caul* k* *Puls*
- **slow**: caul mrr1 kali-p bro1 mit kr1 pituin bro1 *Puls* k*
- **sluggish**: *Puls*
- **soreness**, with: arn k* ars caust
- **spasmodic**: acon bg2* ambr k* arn b2.de* art-v bro1 asaf b2.de* *Bell* k* *Borx* k* *Bry* k* calc b2.de* carb-an b2.de* carb-v b2.de* **Caul** k* **Caust** k* **Cham** k* chin bro1 chlol bro1 cic b7.de *Cimic* k* cinnm bro1 *Cocc* k* coff k* coff-t c1 con cupr k* ferr k* **Gels** k* **Hyos** k* ign k* *Ip* k* kali-c k* kali-p bro1 lob bg2* lyc k* mag-m b2.de* mag-p k* mosch b2.de* nat-m bro1 *Nux-m* k* *Nux-v* k* *Op* k* phos b2.de* pituin bro1 plat k* **Puls** k* sacch bro1 *Sec* k* *Sep* k* stann k* stram b2.de* *Verat* b7a.de vib k* zinc b2.de*
- **stomach** than in uterus; felt more in: borx k*
- **stool** | **urging** to; with: **Nux-v** k* plat
- **suppressed** and wanting: cact carb-v caul cimic *Op* k* *Puls* sec
- **thirst**; with: *Caul* hr1*
- **tormenting**: caul k2*
- **twitching**, with: *Chinin-s*
- **walking** agg.: kali-c k2 thuj kr1
- **wandering** pain: caul bg2*
- **weak**: aeth k* arn k* asaf b2.de* *Bell* k* borx k* bry b2.de* calc b2.de* *Camph* b2.de* cann-i k* cann-s sf1.de carb-an b2.de* *Carb-v* k* *Carbn-s* *Caul* k* *Caust* k* *Cham* k* chin k* **Cimic** k* cinnm hr1* cocc k* coff b2.de* **Gels** k* goss sf1.de *Graph* k* guare hr1 hyos b2.de* ign b2.de* **Kali-c** k* kali-p k* kreos b2.de* lyc k* mag-c b2.de* mag-m b2.de* merc b2.de* mit hr1* mosch b2.de* *Nat-c* k* **Nat-m** k* *Nux-m* k* *Nux-v* k* **Op** k* phos b2.de* plat k* **Puls** k* rhus-t b2.de* *Ruta* k* sabad b2.de* **Sec** k* sep k* stann b2.de* sul-ac b2.de* sulph k* *Thuj* k* ust zinc k*
  - **back**; but pain in the: kali-c k2
  - **shiver**; decreasing with a: caul hr1*

▽ • **extending** to:
  - **Abdomen**; sides of: cimic bro1 kali-c k2
  - **Back**: *Caust* sne *Coff* sne gels bg2* kali-c k2* *Nux-v* sne petr ptk1 **Puls** sne
    - **Down** the back: nux-v ptk1
  - **Groin**, into: cimic thuj
  - **Heart**: cimic
  - **Hip**: cimic k2
  - **Knees** and up to sacrum: phyt
  - **Pelvis**; across: *Cimic* mrr1
  - **Thighs**, into: *Cimic* mrr1 *Kali-c* vib
  - **Throat**, into: lach k2
  - **Upward**: *Borx* k* **Calc** k* **Cham** k* gels k* lach k2* lyc puls

○ • **Back**: *Bell* sne *Caust* sne *Cham* sne cocc sne *Coff* sne dict sne **Gels** sne **Kali-c** sne *Nux-v* sne *Petr* sne **Puls** sne *Sep* sne
  - **paroxysmal**: cham k2 kali-c k2 *Nux-v* *Sep*
  - **through** to back and up the back: *Gels*
  - **extending** to:
    - **Pubes**; from back to: sabin k2*
    - **Rectum**: nux-v bro1
  - **Down** the back into gluteal muscles: kali-c
- **Groin**, felt in: cimic
- **Loins**:
  - **extending** to | **Legs**; down: aloe bro1 *Bufo* bro1 carb-v bro1 caul bro1 cham bro1 *Nux-v* bro1
- **Uterus**:
  - **Cervix**:
    - **extending** to | **Upward**: sep

- **labor**-like: acon k* *Agar* k* *Aloe* k* ant-c b2.de* ant-t b2.de* *Apis* k* *Arn* k* *Asaf* k* aur k* **Bell** k* borx k* bov k* *Bry* k* calc k* calc-sil k2 camph k* *Cann-i* k* canth carb-an k* carb-v k* caul k* caust k* **Cham** k* chin k* *Chlol* hr1 *Cimic* *Cina* k* cocc k* *Coff* k* *Coloc* b4a.de* *Con* k* croc k* cupr k* *Cycl* mrr1 dros k* *Ferr* k* **Gels** k* germ-met srj5• graph k* hydrc hr1 *Hyos* k* *Ign* k* inul br1 iod h* *Ip* k* **Kali-c** k* kali-m k2 kali-p kali-sil k2 *Kreos* k* *Lach* k* *Lil-t* k* lyc k* mag-c k* mag-m k* med merc k* mez bg2 *Mosch* k* mur-ac k* murx k* nat-c k* nat-m k* nit-ac nux-m k* *Nux-v* k* *Op* k* ph-ac k* phos k* phyt bg2 **Plat** k* podo **Puls** k* *Rhus-t* k* ribo rly4• ruta k* sabad b2.de* *Sabin* k* **Sec** k* **Sep** k* *Sil* stann k* sul-ac k* *Sulph* k* tarent ther hr1* thuj k* *Ust* vib k* xan xanth zinc k*
  - **accompanied** by:
    - **dyspnea**: lob bg2
    - **fever**: acon bg2 bell bg2 cham bg2 ferr bg2 ign bg2 nux-v bg2 op bg2 *Puls* bg2 sabin bg2 sec bg2
    - **shrieking** (See MIND - Shrieking - pain - labor-like)
    - **stool** | **urging** to: nux-v bg2 op br1
    - **Urinary** organs; complaints of (See URINARY - Complaints - accompanied - pain)
  - **alternating** with | **Eye** symptoms: kreos bg1
- **lancinating**: aeth k* aur-s k2 clem k* meli sabin k2
- **leukorrhea**:
  - **agg.**: calc ↓ kreos ↓ sep ↓
    - **burning**: calc k2 kreos mrr1
    - **sore**: calc k2
    - **stitching** pain: sep bg2
  - **with**: con ↓ dros ↓ ign ↓ kreos ↓
    - **labor**-like: con b4a.de* dros b7a.de* ign b7.de kreos b7a.de
- **lying**:
  - **agg.**: bell ↓
    - **labor**-like: bell bg2
  - **amel.**: berb ↓

Female

- **amel.**: ...
  - **burning**: berb k*
- **back**; on | **agg.**:
  - **separating** knees as far as possible; and: lac-c ↓
    - **sore**: lac-c kr1
  - **amel.**: sabin c1
- **menses**:
- **after**:
  - **agg.**: *Cham* ↓ chin ↓ iod ↓ *Kali-c* ↓ kreos ↓ plat ↓ puls ↓
    - **bearing** down: chin b7a.de
    - **labor**-like: *Cham* iod kreos plat puls
    - **pressing** pain: kreos b7a.de
    - **sore**: *Kali-c* k*
- **before**:
  - **agg.**: *Alet* ↓ aloe ↓ alum ↓ *Am-c* ↓ am-m ↓ *Apis* ↓ aur ↓ *Bell* ↓ borx ↓ *Bov* ↓ calc ↓ calc-ar k2 *Calc-p* ↓ carb-v ↓ *Caul* ↓ *Cham* ↓ chin cimic ↓ *Cina* ↓ *Cocc* ↓ *Coff* ↓ *Coloc* ↓ con ↓ *Croc* cupr ↓ cycl ↓ *Dig* ↓ dulc fd4.de *Ferr* ↓ ferr-p ↓ *Gels* ↓ germ-met ↓ glycyr-g cte1• *Graph* ↓ *Haem* ↓ helon ↓ *Hyos* ↓ ign ↓ joan ↓ *Kali-c* ↓ kreos ↓ lach ↓ lil-t ↓ lyc mag-c ↓ *Mag-m* ↓ *Mag-p* ↓ med ↓ meli ↓ mosch ↓ mur-ac ↓ nat-m ↓ nit-ac ↓ nux-m ↓ *Nux-v* ↓ phos ↓ plat positr nl2• *Puls* ↓ rhus-t ↓ sabad ↓ *Sabin* ↓ sanic ↓ *Sec* ↓ **Sep** ↓ stann ↓ sulph thlas ↓ thuj ↓ thymol sp1 tritic-vg fd5.de ust ↓ *Verat* ↓ verat-v ↓ vesp ↓ *Vib* ↓ *Xan* ↓ zinc ↓ zinc-p ↓ [brom stj1 kali-br stj1 nat-br stj2]
    - **bearing** down: *Apis* b7a.de cina b7a.de croc b7.de* mag-c b4.de* mosch b7a.de mur-ac b4a.de phos *Plat* b4.de* zinc-p k2
    - **burning**: calc carb-v *Sep*
    - **cramping**: *Apis* b7a.de *Cocc* b7a.de *Coff* b7a.de cupr b7.de* *Nux-v* b7a.de *Puls* b7a.de
    - **labor**-like: *Alet* bro1 aloe bro1 alum k* *Am-c* bro1 am-m bro1 *Apis* k* aur *Bell* k* borx bro1 *Bov* k* brom bro1 calc bro1 *Calc-p* *Caul* bro1 *Cham* k* chin k* cimic k* *Cina* *Cocc* bro1 *Coff* bro1 *Coloc* b4a.de* cupr bro1 cycl k* *Dig* *Ferr* b7a.de* ferr-p bro1 *Gels* bro1 germ-met srj5• *Graph* bro1 *Haem* bro1 helon bro1 *Hyos* k* ign bro1 joan bro1 *Kali-c* bro1 kreos bro1 lil-t bro1 mag-c k* *Mag-m* bro1 *Mag-p* k* med bro1 meli bro1 nat-m bro1 nit-ac bro1 nux-m bro1 *Nux-v* bro1 plat k* *Puls* bro1 rhus-t k* sabad b7.de* *Sabin* bro1 sanic *Sec* bro1 *Sep* k* stann bro1 thlas bro1 thuj ust *Verat* bro1 verat-v bro1 vesp bro1 *Vib* bro1 *Xan* bro1 zinc
    - **pressing** pain: chin *Croc* vesp a1
    - **sore**: con *Kali-c* k* lach **Sep** k*
    - **stinging**: zinc
    - **stitching** pain: con
- **between**: mang-p rly4•
- **during**:
  - **agg.**: *Acon* ↓ agar ↓ *Alet* ↓ all-s ↓ aloe ↓ *Am-c* ↓ am-m ↓ amp rly4• ant-c ↓ apis ↓ arg-n ↓ arist-cl sp1 ars ↓ *Asaf* ↓ bar-c b4.de **Bell** ↓ berb ↓ borx ↓ bov ↓ brom ↓ bufo ↓ cact ↓ *Calc* ↓ *Calc-p* ↓ calc-s ↓ cann-i ↓ canth b7.de *Carb-an* ↓ *Carb-v* ↓ caul ↓ *Caust* ↓ cench ↓ **Cham** ↓ chin ↓ chir-fl ↓ *Cimic* ↓ cina ↓ coc-c ↓ *Cocc* ↓ coff ↓ *Coloc* ↓ *Con* ↓ cupr ↓ *Cycl* ↓ ferr ↓ ferr-p ↓ fum rly4• *Gels* ↓ glycyr-g cte1• *Graph* ↓ *Haem* ↓ helon ↓ hyos ↓ *Ign* ↓ ip ↓ joan ↓ kali-br ↓ *Kali-c* ↓ kali-s ↓ kali-sil ↓ *Kreos* ↓ *Lac-c* ↓ lac-e hrn2• *Lach* ↓ *Lil-t* ↓ lob-e ↓ lyc ↓ *Mag-c* ↓ *Mag-m* ↓ *Mag-p* ↓ mag-s ↓ mand sp1 med ↓ meli ↓ mosch ↓ *Nat-c* ↓ *Nat-m* ↓ nat-sil ↓ nept-m ↓ *Nit-ac* ↓ *Nux-m* ↓ nux-v ↓ phos ↓ *Plat* ↓ *Puls* ↓ *Rhus-t* ↓ ribo ↓ **Sabin** ↓ sal-fr ↓ saroth sp1 *Sec* ↓ *Sep* ↓ *Sil* ↓ stann ↓ sul-ac ↓ sulph ↓ tanac ↓ thlas ↓ thuj ↓ *Thymol* sp1 tritic-vg fd5.de ust ↓ *Verat* ↓ verat-v ↓ vesp ↓ *Vib* ↓ visc sp1 *Xan* ↓ zinc ↓
    - **bearing** down: *Am-c* b4a.de bell b4.de* bov b4.de calc-s carb-an b4a.de *Con* b4a.de *Kreos* b7a.de lob-e c1 med hr1 *Nit-ac* b4a.de nux-m b7a.de plat b4.de* sal-fr sle1• sep gk tanac ptk2 xan c1
    - **biting** pain: *Rhus-t* k* zinc
    - **burning**: *Am-c* bufo k2 *Carb-v* kali-br k* *Kali-c* k* *Kreos* *Sil* k* thuj
    - **congestive**: thymol sp1
    - **cramping**: chir-fl gya2 visc sp1
    - **flow** increases the pain; more: *(↗Menses - painful - flow - more)* cimic k2

- **menses – during – agg.**: ...
    - **labor**-like: *Acon* agar k* *Alet* k* aloe k* *Am-c* k* am-m k* ant-c apis k* arg-n *Asaf* k* *Bell* k* berb borx k* bov k* brom bro1 cact k2 *Calc* k* *Calc-p* k* cann-i k2 *Carb-an* k* caul k* *Caust* cench k2 **Cham** k* chin k* *Cimic* k* cina coc-c k2 *Cocc* bro1 coff k* *Coloc* bro1 *Con* k* cupr bro1 *Cycl* k* ferr k* ferr-p bro1 *Gels* k* *Graph* k* *Haem* bro1 helon bro1 hyos k* *Ign* k* joan bro1 *Kali-c* k* kali-s kali-sil k2 kreos k* *Lac-c* *Lach* k* *Lil-t* k* lyc *Mag-c* bro1 *Mag-m* bro1 *Mag-p* k* med k* meli bro1 mosch *Nat-c* k* nat-m bro1 *Nit-ac* k* *Nux-m* k* nux-v k* *Plat* k* *Puls* k* *Rhus-t* k* ribo rly4• **Sabin** b7.de* *Sec* k* *Sep* k* stann bro1 sulph k* thlas bro1 ust *Verat* b7a.de* verat-v bro1 vesp bro1 *Vib* bro1 *Xan* bro1
    - **pressing** pain: am-c ant-c asaf **Bell** berb bov calc *Cham* chin con ip mag-c mag-s mosch nat-m nept-m lsd2.fr nit-ac nux-m nux-v *Plat* k* puls *Sep* sil sulph zinc
    - **sore**: all-s hr1 am-c k2 bov *Kali-c* k* *Nat-m* k* sil k*
    - **standing** agg.: *Rhus-t* ↓
      - **labor**-like: *Rhus-t*
    - **stinging**: kali-c kreos lyc phos puls sabin sep sul-ac
    - **stitching** pain: ars b4a.de lyc nat-sil fd3.de• sul-ac k* zinc h2*
    - **tearing** pain: am-c k* zinc b4a.de
    - **twisting**: nept-m lsd2.fr
  - **beginning** of menses:
    - **agg.**: haliae-lc ↓ [sol-ecl cky1]
      - **spasmodic**: [sol-ecl cky1]
      - **stitching** pain: haliae-lc srj5•
    - **amel.**: glycyr-g cte1•
- **suppressed** menses; from: cham ↓
  - **labor**-like: cham b7a.de*
- **metrorrhagia**; during: *Bell* ↓ *Caul* ↓ *Cham* ↓ *Cimic* ↓ ham ↓ *Plat* ↓ puls ↓ *Sabin* ↓ sec ↓ thlas ↓ visc ↓
  - **bearing** down: *Bell* b4a.de *Cham* b7a.de *Sabin* b7a.de
  - **labor**-like: *Bell* b4a.de *Caul* bro1 *Cham* bro1 *Cimic* bro1 ham bro1 *Plat* b4a.de puls k2 sabin bro1 sec bro1 thlas bro1 visc bro1
- **motion** agg.: ars ↓ berb caust ↓ ip ↓
  - **burning**: ars k*
  - **cutting** pain: caust ip
- **ovulation**; during | **cutting** pain (See ABDOMEN - Pain - ovulation - cutting)
- **paroxysmal**: *Staph* tritic-vg fd5.de
- **perspiration**; during: rhus-t ↓
  - **cramping**: rhus-t b7.de
- **piercing** (See stitching)
- **pinching** pain: kali-c k* mur-ac plat k*
- **pregnancy**; end of: caul ↓
  - **labor**-like: caul tl1
- **pressing** pain: asaf b7a.de* bar-c **Bell** b4.de* bov b4.de* *Calc* b4a.de* calc-p k* *Cham* bg2 *Chin* b7.de* chinin-s bg2 cimic k2 cina b7a.de* *Con* b4.de* croc b7.de* graph k* ign bg2 ip b7.de* kali-c b4.de* kreos b7a.de mag-c bg2 mag-m b4.de* mang h2* merc b4.de* mosch b7.de* mur-ac bg2 **Nat-c** bg2 nat-m bg2 nux-v b7.de* *Plat* b4.de* podo a1 puls b7.de* ruta fd4.de sabin b7a.de* **Sep** b4.de* spig bg2 sulph b4.de* symph fd3.de• thuj k* vanil fd5.de zinc b4.de*
  - **alternating** with:
    - **Inguinal** region | **dragging**, bearing down in (See ABDOMEN - Pain - inguinal region - dragging - alternating - pressure)
- **pressure**:
  - **amel.**: ign ↓ mag-p mrr1
    - **labor**-like: ign
- **pressure** feet against support:
  - **amel.**: med ↓
    - **pressing** pain: med lp
- **pulsating** pain: calc-p k* tritic-vg fd5.de
- **rising** from sitting agg.: thuj k*
  - **cramping**: thuj k*
- **sharp**: aeth ars clem *Lyc* hr1 meli k* rhus-t

- **shooting** (See stitching)
- **sitting** agg.: berb↓ *Con*↓ *Lac-c* sep↓ staph h1 thuj
  - **burning**: berb k* sep
  - **pressing** pain: *Thuj*
  - **tearing** pain: *Con*
- **sitting** up in bed | **amel.**: coc-c
- **smarting** (See biting; burning)
- **sore** (= tender): agath-a nl2• am-c ambr k* androc srj1• apis ptk1 arg-n k2 am ars *Ars-i* aur-s k2 bar-m bg2 bell bg2* bov *Calc* calc-p calc-sil k2 canth k* **Carb-v** *Carbn-s* *Caust* cham bg2 chin b7.de* *Coc-c* coff k* con k* falco-pe nl2• *Ferr* b7.de* ferr-i *Graph* *Hep* iod kali-bi k* *Kali-c* k* kali-sil k2 **Kreos** k* *Lac-c* *Lach* ptk1 lil-t ptk1 lyc meph mur-ac ptk1 nat-c a1 nit-ac petr phasco-ci rbp2 (non:phos a1) **Plat** k* puls rhus-t k* ruta fd4.de sal-fr sle1• sec *Sep* *Sil* **Staph** k* sul-i k2 *Sulph* k* *Thuj* k* tritic-vg fd5.de vanil fd5.de *Zinc* zinc-p k2 [heroin sdj2]
- **spasmodic**: caul hr1* ign kreos k* nux-v *Staph* h1* thuj
- **squeezed**; as if: *Bell* b4a.de croc b7.de* phyt bg2
- **stabbing** (See stitching)
- **standing** agg.: aloe↓ dict↓ *Rhus-t*↓
  - **labor**-like: aloe k2 dict ptk1 *Rhus-t*
- **stinging**: *Apis* *Ars* k* berb bufo k2 calc-p k* carb-v eupi *Kali-c* kreos lil-t lyc phos puls sabin sep *Staph* urt-u k* zinc
- **stitching** pain: aeth a1 agath-a nl2• alum k* *Ars* k* aur bart a1 *Bell* k* *Borx* *Calc* k* *Calc-p* cann-xyz bg2 caust k* coc-c *Con* k* croc k* dulc fd4.de fl-ac bg2 *Glon* **Graph** k* hydr sne ign inul hr1 *Kali-c* k* kali-n h2* kreos b7a.de* lac-c *Lyc* h2* m-aust b7.de meli merc k* murx nat-p fkr6.de nat-s nit-ac k* pall **Phos** k* *Puls* b7.de* rhus-t k* ruta fd4.de sabin b7.de* sep k* spong fd4.de staph k* sul-ac symph fd3.de• tarent k* tell c1 thuj k* tritic-vg fd5.de vanil fd5.de
- **stool**:
  - **after**:
    - **agg.**: lyc↓
      - **cramping**: lyc b4.de*
  - **before**: carb-an↓
    - **drawing** pain: carb-an
  - **during**:
    - **agg.**: carb-v↓ kali-c↓ *Nat-m*↓ *Nux-v*↓ op↓ podo↓ sulph tl1
      - **bearing** down: podo mrr1
      - **labor**-like: carb-v b4a.de *Nat-m* *Nux-v* op b7.de*
      - **pressing** pain: kali-c
- **stool**; during:
  - ○ **Pudendum**: kali-n↓
    - **stitching** pain: kali-n bg2
- **straining**, from: rhus-t↓
  - **labor**-like: rhus-t k2
- **tearing** pain: aloe bg2 anac *Bar-c* k* bell k2 berb calc-sil k2 *Carb-an* carb-v con *Kali-c* k* lyc h2* nat-c k* *Phos* k* ruta b7.de* sep bg2 sil k* ter
- **tenesmus**:
  - ○ **Uterus** | **Cervix**: bell bro1 ferr bro1
- **ulcerative** pain: ign tl1 phos b4a.de
- **urination** | **after**:
    - **agg.**: canth↓ *Caust*↓ *Coloc*↓ **Kreos**↓ *Lac-c*↓ merc↓ sulph↓
      - **burning**: canth k2 *Caust* k* **Kreos** k* *Lac-c* merc sulph k2
      - **labor**-like: *Coloc* b4a.de
  - **during**:
    - **agg.**: *Ambr*↓ calc↓ canth↓ *Caust*↓ clem↓ *Coloc*↓ con↓ *Eupi*↓ falco-pe↓ hep↓ **Kreos**↓ *Lac-c*↓ nat-m↓ plat↓ sulph tl1 zinc↓
      - **biting** pain: *Caust* hep nat-m
      - **burning**: *Ambr* k* calc canth k2 *Caust* *Eupi* falco-pe nl2• **Kreos** k* *Lac-c* nat-m k* plat k* sulph zinc hr1
      - **cutting** pain: con k*
      - **labor**-like: *Coloc* b4a.de
      - **lancinating**: clem k*
- **walking** agg.: berb↓ caust↓ *Lac-c*↓ merc k2 thuj↓ zinc↓
  - **burning**: berb k* thuj
  - **cutting** pain: caust
  - **sore**: *Lac-c*
  - **stinging**: zinc k*
  - **stitching** pain: thuj
- **warm** applications:
  - **amel.**: ars↓
    - **burning**: ars tl1
- **warmth** agg.: nept-m↓
  - **pressing** pain: nept-m lsd2.fr
- ▽ **extending** to:
  - ○ **Anus**: *Carb-an*↓
    - **tearing** pain: *Carb-an* k*
  - **Back**:
    - **Hips**, and: **Gels**↓ sul-ac↓
      - **labor**-like: **Gels** sul-ac
    - **Pubes**, to: sabin↓
      - **labor**-like: sabin k2
  - **Bladder**: carb-v↓
    - **labor**-like: carb-v h2
  - **Chest**: alum↓ calc-p↓
    - **stitching** pain: alum calc-p
  - **Hips**: phasco-ci↓
    - **sore**: phasco-ci rbp2
  - **Mammae**: lach↓
    - **labor**-like: lach bg2
  - **Outward**: caust bg2
  - **Pelvis**: *Cimic*↓
    - **stitching** pain: *Cimic* mrr1
  - **Rectum**: *Aloe*↓ *Nux-v*↓
    - **labor**-like: *Aloe* *Nux-v*
  - **Sacrum**: carb-v↓
    - **labor**-like: carb-v h2
  - **Thighs**: *Aloe*↓ apis↓ berb bg2 bufo↓ *Calc-p* bg2 *Cham*↓ *Cimic*↓ con↓ kali-c↓ lac-c bg2 lil-t bg2 nat-m↓ nux-v↓ stram↓ ust↓ vib↓
    - **labor**-like: *Aloe* apis *Cham* con kali-c nat-m nux-v stram ust vib
    - **stitching** pain: *Cimic* mrr1
    - **tearing** pain: bufo k2
  - **Upward**: sep bg2
  - **Uterus** | **right**: bell bg2
  - **Vagina**: lil-t↓ puls↓
    - **stitching** pain: lil-t puls
- ○ **Clitoris**: borx↓
  - **night**: borx↓
    - **stinging**: borx k*
    - **stitching** pain: borx
  - **stinging**: borx
  - **stitching** pain: borx b4a.de
- **Labia**: acon↓ am-c↓ aur↓ bov↓ *Canth*↓ carb-v↓ con↓ dulc↓ graph↓ helo↓ helon↓ kreos↓ lyc↓ merc↓ puls↓ *Rhus-t*↓ sep↓ sil↓ spong↓ sulph↓ thuj↓
  - **left**: agath-a↓
    - **stitching** pain: agath-a nl2•
    - **extending** to:
      - **Uterus** to right ovary; through: bell↓ lac-c↓ phos↓ thuj↓
        - **stitching** pain: bell lac-c phos thuj
  - **burning**: acon bro1 am-c bro1 aur bro1 bov bro1 *Canth* bro1 carb-v bro1 graph bro1 helo bg2 helon hr1* kreos bg2* lyc bro1 merc bg2* puls bro1 *Rhus-t* bro1 sep bro1 sil bro1 sulph bg2* thuj bro1
  - **menses** | **before**:
      - **agg.**: calc↓
        - **burning**: calc bro1
    - **during**:
      - **agg.**: calc↓
        - **burning**: calc bro1
  - **stitching** pain: con b4.de* dulc fd4.de graph b4.de* lyc h2* spong fd4.de
  - ○ **Between**: *Acon*↓ ambr↓ *Bell*↓ calc-p↓ caust↓ conv↓ eupi↓ *Graph*↓ *Helon*↓ hep↓ **Kreos**↓ ovi-p↓ *Plat*↓ *Sep*↓ sulph↓ tarent↓ urt-u↓
    - **biting** pain: **Kreos**

Female

- **Between**: ...
  - **sore**: *Acon* bro1 ambr bro1 *Bell* bro1 caust bro1 conv bro1 *Graph* bro1 *Helon* bro1 hep bro1 *Kreos* bro1 ovi-p bro1 *Plat* bro1 *Sep* bro1 sulph bro1 tarent bro1 urt-u bro1
  - **stitching** pain: calc-p hr1 eupi
  - **urination** agg.; during: eupi ↓ falco-pe ↓
    - **sore**: eupi k* falco-pe nl2•
- **Meatus**; region of: berb ↓
  - **tearing** pain: berb k*
- **Ovaries** (= ovarialgia; oophoralgia): abrot k2 absin ↓ acon k* aesc agath-a ↓ *Aids* nl2• alet ↓ alum ↓ am-br hr1 am-m k* *Ambr* ↓ anan ang ↓ *Ant-c* ↓ ap-g ↓ **Apis** k* apom ↓ *Arg-met* *Arg-n* arge-pl ↓ arn ars k* ars-i arum-t ↓ *Atro* k* aur aur-ar k2 aur-br ↓ aur-i k2 aur-s k2 bamb-a ↓ **Bell** k* berb ↓ *Borx* ↓ brom k* *Bry* k* *Bufo* *Cact* k* calc calc-i k2 *Canth* k* caps ↓ carb-ac k* carb-an ↓ *Caul* bg *Cench* k* *Cent* cham k* *Chin* ↓ cimic k* cina ↓ cocc k* coli jl2 coll **Coloc** k* con cop k* corian-s knl6• croc ↓ crot-h k* cub ↓ cupr-ar ↓ cur ↓ dream-p sdj1• dulc fd4.de eup-pur ↓ *Eupi* ↓ *Fago* ↓ ferr ↓ ferr-i ↓ ferr-p k2 fl-ac ↓ gels k* germ-met srj5• goss c2 graph k* guaj *Ham* k* helodr-cal ↓ *Helon* k* hep ↓ heroin ↓ hydrc k* hyper ↓ *Ign* *Iod* k* irid-met ↓ kali-ar ↓ *Kali-br* k* kali-c ↓ kali-i a1 kali-n ↓ kali-p k* kola stb3• kreos k* lac-ac k* *Lac-c* k* lac-d k* lac-lup hrn2• **Lach** k* *Lil-t* k* **Lyc** k* lyss k* mag-c ↓ *Mag-m* ↓ **Mag-p** k* med k* melal-alt gya4 meli ↓ *Merc* merc-c ↓ morg fmm1• mosch ↓ mur-ac ↓ murx *Naja* k* nat-m ↓ nat-sil fd3.de• nept-m lsd2.fr nicc ↓ *Nux-m* ↓ ol-j ↓ onos ovi-p c2 oxyt c2 *Pall* k* *Phos* k* *Phyt* k* pic-ac ↓ pieri-b mlk9.de *Plat* k* plb k* **Podo** k* polyg-h ↓ positr nl2• psor ↓ *Puls* k* pyrog k2 *Ran-b* k* *Rhod* k* rhus-t ↓ rob ↓ ruta fd4.de sabad k* sabal ↓ sabin k2 sal-n ↓ sarr k* (non:sars k*) sec k* senec k* *Sep* k* spong fd4.de stann *Staph* k* still a1 stram ↓ sul-i k2 sulph k* sumb bg syc fmm1• symph fd3.de• syph tarent k* ter k* thea ↓ ther k* thuj k* thymol ↓ tritic-vg fd5.de tub al* tub-r ↓ ulm-c jsj8• urt-u k* *Ust* k* vanil fd5.de vesp k* vib k* vib-t c2 wye k* *Xan* k* *Xanth* zinc k* zinc-p k2 *Zinc-val* ↓ ziz ↓ [bell-p-sp dcm1]
  - **alternating** sides: dulc fd4.de **Lac-c** k* vanil ↓
    - **menses**; after: lac-e hrn2•
    - **stitching** pain: dulc fd4.de lac-c vanil fd5.de
  - **right**: abrom-a ks5 absin bro1 aids nl2• alet ↓ ang ↓ *Apis* k* *Arg-n* ars k* ars-i aur-m-n vh bamb-a ↓ **Bell** k* bell-p-sp ↓ bran bro1 *Bry* k* bung-fa mtf calc k* cench k2* chel c1 coloc bro1 cub dream-p sdj1• dulc fd4.de eupi bro1 fago a1* germ-met ↓ graph k* ham fd3.de• ignis-alc ↓ *Iod* k* kali-i ↓ kali-n ↓ kola stb3• *Lac-ac* ↓ lac-c k2 lac-lup hrn2• lach bro1 lec ↓ lil-t k* loxo-recl knl4• **Lyc** k* lyss hr1 mag-m ↓ **Mag-p** hr1 med c1 murx ↓ nat-m hr1 nat-sil fd3.de• neon ↓ ozone sde2• *Pall* k* phyt bro1 plat tl1 **Podo** k* propr sa3• psor ↓ rhus-t hr1 ruta fd4.de sabal ↓ sarr k* (non:sars k*) sec ↓ *Sep* a1* spong fd4.de symph fd3.de• syph tritic-vg fd5.de ulm-c jsj8• ust bro1 vanil fd5.de vult-gr ↓ xan hr1*
    - **then** left: *Lyc* ↓
      - **cutting** pain: *Lyc*
    - **aching**: aids nl2• *Lac-ac* k* *Pall*
    - **bearing** down: *Apis* bell bg *Bry* hr1
    - **boring** pain: **Lyc**
    - **burning**: *Apis* *Ars* hr1 *Bell* coloc kali-n symph fd3.de• ust ptk1
    - **cutting** pain: *Apis* k* *Arg-n* k* *Bell* bg2 xan c1
    - **drawing** pain: *Apis* k* *Bell* bg dulc fd4.de *Lach* hr1 med pall k* ruta fd4.de spong fd4.de
    - **gnawing** pain: *Lil-t* podo
    - **lying** on right side | **amel.**: *Apis* lyc sne
    - **ovulation**; during: granit-m ↓
      - **cutting** pain: granit-m es1•
    - **pressing** pain: ang k* *Ars* k* *Iod* k* symph fd3.de•
    - **sharp**: ignis-alc es2• *Lac-c* hr1 neon srj5• [bell-p-sp dcm1]
    - **sore**: alet k2 *Apis* *Bry* k* *Iod* mag-m murx bg1 *Pall* plat psor bg1 sec bg1
    - **stinging**: apis sabal c1 vult-gr sze5•
    - **stitching** pain: absin br1 **Ars** k* bamb-a stb2.de• *Bell* *Coloc* hr1 germ-met srj5• lac-c k* lec *Lyc* k* nat-sil fd3.de• *Plat* k* *Podo* k* sep a1 symph fd3.de• vanil fd5.de xan c1
    - **tearing** pain: graph k* kali-i k* *Pall* sne
    - **walking** agg.: lil-t ↓ podo ↓
      - **gnawing** pain: lil-t podo
    - **extending** to:
      - **left**: graph **Lyc** xan

- **Ovaries – right – extending** to – **left**: ...
  - **stitching** pain: *Lyc* k*
  - **Back**: kola stb3• lyc sne positr nl2• xan c1
  - **Hip**: xan c1
  - **Scapula** | **Point** under: aur-m-n vh
  - **Thigh**: xan c1
  - **Uterus**: iod podo
- **left**: abrot k* aesc aln vva1• am-br bro1* ap-g bro1 apis bro1 **Arg-met** k* arg-n k1* arge-pl rwt5• atro hr1 *Brom* k* bros-gau ↓ bung-fa mtf caps bro1 *Carb-ac* k* caul c1 cench k2 cimic k* coloc k* dream-p sdj1• erig br1* eup-pur bro1 falco-pe ↓ frax bro1 graph k* grat mrr1 *Ham* k* hed sp1 hir ↓ iod bro1 irid-met srj5• *Kali-br* k* *Kali-p* kola stb3• *Lac-c* k* lac-d ↓ **Lach** k* lec oss• *Lil-t* k* lyss k* magn-gr bg med k* *Merc* murx bro1 musca-d szs1 *Naja* k* nat-sil ↓ nept-m lsd2.fr ovi-p bro1 *Phos* k* pic-ac bro1 pieri-b mlk9.de *Plat* k* podo c1 puls ↓ ruta fd4.de sabal ↓ sep a1* spong fd4.de sumb ↓ suprar rly4• syc bka1*• symph fd3.de• syph ↓ *Tarent* k* thea bro1 *Ther* *Thuj* k* tritic-vg fd5.de **Ust** k* vanil fd5.de vesp k* vesp-xyz c2 visc ↓ wye k* xan bg1* *Xanth* bg *Zinc* k* zinc-p k2
  - **then** right: apis ↓
    - **cutting** pain: apis
  - **aching**: brom k* med pic-ac k* podo syph
  - **bearing** down: lac-d k* *Lach* k* plat hr1
  - **boring** pain: brom ruta fd4.de sumb thuj **Zinc** k*
  - **burning**: abrot lac-c hr1 *Lach* k* med thuj k*
  - **bursting**: med hr1
  - **cramping**: *Coloc* k* *Naja* nat-sil fd3.de•
  - **cutting** pain: graph hir rsj4• phos k* puls *Thuj* k* ust k*
  - **drawing** pain: *Atro* hr1 coloc k* spong fd4.de
  - **gnawing** pain: coloc
  - **lying**:
    - **amel.**: kali-p
    - **back**; on:
      - **amel.**: kali-p
        - **stitching** pain: kali-p
    - **side**; on:
      - **left**:
        - **agg.**: symph fd3.de• thuj k* visc ↓
          - **stitching** pain: visc c1
  - **menses**:
    - **after** | **agg.**: lac-e hrn2•
    - **amel.**: zinc ↓
      - **boring** pain: zinc
    - **before**:
      - **agg.**: croc ↓ *Thuj* ↓ ust ↓
        - **burning**: croc bro1 *Thuj* bro1 ust bro1
    - **during**:
      - **agg.**: croc ↓ *Thuj* ↓ ust ↓
        - **boring** pain: thuj
        - **burning**: croc bro1 *Thuj* bro1 ust bro1
  - **motion** agg.: croc ↓ *Thuj* ↓ ust ↓
    - **burning**: croc bro1 *Thuj* bro1 ust bro1
  - **ovulation**; during: kola stb3•
  - **pressing** pain: *Lach* k* *Med*
  - **sharp**: musca-d szs1
  - **sore**: *Arg-met* atro bg1 coloc kali-br bg1 **Lach** k* med bg1 ovi-p bg1 plat k* syph bg1* ust bg1 vesp
  - **standing** agg.: brucel sa3•
  - **stinging**: lil-t k* sabal c1 thuj k2 zinc sne
  - **stitching** pain: abrot k* bros-gau mrc1 caps bg1 cench k2 falco-pe nl2• graph **Lach** k* pieri-b mlk9.de ruta fd4.de sep bg1 symph fd3.de• thuj k* tritic-vg fd5.de vanil fd5.de visc c1 zinc sne
  - **tearing** pain: plat k* thuj k2
  - **walking** in open air agg.: carb-ac c1*
  - **extending** to:
    - **right**: apis lac-c **Lach** lil-t naja nept-m lsd2.fr syph thuj k2 ust
    - **Abdomen**: ham lil-t
    - **Downward**: (*↗extending to - limbs)* lil-t thuj c1
    - **Heart**: naja bg3 tarent

- **left – extending** to: ...
  - **Hypochondrium**, left: hist vml3•
  - **Leg | left**: ust mrr1
  - **Lumbar** region: *Aesc* aln vva1• lec oss• merc plat podo syph
  - **Thigh**: hist vml3• thuj k2
  - **Uterus**: naja ust
- **morning**:
  - **bed** agg.; in: visc ↓
    - **sharp**: visc c1
- **evening**: aids nl2• ran-b k2 ruta fd4.de tritic-vg fd5.de
- **night**: bung-fa mtf kali-p lyc sne *Merc* podo k* symph fd3.de• *Syph* k* vanil fd5.de
  - **midnight**: bung-fa mtf
    - **before | 22**.30 h: bung-fa mtf
- **abortion**, during: **Apis** ↓
  - **burning**: **Apis**
- **accompanied** by:
  - **walking**; difficulty in: tub jl2
  - **Heart**; complaints of: cimic bro1 lil-t bro1 naja bro1
    - **difficult** respiration; and: **Tarent** k*
- **aching**: aids nl2• apis brom k* con hydrc a1 iod *Kreos* lac-ac k* lil-t med onos pic-ac k* podo k* positr nl2• sep k* sulph k* syph
- **alternating** with:
  - **headache**: morg fmm1•
  - **Eye**; pain in the: sulph
- **bearing** down: *Apis* canth k* ferr-i k* ham k* lac-d k* *Lach* k* *Lil-t* k* *Mag-m* k* med k* plat k* *Podo*
- **bending | backward | amel.**: *Lac-c*
  - **legs | amel.**: pall mrr1
- **bending** double:
  - **amel.**: *Coloc* kali-p op bg1 symph fd3.de•
    - **boring** pain: *Coloc* k*
- **boring** pain: brom k* *Coloc* k* lach **Lyc** ruta fd4.de sumb thuj **Zinc** k*
- **breathing**:
  - **agg.**: bry k* graph h2* *Lac-c*
    - **stitching** pain: *Bry* graph h2
  - **arresting** breathing: *Canth* ↓
    - **stitching** pain: *Canth*
- **burning**: abrot agath-a nl2• anan k* **Apis** k* **Ars** k* *Bell* k* *Bufo* k* *Canth* k* carb-an coloc con k2* *Eupi* k* *Fago* bro1 goss *Kali-i* k* kali-n k* *Lac-c* k* **Lach** k* *Lil-t* k* lyc med merc k2 nat-m *Plat* k* *Sep* k* symph fd3.de• *Thuj* k* tub c1 ust k* zinc zinc-val bro1
  - **paroxysmal**: *Plat* k*
- **bursting**: graph med thuj k2
- **chronic**: med jl2
- **coition**:
  - **after**: *Apis* lac-c *Plat Staph* thuj
    - **burning**: **Apis** thuj
    - **drawing** pain: *Plat* k*
    - **stinging**: *Apis*
  - **during**: *Apis* sne brom sne nat-sil sne syph k2
    - **cutting** pain: syph ptk1
- **cold**:
  - **amel.**: apis ↓ vesp ↓
    - **stinging**: apis vesp
- **cold** agg.; becoming: pall sne thuj k2
- **company**:
  - **agg.**: **Pall**
  - **amel.**: *Pall*
- **constricting**, contracting pain: *Cact* puls pyrog k2
- **continence**, from: *Apis* kali-br
- **conversation**; animated: **Pall**
- **coughing**; pain in left ovary from: naja k*
- **cramping**: *Bufo* k* *Cact* bro1 cocc k* *Coloc* k* cub helodr-cal knl2• kola stb3• melal-alt gya4 *Naja* k* phos plat ruta fd4.de
- **cutting** pain: absin bro1 acon bro1 ap-g vml3• *Apis Arg-n* arum-t k* atro bell k* *Borx* bry k* canth caps bro1 cocc coll **Coloc** k* *Con* k* croc bro1 cub dream-p sdj1• eup-pur k* graph ham k* *Lil-t* k* *Lyc* merc k2 naja k* nat-m nux-m onos polyg-h ptk1 puls k* *Sabad* k* stram syph *Thuj* k* ust k* xan xanth
- **delivery**; after: **Lach** k*
- **drawing** pain: apis *Ars* k* atro k* bell *Chin* k* coloc k* dulc fd4.de goss k* kali-p fd1.de• lach k* lil-t k* med ptk1 naja gm1 *Pall* k* *Plat* k* podo ruta fd4.de spong fd4.de tritic-vg fd5.de tub-r jl2 vanil fd5.de
- **drawing** up legs | **amel.**: ap-g bro1 coloc bro1
- **dull**: aur-br bro1 hydrc bro1 nicc bro1 sep bro1 thymol sp1 tub-r jl2
- **eating | amel.**: iod
- **excitement** agg.: pall mrr1
- **extending** limbs amel.: *Plb*
- **flexing** thigh amel.: *Coloc Pall* xan sne
- **gnawing** pain: coloc *Lil-t* k* plat k* podo
- **gonorrhea**; with chronic: *Plat*
- **grasping** pain: lil-t
- **grinding** pain: fl-ac graph k*
- **griping** pain: cur lil-t k*
- **hawking**: graph h2*
- **hemorrhagic** subjects, in: crot-h
- **intermittent**: bell cham goss a1 lac-c lach thuj ust hr1 ziz hr1
- **jar** agg.: aln vva1• arg-n *Bell* lil-t pall k*
- **lancinating**: **Apis** bell k* borx coll con cub dream-p sdj1• goss **Lil-t**
- **lifting** agg.: rhus-t
- **lying**:
  - **agg.**: ambr bg1 ferr bg1 murx bg1 ruta fd4.de vanil fd5.de
  - **amel.**: carb-ac bro1 dream-p sdj1• pall k* podo c1* sep bro1 thuj k* ust bro1
  - **back**; on:
    - **agg.**: vanil fd5.de
    - **amel.**: kali-p rhus-t
      - **hard**; on something: rhus-t
  - **side**; on:
    - **left | amel.**: ap-g vh1 op bg1 *Pall* k*
    - **painful** side | **amel.**: *Bry*
    - **right | amel.**: apis
- **menses**:
  - **after**:
    - **agg.**: ant-c ↓ apis bg1 borx bg1 cupr bg1 goss bg1 graph bg1 iod bg1 kali-c ↓ **Lach** *Pall* k* ust bg1 zinc bg1*
      - **burning**: zinc
      - **lancinating**: *Borx*
      - **sore**: ant-c c1 *Iod* kali-c
  - **before**:
    - **agg.**: *Apis* k* *Bell* k* bry bro1 cact bro1 calc-i k2 canth bro1 *Cench* cimic bro1 *Coloc* k* graph ham bro1 iod bro1 joan bro1 *Kali-c* ↓ kali-n bro1 lac-c **Lach** k* *Lil-t* bro1 nat-sil fd3.de• pic-ac bro1 podo sal-n bro1 tarent bro1 thuj k* thymol ↓ tritic-vg ↓ ust vib k* *Zinc*
      - **aching**: thymol sp1
      - **drawing** pain: coloc k* tritic-vg fd5.de
      - **sore**: *Kali-c Lac-c*
      - **stitching** pain: nat-sil fd3.de• *Podo* k* vib k*
  - **during**:
    - **agg.**: aln vva1• *Apis* k* arg-met *Bell* k* *Borx* ↓ bry k* bufo ↓ bung-fa mtf cact bro1 canth bro1 cench cimic bro1 cocc coll ↓ coloc bro1 con crot-h hr1 gels ham bro1 iod k* joan bro1 *Kali-c* ↓ kali-n bro1 kali-p kola stb3• lac-c lac-d k2 **Lach** k* lil-t k* lyc merc k2 *Pall Phos* k* pic-ac bro1 *Plat* podo k* positr nl2• sal-n bro1 syc bka1*• tarent bro1 ther *Thuj* k* thymol ↓ tub c1 ust vib bro1 xan k* xanth [heroin sdj2]
      - **burning**: bufo canth kali-n br1
      - **cramping**: *Cocc* k* kola stb3•
      - **cutting** pain: *Apis Borx* cocc k* *Lyc Phos* k*

- **menses – during – agg.**: ...
  - **lancinating**: *Borx* coll
  - **sore**: *Apis* canth *Iod Kali-c* plat k* thymol sp1
  - **stinging**: *Apis*
  - **stitching** pain: kali-p *Lac-c* phos *Podo* k*
  - **tearing** pain: *Pall* sne plat
  - **extending** to:
    - **Abdomen**: sabal ↓
      - **stinging**: sabal c1
  - **amel.**: *Lac-c Lach* k* mosch ust *Zinc* k*
    - **boring** pain: lach zinc
  - **beginning** of menses | **agg.**: morg fmm1•
  - **suppressed** menses; from: ant-c ↓ bell ↓
    - **sore**: ant-c k* bell bro1
- **mental** exertion agg.: calc
- **motion**:
  - **agg.**: *Ars* **Bell Bry** k* *Cench Lac-c Pall* k* podo c1 ran-b k2 sabal c1 ther
    - **drawing** pain: **Ars** k*
    - **sore**: ther k*
    - **stitching** pain: *Ars* k* **Bry** k* cench
  - **amel.**: iod
  - **feet**; of:
    - **amel.**: *Ars*
      - **burning**: **Ars**
- **music** and excitement: pall k*
- **neuralgic**: am-br bro1 ap-g bro1 apis bg2* arg-met bg2 atro bg2* bell bg2* berb bro1 bry bg2* cact bg2* canth bg2* caul bg2* cimic bg2* coll bg2 coloc bg2* con bg2* ferr bro1 ferr-p bro1 gels bg2* goss bro1* graph bro1 ham bg2* hyper bro1 kali-br bro1 lach bg2* lil-t bg2* mag-p bg2* meli bro1 merc bg2* merc-c bro1 naja bg2* phyt bro1 plat bg2* podo bg2* puls bg2* sabal bg2* sal-n bro1 staph bg2* sumb bg2* thea bro1 ust bg2* vib bg2* *Xan* bro1 *Zinc-val* bro1
  - **intermittent**: *Goss* bro1 ziz bro1
- **ovulation**:
  - **during**: alet zr bung-fa mtf cocc k* dream-p sdj1• ham k* mag-c zr meli zr nux-v zr sep k* vanad dx xan zr [bell-p-sp dcm1 heroin sdj2]
  - **menses**; from ovulation until: lac-h ↓
    - **sharp**: lac-h htj1•
- **paroxysmal**: *Ham*
- **pinching** pain: anan canth k* cham *Plat* k* rob sne
- **pregnancy** agg.; during: kali-p podo xan k* xanth
- **pressing** pain: ang k* arge-pl rwt5• *Ars* k* bell bg2 *Coloc Iod* k* lac-d **Lach** k* *Lil-t* k* plat *Sep* k* symph fd3.de• vanil fd5.de [bell-p-sp dcm1]
  - **menses** would reappear, as though: cina bg2 croc bg2 mag-c bg2 mosch bg2 mur-ac bg2 *Plat*
- **pressure**:
  - **agg.**: pall c1 ther ↓
    - **sore**: ther hr1*
  - **amel.**: coloc k2* pall k* podo ruta fd4.de zinc
    - **boring** pain: zinc k*
- **pulsating** pain: cop onos
- **radiating**: [bell-p-sp dcm1]
- **raising** | **arms**:
  - **agg.**: *Apis* sulph
    - **drawing** pain: *Apis*
  - **leg**: lyc
- **riding** agg.: thuj
  - **burning**: thuj
- **rubbing**:
  - **amel.**: pall k*
    - **drawing** pain: *Pall* k*
- **sexual** desire, during: *Kali-br*
- **sharp**: ap-g vh1 *Apis* cench dream-p sdj1• irid-met srj5• kali-p *Lac-c* k* lac-lup hrn2• *Lach* **Lil-t** k* lyc sep *Staph* ust k* vib xan xanth [bell-p-sp dcm1]
- **sitting** bent forward agg.: *Ars*
  - **drawing** pain: **Ars** k*
- **sleep** agg.; on going to: kali-p
- **sore**: alet k2 alum am-m hr1 *Ant-c Apis* k* arg-met arg-n arn k* *Ars-i* atro bell bg2 **Bry** k* *Bufo Canth Chin* cimic coloc con cupr-ar graph guaj ham k* helon k* hep *Iod* kali-br kali-c kreos c1 *Lac-c* **Lach Lil-t** k* med *Nux-m* k* ol-j k* onos *Pall Plat* k* psor puls rhus-t sep k* *Staph* sul-i k2 syph k* tarent ter ther k* thuj bg1 ust vesp [bell-p-sp dcm1 heroin sdj2]
  - **accompanied** by:
    - **Rectum**; complaints of: onos ptk1
    - **Uterus**; complaints of: ust ptk1
- **squeezed**; as if: coloc *Thuj* k*
- **standing** agg.: apis bamb-a ↓ **Lil-t** ↓ nat-sil fd3.de• pall k*
  - **bearing** down: **Lil-t** k*
  - **stitching** pain: lil-t nat-sil fd3.de•
  - **tearing** pain: bamb-a stb2.de•
- **stepping** agg.: arg-n *Bell* lil-t pall
- **stinging**: **Apis** k* borx bry canth bro1 con bro1 goss k* graph **Lil-t** k* merc k* sabal c1 *Sep* k* vesp zinc sne
- **stitching** pain: abrot k* absin k* *Ambr* k* ap-g br1 *Apis* apom bg *Ars* bamb-a stb2.de• *Bell* borx brom *Bry Bufo* k* *Canth* carb-an *Caul* hr1 cench *Coloc* k* con k* cur dulc fd4.de goss k* graph k* kali-ar kali-c k* kali-p lac-c k* *Lach* k* lil-t k* *Lyc* k* *Mag-p* med k* merc phos pic-ac pieri-b mlk9.de *Plat* k* *Podo* k* ruta fd4.de *Sep* k* *Staph* k* symph fd3.de• syph thuj k* tritic-vg fd5.de tub c1 ust vanil fd5.de *Vib* k* xan xanth zinc sne
  - **needles**; as from | **hot** needles: germ-met srj5•
- **stool**:
  - **urging** to:
    - **with**:
      - **menses**; after: *Plat* ↓
        - **pressing** pain: *Plat*
- **stooping** agg.: apis
- **storm**; before: *Rhod* rhus-t
- **stretching** | **agg.**:
  - **bed**; in: apis k*
    - **cutting** pain: apis
  - **limbs** (See extending limbs)
- **talking**, agg.: bell k2
- **tearing** pain: abrot k* bamb-a stb2.de• con k2 graph k* ham k* kali-i k* lil-t merc *Pall* sne *Plat* k* thuj ptk1
- **touch** agg.: ant-c bro1 *Apis* bro1 bell k2* bry k* canth bro1 carb-an bro1 *Cimic* bro1 graph h2 *Ham* bro1 hep bro1 iod bro1 *Lach* bro1 lil-t bro1 *Plat* bro1 sabal bro1 staph k2 *Tarent* bro1 thea bro1 thuj bro1 ust bro1 zinc-val bro1 [bell-p-sp dcm1]
- **turning** in bed agg.: lyc
- **urination** | **during**:
  - **agg.**: androc srj1• nat-m ↓ sulfonam ↓ thuj
    - **burning**: nat-m sulfonam ks2
    - **cutting** pain: nat-m
  - **urging** to; when: *Thuj*
- **walking**:
  - **agg.**: *Apis* arg-n **Arn** ↓ *Bry* carb-ac bro1 fago a1* lil-t k* med pall podo k* sep bro1 thuj k* ust bro1
    - **bearing** down: *Lil-t* med k*
    - **burning**: thuj
    - **sore**: *Apis* **Arn Bry**
  - **air** agg.; in open: *Carb-ac*
  - **rapidly**:
    - **agg.**: apis ↓ lac-ac
      - **aching**: apis lac-ac k*
- **warm** bed agg.: *Apis Merc* sabal c1
- **weather**:
  - **change** of weather: *Ran-b Rhod* k* *Rhus-t* thuj
  - **windy** and stormy | **before**: rhod mrr1

▽ · **extending** to:
: **right**: med↓
: **stitching** pain: med
: **left**: lac-c↓
: **stitching** pain: lac-c
: **Abdomen**: con ham
: **Back**: abrot aesc lyc$_{sne}$ merc plat podo *Sulph* syph xan
: **Up** the back: arg-met
: **Backward**: bell$_{bg1}$ carb-ac$_{bg1}$ con lil-t$_{bg1}$ sep
: **Other** ovary; from one to the: coloc$_{bg1}$ ust$_{bg1}$
: **Chest**: apis lach murx$_{mrr1}$
: **left**: apis
: **Crural** region, down: podo staph xan
: **Diagonally** upward: apis med *Murx*
: **Downward**: med
: **And** forwards: arg-met
: **Genital**-crural nerve: xan$_{c1}$
: **Genitals**, to: lach
: **Groin**: am-c *Bufo Cub* lil-t podo$_{k2}$ symph$_{fd3.de\bullet}$ ust
: **left**: lil-t ust
: **Hypogastrium**, and: xan
: **Toward** left leg; and through: plat
: **Hips**: apis berb brom con lil-t merc ust xan
: **Knee**: lac-c↓ wye↓
: **stitching** pain: lac-c wye
: **Knees**: lac-c wye
: **Limbs**: *(↗left - extending - downward)* bry↓
: **right**: apis podo
: **left**: apis cham lil-t phos thuj ust$_{k*}$
: **down**: *Apis Calc* ferr-i goss lac-c *Lil-t Pall* podo *Thuj* ust$_{k*}$ xan
: **sore**: bry$_{k*}$
: **Liver**: lach med$_{c1}$
: **stitching** pain: med
: **Lumbar** region: staph tub$_{jl2}$
: **Mamma**, to opposite: murx$_{pd*}$
: **Mammae**: senec$_{vml3\bullet}$
: **Other** ovary; from one to the: coloc$_{bg1}$ **Lac-c** med$_{br1}$ onos ust$_{bg1}$
: **Outward**: sep
: **Sacrum**: *Arg-n*$_{k*}$ tub$_{jl2}$
: **Scapula**: aur-m-n$_{vh}$ borx
: **Side**; up the: cimic↓ lac-c↓ *Sep*↓
: **stitching** pain: cimic lac-c$_{k*}$ *Sep*
: **Stomach**: coloc
: **Thighs**: *Apis* arg-met *Arg-n Ars* berb *Bry Cact Calc* carb-an cham cimic$_{mrr1}$ croc↓ *Lac-c Lil-t Mag-m*$_{hr1}$ nat-m pall *Phos Podo* sabal$_{c1*}$ staph symph$_{fd3.de\bullet}$ *Thuj* ust$_{k*}$ vib$_{mrr1}$ wye xan zinc-val↓
: **right**: xan↓
. **cutting** pain: xan$_{c1}$
: **cutting** pain: *Apis* arg-n bry$_{bro1}$ *Cimic*$_{bro1}$ croc$_{bro1}$ lil-t$_{bro1}$ phos$_{bro1}$ podo$_{bro1}$ wye$_{bro1}$ *Xan*$_{bro1}$ zinc-val$_{bro1}$
: **drawing** pain: ars$_{k*}$
: **stitching** pain: phos staph ust
: **Anterior** surface: cimic$_{br}$ lil-t nat-m$_{bg1}$ podo$_{k2}$ xan
: **Hip**; over region of: xan
: **Inner** surface: arg-n ars *Lil-t Phos*
. **Down** knee; and: podo
: **Outer** surface: lil-t
: **Upward**: cimic con lach lil-t *Murx*$_{mrr1}$ podo$_{fd3.de\bullet}$
: **Uterus**: ham *Iod* lach sep ust
: **Vagina**: sep

○ · **Region** of ovaries: ser-a-c$_{jl2}$

- **Perineum**: | **aching** (See RECTUM - Pain - perineum)
- **Pubic** bones: agath-a↓ calc$_{b4a.de}$ carb-v$_{b4a.de}$ con$_{b4a.de}$ kali-c$_{b4a.de}$ merc$_{b4a.de}$ sulph$_{b4a.de}$
· **right** side: agath-a↓
: **stitching** pain: agath-a$_{nl2\bullet}$
- **Pubic** bones: ...
· **stitching** pain: agath-a$_{nl2\bullet}$
- **Pubis**:

○ · **Symphysis**; pubic | **pregnancy** agg.; during: calc-p$_{mrr1}$

- **Pudendum**: carb-v↓
· **burning**: carb-v$_{tl1}$
· **menses**; before: calc↓ sep↓
: **burning**: calc$_{b4.de}$ sep$_{b4a.de}$
· **urinating**; even when not: ambr↓ carb-v↓ falco-pe↓
: **sore**: ambr carb-v$_{tl1}$ falco-pe$_{nl2\bullet}$
· **urination** agg.; during: thuj$_{bg2}$
· **urine**; from: caust↓ scop↓
: **burning**: caust$_{ptk1}$ scop$_{ptk1}$
- **Uterus**: *(↗ABDOMEN - Pain)* abies-c↓ absin *Acon Aesc*↓ *Agar*↓ agath-a↓ alet$_{c2}$ all-c aloe↓ am-c↓ anac↓ anan androc↓ ant-c *Apis*↓ aq-mar↓ *Aran*↓ arg-met↓ *Arg-n*↓ arge-pl↓ *Arist-cl*$_{sp1}$ arn ars *Ars-i*↓ asaf$_{k2}$ asc-c$_{c2}$ aster *Aur* aur-ar$_{k2}$ aur-i$_{k2}$ aur-m-n↓ aur-s$_{k2}$ bar-m **Bell**$_{k*}$ bell-p$_{sp1}$ bell-p-sp↓ bit-ar$_{wht1\bullet}$ borx↓ bov↓ *Bry* bufo cact calad *Calc* calc-ar↓ calc-i$_{k2}$ *Calc-p* calc-s calc-sil$_{k2}$ cann-i↓ *Canth*↓ carb-an *Carb-v*↓ carbn-s *Caul Caust Cham*$_{k*}$ chelin↓ chin chinin-s↓ *Cimic* cinnm cit-ac↓ *Cocc Coff* coloc$_{bg2*}$ *Con* conv↓ cop↓ croc crot-c cub$_{c1}$ cupr↓ cupr-ar↓ cur cypra-eg↓ *Dios*↓ dream-p↓ elaps↓ falco-pe$_{nl2\bullet}$ *Ferr* ferr-ar ferr-i↓ ferr-p fl-ac frax↓ galla-q-r↓ *Gels Goss*↓ graph ham$_{k2}$ hed$_{sp1}$ hedeo↓ helo↓ helon$_{ptk1}$ *Hep*↓ heroin↓ hura↓ *Hydr*↓ hydrog$_{srj2\bullet}$ hyos ign$_{k*}$ inul↓ iod↓ ip↓ iris kali-ar *Kali-c* kali-i↓ kali-p kola$_{stb3\bullet}$ kreos *Lac-c* lac-d↓ **Lach**$_{k*}$ lap-a↓ lappa↓ led$_{k2}$ *Lil-t* lob$_{mrr1}$ *Lyc* lyss mag-m$_{k*}$ *Mag-p*↓ med↓ *Mel-c-s*↓ *Meli*↓ merc merc-c mosch *Murx*$_{k*}$ nabal↓ nat-ar *Nat-c Nat-m* nicotam↓ *Nit-ac*↓ nux-m↓ **Nux-v**$_{k*}$ onos op pall↓ ped↓ phos↓ pip-n↓ plac$_{rzf5\bullet}$ *Plat*$_{k*}$ plb↓ **Podo**$_{k*}$ polyg-h↓ positr$_{nl2\bullet}$ **Puls**$_{k*}$ puls-n$_{c2}$ ran-b↓ raph↓ rhod↓ *Rhus-t* rob ruta$_{fd4.de}$ *Sabin*$_{k*}$ sal-fr↓ sanic↓ *Sec* senec↓ *Sep* sil↓ spira↓ spong$_{fd4.de}$ *Stann*↓ staph↓ stram↓ stry↓ sul-ac↓ sulph symph$_{fd3.de\bullet}$ syph$_{k2}$ tarent *Ter* tere-la↓ *Thlas*↓ thuj↓ thyr↓ til↓ tril-p↓ tritic-vg$_{fd5.de}$ tub$_{al}$ ulm-c$_{jsj8\bullet}$ ust valer↓ verat-v *Vib*↓ visc↓ xan↓ zinc$_{k2}$ [spect$_{dfg1}$]
· **right** side:
: **extending** to:
: **Mammae**:
. **left**: murx↓
neuralgic: murx$_{bro1}$
· **left**: ulm-c↓
: **sore**: ulm-c$_{jsj8\bullet}$
· **side** to side; from: **Cimic**↓
: **stitching** pain: **Cimic**
· **morning**: bufo *Calc-p*$_{k*}$ puls ruta$_{fd4.de}$
: **aching**: *Calc-p*$_{k*}$
: **pressing** pain: puls
· **afternoon**: sabal$_{c1}$
· **evening**: cact$_{k*}$ pall$_{k*}$ ruta$_{fd4.de}$ symph$_{fd3.de\bullet}$
· **night**: kali-p ruta$_{fd4.de}$
: **23** h: *Cact*
: **midnight** | **before**:
. **23** h: *Cact*↓
cramping: *Cact*
: **after**: *Calad*
. **cramping**: *Calad*
: **menses**; before: *Calc*
· **abdomen**, beginning with coldness in: aur-m-n↓
: **cramping**: aur-m-n$_{vml3\bullet}$
· **accompanied** by:
: **Back**; pain in: bell-p$_{sp1}$
: **Lumbar** region; pain in: des-ac$_{rbp6}$
: **Stomach**; cramping pain in (See STOMACH - Pain - cramping - accompanied - uterine)
· **aching**: arge-pl$_{rwt5\bullet}$ bell$_{bg1}$ *Calc-p*$_{k*}$ calc-sil$_{k2}$ *Con* ferr$_{bg1}$ lach$_{bg1}$ merc$_{k*}$ sal-fr$_{sle1\bullet}$ senec$_{bg1}$ sep spira$_{a1}$ tarent$_{a1}$ ust
· **air** agg.; draft of cold: nux-v$_{k2}$

Female

- **alternating** with:
  - **concentration**; difficult (See MIND - Concentration - difficult - alternating - uterus)
  - **Heart**; pain in (See CHEST - Pain - heart - alternating - uterus)
- **anger**; after: **Cham**
  - **cramping**: **Cham**
- **bathing**; after: crot-c
- **bending**:
  - **agg.**: nept-m lsd2.fr positr nl2•
  - **legs** | **amel.**: lob mrr1
- **bending** double:
  - **amel.**: *Acon Cimic Coloc Nux-v* puls k2
  - **must** bend double: cimic bro1
- **boring** pain: merc k*
- **breath**; at every: **Cocc** ↓
  - **cutting** pain: **Cocc**
- **burning**: acon bro1 anan k* *Arg-n Ars* k* ars-i k2 *Bell* k* *Bry* k* bufo k* calc-ar k2* *Calc-p* calc-sil k2 *Canth* bro1 carb-an k* *Carb-v* k* *Con* k* conv bg cur k* *Hep* k* *Kreos* k* lac-c *Lach* k* lap-a k* *Lyc* murx bro1 *Nux-v* k* pall bro1 pip-n ran-b raph rhod k* *Sec* k* sep k* sul-ac h2* sulph tl1 tarent k* ter k* thuj til bg xan bro1
  - **alternating** with | **Extremities**; pain in: rhod ptk1
- **bursting** pain | **something** hard bursts; as if: elaps k*
- **clothing** agg.; contact of: **Lach** ↓ lil-t ↓
  - **sore**: **Lach** lil-t
- **coition**:
  - **after**: nept-m lsd2.fr *Plat*
    - **drawing** pain: *Plat* k*
  - **during**: *Ferr-p Hep* kreos ↓ merc-c k* nat-p fkr6.de nux-v ↓ **Puls** ↓ sep ↓ syph al*
    - **aching**: merc-c k*
    - **cramping**: nux-v mrr1
    - **cutting** pain: puls
    - **sore**: kreos a1 **Puls** k* sep
- **cold**:
  - **air** agg.: nux-v k2
  - **washing** agg.: crot-c ↓
    - **cutting** pain: crot-c k*
    - **lancinating**: crot-c k*
- **constricting**, contracting pain: **Bell** *Bell-p* bro1 cact k* cham bro1 chin bro1 chinin-s cocc *Gels* bro1 lil-t lyc *Mag-p* bro1 nux-v bro1 plb polyg-h bro1 *Puls* sabin sep k* staph tarent ust bro1
  - **accompanied** by | **metrorrhagia**; clotted (See Metrorrhagia - coagulated - expelled - accompanied - constricting)
- **cough** agg.; during: kola stb3• thlas bg1
- **cramping**: agar k* agath-a nl2• aloe anan k* apis bro1 arg-met bro1 arge-pl rwt5• ars bg2 aur-m-n vml3• *Bell* k* bry k* bufo k* *Cact Calad* k* calc bro1 *Calc-p* cann-i k2* **Caul** k* caust k* **Cham** k* chelin br1 chin cimic bg2* cit-ac rly4• *Cocc* k* coff b7.de* *Coloc* bro1* *Con* k* cop cupr b7.de* cypra-eg sde6.de• dios bro1 ferr bg2* ferr-i bro1 *Gels* k* *Goss* bro1 hedeo bro1 *Hyos* k* *Ign* k* inul bro1 ip bg2* kali-c kreos bg2 *Lach* bro1 lyc k* *Mag-m* k* mag-p bro1 mosch b7.de* nat-m k* nicotam rly4• nux-m b7.de* **Nux-v** k* onos k* op bro1 phos bg2 pip-n c2 *Plat* k* *Puls* k* rhus-t b7.de* rob k* **Sabin** k* sec bg2* *Sep* k* sil bro1 *Stann* bg2 staph bg2 stram bg2 sul-ac b4a.de* sulph bg2 *Tarent* k* tere-la rly4• thlas bro1 thuj bg2 til bro1 tritic-vg fd5.de tub c1 **Ust** k* valer bg2 *Vib* k* xan bro1 zinc b4a.de*
  - **accompanied** by:
    - **metrorrhagia** (See Metrorrhagia - accompanied - uterus - pain - cramping)
    - **rheumatic** complaints (See GENERALS - Pain - rheumatic - accompanied - uterus)
  - **followed** by | **leukorrhea**: *Con Mag-m*
- **cutting** pain: asaf bell bg2* bufo *Calc* k* *Calc-p* k* **Cocc** k* con k* crot-c k* cur dream-p sdj1• ign k* ip ptk1 *Lac-c Meli* a1* *Murx* k* pall k* **Puls** k* sep k* sulph bg1* tarent k* thuj k*
  - **upward**: lac-c
- **delivery**; after: cimic ↓ rhod ↓ til ↓
  - **burning**: rhod k*
  - **cramping**: cimic mrr1
  - **sore**: til c1
  - **stitching** pain: cimic mrr1
- **digging** pain: bufo cur k*
- **double** up; compelling her to: *Cact* ↓ *Cimic* ↓ **Nux-v** ↓
  - **cramping**: *Cact Cimic* **Nux-v**
- **drawing** pain: **Aur** hr1 **Bell** calc-p k* *Cham* k* cop k* goss hr1 lac-d c1 plat k* plb k* *Puls* k* ruta fd4.de sabin k* tritic-vg fd5.de
- **eating**; after: *Caust*
- **exertion** agg.; after: pall k*
- **flow** of blood amel.: arg-n bell cimic tl1 kali-c **Lach** mosch sep sulph ust *Vib* zinc k2
- **gnawing** pain: anan k* thyr bg1*
- **gradually**, comes and goes: *Plat* stann
- **grasping** pain: agath-a nl2•
- **griping** pain: androc srj1• bufo bg2 cham k* con k* nux-v bg2 sal-fr sle1•
- **jar** agg.: *Arg-met* ↓ **Bell** *Lach* lappa ↓ *Lil-t*
  - **sore**: *Arg-met* **Bell** *Lach* lappa **Lil-t**
- **jerking**: aster ptk1
- **lancinating**: acon bro1 *Agar* bro1 anan apis bro1 *Aran* bro1 *Ars* k* *Bell* bro1 bry bro1 bufo k* calc bro1 chin bro1 *Cimic* bro1 *Coloc* bro1 *Con* k* crot-c k* cupr-ar bro1 *Dios* bro1 dream-p sdj1• ferr bro1 graph k* hura ign k* kali-p bro1 lac-c k* lach bro1 *Lil-t* bro1 mag-m bro1 *Mag-p* bro1 merc bro1 murx k* op bro1 ped a1 *Plat* bro1 puls bro1 sec bro1 sep k* tarent k* *Vib* bro1 visc bro1
  - **upward**: lac-c sep
- **leukorrhea** agg.: ambr ↓ sep ↓
  - **stitching** pain: ambr b7.de* sep b4.de*
- **lying** | **back**; on | **amel.**: *Onos*
  - **side**; on | **left** | **amel.**: lob mrr1
    - **right** | **amel.**: sep
- **lying** down agg.: *Ambr* dream-p sdj1• *Ferr*
- **maddening** pain: acon *Bell Cact* cimic *Plat*
- **menopause**; during: agar bro1 *Cimic* bro1 cocc bro1 lach bro1 puls bro1 *Sep* bro1
- **menses**:
  - **after**:
    - **agg.**: bov ↓ canth ↓ chin ↓ *Cocc* ↓ iod ↓ *Kreos* ↓ lac-lup hrn2• plat ↓ puls ↓ tarent ↓
      - **burning**: canth *Kreos*
      - **cramping**: chin b7a.de *Cocc* iod kreos b7a.de plat puls
      - **sore**: bov kreos
      - **stitching** pain: tarent k*
  - **before**:
    - **agg.**: alum apis k2 *Arund* k* *Bell* k* borx ↓ bov ↓ bry bufo cact ↓ **Calc Calc-p** carb-an ↓ **Caul** k* *Caust Cham* coloc con ↓ cur ↓ jug-r ↓ **Kali-c** k* *Lach Lyc* mag-c ↓ *Mag-p* mosch murx ↓ nat-c ↓ nat-m nicotam ↓ *Nux-v Phos* positr nl2• **Puls** pyrid ↓ sec **Sep** *Sil* thymol ↓ ust *Vib Zinc*
      - **burning**: bufo carb-an con cur *Nat-m*
      - **cramping**: cact k2 **Calc-p** *Caust* **Cham** *Mag-p* nicotam rly4• pyrid rly4• thymol sp1 *Vib* k*
      - **cutting** pain: caust mag-c murx nat-c
      - **drawing** pain: jug-r thymol sp1
      - **pinching** pain: *Alum* bry
      - **pressing** pain: jug-r
      - **sore**: bov
      - **stitching** pain: borx
      - **tearing** pain: nat-m
  - **between**: cocc sf1.de ham sf1.de **Sep** kl

- **menses**: ...
  - **during**:
    - **agg.**: *(↗Menses - painful)* *Acon* *Agar* agn alum *Am-c* apis k2 arg-n↓ arge-pl rwt5• *Arist-cl* sp1 arn↓ *Ars*↓ ars-met art-v↓ *Asaf*↓ bamb-a stb2.de• **Bell** bov↓ brom↓ *Bry*↓ **Cact** **Calc** *Calc-p* calc-s canth↓ carb-v↓ carc↓ carneg-g↓ caul k* *Caust*↓ cench↓ *Cham* chin↓ *Cimic* *Cinnb*↓ cit-ac↓ *Cocc* *Coff*↓ *Coloc*↓ *Con*↓ cupr oss• der↓ dream-p↓ ferr k2 form↓ *Gels* **Graph**↓ *Ham* helon↓ hydrog↓ *Ign* *Kali-c* kali-i↓ kali-s *Kreos* *Lac-c* k* *Lach* k* led k2 *Lil-t* luna↓ *Lyc* *Mag-m* *Mag-p*↓ merc k2 mill↓ moni↓ murx↓ nat-c↓ *Nat-m*↓ nept-m lsd2.fr *Nit-ac*↓ *Nux-m*↓ **Nux-v** *Ol-an*↓ onos↓ op ptk ph-ac↓ phos↓ phyt *Plat* podo↓ positr nl2• pseuts-m↓ **Puls** pyrid↓ rhus-t↓ ruta↓ sars *Sec*↓ senec↓ sep k* sil↓ *Stann* staph↓ *Sulph* k* symph fd3.de• syph al *Tarent* thymol↓ tritic-vg fd5.de *Tub* *Ust* *Vib*↓ xan xanth zinc↓
      - **burning**: ars bry *Calc-p* canth carb-v caust merc nat-m nux-v ph-ac phos rhus-t sep k* sulph tarent
      - **constricting**, contracting pain: *Agar* *Bell* **Cact** k* staph
      - **cramping**: acon art-v ptk2 *Bell* brom hr1 **Cact** *Calc* hr1 *Calc-p* carc sst• carneg-g rwt1• *Caust* cench k2 **Cham** *Cimic* *Cinnb* hr1 cit-ac rly4• **Cocc** k* *Coff* k* *Coloc* k* *Con* *Cupr* hr1 der dream-p sdj1• ferr hr1 form hr1 *Gels* hr1 **Graph** hydrog srj2• *Ign* k* *Kali-c* kali-i *Lach* k* luna kg1• *Mag-p* mill k2 moni rfm1• *Nat-m* hr1 *Nit-ac* k* **Nux-v** onos *Plat* pseuts-m oss1• *Puls* pyrid rly4• sec sep k* stann thymol sp1 tritic-vg fd5.de *Tub* *Vib* hr1
      - **cry** out, compels her to: *Acon* *Cact* calc-p k2 *Cham* coff *Coloc* cupr *Mag-m* nux-m *Nux-v* **Puls** senec xan xanth
      - **cutting** pain: apis *Ars* hr1 *Asaf* bell k* *Calc* k* calc-p hr1 canth k* carb-v k* *Caust* k* **Cocc** k* *Coloc* k* ferr k* helon hr1 ign *Kali-c* k* kreos lach *Lil-t* hr1 merc k* murx nat-c k* nat-m *Ol-an* hr1 phos rhus-t k* sec k* senec hr1 sep k* sil k* zinc
      - **digging** pain: *Nux-v*
      - **drawing** pain: thymol sp1
      - **sore**: am-c arg-n arn bov *Bry* canth carb-v *Caust* *Cocc* coff *Con* *Ham* ign kreos nat-m *Nux-m* k* nux-v ruta sil
      - **squeezed**; as if: kali-i ptk1
      - **tearing** pain: *Agar* *Am-c* ars *Bell* calc *Caust* k* chin *Cinnb* hr1 **Lach** hr1 lyc merc nat-c nit-ac podo *Puls* rhus-t *Sec* hr1 *Sep* sil staph sulph zinc
      - **unbearable**: **Op** gm1
        - **accompanied** by:
          - **stool** | **urging** to: op br
    - **amel.**: bell calc-p k2 *Lach* mosch sep sulph *Zinc*
      - **cramping**: calc-p k2
    - **beginning** of menses | **agg.**: *(↗Menses - painful - beginning)* *Calc* *Calc-p* *Caust* dream-p sdj1• graph *Kali-c* *Lach* **Lap-a** lyc spong fd4.de tub br1 *Vib*
  - **should** appear but they do not; when menses: *Cocc*↓ *Kali-c*↓
    - **cramping**: *Cocc* *Kali-c*
  - **suppressed** menses; from: *Cocc* *Kali-c* **Puls**
  - **without**: kali-c↓
    - **cramping**: kali-c ptk1
- **metrorrhagia**, during | **cramping** (See Metrorrhagia - accompanied - uterus - pain - cramping)
- **mortification**; from: *Cocc*
  - **cramping**: *Cocc*
- **motion** agg.: arg-met sne **Bell** **Bry** *Cimic* **Cocc** con kali-c bro1 lil-t pall c1 sabal c1
  - **cramping**: **Cocc**
  - **cutting** pain: **Cocc** k*
  - **sore**: **Bell** **Bry**
- **nervous** persons; in | **cramping** (See MIND - Excitement - nervous - uterus)
- **nursing** the child agg.; when: *Arn* *Cham* puls **Sec** kr1 **Sil**
  - **cramping**: cham k2
  - **sharp**: **Sil** k*
- **ovulation**; during: ulm-c↓
  - **sore**: ulm-c jsj8•
- **palpitation** in heart; with sympathetic | **sore** (See CHEST - Palpitation - accompanied - uterus - pain)
- **paroxysmal**: asaf **Bell** *Caul* caust **Cham** *Cimic* coloc con ign lac-c mag-m nux-m *Nux-v* **Plat** **Puls** **Sabin** *Sec* sep sulph *Vib*
- **periodically**, same time each day: cact
- **pessary**; from: nux-m c1
- **pinching** pain: anan k* bell bry cact canth *Cham* k* con k*
- **pregnancy** agg.; during: aesc k2 arn k2 *Bell-p*↓ bry *Cupr-ar*↓ gels c1 ham↓ kali-p lyss k* plat puls↓ *Sil*↓
  - **cramping**: bry c1 *Cupr-ar* plat hr1
  - **sore**: arn k2 *Bell-p* ham bro1 puls k* *Sil*
- **pressing** pain: *(↗bearing)* *Acon* aloe k2 anac anan *Ant-c* **Bell** k* cact calad calc calc-p canth caul bg2 cham chin *Cocc* ferr-i bg2 frax bg2 *Gels* kreos bg2 *Lil-t* k* murx bg2 *Nat-c* nat-m bg2 *Nit-ac* nux-v pall bg2 *Plat* k* podo *Puls* sabin bg2 sal-fr sle1• *Sec* *Sep* k* stann bg2 tarent ust
- **pressure**:
  - **agg.**: abies-c↓ caul hr1 sep tl1 tarent k2
    - **sore**: abies-c c1
  - **amel.**: abies-c br1 ign lil-t *Mag-p* nux-v k2 *Pall* tl1 sep
  - **back**; on | **amel.**: *Mag-m*
- **pulsating** pain: *Aesc* bro1 ars *Bell* k* *Cact* k* cur *Hep* k* murx k* nabal a1 *Sep*
- **reaching** up with the hands agg.: *Graph* k* *Rhus-t*↓
  - **cramping**: *Rhus-t*
- **rheumatic**: *Bry*
- **rhythmic**: ozone↓
  - **cramping**: ozone sde2•
- **riding**:
  - **agg.**: *Arg-n*↓
    - **stitching** pain: *Arg-n* k*
  - **carriage**; in a:
    - **agg.**: *Arg-met*↓
      - **sore**: *Arg-met* k*
- **sharp**: **Acon** k* androc srj1• apis aq-mar rbp6 *Con* k* syph al
- **sitting** for a long time agg.: *Bufo*
- **sneezing**; when: kola stb3•
- **sore**: abies-c bro1 acon bro1 *Aesc* k* am-c ant-c *Apis* k* arg-met k* arg-n **Arn** k* *Ars-i* **Aur** k* **Bell** k* bell-p bg1* bov **Bry** k* *Bufo* *Calc* k* calc-p k* canth caul k* cham chin *Cimic* k* *Cocc* *Con* k* conv bg2* ferr bg2 *Gels* ptk1 ham k13* helo bg2 *Helon* k* *Hydr* kali-c kreos k* *Lac-c* k* **Lach** k* lappa k* *Lil-t* k* lyss k* mag-m bro1 med hr1 *Mel-c-s* bro1 merc bg1* **Murx** k* nat-m k2 nux-m k* nux-v k* *Onos* plat bro1 podo k2 *Puls* rhus-t k* ruta fd4.de sanic c2* sec k* sep k* tarent *Thlas* bro1 til bg2* tril-p ust ptk1 **Verat-v** k* [bell-p-sp dcm1 heroin sdj2]
- **squeezed**; as if: bell-p ptk1 gels hr1* kali-i ptk1 sep sne tarent a1
- **standing** agg.: lappa↓
  - **sore**: lappa
- **stinging**: *Apis* arg-met ars *Calc* k* caul hr1 *Con* k* lap-a hr1* sabin
- **stitching** pain: **Acon** k* agath-a nl2• anan k* *Apis* *Arg-n* k* ars aur k* **Bell** k* borx k* bufo k* calc k* cimic bg2* **Con** k* cur k* dream-p sdj1• *Ferr* k* fl-ac k* gels k* graph hura ign inul k* *Kali-c* k* kali-p kola stb3• *Lac-c* lap-a hr1* *Lil-t* lyss k* *Merc* k* *Murx* nux-v phos k* plac rzf5• plat k* **Sep** k* syph k2 tarent k*
  - **accompanied** by | **Mammae**; cancer in (See CHEST - Cancer - mammae - accompanied - uterus)
  - **upward**: **Lac-c** murx k* *Sep*
- **stool**:
  - **after**:
    - **agg.**: lyc
      - **cramping**: lyc k*
    - **amel.**: pall↓
      - **cutting** pain: pall k*
  - **during**:
    - **agg.**: *Arg-n* hr1 calc-p carb-v
      - **pressing** pain: *Carb-v* k*
  - **urging** to | **during**: nux-v k2 op br

Female

- **suddenly**, comes and goes: **Bell** vib
- **talking**, agg.: bell$_{k2}$
- **tearing** pain: *Arg-n* calc-sil$_{k2}$ *Cham*$_{k*}$ con$_{k2}$ galla-q-r$_{nl2•}$ lap-a lyss$_{k*}$ nat-m plb$_{k*}$ stry$_{k*}$ tarent$_{k*}$
- **touch**:
  - **agg.**: aur-s$_{c1}$ bell$_{k2}$ ign↓ lil-t$_{tl1}$
    - **lancinating**: ign
  - **clothes** agg.; of: led$_{k2}$ lil-t podo$_{k2}$
- **touching** genitals agg.: *Ign*↓
  - **cramping**: *Ign*$_{k*}$
- **urination** | **during**:
  - **agg.**: con↓ ph-ac↓
    - **cutting** pain: con$_{b4.de*}$
    - **pressing** pain: con$_{b4.de*}$ ph-ac$_{b4.de*}$
  - **urging** to urinate: con tarent
- **walking** agg.: *Arg-n*↓ **Bell Bry** bufo med tarent↓
  - **cramping**: tarent
  - **stitching** pain: *Arg-n*$_{k*}$ **Bell**
- **wandering** pain: arn bell cop$_{hr1}$ lach nux-m **Puls** rhus-t sulph
- **warmth**:
  - **amel.**: caust↓ nux-m↓ nux-v↓ pyrid↓
    - **cramping**: caust nux-m nux-v pyrid$_{rly4•}$
    - **heat** amel.: cham$_{k2}$
- **warmth** amel. (See ABDOMEN - Pain - warmth - amel.)
- **weather** agg.; cold wet: *Calc-p*
  - **cramping**: *Calc-p*
- **wedge**-like: iod$_{bro1}$
- ▽ **extending** to:
  - **Abdomen**; across: cimic$_{bro1}$
  - **Back**: agar↓ aq-mar$_{rbp6}$ arge-pl$_{rwt5•}$ *Bell* carb-ac↓ cham↓ *Cimic*↓ *Gels*$_{k*}$ goss↓ graph hedeo↓ *Helon*↓ inul↓ *Kali-c*↓ kreos↓ nat-m↓ onos↓ senec$_{vml3•}$ tril-p↓ vesp↓ vib↓
    - **cramping**: gels
    - **pressing** pain: agar$_{bro1}$ *Bell*$_{bro1}$ carb-ac$_{bro1}$ cham$_{bro1}$ *Cimic*$_{bro1}$ *Gels*$_{bro1}$ goss$_{bro1}$ hedeo$_{bro1}$ *Helon*$_{bro1}$ inul$_{bro1}$ *Kali-c*$_{bro1}$ kreos$_{bro1}$ nat-m$_{bro1}$ onos$_{bro1}$ tril-p$_{bro1}$ vesp$_{bro1}$ vib$_{bro1}$
    - **stitching** pain: *Gels*
  - **Body**, whole: nux-v$_{k2}$
  - **Chest**: *Lach Murx*$_{k*}$ vesp↓
    - **right** side of: con↓
      - **stitching** pain: con
    - **neuralgic**: lach$_{bro1}$ murx$_{bro1}$ vesp$_{bro1}$
  - **Coccyx** and toes: sec
  - **Diagonally** upward: *Murx*
  - **Downward**: aesc *Apis* ars *Cact* calc calc-p con *Graph* ham hydrog$_{srj2•}$ ip kali-i *Kreos* lac-c mag-m nat-m nit-ac nux-v sec *Sep* ust$_{k*}$
  - **Epigastrium**: iris$_{bg1}$
  - **Feet**: caul$_{mrr1}$
  - **Groin**; back to: **Sabin**
  - **Hip** to hip: *Bell*↓ calc↓ chin↓ *Cimic*↓ *Coloc*↓ pall↓
    - **neuralgic**: *Bell*$_{bro1}$ calc$_{bro1}$ chin$_{bro1}$ *Cimic*$_{bro1}$ *Coloc*$_{bro1}$ pall$_{bro1}$
  - **Hips**: haliae-lc↓
    - **stitching** pain: haliae-lc$_{srj5•}$
  - **Kidneys**: anan↓
    - **burning**: anan$_{k*}$
  - **Knees**: haliae-lc↓
    - **stitching** pain: haliae-lc$_{srj5•}$
  - **Labia**: lyss
  - **Legs**: bufo↓
    - **stitching** pain: bufo$_{k2}$
    - **tearing** pain: bufo$_{k2}$
  - **Mammae**: lyss murx$_{k*}$
    - **left**: murx
    - **Side** of abdomen; and right: lyss

- **Uterus** – **extending** to: ...
  - **Pelvis**: *Cimic*↓
    - **cramping**: *Cimic*$_{mrr1}$
    - **stitching** pain: cimic$_{mrr1}$
  - **Pelvis**; through: bell$_{bro1}$
  - **Pit** of stomach: *Raph*↓
    - **burning**: *Raph*
  - **Rectum**: arge-pl$_{rwt5•}$
  - **Sacrum**: calc-p
    - **cutting** pain: **Calc-p**
  - **Side**; from side to: cimic$_{k2}$
  - **Stomach**: cact elaps ran-b raph
    - **cramping**: *Cact*
  - **Thighs**: carb-an↓ cimic↓ haliae-lc↓
    - **burning**: carb-an
    - **stitching** pain: cimic$_{mrr1}$ haliae-lc$_{srj5•}$
  - **Thighs**; down: apis ars bufo cact *Calc* caul$_{mrr1}$ cham$_{mrr1}$ cimic$_{mrr1}$ con des-ac$_{rbp6}$ graph ham *Kali-c* kali-i kreos *Lac-c* mag-m nat-m nit-ac nux-v ust$_{k*}$ *Vib*$_{mrr1}$ xan$_{mrr1}$
    - **cramping**: *Cimic*$_{mrr1}$ *Kali-i Mag-m*
    - **reading** or writing, when: nat-m
  - **Umbilicus**: nux-v$_{bg1}$ sep
  - **Upward**: lac-c$_{mrr1}$ **Lach** lyc lyss *Murx*$_{k*}$ phos *Sep*
    - **Side** of abdomen; to right: lyss
- ○ **Cervix**: arg-met↓ carb-an↓ caul↓ con↓ *Kreos*↓ musca-d↓ sep↓
  - **burning**: arg-met$_{k2}$ carb-an$_{k2}$ con$_{k*}$ *Kreos* sep
    - **coals**; like burning: carb-an$_{mrr1}$
  - **sharp**: musca-d$_{szs1}$
  - **stinging**: arg-met$_{k2}$
  - **stitching** pain: caul$_{c1*}$
  - **ulcerative** pain: kreos$_{bg2}$
- **Ligaments**; broad: **Cimic**↓
  - **cramping**: **Cimic**
- **Middle** of uterus | **Spot**; in a: plac$_{rzf5•}$
- **Os** uteri: puls↓
  - **cutting** pain: puls$_{bg2}$
- **Ovary** and right hip; against right: ang↓
  - **pulsating** pain: ang$_{c1}$

- **Uterus** and region: aesc↓ **Agar**↓ alet↓ aloe↓ alum↓ alumn↓ *Ant-c*↓ *Ant-t*↓ *Apis*↓ arg-met↓ asaf↓ asc-c↓ asc-t↓ aster↓ aur↓ aur-m-n↓ aur-s↓ **Bell**↓ borx↓ bov↓ bry↓ *Calc*↓ calc-f↓ calc-o-t↓ calc-p↓ calc-s↓ calen↓ canth↓ carb-ac↓ *Carb-an*↓ carb-v↓ **Cham**↓ *Chin*↓ *Cimic*↓ cinnm↓ cocc↓ *Coll*↓ *Con*↓ cop↓ croc↓ crot-h↓ cur↓ der↓ des-ac↓ elaps↓ *Ferr*↓ ferr-br↓ *Ferr-i*↓ ferr-p↓ *Frax*↓ glyc↓ gnaph↓ goss↓ *Graph*↓ helio↓ helon↓ ign↓ inul↓ *Iod*↓ ip↓ irid-met↓ kali-bi↓ kali-c↓ *Kali-fcy*↓ kali-s↓ **Kreos**↓ *Lac-c*↓ lappa↓ **Lil-t**↓ lob↓ lyc↓ lyss↓ mag-c↓ mag-m↓ *Mang*↓ *Merc*↓ mosch↓ mur-ac↓ **Murx**↓ *Nat-c*↓ **Nat-hchls**↓ **Nat-m**↓ *Nit-ac*↓ *Nux-v*↓ onos↓ *Pall*↓ pieri-b↓ **Plat**↓ plb↓ *Podo*↓ polyg-h↓ *Puls*↓ rhus-t↓ **Sabin**↓ sal-fr↓ *Sanic*↓ **Sec**↓ **Sep**↓ *Sil*↓ **Stann**↓ *Sulph*↓ tarent↓ thuj↓ *Til*↓ tril-p↓ tritic-vg↓ ust↓ vib↓ wye↓ *Xan*↓ xero↓ zinc↓ zinc-val↓
  - **morning**: **Bell**↓ **Nat-m**↓ *Nux-v*↓ **Sep**↓
    - **bearing** down: **Bell Nat-m** *Nux-v* **Sep**
  - **forenoon**: sep↓
    - **bearing** down: sep
  - **afternoon**: mag-m↓ **Sep**↓
    - **bearing** down: mag-m **Sep**
  - **night** | **midnight**:
    - **after**: *Bov*↓
      - **bearing** down: *Bov*
    - **bed** agg.; in: **Sulph**↓ urol-h↓
      - **bearing** down: **Sulph** urol-h$_{rwt•}$
  - **ascending** stairs agg.: *Plat*↓
    - **bearing** down: *Plat*

- **bearing** down: (↗*Prolapsus - uterus*) aesc k2 **Agar** k* alet k* aloe k* alum alumn k2 *Ant-c* k* *Ant-t* *Apis* arg-met asaf asc-t aster vh aur aur-m-n bro1* aur-s k2 **Bell** k* borx bov bry *Calc* k* calc-f c1 calc-p calc-s k2 calen bro1 canth carb-ac bro1 *Carb-an* carb-v k2 **Cham** *Chin* k* *Cimic* k* cocc k* *Coll* bro1 *Con* k* cop croc cur der elaps *Ferr* ferr-br bro1 *Ferr-i* ferr-p k2 frax br1* glyc bro1 gnaph bro1 goss c2* *Graph* helon k* ign inul *Iod* ip kali-bi bro1 kali-c *Kali-fcy* kali-s *Kreos* *Lac-c* lappa bro1 **Lil-t** k* lob lyc lyss mag-c k* mag-m k* *Mang* *Merc* k* mosch mur-ac **Murx** k* *Nat-c* k* **Nat-hchls** k* **Nat-m** *Nit-ac* *Nux-v* k* onos *Pall* k* pieri-b mlk9.de **Plat** k* plb bro1 *Podo* k* polyg-h bro1 *Puls* rhus-t **Sabin** sal-fr sle1• **Sec** **Sep** k* *Sil* **Stann** *Sulph* k* tarent thuj *Til* c1* tril-p bro1 tritic-vg fd5.de ust vib c2 wye bro1 zinc zinc-val bro1
  - **come** out; as if everything would: *Agar* bro1 alum hr1 **Bell** k* calc k2 calc-o-t bro1 carb-v k2 cimic bro1 cinnm bro1 *Con* crot-h bro1 des-ac rbp6 ferr bro1 *Ferr-i* bro1 *Frax* bro1 goss bro1 helio bro1 irid-met srj5• kali-fcy bro1 **Kreos** k* *Lac-c* k* **Lil-t** k* lyc bro1 mosch bro1 murx bro1* *Nat-c* k* **Nat-hchls** k* *Nat-m* k* *Nit-ac* nux-v k2* onos bro1 pall bro1* *Plat* k* *Podo* k* puls k2* *Sanic* bro1 **Sep** k* *Stann* bro1 *Sulph* bro1 *Til* bro1 tril-p bro1 vib bro1 *Xan* bro1 xero bro1
  - **intermittent**: asc-c br1
- **cold** agg.: hyos↓
  - **bearing** down: hyos ptk1
- **cough** agg.; during: kola↓
  - **bearing** down: kola stb3•
- **crossing** limbs amel.: **Lil-t**↓ murx↓ **Sep**↓ zinc↓
  - **bearing** down: **Lil-t** k* murx k* **Sep** k* zinc
- **drinking** agg.; after: nux-v↓
  - **bearing** down: nux-v
- **eating**:
  - **amel.**: sep↓
    - **bearing** down: sep
- **jar** agg.: bell↓
  - **bearing** down: bell k2
- **lifting**; after: *Agar*↓
  - **bearing** down: *Agar*
- **lying**:
  - **agg.**: *Puls*↓
    - **bearing** down: *Puls*
  - **amel.**: *Agar*↓ cimic↓ onos↓ pall↓ puls↓ *Sep*↓
    - **bearing** down: *Agar* cimic onos pall puls tl1 *Sep*
  - **side**; on:
    - **left**:
      - **amel.**: pall↓
        - **bearing** down: pall
- **menses**:
  - **after**:
    - **agg.**: *Agar*↓ *Con*↓ pall↓ tarent↓
      - **bearing** down: *Agar* *Con* pall tarent
  - **before**:
    - **agg.**: alum↓ *Apis*↓ aur↓ *Bell*↓ bov↓ *Calc-p*↓ *Chin*↓ chinin-s↓ *Cina*↓ *Con*↓ croc↓ elaps↓ *Kali-c*↓ mosch↓ nux-m↓ *Phos*↓ *Plat*↓ rhus-t↓ sabad↓ sec↓ *Sep*↓ sul-ac↓ tarent↓ ust↓ *Vib*↓ zinc↓
      - **bearing** down: alum *Apis* aur *Bell* bov *Calc-p* *Chin* chinin-s *Cina* *Con* croc elaps *Kali-c* mosch nux-m *Phos* *Plat* rhus-t sabad sec *Sep* sul-ac tarent ust *Vib* zinc
  - **during**:
    - **agg.**: acon↓ *Agar*↓ alet↓ aloe↓ am-c↓ am-m↓ androc↓ ant-c↓ arg-n↓ *Asaf*↓ *Aur*↓ aur-s↓ **Bell**↓ berb↓ borx↓ bov↓ calc↓ *Calc-p*↓ caul↓ caust↓ *Cham*↓ *Chin*↓ chinin-s↓ *Cimic*↓ cina↓ *Con*↓ *Ferr*↓ *Gels*↓ graph↓ hyos↓ ign↓ *Kali-c*↓ kali-i↓ *Kali-p*↓ kreos↓ lac-h↓ *Lach*↓ **Lil-t**↓ lob↓ mag-c↓ mosch↓ murx↓ *Nat-c*↓ *Nat-m*↓ *Nit-ac*↓ nux-m↓ nux-v↓ pall↓ *Plat*↓ *Podo*↓ **Puls**↓ rhus-t↓ *Sec*↓ **Sep**↓ *Sulph*↓ thuj↓ tril-p↓ tritic-vg↓ tub↓ *Vib*↓ zinc↓
      - **bearing** down: acon *Agar* alet aloe am-c am-m androc srj1• ant-c arg-n *Asaf* *Aur* aur-s k2 **Bell** berb borx bov calc *Calc-p* caul caust *Cham* *Chin* chinin-s *Cimic* cina *Con* *Ferr* *Gels* graph hyos

- **Uterus** and region – **menses** – **during** – **agg.** – **bearing** down: ...
ign *Kali-c* kali-i *Kali-p* kreos lac-h htj1• *Lach* **Lil-t** k* lob mag-c mosch murx *Nat-c* *Nat-m* *Nit-ac* nux-m nux-v pall *Plat* *Podo* **Puls** rhus-t *Sec* **Sep** *Sulph* thuj tril-p c1 tritic-vg fd5.de tub k2 *Vib* zinc
  - **nursing**; when child is: ust↓
    - **bearing** down: ust ptk1
  - **perspiration**; with hot: til↓
    - **bearing** down: til ptk1
  - **pregnancy**:
    - **during**:
      - **agg.**: *Kali-c*↓
        - **bearing** down: *Kali-c*
          - **come** out; as if everything would: *Kali-c*
  - **pressing** on vulva amel.: *Bell*↓ **Lil-t**↓ **Murx**↓ sanic↓ **Sep**↓
    - **bearing** down: *Bell* **Lil-t** **Murx** sanic c1* **Sep**
  - **riding** in a carriage agg.: *Asaf*↓
    - **bearing** down: *Asaf*
  - **sitting**: *Ferr-i*↓
    - **bearing** down | **pushing** up; sensation as if something were: *Ferr-i*
    - **bent** forward:
      - **agg.**: *Bell*↓
        - **bearing** down: *Bell*
    - **erect**:
      - **amel.**: *Bell*↓
        - **bearing** down: *Bell*
  - **sneezing**; while: kola↓
    - **bearing** down: kola stb3•
  - **standing**:
    - **agg.**: carb-v↓ *Con*↓ lac-f↓ lil-t↓ *Murx*↓ nat-m↓ *Pall*↓ puls↓ rheum↓ rhus-t↓ **Sep**↓ sulph↓ tril-p↓
      - **bearing** down: carb-v k2 *Con* lac-f c1 lil-t mrr1 *Murx* nat-m *Pall* puls k2 rheum rhus-t **Sep** sulph k2 tril-p c1
    - **amel.**: *Bell*↓
      - **bearing** down: *Bell* k*
  - **stool**:
    - **before**: *Nat-c*↓ nit-ac↓
      - **bearing** down: nat-c nit-ac
        - **come** out; as if everything would: *Nat-c*
    - **during**:
      - **agg.**: arg-n↓ *Bell*↓ iod↓ *Lil-t*↓ *Podo*↓ *Stann*↓
        - **bearing** down: arg-n *Bell* iod *Lil-t* k* *Podo* *Stann*
          - **come** out; as if everything would: lil-t mrr1 *Podo*
    - **urging** to: *Con*↓ *Corn*↓ lil-t↓ **Nux-v**↓ plat↓
      - **bearing** down: *Con* *Corn* lil-t br1 **Nux-v** plat
  - **stooping** agg.: *Lyc*↓
    - **bearing** down: *Lyc*
  - **supports** abdomen with hands: *Bell*↓ fic-m↓ *Lil-t*↓ *Murx*↓ *Sep*↓
    - **bearing** down: *Bell* fic-m gya1 *Lil-t* *Murx* *Sep*
  - **urination**:
    - **urging** to urinate:
      - **with**: nux-v↓ *Pall*↓ **Sep**↓
        - **bearing** down: nux-v *Pall* **Sep**
  - **walking**:
    - **agg.**: alet↓ *Bell*↓ *Chin*↓ coff↓ *Con*↓ kreos↓ *Lil-t*↓ **Nat-hchls**↓ phos↓ *Plat*↓ puls↓ rhus-t↓ **Sep**↓ tril-p↓
      - **bearing** down: alet k2 *Bell* *Chin* coff *Con* kreos *Lil-t* **Nat-hchls** phos *Plat* puls k2 rhus-t **Sep** tril-p c1
    - **air**; in open:
      - **amel.**: *Puls*↓
        - **bearing** down: *Puls*

- **Vagina**: *Acon*↓ agath-a nl2• all-s↓ *Alum*↓ *Am-c*↓ *Ambr*↓ ant-c↓ anthraq↓ antip↓ *Apis*↓ arg-n k2 ars↓ aur↓ aur-m↓ aur-s↓ bell bell-p-sp↓ berb k* bov↓ brom↓ bufo↓ **Cact**↓ *Calc* k* calc-ar↓ *Calc-p* k* cann-s↓ cann-xyz↓ canth k* carb-an↓ carb-v↓ card-m cham k* *Chel*↓ chim↓ chin k*

Female

- **Vagina**: ...
cimic↓ cimx↓ cinnb↓ coc-c↓ *Coff*↓ coli↓ coloc c2 con↓ cop↓ elaps↓ falco-pe nl2• ferr k* *Ferr-i*↓ ferr-p↓ *Graph* k* ham helon↓ hura↓ *Hydrc*↓ *Ign*↓ *Kali-bi*↓ kali-br↓ *Kali-c* k* kali-p↓ kola stb3• *Kreos* lil-t k* *Lyc* k* **Lyss**↓ mag-p↓ merc k* merc-c a1 mur-ac↓ musca-d szs1 nat-c↓ *Nat-m*↓ nat-s↓ nit-ac bg2 nux-v olib-sac↓ *Petr*↓ phos bg2 *Plat*↓ plb↓ plb-xyz↓ podo↓ pop-cand↓ puls k* pulx↓ rhus-t k* ruta fd4.de *Sabin*↓ sal-fr↓ *Sec Sep Sil*↓ spira↓ spong fd4.de stann↓ *Staph* k* stry↓ sul-ac↓ sulph symph↓ tarent k2 thuj k* tritic-vg fd5.de *Ust*↓ vanil fd5.de
  - **left**: brass-n-o↓ rhus-g↓
    - **sharp**: brass-n-o srj5•
    - **stitching** pain: rhus-g tmo3•
  - **morning**: puls↓
    - **pressing** pain: puls
    - **waking**; on: *Sep*↓
      - **stitching** pain: *Sep*
  - **evening**: **Kreos**↓ rhus-t↓
    - **sore**: **Kreos** a1 rhus-t k*
  - **abdomen**, from: *Kreos*↓
    - **stitching** pain: *Kreos*
  - **aching**: **Calc** k* calc-p k* chin bg2* elaps k*
  - **biting** pain: cham k* *Graph* k* thuj k*
  - **burning**: *Acon* bro1 all-s alum bro1 antip bro1 ars k2 aur k* aur-m c2* aur-s k2 *Bell* k* **Berb** k* bov bro1 bufo calc k* calc-ar k2 *Calc-p* k* *Canth* k* carb-an k2* carb-v bro1 card-m *Cham* k* *Chel* k* coli jl2 cop k* falco-pe nl2• ferr-p bro1 *Graph* k* ham bg helon *Hydrc* bro1 *Kali-bi* k* kali-br alj kali-c bg* kali-p kola stb3• *Kreos* k* lyc k* lyss bro1 *Merc* k* *Merc-c* bro1 *Nat-m* k* **Nit-ac** k* olib-sac wmh1 *Petr* k* phos k2 pop-cand c1* *Puls* k* pulx br1* rhus-t bg sabin k* sal-fr sle1• sep k* spira k* spong fd4.de **Sulph** k* tarent ptk1 *Thuj* k* tritic-vg fd5.de vanil fd5.de
  - **coition**: (↗*Coition - painful)*
    - **after**: kola stb3• *Kreos*↓ lyc↓ lyss↓ rhus-v↓ sal-fr↓
      - **burning**: kola stb3• *Kreos* lyc k* lyss bro1* rhus-v a1 sal-fr sle1•
      - **hour**; at a fixed: chel↓
        - **burning**: chel ptk1
      - **sore**: kola stb3•
    - **during**: (↗*Coition - painful)* alumn apis kr1 **Arg-n** k* bell *Berb* k* borx bg calc sf *Calc-p* choc srj3• coff falco-pe nl2• *Ferr* k* *Ferr-m* *Ferr-p* k* ham *Hep* hydr ign *Kali-bi Kali-c* k* *Kreos* k* lyc kr1* **Lyss** *Naja*↓ **NAT-M** k ●* pieri-b mlk9.de *Plat* pneu↓ *Rhus-t* sabin sal-fr↓ **SEP** k ●* sil spira↓ *Staph Sulph* k* *Thuj* k*
      - **burning**: ferr c1 kali-bi *Kreos Lyc* k* nat-m pneu jl2 spira k* *Sulph* k*
      - **cutting** pain: *Berb* k* *Ferr-m*
      - **sore**: bell *Berb* coff falco-pe nl2• *Ferr* ferr-m k* ham k* hydr k2* ign k* *Kali-bi Kali-c* k* *Kreos* **Lyss** *Naja Plat Rhus-t* sal-fr sle1• *Sep Sulph* k* *Thuj*
      - **stitching** pain: *Berb*
    - **preventing**: coff↓ *Plat*↓ rhus-t↓ sep↓ *Thuj*↓
      - **sore**: coff *Plat* rhus-t k* sep *Thuj*
  - **constricting**, contracting pain: bell k2 **Cact** *Plat Puls*
  - **cramping**: bell bg berb bg2 cact bg2 coc-c bg2 ferr-p bg2 *Ham* c2* *Ign* bg2* kreos bg2 mag-p bg2 plat bg2 plb bg2 plb-xyz c2 sep bg2 *Sil* c2 staph bg2 thuj bg2
  - **cutting** pain: anthraq rly4• aur-s c1 sil ptk1
  - **drawing** pain: agath-a nl2• card-m k* cop k* tritic-vg fd5.de
  - **dryness**, from: ferr st lyc k2 *Nat-m* st sep st
  - **epistaxis**; after: calc-p k*
    - **aching**: calc-p k*
  - **gnawing** pain: lyc k*
  - **lancinating**: agath-a nl2• anthraq rly4• berb k* hura
  - **leukorrhea**:
    - **agg.**: aur-m-n vml3•
    - **before**: ambr↓
      - **stitching** pain: ambr c1
  - **lying** on left side agg.: merc↓
    - **burning**: merc k*
  - **menses**:
    - **after**:
      - **agg.**: berb↓ graph↓ kreos↓ lyc↓ *Sulph*↓
        - **burning**: berb graph kreos lyc *Sulph*
    - **before**:
      - **agg.**: alum↓ bell↓ berb bufo↓ con↓ elaps germ-met↓ *Ign*↓ nat-m↓ *Sulph*↓
        - **aching**: elaps
        - **bearing** down: germ-met srj5•
        - **burning**: bufo *Ign* k* nat-m k* *Sulph*
        - **pressing** pain: alum bell con
    - **during**:
      - **agg.**: agath-a↓ all-s↓ ant-c↓ *Ars-met Bell*↓ *Berb*↓ calc calc-p↓ *Con*↓ *Graph*↓ kali-c↓ kreos↓ *Lach*↓ *Lil-t*↓ *Nat-c*↓ *Nit-ac*↓ nux-v↓ plat↓ rhus-t↓ sabin↓ *Sep*↓ sul-ac↓ sulph↓ ust↓
        - **aching**: calc
        - **burning**: all-s berb calc-p k2 *Graph* nux-v sulph
        - **pressing** pain: ant-c *Bell* con *Lach Lil-t Nat-c Nit-ac* plat *Sep* ust
        - **rasping**: *Berb*
        - **raw**; as if: kali-c ptk1
        - **stitching** pain: agath-a nl2• bell berb k* *Con Graph* kreos rhus-t sabin sul-ac k*
  - **paroxysmal**: *Staph*
  - **periodical**:
    - **hour**; every day at the same: *Chel*↓
      - **burning**: *Chel*
  - **pregnancy** agg.; during: borx↓
    - **burning**: borx
  - **pressing** pain: alum ant-c k* *Bell* k* *Calc* k* calc-p a1 chim bro1 cinnb bro1 *Ferr-i* bro1 graph *Lil-t* k* lyc nat-c *Nit-ac Nux-v* k* podo *Sep* k* sil k* stann bro1 symph fd3.de• *Ust*
    - **accompanied** by | **leukorrhea**: cinnb ptk1
  - **pulsating** pain: alum bell bro1
  - **raw**; as if: nat-m bg2
  - **sitting**:
    - **agg.**: ferr-i↓ *Thuj*↓
      - **burning**: *Thuj* k*
      - **pressing** pain | **upward**: ferr-i ptk1
  - **sore**: acon agath-a nl2• alum aur **Berb** k* brom k* calc-p k* chim hr1 cimic bg2* coc-c *Coff* falco-pe nl2• ferr ptk1 ferr-i k* graph k* *Ham* k* ign k* *Kali-bi* k* kali-c k* **Kreos** k* **Lyss** k* merc k* nat-m bg2* nit-ac k* *Plat Puls Rhus-t* k* sep k* *Sil* staph *Sulph* k* tarent ptk1 thuj [bell-p-sp dcm1]
  - **standing** agg.: *Nit-ac*↓
    - **stitching** pain: *Nit-ac*
  - **stinging**: *Apis* bro1 berb cimic bro1 cimx bro1 coloc bro1 ham kreos bro1 puls *Rhus-t* bro1 sabin k* *Sep* bro1 staph
    - **accompanied** by | **leukorrhea**: calc tl1
  - **stitching** pain: agath-a nl2• *Alum* k* am-c *Ambr* k* ars k* aur bg2* *Bell* k* *Berb* k* cann-s a1 cann-xyz bg2 chin k* con k* cop a1 *Graph* k* hydrc k* *Kreos* k* lyss mur-ac k* nat-m k2 nat-s k* *Nit-ac* k* phos k* puls *Rhus-t* k* ruta fd4.de *Sabin* k* sal-fr sle1• *Sep* k* stry k* sul-ac bg2* tarent k* vanil fd5.de
    - **backward**: anthraq rly4•
    - **outward**: berb
    - **upward**: alum am-c berb ign k2 *Lyss Nit-ac Phos* sabin *Sep*
  - **stool** agg.; during: podo↓
    - **pressing** pain: podo
  - **stooping** agg.: lyc↓
    - **pressing** pain: lyc k*
  - **tearing** pain: *Am-c* k* chin k* plb k* sec ptk1
  - **touch**:
    - **agg.**: berb *Murx* mrr1 syph jl2
    - **slight** touch agg.: murx mrr1
  - **urination**:
    - **after**:
      - **agg.**: nat-m↓ sulfonam↓

- **urination – after – agg.**: ...
  - **burning**: nat-m k* sulfonam ks2
  - **agg.**: sil ↓
    - **cutting** pain: sil ptk1
  - **during | agg.**: arg-n k2 kreos a1
- **walking** agg.: berb ↓ *Nit-ac* ↓ *Thuj* ↓
  - **burning**: *Thuj* k*
  - **lancinating**: berb k*
  - **stitching** pain: *Nit-ac* k*

▽ • **extending** to:
  - **Chest**: alum
    - **stitching** pain: alum
  - **Upward**: ign k2 lyss nit-ac sabin k2 sep sil bg1
  - **Urethra**; meatus of: berb

○ • **Around**: bit-ar ↓
  - **burning**: bit-ar wht1•
- **Centres** in vagina from other parts: *Calc-p*

- **Vulva**: acon ↓ apis bro1 ars bro1 bacls-7 fmm1• *Bell* bro1 *Berb* bro1 *Calc* bro1 *Cann-s* bro1 carb-v ↓ caust ↓ *Cimic* ↓ cocc ↓ *Coff* ↓ con bro1 ferr bro1 ferr-i ↓ *Gels* ↓ hep ↓ *Ign* ↓ kali-bi ↓ kali-br ↓ kali-c bro1 *Kreos* bro1 lyc bro1 mag-p ↓ meli bro1 *Merc* ↓ *Merc-c* bro1 *Murx* ↓ *Nit-ac* ↓ nux-v ↓ petr ↓ *Phos* bro1 plat bro1* sabin bro1 *Sep* bro1 sulph bro1 tarent ↓ *Thuj* ↓ til ↓ tritic-vg fd5.de zinc ↓
  - **bursting**: berb
  - **leukorrhea** agg.: sep ↓
    - **stitching** pain: sep b4a.de
  - **menses | after**:
    - **agg.**: kreos ↓
      - **constricting**, contracting pain: kreos b7a.de
    - **during | agg.**: rhus-t ptk1
  - **raw**; as if: carb-v bg2 caust bg2 kali-bi bg2 tarent ptk1
  - **sore**: acon bro1 *Bell* bro1 *Cimic* bro1 cocc bro1 *Coff* bro1 ferr-i bro1 *Gels* bro1 hep bro1 *Ign* bro1 kali-br bro1 *Kreos* bro1 mag-p bro1 *Merc* bro1 *Murx* bro1 *Nit-ac* bro1 nux-v bro1 petr bro1 *Plat* bro1 *Sep* bro1 sulph bro1 *Thuj* bro1 til bro1 zinc bro1

PARTURITION (See Delivery)

PELVIC inflammatory disease: sep mrr1

PERSPIRATION: *Alum* b4a.de* *Aur* bg2 bell b4a.de* *Calc* bg2 *Canth* bg2 carb-v k2 cic bg2 con bg2 cypra-eg sde6.de• dios bg2 dros bg fl-ac bg2 gink-b sbd1• hep bg2 hydr dp• ign bg2 lat-m sp1 *Lyc* k* *Merc* k* *Petr* k* *Puls* b7a.de* **Sel** b7a.de* **Sep** b4a.de* sil bg2 stram sne *Sulph* k* *Thuj* k*

- **offensive**: aster sze10• *Calc* bro1 fago bro1 lyc bro1 *Merc* bro1 petr bro1 *Sars* b4a.de stram sne sulph b4a.de* thuj bro1*

○ - **Pubic** bones: *Sel* bg2 sep bg2 thuj bg2

PESSARY; after: | **Uterus**: ter ptk1

PHYSOMETRA (See Flatus)

PLACENTA: *(↗Delivery - during)*

- **previa**: *Erig* c1* *Ip* ptk1* *Nux-v* hr1* *Sabin* hr1* *Sep* hr1* *Verat* hr1*
- **retained**: *(↗Delivery - after)* *Agn* k* all-s hr1* *Arn* bro1 *Ars* k* art-v k* *Bell* k* **Canth** k* carb-v k2* caul k* chin bro1 cimic k* cimx hr1 croc k* ergot bro1 gels k* *Goss* bg* *Hydr* c1* ign bro1* ip k* *Kali-c* b4a.de* **Lyc** b4a.de mag-p dw1 *Nux-v* k* phos k2 plat bg2 *Puls* k* pyrog lp* *Sabin* k* *Sec* k* **Sep** k* verat-v hr1 visc a1*
  - **abortion**, after: *Sabin* kr1 sec kr1 *Sep* kr1 *Verat-v* kr1
- **septic**: sec ptk1

PLUG; sensation of a: | **Symphysis** pubis and coccyx; between: aloe k2

POLYPUS: *Calc* b4a.de lyc

○ - **Uterus**: *Ars* k* *Aur* k* **Bell** *Bufo* **Calc** k* **Calc-p** k* caust *Con* k* erod c2 hydr k* led k* *Lyc* k* med jl2 merc k* mez k* morg-p pte1*• nit-ac k* petr k* *Ph-ac* k* **Phos** k* *Plat* k* puls k* rhus-t k* *Sang* k* sec k* *Sep* k* *Sil* k* *Staph* k* syc pte1*• **Teucr** k* **Thuj** k*
  - **soft**: *Kali-s*
  - **x-ray** amel.; deep: bacls-7 fmm1•

○ • **Cervix**: med jl2

Polypus: ...

- **Vagina**: bell bro1 **Calc** k* med jl2 merc petr ph-ac *Phos* bro1 psor *Puls* k* staph *Teucr* k* *Thuj* bro1

POSITION of fetus (See Fetus - position)

POSTMENOPAUSAL BLEEDING (See Menses - return - ceased; Metrorrhagia - menopause - during)

POSTPARTUM HEMORRHAGE (See Metrorrhagia - delivery - after)

PRECOCITY; sexual (See Sexual desire - premature)

PREGNANCY: acon b2.de* aesc k13 *Agar* hr1* **Alet** bg2* alum k* am-c k* *Am-m* bg2* ambr k* *Ant-c* bg2* **Ant-t** hr1* arg-n k13 arn k* ars k* asaf k* *Asar* k* bar-c k* **Bell** k* bell-p bg2* *Benz-ac* hr1* *Bism* hr1* *Bry* k* *Calc* k* calc-p k* **Camph** hr1* *Canth* hr1* *Caps* k* carb-ac k* *Carb-v* bg2* *Caul* bg2* *Caust* k* **Cham** k* *Chel* hr1* chin k* chlam-tr bcx2• cic k* **Cimic** bg2* **Cocc** k* coff k* coll coloc k* *Con* b2.de* **Croc** k* cupr k* cycl c1 *Dros* hr1* dulc k* ferr k* ferr-c sf1.de *Ferr-p* hr1* glon k* *Goss* hr1* graph k* *Ham* **Hell** bg2* helon bg hydr bg2* *Hyos* k* ign k* *Ip* k* jab kali-bi k13 kali-br hr1 kali-c k* kali-i bg2* kalm kreos k* *Lac-ac* hr1* *Lach* bg2* *Lam* hr1* *Laur* hr1* *Lyc* b2.de* *Lyss* hr1* mag-c k* mag-m b2.de* mang k* merc k* merc-i-f mill mosch k* mur-ac k* *Murx* hr1* nat-c sf1.de nat-m k* nit-ac bg2 nux-m b2.de* nux-v b2.de* op j5.de* petr k* ph-ac bg2 phos k* *Plat* k* plb j5.de podo bg2* pop bg2* *Psor* hr1* **Puls** k* raph rat bg2* *Rhus-t* k* *Sabad* hr1* **Sabin** b2.de* sang *Sec* k* sel k* **Sep** k* sil k* spig k* *Stann* hr1* staph k* *Stram* bg2 sul-ac k* *Sulph* k* tab *Tarent* hr1* valer k* **Verat** b2.de* viol-o hr1* zinc bg2*

- **accompanied** by:
  - **food**; aversion to (See GENERALS - Food and - food - aversion - pregnancy; GENERALS - Food and - food - aversion - seen; GENERALS - Food and - food - aversion - thinking - pregnancy)
  - **salt**; desire for (See GENERALS - Food and - salt - desire - pregnancy)
  - **sour** food; desire for (See GENERALS - Food and - sour food - desire - pregnancy)
- **after**; complaints: *Acon* ptk1 alet ptk1 arn ptk1 bell ptk1 *Bry* ptk1 calc ptk1 caul ptk1 cham ptk1 chlam-tr bcx2• cimic ptk1 cocc ptk1 con ptk1 *Gels* ptk1 helon ptk1* ign ptk1 ip ptk1 **Kali-c** k1* *Kreos* ptk1 mag-c ptk1 nux-m ptk1 **Nux-v** ptk1 plat ptk1 **Puls** ptk1 pyrog ptk1 *Rhus-t* ptk1 sabin ptk1 sec ptk1 **Sep** ptk1 stram ptk1 sulph ptk1 tab ptk1 verat ptk1 vib ptk1 [ant-m stj2 beryl-m stj2 cadm-m stj2 calc-m stj1 chlor stj2 chr-m stj2 cob-m stj2 cupr-m stj2 lith-m stj2 mang-m stj2 mur-ac stj2 plb-m stj2 stront-m stj2 zinc-m stj2]
  - **recovery**; slow: **Arn** graph
- **conception | easy** (See Conception - easy)
- **during**; complaints: *Acon* kr1* aesc k2 *Agar* kr1* **Alet** kr1* **Alum** kr1* am-c k* **Am-m** kr1 ambr k* **Ant-c** kr1 **Ant-t** kr1 **Apis** kr1 apoc vml3• **Arg-met** kr1 arg-n k2 arge-pl rwt5• arist-cl sp1 **Arn** kr1* ars k* asaf k* *Asar* k* **Bar-c** kr1* **Bell** k* bell-p bg* **Benz-ac** kr1 **Bism** kr1 **Borx** a1* *Bry* k* *Calc* k* calc-p k* **Camph** kr1 **Canth** kr1* *Caps* k* **Carb-ac** kr1* *Carb-v* c1* *Caul* bg* *Caust* k* **Cham** k* **Chel** kr1 **Chin** kr1* chlam-tr bcx2• cic k* **Cimic** bg* **Cocc** k* coff k* coll k* coloc k* con k1* **Croc** k* **Cupr** kr1* cycl c1* **Dros** kr1 dulc k* equis-h k1 **Ferr** bg2* ferr-c sf1.de **Ferr-p** kr1 *Gels* bg* glon k* **Goss** kr1* graph k* *Ham* k* **Hell** bg* helon ptk1 hip-ac sp1 hydr bg* **Hyos** kr1* ign k* *Ip* k* jab k* kali-bi k2 kali-br kr1* **Kali-c** kr1* **Kali-fcy** kr1 kali-i k* kalm k* *Kreos* kr1* **Lac-ac** kr1 *Lach* k2 *Lam* kr1 **Laur** kr1 lyc k1 **Lyss** kr1 mag-c k* mang k* **Merc** kr1* merc-i-f k* mill k* mosch k* mur-ac k* *Murx* kr1* nat-c sf1.de **Nat-m** kr1* nux-m kr1* **Nux-v** kr1* op j5.de petr k* phos k* *Plat* k* plb j5.de* podo br1* pop sf1.de *Psor* kr1 *Puls* kr1* pyrog bg* raph k* rat bg* *Rhus-t* k* **Sabad** kr1 sabin bg* sang k* *Sec* k* sel k* **Sep** k* sil k* spig k* *Stann* kr1 staph k* stram ptk1 sul-ac k* *Sulph* k* tab k* *Tarent* kr1 valer k* verat k1* vib bg* viol-o kr1 zinc bg* [astat stj2 aur stj2 aur-m stj2 aur-s stj2 bar-br stj2 bar-i stj2 bar-met stj2 bism-sn stj2 caes-met stj2 cinnb stj2 hafn-met stj2 irid-met stj2 lanth-met stj2 merc-d stj2 osm-met stj2 plb-p stj2 polon-met stj2 rhen-met stj2 *Senec* stj tant-met stj2 thal-met stj2 tung-met stj2]
  - **sensation** as if beginning: arge-pl rwt5•
- **late** in life: bell ptk1

Female

PREMENSTRUAL syndrome (See GENERALS - Menses - before; MIND - Menses - before)

PREMENSTRUAL tension (See MIND - Menses - before)

PRESSURE: | **agg.** | **Ovaries**: staph ptk1
- **amel.** | **Ovaries**: med ptk1

PROLAPSUS:

O - **Uterus**: *(↗Pain - uterus and - bearing)* *Abel* vh1 *Abies-c* bro1* acon k* *Aesc* k* agar k* agn k2 *Alet* k* *Aloe* k* *Alum* k* alum-p k2 alum-sil k2 *Alumn* k* am-m k* anan k* ang a1 ant-c k2 *Apis* **Arg-met** k* **Arg-n** k* *Arn* k* ars ars-i art-v a1* asper bro1 **Aur** k* aur-ar k2 aur-i k2 aur-m k* *Aur-m-n* bro1 aur-s k2 *Bell* k* *Benz-ac* k* berb k* *Brom* hr1 *Bry* k* bufo *Calc* k* calc-ar k* calc-f c1 *Calc-p* k* calc-s calc-sil k2* calen pd canth k* *Carb-an* k* carb-v b4a.de caul k* cham k* chim hr1 *Chin* k* chinin-ar cimic k* cocc k* coll k* *Coloc* hr1 *Con* k* croc k* erig hr1 *Ferr* k* ferr-ar ferr-br c2* *Ferr-i* k* ferr-p fl-ac mrr1 *Frax* bg* *Graph* k* *Ham* hr1 *Helon* k* hydr k* hydrc k* ign bro1 iod k* *Ip* k* kali-ar *Kali-bi* k* *Kali-br* k* *Kali-c* k* kali-p kali-s kali-sil k2 kreos k* lac-c k* *Lac-d* fr *Lach* k* lappa c2* **Lil-t** k* lyc k* *Lyss* k* mang mel-c-s br1* merc k* *Mill* *Murx* k* **Nat-hchls** k* *Nat-m* k* nat-p k* *Nit-ac* *Nux-m* k* *Nux-v* k* onos c2* op k* ovi-p c2 **Pall** k* *Petr* k* ph-ac k* *Phos* k* **Plat** k* *Podo* k* psor ptk1 **Puls** k* pyrog k2 pyrus c2 **Rhus-t** k* *Sabin* k* sang sanic c2 *Sec* k* senec bg* **Sep** k* *Sil* k* *Stann* k* staph k* sul-ac c2 sul-i k2 *Sulph* k* teucr *Thuj* k* til c2* tril-p br1* *Tub* *Ust* k* zinc k* zinc-p k2 zinc-val bro1
- **morning**: bell bg3* **Nat-m** k* sep k*
- **afternoon**: **Sep**
- **accompanied** by:
  - **constipation**: stann bro1
  - **foul** urine: benz-ac ptk1
  - **hemorrhoids**: podo bro1
  - **weakness**: alet bro1 helon bro1* sul-ac ptk1
- **alternate** days, on: alum
- **coition**:
  - **agg.**: nat-c ptk1
  - **amel.**: merc k*
- **crossing** legs amel.: lil-t k* murx **Sep** k*
- **delivery**; after: bell k* *Helon* k* *Nux-v* hr1 *Podo* k* puls *Rhus-t* k* sec k* **Sep** k ●
  - **forceps**; with: sec ptk1
- **diarrhea**; from constant: petr ptk1
- **electric** shocks down the thighs, with: *Graph* k*
- **fright**; after: gels k* **Op** k*
- **holds** the abdomen: helon mrr1
- **hysteria**; with (See MIND - Hysteria - uterus - prolapse)
- **jar** agg.: bell k2
- **lifting** agg.: agar *Aur* k* **Calc** k* nux-v ptk1 *Podo* k* **Rhus-t** k ●*
- **lumbar** backache; with: nat-m ptk1
- **lying** down | **amel.**: lil-t k2 *Nat-m* k* onos vml3• *Sep* k*
- **lying** on back | **amel.**: nat-m ptk1 onos ptk1
- **menses** | **after** | **agg.**: agar k* aur k* ip k* kreos k*
  - **during** | **agg.**: *Aur* k* *Calc-p* k* *Cimic* kreos *Lach* *Lil-t* k* nat-c **Puls** k* **Sep** k* tub k2
- **myelitis**; in (See spinal)
- **nursing** mother: podo bro1
- **pregnancy**:
  - **after** (See delivery)
  - **during** | **agg.**: ferr b7.de*
- **pressure** | **amel.**: abies-c vml3•
- **reaching** up with the hands agg.: *Aur* k* *Calc* k* nux-v *Sulph* k*
- **sitting** agg.: abies-c vml3•
- **spinal** cord; with inflammation of: *Sil* hr1
- **standing** for a long time agg.: abies-c vml3• lappa ptk1
- **stool**:
  - **after** | **agg.**: *Stann*
  - **during** | **agg.**: *Calc-p* k* con k* dirc c1 eupi a1 nux-v **Podo** k* psor ptk1 puls *Stann* k*

Prolapsus: ...
  - **urging** to | **constant**: inul nux-v
- **storm**; before: rhus-t
- **straining**, from: *Aur* k* **Nux-v** b7a.de* podo lp* *Rhus-t* hr1
  - **holding** the head amel.; and: pyrog ptk1
- **urination** | **during** | **agg.**: *Calc-p* k*
  - **involuntary** | **with**: ferr-i pd*
- **walking**:
  - **agg.**: lappa ptk1 lil-t k2
  - **bent** | **must** walk bent: *Am-m* *Arn* k*
- **weather**; in hot: *Kali-bi* k*

- **Vagina**: alum k* bell k* calc-ar *Carb-v* b4a.de chim k* *Ferr* k* ferr-i bg2 fil a1 gran bro1 *Ign* k2 *Kreos* k* *Lach* k* *Lappa* bro1 *Lyc* b4a.de *Merc* k* *Nux-m* k* *Nux-v* k* oci a1* oci-sa mtf11 op k* plat bg2* plb k* podo bg* psor ptk1 **Sep** k* *Stann* k* staph c2* sul-ac k* *Sulph* k* thlas bg* thuj k* verat k*
  - **lifting** agg.: *Nux-v* k*
  - **pregnancy** agg.; during: calc-ar k* *Ferr* k*
  - **stool** agg.; during: stann k*
  - **weakness**; from: sul-ac ptk1

PUBERTY:
- **ailments** at: calc-p k2
- **never** well since (See GENERALS - Convalescence - puberty)

PUERPERAL fever (See FEVER - Puerperal)

PULSATING: alum k* apis *Bell* k* cact bg2* *Calc-p* k* cench k2 cic bg2 *Coc-c* k* *Lac-c* lyc bg2 *Merc* k* murx bg2* nat-c k* nux-v bg2 prun k*
- **coition**; after: *Nat-c*
- **constant** | **Pubis**; behind: aesc
- **lying** on right side agg.: apis

O - **Ovaries**: *Bell* k* brach bro1 bran bro1 *Cact* k* calc con cop k* hep bro1 *Lach* k* *Onos* k* podo
  - **right**: ignis-alc es2• podo
  - **menses**; during: lac-c
  - **standing** agg.: apis cop k*
  - **walking** agg.: apis
- **Pudendum**: prun ptk1
- **Uterus**: aesc ars k* *Bell* k* *Cact* k* calc-p con cur murx k* sabin k* sarr k*
- **Vagina**: *Alum* k* *Merc* k* stry a1
  - **lying** | **amel.**: merc k*

PUSHES up when she sits down; the uterus: bell-p sp1 ferr-i k* **Nat-hchls**

RAISING: | **arms**:
  - **agg.** | **Ovaries**: apis ptk1
- **legs**:
  - **agg.** | **Ovaries**: lyc ptk1

REACHING UP with the hands agg.: graph bg2

O - **Uterus**: aur ptk1 graph ptk1 sulph ptk1

REDNESS (See Discoloration - red)

RELAXATION: *Alet* br1 hyos b7a.de

O - **Pubis** and in pelvis; muscles around tril-p zr
- **Uterus**: sec bro1
- **Vagina**; sphincter of: *Agar* **Agn** hr1* *Ambr* ars *Calad* *Calc* croc *Ferr* *Kali-c* *Lyc* mag-c merc mur-ac *Nat-c* nat-m sec a1 *Sep* sil staph *Sulph* *Tub* k*

RETENTIO SECUNDINARUM (See Placenta - retained)

RIGIDITY of os during labor (See Os - rigid)

RISING:
- **agg.**: canth bg2 graph bg2 kreos bg2 nux-v bg2 plat bg2 rhus-t bg2 sabin bg2 sulph bg2
- **stooping**; from | **agg.**: calc-p bg2

RISING UP; AS IF: | **Uterus**: nux-m bg2

SALPINGITIS (See Inflammation - oviduct)

SCLEROSIS:

O - **Uterus** | **Cervix**: tub-r jl2

SCRATCHING:

- **agg.**:

O • **Vagina**: tarent ptk1

⁝ **bleeds**; until it: sec ptk1

SENSITIVENESS: acon bg2 aur br1 *Aur-m* k* bamb-a stb2.de• **Bell** k* *Cann-s* b7a.de *Canth* k* chin coc-c *Cocc* b7a.de *Coff* k* con k* dulc fd4.de falco-pe nl2• ferr b7.de* *Hydr* hr1 *Kreos* hr1 merc k* merc-c b4a.de *Mur-ac* k* murx bg2* nux-v k* **Plat** k* sec b7.de* *Sep* k* **Staph** k* sulph k* syph c1 tarent k2* thuj bg2* ust bg1 vanil fd5.de *Zinc* k*

- **menses** | **before** | **agg.**: am-c bro1 cocc bro1 kali-c bro1 *Lach* bro1 *Plat* bro1

• **during** | **agg.**: am-c bro1 cocc bro1 kali-c bro1 *Lach* bro1 *Plat* b4.de*

O - **Ovaries**: ant-c hr1 bell bg2 bufo bg2 *Coloc* hr1 ham hr1 **Lach** hr1 staph hr1 ust hr1

- **Uterus**: lach k2 lyss jl2

• **spot** near os uteri: med br1

O • **Os** uteri: *Chin* bg2

- **Vagina**: acon k* alumn k* aur k* *Bell* *Berb* k* bit-ar wht1• bry calc k* carb-v ptk1 chim hr1 coc-c bg2* *Coff* k* *Ferr* ferr-p graph *Ham* hr1 irid-met srj5• kali-bi bg2 *Kreos* k* **Lyss** k* merc *Nat-m* k* nux-v **Plat** k* plb bg2* sec k* *Sep* k* *Sil* k* **Staph** k* sulph k* tarent ptk1 *Thuj* k* vanil fd5.de zinc bg2

• **coition** agg.: hydr ptk1 sulph ptk1 thuj ptk1

• **urination** agg.: coc-c ptk1

SEPSIS PUERPERALIS (See FEVER - Puerperal)

SEROUS cysts in vagina (See Tumors - vagina - cysts - serous)

SEXUAL AVERSION (See Coition - aversion; Sexual desire - wanting)

SEXUAL DESIRE:

- **diminished**: acon b7.de* *Agar* b2.de* agath-a nl2• *Agn* k* aids nl2• alum k* am-c b2.de* ambr k* amyg-p c2 anac b2.de* anh sp1 ant-c b2.de* anthraci vh1 arg-n bg2 arge-pl rwt5• arn b2.de* *Asar* b7a.de bamb-a stb2.de• *Bar-c* k* bar-s k2 bart a1 bell k* berb k* borx k* brom bg2* *Calad* b2.de* calc b2.de* camph k* cann-s k* canth b2.de* caps b2.de* carb-an k* carb-v b2.de* **Caust** k* chinin-s bg2 chlam-tr bcx2• chlor bg2 clem b2.de* *Cocc* b7.de coff b7a.de con b2.de* conch fkr1• cupr sst3• dam sf1.de* des-ac jl dream-p sdj1• ephe-si hsj1• ery-a c2 ery-m c2 euph b2.de* falco-pe nl2• *Ferr* k* *Ferr-m* bro1* ferr-p fl-ac bg2 *Foll* oss• galeoc-c-h gms1• gast c2 ger-i rly4• *Granit-m* es1• *Graph* k* *Hell* b7.de* *Helon* k* *Hep* k* hydrog srj2• hyos b2.de* *Ign* b2.de* kali-bi mrr1 *Kali-br* bg2* kali-c b2.de* *Kali-chl* a1 kali-i kali-m kr1 kali-p fd1.de* kali-s fd4.de* ketogl-ac rly4• kola stb3• kreos sf1.de lac-e hm2• lac-leo hm2• lac-loxod-a hm2• lac-lup hm2• lach b7.de laur b2.de* lir-o mtf11 *Lyc* k* *Lyss* kr1 m-ambo b2.de* m-arct b7.de *Mag-c* k* mag-m b2.de* mand sp1 melal-alt gya4 meny b2.de* moni rfm1• mur-ac k* *Nat-m* k* nat-pyru rly4• nept-m lsd2.fr *Nit-ac* b2.de* nuph mtf11 nux-m b2.de* oci-sa sp1 *Onos* br1* op b7a.de* orch c2 ozone sde2• pall c2 pegan-ha tpi1• petr b2.de* *Ph-ac* k* phos k* plat b2.de* plb b7.de* plut-n srj7• positr nl2• pot-e rly4• rauw sp1 *Rhod* k* ruta fd4.de sabad b2.de* sabal ptk1 sabin b2.de* *Sanguis-s* hm2• saroth mg1.de sel b2.de* seneg b2.de* *Sep* k* ser-a-c jl2 sil k* spig b2.de* spong bg2 stann b2.de* staph b2.de* suis-pan rly4• sul-ac b2.de* sulph k* teucr b2.de* urol-h rwt• vanil br1 vero-o rly4*• visc sp1 yohim lp2* [heroin sdj2]

• **morning**: bell

• **evening**: *Dios* a1

• **night**: coca a1

• **apathy**, with (See indifference)

• **coition**; during: *Kali-br* st

• **eating**; when: galeoc-c-h gms1•

• **exertion** agg.: galeoc-c-h gms1•

• **gonorrhea**; after dragging: med jl2

• **gradually**: *Aeth* vh1

• **husband** absent; when: galeoc-c-h gms1•

• **indifference**; with: chlam-tr bcx2• falco-pe nl2•

Sexual desire – **diminished**: ...

• **ovulation**; during:

⁝ **accompanied** by | **weakness** (See GENERALS - Weakness - accompanied - sexual - ovulation)

• **sexual** excitement, with: cann-s

• **work**; when: *Galeoc-c-h* gms1•

- **during**:

• **agg.** | **Ovaries**: kali-br ptk1

- **incest**: (↗*MIND - Ailments - abused - sexually)* cupr sst3•

- **increased**: (↗*Excitability; MIND - Amorous; MIND - Nymphomania; MIND - Sensual)* acon b2.de* *Agar* b2.de* agath-a nl2• agn sf1.de* aloe bg2 alum b2.de* am-c *Ambr* b2.de* anac b2.de* androc srj1• ang vh1 *Ant-c* k* anthraq rly4• *Apis* k* arg-n k* arge-pl rwt5• arn b2.de* *Ars* k* *Ars-i* arund bro1 *Asaf* k* aster k* aur k* aur-ar k2 aur-i k2 aur-s k2 bamb-a stb2.de• bar-c k* bar-i k2 *Bar-m* bar-ox-suc rly4• *Bell* k* bit-ar wht1• borx b2.de* bov k* bufo bg2* cact *Calad* k* **Calc** k* calc-i k2 **Calc-p** k* calc-sil k2 **Camph** k* cann-i k* cann-s k* **Canth** k* caps b2.de* *Carb-v* k* carc mrr1 carneg-g rwt1• *Caust* b2.de* cedr kr1* cench k2* cham b2.de* chin k* chir-fl gya2 chlam-tr bcx2• chord-umb rly4• cimic bro1 cina bg2 cinch c2 *Cinnm* j5.de* clem b2.de* coca bro1 cocc b2.de* *Coff* k* coli rly4• coloc b2.de* **Con** k* corv-cor bdg• *Croc* b2.de* cub cur cypra-eg sde6.de• des-ac jl* *Dig* b2.de* dios bg2 dream-p sdj1• dulc k* ephe-si hsj1• falco-pe nl2• ferr b2.de* *Ferul* a1* **Fl-ac** k* form galeoc-c-h gms1• *Gamb* mrr1 gaul br1 *Gels* ger-i rly4• germ-met srj5• gins c2 gran j5.de *Graph* b2.de* **Grat** k* haliae-lc srj5• ham bg2 hep b2.de* hipp jl2 *Hydr* kr1 hydrog srj2• **Hyos** k* *Ign* k* iod k* irid-met srj5• *Kali-bi* kr1 *Kali-br* k* kali-c b2.de* kali-fcy sf1.de kali-n b2.de* *Kali-p* k* kola stb3• *Kreos* k* *Lac-c* k* lac-e hm2• lac-h htj1• lac-leo hm2• **Lach** k* laur b2.de* led b2.de* *Lil-t* k* limest-b es1• *Lyc* k* lyss k* m-ambo b2.de* m-arct b2.de* m-aust b2.de* mag-m b2.de* mag-p bg2 manc br1* mand sp1 mang b2.de* marb-w es1• **Med** vh* medul-os-si rly4• meny b2.de* *Merc* k* merc-c bg2 mez b2.de* morph a1 *Mosch* k* mur-ac b2.de* *Murx* k* musca-d szs1 mygal nad rly4• *Nat-ar* *Nat-c* k* nat-m k* nat-p nat-sil k2 neon srj5• nit-ac k* nux-m b2.de* **Nux-v** k* oci-sa sp1 *Olib-sac* wmh1 *Op* k* *Orig* k* (non:orig-v kr1) orot-ac rly4• oxal-a rly4• par b2.de* pegan-ha tpi1• petr b2.de* ph-ac c1* **Phos** k* *Pic-ac* k* plac-s rly4• **Plat** k* plb k* plut-n srj7• podo k2 positr nl2• propr sa3• psil jl **Puls** k* pyrid rly4• *Raph* k* rhod b2.de* rhus-g tmo3• rhus-t b2.de* rib-ac jl *Rob* a1* ruta b2.de* sabad a1* *Sabin* k* sacch-a fd2.de• *Sal-n* c1* saroth mg1.de sars b2.de* *Sec* b7a.de sel bg2* seneg b2.de* *Sep* b2.de* *Sil* k* sinus rly4• spig b2.de* *Stann* k* *Staph* k* *Stram* k* stry bro1 suis-em rly4• sul-ac k* sul-i k2 *Sulph* b2.de* *Sumb* bg2* *Tarent* k* thlas ptk1 thuj k* tritic-vg fd5.de tub st* urol-h rwt• *Ust* kr1* vanil br1 **Verat** k* verb b2.de* vero-o rly4*• **Vesp** mgm• vip fkr4.de visc sp1 *Xero* bro1 yohim bwa3* *Zinc* k* *Zinc-p* k2* zinc-pic c1 [heroin sdj2 spect dfg1 temp elm1 zinc-n stj2]

• **morning** | **bed** agg.; in: aster bamb-a stb2.de• cedr kreos [heroin sdj2]

• **afternoon**: calc ruta fd4.de

⁝ **17 h**: galeoc-c-h gms1•

• **night**: bell brucel sa3• psil jl *Syph* st vanil fd5.de *Zinc*

⁝ **rousing**: aur kr1 *Galeoc-c-h* gms1• *Med* st vanil fd5.de

• **accompanied** by:

⁝ **gastroenteritis** (See ABDOMEN - Inflammation - gastroenteritis - accompanied - sexual)

⁝ **leukorrhea**: *Canth* k* hydr ptk1 *Ign* kr1* *Orig* k* (non:orig-v kr1) plat k* *Puls* k* senec ptk1*

⁝ **Colon**; inflammation of the (See ABDOMEN - Inflammation - colon - accompanied - sexual)

• **affection**; with: *Olib-sac* wmh1

• **alternating** with:

⁝ **despair** of salvation; religious (See MIND - Despair - religious - alternating - sexual)

⁝ **moral** obliquity; fear of (See MIND - Fear - moral - alternating - sexual)

⁝ **religious** affections (See MIND - Religious - too - alternating - sexual)

⁝ **sadness** (See MIND - Sadness - alternating - sexual)

• **children**; in: (↗*girls)* ambr lmj *Calc-p* lmj *Cann-i* lmj carc lmj *Fl-ac* lmj graph mrr1 **Hyos** lmj **Lach** lmj lyss lmj med lmj **Merc** lmj *Mosch* lmj ph-ac lmj **Phos** lmj plat mtf33 staph lmj tub ggd* *Zinc* lmj

Female

- **coition**:
  - **agg.**: *Tarent* k2*
  - **not** removed after: androc srj1• aster kr1
- **contact** of parts, by least: (↗*touch*) androc srj1• lac-c ptk1 *Murx* kr1* pycnop-sa mrz1
- **cooking**; while: galeoc-c-h gms1•
- **delivery**: (↗*MIND - Nymphomania - puerperal*)
  - **after**: (↗*MIND - Nymphomania - puerperal*) bell k* camph *Chin* k* *Grat Hyos Kali-br* kr1 *Mosch* phos k2 *Plat* k* tarent verat k* zinc k*
  - **during**: *Verat* kr1
- **dreams** sexual:
  - **with**: *Op* kr1
  - **without**: *Galeoc-c-h* gms1• zinc j5.de
- **drunkenness**; during: calc gl1.fr• canth gl1.fr• *Caust* gl1.fr• chin gl1.fr• con gl1.fr• nux-v gl1.fr• phos gl1.fr•
- **dysmenorrhea**; during: cann-i br1 cann-xyz ptk1
- **emotions**; without: polys sk4•
- **excitement** of:
  - **fancy**; without excitement of: *Hyos* kr1 *Lach* b7.de* sulph bg2 tung-met bdx1•
  - **sexual** parts; with extreme excitement of: androc srj1• *Stram* kr1 ulm-c jsj8•
- **girls**, in young: (↗*children*) **Orig** sne plat k2*
- **headache**, during (See HEAD - Pain - accompanied - sexual)
- **itching**; with: calad k2 *Canth* kr1 *Hydr* kr1 kali-bi ptk1 sabin ptk1
- **lactation**; during: phos k2
- **lochia**, with suppressed: *Verat* kr1
- **love**, after disappointed: *Verat* kr1*
- **married**; with obsession of being: bell gl1.fr• *Caust* gl1.fr• plat gl1.fr• verat gl1.fr•
- **masturbation**; with: *Zinc* kr1
- **menopause**; during: arg-n br1* lach sf1.de manc bg2* *Murx* bg2*
- **menses**:
  - **after** | **agg.**: aeth vh1 ars ptk1 calc-p kr1 *Kali-br* kr1* *Kali-p* k* lac-e hrn2• *Med* kr1* plat kr1 *Sul-ac* b4a.de*
  - **before** | **agg.**: ars ptk1 bell k* calc bg2 *Calc-p* k* croc k* cub *Dulc* k* granit-m es1• kali-c k* nux-v k* *Phos* k* plat bro1 stann ptk1 stram k* *Verat* k*
  - **during** | **agg.**: agar k* ars ptk1 bell k* bufo k* camph k* *Canth* k* chin k* chir-fl gya2 cina k* coff k* *Dulc* k* granit-m es1• *Hyos* k* irid-met srj5• kali-br k* kreos bg2 *Lach* k* *Lyc* k1* *Mosch* k* nux-v k* *Orig Plat* k* **Puls** k* *Sep* bg2* sul-ac k* symph fd3.de• tarent verat k* vip fkr4.de
  - **suppressed** menses, from: ant-c kr1*
- **metrorrhagia**, during (See Metrorrhagia - accompanied - sexual)
- **nursing** child, when: calc-p bro1* phos k2*
- **old** women, in: apis st *Mosch* k1*
- **painful**: androc srj1•
- **paralytic** affections, in: *Sil* kr1
- **partner** only; to: galeoc-c-h gms1•
- **parturition**, during (See delivery - during)
- **pregnancy** agg.; during: bell lach merc phos k2* plat k* puls stram verat *Zinc* kr1
- **puberty**; at: manc br1
- **sadness**; with (See MIND - Sadness - sexual excitement - with)
- **scratching** | **arm** | **agg.**: *Stann*
  - **parts**; distant | **agg.**: *Stann* k*
- **sleep**, disturbing: *Aur* kr1 *Galeoc-c-h* gms1•
- **spinal** affection, in: pic-ac br1 *Sil* kr1

- **increased**: ...
  - **tenderness**; with (See affection)
  - **touch** agg.: (↗*contact; MIND - Lascivious - touch*) bamb-a stb2.de• *Plat* mrr1
  - **unsatisfied** passion, in: *Verat* kr1*
  - **urination**; with erection of clitoris after: calc-p kr1*
  - **virgins**; in: *Con* k* **Plat** k*
  - **waking**; on: puls tl1
  - **widows**; in: **Apis** k* cench k2 **Lyc** h2* **Orig** k*
  - **worms**; from: *Sabad* kr1*
- **insatiable**: (↗*MIND - Ailments - sexual excesses*) agath-a nl2• androc srj1• asaf vh aster *Calc-p* canth galeoc-c-h gms1• *Lach* k* olib-sac wmh1 ozone sde2• *Phos* mrr1 *Plat* k* *Sabin* k* stram *Zinc* k*
  - **menses**; after: *Calc-p* kr1
- **lesbian**: olib-sac wmh1
- **oral** sex; for: olib-sac wmh1
- **premature**: orig mrr1 **Orig-v** sne *Plat* kr1
- **suppressed**: (↗*Suppressed - agg.*) *Aeth* vh1 berb j5.de* carc mlr1• **Con** kr1 *Helon* kr1 melal-alt gya4 **Phos** kr1 tritic-vg fd5.de *Zinc* kr1
  - **agg.**: (↗*suppressed; GENERALS - Sexual desire - suppression - agg.; MALE GENITALIA/SEX - Sexual desire - suppressed - agg.*) *Apis* kr1 berb kr1* **Con** kr1* *Helon* kr1 kali-br kr1 op kr1 **Phos** kr1 plat mrr1 zinc kr1
  - **ailments** from suppressed sexual desire: **Con** kr1* positr nl2• sabal br1*
  - **coition**; during: *Kali-br* kr1
  - **widows**, in: *Apis* kr1 *Con* kr1 *Phos* kr1
- **violent**: (↗*MIND - Ailments - sexual excesses; MIND - Impulse - sexual; MIND - Nymphomania*) agar b4.de* **Agn** ptk1 *Alum* b4a.de* anac b4a.de* androc srj1• ang vh1 *Ars* k* arund asaf vh aster k* *Aur* b4a.de *Bar-c* b4a.de bar-m **Calc** k* *Calc-p* camph k2 canth k* coloc b4a.de* con b4.de* cyna k2 dig bg2 ferr bg2 ferul st *Gels Graph* b4.de* grat ptk1 *Hyos* k* ign b7.de *Kali-br* k* kali-c b4.de* kola stb3• *Lach* k* *Lyc* b4.de* lyss k* m-arct b7.de *M-aust* b7.de* merc b4a.de* *Mosch* k* **Murx** k* *Nat-c* b4.de* **Nat-m** b4.de* nat-s mrr1 **Nux-v** b7.de* olib-sac wmh1 *Op* k* **Orig** k* ozone sde2• *Phos* k* plac rzf5• *Plat* k* plb b7a.de* positr nl2• *Puls* b7a.de* *Rhus-t* bg2 ruta b7.de *Sabin* k* seneg bg2 *Sep* bg2* *Sil* k* spig bg2 stann b4.de* *Staph* k* *Stram* k* **Sulph** bg2 sumb ptk1 *Tarent* k* tritic-vg fd5.de *Tub* st* *Verat* b7.de* *Zinc* k*
  - **coition** agg.: *Tarent* kr1
  - **girls**; in: hyos k2
  - **involuntary** orgasm (See Orgasm - involuntary)
  - **irresistible**: *Caust* gl1.fr• chin gl1.fr• galeoc-c-h gms1• mag-c gl1.fr• nux-v gl1.fr• phos gl1.fr• staph gl1.fr• ulm-c jsj8• verat gl1.fr•
  - **itching** of vulva, from: hydr st
  - **masturbation**, driving her to: bamb-a stb2.de• *Gels Grat Nux-v* **Orig** k* phos *Plat* k* raph **Zinc** k*
  - **orgasm**; with involuntary (See Orgasm - involuntary)
  - **ovulation**; during: kola stb3•
  - **suicidal** disposition; with (See MIND - Suicidal - sexual)
  - **yearning** for sex (See violent)
- **wanting**: (↗*Coition - aversion; MIND - Touched - aversion - sexually*) adam srj5• aether a1 agar sf1.de agath-a nl2• aids nl2• alco a1 am-c a1* anh sp1 anthraci vh1* arg-met a1 arg-n zf arum-d a1 asar vh* aster sze10• bar-act a1 bar-c a1* bar-s k2 bell a1 borx k2 calad a1 carb-an a1 carb-v mrr1 carc jl2 carl a1 **Caust** a1* chlam-tr bcx2• chlf a1 chlor a1 cob-n sp1 coff a1 cordyc mp4• des-ac rbp6 dig a1 dios a1 elaps a1 ery-m a1 falco-pe nl2• fl-ac a1 franz a1 gast a1 get a1 gink-b sbd1• *Granit-m* es1• graph a1* hell a1 *Helon* kr1 hep a1 hydrc a1 hydrog srj2• *Ign* a1* indg a1 iod a1 irid-met srj5• jac-c a1 kali-bi a1* kali-c a1 kali-chl a1 kali-p fd1.de• lac-c mrr1 lach a1 lil-s a1 *Lyc* a1* med jl2 merc-c a1 morph a1 myric a1 napht a1 *Nat-m* mrr1 nept-m lsd2.fr nuph a1 onos c1* op a1 osm a1 pen a1 phos a1 plb a1 plut-n srj7• pneu jl2 positr nl2• psor jl2 pycnop-sa mrz1 rhod a1 rumx a1 sabad a1 sal-fr sle1• sep k2* spong fd4.de staph j5.de* *Sulph* a1* sumb a1 syph jl2 tab a1 teucr a1 ther a1 thuj a1 tritic-vg fd5.de upa a1 ust a1 v-a-b jl2* [heroin sdj2 lac-mat sst4 moly-met stj2 nat-caust stj2 tax jsj7]
  - **forenoon**: phys a1
  - **evening**: dios a1

- **night**: bufo a1
- **irritation** of genitalia; with: borx b4a.de
- **married**, with obsession of getting: lyc gl1.fr•
- **menses**; after: nat-m a1

SEXUAL EXCITEMENT (See Sexual desire)

SEXUAL NEURASTHENIA (See Sexual desire - diminished)

SHOCKS in:
○ - **Uterus** on falling asleep stry k*
- **Vagina**: kreos k*

SITTING:
- **agg.**: sulph ptk1
○ • **Vagina**: staph ptk1
• **Vulva**: berb ptk1 kreos ptk1 staph ptk1 sulph ptk1
- **bent**:
• **agg.** | **Ovaries**: ars ptk1

SLEEP: | **after** | **agg.**: mag-c bro1
- **during** | **agg.**: mag-c bro1

SMALL for fetus; sensation as if uterus too: apoc vh1 bar-c bg2* calc-p bg2* chim sf con bg2* ferr bg2* helo bg2 helon sf iod bg2* *Ov* sf phos bg2* plb pd senec bg2*

SMALL OVARIES (See Atrophy - ovaries)

SOFT, uterus: *Arg-n* hr1 op k*
- **sensation** as if: abies-c k*

SPASMS in uterus (See Pain - uterus - cramping)

SPONGY:
○ - **Uterus** | **Cervix**: arg-met ptk1 ust ptk1

STEPPING HARD agg.: *Bell* bg2

STERILITY: *(↗Infantilism)* agn k* *Alet* k* alum bg2* *Am-c* k* anag k* anan k* apis k* apoc vh1 arg-n ptk1 ars zf **Aur** k* *Aur-i* k2* aur-m hr1* aur-m-n c1* *Bamb-a* stb2.de• bar-c k2* *Bar-m* k* bers-l bta1• **Borx** k* bov mrr1 brom k* *Calad* b7a.de *Calc* k* calc-i k2* cann-i a1* cann-s k* *Canth* k* caps b7.de* carbn-s carc sst2• *Caul* k* caust k* chlam-tr bcx2• cic k* cissu-c bta1• cocc bg2* *Coff* *Con* k* *Croc* b7.de* dam c1* dros b7a.de dulc k* erios-co bta1• *Eup-pur* hr1* *Ferr* k* *Ferr-p* *Fil* j5.de* form c1* *Goss* k* *Graph* k* grew-oc bta1• gunn-p bta1• helo bg2 helon k* *Hyos* k* ign sne* *Iod* k* *Kali-bi* *Kali-br* k* kali-c bg2* *Kreos* k* *Lach* k* lappa c1* lec bro1 lil-t bg2* mand sp1* med bg2* *Merc* k* mill c1* mit sf1.de morph c1 **Nat-c** k* **Nat-m** k* nat-p k* *Nux-m* k* nux-v b7.de* oncor-t srj6• *Orig* k* *Ov* st1 *Phos* k* physala-p c1 phyt k* pitu-a vml2• pitu-gl das* *Plat* k* plb b7.de* *Puls* b7.de* pyren-sc bta1• retin-ac mtf11 roye-l bta1• rub-c bta1• ruta k* *Sabal* c1* *Sabin* b7.de* sec a1* *Senec* **Sep** k* *Sil* k* sol-so bta1• *Sul-ac* k* sulph k* *Syph* jl2* tarent sne ther c1* trium-r bta1• vern-co bta1• vib bg2* wies c1* x-ray br1* *Zinc*
- **leukorrhea**; with: alet sne borx a1* caul c1 *Kreos* hr1* lam b7a.de *Nat-c* kr1
- **menses**:
  • **copious** menstrual flow; from: **Borx** b4a.de *Calc* k* cham b7a.de chin b7a.de croc b7a.de ign b7a.de merc k* mill k* *Nat-m* k* nux-v b7a.de phos k* sabin b7a.de sul-ac k* *Sulph* k*
    ⋮ **early**; and too: sulph kr1
    ⋮ **late**; or too: *Phos* kr1
  • **during**:
    ⋮ **agg.** | **convulsions**; with: *Kali-c* b4a.de
  • **early**; too: *Calc* b4a.de *Nat-m* b4a.de sul-ac b4a.de *Sulph* b4a.de
  • **late**; too: caust b4a.de *Graph* b4a.de
  • **scanty**; too: *Am-c* b4a.de
  • **suppressed** menses; from: *Con* b4a.de
- **self**-reproaching; with (See MIND - Reproaching oneself - sterility)
- **sexual** desire:
  • **with** excessive: calc b4a.de cann-xyz ptk1 con b4a.de ign b7a.de *Kali-br* k* lach b7a.de *Orig* k* *Phos* k* *Plat* k* stram b7a.de
  • **without**: agn kr1

STOOL:
- **during** | **agg.**: ambr ptk1 podo ptk1 stann ptk1

STOOPING:
- **agg.** | **Ovaries**: apis ptk1

STRETCHING:
- **legs** | **agg.** | **Ovaries**: podo ptk1
  • **amel.** | **Ovaries**: plb ptk1

SUBINVOLUTION: arn bg2* *Bell* k* bry k* *Calc* k* *Carb-v* *Caul* k* chin k* **Cimic** k* cycl k* *Epiph* br1 frax bg2* ham k2 helo bg2 *Helon* ptk1 *Hydr* k* *Kali-bi* k* **Kali-br** k* kali-c k* *Kali-i* k* *Lil-t* k* mel-c-s br1 mill k* *Nat-hchls* k* nat-m k2 nat-s *Op* plat k* podo k* psor **Puls** k* *Sabin* k* *Sec* k* **Sep** k* staph k* **Sulph** k* ter k* *Ust* k* visc a1*
- **abortion**; after: psor ptk1
- **accompanied** by:
  • **congestion**: epiph br1
  • **menses**; painful: epiph br1
- **sunken** uterus, vagina reddened: berb

SWOLLEN: agath-a nl2• *Am-c* k* *Ambr* k* ang bg2 *Apis* k* arg-n k2 arn k* **Ars** k* ars-i *Asaf* k* aur k* aur-m k* aur-s bell k* bry k* *Calc* k* calc-p k* calc-s cann-s *Canth* k* carb-an *Carb-v* k* chin b7.de* coc-c *Coll* coloc k* con dig k* dulc fd4.de *Ferr* b7a.de *Ferr-i* k* goss k* *Graph* k* *Helon* k* kali-bi k* **Kreos** k* *Lac-c* k* lach k* *Lil-t* k* **Lyc** bg2 mag-p br1 meph k* *Merc* k* merc-c bg2 *Nat-s* **Nit-ac** k* nux-v k* oxal-a rly4* paeon c1* *Phos* *Podo* k* **Puls** k* pyrog c1 **Rhus-t** k* sec k* *Sep* k* spong fd4.de stram hr1 sulph k* tarent bg2 *Thuj* k* tritic-vg fd5.de *Urt-u* k* vanil fd5.de
- **dropsical**: *Apis* b7a.de
- **edematous**: apis apoc k2* *Graph* *Merc* *Nit-ac* *Phos* *Urt-u*
- **leukorrhea**; from: kreos bg2 puls bg2
- **menses** | **before** | **agg.**: agath-a nl2• lyc *Sep*
  • **during** | **agg.**: agath-a nl2• chin graph kreos k2 lyc sep staph sulph zinc
- **phlegmonous**: *Merc* k*
- **pregnancy** agg.; during: *Coll* hr1 *Merc* k* (non:podo k*)
- **sensation** as if: colch bg2 lach bg2 nux-m bg2 sabal bg2 sep b4a.de*
  • **menses**; before: sep b4a.de
○ • **Vulva**: colch ptk1 coll ptk1 merc b4a.de sep b4a.de sulph b4a.de
○ - **Clitoris**: | **as if swollen**: borx a1 colch ptk1 coll ptk1
- **Internal**: canth b7a.de ferr b7a.de kreos b7a.de
- **Labia**: am-c bg2 *Ambr* a1* *Apis* b7a.de* arn hr1 aur-m a1 borx c1* bry bg2* *Carb-v* bg2 chin a1 coll bg2 *Coloc* hr1 *Dig* hr1 dulc fd4.de gast a1 goss hr1 *Ham* hr1 *Helon* a1* kali-bi k2 *Kreos* hr1* lac-c hr1 lach bg2 meph bg2* *Merc* bg2* nit-ac a1 *Phos* hr1 podo hr1 **Puls** hr1 *Sep* hr1 spong fd4.de thuj a1* vanil fd5.de
  • **pregnancy** agg.; during: podo c1
○ • **Minora**: *Apis* chinin-s dulc fd4.de merc k* nit-ac vanil fd5.de
    ⋮ **Between**: eupi
- **Ovaries**: *(↗Enlarged - ovaries)* *Alum* k* *Am-br* bro1 *Apis* k* *Ars* k* ars-i k2 atro k* bell k* *Brom* k* *Bufo* k* *Carb-ac* k* *Carb-an* b4a.de coll *Coloc* k* con k* cub goss *Graph* k* ham k* *Iod* k* irid-met vml3• *Kali-br* k* *Kali-i* k* **Lach** k* **Lil-t** k* lyc bg1* *Med* *Merc* b4a.de nat-hchls nux-m k* *Pall* k* podo bg1 staph k* streptoc rly4• syph k* *Tarent* bro1 thuj tritic-vg fd5.de ust k*
  • **right**: *Apis* *Lach* hr1 lyc *Pall* k*
  • **left**: am-br vh1 *Atro* hr1 *Brom* k* carb-ac k* graph *Ham* hr1 *Kali-br* k* **Lach** k* lil-t k* *Nat-hchls* syph al* tritic-vg fd5.de
  • **dropsical**: *(↗GENERALS - Dropsy - internal)* **Apis** arn **Ars** k* aur-m-n bell k* bry **Calc** carb-an chin *Coloc* con dig b4a.de *Ferr-i* k* graph *Iod* k* kali-br kali-c kreos *Lach* *Lil-t* k* **Lyc** med merc k* nat-s phos plat *Plb* podo prun rhod rhus-t sabin *Sulph* b4a.de ter k* zinc
  • **menses**:
    ⋮ **after** | **agg.**: *Graph* k*
    ⋮ **before** | **agg.**: brom k*
    ⋮ **during** | **agg.**: apis *Atro* hr1 brom k* ham hr1 nat-hchls
- **Pubic** region: ambr br1
- **Pudendum** | **leukorrhea** agg.: *Puls* b7.de*
- **Uterus**: *Agn* k* anan ang bg2* aur bg2* *Bell* bg2 calc-i bg2* canth bg2 con bg2* cub c1 falco-pe nl2* *Iod* k* *Lach* k* lap-a bg* *Lil-t* k* lyc b4a.de* *Lyss* meph k* merc bg2 nux-m tl1 **Nux-v** bg2* *Ph-ac* b4a.de phos bg2 plat bg2* rob hr1 sabin k* sec bg2* *Sep* bg2* *Tarent* k* thuj bg2 ust k* verat hr1
  • **daytime**: *Bry*

Female

- **Uterus**: ...
  - **dropsical**: (↗*GENERALS - Dropsy - internal)* aesc *Apis* ars *Bell* brom *Bry* calc *Camph* canth *Chin Colch* k* con *Dig* dulc *Ferr* ham **Hell** k* iod kali-c lach lact led *Lob* **Lyc** k* merc nat-hchls bro1 phos puls rhus-t ruta sabad *Sep* k* *Sulph*
    - **accompanied** by:
      - **induration** of uterus: aur bro1 aur-m-k bro1 *Aur-m-n* bro1 carb-an bro1 *Con* bro1 graph bro1 *Iod* bro1 kalm bro1 kreos bro1 mag-m bro1 plat bro1 *Sep* bro1
      - **Extremities**; piercing pain in: hell ptk1
  - **menses** | **before** | **agg.**: nux-m ph-ac
    - **during** | **agg.**: kali-bi *Nux-m* hr1 ust
- ○ · **Cervix**: anan bro1 arg-met k2 arg-n aur hr1 calc k* *Calc-p* canth k* *Caul* hr1 hydr k* *Iod* k* *Kreos* k* mit hr1 murx hr1 *Nat-m* k* sarr k* sec b7a.de *Sep* b4a.de ust hr1
  - **accompanied** by | **urinary** complaints: canth bro1
- **Vagina**: *Agar* k* alum hr1 alumn k* calc-p k* cann-s k* coc-c *Cur* k* ferr k* *Ferr-i* k* *Iod* k* kali-bi bg2 *Kreos* k* merc k* **Nit-ac** k* *Nux-v* k* oxal-a rly4• puls k* rad-br c11
  - **pregnancy** agg.; during: borx c1
  - **sensation** of: allox sp1
    - **standing**; after: allox sp1*
- **Vulva**: *Apis* bro1 carb-v tl1* hep ptk1 puls ptk1 senec ptk1 sep ptk1
  - **itching**; with: rhus-t ptk1
  - **leukorrhea**; from: *Kreos* mrr1
  - **menses** | **after** | **agg.**: kreos b7a.de
    - **during** | **agg.**: lyc b4a.de
  - **pregnancy** agg.; during: podo ptk1

SYMPHYSIOLYSIS: tril-p c1*
- **sensation** of: murx hr1*

TENSION: *Graph* b4a.de puls b7.de*
- ○ - **Clitoris**: borx b4a.de

TIGHTNESS in ovarian region on raising arms: *Apis*

TINGLING, voluptuous: (↗*Formication)* agar *Alum* am-m j5.de* apis bov bufo cadm-s a1 calc *Calc-p* cann-i a1 canth cere-s a1 coff elaps fl-ac a1 gink-b sbd1• irid-met srj5• *Kali-br* kreos lach lil-t lyc mosch *Nit-ac* kr1 *Nux-v* **Orig** k* par a1 petr h2* *Phos* **Plat** k* raph rhus-t bg2 *Stann* kr1 staph sul-ac j5.de tarent
- **morning**: *Kreos* j5.de
- **anxiety** and palpitation, with: *Plat* kr1
- **dream**, in: sul-ac j5.de
- **menses**:
  - **before** and during | **agg.**: calc sf1.de kali-c j5.de*
- **orgasm**; with: sul-ac j5.de
- **scratching** the arm, while: *Stann* kr1
- **sitting** agg.: nat-m a1
- **unconsciousness**, during partial: meth-ae-ae a1
- **waking**; on: am-m j5.de* kali-c j5.de
- **walking** | **amel.**: nat-m a1
- ▽ - **extending** to | **Abdomen**; into: plat st
- ○ - **Ovaries**:
  - **left** | **menses**; after: lac-e hrn2•
- **Vulva**: bros-gau mrc1

TREMBLING:
- ○ - **Ovaries** | **left**: bell bg2

TUBERCLES: *Calc* k* *Carb-ac* k* *Kali-i* hr1 *Merc* k* phos
- **stinging** burning: *Calc* k*

TUMORS: arg-met k2 *Calc* k* coc-c **Lyc** k* *Nit-ac* k*
- **encysted**: apis vh bar-c k* calc k* carbn-s *Graph* k* *Kali-br* vh kali-c k* lyc k* nit-ac rhod *Sabin* sep k* *Sil* k* sulph k* *Thuj*
- **erectile**: ars k* *Carb-an* k* *Carb-v* k* kali-bi vh kreos k* *Lach* k* lyc k* *Nit-ac* k* *Phos* k* plat k* sep k* sil k* sulph k* *Thuj* k*
  - **bleeding**: arn k* coc-c k* kreos k* lach k* *Phos* k* puls k* thuj k* vac jl2
  - **blue**: *Carb-v* k*

Tumors – erectile: ...
  - **burning**: calc *Carb-an* k* *Thuj* k*
  - **itching**: graph mtf naja mtf *Nit-ac* k*
  - **pricking**: *Carb-v* k*
  - **sticking**: *Nit-ac*
- **hard**: *Carb-v* k*
- ○ - **Labia**: ozone sde2•
  - **pointed**: ozone sde2•
  - **sensitive** to touch; not: ozone sde2•
- **Ovaries**: **Apis** k* apoc k* arg-met k2 *Ars* k* ars-i aur-m-n bro1* *Bar-m* k* bov bro1 *Brom* lp *Calc* k* calc-i k2 *Coloc* k* con bro1 fl-ac k* graph k* hep k* *Iod* k* kali-br bro1* **Lach** k* **Lyc** k* med mrr1 ov c2* phos mrr1 *Plat* k* *Podo* k* *Sec* c2* staph k* stram k* syph k* tarent mrr1 thuj k* zinc k*
  - **right**: *Apis Ars* hr1 fl-ac *Iod* **Lyc** k* *Pall* k* *Podo* k* rhod c1 xan c1
  - **left**: apis vh arg-met k2 *Ars* sne brom mrr1 grat mrr1 kali-bi vh **Lach** k* phos mrr1 *Podo*
  - **cysts**: am-c mtf am-i mtf am-m mtf *Apis* k* apoc bro1* arg-met k2* arg-n mtf arn bro1 ars bro1 aur ptk1* aur-i bro1 *Aur-m-n* bro1* bar-c mtf bar-i mtf bell bro1* *Bov* k* brom mrr1 bry bro1 *Bufo* calc gk* calc-f mtf calc-i mtf calc-s mtf canth k* carb-an k* carc mrr1* chin bro1 *Coloc* k* con bro1* ferr-i bro1 foll oss• form ptk1 graph bro1* *Iod* k* kali-bi mrr1 *Kali-br* k* kali-c mtf lac-c mtf *Lach* k* lil-t bro1 lyc bro1* mag-i mtf mag-m mtf med bro1* merc k* murx k* naja mrr1* nat-m mtf nit-ac gk* ov br1* *Pall* mrr1* *Phos* mrr1* *Plat* k* podo mrr1* prun k* puls mtf rhod k* *Rhus-t* k* sabin bro1 sec mtf sep mtf sil mtf staph mtf sulph mtf syc pte1* syph k2* ter bro1 thuj k* zinc bro1*
    - **right** side: *Apis* mrr1 *Bell* mrr1 lyc mrr1 pall mrr1 podo mrr1
    - **left** side: kali-bi mrr1 lach mrr1 naja mrr1 pall mtf11 phos mrr1 plat mrr1 thuj mrr1
    - **painful**: syc fmm1•
  - **fibroids**: apis calc k* coloc k* fl-ac k* hep k* iod k* lach k* merc k* plat k* *Podo* k* puls k2 sabin k2 staph k* tarent k2 thuj k* xan c1
- **Uterus**: aur-m c2 **Aur-m-n** bn* bufo dgt1 cadm-met sne *Calc* carc br1* cham sne cocc mrr1 *Crot-h* frax c2* irid-met br1 *Kali-bi* sne sabal c2 sanic c2 **Ter** k* thuj k*
  - **cysts**: mag-c gm1 sabin mrr1
  - **myoma** (= fibroid): abel vh1 *Apis* arb st1 *Arn* sne ars sk1• ars-i vh aur mrr1 *Aur-i* bro1 aur-m bro1* *Aur-m-n* k* bell hr1* brom bry hr1* bufo **Calc** k* **Calc-f** k* *Calc-i* a1* *Calc-p* k* *Calc-s* k* *Calen* bro1 carc sst*• cham sne chin bro1 chol st1 chr-s bro1 cimic gk coenz-q mtf11 *Con* k* erod bro1 ferr bro1* fl-ac mg1.de* foll oss• frax br1* graph bro1* ham bg2* helon mrr1 hydr a1* *Hydrc* bro1 *Hydrin-m* c1* *Hydrinin-m* c1* *Iod* bro1 ip bro1 irid-met vml3• *Kali-bi* sne kali-br k* *Kali-c* k* *Kali-i* k* *Lach* k* lap-a hr1* *Led* k* lil-t k* lyc k* mag-m a2 med a1 merc *Merc-c* k* merc-i-r k* morg-p pte1*• nat-m gk nit-ac k* nux-v parathyr mtf11 **Phos** k* phyt st1 plat k* plb bro1 puls k2* rhus-t sne sabal bro1 sabin k2* sang bro1 *Sec* k* sep bro1 **Sil** k* solid bro1 staph bro1 sul-ac sulph bro1 tarent hr1* ter k* teucr c1* thiosin br1* thlas c1* thuj k* thyr c1* tril-p bro1* tub ust k* vinc viol-o br1 x-ray sp1 xan c1* xanth sne [berb stu1 calc-n stj1]
    - **accompanied** by:
      - **hemorrhage** (See Metrorrhagia - fibroids)
      - **pain**; burning: *Lap-a* br1*
      - **Head**; pain in (See HEAD - Pain - accompanied - myoma)
    - **hard**: *Calc-f* mrr1 merc-i-r ptk1 sil mrr1
    - **hemorrhage**; with (See Metrorrhagia - fibroids)
    - **large**: *Calc-f* mrr1
    - **painful**: viol-o br1
- **Vagina**:
  - **cysts**: *Lyc* k* *Puls* k* rhod k* **Sil** k* thuj mtf11
    - **serous**: rhod c1*

TURNING:
- **amel.**: castm bg2
- **bed**; in:
  - **agg.** | **Ovaries**: lyc ptk1

TWITCHING: bell k2 sep k*

ULCERS: alum alum-p k2 alum-sil k2 **Alumn** am-c k* anan *Arg-n* k* ars *Asaf* bell bell-p sp1 bry calc k* calc-s carb-v con graph *Hep* hydr bg2 hydrc c1 kali-i kreos b7a.de* lac-c k* lacer a1* *Lach* *Lyc* **Merc** k* *Merc-c* k* merc-i-f merc-i-r mez a1 *Mur-ac* k* **Nit-ac** k* ph-ac phos *Psor* k* *Puls* rhus-t rob k* sars b4a.de sec k* *Sep* k* **Sil** staph sulph syph k* *Thuj* k* vesp zinc k*

- **chancres**: (↗*GENERALS - Chancre)* kali-i mrr1 merc k2

○ - **Labia**: kali-bi bg2 med hr1 merc bg2 nit-ac bg2* *Psor* hr1 *Sep* hr1 syph br thuj bg2 zinc hr1

- **Uterus**: arg-met k2 arg-n bg2* *Arn* hr1 ars bg2 ars-i k2 aur k2 bufo k2 *Calc* hr1 carb-an bg2* hydr bg2* *Hydrc* br1 kreos bg2* *Lyss* hr1 *Merc-c* hr1 *Mez* hr1 sep bg2 ust bg2* vesp-xyz c2 *Zinc* hr1
  - · **abortion**; from: aur ptk1

○ · **Cervix**: aln bro1 alum k2 alumn k2* arg-met k2* arg-n k2* *Ars* bro1 *Aur-m-n* bro1 bomh gm1 bufo k2* calc-s k2 *Carb-ac* bg* carb-an bg* fl-ac bg2* *Helon* hr1 hydr bg2* *Hydrc* bro1 kali-ar bro1 kreos bg2* lyc bg* med hr1 *Merc* hr1* merc-c bg2* *Murx* hr1* **Nat-m** hr1 *Phyt* hr1* sang hr1* sep bg2* *Sil* hr1* sul-ac bg* *Thuj* hr1* ust bg2* *Vesp* bg*

: **bleeding** easily: aln bro1 arg-n bro1 carb-an bro1 kreos bro1

: **cancerous**: bufo ptk1 med ptk1 mez ptk1

: **accompanied** by | **prolapse** of uterus: arg-n ptk1

: **deep**: merc-c bro1

: **fetid** discharge; with: ars bro1 carb-ac bro1 carb-an bro1 kreos bro1

: **old** people; in: | **women**; old: sul-ac bro1

: **spongy**: arg-n bro1 kreos bro1

: **superficial**: *Hydr* bro1 merc bro1

: **Os**: calc-sil k2

: **cautery**, after: arg-n k2

- **Vagina**: alumn k2* arg-n bg2 bapt hr1 calc-sil k2 *Hydr* hr1 kali-bi bg2 kreos bg2 *Merc* hr1 merc-c bg2 mez ptk1 *Nit-ac* bg2* rob hr1 *Sep* hr1 sulph bg2 thuj bg2
- **Vulva**: arg-n bro1 *Ars* bro1 *Aur-m-n* bro1 graph bro1 *Hep* bro1 merc bro1 mur-ac bro1 *Nit-ac* bro1 sep bro1 syph bro1* thuj bro1

UNDRESSING:

- **amel.** | **Uterus**: onos ptk1

URINATION:

- **agg.** | **Vagina**: sil ptk1

VAGINISMUS: (↗*Coition - enjoyment - absent)* *Acon* k* aln c1 alumn c1* aq-mar mgm• aur c1 *Bell* k* *Berb* k* **Cact** k* *Canth* k* caul ptk1 coc-c sf1.de cocc k* con k* *Cupr* st ferr *Ferr-p* k* gels *Ham* k* *Ign* k* kali-br k* kreos sf1.de *Lyc* k* lyss c1* mag-p k* med jl2 merc *Nat-m* k* nux-v k* plat k* **Plb** k* plb-xyz c2 *Puls* k* sep sf1.de* *Sil* k* staph sf1.de *Thuj* hr1*

- **coition**:
  - · **during**: cact k* gels ptk1 *Plat* k*
  - · **painful**: alumn apis kr1 **Arg-n** bell *Berb* borx sf1.de calc sf1.de *Calc-p* coff *Ferr* *Ferr-m* *Ferr-p* ham *Hep* hydr ign *Kali-bi* *Kali-c* *Kreos* *Lyc* kr1* **Lyss** **Nat-m** *Plat* *Rhus-t* sabin **Sep** sil *Staph* *Sulph* *Thuj*
  - · **preventing**: **Cact** k* plat
- **sensitiveness** of vagina; from: acon bro1 aur bro1 *Bell* bro1 *Berb* bro1 *Cact* bro1 carb-v bro1 *Caul* bro1 caust bro1 *Cimic* bro1 *Cocc* bro1 *Coff* bro1 con bro1 ferr bro1 ferr-i bro1 ferr-p bro1 *Gels* bro1 ham bro1 *Ign* bro1 kreos bro1 lac-c bro1 lyss bro1 *Mag-p* bro1 mur-ac bro1 *Murx* bro1 nit-ac bro1 nux-v bro1 orig bro1 plat bro1* *Plb* bro1 sil bro1 *Staph* bro1 tarent bro1 *Thuj* bro1

VAGINITIS (See Inflammation - vagina)

VEINS, varicose: ambr k* arn lt1.fr *Calc* k* calc-f bg* calc-sil k2 *Carb-v* k* coll bg fl-ac bg2 *Ham* k* **Lyc** k ●* nux-v k* *Thuj* k* *Zinc* k*

- **accompanied** by | **abortion**: calc bg2 carb-v bg2
- **burning** | **menses**; during: thuj hr1

○ - **Labia**: calc-f bg2 carb-v bg2 coll bg2 ham bg2 lyc bg2 nux-v bg2 zinc bg2

- **Vulva**: calc bro1 carb-v bro1 **Ham** mrr1 lyc bro1

VIRILISM: (↗*GENERALS - Hair - distribution)* chlorpr jl1 cortico jl1* cortiso jl1

VOLUPTUOUS SENSATION, coitus-like (See Tingling)

WARM: | **applications** | **amel.**: mag-p bro1

- **bed**:
  - · **agg.** | **Ovaries**: apis ptk1 merc ptk1

WARMTH; sensation of (See Heat)

WARTS (See Condylomata; Excrescences)

WEAKNESS, sensation of: alum k2 amyg-p c2 sulph b4.de* thlas bg1

○ - **Pelvic** muscles: rhus-t k2

- **Uterus**: alet bg2 alst c2 calc-p bg2 *Chin* b7a.de croc bg2 ferr-i bg2 helo bg2 nat-p kr1 phos bg2 plb bg2 sabin bg2 sep bg2 sulph h2* thlas bg2
  - · **stool** and urine; during passage of: *Calc-p* k* nat-p k2

WEIGHT; sensation of: | **Uterus** (See Heaviness - uterus)

WORMS: | **pinworms**: ferr k* merc b4a.de *Sabad* hr1 *Sil* k* *Sulph* k*

CLITORIS; complaints of: am-c ptk1 coll ptk1

OVARIES; complaints of: acon b2.de* agar b2.de* agn b2.de* ambr b2.de* ant-c b2.de* **Apis** b7a.de* arn b2.de* ars bg2 *Asaf* b2.de* *Aur* b2.de* **Bell** b2.de* calc b2.de* **Canth** b2.de* *Carb-an* b2.de* carb-v b2.de* caust b2.de* chel b2.de* *Chin* b2.de* *Cimic* br1 clem bg2 coloc b2.de* *Con* bg2 dros b2.de* *Dulc* bg2 graph b2.de* guaj ptk1 hyos b2.de* ign b2.de* *Kali-c* b2.de* kali-n b2.de* **Lach** b2.de* laur b2.de* **Lil-t** bg2* *Lyc* b2.de* mag-p ptk1 med jl2 **Merc** b2.de* mez b2.de* nat-c b2.de* nit-ac b2.de* nux-v b2.de* pall bg2* **Plat** bg2 plb b2.de* podo ptk1 puls b2.de* *Ran-b* b2.de* ran-s b2.de* ruta b2.de* sabal br1* *Sabin* bg2 sars b2.de* *Sec* b2.de* *Sep* b2.de* **Staph** b2.de* sulph b2.de* tarent mrr1 **Thuj** b2.de* ust ptk1 viol-t b2.de *Zinc* b2.de* *Zinc-val* br1*

- **alternating** sides: cimic bg2* coloc ptk1 lac-c bg2* lil-t ptk1 onos bg2* ust ptk1
- **right**: **Apis** bg2 bell ptk1 **Lyc** bg2* pall ptk1 podo ptk1 *Staph* bg2
- **left**: arg-met ptk1 coloc bg2 lach ptk1 lil-t bg2 puls bg2 thuj bg2* ust ptk1 zinc ptk1

▽ · **extending** to | **Heart**: brom ptk1 cimic ptk1 lac-c ptk1 lach ptk1 lil-t ptk1 *Naja* ptk1 sulph ptk1 vib ptk1

- **accompanied** by:
  - · **congestion** (See GENERALS - Congestion - blood - accompanied - ovaries)
  - · **convulsions** (See GENERALS - Convulsions - accompanied - ovaries)
  - · **urine**; bloody: diosm br1

○ · **Eyes**, complaints of: onos ptk1

- · **Head** | **complaints** of: sabal ptk1
- · **Heart**; complaints of (See CHEST - Heart; complaints - accompanied - ovaries)
- · **Mammae**; complaints of: sabal ptk1

▽ - **extending** to:

○ · **Back** | **right**: rumx ptk1

- · **Limbs**: lil-t ptk1
- · **Mammae**: lil-t ptk1 murx ptk1 senec ptk1
- · **Shoulder**: podo ptk1
- · **Thigh**: coloc ptk1 graph ptk1 lil-t ptk1 podo ptk1 *Staph* ptk1 ust ptk1 xan ptk1 zinc-val ptk1
- · **Uterus**: iod ptk1

UTERUS; complaints of: acon b2.de* ant-c b2.de* ant-t b2.de* arn b2.de* asaf b2.de* aur b2.de* **Bell** b2.de* borx b2.de* bov b2.de* bry b2.de* calc b2.de* camph b2.de* *Carb-an* b2.de* carb-v b2.de* caust b2.de* **Cham** b2.de* chin b2.de* cina b2.de* *Cocc* b2.de* coff b2.de* **Con** b2.de* *Croc* b2.de* cupr b2.de* dros b2.de* *Ferr* b2.de* ferr-i bg2 frax bg2 *Graph* b2.de* ham bg2 *Hyos* b2.de* *Ign* b2.de* iod b2.de* ip b2.de* **Kali-c** b2.de* *Kreos* b2.de* lach b2.de* **Lil-t** bg2 lyc b2.de* mag-c b2.de* *Mag-m* b2.de* merc b2.de* mosch b2.de* mur-ac b2.de* nat-c b2.de* *Nat-m* b2.de* nux-m b2.de* **Nux-v** b2.de* op b2.de* ph-ac b2.de* phos b2.de* **Plat** b2.de* **Puls** b2.de* *Rhus-t* b2.de* ruta b2.de* sabad b2.de* **Sabin** b2.de* **Sec** b2.de* **Sep** b2.de* stann b2.de* stram bg2 sul-ac b2.de* **Sulph** b2.de* thuj b2.de* verat bg2 zinc b2.de*

- **accompanied** by:
  - · **cough**: graph bg2 ign bg2
  - · **dysuria**: con bro1 nux-m ptk1 staph bro1
  - · **sleeplessness**: senec bro1*
  - · **vertigo**: cycl bg2 lach bg2 lil-t bg2 puls bg2 stann bg2
  - · **vomiting**: caul ptk1 kreos ptk1 lil-t ptk1 senec ptk1

○ · **Head**; pain in: aloe bro1 bell bro1 *Cimic* bro1 *Gels* bro1 helon bro1 ign bro1 joan bro1 lil-t bro1 plat bro1 *Puls* bro1 *Sep* bro1 zinc bro1 zinc-p bro1

Female

- **accompanied** by: ...
  - **Joints**; complaints of: sabin bro1
  - **Lower** limbs; paralysis of (See EXTREMITIES - Paralysis - lower - accompanied - uterus)
  - **Mammae**; complaints of: sil ptk1
  - **Stomach**; pain in: borx bro1
- **alternating** with | **Heart**; complaints of (See CHEST - Heart; complaints - alternating - uterus)

▽ - **extending** to:

O · **Stomach**: borx ptk1
  - **Thigh**:
    - **Anterior**: vib ptk1
    - **Downward**: ust ptk1
  - **Throat**: gels ptk1

VAGINA; complaints of: alum bg2 ambr b2.de* ars b2.de* aur b2.de* *Bell* b2.de* berb ptk1 borx b2.de* bry b2.de* **Calc** b2.de* *Canth* b2.de* caps bg2 carb-an b2.de* carb-v b2.de* caust b2.de* cham b2.de* chin b2.de* cocc b2.de* coff b2.de* **Con** b2.de* croc b2.de* dulc b2.de* *Ferr* b2.de* graph b2.de* hep b2.de* hyos b2.de* ign b2.de* iod b2.de* **Kali-c** b2.de* kreos b2.de* *Lyc* b2.de* mag-c b2.de* mag-m b2.de* *Merc* b2.de* mur-ac bg2 *Nat-c* b2.de* nat-m b2.de* nit-ac b2.de* nux-m b2.de* *Nux-v* b2.de* petr b2.de* phos b2.de* plat b2.de* *Puls* b2.de* rheum b2.de* *Rhus-t* b2.de* sabin b2.de* sars b2.de* sec b2.de* **Sep** b2.de* sil b2.de* stann b2.de* staph b2.de* sul-ac b2.de* **Sulph** b2.de* thuj b2.de* zinc b2.de*

MORNING: am-m bg2 anac bg2 aur bg2 bov bg2 brom bg2 bry bg2 calad bg2 calc bg2 calc-p bg2 cann-xyz bg2 canth bg2 caps bg2 carb-v bg2 caust bg2 cham bg2 cic bg2 clem bg2 coff bg2 dig bg2 fl-ac bg2 graph bg2 kali-bi bg2 kali-c bg2 kreos bg2 lach bg2 lyc bg2 mag-m bg2 mur-ac bg2 nat-c bg2 nat-m bg2 nat-s bg2 nit-ac bg2 nux-v bg2 par bg2 ph-ac bg2 phos bg2 phyt bg2 plb bg2 puls bg2 rhus-t bg2 sabad bg2 sabin bg2 sel bg2 sep bg2 spig bg2 sulph bg2 thuj bg2 valer bg2 verb bg2 viol-t bg2 zinc bg2

NOON: caust bg2 mag-c bg2 sulph bg2 thuj bg2

AFTERNOON: arg-met bg2 arn bg2 calc bg2 calc-p bg2 cann-xyz bg2 caps bg2 cham bg2 gels bg2 kali-n bg2 mag-c bg2 nat-m bg2 nat-s bg2 phyt bg2 podo bg2 sep bg2 thuj bg2

EVENING: arg-met bg2 aur bg2 bar-c bg2 bell bg2 brom bg2 caps bg2 carb-v bg2 chin bg2 con bg2 croc bg2 cycl bg2 euphr bg2 fl-ac bg2 gels bg2 ign bg2 kali-bi bg2 *Kreos* bg2 lach bg2 laur bg2 lyc bg2 mag-c bg2 mag-m bg2 *Merc* bg2 mez bg2 nat-m bg2 nat-s bg2 nit-ac bg2 nux-v bg2 phos bg2 *Puls* bg2 rhod bg2 rhus-t bg2 ruta bg2 sabad bg2 sel bg2 sil bg2 sulph bg2 zinc bg2

NIGHT: agar bg2 am-c bg2 am-m bg2 anac bg2 arg-met bg2 arg-n bg2 arn bg2 aur bg2 bell bg2 bism bg2 bov ↓ brom bg2 bry bg2 calc bg2 camph bg2 cann-xyz bg2 caps bg2 carb-an bg2 carb-v bg2 caust bg2 cham bg2 chin bg2 cic bg2 clem bg2 cocc bg2 coff bg2 colch bg2 coloc bg2 con bg2 cycl bg2 dig bg2 euph bg2 ferr bg2 fl-ac bg2 gels bg2 graph bg2 guaj bg2 ign bg2 kali-bi bg2 kali-c bg2 lach bg2 laur bg2 led bg2 lyc bg2 *Mag-c* bg2 mag-m bg2 *Merc* bg2 nat-c bg2 nat-m bg2 nit-ac bg2 nux-m ↓ nux-v bg2 op bg2 par bg2 ph-ac bg2 phos bg2 phyt ↓ plat ↓ plb ↓ puls bg2 ran-b ↓ ran-s ↓ rhod bg2 rhus-t bg2 ruta bg2 sabin bg2 samb ↓ sars bg2 seneg bg2 sep bg2 sil bg2 stann bg2 staph bg2 sulph bg2 tab bg2 tarax bg2 thuj bg2 verb bg2 zinc bg2
- **midnight**; after: bov bg2 nat-c bg2 nat-m bg2 nit-ac bg2 nux-m bg2 phyt bg2 plat bg2 plb bg2 ran-b bg2 ran-s bg2 *Rhus-t* bg2 samb bg2 tab bg2

AIR; IN OPEN:
- **agg.**: nit-ac bg2 ph-ac bg2 rhus-t bg2
- **amel.**: thuj bg2

ANGER; after: nat-m bg2

BATHING: | **amel.**: sec bg2

BED AGG.; IN: am-m bg2 arg-met bg2 cann-xyz bg2 caps bg2 cham bg2 chin bg2 clem bg2 euph bg2 ign bg2 lyc bg2 *Mag-m* bg2 mur-ac bg2 nat-s bg2 nit-ac bg2 nux-v bg2 ph-ac bg2 phos bg2 plat bg2 puls bg2

BEER agg.: nat-c bg2

BENDING:
- **agg.**: bell bg2
- **amel.**: caust bg2 *Puls* bg2 sep bg2

BENDING DOUBLE: | **amel.**: mag-p bg2

BRANDY: | **amel.**: nux-v bg2

BREATHING agg.: *Cocc* bg2 rhod bg2

CAMPHOR amel.: nux-v bg2

CARESSED agg.; being: arn bg2 *Con* bg2 hep bg2 petr bg2 sabad bg2

COITION: (↗*GENERALS - Coition)*
- **agg.**: arg-met bg2 berb bg2 calc bg2 cann-xyz bg2 caust bg2 clem bg2 ferr bg2 graph bg2 kali-c bg2 kali-n bg2 kreos bg2 lyc bg2 merc bg2 nat-c bg2 nat-m bg2 nit-ac bg2 par bg2 phos bg2 psor bg2 rhus-t bg2 sec bg2 sep bg2 sulph bg2
- **amel.**: merc bg2
- **enjoyment**: chlam-tr bcx2•
  - **insupportable**: stann bg2

COLD; AFTER TAKING A: acon bg2 puls bg2

COLD BATHING: | **amel.**: *Alum* bg2 ang bg2 apis bg2 bell bg2 caps bg2

COMPLAINTS of genitalia: acon b2.de agar b2.de agn b2.de* alum b2.de* am-c b2.de* am-m b2.de ambr b2.de* anac b2.de ang b2.de ant-c b2.de* ant-t b2.de* arg-met b2.de **Arn** b2.de* ars b2.de* asaf b2.de asar b2.de aur b2.de* bar-c b2.de bell b2.de* berb ptk1 bism b2.de borx b2.de bov b2.de bry b2.de* calad b2.de* calc b2.de* camph b2.de cann-s b2.de* canth b2.de* caps b2.de* carb-an b2.de carb-v b2.de* caust b2.de* cham b2.de chel b2.de chin b2.de* cic b2.de cina b2.de clem b2.de* cocc b2.de* coff b2.de* colch b2.de coloc b2.de con b2.de* croc b2.de cupr b2.de cycl b2.de dig b2.de dros b2.de dulc b2.de erig ptk1 euph b2.de euphr b2.de ferr b2.de gels ptk1 graph b2.de* guaj b2.de hell b2.de hep b2.de* hyos b2.de* ign b2.de* iod b2.de* ip b2.de kali-c b2.de* kali-n b2.de kreos b2.de lach b2.de laur b2.de led b2.de lyc b2.de* m-ambo b2.de m-arct b2.de *M-aust* b2.de mag-c b2.de mag-m b2.de mang b2.de meny b2.de **Merc** b2.de* mez b2.de* mosch b2.de mur-ac b2.de nat-c b2.de* nat-m b2.de* nat-p ptk1 **Nit-ac** b2.de* nux-m b2.de **Nux-v** b2.de* op b2.de par b2.de petr b2.de ph-ac b2.de* phos b2.de* plat b2.de plb b2.de* **Puls** b2.de* ran-s b2.de rheum b2.de rhod b2.de* rhus-t b2.de* ruta b2.de sabad b2.de sabal ptk1 sabin b2.de* samb b2.de sars b2.de sec b2.de sel b2.de* seneg b2.de **Sep** b2.de* sil b2.de* spig b2.de spong b2.de* squil b2.de stann b2.de staph b2.de* stram b2.de sul-ac b2.de **Sulph** b2.de* tarax b2.de teucr b2.de **Thuj** b2.de* valer b2.de verat b2.de viol-t b2.de zinc b2.de*
- **right**: acon b7a.de* alum b4a.de **Apis** b7a.de* arn bg2 aur b4a.de* *Bell* bg2 bism b7a.de* **Calc** b4a.de* cann-s b7a.de* canth b7a.de* **Caust** b4a.de* clem b4a.de* coff b7a.de* coloc b4a.de* con b4a.de* croc b7a.de* dig b4a.de* graph b4a.de **Hep** b4a.de* **Iod** b4a.de lach b7a.de* lyc b4a.de* m-arct b7a.de meny b7a.de* **Merc** b4a.de* mez b4a.de mur-ac b4a.de* nat-c b4a.de* nit-ac b4a.de **Nux-v** b7a.de* pall ptk1 petr b4a.de* puls b7a.de* rhod b4a.de* sabin b7a.de* sec b7a.de* sel b7a.de* sil b4a.de spig b7a.de* **Spong** b7a.de* staph b7a.de* **Sul-ac** b4a.de* sulph b4a.de* tarax b7a.de teucr b7a.de valer b7a.de* **Verat** b7a.de* zinc b4a.de*
- **left**: agar b4a.de* alum b4a.de am-m b7a.de ambr b7a.de ang b7a.de* ant-c b7a.de* apis b7a.de* arg-met b7a.de* aur b4a.de* bar-c b4a.de* brom b4a.de* bry b7a.de* calc b4a.de cann-s b7a.de chin b7a.de* clem b4a.de* colch b7a.de* con b4a.de* euph b4a.de* fl-ac b4a.de* graph b4a.de kali-c b4a.de* **Lach** b7a.de* lil-t bg2 lyc b4a.de m-arct b7a.de mag-c b4a.de* meny b7a.de merc b4a.de* mez b4a.de naja ptk1 nat-c b4a.de* nit-ac b4a.de* petr b4a.de ph-ac b4a.de* plb b7a.de* puls b7a.de* rhod b4a.de* rhus-t b7a.de* sabad b7a.de* *Sabin* b7a.de sel b4a.de* sep b4a.de* sil b4a.de spig b7a.de staph b7a.de tarax b7a.de teucr b7a.de **Thuj** b4a.de* *Ust* bg2 zinc b4a.de
- **accompanied** by:
  - **voice**; complaints of: helio bg2
  - ○ **Head**; complaints of (See HEAD - Complaints - accompanied - genitalia)
- ▽ **extending** to | **Abdomen**: coloc ptk1

CONDYLOMATA: nit-ac bro1 thuj bro1

CONSTIPATION agg.: coll bg2 con bg2 fl-ac bg2 graph bg2 lach bg2 mag-m bg2 plat bg2 sep bg2 sulph bg2

COUGH agg.; during: cann-xyz bg2 ign bg2 nat-m bg2

DINNER; after: cham bg2 nat-c bg2

DRINKING: | **amel.**: ferr bg2

DRIVING agg.: am-c bg2 apis bg2 brom bg2 calc bg2 calc-p bg2 eup-per bg2 phos bg2

EATING agg.: aloe bg2 colch bg2 hyos bg2

ERUPTIONS: | **herpes**: aur-m bro1 calc bro1 *Caust* bro1 crot-t bro1 dulc bro1 *Hep* bro1 jug-r bro1 *Merc* bro1 *Nit-ac* bro1 petr bro1 ph-ac bro1 *Sars* bro1 ter bro1

EXERTION agg.: arn bg2 rhus-t bg2 tril-p bg2

FLATUS; PASSING:
- **agg.**: ars bg2 lyc bg2 mag-c bg2
- **amel.**: aloe bg2 canth bg2 gels bg2 merc bg2

FLEXED legs: | **amel.**: sep bg2

FOOT-BATH agg.: mag-c bg2

GONORRHEA; AFTER SUPPRESSED: clem bg2 merc bg2 mez bg2 phyt bg2 **Puls** bg2 sel bg2 staph bg2 sulph bg2 thuj bg2

GRIEF agg.: coloc bg2

HAIR: | **falling**: nat-m ptk1 nit-ac ptk1 sel ptk1 zinc ptk1

HANDLING GENITALS: (↗*MIND - Gestures - tics)* acon ptk1 bell ptk1 bufo bro1* canth bro1* hyos bg2* merc ptk1 sep ptk1 *Stram* ptk1 ust bro1 zinc bro1*

HAWKING agg.: graph bg2

HEATED; when becoming: croc bg2

INDIGNATION agg.: coloc bg2

INSPIRATION AGG.; DEEP: graph bg2 sep bg2

Male and female

ITCHING: *Ambr* bro1 ars-i bro1 borx bro1 *Calad* bro1 carb-ac bro1 carb-v bro1 colch bro1 coll bro1 crot-t bro1 dulc bro1 fuli bro1 guan bro1 helon bro1 kreos bro1 mez bro1 nit-ac bro1 rhus-t bro1 rhus-v bro1 *Sep* bro1 sil bro1 tarent-c bro1

LEANING against something: | **amel.**: ign bg2

LIFTING agg.: croc bg2 podo bg2

LYING DOWN:
- **agg.**: ferr bg2 ign bg2 nit-ac bg2 *Puls* bg2
- **amel.**: bell bg2 sep bg2

LYING: | **abdomen**; on | **amel.**: bell bg2
- **side**; on | **amel.**: sep bg2

MASTURBATION; disposition to:
- **involuntary**: camph ptk1
- **itching**; from: staph bg2
- **puberty**; before: plat ptk1

MOTION:
- **agg.**: asaf bg2 bell bg2 *Cocc* bg2 **Croc** bg2 ferr bg2 nat-m bg2 *Sabin* bg2* spig bg2
- **amel.**: graph bg2 rhod bg2

MUSIC:
- **agg.**: pall bg2
- **amel.**: *Lach* bg2 mag-p bg2 mosch bg2 zinc-val bg2

ORGASM: | **easy**: stann ptk1

PAIN: borx ↓
- **coition**; after: kreos ↓
  - **corrosive**: kreos bg2
- **cutting** pain: borx bg2
- **urination** | **after**:
  - **agg.**: borx ↓
    - **cutting** pain: borx b4a.de
  - **before**: merc ↓
    - **pressing**: merc b4a.de

PERSPIRATION: calc bro1 petr bro1 ph-ac bro1 thuj bro1

PRESSURE:
- **agg.**: aesc bg2 apis bg2 bell bg2 canth bg2 carb-v bg2 cimic bg2 euphr bg2 ferr bg2 nux-m bg2 ph-ac bg2 sep bg2 thuj bg2
- **amel.**: castm bg2 mag-c bg2 plb bg2 sec bg2 staph bg2
- **clothes**; of: | **agg.**: arg-met bg2 *Lach* bg2
- **hand**; of | **amel.**: lil-t bg2

PURGATIVES agg.: sulph bg2

REST agg.: arg-met bg2 ign bg2 sil bg2 teucr bg2 zinc bg2

RIDING agg.: cann-xyz bg2

RISING FROM SITTING agg.: thuj bg2

RUBBING:
- **agg.**: aur bg2 chin bg2 coff bg2 con bg2 cycl bg2 nat-m bg2 staph bg2 thuj bg2
- **amel.**: crot-t bg2 pall bg2 staph bg2

SCRATCHING:
- **agg.**: clem bg2 euphr bg2 *Merc* bg2 nat-c bg2 nat-s bg2
- **amel.**: ang bg2 cann-xyz bg2 crot-t bg2 ign bg2 *Merc* bg2 nat-s bg2

SEXUAL desire:
- **absent**: *Ferr* b7a.de
- **complaints** of: agn ptk1 bar-c ptk1 calc ptk1 **Canth** ptk1 chin ptk1 *Con* ptk1 graph ptk1 *Lil-t* ptk1 **Lyc** ptk1 *Nux-v* ptk1 ph-ac ptk1 **Phos** ptk1 pic-ac ptk1 plat ptk1 sel ptk1 *Staph* ptk1 stram ptk1 sulph ptk1
  - **neurotics**; in: sabal ptk1
- **excessive**: **Phos** ptk1 *Stram* ptk1 tarent ptk1 *Zinc* ptk1
- **increased**: calc ptk1 calc-p ptk1 camph ptk1 cann-xyz ptk1 **Canth** ptk1 carb-v ptk1 con ptk1 fl-ac ptk1 lyc ptk1 lyss ptk1 mosch ptk1 *Nux-v* ptk1 onos ptk1 **Phos** ptk1 **Pic-ac** ptk1 **Plat** ptk1 *Puls* ptk1 sep ptk1 *Sil* ptk1 staph ptk1 stram ptk1 *Tub* ptk1 *Zinc* ptk1
  - **accompanied** by | **respiration**; asthmatic (See RESPIRATION - Asthmatic - accompanied - sexual)
  - **agg.**: con bg2 sabin bg2 *Sel* bg2

Sexual desire – **increased** – **agg.**: ...
  - **children**; in: aloe ptk1
  - **easily** excited: phos ptk1 sumb ptk1 zinc ptk1
  - **fever**; during: *Coff* b7a.de
  - **puberty**; at: manc ptk1
- **suppressed** | **ailments** from suppressed sexual desire: apis ptk1 *Camph* ptk1 *Con* ptk1 kali-br ptk1 lyss ptk1 phos ptk1 *Puls* ptk1
- **unsatisfied**: staph ptk1

SITTING agg.: am-c bg2 apis bg2 bry bg2 calc-p bg2 cann-xyz bg2 cocc bg2 con bg2 euph bg2 euphr bg2 graph bg2 helio bg2 kali-n bg2 lyc bg2 mag-c bg2 mag-m bg2 nat-s bg2 rhod bg2 sep bg2 sil bg2 staph bg2 sulph bg2* teucr bg2 thuj bg2 valer bg2 zinc bg2

SLEEP:
- **after** | **agg.**: canth bg2 caust bg2 clem bg2 dig bg2 fl-ac bg2 iod bg2 kali-c bg2 **Lach** bg2 mag-c bg2 merc bg2 merc-c bg2 nat-m bg2 nit-ac bg2 nux-v bg2 op bg2 phos bg2 plat bg2 plb bg2 rhod bg2 sep bg2
- **back**; when sleeping on:
  - **agg.**: stann bg2 staph bg2 sulph bg2
  - **amel.**: nat-m bg2
- **during** | **agg.**: canth bg2 caust bg2 clem bg2 dig bg2 fl-ac bg2 iod bg2 kali-c bg2 **Lach** bg2 mag-c bg2 merc bg2 merc-c bg2 nat-m bg2 nit-ac bg2 nux-v bg2 op bg2 phos bg2 plat bg2 plb bg2 rhod bg2 sep bg2

STANDING:
- **agg.**: ant-c bg2 ars bg2 bell bg2 carb-an bg2 graph bg2 iod bg2 mag-c bg2 mag-m bg2 ph-ac bg2 rhod bg2 rhus-t bg2 sil bg2 spig bg2 staph bg2 viol-t bg2
- **amel.**: bell bg2

STOOL:
- **after**:
  - **agg.**: ambr bg2 calc-p bg2 caust bg2 lyc bg2
  - **amel.**: mag-m bg2 pall bg2 senec bg2
- **before** | **agg.**: ign bg2 nat-c bg2
- **during** | **agg.**: am-m bg2 ambr bg2 ars bg2 carb-v bg2 ign bg2 iod bg2 nat-m bg2 phos bg2 stann bg2 zinc bg2
- **straining** at stool | **agg.**: carb-v bg2 con bg2 ph-ac bg2

STOOPING:
- **agg.**: staph bg2 zinc bg2
- **amel.**: ant-c bg2 mag-c bg2

STRETCHING agg.: apis bg2

SWELLING hot: | **coition**; after: kreos bg2

TOUCH:
- **agg.**: am-c bg2 ars bg2 asaf bg2 aur bg2 bism bg2 borx bg2 bry bg2 chin bg2 clem bg2 cocc bg2 con bg2* graph bg2 grat ptk1 mag-m bg2 merc bg2 merc-c bg2 nat-c ptk1 nat-m bg2 *Nit-ac* bg2 nux-v bg2 ph-ac bg2 *Plat* bg2* rhod bg2 rhus-t bg2 sabin bg2 sec bg2 sep bg2 staph bg2 thuj bg2 zinc bg2
- **clothes** agg.; of: graph bg2 **Lach** bg2 phos bg2

URINATION:
- **agg.**: am-c bg2 asaf bg2 bell bg2 calad bg2 calc bg2 calc-p bg2 canth bg2 caps bg2 carb-v bg2 caust bg2 clem bg2 con bg2 crot-t bg2 ign bg2 kali-n bg2 *Kreos* bg2 mag-m bg2 merc bg2 mez bg2 nat-c bg2 nat-m bg2 nit-ac bg2 op bg2 ph-ac bg2 phos bg2 plat bg2 puls bg2 rhus-t bg2 sars bg2 seneg bg2 sil bg2 sulph bg2 thuj bg2
- **amel.**: camph bg2 chin bg2 sep bg2

WAKING agg.; on: am-m bg2 anac bg2 arn bg2 borx bg2 calc-p bg2 carb-v bg2 kali-bi bg2 **Lach** bg2 merc-c bg2 nat-c bg2 nat-m bg2 nit-ac bg2 op bg2 par bg2 petr bg2 puls bg2 rhus-t bg2 sel bg2 sep bg2 sil bg2 viol-t bg2 zinc bg2

WALKING:
- **agg.**: ambr bg2 apis bg2 arg-met bg2 *Bell* bg2 cann-xyz bg2 carb-an bg2 caust bg2 chin bg2 clem bg2 crot-t bg2 graph bg2 ign bg2 kali-n bg2 mag-c bg2 mag-m bg2 merc bg2 nat-m bg2 nat-s bg2 nit-ac bg2 ox-ac bg2 ph-ac bg2 phos bg2 podo bg2 rhod bg2 rhus-t bg2 sars bg2 *Sep* bg2 staph bg2 teucr bg2 thuj bg2 zinc bg2
- **amel.**: glon bg2 mag-c bg2 mag-m bg2 nat-c bg2 nat-m bg2 sep bg2 thuj bg2 zinc bg2

WARM:
- **amel.**: bell bg2 castm bg2 caust bg2 laur bg2 mag-p bg2 rhus-t bg2
- **bathing** | **agg.**: clem bg2 nat-c bg2

WEAKNESS of sexual organs and functions: agar b2.de **Agn** b2.de* alum b2.de am-c b2.de ambr b2.de *Ant-c* b2.de apis b7a.de arn b2.de *Bar-c* b2.de* borx b2.de **Calad** b2.de* calc b2.de* *Camph* b2.de cann-s b2.de canth b2.de* caps b2.de carb-an b2.de carb-v b2.de caust b2.de *Chin* b2.de coff b2.de coloc b2.de **Con** b2.de dig b2.de dulc b2.de euph b2.de ferr b2.de **Graph** b2.de hell b2.de hep b2.de hyos b2.de *Ign* b2.de* iod b2.de *Kali-c* b2.de kreos b2.de lach b2.de **Lyc** b2.de m-ambo b2.de m-aust b2.de mag-c b2.de mang b2.de* meny b2.de* merc b2.de* mosch b2.de mur-ac b2.de* nat-c b2.de nat-m b2.de nit-ac b2.de nux-m b2.de* nux-v b2.de op b2.de petr b2.de ph-ac b2.de* phos b2.de plat b2.de plb b2.de rhod b2.de rhus-t b2.de ruta b2.de sabad b2.de sabin b2.de **Sel** b2.de* sep b2.de* sil b2.de* spong b2.de stann b2.de sul-ac b2.de *Sulph* b2.de* teucr b2.de thuj b2.de zinc b2.de

WEATHER: | **thunderstorm**; before: nat-c bg2

WET:
- **feet**: puls bg2
- **getting** wet: calc bg2

WINE agg.: thuj bg2

MORNING: acon b7.de alum b4.de am-m b7.de *Apis* b7a.de arn b7.de aur b4.de bar-c b4.de *Bov* b4.de* calc b4.de cann-s b7.de *Carb-an* b4.de *Carb-v* b4a.de caust b4.de *Cina* b7.de dig b4.de *Iod* b4.de* kali-c b4.de lyc b4.de mag-m b4.de *Mang* b4.de* merc-c b4a.de nat-m b4.de nux-v b7.de par b7a.de phos b4.de rhod b4.de seneg b4.de sep b4.de sulph b4.de zinc b4.de

FORENOON: bar-c b4.de mag-c b4.de phos b4.de sars b4.de seneg b4.de stann b4.de sul-ac b4.de

AFTERNOON: *Alum* b4.de* am-m b7.de lyc b4.de petr b4.de phos b4.de zinc b4.de

EVENING: *Alum* b4.de* *Apis* b7a.de calc b4.de carb-an b4.de *Carb-v* b4.de* caust b4.de ferr b7.de graph b4.de hep b4.de ign b7.de iod b4.de nux-v b7.de par b7a.de petr b4.de sel b7a.de *Spong* b7a.de teucr b7.de *Thuj* b4.de*

NIGHT: *Ant-t* b7a.de bar-c b4.de *Carb-an* b4a.de carb-v b4.de caust b4.de lyc b4.de nit-ac b4.de phos b4.de

ADHESION; sensation of: | **Larynx**: chin b7a.de lach b7.de*

AIR rose through trachea in waves; as if: lyc h2*

ANESTHESIA of larynx: *(↗Numbness; Numbness - trachea)* kali-br k*

APHTHAE: | **Trachea**: apis b4a.de ars b4a.de phos b4a.de

ARSENICAL vapors agg.: *Kali-bi* bg2

BALL; sensation of a (See Lump)

BENDING backward: | **agg.** | **Larynx**: bell ptk1 *Lach* ptk1 rumx ptk1
- **amel.** | **Larynx**: hep ptk1

BLEEDING sensation: adam skp7•
- **forenoon** | **11**-12 h: adam skp7•
- **talking**; when: adam skp7•

BLOWING the nose agg.: caust bg2*

BREATHING DEEP agg.: meny bg2

CANCER: ars bg2 con bg2 hydr bg1 iod bg2 lap-a bg1 nit-ac k* phos phyt bg2 sang k* sil sne thuj k*

○ - **Larynx**: arg-cy gm1 ars k* hydr bg1 lap-a bg1 nit-ac k* phos sang k* sil sne thuj k*

CATARRH: acon k* **All-c** a1* *All-s* k* alum k* alum-p k2 alum-sil k2 *Am-c* k* *Am-m* **Ant-t** k* *Arg-n* hr1 arn **Ars** k* ars-s-f k2 *Asar* hr1 atro vh *Bad* k* *Bar-c* k* bar-m bell k* *Brom* k* *Bry* hr1 **Calc** k* *Calc-p* k* **Calc-s** k* camph cann-s canth carb-an **Carb-v** k* *Carbn-s* *Caust* k* *Cham* k* *Chin* k* chinin-ar *Cinnb* hr1 *Coc-c* k* *Coff* *Colch* k* con k* **Cor-r** hr1 cot br1 crot-t dros k* *Dulc* k* ferr ferr-ar *Ferr-p* gels k* graph *Hep* k* *Hippoz* k* *Hydr* k* hyos ign ip k* **Kali-ar** **Kali-bi** k* *Kali-br* k* **Kali-c** k* kali-i k2 kali-p *Kali-s* k* kali-sil k2 kreos k* *Lac-d* hr1 lob *Lyc* k* **Mang** k* med k2 meph k* **Merc** k* *Nat-ar* *Nat-m* k* **Nux-m** k* **Nux-v** k* *Petr* hr1 *Ph-ac* k* phel *Phos* *Rhod* *Rumx* sal-fr sle1• **Sang** k* **Seneg** k* *Sil* spig k* *Spong* k* **Stann** k* **Sulph** k* *Thuj* hr1 verat k* verb ziz hr1
- **morning**: nux-v k*
- **evening**: carb-an
- **night**: carb-an carb-v spig
- **alternating** with uterine complaints: *Arg-n*
- **chronic**: am-br br1
- **measles**; after: *Carb-v* dulc hr1
- **old** people; in: *Ammc* *Ant-t* k* *Ars* **Bar-c** k* *Carb-v* hr1 **Chin** hr1 *Hydr* k* *Lyc* hr1 **Seneg**
- **snow** melting: calc-p k2
- **speakers**; in: am-br vh1
- **sudden**: **Ars** k*
- **suffocating**: ambr bro1 ant-c tl1 ars bro1* calc bro1 coff bro1 lyc tl1 sang bro1 spong bro1
- **weather**:
  - **change** of; before: *Kali-bi*
  - **wet** | **agg.**: *Calc* calc-p k2 dulc *Kali-bi*
- **winter**: kali-bi k2

○ - **Air** passages; of the: *Caust* br1 diph br1 *Ferr-p* br1 hep br1 *Seneg* br1
- **Larynx**: aesc alum-p k2 alum-sil k2 *Alumn* am-br c2* am-caust mtf11 am-i mtf11 *Arg-n* k* ars k2 bar-m k2 *Brom* bry mtf11 **Calc** k* calc-i k2 **Calc-p** k* **Calc-s** k* calc-sil k2 carb-v k2 *Caust* *Cham* chinin-ar **Coc-c** k* *Con* cot br1 croc dig a1 erio a1 euph mtf11 euphr k2 ferr-ar guaj mtf11 *Ham* k* *Hep* k* hydr k2

Catarrh – Larynx: ...
hyos mtf11 iod k* kali-ar k2 kali-bi br1 kali-c c2 kali-i k2 *Kali-s* *Kreos* hr1 linu-c a1 mang k* merc *Nat-m* osm k* *Ph-ac* k* phos **Rumx** k* **Sang** *Seneg* *Sil* *Spong* k* sul-i k2 **Sulph** *Tarent*
- **Trachea**: *All-s* hr1 alum bro1 alum-p k2 alum-sil k2 *Ammc* anis bro1 *Ant-t* bro1 arg-n bro1 *Ars* k* arum-t k2 *Bar-c* k* bar-m k2 bar-s k2 *Bry* bro1 calc k* calc-i k2 calc-s k2 calc-sil k2 cann-s k* caps a1 carb-v k2* *Caust* bro1 chin chinin-ar coc-c bro1 conv bro1 cot br1* dig a1 euphr k2 ferr-ar ferr-i bro1 hep bro1 hydr k2 iber bro1 kali-ar k2 *Kali-bi* k* kali-i k2 mang-act bro1 merc k* naphtin bro1 *Nat-m* hr1* nux-m nux-v bro1 par bro1 *Ph-ac* positr nl2• **Rumx** k* **Sang** **Seneg** sil bro1 *Stann* bro1 stict bro1 sul-i k2 sulph bro1 tab bro1 tep a1
  - **drunkards**; in old: anis br1
  - **purulent**: anis br1

CHOKING sensation: | **Larynx**: *Cupr* b7.de* *Dros* b7.de* *Puls* b7a.de sul-ac b4.de*

CLOSED, almost: calc-f
- **sensation** as if almost closed by a film: *Mang* a1

○ - **Larynx**: calc-f ptk1
  - **accompanied** by | **salivation**; increased: tarax ptk1

COATED, seems (See Velvety)

COLD sensation: arg-met bg2 brom bg2 chinin-s bg2
- **air**; as from cold | **Air** passages; in: cor-r br1
- **breathing** agg.: arn k* **Brom** k* camph k* chin *Cist* k* cor-r k* iod lith-c *Rhus-t* k* sulph
- **expiration** agg.: rhus-t h1
- **inspiration** cold, expiration hot: *Sulph* k*
- **shaving** | **amel.**: *Brom* k*

○ - **Air** passages: *Arg-met* bg2 arn bg2 *Ars* bg2 bit-ar wht1• brom bg2 *Bry* bg2 camph bg2 *Carb-v* bg2 chin bg2 merc bg2 mur-ac bg2 phos bg2 *Rhus-t* bg2 *Sulph* bg2 *Verat* bg2
- **Larynx**: adam skp7• *Arg-met* b7a.de brom b4a.de* rhus-t bro1 *Sulph* b4a.de* [heroin sdj2]
- **Trachea**: *Ars* b4a.de camph b7.de *Sulph* b4.de*
  - **breathing** agg.: arn b7.de* brom bg2 m-aust b7.de*

COMPLAINTS of larynx and trachea:
- **spots**; in: nat-m bg2

○ - **Air** passages; of: dubo-m br1 eucal br1 hep br1 kali-bi br1
- **Larynx**: **Acon** b2.de* agar b2.de* all-c br1* alum b2.de* am-c b2.de* am-m b2.de* ambr b2.de* anac b2.de* ang b2.de* ant-c b2.de* ant-t b2.de* *Arg-met* b2.de* arg-n bg2 arn b2.de* *Ars* b2.de* asar b2.de* aur bg2 bar-c b2.de* bell b2.de* borx b2.de* bov b2.de* *Brom* bg2* bry b2.de* calad b2.de* calc b2.de* camph b2.de* cann-s b2.de* *Canth* b2.de* caps b2.de* carb-an b2.de* **Carb-v** b2.de* **Caust** b2.de* *Cham* b2.de* chel b2.de* chin b2.de* cic b2.de* cina b2.de* cocc b2.de* coff b2.de* colch b2.de* con b2.de* cupr b2.de* dig b2.de* **Dros** b2.de* dulc b2.de* epil c1 euph bg2 ferr b2.de* graph b2.de* guaj b2.de* hell b2.de* **Hep** b2.de* hyos b2.de* ign b2.de* **Iod** b2.de* ip b2.de* kali-bi bg2* kali-c b2.de* kali-n b2.de* kreos b2.de* *Lach* b2.de* laur b2.de* led bg2 lyc b2.de* mag-c b2.de* mag-m b2.de* *Mang* b2.de* meny b2.de* merc b2.de* mez b2.de* mosch b2.de* mur-ac b2.de* nat-c bg2 nat-m b2.de* *Nit-ac* b2.de* nux-m b2.de* **Nux-v** b2.de* olnd b2.de* op b2.de* *Par* b2.de* petr b2.de* ph-ac b2.de* **Phos** b2.de* plat b2.de* plb b2.de* *Puls* b2.de* rhod b2.de* rhus-t b2.de* *Rumx* bg2* ruta b2.de* sabad b2.de* sabin b2.de* samb b2.de* sars bg2 sel ptk1 *Seneg* b2.de* sep b2.de* sil b2.de* spig b2.de* **Spong** b2.de* squil bg2 *Stann* b2.de* staph b2.de* stram b2.de* stront-c b2.de* sul-ac b2.de* *Sulph* b2.de* tarax b2.de* teucr bg2 thuj b2.de* verat b2.de* verb b2.de* zinc b2.de*
  - **right**: agar ptk1 kali-n ptk1 puls ptk1 stann ptk1 stict ptk1
  - **left**: brom mtf33 caust ptk1 *Crot-h* ptk1 *Hep* ptk1 *Lach* ptk1 rhus-t ptk1 *Sul-ac* ptk1 thuj ptk1 til ptk1
  - **acute**: santin br1
  - **chill**; during: borx bg2 carb-v bg2 caust bg2 dros bg2 *Hep* bg2 mang bg2 phos bg2 spong bg2
- **Trachea** (See Trachea)

CONDYLOMATA:

○ - **Larynx**: *(↗Polypi - larynx)* *Arg-n* calc hep k* *Merc-c* *Nit-ac* *Thuj*
- **Vocal** cords: arg-n vh1 plat ser

Larynx

CONSTRICTION: *(↗THROAT - Choking)* alum alumn asar **Bell** k* brom mrr1 *Calad* calc-i k2 camph canth carc fd2.de• *Cham Cocc* k* coloc convo-s sp1 cyt-l sp1 dros dulc fd4.de *Hell* ictod ign *Ip* k* lach laur **Mang** meny *Mosch Nux-m Nux-v* ol-an ox-ac ph-ac *Phos Plb* positr nl2• *Puls* rhus-t *Sars* sil *Spong* verat [heroin sdj2]

- **night**: *Phos* puls rhus-t
- **lying** agg.: *Kali-bi* puls
- **vapor** | **sulphur**; as from: mosch k2
- **waking**; on: kali-i k2 rhus-t

○ - **Larynx**: *(↗Laryngismus)* **Acon** k* *Agar* k* *All-c Alum* k* *Alumn* k* am-c k* *Ant-c* k* ant-t k* arg-met *Ars* k* asaf bg2 asar k* asc-t atra-r bnm3• *Aur* b4a.de aur-i c2 bar-c **Bell** k* *Brom* k* bufo k* calad k* *Calc* camph k* canth bg2 *Carb-an* k* carbn-s caust k* *Cedr* k* *Cham* k* *Chel* chinin-s bg2 *Chlor* k* coc-c *Cocc* k* coff k* coloc k* *Cor-r Crot-c Cupr* k* dios *Dros* k* dulc fd4.de erio a1 eug k* euphr ferr *Gels Glon* k* gua bro1 hell k* hep hydr-ac bro1 *Hyos Ign* k* **Iod** k* *Ip* k* *Kali-c* k* kali-i kali-n k* *Lach* k* laur k* *Lob* k* lycps-v manc **Mang** k* mang-act bro1 med k* meny k* meph ptk1 merc bg2 *Merc-c* b4a.de mez *Mosch* k* *Naja* k* nat-ar *Nat-m* nit-ac nit-s-d a1 nux-m b7a.de* *Nux-v* k* oena k* ol-an ox-ac k* pert jl2 ph-ac k* **Phos** k* *Phyt* k* plat k* plat-m a1 *Plb* k* plut-n srj7• *Puls* k* rhus-t bg2 samb ptk1 sang sars bg2 *Seneg* sep h2* *Sil* k* *Spong* k* still k* *Stram* k* sul-ac k* sul-i k2 *Sulph* k* tab a1 tarax b7.de* *Tarent* thuj k* tub c1 *Verat* k* vib tl1 *Zinc* zinc-p k2

- **evening**: brom k* dros gk hep kali-c k* lycps-v nux-v ol-an
  - **bed** agg.; in: ferr naja
  - **sleep**; when falling asleep: *Kali-c Spong Sulph*
- **night**: acon bg3 dros gk *Phos*
  - **midnight**, before: *Spong*
- **air**; in open:
  - **agg.**: *Hep* kali-c
  - **amel.**: coloc
- **anger**; after: staph hr1 sulph
- **convulsive**: ign bro1
- **cough**:
  - **during**:
    - **agg.**: *Agar* all-c tl1 *Ars* k* *Bell* carb-an b4a.de carbn-s k2 *Chel* chlor bg2 **Cor-r Cupr** k* **Dros** euphr **Hyos** ign *Ip* meph bg2* mosch bro1 *Puls* stram *Sulph* verat
    - **amel.**: asar
- **crumb**; sensation of a: *Coc-c* lach
- **drinking** | **after** | **agg.**: *Ars* meph mp1•
  - **agg.**: acon bg3
- **eating**; after: *Puls*
- **inspiration** agg.: *Hep*
- **lying** on abdomen and protruding tongue | **amel.**: med hr1
- **scratching** auditory canal, from: agar *Carbn-s* kali-c lach mang psor *Sil Sulph Tarent*
- **singing** agg.: *Agar* k*
- **sitting** agg.: *Spong*
- **sleep** | **during**:
  - **agg.**: *Agar Cench Coff Crot-h* dros gk *Kali-c Kali-i* **Lach** k* *Naja* nit-ac **Nux-v** k* *Sep Sil* **Spong** k* *Sulph Valer*
    - **lying** on either side; while: *Kali-c Spong*
  - **falling** asleep: *(↗THROAT - Choking - sleep; THROAT - Choking - sleep - going - agg.)*
    - **when**: *(↗THROAT - Choking - sleep; THROAT - Choking - Sleep - going)* *Agar Arg-n* **Kali-c** k* **Lach** k* med k2 *Phos Spong Sulph Valer*
      - **lying** on either side; while: *Arg-n Kali-c Spong*
- **spasmodic**: atra-r bnm3• *Chlor* mrr1 dig h2* hydr-ac br1
- **swallowing** agg.: *Dig* k*
- **talking** agg.: *Dros* k* *Mang* k* meph mp1• spong fd4.de
- **touch** agg.: bell
- **waking**; on: *Lach* manc *Phos* thuj
- **walking** | **amel.**: **Dros** k*

- **Throat**-pit: *Apis* **Brom** cot c1 *Ign* k* ph-ac h2* rhus-t k* *Staph* k* valer k* zinc [calc-br stj1 mag-br stj1]
  - **anger**; after: *(↗MIND - Anger - throat-pit)* *Staph* k*

Constriction – Throat-pit: ...

- **bending** neck agg.: ph-ac h2*
- **eating** | **amel.**: rhus-t k*
- **sleep** agg.; on going to: valer k*
- **suddenly**: dol rb2
- **swallowing** agg.: staph k*

- **Trachea**: alum k* *Ant-t* b7a.de **Ars** k* asar b7.de* *Aur* b4a.de bell k* *Brom* k* bry k2 *Calad* k* cann-xyz bg2 canth k* *Cham* k* chel k* *Cist* hr1* cocc k* galla-q-r nl2• gua bro1 hydr-ac ign k* *Iod* b4a.de ip k* *Lach* k* laur k* mag-c k* meny h1 mosch k* *Nux-v* b7.de* osm bg2 *Phos* k* *Puls* k* *Rhus-t* b7.de* sars k* *Spong* k* stann k* staph bg2 verat xero bro1
  - **evening** | **lying** down agg.: *Ars* k*
  - **band**; like a: chel bg2
  - **cough**; during (See COUGH - Constriction - trachea)
- **Vocal** cords: *Maias-l* hm2•

CONTRACTION:

○ - **Larynx**: alum b4.de* bar-c b4.de* calad b7.de* canth b7.de* *Cina* b7.de* con b4a.de dros b7.de* ferr b7.de* hell b7.de* ign bg2 iod b4.de* ip b7.de* lycps-v bg2 meny b7.de* *Nux-v* b7.de* ph-ac b4.de* puls b7.de* rhus-t b7a.de spong b7.de* stram bg2 thuj b4a.de verat bg2 zinc b4.de*

- **cough** agg.; during: arn b7a.de *Calad* b7a.de *Ign* b7a.de
- **sensation** of: alum bg2 cocc b7.de* spong b7.de*

- **Trachea**: bell b4a.de calad b7.de* canth b7.de* cocc b7.de* dros b7.de* iod b4.de* ip b7.de* lach b7.de* mag-c b4.de* mez b4.de* nit-ac b4.de* nux-v b7.de* ph-ac b4.de* *Puls* b7.de* stann b4.de* staph b7.de*
  - **accompanied** by | **respiration**; impeded (See RESPIRATION - Impeded - contraction - trachea)

COUGH:

- **agg.**: **Acon** bg2 all-c bg2 ant-c bg2 *Arg-met* bg2 **Arn** bg2 ars bg2 *Bell* bg2 borx bg2 brom bg2 bry bg2 calc bg2 carb-v bg2 caust bg2 cham bg2 chin bg2 grat bg2 **Hep** bg2 kali-c bg2 lach bg2 mag-m bg2 mang bg2 nat-m bg2 nux-v bg2 phos bg2 sang bg2 sep bg2 **Spong** bg2

○ • **Larynx**: all-c ptk1 arg-met ptk1 arum-t ptk1 bell ptk1 brom ptk1 caust ptk1 kreos ptk1 nux-v ptk1 phos ptk1 puls ptk1 sulph ptk1

- **amel.** | **Larynx**: asar ptk1

CRAWLING:

○ - **Larynx**: am-m ant-t arn bov k* bry calc-s *Caps* k* *Carb-v* k* *Caust* k* colch **Con** k* *Dros* k* graph k* iod k* **Kali-c** k* kreos k* *Lach* laur led lyc k* mag-m meny b7.de* **Nat-m** k* nit-ac k* prun *Psor* k* rhus-t *Sabin* k* sang sep k* stann stram stront-c sul-i k2 sulph k* *Thuj* k* zinc k*

- **morning**: iod k*
- **evening**: carb-v k*
  - **lying**, after: caps
- **night**: lyc
- **cough** agg.: kreos sabin b7.de*
- **eating**; after: nit-ac k*
- **sitting** agg.: *Psor* k*
- **swallowing** agg.: staph

- **Trachea**: *Am-c* b4a.de anac k* arn k* borx b4a.de bov b4.de* calc b4.de* *Caps* k* *Carb-v* b4.de* colch k* dros b7.de* euph b4.de* iod b4.de* kali-c b4.de* kreos bg2 *Lach* led k* lyc k* mag-m k* nit-ac nux-m k* petr b4.de* phos b4.de* plat b4.de* ruta *Seneg* sep b4.de* sil b4.de* spong stann k* *Sulph* b4a.de *Thuj* b4.de*
  - **night**:
    - **midnight**:
      - **after**:
        - **2 h** | **waking** him or her from sleep: lyc h2
  - **lying** down; after | **evening**: caps
  - **cough** agg.: colch k* mag-m k*

CREAKING noise: | **Trachea**: arn b7.de*

CROUP: *(↗COUGH - Croupy; RESPIRATION - Rough - crowing)* acet-ac c2* **Acon** k* all-c alum-sil k* alumn k* anac k* *Ant-t* k* apis b7a.de* arn bg2 *Ars* k* *Ars-i* k* arum-d c2 arum-t k* asaf *Bell* k* **Brom** k* bry b7a.de* bufo bg2 *Calc* k* calc-i k2* **Calc-s** k* *Canth* k* *Carb-ac* k* *Carb-v* k* caust k* *Cham* k* chin k* *Chlor* k* cina bg2 coc-c mrr1 cub c2 *Cupr* k* cupr-act c2 diph c2

Croup: ...
dros k* ferr-p c2 gels **Hep** k* hyos bg2 *Ign* c2 *Iod* k* ip b7a.de* **Kali-bi** k* *Kali-chl* k* kali-i c2 kali-m c2* kali-n br1 *Kali-p* k* lac-ac k* lac-c c2 *Lach* k* *Lob* k* lyc k* *Mosch* bg2* naja *Nat-m* k* *Nit-ac* k* nux-v bg2 **Phos** k* rumx mrr1 *Samb* k* *Sang* k* sangin-act c1 *Seneg* bg2 solid c2 spong b7.de* *Still* k* succ-xyz c2 sulo-ac c2 **Sulph** tub mrr1 verat bg2
- **morning**, early: *Hep* c1
- **evening**: acon c1
- **night**: hep mrr1 **Spong** k*
  - **midnight** | **before**: acon k2 hep k2 **Spong** k*
- **accompanied** by:
  - **choking**: brom tl1
  - **diphtheria** (See THROAT - Diphtheria - accompanied - croup)
  - **hoarseness** (See Voice - hoarseness - croup - with)
  - **respiration**; difficult: acon tl1 spong bg2
  - ○ **Chest**; rattling in: hep tl1
  - **Head** bent back: ant-t tl1
  - **Lungs**; paralysis of (See CHEST - Paralysis - lung - accompanied - croup)
  - **Neck** stretched out: ant-t tl1
- **alternating** with | **urticaria**: ars bro1
- **children**; in light-haired fair: kali-bi tl1
- **chronic**: **Ars** bg2 cham bg2 cupr bg2 lach bg2 mosch bg2 *Phos* bg2
- **cold** dry air; after exposure to: **Acon** k* **Hep** k* kali-bi
- **eating**; after: anac k*
- **gangrenous**: *Ars* k*
- **heated**; from becoming: **Brom** calc-s k2
  - **lying** agg.: *Hep*
- **membranous**: *(↗Membrane)* acet-ac k2* *Acon* bg2* *Alum-sil* bro1 *Alumn* am-c am-caust br1* ammc bro1 ant-t k* *Apis* k* ars bro1 ars-i bro1 *Arum-t* bell bro1 **Brom** k* calc-i bro1 *Carb-ac* caust k* con bro1 diph pd dros bro1 ferr-p bro1 *Hep* k* *Iod* k* **Kali-bi** k* *Kali-br* k* *Kali-chl* k* *Kali-m* bro1 kali-n bro1 kali-perm *Lac-c* k* *Lach* k* *Merc* bro1 *Merc-cy* k* *Merc-i-f* *Naja* *Nit-ac* **Phos** k* samb bro1 *Sang* k* spong k*
  - **accompanied** by:
    - **Esophagus**:
      - **pain** | **burning**: am-caust br1
- **paroxysmal**: *Hep* *Kali-br* k*
- **recurrent** (See GENERALS - History - croup)
- **sequelae** (See GENERALS - Convalescence - croup)
- **sleep** agg.; after: **Lach** k* *Spong*
- **spasmodic**: *Acon* bro1 alum-sil bro1 ant-t bro1 ars bro1 bell bro1 benzo bro1 *Brom* bro1 bry bro1 *Calc-f* bro1 calc-i bro1 *Chlor* bro1 cupr bro1 euph bro1 ferr-p bro1 *Hep* bro1 ictod bro1 ign bro1 *Iod* bro1 ip bro1 *Kali-bi* bro1 kali-br bro1 *Kali-n* bro1 lach bro1 meph bro1 merc-i-f bro1 mosch bro1 naja bro1 petr bro1 *Phos* bro1 samb bro1 sang bro1 *Spong* bro1 *Verat-v* bro1
- **threatening**: **Acon** bg2 cham bg2 chin bg2 cina bg2 *Dros* bg2 **Hep** bg2 hyos bg2 nux-v bg2 *Spong* bg2 verat bg2
- **waking**; on: kali-bi tl1
- **whooping** cough; during: **Brom**
- ▽ **extending** to:
  - ○ **Bronchi**: brom k2
  - **Fauces**: **Brom**
  - **Trachea**: brom k2 *Iod* k* **Kali-bi** k* *Kali-chl* k* *Phos* k*

CRUMB in larynx; sensation of a: *(↗Dryness - larynx; Flesh; Foreign body; Foreign body - larynx; Hair; THROAT - Bread)* *Bry* coc-c **Lach** k* pall plb tril-p c1*

DIPHTHERIA: *(↗Membrane - larynx)* apis bro1 *Brom* bro1 canth bro1 chlor bro1 diph bro1 *Hep* bro1 iod bro1 *Kali-bi* bro1 lac-c bro1 *Merc-cy* bro1 petr bro1 phos bro1 samb bro1 spong bro1

DISCOLORATION:
- **red**:
  - **dark** red | **Larynx**: *Brom* b4a.de
  - **network** | **Larynx**: *Brom* b4a.de
  - **stripes** | **Larynx**: *Brom* b4a.de
  - ○ **Larynx**: *Par* b7a.de strept-ent jl2

DOWNY feeling (See Velvety)

DRAWN: | **backward**:
- ○ **Larynx** | **thread**; sensation as if drawn backward by a: calc-ar ptk1
- **inward** | **Larynx**: apis ptk1

DRYNESS: agar agn hr1 alum ant-c *Ars* calc-s carb-v caust chin coloc dros ferr gels hyos *Kali-ar* kali-bi kali-chl kali-m k2 lact laur lob nat-c nat-m nicc par phos k2 rhod sec k2 sep spong fd4.de stann sul-i k2 ter teucr vanil fd5.de
- ○ **Bronchi**: camph h1
- **Larynx**: *(↗Crumb; Flesh; Hair)* *Acon* aesc k* agar all-s k* *Alum* k* alum-p k2 am-c am-caust bg2 am-m ant-c bg2 ant-t apis k* *Arg-met* bg2 *Ars* k* ars-i ars-s-f k2 atro k* **Bell** k* borx b4a.de *Bry* *Calc* k* calc-ar calc-f k* carb-an k* *Carb-v* k* card-m k* carl k* *Caust* k* chim-m hr1 cina bg2 cist k* *Clem* coc-c k* coch hr1 colch **Con** k* *Cop* k* *Crot-h* cub hr1* cycl *Dros* k* dub bro1 erio a1 ery-m a1 euph bg2 ferr bg2 ferr-p fl-ac k* gels hep k* hura hydr-ac k* hyos k* iber a1* ign bg2 iod k* ip k* kali-ar k2 *Kali-bi* k* *Kali-c* k* kali-chl kali-i bro1 *Kali-s* kalm lac-ac k* **Lach** k* lachn lact a1 laur k* lem-m br1* *Lyc* k* *Mag-m* k* *Mang* k* *Mang-act* bro1 med k* *Merc* merc-c k* *Mez* k* nat-ar nat-c k* *Nat-m* k* nicc nit-ac bg2 nux-m k* *Nux-v* k* op k* osm k* *Par* k* petr k* *Phos* k* *Phyt* k* plac rzf5• plan plut-n srj7• pop-cand bro1 psil ft1 *Puls* k* rhod bg2 *Rhus-t* k* rhus-v k* rumx k2 sabad k* samb-c c2 *Sang* k* sel b7a.de **Seneg** k* *Sep* k* **Spong** k* stann k* *Stict* still k* stram sul-ac k* **Sulph** k* tarent k2 tep k* ter teucr bg2* thuj k* thyr ptk1 *Tub* jl2 vanil fd5.de verat verat-v verb k* *Zinc* k* zinc-p k2 zing hr1
  - **morning**: iod *Nat-m* vh *Nux-v* phyt seneg k* sep k* vanil fd5.de *Zinc* k*
    - **waking**; on: nat-m k* *Par* sars
  - **forenoon**: seneg k*
  - **evening**: carb-v phyt k* *Rhus-t* zinc
  - **night**: *Bell* carb-v graph k2 hep kali-c lach nat-m *Phos* *Sulph*
    - **midnight**:
      - **after**:
        - **2-3 h**: *Kali-c*
        - **5 h**: kali-c
  - **air** agg.; in open: *Mang* nat-c
  - **coryza**; during: nux-v b7.de*
  - **cough** agg.; during: bell k* *Mang* b4a.de osm polyg-h
  - **drink**, aversion to: **Bell** k*
  - **eating**:
    - **after**:
      - **agg.**: zinc h2
      - **amel.**: zinc h2
  - **fever**; during: ars bg2 dros bg2 hep bg2 iod bg2 mang bg2 nux-v bg2 *Op* bg2 par bg2 *Petr* bg2 phos bg2 spong bg2 thuj bg2 zinc bg2
  - **hawking**:
    - **constant**, with: am-m
    - **from**: *Spong*
  - **heat**; during: *Ars* hep nux-v *Petr* phos
  - **perspiration**; during: *Ars* bg2 **Calc** bg2 *Caust* bg2 dros bg2 *Hep* bg2 mang bg2 mez bg2 op bg2 *Phos* bg2 sel bg2 **Spong** bg2 *Sulph* bg2 thuj bg2 **Zinc** bg2
  - **sensation** of: nux-m b7.de* par b7a.de sel b7a.de
  - **singers**; in: sang ptk1
  - **spot**: cimic k* *Cist* **Con** k* crot-h nat-m bg2
  - **waking**; on: am-c *Cist* hep kali-c lach nat-m k* phos spong fd4.de
  - **winter** agg.: mez
  - ○ **Epiglottis**: lach lyss c1 wye k*
- **Trachea**: **Acon** k* alum b4.de* *Ars* k* *Ars-i* bell bro1 brom k* calc-ar carb-an *Carb-v* k* carl a1 caust b4.de* cina b7.de* clem k* cycl k* dros k* fl-ac k* *Hep* b4a.de *Iod* k* kali-bi bg2 laur k* lipp a1 *Lyc* k* mang b4.de* *Merc* merc-c b4a.de* mez k* nat-ar bg2 nat-m k* par b7.de* petr k* phos k* *Phyt* a1* *Puls* k* rheum bg2 rhod b4.de* rhus-t k* rumx k2* sang bg2* seneg b4.de* sep k* *Spong* k* stann sul-ac b4.de* sulph b4.de* tarent k* teucr a1* trif-p a1 verb k* zinc b4.de*
  - **morning**: cina h1 phyt k* rhod k* sul-i a1
    - **waking**; on: *Par* k*

Larynx

- **Trachea**: ...
  - **fever**; during: *Petr* b4a.de
  - **room** agg.; closed: clem k* *Puls* k*
  - **sensation** of: camph b7.de* caust b4.de* *Par* b7a.de phos b4.de* puls b7.de* stann b4.de* teucr b7.de*

DUST, as from: *Agar* *Alumn* k* *Am-c* k* **Ars** k* aur-m bar-c k2 *Bell* *Brom* *Calc* k* calc-s k* *Chel* k* *Chin* k* cina *Coc-c* crot-c cycl **Dros** k* ferr-ma a1 glon *Hep* ictod *Ign* k* iod *Ip* **Lyc** meph nat-ar *Nat-m* ph-ac pic-ac plat bg1 **Puls** k* rumx bg1 **Sulph** teucr

○ - **Trachea**: cina bg2 kali-bi bg2 teucr b7.de*

EDEMA: apis bg2 iod bg2 kali-i bg2 lach bg2 merc-cy bg2

○ - **Glottis**: **Apis** k* ars k* arum-t bell k* chin chinin-ar bro1 chlor bro1 *Crot-h* k* hippoz ign k* iod k* *Kali-bi* nh6 **Kali-i** k* *Lach* k* loxo-recl bnm10• merc k* pilo bro1 *Sang* k* staph *Stram* k* tub c2* vip br1*
  - **accompanied** by | **scarlet** fever: *Apis* bro1 apisin bro1 chinin-s bro1 merc-c bro1
- **Vocal** cords: **Lach** k*

FEATHER; sensation of a: | **Larynx**: *Dros* b7a.de

FISSURES in larynx: bufo k*

FLAPPING sensation, larynx: *Lach* k*

FLESH hanging in larynx, sensation of: *(↗Crumb; Dryness - larynx; Foreign body; Hair)* lach ptk1 **Phos** k •* spong ptk1

FOOD drops into larynx: acon k* anac b4.de* *Arg-met* bg2 *Bell* b4.de* calc b4.de* cann-s k* caust ptk1 cocc bg2 gels k* **Hyos** bg2* ign bg2 kali-bi *Kali-c* k* kali-n bg2 **Lach** k •* *Meph* k* **Nat-m** k •* nux-m bg2 op bg2* plat b4.de* rhus-t b7.de* sil bg2 sul-ac b4.de* verat b7.de*

FOREIGN body; sensation of a: *(↗Crumb; Flesh; Hair; Membrane - sensation; Velvety)*

○ - **Epiglottis**; as if particles of food remained in *Hepat* br1
- **Larynx**: *(↗Crumb)* *Agar* ant-c h2* ant-t bro1 *Arg-met* k* **Bell** k* brom *Bry* *Calc-f* caust bg2 *Coc-c* *Dros* k* *Hep* hydrog srj2• iod h* ip bro1 kali-c ptk1 *Lach* lob med *Nat-m* *Phos* k* ptel k* rumx *Sang* k* *Sil* k* tarent *Thuj* k* tril-p bg2
  - **morning**: caust
  - **hanging** in larynx: ant-c b7a.de
  - **lodged** in larynx: arg-met b7a.de *Lach* b7a.de
  - **soft** body; as if from a: dros b7.de*

○ · **Behind** larynx: *Coc-c*
- **Trachea**: ant-t bro1 cann-s b7.de* cic b7.de* fl-ac bg2 hyos k* ip bro1 *Kali-c* *Lach* b7a.de *Sang* sil bro1 sin-n thuj tt1*

FOREIGN substances drop into larynx when drinking or talking: *Meph*

FULLNESS, larynx: cob naja k*
- **morning**: cob
- **evening**: naja
- **singers**; in: sang ptk1

FURRY larynx: *Phos* b4a.de*

GRASPED (See Constriction)

HAIR in trachea; sensation of a: *(↗Crumb; Dryness - larynx; Flesh; Foreign body)* naja k* sil k*

HEAT: **Acon** bg2 *Am-m* bg2 ant-c bg2 *Apis* bg2 *Ars* bg2 arum-t bg2 bell bg2 bov bg2 brom bg2 bry bg2 bufo bg2 calc-p bg2 cann-xyz bg2 *Canth* bg2 *Carb-v* bg2 caust bg2 *Cham* bg2 chel bg2 clem bg2 elaps bg2 euph bg2 euphr bg2 hep bg2 iod bg2 kali-bi bg2 kali-n bg2 lach bg2 laur bg2 mag-m bg2 mang bg2 *Merc* bg2 merc-c bg2 mez bg2 nit-ac bg2 **Nux-v** bg2 par bg2 ph-ac bg2 **Phos** bg2 phyt bg2 puls bg2 *Rhus-t* bg2 *Sabad* bg2 *Seneg* bg2 *Sep* bg2 *Spong* bg2 stann bg2 *Sulph* bg2 tab bg2 ter bg2 verat bg2 zinc bg2

○ - **Larynx**: alco a1 all-s k* alumn k* anan k* ant-c b7.de* apis b7a.de apoc k* ars ptk1 canth b7.de carbn-s **Iod** k* kali-bi k* laur b7.de mag-m k* merc-sul a1* naja nit-ac ptk1 *Phos* hr1 phyt k* rumx ptk1 sang ptk1 seneg ptk1 spong ptk1
- **Trachea**: cain caj a1 chel k* iod b4.de laur b7.de petr k* phyt k* rhus-t hr1 spong fd4.de
  - **accompanied** by cough (See COUGH - Heat - sensation - trachea)

HEAVINESS; sensation of: phos bg2

Heaviness: ...

○ - **Larynx** | **talking** for a long time; after: flav jl2

HEMMING (See Scraping)

HOARSENESS (See Voice - hoarseness)

HOLDING larynx on coughing (See Pain - larynx - cough - grasps)

INFLAMMATION:

○ - **Larynx** (= laryngitis) **Acon** k* adren mtf11 *Aesc* **All-c** k* *Am-br* vh1 am-i br1 am-m k2 *Ant-c* ant-s-aur c2 *Ant-t* k* *Apis* k* *Arg-met* k* **Arg-n** k* am bg2 *Ars* k* ars-i k* arum-m mtf11 arum-t mrr1 aur-m bar-c bg2 **Bell** k* beryl sp1* *Brom* k* bry k* *Bufo* calad *Calc* k* calc-i k2 calc-s cann-xyz bg2 caps bg2 carb-ac carb-an *Carb-v* k* carbn-s *Caust* k* *Cham* k* *Chel* chin bg2 *Chlor* cina bg2 con bg2 *Crot-c* *Crot-h* cupr bg2 diphtox jl2 **Dros** k* *Dulc* k* ery-a c2 eucal mtf11 euphr bg2 ferr bg2 ferr-p **Gels** k* *Guaj* **Hep** k* hydr-ac hyos bg2 ign bg2 influ jl2* *Iod* k* *Ip* k* **Kali-bi** k* kali-i k* kali-m k2 *Kali-n* bg2 kreos bg2 lac-c mtf11 *Lach* k* *Led* bg2 linu-c c2 luf-op mtf11 lyc bg2 mag-c bg2 *Mang* k* med jl2 mentho br1 *Merc* k* merc-i-r k* mez mtf11 morg-p pte1*• mosch bg2 *Naja* nat-c bg2 nat-i c2 *Nat-m* k* *Nit-ac* k* *Nux-v* k* oscilloc jl2 par b7a.de* ph-ac k* **Phos** k* polyg-xyz c2 *Puls* k* pyrog mtf11 *Rhus-t* k* **Rumx** k* sabad bg2* **Samb** bg2 *Sang* sangin-n c2 sel k* seneg k* sep bg2 ser-a-c jl2 sil bg2 spig bg2 *Spong* k* squil bg2 *Stann* bg2 staph bg2 stict c2 *Still* stram bg2 streptoc jl2 sul-i k2 *Sulph* k* tab thuj bg2 tub mtf11 tub-a mtf11 tub-m jl2* verat bg2 verb bg2 zinc bg2 [buteo-j sej6 *Mang-i* stj2 *Mang-met* stj2]
  - **evening**: *Cedr* kali-bi *Rhus-t*
  - **accompanied** by:
    - **discharge**; ropy: kali-bi tl1
    - **hoarseness**:
      - **evening**: carb-v mtf11
      - **cold** air agg.: phos mtf11
  - **acute**: **Acon** bg2 ant-t bg2 ars bg2 arum-t mtf11 **Bell** bg2 **Bry** bg2 calc bg2 carb-v bg2 caust bg2 **Cham** bg2 *Dros* bg2 **Hep** bg2 iod bg2 *Ip* bg2 kali-n bg2 *Lach* bg2 led bg2 mang bg2 *Merc* bg2 nit-ac bg2 **Nux-v** bg2 **Phos** bg2 *Puls* bg2 seneg bg2 *Spong* bg2 stann bg2 streptoc jl2
  - **blood**-streaked | **expectoration**; with: sel mtf11
  - **catarrhal**: *Acon* bro1 aesc bro1* *All-c* bro1 ant-t bro1 apis bro1 arg-met bro1 ars-i bro1 *Arum-t* bro1 *Bell* bro1 brom bro1 bry bro1 canth bro1 carb-v bro1 *Caust* bro1 cub bro1 dros bro1 *Dulc* bro1 eup-per bro1 *Ferr-p* bro1 guaj bro1 hep br1* iod bro1 ip bro1 *Kali-bi* bro1 kali-i bro1 mentho bro1 *Merc* bro1 osm bro1 *Phos* bro1 *Rhus-t* bro1 *Rumx* bro1 sabal c2 *Samb* bro1 sang bro1 *Spong* bro1 stict bro1 sulph bro1
  - **children**; in: diphtox jl2 influ jl2*
  - **chronic**: am-br bro1 am-i bro1 ant-s-aur bro1 ant-t bro1 *Arg-met* bg2* arg-n bg2* **Ars** bg2 bar-c bro1 bar-m bro1 bry bg2 **Calc** bg2* calc-i bro1 **Carb-v** bg2* **Caust** bg2* *Coc-c* bro1 cot bro1 dros bg2* dulc bg2 gonotox jl2 *Hep* bg2* influ jl2* **Iod** bg2* irid-met bro1 kali-bi bg2* kali-c bro1 *Kali-i* bro1 *Kreos* bg2 lach bg2* led bg2 lyc bg2 *Mang* bg2 *Mang-act* bro1 merc bg2* merc-c bro1 nat-c bg2 nat-m bg2* nat-sel bro1 *Nit-ac* bg2* nux-v bg2* *Par* bro1 petr bg2 ph-ac bg2 **Phos** bg2* puls bg2* rhus-t bro1 sangin-n bro1 *Sel* bro1 seneg bg2* sil bg2 spong bg2 *Stann* bg2* staph bg2 still bro1 streptoc jl2 **Sulph** bg2* syph jl2 thuj bro1 tub jl2
  - **follicular**: arg-n bro1 hep bro1 *Iod* bro1 kali-i bro1 sel bro1 *Sulph* bro1
  - **gangrenous**: apis b7a.de *Ars* k* *Bell* *Chin* b7.de* *Lach* *Nit-ac* b4a.de *Phos*
  - **heated**, from getting: **Brom Puls**
  - **influenza**; from: influ jl2*
  - **over**-use of voice; from (See singers; speakers)
  - **recurrent** (See GENERALS - History - laryngitis)
  - **singers**, in: *(↗Pain - larynx - singers - sore)* *Ant-c* *Arg-met* k* **Arg-n** k* ferr-p tl1 *Mang* mang-act br1
  - **spasmodic**: med jl2 pert jl2
  - **speakers**, in: **Arum-t** k* *Carb-v* k* *Still*
  - **sudden**: bell k2
  - **syphilitic**: *Aur* bro1 cinnb bro1 fl-ac bro1 *Hep* k* *Iod* k* *Kali-bi* bro1 *Kali-i* bro1 kreos bro1 lach bro1 *Merc* k* *Merc-c* bro1 merc-i-f bro1 *Merc-i-r* k* mez bro1 *Nit-ac* k* *Phyt* bro1 sang bro1 *Still* sulph bro1 syph jl2 thuj bro1

- **Larynx**: ...
  - **tubercular**: am-m bro1 *Arg-n* bro1 ars bro1 *Ars-i* bro1 atro bro1 bac jl2 bapt bro1 brom bro1 *Calc* bro1 calc-p bro1 canth bro1 carb-v bro1 *Caust* bro1 chr-o bro1 cist bro1 cupr mtf11 *Dros* bro1 ferr-p bro1 hep bro1 *Iod* bro1 ip bro1 jab bro1 *Kali-bi* bro1 kali-c bro1 kali-i bro1 kali-m bro1 kreos bro1 lach bro1 lyc bro1 *Mang-act* bro1 merc-n bro1 naja bro1 *Nat-sel* bro1 nit-ac bro1 *Phos* bro1 rumx mrr1 sang bro1 sel c1* spong bro1 *Stann* bro1 sulph bro1
  - **urticaria**; suppressed: *Ars*
  - **warm** room; agg.: all-c k2
  - **weather** agg.; wet: *Kali-bi* mang k2
- **Trachea** (= tracheitis): *Acon* k* *Ant-t* k* *Arg-met* bg2 *Arg-n* bg2 am bg2 ars k* ars-i bar-c bg2 *Bell* k* beryl sp1* *Brom* k* bry k* **Calc** bg2 cann-xyz bg2 canth k* caps b7.de* *Carb-v* k* **Caust** bg2 cham k* chin k* cina bg2 con b4.de* cupr bg2 dig k* diph mtf11 diphtox jl2 dros k* *Dulc* k* dys mtf11 eucal mtf11 euphr bg2 ferr bg2 *Hep* k* hyos bg2 ign bg2 *Iod* k* ip k* *Kali-bi* k* *Kali-n* bg2 *Kreos* bg2 lach bg2* *Led* bg2 lob lyc bg2 mag-c bg2 *Mang* k* **Merc** bg2 morg-p pte1* mosch bg2 nat-c bg2 *Nat-m* k* *Nit-ac* bg2 nux-v k* oscilloc jl2 pert jl2 petr bg2 ph-ac bg2 **Phos** b4a.de* pneu jl2* *Puls* k* rhus-t bg2 *Rumx* k* sabad bg2* *Samb* k* *Sang* k* *Seneg* bg2 sep bg2 ser-a-c jl2 sil bg2 spig bg2 *Spong* k* squil bg2 *Stann* bg2 staph bg2 stram bg2 sul-i k2 **Sulph** bg2 syc pte1* thuj bg2 tub-a mtf11 verat k* verb bg2 zinc bg2
  - **croupous**: acon tl1 am-c b4a.de ars b4a.de bar-c b4a.de bell b4a.de **Brom** b4a.de dulc b4a.de euph b4a.de **Hep** b4.de* *Iod* b4a.de merc b4a.de ph-ac b4a.de phos b4.de* seneg b4.de* sep b4a.de *Thuj* b4a.de
  - **winter**: diphtox jl2

INJURIES to air passages: calen hr1

INSENSIBILITY of larynx: (↗*Paralysis - larynx*) *Kali-br* k*

INSPIRATION agg.: bell bg2 hep bg2 ph-ac bg2

IRRITATION: calc-sil k2 sul-i k2

○ - **Air passages**: **Acon** *Agar* agn all-s aloe *Alum* am-br am-c am-m aml-ns *Anac* ant-t aspar bar-c cain *Calc* carb-ac *Carb-v* *Carbn-s* *Caust* **Cham** chinin-s *Chlor* clem coc-c coff colch coll *Con* crot-t dios *Gels* hyos **Iod** ip mtf33 **Kali-bi** *Kali-c* kali-i **Lach** lob lyc mag-s merc-i-r mez *Mosch* mur-ac nat-ar nat-s **Nux-v** osm ox-ac petr-ra shn4• *Ph-ac* **Phos** plan psor *Puls* raph **Sep** *Stann* sul-ac *Sulph*
  - **morning** | **rising** agg.; after: alum alumn nat-ar k2
  - **afternoon**: bapt
  - **evening**: chel cimic dios sulph
    - **19**.30 h: cimic
    - **bed** agg.; in: agn am-c coff hyos kali-c
  - **night** | **waking**; on: thuj
  - **cold** air agg.: acon all-c *Ars* *Bell* brom bry calc-p *Carb-v* caust cimic cupr fl-ac **Hep** ip *Kali-bi* kali-c kali-p *Lach* *Mang* naja nux-v osm ox-ac **Phos** **Rumx** *Sil* spong sulph
  - **heated**; when: *Apis*
  - **increases** the more one coughs: cist **Ign** raph squil teucr
  - **spasmodic**: ip mtf33
- **Larynx**: acet-ac k* **Acon** k* *Aesc* **Agar** k* *Alum* k* alum-sil k2 *Alumn* am-c k* am-m ambr anac anan ant-c ant-t *Aphis* apis **Arg-met** k* **Arg-n** k* *Arn* k* ars k* arum-d a1 asar asc-t br1 astac a1 bar-c k* bar-m **Bell** k* bond a1 bov *Brom* **Bry** calad k* *Calc* *Calc-p* calc-sil k2 camph canth caps carb-ac *Carb-an* **Carb-v** k* *Carbn-s* card-m k* *Carl* **Caust** k* *Cham* k* chel chin *Chlor* k* cimic cina *Cist* **Coc-c** k* coca *Cocc* k* coff colch coloc k* **Com** *Con* k* cop k* *Cor-r* **Crot-c** *Crot-h* crot-t k* *Cupr* dig k* dios k* **Dros** k* echi erio a1 *Euphr* k* ferr ferr-i k* fl-ac k* form k* *Gels* guaj guare k* *Ham* **Hep** k* hipp jl2 hydr-ac *Hyos* hyper **Ign** k* **Iod** k* *Ip* **Kali-bi** k* **Kali-c** **Kali-chl** k* kali-i k* kali-m k2 *Kali-p* *Kali-perm* br1* *Kali-s* kali-sil k2 lac-ac lac-c **Lach** k* lachn laur lith-c *Lob* **Lyc** mag-c mag-m manc **Mang** mang-act bro1 meny *Merc* merc-c k* mez mur-ac myric **Naja** nat-c **Nat-m** nat-p nat-sil fd3.de• nicc nit-ac k* nux-m *Nux-v* k* olnd osm k* *Ph-ac* **Phos** k* *Phyt* plan **Puls** *Rhus-t* *Rumx* k* sabad sabin **Sang** *Seneg* k* *Sep* *Sil* **Spong** k* *Squil* *Stann* k* *Staph* k* stront-c *Sul-i* k* *Sulph* k* sumb tab k* tarax *Tarent* teucr *Thuj* k* thymol sp1 tong a1 trom tub-a jl2 verat verb *Zinc* [ambro stj]
  - **morning**:
    - **bed** agg.; in: *Caust*
    - **waking**; on: kali-bi naja
  - **afternoon**: coca ferr-i k* phos

Irritation – Larynx – afternoon: ...
    - **14** h: coca
  - **evening**:
    - **bed** agg.; in: coc-c cocc *Hyos*
    - **lying** agg.: *Ign*
  - **night**: ambr *Kali-c*
    - **midnight**, before: *Acon* *Spong*
  - **accompanied** by | **sneezing**: carb-v bg2
  - **cold** air agg.: **Acon** k* *Ars* **Bell** calc-p **Carb-v** cimic crot-h fl-ac *Hep* ip *Kali-bi* kali-p k2 mang *Naja* *Nux-m* nux-v osm ox-ac **Phos** **Rumx** sil spong sulph
  - **cough**:
    - **from**: alum-sil k2 cocc b7.de* *Op* b7a.de
    - **suppressing** the cough amel.: *Hyos* ign tl1
  - **eating**; after: nit-ac k* *Rumx* staph
  - **heat**; during: hep
  - **lying** on either side, on going to sleep: *Kali-c* *Spong*
  - **recurrent**: *Calc* **Carb-v**
  - **sleep** agg.; during: **Lach** *Phos* *Spong*
  - **swallowing**, empty: lyc *Nat-m* op
  - **talking** agg.: *Alumn* **Arg-met** *Bell* *Caust* **Dros** *Hep* *Kali-bi* *Mang* *Nat-m* **Phos** psil ft1 *Rhus-t* *Seneg* *Spong* *Sulph*
  - **warm** agg.; becoming: ant-c *Brom* *Carb-v* *Puls*
  - **warm** room agg.: iod
  - **weather** | **warm**:
    - **wet** | **agg.**: *Iod*
    - **wet** | **agg.**: *Kali-bi* *Rhus-t*

○ - **Upper** part: *Spong*
- **Throat-pit**: *Apis* bell card-m *Cham* croc *Hyos* **Ign** k* iod kreos lac-c mang ph-ac rhus-r **Rumx** k* **Sang** k* *Sil* squil
- **Trachea**: acet-ac k* acon *Aesc* bro1 agar k* alum alum-sil bro1 ambro bro1 ang k* ant-t *Apis* c2* *Arg-met* k* *Arg-n* k* *Arn* **Ars** k* asaf bar-c bar-m bell k* bov *Brom* c2* *Bry* k* *Calc* calc-sil k2 cann-s k* carb-an k* **Carb-v** k* carbn-s *Caust* k* *Cham* chel hr1 chin cina *Coc-c* k* cocc colch coloc con k* *Cor-r* croc dig **Dros** erio a1 euph ferr ferr-i ferr-p bro1 *Graph* grat hep hydr-ac hyos k* ign *Iod* **Ip** **Kali-bi** k* **Kali-c** *Kali-i* kali-n *Kali-p* kali-sil k2 ketogl-ac rly4• *Lach* bro1 laur led **Lyc** k* mag-c *Mang* menth bro1 *Merc* k* *Merc-sul* mez k* mur-ac naja nat-ar *Nat-m* nicc *Nit-ac* nux-m **Nux-v** osm a1* *Petr* **Phos** k* plat prun k* psor *Puls* rhod *Rhus-t* *Rumx* k* sabin **Sang** k* seneg **Sep** **Sil** spig k* **Squil** k* **Stann** k* staph *Stict* still bro1 stront-c sul-i k2 **Sulph** k* syph bro1 teucr *Thuj* trif-p k* tub-a jl2 verat xero bro1 zinc
  - **cough** agg.; during: alum-sil k2
  - **hawk**; with disposition to: *Lach* b7a.de teucr b7.de*
- **Vocal** cords: ozone sde2•

ITCHING: (↗*Tickling*) ozone sde2•

▽ - **extending** to | **Bronchia**; into: ozone sde2•

○ - **Larynx**: all-c bg2 alum-p k2 am-c k* am-m b7.de* ambr k* ant-t k* apis bg2 aral bg2 *Arg-n* k* *Ars* bg2 ars-s-f k2 asar bg2 bar-c bg2 bell k* borx bg2 bov b4.de* brom bg2 bry bg2 cact *Calc* k* calc-f carb-an bg2 carb-v k* caust bg2 *Cham* b7a.de* chin bg2 cist k* coff bg1 colch k* con k* cupr bg2 dig k* dros bg2 ferr b7a.de fl-ac k* graph bg2 hep b4.de* ign bg2 *Iod* bg2 *Ip* b7.de* kali-bi bg2 kali-c bg2 kali-n bg2 lach k* laur k* lyc mag-c bg2 mag-m b4a.de* mang meny b7.de* *Merc* b4.de* mur-ac bg2 nat-c bg2 *Nat-m* bg2 *Nux-v* k* olnd b7.de* *Op* b7a.de ozone sde2• *Phos* b4a.de* prun bg2 *Puls* k* rhod b4a.de rumx bg2 sabin b7.de* seneg b4.de* *Sep* bg2 sil spong bg2 stann bg2 *Staph* bg2 sulph bg2 tritic-vg fd5.de vanil fd5.de zinc b4.de*
  - **night**: *Cist* k*
- **Throat-pit**:

○ - **In**: agn a1
  - **Under**: ozone sde2• phos h2
- **Trachea**: acon b7.de* *Agar* *Am-c* b4a.de *Ambr* k* ang b7.de* *Ant-t* b7a.de apis bg2 arn b7.de* cann-xyz bg2 caps b7.de* cham cina b7.de* *Cist* k* colch k* con *Ferr* b7.de* iod bg2 ip b7.de* kali-bi k* ketogl-ac rly4• kreos bg2 laur k* *Led* b7.de* *Nux-v* k* ozone sde2• petr bg2 phos k* **Puls** k* rhus-t b7.de* rumx bg2 sabin b7.de* sel b7a.de squil b7.de* *Stann* b4a.de teucr b7.de* *Verat* b7.de*

JERK, drinking: nat-m h2*

Larynx

LARYNGISMUS stridulus: (↗*Constriction - larynx*)
acon b7a.de* *Agar* k* alum k1* am-caust bro1 *Ant-c* **Ant-t** b7a.de *Ars* k* ars-i k* arum-d k* arum-t bro1 arund c1* *Asaf* k* aur-i c2 **Bell** k* *Brom* k* calc bro1* calc-i bro1 calc-p bro1* cham k2 *Chel* k* chin bro1 chlf hr1 *Chlol* bro1 *Chlor* k* cic bro1 *Coff* k* *Cor-r* k* crot-h k* *Cupr* k* *Cupr-act* bro1 dig k* dros k2 *Form* bro1 **Gels** k* gran br1* guaj guar bro1 guare k* hep bro1 hydr-ac k* hyos k2 ictod br1 **Ign** k* influ jl2 *Iod* k* *Ip* k* irid-met srj5• kali-br k* lac-ac k* *Lach* k* laur k* lob bro1 *Mag-p* k* *Mang* med k2 *Meph* k* morb jl2 **Mosch** k* naja nux-v b7a.de ol-an k* *Op* k* *Phos* k* phyt k* plat k* plat-m c2 plb k* puls b7a.de* *Samb* k* sang sars k* *Sil* *Spong* k* stram k* *Stry* bro1 sul-i k2 sulph k* *Tab* k* *Tarent* k* *Verat* k* vesp bro1 vesp-xyz c2 visc c1 zinc bro1

- **night**: *Samb* hr1* (non:sumb hr1)
  - **midnight**:
    - **7 h**, until: *Chlor*
    - **waking** from sound sleep: *Samb* k*
- **accompanied** by:
  - **diphtheria** (See THROAT - Diphtheria - accompanied - glottis)
  - ○ **Chest**; burning in: iod mrr1
  - **Face**:
    - **pale**: *Ip* b7a.de
    - **red**: *Samb* b7a.de
- **alternating** with contraction of fingers and toes: asaf k*
- **cold**; on becoming: mosch k2
- **cough**, before the: *Ip* k*
- **daily**: chel k*
- **expiration** agg.; during: *Chel* k* *Chlor* k*
- **hysterical**: mosch mrr1
- **inspiration**; on (See Laryngismus)
- **sleep** | **during** | **agg.**: *Chlor* lac-ac *Lach* spong *Sulph* thuj
  - **falling** asleep | **when**: *Phos*
- **swallowing** agg.: *Cupr* k* merc-c k*
- **warm** room agg.: *Iod* k*

LARYNGITIS (See Inflammation - larynx)

LEAF closing up trachea, like a: ant-t ptk1 mang k*

LIQUIDS pass into larynx: *Acon* k* anan k* hyos tl1* *Lach* k* *Meph* k*

LOSS OF VOICE (See Voice - lost)

LUMP; sensation of a: bell bg2 lach bg2

- ○ **Behind** larynx: ozone sde2•
  - **swallowing**; compels: *Coc-c* *Lach* ozone sde2• ust
- **Larynx**, in: (↗*Plug - larynx*) carc tpw2* *Coc-c* epil a1* *Kali-c* lac-v-c c1 *Lob* *Med* *Nat-m* ozone sde2•
- **Throat**-pit; in: benz-ac rb2 dol rb2 **Lach** *Lob*

LYING agg.: bell bg2 sang bg2 teucr bg2

MEMBRANE: (↗*Croup - membranous*) bufo

- **sensation** of: (↗*Foreign body; Velvety*)
  - **move** about in larynx; seems to: *Kali-c*
  - **skin**; sensation of: *Alum* *Alumn* caust iod bg2 kali-c *Lach* k* *Phos* k* *Thuj* k*
    - **cough** agg.; during: *Phos* b4a.de
    - **loose** skin: *Kreos* b7a.de
- ○ **Larynx**: (↗*Diphtheria*) **Apis** b7a.de *Bry* b7a.de
  - **accompanied** by | **mucus**; profuse: *Phos* b4a.de *Seneg* b4a.de
  - **extending** to | **Lungs**; downward to: ars b4a.de dig b4a.de *Samb* b7a.de
  - **false** membrane in: brom tl1 chlor tl1 cub c1 iod tl1
  - **thick**: kali-bi tl1

MOVEMENT up and down of larynx: lach a1 lyc k* op k* *Spong* b7a.de stram ptk1 sul-ac k* *Sul-i* ptk1

- **cough** agg.; during: lach ptk1

MUCUS:

- **stringy**: asaf bg2

Mucus: ...

- ○ **Air** passages, in the: (↗*MIND - Anxiety - mucus - bronchi; RESPIRATION - Difficult - mucus*) acon aeth all-c bg2 *Alum* am-c k* am-m bg2 *Ambr* k* ang k* ant-ar bg2 ant-t k* *Arg-met* k* *Arg-n* k* am *Ars* k* arum-d ptk2 arum-t **Aur** k* **Bar-c** k* bell k* bov k* *Brom* bry k* calc k* calc-i k2 **Calc-s** *Camph* k* cann-s caps carb-v k* carbn-s **Caust** k* cham k* chin k* cina k* cist bg2* *Coc-c* cocc croc k* crot-t *Cupr* k* dig k* diphtox jl2 **Dros** bg2 *Dulc* k* *Euphr* *Ferr* ferr-ar ferr-p graph bg2 *Hep* k* hydr k2 **Hyos** k* **Iod** k* ip bg2* kali-ar **Kali-bi** k* *Kali-c* k* kali-p kali-s kali-sil k2 kreos lach k* laur **Lyc** k* mag-m k* *Mang* med **Nat-m** k* nit-ac h2* *Nux-v* k* olnd k* osm ox-ac ozone sde2• par phel phos bg3 plb k* *Puls* k* *Rumx* samb k* sang bg2 **Seneg** k* sep bg2 *Sil* *Spong* *Stann* k* staph k* sul-ac k* *Sulph* k* tanac ptk2 teucr bg2 vanil fd5.de verat bg2 verb bg2 zinc bg2
  - **diminished**: imp c1
  - **type** of mucus (See EXPECTORATION - Mucous)
- **Larynx**: acon *Aesc* *All-c* alum k* alum-p k2 alum-sil k2 *Alumn* am-br am-c k* am-m *Ambr* k* amyg anan *Ang* b7.de* **Ant-t** k* *Arg-met* k* **Arg-n** k* *Ars* k* ars-i *Arum-t* asaf asar *Aur* k* aur-ar k2 aur-s k2 bamb-a stb2.de• *Bar-c* k* bell k* bov b4a.de **Brom** k* *Bry* bro1 bufo calc k* *Calc-p* *Camph* *Canth* k* carb-an k* *Carb-v* k* carbn-s k2 *Caust* k* *Cham* k* chin k* chinin-s cina k* cist **Coc-c** cocc k* coff b7.de *Con* croc b7a.de *Crot-t* dig k* diph jl2 *Dros* k* echi ephe-si hsj1• *Euphr* *Ferr* ferr-ar ferr-i ferr-p *Form* *Graph* k* grat *Hep* k* hydr k2 hydr-ac **Hyos** k* **Iod** k* iris **Kali-bi** k* **Kali-c** k* *Kali-chl* kali-i kali-m k2 kali-n *Kali-p* *Kali-s* kali-sil k2 kreos k* lac-ac *Lach* k* laur k* **Lyc** k* mag-c b4.de mag-m b4a.de *Mang* *Mang-act* bro1 med c1 *Merc* mill *Naja* nat-ar **Nat-m** k* nat-s *Nux-v* k* *Ol-j* *Olnd* k* osm ox-ac k2* *Par* k* *Ph-ac* phel **Phos** k* plb b7a.de psor *Puls* **Rumx** k* ruta fd4.de **Samb** k* *Sang* k* *Sel* k* *Seneg* k* sep k* *Sil* spong fd4.de *Stann* k* *Staph* k* sul-i k2 *Sulph* *Tarent* *Thuj* k* vanil fd5.de verb *Zinc* zinc-p k2
  - **morning**: *Alumn* am-m dig *Kali-bi* k* *Mang* **Nat-m** k* *Nux-v* *Ol-j* *Olnd* par *Sel* *Seneg* *Sil* *Sulph* tarent thuj
    - **rising** agg.; after: *Cina* *Olnd* sil
    - **waking**; on: sars sulph
  - **evening**: *Carb-v* crot-t iod h *Puls* *Rumx* spong fd4.de tarent *Zinc*
  - **night**: *Puls* *Rumx* spong fd4.de thuj
    - **talking** agg.: ox-ac
  - **ascending** stairs agg.: arg-met h1
  - **blood**-streaked: am-c anan sol-ni
  - **blue**: *Kali-bi* k* nat-ar
  - **cold** air agg.: *Rumx* seneg
  - **copious**: alumn anan calc-sil k2 *Carb-v* *Coc-c* mang-act br1 *Nat-m* **Rumx** k* sel mrr1 *Seneg*
  - **cough**, after each paroxysmal: *Agar* **Coc-c** kali-bi *Nat-m* *Seneg* sulph
  - **eating**; after: bell caust graph hep kali-bi *Lyc* *Nat-s* nux-m ol-an *Olnd* ph-ac phos puls ruta fd4.de sanic *Sil* thuj tub bg3
  - **ejected** with difficulty: alum alumn ang bg2 *Aur* bar-c bov *Calc* *Canth* carl *Caust* *Cham* cina coc-c k2 cocc crot-t *Form* *Kali-bi* *Kali-c* *Lyc* *Mang* mosch naja nat-ar *Nat-m* *Nux-v* ozone sde2• *Par* rumx sars *Seneg* sep *Sil* spong k2 staph *Sulph* *Tarent*
    - **impossible**: alum bg2
  - **green**: calc-sil k2 *Hep* k* par
  - **laughing** agg.: *Arg-met* kali-bi
  - **milky**: kali-m k2
  - **overheated**, from being: *Brom*
  - **rattling**: sul-ac
    - **evening**: crot-t
  - **saltish**: *Am-c*
  - **sensation** of: dulc fd4.de
  - **stooping**, comes up when: *Arg-met*
  - **stringy**: *Kali-bi* br1
  - **sweetish**: dig br1
  - **talking** agg.: kali-bi ox-ac k2
  - **tenacious**: *Kali-bi* nh6* med c1
  - **thick**: kali-m k2 rumx mrr1
  - **viscid**: ars-s-f k2 *Kali-bi* br1

- **Trachea**: aeth agn k* alum b2.de* alum-sil k2 *Am-c* k* am-m b2.de* ambr k* *Ammc Ang* k* ant-c b2.de* **Ant-t** k* *Arg-met* k* arn b2.de* *Ars* k* ars-i **Arum-t** k* asaf asar b2.de* *Aur* k* aur-ar k2 aur-s k2 **Bar-c** k* bar-i k2 bar-s k2 bell k* bism b2.de* borx b2.de* bov k* brom k2 *Bry* k* bufo bg2 cain **Calc** k* *Camph* k* *Cann-s* k* canth b2.de* caps k* carb-an b2.de* carb-v b2.de* carl caust k* *Cham* k* chin k* *Cina* k* coc-c cocc k* coff b2.de* colch b2.de* con b2.de* croc k* crot-t cupr k* dig k* diph jl2 dros k* *Dulc* k* euphr k* ferr ferr-ar ferr-i ferr-p gels graph b2.de* guaj b2.de* **Hep** k* hydr k2 *Hyos* k* ign b2.de* *Iod* k* iris **Kali-bi** k* *Kali-c* b2.de* kali-n b2.de* kali-s kreos k* lach k* laur k* **Lyc** k* m-ambo b2.de* mag-c b2.de* mag-m k* mang b2.de* *Merc* k* merc-c b4a.de merc-sul mez b2.de* naja nat-c b2.de* *Nat-m* k* *Nat-s* nit-ac b2.de* nux-m b2.de* *Nux-v* k* *Olnd* k* op b2.de* osm ox-ac *Par* k* petr b2.de* *Ph-ac* k* phel **Phos** k* plat b2.de* plb k* *Puls* k* ran-b b2.de* rhod b2.de* rhus-t b2.de* *Rumx* ruta b2.de* sabad b2.de* sabin b2.de* *Samb* k* **Sang** sars b2.de* sel b2.de* senec *Seneg* k* sep b2.de* *Sil* k* spig b2.de* **Squil** k* **Stann** k* staph k* sul-ac b2.de* sul-i k2 *Sulph* k* tarax b2.de* tarent k2 teucr k* thuj k* valer b2.de* verat b2.de* verb b2.de* zinc b2.de*
  - **morning**: *Cann-s* caust olnd
  - **forenoon**: **Stann** k*
  - **evening**: crot-t *Puls*
  - **night**: *Puls* thuj
  - **ascending** and descending: *Coc-c Lach*
  - **ejected** with difficulty: ang bg2 *Cann-s Caust* spong k2
    - **impossible**: alum bg2
  - **sensation** of, which he cannot get up: rhod rb2

NARROW sensation: mez h2 phos h2

○ - **Trachea**: cist ptk1

NECROSIS of cartilages of larynx: *Calc* crot-h *Kali-bi* syph c1 x-ray sp1

NODES: | **Vocal** cord: sel ptk1

NUMBNESS: *(↗Anesthesia)*

○ - **Air** passages: sil ptk1
- **Larynx**: kali-br ptk1
- **Trachea**: *(↗Anesthesia)* acon b7.de*

OBSTRUCTION; sensation of:

○ - **Larynx**: *Spong* b7a.de *Verb* b7.de*
- **Trachea**: rhus-t b7.de* verb bg2

OEDEMA (See Edema)

PAIN: acon↓ all-c↓ alum↓ alum-sil↓ am-c↓ *Am-m*↓ ambr↓ ant-c↓ *Arg-met*↓ arg-n↓ *Ars*↓ ars-i↓ ars-s-f↓ bac↓ bamb-a↓ bar-c↓ *Bell*↓ borx↓ bov↓ brom↓ *Bry*↓ bufo↓ *Cact*↓ calc↓ *Calc-s*↓ canth↓ carb-an↓ **Carb-v**↓ **Carbn-s**↓ *Caust*↓ *Cham*↓ chin↓ cina↓ cot↓ cub↓ cycl↓ dendr-pol↓ dros↓ ferr-ar↓ gels↓ graph↓ ham↓ hep↓ hydr-ac↓ ign↓ *Iod*↓ kali-ar↓ kali-bi↓ kali-c↓ kali-p↓ lach↓ lact↓ *Lob*↓ lyc↓ mag-m↓ merc↓ merc-c↓ mez↓ myric↓ nat-c↓ nat-m↓ nit-ac↓ nux-m↓ *Nux-v*↓ ol-an↓ ox-ac↓ par↓ ph-ac↓ **Phos**↓ *Puls*↓ *Rumx*↓ ruta↓ sec↓ *Seneg*↓ sep↓ sil↓ spig↓ *Spong*↓ **Stann**↓ staph↓ stram↓ sul-ac↓ sul-i↓ **Sulph**↓ tab↓ ter↓ thuj↓ tritic-vg↓ vanil↓ verat↓ zinc↓

- **night**: *Puls*↓
  - **burning**: *Puls*
- **burning**: *Am-m* k* ant-c *Ars* k* ars-s-f k2 bamb-a stb2.de• bar-c *Cact* nh6 canth *Carb-v* k* caust cham cina cub c1 cycl dros k2 ferr-ar gels graph ham fd3.de• hydr-ac iod lach lact *Lob* lyc mag-m merc merc-c mez myric nux-v k2 par phos *Puls Rumx* sec k2 *Seneg* sep *Spong* k* staph sulph ter zinc
- **bursting** pain: cot c1 kali-ar
- **cold** air:
  - **amel.**: *Puls*↓
    - **burning**: *Puls*
- **compressed**; as if: acon k* bufo bg2 ol-an bg2
- **constricting** pain: brom bg2 iod bg2 phos bg2 thuj bg2
- **contracting**: bell k2 brom k* dros ign *Iod* ox-ac ph-ac spong staph stram sul-ac tab thuj tritic-vg fd5.de verat
- **cough** agg.; during: ant-c↓ bamb-a↓ carb-v↓ *Caust*↓ cina↓ coc-c↓ ham↓ iod↓ lach↓ mag-m↓ pyrog↓ **Spong**↓ staph↓ sulph↓ zinc↓
  - **burning**: ant-c bamb-a stb2.de• carb-v *Caust* cina coc-c k2 ham fd3.de• iod lach mag-m pyrog k* **Spong** k* sulph zinc
  - **torn** asunder; as if: staph b7.de*

Pain: ...

- **drawing** pain: borx bg2
- **expiration** agg.; during: coc-c↓
  - **burning**: coc-c k2
- **lying** agg.: *Puls*↓ seneg↓
  - **burning**: *Puls* seneg
- **pricking** pain: bac jl2
- **shooting** (See stitching)
- **sore**: alum alum-sil k2 am-c bg2 am-m ambr k* *Arg-met* k* ars ars-i ars-s-f k2 bar-c *Bell* bov k* brom k* *Bry* k* bufo bg2 calc *Calc-s* carb-an bg2 **Carb-v** k* **Carbn-s** *Caust* k* chin k* cina dendr-pol sk4• graph k* hep ign k* iod k* kali-ar kali-bi bg2 kali-c bg2 kali-p lach lyc mag-m k* merc nat-c nat-m bg2 nux-m *Nux-v* **Phos** k* puls bg2 rumx ruta seneg sep k* sil spig spong **Stann** k* sul-i k2 **Sulph** k* vanil fd5.de
- **split**; as if: all-c bg2
- **squeezed**; as if: *Cham* bg2 nux-v bg2
- **stitching** pain | **splinter**; as from a: arg-n bg2 hep bg2 nit-ac bg2
- **talking**:
  - **agg.**: dros↓
    - **contracting**: dros

○ - **Air** passages: *Acon*↓ *Agar*↓ alum-sil↓ am-c↓ ambr↓ anac↓ ant-c↓ **Arg-met**↓ arn↓ ars-i↓ ars-s-f↓ calc↓ calc-s↓ *Carb-v*↓ *Caust*↓ *Coc-c*↓ coff↓ ferr-p↓ grat↓ hep↓ hydr↓ kali-ar↓ kali-c↓ kreos↓ laur↓ mag-c↓ *Mez*↓ naja↓ *Nat-m*↓ nux-m↓ petr↓ **Phos**↓ ruta↓ sang↓ seneg↓ sep↓ sil↓ stann↓ vanil↓
  - **burning**: ars-i ptk1 sang ptk1 seneg ptk1
  - **cough** agg.; during: ambr↓ anac↓ ant-c↓ arg-met↓ arn↓ calc↓ carb-v↓ caust↓ cina↓ *Coc-c*↓ grat↓ iod↓ kali-c↓ kreos↓ lach↓ laur↓ mag-c↓ mag-m↓ mez↓ nux-m↓ petr↓ phos↓ ruta↓ sep↓ sil↓ *Spong*↓ stann↓ sulph↓ zinc↓
    - **burning**: ant-c bg2 carb-v bg2 caust bg2 cina bg2 iod bg2 lach bg2 mag-m bg2 *Spong* bg2 sulph bg2 zinc bg2
    - **rawness**: ambr bg2 anac bg2 ant-c bg2 arg-met bg2 arn bg2 calc bg2 carb-v bg2 *Coc-c* k* grat bg2 kali-c bg2 kreos bg2 laur bg2 mag-c bg2 mez bg2 nux-m bg2 petr bg2 phos k* ruta bg2 sep bg2 sil bg2 stann
  - **rawness**: *Acon Agar* alum-sil k2 am-c ambr anac ant-c **Arg-met** k* arn ars-s-f k2 calc calc-s *Carb-v* k* *Caust* k* *Coc-c* k* coff ferr-p grat hep k2 hydr k2 kali-ar kali-c kreos laur mag-c *Mez* naja k2 *Nat-m* nux-m petr **Phos** k* ruta sep sil stann vanil fd5.de
- **Larynx**: *Acon* k* adam↓ *Aesc*↓ *Agar*↓ **All-c** k* *All-s*↓ alum bro1 alum-p↓ alum-sil↓ *Alumn*↓ am-c am-caust↓ *Am-m*↓ ambr anac hr1 anan↓ ang↓ ant-c↓ ant-s-aur↓ ant-t k* aphis↓ apis b7a.de aran↓ arg-met arg-n bro1 arn↓ **Ars** k* ars-i↓ ars-s-f↓ *Arum-t* k* asar↓ asc-t bamb-a stb2.de* bapt↓ *Bar-c*↓ **Bell** k* benzo↓ borx↓ bov↓ *Brom* bry k* bufo↓ calad k* *Calc* k* calc-caust↓ calc-i k2 *Calc-p*↓ *Calc-s*↓ calc-sil↓ camph bg2 *Cann-s*↓ canth k* caps↓ carb-an *Carb-v* k* carbn-s carl↓ castm↓ caust k* **Cham**↓ *Chel* k* chen-a↓ *Chin*↓ chinin-ar↓ chinin-s↓ *Chlor*↓ cic bg2 *Cist Clem*↓ cob k* coc-c k* *Coff*↓ colch k* colum-p sze2• *Con*↓ cop↓ croc↓ crot-c k* crot-h↓ crot-t cupr h2* cur↓ cycl k* cer k* dig↓ digin↓ dirc k* dros k* dulc fd4.de elaps↓ ephe-si↓ epil↓ eup-per↓ euphr ferr k* ferr-i ferr-p↓ fl-ac k* flor-p↓ gels graph grat guaj↓ *Hep* k* hipp↓ hura *Hydr*↓ *Hydr-ac*↓ hyos↓ *Ign*↓ *Indg*↓ inul br1 *Iod* k* ip just bro1 kali-ar↓ *Kali-bi* k* kali-c kali-chl k* kali-i k2 kali-n k* kali-p↓ kali-perm *Kali-s*↓ kola stb3• kreos bro1 lac-ac↓ lac-c↓ **Lach** k* lact↓ laur↓ lec↓ led↓ *Lob*↓ lyc k* mag-c↓ mag-m↓ mag-p↓ mag-s↓ manc↓ mang *Mang-act* bro1 med bro1 meny↓ *Merc*↓ merc-c bro1 merc-cy bg2 *Mez*↓ mur-ac↓ myric↓ **Naja**↓ *Nat-ar*↓ nat-c↓ nat-m *Nicc*↓ nit-ac k* nit-s-d↓ nitro-o↓ *Nux-m*↓ *Nux-v* k* oena↓ ol-an↓ olib-sac↓ olnd↓ osm k* ox-ac k2 *Par*↓ *Ph-ac*↓ phel↓ **Phos** k* phyt↓ plac rzf5• plb↓ plut-n↓ podo↓ prun-p↓ *Puls*↓ pyrog↓ rhod↓ *Rhus-t*↓ rhus-v k* *Rumx* ruta sabad k* *Samb*↓ sang bro1 sarr sars k* **Seneg**↓ sep↓ *Sil*↓ spig↓ spira↓ spong k* stann *Staph*↓ *Stict*↓ *Still*↓ stram stront-c↓ sul-ac k* sul-i k2 sulph symph fd3.de• syph k2* tab tarax *Tarent*↓ tell↓ tep k* teucr↓ thuj k* *Til*↓ tong↓ urt-u↓ vanil fd5.de vinc↓ *Zinc*↓ zinc-p↓ zing↓
  - **right**: lachn↓
    - **burning**: lachn c1
  - **left**: tub jl2
  - **morning**: arg-met↓ *Arg-n*↓ calc↓ *Carb-an*↓ carb-v↓ carl↓ *Caust*↓ chinin-s↓ cob↓ *Iod*↓ *Nux-v Rhus-t*↓ sep *Sil*↓ *Stann*↓ **Sulph**↓ symph fd3.de• zinc↓
    - **pressing**: carb-v h2* sep k*

Larynx

- **morning**: ...
  - **rawness**: calc *Carb-an* carl *Caust* cob *Iod* *Rhus-t* *Sil* *Stann* **Sulph** zinc
  - **sore**: arg-met nh6 *Arg-n* chinin-s
  - **waking**; on: ephe-si ↓ ferr a1 kali-bi rhus-t ↓
    - **rawness**: rhus-t
    - **sore**: ephe-si hsj1 • kali-bi
- **afternoon**: am-m ↓
  - **burning**: am-m
- **evening**: borx ↓ *Carb-v* ↓ indg ↓ kali-bi ↓ *Nux-v* **Phos** ↓ podo ↓ spong symph fd3.de • syph k2
  - **rawness**: *Carb-v* **Phos** k*
  - **sore**: kali-bi *Phos*
  - **stitching**: indg k* podo fd3.de • syph k2
  - **tearing**: borx
  - **toward**: all-c br1
- **night**: anac ↓ plac rzf5 • *Puls* ↓ syph jl2
  - **burning**: *Puls*
  - **cough** agg.; during: phos ↓
    - **stitching**: phos
  - **rawness**: anac
- **acute**: syph jl2
- **air** agg.; draft of: arg-met
- **air**; in open:
  - **agg.**: ox-ac ↓
    - **stitching**: ox-ac
  - **amel.**: all-c br1
- **bed** agg.; in: iod ↓
  - **sore**: iod h
- **bending** head backward agg.: *Bell* bry **Lach** k* *Rumx* sil
- **blow**; as from a: ruta b7.de*
- **blowing** the nose agg.: *Caust* k*
  - **pressing**: *Caust*
- **boring**: coc-c k*
- **breathing** agg.: *Bell* *Carb-v* *Hep* kali-n sil ↓
  - **sore**: sil
- **burning**: **Acon** k* *Aesc* *Alumn* k* am-caust bro1 *Am-m* k* ambr h1* ant-s-aur mtf11 aphis apis k* arg-met bro1 *Arg-n* *Ars* k* ars-i ars-s-f k2 *Bell* k* bov brom bry k2 bufo *Calc-p* k* *Canth* k* *Carb-v* carbn-s *Caust* *Cham* k* chel k* *Clem* coc-c cur elaps ferr ferr-i ferr-p *Gels* k* *Graph* hipp jl2 *Hydr-ac* *Iod* k* ip k* *Kali-bi* *Kali-i* kali-n k* lac-ac k* *Lob* mag-s mang k2 mang-act bro1 *Merc* k* *Mez* k* myric *Nat-ar* **Nit-ac** k* oena k* *Par* k* *Ph-ac* *Phos* k* phyt plut-n srj7 • *Puls* pyrog *Rhus-t* *Rumx* k* sang k2* **Seneg** spira a1 *Spong* k* *Stict* tab k* *Tarent* thuj k* tong a1 urt-u zinc-p k2 zing bro1
  - **accompanied** by | **hoarseness**: am-m ptk1
- **chill**; during: borx b4a.de *Hep* b4a.de
- **cold**:
  - **air** agg.: **Acon** ↓ calc-p ↓ *Carb-v* ↓ **Hep** nat-ar k2 *Nat-m* ↓ *Nux-v* ↓ *Phos* ↓ **Rumx** ↓ *Sil* *Sulph* ↓ *Tub* ↓
    - **rawness**: **Acon** calc-p *Carb-v* *Nat-m* *Nux-v* *Phos* **Rumx** k* sil *Sulph* *Tub*
  - **drinks** | **agg.**: calc *Hep*
- **coryza**; during: am-m ↓ *Seneg* ↓
  - **burning**: am-m *Seneg*
- **cough** agg.; during: *Acon* k* **All-c** k* aloe ↓ am-c ↓ ambr ↓ ant-t bro1 arg-met k* *Arg-n* ↓ arn ↓ *Ars* ↓ arum-t bro1 asc-t bro1 **Bell** k* borx *Brom* k* *Bry* bufo ↓ *Calc* *Caps* ↓ carb-an ↓ *Carb-v* k* *Caust* k* cham ↓ *Chel* k* chin chlor ↓ *Cina* hr1 *Cist* ↓ coc-c dros fl-ac ↓ *Gels* ↓ *Hep* k* ign ↓ inul bro1 iod k* *Kali-bi* k* *Kali-c* kali-i ↓ *Lach* k* mag-m h2* med mur-ac ↓ *Naja* ↓ nat-m nit-ac bro1 *Nux-m* ↓ **Nux-v** ↓ *Osm* k* *Phos* k* plac ↓ *Puls* pyrog k2 rauw tpw8* rumx k* sars *Seneg* ↓ sep ↓ sil ↓ *Spong* k* *Stann* *Staph* ↓ **Sulph** ↓ tarent k2 ziz ↓
  - **burning**: acon b7a.de ars bell bufo *Carb-v* *Caust* cham *Chel* coc-c *Dros* *Gels* k* iod mag-m phos k* pyrog rumx *Seneg* spong ptk1
  - **cutting**: **All-c** k* *Staph* k* sulph
- **cough** agg.; during: ...
  - **grasps** the larynx: **Acon** k* **All-c** k* ant-t k* *Bell* k* *Dros* k* **Hep** k* iod k* lach k* *Phos* k*
  - **rawness**: *All-c* ambr a1 **Arg-met** k* *Arg-n* k* *Ars* *Bell* **Brom** k* bry bufo carb-v **Caust** k* cham chlor iod *Kali-c* mag-m *Naja* **Nux-v** osm phos **Puls** k* *Rumx* k* *Seneg* sep sil h2 spong **Sulph** k* ziz
  - **sore**: am-c b4.de* ambr **Arg-met** k* **Bell** *Brom* k* bry b7.de* *Caps* carb-an *Carb-v* k* *Caust* chin *Dros* k* fl-ac hep b4.de* ign k* kali-c k* kali-i med hr1 nat-m k* *Nux-m* **Phos** k* plac rzf5 • *Puls* rumx sep k* *Stann*
  - **stitching**: aloe arn k2 borx c1 bufo dros kali-c k* mur-ac *Phos* k* sulph
  - **tearing**: **All-c** k* *Bell* borx *Calc* *Cist* med *Phos* *Staph*
  - **torn** loose; as if something was: **All-c** k* calc b4a.de*
  - **ulcerative**: carb-v b4.de*
- **cutting**: all-c *Arg-met* k* bufo bg2 canth kali-n k* manc k* merc-c ptk1 *Merc-cy* ptk1 nit-ac bg2* thuj bg2 vinc ptk1
- **drawing** pain: am-c h2* borx c1 caust h2* kali-c h2* kali-p fd1.de • plut-n srj7 • sulph h2*
- **eating**; while: rumx
- **excitement** agg.: *Cist* ↓
  - **stitching**: *Cist*
- **fever**; during: *Acon* bg2 am-m bg2 ant-c bg2 apis bg2 arg-met bg2 bar-c bg2 *Bell* bg2 brom bg2 bry bg2 canth bg2 carb-v bg2 caust bg2 cham bg2 **Dros** bg2 *Hep* bg2 **Iod** bg2 lach bg2 mang bg2 merc bg2 **Mosch** bg2 **Nux-v** bg2 **Op** bg2 par bg2 *Phos* bg2 **Puls** bg2 sabad bg2 samb bg2 seneg bg2 *Spong* bg2 sulph bg2 verat bg2 zinc bg2
- **grasping**: bell b4a.de
- **hawking** up mucus agg.: cham h1 cina h1 lyc h2 nux-v h1
- **heat**; during: bell hep *Iod* mosch **Nux-v** *Phos* **Puls**
- **inspiration**:
  - **agg.**: **Acon** ↓ brom ↓ dros ↓ **Hep** ↓ hipp ↓ **Phos** ↓ *Rumx* ↓ sil ↓
    - **rawness**: **Acon** brom **Hep** hipp **Phos** *Rumx* sil
    - **sore**: brom k2 dros
  - **deep**:
    - **agg.**: *Rumx* ↓
      - **burning**: *Rumx*
  - **forced** inspiration: hep ↓
    - **stitching**: hep
- **lifting** a weight: sil k*
- **measles**; during: *Carb-v* b4a.de
- **motion**:
  - **agg.**: *Bell* spong
  - **head**; of | **agg.**: bell k2 hura
- **nail**; as from a: spong
- **perspiration**; during: acon bg2 apis bg2 **Bell** bg2 bov bg2 con bg2 *Dros* bg2 *Hep* bg2 kali-c bg2 lach bg2 nux-v bg2 ph-ac bg2 *Phos* bg2 puls bg2 **Sep** bg2 spong bg2 *Sulph* bg2
- **piercing**: brom cham kali-c nit-ac phos
- **pressing**: (↗COUGH - Pressure - larynx) acon agar k* anac k* bar-c b4.de* bell b4.de* caps b7.de* carb-v b4.de* *Caust* k* **Chel** k* cic b7.de* colch b7.de* crot-t bg2 euphr k* graph b4.de* hep b4.de* *Iod* k* kali-bi k* lach bg2 mag-c b4.de* *Mang* b4a.de nat-m bg2 olib-sac wmh1 phos b4.de* sep k* *Spong* b7.de* tarax b7.de* tell c1 thuj k* *Zinc* b4.de*
  - **accompanied** by | **salivation**: tarax ptk1
- **pressing** pain | **inward**: *Spong* b7a.de
- **pressure** agg.: *Ars* k* card-m *Hep* **Phos** k*
- **rawness**: *Acon* k* *Aesc* *Agar* *All-c* *All-s* *Alum* k* alum-p k2 alum-sil k2* *Alumn* am-c am-caust bro1 *Ambr* anac anan apis **Arg-met** k* **Arg-n** arn bro1 **Ars** ars-i ars-s-f k2 *Arum-t* bro1 asar *Bar-c* bro1 *Bell* k* benzo bro1 borx a1 bov **Brom** k* *Bry* k* bufo *Calc* calc-sil k2 *Cann-s* *Carb-an* *Carb-v* carbn-s carl *Caust* k* **Cham** k* chin chinin-ar *Chlor* *Cist* k* *Coc-c* *Coff* dirc bg1 dros bro1* dulc eup-per bro1 *Gels* graph *Hep* bro1 *Hydr* k* hydr-ac *Iod* k* kali-ar k2 *Kali-bi* k* kali-c **Kali-i** k* kali-n kali-perm k* *Kali-s* kreos lac-ac **Lach** k* lact laur lec lyc k* mag-m mag-p br1* *Mang* k* *Mang-act* bro1 med k* *Merc* k* **Naja** *Nat-m* **Nux-v** k* ol-an osm k* ox-ac *Ph-ac* k* phel **Phos** k* *Puls* k* *Rhus-t* k* **Rumx** k* *Samb* *Sang* k* sars

- **rawness**: ... *Seneg Sep Sil* spong k2* *Stann Staph* stront-c **Sulph** k* *Tarent* vanil fd5.de *Zinc* k* zinc-p k2
- **reading**; after: euphr nit-ac *Spong* stann
- **scraping** the throat agg.: agar↓ *Cann-s*↓ *Canth*↓ *Carb-v*↓ *Kali-bi*↓ *Rumx*↓
  - **burning**: *Canth Kali-bi*
  - **rawness**: agar *Cann-s Carb-v Rumx*
- **singers**: all-c↓ alum↓ *Arg-n*↓ arn↓ **Arum-t**↓ caps↓ cupr↓ ferr-p↓ *Lach*↓ *Rhus-t*↓ sil↓ *Stann*↓ wye↓ zinc↓
  - **sore**: (↗*Inflammation - larynx - singers*) all-c br1 alum *Arg-n* arn **Arum-t** caps cupr ferr-p k* *Lach Rhus-t* sil h2 *Stann* wye br1 zinc
- **singing** agg.: *Acon* k* arg-met↓ dros↓ sal-fr sle1• **Spong** k* *Stann*↓
  - **pressing**: spong h1*
  - **rawness**: arg-met dros *Stann*
- **smoking** agg.: osm↓
  - **rawness**: osm
- **sneezing** agg.: aphis borx phos
  - **stitching**: borx c1
- **sore**: **Acon** *Agar* b4a.de all-c bg2 all-s alum k* alum-p k2 am-c b4.de* am-caust bg2 *Ambr* ang bg2 ant-c k* aphis apis **Arg-met** k* *Arg-n Ars* ars-i ars-s-f k2 arum-t bg2 bamb-a stb2.de• bapt bar-c **Bell** k* bov b4.de *Brom* k* bry k* calad *Calc-s Cann-s* carb-an *Carb-v* k* **Carbn-s** castm *Caust* k* chen-a hr1 *Chin* k* chinin-ar cic *Con* cop crot-h **Dros** k* ephe-si hsj1• epil a1* fl-ac flor-p rsj3• *Graph* k* *Hep* k* *Ign* k* iod k* kali-ar k2 *Kali-bi* k* kali-c k* *Kali-i Kali-s* lac-c **Lach** mag-m k* mag-p bg2* mang bg2 *Med Mez* nat-ar nat-c bg2 *Nat-m* k* *Nicc* nit-ac h2 *Nux-m* osm ox-ac **Phos** k* *Puls* b7.de* *Rumx Ruta* k* sang *Sep* k* *Sil* k* **Spong** k* **Stann** k* *Still* sul-ac sul-i k2 **Sulph** syph ptk1 teucr vanil fd5.de zinc zinc-p k2
  - **intubation**; as after: bamb-a stb2.de•
- **speaking**, on (See talking - agg.)
- **squeezed**; as if: *Cham* b7.de nux-v b7.de ruta b7.de*
- **stinging**: *Alumn* am-c k* bufo k* canth cham dirc *Iod* mang k2 **Nit-ac** k* *Seneg*
- **stitching**: acon am-m k2 ang k* aphis aran bg2* *Arg-met* asar k* asc-t bg2* bar-c bell borx k* *Brom* k* bufo k* *Calc* k* calc-caust canth k* caps k* caust b4a.de cham k* *Chel* k* chin k* *Cist* cob coc-c k* croc k* cur dig k* digin a1 dirc k* dros k* dulc fd4.de guaj b4.de hep hydr-ac k* hyos k* *Indg* k* *Iod* k* *Kali-c* k* *Kali-s* laur k* led *Mang* k* meny b7.de* merc-c k* *Mez* b4a.de mur-ac naja k* *Nit-ac* k* nit-s-d a1 nitro-o a1 olnd k* ox-ac k* *Phos* k* podo fd3.de• prun-p a1 *Puls* b7a.de sars k* seneg spig b7.de* spong h1* stann sul-ac k* sul-i k2 syph k2 *Thuj Til* k* zinc k*
- **stitching** pain | **pressing** pain: sars h2*
- **supper** agg.; after: *Hep*↓
  - **pressing**: *Hep*
  - **stitching**: *Hep*
- **swallowing**:
  - **agg.**: bapt *Bell* k* *Brom*↓ calc card-m chel chinin-s↓ **Dros**↓ fl-ac a1 gels↓ hep ign iod↓ kali-bi kali-cy kali-perm lyc k* mag-m↓ **Mang**↓ med hr1* *Merc-c* merc-cy↓ ph-ac h2* phos **Spong** k* *Sul-ac* symph fd3.de• tub jl2 [tax jsj7]
    - **cutting**: merc-cy
    - **food** passed over sore spot; as if: *Kali-bi*
    - **pressing**: *Chel* lyc
    - **rawness**: calc
    - **sore**: **Bell** calc chinin-s **Dros** k* fl-ac gels mag-m **Spong**
    - **stitching**: *Brom* k* iod h* **Mang** k*
    - **tearing**: ign k*
  - **amel.**: spig↓ tarax↓
    - **pressing**: tarax h1
    - **stitching**: spig h1*
  - **hindering** swallowing: meny↓
    - **stitching**: meny h1*
- **talking**:
  - **after**: *Ferr*↓ *Kali-bi*↓ phos↓
    - **burning**: *Ferr Kali-bi* phos k2

- **Larynx – talking**: ...
  - **agg.**: *Acon* k* *Alumn*↓ am-c apis arg-met *Arg-n*↓ *Ars*↓ bamb-a stb2.de• bapt *Bell* k* bry *Calc*↓ carb-v k* card-m carl↓ coc-c k* *Hep* kali-bi merc-cy k* *Nat-m*↓ **Nicc** nit-ac osm **Phos** k* rumx sang **Spong** k* *Stann*↓ *Staph*↓ sul-ac k* sulph **Tarent**↓ vanil fd5.de
    - **pressing**: *Kali-bi* k*
    - **rawness**: *Alumn* **Arg-met** *Arg-n Ars Calc* carl coc-c *Kali-bi Nat-m Rumx Stann Staph* **Tarent**
- **tearing**: adam skp7* alum bg2 am-c bg2 am-m bg2* ambr bg2 anac bg2 anan apis b7a.de ars bg2 bell k* borx k* bov bg2 canth bg2 caps bg2* carb-an bg2 carb-v bg2 *Caust* b4a.de* chin bg2 coff bg2 dros bg2 ferr bg2 hep bg2 ign k* kali-c bg2 kali-n bg2 kreos bg2 lac-ac laur bg2 mag-c bg2 mag-m bg2 mang bg2 mur-ac bg2 nat-m bg2 nux-v bg2 par bg2 ph-ac bg2 **Phos** bg2 plb bg2 *Puls* bg2 rhod bg2 *Rhus-t* bg2 sabad bg2 seneg k* sep bg2 sil bg2 spong bg2 *Stann* bg2 staph bg2 stront-c bg2 sul-ac bg2 *Sulph* bg2 *Zinc* bg2
- **tobacco** smoking, from: bry k*
- **torn** asunder; as if: staph b7.de
- **torn** loose; as if something was: calc bg2
- **touch** agg.: acon k2 alum h2* *Ant-t* k* apis↓ bapt↓ bar-c↓ *Bell* brom bry↓ carb-v k2 caust chinin-s↓ cic↓ *Con*↓ crot-h *Graph*↓ hep lac-c↓ **Lach** mez↓ nat-m h2* *Nicc*↓ **Phos** k* rumx k2 sil↓ **Spong** k* *Sul-ac*↓ sulph↓ syph jl2 teucr↓ zinc↓
  - **sore**: **Acon** k* alum apis bapt bar-c **Bell** brom bry carb-v k2 *Caust* k* chinin-s cic *Con Crot-h Graph* hep lac-c **Lach** mez *Nicc* **Phos** k* rumx **Spong** k* *Sul-ac* sulph teucr zinc
  - **stitching**: sil h2
- **turning** head agg.: *Bell Bry Carb-v*↓ lach spong
  - **sore**: *Carb-v* lach *Spong*
- **ulcerative**: bell bg2 caps b7.de* carb-v b4.de* kali-bi bg2 nat-m bg2
- **waking**; on: alum↓
  - **rawness**: alum
- **walking** in open air agg.: ox-ac↓
  - **stitching**: ox-ac
- **warm** room agg.: *All-c* br1
- **weather** agg.; cold wet: *All-c* br1
- **wedge**; as if from a: caust b4.de*
- ▽ **extending** to:
  - **Abdomen**: ambr↓ crot-c
    - **burning**: ambr k*
  - **Chest**: borx a1 carb-v k2
    - **drawing** pain: borx c1
  - **Ear**: arg-met↓ nat-m↓
    - **stitching**: arg-met nat-m
    - **swallowing** agg.: **Mang**↓
      - **stitching**: **Mang** k*
  - **Ears**: mang k2
    - **burning**: mang k2
  - **Mouth**; roof of: plut-n srj7•
  - **Nostrils**: *Kali-bi*↓
    - **burning**: *Kali-bi*
  - **Pharynx**: dros↓
    - **stitching**: dros
  - **Teeth**: crot-h k*
  - **Vertex**: arg-met↓
    - **stitching**: arg-met
- ○ **Back** of: nat-m↓
  - **pressing**: nat-m bg2
- **Epiglottis**: bell↓ wye↓
  - **burning**: wye
  - **rawness**: bell h1*
- **Spot**; in a small: *Hep Lach*
- **Spots**; in: cimic bg2 con bg2 hep bg2 hyos bg2 nit-ac bg2 nux-v bg2
- **Throat**-pit: *Apis*↓ arg-met↓ *Arg-n*↓ ars↓ borx↓ brom↓ calc-p↓ caust h2 chel↓ graph↓ *Lach* lap-la↓ mag-c↓ phos↓ spong↓
  - **breathing** deep agg.: caust↓

- **breathing** deep agg.: ...
  - ⁝ **pressing**: caust h2
- **burning**: ars k* calc-p bg2 chel bg2 lach bg2 lap-la sde8.de•
- **cough** agg.; during: *Ant-t* b7a.de ars b4a.de borx↓ *Cham* b7a.de iod b4a.de *Nux-v* b7.de*
  - ⁝ **rawness**: borx a1
  - ⁝ **stitching**: borx a1
- **eating**; after: ambr↓
  - ⁝ **pressing**: ambr h1
- **pressing**: graph h2* mag-c h2* phos h2*
- **rawness**: arg-met borx a1
- **sneezing** agg.: borx↓
  - ⁝ **rawness**: borx a1
  - ⁝ **stitching**: borx a1
- **sore**: *Apis* k* *Arg-n* k* brom k2
- **stitching**: borx h2 phos h2* spong ptk1

▽ • **extending** to | **Root** of tongue and into hyoid bone: *Lach*

○ • **Back** of: lach↓
  - ⁝ **sore**: lach ptk1

- **Trachea**: *Acon* aesc k* *Agar*↓ alum-p↓ alum-sil↓ *Ambr*↓ *Anac*↓ ant-c↓ *Ant-t*↓ apis↓ aral↓ arg-met arg-n↓ arn↓ ars↓ ars-i↓ arum-t↓ *Asaf*↓ bar-c↓ *Bell*↓ borx↓ bov↓ brom↓ **Bry** k* calad k* *Calc*↓ *Calc-s*↓ calc-sil↓ camph b7.de* cann-s↓ *Canth*↓ caps b7.de* carb-an b4.de* carb-v bg2 *Carbn-s*↓ caust bg2 *Cham*↓ chel↓ chin b7.de* cic bg2 cina↓ *Cist* clem↓ cob bg2 coc-c bg2 coff↓ dig↓ *Dros*↓ eup-per bg2 euph↓ fl-ac↓ galla-q-r↓ gels↓ graph↓ hep ign b7.de* *Iod*↓ ip *Kali-bi*↓ kali-c↓ kali-i↓ kali-m k2 kali-n↓ ketogl-ac↓ kola stb3• kreos↓ lach k* lact↓ laur b7.de led br1 lyc bg2 mag-c↓ mag-s↓ *Mang*↓ *Merc-c*↓ mez k* myric↓ nat-c↓ *Nat-m*↓ nat-p k2 nit-ac↓ nux-m↓ nux-v b7.de* *Osm* c2* par↓ *Petr*↓ petr-ra↓ ph-ac↓ phos b4.de* phyt↓ plb↓ psor↓ puls b7.de* rhod↓ rhus-t↓ rumx bg2* ruta↓ *Sang*↓ sars *Seneg*↓ sep↓ *Sil*↓ spong k* stann staph↓ *Stram*↓ stront-c↓ *Sulph*↓ symph fd3.de• tep↓ ter↓ thuj k* zinc↓ zinc-p↓
  - **18**-20 h: thuj↓
    - ⁝ **burning**: thuj
  - **morning**: *Carb-an*↓ mez k*
    - ⁝ **rawness**: *Carb-an*
  - **night**: calc↓ canth↓ sulph↓
    - ⁝ **rawness**: calc sulph
    - ⁝ **stitching**: canth k*
  - **air** agg.; in open: rumx↓
    - ⁝ **rawness**: rumx mrr1
  - **blow**; as from a: bry b7.de* cina b7.de* *Spong* b7a.de
  - **breathing** agg.: ant-c↓ thuj↓
    - ⁝ **stitching**: ant-c h2* thuj k*
  - **burning**: *Acon* k* *Ant-t* ars k* ars-i arum-t k2 *Asaf* bov k* *Canth* b7a.de *Carb-v* k* *Caust* k* *Cham* clem k* *Coc-c* *Dros* euph k* galla-q-r nl2• gels *Iod* k* *Kali-bi* k* kali-n k* *Lach* k* mag-s mang k* *Merc-c* k* mez k* myric ph-ac *Phos* k* phyt rhod kgp5• rhus-t b7.de rumx k2 *Sang* k* *Seneg* k* *Spong* k* sulph k* tep k* thuj k* zinc k* zinc-p k2
  - **constricting** pain: staph bg2
  - **corrosive**: nat-c b4.de
  - **cough**:
    - ⁝ **agg.**: carb-an↓ laur↓ naja↓ *Staph*↓
      - ⁝ **rawness**: carb-an laur naja *Staph*
    - ⁝ **during**:
      - ⁝ **agg.**: am-c↓ ant-c↓ *Arg-met*↓ *Arg-n*↓ arn↓ bell **Bry** k* *Calc*↓ camph k* cann-s↓ carb-an↓ *Carb-v*↓ **Caust** k* *Chel* *Chin* k* cina↓ cor-r *Gels*↓ *Graph*↓ hep↓ ign k* iod↓ iris↓ **Kali-bi** k* *Kali-i* kali-n *Kreos* lac-h↓ laur k* naja↓ nat-c↓ nat-m *Nux-v* k* osm ox-ac petr-ra↓ ph-ac **Phos** k* *Phyt* plac rzf5• plb↓ psor *Puls* *Rumx* k* *Sang* k* sep↓ spong k* **Stann**↓ staph *Sulph* thuj
        - . **as** after long coughing (= much coughing): carb-an h2
        - . **blow**; as from a: bry b7.de* cina b7.de*
        - . **rawness**: *Arg-met* arg-n k* arn *Calc* *Carb-v* *Caust* *Gels* *Graph* hep k2 laur naja nat-c nux-v **Phos** *Rumx* stann *Staph* *Sulph*

Pain – Trachea – cough – during – agg.: ...
- . **sore**: am-c ant-c b7.de* *Arg-n* k* **Bry** k* cann-s b7.de* **Caust** k* chel chin b7.de* cina hep k2 iod iris kali-i lac-h htj1• nat-m b4.de* nux-v k* osm petr-ra shn4• plac rzf5• plb b7.de* psor *Rumx* sep **Stann** k* sulph
- . **streak** down; pain goes in a: **Caust** k*
- . **torn** asunder; as if: staph b7.de*
- . **ulcerative**: *Carb-v* b4a.de
- ⁝ **with**: ars↓ arum-t↓ carb-v↓ *Caust*↓ *Ferr*↓ gels↓ mag-s↓ phyt↓ **Spong**↓
  - ⁝ **burning**: ars k2 arum-t k2 carb-v k2 *Caust* *Ferr* gels mag-s phyt **Spong**
- **cutting**: arg-met b7.de* camph bg2 canth b7a.de* iod bg2
- **exertion**; on slightest: manc↓
  - ⁝ **stitching**: manc
- **hawking**: camph h1*
- **hawking** up mucus agg.: cham h1 cina h1 lyc h2 nux-v h1 petr-ra↓
  - ⁝ **sore**: petr-ra shn4•
- **inspiration** agg.: *Bry* caps carb-v↓ *Caust* *Chel* *Hep* *Kali-c* laur lyc *Manc* nat-m psor
  - ⁝ **rawness**: carb-v
- **lancinating**: *Iod*
- **measles**; during: *Carb-v* b4a.de
- **motion** agg.: clem↓ seneg↓
  - ⁝ **burning**: clem a1 seneg
- **piercing**: kali-c nit-ac
- **pressing**: ant-c h2* bar-c b4.de* carb-v h2* caust bg2 graph b4.de* mag-c b4.de* phos b4.de* thuj b4.de*
- **pressing** pain | **asunder**: cic b7.de*
- **rawness**: *Acon* *Agar* alum-p k2 alum-sil k2 *Ambr* *Anac* **Arg-met** k* arg-n arn ars-i k2 bry k2 *Calc* *Calc-s* calc-sil k2 *Carb-an* *Carb-v* *Carbn-s* **Caust** k* *Coc-c* coff dig fl-ac graph *Iod* *Ip* ketogl-ac rly4• kreos lact laur **Lyc** *Mang* *Mez* nat-c *Nat-m* nit-ac **Nux-v** osm par *Petr* **Phos** k* psor *Puls* **Rumx** k* *Sang* *Sars* *Seneg* spong k2 **Stann** staph k* *Stram* stront-c *Sulph* zinc zinc-p k2
- **sore**: alum-p k2 *Ambr* k* anac b4.de* ant-c k* apis k* aral bg2 arg-met b7a.de ars-i k2 *Bell* borx bg2 bov b4.de* brom k* *Bry* k* cann-s b7.de* carb-an k* carb-v k* carbn-s *Caust* k* cham k* *Chin* k* eup-per bg2 *Hep* iod b4.de* kali-bi bg2 kali-c k* kali-i bg2 lyc nat-c k* *Nat-m* k* nat-p nux-m b7.de* nux-v k* petr-ra shn4• *Phos* k* plb b7.de* puls b7.de* rhus-t b7.de* **Rumx** k* ruta bg2 sang k2 *Seneg* b4.de* sep k* *Sil* k* stann k* staph b7a.de* sulph ter bg2 zinc k* zinc-p k2
- **stitching**: aesc bg2* ant-c b7.de* *Arg-met* k* bar-c b4.de* bell k* borx b4a.de canth k* caps b7.de* chel bg2 chin bg2 ip b7.de kali-c bg2 lach k* merc-c b4a.de nit-ac b4a.de* phos bg2 sars bg2 **Stann** k* thuj k*
- **swallowing** agg.: puls↓ thuj↓
  - ⁝ **rawness**: puls
  - ⁝ **stitching**: thuj h1*
- **talking** agg.: **Arg-met**↓ bry k* merc-cy bg2 phos bg2 sang k2
  - ⁝ **rawness**: **Arg-met** k*
- **tearing**: borx b4a.de ign bg2 staph bg2
- **torn** asunder; as if: staph b7.de*
- **torn** loose; as if something was: osm bg2
- **ulcerative**: carb-v bg2 kali-c bg2 *Lach* b7a.de

PARALYSIS:

○ - **Larynx**: (↗*Insensibility; NOSE - Liquids - come; THROAT - Paralysis*) absin a1 *Alum* k* am-c k* arg-met k2 **Caust** k* *Cina* *Crot-h* k* *Gels* k* *Hydr-ac* hr1 *Iod* hr1 kali-p hr1 **Lach** k* *Naja* *Phos* k* *Plb* k* *Stram* k*
- **sensation** of: *Caust* b4a.de

○ • **Epiglottis**: acon k* gels k*

- **Vocal** cord: acon b7.de* ars bg2 *Bell* bg2* both bro1 canth bg2* carb-v bg2 caust bg2* chin bg2 cocain bro1 **Cocc** b7.de* diphtox jl2 *Dulc* bg2 *Euph* bg2 *Euphr* b7a.de **Gels** bg2* *Graph* bg2 *Hyos* b7.de* ip b7.de* kali-i bg2 kali-p bro1* *Lach* b7a.de* *Laur* b7.de* mur-ac bg2 nat-m bg2 nux-m b7.de* *Nux-v* b7.de* *Op* b7.de* ox-ac bro1* phos bg2 plb b7a.de* *Rhus-t* b7.de* ruta b7.de* sec b7.de* seneg ptk1 stann bg2 staph bg2 *Stram* b7.de* zinc bg2
  - **catching** cold, from: *Cina* hr1

PHTHISIS:

○ - **Larynx**: *Agar* am-c b4a.de *Am-m* b7.de* ambr b7.de* anan ant-c *Arg-met* k* ars k* ars-i ars-s-f c2 bufo *Calc* calc-i k2 calc-p k2 calc-s k2 calc-sil k2 *Carb-an Carb-v* k* *Carbn-s Caust* k* chr-o c2 *Con* b4a.de cupr b7.de* *Dros* k* elaps *Hep* k* ign b7.de* inul br1 *Iod* k* *Kali-bi* k* *Kali-i* k* kali-n b4.de* kreos k* *Lach* k* *Laur* b7a.de led lob-e c1 **Mang** k* merc k* *Merc-i-r* nat-sel c1* *Nit-ac Nux-v* b7.de* par b7.de* *Phos* k* puls b7.de* *Sel* k* *Seneg* k* *Sil* **Spong** k* **Stann** k* sul-i k2 sulph k* tub

- **short** hacking cough and loss of voice: **Stann** k*
- **singers** and public speakers: *Ant-c Arg-met* k*

- **Trachea**: acon b7.de* *Am-c* b4a.de arg-met b7.de* am b7.de* *Ars* k* *Calc* k* *Carb-an Carb-v* k* caust k* cham b7.de* chin coloc con k* cupr b7.de* *Dros* k* ferr b7.de* hep k* iod *Kali-c* b4a.de kali-n k* kreos b7a.de *Lach* b7a.de *Laur* b7.de* led b7.de* lyc k* mang k* *Nat-m* b4a.de nit-ac k* *Nux-v* b7.de* par b7.de* phos b4.de* puls b7.de* rhus-t b7.de* seneg k* spong k* squil b7.de* *Stann* k* *Sulph* b4.de* teucr b7.de* verat b7.de*
  - **accompanied** by | **mucus**; profuse: *Phos* b4a.de *Seneg* b4a.de

PLUG:

○ - **Larynx**: *(↗Lump - larynx)* anac bg2 *Ant-c* k* arg-met k* bar-c b4.de* bell k* *Calc* caust bg1 dros k* *Hep* k* kali-c k* *Lach* k* *Lob* k* nat-m h2* phos ptk1 sep **Spong** k* sulph k*

- **Trachea**: *Ant-c* b7a.de* *Bell* bg2 dros bg2 kali-c bg2 *Lach* k* spong bg2 sulph bg2

POLYPI:

○ - **Larynx**: *(↗Condylomata - larynx; Tumors - benign)* *Arg-n* ars bg1 berb k* calc k* hep k* kali-bi bg2 kali-br nit-ac phos bg2 psor bro1 *Sang* k* *Sangin-n* bro1 syph jl2 teucr bg2* *Thuj* k*

- **Vocal** cords: arg-met mtf arg-n mtf berb k* *Thuj* k*

PRESSURE:

○ - **Larynx**, on: chel ptk1 ol-an bg1

- **Throat**-pit: aesc anac k* **Brom** carc fd2.de• *Caust* k* cic graph **Lach** *Lob* k* phos *Rumx* sarr k* sars k* spong fd4.de
  - **anger**, after: staph
  - **inspiration**, on: caust
  - **swallowing** agg.: staph

PRICKLING:

○ - **Larynx**: bufo bg2 *Calc*

- **Trachea**: ter bg2 vero-o rly3•

PULSATING: bufo bg2 chel bg2 lach bg2

○ - **Larynx**: *All-c* k*

- **Throat**-pit; in: bell dgt

PURRING sound:

○ - **Trachea**; from | **cough** agg.; during: nat-c h2*

RATTLING:

○ - **Larynx**: acon bg2 alum bg2 am-c k* *Anac* bg2 *Ant-t* k* *Arg-n Bell* bg2 **Brom** k* calc bg2 carb-an bg2 carb-v bg2 carbn-s caust bg2 cham bg2 chin bg2 cina bg2 *Con* crot-t cupr bg2 euphr bg2 ferr-p *Hep* bg2* hydr bg1 hyos bg2 iod bg2 ip bg2* kali-bi k* kali-c bg2 lach bg2 laur bg2 **Lyc** bg2 merc bg2 nat-m bg2 nit-ac bg2 **Op** bg2 *Petr* bg2 phos bg2 *Puls* bg2 samb bg2 sep bg2 sil bg2 spong k* squil bg2 *Stann* bg2 sul-ac **Sulph** bg2

- **Trachea**: *(↗RESPIRATION - Rattling)* acon k* alum bg2 am-c k* *Anac* bg2 **Ant-t** k* bar-c bell k* calc bg2 carb-ac carb-an k* carb-v k* carbn-s k2 caust k* cham k* chen-a c1* chin bg2 cina bg2 cupr bg2 euphr k* ferr-p **Hep** k* hyos k* iod bg2 **Ip** k* kali-bi bg2* kali-c k* *Kali-s* lach bg2 *Laur* k* **Lyc** bg2 merc k* nat-m k* nit-ac k* oena op k* ox-ac petr k* phos bg2 puls k* samb k* *Sep* k* sil k* spong bg2 squil k* *Stann* bg2 sul-ac sulph k*
  - **ball** rolling loose, as if: chen-a vml3•
  - **cough**:
    - **before**: kali-c h2
    - **during** (See COUGH - Accompanied - trachea)
  - **expiration** agg.; during: *Calc* b4a.de
  - **lying** on left side agg.: anac c1

READING aloud agg.: nit-ac bg2

RELAXATION: | **Vocal** cords: pen br1

REMOVED; as if larynx were: spong

RISING; sensation of something:

○ - **Larynx** | **air** rising; sensation of: lyc b4.de*

ROUGHNESS: *Agar* am-c ambr anac k* ant-c apis ars ars-i borx bov k* brom *Calc* k* canth caps *Carb-an* **Carb-v** k* *Caust* k* chin cimic cist coc-c coff colch cur dig dros *Ferr* k* ferr-ar gels graph *Hep* hipp hydr-ac iod kali-ar *Kali-bi* kali-c kali-i kali-n kreos lach lact *Laur* lyc mag-m *Mang* k* meny merc merc-sul mur-ac nat-c nit-ac nux-m ol-an ox-ac *Ph-ac* phel *Phos* k* plb prun puls rhod rhus-t sabad sang *Seneg* k* sep *Sil Stann* k* stront-c *Sul-ac* k* *Sulph* k* verat zinc

- **morning**: borx h2 calc k* *Carb-an* zinc
- **evening**: cimic k*
- **cough** agg.: anac h2*
- **eating**:
  - **after**:
    - **agg.**: anac zinc
    - **amel.**: zinc h2
- **talking** agg.: am-c h2* lyc h2*
- **walking** in open air agg.; after: *Sil*
- **weather**; in wet: phos h2

○ - **Larynx**: *Alum* k* alumn k* am-c b4.de am-m b7.de ambr b7.de* anac b4.de apis k* aq-pet a1 ars b4.de aster hr1 bell b4.de borx b4a.de bov b4.de *Brom* b4a.de calc k* *Cann-s* b7a.de canth b7.de* caps b7.de *Carb-an* **Carb-v** k* card-b a1 carl a1 castm *Caust* k* *Cham* b7a.de chin b7.de* cimic k* *Coff* b7.de* con cop hr1 dig b4a.de dros k* *Ferr* k* ferr-p graph *Hep* k* ign b7a.de iod hr1 ip b7a.de* *Kali-c* k* kali-i *Kali-n* b4.de* kali-s k2 kreos *Lach* laur k* lyc h2* mag-c b4.de mag-m k* mag-s **Mang** k* merc k* merc-sul hr1 mur-ac b4.de nat-ar nat-m b4.de nat-s nicc *Nux-m* b7a.de **Nux-v** k* ol-an par b7.de *Ph-ac* b4.de* *Phos* k* plb k* *Puls* k* rhod k* **Rhus-t** k* sabad k* sars *Seneg* k* *Sep* k* *Sil* k* spig b7a.de **Spong** k* *Stann* k* stront-c b4.de* sul-ac k* sul-i k2 *Sulph* k* tarent k* tep k* *Tub* jl2 verat b7a.de *Verb* b7a.de *Zinc* b4.de
  - **morning**: bov hr1 *Calc* k* coff k* kali-bi k*
  - **cough**:
    - **agg.**: bar-c carb-an *Carb-v Caust* dig *Hep* **Kali-c** kreos *Mang* k* *Nux-v Phos* sabad *Seneg* spong
    - **during** | **amel.**: nicc stann k*
  - **talking**; after: arg-met ptk1 carl a1 coc-c lyc staph tarent ptk1
  - **uncovering**: kali-c h2*

- **Throat**-pit: borx b4a.de*
- **Trachea**: agar b4.de* alum b4.de* am-c b4.de* apis aq-pet a1 bar-c *Cann-s* b7a.de carb-an carb-v b4.de* carl a1 caust b4.de* dig k* dros k* graph b4.de* hep k* *Hyos* b7a.de iod b4.de* kali-c k* *Kali-i* hr1 kali-n b4.de* kreos k* laur k* led b7.de* mag-c b4.de* mang b4.de* mur-ac b4.de* nat-c b4.de* nat-m b4.de* nit-ac b4.de* nux-v b7.de* par b7.de* phos k* phyt k* plb b7.de* puls b7.de* rhod b4.de* rhus-t k* sabad sars b4.de* *Seneg* b4.de* sep k* sil hr1 spong k* *Stann* b4.de* stront-c b4.de* *Sul-ac* b4a.de sulph b4.de* tarent k* verb k* zinc b4.de*
- **Vocal** cord | **right**: tub jl2

SCRAPING, clearing larynx: *(↗THROAT - Hawk; disposition)* *Aesc Agar* alco a1 all-s k* aloe alum alum-sil k2 *Alumn* k* *Am-c* am-m *Ambr* k* amyg a1 anac k* **Ant-t** aphis *Apis* aq-pet a1 *Arg-met* **Arg-n** *Ars* aur-m-n k* bar-c **Bell** k* borx bov k* **Brom** k* *Bry* k* cain *Calc Calc-f Calc-p Calc-s* calc-sil k2 camph *Cann-s Carb-v* k* *Carbn-s* card-m *Carl* **Caust** k* **Cham** k* chel k* chinin-s *Chlor* cimic k* *Coc-c* k* cocc colch k* *Con* k* crot-t *Cycl* k* *Dig* k* *Dros* k* dulc fd4.de *Echi* **Euphr** ferr ferr-i k2 *Fl-ac* k* graph k* grat k* *Hep* k* hydr k* hydr-ac k* *Iod* ip k* kali-ar *Kali-bi* k* *Kali-c* k* *Kali-i Kali-p Kali-s* kali-sil k2 kalm *Kreos Lach* k* laur k* led linu-c a1 lob k* *Lyc* mag-c mag-m manc hr1 *Mang* mang-act br1 *Merc* mur-ac *Naja* nat-ar nat-c k* *Nat-m* k* nat-s k* nat-sil fd3.de• nit-ac k* nux-m **Nux-v** k* *Olib-sac* wmh1 op k* osm a1 paeon *Par* petr k* petr-ra shn4• *Ph-ac* **Phos** phyt plat prun **Puls** k* **Rhus-t** k* **Rumx** ruta fd4.de *Sabad Sang* sanic *Sel* k* *Seneg* k* *Sep* k* *Sil Spong* k* *Stann* k* sul-i k2 **Sulph** symph fd3.de• syph *Tarent* k* thuj k* tritic-vg fd5.de vanil fd5.de *Zinc* k* zinc-p k2 [tax jsj7]

- **daytime**: arg-met k2 *Caust* con k* dulc fd4.de *Stann*
- **morning**: *Cann-s* **Caust** chinin-s *Cina* iod h* kali-bi kali-c h2* nat-m nat-sil fd3.de• *Op* k* ruta fd4.de *Sel Stann* symph fd3.de• *Tarent* tritic-vg fd5.de vanil fd5.de
- **evening**: *Arg-met* **Brom** *Carb-v* k* **Caust** chel k* cimic k* *Coc-c* k* *Con* k* dulc fd4.de kali-p fd1.de• *Lyc* nat-ar *Rumx* stann *Tarent* tritic-vg fd5.de *Zinc*
  - **19** h: bry grat

- **night**: am-c h2* **Ant-t** *Cycl* k* kali-p fd1.de• kali-s k2 mag-c *Merc* *Rumx* ruta fd4.de tritic-vg fd5.de
- **eating**; after: bell carb-v dros k2 *Graph* hep *Kali-bi* kali-s *Lyc* *Nat-s* nit-ac nux-m phos plat puls sanic *Sil* thuj
- **ice** cream agg.: thuj
- **incessant**: brom k2 nat-sil fd3.de• **Phos** k ● spong fd4.de
- **lying** | **amel.**: nat-c
- **reading** aloud, from: *Arg-met* *Seneg*
- **talking**:
  - **agg.**: *Mang* petr-ra shn4• *Stann* symph fd3.de•
  - **before**: bung-fa mtf
- **wind** agg.: kali-c

SCRATCHING:

○ - **Larynx**: acon *Agar* b4a.de all-s mtf11 alum k* alumn k* am-c ambr bg2 anan ang a1 ant-c k* arg-n k* arn b7.de* bell bg2 bov k* brom bg2 calc camph bg2 carb-v k* cist k* coloc h2* dros b7a.de gamb k* gels bg2 *Graph* k* hep b4a.de ign k* kali-bi bg2 kali-c k* kali-n k* *Laur* k* lyc k* mag-c k* mag-m nat-m k* nit-ac k* nux-v k* olib-sac wmh1 *Op* b7a.de *Ph-ac* b4a.de phos psor puls b7.de* rhod b4a.de rhus-t b7.de* sabad b7.de* *Seneg* k* *Spong* b7.de* stann h2* staph b7.de* stict bg2 verat k* zinc k* zing k*
  - **2 h** | **wakens** him: lyc
  - **accompanied** by cough: am-m b7.de*
  - **inspiration** agg.: coloc h2*
  - **singing** agg.: agar
  - **wind** agg.: kali-c h2*
- **Trachea**: agar b4.de* alum b4.de* ambr bg2 ant-c b7.de* bov b4.de* canth b7.de* carb-v b4.de* caust b4.de* *Dros* b7a.de graph b4.de* *Hep* b4.de* kali-c b4.de* kali-n b4a.de kreos b7a.de* laur b7.de* led b7.de* lyc b4.de* mag-c b4.de* mur-ac b4.de* nat-m bg2 nit-ac b4.de* *Nux-v* b7.de* puls b7.de* rhus-t b7.de* sel b7a.de stann b4.de* sulph b4.de* verat b7.de*

SENSITIVE:

○ - **Larynx**: *Acon* k* apis b7a.de **Bell** k* borx bg2 *Brom* bg2 bry bg2 *Calad* canth bg2 carbn-s *Caust* k* cedr k* cor-r erio a1 fl-ac k* *Graph* k* hep k* lac-c **Lach** k* merc-c b4a.de **Naja** nit-ac bg2 *Phos* k* rumx br1 sang bg2 *Spong* k* sul-ac k* sulph k* vip bg2
  - **morning**: kali-bi k*
  - **cold** air, to: **Acon** k* *Ars* *Bell* calc-p *Carb-v* carl cimic k* crot-h erio a1 fl-ac **Hep** k* ip *Lac-ac* hr1 *Mang* *Naja* nux-m nux-v osm k* ox-ac *Phos* k* **Rumx** sil spong stann sulph
  - **cough** agg.: phos mrr1
  - **pressure**, to: *Ars* k* lac-c hr1 **Phos** k*
    - **slightest** pressure, to: bell k1
  - **sound** of the piano, to: **Calc** k*
  - **touch**; to: **Acon** k* *Caust* k* *Con* k* crot-h k* *Graph*. *Hep* k* kali-m k2 **Lach** k* *Naja* **Phos** k* **Spong** k* syph br
- **Trachea**: kali-bi bg2 *Lach* b7a.de laur b7.de* nat-c b4.de* phos b4.de* rumx br1
  - **cold** air, to: hep bg2 *Rumx* k*
  - **touch**; to: *Hep* k* syph br ziz hr1

SHOCKS:

○ - **Larynx**:
  - **cough** agg.; during: sulph h2
  - **waking**; on: manc
- **Trachea**: bry cina spong
  - **sleep** agg.; during: spong

SINGERS; complaints of: | **Larynx**: arum-t ptk1 ferr-p ptk1

SINGING:

- **agg.**: all-c ptk1 *Arg-met* bg2 phos ptk1 spong bg2*
- **amel.**: rhus-t ptk1 sel ptk1

SKIN in larynx; sensation of a (See Membrane - sensation - skin)

SMOKE; sensation of:

○ - **Larynx**: **Ars** k* **Bar-c** k* bell bg2 *Brom* k* ign bg2 nat-ar k2
  - **sleep**; before: *Ars* k*
- **Trachea**: bry bg2 ferr bg2 puls bg2

SNEEZING agg.: borx bg2

SPASMS:

○ - **Glottis** (See Constriction - larynx; Laryngismus)
- **Larynx**: acon bg2 ant-c b7a.de* ars bg2 asaf bg2 *Bell* bg2 brom bg2 calc bg2 calc-p bg2 cham bg2 chlor bg2 crot-h bg2 cupr b7a.de* dig bg2 ferr bg2 gels bg2 hep bg2 hyos bg2 ign bg2 iod bg2 ip bg2 lach bg2 laur b7.de* mag-p bg2 meny b7.de* meph bg2 **Mosch** b7.de* *Nux-v* b7a.de op bg2 pert jl2 phos bg2 phyt bg2 plat bg2 plb bg2 **Samb** bg2 sil bg2 spong bg2 stram bg2 sulph bg2 ter bg2 verat b7.de* visc bg2
  - **accompanied** by cough: cupr bg2
  - **epilepsy**; during (See GENERALS - Convulsions - epileptic - during - larynx)
  - **mental** symptoms; from: ign tl1

○ · **Thyroid** gland; from enlargement of the (= asthma thymicum): **Acon** bg2 am-c bg2 ambr bg2 *Ant-t* bg2 asaf bg2 aur bg2 *Bell* bg2 *Con* bg2 cupr bg2 ferr bg2 *Hep* bg2 ign bg2 **Ip** bg2 lach bg2 *Merc* bg2 phos bg2 *Seneg* bg2 **Spong** bg2 *Verat* bg2 zinc bg2
- **Vocal** cords: ip ptk1

SPONGE; sensation of a: brom bg2 spong bg2

STOPPAGE, sensation of: *Ambro* vh1 aur-m h2* mang bg2 rhus-t spong k* verat verb k*

SULPHUR vapor, as from: am-c aml-ns **Ars** k* asaf bar-c k2 *Brom* *Bry* calc *Carb-v* *Chin* croc **Ign** ip k* kali-chl *Lach* **Lyc** k* mosch k* par k* **Puls** k*

- **cough** agg.; during: brom lyc *Puls* k*

○ - **Larynx**: *Mosch* b7.de*
- **Trachea**: ars bg2 mosch bg2 puls b7.de

SUPPORTING larynx (See Pain - larynx - cough - grasps)

SWALLOWING:

- **agg.** | **Larynx**: spong ptk1

SWELLING:

- **sensation** of: caps bg2 chel bg2 chinin-s bg2 hydr-ac bg2 iod bg2 lach bg2 laur bg2 sulph bg2

○ - **Arytenoids**: tub c1
- **Below**: hep bg2
- **Larynx**: anan apis mrr1 arn **Bell** k* calad chel coc-c *Hep* k* *Iod* k* kali-i k* lac-c *Lach* k* led ptk1 ox-ac sil b4.de* spong sulph tub c1
  - **evening**: coc-c
  - **angioedema**: (↗*SKIN - Eruptions - angioedema)* apis mrr1
  - **sensation** of: *Apis* b7a.de caps b7.de carb-v *Chel* hep b4a.de hydr-ac iod b4.de ip *Kali-bi* kola stb3• *Lach* laur k* merc-c b4a.de ox-ac ozone sde2• sang k* *Spong* b7a.de sulph

○ · **Below**: *Hep* b4a.de
  - **Epiglottis**: mur-ac a1 tub jl2
    - **morning**: bapt a1*
    - **accompanied** by | **bleeding** slightly: tub jl2
- **Throat**-pit: *Ip* b7a.de *Lach* k*
- **Vocal** cords: apis bg2 bell bg2 canth bg2 kali-i bg2 sang bg2
  - **left**: tub jl2

TALKING:

- **agg.**: all-c ptk1 **Arg-met** bg2 bell bg2 bry bg2 hep bg2 lach bg2 nit-ac bg2 phos bg2* spong ptk1 sulph bg2
- **amel.**: rhus-t ptk1 sel ptk1

TENSION:

○ - **Larynx**: chin *Cocc* k* iber a1* *Iod* k* kali-n k* lach k* manc k* mez k* naja k* *Nux-v* hr1 spong b7.de* sul-ac hr1 [tax jsj7]
  - **evening**: naja
  - **bed** agg.; in: naja
  - **menses**; during: cop
- **Trachea**: buth-a sp1 kali-n bg2 lach bg2 naja bg2 spong bg2

THINGS go down the wrong way (See Food)

TICKLING: *(↗Itching; THROAT - Tickling)* androc srj1• dulc fd4.de mim-p skp7• sabin bg2 streptoc rly4• thiam rly4• tritic-vg fd5.de

- **eating**; while: form bg2

▽ - **extending** to | **Downward**: ambr bg2

○ - **Air** passages: acet-ac **Acon** k* *Alum* alum-sil k2 *Alumn* am-c k* am-m k* *Ambr* anac ang k* ant-t k* apis bg3 *Arg-met* arg-n k* arge-pl rwt5• *Arn* k* ars arum-t *Asaf* k* atro aur-m bac al2 bamb-a stb2.de• bar-c k* bell k* borx bg2 bov k* *Brom* k* *Bry* k* cadm-s c1* cain *Calc* **Calc-f** calc-p canth caps bg2* *Carb-an* k* *Carb-v* k* carbn-s carc fd2.de• *Caust* k* **Cham** k* chin k* cimic cina k* *Coc-c* *Coca* cocc colch k* coloc **Con** *Cupr* k* dig k* *Dros* *Euphr* *Ferr* k* ferr-i graph h2* ham hep k* **Hyos** ign k* inul *Iod* k* **Ip** k* iris *Kali-bi* k* **Kali-c** k* kali-n kali-perm kali-s lac-del hrn2• **Lach** k* lact laur k* led k* **Lyc** mag-c k* mag-m k* *Merc* k* mur-ac k* *Naja* nat-c k* **Nat-m** k* nat-p nicotam rly4• nit-ac **Nux-v** k* ol-an ol-j olnd k* op petr *Ph-ac* *Phos* k* prun k* psor bg3 *Puls* k* *Rhus-t* rumx sabad *Sabin* k* **Sang** sars *Seneg* k* **Sep** k* *Sil* k* *Spong* k* *Squil* *Stann* k* **Staph** k* sulph k* *Tab* tell c1 teucr thuj verat k* zinc k*

- **daytime**: coloc *Euphr* lyc nat-m staph
  - **and** night: nat-m
- **morning**: *Alumn* cain *Carb-v* coloc **Iod** lyc nat-m *Op* thuj
  - **rising** agg.; after: alumn *Arn*
  - **waking** | **after** | **agg.**: *Carb-v*
    - **on**: nat-c h2
- **forenoon**: calc-f
- **afternoon**: naja nat-c h2
  - **14** h: arg-n **Coc-c**
  - **15** h: hep naja
  - **15**-16 h: calc-f
- **evening**: alumn *Bell* bry calc-p *Caps* *Carb-v* chin chinin-s cimic coloc graph **Lyc** merc nat-m rhus-t sulph
  - **18** h | **expectoration** of mucus, amel.: sulph
  - **midnight**, until: rhus-t
  - **bed** agg.; in: *Bell* calc-p *Caps* graph **Sang**
  - **sleep**:
    - **going** to sleep; before: merc
    - **going** to sleep; on | **agg.**: *Carb-v* lyc
- **night**: am-c arg-n *Asaf* *Bry* *Calc* coc-c *Coloc* *Cycl* *Dros* kali-bi kali-c lyc mag-m myric nat-m rhus-t rumx sanic zinc
  - **midnight** | **before** | **23**.30 h: **Coc-c**
    - **after**: chinin-s
      - **2** h: nat-m
      - **3** h: *Am-c* *Bufo* cain
- **accompanied** by | **cough** (See COUGH - Tickling - bronchi)
- **air** agg.; draft of: merc
- **air** agg.; in open: *Lach* ox-ac **Phos**
- **blood**; with taste of: ham
- **coughing**; with: nicotam rly4•
- **inspiration** agg.: bamb-a stb2.de• brom hipp
- **lying**:
  - **agg.**: **Hyos** kali-bi bg1 lac-c ph-ac seneg
  - **amel.**: *Euphr* **Mang**
  - **side**; on:
    - **left** | **agg.**: *Phos*
- **smoking** agg.: atro coloc
- **talking** agg.: *Alum* *Alumn* atro *Hep* *Kali-bi* lac-c lac-del hrn2• *Phos*
- **tobacco**: acon
- **waking**; on: carb-v ham
- **walking** in open air agg.: *Ox-ac*
- **warm** room agg.: all-c ambr *Arn* *Brom* *Bry* carc fd2.de• dig **Dros** **Iod** *Ip* kali-p fd1.de• *Lyc* mez *Nat-c* **Puls** seneg spong sul-i k2 sulph

- **Fauces**; in: asc-c c1 bac tl1
- **Larynx**, in: (*↗THROAT - Tickling*) *Acon* k* *Aesc* k* aeth *Agar* k* **All-c** k* *Alum* k* alum-sil k2 *Alumn* k* am-br k* *Am-c* k* am-caust a1 *Am-m* *Ambr* k* anac k* ang k* ant-s-aur bro1 ant-t aphis apis k* *Arg-met* *Arg-n* k* *Arn* k* **Ars** k* arum-i a1 asaf aspar astac a1* aur-m aur-m-n *Bad* k* bapt bar-c bar-m k2 **Bell** k* borx bov k* *Brom* k* *Bry* k* bufo cact cadm-s *Calc* k* calc-ar *Calc-f* k* calc-i k2 *Calc-p* calc-sil k2 *Caps* k* *Carb-ac* *Carb-an* k* *Carb-v* k* *Carbn-s* *Carl* k* *Caust* *Cham* k* *Chel* k* chinin-s chlor k* *Cimic* k* *Cimx* hr1 cina cinnb *Cist* clem k* **Coc-c** k* coca *Cocc* k* colch k* coloc k* com **Con** k* cop k* *Crot-c* *Crot-h* *Cupr* *Cycl* k* daph dig dios k* dream-p sdj1• **Dros** k* *Dulc* k* euph k* *Euphr* k* eupi a1 ferr k* ferr-i fl-ac glon graph k* gymno **Hep** k* hipp hydr k2

Tickling – Larynx, in: ...
hydr-ac hr1 hyos *Ign* ptk1 ind indg k* inul k* **Iod** k* **Ip** k* *Iris* *Kali-bi* k* **Kali-c** k* *Kali-i* k* kali-m k2 kali-n *Kali-p* kali-s k2 kali-sil k2 kalm k* kreos lac-c k* **Lach** k* lact laur k* led k* lipp a1 lob k* **Lyc** k* *Mag-c* k* mag-m **Mang** k* meny h1* *Merc* k* merc-c *Merc-i-f* hr1 mez k* mur-ac *Naja* nat-c **Nat-m** k* nat-p nat-s nicc *Nit-ac* k* nit-s-d a1* **Nux-v** k* oena ol-an olnd k* onos **Op** k* osm a1* ox-ac k* par *Ph-ac* **Phos** k* phys phyt k* plan *Prun* *Psor* k* **Puls** k* raph a1* rat a1* rhod *Rhus-t* k* **Rumx** k* *Sabin* k* **Sang** k* sarcol-ac sp1 sarr hr1 *Sars* *Seneg* k* *Sep* k* *Sil* k* sol-ni sol-t-ae spira k* **Spong** k* *Squil* *Stann* k* **Staph** *Stict* k* still hr1 sul-i a1* *Sulph* k* sumb symph fd3.de• tab tarax *Tarent* tell k* thuj uva vanil fd5.de *Verb* hr1 *Vinc* k* zinc k* zinc-p k2 zing k*

- **daytime** only: nat-m
- **morning**: iod h* vanil fd5.de
- **evening**: sang hr1
- **drawing** in cold air: all-c k2
- **eating** | **amel.**: carb-an *Euphr* hr1 kali-bi a1
- **fever**; during: *Cimx* k*
- **lying** | **amel.**: *Euphr* *Mang*

- **Throat**-pit, in: (*↗COUGH - Tickling - throat-pit*) **Apis** aspar bell cann-s caust **Cham** k* cinnb cocc coloc *Con* crot-h dream-p sdj1• ign inul mtf11 *Iod* kreos lac-c lach lith-c mag-m nat-c nat-m ph-ac phos plut-n srj7• *Puls* rhus-r **Rumx** **Sang** *Sil* squil tarax
  - **night**: plut-n srj7•
- **Trachea**, in: *Acon* aesc k* *Agar* k* ail alum-sil k2 am-m ambr k2* ambro bro1 anac k* ang ant-t k* *Arn* k* ars k* arum-t asaf aur-m k* bar-c bell bov k* brom k* bry *Calc* k* calc-sil k2 *Caps* k* carb-ac carb-an k* *Carb-v* k* *Carbn-s* casc k* caust *Cham* chin chinin-s cina cist coc-c k* colch hr1 coloc com *Con* cop k* crot-h hr1 dig k* dulc *Euphr* eupi *Ferr* ferr-i gymno hyos indg **Iod** *Ip* hr1* iris iris-fl *Kali-bi* k* **Kali-c** kali-p kali-sil k2 *Kalm* k* ketogl-ac rly4• kreos lac-c lach k* lact laur k* led hr1 mag-c mag-m *Med* mez nat-ar nat-m nat-s k* nicc k* nit-ac *Nux-v* k* ol-an k* osm k* ox-ac k* petr k* **Ph-ac** phel hr1 *Phos* k* plat prun k* *Psor* k* **Puls** k* rhod k* rhus-r **Rhus-t** **Rumx** k* sabin k* **Sang** sanic *Seneg* *Sep* k* sil spig k* *Spong* k* squil **Stann** k* staph *Stict* k* *Still* k* sul-i k2 sulph tarent *Ter* hr1 teucr k* thuj verat k* zinc
  - **cough** agg.; during: *Ant-t* b7a.de *Cham* b7.de* kreos b7a.de sabin b7.de*

TIGHTNESS: (*↗CHEST - Constriction*) bar-c carb-v *Cocc* graph kali-bi mez h2 nat-m phos h2 teucr verat verb

○ - **Larynx** (See Tension)

TINGLING: | **Larynx**: *Agar* *Caps* *Iod* *Mag-m* sep

TOBACCO agg.: bry bg2

TOUCH agg.: *Bell* bg2 chinin-s bg2 *Hep* bg2 *Lach* bg2 seneg bg2 *Spong* bg2

○ - **Larynx**: acon ptk1 bell ptk1 **Lach** ptk1 *Phos* ptk1 *Spong* ptk1 syph ptk1

TUBERCULOSIS (See Phthisis)

TUMORS:
- **benign**: (*↗Polypi - larynx*) caust bro1 kali-bi bro1 sang bro1 thuj bro1
- **malignant**: *Ars* bro1 ars-i bro1 bell bro1 carb-an bro1 clem bro1 *Con* bro1 hydr bro1 iod bro1 kreos bro1 lach bro1 morph bro1 *Phyt* bro1 sang bro1 thuj bro1

TURNING HEAD agg.: *Lach* bg2 **Spong** bg2

○ - **Larynx**: lach ptk1 spong ptk1

ULCERATION:

○ - **Larynx**: ant-t k2 arg-met bg2* arg-n bg2 **Ars** bg2 ars-i bg2 bufo *Calc* k* *Carb-v* k* *Caust* k* *Cinnb* k* crot-h k* dros bg2 *Hep* bg2 *Hippoz* k* hydr k2 iod bg2 kali-bi k* kreos bg2 led bg2 lyc bg2 mang bg2* merc bg2 *Nit-ac* k* *Phos* k* sil bg2 *Spong* k* sulph bg2 *Syph* k* tub jl2
- **Vocal** cords: aur-i bro1 iod bro1 lyc br1* merc-n bro1 syph jl2
  - **tuberculous**: lac-ac br1

VALVE; sensation of a: spong bg2

○ - **Larynx**: *Spong* b7a.de

VAPOR; sensation of hot: | **Larynx**: rhus-t b7a.de

VELVETY sensation: (*↗Foreign body; Membrane - sensation*) brom calc chen-a cina *Dros* *Hep* k* *Ph-ac* **Phos** k* sulph

○ - **Larynx**: coff bg2
- **Trachea**: teucr b7.de*

Larynx

VOICE:

- **morning**: acon bg2 aloe bg2 alum bg2 am-m bg2 apis bg2 am bg2 ars bg2 aur bg2 bar-c bg2 bov bg2 calc bg2 cann-xyz bg2 carb-an bg2 **Carb-v** bg2 caust bg2 *Cina* bg2 coff bg2 colch bg2 dig bg2 **Iod** bg2 kali-bi bg2 kali-c bg2 kreos bg2 lyc bg2 mag-m bg2 mang bg2 nat-m bg2 *Nux-v* bg2 phos bg2 rhod bg2 seneg bg2 sep bg2 sulph bg2 zinc bg2
  - **bed** agg.; in: alum bg2 coff bg2 kali-bi bg2 par bg2
- **forenoon**: bar-c bg2 mag-c bg2 phos bg2 sars bg2 seneg bg2 stann bg2 sul-ac bg2
- **noon**: sulph bg2
- **afternoon**: alum bg2 am-m bg2 lyc bg2 petr bg2 phos bg2 zinc bg2
- **evening**: alum bg2 calc bg2 carb-an bg2 **Carb-v** bg2 caust bg2 ferr bg2 graph bg2 hep bg2 ign bg2 iod bg2 kali-bi bg2 *Lach* bg2 mag-c bg2 nux-v bg2 petr bg2 rumx bg2 sulph bg2 teucr bg2 thuj bg2
  - **bed** agg.; in: nux-v bg2
- **night**: arg-n bg2 bar-c bg2 calc bg2 calc-f bg2 carb-an bg2 carb-v bg2 caust bg2 kali-bi bg2 lyc bg2 naja bg2 nit-ac bg2 phos bg2 sil bg2 sumb bg2
- **air** | **wet** air agg.: carb-v bg2 hep bg2
- **air**; in open:
  - **agg.**: mang bg2
  - **amel.**: alum bg2
- **anger** agg. (See MIND - Anger - voice; with)
- **anxious**: ang b7.de* canth b7.de
- **barking**: bell k* brom k* *Canth* bg2* dros k* hep k2 lyc bg3* nit-ac k* spong k* stann k* stram k*
- **bass**: *(↗deep)* carbn-s **Dros** k* *Hydrog* srj2• kola stb3• laur k* mag-s k* par a1 plac rzf5• sulph h2* sumb k*
- **bi**-tonal: diphtox jl2
- **bleating**: *Camph* hr1 nux-m k*
- **blowing** the nose agg.: caust bg2
- **broken**: ant-c ptk1 ars-h hr1 arum-t bg3* bell ptk1 camph k* choc srj3• con ptk1 cupr-n a1 graph ptk1 iod k* merc k* plb k* sep ptk1 spong bg3* stram ptk1 tab k*
  - **sing** high; when attempting to: phos stram ptk1
- **changeable**: alumn k* ant-c bro1 *Arg-met* k* *Ars* k* **Arum-t** k* bell k2* carb-v bro1 caust bro1 choc srj3• dros bro1 ferr ptk1 kola stb3• lach bg2* mang ptk1 plac rzf5• rumx k* seneg ptk1
- **changed**: asaf hr1 bar-c k2 bell k* carbn-s chlf k* cupr-ar a1 fic-m gya1 kali-br a1* lyc k* lyss hr1 merc k* murx k* narcot a1 nat-m k* *Ox-ac* c2* pitu-gl skp7• ric a1 tab k* [tax jsj7]
  - **warm** water | **amel.**: pitu-gl skp7•
- **chilliness** agg.: **Merc** bg2 nat-c bg2 nux-v bg2
- **cold**; after taking a: am-m bg2 bell bg2 bry bg2 *Carb-v* bg2* caust ptk1 *Cham* bg2 **Dulc** bg2 mang ptk1 merc bg2* phos ptk1 sel ptk1 sulph bg2
- **cold** agg.; becoming: viol-o bg2
- **cold** air | **inspiration** of cold dry air agg.: cupr bg2
- **complaints**: acon ptk1 *Bell* ptk1 brom ptk1 canth ptk1 *Carb-v* ptk1 *Caust* ptk1 **Dros** ptk1 hep ptk1 *Iod* ptk1 mang ptk1 *Merc* ptk1 **Phos** ptk1 puls ptk1 *Spong* ptk1 stann ptk1 *Stram* ptk1 verat ptk1
  - **accompanied** by:
    - **chilliness** (See CHILL - Chilliness - accompanied - voice)
    - **coryza** (See NOSE - Coryza - accompanied - voice)
    - **emotions** (See MIND - Emotions - voice)
    - **measles** (See SKIN - Eruptions - measles - accompanied - voice)
    - **mental** disturbances (See MIND - Mental symptoms - voice)
    - **Throat**; sore (See THROAT - Pain - accompanied - voice)
  - **diphtheria**; after (See THROAT - Diphtheria - followed - voice)
  - **ears**; obstructed (See EAR - Stopped - accompanied - voice)
- **coryza** | **after** coryza agg. (See NOSE - Coryza - followed - voice)
- **cough**:
  - **agg.**: am-c bg2 ambr bg2 ant-t bg2 arg-n bg2 bell bg2 *Bry* bg2 calc bg2 caps bg2 *Carb-v* bg2 **Cham** bg2 **Dros** bg2 *Dulc* bg2 hep bg2 kali-bi bg2 mang bg2 **Merc** bg2 nat-c bg2 nat-m bg2 nit-ac bg2 *Nux-v* bg2 phos bg2 *Puls* bg2 *Rhus-t* bg2 *Samb* bg2 seneg bg2 *Spong* bg2 *Sulph* bg2 thuj bg2
  - **during** | **amel.**: stann bg2
- **cracked**: arum-t bg2 camph bg2 cann-xyz bg2 dros k* graph bg2* hep k2 lach bg2 sil k2 *Spong* k* symph fd3.de•
  - **evening**: *Spong* k*
  - **singing** agg.: *Graph* k*
- **creaky**: acon ptk1 *Stram* ptk1
- **croaking**: acon k* ars b2.de* chin bg2 cina b2.de* cupr b7.de* dream-p sdj1• lac-ac k* lach b2.de* melal-alt gya4 plac rzf5• ruta b2.de* **Stram** k* sul-ac k* [heroin sdj2]
- **croupy**: *Acon* k* *Ail* k* hep spong k* sul-ac k*
- **crowing**: *(↗RESPIRATION - Rough)* *Acon* k* ars k* chin k* cina k* dros bg2 hep bg2 lach bg2 samb k* **Spong** k* stram bg2*
- **deep**: *(↗bass)* am-caust k* ambr k* anac k* ant-c k* arizon-l nl2• am k* *Arum-t* k* aur-m bar-c k* *Brom* k* camph bro1 **Carb-v** k* *Caust* bro1 cham b2.de* *Chin* k* chinin-s choc srj3• coc-c k* *Colch* k* conch fkr1• dig k* **Dros** k* franz a1 gins a1 haliae-lc srj5• hep k* hydrog srj2• iod k* lac-ac k* laur k* mag-m mag-s k* nux-v k* op k* par k* *Phos* k* plac rzf5• pop-cand br1* sacch-a fd2.de• samb k* sangin-n bro1 spong k* *Stann* k* sulph k* verat k* *Verb* k* vip a1
  - **air** agg.; in open: coc-c
  - **alternating** with high voice: plac rzf5•
  - **coryza**; during: bar-c b4a.de
  - **eating**; after: anac k*
  - **wet** cold air; in: sulph
- **dumb**: cic bg2 stram bg2
- **exerting** voice agg.: alum bg2 am-br bg2 ant-c ptk1 arg-met ptk1 arg-n bg2* am bg2* arum-t bg2* bar-c ptk1 camph bg2 caps ptk1 carb-v bg2 caust ptk1 *Ferr-p* ptk1 *Graph* ptk1 merc ptk1 rhus-t bg2* *Sel* ptk1 seneg ptk1 stann ptk1
- **expectoration** | **amel.**: *Stann* bg2 zinc bg2
- **failing**: dros b7a.de *Spong* b7a.de
- **finer** than usual: bell bg2 camph bg2 cupr bg2 phos bg2 stann bg2 *Stram* k* stront-c bg2
- **full** mouth; as if talking through a: nux-v hr*
- **guttural**: ars k* gels k*
- **heated** agg.; becoming: ant-c bg2
- **higher**: acon k* alumn k* ars k* **Arum-t** hr1 *Bell* bg2 bry k* cann-i k* cann-xyz bg2 choc srj3• cupr k* dros k* lac-ac stj5• pieri-b mlk9.de *Rumx* stann b2.de* **Stram** k*
  - **alternating** with deep voice (See deep - alternating)
  - **hawking** up mucus; after: stann k*
- **hissing**: bell k* *Nux-v* k* *Phos* k* spong k2
- **hoarseness**: abrot mrr1 acet-ac k* **Acon** k* acon-c a1 *Aesc* k* agar k* agar-ph a1 agn b2.de* aids nl2• ail hr1 alco a1 **All-c** k* all-s c2 aloe k* *Alum* k* alum-sil k2 alumn k* am-br bg2* *Am-c* k* am-caust a1 *Am-m* k* *Ambr* k* ammc a1 ampe-qu c2 amyg a1* anac k* anag hr1 anan k* ang k* *Ant-c* k* *Ant-t* k* antip vh1 *Apis* k* apoc hr1 arg-i c2 **Arg-met** k* **Arg-n** k* arge-pl rwt5• arist-cl sp1 am k* *Ars* k* ars-i k* ars-met ars-s-f k2 ars-s-r hr1 arum-d c2* arum-i c2 arum-m k* **Arum-t** k* asaf k* asc-t c1 *Asim* k* atro k* aur k* aur-ar k2 aur-i k2 aur-m k* aur-s bad bamb-a stb2.de• bapt k* *Bar-c* k* bar-i k2 bar-m bar-s k2 bart a1 **Bell** k* bell-p sp1 benz-ac k* berb k* beryl sp1 borx c1 bov k* **Brom** k* **Bry** k* bufo bung-fa mtf *Cact* k* cain caj k* calad hr1 **Calc** k* calc-caust c2 calc-f k* calc-i k2 *Calc-p* k* *Calc-s* k* *Camph* k* cann-i k* cann-s b2.de* *Canth* k* **Caps** k* *Carb-an* k* **Carb-v** k* *Carbn-s* carc mlr1• card-b a1 *Carl* k* cassia-s ccrh1• castm caul c1 **Caust** k* cench k2 **Cham** k* *Chel* k* chen-a vml3• *Chin* k* chinin-ar chinin-s k* *Chlor* k* cic k* cimic k* cina k* cinch a1 cinnb clem k* *Coc-c* k* coca coch hr1* *Coff* k* *Colch* k* *Coll* coloc c2 *Con* k* cop k* corv-cor bdg• croc b2.de* *Crot-c* *Crot-h* k* *Crot-t* k* cub k* *Cupr* k* cystein-l rly4• dendr-pol sk4• der k* *Dig* k* *Digin* a1 **Dros** k* *Dulc* k* elaps eup-per k* eup-pur hr1 euph-a a1 *Euphr* k* *Ferr* k* ferr-ar *Ferr-i* ferr-p k* flor-p rsj3• franz a1 galeoc-c-h gms1• gamb hr1 gast a1 *Gels* k* gent-c a1* gent-l a1 gins k* *Graph* k* grat k* *Ham* k* helio c2 helo-s bnm14• *Helx* c1 **Hep** k* hepat br1 *Hippoz* k* hir skp7• hydr k* hydr-ac k* hydroph rsj6• *Hyos* k* hyper k* ign b2.de* ind a1 inul k* **Iod** k* ip k2 irid-met srj5• iris kali-ar **Kali-bi** k* kali-br a1 *Kali-c* k* *Kali-chl* k* kali-cy a1 *Kali-i* k* kali-m bg3* kali-n k* *Kali-p* *Kali-s* k* kali-sil k2 kiss a1 kreos k* *Lac-ac* k* lac-c hr1 lac-cp sk4• **Lach** k* lachn c1 lact k* lap-la rsp1* lat-m bnm6• *Laur* k* led k* lepi a1 limest-b es1• linu-c a1 lipp a1 lob k* loxo-recl knl4• *Lyc* k* lyss hr1* mag-c k* *Mag-m* k* mag-p br1* mag-s mand a1* **Mang** k* *Med* k* menth c2 meny k* meph **Merc** k* *Merc-c* k* merc-cy bg2 merc-i-f k* *Merc-i-r* k* merc-sul k* merl k* *Mez* k* morph a1 *Mur-ac* k* murx k* *Naja* k* narcot a1 nat-ar *Nat-c* k* **Nat-m** k* nat-p k* nat-s k* nat-sal a1 nat-sel br1 nicc k* nicc-s br1 nicotam rly4• *Nit-ac* k* *Nux-m* k* *Nux-v* k* oena k* ol-an k* ol-j hr1 olnd b2.de* *Op* k* *Osm* k* ox-ac k* ozone sde2• *Par* k* paull a1 pen br1 *Petr* k* petr-ra shn4• *Ph-ac* k* phel k* **Phos** k* *Phyt* k*

- **hoarseness**: ...
pic-ac k* pin-s a1 pitu-gl skp7• plac rzf5• plac-s rly4• plan k* plat k* plb k* (non:pop bro1) pop-cand c1* prun k* psor k* ptel k* *Puls* k* pyrog k2 raph k* *Rhod* k* rhus-g tmo3• *Rhus-t* k* *Rhus-v* k* ribo rly4• rosm lgb1 *Rumx* ruta b2.de* sabad k* sabal c2 sacch c2 sal-al blc1• salin a1 *Samb* k* *Sang* k* sarr sars k* sec k* **Sel** k* senec k* *Seneg* k* *Sep* k* *Sil* k* sol-ni *Spig* k* **Spong** k* **Stann** k* *Staph* k* *Still* k* **Stram** k* stront-c k* stry succ-ac rly4• suis-em rly4• *Sul-ac* k* *Sulph* k* sumb k* symph fd3.de• syph c2* tab k* tarax k* tarent k2 tart-ac a1 **Tell** k* tep k* tet a1 thea thres-a sze7• *Thuj* k* til k* tong a1 trios rsj11• tritic-vg fd5.de trom k* tub bg *Tub-a* jl2 vanil fd5.de *Verat* k* verb k* vesp k* vinc k* viol-o c2 voes a1 x-ray sp1 xan k* *Zinc* k* zinc-p k2 zing k* [*Mang-act* stj2 *Mang-m* stj2 *Mang-n* stj2 *Mang-p* stj2 *Mang-s* stj2 *Mang-sil* stj2 tax jsj7]
  - **daytime**: *Acon* k* *Ars* k* hir skp7• med hr1 tarent k*
  - **morning**: *Acon* k* alum k* alum-sil k2 ant-t k* *Apis* arn k* ars h2* *Arum-t* bro1 arund k* asim k* bar-ox-suc rly4• benz-ac k* *Bov* k* **Calc** k* **Calc-p** k* *Carb-an* k* carb-v k* carbn-s cassia-s ccrh1• castm **Caust** k* cinnb k* coc-c k* coca *Coff* colch k* cop k* cupr k* *Dig* k* dios k* eup-per bro1 *Euphr* k* hep k2* hydroph rsj6• *Iod* k* *Kali-bi* k* kreos k* lach k* lob-s a1 lyc k* mag-m k* *Mang* k* *Mang-act* bro1 naja *Nat-m* k* nat-sil fd3.de• nicc *Nit-ac* k* nux-v k* petr-ra shn4• **Phos** k* plan k* sacch-a fd2.de• *Sil* k* stry a1 sul-i k2 **Sulph** k* tell c1 thuj tritic-vg fd5.de upa k*
    - **evening**; and: *Calc* b4a.de caust ptk1
    - **menses**; during: cop k*
    - **rising** agg.; after: *Carb-an* k* *Ham* k* ind k* iod h* *Mag-m* k* phos bg1 plan k* sacch-a fd2.de•
    - **waking**; on: aloe *Coff* k* dig *Ham* interf sa3• kali-bi a1 kali-p fd1.de• ozone sde2• *Par* k* petr-ra shn4• sars k*
  - **forenoon**: lachn c1 mag-c k* spong fd4.de sumb k*
  - **noon**: carbn-s
  - **afternoon**: alum k* *Am-m* k* brom k* carb-v k2* coc-c k* kali-bi bro1 lipp a1 petr k* phos bro1 *Rumx* bro1 sulph k*
    - **16** h: chin
    - **17** h: chel
  - **evening**: alum k* alum-p k2 alumn a1 arg-met brom calc-p k* calc-s k* *Carb-an* k* **Carb-v** k* *Carbn-s* **Caust** k* cimic k* cinnb k* coc-c k* coloc k* crot-t gast a1 *Graph* k* *Kali-bi* k* lach lact mag-c k* *Mang* melal-alt gya4 nicc olib-sac wmh1 **Phos** k* raph k* *Rumx* k* sep k* spong fd4.de *Sulph* k* symph fd3.de• thuj
    - **bed** agg.; in: nux-v
    - **reading**; after: calc-f k* cupr k*
    - **sunset**, after: cupr a1 stram k*
  - **night**: alum k* arg-n k* calc k* calc-f k* calc-s k* carb-an cassia-s ccrh1• cench k2 cimic k* hir skp7• lyc k* naja spig sumb k*
  - **accompanied** by:
    - **cold** drinks; desire for (See GENERALS - Food and - cold drink - desire - accompanied - hoarseness; GENERALS - Food and - cold drink - desire - ice-cold)
    - **leukorrhea**: nat-s ptk1
    - **perspiration**: bry b7a.de
    - **salivation**: stram kr1*
    - **Ear**; obstruction of: meny b7a.de
    - **Heart**; complaints of (See CHEST - Heart; complaints - accompanied - hoarseness)
    - **Lips**; cracked (See FACE - Cracked - lips - accompanied - hoarseness)
    - **Tongue**; cancer and atrophy of (See MOUTH - Cancer - tongue - accompanied - atrophy of tongue and)
    - **Tonsils**; inflammation of (See THROAT - Inflammation - tonsils - accompanied - hoarseness)
  - **air** agg.; draft of: merc k*
  - **air** agg.; dry: *Cupr* k*
  - **air**; in open:
    - **agg.**: bry *Calc* b4a.de **Mang** k* *Nux-m* *Phos* b4a.de trios rsj11•
    - **amel.**: calc-s
    - **going** into; when | **warm** room; from a: *Coc-c*
  - **alternating** with | **Heart**; complaints of (See CHEST - Heart; complaints - alternating - hoarseness)
  - **calling** aloud, when: am-c k*
  - **changing**, once loud, once weak: ars h2
  - **children**; in: cham k* stram mtf33
  - **chill**; during: acon bg2 caust bg2 dros bg2 hep k* nux-v b7a.de* phos bg2 puls b7a.de *Sep* b4.de*
  - **choking**: iod ptk1
  - **chronic**: ampe-qu br1* ant-c bg2 arg-met bg2 arg-n bg2* arum-t mrr1 bar-c bg2* bell bg2 calc b4a.de* caps k2 **Carb-v** b4a.de* **Caust** bg2* cupr b7a.de dros b7a.de* dulc bg2 graph bro1 helx gm1 *Hep* bg2 kali-bi k2 *Mang* b4a.de* *Mang-act* bro1 merc bg2 *Mur-ac* b4a.de *Petr* bg2 **Phos** b4a.de* plb b7a.de psor mtf11 rhus-t bg2 *Sil* bg2* stann bg2 **Sulph** bg2*
  - **cold**:
    - **air** agg.: con ptk1 *Cupr* k* *Hep* *Nux-m* thuj
    - **bathing** | **after**: *Ant-c* k*
    - **drinks** | **amel.**: caust mrr1
  - **cold**; after taking a: bry b7a.de *Cham* b7a.de
  - **continuous** (See chronic)
  - **coryza**:
    - **during**: acon k* all-c k2* aloe hr alum alum-p k2 am-c h2* am-m k* *Ars* k* ars-i ptk1 ars-met bar-c *Benz-ac* k* *Bry* k* calc k* **Carb-v** k* carbn-s **Caust** k* cham k* *Dig* k* dulc k* eup-per eup-pur hr1 euphr bg2 ferr-p graph k* hep k* ign bg2 *Kali-bi* k* kali-c k* *Kalm* k* *Lach* bg2 *Mag-m* mag-s **Mang** k* **Merc** k* *Merc-i-r* k* nat-ar *Nat-c* k* nat-m k* *Nit-ac* k* nux-v b7.de* osm bro1 *Petr* k* phel **Phos** k* phys hr1 pop-cand br1* puls k* *Ran-b* *Rhus-t* b7a.de *Rumx* samb b7a.de *Sang* bg2 *Sep* k* *Spig* k* *Spong* k* sul-ac k* sulph k* *Tell* k* thuj k* vanil fd5.de verb bro1 zinc k* zinc-p k2
    - **end** of; at: ip bro1
    - **preceding**: kali-c h2
  - **cough**:
    - **after**: acon b7.de *Alum* b4a.de *Am-c* b4a.de *Ambr* b7.de asaf b7.de bry b7a.de calc b4a.de *Chin* b7.de cina b7.de cupr b7a.de* *Dros* b7.de **Dulc** b4a.de *Hep* b4a.de laur b7.de *Mang* b4a.de *Merc* b4a.de nat-c b4.de nat-m b4a.de nit-ac b4a.de **Phos** b4a.de *Samb* b7.de* seneg b4a.de *Sil* b4a.de *Spong* b7.de stann b4.de thuj b4a.de verat b7.de
    - **amel.**: mang ptk1 *Stann* k*
    - **during** (See COUGH - Hoarse)
  - **croup**:
    - **after**: *Carb-v* k* *Lyc* k*
    - **with**: acon bro1 ail bro1 all-c bro1 brom bro1 caust bro1 *Hep* bro1 kali-s bro1 spong bro1*
  - **crying**, when: acon bro1 **Bell** k* coff hr1 cupr hr1 phos bro1 spong bro1
  - **dinner**, after amel.: mag-c
  - **diphtheria**; after: phyt ptk1
  - **drinks**:
    - **cold** drinks | **desire** for (See GENERALS - Food and - cold drink - desire - accompanied - hoarseness)
  - **dust**; agg.: brom k2
  - **eating**:
    - **after**:
      - **agg.**: anac k*
      - **amel.**: nat-ox rly4•
  - **exertion** agg.: arn ptk1
  - **expectoration** | **amel.**: mang ptk1 stann ptk1
  - **fever**; during: puls b7a.de
  - **fright**; from: gels mrr1
  - **hawking** up mucus | **amel.**: cham tl1 chen-a vml3• phos tl1
  - **hay** fever, in: ran-b hr1
  - **heat**; during: *Hep* *Puls* k* sep k* sulph k*
  - **hysterical**: cocc bro1 *Gels* bro1 *Ign* bro1 nux-m bro1 plat bro1
  - **laughing** agg.: calc-f k*
  - **lost** on exertion of voice: carb-v h2
  - **measles**; after: bell b4a.de *Bry* k* *Carb-v* k* *Dros* k* dulc hr1 sulph k*

Larynx

- **menses** | **before** | **agg.**: gels st graph k* lac-c st mang k* syph k*
  - ⁝ **during** | **agg.**: calc k* gels ptk1 Graph k* lac-c ptk1 spong k* syph ptk1
- **mucus** in larynx: ambr hr1 ang h1* ant-t bg2 aphis arg-n sne **Arum-t** lp Bar-c bell bg2 calc bg2 Calc-p camph caps bg2 **Carb-v** bg2 Caust k* Cham k* chin **Dros** bg2 **Dulc** bg2 ham fd3.de• hep bg2 hydrog srj2• Kali-bi kali-s Mang k* **Merc** bg2 nat-c bg2 Nux-v bg2 Phos k* Psor Puls bg2 Rhus-t bg2 Rumx **Samb** k* **Sel** sil bg2 Stann Staph stram k* Sulph bg2 tarax h1* zinc k*
- **overheated**, from being: Ant-c k* ant-t bro1 Brom k* haem phos k2
- **overuse** of the voice: acon k* alum k* Arg-met k* Arg-n bro1 Arn k* **Arum-t** k* **Caps** k* carb-v bro1 **Caust** k* Coca bro1 coll ferr-p k* ferr-pic bro1 Hep bro1 iod bro1 Kali-p k* Mang mang-act bro1 med bro1 merc bro1 merc-cy bro1 Nat-m nat-sel bro1 petr-ra shn4• Phos k* **Rhus-t** k* Sel k* seneg spong bro1 Still k* sulph bro1 tab bro1 ter bro1
- **painful**: all-c bg2 Arg-met **Bell** Brom Iod k* Kali-bi k* kali-br k* lac-ac bg2 **Phos** k* Stann stict nh6
- **painless**: Ant-c bell bro1 **Calc** k* calc-p bg2 Calc-sil **Carb-v** k* Caust k* Dig k* ferr bg2 ip ptk1 nicotam rly4• op b7a.de Par k* Phos k*
- **paretic**: am-caust bro1 bell bro1 Caust bro1 Gels bro1 lach bro1 Ox-ac bro1 phos bro1 rumx bro1 sil bro1
- **paroxysmal**: Gels k* hep bro1 par k* puls bro1
- **periodical**: Calc hr1 Nux-v par k*
  - ⁝ **year** at same time; every: nicc
- **perspiration**; during: acon bg2 carb-v bg2 Cham bg2 dros bg2 Hep bg2 **Nux-v** bg2 phos bg2 sil bg2 spong bg2 Sulph bg2 thuj bg2
- **reading** aloud, while: Arg-met b7a.de Calc-f k* cupr k* med k* naja seneg k* verb k*
- **riding** in open air: osm
- **rising** | **after** | **agg.**: cimic k* ham k* iod k* plan k* sol-t-ae k* sumb k*
  - ⁝ **bed**; from | **amel.**: nux-v
- **singing**:
  - ⁝ **agg.**: **Agar** alum Arg-met k* Arg-n arn **Arum-t** Bry caps ptk1 Caust hep ptk1 Mang Nat-m Nit-ac osm **Sel** k* sep Stann tritic-vg fd5.de
  - ⁝ **amel.**: rhus-t
- **smokers**: caps fkm1•
- **smoking** | **amel.**: mang ptk1
- **sneezing**; after | **amel.**: kreos a1*
- **speech**, preventing: arum-t k2 Calc hr1 Caust k* cupr k* Mag-m k* par k* **Phos** k*
- **spring** agg.: all-c k*
- **stooping** agg.: caust ptk1
- **straining**, from (See overuse)
- **sudden**: abrot k* alum h2* Bell k* carb-v kali-bi a1 mag-m k* nux-m bg2 seneg k* sep k* Spong k*
- **talking**:
  - ⁝ **agg.**: Alum alum-p k2 alumn am-c ant-t **Arg-met** k* **Arg-n** arn **Arum-t** k* Calc **Caps** Carb-v cassia-s ccrh1• **Caust** Coc-c coca ptk1 Ferr hydroph rsj6• Kali-bi lach Mang morph naja Nat-m Nit-ac ozone sde2• Ph-ac Phos k* psor **Rhus-t** k* sel Sep sne spong bro1 Stann staph stram trios rsj11•
  - ⁝ **amel.**: caust ptk1 coc-c graph ptk1 Rhus-t k* tub bg3*
  - ⁝ **beginning** to talk: sel k2
  - ⁝ **long** time; talking for a: Carb-v b4a.de Phos b4a.de
  - ⁝ **painful**: merc-cy ptk1
- **waking**; on: aloe arund hr1 coff dig k* interf sa3• iod k* loxo-recl knl4• Par plan k* sars sol-t-ae k* tarent k*
- **walking**:
  - ⁝ **air**; in open:
    - **agg.**: bry calc calc-p Nux-m osm symph fd3.de•
    - **amel.**: alum
  - ⁝ **wind**; against the: acon bro1 arum-t bro1 euphr bro1* hep bro1 Nicc k* **Nux-m** k*
- **warm** | **drinks** | **amel.**: cassia-s ccrh1•
  - ⁝ **room** | **agg.**: alum ant-c c1 bry iod Kali-s Puls
- **warm** agg.; becoming: brom ptk1 Phos b4a.de

Voice – hoarseness: ...

- **weather**:
  - ⁝ **change** of weather: phos k2 rhus-t h1
  - ⁝ **cold**:
    - **wet** | **agg.**: Carb-v k* caust bro1 Dulc Mang Rumx k* Sil sulph k*
  - ⁝ **wet** | **agg.**: Carb-v k* carbn-s chlor hep bg1 Kali-bi mang bg1* sulph
- **wet**; after getting: arn ptk1 merc-i-r k* Rhus-t

○ • **Low** down in larynx: aloe bg2

- **hollow**: Acon k* alum k* alum-p k2 ant-c ant-t k* Ars k* Arum-t k* bar-c k* bell k* cain camph k* canth carb-v k* Caust k* cham chin k* cina b2.de* colch k* conch fkr1* crot-t k* dig k* **Dros** k* euph b2.de* hep k* ign k* Iod hr1 Ip k* Kali-bi k* kreos k* lach k* Led k* lyc mag-s k* nux-m b2.de* op k* par bg2 phos k* plb k* puls Samb k* sec k* sil b2.de* spig b2.de* **Spong** k* Stann k* staph k* stram b2.de* sul-ac a1 Thuj **Verat** k* verb k*
  - **coryza**; during: bar-c b4a.de
- **husky**: Acon k* agar b2.de* aloe alum k* alum-sil k2 am-c b2.de* Am-m k* anac b2.de* ant-c b2.de* asc-t br1 atro a1* aur k* Bar-c k* bar-m k* bar-ox-suc rly4• bell k* Brom k* bry b2.de* calc k* Calc-sil camph k* carb-an b2.de* carb-v b2.de* Caust k* cham b2.de* Chin k* Coc-c k* coli mtf11 Cop hr1 croc k* cupr b2.de* cupr-s hr1 **Dros** k* dulc fd4.de echi ephe-si hsj1• gast a1 graph k* hep b2.de* Hyos k* irid-met srj5• Kali-bi hr1 Kali-n kali-p fd1.de• Lac-c k* lac-h htj1* Lyc k* mang k* merc k* merc-i-r k* Mez hr1 nat-m k* nat-s nat-sil fd3.de• nit-ac bg2 nux-m b2.de* nux-v b2.de* onos ozone sde2• **Phos** k* podo fd3.de• pyrog k2 ribo rly4• rumx sabad k* salin a1 sars b2.de* Sel k* sil k* Spong k* Stann k* streptoc rly4• sul-ac a1 Sulph k* tritic-vg fd5.de Tub-d jl2 vanil fd5.de **Verat** hr1 verb b2.de* xan c1
  - **morning**: chir-fl gya2 dulc fd4.de Sil k*
    - ⁝ **waking**; on: alum k*
  - **evening**: carb-v k2 dulc fd4.de kali-p fd1.de• olib-sac wmh1
  - **air** agg.; in open: coc-c
  - **coryza**; during: Merc b4a.de
  - **cough** | **amel.**: ozone sde2•
  - **mucus**; from tough: ozone sde2•
  - **singing**; from: ozone sde2•
  - **sudden**: tub-d jl2
  - **talking** agg.: ephe-si hsj1•
- **increasing** and decreasing: puls bg2
- **indistinct**: agar bg2 am-caust k* atro a1 **Brom** k* Bry b7.de* calc b4a.de* cann-s b7.de* Canth b7a.de* **Caust** bg2* cocc b7.de* dulc fd4.de gels bg2 hyos b7.de* ix bnm8• kali-s fd4.de lach b7a.de* Lyc b4a.de* merc b4a.de* nit-ac hr1 olnd bg2 Sec b7.de* seneg bg2 spong fd4.de Stram b7.de* stry a1 Verat b7.de*
  - **dryness** of throat; from: bry b7a.de
- **inflexible**: nat-m a1 **Stram** k*
- **interrupted**: Alum am-caust a1 Ars camph bg2 cic k* cupr bg2 dros k* euphr k* graph bg2 iod bg2 mag-c k* merc bg2* phos bg2 plb bg2 Spong k* tab bg2
- **lost**: Acon k* Aeth hr1* ail k* Alum k* alum-p k2 **Alumn** k* am-c k* **Am-caust** k* am-m k* ambr b2.de* amyg a1 anan k* **Ant-c** k* Ant-t k* antip bro1* arg-i bro1 **Arg-met** k* **Arg-n** k* arn b7.de* Ars k* ars-i k* ars-s-f k2 Arum-t k* arund k* asc-t bro1 atro a1 aur b4a.de Bapt k* Bar-c k* bar-i k2 bar-s k2 Bell k* benzo bro1 both bg2 bov b2.de* **Brom** k* bry k* cain calad calc b2.de* calc-ar calc-caust bro1 camph k* cann-i cann-s b2.de* canth k* Carb-ac k* carb-an k* **Carb-v** k* Carbn-s **Caust** k* cedr k* cham b2.de* chin b2.de* chinin-s chlf a1* Chlor k* cic b7.de* Cina k* coc-c bro1 Coca br1* Coch hr1* colch bg2* con k* Crot-c k* Crot-h hr1 crot-t k* cub bro1 Cupr k* der a1 dig k* digin a1 diph mtf11 diphtox jl2 Dros k* dub bro1 Dulc b4a.de* elaps Eup-per bro1 Euphr bg2 Ferr k* ferr-ar ferr-i Ferr-p k* ferr-pic c2 flav jl2 fuma-ac rly4• Gels k* gent-c a1 glon bg2 graph k* helo-s bnm14• Hep k* hydr-ac hr1 Hyos k* Ign k* iod k* Ip bro1 ix bnm8• just bro1 Kali-ar k* Kali-bi k* kali-br bg2* Kali-c k* kali-chr bro1 Kali-i k* kali-m k2 kali-n k* Kali-p k* kali-s kreos bro1 Lac-ac k* lac-c hr1* Lach k* lat-h bnm5• lat-m bnm6• Laur b2.de* lepr mtf11 limest-b es1• lyc b4.de* mag-p bro1 mang b2.de* Mang-act bro1 med mtf11 meny b2.de* Merc k* Merc-c k* merc-cy bg2 Merc-i-f k* **Mez** b4a.de mosch bg2 mur-ac b2.de* Naja k* nat-ar nat-c k* Nat-m k* nat-p nicc Nit-ac k* Nux-m k* Nux-v k* ol-an k* olnd b2.de* Op b7.de* oscilloc jl2* osm bro1 ox-ac k* ozone sde2• paeon k* par k* pen br1* petr b2.de* **Phos** k* Phyt k* plac rzf5• plat k* plb k* pop-cand bro1* prot jl2 Puls k* pyrus Rhus-t k* Rumx k* ruta b2.de* sabad b2.de* samb b2.de* Sang k* sangin-n bro1 sec b7.de* Sel k* Seneg k* sep k* sil b2.de* Spong k* Stann k* stict bro1 Still bro1 **Stram** k* strept-ent jl2 stry k* sul-ac k* sul-i k2 Sulph k* syph k2* tarent k* ter k* thuj bro1

- **lost**: ...
Tub jl2 *Verat* k* verat-v bro1 verb b2.de* vesp k* viol-o bro1 vip k* xan br1 zinc bg2 zinc-m k*
  - **morning**: alum k* *Brom* k* *Carb-v* k* *Caust* k* dig k*
    - **waking**; on: *Ail* k*
  - **evening**: brom k* **Carb-v** k* *Phos* k*
  - **night**: *Carb-an* k* *Carb-v* k*
  - **accompanied** by:
    - **Nostrils**; sensitive: *Ant-c* bg2
    - **Stomach**; pain in: laur br1
    - **Tongue**; without complaints of: both ptk1
  - **air** agg.; wet: *Chlor* k*
  - **alternating** with:
    - **complaints** of the heart (See CHEST - Heart; complaints - alternating - aphonia)
    - **palpitation** of the heart (See CHEST - Palpitation - alternating - aphonia)
  - **anger**; after: mag-m dgt staph
  - **chronic**: lepr mtf11 phyt ptk1 psor mtf11 strept-ent jl2*
  - **cold**:
    - **air** agg.: carb-v nux-m k2 *Rumx* k* sulph
    - **exposure** to | **agg.**: ant-c k2 arum-t bnt *Caust* k* choc srj3• *Rumx* k* xan c1
  - **cold**; taking a:
    - **after**: alum ptk1 *Alumn* vh1 seneg k2
    - **agg.**: *Pop-cand* br1
  - **convulsions**; before epileptic: calc-ar k*
  - **coryza**; during: puls b7a.de
  - **cough**; with: mang ptk1
  - **drinking** cold water when overheated: *Crot-t* k*
  - **drunkenness**; during: op bg2
  - **excitement** agg.: lac-del hrn2•
  - **exertion** agg.: ant-c bg1 **Carb-v** k* lac-c bg1
  - **fright** agg.: *Acon* k* *Gels* k* hyos k13* *Op* k*
  - **heart** complaints: ox-ac k2
  - **heated**; from becoming: *Ant-c* k* haem
  - **hysterical**: gels hr1* *Hyos* k* *Ign* k* *Nux-m* k* plat k* sep k*
  - **injuries** of the head; from: acon bg2 *Arn* bg2 bell bg2 hyos bg2
  - **intermittent** in singers: cupr k*
  - **menses** | **before** | **agg.**: *Gels* bro1 graph bro1 syph k2*
    - **during** | **agg.**: *Gels* k* graph bro1 helio bnt
  - **momentarily**: alum choc srj3• dros spong
  - **motion** agg.: ant-c
  - **mucus** in larynx, from: *Bar-c* k*
  - **nervous** aphonia: acon tl1 arg-n ry1 caust tl1 coll tl1 crot-h hr1* gels hr1* hydr-ac mta1 ign ry1 merc hr1* nux-m btw2* ox-ac mta1 phos hr1* pop-cand c1 puls vml4 spong tl1
    - **accompanied** by | **Heart**; complaints of the: coca bro1 hydr-ac bro1 nux-m bro1 ox-ac bro1*
  - **overheated**; from becoming: ant-c nh6* brom k2 phos k2
  - **overuse** of: alum k2 arg-met k2 *Caust* k* *Merc* k* *Seneg* k*
  - **painful**: tub mtf11
  - **painless**: ant-c k2 *Phos* k*
  - **paralysis**; from: alum k2 bar-c k2* **Caust** k* *Gels* k* kali-p ptk1 *Lach* k* merc ox-ac ptk1 *Plb* k*
  - **periodical**: gels
    - **singers**, in: cupr ptk1
  - **reading** agg.: plb k*
  - **shivering**; during: chin b7.de
  - **singers**: arg-met k2* **Arg-n** k* arn bnt *Arum-t* bg1 bry k2 **Caust** k* graph bg1 mang ptk1 mang-act br1 sel ptk1
  - **sudden**: alum k* arund hr1 *Bell* k* **Caust** k* *Phos* hr1 seneg bg1 *Spong* hr1 sulph hr1

- **lost**: ...
  - **talking**; from prolonged: ferr-pic br1 *Phos* k* spong fd4.de
  - **temporary**: *Tub* jl2
  - **tobacco**; by: strept-ent jl2
  - **waking**; on: nux-m k* ptel k*
  - **warm** | **air** | **amel.**: seneg k*
    - **room** agg.: *Ant-c* puls
  - **weakness**; general: canth ptk1 xan c1
  - **weakness** of vocal cords; from: canth bg1
  - **weather**:
    - **change** of weather: phos k2
    - **wet** | **agg.**: *Bar-c* bg1 chlor strept-ent jl2
  - **wind**, after exposure to north-west: *Arum-t* hep bg1* nux-m bg1
- **loud**: bell cann-i dream-p sdj1• hyos ptk1 lac-leo sk4• lach mosch nux-m bg1* sulph *Verat* sne
- **low**: aloe sne alumn k* am-caust k* ang k* ant-c k* *Arn* k* *Ars* k* bell b2.de* *Cact* k* *Calc* camph h1* cann-i k* cann-s b2.de* *Canth* k* carb-an bg2* caust b2.de* cham k* chin k* crot-t k* gels vh hep k* hydrog srj2• *Ign* k* kali-i hr1 laur b2.de* lyc k* mang-act br1* mang-o bro1 mosch b2.de* **Nit-s-d** h nux-v b2.de* op b2.de* osm k* ox-ac k* ozone sde2• par b2.de* *Ph-ac* b4a.de phos mtf33 puls k* sec k* *Spong* k* stann b2.de* staph k* stry a1 sul-ac k* symph fd3.de• tab k* thuj hr1 verat k* viol-o b7a.de*
- **measles**; after (See SKIN - Eruptions - measles - followed - voice)
- **medium** height are missing; tones of: arg-met b7a.de
- **men**; complaints of voice in (= male persons): bar-c ptk1 *Nit-ac* ptk1
- **menses** | **after** | **agg.**: carb-an bg2 stram bg2
  - **during** | **agg.**: bell bg2 berb bg2 calc bg2 carb-an bg2 caul bg2 cocc bg2 *Gels* bg2 **Graph** bg2 kali-n bg2 mang bg2 plb bg2 spong bg2
- **monotonous**: bry b7.de* dros bg2 graph bg2 nat-m bg2 spong bg2 stram bg2
- **mucus** agg.: ang bg2 bar-c bg2 mez bg2
- **muffled**: cere-b a1 gels k* lach lyc k* merc-i-r a1 ric a1 rumx sul-ac k* sumb k*
  - **linen**; as if talking through a piece of: nux-m b7a.de
- **murmuring**: hyos b2.de lach b2.de op b2.de stram b2.de
- **nasal**: all-c k* alum k* aur k* bar-i sf1.de bar-m br1* bell k* bov k* bry k* *Caust* k* diphtox jl2 ferr *Fl-ac* k* gels k* *Ham* hr1 hippoz jl2 influ jl2* *Iod* k* **Kali-bi** k* *Kali-i* k* kali-n k* kali-p hr1 *Lac-c* k* *Lach* k* lap-la sde8.de• *Lyc* k* mag-m k* mag-s k* *Manc* k* merc k* *Merc-c* hr1 *Mez* hr1 morb jl2 *Mur-ac* hr1 *Nat-c* k* nat-m nux-v h1* oscilloc jl2 ozone sde2• petr b4a.de* ph-ac k* *Phos* k* plb k* psor jl2 rumx k* sang k* sep k* sil bg2 sin-n k* spong k* *Staph* k* sul-i bg2* sulph k* sumb k* teucr bg2* thuj k* tub jl2 [calc-n stj1]
  - **morning**: bov k* sulph k*
  - **evening**: sep k* sumb k*
  - **catarrhal**: kali-i k* mag-m h2* ph-ac staph b7.de*
  - **children**; in: bar-m ptk1 lac-c ptk1
  - **intermittent**: *Tub* jl2
  - **tonsils**; with enlarged: staph ptk1
- **nausea** agg.: phos bg2
- **old** people; complaints of: bar-c bg2
- **periodicity**: carb-v bg2 nux-v bg2 par bg2
- **piping**: bell k* *Spong*
- **powerful**: hydr-ac nat-sil fd3.de•
- **reading** agg.: verb bg2
- **reverberating**: bar-m bg2 caust bg2 iod bg2 phos bg2
- **rough**: acon k* acon-c a1 *All-s* k* *Alum* k* alum-p k2 alum-sil k2 am-c k* am-caust a1 ambr k* ant-c k* apis arg-met k2 ars k* ars-i aur bg2 aur-m hr1 *Bar-c* k* bar-i k2 bar-s k2 **Bell** k* borx b2.de* *Brom* k* *Bry* k* cain *Calc* k* calc-ar k* canth k* *Caps* bg2 *Carb-an* bg2 **Carb-v** k* *Carbn-s* card-b a1 carl a1 *Caust* k* *Cham* k* *Chin* k* chinin-ar chinin-s bg2 *Coc-c* k* *Coff* k* conch fkr1• croc bg2* *Crot-h* a1* crot-t k* cub hr1* cupr cycl k* dig dros k* dulc bg2* eup-per hr1 eup-pur hr1 franz a1 gins a1 *Graph* k* hep k* hydrog srj2• **Hyos** k* *Iod* k* kali-ar **Kali-bi** k* *Kali-br* hr1 kali-c k* kali-n k* kali-sil k2 kola stb3• kreos b2.de* lach b2.de* lat-m bnm6• laur b2.de* lyss hr1* mag-m k* mag-s k* *Mang* k* *Meny* k* *Merc* k* merc-c k* merc-i-r k* mez k* *Nat-c* bg2 nat-m k* nat-sil fd3.de• nit-ac k* nux-m b2.de* *Nux-v* k* op k* ox-ac k* ozone sde2• *Petr* bg2 ph-ac b2.de* **Phos** k* plb k* prun k* **Puls** k* rhus-t b2.de* ribo rly4• sacch-a gmj3 *Samb* bg2 sars b2.de* *Seneg* k* *Sil* k* *Spong* k* stann b2.de*

Larynx

- **rough**: ...
staph b2.de* stram k* stront-c b2.de* sul-ac b2.de* sul-i k2 *Sulph* k* sumb k* thuj k* til a1 vanil fd5.de verat bg2 verb b2.de* zinc k* zinc-p k2
  - **morning**: *Calc* k* coc-c k* coff *Mang* k* nat-sil fd3.de• sacch-a fd2.de•
  - **forenoon**: sulph k*
  - **afternoon**: alum k* coc-c k* sulph h2*
  - **evening**: alum k* coloc k* kali-bi k* sulph k*
  - **air** agg.; draft of: *Merc* k*
  - **air**; when going into open: **Mang** k*
  - **bed**; before going to: ox-ac k*
  - **smoking** amel.: *Mang* k*
  - **talking** agg.: am-c *Coc-c* k*
- **shrieking**: alum **Arum-t** k* aur-m hr1 bell bg2 camph bg2 cann-xyz bg2 cupr k* dig hr1 ozone sde2• samb ptk1 *Stram* k*
- **shrill**: acon ptk1 alumn a1* bell a1 cann-i sf1.de cupr sf1.de lyss hr1* samb ptk1 spong ptk1 stram kr1*
- **singing** agg.: alum bg2 ant-c bg2 *Arg-met* bg2 arum-t bg2 caust bg2 ferr-p bg2 graph bg2 sel bg2
  - **beginning** to sing: *Stann* bg2
- **squeaking**: ars k* ars-h hr1 bell k2 lac-ac k* **Stram** k*
- **strange**: conch fkr1•
- **talking** agg.: *Arg-met* bg2 carb-v bg2 staph bg2
- **toneless**: agn k* ambr k* arg-met bg2 ars a1 asaf bg2 *Calad* k* carb-an k* chin k* cina b2.de* cupr bg2 **Dros** k* hep k* kali-p fd1.de• lyc bg2 *Mang* b4a.de nat-c k* *Nit-ac* hr1 rhod k* samb k* spong k* **Stram** k* sulph bg2 thuj k* verat bg2
- **tremulous**: absin vh1 acon k* agar *Ars* k* *Camph* k* canth k* *Cocc* cupr k* gels *Ign* k* iod k* kali-i k* kali-s fd4.de laur k* **Merc** k* mez k* *Nux-m* k* op k* *Phos* k* plb bg2 psor k* xan c1 [tax jsj7]
- **trumpet** toned: verb bg2*
- **unsteady**: seneg ptk1
- **using** voice amel.: ant-c ptk1 caust ptk1 graph ptk1
- **waking** agg.: ail bg2
- **walking**:
  - **air** agg.; in open: carb-v bg2
  - **wind**; against the: *Nux-m* bg2
- **warm** | **bathing** | **amel.**: lat-m bnm6•
  - **room** | **agg.**: **Bry** bg2
- **weak**: *(↗MOUTH - Speech - difficult - weakness - organs)* abrot k* absin k* acon k* aloe bg2 alum bg2* am-caust k* ang b7.de* *Ant-c* k* **Ant-t** k* arg-met bg2 *Arg-n* ars k* ars-i ars-s-f k2 arum-t hr1 asaf hr1 atro a1 bar-c k* bar-i k2 bar-m k* bar-s k2 *Bell* k* *Brom* k* *Calc* *Calc-s* *Camph* k* cann-s b7a.de* **Canth** k* carb-an bg2* *Carb-v* k* *Caust* k* *Cham* k* chel hr1 *Chin* k* clem k* coc-c k* coca c2 cocc ptk1 *Coll* *Crot-h* k* cupr *Cycl* k* daph k* der a1 dig dream-p sdj1• dros bg2 *Ferr* *Ferr-p* fl-ac hr1 fuma-ac rly4• gad a1 *Gels* k* get a1 *Hell* hr1 **Hep** k* hydrc a1 hydrog srj2• *Ign* k* iod k* ix bnm8• kali-bi bg2 kali-br a1 kali-i k* lach k* laur k* limen-b-c hrn2* *Lyc* k* lyss hr1* menth c2 merc-n a1 *Naja* nat-ar nat-c k* *Nat-m* k* nit-ac k* *Nux-v* k* op k* osm k* ox-ac k* par k* petr k* *Ph-ac* k* *Phos* k* plb k* prun k* psor k* *Puls* k* pyrog k2 *Rhus-t* *Sec* k* sel k2 seneg hr1 *Spong* k* **Stann** k* *Staph* k* *Stram* k* stry sul-ac k* sul-i k2 *Sulph* k* tab k* thal-xyz srj8• thuj **Verat** k* zinc k* zinc-m a1 zinc-p k2 [tax jsj7]
  - **evening** | **bed** agg.; in: phos
  - **anger**; after: *Staph* k*
  - **headache**; after: gels vh
  - **heat**; during: *Hep* k*
  - **menses**; during: plb k*
  - **singers**: alum k2
  - **talking**; after: carb-v k2 *Coc-c* daph bg1* fuma-ac rly4• *Ph-ac* psil ft1 **Stann** sul-ac *Sulph*
- **weather**:
  - **stormy**:
    - **agg.**: nux-m bg2
    - **before**: agar bg2
  - **wet** | **agg.**: carb-v bg2 sulph bg2
- **wet** | **getting** wet agg.: merc-i-r bg2
- **wheezing**: bell hr1 cist tl1 cub hr1*
- **whining**: *Alum* k* ambr k* borx carb-an k* *Cina* k* ip k* mang bg2 nux-v k* plb k* squil k* stram k*

Voice – whining: ...
  - **morning**: *Borx*
  - **menses**; after: stram
  - **sleep** agg.; during: verat k*
- **whispering**: *(↗MIND - Speech - whispering)* aloe sne am-caust k* arg-met bro1 ars k* ars-h hr1 *Calc* k* camph k* canth bro1 carb-v bro1 *Caust* bro1 coch hr1 *Coloc* hr1 cupr ptk1 dub bro1 *Ferr* k* ign bg2* iod k* kali-br a1* lac-ac a1 limen-b-c hrn2* *Merc* k* nit-ac k* **Nit-s-d** h ol-an ptk1 phos bg1* phyt k* *Pop-cand* bro1 prim-v bro1 puls bg2* rumx stram k* sul-ac k* *Sulph* hr1 tab k* verat bro1 zinc-m k*

WARMTH (See Heat)

WARTS (See Condylomata - larynx)

WEAKNESS: alum ptk1 bar-c ptk1 calc k2 canth bg2 caust bg2* gels ptk1 limen-b-c hrn2* plb ptk1 sulph ptk1

○ - **Larynx** | **sensation** of: *Canth* b7a.de *Caust* b4a.de
- **Vocal** cords: *Carb-v* bro1 *Caust* bro1 coca bro1 dros bro1 graph bro1 pen bro1 phos bro1

WHISTLING: acon k* alum h2* ars k* bell k* brom k* *Calc* k* *Cham* k* chin k* graph h2* hep k* iod h* kreos k* laur k* lyc bg2 mag-m a1 sabad k* spong bg2*
- **morning**: coloc h2*
- **evening**: *Calc* k*
- **inspiration** agg.: coloc h2*
- **lying** down agg.; after: *Calc*
- **lying** on left side agg.: arg-n

EPIGLOTTIS; complaints of: all-c bro1 chlor bro1 hepat bro1 wye bro1

LARYNX; complaints:
- **accompanied** by | **Mouth**; complaints of: **Acon** bg2 ars bg2 bell bg2 bry bg2 carb-v bg2 *Dros* bg2 **Hep** bg2 *Iod* bg2 nux-v bg2 *Phos* bg2 *Spong* bg2
- **menses** | **after** | **agg.**: carb-an bg2 stram bg2
  - **during** | **agg.**: bell bg2 berb bg2 calc bg2 carb-an bg2 caul bg2 cocc bg2 *Gels* bg2 **Graph** bg2 kali-n bg2 mang bg2 plb bg2 spong bg2

▽ - **extending** to:
- ○ **Downward**: cham ptk1 glon ptk1 ip ptk1 verat ptk1
- **Ear** | **left**: zinc-chr ptk1
- **Upward**: stann ptk1

TRACHEA; complaints of: **Acon** b2.de* agar b2.de* alum b2.de* am-c b2.de* am-m b2.de* ambr b2.de* anac b2.de* ang bg2 ant-c b2.de* ant-t bg2 arg-met b2.de* arg-n bg2 arn b2.de* *Ars* b2.de* asar b2.de* aur bg2 bar-c b2.de* bell b2.de* borx b2.de* bov b2.de* *Brom* bg2* bry b2.de* calad b2.de* calc b2.de* camph b2.de* cann-s b2.de* *Canth* b2.de* caps b2.de* carb-an b2.de* **Carb-v** b2.de* **Caust** b2.de* *Cham* b2.de* chel bg2 chin b2.de* cic b2.de* cina b2.de* cocc b2.de* coff b2.de* colch bg2 con b2.de* cupr b2.de* dig b2.de* **Dros** b2.de* dulc bg2 euph b2.de* ferr b2.de* graph b2.de* guaj bg2 hell bg2 **Hep** b2.de* hyos b2.de* ign b2.de* **Iod** b2.de* ip b2.de* kali-bi bg2 kali-c b2.de* kali-n b2.de* kreos b2.de* *Lach* b2.de* laur b2.de* led b2.de* lyc b2.de* mag-c b2.de* mag-m b2.de* *Mang* b2.de* meny bg2 merc b2.de* mez b2.de* mosch b2.de* mur-ac b2.de* nat-c b2.de* nat-m b2.de* *Nit-ac* b2.de* nux-m bg2 **Nux-v** b2.de* olnd bg2 op bg2 *Par* b2.de* petr b2.de* ph-ac b2.de* **Phos** b2.de* plat b2.de* plb b2.de* *Puls* b2.de* rhod b2.de* rhus-t b2.de* *Rumx* bg2 ruta bg2 sabad b2.de* sabin b2.de* samb b2.de* sars b2.de* *Seneg* b2.de* sep b2.de* sil b2.de* spig bg2 **Spong** b2.de* squil b2.de* *Stann* b2.de* staph b2.de* stram bg2 stront-c b2.de* sul-ac b2.de* *Sulph* b2.de* tarax bg2 teucr b2.de* thuj b2.de* verat b2.de* verb b2.de* zinc b2.de*

DAYTIME: *Sep* b4a.de

MORNING: am-m b7.de* ambr b7.de* ant-t b7.de* *Ars* bg2 bell b4a.de* *Bry* b7a.de calc b4.de* *Carb-an* b4a.de carb-v b4.de* caust b4.de* cham b7.de* chin b7.de* coff bg2 coloc b4a.de con b4.de* dig b4a.de* graph b4.de* hyos b7.de* *Kali-bi* bg2 kali-c b4.de* kali-n b4.de* merc b4.de* nat-c b4.de* nux-v b7.de* phos b4.de* puls b7.de* rhod b4.de* sars b4.de* seneg bg2 sep b4.de* sil b4.de* squil bg2 *Staph* b7a.de sul-ac b4.de* sulph b4.de* valer b7.de* zinc b4.de*
- **bed** agg.; in: ant-t bg2 carb-an bg2 con bg2

FORENOON: alum b4.de* calc b4.de* chin b7.de* ferr b7.de* ip b7.de* nat-c b4.de* phos b4.de* sep b4.de*

AFTERNOON: ant-c b7.de* asaf b7.de* bell b4.de* calad b7.de* *Caps* b7a.de *Carb-an* b4a.de caust b4.de* chel b7.de ip b7.de* lach b7a.de *Nux-v* b7.de* petr b4.de* *Puls* b7.de* rhus-t b7.de* sabad b7.de* sars b4.de* staph b7.de* sulph b4.de* viol-t b7.de* zinc b4.de*
- **14** h: chel bg2

EVENING: *Am-c* b4a.de ang b7.de* ant-c b7a.de ant-t b7.de* *Ars* b4.de* bell b4.de* borx b4a.de *Calc* b4a.de *Caps* b7a.de carb-an b4a.de* carb-v bg2 chin b7.de* *Colch* b7a.de con b4.de* cycl b7.de* ferr b7.de* *Graph* b4.de* ip b7.de* *Kali-c* b4a.de lach bg2 *Lyc* b4a.de m-aust b7.de merc bg2 merc-c b4a.de nat-c b4.de* nat-m b4a.de* nux-m b7.de* nux-v b7.de* petr b4.de* phos b4.de* *Puls* b7.de* ran-b b7.de* rhus-t b7.de* sars b4.de* sep b4.de* *Spong* b7a.de *Stann* b4.de* *Sulph* b4.de* verb bg2 zinc b4.de*
- **17-19** h: nat-m bg2

NIGHT: acon b7a.de* alum bg2 am-c b4.de* am-m b7a.de* arg-n bg2 arn b7.de* **Ars** b4.de* asaf b7a.de asar b7.de* aur b4.de* bell b4.de* bry b7.de* *Calc* b4.de* **Carb-v** bg2 *Cham* b7.de* chin b7.de* coloc b4.de* cupr bg2 dig b4a.de* *Ferr* b7.de* *Graph* b4a.de* guaj b4.de* ign b7.de* ip b7.de* kali-ar ptk1 kali-bi bg2 kali-br bg2 kali-c b4a.de* lach b7.de* lyc b4.de* *M-ambo* b7a.de meph bg2 merc bg2 naja ptk1 nat-c b4.de* **Nux-v** b7.de* *Op* b7.de* ox-ac ptk1 petr b4.de* ph-ac b4a.de phos b4.de* plb b7a.de* podo bg2 **Puls** b7.de* ran-b bg2 ran-s bg2 rhus-t b7.de* ruta bg2 sabad bg2 *Samb* b7.de* sel b7.de* seneg bg2 sep b4.de* sil b4.de* spig b7a.de spong b7.de* stann b4a.de* sul-ac b4.de* sulph b4.de* verat b7a.de vib ptk1
- **midnight**:
  - **before**: *Am-c* b4a.de *Cann-s* b7a.de nux-v b7.de* *Puls* b7.de* *Spong* b7a.de
  - **at**: ars bg2* ferr ptk1 graph ptk1 samb bg2* spong bg2
  - **after**: acon b7.de* *Ars* bg2 bry b7.de* ferr b7.de* ign b7.de* *Kali-bi* bg2 m-ambo b7.de *Nux-v* b7.de* *Op* b7a.de samb b7.de* squil b7.de*
    - **3** h: bufo bg2
- **bed** agg.; in: *Ars* bg2 bell bg2 carb-an bg2 carb-v bg2 chin bg2 con bg2 ferr bg2 *Graph* bg2 lach bg2 merc bg2 nat-m bg2 nux-v bg2 sep bg2 verb bg2

ABDOMINAL: (↗*Asthmatic; Difficult*) am-m **Ant-t** k* arg-n k* *Aur-m* k* bry k* choc srj3• *Ferr* k* *Mur-ac* k* *Phos* k* *Spong* k* *Stram* k* ter thuj

ACCELERATED: (↗*Asthmatic; Difficult; Panting*) absin k* acet-ac k* **Acon** k* acon-f a1* aesc k* aethyl-n a1 *Agar* k* *Ail* k* alco a1 alum b2.de* alumn k* am-c k* am-caust a1 ambr b2.de* aml-ns ammc a1* amyg a1* anac b2.de* anil a1 **Ant-t** k* anthraci apis k* *Apoc* k* apom a1* aral bro1 *Arg-n* k* *Arn* k* **Ars** k* ars-h a1* ars-i k* *Asaf* k* asar b2.de* *Aspar* k* atro a1 *Aur* k* aur-ar k2 aur-i k2 aur-s k2 bar-c k* bar-i k2 bar-m bar-s k2 **Bell** k* borx k* bov b2.de* *Brom* k* **Bry** k* calad a1 calc k* calc-i k2 *Calc-p* k* calc-sil k2 *Camph* k* cann-i k* cann-s k* *Canth* k* carb-ac k* carb-an b2.de* **Carb-v** k* carbn-s card-b a1 caru a1 castm caust b2.de* *Cedr* k* *Cham* k* **Chel** k* *Chin* k* chinin-ar *Chinin-s* chir-fl bnm4• chlor k* cic b2.de* cimic k* *Cina* k* cinch a1 clem k* *Coc-c* *Coca* cocc k* coch hr1 cod a1 coff k* coff-t a1 *Colch* k* coloc k* con k* *Cop* k* crot-h k* cryp a1 cub k* **Cupr** k* cupr-act bro1 cupr-ar a1 cupr-n a1 cur bro1 cycl k* cyt-l a1* *Dig* k* dros b2.de* dubo-h a1* dulc k* esch br1 eucal hr1 euph b2.de* euphr b2.de* ferr b2.de* *Ferr-p* bro1 gad a1 **Gels** k* gent-c a1 *Glon* k* guaj b2.de* *Ham* hr1 hell k* helo-s bnm14• *Hep* k* hippoz bro1 hydr k* hydr-ac k* *Hyos* k* iber hr1 *Ign* k* *Iod* k* **Ip** k* ix bnm8• jab a1 jac-c a1* kali-ar *Kali-bi* k* kali-c k* *Kali-i* k* kali-m k2 kali-n k* kreos b2.de* lach b2.de* *Lact* k* lat-m sp1* laur k* led k* lob a1* lob-p bro1 loxo-lae bnm12• loxo-recl bnm10• **Lyc** k* lyss k* m-arct b2.de m-aust b2.de mag-c b2.de* mag-m b2.de* mag-p bro1 mec a1 meny b7.de* *Merc* k* merc-c k* merc-cy br1* *Merc-sul* k* mez k* morph a1 mosch b2.de* *Mur-ac* k* naja nat-ar nat-c k* *Nat-m* k* nat-s bro1 nat-sal a1 nat-sil fd3.de• nicot a1 nit-ac b2.de* *Nux-m* k* *Nux-v* k* oena a1 *Op* k* ox-ac k* paull a1 peri br1 petr k* ph-ac b2.de* **Phos** k* *Phyt* k* *Plan* k* plat b2.de* plb k* plumbg a1 plut-n srj7• positr nl2• prun hr1* *Puls* k* pyrog jl2 ran-b b2.de* rhod k* *Rhus-t* k* ruta b2.de* sabad b2.de* sabin b2.de* sal-ac hr1 *Samb* k* *Sang* k* sars b2.de* sec b2.de* sel seneg k* **Sep** k* *Sil* k* sol-t a1 spig b2.de* spong k*

Accelerated: ...
squil k* stann k* staph b2.de* *Stram* k* stry a1* sul-ac k* sul-h a1 sul-i k2 **Sulph** k* tab k* tanac a1 tart-ac a1 tax a1 ter a1* thiosin c1 tub k* *Verat* k* *Verat-v* k* *Vesp* k* vinc k* viol-o b2.de* voes a1 wies a1 *Zinc* k* zinc-m a1 zinc-p k2 ziz a1*
- **morning**: (non:arg-met kl) **Ars-met** asaf k* upa a1
- **evening**: merc-c k* oena a1 petr h2 stann k*
- **night**: apis menis a1 spong k* thuj k*
- **anxiety**, during: ars nux-v k* seneg k*
- **ascending** agg.: lycps-v
- **bed**, first lying down in: sulph h2*
- **chill**; during: acon bg2 ars bg2 bell bg2 carb-v bg2 cupr bg2 ign bg2 ip bg2 lyc bg2 nat-m bro1 nux-v bg2 phos bg2 puls bg2 rhus-t bg2 sep bg2 sulph bg2 zinc bg2
- **coma**; during: (↗*MIND - Coma - respiration - accelerated*) stram
- **convulsions**; during: cocc kr1
- **cough**, during paroxysm of: **Dros** k*
- **disturbed**; when: ant-t k2
- **drinking** agg.: nat-m k*
- **dyspnea**; without: tub c1
- **epigastrium**; from pressure with dull stitches in: coloc h2
- **exertion** agg.: calc nh6 lycps-v
- **expiration**: chin b7.de* ign b7.de* stram b7.de*
- **headache**; during: **Nux-m**
- **inspiration**: *Acon* b7a.de am b7.de* camph b7.de* *Cham* b7.de* ign b7.de* *Ip* b7a.de
- **lying** down agg.: ant-t carb-v k* tarent k*
- **mental** exertion agg.: *Plan* k*
- **rising** from sitting agg.: agar k*
- **short** walk, from: nit-s-d sf1.de
- **sleep** | **during**:
  - : **agg.**: chel k* cocc k* con k* merc k* sep sne
  - : **alternating** with slow respiration (See Slow - alternating - short - sleep)
  - • **going** to: *Hydr-ac* k*
- **spoken** to; when | **amel.**: tub c1
- **standing** agg.: nat-m k*
- **waking**; on: *Cimic* k* coca-c sk4• frax a1

ACCOMPANIED BY: | **complaints**; other: acon b2.de* alum b2.de* am-c b2.de* am-m b2.de* anac b2.de* ang b2.de* ant-c b2.de* ant-t b2.de* arg-met b2.de* arn b2.de* **Ars** b2.de* asaf b2.de* asar b2.de* aur b2.de* bar-c b2.de* bell b2.de* bism b2.de* borx b2.de* bov b2.de* *Bry* b2.de* calad b2.de* *Calc* b2.de* camph b2.de* cann-s b2.de* canth b2.de* caps b2.de* carb-an b2.de* *Carb-v* b2.de* caust b2.de* cham b2.de* chel b2.de* *Chin* b2.de* cic b2.de* cina b2.de* cocc b2.de* coff b2.de* colch b2.de* coloc b2.de* con b2.de* croc b2.de* **Cupr** b2.de* cycl b2.de* dig b2.de* dros b2.de* dulc b2.de* euph b2.de* euphr b2.de* ferr b2.de* graph b2.de* guaj b2.de* hell b2.de* hep b2.de* hyos b2.de* *Ign* b2.de* iod b2.de* **Ip** b2.de* kali-c b2.de* kali-n b2.de* kreos b2.de* lach b2.de* laur b2.de* led b2.de* lyc b2.de* m-ambo b2.de m-arct b2.de m-aust b2.de mag-c b2.de* mag-m b2.de* mang b2.de* meny b2.de* merc b2.de* mez b2.de* mosch b2.de* mur-ac b2.de* nat-c b2.de* nat-m b2.de* nit-ac b2.de* *Nux-m* b2.de* *Nux-v* b2.de* olnd b2.de* op b2.de* par b2.de* petr b2.de* ph-ac b2.de* **Phos** b2.de* plat b2.de* plb b2.de* **Puls** b2.de* ran-b b2.de* ran-s b2.de* rheum b2.de* *Rhod* b2.de* *Rhus-t* b2.de* ruta b2.de* sabad b2.de* sabin b2.de* samb b2.de* sars b2.de* sec b2.de* sel b2.de* *Seneg* b2.de* **Sep** b2.de* sil b2.de* *Spig* b2.de* spong b2.de* squil b2.de* stann b2.de* staph b2.de* stram b2.de* stront-c b2.de* sul-ac b2.de* *Sulph* b2.de* tarax b2.de* teucr b2.de* thuj b2.de* valer b2.de* *Verat* b2.de* verb b2.de* viol-o b2.de* viol-t b2.de* zinc b2.de*

AIR; IN OPEN:
- **agg.**: ars b4.de* aur b4.de* calc b4.de* carb-v b4.de* cocc b7.de* graph bg2 lyc b4a.de* *Mag-m* b4a.de nit-ac b4.de* nux-v b7.de* psor bg2* puls bg2 *Sel* b7a.de seneg b4.de* sep b4.de* sulph b4.de* zinc b4.de*
- **amel.**: am-c b4.de* anac b4a.de ant-t ptk1 *Apis* bg2* arg-n bg2 *Bapt* bg2 bell b4a.de* bufo bg2 *Cann-s* b7a.de *Caps* b7a.de croc b7.de* *Ip* bg2 nat-m b4a.de* plb b7.de* puls b7.de* sulph ptk1

ANGER agg.: *Cham* b7a.de *Cupr* b7a.de *Ign* b7a.de *Ran-b* b7a.de

ANXIOUS: (↗*MIND - Anxiety*) abrot **Acon** k* aeth k* agath-a nl2• alumn *Am-c* k* *Aml-ns* vh1 ammc hr1 *Anac* k* anan hr1 ant-t k* *Apis* k* arg-n bg2 *Arn* k* **Ars** k* aur-m bar-c **Bar-m** k* *Bell* k* bov k* bry k* bufo cact bg2 calc k* calc-ar *Camph* k* cann-s k* caps bg2* *Carb-an* k* carb-v bg2 cench k2 *Cham* k*

Respiration

Anxious: ...
Chel k* chinin-s *Chlor* k* cina k* cist bg2 *Cocc* k* *Coff* k* colch k* *Coloc* k* corv-cor bdg• croc b2.de* *Crot-c* *Crot-h* k* crot-t k* cupr cupr-s hr1 *Dig* ferr k* gins k* glon bg2 hell *Hep* k* hydr-ac k* *Hyos* k* ictod bg2 *Ign* k* **Ip** k* kali-ar kali-bi k* kali-br a1 *Kali-c* k* kalm bg2 kreos k* *Lach* k* *Laur* k* lob lyc b2.de* m-ambo b2.de* m-arct b2.de* mang k* marb-w es1• merc bg2 *Mez* h2* mosch mrr1 nat-c bg2 **Nat-m** k* nit-ac k* nux-v k* olnd k* *Op* k* osm bg2 ph-ac **Phos** k* *Plat* k* plb k* positr nl2• **Prun** k* psil ft1 *Psor* **Puls** k* ran-b ptk1* *Rhus-t* k* ruta b2.de* sabad k* *Samb* k* sars **Sec** k* spig k* **Spong** k* **Squil** k* **Stann** k* staph k* *Stram* k* *Sulph* bg2 tab k* ter k* thuj k* valer k* verat k* viol-o k* viol-t b2.de* vip bg2* zinc k* zinc-p k2 [heroin sdj2]
- **morning**: *Phos*
  - **bed** agg.; in: nat-c
- **afternoon**: bell k*
- **evening**: bar-c mez k* *Phos* psil ft1 stann
  - **formication**, after: cist
- **fever**; during: **Acon** bg2 *Apis* bg2 am bg2 ars bg2 bell bg2 **Bry** bg2 camph bg2 cham bg2 coff bg2 hep bg2 ign bg2 **Ip** bg2 kali-c bg2 lach bg2 *Phos* bg2 plat bg2 *Puls* b7.de* rhus-t bg2 samb bg2 sec bg2 spong bg2 squil bg2 stann bg2 stram bg2 viol-t bg2
- **headache**; during: **Nux-m**
- **hyperventilation** (See Hyperventilation)
- **lying**:
  - **agg.**: apis *Puls*
  - **back**; on | **agg.**: aeth
- **mental** exertion agg.: phos k*
- **oppression** in region of heart; with: bell h1
- **perspiration**; during: acon bg2 *Ars* bg2 bell bg2 *Bry* bg2 **Cham** bg2 ign bg2 ip bg2 op bg2 phos bg2 *Puls* bg2 *Rhus-t* bg2 samb bg2 spong bg2 stram bg2
- **pulsating** in epigastrium, from: chel h1*

APNEA (See Arrested)

ARRESTED: *(↗Asphyxia; Interrupted)* acet-ac k* acon b2.de* alum k* am-br a1 am-c b2.de* anac k* ang ant-c b7a.de ant-t b2.de* apis apom a1 arn k* ars k* asaf b7.de* atra-r bnm3• bar-c k* bell k* bism b2.de* borx k* bov bro1 brass-n-o srj5• *Brom* b4a.de **Bry** k* *Cact* calad b2.de* *Calc* k* *Calc-p* vh *Camph* k* cann-s k* canth b2.de* caps k* carb-an k* carb-v k* carbn-s castm *Caust* k* cham b2.de* chin k* chir-fl bnm4• *Cic* k* *Cina* k* cit-v a1 cocc k* coff b2.de* con k* croc b2.de* crot-c k* **Cupr** k* cycl bg2 der a1 dios br1 diphtox jl2 dros b2.de* dulc fd4.de euphr k* grat bg2 guaj k* ham fd3.de• hep b2.de* hydr-ac k* hyos bg2 *Ign* k* iod k* *Ip* b2.de* kali-c k* kali-i k* kali-n b2.de* kalm k* kreos b2.de* *Lach* k* *Lat-m* k* laur b2.de* *Led* k* lepi a1 *Lyc* k* lyss br1* m-arct b2.de* m-aust b2.de* mag-m b2.de* merc k* merc-c k* mez b4.de* mim-h a1 *Mosch* k* mur-ac b2.de* naja nat-m k* nat-s k* nit-ac k* *Nux-m* k* nux-v k* oena k* **Op** k* petr bg2 *Phos* k* plat k* plb k* *Psor* jl2 *Puls* k* ran-b b2.de* ran-s b2.de* rhus-t b2.de* *Ruta* k* sabad b2.de* sabin b2.de* **Samb** k* sars k* *Sec* b7a.de sel b2.de* sep k* *Sil* k* sol-t-ae a1 spig b2.de* spong b2.de* squil b2.de* stann k* staph b2.de* stram k* stry a1 sul-ac b2.de* *Sulph* k* syc pte1• tab k* tanac k* tarax b2.de* ter thea ther tritic-vg fd5.de upa bro1 valer b2.de* vanil fd5.de *Verat* k* verb k* zinc b4.de* [heroin sdj2 **Spect** dfg1]
- **morning**: lyc k*
- **forenoon** | **stitches** in side: stann k*
- **afternoon**: cham k* dios k* kreos k* thuj k*
  - **15 h** | **stitches** under right scapula; from: kreos k*
  - **16 h**: dios
- **evening**, griping in inguinal region: nat-m nicc plan
- **night**: der a1 guaj *Kali-c* **Lyc** k* ruta samb k*
  - **midnight**: cinnb k*
  - **cough** agg.; during: nat-m k*
- **air** agg.; in open: caust h2 **Psor** k*
- **as** if he could not breathe again: apis bg2 bell bg2 helo bg2
- **ascending** stairs agg.: beryl tpw5 gaba sa3• glycyr-g cte1• mag-c nit-ac thuj
- **children**; in: | **lifted**; when they are: borx ptk1 calc-p br3*
- **constriction** of:
  - ○ **Chest**: carb-v h2* hell k* sep k* spig h1*
  - **Larynx** (See LARYNX - Constriction - larynx)
- **convulsions**; during: *Cic* *Cina* coff k* **Plb** a1 *Santin* sars k* *Stry* k*

Arrested: ...
- **cough**:
  - **before**: led h1*
  - **during**:
    - **agg.**: acet-ac *Acon* k* **Alum** k* alum-p k2 alum-sil k2 alumn nh6 am-c k* anac k* **Ant-t** k* aral arg-n k* arn k* **Ars** k* bar-c k* bell k* brom bry k* cain calad k* calc k* canth carb-an k* carb-v k* caust k* chlor bg2 **Cina** k* clem coc-c cocc con k* cop *Cor-r* k* **Cupr** k* diphtox jl2 dol **Dros** k* euphr k* ferr ferr-ar guaj hep k* hyos iod **Ip** k* kali-bi kali-c kali-chl kali-n k* *Kreos* k* lach k* lact led k* lob *Lyc* k* merc k* mosch mur-ac k* nat-m k* nat-s nicc nit-ac k* *Nux-m* k* **Nux-v** k* op k* pert jl2 petr h2* phel phos puls k* rhus-t *Samb* k* sang sarr *Sep* k* *Sil* k* spig k* spong squil k* staph sul-ac sulph verat zinc ziz
    - **drinking**; or: am-m ptk1 anac ptk1
- **desire** to arrest: calc h2*
- **drinking** agg.: anac k* *Cimx*
- **eating**; after: cham b7a.de
- **eruptions**; suppressed: *Ars* *Sulph*
- **fall** in a child; after a: petr h2*
- **fever**; during: ruta k*
- **forgets** to breath: plut-n srj7•
- **knocking** against something: petr h2*
- **lying**:
  - **agg.**: apis *Borx* k* dros k2 nat-m k* *Puls* k*
  - **amel.**: *Psor*
  - **back**; on | **agg.**: dulc fd4.de sil
- **pain**; during: aesc vh1 ars st kalm bg3 nat-m st nux-v h1 plb st prun bg3 puls st ran-s bg3 sep st sulph st
- **rubbing** | **amel.**: *(↗Difficult - rubbing; Difficult - rubbing - back - amel.; Difficult - rubbing - chest - amel.)* mur-ac k*
- **sitting** agg.: *Caust* nat-s k* psor k*
- **sleep**: *(↗Difficult - sleep)*
  - **during** | **agg.**: am-c *Ant-t* b7a.de cadm-s *Carb-v* **Cench** dig **Grin** k* guaj *Hep* b4a.de *Kali-c* *Lac-c* **Lach** k* lyc **Op** k* phos b4a.de samb k* *Sulph* k*
  - **going** to sleep; on | **agg.**: *Am-c* bro1 cadm-s br1* carb-v cench *Dig* nh6* dulc fd4.de graph k2 **Grin** k* lac-c bro1 **Lach** k* merc-pr-r bro1 *Op* k* *Samb* bro1
  - **preventing** (See SLEEP - Sleeplessness - respiration - arrested)
  - **side**; when going to sleep on the right: bad
- **smoking** agg.: tarax h1*
- **standing** | **still** | **agg.**: sep k*
  - **water** agg.; in: nux-m
- **stool** agg.; during: *Alum* b4a.de carb-an b4.de*
- **stooping** agg.: psor k* sil
- **suddenly**, in children: cham
- **swallowing** agg.: anac ptk1
- **talking** agg.: *Caust* dig br1 mez h2* plan *Sulph*
- **turning** in bed agg.: carb-v
- **walking**:
  - **agg.**: am-m *Calc* k* *Caust* cham *Chin* ign nat-c *Nit-ac* psor jl2 sep thuj
  - **wind**; against the: *Calc* k* plat

ARSENICAL vapors agg.: camph bg2 cupr bg2 **Hep** bg2 *Ip* bg2 kali-bi bg2 merc b4a.de*

ASCENDING:
- **agg.**: aesc bg2 am-c b4a.de* ang b7.de* ars b4a.de* aur b4.de* bar-c bg2 borx b4a.de* *Brom* b4a.de *Calc* b4a.de* canth b7.de* cupr b7.de* *Euph* b4a.de ferr bg2 graph bg2 hyos b7.de* iod bg2 *Kali-c* b4a.de kali-i bg2 kali-n b4.de* led bg2 lyc bg2 lycps-v bg2 mag-c b4.de* mag-m b4.de* **Merc** b4.de* nit-ac b4a.de* nux-v b7.de* ox-ac bg2 ran-b b7.de* rhus-t b7.de* ruta bg2 seneg b4.de* sep b4a.de* spig b7.de* **Spong** b7a.de *Squil* b7a.de stann b4.de* zinc b4.de*
- **amel.**: ran-b b7.de*
- **stairs** | **agg.**: *Ang* b7a.de *Apis* b7a.de *Bry* b7a.de hyos b7a.de iod ptk1 *Kreos* b7a.de led b7.de* m-arct b7.de merc ptk1 nux-v b7.de* ruta b7a.de spig b7.de*

ASPHYXIA: *(↗Arrested; Interrupted)* am-c bg2* **Ant-t** k* arn bg2 bell bg2 *Camph* carb-v k* *Carbn-s* chin k* *Chlor* k* *Coch* k* con tl1 crot-h bg2 hydr-ac bg2* hyos bg2 **lat-m** sp1 laur bg2 loxo-recl bnm10• mosch mrr1 *Op* k* petr a1 plut-n srj7• rhus-t k* *Sin-n* k* sul-h c2* tab k* *Upa* br1* vip bg2

- **children**, newborns: *(↗Difficult - children - newborns)* acon k* am-c sf1.de *Ant-c* k* **Ant-t** k* *Arn* *Bell* k* **Camph** k* chin k* crot-h sf1.de hydr-ac sf1.de hyos sf1.de *Laur* k* *Op* k* vip sf1.de
  - **mother**; from loss of blood of: chin ptk1
- **cholera**: *Hydr-ac* k* *Laur* k*
- **coal** gas: *(↗GENERALS - Coal gas)* bov br1* carb-v *Carbn-s*
- **coma**; with (See MIND - Coma - asphyxia)
- **lightning**; after: nux-v k*
- **paralysis** of diaphragm and respiratory muscles: con tl1
- **shivering**; during: *Carb-v* b4a.de

ASTHMATIC: *(↗Abdominal; Accelerated; Difficult; Wheezing; Whistling)* abies-c oss4• acet-ac a1 acetan c2 acetylch mtf11 *Acon* k* acon-ac mtf11 adam skp7• *Adren* br1 *Agar* k* agath-a nl2• alco a1 alis-p mtf11 all-c k* aloe alum alum-p k2 alum-sil k2 alumn bro1 *Am-c* k* **Ambr** k* ambro bro1 aml-ns bro1* ammc c2 amyg c2 anac k* anis bro1 ant-ar bro1* ant-c k* ant-i c1* ant-s-aur mtf11 *Ant-t* k* *Apis* k* aral a1* arg-cy c2 **Arg-n** k* arist-cl sp1 arn k* **Ars** k* **Ars-i** k* arum-d c2 arum-m c2 arum-t k* *Asaf* k* asar asc-c hr1 asc-t a1* *Aspidin* br1 asthm-r mtf11 atro bro1 *Aur* k* aur-i k2 aur-m c2 *Aur-m-n* wbt2• aur-s k2 bac bro1* bacls-10 pte1* bacls-7 fmm1* *Bar-c* k* bar-i k2 bar-m k* bar-s k2 *Bell* k* benz-ac c2* *Bit-ar* wht1• *Blatta-a* k* blatta-o c2* *Bov* k* *Brom* k* *Bry* k* *Cact* k* *Calad* k* *Calc* k* calc-ar c2* calc-hp c2 calc-i k2 calc-ln c1 calc-s k2 calc-sil k2* camph k* *Cann-s* k* *Caps* k* carb-an *Carb-v* k* carbn-s carc sp1* card-m k* cassia-s zzc1• caust k* cham k* chel k* chen-a c2 *Chin* k* *Chinin-ar* k* chinin-s c2 *Chlol* k* *Chlor* c2* *Cic* k* cina k* cist k* coc-c k* coca c2* cocain bro1 cocc k* coch c2 coenz-q mtf11 *Coff* k* *Colch* k* coloc *Con* k* cordyc mp4• cortiso sp1 coxs mtf11 croc *Crot-h* k* crot-t k* cumin hsa1 **Cupr** k* *Cupr-act* bro1* cupr-ar bro1 *Cyt-l* sp1 daph der c2 des-ac rbp6 *Dig* k* digin c2 diph-pert-t mp4• *Dros* k* *Dulc* k* eos mtf11 ephe mtf11 erio a1* eucal c2 eup-per k* *Euph* k* euph-hi jsx1.fr euph-pi c2 fel c2 *Ferr* k* *Ferr-ar* ferr-i ferr-p form-ac mtf11 fuma-ac mtf11 gad c2 gal-ac c1* galph mtf11 galv c2 *Gels* k* glon bro1 *Graph* k* grat grin k* hed sp1 *Hep* k* *Hippoz* hist sp1* hydr c2 hydr-ac k* hyos k* hyper c2 hypoth mtf11 iber c2 ictod c2* *Ign* k* *Iod* k* **Ip** k* junc-e c2* **Kali-ar** k* kali-bi c2* *Kali-br* k* **Kali-c** k* *Kali-chl* k* kali-chls c2 kali-cy c2 *Kali-i* k* kali-m k2 **Kali-n** k* *Kali-p* k* *Kali-s* k* kali-sil k2 kola br1* lac-d k* lac-e hrn2• *Lach* k* lact k* lact-v c1* *Laur* k* *Led* k* lem-m c2 limen-b-c hrn2* linu-u c2* **Lob** k* lob-s c2 luf-op mtf11 *Lyc* k* lyss jl2 magn-gl c2 magn-gr bro1 mal-ac mtf11 manc k* mang c2 *Med* k* meny *Meph* k* merc k* merc-d a1 merc-i-r c2 mez k* mill c2 morg fmm1• morg-g pte1* morg-p pte1*• morph bro1 *Mosch* k* mut fmm1• *Naja* k* naphtin c2* nat-ar k* nat-c *Nat-m* k* nat-ox-act mtf11 nat-p k* *Nat-s* k* nig-s mp4• *Nit-ac* k* nux-m k* *Nux-v* k* oci-sa sp1 ol-an k* ol-j a1* onis br1 *Op* k* osm c2 par *Passi* br1* pect c2 penic mtf11 pert jl2* petr k* ph-ac c2 phel k* *Phos* k* phos-pchl c1 *Phyt* k* pisc mtf11 pitu-p mtf11 plat plb k* plb-xyz c2 podo pop-cand c2 positr nl2• pseuts-m oss1• *Psor* k* ptel c2* pulm-v c1* **Puls** k* pycnop-sa mrz1 queb c1* ran-s raph rhod rhus-t mrr1 rumx k* *Ruta* sabad a1* sabin **Samb** k* samb-c c2 *Sang* k* sangin-n c2 sanic c2 saroth sp1 sars k* scroph-n bro1 sec k* sel *Seneg* k* *Sep* k* **Sil** k* silphu c2* sin-n k* sol-x mtf11 spig **Spong** k* squil k* *Stann* k* stict c2* *Still* k* **Stram** k* stront-c stry bro1 stry-xyz c2 succ br1 succ-ac br1 succ-xyz c2 *Sul-ac* k* sul-h c2 sul-i k2 sulfa sp1 **Sulph** k* sumb c2* syc pte1* syph a1* tab c2* tela bro1 ter c2 thala mtf11 *Thuj* k* trach-xyz c2 trios c2 tub bg* uncar-tom mp4• vario c2* *Verat* k* verat-v k* verb br1 viol-o viol-t visc br1* wye c2 x-ray sp1 xan c1* zinc k* zinc-p k2 zinc-val c2 zing c2* ziz a1* [bell-p-sp dcm1 calc-br stj1 *Cupr-f* stj2 *Cupr-m* stj2 *Cupr-p* stj2 lith-p stj2 mag-br stj1]

- **morning**: am-c bro1 ant-t bro1 *Ars* bro1 *Aur* k* *Calc* k* carb-an *Carb-v* k* carc gk6* *Cassia-s* zzc1• *Coff* k* *Con* k* dig grin bro1 kali-bi bro1 **Kali-c** k* *Meph* k* nat-s bro1 nux-v bro1* phos *Verat* k* zing k*
  - **bed** agg.; in: alum con k*
  - **waking**; on: alum *Con* k* des-ac rbp6 lach mrr1 pitu-a vml2• sep
- **forenoon**:
  - **10** h: carc gk6*
    - **10**-11 h: *Ferr*
- **noon**: *Lob*
- **evening**: bell bit-ar wht1• *Cist* k* ferr *Kali-s* mrr1 nat-m mrr1 nat-p mrr1 nux-v petr h2 *Phos* k* **Puls** k* stann *Sulph* k* *Zinc* k*
  - **21** h: bry
  - **bed** agg.; in: am-c graph sep

Asthmatic – evening: ...

  - **lying** down agg.; after: aral ars *Cist* *Meph*
- **night**: am-m *Ant-t* k* *Arg-n* hr1 **Ars** k* ars-s-f k2 arum-d a1* aur aur-ar k2 bit-ar wht1• *Brom* k* bry k* calc-ar hr1 *Carb-v* k* carc cd cham bg1 **Chel** k* *Chlol* k* *Cist* k* coff k* coloc k* daph des-ac rbp6 *Dig* k* *Ferr* k* ferr-ar *Ip* kali-ar k* *Kali-c* k* *Kali-s* mrr1 lach k* limen-b-c mlk9.de meph naja mrr1 nux-v k* *Op* k* phos **Puls** k* *Samb* mrr1 sang *Sep* k* spong mrr1 *Sulph* k* *Syph* *Thuj* k* *Tub* jl2 zinc zinc-p k2
  - **midnight**:
    - **before**:
      - **22** h: limen-b-c hrn2• meph
      - **23** h:
        - **23**-2 h: *Ars-i*
        - **urination** agg.; during: chel
    - **at** | **0**-2 h: *Ars* mrr1
    - **after**: **Ars** k* calc-ar *Carb-v* des-ac rbp6 *Ferr* ferr-ar *Graph* *Lach* **Samb** k*
      - **1** h:
        - **1**-2 h: *Kali-bi* mrr1
        - **1**-3 h: *Kali-ar* mrr1
        - **1**-4 h: syph ptk1
      - **2** h: ambro vh1 **Ars** k* *Kali-bi* med c1 *Rumx* k*
        - **2**-2.30 h: adam skp7•
        - **2**-3 h: **Kali-ar** **Kali-c** k*
        - **2**-4 h: **Kali-c** mrr1 med c1
      - **3** h: *Chin* *Cupr* k* **Kali-c** k* **Kali-n** k* nux-v mrr1
      - **4** h: cupr sst3• nux-v mrr1
        - **4**-5 h: *Nat-s* k* stann
      - **5** h: des-ac rbp6 kali-i k*
      - **jump** out of bed; must: **Ars** k* *Graph* **Samb** k* sulph mrr1
      - **sitting** up in bed | **must** sit up: **Kali-n** mrr1
  - **lying** agg.: *Aral* bro1 ars bro1 cist bro1 con bro1 ferr-act bro1 *Grin* bro1 lach bro1 merc-pr-r bro1 naja bro1 puls bro1 *Samb* bro1 sulph bro1
  - **sitting** up in bed | **must** sit up: limen-b-c hrn2•
- **accompanied** by:
  - **anxiety** (See MIND - Anxiety - asthma)
  - **blushing**; violent (See MIND - Blushing - asthmatic)
  - **burning**; internal: carb-v tl1
  - **catarrh**: cassia-s zzc1•
  - **chlorosis**: calc-p tl1
  - **coldness**; external: carb-v tl1
  - **collapse**; state of: verat mtf11
  - **convulsions**: *Cupr* mrr1
  - **coryza**: ant-t bro1 *Aral* bro1 arg-n ptk1 *Ars-i* bro1 bad bro1 *Ip* bro1 just ptk1 naphtin bro1 nat-s ptk1 spong ptk1
    - **chronic**: sil ptk1
  - **cramps** or spasms in various parts: cupr bro1
  - **cyanosis**: ars bro1 cupr bro1 samb bro1
  - **diabetes** (See GENERALS - Diabetes mellitus - accompanied - respiration)
  - **diarrhea** | **morning**; early: nat-s hr
  - **eczema**: *(↗Difficult - eruptions - with; CHEST - Complaints - bronchial tubes - accompanied - urticaria)* med mrr1 petr mrr1 rhus-t mrr1
  - **edema**: ant-ar mtf11
  - **emphysema**: lac-d mtf11
  - **eructations**: *Caps* hr1
    - **acrid**: sang mrr1
  - **expectoration**; yellow: kali-s tl1
  - **expiration**; difficult: brom tl1 chlor tl1 med jl2
  - **fever**: tub-a jl2
  - **goitre**: spong ptk1
  - **gout**: led bro1 sulph bro1 *Visc* bro1

Respiration

- **headache** (See HEAD - Pain - accompanied - asthma)
- **heartburn**: sang mrr1
- **hemorrhoids**: *Junc-e* br1* nux-v bro1
- **husky** voice: hippoz mtf11
- **inspiration**; difficult: brom tl1 iod tl1
- **itching**: bit-ar wht1• calad ptk1 cist ptk1 sabad ptk1
- **menses**; scanty: arg-n ptk1
- **nausea**: ip tl1 kali-n br1 lob bro1
- **obesity**: blatta-o mrr1
- **palpitation**: ars bro1 cact bro1 eucal bro1 puls bro1
- **perspiration**; profuse: *Samb* mrr1
- **phthisis** pulmonalis (See CHEST - Phthisis - accompanied - respiration)
- **pulsatilla** symptoms: puls tl1
- **respiration**:
  - **difficult** and slow: ferr tl1
  - **painful**: ars tl1
- **retching**: dros mtf11
- **rheumatic** pains: benz-ac ptk1 led bro1 sulph bro1 tub mrr1 *Visc* bro1
- **salivation**: *Carb-v* kr1*
- **sexual** desire; increased: nat-c a1*
- **sleeplessness**: carc mlr1• chlol bro1 tela bro1
- **speak**; inability to: cupr tl1
- **suffocation**: am-c tl1 ip tl1
- **swallowing**; difficult: cupr tl1
- **thirst**: ars mrr1 kali-n bro1
- **uremia** (See GENERALS - Uremia - accompanied - respiration - asthmatic)
- **urination**:
  - **dysuria** | **night**: solid bro1*
- **urine**:
  - **discharge** of: kreos tl1
  - **sediment** in: nat-n br1*
- **vertigo**: cupr ptk1
- **water**; desire of: bit-ar wht1•
- **weakness** (See GENERALS - Weakness - accompanied - asthma)
- ○ **Abdomen**; pain in: mosch mrr1
- **Bronchial** tubes:
  - **catarrh** (See CHEST - Catarrh - bronchial - accompanied - respiration)
  - **inflammation** (See CHEST - Inflammation - bronchial - accompanied - respiration)
- **Chest**:
  - **burning** pain: aral bro1
  - **constriction**; sensation of: ars tl1 chel tl1
  - **oppression**: ars tl1 chel tl1
  - **sink** in; sensation chest would: ptel tl1
  - **stitches** beneath right ribs: chel tl1
- **Colon**; inflammation of: lyc mtf nat-s mrr1
- **Diaphragm**; spasms of: staph tl1
- **Epigastrium**; swelling of: lac-d mtf11
- **Epiglottis**:
  - **spasms**: med bro1
  - **weakness**: med bro1
- **Heart**; complaints of (See heart - complaints; CHEST - Heart; complaints - accompanied - respiration)
- **Lids**; twitching of: cupr ptk1
- **Nose**; obstruction of: bit-ar wht1•

- **accompanied** by: ...
  - **Rectum**:
    - **cancer** of (See RECTUM - Cancer - accompanied - respiration)
    - **polypi**: nat-s mrr1
  - **Skin**; complaints of: naja ptk1
  - **Stomach**:
    - **complaints**: arg-n mtf *Bry* mtf carb-v mtf ip mtf kali-m mtf *Lob* mtf lyc mtf *Nux-v* mtf puls mtf sang mtf verat-v mtf zing mtf
    - **disordered**: arg-n bro1 *Bry* bro1 carb-v bro1 ip bro1 kali-m bro1 *Lob* bro1 lyc bro1 *Nux-v* bro1 puls bro1 sang bro1 verat-v bro1 zing bro1
    - **hyperchlorhydria** of: grin br1
  - **Testes**; pain in: spong mrr1
  - **Throat**:
    - **burning** pain in: aral bro1
    - **choking** of: hydr-ac ptk1
  - **Thyroid**; complaints of: spong mrr1
- **air** | **mountain** air amel.: syph mtf11
- **air** agg.; draft of: *Sil* k*
- **air**; in open:
  - **agg.**: calad al1 nat-m al1 psor al1
  - **amel.**: *Am-c* k* bry k2 ip tl1 kali-s k2* lach mrr1 naphtin bro1 puls mrr1 tub mrr1
- **alcoholics**; in (See drunkards)
- **allergic**: *(↗hay; from; GENERALS - Allergic)* ambr mtf *Ars* mtf *Ars-i* mtf blatta-o mtf *Brom* mtf carc mlr1• cortiso mtf11 dulc mtf euphr mrr1 *Iod* mtf kali-bi mtf kali-c mtf kali-i mtf kali-s mtf lyc mtf *Med* mtf moni jl2* *Morg-p* mtf naja mtf naphtin mtf *Nat-ar* mtf nat-c mtf nat-m mtf *Nat-s* mtf nux-v mtf psor mtf *Puls* mrr1 sabad mrr1 sang mrr1* sin-n mtf stict mrr1 *Sul-ac* mtf *Thuj* mtf tub mtf11
  - **hay** fever; with: carc mlr1•
- **alternating** with:
  - **diarrhea**, nocturnal: *Kali-c* k*
  - **eczema**: ars mtf11 cupr sst3• *Psor* jl2
  - **eruptions**: *(↗COUGH - Alternating - eruptions)* apis dx1 ars tl1* calad k* calc kr1 carc gk caust bro1 *Crot-t* k* cupr sht*• dulc wt *Hep* k* *Kalm* k* lach med hu mez mut ptj*• phenob jl *Psor* jl rat dx1 rhus-t k* *Sulph* k* syph a
  - **gout**: benz-ac lyc *Sulph*
  - **pain**; rheumatic: *(↗EXTREMITIES - Pain - rheumatic - alternating - dyspnea; EXTREMITIES - Pain - rheumatic - alternating - pulmonary)* dulc gma *Med* gg
  - **rash**: calad k*
  - **urticaria**: calad k*
  - **vomiting**: kali-c ptk1
    - **periodical** | **convulsive**, spasmodic: cupr bro1 ip bro1
  - ○ **Chest**; rash: *Calad*
  - **Forearm**:
    - **pimples**: calad
    - **rash**: calad
  - **Head**; pain in: ang k* glon kali-br
  - **Stomach** | **complaints**: **Kali-bi** mrr1
  - **Upper** limbs; rash: calad mez
- **anesthesia**; ailments from: aral mtf11
- **anger**; after (See MIND - Anger - asthmatic)
- **arms** away from the body amel.; holding the: psor br1*
- **ascending** | **hills** | **agg.**: nux-v tl1
  - **stairs** | **agg.**: saroth sp1
- **autumn** agg.: *Chin* k* lach gg med gg
- **bathing**; after: mosch mrr1
- **bending**:
  - **forward** | **amel.**: oci-sa sp1
  - **head**:
    - **backward** | **amel.**: bell hr1 cham k* **Spong** k* *Verat* k*
  - **shoulders**:
    - **backward** | **amel.**: calc-act ptk1

- **bronchial**: acon ptk1 ambr ptk1 ant-t bg2 arg-n ptk1 arist-cl sp1 **Ars** bg2* ars-i ptk1 bar-c bg2 bell bg2 *Bry* bg2 *Calc* bg2 *Camph* bg2 **Chin** bg2 con bg2 cortiso sp1 *Cupr* bg2* cupr-ar br1 **Dulc** bg2 *Ferr* bg2 *Graph* bg2 hed sp1 hep bg2 hippoz jl2 *Influ* jl2 ip bg2* kali-ar ptk1 *Kali-c* ptk1 kali-n ptk1 *Lach* bg2* *Lob* ptk1 merc bg2 merc-i-r ptk1 nux-v bg2* *Phos* bg2 **Puls** bg2* *Samb* ptk1 **Seneg** bg2 **Sep** bg2 sil bg2* **Spong** ptk1 **Stann** bg2* stram ptk1 *Sulph* bg2* tab ptk1 ter ptk1 thuj ptk1 tub ptk1 visc ptk1 zinc bg2
  - **children**; in: hed sp1
- **cardiac** (See heart - complaints)
- **children**; in: *Acon* k* ambr k* *Ant-t* hr1 ars tl1* *Bell* hr1 camph hr1 *Carc* vh* **Cham** k* chin hr1 coff hr1 cupr hr1 hep hr1 ign hr1 **Ip** k* kali-br k* kali-c mtf33 kali-i lach hr1 lyc hr1 med k2* merc-sul c1 *Mosch* k* **Nat-s** k* nux-m hr1 nux-v k* op hr1* phos hr1 psor **Puls** k* **Samb** k* sil k2* stram k* sulph k* syph mtf33 thuj mtf33 tub-a vs* zinc mtf33
  - **fail** to act; where indicated remedies: morg-p mtf11
  - **infants**; in: med ptk1 naphtin mtf11 tub-a jl2 v-a-b jl2 vib tl1*
  - **sycotic**: nat-s tl1 thuj mtf33
  - **vaccination**; after: carc mlr1• thuj
- **chronic**: anis br1 ant-s-aur mtf11 sul-ac mtf11 syph jl2*
- **coition**:
  - **after**: *Asaf* k* cedr kali-bi
  - **during**: aeth ambr k* asaf ptk1 kali-bi ptk1
- **cold**:
  - **agg.**: nux-v mrr1 sil mrr1
  - **air**:
    - **agg.**: agar mtf all-c mtf am-c mtf ant-t mtf apis mtf *Arg-n* hr1 *Ars* mtf aur mtf bell mtf brom mtf bry mtf *Calc* mtf calc-sil mtf campan-ra mtf carb-v mtf chin mtf chinin-ar mtf *Cist* mtf cupr mtf dulc mtf *Hep* mtf ip mtf kali-ar mtf *Kali-c* mtf kali-n mtf *Lob* mosch mrr1 *Nux-v* k* petr *Psor* mtf puls mtf rhus-t mtf rumx mtf sabad mtf sep mtf sil mtf sulph mtf
    - **amel.**: am-c k2 bry *Carb-v* k* *Cham* k* *Merc* *Puls* nh6
    - **entering** cold air from a warm room agg.: ars b
  - **amel.**: lach mrr1
  - **drinks**:
    - **agg.**: *Cassia-s* zzc1•
      - **ice**-cold: meph ptk1
  - **water**:
    - **agg.**: *Meph* k*
    - **amel.**: cham k*
- **cold**; after taking a: acon *Arg-n* hr1 dulc *Lob* nat-s bro1 *Podo* *Puls* k* sil **Spong** k* *Stann* sulph ptk1*
  - **heated**; when: *Sil*
  - **summer** agg.: (↗*summer*) arg-n ptk2 *Ars* k*
- **company** | **amel.**: bit-ar wht1•
- **congestive**: morg fmm1•
- **constriction** | **Larynx**; of: dros k2
- **coryza**; after: aral bro1 just ptk1 naja bro1* nux-v bro1
- **cough** agg.; during: *Meph* nux-v k2 pert mtf11 phos ptk1
- **dampness**; from: carc mlr1• nat-s tl1 syc fmm1•
- **die**; with sensation he is going to (See MIND - Death - presentiment - respiration)
- **dinner**; after: thuj k*
- **drunkards**: *Ars* hr1 coca mtf11 *Meph* k*
- **dry**: morg-p fmm1• thymu br1
- **dust**; from inspiration of: (↗*GENERALS - Dust - agg.*) bit-ar wht1• *Cassia-s* zzc1• ictod k* *Ip* bro1 kali-c bro1 sul-ac mrr1
- **earlier** illness; after: carb-v tl1
- **eating** | **after** | **agg.**: (↗*meal*) *Asaf* hr1 asc-t c1 *Kali-p* k* manc rb2 *Nux-v* k* *Puls* k* sars hr1
  - **amel.**: ambr k* *Graph* k* iod hr1
- **eczema**; after suppressed: ars tl1
- **emotions**:
  - **after**: (↗*nervous; Hyperventilation*) *Acon* k* ambr caust mrr1 cham k* *Coff* k* cupr k* *Gels* k* *Ign* k* lach mrr1 nux-v k* pall puls hr1* thyreotr mtf11 verat k*
  - **suppressed** emotions; after: caust mrr1
- **endocrine** imbalance; from: pitu-gl mtf11
- **eructations** | **amel.**: carb-v k* nux-v k*
- **eruptions**; after suppressed: (↗*Difficult - eruptions - suppressed*) ant-c bl1 *Apis* *Ars* k* calc gk1 *Carb-v* k* cupr sst3* *Dulc* k* *Ferr* k* graph mrr1 hep k* *Ip* k* mez gk* *Psor* k* **Puls** k* rhus-t mrr1 sec k* *Sulph* k*
- **erysipelas**; from suppressed: ptel hr1
- **excitement**: ambr carc mlr1•
- **exertion**; from slight: blatta-o mrr1 bry vh calc vh* *Cassia-s* zzc1• caust mrr1 nat-p mrr1 *Nat-s* mrr1 nux-v mrr1 sil mrr1 stann vh* [tax jsj7]
- **expectoration** | **amel.**: ant-t bg1* aral bro1 calad ptk1 erio c1* grin bg1* hyper k* ip bro1* kali-bi bro1 sep bg1 stann ptk1 zinc bg1*
- **face**, after disappearance of tetter on face; with pain in: *Dulc* k*
- **feather** pillow agg.: mang-act br1
- **fever**; with intermittent: mez
- **flatulence**; from: (↗*stomach - fullness; Difficult - flatulence; Impeded - flatulence*) *Carb-v* k* *Cham* k* *Chel* bg1 *Chin* k* *Lyc* k* mag-p k* *Nux-v* k* op k* phos k* *Sulph* k* zinc k*
- **flowers**; from: sang mrr1
- **followed** by | **diarrhea**: kali-c ptk1 nat-s ptk1
- **formication**; after: cist bro1 lob bro1
- **fright** agg.: carc fb* samb ptk1
  - **children**; in: carc mlr1•
- **frost** | **agg.**: syc fmm1•
- **fumes**; from: sul-ac mrr1
- **grief**; from: **Nat-s** mrr1
- **hay** fever, during (See NOSE - Hay - asthmatic)
- **hay**; from: (↗*allergic; NOSE - Hay - asthmatic; NOSE - Heat - bleed*) *Ambr* aral bro1 *Ars* k* *Ars-i* k* arum-t st *Bad* *Carb-v* k* chinin-ar bro1 *Dulc* *Euphr* k* **Iod** k* *Ip* bro1 *Kali-i* k* kali-s-chr c1 *Lach* lob c2* *Naja* k* *Naphtin* c2* *Nat-s* k* *Nux-v* k* *Op* phle bg1 *Sabad* k* sang k2* *Sil* *Sin-n* k* *Stict* k* sul-i c2*
- **head** on knee-position: (non:kali-c h2)
  - **amel.**: kali-c lpc2*
- **heart**:
  - **complaints**; from heart: (↗*CHEST - Heart; complaints - accompanied - respiration; CHEST - Heart; complaints - accompanied - respiration - difficult*) adon mtf11 *Aspidin* br1 aur k2 cact bro1* chinin-ar ptk1 digin bro1 grin hr1* kali-n br1 laur ptk1 naja bg* psor ptk1* queb c1* spong ptk1 stroph-h bro1 sumb ptk1
  - **fatty** degeneration of heart; from: **Arn** k*
- **hiccough**; after (See STOMACH - Hiccough - followed - asthma)
- **hives**, from: apis ptk1 puls ptk1
- **horse**; when coming in contact with a: castor-eq vh
- **humid** (See Rattling)
- **hysterical**: (↗*Difficult - hysterical; Hyperventilation; MIND - Hysteria*) acon hr1 ambr c1 asaf hr1* aur hr1 bell hr1 caul hr1 caust hr1 cham hr1 cocc hr1* coff hr1 con hr1 cupr hr1 ign hr1* ip hr1 *Lach* hr1 lob ptk1 **Mosch** k* **Nux-m** k* nux-v k* phos k* **Puls** k* stann k* stram k* sulph k*
- **injury** of spine, after: *Hyper* k*
- **jealousy**; after: **Lach** mrr1
- **laughing**:
  - **agg.**: ars ptk1
  - **with** (See MIND - Laughing - asthma)
- **leaning** | **backward** | **agg.**: psor k*
  - **forward** | **amel.**: kali-c tl1 spong mrr1
- **lying**:
  - **abdomen**; on: (↗*COUGH - Lying - Abdomen - amel.*)
    - **amel.**: *Med* hr1*
  - **agg.**: des-ac rbp6
  - **back**; on | **amel.**: psor tl1
  - **face**; on the | **amel.**: med bro1*
  - **knees** and chest; on | **amel.**: carc cd med mtf33
- **meal**, after every satisfying: (↗*eating - after - agg.*) asaf k1*
- **measles**; after: brom k* *Carb-v* k*
- **menses**:
  - **before** | **agg.**: cupr bro1 *Iod* bro1 *Lach* bro1 spong bro1 sulph
  - **during** | **agg.**: cupr bro1 *Iod* bro1 kali-c k* *Lach* bro1 spong bro1*
  - **suppressed** menses; from: *Puls* k* spong k* zinc mrr1
- **mental** exertion agg.: kali-c gm1 sep k*
- **mercury**; after abuse of: aur

Respiration

- **Millar's** asthma (See LARYNX - Laryngismus)
- **miner's** asthma, from coal dust: card-m br1* nat-ar k* sulph ptk1
- **moon**; full: calc nh6 spong nh6*
- **motion** | **amel.**: ferr bro1 lob bro1
- **mountains** | **amel.** (See air - mountain)
- **music** agg.: ambr
- **nervous**: *(↗emotions - after)* acon bro1 ambr bro1 aml-ns bro1 *Asaf* bro1 cham ptk1 chinin-s bro1 cina bro1 coff bro1 *Cupr* bro1 form pd grin bro1 *Hydr-ac* bro1 *Ip* bro1 kali-br hr1 kali-p bro1* lob bro1 mag-p tl1* *Mosch* bro1 nux-m bro1 *Nux-v* bro1 stram ptk1 sumb bro1 tela bro1 thymu br1* valer c2* verat bro1
- **obstruction**, from nasal: lem-m c1*
  - **weather** agg.; wet: lem-m c1*
- **odors** agg.: asar ptk1 sang hr1*
- **old** people; in: am-c hr1 *Ambr* k* ant-c hr1 **Ars** k* aur hr1 *Bar-c* k* bar-m bro1* camph hr1 *Carb-v* k* *Coca* ptk1 *Con* k* phel *Seneg* ptk1* sulph
  - **athletes**: coca mtf11
- **overheated**; when: bry k2 sil ptk1
- **paroxysmal**: meph br1
- **periodical**: all-s k* *Alum* ant-t **Ars** k* *Asaf* *Carb-v* *Chel* *Chin* bro1 chinin-ar br1* *Hydr-ac* ip bro1 nux-v *Phos* *Plb* *Seneg* sulph tab thuj
  - **days**; every eight: chin bro1 ign bro1 sulph
  - **week**; every: chin ptk1 ign ptk1 sulph ptk1
- **perspiration** | **suppressed** perspiration of feet: ol-an bro1*
- **position** knee-elbow | **amel.**: med jl2
- **protruding** tongue | **amel.**: med hr1*
- **puberty** | **stops** at puberty and recurs later in life: nat-s mrr1
- **rash**; after suppression of acute: acon *Apis* *Puls*
- **reading**; constant | **amel.**: ferr tl1
- **recurrent**: am-c bg2 *Ant-c* bg2 *Ars* bg2 **Calc** bg2 carb-v bg2 caust bg2 cupr bg2 ferr bg2 graph bg2 **Kali-c** bg2 lach bg2 lyc bg2 *Nit-ac* bg2 *Nux-v* bg2 phos bg2 sep bg2 sil bg2 stann bg2 *Sulph* bg2 zinc bg2
- **riding** agg.: meph k*
- **rocking** amel.: kali-c k*
- **rose** cold, following: *Sang* k*
- **sadness**, with (See MIND - Sadness - respiration - asthmatic)
- **sailors** as soon as they go ashore: *(↗seaside - amel.)* **Brom** k* kali-br tl1
- **seaside**; at the:
  - **agg.**: brom tl1 med tl1 nat-m tl1
  - **amel.**: *(↗sailors)* brom bro1 carc fb* med gg* syc ptj*
- **sitting**:
  - **erect**:
    - **agg.**: ferr-act bro1 laur bro1 psor bro1
    - **amel.**: *Ars* bro1* ip ptk1 kali-c bro1* merc-pr-r bro1 nux-v bro1 *Puls* bro1
      - **head** bent backward: hep bro1
- **sleep**:
  - **after** | **agg.**: aral bro1 grin bro1 *Lach* bro1 samb bro1
  - **during**:
    - **agg.**: *Acon* *Ars* k* *Carb-v* k* *Hep* k* *Kali-c* k* kali-i mrr1 *Lach* k* meph k* nat-s k* op sep k* spong mrr1 *Sulph* k*
      - **menses**:
        - **during** | **agg.**: cupr ptk1 *Iod* ptk1 *Lach* ptk1 spong ptk1
  - **falling** asleep agg.: am-c bro1 *Grin* bro1 lac-c bro1 *Lach* bro1 *Merc-pr-r* bro1 op bro1
- **smoke**: *Cassia-s* zzc1• mosch mrr1 sul-ac mrr1
- **smokers**; of: naphthoq mtf11
- **smoking**:
  - **after** | **agg.**: asc-t c1 **Nat-ar** mrr1
  - **agg.**: puls h1*
  - **amel.**: merc ptk1
- **spasmodic**: agar bg1 am-c ambr bg1 ammc hr1 ant-c bg2 *Ant-t* k* aral nh6 arg-n k* **Ars** k* *Asaf* bapt bg1 *Bell* k* bry bg2 *Cact* k* camph bg2* caust k* cham bg1 cic bg1 *Cocc* k* coff coff-t hr1 con *Cupr* k* *Dros* *Ferr* k* ferr-p *Gels* k* *Graph* k* guaj bg1 *Hydr-ac* k* *Hyos* k* hyper br1 **Ip** k* *Kali-br* k* *Kali-c* k* *Lach* k* laur led lil-t bg1 **Lob** k* lyc bg2 *Mag-p* k* *Meph* k* merc *Mez* k* *Mosch* k* nat-s bg1* nux-m bg1 *Nux-v* k* *Op* k* ph-ac phos k* plat bg1 *Plb* *Puls* raph rumx bg1 samb k* *Sars* k* *Sep* k* **Spong** k* stann bg2 *Stram* k* sulph k* *Sumb* k* syph mtf11 *Tab* k* **Valer** k* zinc k* zinc-p k2

Asthmatic: ...

- **spring**; in: aral bro1
- **status** asthmaticus: ant-t mtf cann-s mtf kali-c mtf lach mtf laur mtf
- **stomach**: *(↗Difficult - stomach - disorders)*
  - **disordered**; from: nux-v k2*
  - **fullness** of; from: *(↗flatulence)* nux-v mtf33
- **stool** | **amel.**: ictod k*
- **sudden** attacks: *Acon* bg2 *Ant-t* bg2 *Ars* bg2 bell bg2 bry bg2 **Camph** bg2 *Cham* bg2 chin bg2 cupr k* ip k* *Lach* bg2 **Mosch** bg2* nux-m bg2 nux-v bg2 **Op** bg2 pitu-a vml2• puls bg2 *Samb* bg2
- **summer**; in: *(↗cold; after - summer; weather - warm - wet - agg.)* arg-n hr1* syph hr1*
- **sycotic**: med ptk1 nat-s ptk1 sil ptk1*
- **talking**:
  - **agg.**: *Dros* k* **Lach** hr1 meph bro1 **Stann** mrr1
  - **amel.**: ferr k*
- **temperature**; from a slight change of: rumx vh
- **thunderstorm**; during: phos ptk1 sep k* *Sil* k* syph k*
- **tuberculosis** family history: dros tl1
- **turning** in bed agg.: ars ptk1
- **uncovering** chest | **amel.**: ferr c1
- **urination** agg.; during: chel k* dulc bg1*
- **vaccination**; after: carc mlr1• thuj k*
- **vexation** agg.: ars
- **violent**: nat-s tl1
- **vomiting** | **amel.**: cupr bro1
- **walking**:
  - **amel.**: ferr tl1 nux-v tl1
  - **wind**; against the: cupr k* nat-m bg1
- **warm**:
  - **air** agg.: aur k13
  - **drinks** | **amel.**: spong mrr1
  - **food**:
    - **agg.**: *Cham* *Lob*
    - **amel.**: spong mrr1
  - **room**:
    - **agg.**: *Am-c* k* bry k2 carb-v kali-s lach mrr1 puls mrr1 tub jl2
    - **entering** a warm room; when | **air**; from open: *Bry* *Lob* st
- **weather**:
  - **change** of weather: *Ars* *Cassia-s* zzc1• chel dulc hyper br1 pitu-a vml2•
  - **cold**:
    - **agg.**: arg-n ptk1 *Hep* tl1
    - **wet** | **agg.**: ant-t gm1 ars bro1 aur sne **Dulc** k* *Med* *Nat-s* k* thuj mrr1 verat hr1*
  - **dry** | **agg.**: acon bro1 caust bro1 cham ptk1 *Hep* bro1*
  - **foggy**: hyper ptk1 nat-s mtf11 [bell-p-sp dcm1]
  - **frosty**: syc bka1•
  - **warm**:
    - **agg.**: nat-s k2 syph jl2*
    - **wet**:
      - **agg.**: *(↗summer)* bar-c bg3* *Bell* k* *Carb-v* k* ip hr1* lach svr7 syc bka1• syph c1*
      - **amel.**: caust bro1 *Hep* bro1*
  - **wet**:
    - **agg.**: ant-t gm1 *Aur* bar-c ptk1 carc fb* *Chin* con *Dulc* k* hep br1 ip k2 kali-c k2 lem-m c1* *Nat-s* k* sil syph ptk1 verat
    - **amel.**: caust ptk1 hep ptk1
  - **windy**: carc gk6*
    - **before**: hyper br1
- **whooping** cough: carb-v tl1
- **winter** attacks: *Carb-v* k* *Cassia-s* zzc1• nat-m ptk1 *Nux-v* k* parth vml3• phel
- **writing**; constant | **amel.**: ferr tl1

AWAKE; agg. while: nux-v b7.de

BED: | **going** to bed | **when**: *Nux-v* b7a.de

- **in** bed:
  - **agg.**: ant-t b7a.de* ars b4a.de* bell bg2 carb-an b4a.de* carb-v bg2 chin b7a.de* con b4a.de* ferr b7a.de* *Graph* b4a.de* lach bg2 merc bg2 nat-m b4a.de* nux-v b7a.de* sep b4a.de* spig bg2 sulph bg2 verb bg2
  - **amel.**: nux-v bg2

BENDING:
- **backward**:
  - **agg.**: cupr bg2* nit-ac b4a.de psor ptk1
  - **amel.**: hep bg2
- **forward** | **amel.**: *Ant-t* b7a.de ars b4a.de *Calc* b4a.de *Cann-s* b7a.de *Colch* b7a.de hell b7a.de *Kali-bi* bg2 *Lach* b7a.de *Nit-ac* b4a.de *Phos* b4a.de sep bg2 *Spong* b7a.de
- **head** | **backward** | **amel.**: *Hep* b4a.de* lach ptk1 *Spong* ptk1 verat ptk1
  - **forward** | **amel.**: *Cann-s* b7a.de
- **shoulders**:
  - **backward** | **amel.**: *Calc* b4a.de

BLOWING: (↗*MOUTH - Blowing)* chin bg1 lach bg1
- **expiration**: *Chin* b7.de* naja bg2 *Op* bg2 stram bg2
  - **perspiration**; during: *Chin* bg2
  - **sleep**; during: chin b7.de*

BREAKFAST agg.; after: cham b7.de* valer b7.de*

BREATHING:
- **deep**:
  - **agg.**: am-m b7a.de ars bg2 bry b7.de* calad b7.de* canth b7.de* kalm bg2 merc bg2 ran-s b7.de* rhus-t b7.de*
  - **amel.**: chin b7.de* *Cupr* b7.de* osm bg2 stann b4.de*
- **holding** breath:
  - **agg.**: spig b7.de*
  - **amel.**: bell bg
  - **anger**; from | **children**; in: cham mrr1

BREATHLESS (See Arrested)

CATARRH agg.: **Ant-t** bg2 **Ars** bg2 *Camph* bg2 *Carb-v* bg2 graph bg2 *Ip* bg2 lach bg2 *Nux-v* bg2 *Puls* bg2 *Samb* bg2

CATCHING: (↗*Gasping; Panting)* *Arg-n* k* *Brom* k* calad *Calc* k* carb-ac k* *Caust* k* cina gels k* kreos k* *Led* k* lil-t k* merc-c k* nit-ac k* *Phos* k* santin **Sil** k* stry k* sulph k* thioc-ac rly4•
- **morning**: sars k*
- **night**: **Sil** k*
- **bending** agg.: *Calc*
- **cough**:
  - **after**: arn k* *Ars* k* bry k* hep k* *Nat-m* k* *Puls* k*
  - **before**: ant-t kl bry h1*
  - **during** | **agg.**: bry *Cina*
- **dancing**; after: *Spong* k*
- **fever**; during: **Sil**
- **menses**; before: borx
- **sleep** agg.; during: lyc k*
- **stitching**, from:
  - **hemorrhoids**, in: **Sulph**
  - ○ **Abdomen** to back; in: *Calc*
- **working**: sars k*

CELLARS agg.; air of: *Ars* b4a.de *Sep* b4a.de

CHEYNE-STOKES breathing (See GENERALS - Cheyne-stokes)

CHILDREN; in: **Acon** bg2 *Ambr* b7a.de *Ant-t* bg2 ars bg2 **Bell** bg2 *Calc* b4.de* camph bg2 **Cham** bg2 chin bg2 *Coff* bg2 cupr bg2 hep bg2 ign bg2 **Ip** bg2 lach bg2 lyc b4.de* **Mosch** bg2 *Nux-m* bg2 **Nux-v** bg2 *Op* bg2 phos bg2 puls bg2 **Samb** bg2 stram bg2 sulph bg2
- **infants**: acon bg2 ars bg2 **Cham** bg2 *Ip* bg2 lach bg2 mosch bg2 samb bg2

CHILL; during: acon bg2 anac bg2 apis bg2 arn bg2 **Ars** b4.de* bov bg2 bry bg2 caps bg2 chin bg2 *Cina* bg2 *Ferr* bg2 *Ign* bg2 *Ip* bg2 **Kali-c** b4a.de* lach bg2 lyc bg2 **Mez** b4.de* nat-m b4.de* nux-m bg2 *Nux-v* bg2 phos bg2 **Puls** bg2 *Rhus-t* bg2 **Seneg** b4a.de* sep bg2 stram bg2 sulph bg2 verat bg2 *Zinc* b4a.de*

CHRONIC OBSTRUCTIVE PULMONARY DISORDER (See CHEST - Emphysema; CHEST - Fibrosis; CHEST - Sarcoidosis)

CLOSING the eyes agg.: carb-an ptk1 *Carb-v* ptk1

CLOTHING:
- **agg.**: ars ptk1 chel ptk1 lach ptk1
- **loosening** of | **amel.**: apis bg2 caps b7.de* nux-v b7.de* sars b4a.de* stann b4a.de*

COAL GAS; from: bov b4a.de

COFFEE:
- **agg.**: bell b4.de* caps bg2 *Cham* b7.de* cocc b7.de* ip b7.de* nux-v b7.de*
- **amel.**: *Ars* b4a.de

COITION agg.; during: ambr bg2* asaf b7a.de* cedr ptk1 con bg2 dig ptk1 kali-bi bg2 phos ptk1 staph b7.de*

COLD:
- **air** agg.: *Act-sp* bg2 *Ars* b4.de* bar-c bg2 bry b7a.de* *Calc* b4a.de carb-v bg2 dig bg2 *Hep* b4a.de *Ign* b7a.de *Lob* bg2 nux-v b7a.de petr b4a.de* puls bg2
- **drinks**:
  - **agg.**: ars bg2 thuj bg2
  - **amel.**: cupr bg2

COLD AGG.; BECOMING: **Mosch** b7a.de

COLD AGG.; TAKING A: *Acon* b7.de* apis b7a.de ars b4a.de* *Bell* bg2 *Bry* b7.de* cham b7.de* chin b7.de* *Cupr* b7a.de cycl b7.de* **Dulc** b4a.de* **Ip** b7.de* nux-m bg2 *Nux-v* b7.de* puls b7.de* rhus-t b7.de* samb b7.de* spong bg2 *Staph* b7.de*

COLDNESS of breath: acon ant-t bro1 ars bro1 asar bg2 **Camph** k* **Carb-v** k* carbn-o *Cedr* *Chin* k* chinin-s cist k* cocc-s bro1 colch *Cop* cor-r cupr bro1 euph-l bro1 *Helo* bg2* *Helo-s* c1* hyper k2 jatr-c bro1 merc mur-ac b2.de* *Phos* k* rhus-t k* sin-n bro1 *Tab* bro1 tell bg2 ter k* **Verat** k*
- **accompanied** by | **rattling** respiration and cold extremities (See Rattling - accompanied - cold)
- **chill**; during: **Carb-v** k* chin bg2 verat k*
- **inspiration** agg.: brom bg2
- **perspiration**; during: carb-v bg2 chin bg2 mur-ac bg2 *Rhus-t* bg2 **Verat** bg2

COMPANY agg.: arg-n bg2

COMPLAINTS of respiration: acon ptk1 *Ant-t* ptk1 *Apis* ptk1 **Ars** ptk1 *Bell* ptk1 bry ptk1 carb-v ptk1 cupr ptk1 dig ptk1 dros ptk1 grin ptk1 hep ptk1 ip ptk1 *Kali-c* ptk1 **Lach** ptk1 lob ptk1 *Lyc* ptk1 nat-s ptk1 **Op** ptk1 **Phos** ptk1 **Puls** ptk1 ran-b ptk1 *Samb* ptk1 **Spong** ptk1 stann ptk1 **Sulph** ptk1 tarent ptk1 vib ptk1
- **accompanied** by:
  - **anger** (See MIND - Anger - respiration)
  - **coition**; desire for: nat-c bg2
  - **coldness**; general sensation of (See GENERALS - Heat - lack - accompanied - respiration - complaints)
  - **emotions** (See MIND - Emotions - respiration)
  - **heat**; general sensation of: anac bg2 ant-t bg2 plat bg2
  - **hysteria** (See MIND - Hysteria - respiration)
  - **miliaria** rubra: *Bar-c* b4a.de
  - **nausea**: canth bg2 cham bg2 hyos bg2 lach bg2 lob ptk1 petr bg2 rhus-t bg2 samb bg2 sang bg2
  - **palpitations** (See CHEST - Palpitation - accompanied - respiration - complaints)
  - **perspiration**: m-arct b7.de samb ptk1
  - **short** respiration: sec bg2
  - **sighing** (See MIND - Sighing - respiration)
  - **thirst** (See STOMACH - Thirst - accompanied - respiration)
  - **urination**; complaints of: con bg2
  - **vertigo**: cham bg2 puls bg2
  - **weakness**; general (See GENERALS - Weakness - accompanied - respiration - complaints)

Respiration

- **accompanied** by: ...
  - ○ **Abdomen**; complaints of: am-m bg2 ars bg2 caps bg2 *Carb-v* bg2 cham bg2 chin bg2 cocc bg2 ign bg2 kali-c bg2 kreos bg2 lach bg2 lyc b4a.de* mez b4a.de* mosch bg2 prun bg2 **Puls** bg2 rhod b4a.de* staph bg2 *Sulph* bg2
  - **Chest**:
    - **congestion** (See CHEST - Congestion - accompanied - respiration)
    - **pain** (See CHEST - Pain - accompanied - respiration - complaints)
    - **pain** in sides (See CHEST - Pain - sides - accompanied - respiration)
    - **tightness** (See CHEST - Constriction - accompanied - respiration - complaints)
  - **Ears**; noises in: nux-v bg2 *Puls* bg2
  - **Epigastrium**:
    - **complaints** of: *Ars* ptk1 chin ptk1 cocc ptk1 guaj ptk1 lach ptk1 nat-m ptk1 *Phos* ptk1 rhus-t ptk1 sulph ptk1
    - **pain** in (See STOMACH - Pain - epigastrium - accompanied - respiration)
  - **Face**:
    - **cyanotic**: ant-t mrr1 brom tl1
    - **heat**: kreos bg2 puls bg2 stront-c bg2
  - **Head**; pain in: ferr bg2
  - **Heart**; complaints of (See CHEST - Heart; complaints - accompanied - respiration - complaints)
  - **Hypochondria**; pain in (See ABDOMEN - Pain - hypochondria - accompanied - respiration)
  - **Lips**; red discoloration of: spig bg2*
  - **Liver**; pain in: ran-b bg2 sep bg2
  - **Lumbar** region; pain in: **Nux-v** bg2 *Puls* bg2 sel bg2
  - **Nose**; dry: canth bg2
  - **Pupils**; dilated: *Bell* bg2 **Calc** bg2 mosch bg2
  - **Rectum**; pain in: nux-v bg2
  - **Scapulae**; pain in: petr bg2 puls bg2 rhus-t bg2 sars bg2 sep bg2
  - **Spleen**; complaints of (See ABDOMEN - Spleen - accompanied - respiration)
  - **Stomach**; complaints of: *Ars* ptk1 chin ptk1 cocc ptk1 guaj ptk1 lach ptk1 nat-m ptk1 *Phos* ptk1 rhus-t ptk1 sulph ptk1
  - **Teeth**; complaints of: ars b4a.de *Nat-m* b4a.de *Puls* b7a.de sep b4a.de
  - **Tongue**; red discoloration of: mosch bg2*
- **alternating** with:
  - **convulsions**: *Ign* b7a.de
  - **cough**: ant-t ptk1
  - **diarrhea**: *Rhus-t* b7a.de
  - **eruptions**: *Calad* b7a.de crot-t lach *Rhus-t* b7a.de
  - ○ **Head**; pain in (See HEAD - Pain - alternating - respiration)
  - **Skin**; complaints of: calad bg2
- **weeping**; with (See MIND - Weeping - respiration - complaints)

CONVULSIVE (See Paroxysmal)

COPD (See Chronic)

COPPER agg.; fumes of: ars bg2 camph bg2 **Hep** bg2 *Ip* bg2 merc b4a.de*

CORYZA:
- **after**: ant-t bg2 *Ars* bg2 **Camph** bg2 carb-v bg2
- **suppressed**: *Ars* b4a.de* bry b7a.de* **Ip** b7a.de* nux-v b7a.de* puls bg2 sulph bg2

COUGH:
- **after**:
  - **agg.**: ars bg2 *Cupr* b7a.de ferr b7.de* merc bg2
  - **amel.**: *Ant-t* b7a.de m-ambo b7.de *Nux-v* b7a.de
- **before** | **agg.**: ant-t ptk1 caust ptk1 led b7.de*

Cough: ...
- **during** | **agg.**: am-m ptk1 ant-t bg2* ars bg2* asar bg2 bry bg2 cocc bg2 *Con* bg2 **Cupr** bg2* **Dros** bg2* *Ip* bg2* just ptk1 kali-bi bg2 lach bg2 *Meph* bg2 merc-cy ptk1 mez bg2 mosch bg2 naja ptk1 *Nux-v* bg2* op ptk1 petr bg2 *Phos* ptk1 **Puls** bg2 *Rhus-t* bg2 sil bg2 spig bg2 stann ptk1 tarent ptk1 tub ptk1 *Verat* bg2

COVERING agg.: *Lach* b7.de*

COVERING THE MOUTH OR NOSE agg.: arg-n ptk1 cupr ptk1 lach bg2*

CRACKLING: ant-t bg2 bell bg2 carb-an bg2 carb-v bg2 caust bg2 cupr bg2 hep bg2 hyos bg2 ip bg2 laur bg2 nat-m bg2 puls bg2 samb bg2 sep bg2 sil bg2 squil bg2

CROAKING: (↗*Rough - crowing)* am-caust a1 cham lach [bell-p-sp dcm1]

CROWING (See Rough - crowing)

DANCING; after:
- **agg.**: spong b7.de*
- **alternating** with | **jumping**: bell bg2

DEEP: *Acon* k* *Agar* k* *Ail* am-c b2.de* am-m k* ant-c k* ant-t k* **Arg-n** k* arn k* ars **Aur** k* bar-c k* bar-m bell k* borx k* bov *Brom* k* **Bry** k* *Cact* *Calc* k* calc-p k* calc-sil k2 *Camph* k* cann-i c1 cann-s k* **Caps** k* carb-v k* carl a1 *Castm* *Caust* cham k* chel chin k* chinin-ar chlor k* choc srj3• cic k* cimx coca ptk1 cocc b2.de* colch croc k* *Cupr* k* *Dig* k* dros k* euon k* *Euph* k* fl-ac k* gamb glon k* hell k* **Hep** k* *Hydr-ac* k* hyos k* ictod **Ign** k* *Ind* **Ip** k* kali-ar kali-c k* kali-m k2 kreos k* **Lach** k* lachn lact laur k* lil-t bg3* lob k* *Lyc* k* m-arct b2.de m-aust b2.de* mag-c h2* merc k* mez k* mosch b2.de* *Mur-ac* k* nat-ar nat-c k* nat-m k* **Nat-s** k* nicc k* nux-m b2.de* nux-v k* *Olib-sac* wmh1 olnd k* **Op** k* ox-ac k* par k* **Phos** k* *Plat* k* plb b2.de* podo prun puls b2.de* *Ran-b* k* ran-s k* *Rhus-t* k* sabin b2.de* sars k* *Sec* k* **Sel** k* seneg b2.de* **Sil** k* spig k* spong k* squil k* stann k* *Stram* k* stry sul-ac k* *Sulph* k* tab k* ther thuj k* *Zinc* k* [spect dfg1]
- **evening**: eupi k* *Ran-b*
- **night**:
  - **midnight** | **waking**; on: cann-i k*
- **abdomen**, from: alumn k* cann-s k*
- **amel.**: acon asaf aur-m-n wbt2• bar-c *Cann-i* caps ptk1 chin *Colch* *Cupr* k* dig dros *Ign* k* iod kali-p fd1.de• *Lach* meny olnd osm plut-n srj7• puls rhus-t h1 *Seneg* k* sep *Spig* k* **Stann** k* staph sulph ptk1 ter viol-t
- **chill**; during: bry bg2 caps bg2 cimx ip bg2 *Ph-ac* bg2
- **convulsion**; during: op bro1
- **desire** to breathe: acet-ac acon k* adon vh1 agar bg2* alum k* alum-p k2 alumn am-br k* aml-ns bg2 androc srj1• anh sp1 ant-c sf apis bg2 arg-n ptk1 *Aur* k* *Aur-m-n* wbt2• bapt k* bit-ar wht1• *Borx* brass-n-o srj5• brom k* **Bry** k* **Cact** k* **Calc** k* *Calc-p* k* camph sf cann-i sf *Caps* k* *Carb-ac* k* *Carb-v* k* carc fb* *Card-m* k* *Caust* k* cedr k* *Chin* k* chir-fl gya2 cimx clem a1 coca croc k* *Crot-t* **Cupr** b7.de* cypra-eg sde6.de• *Dig* k* euon eup-per *Glon* k* hell b7.de* hep c1 hydr k* *Hydr-ac* bg1* iber hr1 ictod **Ign** k* *Ind* k* *Ip* bg2* irid-met srj5• kali-bi bg2 *Kali-c* *Kali-n* bg2* kali-p fd1.de• kola stb3• *Kreos* k* **Lach** k* *Lact* laur b7.de* lil-t k* lob bg2* *Lyc* m-arct b7.de mag-p bg2 malar jl2 med hr1* *Merc* k* mez k* mosch k* **Nat-s** k* nux-m k* olib-sac wmh1 op bg2* ozone sde2• *Par* *Phos* k* plan bg1 *Plat* bg2 podo k* prun ran-b k* rauw sp1 rhus-t b7.de* sabin b7.de* sacch-a fd2.de• samb k* *Sang* k* **Sel** k* *Seneg* k* sep k* sil bg2* squil b7.de* stann k* stram k* stroph-s sp1 sulfa sp1 **Sulph** k* tab bg2 ther k* trios rsj11• tub c1* vanil fd5.de verb xan k* [tax jsj7]
  - **accompanied** by | **Head**; heat of (See HEAD - Heat - accompanied - breath)
  - **chill**; during: cimx
  - **dinner**; after: hep h2*
  - **lying** agg.: *Ind* k*
  - **oppression** in stomach, with: nat-m h2*
- **dinner**; before: chin k* rhus-t k*
- **eating**; after: ant-c h2* hep b4a.de rhus-t h1* sars
- **epileptic** convulsions; after: ign gk
- **fever**; during: aur bg2 *Borx* b4a.de* bry bg2 caps bg2 cupr bg2 ip bg2 mur-ac bg2 op bg2 *Ph-ac* b4.de* plat bg2 sel bg2 sil bg2 stann bg2
- **heart**, from heaviness at: *Adon* vh1 croc
- **heat**; with: ph-ac h2*

- **impossible**: alumn ambr h1* ant-c apoc vh **Ars** k* ars-i sne *Aur* aur-m-n wbt2• bry calc-p *Caps* hr1 *Cocc* *Crot-t* dig euph h2* euphr ferr kali-cy mtf11 kali-n h2* lach bg1 *Lob* morph plat sep h2* sil h2* stann sulph
- **lying** | **back**; on | **amel**.: ind
  - **side**; on:
    - **left** | **agg**.: ind
- **lying** down agg.: *Ind* k*
- **menses**; before: sulph
- **oppression** in epigastrium, from: bell h1*
- **perspiration**; during: *Bry* bg2 ip bg2 *Op* bg2 **Ph-ac** bg2 *Phos* bg2 ran-b bg2 *Sel* bg2 sil bg2 stram bg2
- **running**; after: *Hep* k*
- **sitting** agg.: cic lach k*
- **sleep** agg.; during: ign
- **slow**, wheezing: sep
- **walking** agg.: bell h1*
- **writing** agg.: fl-ac

DENTITION; during: | **agg**.: cham b7.de* ign b7.de* ip b7.de* op b7.de*

DESCENDING agg.: *Borx* bg2

DIFFICULT: (↗*Abdominal; Accelerated; Asthmatic*) abies-c br1 abies-n k* abrot absin acet-ac k* *Acetan* br1* *Acon* k* *Acon-f* bro1 adon mtf11 adren bro1 *Aeth* k* *Agar* k* *Agath-a* nl2• *Agn* aids nl2• ail *All-c* bro1 all-s allox tpw4* aloe alum k* alum-sil k2 alumn *Am-c* k* am-m k* *Ambr* k* aml-ns bro1 **Anac** k* ancis-p tsm2 ang b7.de* anh br1 *Ant-ar* k* *Ant-c* k* ant-i bro1 **Ant-t** k* **Apis** k* apoc k* *Aral* k* arg-met k* *Arg-n* k* arge-pl rwt5• *Arn* k* **Ars** k* *Ars-i* k* ars-s-f k2* arum-t arund *Asaf* k* *Asar* k* *Asc-t* aspar astac atra-r bnm3• *Aur* k* aur-ar k2 aur-i k2 aur-m aur-m-n aur-s k* *Bac* br1* *Bad* bar-c k* bar-i k2 *Bar-m* bar-ox-suc mtf11 *Bell* k* *Benz-ac* beryl sp1 bism k* *Blatta-o* k* borx both tsm2 both-ax tsm2 botul br1 *Bov* k* brass-n-o srj5• *Brom* k* bros-gau mrc1 **Bry** k* bufo bung-fa tsm2 buth-a sp1 **Cact** k* cadm-met sp1 cain caj bro1 calad k* *Calc* k* *Calc-ar* k* *Calc-f* calc-i k2 *Calc-p* *Calc-s* calc-sil k2 *Camph* k* cann-i k* cann-s k* canth k* *Caps* k* carb-ac k* carb-an k* **Carb-v** k* *Carbn-o* *Carbn-s* *Carl* cassia-s ccrh1*• castm **Caust** k* *Cedr* *Cench* k* *Cham* k* **Chel** k* chen-a **Chin** k* *Chinin-ar* *Chinin-s* chir-fl bnm4• chlam-tr bcx2• chlol **Chlor** k* chord-umb rly4• *Cic* k* cimic *Cimx* **Cina** k* cist *Coc-c* *Coca* k* *Cocc* k* coff k* *Colch* k* coll k* *Coloc* k* *Con* k* conv br1* cop cor-r k* cordyc mp4• cortiso sp1 cot br1 *Crat* bro1 croc k* *Crot-c* *Crot-h* **Crot-t** k* *Cub* **Cupr** k* cupr-act nh6* **Cupr-ar** k* cupr-n a1 cupr-s cur k* *Cycl* k* cyt-l sp1 dendr-pol tsm2 *Dig* k* dios bro1 diph-pert-t mp4• diph-t-tpt jl2 diphtox jl2 dirc dream-p sdj1• *Dros* k* *Dulc* k* dys pte1*• eberth jl2 elaps tsm2 ephe mtf11 equis-h ery-a eup-per euph k* euphr k* falco-ch sze4• **Ferr** k* *Ferr-ar* *Ferr-i* *Ferr-p* k* *Fl-ac* k* foll mtf11 *Formal* bro1 fuma-ac rly4• galla-q-r nl2• gard-j vlr2• *Gels* ger-i rly4• gins *Glon* k* *Graph* k* *Grin* k* *Guaj* k* ham *Hell* k* helo ptk1 helodr-cal knl2• **Hep** k* hippoz k* hist sp1* hura hura-c a1 hydr hydr-ac k* hydrc hydrog srj2• hydroph rsj6• hyos k* hyper ictod bro1 *Ign* k* indg *Iod* k* **Ip** k* irid-met srj5• *Iris* ix bnm8• jab jatr-c jug-c *Just* bro1 **Kali-ar** k* *Kali-bi* k* kali-br a1 **Kali-c** k* *Kali-chl* **Kali-i** k* kali-m k2* kali-n k* *Kali-p* *Kali-s* kali-sil k2 kali-sula a1* *Kalm* k* ketogl-ac rly4• kreos k* lac-c lac-e hrn2• **Lach** k* *Lact* lat-h bnm5• *Lat-m* k* *Laur* k* lavand-a ctl1• lec br1 led k* *Lil-t* k* limest-b es1• *Lith-c* **Lob** k* lob-e c1 loxo-lae bnm12• loxo-recl bnm10• luna kg1• **Lyc** k* *Lycps-v* k* *Lyss* *M-ambo* b7.de* m-arct b7.de *M-aust* b7.de mag-c k* mag-m k* mag-s k* malar jl2 manc mand sp1 mang *Med* k* meli k* meny k* **Meph** k* *Merc* k* **Merc-c** k* *Merc-cy* br1* *Merc-pr-r* bro1 *Merc-sul* k* merl *Mez* k* moni rfm1• morg-g pte1*• morg-p pte1*• morph k* *Mosch* k* mucor jl2 *Mur-ac* k* murx musca-d szs1 mygal **Naja** k* *Naphtin* bro1 nat-ar k* *Nat-c* k* nat-f sp1 *Nat-m* k* nat-n mtf11 *Nat-p* **Nat-s** k* nat-sil fd3.de• nicc nicc-met sk4• nicotam rly4• *Nit-ac* k* **Nux-m** k* *Nux-v* k* oena ol-j *Olib-sac* wmh1 **Op** k* osm *Ox-ac* oxyd br1 oxyurn-sc mcp1• ozone sde2• p-benzq mtf11 par k* petr k* petr-ra shn4• *Ph-ac* k* phel **Phos** k* *Phos-pchl* c1 *Phys* physala-p bnm7• *Phyt* k* pin-con oss2• pitu-gl skp7• plac rzf5• *Plat* k* *Plb* k* plut-n srj7• podo polys sk4• *Positr* nl2• prot pte1* *Prun* k* pseuts-m oss1• *Psor* k* ptel pulm-v bro1 **Puls** k* pycnop-sa mrz1 *Queb* bro1 *Ran-b* k* ran-s k* raph rat rauw tpw8* rheum k* rhod k* rhus-g tmo3• *Rhus-t* k* rumx k* ruta k* sabad k* sabin k* sal-fr sle1• *Samb* k* *Sang* k* sarcol-ac sp1 sarr sars k* scol a1* *Sec* k* **Sel** k* senec bro1 *Seneg* k* *Sep* k* ser-ang bro1 **Sil** k* sinus rly4• *Spig* k* **Spong** k* **Squil** k* **Stann** k* staph k* *Stram* k* stront-c b4.de* *Stroph-h* bro1 stroph-s sp1 **Stry** k* suis-pan rly4• sul-ac k* sul-i k2 sulfa sp1 **Sulph** k* *Sumb* ptk1 suprar rly4• syc fmm1• syph k2 *Tab* k* tarax b7.de* **Tarent** k* tax *Ter* thal-xyz srj8• thiam rly4• thuj k* thymol sp1 til ban1• *Toxo-g* jl2 trad a1* trif-p bro1 tril-p c1 trinit br1 tritic-vg fd5.de *Tub* k* tub-a jl2 tub-r jl2 tung-met bdx1• uva br1 vac jl2 valer k* vanil fd5.de **Verat** k*

Difficult: ...
verat-v k* vero-o rly4*• vesp vib ptk1 viol-o k* viol-t b7a.de vip visc bro1* xan c1 yers jl2 *Zinc* k* zinc-p k2 zing [*Buteo-j* sej6 calc-br stj1 heroin sdj2 mag-br stj1 **Spect** dfg1]

- **daytime**: *Chel*
- **morning**: ambr ant-t k* aur bell k* *Brom* k* carb-an carb-v cassia-s ccrh1• *Caust* k* chel k* *Con* k* *Dig* k* euphr k2 *Kali-bi* k* *Kali-c* k* kali-chl k* kali-i *Lach* k* lyc k* mang h2* merc k* nat-s bro1 nicc-met sk4• nit-ac k* *Nux-v* k* petr-ra shn4• *Phos* k* puls k* rhod k* *Sang* k* *Sep* k* *Sil* k* sulph h2* tritic-vg fd5.de
  - **8** h: dios
  - **bed** agg.; in: alum ant-t carb-an com k* con k* led mag-s nat-c h2 nux-v k* puls sulph
  - **chest**, from anxiety in: puls k*
  - **exertion** agg.: lyc k*
  - **expectoration** | **amel**.: *Sep*
  - **rising**:
    - **after**:
      - **agg**.: bell k* carb-v h2* caust h2* (non:con kl) dig k* ran-b
      - **amel**.: con h2 led puls sulph
    - **agg**.: calc-p k* *Kali-bi*
  - **standing** agg.: con k*
  - **waking**; on: con kali-i nit-ac h2* seneg k* *Sep* sil k* tung-met bdx1•
- **forenoon**: alum bry chinin-ar dulc fd4.de hyper *Ip* nat-c *Nat-s* ox-ac sulph
  - **9** h: chel chin chinin-ar k2 nat-ar tarent valer
    - **breakfast** agg.; after: valer
  - **10** h: *Ferr* iod
  - **11** h: agar squil
  - **standing** agg.: kali-n
  - **walking**:
    - **agg**.: cocc
    - **air** agg.; in open: ferr
  - **writing** agg.: mag-s
- **noon**: gels k* hura tritic-vg fd5.de
- **afternoon**: act-sp bro1 all-s alumn *Ars* bro1 asar hr1 aur bro1 bapt k* bell k* cain bro1 calc bro1 carb-v bro1 chel k* dig k* dulc fd4.de elae a1 elaps *Fl-ac* k* *Lach* k* lyc *Merc-sul* k* nat-m k* op k* phos bro1 puls bro1 ruta fd4.de sabad *Samb* bro1 *Sang* k* sep bro1 spong fd4.de sulph k* trif-p bro1 tritic-vg fd5.de
  - **13** h: cact squil
  - **14** h: chel
  - **15** h | **running**; when: am-c lyc
  - **15**.30 h | **sitting** agg.: mag-c
  - **16** h: phos
    - **after**: polys sk4•
  - **17** h: med c1
    - **17**-19 h: nat-m k*
    - **sudden**: ign
- **evening**: acon k* aeth agath-a nl2• agn *All-c* k* anac ant-t *Ars* k* ars-s-f k2 bell k* *Calc-p* calc-s carb-an k* *Carb-v* k* *Carbn-s* cassia-s ccrh1• cench k2 *Chin* chinin-ar cist k* clem coloc con k* cycl dig digin a1 dulc fd4.de elaps *Ferr* k* ferr-ar ferr-p *Fl-ac* k* graph k* *Hell* k* hyper ip k* *Kali-ar* *Kali-c* kali-s *Lach* *Lob* mag-c h2* merc mez nat-m nux-m k* *Nux-v* k* oena a1 ox-ac k* petr k* *Phos* k* *Psor* k* *Puls* k* *Ran-b* k* raph k* rhod k* *Rhus-t* ruta fd4.de sep k* spong fd4.de *Stann* **Sulph** k* tritic-vg fd5.de verb *Zinc* zinc-p k2
  - **18** h: bapt mag-c **Rhus-t** k*
    - **18**-21 h: castm
  - **18**.30 h: chel
  - **21** h: androc srj1• bry
  - **amel**.: lyc
  - **bed**:
    - **in** bed:
      - **agg**.: am-c h2* ant-t *Ars* k* bell h1* borx carb-an *Carb-v* k* chin *Cist* k* con k* crot-h k* *Ferr* k* *Graph* merc k* nat-m *Nat-s* par k* *Phos* k* podo *Sep* k* sul-ac h2* *Sulph* k* zinc
      - **amel**.: *Chel*

- **night**: acon aeth$_{mtf33}$ agath-a$_{nl2}$• alum alum-p$_{k2}$ am-c am-m androc$_{srj1}$• *Ant-t*$_{k*}$ apis arg-n **Ars**$_{k*}$ ars-i ars-s-f$_{k2}$ arum-d$_{ptk2}$ asar aspar *Aur* aur-ar$_{k2}$ aur-i$_{k2}$ aur-m aur-s *Bac*$_{br1}$ bapt$_{a1}$ bar-c bar-i$_{k2}$ bar-s$_{k2}$ bell berb brom bry bufo cact *Calc* calc-i$_{k2}$ calc-s cann-i carb-ac carb-an$_{h2}$ *Carb-v* **Carbn-s** cassia-s$_{ccrh1}$• castm *Cench* cham chel *Chin* *Chinin-ar* *Coca* *Colch* coloc con *Crot-t* cupr$_{k*}$ daph *Dig*$_{k*}$ dros$_{gk}$ dulc$_{fd4.de}$ elaps *Ferr* ferr-ar *Ferr-i* *Ferr-p* flav$_{jl2}$ *Graph* *Guaj* ign *Iod* *Ip* **Kali-ar** *Kali-bi* *Kali-c* kali-i kali-p kali-s **Lach**$_{k*}$ lact *Lob* *Lyc* mag-s mang-p$_{rly4}$• med merc morg-p$_{fmm1}$• **Naja**$_{k*}$ nat-c nat-m nit-ac *Nux-v* *Op* petr petr-ra$_{shn4}$• ph-ac **Phos**$_{k*}$ plb podo *Psor* *Puls*$_{k*}$ ran-b ran-s *Rhus-t* sal-fr$_{sle1}$• **Samb**$_{k*}$ sang$_{hr1}$ sel seneg *Sep* *Spong*$_{k*}$ *Stann* stict stront-c$_{br1}$ *Sul-ac* sul-i$_{k2}$ **Sulph**$_{k*}$ syph$_{jl2}$ *Ter* *Thuj* tritic-vg$_{fd5.de}$ *Tub* zinc zinc-p$_{k2}$ zing
  - **midnight**:
    - **before**: coloc ham$_{fd3.de}$• *Squil*
      - **22** h: ip *Phos* phys valer
        - **22-10** h: ip
      - **23** h: cact nat-m spong$_{k2}$ *Squil* [tax$_{jsj7}$]
        - **23-3** h: colch
    - **at**: *Acon* aral$_{vh1}$ **Ars**$_{k*}$ calc *Chin* puls *Rhus-t*
    - **after**: **Ars**$_{k*}$ *Dros*$_{k*}$ ferr *Graph* ham$_{fd3.de}$• lyc nat-sil$_{fd3.de}$• psor$_{al2}$ **Samb**$_{k*}$ *Spong*$_{k*}$
      - **1** h:
        - **1-2** h: ars$_{k2}$ *Spong*
        - **1-4** h: *Syph*$_{k*}$
      - **2** h: **Ars**$_{k*}$ flav$_{jl2}$ *Kali-bi* med$_{c1}$ rumx
        - **2-3** h: **Kali-ar** **Kali-c**
      - **3** h: am-c **Ant-t**$_{k*}$ bufo cupr **Kali-c**$_{k*}$ nat-m **Samb**$_{k*}$
      - **4** h: kali-bi lil-t
        - **until** 4 h; frequent attacks: **Samb**$_{k*}$
      - **5** h: ham$_{fd3.de}$• kali-i
      - **waking**; on: arund cann-i sil$_{h2}$
  - **bed**:
    - **in** bed:
      - **agg.**: ant-t$_{tl1}$ apis **Ars**$_{k*}$ calc-ar$_{k2}$ *Graph* plb sal-fr$_{sle1}$• sep$_{gk}$ spong$_{k*}$
      - **amel.**: *Chel*
- **abortion**; during: puls$_{bro1}$
- **accompanied** by:
  - **anemia** (See GENERALS - Anemia - accompanied - respiration)
  - **bronchopneumonia** (See CHEST - Inflammation - lungs - accompanied - breathlessness)
  - **coryza**: aral$_{pd}$ ars$_{ptk1}$ ars-i$_{ptk1}$ calc$_{ptk1}$ ip$_{ptk1}$ kali-i$_{pd*}$ m-aust$_{b7a.de}$ mang$_{h2*}$ naja$_{pd}$ nat-m$_{h2*}$ nit-ac$_{h2*}$ nux-v$_{pd}$ phos$_{ptk1}$ *Rhus-t*$_{b7a.de}$ samb$_{bat1}$• stict$_{pd}$ sulph$_{ptk1}$
  - **cough**: acon all-s **Alum**$_{k*}$ alum-sil$_{k2}$ am-c am-m ambr$_{hr1}$ anac$_{k*}$ **Ant-t** aral arg-n$_{hr1}$ arn **Ars** *Ars-i* aspar bamb-a$_{stb2.de}$• bar-c bar-m *Bell* *Blatta-o*$_{br1}$ brom$_{k*}$ bry$_{k*}$ calad calc calc-p$_{k*}$ calc-s calc-sil$_{k2}$ carb-an$_{h*}$ *Carb-v* carbn-s$_{k2}$ *Caust*$_{k*}$ cench$_{k2}$ chin chinin-ar *Cina* coc-c con$_{k*}$ cop$_{hr1}$ cor-r **Cupr**$_{k*}$ dig$_{k*}$ dol **Dros** eup-per euphr$_{k*}$ *Ferr*$_{k*}$ ferr-ar ferr-p guaj *Hep* hydr-ac ign **Ip**$_{k*}$ kali-ar *Kali-bi*$_{k*}$ kali-c kali-n$_{h*}$ *Kali-s* kali-sil$_{k2}$ *Kreos* lac-c *Lach* lachn$_{bg1}$ lact laur led lob *Lyc*$_{k*}$ merc$_{k*}$ mez mur-ac$_{k*}$ nat-m *Nat-s* nicc nit-ac *Nux-m*$_{k*}$ **Nux-v** **Op** phel$_{k*}$ **Phos**$_{k*}$ pycnop-sa$_{mrz1}$ rhus-t samb$_{k*}$ *Sep* *Sil* spig spong squil **Stann**$_{k*}$ sul-ac sulph syc$_{fmm1}$• tub$_{bg}$ viol-o visc$_{sp1}$ zinc zing$_{a1}$
  - **croup** (See LARYNX - Croup - accompanied - respiration)
  - **diphtheria**: apis$_{tl1}$
  - **dropsy** (See GENERALS - Dropsy - general - accompanied - respiration)
  - **eructation** (See STOMACH - Eructations - accompanied - dyspnea)
  - **fever**; intense: diph$_{mtf11}$
  - **heat**; lack of vital (See GENERALS - Heat - lack - accompanied - respiration)
  - **menses**; absent: ars-i$_{br1}$
  - **mental** symptoms (See MIND - Respiration)
  - **nausea**: cham$_{bg2}$ ip$_{ptk1}$ kali-n$_{ptk1}$ lac-ac$_{stj5}$•

- **accompanied** by: ...
  - **obesity**: am-c$_{br1}$
  - **palpitations** (See palpitations)
  - **perspiration**: bapt$_{ptk1}$
  - **pricking**: lob$_{ptk1}$
  - **salivation**; increased: lob$_{ptk1}$
  - **stool**; loose: lycps-v$_{mrr1}$
  - **ulcers**: kali-n$_{ptk1}$
  - **uremia** (See GENERALS - Uremia - accompanied - respiration)
  - **urinary** and heart complaints (See BLADDER - Urinary - accompanied - heart)
  - **urine** | **albuminous** (See URINE - Albuminous - accompanied - respiration)
  - **urticaria**: apis$_{ptk1}$
  - **vertigo**: acon$_{b7.de*}$ cur$_{bg2}$ kali-c$_{ptk1}$ lac-ac$_{stj5}$• laur$_{bg2}$
  - ○ **Back**; pain in: ozone$_{sde2}$• polys$_{sk4}$•
  - **Brain** congestion: cimic$_{tl1}$
  - **Chest**:
    - **catarrh** (See CHEST - Catarrh - accompanied - respiration)
    - **constriction** (See CHEST - Constriction - accompanied - respiration)
    - **oppression** (See CHEST - Oppression - respiration - difficult)
    - **pain** (See CHEST - Pain - accompanied - respiration)
  - **Face**:
    - **heat**: kreos$_{bg2}$ puls$_{bg2}$ stront-c$_{b4a.de*}$
    - **redness**: phos$_{bg2}$ spig$_{bg2}$
  - **Head**; complaints of (See HEAD - Complaints - accompanied - respiration)
  - **Heart**:
    - **complaints** of the heart (See CHEST - Heart; complaints - accompanied - respiration)
    - **dropsy** (See CHEST - Dropsy - cardiac - dyspnea)
    - **pain** in the heart (See CHEST - Pain - heart - accompanied - respiration)
    - **weakness** of (See CHEST - Weakness - heart - accompanied - respiration)
  - **Kidneys**; inflammation of (See KIDNEYS - Inflammation - accompanied - respiration)
  - **Lips**:
    - **cyanotic** (See Complaints - accompanied - face)
    - **red** discoloration of: spig$_{ptk1}$
  - **Lower** limbs; complaints of: thuj$_{bg2}$
  - **Lungs**; cancer of the: | **Heart**; weakness of (See CHEST - Weakness - heart - accompanied - lungs - cancer - dyspnea)
  - **Mouth**; complaints of: *Bell*$_{bg2}$ *Hep*$_{bg2}$ **Lach**$_{bg2}$
  - **Nose**; obstruction of (See NOSE - Obstruction - suffocating; NOSE - Obstruction - swelling)
  - **Ovary** and heart complaints; pain in left (See FEMALE - Pain - ovaries - accompanied - heart)
  - **Shoulders**; raised: ant-c$_{k*}$ (non:eup-per$_{hr1}$)
  - **Stomach**:
    - **complaints**: *Carb-v*$_{b4a.de}$ *Guaj*$_{b4a.de}$ *Kali-c*$_{b4a.de}$ *Rhod*$_{b4a.de}$ stann$_{b4a.de}$
    - **congestion**: grin$_{br1}$
    - **pain**: arg-n$_{ptk1}$
  - **Testes**; pain in: spong$_{mrr1}$
  - **Throat**; constriction in: bell$_{bg2}$ cham$_{bro1}$ cocc$_{bg2}$ dig$_{bg2}$ dros$_{bro1}$ *Hydr-ac*$_{bro1}$ lob$_{bro1}$ *Mosch*$_{bro1}$ sabad$_{bg2}$
- **air** agg.; draft of: lob$_{mrr1}$

- **air**; in open:
  - **agg.**: *Borx* caust crot-c dulc fd4.de phys plat **Psor** k* rhus-t sel seneg sulph
  - **amel.**: *(↗open - doors; open - window)* aeth mtf33 alum *Am-c* aml-ns vh1 **Apis** k* arg-n bg1 ars-i bapt bell *Bry Cact* calc bro1 cann-s k2 carbn-s k2 chel *Chinin-ar* cist dig fl-ac *Gels* graph gk *Ip Kali-i Kali-s* kola stb3• *Lach* k* lil-t **Nat-m** k* nicc-met sk4• nux-v psor al2 **Puls** k* *spong* fd4.de stram **Sulph** k* tarent mtf33 tritic-vg fd5.de *Tub* vanil fd5.de
- **alternating** with:
  - **convulsions**: plat pd*
  - **long** respiration: ign bg2
  - **metrorrhagia** (See FEMALE - Metrorrhagia - alternating - dyspnea)
  - **sleep**; deep: plb k*
  - **slow** respiration (See Slow - alternating - suffocation)
  - **sopor**: plb k*
  - **urticaria**: *Calad*
  - **uterine** hemorrhage: fl-ac
  - ○ **Hypochondria**; pain in: *Zinc*
- **anger**; after (See MIND - Anger - respiration)
- **anxiety**; from (See MIND - Anxiety - respiration; with)
- **arms** away from the body amel.; holding the: lach ptk1 laur ptk1 nux-v ptk1 psor hr1* spig ptk1 tarent ptk1
- **ascending**:
  - **agg.**: acet-ac k* agn aloe *Am-c* k* ang *Apis Arg-n* **Ars** k* *Ars-i* ars-s-f k2 arund k* aspar k* aur aur-ar k2 aur-i k2 *Aur-m* aur-s k2 bar-c k* bar-i k2 bar-m k2 bar-s k2 berb k* beryl tpw5 *Borx* k* *Brom* bros-gau mrc1 bufo *Cact* k* **Calc** k* **Calc-ar** calc-i k2 calc-p k2 calc-s calc-sil k2 cann-i canth *Caps Carb-ac* k* carbn-s carl k* castm chinin-ar bro1 cist *Clem* k* coc-c k2 **Coca** crot-t k* cupr dirc k* *Elaps* ferr k2 gaba sa3• glon k2 glycyr-g cte1• graph k* grat helx gm1 hyos iber hr1* *Iod* k* **Ip** k* irid-met srj5• kali-ar k2 kali-c k2 kali-n k* *Kali-p* k* led k* lil-t *Lob* k* *Lyc Lycps-v* mag-m h2* **Merc** k* nat-ar **Nat-m** k* *Nat-s* nat-sil fd3.de• **Nit-ac** k* nux-v ol-an petr k* *Pic-ac Plb* k* positr nl2• puls ran-b rat rauw tpw8 *Rhus-t* k* *Ruta Sars* k* *Seneg* k* sep k* spig k* *Spong* squil k* *Stann* k* sul-i k2 sulph tab k* ter hr1 tere-la rly4• ther k* thuj k* til k* tritic-vg fd5.de vanil fd5.de zinc
  - **stairs** | **agg.**: iod br1
- **athletics**, in: coca ptk1
- **autumn** agg.: chin
- **bathing**; while: petr-ra shn4•
- **beer**; after: cocc graph gk
- **bending**:
  - **arms** | **backward** agg.: **Sulph** k*
  - **backward**:
    - **agg.**: apis cupr k* psor *Sulph* nh6
    - **amel.**: cupr fl-ac
  - **forward**:
    - **agg.**: apis seneg *Spig*
    - **amel.**: *Arg-n* hr1 *Ars* k* *Cench* coc-c colch *Kali-bi Kali-c* k* *Lach Spong* k*
  - **head**:
    - **backward**:
      - **agg.**: bell cham hep bg1
      - **amel.**: spong mrr1
      - **must** rise up and bend head backward: hep k*
    - **forward** | **amel.**: sep bg1 tritic-vg fd5.de
  - **shoulders**:
    - **backward** | **amel.**: calc bro1* calc-act ptk1
- **blow**; as from a: sal-fr sle1•
- **breakfast** | **amel.**: sulph h2*
- **breathing**:
  - **deep**:
    - **agg.**: phos thuj ptk1
    - **amel.**: ham fd3.de• seneg mrr1 spong fd4.de sulph bg1 tritic-vg fd5.de
  - **last**; as if the next would be the: apis k* helo-s rwt2•
- **breathing**: ...
  - **want** of breath (See Arrested)
- **chest** muscles fail to act; as if: vib tl1
- **children**; in: *Ambr* k* *Ant-t* mrr1 calc calc-p **Ip** mtf33 lyc k* med k2 **Nat-s** *Op* wbt• *Puls* k* samb bro1 thuj mtf33
  - **newborns**: *(↗Asphyxia - children)* ant-t mrr1 laur mrr1
- **chill**; during: ant-t bg2 **Apis** k* arg-n bro1* ars k* bry caps b7.de cimx con bg2 gels gins guare hep bg2 ign b7a.de* ip bg2 kali-c k* mag-p bro1* mez *Nat-m* k* nux-m k* nux-v k* puls k* seneg sep h2* stram b7.de *Thuj* zinc
- **closing** the eyes agg.: ang hr1 carb-an k* *Carb-v*
- **clothes**:
  - **loosening** clothes: *(↗Impeded - pressure - clothes)*
    - **amel.**: *(↗Impeded - pressure - clothes)* aur-m k2* *Caust* a3 lach mrr1 **Nux-v** h1* stann h2* **Sulph** a1
      - **neckcloth** amel.; loosening: ham a1 sars bg2
- **coffee** agg.: *Bell* k* *Cham* dig digin a1
- **coition**:
  - **after**: ambr k2 arund c1 asaf b7a.de* *Cedr Dig* ph-ac b4a.de *Sep* b4a.de staph b7.de*
  - **during**: aeth *Ambr* k* arund k* asaf con sep *Staph* k*
  - **end** of; towards: *Staph* k*
- **cold**:
  - **air**:
    - **agg.**: *Act-sp* bg1* all-c k2 alum bg1 apis *Ars* aur graph **Lob** k* *Lyc Merc* nux-v petr puls sel seneg *Spong* sulph
    - **amel.**: *Am-c* k* apis mtf *Arg-n* k* bell *Bry* k* *Carb-v* k* *Carbn-s* cham cist graph gk ham fd3.de• *Kali-c* mtf kali-s mtf lac-c lach mtf *Med* mtf *Op* k* *Puls* k* spong fd4.de tritic-vg fd5.de tub mtf33 ust vanil fd5.de
  - **applications** | **agg.**: cassia-s ccrh1•
  - **drinks**:
    - **agg.**: cassia-s ccrh1•
    - **amel.**: lavand-a ctl1•
  - **food** | **agg.**: ars bg1
- **cold**; after taking a: acon bg2* ars bg2 arum-d ptk2 *Bell* bg2 carb-v k2 cham bg2 chin bg2 dulc k* ip k* *Kali-i* lob mrr1 puls k*
- **coma**; with (See MIND - Coma - respiration - difficult)
- **constriction**:
  - ○ **Diaphragm**; of: cact a1*
  - **Larynx**; of: **Apis** bell cocc **Crot-h** dros gk hell **Lach** ox-ac k2 sars spong tritic-vg fd5.de
  - **Stomach**; of: guaj k2
  - **Throat**-pit; at: cocc physala-p bnm7•
  - **Trachea**; of: petr spong fd4.de
- **contraction**; from | **Abdomen**; in: bry bg1 nat-s bg1*
- **convulsions**; during: glon k2 *Lyss* nux-v k2 *Op* stry tanac
  - **tetanic**: mill
- **coryza**; during: sep b4.de*
- **cough**:
  - **before**: caust h* cor-r br1 lyc h*
  - **during** | **agg.**: alumn nh6 am-c b4.de* *Ambr* b7a.de anac bg2 *Apis* b7a.de *Arn* b7.de* ars b4a.de* bell b4a.de *Bry* b7.de* carb-v b4.de* caust b4.de* cham b7a.de *Chin* b7a.de *Cina* b7a.de cocc b7.de* **Cupr** b7a.de dig b4.de* *Dros* b7a.de* euph b4.de* *Euphr* b7a.de ferr b7.de* guaj b4a.de iod b4a.de *Ip* b7.de* kali-bi bg2 *Kreos* b7a.de led b7.de* lyc b4a.de* m-arct b7.de m-aust b7a.de nat-m b4.de* *Nux-v* b7a.de ozone sde2• ph-ac b4a.de phos b4.de* *Puls* b7a.de rhod b4.de* rhus-t b7.de* sabad b7a.de *Samb* b7a.de seneg b4.de* sep b4.de* squil b7a.de* *Stann* nh6 sulph b4a.de* verat b7.de* zinc bg2
- **covering** nose or mouth: *(↗handkerchief)* am-c h2* *Arg-n* k* cupr bg3* *Lach* k*
- **crowded** room; in a: *Arg-n* k* dulc fd4.de lil-t br1*
- **dancing**: | **alternating** with jumping (See Dancing - alternating - jumping)
- **darkness** agg.: aeth carb-v gm1
- **diarrhea**, profuse: merc-sul c1
- **dinner**; after: chel nat-m *Nux-v Puls* sars

Respiration

- **diseased** conditions of distant parts not involved in act of breathing: berb ptk1 puls k*
- **dreams**:
  - **after** frightful: bapt a1 *Chel*
  - **during**: sang k* zinc h2*
- **dressing**; while: **Stann** k ●
- **drinking**:
  - **after** | **agg.**: *Mur-ac* hr1 nux-v k* thuj
  - **agg.**: anac k* apis bg2 *Arg-n* bell *Cimx* k* *Kali-c* k* kali-n k* lim bg1 meph nat-m plb squil bg2 thuj
  - **amel.**: lavand-a ctl1•
  - **cold** water | **agg.** | **heated**; when: *Kali-c*
    - **amel.**: cham
  - **diffcult**: squil k2
  - **impossible**: *Kali-n* mrr1
- **driving**; when: falco-pe nl2•
- **dust**, as from: agath-a nl2• **Ars** k* aur-m bell *Brom Calc* k* cassia-s ccrh1*• cycl *Hep* k* ip nux-v petr-ra shn4• phos podo fd3.de• **Sil** k* sulph
- **eating**:
  - **after** | **agg.**: allox tpw4* *Anac* k* ant-ar ant-c k* apoc arge-pl rwt5• ars k* ars-s-f k2 *Asaf* asc-t *Aur* bry k2 calad calc carb-an k* *Carb-v* carbn-s k2 cham chel chin con b4a.de dig digin a1 ignis-alc es2• kali-p **Lach** k* *Mag-m* marb-w es1• merc k* nat-m *Nux-m* k* *Nux-v* k* **Phos** k* **Puls** k* ran-b rhus-t ruta fd4.de sang k* sanic sars k* sol-t-ae a1 *Sulph* k* syph viol-t *Zinc* k* zinc-p k2
  - **amel.**: cedr *Graph* iod med bg1 *Spong* k*
  - **overeating** agg.; after: **Carb-v** mrr1
  - **while** | **agg.**: ant-ar br1 cann-i c1 kali-c k2 mag-m streptoc rly4•
- **edema**, pulmonary: adon vh1 **Am-c** *Carbn-s Ferr-i*
- **effort**, after an (See exertion - agg. - slight)
- **emissions** agg.; after: *Phos* k* **Staph** k*
- **emphysema**, in: am-c k* **Ant-ar** br1 carb-v mtf11 cortico mtf11 cupr-ar br1 ephe mtf11 grin mtf11 hist mtf11 ip mtf11 morg-p pte1* penic mtf11 pneu mtf11 psor mtf11 queb mtf11 sars ptk1 seneg mtf11 tub mtf11 tub-r mtf11
  - **old** people; in: naphtin mtf11
- **epistaxis**; with: acon bg1 bell bg1 bry bg1 carb-v bg1 ip bg1 phos bg1 puls bg1 spong bg1 sulph bg1
- **eructations** | **amel.**: ambr bro1 ant-t bro1 *Aur* **Carb-v** k* *Nux-v* psor al2
- **eruptions**:
  - **suppressed** eruptions; after: (↗*Asthmatic - eruptions*) **Apis** k* mez gk puls mrr1
  - **with**: (↗*Asthmatic - accompanied - eczema*) *Apis*
- **excitement** agg.: (↗*Hyperventilation*) ambr ars aur-m-n wbt2• caj br1 *Coc-c* cupr mrr1 ferr lac-ac stj5• *Puls* k* ruta fd4.de *Sep* tritic-vg fd5.de vanil fd5.de
- **exertion**: (↗*manual*)
  - **after** | **agg.**: (↗*manual*) acetan vh1 aids nl2• am-c k* am-m ambr k2 *Apis Arg-n* arn tl1 **Ars** k* *Ars-i* ars-s-f k2 asaf *Aspidin* br1 *Aur-m* benz-ac beryl tpw5 borx bov brass-n-o srj5• brom **Calc** k* calc-p k2 *Camph Carb-v* k* carbn-s *Cench* chlf br1 cimic cist tl1 **Coca** colch k2 con conv br1 crat br1 *Dig* dirc *Ferr-m* fuma-ac rly4• glon k2 glycyr-g cte1• ham fd3.de• *Iod* **Ip** k* irid-met srj5• *Kali-ar Kali-c Kali-i* kali-sil k2 kalm k2 kola stb3• **Lach** *Laur Led* **Lob** k* **Lyc** k* **Lycps-v** k* mag-s sp1 med k2 *Merc* **Nat-m** *Nat-s* nat-sil fd3.de• *Nit-ac Nux-m Nux-v* olib-sac wmh1 ox-ac ozone sde2• ph-ac *Phos* k* *Puls* k* rat rauw sp1 rhus-t k2 ruta fd4.de sacch-a fd2.de• sars sel k2 sep *Sil Spig* **Spong** k* squil *Stann* k* *Staph* sul-i k2 *Sulph* k* tell rsj10• ter tub *Verat* vero-o rly4• [bell-p-sp dcm1]
  - **agg.**:
    - **slight** exertion: calc br1 cassia-s ccrh1• coca mrr1 crat gm1 laur mrr1 nat-sil fd3.de• positr nl2• spong fd4.de **Stann** mrr1 tritic-vg fd5.de
      - **pulse**; without much increase of: crat br1 tell rsj10•
    - **two** distinct efforts; by: led bg2
  - **arms** agg.; of the: am-m bov **Lach** k* *Nat-m Nit-ac Sil*
- **expectoration**:
  - **amel.**: ail **Ant-t** k* ars bro1 aur h2* *Grin* k* guaj ip k* kali-bi bro1 manc nit-ac *Sep Zinc* k*
  - **checked**, after: **Ant-t** hr1 *Sep*
- **expiration**: am-c anac b4a.de aq-mar rbp6 *Arg-met* ars brom tl1 *Caust* chin h1* **Chlor** k* dros h1* *Ip* k* *Med* k* *Meph* k* physala-p bnm7• puls k* **Samb** k* seneg sep hr1 viol-o b7.de*
  - **cough**, during: meph
- **extreme** (= orthopnea): ant-t tl1 carb-v tl1 conv br1
- **fanned**, wants to be: ant-t apis bapt bg1 bit-ar wht1• cann-i c1 **Carb-v** k* chin k* chlor bg1 *Ferr* k* kali-n bg1 lach bro1 *Med* k* naja bg1 parth vml3• sec bg1 sulph tab k2 zinc bg1
- **fever**; during: (↗*FEVER - Intense - dyspnea*) **Acon** b7a.de* am-c bg2 ambr bg2 *Anac* b4.de* ant-t bg2 *Apis* b7a.de* am bg2 **Ars** b4a.de* aur bg2 bell bg2 **Bry** b7a.de* *Calc* b4a.de* *Camph* b7.de* carb-v bg2 caust bg2 chel bg2 chin bg2 *Cina* b7.de* *Cocc* b7.de* con bg2 conv br1* cupr bg2 *Ferr* b7.de* hep bg2 *Ign* b7.de* ip bg2* *Kali-c* b4.de* lach bg2 **Lyc** b4.de* merc bg2 nat-c bg2 nat-m bg2 nit-ac bg2 nux-m bg2 nux-v bg2 ph-ac bg2 **Phos** b4.de* plat bg2 **Puls** b7.de* rhus-t bg2 **Ruta** bg2 sabad bg2 samb bg2 seneg bg2 *Sep* b4.de* sil bg2 spig bg2 squil bg2 stann bg2 sulph bg2 **Zinc** b4a.de*
- **flatulence**; from: (↗*Asthmatic - flatulence; Impeded - flatulence*) abies-c vml3• arg-n ptk1 brass-n-o srj5• **Carb-v** k* castm cham chin k13 dios br1 lac-d k2 *Lyc Mez* b4a.de *Nat-s* k* **Nux-v** bg1* ol-an osm bg1 puls bg1 sang *Zinc* k*
- **foreign** bodies, from: ant-t bro1 sil bro1
- **fright**; after: acon k2 *Cupr* k* *Samb* k* vanil fd5.de
- **fullness** of abdomen from difficult respiration: puls k2
- **gasping**, with: hydr-ac bg1
- **handkerchief** approach the mouth as it will cause dyspnea; cannot bear to have: (↗*covering*) am-c h2 *Arg-n Lach*
- **hang** down amel.; letting legs: *Sul-ac*
- **headache**; during: glon bg1 lact-v bro1 pitu-a vml2• sep h2*
- **heart**:
  - **complaints**; with heart (See CHEST - Heart; complaints - accompanied - respiration)
  - **pain** in heart; during (See CHEST - Pain - heart - accompanied - respiration)
- **heat**; with: anac **Apis** k* am ars k* *Cact* carb-v chel k* cimx cina cinnb k* con conv br1 ferr c1 **Kali-c** k* *Lach* lyc h2* nat-m phos k* *Sep Sil* spong fd4.de *Tub* zinc
- **hemoptysis**, with: am br1*
- **hiccoughs**; interrupted by: aeth ptk1*
- **high** altitudes; at (See mountains)
- **hurried**, if: caust [heroin sdj2]
- **hydrothorax** from difficult respiration: lyc k2
- **hysterical**: (↗*Asthmatic - hysterical; Hyperventilation*) ars asaf *Cedr* hr1 gels *Ign* k* lac-ac stj5• *Lob* k* mosch k*
- **injuries**; after: petr bg1
- **inspiration**: *Acon* k* anthraq rly4• *Arg-n* am h1* *Ars Brom* k* *Bry* b7a.de cact bro1 calad *Calc* k* camph h1* **Caust** k* chel bro1 chin k* chlor k* chord-umb rly4• cina b7.de* cocc b7.de* con h2* crot-t bg2 cystein-l rly4• dros gk dulc fd4.de euphr *Ferr* k* fuma-ac rly4• ger-i rly4• hep h2* hydrog srj2• *Ign* k* *Iod* k* irid-met srj5• kali-c k* ketogl-ac rly4• meph mur-ac a1 nicot bro1 *Nux-m Ox-ac* bro1 *Phos* k* *Ran-b* b7a.de ruta fd4.de sal-fr sle1• **Samb** k* sinus rly4• *Spong* b7a.de staph b7.de* verat b7.de* viol-o b7.de* zinc
  - **double** (See Double)
  - **nose**; through: acon vh1
  - **rapid** expiration: chin gels hr1 ign *Kali-c* k* meph *Nux-m* nux-v *Sang* k*
- **itching**; after | **Nose**; in: sabad ptk1
- **jumping** | **alternating** with dancing (See Dancing - alternating - jumping)
- **kneeling**: | **amel.**: caust bg1
- **labor** pain; with every: **Lob** k*
- **laughing** agg.: (↗*MIND - Laughing - asthma*) *Ars* k* aur k* *Bry* cupr k* lach lyc plb
- **liver**, from stitches in: acon k* con k*
- **lump** in | **throat**-pit: lob
- **lung**:
  - **contraction** of lungs; as from: mez tl1
  - **expand** the lung; cannot: *Crot-t*
    - **sensation** of: acon vh1 asaf tl1
  - **heaviness** in left; from: ferr
  - **water** in lungs; as if: ozone sde2•

- **lying**:
  - **agg.**: abies-n br1 acet-ac k* acon k* alum-p k2 *Ant-ar* k* ant-c c1 *Ant-t* k* antip vh1 **Apis** apoc k* **Ars** k* *Ars-i* k* ars-s-f k2 asaf k* *Aur* aur-ar k2 aur-s k2 *Bapt* k* bar-m borx brom k* bufo cact k* cain br1 calc calc-s calc-sil k2 *Cann-s* k* carb-ac c1 **Carb-v** k* *Carbn-s* castm caust k* cedr k* cench cham *Chin* k* chinin-ar cist k* con *Crot-t Dig* dros k2 euph euphr k* *Ferr* k* *Ferr-ar* ferr-p *Fl-ac* k* **Graph** k* grin pd *Ham* k* hell *Hep* k* iber bg1 *Kali-ar Kali-bi* k* **Kali-c** k* *Kali-n* k* kali-s kali-sil k2 *Lac-c Lach* k* lact **Lob** *Lyc* k* lyss c1 *Meph Merc* k* *Naja* nat-m nux-v olnd phel *Phos* k* *Plb* k* podo positr nl2• *Puls* k* rumx *Samb* k* sang sars k* sel c1 *Seneg* k* *Sep Sil* k* *Spig Spong* k* stann k2 *Sulph* k* syph k* tab hr1 tarax *Tarent* ter tritic-vg fd5.de **Tub** verat-v hr1 zinc zing k*
    - **night**: cain br1
    - **enlargement** of tonsils; from: bar-c
  - **amel.**: bry k* *Calc-p* k* *Chel* k* *Dig* k* euphr ham fd3.de• *Hell* kali-bi bro1 kali-c bg1 lach bg1 *Laur* k* nat-s *Nux-v* k* **Psor** k* sabad bg1
  - **back**; on:
    - **agg.**: acet-ac aeth alum *Ars Aur* castm dros gk *Hyper Iod* **Lyc** k* med nat-m ol-an *Phos* k* ptel *Puls* k* sang bg1* *Sil Spig Sulph* k*
    - **amel.**: **Cact** k* dig ind kali-i *Kalm* k* nux-v polys sk4•
      - **arms** outstretched; with: *(↗CHEST - Oppression - arms)* *Psor* k* spig bg sulph bg
      - **shoulders** elevated; with: **Cact** spig nh6
  - **head** high; with the | **must** lie with the head high: eup-per hr1
  - **head** low; with the | **agg.**: **Apis Cact** *Carb-v Chin* k* colch cop eup-per *Hep* **Kali-c** k* kali-n k* puls k* rumx *Spig* k* *Spong* k*
  - **impossible**: acon *Ant-t* k* **Apis** k* *Apoc* k* **Ars** k* *Aur* bar-m borx brom bufo *Cact* k* cann-s chin *Crot-t Hep Kali-c* k* *Lac-c Lach* k* *Lyc Merc* moni rfm1• naja k2 *Nux-v* k* psor al2 *Puls* k* *Seneg Sep* stann staph k* *Sulph* k* *Tab Ter Tub*
  - **knees** and elbows; on | **amel.**: med k* polys sk4•
  - **side**; on:
    - **agg.**: *Ars* carb-an *Puls*
    - **amel.**: alum lyss bg1 ozone sde2• sang bg1
    - **left**:
      - **agg.**: absin am-c bg1 *Apis* cann-i elaps gk *Hydr* ind *Kali-c* lyc gk med merc naja k* nat-m gk *Phos* plb *Puls Spig* k* sulph bg1 tab bro1 *Tarent* visc k*
      - **amel.**: castm lach sne
    - **right**:
      - **agg.**: castm lycps-v mrr1 squil visc bro1
        - **sleep**; going to: bad
      - **amel.**: ant-t bro1 naja gm1 *Spig*
        - **head** high; with the: cact bro1 spig bro1 spong bro1
- **lying** down agg.: abies-n bro1 act-sp bro1 antip vh1 aral bro1 *Ars* bro1 cain bro1 dig bro1 grin bro1 lach bro1* merc-sul bro1 nat-m h2 positr nl2• puls bro1 sep bro1 stry-ar bro1 sulph bro1
- **manual** labor: *(↗exertion; exertion - after - agg.)* am-m *Bov Lach Nat-m Nit-ac* ruta fd4.de *Sil* k*
- **measles**; after suppressed: **Cham** k* **Puls** *Zinc*
- **menorrhagia** (See menses - during - agg.)
- **menses**:
  - **after** | **agg.**: am-c ptk1 ferr *Nat-m* k* *Puls* k* *Spong* bg2
  - **amel.**: puls k2
  - **before** | **agg.**: asar bg2 borx k* brom k* *Cupr* k* lac-c bg2 lach bg2 laur bg2 mosch mrr1 *Nat-s* k* pitu-a vml2• puls bg2* spong bg2 *Sulph* k* **Zinc** k*
  - **during** | **agg.**: borx bg2 cact k* *Calc* k* chin k* cocc k* *Coff* b7a.de *Coloc* k* **Cupr** bg2 dig bg2 fl-ac ptk1 graph k* ign k* *Iod* k* ip k* kali-c *Lach* k* laur lyc k* mosch bg2* nat-s bg2 phos bg2 plat k* puls k* rhod b4.de* sep k* **Spong** k* sulph k* zinc k*
  - **suppressed** menses; from: chen-a hr1* fl-ac lob mrr1 **Puls** k* spong
- **mental** exertion agg.: agath-a nl2• ferr nat-m nh6 phos sep
- **mortification**; from: *(↗MIND - Ailments - mortification)* puls
- **motion**:
  - **agg.**: am-c k2 *Apis Arg-n* arn k* *Ars* k* ars-i aspar k* bapt beryl sp1 **Bry** k* cadm-met sp1 calc k* cann-s k* caps k* *Carb-v* cassia-s ccrh1• *Con* k* conv br1 euphr k2 ferr k* ferr-i gard-j vlr2• graph k* ham fd3.de• iod k* ip k* kali-ar *Kali-c* k* *Kali-i Led Lob* k* *Lyc* k* merc k* *Nat-s* k* nux-v k* olib-sac wmh1 ox-ac *Phos* k* plb psil ft1 puls k* rhod k* rhus-t k* sabad sal-fr sle1• seneg k2 *Sep* k* *Spig* k* **Spong** k* **Stann** k* sulph h2* *Tarent* tritic-vg fd5.de *Verat* k*
    - **slow** motion: *Sep*
  - **amel.**: arg-n bg1 arge-pl rwt5• *Aur* bell bg1 brom bg1 calc coff bg1 dros gk **Ferr** k* lob bg1* nat-m phos bg1 puls bg1 rhus-t bg1 samb bg1 seneg k* sep k* sil sulph
    - **rapid** motion: lob ptk1 sep bro1
  - **arms**; of | **agg.**: *Am-m* berb pd **Lach** k* nat-m *Nit-ac* st *Sil* st spig k* sulph tarent pd
- **mountain**; when ascending a (See ascending - agg.)
- **mountains**; when being in the: coca br1*
- **movies**; looking at: cadm-met gm1
- **mucus**; from: *(↗CHEST - Mucus - lungs; LARYNX - Mucus - air)* ip mtf33 tritic-vg fd5.de
  - ○ **Bronchi**; in: nat-m h2
  - **Trachea**; in: alum ammc **Ant-t** k* **Ars** asar h1 aur h2 bov *Cact* camph cina **Hippoz** *Ip* sel thuj verat h1
- **muscles** of respiration; must use accessory: ant-t dw5* *Ars* b4a.de *Bell* b4a.de *Bry* b7a.de *Cann-s* b7a.de *Cupr* b7a.de *Spong* b7a.de
- **music** agg.: ambr k2
- **nervous**: ambr bro1 *Arg-n* bro1* ars bro1* asaf bro1 *Caj* bro1 carb-an ptk1 lob ptk1 mosch bro1* nux-m bro1 puls bro1 *Valer* bro1 viol-o bro1
- **nose**, felt in (See NOSE - Dyspnea)
- **odors** agg.; strong: ph-ac k* *Phos* b4.de* sang k*
- **old** people: ammc vml3• *Bac* br1 *Bar-c* k* carb-v nh6 *Chin* k* coca bro1* seneg k*
- **open**: *(↗GENERALS - Cold - air - amel. - windows)*
  - **clothes** to be able to breathe freely; must open (See clothes - loosening; clothes - loosening - amel.)
  - **doors** and windows open; wants: *(↗air; in open - amel.; GENERALS - Cold - air - amel. - windows)* acon mrr1 aeth mrr1 **Apis** k* **Arg-n** k* ars-i sne aspar *Bapt* k* *Cann-s Carb-v Chel* chinin-ar cist crat br1 *Dig* grin mrr1 *Ip* **Lach** k* *Nat-s* petr-ra shn4• plb **Puls** k* **Sulph** k*
  - **mouth** during inspiration: acon squil k*
    - **coryza**; during: am-c tl1
  - **window**; must sit by the open: *(↗air; in open - amel.; GENERALS - Cold - air - amel. - windows)* *Cann-s Chel* k* tritic-vg fd5.de
- **overheated**; when: **Apis** k* bry k2 kali-c ptk1 lyc k2
- **pain**; during: cact k2 dulc fd4.de ruta fd4.de spong fd4.de tritic-vg fd5.de vanil fd5.de
  - **blood** boil; from a: nat-m h2
  - ○ **Axilla**; in: jug-c br1
  - **Back**:
    - **Dorsal** region | **Scapulae**: jug-c br1
  - **Chest**; in: jug-c br1
  - **Heart**; in (See CHEST - Pain - heart - accompanied - respiration)
  - **Hypochondrium**; in right: sep h2
  - **Ovaries**; in (See FEMALE - Pain - ovaries - accompanied - heart)
  - **Shoulder**; in: muru a1
- **palpitations**; during: acon bg2* aids nl2• am-c k* ambr k2 ars-i **Aur** k* bell h1* beryl tpw5* brom *Bry* bg2 *Cact* k* cadm-s *Calc* k* calc-ar carb-ac c1 *Carb-v* caust h2* chin kr1* *Colch* k* dig bro1 dulc fd4.de ferr tl1 gard-j vlr2• *Glon* bro1 glyc bro1 grat ham fd3.de• iber hr1 iod *Kali-c* k* kali-n bg2 kalm bg1 lac-ac stj5• lach k* manc bg1 med jl2 merc-i-f ptk1 naja bro1 nat-sil fd3.de• nit-ac olnd bro1 ox-ac bro1 *Phos* bro1 plb k* *Psor* k* puls k* sep *Spig* k* *Spong* k* stroph-h ptk1 tab vanil fd5.de *Verat* k* verat-v k* viol-o k* zinc bro1
  - **forenoon** | **11**-3 h: colch
- **paroxysmal**: ip tl1
- **periodical**: agath-a nl2• *Ars* **Cact** k* *Calc-p* colch plb sulph
  - **days**; every seven: sulph

Respiration

- **perspiration**: *(↗PERSPIRATION - Dyspnea)* acon bg2 *Anac* b4.de* *Ars* k* arund bry bg2 cina bg2 ferr bg2 iber bg2 ign bg2 *Ip* bg2 kali-c bg2 lach lyc bg2 *Mang* b4a.de* nat-c bg2 nux-v k* op bg2 **Phos** bg2 puls bg2 *Rhus-t* bg2 samb bg2 *Sep* k* spong fd4.de *Sulph* k* verat bg2 *Zinc* bg2
  - **anxious** face and sleeplessness: eup-per k*
  - **with** (See accompanied - perspiration)
- **pork**, after: nat-c
- **pregnancy** agg.; during: apoc bro1 lyc bro1 nux-v bro1 puls bro1 viol-o bro1*
- **pressure**:
  - **spine** agg.; on: *Chinin-s*
  - **stomach**; on | **agg.**: kali-c h2 rhus-t h1
- **raising**:
  - **agg.**: calc-p bg1
  - **arms** | **agg.**: *(↗Impeded - raising - arm - agg.)* am-m ptk1 ant-c bg2 **Berb** k* cupr bg2* lach ptk1 led bg2 pop bg1 pop-cand c1 **Spig** k* sulph bg2 tarent ptk1
- **reading**:
  - **agg.**: hell kola stb3•
  - **amel.**: ferr
- **rest** agg.: sil bro1
- **restlessness**; with: apis bg1 tarent mtf33
  - **tossing** arms about: *Kali-br* hr1
- **retraction** of shoulders amel.: am-c ars *Calc*
- **rheumatic**:
  - **inflammatory**: benz-ac k2
  - ○ **Heart**; of: *Abrot* adon vh1 aur *Cact* cimic *Kalm* *Psor* sep *Spong*
- **riding**:
  - **agg.**: falco-pe nl2• lyc
  - **amel.**: *Psor* k*
  - **horse**; a: | **agg.**: *Meph* k*
- **rising**:
  - **after** | **agg.**: coc-c irid-met srj5•
  - **agg.**: lyc
  - **amel.**: meph br1 olnd
- **rocking** | **amel.**: sec bg1
- **rubbing**: *(↗Arrested - rubbing - amel.)*
  - **back** | **amel.**: *(↗Arrested - rubbing - amel.)* kali-c mtf mur-ac mtf
  - **chest** | **amel.**: *(↗Arrested - rubbing - amel.)* kali-c mtf
- **running**:
  - **after**: borx carc tpw2* hyos k* ozone sde2• rauw sp1 *Sil* k*
    - **short** running: ozone sde2•
  - **agg.**: bit-ar wht1•
  - **as** from running: hyos bg2
  - **does** not agg., slow motion agg.: *Sep*
- **sea**; on the | **amel.**: med jl2
- **serum** in pleura and pericardium; from: lyc mtf33
- **shivering**; during: rhus-t b7.de
- **singing** agg.: arg-met
- **sinking** sensation in abdomen agg.: acet-ac bro1
- **sitting**:
  - **agg.**: alum alumn k* anac calc carb-v k* caust k* cedr dig digin a1 dros dulc fd4.de euphr *Ferr* gins k* indg *Lach* k* *Laur* k* led *Lyc* k* mag-c h2* mez h2* nat-s k* nicc petr k* *Phos* k* *Psor* k* rhus-t sep k* sulph h2* tritic-vg fd5.de verat
  - **amel.**: acon-f bro1 *Ant-t* k* *Apis* apoc *Ars* bro1 asaf aspar k* bar-m k2 bit-ar wht1• cann-s k* *Carb-v* mrr1 *Crot-t* dig bro1 hep ip k* *Kali-c* laur bro1 merc-sul bro1 moni rfm1• nat-s bro1 nat-sal a1 psor al2 puls mrr1 *Samb* bro1 sulph bro1 ter bro1 *Verat*
  - **bent** backward | **agg.**: psor
  - **bent** forward:
    - **agg.**: dig rhus-t sep
    - **amel.**: aral vh *Ars* k* bufo chinin-ar iber bg1 kali-c k2* **Lach** k* *Spong* k*
      - **elbows** resting on knees: **Kali-c** mrr1
- **sitting**: ...
  - **erect**:
    - **amel.**: *Am-m* b7a.de *Ant-t* b7.de* ars b4a.de* asaf b7.de* bar-m bit-ar wht1• borx b4a.de *Bry* b7a.de cact k2 caps h1* carb-v b4.de* cham b7.de* der vml3• ferr b7.de* ham a1 hyos bg2 ip k2 **Kali-c** k* *Lach* *Laur* *Lyc* k* nat-c *Nux-v* b7a.de parth vml3• phos b4.de* puls b7.de* rhus-t b7.de* samb b7.de* *Seneg* k* sulph *Ter*
      - **bent** forward; and: acon bg2 aur bg2 bufo bg2 *Lach* bg2 spong bg2
  - **half** sitting position | **amel.**: *Kali-c* mrr1 spig
  - **head** on knees; with | **amel.**: coc-c **Kali-c** k*
  - **room**; in a: sep bro1
- **sitting** up in bed:
  - **agg.**: laur lyc nat-c
  - **must** sit up: merc-sul br1
- **sleep**: *(↗Arrested - sleep)*
  - **after**:
    - **agg.**: alum apis bell cedr lac-c k* **Lach** k* nit-ac *Phos* k* *Sep* k* **Spong**
      - **short** sleep: aral vh1
  - **awakened** to avoid suffocation, must be: **Op** k* sulph
  - **during**: *(↗MIND - Starting - waking - suffocated)*
    - **agg.**: *(↗waking; MIND - Starting - Waking - suffocated; SLEEP - Waking - Breath to)* acon k* agar bell brom mtf33 calc h2* *Carb-v* k* *Cench* cham k* chlor mrr1 con k* dig k* dros gk *Grin* k* guaj k* hep k* hyos h1* ign *Kali-bi* k* *Kali-c* k* kali-i mrr1 **Lach** k* *Lact* *Lyc* k* manc k* meph merc naja mrr1 nat-sil fd3.de• nux-v *Op* k* phos h2* positr nl2• pyrog k2 rhus-t k* sal-fr sle1• samb k* sep spong k2* stram h1* *Sulph* k*
      - **jump** out of bed; must (See Asthmatic - night - midnight - after - jump)
  - **falling** asleep; when: am-c k* ant-t c1 ars bro1 *Arum-t* bad c1 bapt k* bell bg1 bry cadm-s br1 calc b4a.de carb-an bg1* *Carb-v* *Carbn-s* *Cench* *Crot-h* *Cur* bro1 dig k* gels bg1 *Graph* k* **Grin** k* hep k* *Kali-c* bg1 kali-i bro1 *Lac-c* k* **Lach** k* merc-i-r bg1 *Merc-pr-r* bro1 morph bro1 naja bro1 nux-m **Op** k* phos ran-b c1 *Samb* bro1 *Spong* k* stict lp stront-c bro1 sulph k* tab teucr bro1 valer
    - **lying** on right side agg.: *Bad*
- **smoke** | **as** from: ars ptk1 bar-c k* *Brom* k* cassia-s ccrh1• chin ptk1 cocc *Ign* ptk1 lach ptk1 lyc ptk1 nat-ar ozone sde2• petr-ra shn4• puls ptk1
- **smoke** agg.: ozone sde2•
- **sneezing**:
  - **agg.**: naja ptk1 phos ptk1
  - **amel.**: sul-ac vh
  - **with**: ambro ptk1 ars-i ptk1 phos ptk1 tril-p br1
- **spasmodic**: acon b7.de* ambr b7.de* asaf k* caust k* *Cham* b7.de* chin b7.de* *Chlor* coff b7.de* *Cupr* k* ferr b7.de* ip b7.de* *Kali-c* b4.de* *Laur* k* *Led* b7a.de lyss jl2 *Merc* b4a.de *Mosch* b7.de* nux-v b7.de* *Op* b7.de* ph-ac b4a.de phos b4a.de* plb k* *Puls* k* **Samb** b7.de* *Sars* b4a.de *Sec* b7a.de sep b4a.de verat b7.de* *Zinc* b4a.de
  - **children**; in: androc bnm2•
- **spasms** of larynx (See LARYNX - Laryngismus)
- **sponge**; as through a: am-i bg2 brom bg2 phos bg2 phyt bg2* spong bg2*
- **standing**:
  - **agg.**: aur-m k* cina kali-n merc-act bg1 phel psor jl2 *Sep*
  - **amel.**: ars-i sne bapt bg1 cann-s bro1 ham a1 sep ptk1 sil bg1 spig bg1
  - **erect** | **must** stand erect: cedr
  - **must** stand: cann-s
  - **water** agg.; in: *Nux-m* k*
- **sternum**:
  - **pressure** on; from: all-s cann-s ph-ac phos rhus-t squil thuj
  - ○ **Upper** part of: bry
- **stimulants** agg.: lach
- **stomach**:
  - **disorders**; from stomach: *(↗Asthmatic - stomach)* nux-v k2 sang k2
  - **from**; as: *Ars* nh6 caps h1* nux-v bg2 rhus-t bg2 thuj bg2 zing bg2

- **stool**:
  - **after** | **agg.**: calc bg2 caust k* con b4.de* crot-t kali-c b4a.de* rhus-t sep h2*
  - **amel.**: ictod
  - **before**: ictod *Nat-s* bg2 *Rhus-t* b7.de*
  - **bloody** stool | **after**: kali-c h2*
  - **during** | **agg.**: *Alumn* k* ars b4a.de* *Calc* *Cocc* hr1 gamb bg2 nat-m bg2 *Puls* b7a.de *Rhus-t* k* *Sulph* hr1
- **stooping** agg.: *Am-m* *Calc* k* caust chin dig digin a1 laur mez h2* phos k* seneg sep k* sil k* sulph k*
- **sudden**: cupr bg1* *Gels* graph k* ign k* iod k* kola stb3• *Sulph*
  - **afternoon** | **17** h: ign
  - **night**:
    - **midnight**:
      - **after** | **3** h: cupr mrr1
  - **emotions** agg.: cupr mrr1
- **sulphur**; as if he inspired fumes of: brom camph canth croc kali-chl **Lyc** meph *Mosch* **Puls** sulph
- **supper** | **after** | **agg.**: alumn ant-c k* arg-n hr1 mag-m h2* nat-sil fd3.de• sanic
  - **during**: ant-c k*
- **swallowing** agg.: anac ptk1* atro *Bell* k* **Brom** *Calc* chen-a *Cupr* k* thuj
- **talking**:
  - **after**: apoc k* *Ars* bry *Caust* k* cench k2 *Dros* k* irid-met srj5• **Lach** laur meph *Mur-ac* hr1 (non:nat-c a1) *Nit-ac* k* ph-ac k* *Sil* *Spig* k* **Spong** k* **Sulph** k*
  - **agg.**: botul jl2 caust nh6 dig br1 irid-met srj5• *Lach* nh6 ph-ac bg2 *Spong* nh6 **Stann** mrr1
    - **rapidly**: caust
  - **amel.**: *Ferr* k*
  - **loudly** agg.: petr
- **tension** in epigastrium, from: phos h2*
- **thinking** of anything that has gone wrong: hura c1
- **thunderstorm**; before: sep *Sil* syph
- **tickling** in; from | **throat**-pit: sil h2
- **touch**:
  - **abdomen** agg.; of: stann bg2
  - **back** agg.; of: adon bg1*
  - **face** agg.; of: cupr mtf33
  - **larynx** agg.; of: apis bell **Lach**
- **travelling**; while | **amel.**: psor jl2
- **turning** | **bed**; in | **agg.**: **Ars** k* *Carb-v* *Sulph* k*
  - **side**; to | **left**:
    - **sitting** up | **amel.**: *Sulph*
    - **right**: euph
- **undressing**: kali-bi bg2
- **urinary** complaints with difficult respiration: cann-s k2
- **urination**:
  - **after** | **agg.**: lyc bg2
  - **agg.**: chel bg1 cimic bg1 dulc bg1 laur bg2 sars bg2
  - **during** | **agg.**: con bg2
- **vexation**; after: agath-a nl2• ars k* *Cupr* k* dulc fd4.de lob mrr1 nat-sil fd3.de• spong fd4.de
- **violent**: ip tl1
- **waking**; on: *(↗sleep - during - agg.; SLEEP - Waking - breath to)* alum am-c k* *Ant-t* k* *Apis* *Arg-n* *Arn* k* *Arum-t* bad bapt k* bell benz-ac k* *Cadm-s* calc k* *Carb-v* carbn-s k2 *Cench* *Chel* *Chin* crot-h cur *Dig* dros k2 euphr flav jl2 *Graph* **Grin** k* guaj *Hep* irid-met srj5• *Kali-bi* k* *Kali-c* k* *Kali-i* k* *Lac-c* **Lach** k* lact med *Naja* k* nit-ac h2* *Nux-m* nux-v **Op** k* ph-ac h2* *Phos* k* puls h1* rhus-t sal-fr sle1• *Samb* k* seneg sep sil spong squil b7.de* suis-pan rly4• sulph k* syc fmm1• tab valer vesp
- **walking**:
  - **agg.**: *Acon* bro1 agar *Am-c* k* am-m *Apis* apoc **Ars** k* arund k* aur k* aur-ar k2 aur-m k2 aur-s k2 bell botul jl2 *Brom* *Cact* k* **Calc** k* *Calc-s* *Caps* k* *Carb-v* k* cassia-s ccrh1• castm *Caust* k* chel k* coc-c k* coca *Con* k* conv br1 *Dig* k* dirc c1 dulc fd4.de glon k2 *Ign* k* *Ip* bro1 *Kali-ar* *Kali-c* k* *Kali-i* kali-s *Lach* lact *Laur* led lil-t k* lyc k* lycps-v mag-c *Merc* k*
- **walking – agg.**: ... nat-c h2* nat-m k* *Nat-s* k* nat-sil fd3.de• nicc-met sk4• *Nit-ac* k* *Nit-s-d* a1* nux-v olnd ozone sde2• petr phel k* *Phos* plat k* *Prun* k* psil ft1 *Psor* k* *Puls* k* ran-b rhus-t k* sel k* seneg k* *Sep* k* sil bro1 **Stann** stront-c **Sulph** k* thuj tritic-vg fd5.de vanil fd5.de [spect dfg1]
    - **level** ground but not when ascending; on: *Ran-b*
  - **air** agg.; in open: *Am-m* *Ars* k* *Aur* *Carb-v* caust graph ham fd3.de• *Lyc* *Merc* hr1 nit-ac h2* psor hr1* **Sulph** hr1* tritic-vg fd5.de zinc h2*
  - **amel.**: brom k* bry k* carb-v bg1 *Dros* k* *Ferr* indg nicc sep k* tritic-vg fd5.de
  - **beginning** to walk: petr ph-ac plat h2*
  - **rapidly**:
    - **agg.**: ang **Ars** hr1 *Aur* aur-m k2 bros-gau mrc1 *Caust* k* *Cupr* k* ign kali-ar k2 *Kali-c* k* *Lob* lyc k2 merc **Nat-m** k* *Nat-s* **Phos** k* **Puls** k* seneg *Sil* k* *Sulph* k* vanil fd5.de
    - **amel.**: *Sep*
  - **slowly** | **amel.**: **Ferr** k*
  - **uneven** ground agg.; on: clem dulc fd4.de
  - **wind**; against the: *Calc* k* coc-c pd *Cupr* lyc nat-m bg nux-m nh6 *Phos* plat k* psor rhus-r rhus-t sel seneg k2
- **warm**:
  - **air** agg.: arg-n ptk1
  - **applications** | **amel.**: ars mtf kali-c mtf sil mtf spong mtf
  - **bathing** | **agg.**: *Iod* nit-ac
  - **bed** | **agg.**: puls k2
  - **clothes** agg.: *Ars*
  - **drinks**:
    - **after**: lach k2 phos
    - **amel.**: spong k2*
  - **food**:
    - **agg.**: *Lob* k*
    - **amel.**: spong k2*
  - **room**:
    - **agg.**: am-c k* ant-c k2 ant-t **Apis** k* *Arg-n* ars k* ars-i sne aur-m k2 bry k2 *Carb-v* *Carbn-s* chlor cortiso tpw7* fl-ac *Iod* ip *Kali-i* **Kali-s** kreos lach k2* *Lil-t* *Lyc* **Puls** k* sep bro1 **Sulph** k* thuj tritic-vg fd5.de tub
      - **pale** and must remain quiet; becomes deathly: *Am-c* k*
    - **entering** a warm room; when | **air**; from open: *Bry*
- **water**:
  - **lungs**; as if water in (See lung - water)
  - **standing** in water (See standing - water)
- **weakness**: *(↗Superficial)* ars k* cupr-n a1 lach sep h2*
  - **respiratory** organs, of: act-sp bapt a1 cic a1 plat **Stann** k*
- **weather**:
  - **change** of weather: cassia-s ccrh1• chel ip tritic-vg fd5.de
  - **cloudy** weather: | **agg.**: nat-s tl1
  - **cold**:
    - **agg.**: apis
    - **wet** | **agg.**: ars *Dulc* *Mang* *Sil*
  - **stormy** | **agg.**: *Ars* k* calc *Nat-s* *Sep*
  - **warm** wet: *Aur* sne bell k2 tritic-vg fd5.de
  - **wet** | **agg.**: am-c ars mtf ars-i sne cassia-s ccrh1• chin cupr bg1 dulc mtf i p k2 kali-c k2 mang mtf **Nat-s** k* sil mtf
- **whooping** cough: am-c bro1 ambr bro1 *Ant-t* bro1 bell bro1 brom bro1 *Carb-v* bro1 cina bro1 cor-r bro1 *Cupr* bro1 *Dros* bro1 euph bro1 hep bro1 hipp bro1 iod bro1 *Ip* bro1 kali-bi bro1 *Lob* bro1 *Meph* bro1 naphtin bro1 op bro1 *Samb* bro1 senec bro1 *Verat* bro1 *Viol-o* bro1
- **winter**: *Cassia-s* ccrh1*•
- **working**; while: am-m bro1 calc bro1 lyc bro1 nat-m bro1 nit-ac h2* nux-m nh6 sep bro1 sil bro1 sumb bro1
- **writing**:
  - **agg.**: aspar dig k* kali-c h2* vanil fd5.de
  - **amel.**: *Ferr*
- **yawning**:
  - **agg.**: brom ptk1

- **amel.**: croc k*

○ - **Heart**; felt about: stront-c bg2 sulph bg2
- **Lower** chest; felt in: lob-s bro1 nux-v bro1
- **Throat**; felt in: am-m bg1 apis bg1 caust bg1 cocc bg1 dulc fd4.de lyc bg1 spong bg1
- **Trachea**; felt in: kali-n bg2

DOUBLE inspiration: *(↗Paroxysmal - double)* *Cina* bg2 led ptk1

DRINKING:
- **agg.**: acon bg2 anac b4a.de* apis b7a.de arn bg2 bell bg2 *Brom* b4a.de *Chin* b7.de* cocc b7.de* euphr bg2 hyos b7.de* kali-bi bg2 kali-c bg2 nat-m b4.de* nux-v b7.de* puls b7.de* rhus-t b7.de* thuj bg2 verat b7.de*
- **amel.**: bry b7.de* cupr b7a.de mosch b7a.de rhus-t b7.de* spig b7.de* tarax b7.de*

DUST agg.: ars bg2 ars-i ptk1 bell bg2 brom ptk1 **Calc** bg2 chin bg2 dulc ptk1 *Hep* bg2 *Ictod* ptk1 ip bg2 nat-ar ptk1 nux-v bg2 phos bg2 *Rhus-t* b7a.de sep b4a.de **Sil** bg2* *Sulph* bg2

EATING:
- **after** | **agg.**: anac b4a.de ant-c b7.de* arn bg2 ars b4a.de* asaf b7.de* bry b7.de* calad b7.de* caps b7.de* carb-an b4.de* cham b7a.de* chel b7.de* chin b7.de* cocc b7.de* ferr b7.de* ign b7.de* ip b7.de* kali-bi bg2 lach b7.de* *Lyc* b4a.de merc b4.de* nat-c b4.de* nat-s bg2 nux-m b7.de* nux-v b7.de* petr b4.de* phos b4.de* *Puls* b7.de* ran-b b7.de* rhus-t b7.de* ruta b7.de* sars b4.de* *Sil* b4.de* *Sulph* b4.de* thuj bg2 verat b7.de* viol-t b7.de* zinc b4.de*
- **agg.**: kali-p ptk1 lach ptk1 nat-s ptk1 *Phos* ptk1 puls ptk1 zinc-val ptk1
  - **evening**: *Ant-c* b7a.de
- **amel.**: ambr b7.de* graph bg2* iod ptk1 laur b7.de* lyc bg2 med ptk1 rhus-t b7.de* sabad b7.de* spong bg2* staph bg2
- **before** | **agg.**: chin b7.de* sabad b7.de*
- **while** | **agg.**: cocc b7.de* lach b7a.de* *Mag-m* b4a.de

ERUCTATIONS: | **amel.**: ambr ptk1 ant-t ptk1 aur ptk1 calc bg2 *Carb-v* bg2* *Chel* bg2 kali-c bg2 lach b7a.de *Lyc* b4a.de mosch ptk1 *Nux-v* ptk1 *Phos* b4a.de puls bg2

EXERTION:
- **agg.**: am-c b4a.de* am-m b7a.de ars b4.de* *Asaf* b7a.de borx bg2 *Bry* b7a.de calc ptk1 camph bg2 coca ptk1 *Dulc* b4a.de ip ptk1 lach b7a.de* lob ptk1 lyc ptk1 lycps-v ptk1 nat-m ptk1 rhus-t b7.de* spong b7.de* *Squil* b7a.de
  - **slight** exertion: calc ptk1 con ptk1 kali-c ptk1 nat-s ptk1
- **mental** | **agg.** (See MIND - Mental exertion - respiration)

EXPECTORATION; after: | **amel.**: ant-t b7.de* aral ptk1 calc b4a.de grin ptk1 *Guaj* b4a.de hyper ptk1 ip ptk1 lach ptk1 *Nit-ac* b4a.de *Nux-v* b7a.de *Phos* b4a.de *Sep* b4a.de* *Spong* b7a.de squil bg2 sulph bg2 zinc ptk1

EXPIRATION:
- **during**:
  - **agg.**: *Calc* b4a.de dros b7.de* *Dulc* b4a.de *Nat-m* b4a.de olnd b7.de* staph b7.de*
  - **amel.**: cina b7.de*

FALSE STEP; at a: *Bry* b7a.de

FANNING: | **amel.**: apis bg2 carb-v ptk1 med ptk1 naja ptk1

FASTING agg.: *Staph* b7a.de

FEEBLE (See Difficult - weakness; Superficial)

FLATULENCE:
- **agg.**: *Carb-v* bg2 mez bg2 **Puls** bg2
- **obstructed** flatulence agg.: ars bg2 caps bg2 *Carb-v* bg2 *Cham* bg2 *Chin* bg2 hep bg2 nat-c bg2 **Nux-v** bg2 *Op* bg2 phos bg2 **Sulph** bg2 verat bg2 *Zinc* bg2

FLATUS; PASSING: | **amel.**: *Lyc* b4a.de

FORCIBLE: acon b7.de* brom k* cann-s k* gels bg2 helo-s bnm14• hydr-ac k* ign b7.de* nux-v bg2 olnd bg2 op bg2 spong b7.de* sul-ac bg2 verat bg2
- **expiration**: bell caps k* card-b a1 cham *Chin* k* *Gels* k* ign *Ox-ac* k* stram

FRIGHT agg.: *Acon* b7a.de *Cupr* b7a.de

GASPING: *(↗Catching; Panting)* acet-ac k* *Acon* k* acon-c a1 *Am-c* k* am-caust a1 anil a1 *Ant-t* k* **Apis** k* *Apoc* k* *Arg-n* *Ars* k* ars-h k* *Brom* k* camph k* canth k* carb-an k* carb-v ptk1 castm chir-fl bnm4• chlol hr1

Gasping: ...
Chlor k* *Cic* k* cit-l a1* *Coff* k* *Colch* k* *Coloc* k* cor-r ptk1 cub k* cupr cupr-ar a1 *Dig* k* *Dros* gels k* *Hell* k* *Hydr-ac* k* hydrc k* *Hyper* k* *Ign* hr1 *Ip* k* irid-met srj5• kali-n ptk1 lat-m k* *Laur* k* lob ptk1 **Lyc** k* lyss c1 *Med* k* meph ptk1 merc k* methyl a1 *Mosch* k* *Naja* k* op k* petr hr1 *Phos* k* phyt k* puls k* samb k* *Spong* k* *Stram* k* stry k* syc pte1• *Tab* k* tarent k* thuj k*
- **afternoon**: nicc k*
- **night**: lach
  - **midnight**:
    - **after** | **2** h | **cough**; with: chinin-s
    - **5** h: tarent
- **convulsions**:
  - **after**: caust ptk1 laur ptk1
  - **before**: caust ptk1 laur ptk1
  - **during**: caust ptk1 laur ptk1
- **cough**:
  - **after**: cor-r br1
  - **before**: ant-t k* *Brom* k* bry coc-c
  - **during** | **agg.**: *Ant-t* k* chin bg2 **Cina** bg2 *Cor-r* k* *Cupr* bg2 **Dros** bg2 *Dulc* bg2 *Hyos* bg2 ip bg2 kreos bg2 mur-ac bg2 phos bg2 *Puls* bg2 rhus-t bg2 sep bg2 sul-ac k* sulph bg2 *Verat* bg2
- **dozing**, when: naja
- **heart** complaints; in: laur k2
- **inspiration**, expiration long and slow: *Ant-t* k* *Op*
- **lying** | **amel.**: laur k2
- **running**; as from: hyos bg2
- **sleep**; during: dig k2
- **talking** agg.: cench k2

GRIEF agg.: *Cham* bg2 laur bg2 mag-c bg2 nux-v bg2 petr bg2

GROANING (See Moaning)

HANG DOWN; letting legs: | **amel.**: sul-ac ptk1

HEAT; during: | **agg.**: *Ruta* b7a.de

HICCOUGH agg.: puls bg2

HICCOUGHING respiration: nux-v bg2

HISSING: acet-ac bro1 arg-n bg2 led b7.de*

HOLDING: | **sides** | **amel.**: kali-bi bg2
- **something** | **amel.**: graph ptk1

HOT breath: **Acon** k* aeth k* agar k* anac k* anac-oc hr1 *Ant-c* k* apis *Ars* k* arum-m a1* asaf k* asar b2.de* *Bad* hr1 *Bell* k* calc k* calc-p k* *Camph* hr1 cann-i a1 cann-s **Carbn-s** card-b a1 *Cham* k* chel k* coc-c k* coff k* *Ferr* k* kali-bi ptk1 kali-br k* lyss hr1 mag-m k* *Mang* k* med k* merc a1 merl mez k* naja *Nat-m* k* *Nux-v* bg2 *Phos* k* plat b2.de* ptel k* raph k* *Rhus-t* k* *Rhus-v* k* *Sabad* k* squil k* *Stront-c* k* *Sulph* k* sumb k* til a1 *Trif-p* ptk1 *Verat* b7a.de *Zinc* k*
- **morning** | **waking**; on: sulph
- **afternoon**: *Bad* k* *Rhus-t* k*
- **evening**: mang k* sumb k*
- **accompanied** by:

○ - **Limbs**; cold: cham k*
  - **Mouth**; heat of the (See MOUTH - Heat - accompanied - hot)
- **chill**; during: acon bg2 anac k* camph cham k* **Rhus-t** k* sabad bg2 *Zinc* bg2
- **coryza**; during: mag-m h2*
- **cough** agg.; during: ant-c b7.de*
- **fever**; during: zinc k*
- **perspiration**; during: **Cham** bg2 *Rhus-t* bg2 sabad bg2 stront-c bg2 *Zinc* bg2
- **sensation** as if: rad-br ptk1

HYPERVENTILATION: *(↗Asthmatic - emotions - after; Asthmatic - hysterical; Difficult - excitement; Difficult - hysterical)* **Acon** vh* arg-n vh* camph mtf cupr sst3* grin mtf hydr-ac mtf lac-ac stj1*• lach mtf lob vh* op mtf phos vh3* zinc mtf zinc-cy mtf [calc-p stj1 kali-p stj1 mag-br stj1 mag-p stj1 ph-ac stj1]
- **riding** on a streetcar agg.: cupr sst3•

HYSTERICAL (See Paroxysmal)

IMPEDED, obstructed: *(↗Stridulous)* *Abrot* acon anac ant-t arn *Ars* ars-h atra-r bnm3• aur-m bar-c bell berb bism brom *Bry* *Cact* k* calc calc-p *Camph* cann-s canth caps k* carb-an carb-v caust cham chin k* chlor cimx **Cina** clem *Cocc* con *Croc* crot-c cub *Cupr* k* dig dios br1 dol dros gk euph grat *Hell* hydr-ac *Ign* *Iod* kali-bi kali-s fd4.de *Lach* lap-la sde8.de• laur *Led* lob br1 lyc *Merc* *Merc-c* nat-m nicc **Nit-ac** *Nux-m* nux-v *Ol-an* *Olib-sac* wmh1 *Op* k* phos pic-ac plb *Podo* propr sa3• *Psor* k* puls rad-br c11 ran-b c1 ran-s rumx ruta sabad **Samb** santin sel *Sil* *Spong* squil *Stann* stram sul-ac *Sulph* syc bka1• tetox pin2• trad a1* tritic-vg fd5.de *Tub* jl2 valer vanil fd5.de *Verat* verb vesp [spect dfg1]

- **midnight**: ign
- **morning**: bufo sars h2
  - **bed** agg.; in: ant-t
  - **waking**; on: syc bka1•
- **forenoon**: nat-m *Phos*
- **noon**: hura
- **afternoon**: nux-v tritic-vg fd5.de
- **evening**: dig sars h2
  - **bed** agg.; in: *Ant-t*
  - **eating**; after: lach
- **night**: *Kali-c* sel stann *Sulph*
  - **sleep** agg.; during: *Guaj*
- **accompanied** by:
  - **convulsions**: bry b7a.de ip b7a.de nux-v b7a.de puls b7a.de verat b7a.de
  - **dropsy**: *Am-c* b4a.de
  - **eructations** (See STOMACH - Eructations - respiration)
  - **heartbeat**; intermittent: *Phos* b4a.de *Zinc* b4a.de
  - **speech**; loss of: *Ph-ac* b4a.de
  - **swallowing**; constant: *M-aust* b7a.de
  - **urination** | **urging** to urinate: *Bry* b7a.de squil b7.de*
  - **vertigo**: *Phos* b4a.de
  - **vomiting**: asar bg2 cocc bg2 lob ptk1
  - **whistling** | **Trachea**; in: *Cann-s* b7a.de
  - ○ **Abdomen**; constriction of: kali-bi bg2
  - **Chest**:
    - **contraction**: *(↗CHEST - Contraction - intercostal - respiration)* *Verat* h1
    - **pain**:
      - **bruised**; as if (See CHEST - Pain - sore - accompanied)
      - **burning** (See CHEST - Pain - burning - accompanied - respiration)
  - **Ears**; roaring in: *Phos* b4a.de
  - **Hypochondrium**; constriction of: staph bg2 thuj bg2
  - **Mouth**; open: *Acon* b7a.de *Bell* b4a.de *Op* b7a.de *Squil* b7a.de
  - **Neck**; pain at nape of: lyc bg2
  - **Stomach**; pain in: alum bg2 cham bg2 chel bg2 cocc bg2 cupr bg2 dulc bg2 guaj bg2 hell bg2 lyc bg2 *Nux-m* bg2 *Nux-v* bg2 *Phos* bg2 puls bg2 rhod bg2 *Rhus-t* bg2 spig bg2 stram bg2
  - **Teeth**; pain in (See TEETH - Pain - accompanied - respiration)
- **adhesion**; from sensation of:
  - ○ **Epigastrium**: *Sulph* b4a.de
  - **Lungs**; of: *Mez* b4a.de *Thuj* b4a.de
- **air** | **lack** of air; from: *Asar* b7a.de
- **alternating** with | **convulsions**: *Ign* b7a.de
- **anxiety**; from (See MIND - Anxiety - respiration; with)
- **anxiety** in chest; from (See CHEST - Anxiety - accompanied - respiration)
- **arising** from abdomen: lyc bg2 merc-c bg2
- **bending**:
  - **arms** | **forward** agg.: *Sulph* b4a.de
  - **backward** | **agg.**: psor bg2
  - **forward** | **agg.**: psor bg2*
- **blows**, injuries: petr bg2

Impeded, obstructed: ...

- **burrowing**; from | **Epigastrium**; in: chin b7.de*
- **chest**; thrusts in left side of:
  - ▽ **extending** to | **Heart**: *Sulph* k*
- **coffee** agg.: *Cham* k*
- **coition** agg.: cub bg2
- **coming** near mouth; anything: arg-n bg2 cupr bg2 lach bg2
- **congestion**; from: | **Chest**; of: *Calc* b4a.de *Nux-m* b7a.de puls b7a.de *Spong* b7a.de
- **constriction**:
  - ○ **Chest**, of: bell brom bry bg2 **Cact** k* *Caps* *Chel* cic *Cupr-act* medul-os-si rly4• staphycoc rly4• tritic-vg fd5.de
  - **Epigastrium**: *Cupr* b7a.de ign b7a.de staph bg2 sulph bg2 thuj bg2
  - **Larynx**; of: meny b7.de* sabad b7.de* **Spong** b7.de*
  - **Stomach**, in: anan guaj b4a.de*
  - **Throat**; of: *Apis* b7a.de asar b7.de* *Camph* b7a.de canth b7.de* cham b7.de* cocc b7.de* *Hell* b7a.de *Hyos* b7a.de *Ip* b7a.de lac-e hrn2• *Nux-v* b7.de* *Puls* b7.de* sars b4.de* **Verat** b7.de*
  - **Throat**-pit; in: cham b7a.de* cocc b7a.de ign b7a.de lach b7a.de *Rhus-t* b7.de*
- **contraction**:
  - ○ **Chest**; in: *Acon* b7a.de arn b7.de* asaf b7.de* bism b7.de* camph b7a.de canth b7.de* caps b7.de* chin b7.de* cocc b7.de* *Cupr* b7.de* dros b7a.de *Ferr* b7a.de hell b7.de* ip b7.de* kali-n b4.de* kreos b7a.de laur b7.de* *Led* b7.de* m-arct b7.de m-aust b7.de mez b4.de* mosch b7.de* nux-m b7.de* *Nux-v* b7.de* op b7.de* podo bg2 *Puls* b7a.de sars b4.de* sep b4.de* spig b7.de* **Spong** b7a.de staph b7.de* stram b7a.de *Verat* b7.de*
  - **Epigastrium**; in: kali-n b4a.de
  - **Hypogastrium**; in: staph b7.de*
  - **Nose**; of: *Hell* b7a.de
  - **Stomach**; in: sulph h2
  - **Trachea**; in: canth b7.de* *Coff* b7a.de ip b7.de* *Nux-v* b7a.de *Puls* b7.de*
- **cough** agg.; during: acon b7a.de ant-t b7.de* *Apis* b7a.de *Arn* b7a.de ars b4.de* asar b7.de* bry b7.de* calad b7a.de *Chin* b7a.de *Cina* b7a.de cocc b7.de* *Cupr* k* cupr-s dig **Dros** b7.de* euphr b7a.de ferr k* ign k* *Ip* k* just bg2 m-ambo b7.de m-aust b7a.de merc bg2 mez b4.de* *Nux-m* k* nux-v b7.de* op b7a.de petr b4.de* phos bg2 rhus-t b7.de* ruta fd4.de sil k* spig b7.de* squil k* syc bka1• *Verat* b7.de*
  - **dry**: ant-t b7.de* *Carb-v* b4a.de *Cupr* b7.de* *Ip* b7.de* *Nux-v* b7.de* *Rhus-t* b7.de* sep b4.de*
- **cramps**; from:
  - ○ **Tongue**; of: borx b4a.de
  - **Trachea**; in: bell b4a.de
- **crusts** in nose; from: ozone sde2•
- **descending**, on: **Borx**
- **disagreeable** feeling; from | **Abdomen**; in: ars b4.de* op bg2
- **distention**; from | **Hypogastrium**; of: caps b7.de* *Carb-v* b4a.de cham b7.de* *Colch* b7a.de *Ign* b7.de* *Iod* b4a.de kreos b7a.de mez b4.de* *Rhod* b4a.de *Zinc* b4a.de
- **drawing** and stitching; from | **Nape** of neck; in: sep b4.de*
- **dreams**; from anxious: *(↗DREAMS - Abdomen - someone - respiration)* graph h2
- **dryness**; from:
  - ○ **Nose**; in: canth b7.de*
  - **Throat**; in: petr b4.de*
  - **Trachea**; in: merc-c b4a.de *Phos* b4a.de
- **dust**; as if from: am-c bg2 *Ars* b4a.de* bell bg2 calc b4a.de* *Chin* bg2 cycl bg2 *Ign* bg2 ip b7.de* merc bg2 *Puls* bg2
  - ○ **Trachea**; in: **Ip** b7a.de
- **eating** | **after** | **agg.**: cham
  - **while** | **agg.**: mag-m k*
- **edema**; from pulmonary: *Bar-c* b4a.de seneg b4a.de
- **emotional** excitement; from: *Acon* bg2 ars bg2 **Cham** bg2 coff bg2 **Ign** bg2 **Nux-v** bg2 *Staph* bg2 verat bg2
- **emptiness**; sensation of:
  - ○ **Chest**; in: stann b4.de*
  - **Epigastrium**: stann b4a.de

- **exhaustion**; from (See MIND - Prostration - respiration)
- **expanding** lungs impossible: *Asaf* b7a.de *Laur* b7a.de *Op* b7a.de
- **expectoration**; from:
  - · **obstructed** expectoration; from: *Ant-t* b7a.de
  - · **profuse**; too: *Sep* b4a.de *Stann* b4a.de
- **flatulence**; from: *(↗Asthmatic - flatulence; Difficult - flatulence)* ars bg2 caps h1* **Carb-v** k* *Cham* b7.de* chin bg2 *Colch* b7a.de hep bg2 *Kali-c* b4a.de lach b7a.de mez b4a.de nat-c bg2 **Nux-v** b7.de* ol-an **Op** bg2 osm bg2 phos bg2 puls b7.de* *Rhod* b4a.de **Sulph** bg2 *Thuj* bg2 verat bg2 zinc k*
- **foreign** body; from a:
  - ○ · **Chest**; in: chel bg2
  - · **Throat**; in: cic b7.de* *Lach* b7a.de
    - ⋮ **skin** hanging loose in throat; sensation of a: *Phos* b4a.de
- **fullness**; from:
  - ○ · **Abdomen**; in: phos h2*
  - · **Body**; of whole: ruta b7.de*
  - · **Chest**; in: *Acon* b7.de* ant-c b7.de* *Apis* b7a.de caps b7.de* lach b7a.de mez b4.de* nux-m b7.de* *Puls* b7.de* ran-b b7.de* ruta b7.de* sep b4.de* verat b7.de*
  - · **Epigastrium**: staph bg2 thuj bg2
  - · **Hypochondria**: staph bg2 thuj bg2
  - · **Hypogastrium**: cann-s b7.de* caps b7.de* cham b7.de* *Chin* b7.de* m-aust b7.de phos b4.de*
  - · **Stomach**; in: *Chin* b7.de* *Cocc* b7.de* laur b7.de* nux-m b7.de*
- **fumes**; from toxic | **arsenic** or copper: *Camph* b7a.de
- **gagging** | **Esophagus**; in: *Cimx* k*
- **heat**; by: carb-v b4a.de merc b4a.de ruta b7.de* *Sil* b4a.de
  - · **internal**: *Anac* b4a.de
  - · **sensation** of | **Heart**; region of: *Ant-t* b7a.de
  - ○ · **Chest**; in: *Apis* b7a.de
- **heaviness**; from:
  - ○ · **Chest**: am-m b7.de* borx b4a.de cann-s b7.de* ign b7.de* iod b4a.de *Kreos* b7a.de phos b4.de* plat b4.de* rhus-t b7.de*
  - · **Heart**; at: croc b7a.de
  - · **Hypogastrium**: nux-v b7.de*
- **irritation**; from | **Larynx**; in: apis b7a.de
- **lifting** a heavy weight; when: *Bry* b7a.de
- **lying**:
  - · **agg.**: antip vh1 dig c1 *Samb*
  - · **amel.**: psor jl2
  - · **back**; on:
    - ⋮ **agg.**: ol-an sil *Sulph*
    - ⋮ **amel.**: sumb
  - · **side**; on:
    - ⋮ **left** | **agg.**: *Puls*
- **menses**; from suppressed: *Puls* b7a.de *Spong* b7a.de
- **mortification**; from: ign b7.de* ran-b b7.de* staph b7.de*
- **mucus**; from:
  - ○ · **Chest**; in: **Ant-t** bg2 cina b7.de* *Dulc* b4a.de *Ip* b7a.de* m-ambo b7.de *Seneg* b4a.de sep b4a.de *Sulph* b4a.de thuj b4a.de zinc b4a.de
  - · **Larynx**; in: chin b7.de* cupr b7.de* puls b7a.de
  - · **Throat**; in: asar b7.de* aur b4.de* puls b7a.de spong b7a.de
  - · **Trachea**; in: chin b7a.de cupr b7.de* *M-ambo* b7a.de merc-c b4a.de ruta b7.de* sel bg2 *Seneg* b4a.de thuj b4a.de* verat b7.de*
- **nausea**; from: alum bg2 canth b7a.de cham bg2 dig bg2 olnd bg2 petr bg2 rhus-t b7.de* samb b7.de* stram bg2 thuj bg2
- **nightmares**; from: *Op* b7a.de
- **nose** is impeded; breathing through: euph bg2 lach bg2 puls b7.de*
- **obstruction**; from:
  - ○ · **Epigastrium**; in: guaj bg2 lach bg2 nat-m bg2 sulph bg2
  - · **Lungs**; of: *Seneg* b4a.de
  - · **Trachea**; in: cann-s b7.de* spong b7.de*
- **oppression**; from:
  - ○ · **Chest**: *(↗CHEST - Oppression - respiration - difficult)* *Acon* b7.de* anac b4a.de *Ant-t* b7a.de *Apis* b7a.de *Arn* b7.de* *Asaf* b7a.de *Aur* b4a.de borx b4a.de cann-s b7.de* cic b7.de* cina b7.de* cocc b7.de*

- **oppression**; from – **Chest**: ...
  coff b7.de* dros b7.de* ign b7.de* m-aust b7.de merc b4.de* nux-v b7.de* *Olnd* b7a.de *Phos* b4a.de *Plat* b4a.de *Puls* b7.de* *Ran-b* b7.de* rhus-t b7.de* sabad b7.de* sars b4.de* seneg b4.de* spig b7.de* squil b7.de* *Sulph* b4a.de teucr b7.de* thuj b4a.de *Verat* b7.de*
  - · **Epigastrium**; in: chin h1 guaj h2 lac-e hrn2•
  - · **Heart**; in: olib-sac wmh1
  - · **Occiput**; in: kali-n h2
- **orgasm** of blood; from | **Hypogastrium**; in: rhod b4.de*
- **pain**; from: *Acon* bg2 arg-n bg2 **Bry** bg2 *Cupr* bg2 kalm bg2 lach bg2 lyc bg2
  - · **night**: *Nat-m* b4a.de
  - · **takes** away the breath: berb **Bry** k* dios
  - ○ · **Abdomen**; in: arn bg2 ars h2* bry bg2 calc bg2 cann-xyz bg2 caps bg2 cham bg2 *Chin* bg2 *Cocc* bg2 croc bg2 dros bg2 hell bg2 **Ign** bg2 kali-bi bg2 led bg2 lyc bg2 mez bg2 mosch bg2 *Nux-v* bg2 phos bg2 puls bg2 rhod bg2 rhus-t bg2 ruta bg2 spig bg2 stann b4.de* staph bg2
    - ⋮ **cramping**: *Coloc* b4a.de mez b4a.de
    - ⋮ **Lower** abdomen | **pinching**: am-m b7a.de *Coloc* b4a.de *Lyc* b4a.de rhus-t b7.de* spig b7.de*
    - ⋮ **Upper** abdomen: ars b4.de* *Cham* b7a.de *Cocc* b7.de* hell b7.de* lach b7a.de puls b7.de* sep b4.de* staph b7.de*
  - · **Back**; in: *Apis* b7a.de arg-met b7.de* asar ptk1 calc b4a.de cann-s b7.de* lach b7.de* led b7a.de lyc bg2 ox-ac bg2 petr bg2 *Ruta* b7.de* *Sars* b4a.de sep b4.de* staph b7.de* sulph b4a.de* tarax b7.de*
    - ⋮ **dislocated**; as if: petr b4.de*
  - · **Chest**; in the: *Apis* b7a.de ars nh6 brom *Bry* caps carb-v h2 colch croc k* dig c1 lat-m bnm6• merc nux-m b7.de* ozone sde2• plb k* ran-s ruta sel b7.de* *Spig* b7a.de spong k* sulph valer verb
    - ⋮ **drawing**: nux-v b7.de*
    - ⋮ **gnawing**: ran-s b7.de*
    - ⋮ **pinching**: *Spig* b7a.de
    - ⋮ **stitching**: arg-m•: ptk1
    - ⋮ **ulcerative**: staph b7.de*
  - · **Diaphragm**; in: ip spig
  - · **Epigastrium**; in: arn b7.de* ars h2* cina b7.de* *Cocc* b7a.de hell b7.de* laur bg2 *M-aust* b7.de* nux-m b7.de* nux-v b7.de* puls b7.de* *Rhus-t* b7a.de ruta b7.de* sabad b7.de* sulph bg2
    - ⋮ **cramping**: cocc ptk1 guaj b4.de* sulph b4.de*
  - · **Head**; of: arn b7.de*
  - · **Heart**; in region of: apis b7a.de laur b7.de* nux-v b7.de* puls b7.de*
  - · **Hypochondria**; in: chin b7.de* ign b7a.de led b7.de* puls b7.de* staph b7.de* *Valer* b7a.de
  - · **Hypogastrium**; in: arn b7.de* bry b7.de* *Ign* b7.de* ruta b7.de*
    - ⋮ **cramping**: led b7.de*
    - ⋮ **cutting**: *Cham* b7a.de puls b7.de*
  - · **Liver**; in: acon bg2 *Bry* b7a.de con h2* laur bg2 *Nux-v* b7a.de ran-b b7.de* sep h2
    - ⋮ **riding** in a carriage agg.: sep b4.de*
  - · **Loins**; in: *Asar* b7a.de ran-s b7.de*
  - · **Lumbar** region; in: puls b7.de* ruta b7a.de sel b7.de* *Tarax* b7a.de
  - · **Ribs**; under the: sep b4.de*
  - · **Scapulae**; in:
    - ⋮ **dislocated**; as if: petr b4.de*
    - ⋮ **drawing**: rhus-t b7.de* ruta b7.de*
  - · **Shoulder**; in: graph b4a.de sulph b4a.de
  - · **Side**; in: sel b7.de*
    - ⋮ **left** | **squeezed**; as if: merc b4.de*
  - · **Spleen**; in: *Am-m* b7a.de *Apis* b7a.de ruta b7.de*
  - · **Stomach**; in: ars bg2 calad b7.de* cann-s b7a.de caps b7.de* cham b7.de* *Cocc* b7a.de ferr b7a.de guaj bg2 *Nux-v* b7a.de *Phos* bg2 *Rhus-t* b7.de* *Samb* b7a.de stann bg2
    - ⋮ **cramping**: sep b4a.de
    - ⋮ **griping**: guaj b4.de* *Phos* b4.de*
    - ⋮ **stitching**: kali-c b4a.de kali-n b4a.de

- **palpitations**; from: *Am-c* b4a.de *Bry* b7a.de nat-m bg2 *Nit-ac* b4a.de *Phos* b4a.de puls b7a.de spig b7.de* *Spong* b7a.de *Sulph* b4a.de *Verat* b7a.de *Viol-o* b7a.de *Zinc* b4a.de
- **plug**; from sensation of a | **throat**; in: *Spong* b7.de*
- **pressure**; from:
  - **clothes**; of: (↗*Difficult - clothes - loosening; Difficult - clothes - loosening - amel.*) nux-m bg2
  - **weight**; as from a | **Chest**; in: *Asaf* b7a.de *Cann-s* b7a.de ign b7a.de *Nux-m* b7.de* rheum b7.de* sabad b7.de* spig b7.de* viol-o b7.de*
  - **Abdomen**; in: mez b4.de* sep b4a.de
  - **Chest**; in: all-c bg2 am-m b7.de* anac b4.de* ang b7.de* *Ant-t* b7a.de apis b7a.de arg-met b7.de* arn b7.de* ars b4a.de asaf b7.de* bell b4.de* borx b4a.de *Bry* b7a.de camph b7.de* cann-s b7.de* caust b4.de* cham b7.de* chel b7.de* chin b7.de* *Cic* b7.de* *Colch* b7a.de ign b7.de* kreos b7a.de laur b7.de* m-arct b7.de mosch b7a.de nux-m b7.de* nux-v b7.de* olnd b7.de* ph-ac b4a.de ran-b b7.de* ran-s b7.de* rheum b7.de* *Rhod* b4a.de ruta b7.de* sabad b7.de* samb b7.de* spig b7.de* *Staph* b7.de* stram b7.de* teucr b7.de* valer b7.de* verat b7.de* viol-o b7a.de *Zinc* b4a.de
  - **Epigastrium**; in: arn b7.de* ars b4a.de bry b7.de* calad b7.de* camph b7.de* *Caust* b4a.de cham b7.de* chin b7.de* cic b7.de* cocc b7.de* hell b7.de* hyos b7.de* ign b7.de* mosch b7.de* *Nux-v* b7.de* olnd b7.de* *Rhod* b4a.de *Rhus-t* b7.de* samb b7.de*
  - **Heart**; sensation of pressure at: bell h1
  - **Hypochondria**; in: *Rhod* b4a.de
  - **Hypogastrium**; on: *Cham* b7a.de
  - **Scapulae**; in: rhus-t b7.de*
    - **leaning** against something; when: *Calc* b4a.de sep b4.de*
  - **Throat**; in: olnd b7.de*
  - **Uterus**; in: *Sep* b4a.de
- **pulsation**; from:
  - **Chest**; in: asaf b7.de*
  - **Epigastrium**; in: chel b7.de* nux-v b7a.de
  - **Tonsils**; of: *Am-m* b7a.de
- **raising** | **arm** | **agg.**: (↗*Difficult - raising - arms - agg.*) berb
  - **arm** above head agg.: *Cupr* b7.de*
- **rising**; as if something was | **falling**; and | **Chest**; in: ip b7a.de
  - **Throat**; in: cann-s b7.de* *Cham* b7a.de stann b4.de*
    - **warm**; something: *Plat* b4a.de
- **sadness**; with (See MIND - Sadness - respiration - impeded)
- **salt**; as from: phos b4a.de
- **scabs** in nose; from: ozone sde2•
- **scratching**; from | **Throat**; in: sabad b7.de*
- **shooting** in chest: canth nux-m *Ox-ac*
- **sitting** agg.: dig c1 psor jl2
- **spasms** of chest: ars b4a.de asaf b7.de* *Bell* b4a.de **Bry** b7a.de *Carb-v* b4a.de *Caust* b4a.de *Cic* b7a.de *Cina* b7a.de cupr b7.de* guaj b4.de* hyos k* **Ip** b7a.de* *Kali-c* b4a.de kali-n b4a.de merc-c b4a.de mosch b7a.de op b7a.de petr b4.de* *Phos* b4a.de plb b7.de* *Puls* b7a.de *Samb* b7a.de sars b4.de* stram k* *Sulph* b4a.de *Verat* b7a.de *Zinc* b4a.de
- **stitches**; from:
  - **Abdomen**: calc h2 mez h2 ruta fd4.de
  - **Back**: cann-s h1 mez h2
  - **Bladder**; in: aur b4.de*
  - **Cervical** region: sep h2
  - **Chest**; in: **Acon** b7.de* aloe ang b7.de* arg-met k* arn asaf b7.de* asar b7.de* aur b4.de* berb **Borx** b4a.de *Bry* k* calc b4a.de canth b7.de* caps b7.de* carb-an h2 carb-v b4.de* chin b7.de* chinin-s *Cycl* b7.de* dros b7.de* graph h2 kali-n b4a.de* *Kreos* k* laur b7.de* lyc h2 m-aust b7.de merc b4.de* mez mosch b7a.de nat-m h2 nit-ac h2 nux-m b7.de* ph-ac h2 plb b7.de* ran-b b7.de* rhod ruta b7.de* *Sel* b7a.de spig b7.de* squil b7.de* stann k* staph b7.de* sul-ac thuj verat b7.de* verb k* viol-t b7.de*
  - **Epigastrium**; in: *Bry* b7a.de *Cham* b7a.de chin b7.de* phos b4.de* spig b7.de*
  - **Heart**, in: apis b7a.de bac c1 *Cact* k* *Calc* calc-p cham b7.de* mag-m b4.de* merc-i-f *Naja* k* petr b4.de* puls b7.de* *Staph*
  - **Hypochondria**: arn h1 *Kali-c* b4a.de
    - **Epigastrium**; and: kali-c h2
- **stitches**; from: ...
  - **Hypogastrium**; in: croc b7.de* dros b7.de* kreos b7a.de mosch b7.de* nux-v b7.de* puls b7.de* ruta b7.de* *Sep* b4a.de sil b4a.de
  - **Kidneys**; region of: cycl b7.de*
  - **Larynx**; in: laur b7.de*
  - **Liver**: nat-m h2
  - **Lumbar** region; in: arn b7a.de *Carb-an* b4a.de m-aust b7.de merc b4a.de nux-v b7.de* puls b7.de* tarax b7.de*
  - **Occiput**: nit-ac h2
  - **Rectum**; in: sulph b4.de*
  - **Scapulae**: *Am-m* b7a.de *Cann-s* b7a.de *Kali-n* b4a.de kreos b7a.de *Myrt-c* b7a.de puls b7.de* sars b4.de* sep b4.de* sil b4a.de
    - **Between**: nit-ac h2
    - **Under**: sulph h2
  - **Shoulder**; in: graph b4.de* laur bg2
  - **Side**; in | **right**: calc b4a.de graph b4.de*
  - **Spleen**; in: *Am-m* b7a.de arn b7.de* *Kali-c* b4a.de rhod b4a.de
  - **Sternum**: nat-m h2 phos h2
- **stooping**:
  - **agg.**: *Calc* k* sil
  - **amel.**: petr h2
- **sulphur** fumes; as if from: *Camph* b7a.de croc b7.de* lyc bg2 mosch b7.de* *Puls* b7a.de
- **swallowing** agg.: **Brom**
- **swelling**; from:
  - **Abdomen**; of: *Iod* b4a.de
  - **Hypochondria**; of: *Cham* b7.de* *Ign* b7.de*
  - **Hypogastrium**; of: bry b7.de*
  - **Pharynx**; of: *Bell* b4a.de *Merc* b4a.de *Merc-c* b4a.de verat b7.de*
  - **Throat**; of: merc-c b4a.de
  - **Tongue**; of: *Apis* b7a.de *Dulc* b4a.de
  - **Tonsils**; of: bar-i bg2
- **swelling**; from sensation of:
  - **Epigastrium**; of: rhus-t b7.de*
  - **Throat**; in: *Am-m* b7a.de
- **talking** agg.: *Caust* k*
- **tearing**; from | **Chest**; in: cycl b7.de*
- **tension**; from:
  - **Abdomen**; in | **Lower** abdomen: *Ars* b4a.de bell b4a.de *Caps* b7a.de *Ferr* b7a.de *Sulph* b4a.de
  - **Chest**; in: *Calc* b4a.de cann-s b7.de* *Cic* b7.de* cocc b7.de* colch b7a.de *Con* b4a.de *Euph* b4a.de merc b4.de* mur-ac b4.de* *Nat-c* b4a.de puls b7.de* rhus-t b7.de* *Sep* b4a.de staph b7.de*
  - **Epigastrium**: *Cupr* b7a.de
  - **Hypochondria**; in: ign b7a.de *Puls* b7a.de *Staph* b7a.de
- **thinking** of past troubles: sep h2
- **thrusts**; from:
  - **Abdomen**; in: calc b4.de*
  - **Chest**; in: cann-s b7.de*
  - **Heart**: *Zinc* b4a.de
  - **Lumbar** region; in: m-ambo b7.de
- **tickling**; from:
  - **Throat**; in: *Brom* b4a.de
  - **Trachea**; in: rhus-t b7.de*
- **touch**; from | **Throat**; of external: lach b7.de*
- **trembling**; from | **Chest**; in: ang b7.de*
- **walking** agg.: dig c1 *Phos* bg2*
- **warmth**; from:
  - **rising** from upper abdomen: valer b7.de*
  - **Chest**: *Mang* b4a.de *Plat* b4a.de
  - **Epigastrium**; in: bry b7.de*
- **weakness**; from: ars b4a.de
  - **Chest**; in: *Canth* b7a.de *Cycl* b7a.de *Ph-ac* b4a.de **Plat** b4a.de stann b4.de*
  - **Lungs**; of: carb-v b4a.de stann b4.de*
- **weariness**; from: cycl b7.de*

Respiration

○ - **Throat-pit**; felt in: kali-n b4a.de

IMPERCEPTIBLE: *(↗Superficial)* acon k* amyg k* *Ars* k* benz-ac carb-ac k* cass a1 chlor k* cic k* *Cocc* gels k* hydr-ac k* m-ambo b7.de merc morph k* naja nit-s-d a1 nux-v k* oena a1 op k* petr k* stram verat b7.de*
- **sleep** agg.; during: caust h2*

INFLAMMATION: | **Respiratory** tract (See CHEST - Inflammation - bronchial)

INJURY agg.; after: petr ptk1

INSPIRATION:
- **agg.**: acon b7.de* *Apis* b7a.de bry b7.de* caps b7.de* caust b4a.de cham b7a.de chin b7a.de cina b7.de* cocc b7a.de coloc b4a.de ign b7.de* *Ip* b7.de* *Lob* bg2 mosch b7.de* op b7a.de ran-b b7.de* rhus-t b7.de* *Sabad* b7a.de sabin b7.de* *Sep* b4a.de spig b7.de* *Spong* bg2 squil b7.de*
- **deep** | **amel.**: chel bg2

INTERMITTENT, unequal: *(↗Irregular; Jerking; GENERALS - Cheyne-stokes)* ang k* **Ant-t** k* bell calad camph b7.de* carb-ac carb-an carbn-h *Cham* chlor cina k* coc-c cocc c1 *Colch* ign laur b7.de* **Nit-ac** k* *Op* k* plb stry ter *Verat* k*
- **night**: bell
  - **midnight** | **waking**; on: cann-i
- **lying** down agg.: ant-t k*
- **sleep** agg.; during: *Ant-t* k* bell h1 op
- **waves**; like in: *Iod* b4a.de

INTERRUPTED: *(↗Arrested; Asphyxia)* acon b7.de* ang b7.de* ant-t b7.de* bell b4a.de *Camph* bg2 *Cham* b7.de* cic b7.de* cina b7.de* **Cupr** b7.de* dig bg2 euph bg2 *Hydr-ac* bg2 ign b7.de* *Laur* b7.de* m-arct b7.de merc-c b4a.de *Op* b7.de* puls b7.de*
- **expiration**: ars k*
- **inspiration**: **Cina** *Led*

INTOXICATION agg.: bry b7a.de puls b7a.de *Spig* b7a.de

IRREGULAR: *(↗Intermittent; GENERALS - Cheyne-stokes)* absin k* acet-ac k* acon b2.de* agar-cps a1 agath-a nl2• **Ail** k* alco a1 ambr k* **Ang** k* *Ant-t* k* apom vh1 *Ars* k* ars-i asar b2.de* atra-r bnm3• aur aur-ar k2 aur-i k2 aur-s k2 **Bell** k* calad k* *Camph* k* canth k* *Cham* k* chin b2.de* chinin-s chir-fl bnm4• chlf hr1 chlor k* cic k* *Cina* k* clem k* coca cocc k* coff b2.de* *Colch* k* convo-s sp1 crat br1* *Crot-h* k* **Cupr** k* **Dig** k* dros k* gels k* hell bro1 hippoz k* hydr-ac k* hyos k* *Ign* k* *Iod* k* ip b2.de* lat-m bnm6• laur k* led k* lyss c1 m-arct b2.de merc merc-c b4a.de* mez b2.de* **Morph** k* mosch k* nicc k* nitro-o a1 *Nux-v* k* olnd k* **Op** k* phos k* physala-p bnm7• plb k* psil ft1 *Puls* k* ruta b2.de* sec b2.de* sep k* sol-t-ae k* stram k* *Stry* k* sul-ac k* sul-i k2 sulph ptk1* tab k* tax k* ter k* tril-p bro1 valer st verat b2.de* verat-v k* zinc k* zinc-p k2
- **chill**; during: ang bg2 bell bg2 cina bg2 cupr bg2 ign bg2 mosch bg2 op bg2 puls bg2
- **cough** agg.; during: clem cupr-s k*
- **drinking** agg.: anac k*
- **sleep** agg.; during: ant-t k* cadm-s *Ign* k*
- **slow**, at another time hurried; at one time: acon bell grin st *Ign* k* nux-v op k* spong
- **sneezing**; with: tril-p br1
- **standing** agg.: arn k*

JERKING: *(↗Intermittent)* asar k* bell bg2* *Cact* k* *Calad* k* crot-h k* *Cupr* k* gels k* *Ign* ptk1 *Iod* k* ix bnm8• laur bg2* merc k* nicc k* op k* ox-ac ptk1 pyrog jl2 tab bg2*
- **expiration**: ars
- **inspiration**: **Ox-ac** k*
  - **two** distinct efforts; by: led
- **two** jerks; in: acon bg2 ang b7.de* ant-t b7.de* asar b7.de* led b7.de* tab bg2

KNEELING: | **amel.**: caust bg2*

LABORED (See Difficult)

LARGELY: lat-m bnm6•

LAUGHING agg.: ars b4a.de* aur b4.de* cupr b7a.de* lyc bg2 manc bg2 plb bg2

LEANING AGAINST SOMETHING agg.: *Apis* b7a.de *Cupr* b7a.de

LIFTING agg.: *Bry* b7a.de *Calc* bg2 **Rhus-t** bg2 *Sulph* bg2

LONG: ant-t cham *Chlor* lil-t ptk1 lob *Op* k*
- **alternating** with | **difficult** respiration (See Difficult - alternating - long)

LOUD: *(↗Moaning; Panting; Snoring; Stertorous)* acon k* agar k* alum k* am-c k* ambr b2.de* ant-c b2.de ant-t k* aral vh1 *Arn* k* ars k* asar b2.de* bell b2.de* bov k* *Brom* k* bry b2.de* bufo bg2 calad b2.de* **Calc** k* camph b2.de* cann-s b2.de* caps b2.de* *Carb-v* k* carbn-s **Cham** k* **Chin** k* chinin-s *Chlor* *Cina* k* *Cocc* b2.de* *Colch* k* coloc b2.de* con k* *Cor-r* cub c1 cupr dros b2.de* dulc b2.de* ferr k* ferr-m k* gamb k* gard-j vlr2• graph b2.de* guare k* *Hep* k* hippoz jl2 hydr-ac k* *Hyos* k* *Ign* k* iod b2.de* **Kali-bi** k* *Kali-c* k* kali-cy a1 *Kalm* k* **Lach** k* laur b2.de* loxo-lae bnm12• lyc b2.de* m-ambo b2.de m-aust b2.de mag-m b2.de* merc merc-c b4a.de* morph k* mur-ac b2.de* nat-m k* *Nat-s* nat-sal a1 nit-ac b2.de* nux-v k* *Op* k* petr b2.de* **Phos** k* plb b2.de* plut-n srj7• *Puls* k* rheum b2.de* *Rhus-t* k* sabad b2.de* sabin b2.de* **Samb** k* *Seneg* sep b2.de* sil b2.de* **Spong** k* squil k* stann b2.de* *Stram* k* sul-ac k* **Sulph** k* **Verat** k*
- **forenoon**: hell k*
- **night**:
  - **midnight** | **waking**; on: ant-s-aur
- **chill**; during: *Calad* bg2 cham bg2 chin bg2 cina bg2 ign bg2 kali-c bg2 nux-v bg2 phos bg2 samb bg2 spong bg2 sulph bg2 thuj bg2
- **expiration**: ant-t bell h1* kali-cy a1 lat-m bnm6• mag-s meph *Nux-v* op
- **inspiration** agg.: *Bell* k* caps cham *Chin* cina coloc hyos *Ign* mag-s *Nux-v* puls rheum sep h2*
- **lying** on right side agg.: sulph k*
- **open** mouth: acon bg2 *Squil* bg2
- **paroxysms**; during: plb k*
- **sitting** quiet, while: *Ferr* k*
- **sleep** agg.; during: *Arn* h1* carb-v k* cham ign **Puls** k* rheum
  - **nose**, through: arn h1
- **spasms** of glottis, as from: kalm k*
- **walking** agg.: calc k*
  - **nose**; respiration through: calc h2

LYING:
- **agg.**: am-m b7a.de ant-t b7a.de* apis b7a.de* ars b4.de* asaf b7.de* bapt bg2 bell b4.de* borx b4a.de* calc b4a.de* *Cann-s* b7a.de* carb-v b4.de* caust bg2 chin b7.de* coll bg2 *Con* b4a.de *Dig* b4.de* euphr bg2 ferr b7.de* graph b4.de* ham bg2 hep b4a.de* *Ip* bg2 kali-c ptk1 *Kali-n* b4.de* lach b7.de* lob ptk1 *Nat-m* b4a.de *Nux-v* b7.de* olnd b7.de* *Phos* b4.de* podo bg2 puls b7.de* rhus-t b7.de* rumx bg2 sabad b7.de* samb b7a.de* sang bg2 sel b7.de* sep b4a.de* *Spong* b7a.de *Stann* b4a.de sulph bg2 tarax bg2 tarent bg2 tub ptk1
- **amel.**: bry b7.de* calc-p bg2* chel ptk1 dig ptk1 hell ptk1 kali-bi bg2* laur ptk1 *Nux-v* b7.de* psor bg2* sabad b7.de* ter ptk1
- **back**; on:
  - **agg.**: alum bg2 lyc bg2* nux-v b7.de* *Phos* b4.de* *Plb* b7a.de puls b7.de* sil b4.de*
  - **amel.**: borx bg2 bry b7.de* *Cact* ptk1 ign b7.de* kalm ptk1 puls b7.de*
- **head** high; with the | **amel.**: *Ant-t* b7a.de *Apis* b7a.de cann-s b7.de* caps b7.de* *Chin* b7.de* *Kali-n* bg2 *Puls* b7.de* *Spig* b7.de*
- **head** low; with the | **agg.**: ant-t b7.de* *Apis* b7a.de* *Ars* b4a.de cact ptk1 cann-s b7.de* caps b7.de* chin b7a.de* colch b7a.de* hep b4.de* kali-c ptk1 kali-n b4a.de* lach b7a.de nux-v b7a.de *Puls* b7.de* spig b7.de*
- **horizontal** position; in a | **amel.**: arn b7.de* spong b7.de*
- **side**; on:
  - **affected** side | **agg.**: borx bg2 calc bg2 lyc bg2 sabad bg2 sulph bg2
  - **agg.**: ars ptk1 bry b7.de* carb-an bg2 ign b7.de* plat bg2 puls b7a.de* sabad bg2 sang bg2 scroph-n bg2 sulph bg2
  - **amel.**: alum bg2* lyc bg2 *Phos* b4.de*
  - **left**:
    - **agg.**: acon b7.de* am-c bg2 anac b4a.de ant-t b7a.de apis bg2 bry b7.de* carb-an b4a.de ip b7.de* kali-c bg2 lyc b4a.de merc b4.de* *Phos* bg2 plb bg2 *Puls* b7.de* rumx bg2 sulph b4.de*
    - **amel.**: castm ptk1 sulph b4.de*
  - **right**:
    - **agg.**: acon b7.de* am-m b7a.de anac b4a.de bry b7a.de carb-an b4a.de castm bg2 kali-c bg2 *Nux-v* b7a.de ran-b b7.de* scroph-n bg2 *Sil* b4a.de spig b7.de* spong bg2 squil bg2 sulph b4.de*

- **side**; on – **right**: ...
  - **amel.**: ant-t b7a.de colch b7.de* naja ptk1 spig b7.de*
  - **head** high; with the: cact ptk1 spig ptk1 spong ptk1
- • **unaffected** side | **agg.**: stann bg2

LYING DOWN agg.; after: apis bg2 **Ars** b4a.de m-ambo b7.de m-aust b7.de podo bg2 puls b7.de* rhus-t b7.de* squil bg2 _Thuj_ b4a.de

MEASLES; after: _Brom_ b4a.de

MENSES:
- **before** | **agg.**: borx b4a.de cupr bg2 _Kali-c_ b4a.de nat-m b4.de* ph-ac b4a.de phos b4.de* sulph b4a.de thuj b4a.de
- **during**:
  - • **agg.**: _Sep_ b4.de*
  - • **beginning** of menses | **agg.**: _Asar_ b7a.de
- **suppressed** menses; from: phos b4a.de

MILK CRUST; after: cupr b7a.de

MOANING: (_↗Loud_) acon k* aeth _Ant-t_ k* _Ars_ k* bell k* _Bry_ b7.de* _Calad_ b7.de* carb-v k2 cham b7.de* cina k* _Cocc_ b7.de* coff _Colch_ k* con h2* cupr k* _Graph_ b4a.de _Hydr-ac_ k* ign b7.de* _Ip_ b7a.de kali-c k* _Lach_ k* laur k* _Lyss_ k* m-ambo b7.de _Mur-ac_ k* _Nux-v_ b7.de* olib-sac wmh1 _Op_ k* phos k* phyt plb _Puls_ k* rhus-t k* sec k* sel spong k* squil k* _Stram_ b7.de* tab k*
- **acute**: _Ip_ b7.de*
- **expiration**: bell h1*

MORTIFICATION agg.: ars bg2 **Ign** bg2 ran-b bg2 _Staph_ bg2

MOTION:
- **agg.**: agar b4.de* _Am-c_ b4a.de am-m b7a.de anac b4.de* _Apis_ b7a.de arn b7.de* _Ars_ b4.de* _Aur_ b4a.de borx bg2 _Bry_ b7.de* calc b4.de* cann-xyz bg2 caps b7.de* carb-v b4.de* chin b7.de* cocc b7.de* colch bg2 _Con_ b4.de* _Euph_ b4a.de ferr bg2 ferr-p bg2 graph bg2 ign b7.de* ip b7.de* _Kali-c_ b4a.de* led b7.de* lyc bg2 meph bg2 mur-ac bg2 nat-m b4.de* nit-ac b4.de* nux-m b7.de* nux-v b7.de* petr b4.de* _Phos_ b4.de* puls bg2 rhus-t bg2 _Samb_ b7a.de seneg bg2 sep b4.de* _Spig_ b7.de* spong b7.de* _Stann_ b4.de* sulph b4.de* verat b7.de* zinc b4.de*
  - • **rapid** motion: merc ptk1
- **amel.**: arg-n ptk1 aur ptk1 bell bg2 brom bg2* _Caps_ b7a.de coff bg2 euph bg2 ferr bg2* lob bg2* phos ptk1 puls b7.de* rhus-t b7.de* samb b7.de* seneg bg2 sil bg2
  - • **rapid** motion: sep ptk1
- **arms**; of:
  - • **agg.**: _Am-m_ b7a.de ang bg2 camph bg2 led bg2 plb b7.de* spig b7a.de*
  - • **amel.**: nat-m ptk1
- **beginning** of | **agg.**: thuj bg2
- **gentle** motion | **amel.**: carb-v bg2 psor bg2
- **hands**; of | **agg.**: bov ptk1
- **head**; of | **agg.**: gels bg2

MOUTH; through: elaps mtf11

MUCUS agg.; accumulation of: _Ant-t_ bg2 ars bg2 bar-c bg2 bell bg2 bry bg2 calc bg2 camph bg2 chin bg2 con bg2 cupr bg2 dulc bg2 ferr bg2 graph bg2 hep bg2 ip bg2 lach bg2 merc bg2 nux-v bg2 phos bg2 puls bg2 seneg bg2 sep bg2 sil bg2 sulph bg2 zinc bg2

NOISY (See Loud)

OBSTRUCTED (See Impeded)

ODORS AGG.; STRONG: ars ptk1 ph-ac bg2* sang bg2*

OPENING THE MOUTH: | **amel.**: op bg2

OPPRESSION (See CHEST - Oppression)

PAINFUL: (_↗CHEST - Inflammation - lungs; CHEST - Inflammation - pleura_) _Acon_ b7.de* aeth gsy1* aethyl-n a1 apis _Arn_ b7.de* ars b4.de* asc-t k* bell k2 brom k* _Bry_ k* chin k* cimx k* coff coff-t a1 crot-t k* dream-p sdj1• gad a1 ger-i rly4• guaj bg2 jug-c k* led k* _Mez_ bg2 nit-ac k* nit-s-d a1 ol-j plb k* **Ran-b** k* ruta fd4.de sang k* trad a1* verat-v tl1 viol-o k* zing k*
- **morning**: phos k*
- **night**: dig c1 sang k*
- **accompanied** by | **Abdomen** | **distension** (See ABDOMEN - Distension - accompanied - respiration)
  - • **Hypochondrium**; fullness of: but-ac sp1

Painful: ...
- **inspiration** agg.: aesc apis mrr1 chin a1 ger-i rly4• kali-n a1 olib-sac wmh1 plect a1
- **lying** down agg.: dig c1
- **metallic** tube; as if hot water is running through: ter ptk1

PAINS:
- **general** pains agg.: **Ars** b4.de* berb bg2 bry ptk1 cact bg2 caps bg2 carb-v bg2* cham b7.de* _Cocc_ bg2* con bg2 glon bg2 kalm ptk1 lach bg2 lob bg2 lyc bg2 **Nat-m** b4a.de* nat-s bg2 nux-v bg2 plb bg2 prun ptk1 _Puls_ b7.de* ran-s ptk1 _Sep_ bg2* sil b4.de* staph bg2 sulph bg2* verat bg2
- **stomach** pains agg.: arg-met ptk1 arg-n ptk1 berb ptk1

PANTING: (_↗Accelerated; Catching; Gasping; Loud; Puffing_) acon k* alum b2.de* aml-ns bg2 amyg a1* anac k* ant-ar bg2 _Ant-t_ k* _Apoc_ k* arg-n k* _Arn_ k* ars k* bar-c b2.de* bell b2.de* brom bg2 _Bry_ k* bufo k* cact br1 calad k* **Calc** gk calc-p bg2 camph k* _Carb-an_ k* caul k* cham k* chin k* chlor k* _Cina_ k* _Cocc_ k* con cop k* cor-r bg2 cupr b2.de* _Dig_ bg2 dros bg2 ferr k* graph b2.de* grin bg2 hell bg2 hydr-ac bg2 hyos k* ign b2.de* _Ip_ k* jatr-c kali-bi k* kali-c b2.de* kreos b2.de* laur k* limest-b es1• _Lob_ bg2 _Lyc_ k* m-ambo b2.de merc b2.de* mur-ac b2.de* naja bg2 _Nat-m_ b4a.de _Nit-ac_ k* nitro-o a1 _Nux-m_ k* nux-v b2.de* op k* **Phos** k* _Phyt_ k* plan k* plb k* prun k* puls b2.de* _Samb_ b7a.de* sec k* senn a1 _Sil_ k* spira a1 _Spong_ k* squil b2.de* stann b2.de* stram k* sulph b4a.de* _Tarent_ k* **Verat-v** k* vip bg2 zinc bg2
- **ascending** stairs agg.: **Calc** k* phos h2* plan k* [tax jsj7]
- **children**; in: androc bnm2•
- **chill**; during: calad b7a.de
- **motion** agg.: tarent
- **reading**; when: nit-ac ptk1
- **running** rapidly; as from: hyos ptk1
- **sleep**; during: m-aust b7a.de nux-v b7a.de sabin b7a.de
- **stooping** agg.: nit-ac ptk1
- **waking**; on: coca-c sk4• kali-bi rad-br ptk1
- **walking** rapidly agg.: sil h2*

PARALYSIS (See Asphyxia - paralysis; CHEST - Paralysis - lung)

PAROXYSMAL: ang b7.de* _Arg-n_ ptk1 ars k* arund bell k2 brom k* con bg2 _Cor-r_ _Cupr_ k* _Gels_ k* hydr-ac k* _Ign_ _Ip_ k* kali-c kali-cy k* lach bg2 lat-m bnm6• led k* m-arct b7.de _Mag-p_ meli a1 mez mill mosch mur-ac nat-m k* nux-m ptk1 oena k* op k* _Ox-ac_ k* phos plb puls k* pyrus _Samb_ spig hr1 stann sulph tab k* **Valer** k* _Verat_ k* verat-v k*
- **evening**: stann
- **night**: nat-m
- **double** inspiration: (_↗Double_) led br1*

PERIODICITY: alum bg2 asaf bg2 cact bg2 _Cann-s_ b7a.de carb-v bg2 chel bg2 chin bg2 colch b7a.de kali-c bg2 nat-s bg2 plb b7a.de* sulph bg2

PERSPIRATION:
- **after**:
  - • **agg.**: _Op_ b7a.de
  - • **amel.**: chel bg2
- **agg.**: ars bg2 lach bg2 nux-v bg2

PORK agg.: ip b7.de* nat-c b4.de* puls b7.de*

PRESSURE:
- **abdomen**; on | **agg.**: cham b7a.de
- **amel.**: asaf b7.de* bry b7.de* puls b7.de*
- **clothes**; of: | **agg.**: am-m bg2 **Bry** bg2 _Calc_ bg2 carb-v bg2 _Caust_ b4a.de* coff bg2 **Hep** bg2 kreos bg2 lach b7a.de* **Lyc** bg2 **Nux-v** bg2 sars b4a.de* _Spig_ bg2 spong bg2 **Sulph** bg2
- **spine** agg.; on: chinin-s ptk1

PUFFING: (_↗Panting; Stertorous_)
- **expiration**: (non:cham h1) chen-a bg2 _Chin_ k* lyc bg2 op bg2* stram

QUICK (See Accelerated)

RAISING ARMS agg.: _Spig_ b7a.de

RASPING: (_↗Rough; Rough - sawing_) brom k2

Respiration

RATTLING: (*↗LARYNX - Rattling - trachea; NOSE - Rattling*) acet-ac *Acon* k* adam skp7• agar *All-c* k* all-s bro1 alum k* alum-p k2 alum-sil k2 *Am-c* k* am-caust bro1* *Am-m* k* *Ammc* k* *Anac* b2.de* anan ang b2.de* ant-ar bg2* ant-c b2.de* *Ant-i* bro1 ant-o **Ant-t** k* *Apis* **Apoc** k* aral sne arg-met bg2 arg-n k* arn b2.de* **Ars** k* *Ars-i* ars-s-f k2 *Art-v* k* asaf k* *Asc-t* bac bro1* bals-p bro1 *Bar-c* k* bar-i k2 *Bar-m* k* bar-s k2 *Bell* k* bism bg2 bit-ar wht1• *Brom* k* bry k* bufo **Cact** k* *Calc* k* calc-act bro1 calc-i k2 *Calc-p* *Calc-s* k* calc-sil k2 camph k* cann-i br1* *Cann-s* k* cann-xyz ptk1 canth bg2 carb-ac bg2 *Carb-an* k* *Carb-v* k* *Carbn-h* carbn-s **Caust** k* *Cham* k* *Chel* k* chen-a c1* **Chin** k* *Chinin-ar* chinin-s chlor k* cic k* *Cina* k* *Coc-c* k* cocc b2.de* coch bro1 cod bg2 con sne cop croc b2.de* crot-t cub **Cupr** k* cupr-n a1 *Dig* k* **Dulc** k* eucal bg2* euph sne euph-pi bro1 *Euphr* *Ferr* k* ferr-ar ferr-i ferr-p k* fl-ac bg2 galv c1 *Graph* k* grin bg2* **Hep** k* **Hippoz** k* hydr-ac k* *Hyos* k* hyper bro1 ign b2.de* *Iod* k* **Ip** k* ix bnm8• jab sne kali-ar *Kali-bi* k* kali-br sne *Kali-c* k* *Kali-chl* kali-hox tl1 kali-i k* kali-m k2* kali-n bro1 kali-p **Kali-s** k* kali-sil k2 kola stb3• *Lach* k* lact laur k* led b2.de* lob k* **Lyc** k* lyss k* *Manc* k* med k2 meph br1* merc k* *Merc-c* b4a.de morb jl2 morph k* mosch k* mucor jl2* *Mur-ac* k* nat-ar mrr1 nat-c k* *Nat-m* k* *Nat-s* k* *Nit-ac* k* *Nux-m* k* *Nux-v* k* oena bro1 *Op* k* ox-ac k* par b2.de* parathyr jl2 *Pect* c1 petr k* *Ph-ac* phel bg2 **Phos** k* phyt pix bro1 plb k* podo c1 pulm-v bro1* **Puls** k* *Pyrog* k* *Ran-b* k* rhus-t bg2 rumx **Ruta** bg2 sabal bro1 sabin c1 samb k* *Sang* k* sanic santin sars sel senec **Seneg** k* *Sep* k* *Sil* k* sin-n sne *Spong* k* squil b2.de* *Stann* k* *Stram* k* stry k* sul-ac k* sul-i k2 *Sulph* k* syc fmm1• syph tab ter sne thuj k* *Tub* k* *Verat* k* yers jl2 *Zinc* k* zinc-p k2 zing k* [bell-p-sp dcm1]

- **day** and night: **Cact**
- **morning**: agar
- **evening**:
  - **bed** agg.; in: carb-an h2 petr sul-ac h2
  - **lying** down agg.: con h2*
- **midnight**, before: *Stram* k*
- **accompanied** by:
  - **cold** breath and coldness of lower extremities: ant-t tl1 carb-v tl1
  - **croup**: hep tl1
- **children**; in: ant-t mrr1 cham mtf33 chin mtf33 cupr mtf33 kali-s mrr1 *Nat-s* bro1 samb bro1 sil mtf33 sulph mtf33 thuj bro1 tub mtf33 verat mtf33
- **chill**; during: chin bg2 cupr bg2 hep bg2 lyc bg2 nux-m bg2 stram bg2
- **cold** drinks agg.: phos ptk1
- **coma**; with (See MIND - Coma - respiration - rattling)
- **convulsions**; during: tab k*
- **cough**:
  - **after**: ant-t hr1 carb-v hr1 *Mur-ac* hr1
  - **before**: dros h1* sep h2*
  - **during**:
    - **agg.**: adam skp7• *Bell* b4.de *Chin* b7a.de kali-s tl1
      - **daytime**: adam skp7•
      - **air**; in open | **amel.**: adam skp7•
    - **amel.**: squil h1
      - **night**: adam skp7•
- **drinking** agg.; after: *Mur-ac* hr1
- **expectoration**:
  - **amel.**: sulph h2*
  - **before**: sep h2*
  - **scanty** expectoration; with: am-c bg2 *Ant-t* bg2 ip bg2
  - **without**: am-c ptk1 **Ant-t** br1* carb-v ptk1 caust ptk1 con ptk1 hep ptk1 *Ip* ptk1 kali-s ptk1 *Lob* ptk1 phos ptk1 sep ptk1 sulph ptk1 tub ptk1 verat bg2*
- **expiration** agg.; during: calc chin h1
- **fever**; during: *Acon* bg2 *Ars* bg2 carb-v bg2 cham bg2 hep bg2 ip bg2 lyc bg2 **Nux-m** b7.de* **Op** b7.de* spong bg2 squil bg2 stann bg2
- **fine**: ip ptk1
- **lying**:
  - **agg.**: **Cact** calc puls k2
  - **back**; on | **agg.**: agar kali-c
  - **side**; on | **agg.**: anac h2
- **old** people●: *Ammc* *Bar-c* **Hippoz** **Kali-bi** **Lyc** *Seneg* k*
- **perspiration**; during: ant-t bg2 **Cham** bg2 ferr bg2 hyos bg2 ip bg2 *Lyc* bg2 op bg2 stram bg2
- **phlegm** (See Mucus)
- **rough**: *Am-c* bg2 ant-t ptk1 cupr ptk1 kali-s ptk1

Rattling: ...

- **sitting** erect | **amel.**: nat-c k*
- **sleep** agg.; during: alco a1 bell h1* con h2* *Hep* k* kali-bi mrr1 *Kali-s* mrr1 lach b7a.de op b7.de* stram k* tab k*
  - **children**; in: ant-t mrr1 kali-bi mrr1 *Kali-s* mrr1
- **talking**; after: *Mur-ac* hr1
- **walking**:
  - **agg.**: cina
  - **air** agg.; in open: ang cina
- ○ - **Bronchi**; in: ip tl1 *Morb* jl2 parathyr jl2
- **Sternum**; under: cob-n sp1

READING:
- **agg.**: nit-ac ptk1
- **aloud** | **agg.**: ph-ac bg2
- **amel.**: ferr b7.de*

REFLECTING agg.: m-ambo b7.de nux-v b7.de* phos b4.de*

RELIEVED (See Deep)

REST:
- **agg.**: ars b4a.de *Calc* b4a.de caps b7.de* ferr b7.de* puls b7.de* rhus-t b7.de* samb b7.de* seneg b4.de* *Sep* b4a.de **Sil** b4.de*
- **amel.**: nux-v b7.de* verat b7.de*

RIDING a carriage:
- **agg.**: borx b4a.de graph bg2 sep b4.de* sulph b4a.de
- **amel.**: psor bg2

RISING:
- **after** | **agg.**: am-m bg2 coc-c bg2 graph bg2 verat bg2
- **agg.**: acon b7a.de* calc-p bg2 caps b7.de* cina b7.de* hyos b7.de* nux-v b7.de* staph b7.de*
- **stooping**; from | **amel.**: *Ant-t* b7a.de *Cann-s* b7a.de chin b7.de* *Hep* b4a.de kali-c bg2 olnd b7.de* puls b7.de*

ROCKING: | **amel.**: kali-c bg2

ROUGH: (*↗Rasping; LARYNX - Voice - crowing*) am-c k* am-caust a1 *Ant-t* k* **Bry** k* *Hep* k* *Kali-bi* nit-ac k* plb k*
- **crowing**: (*↗Croaking; LARYNX - Croup*) **Bry** k* *Chin* *Chlor* cor-r *Cupr* k* *Gels* k* **Samb** k* **Spong** stann verat
  - **cough** agg.; during: chin b7a.de samb b7a.de
- **inspiration**: camph h1 *Op*
- **sawing**: (*↗Rasping*) *Alum-sil* k* *Ant-t* k* **Brom** k* *Con* k* **Iod** k* lac-ac k* lac-c samb bro1 *Sang* **Spong** k*
  - **coughs**, between: *Spong*

RUNNING; after: | **agg.**: *Bry* b7a.de cupr b7.de* hyos b7.de* *Ign* b7a.de phos b4.de* *Sil* b4.de*

SADNESS agg.: caust bg2 lach bg2

SAWING (See Rough - sawing)

SEA; on the: | **amel.**: brom bg2

SEASONS:
- **autumn** agg.: *Aur* b4.de*
- **spring** agg.: *Aur* b4.de*
- **summer** agg.: arg-n ptk1 syph ptk1
- **winter** agg.: *Ant-t* b7a.de carb-v bg2

SHAKING THE BODY; on: | **amel.**: ars b4a.de phos b4a.de

SHALLOW (See Superficial)

SHORT (See Difficult)

SHRILL: bell ptk1 gels ptk1 ign ptk1 mosch ptk1

SIBILANT: bros-gau mrc1 calc b4.de*

SIGHING: (*↗MIND - Sighing*) *Acon* k* agar k* ail bro1 am-c k* aml-ns bg2 ant-c k* apis apoc k* *Arg-met* k* *Arg-n* k* *Ars* k* ars-s-f k2 *Aspar* k* *Aur-m-n* wbt2• bell k* bit-ar wht1• *Borx* bov bg2 **Bry** k* cact bro1 **Calad** k* *Calc* **Calc-p** k* calc-sil k2 *Camph* k* caps b2.de* carb-ac bro1 carb-an **Carb-v** k* carc mlr1• *Caust* cench k2 cere-b a1* *Cham* k* chin b2.de* *Chinin-s* chlf hr1 *Cimic* k* cina bg2 clem a1 cob a1 cocc b2.de* colch bg2 crot-c sk4• cupr k* cystein-l rly4• der a1 **Dig** k* elae a1 euon a1 eup-pur k* euph b2.de* *Ferr-m* k*

Sighing: ...
gard-j vlr2• gast a1 *Gels* k* *Glon* k* gran a1* graph bg2 *Hell* k* hura hydrog srj2• **Ign** k* iod bg2 **Ip** k* irid-met srj5• jab br1 kali-br a1* kali-c bg2 kali-cy a1 lac-ac lach k* lact k* laur bg2 led bro1 lil-t k* lob hr1 *Lyc* k* lycps-v bg2 *Lyss* k* m-aust b2.de* merc bg2 *Merc-c* k* mit a1 morph k* mur-ac h2* naphtin bro1 nat-ar nat-c b2.de* nat-m mrr1 nat-p k* nit-ac k* nux-m k* nux-v k* olib-sac wmh1 **Op** k* phase bro1 phase-vg a1 *Phos* phys k* *Phyt* k* pilo bro1 plb k* plut-n srj7• podo k* prun *Puls* k* ran-b k2 ran-s k* rhus-t hr1 samb bro1 sang **Sec** k* **Sel** k* sep hr1 sil k* *Spong* squil bg2 stann bg2 **Stram** k* sulfon bro1 sulph k* tab k* taosc iwa1• tarent tax k* ther k* til a1 trad a1* verat-v k* vip k*

- **morning**: sang
  - **running**; after: adam skp7•
- **forenoon** | 9.30 h: hura
- **afternoon**: ant-c k*
- **evening**: chin k*
  - **19** h: lycps-v
- **night**: bry k*
  - **midnight**:
    - **after** | **2** h: ign
- **ascending** agg.: ther k2
- **chill**; during: acon bg2 bry bg2 caps bg2 cocc bg2 ign bg2* *Ip* bg2 op bg2 sil bg2
- **convulsions**; after: *Cocc* plb a1
- **convulsive**: aml-ns bg2
- **cough**; after: led ptk1
- **dinner**; after: arg-n k*
- **eating**; after: *Ant-c* k*
- **fever**; during: acon b7.de ail bg2 bry b7a.de cocc b7.de ign b7.de ip b7.de* lach bg2
- **jerks**; in: plut-n srj7•
- **leukorrhea**; with: phys ptk1
- **menses**; during: nat-p k*
- **sleep** | **during** | **agg.**: anac k* *Aur* ptk1 calc ptk1 camph k* cortico sp1 puls h1* *Sulph* k* [zirc-met stj2]
  - **quickened** on waking; respiration: cimic
- **swimming**; after: adam skp7•
- **typhoid** fever; sighing in jerks in: calad
- **unconsciousness**, during: glon k*

SINGING agg.: am-c bg2 arg-met ptk1 sulph bg2

SITTING:
- **agg.**: alum b4a.de* anac b4a.de ant-t b7.de* aur b4.de* calc b4.de* carb-v b4.de* chin b7.de* dig b4a.de* dros b7a.de* ferr b7.de* lach b7.de* led bg2 meny b7.de* nit-ac b4.de* petr b4.de* phos b4a.de* psor bg2 puls b7.de* rhus-t b7.de* ruta b7.de* sabad b7.de* samb b7a.de* spong b4a.de* staph b4a.de* *Sulph* b4a.de tarax b7.de tarent bg2 verat bg2
- **amel.**: *Apis* b7a.de nux-v b7.de* verat b7.de*
- **bent** backward | **agg.**: psor bg2
- **bent** forward:
  - **agg.**: *Ars* b4a.de chin b7.de* dig bg2 rhus-t bg2 *Sulph* b4a.de
  - **amel.**: kali-c ptk1
- **erect** | **amel.**: acon ptk1 *Kali-c* ptk1 lach ptk1 laur ptk1 lyc ptk1 nat-c ptk1 seneg ptk1 ter ptk1

SLEEP:
- **after** | **agg.**: bry b7.de* calad b7.de* *Cann-s* b7a.de chin b7.de* lach b7a.de m-ambo b7.de op b7.de* samb b7.de* sel b7.de* *Sulph* b4a.de
- **during** | **agg.**: *Acon* b7.de* anac bg2 ant-t bg2 arn b7.de* bell b4.de* calc bg2 camph bg2 carb-v bg2 cham b7.de* chel bg2 chin b7.de* cocc bg2 con bg2 dulc bg2 graph bg2 guaj b4.de* hep b4a.de *Hyos* b7a.de ign b7.de* kali-bi bg2 kali-c bg2 lach b7a.de* lyc b4a.de* merc bg2 nux-v b7.de* *Op* b7.de* puls b7.de* rheum b7.de* rhod b4.de* rhus-t b7.de* samb bg2 stram b7a.de* sulph b4a.de* tab bg2
- **falling** asleep; when | **agg.**: am-c ptk1 ars b4a.de* bell bg2 bry b7.de* cadm-s ptk1 carb-an bg2 carb-v bg2* *Dig* bg2 gels ptk1 *Grin* bg2* kali-c bg2* *Lach* bg2* manc bg2 merc bg2 nux-m b7.de* nux-v b7a.de petr bg2 phos bg2* *Puls* b7a.de ran-b b7.de* spong ptk1 sulph bg2* tab ptk1 valer bg2

SLOW: *Acon* k* acon-c a1 agar b2.de* agath-a nl2• alco a1 am-c bro1 amyg a1* ant-c b2.de* ant-t k* *Apis* k* arn k* ars k* *Asaf* k* aur b2.de* **Bell** k* ben-d bro1 ben-n c2 *Brom* bry k* cact bro1 calc b2.de* *Camph* k* cann-i k* cann-s b2.de* *Caps* k* cass a1 *Castm* cham b2.de* chin k* chinin-s chlf hr1 chlol k* choc srj3• cic k* cinch a1 clem k* *Cocc* k* coff b2.de* *Colch* k* *Coloc* k*

Slow: ...
con k* cop k* croc b2.de* *Crot-c* crot-h crot-t cub c1 cupr k* cyt-l a1 der a1 *Dig* k* *Dios* k* dros k* ferr k* gad bro1 *Gels* k* *Glon* k* *Hell* k* *Hep* k* *Hydr-ac* k* *Hyos* k* *Hyper* k* *Ign* k* *Ip* k* jab br1 kali-c b2.de* kali-cy a1 kreos b2.de* *Lach* k* *Lact* *Laur* k* lob-p bro1 lyc k* m-ambo b2.de *M-aust* b2.de merc b2.de* *Merc-c* k* mez b2.de* morph k* mosch b2.de* mur-ac b2.de* naja bg2* narcin a1 nat-c b2.de* nit-ac k* nux-m k* *Nux-v* k* oena k* *Olnd* k* **Op** k* ox-ac k* ozone sde2• par b2.de* phase bro1 phase-vg a1 phos k* *Phyt* k* pilo bro1 plat k* plb k* puls b2.de* ran-b b2.de* ran-s b2.de* rhus-t b2.de* ruta b2.de* sang bg2 sars b2.de* sec k* sel b2.de seneg b2.de* sil b2.de* *Spong* k* squil k* stann b2.de* staph b2.de* stram k* sul-ac k* sulph b2.de* tab k* thuj b2.de* verat-v k* visc a1* zinc b2.de* [tax jsj7]

- **morning**: *Lach* k* merc merc-c a1
- **evening** | **lying** quiet agg.; while: con ferr
- **night**: coloc k* *Lach* k*
- **alternating** with:
  - **short** respiration: ign bg2
    - **sleep**; during: ign
  - **suffocation**: cocc
- **chill**; during: bell bg2 caps bg2 hell bg2 ign bg2 op bg2 spong bg2
- **coma**; with (See MIND - Coma - respiration - slow)
- **concussion** of brain, from: hell hr1
- **convulsions**; during: **Op** k*
- **cough** agg.; during: clem k*
- **expiration**: ant-t k* apis *Arn* k* borx camph b7.de* cham b7.de* chin b7.de* hell b7.de* ign b7.de* *Ip* b7a.de kali-cy a1 lob k* *M-aust* b7.de* *Op* k* *Sep* squil b7.de*
  - **sleep**, during: chin ign
- **inspiration**: cham k* chin k* **Cupr** hr1 ferr b7.de* *Ign* k* *M-aust* b7.de* olnd b7.de* op b7.de* squil b7.de* staph b7.de* stram k*
  - **expiration**; with quick: stram ptk1*
- **palpitations**; during: bell h1*
- **sleep** agg.; during: acon k* chin **Op**
- **walking** | **amel.**: *Ferr* k*

SMOKE; sensation as if inhaling only: bar-c b4a.de

SMOKING agg.: puls b7.de* spong b7.de* staph b7.de* tarax b7.de*

SNEEZING:
- **agg.**: dros bg2 meph bg2 merc bg2 naja ptk1 phos ptk1 sec bg2 sil bg2 sulph bg2
- **amel.**: naja ptk1

SNORING: *(↗Loud; Stertorous)* acon aeth alco a1 alum b4.de* amp rly4• amyg k* *Anac* b4a.de **Ant-t** b7a.de arge-pl rwt5• arn k* ars k* bapt k* bar-c bg2 bar-i bg2 bell k* benz-ac *Brom* k* bros-gau mrc1 calc k* *Camph* k* caps b7.de* carb-v bg2 *Carl* k* *Cham* k* *Chin* k* chinin-s bg2 chlol c1 *Cic* k* cocc b7.de* con k* cund k* *Cupr* k* cycl des-ac rbp6 dros k* dulc k* fl-ac glon k* *Graph* b4a.de guare a1 *Hep* k* hydr-ac hyos k* *Ign* k* kali-bi k* kali-c b4.de* kali-chl k* kali-m k2 *Kali-s* mrr1 **Lac-c** k* *Lach* k* *Laur* k* lyc k* m-ambo b7.de* mag-c bg2 mag-m k* merc b4a.de merc-c bg1* mez morb jl2 mur-ac k* nat-m k* nit-ac k* nux-m k* *Nux-v* k* oena a1* **Op** k* petr k* puls b7.de* rat k* rheum k* *Rhus-t* k* sabad sabin b7.de* samb k* sep k* sil k* stann k* *Stram* k* stry k* *Sulph* k* teucr k* tub bro1 *Zinc* bro1 [aur-s stj2 cinnb stj2 gal-s stj2]

- **midnight**: mur-ac k* nux-v k*
- **morning** | **sleeping**; while: petr k*
- **afternoon** | **nap**; during: alum
- **evening** | **bed** agg.; in: sil k*
- **adenoids** removed; after: carc mlr1• kali-s ptk1
- **awake**, while: chel k* sumb k*
- **children**; in: chin mtf33 dros mtf33 dulc fd4.de mez ptk1 op wbt•
- **chill**; during: bell bg2 camph bg2 *Chin* laur **Op** k* stram bg2
- **cough**; during (See COUGH - Snoring)
- **delirium**; after: sec k*
- **expiration**, during: arn camph chin lat-h bnm5• *Nux-v* *Op* k*
- **heat**; during: anac bg2 apis chin bg2 con graph bg2 ign k* laur mur-ac bg2 *Nux-v* bg2 **Op** k* sil bg2 stram bg2
- **inspiration**: nux-v b7.de* *Op* b7.de* puls b7.de* rheum b7.de*
  - **sleep**; in: bell h1* caps h1* cham h1* chin h1* hyos h1* ign h1* musca-d szs1 myos-a rly4• rheum h teucr hr1
- **lying** on back agg.: dros k* dulc kali-c mag-c sulph
- **nose**, through: puls h1*

Respiration

- **sleep**; during:
  - **children**; in: chin ptk1
  - **perspiration**; during: anac bg2 *Chin* bg2 graph bg2 hyos bg2 ign bg2 *Mur-ac* bg2 nux-v bg2 **Op** bg2 *Sil* bg2 stram bg2
- **swoon**, during: stram k*
- **unconscious**, while: *Op*

○ - **Larynx** and trachea cham b7a.de* chin bg2 hyos bg2 nat-m bg2 stann bg2 sulph bg2

SNUFFLING: ant-t b7.de* *Arn* b7.de* bell bg2 chin b7.de* elaps bg2 hydr bg2 iris bg2 kali-bi bg2 m-aust b7.de merc-i-r bg2 nux-v b7.de* rhus-t b7.de* sabad bg2 sabin b7.de* *Samb* bg2 sep bg2
- **expiration**: *M-aust* b7a.de rhus-t b7.de*
- **sleep**; during: am b7.de* rhus-t b7.de*

SOBBING: (↗*MIND - Grief; MIND - Sighing; MIND - Weeping; MIND - Weeping - sobbing)* acon aeth am-m k* ang k* ant-c asaf k* *Aur* k* *Bry* k* *Calc* k* *Cupr-act* gels k* *Guare* k* *Ign* k* laur k* *Led* k* m-ambo b2.de* *Mag-p* k* *Merc* k* merc-c hr1 nit-ac k* op b2.de* petr a1 ran-s *Sec* k* sil k* stram sul-ac bg2 ther
- **dancing**; after: spong h1*
- **paroxysmal**: *Mag-p* k*
- **sleep** agg.; during: **Aur** k* *Calc*
- **spasmodic**: *Mag-p* c2
  - **inspiration** in two jerks; with: acon b7.de ang b7.de ant-t b7.de asaf b7.de *Led* b7.de*
  - ⁝ **sleep**; during: acon b7.de*
- **sudden** (See paroxysmal)

SPASMODIC (See Paroxysmal)

STANDING:
- **agg.**: olnd b7.de* puls b7.de* *Sep* b4.de*
- **amel.**: bapt ptk1 cann-xyz ptk1 sil ptk1 spig ptk1
- **erect** | **amel.**: *Cann-s* b7a.de
- **water** agg.; in: nux-m ptk1

STERTOROUS: (↗*Loud; Puffing; Snoring)* absin k* acon k* agath-a nl2• **Am-c** k* am-caust a1 ambr c1 amyg k* anac k* ang b7.de* ant-c b7a.de *Ant-t* k* *Apis Arn* k* *Ars* k* asaf bg2 bapt hr1 bell k* *Bry* b7.de* bufo *Calc* b4.de* *Camph* k* cann-i k* *Cann-s* b7.de* *Carb-ac* k* carb-an k* *Carb-v* b4a.de caust b4.de cham k* chen-a k* *Chin* k* chlf hr1* chlol k* cic k* cic-m a1 *Cina* b7.de cocc croc b7.de cupr k* cyt-l sp1 dros gk dulc fd4.de euph-l bro1 ferr b7.de ferr-m k* *Gels* k* *Glon* k* *Hell* bro1 **Hep** b4a.de hippoz bro1 hydr-ac k* hyos k* **Ip** b7.de* ix bnm8• kali-bi k* kali-br br1 kali-cy a1 *Lach* k* *Laur* k* led bg2 lob-p bro1 loxo-lae bnm12• *Lyc* k* merl k* naja k2* nat-c b4.de nat-sal bro1 *Nit-ac* k* nit-s-d bg nitro-o a1 *Nux-m* k* *Nux-v* k* *Oena* k* olnd k* **OP** k ●* petr k* phase bro1 phos k* pilo bro1 plb k* *Puls* k* sabad k* *Samb* b7.de sarr sec bro1 sep b4.de *Spong* k* *Squil* b7.de* stann k* *Stram* k* sul-ac k* *Sulfon* bro1 *Sulph* b4a.de tab k* tanac bro1* tax a1 tell sne ter k* thuj b4a.de trion bro1 verat-v bro1 visc a1*
- **evening** | **bed** agg.; in: carb-an
- **accompanied** by | **cough**: samb
- **children**; in: androc bnm2•
- **coma**; with (See MIND - Coma - respiration - stertorous)
- **concussion** of brain: hyos hr1
- **convulsions**:
  - **after**: cupr sne *Oena* **Op** k*
  - **during**: op bro1
- **lying** on affected side agg.: anac
- **puffing** expiration, with: *Am* sne bufo *Chin* chlol st *Lach* k* *Nux-v* **Op** k●* plb tab
  - **lying** on back agg.: chlol hr1*
- **sleep** agg.; during: *Brom* k* chin gt1 dulc fd4.de ign gt1 nux-v k* **OP** k ●* **Puls** k*
- **stools** and urine; with involuntary: amyg
- **stupefaction** and crying out as from a sharp pain: **Apis** k*

STONE CUTTERS; complaints of (See Dust)

STOOL:
- **after**:
  - **agg.**: caust bg2 crot-t bg2
  - **amel.**: ictod bg2*

Stool: ...
- **before** | **agg.**: puls b7a.de *Rhus-t* b7.de*
- **during** | **agg.**: puls b7a.de *Rhus-t* b7.de* sulph bg2
- **urging** to: bry bg2 *Ip* b7a.de

STOOPING agg.: alum bg2 am-c bg2 am-m b7a.de arg-met bg2 *Ars* b4a.de bell bg2 calc b4.de* caust b4.de* chin b7.de* con b4a.de dig bg2 laur b7.de* m-aust b7.de nit-ac ptk1 olnd bg2 phos bg2 psor bg2 seneg b4.de* sil b4.de* sulph b4.de*

STRIDULOUS: (↗*Impeded)* am-caust k* atra-r bnm3• **Bell** k* *Chlor* k* dros gk **Gels** k* **Ign** k* ix bnm8• *Kali-bi* hr1 *Lach* lat-m bnm6• laur *Meph* morb jl2 **Mosch** k* nit-ac k* *Nux-v* k* *Op* k* plb *Samb* k* *Sang* k* sarr verat
- **evening** | **sleep**; when falling asleep: **Phos** k*

SUDDENLY; complaints appearing: *Sep* b4a.de

SUFFOCATION; attacks of: **Acon** b2.de* *Am-c* bg2 anac b2.de* ant-c b2.de* **Ant-t** b2.de* *Apis* b7a.de* arg-n bg2 **Ars** b2.de* asar b2.de* *Aur* b2.de* *Bar-c* b2.de* bell b2.de* brom b4a.de* bry b2.de* bufo bg2 calc b2.de* *Calc-p* bg2 *Camph* b2.de* cann-s b2.de* canth b2.de* carb-an b2.de* **Carb-v** b2.de* caust b2.de* *Cham* b2.de* **Chin** b2.de* chlor bg2 cic b2.de* cina b2.de* cocc b2.de* coff b2.de* *Colch* b7a.de con b2.de* *Cor-r* bg2 cupr b2.de* cycl b2.de* dig b2.de* dros b2.de* euphr b2.de* ferr b2.de* gels bg2 *Graph* b2.de* *Grin* bg2 hell b2.de* **Hep** b2.de* hyos b2.de* ign b2.de* iod b2.de* **Ip** b2.de* kali-c bg2 kali-n b2.de* kreos b2.de* **Lach** b2.de* laur b2.de* led b2.de* lil-t bg2 lyc b2.de* *M-arct* b2.de* m-aust b2.de* mag-m b2.de* *Meph* bg2 merc b2.de* merc-c b4a.de mosch b2.de* nat-m b2.de* nit-ac b2.de* nux-m b2.de* *Nux-v* b2.de* **Op** b2.de* petr b2.de* *Phos* b2.de* plat b2.de* plb b2.de* podo bg2 psor bg2 **Puls** b2.de* ran-b b2.de* rhus-t b2.de* sabad b2.de* **Samb** b2.de* *Sec* b2.de* seneg b2.de* sep b2.de* sil b2.de* **Spig** b2.de* **Spong** b2.de* stann b2.de* staph b2.de* stram b2.de* **Sulph** b2.de* tab bg2 **Verat** b2.de* zinc bg2
- **coal**; as if from fumes of: *Bov* b4a.de
- **coryza**; during: coff b7a.de *Ip* b7a.de *Samb* b7a.de
- **sulfur**; as if from fumes of: *Brom* b4a.de

SUFFOCATIVE (See Difficult)

SULFUR; as from fumes of: am-c bg2 **Ars** bg2 brom bg2 bry bg2 calc bg2 camph bg2 *Chin* bg2 cina bg2 croc bg2 **Ign** bg2 lach bg2 lyc bg2 par bg2 **Puls** b7a.de*

SUPERFICIAL: (↗*Difficult - weakness; Imperceptible)* acon bro1 *Acon-f* bro1 am-c bro1 androc bnm2• ant-c bg2 *Ant-t* bro1 apis bro1 *Apoc* bro1 aral bro1 *Ars* bro1 atro hr1 **Bell** b2.de* bit-ar wht1• brass-n-o srj5• *Bry* bro1 calc bro1 cann-xyz bg2 canth b2.de* carb-v bro1 *Chin* k* chir-fl bnm4• chlf br1 cob-n sp1 coenz-q mtf11 colum-p sze2• cupr bro1 cupr-act bro1 cur bro1 dubo-h hs1 *Ferr-p* bro1 gels bg2 helo-s bnm14• hep b2.de* hippoz bro1 ign b2.de* ix bnm6*• kali-bi bro1 lach bro1 lat-m bnm6• laur b2.de* lob bg2 lob-p bro1 lyc bro1 m-ambo b2.de mag-p bro1 malar jl2 merc-cy bro1 merc-sul bro1 mez b2.de* naja bg2 nat-s bro1 nicotam rly4• nit-ac b2.de* *Nux-m* k* *Nux-v* bro1 *Olnd* b2.de* op b2.de* ox-ac bro1 ph-ac k* **Phos** k* positr nl2• prun bro1 psil ft1 puls k* seneg bro1 sil bg2* sinus rly4• *Spong* bro1 stann bg2* sul-ac bro1 sulph b2.de* verat b2.de* *Viol-o* b2.de*
- **old** people; in: *Bac* br1
- **sensation** as of superficial respiration: prun ptk1
  - **sleep**; on going to: grin mtf11

SWALLOWING:
- **agg.**: ant-t bg2 bell b4.de* *Brom* ptk1 calc ptk1 cinnb bg2 cupr ptk1 dig bg2
- **food** | **agg.**: *Lach* b7a.de

SYNCHRONOUS with: | **twitching** of extremities (See EXTREMITIES - Twitching - synchronous)

TALKING:
- **agg.**: borx bg2 canth b7.de* caust b4a.de* *Chin* b7a.de *Dros* b7.de* hyos b7.de* kali-c b4a.de* lach ptk1 lyc bg2 mez b4.de* **Ph-ac** b4a.de rhus-t bg2 *Sil* b4a.de spig b7.de* spong ptk1 stram bg2 **Sulph** b4a.de* thuj ptk1 zinc bg2
  - **rapidly**: caust b4.de* ph-ac b4a.de sil b4a.de
- **amel.**: ferr b7.de*
- **loudly** agg.: petr b4.de* ph-ac b4a.de

TEMPERATURE; change of: | **agg.**: ars b4a.de

TIGHT (See CHEST - Oppression)

TOBACCO agg.: aloe bg2 tarax bg2

TOUCH:
- **back** agg.; touching: adon ptk1
- **mouth** agg.; touching: apis bg2 *Bell* bg2 *Lach* b7.de*
- **nose** agg.; touching: lach b7a.de
- **stomach** agg.; touching: am bg2
- **throat** agg.; touching: apis bg2 **Bell** b4.de* *Hep* bg2 *Lach* b7.de* **Spong** bg2

TREMULOUS: *Ant-t* k* m-arct b7.de m-aust b7.de* zinc h2*

TUBE; as if through a metallic: merc-c ptk1* tub gk

TURNING:
- **bed**; in:
  - **agg.**: ars b4a.de* carb-v bg2 spig bg2 sulph bg2
  - **amel.**: *Nux-v* b7a.de
- **head** | **agg.**: **Bell** b4.de* *Hep* bg2 **Spong** bg2

URINATION:
- **amel.**: nat-ar bg2
- **during** | **agg.**: chel bg2* dulc bg2*

VEHEMENT expiration (See Forcible - expiration)

VOMITING:
- **agg.**: asar b7.de* cann-xyz bg2 cic bg2 lach bg2
- **amel.**: *Ars* b4a.de *Ip* b7a.de phos b4a.de

WAKING; on: alum bg2 *Am-m* b7a.de ant-c bg2 *Ant-t* b7a.de bapt bg2 bell bg2 bry b7.de* *Cann-s* b7a.de chin b7.de* con b4a.de* *Dig* bg2 kali-bi bg2 kali-c bg2 **Lach** bg2 led bg2 meph bg2 naja bg2 nux-v b7.de* op bg2 phos bg2 puls b7.de* *Samb* b7a.de* sep bg2 spong bg2 squil b7.de*

WALKING:
- **after** | **agg.**: puls b7.de* rhus-t b7.de* valer b7.de*
- **agg.**: agar b4.de* ang bg2 apis b7a.de arg-n bg2 am b7.de* *Ars* b4a.de aur b4.de* bell b4.de* borx bg2 bry b7.de* calc b4a.de caps b7.de* *Carb-v* b4.de* *Caust* b4a.de* chin b7.de* *Con* b4a.de *Dig* b4a.de ign b7.de* *Kali-c* b4a.de lach b7a.de led b7.de* *Lyc* b4a.de mag-c b4.de* mag-m b4.de* merc b4.de* nat-m bg2 *Nit-ac* b4a.de *Nux-v* b7.de* olnd b7.de* *Ph-ac* b4a.de *Phos* b4a.de plat b4.de* puls b7a.de* ran-b b7.de* rhus-t b7a.de sel b7a.de *Seneg* b4a.de *Sep* b4a.de **Sil** b4a.de* spig b7.de* squil b7.de* *Stann* b4.de* stront-c b4.de* sulph b4.de* viol-t b7.de*
- **air**; in open | **after** | **agg.**: ferr b7.de* rhus-t b7.de* spong b7.de*
  - **agg.**: carb-v bg2 cina b7.de* hell b7.de* kali-n bg2 nux-m b7.de* nux-v b7.de* *Sel* b7a.de tarax b7.de*
- **amel.**: bry bg2 carb-v bg2 ferr b7.de* mosch b7.de* puls b7.de* rhus-t b7.de* staph b7.de* tarax b7.de*
- **level** ground agg.; on: ran-b b7.de*
- **rapidly** | **agg.**: ang b7.de* *Ars* b4a.de* aur b4.de* borx bg2 *Brom* b4a.de *Bry* b7a.de *Caust* b4.de* *Cupr* b7.de* ign bg2 *Kali-c* b4a.de **Nat-m** b4.de* *Nit-ac* b4a.de seneg b4.de* *Sil* b4.de* spig b7.de* squil b7.de*
- **wind**; against the: *Cupr* b7a.de

WARM:
- **amel.**: bar-c bg2
- **bathing** | **amel.**: lat-m bnm6•
- **bed** | **amel.**: kali-bi bg2
- **room** | **agg.**: am-c b4.de* anac b4a.de *Apis* bg2 ars b4a.de* bell b4a.de* bry b7.de* *Calc* b4a.de *Caps* b7a.de kali-i bg2 *Puls* b7.de* sec bg2 spig b7.de* verb b7.de*
- **warm** agg.; becoming: *Euph* b4a.de lach bg2
- **wraps**: ars bg2

WEAKNESS agg.: **Ars** bg2 cycl bg2 *Lach* bg2

WEATHER:
- **cold**:
  - **wet** | **agg.**: *Ant-t* b7a.de
- **stormy** agg.: ars b4a.de* calc bg2 plat bg2 rhus-t bg2
- **wet** | **agg.**: aran ptk1 aur ptk1 bar-c bg2* cupr bg2 *Dulc* b4a.de kali-bi bg2 *Nat-s* ptk1

WEEPING: | **amel.**: anac b4a.de

WET; from becoming: *Phos* b4a.de sep b4a.de

WHEEZING: (↗*Asthmatic; Whistling*) acon bg2 agar bg2 aids nl2• ail k* aloe k* *Alum* k* alum-p k2 alum-sil k2 am-c bg2* *Ambr* k* anac bg2 ang bg2 ant-i bro1 *Ant-t* bro1 apis bg2 *Apoc* k* aral k* arg-met bg2 arg-n k* arn bg2 **Ars** k* *Ars-i* k* ars-s-f k2 *Asaf* bg2 *Aur* bg2 **Bell** bg2 bit-ar wht1• blatta-o mrr1 bov bg2 *Brom* k* bry bg2 calad k* calc k* calc-s camph bg2 *Cann-s* k* *Caps* k* carb-an bg2 **Carb-v** k* carbn-s card-m bro1 caust bg2 *Cham* k* *Chin* k* *Chinin-ar* chlol k* *Cic* bg2 *Cina* k* *Cocc* bg2 coloc bg2 con bg2 croc bg2 crot-t *Cupr* k* cycl a1 des-ac rbp6 *Dig* bg2 dol *Dros* k* dulc bg2 erio bro1 euphr bg2 ferr k* ferr-i *Fl-ac* k* form bg2 graph *Grin* bro1 hell bg2 helodr-cal knl2• hep k* hydr-ac k* *Hyos* bg2 ign bg2 *Iod* k* iodof hr1* **Ip** k* irid-met srj5• just bro1 *Kali-ar* k* *Kali-bi* k* **Kali-c** k* *Kali-i* bg2 kali-n bg2 *Kali-s* k* lac-e hrn2• *Lach* k* laur bg2 *Led* bg2 limest-b es1• lob bro1 loxo-recl bnm10• *Lyc* k* *Lycps-v* k* mag-m bg2 manc mang-p rly4• melal-alt gya4 merc k* mez bg2 mosch bg2 mur-ac bg2 murx k* naja nat-c a1 *Nat-m* k* *Nat-n* bg2 *Nat-s* k* neon srj5• *Nit-ac* k* *Nit-s-d* hr1 *Nux-m* k* nux-v k* op bg2 ox-ac k* par bg2 ph-ac bg2 phos k* plb bg2 positr nl2• prun bro1 *Puls* bg2 ran-b bg2 ran-s bg2 *Rhod* bg2 rhus-t bg2 ruta bg2 sabad k* *Samb* k* sang sanic sars bg2 seneg bg2* sep k* *Sil* bg2 spong k* squil k* stann k* staph bg2 stram bg2 suis-pan rly4• sul-ac bg2 sul-i k2 sulph k* syc bka1*• *Syph* k* teucr bg2 *Thuj* bg2 tritic-vg fd5.de tung-met bdx1• *Verat* bg2 vero-o rly3• *Visc* bg2 *Zinc* bg2 [ambro stj]
- **daytime**: irid-met srj5• *Kali-bi* hr1 *Lyc* k* suis-pan rly4•
- **afternoon**: fl-ac k*
- **evening**: lycps-v murx k*
  - **bed** agg.; in: nat-m
  - **lying** down agg.: aral vh1 *Ars* k*
- **night**: kali-bi k* limen-b-c hm2*
  - **midnight**: aral vh1
    - **after**: *Samb* k*
      - **2-2.30 h**: adam skp7•
      - **2-3 h**: syc fmm1•
- **accompanied** by | **obesity**: am-c br1
- **cold**; after taking a: carb-v k2
- **cold** air | **amel.**: kali-s mrr1
- **expectoration** | **amel.**: ip k*
- **expiration** agg.; during: bit-ar wht1• *Lyc* k* nat-m pyrog k2 *Sep*
- **inspiration** agg.: *Alum* *Caps* k* *Chin* k* cupr sst3• *Kali-c* k* melal-alt gya4 mur-ac a1 spong
- **lying** agg.: bit-ar wht1•
- **pressure** on chest agg.: bit-ar wht1•
- **seasons** | **autumn** agg.: mucor-a-p bc2
- **sitting** up in bed agg.: nat-c k*
- **sleep** agg.; during: *Kali-s* mrr1 nux-v
  - **children**; in: ant-t mrr1 kali-bi mrr1 *Kali-s* mrr1
- **smoking** agg.: kali-bi
- **waking**; on: hydrog srj2• syc bka1*•
- **warm** room agg.: *Kali-s* k*

WHISTLING: (↗*Asthmatic; Wheezing; MIND - Sighing*) acet-ac acon k* aeth k* aloe k* alum k* am-c bg2 *Ambr* k* ant-ar bg2 *Ant-c* b7a.de *Ant-t* k* arg-n k* *Ars* k* arund k* asar b7.de* aur ptk1 bell k* benz-ac k* brom k* bry bg2 bufo k* cact bg2 calad bg2 calc k* cann-s k* *Carb-v* k* carbn-s card-b a1 caust bg2* *Cham* k* chel bg2 **Chin** k* chinin-ar cina b7.de* cocc b7.de* coloc k* cupr k* graph k* *Hep* k* *Iod* k* ip bg2* kali-ar *Kali-c* k* kali-i ptk1 kali-s kali-sil k2 kreos k* *Lach* bg2 lat-m sp1 laur k* lob bg2 *Lyc* k* mag-m h2* *Manc* k* med mtf11 nat-m k* nit-ac k* nux-v k* osm k* ph-ac phos k* plb b7.de* psor bg2 puls b7a.de* rhus-t b7a.de sabad k* *Samb* k* sang k* seneg ptk1 sep b4.de* *Sil* k* *Spong* k* stann k* stram bg2* sul-ac k* sul-i k* *Sulph* k* thuj k* vanil fd5.de
- **morning**: *Lach* k*
- **evening**: *Calc* carb-v k* psor k* spong fd4.de vanil fd5.de
  - **bed** agg.; in: *Calc* b4a.de carb-an b4a.de
  - **lying** down agg.; after: ars h2 *Calc* vanil fd5.de
- **night**:
  - **midnight**:
    - **after**:
      - **3 h** | **sleep**; in: sulph
- **ascending** agg.: sulph
- **cough**:
  - **beginning** of: asar h1
  - **during** | **agg.**: acon b7a.de dros bg2 *Kali-c* bg2 kreos b7a.de lyc k* mag-m bg2 *Samb* b7a.de spong fd4.de
- **expiration** agg.; during: ars hr1 nat-m
- **inspiration** agg.: aral k* card-b a1 cina crot-t k* graph h2* *Kali-c* k* moni rfm1• nit-ac sulph

Respiration

- **lying**:
  - **agg.**: *Calc* vanil fd5.de
  - **back**; on | **agg.**: aeth
  - **side**; on:
    - **left** | **agg.**: arg-n
- **sleep** in: chel sulph
- **waking**; on: psor k*
- **whooping** cough; in: *Brom* k* *Carb-v* k* *Cupr* k* *Hep* k* samb k* spong k*

WIND: | **north** wind agg.: *Spong* b7a.de

WORKING agg.: bov b4.de* *Lyc* b4.de* *Nat-m* b4a.de *Nit-ac* b4a.de sars b4.de* *Sil* b4.de*
- **manual** work | **agg.**: *Am-m* b7a.de bov b4a.de* lach bg2 **Nat-m** b4.de* nit-ac b4a.de sil b4a.de*

WRITING: | **amel.**: ferr b7.de*

YAWNING: | **after** | **amel.**: coc-c bg2 croc b7.de* staph b7.de*
- **agg.**: cocc bg2 croc b7.de ign b7.de nux-v bg2

COUGH in general: *Acal* bro1 *Acet-ac* bro1 **Acon** b2.de* agar b2.de* agn b2.de* alchor-c jsx1.fr *All-c* bro1 all-s br1* alum b2.de* am-br bro1 am-c b2.de* am-caust bro1 *Am-m* b2.de* ambr b2.de* anac b2.de* ang b2.de* ant-ar bro1 ant-c b2.de* ant-s-aur bro1 ant-t b2.de* aral bro1 arg-met b2.de* arg-n bg2 arn b2.de* **Ars** b2.de* *Ars-i* bro1 asaf b2.de* asar b2.de* asc-t bro1 aur b2.de* bac jl2 bals-p bro1 bar-c b2.de* **Bell** b2.de* bism b2.de* borx b2.de* bov b2.de* brid-at jsx1.fr brom bro1* **Bry** b2.de* cadm-met sp1 calad b2.de* *Calc* b2.de* calc-f sp1 camph b2.de* cann-s b2.de* canth b2.de* caps b2.de* carb-ac bro1 carb-an b2.de* **Carb-v** b2.de* carc mrr1 caust b2.de* *Cham* b2.de* chel bro1 *Chin* b2.de* cic b2.de* *Cimic* bro1 cina b2.de* clem b2.de* coc-c nh6* cocc b2.de* *Cod* bro1 coff b2.de* colch b2.de* coloc b2.de* *Con* b2.de* *Cor-r* bro1 cortiso tpw7 croc b2.de* *Crot-h* bro1 cupr b2.de* cupr-act bro1 cupr-n a1 cycl b2.de* dig b2.de* diph-pert-t mp4• **Dros** b2.de* *Dulc* b2.de* *Eup-per* bro1 euph b2.de* euphr b2.de* ferr b2.de* *Ferr-p* bro1 fic-c mtf11 flav jl2 galla-q-r nl2• *Glycyr-g* cte1• graph b2.de* guaj b2.de* hell b2.de* *Hep* b2.de* hetrt-r jsx1.fr hydr mtf11 hydr-ac bro1 *Hyos* b2.de* hyosin-hbr bro1 *Ign* b2.de* *Iod* b2.de* **Ip** b2.de* **Kali-bi** bg2* kali-c b2.de* kali-chl bro1 kali-n b2.de* *Kreos* b2.de* lach b2.de* *Lact-v* bro1 lant-c jsx1.fr lant-t jsx1.fr lat-m sp1* laur b2.de* led b2.de* *Lob* bro1 *Lyc* b2.de* m-ambo b2.de m-arct b2.de* m-aust b2.de mag-c b2.de* mag-m b2.de* *Mag-p* bro1 malar jl2 mang b2.de* mang-act bro1 *Menth* bro1 meny b2.de* meph bro1* merc b2.de* mez b2.de* mosch b2.de* mur-ac b2.de* myrt-c bro1 *Naja* bro1 narc-ps c1* nat-c b2.de* nat-m b2.de* nit-ac b2.de* nux-m b2.de* **Nux-v** b2.de* oci-sa sp1 olib-sac wmh1 olnd b2.de* op b2.de* *Osm* bro1 par b2.de* pentad-b jsx1.fr petr b2.de* ph-ac b2.de* *Phel* br1* **Phos** b2.de* phyt bg2 pip-g jsx1.fr pix br1 plat b2.de* plb b2.de* pop-cand bro1 prot jl2* *Psor* jl2* **Puls** b2.de* pycno-e jsx1.fr quill br1 rad-br sze8• ran-b b2.de* ran-s b2.de* rheum b2.de* rhod b2.de* *Rhus-t* b2.de* rumx nh6* ruta b2.de* *Sabad* b2.de* sabin b2.de* sal-ac mtf11 samb b2.de* sang nh6* *Santin* bro1 sars b2.de* sec b2.de* sel b2.de* seneg b2.de* **Sep** b2.de* *Sil* b2.de* spig b2.de* *Spong* b2.de* *Squil* b2.de* *Stann* b2.de* *Stann-i* bro1 staph b2.de* stict bro1* stram b2.de* stront-c b2.de* sul-ac b2.de* **Sulph** b2.de* syc fmm1• tab bg2 tarax b2.de* tetrad-r jsx1.fr teucr b2.de* thuj b2.de* toxo-g jl2 trem-or jsx1.fr trif-p bro1 tub bro1 ursin-t bta1• vario jl2 **Verat** b2.de* verb b2.de* vero-o rly4*• *Viol-o* bro1 wye bro1 xylop-a jsx1.fr *Zinc* b2.de* zizyp-m bta1• [bryo-p dbx1.fr heroin sdj2]

DAYTIME: *Agar* k* ail alum k* alum-sil k2 **Am-c** k* am-m k* anac k* ang k* ant-t k* *Arg-met* k* *Arn* k* *Ars* hr1 arum-d bamb-a stb2.de• bar-c k* bar-m *Bell* k* bism k* bov k* brom *Bry* k* bufo calc k* calc-p k* cham k* chin k* cic k* coc-c coloc k* com con k* cot k* cupr **Euphr** k* ferr k* ferr-p gamb graph k* guaj hep k* kali-bi kali-br *Kali-c* k* kali-m k2 kali-n k* kali-p kali-sil k2 **Lach** k* laur k* lyc k* manc k* merc hr1 mez k* mur-ac k* nat-ar nat-c k* nat-m **Nat-s** k* nicc nit-ac k* nux-v k* **Phos** k* rhus-t k* sars k* sep sil k* sol-t-ae spong stann k* *Staph* k* sulph k* sumb thuj k* viol-o k* zinc k* zinc-p k2

- **6**-18 h: calc-p
- **night**, and: ars-i *Bell* k* bism k* calc calc-p k* carb-an k* cham k* chin chinin-s bg2 cina bg2 cupr k* dulc k* euph k* hep k* *Ign* k* indg kali-bi *Kali-c* hr1 kali-m k2 kali-n k* *Lyc* k* mez mur-ac k* nat-c k* *Nat-m* k* nit-ac *Phos* k* rhus-t k* *Samb* b7a.de *Sep* k* sil k* **Spong** k* *Squil* stann k* sulph k* *Verb* b7a.de xan hr1 zinc k* zinc-p k2
  - **breathless**; which makes boy quite: nat-m
  - **expectoration**; with: dulc sil
- **only**: *Am-c* k* *Arg-met* brom bry h1* *Calc* k* chin cic *Cocc* b7a.de dulc **Euphr** k* *Ferr* k* graph hep kali-bi hbh kali-n k* *Lach* laur lyc *Mang* merc nat-m bro1 nit-ac k* nux-m *Phos* k* *Rumx* k* sep sin-n stann k* *Staph* k* thuj k* viol-o k*
  - **long** lasting spells, dry short violent cough with much dyspnea: viol-o k*
  - **or**:
    - **morning** after rising, and evening after lying down: thuj
    - **night**:
      - **only**: merc
      - **wakens** him; cough: sep
- **amel.**: bell *Caust* con dulc euphr hydrog srj2• ign lach lyc meph mrr1 merc nit-ac sep spong
- **every** day (See Periodical - day - every)
- **expectoration**; copious, greenish, salty:
  - **morning** | **agg.**: acal br1 *Stann* k*
- **menses**; before: graph k*
- **periodical** (See Periodical - day - every)

MORNING (= 6-9 h): abrom-a ks5 acal bro1 acon k* *Agar* k* agn ail k* all-c k* all-s k* **Alum** k* alum-p k2 alum-sil k2 alumn k* am-br a1 am-c k* am-m k* ambr k* anac k* ang k* ant-c k* ant-t k* apoc arg-met k* arge-pl rwt5• arist-cl sp1 arn k* **Ars** k* *Ars-i* ars-s-f k2 arum-d k* astac a1* aur k* aur-ar k2 aur-s k2 bacls-10 pte1*• bad k* bar-c k* bar-i k2 bar-m bell k* borx k* bov k* brom k* bry k* calad k* **Calc** k* calc-i k2 *Calc-p* k* *Calc-s* canth k* *Carb-an* k* carb-v k* carbn-s carc tpw2* *Caust* k* *Cetr* hr1 cham k* *Chel* k* **Chin** k* *Chinin-ar* chinin-s cina k* cob-n sp1 *Coc-c* k* coca cod k* colch colocin a1 con k* cop k* cor-r k* cortico sp1 cortiso tpw7* crot-h a1 crot-t k* cupr k* cur k* dig k* dios k* dirc k* dros k* dulc k* elaps bg2 erig erio a1 eup-per bg2 euph bg2* **Euphr** k* ferr k* ferr-ar ferr-i ferr-m ferr-p graph k* grat k* gymno hep k* hydrog srj2• hyper k* ign k* indg k* *Iod* k* ip k* iris **Kali-ar** **Kali-bi** k* **Kali-c** k* kali-i k* kali-n k* kali-p *Kali-s* kali-sil k2 kola stb3• kreos k* lac-h sk4• lach k* lachn laur *Led* k* *Lyc* k* *M-ambo* b7.de* mag-c k* *Mag-s* k* mang k* meny k* *Meph* merc k* mill morg-p fmm1• **Mosch** k* mur-ac k* *Myrt-c* b7a.de naja nat-ar nat-c k* *Nat-m* k* nat-p nat-s k* nit-ac k* nux-m k* **Nux-v** k* oci-sa sp1 ol-an k* ol-j k* op k* osm k* ox-ac par k* petr-ra shn4• *Ph-ac* k* phel k* **Phos** k* phyt k* plb k* podo fd3.de• polys sk4• *Psor* k* **Puls** k* pyrus rhod k* rhus-t k* **Rumx** k* ruta fd4.de sabad b7a.de sang k* sars k* sel k* seneg k* *Sep* k* *Sil* k* spig k* spong hr1 **Squil** k* stann k* staph k* stict bro1 stram k* stront-c sk4• sul-ac k* sul-i k2 **Sulph** k* sumb k* tab k* tarent k* tell k* thuj k* tritic-vg fd5.de urol-h rwt• vanil fd5.de verat k* vib vichy-g a1 x-ray sp1 zinc k* zinc-p k2 zing k* [spect dfg1]

- **6** h: *Alum* *Cedr* *Coc-c* k* petr
  - **6**-7 h: arum-t calc-p *Coc-c* mez
  - **6**-8 or 6-9 h: *Cedr*
  - **6**-9 h: mez b4a.de
  - **6**-18 h: calc-p
- **7** h: coc-c dig
  - **7**-10 h: sil
- **8** h: dios ham ol-an
  - **8**-9 h: sil
- **9** h; until: abrom-a ks5
- **noon**; until: **Mang** k*
- **evening**; and: acon bg1* *Alum* bg1 asc-t bg1 borx bg1* bov bg1 bufo bg2 calc bg1* carb-v bg1* *Caust* bg1* cina bg1* ferr bg1* ferr-p ptk1 ign bg1* *Lyc* bg1* **Merc** bg1* **Nat-m** bg1* *Phos* bg1* *Rhus-t* bg1* *Sep* bg1 sil bg1* stram bg1 verat bg1*
- **night**; and: *Caust* k*
- **amel.**: agar *Aur* sne coc-c grat k*
- **bathing**; after: calc-s
- **bed** agg.; in: am-c aster k* bry k* *Caust* k* coc-c ferr kali-n nat-sil fd3.de• **Nux-v** k* *Phos* k* rhus-t
- **daybreak** amel.: syph
- **dressing**; while: carc tpw2* seneg k* sulph hr1
- **early**: *Am-br* bro1 *Am-c* bro1 arist-cl sp1 *Ars* bro1 cassia-s cdd7• caust bro1 cupr bro1 hep bro1 *Kali-c* bro1 *Nux-v* bro1 oci-sa sp1 phel bro1 puls bro1 sulph bro1
- **rising** | **after**:
  - **agg.**: ail all-s alum k* alumn k* am-br k* ang ant-c k* arg-met arn k* *Ars* bar-c bar-s k2 borx bov bry calc k* calc-sil k2 canth carb-an carb-v k* *Chel* chin chinin-s **Cina** coc-c cortico tpw7 dig *Euphr* k* **Ferr** k* ferr-ar ferr-p grat *Hep* hr1 ina-i mlk9.de indg k* irid-met srj5• lach melal-alt gya4 *Nat-m* nat-s nit-ac nux-v osm k* par **Phos** k* plb psil ft1 sep *Sil* k* *Spong* staph sulph thuj k*
    - **lying** down again; continuing until: euphr
  - **agg.**: ars nh6 cina nh6 cortico sp1 ferr nh6 phos nh6
- **sleep** agg.; on going to: lyc
- **sunrise**; before: lyc bg2
- **waking**; on: agar ail k* alum bro1 am-br vh ambr br1* arn aur *Bry* bro1 calc-sil k2 carb-v k* carc fd2.de• *Caust* k* *Chel* *Coc-c* k* cod k* dulc fd4.de ferr k* hep h2* hydrog srj2• *Ign* irid-met srj5• **Kali-bi** k* kali-c mrr1 limest-b es1• mag-s k* myos-a rly4• **Nux-v** phos plb k* podo fd3.de• *Psor* k* pyrid rly4• rhus-t k* **Rumx** k* **Sil** k* spong fd4.de sul-ac h2* sulph k* tarent k* thuj tung-met bdx1• vanil fd5.de [spect dfg1]

FORENOON (= 9-12 h): agar k* alum k* am-c k* *Am-m* k* astac a1 aur-m hr1 *Bell* k* bry k* camph k* chinin-s coc-c k* dios k* dros dulc fd4.de glon k* grat k* hell k* kali-c k* kali-sil k2 lact mag-c k* nat-ar nat-c k* nat-m rhus-t k* sabad k* sars k* seneg k* sep k* sil k* spong fd4.de stann k* staph k* sul-ac k* sulph k* tritic-vg fd5.de zing k*

- **9** h: sep tarent

- **9** h: ...
  - • **9**-10 h: ars-h
  - • **9**-11 h: nat-c pd
  - • **9**-12 h: staph
  - • **9**-17 or 9-18 h: merc
  - • **until**: sep
- **10** h:
  - • **10**-12 h: coc-c nat-m
  - • **rawness** in air passages while lying; from: coc-c
- **11** h: lach nat-m
  - • **blood** to chest; from rush of: raph
  - • **dry** cough from tickling behind upper half of sternum | **sitting** bent forward; while: *Rhus-t*
- **waking** | **after** | **agg.**: rhus-t k*
  - • **on**: dios k* nat-m k*

NOON (= 12-13 h): agar k* arg-n k* arund k* bell k* euphr k* naja sil staph k* sulph k*

- **until** noon: nicc-met sk4•
- **evening**; until: dendr-pol sk4•
- **sleep** agg.; during: euphr k*

AFTERNOON (= 13-18 h): agar k* agath-a nl2• all-c alum k* alum-p k2 am-c k* am-m k* anac h2* ant-t k* anth k* arn k* ars k* ars-i sne ars-s-f k2 asaf k* astac k* bad k* bapt k* *Bell* k* bov k* bry k* calc k* calc-p k* caps k* *Chel* k* chin k* chinin-ar coc-c coca cupr dulc fd4.de fago k* ferr-i gamb k* hip-ac sp1 kali-ar kali-bi k* kali-c k* laur k* lim a1 lyc k* mag-c k* mez k* mosch k* mur-ac k* nat-ar nat-c k* nat-m k* nat-p nux-v k* ol-an phel k* phos k* rein a1 ruta fd4.de *Sang* k* spong fd4.de stann staph k* sulph k* thuj k* vanil fd5.de zinc k* zinc-p k2

- **13** h: nat-s
  - • **13**-1 h: hep
  - • **13**-14 h: ars
- **13**.30 h: phel
- **14** h: ars-i sne coca dios laur ol-an
- **15** h: agath-a nl2• ang calc-f cench hep phel [heroin sdj2]
  - • **15**-16 h: agath-a nl2• calc-f lyc
  - • **15**-17 h: sal-ac
  - • **15**-22 h: bell
  - • **bedtime**; until: cench k2
- **16** h: calc-f cench *Chel* coca kali-bi naja bg2
  - • **16**-18 h: lyc
  - • **16**-20 h: *Lyc* k* phel
  - • **morning**; until: dol
  - • **bedtime**; until: *Mang* k*
- **17** h: cupr mang nat-m sol-t-ae
  - • **17**-21 h: caps
- **evening**, until: nux-m
- **midnight**, until: bell k* sulph k*
- **bathing**; after: calc-s

EVENING (= 18-22 h): acal bro1 acet-ac k* acon k* agar k* agn k* ail k* *All-c* k* alum k* alum-p k2 alum-sil k2 alumn k* am-br k* am-c k* am-m k* *Ambr* k* anac k* anan ant-c ant-t k* apis k* apoc k* *Arg-n* k* arn k* **Ars** k* ars-i arum-d arund k* aspar k* bad k* bar-c k* bar-i k2 bar-m bar-s k2 *Bell* k* bism borx k* bov k* *Brom* k* bry k* **Calc** k* calc-i k2 calc-s **Caps** k* carb-an k* **Carb-v** k* carbn-s cassia-s cdd7• *Caust* k* cent a1 cham k* chel k* chin k* *Chinin-ar* chinin-s chlor k* cimic k* cina k* cinnb coc-c k* coca cocc k* *Cod* bro1 coff k* *Colch* bro1 coloc k* com a1 con k* cop k* crot-t k* cub *Cupr* hr1 dios k* dol dream-p sdj1• *Dros* k* dulc fd4.de eug k* *Eup-per* k* eup-pur euphr k* *Ferr* k* ferr-ar ferr-i ferr-p *Fl-ac* k* graph k* grat a1 gymno ham fd3.de• **Hep** k* hip-ac sp1 hydr-ac k* *Hyos* bro1 **Ign** k* indg k* iod k* ip k* iris-foe kali-bi k* kali-br bro1 *Kali-c* k* kali-i k* kali-n hr1 *Kali-s* kali-sil k2 kalm kreos k* lach k* lact laur k* led k* lipp a1 lith-c **Lyc** k* lycps-v *M-ambo* b7.de* *M-arct* b7.de* mag-c k* *Mag-m* k* mag-s k* menth bro1 meph bro1 **Merc** k* merc-c k* merc-i-r k* mez k* mosch k* mur-ac k* naja nat-ar nat-c k* *Nat-m* k* nicc **Nit-ac** k* nit-s-d a1 nux-m nux-v k* oci-sa sp1 ol-an k* olnd k* op bro1 ox-ac k* par k* passi bro1 *Petr* k* ph-ac k* phel k* *Phos* k* prun k* *Prun-v* bro1 *Psor* k* **Puls** k* ran-b k* rheum k* rhod k* rhus-t k* rumx k* ruta k* *Sabad* b7a.de

Evening: ...
Samb bro1 *Sang* k* *Sanic* bro1 santin bro1 *Sec* b7a.de sel b7a.de *Seneg* k* *Sep* k* sil k* *Sin-n* k* sol-t-ae k* spong k* squil k* **Stann** k* staph k* stict k* still k* stram a1* stront-c k* sul-ac k* sul-i k2 sulph k* sumb k* tab k* tarent ter hr1 teucr k* thuj k* trios rsj11• tritic-vg fd5.de tub bro1* tung-met bdx1• upa k* vanil fd5.de verat k* verat-v *Verb* k* zinc k* zinc-p k2 zing k*

- **18** h: am-m bapt a1 chel con nat-m phys *Rhus-t* sulph sumb
  - • **18**-19 h: ip
  - • **18**-22 h: hyper
- **18**.15 h: ol-an
- **18**.30 h: dios
- **19** h: bry cimic com grat *Ip* iris-foe polys sk4• spira
  - • **19**-1 h: *Cain*
  - • **19**-20 h: sin-n
  - • **after**: ip rumx
- **19**.30 h: cimic raph
- **19** or 20 h: sin-n
- **20** h: dios nat-m polys sk4• sep
  - • **20**-21 h: plut-n srj7• *Sep*
  - • **20**-23 h: carc tpw2* nat-m
- **20**.30 h: coca
- **21** h: apis dios lyc *Sil*
  - • **21**-4 h: *Apis*
  - • **21**-23 h: acon k2
  - • **21**-0 h: cham mrr1
  - • **morning**; until: *Kali-c*
  - • **midnight**; until: cham k2
  - • **fever**, followed by burning heat of head; with | **cramps** in legs, feet, hands and arms and rapid pulse: lyc
- **midnight**; until: am *Bar-c* bell carb-v *Caust* ferr **Hep** k* led mag-m merc mez nit-ac nux-v **Phos** *Puls* k* *Rhus-t* k* *Sep* spong stann sul-ac sulph verat zinc
  - • **increasing** until midnight: hep bg2 mez bg2
- **midnight**; until after: mag-m
- **bed** agg.; in: acon agn k* **Alumn** k* *Am-c* k* am-m anac k* ant-t **Ars** k* ars-s-f k2 bell k* borx k* *Calc* k* calc-sil k2 *Caps* k* carb-an k* *Carb-v* k* *Caust* k* coca cocc k* coff k* **Con** k* dol *Dros* k* ferr k* ferr-ar graph k* **Hep** k* hyos **Ign** k* indg ip k* kali-ar *Kali-c* k* kali-p *Kali-s* *Kreos* k* *Lach* k* lact **Lyc** k* mag-c mag-s k* **Merc** k* *Mez* hr1 naja nat-c **Nat-m** k* nat-p nicc *Nit-ac* k* *Nux-m* *Nux-v* k* par petr k* ph-ac *Phos* k* phyt *Puls* k* rhus-t k* ruta k* **Sep** k* *Sil* k* *Stann* k* staph k* still **Sulph** k* teucr k* thuj k* vanil fd5.de verat verb k*
  - • **menses**; before: sulph k*
- **going** out; when: naja
- **sleep**:
  - • **going** to sleep; after: carb-an *Caust* dol c1 *Lach* k* petr
  - • **going** to sleep; on | **agg.**: carb-v h2 *Con* k* *Hep* k* ign **Lyc**
- **sunset** to sunrise: aur k*

NIGHT (= 22-6 h): acal hr1* acet-ac hr1 **Acon** k* aeth *Agar* k* aids nl2• alum k* alum-p k2 alum-sil k2 **Am-br** k* **Am-c** k* *Am-m* k* *Ambr* k* **Anac** k* anan ant-t k* apis apoc k* aq-pet a1 aral *Arg-n* k* arge-pl rwt5• arn k* **Ars** k* ars-s-f k2 *Arum-d* k* *Asaf* asar *Aur* k* aur-ar k2 aur-m k* aur-s k* bac jl2 bad bamb-a stb2.de• **Bar-c** k* bar-m bar-s k2 **Bell** k* bism k* borx k* bry k* cact calad k* **Calc** k* calc-f calc-s calc-sil k2 *Caps* k* *Carb-an* k* carb-v k* **Carbn-s** carc tpw2 card-m k* castm *Caust* k* cench **Cham** k* *Chel* k* *Chin* k* *Chinin-ar* chinin-s chr-ac hr1 cimic k* cina *Coc-c* k* cocc k* cod k* coff k* *Colch* k* coloc k* com k* *Con* k* cor-r k* cortico sp1 crot-c sk4• crot-t k* *Cupr* k* cur *Cycl* k* dig k* *Dros* k* dulc k* erig eug k* eup-per k* ferr k* ferr-ar *Ferr-p* k* *Form* hr1 gaert pte1*• gamb k* gels **Graph** k* *Grat* k* guaj *Hep* k* hydr-ac bro1 hydrog srj2• **Hyos** k* *Ign* k* indg k* *Ip* k* iris-foe **Kali-ar** kali-bi k* kali-br k* **Kali-c** k* kali-chl hr1 kali-i bg2 kali-n k* kali-p **Kali-s** kali-sil k2 kalm *Kreos* k* lac-ac lac-h sk4• **Lach** k* lachn k* laur bg2* led k* lepi k* linu-c a1 **Lyc** k* *M-ambo* b7.de* *M-arct* k* m-aust k* *Mag-c* k* *Mag-m* k* mag-p mag-s k* *Manc* k* med hr1* menth bro1 meph k* **Merc** k* merc-c k* *Merc-i-f* hr1 *Mez* k* mur-ac naja *Nat-ar* nat-c k* *Nat-m* k* nat-p nat-s nicc a1* *Nit-ac* k* nux-v k* oena k* ol-an ol-j k* op k* par k* passi bro1 *Petr* k* petr-ra shn4• phel k* phos k* *Phyt* k* positr nl2• *Prun-v* bro1 psor k* **Puls** k* rhod k* *Rhus-t* k* *Rumx* k* ruta k* *Sabad* k* samb k* *Sang* k* *Sanic* bro1 *Santin* br1* sarcol-ac sp1 senec k*

Night: ...
seneg k* **Sep** k* **Sil** k* sol-t-ae k* spig k* spong k* squil k* stann k* staph k* stict k* stront-c k* sul-ac **Sulph** k* syc fmm1• *Syph* k* tab k* tarent k* ther k* thuj k* tub hr1* urol-h rwt• vanil fd5.de *Verat* k* *Verb* k* vib vichy-g a1 vinc *Zinc* k* zinc-p k2 zing k* ziz [bell-p-sp dcm1]

- **midnight**: am-c ant-t k* apis k* aral ptk1 arg-n ars k* bar-c k* bell k* bry calc h2 caust *Cham* chin cocc k* coff k* dig k* dros k* grat hep kali-c k* kali-n lach ptk1 lyc mag-c bg2 mag-m k* manc k* mez mosch naja nit-ac k* nux-v k* phos puls rhus-t ruta samb k* sep k* *Sulph* k* zing k*
  - **before**: acon k2 alum k* alum-p k2 ant-t k* apis k* aral k* *Arg-n* arn k* ars k* bar-c k* bar-m bell k* brom calc k* **Carb-v** k* carbn-s caust k* ferr k* ferr-ar graph k* hep k* irid-met srj5• kali-c k* lach led k* *Lyc* k* *M-ambo* b7.de* *M-arct* b7a.de mag-c k* mag-m k* mez k* mosch k* mur-ac k* nat-m k* *Nit-ac* k* nux-v k* osm k* *Phos* k* puls k* rhus-t k* rumx sabad k* samb bro1 sep k* spong k* squil k* **Stann** k* staph k* sul-ac k* sulph k* verat k* zinc k* zing hr1
    - **22** h: *Bell* dios nat-m
      - **22**-1 h: *Ant-t* calad cupr hep lach
      - **22**-0 h: cortico tpw7*
    - **22**.30 h: carbn-s ham fd3.de• sol-t-ae
    - **23** h: *Ant-t* aral c1 *Bell* cact vh *Coc-c* mrr1 hep lach rhus-t *Rumx* k* verat
      - **23**-1 h: cupr
      - **23**-3 h: squil
      - **23**-0 h: hep k*
    - **23**.30 h: **Coc-c** k*
  - **after**: *Acon* k* am-br bro1 am-c k* am-m ant-t k* *Ars* k* ars-i arum-d bar-c k* *Bell* k* bry k* calc k* calc-i k2 caust k* cham k* chin k* chinin-ar coc-c k* cocc k* coff k* cupr bro1 dig k* **Dros** k* grat k* hep k* *Hyos* k* iod k* *Kali-ar* kali-c k* *Led* b7a.de lyc k* *M-ambo* b7.de* mag-c k* mag-m mang k* merc k* mez k* nat-m bg2* nit-ac k* *Nux-v* k* ph-ac k* phel bro1 phos k* *Rhus-t* k* rumx samb k* sep spong squil sulph b4a.de
    - **1** h: ars mrr1 coc-c sulph
      - **1**-1.30 h: flav jl2
      - **1**-2 h: rumx zing
      - **1**-4 h: bufo syph jl2
    - **1**.30 h: chel sys flav jl2
    - **2** h: am-c am-m *Ars* caust chin k* chinin-s cocc *Dros* glon **Kali-ar** *Kali-c* kali-n nat-m op petr phos rumx sulph syc fmm1•
      - **2**-2.30 h: kali-p
      - **2**-3 h: am-c *Kali-bi* k* kali-c bg2
      - **2**-3.30 h: coc-c
      - **2**-4 h: arist-cl sp1 eup-per kali-c mrr1
      - **2**-5 h: kali-c tl1 nat-m gk rumx
      - **until**: *Cocc* b7a.de sulph
    - **2** or 3 h: ant-t ars *Kali-c* merc
    - **3** h: am-br vh *Am-c* k* ant-t *Ars* bapt bry sys bufo cain chin cupr k* **Kali-ar** **Kali-c** k* kali-n kali-p fd1.de• mag-c mur-ac nux-v op rhus-t sanguis-s hrn2• sulph h2 thuj tub jl2
      - **3**-4 h: *Am-c* k* *Bufo* cain *Kali-c* k* lyc op rhus-t rumx gm1
      - **until**: acon
    - **4** h: *Anac* ant-t asc-t chin k* choc srj3• kali-c lyc nat-s nit-ac nux-v petr phos
      - **until**: *Apis* nicc sil
    - **5** h: ant-c arum-t chinin-m kr1 *Kali-c* rumx
      - **5**-6 h: kali-i
      - **5**-12 h: kali-c
    - **5**.30 h: ars
    - **morning**, until: nux-v rhus-t ptk1 sep stict
    - **amel.**: brom rhus-t
    - **daybreak**, until: **Nux-v**
    - **waking** from cough: samb ptk1
- **amel.**: bufo bg2
- **bed**:
  - **in** bed:
    - **agg.**: sulph mrr1
    - **amel.**: euphr mrr1
- **children**; in: *Puls* mrr1 *Santin* br1

Night: ...
- **only**: *Ambr* k* *Caust* k* petr ptk1
- **perspiration**; with: acal vh1 chin dig eug kali-bi lyc *Merc* nat-c k* nit-ac psor sulph
- **rising** agg.; after: sulph
- **waking** from the cough: (↗*Sleep - wakens)* am-m *Bell* *Calc* k* *Caust* coc-c k* cocc k* coff dros k2 hep **Hyos** k* **Kali-c** kali-n lach limest-b es1• mag-m nat-sil fd3.de• nit-ac phos *Puls* ruta sang **Sep** k* sil squil stront-c **Sulph** zing
  - **1** h: coc-c
  - **2** h: cocc *Dros* *Kali-c* kali-n
    - **2**-5 h: am-c c1
  - **3** h: dros k2 kali-n tub jl2
  - **4** h: choc srj3• nit-ac
  - **not** waking from the cough (See Sleep - wakens - not)

ABDOMEN, seems to come from: ant-c b7a.de* arg-n ptk1 bell ptk1 bry bg2* carb-v bg2 con bg2 dros bg2* ign ptk1 kali-bi bg2* *Kali-m* ptk1 lach ptk1 nat-m ptk1 *Nit-ac* ptk1 ph-ac ptk1 phos bg2* puls ptk1 rumx bg2* sang ptk1 sep h2* verat b7.de*

O - **Hypogastrium**: verat bg2

ACCOMPANIED BY:
- **angina** pectoris (See CHEST - Angina - accompanied - cough)
- **breathing**; short (See Suffocative)
- **cachexia** (See GENERALS - Cachexia - accompanied)
- **complaints**; other: *Acon* b2.de* alum b2.de* am-c b2.de* am-m b2.de* ambr b2.de* anac b2.de* ang b2.de* ant-c b2.de* ant-t b2.de* arg-met b2.de* *Arn* b2.de* *Ars* b2.de* asaf b2.de* asar b2.de* aur b2.de* bar-c b2.de* **Bell** b2.de* bism b2.de* borx b2.de* **Bry** b2.de* calad b2.de* *Calc* b2.de* camph b2.de* cann-s b2.de* canth b2.de* *Caps* b2.de* carb-an b2.de* *Carb-v* b2.de* caust b2.de* cham b2.de* chel b2.de* *Chin* b2.de* *Cina* b2.de* cocc b2.de* coff b2.de* colch b2.de* coloc b2.de* con b2.de* croc b2.de* cupr b2.de* dig b2.de* **Dros** b2.de* dulc b2.de* euph b2.de* euphr b2.de* ferr b2.de* *Fl-ac* bg2 graph b2.de* guaj b2.de* hell b2.de* *Hep* b2.de* hyos b2.de* ign b2.de* iod b2.de* **Ip** b2.de* kali-c b2.de* kali-n b2.de* kreos b2.de* lach b2.de* laur b2.de* led b2.de* lyc b2.de* m-ambo b2.de m-arct b2.de m-aust b2.de mag-m b2.de* mang b2.de* meny b2.de* merc b2.de* mez b2.de* mosch b2.de* mur-ac b2.de* nat-c b2.de* *Nat-m* b2.de* nit-ac b2.de* nux-m b2.de* **Nux-v** b2.de* olnd b2.de* op b2.de* par b2.de* petr b2.de* ph-ac b2.de* **Phos** b2.de* plb b2.de* **Puls** b2.de* rhod b2.de* *Rhus-t* b2.de* ruta b2.de* sabad b2.de* sabin b2.de* samb b2.de* sars b2.de* sec b2.de* sel b2.de* seneg b2.de* **Sep** b2.de* sil b2.de* spig b2.de* spong b2.de* *Squil* b2.de* stann b2.de* staph b2.de* stront-c b2.de* sul-ac b2.de* *Sulph* b2.de* teucr b2.de* thuj b2.de* valer b2.de* *Verat* b2.de* verb b2.de* zinc b2.de*
- **constipation** (See RECTUM - Constipation - accompanied - cough)
- **coppery** taste (See MOUTH - Taste - coppery - cough)
- **coryza** (See NOSE - Coryza - cough - with)
- **emaciation** (See GENERALS - Emaciation - accompanied - cough)
- **emphysema** (See CHEST - Emphysema - accompanied - cough)
- **epistaxis**: acon k* agn hr1 arn k* bell k* bry caps bg2* carb-an carb-v cina k* cor-r gk cupr k* cyn-d zzc1• **Dros** k* dulc ferr ferr-i ferr-p k* hyos *Ign* sne *Indg* k* iod ip k* kali-bi kali-c k2 kreos lach bg2* *Led* k* merc k* mosch mur-ac nat-m k* nit-ac nux-v k* phos k* *Puls* k* rhus-t sabad sarr a1* sep sil spong sul-ac *Sulph* k*
  - **night**: nat-m k*
- **eructations**; foul (See STOMACH - Eructations; type - foul - cough)
- **falling** down (See MIND - Unconsciousness - cough - during)
- **fanned**; desire to be: carb-v bg2
- **flatulence** (See ABDOMEN - Flatulence - cough)
- **hemorrhage** (See GENERALS - Hemorrhage - cough)
- **lachrymation** (See EYE - Lachrymation - cough)
- **nausea** (See STOMACH - Nausea - cough)
- **orgasm** of blood (See GENERALS - Orgasm - cough)
- **palpitations** (See CHEST - Palpitation - cough)
- **perspiration**; cold: ant-t bg2* ars bg2 dros bg2* hep bg2 verat bg2* verat-v bg2

- **respiration**; difficult (See RESPIRATION - Difficult - accompanied - cough)
- **saliva**:
  - **bloody** (See MOUTH - Saliva - bloody - cough)
  - **frothy**: *Cupr* kr1*
- **salivation**: *Am-m* k* ambr k* ars k* **Bar-c** st1 bell b4a.de* bry bg2 carb-v k* cycl k* iod bg2 lach k* merc k* mez k* nat-m bg1 psor bg2 spig k* staph k* thuj ptk1 verat b7.de*
  - **profuse**: am-m ptk1 lach ptk1 thuj ptk1 verat ptk1
- **sighing**: tell rsj10•
- **sleep**; comatose: **Ant-t** mrr1
- **sleepiness**: **Ant-t** mrr1
- **stiffness**; general (See GENERALS - Stiffening - cough; GENERALS - Stiffness - accompanied - cough)
- **taste**; altered (See MOUTH - Taste - altered - cough)
- **urination**:
  - **copious**: squil bro1
  - **retention** of (See BLADDER - Retention - cough)
- **vision** before the eyes; dark (See VISION - Colors - dark - cough)
- **water** brash (See STOMACH - Eructations; type - water brash - cough - during)
- **yawning**: *(↗Yawning)* am-m b7a.de anac b4a.de* *Ant-t* bg2 am b7.de* bell ptk1 brom bg2 cham bg2 ign bg2 kreos bg2 lyc b4a.de* nat-m bg2 nux-v b7.de* op b7.de* phos b4a.de* puls b7a.de* rhus-t bg2 zinc bg2

○ - **Abdomen**:
  - **contraction** (See ABDOMEN - Contraction - cough)
  - **distension** (See ABDOMEN - Distension - cough)
- **Brain**; complaints of (See HEAD - Brain; complaints of - accompanied - cough)
- **Chest**:
  - **coldness**; internal (See CHEST - Coldness - internal - accompanied)
  - **gurgling**: *Cina* b7a.de*
  - **pain**: cassia-s zzc1•
    - **right** side (See CHEST - Pain - sides - right - cough)
    - **left** side: cassia-s ccrh1•
      - **morning**: cassia-s ccrh1•
      - **evening**: cassia-s ccrh1•
  - **weakness** (See CHEST - Weakness - cough)
- **Ears**; stopped sensation of (See EAR - Stopped - accompanied)
- **Epigastrium**; contraction of (See STOMACH - Contraction - epigastrium - cough)
- **Extremities**; pain in (See EXTREMITIES - Pain - accompanied - cough)
- **Eyes**:
  - **complaints** of (See EYE - Complaints - accompanied - cough)
  - **heat** in (See EYE - Heat in - cough)
- **Forehead**; cold perspiration on (See HEAD - Perspiration of - forehead - cold - cough)
- **Hypochondria**; pain as from weariness in (See ABDOMEN - Pain - hypochondria - cough - during - agg. - exertion)
- **Hypogastrium**; contraction of (See ABDOMEN - Contraction - hypogastrium - cough)
- **Kidneys**; pain in (See KIDNEYS - Pain - accompanied - cough)
- **Larynx**; scratching in (See LARYNX - Scratching - larynx - accompanied)

Accompanied by: ...
- **Liver**; complaints of (See ABDOMEN - Liver - accompanied - cough)
- **Lungs** | **pain** | **Base** (See CHEST - Pain - lungs - lower - cough)
  - **weakness** of (See CHEST - Weakness - lungs - accompanied - cough)
- **Mouth**:
  - **bleeding** (See MOUTH - Bleeding - accompanied - cough)
  - **dry**: cocc b7.de* laur b7.de*
- **Neck** | **pain** | **Nape** of neck (See BACK - Pain - cervical - nape - cough)
  - **swelling** (See Swelling - neck)
- **Nose**:
  - **dryness** inside (See NOSE - Dryness - inside - accompanied)
  - **itching**: kali-n bg2
- **Spermatic** cords | **stitching** pain (See stitching)
- **Stomach**; complaints of (See STOMACH - Complaints - accompanied - cough)
- **Teeth**:
  - **complaints** of: ars b4a.de lyc b4a.de sep b4a.de
  - **grinding** of: *Bell* b4.de*
  - **pain** (See RESPIRATION - Difficult - accompanied - cough; TEETH - Pain - accompanied - cough)
- **Testes**; pain in: spong mrr1
- **Throat**:
  - **constriction** of (See THROAT - Constriction - cough)
  - **inflammation** (See THROAT - Inflammation - accompanied - cough)
  - **red** discoloration of: *Bell* bg2 carb-v b4a.de *Kali-c* b4a.de lyc b4a.de
  - **rising** in throat; sensation as if something is (See ABDOMEN - Lump in - rising)
- **Tongue**:
  - **dark**: bapt kr1*
  - **white**: chin kr1*
- **Tonsils**; enlarged (See THROAT - Swelling - tonsils - accompanied - cough)
- **Trachea**; rattling in: sep bg2
- **Uterus**; complaints of (See FEMALE - Uterus - accompanied - cough)

ACIDS: | **agg.**: ant-c brom *Con* k* lach k* mez k* nat-m k* nux-v sep k* sil sulph k*

ACRID fluid through posterior nares; cough from sensation of: kali-bi k*

ADHERES; from something which: | **Trachea**, in: staph h1

AGGRAVATES symptoms (See GENERALS - Cough - during - agg.)

AGITATION, from: *Cist* k*

AIR:
- **night**: calc-p *Hep* k* *Merc* k* phos spig sul-ac sulph trif-p
- **close** air agg.: brom nat-ar
- **cold** (See Cold - air - agg.)
- **dry** air agg.: acon bg2 caust cham bg2 loxo-recl knl4• samb bg2 sep sulph sne
- **evening** | **agg.**: merc bg2

AIR AGG.; DRAFT OF: *Acon* k* *Calc* caps k* *Caust* k* *Chin* k* cortico tpw7* hep tl1 ol-j hr1 *Ph-ac* rhus-t gk sep symph fd3.de• xanth bg2

AIR; IN OPEN:
- **agg.**: *Acon* k* all-s k* alum k* ang aphis **Ars** k* ars-s-f k2 bar-c k* bar-s k2 bry k* calc k* calc-p a1 carb-v k* cham k* cina k* cocc k* *Coff* con k* cor-r bg2 cortiso tpw7* cub hr1* cycl k* dig b4a.de* dulc bg2 euphr ferr ferr-ar ferr-p *Hep* ip k* kali-bi k* kali-c bg2 **Kali-n** k* *Lach* k* linu-c a1 lyc k* m-arct k* mag-m h2* mosch k* *Naja* nit-ac k* nux-v k* osm k* ph-ac k* **Phos** k* phyt podo fd3.de•

- **agg.**: ...
psil ft1 psor mrr1 *Rhus-t* k* **Rumx** k* sang k* seneg k* sil k* sin-n a1 spig k* spong fd4.de squil staph k* stram *Sul-ac* k* *Sulph* k* trif-p a1
- **amel.**: (↗*Warm - room - agg.)* *All-c* ambr ant-c anth apis *Arg-met* *Arg-n* bov *Brom* **Bry** k* calc-s cench chel **Coc-c** k* cycl dros *Dulc* k* hed sp1 **Iod** k* *Kali-s* kola stb3• *Lil-t* **Mag-p** k* *Nat-s* nux-v olib-sac wmh1 op wbt• podo fd3.de• **Puls** k* pyrog rad-br ptk1* rauw sp1 sanic sul-i k2 sulph tub jl2 visc sp1
- **going** into; when: ip b7a.de*

ALCOHOL: (↗*Beer; Brandy; Wine)* arn k* ferr k* ign k* lach k* led k* *Spong* stann stram k* zinc k*

ALLERGIC: ozone sde2• stict mrr1

ALTERNATING with:
- **bronchitis**: lac-f wza1•
- **colds**: lac-f wza1•
- **eruptions**: (↗*RESPIRATION - Asthmatic - alternating - eruptions)* ars *Crot-t* mez *Psor* *Sulph*
- **hemorrhoids**: berb dgt1
- **leukorrhea** (See FEMALE - Leukorrhea - alternating - cough)
- **sciatica** in summer: staph k*

○ - **Head**; pain in (See HEAD - Pain - alternating - cough)
- **Pleura**; pain in: dros mtf11

ANGER; after: (↗*MIND - Anger)* acon k* adam srj5• agar sne anac br1 *Ant-t* k* *Arg-met* k* arg-n k* *Arn* k* ars asar b7.de bell k* bry *Caps* k* *Cham* k* chin *Coloc* *Ign* kali-s fkr2.de nux-v sabad ptk1* sep spong bg **Staph** k* verat k* [ant-c stj2 ant-met stj2]
- **children**; in: anac bro1* ant-t bro1* *Arn* h1* cham mtf33

APPREHENSION and discouragement; after feelings of: rhus-t tl1

ARMS:
- **cold**, becoming (See Cold; becoming - agg. - arm)
- **raising** agg. (See Raising)
- **stretching** agg.: lyc ptk1
- **thighs** when coughing; must put arms on: nicc c1*

ARSENICAL wall paper; from: calc bro1

ASCENDING STAIRS agg.: am-c gsy1* arg-met k* arg-n k* *Ars* k* bar-c k* *Bry* cench iod k* kali-ar k2 kali-n k* lyc k* mag-c k* mag-m k* merc k* nux-v k* puls hr1 seneg k* sep k* spong k* squil k* stann k* staph k* tell a1 zinc k*

ASTHMATIC: *Acon* *Alum* alum-p k2 alum-sil k2 *Am-c* k* am-m ambr ambro bro1 anac **Ant-t** k* antip vh aral arg-n arn **Ars** k* *Ars-i* ars-s-f k2 asaf k* aspar bar-c k* bar-i k2 bar-m bar-s k2 *Bell* k* benz-ac bro1 bit-ar wht1• *Brom* k* bry k* calad calc calc-i k2 calc-s calc-sil k2 carb-an *Carb-v* k* carbn-s cassia-s ccrh1• caust cetr hr1 cham k* *Chin* k* chinin-ar chlor cic **Cina** k* coc-c cocc con cor-r croc k* *Crot-t* k* **Cupr** k* des-ac rbp6 dig dol **Dros** k* dulc *Euph* k* euphr ferr ferr-ar ferr-i ferr-p guaj helodr-cal knl2• *Hep* k* hydrog srj2• hyos ign iod k* **Ip** k* irid-met srj5• *Kali-ar* *Kali-bi* k* *Kali-c* k* kali-chl kali-m k2 kali-n kali-p kali-sil k2 *Kreos* *Lach* lact laur *Led* lob k* lyc k* meph bro1* merc merc-c hr1 mez moni rfm1• morg-p pte1• mosch mur-ac nat-m nat-s k* nicc nit-ac k* *Nux-m* **Nux-v** k* op petr k* phel *Phos* k* podo hr1 prun psor *Puls* pycnop-sa mrz1 rhodi br1* rhus-t sabad k* *Samb* k* *Sang* k* seneg bro1 *Sep* k* *Sil* spig *Spong* k* squil stann *Stram* sul-ac k* sul-i k2 sulph syc pte1*• verat viol-o zinc zing
- **morning** | 6h: syc bka1•
- **night**: syc bka1•
  - **midnight**:
    - **after**:
      - **2** h: syc bka1•
      - **2-3** h: syc fmm1•
      - **4** h: syc bka1•

AUTUMN (See Seasons - autumn)

BACK; as if coming from the: agar bg2 nux-m bg2 tell bg2

BARKING: **Acon** k* all-c k* ambr hr1* ant-t aur-m bamb-a stb2.de• **Bell** k* brom k* bry hr1 caps carc gk *Caust* b4a.de* cimx clem k* cob-n sp1 *Coc-c* k* cor-r k* cub k* **Dros** k* *Dulc* k* gels bg2 germ-met srj5• **HEP** k ●* hipp k* hydrog srj2• *Hyper* hr1 *Iod* hr1* *Kali-bi* k* kali-br bg2 kali-m k2 kali-s fd4.de kreos hr1 lac-c k* lac-h htj1• lact k* lyc lyss k* med hr1* meph gk1 merc k*

Barking: ...
Merc-cy hr1 mur-ac *Nit-ac* k* nux-m k* ol-j hr1 op wbt• ozone sde2• phos k* phyt k* puls gk rosm lgb1 *Rumx* k* *Sal-ac* hr1 *Samb* hr1* sanguis-s hrn2• sin-n bro1 spig hr1 **Spong** k* stann k* staph hr1 stict k* **Stram** k* sulph k* thuj bg2 tub gk1 urol-h rwt• verat k* verb bg2 visc sp1 [bell-p-sp dcm1]
- **day** and night: *Spong* k*
- **morning**: *Coc-c* hr1 kali-bi thuj k*
- **evening**: *Nit-ac* k*
- **night**: bell k* *Coc-c* hr1 *Merc-cy* hr1 nit-ac phyt hr1 sanguis-s hrn2•
  - **23** h | **wakes** suddenly face fiery red, crying: bell k*
- **accompanied** by | **eructations**: verat ptk1
- **breathing** deep; after: *Dulc* k*
- **children**; in: iod mtf33
- **dog**, like a: bell k* lyss k*
- **drinking** cold water | **amel.**: caust nh6 *Coc-c* k*
- **loud**: **Acon** k* aur-m kali-bi kali-chl hr1 lyc stann verat k*
- **sleep** agg.; during: hipp k* lyc nit-ac

BATHING:
- **agg.**: ant-c k* ars *Calc* k* calc-f *Calc-s* k* carc tpw2* *Caust* dulc lach *Nit-ac* k* nux-m k* *Psor* **Rhus-t** k* sep stram sul-ac sulph verat zinc k*
- **amel.**: positr nl2•
- **sea**; in the: mag-m bg2

○ - **Chest**, in cold water amel. borx k*

BED:
- **changing** position: ars con **Kreos** k*
  - **amel.**: borx ign
- **foot** out of bed; putting: hep tl1
- **hand** out of bed; putting: hep tl1 *Rhus-t* hs
- **in** (See Lying - bed - agg.)
- **rising** from; on (See Rising - bed - agg.)
- **sitting** erect | **amel.**: phos tl1
- **warm**:
  - **evening**: nux-m
  - **amel.**: cham *Kali-bi*
  - **becoming** warm in bed; on (See Warm; becoming - bed)

BEER agg.: (↗*Alcohol)* mez k* nux-v k* rhus-t k* spong k*

BENDING: (↗*Stooping)*
- **backward** | **agg.**: beryl sp1* cupr bg2
- **forward**:
  - **agg.**: **Caust** k* dig k* podo fd3.de•
  - **amel.**: eup-per ruta fd4.de *Spong* k* tritic-vg fd5.de
- **head**:
  - **backward** | **agg.**: ars-i sne *Bry* cupr hep kali-bi lyc psor *Rumx* *Sil* spong

BENDING DOUBLE: | **must** bend double: agar k* choc mp1*• coff k* hydrog srj2• *Kali-bi* sne pneu jl2 ther k*

BLANKET; as if head in a: sang tl1

BLOOD:
- **rush** of blood to chest; cough from: aloe k* calc-f sp1
  - **11** h: raph

BLOWING THE NOSE agg.: arn bg2

BLOWING wind instruments: rhus-t bg2

BRANDY: (↗*Alcohol)* ferr k*

BRASSY: kali-bi vk

BREAD: kali-c k*
- **black**: ph-ac k*

BREAKFAST:
- **after**:
  - **agg.**: pneu jl2
  - **amel.**: alumn aspar bar-c coc-c kali-c k* lach murx
- **before** | **agg.**: alumn k* kali-c murx seneg sulph
- **during**: alum k* alumn k* kola stb3• seneg k*

BREATH: | **want** of (See Breathing - deficient)

BREATHING:

- **agg.**: am-c k* asar k* bell k* beryl tpw5 calc b4a.de coloc k* dulc k* graph k* hep k* ip k* kali-n k* mag-m k* nat-m k* sang mtf11 spong fd4.de stann k2 sulph k*
- **deep**:
  - **agg.**: *Acon* k* *Aesc* am-c am-m k* apis arn k* ars k* asar k* **Bell** k* bism k* *Brom* k* **Bry** k* calc bg2 carb-an k* chin chinin-ar cina k* coc-c **Con** k* *Cor-r* k* croc bg2 crot-h cupr k* dig dros *Dulc* k* euphr k* *Ferr* ferr-ar ferr-p graph k* *Hep* k* *Iod* ip k* kali-ar *Kali-bi* k* **Kali-c** k* kali-m k2 kali-n h2* kali-p *Lac-c* k* lach k* lec *Lyc* k* mag-m k* mang k* meny k* *Merc* mez k* mur-ac k* naja k* nat-ar nat-m k* nit-ac k* oci-sa sk4• olnd bg2 ozone sde2• ph-ac phos plb k* *Puls* k* *Rhus-t* *Rumx* k* sabad samb seneg k* sep k* serp sil k* *Squil* k* stann stram k* *Sulph* k* verb bg2* zinc ziz
    - **morning** | **lying** down agg.; after: ip k*
  - **amel.**: kali-n bg2 lach olib-sac wmh1 osm bg2 *Puls* k* *Verb* k*
- **deficient**, being: (↗*Suffocative*) am-c *Ars* *Aur* k* aur-m cina cocc coloc k* con *Cur* dros k* euphr ferr guaj hep ign *Ip* lyc nux-v op spig
  - **night**: aur k* coloc h2*
- **holding** breath:
  - **agg.**: kali-n k* prun
  - **amel.**: bry bg2
- **irregular** breathing agg.: **Rumx**

BRIGHT objects: stram k*

BRONCHIAL (See Irritation - bronchi)

BRUSHING teeth: carb-v bg3* coc-c k* cocc tl1 dig bg3* euphr bg3* podo fd3.de• sep bg3* spong fd4.de staph k*

BURNING; from:

- ○ **Chest**; in: am-c k* *Carb-v* b4a.de caust coc-c k* euph k* euphr led k* mag-m ph-ac k* phos b4a.de*
- **Larynx**; in: acon k* aphis arg-n ars bell bov brom bufo caust mag-s ph-ac phos k* phyt seneg k* *Spong* stict tarent urt-u zing
- **Throat**-pit; in: ars k*
- **Trachea**; in: acon ars k* euphr

CARBON, as from vapor of: (↗*Vapor*) arn k* *Puls*

CARDIAC (See Heart affections)

CATARRHAL cough (See Loose)

CELLARS, air of: (↗*MIND - Fear - narrow*) ant-t k* *Dulc* hr1 nux-m k* *Sep* k* stram k*

CHAGRIN (See Mortification)

CHICKENPOX:

- **after**: ant-c k* calc ptk1
- **during**: plat ptk1

CHILDREN; in: cupr tl1

CHILL:

- **after**: apis cimx nux-m ph-ac phos *Samb*
- **before**: apis eup-per mag-c k2 puls hr1 **Rhus-t** k* rumx *Samb* k* *Tub* k*
- **during**: acon k* apis *Ars* k* bell borx k* *Bry* k* calc k* calc-p k* carb-v k* cham k* *Chin* k* *Chinin-ar* chinin-m kr1 cimx con k* cupr b7a.de *Ferr* hep k* hyos k* ip k* kali-ar kali-c k* kali-p kreos k* lach k* lyc k* mez b4a.de nat-c nat-p nux-m k* nux-v k* ph-ac **Phos** k* pitu-gl skp7• *Psor* k* *Puls* k* **Rhus-t** k* *Rumx* **Sabad** k* samb xxb1 *Sep* k* sil spong k* sulph k* thuj k* *Tub* k* *Verat* b7a.de

CHOKING: (↗*Suffocative*) acon k2 *Agar* **Alum** ars bell k2 carb-v k* cina **Coc-c** k* crot-h dros k* dulc fd4.de *Hep* k* iod **Ip** k* kali-ar *Kali-bi* *Kali-c* k* *Lach* k* lyc mag-p maias-l hrn2• merc mez bg2* nat-m nux-v bg2 **Puls** bg2* *Ruta* *Sep* k* spong sul-i k2 *Sulph* k*

- **morning** | **rising** agg.; after: **Cina** k*
- **evening**: cina
- **night**: carb-v hep ip ruta
  - **midnight**: dros *Ruta*
- **from**: meph a1
- **inspiration** agg.: cina

Choking: ...

- **sensation** | **Fauces** to bifurcation of bronchia; from: syph
- **sleep**:
  - **lying** on side agg.: kali-c
  - **sound** sleep; as soon as one falls into a: **Lach** k* *Sulph*

CHRONIC: (↗*Constant*) adam srj *All-s* bro1 am-c mrr1 am-m bg2 ant-c mrr1 *Ant-t* bro1 ars-i bro1 ast-a bta1• bar-c bro1 bry bro1 calc ptk1 calc-i bro1 calc-p bro1 capp-crm bta1• caust bg2 cham bro1 *Cod* bro1 crot-h bro1 cucum-h bta1• *Dros* bro1 dulc bro1 eup-per bro1 form bg2 hyosin-hbr bro1 ign bg2 kali-i bg2 kreos bro1 laur bro1* lich-i bta1• lob bro1 lyc bg2* mang-act bro1 merc bro1 naja bro1 nat-m bg2 *Nit-ac* bro1 phel bro1 *Phos* bro1* psor bro1 puls bro1* rumx bro1 *Sang* bro1 sil bg2* spong bg2* squil bro1 staph mrr1 stict bro1 stram mrr1 streptom mtf11 sulph bro1 teph-k bta1•

CHURCH agg.; air in (See Cellars)

CLEANING the teeth (See Brushing)

CLEAR, bright sound: *Ars* b4a.de

CLOCK (See Periodical - clock)

CLOSING eyes at night excites cough: **Hep** k*

CLOTHES AGG.; TIGHT: carc mlr1• stann k*

COAL (See Carbon)

COBWEBS in the throat; from sensation of: pop-cand c1

COFFEE:

- **agg.**: caps k* caust k* cham k* cocc k* hep b4a.de ign k* kali-bi bg2 nux-v k* sul-ac
- **odor** of coffee: sul-ac k*
  - **amel.**: [tax jsj7]

COITION; after: tarent k*

COLD:

- **air**:
  - **agg.**: (↗*Covering*) acon k* adam srj5• agar agn k* **All-c** k* all-s alum k* alum-p k2 alum-sil k2 am-c bro1 am-m k* aphis **Ars** k* ars-s-f k2 aur aur-ar k2 aur-s k2 *Bad* k* *Bar-c* k* bar-s k2 bell b4a.de* beryl sp1 bov *Brom* k* bry k* *Calc* calc-sil k2* caps tl1 *Carb-an* k* *Carb-v* k* carbn-s carc mg1.de* **Caust** k* cham k* cimic k* cina k* cist *Coca* cocc coff *Con* cor-r bg2 cortico tpw7* crot-h hr1 cub k* *Cupr* k* cur k* cycl dulc k* *Ferr* *Ferr-ar* ferr-p **Hep** k* **Hyos** k* hyper k* ip k* *Kali-ar* *Kali-bi* *Kali-c* k* kali-i **Kali-n** k* kali-p lac-ac lac-d k2 *Lach* k* lyc *Menth* bro1 mez k* mosch k* naja nat-s nit-ac k* nux-m k* **Nux-v** osm ph-ac k* **Phos** k* *Phyt* k* plan k* plat hr1 plut-n srj7• psor mrr1 rauw tpw8* *Rhus-t* k* **Rumx** k* sabad k* samb sang k* *Seneg* k* *Sep* k* *Sil* k* sin-n k* spig spong k* squil k* staph stram k* *Sul-ac* sulph k* symph fd3.de• trif-p bro1 tub dp• vanil fd5.de verat k* verat-v zinc hr1
  - **amel.**: arg-n bg2 calc-s *Coc-c* k* kali-s mag-p pd
  - **entering** cold air from a warm room agg.: *Acon* *Carb-v* k* nat-c *Nux-v* **Phos** k ● **RUMX** k ● *Sang* sep
  - **sensation** of icy cold air in air passages; from: *Cor-r* k*
  - **wet**: ant-t k* bar-c bar-s k2 *Calc* k* calc-sil k2 carb-an k* carb-v k* *Chin* k* cur **Dulc** k* *Iod* *Lach* k* mag-c k* mang k2 merc mosch k* mur-ac k* *Nat-s* bro1 *Nit-ac* k* nux-m k* phyt k* rhus-t k* sep k* sil spong fd4.de sul-ac k* *Sulph* k* verat k* zinc k*
- **applications** | **agg.**: carc tpw2
- **bathing**:
  - **agg.**: borx psor
  - **amel.**: hed sp1
- **drinks**:
  - **agg.**: acon bg2 adam srj5• am-c bg2 am-m k* ant-c **Ars** k* bad hr1 *Bar-c* k* bry k2 calc k* calc-p bg2 calc-sil k2 *Carb-v* k* (non: caust hr1) cimic hr1 coc-c ptk1 dendr-pol sk4• dig k* dros k2 dulc hr1 germ-met srj5• ham fd3.de• *Hep* k* kali-ar kali-c lyc k* manc ptk1 *Merc* k* nit-ac hr1 *Ph-ac* *Phos* k* psil ft1 **Psor** k* puls b* rhus-t k* rumx sabad hr1 sep hr1 *Sil* k* *Spong* k* *Squil* k* staph k* stram k* sul-ac k* symph fd3.de• *Thuj* k* *Tub* verat k*
    - **icy** cold: acon vh1
    - **overheated**; when: bry k2

- **drinks**: ...
  - **amel.**: am-caust borx brom bros-gau$_{mrc1}$ caps$_{k}$* **Caust**$_{k}$* cina$_{bg2}$* *Coc-c*$_{k}$* cocc$_{tl1}$ **Cupr**$_{k}$* euphr glon iod ip$_{k}$* irid-met$_{srj5}$• kali-c kali-s onos$_{k}$* *Op*$_{k}$* phos$_{bro1}$ sal-fr$_{sle1}$• sulph tab$_{bg2}$* (non: tub$_{lmj}$) verat
- **dry** | **air**: **Acon** brom caps cham crot-h$_{k}$* **Hep** nux-m *Phos* rumx samb *Spong*
- **food** | **agg.**: am-m *Carb-v*$_{k}$* dros$_{k}$* dulc$_{fd4.de}$ *Hep*$_{k}$* lyc$_{k}$* mag-c$_{k}$* *Ph-ac* rhus-t$_{k}$* *Sil*$_{k}$* thuj$_{k}$* verat$_{k}$*
- **milk** agg.: ant-t$_{k}$* spong$_{ptk1}$
- **room** | **agg.**: cortico$_{tpw7}$* sang$_{mtf11}$
- **warm** | **room**; going from or to warm (See Warm - room - entering - cold - or)
- **water**:
  - **agg.**: calc$_{bg2}$ rhus-t$_{bg2}$ stram$_{bg2}$ sul-ac$_{bg2}$ verat$_{bg2}$
    - **standing** in cold water: nux-m
- **wet** air (See air - wet)

○ - **Trachea**; cold sensation in camph$_{b7.de}$*

COLD; AFTER TAKING A: acon$_{b7a.de}$* arn$_{b7a.de}$ *Bell*$_{b4a.de}$ *Bry*$_{b7.de}$* calc$_{b4a.de}$ carb-v$_{b4.de}$* caust$_{bg2}$ cham$_{b7a.de}$* chin$_{bg2}$ cupr$_{b7.de}$* *Dros*$_{b7.de}$* dulc$_{b4.de}$* ferr$_{b7a.de}$ hep$_{b4.de}$* hyos$_{bg2}$ *Ip*$_{b7.de}$* nat-c$_{b4.de}$* *Nux-m*$_{b7.de}$* **Nux-v**$_{b7.de}$* *Op*$_{b7.de}$* petr$_{b4.de}$* phos$_{b4.de}$* puls$_{b7a.de}$* *Rhus-t*$_{b7.de}$* sep$_{b4a.de}$* sil$_{bg2}$
- **water**; in: *Nux-m*$_{b7a.de}$ rhus-t$_{b7a.de}$

COLD; BECOMING:
- **agg.**: (↗*Uncovering - agg.*) am$_{k}$* **Ars**$_{k}$* ars-s-f$_{k2}$ *Bad* *Bell*$_{bg2}$ borx$_{b4a.de}$* *Bry Calc Calc-p Carb-v*$_{k}$* carbn-s *Caust*$_{k}$* *Cham*$_{bg2}$ *Coc-c*$_{mrr1}$ *Con Dulc*$_{k}$* ham$_{fd3.de}$• **Hep**$_{k}$* kali-ar *Kali-bi* **Kali-c**$_{k}$* *Lach* lycps-v$_{bg2}$ *Mosch*$_{k}$* mur-ac$_{k}$* nat-c$_{bg2}$ nit-ac$_{bg2}$ *Nux-m*$_{bg2}$ **Nux-v**$_{k}$* **Phos**$_{k}$* psil$_{ft1}$ **Psor**$_{k}$* **Puls**$_{bg2}$ **Rhus-t**$_{k}$* **Rumx** *Sabad*$_{k}$* *Sang* **Sep**$_{bg2}$ **Sil** spong$_{k}$* *Squil* *Staph* sul-ac *Sulph* thuj **Tub**

○ • **Arm** or hand: ars bar-c calc *Con* ferr **Hep**$_{k}$* kali-c **Rhus-t**$_{k}$* *Sil* sulph
  - **Feet**: *Bar-c*$_{k}$* *Bufo*$_{k}$* *Sil*$_{k}$* sulph
    - **standing** in water, from: nux-m$_{ptk1}$
  - **Single** part: bar-c **Hep**$_{k}$* **Rhus-t**$_{k}$* sil$_{k}$*
- **amel.**: sul-i$_{k2}$

COMPANY: (↗*Strangers; Strangers - presence*) *Ambr*$_{k}$* ars$_{ptk1}$ bar-c$_{k}$*

CONCUSSIVE (See Racking)

CONDIMENTS (See Spices)

CONSCIOUSNESS; with loss of: cadm-s cina *Cupr*$_{k}$*

CONSOLATION agg.: ars$_{k}$*

CONSTANT: (↗*Chronic*) acon$_{k}$* adam$_{srj}$ *Agar*$_{k}$* ail$_{k}$* **Alum**$_{k}$* am-br$_{k}$* am-c ant-s-aur$_{bg1}$ ant-t$_{k}$* apoc$_{k}$* arg-cy *Arn Ars*$_{k}$* bell benz-ac$_{k}$* both-ax$_{tsm2}$ brom$_{k2}$ bry$_{k}$* calad$_{k}$* calc$_{k}$* cann-s carb-ac$_{k}$* *Carb-v* **Caust**$_{k}$* cham$_{bg3}$* **Chin**$_{k}$* chlor$_{k}$* cimic cimx$_{k}$* cina *Coff*$_{k}$* *Con* cor-r$_{k}$* crot-c$_{sk4}$• crot-h$_{ptk1}$ cub$_{k}$* *Cupr*$_{k}$* cupr-s$_{k}$* dol$_{k}$* dros$_{k}$* elaps euph$_{k}$* *Ferr* ferr-p glycyr-g$_{cte1}$• guare *Hep Hyos*$_{k}$* hyper *Ign*$_{k}$* *Ip*$_{k}$* irid-met$_{srj5}$• kali-bi$_{k}$* kali-c$_{bg3}$* kali-chl$_{k}$* kali-i$_{k}$* kali-n$_{k}$* kali-perm kalm$_{k}$* kreos$_{k}$* lac-ac *Lac-c* *Lach*$_{k}$* lact$_{k}$* laur lob$_{hr1}$ lob-s **Lyc**$_{k}$* m-arct malar$_{jl2}$ mang$_{k}$* med$_{k}$* merc$_{k}$* *Mez* narc-ps$_{br1}$* nat-m nat-p$_{k}$* *Nux-v*$_{bg3}$* *Op*$_{hr1}$ petr-ra$_{shn4}$• *Ph-ac*$_{k}$* phel$_{k}$* phos$_{k}$* phyt$_{k}$* plan$_{k}$* *Pneu*$_{jl2}$ podo *Puls*$_{k}$* *Rhus-t*$_{k}$* rosm$_{lgb1}$ **Rumx**$_{k}$* sang$_{k}$* *Seneg* sep$_{k}$* **Spong**$_{k}$* *Squil*$_{k}$* staph$_{mrr1}$ stict$_{k}$* sulph$_{bg3}$* syph$_{sne}$ tab thuj$_{k}$* tril-p$_{c1}$ tritic-vg$_{fd5.de}$ *Tub*$_{mrr1}$ tub-a$_{br1}$* ust$_{hr1}$ verat$_{ptk1}$* zinc$_{k}$*
- **day** and night: *Ant-t*$_{hr1}$ brom$_{hr1}$ *Calc-p*$_{hr1}$ *Carb-v*$_{hr1}$ euph$_{hr1}$ *Hydr*$_{hr1}$ ign *Kali-c*$_{hr1}$ lyc$_{k}$* nat-m phos plb$_{hr1}$ samb$_{hr1}$ spong squil
- **day** or night: *Squil*
- **morning**: cupr-s$_{k}$* phel tritic-vg$_{fd5.de}$
- **evening**: acon$_{k}$* *Caust*$_{k}$* cub$_{k}$* **Puls**$_{k}$* tritic-vg$_{fd5.de}$
- **night**: anac calc$_{h2}$* *Con* dros$_{gk}$ laur lyc med$_{k}$* rosm$_{lgb1}$ **Sep**$_{k}$* stict stront-c zinc
  - **midnight**:
    - **before**:
      - **22** h: rosm$_{lgb1}$
        - **sleep**; till falling to: rosm$_{lgb1}$
  - **lying** down agg.: am-br$_{hr1}$ **Sep**$_{k}$* zinc
  - **sleep**, on falling to: med

Constant – **night**: ...
  - **waking**; on: **Sep**$_{k}$*
- **irritation** in lower chest; from: kreos$_{k}$*
- **lying** | **agg.** | **sitting** up amel.; and: **Hyos**$_{k}$* *Laur* **Puls**$_{k}$* rhus-t sang **Sep**
  - **amel.**: mang
- **maddeningly** frequent but soft cough: staph$_{mrr1}$
- **pregnancy**: *Kali-br*$_{hr1}$
- **vomiting** | **amel.**: *Mez*

CONSTIPATION agg.: con$_{ptk1}$ graph$_{ptk1}$ sep$_{h2}$*

CONSTRICTION; from: (↗*Smothering*)

○ - **Chest**; in: agar$_{tl1}$ bell$_{bg2}$ carb-v clem dros hep$_{tl1}$ iod$_{tl1}$ ip$_{k}$* mosch$_{k}$* phos$_{tl1}$ samb$_{k}$* stram$_{k}$* sulph suprar$_{rly4}$•

○ • **Diaphragm**: cench$_{k2}$
- **Epigastrium**; in: ferr$_{bg2}$
- **Larynx**; in: **Agar** ambr$_{k2}$ *Ant-t Arg-n Ars Asc-t Bell*$_{k}$* *Brom Calc Carb-an* carbn-s *Cham* chlor *Coc-c Coff*$_{k}$* *Cor-r* **Cupr**$_{k}$* *Dros* euphr *Gels Hep* hyos ign$_{k}$* *Iod Ip*$_{k}$* *Kali-c Lach* laur *Lob Mang*$_{k}$* meny$_{k}$* naja$_{k}$* nit-ac **Phos** *Puls*$_{k}$* *Sil Spong* stram$_{k}$* *Sulph*$_{k}$* verat
  - **night**:
    - **sleep** | **during** | **agg.**: *Agar Lach Nit-ac Phos Sulph*
      - **first** sleep while lying on the side: *Kali-c Phos Spong*
  - **eating** agg.: *Puls*
  - **sleep** agg.; on going to: agar *Arg-n* **Lach** *Phos Spong Sulph*
- **Throat**; of: aesc$_{bg2}$ ars$_{bg2}$ carb-an$_{bg2}$ cocc$_{b7.de}$* *Coff*$_{b7a.de}$ ign$_{b7.de}$* ip$_{bg2}$ nit-ac$_{bg2}$
- **Throat-pit**: ign$_{b7a.de}$*
- **Trachea**; in: *Cocc*$_{k}$* galla-q-r$_{nl2}$• ign$_{bro1}$ *Ip*$_{b7a.de}$ mosch$_{k}$* nux-v$_{bg2}$ osm$_{bg2}$ stann$_{k}$* staph$_{h1}$

CONTINUED coughing agg. (See Cough agg.)

CONTINUOUS (See Constant)

CONVULSIONS; with: (↗*CHEST - Spasms - Cough*) agar$_{tl1}$ ars *Bell* brom calc *Cham* *Cina*$_{k}$* croc **Cupr**$_{k}$* *Dros*$_{k}$* *Hyos* iod$_{tl1}$ kali-c$_{bg2}$ lach$_{bg3}$* led *Meph*$_{k}$* *Stram*$_{k}$* stront-c$_{bg2}$ sulph ther$_{c1}$ verat

○ - **Chest**; in: (↗*CHEST - Spasms - Cough*) samb$_{b7a.de}$*
- **Larynx**; in (See LARYNX - Spasms - larynx - accompanied)

COUGH agg.; during: acon$_{bg2}$* agar$_{bg2}$* *Bell*$_{k}$* caust$_{dgt2}$ cist cocc coff$_{bg2}$* *Hep*$_{k}$* **Ign**$_{k}$* *M-arct*$_{b7.de}$* raph$_{k}$* squil$_{k}$* stict$_{bg2}$* teucr$_{k}$* thyr$_{bg3}$* zinc-i$_{bg3}$*

COVERING: (↗*Cold - air - agg.; Uncovering*)
- **head** | **amel.**: rumx$_{br1}$
- **mouth** | **amel.**: rumx$_{bg2}$*

CRAMPS in chest, from: bell$_{k}$* cob-n$_{sp1}$

CRAWLING, sensation of: aeth$_{k}$* apis cain caust$_{k}$* con$_{k}$* kreos$_{k}$* nux-m *Psor*$_{k}$* rhus-t squil
- **evening** | **bed** agg.; in: kreos
- **night**: aeth
  - **midnight**, before: apis

○ - **Air** passages, in: aeth$_{k}$*
- **Bronchi**: eupi kreos
- **Chest**: cain caust colch$_{a1}$ con$_{k}$* kreos$_{k}$* nux-m$_{k}$* rhus-t$_{k}$* sang$_{hr1}$ sep$_{h2}$* squil$_{k}$*
- **Larynx**: am-m$_{k}$* ant-t$_{k}$* bry$_{k}$* calc-p$_{k}$* carb-v$_{k}$* *Caust*$_{k}$* colch$_{k}$* **Con**$_{k}$* *Dros*$_{k}$* euph$_{k}$* iod$_{k}$* **Kali-c**$_{k}$* kreos$_{k}$* lach$_{k}$* lact led$_{k}$* mag-m$_{k}$* nux-m prun$_{k}$* *Psor*$_{k}$* rhus-t$_{k}$* *Sabin*$_{k}$* sang stann$_{k}$* stict sulph
- **Throat**, in: bry$_{bg2}$ carb-v$_{h2}$ euph$_{h2}$ kreos$_{bg2}$ lach$_{bg2}$ stann$_{bg2}$
- **Throat-pit**: apis$_{k}$* kreos$_{k}$* mag-m$_{k}$* **Sang**$_{k}$*
- **Trachea**, in: anac$_{k}$* am$_{k}$* carb-v$_{k}$* caust$_{k}$* colch$_{a1}$ kreos$_{k}$* mag-m$_{h2}$* prun$_{k}$* rhus-t$_{k}$*

CROAKING: acon$_{k}$* ant-t lach$_{k}$* nit-ac$_{k}$* ruta$_{k}$* *Spong*
- **daytime**: nit-ac$_{k}$*

CROUP; after: *Bell*$_{b4a.de}$ ip$_{b7a.de}$

CROUPY: *(↗LARYNX - Croup)* *Acet-ac* k* **Acon** k* all-c k2* anac ant-t k* apis *Ars* k* *Ars-i* arum-d k* asc-t hr1 aur-s wbt2• *Bell* k* *Brom* k* *Calc-s* k* *Canth* hr1 *Carb-ac* k* cham k* *Chin* k* *Chlor* *Cina* k* cinnb k* cor-r cub k* cupr-s k* dros k* euph bg2 *Gels* k* **Hep** k* **Iod** k* *Ip* k* **Kali-bi** k* *Kali-chl* k* kali-i ptk1 *Kali-m* kali-n c1 kali-s k* kola stb3• kreos bg2 *Lac-c* k* **Lach** k* merc-cy ptk1 *Nit-ac* hr1* oci-sa sp1 op wbt• **Phos** k* *Phyt* k* *Rumx* k* ruta **Samb** k* *Sang* k* sarcol-ac sp1 **Spong** k* staph k* stict k* **Stram** k* syc bka1•
- **morning**: *Calc-s* hep k2
- **evening**: cinnb k* hep k2
- **night**: ars k* *Bell* hr1 carb-ac k* *Hep* k* *Ip* k* kali-br hr1 kali-s k2 op wbt• phyt k* *Spong* k*
  - **midnight**:
    - **before**: acon k2 spong k2*
    - **after**: *Ars*
- **eating**; after: anac
- **expiration** agg.; during: acon
- **sopor**; with (See Sleep - during - agg. - deep)
- **waking**, only after: **Calc-s**
- **winter**:
  - **alternating** with | **sciatica** in summer: staph

CROWING (See Croupy)

CRUMB in larynx; from sensation of a: *(↗THROAT - Bread)* *Bry* coc-c **Lach** k* limest-b es1• pall plb tritic-vg fd5.de

CRYING agg.: ant-t k* **Arn** k* ars *Bell* k* brom bg2 *Bry* ptk1 cain c1 cham k* cina k* dros ferr guare *Hep* k* lyc phos k* samb sil sulph *Verat* k*
- **children**; in: ant-t b7a.de* **Arn** b7.de* bell b4a.de* *Cham* b7a.de* dros b7a.de* hep b4a.de* lyc b4a.de* phos b4a.de* verat b7a.de*

CUTTING, stinging: beryl sp1 tub jl2

○ - **Larynx**; from cutting in ang *Arg-met*
- **Thyroid** gland; in: arg-n

DAMP room (See Wet room)

DANCING; after: puls k*

DEBAUCH, after: *(↗MIND - Libertinism)* *Nux-v* k* stram k*

DEEP: ail k* all-s k* am-br k* am-c b4.de* am-m b7a.de* *Ambr* k* ammc anac k* ang k* ant-c k* apoc hr1 arg-met k2 *Ars* k* ars-i bufo *Carb-v* *Caust* mrr1 chr-ac k* cystein-l rly4• *Dig* k* dios k* **Dros** k* dulc fd4.de eug k* graph bg2 guare k* *Hep* k* hydrog srj2• iod k* kali-bi k* *Kali-c* *Kali-i* *Kali-n* b4a.de kali-p fd1.de• *Lach* k* limest-b es1• lob lyc ptk1 lycps-v k* mag-m k* *Mang* k* med k* meph nat-ar nat-sil fd3.de• *Nux-v* k* petr k* phos k* podo fd3.de• ruta fd4.de *Sabad* k* sal-fr sle1• *Samb* k* sanic sel sep k* sil k* spong k* squil **Stann** k* *Still* k* suis-hep rly4• vanil fd5.de **Verat** k* *Verb* k*
- **morning**: ang k* dios k* spong fd4.de vanil fd5.de
- **afternoon** and evening: am-br k*
- **evening**: eug k* vanil fd5.de **Verat** k*
- **midnight**, after: ars k* spong fd4.de
- **alternating** with short cough (See Short - alternating - deep)
- **breathing** agg.: bell ptk1 brom ptk1 con ptk1 cupr ptk1 graph ptk1 lyc ptk1 stict ptk1
  - **accompanied** by croup: *Hep* tl1
- **inspiration**:
  - **agg.**: hep k* ip squil k2
  - **deep** | **amel.**: *Verb*
- **lower** and lower down in throat; coming from: *(↗Tickling - throat; in - extending - lower)* ip bg2 lach bg2 rumx bg2 sil bg2
- **lying** | **amel.**: **Mang** k* sep squil
- **not** cough deep enough to start mucus; sensation as though he could: ars bell beryl tpw5* bit-ar wht1• **Caust** k* dros kali-c ptk1* lach med *Mez* rumx k*

DEEP-SOUNDING: *(↗Sonorous)* aloe *Kali-bi* kali-s fd4.de mang **Stram** k* verb
- **night**: verb k*

DELIVERY: | **after**: acon b7a.de arn b7a.de dulc b4a.de puls b7a.de rhus-t k* sulph b4a.de

DENTITION; during: acon bro1 *Ant-t* hr1 bell b4a.de* calc k* calc-p k* *Cham* k* cina k* cupr st ferr-p bro1 hyos k* ip b7.de* kali-br hr1 kreos k* **Nux-v** bg2 phos gk podo k* rhus-t k* ter hr1

DESCENDING, on: lyc k*

DIARRHEA:
- **after** | **agg.**: abrot bro1
- **amel.**: bufo k* hydrog srj2• sang hr1
- **during**: *Cham* b7a.de *Merc* b4a.de *Puls* b7a.de *Sulph* b4a.de verb c1

DIFFICULT: ant-t k* arg-met k2 ars *Bac* br1 brom chin k* chlor k* cocc k* dig k* kali-br k*

DINNER: | **after**:
- **agg.**: aeth k* agar k* anac k* arg-n k* bar-c bry calc-f k* carb-v coc-c *Cocc* hr1 ferr ferr-ma a1 hep *Ip* k* kali-bi k* lach mur-ac k* nux-v phos k* sil k* sulph k* syph k* tab tax k* thuj zinc
  - **sleeping**, when: puls staph k*
- **before**: arg-n k*

DISAPPEARING slowly: ant-c bg2

DISTRACTING: ant-t
- **day** and night: ant-t

DISTRESSING: *(↗Painful; Tormenting)* agn *Arum-t* k* aspar k* *Brom* carc gk6 **Caust** k* iris *Lach* limest-b es1• lyc k* meli k* *Nit-ac* **Nux-v** *Sang* k* *Seneg* k* *Sep* k* *Squil* *Stann*
- **daytime**: lyc k*
- **morning**:
  - **evening**; and | **sleep**; on going to: agn k* *Brom* k* *Lach* k* lyc k* nit-ac k*

DOWN in throat-pit; cough from sensation of: calc cina *Ph-ac* *Sulph*

DRAFT of air (See Air agg.)

DRAWING In abdomen; from: *Dros* b7.de*

DREAMS; as if caused by: arn bg2 mill bg2

DRESSING agg.: carc mg1.de*

DRINKING:
- **acids** (See Acids)
- **after** | **agg.**: acon k* am-caust k* am-m k* anac hr1 ant-t k* arn k* **Ars** k* *Bry* k* calc k* carb-v k* *Chin* k* *Cimx* k* cina k* cocc k* con dig **Dros** k* dulc fd4.de ferr k* ferr-ar *Hep* k* hyos k* kali-ar kali-bi kali-c k* lac-c *Lach* k* laur k* lyc k* *Manc* k* mang ptk1 meph k* nat-m k* nat-p k* nux-m k* nux-v k* op k* *Phos* k* **Psor** k* rhus-t k* sang ptk1 sil k* squil k* staph k* stram k* sul-ac k* tell k* verat k* zinc hr1
- **agg.** | **rapidly**: sil k*
- **alcohol** (See Alcohol)
- **amel.**: am-c ptk1 arizon-l nl2• brom k* bry *Caust* choc srj3• *Coc-c* k* cupr b7a.de* euphr glon bg2 hydrog srj2• iod kali-c nat-sil fd3.de• *Op* k* *Rumx* mrr1 sal-fr sle1• **Spong** k*
- **beer** (See Beer)
- **brandy** (See Brandy)
- **cold** fluids (See Cold - drinks - agg.)
- **milk** (See Milk)

DRIVING in an open wagon: staph bg2 sul-ac bg2 sulph bg2*

DRUNKARDS, of: *Ars* k* *Coc-c* k* lach *Nux-v* hr1 *Op* hr1 *Sel* hr1 *Stram* k*

DRY: *(↗Dry; Ringing)* acal k* acet-ac k* achy-a bnj1 **Acon** k* aesc k* *Agar* k* agath-a nl2• ail k* alco a1 *All-c* bro1 all-s k* aloe **Alum** k* *Alumn* k* am-br k* *Am-c* k* *Am-m* k* *Ambr* k* anac k* anag k* anan k* androc srj1• ang k* ant-c k* ant-s-aur bro1 ant-t k* anth aphis apis k* apoc k* aq-pet a1 arg-cy arg-met k* arg-n k* arge-pl rwt5• *Arn* k* **Ars** k* **Ars-i** k* ars-s-r hr1 arum-i a1 arum-t k* asaf k* asar k* *Asc-t* k* asim k* atro k* aur k* aur-i k2 aur-m aur-m-n k* aur-s bamb-a stb2.de* *Bar-c* k* *Bar-m* k* **Bell** k* ben benz-ac k* berb k* beryl tpw5* bit-ar wht1• bond a1 borx k* bov k* brass-n-o srj5• **Brom** k* bros-gau mrc1 **Bry** k* *Bufo* cact k* calad k* **Calc** k* *Calc-i* k2* calc-p k* **Calc-s** k* camph k* cann-i k* cann-s k* *Canth* k* *Caps* k* *Carb-ac* k* **Carb-an** k* *Carb-v* k* *Carbn-s* card-b a1 card-m k* carneg-g rwt1• casc k* cassia-s ccrh1• castm castn-v br1 *Caust* k* *Cedr* hr1 cench cent a1 *Cham* k* *Chel* k* **Chin** k* chin-b hr1 chinin-ar chlf hr1 chlor k* choc srj3• chr-ac k* cimic k* cimx k* *Cina* k*

Dry: ...
cinnb cit-ac rly4• clem K* cob ptm1• cob-n sp1 *Coc-c* K* cocc K* cod K* *Coff* K* colch K* coloc K* colocin a1 colum-p sze2• *Con* K* conch fkr1• cop K* cor-r br1* corn K* cortico sp1 *Croc* K* *Crot-c* crot-h K* *Cupr* K* cur K* cycl K* der K* dig K* dios K* dream-p sdj1• dros K* *Dulc* K* elaps eucal bg2 eup-per K* euph K* euphr K* eupi K* falco-pe nl2• *Ferr* K* *Ferr-ar* *Ferr-i* K* *Ferr-p* K* ferul a1 fic-m gya1 fl-ac K* flav jl2 *Form* fuma-ac rly4• gaba sa3• gamb K* gels K* germ-met srj5• gink-b sbd1• gins a1 glyc bro1 glycyr-g cte1• gran a1 graph K* grat K* *Guaj* K* guare K* guat sp1 gymno ham K* *Hell* K* helodr-cai knl2• helx c1* *Hep* K* hera a1 hip-ac sp1 hir skp7• hist sp1 hura hydr K* hydr-ac K* hydrog srj2• **Hyos** K* hyosin a1 hyosin-hbr bro1 *Hyper* K* **Ign** K* *Indg* K* influ jl2* inul K* **Iod** K* *Ip* K* iris iris-foe jac-c a1 just bro1 *Kali-ar* *Kali-bi* K* *Kali-br* K* **Kali-c** K* *Kali-i* K* kali-m K2* *Kali-n* K* *Kali-p* kali-s ketogl-ac rly4• kreos K* lac-ac K* lac-c lac-d K* lac-del hrn2• lac-e hrn2• lac-h htj1*• lac-loxod-a hrn2• **Lach** K* *Lachn* K* lact K* lap-la rsp1* laur K* lec led K* lepi a1 lil-t K* limest-b es1• linu-c a1 lipp a1 lob K* lob-s hr1 loxo-recl knl4• *Lyc* K* lycpr bro1 lycps-v bro1 m-ambo b2.de* m-arct b2.de* m-aust b2.de mag-c K* mag-m K* *Mag-p* mag-s K* *Manc* hr1 **Mang** K* mang-act bro1 mang-p rly4• med K* melal-alt gya4 meli K* *Menth* c2* *Mentho* bro1 meph bg2 *Merc* K* merc-c K* *Merc-cy* hr1 *Mez* K* mim-p skp7• moni rfm1• morg-p pte1*• *Morph* bro1 mosch K* mur-ac K* murx K* myos-a rly4• *Myrt-c* K* naja K* **Nat-ar** *Nat-c* K* **Nat-m** K* nat-p K* nat-s K* nat-sil fd3.de• nicc K* nicotam rly4• nig-s mp4• *Nit-ac* K* nit-s-d a1* *Nux-m* K* **Nux-v** K* oci-sa sp1* ol-an K* *Ol-j* hr1* ol-sant br1 olib-sac wmh1 olnd K* *Onos* bro1 *Op* K* oscilloc jl2 osm K* *Ox-ac* ozone sde2• *Par* K* parathyr jl2 paull K* ped a1 pert jl2 **Petr** K* petr-ra shn4• **Ph-ac** K* phal a1 phel K* **Phos** K* *Phyt* K* pic-ac K* pin-con oss2• pin-s a1 pitu-gl skp7• plac-s rly4• plan K* *Plat* K* *Plb* K* plut-n srj7• *Pneu* jl2 podo K* polyg-h positr nl2• propr sa3• psil ft1 *Psor* K* ptel K* **Puls** K* pyrus rad-br c11 ran-s K* rat K* rauw sp1 rheum K* *Rhod* K* rhus-r *Rhus-t* K* *Rhus-v* a1* ros-d wla1 rosm lgb1 **Rumx** K* ruta K* sabad K* sabin K* sal-ac K* salv bro1 *Samb* K* *Sang* K* *Sangin-n* bro1 *Sapin* a1 sarr sars K* sel K* senec K2 *Seneg* K* *Sep* K* *Sil* K* sinus rly4• sol-t-ae K* spig K* spira a1 **Spong** K* squil K* *Stann* K* *Staph* K* stict K* still K* stram K* stront-c K* stry K* suis-hep rly4• sul-ac K* **Sulph** K* sumb K* suprar rly4• symph fd3.de• syph K* tab K* taosc iwa1• tarax K* *Tarent* K* tela bro1 tep K* ter K* teucr K* thea K* *Thuj* K* thymu br1 til trif-p a1 tril-p *Trios* rsj11• tritic-vg fd5.de **Tub** K* *Tub-a* bro1* tub-r jl2 urol-h rwt• *Ust* hr1 v-a-b jl2 valer K* vanad br1* vanil fd5.de verat K* verat-v K* verb K* viol-o K* voes a1 wye K* x-ray sp1 xan c1* *Zinc* K* zing K* ziz a1* [bell-p-sp dcm1 heroin sdj2 pop dhh1]

- **day** and night: acon K* bell K* brom K* calc-p K2 carb-an cimic *Euph* K* ign K* *Kali-c* kreos K* laur K* *Lyc* K* mez mosch K* mur-ac *Nat-m* *Spong* K* stram K* verb K* xan c1*
- **daytime**: *Alum* K* bar-c bell calc chel K* coloc K* con K* cot a1 euph gamb K* ign *Kali-bi* lyc nat-ar K2 nat-m a1 op petr-ra shn4• phos K* pitu-gl skp7• puls K* *Sep* K* sol-t-ae K* **Spong** K* stront-c sk4• sulph K*
  - **loose** at night: alum b2.de* am-m b2.de* arn b2.de* calc b2.de* caust K* euphr b2.de* led b2.de* m-aust b2.de phos b2.de* rhod b2.de* sep K* staph K* sulph b2.de*
  - **lying** down | **amel**.: sep
  - **menses**; before: graph
- **morning**: agar K* alum b4a.de* alum-sil K2 *Alumn* am-m K* ant-c K* ant-t arg-met *Arn* K* asc-t c1 bamb-a stb2.de* bar-c K* bar-i K2 bar-s K2 borx bov K* brom K* bry K* carb-an K* *Carb-v* carbn-s caust K* chin K* *Coc-c* K* con K* cop K* cur dios K* dulc fd4.de flav jl2 gink-b sbd1• grat K* gymno hep hyper K* ign K* **Iod** K* *Kali-c* K* kali-n c1 kreos lec lyc K* mag-s K* mim-h a1 mit a1 *Mosch* K* **Nat-ar** nat-c K* nat-s K* nux-v K* ol-an *Op* K* pitu-gl skp7• propl ub1• rhod K* *Rhus-t* sang K* sel K2 sep sil K* spong fd4.de stann K* sul-ac K* sul-i K2 sulph K* symph fd3.de• tab K* tarent K* thuj K* tritic-vg fd5.de vanil fd5.de verat K*
  - **early**: alum am-m ant-c chin graph grat lyc nux-v ol-an op rhod stann sul-ac verat
  - **loose** in:
    - **afternoon**: am-m
    - **evening**: arn bov chin cina crot-t dig ign iod nux-v
  - **menses** | **before** | **agg**.: graph **Zinc** K*
    - **suppressed** menses; from: *Cop*
  - **rising** agg.; after: alum K* ang K* arg-met arn bar-c K* borx bov K* *Carb-an* K* *Chin* cina mtf33 cortico tpw7 dig K* dulc fd4.de grat K* nat-s K* plb sul-ac h2*
  - **waking**; on: caust K* ign K* mag-s K* sil K* spong fd4.de
- **forenoon**: agar K* alum K* *Am-m* K* *Camph* K* coc-c K* grat a1 podo fd3.de• sars K* zing
- **forenoon**: ...
  - **11** h: bros-gau mrc1 *Rhus-t*
- **noon**: arg-n K* naja sulph K*
- **afternoon**: agath-a nl2• am-m anth K* asaf hr1 calc-p K* cench *Chel* K* ham fd3.de• kali-bi K* mez K* nat-c K* nat-m K* *Nux-m* K* petr-ra shn4• phel K* *Sang* K* spong fd4.de sulph K* thuj K*
  - **13** h: aesc
  - **15** h: agath-a nl2• calc-p
  - **16** h: cench *Chel*
  - **17** h: bov nat-m
  - **entering** warm room: anth K* nat-c K*
  - **walking** agg.: *Thuj*
- **evening**: agn aloe alum K* alum-p K2 alum-sil K2 *Alumn* K* am-br am-m K* *Arg-n* K* *Ars* K* arund K* bals-p bar-c K* bar-s K2 *Bell* beryl tpw5 borx bov K* **Brom** K* bry K* *Calc* K* *Caps* K* carb-an carb-v K* carc fd2.de• cent a1 chin choc srj3• cimic K* coca com K* *Con* K* cop K* dig K* dulc fd4.de *Ferr* K* ferr-ar *Grat* K* gymno ham fd3.de• **Hep** K* **Ign** K* indg K* iod h* kali-ar kali-bi K* *Kali-c* K* kreos lach K* lec lipp a1 lith-c **Lyc** K* mag-c K* *Mag-m* K* mag-s K* merc K* merc-i-r K* mez K* nat-ar nat-c K* nat-m nat-p nat-sil fd3.de• nicc nit-ac K* nit-s-d a1 *Nux-m* *Nux-v* K* petr K* *Ph-ac* K* phel K* *Phos* K* phyt psor **Puls** K* rheum *Rhus-t* K* *Sang* *Seneg* K* *Sep* K* sol-t-ae K* *Spong* **Squil** K* stann K* *Stict* K* still K* stront-c **Sulph** K* symph fd3.de• tab K* tarent K2 teucr K* thuj K* vanil fd5.de verat K* zinc K* zing
  - **18** h: am-m carc fd2.de• *Con* *Nat-m*
  - **19** h: grat spira
  - **and** night; can neither sleep nor lie down evening: stict K*
  - **midnight**, until: *Hep* *Phos* K* *Rhus-t* K* sep stann
  - **bed** agg.; in: dulc fd4.de petr h2* phos h2* sep h2* sulph h2* vanil fd5.de
  - **entering** warm room: com a1 nat-c K* *Puls*
  - **inspiration** agg.: dig K*
  - **loose** in morning: acon K* alum K* alum-p K2 *Am-c* b2.de* am-m b2.de* *Ambr* K* *Ang* b2.de* ant-c K* ant-t K* arn b2.de* ars b2.de* aur b2.de* bar-c K* bell b2.de* brom bg2 *Bry* K* **Calc** K* caps b2.de* carb-an b2.de* *Carb-v* K* caust b2.de* cina b2.de* colch b2.de* cupr K* dig b2.de* dros K* euph *Euphr* b2.de* *Ferr* K* **Hep** K* *Hyos* K* ign b2.de* ip K* kali-c K* kali-n b2.de* kreos b2.de* lach K* led K* lyc K* m-ambo b2.de mag-c K* mag-m K* *Mang* b2.de* mez K* mur-ac K* nat-c b2.de* nat-m K* nat-p K2 nit-ac K* nux-v K* **Par** b2.de* *Ph-ac* K* *Phos* K* *Puls* K* rheum b2.de* rhod b2.de* rhus-t K* seneg K* *Sep* K* *Sil* K* spong K* **Squil** K* stann K* staph b2.de* stram *Stront-c* b2.de* *Sul-ac* K* sulph K* verat b2.de* zinc K*
  - **lying** down:
    - **agg**.: *Alumn* K* *Bell* K* borx *Caps* K* carb-v ferr K* *Hyos* nh6 indg **Kali-c** moni rfm1• nat-m nicc *Nux-v* **Ph-ac** **Puls** K* **Sang** K* **Sep** spong fd4.de **Stann** hr1 *Stict* **Sulph** teucr K*
    - **amel**.: am-m K* zinc K*
  - **sleep** agg.; on going to: *Hep* K* *Sulph*
  - **smoking** agg.: thuj K*
- **night**: acon K* agar K* agath-a nl2• aloe *Alum* K* alum-p K2 alum-sil K2 **Am-c** K* *Am-m* K* *Arg-n* K* **Ars** K* *Asaf* asc-t c1 aur-ar K2 aur-m K* bar-c K2 **Bell** K* bros-gau mrc1 bry K* calad **Calc** K* calc-s calc-sil K2 *Caps* **Carb-an** K* *Carb-v* *Carbn-s* card-m cassia-s ccrh1• caust h2* cent a1 *Cham* K* *Chel* chin K* chinin-ar chlf br1 *Cimic* K* coc-c K* coloc K* *Con* K* *Crot-c* *Cupr* K* **Dros** euph K* *Euphr* falco-pe nl2• form gamb K* graph K* grat K* *Hell* K* **Hep** **Hyos** K* *Ign* inul br1 *Ip* K* *Kali-ar* kali-br K* *Kali-c* K* kali-p kali-sil K2 **Lach** laur lec linu-c a1 *Lyc* K* *Mag-c* K* *Mag-m* K* mag-s mang *Med* *Merc* K* *Mez* K* nat-ar nat-m K* nat-s *Nit-ac* K* *Nux-m* *Nux-v* K* ol-an ol-j op K* petr K* **Phos** K* *Phyt* *Pneu* jl2 **Puls** K* rhod K* *Rhus-t* K* *Rumx* *Sabad* K* samb *Sang* sep h2* *Sil* K* sol-t-ae K* spira a1 **Spong** K* squil K* *Stict* K* stront-c K* **Sulph** K* syph tab K* tarent K* tub c1 vanil fd5.de *Verat* K* verb K* vichy-g a1 zinc K* *Zing*
  - **midnight**: *Am-c* grat K* nicc *Nux-v* K* phos K*
    - **before**: acon K2 arg-n **Calc** K* *Lyc* *Nit-ac* K* phos rhus-t K* spong K2* *Stann*
      - **22** h | **22**-22.30 h: adam skp7•
      - **22**.30 h: sol-t-ae
      - **23** h: squil K2
      - **sleep** agg.; during: *Nit-ac* K* *Rhus-t*
    - **at**:
      - **daybreak**, until: **Nux-v** K*

Cough

- **midnight – at**: ...
  - **lying** | **back**; on | **agg.**: *Nux-v* k*
    - **side**; on | **amel.**: *Nux-v* k*
  - **after**: *Ars* k* bell *Calc* k* hyos lec nicc **Nux-v**
    - **1**-2 h: zing
    - **2** h: *Kali-c Op Rumx*
    - **3** h: **Am-c** k* *Kali-c* k* op
    - **4** h, until: nicc
    - **loose**: *Calc* k*
- **sunset** to sunrise: aur
- **fever**; during: *Hyos* b7a.de
- **followed** by:
  - **salty** expectoration | **pain** as if something were torn loose from larynx; with: calc
- **inspiration** agg.: nat-ar
- **loose** by day: acon k* alum b2.de* am-c b2.de* anac k* ang b2.de* ant-t b2.de* arg-met b2.de* arn b2.de* ars k* asaf b2.de* bell b2.de* bry k* *Calc* k* caps b2.de* carb-an k* caust k* cham k* chin k* cocc b2.de* colch b2.de* con k* euphr k* *Graph* b2.de* guaj b2.de* *Hep* k* hyos k* kali-ar k2 kali-c k* lach k* *Lyc* k* m-ambo b2.de mag-c k* mag-m k* mang b2.de* merc k* nit-ac k* nux-v k* op b2.de* petr b2.de* phos k* *Puls* k* rhus-t b2.de* sabad k* samb k* sil k* squil b2.de* stann b2.de* *Stront-c* b2.de* **Sulph** k* taosc iwa1• verat k* zinc k*
- **lying**:
  - **agg.**: *Con Hyos* kali-br laur ol-j *Phyt Puls* **Sulph** vanil fd5.de zinc
  - **amel.**: *Mang* vh
  - **side**; on:
    - **right**:
      - **agg.** | **only** while lying on right side: carb-an
- **lying** down agg.: petr hr1
- **motion** agg.: bell *Seneg*
- **sitting** up in bed | **amel.**: **Hyos** k* **Puls** k* sang
- **sleep**; on going to: med
- **smoking** amel.: tarent k*
- **waking**; on: graph *Puls* k* *Sil* **Sulph** k* zinc h2*

- **accompanied** by:
  - **emaciation** (See GENERALS - Emaciation - accompanied - cough - dry)
  - ○ **Heart**; complaints of the | **Valves** (See CHEST - Heart; complaints - valves - accompanied - cough)
- **air**; in open:
  - **agg.**: *Coff* kali-c m-arct *Seneg* spig
  - **amel.**: iod lil-t
  - **going** into; when | **warm** room; from a: *Acon Con*
- **alternating** with:
  - **diarrhea**: abrot br1
  - **loose** cough: ars ptk1
- **bending** backward agg.: beryl tpw5
- **blood**:
  - **discharge** of; with: acal c1* zinc
  - **ends** in raising black blood: elaps
- **breath**; with sudden loss of: *Nux-m*
- **children**; in: cina mtf33 iod mtf33
  - **emaciated** boys, in: **Lyc** k*
- **chill**:
  - **after**: nux-m samb
  - **before**: mag-c **Rhus-t** *Samb Tub*
  - **during**: *Acon* bg2 ars bg2 bell bg2 bry bg2 carb-v bg2 cham bg2 chin bg2 *Ferr* hep bg2 hyos bg2 *Ip* bg2 kali-c bg2 lach bg2 nux-m bg2 nux-v bg2 *Phos* bg2 puls bg2 *Rhus-t* k* sabad bg2 samb xxb1 sep bg2 *Spong* bg2 sulph bg2
- **chronic** dry cough: alum tl1 am-c tl1 bry tl1 cimic tl1 flav mtf11 hyos tl1 lyc mrr1
  - **pining** boys; in: **Lyc** k*
  - **scrofulous** children; in: **Bar-m**
- **cold**:
  - **air** agg.: beryl tpw5 kali-c phos pneu jl2 sang *Seneg* spong fd4.de squil k2
  - **drinks** | **agg.**: *Sil* squil k2
  - **dry** | **air**: crot-h hep c1
- **constant**, almost: **Alum** *Arn Ars* euph glycyr-g cte1• *Ign* med c1 rhus-t sne syph sne
- **constriction** in throat; from: aesc
- **coryza**; during: bell graph merc merc-sul hr1 nat-c h2* nat-m k* nit-ac sel k* sep k*
  - **evening**: *Dig*
- **dinner** | **after** | **agg.**: aeth k* agar k* *Kali-bi* k* lach nux-v
  - **amel.**: bar-c
- **drinking** | **after**:
  - **agg.**: ars hyos kali-c *Nux-m* phos staph
    - **loose** after eating: nux-m staph
  - **amel.**: brom bry *Caust Coc-c* k* iod kali-c mang-p rly4• *Op* k* **Spong** k*
- **dyspnea**; as from | **day** and night: euph
- **eating**:
  - **agg.**: aeth agar all-s k* ferr-ma *Hyos Kali-c* nux-v sang hr1 *Sep* sulph ter
    - **night**: ter
  - **amel.**: mang-p rly4• **Spong** k*
- **exertion**; from violent: *Ox-ac* petr-ra shn4•
- **expectoration**:
  - **morning**, only in: *Alum* alum-sil k2 *Am-c* bell *Bry Calc Carb-v* k* coc-c euph *Ferr Hep* kali-c led lyc *Mag-c Mang* mur-ac nat-c *Nat-m* nit-ac nux-v ph-ac *Phos* **Puls** *Sep Sil* **Squil** stann *Sul-ac*
  - **hawking** copious green sputum; later: kali-i
- **expiration** with flush of heat and sweat; after every: carb-v
- **fever** | **during**:
  - **agg.**: **Acon** k* ang k* ant-c k* *Apis* k* *Arn* k* *Ars* k* bell k* brom k* **Bry** k* calc k* carb-v k* caust k* cham k* chin k* chinin-ar cina k* coff k* **Con** k* cupr k* dros k* hep k* *Hyos* k* ign k* **Ip** k* **Kali-c** k* kali-p lach k* lyc k* **Nat-m** k* nit-ac k* nux-m k* **Nux-v** k* op k* petr k* **Phos** k* plat k* puls k* rhus-t k* **Sabad** k* samb k* sep k* spig k* spong k* squil k* staph k* sul-ac k* sulph k* tarent verat k* verb k*
    - **thirstlessness**; with: ars bg2* con bg2* phos bg2* puls bg2* sabad bg2* squil bg2*
  - **intermittent**, before: eup-per eup-pur hr1 *Rhus-t Tub*
- **flatus** discharges up and down, which amel.; must sit up and: **Sang** k*
- **gonorrhea**; after suppressed: benz-ac sel
- **hacking** (See Hacking - dry)
- **inspiration**:
  - **agg.**: bell brom dig *Hep* lach nat-ar plb rumx
    - **evening** (See evening - inspiration)
    - **sleep** agg.; during: sep
  - **deep** | **agg.**: aesc *Brom* dig *Ferr-p Hep* nat-ar plb squil
- **irritation** in larynx: aphis bar-m k2 bell k* carb-ac k* cassia-s ccrh1• cimic fic-m gya1 kali-i k* lach lith-c lyc *Phos* hr1 positr nl2• ros-d wla1 *Rumx Seneg* sulph k* tab k* thuj k* *Zinc*
- **lying**:
  - **agg.**: alum cinnb *Con* cortiso gse **Hyos** k* inul br1 ip *Kali-br* lac-h htj1• lyc nit-ac *Ph-ac* phos **Puls** k* rhus-t sabad *Sang* sep sil sulph ter vanil fd5.de
  - **amel.**: am-c cassia-s ccrh1• **Mang** sep zinc
  - **back**; on:
    - **agg.**: am-m iod nux-v *Phos* k* rhus-t sil
      - **midnight**: *Nux-v* k*
    - **amel.**: *Mang* k*
  - **side**; on:
    - **amel.**: *Nux-v*
    - **left** | **agg.**: acon bry eup-per kali-bi par **Phos** k* puls rumx
    - **right** | **agg.**: acon carb-an ip merc phos *Puls* vh syph k2
- **measles**; after: acon tl1 cham *Dros* k* euphr k2 hyos ign stict nh6
- **menses**:
  - **before**:
    - **agg.**: graph hyos lac-c plat *Sulph* k* **Zinc** k*
      - **morning**: **Zinc** k*

- **during**:
  - **agg.**: *Bry* k* castm cop cur *Graph* k* lac-c phos **Zinc** k*
    - **perspiration**; with profuse: graph
- **suppressed** menses; from: *Cop* k*

- **motion**:
  - **agg.**: bell iod seneg
  - **amel.**: kali-c phos
- **perspiration**; during: acon bg2 ant-t bg2 apis bg2 **Ars** bg2 bell bg2 bry bg2 *Caust* bg2 **Cham** bg2 coff bg2 con bg2 *Dros* bg2 *Hep* bg2 hyos bg2 ign bg2 *Ip* bg2 kali-n bg2 led bg2 lyc bg2 *Merc* bg2 mur-ac b4a.de nit-ac bg2 *Nux-v* bg2 phos bg2 puls bg2 **Rhus-t** bg2 sabad bg2 *Samb* bg2 **Sep** bg2 *Spong* bg2 stront-c bg2 **Sulph** bg2 *Verat* bg2
- **reading** aloud agg.: anag hr1 *Mang* k* meph **Phos** k*
- **rising** agg.: cortico tpw7 dulc fd4.de grat
- **room** | **in**: alum h2*
- **scraping**; from:

○ - **Larynx**; in: alumn aur-m-n *Bell* k* borx h2 bov **Brom** k* bry chel *Coc-c* k* *Con* dig gamb hep hydr-ac laur led mang naja nit-ac nux-v op osm **Puls** k* *Sabad* seneg til
  - **Throat**; in: graph h2
- **sitting**:
  - **agg.**: agar lach phos rhus-t
  - **amel.**: arg-n cinnb *Sang* k*
- **sleep**:
  - **after** every: puls k*
  - **disturbing**: alum calad caust h2* irid-met srj5• *Kali-c* nux-v ol-j phos rhod rhus-t *Sang* spong squil stict sulph syph zinc
  - **during** | **agg.**: abrom-a ks5 **Cham** k* coff k* hipp jl2 *Lach* nh6 mag-s *Nit-ac* k* *Rhus-t* k* sep k* tub cp*
- **smoke**; from inspiration of: kali-bi menth a1
- **smoking** agg.: acon all-s k* atro k* beryl tpw5 coc-c k* coca hell k* petr rad-br c11 thuj
- **sneezing**, and: *Cina* k*
- **spasmodic**, exhausting cough especially in children:
  - **night** | **lying** down and going to cold room to sleep: sang
- **stopped** up feeling in stomach, from: guaj h2
- **talking** agg.: atro k* bell cimic k* crot-h k* dig k* *Hep* k* *Hyos* lach *Mang* k* *Rumx* stann
- **temperature**, from change of: *Acon* k*
- **thirst**; with: cassia-s ccrh1•
- **tickling**, from:

○ - **Larynx**; in: *Agar* agath-a nl2• *Am-m* *Arg-n* ars-s-f k2 asaf aur-m aur-m-n bar-c *Bell* k* borx h2 bov *Brom* k* cact calc-f carb-ac carb-an *Caust* cimic coc-c mrr1 coca colch coloc **Con** k* cot c1 *Crot-c* cycl falco-pe nl2• hydr hydr-ac hyos ptk1 iod ip iris iris-foe kali-bi *Kali-c* *Lach* k* *Lachn* led **Lyc** k* mang mez mur-ac h2 *Nat-m* k* nat-s nit-ac nux-v *Op* *Ox-ac* ozone sde2• phos h2 *Phyt* *Psor* **Puls** k* rat ros-d wla1 rumx sabin c1 *Sang* *Seneg* *Sep* *Zinc* zing [heroin sdj2]
  - **Throat**; in: trios rsj11•
  - **Throat**-pit; in: plut-n srj7•
  - **Trachea**; low down in: arn br1
  - **Upper** sternum: beryl tpw5
- **vomiting**, until: mez ptk1 stict ptk1
- **waking**; on: *Agar* k* bry k* calc caust coc-c k* dig digin a1 ign *Kali-br* hr1 *Lach* hr1 mag-s medul-os-si rly4• melal-alt gya4 *Puls* k* *Sang* k* sil sol-t-ae k* **Sulph** k* *Thuj*
- **walking**:
  - **agg.**: cassia-s ccrh1• *Lach* hr1 phel k* *Seneg* thuj verat k*
  - **air** agg.; in open: alum h2 sulph h2
  - **cold** air; in | **agg.**: verat
- **warm** | **drinks** | **amel.**: cassia-s ccrh1• glycyr-g cte1•
  - **room**:
    - **agg.**: coc-c nat-ar pneu jl2
    - **amel.**: beryl tpw5
    - **entering** a warm room; when: anth *Bry* nh6 carc fd2.de• com *Nat-c* k*
- **weather**: caps tl1 hep tl1

Dry – weather: ...
  - **wet** | **agg.**: calc-p k2 cur

○ - **Stomach**, as if from **Bry** **Sep**

DRYNESS, from:

○ - **Air** passages; of: carb-an k* kola stb3• lach k* merc k* ozone sde2• petr k* *Puls* k* [tax jsj7]
- **Chest**; in: bell k* benz-ac fic-m gya1 kali-chl lach laur merc k* *Puls* k*
- **Fauces**; in: **Dros** k* *Mez* *Phyt* k*
- **Larynx**; in: ant-t arg-n bg2 atro bell k* bry *Calc* carb-an k* carbn-o caust colch *Con* k* cop *Crot-h* *Dros* k* eug hura c1 ip *Kali-c* kali-chl kalm lach lachn laur k* *Mang* mez h2 *Nux-v* petr phyt plan *Puls* raph rhus-t **Sang** seneg spong stann stict mrr1 stram *Sulph* verat verat-v
  - **morning**: phyt
  - **spot**, dry: cimic **Con** k* crot-h nat-m h2* nit-ac ptk1*
- **Palate**: thuj bg2
- **Pharynx**: *Stict* bg2*
- **Throat**; in: borx b4a.de bry b7.de* carb-an b4a.de* caust bg2 cimic bg2 coc-c bg2 cortiso tpw7 dros b7.de* dulc fd4.de hydroph rsj6• kali-bi bg2 mang b4.de* med jl2 nat-m bg2 nat-sil fd3.de• petr b4a.de* phyt bg2 puls b7.de* rhus-t b7.de* seneg b4.de* stann b4.de* stict mrr1 [tax jsj7]
  - **spot**: cimic hr1*
- **Trachea**; in: carb-an k* *Cycl* k* *Dros* b7a.de laur k* ozone sde2• *Puls* k* stann k*

DULL: (↗*Toneless*) asaf b7.de* bry b7.de* cham b7.de* cocc b7.de* iod bg2 *M-arct* b7.de* *Sabad* b7.de*

DUST, as from: a-dnitroph fkm1• agar *Alumn* k* *Am-c* k* **Ars** k* aur bg2 aur-m *Bell* k* *Brom* k* *Calc* k* calc-s caps bro1 *Carb-v* bro1 caust bro1 chel k* *Chin* k* cina k* *Coc-c* k* crot-c cycl k* **Dros** k* euph-l bro1 ferr-ma k* glon *Hep* k* ictod *Ign* k* iod *Ip* lac-c bro1 lach bro1 *Lact-v* bro1 **Lyc** k* meph *Mez* b4a.de nat-ar nat-m bro1 nept-m lsd2.fr nux-v bro1 par bro1 ph-ac k* *Phos* bro1 pic-ac k* podo fd3.de• **Puls** k* rumx bro1* sep bro1 sil sne **Sulph** k* teucr k*

○ - **Throat**; in: *Phos* b4a.de
- **Throat**-pit; in: *Ign* k*
  - **evening** | **21** h: brucel sa3•
- **Trachea**; in: ferr-ma
  - **coughing** does not amel.: chel bg2

DUST; from: *Bell* hr1 nat-m bg2

EATING:
- **after** | **agg.**: agar bg2 am-m b7a.de* anac b4.de* *Ant-t* b7.de* arg-n bg2 *Ars* bg2 bell b4.de* **Bry** b7.de* calc bg2 carb-v bg2 cham b7a.de* chin b7.de* dig b4.de* ferr b7.de* hep b4a.de* kali-bi bg2 kali-c b4a.de* lach bg2 laur bg2 mag-c bg2 *Mez* b4a.de nux-m b7a.de* **Nux-v** b7.de* op b7.de* *Phos* bg2 puls b7.de* rhus-t bg2 ruta b7.de* sep b4a.de* sil b4a.de* staph b7.de* sulph bg2 ter bg2 thuj b4a.de* *Zinc* b4.de*
- **agg.**: acon k* aeth agar k* all-s k* alum-sil k2 am-m gsy1 ambr k* *Anac* k* ant-ar c1* *Ant-t* k* arn *Ars* k* ars-s-f k2 bar-c bell k* brom *Bry* k* bufo k* *Calc* k* calc-f caps k* *Carb-v* k* carbn-s carc tpw2* caust k* cham k* *Chin* k* *Coc-c* *Cocc* b7.de* cor-r k* *Cupr* *Cur* k* dig k* dros k* dulc fd4.de euphr *Ferr* k* ferr-ar ferr-ma ferr-p ham fd3.de• *Hep* k* hyos k* *Ip* k* **Kali-bi** k* kali-c k* kali-m k2 kali-p kali-s kali-sil k2 lac-c lach k* laur k* lyc mag-c mag-m k* med k* meph mrr1 *Mez* k* mosch k* myos-a k* myos-s bro1 nat-m nit-ac nux-m **Nux-v** k* op ph-ac phos k* plut-n srj7• puls k* rhus-t k* *Rumx* k* ruta sang k* *Sep* k* sil k* squil k* staph k* sulph k* tarax k* tax bro1 ter k* *Thuj* k* trios rsj11• vanil fd5.de verat zinc k*
  - **hastily** agg.: sil k*
  - **until** he vomits: *Mez* k*
- **amel.**: all-s am-c ammc k* anac k* bar-c bg2 bism bro1 carb-an *Euphr* k* ferr k* ferr-m k* ham fd3.de• hydrog srj2• kali-c k* rad-br ptk1* sin-n **Spong** k* tab k*
- **before** | **agg.**: bufo bg2
- **satiety** agg.; after eating to: carb-v b4a.de*
- **seasoned** food agg.; highly (See Spices)
- **sweets** (See Sugar)
- **warm** food (See Warm - food - agg.)
- **while** | **beginning** to eat: seneg gm1

ELONGATED Palate; from: hyos bg2* merc-i-r a1*

ELONGATED Uvula; from: alum k* bapt k* bar-c bro1 brom bry bg2 *Hyos* k* kali-c bro1 merc-i-r k* nat-m k*

- **morning**: brom k*
- **sensation** of elongated uvula: alum bnu2
  - **morning**: alum bnu2 brom vh1

EMOTIONS agg.: *(↗Excitement)* acon b7.de* ambr ptk1 ant-t b7.de* arg-n bg2 arn b7.de* ars bg2 asar b7.de* bry b7.de* bufo bg2 caps bg2* cham b7.de* chin bg2 cina bg2 cist bg2 ign bg2* *Lach* bg2 nat-m bg2 *Nux-v* b7.de* op b7.de* rhus-t b7.de* *Spong* bg2* staph b7.de* verat bg2 verb ptk1
- **night**: aur ptk1

EPIGASTRIUM; cough seems to come from the (See Stomach - come)

ERUCTATIONS:
- **after**: ambr bg2 lob bg2 sang bg2* sul-ac bg2 verat bg2
- **amel.**: ambr bro1 ang bro1 ant-t c1* **Sang** k*
- **excite** cough; eructations: *(↗STOMACH - Eructations - cough - during - agg.)* *Ambr* k* bar-c k* carb-v ptk1 lac-ac lob ptk1 sol-t-ae staph k*

ERUCTATIONS and FLATUS both amel.: **Sang** k*

ERUPTIONS:
- **alternating** with (See Alternating - eruptions)
- **cough**; from suppressed: dulc k* mez gk psor al2*
- **receding**; when eruptions are: dulc ptk1 led ptk1 phys pd puls ptk1

EXCESSES agg.: ip bg2

EXCITEMENT: *(↗Emotions)* acon ambr k2* ant-t ars asar bry bufo *Cham* *Cist* k* con cor-r bro1 cortiso tpw7 dig dros k* hyos ign bro1 lach lob mag-c nux-v op ph-ac rhus-t **Spong** k* tarent bro1 tritic-vg fd5.de

EXERTION:
- **agg.**: *(↗Manual)* ail am k* **Ars** hr1 ars-i k* *Bar-c* bell hs *Brom* k* bry k* camph *Chin* hr1 coc-c cocc k* *Dros* hr1 dulc k* *Ferr* k* ham fd3.de• hep hr1 iod k* ip k* *Kali-c* k* lach hr1 led *Lyc* k* *Manc* k* merc k* mur-ac k* naja nat-ar *Nat-m* k* *Nux-v* k* op wbt• *Ox-ac* k* oxyt ptk2 phos k* pieri-b mlk9.de **Puls** rhus-t bg2 sil k* spong squil k* stann ptk1 sulph verat k*
  - **violent**: *Brom* carb-v *Ferr* k* ox-ac k* **Puls** k* verat
- **amel.**: dros gk rad-br ptk1* rhus-t gk stront-c ptk1

EXHAUSTING: *Acon* bro1 ail k* alum k* am-c bro1 *Am-m* b7a.de anan ang b7a.de ant-i bro1 ant-t k* aq-pet a1 arg-met arg-n k* arn bg2 **Ars** k* ars-i *Arum-t* bro1 bac jl2 bals-p bro1 **Bell** k* benz-ac k* *Brom* k* bry bro1 bufo bg2 calc bro1 *Camph* k* *Carb-v* k* **Caust** k* cham k* chel k* chin chinin-ar chinin-m kr1 chlor *Coc-c* *Cocc* k* *Cod* bro1 coff colch k* coll bro1 *Con* hr1* cor-r k* *Croc* k* *Cupr* k* daph dig k* *Dros* k* eucal bro1 eup-per k* ferr ferr-ar ferr-p graph k* hep bro1 hydr-ac bro1 *Hyos* k* ign k2* iod k* *Ip* k* irid-met bg2 *Kali-ar* kali-bi kali-br a1* *Kali-c* k* kali-s *Kreos* k* *Lach* k* lact-v bro1 laur bro1 *Led* b7.de* lipp a1 *Lob* bro1 lyc k* m-arct b7.de mag-m h2 mag-s k* *Menth* bro1 mentho bro1 *Merc* k* merc-c k* myrt-c bro1 *Naja* bro1 nat-ar nat-c k* nit-ac bro1 *Nux-v* k* op bro1 ozone sde2* par b7.de* phel bro1 *Phos* k* plb k* psor bro1 *Puls* rhod k* *Rhus-t* k* *Rumx* rumx-act bro1 sang k* sarr senec hr1 seneg k* **Sep** k* *Sil* k* silphu bro1 spong k* squil k* **Stann** k* stict k* *Still* stram stry bro1 sul-ac k* sul-i k2 sulph k* tarent k* tax k* tela bro1 thuj k* tub-a bro1 v-a-b jl2 verat k* zinc k* zinc-p k2
- **daytime**: lyc k*
- **morning**: rhod k* squil sulph k* thuj k*
  - **going** to sleep, on: lyc k*
  - **waking** agg.; after: mag-s k* thuj k*
- **noon**: arg-n k*
- **evening**: arg-n k* ip k* *Kali-c* k* lyc k* rhod *Sil* k* *Still*
  - **going** to sleep, on: lyc k*
- **night**: *Caust* k* *Hyos* hr1 nat-c k* **Puls** k* rhod k* tarent k*
  - **bed** agg.; in: *Caust* k* tarent k*
  - **sitting** up in bed | **amel.**: nat-c k*
  - **sleep**, disturbing: **Puls** k*

EXPECTORATION:
- **agg.**: coc-c ptk1 tarent ptk1
- **amel.**: ail alum alumn k* ant-t bg3* apis b7a.de* aral bg3* bell calc carb-an k* caust chin bg3* cist k2* coc-c bg3* grin bg3* *Guaj* k* *Hep* *Iod* k* *Ip* kali-bi bg3* kali-c bg3* kali-n kreos *Lach* lob meli mez k* *Phos* k* phyt plan k* psil ft1 *Sang* *Sep* k* *Stann* ptk1 sul-i k2 sulph k* zinc k*
- **impossible**: caust tl1 con tl1

Expectoration
- **with** (See Loose)
- **without** (See Deep - not; Dry; Loose - expectoration - without)

EXPIRATION agg.: acon k* cann-i cann-s k* canth bg2 *Carb-v* k* *Caust* k* dros iod k* kreos k* lach meph mrr1 merc nux-v k* ph-ac k* staph k*

EXPLOSIVE: adam skp7• *Caps* k* dros bro1 lycpr bro1 malar jl2 nit-s-d a1 *Osm* bro1 plut-n srj7• rumx sil k* stry k*
- **evening**: sil k*
- **escape** of fetid, pungent air; with: caps

FASTING agg.: kali-c k* mag-m staph bg2

FAT FOOD agg.: ip bg2 mag-m k* puls bg2*

FATIGUING (See Exhausting)

FEAR to cough, seem to avoid it as long as possible (See MIND - Fear - coughing)

FEATHER:
- **as** from (See Dust, as; Tickling)
- **sensation** of feather or awn of barley in trachea: *Am-c* bg2 bell bg2 *Calc* bg2 cina bg2 dros bg2 glon bg2 hep bg2 *Ign* bg2 *Ip* bg2 ph-ac bg2 plat bg2 rumx k* sulph bg2

FEVER:
- **after**: bell b4a.de puls b7a.de
- **before**: ars b4a.de bell b4a.de hep b4a.de kali-c b4a.de phos b4a.de puls b7a.de rhus-t b7a.de samb ptk1 sil b4a.de
- **comes** on; cough amel. when fever: ol-j c1*
- **during** | **agg.**: **Acon** k* alum alum-sil k2 am-c b4a.de *Ambr* b7a.de anac ang ant-c ant-t k* *Apis* k* *Aran* hr1 arg-met *Arn* k* **Ars** k* ars-i bapt *Bell* k* bism brom *Bry* k* **Calc** k* *Calc-p* hr1 calc-sil k2 carb-v caust cham *Chin* k* *Chinin-ar* cic cimx k* cina coff **Con** k* cub cupr dig dros dulc eup-per k* *Ferr* k* ferr-ar ferr-i ferr-p k* guaj k2 hep *Hyos* k* ign iod **Ip** k* *Kali-ar* **Kali-c** k* kali-p *Kali-s* kali-sil k2 kreos k* lach lyc m-arct b7.de nat-c b4.de **Nat-m** k* nit-ac k* nux-m **Nux-v** k* op petr ph-ac **Phos** k* plat podo k* puls k* rhus-t k* ruta **Sabad** k* samb sang seneg sep sil spig spong squil k* staph sul-ac sul-i k2 sulph k* tarent k* thuj k* *Tub* verat verb
- **hectic**; during: nit-ac k2
- **intermittent**:
  - **after**: nat-m k*
  - **before**: eup-per *Rhus-t* samb
  - **suppressed**; from: eup-per
- **remittent**, during (See Remittent)
- **scarlet** fever; after (See Scarlatina)

FILLING up in throat; from sensation as of: apis ars sil

FIRE; when looking into: *Ant-c* k* *Stram* k*

FISH, from eating: lach k*

FLATUS; PASSING: | **amel.**: **Sang** k*

FLUIDS; from loss of: *Chin* k* cina k* con b4a.de* ferr k* ph-ac k* staph k*

FOLLOWED BY:
- **swallowing** (See THROAT - Swallowing - must - cough)

FOOD:
- **irritating** food: *Stann* b4.de*
- **warm** (See Warm - food - agg.)

FORCIBLE: acon k* alum k* am-m bg2 ambr b7.de* **Anac** b4a.de* ang bg2 apis bg2 arg-met b7a.de ars bg2 brom bg2 bry k* calc b4a.de* cann-s b7a.de* *Caps* b7a.de carb-v bg2 caust bg2 cench k2 chel bg2 chin b7a.de* cina b7.de cocc b7a.de* con k* croc b7a.de* cupr bg2 dros bg2 *Dulc* bg2 graph bg2 hep k* *Hyos* bg2 *Ign* b7.de* ip b7.de* kali-c bg2 lac-h sk4• **Lach** bg2 led b7.de* lyc k* **Merc** b4.de* *Mez* b4.de* mur-ac b4a.de* nat-c bg2 nit-ac b4a.de **Nux-v** b7.de* op b7a.de* par b7.de* *Phos* k* **Puls** bg2 rhod bg2 rhus-t bg2 ruta k* sabad b7.de* sel b7a.de seneg b4.de* spig b7.de* spong b7.de* squil b7a.de* *Stann* b4.de* **Sulph** bg2 *Verat* bg2 verb bg2 zinc bg2
- **morning**: cina a1
- **evening** and night: ruta

FOREIGN body; sensation of a:

○ - **Larynx**; in: am-caust *Arg-met* **Bell** brom *Dros Hep Lach* lob *Phos* ptel *Rumx Sil*

- • **awn** of barley swaying in larynx: rumx
- • **swallowing** agg.: bell bg2 lach bg2

- **Throat**; in: ign b7a.de

- **Trachea**; in: hyos *Kali-c* **Sang** sin-n staph h1 ter bg2

FRETTING: *Cina* k*

FRIGHT agg.: *(↗MIND - Ailments - fright)* acon k* bell cina bg2 ign k* rhus-t samb k* stram k*

FRIGHTENING:

- **children**; in weak nervous:
  - • **arousing** with a dry, spasmodic cough | **cry** out in terror; which causes them to: *Kali-br* k*

FRUIT agg.: arg-met k* mag-m k*

FULLNESS; from feeling of:

○ - **Chest**; in: aml-ns bg2 chinin-ar ph-ac h2* sabin b7.de* sulph k*

- • **morning**: chinin-ar ph-ac h2* sulph

- **Sternum**; under: kali-n bg2

GAGGING (See STOMACH - Nausea - cough)

GASTRIC: borx card-m ferr ip kali-ar k* lob nux-v

GLISTENING objects (See Bright)

GONORRHEA; after suppressed: benz-ac k* *Med* k* sel *Thuj* k*

GOUT, before an attack of: led k*

GRASPING: *(↗Hold)*

○ - **Larynx**; cough impels one to grasp the all-c k*

- **Throat** during cough: *Acon* k* all-c k* ant-t arum-t bg3 bell k* dros hep iod k* lach lob bro1

GRASPING something agg.: | **genitalia** during cough: zinc h2*

GREASE, sensation as if throat irritated by smoke of rancid: hep

GRIEF: *(↗MIND - Admonition - agg.; MIND - Ailments - grief)* arn asar *Cham* nat-m gk ph-ac k* phos

HACKING: acet-ac k2 acon k* aesc k* aeth k* agar k* agn k2 ail k* alco a1 *All-c* k* *Aloe* **Alum** k* alum-p k2 alum-sil k2 am-c k* am-m k* am-t br1 anac k* ang k* *Ant-c* k* ant-t k* apoc k* arg-met k* arg-n bg2* arizon-l nl2• arn k* **Ars** k* *Ars-i* k* ars-s-f k2 arum-t asaf k* *Asar* k* asc-t k* aur ptk1 *Bell* bg2* benz-ac k* berb hr1 *Borx* k* both-ax tsm2 bov k* brom k* *Bry* k* bufo k* *Calc* k* *Calc-f* k* calc-p k* calc-s calc-sil k2 camph k* cann-i cann-s k* *Canth* k* *Caps* k* *Carb-ac* k* carb-an k* carb-v k* carbn-s card-m hr1 caust k* cench k2 cham k* *Chin* k* chinin-ar chr-ac a1* cimic k* *Cina* k* cit-ac rly4• clem k* cob k* coc-c k* cocc coff k* colch k* coloc k* *Con* k* cor-r bg2 cupr b7.de* *Cupr-s* k* cycl k* dendr-pol sk4• dig k* digin a1 dios k* *Dros* k* dulc k* eup-per k* eup-pur hr1 euph k* eupi k* ferr-i ferr-p flor-p rsj3• franz a1 gels k* graph hr1 grat k* guare k* ham hr1* hell k* hell-o a1 hep k* hip-ac sp1 hydr-ac *Hyos* k* *Hyper* k* *Ign* k* iod hr1 ip k* irid-met srj5• iris jatr-c kali-ar k2 kali-bi k* kali-br k* kali-c k* *Kali-i* k* kali-m k2 kali-n k* kali-p kali-perm kali-s kreos hr1 *Lac-c* hr1 *Lac-d* hr1 **Lach** k* lact k* laur k* lil-t linu-c a1 lob-s k* lyc k* mag-c k2 mag-s k* malar jl2 mang k* med hr1 merc k* merc-i-f k* **Mez** hr1 mur-ac k* naja bg2* **Nat-ar** nat-c k* **Nat-m** k* nat-p nicc k* nit-ac k* *Nux-v* b7a.de* oci-sa sp1 ol-an a1* ol-j k* ol-sant br1 olib-sac wmh1 onos op k* osm k* *Par* k* petr k2* petr-ra shn4• ph-ac b4a.de* **Phos** k* phyt k* plan plb k* podo k* prun *Psor* k* ptel k* puls hr1 ran-s k* *Rhus-t* k* *Rumx* k* ruta k* sabin k* sal-ac samb hr1* **Sang** k* senec k2 *Seneg* k* **Sep** k* *Sil* k* sin-n k* *Spong* hr1 squil k* *Stann* k* staph k* stict k* *Still* k* stront-c k* sul-ac k* sul-i k2 *Sulph* k* *Sumb* k* syph hr1 taosc iwa1• tarax k* ter k* *Thuj* k* til k* trif-p a1 tritic-vg fd5.de trom k* **Tub** k* ust k* v-a-b jl valer k* vanil fd5.de verat-v k* xan k* zinc k* zinc-p k2 zing a1*

- **day** and night: euph
- **daytime**: *Calc* com k* gamb k* nat-m k* *Sumb* k*
- **morning**: all-c k* ant-t k* arg-met arn k* *Ars* k* calc k* *Calc-p* hr1 cina con k* iris kali-c k* kali-i k* laur k* mang k* mit a1 nit-ac k* ol-an k* par k* phos sel k2 sil k* sumb k* thuj tritic-vg fd5.de vanil fd5.de

Hacking – morning: ...

- • **mucus**, from: laur k*
- • **rising** agg.; after: arg-met *Arn* k* *Chin* k* euph *Ferr* lach k* nit-ac ox-ac par k* staph thuj tritic-vg fd5.de vanil fd5.de
- • **talking** agg.: sumb k*
- • **waking**; on: fic-m gya1 phos sil k*

- **forenoon**: am-m k*
- **noon**: arg-n k* naja olib-sac wmh1
- **afternoon**: calc-f k* calc-p k* cench kali-ar k2 kali-c k* laur k* **Sang** k*
  - • **14** h: laur
  - • **15** h: calc-p
  - • **15**-16 h: calc-f calc-p cench
- **evening**: alum alum-p k2 alum-sil k2 am-br k* am-m k* *Borx* bry k* *Calc* hr1 caps k* carb-an k* coloc k* com k* digin a1 dulc fd4.de eup-per k* eup-pur k* **Ign** k* kali-ar k2 kali-bi k* lach lil-t k* nit-ac k* ol-an phos k* phyt k* *Rhus-t* k* rumx **Sang** k* **Sep** k* sil k* sin-n k* stront-c *Sulph* k* sumb k* tritic-vg fd5.de vanil fd5.de zinc k*
  - • **18** h: sumb
  - • **19** h: com
  - • **bed** agg.; in: bry k* *Calc* hr1 carb-an **Ign** k* lact k* nit-ac k* *Rhus-t* k* **Sep** k* *Sulph* k*
  - • **lying** down:
    - **after**:
      - **agg.**: caps **Ign** k* kali-bi phyt *Rhus-t* rumx **Sang** k* **Sep** k* sil
      - **amel.**: am-m
  - • **smoking** agg.: coloc k*
  - • **warm** room agg.: com k*
- **night**: aeth arizon-l nl2• asc-t c1 calc k* *Cina Con* graph k* kali-bi *Kali-c* k* kali-sil k2 mag-s k* nat-m k* phyt senec k* *Sil* k* taosc iwa1•
  - • **midnight** | **wakening**: ruta
  - • **and** day (See day and)
  - • **smothered** feeling: asaf k*
- **accompanied** by | **coryza**: pert c1
- **air**; in open:
  - • **agg.**: kali-c k2 osm k* *Seneg* k* sulph a1 xan c1
  - • **amel.**: lil-t
- **chill**; during: tub k2
- **cold** air agg.: **All-c** calc-f k2 hyper
- **crawling** in the larynx, from: carb-v caust colch euph lach prun *Psor* hr1
- **dinner**; after: agar calc-f k* **Hep** k*
- **dry**: agar b4.de* alum b4.de* am-m b7.de* arg-met b7.de* *Arn* b7.de* ars b4.de* bell b4.de* *Calc* b4a.de canth b7.de* *Caps* b7.de* carb-an b4.de* carb-v b4a.de caust b4.de* *Chin* b7a.de *Cina* b7.de* *Coff* b7a.de colch b7.de* *Coloc* b4a.de con b4.de* graph b4.de* *Hell* b7a.de *Ign* b7.de* kali-n b4.de* *Laur* b7a.de m-aust b7.de mang b4.de* *Phos* b4.de* ran-s b7.de* sabad b7.de* sabin b7.de* stront-c b4.de* sulph b4.de* verat b7.de* zinc b4.de*
- **dryness** in larynx, from: carb-an **Con** *Dros* kali-c laur mang plan *Puls* **Sang** k* *Seneg* spong
- **eating** | **after** | **agg.**: anac calc-f k2 *Hep* k*
  - • **while** | **agg.**: hep nh6 nit-ac sang k*
- **heat**: hyper
  - • **during**: tub k2
- **inspiration** agg.; deep: nat-ar
- **irritation** in larynx; from: hep hydrog srj2• hyper *Seneg Sumb* thuj trom vanil fd5.de
- **lying** down agg.: *Ars Bry Con* **Hyos** *Ign* k* *Lach* nat-m par phos rhus-t k* *Rumx* **Sang** sep sil stann sulph vesp
- **menses**; during | **beginning** of menses: phos k*
- **motion** agg.: osm k* *Seneg* k*
- **rawness** in larynx; from: alum bry *Caust Coc-c Dulc* kali-bi kali-i laur *Phos* rumx sil stront-c sulph
- **rising**:
  - • **agg.**: benz-ac
  - • **amel.**: rhus-t k*
- **sleep**; on going to: agar arn brom hep lach lyc nit-ac sep sulph
- **smoking** agg.: clem k* coc-c coloc hell k* ign lach nux-v petr

Cough

- **tickling** in larynx, from: acon k* **All-c** k* *Alum* ang **Ars** borx *Bry* *Calc* calc-f hr1* *Carb-an* k* carb-v caust **Coc-c** k* colch *Con* dig **Dros** hyos ip kali-bi kali-c kali-n lac-c **Lach** k* laur k* lob-s k* lyc k* nat-c **Nat-m** nit-ac **Phos** k* phyt k* psor rhus-t *Rumx* sabin *Sang* k* *Seneg* sep sil k* spira k* spong **Stict** hr1 sumb k* taosc iwa1•
- **waking**; on: arum-t **Lach** hr1 phos k* sil
- **walking**:
  - **air** agg.; in open: ang
  - **rapidly** | **agg.**: seneg k*
- **weather** | **cold**:
  - **wet** | **agg.**: calc-p k*
  - **wet** | **agg.**: calc-p k2

HAIR; sensation of a:

○ - **Throat**; in: arg-n br1
- **Tongue**; on: *Sil* b4.de*
- **Trachea**; in: naja bg2 sil k*

HANDS (See Hold - chest)

HANDS AND KNEES; ON: | **amel.**: eup-per

HAPPY surprise; from a: acon k* merc k*

HARASSING (See Tormenting)

HARD: acal br1* **Acon** hr1 alum k2 alumn k* apoc k* ars asc-t k* aur-m k* aur-s k* **Bell** k* *Borx* *Bry* mrr1 calc k* cann-i k* caps k* *Carb-v* k* *Caust* k* cench *Chlf* hr1 chlol hr1 chlor chr-ac k* cina *Coc-c* coch hr1 coll k* *Cupr* k* eup-per k* euphr k2 eupi k* *Gels* hr1 guaj k2 gymno hep bg3* *Kali-bi* k* **Kali-c** k* kali-m k2 *Lac-c* k* *Lach* k* laur linu-c a1 *Lyc* k* naja **Nit-ac** hr1 *Nux-v* osm k* ph-ac bg3* *Phos* k* *Phyt* k* pitu-gl skp7• *Puls* k* rhus-t k* rumx k2 ruta fd4.de sal-ac hr1 *Samb* hr1 sarr k* sec k* seneg *Sep* k* *Spig* hr1 spong k* squil k2* **Stann** k* stict k* sulph hr1 syc fmm1• syph k* tub k2* verb bg3* ziz k*
- **morning** | **waking**; on: kali-bi k2
- **evening**: apoc k* caps k* choc srj3• *Puls* k*
- **night**: apoc k* ars sal-ac hr1 sul-i k2 syph
  - **1** h, after: ars
- **pneumonia** | **after**: calc-i k2
- **sleep**; during: tub br1
- **smoking** agg.: all-s k* nux-v
- **spells** of cough not ceasing until masses of offensive sputa are raised: *Carb-v*

HAWKING: eug k* lat-m sp1 olib-sac wmh1
- **morning** | **waking**; on: fic-m gya1
- **agg.**: am-m k* arg-n ptk1 coc-c ptk1 nux-v ptk1 raph a1 sil ptk1
- **choking** and vomiting, when hawking up phlegm in morning: ambr hr1*

HEART affections, with: adon bg3* arn bg2* aur-m k2 both-ax tsm2 cact k2* crat br1 dig bg2* guaj bg2 hydr-ac bro1 **Lach** k* *Laur* k* lycps-v bg2* **Naja** k* nux-v bg3* ox-ac k1* phos bg2 *Rhus-t* h1 spong bg2* *Tab*

HEARTBURN, from: carbn-s choc srj3• staph h1*

HEAT:
- **after**: bell spong fd4.de
- **sensation** of:

○ • **Bronchi**: aeth eup-per
  - **Chest**: carb-v
  - **Trachea**; in: chel bg2

HECTIC: bov nux-v *Phos* k* puls sil *Stann* k*
- **fever**; after suppressed: eup-per

HEMORRHOIDS:
- **appearance** of; after: berb k* (non: euphr hr1) sulph
- **disappearance** of; after: (↗*RECTUM - Hemorrhoids - suppressed*) euphr hr1 mill bro1
- **suppressed**; after: carb-v b4a.de lyc b4a.de *Nux-v* b7a.de phos b4a.de sulph b4a.de

HIGHLY SEASONED FOOD, from (See Spices)

HISSING: *Ant-t* *Caust* k*

Hissing: ...
- **hoarseness**, raises hand to larynx which is sensitive to touch; with: *Ant-t*

HOARSE: **Acon** k* agar agn **All-c** k* aloe k* am-c bro1* am-p bro1 ambr k* anan ant-t k* apis k* apoc k* ars bg2* *Ars-i* bg2* *Arum-t* bro1 asaf k* asc-t k* bar-c k2 **Bell** k* bov **Brom** k* bry bro1 bufo k* calad k* *Calc* k* calc-p hr1 calc-s calc-sil k2 calen bro1 camph k* cann-i caps tl1 carb-an k* **Carb-v** k* carbn-s **Caust** k* cench cham b7a.de* chin k* cina k* cop croc bg2 dirc bg3* **Dros** k* *Dulc* k* *Eup-per* k* euph bro1 euphr bro1 gels graph k* **Hep** k* hydr ign k* iod bro1 irid-met bro1* **Kali-bi** k* *Kali-i* k* kali-s kreos k* lac-ac k* *Lac-c* *Lach* k* laur k* lip bro1 *Lyc* k* mang-act bro1 med bro1 meph c1* merc k* myrt-c bro1 naja k* nat-c k* nat-m k* nit-ac bg2* nux-v k* *Phos* hr1* phyt k* *Puls* hr1 rhod b4a.de* *Rhus-t* k* *Rumx* sabad k* samb k* sang hr1 sec k* *Sil* k* sol-x gsb1 *Spong* k* **Stann** k* stict hr1 sul-ac k* sulph hr1* urol-h rwt• v-a-b jl verat k* *Verb* k*
- **morning**: calc-sil k2 carb-an k* *Caust* k* hep
- **evening**: *Caust* k* cina phos tl1
  - **until** midnight: **Hep**
- **night**: apoc hr1 dros rumx verat a1 verb k*
  - **midnight**: dros
    - **before**:
      - **23** h | **barking**: rumx
    - **after**: **Dros** k* rumx k*
      - **2-5** h | **barking**: rumx

HOLD: (↗*Grasping*)
- **abdomen** amel.: carb-an h2 con dros mtf33 nux-v mtf33 phos h2* plb gk
- **chest** with both hands; while coughing must hold●: **Arn** k* *Borx* k* **Bry** k* caps bro1 cimic cina bro1 **Dros** k* *Eup-per* k* kreos k* lact-v bro1 merc nat-m nat-p nh6 *Nat-s* k* *Phos* k* *Sep* k* stann mrr1 tub gk
- **hypochondria**: dros h1*
- **inwardly**; cough obliges him to hold himself (See Bending double - must)
- **larynx**: acon k2 **All-c** k2* dros gk
- **stomach**; pit of: lach bg2 phos h2*
  - **amel.**: arg-n pd* *Croc* k* *Dros* k* lach bg2 phos h2
- **testes** while coughing; must hold: zinc c1*
- **thighs**, must: nicc ptk1*
- **up** the child or it will go into convulsions; must hold: nicc c1

HOLLOW: *Acon* k* all-s k* aloe bg2 *Ambr* k* anac k* ant-t k* apis k* arge-pl rwt5• **Bell** k* brom k* bry k* bufo calc bg2 carb-v k* **Caust** k* chel k* *Chin* hr1 cina k* *Dig* k* dros k* euph b4.de* euphr k* hep k* *Ign* k* *Ip* k* jatr-c *Kali-c* hr1 *Kali-i* k* kreos k* lach lact k* led k* lyc ptk1 *Mag-c* k* med k* meph merc merc-c k* myrt-c k* nat-c k* nat-m bg2 nat-p nit-ac k* nux-v k* op k* osm *Phos* k* samb k* sanic sil k* spig k* **Spong** k* stann b4.de* staph k* *Stram* sulph hr1 **Verat** k* *Verb* k*
- **daytime**: spong k*
- **morning**: *Caust* k* cina *Ign* k* *Phos* k*
  - **bed** agg.; in: *Phos* k*
  - **rising** agg.; after: cina
  - **waking**; on: **Ign** k*
- **noon**, toward: sil k*
- **evening**: *Caust* **Ign** k* lact k* verat k*
  - **midnight**, until: bry caust
  - **lying** down agg.; after: lact k*
- **night**: acon k* anac ant-t *Caust* k* nat-c h2* *Phos* k* samb spong k* verb
- **breathing** deep | **amel.**: *Verb*
- **sitting** up in bed | **amel.**: med nat-c k* nit-ac phos sil
- **stooping** agg.: spig k*

HOUSE: | **inside**: cench k2

HUMID (See Loose)

HUNGER:
- **from**: ant-t tl1 kali-c mag-c
- **violent**, with: nux-v sul-ac

HYSTERICAL attack of:
- **followed** by crying, night: form
- **women**: cocc der *Gels* *Ign* k* *Kali-br* hr1 nux-m plat verat

ICE CREAM, at first amel., then agg.: ars-h

ICY (See Cold - air - agg.)

INABILITY to: ant-t k* bar-c hr1 *Dros* k* *Iod* hr1 nat-s k* ox-ac k* sulph k*
- **pain**; from: dros h1 nat-s
  - **pressure** of hand on pit of stomach amel.: *Dros* k*
  - ○ **Side**; in: ox-ac

INCESSANT (See Constant)

INFLUENZA:
- **after**: all-c bro1 am-c tl1* atro vh bry tl1 coch mtf11 *Erio* br1* hyos bro1 *Kali-bi* bro1 kali-s bro1 *Kreos* bro1 *Pix* bro1 sang bro1* seneg bro1 stann bro1 stict c1 stry bro1
- **during**: am-c tl1 sang br1
  - **sensation** as if: ozone sde2•

INHALING (See Inspiration)

INJURIES: arn bro1 mill bro1

INSANITY; with (See MIND - Insanity - cough)

INSPIRATION agg.: *Acet-ac* bro1 acon k* all-c bg2 apis asaf k* asar k* bamb-a stb2.de• bell k* benz-ac k* *Brom* k* bry bro1 *Calc* k* *Camph* k* carc tpw2* chlor cina k* cist st coff con cor-r croc k* *Cupr* b7a.de dig k* dulc k* graph k* *Hep* k* iod bro1 ip k* irid-met srj5• *Kali-bi* k* lach k* mag-m k* menth k* meny k* meph merc-i-f *Nat-m* hr1* nat-s olnd k* op k* *Phos* bro1 phys a1 plb k* prun k* *Puls* k* **Rumx** k* sep hr1 *Spong* bro1 squil k* staph bg2 stict k* sulph bg2 ter verb
- **crowing**, violent, spasmodic cough:
  - **beginning** with gasping for breath:
    - **followed** by repeated crowing inspirations:
      - **face** becomes black or purple and patient exhausted; till | **night** and after a meal agg.: *Cor-r* k*
- **deep** (See Breathing - deep - agg.)

INTERMITTING:
- **6** h; at:
  - **drinking** cold water | **amel.**: *Coc-c* k*

INTERRUPTED: agar k* coff k* eup-per bro1 (non: kreos a1) sul-ac k* thuj k*
- **evening** | **smoking**; from: thuj
- **dinner**; after: agar k*

IRREPRESSIBLE, sudden, violent:
- **evening** | **sitting** agg.: alum k*

IRRESISTIBLE: | **short**, hawking: osm k*

IRRITABLE: arg-met chlor clem k* cocc cod k* coff k* conch fkr1• dros mtf11 dulc fd4.de flor-p rsj3• hippoz ign k* kali-c k* lach laur k* m-arct b7.de moni rfm1• ol-j olib-sac wmh1 oxyg ozone sde2• par b7.de* petr-ra shn4• ph-ac k* phos k* phyt k* pieri-b mlk9.de plan k* spong fd4.de syc fmm1• teucr k* tritic-vg fd5.de tub jl2 vanad br1
- **morning**: spong fd4.de
  - **rising** agg.; after: arg-met
- **evening**: *Tub* jl2
- **night**: *Cod* k* phos tub c1

IRRITATING things (= salt, wine, pepper, vinegar, ...): petr-ra shn4•
- **immediately**; start cough: alum k* psor

IRRITATION; from:
- **morning** | **rising** agg.; after: alumn
- **forenoon**: mag-c h2
- **afternoon**: bapt
- **evening**: chel cimic dios petr h2 sulph
  - **19.30** h: cimic
  - **bed** agg.; in: agn am-c coff kali-c
- **night** | **waking**; on: thuj
- **increases** the more one coughs: *Bell* cist cocc hep st **Ign** k* raph squil teucr
- ○ **Air** passages; in: acet-ac br1 **Acon** *Agar* agn all-s aloe alum am-br am-c am-m aml-ns *Anac* ant-t arge-pl rwt5• aspar bar-c cain *Calc* carb-ac *Carb-v* carbn-s carneg-g rwt1• *Caust* k* cench k2 **Cham** k* chinin-s chlor clem coc-c coff colch coll con crot-t cypra-eg sde6.de• dios ferr-ar ferr-p *Gels* hyos **Iod** kali-bi kali-c kali-i kola stb3• lob lyc mag-s merc-i-r mez mosch mur-ac nat-ar nat-s **Nux-v** osm ox-ac petr-ra shn4• ph-ac phos plan psor *Puls-n* pycnop-sa mrz1 raph sabad mrr1 **Sep** sul-ac *Sulph* vero-o rly4•
  - **night**: kola stb3•
- **Bronchi**; in: aesc *Anac* arg-met asc-t k* carbn-s chlor cocc con cub *Dros* ind ip *Kali-bi* k* kali-n ketogl-ac rly4• *Lach* *Lyc* phyt *Sang* squil trif-p verat *Vero-o* rly3•
  - **right**: kali-n
  - ○ **Bifurcation** of: (↗ *Tickling - bronchi - bifurcation*) bry carbn-s dub *Kali-bi* k* *Spong*
  - **Low** in bronchi: verat bg2
- **Cardiac** region; in: bar-c
- **Chest**, in: acon bg2 *Anac* ant-o arn k* ars k* ars-h *Bell* k* bov k* bry bg2 *Calc* *Carb-v* k* carbn-s *Cham* k* *Cocc* bg2 colch k* con b4a.de* dros k* euph k* *Ferr-p* graph k* grat k* guaj k* guare ign bg2 iod b4a.de* kali-bi bg2 kali-n k* kreos k* lach bg2 m-arct k* mag-c k* merc k* mez k* mur-ac k* nat-c k* nat-p nux-m k* **Nux-v** bg2 ol-j osm petr k* *Ph-ac* k* **Phos** k* positr nl2• puls k* rhus-t k* *Sang* sanic **Sep** k* spong k* **Stann** k* sul-ac k* thuj k* verat k* verb bg2 zinc k*
  - **right**: kali-c bg2
  - **left**: chin bg2 rumx bg2
  - ○ **Lower**: kreos
  - **Upper**: ars-h carb-v myrt-c nux-m ol-j
- **Epigastrium**; in: bar-c bell *Borx* **Bry** cann-s cench cham guaj *Hep* ign *Lach* merc nat-m nit-ac nux-v ph-ac **Puls** raph **Sep**
- **Fauces**, in: aloe bg2 dios dros b7.de* lycps-v mag-s *Mez* sul-ac
- **Hypochondria**; in: thuj b4.de*
- **Larynx**; in: *Acon* k* **Agar** agath-a nl2• **All-c** k* *Alum* k* alum-p k2 *Alumn* am-c k* am-m k* ambr k* anac ang k* ant-c ant-t k* aphis *Apis* b7a.de *Arg-met* *Arg-n* k* *Arn* b7.de* ars k* ars-i asaf asar k* asc-t c1 bar-c k* bar-i k2 bar-m bar-s k2 **Bell** k* borx b4a.de* bov k* *Brom* k* *Bry* k* *Calad* k* *Calc* k* calc-f calc-i k2 camph canth k* caps k* carb-ac *Carb-an* k* *Carb-v* k* carbn-s card-m *Caust* k* **Cham** k* chel chin chinin-ar chlor bg2 cimic k* cina k* **Coc-c** k* coca *Cocc* k* coff k* colch k* *Coloc* k* **Con** k* crot-h crot-t bg2 *Cupr* dig dios **Dros** k* euph k* *Euphr* ferr k* ferr-i ferr-p k2 form *Gels* graph k* guare **Hep** k* hydr-ac k* hyos hyper **Ign** k* *Iod* k* **Ip** k* irid-met vml3• *Kali-ar* *Kali-bi* k* **Kali-c** k* kali-chl kali-i kali-m k2 kali-p kali-sil k2 kreos b7a.de lac-ac lac-c **Lach** k* lachn laur k* lith-c *Lyc* k* mag-c k* mag-m bg2 manc mang k* meny k* *Merc* k* merc-c k* mez k* mur-ac k* myric *Naja* k* nat-ar nat-c k* **Nat-m** k* nat-p nat-s bg2* nicc nit-ac **Nux-v** k* olnd k* *Op* b7a.de osm par b7a.de* *Petr* *Ph-ac* k* **Phos** k* *Phyt* plan prun bg2 *Psor* **Puls** k* *Rhus-t* k* *Rumx* k* sabad k* sabin k* sal-fr sle1• sang k* *Seneg* k* *Sep* k* *Sil* k* **Spong** k* *Squil* k* stann k* *Staph* k* stront-c sul-i **Sulph** k* sumb tab tarax k* teucr k* thuj trom tub-a vs verat verb zinc k* zinc-p k2
  - **right** side: kali-n a1
  - **morning**: *Sil*
  - **afternoon**: carc fd2.de• coca ferr-i phos
    - **14** h: coca
  - **evening**:
    - **bed** agg.; in: coc-c cocc
    - **lying** agg.: *Ign*
  - **midnight**, before: *Spong*
  - **eating**; while: *Rumx* k*
  - **fluid** had gone the wrong way; as if some: **Lach**
  - **severe**: chel a1
  - **sleep**; when lying on side in first: *Kali-c* *Spong*
  - **spot**; on a dry: *Con* a1*
  - ○ **Above** larynx: calad b7.de*
  - **Below** larynx: *Carb-v* b4a.de
  - **Low** in Larynx: ang bg2* phos hr1
- **Lungs**; in: dios lach lycps-v
  - **right**: carb-an nux-m
  - **20** h: dios
- **Mucous** membranes; of: *Bell* bro1 con bro1 *Hyos* bro1 lach bro1 phos bro1 *Rumx* bro1 stict bro1
- **Palate**; in: cham bg2 dig b4.de* *Nux-v* bg2 phos bg2

- **Stomach**; in: bell b4.de* bism bg2 *Bry* b7.de* calad bg2 con bg2 ign bg2 lach b7a.de* lob bg2 lyc bg2 merc b4.de* nat-m bg2 nux-v bg2 ph-ac bg2 phos bg2 puls b7a.de* rumx bg2 sang bg2 sep b4a.de* sulph bg2 verat bg2
- **Throat**; in: am-m b7a.de *Ambr* b7a.de anac b4a.de ant-t b7a.de asar b7a.de bov b4a.de bry b7a.de *Calad* b7a.de *Calc* b4a.de carb-an b4a.de carb-v b4a.de caust b4a.de cocc b7a.de coff b7.de* *Coloc* b4a.de *Con* b4a.de dros b7a.de graph b4a.de hep b4a.de iod b4a.de lach b7a.de laur b7.de* mag-c b4a.de mag-m b4a.de mang b4a.de *Merc* b4a.de mez b4a.de *Nat-m* b4a.de nux-v b7a.de par b7a.de petr b4a.de* puls b7a.de rhod b4a.de sabad b7a.de sars b4a.de sep b4a.de* sil b4a.de stront-c b4a.de sul-ac bg2 sulph b4a.de*
  - **right**: agar bg2 dios bg2 dros bg2 ferr bg2 iris bg2 lappa bg2 stann bg2 stict bg2
  - **left**: *Caust* bg2 coca bg2 hep bg2 kali-n bg2 ol-an bg2 phyt bg2 rhus-t bg2 sal-ac bg2 thuj bg2 til bg2 verat bg2
  - **coryza**; during: petr b4.de* sep b4.de* sil bg2 sul-ac b4.de* sulph b4.de
  - ○ **Posterior** part: carb-v bg2
- **Throat-pit**; in: *Apis* bell *Cann-s* card-m *Cham* croc dros mrr1 **Ign** k* iod kreos lac-c mag-c nat-m ph-ac rhus-r **Rumx** k* **Sang** k* *Sil* spong mrr1 squil thymol sp1
- **Thyroid** gland; in region of: iod b4.de* mag-c k* spong b7.de squil b7.de
- **Tonsils**; in: am-br bg2 kali-bi bg2 nux-v bg2
- **Trachea**; in: acon k* agar k* alum k* alum-p k2 *Am-c* b4a.de anac b4a.de ang k* ant-c bg2 ant-t k* apis b7a.de *Arg-met* k* arg-n *Arn* k* ars k* ars-i asaf k* bar-c k* bar-i k2 bar-m bar-s k2 *Bell* k* borx b4a.de *Bov* k* brom bg2 *Bry* k* *Calc* k* calc-i k2 *Cann-s* k* carb-an k* *Carb-v* k* carbn-s *Caust* k* *Cham* k* chin k* chinin-ar cina k* *Coc-c* cocc k* colch k* coloc k* *Con* k* croc k* dig k* **Dros** euph k* *Ferr* k* *Ferr-ar* ferr-i ferr-ma *Ferr-p* graph k* grat hep k* hydr-ac hyos k* ign k* *Iod* k* ip k* *Kali-ar* kali-bi k* **Kali-c** k* *Kali-i* kali-m k2 kali-n kali-p kali-sil k2 kreos b7a.de lach bg2 laur k* led k* **Lyc** k* m-arct b7.de mag-c k* mag-m bg2 *Mang* *Merc* mez k* mur-ac naja bg2 nat-ar *Nat-m* k* nicc *Nit-ac* k* nux-m k* nux-v k* ol-an bg2 *Petr* k* ph-ac b4a.de* **Phos** k* plan positr nl2• prun psor *Puls* k* rhod k* **Rhus-t** k* *Rumx* k* sabin k* seneg k* **Sep** k* **Sil** k* spig k* *Spong* squil k* **Stann** k* staph k* *Stict* stront-c k* sul-i k2 **Sulph** k* teucr k* *Thuj* k* trif-p verat k* verb b7a.de* zinc k* zinc-p k2
  - ○ **Bifurcation**; at: kali-bi bg2
- **Uvula** elongated (See Elongated palate)

ITCH; after suppressed: calc-f c1 psor

ITCHING:

- ○ **Chest**; in: agar ambr k* ars bamb-a stb2.de• carb-v coc-c con k* iod k* kali-bi kali-c mag-m k* mez *Nux-v* ph-ac k* phos k* polyg-h puls k* sep k* spig stann k*
  - ▽ **extending** to | **Nose**; through trachea to tip of: iod
- **Larynx**; in: ambr ant-t ars-s-f k2 bamb-a stb2.de• bell k* cact *Calc* calc-f carb-v k* *Con* k* dig lach laur lyc bg2 mang *Nux-v* k* ozone sde2• puls k* sil
  - **drinks** amel.; warm: bamb-a stb2.de•
  - **lying** on back agg.: bamb-a stb2.de•
- **Throat**; in: (↗*THROAT - Itching - cough)* bamb-a stb2.de• dulc fd4.de nux-v b7a.de puls b7a.de* spig bg2
- **Throat-pit**: (↗*THROAT - Itching - cough)* phos bg2
- **Trachea**; in: ambr b7.de* cham con k* kali-bi laur *Nux-v* k* phos bg2 puls k*

JERKING of head forward and knees upward; with: pert jl2 ther bg3*

JUMPING up: bry tl1 nat-s tl1

- **children**; in:
  - **clinging** to those around, calling for help in a hoarse voice; and | **or** bending backward and grasping at larynx: *Ant-t* k*

KNEELING with face toward pillow amel.: eup-per k*

LABOR:

- **difficult** labor or abortion; following: | **backache** and sweat; with: kali-c k*

LACTATION; during: ferr k*

LAMENTING; from: (↗*Weeping)* arn a1*

LATE; when going to bed: ambr bg2

LAUGHING agg.: alum bro1 *Ambr* bro1 anac bro1 *Arg-met* k* *Arg-n* k* ars arum-t bro1 **Bry** k ●* calc bg2 carb-v bro1 carc mg1.de* *Caust* bro1 **Chin** k* cimic bro1 coll bro1 con k* cortiso tpw7* cupr k* cur k* cycl kr1 dros k* dulc *Hep* bro1 hyos k* irid-met bro1 kali-c k* lach k* limest-b es1• mang k*

Laughing agg.: ...
Mang-act bro1 menth bro1 merc-i-f mur-ac k* nat-m zf nit-ac k* nux-v bro1 ol-j k* *Petr* **Phos** k ●* raph c1 rhus-t *Rumx* bro1* *Sanic* sil k* sin-n k* spong bg3* *Stann* k* staph sulph bro1 tell c1 zinc k*

LAYING hands on the part: | **amel.**: *Croc* b7a.de dros b7a.de

LIE DOWN: | **not** lie down; sat bent forward could: iod

LIFTING heavy weight: ambr k*

LIGHT, looking at: stram k2*

LIQUIDS:

- **swallowing**, night: sul-ac
- **touching** back part of mouth, from: am-c k*

LOOSE: abrom-a ks5 acet-ac k* **Acon** b2.de* adam skp7• agar k* agn b2.de* agri mtf11 all-c ptk1 all-s ptk1 alum k* am-br bro1 am-c k* am-caust a1 am-m k* ambr b2.de* ammc k* anac k* ang b2.de* ant-c b2.de* ant-s-aur bro1 ant-t k* apis apoc k* *Arg-met* k* arn b2.de* **Ars** k* *Ars-i* k* ars-s-f k2 arum-d k* arum-t asaf k* asar b2.de* asc-t bro1 atp rly4• atra-r skp7*• aur b2.de* aur-m k* bac ptk1 *Bad* hr1 bals-p bro1 bamb-a stb2.de• bar-c b2.de* bell k* bism k* borx b2.de* bov b2.de* brom k* bry k* calad b2.de* *Calc* k* *Calc-act* bro1 calc-s cann-s b2.de* canth b2.de* *Caps* b2.de* carb-an k* *Carb-v* k* carbn-s carl k* caust b2.de* cench cham k* *Chel* k* chen-a hr1 chin k* chinin-ar chinin-s choc srj3• cic k* cina k* cinch a1 *Coc-c* k* cocc k* coch hr1 colch b2.de* coloc k* colocin a1 *Con* k* cop ptk1 cortiso mtf11 croc b2.de* cub cupr b2.de* cupr-n k* dig k* diph mtf11 diphtox jl2 dros k* *Dulc* k* elaps ephe-si hsj1• eucal ptk1 eug a1* eup-per k* euph k* euphr b2.de* eupi k* ferr k* ferr-ar ferr-i ferr-p ferul a1 granit-m es1• graph k* grin ptk1 guaj b2.de* helo-s rwt2• hep k* hippoz mtf11 hydr k* hyos b2.de* ign k* ina-i mlk9.de iod k* *Ip* b2.de* irid-met srj5• jab k* kali-ar *Kali-bi* bg2* kali-c k* kali-m k2* kali-n b2.de* kali-p kali-s k* kreos k* lac-h htj1• lach b2.de* lappa lat-m bnm6• *Laur* b2.de* led b2.de* linu-c a1 lyc k* m-ambo b2.de* m-aust b2.de* mag-c b2.de* mag-m b2.de* mag-s k* mang b2.de* meph bg2 merc k* merc-c k* merc-i-f mez b2.de* mucor jl2 mur-ac k* nat-ar nat-c k* nat-m b2.de* nat-s k* nit-ac k* nux-m k* *Nux-v* b2.de* ol-j k* olnd b2.de* op b2.de* oscilloc jl2 par b2.de* pert jl2 petr b2.de* ph-ac k* *Phel* bg2* *Phos* k* pilo a1 pitu-gl skp7• plb b2.de* podo k* positr nl2• prot pte1* **Puls** k* pyrog jl2 rheum b2.de* rhod b2.de* **Rhus-t** b2.de* ruta k* sabad k* sabin b2.de* sacch samb b2.de* *Sang* hr1* sec k* sel b2.de* *Senec* k* seneg k* *Sep* k* *Sil* k* spig b2.de* spong k* squil k* *Stann* k* staph k* stict k* still k* stront-c b2.de* sul-ac k* sulph k* syc bka1*• taosc iwa1• tarax b2.de* tarent k* tell k* ter bro1 thuj k* tritic-vg fd5.de tub ptk1 ulm-c jsj8• vanil fd5.de vario jl2 *Verat* b2.de* verat-v k* *Verb* bg2 viol-t hr1 zinc b2.de*

- **day** and night: dulc k* sil
- **daytime** (See Dry - night - loose; EXPECTORATION - Daytime)
- **morning**: *Agar* *Alum* k* alum-p k2 *Am-c* b4a.de* *Am-m* b7a.de ars k* bad k* bell bg2 borx b4a.de **Bry** k* *Calc* k* carb-an b4a.de* **Carb-v** k* *Carbn-s* cench cham k* *Chel* k* coc-c k* cupr b7a.de* dros b7a.de* dulc fd4.de euph b4a.de* euphr b7a.de* *Ferr* bg2 franz a1 **Hep** k* iod b4a.de kali-c b4a.de* kali-s fd4.de led b7a.de* lyc b4a.de* *Mag-c* b4a.de* *Mang* b4a.de* meph k* morg-p pte1*• mur-ac k* nat-c b4a.de* nat-m k* nat-p nat-s nit-ac k* nux-m a1 nux-v k* *Par* ptk1 *Ph-ac* k* *Phos* k* *Psor* **Puls** k* **Sep** k* *Sil* k* **Squil** k* **Stann** k* stict k* stram k* **Sul-ac** k* **Sulph** k* syc pte1• tarent k2 tritic-vg fd5.de vanil fd5.de wies a1
  - **8** h: tell rsj10•
  - **tight**, afternoon: bad
- **forenoon**: alum b4a.de beryl tpw5 **Stann**
  - **9-11** h: nat-c ptk1
- **afternoon**: am-m k* beryl tpw5 vanil fd5.de
  - **dry** in morning: am-m
- **evening**: *Arn* bg2 ars-h hr1 bov k* calc b4a.de* *Cina* bg2 eug k* *Graph* b4a.de* kali-c b4a.de* kali-n bg2 lyc bg2 mur-ac k* nat-c bg2 nux-v bg2 phos b4a.de* ruta b7a.de* sep b4a.de* stann bg2 staph b7a.de*
  - **19** h: spira
  - **dry** in morning: alum b2.de* ant-c b2.de* arg-met b2.de* *Arn* b2.de* ars b2.de* aur b2.de* bar-c b2.de* bell b2.de* bov k* bry b2.de* calc b2.de* cann-s b2.de* canth b2.de* caust b2.de* chin b2.de* *Cina* b2.de* crot-t bg2 dig b2.de* *Graph* b2.de* ign b2.de* iod bg2 kali-c b2.de* kali-n b2.de* kreos b2.de* lyc b2.de* mur-ac b2.de* nat-c b2.de* nux-v b2.de* rhod b2.de* rhus-t b2.de* *Ruta* b2.de* sep b2.de* sil b2.de* stann b2.de* staph b2.de* sul-ac b2.de* thuj b2.de* verat b2.de*

- **night**: am-m k* ant-t b7a.de* *Bell* b4a.de* calc k* caust bg2 eug k* eup-per hep bg2 led bg2 lyc bg2 mez bg2 puls k* *Sep* k* sil staph b7a.de* stict vanil fd5.de
  - **midnight**: phos k* sep
    - **after**: *Calc* hep
    - **sitting** up in bed | **amel.**: phos
  - **less** free during day: stict
  - **lying** agg.: arum-d
- **alternating** with | **dry** cough (See Dry - alternating - loose)
- **apyrexia**, during: eup-per k*
- **breakfast** agg.; after: coc-c k*
- **chill**; during: *Ars* bg2 bry bg2 *Calc* bg2 chin bg2 kali-c bg2 kreos bg2 *Lyc* bg2 ph-ac bg2 *Phos* bg2 *Puls* bg2 *Sep* bg2 sil bg2 sulph bg2 thuj bg2
- **drinking** cold water | **amel.**: *Coc-c*
- **eating** | **after**:
  - **agg.**: bell nux-m k* *Phos* k* sanic sil staph thuj
    - **dry** cough after drinking: nux-m staph
  - **while** | **agg.**: phos h2*
- **exertion** agg.: brom k*
- **expectoration**:
  - **with** (See Loose)
  - **without**: ambr bg2 ammc k* arn k* arum-t brom *Caust* k* *Con* crot-t dros hep ptk1 ip mtf33 kali-c bg2 *Kali-s* lach melal-alt gya4 *Phos* *Sep* k* stann sulph
- **fever**; during: alum k* anac k* apis arg-met k* **Ars** k* bell k* bism k* brom bry k* **Calc** k* carb-v k* *Chin* k* cic k* cub dig k* dros k* dulc k* ferr k* iod k* **Kali-c** k* kreos k* lyc k* ph-ac k* phos k* puls k* ruta k* seneg k* sep k* *Sil* k* spong k* squil k* stann k* staph k* *Sulph* k* thuj k*
- **painful** cough in chest; very: arg-met k2
- **perspiration**; during: ant-t bg2 **Ars** bg2 bell bg2 brom bg2 *Bry* bg2 *Calc* bg2 *Dig* bg2 *Dros* bg2 ferr bg2 kali-n bg2 *Merc* bg2 *Nat-c* bg2 ph-ac bg2 **Phos** bg2 puls bg2 **Sep** bg2 sil bg2 *Spong* bg2 squil bg2 *Sulph* bg2 thuj bg2 verat bg2
- **skin** hanging in throat; from sensation of: alum
- **tickling** deep in chest, from: graph k*
- **warm** room; going into a: brom k*

LUMP; from: | **sensation** | **Chest**; in: abies-n bro1

○ - **Throat**; in: *Bell* k* calc k* coc-c k* lach k* ozone sde2•

LYING:

- **daytime** amel.: *Dros* nit-ac sep k*
- **afternoon**: calc-p laur
  - **14** h: laur
  - **15** h: calc-p
- **evening**: alum **Ars** k* *Bell* k* borx bry carb-an carbn-s **Con** k* **Dros** k* graph k* *Hyos* nh6 ign kali-ar **Kali-c** k* kali-n h2* lach k* lact mez nat-m k* nicc nux-v k* petr *Ph-ac* *Psor* **Puls** k* rumx **Sang** *Seneg* **Sep** k* *Sil* k* staph k* stict *Sulph* teucr thuj tritic-vg fd5.de vanil fd5.de
- **night**: all-c k2 am-br hr1 am-m k* arg-n a1 *Ars* arum-d *Bell* borx *Carb-an* k* carbn-s *Con* k* dol k* **Dros** k* *Dulc* gamb kali-bi kali-br **Kali-c** *Laur* lyc *Meph* nat-s nit-ac ol-j *Ph-ac* *Phyt* psor a1 **Puls** rhus-t **Rumx** **Sang** sanic **Sep** k* sil k* sulph *Thuj* tritic-vg fd5.de zinc
  - **midnight**:
    - **before**: *Aral* k* *Spong*
    - **after**: nux-v
- **abdomen**; on | **amel.**: (↗*RESPIRATION - Asthmatic - lying - abdomen)* aloe alum am-c bar-c k* calc caust eup-per k* *Med* k* phos podo rhus-t syph
- **agg.**: (↗*Sit up)* acon k* aeth k* agar k* all-c k* am-br k* am-m k* *Ambr* k* ant-ar c1* ant-t k* **Apis** k* aq-pet a1 aral k* arg-n k* *Arn* k* *Ars* k* ars-s-f k2 bar-c k* bell k* borx *Bry* k* calc k* calc-f sp1 calc-s calc-sil k2 caps k* carb-an k* *Carb-v* k* carbn-s **Caust** k* cham k* chin hr1 cinnb k* *Coc-c* k* cocc k* coch bro1 colch **Con** k* corn croc br1* crot-c sk4• *Crot-t* k* dol k* *Dros* k* *Dulc* k* ephe-si hsj1• euph gm1 eupi k* ferr b7.de* ferr-ar ferr-p guat sp1 hep k* **Hyos** k* ign k* inul bro1 *Iod* ip k* kali-bi bg2 kali-br k* *Kali-c* k* kali-p *Kali-s* kali-sil k2 kola stb3• **Kreos** k* lac-c *Lach* k* lact *Laur* k* lith-c k* *Lyc* k* m-ambo b7.de m-arct b7.de mag-c k* mag-m k* mag-p mag-s k* mang bg2 med k* *Meph* k* merc k* *Mez* k* nat-c nat-m k* nat-s k* nicc nit-ac k* nux-v k* ol-j k* olib-sac wmh1 par k* petr k* ph-ac k* phel bro1 *Phos* k* phyt k* plan plut-n srj7• *Prun-v* bro1 psor k* **Puls** k* pyrog rad-br ptk1 rauw sp1 *Rhus-t* k* **Rumx** k* ruta *Sabad* k* **Sang** k* sanic *Seneg* k* *Sep* k* *Sil* k* *Spong* stann k* staph stict k*

- **Lying – agg.**: ... sul-i k2 *Sulph* k* tarent k* ter k* teucr k* thuj tritic-vg fd5.de tub bro1 verb k* vesp vib vip visc sp1 zinc k* [heroin sdj2]
  - **night**:
    - **midnight** | **wakens** him: **Apis** k*
    - **sleep** | **amel.**: dulc kali-bi
    - **waking**; on: sanic
  - **as** soon as head touches pillow | **night**: caps *Con* **Dros** k*
  - **sit** up; must | **evening**: **Ars** **Con** k* **Puls** k* **Sang** **Sep**
- **amel.**: acon k* am-c am-m k* arg-met k* bry calc-p bro1* coca **Euphr** k* *Ferr* k* *Hydr* ichth sne indg kali-bi k* **Mang** k* *Mang-act* bro1 nit-ac ozone sde2• sep k* sin-n k* squil sulph k* *Thuj* k* verat k* zinc k*
  - **evening**: am-m k* zinc a1*
- **back**; on:
  - **agg.**: agar k* am-c bg2 *Am-m* k* *Ars* k* bamb-a stb2.de• crot-t eup-per iod k* kali-bi kali-c bg2 *Nat-m* k* nat-s *Nux-v* k* *Phos* k* plb k* rhod rhus-t k* *Sep* sil k* spong
  - **amel.**: *Acon* k* bry *Lyc* *Mang* k*
    - **better** than on either side, though worse lying on left side: *Phos* k*
- **bed**; in:
  - **agg.**: agn k* all-c vh1 *Alumn* am-c k* am-m k* anac k* ant-t k* aral aran-ix sp1 arg-n *Ars* k* bry cact calc k* *Caps* carb-v b4a.de caust bg2 cham k* coc-c coca coff k* **Con** k* *Crot-t* dol *Dros* k* euphr k* ferr b7.de* ferr-ar ferr-p graph b4a.de hep k* *Hyos* k* ign k* indg iod ip k* *Kali-c* kali-n k* kali-s kreos k* lach lachn k* lact lyc k* *M-arct* b7a.de mag-c k* mag-m k* mag-s meph merc b4a.de mez nat-c nat-m k* nit-ac nux-v k* petr b4a.de* **Phos** k* positr nl2• psor *Puls* k* *Rhus-t* k* ruta b7a.de sabad samb k* sang k* seneg bg2 *Sep* k* *Sil* k* squil k* staph b7a.de* *Still* **Sulph** k* vanil fd5.de verb k*
    - **children**; in: *Puls* mrr1
    - **sit** up, or sleep in chair from sense of suffocation; must: crot-t
- **face**; on the | **agg.**:
  - **rattling** of mucus, which appears to be low down in chest; with:
    - **reach** there, but only to throat-pit; while cough does not seem to:
      - **hard** cough does not reach phlegm unless he lies on his face; consequently | **expectorating** greenish yellow, gelatinous mucus without taste: *Med* k*
  - **amel.**: med tl1
- **head** high; with the | **amel.**: aral vh1 *Carb-v* k* **Chin** k* rumx sep
- **head** low; with the | **agg.**: am-m k* *Bry* carb-v **Chin** k* hyos puls k* rumx samb k* sang spong k*
- **knees** and hands; on:
  - **amel.** | **head** on pillow; with: eup-per ptk1
- **only** when lying: *Caust*
  - **first** lying down; only when | **sit** up and cough it out, then had rest; was obliged to: **Con** k*
- **side**; on:
  - **agg.**: *Acon* am-m h2 bar-c k* bry carb-an k* erig kali-c k* kreos k* lyc k* merc k* phos k* puls k* seneg k* sep k* *Spong* *Stann* k* sulph k*
  - **left**:
    - **agg.**: *Acon* b7.de* am-c apis k* arg-n ars *Bar-c* bry k* calc b4a.de chin dros bro1 eup-per ip k* kali-bi kali-c b4a.de* kreos b7a.de lyc k* merc k* par k* *Phos* k* ptel bro1 puls k* rhus-t *Rumx* k* *Seneg* *Sep* k* stann bro1 *Sulph* *Thuj* k*
      - **turning** to right side amel.: ars kali-c *Phos* *Rumx* *Sep* *Sulph* *Thuj* k*
  - **painful** side | **agg.**: acon
  - **right**:
    - **agg.**: *Acon* b7.de* alum k* alum-sil k2 am-m k* benz-ac bg2* *Carb-an* k* *Cina* k* guat sp1 ip k* kali-c k* kreos b7a.de lyc k* **Merc** k* phos k* plb puls vh sabad bg2 seneg bg2* sil *Spong* **Stann** b4a.de* staph ptk1 syph k* tub
      - **night**: *Carb-an*
    - **amel.**: ant-t bro1 phos mrr1

Cough

- **still**:
  - **long** time; for a | **change** position | **amel.**: ign bg2
    - **sitting**; or: con ph-ac
- **stomach**; on (See abdomen - amel.)

LYING DOWN agg.●: *Am-m* b7a.de ambr bg2 *Apis* b7a.de arg-n *Ars* k* bry b7a.de* calc bg2 caps carb-v bg2 caust bg2 con k* *Dros* k* euphr bg2 hyos ign bg2 kali-c bg2 laur lyc b4a.de* *M-arct* b7.de* nit-ac b4a.de* *Nux-v* b7.de* *Par* b7a.de phyt psor bg2 puls k* rhus-t b7.de* *Rumx* bg2 ruta b7.de* sabad k* sang k* staph b7.de* teucr b7.de* tritic-vg fd5.de verb bg2 [heroin sdj2]

MANUAL LABOR agg.: *(↗Exertion - agg.)* led k* nat-m k*

MEASLES:
- **after**: am-c b4a.de ant-c k* *Arn* k* bell b4a.de bry k* *Calc* k* camph k* *Carb-v* cham k* chel chin k* cina b7a.de coff k* con k* cop k* cupr k* **Dros** k* dulc k* *Eup-per* k* euphr bg2* gels graph b4.de* hep k* *Hyos* k* ign k* ip bg2* kali-bi bg2* *Kali-c* k* merc bg2* murx k* *Nat-c* nux-v k* **Puls** k* sang bg2* squil k* stict k* *Sulph* tub-a c
- **during**: *Acon* b7a.de calc bro1 cham b7a.de coff k* *Cop* k* dros b7a.de* dulc bro1 eup-per k* euphr bro1 ip bro1* kali-bi bro1 puls bro1* sang bro1 spong squil k* stict c2*
  - **daytime**: cupr
    - **eruption** develops amel.; when: cupr

MEAT agg.: *Staph* k*

MENOPAUSE; during: sang bro1

MENSES:
- **before**:
  - **agg.**: alet bg2 *Arg-n* k* dig bg2 *Graph* k* hyos k* lac-c k* phos bg2 plat k* senec bg2 *Sulph* k* zinc k*
    - **daytime**: graph k* sulph zinc
    - **morning**: graph **Zinc** k*
      - **early**: graph
    - **evening**: *Sulph* k* zinc k*
      - **bed** agg. and getting up amel.; in: *Sulph* k*
    - **hysterical**: plat k*
  - **amel.**: graph bg2
- **during**:
  - **agg.**: am-c b4.de* am-m atro bry k* cact *Calc-p* k* castm k* cham k* coff cop cub k* cur *Graph* k* iod k* kali-n h2* lac-c k* lachn k* nat-m phos k* plat bg2 puls bg2 rhod k* senec k* *Sep* k* sulph k* thuj *Zinc* k*
    - **morning**: cop k* **Zinc** a1
    - **evening**, every: *Sulph* k*
    - **coryza**; during: cub *Graph*
    - **hysterical**: hyos plat
    - **roughness** in throat, from: castm
  - **amel.**: senec ptk1
  - **beginning** of menses | **agg.**: *Alet* vh1 *Phos* k* senec bg2
- **suppressed** menses; from: bell b4a.de calen vml3• dig ptk1 mill k* puls k* senec bg2* sulph b4a.de tub k2

MENTAL EXERTION:
- **agg.**: *(↗Reflecting; Thinking)* ambr k2 arn k* *Ars* asar k* cina cist cocc colch k* ign k* m-ambo b7a.de *Nux-v* k*
- **amel.**: ign bg2

METALLIC: *Dros* gk eupi k* iod k* *Kali-bi* k* lac-c k* rumx sang k* spong

METASTATIC, with the sound of croup: cupr k*

MILK agg.: ambr k* ant-c ant-t k* brom k* kali-c k* spong k* sul-ac k* zinc k*

MINUTE guns; short, hacking cough like: cor-r k*

MOIST (See Loose)

MOON:
- **full**: kali-n b4a.de sabad bg2
- **new**: sabad bg2 sil bg2

MORTIFICATION; from: ign ph-ac

MOTION:
- **after** | **agg.**: ars bg2 zinc bg2

Motion: ...
- **agg.**: arn k* *Ars* k* ars-i bar-c k* bell k* brom k* *Bry* k* bufo k* *Calc* *Carb-v* k* carbn-o chel bg2 *Chin* k* chinin-ar choc srj3• cina k* coc-c cur k* dros k* eup-per **Ferr** k* ferr-ar ferr-i k2 form k* hep bg2* iod k* ip k* kali-ar kali-bi *Kali-c* k* kali-n k* kreos k* lach k* laur k* led k* lob lyc mag-p bg2 melal-alt gya4 merc k* mez k* mosch k* mur-ac k* nat-m k* nat-s k* nit-ac *Nux-v* k* osm ox-ac bg2 *Phos* k* plan k* psor puls bro1 pyrog k* rumx k2 *Seneg* k* sep *Sil* k* spong k* squil k* *Stann* k* staph k* sul-ac k* vanil fd5.de verat bro1 zinc k*
  - **13** h: nat-s
  - **16** h: calc-f kali-bi
  - **rapid** motion: *Nat-m* puls
  - **violent** motion: stann bg2
- **amel.**: ambr arg-met k2 arg-n ars ars-i sne caps coc-c dros dulc euph euphr grat hyos *Kali-bi* *Kali-i* mag-c mag-m k* nux-v ph-ac phos k* podo fd3.de• psor puls rhus-r *Rhus-t* k* sabad samb sep sil stann sulph verb zinc zinc-p k2
- **arms**; of | **agg.**: ars calc *Ferr* kali-c led k* lyc **Nat-m** k* nux-v
- **beginning** of | **agg.**: nit-ac k* plan k* sil k*
- **chest**; of: anac k* bar-c k* **Chin** k* cocc k* dros k* *Lach* k* mang k* merc k* mur-ac k* nat-m k* **Nux-v** k* *Phos* k* sil k* **Stann** k*
- **head**; of | **backward** or sideways: bell k2

MUCUS:

○ - **Chest**; in: ant-t aral bg2 arg-met k* ars k* arum-t asar k* bamb-a stb2.de• bar-c k* *Calc* caust k* cham k* *Chin* b7a.de cina k* coc-c bg2 euphr k* graph guare helodr-cal knl2• iod ip **Kali-bi** k* kali-n kreos k* maias-l hm2• med nat-m plb **Puls** k* pyrid rly4• ruta fd4.de sep k* *Spong* **Stann** k* suis-hep rly4• sulph k* vanil fd5.de

○ • **Upper**; in: maias-l hrn2• plb

- **Larynx**: aesc am-br am-c k* am-caust arg-met arg-n *Arum-t* asaf asar atro bamb-a stb2.de• brom caust k* cham chinin-s cina coc-c cocc crot-t k* *Cupr* dig dulc k* euphr k* grat hyos **Kali-bi** k* kali-s fd4.de kreos k* **Lach** laur mang *Nux-v* osm ozone sde2• par phel plan pycnop-sa mrz1 pyrog k2 raph seneg spong fd4.de *Stann* staph h1 stram tritic-vg fd5.de vanil fd5.de zinc
- **Posterior** nares: calc b4a.de hydr bro1 *Nit-ac* b4a.de pop-cand bro1 spig bro1 *Thuj* b4a.de
- **Throat**; in: arum-t bg2 asar b7.de* caust b4.de* cham b7.de* cocc b7.de* con b4a.de *Euphr* b7.de* graph b4a.de kreos b7a.de laur b7.de* mang b4a.de rhod b4a.de seneg b4.de* sep bg2
- **Trachea**: arg-met *Arum-t* caust k* cham cina k* crot-t cupr k* dulc k* euphr k* gels hyos *Nux-v* k* phos bg2 seneg *Spong* squil k* **Stann** k*
  - **ascending** or descending mucus; as from: coc-c
  - **sensation** of mucus in trachea; from: kali-c **Stann** k*

MUSIC:
- **agg.**: **Ambr** k* *Calc* k* cham k* kali-c k* kreos k* ph-ac k*
- **piano**; when playing (See Piano - playing)
- **violin**; when playing (See Violin)

NERVOUS: *(↗MIND - Excitement)* *Acon* hr1* ambr h1* asar bro1 aur k* *Bell* hr1* *Brom* bro1 **Caps** k* carb-v bro1 *Caust* bro1 cimic ptk1 cina k* cocc con bg2 cor-r k* crot-h k* cupr k* *Dros* k* gels bro1 *Hep* k* hydr-ac k* *Hyos* k* *Ign* k* *Ip* hr1* kali-br k* kali-m bro1 lach k* med bro1 merc bro1 narc-ps ah1 *Nit-ac* bro1 nux-m k* nux-v k* ozone sde2• phel phos k* *Plb* a1* puls bro1 *Rumx* bro1 *Santin* bro1 *Spong* bro1 staph mrr1 sulph bro1 tarent bro1 ter bro1 vanil fd5.de verat bro1 verb ptk1 viol-o bro1 zinc-p k2
- **evening**, sunset to sunrise | **women**; peculiar to: aur
- **night**; all: *Hep*
- **chronic**: tann-ac br1
- **enters** the room; when anyone: *(↗Persons - coming; Strangers; Strangers - presence)* phos k*
- **lying** agg.: **Hyos**

NOISE agg.: arn k* ph-ac k* tarent ptk1

NURSING the infant; while: chin b7.de* ferr b7.de*

ODORS AGG.; STRONG: irid-met srj5• merc-i-f ptk1 *Phos* k* podo fd3.de• sil sne sul-ac k* vanil fd5.de

OLD people: alum k* alumn k* *Am-c* k* *Ambr* *Ammc* ant-c ant-i bro1 *Ant-t* k* *Bar-c* k* bar-m bro1 camph *Carb-v* bro1 con k* **Dulc** hr1 hydr k* hyos k* ichth br1 ip k* kreos k* myrt-c bro1 *Psor* rhus-t bro1 sal-ac hr1 *Seneg* k* sil bro1 stict bro1
- **morning** | **chronic**: alumn
- **night**: hyos

- **winter** (See Seasons - winter - old)

ONIONS agg.: all-c tl1

OPERATION; after: | **fistulae**; for: berb bro1 calc-p bro1 sil bro1

OPISTHOTONOS; after (See GENERALS - Stiffening - cough)

OPPRESSION; from:

○ - **Chest**; in: *(↗CHEST - Oppression - Cough - during - agg.)* *Cocc* b7a.de* lap-la sde8.de• lyc h2*
- · **left** chest and hypochondrium: thuj h1
- **Epigastrium**: kali-bi k*

OPPRESSIVE: ail k* phal k* phel

OVERPOWERING, as if larynx were tickled by a feather: | **evening**, before sleep: **Lyc** k*

OYSTERS agg.: lyc tl1

PAIN:

○ - **Abdomen**; from cramping pain in ozone sde2•
- **Chest**; cough from pain in (See CHEST - Pain - cough)
- **Epigastrium**; cough from pain in: *(↗Stomach - come; STOMACH - Pain - epigastrium - cough)* lob ptk1 mim-p skp7• nux-v tl1 rhus-t↓
- · **stitching** pain: rhus-t
- **Larynx**; cough from pain in: acon ang arg-met bry calad caust chinin-s euphr ferr grat hep iod kali-c rauw tpw8 sars *Spong* *Stann*
- · **piercing** pain; from: acon bg2
- · **pressing** pain; from: agar
- **Throat**; cough from pain in: *Caps* hr1
- **Throat**; in: calc-f↓ carc↓ cortico↓ cortiso↓ hist↓ mag-s↓ mand↓
- · **tearing** pain: calc-f sp1 carc sp1 cortico sp1 cortiso sp1 hist sp1 mag-s sp1 mand sp1
- **Throat-pit**; cough from pain in: nux-v b7.de*
- **Trachea**; cough from pain in: acon ang arg-met bry calad euph grat hep indg ip lach↓ sars *Spong* stann
- · **stitching** pain; from: acon bg2 *Arg-met* lach stann k*

PAINFUL: *(↗Distressing; Tormenting; MIND - Weeping - cough - during)* *Acon* bg2* adam srj5• *Agar* k* *Ail* k* **All-c** k* anis ant-o ant-t k* apis arn bg2* arum-t bg2 **Bell** bg2* beryl sp1 borx bg2 brom **BRY** k ●* calad k* calc-p bg2 *Caps* k* caust k* chel mrr1 chin cit-ac rly4• coc-c k* cop cor-r k* crot-h bg2 dros bg2* dulc fd4.de elaps bg2* eup-per bg2* ferr-p k* influ jl2* iod bg2* irid-met srj5• kali-bi bg2 kali-c bg2* kali-n mrr1 kali-s fd4.de kreos k* lact k* lob bg2 med jl2 *Merc* k* merc-c k* nat-c nat-m bg3* nat-s k* **Nux-v** bg3* oscilloc jl2 phos bg2* *Puls* b7a.de ran-b bg2 rhus-t k* rumx bg2 sang mrr1 seneg bg2* spong bg3* *Squil* b7a.de* stann bg3* staph bg2 stict bg2* sulph bg3* tarent k* *Tub-a* jl2 ust k* visc sp1
- **evening** | **bed** agg.; in: bry k*
- **night**: caust k* kali-s fd4.de *Rhus-t* k*
- · **midnight**, waking before: *Rhus-t* k*
- **causes** pains in distant parts: agar bro1 am-c bro1 bell bro1 *Bry* bro1 caps bro1* *Caust* bro1 chel bro1 lach bro1 nat-m bro1 seneg bro1

PAINLESS: mag-s sp1

PALPITATION; from tumultuous: phos h2

PANTING: calad *Dulc* k* mur-ac phos rhus-t sul-ac
- **rumbling** in chest from above downward; audible: acon ars h2 bry caps hr1 mur-ac nit-ac nux-v rhus-t
- **sleep**; preventing: calad caps h1

PAROXYSMAL: *(↗Spasmodic)* acon adam skp7• aeth *Agar* k* alum k* alum-p k2 alum-sil k2 *Ambr* k* *Anan* k* ang *Ant-c* k* anth k* aq-pet a1 *Arg-n* *Arn* k* *Ars* arum-i a1 arum-t aur-m k2 *Bad* k* bamb-a stb2.de• **Bell** k* brom k* bry k* calad k* *Calc* calc-f calc-s k2 calc-sil k2 cann-s k* *Caps* k* **Carb-v** k* *Carbn-h* *Carbn-s* castn-v mtf11 *Caust* k* *Cham* k* *Chel* k* *Chin* k* choc srj3• cimx k* **Cina** k* **Coc-c** k* coca cocc coff k* *Con* k* *Cor-r* k* croc k*

Paroxysmal: ...
Crot-c **Cupr** k* cupr-act br1 cycl del a1 dig digin a1 **Dros** k* elaps *Euphr* ferr ferr-m k* ferr-p gins k* graph k2 ham fd3.de• **Hep** k* hydr-ac k* **Hyos** k* ign k* indg iod k* **Ip** irid-met srj5• jatr-c kali-bi k* *Kali-br* k* *Kali-c* k* *Kali-chl* k* kali-m k2 kali-n k* *Kali-p* kali-s kali-sil k2 *Kreos* lac-h sk4• lac-leo sk4• *Lach* lact k* laur k* lina a1 lob lyc k* *Mag-c* *Mag-m* k* mag-p mang k* **Meph** k* merc k* merc-c k* merc-i-r k* moni rfm1• morph k* naja nat-m k* nat-s k2 nat-sil fd3.de• nicc k* nit-ac k* **Nux-v** k* op k* pert c1* ph-ac phos k* phyt k* plb k* podo fd3.de• *Psor* k* **Puls** k* rhus-t k2 **Rumx** k* ruta fd4.de sabad k* sang k* sarr senec hr1 *Seneg* **Sep** sil k* *Spong* k* squil k* **Stann** k* staph *Sul-ac* k* sul-i k2 *Sulph* k* symph fd3.de• taosc iwa1• **Tarent** k* thuj k* tritic-vg fd5.de vanad br1 vanil fd5.de **Verat** k* x-ray sp1 zinc k* zinc-p k2
- **daytime**: *Agar* *Euphr* *Hep* kali-s fd4.de nit-ac k* staph
- · **amel.**: bell ign lyc spong
- **morning**: *Agar* k* *Alumn* vh1 *Ant-c* k* carb-v coc-c k* dig ferr ferr-m k* ferr-p ign iod ip kali-c kreos limest-b es1• nat-ar nat-m nat-p *Nux-v* k* ol-j k* ph-ac puls sang k* squil stram sul-ac k* sulph symph fd3.de• thuj vanil fd5.de
- · **8** h: lac-h htj1•
- · **bed** agg.; in: coc-c k* ferr **Nux-v**
- · **eating** | **amel.**: ferr k* ferr-m hr1
- · **rising** agg.; after: *Ant-c* ferr-p symph fd3.de•
- · **waking** agg.; after: *Agar* *Ambr* *Con* nh6 **Rumx** k* thuj
- **forenoon**: *Agar* cact coc-c k* grat k* sabad *Sep* tritic-vg fd5.de
- · **11** h: ozone sde2•
- **noon** until midnight: mosch
- **afternoon**: agar all-c anth a1 bad k* *Bell* bry caps *Chel* k* coca cupr k* mosch mur-ac nat-sil fd3.de• ol-an k* phel k*
- · **13**.30 h: phel
- · **14** h: ol-an
- · **16** h: *Chel* k* coca
- · **17** h: cupr
- · **17-21** h: caps
- **evening**: all-c anan bad bar-c *Bell* bry calc *Carb-v* chel k* chlor k* *Coc-c* coca grat k* *Hep* k* ign indg ip lach laur led mag-c merc mez nat-ar nat-m k* nit-ac *Nux-v* k* ol-an k* ph-ac *Phos* puls rhus-t *Sep* sil stann still stram tarent tritic-vg fd5.de verat-v
- · **18**.15 h: ol-an
- · **19** h: grat
- · **21**-22 h: brucel sa3•
- · **till** midnight: bar-c carb-v ferr *Hep* led mag-c mez nit-ac *Puls* rhus-t sep stann zinc
- · **bed** agg.; in: cocc k* nat-m k*
- · **cool** wind, in: coca
- · **lying** down agg.; after: *Nux-v* k*
- **night**: *Agar* anac anan ant-t apis aral arg-n k* arn k2 aur aur-m k* aur-s k* **Bell** bry calc calc-i **Carb-v** k* *Chel* chin choc srj3• *Coc-c* k* *Con* k* cor-r *Dros* ferr *Ferr-p* hr1 *Hep* k* **Hyos** k* ign *Ip* kali-br kali-c *Lach* lyc *Mag-c* mag-m *Meph* *Merc* k* merc-c k* naja *Op* k* *Phos* *Puls* k* **Rumx** k* sang sil *Spong* squil sulph tarent thuj vanil fd5.de vinc
- · **midnight**: *Cham* k* dig mosch naja phos *Sulph*
  - : **before**: ant-t apis aral bell *Cham* hr1 *Hep* lach mosch mur-ac rhus-t **Rumx** k* *Spong* squil sulph
    - : **22** h | **22**-22.30 h: adam skp7•
    - : **23** h: ant-t bell lach **Rumx** k* spong squil
      - . **lying** down agg.; after: **Rumx** k*
      - . **sleep** agg.; after: aral *Lach* k*
    - : **23.30** h: **COC-C** k●
    - : **on** falling asleep on either side: *Spong*
    - : **swallowing** mucus, amel.: apis
  - : **after**: bell *Cocc* dig **Dros** k* hyos kali-c meph mrr1 squil
    - : **2** h: **Dros**
    - : **2** and 3.30 h: coc-c
- · **bed**; before going to: *Coc-c* k* propr sa3•
- · **every** other; on going to sleep: merc
- · **warm** in bed agg.; becoming: *Coc-c* naja
- **accompanied** by | **breathing**; rapid: androc bnm2•

- **attacks** follow one another quickly: *Agar* ant-t k* cina coff *Cor-r* k* **Dros** k* hep k* ign br1 *Ip* k* merc sep k* sulph k*
  - **strongest**, following attacks weaker and weaker; first the: *Ant-c* k*
- **bread** or cake, from eating: kali-n k*
- **chill**; after: irid-met srj5• phos k*
- **consisting** of:
  - **few** coughs: bell k* calc k* laur k*
  - **long** coughs: alum bg1 ambr carb-v **Cupr** k* dros bg3* ip lob rumx bg1
  - **one** cough: calc bg2*
  - **short** coughs: alum k* ant-t k* asaf k* bell calc k* carb-v k* *Coc-c* cocc *Cor-r* k* *Dros* kali-bi k* *Kali-c* lact squil
  - **three** coughs: *Carb-v* *Cupr* k* phos k* stann k*
    - **or** four coughs: bell bg2* carb-v bg2* cupr ptk1 stann bg2 verat bg2*
  - **two** coughs: agar bamb-a stb2.de• bell bg3* cocc grat laur merc k* phos k* plb k* puls k* sul-ac sulph thuj tritic-vg fd5.de
    - **or** three coughs: *Merc* ptk1 phos bg2* plb ptk1 puls ptk1 stann ptk1 sulph bg2* thuj ptk1
    - **quick** succession; in: merc bg2 merc-sul sulph bg2
- **convulses** the whole body; in sudden paroxysms which: caps k*
- **crawling** in larynx, from: *Psor*
- **dinner**; after: aeth k* calc-f k* phos k*
- **followed** by copious mucus: *Agar* alumn *Anan* *Arg-n* **Coc-c** kali-bi kali-c mtf33 seneg spong fd4.de stann sulph
- **gasping** for breath; beginning with: ant-t cor-r
- **hard** spells of coughing, not ceasing until masses of offensive sputa are raised: carb-v
- **irresistible** paroxysms without illness: **Ign** mrr1
- **lachrymation** is profuse with every paroxysm: am k1
- **long** paroxysms: alum bg2 ambr bg2 carb-v bg2 chel bg2 cupr bg2 hyos bg2 ip bg2 sep bg2
- **rinsing** mouth with cold water, amel.: coc-c
- **short** paroxysms: bell bg2* calc bg2 dros bg2 kali-c bg2 squil bg2
- **sitting** up in bed | **amel.**: cinnb k* phos h2*
- **smoking** agg.: all-s k*
- **sneezing**; with: **Agar** k* carb-v lyc
- **stomach** amel.; laying hand on pit of: *Croc* k*
- **suffocation**, suddenly on swallowing: **Brom** k*
- **sun**, walking in hot: coca
- **temperature**; change of: *Spong*
- **three** coughs (See consisting - three)
- **two** coughs (See consisting - two)
- **two** paroxysms: cocc b7.de* laur b7.de* **Op** b7a.de phos bg2 puls b7.de* sulph b4a.de
- **uninterrupted** paroxysms: **Cupr**

○ • **Chest** would fly to pieces; as if: lact br1
- **vomiting**; with: meph mrr1
- **walking** in the cool wind: coca

PEPPER, from: alum k* cina k*

PERIODICAL: am-m k2 ambr bg2 anac k* arn bg2 ars k* aur k* bell bg2 carb-v b4.de* cina b7.de* coc-c k* cocc k* colch k* con bg2* cupr bg2 dros bg2 euphr bg2 hep bg2 ip bg2 kali-c bg2 lach k* lact k* lyc k* mag-m bg2 merc k* mur-ac bg2 *Nux-v* k* par bg2 phos b4.de* *Psor* hr1 *Sang* hr1 sep k* squil bg2 stann b4.de* staph bg2 stram k* sul-ac bg2 sulph bg2 verat bg2 verb bg2
- **day**:
  - **alternate**: anac k* lyc k* nux-v sep
    - **coughs**; violent: *Anac* lyc *Nux-v*
  - **every**: anac
    - **hour**; at the same: kali-c bg2 lyc k* sabad k*
  - **third**; every: anac k* lyc
- **morning**: stram
- **evening**, sunset to sunrise: aur
- **night**: acon k* cocc k* merc k*
  - **midnight**: cocc k*
    - **after**: acon k* cocc k*
      - **hour**; every half: acon
      - **2 h**: cocc
  - **alternate**: merc

Periodical – night: ...
  - **fourth**; every: cocc k*
- **year**; every: nicc bg2
- **clock**; in its regularity like tick of a: nicc k*
- **hour**:
  - **three** hours; every: anac dros
  - **same**; every day: lyc k* sabad k*
- **speaking** or smoking, from: atro k*

PERSISTENT: acon adam srj agath-a nl2• am-caust k* **Bell** cact crot-t cub **Cupr** k* dios diphtox jl2 hydrog srj2• *Hyos* k* ip jatr-c kali-n k* limest-b es1• lyc k* mag-p merc mez *Nux-v* k* positr nl2• prot jl2 rumx sang squil
- **night**:
  - **midnight** | **lying** on back agg., lying on side amel.: *Nux-v* k*

PERSONS:
- **approaching** or passing, agg.: carb-v k*
- **coming** into room; other persons: *(↗Nervous - enters; Strangers; Strangers - presence)* **Phos** k ●
- **present**; when many persons are: *Ambr*

PERSPIRATION:
- **after** | **agg.**: sil b4a.de*
- **amel.**; breaking out of perspiration: eupi c1
- **during**: bry b7a.de sabad b7.de

PERTUSSIS (See Whooping)

PIANO:
- **note** she struck seemed to vibrate in her larynx; every: *Calc*
- **playing**; when: ambr **Calc** k* cham kali-c k* kreos ph-ac

PLEURITIS, in: acon *Ars* bry ip *Lyc* *Sulph* syc bka1•

PLUG:

○ - **Larynx**; from sensation of a plug in spong k*
- **Throat**; sensation of a plug in: calc b4a.de*
- **Trachea**; from sensation as of a plug moving up and down in: *Calc* k*

PNEUMONIA, after: calc-i k2

POSITION:
- **changing** position agg.: kreos ptk1
- **knee**-chest | **amel.**: eup-per bro1 med jl2

POTATOES agg.: alum k*

PREGNANCY agg.; during: acon bro1 apoc bg2* *Bell* bg2* bry bro1 calc k* *Caust* k* cham bg2* *Con* k* cor-r bro1 dros bg2* glon bro1 hyos bg2* ip k* kali-br k* nat-m hr1 *Nux-m* k* nux-v bro1 **Phos** k ●* puls k* sabin **Sep** k ●* stann hr1 vib k* vib-od bro1
- **night**: *Con* k*
- **early** pregnancy, causing abortion; during: rumx ptk1

PRESSURE: *(↗Touched)*
- **abdomen**; on | **amel.**: con ptk1
- **chest**; on | **amel.**: *Hep* b4a.de phos b4.de* *Sep* b4a.de
- **goitre**; from pressure of: ars-i bg2 brom bg2 iod bg2 kali-i bg2 psor k* *Spong* bg2*
- **larynx** agg.; on: *(↗LARYNX - Pain - larynx - pressing)* apis *Bell* *Chin* cina k* crot-h ferr **Lach** k* rumx k* tarax
- **stomach**; on:
  - **agg.**: *Calad* b7.de*
  - **amel.**: croc ptk1 dros ptk1
- **temples**; on | **amel.**: petr bg3*
- **throat**-pit agg.; on: rumx k*
- **trachea** agg.; on: bell hydr k* *Lach* k* rumx k*

PRESSURE; from a sensation of: *(↗Touched)*

○ - **Chest**; in: *(↗CHEST - Pain - Cough - during - agg. - pressing)* iod k* op
- **Epigastrium**; in: *Calad* a1

- **Larynx**; in:
  - **pain** in larynx; from pressing (See Pain - larynx - pressing)
  - **roughness** and pressure; from a sensation between | **tickling** sensation; which gradually becomes a: tell k*
- **Stomach**; in: calad k*

PRICKLING; from: *(↗Tingling - trachea)*
○ - **Larynx**; in: bac jl2 bufo bg2
- **Tongue**; on: lach bg2
- **Trachea**; in: *(↗Tingling - trachea)* hydr-ac

PRODROME, as a: bry ptk1 rhus-t ptk1 sabad ptk1 samb ptk1 tub ptk1

PROSTRATION with (See Exhausting)

PROTRUDING tongue agg.: *(↗MOUTH - Protruding - tongue - cough - during; MOUTH - Protruding - Tongue - cough - during - agg.)* *Lyc* hr1*

PUFFING: naja bg2

PUNGENT food: *(↗Spices)* sulph bg2 thuj a1

PURRING: nat-c h2*

PUTTING out the tongue, from: lyc k*

QUININE; abuse of: arn bg2 *Con* b4a.de ferr bg2

RACKING: *(↗Shaking; Tormenting)* acal br1* **Agar** k* ail hr1 alum-sil k2 alumn k* am-m anac k* anan k* ang ant-c k* arg-n k* *Arn* k* ars k* ars-i br1 ars-s-f k2 arum-t aur k* aur-s k2 **Bell** k* benz-ac hr1 brom k* **Bry** k* calc k* calc-ar calc-s calc-sil k2 cann-i *Caps* k* *Carb-an* k* **Carb-v** k* **Caust** k* cench *Chel* k* chin k* chinin-s cinch a1 **Coc-c** k* cocc k* coll k* *Con* k* cop croc cupr k* cur k* daph *Dulc* eup-per k2 graph k* gymno *Hyos* k* **Ign** k* *Ip* k* iris-foe kali-bi k* **Kali-c** k* kali-m k2 kali-n bg2 *Kali-p* kali-s kali-sil k2 kreos k* lac-c *Lach* k* *Lact* led k* lob hr1 *Lyc* k* m-ambo b7.de *M-arct* b7.de* mag-m k* mag-s mang bg2* **Merc** k* merc-c *Mez* mur-ac nat-ar nat-c nat-m k* nat-p nicc k* nit-ac k* **Nux-v** k* olnd k* op k* osm k* petr-ra shn4• *Ph-ac* ptk1 **Phos** k* psor k2 **Puls** k* rhod *Rhus-t* k* rob rumx bg2* sal-ac hr1 samb xxb1 sang hr1 sarr *Sec* k* sel *Seneg* k* *Sep* k* *Sil* k* spig *Spong* k* squil k* **Stann** k* staph stict k* sul-ac k* **Sulph** k* sumb k* syph k* tub k2 *Verat* k* zinc k* zinc-p k2
- **morning**: caust k* *Chel* k*
  - **waking**; on: caust k*
- **afternoon** | **15** h: cench
- **evening**: anan k* cench *Ip* k* iris-foe led lyc h2* nat-m k* nit-ac petr h2* *Puls* rhus-t stict
  - **until** midnight: led nit-ac *Puls* rhus-t
- **night**: agar anac a1 anan k* aur **Bell** chinin-s *Hyos* iris-foe merc k* nat-c h2* nat-m a1 nit-ac sal-ac hr1 stict
  - **22** h: nat-m
  - **midnight**, after: hyos
- **drinking** water amel.: *Op* k*
- **inspiration** agg.; deep: con
- **sitting** up in bed | **amel.**: arg-n k* **Hyos Puls**

RAISED, gets blue in face cannot exhale; child must be: meph k*

RAISING ARMS agg.: *Bry* k* *Ferr* k* lyc ol-j k* tub bg*

RAPID, until patient falls back as limp as a rag: *Cor-r* k*

RASPING: ars k2 calc k* calc-s a1 phos k2 **Spong** stram k* syph hr1*

RATTLING: alum alum-p k2 am-c mrr1 *Ammc* ang k* **Ant-t** k* *Apoc* hr1 aral *Arg-met* k* *Arg-n* k* ars sne ars-s-f hr1 arum-d arund k* *Bar-c* bar-i k2 bar-m bar-s k2 *Bell* k* brom k* *Bry* k* *Cact* cain *Calc* k* *Calc-s* *Carb-an* *Carb-v* **Caust** k* *Cham* k* *Chel* k* chen-a k* chinin-m kr1 *Cina* *Coc-c* k* con k* cupr dig c1 dros sne *Dulc* hr1 eug ferr ferr-p gamb *Hep* k* *Hippoz* *Hydr* k* hydr-ac *Iod* k* **Ip** k* *Kali-bi* k* *Kali-chl* kali-p **Kali-s** k* ketogl-ac rly4• *Lach* *Lyc* k* med k* meph k* merc merc-c k* merc-i-f k* merc-i-r mur-ac nat-ar mrr1 nat-c k* *Nat-m* k* *Nat-s* k* *Nux-v* k* oena *Op* k* phos k* podo k* *Puls* k* rumx samb *Sang* *Sanic* sars k* **Sep** k* *Sil* k* spong fd4.de *Squil* k* *Stann* k* sul-ac k* sul-i k2 *Sulph* k* teucr-s gm1 verat k* verat-v k* yuc a1
- **daytime**: *Arg-met* ferr nit-ac k2
- **morning**: aral dulc fd4.de hep k* meph stram
- **evening**: caust sil
- **night**: anac gamb spong fd4.de

Rattling: ...
- **air**; in open | **amel.**: arg-met *Kali-s*
- **eating** | **after** | **agg.**: hep k*
  - **while** | **agg.**: dulc fd4.de *Phos* k*
- **hoarseness**:
  - **with**: *Kali-chl*
  - **without**: **Kali-s**
- **old** people: *Ammc* bar-c k2 *Hippoz* *Kali-bi* *Seneg* k*
- **shaking** the body: phos k2
- **spells** in: cina k*
- **weather**; warm wet agg.: ip mrr1
- **wheezing** or whistling while lying on back, or on either side; with: med
  - **right** side: cassia-s ccrh1•

RAWNESS: bell-p sp1
○ - **Larynx** excites cough; rawness in acon *Alum* ambr bar-c brom k* *Bry* carbn-s k2 castm *Coc-c* dulc *Hep* kali-i laur **Nux-v** ol-an **Phos Rumx** sang *Sil* **Sulph** k*
- **Sternum** excites cough; rawness behind: kali-n h2

READING ALOUD agg.: alum bro1 *Ambr* k* anac bro1 anag hr1 *Arg-met* bro1 *Arg-n* bro1 arum-t bro1 carb-v bro1 *Caust* bro1 cimic bro1 cina coll bro1 *Con* bro1 *Dros* k* *Hep* bro1 *Hyos* bro1 irid-met bro1* lach bro1 mag-p bg2 *Mang* k* *Mang-act* bro1 menth bro1 meph k* nit-ac k* *Nux-v* k* par k* **Phos** k* *Rumx* bro1 sil bro1 spong nh6* *Stann* k* sulph bro1 *Tub* verb k*
- **evening**: *Phos*
- **oneself**; to: *Ambr* b7a.de cina bg2* *Nux-v* b7.de*

RE-ECHO in stomach; seems to: *Chel* hr1 cupr k*

REFLECTING agg.: *(↗Mental - agg.)* asar b7.de* cocc b7.de* m-ambo b7.de* *Nux-v* b7.de*

REFLEX: ambr bro1 apis bro1 cer-ox c2 ign br1 phos bro1

REMITTENT fever, during: podo k*

REPOSE, amel.: ip ptk1

REPRIMANDS agg.: cina bg2

RESONANT: cor-r ptk1 kali-bi k* *Stram* ptk1 verb pd*

REST:
- **after** (See Lying - bed - agg.)
- **agg.**: ambr bg2 apis b7a.de ars bg2 caps b7.de* dros b7.de* dulc bg2 euph b4.de euphr bg2 ferr b7.de* hyos b7.de* mag-c bg2 mag-m bg2 nux-v b7.de* ph-ac bg2 phos b4.de* **Puls** b7.de* *Rhus-t* b7.de* sabad bg2 samb b7.de* seneg bg2 sep bg2 stann bg2 sulph bg2 verb bg2 zinc bg2
- **amel.**: psor bg2

RESTING hands on thighs: | **amel.**: nicc bro1

RETCHING (See STOMACH - Retching - cough)

RIDING agg.: staph sul-ac k* sulph

RINGING: *(↗Dry)* acon k* all-c k* apis arn bg2 *Ars* asaf castn-v br1 dol **Dros** k* *Kali-bi* lac-c spong stram k*

RINSING mouth:
- **agg.**: *Coc-c* k* polys sk4•
- **cold** water | **amel.**: coc-c bg2*

RISING:
- **agg.**: acon k* alum k* alumn k* ang k* arg-n arn k* ars bar-c k* benz-ac k* bov k* bry calc-s k* canth carb-an k* carb-v k* chel k* chinin-s cina cocc con cortico tpw7 dig k* euph euphr k* *Ferr* k* ferr-ar ferr-p grat k* ign indg k* *Lach* k* mag-c k* nat-s k* nit-ac osm k* ox-ac par k* phos k* plb sep staph stram sul-ac sulph k* tarent k* thuj vanil fd5.de verat k*
- **amel.**: hyos bg2 mag-c mag-s k* puls bg2 rhus-t
- **bed**; from:
  - **agg.**: acon alum bg2 arn bg2 ars bar-c bry calc bg2 calc-s canth k* carb-an carb-v k* chel cocc con elaps bg2 eup-per bg2 *Euphr* k* ferr-p ign k* **Lach** k* mag-s nat-s nux-v bg2 phos k* plb sep spong hr1 sul-ac k* tarent k* thuj k* vanil fd5.de verat
  - **amel.**: puls bg2
- **before**: ail **Nux-v** k*

Cough

- **stooping**; from | **agg.**: chel a1 phos

RISING; from sensation of something: | **Throat**; in: cham b7.de* mur-ac bg2

ROOM agg.: adam skp7• arg-met k* brom k* bry k* bufo bg2 coc-c bg2 croc k* *Kali-c* b4a.de kali-n h2* laur k* mag-c k* mag-m k* nat-c nat-m k* *Phos* b4a.de podo fd3.de• puls k* spig k* spong k* *Verat* b7a.de

ROUGH: acon k* am-m bg2 bell k* brom k* cann-i k* carb-an k* carb-v k* card-b k* caust bg2 cop k* diphtox jl2 dros k2 dulc k* *Eup-per* k* eupi k* *Hep* k* ign hr1 iod k* ip k* kali-c bg2 kola stb3• kreos b7a.de* laur bg2 mag-m k* meli k* *Merc* k* *Merc-cy* hr1 morb jl2 *Mur-ac* k* nat-c k* nat-m h2* nux-v b7.de* ozone sde2• petr bg2 *Phos* hr1 puls b7.de* *Rhus-v* k* rumx bg2 sabad b7.de samb hr1* sep k* sil k* *Spong* hr1 tarent k* ust k* v-a-b jl2 verb c1

- **night**: bros-gau mrc1 *Cham* k* lyc k* nat-c h2* *Nit-ac* k* *Verb* hr1
  - • **midnight**: *Nit-ac*

ROUGHNESS; from:

○ - **Chest**; in: *Alum* b4a.de am b7.de* calc b4a.de carb-v b4.de* kali-c b4.de* kreos b7a.de lyc b4.de* m-arct b7.de nat-c b4.de* nux-m b7.de* *Nux-v* b7a.de **Phos** b4a.de sep b4.de* sulph b4a.de zinc b4a.de

- **Larynx**; in: *(↗throat)* *Alum* ang aur-m bar-c k* *Bry* carb-an k* *Carb-v* carbn-s castm *Caust* coloc con dig k* graph *Kali-c* kali-i kalm kreos k* *Lach* laur mang nat-s **Nux-v** ol-an plb *Puls* rhod *Rhus-t* sabad k* sars *Seneg* *Spong* stront-c *Sulph* verat-v
- **Palate**; in: calc h2
- **Throat**; in: *(↗larynx; THROAT - Roughness - cough)* bry b7.de* coc-c bg2 kreos bg2 laur b7.de* nux-v b7.de* phos h2* plb b7.de* rhod bg2 rhus-t b7.de* sabad b7.de* sars b4.de* seneg b4.de* stront-c b4.de*
- **Trachea**; in: bar-c k* carb-an k* dig k* kreos k* laur sabad k*

RUNNING agg.: cina k* *Con* hr1 iod k* merc k* seneg k* sil k* stann k* sul-ac k*

SALIVATION; from: nat-m bg2 valer b7.de*

SALT food: alum k* *Con* k* lach k*

- **pepper** in larynx; as if from salt food and: crot-h
- **throat**; as if from salt food in: cann-xyz bg2

SAW; like a (See Sibilant - dry)

SCARLATINA; following: *Am-c* b4a.de ant-c k* con k* hyos k*

SCRAPING: *Alumn* k* bell k* bry bg2* calc k* *Caust* cham cimx k* coff k* dros eup-per *Euphr* eupi k* grat k* *Hep* k* kali-c k* kreos k* lyc k* merc nat-c k* nicc k* nit-ac *Nux-v* k* plan k* puls k* rhod k* sabad samb *Sel* sep k* sil k* spong **Stann** k* zing k*

- **evening**: bry k* rhod k* stann h2*
  - • **lying** down agg.; after: bry k*
- **night**: calc k* cham nat-m k* rhod k*
  - • **waking**; on: calc k*

○ - **Chest**: *Ang* b7a.de arg-met bry con kali-bi k* kreos k* *Puls* ruta k* staph k* *Thuj*

○ • **Upper**, in: ruta

- **Fauces**: **Dros** k* kali-bi a1
- **Larynx**; in: aesc agn aloe alum *Alumn* *Am-c* ambr arg-n aur-m-n bar-c *Bell* k* borx bov **Brom** k* *Bry* k* cain camph **Carb-v** *Carbn-s* card-m *Caust* chel chinin-s *Coc-c* k* colch *Con* croc *Cycl* k* dig **Dros** graph **Hep** hydr-ac kali-bi kalm kreos laur led mag-c mag-m mang naja nit-ac **Nux-v** ol-an op osm paeon petr ph-ac phyt plat prun **Puls** k* *Sabad* **Sel** *Seneg* sil sin-n syph ter thuj til upa
- **Pharynx**; in: arg-n cycl graph h2 hep h2 kali-bi
- **Sternum**; under: cann-i c1
- **Throat**: am-c bg2 bry bg2 graph bg2 kreos b7a.de *Nux-v* b7a.de phyt bg2 puls b7.de* sabad b7.de* sul-ac bg2
- **Trachea**; in: bry cycl *Puls* sabad thuj

SCRATCHING: brom a1 cann-i tl1 kali-c k* nat-c h2 rhodi br1 ribo rly4• zing k*

○ - **Chest**; in: bry bg2 kreos bg2 puls b7a.de*

- **Larynx**; in: *Acon* alum alumn *Am-c* ang arg-n arn bart con bg2 dig k* kreos k* mag-m nux-m petr *Phos* psor puls sabad sil staph sul-ac zing
- **Throat**; in: acon bg2 agn b7.de* ambr b7.de* carb-v h2 croc b7.de* kali-bi bg2 kreos b7a.de* mag-m h2 petr bg2* phos h2 sabad bg2
- **Trachea**; in: acon agar bry bg2 cimx cycl bg2 dig k* kreos k* puls k*

SCREAMING (See Crying)

SCREECHING shrill, in painless paroxysmal: *(↗Shrill)* stram k*

SEA wind, from (See Wind; in - sea)

SEASONS:

- **autumn** agg.: caps *Cina* k* *Iod* k* kreos k* lac-ac k* mucor-a-p bc2 verat k*
  - • **spring**; and (See spring - autumn)
- **spring** agg.: ambr k* *Cina* k* *Gels* kreos k* lac-ac k* syph hr1 verat k*
  - • **autumn**; and: cina k* kreos lac-ac
- **summer** agg.: sang hr1
- **winter**; in: acon k* aloe bro1 am-c bg2 *Ant-s-aur* bro1 ant-t ptk1 ars h2* bry bro1 cham k* *Coc-c* dulc eupi ichth br1 ip bro1 kali-bi k2 kali-c bg2 kali-m ptk1 *Kreos* k* lip bro1 nat-m ptk1 *Nit-ac* k* nux-m bg2 *Petr* b4a.de plan *Psor* k* *Rumx* sep h2* *Stann* k* staph k* *Syph* hr1
  - • **alternating** with sciatica in summer: staph
  - • **old** people: am-c k* ammc mrr1 ant-c ptk1 **Ant-t** mrr1 *Kreos* k* psor

SERIES, in: phos k* sumb k*

- **10**-11 h: sumb

SEVERE (See Violent)

SHAKING the body: *(↗Racking)* ant-c b7.de* *Bell* b4a.de *Ip* b7.de* *Led* b7.de* m-ambo b7.de m-arct b7.de *Merc* b4a.de olnd b7.de* **Puls** b7.de* rhus-t b7.de*

SHARP: arn k* calc-s k* *Lach* hr1 *Phos* hr1 staph k* syph hr1

- **eating**; after: staph k*

SHATTERING (See Racking)

SHAVING agg.: carc tpw2* cortiso tpw7*

SHIVERING; during: rhus-t b7.de

SHOCKS; from:

○ - **Chest**; in: nux-v b7.de*

- **Heart**; of (See Palpitation)

SHORT: **Acon** k* *Aesc* k* aeth k* agar k* *Alum* k* alum-p k2 am-c k* anac k* ang k* ant-c k* ant-t k* *Apoc* k* arg-met k* arg-n k* arn k* *Ars* k* ars-s-r hr1 asaf b7a.de* asar k* aur k* aur-ar k2 aur-i k2 aur-m k* aur-s k2 *Bell* k* berb k* bism hr1 both-ax tsm2 brom k* *Bry* k* cadm-s *Calc* k* calc-i k2 calc-s k* camph k* canth k* carb-ac k* carb-v k* carbn-o carbn-s card-m k* casc k* *Caust* k* *Chel* k* *Chin* k* chinin-ar chinin-s chr-ac hr1 cimic k* cimx a1* cina cinnb cob k* coc-c k* cocc *Cod* k* **Coff** k* colch k* *Coll* hr1 coloc k* con k* cop croc cupr k* cur k* cycl h1 dig k* digin a1 dros k* dulc k* eup-per k* euph k* eupi k* *Ferr-i* ferr-p k* fl-ac k* granit-m es1• *Graph* k* *Ham* hr1 hep k* hydr a1 hydr-ac hyos k* hyper k* **Ign** k* iod k* ip k* iris jatr-c kali-ar kali-bi k* kali-c k* kali-chl k* kali-i k* kali-m k2 kali-n k* *Kali-p* kali-perm kola stb3• kreos k* lac-d k* lac-del hrn2• *Lach* k* lachn k* lact k* laur k* led k* linu-c a1 lob k* *Lyc* k* m-arct b7.de mag-c mag-m h2* *Merc* k* merc-c hr1 *Mez* k* mur-ac k* naja nat-ar nat-c k* *Nat-m* k* nat-p *Nit-ac* k* nit-s-d a1* *Nux-m* hr1 *Nux-v* k* oena k* olnd k* osm k* ozone sde2• paull k* *Petr* k* *Phos* k* pin-s k* plac-s rly4• *Plat* k* *Plb* k* podo puls k* **Rhus-t** k* rumx ruta fd4.de sabad k* samb hr1* sang ptk1 seneg k* **Sep** k* sin-n k* spig k* *Spong* k* *Squil* k* **Stann** k* stict *Still* k* stront-c k* *Sul-ac* k* sul-i k2 sulph k* tab k* *Tell* k* tep k* ter a1* teucr k* *Thuj* k* tub ptk1* vanil fd5.de verat-v k* viol-o k* zinc k* zinc-p k2 zing ziz k*

- **daytime**: arg-met cot a1 kali-bi nat-c k* phos k*
  - • **and** night: *Lach* hr1 mez
- **morning**: agar k* am-br k* arn k* ars k* croc dulc fd4.de kali-bi k* lyc k* nit-ac thuj k* vanil fd5.de
  - • **rising** agg.; after: am-br k* arn k* dulc fd4.de vanil fd5.de
  - • **tea** drinking, after: ars k*
  - • **waking**; on: (non: dig slp) digin a1* dulc fd4.de vanil fd5.de
- **forenoon**: agar k* alum k* coc-c k* dulc fd4.de rhus-t k*
  - • **11** h: rhus-t
- **afternoon**: anac k* cench k2 chinin-s laur k* nat-m k* ruta fd4.de vanil fd5.de
  - • **14** h: laur
  - • **16** h: cench k2
  - • **17** h: nat-m
- **evening**: alum k* bar-c k* *Bell* carb-v k* carc fd2.de• chel k* cimic k* **Ign** k* kali-bi k* lyc k* phos k* ruta fd4.de *Sep* k* sulph thuj k* vanil fd5.de

- **evening**: ...
  - **bed** agg.; in: lyc k* *Sep* k* vanil fd5.de
  - **sleep** agg.; during: sulph
  - **smoking** agg.: thuj k*
  - **undressing**, on: chel k*
- **night**: arg-n k* bell k* *Calc Cod* a1 coloc a1 mez rhus-t k* vanil fd5.de
  - **midnight**:
    - **before**: *Rhus-t* k*
    - **23** h: rhus-t
    - **after**: acon k* *Ars* k*
    - **wakens**: *Rhus-t*
  - **bed** agg.; in: arg-n k* *Calc*
- **air** agg.; in open: ang seneg spig
- **alternating** with | **deep** cough: apoc
- **breathing** deep agg.: *Aesc* k* con a1
- **dinner**; after: agar k*
- **eating**; after: anac k* caust k* ter k*
- **frequent**: fl-ac
- **inspiration** agg.: nat-ar
- **irritation** in larynx; from: am-c seneg spong
- **lying**, after eating: caust ter k*
- **motion** agg.: carbn-o
- **sitting** up in bed | **amel.**: *Arg-n* k* cinnb nat-c k*
- **sleep** | **siesta** agg.; after: rhus-t k*
- **smoking** agg.: coca thuj
- **swallowing** agg.: *Aesc* k*
- **talking** agg.: ant-t k*
- **tickling** in larynx, from: *Acon* agar *Ang* carb-an h2 carc fd2.de• cimic fic-m gya1 graph iris kali-bi laur led mag-c h2 mez *Spong*
- **walking**:
  - **rapidly**:
    - **agg.**: seneg
    - **air**; in open: ang sulph h2

SHRILL: *(↗Screeching)* ant-t med hr1 sol-t-ae k* stram k* tab bg2
- **waking**; on: sol-t-ae k*

SIBILANT: bros-gau mrc1 kreos prun *Spong* k*
- **dry**, like a saw driven through a pine board; sibilant and: *Spong* k*

SINGING agg.: alum k* *Ambr* bro1 anac bro1 *Arg-met* k* *Arg-n* k* arge-pl rwt5• arum-t bro1 carb-v bro1 carc tpw2* *Caust* bro1 cimic bro1 coll bro1 *Con* bro1 *Dros* k* dulc fd4.de ferr-p bg2 *Hep* bro1 hyos k* irid-met bro1 kali-bi bg3* lach bro1 mang *Mang-act* bro1 menth bro1 meph k* nux-v bro1 **Phos** k ●* rhus-t k* rumx k* sil k* spong k* *Stann* k* stram k* sulph bro1 tritic-vg fd5.de vanil fd5.de
- **raising** the voice, from: **Arg-n** k*

SIT UP, must: *(↗Lying - agg.)* acon vh1 *Agar Ant-t* k* aral *Ars* k* arum-t lp **Bry** k ●* caust chinin-s choc srj3• *Coc-c* colch **CON** k ●* crot-t eupi *Ferr* ferr-ar gamb hep hyos b7a.de* *Iod Kali-bi* k* kali-i bg2 kreos lach mag-m mag-s mang bg2 nat-s k* nicc k* olib-sac wmh1 phel bg2* **PHOS** k ●* plan **PULS** k ●* ruta fd4.de *Sang* k* *Seneg* **Sep** k ●* sil sne staph k* sul-i k2 tarent bg2
- **commences**; as soon as cough: ars *Bry* k* caust *Coc-c* colch **Con** hep lach plan
- **cough** it out, after which he can rest: **Con** k*

SITTING:
- **agg.**: agar aloe alum astac caps tl1 euphr k* ferr k* guaj hell k* kali-c mag-c k* mag-m k* mur-ac nat-c nat-p k* ph-ac k* phos k* puls k* *Rhus-t* sabad k* *Seneg* k* sep k* spig stann zinc k* zinc-p k2
- **bent** forward:
  - **agg.**: rhus-t k* spig stann k*
  - **amel.**: aral vh1 choc srj3• iod k* stann c1
- **erect**:
  - **agg.**: acon bg2 kali-c k* nat-m k* spong k* stram bg2
  - **amel.**: ant-t k* hyos tl1 puls tl1 spong fd4.de
- **long** time agg.; for a: coc-c ph-ac
- **still**:
  - **agg.**: coca rhus-t
    - **afternoon**: coca

Sitting – **still**: ...
  - **amel.**: verat

SITTING UP in bed:
- **agg.**: con h2 spong fd4.de
- **amel.** (See Lying - agg.; Sit up)

SLEEP:
- **after** | **agg.**: acon bg2 aeth bg3* ambr bg2 *Apis* k* *Aral* arum-i a1 bell bg3* brom bro1 calc bg2 *Caust* k* chin bg2 cina bg2 coc-c bg2 dig bg2 euphr bg2 ign bg2 ip bg3* *Kali-bi* kreos bg2 **Lach** k* lachn lyc bg2 nit-ac k* nux-v bg2 ph-ac bg2 puls k* rhus-t bg2 *Sep* spong bg2* squil bg2 stram bg2 sul-ac bg2 sulph k* verat bg3*
- **before**: *Coc-c* lyc merc **Sulph** k*
- **disturbing**●: *(↗preventing; SLEEP - Disturbed - cough)* *Agar* k* alum bism h1* calad *Cina* hr1 cortiso gse irid-met srj5• mez nat-sil fd3.de• nux-v ol-j *Osm* hr1 phos *Puls* mrr1 rhod rhus-t samb pd sang sep h2* spong k* squil k* stict k* **Sulph** k* syph zinc
  - **children**; in: **Puls** mrr1 sulph mtf33
- **during**:
  - **agg.**●: *Acon* k* *Agar* k* alum h2* *Apis Aral* bro1 *Arn* k* ars arum-t bac pd* *Bell* k* calc k* carb-an k* **Cham** k* cina tl1 coff k* *Con* b4a.de *Cycl* k* hipp k* hyos k* ip gsy1 kali-p fd1.de• ketogl-ac rly4• kreos **Lach** k* lachn bg2 lyc k* lycps-v m-ambo b7.de m-aust b7.de mag-s merc k* murx nit-ac k* op b7a.de *Petr* phos psor mtf33 rhod *Rhus-t* k* samb k* sang sep k* sil stram k* *Sulph* k* tritic-vg fd5.de tub k* vanil fd5.de verb k*
    - **deep** sleep: samb
    - **first** sleep; after: aral bg2*
    - **short** sleep; after: *Aral* vh1
- **falling** asleep:
  - **before**: *Agn* b7a.de
  - **when**: carb-an bg2 nit-ac bg2 nux-v bg2 puls bg2 sep bg2
- **falls** asleep during dry cough: mag-s
- **going** to, on: *Agar* agn apis b7a.de aral lp arn brom *Carb-v* coff b7a.de *Con* guare *Hep* k* ign *Kali-c* **Lach Lyc** m-arct b7.de med merc k* nat-sil fd3.de• nit-ac petr-ra shn4• *Phos* sep **Sulph**
  - **hour** after; one: aral arn calc
  - **lying** on side, when: *Arg-n* kali-c *Lyc Psor Spong*
- **preventing**●: *(↗disturbing)* am-m gsy1 anac h2* apis bell k2 calad k* carb-v k* caust h2* *Cupr* hr1 daph k* helx gm1 kali-bi k* kali-c kali-cy k* kola stb3• laur **Lyc** k* *Nux-v* hr1 *Ol-j* hr1 phos **Puls** k* *Rhus-t* k* sang **Sep** k* spong fd4.de stict k* sulph h2* tritic-vg fd5.de tub c1 zinc k*
  - **children**; in: lyc mtf33 **Puls** mrr1
- **starting** from sleep; when: apis k* cina hep k*
- **wakens** from●: *(↗Night - waking)* acon k* *Agar* k* alum k* *Apis Aral* arizon-l nl2• arn *Ars* k* bell k* bism a1 calc carb-v k2 carbn-s **Caust** k* cham *Coc-c* k* cocc coff con k* daph dros graph hep k* hipp *Hyos* k* kali-c k* kali-n *Lach* k* mag-m k* med merc nat-sil fd3.de• nit-ac op *Petr* **Phos** k* positr nl2• puls ptk1 rhod *Rhus-t* k* ruta kr1 samb ptk1 *Sang* k* sanguis-s hm2• *Sep* k* *Sil* k* sol-t-ae spong ptk1 squil **Sulph** k* tritic-vg fd5.de verb zinc k* zing
  - **not** waking from the cough: arn ptk1 bac ptk1 cham ptk1* cycl br1* lach ptk1 lycps-v ptk1 nit-ac ptk1* verb ptk1
    - **children**; in: cham br1* *Cycl* br1 nit-ac br1*

SLIGHT: loxo-lae bnm12•

SMARTING (See Burning - chest)

SMOKE:
- **all** kinds; of: euphr kola stb3• limest-b es1• menth
- **as** from: ars bg2 euphr bg2 nat-ar bg2 ol-an bg2
- **sensation** of smoke; from | **Trachea**; in: *Ars* bry nat-ar ozone sde2•
- **tobacco** smoke (See Tobacco - agg.)

SMOKING:
- **agg.**: *(↗Tobacco - agg.)* *Acon* k* agar all-s aral vh1 arg-n k* ars ptk1 atro brom bry k* *Calc* b4a.de carb-an cham clem k* coc-c coca cocc *Coloc* k* *Dros* k* *Euphr* k* ferr k* hell k* hep hydrog srj2• ign k* iod k* irid-met srj5• lac-ac lach *M-arct* b7.de* mag-c menth merc ptk1 nux-v k* osm petr k* psil ft1 puls k* queb mtf11 rad-br ptk1* spig spong k* staph k* sul-ac sul-i k2 taosc iwa1• tarent thuj
  - **evening**: *Arg-n* k* coloc thuj
  - **dinner**; after: acon bry coc-c dros *Lach* petr

Cough

- **amel.**: *Arg-n* ptk1 euphr ptk1 hep ptk1 ign ptk1 merc ptk1 sep ptk1 tarent ptk1
  - **night**: tarent

SMOTHERED: meli k*

SMOTHERING in throat; from: *(↗Constriction)* lach

SNEEZING:
- **agg.**: agar ptk1 alum ptk1 bell ptk1 bry ptk1 cina bg2* lob ptk1 petr a1 psor ptk1 seneg k* *Squil* ptk1
- **amel.**: osm k*
- **ends** in sneezing; cough: **Agar** k* *Arg-n* k* bad k* *Bell* k* bry caps h1* *Carb-v* st cina bg2* dros bro1 hep k* just bro1* lyc k* psor *Rumx* lp seneg k* *Squil* k* *Sulph* k*
- **preceded** by sneezing: ip bg2
- **with**: *(↗NOSE - Coryza - cough - with)* agar bg2 all-c alum k* anac k* ant-t k* aspar bad k* *Bell* k* *Bry* k* carb-an carb-v k* chel bg2 chin *Cina* k* *Con* cortiso tpw7 dulc fd4.de eup-per hep k* iod just br1 kali-c kreos lach bg2 lob k* lyc bg2 merc *Nat-m* nit-ac k* nux-v k* osm ozone sde2• psil ft1 *Rumx* lp sabad bg2 sal-ac k* seneg bg2 sep k* sil spong fd4.de squil staph *Sulph* suprar rly4• vanil fd5.de
  - **morning**: cortiso tpw7*

SNORING, with: ant-t arg-met bell caust *Chin* b7.de* hyos b7a.de ip nat-c nat-m nux-v puls sep squil b7a.de

SNOWFALL; cough in children from exposure to: sep

SOLID food agg.: cupr b7a.de*

SONOROUS: *(↗Deep-sounding)* **Stram**

SOUNDLESS (See Toneless)

SOUR FOOD agg.: alum ptk1 ant-c k* brom k* con b4a.de* lach k* nat-m k* nux-v k* **Sep** k ●* sulph k*

SPASM (See Convulsions)

SPASMODIC: *(↗Paroxysmal)* acon k* **Agar** k* *All-c* alum bg2 am-br k* am-caust **Ambr** k* aml-ns vh1 anac k* *Anan* ant-ar bro1 ant-c bg2 *Ant-t* b7a.de* apis aral bro1* *Arg-n* arn bg2* *Ars* k* ars-i ars-s-f k2 arum-t asar bro1 asc-t aur k* aur-i k2 aur-s k2 bac jl2 *Bad* bar-c k* bar-i k2 bar-s k2 **Bell** k* borx bg2 bov brom k* **Bry** k* *Cact* *Calc* k* calc-f calc-i k2 calc-s calc-sil k2 *Caps* k* carb-ac c1* *Carb-an* **Carb-v** k* carbn-s castm castn-v br1 *Caust* k* cer-ox br1 *Cham* bg2* *Chel* k* **Chin** k* chinin-ar chlf *Chlol* *Chlor* cimic **Cina** k* *Coc-c* k* **Cocc** coff k* coll coloc *Con* k* **Cor-r** k* corn croc bg2 *Crot-c* crot-t bro1 **Cupr** k* *Cupr-act* bro1 cur *Dig* k* diphtox jl2 **Dros** k* *Dulc* k* euph euphr bg2 *Ferr* k* ferr-ar ferr-i ferr-m ferr-p *Gels* k* glyc bro1 *Hep* k* hippoz jl2 hydr-ac k* **Hyos** k* *Ign* k* indg *Iod* k* **Ip** k* *Just* bro1 kali-ar kali-bi k* **Kali-br** k* *Kali-c* k* *Kali-chl* kali-p kali-sil k2 ketogl-ac rly4• *Kreos* k* **Lac-ac** lac-leo sk4• lach k* *Lact* *Lact-v* bro1 laur k* *Led* k* *Lob* lyc k* lyss jl2 *M-ambo* b7.de *M-arct* b7.de* *Mag-c* k* *Mag-m* k* mag-p k* meli *Meph* k* *Merc* k* merc-c k* mez k* mosch k* naphtin bro1 nat-ar *Nat-m* k* nat-sil fd3.de• nit-ac k* nux-m bro1 **Nux-v** k* oena op k* osm k* pert br1* petr ph-ac k* *Phos* k* *Plb* k* *Psor* **Puls** k* rad-br c11* *Rhus-t* k* **Rumx** k* ruta fd4.de sabad bg2 sal-ac *Samb* k* *Sang* k* santin bro1 **Sep** k* ser-a-c jl2 sil k* spig bg2 **Spong** k* *Squil* k* stann bg2* staph k* stict bro1 still stram k* stry sul-ac sul-i k2 *Sulph* k* syc bka1*• tab *Tarent* *Thuj* k* trif-p bro1 tritic-vg fd5.de *Verat* k* verat-v verb k* vinc viol-o c2* xan c1 *Zinc* k* zinc-p k2
- **daytime**:
  - **amel.**: bell euph ign lyc spong
  - **only**: *Agar* staph
- **morning**: *Agar* carb-v dig ferr k* ferr-m k* ferr-p k* ign iod ip kali-c kreos k* nat-ar nat-m ph-ac puls spong fd4.de squil stram k* sulph thuj k* tritic-vg fd5.de
  - **bed**: ferr
  - **eating** | **amel.**: ferr ferr-m k*
  - **rising** agg.; after: cina mtf33 ferr-p
  - **waking**; on: *Agar* thuj k*
- **forenoon**: *Agar* k* lact k* nat-sil fd3.de• sabad sep
- **noon**, until midnight: mosch
- **afternoon**: agar all-c bad **Bell** bry mur-ac zinc
- **evening**: all-c bad bar-c bell bry calc k* *Carb-v* k* carbn-o *Coc-c* *Ferr* k* ign *Ip* lach laur led mag-c k* *Mag-m* hr1 merc mez nat-ar nat-m nit-ac ph-ac *Phos* *Puls* k* rhus-t **Sep** k* sil spong fd4.de stann **Still** k* stram k* tarent k* verat-v k*
  - **midnight**; until: bar-c carb-v ferr led mag-c mez nit-ac *Puls* rhus-t *Sep* stann zinc

Spasmodic: ...
  - **after** midnight; until: mag-c mag-m
  - **sunset** to sunrise: aur
- **night**: *Agar* k* ambr mtf11 anac apis arg-n aur k* aur-ar k2 bad **Bell** *Bry* calc calc-f k* carb-v k2 **Chin** hr1 cina *Coc-c* coll com hr1 con k* cor-r k* **Dros** euph *Ferr* *Hep* hyos ign *Ip* k* kali-c k* lyc *Mag-c* k* *Mag-m* k* *Mag-p* hr1 meph merc *Op* petr k* *Phos* *Puls* k* *Sang* k* sil spong sulph k* tarent k* thuj k* *Verb* hr1 vinc
  - **midnight**: dig mosch *Sulph*
    - **before**: mur-ac rhus-t sabad *Spong*
    - **22.30 h**: carbn-s **Coc-c**
    - **after**: bell dig *Hyos* *Kali-c* squil syc pte1•
    - **afternoon**; until: mosch *Sulph*
  - **waking**; on: thuj k*
- **autumn**: caps
- **bronchitis**; people suffering from: pert jl2
- **chill**; during: *Puls* b7a.de sabad b7a.de
- **cold** drinks | **amel.**: *Ip* k*
- **drinking** agg.; after: *Bry* k* *Ferr* k*
- **eating** | **after** | **agg.**: bry b7a.de carb-v cocc **Ferr** k* hyos
  - **amel.**: *Ferr-m* k*
- **herpes**; with facial: am br1
- **inspiration**; deep | **amel.**: verb
- **laryngotracheitis**; with acute: naphtin ctb*
- **lying** agg.: **Coc-c** *Con* *Hyos* mag-p br1 meph puls ruta fd4.de *Sang* k*
- **old** people: *Ambr* *Ip*
- **reprimands**; after: mosch k2
- **slowly** growing weaker, as if from increasing closure of throat: ant-c bg2
- **smoking**:
  - **agg.**: lac-ac k* lac-c rad-br c11
  - **amel.**: tarent k*
- **summer** heat amel.: ars k*
- **swallowing** liquids agg.: caust tl1 sul-ac k*
- **talking**; after: ambr hr1 dig k*
- **temperature**; change of: *Spong*
- **touching** the ear canal: lach k2
- **tuberculosis**; in people suffering from: pert jl2
- **vomiting**; with: bry carb-v dros mtf33 ferr ip kali-c mtf33 puls
- **waking**; on: *Thuj* k*
- **whooping** cough; after●: **Sang** k*
- **winter**: ars psor
- **women**, peculiar to: aur k* *Cocc* *Hyos* *Ign*

SPEAKING (See Talking - agg.)

SPICES, from: *(↗Pungent)* alum bro1* stann bg2 sulph k* thuj b4.de*

SPINE, from: agar bg2* nux-m ptk1 tell ptk1

SPIRITS; drinking (See Alcohol)

SPLEEN:
- **complaints** of; from: card-m squil c2
- **enlarged** spleen or pain in spleen; with: squil ptk1

SPLITTING: aur k*
- **night**: aur k*

SPOKEN to, on being: ars k*

SPOT:
- **chest**; excited at a small spot in right: carb-an h2*
- **larynx**; as if from a dry spot in: cimic **CON** k ● crot-h *Nat-m* bg1
- **starting** from a spot: con bg2 crot-h bg2 lith-c bg2 nat-m bg2

SPRING; in the (See Seasons - spring)

SPRINGS (See Jumping)

STAGNATION; from sensation of: | **epigastrium**; in: guaj b4a.de

STANDING:
- **agg.**: acon aloe euphr k* ign k* mag-s nat-m nat-s sep k* stann sulph k* zinc k*
- **amel.**: mag-s
- **erect** | **agg.**: acon nat-m k* stann

- **sitting** agg.; after | **vice** versa; and: aloe[k*]
- **still**:
  - **agg.** | **walk**; during a: astac[bro1] ign[k*]

STERTOROUS: cact[k*]
- **night**: cact[k*]

STICKING:
- ○ - **Chest**; in: borx[tl1] iod
- **Larynx**; in: bapt[bg2] bufo lyc mur-ac naja[bg2] *Phos* *Sil* spir-n-d[bg2]
  - **1-4** h: bufo
- **Throat**; in: *Cham*[b7.de*] stann[b4.de*]

STIMULANTS (See Alcohol)

STINGING or burning tickling in larynx; from: *Agar* aphis bufo

STITCHING:
- ○ - **Chest**; in: *(↗CHEST - Pain - Cough - during - agg. - stitching)* acon ars[h2] bry nit-ac nux-v
- **Epigastric** region: rhus-t
- **Epigastrium**; in: am-c[b4a.de] ars[b4.de*] *Bry*[b7.de*] phos[b4.de*] sulph[b4.de*]
- **Epiglottis**: caps[hr1]
- **Hypochondria**: *Acon*[b7.de*] am-c[b4a.de] am-m[b7.de*] ars[b4.de*] aur[b4a.de] bry[b7.de*] *Lyc*[b4a.de] *Nit-ac*[b4a.de] phos[b4.de*] sabad[b7.de*] *Samb*[b7a.de] sep[b4a.de] sulph[b4.de*]
- **Larynx**; in: acon aphis bufo cham *Cist* hydr-ac indg kali-c naja ox-ac sol-t-ae stann
  - **evening**: bufo
- **Pharynx**; in: caps[h1*]
- **Throat**; in: lyc[h2] phos[h2]
- **Trachea**; in: *Arg-met* lach stann

STOMACH:
- **come** from the stomach; seems to: *(↗Pain - epigastrium)* all-s ant-t *Am*[c1] bar-c[bg2*] bell[k*] bism[bro1] **Bry**[k*] calad[bg2*] cann-s carc[mg1.de*] cench[k2] cer-o[bro1] cham[bg2*] con[bg1] ery-a ferr[bg1] guaj[bg2*] hep[bg2*] ign[bg2*] kali-bi[bg2*] kali-m[bg1*] lach[k*] *Lob*[bro1] lob-s[c2*] merc nat-m[bg2*] nit-ac[bg2*] *Nux-v*[k*] ph-ac[bg2*] phos[bg2*] plat[bg1] puls[k*] ribo[rly4•] rumx[mrr1] sang[bg2*] **Sep**[k*] sul-ac[bg2] sulph[bro1] tax[bro1] verat[bro1]
- **fullness** in stomach rises to throat and triggers coughing: rumx[mrr1]
- **turned** inside out; feeling as if stomach were: *Puls*[k*] ruta tab

STOOL: | **after** | **amel.**: bufo[bg2]
- **frequent** | **amel.**: bufo

STOOPING agg.: *(↗Bending)* all-s arg-met[k*] arg-n[k*] arn[k*] bar-c[k*] **Caust**[k*] chel dig *Hep*[k*] kali-c[k*] laur[k*] lyc[k*] phos *Sel*[b7a.de] seneg[k*] sil[k*] *Spig*[k*] spong[k*] staph[k*] verat[k*]

STORM with thunder (See Thunderstorm)

STORMY weather (See Weather - stormy - agg.)

STRAINING: aspar[k*] caust[k*] *Chel*[k*] cocc croc *Cupr*[k*] ip lach led nux-v par phos rhod rhus-t sel thuj[k*]
- **children**; in irritable: bell[h1*]

STRANGERS: *(↗Company; Nervous - enters; Persons - coming; MIND - Stranger - presence - agg.)*
- **presence** of; in the: *(↗Company; Nervous - enters; Persons - coming; MIND - Stranger - presence - agg.)* ambr[bg2] bar-c[bg2] caust[bg2] phos[bg2*]
  - **children**; in: bar-c[vh1] phos[mtf33]
- **sight** of; at: *Ars*[ptk1] bar-c[ptk1] phos[ptk1]
  - **children**; in: ambr[k*] *Ars* bar-c[k*] phos[k*]

STRANGLING (See Choking)

STRETCHING:
- **agg.**: merc
- **arms** | **agg.**: lyc[k*]

STRETCHING OUT: | **throat**; stretching the: lyc[h2*]

STUDENTS, of: nux-v[k*]

SUCKING:
- **candy**; on | **amel.**: *Rumx*[mrr1]

SUCKLING (the infant) (See Nursing)

SUDDEN: *Agar*[k*] alum[k*] am-br[k*] apoc[k*] calad[k*] coloc[k*] *Cupr* *Ip*[k*] kali-bi[k*] kali-c[k*] kali-p kali-s[fd4.de] naja nat-sil[fd3.de•] pert[jl2] polys[sk4•] positr[nl2•] *Sep*[k*] **Squil**[k*]
- **daytime**: agar coloc[k*]
- **morning**: am-br[k*] **Squil**[k*]
  - **rising** agg.: am-br[k*]
- **forenoon**: agar
- **evening**: alum[k*] *Am-br*[k*] apoc[k*]
  - **sitting** agg.: alum
- **night**: apoc[k*]

SUFFOCATIVE: *(↗Breathing - deficient; Choking)* acon[k*] adam[srj5•] *Agar* **Alum**[k*] alum-sil[k*] am-c[bg2] am-m[k*] ambr[h1*] aml-ns[vh1] anac[k*] anan[k*] *Ant-t*[k*] *Apis*[k*] apoc[k*] aq-pet[a1] *Arg-n*[k*] *Ars*[k*] ars-i ars-s-f[k2] aur[b4.de*] bar-c[k*] bar-i[k2] bar-s[k2] bell[k*] *Borx*[ptk1] *Brom*[k*] *Bry*[k*] calc[bg2] *Carb-an*[k*] **Carb-v**[k*] carbn-s *Caust*[k*] *Cham*[k*] chel **Chin**[k*] *Chinin-ar* **Cina**[k*] coc-c[k*] cocc[k*] coloc[bg2] *Con*[k*] cor-r[br1] crot-h[k*] **Cupr**[k*] *Cycl*[k*] del[a1] der[k*] **Dios**[bg2] **Dros**[k*] euph[b4a.de*] euphr[k*] eupi[k*] guaj[b4a.de*] guare[k*] **Hep**[k*] hydr-ac[k*] **Hyos**[k*] ign[k*] indg[k*] *Iod*[k*] **Ip**[k*] kali-ar kali-bi[k*] *Kali-c*[k*] kali-i[k*] kali-n[bg2] kali-s kali-sil[k2] kreos[k*] *Lach*[k*] lact[k*] *Led*[k*] lyc[k*] *M-arct*[b7.de*] mag-p mang meph[k*] *Merc*[k*] merc-c[bg2] nat-m[k*] nit-ac[bg2] *Nux-m*[k*] **Nux-v**[k*] *Op*[k*] petr[k*] phel[k*] plb[bg2] psor[bg2] *Puls*[k*] rumx[bg2] ruta salv[br1] **Samb**[k*] *Sang*[ptk1] *Seneg*[ptk1] *Sep*[k*] sil[k*] spig[k*] *Spong*[k*] squil[k*] stram[k*] sul-i[k2] **Sulph**[k*] *Tab*[k*] tarent[k2] tep[k*] thuj *Tub* verat[k*] zinc[k*]
- **daytime**: anac[k*]
- **morning**: coc-c ruta[fd4.de]
  - **lying** down agg.: coc-c
  - **rising** agg.; after: **Cina**[k*]
- **noon**: *Arg-n*[k*]
- **evening**: *Carb-an*[k*] cina indg[k*] *Ip*[k*] *Lach* nat-m[k*]
  - **18** h: am-m
  - **19** h: **Ip**[k*]
  - **bed** agg.; in: indg[k*] nat-m[h2*]
- **night**: ars[k*] bell[k*] bry carb-an *Carb-v* cham *Chin*[k*] coc-c[k*] *Cupr*[k*] **Hep**[k*] indg ip lyc petr[h2*] ruta sil thuj
  - **midnight**: cham *Dros* *Ruta* **Samb**
    - **after**: ars[h2*] chin *Kali-c*[k*] *Samb*
      - **2** and **4** h: chin
      - **5** h: *Kali-c*[k*]
- **children**; in:
  - **appears** dead during paroxysm; child: cupr[mtf33] meph[br1]
  - **stiff** and blue in the face; child becomes: *Cupr*[k*] **Ip**[k*]
- **eating** and drinking, after: bry
- **gurgling** down in throat, then: cina[ptk1]
- **inspiration** agg.. cina
- **lying** agg.: spong
- **sleep** agg.; during: aral carb-an **Lach**
- **stiff** and blue in face; child becomes (See children - stiff)
- **swallowing** agg.: **Brom**
- **walking** agg.: ars[k*]

SUGAR:
- **agg.**: med[bro1] *Spong*[bro1] zinc[k*]
- **amel.**: spong[mrr1] sulph
- **dissolving** in larynx; as if sugar was: bad

SULPHUR fumes or vapor; cough agg. by a sensation of: am-c[k*] am-m[vh1] aml-ns[k*] **Ars**[k*] asaf *Brom*[k*] bry[k*] calc[k*] *Carb-v*[k*] *Chin*[k*] cina[k*] **Ign**[k*] ip[k*] kali-chl[k*] *Lach*[k*] **Lyc**[k*] mosch[k*] naja[bg2] *Par*[k*] **Puls**[k*]
- **evening** before sleep: ars[h2]

SUN agg.: ant-c[bg2*] *Ant-t*[k*] coca

SUPPER: | **after** | **agg.**: nat-ar
- **during**: carb-v[k*]

SUPPORT, must (See Hold)

SUPPRESSING the cough: | **amel.**: ign[bg2]

SUPPRESSION of complaints or discharges agg.: lach bg2 senec bg2

SURPRISE, happy (See Happy)

SWALLOWING:
- **agg.**: *Aesc* k* **Brom** k* choc srj3• *Cupr* k* eug k* kali-perm lyc k* lyss k* *Nat-m* k* op k* phos k* puls k* spong bro1 sul-ac k*
  - **wrong** way; from swallowing the: acon bg2 spig b7.de*
- **amel.**: apis k* eug k* hydrog srj2• spong k* verat bg2
- **empty**:
  - **agg.**: caust lyc k* *Nat-m* k* op
  - **amel.**: bell k*
- **must** swallow | **cough**; after (See THROAT - Swallowing - must - cough)

SWEETMEATS:
- **agg.**: bad bg3* med k* spong k* sulph hr1 zinc k*
- **amel.**: psil ft1 sulph ptk1

SWEETS (See Sugar)

SWELLING:
- **larynx**; from swelling of: *Kali-i*
  - **sensation** of swelling; from: ars ox-ac
- **neck**; from swelling of: ars bg2 *Coff* bg2 kali-bi bg2
- **throat** | **sensation** of swelling; from: ars b4.de*

SYMPATHETIC: ambr bg2 apis bg2 cadm-s bg2 carb-v bg2 carc mlr1• card-m cimic bg2 cina bg2 dros ign bg2 kali-bi bg2 kali-br bg2 **Lach** k* **Naja** nat-m bg2 nux-v bg2 phos bg2 plat bg2 plb bg2 sep bg2 sul-ac bg2 verb bg2
- **night**: card-m k*

TALKING:
- **agg.**: acon k* alum k* alum-p k2 *Alumn* k* *Ambr* k* anac k* ant-t arg-met k* *Arg-n* k* arn k* ars k* ars-i k2 arum-t bro1 atro k* bar-c k* bar-i k2 bar-s k2 *Bell* k* brom bry k* calad k* calc k* *Calc-s* calc-sil k2 *Carb-v* k* carbn-s carc mg1.de* *Caust* k* cham k* *Chin* k* chinin-ar *Cimic* k* cina coc-c k* *Cocc* k* coll bro1* con k* crot-c sk4• crot-h k* *Cupr* k* dig k* **Dros** k* dulc k* erig erio a1 *Euphr* k* ferr k* ferr-ar ferr-i ferr-p ham fd3.de• hed sp1 *Hep* k* hyos k* ign k* iod k* ip k* irid-met bro1* kali-bi kali-s fkr2.de lac-c *Lach* k* mag-c k* mag-m k* mag-p malar jl2 mang k* *Mang-act* bro1 menth k* meph k* *Merc* k* merc-c hr1 mez k* mur-ac k* myric k* nat-m k* nit-ac k* nux-v bro1 ozone sde2• par ph-ac k* *Phos* k* phys hr1 *Phyt* psil ft1 *Psor* k* rauw sp1 rhus-t k* **Rumx** k* sang mtf11 **Sanic** k* *Sil* k* *Spong* k* squil k* *Stann* k* stram k* stront-c sk4• sul-ac k* sul-i k2 sulph k* sumb k* tritic-vg fd5.de *Tub* vanil fd5.de verb k* [heroin sdj2]
  - **evening**: psor
  - **night**: puls
- **impossible**: *Am-m* k* brom calad *Cimic* k* *Cupr* k* *Lach* mag-p *Merc* *Rumx*
- **loudly** agg.: (↗*Voice - overuse)* *Ambr* *Arg-n* *Coc-c* k* cocc tl1 mang *Phos* puls hr1 *Tub*

TALL, slender, tuberculous subjects; in: (↗*Tuberculous)* phos k*

TEA agg.: ferr k* spong k*
- **hot**: spong

TEARING: all-c *Bell* borx calc castn-v tl1 ip tl1 med phos rhus-t ptk1 senec syph jl2 tarent tl1 x-ray sp1
- **night**: *Bell* senec
- **menses**; during: senec

○ - **Cardiac** region; tearing sensation in elaps
- **Throat**; from: carc gk6

TEASING (See Tormenting)

TEA-TASTERS; in: | **fungus**; from inhaling the: kali-i br1

TEDIOUS: form tub

TEMPERATURE, change of: (↗*Warm - room - agg.; Warm - room - agg. - cold; Warm - room - entering - air)* acon sne aran-ix sp1 carb-v bg2 cur sne dulc fd4.de graph sne ichth sne ip bg2 kali-c bg2* lach bg2* lact sne *Phos* bg2* polyg-h sne rumx bg2* seneg mrr1* sep bg2* sil bg2 verb bg2*

TENSION in chest: (↗*CHEST - Tension - cough)* apis tl1 ars k* thuj

THINKING of it agg.: (↗*Mental - agg.)* bar-c k* nat-sil fd3.de• nux-v k* *Ox-ac*

THREE coughs in paroxysm (See Paroxysmal - consisting - three)

THUNDERSTORM; before: phos k* sil k*

TICKLING: (↗*Titillating)* acet-ac k* **Acon** k* agath-a nl2• aids nl2• alum k* alumn k* am-c k* am-m k* *Ambr* k* anac k* androc srj1• ang k* ant-c mrr1 ant-t k* apeir-s mlk9.de apis b7a.de* *Arg-met* arg-n k* arge-pl rwt5• *Arn* k* ars k* arum-t k* *Asaf* k* atro k* bamb-a stb2.de• bar-c bar-s k2 *Bell* k* bov k* *Brom* k* *Bry* k* cain *Calc* k* calc-p k* canth k* *Carb-an* k* *Carb-v* k* *Caust* k* **Cham** k* chin k* chinin-ar cimic k* cina *Coc-c* k* *Coca* cocc k* colch k* coloc k* **Con** k* **Crot-c** crot-h hr1 cupr k* cypra-eg sde6.de• dig *Dros* k* erio a1 *Euph* b4a.de *Euphr* falco-pe nl2• ferr k* ferr-ar ferr-i k2 *Ferr-p* granit-m es1• graph k* ham k* helodr-cal knl2• helx c1* hep k* hydr-ac bg2 *Hydrog* srj2• **Hyos** k* *Ign* k* inul k* *Iod* k* **Ip** k* irid-met srj5• *Iris* *Kali-bi* k* **Kali-c** k* kali-n k* kali-p kali-perm kali-s **Lach** k* lact laur k* led linu-c a1 **Lyc** k* mag-c k* mag-m k* mag-p br1 merc k* morg-g fmm1• morg-p pte1*• mur-ac k* naja nat-c k* **Nat-m** k* nat-p k* nit-ac k* nit-s-d a1 **Nux-v** k* ol-an ol-j k* *Olib-sac* wmh1 olnd op k* petr k* *Ph-ac* k* *Phos* k* plut-n srj7• positr nl2• prun *Puls* k* *Rhus-t* k* *Rumx* k* ruta fd4.de sabad k* *Sabin* k* salv c2* **Sang** k* sars k* senec bg2 *Seneg* k* **Sep** k* sil k* *Spong* k* *Squil* k* *Stann* k* **Staph** k* stict bg2 sulph k* symph fd3.de• *Tab* k* tarax b7.de* teucr *Thuj* k* tub c tub-a br1 verat k* zinc k* zinc-p k2 [bell-p-sp dcm1 heroin sdj2]
- **daytime**: coloc k* lyc k* nat-m staph h1*
  - **and** night: nat-m
- **morning**: alumn k* bov a1 cain carb-v k* coloc iod h lyc k* morg-g pte1*• nat-m k* olib-sac wmh1 ruta fd4.de spong fd4.de sumb thuj
  - **rising** agg.; after: alumn k* *Arn* ruta fd4.de
  - **waking**; on: limest-b es1•
  - **walking** agg.; after: carb-v
- **afternoon**: ruta fd4.de
  - **15 h**: agath-a nl2• hep
- **evening**: alumn k* calc-p k* carb-v chin k* cimic coloc k* lyc k* merc nat-m k* *Ph-ac* rhus-t sulph k*
  - **18 h** | **expectoration** of mucus amel.: sulph
  - **midnight**, until: rhus-t
  - **bed** agg.; in: calc-p k*
  - **falling** asleep, before: merc
  - **going** to sleep, on: lyc k*
- **night**: aids nl2• arg-n k* *Asaf* *Calc* carc tpw2* chlf br1 coc-c *Coloc* k* *Dros* fic-m gya1 kali-bi kali-c lyc morg-g pte1*• myric nat-m k* rhus-t ros-d wla1 rumx sanic sep h2* zinc k*
  - **midnight**:
    - **after** | **3** h: cain
  - **lying** agg.: hyos mrr1
- **air** agg.; in open: *Lach* k* ox-ac k* **Phos**
- **breathing** deep agg.: nat-m h2
- **constant**: nat-c ptk1 op ptk1
- **eating**; after: kali-c h2*
- **lying** down agg.: limest-b es1• morg-g pte1*• [heroin sdj2]
- **overheated**; from being: *Brom* mrr1
- **smoking** agg.: atro k* coloc
- **talking** agg.: alumn k* atro k* **Ph-ac** phos hr1*
- **waking**; on: carb-v k* ham morg-g pte1*•
- **walking** agg.: nat-m h2*

○ - **Bronchi**: *Ant-t* arg-met bar-c cop dios ip kali-bi kali-n lac-del hm2• merc mez bg2 phos rhus-t sep stict tarent tritic-vg fd5.de *Verat* verat-v [tax jsj7]

○ • **Bifurcation**: (↗*Irritation - bronchi - bifurcation)* kali-bi k* **Ph-ac** rumx br1
- **Chest**: am-br bro1 *Ambr* bro1 *Ant-c* bro1 apis bro1 arn k* ars bro1 bar-c borx bov k* brom bro1 bry k* *Calc* bro1 caps bro1 *Carb-an* k* *Carb-v* bro1 *Caust* bro1 *Cham* k* chin k* cist k2 coc-c k* *Con* k* *Com* hr1 eup-per k* euph k* ferr-act bro1 graph ign k* iod k* ip bro1 irid-met srj5• *Kali-bi* k* kali-n k* kali-s kreos k* lach k* *Menth* bro1 *Merc* k* mur-ac k* myrt-c k* nat-c nat-m k* nat-p nat-sil fd3.de• *Nux-m* hr1 *Nux-v* k* *Osm* bro1 par bro1 **Ph-ac** k* **Phos** k* polyg-h puls bro1 pycnop-sa mrz1 rad-br bro1 rhus-t k* *Rumx* bro1 sang bro1 sars k* sep k* *Sil* bro1 *Spong* bro1* squil **Stann** k* sul-ac sulph k* tell *Verat* k* verat-v verb k* zinc k*

○ • **Upper**; in: merc k* *Nux-m* hr1 polyg-h zinc
- **Epigastrium**; in: ant-t hr1 bar-c k* bell k* bry k* guaj k* hep k* *Ign* b7a.de *Lach* k* *Nat-m* k* *Nit-ac* k* *Ph-ac* k* *Phos* sang k* tarax thuj k*

- **Fauces**; in: aloe carb-ac *Gels* k* lact k* til k*
- **Larynx**; in: *Acon Aesc Agar* agath-a nl2• **All-c** k* alum k* alum-sil k2 *Alumn* am-br *Am-c Am-m Ambr* anac *Anan* ang ant-t anth apis *Arg-met* k* *Arg-n Arn* **Ars** ars-i k2 *Asaf* aspar astac aur-m *Bad Bapt* a1* bar-c bar-i k2 bar-s k2 **Bell** k* borx bov *Brom* k* *Bry* bufo cact cadm-s cain calad *Calc* k* **Calc-f** k* calc-i k2 *Caps* k* *Carb-ac Carb-an Carb-v* k* *Carbn-s* carl *Caust* k* *Cham Chel* chlor cimic cimx cinnb *Cist* **Coc-c** k* cocc coch bro1 coff bg1 colch coloc **Con** k* cop **Crot-c** crot-h k* crot-t *Cupr Cycl* dig dios **Dros** k* *Dulc* k* ephe-si hsj1• ery-a bro1 euph *Euphr* eupi ferr-ar fic-m gya1 glon graph *Hep* k* hist sp1 hydr hydr-ac hydrog srj2• *Hyos Ign* k* **Iod** k* **Ip** k* *Iris Iris-foe Kali-bi Kali-c* kali-n kali-p kali-s kali-sil k2 kola stb3• kreos k* *Lac-c* **Lach** k* lact laur led limest-b es1• lob lob-s **Lyc** mag-c mag-m mang menth bro1 merc merc-c mez mur-ac naja nat-ar nat-c **Nat-m** nat-p nat-s nat-sil fd3.de• nicc *Nit-ac* k* **Nux-v** olnd onos op osm ox-ac par *Ph-ac* **Phos** k* *Phyt* plan podo fd3.de• *Prun Psor* k* **Puls** k* rad-br sze8• rat rhus-t *Rumx* k* *Sabin Sang* k* sars *Seneg Sep Sil* k* sol-ni spira **Spong** k* *Squil* stann **Staph** *Stict* k* sulph k* sumb symph fd3.de• tab tarent tep thuj til tritic-vg fd5.de verb *Vinc* zinc zing
  - **right** side: eupi c1 *Iris* bg2* stann bg2
  - **morning** | **rising** agg.; after: alumn arn *Op*
  - **afternoon**: agath-a nl2• anth mag-c naja
    - **14** h: arg-n **Coc-c**
  - **evening**: ambr carb-an h2 *Carb-v* cimic graph lyc nat-m
  - **night**: agar h2 cycl a1 *Dros*
    - **midnight**:
      - **before** | **23**.30 h: **Coc-c**
      - **at**: hep h2 phos h2
      - **after** | **3-4** h: *Bufo*
  - **down**; as from: calc *Cina* hr1 *Ph-ac* sulph
  - **insupportable**: arn hr1 kali-bi bg2
  - **lying** agg.: **Dros**
  - **severe**: chel bg2
  - **spot**; in a small: apis k* cimic con k*
  - **touching** the ear canal; from: lach k2
  - ▽ **extending** to:
    - **Chest**: sil
    - **Lungs**: ip bg2 stict hr1
    - **Midsternum**: rumx
  - ○ **Above**: calad c1
  - **Back** part of; in: apis bg2 *Bell* h1*
  - **Low** down in larynx: bry wl1 cina a1 hydr-ac a1
  - **Upper** part: acon bg2 ip h1*
- **Palate**; in: cham h1 dig h2 lach b7a.de nux-v b7.de* phos h2 rein a1
- **Pharynx**; in: anac arg-n ars carbn-s cham coc-c coca dulc fd4.de hydr-ac kali-s fkr2.de lact mag-s olnd plut-n srj7• sil
  - **night**: anac mag-s *Sil*
- **Precordial** region: bar-c verat
- **Sternum**; behind: ang bg2 caust bg2 cina a1 con bg2 hydrog srj2• iris bg2 polyg-h bg2 polyg-pe vml2• rad-br c11 rhus-t bg2* *Rumx* bg2 verat bg2 zinc h2*
- **Throat**; in: **Acon** bg2* agar bg2 alum b4.de* am-br bro1 am-c b4a.de* am-m b7.de* ambr b7.de* anac b4a.de* ang bg2 ant-t b7a.de* aral bro1* arg-met vh1 arg-n bg2* arn b7a.de* **Ars** b4a.de* bell b4a.de* borx b4a.de* bov b4a.de* brom bg2 **Bry** b7.de* calad bg2 calc b4.de* *Caps* bro1 carb-an bg2 carb-v b4a.de carc mrr1 *Caust* b4.de* **Cham** b7a.de* **Chin** b7.de* cimic bro1 cina bg2* colch b7.de* *Con* b4a.de* cortico tpw7 *Dros* b7a.de* euph b4.de* ferr bg2 hep b4.de* hepat bro1 hist sp1 *Hyos* b7a.de* **Ign** bg2* iod b4.de* ip b7a.de* kali-c b4.de* kreos b7a.de* **Lach** b7a.de* lact-v bro1 *Laur* b7.de* *Lob* bro1 lyc bg2* m-ambo b7a.de mag-c b4a.de* mag-m b4a.de* meli bro1 menth bro1 *Merc* bg2 nat-c b4a.de* **Nat-m** b4a.de* nux-v b7a.de* olib-sac wmh1 olnd b7a.de* pert c1* *Petr* b4a.de ph-ac b4a.de* *Phos* bg2* phyt bg2 prun bg2 psor jl2 **Puls** bg2 rhod bg2 rhus-t b7a.de* *Rumx* bg2* sang bg2 sars bg2 seneg b4.de* *Sep* b4a.de *Sil* b4a.de spong mrr1 squil b7a.de **Stann** b4a.de* stann-i bro1 **Staph** bg2 stict mrr1 sulph bg2* teucr bg2 thuj bg2 *Trios* rsj11• tritic-vg fd5.de vanil fd5.de *Verb* b7a.de wye bro1 *Zinc* b4.de* zinc-i ptk1
  - **right**: bapt bg2 dios bg2* stann h1
  - **left**: bell bg2 **Con** bg2 hep bg2* ol-an a1
  - ▽ **extending** to:
    - **upward**: coc-c bg2

Thickling – Throat; in – **extending** to: ...
- **Lower** and lower down: *(↗Deep - lower)* apis bg2* ip bg2 rumx bg2 sil bg2
- ○ **Back** of throat: dulc ptk1*
- **Throat**-pit; in: *(↗LARYNX - Tickling - throat-pit)* *Apis* k* ars b4a.de arum-t bg2 aspar bell k* brom bg2 cann-s k* carc mg1.de* *Caust* **Cham** k* chin bg2 cinnb cocc k* coloc *Con* cortico tpw7* crot-h hep bg1 *Hydrog* srj2• *Ign* k* *Inul Iod* k* kali-bi bg2* lac-c lach lith-c mag-m bg2 nat-c nat-m petr bg2 ph-ac k* phos bg1 puls k* pycnop-sa mrz1 rhus-r **Rumx** k* **Sang** k* *Sep* bg2* *Sil* k* squil k* sul-ac bg2 sulph bg2* tarax k* tub c1
  - **warm** room agg.: cortico tpw7*
- **Tonsils**; below: *Am-br* k*
- **Trachea**; in: *Acon* k* agar ail am-m ambr gsy1 anac ang *Ant-t* k* *Arn* ars ars-i k2 arum-t asaf aur-m bac al2 bar-c bar-i k2 bar-s k2 bell bov *Brom* bry *Calc Caps* carb-ac *Carbn-s* casc caust cham chin chinin-s cina coc-c coloc com con cop dig dulc euph *Euphr Ferr* ferr-ar ferr-i graph k2 gymno hyos indg **Iod** iris iris-foe *Kali-bi* k* **Kali-c** kali-n h2 kali-p kali-s kali-sil k2 kreos lac-c lach lact laur mag-c mag-m med *Merc* mez nat-ar nat-m nicc nit-ac **Nux-v** ol-an ox-ac petr **Ph-ac** *Phos* plat prun *Psor Puls* rhod rhus-r **Rhus-t** rumx sabin **Sang** sanic *Seneg Sep* **Sil** spig squil *Stann* staph stict *Still* sulph tarent teucr thuj tritic-vg fd5.de verat zinc

TIGHT: *Bapt* hr1 calc-s k* *Caust Chin* hr1 cimx *Con Cupr Form* guaj k* *Hell Mag-p* merc *Mosch* myrt-c nat-ar **Phos** k* *Puls* stann ptk1 stram *Sulph* xan hr1 ziz k*
- **daytime**: nat-ar
- **evening**: calc-s k*

TIGHTNESS, chest (See Constriction)

TIMIDITY agg.: ambr bg2

TINGLING:
- ○ **Chest**; in: acon bro1 sep squil
- **Larynx**; in: *Agar* caps *Iod* mag-m sep
- **Trachea**; in: *(↗Prickling; Prickling - trachea)* stann

TIRED; agg. when: stict ptk1

TITILLATING: *(↗Tickling)* acet-ac asaf coloc dros

TOBACCO smoke: | **agg.**: *(↗Smoking - agg.)* acon bg2* arg-n bg2* brom bg2* bry bg2 carb-an bg2 clem bg2 coc-c bg2 coloc bg2 dros bg2 dulc fd4.de euphr bg2 ferr bg2 hep bg2 ign bg2 iod bg2 irid-met srj5• *Lach* bg2 mag-c bg2 menth a1* merc br1* nux-v bg2 petr bg2 spong bg2* staph bg2* sul-ac bg2 thuj bg2

TONELESS: *(↗Dull)* calad k* card-b k* cina dros k*

TORMENTING: *(↗Distressing; Painful; Racking)* alum alum-p k2 am-c anac ang arg-met k2 arg-n k* **Ars** arum-t asaf bar-c bar-s k2 **Bell** benz-ac k* berb borx brom *Calc* k* calc-caust bg2 cann-s carb-an carb-v **Caust** k* chel chin cina *Cocc* coloc a1 *Con* k* cor-r *Croc Cupr* daph **Dros** k* dulc eup-per k2 ferr-p k* hep hydr-ac iod bg2 **Ip** *Kali-c* k* kali-n kreos k* *Lach* k* lact led lob k* lyc bg2 mang bg2 meli a1 merc merc-c *Mez* k* mur-ac naja bg2 *Nat-ar* nat-c *Nat-m* nit-ac *Nux-v* k* op *Petr* k* *Phos* k* phyt k* psor bg2* pyrog bg2 rhod rhus-t k* rumx *Sang* k* sel sep spig spong k2 *Squil* k* *Stann Sulph* k* ter bg2 verat zinc hr1

TOUCHED; from being: *(↗Pressure; Pressure; from)* arn bg2 bell bg2 chin bg2 lach bro1 *Rumx* bro1
- **ear** canal; at the: *Agar Arg-n Carbn-s* kali-c k* **Lach** k •* lyc dgt mag-m dgt mang k* nat-s dgt *Psor* k* sil k* *Sulph* tarent
- **larynx** agg.; slightly at the: *Bell* k* chin k* ferr-p **LACH** k •* *Rumx* k* staph k* stram k*
- **neck** agg.: bell ptk1 brom ptk1 *Lach* ptk1
- **parotid** glands, with wool: merc b4.de*
- **tonsils**: phos h2*

TRUMPET-TONED: verb k*

TUBE, sounds as if he coughed in a: osm k*

TUBERCULOUS persons, in: *(↗Tall)* all-s bro1 ars bro1 *Ars-i* bro1 bapt bro1 *Bell* bro1 calc bro1 caust bro1 chin bro1 *Cod* bro1 con bro1 *Cor-r* bro1 crot-h bro1 *Dros* bro1 ferr-act bro1 *Hep* bro1 *Hyos* bro1 ip bro1 *Kali-c* bro1 lach bro1 laur bro1 lob bro1 myos-s bro1 *Nit-ac* bro1 phos k* rumx bro1 sang bro1 *Sil* bro1 silpho bro1 spong bro1 stann bro1* stict bro1 tub-a bro1

TURNING:
- **bed**; in:
  - **agg.**: ars bg2 kreos k* malar jl2 tritic-vg fd5.de vanil fd5.de
    - **left** side; on: rumx bg2
    - **side**; on: am-m
  - **amel.** | **right**; to: ars kali-c *Phos Rumx Sep* sulph pd *Thuj*
- **head** | **agg.**: spong k*
- **single** parts agg.: hep hr1 rhus-t hr1

TWITCHING in hip: ars b4.de*

TWO coughs in a paroxysm (See Paroxysmal - consisting - two)

ULCERATION deep in trachea; as if from an: stann h2*

UNCONSCIOUSNESS, with (See Consciousness)

UNCOVERING: *(↗Covering)*
- **agg.**: *(↗Cold; becoming - agg.)* ars bar-c bro1 carc mg1.de* chel **Hep** k* ign sne *Kali-bi* nux-v k* **Rhus-t** k* **Rumx** k* sil k* squil k2
- **feet** or head | **agg.**: **Sil** k*
- **hands** | **agg.**: bar-c **Hep** k* **Rhus-t** k* sil
- **head** | **agg.**: rumx pd
- **single** parts | **agg.**: hep bg2* rhus-t bg2*

UNDRESSING: bar-c bro1 carc sp1* cortiso tpw7* *Hep* bro1 kali-bi bro1 *Rhus-t* bro1 *Rumx* bro1

UNINTERRUPTED (See Constant)

VACCINATION; after: carc mlr1• sil gk *Thuj* k*

VAPOR; as from: *(↗Carbon)* brom ptk1 lyc ptk1

VARIOLA:
- **after**: *Ant-t* hr1 calc k*
- **during**: plat

VAULTS, air of (See Cellars)

VEXATION; after: acon k* ant-t k* arn bg2 ars k* bry k* **Cham** k* chin *Cina* coloc b4a.de **Ign** k* iod *Nat-m* k* nux-v k* ph-ac sep k* **Staph** k* verat k*

VINEGAR agg.: alum k* ant-c k* **Sep** k ●* sulph k*

VIOLENT: **Agar** k* alum k* alum-p k2 alum-sil k2 am-c h2* am-m ambr k* anac anan k* ang ant-t k* *Antip* vh1 apis arg-n ars arum-d hr1 bad bg3* **Bell** *Borx* k* brom bry bufo *Calc* calc-i k2 camph carb-an **Carb-v** castn-v br1 **Caust** k* *Cham Chel* k* chin chlor hr1 *Cimx* k* *Cina* k* clem **Coc-c Con** cop cor-r k* croc cub hr1 **Cupr** k* *Cycl* k* **Dros** k* elaps *Eup-per Euphr Form* gamb gels k* graph k2 guare **Hep** k* hydr-ac **Hyos Ign** indg iod k2 **Ip** k* irid-met srj5• kali-bi k* **Kali-c** k* kali-chl k* kali-m k2 kali-sil k2 *Kreos* lac-h sk4• lac-leo sk4• **Lach** lact led lith-c *Lob* lycps-v *Mag-c* mag-p manc *Meph* k* *Merc* **Mez** mur-ac k* *Nat-ar Nat-c* k* nat-p nat-s mtf33 nicc nit-ac *Nux-v* k* ol-j olnd *Op* ozone sde2• par petr **Ph-ac Phos** plat **Puls** *Rhus-t* k* rumx ruta sabad sang seneg **Sep** k* *Sil* spig k* *Spong* **Squil** k* **Stann** k* staph stict stram fry stront-c sulph k* symph fd3.de• ther urol-h rwt• vanil fd5.de verat k* viol-o k* *Zinc* k* zinc-p k2
- **daytime**: *Agar* alum h2* *Euphr*
- **morning**: ars h2* bry cina nux-v *Puls* rumx k2 **Squil** k* symph fd3.de• verat h1*
  - **early**, in bed: bry *Mez* **Nux-v**
  - **rising**, before: **Nux-v**
  - **waking**; on: *Agar* **Lach**
- **noon**: bell staph a1
- **afternoon**: mur-ac *Nat-c* k*
- **evening**: alum anac borx h2 *Calc* con indg irid-met srj5• *Kali-c* k* *Mez Nat-c* k* verat
  - **lying**, after: am-m h2* *Kali-c* k* *Mez* **Sep** k* staph a1
- **night**: am-c h2* ammc vh1 arg-n bell h1* calc h2* *Con* cupr *Cycl* k* dros sne graph k2 *Hep Merc* nicc petr vanil fd5.de verat h1*
  - **midnight**:
    - **after** | **3** h: **Kali-c** k* mur-ac
- **children**; in: | **throwing** the child down: nux-v mtf33
- **dinner**; after: anac mur-ac k*
- **jerking** of head forward and knees upward; spasmodic: bac jl2 ther

Violent: ...
- **laughing** agg.: mur-ac k*
- **pneumonia**; after: calc-i k2
- **sitting** or lying, not during motion; while: phos
- **sleep** agg.; during: apis cham *Cycl* k* *Sulph* k*
- **talking** agg.: mur-ac k* vanil fd5.de
- **uninterrupted** until relieved by vomiting: *Mez*
- **waking**; on: *Agar* calc carb-v rhus-t k*
- **yawning** agg.: mur-ac k*

VIOLIN; when playing: calc b4.de* kali-c k*

VOICE: | **overuse** of the voice: *(↗Talking - loudly)* coll ptk1

VOMITING: | **amel.**: coc-c bg2 mez ptk1 **Sang** mrr1 syc bka1•

WAKENS (See Sleep - wakens)

WAKING; on: acon k* ail ambr k* apis *Aral* arg-n arum-t bamb-a stb2.de• bell k* calc k* carb-v caust k* *Chel* k* *Chin* k* cina k* **Coc-c** k* cod coff cot a1 crot-h dig k* digin a1 euphr k* ferr k* ferr-p ign k* *Kali-bi* k* kali-n kreos lac-c **Lach** k* lachn lyc bg2 mag-s k* nat-ar nat-sil fd3.de• nit-ac nux-v k* ph-ac k* phos psor puls k* *Rhus-t* k* rumx *Sang* k* sanic sep k* sil k* sol-t-ae k* spong squil k* stram k* sul-ac k* sulph k* syc bka1*• tarent k* tell rsj10• thuj k*

WALKING:
- **agg.**: alum k* ars k* bell b4a.de *Calc* k* carb-v k* cina *Con* hr1 cortiso sp1 dig k* dulc fd4.de **Ferr** k* ferr-p k2 hep k* iod k* ip k* *Kali-n* b4a.de* lach k* mag-m k* mang k* mez k* nat-ar nat-m k* phos bg2 rumx *Seneg* k* sil b4a.de stann k2 stram k* stront-c k* sul-ac k* sulph bg2 tell a1 *Thuj* k*
- **air**; in open | **after** | **agg.**: ferr b7.de* *Ip* b7.de* *Lach* b7a.de
  - **agg.**: acon k* alum k* ang **Ars** k* carb-v k* cina k* cortiso tpw7 dig k* dulc fd4.de ferr k* ferr-ar ip k* kali-n k* lyc mag-m k* nux-v osm ox-ac ph-ac k* **Phos** k* *Rhus-t* k* *Seneg* k* sep spig staph k* stram k* sul-ac k* *Sulph* k*
- **amel.**: ars-i sne astac k* *Dros* k* grat k* ign phos
- **cold** air; in | **agg.**: *Ars* k* cist ip *Kali-n* **Phos** k* **Rumx** k* *Seneg* spig spong fd4.de *Sul-ac* verat
- **rapidly**:
  - **after**: sep bg2
  - **agg.**: carb-v bg2 cench coca merc k* nat-m k* *Puls* k* *Seneg* k* sep k* sil k* squil k* stann k*
- **slowly** | **amel.**: ferr mrr1

WARM:
- **abdomen**; warming | **amel.**: sil k*
- **air**:
  - **agg.**: ant-c bg2 iod bg2
    - **hot** air: kali-s kr1*
  - **amel.**: hep bro1 rhus-t bro1 *Rumx* bro1
- **applications**:
  - **agg.**: all-c bg2 brom bg2 bry bg2 caust bg2 coc-c bg2 dros bg2 iod bg2 lach bg2 laur bg2 nat-c bg2 puls bg2 seneg bg2 verat bg2
  - **amel.**: acon bg2 alum bg2 aral bg2 ars ptk1 bad bro1 bell bg2 caust bg2 cupr bg2 hep bg2* ip ptk1 lyc bg2* lyss ptk1 nux-v bg2* phos bg2* rhus-t ptk1 rumx bg2* sil bg2* spong bg2 stict bg2
- **bed** (See Bed - warm - becoming)
- **drinks**:
  - **agg.**: ambr k* ant-t k* caps k* *Coc-c* k* ign k* laur k* mez k* phos *Stann* k*
  - **amel.**: alum **Ars** k* *Bry* k* cassia-s cdd7• eupi k* germ-met srj5• **Lyc** k* **Nux-v** k* **Rhus-t** k* **Sil** k* *Spong* k* verat k*
- **food**:
  - **agg.**: *Bar-c* k* *Coc-c* k* *Kali-c* k* laur k* *Mez* k* *Puls* k*
    - **hot**: mez bg2*
  - **amel.**: lyc bg2 nux-v bg2 *Spong* k*
- **room**:
  - **agg.**: *(↗Air; in - amel.; Temperature)* acon k* *All-c* k* ambr k* anan ant-c k* anth bro1 *Apis* k* arg-met k2 arn k* ars k* ars-i k2 bell bg2 bov bg2 brom k* *Bry* k* carc mg1.de* *Caust* bro1 cham bro1 **Coc-c** k* com cub dig k* *Dros* k* *Dulc* k* *Iod Ip* k* kali-n bg2 *Kali-s* laur k* *Lyc* k* mag-p med *Merc* bro1 mez k* nat-ar *Nat-c* k* nat-m gk nit-ac nux-m bro1 phos pneu jl2 **Puls** k* pyrog k* ran-b bro1 sanic *Seneg* k* spig hr1 *Spong* k* squil bro1 sulph k* trios rsj11• *Tub* k* verat k*

- **room** – **agg.**: ...
  - ⁝ **cold** air, or vice versa; going from warm room to: *(↗Temperature) Phos* ptk1 rumx ptk1
  - **amel.** | **hot** room: beryl sp1
  - **entering** a warm room; when:
    - ⁝ **air**; from open: *(↗Temperature) Acon All-c* **Ant-c** k* anth k* bov *Brom* **Bry** k ●* carb-v carc tpw2* *Coc-c* k* com con cupr dig ip bro1 med k* *Nat-c* k* *Nat-m Nux-v* op wbt• *Pneu* jl2 **Puls** k ● rumx k2 sep squil k* *Sulph* thyr ptk1 verat k* verb
    - ⁝ **cold** air; from | **or** vice cersa: acon k* all-c k* bry bg2 carb-v k* carc tpw2* kali-n bg2 lach nat-c k* nat-m gk nux-v **PHOS** k ●* *Rumx* k* sep k* tub gk verat bg2 verat-v verb bg2
- **stove** | **agg.**: ant-c hbh coc-c

WARM; BECOMING:
- **agg.**: acon k* ant-c k* *Brom* k* *Bry* k* carb-v caust k* *Coc-c* k* cortiso tpw7 *Dig* k* iod k* ip b7.de* kali-c k* laur mag-c k* mur-ac b4a.de nit-ac nux-m k* nux-v k* phos a1 **Puls** k* rhus-t k* sil k* thuj k* zinc k*
  - **exertion** agg.; after: cortiso sp1
- **bed**; in:
  - **agg.**: ant-t k* apis b7a.de brom k* **Caust** k* *Cham* k* coc-c k2 dros led k* m-arct b7.de merc k* naja nat-m k* *Nux-m* k* nux-v k* **Puls** k* *Verat* k*
  - **amel.**: arg-n ptk1 cham k* *Kali-bi* k* *Rhus-t* b7a.de

WARMTH; sensation of (See Heat - sensation)

WATER: | **Trachea** from mouth; from water running into: spig b7.de*

WEAK cough: calad b7.de*

WEATHER:
- **change** of weather: atro vh *Dulc* erig erio bg3* lach k* nit-ac k* petr-ra shn4• phos k* rumx sil spong syc bka1• verat k* verb
- **fog**:
  - **agg.**: menth c1 **Sep** k ●*
  - **cold** fog amel.: spong ptk1
- **frosty** | **amel.**: spong
- **hot**: lach
- **stormy**:
  - **agg.**: mag-m phos *Rhod Sep Sil* sulph
  - **before**: phos k* syph jl2
- **warm**:
  - **agg.**: caps tl1 kali-bi k2
  - **wet** | **agg.**: iod
- **wet**:
  - **agg.**: bar-c calc carb-v cur *Dulc* k* iod lach k* *Mang* nat-s phyt rhus-t k* sep bg2 sil spong sulph
    - ⁝ **cold** (See Cold - air - wet)

WEEPING: *(↗Lamenting)*
- **agg.** cough (See Crying)
- **during** cough (See MIND - Weeping - cough - during)
- **from**: arn a1*

WET cough (See Loose)

WET; GETTING:
- **agg.**: ant-c calc k* *Calc-s* **Dulc** k* lach k* nit-ac k* *Nux-m* bg2 psor *Puls* bg2 rhus-t k* sep k* sulph tub c1
  - **feet**: nux-m bg2
- **amel.** | **chest** getting wet: borx ptk1

WET room: bry

WHEEZING (See Asthmatic)

WHINING, during: acon ars cina

WHISPERING sound; has a: card-b k*

WHISTLING: acon k* ars k* brom k* carb-v chlor cina bg2 croc br1 **Dros** bg2 euphr bg2 *Hep* k* kali-bi **Kali-c** bg2 kali-i kali-p kreos k* *Laur* k* lyc k* mur-ac bg2 phos bg2 prun k* rhus-t bg2 samb *Sang* k* seneg *Spong* k* sul-ac bg2 sulph bg2
- **diarrhea** | **amel.**: sang hr1

WHOOPING: acon k* all-c k* alumn bro1 am-br c2* am-c am-m bro1 am-pic c1* *Ambr* k* ambro br1* *Anac* k* *Anan* ang c1* ant-c k* *Ant-t* k* *Arg-n* k* *Arn* k* *Ars* k* ars-i k2 ars-s-f k2 arum-t k* asaf k* asar asc-c k* atro-s mtf11 bad k* *Bar-c* k* bar-m bar-s k2 *Bell* k* *Brom* k* *Bry* k* *Calc* k* *Calc-p* caps k* *Carb-ac* k* *Carb-an* k* **Carb-v** k* carbn-h c2 *Carbn-s* carc fb* *Castn-v* k* *Caust* k* cer-ox br1* *Cham* k* chel c2* *Chin* k* chlol k* *Chlor Cina* k* *Coc-c* k* cocain bro1 con k* *Cor-r* k* *Crot-h* k* *Cupr* k* cupr-act c2* cupr-ar cur c2 *Cyt-l* sp1 dig k* **Dirc Dros** k* *Dulc* k* dys pte1*• erio br1 eucal bro1 euph-l bro1 *Euphr* k* *Ferr* k* ferr-ar *Ferr-p* k* flf br1 *Form* bro1 formal br1 *Graph* k* grin bro1* guare k* *Hep* k* *Hippoz* k* hist mtf11 hydr-ac k* *Hyos* k* hyper k* ign k* indg iod b4a.de* *Ip* k* *Just* bro1 *Kali-bi* k* kali-br k* *Kali-c* k* kali-chl kali-i k* kali-m k2* *Kali-p* k* **Kali-s** k* kali-sil k2 *Kreos* k* lach b7a.de* *Lact* k* lact-v c1* laur k* *Led* k* *Lob* k* *Lyc* k* *Mag-m* k* mag-p k* *Meph* k* merc k* *Mez* k* mosch k* mur-ac k* *Naphtin* c2* narc-ps ah1* *Nat-m* k* nicc k* nig-s mp4• *Nit-ac* k* *Nux-v* k* ol-j bro1 op k* ouabin br1 oxyg c2 par k* passi br1* pert c1* phel *Phos* k* podo k* psor al2 *Puls* k* rhus-t k* *Rumx* k* ruta k* sabal c2 *Samb* k* *Sang* k* sangin-n bro1 sec *Seneg* k* *Sep* k* *Sil* k* sol-crl bro1 spig *Spong* k* *Squil* k* stann stict k* stram succ-xyz c2 sul-ac k* *Sulph* k* syph *Tab* k* terp-h bwa3 thuj b4a.de* thymol br1* thymu bro1 tong br1* *Trif-p* bro1 tub c1 urt-u c2 vac c2* *Verat* k* viol-o k* *Visc* k* zinc k* zinc-p k2 [calc-br stj1 mag-br stj1]
- **daytime**: brom cupr *Euphr*
- **morning**: ant-c *Calc* k* cina mur-ac hr1 verat
- **forenoon**: sep
- **afternoon**: lyc mur-ac k* sulph
  - **midnight**, until: sulph
- **evening**: ambr arn ars bar-c bell bry carb-v chin cina coc-c dros hep ign *Laur* k* lyc mez k* mur-ac hr1 nat-m puls seneg sep spong sul-ac verat
  - **18**-22 h: hyper
  - **and** night: ars bry
  - **midnight**, until: arn bar-c carb-v hep mez puls sep spong sul-ac verat
- **night**: ambr anac ant-t arn ars bar-c bell bry carb-v *Cham* chin coc-c con h2* cor-r k* cupr k* dros dulc *Hep* hyos meph *Merc* k* mez k* mur-ac nat-m nit-ac k* puls samb seneg k* sep sil spong stann k* sul-ac sulph verat
  - **midnight**:
    - ⁝ **before**: lyc mur-ac *Spong*
    - ⁝ **after**: acon am-m bell chin dros *Hyos Kali-c* k* samb stict c1
      - ⁝ **2** h: dros
      - ⁝ **3** h: *Kali-c* k*
- **accompanied** by:
  - **fever**: kali-c b4.de*
  - **hemorrhage**: cer-ox br1
  - **salivation**: *Bry* kr1* *Iris* kr1* spong kr1*
  - **sneezing**: cina ptk1
  - **stiffness**: am-c bro1 *Ant-t* bro1 carb-v bro1 cina bro1 cor-r bro1 *Cupr* bro1 *Cupr-act* bro1 iod bro1 *Ip* bro1 mag-p bro1 meph bro1 op bro1 samb bro1 *Verat* bro1
  - ○ **Face** | **cyanosis**: am-c bro1 *Ant-t* bro1 carb-v bro1 cina bro1 cor-r bro1 *Cupr* bro1 *Cupr-act* bro1 iod bro1 *Ip* bro1 mag-p bro1 meph bro1 op bro1 samb bro1 *Verat* bro1
  - **Tongue**; ulcers under: nit-ac bro1
- **after** whooping cough; cough: *Puls* b7a.de
- **breathing** | **agg.** | **rapid**; during paroxysm: *Led* kr1
  - **deep** | **agg.**: *Mag-m* kr1
- **catarrhal** phase: **Acon** bg2* ant-t bg2* carb-v bg2 chin bro1 *Dulc* bg2* hep bro1 ip bg2* nux-v bg2* puls bg2*
- **chest**:
  - **constriction** of chest, supports with hands; worse after midnight: **Dros** kr1
  - **deep** in chest; seemingly from: *Lob* kr1
  - **shattered** during paroxysm: *Led* kr1
- **child**: carc jl2
  - **bends** backward then expectoration of clear frothy blood: *Led* kr1
  - **chubby**: *Seneg* kr1
  - **cries** before coughing: arn br1
  - **grasps** genitals when coughing: *Zinc* kr1

- **child**: ...
  - **infants**: carc jl2*
  - **stiff** before paroxysm: *(↗EXTREMITIES - Stiffness - cough - before)* cina mtf33 cupr mtf33 *Led* kr1
- **chronic**: calc-p ptk1 sep ptk1
- **cold**:
  - **air**:
    - **agg.**: *Cina* kr1
    - **amel.**: mag-p ptk1
- **cold**; after taking a: caust bro1 sang bro1
- **convulsions**; with: arg-n kr1 *Bell* bro1 cina bro1 **Cupr** kr1* *Cupr-act* kr1* *Hydr-ac* kr1* hyos bro1 **Kali-br** kr1* mag-p bro1 **Meph** kr1 narc-ps bro1 seneg kr1 *Sep* kr1 *Sol-crl* bro1 *Stict* kr1 *Verat* kr1
  - **attack** ending in convulsions, appears as if dead; each: *Cupr* kr1
- **croup**; symptoms of: **Brom** kr1
- **crowing** inspiration; without: ambr bro1
- **defervescent** stage: ant-t ptk1 *Arn* bg2 carb-v bg2 dulc bg2 hep bg2 phos ptk1 **Puls** bg2*
- **dentition**; during: *Calc* kr1 *Cham* kr1
- **diaphragm** after paroxysm; spasmodic contraction of: *Led* kr1
- **early** in life: carc gk6
- **eating** agg.: bry k2
- **epidemic**: *Dros* tl1 kali-c tl1
- **esophagus** excites cough; feeling of cramps in: *Cupr* kr1 *Iris* kr1
- **eyes**:
  - **baglike** swelling between upper lids and eyebrows: *Kali-c* kr1*
  - **protrude** from sockets with burning and lachrymation: *Caps* hr1
  - **sclerotic** appears as one gore of blood: *Bell* kr1
- **first** stage; inflammatory cough: *Acon* kr1 *Ant-t* kr1 **Bell** kr1 *Castn-v* br1 *Cham* kr1 *Ferr-p* kr1
- **heart** would break after paroxysm; as if: arn k1
- **herpes**; with facial: arn ptk1
- **neglected**, with complications: verat ptk1*
- **prophylaxis**: carb-v gm1 cupr gm1 dros bro1* pert gm1 vac bro1*
- **sequelae** (See GENERALS - Convalescence - whooping)
- **spasmodic** phase: *Acon* bro1 agar ptk1 bell bg2* calc bg2 carb-ac bro1 *Carb-v* bg2* *Castn-v* bro1 caust ptk1 cham ptk1 chel bro1 **Cina** bg2* *Coc-c* bro1* con ptk1 *Cor-r* bro1* cupr bg2* **Dios** bg2 *Dros* bro1* hep bg2* hyos bro1 ign ptk1 *Ip* bro1* *Kali-c* bg2* kali-s ptk1 lach ptk1 mag-p bro1 *Meph* bro1* merc bg2 mez ptk1 naphtin bro1 narcin bro1 nux-v bg2* ph-ac ptk1 phos ptk1 puls bg2* samb bro1 sep ptk1 squil ptk1 stann bro1* stict ptk1 *Stram* ptk1 thymu bro1 tub ptk1 verat bg2* verat-v ptk1
- **terminal** stage: v-a-b jl2
- **tickling** | **Chest**: *Mur-ac* kr1
- **torn** loose feeling, with: osm ptk1
- **violent**: agar ptk1 **Bell** ptk1 **Carb-v** ptk1 caust ptk1 cham ptk1 *Cina* ptk1 *Coc-c* ptk1 con ptk1 *Cor-r* ptk1 cupr tl1* *Dros* ptk1 ferr tl1 hep ptk1 ign ptk1 *Ip* ptk1 *Kali-c* ptk1 kali-s ptk1 lach ptk1 *Meph* ptk1 mez ptk1 **Nux-v** ptk1 ph-ac ptk1 phos ptk1 *Puls* ptk1 sep ptk1 squil ptk1 stann ptk1 stict ptk1 *Stram* ptk1 tub ptk1 *Verat* ptk1 verat-v ptk1
- **walking** in cold air agg.: *Cina* kr1
- **weeping** after paroxysm, as if heart would break: arn k13 calc hbh

WIND; in: *Acon* caps cham k* coca cupr euphr k* **Hep** lyc k* lycps-v k* samb sep spong stram k*
- **amel.**: tub hbh
- **cold**: coca **Hep** lyc lycps-v spong fd4.de tub jl2
  - **dry**: **Acon** k* caust bg2 cham k* cupr bg2 **Hep** k* samb bg2 spong k*
- **east**: **Acon** cham cupr **Hep** samb sep spong
- **north**: **Acon** k* caps cham k* cupr k* **Hep** k* samb bg2 sep k* spong k*
- **sea**, at the: *Cupr* k* mag-m
- **sharp**: caps
- **south**: euphr
- **west**: **Hep**

WIND ON CHEST AGG.; COLD: *Phos* k* *Rumx* k*

WINE: *(↗Alcohol)* acon alum bro1 ant-c arn borx k* ferr ign lach k* led *Stann* k* stram **Zinc** k*
- **amel.**: sulph k*

Wine: ...
- **sour**: ant-c bg2

WINTER (See Seasons - winter)

WORM crawled up from pit of stomach in throat; from sensation as if a: zinc

WORMS: cina b7a.de* ter bro1

WRITING agg.: cina k*

YAWNING agg. or excites the cough: *(↗Accompanied - yawning)* arn k* asaf k* *Bell* hr1* *Carc* mg1.de* cina k* kreos mrr1 mur-ac k* *Nat-s* c1 nux-v k* oci-sa sk4• puls k* staph k*
- **and** coughing consecutively: ant-t k* *Nat-m* k*

DAYTIME only: acon adam skp7• ail alum k* alum-sil k2 *Alumn* am-c ambr bro1 anac ang ant-t *Arg-met* k* arn **Ars** k* asaf *Bell* borx bry k* *Calc* k* caps carb-an carbn-s *Caust* **Cham** k* chin cic k* coc-c cocc colch *Con* k* dig euph bg2 euphr k* ferr ferr-ar ferr-p *Graph* k* guaj **Hep** k* *Hyos* k* kali-c k* lach *Lyc* k* mag-c mag-m *Mang* **Merc** k* *Nit-ac* k* *Nux-v* k* op petr phos **Puls** k* rhus-t *Sabad* k* samb sanic **Sil** k* squil *Stann* k* staph *Stront-c* **Sulph** k* taosc iwa1• verat zinc zinc-p k2

MORNING (= 6-9 h): acal k* acon *Agar* agath-a nl2• ail *Alum* k* alum-p k2 alum-sil k2 *Alumn* *Am-c* am-m k* ambr *Ang* *Ant-c* *Ant-t* apis aq-mar skp7• aral arn ars ars-i k2 arund aur aur-ar k2 aur-i k2 aur-s k2 bamb-a stb2.de• bar-c bar-i k2 bar-m bar-s k2 bell borx **Bry** k* bufo *Calc* k* calc-i k2 calc-p calc-s k* calc-sil k2 caps carb-ac carb-an **Carb-v** *Carbn-s* *Caust* cina cob coc-c colch crot-c sk4• crot-t k* cub cupr *Dig* dios dros k* euph *Euphr* k* *Ferr* ferr-ar ferr-i *Ferr-p* **Hep** k* hyos ign ind iod ip kali-ar kali-c k* kali-m k2 kali-n a1 kali-p kali-s kali-sil k2 kola stb3• kreos lac-ac lac-h sk4• lach led lyc k* *Mag-c* mag-m mag-s a1 *Mang* meph mez mur-ac nat-ar nat-c *Nat-m* *Nat-p* nat-s *Nit-ac* nux-v **Par** *Ph-ac* phel **Phos** k* phyt psor k* **Puls** k* rein a1 rheum rhod *Rhus-t* ruta fd4.de sanic sel seneg **Sep** k* **Sil** sol-t-ae spong **Squil** k* *Stann* staph stram a1 stront-c **Sul-ac** k* sul-i k2 **Sulph** k* thuj k* tub c1 verat zinc zinc-p k2 zing k*

- **8.30 h**: spong
- **8-9 h**: sil
- **evening**; and: squil ptk1
- **bathing**; after: calc-s
- **bed** agg.; in: *Calc* k* nit-ac
- **rising** | **after** | **agg.**: chinin-s coca mag-m *Puls* k* sep sulph
  - **agg.**: calc calc-s a1 ferr *Phos* **Puls**
- **waking** agg.; after: *Agar* aur carb-v hydrog srj2• lyc psor *Sulph* k* thuj tung-met bdx1•

FORENOON (= 9-12 h): bry k* calc-s chinin-s coc-c iris lyc oena *Sil* **Stann** sulph zinc

- **9 h**: agath-a nl2• cob phyt
- **10 h**: iris

NOON (= 12-13 h): bell calc-s sil

- **12-15 h**: calc-s

AFTERNOON (= 13-18 h): alum am-m anac ars *Bad* caust chin chinin-s clem coc-c k* eucal hydr lyc mag-c mill naja nux-v op phos k*

- **16 h**: op
- **17 h**: caust hydr mag-c

EVENING (= 18-22 h): agn all-c alum alum-sil k2 *Alumn* ambr c1 ant-c *Arg-met* *Arn* ars ars-br vh aur aur-ar k2 aur-s k2 bar-c bar-i k2 bar-s k2 *Bell* borx bry bufo calc k* cann-s canth carbn-s *Caust* cench k2 chin chinin-s *Cina* coc-c k* crot-t cub dig galeoc-c-h gms1• *Graph* hydr hydr-ac *Ign* iod kali-ar kali-c k* kali-n k* kali-s *Kalm* k* kreos lach *Lyc* mur-ac naja nat-ar nat-c nat-m nux-m nux-v oena k* rhod rhus-t *Ruta* sep sil stann staph sul-ac sul-i k2 sulph thuj verat

- **bed** agg.; in: calc *Nux-m* sep
- **lying** down agg.; after: graph kali-n h2 psor sep
- **warm** agg.; becoming: *Nux-m*

NIGHT (= 22-6 h): alum alum-sil k2 am-m ammc vh1 ant-t a1 arn ars calc calc-s carb-v carbn-s *Caust* k* chinin-s coc-c k* cycl dulc euphr ferr ferr-ar gamb hep kali-c k* kali-s led lyc k* m-aust meli mez phos puls pyrog raph k* rhod rhus-t ruta fd4.de sabad k* sang hr1 **Sep** k* sil *Staph* stront-c sk4• sulph

- **midnight** | **before** | **bed**; on getting into: *Sep* k*
  - **after**: *Led*
- **bed** agg.; in: sulph

ACRID: *Alum* k* alum-sil k2 am-c k* *Am-m* k* anac k* *Ars* k* asaf bg2 aur bg2 bell bg2 carb-v k* *Caust* k* cham k* coc-c con k* ferr k* fl-ac bg2 ign k* iod k* kreos k* lach k* laur bg2 lyc k* mag-m k* *Merc* k* mez k* nat-c b2.de* nat-m k* nit-ac k* nux-v k* phos k* *Puls* k* rhus-t k* sep k* *Sil* k* spig k* squil k* staph bg2 sul-ac k* sulph k* thuj bg2 verat bg2

AGG. (See GENERALS - Expectoration - agg.)

AIR agg.: chinin-s cob merc nux-v k* plan sacch sep

AIR; IN OPEN:

- **agg.**: chinin-s cob *Lach* merc nux-v k* *Sacch* sep
- **amel.**: adam skp7• arg-n calc-s k*

ALBUMINOUS (See White)

ALTERNATING with: | **Pleura**; pain in: dros mtf11

AMEL. (See GENERALS - Expectoration - amel.)

ASH-COLORED clots; round: (↗*Balls*) arund k*

BALL and rushes into mouth; feels like a round: syph k*

BALLS, in shape of: (↗*Ash-colored; Globular*) agar k* *Arg-n* k* calad b7.de* cob-n sp1 *Coc-c* k* croc bg2 ham fd3.de• kali-c b4a.de kola stb3• kreos b7a.de lyc k* *Mang* b4a.de med ph-ac k* *Rhus-t* b7a.de sang ptk1 *Sil* k* squil k* **Stann** k* sulph k* *Thuj* b4.de* tritic-vg fd5.de

- **agg.**: *Coc-c* *Nux-v* pd
- **albuminous**, little: ph-ac
- **bitter**, green: med k*

BATTER, breaks and flies like thin: phos k*

BED: | **in** bed | **agg.**: am-c *Calc* ferr *Phos* k* sep

- **sitting** up in bed agg.: *Phos* k*

BILIOUS: bar-c dig puls k* samb

BLACKISH: arn k* aster bell k* *Chin* k* crot-c sk4• cur *Elaps* k* hydr-ac k* *Kali-bi* k* kali-c b4a.de led h1 lyc k* *Nux-v* k* ox-ac phos b4a.de puls k* rhus-t k*

- **grains**; with blackish: chin
- **lumps** in centre: arn ox-ac
- **yellow**: hydr-ac k*

BLOODY (= spitting of blood): (↗*CHEST - Hemorrhage*) *Acal* k* acet-ac **Acon** k* aesc agn ail all-s k* aloe alum k* alum-p k2 alum-sil k2 alumn k2 am-br **Am-c** k* am-m k* ambr k* anac k* *Anan* anis ant-c k* ant-s-aur ant-t tl1 *Apis* *Aran* *Arg-n* k* **Arn** k* **Ars** k* ars-i k2 ars-s-f k2 arum-m asar k* aspar atra-r bnm3• aur k* aur-ar k2 aur-s c1* bad bamb-a stb2.de• bapt bg2 *Bell* k* bell-p sp1 beryl sp1 bism k* *Borx* k* both fne1• brom *Bry* k* bufo k* *Cact* k* cadm-met sp1 *Calc* k* calc-i k2 calc-p k2 calc-s calc-sil k2 **Cann-s** *Canth* k* capp-g bta1• caps k* carb-an k* *Carb-v* k* carbn-h carbn-o *Carbn-s* carc mlr1• *Card-m* k* casc *Cench* *Cham* k* chel bg2* *Chin* k* chinin-ar chlor cimic bg2 cina k* cinnm br1 cist cob coc-c coll *Con* k* cop *Cor-r* br1 *Croc* k* **Crot-h** k* *Crot-t* *Cupr* k* cur daph der *Dig* k* dios *Dros* k* *Dulc* k* dys fmm1• elaps k* erig k* eug euphr k* **Ferr** k* *Ferr-ar* *Ferr-i* **Ferr-p** k* fl-ac gamb gels graph guaj k* *Ham* k* hell helx gm1 hep k* hippoz hydr-ac *Hyos* k* ind iod k* **Ip** k* jug-c just-r gsb1 kali-ar *Kali-bi* k* kali-c k* kali-i k* kali-m k2 kali-n k* kali-p kali-perm kali-s kali-sil k2 *Kreos* k* lach k* lachn lam br1 lat-h bnm5• **Laur** k* **Led** k* loxo-lae bnm12• *Lyc* k* lycps-v m-ambo b2.de* *Mag-c* k* mag-m k* manc *Mang* k* *Merc* k* merc-c k* *Mez* k* *Mill* k* mur-ac k* myrt-c mtf11 naja bg2 *Nat-ar* nat-c k* *Nat-m* k* nat-p nat-s k2 nat-sel br1 **Nit-ac** k* nux-m k* nux-v k* oena *Op* k* ph-ac k* **Phos** k* *Plb* k* psor **Puls** k* pyrog k2 *Rhus-t* k* ruta sabad k* *Sabin* k* sal-ac sang k* sarr **Sec** k* sel k* senec k2 *Sep* k* *Sil* k* sol-mm spong fd4.de squil k* **Stann** k* staph k* stram b7.de* *Sul-ac* k* sul-i k2 **Sulph** k* tarax k* *Ter* k* thlas bg2 thuj k* tril-p br1 tub al2 vanil fd5.de vario br1* verat verat-v bg2 verb b7a.de *Zinc* k*

- **morning**: acal k* acon k* aesc ail alum k* ant-c bell k* cupr *Ferr* indg ip laur mez k* nit-ac k* ozone sde2• ph-ac sel sep k* sil k* sol-t-ae k* sul-ac zinc
  - **bed** agg.; in: nit-ac k* **Nux-v** k*
  - **cough** agg.; during: bell k* sep k* sil h2
  - **lying** down agg.: merc k*
  - **menses**; during: **Zinc** k*
  - **pure** blood morning:
    - **dark** clotted | **evening**: acal c1*
  - **rising** agg.: aesc *Ferr*
- **noon**: sil k*
- **afternoon**: alum k* clem k* kali-n h2 lyc k* mag-c k* mez mill nux-v k*
  - **13 h**: clem
  - **14 h**: nux-v
  - **16 h**: mill
  - **17 h**: mag-c
- **evening**: cub nat-c k* sep k*
  - **cough** agg.; during: nat-c k* sep h2
  - **lying** down agg.; after: sep k*
- **night**: arn ars *Ferr* k* mez k* puls rhus-t sulph k*

- **accompanied** by | **palpitations** (See CHEST - Palpitation - accompanied - expectoration)
- **acrid**: Am-c k* Ars k* Canth k* carb-v k* hep k* **Kali-c** k* Kali-n k* rhus-t k* sars b4a.de* **Sil** k* sul-ac k* sulph k* tarax bg2 zinc k*
- **alternating** with:
  - **epistaxis** (See NOSE - Epistaxis - alternating - blood)
  - **rheumatism**: led tl1*
- **bathing** | **sea**; in the: mag-m h2*
- **black**: Am-c b4a.de arn k* ars k2 bism k* Bry b7a.de canth k* chin k* croc k* crot-c dig dros k* **Elaps** k* kali-bi Kali-c b4a.de Led b7a.de Lyc b4a.de Mag-c b4a.de Nit-ac k* nux-v k* ph-ac k* puls k* Sec b7a.de Sep b4a.de Sul-ac b4a.de zinc
- **blowing** a wind instrument: rhus-t hr1
- **bluish**: con bg2
- **bright**-red: acal k* **Acon** am-c k* Arn k* ars k* **Bell** k* borx b2.de bry k* Calc k* canth k* carb-an k* Carb-v k* cench chin k* cob dig k* dros k* **Dulc** k* ferr k* ferr-p k* **Hyos** k* Ip k* Kali-bi kali-n k* kreos b2.de laur k* Led k* mag-m b2.de Merc k* mill nat-c b2.de nux-m k* nux-v Phos k* puls k* Rhus-t k* sabad k* **Sabin** k* Sec k* sep k* sil k* sulph b2.de Zinc k* zinc-p k2
  - **morning**: acal br1
  - **few** clots; with: methyl gm1
- **brown**: **Bry** k* Calc k* **Carb-v** k* con k* puls k* Rhus-t k* sil
- **burning** in chest, with: psor ptk1
- **chronic**: sul-ac k*
- **clearing** the throat, when: am-c k*
- **clotted**: acon bg2 arn b2.de* Bell b2.de* bry b2.de* canth b2.de* carb-an b2.de* caust bg2 **Cham** b2.de* Chin b2.de* con bg2 croc b2.de* dros b7a.de* elaps gk Ferr b2.de* Hyos b2.de* ign bg2 Ip b2.de* kali-bi k2 kreos b2.de* mag-m b2.de* merc b2.de* nit-ac b2.de* nux-v b2.de* ph-ac b2.de* plat bg2 Puls b2.de* **Rhus-t** b2.de* Sabin b2.de* sec b2.de* sep b2.de* spong bg2 stram bg2 stront-c bg2 sulph bg2 tub gk
- **coughing**; after: am-c ptk1
- **dark**: acal k* acon k* Am-c k* am-m Ant-c k* Arn k* Asar k* bell k* Bism k* Bry k* Cact Canth k* carb-v k* caust bg2 cench **Cham** k* Chin k* coc-c cocc bg2 coll con k* **Croc** k* Cupr k* dig k* dros k* Elaps erig ferr k* ferr-p graph bg2 ham ign bg2 kali-c bg2 kali-i kali-n k* Kreos k* lach bg2 led k* Lyc k* Mag-c k* mag-m k* merc mur-ac k* Nit-ac k* Nux-m k* **Nux-v** k* Ph-ac k* Phos k* plat k* Puls k* sec k* Sel k* Sep k* sil bg2 stict stram bg2 sul-ac k* sulph k* tub gk
  - **afternoon**: acal br1
- **drinking** agg.; after: calc
- **eating**; after: sep k*
- **erection**, after a violent: nat-m k*
- **exertion** agg.; after: ip mill urt-u pd*
- **falling**; after: Ferr-p k* Mill k*
- **fever**; during: arn b7.de* Ars b4a.de nux-m b7.de*
- **fluids**; after loss of vital: ars bg2 brom bg2 bry bg2 calc bg2 carb-v bg2 **Chin** bg2 con bg2 dros bg2 ferr bg2 hep bg2 kali-c bg2 led bg2 lyc bg2 nat-c bg2 nit-ac bg2 ph-ac bg2 phos bg2 plb bg2 puls bg2 rhus-t bg2 samb bg2 sep bg2 sil bg2 stann bg2 sulph bg2
- **hawking** up mucus agg.: calc bg1 cham k* Ferr k* hyper k* kali-n k* Nit-ac
- **heart** complaints; in: aur-i k2
- **lactation**; during: chin kr1 Ferr k*
- **liver**-colored: puls h1
- **lumps**: mag-c h2 sang ptk1 sel ptk1
- **masturbation**; from: ferr pd*
- **menses**:
  - **before** | **agg.**: dig ptk1 phos b4.de* **Zinc** k*
  - **during** | **agg.**: iod kali-n h2 nat-m k* Phos k* sep **Zinc** k*
  - **suppressed** menses; from: acon ars ptk1 bell bg2 Carb-v k* crot-h bg2 cupr bg2 Dig k* ham bg2* ip bg2 kali-c bg2 Led k* Lyc k* nat-s bg2 **Nux-v** k* Phos k* puls k* sabad bg2 sang hr1 sec bg2 senec c1* sulph k* tril-p bg2 ust bg2 verat bg2 Zinc bg2
- **moon**; full: kali-n h2
- **offensive** odor: bell bg2 bry b7a.de* carb-an bg2 Carb-v bg2 caust bg2 cham b7a.de* croc b7a.de* ign b7a.de* kali-c bg2 kreos b7a.de* merc bg2 phos bg2 plat bg2 sabad bg2 sabin b7a.de sec b7a.de* sil bg2 Stann bg2
- **pale**: am-c k* ant-t bg2 arn k* ars k* bell k* borx k* Bry k* calc k* canth k* carb-an k* carb-v k* chin k* dig k* dros k* dulc k* ferr k* graph k* Hyos k* ip k* kali-n k* kreos k* laur k* led k* mag-m k* Mang merc k* nat-c k* nux-m k*

Bloody – pale: ...
ph-ac bg2 phos k* puls k* rhus-t k* sabad k* sabin k* sec k* sel b7a.de* sep k* sil k* stram bg2 stront-c bg2 sulph k* zinc k*

- **purulent**: Arg-n k* calc bg2 carb-v bg2 chin con bg2 kali-c bg2 kreos bg2 lyc bg2 Nit-ac bg2 Phos bg2 sil bg2 sulph
- **respiration**, from violent effort at: Sec k*
- **sour**: tarax b7a.de
- **speckled**: am-c bg2 laur bg2 sel bg2 sulph bg2
- **sticky** (See viscid)
- **streaked**: Acon k* alum k* Am-c k* am-caust vh1 anac k* ant-c k* Arg-n k* Arn k* **Ars** k* bapt bg2 Bell bro1 bism k* Borx k* **Bry** k* bufo bg2 Cact calc k* cann-s bro1 canth bro1 Caust k* Cetr bro1 Chel Chin k* cina k* cocc k* con k* cor-r bro1 crot-h k* cub cupr k* daph dig k* dros k* dulc k* Elaps bro1 erig eug euphr k* **Ferr** k* Ferr-ar Ferr-p bg2* hep k* hyos k* iod k* Ip k* kali-bi k* kali-c k* kali-n b2.de* kreos k* lach lachn Laur k* led bg2* Lyc k* **mag-m** k* merc k* Merc-c k* methyl gm1 mez k* Mill bro1 nat-c bg2 Nat-m k* nit-ac k* nux-m k* nux-v bro1 Op k* Phos k* psor bg2 puls k* Rhus-t bro1 Sabin k* sang sec k* Sel k* senec seneg k* sep k* sil k* spong k* squil k* sul-ac k* sulph bro1 ter Tril-p bro1 Zinc k* zinc-p k2
- **stringy**: Croc
- **talking**; after: hura
- **tenacious** (See viscid)
- **thick**: arn b7a.de* asar bg2 carb-v bg2 croc bg2 cupr k* dig bg2 ferr bg2 graph bg2 kreos bg2 lach bg2 nux-m bg2 nux-v b7a.de* plat bg2 puls bg2
- **thin**: carb-an bg2 carb-v bg2 dig c1 ferr k* ferr-p sne Gels bg2* graph bg2 kreos bg2 laur bg2 merc bg2 nux-m k* puls bg2 sabin k* sec bg2 stram bg2 sul-ac k2
- **threads** of blood mixed with white sputa: aur-m
- **uncoagulated**: alum k* ant-t k* bov k* bry k* dulc k* m-aust b7a.de mag-m bg2 ph-ac k* Phos k* sec k* stram k* stront-c bg2 sulph k*
- **viscid**: agn b7a.de* cann-s b7a.de* **Croc** k* Cupr k* mag-c k* ph-ac bg2 phos bg2 plat bg2 ran-b b7a.de* rhus-t b7a.de* samb b7a.de* sec k* seneg bg2 squil b7a.de*
- **walking** agg.: cham merc sul-ac zinc
- **whooping** cough; in: cor-r br1
- **working**; while: merc k*

BLUISH: am-c bg2 ambr bg2* arund k* brom dig bg2* Kali-bi k* Kali-c b4a.de* laur b7a.de nat-ar nux-v b7a.de* phos ptk1 plb b7a.de* sulph k*
- **alternating** with | **white**: arund k*
- **gray**: coc-c k*

BREAKFAST agg.; after: sep k*

BRICK-DUST color: (↗Rusty) bry Phos k* rhus-t

BROWNISH: agar k* Ars bamb-a stb2.de• bism b7a.de* bry k* calc b4a.de* caps Carb-an Carb-v k* con b4a.de hyos lyc k* mag-c k* nit-ac b4a.de* phos k* puls k* rhus-t b7a.de sil k* spong fd4.de symph fd3.de• thuj b4a.de [spect dfg1]
- **frothy**: carb-an h2
- **lumps**: agar phos
- **yellow**: lyc k* symph fd3.de•

BURNED; when dry on the floor looks as if: Phos k*

BURNING (See Hot)

CALCAREOUS tubercles: sars k*

CASTS (See Membranous)

CHEESE, like: chin fago k* kali-c ptk1 lyc puls k* sal-ac k* sanic k* thuj ptk1

COLD:
- **air**:
  - **agg.**: Lach plan k*
  - **amel.**: calc-s k*

CONSTANT, almost day and evening: Arg-met mang ptk1 spong ptk1 **Squil**

COOL (= cold): aq-mar skp7• asaf b7a.de* bry k* calad cann-s k* caust bg2 Cor-r k* irid-met srj5• Kali-c bg2 lach merc k* nit-ac k* nux-v k* Phos k* rhus-t k* sacch k* sin-a bg1 sin-n ptk1 sulph k* Verat b7a.de*

COPIOUS: acet-ac br1 agar agath-a nl2• ail all-s bro1 alum k* alum-p k2 alum-sil k2 *Alumn* am-c k* am-caust vh1 *Am-m* bro1 ambr k2 **Ammc** k* ant-ar br1* ant-c k* *Ant-i* bro1 ant-t k* antip vh arg-met bro1 **Ars** k* ars-i k2* ars-s-f k2 asar k* asc-t bro1 aspar k* bac br1* bals-p br1* bar-c b4a.de bar-m *Bism* k* bry k* **Cact** k* cadm-met sp1 **Calc** k* calc-p **Calc-s** k* calc-sil k2* canth bro1 carb-ac *Carb-v* k* carbn-s *Caust* k* cean br1* *Chel* k* *Chin* k* chinin-ar chir-fl bnm4• cic k* cina k* cob k* **Coc-c** k* cod k* coloc b4a.de cop k* cupr cupr-n a1 cycl k* daph k* dig k* dios k* *Dros* k* *Dulc* k* eucal bro1 eup-per k* euph k* **Euphr** k* *Ferr* k* *Ferr-ar* *Ferr-i* ferr-p gal-ac c1* gast a1 graph k* grin bro1 guaj k* **Hep** k* hepat br1* hippoz k* hydr k* ina-i mlk9.de indg inul br1 *Iod* k* *Ip* bro1 jab br1 kali-ar *Kali-bi* k* *Kali-br* hr1 *Kali-c* k* kali-i k* *Kali-n* b4a.de kali-sil k2 kreos k* lach k* *Laur* k* led k* lob **Lyc** k* mag-c ptk1 merc k2* merc-i-f k* merc-i-r k* myos-s bro1 myric k* myrt-ch bro1 nat-ar bro1 nat-s k2* oci-sa sp1 oena k* ol-car vs petr k* *Ph-ac* k* phel bro1* **Phos** k* phyt k* pilo bro1 *Pix* bg2 plb k* psil ft1 *Psor* **Puls** k* pyrog jl2 *Rumx* k* ruta k* *Samb* k* sang bg2* sanic sel br1 *Senec* *Seneg* k* **Sep** k* *Sil* k* silphu bro1 spong fd4.de *Squil* k* **Stann** k* stict stront-c b4a.de sul-ac k* sul-i k2 *Sulph* k* taosc iwa1• ter k* tere-la rly4• *Thuj* trif-p k* tril-p k* tritic-vg fd5.de tub ptk1* (non:uran-met k) *Uran-n* verat k* viol-o k* wies k* zinc k* zing k* [bell-p-sp dcm1 tax jsj7]

- **daytime**: cic *Sil*
- **morning**: agar *Alum* calc *Calc-s* k* *Carb-v* cob k* *Coc-c* dig k* euph k* euphr k* kali-bi *Ph-ac* *Phos* psor sanic squil *Stann*
- **forenoon** | **9**h: cob
- **evening**: *Carb-v* graph k*
  - **lying** down agg.: graph k*
- **night**: carb-v *Kali-bi*
- **accompanied** by | **Nose**; discharge from: sabal ptk1
- **coryza**; during: euphr k2
- **cough** | **after** each paroxysmal: *Agar* *Alumn* *Anan* *Arg-n* **Coc-c** kali-bi psor jl2 spong fd4.de stann c1 sulph
- **meals**, after: sanic
- **mouthful** at a time: **Euphr** k* lyc *Phos* k* rumx k*
- **moving**, while: *Ferr* k*
- **old** people: alum ptk1 *Ammc* *Ant-t* *Ars* **Bar-c** k* caust st *Kreos* senec c1
- **warm** room agg.: *Kali-c*

CORROSIVE: iod k* kali-c ptk1 sil ptk1 thuj ptk1

COTTON, like: aq-mar vml3•

CREAM-LIKE, yellowish white: ambr k* beryl tpw5 galeoc-c-h gms1• hepat br1 oci-sa sk4• petr-ra shn4•

CRUMBLY: ox-ac k*

CRUSTY: galeoc-c-h gms1•

DARK: aq-pet a1 *Ars* bism *Carb-an* cench k2 crot-c sk4• cupr k* galeoc-c-h gms1• hydrog srj2• kali-bi k* med naja nux-m oena k* petr-ra shn4• sul-i k2

DEFICIENT: bell-p sp1

DIFFICULT: aesc bro1 agn ail k* *All-s* k* aloe bro1 alum k* alum-p k2 alumn k2 am-br bro1 am-c k2 am-m bro1* ambr k* *Ammc* ang k* *Ant-t* b7a.de* apis aq-mar skp7• aq-pet a1 aral *Arg-n* bro1 *Arn* k* *Ars* k* ars-i k2 arum-d ptk2 arum-t k* arund k* asc-t k* aspar k* atro k* aur k* aur-i k2 aur-s k2 bacls-10 pte1*• bacls-7 fmm1• *Bar-c* k* bar-i k2 bar-s k2 borx k* *Bov* k* *Brom* bry k* *Calc* calc-p k2 camph k* cann-s k* canth k* carb-an h2 *Carb-v* b4a.de* **Caust** k* cham k* *Chel* k* chin k* chinin-ar chinin-s k* chlor k* cina k* cist bro1 *Coc-c* k* coca k* con k* cop k* cor-r crot-h crot-t a1 cub *Cupr* k* der k* dig k* digin a1 diphtox jl2 dros k* *Dulc* euphr k* ferr ferr-ar ferr-i ferr-p gels bg2 grin br1 *Hep* hepat br1 *Hydr* bro1 hydrc k* hydrog srj2• hyos k* iber bro1 ign k* *Iod* k* **Ip** k* irid-met srj5• jatr-c just ptk1 kali-ar *Kali-bi* k* *Kali-c* k* *Kali-s* kreos k* lac-h htj1• *Lach* k* limest-b es1• lob lyc k* m-arct b7.de mag-c k* mag-m k* *Mang* k* marr-vg mtf11 med k* melal-alt gya4 *Merc-i-f* bro1 *Merc-i-r* bro1 mosch k2 mur-ac bg2 myric bro1 nat-ar nat-c bro1 nat-m bro1 nat-s bro1 *Nit-ac* k* nux-m k* nux-v k* oci-sa sk4• oena k* op osm ox-ac k* par k* paull a1 petr bro1 ph-ac bro1 *Phos* k* *Phyt* bro1 plan k* plb k* psil ft1 *Psor* k* **Puls** k* quill br1 rat k* *Rumx* k* sang bro1* sapin a1 *Sel* bro1 **Seneg** k* sep k* silphu bro1 spong b7a.de* *Squil* k* *Stann* b4.de* staph k* stram sul-ac k* sul-i k2 sulph k* syph sne tarent k* *Thuj* b4a.de tritic-vg fd5.de tub-r jl2 vichy-g a1 zinc k* zinc-p k2

- **afternoon**: chin k* chinin-s
- **night**: diphtox jl2 melal-alt gya4

Difficult – **night**: ...

  - **midnight**:
    - **after** | **2** h: chinin-s k*
- **adhering** to throat, teeth and lips: **Kali-bi**
- **children**; in: caust mtf33 diphtox jl2 zinc mtf33
- **loose**; although it is (See COUGH - Loose - expectoration - without)
- **old** people: *Ammc* diphtox jl2 *Seneg* mrr1
- **swallow**, must (See Swallow)
- **tongue**, from where it must be removed by wiping; can raise sputa only to: apis
- **weak** to cough out; too: caps ptk1

DINNER; after: alumn k*

DIRTY-LOOKING: adam skp7• calc nit-ac k2 petr-ra shn4•

DRINKING amel.: am-c am-caust k* coc-c sne

DRY: galeoc-c-h gms1•

DUST, as if mixed with: ambr b7a.de* kreos b7a.de* nux-v b7a.de* phos k*

EASIER after each cough: aspar

EASY: *(↗Hawked)* acon agar b4a.de* ail ant-t **Arg-met** k* arund atra-r skp7*• aur bac c1 carb-v bro1 cimic *Coc-c* coloc dig dol dulc k* erio bro1 euphr k* flav jl2 hep iod ip kali-bi kali-s bro1 kalm kreos k* lach lact *M-ambo* b7.de mag-m mang meli nat-s bro1* oena phos ptk1* plb k* *Puls* k* ruta k* sang bg2 sil squil bro1* **Stann** k* staph k* sulph syc fmm1• tell tub al* ulm-c jsj8• verat k*

- **daytime**: ail k* *Arg-met* coc-c k* dig k* euphr ptk1 mang ptk1 phos ptk1 sil k* staph k*
- **morning**: ail a1 arg-met vh arund k* mang *Sil* b4a.de
- **evening**: *Arg-met* dig digin a1
- **night**: meli
- **lying** agg.: thuj bg2*
- **motion** agg.: ip k*
- **turning**; after (See Side)
- **waking**; on: meli k*

EATING; after: bell k* *Lyc* nux-m *Phos* sanic sep bg2 sil k* staph thuj k* tub ptk1

EPITHELIUM; exfoliated: chinin-s

FEEBLE POWER of expectoration (See Difficult)

FLAKES: agar hr1 ail k* phos k*

FLIES forcibly out of mouth: *(↗MOUTH - Mucus - flies)* arg-n ptk1 *Bad* k* *Chel* k* kali-c k* *Kali-m* bg3* mang ptk1 mez ptk1

FLOATING (See Trail)

FLOCCULENT: agar bg2 phos bg2 stann bg2 *Sulph* bg2

FREQUENT: agar aphis asar cina daph *Euphr* hep iod lact laur lyc mand sp1 *Puls* k* ruta samb *Seneg* *Sep* k* sil *Stann* k* sulph verat

FROTHY: *(↗Soapsuds)* *Acon* k* alet all-c k* am-c k* *Ant-ar* bro1 *Ant-i* c1 ant-t k* *Apis* k* aq-pet a1 aral arg-n *Arn* **Ars** k* ars-s-f k2 asc-t atra-r bnm3• atro k* bamb-a stb2.de• bapt bg2 bell b4a.de* bry bg2* bufo k* cadm-met sp1 calc canth k* carb-v bro1 cench chir-fl bnm4• chlor k* clem a1 cob k* cortico tpw7* cot a1 croc bro1 cub k* daph dios k* dros eucal *Ferr* k* ferr-p k* fl-ac gad a1 gast a1 grin bro1 hep k* hura hydrog srj2• iber bg1 iod bg2 ip bg2* *Kali-i* k* kali-p k* lach k* lat-m bnm6• led linu-c a1 lyc mrr1 merc bro1 mill k* nat-m k* nat-sil fd3.de• nux-v k* oena k* op k* paull k* petr k* *Phos* k* pilo bro1 plb k* podo fd3.de• *Puls* k* rumx k* sec k* sil k* silphu bro1 stict stram k* sul-ac bg2 sulph k* tanac bro1* ter thuj k* (non:uran-met k) uran-n urt-u k* vanil fd5.de verat mrr1 zinc zinc-p k2

- **morning**: cub k* dios k* sulph k* thuj k*
  - **8** h: dios
- **forenoon** | **9**h: cub
- **blood** and mucus; containing: acon bg2 **Arn** b7.de* ars bg2 *Dros* b7.de* ferr b7.de* hep bg2 led b7a.de* op k* phos bg2 sil bg2
- **threads** like fine twine; containing: croc br1

GELATINOUS: *(↗Viscid)* acon bg2 adam skp7• agar aloe bg2 *Alumn* **Arg-met** k* *Arg-n* arn k* bar-c k* bry *Cact* chin k* chinin-s coc-c k2 cortiso tpw7* cupr cur dig k* *Ferr* k* hyper bg2* kreos laur k* lyc bg2 med **Samb** sel bg2 *Sil* sulph viol-o

GLAIRY: *Arn* k* carbn-h cist ptk1 linu-c a1 lipp a1 med jl2 **Nat-m** *Nat-s* pall ptk1 sang hr1 tritic-vg fd5.de

GLOBULAR: *(↗Balls)* agar k* *Alumn* am-m bro1 ant-t bro1 arg-met bro1 *Bad* bro1 calad calc bro1 calc-f bro1 *Chel* bro1 chin-b coc-c k* *Kali-c* bro1 mang-act bro1 nat-sel bro1 podo fd3.de• rhus-t bro1 sel sil k* **Stann** thuj

GLUTINOUS (See Viscid)

GRANULAR: agar arg-n bg2 *Bad* k* *Calc* k* *Chin* k* hyper k* *Kali-bi* k* lach lyc k* mang mez k* nit-ac bg2 *Phos* k* *Rhus-t* b7a.de sel sep k* *Sil* k* spong k* *Stann* bg2 thuj

- **morning**: lyc
- **afternoon**:
  - **16** h | **23** h; until: lyc
- **night**:
  - **midnight**:
    - **after** | **3-4** h: lyc
- **offensive**: *Sil* k*
- **sneezing** agg.: mez k*

GRAYISH: alum-sil bro1 am-p bro1 **Ambr** k* anac k* ant-s-aur bro1 **Arg-met** k* *Ars* k* arum-t k* *Benz-ac* bro1 bufo k* cain *Calc* k* calc-i bro1 calc-p bro1 calen bro1 cann-s bro1 carb-an k* *Carb-v* bro1 chel chin k* *Cina* coc-c k* cop k* cortiso tpw7* cur dig k* dros k* dulc bro1 eupi k* ferr-act bro1 ferr-i k2 gast a1 ham k* iod *Kali-bi* k* kali-c k* *Kali-i* bro1 kali-m k2* kali-s bro1* kalm k* *Kreos* k* lac-ac k* lac-del hrn2• lach k* **Lyc** k* mag-m k* mang k* med k* merc-c k* nat-ar nat-c bro1 nat-m k* *Nat-s* bro1 *Nux-v* k* *Par* bro1 petr k* *Phos* k* psil ft1 psor bro1 *Puls* bro1 rhus-t k* *Seneg* k* *Sep* k* silphu bro1 sol-t-ae k* spong bro1* **Stann** k* sulph bro1 syph tab k* tep k* *Thuj* k* vanil fd5.de visc sp1

- **whitish**: am-i mtf11

GREENISH: adam skp7• anan anthraq rly4• *Arg-met* *Arn* *Ars* k* ars-i arum-t asaf k* atra-r skp7*• aur k* aur-s k2 bamb-a stb2.de• benz-ac k* borx k* bov k* bry k* bufo k* cain *Calc* k* calc-i k2 *Calc-s* **Calc-sil** *Cann-s* k* *Carb-an* k* **Carb-v** k* **Carbn-s** cob-n sp1 coc-c k* colch k* *Coloc* *Cop* *Crot-c* k* cub cur dig k* dros k* *Dulc* elaps gk eupi *Ferr* k* *Ferr-ar* ferr-i *Ferr-p* grin k2 ham k* hyos k* iod k* kali-ar *Kali-bi* k* kali-c k* **Kali-i** k* kali-p *Kali-s* kali-sil k2 kola stb3• kreos k* led k* **Lyc** k* m-aust b2.de* mag-c k* *Mang* k* med **Merc** k* *Merc-i-f* *Merc-i-r* k* *Nat-c* k* nat-m k* nat-p **Nat-s** k* nat-sil fd3.de• neon srj5• nit-ac k* nux-v k* oena k* ol-j k* ox-ac k* **Par** k* *Petr* petr-ra shn4• **Phos** k* plb k* psil ft1 **Psor** k* **Puls** k* raph k* rhus-t k* ruta fd4.de *Sep* k* *Sil* k* spong fd4.de **Stann** k* sul-i k2* **Sulph** k* syph k* thuj k* *Tub* k* vanil fd5.de x-ray sp1 zinc k* zinc-p k2 [spect dfg1]

- **morning**: ars k* crot-c k* elaps gk *Ferr* k* *Lyc* k* mang k* nat-m k* *Nit-ac* *Par* petr-ra shn4• *Psor* k* *Sil* k* spong fd4.de *Stann*
  - **7-10** h: sil
  - **waking**; on: ferr k* *Psor*
- **evening** | **lying** down; while: *Psor*
- **yellow**: musca-d szs1 petr-ra shn4• psor tl1* taosc iwa1•

HARD: agar k* am-m k* ant-c k* bry k* calad k* *Con* k* dig k* digin a1 fago k* hep b4a.de* iod k* kali-bi k* kali-c k* kreos k* lach k* mang k* **Nat-c** k* nat-s ox-ac k* phos k* sep k* *Sil* k* *Spong* k* *Stann* staph k* stront-c k* sul-i sulph k* thuj k*

HAWKED up, mucus: *(↗Easy)* agar all-c *Alum* am-c am-m ant-c *Ant-t* aphis bism calc caps carb-an *Carb-v* *Caust* *Cham* cina con croc crot-t dros **Euphr** k* ferr-i ferr-ma glycyr-g cte1• hep iod *Kali-bi* kali-c lach lam laur *Lyc* meph naja *Nat-m* *Nux-v* ol-an k* osm ox-ac *Par* k* petr ph-ac *Phos* *Plat* plb rhod rhus-t **Rumx** *Sel* *Seneg* *Sep* *Sil* *Stann* sulph h2 tarax thuj

- **morning**: ant-t *Nat-m* *Sel*
- **bloody**: am-c anac b4a.de cham ferr hyper kali-n *Sabad* b7a.de *Sel* b7a.de
  - **water**: **Gels**
- **cough** agg.; during: kali-bi bg2

HEAVY: kali-bi bg2 kali-n bg2 squil ptk1

HEMOPTYSIS (See Bloody)

HOT: aral ptk1* asar b7a.de* ictod bg1 mosch b7a.de* sabad bg2 sabal b7a.de sil bg2

HOUSE, in the: calc-s

IMPOSSIBLE (See Swallow)

INFREQUENT: acon k* alum k* arn k* bell k* caps ign k* tub-r jl2

JELLYLIKE (See Gelatinous)

KNOTS; in little (See Tubercles)

LEMON-COLORED (See Yellow)

LIQUIDS at back part of mouth; from contact of: am-caust k*

LIVER-COLORED: graph bro1 lyc bro1 puls k* sep bro1 stann bro1

LUMPY: acon agar k* ail k* aloe am-m k* apeir-s mlk9.de arg-n k* *Arn* k* ars k* bamb-a stb2.de• borx bry k* calad k* **Calc-s** k* carb-ac k* carb-v cent cetr chel k* cob k* coc-c k* coca colch k* coll dig k* gink-b sbd1• ham fd3.de• *Hep* k* indg kali-ar kali-bi k* *Kali-c* k* kali-s fd4.de kreos k* lac-d lach k* lyc k* *Mang* k* nat-ar nat-m k* ol-an bg2 osm k* ox-ac pall c1 par k* petr-ra shn4• phos k* pimp a1 plb b7a.de* podo fd3.de• puls ruta fd4.de *Sel* **Sil** k* sin-n k* sol-t-ae k* spong k* stann bg2 sulph k* thuj k* verat k* wies k*

- **morning**: carb-ac k* cob k* ham fd3.de• kali-s fd4.de lyc k* mang k* nat-ar petr-ra shn4•
- **forenoon** | **9**h: cob
- **evening**: kreos k*
- **core** of boil; lump, like: menth
- **smoke**-colored lumps, streaked with blood: kali-c

LYING: | **amel.**: cist ptk1 thuj ptk1

MASSES, in: ars k* coc-c k* kali-n k* sin-n k*

MEMBRANOUS: alum-sil k1 am-caust a1 *Brom* k* calc-act c1* chinin-s hep k* iod bg2* ip tl1 *Kali-bi* k* kali-n h2 *Merc-c* k* ozone sde2• **Spong** k*

MILKY: am-c k* *Ars* k* aur k* carb-v k* ferr k* **Kali-chl** k* kali-m k2 phos k* plb k* puls k* ruta fd4.de *Sep* k* *Sil* k* *Sulph* k* zinc k*

- **slimy**: *Sep* b4a.de

MUCOUS: acon k* aesc k* aeth k* agar k* agn k* *All-c* k* all-s k* aloe alum k* alum-p k2 *Alumn* k* am-c k* *Am-m* k* *Ambr* k* *Ammc* anac k* ang k* *Ant-c* k* *Ant-i* c1 *Ant-t* k* antip vh1 aral k* aran k* **Arg-met** k* **Arg-n** k* arn k* **Ars** k* ars-i k2 ars-s-f k2 *Arum-t* asar k* aspar k* atro k* aur k* aur-ar k2 aur-i k2 bac jl2 bad k* bapt a1 **Bar-c** k* bar-i k2 **Bar-m** bar-s k2 bell k* benz-ac k* bism k* *Borx* k* bov k* **Bry** k* bufo *Cact* calad k* **Calc** k* calc-i k2 *Calc-s* k* cann-s k* *Canth* k* *Caps* k* carb-ac carb-an k* *Carb-v* k* carbn-s carl a1 cassia-s ccrh1• **Caust** k* cham k* chel k* **Chin** k* **Chinin-ar** chinin-s cimic cimx k* *Cina* k* cob k* **Coc-c** k* coca cocc k* cod coloc b4a.de con cop corn croc k* crot-t k* cub k* cupr k* cycl k* der k* dig k* diph jl2 *Dirc* k* dor k* **Dros** k* **Dulc** k* erig erio a1 ery-a k* eug **Euphr** k* eupi k* ferr k* ferr-ar ferr-i ferr-p fl-ac k* franz a1 gamb gast a1 *Graph* k* guaj k* ham k* **Hep** k* hipp k* hydr k* hydr-ac k* hydrog srj2• hyos k* hyper k* iber k* ign k* indg k* *Iod* k* ip k* iris kali-ar **Kali-bi** k* *Kali-c* k* *Kali-chl* *Kali-i* k* kali-m k2 kali-n k* kali-p *Kali-s* kali-sil k2 kiss a1 kreos k* lac-ac k* lac-d **Lach** k* lact laur k* linu-c a1 **Lob** *Lob-s* k* loxo-lae bnm12• **Lyc** k* m-ambo b2.de m-aust b7.de* mag-c k* mag-m k* mag-s k* mand sp1 *Mang* k* *Med* merc k* merc-c k* mez k* mur-ac k* naja nat-ar *Nat-c* k* **Nat-m** k* nat-p *Nat-s* k* nat-sil fd3.de• nicc k* **Nit-ac** k* nux-m k* *Nux-v* k* oena k* ol-an a1 ol-j k* olib-sac wmh1 olnd k* op k* oscilloc jl2 osm k* ox-ac ozone sde2• **Par** k* pert jl2 *Petr* k* *Ph-ac* k* phel **Phos** k* phys k* pimp a1 plan k* plb k* **Psor** k* **Puls** k* pyrog jl2 raph k* rat k* rein a1 rheum k* rhod k* rhus-r *Rhus-t* k* rumx ruta k* sabad k* sabin k* samb k* **Sang** k* sec k* sedi a1 sel k* *Senec* *Seneg* k* *Sep* k* ser-a-c jl2 **Sil** k* sin-n k* spig k* *Spong* k* **Squil** k* **Stann** k* *Staph* k* stict stram a1 suis-hep rly4• sul-ac k* sul-i k2 sulph k* syph k2 tab k* tarax k* tep a1 ter *Thuj* k* trif-p a1 upa a1 (non:uran-met k) uran-n ust k* vanil fd5.de verat k* vinc visc sp1 wies a1 xan k* *Zinc* k* zinc-p k2

- **daytime**: *Ars* borx hr1 calc-s k* *Caust* mag-s k* *Spig* k*
- **morning**: *Agar* k* *All-c* k* *All-s* k* alum k* *Alumn* am-c h2 am-m k* ant-c k* *Ant-t* aral k* aran k* bell k* borx *Calc* k* chel cimx k* dig k* fl-ac k* franz a1 hipp k* ip k* *Kali-i* k* kali-s fd4.de lyc k* *Mang* k* mur-ac k* nat-m k* nat-sil fd3.de• ol-j k* ph-ac h2 *Phos* k* puls rein a1 sel k* sil k* *Stann* sul-ac h2 **Sulph** k* tab k* thuj k* vichy-g a1
  - **8.30** h: spong
  - **8-9** h: sil

- **morning**: ...
  - **bed** agg.; in: ferr$_{k*}$
  - **rising** agg.; after: chinin-s iod$_{h}$ mag-m$_{k*}$ sulph$_{k*}$
  - **waking** agg.; after: sulph$_{k*}$ thuj$_{k*}$
- **forenoon**: calc-s$_{k*}$ chinin-s coc-c$_{k*}$ iris lyc$_{k*}$ **Stann** sulph$_{k*}$ zinc$_{k*}$
  - **9** h: cob phyt
  - **10** h: iris
- **afternoon**: am-m$_{k*}$ *Bad*$_{k*}$ caust$_{k*}$ hydr$_{k*}$ hydr-ac$_{a1}$ mag-c$_{k*}$
  - **17** h: caust hydr mag-c
- **evening**: agn all-c$_{k*}$ *Calc*$_{k*}$ chinin-s crot-t$_{k*}$ dig$_{c1}$ hydr hydr-ac$_{k*}$ naja nat-m$_{k*}$ sulph$_{k*}$
- **night**: agar$_{k*}$ bell calc$_{k*}$ cycl$_{k*}$ hep kali-c$_{h2}$ op$_{k*}$ phos$_{k*}$ sep$_{k*}$ sil$_{k*}$ sulph$_{k*}$
  - **midnight**:
    - **after**:
      - **2** h; after: phos
      - **3** h: op
- **blackish**: lyc$_{b4.de*}$ thuj$_{b4a.de}$
- **bloody**: *Acon*$_{k*}$ ail alum$_{k*}$ alum-p$_{k2}$ **Am-c**$_{k*}$ anac ant-t *Apis*$_{k*}$ *Arg-n* **Arn**$_{k*}$ **Ars**$_{k*}$ ars-i$_{k2}$ aur-m$_{bg2}$ bell$_{k*}$ bism$_{k*}$ *Borx*$_{k*}$ *Bry*$_{k*}$ bufo$_{bg2}$ cact *Calc* *Calc-s* card-m *Caust*$_{b4a.de}$ chin$_{k*}$ cina cob coll con$_{k*}$ cupr daph dig$_{k*}$ *Dros*$_{k*}$ *Dulc* eug euphr$_{k*}$ **Ferr**$_{k*}$ ferr-i fl-ac$_{k*}$ **Gels** hep iod$_{k*}$ **Ip**$_{k*}$ kali-ar *Kali-bi*$_{k*}$ kali-c kali-n$_{h2}$ *Lach* lachn **Laur**$_{k*}$ lyc mag-m manc med *Merc* *Merc-c*$_{k*}$ *Nat-m*$_{k*}$ nat-sel$_{br1}$ nit-ac$_{k2}$ nux-m$_{k*}$ ol-j op$_{k*}$ **Phos**$_{k*}$ sabin$_{k*}$ **Sec**$_{k*}$ sel$_{k*}$ senec *Sep*$_{b4a.de}$ sil$_{k*}$ spong$_{k*}$ squil$_{k*}$ stict sul-ac$_{k*}$ zinc$_{k*}$
- **dry**: bry$_{b7.de*}$ plb$_{b7.de*}$
- **grayish**: *Ambr*$_{b7.de*}$
- **green**: psor$_{bg2}$
- **old** people: *Ammc*
- **reddish**: apis$_{bg2}$ kali-bi$_{bg2}$
- **tenacious**: agn$_{b7.de*}$ ant-c$_{b7.de*}$ **Ant-t**$_{b7a.de}$ *Ars*$_{b4.de*}$ bell$_{b4.de*}$ bry$_{b7.de*}$ *Cann-s*$_{b7.de*}$ canth$_{b7.de*}$ carb-v$_{b4.de*}$ caust$_{b4.de*}$ *Cham*$_{b7.de*}$ chin$_{b7a.de}$ cocc$_{b7.de*}$ euphr$_{b7.de*}$ iod$_{b4.de*}$ **Kali-bi**$_{bg2}$ laur$_{b7a.de}$ m-ambo$_{b7.de}$ nux-v$_{b7.de*}$ olnd$_{b7a.de}$ *Par*$_{b7.de*}$ *Ph-ac*$_{b4a.de}$ phos$_{b4.de*}$ plb$_{b7a.de}$ puls$_{b7.de*}$ ruta$_{b7.de*}$ *Samb*$_{b7.de*}$ *Seneg*$_{b4a.de}$ sep$_{b4.de*}$ *Spong*$_{b7a.de}$ squil$_{b7.de*}$ staph$_{b7.de*}$ vario$_{jl2}$ verat$_{b7.de*}$ zinc$_{b4.de*}$
- **thick**: *Ambr*$_{b7a.de}$
- **transculent**: *Ars*$_{b4.de*}$ *Chin*$_{b7.de*}$ *Ferr*$_{b7a.de}$ laur$_{b7.de*}$ seneg$_{b4a.de}$ sil$_{b4.de*}$
- **viscid** (See tenacious)
- **weather** agg.; cold: *Ammc*
- **white**: *Acon*$_{b7a.de}$ *Am-m*$_{b7a.de}$ ambr$_{b7.de*}$ arg-met$_{b7.de*}$ cina$_{b7.de*}$ *Kreos*$_{b7a.de}$ *Lyc*$_{b4a.de}$ par$_{b7.de*}$ phos$_{b4.de*}$ rhus-t$_{b7.de*}$ sep$_{b4.de*}$ sil$_{b4a.de}$ spong$_{b7.de*}$ *Squil*$_{b7a.de}$ suis-hep$_{rly4•}$ sulph$_{b4a.de}$
- **yellow**: ang$_{b7.de*}$ *Bism*$_{b7.de*}$ bry$_{b7.de*}$ cist$_{tl1}$ dig$_{c1}$ dros$_{b7.de*}$ plb$_{b7a.de}$ *Puls*$_{b7.de*}$ *Ruta*$_{b7a.de}$ *Staph*$_{b7a.de}$ ther$_{tl1}$ *Verat*$_{b7a.de}$

MUDDY-LIKE pus, flies like batter: phos$_{k*}$

ODOR:
- **burnt**: cycl$_{k*}$ dros$_{k*}$ nux-v$_{k*}$ puls$_{k*}$ ran-b$_{k*}$ sabad$_{k*}$ squil$_{k*}$ sulph$_{k*}$
- **cadaverous**: canth$_{k2}$
- **catarrh**; of an old: *Bell* *Ign*$_{k*}$ mez nux-v$_{b7a.de}$ **Puls**$_{k●*}$ sabin$_{k*}$ **Sulph**$_{k●*}$ zinc
- **fetid**: arn ars bell bry *Calc*$_{k*}$ **Caps**$_{sne}$ carb-ac carb-v$_{k*}$ cocc cop diphtox$_{jl2}$ ferr$_{c1}$ *Guaj* kali-p led lyc mag-c nat-c nit-ac ph-ac phos puls sacch *Sang*$_{k*}$ sep$_{k*}$ sil stann$_{k*}$ sulph thuj
- **garlic**, like: ars$_{k*}$ petr$_{b4a.de*}$
- **herbaceous**: ph-ac$_{h2}$
- **leather**; like that of Russian: arn$_{b7a.de*}$
- **milky**: aur dros$_{k*}$ phos sep spong$_{k*}$
  - **fresh** milk; like: dros$_{b7a.de}$ spong$_{b7a.de}$
- **musty**: **Borx**$_{k*}$ jug-c
- **odorless**: arg-met$_{b7.de*}$ calc$_{b4a.de*}$
- **offensive**: all-s alum$_{k*}$ alum-sil$_{k2}$ *Arn* **Ars**$_{k*}$ ars-i$_{k2*}$ ars-s-f$_{k2}$ asaf$_{k*}$ asar aur$_{k*}$ aur-ar$_{k2}$ aur-i$_{k2}$ aur-s$_{k2}$ bell$_{k*}$ **Borx**$_{k*}$ bry$_{k*}$ **Calc**$_{k*}$ calc-i$_{k2}$ calc-sil$_{k2}$ *Caps*$_{k*}$ *Carb-an* carb-v$_{k*}$ carbn-s caust$_{k*}$ cham$_{k*}$ chin$_{k*}$ chinin-ar cinnb$_{bg2}$ con$_{k*}$ cop$_{k*}$ cortico$_{tpw7}$ *Cupr*$_{k*}$ dig$_{k*}$ diphtox$_{jl2}$ dirc$_{k*}$ dros euphr$_{br1*}$ eupi$_{k*}$ fago$_{k*}$ ferr$_{k*}$ ferr-ar ferr-i ferr-p graph$_{k*}$ **Guaj**$_{k*}$ hep$_{k*}$ hura ign$_{k*}$ iod *Kali-c*$_{b4a.de*}$ *Kali-hp*$_{bro1}$ kali-i *Kali-p* kreos$_{k*}$ lach$_{bg2}$ led$_{k*}$ lipp$_{a1}$ **Lyc**$_{k*}$ m-aust$_{b2.de*}$ mag-c mag-m$_{k*}$ meph$_{ptk1}$ merc$_{k*}$ **Nat-ar** **Nat-c**$_{k*}$ nat-m *Nat-p*

Odor – offensive: ...

Nit-ac$_{k*}$ nux-v$_{k*}$ *Ph-ac*$_{k*}$ **Phel**$_{k*}$ *Pix*$_{bro1}$ *Psor*$_{k*}$ puls$_{k*}$ pyrog *Rhus-t*$_{k*}$ sabin$_{k*}$ sacch samb$_{xxb1}$ **Sang**$_{k*}$ seneg$_{k*}$ *Sep*$_{k*}$ *Sil*$_{k*}$ squil$_{k*}$ **Stann**$_{k*}$ sul-i$_{k2}$ sulph$_{k*}$ thuj$_{k*}$ tritic-vg$_{fd5.de}$ tub$_{al2}$ zinc$_{h2}$
  - **bedbugs**; smelling like: phel$_{ptk1}$
- **sour**: arn$_{b7a.de}$ *Borx*$_{b4a.de}$ calc$_{k*}$ cham$_{k*}$ dulc$_{k*}$ kali-n$_{b4a.de*}$ merc$_{k*}$ nit-ac$_{k*}$ nux-v$_{k*}$ sul-ac$_{k*}$ sulph$_{k*}$
- **sweetish**: squil
- **violets**, of: phos$_{k*}$ puls$_{k*}$ valer$_{b7a.de*}$

OLEAGINOUS: petr$_{k*}$

OPAQUE: aq-pet$_{a1}$ chinin-s **Kali-chl**

ORANGE: *Kali-c*$_{ptk1}$ puls$_{ptk1}$

PAINFUL: agath-a$_{nl2•}$ ars$_{k*}$ cub elaps iod$_{bg2}$ lach$_{bg2}$ lyc$_{bg2}$ merc-c$_{k*}$ nat-m$_{bg2}$ psil$_{ft1}$ zinc$_{bg2}$
- **heart**; as if from: elaps

PALE: kali-bi$_{k*}$ lycps-v

PASTY: kali-bi$_{k*}$

PHOSPHORESCENT: phos$_{k*}$

PIECES, in: alum$_{k*}$ nit-ac rhus-t sep sinus$_{rly4•}$

POLYPOID masses; of: kali-bi$_{bg2}$

PROFUSE (See Copious)

PRUNE juice: *Ars*$_{k*}$ carb-v$_{gm1}$ dig$_{bg2*}$ phos$_{bg2}$

PURULENT: acet-ac acon$_{k*}$ agar ail$_{k*}$ all-s$_{k*}$ am-c$_{k*}$ ammc$_{k2*}$ *Anac*$_{k*}$ anan anis ant-i$_{bro1}$ *Ant-t* antip$_{bro1}$ arg-met$_{k*}$ *Arn* *Ars*$_{k*}$ ars-i$_{k*}$ ars-s-f$_{k2}$ asaf$_{k*}$ asc-t$_{bro1}$ aur$_{k*}$ aur-ar$_{k2}$ aur-s$_{k2}$ bac$_{br1*}$ bals-p$_{br1*}$ bar-c bar-i$_{k2}$ bar-s$_{k2}$ bell$_{k*}$ blatta-o$_{br1}$ brom$_{k*}$ bry$_{k*}$ bufo **Calc**$_{k*}$ calc-i$_{k2}$ calc-p$_{bro1}$ *Calc-s*$_{k*}$ calc-sil$_{k2*}$ *Carb-an*$_{k*}$ carb-v$_{k*}$ *Carbn-s* cham$_{k*}$ **Chin**$_{k*}$ *Chinin-ar* cic$_{k*}$ *Cimx* cina$_{k*}$ cocc$_{k*}$ *Cod*$_{k*}$ **Con**$_{k*}$ cop$_{k*}$ cupr$_{k*}$ *Dig* *Dros*$_{k*}$ dulc$_{k*}$ elaps$_{gk}$ *Ery-a*$_{bro1}$ eucal$_{bro1}$ *Ferr*$_{k*}$ ferr-ar ferr-i ferr-p gels graph$_{k*}$ grin$_{k2}$ guaj$_{k*}$ hep$_{k*}$ hepat$_{bro1}$ *Hydr*$_{bro1}$ hyos$_{k*}$ ign$_{k*}$ iod$_{k*}$ ip$_{k*}$ kali-ar kali-bi$_{k*}$ *Kali-br*$_{hr1}$ **Kali-c**$_{k*}$ kali-i$_{k*}$ *Kali-n*$_{k*}$ *Kali-p*$_{k*}$ *Kali-s*$_{k*}$ kali-sil$_{k2}$ kalm *Kreos*$_{k*}$ lach$_{k*}$ laur$_{bg2*}$ led$_{k*}$ loxo-lae$_{bnm12•}$ **Lyc**$_{k*}$ mag-c$_{k*}$ mag-m$_{k*}$ *Merc*$_{k*}$ *Myos-s*$_{bro1}$ myrt-c$_{bro1}$ myrt-ch$_{bro1}$ **Nat-ar** *Nat-c*$_{k*}$ nat-m$_{k*}$ nat-p nat-s *Nit-ac*$_{k*}$ nux-m$_{k*}$ nux-v$_{k*}$ oena$_{k*}$ op oscilloc$_{jl2}$ *Ph-ac*$_{k*}$ phel$_{vml3•}$ **Phos**$_{k*}$ *Pix*$_{bro1}$ *Plb*$_{k*}$ podo$_{fd3.de•}$ psor$_{k*}$ ptel *Puls*$_{k*}$ pyrog$_{k2}$ *Rhus-t*$_{k*}$ ruta$_{k*}$ sabin$_{k*}$ samb$_{k*}$ sang$_{k*}$ sangin-n$_{bro1}$ sec$_{k*}$ **Sep**$_{k*}$ **Sil**$_{k*}$ sol-ni$_{bro1}$ squil$_{bro1}$ *Stann*$_{k*}$ *Staph*$_{k*}$ stront-c$_{b2.de*}$ sul-i$_{k2}$ *Sulph*$_{k*}$ symph$_{fd3.de•}$ syph ter$_{bro1}$ *Teucr-s*$_{bro1}$ tril-p$_{k*}$ tub$_{gk}$ verat vichy-g$_{a1}$ zinc$_{k*}$ zinc-s$_{k*}$
- **old** people; in: nat-s$_{k2}$

REDDISH (See Bloody)

ROPY: all-s$_{k*}$ alumn *Ant-t*$_{sne}$ apis *Coc-c*$_{k*}$ crot-c$_{sk4•}$ cystein-l$_{rly4•}$ hydr$_{k*}$ ip **Kali-bi** kali-s$_{fd4.de}$ *Lach* lob med *Merc* *Nat-s* rumx$_{k2}$ sang$_{k2}$ *Seneg* stict viol-o

ROSY: yers$_{jl2}$

RUSTY: *(↗Brick-dust)* *Acon*$_{k*}$ aq-mar$_{skp7•}$ arn *Ars* atro$_{k*}$ **Bry**$_{k*}$ canth$_{k2}$ carb-v$_{bg2}$ ferr-p$_{bro1}$ **Lyc**$_{k*}$ *Phos*$_{k*}$ pyrog *Rhus-t*$_{k*}$ *Sang*$_{k*}$ *Squil*$_{k*}$

SALIVA-LIKE: ars astac$_{k*}$ eug med merc mez thuj$_{k*}$

SCABS coughed up every few weeks: ferr

SCANTY: acon$_{k*}$ ail$_{k*}$ alum$_{bro1}$ alumn$_{k*}$ am-m$_{bro1}$ ant-t$_{k2*}$ apis apoc ars$_{k*}$ asc-t$_{bro1}$ aur-s$_{k2}$ bar-s$_{k2}$ brom$_{k*}$ bry$_{bro1}$ calc-s$_{k*}$ cassia-s$_{ccrh1•}$ *Caust*$_{bro1}$ cham$_{k*}$ cimic$_{bro1}$ clem$_{k*}$ cot$_{a1}$ cupr$_{k*}$ dig$_{k*}$ ery-a$_{k*}$ *Ferr*$_{k*}$ ferr-p ign$_{br1*}$ kali-bi$_{k*}$ kali-c$_{bro1}$ kali-hp$_{bro1}$ ketogl-ac$_{rly4•}$ lach$_{k*}$ lipp$_{a1}$ lyc$_{k*}$ *Mang*$_{hr1}$ med$_{jl2}$ mez$_{h2}$ morph$_{bro1}$ nit-ac$_{bro1}$ *Nux-v*$_{bro1}$ ol-sant$_{br1}$ op$_{k*}$ paeon$_{k*}$ **Phos**$_{k*}$ phyt$_{k*}$ *Puls*$_{k*}$ rumx$_{k*}$ samb$_{k*}$ sang$_{k*}$ sep$_{k*}$ sil spong$_{k*}$ squil$_{bro1}$ **Stann**$_{k*}$ stict syph$_{sne}$ tarent$_{k*}$ tub-r$_{jl}$ zinc$_{bro1}$
- **accompanied** by much rattling (See RESPIRATION - Rattling - expectoration - scanty)

SEA BATHING, after: mag-m

SEDIMENT; looks like a: sil$_{bg2}$

SIDE; is easier after turning from left to right: ars kali-c$_{k*}$ lyc$_{k*}$ *Phos*$_{k*}$ *Rumx* *Sep*$_{k*}$ *Thuj*$_{k*}$

SIT up at night to raise it; must: ferr k*

SITTING up in bed; on (See Bed - sitting)

SKIN, like dead: merc-c k*

SLATE-COLORED: kali-bi k* nat-ar

SLEEP; during: nat-m b4.de*

SLIMY (See Mucous)

SLIPS back again: arn bro1 **Caust** bro1* **Con** bro1* iod bro1 *Kali-c* bro1 *Kali-s* ptk1 lach bro1 nux-m bro1 sang ptk1 seneg ptk1 spong bro1 zinc-chr ptk1

SOAP-LIKE: arg-n k* caust bro1 ph-ac k*

SOAPSUDS, like: (↗*Frothy)* kali-i kali-p mez kh

SOUR (See Taste - sour)

STARCH, like: *Agar* k* *Arg-met* k* arn bg2 ars bg2 bar-c k* cact k* chin bg2 coca dig k* ferr bg2 laur k* nat-ar *Phyt Sel* seneg bg2 sil b4a.de* stann ptk1 sulph

- **yellow**: calc-f ptk1

STICKY (See Viscid)

STRINGY: (↗*Viscid)* aesc agar k* alum **Alumn** ammc vh1 *Arg-met* arg-n ptk1 ars-i arum-i asaf k* calc-s cassia-s ccrh1• *Caust* chinin-s cimic cinnb ptk1 cob-n sp1 *Coc-c* k* cupr-n a1 ery-a ferr hydr k* iber **Kali-bi** k* lac-h sk4• *Lach* k* lob mag-m ptk1 *Phos* phyt bg2* polys sk4• rumx k* ruta sang sanic seneg stann sne stict tritic-vg fd5.de vario jl2

SWALLOW what has been loosened; must: ambr *Arn* k* beryl tpw5 calad k* *Cann-s* k* **CAUST** k ●* chr-ac coca **Con** k* dig k* dros k* eug gels iod *Kali-c* k* kali-i nh6 **Kali-s** k* lach k* lyc k* m-aust b2.de mur-ac k* *Nux-m* k* osm k* pall c1 podo fd3.de• rumx seneg *Sep* k* **Spong** k ●* *Staph* k* tritic-vg fd5.de vanil fd5.de zinc k* zing

SYRUP-LIKE: carb-an k*

TASTE:

- **almonds**; like taste of: caust k* coff b7a.de* dig k*
- **bad**: anthraq rly4• carb-an lach k* lycps-v nat-m h2 puls k* sep
- **bilious**: puls k*
- **bitter**: acon k* ail arn k* *Ars* k* bry k* calc k* canth k* **Cham** k* chin k* chinin-ar *Cist* k* coloc k* con k* *Dros* k* ign k* irid-met srj5• kali-ar kali-bi kali-c k* kali-n bro1 lyc k* med menis ptk1 *Merc* k* nat-ar nat-c k* nat-m k* *Nit-ac* k* *Nux-v* k* paull a1 **Puls** k* sabad k* *Sep* k* stann k* sulph k* thuj b4a.de *Verat* k*
- **broth**, like meat: iod k*
- **burnt**: ang bry k* *Cycl* b2.de dros k* nux-v k* *Puls* k* *Ran-b* b2.de rhus-t *Sabad* b2.de squil k* sulph k* zinc
- **cabbage**, like boiled: sulph k*
- **catarrh**; of an old: *Bell* k* *Ign* k* mez k* nux-v k* phos k* **Puls** k* sabin k* *Sulph* k* zinc k*
- **chalk**, like: am-c b4a.de* ign k* nux-v k*
- **cheese**; like: chin b7a.de* kali-c mrr1 lyc b4a.de*
  - **old**: *Chin Kali-c Lyc* phos *Thuj* k* zinc
  - **putrid**: aur k* kali-c k* phos k* thuj bg2 zinc k*
- **clay**, like: cann-s k* chin k* phos k* puls k*
- **copper**, like: cupr k* kali-c k* lach k* nat-m k*
- **dung**; like: calc b4a.de* carb-an b4a.de* cham bg2 rhus-t b7a.de sep b4a.de* teucr b7a.de verat bg2
- **earthy**: ars k* cann-s b7a.de* caps k* chin k* ferr k* hep k* ign k* mang k* merc k* nux-m k* nux-v bg2 phos k* puls k* stront-c k*
- **eggs**; like:
  - **bad**: acon k* arn k* carb-v k* con eupi graph k* hep k* merc k* mez k* mur-ac k* ph-ac k* phos k* psor jl2 sep k* stann k* sulph k*
  - **raw**; like: *Psor* b4a.de
  - **yolk** of: kali-c k* ph-ac k* phos k* sep k* staph k* sulph k* thuj k*
- **empyreumatic** (See burnt)
- **fatty** (See greasy)
- **feces**; like: merc b4a.de*
- **fish**; like: acon k*

Taste: ...

- **flat**: alum am-m anac *Ant-c* ant-t arg-met arn ars aur aur-s bell *Bry Calc* cann-s k* caps *Chin* chinin-ar cop k* euphr *Ign* ip kali-ar kali-c kali-s fd4.de kreos *Lyc* nat-ar nat-c nat-m nat-p nat-s op *Par* petr ph-ac phos puls rhus-t sabad k* sabin sep stann *Staph* stront-c sulph thuj
- **flour**: lach b7a.de*
- **food**; of the ingested: am-c b4a.de* ant-c b7a.de* ant-t b7a.de* bell b4a.de* bry b7a.de* carb-v b4a.de* chin b7a.de* cocc b7a.de* con b4a.de* hep b4a.de* ign b7a.de* lyc b4a.de* mag-m b4a.de* nux-m bg2 nux-v b7a.de phos b4a.de* puls b7a.de* rhus-t b7a.de* sep b4a.de* sil b4a.de* sulph b4a.de* teucr b7a.de* thuj b4a.de*
- **fruit**; like unripe: alum b4a.de* apis b7a.de* ars b4a.de* caps b7a.de* euph b4a.de* lach b7a.de* mur-ac b4a.de* sabad b7a.de*
- **greasy**: alum k* ambr b7a.de *Asaf* k* bar-c b4a.de bry b7a.de carb-v b4a.de **Caust** k* cham k* euph b4a.de fl-ac k* ign b7a.de ip b7a.de kali-c k* laur b7a.de lyc k* *Mag-m* k* mang k* merc b4a.de merc-c k* mur-ac k* petr k* ph-ac b4a.de* phos k* **Puls** k* rhod b4a.de rhus-t k* sabad b2.de* sabin b2.de* sarr *Sil* k* thuj k* valer b7a.de
- **hair**; like: con b4a.de
- **herbaceous**: borx bro1 calad k* gels k* *Nux-v* k* *Ph-ac* k* puls k* sars k* stann k* verat k*
- **herring**; like: anac k* nux-m k*
- **inky**: calc b4a.de* fl-ac b4a.de*
- **iron**; like: calc b4a.de* cupr b7a.de* sulph bg2
- **leather**, like that of Russian: arn
- **meal**, like: lach k*
- **meat**; like putrid: ars k* aur b4a.de bell k* bry k* carb-v k* dulc k* kali-c k* lach k* nit-ac k* phos k* puls k* rhus-t k*
- **metallic**: agn k* alum k* am-c b2.de* bism b2.de* *Calc* k* cench cocc k* coloc b2.de* *Cupr* k* *Ferr* hep k* *Ip* k* kali-bi k* kali-c kreos lac-h htj1• lach k* *Merc* b2.de* merc-c b4a.de* nat-c k* nat-m k* nux-v k* plb bg1 ran-b k* *Rhus-t* k* sars k* seneg k* sulph k* vanil fd5.de zinc k*
- **milky**: ars bg2 phos k* sulph bg2
- **musty**: **Borx** k* led k* lyc k* m-ambo b2.de mag-c b4a.de merc k* ph-ac k* rhus-t k* teucr k* thuj k*
- **nauseous**: all-c a1 *Ars* k* asaf k* bry k* calc k* canth k* carb-an chin k* cina k* coc-c k* cocc k* cop k* dig *Dros* k* ferr k* ferr-ar iod k* *Ip* k* kali-ar kali-c k* *Lach* bg2 led k* *Merc* k* nat-m k* nit-ac nux-v k* phos k* psor **Puls** k* sabad k* samb k* sel k* sep k* sil squil k* *Stann* k* sulph k* tarent k* zinc k*
- **nuts**; like: caust b4a.de coff b7a.de dig b4a.de
- **offensive**: arn bg2 *Ars* b4.de* asaf ptk1 bell bg2 carb-v bg2 cham bg2 con bg2 cupr bg2 ferr bg2 *Graph* bg2 *Iod* b4a.de kali-c b4a.de lach bg2* **Puls** bg2* sep bg2 *Stann* b4.de*
- **oil**; tasting like (See greasy)
- **onions**; like: ars *Asaf* k* mag-m k* petr sul-ac k* sulph k*
- **oranges**, like: phos k*
- **peach** kernels, like: laur k*
- **peas**, like raw: puls k* zinc k*
- **pepper**, like: acon k* ars k* mez k* sabad k* sulph k*
- **pitch**; like: canth b7a.de*
- **putrid**: acon k* all-s k* alum k* alum-p k2 *Arn* k* *Ars* k* ars-i bell k* bov k* bry k* *Calc* k* carb-an k* *Carb-v* k* carbn-s caust k* *Cham* k* cocc k* con k* cupr k* dig dros k* dulc ferr k* ferr-ar k2 ferr-i ferr-p *Graph* b4a.de ham hep iod k* ip k* *Kali-ar* kali-c k* kali-p k2 kalm k* kreos lach led lyc k* merc k* *Nat-ar* *Nat-c* nat-p nit-ac nux-v k* ph-ac phos k* *Puls* k* *Pyrog* jl2 rhus-t k* samb k* *Sang* bg2 sarr sep k* sil *Stann* k* staph k* sulph k* tritic-vg fd5.de verat k* zinc k* zinc-p k2
- **rancid**: alum k* ambr k* asaf k* bar-c k* bry k* caust k* cham k* euph b4a.de* ip k* lach k* merc k* mur-ac k* nux-v k* petr k* phos k* puls k* rhod b4a.de* thuj k*
- **resinous**: thuj bg2
- **salty**: acon k* agar k* alum k* alum-p k2 am-c k* *Ambr* k* ang k* ant-t k* aq-mar skp7• aral k* **Ars** k* ars-i bar-c k* bar-i k2 bell k* bov k* bry sne *Calc* k* *Cann-s* k* *Carb-v* k* carbn-s cassia-s ccrh1• *Chin* k* chinin-ar coc-c cocc k* coloc con k* cop k* dros k* euph k* *Graph* k* hyos k* iod k* irid-met srj5• kali-bi k* kali-c bg2 *Kali-i* nh6* kali-p kalm k* lac-ac lac-h sk4• lach k* lepi k* **Lyc** k* macro a1 *Mag-c* k* mag-m k* *Merc* k* *Merc-c* k* mez k* *Nat-c* k* *Nat-m* k* nat-p nit-ac k* *Nux-m* k* nux-v k* petr-ra shn4• *Ph-ac* k* **Phos** k* plan k* podo fd3.de• psor k* **Puls** k* raph k* rhus-t k* sacch samb k* **Sep** k* sil k* spong k* squil bro1 *Stann* k* staph stram bg2 sul-ac k* sulph k* tarax k* tarent k* tell ptk1 ther verat k* wies k* [spect dfg1]
  - **morning**: *Ph-ac* a1 (non:phos kl) puls a1

- **sea**-weed, like: spong
- **smoky**: bry k* kali-c mtf33 nux-v k* puls k* rhus-t k* sep k*
- **soapy**: bar-c bry b7a.de* dulc k* iod k* merc k*
- **sour**: ambr k* ang k* ant-t k* ars k* *Bell* k* borx bg2 bry k* **Calc** k* cann-s carb-an k* carb-v k* cham k* chin k* coc-c k* con k* crot-t k* dros dulc bg2 ferr k* graph k* hell bg2 hep k* hyos ign k* iod ip k* iris bro1 kali-ar *Kali-c* k* kali-n k* lach k* lat-m sp1 laur k* lyc k* mag-c mag-m k* mag-s k* *Merc* k* nat-c k* nat-m k* nit-ac k* **Nux-v** k* petr k* ph-ac k* **Phos** k* plan k* plb k* psor jl2 *Puls* k* rhus-t k* sabin k* sep k* spong k* stann k* sul-ac k* *Sulph* k* tarax k* verat k* zinc bro1
- **sugar**; like: (↗*sweetish)* calc b4a.de* lyc b4a.de* sep b4a.de*
- **sulphur**, like: cocc k* nux-v k* ph-ac k* phos k* plb k* sulph k*
- **sweetish**: (↗*sugar)* acon k* aesc ptk1 all-c a1 alum k* alum-p k2 am-c k* anac k* ant-s-aur ant-t k* apis k* ars k* ars-i asar k* astac aur k* aur-ar k2 beryl tpw5* **Calc** k* calc-s cann-s k* canth k* carb-an chin k* cob k* coc-c k* cocc k* cop *Dig* k* dirc ferr k* ferr-ar gink-b sbd1• hep k* hepat br1* iod k* ip k* iris kali-ar kali-bi k* *Kali-c* k* kali-n h2 kali-p kreos k* lach bg2 laur k* limest-b es1• lyc k* lycps-v k* mag-c k* mag-m mag-p ptk1 merc k* mez k* nat-p fkr6.de nux-m b2.de nux-v k* oci-sa sk4• **Phos** k* *Plb* k* ptel *Puls* k* rhus-t k* *Sabad* k* samb k* sangin-n bro1 *Sanic* sel k* senec sep k* *Squil* k* **Stann** k* sul-ac k* sul-i k2 sulph k* sumb symph fd3.de• thuj b4a.de tritic-vg fd5.de zinc k* zinc-chr ptk1 zinc-p k2
  - **salty**: acon bg2
- **tallow**; like: valer b7a.de*
- **tar**, like: con k*
- **tasteless**: alum b2.de* am-m b2.de* anac bg2 ant-c b2.de* ant-t bg2 arg-met b2.de* arn b2.de* ars b2.de* aur b2.de* bell b2.de* *Bry* b2.de* *Calc* b2.de* caps b2.de* *Chin* b2.de* cina bg2 dulc bg2 euphr b2.de* *Ign* b2.de* ip b2.de* kali-c b2.de* kali-n bg2 kreos b2.de* lyc b2.de* nat-c b2.de* nat-m b2.de* *Par* b2.de* petr b2.de* ph-ac b2.de* phos b2.de* puls b2.de* rhus-t b2.de* sabin b2.de* sep bg2 stann b2.de* *Staph* b2.de* stront-c b2.de* sulph b2.de* thuj b2.de*
- **tobacco** juice, like: *Puls* k*
- **urine**, like: graph k* phos k* seneg k*
- **water**; like putrid: acon b7a.de*
- **wine**, like: bell k* bry k*
- **wood**; like: ars k* ign k* stram k* sulph k*
  - **rotten**: sulph bg2

TASTELESS (See Taste - tasteless)

TENACIOUS (See Viscid)

THICK: (↗*Viscid)* abrom-a ks5 acon k* adam skp7• agar k* aloe *Alumn* am-m k* ambr ant-c bg2 *Ant-i* c1 ant-t k* anthraq rly4• aq-pet a1 *Arg-met* k* **Arg-n** k* *Ars* k* ars-s-f k2 arum-d ptk2 arum-i a1 asaf bg2 atra-r skp7*• atro k* aur-m k* bar-c bg2 bell bg2 borx bg2 brom k2* bry k* *Cact* *Calc* k* calc-s calc-sil k2 canth mrr1 carb-ac k* carb-an carb-v b4a.de* cassia-s cdd7*• *Caust* k* chlor k* *Cist* k* cob *Coc-c* k* cot a1 *Cycl* k* dig b4a.de *Dulc* erio a1 ery-a k* eucal k* eupi k* ferr k* ferr-ar ferr-i ferr-p ferul a1 fuma-ac rly4• glon graph bg2 grin k2 ham **Hep** k* hepat br1 hura **Hydr** k* hydrog srj2• inul br1 iod h* ip k* **Kali-bi** k* kali-c k2* kali-chl kali-i k2 *Kali-m* br1 kali-p kali-s k2* kalm kreos k* *Lac-c* lac-h htj1*• laur k* lepi a1 *Lyc* k* mag-m mang bg2 *Merc* b4a.de merc-i-r k* mur-ac bg2 naja nat-c bg2 nat-p nat-s k2 nit-ac bg2 oena ol-j k* op k* ox-ac pert jl2 petr-ra shn4• phos k* *Phyt* psil ft1 *Puls* k* pyrid rly4• pyrog raph k* rhodi br1* rumx k2 ruta k* sabad bg2 sacch samb bg2 sang k* sars bg2 sel bg2 senec seneg k* *Sep* **Sil** k* *Spong* b7a.de squil *Stann* k* staph bg2 stram sulph k* syph tarent k* ther tl1 thuj k* tritic-vg fd5.de **Tub** k* tung-met bdx1• ust k* vario br1* yers jl2 zinc k*
- **morning**: agar k* cassia-s ccrh1• franz a1 lyc k* *Phos* *Puls* *Sil* **Stann** sulph k* tarent tere-la rly4• thuj k*
  - **rising** agg.; after: *Phos* puls sulph k*
  - **waking** agg.; after: lyc k*
- **afternoon**: eucal k*
- **evening**: cassia-s ccrh1• kreos k* sulph k*
- **night**: calc h2 *Cycl* k* lyc k* sacch
- **warm** applications | **amel**.: cassia-s ccrh1•

THIN: (↗*Watery)* acon bg1 all-s am-c ant-c ars k2 bry k* canth k2 cassia-s ccrh1• colch cupr daph dig c1 *Ferr* gels bg1 iber jab br1 kali-n mag-c k* sacch sul-ac k2 tritic-vg fd5.de

TICKLING: caust b4.de*

TOUGH: (↗*Viscid)* acon k* aesc k* agn k* *All-c* *Alumn* ambr anac anis c1 ant-c *Ant-t* aral vh1 *Ars* k* ars-i atro k* aur aur-ar k2 aur-i k2 *Bac* br1 bamb-a stb2.de• bell bov k* *Bry* k* **Calc** *Cann-s* canth *Carb-an* carb-v carl k* *Caust* k* cham cist cob *Coc-c* k* cocc cupr cupr-act br1 *Dulc* euphr grin br1 **Hep** indg *Iod* iris **Kali-bi** k* kali-c k* kali-sil k2 *Lac-c* mag-c mag-m mang merc-i-r k* mez nux-m nux-v ol-an ptk1 ozone sde2• par k* petr ph-ac phos phyt k* puls *Rumx* k* ruta samb sang k* sanic senec k* seneg k* *Sep* sil k* spong squil **Stann** staph sul-i k2 syc bka1• tarent k* thuj k* verat vinc *Zinc* [nicc stj1]
- **morning**: calc k* *Cann-s* kali-bi petr k* *Phos* phyt sars *Sil*
  - **bed** agg.; in: calc k*
- **forenoon** | **9h**: phyt

TRAIL in water; like a: calc bg2*

TRANSPARENT: agar k* alum k* alumn k* am-c am-m ant-t k* *Apis* k* aq-pet a1 **Arg-met** arn k* *Ars* k* asaf bamb-a stb2.de• *Bar-c* borx bry k* bufo bg2 calc-s k* *Caust* chin *Ferr* k* galeoc-c-h gms1• hydrog srj2• *Kali-bi* k* kali-s fd4.de kola stb3• kreos lac-h htj1• laur *Med* *Mez* **Nat-m** petr *Ph-ac* **Phos** k* puls ruta fd4.de *Sel* k* senec k* **Seneg** k* *Sil* k* spong fd4.de *Stann* sulph tritic-vg fd5.de vanil fd5.de
- **morning**: sel br1*

TUBERCLES: hep mag-c *Phos* *Sil* *Spong*
- **brown**: phos k* *Thuj* b4a.de
- **offensive**: mag-c phos sil

TURNING on side (See Side)

VISCID: (↗*Gelatinous; Stringy; Thick; Tough)* acet-ac k* acon k* *Agar* agn k* ail k* *All-c* all-s k* aloe alum k* alum-p k2 alum-sil k2 **Alumn** *Am-br* *Am-c* bro1 am-m k* *Ambr* ammc bro1 anac k* ant-c k* ant-i bro1 ant-s-aur bro1 ant-t k* apeir-s mlk9.de aq-pet a1 aral bro1* **Arg-met** **Arg-n** *Ars* k* ars-i ars-s-f k2 arum-i a1 asaf bg2 asar asc-t bro1 aspar k* aur *Bac* br1 bacls-7 fmm1• *Bad* k* bals-p bro1 *Bar-c* k* bar-i k2 bar-m bro1 bar-s k2 bell k* borx k* *Bov* k* *Bry* k* bufo k* *Cact* *Calc* k* calc-i k2 calc-s calc-sil k2 *Cann-s* k* canth k* carb-ac *Carb-v* k* *Carbn-s* *Caust* k* *Cham* k* chel bro1 chin k* chinin-ar chion ptk1 cimic cob **Coc-c** k* coca cocc b2.de* colch k* crot-t a1 *Cupr* k* cupr-act br1 cystein-l rly4• dig k* *Dulc* k* eucal bro1 euphr k* ferr k* ferr-ar *Ferr-i* ferr-p graph k* grin k* hell **Hep** k* hepat br1 **Hydr** k* hyper k* iber indg k* *Iod* k* *Ip* bro1 jug-c kali-ar **Kali-bi** k* *Kali-c* k* *Kali-hp* bro1 kali-m bro1 kali-n a1 kali-p kali-s kali-sil k2 kreos lac-ac k* *Lac-c* lac-h sk4• lach k* laur bro1 lepi a1 lyc k* m-ambo b2.de mag-c k* mag-m k* *Mang* k* mang-act bro1 med k* merc k* *Merc-c* merc-sul k* *Mez* k* morg-p pte1• morph bro1 myrt-c bro1 naja k* naphtin bro1 *Nat-ar* nat-c k* nat-m k* nat-p nat-s k2* *Nit-ac* *Nux-v* k* oena ol-j bg2 *Olnd* onos op k* osm bg2* *Paeon* k* *Par* k* petr k* ph-ac k* **Phos** k* *Phyt* k* pitu-gl skp7• plb k* psil ft1 *Psor* k* **Puls** k* *Pyrog* quill bro1 raph a1 rhus-t k* *Rumx* k* ruta sabad k* sabin k* **Samb** k* sang k* sangin-n bro1 sec k* **Seneg** k* *Sep* k* ser-a-c jl2 *Sil* k* silphu bro1 spig k* *Spong* k* squil k* **Stann** k* *Staph* k* sul-ac k* sul-i k2* sulph k* syc fmm1• tep thuj k* tub c1 ust vario jl2 verat k* visc sp1 wies k* x-ray sp1 *Zinc* k* zinc-chr ptk1 zinc-p k2 [*Nicc* stj1]

WALKING:
- **after** | **agg**.: ferr
- **agg**.: cham merc nat-m nux-v bg2 sul-ac zinc
- **air** agg.; in open: merc nux-v *Sacch*

WATERY: (↗*Thin)* acon acon-l a1 agar k* am-c k* am-m k* ang k* aq-mar jl* aq-pet a1 arg-met k* *Ars* k* bell bov k* calc b4a.de* calc-f sp1 canth k2 caps bg2 carb-an k* *Carb-v* k* cham k* chin k* cupr bg2 *Daph* elaps br euphr k* ferr k* *Graph* k* guaj k* hydrog srj2• ign bg2 jac-c k* *Kali-s* *Lach* k* lyc k* *Mag-c* k* mag-m k* melal-alt gya4 *Merc* k* mez k* mur-ac k* nat-c nat-m b4a.de* nit-ac k2 nux-v k* op k* par bg2 phos k* phys k* plb k* puls k* ran-s k* rumx sacch sep k* squil k* *Stann* k* sul-ac k* sulph k* thuj k* tritic-vg fd5.de tub c1

WHITE: abrom-a ks5 *Acon* k* adam skp7• *Agar* k* ail k* alum alum-p k2 alum-sil k2 *Alumn* *Am-br* am-c am-m k* ambr k* *Ant-i* c1 ant-t k* *Apis* apoc *Arg-met* k* arn *Ars* k* arund k* aur-m k* bamb-a stb2.de• bar-c *Borx* bov brom k2 bry bro1 cadm-met sp1 *Calc* calc-s k* calc-sil k2 caps k* carb-ac carb-an k* *Carb-v* k* cassia-s ccrh1• *Caust* k* cench chin k* chinin-ar chinin-s chlor k* cina k* cob *Coc-c* k* crot-t k* cupr k* cur dulc erio a1 eucal k* ferr k* ferr-ar ferr-i ferr-p fl-ac gad a1 graph k2 hydrog srj2• hyper iber a1 *Iod* ip irid-met srj5• *Kali-bi* k* kali-c mtf33 **Kali-chl** kali-i k* kali-m k2* kali-p kali-s k2 *Kreos* k* *Lac-c* lac-h htj1• laur k* **Lyc** k* manc k* *Med* merc-i-r k* mez naja bg2 **Nat-m** nat-s k2 nat-sil fd3.de• nicc oena k* ol-j k* onos ox-ac par k* petr

White: ...
petr-ra shn4• ph-ac k* **Phos** k* phys k* pitu-gl skp7• plumbg a1 podo fd3.de• *Puls* k* puls-n raph k* rhus-t k* rumx k2 sacch sang *Sel* k* senec k* **Seneg** k* **Sep** k* sil k* *Spong* k* *Squil* k* *Stann* k* stront-c k* *Sulph* k* syph tarent k* tell k* thuj k* vanil fd5.de [spect dfg1]
- **daytime**: *Arg-met Stann*
- **morning**: *Agar Alumn* carb-v k* **Kali-bi** *Nat-m Phos* puls *Sulph* k*
- **evening**: *Arg-met Arg-n* calc-s k* crot-t k*
- **night**: sep h2
- **albuminous**: *Agar* alum **Alumn** am-c am-m k* ant-t *Apis* **Arg-met** am k* *Ars* k* asaf *Bar-c* k* borx k* bov k* bry calc-s *Caust* chin k* **Coc-c** k* cur *Ferr* k* hydrog srj2• ip *Kali-bi* k* *Laur* k* *Med Mez* k* **Nat-m** *Nat-s* petr k* *Ph-ac* **Phos** podo fd3.de• ruta fd4.de *Sel* **Seneg** k* *Sil* k* *Stann* k* sulph k*
- **blue** alternately; and (See Bluish - alternating - white)
- **eating**; after: sil
- **opaque**: **Kali-chl**
- **tough**: **Anis** c1 caust mtf33 podo fd3.de•
- **yellowish** white: *Carb-an* b4a.de *Carb-v* b4a.de lyc b4.de* ph-ac b4.de* *Phos* b4a.de sep b4a.de stront-c b4a.de **Sulph** b4a.de

WIND:
- **cold** | **agg.**: lycps-v

YELLOW: abrom-a ks5 *Acon* k* adam skp7• ail aloe alum k* alum-p k2 alum-sil k2 alumn k2 am-c k* *Am-m* k* ambr k* ammc k2* anac k* anan *Ang* k* ant-c k* *Ant-i* c1 ant-t tl1 apeir-s mlk9.de arg-met k* *Arg-n Ars* k* *Ars-i* ars-s-f k2 arum-m arum-t asc-t astac aur k* aur-ar k2 aur-i k2 aur-m aur-s *Bad* k* bar-c k* bar-i k2 bar-m bar-s k2 bell k* bism k* borx k* bov k* brom k* *Bry* k* bufo *Cact* cadm-met sp1 **Calc** k* calc-i k2 **Calc-p** **Calc-s** k* calc-sil k2 cann-s k* *Canth* carb-an k* *Carb-v* k* carbn-s cassia-s cdd7*• caust k* cench cham k* chlol chlor k* cic k* cist *Coc-c* k* coca coloc k* con k* cop cub cupr k* cupr-n a1 cur cystein-l rly4• daph dig k* digin a1 *Dros* k* elaps gk eug k* eupi k* ferr k* ferr-ar ferr-i *Ferr-p* ferul a1 fuma-ac rly4• gels a1 graph k* grin k2 ham hed sp1 **Hep** k* hura **Hydr** hydr-ac hydrog srj2• *Ign* k* ina-i mlk9.de iod k* ip k* irid-met srj5• kali-ar *Kali-bi* k* *Kali-c* k* *Kali-chl Kali-i* bg2 kali-m k2 *Kali-p Kali-s* k* kali-sil k2 ketogl-ac rly4• kola stb3• *Kreos* k* lac-ac lac-h sk4• lach lat-m sp1 linu-c k* **Lyc** k* mag-c k* mag-m k* *Mang* k* med *Merc* k* merc-i-f *Merc-i-r* k* mez k* mur-ac k* musca-d szs1 *Nat-ar Nat-c* k* nat-m k* *Nat-p* nat-s k2 neon srj5• *Nit-ac* k* nux-v k* oena k* *Ol-j* k* op k* ox-ac ozone sde2• par k* paull a1 *Petr* k* petr-ra shn4• *Ph-ac* k* **Phos** k* phyt plb k* podo fd3.de• polys sk4• *Psor* k* **Puls** k* pyrid rly4• pyrog rhodi br1* rumx *Ruta* k* sabad k* sabin b2.de* sacch samb sang *Sanic* sel k* senec seneg k* **Sep** k* **Sil** k* spig k* *Spong* k* **Stann** k* *Staph* k* sul-ac k* sul-i k2* *Sulph* k* symph fd3.de• syph tarent k* tere-la rly4• *Thuj* k* tritic-vg fd5.de **Tub** k* tung-met bdx1• vanil fd5.de verat k* visc sp1 *Zinc* k* zinc-p k2 [bell-p-sp dcm1 spect dfg1]
- **morning**: ail aur bamb-a stb2.de• *Calc* k* *Calc-p* k* cassia-s ccrh1• cench franz a1 gink-b sbd1• *Kali-bi* lyc k* mag-c mang k* melal-alt gya4 *Ph-ac* k* *Phos* **Puls** *Sil* k* **Stann** tarent tub c1
  - **7**-10 h: sil
  - **waking**; on: aur
- **forenoon**: staph
- **noon** | **12**-15 h: calc-s
- **afternoon**: anac k* calc-s k*
- **evening**: cassia-s ccrh1•
- **night**: lyc a1 staph
- **frothy**: hura bg2
- **greenish**: ars-i ptk1 kali-bi bg2 lyc ptk1 puls bg2 stann bg2
- **lemon**-colored: kali-c k* lyc k* melal-alt gya4 petr-ra shn4• phos k* puls k*
- **mucous** | **evening**: dig c1
- **orange**-colored: hydrog srj2• *Kali-c* petr-ra shn4• phos puls
- **warm** applications | **amel.**: cassia-s ccrh1•

MORNING: agar bg2 *Am-m* b7.de* ang b7.de* ant-c b7.de* apis b7a.de arn b7.de* bov b4a.de bry b7.de* calad b7.de* calc bg2* canth b7.de* carb-an b4a.de *Carb-v* b4.de* caust bg2 cham bg2 chel bg2 chin b7.de* cina b7.de* coff b7.de* colch b7.de* croc b7.de* cycl b7.de* dig b4.de* elaps bg2 euphr b7.de* hep b4a.de ign b7.de* kali-bi bg2 kali-c b4.de* kali-n b4.de* kreos b7a.de led b7.de* *Lyc* b4.de* m-ambo b7.de m-arct b7.de m-aust b7.de mag-m b4a.de mang b4.de* merc-c b4a.de mez bg2 nat-c b4.de* nat-m b4.de* nit-ac b4.de* nux-m b7.de* nux-v b7.de* petr b4.de* phos b4a.de* podo bg2 puls b7.de* *Ran-b* b7.de* ran-s b7.de* rheum b7.de* rhus-t b7.de* sars b4.de* sel b7a.de seneg b4.de* sep b4.de* sil b4.de* spig b7.de* squil b7.de* stann b4.de* *Staph* b7.de* stram b7.de* sul-ac b4.de* sulph b4.de* tarax b7.de* thuj b4a.de* verat b7.de* verb b7.de* zinc b4.de*

- **bed** agg.; in: ant-t bg2 carb-an bg2 con bg2 kali-bi bg2

FORENOON: acon bg2 anac b4a.de *Cann-s* b7.de* carb-an b4.de* caust b4.de* gels bg2 kali-c b4.de* laur b7.de* mang b4.de* merc b4.de* nat-m bg2 nit-ac b4.de* nux-m b7.de* par b7.de* petr b4.de* phos b4.de* ran-b b7.de* sabad b7.de* sep bg2 stann b4.de* sul-ac b4.de* sulph bg2 zinc b4.de*

AFTERNOON: alum b4.de* am-c b4.de* am-m b7.de* ant-c b7.de* asaf b7.de* bov b4.de* calc b4.de* canth b7.de* chel bg2 colch bg2 euphr bg2 gels bg2 ign b7.de* kali-bi bg2 kali-c b4.de* kali-n b4.de* laur b7.de* lyc b4.de* m-aust b7.de mag-c b4.de* meny b7.de* mur-ac b4.de* nat-c b4.de* nat-m b4.de* nux-m b7.de* nux-v b7.de* petr b4.de* ph-ac b4.de* phos b4.de* phyt bg2 plb b7.de* puls b7.de* *Ran-b* b7.de* rhod b4.de* rhus-t bg2 sars b4.de* seneg b4.de* sep b4.de* sil b4.de* spig b7.de* staph b7.de* valer b7.de* viol-t b7.de* zinc b4.de*

EVENING: acon b7.de* agar bg2 alum b4.de* am-c b4.de* am-m b7.de* ang b7.de* ant-t b7.de* arg-met b7.de* arg-n bg2 arn b7.de* ars b4.de* bar-c b4.de* bell b4.de* bry b7.de* bufo bg2 calad b7.de* calc b4.de* canth b7.de* carb-an b4.de* carb-v b4.de* caust b4.de* chel bg2 chin b7.de* cocc b7.de* colch b7.de* coloc b4.de* cycl bg2 dig bg2 dulc b4.de* ferr b7.de* graph b4.de* hell b7.de* hep bg2 hyos b7.de* ign b7.de* ip b7.de* kali-bi bg2 kali-c b4.de* kali-n b4.de* lach b7.de* laur b7.de* led b7.de* *Lyc* b4a.de m-arct b7.de m-aust b7.de mag-m b4.de* mang b4.de* merc b4.de* mez b4.de* mur-ac b4.de* nat-c b4.de* nat-m bg2 nit-ac b4.de* *Nux-m* b7.de* nux-v b7.de* par b7.de* petr b4.de* phos b4a.de plb b7.de* **Puls** b7.de* ran-b b7.de* *Ran-s* b7.de* rhus-t b7.de* sabad b7.de* sabin b7.de* sars b4.de* *Sel* b7a.de seneg b4.de* sep b4.de* sil bg2 spig b7.de* stann b4.de* stront-c b4.de* sul-ac b4.de* *Sulph* b4.de* tab bg2 thuj bg2 valer b7.de* verb b7.de* zinc b4.de*

NIGHT: agar b4a.de* *Alum* b4.de* am-c b4.de* am-m b7.de* *Ambr* b7.de* anac bg2 ant-t b7a.de *Apis* b7a.de arg-n bg2 **Ars** b4.de* aur bg2 bar-c bg2 benz-ac bg2 borx b4a.de bry b7.de* calc b4.de* cann-xyz bg2 canth b7.de* **Cham** b7.de* **Chin** b7.de* dig bg2 *Dulc* b4.de* ferr b7.de* *Graph* b4a.de ign b7.de* kali-bi bg2 kali-c b4.de* *Kali-n* b4a.de lach b7.de* lyc b4.de* m-ambo b7.de m-arct b7.de mag-m b4.de* *Merc* b4.de* merc-c b4a.de* *Mur-ac* b4a.de nat-c b4.de* nat-m b4.de* *Nit-ac* b4.de* nux-v b7.de* op b7.de* ox-ac bg2 petr b4.de* ph-ac b4.de* phos b4.de* *Puls* b7.de* ran-b b7.de* ran-s b7.de* rhus-t b7.de* *Ruta* b7.de* *Sabad* b7a.de sars b4.de* sec b7.de* sel b7.de* seneg b4.de* sep b4.de* *Sil* bg2 *Spong* b7.de* stram b7.de* stront-c b4.de* **Sulph** b4.de* tab bg2 viol-t bg2 zinc b4.de*

- **midnight**:
  - **before**: led b7.de* puls b7.de* rhus-t b7.de* spong b7.de*
  - **after**: ambr b7.de* kali-c b4a.de* *Nux-v* b7.de* phyt bg2 ran-s b7.de*

○ - **Mammae**: bufo ptk1

ABORTION; after: sec bg2

ABSCESS:

○ - **Axillae**: am-c *Apis* ars bell bov bg2 bufo cadm-s k* *Calc* k* calc-s calc-sil k2* cedr coloc k* *Crot-h* k* **Hep** k* irid-met c2* *Jug-r* bro1* kali-bi k* kali-c kali-p k2 kali-sil k2 lac-c *Lyc* bg2* **Merc** k* *Merc-i-r* k* nat-m *Nat-s* k* **Nit-ac** k* petr k* ph-ac k* *Phos* ptk1 prun k* **Rhus-t** k* *Sep* k* **Sil** k* *Sulph* k* tarent tl1 thuj k*
  - **right**: plut-n srj7•
  - **delivery**; after: rhus-t ptk1
- **Lungs**: acon bro1 *Ars* b4a.de ars-i bg2* bac jl2 bell bro1 *Brom* b4a.de bry b7a.de **Calc** k* calc-s bg2* calc-sil k2* caps bg2* carb-an b4a.de carb-v b4a.de* chin b7a.de* chinin-ar bro1 *Crot-h* k* dros b7a.de guaj b4a.de **Hep** k* *Hippoz* k* hyos b7a.de iod b4a.de* *Kali-c* k* kali-n k* kali-p kali-sil k2 kreos b7a.de *Lach* k* *Led* k* *Lyc* k* *Mang* k* *Merc* k* nat-m b4a.de *Nit-ac* b4a.de nux-m b7a.de parathyr jl2 phel bg2 **Phos** k* *Plb* k* *Psor* k* *Puls* k* pyrog k2* sang bg2 sep k* **Sil** k* **Stann** b4a.de staphycoc jl2 stram tl1 sul-ac *Sulph* k* ter bg2 *Tub* k*
  - **left**: *Calc* k*

Abscess – Lungs: ...

  - **accompanied** by | **Lungs**; inflammation of: ars-i br1
- **Mammae**: apis *Am* hr1 *Ars* bg2 *Bell* k* *Bry* k* bufo k* *Camph* k* carb-an mrr1 cham b7a.de *Cist* k* con k2 *Crot-h* k* crot-t bro1* graph k* **Hep** k* kali-chl hr1 kali-i mrr1 kreos *Lach* k* **Merc** k* paeon gm1 **Phos** k* **Phyt** k* pyrog jl2 sars k* **Sil** k* **Sulph** k* tarent-c
  - **left**: *Am* mp1• carb-an mrr1 *Cist* mp1•
  - **fistula** discharging serum or milk: *Sil* mp1•
  - **sensation** as from: calc bg2 clem bg2 phos bg2 plb bg2
  - **threatening**, in old cicatrices: (↗*SKIN - Cicatrices*) acet-ac ptk1 calen mp1• **Graph** k* **Phyt** k* *Sil* mp1•

○ - **Nipples**: castor-eq cham k* *Merc* k* nat-m b4a.de plb bg2 puls b7a.de *Sil* k*

- **Pectoralis** major and minor; between | **sensation** of abscess: med c1

ADAMS-STOKES syndrome: reser mtf11

ADHESIONS:

- **pleuritis**; after: abrot bro1 acon tl1 bry tl1 carb-an bro1 hep bro1 ran-b c2* sulph bro1
- **sensation** of: arn aur aur-m bry k* cadm-s k* coloc dig euph k* hep kali-c k* kali-n k* *Merc Mez* k* nux-v par petr phos *Plb* puls *Ran-b* k* **Rhus-t** seneg k* *Sep Sulph* k* *Thuj* k* verb
  - **respiration**; with difficult: kreos b7a.de *Mez* b4a.de *Thuj* b4a.de

○ - **Lungs**:
  - **chest**; to: cadm-s a1*
  - **ribs**; to: *Euph* b4a.de kali-c ptk1 kali-n b4a.de *Mez* b4a.de ran-b b7a.de seneg b4a.de *Thuj* b4a.de

○ - **Pericardium**; of the *Graph*

AFFECTIONS:

○ - **Cartilages**; of the (See Cartilages)

- **Heart** (See Heart; complaints)

AGALACTIA (See Milk - absent; Milk - decreased)

AIR:

- **cold** (See Cold - air)
- **sensation** as if too much air enters the chest: chlor bg3* sabin ptk1 ther ptk1
- **sensitive** to air: helon c1 *Ph-ac* k*

○ - **Mammae** | **cold** air; sensitive to: cact

- **streaming** from chest; sensation of air | **Nipples**; from: cycl k*

AIR; IN OPEN:

- **agg.**: am-m b7.de* ambr b7.de* bry b7.de* caust b4.de* chin b7.de* cocc b7.de* coff b7.de* con b4.de* euph b4.de* graph b4.de* ign b7.de* lyc b4.de* mag-m b4.de* mang b4.de* merc b4.de* mez b4.de* nat-m b4.de* nux-m b7.de* nux-v b7.de* ran-b b7.de* rhus-t b7.de* sabad b7.de* sars b4.de* seneg b4.de* sep b4.de* spig b7.de* stann b4.de* staph b7.de* stront-c b4.de*

○ - **Clavicles**: chlor ptk1 rumx hs1*
  - **Mammae** | **Nipples**: cycl ptk1
- **amel.**: bry b7.de* kali-n b4.de* nat-m b4.de* phyt bg2 puls b7.de* rhus-t bg2 *Seneg* b4.de*

ALIVE; sensation of something (= moving): *Croc* k* led k*

- **evening**: colch
  - **eating**; after: colch
- **jumping**; something: *Croc* b7.de*

○ - **Heart**: aur ptk1 croc mrr1 cycl k* merc-i-f ptk1 tarent ptk1 thyr ptk1

- **Mammae** | **right**: croc br1*

ALTERNATING with:

- **diarrhea** and bronchitis: *Seneg*

○ - **Eye** symptoms: ars *Sil* nh6

- **Rectal** symptoms: calc-p **Sil** verat
- **Skin** symptoms: crot-h

ANEURYSM of: (↗*GENERALS - Aneurysm*) calc-f sp1 syph mrr1

○ - **Aorta**: aur-i mtf11 ign sne spong ptk1
  - **painful**: cact bro1 gal-ac ptk1* sec ptk1

- **Arteries**; large: acon bro1 ars-i bro1 *Bar-c* k* *Bar-m* bro1 cact bro1 *Calc* calc-f bro1 calc-p bro1 carb-v glon bro1 iod bro1 *Kali-i* bro1 kalm bro1 lach bro1 lith-c bro1 *Lyc* k* lycps-v k* morph bro1 *Nat-i* bro1 plb bro1 puls bro1 ran-s spig bro1 *Spong* k* syph jl2 *Verat-v* bro1
- **Heart**: ambr bg2 arn bg2 ars bg2 **Cact** k* calc bg2 carb-an c1 *Carb-v* k* caust bg2 ferr bg2 graph bg2 guaj bg2 **Lach** bg2 *Lyc* bg2 nat-m bg2 puls bg2 rhus-t bg2 spig bg2 zinc bg2

ANGER agg.: agar bg2 anac bg2 arg-n bg2 **Cham** b7a.de cupr b7a.de* lyc bg2 sep bg2 *Staph* b7a.de thuj bg2 *Verat* b7a.de

ANGINA pectoris: (↗*Pain - heart)* acet-ac k* acetylch-m mtf11 *Acon* k* acon-ac mtf11 adren br1* *Agar* hr1* **Am-c** k* *Aml-ns* k* anac k* ang k* **Apis** k* arg-col mp1• arg-cy c2* **Arg-n** k* **Arn** k* **Ars** k* ars-i bro1* asaf hr1 asar j5.de *Asim* c2 **Aur** k* **Aur-m** k* *Bar-m* hr1 bell j5.de bism c2* **Cact** k* calc-hp c2 camph c2* *Carb-v* c2 carneg-g rwt1• caust k* cere-b bro1* *Chel* k* chim-m c2 chin j5.de **Chinin-ar** k* *Chinin-s* k* chlol c1* chr-ac k* chr-o c2 *Cimic* k* cit-ac mtf11 coca k* cocain bro1* conv br1* crat c1* crot-h hr1* crot-t hr1 *Cupr* k* cupr-act c2* *Cupr-ar* k* des-ac mtf11 *Dig* k* *Dios* k* diph mtf11 diphtox jl2 elaps mrr1 foll mtf11 form-ac mtf11 fuma-ac mtf11 gels hr1 germ-met srj5• glon bg2* haem c2* *Hep* k* hist mtf11 *Hydr-ac* c2* ign hr1 iod j5.de ip k* *Jug-c* k* *Kali-c* k* kali-i bro1 kali-p *Kalm* k* kola stb3• *Lach* k* lact k* lact-v c1* **Lat-m** k* *Laur* k* lil-t c2* *Lith-c* c2* lith-met mp1• lob c2* *Lyc* k* lycps-v mrr1 *Mag-p* k* magn-gr c2* mal-ac mtf11 **Med** vh* merc j5.de morg-g mtf11 morg-p pte1* morph bro1* *Mosch* k* mucor mtf11 **Naja** k* nat-i bro1* nat-n bg2* nat-ns c2 nat-pyru mtf11 *Nux-v* k* olnd bro1* **Ox-ac** k* penic mtf11 petr k* **Phos** k* phyt k* pip-n bro1* pitu-gl mtf11 plb bg2* prot jl2* prun bro1* psor hr1 **Rhus-t** k* sacch-l c2 *Samb* k* samb-c c2 saroth bro1* scarl jl2 scol c1* sep k* **Spig** k* spir-aeth-c br1 **Spong** k* squil c2 staph bro1* stict c1* *Stram* k* stront-c c2* stront-i bro1* stry mp1• sulph mrr1 *Syph* hr1* *Tab* k* *Tarent* k* thala mtf11 *Ther* k* thuj c2 thyr c2* *Verat* k* verat-v bro1* verb hr1 vib hr1 wies c2 *Zinc* bg2* zinc-val c2* [kali-n stj1]

- **night**: arg-n br1
- **accompanied** by:
  - **cough**: ars bg2 chlor bg2 lach bg2 sulph bg2
  - **myocardial** infarction (See Infarction - accompanied - angina)
  - **warm** drinks; desire for (See GENERALS - Food and - warm drinks - desire - accompanied - angina)
  - ○ **Throat**; constriction of: tab ptk1
- **children**; in: *Med* mrr1
- **coffee** agg.; abuse of: coff mp1•
- **coition**; agg.: dig mrr1
- **drinking** water agg.: ars h2
- **heart** disease; from organic: *Ars-i* mp1• *Cact* mp1• calc-f mp1• crat mp1• kalm mp1• nat-i mp1• tab mp1•
- **hot** drinks amel.: spig ptk1*
- **lies** on knees with body bent backwards: nux-v ptk1*
- **pain**; excessive: agar ptk1* arn tl1 aur tl1 gels tl1 spig tl1
- **pain** in left elbow; with: arn br1
- **periodical** | **winter**; every: mez bg2
- **pseudo** angina pectoris: aconin bro1* cact bro1* *Lil-t* bro1* *Mosch* bro1* nux-v bro1* tarent bro1* [bell-p-sp dcm1]
- **rest** | **not** amel.: agar mtf haem mtf lat-k mtf *Lat-m* mtf
- **rheumatism**; from: cimic mp1• lith-met mp1•
- **standing** | **amel.**: ars h2
- **stimulants**; from abuse of: nux-v mp1• spig mp1•
- **straining**; from: *Arn* mp1• carb-an mp1• caust mp1•
- **tobacco**; from: calad mp1• conv mp1• kalm mp1• lil-t mp1• nux-v mp1• spig mp1• staph mp1• tab mp1•
- **walking** agg.: jug-c c1
- ○ **Muscular** origin; from cupr mp1• hydr-ac mp1•

ANGUISH in: | **Heart**; region of: arn bg2 *Ars* bg2 aur bg2 camph bg2 cann-xyz bg2 olnd bg2 rhus-t bg2 sabad bg2 sulph bg2 tab bg2

ANXIETY in: (↗*MIND - Anxiety)* **Acon** k* acon-f k* aeth k* agar k* *Agath-a* nl2• am-c k* ammc a1 anac k* anag hr1* androc srj1• *Ant-c* ant-t b7.de* *Apis* bg2 aran hr1 arg-n k* arn k* **Ars** k* *Ars-i* ars-s-f k2 asaf k* astac a1* aster k* **Aur** k* aur-ar k2 *Aur-m* k* aur-m-n wbt2• aur-s k2 bamb-a stb2.de• bell k* benz-ac hr1 bism hr1 borx brom k* *Bry* k* *Cact* k* **Calc** k* calc-i k2 calc-p bg2 *Camph* b7.de* cann-i k* cann-s k* canth caps k* carb-an k* *Carb-v* k* carbn-s caust k* *Cench* *Chel* k* chin k* chinin-ar chir-fl gya2 cinnm k* cocc k* *Colch* k* con cop crot-t cupr bg2 *Cupr-act* cupr-s k* *Dig* k* ferr k* ferr-ar ferr-i ferr-p

Anxiety in: ...
Graph k* guaj k* *Guare* k* hep gl1.fr• hydrog srj2• hyos k* hyper k* iber hr1 ign k* iod *Ip* k* irid-met srj5• jab k* *Kali-ar* kali-bi k* kali-c k* kali-cy k* kali-n k* kali-p *Kali-s* *Kreos* k* lac-cp sk4• lach k* laur k* limest-b es1• lipp a1 *Lob* k* *Lyc* k* m-arct b7.de *M-aust* b7.de* marb-w es1• med ser **Merc** k* merc-c k* merl hr1 mez k* mosch k* *Nat-ar* *Nat-c* k* nat-m k* nat-p *Nit-ac* k* *Nux-v* k* ol-an k* olnd op petr k* petr-ra shn4• ph-ac k* **Phos** k* plat k* *Plb* k* plut-n srj7• positr nl2• prun k* psil ft1 *Psor* k* *Puls* k* *Ran-b* k* rhus-t k* samb k* sec k* seneg k* sep k* *Spig* k* spong k* stann k* staph k* sul-i k2 *Sulph* k* tab k* teucr k* *Ther* thiam rly4• thuj b4a.de valer k* vanad br1 verat k* viol-o k* *Zinc* k* zinc-p k2 [heroin sdj2 spect dfg1]

- **morning**: bry carb-an k* hyper k* kali-p k2 petr-ra shn4• puls k*
- **forenoon**: ol-an k*
- **afternoon**: petr-ra shn4•
- **evening**: anag k* borx chel k* kali-c k* kali-p *Phos* k* psil ft1 **Puls** k* seneg k* stann
  - **amel.**: *Zinc* k*
  - **bed** agg.; in: anag k* borx
  - **undressing**: chel k*
- **night**: *Ars* k* aster k* ign k* lyc k* **Puls** k* *Ran-b* k* sulph k*
  - **midnight**:
    - **after**:
      - **2** h: kali-c
      - **4** h | **4-5** h: alum
- **accompanied** by | **respiration**; impeded: phos b4a.de*
- **agg.**: *Spig* bg2 *Verat* b7a.de
- **air**; driving him into open: anac
- **ascending** stairs agg.: hyos
- **bending** forward | **amel.**: *Colch*
- **breakfast** agg.; after: valer k*
- **cough** agg.; during: arund k*
- **eating**; after: caps k* carb-an k* scroph-n c1
- **excitement** agg.: **Phos**
- **exertion** agg.: ferr
- **inspiration**; after deep: chel nat-m
  - **amel.**: petr-ra shn4•
- **lying**:
  - **agg.**: *Cench* *Graph* k* petr-ra shn4• *Tarent*
  - **back**; on | **agg.**: *Sulph* k*
  - **side**; on:
    - **left** | **agg.**: **Puls** k*
- **motion** | **amel.**: seneg k*
- **piano**; from playing: nat-c k*
- **pressing** on left side agg.: plb k*
- **rising** from chest: cact bg2 kali-bi bg2
- **sitting**:
  - **agg.**: cupr kali-c k* meny h1*
  - **bent** forward | **agg.**: chin
  - **erect** | **amel.**: chin k*
- **standing** agg.: meny k*
- **stool** agg.; after: calc h2 *Caust* k* cund k*
- **walking** agg.: meny k*
- ○ **Heart**, region of: **Acon** k* adon mtf11 *Aeth* agar k* agath-a nl2• alum k* alum-p k2 am-c k* *Ambr* k* *Aml-ns* anac k* **Ant-t** k* apis apom vh1 *Arg-n* k* arn k* **Ars** k* *Ars-i* aster k* **Aur** k* aur-ar k2 aur-i k2 *Aur-m* **Bell** k* bov *Brom* *Cact* k* *Calc* k* calc-i k2 calc-s k2 **Camph** k* cann-s k* *Canth* k* **Carb-v** k* *Carbn-o* *Carbn-s* carl k* *Caust* k* **Cench** *Cham* k* chel k* chin chinin-ar chinin-s cic cina k* cob ptm1• *Cocc* k* *Coff* k* colch k* *Con* k* croc k* *Crot-c* k* *Cupr* k* cycl k* *Dig* k* echi elaps elec j *Euon* k* *Ferr* k* *Ferr-i* ferr-p *Gels* *Glon* gran graph k* hed sp1 hell k* helo bg2 *Helo-s* rwt2• hep gl1.fr• hydr hydr-ac k* hyos **Ign** k* indg a1 *Iod* k* **Ip** k* kali-c bg2 kali-m k2 **Kalm** k* kou br1 *Kreos* k* *Lach* lachn c1 *Lact* lat-m bg led b7.de* lipp a1 lob *Lyc* k* m-aust b7a.de **Meny** k* *Merc* k* *Merc-c* k* mez k* mosch k* *Naja* k* nat-m bg2 nat-s nit-ac k* *Nux-v* k* olnd k* op k* ox-ac petr **Phos** k* *Plat* k* *Plb* k* pneu jl2 *Prun* psil ft1 *Psor* k* *Puls* k* pyrog k2 ran-b k* *Rhus-t* k* sabad k* sal-n sec k* sep k* sil k* *Spig* k* *Spong* k* stann stict stram k* stroph-h ptk1 sulph k* *Tab* k* *Tarent* **Ther** k* thuj k* *Verat* k* viol-t k* vip k* zinc b4a.de
  - **morning**: alum k* aster k*
    - **rising**; after | **amel.**: alum

- **Heart**, region of: ...
  - **afternoon**: canth rhus-t k*
  - **evening**: bell brom cench k2 hydrog srj2• *Puls* k*
  - **night**: alum k* **Ars** k* aster k* calc cench k2 lyc k* rhus-t
    - **midnight** | **before** | **23** h, after lying down: kali-bi
      - **after**:
        - 2 h: *Kali-c* k*
        - 4 h: alum
          - 4-5 h: *Alum*
    - **bed** agg.; in: cann-s thuj viol-t
    - **nausea**; during: plb
  - **accompanied** by:
    - **coryza**: anac bg2
    - **sciatica**: spig bro1
  - **clutches** at heart: laur br1
  - **dinner**; after: arg-n bell
    - **leaning** back in a chair; when: glon
  - **epilepsy**, with: *Lyc*
  - **exertion** agg.; after: *Lyc*
  - **expectoration**; copious | **amel.**: *Ip*
  - **fever**; during: **Acon** bg2 *Ars* bg2 *Aur* bg2 **Calc** bg2 chin bg2 *Lyc* bg2 *Nat-m* bg2 nit-ac bg2 nux-v bg2 *Phos* bg2 plat bg2 **Puls** bg2 sep bg2 *Spig* bg2 sulph bg2 thuj bg2 viol-o bg2
  - **headache**:
    - **after**: sep h2
    - **before**: plat
  - **lying**:
    - **agg.**: cench k2
    - **side**; on:
      - **left** | **agg.**: bell glon *Nat-m Phos Spig*
  - **menses**; during: bell
  - **moving** about:
    - **agg.**: *Dig* k*
    - **amel.**: *Aur* caust op
  - **paroxysmal**: arg-n k* **Kalm** lach verat k*
  - **puts** hands on heart: laur br1
  - **rising** and walking about; after | **amel.**: glon k*
  - **sight** of decisive colors: *Tarent* k*
  - **sitting** agg.: agar k* *Caust* k* kali-c
  - **stool** agg.; during: *Rheum* b7a.de
  - **stretching** out body after physical exertion: lyc
  - **supper** agg.; after: bell
  - **thinking** of it agg.: bar-c ox-ac
  - **vexation**; after: lyc
  - **walking**:
    - **air** agg.; in open: cina spong
    - **amel.**: *Caust* glon indg a1
  - O **Precordial** region: scol a1*

AORTIC disease (See Heart; complaints - aorta)

APHTHAE; bleeding: *(↗GENERALS - Aphthae)*
- O **Mammae** | **Nipples**: *(↗GENERALS - Aphthae)* *Borx* k*

APPREHENSION: *(↗MIND - Anxiety; MIND - Clairvoyance; MIND - Excitement; MIND - Fear - happen)* astac vh carl k* irid-met srj5• nat-m k* ph-ac k*
- O **Heart**, region of: ant-t *Aur* carl melal-alt gya4 meny mez plat plb *Rhus-t* k*

ARRHYTHMIA (See Palpitation - irregular)

ARSENIC poisoning: | **fumes** of arsenic agg.: camph b7a.de ip b7a.de merc b4a.de nux-v b7a.de

ARTERIOSCLEROSIS of coronaries: *(↗Weakness - heart - arteriosclerosis; GENERALS - Arteriosclerosis)* ars-i mtf aur ptk1 *Bar-c* br1 bar-i mtf11 cact br1 calc-f mtf *Crat* br1* squil mtf stront-i mtf sumb mtf tab br1
- **old** people; in: | **men**; old: bar-c br1

Arteriosclerosis: ...
- **tobacco**; from: tab mrr1

ASCENDING:
- **agg.**: am-c bg2 ang b7.de* *Bar-c* b4a.de bell b4.de* bufo bg2 cham bg2 conv bg2 graph b4.de* kali-bi bg2 kali-i bg2 kalm bg2 nat-m bg2 **Nux-v** b7.de* rhus-t bg2 ruta bg2 sep b4.de* spong bg2 staph bg2 sulph b4a.de tab bg2 thuj b4.de* *Zinc* b4.de*
- **stairs** | **agg.**: acon b7a.de dig bg2 lyc bg2 nat-c b4a.de* nit-ac b4a.de* *Nux-v* b7.de* ox-ac bg2 ph-ac bg2 plb bg2 rhus-t b7.de* ruta b7.de* spig b7a.de spong b7.de* staph b7.de* *Thuj* b4a.de

ASTHMATIC BRONCHITIS (See RESPIRATION - Asthmatic)

ATELECTASIS: *(↗Pneumothorax)* **Ant-t** k* **Calc** sne *Calc-p* sne *Hyos* stry-p br1 sulph c2

ATROPHY:
- O **Mammae**: *(↗Emaciation - mammae)* anac mp1• anan ars bar-c cham bg1* *Chim* k* chin bg1* **Coff** mp1• **Con** k* dulc mp1• fago bg1* ferr bg1* **Iod** k* **Kali-i** k* *Kreos* k* lac-d lach mp1• *Nat-m Nit-ac* k* *Nux-m* k* onos bg1* plb sabal bg3* sacch sars *Sec Sep* mrr1 sil bg1 **Staph** gl1.fr•
  - **dropsy**, ovarian: *Iod* mp1•
  - **enlargement**; after: iod mrr1
  - **goitre**; with: calc gl1.fr• iod gl1.fr•
  - **infertility**, with: *Iod* mp1•
  - **lumps**, with small hard: *Kreos* mp1•
  - **rapid**: *Chim* mp1•
  - O **Skin**, leaving a flaccid bag-like: *Con* mp1•
- **Nipples**; of: *Iod* k* *Puls* b7a.de sars k*

AWARENESS of heart (See Conscious)

BALL; sensation of a:
- O **Heart**: agar bg2 ambr bg2 asaf bg2 calc bg2 hydr-ac bg2 lil-t bg2* nat-p bg2 rhus-t bg2 spig bg2
- **Mamma**; under left: hura k*
- **Ribs**:
  - **moving** to and from: cupr ptk1
  - O **Under**: cupr ptk1

BAND (See Constriction)

BAR of iron; sensation of a:
- O **Around** the chest: arg-n mand sp1 olib-sac wmh1
- **Centre** of chest; across the: haem k* kali-bi bg1* vichy-g sfa

BEATEN; sensation as if: ozone sde2•
- O **Ribs**; in (See Smashed)

BEER agg.: sep b4.de*

BENDING:
- **backward**:
  - **agg.**: am-c b4a.de *Nit-ac* b4a.de puls b7.de* rhod b4a.de teucr b7.de*
  - **amel.**: acon b7.de* cann-s b7.de* caust b4a.de fl-ac ptk1 nux-v b7.de* phos b4a.de puls b7.de*
- **forward** | **amel.**: asc-t bg2* colch bg2 kali-bi bg2 lach bg2 ran-b bg2 spig b7a.de teucr b7.de*
- **side**; to | **agg.**: borx b4a.de *Calc* b4.de* canth b7.de* cocc b7.de* staph b7.de*

BLEEDING: | **Heart**:
  - **sensation** of bleeding | **evening**: adam skp7•
- **Mammae**:
  - O **Nipples**: bufo ptk1 *Ham* k* *Lyc* k* med c1* *Merc* k* *Merc-c* mp1• *Sep* k* sil bg1* *Sulph* k*
    - **discharge** of blood and water: *Lyc* ptk1* phyt ptk1
    - **easily**: *Lyc* mp1•
    - **nursing**, when: *Sulph* mp1•
    - **soreness**, with great: *Ham* mp1•
    - **suppurate**, seems about to: *Sep* mp1•

BLOWING THE NOSE agg.: chel ptk1 kali-n b4.de* sumb ptk1

BOILING sensation: canth b7.de* lachn vml3•

BOILS (See Eruptions - boils)

BREATHING:

- **agg.**: *Acon* b7.de* am-c b4.de* anac bg2 ant-c b7.de* arg-met b7.de* arn b7.de* ars b4.de* asaf b7.de* aur b4.de* bell bg2 bism b7.de* borx b4a.de* *Bry* b7.de* *Calc* b4.de* *Cann-s* b7.de* caps b7.de* cham b7.de* chin b7.de* cina b7.de* cocc b7.de* colch b7a.de dros b7.de* dulc b4.de* graph b4.de* hep b4.de* hyos b7.de* kali-c b4a.de* kali-n b4.de led b7.de* lyc b4.de* merc b4.de* mez b4.de* *Mur-ac* b4a.de *Myrt-c* b7a.de nat-c b4.de* *Nat-m* b4.de* nit-ac b4.de* nux-v bg2 plat b4a.de *Puls* b7.de* ran-b b7.de* *Rhus-t* b7a.de sabad b7.de* sars b4.de* *Sep* b4.de* spig b7.de* squil b7.de* *Stann* b4.de* sulph b4a.de* verat b7a.de
- **amel.**: asaf b7.de* cina b7.de* tarax b7.de*
- **deep**:
  - **agg.**: *Acon* b7.de* agn b7.de* aloe bg2 arg-met b7.de* arn b7.de* asaf bg2 bapt bg2 **Borx** b4a.de **Bry** b7.de* *Calc* b4.de* calc-p bg2 canth b7.de* caps b7.de* caust b4a.de cina b7.de* con bg2 dros b7.de* fl-ac bg2 ign b7.de* kali-bi bg2 *Kali-c* b4a.de kali-n b4.de* kreos b7a.de laur b7a.de mag-m b4.de* mag-p bg2 merc b4.de* merc-c b4a.de mez bg2 mur-ac bg2 nat-m b4.de* nat-n bg2 nat-p ptk1 nux-m b7.de* *Olnd* b7a.de *Plb* b7a.de puls b7.de* rhus-t b7.de* *Sabad* b7a.de sabin b7.de* seneg b4.de* spig b7.de* spong b7.de* *Sulph* b4a.de valer b7.de*
  - **amel.**: aur bg2 chel ptk1 dig b4.de* hyos bg2 ign b7.de* seneg bg2 stann b4.de* tab bg2 *Verat* b7a.de verb bg2
- **holding** breath | **agg.**: apis b7a.de dros b7.de* led b7.de* meny b7.de* merc b4.de* spig b7.de*
- **not** breathing; when: dros bg2 ign b7.de led bg2 meny bg2 merc b4.de* merc-c b4a.de spig b7.de* *Sulph* b4a.de

BRONCHIECTASIS: acet-ac bro1 all-s bro1 alumn bro1 am-c hr1 **Ant-t** hr1* bac bro1* bals-p bro1* benz-ac bro1 beryl mtf11 *Calc* hr1* cop hr1 crot-h hr1 dios hr1 eucal bro1 ferr-i bro1 grin bro1 *Hep* hr1* ichth bro1 **Kali-bi** hr1* *Kali-c* bro1 kreos bro1* *Lyc* bro1 med hr1 mucot mtf11 myos-s bro1 myrt-ch bro1 nat-pyru mtf11 pert jl2* phel mtf11 *Phos* hr1 psor jl2* *Puls* bro1 sang bro1 sangin-n mtf11 *Sil* bro1 *Stann* hr1* sulph bro1 tub bro1*
- **chronic**: med mrr1
- **old** people: eucal ptk1

BRONCHITIS (See Inflammation - bronchial)

BRONCHORRHEA (See COUGH - Loose)

BUBBLE starts from heart and passes through the arteries: nat-p k*

BUBBLING: *(↗Clucking; Eruptions - vesicles - bursting; Gurgling)* ant-t tl1 *Cina* b7.de* kali-c b4.de* *Lyc* b4a.de merc ptk1 nat-m b4.de* ol-an bg2 rheum h* ruta b7.de* tub gk
- **left**: sep h2
- ○ - **Axillae**: colch k*
- **External** chest: *Rheum* b7a.de
- **Heart**; in region: bell ptk1 lach rb2* lachn ptk1 lyc rb2*
- **Lungs** | **right**: tell ptk1
- **Middle** of chest:
  - ▽ **extending** to | **Stomach**: ol-an a1
- **Muscles**: rheum b7.de*
- **Sternum**: nad rly4•

BUZZING noise: | **Heart**; in region of: cycl hr1* glon bg2 iod bg2 *Spig* b7.de* sulph bg2 tab bg2

CANCER:
- ○ - **Axillae**: *Ars* b4a.de *Aster* k*
- **Clavicles**: | **fungus** haematodes: *(↗SKIN - Excrescences - fungus haematodes)* sep
- **Heart**: cact gm1 kreos tl1
- **Lungs**: acal sne* aran sne* arg-met gm1 ars sne ars-i sne* bry sne* cadm-bi gm1 cob-m sne* con sne crot-h sne germ-met srj5• guaj gm1 hydr sne* kali-bi sne **Lyc** mk1• methyl gm1 phos sne* *Sang* mk1• *Scir* mk1• ther sne*
  - **accompanied** by:
    - **arthritis** (See joints)
    - **hemorrhage**: acal gm1 aran gm1
    - **Heart**; weakness of | **dyspnea**; and (See Weakness - heart - accompanied - lungs - cancer - dyspnea)
    - **Joints**; inflammation of: guaj gm1

Cancer: ...
- **Mammae**: acon gm1 aids nl2• alum kr alumn k* *Apis* k* *Arg-n* k* arn k* *Ars* k* *Ars-i* k* ars-s-f k2 *Aster* k* *Aur-ar* aur-m ptk1 aur-m-n k* *Bad* k* bapt bro1 bar-i c1* *Bell* k* *Bell-p* *Brom* k* bry k* **Bufo** k* cadm-met sne* calc k* calc-i bro1 calc-sil k2 *Carb-ac* k* *Carb-an* k* carb-v k* carbn-s carc br1* caust k* cham *Chim* k* cic bro1 cist k* *Clem* k* coloc k* **Con** k* congo-r gm1 *Cund* k* cupr b7a.de cypr sne ferr b7a.de ferr-i form-ac bro1 formal gm1 gaert sne *Gali* bro1 **Graph** k* *Hep* k* hip-ac sne hippoz gm1 *Hydr* k* ign sne iod gm1 kali-br sne kali-c k* *Kali-i* bro1 kreos k* lac-c sne *Lach* k* lap-a gm1 lob-e c2* *Lyc* k* mag-c sne **Merc** k* *Merc-i-f* naja gm1 nat-cac bro1 nat-tmcy gm1 *Nit-ac* k* ol-an *Ox-ac* k* ph-ac b4a.de* *Phos* k* *Phyt* k* *Plb-i* bro1 *Psor* k* *Puls* k* rad-br sne rhus-t b7.de* *Sang* k* sars c2* scir c1* scroph-n gm1 sed-r sne semp br1* *Sep* k* **Sil** k* strych-g bro1 sul-i k2 *Sulph* k* tarent bro1 thuj k* tub k* zinc b4a.de [*Merc-d* stj2]
  - **right**: ars-i sne bac sne *Con* sne ferr-i k2 gaert sne **Graph** sne **Hydr** sne **Phyt** sne sars sne *Sil* sne
  - **left**: aids nl2• ars-i sne aster vh *Caust* sne clem k2 **Con** sne *Hydr* sne ign sne nit-ac sne puls sne scroph-n sne *Sil* sne thuj sne
  - **nightly** pains: *Aster* k*
  - **accompanied** by:
    - **discharge** | **offensive**: carb-an mrr1
    - **hemorrhage**: kreos bro1 lach bro1 *Phos* bro1 sang bro1 strych-g bro1 thuj bro1
      - **bright** red blood: bell gm1
      - **copious** with serum and blood: plb gm1
      - **dark** thick clots: elaps gm1
      - **pain**; with: durb gm1
    - **induration** of the mammae: alum-sil gm1 aur-n-f gm1 cadm-calc-f gm1 carc br1 **Con** mrr1
    - **itching**: sil ptk1
    - **pain**: cadm-met gm1 carc br1 hippoz gm1 lap-a gm1 lob-e c1 phyt gm1
      - **burning** pains: carb-an mrr1 lap-a gm1 ol-an gm1
      - **operation**; after surgical: hippoz gm1 streptom gm1
      - **radiation**; after: hippoz gm1 streptom gm1
      - **stitching** pains: lap-a gm1 ol-an gm1
      - **violent** pain: nat-tmcy gm1
    - **swelling** of mammae: cadm-calc-f gm1
    - **ulcers**: coenz-q mtf11
      - **small** ulcers: alum-sil gm1 aur-n-f gm1
      - **tubercular** ulcers: bell-p gm1
    - **Axillary** gland; enlarged: alum-sil gm1 *Aster* gm1 aur-n-f gm1 carb-an mrr1 **Con** mrr1 goss ptk1
    - **Uterus** and shoulders; stitching pain in: clem ptk1
  - **cicatrices**, in old: *(↗SKIN - Cicatrices)* **Graph** k*
  - **contusion**; from: *(↗injuries)* arn sne* *Bell-p* calen sne* *Con* ruta sne
    - **gangrene**; with: carb-an gm1
  - **epithelioma**: *Arg-n* *Ars* *Ars-i* brom **Bufo** calc calc-p *Clem* **Con** *Hydr* k* *Kreos* *Lach* merc *Merc-i-f* *Phos* *Phyt* *Sep* *Sil* sulph thuj
  - **fungous**: **Carb-an** b4a.de **Thuj** b4a.de
  - **injuries**; after: *(↗contusion)* bell-p mrr1 hyper c1
  - **last** stage: carb-an gm1
    - **mastectomy** of opposite cancerous mamma; after: lac-c gm1
  - **metastasis** | **Bones**; to: aster mtf calc mtf carb-ac mtf carb-an mtf con mtf lach mtf merc mtf nit-ac mtf phos mtf
  - **old** people: carb-an gm1
  - **scirrhus**: ars bro1 carb-an bro1 **Con** bro1* cund bro1 **Graph** sne *Hydr* bro1* kreos bro1 lap-a bro1 phyt bro1 sars gm1 *Scir* bro1 *Sil* bro1
    - **accompanied** by | **menses**; absent: brom ptk1
- **Sternum**: ars-s-r sne* sulph

CAPILLARY network: carb-v

CAPPED; sensation as if: | **Heart**: zinc bg2

CARDIALGIA (See STOMACH - Heartburn)

CARDIOMEGALY (See Hypertrophy - heart)

CARIES:
- ○ - **Bones**: *Con* b4a.de
- **Clavicles**: sil

- **Sternum**: con k* mez kh

CATARRH: *Acon* k* agar k2* alum h2 alumn k2 am-c k2 am-m k2 *Ammc* *Ant-c* **Ant-t** k* *Apis* *Arn* k* **Ars** k* ars-i ars-s-f k2 *Aur-m* **Bar-c** k* bar-i k2 **Bar-m** bar-s k2 bell bg2 benz-ac brom k2 **Bry** k* **Cact** **Calc** k* calc-i k2 *Calc-s* calc-sil k2* cann-s b7.de* canth *Caps* bg2 carb-v k* carbn-s *Caust* k* **Cham** bg2 chel chin bg2* choc srj3• cina bg2 cist k2 *Coc-c* con bg2 cop *Dros* k* **Dulc** k* euphr bg2 falco-pe nl2• ferr k* ferr-ar ferr-i *Ferr-p* grin br1 *Guaj* **Hep** k* *Hippoz* *Hydr* *Hyos* b7a.de* ign b7.de* *Iod* *Ip* bg2 *Kali-ar* **Kali-bi** k* kali-br a1 *Kali-c* **Kali-chl** kali-i k2 kali-m k2 kali-p **Kali-s** kali-sil k2 *Kreos* lac-d *Lach* k* *Lact* **Lyc** k* mag-c bg2 mang bg2 **Merc** k* nat-c bg2 *Nat-m* k* *Nat-s* **Nux-v** k* *Petr* k* ph-ac bg2* phel **Phos** k* plut-n srj7• *Psor* **Puls** k* *Rhus-t* k* *Rumx* sabad bg2 *Samb* **Sang** k* sel k2 *Senec* **Seneg** sep bg2* **Sil** k* sin-n *Spig* bg2 *Spong* k* squil bg2* **Stann** k* staph bg2 stram bg2 sul-i k2 **Sulph** k* *Ter* thuj k2 *Tub* verat bg2* *Verb* b7.de*

- **morning**: aur h2 sul-ac h2
- **accompanied** by | **respiration**; difficult: bac br1
- **alternating** with diarrhea: kali-bi k2 seneg
- **children**; in: nat-s mtf33
- **chronic**: *Bac* br1
- **dentition**; during: podo c1
- **old** people: *Ammc* *Ant-t* *Bac* br1 **Bar-c** *Chin* hydr k2 *Nat-s* phel **Seneg** k* *Tub*
- **winter**: kali-bi k2

○ - **Bronchial** tubes: ant-s-aur mtf11 bals-p br1 kali-bi br1 mucot jl2 myrt-ch mtf11 onis br1 stict br1

- **accompanied** by | **respiration**; asthmatic: acon bro1 *Ant-t* bro1 *Ars* bro1 blatta-a bro1 *Bry* bro1 calad ptk1 caps ptk1 cupr-act bro1 *Erio* bro1 eucal bro1 *Grin* bro1 *Ip* bro1 kali-i bro1 lob bro1 nat-s bro1 onis bro1 sabal bro1 sulph bro1
- **children**; in: phos mtf33
- **chronic**: *Ant-s-aur* br1
- **old** people; in: *Alumn* br1

CAVITIES; tubercular (= caverns): calc-p bg3 kreos lsr6 led ll1 nit-ac bg3 sil hr1 teucr-s gm1

CEASES to beat; as if heart: (↗*MIND - Delusions - heart - stops; MIND - Fear - heart - cease; MIND - Fear - heart - disease - stop)* ant-t bg2 arn bg2 ars bg2 asaf bg2 aur b4a.de* bell bg2 carb-ac bg2 carb-v bg2 chinin-ar ptk1 cic bg2* cimic bg2* colch bg2 conv bg2* *Dig* bg2* gels bg2* glon bg2 lob bg2* lyc bg2 onos bg2 op bg2 pip-n bg2 rumx bg2* spig bg2 tab bg2 vib bg2*

- **followed** by:
  - **one** violent throb: aur bg2 lach bg2 lil-t bg2
  - **palpitation**: aur bg2 rumx bg2
- **had** ceased: *Arg-met* *Arg-n* am bg1 aster *Aur* *Cact* chinin-ar choc srj3• **Cic** k* cimic gk conv br1 **Dig** k* falco-pe nl2• *Lach* *Lil-t* *Lycps-v* mag-p sne pot-e rly4• pyrus rb2 *Rumx* sal-fr sle1• **Sep** k ● sil sne spig tarent zinc
  - **dinner**; after: sep
  - **pregnancy** agg.; during: arg-met
  - **starting** very suddenly; then: *Aur* bro1 conv br1* lil-t bro1 sal-fr sle1• sep bro1
- **rush** of blood; after violent: lyc bg2
- **will** cease; fears unless constantly on the move the heart: (↗*MIND - Delusions - heart)* **GELS** k ●* trif-p bro1
  - **jump** up; has to: **Gels** mrr1
- **would** cease: (↗*MIND - Fear - heart - disease - stop)* antip bro1 aur both-ax tsm2 bros-gau mrc1 *Calc* vh chinin-ar bg3* cimic bg3* conv bg3 crat bro1 dig k2* *Gels* tl1* kali-s fkr2.de lap-la sde8.de• **Lob** k* magn-gr mrr1 nux-m k* onos *Phase* bro1 sep tl1 sulph c1 trif-p bro1 vib bg3* visc c1
  - **exertion** agg.: cocain bro1 dig bro1*

CELLARS; air of: | **agg.**: (↗*Church)* ars b4a.de

CHICKEN BREAST: kali-c b4a.de lac-ac hr1*

CHILL:

- **begins** in chest (See CHILL - Beginning - chest)
- **during**: bry b7.de calad b7.de ip b7.de nux-m b7.de nux-v b7.de puls b7.de rhus-t b7.de

CHILLINESS in: alum k* *Ars* k* bamb-a stb2.de• bry k* kali-bi k2 mez h2 nat-c k* *Nat-m* b4a.de *Olnd* b7a.de par plut-n srj7• *Ran-b* ruta h1

Chilliness in: ...

- **left** side: nat-c nat-m
- **evening**: *Ars*
- **eruptions**; with: staph h1*
- **stool** agg.; after: plat
- **walking** in open air agg.: chin *Ran-b* k*

○ - **External** chest: calc bg2 chin b7.de* *Cic* bg2 cina b7.de* coff bg2 *Dig* bg2 hep b4a.de kali-n b4.de* merc bg2 nat-c bg2 nux-v b7.de* par b7.de* plat b4.de* *Ran-b* b7.de* ruta b7.de* *Spig* b7.de* staph b7.de* sulph bg2

- **Heart**: helo-s rwt2•
- **Mammae**, shivering in: cimic bg2 *Cocc* k* con bg2 dig b4a.de* *Guaj* k* nux-v b7.de* petr rhus-t bg2
- **Sternum**: alum h2

CHOKING (See THROAT - Choking)

CHOREA CORDIS (See Palpitation - tumultuous - accompanied - chorea)

CHRONIC OBSTRUCTIVE PULMONARY DISEASE: ant-t mrr1

CHURCH agg.; in: (↗*Cellars - agg.)* ars b4a.de carb-an b4a.de *Puls* b7a.de

CICATRICES; old: (↗*SKIN - Cicatrices)*

- **suppurating**: asaf tl1 **Sil**

○ - **Mammae**; in: carb-an k* **Graph** k* *Phyt* k*

- **suppurating**: sil ptk1

CLAWING sensation in chest: arg-n a1 samb stront-c

CLOTHING agg.: ail arn bg2 ars ptk1 aur-m benz-ac bov calc **Caust** k* *Chel* k* *Con* graph h2 *Kali-bi* **Lach** k* lact *Lycps-v* mag-p bg2 meli pd *Merc* naja k2 nux-v b7.de* ovi-p br1 ozone sde2• ran-b b7.de* spong b7.de* *Tarent* vip bg2 zinc

- **bra** feels tight: lavand-a ctl1•

CLUCKING sound: (↗*Bubbling; Eruptions - vesicles - bursting; Gurgling)* cina kali-c nat-m

○ - **Chest**; in: ruta h1

- **Heart**: bell bg2 **Lyc** ●*

CLUTCHING at heart and palpitation: laur br1 thyr ptk1

COATED, sensation as if: ant-t bar-c bry bg1 caust *Nat-m*

COITION; after: am-c bg2

COLD:

- **agg.** | **Mammae**: sabal ptk1
- **air**:
  - **agg.**: *Acon* b7.de* act-sp ptk1 bar-c bg2 bell bg2 bry b7.de* *Calc-p* ptk1 *Carb-v* b4.de* chin bg2 cocc b7.de* hep b4a.de* mur-ac bg2 nux-m b7.de* *Petr* b4a.de* ph-ac ptk1 *Phos* bg2 phyt bg2 ran-b ptk1 rhus-t b7.de* sabad b7.de* *Spong* b7.de* staph bg2 sul-ac bg2 sulph bg2
  - **amel.**: ferr ptk1
- **applications** | **agg.**: apis bg2 nux-m b7.de* *Rhus-t* b7.de* *Sabad* b7.de*
- **drinks** | **agg.**: phos ptk1 psor ptk1 rhus-t bg2 staph bg2 *Thuj* b4.de*
- **snow** or ice agg.: ant-c bg2 dros bg2 iod bg2 laur bg2 puls bg2 seneg bg2 verat bg2 verb bg2
- **washing** | **amel.**: borx ptk1 sulph bg2
- **water**:
  - **amel.**: borx bg2
  - **putting** hands in cold water agg.: tarent bg2

COLD; AFTER TAKING A: **Acon** b7.de* bell bg2 *Bry* b7.de* camph b7a.de *Carb-v* b4.de* cham b7.de* **Dulc** bg2 ip b7a.de merc bg2 *Nux-v* b7.de* *Phos* bg2 *Puls* bg2 rhus-t b7.de* sulph bg2

COLD AGG.; BECOMING: bar-c bg2 mosch b7a.de*

COLDNESS: abies-c bro1 aesc am-c k* *Am-m* bro1 ambr *Apis* arn **Ars** k* ars-s-f k2 bamb-a stb2.de• berb *Brom* bro1 bry k* bufo *Camph* *Carb-an* k* carbn-s chel sne cic k* cist bro1 cocc ptk cor-r k* culx dig **Elaps** bg2* falco-pe nl2• graph helo bro1 helo-s rwt2• hydr ign kali-c bg1* lact lil-t ptk1 lith-c bro1 lyc med k* merc bg2 merc-c bg2 merl morg-g fmm1• nat-c k* nat-m nat-p olnd k* *Par* petr *Ph-ac* *Ran-b* rhus-t ruta sabad sep spong suis-pan rly4• sul-ac **Sulph** k* tep tub jl2 *Zinc* [thuj xyz62]

- **right**: med *Sulph*
- **evening** | **22** h: cench k2
- **breathing** agg.: arn *Brom* camph chin *Cist* *Rhus-t* sulph
- **chill**; during: *Caps* k*
- **cold** air | **breathing**: *Cor-r* k* lith-c k* **Ran-b** k*
- **drinking** agg.; after: *Elaps* k*
- **expectoration**; after: *Zinc* k*
- **ice**, as if full of: corn br1
- **pain**; at seat of: *Cact* k*
- **walking** in open air agg.: **Ran-b**
- **warm** bed | **amel**.: nat-c
- **wet** cloth; as from a: ran-b ptk1*
- **wind** on the chest; from: chinin-s *Ph-ac* phos
- **wrap** up the chest, must: bov k* nux-v *Ph-ac*

○ - **Anterior** part:
  - **cold** water; sensation as of:
    - **running** down the chest when drinking; sensation of cold water: verat
    - **Clavicle**:
      - **Below** | **running** to the toes; sensation of cold water: *Caust*
- **Axillae**: agar lact
- **External** chest: *Calc* b4a.de* dig b4a.de* *Merc-c* b4a.de nat-m bg2 par bg2 **Ran-b** k*
  - **left** side: visc c1

○ • **Ribs**; last: spong bg2
- **Heart**: *Ars* bg2 brom bg2 carb-an bg2 graph bg2 helo bg2 kali-bi bg2 kali-c bg2 lach bg2 lil-t bg2 *Nat-m* bg2 nux-m bg2 olnd bg2 petr bg2 rhus-t bg2 ruta bg2 sec bg2 spig bg2 sulph bg2 verat bg2 zinc bg2
  - **icy** coldness during chill: arn camph kali-c **Nat-m** k* olnd petr pyrog k2
  - **sensation** as if heart were cold: *Helo-s* rwt2•
  - **stone** in; sensation of: petr hr1

○ • **Region** of: **Acon** ptk1 alum bg2 arn k* ars ptk1 bov bg2* calc bro1 camph bg2 *Carb-an* k* cic bg2* graph k* *Helo* k* *Helo-s* rwt2• *Kali-bi* k* *Kali-chl* k* *Kali-m* k* kali-n bg2* lil-t k* *Nat-m* k* nux-m bg2 olnd bg2 *Petr* k* pyrog k* rhus-t ptk1 sec bg2 spig bg2 spong bg2 sul-i ptk1 *Verat* ptk1
    - **mental** exertion agg.: *Nat-m*
- **Internally**: alum bg2 am-br *Apis* b7a.de* arn b7.de* **Ars** k* brom bg2 **Bry** b7a.de* *Calc* b4a.de* camph b7.de* carb-an b4.de* carb-v bg2 choc srj3• cic bg2 corn-a br1 dig bg2 *Elaps* bg2 graph bg2 helo br1 helo-s br1* kali-c mrr1 *Lach* b7a.de* laur mrr1 *Lil-t* bg2 **Nat-c** bg2 nux-v b7a.de* *Olnd* b7.de* *Par* bg2 petr bg2* pic-ac bg2 plut-n srj7• *Ran-b* bg2* rhus-t bg2 ruta b7.de* spig bg2 *Sulph* k* zinc b4.de* [heroin sdj2]
  - **accompanied** by cough: zinc b4.de*
  - **air**; inspiring cold: ran-b mrr1
  - **ice** water were rising and descending through a cylindrical tube; as if: elaps
  - **pleasant** cooling; sensation of a: ruta b7.de*

○ • **Sides** | **left**: *Nat-m* bg2
- **Lungs**: bit-ar wht1• ran-b mrr1
  - **right**: med hr1
  - **expectoration**; after: zinc ptk1
- **Mammae**: *Bry* b7a.de chin bro1 cimic k* *Cocc* k* dig k* *Med* k* rhus-t
  - **left**: nat-c ptk1
    - **coughing** while: nat-c bro1*
  - **icy** cold:
    - **menses** | **before** | **agg**.: med bro1
      - **during** | **agg**.: med bro1
  - **touch**; to: med tl1

○ • **Nipples**: med k*
    - **icy** cold:
      - **menses** | **before** | **agg**.: med bro1
        - **during** | **agg**.: med bro1
  - **Region** of: chinin-s
- **Middle** of chest: raph
- **Sides**: olnd

Coldness – Sides: ...
  - **right**: berb merc sulph
  - **left**: ferr-ma nat-c nat-m
    - **ice**; as if a lump of: sulph
- **Sternum**: apis *Camph* k* cupr-act **Ran-b** k*

COMPLAINTS of chest (= Thorax): *Acon* b2.de* agar b2.de* agn b2.de* alum b2.de* am-c b2.de* am-m b2.de* ambr b2.de* anac b2.de* ang b2.de* ant-c b2.de* **Ant-t** b2.de* arg-met b2.de* *Arn* b2.de* *Ars* b2.de* asaf b2.de* asar b2.de* aur b2.de* bar-c b2.de* *Bell* b2.de* bism b2.de* borx b2.de* bov b2.de* **Bry** b2.de* calad b2.de* *Calc* b2.de* camph b2.de* cann-s b2.de* canth b2.de* caps b2.de* carb-an b2.de* *Carb-v* b2.de* *Caust* b2.de* *Cham* b2.de* chel b2.de* chin b2.de* cic b2.de* cina b2.de* clem b2.de* *Cocc* b2.de* coff b2.de* colch b2.de* coloc b2.de* con b2.de* croc b2.de* cupr b2.de* cycl b2.de* dig b2.de* dros b2.de* *Dulc* b2.de* euph b2.de* euphr b2.de* ferr b2.de* *Ferr-p* ptk1 graph b2.de* guaj b2.de* hell b2.de* helodr-cal knl2• hep b2.de* hyos b2.de* ign b2.de* iod b2.de* ip b2.de* **Kali-bi** bg2 *Kali-c* b2.de* kali-n b2.de* kreos b2.de* lach b2.de* lachn br1 laur b2.de* led b2.de* *Lyc* b2.de* m-ambo b2.de m-arct b2.de m-aust b2.de mag-c b2.de* mag-m b2.de* mang b2.de* meny b2.de* merc b2.de* mez b2.de* morg fmm1• mosch b2.de mur-ac b2.de* nat-c b2.de* nat-m b2.de* nit-ac b2.de* nux-m b2.de* *Nux-v* b2.de* olnd b2.de* op b2.de* par b2.de* petr b2.de* ph-ac b2.de* phel ptk1 **Phos** b2.de* plat b2.de* plb b2.de* **Puls** b2.de* *Ran-b* b2.de* ran-s b2.de* rheum b2.de* rhod b2.de* *Rhus-t* b2.de* *Ruta* b2.de* sabad b2.de* sabin b2.de* samb b2.de* sang ptk1 sars b2.de* sec b2.de* sel b2.de* senec ptk1 **Seneg** b2.de* *Sep* b2.de* sil b2.de* **Spig** b2.de* spong b2.de* squil b2.de* **Stann** b2.de* staph b2.de* stram b2.de* stront-c b2.de* sul-ac b2.de* **Sulph** b2.de* syc fmm1• tarax b2.de* teucr b2.de* thuj b2.de* tub ptk1 valer b2.de* verat b2.de* **Verat-v** bg2* verb b2.de* viol-o b2.de* viol-t b2.de* *Zinc* b2.de* [bell-p-sp dcm1]
- **accompanied** by:
  - **coryza**: *Acon* bg2 bell bg2 *Cham* bg2 *Merc* bg2 **Nux-v** bg2 **Puls** bg2 rhus-t bg2 sulph bg2
  - **epistaxis**: ham bro1 nit-ac bro1
  - **nausea**: bell b4.de* sul-ac b4.de*
  - **reaction**; lack of (See GENERALS - Reaction - lack - accompanied - chest)
  - **waking**; frequent: alum b4a.de am-m b7.de* ant-c b7.de* arn b7.de* *Ars* b4a.de calc b4.de* euphr b7.de* ign b7.de* kali-c b4.de* nit-ac b4.de* nux-m b7.de* nux-v b7.de* petr b4.de* phos b4.de* puls b7.de* ran-b b7.de* rhus-t b7.de* sabad b7.de* seneg b4.de* sep b4.de* sil b4.de* squil b7.de*

○ • **Abdomen**; cramping pain in: plb bg2
  - **Abdomen**; pressing pain in: asaf b7.de*
  - **Rectum**; fistula in: berb hr1*
  - **Uterus**; complaints of: stann ptk1
- **alternating** with:
  - **herpes**: rhus-t

○ • **Abdomen**; complaints of (See ABDOMEN - Complaints - alternating with - chest)
  - **Head**; complaints of: chel bg2
  - **Rectum**; fistula in: berb bro1* calc-p al1* sil al1*
- **followed** by | **Head**; pain in: plat bg2
- **increasing** and decreasing gradually: mur-ac bg2
- **spots**; in: agar ptk1 anac ptk1 bufo ptk1 nat-m ptk1 ol-j ptk1 seneg ptk1 thuj ptk1 tub ptk1
  - **inflammation**; after: seneg bro1
- **wandering**: *Acon* ptk1 alum ptk1 arg-n ptk1 bell ptk1 cact ptk1 caust ptk1 colch ptk1 ferr ptk1 *Lyc* ptk1 mag-m ptk1 merc ptk1 nat-c ptk1 phos ptk1 *Puls* ptk1 seneg ptk1

▽ - **extending** to:

○ • **Axillae**: bell bg2 kali-c bg2 kali-n bg2 seneg bg2 thuj bg2
    - **right**: carb-an bg2
  - **Backward**: ars ptk1 bry ptk1 *Calc* ptk1 caps ptk1 carb-v ptk1 *Chel* ptk1 con ptk1 cupr ptk1 kali-bi ptk1 kali-i ptk1 lil-t ptk1 *Merc* ptk1 nat-m ptk1 phos ptk1 sep ptk1 spig ptk1 *Sulph* ptk1 ther ptk1
    - **right**: acon ptk1 ars ptk1 *Carb-v* ptk1 *Chel* ptk1 dulc ptk1 guaj ptk1 kali-bi ptk1 nit-ac ptk1 phel ptk1 phyt ptk1 sep ptk1 *Sulph* ptk1
    - **left**: bry ptk1* kali-n ptk1 lil-t ptk1 *Lyc* ptk1 mur-ac ptk1 nat-m ptk1 phys ptk1 rhus-t ptk1 spig ptk1 sul-ac ptk1 ther ptk1
  - **Downward**: agn ptk1 kali-bi ptk1

- **Downward**: ...
  - **right**: dulc ptk1 nit-ac ptk1 sang ptk1 sep ptk1
  - **left**: *Kali-c* ptk1 laur ptk1 phos ptk1 puls ptk1 squil ptk1 zinc ptk1
- **Elbow** | **right**: thuj bg2
- **Epigastrium**: caust bg2 ox-ac ptk1 thuj bg2
- **Forward**: berb ptk1 borx ptk1 **Bry** ptk1 castm ptk1 *Kali-c* ptk1 kali-n ptk1 psor ptk1 rat ptk1 *Sep* ptk1 sulph ptk1
  - **right**: acon ptk1 coloc ptk1 merc ptk1
  - **left**: agar ptk1 bar-c ptk1 *Bry* ptk1 lac-c ptk1 naja ptk1 phos ptk1 *Sulph* ptk1 thuj ptk1 zinc ptk1
- **Lumbar** region: acon bg2 dulc bg2 thuj bg2
- **Neck**: calc bg2 dios bg2 mur-ac bg2 sulph bg2 ther bg2 zinc bg2
- **Nose**: iod bg2
- **Outward**: staph bg2 valer bg2
- **Scapulae**: sulph bg2 ther bg2
  - **right**: acon bg2 nit-ac bg2 phos bg2
  - **left**: gels bg2 lil-t bg2 lyc bg2 spig bg2 sul-ac bg2
- **Shoulders**: ant-t bg2 sang bg2 squil bg2
- **Stomach**: thuj bg2
- **Throat**: apis ptk1 bell bg2* calc ptk1 laur ptk1 phos ptk1 *Plb* bg2 sulph ptk1 thuj ptk1 zinc bg2*
- **Transversely**: nux-v bg2
- **Upper** limbs: act-sp bg2 alum bg2 bar-c bg2 bry ptk1 carb-ac bg2 carb-v bg2 dig ptk1 dios bg2* glon bg2 kali-i bg2 lat-m bg2* led bg2 nat-m bg2 phys bg2 plat bg2
  - **right**: hydr ptk1 kreos bg2* lob ptk1 phos bg2* phyt bg2* plb bg2* sang ptk1
  - **left**: hell bg2
- **Upward**: ars ptk1 calc ptk1 caust ptk1 lach ptk1 mang ptk1 mur-ac ptk1 thuj ptk1
  - **right**: arn ptk1 plat ptk1 thuj ptk1
    - **left**; then: petr ptk1
  - **left**: am-m ptk1 bov ptk1 *Coc-c* ptk1 kali-c ptk1 laur ptk1 med ptk1 spig ptk1 *Squil* ptk1 stann ptk1 zinc ptk1
    - **right**; then: calc ptk1 carb-v ptk1 graph ptk1 ign ptk1 lil-t ptk1

○ - **Axilla** (See Axilla)

- **Bronchial** glands: bell bro1 calc bro1 calc-f bro1 *Iod* bro1 merc-c bro1 tub bro1
- **Bronchial** tubes: erio br1 *Eup-per* br1 pin-s br1
  - **accompanied** by:
    - **rheumatic** complaints: pin-s br1
    - **urticaria**: *(↗RESPIRATION - Asthmatic - accompanied - eczema)* pin-s br1
  - **chronic**: strept-ent jl2
- **Deep** in: all-c bg2* arn bg2* bry bg2* dros bg2* eup-per bg2* kali-c bg2* kreos ptk1
- **External** chest: acon b2.de* agar b2.de* alum b2.de* am-c b2.de* am-m b2.de* ambr b2.de* anac b2.de* ang b2.de* ant-c b2.de* ant-t b2.de* arg-met b2.de* **Arn** b2.de* ars b2.de* asaf b2.de* asar b2.de* aur b2.de* bar-c b2.de* bell b2.de* bism b2.de* borx b2.de* bov b2.de* *Bry* b2.de* calad b2.de* *Calc* b2.de* camph b2.de* cann-s b2.de* *Canth* b2.de* caps b2.de* carb-an b2.de* carb-v b2.de* caust b2.de* cham b2.de* chel b2.de* *Chin* b2.de* cic b2.de* cina b2.de* clem b2.de* cocc b2.de* colch b2.de* coloc b2.de* con b2.de* croc b2.de* cupr b2.de* dig b2.de* dros b2.de* *Dulc* b2.de* euph b2.de* euphr b2.de* ferr b2.de* graph b2.de* guaj b2.de* hell b2.de* hep b2.de* hyos b2.de* ign b2.de* iod b2.de* ip b2.de* kali-c b2.de* kali-n b2.de* kreos b2.de* lach b2.de* laur b2.de* *Led* b2.de* *Lyc* b2.de* m-ambo b2.de m-arct b2.de m-aust b2.de mag-c b2.de* mag-m b2.de* mang b2.de* meny b2.de* merc b2.de* *Mez* b2.de* mosch b2.de* mur-ac b2.de* nat-c b2.de* nat-m b2.de* nit-ac b2.de* nux-m b2.de* *Nux-v* b2.de* *Olnd* b2.de* op b2.de* par b2.de* petr b2.de* ph-ac b2.de* **Phos** b2.de* plat b2.de* plb b2.de* *Puls* b2.de* **Ran-b** b2.de* **Ran-s** b2.de* rheum b2.de* rhod b2.de* *Rhus-t* b2.de* ruta b2.de* sabad b2.de* sabin b2.de* samb b2.de* sars b2.de* sec b2.de* sel b2.de* seneg b2.de* sep b2.de* sil b2.de* **Spig** b2.de* spong b2.de* squil b2.de* stann b2.de* *Staph* b2.de* stram b2.de* stront-c b2.de* sul-ac b2.de* **Sulph** b2.de* tarax b2.de* teucr b2.de* thuj b2.de* valer b2.de* *Verat* b2.de* verb b2.de* viol-t b2.de* zinc b2.de*
  - **right** side: *Acon* fse1.de agar fse1.de *Agn* fse1.de *Alum* fse1.de *Am-c* fse1.de am-m fse1.de ambr fse1.de anac fse1.de ang fse1.de ant-c fse1.de ant-t fse1.de *Arg-met* fse1.de **Arn** fse1.de *Ars* fse1.de *Asaf* fse1.de

- **External** chest – **right** side: ...
  asar fse1.de *Aur* fse1.de bar-c fse1.de **Bell** fse1.de bism fse1.de *Borx* fse1.de bov fse1.de **Bry** fse1.de calad fse1.de *Calc* fse1.de camph fse1.de *Cann-s* fse1.de *Canth* fse1.de caps fse1.de **Carb-an** fse1.de *Carb-v* fse1.de caust fse1.de *Cham* fse1.de chel fse1.de chin fse1.de cic fse1.de cina fse1.de clem fse1.de *Cocc* fse1.de *Colch* fse1.de **Coloc** fse1.de con fse1.de croc fse1.de cupr fse1.de cycl fse1.de *Dig* fse1.de dros fse1.de *Dulc* fse1.de euph fse1.de *Graph* fse1.de *Hep* fse1.de *Hyos* fse1.de ign fse1.de **Iod** fse1.de *Ip* fse1.de kali-c fse1.de kali-n fse1.de kreos fse1.de **Lach** fse1.de laur fse1.de *Led* fse1.de *Lyc* fse1.de *M-ambo* fse1.de m-arct fse1.de m-aust fse1.de *Mag-m* fse1.de mang fse1.de meny fse1.de *Merc* fse1.de mez fse1.de *Mur-ac* fse1.de nat-c fse1.de *Nat-m* fse1.de *Nit-ac* fse1.de *Nux-m* fse1.de *Nux-v* fse1.de olnd fse1.de *Op* fse1.de *Par* fse1.de petr fse1.de *Ph-ac* fse1.de *Phos* fse1.de plat fse1.de plb fse1.de **Puls** fse1.de *Ran-b* fse1.de *Ran-s* fse1.de rheum fse1.de *Rhus-t* fse1.de ruta fse1.de *Sabad* fse1.de sabin fse1.de sars fse1.de seneg fse1.de *Sep* fse1.de *Sil* fse1.de *Spig* fse1.de spong fse1.de *Squil* fse1.de stann fse1.de staph fse1.de stront-c fse1.de sul-ac fse1.de *Sulph* fse1.de *Tarax* fse1.de *Teucr* fse1.de thuj fse1.de valer fse1.de *Verat* fse1.de *Viol-t* fse1.de zinc fse1.de
  - **left** side: *Acon* fse1.de *Agar* fse1.de agn fse1.de alum fse1.de *Am-c* fse1.de **Am-m** fse1.de ambr fse1.de *Anac* fse1.de ang fse1.de *Ant-c* fse1.de *Ant-t* fse1.de arg-met fse1.de *Arn* fse1.de ars fse1.de *Asaf* fse1.de asar fse1.de *Aur* fse1.de *Bar-c* fse1.de *Bell* fse1.de *Bism* fse1.de borx fse1.de *Bov* fse1.de *Bry* fse1.de *Calad* fse1.de **Calc** fse1.de *Camph* fse1.de *Cann-s* fse1.de *Canth* fse1.de *Caps* fse1.de *Carb-an* fse1.de *Carb-v* fse1.de *Caust* fse1.de *Cham* fse1.de *Chel* fse1.de *Chin* fse1.de cic fse1.de *Cina* fse1.de clem fse1.de *Cocc* fse1.de colch fse1.de coloc fse1.de *Con* fse1.de *Croc* fse1.de *Cupr* fse1.de *Cycl* fse1.de dig fse1.de *Dros* fse1.de *Dulc* fse1.de **Euph** fse1.de *Graph* fse1.de *Guaj* fse1.de *Hep* fse1.de hyos fse1.de *Ign* fse1.de **Kali-c** fse1.de *Kali-n* fse1.de *Kreos* fse1.de lach fse1.de **Laur** fse1.de led fse1.de **Lyc** fse1.de m-ambo fse1.de *M-arct* fse1.de *M-aust* fse1.de *Mag-c* fse1.de mang fse1.de *Meny* fse1.de *Merc* fse1.de mez fse1.de *Mosch* fse1.de mur-ac fse1.de *Nat-c* fse1.de *Nat-m* fse1.de **Nit-ac** fse1.de nux-m fse1.de **Nux-v** fse1.de *Olnd* fse1.de par fse1.de petr fse1.de *Ph-ac* fse1.de *Phos* fse1.de *Plat* fse1.de *Plb* fse1.de *Puls* fse1.de *Ran-b* fse1.de ran-s fse1.de *Rheum* fse1.de *Rhod* fse1.de **Rhus-t** fse1.de *Ruta* fse1.de sabad fse1.de *Sabin* fse1.de sars fse1.de **Seneg** fse1.de *Sep* fse1.de *Sil* fse1.de *Spig* fse1.de *Spong* fse1.de *Squil* fse1.de **Stann** fse1.de *Staph* fse1.de stront-c fse1.de *Sul-ac* fse1.de **Sulph** fse1.de *Tarax* fse1.de teucr fse1.de *Thuj* fse1.de *Valer* fse1.de *Verat* fse1.de *Verb* fse1.de *Viol-t* fse1.de *Zinc* fse1.de
- **Heart** (See Heart; complaints)
- **Lower** part: acon b2.de* agar b2.de* agn b2.de* alum b2.de* *Am-c* b2.de* ambr b2.de* anac b2.de* arg-met b2.de* arg-n bg2 *Arn* b2.de* ars b2.de* asaf b2.de* asar b2.de* asc-t bg2 aur b2.de* bell b2.de* bism b2.de* bov b2.de* bry b2.de* calc b2.de* calc-p bg2 cann-s b2.de* canth b2.de* *Carb-v* b2.de* *Caust* b2.de* cham b2.de* **Chel** bg2 **Chin** b2.de* cic b2.de* cocc b2.de* colch b2.de* croc b2.de* *Cupr* bg2 dig b2.de* dros b2.de* dulc b2.de* guaj b2.de* hell b2.de* hep b2.de* hyos b2.de* iod b2.de **Kali-c** b2.de* kali-n b2.de* kreos b2.de* laur b2.de* led b2.de* m-aust b2.de mag-c b2.de* mang b2.de* *Merc* b2.de* *Mez* b2.de* *Mosch* b2.de* mur-ac b2.de* *Nat-c* b2.de* nat-m b2.de* **Nat-s** bg2 olnd b2.de* op b2.de* ox-ac bg2 par b2.de* petr b2.de* **Ph-ac** b2.de* **Phos** b2.de* plat b2.de* plb b2.de* puls b2.de* ran-b b2.de* rheum b2.de* rhus-t b2.de* ruta b2.de* sabad b2.de* **Sabin** b2.de* samb b2.de* sang bg2 sars b2.de* *Seneg* b2.de* *Sep* b2.de* sil b2.de* *Spig* b2.de* **Squil** b2.de* stann b2.de* staph b2.de* stront-c b2.de* sulph bg2 tarax b2.de* teucr b2.de* thuj b2.de* *Valer* b2.de* verat b2.de* verb b2.de* viol-t b2.de* *Zinc* b2.de*
  - **left**:
    - **extending** to | **Epigastrium**: ox-ac ptk2
- **Lungs** (See Lungs; complaints)
- **Mammae** (See Mammae)
- **Middle** of chest: calc ptk1 dulc bg2* kali-bi ptk1 **Phel** bg2* **Sep** bg2*
- **Muscles**: *Asc-t* br1
- **Sides**:
  - **alternating** sides: *Agar* ptk1 apis ptk1 ars ptk1 *Calc* ptk1 *Cimic* bg2* dulc ptk1 graph ptk1 hyper bg2* lyc ptk1 mang ptk1 mosch ptk1 **Phos** ptk1 plb bg2* ran-b ptk1 rumx bg2* thuj ptk1
  - **right**: acon b7a.de* agar b4a.de* agn b7a.de* alum b4a.de* am-c b4a.de* am-m b4a.de* ambr b7a.de* anac b4a.de* ang b7a.de* ant-c b7a.de* ant-t b7a.de* apis bg2 arg-met b7a.de* **Arn** b7a.de* **Ars** b4a.de* *Asaf* b7a.de* asar b7a.de* *Aur* b4a.de* bar-c b4a.de* **Bell** b4a.de* bism b7a.de* **Borx** b4a.de bov b4a.de* *Brom* b4a.de* **Bry** b7a.de* calad b7a.de*

Chest

- **Sides – right**: ...
calc b4a.de* camph b7a.de* cann-s b7a.de* *Canth* b7a.de* caps b7a.de* **Carb-an** b4a.de* carb-v b4a.de* caust b4a.de* cham b7a.de* *Chel* b7a.de* chin b7a.de* cic b7a.de* cina b7a.de* clem b4a.de* cocc b7a.de* *Colch* b7a.de* **Coloc** b4a.de* con b4a.de* croc b7a.de* cupr b7a.de* cycl b7a.de* *Dig* b4a.de* dros b7a.de* dulc b4a.de* euph b4a.de* fl-ac b4a.de* graph b4a.de* *Hep* b4a.de* *Hyos* b7a.de* ign b7a.de* **Iod** b4a.de* ip b7a.de* *Kali-bi* bg2 **Kali-c** b4a.de* kali-n b4a.de* kreos b7a.de* **Lach** b7a.de* laur b7a.de* led b7a.de* **Lyc** b4a.de* lycps-v bg2 *M-ambo* b7a.de m-arct b7a.de m-aust b7a.de *Mag-m* b4a.de* mang b4a.de* meny b7a.de* *Merc* b4a.de* mez b4a.de* mill b7a.de **Mur-ac** b4a.de* *Nat-c* b4a.de* *Nat-m* b4a.de* nit-ac b4a.de* nux-m b7a.de* nux-v b7a.de* olnd b7a.de* *Op* b7a.de* par b7a.de* petr b4a.de* ph-ac b4a.de* *Phel* bg2 *Phos* b4a.de* plat b4a.de* plb b7a.de* psor b4a.de* **Puls** b7a.de* ran-b b7a.de* ran-s b7a.de* rheum b7a.de* rhus-t b7a.de* ruta b7a.de* sabad b7a.de* sabin b7a.de* *Sang* bg2 sars b4a.de* seneg b4a.de* sep b4a.de* **Sil** b4a.de* spig b7a.de* spong b7a.de* *Squil* b7a.de* stann b4a.de* staph b7a.de* stront-c b4a.de* sul-ac b4a.de* sulph b4a.de* *Tarax* b7a.de* teucr b7a.de* thuj b4a.de* valer b7a.de* *Verat* b7a.de* viol-t b7a.de* zinc b4a.de*
  - **extending** to | **left**: acon ptk1 lach ptk1 petr ptk1
- • **left**: *Acon* b7a.de* agar b4a.de* agn b7a.de* alum b4a.de* am-c b4a.de* **Am-m** b4a.de* ambr b7a.de* anac b4a.de* ang b7a.de* ant-c b7a.de* *Ant-t* b7a.de* *Apis* b7a.de* arg-met b7a.de* *Arg-n* bg2 *Arn* b7a.de* ars b4a.de* asaf b7a.de* asar b7a.de* asc-t bg2 aur b4a.de* bar-c b4a.de* bell b4a.de* bism b7a.de* borx b4a.de* bov b4a.de* brom b4a.de* bry b7a.de* calad b7a.de* **Calc** b4a.de* calc-p bg2 camph b7a.de* *Cann-s* b7a.de* canth b7a.de* *Caps* b7a.de* carb-an b4a.de* *Carb-v* b4a.de* *Caust* b4a.de* *Cham* b7a.de* chel b7a.de* *Chin* b7a.de* cic b7a.de* *Cimic* bg2 *Cina* b7a.de* clem b4a.de* *Cocc* b7a.de* colch b7a.de* coloc b4a.de* **Con** b4a.de* croc b7a.de* cupr b7a.de* cycl b7a.de* dig b4a.de* dros b7a.de* *Dulc* b4a.de* **Euph** b4a.de* **Fl-ac** b4a.de* *Graph* b4a.de* *Guaj* b4a.de* *Hep* b4a.de* hyos b7a.de* *Ign* b7a.de* **Kali-c** b4a.de* **Kali-n** b4a.de* *Kreos* b7a.de* lach b7a.de* **Laur** b7a.de* led b7a.de* **Lyc** b4a.de* m-ambo b7a.de *M-arct* b7a.de *M-aust* b7a.de mag-c b4a.de* mang b4a.de* *Meny* b7a.de* *Merc* b4a.de* mez b4a.de* mill b7a.de mosch b7a.de* mur-ac b4a.de* *Myrt-c* b7a.de nat-c b4a.de* *Nat-m* b4a.de* *Nat-s* bg2* **Nit-ac** b4a.de* nux-m b7a.de* **Nux-v** b7a.de* *Olnd* b7a.de* ox-ac bg2 par b7a.de petr b4a.de* *Ph-ac* b4a.de* **Phos** b4a.de* plat b4a.de* *Plb* b7a.de* psor b4a.de* puls b7a.de* *Ran-b* b7a.de* ran-s b7a.de* rheum b7a.de* *Rhod* b4a.de* **Rhus-t** b7a.de* rumx bg2 *Ruta* b7a.de* sabad b7a.de* *Sabin* b7a.de* sars b4a.de* **Seneg** b4a.de* *Sep* b4a.de* sil b4a.de* *Spig* b7a.de* *Spong* b7a.de* squil b7a.de* **Stann** b4a.de* staph b7a.de* stront-c b4a.de* *Sul-ac* b4a.de* **Sulph** b4a.de* *Tarax* b7a.de* teucr b7a.de* ther bg2 thuj b4a.de* valer b7a.de* verat b7a.de* *Verb* b7a.de* *Viol-t* b7a.de* *Zinc* b4a.de*
  - **extending** to:
    - **right**: apis ptk1 calc bg2* graph ptk1 kreos ptk1 phos ptk1 plb ptk1 zinc ptk1
    - **Epigastrium**: ox-ac ptk1
- **Transversely**: caust ptk1 thuj ptk1

▽ • **extending** to | **Arms**: *Alum* ptk1

- **Upper** part: acon b2.de* agn b2.de* alum b2.de* ambr b2.de* *Anac* b2.de* ang b2.de* ant-c b2.de* arg-met b2.de* *Ars* b2.de* asaf b2.de* aur b2.de* bar-c b2.de* *Bell* b2.de* bry b2.de* **Calc** b2.de* cann-s b2.de* *Canth* b2.de* carb-v b2.de* caust b2.de* cham b2.de* chel b2.de* chin b2.de* cic b2.de* cina b2.de* cocc b2.de* colch b2.de* con b2.de* cycl b2.de* dulc b2.de* graph b2.de* guaj b2.de* hyos b2.de* **Iod** b2.de* kali-c b2.de* laur b2.de* lyc b2.de* m-arct b2.de **Mang** b2.de* meny b2.de* merc b2.de* mez b2.de* nat-m b2.de* nit-ac b2.de* olnd b2.de* petr b2.de* ph-ac b2.de* *Phos* b2.de* *Plat* b2.de* plb b2.de* puls ptk1 ran-b b2.de* rhus-t b2.de* ruta b2.de* sars b2.de* seneg b2.de* *Sep* b2.de* sil b2.de* spig b2.de* **Stann** b2.de* staph b2.de* sul-ac b2.de* *Sulph* b2.de* tarax b2.de* ther bg2 thuj b2.de* tub bg2 verat b2.de* viol-t b2.de* zinc b2.de*
- **Wall**; Chest: *Ran-b* br1

COMPRESSION: | **Diaphragm**: op bg2

CONGESTION (= hyperemia of chest): **Acon** k* *Adren* vh1 agar tl1 aloe k* alum k* alum-sil k2 *Am-c* k* am-m bg2 ammc anac bg2 *Apis* k* *Arn* k* ars bg2* asaf bg2* *Aur* k* aur-i k2 aur-s k2 bar-c bg2 **Bell** k* bit-ar wht1• borx c1 bov bg2 brom k* **Bry** k* bufo bg2 **Cact** k* calad bg2 *Calc* k* **Camph** k* cann-xyz bg2 canth bg2 caps bg2* *Carb-v* k* carbn-s caust tl1 cham bg2 *Chin* k*

Congestion: ...
chlor cimic *Coc-c* cocc b7.de* coff bg2 colch tl1 conv br1 *Cupr* k* cycl k* **Dig** k* dulc bg2 ferr k* ferr-i ferr-p k* *Gels* *Glon* k* *Graph* k* guaj b4a.de* helodr-cal knl2• *Hyos* b7.de* ign bg2 *Iod* k* **Ip** k* *Kali-c* k* kali-chl kali-m k2 kali-n k* **Lach** k* lact limest-b es1• *Lyc* k* mag-m k* maias-l hrn2• mang bg2 meny bg2 *Merc* k* merl *Mill* mur-ac bg2 naja k2 nat-c bg2 nat-m b4.de* *Nit-ac* k* **Nux-v** k* ol-an olnd bg2 *Op* par bg2 ph-ac bg2 **Phos** k* positr nl2• *Puls* k* ran-b b7.de* rat rhod k* **Rhus-t** k* sabad bg2 sang bg2* sarr sec *Seneg* k* **Sep** k* *Sil* k* **Spig** bg2 **Spong** k* squil k* stram bg2 **Sulph** k* suprar rly4• **Ter** k* thiam rly4• *Thuj* k* verat bg2 *Verat-v* k* zinc bg2 [spect dfg1]

- **morning**: elaps pall
  - • **waking**; on: carb-v h2 phos h2 sulph h2
- **afternoon**: seneg
- **night**: *Ferr* k* nit-ac h2 *Puls* k*
- **accompanied** by:
  - • **menses**; suppressed: acon bro1 calc bro1 sep bro1
  - • **palpitations**: glon tl1
  - • **respiration**; complaints of: **Acon** bg2 am-c bg2 *Aur* bg2 **Bell** bg2 calc bg2 carb-v bg2 cupr bg2 ferr bg2 *Merc* bg2 **Nux-v** bg2 **Phos** bg2 puls bg2 *Spong* bg2 **Sulph** bg2
- **alternating** with | **congestion** of head (See HEAD - Congestion - alternating - chest)
- **bathing**; sea: *Mag-m*
- **cold** air agg.: cimic *Phos*
- **coldness** of body, with: carb-v h2
- **epistaxis**; with: mill c1
- **excitement**: *Phos*
- **exertion** agg.; after: *Spong* k*
  - • **slight**: *Spong* br1
- **fever**; during: *Acon* bg2 aur bg2 *Bell* bg2 bry bg2 chin bg2 merc bg2 **Nit-ac** b4a.de* *Nux-v* bg2 phos bg2 *Puls* bg2 seneg bg2 spong bg2 squil bg2 sulph bg2 thuj bg2
- **lying** down | **impossible**: *Bell* nh6 **Cact** k*
- **measles**; after: camph tl1
- **menopause**; during: arg-n **Lach**
- **menses**:
  - • **before** | **agg.**: kali-c
  - • **delayed**: graph nux-m *Puls*
  - • **during** | **agg.**: glon
- **motion**; after: *Spong* k*
- **perspiration**; during: acon bg2 apis bg2 *Bell* bg2 bry bg2 *Chin* bg2 **Nux-v** bg2 phos bg2 puls bg2 rhus-t bg2 *Sep* bg2 *Sulph* bg2
- **pregnancy** agg.; during: *Glon* k* *Nat-m* k* *Sep* k*
- **pressure** | **amel.**: calc-f sp1
- **recurrent**: morg-p mtf11 pneu mtf11 streptoc mtf11 tub-a mtf11 tub-m mtf11
- **running** agg.: bit-ar wht1•
- **sleep** agg.; during: mill puls k*
- **stopped** to flow; sensation as if blood: sabad k* *Seneg* k*
- **urinate** is not obeyed; if desire to: **Lil-t** k*
- **uterine** hemorrhage, after: **Aur-m** k* *Chin* k* *Phos*
- **waking**; on: **Lach**
- **walking** in open air agg.: mag-m *Phos*
- **weakness** and nausea: *Spong*
- **writing**; after: am-c

▽ - **extending** to | **Head**: sulph bg2

○ - **Heart**: (↗*Heart failure - congestive*) **Acon** k* am-c b4.de* *Asaf* k* asar bg2 *Aur* b4a.de bell mtf11 *Calc* b4a.de carb-v b4.de* cham b7.de* cupr b7a.de cycl k* cyt-l sp1 *Ferr* b7.de* ferr-i k2 **Glon** k* hyper *Kali-c* b4a.de laur b7.de* *Lil-t* lyc b4.de* merc-c b4a.de* nat-m b4a.de nit-ac b4.de* *Nux-m* k* nux-v b7.de* phos b4.de* *Puls* k* rhod b4a.de seneg b4a.de sep b4.de* sil b4.de* spig bg2 sulph k* thuj b4a.de
  - • **night**: nit-ac h2 *Puls*
  - • **alternating** with | **Head**; congestion of (See HEAD - Congestion - alternating - heart)
  - • **convulsions**, in: *Glon*
  - • **menses**; after: *Ign*
  - • **walking** rapidly agg.: nux-m

- **Lungs**: *Acon* bro1 adren br1* ars-i bro1 *Bell* bro1 both br1* *Cact* bro1 conv bro1 eberth jl2 ferr br1 *Ferr-p* bro1 glycyr-g cte1• ign mtf33 iod bro1 kali-n bro1 lyc bro1 meli mtf11 *Morg* fmm1• nux-v bro1 op bro1 parathyr jl2 phos bro1 *Seneg* b4a.de stroph-h bro1 sulfon bro1 tub-a jl2 tub-m jl2 upa bro1 *Verat-v* br1*
  - **right**: chel tl1
  - **left**: glycyr-g cte1•
  - **accompanied** by:
    - **hepatization** of lungs (See Hepatization - accompanied - congestion)
    - **nausea**: verat-v br1
    - **vomiting**: verat-v br1
  - **hemoptysis** amel.: meli mtf11
  - **passive** congestion: carb-v bro1 *Dig* bro1 ferr bro1 hydr-ac bro1 nux-v bro1 phos bro1 *Sulph* bro1
  - **violent**: iod mtf33
- **Mammae**: acon ptk1 apis ptk1 ferr ptk1 phos ptk1 yohim br1*

○ · **Nipples** | **sensation**: gard-j vlr2•

CONGESTIVE HEART FAILURE (See Heart failure - congestive)

CONSCIOUS of heart's action: bamb-a stb2.de• iber c1* lac-loxod-a hrn2• luf-op rsj5• olib-sac wmh1 pyrog c2* [heroin sdj2 tax jsj7]
- **accompanied** by | **Body** had changed into a big soft bag; sensation as if: lac-loxod-a hrn2•
- **slower**; as if beating: bit-ar wht1•

CONSTRICTION: *(↗Pain - constricting; Tension; LARYNX - Tightness)* abies-n bro1 **Acon** k* adren bro1 *Aesc* aeth c1* *Agar* k* agath-a nl2• aids nl2• ail k* *All-c* *Alum* k* alum-sil k2 alumn am-c k* am-m am-p br1 ambr *Ambro* bro1 anac k* *Ang* k* anh sp1 *Ant-t* k* anthraq rly4• antip vh1 *Ap-g* bro1 apis k* *Apoc* bro1 aral k* *Arg-n* k* arge-pl rwt5• *Arn* k* **Ars** k* *Ars-h* *Ars-i* ars-s-f k2 *Asaf* k* asar k* asc-t aspar **Aur** k* aur-ar k2 aur-i k2 *Aur-m* *Aur-m-n* wbt2• *Bac* bro1 *Bapt* *Bar-c* bar-i k2 bar-s k2 **Bell** k* beryl sp1 bism k* bit-ar wht1• *Borx* bov k* **Brom** k* bros-gau mrc1 **Bry** k* bufo **Cact** k* *Cadm-s* k* cain calad bg2 **Calc** k* calc-ar bro1 *Calc-p* k* calc-s calc-sil k2 *Camph* k* cann-i cann-s k* canth k* *Caps* k* *Carb-ac* *Carb-an* k* **Carb-v** k* *Carbn-o* **Carbn-s** carc sp1 *Cardios-h* rly4• carl **Caust** k* *Cham* k* **Chel** k* chin chinin-ar chinin-s bg2 chlol *Chlor* k* *Cic* k* *Cimx* cina cinnb clem *Coc-c* coca bro1 *Cocc* k* coff k* *Colch* k* *Coloc* k* **Con** k* cop *Crot-c* crot-h *Crot-t* *Cupr* k* *Cupr-act* bro1 cupr-s cycl cyt-l sp1 *Dig* k* dios k* *Dros* k* *Dulc* k* elaps *Euph* falco-pe nl2• *Ferr* k* ferr-ar ferr-i ferr-p k* gamb *Gels* germ-met srj5• gins *Glon* k* glyc bro1 **Graph** k* *Grin* bro1 haem bro1 hed sp1 *Hell* k* helon ptk1 *Hep* k* hydr-ac k* hydrog srj2• *Hyos* k* *Hyper* ictod **Ign** k* *Iod* k* *Ip* k* irid-met srj5• iris jatr-c *Just* bro1 *Kali-ar* *Kali-bi* k* *Kali-c* k* *Kali-chl* k* kali-i kali-m k2 *Kali-n* k* kali-p kali-s kali-sil k2 ketogl-ac rly4• kola stb3• kreos k* lac-h htj1• lac-loxod-a hrn2• **Lach** k* *Lact* *Lact-v* br1* lap-la sde8.de• lappa bg1 lat-h bnm5• lat-m br1* *Laur* k* lavand-a ctl1• lec *Led* k* lith-c **Lob** k* loxo-recl bnm10• luna kg1• **Lyc** k* *Lycps-v* *Mag-c* k* *Mag-m* k* *Mag-p* k* magn-gr bro1 *Manc* mand sp1 mang mang-p rly4• med bro1 melal-alt gya4 meny b7.de* *Merc* k* *Merc-c* k* merc-i-r *Mez* moni rfm1• morg-g fmm1• morph k* mosch k* mur-ac k* *Naja* k* naphtin bro1 *Nat-ar* k* *Nat-c* **Nat-m** k* nat-p *Nat-s* bro1 neon srj5• *Nit-ac* k* *Nit-s-d* bro1 *Nux-m* k* *Nux-v* k* olib-sac wmh1 olnd *Op* k* orni bro1 osm ox-ac k* ozone sde2• petr ph-ac k* **Phos** k* phys physala-p bnm7• pic-ac pin-con oss2• pitu-p sp1 plac-s rly4• *Plat* k* plb k* podo positr nl2• prot jl2* psil ft1 psor k* *Puls* k* pycnop-sa mrz1 rad-br c11 ran-b c1* rat rauw sp1 *Rhod* k* *Rhus-t* k* ruta k* sabad b7a.de* sabin sal-fr sle1• samb k* sang bro1 saroth sp1 *Sars* k* sel rsj9• **Seneg** k* *Sep* k* **Sil** k* silphu bro1 sinus rly4• sol-ni bro1 *Spig* k* *Spong* k* squil k* **Stann** k* *Staph* k* *Stram* k* stront-c k* stry k* suis-em rly4• suis-hep rly4• suis-pan rly4• sul-ac k* sul-i k* **Sulph** k* sumb suprar rly4• symph fd3.de• *Tab* k* tarent ter k* thea thiam rly4• thuj tril-p c1 tub c1 tung-met bdx1• upa **Verat** k* verat-v bro1 verb k* vero-o rly4• visc sp1 xan zinc k* [bell-p-sp dcm1 heroin sdj2]
- **daytime**: mez phos
- **morning**: *Arg-n* calc carb-v cycl kali-n br1 lyc melal-alt gya4 nat-m phos *Puls* sars sep
  - **fasting**: sulph
  - **lying** agg.: kali-n h2
  - **waking**; on: dig h2 sep
- **forenoon**: kali-n h2
- **noon**: agar
- **afternoon**: bapt eupi kali-n h2 lac-c mag-c nat-m petr ph-ac h2 sulph

Constriction: ...
- **evening**: *Ars* k* *Bry* calc-p carb-v carbn-s hyper kali-n h2 lyc h2 mag-c h2 phos h2 positr nl2• *Puls* k* ran-b k2 raph rhus-t sep h2 *Stann* k* sulph symph fd3.de• verb *Zinc*
  - **bed** agg.; in: *Ars* k* bell symph fd3.de• verb
- **night**: alum androc srj1• aral *Bry* coloc *Ferr* k* kali-n kola stb3• *Lach* *Mez* k* myric petr h2 *Puls* k* seneg sep sil stram *Tab*
  - **bed** agg.; in: *Ferr* *Nux-v*
- **accompanied** by:
  - **respiration**:
    - **complaints**: alum bg2 *Am-c* bg2 *Am-m* bg2 ant-c bg2 **Ars** bg2 asaf bg2 aur bg2 *Bry* bg2 *Calc* bg2 caps bg2 carb-an bg2 **Carb-v** bg2 *Caust* bg2 cham bg2 *Chin* bg2 cina bg2 cocc bg2 colch bg2 coloc bg2 *Con* bg2 **Cupr** bg2 *Dig* bg2 *Dros* bg2 **Ferr** bg2 *Graph* bg2 *Hyos* bg2 ign bg2 **Ip** bg2 **Kali-c** bg2 *Kali-n* bg2 **Lach** bg2 *Led* bg2 lyc bg2 merc bg2 mez bg2 nat-c bg2 *Nat-m* bg2 *Nit-ac* bg2 **Nux-v** bg2 op bg2 petr bg2 **Phos** bg2 plat bg2 plb bg2 **Puls** bg2 rheum bg2 ruta bg2 sabin bg2 **Samb** bg2 sars bg2 sec bg2 **Sep** bg2 **Sil** bg2 *Spig* bg2 spong bg2 *Squil* bg2 **Stann** bg2 stront-c bg2 **Sulph** bg2 thuj bg2 verat bg2 viol-o bg2 zinc bg2
    - **difficult**: ign mrr1

○ · **Throat**; lump sensation in: kola stb3•
- **alternating** with:
  - **drawing** in occiput and nape of neck: kali-n h2
  - **expansion**; sudden: sars

○ · **Abdomen**:
  - **distension**: lyc h2
  - **pain**: *Calc*
- **anger**; after: *Cupr* k*
- **anguish**, with: adren br1*
- **armor**, as if from an: aur mrr1 **Cact** *Crot-c* k* nept-m lsd2.fr

○ · **Heart**: aur mrr1
- **arms**:
  - **stretching** out: mez h2
  - **together** in front; from bringing: *Sulph* k*
- **ascending** agg.: ang **Ars** k* borx a1 **Calc** led *Mag-c* nux-v
- **asthmatic**: aids nl2• ang cact bg1 cadm-s bg1 coff kali-chl bg1 *Led* mez naja nux-v sulph verat mtf11 zinc bg1
- **band**; as from a: **Acon** k* aeth a1* *Aml-ns* k* *Anac* bg2 ant-c b7a.de* arag br1* *Arg-n* *Ars* k* bell bg2 bry **Cact** k* chlor ham fd3.de• led k* lepi br1 *Lob* k* *Lyc* mag-c bg2 mang-p rly4• nat-m bg2 nit-ac bg2 *Nux-v* b7a.de op **Phos** k* pic-ac *Puls* b7a.de sabad b7.de* sabin b7.de* sil thuj bg2 zinc h2* zinc-p k2
  - **accompanied** by | **yawning**: stann ptk1
  - **hot**: eucal bg2
  - **iron**: cact tl1 kola stb3• merc tl1
    - **Heart**: cact nh6* iod tl1 lil-t tl1 mand sp1 nux-m tl1

○ · **Lower** part of chest: agar chlor thuj
- **bending**:
  - **amel.**: caust
  - **backward** | **agg.**: nit-ac
  - **forward** | **agg.**: dig
- **breakfast** agg.; after: agar ozone sde2• sulph
- **breathing**:
  - **agg.**: borx h2 positr nl2•
  - **amel.**: sulph
  - **deep** | **agg.**: agar aspar *Caust* cham *Cic* *Coc-c* k* dulc euon *Ferr* ham kali-bi kali-n lact lyc mag-m mosch nat-c nat-m h2 nept-m lsd2.fr nux-v *Puls* rauw tpw8 sang seneg stry *Sulph* tab tarax thuj visc c1
- **burning**: bism h1 mag-m h2
- **chill**; during: *Ars* k* *Cimx* *Kali-c* mez h2 **Nux-v** k* *Phos*
- **clothes** are too tight; sensation as if: meli ptk1
- **coat** of mail, as from: chel
- **coition**; after: staph k* [heroin sdj2]
- **cold**:
  - **air** agg.: bry *Phos* sabad
  - **bathing** | **agg.**: nux-m
- **cold** agg.; becoming: mosch *Phos*
- **convulsive**: **Asaf** k* **Bell** k* **Cupr**

- **coryza**; during: **Ars**[bg2] bov[bg2] *Bry*[bg2] calc[bg2] **Ip**[bg2] kali-c[bg2] *Nux-v*[bg2] phos[b4.de*] sulph[bg2]
- **cough**:
    - **amel.**: con[ptk1]
    - **during** | **agg.**: am-c[b4.de*] calc *Cham* cimx *Con*[k*] *Cupr* *Dros*[b7.de*] *Form* *Hell* kali-n[b4.de*] lyc *Mag-p*[k*] merc *Myrt-c*[k*] **Phos**[k*] *Puls* sep[bg2] stram *Sulph*[k*]
    - **inclination** to; from: *Sep*[k*]
    - **spasmodic**, during: *Mosch*[k*]
- **covers** of bed agg.: *Ferr*
- **dinner**; after: am-m[h2] carbn-s hep phel
- **drawing** shoulders back amel.: **Calc**[k*]
- **drinking** agg.; after: *Cupr*
- **eating** | **after** | **agg.**: am carb-an cupr hep phel *Puls* sil[h2]
    - **amel.**: sulph
- **eructations** | **amel.**: lyc[h2] mag-c[h2]
- **exertion** agg.: *Ars*[k*] *Calc* ferr ham[fd3.de•] *Nat-m*[k*] nux-v *Spong* *Verat*
- **expectoration** | **amel.**: *Calc* *Manc*
- **expiration** agg.; during: borx *Caust* chel *Kali-c*
- **fever**; during: *Acon*[bg2] am[bg2] *Ars*[bg2] asaf[bg2] cupr[bg2] *Ip*[bg2] kali-c[bg2] kali-n[bg2] **Merc**[bg2] **Mosch**[bg2] nit-ac[bg2] *Nux-v*[bg2] ph-ac[bg2] *Phos*[bg2] *Plat*[bg2] *Puls*[bg2] rhus-t[bg2] sep[h2*] spig[bg2] spong[bg2] *Stann*[bg2] staph[bg2] stram[bg2] sul-ac[bg2] *Sulph*[bg2] thuj[bg2] verat[bg2]
- **flatulence**; from: *(↗Oppression - flatulence - from)* lyc[h2] **Nux-v** *Rheum* sil
- **heart** disease; with acute rheumatic (See Pain - heart - rheumatic - accompanied - constriction)
- **hot**: bism[h1]
- **hydrothorax**, in: *Apis* apoc asaf[hr1*] colch lact merc psor *Spig* stann
- **inspiration** agg.: agar asaf[hr1] aspar beryl[tpw5*] bit-ar[wht1•] cham chel con dros mez raph sabad seneg *Sulph* tung-met[bdx1•]
- **lumbar** pain; from: lyc[h2]
- **lying**:
    - **agg.**: aral lach nat-m nux-v verb[c1]
    - **amel.**: *Calc-p* cardios-h[rly4•]
    - **head** high; with the | **amel.**: *Ferr*
    - **quietly** | **agg.**: caps
    - **side**; on | **left** | **agg.**: myric
        - **right** | **agg.**: *Lycps-v* symph[fd3.de•]
- **manual** labor agg.: *Calc*[k*]
- **menses** | **before** | **agg.**: phos
    - **during** | **agg.**: sep
- **motion**:
    - **after** | **agg.**: acon[vh1]
    - **agg.**: agar ang *Ars* caps[h1] *Ferr* ip[ptk1] *Led* lyc nux-v *Spong* *Verat*
    - **amel.**: *Seneg*
- **painful**: cupr[h2] dig[h2] ham[fd3.de•] sars[h2] *Sulph* tell[rsj10•] *Verat*
- **paroxysmal**: sep[h2]
- **perspiration**:
    - **amel.**: sulph
    - **feet**; after suppressed perspiration of: **Sil**
- **restlessness**; with (See MIND - Restlessness - chest - constriction)
- **running** short distances: rauw[sp1]
- **sighing** agg.: [heroin sdj2]
- **sitting**:
    - **agg.**: agar ars mag-c[h2] mez nit-ac
    - **amel.**: nux-v
    - **bent** forward:
        - **agg.**: alum
        - **amel.**: lach
    - **erect**:
        - **agg.**: sars
        - **amel.**: mez
- **sitting** up in bed | **must** sit up: acon[vh1] dig[h2]
- **sleep**; when falling asleep: bry *Graph* *Lach*[k*]
- **sneezing** agg.: phos[h2]
- **spasmodic**: am-c **Asaf**[k*] *Aur* aur-s[k2] calc carb-v carbn-s *Caust* *Cupr*[k*] glon *Hep* **Ign**[k*] ip *Kali-c* kali-p lact led lyss[c1*] nat-m *Op* *Phos* sars sec *Sep* *Spong* *Sulph* verat[k*]
- **spots**; in: arge-pl[rwt5•] thuj[bg2]
- **standing**:
    - **agg.**: am-m[h2] kali-n[h2] spig[h1] verat
    - **amel.**: mez
- **stitching**: spig[h1]
- **stool** agg.; during: coloc
- **stooping** agg.: alum laur merc mez[k*] seneg
- **stretching** out: nat-m
- **sudden**, violent: tab[bg2]
- **sulphur**, as from: kali-chl[k*]
- **supper** agg.; after: mag-m[h2] mez
- **swallowing** agg.: *Kali-c*[k*]
- **talking**:
    - **after**: *Hep*[k*]
    - **impossible**: ars[h2] *Cact*[k*]
- **touch** agg.: am cupr
- **vomiting**:
    - **after**: verat-v
    - **before**: *Cupr*
- **waking** | **after** | **agg.**: dig psor
    - **on**: alum carb-v[bg1] dig *Graph* hydrog[srj2•] **Lach**[k*] *Lact*[k*] lap-la[sde8.de*] seneg sep
        - **wheezing**; with: hydrog[srj2•]
- **walking**:
    - **agg.**: am-c *Anac* ang **Ars**[k*] cocc[vh] *Dig*[k*] ferr *Jug-c* *Kali-c*[k*] led *Lyc* mag-c[h2] nit-ac[h2] nux-v ozone[sde2•] puls sil[h2] sulph tung-met[bdx1•] *Verat*
    - **air**; in open:
        - **agg.**: am-c *Calc* lith-c lyc[h2] mez[bg1] sulph[bg1] zinc[h2]
        - **amel.**: alum chel dros ozone[sde2•] *Puls*[k*]
    - **amel.**: arge-pl[rwt5•] ferr
    - **rapidly** | **agg.**: *Puls*[k*]
- **warm** | **applications** | **amel.**: kola[stb3•]
    - **bed** | **amel.**: phos
- **weeping** | **amel.**: anac moni[rfm1•]
- **whooping** cough; during: *Caust*[k*] mur-ac spong[k*]
- ▽ **extending** to:
    - ○ **Back**: lat-m[br1]
    - **Lower** ribs: dys[fmm1•] morg-g[fmm1•]
    - **Shoulders**: lat-m[br1]
    - **Stomach**: lac-h[htj1•]
    - **Throat**: [heroin sdj2]
    - **Upper** limbs | **left**: morg-g[fmm1•]
- ○ **Bifurcation** of trachea kali-bi[k2]
- **Clavicle** | **left**: zinc[h2]
- **Diaphragm**: *(↗Spasms - diaphragm)* asar[h1*] cact[bg2] mez[h2*] nux-v[b7a.de*] petr[a1] tarax[h1]
    - **cough** agg.; during: cench[k2]
- **Heart**: aeth agar *Ail* alum[k*] alum-p[k2] am-c[ptk1] aml-ns[k*] ang[k*] anh[sp1] *Anth* anthraci[vh] apis *Arn*[k*] **Ars**[k*] **Ars-i**[k*] asaf[k*] asc-t aur aur-ar[k2] aur-i[k2] berb bufo **Cact**[k*] cadm-s calad[bg2] calc[k*] *Calc-ar* calc-i[k2] cann-i cann-s cann-xyz[bg2] carbn-s[k2] carc[tpw2*] caust[bg2] cench[bg1] chlor coca[bg2] cocc colch[bg2*] cund *Dig*[k*] ferr ferr-ar ferr-i ferr-p galla-q-r[nl2•] glon[bg2] graph hed[sp1] hydr *Ign* **Iod**[k*] *Kali-ar* kali-bi *Kali-c*[k*] kali-chl kali-m[k2] kali-p kola[stb3•] lac-ac *Lach*[k*] *Laur* **Lil-t**[k*] lyc *Lycps-v*[k*] lyss mag-p[bg2*] mand[sp1] merl mur-ac[k*] *Naja* *Nat-m*[b4a.de*] nat-n[bg1] nit-ac[k*] *Nux-m* nux-v phos phyt[k*] *Plat*[b4a.de] *Plb* plut-n[srj7•] rad-br[c11*] ran-s[bg2] rauw[sp1] rhus-t samb sanguis-s[hm2•] saroth[sp1] *Spig*[k*] *Spong*[k*] sul-i[k2] tab[bg2] tarent tell[rsj10•] tub[c] vanad[dx] verat zinc zinc-p[k2]
    - **night**: *Lil-t*
        - **midnight**; after | **3**-**4** h: saroth[sp1]
    - **alternating** with | **release**: lil-t[tl1]
    - **band**; as from a: | **iron**: *Cact*[br1]
    - **bending** chest forward amel.: lac-ac lil-t

- **convulsions**; before epileptic: *Calc-ar Lach*
- **drinking** water amel.: *Phos* k*
- **eating** agg.: alum
- **epistaxis**; with: verat bg1
- **exertion** agg.: asaf bry
- **grasping** sensation: arn **Cact** k* **Iod** k* *Lach Laur* **Lil-t** k* *Nux-m* k* rhus-t sanguis-s hrn2• *Spig* k* *Tarent*
  - ⁝ **right** side; and on: borx k*
  - ⁝ **iron** hand; as if grasped by an: arn bro1 *Cact* bro1 iod bro1 lil-t bro1* sulph bro1 vanad bro1 visc bro1
- **grief**; from: *Ign* k*
- **hand**; like a hand around her heart: *Cact* nh6 *Iod* nh6 laur nh6 sanguis-s hrn2•
- **heartbeat** amel.; a strong: nit-ac h2
- **lying** on side agg.: saroth sp1
- **sigh**; as if one wants to: carc mg1.de*
- **stool** | **urging** to; with: calc-ar
- **sulphur** fumes; as from: kali-m k2
- **walk** erect, inability to: *Lil-t* k*

▽ • **extending** to | **Back**: lat-m br1 *Lil-t* k*

○ • **Above** heart: ars bg2

- **Apex**: rauw sp1
- **Behind** the heart: choc srj3•

– **Lower** part: aesc agar agath-a nl2• am-m bry **Cact** k* calc h2 chlor cocc ptk1 cupr ptk1 *Dros* k* *Gels* k* *Ham* lact lil-t lycps-v med c1 nept-m lsd2.fr *Nux-v* k* phos h2 *Plat* ptk1 *Puls Ran-b* sep h2 *Spig* k* *Sulph* thuj
- **night**: ruta c1
- **lying** on the right side agg.: lycps-v

– **Lungs**: abies-n hs1* corv-cor bdg• nat-m tl1
- **wire**; as with a: asar k* dig c1 kali-n c1

○ • **Upper** part | **left**: visc c1

– **Mammae**: lil-t sang stram verat
- **right** | **Below**: alum h2 am-m h2
- **left** | **child** nurses from right; when: *Borx* k*
- **inspiration** agg.; deep: sang

– **Middle** of chest: cassia-s ccrh1• lob mag-c h2 melal-alt gya4 ol-an
- **evening** | **18** h: mag-c
- **cough** agg.; during: cassia-s ccrh1•
- **inspiration** agg.: graph h2
- **string**, as from a: led
- **walking** in open air agg.: lyc h2

– **Sides**: *Acon* aeth agath-a nl2• aloe alum asar aur bg2 bell k* carb-v h2 colch kali-n lil-t lyc h2 meny h1 mez myric nat-m h2 nit-ac plat puls sil h2 spig h1 thuj
- **one** side: cocc zinc
- **right**: am-m ptk1 cina h1 cocc k* flor-p rsj3• irid-met srj5• lyc h2 mag-m h2 nat-m h2 puls h1 sulph h2* zinc
  - ⁝ **followed** by | **left**: flor-p rsj3•
- **left**: agath-a nl2• aids nl2• graph ptk1 lyc ptk1 nat-m h2 plat h2 sep h2 sil h2 sul-ac h2* sumb ptk1 zinc h2 [heroin sdj2]
  - ⁝ **sitting** erect agg.: dig h2
- **forenoon**: nat-m h2
- **inspiration** agg.: lyc h2
- **lying** down agg.: lil-t plat
- **sitting** agg.: nit-ac
- **turning** body: nat-m h2
  - ⁝ **right**, to: euph h2

– **Sternum**: acon k* agar bg2 ap-g br bov bg2 bry bg2 *Cact* bg2 cann-s castm bg2 choc srj3• croc bg2 dig bg2* dios br1 ham fd3.de• led bg2 lob k* melal-alt gya4 mur-ac nux-m k* op bg2 *Phos* k* puls h1 rhus-t k* sabin staph h1 sulph k* trios rsj11• zinc
- **cough** agg.; during: **Phos**
- **eating**; while: led
- **hindering** breathing: mang-p rly4• mur-ac h2

Constriction – Sternum: ...
- **motion** agg.: **Cact** op

– **Upper** part: ang gsy1 carb-an h2 cham nit-ac h2 phos rhus-t k* spig h1 stann h2 suis-pan rly4• symph fd3.de• tab hr1
- **left**: phos h2

CONTRACTION: acon b7.de* alum b4.de* ars b4.de* asaf b7.de* aur b4a.de* bism b7.de* borx b4a.de canth b7.de* *Carb-v* b4a.de caust b4.de* cham b7.de* chin b7.de* cina b7.de* cocc b7.de* coloc b4.de* *Cupr* b7.de* dig b4.de* *Dros* b7a.de ferr b7.de* hell b7.de* *Hep* b4a.de ign b7.de* ip b7.de* kali-n b4.de* *Kreos* b7a.de *Lyc* b4.de* m-arct b7.de mag-c b4.de* mag-m b4a.de* mang b4.de* meny b7.de* merc b4.de* merc-c b4a.de *Mosch* b7.de* nit-ac b4a.de nux-v b7.de* op b7.de* ph-ac b4.de* phos b4a.de *Plat* b4a.de *Puls* b7.de* ran-s b7.de* rheum b7.de* rhod b4.de* samb b7.de* sars b4.de* seneg b4.de* spig b7.de* stann b4.de* staph b7.de* stront-c b4.de* sulph b4.de* verat b7.de*

– **accompanied** by | **respiration**; asthmatic: cadm-s bg3*

– **tearing** | **External** chest: am-m bg2 cham bg2 mez bg2

○ – **Diaphragm**: asar b7a.de* canth b7.de* dros b7a.de mez b4.de* *Nux-v* b7a.de

– **External** chest: arn b7.de* bry b7.de* *Coloc* b4a.de *Cupr* b7a.de dig b4.de* led b7.de* mez b4.de* nux-m b7.de* nux-v b7.de* op b7.de* plat b4.de* rhod b4.de* rhus-t b7.de* spig b7.de* stram bg2 *Sulph* b4a.de verat b7a.de

– **Heart**; of | **increased**: adon br1 arec br1 dig br1 spartin bwa3 *Stroph-h* br1

– **Intercostal** muscles towards left side; spasmodic contraction of | **respiration**; hindering: *(↗RESPIRATION - Impeded - accompanied - chest - contraction)* verat h1

CONTUSIONS:

– **agg.**: apis b7a.de **Arn** b7.de* puls b7.de* *Rhus-t* b7.de* ruta b7.de*

○ – **Mammae**: arn b7.de

CONVEX: limen-b-c hrn2•

CONVULSIONS: acon ang **Ars** bell k* *Calc* cic **Cupr** *Hydr-ac* hyos ip merc-n merc-ns *Nat-s* op phos sep stram stry sul-ac verat

– **night**: phos sep
- **waking**; on: *Ars*

– **before**; agg.: ars bg2 glon bg2

– **epileptic** | **Lower** part; beginning in (See GENERALS - Convulsions - begin - lower)

COPPER poisoning: | **fumes** of copper agg.: camph b7a.de ip b7a.de merc b4a.de nux-v b7a.de

CORROSIVE gnawing in axilla: mez h2

COTTON; sensation as if stuffed with: | **Lungs**: kali-bi ptk1 med ptk1

COUGH: | **after** | **agg.**: cina b7.de* ferr b7.de* *Mur-ac* b4a.de

– **during**:
- **agg.**: **Acon** b7.de* agar bg2 alum b4.de* am-c b4.de* am-m b7.de* ambr b7.de* *Ang* b7a.de ant-c b7.de* apis bg2 *Arn* b7.de* *Ars* b4.de* bar-c b4.de* bell bg2 borx b4a.de* **Bry** b7.de* *Calc* b4.de* cann-s b7.de* *Caps* b7.de* carb-v b4.de* caust b4.de* *Cham* b7.de* *Chin* b7.de* *Cina* b7.de* cocc bg2 coff b7.de* colch b7.de* con b4.de* dig b4.de* *Dros* b7.de* elaps ptk1 ferr b7.de* gels bg2 iod b4.de* kali-bi bg2 *Kali-c* b4.de* kali-n b4.de* *Led* b7.de* lyc b4.de* m-ambo b7.de m-arct b7.de mag-c b4.de* mag-m b4.de* mang b4.de* *Merc* b4.de* mez b4.de* mur-ac b4.de* *Myrt-c* b7a.de nat-c b4.de* *Nat-m* b4.de* nit-ac b4.de* nux-m b7.de* nux-v b7.de* *Ph-ac* b4.de* phos b4.de* psor bg2 puls b7.de* *Rhus-t* b7.de* ruta b7.de* sabad b7.de* sabin b7.de* *Sel* b7a.de seneg b4a.de* *Sep* b4.de* *Sil* b4.de* spig b7.de* *Spong* b7.de* *Squil* b7.de* *Stann* b4.de* staph b7.de* stront-c b4.de* sulph b4.de* verat b7.de* zinc b4.de*
  - ⁝ **Mammae**: con ptk1
  - ⁝ **Sternum**: *Bry* ptk1 *Caust* ptk1 kali-bi ptk1
- **amel.**: con bg2

CRACKING: *Arn* b7a.de *Phos* b4a.de *Rheum* b7a.de sabin b7.de*

– **motion** agg.: irid-met srj5• nat-m sulph

○ – **External** chest: am-c b4a.de arn b7a.de rheum b7.de*

– **Heart**, in region of: mag-c h2 *Nat-c* k* spig ptk1 spong ptk1

– **Sternum**: calc-p bg2
- **backward**; on bending the chest: am-c
- **motion** agg.: irid-met srj5•

CRACKS (= fissures): graph bg2 *Sulph* bg2

○ – **Mammae**: *Caust* bg2 graph bg2 *Sulph* bg2

Cracks: ...
O • **Nipples**: aesc ptk1 anan bro1 arn k* aur bg2 aur-s c1* calc-ox bro1 calc-sil k13 calen bro1 carb-an ptk1 carb-v bro1 *Castm* bro1 **Castor-eq** k* **Caust** k* cham bro1 collod btw2 *Con* bro1 *Crot-t* bro1 *Cund* bro1 cur eup-a br1* *Fl-ac* gali bro1 ger bro1 **Graph** k* ham bro1 hep bro1 hipp bro1 *Hydr* k* *Lyc* k* merc bro1 *Merc-c* *Mill* nit-ac k2* *Paeon* bro1 **Petr** bg2* *Phel* bro1 phos bro1 **Phyt** k* **Rat** k* **Sars** ptk1 *Sep* k* *Sil* k* *Sulph* k*
⁝ **deep** cracks: *Castor-eq* mrr1
⁝ **nursing**, from: graph bro1 hydr ptk1 nit-ac gk rat bro1 sep bro1
⁝ **painful**: *Castor-eq* mrr1 graph nit-ac gk phyt

CRAMP (See Pain - cramping)

CRAWLING (See Formication)

CROSSED; sensation as if:
O - **Deep** in chest: kreos bg2
- **Ribs**: merc-c bg2

CROUP, cardiac: *Spong*

CYANOSIS: *(↗GENERALS - Cyanosis)* *Ant-t* k* *Borx* carb-an *Dig* k* *Ip* k* **Lach** k* **Laur** k* naphthoq mtf11
O - **Clavicle**; region of the thuj

DA COSTA'S SYNDROME (See Palpitation - irritable)

DANCING amel.: caust ptk1

DECOMPENSATION of heart (See Heart failure)

DEFORMED: nat-m h2
O - **Mammae** | **Nipples**: merc k*

DELIVERY; after: *Carb-an* b4a.de

DIGESTION; during: | **agg.**: *Lyc* b4.de* sep bg2

DILATATION of heart: *(↗Hypertrophy - heart)* adon bro1* *Alum* am-c k* *Ant-t* *Apis* k* *Ars* b4a.de* ars-i bro1 aur b4a.de *Bar-c* b4a.de* *Brom* b4a.de **Cact** k* calc b4a.de carb-v gm1 cench k2 chlol ptk1 cimic bro1 coff conv br1* crat br1* cupr dig b4a.de* gels bro1 grin ptk1 hydr-ac iber bro1 *Iod* kali-bi br1 *Kali-i* *Lach* k* *Laur* lil-t *Lyc* *Lycps-v* merc-c b4a.de morg-g mtf11 *Naja* k* *Nat-m* k* *Nux-v* ph-ac *Phase* bro1 *Phos* k* phys bro1 plb k* prun bro1 *Psor* *Puls* rhus-t tl1 saroth bro1 seneg b4a.de spig bro1* stroph-h bro1 sulph zf tab k* thyr mtf11 verat-v bro1
- **accompanied** by | **hypertension**: crat mtf11
- **painful** | **stool**; before: asaf bg2
- **sensation** of dilatation: ang c1 ars bg2 asaf b7.de* bufo bg2 cadm-s gm1 glon bg2 med bg2 nat-m bg2 petr bg2 phos bg2 sabin bg2
  • **lying** left side | **amel.**: ang c1
  • **pushing** against back, spreading up and out: choc srj3•
O - **Myocardium**: *Dig* br1
- **Ventricles**: con br1 conv br1
  • **left**: toxo-g jl2

DINNER: | **after** | **agg.**: arg-n bg2 bell bg2 glon bg2 kali-bi bg2 nat-m bg2 nit-ac bg2 nux-v bg2
- **during** | **agg.**: calc bg2 chin bg2 crot-t bg2 hep bg2 ign bg2 puls bg2 sil bg2 sulph bg2

DISAGREEABLE sensation: spig b7.de

DISCHARGE from nipple: bell-p sne *Graph* sne ham bg2 *Lyc* b4.de* med c1 phel phos phyt k* plb b7.de *Puls* b7a.de sel bg2 sep bg2 sil bg2 *Sulph* bg2
- **bathing** agg.: kali-cy gm1
- **blood**: carc mlr1• ham bg2 kali-cy gm1 *Lyc* b4.de* phyt bg2 sel bg2 sep bg2 sil bg2 *Sulph* bg2
  • **nursing**; pure blood at every: **Sil** hr1
- **bloody** water: kali-cy gm1 *Lyc* *Phyt* sil mp1•
- **brown**; dark: kali-cy gm1
- **gummy** | **drying** on orifice, when picked off nipple bleeds freely: med c1
- **milky**:
  • **right** nipple; from: thlas mp1•
  • **male**; in: lac-h sk4•
- **oozing**: lyc bg2 plb bg2 thlas bg2
- **watery**: lyc bg2 phos bg2 thlas bg2

DISCOLORATION:
- **blueness**, near clavicle: *Ars* *Cupr* lach k* thuj k*
- **copper** colored: stram
- **livid**: ars
- **redness**: am-c h2 aster aur k* bar-c bell k* bomb-chr a1 canth b7a.de chinin-s *Graph* iod kali-ar *Lac-c* rhus-t rhus-v sulph tarax tritic-vg fd5.de vesp
  • **blotches**: apis chlol cinnb
  • **burning**: am-m h2 mez h2
  • **coppery**: stram
  • **erythematous**: *(↗SKIN - Eruptions - erythema)* *Apis* eberth jl2
  • **itching**: am-m h2
  • **spots**: am-m b7.de* ant-c arn *Bell* k* carb-v b4.de* chel bg2 cinnb cocc k* guaj ptk1 *Ip* bg2 lach bg2 led k* lyc b4.de* mag-c k* manc *Merc* mez k* phos bg2 puls raph rhus-t hr1 ros-d wla1 sabad k* sil squil b7.de* sulph ptk1 tab tritic-vg fd5.de visc c1
- **spots**: agar bg3 am-c am-m ars *Bell* carb-v cinnb cocc colch rsj2• crot-c k* *Crot-h* ery-a ip *Lach* **Led** lyc *Mag-c* mez nat-m bg3 nat-s bg2 *Nit-ac* **Phos** phyt sabad sars bg2 seneg bg3 *Sep* squil sulph thuj bg3 vip
  • **black**, mottled: vip
  • **brown**: cadm-s *Carb-v* k* *Lyc* k* *Mez* *Petr* *Phos* k* **Sep** k* sulph bg2* thuj k*
    ⁝ **itching**: hydr lyc sulph
    ⁝ **Axillae**: ozone sde2• thuj b4a.de
    ⁝ **Mammae**; on: cadm-s carb-v lyc phos *Sep*
  • **dark**: phos
  • **ecchymoses** (See Ecchymoses - spots)
  • **freckles**: nit-ac
  • **itching**: nit-ac h2
  • **mottled**: **Crot-h** k* **Lach** k* naja vip
  • **white**: ozone sde2•
    ⁝ **Axillae**: ozone sde2•
  • **yellow**: ars k* chel bg2 lyc b4a.de merc bg2 *Phos* k*
    ⁝ **become** dark: mez
    ⁝ **itching** | **evening**: sulph
O • **Liver**: **Lyc** k*
- **yellow**: *Thuj* b4a.de
O - **Axillary** glands | **blueness**: carb-an k2
- **Mammae**:
  • **blue** | **ulcerated** mammae; of: bell-p sne *Lach* k* phos
  • **bluish** red: *Apis* b7a.de kreos *Lach*
  • **livid**: plb
  • **pale**: bry tl1
  • **redness**: am-c bell k2* cocc led sabad samb xxb1
    ⁝ **streaks**: bell phos rhus-t sulph
    ⁝ **Nipples**: agar castor-eq *Colch* *Fl-ac* psor k*
  • **yellow**: chel thuj
    ⁝ **spots**: *Ars* carb-v chlor kali-c h2 lyc manc *Phos* *Sep* sulph tab
- **Sternum** | **redness**: cortiso sp1

DISLOCATED: | **Ribs** seem: agar ptk1 caps ptk1* kali-bi ptk1 naja ptk1 petr ptk1 psor ptk1 stram ptk1

DISTENSION: apoc k2 ars ptk1 bell k* benz-ac cadm-s carb-v bg1 cench k2 **Lach** k* lil-t petr rhus-t thuj ptk1 vip
- **convulsions**; during: ars
- **sensation** of distension: alum h2 *Ars* k* asar b7.de* brom bry b7.de* cadm-s caps k* chin coca ignis-alc es2• nat-ox rly4• olnd k* sil k* stann k* ter bro1 thuj k* zinc k*
  • **breathing** agg.: bry
  • **cough** agg.: tarent
O - **Heart** (See Dilatation)
- **Mammae**: aster zinc
  • **sensation** of: olnd bg2 sabin b7.de* zinc b4.de*

DRAWING on boots agg.: arg-n ptk1

DRAWN: *(↗Pain - drawing pain)*
- **back**; chest as if drawn towards the: ind syph
O - **Heart** | **downwards**; as if drawn: thuj k*

- **Lungs**:
  - **backwards**; as if drawn: laur bg2 seneg bg2
  - **downwards**; as if drawn: am-c gsy1
- **Nipples** | **backward**; as if drawn: crot-t k2

DREAMS agg.: merc bg2 sulph bg2

DRINKING:
- **after**:
  - **agg.**: ant-t b7.de* arn b7.de* chin b7.de* cocc b7.de* con b4.de* cupr b7.de* nat-m bg2 nux-v b7.de* thuj b4a.de* verat b7.de*
  - **amel.**: bry b7.de* ferr b7.de*
- **agg.**: chin b7.de*

DRIPPING; as if water: | **Heart**; region of: cann-xyz bg2 nux-m bg2

DRIVING: | **agg.**: coc-c bg2 phos bg2

DROPS (See Falling - drops)

DROPSY: (↗*GENERALS - Dropsy - internal*) **Abrot** sne acet-ac acon b7.de* adon br1* *Am-c* k* *Ambr* b7.de* *Ant-t* k* **Apis** k* **Apoc** k* arn b7.de* **Ars** k* *Ars-i* c2* ars-s-f k2 *Asaf* *Aspar* k* aur bg2* *Aur-m* **Borx** sne **Bry** k* cact k2 calc k* *Canth* k* caps b7.de* *Carb-v* k* *Carbn-s* chin k* chinin-ar **Colch** k* coloc b4.de* con b4.de* *Crot-h* *Dig* k* *Dulc* k* elat hr1 ferr b7.de* ferr-m *Fl-ac* k* **Hell** k* hep b4a.de *Iod* k* *Ip* b7.de* jug-c c2* *Kali-ar* **Kali-c** k* *Kali-i* k* kali-sil k2 *Lach* k* *Lact* k* lact-v br1* *Led* b7.de* **Lyc** k* *Merc* k* **Merc-sul** k* mez k* mur-ac k* *Nat-m* *Nit-ac* b4a.de* op k* phase bro1 phase-xyz c2 phos bro1 pilo bro1 *Psor* k* *Ran-b* k* rat k* rhus-t b7.de* sabad b7.de* *Sang* sars b4.de* *Seneg* k* *Sep* b4a.de *Sil* *Spig* k* *Squil* k* stann k* sul-i k2 *Sulph* k* *Ter* teucr b7.de* tub c1 (non:uran-met k) uran-n verat b7.de* *Zinc*
- **accompanied** by:
  - **albuminuria**: *Lach* kr1
  - **anasarca**: phos b4a.de
  - **impeded** respiration: **Am-c** b4a.de *Apis* b7a.de **Ars** b4a.de *Carb-v* b4a.de *Colch* b7a.de *Hell* b7a.de **Nit-ac** b4a.de *Psor* b4a.de *Seneg* b4a.de
  - ○ **Feet**; swelling of: ars b4a.de bry b7a.de chin b7a.de colch b7a.de hell b7a.de ip b7a.de lach b7a.de nux-v b7a.de op b7a.de
  - **Heart** disease; organic: *Apoc* k*
  - **Heart**; complaints of the: spig k*
  - **Skin**; swelling of: hell b7a.de
- **asthma**, with: colch bro1 psor
- **cardiac**: arn br1
  - **dyspnea**; with distressing: adon vh1 arn br1
- **operation**; after: abrot bro1
- ○ **Pericardium**: adon vh1 ant-ar bro1* *Apis* k* *Apoc* k* **Ars** k* ars-s-f k2 asc-t ptk1 aur k2 **Colch** k* **Dig** k* iod bro1* *Lach* k* **Lyc** k* *Sulph* k* *Zinc*
- **Pleurae**: colch tl1
- **Side** | **right**:
  - ⁝ **head** low; with | **only**; can lie: *Spig*
  - **affected** | **only** on; can lie: *Ars* k*

DRUMMING heart sounds: lob-p bg1*

DRYNESS: acon k2 agath-a nl2• agn hr1 alum h2 bell k2 chel bg2 con h2 *Ferr* k* flor-p rsj3• hydroph rsj6• kali-c k2 kali-chl *Lach* k* mand rsj7• *Merc* k* osm phos h2* *Puls* k* sang k2 stram zinc
- **left**: naja ptk1
- **warm** room agg.: hydrog srj2•
- ○ **Axillae**: hep
- **Internally** | **sensation** of: alum b4.de* bell bg2 canth b7.de* ferr b7.de* kali-bi bg2 merc bg2 *Phos* b4.de* puls b7a.de* stann bg2 stram b7.de* zinc bg2
- **Mammae** | **Nipples**: castor-eq k*

EATING:
- **after**:
  - **agg.**: acon b7.de* am-m b7.de* ambr b7.de* ant-c b7.de* arn b7.de* asaf b7.de* *Aur* b4a.de bell bg2 bry b7.de* calc b4a.de* camph b7a.de* canth b7.de* caps b7.de* carb-an b4.de* carb-v b4.de* caust b4.de* cham b7.de* chin b7.de* cinnb bg2 cocc b7.de* con b4.de* ferr b7.de* hyos b7.de* ign b7.de* kali-bi bg2 kali-c b4a.de lach bg2 laur bg2 lil-t bg2 *Lyc* b4.de* mag-c b4.de* meny b7.de* merc b4.de* nat-c b4.de* nat-m bg2

Eating – after – agg.: ...
nat-s bg2 nit-ac b4a.de* nux-v b7.de* phos b4.de* puls b7.de* ran-b b7.de* rhus-t b7.de* ruta b7.de* sep b4.de* *Sil* b4a.de spig b7a.de sulph b4a.de* thuj b4.de* valer b7.de* verat b7.de* viol-t bg2 zinc b4.de*
  - **amel.**: bry b7.de* nat-c b4.de* rhus-t b7.de* sabad b7.de*
- **before** | **agg.**: mez bg2
- **fast** agg.: led b7.de*
- **while** | **agg.**: *Arn* b7.de* bov b4.de* chin b7.de* cocc b7.de* ign b7.de* led bg2 mag-m b4.de* olnd bg2 phos b4.de*

EBULLITION (See Orgasm)

ECCHYMOSES: | **spots**: *Lach* phos *Sul-ac*

EDEMA; PULMONARY: acon bg2 adon vh1 *Adren* vh1 *Am-c* k* am-i br1* **Ant-ar** st ant-c b7a.de **Ant-t** k* *Apis* k* apoc **Ars** k* ars-i bg2 aspar atra-r bnm3• aur bg2 *Aur-i* *Bar-c* b4a.de* bell bg2 beryl sp1 brass-n-o srj5• bry bg2 cadm-s bg2 camph b7a.de* *Carb-v* k* cham b7a.de* chel chin bg2 chir-fl bnm4• coch k* coff b7a.de colch con bg2 cortico sp1 crot-h crot-t *Dig* k* dros bg2 *Graph* bg2 hep bg2 *Hyos* k* ign b7a.de* iod b4a.de *Ip* k* jab br1 kali-c k* *Kali-i* k* *Kali-p* k* **Lach** k* lat-m sp1 laur b7.de* loxo-lae bnm12• *Lyc* k* merc bg2* **Merc-sul** k* mosch b7a.de *Nat-m* k* *Nux-v* bg2 **Op** b7a.de* *Phos* k* pilo bro1 plb b7a.de* pulm-v c2* puls k* *Samb* b7a.de* *Sang* bro1 *Sec* b7a.de senec bro1 seneg spong bg2 squil stront-c bg2 stroph-h br1* sulph k* thal-xyz srj8• tub c2* verat k*
- **accompanied** by:
  - **scarlet** fever: *Ant-t* bro1 cann-s bro1 phos bro1 squil bro1
  - ○ **Heart** failure (See Heart failure - accompanied - lungs)
  - **Kidneys**; complaints of (See KIDNEYS - Complaints - accompanied - lungs)
- **drunkards**; in: crot-h
- **sudden**: rhus-t ptk1

EFFUSION: colch tl1
- ○ **Endocardium**: ars tl1
- **Pericardium**: ant-ar br1* asc-t ptk1 psor mtf11 sulph mtf33
  - **inflammation** of heart; after: colch tl1
- **Pleural** exudate: ant-ar mtf11 ars mtf11 erio br1 ign mtf33 iod mtf33 sulph mtf33
  - **accompanied** by | **renal** failure (See KIDNEYS - Renal - accompanied - pleural)

ELEVATED; as if: | **Diaphragm**: bism bg2 caps bg2 carb-an bg2 carb-v bg2 card-m bg2

EMACIATION: (↗*Narrow*) calc-p k2 kali-i k* petr bg2* phos k2 senec bg1* sulph k2 tub gk*
- ○ **Clavicles**, about the lach mtf *Lyc* k* *Nat-m* k* plb a1 tub gk
- **Mammae**: (↗*Atrophy - mammae*) ars-i ptk1 bar-c ptk1 cench k2 cham bg2* chin bg2* **Coff** k* *Con* bg2* ferr bg2* iod bg2* *Kali-i* ptk1 kreos bg2 lac-d k2 nat-m k2* nit-ac bg2* *Nux-m* k* *Onos* c1* sabal ptk1 sec bg2* sep mtf33 sil bg2*
  - **one** smaller than the other: **Sabal** vh
- **Ribs**: tub gk

EMBOLISM: | **Lungs**; of: both mrr1

EMOTIONS agg.: arg-n bg2 asaf bg2 *Aur* b4a.de bad bg2 cocc bg2 cupr bg2 ip bg2 kreos bg2 lach bg2 lith-c bg2 nit-ac b4a.de* phos b4.de* podo bg2 puls bg2 sep bg2

EMPHYSEMA: **Am-c** k* **Ant-ar** k* **Ant-t** k* *Ars* k* *Aur-m* bro1 *Bell* k* blatta-o cpy *Brom* k* bry bro1 calc bro1 *Calc-p* bro1 *Camph* *Carb-v* k* carbn-s chin bro1 chinin-ar bro1 *Chlor* coca br1* cupr cupr-ar br1 cur k* *Dig* k* dros k* eucal bro1 glon bro1 grin c2* **Hep** k* hist sp1 *Ip* k* kali-c bro1 lac-d **Lach** k* led br1 **Lob** k* loxo-lae bnm12• *Lyc* bro1 *Merc* morg-p pte1*• myrt-c br1* naphtin bro1 *Nat-m* nit-ac nux-v bro1 op *Phel* k* *Phos* k* pneu jl2 psor jl2 puls bro1 queb br1 sars sec a1 seneg k* sep k* spong bro1 *Stry* bro1 sulph k* ter tub-r jl2 verat c2 [am-m stj1 am-p stj1]
- **accompanied** by:
  - **bronchitis** (See Inflammation - bronchial - accompanied - emphysema)
  - **cough**: ant-ar br1
  - **respiration**; difficult (See RESPIRATION - Difficult - emphysema)
- **dilated** heart; with: grin c1
- **old** people; in: lob ptk1

- **pleuritis**; after: sil mtf33

EMPTINESS, sensation of: adam skp7• all-s aspar bov *Calad* k* carb-an ptk1 chin k* chr-ac coc-c nh6 *Cocc* k* crot-t k* falco-pe nl2• ferr-ma fuma-ac rly4• galla-q-r nl2• gels mrr1 graph k* *Guare* ictod bg2 *Ign* k* *Kali-c* k* kali-sil k2 kola stb3• med bg2* *Moni* rfm1• *Myrt-c* b7a.de nat-p k* nat-s k* olib-sac wmh1 olnd k* phos b4a.de* phyt k* plat rhus-t sars k* *Sep* k* **Stann** k* sulph k* vinc zinc k*
- **night**: *Sep* k*
- **asthma**, during: nat-s vh
- **breathing** agg.: kola stb3•
- **cough**:
  - **after**: anis kali-c nat-s sep stann zinc
  - **during** | **agg.**: *Calad* b7a.de ph-ac bro1 *Phos* b4a.de *Sep* k* *Stann* k* sulph zinc b4.de*
- **eating**; after: nat-p k* olnd ptk1
- **exertion** agg.: **Stann** mrr1
- **expectoration**; after: calad ruta ptk1 *Stann* k* *Zinc* k*
- **faint** feeling: sulph
- **inspiration** agg.: nat-s k2
- **palpitations**; during: olnd bro1
- **sing**, on beginning to: *Stann* k*
- **talking**; when: **Stann** mrr1

O - **Heart**: bar-m bg2 cocc k* croc bg2 gels k2 graph bg2* lach k2 lil-t c1 med k* nux-m bg2 olnd bg2 sulph k* tab bg2

O · **Region** of: chr-o bg1 con graph med hr1 naja nux-m bg1 sulph
- **Mammae**: **Borx** b4a.de*
  - **after** child nurses: *Borx* k*
- **Sides**:
  - **left**: naja k2*
    - ⁝ **Lower** part: gels k2
- **Sternum**, behind: zinc

EMPYEMA: apis arn bro1* **Ars** k* *Ars-i* *Calc* k* **Calc-s** k* carb-an c2 *Carb-v* *Carbn-s* *Chin* k* *Chinin-ar* croc xyz61 dig echi bro1 ferr k* *Hep* k* iod ip bro1 *Kali-c* k* **Kali-s** k* kali-sula hsa1 *Lach* lyc **Merc** k* *Nat-ar* nat-s bro1 *Nit-ac* *Phos* k* pyrog mtf11 *Sep* **Sil** k* **Sulph** k* tub c1*
- **pleura**; after inflammation of: sil ptk1

ENDOCARDITIS (See Inflammation - heart - endocardium)

ENLARGED sensation: galla-q-r nl2• ulm-c jsj8•

O - **Heart**: *(↗Swelling - heart - sensation)* acon bg3 bell bg2 bov sf1.de bufo a1 cench gm1 cent a1 ham fd3.de• kali-i a1 lach k* med hr1* pyrog al2 spig b7a.de stroph-h br1 stroph-s sp1 sulph st*
  - **bulging** through ribs when lying: choc srj3•
- **Mammae**: cycl bg2

ENLARGEMENT (See Hypertrophy)

EPISTAXIS:
- **agg.**: carb-v b4.de*
- **amel.**: bov bro1 brom bg2* carb-v ptk1

ERUCTATIONS:
- **agg.**: *Cann-s* b7.de* cocc b7.de* nit-ac b4.de* par b7.de* phos b4.de* rhus-t b7.de* staph b7.de* zinc b4.de*
- **amel.**: aloe bg2 am-m bg2 ambr b7.de* aml-ns bg2* asaf bg2 *Aur* b4a.de bar-c b4a.de* canth b7.de* carb-v bg2 gels bg2 kali-c b4.de* lach ptk1 lyc bg2 lycps-v bg2 nux-v b7.de* petr b4.de* phos bg2* *Sep* b4.de* thuj bg2 zinc b4.de*

ERUPTIONS: agar ail k2 alum bg2 *Alumn* am-c am-m amp rly4• anac ant-c ant-t bg2 **Ars** k* ars-s-f k2 arund bro1 asar aur b4a.de *Bar-c* bell bg2 berb bov k* cadm-s *Calad* b7a.de *Calc* k* calc-s calc-sil k2* camph cann-s canth b7a.de* **Carb-an** *Carb-v* *Carbn-s* *Caust* chel chin chord-umb rly4• cic *Cinnb* cist cocc con k* cupr b7a.de cycl des-ac rbp6 dream-p sdj1• dulc fl-ac **Graph** k* grat bg2 haliae-lc srj5• *Hep* k* hippoz hydr hydr-ac hydrc hyper iod jug-c bro1 kali-ar kali-bi kali-br bro1 *Kali-c* *Kali-i* kali-s lach k* lap-la sde8.de• *Led* k* luna kg1• *Lyc* k* mag-c *Mag-m* merc bg2 *Merc-c* mez k* morg-p pte1• nat-ar nat-c nat-p *Nat-s* k* **Petr** k* petr-ra shn4• ph-ac k* *Phos* pin-con oss2• plac-s rly4• plb k* **Psor** k* puls ran-b k2 rhus-t k* ruta fd4.de sec bg2 *Sep* sil spong fd4.de staph k* stram stront-c bg2 sul-i k2 **Sulph** k* symph fd3.de• *Syph* tab thuj tritic-vg fd5.de urt-u valer k* vanil fd5.de zinc
- **acne**: amph a1 bar-c carc mrr1 des-ac rbp6 tritic-vg fd5.de
- **blood** blisters: *Ars* k*

Eruptions: ...
- **blotches**: chord-umb rly4• dulc fd4.de nat-c podo fd3.de• sars
- **blue**: ran-b k2
- **boils**: am-c k* *Am* bg2 chin k* *Hep* k* **Kali-i** k* lach mag-c mag-m h2 phos **Psor** **Sulph**
  - **blood** boils: *Arn* b7.de *Chin* b7.de graph b4a.de
- **burning**: alum bov *Cic* mez *Rhus-t* ruta fd4.de
- **comedones**: *Dros* b7a.de
- **crusts**: anac ars *Fl-ac* *Hep* *Mez* *Nat-s*
- **desquamating**: *Led* mag-c h2 mang hr1 mez sulph
- **dry**: *Carb-v* *Petr* **Psor** k* *Sep* *Sulph*
- **eczema**: anac ars bg2 aur-i k2 *Calc* calc-s *Carb-v* cycl **Graph** hep kali-s moni jl2 *Petr* k* **Psor** staph bg2 **Sulph**
- **hay** causes: *Graph* vh
- **herpes**: *Ars* ars-br vh dys pte1*• *Graph* k* *Hep* k* lyc mag-c nat-m bro1 *Petr* k* petr-ra shn4• *Ran-b* hr1 *Staph* syc pte1*• *Syph* k*
  - **zona**●: dol c1* *Graph* k* *Lach* k* *Mez* k* *Ran-b* hr1* *Rhus-t* k* staph bg1 thuj k2
    - ⁝ **left** side: ran-b mrr1
- **itching**: amph a1 cann-s corian-s knl6• gink-b sbd1• *Graph* lap-la sde8.de• led luna kg1• mang-p rly4• medul-os-si rly4• morg-p pte1• plac-s rly4• *Rhus-t* ruta fd4.de sal-fr sle1• stram urt-u
- **menses**; before: *Sulph* b4a.de
- **miliary**: am-c b4a.de* amph a1 ant-c b7.de* ant-t b7a.de* bry bg2 calad b7.de* *Canth* b7a.de cupr b7a.de* hydrc lach bg2 *Led* b7.de* merc bg2 mez sep b4a.de sil bg2 staph b7.de* stram bg2 valer b7.de* verat b7.de*
- **nodules**: *Bar-c* *Carb-an* hippoz hydr *Merc-c* nat-c h2 *Nat-s* ruta fd4.de
- **painful**: arizon-l nl2• luna kg1• lyc h2 mang-p rly4• petr-ra shn4• positr nl2• tritic-vg fd5.de
  - **spots**: luna kg1•
- **pimples**: am-c b4.de* am-m k* *Ant-c* k* arg-n *Ars* aur b4.de* bell b4.de* berb borx k* bov k* bry b7.de* calc k* cann-s canth k* chin k* cinnb *Cist* cocc k* con k* des-ac rbp6 dulc k* fl-ac gins br1 *Graph* ham fd3.de• *Hep* k* hura hyper iod k* kali-ar *Kali-c* kali-p fd1.de• *Lach* k* led k* lyc b4a.de m-ambo b7.de mag-c b4a.de mag-m k* mang a1 mez k* nat-ar nat-c k* nat-p ph-ac k* plb k* puls *Rhus-t* k* spong fd4.de squil k* staph k* stront-c k* *Sulph* b4a.de symph fd3.de• tab tritic-vg fd5.de valer k* vanil fd5.de verat zinc k* zinc-p k2
  - **acne** (See acne)
  - **angry**: sep k*
  - **bleed** easily: *Cist*
  - **burning**: agar bov staph
  - **elevated**: valer
  - **flattening**: rhus-t
  - **hard**: bov valer
    - ⁝ **Under** the skin: alum
  - **indolent**: cund
  - **itching**: allox tpw3 ant-c h2 arg-n a1 cann-s dulc gins iod h mag-m nat-c spong fd4.de tab vanil fd5.de
  - **painful**: cist tritic-vg fd5.de
    - ⁝ **touch** agg.: con h2
  - **pointed**, with whitish semi-transparent vesicles on it: bry
  - **red**: am-c apis arund bov cocc ham fd3.de• iod mang-p rly4• *Mez* ph-ac plb stram tritic-vg fd5.de vanil fd5.de zinc
    - ⁝ **evening**: ph-ac
    - ⁝ **lichen** simplex; like: ant-t
  - **white**: valer
    - ⁝ **red** areola, with: *Borx* k* bov
- **pustules**: agar alum bg2 *Ant-t* k* *Ars* arund asar aur bar-c bar-s k2 *Calc* chel chlor cocc euon fl-ac graph *Hep* k* hydr *Hydrc* kali-bi kali-s *Led* bg2 mag-m merc-c petr *Psor* *Rhus-t* ros-d wla1 *Sil* stront-c k*
- **rash**: ail k2 *Am-c* ant-t *Bry* calad *Calc* calc-s **Chel** coca-c sk4• cupr ferr germ-met srj5• *Ip* lach **Led** k* merc mez musca-d szs1 plac-s rly4• plb sal-fr sle1• *Sil* *Staph* *Sulph* syph ter
  - **alternating** with asthma (See RESPIRATION - Asthmatic - alternating - chest)
  - **flat**: musca-d szs1
  - **itching**: calad caust sal-fr sle1• sil h2 staph vanil fd5.de
  - **pink**: musca-d szs1

- **red**: am-c calc *Camph* **Chel** k* corn staph staphycoc rly4• stram sulph [spect dfg1]
  - **itching** rash over region of liver: *Sel*
  - **Sternum**; lower: cortiso tpw7
- **warmth** agg.: stram
- **whitish** in typhus fever: *Apis* valer

- **red**: chord-umb rly4• mag-c h2 *Merc* merc-i-f nat-s k2 oci-sa sk4• petr-ra shn4• positr nl2• tritic-vg fd5.de ust valer vip
  - **coppery**: merc stram
  - **spots** (See Discoloration - redness - spots)
- **roseola** after abuse of mercury: *Kali-i*
- **scaly**: musca-d szs1
- **sore** (See painful)
- **spots**; in: am-m bg2 ars bg2 bell bg2 *Carb-v* bg2 *Cocc* bg2 *Ip* bg2 lach bg2 led bg2 mag-c bg2 mez bg2 nit-ac bg2 *Phos* bg2 *Sep* bg2 squil bg2 sulph bg2
- **spring**, every: *Nat-s*
- **suppressed**; after: hep bro1
- **tetters**: *Ars* b4.de* *Dulc* b4a.de lyc b4.de* mag-c b4.de* *Petr* b4.de* phos b4a.de staph b7.de*
- **tubercles**: am-c caust mang nicc
- **urticaria**: atra-r bnm3• *Calad* hydrc ina-i mlk9.de sars sulph tub c1 urt-u
- **varicella**: *Led* b7.de*
- **vesicles**: alum arund calc calc-s camph carbn-s caust dulc fd4.de *Graph* k* kali-i led medus br1 *Merc* ran-b k2 rhus-t sep stram sulph
  - **burning**: alum
  - **bursting** sensation: (↗*Bubbling; Clucking; Gurgling)* sulph h2
  - **painful**: caust h2
- **yellow**, scaly, itching spots: kali-c

○ - **Axillae**: brom calc k* **Carb-an** bg2* elaps k* graph mrr1 *Hep* jug-r lac-c bg2 lac-h htj1• lyc k* *Merc* k* nat-m k* nicc nit-ac bg2 petr k* petr-ra shn4• phos b4a.de* psor k* *Rhus-t* sal-fr sle1• *Sep* k* *Sulph* thuj
  - **right**: lac-h sk4• musca-d szs1
  - **left**: musca-d szs1 nat-f sp1
  - **acne**: carb-v bro1*
  - **bathing**; after: musca-d szs1
  - **blotches**: | **red**: ros-d wla1
  - **boils**●: borx k* **Hep** k* *Lyc* k* *Merc* k* *Nat-s* k* petr ph-ac k* *Phos* k* prot pte1*• sal-fr sle1• sep k* *Sil* k* *Sulph* k* thuj
    - **right**: petr-ra shn4• thuj
    - **left**: borx lyc k* petr-ra shn4• *Phos* k* sal-fr sle1• *Sep* k*
    - **painful**, small: sep
    - **recurrent**●: lyc k* petr-ra shn4•
    - **tearing** pain: petr h2
  - **burning**: *Merc* k*
    - **scratching**; after: phos h2
  - **cracks**: *Hep* k*
  - **crusts**: anac jug-r **Nat-m** k*
  - **dry**: *Hep* k*
  - **eczema**: *Carb-an* bg2 elaps bro1 *Hep* jug-r **Lyc** bg2 merc moni jl2 *Nat-m* k* petr **Psor** k* sep k*
  - **herpes**: *Carb-an* k* elaps graph k2 *Lac-c* *Lyc* mez *Nat-m* petr-ra shn4• *Rhus-t* *Sep*
    - **zona**: dol st
  - **indurated**: psor mtf33
  - **itching**: elaps *Hep* lac-h sk4• nat-f sp1 oxal-a rly4• phos h2 *Psor* k* sal-fr sle1•
  - **moist**: brom carb-v jug-r nat-m *Sep* sulph
  - **painful**: *Merc*
  - **pimples**: cocc phos sal-fr sle1•
  - **pustules**: crot-c k* viol-t
  - **rash**: *Hep* musca-d szs1 sal-fr sle1• *Sulph*
  - **scabs** (See crusts)
  - **scaly**: jug-r
  - **tetters**: calc b4a.de *Carb-an* b4a.de lyc b4a.de nat-m b4a.de *Sep* b4a.de

- **Axillae**: ...
  - **tubercles**: nit-ac phos
- **External** | **vesicles**: am-m b7.de* bell b4.de* caust bg2 *Hep* b4a.de
- **Mammae**: amp rly4• arge-pl rwt5• ars bg2 aster bufo k2 *Caust* k* falco-pe nl2• graph k* grat hep led lyc nat-m bg2 phos bg2 pip-n c2 psor ptk1 rhus-t bg2 sinus rly4• staph tab valer
  - **blisters**: bufo k2
  - **boils**: chin mag-c phos
  - **burning**: ars grat phos rhus-t
    - **scratching** agg.; after: grat
  - **eczema**: anac *Caust* bg2 dulc bg2
  - **furfuraceous**, between mammae: aster
  - **herpes**: ars *Caust* dulc k* graph *Lach* petr psor staph
  - **itching**: kali-c sil hr1 staph tab
    - **warmth** agg. | **heat** agg.: staph
  - **mealy**: petr
  - **miliary**: ant-t led staph
  - **nursing** women, tetters on: dulc c1*
  - **painful**: falco-pe nl2• lyc ulm-c jsj8•
    - **right** side: ulm-c jsj8•
    - **touch**; to: falco-pe nl2• hep ph-ac
  - **pimples**:
    - **itching**: bell h1
    - **stinging**: hep
  - **pustules**: euon falco-pe nl2• hep
  - **rash**: dulc mtf11
  - **red**: staph
  - **rubbing** agg.: kali-c h2
  - **scaly**: petr bg2
  - **squamous**: kali-c *Kreos* petr
  - **stinging**: hep
  - **vesicles**: aeth

○ · **Nipples**: caust falco-pe nl2• *Graph* k* lach c1 petr k2 psor rhus-t tell
    - **crusts**: fl-ac bg2
    - **desquamating**: *Puls* b7a.de
    - **eczema**: *Graph* k* morg-p pte1• sars bg2 sulph bg2
      - **left**: morg-p fmm1•
    - **herpes**: **Caust** k*
    - **itching**: petr k2
    - **mealy**: *Petr*
    - **moist**, itching: *Sulph*
    - **pimples**: agar k* falco-pe nl2• *Graph* b4a.de* sulph b4a.de
    - **scabs**: *Lyc* bg2
    - **scaly**: *Lyc* k*
    - **scurfy**: *Lyc* *Petr*
    - **tetters**: kali-c b4a.de
    - **vesicles**: *Graph* k*
  - **Under** | **eczema**: lac-ac stj5• moni jl2
- **Side**:
  - **right**: oci-sa sk4•
  - **left**: vac jl2
- **Sternum**: petr-ra shn4• [card-m stj]
  - **circinate**: gaert fmm1•
  - **eczema**: carc mlr1•
  - **pustules**: sil tl1
    - **variola**-like:
      - **painful**: sil tl1
      - **ulcers**; join to form: sil tl1
  - **rash**: cortiso tpw7
  - **undressing** agg.: carc tpw2*
- **Upper** chest | **acne**: carc mlr1•

ERYSIPELAS of mammae: acon b7.de* anan **Apis** k* arn k* *Bell* k* *Bry* b7.de* cadm-s *Carb-an* k* *Carb-v* k* *Carbn-s* *Cham* k* coll graph *Phos* k* plan k* *Sulph* k*
- **bluish**: *Carb-an* b4a.de

EXCORIATION:
○ - **Axillae**: ars k* aur k* carb-v k* con *Graph* k* kola stb3• *Mang* b4a.de mez k* sanic *Sep* k* *Sulph* k* teucr bg2 zinc k*
- **Mammae**:
  - **rubbing**; from: con h2
○ • **Nipples**: alumn anan arg-n *Arn* k* calc k* calc-p calc-sil k2 castor-eq **Caust** k* *Cham* k* crot-t dulc **Fl-ac** k* *Graph* k* *Ham* k* *Hell* hyper ign k* lil-t bg2 *Lyc* k* *Merc* k* *Nit-ac* k* nux-v bg2 petr b4a.de phos k* **Phyt** k* psor bg2 puls k* *Sang* k* *Sep* k* *Sil* k* *Staph* b7a.de *Sulph* k* zinc

EXERTION agg.: alum b4.de* am-c bg2 arg-n bg2 asaf bg2 aur bg2 caust b4a.de chel bg2 gels bg2 iod b4a.de* kali-bi bg2 kali-c bg2 lach bg2 lyc bg2 merc bg2 nux-v b7.de* podo bg2 rhus-t b7.de* spong b7.de* stram bg2
○ - **Heart**: ant-t bg2 *Arn* bg2 cact ptk1 dig ptk1 lil-t ptk1 nit-ac ptk1 stroph-h ptk1 tab ptk1

EXHAUSTION agg.; after: lyc bg2

EXOSTOSIS: *Calc* b4a.de *Sil* b4a.de *Sulph* b4a.de
○ - **Ribs**; on: calc-f k2 merc-c k*
- **Sternum**: merc-c ptk1

EXPANDING:
- **impossible**: con b4a.de
○ - **Lungs** | **impossible**: asaf b7.de* bry b7.de* cina b7.de* crot-t bg2* laur b7.de* mosch b7a.de

EXPANSION; sensation of:
○ - **Bronchi**: limen-b-c hm2•
- **Heart**: limen-b-c hm2•
- **Vessels**: asaf hr1

EXPECTORATION:
- **agg.**: calad b7.de* kreos bg2 *Stann* bg2 *Zinc* b4.de*
- **amel.**: asaf b7.de* *Bry* b7a.de ip bg2 kali-n b4.de* *Nit-ac* b4a.de *Sep* b4a.de *Zinc* b4a.de

EXPIRATION:
- **agg.**: agn b7.de* am-c bg2 ambr b7.de* anac b4.de* ang b7.de* ant-c b7.de* arg-met b7.de* ars b4.de* aur b4.de* bell bg2 bry b7.de* carb-v b4.de* cham b7.de* chel b7.de* chin b7.de* cic b7.de* cina b7.de* clem b4.de* colch b7.de* crot-t bg2 dulc b4a.de ign b7.de* iod b4.de* kreos b7a.de* laur b7.de* led b7.de* mag-p bg2 mang b4.de* meny b7.de* mur-ac b4.de* nat-c b4.de* *Olnd* b7.de* ph-ac b4.de* ruta b7.de* sabad b7.de* sep b4.de* *Spig* b7.de* squil b7.de* stann b4.de* *Staph* b7.de* tarax b7.de* *Viol-t* b7.de* zinc b4.de*
- **amel.**: borx b4a.de cina b7.de* merc b4.de* tarax b7.de*

EXPULSIVE POWER:
○ - **Lungs**:
  - **great**: (non:ant-t tl1) ip tl1
  - **wanting**: ant-t cda1*

EXUDATION: *(↗Heart; complaints - valves)*
○ - **Lungs**; in | **pneumonia**; after: ferr mtf33
- **Pleura**:
  - **accompanied** by | **Pleura**; inflammation of (See Inflammation - pleura - exudative)
- **Valves** of heart; in: *(↗Heart; complaints - valves)* *Spong*

EYES:
- **exertion** of eyes agg.: cina bg2
- **opening** the eyes agg.: carb-an bg2

FAILURE of heart; incipiency of (See Heart failure - beginning)

FAINT feeling about heart (See Weakness - heart - about)

FALLING, sensation of:
- **down** in: bry bg1 nux-v b7.de* *Sulph* b4a.de*
- **drops** were falling; as if:
○ • **Chest**, in the: thuj k*
  - **Heart**, from the: cann-i c1 cann-s k*

Falling, sensation of: ...
- **dry** body were falling down; as if a: bar-c b4a.de
- **forward** in chest when turning in bed; sensation of something falling: bar-c sulph k*
- **hard** falling into chest; as of something: bar-c bg2
- **weight** falling from pit of chest to abdomen; a: nat-hchls
○ - **Heart** feels as thought it would fall down hyper ptk1 laur ptk1
  - **evening**: hyper c1

FALSE STEP; at a: | **agg.**: bry b7.de* puls b7.de* seneg b4.de* spig b7.de*

FASTING:
- **agg.**: iod ptk1
- **sensation** as if: plat b4.de*

FAT about the heart with nervous irritability: **Aur** crat br1

FATTY degeneration of heart: adon br1* adon-ae bro1 **Arn** k* **Ars** k* *Ars-i* k* **Aur** k* **Aur-m** k* *Bar-c* bro1 **Cact** k* *Calc* caps k* carb-v bg2 cimic bro1 crat br1* crot-h cupr h2 cupr-act bro1 *Ferr* fuc bro1 *Iod* k* **Kali-c** k* kali-fcy c2* kali-p kali-s k2 *Kalm* k* lac-d k2 *Naja* *Ph-ac* bro1 **Phos** k* phys bro1 phyt k* sacch bro1 stroph-h br1* stry-ar bro1 stry-p br1* vanad br1*
○ - **Myocardium**: spartin bwa3

FEATHERS or petals; sensation of: limen-b-c hrn2•
- **overlaying** chest: limen-b-c hm2•

FERMENTATION; sensation of: *Phos* b4.de*

FEVER:
- **after** | **agg.**: bell b4a.de
- **before** | **agg.**: chin b7.de*
- **during** | **agg.**: acon b7.de bry b7.de chin b7.de ip b7.de

FIBROSIS; pulmonary: *(↗Phthisis - fibrosis; Sarcoidosis; GENERALS - Besnier-boeck-schaumann)* med mrr1 penic jl1

FISTULOUS openings:
○ - **Axillae**, in: *Calc* *Sulph*
- **Mammae**; in: alum sne *Caust* *Hep* *Merc* *Phos* k* *Phyt* **Sil** k*

FLABBY mammae: bell calc lp cham k* **Con** k* graph gl1.fr• hydr bg2 **Iod** k* kali-i bg2 kreos bg2 nit-ac b4a.de* nux-m b7.de* nux-v sne onos st sars b4a.de
- **except** during menses: con

FLATULENCE: | **agg.**: *Carb-v* bg2 *Cocc* b7a.de *Ign* b7a.de *Kali-c* b4a.de nux-m b7.de* nux-v b7.de* rheum b7.de*

FLATUS; PASSING: | **amel.**: bry bg2 caust bg2 kali-c b4a.de mur-ac bg2 ph-ac bg2 sep bg2 spig b7.de* stram b7.de* verat b7.de*

FLOATING; as if heart were: bov ptk1 *Bufo* bg1* crot-c bg1 kali-i ptk1 sumb ptk1

FLUCTUATION, feeling of: plb

FLUTTERING: *(↗Trembling - heart)* acon k* *Alumn* *Ambr* *Apis* bg2 apoc arg-met k2 *Arg-n* *Arn* ars-i *Asaf* k* aur aur-ar k2 *Aur-m* aur-s k2 *Bry* *Cact* calad *Calc* calc-s carb-v cartl-s rly4• *Cench* cinnb bg2 crot-h bg2 cupr-ar daph *Dig* k* eup-pur falco-pe nl2• form gels k* ger-i rly4• glon k2 hydr-ac iber vml3• ignis-alc es2• irid-met srj5• *Kali-bi* *Kali-br* *Kali-i* *Kali-p* *Kalm* lac-c *Lach* k* *Laur* lec **Lil-t** k* *Lith-c* lyss *Med* mosch **Naja** k* **Nat-m** k* **Nat-s** k* **Nux-m** k* nux-v k* olib-sac wmh1 *Ox-ac* oxal-a rly4• **Ph-ac** k* phos bg2 *Pic-ac* positr nl2• rat *Rhus-t* *Samb* *Sep* *Spig* k* stry *Sulph* k* sumb thea tung-met bdx1• verat-v zing
- **morning**: naja stry
- **afternoon**: form k* sumb k*
  - **exertion**; after quick: sumb
  - **headache**; during: form sumb
- **evening**: pic-ac k*
- **night**: marb-w es1• naja
  - **wakens** her: *Lil-t*
- **air**; in open | **amel.**: **Nat-m** **Nat-s**
- **alternating** with | **soreness**: aur-m
- **ascending** stairs agg.: *Bry* **Calc** k*
- **audible**: dig br1
  - **rheumatic** fever; after: *Dig* br1
- **dinner**; after: *Sep*
- **excitement** after slight: *Aml-ns* k* **Lil-t** *Lith-c*

- **exertion** agg.: conv mtf11
- **faintness**; after: asaf k* *Calc Gels Lil-t Mosch* **Nat-m Nat-s** ph-ac stry
- **lying**:
  - **agg.**: marb-w es1• **Nat-m** k*
  - **side**; on | **left** | **agg.**: cact nh6 *Daph Dig* k* *Gels Nat-m* k* spig
    - **right** | **agg.**: *Alumn*
- **menses**; after: dig k2 nat-p ptk1 spig
- **raising** arms agg.: dig *Sulph*
- **rest** agg.: **Lil-t**
- **sensation**; of: falco-pe nl2•

○ • **Heart**: absin bro1 *Acon* bro1 aml-ns bro1 apoc bro1 asaf bro1 *Cact* bro1 *Cimic* bro1 conv bro1 crot-h bro1 ferr bro1 flor-p rsj3• glon bro1 *Iber* bro1 *Kalm* bro1 lach bro1 *Lil-t* bro1 lith-c bro1 *Mosch* bro1 naja bro1 *Nat-m* bro1 nux-m bro1 *Ph-ac* bro1 phase bro1 *Phys* bro1 pyrog bro1 *Spig* bro1 sul-ac bro1 thea bro1
  - **excitement** agg.: galeoc-c-h gms1•
  - **lying** in bed; while: flor-p rsj3•
- **sitting** agg.: *Asaf*
- **thinking** of it agg.: *Arg-n*
- **waking**; on: *Kali-i* k* naja
- **writing** agg.: naja

○ - **Mammae**: plut-n srj7•

FOLDING arms: | **agg.**: staph b7.de*

FOOD: | **irritating** food agg.: *Stann* b4.de

FOREIGN BODY; sensation of a: ambr b7a.de chel bg2 cic b7.de* fl-ac bg2 zinc bg2
- **ascending** body; of an: zinc h2

○ - **Heart** | **bubble** were hanging at heart; as if a: *Aur* b4a.de
- **Sternum**; behind: nat-m h2
- **Throat**; up into: zinc h2

FORMICATION: acon agar k2 alum am-m arn b7.de* ars arund cadm-s cain calc bg2 *Carl* chin k* colch b7a.de coloc cycl k* dros b7.de* guaj laur b7.de* m-aust b7.de mag-m nux-v bg1 olnd b7.de* *Ran-s* k* rhus-t b7.de* *Seneg Sep* spig bg1 spong bg2 *Sulph* b4a.de thuj h1 tritic-vg fd5.de urt-u
- **ants** running over chest; as if: mez tl1 ph-ac tl1
- **entering** the house: phos
- **warm** | **food** | **agg.**: *Mez*
  - **room** | **agg.**: *Mez*

○ - **Axillae**: berb *Bry* bg2 cocc h1 con k* mang bg2 mez bg2

○ • **Glands**: canth b7.de*
- **Clavicles**; region of: alum arund mez
- **Heart**; region of: canth b7.de* kalm ptk1 nux-v bg2* spig h1*
- **Internal** chest: acon b7.de* am-m b7a.de ars b4.de* colch b7.de* coloc b4.de* guaj b4.de* kreos bg2 nux-m b7.de* ph-ac b4.de* rhus-t b7a.de* seneg b4.de* sep b4.de* spig b7.de* spong b7.de* squil bg2 stann b4.de* thuj b4.de*
- **Mammae**: calc chin b7.de* con k* mang ran-s sabin b7a.de*
  - **left**: ant-t ptk1
  - **cold** crawling: guaj ptk1

○ • **Nipples**: sabin b7.de*
- **Rib** muscles | **left**: dros h1
- **Sides** | **left**: am-m h2 spong h1
- **Sternum**: *Ran-s* k*

FRIGHT; after: | **agg.**: acon b7.de* camph bg2 cham b7.de* *Cupr* b7a.de ign b7.de* kali-c bg2 nat-m bg2 op b7.de*

FULLNESS: *(↗Large)* **Acon** k* aesc agar k* aids nl2• *Ail* aml-ns anac b4.de* ang c1 ant-c b7.de* **Apis** k* apoc k2 arg-n k* *Arn* b7.de* *Ars* k* arum-t *Asaf Aspar* aster **Aur** bg2* *Bar-c* k* bar-s k2 bell bg2 benz-ac brom bry k* *Cact* cadm-s calc k* calc-ar *Canth* k* *Caps* k* *Carb-v* k* *Carbn-s* carl caust cench k2 chel b7.de* chin *Cist Coff* colch con k* cop cot br1 croc *Crot-t* cub cycl b7.de* *Dig* bg2 echi ery-a *Ferr* k* ferr-ar *Ferr-p* k* *Gels* gent-l k* *Glon* k* *Hydr* ign k* *Kali-bi* **Lac-c** sne **Lach** k* lachn c1 lact lil-t k* *Lob* lyc k* med merc mez b4.de* mosch k* naja bg2 *Nat-ar* nat-m nat-p *Nit-ac* k* *Nux-m* k* nux-v *Phos* k* **Phyt** sne *Puls* k* pyrog pd *Rhus-t* k* rumx ruta k* sabad b7.de sabin k* sacch sang k* sel sep k* spong k* sul-ac k* *Sulph* k* sumb tax ter verat k*
- **morning**: calc h2 con k* gent-l a1 lyc k* *Sulph* k*
  - **smoking** agg.; after: cycl k*

Fullness – morning: ...
  - **waking**; on: ph-ac h2
- **forenoon**:
  - **walking** agg.: acon k*
  - **writing** agg.: fl-ac k*
- **noon**: lyc h2
- **afternoon**: alumn k* coca
  - **17 h**: phos
- **evening**: *Carb-v* k* eupi k* lact k* **Puls** k* *Sulph* k*
  - **bed** agg.; in: nat-p nh6 *Nat-s* sulph
  - **eating**; after: alumn
  - **sleep**; preventing: puls k2
- **accompanied** by:
  - **cough** (See COUGH - Fullness - chest)

○ • **Heart**; weakness or dilatation of: chlol ptk1
- **air** agg.; in open: lyc k*
- **ascending** agg.: bar-c k*
- **bending** agg.: stroph-s sp1
- **coffee** agg.: *Canth* k*
- **eating**; after: ant-c caps k* con b4a.de *Lyc* k* melal-alt gya4 phos k2
- **eructations**; from incomplete: ang h1
- **exertion** agg.: nat-ar
- **expectoration** | **amel.**: *Ail* calc h2
- **hard** mass in chest; feeling of a: stict c1
- **inspiration** agg.; deep: kali-n k* nat-ar sulph
- **menses**; before: brom **Sulph** k*
- **sitting** agg.: anac h2 *Caps* k*
- **urination** | **delayed**; if desire to urinate is: **Lil-t**
- **waking**; on: con ph-ac k*
- **walking** agg.: ferr verat h1

○ - **Heart**: *Acon Aesc* k* aml-ns bro1 ang bg1 ant-t bg2* arg-met arg-n k* *Asaf* k* **Aur** k* **Aur-m** k* bamb-a stb2.de• *Bell* bro1 *Bov* k* bufo k* *Cact* bro1 caust *Cench* k* colch k* coll bro1 conv bro1 cot br1 cycl bg2 *Glon* k* glyc bro1 iber bro1 **Lach** k* lact-v bro1 *Lil-t* k* *Lycps-v* med naja bg2 *Puls* pyrog k* sel bg2 sep k* *Spig* bro1 spong k2 stroph-h bro1 **Sulph** k* vanad bro1 verat-v ptk1
  - **evening**: **Puls**
  - **night**: colch
    - **side**; while lying on left: colch
  - **ascending** stairs agg.: **Aur** aur-m
  - **menses**; during: *Puls*
  - **obstruction**, as if, from: cot br1
- **Lower** part: puls h1
- **Mammae**: bell *Bry* k* calc *Calc-p* choc srj3• clem k* cycl *Dulc Kali-c Lac-c* lact merc nux-v phos k2 *Phyt* plut-n srj7• sabal bg3 sec *Sep* zinc [spect dfg1]
  - **menses**; during: *Con*
  - **sensation** of fullness: carb-an clem a1 sal-fr sle1• *Sep*
    - **milk** in mammae; as if: choc srj3•
- **Sternum**:

○ • **Below**: rhus-t bg2
  - **Under**:
    - **accompanied** by | **cough** (See COUGH - Fullness - sternum)

GALACTORRHEA (See Milk - increased; Milk - pregnancy; in)

GANGRENE of lungs: arn bg2* **Ars** k* bufo k2 caps bg2* carb-ac *Carb-an* k* *Carb-v* k* *Chin* k* crot-h k* dulc bro1 eucal bro1 hep bg2* **Kreos** k* *Lach* k* lyc bg2* lyss osm *Phos* k* *Plb* pyrog jl2 sec k* sil bg2* sul-ac tarent ter bg2
- **inflammation** of lobes; after: phos tl1

GOUTY heart: aur aur-m bro1 *Benz-ac* cact bro1 *Calc Carb-v Caust Colch* k* conv bro1 cupr bro1 *Kalm* k* *Led* **Lyc** *Puls Spong*

GRANULOMA lungs: beryl sp1

GRASPING (See Constriction)

GREASY, as if: nux-m bg1

GRIEF: kola stb3•

GROWLING: aur b4.de* calad b7.de* coloc b4.de*

GURGLING: *(↗Bubbling; Clucking; Eruptions - vesicles - bursting)*
- **accompanied** by | **cough** (See COUGH - Accompanied - chest - gurgling)
- **breathing** agg.: cina cocc c1 ind lac-del hm2• mur-ac puls bg1 [bell-p-sp dcm1]
- O - **Heart**: bell k* cact bg2 lyc bg2 *Psor* k* rhus-t
  - **lying** agg.: *Psor*
- **Mammae**: crot-t
- **Sides** | **right**: nat-m

HAIR:
- **falling**: *(↗SKIN - Hair - falling)* ph-ac mrr1
- O • **Axillae**: sel mrr1 thal dx thal-xyz srj8•

HANG DOWN; letting legs: | **amel.**: sul-ac ptk1

HANGING by a thread; as if heart was (See Thread)

HARD body:
- **coughing**; sensation of hard body falling after: bar-c h2
- O - **Heart**:
  - **were** a hard body; as if heart: nat-c k*
  - O • **Region** of | **lying** there; as if a hard body where: nat-c b4.de*
- **Lung** were small and hard; sensation as if right: abies-c c1*

HARDNESS, mammae (See Induration - mammae)

HAWKING:
- **agg.**: calc ptk1 rumx ptk1 spig b7.de*
  - O • **Clavicles**: rumx ptk1

HEART failure: *Acetan* mtf adon ah1* adren bro1 aether bro1 agarin bro1 *Alco* bro1 am-c tl1 am-caust mtf aml-ns bro1 ant-t bro1* arg-n mtf *Ars* mtf atro bro1 calc mrr1 camph bro1 carb-v mrr1* cench mtf cocain bro1 *Coffin* bro1 conv bro1* *Crat* br1* crot-c mtf *Crot-h* mtf11 *Dig* br1* *Digin* bro1 eberth jl2 *Elaps* mtf elat mtf gala br1 *Glon* bro1 *Helo* ah1 *Hydr-ac* mtf iber c1 *Kali-c* mtf *Lach* mtf lat-m bnm6* *Merc-cy* bwa3 naja mtf11 nat-f sp1 nux-m br1 oxyg bro1 *Phase* ah1 sacch br1* saroth bro1 ser-ang br1* stroph-h br1* *Stry-ar* mtf *Stry-s* bro1 verat bro1 verat-v hl1 vip mtf
- **accompanied** by:
  - **faintness**: nux-m br1
  - **hyperthyroidism**: iod mtf lycps-v mtf nat-i mtf nat-m mtf
  - **hypotension**: elat mtf
  - **indigestion**: crat br1
  - **nausea**: *Adren* vh1 crat gm1
  - **prostration**; nervous (See MIND - Prostration - heart)
  - **pulse**; soft: glon mtf
  - **septicemia**: carb-v mtf crot-h mtf pyrog k2
  - **shock**: adren mtf carb-v mtf kali-c mtf lach mtf
  - **weakness**; general: adon vh1 am-c k2* ars mrr1
  - O • **Lungs**; edema of: dig mtf sulfon mtf thyr mtf
  - • **Valves**; complaints of the: *(↗Heart; complaints - valves; Murmurs - cardiac - valvular)* naja mtf thyr mtf
- **anesthesia**; during: adren br1
- **beginning** of: cact br1 crat br1 nat-f sp1
- **congestive**: *(↗Congestion - heart)* am-c mrr1 ant-t mrr1 ars mrr1 carb-v mrr1* dig mrr1 gels mrr1 glon mrr1 hydrc mrr1 kali-c mrr1 kalm mrr1 lach mrr1 laur mrr1 lyc mrr1 lycps-v mrr1 naja mrr1 ox-ac mrr1 phos mrr1 stry-ar mtf sulph mrr1
  - **anxiety**; with (See MIND - Anxiety - heart failure)
- **incipient** (See beginning)
- **pneumonia**; after: ferr-p tl1
- **threatening**:
  - **fever**:
    - ⁝ **septic** fever: pyrog br1
    - ⁝ **zymotic** fever: pyrog br1
- O - **Mitral** valve: gala br1 ser-ang br1
- **Ventricles** | **left**: acon-f mtf arn mtf *Coffin* mtf digox mtf gels mtf grin mtf

HEART hung by a thread; as if (See Thread)

HEART is on right side; sensation as if (See Right)

HEARTBEAT:
- **each** heartbeat agg.: spig bg2
- **heavy**: lycps-v bg2* rhod ptk1
- **jerks**; in: *Arn* b7a.de
- **lower** down in chest; felt as if the heart would beat: *Cann-s* b7a.de
- **shaking**: alum bg2 seneg bg2
  - **body**; whole: apis ptk1 arn ptk1 bell ptk1 ferr ptk1 glon bg2* graph bg2 *Kali-c* ptk1 lach ptk1 lyc bg2 mur-ac ptk1 nat-m bg2* rhod bg2 rhus-t ptk1
- **shocks**; sudden: ant-t bg2 aur bg2 calc bg2 caust bg2 lith-c bg2 zinc bg2
- **violent** beat; single: aur bg2 lil-t bg2 sep ptk1 visc bg2 zinc ptk1

HEAT: **Acon** k* aesc all-c alum k* alum-p k2 alum-sil k2 am-c k* anac *Ant-t* k* *Apis* k* arg-n *Arn* k* *Ars* k* ars-h ars-i k2 *Arum-t* bg2 arund asaf k* asc-t aster aur k* aur-ar k2 aur-i k2 aur-m-n aur-s k2 bamb-a stb2.de• bar-c bg2 bar-m k* **Bell** k* bism k* bit-ar wht1• bomb-chr a1 both-ax tsm2 bov k* brom *Bry* k* bufo bg2 cact k2 *Calc* k* calc-ar k2 *Calc-p* calen oss• *Camph* bg2 *Canth* bg2 carb-an bg2 carb-v k* carbn-s castm caust k* cham k* chin k* chlol *Cic* k* clem coc-c k* cocc k* *Coff* bg2 colch bg2 conch fkr1* cop crot-t cupr bg2 dig k* dream-p sdj1• dros dulc bg2* eup-per euph bg2 falco-pe nl2• *Ferr* ferr-ar ferr-i ferr-p glon k* graph bg2 grat helo-s rwt2• *Hep* k* hyos hyper iod k* kali-bi bg2 kali-c bg2 kreos bg2 *Lach* k* lachn lact laur bg2 *Led* bg2 *Lil-t* *Lyc* k* m-arct b7.de mag-m bg2 manc k* mang k* *Med* melal-alt gya4 meny merc k* merc-c bg2 mez bg2 nat-m k* nit-ac k* *Nux-v* k* ol-an k* ol-j *Op* k* osm k* paeon petr petr-ra shn4• ph-ac bg2 **Phos** k* plat bg2 plb polyg-h bg2 *Psor* k* puls k* pyrog c1 *Ran-b* bg2 ran-s rat rhus-t k* rumx k* ruta k* sabad bg2 samb *Sang* bg2 *Sars* k* sel *Seneg* k* *Sep* k* sil k* spig k* *Spong* k* *Stann* k* sul-ac bg2 sul-i k2 **Sulph** k* tax tep *Ter* bg2 thuj k* ust verat zinc bg2 [bell-p-sp dcm1 heroin sdj2]
- **left** side hot:
  - **right** side cold; and | **sun** agg.; walking in the: *Med* k*
- **morning** | **waking**; on: apis bamb-a stb2.de• nat-m sulph
- **afternoon**:
  - **13** h:
    - ⁝ **13**-15 h: plan
    - ⁝ **ascending** a hill; on: clem
  - **14** h: hura
  - **14**.30 h: laur
  - **walking** agg.: thuj
- **evening**: arge-pl rwt5• mang k* puls h1
- **night**: ant-c k* arg-n carb-an h2 sars h2
- **alternating** with | **pain** on internal surface of thigh: coc-c k*
- **bed** agg.; in: sars k*
- **burning**: *Acon* ptk1 apis k* *Ars* ptk1 bell ptk1 canth ptk1 *Carb-v* ptk1 euph ptk1 kali-m ptk1 lavand-a ctl1• lyc ptk1 naja ptk1 paeon *Phos* ptk1 puls h1 raph sang ptk1 spong ptk1 *Sulph* k* *Tub* ptk1 verat-v ptk1
- **chill**; during: sars h2 sil h2
- **during** | **agg.**: acon b7.de caps b7.de chin b7.de ip b7.de nux-v b7.de puls b7.de
- **eating**; after: clem k* sel k*
- **expectoration** | **amel.**: cham k*
- **fever**; during: am-m b7a.de
- **fire**; sensation as if on:
  - O • **Lungs**: pyrog tl1
    - ⁝ **air**; in open | **amel.**: pyrog tl1
- **flushes**: *(↗Orgasm)* alum arg-n bamb-a stb2.de• bism cact k2 calc-s k2 clem *Coc-c* *Cupr* *Ferr* *Glon* k* kali-m k2 lact *Lil-t* merc k2 mill k2 nit-ac nux-v ol-an *Phos* plb podo fd3.de• psil ft1 rhod **Seneg** *Sep* k* *Spong* **Sulph** *Thuj* [heroin sdj2]
  - ▽ • **extending** to:
    - ⁝ **Face**: bamb-a stb2.de• **Sulph**
    - ⁝ **Head**: cinnb ptk2 glon mill k2 phos k2 ulm-c jsj8•
    - ⁝ **Upward**: phos k2
  - O • **Upper** chest | **excitement** agg.: merc mrr1 nat-m mrr1
- **glowing**: bell lach k* *Spong*
- **holds** left arm during: aur mtf33
- **itching**; with: cic h1
- **motion** agg.: *Spong*
- **rising** from stooping agg.: rhus-t

- **rising** upward; heat: (↗*Rising; sensation - Heart; Rising; sensation - Heart - throat)* caust k* *Sulph* k* thuj
  - **fever**; during: am-m b7a.de *Nux-v* b7a.de
- **sensation** of: acon bg2 alum k* *Arn* b7a.de *Ars* bg2 asc-t a1* bell bg2 *Bry* b7.de* *Caust* bg2 coff b7.de* euph k* falco-pe nl2• ferr bg2 galla-q-r nl2• hell k* *Iod* b4a.de lact *Mang* k* merc b4.de* nat-m k* *Nux-v* b7.de* ol-an *Plat* b4a.de rhod rhus-t h1 **Sulph** k* verat b7.de* [bell-p-sp dcm1]
  - **chill**; during: sars bg2
  - **cough** agg.; during: *Arn* b7a.de
  - ○ **Heart**:
    - **About** the: acon bg2 ant-t b7.de* arg-n bg2 ars bg2 bar-m bg2 cann-s k* chinin-s bg2 croc k* dig bg2 kali-c bg2 kalm c1 merc bg2 mur-ac bg2 phos bg2 rhod k* sulph bg2 ter bg2* verat b7.de*
    - **In**: *Ant-t* bg1 verat h1 visc bg1
  - **Lungs**: *Acon* bro1*
  - **Sternum**; behind: chlam-tr bcx2•
    - **drinking** | **amel**.: chlam-tr bcx2•
- **sleep** | **during** | **agg**.: arg-n
  - **siesta**:
    - **after** | **agg**.: clem k*
- **smoking** agg.: cic h1 spong
- **sun** agg.; walking in the: med
- **talking** agg.: phos h2
  - **excitedly**: phos
- **urination** | **delayed**; if desire to urinate is: lil-t
- **walking**:
  - **agg**.: naja
  - **air**; in open | **after** | **agg**.: stann h2
    - **agg**.: rhus-t
- **water**; hot:
  - **sensation** as from: hep bg2
  - ○ **Abdomen** from chest; as if hot water poured into: sang ptk1
    - **stool**; before: sang k*
  - **Lungs** | **as** if hot water poured into: acon *Hep*
- ○ **Axillae**: aur *Carb-an* bg2 *Carb-v* bg2 caust bg2 clem bg2 **Kali-c** bg2 laur bg2 lyc bg2 *Nat-m* bg2 nit-ac bg2 ol-an bg2 phos bg2 *Rhus-t* bg2 sep bg2 sil bg2 *Spig* bg2 sul-ac bg2 sulph bg2 zinc bg2
  - **right**: lavand-a ctl1•
- **Diaphragm**: acon vh1
- **External** chest: ambr bg2 *Apis* b7a.de* **Arn** bg2 **Ars** bg2 bar-c bg2 *Bell* bg2 **Bism** b7.de* *Bry* bg2 *Calc* bg2 canth bg2 carb-v bg2 *Caust* bg2 cham b7.de chin bg2 cic b7.de* dig k* dros b7.de dulc bg2 euph bg2 iod bg2 laur bg2 led bg2 **Lyc** bg2 **Mang** b4a.de* merc bg2 merc-c bg2 mez bg2 mur-ac bg2 nat-c bg2 *Nux-v* b7.de* olnd bg2 ph-ac bg2 phos k* plat bg2 *Puls* b7.de* *Rhus-t* b7.de* *Sars* b4a.de *Sel* bg2 seneg bg2 sep bg2 **Spig** bg2 stann bg2 *Staph* bg2 stront-c bg2 **Sulph** bg2 tarax bg2 thuj k* verat bg2
  - **left**: sul-ac bg2
- **Heart**, in region of: **Acon** bg2 *Ant-t* k* arg-met bg2 arn bg2 ars bg2 aur bg2 bell bg2 brom bg2 bry bg2 *Calc* bg2 *Cann-s* cann-xyz bg2 canth bg2 carb-v bg2 caust bg2 cic bg2 coc-c bg2 cocc bg2 cot c1 croc k* ferr bg2 **Glon** k* kali-c bg2 lach bg2 lachn k* lyc bg2 lycps-v bg2 lyss m-aust b7.de med merc bg2 naja bg2 nit-ac bg2 nux-v bg2 op k* **Phos** bg2 plan *Puls* bg2 rhod bg2* rhus-t bg2 sabad k* *Sep* bg2 *Spig* bg2 *Spong* sul-i **Sulph** bg2 verat bg2 **Verat-v** bg2
  - **evening**: naja
  - **flushes** of: ars cact k2 carb-v **Glon** lyc merl mill k2 nit-ac *Nux-m* **Phos** plb sep sil *Sulph* yohim c1*
  - ▽ **extending** to:
    - **Body**; over: ars *Nux-m*
    - **Head**: **Glon** lachn c1
- **Lower** part: calc-p kr1 hell h1
- **Mammae**: *Acon* bg2 *Apis* bg2 arn bg2 **Ars** bg2 bar-c bg2 bell bg2* benz-ac bg2 bry bg2* calc b4a.de* calc-p bg2 *Cann-s* b7.de* *Carb-an* bg2 carb-v bg2 cham bg2 clem bg2 cocc bg2 con bg2 graph bg2 hep bg2 laur bg2 lyc bg2 *Merc* bg2 nit-ac bg2 phos bg2* phyt k2 *Puls* bg2 rhus-t bg2 sep bg2 *Sil* bg2 **Sulph** bg2
  - **right**: calc h2
  - **left**: ign gk
  - ○ **Below** | **left**: tab bg2

Heat – Mammae: ...

  - **Nipples**: phos ptk1 plut-n srj7•
    - **left**: senec bg2
- **Skin**; under: bamb-a stb2.de•
- **Sternum**: bell pyrid rly4• [bell-p-sp dcm1]
  - ▽ **extending** to | **Shoulders**: [bell-p-sp dcm1]
  - ○ **Behind**: cob ptm1• lach bg2
  - **Xiphoid** cartilage: ol-an bg2
- **Upper** part: nit-ac h2

HEAVINESS (See Oppression)

HEMOPTYSIS (See Hemorrhage)

HEMORRHAGE of lungs: (↗*EXPECTORATION - Bloody)*
Acal k* *Acet-ac* k* *Achil-m* bro1 **Acon** k* *All-s* bro1 aloe *Alum* alum-sil k2 am-c k* *Anan* *Ant-t* *Apoc* *Aran* arg-n **Arn** k* **Ars** k* ars-s-f k2 arum-m aspar *Bapt* hr1 *Bell* k* brom *Bry* k* bufo **Cact** k* *Calc* *Calc-p* calc-s calc-sil k2 canth carb-an carb-v k* carbn-s *Card-m* casc caust cham **Chel** k* **Chin** k* chinin-ar k* chinin-s chlor cinnm br1* *Coc-c* cocc bg2 coff bg2 *Colch* *Coll* k* con k* *Cop* *Croc* k* crot-h cupr k* cupr-s *Dig* k* dros k* dulc k* elaps *Erech* br1* ergot bro1 *Erig* k* **Ferr** k* *Ferr-act* bro1 **Ferr-ar** *Ferr-i* ferr-p k* fic-r br1 fic-v mtf11 gelin bro1 *Ger* br1* **Ham** k* helx bro1 *Hydrin-m* bro1 hyos k* ign bg2 **Ip** k* jug-c cda kali-ar kali-bi *Kali-c* k* *Kali-chl* *Kali-i* kali-m k2 kali-n kali-p kali-s kali-sil k2 *Kreos* k* *Lach* k* lam br1* *Led* k* lyc k* *Lycps-v* mag-c mag-m mang *Mangi* br1* meli k* merc k* *Merc-c* **Mill** k* *Nat-ar* nat-n br1* **Nit-ac** k* *Nux-m* *Nux-v* k* ol-j op k* oxyurn-sc mcp1• *Ph-ac* phel br1 *Phos* k* *Plb* *Puls* k* *Rhus-t* k* *Sabin* *Sang* k* sarr **Sec** *Senec* sep k* sil **Stann** k* staph *Stram* stront-c stroph-h bro1 *Sul-ac* k* sulph k* tab *Ter* k* tril-p k* tub c1* *Urt-u* verat *Verat-v* bro1

- **accompanied** by:
  - **congestion**: erech br1
  - **convulsions**: hyos ptk1
  - **phthisis** (See Phthisis - accompanied - hemorrhage)
  - **pneumonia** (See EXPECTORATION - Bloody)
  - **respiration**; difficult: arn ptk1
  - ○ **Chest**; heat in: psor ptk1
  - **Heart** | **Valves**; complaints of the (See Heart; complaints - valves - accompanied - lungs)
  - **Lung**; cancer in (See Cancer - lungs - accompanied - hemorrhage)
  - **Valvular**; complaints of: cact bro1 lycps-v bro1
- **ailments** from hemorrhage: ars bg2 **Carb-v** bg2 *Chin* b7a.de* coff bg2 ign bg2 *Squil* b7a.de sulph bg2
- **alcoholics**; in: ars k* hyos k* *Led* bro1 **Nux-v** k* op k*
- **alternating** with | **rheumatism**: led
- **anger**; after: *Nux-v*
- **black**: ars k2 elaps al
- **bright** red blood: acal bro1 *Acon* bro1 aran bro1 cact bro1 ferr-act bro1 *Ferr-p* bro1 ger bro1 led bro1 *Mill* bro1 nit-ac bro1 rhus-t bro1 tril-p bro1
  - **accompanied** by | **Mammae**; cancer in (See Cancer - mammae - accompanied - hemorrhage - bright)
- **coagulated**: acal acon *Arn* *Bell* brom bry canth carb-an caust **Cham** *Chin* coc-c coll con *Croc* dros erig *Ferr* ham *Hyos* *Ip* jug-c vml3• kali-n kreos mag-m *Merc* *Nit-ac* nux-v ph-ac *Puls* **Rhus-t** *Sabin* sec sep stram stront-c
  - **black**: kreos
  - **brown**: bry rhus-t
  - **dark**: arn coc-c k2 coll ham jug-c vml3• mag-c puls
- **convulsions**; after: dros ptk1*
- **copious**: *Ger* br1
  - **serum** and blood; with:
    - **accompanied** by | **Mammae**; cancer in (See Cancer - mammae - accompanied - hemorrhage - copious)
- **cough**:
  - **with**: acal bro1 *Acon* bro1 *Ferr-act* bro1 ferr-p bro1 *Ip* bro1 *Led* bro1 phos bro1
    - **whooping** cough: *Arn* bro1 *Cer-ox* bro1 con mlb cor-r br1* cupr bro1 *Dros* bro1 ind bro1 *Ip* bro1 merc bro1
  - **without**: *Acon* bro1 *Ham* bro1 mill bro1 sul-ac bro1

- **dark** thick clots: arn bro1 crot-h bro1 *Elaps* bro1 ferr-m bro1 *Ham* bro1 sul-ac bro1
  - **accompanied** by | **Mammae**; cancer in (See Cancer - mammae - accompanied - hemorrhage - dark)
- **delivery**:
  - **after**: arn ptk1 chin ptk1 puls ptk1
  - **during**: *Acon* *Arn* *Chin* hyos ip *Puls* sulph tril-p
    - **puerperal** fever; in: ham bro1*
- **excitement** agg.: rhus-t k2
- **exertion** agg.; after: acon *Arn* coc-c k2 ferr ip *Mill* puls *Rhus-t* *Urt-u* verat bg1
- **falling** from a height, after: *Mill* c1
- **frothy**, foaming: acon *Arn* dros ferr ip *Led* mill op ph-ac *Phos* sec *Sil*
- **hemorrhoidal** flow; after suppression of: acon *Carb-v* *Led* *Lyc* mez bro1 **Nux-v** k* phos *Sulph*
- **hot** blood: acon *Bell* mill psor
- **injuries**; after: mill bro1
- **intermittent**: kreos ptk1
- **mechanical** injuries; after: ip tl1
- **menopause**; during: lach bro1 sang hr1 sul-ac k2
- **menses** | **before** | **agg.**: *Dig* k*
  - **suppressed** menses; from: *Acon* ars *Bell* k* *Bry* con *Dig* ferr graph ham mill *Phos* **Puls** *Sang* *Senec* sep sulph k* ust
- **moon**; full: kali-n h2
- **nursing** mothers: *Chin*
- **painful**: ferr mtf11
- **periodical**: kreos bro1*
- **pneumonia**, results of: calc-s k* *Sul-ac* k*
- **profuse** (See copious)
- **recurrent**: apoc vh ars bg2 nux-v bg2 phos ptk1* sulph bg2
- **vicarious**: bry bro1 ham bro1 phos bro1
- **walking** slowly | **amel.**: *Ferr*
- **watery**: elaps al
- **whiskey**; after: merc puls
- **wine** agg.: acon

HEPATIZATION of lungs: ant-t k* *Brom* k* bry k2 *Cact* calc k2 calc-s *Camph* *Chel* k* emetin mp4• ferr *Hep* b4a.de ign mtf33 *Iod* k* *Kali-c* *Kali-chl* *Kali-i* k* kali-m k2 kali-p *Lach* k* *Lob* *Lyc* k* merc *Myrt-c* b7a.de *Nit-ac* b4a.de *Nux-v* op **Phos** k* *Sang* *Seneg* b4a.de *Spong* b7a.de **Sulph** k* *Ter* *Tub* verat-v br1

- **right**: *Kali-c* **Kali-i** *Phos*
  - ○ **Upper** right half: *Chel*
- **left**: *Lach* *Lyc* *Myrt-c* phos *Sulph*
- **accompanied** by | **congestion** of lungs: verat-v br1
- **incipient**: verat-v br1
- **lying** | **back**; on | **agg.**: *Phos*
  - **side**; on | **left** | **agg.**: **Phos**
    - **right**:
      - **agg.**: kali-c *Merc*
      - **amel.**: **Phos**
- **painless**: ign mtf33 iod mtf33
- **pneumonia**; after: ant-t tl1
- **rapid**: ign mtf33 iod mtf33
  - **accompanied** by | **fever**; high: ign mtf33 iod mtf33

HICCOUGH agg.: am-m b7.de* stront-c b4.de* teucr b7.de*

HOLD chest with hand during cough; must (See COUGH - Hold - chest)

HOLDING CHEST amel.: bry bg2 dros bg2 eup-per bg2 nat-s bg2 phos bg2 sep bg2

HOLDS hands over the heart, as if there was some trouble there: bufo ptk1 cupr ptk1 hydr-ac ptk1 laur bg2* lil-t ptk1 naja ptk1 nat-m bg2* puls ptk1 tarent ptk1

- **exertion** amel.; any: laur pd

HOLLOW (See Emptiness)

HUNGER: | **agg.**: kali-c b4.de* rhus-t b7.de* spig b7.de*

HUNGER; sensation as if from: spig b7.de*

HYDROPERICARDIUM (See Dropsy - pericardium)

HYDROTHORAX (See Dropsy)

HYPERTROPHY: cench k2

- ○ **Bronchial** tubes (= bronchiectasis) am-c tl1 pert jl2 psor jl2
  - **edematous**: am-c tl1
- **Heart**; of: (↗*Dilatation*) **Acon** k* aethyl-n c1* *Aml-ns* *Arn* k* *Ars* k* aspar **Aur** k* aur-br vh1 **Aur-i** k* *Aur-m* bell bro1 *Brom* k* **Cact** k* *Caust* bro1 cere-b bro1 chlol c1* cimic k2 coffin bro1 *Conv* bro1 crat c1* *Dig* k* *Ferr* *Glon* k* *Graph* *Hep* *Iber* k* *Iod* k* kali-bi k* **Kali-c** k* **Kalm** k* *Lach* lil-t bro1 **Lith-c** k* *Lyc* k* *Lycps-v* k* morg-g pte1• *Naja* k* *Nat-m* nux-v *Phos* k* phyt c2* plb prun ptk1 prun-v c2 *Puls* *Rhus-t* k* *Spig* k* **Spong** k* staph stroph-h bro1 stry-ar bro1 stry-p br1 thyr ptk1 *Verat-v* bro1 visc bro1
  - **accompanied** by:
    - **hypertension**: crat mtf11
    - **Liver**; complaints of the: mag-m mtf33
  - **numbness** and tingling of left arm and fingers; with: (↗*Heart; complaints - accompanied - upper - left - numbness*) **Acon** cimic c1 puls c1 **Rhus-t**
  - **overexertion**, from: arn bro1 brom bro1* *Calc* *Caust* k* crat c1 *Kali-c* **Rhus-t** k* thyr ptk1
  - **sensation** of (See Enlarged - heart)
- **Mammae**: (↗*Swelling - mammae*) bell gl1.fr• bell-p sp1 bry gl1.fr• *Calc* k* calc-p tl1* chim br1* *Con* k* cycl ptk1 hep gl1.fr• hydrog srj2• iod tl1 kali-i bg2 med tl1 nat-m gl1.fr• *Nux-v* gl1.fr• petr-ra shn4• phos gl1.fr• *Phyt* k* sep ptk1 sulph gl1.fr•
  - **menopause**; during: sang hr1*
  - **sensation** as if: plac rzf5•
  - ○ **Areola**: *Sil* hr1
- **Mediastinal** ganglion: v-a-b jl2

HYPERVENTILATION (See RESPIRATION - Hyperventilation)

IMMOVABLE: ox-ac ptk1 **Phos** k* stry ptk1

IMPULSE of heart; excessive: aethyl-n a1 cact hr1* melal-alt gya4

INDURATION: tritic-vg fd5.de

- **sensation** of:
  - ○ **External** chest: ferr-p bg2
  - **Mammae** | **left**: arist-cl sp1
- ○ **Axillae**: *Carb-an* b4a.de iod b4.de*
  - **boil**; as from a: psor bg2
- **Axillary** glands: am-c aster ptk1 bufo calc **Carb-an** k* clem hep k2 **Iod** k* *Kali-c* lac-c nat-c k2 plut-n srj7• **Sil** k*
  - **right**: plut-n srj7•
- **Mammae**: (↗*Lumps - mammae; Lumps - sensation; Nodules - mammae*) alum-sil gm1 alumn k* ambr b7.de* anan bro1 apis k* ars b4a.de *Ars-i* sne *Aster* k* *Aur* bg2 **Bar-i** bg2* *Bell* k* *Bry* k* bufo k* *Calc* k* calc-f bg2* calc-i k2 calc-p **Carb-an** k* *Carb-v* bg2* *Carbn-s* **Cham** k* chim bg2 *Cist* k* *Clem* k* coloc **Con** k* *Crot-h* *Crot-t* cund sne *Cupr* cycl bg2* dulc *Graph* k* hep k2 *Hydr* k* hyos sne ina-i mlk9.de *Iod* k* **Kali-chl** sne *Kali-m* bg2 *Kreos* k* *Lac-c* k* lap-a br1* *Lyc* mang b4a.de *Merc* k* nit-ac k* petr b4a.de *Phos* k* *Phyt* k* plb k* *Plb-i* bro1 puls k* *Rhus-t* b7a.de* ruta sabin bg2 *Sep* k* **Sil** k* spong b7a.de* sul-i bg2* *Sulph* k* *Thuj* k* tub ust vip
  - **right**: *Arn* **Con** k* graph sne hydr sne irid-met srj5• kali-chl sne lyc sne *Phyt* k* thuj sne vip
  - **left**: *Aster* sne calc sne carc sne **Con** sne *Cund* sne **Kali-chl** sne lap-a sne phyt sne **Sil**
  - **abscess**, after: *Con* k* *Graph*
  - **accompanied** by | **cancer** of mammae (See Cancer - mammae - accompanied - induration)
  - **blows**; after: arn bg2 bell-p tl1 carb-an bg2 *Con* bg2
  - **children**; in: | **infants**: cham bg2
  - **cicatrices**, in: (↗*SKIN - Cicatrices*) **Graph** phyt k2
  - **contusion**, after: arn sne ars-i sne *Bell-p* carb-an sne *Con* k* cund sne kali-chl sne
  - **delivery**; after: phyt c1

- **Mammae**: ...
  - **menses**:
    - **absent**: dulc ptk1
    - **before** | **agg.**: bry k2 *Con* lac-c sang
    - **during** | **agg.**: carb-an con
  - **painful** on touch: clem sne con h2* cund sne hydr sne *Kali-chl* sne *Phyt* sne thuj sne
  - **red**; but not: calc tl1 con tl1
  - **stone**; like: phyt mtf11
  - ○ **Nipples**: agar bg2 *Bry* k* *Calc* k* *Carb-an* k* graph bg2 *Merc* k* sulph k* thuj b4a.de

INFARCTION; myocardial: am-c tl1 ars mtf11 cimic tl1 crot-h mrr1 hist mtf11 lach mrr1* lat-m mrr1* *Naja* mtf parathyr mtf11 tab mtf
- **accompanied** by | **angina** pectoris: acon mtf11
- **acute**: hist-m mtf11

INFLAMMATION: ars tl1 kali-c tl1
- **accompanied** by | **cough**: *Kali-c* b4a.de
- **agg.**: *Seneg* b4a.de
- **menses** | **before** | **agg.**: senec bro1
  - **during** | **agg.**: senec bro1
- **rheumatic**: *Arn* b7a.de bry b7a.de nux-v b7a.de sabad b7a.de
- ○ **Aorta**: acon bro1 adren br1 apis bro1 glon bro1 syph jl2 tub bro1
  - **chronic**: adon bro1 adren br1* *Ant-ar* bro1 ars-i br1* aur bro1 aur-ar bro1 cact bro1 chinin-s bro1 crat bro1 cupr bro1 glon bro1 kali-i bro1 lyc bro1 *Nat-i* bro1 spig bro1 stroph-h bro1
  - **syphilitic**: syph jl2
  - **ulcerative**: acon bro1 ars bro1 chinin-s bro1
- **Axilla**, glands: con k2 hep b4a.de* jug-c vml3• jug-r vml3• merc k2 **Nit-ac** k* petr k* phos k* raph c2 sulph b4.de* [heroin sdj2]
  - **right**: [heroin sdj2]
- **Bronchial** tubes (= bronchitis): *Acet-ac* *Acon* k* **Aesc** aeth mrr1 aether c2 *All-c* all-s c2 aloe c2 *Alum* alum-p k2 alum-sil k2 *Alumn* k* am-br mtf11 am-c k* am-caust vh1 am-i br1 *Am-m* k* am-p br1 ammc c2* *Ant-c* k* ant-i c1* ant-s-aur c2 **Ant-t** k* *Apis* *Arn* k* **Ars** k* ars-i k* asc-c c1* *Asc-t* k* *Aur-m* bac br1* bacls-7 pte1*• bals-p c2 bar-c k* bar-i k2 **Bar-m** bar-s k2 *Bell* k* bell-p sp1 *Benz-ac* blatta-o c2* brom k2* **Bry** k* *Cact* k* cadm-met sp1 *Calc* k* calc-i k2* calc-sil k2 *Camph* *Cann-s* cann-xyz bg2 canth mrr1 caps bg2* *Carb-v* k* *Carbn-s* carc cd* card-m k* *Caust* k* cetr mtf11 *Cham* k* *Chel* chin bg2* chlol k* chlor *Cina* k* *Cist* *Coc-c* k* colch tl1 *Con* bg2* cop k* cordyc mp4• dig k* diphtox br1* **Dros** k* *Dulc* k* erio c2 eucal c2 eup-per k2 euphr k* ferr bg2 *Ferr-i* **Ferr-p** k* *Gels* grin c2 *Guaj* k* hed sp1 **Hep** k* hepat c2* *Hippoz* k* hist sp1 hydr ptk1* *Hyos* k* hyss-o vs1.fr iber c2 ign bg2 influ jl2* inul br1 *Iod* k* **Ip** k* jab c2 kali-ar *Kali-bi* k* *Kali-c* k* *Kali-chl* kali-m k2 kali-n br1 kali-p kali-s mrr1 kali-sil k2 kola stb3• *Kreos* k* lac-f wza1• *Lach* k* laur mrr1 led br1* linu-c c2 *Lob* lob-a mtf11 **Lyc** k* mag-c bg2 malar jl2 manc mrr1 mang bg2* meph mrr1 *Merc* k* morg fmm1• morg-p pte1*• mucot jl2 myrt-ch mtf11 *Naja* naphtin c2 narc-ps c1* nat-c bg2 *Nat-m* k* **Nat-s** k* nig-s mp4• *Nit-ac* k* *Nux-v* k* oci-sa sp1 oscilloc jl2 osm c2 parathyr jl2 pert jl2 petr bg2 *Ph-ac* k* phel c2* **Phos** k* pin-s c2 pix c2* *Plb* pneu jl2 podo c2 prot fmm1• *Psor* k* pulm-v c1* **Puls** k* pyrog mrr1 ran-b mrr1 *Rhus-t* k* *Rumx* k* sabad bg2 sabal c2 samb mrr1 **Sang** k* sangin-n c2 sec a1 **Senec** k* *Seneg* k* *Sep* k* **Sil** k* silphu c2* *Spig* bg2 **Spong** k* *Squil* k* **Stann** k* stann-i mtf11 staph bg2 stict c2* stram bg2* streptom mtf11 succ-ac br1 sul-i k2 *Sulph* k* syc pte1*• *Ter* k* thal-xyz srj8• thuj k2 tub c2* tub-a c2 *Tub-d* jl2 tub-m jl2 (non:uran-met k) uran-n *Urin* c1 *Verat* k* verb k* visc sp1 [alumin-p stj2 bell-p-sp dcm1]
  - **accompanied** by:
    - **cough**; constant urging to: stann-i mtf11
    - **emphysema**: led tl1
    - **fever**; little: ant-t tl1
    - **perspiration**; cold: ant-t tl1
    - **respiration**; asthmatic: *Blatta-o* br1 cassia-s zzc1•
    - **sleep**; comatose: **Ant-t** mrr1
    - **sleepiness**: **Ant-t** mrr1 tub ptk1
    - **violent** complaints: acon tl1 ant-t tl1 bell tl1 bry tl1
    - **weakness**: *Ammc* br1
  - **acute**: *Acon* bro1 am-c bro1 am-i bro1 am-p bro1 ant-ar bro1 ant-i bro1 ant-t bro1* ars bro1 ars-i bro1 asc-t bro1 *Bell* bro1 blatta-o bro1 *Brom* bro1 *Bry* bro1 *Caust* bro1 cham bro1 colch bro1 cop bro1 *Dulc* bro1 eup-per bro1

Inflammation – Bronchial tubes – **acute**: ...
euphr bro1 *Ferr-p* bro1 gels bro1 grin bro1 *Hep* bro1 hyos bro1 *Ip* bro1 *Kali-bi* bro1 lob bro1 mang-act bro1 *Merc* bro1 morg-p mtf11 mucot jl2 naphtin bro1 nat-ar bro1 nit-ac bro1 *Phos* bro1 pilo bro1 *Puls* bro1 rhus-t bro1 *Rumx* bro1 *Sang* bro1 *Sangin-n* bro1 solid bro1 spong bro1 *Squil* bro1 stict bro1 sul-ac bro1 sulph bro1 thuj bro1 tub bro1 tub-a bro1 verat bro1 verat-v bro1 zinc bro1

- **alternating** with:
  - **colds**: lac-f wza1•
  - **cough**: lac-f wza1•
  - **diarrhea**: seneg
- **asthmatic**: ephe mtf11
- **bronchopneumonia**: *Acon* bro1 am-i bro1 ant-ar bro1 *Ant-t* bro1* ars bro1 *Ars-i* bro1 bell bro1* bry bro1 cadm-met sp1 carb-v ptk1 *Chel* bro1 *Ferr-p* bro1* glyc bro1 influ jl2 iod bro1 *Ip* bro1* kali-c bro1 *Phos* bro1 puls bro1 seneg ptk1 solin bro1 *Squil* br1* ter ptk1 *Tub* bro1 tub-a jl2* tub-k bro1 tub-m jl2
  - **children**; in: ant-t tl1 bry tl1 thymu br1
  - **neglected**: ferr mtf33
- **capillary** (See bronchopneumonia)
- **children**; in: ant-t tl1* *Cina* hr1 *Dulc* **Ip** k* **Kali-c** morg-p mtf11 narc-ps ah1 nat-ar br1 pneu mtf11 tub ptk1* tub-a c*
  - **infants**: ferr-p br1
- **chronic**: alum bro1 alumn bro1 am-c bro1* am-caust bro1 am-i bro1 am-m bro1 ammc bro1* ant-ar bro1 ant-i bro1 *Ant-s-aur* bro1 *Ant-t* bro1 *Ars* bro1 *Ars-i* bro1 bac bro1* *Bals-p* bro1 bals-t br1 bar-c bro1 *Bar-m* bro1 *Calc* bro1 calc-i bro1 calc-sil bro1 canth bro1 carb-an bro1 *Carb-v* bro1 cean br1* chel bro1 *Chin* bro1 coc-c bro1 con bro1 *Cop* bro1 cortiso mtf11 cub bro1 dig bro1 diphtox jl2 dros bro1 *Dulc* bro1 erio bro1 eucal bro1 eup-c lsr4.de• grin br1* hep bro1* hydr bro1 hyos bro1 ichth bro1 ilx-a mtf11 iod bro1 *Ip* bro1 *Kali-bi* bro1 kali-c bro1 kali-hp bro1 *Kali-i* bro1 kali-s bro1 kreos bro1 lach bro1 *Lyc* bro1 marr-vg br1 med mrr1 *Merc* bro1 morg fmm1• mucot jl2 myos-a br1 myos-s bro1 myrt-ch bro1 nat-m bro1 nat-s bro1* *Nit-ac* bro1 nux-v bro1 pert jl2 phos bro1* pix bro1 pneu jl2 *Puls* bro1 rumx bro1 sabal bro1 sang bro1 sec bro1 *Seneg* bro1* sep bro1 *Sil* bro1 silphu br1* spong bro1 *Squil* bro1 *Stann* bro1 stram mrr1 stry bro1 *Sulph* bro1 tax bro1 ter bro1 tub bro1* tub-d jl2 tub-r jl2* verat bro1
  - **old** people; in: hippoz mtf11 squil br1
- **congested**: *Morg* fmm1•
  - **children**; in: *Morg* fmm1•
- **coryza**; begins as: bry k2
- **descending** agg.: ant-t mtf11 coenz-q mtf11
- **expectoration** difficult: canth mtf11
- **fibrinous**: brom bro1 bry bro1 *Calc-act* bro1 *Kali-bi* bro1 phos bro1
- **old** people: all-c ptk1 *Am-c* k* *Ammc* br1 ant-c ptk1 **Ant-t** ptk1* ars ptk1 *Camph* k* *Carb-v* diphtox jl2 *Dros* **Hippoz** *Hydr* kreos ptk1 led br1 *Lyc* k* *Nux-v* prot fmm1• *Seneg* ptk1* squil br1 verat hr1
- **painful**: ran-b mrr1
- **purulent**: prot jl2
- **recurrent** (See GENERALS - History - bronchitis)
- **seaside** | **amel.**: syc bka1*•
- **toxemic**: am-c bro1 ant-t bro1 bry bro1 colch bro1 diphtox bro1 *Merc-c* bro1
- **weather**:
  - **cold** weather; from: dulc k2* hep bg3* ip k2 mang k2* mang-act br1
  - **frosty** | **agg.**: syc bka1*•
  - **wet** | **agg.**: syc bka1*
- **winter**; in: kali-s mrr1 morg-p pte1*• psor jl2 sil mrr1 syc pte1*
- ○ **Bronchioles** (= bronchiolitis): *Alum-sil* bro1 am-c bro1 am-i bro1* ant-ar bro1* *Ant-t* bro1 ars bro1 bac bro1 *Bell* bro1 bry bro1 calc bro1 camph bro1 *Carb-v* bro1 chel bro1 cupr-act bro1 eucal mtf11 *Ferr-p* bro1 ip bro1* kali-c bro1 kali-i bro1 lyc gk2 nit-ac bro1 ph-ac bro1 phos bro1 *Seneg* bro1 sep gk5 *Solin* bro1 sulph bro1 *Ter* bro1 verat bro1
  - **accompanied** by | **Heart**; weak (See Weakness - heart - accompanied - bronchiolitis)
- **Costal** cartilages: am mrr1

- **Diaphragm**: acon b7a.de* atro bro1 bell b4a.de* bism bro1 bry k* cact k* calc b4a.de cham b7a.de cocc b7a.de *Cupr* bro1 dulc k* ham hr1 *Hep* k* hyos b7a.de* ign bro1 lyc mosch bro1 *Nux-m* *Nux-v* k* puls b7a.de *Ran-b* k* *Stram* k* *Verat* verat-v bro1
- **Heart** (= carditis): *Acon* k* ant-t bg2 apis k* ars k* asc-t a1 **Aur** aur-i k2 bism bg2 *Brom* b4a.de *Bry* k* *Cact* *Cann-s* k* *Carb-v* k* *Carbn-s* *Caust* k* cocc k* *Colch* crat br1 *Dig* kali-i *Kalm* *Lach* k* *Led* mang bg2 merc-c bg2 *Naja* *Phos* k* plb bg2 *Psor* *Puls* k* rheum b7.de* rhus-t **Spig** k* sulph sumb *Verat-v*
  - **Bright's** disease, with: adon vh1 *Apis* apoc *Ars* asc-t cact k2 cann-s colch *Dig* kali-n phos
  - **influenza**; after: adon vh1
  - **lie** on the back with head raised; compelled to: *Acon*
  - **lying** on side impossible: *Cact*
  - **malignant**: acon bro1 ars bro1 *Chinin-s* bro1 crot-h bro1 lach bro1 vip bro1
  - O **Coronaries**: tab br1
  - **Endocardium** (= endocarditis): *Abrot* *Acet-ac* **Acon** k* adon mtf11 **Ars** k* ars-i **Aur** k* aur-i k2 *Aur-m* bell bro1 bism *Bry* *Cact* k* *Calc* carb-v tl1 coc-c cocc *Colch* k* conv br1* dig k* diph mtf11 ferr *Iod* kali-ar *Kali-c* k* *Kali-i* **Kalm** k* *Lach* k* led magn-gr bro1 *Naja* k* nat-m ox-ac *Phos* k* phyt plat plb *Sep* **Spig** k* *Spong* k* staphycoc jl2* streptoc jl2* tab bro1 tarent *Verat-v* k* *Zinc-i* ptk1
    - **accompanied** by:
      - **pericarditis**: *Apis* b7a.de carb-v tl1 iber mtf11
        - **rheumatic**: psor mtf11 staphycoc mtf11 streptoc mtf11
      - **rheumatism**: kalm mtf11
      - **Joints**; rheumatism of: kalm mtf11
      - **Tongue**; dry and white: *Aur* kr1*
    - **acute**: ars tl1 spig mtf11
    - **mitral** insufficiency and violent, rapid action; with: adon vh1 cact br1
    - **orthopnea**; with extreme: conv br1
    - **pain** and great anxiety: *Aur* *Kalm*
    - **purulent**: cupr-ar br1
    - **rheumatic**: acon bro1 adon bro1 *Ars* **Aur** k* *Aur-m* aven br1 bell bro1 *Bry* bro1 *Cact* colch lp* dig *Hyos* kali-c bro1 *Kali-n* **Kalm** k* **Lach** *Phos* plat rhus-t bro1 *Spig* k* *Spong* *Sumb* verat
    - **scanty** menses, with: nat-m
  - **Endocardium** and myocardium (= endomyocarditis): adon vh1 ant-ar br1 ars-i br1 crat br1* diph mtf11 diphtox jl2 eberth jl2 *Gala* br1 iod mtf33 morg-g mtf11 p-benzq mtf11 streptoc jl2* toxo-g jl2*
    - **toxic**: eberth jl2
  - **Pericardium**: **Acon** k* adon bro1* anac ant-ar c2* *Ant-t* *Apis* k* apoc **Ars** k* *Ars-i* ars-s-f k2 *Asc-t* k* aur mrr1 bell bro1 *Bry* k* *Cact* k* cann-s bro1 canth br1* carb-v tl1 chlor *Cimic* *Colch* k* *Dig* k* eberth jl2 franc c2 *Iod* k* kali-ar *Kali-c* k* kali-chl *Kali-i* k* *Kalm* k* *Lach* lycps-v c2 magn-gr bro1 *Merc* bro1 *Merc-c* bro1 naja bro1 nat-m bro1 ox-ac phase bro1* phase-xyz c2 plat **Psor** seneg mtf11 **Spig** k* *Spong* k* squil bro1 staphycoc jl2 streptoc jl2 **Sulph** k* *Verat* k* *Verat-v* k*
    - **accompanied** by:
      - **endocarditis** (See endocardium - accompanied - pericarditis)
      - **rheumatism**: franc br1
      - **Bladder** irritation: canth br1
    - **chronic**: apis bro1 *Aur-i* bro1 calc-f bro1 kali-c bro1 spig bro1 squil bro1 sulph bro1
    - **lying** | **amel**.: *Psor*
    - **perspiration**, with profuse: asc-t vh
    - **rheumatic**: acon bro1 anac bro1 bry bro1 colch bro1 *Colchin* bro1 crat bro1 kalm bro1 rhus-t bro1 *Spig* bro1
- **Joints** | **Intercostal** region: arn bro1 *Cimic* bro1 phyt bro1 *Ran-b* bro1 rhus-t bro1
- **Lobes**: morg fmm1•
- **Lungs** (= pneumonia/pneumonitis): (↗*RESPIRATION - Painful*) **Acon** k* aesc *Agar* *All-c* k* am-c am-i mtf11 am-m c2* *Ammc* vh1 anac b4a.de ant-ar c2 *Ant-c* ant-i c1* **Ant-t** k* *Apis* *Arg-n* *Arn* k* **Ars** k* *Ars-i* k* ars-s-f k2 arum-t k2 aur-m *Bad* *Bapt* hr1 bar-c bar-i k2 *Bell* k* *Benz-ac* beryl sp1 both fne1• brass-n-o srj5• *Brom* k* **Bry** k* *Cact* k* cadm-met sp1 *Calc* k* calc-s c2* calc-sil k2* camph k* *Cann-s* k* canth k* caps carb-ac c1* *Carb-an* **Carb-v** k* *Carbn-s* carc jl2* cham bg2 **Chel** k* *Chin* k* chin-b kr1* *Chlor* coff bg2 colch b7.de*

- **Lungs**: ... *Con* cop corn corn-f c2 corv-cor bdg• crot-h *Cupr* k* *Dig* dulc k* eberth jl2 *Elaps* k* eup-per k2 *Ferr* k* *Ferr-ar* *Ferr-i* k* **Ferr-p** k* *Gels* **Hep** k* *Hippoz* *Hyos* k* ign bg2 *Iod* k* *Ip* k* kali-ar *Kali-bi* k* *Kali-br* *Kali-c* k* *Kali-chl* *Kali-i* k* kali-m k2 *Kali-n* k* *Kali-p* k* *Kali-s* *Kreos* lac-del hm2• *Lach* k* *Lachn* lat-m bnm6• *Laur* k* **Lob** k* **Lyc** k* lycps-v meli-xyz c2 **Merc** k* *Mill* morb mtf11 morg fmm1• morg-p pte1*• myrt-c nat-ar k2 *Nat-m* nat-ox-act mtf11 *Nat-s* k* *Nit-ac* k* nux-v k* oci-sa sp1 ol-j c2 op k* parathyr jl2 *Ph-ac* k* **Phos** k* plut-n srj7• podo c1* *Psor* **Puls** k* pyrog mrr1* ran-b k* **Rhus-t** k* rumx ruta b7.de* *Sabad* k* *Sang* k* sec b7.de* **Seneg** k* **Sep** k* *Sil* k* skat mtf11 spig spong k* *Squil* k* stann b4a.de* *Stram* k* stroph-h br1 sul-ac c2 sul-i k2 **Sulph** k* sumb c2 *Ter* thal-xyz srj8• thiam rly4• toxo-g jl2 tub c2* tub-a mtf11 *Verat* k* **Verat-v** k* x-ray sp1
  - **right**: *Bell* *Brom* **Bry** k* *Carb-an* *Chel* k* elaps ferr-p mrr1 gink-b sbd1• iod mtf33 *Kali-c* k* kali-i k* *Lyc* k* *Merc* k* petr a1 *Phos* k* *Sang* k* squil stram tub gk
    - **Lower** lobe: bell lp* bry sne *Chel* sne *Kali-c* k* lyc mtf33 *Merc* k* *Phos* k*
      - **accompanied** by:
        - **perspiration**: merc tl1
        - **thirst** for cold drinks: phos tl1
        - **Mouth**; offensive odor from: merc tl1
    - **Upper** lobe: bell sne **Calc** *Chel*
  - **left**: *Acon* arn sne *Calc* ferr-p sne *Kali-c* mrr1 *Lach* k* *Nat-s* k* *Ox-ac* phos k* *Sang* sulph tub gk
    - **Lower** lobe: arn sne *Chel* *Nat-s* k* phos lp* sulph k* tub gk
    - **Upper** lobe: *Acon* ferr-p sne sulph mtf33
  - **afternoon** | **16** h: lyc tl1
  - **night**:
    - **midnight** | **4**-5 h: *Nat-s* tl1
  - **abuse** of aconite, after: *Bry* k* sulph
  - **accompanied** by:
    - **breathlessness**: benz-ac mtf11
    - **cramps**: cupr tl1
    - **fever**: eberth jl2
      - **noon**: stram tl1
    - **heat**: verat-v tl1
    - **hemoptysis** (See EXPECTORATION - Bloody)
    - **influenza**: bapt tl3* ferr-p ry1* gels tl2 glyc mp4• merc tl1
    - **nephritis** (See kidneys)
    - **pulse**; frequent: **Verat-v** mrr1
    - **restlessness** (See MIND - Restlessness - pneumonia)
    - **sleep**; deep: phos mtf33
    - **sticking** pain: kali-c tl1
      - **motion** agg.: bry tl1
    - **vomiting**: apom br1 verat-v mrr1
    - **warm** drinks; desire for (See GENERALS - Food and - warm drinks - desire - accompanied - lungs)
    - **weakness**: lyc mrr1
    - **Chest**:
      - **oppression** of: phos mtf33
      - **pressure** in: *Phos* tl1
    - **Extremities**; burning of: sang mrr1
    - **Face**:
      - **cyanotic**: ant-t tl1
      - **pale**: ant-t tl1
      - **red** discoloration of: verat-v tl1
    - **Forehead**; frowning (See MIND - Frown - contraction - pneumonia)
    - **Kidneys**; acute inflammation of: chel bro1 phos bro1 pyrog gm1
    - **Lids** covered with mucous; sides of: ant-t tl1
    - **Liver**; complaints of: ant-t bro1 *Chel* bro1 lept bro1 merc bro1 phos bro1 podo bro1
    - **Pleura**; inflammation of (See pleuropneumonia)
    - **Skin**; yellow discoloration of: phos mtf33
    - **Tongue**:
      - **brown** discoloration: *Ant-t* kr1* *Chel* kr1* lyc kr1*

- **accompanied** by – **Tongue** – **brown** discoloration: ...
  - **yellowish** brown: *Lachn* kr1*
  - **cracked**: chel kr1*
  - **dirty** discoloration: calc kr1*
  - **dryness** of tongue: *Ant-t* kr1* *Lachn* kr1*
  - **red** streak | **Centre** of tongue: verat-v tl1
  - **white** discoloration of the: chel kr1* puls kr1*
    - **moist**; and: puls kr1*
    - **streak** | **Centre** of tongue: verat-v tl1
- **acute**: ant-t tl1 bell tl1 ferr-p tl1 kali-i mrr1 merc-cy br1 sulph mtf11
- **alternating** with | **sadness** (See MIND - Sadness - alternating - lungs)
- **anxiety**; with (See MIND - Anxiety - pneumonia)
- **appearing** suddenly: acon mrr1
- **aspiration** pneumonia: kali-c mtf33 sang mrr1
- **asthenic** type (See old)
- **blennorrhea**; chronic (See catarrhal)
- **catarrhal**: am-i br1 ant-ar br1 **Ant-t** bg2* *Ars* bg2 bar-c bg2 camph bg2 carb-v bg2 chin bg2 graph bg2 *Ip* bg2 lach bg2 *Op* bg2 psor tl1 puls bg2 samb bg2
  - **accompanied** by | **influenza**: ant-ar br1
- **cerebral** type: acon bg2* arn ptk1 bell bg2* bry bg2* cann-xyz bg2* canth bg2* hyos bg2* lach bg2* merc bg2* nux-v bg2* phos bg2* puls bg2* rhus-t bg2* stram bg2* sulph bg2*
- **children**; in: acon gsy bell gsy bry gsy calc gsy carc sp* hep gsy lob c1 lyc gsy merc gsy morg fmm1• phos gsy sulph gsy thymu br1 tub gk* verat mtf33
  - **infants**: *Acon* k* *Ant-t* k* *Bry* k* carc fb* *Ferr-p* k* **Ip** k* *Kali-br* hr1 *Kali-c* k* *Lob* *Lyc* *Merc* k* *Nux-v* op *Phos* k* tub br1
- **chilled** | **overheated**; when: ran-b k2
- **chronic**: ars-i br1 carc fb* nat-ox-act mtf11
  - **accompanied** by | **Lungs**; abscess of (See Abscess - lungs - accompanied - lungs)
- **congestive**: *Acon* bro1 aesc bro1 bell bro1 bry bro1 *Ferr-p* bro1 *Iod* bro1 lac-del hrn2• sang bro1 *Verat-v* bro1
- **coryza**; from suppressed: acon bg2 *Bry* bg2 merc bg2 **Nux-v** bg2 puls bg2 rhus-t bg2 sulph bg2
- **croupous**: *Acon* bro1 agar bro1 am-i bro1 ant-ar bro1 ant-i bro1 ant-s-aur bro1 *Ant-t* bro1 apom bro1 arn bro1 ars bro1 *Bell* bro1 brom k2* *Bry* bro1 camph bro1 carb-ac bro1 carb-v bro1 *Chel* bro1 chin bro1 coffin bro1 dig bro1 *Ferr-p* bro1 gels bro1 hep bro1 *Iod* bro1 ip bro1 kali-bi bro1 *Kali-c* bro1 kali-i bro1 lach bro1 *Lyc* bro1 *Merc* bro1 mill bro1 nat-s bro1 nit-ac bro1 op bro1 ox-ac bro1 *Phos* bro1 pyrog bro1 ran-b bro1 rhus-t bro1 *Sang* bro1 seneg bro1 squil bro1 stry bro1 *Sulph* bro1 tub bro1 verat bro1 *Verat-v* bro1
- **drunkards**: *Hyos* k* *Kali-br* *Nux-v* k* *Op* k*
- **fear**; with (See MIND - Fear - pneumonia - during)
- **first** stage: **Acon** bg2 **Bry** bg2 chin bg2 lach bg2 lyc bg2 *Phos* bg2 sil bg2 *Sulph* bg2
- **followed** by | **hepatization** (See Hepatization - pneumonia)
- **gangrenous**: ars k2 canth k2
- **gram**-negative bacilli: (*↗klebsiella*) ammc mtf bac mtf camph mtf carb-v mtf ferr-p mtf hep mtf hippoz mtf lob mtf lyc mtf nat-s mtf parat mtf phos mtf puls mtf seneg mtf solin-act mtf sulph mtf tub mtf tub-a mtf
- **hemorrhage**; after: *Chin* k* *Ph-ac* k* squil k2
- **hemorrhoids**; after: hyper c1
- **incipient** stage: am-c tl1 chel tl1 verat-v mrr1
- **infants** (See children - infants)
- **influenza**; after: tub ptk1*
- **klebsiella**: (*↗gram-negative*) apis mtf aur mtf bac mtf carb-v mtf hep mtf hippoz mtf kali-c mtf lach mtf lyc mtf nat-s mtf parat mtf phos mtf seneg mtf solin-act mtf sulph mtf tub mtf tub-a mtf
- **last** stage: ant-s-aur bro1 *Ant-t* bro1 ars bro1 ars-i bro1 carb-v bro1 *Hep* bro1 iod bro1 *Kali-i* bro1 kali-s bro1 lach mtf33 *Lyc* bro1 nat-s bro1 *Phos* bro1 *Sang* bro1 sil bro1 stann-i bro1 *Sulph* bro1
- **lie** on the back, must: acon *Cact* sulph

- **Lungs**: ...
- **low** forms (See typhoid)
- **lying**:
  - **back**; on:
    - **amel.**: acon phos sulph
    - **head** thrown back; with: phos
  - **side**; on:
    - **affected** side:
      - **agg.**: bry tl1
      - **amel.**: bell tl1
    - **left** | **agg.**: acon mrr1
    - **right** | **agg.**: *Kali-c* merc k2
- **measles**; after: *Kali-c*
- **menses** | **suppressed** menses; from: **Puls**
- **motion**; continual | **agg.**: pyrog tl1
- **neglected**: *Am-c* bg2* ant-i bro1 ant-s-aur bro1 *Ant-t* bro1 ars bg2 ars-i bro1* aur bg2 bry bro1 calc bg2 calc-s k2 carb-v k2* chin bro1 hep bg2* kali-c bg2* kali-i bro1 kali-n bg2 *Lach* bg2* *Lob* **Lyc** k* nit-ac bg2 *Phos* k* plb bro1 pyrog ptk1 *Sang* *Sep* k* **Sil** k* stann bg2 sul-ac bg2 sul-i ptk1 **Sulph** k* thuj mtf33
- **nervous**: bry b7a.de *Chin* b7a.de *Hyos* b7a.de laur b7a.de puls b7a.de *Rhus-t* b7a.de stram b7a.de verat b7a.de
- **old** people: **Acon** bg2 ant-ar bro1 *Ant-t* bro1 ars bg2 *Bell* bg2 *Bry* k* cham bg2 *Dig* k* *Ferr* **Ferr-p** bg2* gels bg2 *Hyos* k* ip bg2 **Merc** bg2 *Nat-s* k* *Nit-ac* *Nux-v* k* *Op* k* *Seneg* k* verat bg2
- **painful**: ran-b mrr1
  - **extending** to | **Back**: chel mrr1
- **paralysis**, approaching: ant-t tl1 arn br1
- **pleuropneumonia**: **Ant-t** k* *Asaf* **Bry** k* *Calc* *Camph* *Caps* k* *Chin* *Dulc* *Ferr* *Hep* *Iod* *Kali-i* *Lach* **Phos** k* *Ran-b* bg1 *Rhus-t* *Seneg* *Sulph* k* tub bg* tub-a c1*
  - **alternating** with | **sadness** (See MIND - Sadness - alternating - pleuropneumonia)
- **pneumococcal**: aur mtf carb-v mtf kali-c mtf lach mtf lyc mtf nat-s mtf phos mtf puls mtf sulph mtf tub mtf
- **pneumocystis**: stann mrr1
- **putrescent**:
  - **accompanied** by | **typhoid** fever: ars bro1 mur-ac bro1
- **recurrent** (See GENERALS - History - lungs - inflammation)
- **second** stage: ant-ar bro1 *Ant-t* bro1 ferr-p bro1* phos bro1*
- **staphylococcal**: aur mtf bac mtf carb-v mtf kali-c mtf lach mtf lyc mtf nat-s mtf phos mtf staphycoc mtf sulph mtf thuj mtf tub mtf
- **sycotic** pneumonia: **Nat-s** k*
- **typhoid** fever: acon bg2 **Ant-t** k* **Arn** bg2 **Ars** bg2* *Bad* bell bg2* *Benz-ac* **Bry** k* cann-xyz bg2 *Carb-v* mtf33 chin bg2 eberth jl2 *Hyos* k* ip bg2* lach bg2* lachn c1* *Laur* k* **Lyc** k* merc bg2 merc-cy br1* nat-m bg2 *Nit-ac* nux-v bg2 **Op** bg2* **Phos** k* puls bg2* *Rhus-t* k* *Sang* k* *Stram* bg2 **Sulph** k* *Ter* k* tub gk **Verat** bg2
- **viral**: achy mtf acon mtf ant-s-aur mtf ant-t mtf apis mtf ars mtf asc-t mtf bry mtf carb-v mtf hep mtf influ mtf ip mtf lob mtf lyc mtf nat-s mtf parat mtf phos mtf puls mtf solin-act mtf squil mtf sulph mtf
- **weakness**, from loss of fluids: *Chin* k*
- **weather**:
  - **wet** damp | **agg.**: nat-s tl1
- ○ **Alveoli**: influ jl2

- **Mammae** (= mastitis): *Acon* k* acon-l c2 anan ant-t bro1 *Apis* k* arn b7.de* ars bro1 **Bell** k* bell-p dp• **Bry** k* bufo k* *Cact* calc k* **Camph** b7a.de *Carb-an* k* *Carb-v* k* *Carbn-s* carc mlr1• *Card-m* *Castor-eq* mrr1* *Cham* k* *Cist* k* clem *Con* k* *Crot-t* k* cur dulc k2 ferr bg2 ferr-p bro1 galeg bro1 graph bro1 **Hep** k* lac-ac stj5• lac-c bg2* *Lach* k* laur b7.de* *Lyc* *Merc* k* naphthoq mtf11 op b7a.de petr b4a.de phel bg2* *Phos* k* **Phyt** k* plan hr1* plb *Puls* k* pyrog jl2 rhus-t sabad bro1 sabal c2 *Samb* b7a.de **Sil** k* **Sulph** k* ust verat-v x-ray sp1 [*Merc-d* stj2]
  - **right**: bell mrr1 phel mrr1
  - **left**: cist k2 **Phyt** mrr1

- **bronchitis**, with: phel vml3•
- **bruises**, from: *Arn* bell-p sne con sne hep sne
- **chronic**: carc fb* fl-ac
- **delivery**:
  - **after**: arn bg2 **Bell** bg2 bry bg2 calc bg2 carb-an bg2 carb-v bg2 con bg2 graph bg2 merc bg2 *Phos* bg2 puls bg2 **Sil** bg2 sulph bg2
  - **during**: bell k2
- **excitement** agg.: phyt k2
- **motion** agg.: bry tl1
- **nursing** mothers; in: bamb-a stb2.de• *Phyt* mrr1 sil mrr1
- **pregnancy** agg.; during: *Bell* bro1 *Bry* bro1
- **recurrent** (See GENERALS - History - mammae)

O · **Nipples**: acon b7.de* arn bell b4a.de *Bry* b7.de* *Cadm-s* k* calc b4a.de* cann-s carb-an b4a.de *Castor-eq* mrr1 *Cham* k* graph b4a.de helon bro1 lyc b4a.de petr k2 *Phos* k* *Phyt* bg2* pic-ac puls b7.de* sep b4a.de *Sil* k* sulph k*
- **Skin**: morg-p fmm1•

\- **Nerves** | **Circumflex** nerve: sang bro1

\- **Pleura** (= pleuritis): (↗*RESPIRATION - Painful*) abrot k* **Acon** k* act-sp c2 ant-ar c2* ant-t k* anthraq mtf11 *Apis* k* *Arg-n* *Arn* k* *Ars* k* ars-i ars-s-f k2 arum-t asc-c c1* asc-t k* bad *Bell* k* bell-p tl1 *Borx* k* **Bry** k* *Cact* *Calc* calc-i k2 *Cann-s* k* *Canth* k* **Carb-an** k* *Carb-v* k* *Carbn-s* card-m k* caust bg2 cham bg2 *Chel* chin k* chlor c2 *Colch* k* *Dig* k* diph mtf11 *Dulc* eberth jl2 erio bro1 eucl-n bta1• *Ferr-m* c2* *Ferr-p* k* form bro1 gaul br1 guaj c2* *Hep* k* *Iod* k* *Kali-ar* *Kali-c* k* *Kali-chl* *Kali-i* k* kali-m k2 kali-n c2 kali-p *Kali-s* *Lach* bg2 lat-m bnm6• *Laur* led bro1 lob c2 lon-c bro1 *Merc* k* merc-d ptk1 methyl c2 morb jl2 mucot mtf11 *Mur-ac* nat-m nat-s bro1 *Nit-ac* nux-v bg2 op bro1 ox-ac mrr1 parathyr jl2 phase-xyz c2 *Phos* k* puls bg2* *Ran-b* k* rat c2 rhus-t k* sabad k* sang **Seneg** k* sep k* *Sil* c2* spig bro1 *Squil* k* *Stann* sul-ac sul-i k2 **Sulph** k* syc pte1*• tub c2* tub-m jl2 v-a-b jl2 verat bg2 verat-v ziz c2
- **right**: borx *Bry* ferr-p k2
- **left**: *Ant-ar* br1 *Kali-i* k* tub gk
- **accompanied** by:
  - **pain** | **breaths**; between: kali-c tl1
  - **weakness**; paralytic: sabad ptk1
  - **Back**; pressing pain in: abrot tl1
  - **Bladder** irritation: canth br1
  - **Kidneys**; inflammation of (See KIDNEYS - Inflammation - accompanied - pleura)
  - **Lungs**; inflammation of the (See lungs - pleuropneumonia)
  - **Tongue** | **dryness** of tongue: *Hep* kr1*
- **acute**: **Acon** bg2 arn bg2 **Bry** bg2 chin bg2 kali-c bg2 lach bg2 nux-v bg2 *Squil* bg2 *Sulph* bg2
- **alternating** with | **sadness** (See MIND - Sadness - alternating - pleuropneumonia)
- **beginning** stage: ferr-p tl1
- **breathing** deep agg.: guaj ptk1
- **chilled** when overheated: acon tl1 arn tl1 ran-b k2* sulph tl1
- **chronic**: ars-i bro1 *Hep* bro1 *Iod* bro1 kali-i bro1 squil bro1 *Sulph* bro1
- **cold** ground; after standing on: rhod tl1
- **dry**: tub-r jl2 v-a-b jl2
- **exudative**: *Abrot* br1* *Ant-ar* br1 ferr ptk1 iod ptk1 kali-i ptk1 seneg ptk1
- **injuries**; after mechanical: arn tl1
- **neglected**: **Ars** k* *Ars-i* *Calc* camph canth *Carb-v* chin ferr *Hep* *Iod* lach lyc *Nat-m* *Seneg* *Sep* *Sil* sul-i k2 **Sulph** k*
- **old** people: *Nit-ac* k*
- **painful**: gaul br1
- **perspiration**, with profuse: asc-t vh
- **phthisical** patients, in: *Arg-n* ars-i bro1 bry bro1 *Calc* hep bro1 *Iod* bro1 iodof bro1 kali-c bro1 *Seneg* tub gk
- **purulent**: pyrog jl2
- **recurrent**: guaj ptk1 kali-c mtf33 phos mtf33
- **rheumatic**: acon bro1 *Ant-t* k* *Arn* k* ars nh6 **Bry** k* *Dulc* iod sne nux-v ran-b bro1 rhod bro1 rhus-t bro1 sabad *Sulph* k*

INJURIES:

\- **after**: apis b7a.de ruta ptk1

O - **Heart**; to: arn st1 cact st1

\- **Mammae**; to: arn k1* ars-i sne *Bell-p* k1* calen sne carb-an sne con k1* *Cund* sne kali-chl sne phos sne ruta sne

INSENSIBILITY of nipples: lac-ac stj5• sars

INSPIRATION:

\- **agg.**: **Acon** b7.de* agar b4.de* am-c b4.de* anac b4.de* ang b7.de* *Arg-met* b7.de* *Arn* b7.de* *Asar* b7.de* aur b4.de* bar-c b4.de* bell bg2 borx bg2 bov b4.de* **Bry** b7.de* calc b4.de* camph b7.de* cann-s b7.de* canth b7.de* *Caps* b7.de* carb-an b4a.de carb-v b4.de* caust b4.de* cham b7.de* chel b7.de* *Chin* b7.de* cic b7.de* cina b7.de* clem b4.de* cocc b7.de* colch b7.de* coloc b4.de* con b4.de* croc bg2 dulc b4.de* euphr b7.de* guaj b4.de* hell b7.de* hyos b7.de* iod b4.de* kali-bi bg2 kali-c b4.de* *Kali-n* b4a.de* *Kreos* b7a.de laur b7.de* led b7.de* *Lob* bg2 lyc b4.de* mag-c b4.de* mag-m b4.de* *Meny* b7.de* merc b4.de* *Mez* b4.de* mur-ac b4.de* nat-c b4.de* nat-m b4.de* nit-ac b4.de* nux-m b7.de* olnd b7.de* op b7.de* par b7.de* ph-ac b4.de* phos b4.de* plat b4.de* plb b7.de* puls b7.de* *Ran-b* b7.de* **Rhus-t** b7.de* ruta b7.de* *Sabad* b7.de* *Sabin* b7.de* sars b4.de* scroph-n bg2 seneg b4.de* sep b4.de* sil b4.de* *Spig* b7.de* *Spong* b7.de* **Squil** b7.de* stann b4.de* stront-c b4.de* sul-ac b4.de* sulph b4.de* tarax b7.de* teucr b7.de* *Valer* b7.de* verat b7.de* verb b7.de* viol-t b7.de* zinc b4.de*

\- **amel.**: borx b4a.de cina b7.de* colch b7.de* merc b4.de* tarax b7.de*

INTERCOSTAL neuralgia (See Pain - intercostal - neuralgic)

INTERTRIGO:

O - **Mammae**: syc fmm1•

O · **Beneath**: morg-p pte1• syc pte1•
- **Between**: syc bka1•

INVERSION: (↗*Retraction*)

O - **Nipples**; of: (↗*Retraction*) apis gsy1 **Con** sne graph bg3 nat-s bg3 phyt bg3 sars bg3*

IRRITABLE HEART (See Palpitation - irritable)

IRRITATION:

\- **spasmodic**: ip br1

O - **Bronchial** tubes: acet-ac bro1 *Acon* bro1 alumn bro1 ambro bro1 brom bro1 *Bry* bro1 chlor bro1 ferr-p bro1 *Hep* bro1 jab br1 *Phos* bro1 pilo bro1 *Rumx* bro1 sangin-n bro1 spong bro1 verb br1
- **influenza**; after: kali-bi br1 kreos br1 pix br1

ITCHING: agar k* *Alum* k* alum-p k2 alumn am-m k* *Ambr* k* anac k* ang b7.de* **Ant-c** k* apis bg2 arg-n arn ars k* ars-i arund br1* aster bamb-a stb2.de• bar-c k* bar-s k2 bell bg2 berb borx *Bov* k* bufo bg2* cact *Calc* k* calc-s canth b7.de* caps k* carb-v k* carbn-s carneg-g rwt1• caust k* chel chin k* cic h1 clem cocc k* con k* corn dios dulc fd4.de fl-ac ham fd3.de• iod k* jug-r kali-ar kali-bi k* kali-br k* kali-c k* kali-n kali-p kali-s *Led* b7.de* *Lyc* k* mag-m k* manc mand rsj7• merc-i-f *Mez* k* nat-c k* nat-m k* nat-n nit-ac op k* ph-ac bg2 phos k* phyt podo fd3.de• positr nl2• pot-e rly4• puls k* ran-s b7.de* rhus-t ribo rly4• ruta fd4.de sabad bg2 sep k* sil bg1 spong b7.de* squil bg2 stann bg2 staph b7.de* stram bg2 stront-c k* sul-i k2 **Sulph** k* symph fd3.de• tell rsj10• thuj *Til* tritic-vg fd5.de *Urt-u* vanil fd5.de *Verat* b7.de* viol-t b7.de* [tax jsj7]

\- **morning**: brom
- **bed** agg.; in: rhus-t

\- **afternoon**: nicc tritic-vg fd5.de

\- **evening**: am-m h2 cact carneg-g rwt1• chin mez podo fd3.de• stront-c *Sulph* symph fd3.de•
- **walking** agg.: fl-ac
- **warm** in bed, on becoming: puls rhus-v

\- **night**: ant-c h2 ham fd3.de• lith-c tritic-vg fd5.de

\- **air** agg.; in open: nat-m h2

\- **biting**: *Laur* nicc a1 spong
- **cold** agg.: nicc

\- **burning**: calc-s k2 caps a1* hir rsj4•
- **then**: agar h2

\- **fleas**, as from: alum cact led nat-c

\- **scratching**:
- **agg.**: con

- **scratching**: ...
  - **amel.**: alum h2 nicc phos h2
  - **returns** after scratching: berb bov chin grat mez squil h1
- **spots**, in: aster hydr-ac luna kg1• lyc nit-ac sulph
- **sticking**: caps con h2 staph
- **tingling** and: con
- **warm**; when: bov cocc

▽ - **extending** to:
- ○ • **Nose**: con ptk1 *Ip* ptk1
  - **Posterior** nares: coc-c bro1 con bro1 iod bro1 *Ip* bro1 puls bro1

○ - **Axillae**: agn k* *Anac* k* androc srj1• arg-n asar b7.de* aster berb calc-p carb-an k* *Carb-v* k* *Carbn-s* caust k* cocc con k* cop cycl dig k* dulc fd4.de elaps k* falco-pe nl2• form graph bg2 grat ham *Hep* hura jug-r kali-bi bg2 kali-c k* kali-n mag-c k* maias-l hm2• nat-m *Nit-ac* k* oxal-a rly4• ozone sde2• *Phos* k* pot-e rly4• prot pte1• sal-fr sle1• sang bg2* sep k* spig k* spong k* squil h1 stann k* *Staph* b7.de* **Sulph** k* valer b7.de* vanil fd5.de viol-o bg2 viol-t k*
  - **left**: maias-l hm2•
  - **morning**: form
  - **heated**; when body becomes: arg-n *Hep*
  - **menses** | **before** | **agg.**: sang k*
    - **during** | **agg.**: sang bro1
  - **perspiration** agg.: jug-r sal-fr sle1•
  - **sitting** agg.: spong h1
  - ○ **Below**: asar h1 cycl a1
  - **Glands**: cocc b7.de*
- **Clavicles**; region of: nicc k*
  - **scratching** | **amel.**: grat
- **Costal** cartilages | **Between**: staph h1
- **Heart**: aur bg2
- **Internally**: agar b4.de *Am-c* b4a.de ambr b7.de* bar-c b4.de bufo bg2 calc b4a.de carb-v b4.de* *Cham* b7.de chin b7.de *Con* b4a.de *Iod* b4a.de kali-c b4.de meny b7.de* mez b4.de nux-m b7.de ph-ac b4.de* phos b4.de* sep b4a.de spig b7.de* *Stann* b4.de *Verat* b7.de
- **Mammae**: *(↗Rubbing - mammae)* agar alum k* alum-p k2 anac ang ant-c arge-pl rwt5• am ars k* bar-c bar-s k2 berb bov calc canth carb-v carbn-s castor-eq *Caust* k* **Con** k* *Dulc* k* hipp jug-r *Kali-c* k* led lyc mez nat-m nicc nux-v b7.de* phel *Phos* plb k* ran-s b7.de* rhus-t k* ribo rly4• sabad sep sil bg1 spong squil staph sulph
  - **left**: carbn-dox knl3•
  - **accompanied** by:
    - **cancer** of mammae (See Cancer - mammae - accompanied - itching)
    - **stabbing** pain (See Pain - mammae - stitching - accompanied - itching)
  - **nursing** women; in: caust pd
  - **warm**; on becoming: aeth ptk1
  - ○ **Between**: irid-met srj5• ozone sde2• ph-ac puls h1 vanil fd5.de
  - **Nipples**: agar k* anag con k* fl-ac k* form *Graph* k* hep k* m-arct b7.de m-aust b7.de mang b4.de* onos k* orig c1 *Petr* k* psor jl2 puls b7.de* rhus-t b7.de* ribo rly4• sabad b7.de* sabin hr1 sars *Sep* k* stann *Sulph* k* tarent verat c1 zinc k*
    - **left**: olib-sac wmh1
    - **menses**; during: hep ptk1
    - **voluptuous**: sabin hr1*
- **Ribs** | **corrosive**: ph-ac h2
- **Sides**: alum b4.de* am b7.de* canth b7.de* cic b7.de* nit-ac b4.de* spong b7.de* squil b7.de*
- **Sternum**: alum h2 kali-p fd1.de• puls h1 sep h2 symph fd3.de• vanil fd5.de
  - ○ **Behind**: iod ptk1
    - **cough** agg.; during: kali-bi tl1

JERKS: *(↗Shocks)* *Agar* k* anac arg-met calc-p cina *Con* k* graph ptk1 lyc k* plat ptk1 spong squil sulph ptk1 valer
- **night**: am-c h2
- **breathing** agg.: lyc
- **moving** the arm: anac

○ - **Axillae**: dulc bg2 valer bg2

Jerks: ...
- **Heart**: acon bg2 agar arg-met arg-n am bg2 *Calc* fl-ac k* nat-m k* **Nux-v** k* plb bg2 sumb k* tarent
  - **evening**: sumb k*
- **Mammae**: croc k*

JUMPING: | **sensation** of (See Alive)

LACTATION; complaints of (See GENERALS - Lactation)

LAMENESS: | **Heart**: phyt bg2

LARGE: *(↗Fullness)*

○ - **Clavicles**: nat-m mtf33
- **Mammae**: chim ptk1

LAUGHING agg.: acon bg2 borx b4a.de bry ptk1 laur b7.de* lyc bg2 mez b4.de* mur-ac b4.de* nicc bg2 plb b7a.de* psor bg2 stann b4.de*

LEANING: | **backward** against something | **agg.**: glon bg2 staph b7.de*
- **forward** resting on arms agg.: sul-ac bg2

LIFTING a weight: | **agg.**: *Alum* b4a.de* bar-c b4.de* kali-c b4.de* kali-n bg2 lyc b4.de* psor ptk1 sul-ac b4.de* sulph bg2* zinc bg2

LIGHTNESS; sensation of: stann bg2
- **expansive**: chir-fl gya2

○ - **Heart**: graph bg2

LIVING; sensation of something (See Alive)

LOOSE, sensation: bry b7.de* kali-n b4.de* mez bg2 phos bg2 rhus-t h1 *Sulph* b4a.de
- **cough** agg., during: kali-n b4.de*
- **flesh** were loose; as if: squil b7.de*
- **ribs** rubbing; of loose: ign bg2

○ - **Heart** were loose; as if am bg2 aur b4.de* *Bell* bg2 crot-h bg2* dig c1 gels bg2 lil-t bg2 plb bg2
- **Sternum**; behind: chlam-tr bcx2•

LOSS of fluids agg.: *Chin* b7a.de squil b7a.de

LUMPS:
- **sensation** of: *(↗Induration - mammae; Nodules - mammae)* abies-n br1 alum bg2 **Am-m** bg2* ambr k* anac bg2 chin bg2 cic k* cupr bg2 falco-pe nl2• lil-t bg2* melal-alt gya4 nat-c bg2* nat-p bg2 nux-m bg2* stict bg2 sulph k* *Tarax* bg2* tritic-vg fd5.de zinc bg2*
  - **moving** up and down on empty swallowing: lil-t a1*

○ - **Axillae**: *Petr* bg2
  - **brown**: *Thuj* b4a.de
- **Clavicles**: *Caust* b4a.de *Fl-ac* b4a.de
- **External** chest: cann-s b7.de* caust b4.de* mang b4.de*
- **Mammae**; between●: *(↗Induration - mammae; Nodules - mammae)* raph k*
- **Sternum**:
  - **left**:
    - **sensation** of lumps | **pushing** everything there away: bamb-a stb2.de•
  - ○ **Behind** | **sensation** of a lump: gels bg3*
  - **Middle** of sternum: *Chin Puls*
  - **Under**: aur bg1* bell bg2* chin bg2* echi ptk1 gels bg2* kola stb3• lec melal-alt gya4 *Phos* ptk1 *Puls* bg2* ran-s bg1 sil bg1* thlas bg2*
    - **sensation** of lumps: choc srj3• melal-alt gya4

LUNGS touched back on coughing; as if: sulph b4a.de*

LYING:
- **abdomen**; on:
  - **agg.**: asc-t ptk1
  - **amel.**: bry ptk1
- **agg.**: am-c b4.de* am-m b7.de* ang b7.de* ant-c b7.de* arg-n bg2 ars b4a.de asaf b7.de* calc b4.de* canth b7.de* carb-v b4.de* cham b7.de* chel bg2 ferr b7.de* *Kali-n* b4.de* lil-t bg2 lyc bg2 lycps-v bg2 meny b7.de* nat-c bg2 nat-m b4.de* nit-ac b4.de* olnd b7.de* puls b7.de* rhus-t b7.de* sel b7.de* sulph b4.de* viol-t b7.de*

- **amel.**: alum b4.de* arg-n bg2 bry b7.de* calc-p bg2 canth b7.de* iod b4.de* nux-v b7.de* olnd b7.de* psor bg2 sabad b7.de* *Sulph* b4a.de *Verat* b7a.de zinc b4.de*
- **arms** near chest amel.; with: lac-ac a1*
- **back**; on:
  - **agg.**: alum b4.de* ars b4.de* asaf bg2 aur bg2 chin b7.de* kali-c b4.de* nux-v b7.de* sep b4.de* sulph bg2
  - **amel.**: *Acon* b7a.de arn b7.de* borx ptk1 *Bry* b7.de* *Cact* ptk1 *Ign* b7.de* kalm bg2 par b7.de* phos ptk1 *Puls* b7.de* sabad b7.de* spig b7a.de sulph ptk1
- **bed**; in:
  - **agg.**: ambr b7.de* ang b7.de* calc bg2 cham b7.de* chin b7.de* colch b7.de* ferr b7.de* ign b7.de* kali-bi bg2 *Kali-c* b4a.de kali-n bg2 led b7.de* lyc b4a.de* mag-m b4a.de nit-ac bg2 nux-v b7.de* phos b4a.de* puls b7.de* *Rhus-t* b7.de* seneg b4a.de sep b4a.de* sil bg2 spong b7.de* squil b7.de* stram b7.de* *Sulph* bg2 valer b7.de* verb b7.de*
  - **amel.**: arg-n bg2
- **head** low; with the | **agg.**: cinnb bg2 glon bg2
- **impossible**: acon-f bro1 *Ars* bro1 *Conv* bro1 dig bro1 grin bro1 lach bro1 mag-p bro1 puls bro1 visc bro1
- **side**; on:
  - **affected** side | **agg.**: dros b7.de* ign b7.de* kali-c bg2 *Phos* b4.de* rhus-t b7.de* sabad b7.de* tarax b7.de*
  - **agg.**: am-m b7.de* ang b7a.de* bry b7.de* con b4.de* ign b7.de* kali-c b4.de* kreos bg2 nat-c b4.de* phos b4a.de* puls b7.de* ran-b b7.de* sabad b7a.de seneg b4a.de sulph b4a.de viol-t b7a.de
  - **amel.**: alum b4.de*
  - **left**:
    - **agg.**: **Acon** b7.de* am-c b4.de* ang b7.de* ant-c bg2 bar-c b4a.de* brom bg2 bry b7.de* *Cact* bg2 calc b4.de* camph bg2 canth b7.de* chin b7.de* cinnb bg2 clem bg2 crot-t bg2 dig bg2 glon bg2 graph bg2 ip b7.de* kali-c b4a.de* kali-n bg2 kalm bg2 lil-t bg2 lyc b4.de* mag-p bg2 med bg2 naja bg2 nat-c b4.de* nat-m b4.de* *Phos* b4.de* puls b7.de* rumx bg2 seneg b4.de* sep b4.de* *Sil* b4.de* spig b7a.de *Stann* b4a.de sulph b4.de* tab bg2 visc bg2
    - **impossible**: *Phos* bro1 puls bro1
  - **painful** side:
    - **agg.**: borx bg2 *Calc* b4a.de caps b7.de* ign b7.de* kali-c b4a.de laur b7a.de nux-v b7.de* ran-b bg2 *Sabad* b7a.de spong b7.de* tarax b7.de*
    - **amel.**: ambr b7.de* arn b7.de* *Bry* b7.de* cham b7.de* ign b7.de* naja bg2 nux-v b7.de* *Puls* b7.de*
  - **painless** side:
    - **agg.**: ambr bg2 arn bg2 bry b7.de* cham b7.de* ign b7.de* nux-v b7.de* puls b7.de* *Stann* b4a.de
    - **amel.**: ign b7.de* *Nux-v* b7.de*
  - **right**:
    - **agg.**: acon b7.de* alum bg2 arg-n bg2 bad bg2 borx b4a.de* chinin-s bg2 ip b7.de* kali-n bg2 lil-t bg2 lycps-v bg2 mag-m bg2 merc b4.de* puls b7.de* rumx bg2 seneg b4.de* spig b7.de* stann b4.de*
    - **amel.**: glon bg2 graph bg2 kali-c b4a.de lach bg2 naja bg2 nat-m bg2 spig bg2 tab bg2
    - **impossible**: merc bro1

LYING DOWN: | **after** | **agg.**: ang b7.de* ant-t b7.de* hell b7.de* ign b7.de* kali-bi bg2 m-ambo b7.de nux-v b7.de* ox-ac bg2 par b7.de* puls b7.de* rhus-t b7.de* sabad b7.de* stann bg2 stram b7.de verb b7.de*
- **amel.**: psor tl1

MASTITIS (See Inflammation - mammae)

MEALY coating nipples: petr h2*

MENSES:
- **after**:
  - **agg.**: ars-i bg2 chin bg2 iod bg2 lac-c bg2 mag-c bg2 puls bg2 sep bg2 stann bg2 thuj bg2 ust bg2
    - **Mammae**: berb bg2 cycl bg2

Menses: ...
- **before**:
  - **agg.**: alum bg2 ars-i bg2 bell bg2 borx bg2 brom bg2 bry bg2 caul bg2 chin bg2 cocc bg2 con bg2 *Cupr* b7.de* dig bg2 graph bg2 grat bg2 iod bg2 lac-c bg2 lach bg2 mag-c bg2 mag-m bg2 merc bg2 nat-m bg2 puls b7.de* sang bg2 spong b7.de* sulph bg2 verat-v bg2 vib bg2
    - **Axillae**: aur bg2 calc bg2 sang bg2*
    - **Mammae**: bry ptk1 calc ptk1 *Con* ptk1 **Kali-m** ptk1 **Lac-c** ptk1 lyc ptk1 ol-an ptk1 *Phyt* ptk1 puls ptk1
- **during**:
  - **agg.**: acon bg2 am-c b4.de* am-m b7.de* bell b4.de* berb bg2 *Cact* bg2 caust b4.de* cham b7.de* **Chin** bg2 **Cocc** bg2 *Con* bg2 glon bg2 *Graph* b4.de* kali-n bg2 **Kreos** bg2 **Lach** bg2 laur bg2 lob bg2 mag-c bg2 mang bg2 mosch bg2 nat-m bg2 phos b4.de* *Puls* b7.de* rhod bg2 sang bg2 sep bg2 verat bg2 verat-v bg2 vib bg2
    - **Mammae**: berb bg2 bry bg2* *Calc* bg2* carb-an bg2 *Caust* bg2 *Cham* bg2 **Con** bg2* dulc bg2 grat bg2 *Helo* bg2 helon ptk1 *Iod* bg2 *Lac-c* bg2* merc bg2* murx bg2* phel ptk1 **Phos** bg2* **Phyt** bg2* rhus-t bg2 sang bg2 thuj bg2 vib bg2 zinc bg2*
  - **beginning** of menses | **agg.**: phos bg2

MENTAL EXERTION agg.: colch b7.de* ign b7.de* nat-c b4.de* nat-m bg2 nux-v b7.de* *Sep* b4.de* staph b7a.de*

MILK: (↗*GENERALS - Lactation)*
- **absent**: acon k* *Agn* k* alf ptk1* apis *Asaf* k* *Bell* borx *Bry* k* **Calc** k* calc-sil k2* carb-an card-m *Caust* k* cham bro1* *Chel* bro1* *Coff* dulc k* *Form* k* frag br1* *Ign* *Lac-c* k* *Lac-d* k* lach lact br1 *Lact-v* br1* lec br1* medus c1 merc *Mill* k* nux-m c1 nux-v ph-ac bro1* phos bro1* phyt k2* pilo bro1* puls k* rheum rhus-t *Ric* bro1* samb *Sec* k* *Sil* bro1* spira br1 stict bro1* sulph *Thyr* br1* *Urt-u* k* ust x-ray bro1* yohim br1 **Zinc** k*
  - **delivery**; after: acon bg2 agn mrr2* bell bg2 bry bg2 **Calc** bg2 *Caust* bg2 cham bg2 coff bg2 merc bg2 *Puls* bg2 rhus-t bg2 stict pd sulph bg2 urt-u ptk1
  - **night** watching; from: caust ptk1
- **altered**: bell ptk1 merc ptk1
- **bad**: acet-ac k* **Aeth** bg1* asaf vh *Borx* k* bufo **Calc** k* calc-p k* carb-an k* **Cham** k* cina crot-t lach lec br1 *Merc* k* nat-m k2 nux-v op *Ph-ac* bro1 puls sabal bro1 **Sil** bg1* stann k* sulph bro1
- **bitter**: phos b4a.de rheum k* samb b7a.de sulph b4a.de
- **bloody**: *Apis* b7a.de bufo k* *Cham* k* hep ip b7a.de *Lyc* *Merc* *Phyt* k* *Sep* *Sulph*
- **boys**, in: merc ptk1
- **cheesy**: *Borx* k* bov b4a.de *Cham* k* *Phyt*
- **child** refuses mother's milk● (See GENERALS - Food - milk - aversion - mother - child)
- **complaints** of milk: (↗*GENERALS - Lactation)* acon bg2 ars bg2 **Bell** bg2 borx bg2 bry bg2 *Calc* bg2 carb-an bg2 carb-v bg2 *Cham* bg2 chin bg2 cina bg2 con bg2 dulc bg2 graph bg2 ign bg2 ip bg2 kali-c bg2 lach bg2 lyc bg2 **Merc** bg2 nat-m bg2 nux-v bg2 ph-ac bg2 phos bg2 *Puls* bg2 rheum bg2 rhus-t bg2 samb bg2 *Sep* bg2 *Sil* bg2 stann bg2 staph bg2 zinc bg2
- **decreased**: agn c2 alf br1 caust c2 urt-u c2 ust c2
- **disappearing**: acon bg2* agar k* **Agn** k* alf qqh *Arn* *Asaf* k* *Asar* aur aur-s k2 bell b2.de* bry k* *Calc* k* *Camph* k* *Caust* k* cham k* *Chel* k* chin k* *Chion* cocc bg2 coff **Dulc** k* *Form* bg2* gou-l jsx1.fr hecla **Hyos** b7a.de *Ign* k* iod bg2 jab bg2 kali-i bg2 *Lac-c* k* *Lac-d* lec br1 lyc medus br1* merc k* merc-c bg2 mill musan-c jsx1.fr nat-m k2 nux-m bg2 ph-ac k* *Phel* phos k* phyt *Plan* *Plb* k* *Puls* k* *Rhus-t* k* ric plr1 sabal plr1 samb b2.de* *Sec* k* sep k* sil bg2 spira br1 stict c1 sulph k* tabern-s jsx1.fr *Tub* **Urt-u** k* *Ust* *Verat-v* *Zinc* k*
  - **brain** troubles, with: *Agar* k*
  - **cold**; after taking a: acon bg2 **Bell** bg2 *Cham* bg2 dulc k* merc bg2 *Puls* *Sulph* bg2
  - **delivery**; less milk since (See decreased)
  - **excitement**; after: caust
  - **fever**; during: *Agn* bg2 bell bg2 *Bry* bg2 *Calc* bg2 cham bg2 dulc bg2 *Hyos* bg2 ign bg2 *Puls* bg2 **Rhus-t** b7a.de* zinc bg2
  - **perspiration**; during: agn bg2 bry bg2 *Calc* bg2 cham bg2 chin bg2 *Dulc* bg2 ign bg2 puls bg2 rhus-t bg2 *Sep* bg2 zinc bg2
- **drying** off (See disappearing)
- **emotions** agg.: acon bg2 bell bg2 *Bry* bg2 **Cham** bg2 *Coff* bg2
- **failing** to release the milk: acon bg2 *Bell* bg2 **Bry** bg2 calc bg2 cham bg2 coff bg2 *Dulc* bg2 merc bg2 **Puls** bg2 rhus-t bg2 sulph bg2

- **flowing** spontaneously: acon k* ant-t arn bg2 *Bell* k* *Borx* k* *Bry* k* **Calc** k* cham chin k* *Coff* bg2 *Con* k* *Iod* k* *Kali-i* kreos lac-c *Lach* *Lyc* k* nux-v *Phos* k* *Puls* k* rhod bg2 *Rhus-t* k* *Sil* stann staph stram bg2 ust
  - **sensation**: dict bg2* kreos bg2* nux-v bg2* puls bg2*
- **increased**: *Acon* k* anan arund c1 asaf k* **Bell** k* *Borx* k* **Bry** k* **Calc** k* cham bro1 chim bro1 chin k* con k* erig bro1 iod k* kali-i bg2 lac-c bg2* lact a1* *Medus* bro1 nux-v k* parth c2* phos k* phyt bg2* pip-m bro1 pitu-p sp1 plac bwa3 **Puls** k* rheum bg2* *Rhus-t* k* *Ric* br1* sabal bro1 *Sabin* ptk1 salv br1* sec bro1 *Sol-o* bro1 spira bro1 spirae a1 stram k* tritic-vg fd5.de urt-u bg2 ust bro1
  - **menses**; before: con ptk1
  - **mental** symptoms; with (See MIND - Mental symptoms - milk)
  - **perspiration**; during: acon bg2 *Bell* bg2 *Bry* bg2 calc bg2 chin bg2 con bg2 phos bg2 *Puls* bg2 rhus-t bg2 stram bg2
- **menses**:
  - **absent**: bell ptk1 bry ptk1 calc ptk1 lyc ptk1 phos ptk1 puls ptk1 rhus-t ptk1 sabin ptk1 stram ptk1
  - **before** | **agg.**: cycl *Tub* k*
  - **during** | **agg.**: calc bro1* merc k* pall bro1* *Puls* k* *Tub* k*
  - **instead** of: merc bro1* rhus-t bg2
  - **suppressed** menses; from: *Chin* cycl lyc *Merc* phos puls rhus-t *Tub* k*
- **obstructed** (See failing)
- **pregnancy**; during false (See pregnancy; in) *(↗Pregnancy; in)*
- **pregnancy**; in women when not related to: *(↗pregnancy; during; MIND - Delusions - Pregnant)* apis mmj* ars k* *Asaf* k* atro mmj bamb-a stb2.de• bell k* borx bry bg2 calc bg2* calc-i mtf11 caul mmj cham mld5* con mmj croc mmj* *Cycl* k* helon mmj ign bnf1.es* kola stb3• lac-c bnf1.es* lach itm lyc k* *Merc* k* nux-m mmj* nux-v mmj* op mmj phos k* phyt itm **Puls** k* reser mtf11 rhus-t k* sabad mmj sabin bg2 sep qqh stram h1* sulph mmj* thlas bg3* thuj mmj* *Tub* k* *Urt-u* k* vip fkr4.de
- **puberty**; at: *Puls*
- **pus**; containing: *Cham* b7a.de
- **robust** women; in: *Acon* bg2 bell bg2 **Bry** bg2 *Cham* bg2 merc bg2
- **sour**: acet-ac br1* calc-p bg2
- **spoiled**: acet-ac bg2 **Aeth** bg2 bell b2.de* borx b2.de* calc bg2 calc-p bg2 carb-an b2.de* *Cham* b2.de* **Cina** bg2 ip b2.de* lach b2.de* *Merc* b2.de* nux-v b2.de* ph-ac bg2 puls b2.de* rheum b2.de* samb b2.de* **Sil** bg2 stann bg2 sulph bg2
- **stringy**: borx *Kali-bi* k* kali-c *Phyt* k*
- **suppressed**: acon bg2* agar k* *Agn* k* aur k* aur-i k2 aur-s k2 bell bro1 **Bry** k* calc k* calc-sil k2* camph-br br1 camph-mbr bro1 *Carb-v* k* **Caust** k* *Cham* k* chel bg2 chim k* cimic k2* cycl sf1.de dulc k* frag a1 *Hyos* k* ign a1 *Iod* k* lac-d k* *Lach* k* *Merc* k* merc-c a1 mill c1* phyt bro1 **Puls** k* *Rhus-t* k* *Sec* k* senec sf1.de *Sil* k* stict c1 sul-i k2 *Sulph* k* *Urt-u* k* verat k* zinc b4a.de*
  - **anger**; after: *Cham* k*
  - **cold**; from: **Bry** hr1 dulc hr1*
  - **metastasis** from suppressed milk: agar k*
  - **remedies** to suppress milk flow: asaf bro1 borx bg2 bry bro1 *Calc* bro1 con bro1 *Lac-c* bg2* *Puls* bro1 urt-u bro1
- **thick** and tastes bad: *Borx* k* *Kali-bi* k* lyc *Phyt*
- **thin**: alf br1 asaf vh *Calc-p* k* carb-an cham *Con* cycl bg2 *Lach* lec br1 lyc merc nux-v sanic c2 *Sil* *Tub*
  - **blue**; and: acet-ac asaf vh *Calc* *Lach* k* lyc nux-v b7a.de puls k*
  - **salty**; and: carb-an
  - **watery**; and: *Bell* b4a.de *Calc* k* cham b7a.de *Con* *Iod* *Merc* b4a.de *Plb* *Puls* sulph b4a.de *Tub*
    - ⁝ **long** after weaning: *Con*
- **weak** women; in: calc bg2 caust bg2 puls bg2 rhus-t bg2
- **weaning** | **complaints** after (See GENERALS - Ailments - weaning)
- **yellow**: phyt rheum k*

MILK FEVER: **Acon** bg2* arn bg2 bell bg2 bry bg2* calc ptk1 cham ptk1 *Coff* bg2 rhus-t bg2

MOISTURE from humor in axilla: carb-an b4.de* *Carb-v* k* *Sulph* k*

MOTION:
- **agg.**: *Acon* b7.de* agar bg2 agn b7.de* alum b4.de* am-c b4.de* am-m b7.de* ang b7.de* ant-t bg2 arg-met b7.de* arg-n bg2 arn b7.de* ars b4a.de* aur bg2 bell b4.de* borx b4a.de bov bg2 **Bry** b7.de* **Calc** b4.de* camph b7.de* cann-s b7.de* caps b7.de* carb-v b4.de* caust bg2 cham b7.de* chin b7.de* cocc b7.de* colch b7.de* con b4.de* cycl b7.de* dig b4.de* euph b4.de euphr bg2 ferr b7.de* glon bg2 graph b4.de* hep b4.de* ign b7.de* iod b4.de* kali-bi bg2 kali-c bg2 kali-n b4.de* kreos bg2 laur bg2 led b7.de* lyc b4.de* m-aust b7.de mag-m b4.de* manc bg2 mang b4.de* meny b7.de* merc b4.de* mez b4.de* mur-ac b4a.de* naja bg2 nat-c b4.de* nat-m b4.de* nit-ac b4.de* nux-m b7.de* nux-v b7.de* op b7.de* ph-ac b4.de* *Phos* b4.de* phyt bg2 puls b7.de* ran-b b7.de* rhod b4.de* rhus-t b7a.de ruta b7.de* sabin b7.de* samb b7.de* sars b4.de* *Seneg* b4.de* sep b4.de* sil bg2 spig b7.de* spong b7.de* squil b7.de* stann b4.de* staph b7.de* stront-c b4.de* sulph b4.de* verat b7.de* viol-t b7.de* zinc b4.de*
- **amel.**: arg-met b7.de* arn b7.de* bell bg2 borx b4a.de caust bg2 cham b7.de* cina b7.de* cycl b7.de* dros b7.de* euph b4.de* kali-n b4.de* mag-m b4a.de* meny b7.de* mez b4.de* mur-ac b4.de* nat-c b4.de* ph-ac b4.de* plb b7.de* puls b7.de* pyrog bg2 rhus-t b7.de* sabad b7.de* seneg ptk1 sep b4.de* teucr b7.de*
- **arm**; of | **left** arm agg.; of: phos bg2
- **arms**; of | **agg.**: *Acon* b7a.de *Anac* b4a.de *Ang* b7a.de ant-c b7a.de asc-t bg2 borx b4a.de camph b7a.de carb-an bg2 dig b4.de* led b7.de* m-arct b7.de nux-m b7.de* plb b7.de* puls b7.de* ran-b b7.de* rhus-t ptk1 sulph b4a.de thuj b4a.de viol-t b7.de*

MOTIONS OF FETUS: | **agg.**: sulph b4a.de

MOVEMENT:
- **sensation** of:
  - ○ **Lungs** | **waves**; as if lung moved in: dulc hr1*
- ○ **Heart**: phyt bg2 zinc h2
  - **sensation** of: nat-m b4.de* sulph b4.de*
  - **upward**: neon srj5•
- **Region** of heart: sulph h2

MUCUS:
- **right** chest: caust h2
- **chronic**: *Ars* b4a.de* *Bar-c* b4a.de bry bg2 *Calc* b4a.de* **Carb-v** b4a.de* *Caust* bg2 *Dulc* bg2 iod b4a.de* lach bg2 lyc b4a.de* mang bg2 nat-c bg2 nat-m bg2 petr bg2 ph-ac bg2 *Phos* b4a.de* **Psor** b4a.de *Seneg* b4a.de *Sil* bg2 *Stann* b4a.de* staph bg2 **Sulph** b4a.de* **Thuj** b4a.de *Zinc* b4a.de
- ○ **Air** passages; in (See LARYNX - Mucus - air)
- **Bronchial** tubes: grin br1 jab br1
- **Lungs**: *(↗RESPIRATION - Difficult - mucus)* *Ant-t* tl1 phos tl1

MUFFLED: | **Heart** sound: coli jl2

MURMURS: *(↗BACK - Murmurs - respiratory - scapula - rough)* tritic-vg fd5.de
- **cardiac** murmurs: *(↗Heart; complaints - valves)* agar *Aml-ns* *Apis* k* apoc k* *Ars* *Ars-i* aspar *Aur* aur-br vh1 aur-i k2* *Aur-m* bar-c **Cact** k* *Calc* calc-f dgt1 carb-ac *Chel* chinin-ar *Cocc* *Colch* **Coll** crat br1 *Crot-h* cupr-s *Cycl* hr1 **Dig** **Ferr** ferr-ar k* ferr-i k* *Glon* k* hep *Hydr* hydr-ac iber *Iod* ip kali-ar k* kali-br *Kali-c* **Kalm** k* *Lach* k* lat-m bnm6• laur k2 *Lith-c* lob *Lyc* *Lycps-v* *Merc* **Naja** k* nat-ar nat-c *Nat-m* *Nit-ac* ox-ac k2 *Phos* k* plb *Psor* k* puls **Rhus-t** k* **Spig** k* **Spong** k* stann stram *Sumb* tab tarent thyr c1* toxo-g jl2 tub
  - **loud**: kalm mrr1 lycps-v mrr1 *Naja* mrr1
  - **valvular**: *(↗Heart failure - accompanied - valves; Heart; complaints - valves)* acon mtf *Adon* mtf apoc mtf *Ars* mtf ars-i mtf aur mtf aur-br mtf aur-i mtf *Bar-c* mtf *Cact* hr1* calc mtf calc-f mtf camph mtf *Conv* mtf crat br1* *Dig* mtf ferr mtf *Glon* mtf iod mtf *Kali-c* mtf kalm mtf lach mtf laur mtf lith-c mtf *Lycps-eu* mtf lycps-v mrr1 **Naja** mtf ox-ac mtf phos mtf plb mtf *Puls* mtf rhus-t mtf sang mtf *Spig* mtf *Spong* mtf *Stroph-h* mtf *Tarent* mtf thuj mtf
    - ⁝ **Aortic** valve: *(↗Heart; complaints - valves - aortic)* cact vh1 onos c1
    - ⁝ **Mitral** valve: *(↗Heart; complaints - valves - mitral)* carb-ac hr1 coll hl9 dig btw2 kali-c fr2 onos c1
  - ○ **Apex** of heart: gala br1 laur he1
- **respiratory** murmurs: arg-n hr1 asc-t hr1 bapt nh4 bell a1 *Cact* hr1 carbn-o a1 *Dig* a1* *Gels* hr1 *Hep* hr1 loxo-lae bnm12* *Phos* a1 sang hr1 sulph hr1

MUSIC agg.: carb-an b4a.de nux-v b7.de* staph b7.de*

NARROW: (↗*Emaciation*) calc-p mtf33 cypra-eg sde6.de• phos k2* sep mtf33 *Tub* br1*

- **sensation** as if too: agar bg2* asar bg2 aur bg2 bell bg2 bry bg2 cact bg2 calc b4a.de *Caust* b4a.de cina bg2 *Euph* b4a.de hell b7.de* ign bg2 kali-c bg2 mez b4a.de* nat-m bg2 nux-m tl1 olnd b7.de* *Petr* b4a.de phos bg2 puls b7.de* ran-b b7.de* seneg b4a.de* spig b7.de* squil b7.de* *Sulph* b4a.de *Teucr* b7a.de tritic-vg fd5.de
  - • **respiration**; with difficult: *Euph* b4a.de *Mez* b4a.de *Petr* b4a.de *Seneg* b4a.de *Sulph* b4a.de

○ - **Coronaries**: aur mtf aur-i mtf cact mtf calc-f mtf lat-m mtf syph mtf

NAUSEA in chest: *Rhus-t* c1

NECROSIS: | **Sternum**: con bro1

NEUROCIRCULATORY ASTHENIA (See Palpitation - irritable)

NODULES, sensitive: **Carb-an** caust mang

○ - **Axillae**: lyc h2 mag-c nit-ac bg2 phos bg2

- **Mammae**: (↗*Induration - mammae; Lumps - mammae; Lumps - sensation)* aids nl2• am bg2 **Ars** b4a.de aur k2 *Bell* b4a.de* *Bell-p* k* *Bry* k* *Bufo* k* calc-f k* calc-i k2 calc-p **Carb-an** k* *Carb-v* cham k* *Chim* chin cist pd clem k* *Coloc* k* **Con** k* croc b7a.de crot-t ptk1 cund cupr sst3• dulc k* *Graph* k* *Iod* k* kali-c b4a.de* kreos k* *Lac-c* k* lac-h sze9• *Lyc* k* mang merc bg2 nat-m bg2 *Nit-ac* k* *Phos* k* **Phyt** k* *Puls* k* rhus-t bg2 ruta k* sang gk scir br1 scroph-n br1 sep bg2 **Sil** k* *Sulph* k* thuj tl1 tub br1* vanil fd5.de [*Merc-d* stj2]
  - • **right**: pitu-a vml2• sang gk *Sil*
  - • **left**: *Arum-t* *Calc-p* **Lyc** k ●*
  - • **arm**; moving: calc-i k2
  - • **children**; in: | **newborns**: cham st
  - • **excitement** agg.: phyt k2
  - • **girls**, before puberty: puls ptk1
  - • **hard**: aster ptk1 nit-ac ptk1
  - • **menses**; during: *Lac-c*
  - • **milk** flow; from suppressed: agn bg2 bell bg2 cham bg2 *Dulc* bg2 rhus-t bg2
  - • **painful**: kreos pd phos k2 phyt tl1
    - ⁝ **old** fat men; in: bar-c vml
  - • **points** at tip; dry black: *Iod* k*
  - • **pregnancy** agg.; during: *Fl-ac*
  - • **purple**: *Carb-an*
  - • **weather** agg.; cold wet: phyt k2

NOISES: (↗*Purring; Purring - region - noise)*

- **abnormal**: acon bg2 apoc bg2 ars bg2 aur bg2 cact bg2 dig bg2 kali-c bg2 kalm bg2 laur bg2 lycps-v bg2 naja bg2 phos bg2 puls bg2 spig bg2 spong bg2 stroph-h bg2 verat bg2 verat-v bg2
- **blowing**; of | **Heart**: ars bg2 colch bg2 cupr bg2 dig bg2 ferr bg2 lycps-v bg2 merc-c bg2 nat-c bg2 phos bg2 plb bg2
- **creaking**: calc-p bg2

○ • **Heart**: mag-c bg2

- **rasping** | **Heart**: plb bg2 zinc bg2
- **ringing** | **Heart**: dig bg2 plb bg2
- **rubbing** | **Heart**: benz-ac bg2 mez bg2 mur-ac bg2
- **rushing**:

○ • **Heart**; region of:
  - ⁝ **morning**:
    - ⁝ **rising** from bed; after | **amel.**: caust h2

○ - **Heart** | **Deep** in heart: bar-c bg2 dig bg2 gels bg2 mez bg2

NUMBNESS: bufo bg2* carbn bg1 chel k* cupr-ar ferr bg2 *Glon* k* graph b4a.de* lat-m bg1 merc k* nux-m physal-al bg1 rhus-t k* stict ptk1 urt-u

▽ - **extending** to:

○ • **Arms**; down | **left**: glon ptk1

○ - **Axillae**: cann-xyz bg2

- **Clavicles**: ferr
- **Heart**: bufo bg2 kalm ptk1 nux-m bg2
- **Mammae**: graph k*

○ • **Nipples**: sars k*

- **Precordial** region: cact br1

Numbness: ...

- **Sides**:
  - • **right**: chel k*
  - • **left**: cupr bg2 cupr-ar *Cur* plb

NURSING:

- **agg.**: borx b4a.de bry bg2 crot-t bg2 *Ferr* bg2 graph bg2 lil-t bg2 nux-v b7a.de phel bg2 *Sil* bg2

○ • **Mammae**: ant-t ptk1 borx bg2* bry ptk1 crot-t ptk1 lac-c ptk1 lil-t ptk1 phel ptk1 phyt ptk1 *Puls* ptk1 sil ptk1
  - ⁝ **Opposite** mamma: borx bg2

- **amel.** | **Mammae**: phel ptk1

NURSING THE CHILD agg.; after: borx bg2 puls bg2

OBSTRUCTION; sensation of: ambr ptk1 bry b7.de* guaj b4a.de lach ptk1 med ptk1 rad-br ptk1

- **cough** agg.; during: guaj b4a.de

OEDEMA (See Edema)

OPEN; sensation as if: (non:guar vml3)

- **chakra**; heart: limen-b-c hm2•

OPERATION on chest; after: abrot ptk1

- **fistula**; for: berb bro1* calc-p bro1* sil bro1*

OPPRESSION: *Absin* **Acon** k* act-sp bg2 adam skp7• *Aesc* aeth *Agar* k* agath-a nl2• aids nl2• *Ail* *All-c* *Alum* k* alum-sil k2 *Alumn* **Am-c** k* *Am-caust* vh1 *Am-m* k* *Ambr* k* ammc vh1 *Anac* k* androc srj1*• *Ang* k* anh sp1 *Ant-c* k* *Ant-t* k* **Apis** k* **Apoc** k* apom vh1 arag br1 aran-ix sp1 arg-met b2.de* *Arg-n* k* arizon-l nl2• *Arn* k* **Ars** k* **Ars-i** k* ars-s-f k2 *Asaf* k* asar k* asc-t aspar **Aur** k* aur-ar k2 aur-i k2 aur-m aur-s k2 *Bapt* bapt-c c1 bar-c k* bar-i k2 bar-m bar-s k2 **Bell** k* benz-ac berb bism k* *Bit-ar* wht1• borx k* both-ax tsm2 *Bov* k* brach k* brom k* bros-gau mrc1 **Bry** k* bufo k* **Cact** k* cadm-s cain *Calad* k* **Calc** k* *Calc-ar* calc-i k2 *Calc-s* calc-sil k2* calen oss• *Camph* k* cann-i *Cann-s* k* canth k* caps b2.de* carb-ac carb-an k* **Carb-v** k* **Carbn-s** carc jl2* *Carl* caul *Caust* k* *Cedr* *Cham* k* chel k* *Chin* k* *Chinin-ar* **Chinin-s** k* chlam-tr bcx2• chlf chlol chlor k* *Cic* k* *Cimx* *Cina* k* cinnb cit-v br1 *Clem* coc-c *Cocc* k* *Coff* k* **Colch** k* *Coloc* k* *Con* k* cop cor-r cot br1 croc k* **Crot-c** k* *Crot-h* k* *Crot-t* **Cupr** k* *Cupr-ar* *Cupr-s* *Cycl* k* cypra-eg sde6.de• cystein-l rly4• *Dig* k* dor dream-p sdj1• *Dros* k* *Dulc* k* *Elaps* euon *Eup-per* euph b2.de* euphr b2.de* falco-pe nl2• **Ferr** k* **Ferr-ar** ferr-i ferr-p *Fl-ac* k* galeoc-c-h gms1• *Galla-q-r* nl2• gamb k* gard-j vlr2• *Gels* k* *Glon* k* gran *Graph* k* grat k* guaj b2.de* *Ham* hell b2.de* *Hep* k* hist sp1 hura hydr-ac hydrang br1 hydrc hydrog srj2• hyos k* **Ign** k* *Iod* k* **Ip** k* jab jug-c jug-r **Kali-ar** **Kali-bi** k* kali-br **Kali-c** k* kali-chl *Kali-i* kali-m k2* *Kali-n* k* kali-p *Kali-s* kali-sil k2 *Kalm* *Kreos* k* lac-ac stj5• lac-d k2 *Lach* k* lachn *Lact* lat-m bnm6• laur k* lavand-a ctl1• led k* lil-t k* limest-b es1• *Lob* k* *Lyc* k* lyss m-ambo b2.de* m-arct b2.de* m-aust b2.de* *Mag-c* k* *Mag-m* k* mag-s *Manc* mang b2.de* med medul-os-si rly4• meli meny k* *Merc* k* merc-c k* merc-i-f *Mez* k* mill moni rfm1• mosch k* mur-ac k* *Mygal* *Naja* k* nat-ar nat-c k* *Nat-m* k* nat-p nat-pyru rly4• **Nat-s** k* nat-sil fd3.de• *Nicc* *Nit-ac* k* **Nux-m** k* **Nux-v** k* ol-j olnd k* onos *Op* k* osm bg2 ox-ac ozone sde2• par k* *Petr* k* ph-ac k* **Phos** k* physala-p bnm7• *Phyt* pieri-b mlk9.de pin-con oss2• plac rzf5• *Plat* k* plb k* plut-n srj7• podo k* polys sk4• *Positr* nl2• prot pte1* *Prun* k* *Psor* k* **Puls** k* pyrog k2 *Ran-b* k* ran-s b2.de* raph rheum k* rhod k* *Rhus-t* k* ribo rly4• ruta k* sabad k* sabin k* *Samb* k* *Sang* k* sanic sars k* sec k* **Sel** k* **Seneg** k* **Sep** k* *Sil* k* sinus rly4• solid br1 *Spig* k* *Spong* k* squil k* *Stann* k* staph k* stict *Stram* k* stront-c b2.de* stry sul-ac k* sul-i k2 **Sulph** k* sumb suprar rly4• symph fd3.de• syph *Tab* tarax b2.de* *Tarent* teucr k* *Thuj* k* til k* tritic-vg fd5.de **Tub** k* tung-met bdx1• valer k* vanad br1* vanil fd5.de **Verat** k* verat-v k* verb k* vesp vib tl1 viol-o k* viol-t k* vip visc sp1 xan br1 *Zinc* k* zinc-p k2

- **morning**: *Alum* k* am-m ant-c h2 *Ars* asaf k* bapt bry k* calc-s carb-v chel chin h1 ham fd3.de• *Ip* k* lyc k* mang k* marb-w es1• nat-c h2 *Nat-s* k* nit-ac *Nux-v* *Phos* k* plb k* *Psor* *Puls* k* rhod sars k* **Sep** k* sul-ac k* *Sulph* tritic-vg fd5.de vanil fd5.de verat c1 zinc k*
  - • **rising** agg.: calc h2 clem graph k* puls k* verat k*
- **forenoon**: bry k* calc h2 *Ip* sulph k* thuj k* tritic-vg fd5.de vanil fd5.de
  - • **9-15 h**: sulph
  - • **10** or **11 h**: cham
  - • **talking** agg.: bry coc-c
- **afternoon**: agar k* alum bufo caust k* coloc k* franz a1 gels ham fd3.de• kali-s fd4.de lyc nat-m h2 nat-sil fd3.de• nicc petr h2 ph-ac k* pitu-gl skp7• seneg k* spong fd4.de staph h1 sulph k* thuj tritic-vg fd5.de

- **14** h: chin sulph
- **15** h: am-c k1 arn
- **16** h: plan
- **17** h: ham fd3.de• med
- **18** h: chel
- **sleep** agg.; after: calad k*

- **evening**: *All-c* am-m ars k* *Bry* chin k* clem k* *Coloc* k* crot-t k* digin a1 *Elaps* ferr k* ferr-ar gink-b sbd1• ham fd3.de• hyper k* kali-p fd1.de• kali-s fd4.de lact lyc h2 *Mag-c* mur-ac nat-c h2 nat-m k* nux-m k* nux-v k* *Phos* **Puls** k* ran-b k* rhod k* sars h2 seneg k* **Sep** k* spong fd4.de *Stann* stront-c sulph k* tritic-vg fd5.de vanil fd5.de *Zinc*
  - **21** h: hura
  - **sunset**, after: nat-s
  - **bed** agg.; in: *Apis* k* borx chel k* *Chin* galla-q-r nl2• *Sep* k* zinc
- **night**: *Alum* k* alum-p k2 ambr k* *Apis* ars-met *Aur* aur-m aur-s k2 berb k* *Bry* *Calc* chin k* *Coca* *Coloc* gamb *Lact* lyc mang-p rly4• nat-c h2 nat-s nit-ac *Nux-v* k* *Op* k* petr k* ph-ac *Phos* k* polys sk4• *Puls* mrr1 *Rhus-t* k* ruta sars h2 sin-n spong fd4.de sulph k* tritic-vg fd5.de vanil fd5.de
  - **midnight**: ign k* *Lach*
    - **before**: *Coloc* k* grat k* ham fd3.de•
    - **after**:
      - **2** h: am-c *Kali-bi* lach
      - **3** h: am-c am-m ant-t
      - **4** h: chel lil-t
    - **waking**; on: cinnb op k*
  - **bed** agg.; in: am-m k* *Nux-v* tritic-vg fd5.de vanil fd5.de
  - **chill**; during: ol-j
  - **dreaming**: mag-m
  - **falling** asleep: *Nux-m*
- **accompanied** by:
  - **coryza**: samb bat1•
  - **respiration**; difficult: cact mtf11
  - ○ **Lungs**; inflammation of (See Inflammation - lungs - accompanied - chest - oppression)
- **air**; in open:
  - **agg.**: am-m k2 carbn-s *Lyc* nux-v *Psor* seneg
  - **amel.**: anac chel *Nat-m* **Puls** k* sep
- **alternating** with:
  - **coryza** with discharge: samb bat1•
  - **eruptions**: calad k* kalm rhus-t
  - **palpitation** after eating: alum k*
  - **urticaria**: *Calad*
  - ○ **Back**; pain in: sil h2
  - **Face**; pain in (See FACE - Pain - alternating with - chest)
  - **Head**; pain in: glon k*
  - **Hypochondria**; pain in (See ABDOMEN - Pain - hypochondria - alternating with - chest)
- **anger**; after: dulc fd4.de *Staph*
- **anxious**: *Acon* b7a.de *Arn* b7a.de *Bry* b7a.de *Cina* b7a.de *Coloc* b7a.de *Ferr* b7a.de *Op* b7a.de *Puls* b7a.de *Rhus-t* b7a.de *Spig* b7a.de *Squil* b7a.de *Viol-o* b7a.de
- **arms** away from the body amel.; holding the: (↗*RESPIRATION - Difficult - lying - back - amel. - arms*) psor tl1
- **ascending**:
  - **agg.**: **Acon** k* agn k* apis **Ars** k* ars-s-f k2 bar-c borx c1 bufo cact **Calc** k* cann-i k* *Elaps* gran k* graph h2* grat k* lyc ol-an k* ran-b k* *Seneg* k* sulph tep a1 til vanil fd5.de
  - **hills** | **agg.**: ars tl1
- **bed** agg.; in: *Alum* k* am-c k* *Phos* k*
- **bending**:
  - **arms** | **backward** agg.: **Sulph** k*
  - **backward** | **amel.**: fl-ac *Sulph* nh6
  - **forward** | **amel.**: *Colch*
- **bending**: ...
  - **head**:
    - **forward** | **agg.**: **Alum** k*
- **breathing**:
  - **amel.**: op k* tab k*
  - **deep** | **agg.**: agn k* chel tl1 ham fd3.de• *Lyc* k* nat-ar k2 nept-m lsd2.fr plb rauw tpw8
  - **deep** and labored: cann-i c1*
- **chill**; during: **Apis** k* ars k* *Bry* cimx cina b7a.de daph *Eup-per* gels *Ip* *Kali-c* lach k* merl *Mez* k* nat-m *Puls* k* sep
- **clothing** agg.: **Ars** k* aur-m bov **Chel** k* **Lach** k* meli *Merc-c* mez h2 phos *Sep* tarent
- **cold air agg.** | **sitting** in cold air; after: *Petr*
- **conversation**, from: *Ambr* k*
- **coryza**; during: berb *Calc* *Carb-v* graph k* lyc h2 nat-c a1 *Puls* mrr1
- **cough**:
  - **after**: ars cocc
  - **desires** to cough to be relieved: am-c h2*
  - **during**:
    - **agg.**: (↗*COUGH - Oppression - chest*) am-c k* *Ant-t* b7a.de *Ars* k* ars-s-f k2 aur k* bapt calad b7a.de cocc k* con b4a.de* **Dros** k* graph b4a.de* grat bg2 *Ip* b7a.de *Kali-bi* k* kali-n b4.de* m-ambo b7.de *Nit-ac* **Phos** k* *Psor* k* puls b7a.de rhod b4a.de* rhus-t b7.de* *Seneg* *Sil* *Stann* **Sulph** k* tarent k* *Verat* k* zinc b4.de*
    - **amel.**: bit-ar wht1•
- **dancing** amel.: caust k*
- **delivery**; during: *Chinin-s*
- **dinner** | **after** | **agg.**: mag-m h2 *Phos* k* stram k*
  - **during** | **agg.**: *Mag-m* h2*
- **drawing** shoulders back amel.: **Calc** k*
- **drinking** agg.: cimx *Verat*
- **eating** | **after** | **agg.**: alum h2 aran ars ars-s-f k2 asaf k* calad k* *Caust* chin chinin-s chlol k* cinnb coloc k* con b4a.de* elaps hep b4a.de ip k* lyc k* *Mag-m* k* nat-c k* nat-s k* *Nux-v* k* petr b4a.de phos b4a.de ran-b *Rhus-t* ruta sars sil h2 stry k* *Sulph* k* thuj *Verat* viol-t k* *Zinc*
  - **amel.**: ambr k*
- **erect**; sitting (See sitting - erect - bent)
- **eructations** | **amel.**: *Am-m* k* **Carb-v** k* castm bg grat k* *Lach* **Lyc** k* *Phos* k*
- **exertion** agg.: nat-ar k2 pieri-b mlk9.de puls mrr1
  - **slight** exertion: laur mrr1 stann mrr1
- **expectoration** | **amel.**: *Asaf* calc *Manc* nit-ac k2
- **expiration**:
  - **amel.**: chir-fl gya2 staph k* tung-met bdx1•
  - **deep** | **amel.**: chir-fl gya2
  - **during** | **agg.**: am-c k* ambr hr1 anac h2 chel k* cina
- **explode**; as if heart will: *Acon* vh1
- **fever**:
  - **before**: **Ip** b7a.de
  - **during** | **agg.**: **Acon** b7.de* ambr bg2 *Anac* b4a.de* ant-t bg2 *Apis* k* arn bg2 ars k* aur bg2 bell bg2 **Bov** k* brom bg2 **Bry** b7a.de* cact *Calc* b4a.de* carb-v k* cham bg2 chin bg2 cimic cocc bg2 cupr bg2 dulc bg2 elaps graph bg2 guare a1 hep bg2 ign bg2 *Ip* k* **Kali-c** k* kali-n bg2 lach k* lyc bg2 *Merc* b4.de* mez bg2 *Nat-m* nux-v bg2 op bg2 phos bg2 plan plat bg2 puls k* ran-b bg2 rhod bg2 rhus-t bg2 **Ruta** bg2 samb bg2 seneg bg2 sep k* sil bg2 spig bg2 stann bg2 sulph bg2 thuj bg2 verat bg2 **Viol-t** b7a.de* zinc bg2
- **flatulence**:
  - **as** from: con h2 nat-c h2
    - **Upper** abdomen; in: cham h1
  - **from**: (↗*Constriction - flatulence*) phos h2
- **flatus**; passing | **amel.**: bry ol-an ph-ac h2
- **food** agg.; dry: bov bg1
- **hang** down; unless his legs: *Sul-ac*
- **headache**; during: sep h2
- **inspiration**:
  - **after**: zinc h2

- **agg.**: asc-t k* chir-fl gya2 cina crot-t k* ferr k* ferr-m galla-q-r nl2• graph h2* grat k* nat-ar *Phos* k* **Spig** k* tung-met bdx1• zinc h2
- **amel.**: acon k* *Chel* chin k* [tax jsj7]
- **deep** | **desire** for deep inspiration: carc hbh* ign hbh

- **jerking**: mez h2
- **laughing** agg.: plb
- **load**; as if a:
  - **accompanied** by | **respiration**; complaints of: cann-xyz bg2 ign bg2 rheum bg2 sabad bg2
- **lying**:
  - **agg.**: alum am-c ambr k1 asaf aur-ar k2 bar-c cact *Chin* *Colch* fl-ac *Graph* kali-p fd1.de• *Olnd* *Phos* positr nl2• *Puls* mrr1 sabad *Sep* *Spong* *Stann* thuj tritic-vg fd5.de vanil fd5.de
  - **amel.**: alum laur k2 *Nat-s* zinc
  - **back**; on | **agg.**: alum am-c chin
  - **head** low; with the | **agg.**: *Chin* **Spong** k*
  - **side**; on:
    - **affected** side | **agg.**: phel
    - **left** | **agg.**: both-ax tsm2 *Cact* corn *Lach* mrr1 naja phos mtf33 *Puls* tarent k2
    - **right** | **agg.**: kali-c
- **lying** down agg.: nat-m h2 tritic-vg fd5.de
- **menses**:
  - **appearance** of, on: phos k*
  - **before** | **agg.**: borx k* *Lach*
  - **during** | **agg.**: *Ign* b7a.de
- **motion**:
  - **agg.**: bapt carl led nat-m plb *Stann* sulph tarent
    - **rapid** motion: **Acon** k* **Ars** k* aur-ar k2 *Puls* k*
  - **amel.**: *Seneg* k*
  - **arm**; of | **agg.**: am-m
- **painful**: aids nl2• ambr b7a.de ham fd3.de• hist sp1 lat-m bnm6• nat-m h2 spong fd4.de
- **palpitations**; with: ambr h1 aspar vh **Aur** bg2 *Bry* bg2 calc bg2 chel ptk1 coca bro1 grat bg1 ham fd3.de• hyos h1 kali-n h2* phos h2 sep h2 spig h1* tritic-vg fd5.de [tax jsj7]
- **paroxysmal**: mur-ac h2 sep h2
- **perspiration**; during: acon bg2 **Ars** bg2 *Bell* bg2 **Bry** bg2 **Cham** bg2 ign bg2 **Ip** bg2 *Merc* bg2 *Nux-v* b7.de* op bg2 phos bg2 psor puls bg2 **Rhus-t** bg2 sabad bg2 samb bg2 sep k* **Sulph** bg2 thuj bg2 **Verat** bg2
- **pressure** of hand | **amel.**: sep
- **prolapse** of uterus: agar zr bell zr lil-t zr murx zr sep zr
- **raising** arms agg.: tarent k*
- **reclining**, when: fl-ac k*
- **respiration**: ars tl1 bit-ar wht1• chel dulc k* ferr k* glon tl1 kali-c kali-n kali-s fd4.de *Lyc* med tl1 sep tl1 *Sil* spong fd4.de squil tritic-vg fd5.de vanil fd5.de
  - **difficult**; with: *(↗RESPIRATION - Impeded - oppression - chest)* cic c1 ign mrr1 lac-ac stj5• nux-m tl1 positr nl2• spong fd4.de tritic-vg fd5.de vanil fd5.de
- **rising**:
  - **after** | **agg.**: am-m k*
  - **amel.**: nux-v olnd k*
  - **bed**; from:
    - **after**:
      - **walking** about; and | **amel.**: kali-bi
- **rising** in throat; as from: stann h2
- **room** full of people: lil-t ptk1
- **shivering**; during: puls b7.de
- **sitting**:
  - **agg.**: agar anac calad carb-an cham k* cic crot-h k* crot-t gins a1 indg a1 kali-c k* kali-n h2 laur k2 mang mez h2 *Nat-s* k* nat-sil fd3.de• phos h2 psor sabad k* staph k* vanil fd5.de
  - **amel.**: alum puls mrr1 vanil fd5.de
  - **bent** forward | **agg.**: alum coloc h2 dig
  - **erect** | **bent**; after sitting: nat-m k*
  - **motion**; after: acon k*
- **sitting** up in bed | **must** sit up: sulph h2
- **sleep**:
  - **before**: berb
  - **during**: all-s k* **Lach** k* lact nux-m positr nl2• psor al2 pyrog k2 ran-b b7.de
  - **falling** asleep | **when**: *Nux-m*
- **smoking** agg.: asc-t k* [tax jsj7]
- **sneezing** agg.: sil sulph
- **spasmodic**: cann-i k2
- **standing** agg.: mang olnd phel sep verat c1
- ○ **Lower** part of chest: am-m
- **stool** agg.; after: calc k* **Caust** k* sil k*
- **stooping** agg.: alum am-m cop mez h2 *Samb*
- **talking** agg.: ambr caust ptk1 **Dros** k* lach nat-m h2 spong fd4.de stram
  - **long** time; talking for a: *Chin*
- **thinking** of it agg.: gels ox-ac k2
- **turning** in bed agg.: *Calc*
- **vomiting** green amel.: *Cocc* k*
- **waking**; on: *Alum* ant-c k* *Ars* k* *Carb-v* k* chin *Cinnb* *Con* ham fd3.de• kali-bi **Kali-i** k* *Lach* k* *Lact* *Nat-s* k* *Nux-m* op phos k* sep tarent vanil fd5.de
- **walking**:
  - **after** | **agg.**: *Calc* k* nux-m **Phos** k*
  - **agg.**: agar h2 alum aml-ns **Ars** k* ars-s-f k2 aur-ar k2 bry bufo cact calc h2 carb-an k* chel k* clem k* colch k* dig digin a1 *Kali-c* lach led lipp a1 lyc mag-s k* mang naja olnd paeon ph-ac k* phos h2 puls ran-b k* seneg k* *Sep* k* sil k* staph sulph thuj verat h1
  - **air**; in open:
    - **agg.**: am-c am-m *Aur* k* calc h2 dulc fd4.de lact lyc h2 *Phos* k* spig h1 zinc h2
    - **amel.**: *Alum* anac *Lyc*
  - **amel.**: gins k* staph k*
  - **beginning** to walk: ph-ac h2
  - **cold** air; in | **agg.**: *Lyc* nux-m
  - **rapidly** | **agg.**: ang **Ars** k* ham fd3.de• lipp a1 meli ptk1 nat-m h2 nit-ac h2 *Puls* k* ruta *Spig* vanil fd5.de
- **warm** | **covers** | **amel.**: bit-ar wht1•
  - **room** | **agg.**: alum anac **Apis** k* ars-i k* nat-m puls mrr1
- **weather**:
  - **changes** to cold; when: **Ars** k* phos k2
  - **stormy** | **agg.**: **Ars** k*
  - **wet** | **agg.**: *Dulc* *Kali-c* nat-s
- **weight** on chest; as from a: abrom-a bnj1 bar-ox-suc rly4• cact br1 fuma-ac rly4• kali-p fd1.de• olib-sac wmh1 suprar rly4• tritic-vg fd5.de
- **wine** | **amel.**: acon k*
- **writing** agg.: alum k*
- **yawning**:
  - **agg.**: stann c1 sulph
  - **amel.**: croc k*
- ▽ **extending** to:
  - ○ **Scapula**:
    - **left** | **Under**: plut-n srj7•
- ○ **Axillary** gland: cupr b7.de*
- **Clavicles**: plut-n srj7•
  - **left**: ephe-si hsj1•
  - ○ **Below**: ephe-si hsj1•
- **Diaphragm**, in region of: *Agar*
- **Heart**: abel vh1 abies-n vh1 *Acon* k* adam skp7*• *Agar* k* am-c k* *Ambr* k* *Aml-ns* k* anac ant-t k* *Apis* aran-ix sp1 **Ars** k* *Ars-i* arund **Aur** k* aur-ar k2 aur-i k2 **Aur-m** bapt bell k* brass-n-o srj5• *Brom* k* bry bufo k* **Cact** k* *Calc-ar* calc-f sp1 cann-i cann-s k* *Carb-v* card-m *Caust* k* cham k* *Chin* chlor cimic clem coff bg2 colch k* coll croc k* cupr *Dig* k* dioxi rbp6 eup-per k* fago falco-pe nl2• galla-q-r nl2• *Gels* *Glon* k* graph hell k* helo hyos ignis-alc es2• *Iod* **Ip** k* kali-ar kali-bi bg2 *Kali-c* kali-i kalm lac-h htj1• *Lach* *Laur* *Lil-t* k* *Lycps-v* k* mag-m k* mand sp1 med *Merc* merc-c merc-i-r bg2 mez k* mosch bg2* *Naja* *Nat-ar* nat-c *Nat-s* nat-sil fd3.de• *Nux-m* *Nux-v* k* ol-j olib-sac wmh1 op k* ovi-p c2 ox-ac ozone sde2• *Phos* k* plb podo fd3.de•

- **Heart**: ...
Prim-vl c1 **Puls** k* pyrog k2 ran-b k2 saroth sp1 sarr scop ptk1 sil h2* sin-n **Spig** k* spong k2 stict stram sumb *Tab Tarent* ter thuj trios rsj11• tritic-vg fd5.de tub bg* viol-t k* vip zinc bg2
  - **morning**: graph h2 kalm nat-s ozone sde2• *Tarent*
  - **afternoon**: bapt nat-sil fd3.de• tritic-vg fd5.de
  - **evening**: brom bufo cact kalm **Puls** ran-b k2 ulm-c jsj8•
  - **night**: *Aur* colch kali-c olib-sac wmh1
  - **accompanied** by | **sleep**; desire for: ulm-c jsj8•
  - **ascending** stairs agg.: **Aur Aur-m**
  - **breathing** deep agg.: aur-m nat-ar rumx
  - **drawn** downwards: thuj k*
  - **eating**; after: bufo
  - **exertion**, on least: *Brom Laur Nat-ar*
  - **inspiration** agg.: ulm-c jsj8•
  - **lying**:
    - **abdomen**; on | **amel**.: ulm-c jsj8•
    - **agg**.: aran-ix sp1
    - **amel**.: *Laur Psor*
    - **head** low; with the | **agg**.: colch **Spong**
    - **side**; on:
      - **left** | **agg**.: *Colch Lach Naja* **Spig** trios rsj11•
  - **melancholy**: aur caust
  - **motion** agg.: bufo coll eup-per
  - **obstruction**; as if from: cot br1
  - **pressure** | **amel**.: ulm-c jsj8•
  - **rest** agg.: olib-sac wmh1
  - **sitting** agg.: agar **Nat-s**
  - **standing** agg.: prun
  - **thinking** of it agg.: *Gels*
  - **walking** | **amel**.: colch k*
  - **warm** room agg.: ars-i k2
  - ▽ **extending** to | **Throat**: nux-m c1
- **Lower** part: kreos bg2 nept-m lsd2.fr puls h1* rhus-t bg2
- **Mammae**: allox tpw4 bry bg2* calc bg2 chin ptk1 clem bg2 hyos bg2 *Iod* bg2* lac-c bg2* lil-t bg2 petr-ra shn4• phyt bg2* plut-n srj7• thuj bg2 tritic-vg fd5.de [tax jsj7]
- **Precordial** region: prot jl2 v-a-b jl2 vac jl2
- **Sides**: arg-met bg2 asaf aur bg2 carb-v bg2 caust chin bg2 con bg2 mag-s *Ox-ac* par bg2 plb bg2 sul-ac bg2
  - **right**: acon aloe bg2 *Bry* euph mag-s mur-ac *Ox-ac* psor jl2 staph h1
    - **Upper**: con h2
  - **left**: am-m h2 arg-met h1 both-ax tsm2 calc crot-t graph h2 ham fd3.de• kali-s fd4.de lil-t bg2 samb seneg thuj h1
  - **evening** | **lying** agg.: calc
- **Sternum**: arg-met bg2 arg-n ars h2* asaf bg2 aur k2 bell bg2 brass-n-o srj5• bry k* calc cina ptk1 con bg2 cypra-eg sde6.de• kali-p fd1.de• kali-s fd4.de melal-alt gya4 merc bg2 olib-sac wmh1 *Phos* ran-s rhus-t *Sep* bg2 *Sulph* bg2 tab bg2
  - **night**: am-c
  - **eating**; after: con lac-ac
  - ○ **Behind**: chlam-tr bcx2• ph-ac h2 samb h1 symph fd3.de• zinc h2
    - **rubbing** | **amel**.: chlam-tr bcx2•
    - **sitting** erect | **amel**.: chlam-tr bcx2•
  - **Under**: aur ptk1
    - **ascending** agg.: aur ptk1
- **Upper** part: hyos h1 vanil fd5.de

ORGASM of blood: *(↗Heat - flushes)* acon k* alum k* alum-sil k2 **Aml-ns** k* anac *Ars* b4a.de aur k* aur-s k2 bov calc-ar k2 carb-an k2 *Carb-v* k* chel chlor cocc b7a.de* colch dig bg2 elaps *Ferr* **Glon** k* indg iod k* *Kali-n* bg2* **Lach** lachn *Lil-t* mag-m *Merc* merl *Mill* k* nat-m *Nit-ac Nux-v* b7.de* ol-an ph-ac **Phos** k* phyt plat b4.de* plb b7.de* rhod k* *Seneg* k* **Sep** k* sil spig bg2 spong b7.de* **Sulph** k* *Thuj* k*
- **left**: sep h2
- **morning**: nux-v sep h2

Orgasm: ...
- **evening**: carb-v caust tl1 kali-c
- **anticipation**; from: phos k2
- **excitement** agg.: phos k2
- **exertion**, least: **Spong**
- **flatus**; from obstructed: carb-v h2
- **menses**; during: *Merl*
- **motion** agg.: *Spong*
- **worries**; from: phos k2
- ○ **Heart**; region of: carb-v b4.de* cham bg2 nux-v b7.de* sulph b4.de*

OVERLIFTING agg.: *Rhus-t* b7.de* *Sulph* b4a.de

PAIN: *Abies-n* ↓ abrot bro1 acal br1* *Acet-ac Acon* k* acon-ac ↓ adon ↓ *Aesc* aeth ↓ *Agar* agath-a nl2• agn a1 aids nl2• ail all-c all-s ↓ allox ↓ aloe ↓ alum k* alum-p ↓ alum-sil ↓ alumn am-br ↓ **Am-c** k* am-m k* ambr **Aml-ns** ampe-qu ↓ *Anac* ↓ anag ↓ anan ↓ *Ang* ↓ anh ↓ **Ant-c** *Ant-t* ap-g ↓ **Apis** k* apoc ↓ aq-mar ↓ aral ↓ *Arg-met Arg-n* k* arge-pl rwt5• **Arn** k* **Ars** k* ars-h ↓ ars-i ars-s-f ↓ arum-t *Asaf* ↓ *Asar* ↓ asc-t aspar ↓ *Aster* ↓ **Aur** aur-ar k2 aur-i k2 **Aur-m** aur-s k2 bacls-7 pte1*• *Bad* ↓ *Bamb-a* stb2.de• bapt bar-c k* bar-i k2 *Bar-m* bar-s ↓ **Bell** k* bell-p ↓ bell-p-sp ↓ benz-ac ↓ berb ↓ beryl ↓ *Bism Borx* k* both fne1• *Bov* ↓ brass-n-o srj5• brom k* bros-gau mrc1 **Bry** k* bufo ↓ **Cact** k* cadm-met sp1 *Cadm-s* cain calad ↓ **Calc** k* calc-ar mrr1 calc-i ↓ **Calc-p Calc-s** calc-sil ↓ camph cann-i cann-s *Canth Caps* k* carb-ac ↓ *Carb-an* k* *Carb-v* k* carbn-h ↓ carbn-s *Card-m* cardios-h rly4• cartl-s rly4• cassia-s ↓ castm castor-eq ↓ caul bro1 **Caust** k* cedr ↓ cench k2 *Cham* k* *Chel* k* chin k* chinin-ar chinin-s chir-fl gya2 chlor chlorpr pin1• *Cic* ↓ *Cimic* k* *Cimx* ↓ cina b7.de* cinnb ↓ *Cist* cit-ac ↓ *Clem* ↓ cob-n ↓ *Coc-c* ↓ *Cocc* ↓ *Coff* ↓ colch coli ↓ coll bro1 coloc k* com k* con k* *Cop* ↓ cor-r ↓ corn corn-f br1 cot ↓ croc b7.de* *Crot-c* k* crot-h crot-t k* cub ↓ *Cupr* cupr-ar cupr-s ↓ *Cur* ↓ cycl ↓ cystein-l rly4• dendr-pol sk4• *Dig* k* digin ↓ *Dios* ↓ dor ↓ dream-p ↓ *Dros* b7a.de *Dulc* k* dys fmm1• echi elaps bro1 elat ↓ ephe-si ↓ erio bro1 euon *Eup-per* ↓ *Euph* ↓ euphr ↓ eupi ↓ falco-pe ↓ *Ferr* k* *Ferr-ar* ferr-i ↓ ferr-m ↓ ferr-p fic-m ↓ fl-ac flor-p ↓ form ↓ fum ↓ fuma-ac rly4• gad bro1 galeoc-c-h gms1• gamb ↓ gels ger-i rly4• glon ↓ gnaph ↓ gran *Graph* k* grat ↓ guaj gymno ↓ haem ↓ *Ham* ↓ *Hecla* hed ↓ *Hell* ↓ helo ↓ *Hep* heroin ↓ hippoc-k szs2 hir skp7• hist ↓ hura *Hydr* hydr-ac k* hydrog ↓ *Hydroph* ↓ *Hyos* ↓ hyper ↓ ictod k* *Ign* ↓ indg ↓ inul ↓ *Iod* k* *Ip* ↓ irid-met ↓ iris ↓ jab jac-c jac-g *Jug-c* c2* jug-r ↓ kali-ar kali-bi k* kali-br ↓ *Kali-c* k* kali-chl *Kali-i* kali-m k2 kali-n k* kali-p kali-s kali-sil ↓ *Kalm* ketogl-ac ↓ kola ↓ kreos k* lac-ac ↓ lac-c ↓ lac-d k2 lac-h ↓ lac-loxod-a ↓ *Lach* lachn *Lact* lat-m bnm6• *Laur* k* *Led* b7a.de *Lil-t* ↓ lith-c ↓ *Lob Lob-c* ↓ loxo-recl ↓ luf-op rsj5• *Lyc* k* lycpr bro1 lyss ↓ m-ambo ↓ m-arct ↓ *M-aust* ↓ *Mag-c* ↓ *Mag-m* ↓ *Mag-p* mag-s maias-l hrn2• manc ↓ mand ↓ *Mang* ↓ mang-act ↓ mang-p ↓ marb-w ↓ med k2* melal-alt ↓ meli mentho ↓ *Meny* ↓ meph ↓ *Merc* **Merc-c** ↓ merc-i-f merc-i-r *Merc-sul* ↓ merl ↓ *Mez Mill* ↓ moni ↓ morg-g pte1*• morph bro1 mosch b7.de* *Mur-ac* k* murx ↓ musca-d ↓ myos-a ↓ myric ↓ *Myrt-c* k* nad ↓ *Naja* nat-ar *Nat-c* ↓ nat-m *Nat-n* ↓ nat-p nat-pyru rly4• *Nat-s* ↓ nat-sil ↓ nept-m ↓ *Nicc* ↓ nit-ac k* *Nux-m* k* *Nux-v* ol-an ol-j olib-sac ↓ olnd ↓ op **Ox-ac** k* oxal-a ↓ ozone ↓ paeon pall ↓ par ↓ pert-vc ↓ petr k2 petr-ra ↓ *Ph-ac* phase ↓ phel ↓ **Phos** k* *Phos-pchl* ↓ *Phyt Pieri-b* ↓ pitu-gl skp7• plac-s ↓ plan *Plat* ↓ plb podo polyg-h ↓ positr nl2• pot-e rly4• prim-v ↓ propl ↓ propr ↓ prot pte1*• prun-p ↓ psil ↓ *Psor* k* ptel ↓ *Puls* k* pycnop-sa ↓ pyrog ↓ **Ran-b** k* *Ran-s* raph rat ↓ rauw ↓ rheum ↓ rhod k* rhus-r ↓ rhus-t *Rhus-v* ↓ ribo rly4• *Rumx* k* ruta b7.de* sabad k* sabin ↓ sal-fr ↓ *Samb* ↓ *Sang* k* sangin-n br1 sanic ↓ saroth ↓ *Sars* scroph-n ↓ sec sel b7.de* **Seneg** k* *Sep* k* *Sil* k* sin-n sol-t-ae ↓ sphing a1 **Spig** k* **Spong** k* *Squil* **Stann** k* *Staph* ↓ stict bro1 still ↓ *Stram Stront-c* ↓ stroph-s ↓ stry ↓ stry-p bro1 succ bro1 succ-ac br1 suis-em ↓ suis-hep ↓ suis-pan rly4• sul-ac sul-i ↓ sulfa sp1 *Sulph* k* sumb suprar ↓ symph ↓ syph ↓ *Tab* taosc iwa1• tarax ↓ *Tarent* k* tell ↓ tep *Ter* ↓ tetox pin2• teucr ↓ *Ther Thuj* ↓ tril-p ↓ *Trios* rsj11• tritic-vg fd5.de tub k* tub-m vn* valer k2 vanil fd5.de *Verat* k* *Verat-v* ↓ verb k* vero-o ↓ vinc viol-o ↓ viol-t ↓ vip visc wye ↓ x-ray ↓ xan ↓ *Zinc* k* zinc-m ↓ zinc-p k2 zinc-s zing ↓ ziz [*Buteo-j* sej6 spect dfg1]
- **right**: x-ray ↓
  - **wandering** pain: x-ray sp1
- **morning**: acon alum ↓ am-c ↓ am-m ang ↓ arn ↓ bamb-a ↓ borx ↓ bov *Bry* calad ↓ carb-v h2 cassia-s ↓ caust chel chin con corn ↓ crot-h ↓ dulc ↓ ferr-p gal-ac ↓ hep *Kali-bi* ↓ kali-c h2 kali-n ↓ lac-h ↓ lyc mang melal-alt gya4 merc merc-c mur-ac ↓ nat-ar ↓ nat-c ↓ nat-s nit-ac ox-ac ozone ↓ phos pitu-gl skp7• puls *Ran-b* rhus-t ruta fd4.de *Sang* sars ↓ seneg ↓ sep spong fd4.de *Squil* staph ↓ sulph thuj tritic-vg fd5.de vanil fd5.de zinc ↓
  - **8 h**: naja ↓ pitu-gl skp7•

- **8** h: ...
  - **aching**: naja
  - **Anterior** part: naja ↓
    - **aching**: naja
- **aching**: melal-alt gya4 sulph k*
- **beaten**; as if: ozone sde2•
- **bed** agg.; in: colch lact mag-s phel rhus-t ↓ *Rumx* seneg sil spong fd4.de sulph ↓ tritic-vg fd5.de
  - **aching**: lact k*
  - **drawing** pain: lact
  - **pressing** pain: mag-s phel rhus-t seneg sil h2 sulph k*
- **burning**: bamb-a stb2.de• caust k* kali-n h2 ruta fd4.de spong fd4.de tritic-vg fd5.de zinc k*
- **cutting** pain: caust k* **Kali-c** k* tritic-vg fd5.de
- **drawing** pain: dulc fd4.de nat-c h2 spong fd4.de tritic-vg fd5.de vanil fd5.de
- **eating**; after: sulph ↓
  - **aching**: sulph
  - **sore**: sulph
- **motion** agg.: kali-c ↓
  - **cutting** pain: kali-c
- **pressing** pain: *Ran-b* k* ruta fd4.de sars h2 spong fd4.de sulph k* tritic-vg fd5.de vanil fd5.de
- **raw**; as if: borx caust k* nat-c k*
- **rising** | **after**:
  - **agg.**: lact ↓
    - **drawing** pain: lact
  - **agg.**: ran-b ↓
    - **stitching** pain: ran-b
- **sore**: alum h2 am-c h2 ang h1 arn br1 bamb-a stb2.de• calad cassia-s ccrh1• corn crot-h gal-ac a1 mur-ac nat-ar ozone sde2• seneg staph k* thuj
- **stitching** pain: chin k* hep *Kali-bi* lac-h htj1• mang k* merc k* rhus-t spong fd4.de *Squil* vanil fd5.de
- **waking**; on: ant-c ↓ cupr ↓ ozone ↓ petr-ra shn4• *Seneg* ↓ sulph ↓ tritic-vg ↓
  - **aching**: *Seneg* k*
  - **beaten**; as if: ozone sde2•
  - **pressing** pain: ant-c h2 cupr h2 tritic-vg fd5.de
  - **raw**; as if: sulph k*
  - **sore**: ozone sde2•

- **forenoon**: agar alum ↓ am-m bros-gau mrc1 *Bry* ↓ caust cham coloc dulc ↓ **kali-s** ↓ mag-s ↓ malar ↓ mang ↓ nit-ac ↓ puls puls-n ↓ *Ran-b* ruta fd4.de stann ↓ tritic-vg fd5.de vanil fd5.de
  - **9** h: chel
  - **10** h: cham kali-cy
    - **10**-11.30 h: hir skp7•
  - **10**-11 h: aesc ↓
    - **cramping**: aesc
  - **11** h: cact k2 cham lac-lup hrn2•
  - **aching**: (non:puls slp) puls-n slp
  - **burning**: mag-s k* malar jl2 vanil fd5.de
  - **pressing** pain: alum h2 dulc fd4.de
  - **sore**: alum *Bry*
  - **stitching** pain: caust k* kali-s fd4.de mang h2 nit-ac h2 stann h2 tritic-vg fd5.de
- **noon**: agar ↓ dig naja
  - **12**-13 h: pitu-gl skp7•
  - **stitching** pain: agar
  - **walking** agg.: bry ↓
    - **aching**: bry k*
- **afternoon**: alum ↓ am-m bad bar-c canth chel coloc dulc fd4.de eupi fago gamb ham ↓ iod kali-bi kali-n kali-s fd4.de led lyc nicc op sang spong fd4.de sulph tarent tritic-vg fd5.de vanil fd5.de
  - **13** h: sars

- **afternoon**: ...
  - **14** h: alum chel elaps rhus-t
    - **stitching** pain: chel
  - **15** h: dendr-pol sk4• hura nat-m ol-an
  - **16** h: aq-mar skp7• asc-t
    - **16**-17 h | **right** side: merc-sul
  - **16**.10 h: aq-mar skp7•
  - **17** h: hyper ↓
    - **17**-19 h: luf-op rsj5•
    - **burning**: hyper
  - **18** h lasting all evening: phos
  - **aching**: kali-n k*
  - **cutting** pain: bad
  - **drawing** pain: chel dulc fd4.de tritic-vg fd5.de vanil fd5.de
  - **griping** pain: sulph
  - **inspiration** agg.; deep: sang ↓
    - **tearing** pain: sang
  - **sore**: alum h2 nicc
  - **speaking**; after: lyc ↓
    - **raw**; as if: lyc
  - **stitching** pain: alum h2 coloc k* dulc fd4.de ham fd3.de• iod k* spong fd4.de sulph vanil fd5.de
  - **walking** agg.: sulph ↓
    - **griping** pain: sulph
  - **yawning** agg.: sang ↓
    - **tearing** pain: sang k*
- **evening**: acon agath-a nl2• alum ambr ant-t *Ars* ↓ bad bar-c bar-s k2 cain calad calc cassia-s ↓ chel coc-c ↓ coloc dig dios dulc fd4.de euphr gal-ac a1 gamb graph ↓ hyper kali-bi **Kali-c** kali-i kali-n kali-s ↓ kreos ↓ lyc lyss ↓ *Mag-c* ↓ mez mur-ac murx ↓ nat-c ↓ nat-m ↓ nicc nux-m ol-an ↓ olnd *Phos* *Ran-b* ran-s rumx ruta fd4.de seneg spig ↓ spong fd4.de sulph tab tetox pin2• thuj tritic-vg fd5.de vanil ↓ verat ↓ verb zinc zinc-p k2
  - **18** h: bry hir rsj4• puls ↓
    - **burning**: puls
    - **retiring**; lasting until: phos
    - **stitching** pain: bry
  - **19** h: ol-j zing
    - **drawing** pain: zing
  - **19**.30-22 h: adam skp7•
  - **20** h: am-m ↓ canth kali-n
    - **raw**; as if: am-m
    - **stitching** pain: canth
  - **21** h: lyss
  - **aching**: coloc k* nux-m k* ran-b k* sulph k*
  - **bed** agg.; in: agath-a nl2• bell ↓ benz-ac cain con ↓ *Kali-c* nat-c nat-p ↓ nit-ac ran-b sep
    - **burning**: bell k* nat-p k*
    - **drawing** pain: cain con h2
    - **pressing** pain: sep k*
    - **stitching** pain: benz-ac k* nat-c k*
    - **tearing** pain: con h2
  - **boring** pain: alum k*
  - **breathing** deep agg.: ran-b ↓
    - **aching**: ran-b
  - **burning**: kali-n h2 kreos k* murx k* vanil fd5.de verat k* zinc k*
  - **cramping**: phos h2 spong fd4.de
  - **cutting** pain: agath-a nl2• bad cain **Kali-c** k* kali-i k* kali-n h2 *Mag-c* nicc k* ol-an k*
  - **drawing** pain: dulc fd4.de nat-c h2 spong fd4.de tritic-vg fd5.de
  - **lying** down agg.; after: **Kali-c** ↓
    - **cutting** pain: **Kali-c** k*
  - **lying** on left side agg.: cain ↓
    - **drawing** pain: cain

- pressing pain: dulc fd4.de graph h2 lyc h2 nat-m h2 *Ran-b* ruta fd4.de spig h1 spong fd4.de tritic-vg fd5.de
- **raw**; as if: *Ars* calc k* murx k* nat-c h2*
- **riding** agg.: phos↓
  - **cramping**: phos
- **sore**: cassia-s ccrh1• coc-c dig *Kali-i* lyss mur-ac murx nat-m ran-b
- **stitching** pain: agath-a nl2• calad k* dulc fd4.de kali-bi k* *Kali-i* kali-n k* kali-s fd4.de *Mag-c* ran-s rumx ruta fd4.de spong fd4.de tritic-vg fd5.de vanil fd5.de verb
- **tearing** pain: ambr kali-n h2
- **warm** room agg.: sulph↓
  - **cramping**: sulph

- **night**: agath-a nl2• **Alum** alum-p k2 alum-sil k2 am-c ant-t apis aq-mar rbp6 arg-n **Ars** asaf↓ bamb-a↓ borx h2 *Caust* cench↓ chel con graph *Ip*↓ kali-c↓ kali-p↓ kali-s fd4.de *Lach*↓ *Lyc* mag-s melal-alt↓ *Merc*↓ merc-c nit-ac *Nux-v* pant-ac↓ ph-ac↓ phos↓ ran-b ran-s rhus-t ruta fd4.de sabad sars↓ seneg sep↓ sil sin-n spong fd4.de *Syph*↓ tritic-vg fd5.de tub↓ vanil fd5.de zinc↓
  - **midnight**:
    - **before**:
      - **22.30 h**: cench k2
      - **23 h**: cact k2
    - **after**: rhus-t
      - **1.30 h**: nat-ar↓ sep↓
        - **cramping**: nat-ar sep h2
      - **2 h**: lachn hr1
      - **4 h**: asc-t
      - **5 h**: ars-s-f↓
        - **cough**; with: kali-c↓
          - **cramping**: kali-c
        - **cutting** pain: ars-s-f k2
    - **morning**; till: *Ars*↓
      - **burning**: *Ars*
  - **aching**: melal-alt gya4 ran-b k*
  - **air**; going into open: am-m
  - **bed** agg.; in: phos↓
    - **stitching** pain: phos k*
  - **bending** to right agg.: rhod↓
    - **cutting** pain: rhod
  - **boring** pain: sil
  - **burning**: bamb-a stb2.de• *Lach* k* vanil fd5.de
  - **bursting** pain: asaf *Merc*
  - **cough** agg.; during: *Calc*↓
    - **raw**; as if: (non:alum a4) *Calc* k* (non:carb-v a4) (non:nit-ac a4) (non:nux-v a4)
  - **cramping**: alum h2 kali-c h2 lyc h2 nit-ac h2 phos h2 sep a1
  - **cutting** pain: agath-a nl2• pant-ac rly4• *Syph*
  - **digging** pain: graph h2
  - **drawing** pain: cench k2
  - **lying**:
    - **agg.**: calc bro1 sep bro1
    - **back**; on:
      - **agg.**: alum↓ chin↓
        - **pressing** pain: alum k* chin h1
  - **pressing** pain: **Alum** chel kali-p fd1.de• mag-s k* ph-ac h2 sars h2 seneg spong fd4.de tritic-vg fd5.de vanil fd5.de
  - **raw**; as if: zinc k*
  - **sleep**; on going to: *Nux-m*↓
    - **pressing** pain: *Nux-m*
  - **sleep**; when falling asleep: *Nux-m*
  - **sore**: borx a1
  - **stitching** pain: agath-a nl2• alum am-c *Apis* bamb-a stb2.de• *Ip* *Lyc* k* merc-c nit-ac phos k* ran-s *Rhus-t* k* ruta fd4.de sabad k* seneg k* tub gk vanil fd5.de
  - **tearing** pain: am-c h2 nit-ac k* sil

- **night**: ...
  - **waking**; on: *Seneg*↓
    - **aching**: *Seneg*
    - **stitching** pain: seneg
- **accompanied** by:
  - **anxiety** (See MIND - Anxiety - chest - pain)
  - **coryza**: hydrog srj2•
  - **nausea**: merc bg2 mosch bg2
  - **respiration**:
    - **complaints**: **Acon** bg2 agn bg2 am-c bg2 ant-c bg2 arg-met bg2 asar bg2 bar-c bg2 *Bell* bg2 borx bg2 **Bry** bg2 *Calc* bg2 *Cann-xyz* bg2 caps bg2 carb-an bg2 *Carb-v* bg2 caust bg2 *Chin* bg2 clem bg2 colch bg2 dulc bg2 graph bg2 hep bg2 iod bg2 kali-bi bg2 kali-c bg2 kali-n bg2 kreos bg2 lach bg2 led bg2 lyc bg2 meph bg2 merc bg2 mez bg2 mur-ac bg2 nat-c bg2 nat-m bg2 *Nit-ac* bg2 nux-v bg2 olnd bg2 plat bg2 plb bg2 puls bg2 rhus-t bg2 *Sabad* bg2 sabin bg2 *Sep* bg2 spig bg2 **Squil** bg2 stann bg2 **Sulph** bg2 valer bg2
    - **difficult**: ant-t tl1 helo-s bnm14• kreos tl1 phos tl1 psor tl1*
  - **weakness**: nept-m lsd2.fr
  - ○ **Abdomen**; complaints of: bell bg2 caps bg2 carb-v bg2 lach bg2 lyc bg2 nux-v bg2 phos bg2 plb bg2 sulph bg2
  - **Head**; complaints of (See HEAD - Complaints - accompanied - chest)
  - **Spine**; irritation of: agar bro1 ran-b bro1
  - **Stomach**; pain in: *Arn* bg2 lyc bg2 nux-v bg2 *Sulph* bg2
- **aching**: acon k* agar k* *Ail* alum k* alum-p k2 ambr hr1 ant-c k* arg-n *Arn* k* *Asaf* k* bapt *Bell* k* borx *Bry* k* cact k* *Calc-p* k* cann-i k* cann-s k* carb-ac *Carb-an* k* *Carb-v* carbn-s cham k* chel k* chin k* *Clem* *Coc-c* k* colch k* crot-t k* cupr-s k* cycl k* cystein-l rly4• dig k* flor-p rsj3• hydr-ac k* iod k* kreos k* lach k* *Lact* k* lat-m bnm6• led k* *Lyc* k* mag-m k* melal-alt gya4 merc k* merc-c k* musca-d szs1 naja nat-m k* nat-p k* nat-pyru rly4• *Phos* *Phyt* plac-s rly4• psor k* *Ran-b* k* rauw sp1 rhod k* rhus-t k* ribo rly4• *Rumx* sang k* *Seneg* k* sep k* stict stram k* stront-c stroph-s sp1 sul-i k2 sulph k* tarent k* zinc k* zinc-p k2
- **air**; in open:
  - **agg.**: caust↓ iod↓ mez↓ spig↓ sulph↓
    - **cramping**: iod mez bg1 sulph bg1
    - **pressing** pain: caust h2
    - **sore**: spig
    - **tearing** pain: caust
  - **amel.**: anac bro1 nat-m puls bro1 sang hr1 sul-ac↓
    - **pressing** pain: sul-ac h2
    - **stitching** pain: sul-ac h2
- **alternating** with:
  - **complaints**; other: *Ran-b* b7a.de
  - **rheumatism**: abrot k2
  - ○ **Abdomen**; pain in: aesc hir skp7• rad-br c11 *Ran-b*
    - **cramping** (See ABDOMEN - Pain - cramping - alternating - chest)
    - **stitching** pain: ran-b c1
  - **Stomach**; pain in: *Caust*
- **anger**; after: arg-n k2 caust↓
  - **stitching** pain: arg-n caust
- **anticipation**; from: stroph-s sp1
- **anxiety**; with: thuj↓
  - **aching**: thuj a1
- **appearing** suddenly:
  - **disappearing** suddenly; and: hir skp7• pert-vc↓
    - **stitching** pain: pert-vc vk9
- **arms** near chest:
  - **agg.**: psor spig bg sulph bg
  - **amel.**: lac-ac
- **ascending**:
  - **agg.**: acon arg-n↓ ars bro1 borx cact crot-h k* graph kali-bi ran-b rat sep bro1 staph stram
    - **aching**: cact k*

• **agg.**: ...
⁝ **bursting** pain: arg-n
• **stairs**:
⁝ **agg.**: borx↓ rat↓ ruta↓ stram↓
: **stitching** pain: borx rat ruta h1 stram
- **autumn**: *Kali-c*↓
• **stitching** pain: *Kali-c*
- **bed** agg.; in: allox↓ iod↓
• **sore**: iod h
• **sticking** pain: allox sp1
- **bending**:
• **amel.**: chinin-s↓
⁝ **cutting** pain: chinin-s
• **backward**:
⁝ **agg.**: mez h2 rhod
⁝ **must** bend backward or forward: agar↓ cassia-s↓
: **stitching** pain: agar cassia-s ccrh1•
• **forward**:
⁝ **agg.**: aloe alum alumn arg-met borx h2 brom cardios-h rly4• lact bg1 mang↓ nat-m seneg↓ spong fd4.de stann h2 stroph-s↓ sulph bro1 [lach xyz62]
: **cutting** pain: arg-met
: **gnawing** pain: stroph-s sp1
: **sore**: mang seneg
⁝ **amel.**: *Asc-t* k* cassia-s↓ chel chin↓ chinin-s hyos bro1 mag-c h2 **Puls**
: **stitching** pain: cassia-s ccrh1• *Chel* chin
• **head**:
⁝ **forward**:
: **agg.**: alum↓ psor↓
. **pressing** pain: alum psor al2
• **must** bend: sars↓
⁝ **stitching** pain: sars
• **right**; to | **agg.**: rhod
• **side**; to:
⁝ **agg.**: acon borx h2
⁝ **must** bend to side: acon↓
: **stitching** pain: acon
- **biting** pain: kali-c h2
- **blow**; pain as from a: borx h2 cadm-s bg2 cann-s b7.de* chin b7.de* cic b7.de* hep bg2 lyc bg2 nux-m b7.de* nux-v bg2 sep bg2 sulph bg2
- **blowing** the nose agg.: chel sumb↓
• **cramping**: sumb
- **boring** pain: acon b7.de* alum k* asaf b7.de* *Bism* k* *Brom* cina k* cupr *Ferr* indg kali-c k* lob k* mag-m h2 med meny b7.de* *Mur-ac* k* ph-ac k* psor k* rhus-t k* ruta fd4.de *Seneg* k* sil spig b7.de* staph b7.de* tarax k* thuj k* [*Buteo-j* sej6]
• **drawing** pain: colch k*
• **paroxysmal**: plb
- **breathing**:
• **agg.**: arg-met↓ ars-s-f↓ bapt↓ cob-n↓ *Colch*↓ kali-c↓ mur-ac↓ raph↓
⁝ **boring** pain | **tensive**: mur-ac k*
⁝ **burning**: kali-c
⁝ **cutting** pain: arg-met ars-s-f k2 bapt *Colch* raph
⁝ **sticking** pain: cob-n sp1
• **deep**:
⁝ **agg.**: acon aesc aeth↓ agar↓ *All-c*↓ aloe ant-c↓ arg-met arn asar↓ aur↓ bapt bar-c benz-ac *Berb* *Borx* k* bov↓ brom↓ **Bry** k* *Calc* *Calc-p* calc-sil k2* caps↓ carb-an carb-v carbn-s↓ card-m↓ *Caust* k* cench k2 *Cham*↓ chel cob crot-t *Cupr*↓ cycl dros↓ dulc fd4.de ferr-p k2 fl-ac flor-p↓ form graph *Guaj* hell iod h irid-met↓ *Kali-bi* **Kali-c** k* *Kali-n* kali-sil k2 lyc mang↓ merc↓ merc-c mez mur-ac naja **Nat-m** k* nat-p nat-pyru↓ nat-s↓ nit-ac nux-v↓ olnd pall ph-ac *Phos* k* phyt plat plut-n srj7• puls **Ran-b** k* ran-s raph rhus-t rumx ruta fd4.de sabin↓

- **breathing – deep – agg.**: ...
Sang k* seneg sep↓ sil *Spong* *Stann* stroph-s↓ *Sulph*↓ sumb tax↓ thuj valer vanil↓ visc c1 zinc zinc-p k2 zing
: **aching**: flor-p rsj3•
: **cramping**: stroph-s sp1
: **pressing** pain: caps h1 sep h2 vanil fd5.de
: **sprained**; as if: agar *Arn*
: **stitching** pain: *Acon* k* aesc aeth *All-c* ant-c h2 arg-met arn asar h1 aur bapt benz-ac k* *Berb* **Borx** k* bov brom **Bry** k* *Calc* *Calc-p* carbn-s card-m *Caust* k* *Cham* chel *Cupr* dros h1 dulc fd4.de ferr-p *Guaj* hell k* irid-met srj5• **Kali-c** k* *Kali-n* k* mang h2 merc sne merc-c mez *Mur-ac* **Nat-m** k* nat-pyru rly4• nat-s k2 nit-ac nux-v olnd pall *Phos* k* *Puls* k* *Ran-b* raph k* *Rhus-t* *Rumx* ruta fd4.de sabin c1 sep sil h2 *Spong* *Sulph* k* valer zinc k* zinc-p k2 [tax jsj7]
: **Heart**: berb↓ borx↓ *Iod*↓ *Spig*↓
. **sprained**; as if: berb hr1 borx hr1 *Iod* hr1 *Spig* hr1
⁝ **amel.**: ign kali-bi bg1 seneg vanil fd5.de verb
• **holding** breath:
⁝ **agg.**: merc↓
: **aching**: merc k*
- **bruised** (See sore)
- **burning**: acet-ac k* *Acon* k* aesc agar k* ail alum k* alum-p k2 alum-sil k2 am-c k* am-m k* ambr k* anan ant-c k* *Ant-t* k* **Apis** k* aral bro1* arg-met b7.de arg-n k* *Arn* k* **Ars** k* ars-i ars-s-f k2 arum-t *Asaf* k* asar b7.de aur k* aur-ar k2 aur-i k2 aur-s k2 bamb-a stb2.de• bar-c b4.de* *Bell* k* bell-p k* berb beryl sp1 *Bism* k* bov b4.de brom k* bry k* bufo *Calc* k* *Calc-ar* calc-i k2 calc-p calc-s calc-sil k2* cann-i k* **Canth** k* caps *Carb-an* k* **Carb-v** k* *Carbn-s* castor-eq *Caust* k* *Cham* k* chel k* chin b7.de *Cic* k* cina k* clem k* coc-c k* cocc k* *Coff* b7.de colch k* con b4.de *Cop* k* croc k* *Crot-h* crot-t k* cub cupr k* dream-p sdj1• *Dros* k* euph k* ferr b7.de gels k* ger-i rly4• *Graph* k* ham k* hep k* *Hydr* k* hydroph rsj6• hyos b7.de hyper k* ign k* iod k* irid-met srj5• kali-ar *Kali-bi* kali-br kali-c k* kali-n b4.de* kali-p kali-s kali-sil k2 kola stb3• *Kreos* k* *Lach* k* lact laur k* *Led* k* lob *Lyc* k* m-ambo b7.de m-arct b7.de mag-m k* mag-s k* manc *Mang* k* mang-act bro1 mang-p rly4• *Med* melal-alt gya4 *Merc* k* *Merc-sul* k* mez k* mosch k* *Mur-ac* k* murx k* myrt-c bro1 *Nat-ar* nat-c k* nat-m b4a.de nat-p nat-pyru rly4• nat-s nit-ac k* *Nux-m* k* *Nux-v* k* ol-j bro1 op k* petr-ra shn4• *Ph-ac* k* *Phos* k* *Plat* k* polyg-h prim-v bro1 psor k* puls k* ran-b k* ran-s bro1 raph k* rat rhod b4a.de rhus-t k* ruta b7.de* *Sabad* k* sabin b7.de *Sang* k* sangin-n br1* sec b7.de* *Seneg* k* sep k* *Sil* k* spig *Spong* k* stann k* stry k* suis-hep rly4• sul-ac b4.de* sul-i k2 *Sulph* k* suprar rly4• tab *Ter* tetox pin2• thuj k* tritic-vg fd5.de vanil fd5.de vero-o rly3• vip k* visc sp1 wye bro1 *Zinc* k* zinc-m k* zinc-p k2 [heroin sdj2 spect dfg1]
• **accompanied** by:
⁝ **epistaxis**: thuj ptk1
⁝ **expectoration**; bloody: psor ptk1
⁝ **laryngismus** (See LARYNX - Laryngismus - accompanied - chest)
⁝ **respiration**; impeded: *Bism* b7a.de *Phos* b4a.de *Plat* b4a.de ran-b b7.de*
⁝ **Mammae**; cancer in (See Cancer - mammae - accompanied - pain - burning)
⁝ **Stomach**; cold sensation in: polyg-h ptk1
• **currents**; as from burning: m-ambo b7.de
• **hot** stream; as from: kreos ptk1 merc ptk1 sang a1*
• **upward**: lob **Sulph** k*
- **burrowing**: arn b7.de* cann-s b7.de* cina b7.de* dulc b4.de* ferr b7.de* *Graph* b4a.de petr b4.de* stann b4.de*
- **bursting** pain: arg-n a1 ars bg2 *Aur-m* brom ptk1 bry k* carb-an k* cham k* cina k* coff cot br1 kali-s fd4.de lach lyc med c1 merc k* mur-ac k* ol-an bg2 rhus-t k* sanic tl1 seneg k* spong fd4.de sulph k* tarent zinc k*
• **bubbles**; like: *Sulph* b4a.de
- **carrying** a load, from: alum
- **chill**:
• **after**: **Acon**↓ *Iod*↓
⁝ **cutting** pain: **Acon** k*
⁝ **pressing** pain: *Iod*
• **before**: ars plan
⁝ **cutting** pain: ars

- **during**: *Acon* bg2 am-c↓ arn bg2 ars k* bell k* borx b4a.de* bov b4.de* brom bg2 **Bry** k* calad b7.de* calc bg2 cham bg2 *Chin* b7a.de* *Chinin-s* eup-per↓ *Ip* b7.de* **Kali-c** k* lach med↓ merc bg2 *Mez* b4.de* nux-m b7.de* nux-v b7.de* ph-ac bg2 phos bg2 puls k* *Rhus-t* k* *Rumx*↓ *Sabad* k* seneg k* sep bg2 sil bg2 spig bg2 sulph bg2
  - **boring** pain: med
  - **cramping**: ars h2
  - **sore**: lach
  - **stinging**: bell h1
  - **stitching** pain: *Acon* bg2 am-c bg2 **Bry** k* chin bg2 eup-per kali-c k* lach *Nux-v* bg2 phos k* puls bg2 *Rhus-t Rumx* sabad sep bg2 sil bg2
- **chilliness**; during: eupi sep
  - **drawing** pain: sep
  - **stitching** pain: eupi k*
- **clawing** pain: arg-n bg2* meny b7.de* samb b7.de* **Seneg** k* sil b4a.de stront-c b4.de*
- **clearing** throat agg.: spig
  - **aching**: spig k*
- **cold**:
  - **air** agg.: acon tl1 apis↓ bry tl1 *Kali-c*↓ petr bro1 *Ph-ac* phos bro1 prot pte1*• ran-b k2*
    - **cutting** pain: ran-b k2
    - **raw**; as if: apis **Phos**
    - **sore**: ph-ac ptk1
    - **stitching** pain: *Kali-c*
  - **applications**:
    - **agg.**: cassia-s↓
      - **pressing** pain: cassia-s ccrh1•
  - **drinks**:
    - **agg.**: *Carb-v* nit-ac *Psor* k* rhus-t a1 staph thuj k*
      - **stitching** pain: staph thuj
    - **amel.**: *Phos* mrr1
- **compressed**; as if: acon b7a.de *Arn* b7a.de coloc b4a.de dulc fd4.de *Meny* b7a.de olnd b7a.de ruta b7a.de
- **constant**: *Lyc*↓
  - **pressing** pain: *Lyc*
- **constricting** pain: (↗*Constriction)* adon bro1 allox tpw3 am-br br1 asaf bro1 bamb-a stb2.de• *Bry* bro1 **Cact** mrr1* cadm-met sp1 *Caps* a1* *Dig* bro1 hist sp1 ign bro1 iod bro1 lach bro1 lat-m bnm6• mang-p rly4• meli bro1 mill bro1 *Mosch* bro1 musca-d szs1 nat-s bro1 *Phos* bro1 rauw sp1 squil bro1 tell rsj10• tritic-vg fd5.de xan bro1 [bell-p-sp dcm1]
- **contracting**: chin h1 mag-m h2 mang h2 mez h2 nit-ac h2 ruta fd4.de spong fd4.de stann h2 sulph h2 tritic-vg fd5.de vanil fd5.de verat h1
- **corrosive**: bell b4.de* lyc b4a.de ruta b7.de* sulph b4a.de
- **coryza**; during: *Acon* b7.de* ant-t b7.de* bell b4a.de* borx↓ **Bry** b7.de* carb-v bg2 caust b4.de* cina↓ kreos bg2 lach b7a.de meph bg2 *Merc* bg2 mez b4a.de *Nux-v* bg2 ph-ac b4a.de* *Puls* bg2 *Rhus-t* bg2 *Sang* bg2 seneg b4a.de sep↓ sil↓ **Sulph** b4a.de* zinc bg2
  - **burning**: zinc b4a.de
  - **bursting** pain: cina b7.de* sil b4.de*
  - **raw**; as if: carb-v h2* kreos meph sep k* sulph
  - **sore**: mez b4.de*
  - **stitching** pain: borx b4a.de* merc b4.de*
- **cough**:
  - **after**: *Arn*↓ *Carb-v*↓ lach↓ lyc↓ mag-m↓ mag-s↓ *Nat-m*↓ *Phos*↓ *Seneg*↓ sep↓ spong↓ *Stann*↓ staph↓ zinc↓
    - **burning**: *Carb-v* mag-s *Seneg*
    - **pressing** pain: mag-m h2
    - **raw**; as if: *Arn Carb-v* lach lyc *Nat-m Phos* sep spong *Stann* staph zinc
  - **agg.**: abrom-a↓ acon↓ alum↓ alum-p↓ alum-sil↓ am-c↓ ambr↓ ant-s-aur↓ **Apis**↓ arg-met↓ **Arn**↓ ars↓ ars-s-f↓ bamb-a↓ bar-c↓ *Bell*↓ berb↓ borx↓ brom↓ **Bry**↓ *Calc*↓ calc-s↓ **Carb-v**↓ *Carbn-s*↓ *Caust*↓ chin↓ chlor↓ cina↓ cocc↓ colch↓ *Cop*↓ *Cur*↓ dig↓ **Dros**↓ eug↓ *Eup-per*↓ *Ferr*↓ ferr-ar↓ *Ferr-m*↓ ferr-p↓ gal-ac↓ gamb↓ *Gels*↓ graph↓ guare↓ ham↓ hep↓ hydr↓ ip↓ *Kali-bi*↓ kali-n↓

- **cough – agg.**: ...
  Kreos↓ lach↓ lact↓ lec↓ lyc↓ mag-c↓ *Mag-m*↓ meph↓ merc↓ mez↓ mur-ac↓ nat-ar↓ *Nat-c*↓ *Nat-m*↓ *Nat-s*↓ *Nit-ac*↓ nux-m↓ *Nux-v*↓ ol-j↓ **Phos**↓ psor↓ **Ran-b**↓ rat↓ rumx↓ sanic↓ **Seneg**↓ sep↓ *Sil*↓ spig↓ **Spong**↓ **Stann**↓ *Staph*↓ stram↓ stront-c↓ *Sulph*↓ syph↓ thuj↓ verat↓ zinc↓ zinc-p↓
    - **sore**: abrom-a ks5 acon alum k* alum-p k2 alum-sil k2 am-c k* ambr ant-s-aur bg1 **Apis** arg-met **Arn** k* ars ars-s-f k2 bamb-a stb2.de• bar-c k* *Bell* berb borx brom **Bry** k* *Calc* k* calc-s **Carb-v** k* *Carbn-s* *Caust* k* chin chlor cina k* cocc colch *Cop Cur* dig k* **Dros** k* eug *Eup-per* k* *Ferr* ferr-ar *Ferr-m* ferr-p gal-ac a1 gamb *Gels* graph guare ham fd3.de• hep k* hydr ip k* *Kali-bi* kali-n k* *Kreos* lach lact lec lyc k* mag-c *Mag-m* k* meph merc k* mez mur-ac k* nat-ar *Nat-c* k* *Nat-m* *Nat-s* k* *Nit-ac* k* nux-m k* *Nux-v* k* ol-j **Phos** k* psor **Ran-b** k* rat rumx sanic **Seneg** k* sep k* *Sil* k* spig b7.de* **Spong** k* **Stann** k* *Staph* stram stront-c *Sulph* k* syph thuj verat k* zinc k* zinc-p k2
  - **desiring** to; when: sil↓
    - **pressing** pain: sil
  - **during**:
    - **agg.**: abies-n bro1 abrom-a ks5 *Acon* k* aeth agar↓ ail alum alum-p k2 alum-sil k2 alumn↓ am-c am-m k* *Ambr* k* amyg↓ *Anac* ant-c k* ant-s-aur↓ ant-t apis k* *Arg-met*↓ arn k* ars k* ars-i↓ ars-s-f k2 arum-t↓ *Asaf*↓ asc-t a1 aur aur-ar k2 aur-i k2 aur-s k2 **Bell** k* bell-p↓ berb↓ bism↓ **Borx** k* brom k* **Bry** k* *Bufo*↓ cact↓ *Calc* k* calc-i k2 *Calc-p*↓ calc-s k2 calc-sil k2* *Camph* cann-s↓ canth caps k* carb-an k* **Carb-v** k* carbn-s k2 card-m↓ cassia-s cdd7*• **Caust** k* cetr mtf11 *Cham* k* chel k* *Chin* k* chin-b↓ chinin-ar chinin-s↓ cina k* clem↓ *Coc-c*↓ coff k* colch↓ com bro1 *Con* k* cor-r↓ *Corn*↓ crot-h↓ crot-t cupr cur↓ *Dig* k* dream-p sdj1• **Dros** k* dulc bro1* elaps k* eup-per k* euph bro1 eupi ferr k* ferr-ar ferr-i ferr-m ferr-p gal-ac a1* gels *Graph*↓ grat↓ guaj↓ ham↓ *Hep*↓ hydrog srj2• ign bro1 iod k* ip↓ irid-met srj5• just bro1 kali-ar kali-bi k* kali-c k* kali-i k* **Kali-n** k* kali-p kali-sil k2 ketogl-ac↓ kreos k* lac-del hrn2• lach k* lachn↓ **Lact**↓ *Lact-v* bro1 laur↓ led k* **Lyc** k* m-ambo↓ mag-c↓ *Mag-m* k* *Mag-s*↓ mang k* med k2 meph k* *Merc* k* mez mosch k* mur-ac k* myric↓ myrt-c bro1 naja nat-ar nat-c k* *Nat-m* k* nat-n nat-p *Nat-s* k* *Nicc* bro1 nit-ac k* nux-m nux-v k* oci-sa sk4• ol-j ox-ac petr k* ph-ac k* phel bro1 **Phos** k* *Phyt* k* psor **Puls** k* pycnop-sa mrz1 pyrog k2 ran-b k* raph *Rhus-t* k* rumx k* ruta↓ sabad k* samb *Sang* k* sanic↓ sec *Sel* b7a.de **Seneg** k* *Sep* k* *Sil* k* sphing a1* spig k* **Spong** k* **Squil** k* **Stann** k* staph k* *Stict* bro1 stram stront-c suis-hep↓ sul-i k2 **Sulph** k* symph fd3.de• syph↓ tarent tell↓ thuj↓ tritic-vg fd5.de tub gk upa *Verat* k* *Zinc* k* zinc-p k2 zing ziz bro1 [heroin sdj2]
      - **morning**: cassia-s ccrh1•
      - **evening**: cassia-s ccrh1•
      - **aching**: chin k* kali-c mag-m mang k* phyt raph samb stront-c
        - **paroxysmal**: mag-m k*
      - **blow**; pain as from a: *Hep* b4a.de m-ambo b7.de *Sep* b4a.de
      - **burning**: agar ail am-c k* ambr *Ant-c* k* arn b7a.de ars k* arum-t bry *Bufo* cann-s carb-v k* *Caust* k* cina k* dig ferr k* gels ham fd3.de• hep k* **Iod** k* kali-c kali-n b4a.de *Lach* led k* lyc *Mag-m* k* *Mag-s* k* ph-ac k* phos k* phyt *Puls* b7a.de pyrog k* rumx *Seneg* k* sep **Spong** k* suis-hep rly4• sulph syph thuj ptk1 zinc k* zing
      - **bursting** pain: ars k* *Bry* k* caps k* cham k* **Lact** *Merc* k* mur-ac *Rhus-t* b7a.de *Sulph* k* zinc k*
      - **cold** pain in chest: *Med* k*
      - **cramping**: am-c b4.de* bell carb-an b4a.de *Kali-c* k* laur *Sulph* b4a.de
      - **cutting** pain: *Bry* k* calc colch kali-n k* lachn mag-c mag-s mang k* *Nat-m* k* (non:nat-n a4) ox-ac phos k2 raph *Sulph* k* [heroin sdj2]
      - **drawing** pain: caps k* crot-t dig merc
      - **dry** cough: bry↓ *Caust*↓ **Iod**↓ *Kali-c*↓ *Mag-m*↓ **Spong**↓
        - **burning**: bry *Caust* **Iod** k* *Kali-c Mag-m* **Spong** k*
      - **griping** pain: *Sulph*
      - **pressing** pain: (↗*COUGH - Pressure; from - chest)* alum am-c k* *Anac* ars-i aur b4a.de bism k* borx k* **Bry** *Calc* canth carb-v b4.de* chin k* *Con* cupr dig h2 iod k* *Kali-n* k* mag-m nicc ph-ac k* *Samb* b7a.de sil b4.de* squil k* stann b4a.de stront-c k* *Sulph* k* tell c1

Chest

- **during – agg.**: ...
  - **raw**; as if: alum alum-p k2 alum-sil k2 alumn k* ambr amyg bro1 anac ant-c ant-s-aur bro1 *Arg-met* arn *Ars* k* arum-t k2 borx h2 *Bry* bro1 *Calc* k* *Carb-v* k* carbn-s k2 *Caust* k* chinin-s *Coc-c* cor-r bro1 dig br1* *Eup-per* bro1 ferr-p bro1 gels bro1 *Graph* k* grat ip kali-c kali-sil k2 ketogl-ac rly4• kreos lach laur mag-c mag-m k* mag-s meph k* merc k* mez nat-c k* *Nat-m* nat-p nat-s nit-ac k* nux-m k* nux-v petr *Phos* k* rhus-t bro1 *Rumx* k* ruta sanic sel bro1 seneg bro1 *Sep* sil spig *Spong* *Stann* k* *Staph* sulph thuj k* zinc zinc-p k2
  - **smarting**: carb-v b4.de* *Dig* b4a.de hep b4a.de lyc b4.de* phos b4.de* sep b4.de* spong b7.de*
  - **sore**: ant-s-aur bg1 *Arn* nh6 *Bry* nh6 calc nh6 dig br1 eup-per nh6 gal-ac a1 ham fd3.de• nat-s nh6 phos nh6
  - **sticking** pain: bell-p sp1
  - **stitching** pain: (↗*COUGH - Stitching - chest)* *Acon* k* alum-sil k2 am-c am-m k* ant-c k* arg-met *Arn* k* *Ars* k* ars-i k2 ars-s-f k2 *Asaf* asc-t aur k* **Bell** k* berb **Borx** k* **Bry** k* cact calc k* calc-i k2 *Calc-p* cann-s k* caps carb-an k* carb-v k* card-m cassia-s ccrh1• caust k* *Chel* *Chin* k* chin-b c1 chinin-ar clem *Coff* k* con k* *Corn* crot-h cupr cur **Dros** k* dulc *Ferr* ferr-ar ferr-i *Ferr-m* ferr-p k2 guaj **Iod** k* irid-met srj5• kali-ar *Kali-bi* k* *Kali-c* k* kali-n k* kali-p kali-sil k2 *Kreos* *Lach* k* *Lyc* k* **Merc** k* mez k* myric *Myrt-c* b7a.de nat-c bg2 nat-m k* nat-s nit-ac k* nux-m k* nux-v k* petr k* *Phos* k* *Psor* k* *Puls* k* ran-b rhus-t k* rumx ruta sabad k* sel seneg k* *Sep* k* sil k* **Squil** k* *Stann* k* stront-c k* sul-i k2 *Sulph* k* thuj bg2 tub c1* verat zinc k* zinc-p k2
  - **tearing** pain: aeth k* *Ambr* bell b4a.de borx b4a.de bufo k* *Calc* elaps eupi k* irid-met srj5• kali-c k* *Nat-m* nit-ac nux-v phos k2 psor *Rhus-t* seneg k2 suis-hep rly4• sulph tl1
  - **torn** loose; as if: *Nux-v* b7a.de
  - **ulcerative** pain: kali-bi bg2 mag-m k* psor staph b7.de*
  - **warm** applications | **amel.**: cassia-s ccrh1•
- **cramping**: (↗*Spasms)* aesc agath-a nl2• allox sp1 alumn ang c1 arg-n ars bell bov *Cact* calc cartl-s rly4• cit-ac rly4• *Cocc* coff con cupr dig *Ferr* k* fic-m gya1 graph ham iod *Kali-c* kali-i lact lat-m bnm6• *Lyc* marb-w es1• *Mez* k* nit-ac *Petr* phos bg1 *Plat* plb pot-e rly4• propr sa3• *Puls* k* pycnop-sa mrz1 rauw sp1 ruta fd4.de *Sang* *Sars* sec sep h2 *Spong* stroph-s sp1 *Sulph* tarent vanil fd5.de verat b7.de *Zinc* [spect dfg1]
  - **accompanied** by | **nausea**: cic bg2
  - **alternating** with | **Forehead**; pain in (See HEAD - Pain - forehead - alternating with - chest - followed)
- **cramps**; during: sulph bg2
- **crawling**: acon h1 ph-ac h2
- **crossing** arms: ang ↓
  - **sore**: ang h1
- **crushing**: stroph-s sp1
- **cutting** pain (= sudden sharp pain): *Acon* acon-ac rly4• agath-a nl2• aloe alum b4.de* ang k* *Ant-t* *Apis* k* arg-met k* arn b7.de* *Ars* ars-i ars-s-f k2 asar b7.de* *Asc-t* *Aur* k* aur-i k2 aur-s k2 *Bad* bapt *Bell* k* benz-ac bov k* *Bry* k* bufo bg2 *Cact* cain *Calc* k* calc-i k2 *Calc-p* calc-s cann-s carb-v carbn-s cartl-s rly4• caust b4.de* cedr chel chin b7.de* chinin-s cimic *Colch* con k* crot-c dig k* *Dios* dros h1 dulc k* falco-pe nl2• ferr a1 fum rly4• glon hell hyos *Iod* kali-ar kali-bi bg2 **Kali-c** k* *Kali-i* kali-m k2 *Kali-n* k* kali-s lac-ac laur led *Lyc* k* m-ambo b7.de *Mag-c* k* manc mand rsj7• mang b4.de* *Merc* k* merc-i-r *Mur-ac* k* myos-a rly4• myrt-c b7a.de naja bg2 nat-ar nat-c **Nat-m** k* nat-p nept-m lsd2.fr nux-v b7.de* ol-an par b7.de* petr ph-ac b4.de* phos k* pitu-gl skp7• plat b4.de* plb podo fd3.de• *Psor* k* *Puls* k* pycnop-sa mrz1 *Ran-b* rat rhus-v *Rumx* ruta k* sabin k* samb b7.de* seneg sep spig k* spong k* *Stann* k* stry sul-i k2 *Sulph* k* sumb tab tarax thuj tritic-vg fd5.de verat k* viol-t b7.de* xan zinc k* zinc-p k2 [heroin sdj2]
  - **flatulence**; as from: dulc h2 kali-c h2
  - **upward**: scroph-n bg2 stann h2
- **darting** (See stitching)
- **descending** stairs agg.: alum ↓
  - **stitching** pain: alum
- **digging** pain: acon cann-s k* carb-an h2 carbn-s cina **Dulc** k* lach mang h2* meny olnd petr k* seneg stann stram tarax
- **dinner**; after: agar ↓ bry canth carbn-s caust ↓ cimic lob meny ↓ mez nat-c ↓ nat-p orot-ac ↓ rat sulph zinc
- **dinner**; after: ...
  - **aching**: sulph k*
  - **burning**: agar k* orot-ac rly4•
  - **pressing** pain: caust h2 meny h1
  - **raw**; as if: nat-c k*
  - **stitching** pain: carbn-s
- **dragging** | **downward**: am-c bg2
- **drawing** on boots; when: arg-n
- **drawing** pain: (↗*Drawn)* abrot acon k* agar k* *Anac* k* apis bg2 arn k* asaf k* aster k* aur-m *Borx* k* *Cadm-s* camph k* cann-s b7.de* *Caps* k* carb-v k* card-m k2 *Cham* k* chel k* *Chin* k* cocc b7.de* com con k* crot-t dig k* dulc k* euon *Ferr* k* iod *Kali-c* k* kali-s fd4.de kreos b7a.de lact k* led b7.de* lyc k* m-ambo b7.de m-aust b7.de* meny b7.de* *Mur-ac* nat-c h2 nit-ac k* **Nux-v** k* olnd k* op b7.de* par b7.de* petr h2 phos bg2 plat k* plb mrr1 psil ft1 *Puls* b7.de* ruta b7.de* *Seneg* k* sep k* sil b4.de* spig b7.de* spong b7.de* squil k* *Stann* k* stront-c k* tritic-vg fd5.de vanil fd5.de zinc zing k*
  - **cramping**: nit-ac h2*
  - **downward**: am-c bg1
  - **inward**: *Aster* k* cham b7.de*
  - **paroxysmal**: nit-ac stront-c
  - **upward**: lach mang
- **drawing** shoulders back; when | **amel.**: aster
- **drinking**:
  - **after**:
    - **agg.**: chin b7a.de nit-ac ↓ thuj b4a.de verat b7a.de
      - **sore**: nit-ac h2
      - **tearing** pain: nit-ac k*
  - **agg.**: kali-c ↓
    - **cutting** pain: kali-c mrr1
    - **stitching** pain: kali-c mrr1
  - **milk**:
    - **hot** milk:
      - **amel.**: cassia-s ↓
        - **pressing** pain: cassia-s ccrh1•
- **dull** pain: agn b7.de* *Apis* b7a.de tritic-vg fd5.de vanil fd5.de [*Buteo-j* sej6]
- **eating**:
  - **after**:
    - **agg.**: agar ↓ alum alum-p k2 anac ↓ anag *Arg-n* k* *Asaf* ↓ aspar bov ↓ caust k* chin k* cimic con ↓ *Kali-c* laur mang-p ↓ melal-alt ↓ mez nat-c nat-m ↓ nux-v petr b4a.de phos k* sulph sumb thuj k* verat k* zinc
      - **aching**: alum k* melal-alt gya4 nux-v k*
      - **burning**: mang-p rly4•
      - **cramping**: nat-m k* petr b4a.de*
      - **cutting** pain: *Nux-v* k* sumb k*
      - **pressing** pain: agar h2 anac c1 caust b4a.de con k* nat-c b4a.de* phos b4a.de*
      - **stitching** pain: *Asaf* bov caust b4a.de nat-c k* sulph
    - **amel.**: chel rhod
  - **agg.**: alum ↓ ars ↓ kali-c ↓ nit-ac ↓ spong ↓
    - **cutting** pain: kali-c mrr1
    - **pressing** pain: alum h2 ars h2 spong fd4.de
    - **sore**: nit-ac h2
  - **amel.**: nat-c ↓
    - **raw**; as if: nat-c h2
  - **while**:
    - **agg.**: bov ↓ kali-bi kali-c ↓ led k* mag-m b4a.de ol-an spong fd4.de
      - **stitching** pain: bov k* kali-c mrr1
- **epistaxis**:
  - **after**: calc hr1
  - **amel.**: brom bg1 carb-v bg1
- **erect**; becoming:
  - **agg.**: nicc ↓
    - **stitching** pain: nicc

- **eructations**:
  - **agg.**: *(↗STOMACH - Eructations - accompanied - chest)* cocc phos staph
    - **cramping**: (non:dig slp)
    - **sore**: phos
  - **amel.**: ambr h1 bar-c k* digin ↓ gels bg1* kali-c k* lyc melal-alt ↓ petr h2 sep ↓ zinc ↓
    - **aching**: ambr a1 lyc k* melal-alt gya4
    - **cramping**: (non:dig slp) digin a1* kali-c h2
    - **pressing** pain: ambr h1 kali-c h2 lyc h2 sep h2 zinc h2
    - **sore**: ambr h1
    - **tearing** pain: sep h2
- **excitement**:
  - **after**: stroph-s ↓
    - **needles**; as from: stroph-s sp1
  - **agg.**: *Phos* mrr1 *Rhus-t* hr1 ruta fd4.de spong fd4.de stann stram stroph-s sp1 trios ↓ vanil fd5.de
    - **dull** pain: trios rsj11•
    - **gnawing** pain: stroph-s sp1
- **excoriated**; as if: bamb-a stb2.de• hyos bg2 lach bg2 mez bg2
- **exertion**:
  - **after**:
    - **agg.**: plb ↓ rauw ↓
      - **aching**: rauw sp1
      - **cramping**: plb
  - **agg.**: alum am-m bro1 ang borx ↓ cact mrr1 caust colch ↓ dys pte1• ferr kali-s fd4.de laur led ↓ lob ↓ lyc bro1 plb prot pte1• ran-b rauw tpw8 sep bro1 vanil fd5.de
    - **sore**: colch lob
    - **stitching** pain: alum borx caust ferr led
  - **arms** agg.; of the: ang ant-c kali-s fd4.de led
- **exhaling** | **burning** (See expiration - agg. - burning)
- **expanding** chest: carb-v h2
- **expectoration**: asaf ↓ puls ↓
  - **aching**: asaf k*
  - **after**: cist ↓
    - **raw**; as if: cist k2*
    - **sore**: cist ptk1
  - **amel.**: chel euon kali-n ↓ mag-s
    - **burning**: kali-n
    - **pressing** pain: mag-s
  - **before**: lyc h2
  - **bursting** pain: puls
  - **during**: lyc ↓ zinc ↓
    - **sore**: lyc zinc
- **expiration**:
  - **agg.**: *Ant-c* ↓ arg-met ↓ calc ↓ clem ↓ coc-c ↓ *Colch* ↓ crot-t ↓ mang ↓ spong ↓
    - **burning**: coc-c k2 mang h1*
    - **stitching** pain: *Ant-c* arg-met c1 calc h2 clem h2 *Colch* crot-t mang h2 spong
  - **during**:
    - **agg.**: am-c ↓ chin coloc ↓ crot-t *Puls* b7a.de ruta ↓ spig staph tarax verat a1 *Viol-o* k* zinc
      - **drawing** pain | **downward**: am-c h2
      - **pressing** pain: coloc h2 ruta h1
  - **must** expire: chin ↓
    - **stitching** pain: chin h1
- **fasting** agg.: *Iod* k*
- **fever**:
  - **before**: ars b4a.de bell b4a.de hep b4a.de
  - **during**:
    - **agg.**: acon ↓ *Am-c* ↓ apis ↓ arn ↓ **Ars** ↓ asaf ↓ bell ↓ borx ↓ **Bry** ↓ calc ↓ camph ↓ carb-v ↓ caust ↓ chin ↓ cocc ↓ colch ↓ cupr ↓ hyos ↓ ign ↓ *Ip* ↓ *Kali-c* ↓ kali-n ↓ merc ↓ mosch ↓ *Nat-m* ↓ *Nux-v* ↓ *Phos* ↓

- **fever – during – agg.**: ...
  Puls ↓ *Rhus-t* ↓ sep ↓ sil ↓ spig ↓ squil ↓ stann ↓ sulph ↓ tub ↓ valer ↓
      - **cramping**: **Ars** b4.de* asaf bg2 camph bg2 caust bg2 cocc bg2 colch bg2 cupr bg2 hyos bg2 ign bg2 *Ip* bg2 mosch bg2 *Nux-v* bg2 **Puls** b7.de* sep bg2 stann bg2 sulph bg2
      - **stitching** pain: acon k* *Am-c* b4.de* apis bg2 arn bg2 ars bg2 asaf bg2 bell bg2 borx bg2 **Bry** k* calc bg2 carb-v bg2 chin bg2 ign bg2 *Kali-c* k* kali-n bg2 merc bg2 *Nat-m* bg2 nux-v *Phos* bg2 *Puls* bg2 *Rhus-t* bg2 sep bg2 sil bg2 spig bg2 squil bg2 stann bg2 sulph bg2 tub gk valer bg2
- **flatulence**; from: glycyr-g cte1•
- **flatus**; from obstructed: carb-v h2 lyc bg2 spong fd4.de verat h1
- **flatus**; passing:
  - **amel.**: ph-ac ↓
    - **pressing** pain: ph-ac h2
- **gnawing** pain: acon bg2 ail bg2 arg-met b7.de* bell bg2 berb bg2 calc k* calc-p k* *Colch* lil-t bg2 mang k* mosch k* nat-m h2* olnd bg2 par bg2 ran-s k* ruta k* stann bg2
- **gouty**: | **Joints**: colch bro1
- **griping** pain: aesc *Cact* castm *Caul* cocc coloc bg2 *Dig* *Graph* k* led bg2 *Nit-ac* pall petr-ra shn4• plat spig sulph verat b7.de zinc k* [heroin sdj2]
- **hard** bed; as from a: borx b4a.de*
- **hawking**: *Calc* ↓
  - **after**: asaf
  - **sore**: *Calc*
- **hawking** up mucus:
  - **after**: asaf ↓ spig ↓
    - **aching**: spig k*
    - **pressing** pain: spig h1*
    - **stitching** pain: asaf k*
  - **agg.**: camph h1 kali-n h2 plb rumx ↓ spig
    - **raw**; as if: rumx
- **heartbeat**, at every: calc-act ↓
  - **stitching** pain: calc-act h1
- **heat**; during: **Acon** b7.de* *Am-c* bg2 **Ant-c** k* apis bg2 arn bg2 ars k* bell bg2 borx bg2 *Bov* b4.de* **Bry** b7.de* calad b7a.de* calc bg2 canth caps k* carb-v k* **Chin** b7.de* cina k* cocc bg2 con bg2 dulc bg2 *Guare* *Ip* b7.de* kali-c k* kali-p fd1.de• *Kalm* kreos tl1 lyc bg2 med tl1 *Merc* b4.de* mez b4.de* mur-ac bg2 nit-ac bg2 nux-v k* ph-ac bg2 *Phos* bg2 **Puls** b7.de* ran-b bg2 *Rhus-t* bg2 ruta bg2 sabad b7a.de* seneg bg2 sep bg2 *Spig* bg2 stann bg2 sulph bg2 thuj bg2 zinc bg2 [heroin sdj2]
- **herpes** zoster: *(↗BACK - Pain - herpes - stitching)*
  - **after**: kalm k2 *Mez* k* morg-p pte1*• *Ran-b* k* zinc bg1
    - **burning**: mez hr1
  - **before**: staph bg
- **hiccough** agg.: am-c bg2 am-m stront-c k*
  - **stitching** pain: am-m
- **holds** chest with hands during cough: abrom-a ↓ **Arn** ↓ *Borx* ↓ **Bry** ↓ cimic ↓ **Dros** ↓ *Eup-per* ↓ kreos ↓ merc ↓ nat-m ↓ *Nat-s* ↓ *Phos* ↓ *Sep* ↓
  - **sore**: abrom-a ks5 **Arn** k* *Borx* k* **Bry** k* cimic **Dros** *Eup-per* kreos merc nat-m *Nat-s* k* *Phos* *Sep*
- **hysterical**: *(↗Spasms - hysterical)* aqui br1
- **inflammation** of lungs, after: am-c *Ars* *Lach* **Lyc** **Phos** **Sulph**
- **inspiration**:
  - **agg.**: **Acon** k* aesc aeth ↓ agar alum alum-p k2 alum-sil ↓ alumn am-m bro1 anac ↓ apis mrr1 aq-mar rbp6 arg-met arn k* *Ars* k* asaf asar *Asc-t* ↓ aspar aster aur aur-ar k2 aur-m aur-s k2 bamb-a ↓ bapt bar-c bell-p sp1 **Borx** k* bros-gau mrc1 **Bry** k* calad **Calc** k* calc-p ↓ calc-s k2 calc-sil k2* camph canth caps ↓ carb-an carb-v card-m cassia-s ↓ caust *Cham* *Chel* cina cinnb ↓ clem cob ↓ cocc colch k* coloc com con cupr-ar *Dros* ↓ dulc a1 euon *Eup-per* ↓ ferr ferr-p gal-ac a1* ger-i rly4• gink-b sbd1• grat guaj ↓ *Guare* ↓ hell ↓ hippoc-k szs2 hyos inul iris jatr-c *Kali-ar* kali-bi k2 kali-c k* kali-n kali-p kali-sil ↓ kola stb3• *Kreos* lac-lup hrn2• lact *Laur* ↓ led *Lyc* lyss ↓ *Mag-c* ↓ mentho bro1 *Merc* *Merc-c* ↓ merc-sul mez mur-ac nad rly4• *Naja* nat-ar ↓ nat-m k* nat-s nicc nit-ac ↓ *Nux-m* op *Phos* k* plat plb plut-n srj7• podo *Psor* *Ran-b* k* raph rhus-t ↓ ros-d ↓ rumx ruta fd4.de sabad samb sang *Seneg* k* sep k* *Sil* k*

- **agg.**: ...
  Spig k* spong fd4.de **Squil** k* stann stront-c stroph-s↓ succ-ac rly4• sul-ac sulph k* symph↓ tarax tarent thuj tritic-vg fd5.de tub gk valer vanil fd5.de viol-t zinc [heroin sdj2]
  - **aching**: bapt calc jatr-c
  - **boring** pain: alum k*
  - **burning**: asc-t a1 ger-i rly4• *Laur* k* sep
  - **cutting** pain: *Asc-t* aur **Bry** *Calc* k* con *Guare* k* hell kali-c mrr1 naja phos ran-b k2 stann [heroin sdj2]
  - **deep** | **stitching** pain (See breathing - deep - agg. - stitching)
  - **drawing** pain: calad *Camph* lact led h1 raph spong fd4.de stann tritic-vg fd5.de
  - **griping** pain: cina mur-ac
  - **pinching** pain: cina a1 dulc h1
  - **pressing** pain: asaf aur-m *Borx* *Calc* con h2 kali-c h2 ran-b ros-d wla1 stann h2 tritic-vg fd5.de
  - **raw**; as if: *Acon* anac h2* *Calc* carb-v k2
  - **sore**: anac h2 **Bry** k* **Calc** k* calc-s k2 *Camph* cinnb *Eup-per* k* kali-c h2 nat-ar nat-m nit-ac nux-m sang seneg sil h2
  - **sticking** pain: stroph-s sp1
  - **stitching** pain: **Acon** k* aeth a1 alum alum-p k2 alum-sil k2 am-m *Arg-met* *Ars* asaf *Asar* *Aur* aur-ar k2 aur-m aur-s k2 bamb-a stb2.de• bar-c **Borx** k* **Bry** k* *Calc* calc-p calc-sil k2 canth caps a1 carb-an card-m cassia-s ccrh1• *Chel* clem cob coloc *Con* *Dros* dulc fd4.de ger-i rly4• grat guaj *Hyos* **Kali-c** k* kali-sil k2 kola stb3• *Kreos* *Lyc* lyss *Mag-c* *Merc* *Merc-c* mez **Nat-m** nat-s op *Phos* k* plat *Ran-b* rhus-t h1 ruta fd4.de seneg sep *Sil* spong **Squil** k* stront-c sulph symph fd3.de• tarax tub gk valer
    - **inward**: tarax
  - **tearing** pain: aur-m *Psor*
- **amel.**: chir-fl gya2 mang↓ merc thuj bg1
  - **aching**: merc k*
  - **burning**: mang a1
- **deep**:
  - **agg.**: aesc↓ agn↓ aloe↓ arg-met↓ bapt↓ com↓ eup-per↓ ferr↓ ferr-i↓ gal-ac↓ guare↓ hydr↓ iod↓ kali-bi↓ **Kali-c**↓ kali-n↓ meph↓ mez↓ naja↓ nat-ar↓ *Ran-b*↓ ran-s↓ sang↓ *Spong*↓ *Stann*↓ tritic-vg↓ zing↓
    - **cutting** pain: bapt com guare hr1 kali-n h2 naja spong
    - **drawing** pain: spong fd4.de tritic-vg fd5.de zing
    - **pressing** pain: agn c1 arg-met **Kali-c** k* mez h2 ran-s *Spong* k*
    - **sore**: aesc aloe eup-per ferr ferr-i gal-ac a1 hydr iod kali-bi k2 kali-c meph a1 nat-ar *Ran-b* sang *Stann*
    - **tearing** pain: kali-n h2
  - **amel.**: *Ign*↓ vanil↓
    - **pressing** pain: *Ign* vanil fd5.de

- **jar** agg.: alum k2 bell k2
- **jerking** pain: *Ang* b7a.de calc b4a.de calc-p cann-s b7.de* clem b4a.de con k* croc b7.de* dulc b4a.de lac-c lyc b4.de* m-arct b7.de mang b4a.de mur-ac b4a.de nux-m b7.de* plat b4a.de spig h1 valer b7.de*
- **lancinating** (See cutting)
- **laughing** agg.: acon laur mez nicc psor tub↓
  - **stitching** pain: acon mez k* nicc tub c1
- **leaning** against the chair: kali-p↓
  - **stitching** pain: kali-p k2
- **lifting** agg.: alum bar-c brom bg1 dys fmm1• gamb bg1 *Kali-c* bg1 nat-m bg1 phos prot fmm1• *Psor* *Sulph* zinc h2*
  - **sore**: alum gsy1 kali-c h2
  - **tearing** pain: *Psor* k*
- **lifting**; as from: plat h2
- **liver** pain; with: card-m k2
- **lying**:
  - **abdomen**; on | **amel.**: *Bry* k* vanil fd5.de
  - **agg.**: alumn am-c↓ asaf bry calc caps caust chel↓ **Chin**↓ cit-ac↓ coc-c↓ con dulc↓ kali-n kali-p↓ lac-h sk4• psor puls seneg spong fd4.de tritic-vg fd5.de vanil fd5.de
    - **pressing** pain: am-c h2 kali-p fd1.de• spong fd4.de tritic-vg fd5.de

- **lying** – **agg.**: ...
    - **raw**; as if: coc-c
    - **sore**: **Chin** k*
    - **stitching** pain: asaf bry chel cit-ac rly4• dulc fd4.de kali-n psor
  - **amel.**: alum borx c1 bry bg3 gal-ac a1* graph↓ mang bg3 nat-c↓ ox-ac petr-ra↓ psor al2*
    - **griping** pain: graph petr-ra shn4•
    - **pressing** pain: alum
    - **raw**; as if: nat-c
    - **sore**: alum
  - **arms** close to side; with:
    - **amel.**: lac-ac↓
      - **cutting** pain: lac-ac
  - **back**; on:
    - **agg.**: alum kali-c↓ kali-p↓ rumx↓ spong fd4.de sulph tritic-vg fd5.de
      - **stitching** pain: kali-c h2 kali-p k2 rumx sulph
    - **amel.**: ambr borx h2 *Cact* *Kalm* mrr1
      - **can** only lie on the back: *Acon* k* bry *Phos* k* plat↓
        - **stitching** pain: *Acon* k* *Bry* k* *Phos* k* plat
  - **face**; on the:
    - **amel.**: bry↓
      - **stitching** pain: bry
    - **must** lie on the face: bry↓
      - **stitching** pain: bry
  - **side**; on:
    - **affected** side:
      - **agg.**: *Ant-t* *Bell* *Calc* *Kali-c*↓ nux-v bro1 phos bro1 sabad stann bro1 tub gk
        - **stitching** pain: *Calc* *Kali-c* sabad
    - **agg.**: acon↓ *Canth* con↓ *Hydr* ran-b [heroin sdj2]
      - **drawing** pain: con h2
      - **stitching** pain: acon
      - **tearing** pain: con
    - **amel.**: alum *Bry* nh6 tritic-vg↓
      - **pressing** pain: alum tritic-vg fd5.de
    - **left**:
      - **agg.**: *Agar* am-c asc-t hr1 cact mrr1 cain calad↓ calc crot-h mrr1 kalm k* lyc h2 *Naja* **Phos** k* **Spig** k* *Stann*↓
        - **cutting** pain: *Phos* k*
        - **stitching** pain: am-c calad **Phos** k* **Spig** k* *Stann*
    - **painful** side:
      - **agg.**: am-c↓ **Bell** bry *Nux-v* *Ran-b* k* rhus-t↓ rumx stann↓
        - **stitching** pain: am-c rhus-t a1 stann
      - **amel.**: *Ambr* **Bry** k* calad *Nux-v* puls h1* stann
        - **stitching** pain: **Bry** calad
    - **painless** side:
      - **agg.**: ambr **Puls** k* stann
        - **stitching** pain: stann
    - **right**:
      - **agg.**: *Borx* k* cench↓ *Kali-c* k* lyc **Merc** k* phyt rumx↓ *Seneg*
        - **cutting** pain: *Kali-c* k*
        - **drawing** pain: cench k2
        - **stitching** pain: *Borx* rumx seneg
      - **amel.**: cassia-s↓
        - **can** only lie on right side: *Kali-c* k* *Naja* k* **Spig** k*
          - **stitching** pain: **Spig** k*
        - **pressing** pain: cassia-s ccrh1•
- **lying** down:
  - **agg.**: puls↓
    - **burning**: puls
  - **amel.**: sulph↓
    - **cramping**: sulph
  - **impossible**: tub↓
    - **stitching** pain: tub gk
- **menopause**; during: sang↓
  - **burning**: sang bro1

- **menses**:
  - **before**:
    - **agg.**: aln vva1• borx↓ *Kali-c*↓ puls *Zinc*↓
      - **burning**: *Zinc* k*
      - **stitching** pain: borx hr1 *Kali-c* puls b7.de*
  - **before** and during:
    - **agg.**: aln↓ carc↓ **Zinc**↓
      - **sore**: aln vva1• carc mlr1• **Zinc** k*
  - **during**:
    - **agg.**: am-c↓ am-m↓ borx↓ caust↓ cocc *Croc*↓ *Graph* kali-n↓ kreos↓ phos *Puls*↓ *Sep*↓
      - **cramping**: *Cocc*
      - **drawing** pain: *Sep*
      - **griping** pain: *Cocc*
      - **pressing** pain: am-c b4.de cocc graph b4.de* sep b4a.de
      - **stitching** pain: am-c b4.de am-m b7.de borx k* caust b4.de *Croc* kali-n kreos b7a.de *Puls* k*
  - **suppressed** menses; from: *Cocc*↓ cupr↓
    - **cramping**: cupr bro1
    - **pressing** pain: *Cocc* b7a.de
- **mental** exertion agg.: cham sep tritic-vg fd5.de
  - **stitching** pain: sep
- **motion**:
  - **after**:
    - **agg.**: stroph-s↓
      - **needles**; as from: stroph-s sp1
  - **agg.**: abrot alum h2 ang↓ *Arn* k* ars bro1 ars-s-f k2 asc-t vh aur-m↓ bad bapt **Bell** borx↓ **Bry** k* **Calc** k* caps carbn-s card-m k* cardios-h rly4• *Chel* chin chinin-s↓ *Cimic* crot-h↓ equis-h ferr↓ flor-p↓ gamb *Graph* guaj k2 *Hep* hyos hyper↓ jug-r bro1 kali-c k* kali-n↓ kali-p *Kalm* lac-ac lac-lup hrn2• *Laur* lyc mag-c bro1 manc mang↓ meny meph↓ *Merc* mur-ac↓ *Naja* nat-m nit-ac *Nux-v* ol-j↓ ox-ac↓ pant-ac rly4• *Phos* k* psil↓ psor puls↓ *Ran-b* k* sabad sars sec seneg bro1 sep h2* sil h2 **Spig** k* spong fd4.de *Squil* staph↓ stront-c sulph k* symph fd3.de• thuj↓ tub↓ viol-t zinc h2 [heroin sdj2]
    - **aching**: bapt bry flor-p rsj3• sep k* stront-c
    - **burning**: crot-h mang a1
    - **constricting** pain: *Caps* a1
    - **cramping**: ferr spong fd4.de sulph
    - **cutting** pain: ars-s-f k2 bad **Bry** chinin-s lac-ac k* ox-ac ran-b k2
    - **drawing** pain: abrot psil ft1 seneg spong fd4.de
    - **sore**: alum ang h1 *Arn* mag-c meph a1 ol-j *Phos* *Ran-b* *Seneg* squil k2 staph k* thuj
    - **stitching** pain: alum aur-m bad borx hr1 **Bry** k* *Calc* *Chel* chin k* guaj k2 hyos hyper c1 kali-n h2 meny k* merc mur-ac h2 nit-ac k* ox-ac phos k* puls h1 *Ran-b* **Spig** k* *Sulph* tub c1
    - **tearing** pain: aur-m bry nit-ac h2
  - **amel.**: con↓ *Dros*↓ *Euph*↓ ign bro1 indg↓ irid-met↓ *Kali-c*↓ lob phos puls bro1 rhod k2 rhus-t ruta fd4.de *Seneg* tab↓ tritic-vg fd5.de tub↓
    - **aching**: *Seneg* k*
    - **burning**: euph
    - **cutting** pain: phos tritic-vg fd5.de
    - **digging** pain: *Seneg*
    - **pressing** pain: dros h1 *Seneg*
    - **sore**: tab
    - **stitching** pain: con *Dros* *Euph* indg irid-met srj5• *Kali-c* phos rhod k2 **Rhus-t** *Seneg* tritic-vg fd5.de tub gk
  - **arm**; of:
    - **agg.**: carb-an↓
      - **tearing** pain: carb-an
  - **arms**; of:
    - **agg.**: ang↓ *Asc-t*↓ *Camph*↓ carb-an card-m caust cench k2 mez h2 nat-c↓ *Nux-m* *Seneg* sulph sumb↓
      - **cutting** pain: *Asc-t* sumb
      - **sore**: ang c1 nat-c h2 *Seneg*
      - **stitching** pain: *Camph* *Sulph* sumb
      - **Anterior** part of chest: carb-an↓
- **motion – arms**; of – **agg.** – **Anterior** part of chest: ...
  - **aching**: carb-an
  - **certain** motions; during: cassia-s↓ sep↓
    - **pressing** pain: cassia-s ccrh1• sep h2
  - **head**; of | **agg.**: *Guaj* spong fd4.de
- **needles**; as from: cham tl1 hed sp1 stroph-s sp1
  - **outwards**; from within: ars-s-f br1
- **neuralgic**: corn-f br1 *Ran-b* mrr1
- **operation** for hydrothorax or empyema; after: abrot↓
  - **pressing** pain: abrot br1
- **palpitations**; during: hep bg2 **Ign** bg2 nux-v bg2 sep *Spig* *Spong* *Tell* rsj10• vanil fd5.de
- **paralyzed**; as if: alum bg2
- **paroxysmal**: ambr h1 caul kola stb3• nit-ac *Ox-ac* plb sep stront-c stry tritic-vg fd5.de
- **pecking**: ruta h1
- **percussion** agg.: **Chin**↓ myos-a mtf11 seneg↓
  - **sore**: **Chin** k* seneg
- **periodical**: acon↓ aloe↓ dig↓
  - **menopause**; during: sang↓
    - **neuralgic**: sang bro1
  - **stitching** pain: acon k* aloe dig c1
- **perspiration**; during: acon bg2 apis bg2 *Ars* bg2 **Bell** bg2 bov bg2 **Bry** b7a.de* calad bg2 calc bg2 **Cham** bg2 chin bg2 dulc bg2 ip bg2 *Kali-c* bg2 lyc bg2 mez bg2 nux-v bg2 phos bg2 puls bg2 rhus-t bg2 sabad bg2 *Sep* bg2 spig bg2 *Sulph* bg2
  - **cramping**: ars b4a.de
- **piercing** (See stitching)
- **pinching** pain: agar k* alum k* ang b7.de* ant-c h2 bell k* bism b7.de* borx h2 carb-an carb-v k* cina k* cupr *Dulc* k* graph h2 ign b7.de* ip k* *Kali-c* k* lact lyss mag-c h2 melal-alt gya4 mur-ac h2 olnd b7.de* par k* ph-ac k* *Phos* ran-s k* rhod samb b7.de* *Seneg* k* sil h2 spig b7.de* spong k* stann h2 suprar rly4• thuj k* tub zinc h2
- **pleuritis**:
  - **after**: carb-an↓ tub↓
    - **stitching** pain: carb-an al1* tub gk
  - **during**: tub↓
    - **stitching** pain: tub gk
- **pneumonia**; after: ran-b↓
  - **sore**: ran-b tl1
- **pork**; after: ham↓
  - **cramping**: ham
- **pressing** pain: *Abies-n* bro1 abrot bro1 acon b7.de* agar k* agath-a nl2• agn b7.de* *Ail* *Alum* k* alum-p k2 alum-sil k2 am-c k* am-m b7.de* *Ambr* k* *Anac* k* anag ang b7.de* ant-c b7.de* ant-t bg2 apis k* apoc k2 arg-met k* arg-n bg2* arn k* ars k* ars-i ars-s-f k2 *Asaf* k* asar k* *Aur* k* aur-ar k2 aur-s k2 bar-c k* bar-s k2 *Bell* k* berb bism k* *Borx* k* *Bov* k* brom k* *Bry* k* bufo bg2 *Cact* bro1 cain *Calc* k* calc-i k2 calc-p calc-sil k2* camph b7.de* cann-s b7.de* canth b7.de* caps k* carb-ac carb-an k* *Carb-v* k* *Carbn-s* *Caust* k* *Cham* b7.de* *Chel* k* *Chin* k* chlor k* cic k* *Cimx* *Cist* k* clem b4.de* coc-c cocc k* colch k* *Coloc* k* con k* cor-r corn crot-t k* cupr k* *Cur* k* cycl k* *Dig* k* digin a1 dream-p sdj1• *Dulc* k* euphr b7.de* ferr b7.de* ferr-i bro1 fl-ac k* gamb bg2 graph k* grat k* gymno haem bro1 *Hell* hep b4a.de *Hydr-ac* k* hyos k* hyper k* ign k* *Iod* k* ip b7.de* kali-bi k* **Kali-c** k* kali-m k2 *Kali-n* k* kali-p fd1.de• kali-s fd4.de kali-sil k2 kreos bro1* *Lac-d* lac-loxod-a hrn2• *Lach* k* *Lact* k* laur k* led b7.de* *Lil-t* bro1 lith-c *Lob* bro1 lyc k* lyss m-ambo b7.de m-arct b7.de *M-aust* b7.de* mag-c b4.de* *Mag-m* k* *Mag-s* k* mang b4.de* mang-p rly4• *Meny* b7.de* *Merc* k* merc-c b4a.de merc-sul merl *Mez* k* *Mill* mosch b7.de* *Mur-ac* k* nat-ar *Nat-c* k* *Nat-m* k* *Nat-p* *Nat-s* k* *Nicc* k* nit-ac b4.de* *Nux-m* k* *Nux-v* k* olib-sac wmh1 olnd k* op k* par b7.de* petr k* *Ph-ac* k* *Phos* k* *Plat* k* plb k* positr nl2• propl ub1• prun-p bro1 psor k* ptel br1* puls k* *Ran-b* k* ran-s k* rheum b7.de* *Rhod* k* rhus-t b7.de* *Ruta* k* sabad k* sabin k* *Samb* b7.de* sang k* sangin-n bro1 *Sars* k* **Seneg** k* *Sep* k* *Sil* k* spig k* spong k* *Squil* b7.de* **Stann** k* staph k* stram k* *Stront-c* k* suis-em rly4• *Sul-ac* k* **Sulph** k* symph fd3.de• tab k* tarax k* teucr b7.de* *Thuj* k* tritic-vg fd5.de tub c1* **Valer** k* vanil fd5.de verat k* verat-v bro1 verb k* viol-o k* viol-t b7.de *Zinc* k* zinc-p k2

Chest

- **accompanied** by | **pneumonia** (See Inflammation - lungs - accompanied - chest)
- **alternating** with | **Abdomen**; distension of: lyc h2
- **asunder**: euph b4.de*
- **burning**: chin h1
- **drawing** downward: phos h2
- **flatulence**; as from: zinc h2
- **inward**: acon bg2 ang bg2 apis bg2 bell h1 cann-s b7.de* chin b7.de* cocc b7.de* ign b7.de* kreos b7a.de laur b7.de* nux-m b7.de* nux-v b7.de* op bg2 spong fd4.de tritic-vg fd5.de
- **lump**; as from a: ambr b7a.de *Ars* b4a.de cic b7a.de *Phos* b4a.de *Puls* b7a.de *Sulph* b4a.de
- **outward**: ang b7.de* arg-met b7.de* *Asaf* b7.de* bell k* bry b7.de* cina b7.de* dulc k* led b7.de* nux-m b7.de* seneg k* tarax b7.de* **Valer** k* zinc k*
- **paroxysmal**: nat-m h2
- **plug**; as from a: (↗*Plug*) *Am-c* bg2 anac b4a.de* ang bg2 aur b4a.de* cina bg2 cocc bg2 *Ran-s* bg2
  - **ribs**; as if forced between: ran-s bg2
- **stone**; like a: borx h2 cocc c1 cor-r
- **upward**: nat-m bg2
- **vise**; as if in a: am-m gsy1*
- **weight**; as from a: *Am-c* bg2 aml-ns bg2 **Ant-t** bg2 aral bg2 arg-met b7.de* arn bg2 ars bg2 asaf bg2 aur bg2 bell bg2 bry b7a.de* **Cact** bg2 calc bg2 carb-ac bg2 carb-v bg2 caust bg2 glon bg2 *Kali-n* bg2 kreos bg2 laur b7.de* lob bg2 naja bg2 *Nux-m* b7.de* *Nux-v* b7.de* olnd b7.de* **Phos** bg2 plat bg2 plb bg2 psor bg2 puls bg2 rheum b7.de* rhus-t b7a.de* sabad b7.de* *Samb* b7.de* *Seneg* bg2 spig b7.de* stann bg2 sulph bg2 *Verat* b7a.de *Verat-v* bg2 viol-o b7.de*

- **pressure**:
  - **agg.**: agath-a nl2• am-c h2 ang↓ ant-c aq-mar↓ arn bro1 ars bro1 *Bar-c*↓ *Bry* bro1 cassia-s↓ cench k2 cina a1 colch bro1 *Crot-t*↓ dros↓ falco-pe↓ meny merc-i-f nat-m↓ nat-p nux-v bro1 *Phos* bro1 ran-b k* ran-s↓ seneg stann h2 sul-ac tarax
    - **cutting** pain: ran-b k2
    - **desire** to press; but: stroph-s sp1
    - **sore**: ang **Arn** *Bar-c* cassia-s ccrh1• *Crot-t* dros falco-pe nl2• nat-m h2 phos h2
    - **stitching**: aq-mar skp7• ran-b ran-s k*
  - **amel.**: adam skp7• **Arn** asaf↓ *Borx* **Bry** k* caust↓ cimic **Dros** dulc h1 *Eup-per* kreos lac-lup hrn2• merc nat-m *Nat-s* pant-ac rly4• petr-ra↓ *Phos* ran-b k* *Sep* symph fd3.de• tritic-vg fd5.de
    - **griping** pain: petr-ra shn4•
    - **sore**: *Bry* k* *Dros* k* *Eup-per* k* *Nat-m* k* *Nat-s* k*
    - **stitching**: arn ptk1 asaf *Borx* k* **Bry** k* **Dros** k*
    - **wandering** pain: caust ptk1*
  - **clothes**; of: | **agg.**: ail bg1 benz-ac lach bg1 ran-b
  - **not** amel.: pert-vc↓
    - **stitching**: pert-vc vk9
- **pulsating** pain: bell lp *Caps* com *Kali-c* podo fd3.de• zinc
- **raising**:
  - **arm** | **agg.**: ang ant-c h2 berb *Ran-b* sel sep spig *Sulph* tarent thuj tritic-vg fd5.de
  - **arm** to head agg.: spig↓
    - **tearing** pain: spig
  - **arms**:
    - **agg.**: berb↓ borx↓ ol-j↓ puls↓ rhus-t↓ *Sulph*↓ thuj↓
      - **stitching** pain: berb borx ol-j puls rhus-t *Sulph* thuj
- **rasping**: carb-v
- **raw**; as if: abrot st acon k* *Aesc* *Agar* all-c k2 alum alum-sil k2 alumn am-c k* am-m *Ambr* k* *Anac* k* anan ant-c bg2 ant-t k* apis aral vh1 **Arg-met** k* *Arn* b7.de* *Ars* k* ars-i k2 arum-t bell bg2 berb bov bg2 bry b7.de* *Calc* k* calc-i k2 calc-s calc-sil k2 cann-s carb-v *Carbn-s* **Caust** k* cham chin k* *Chinin-ar* *Cist* clem *Coc-c* cocc b7.de* colch b7a.de *Cop* dig k* dulc fd4.de fl-ac bg2 gamb *Gels* *Graph* k* hell b7.de* *Hydr* iod k* *Ip* k* irid-met srj5• kali-bi bg2 kali-c bg2 kali-i kali-m bg2 kali-n k* ketogl-ac rly4• kreos b7a.de* lac-h htj1• lach bg2 *Laur* bg2 led **Lyc** m-arct b7.de mag-p bg2 meph merc k* *Mez* mur-ac bg2 naja nat-ar
- **raw**; as if: ...
  nat-c k* *Nat-m* k* nat-p nit-ac nux-m b7.de* **Nux-v** k* *Petr* **Phos** k* *Phyt* psor *Puls* k* rhus-t b7.de* *Rumx* sang bg2* seneg bg2 sep sil k* *Spong* **Stann** k* *Staph* k* suis-hep rly4• *Sulph* k* syph k2 thuj zinc k*
- **reading** agg.: euph↓ stann
  - **aching**: stann
  - **stitching** pain: euph
- **respiration**: acon aesc aloe↓ am-c *Anac* *Ant-c*↓ ant-t arg-met **Arn**↓ ars tl1 ars-s-f k2 aur bapt **Borx** k* bov **Bry** k* *Calc* calc-p cann-s caps k* card-m cench k2 *Cham* *Chel*↓ chin colch *Coloc*↓ crot-t *Dig* dros dulc fd4.de elaps eup-per↓ euph↓ ferr-p↓ guaj k2 helo-s bnm14• *Hep*↓ hydrog srj2• **Kali-c** k* kali-m k2 *Kali-n*↓ *Kali-p* *Kalm* *Kreos* lob *Lyc* k* mag-c↓ *Manc* med k2 meny merc-sul mez mur-ac nat-c↓ nat-m nat-s↓ nicc nit-ac↓ *Nux-m*↓ ox-ac↓ ozone↓ ph-ac *Phyt* pieri-b mlk9.de pitu-gl skp7• psil↓ **Psor** k* raph ruta fd4.de sabad seneg↓ *Sep* *Spig* k* spong squil *Stann* k* sulph tab tritic-vg fd5.de tub↓ vanil fd5.de verat verb↓
  - **menses**; before: puls
  - **sitting** agg.: chin
  - **sore**: **Arn** k* *Calc* k* eup-per *Kali-c* k* lob nit-ac psil ft1
  - **stitching** pain: acon k* aloe am-c k* *Anac* *Ant-c* arg-met arn *Aur* k* **Borx** k* bov k* **Bry** k* *Calc* k* cann-s caps k* card-m cham *Chel* chin k* colch *Coloc* *Dros* dulc fd4.de elaps euph ferr-p k2 guaj k2 *Hep* **Kali-c** k* kali-m k2 *Kali-n* kali-p *Kreos* *Lyc* k* mag-c meny mez k* mur-ac k* nat-c h2 nat-s nicc *Nux-m* ox-ac ozone sde2• ph-ac k* pieri-b mlk9.de *Psor* k* ruta fd4.de sabad seneg *Sep* k* *Spig* k* *Spong* *Squil* k* *Stann* k* tab k* tub gk verat verb
- **rest** | **amel.**: bry bro1
- **rheumatic**: *Abrot* *Acon* bg2 ambr ant-t k* *Arg-n* arn k* berb **Bry** k* *Cact* cadm-s carb-v caust *Chin* k* *Cimic* k* *Colch* k* con *Corn* ferr-p k2 guaj hydr iod h *Kali-i* **Kalm** **Lac-ac** lac-d k2 lach k* lyc med k2 meph a1 merc k2 mez h2 *Nux-v* k* *Phos* plb puls bg2 **Ran-b** k* *Rhod* **Rhus-t** k* *Rumx* k* sang a1 **Spig** k* sulph bg2 *Tarent* verat bg2
  - **right**: meph a1
  - **subcutaneous** ulceration; as from: ran-b br1
  - ○ **Diaphragm**: *Bry* bro1 cact bro1 *Cimic* bro1 spig bro1 stict bro1
  - **External** chest: ambr b7.de* ant-t b7.de* **Arn** b7a.de* *Bry* b7.de* carb-v b4a.de* kali-bi bg2 nux-v b7a.de ran-b b7.de* *Spig* b7.de*
- **riding**:
  - **air**; in open: guaj k2
  - **carriage**; in a:
    - **agg.**: alum dig spong fd4.de tritic-vg fd5.de zinc↓
      - **sore**: zinc
  - **horse**; a: | **agg.**: nat-c ol-j
- **rising**:
  - **after** | **agg.**: agar lact
  - **agg.**: agar chinin-s lach ran-b
    - **aching**: agar k* chinin-s *Lach* k*
  - **sitting**; from | **after**: kali-c nat-c sil
  - **stooping**; from:
    - **after**:
      - **agg.**: aloe nicc
      - **amel.**: kali-c
    - **agg.**: aloe↓ nat-c↓
      - **cutting** pain: aloe
      - **stitching** pain: nat-c h2
- **rubbing** | **after**:
  - **agg.**: ant-c↓
    - **sore**: ant-c h2
  - **amel.**: calc melal-alt gya4 *Phos* k*
    - **stitching** pain: calc *Phos* k*
- **running**:
  - **after**: stroph-s↓
    - **cramping**: stroph-s sp1
  - **agg.**: borx↓ lyc↓
    - **stitching** pain: borx lyc k*

- **sadness**; with | **pressing** pain (See MIND - Sadness - pressure)
- **salt** agg.: nit-ac↓
  - **burning**: nit-ac$_{h2}$
- **scraped**; as if: seneg$_{ptk1*}$
- **scraping** the throat; after | **pressing** pain (See hawking up - after - pressing)
- **scratching** pain: anac$_{bg2}$ *Ang*$_{b7a.de}$ arg-met$_{b7.de*}$ caust$_{h2}$ kali-c$_{h2}$ puls$_{bg2}$ *Ruta*$_{b7a.de}$ sep$_{bg2}$ sil$_{h2}$ staph$_{b7a.de*}$ thuj$_{bg2}$
- **screwing** together: sulph$_{h2}$
- **sharp** (See cutting)
- **shattering** pain: seneg
- **shooting** (See stitching)
- **singing** agg.: am-c *Arg-met*↓ asc-t$_{a1}$
  - **raw**; as if: *Arg-met*
  - **stitching** pain: am-c$_{k*}$
- **sitting**:
  - **agg.**: agar alum alumn anac↓ bell *Bry*$_{k*}$ cact *Caps* chin *Con* dig dros dulc$_{fd4.de}$ graph indg↓ kali-i kali-p↓ mag-c mez nat-s nat-sil$_{fd3.de•}$ paeon ph-ac *Phos* psor$_{jl2}$ **Seneg**$_{k*}$ spong stann↓ staph tritic-vg$_{fd5.de}$
    - **aching**: bell$_{k*}$ con$_{k*}$
    - **burning**: phos$_{k*}$
    - **cramping**: mez
    - **drawing** pain: *Chin*
    - **griping** pain: graph
    - **pressing** pain: anac$_{h2}$ cact *Chin* dulc$_{fd4.de}$ mez *Seneg* stann$_{h2}$
    - **sore**: nat-sil$_{fd3.de•}$
    - **stitching** pain: agar chin$_{h1}$ *Con* indg kali-p$_{k2}$ phos
  - **amel.**: alum am-m asaf bry$_{bg1}$ chel↓ limest-b$_{es1•}$ tub↓
    - **cutting** pain: alum$_{k*}$
    - **pressing** pain: alum$_{k*}$
    - **stitching** pain: asaf$_{k*}$ chel tub$_{gk}$
  - **bent** forward:
    - **agg.**: am-m borx↓ calc-f↓ chel↓ chin↓ dig dulc$_{a1}$ hir$_{rsj4•}$ lac-loxod-a↓ meny$_{h1}$ *Rhus-t*↓ stroph-s↓
      - **cutting** pain: chin
      - **gnawing** pain: stroph-s$_{sp1}$
      - **pressing** pain: borx$_{h2}$ chin$_{h1}$ *Dig* lac-loxod-a$_{hrn2•}$
      - **sore**: meny$_{h1}$
      - **stitching** pain: am-m borx$_{h2}$ calc-f$_{sp1}$ chel *Rhus-t*
  - **erect**:
    - **agg.**: acon aloe nicc
      - **aching**: acon
    - **amel.**: **Bry**↓ nat-c↓ *Nat-s*↓
      - **sore**: **Bry** nat-c *Nat-s*
- **sitting** a long time; as from: ph-ac$_{h2}$
- **sitting** up in bed agg.: am-c bry$_{mrr1}$ ph-ac **Phos**$_{k*}$ *Staph*$_{a1}$
- **sleep**:
  - **after**:
    - **agg.**: nux-m↓
      - **burning**: nux-m$_{k*}$
  - **agg.**: kali-c↓
    - **cutting** pain: kali-c$_{mrr1}$
  - **before** going to sleep: carb-v sulph
  - **during**: cupr *Ran-b*$_{b7.de*}$
    - **agg.**: bell↓
      - **cramping**: bell$_{h1}$
  - **going** to sleep; on:
    - **agg.**: carb-v↓
      - **stitching** pain: carb-v$_{k*}$
- **smarting**: thuj$_{bg2}$
- **smoking** agg.: asc-t$_{vh}$ merc↓ *Seneg* *Spig*$_{vh}$
  - **cutting** pain: merc$_{k*}$
- **sneezing**:
  - **agg.**: acon *Borx* **Bry**$_{k*}$ carbn-s↓ *Caust*$_{k*}$ *Chel* cina↓ coc-c crot-h *Dros*$_{k*}$ hydr$_{bg1}$ lact *Merc* mez↓ ol-an↓ rhus-t ruta$_{fd4.de}$ seneg sil$_{h2}$ spong$_{fd4.de}$ thuj tub↓ vanil$_{fd5.de}$
- **sneezing – agg.**: ...
    - **bursting** pain: cina$_{h1}$ ol-an$_{k*}$ sil$_{k*}$
    - **pressing** pain: sil$_{h2}$
    - **sore**: carbn-s lact mez *Seneg*
    - **stitching** pain: acon *Borx* *Bry* chel **Dros**$_{k*}$ **Merc**$_{k*}$ rhus-t tub$_{gk}$
  - **amel.**: seneg$_{bg1}$
- **sore**: (↗*Sensitive)* acon$_{k*}$ aesc agar agath-a$_{nl2•}$ alum$_{k*}$ alum-sil$_{c2*}$ *Am-c*$_{b4a.de}$ *Am-m*$_{k*}$ ambr$_{k*}$ ampe-qu$_{bro1}$ anac$_{k*}$ ant-t$_{k*}$ **Apis**$_{k*}$ *Arg-met*$_{b7a.de}$ **Arn**$_{k*}$ *Ars*$_{k*}$ arum-t asc-t aur-s$_{k2}$ *Bad* bamb-a$_{stb2.de•}$ bapt bar-c$_{k*}$ bar-s$_{k2}$ bell$_{k2}$ berb brom **Bry**$_{k*}$ bufo$_{bg2}$ **Calc**$_{k*}$ calc-p calc-s calc-sil$_{k2}$ camph$_{b7.de*}$ canth carb-an *Carb-v*$_{k*}$ *Carbn-s* cartl-s$_{rly4•}$ **Caust**$_{k*}$ cham$_{k*}$ **Chel**$_{k*}$ **Chin**$_{k*}$ chlor *Cic*$_{k*}$ cimic$_{k*}$ *Cina*$_{k*}$ *Coc-c* cocc$_{k*}$ colch$_{k*}$ coli$_{rly4•}$ con$_{b4.de*}$ *Cop* corn crot-t *Cur* dig$_{k*}$ dor echi *Euon* *Eup-per*$_{k*}$ *Ferr*$_{k*}$ ferr-ar ferr-m ferr-p fl-ac gamb *Gels*$_{k*}$ graph$_{k*}$ *Guaj* *Ham* **Hep**$_{k*}$ hist$_{sp1}$ *Hydr* *Hyos* ign iod$_{b4a.de}$ ip$_{k*}$ iris kali-ar **Kali-bi**$_{k*}$ *Kali-c*$_{k*}$ kali-m$_{k2}$ kali-n$_{k*}$ kali-p kali-s kali-sil$_{k2}$ *Kreos*$_{k*}$ *Lac-d* *Lach*$_{k*}$ lact laur *Led*$_{k*}$ lob *Lyc*$_{k*}$ lyss *Mag-c*$_{k*}$ *Mag-m*$_{k*}$ manc$_{k*}$ mang$_{k*}$ med meny$_{b7.de*}$ meph$_{k*}$ *Merc*$_{k*}$ *Mez*$_{k*}$ *Mur-ac*$_{k*}$ nad$_{rly4•}$ nat-ar *Nat-c*$_{k*}$ *Nat-m*$_{k*}$ nat-p nat-s$_{k*}$ nat-sil$_{fd3.de•}$ nicc *Nit-ac*$_{k*}$ *Nux-m*$_{k*}$ nux-v ol-j$_{k*}$ olnd ox-ac oxal-a$_{rly4•}$ ozone$_{sde2•}$ *Petr* ph-ac$_{b4.de*}$ phase$_{bro1}$ **Phos**$_{k*}$ *Phos-pchl*$_{c1}$ *Phyt* pot-e$_{rly4•}$ psor$_{k*}$ **Puls**$_{k*}$ pyrog$_{bg2}$ **Ran-b**$_{k*}$ ran-s$_{k*}$ rat rhod$_{k*}$ *Rhus-t*$_{k*}$ ribo$_{rly4•}$ rumx sabin$_{b7.de*}$ sal-fr$_{sle1•}$ samb sang$_{k*}$ sanic **Seneg**$_{k*}$ *Sep*$_{k*}$ *Sil*$_{k*}$ spig$_{b7.de*}$ *Spong*$_{k*}$ squil$_{k2}$ **Stann**$_{k*}$ *Staph*$_{k*}$ stram$_{bg2}$ stront-c$_{k*}$ sul-ac$_{k*}$ *Sulph*$_{k*}$ syph tab tarent thuj$_{k*}$ tub$_{bg}$ valer$_{b7.de*}$ verat$_{b7a.de*}$ viol-t$_{b7.de*}$ *Zinc*$_{k*}$ [spect$_{dfg1}$]
  - **accompanied** by:
    - **respiration**; impeded: *Cham*$_{b7a.de}$ kreos$_{b7a.de}$ nux-v$_{b7.de*}$
    - **Scapulae**; sore pain between: chin$_{ptk1*}$
  - **alternating** with | **fluttering** (See Fluttering - alternating - soreness)
  - **throbbing**: agar$_{h2}$
- **splinter**; as from a: **Arg-n**$_{k*}$ nit-ac$_{k2}$
- **sprained**; as if: agar$_{k*}$ *Arn*$_{k*}$ aur$_{bg2}$ aur-m caps$_{bg2}$ caust$_{b4.de*}$ cocc$_{bg2}$ dulc$_{b4.de*}$ *Kalm*$_{k*}$ lyc$_{b4.de*}$ petr$_{b4.de*}$ plat$_{b4.de*}$ rhod$_{b4.de*}$ spig$_{b7.de*}$ sulph$_{b4.de*}$ tell$_{ptk1}$ thuj$_{b4.de*}$
- **squeezed**; as if: acon$_{b7.de*}$ aeth$_{bg2}$ am-m$_{bg2}$ *Asar*$_{b7a.de}$ bell$_{b4.de*}$ bism$_{b7.de*}$ borx$_{b4a.de}$ brom bry$_{b7.de*}$ bufo$_{bg2}$ *Cact*$_{bg2}$ *Camph*$_{b7a.de}$ canth$_{b7.de*}$ carb-an$_{b4.de*}$ *Caust*$_{bg2}$ cham$_{b7.de*}$ cina$_{k*}$ colch$_{b7.de*}$ dros$_{k*}$ dulc$_{b4.de*}$ graph$_{k*}$ helo$_{bg2}$ hydrog$_{srj2•}$ hyos$_{b7.de*}$ kali-c$_{b4.de*}$ lact mag-c$_{b4.de*}$ mang-p$_{rly4•}$ merc$_{k*}$ mur-ac$_{b4.de*}$ nux-v$_{b7.de*}$ *Ph-ac*$_{k*}$ *Plat*$_{k*}$ rhod$_{b4.de*}$ *Sars*$_{bg2}$ seneg$_{k*}$ stann$_{b4.de*}$ sulph$_{bg2}$ teucr$_{k*}$ thuj$_{k*}$ verat$_{k*}$
- **stabbing** (See stitching)
- **standing**:
  - **after**: nat-m↓
    - **pressing** pain: nat-m$_{h2}$
  - **agg.**: aur-m bov calc lac-loxod-a↓ nat-m *Nat-s* ran-b spig spong$_{fd4.de}$ stann zinc
    - **aching**: nat-m$_{k*}$
    - **drawing** pain: calc spig
    - **pressing** pain: aur-m lac-loxod-a$_{hrn2•}$ *Ran-b* spig$_{k*}$
    - **sprained**; as if: aur-m
    - **tearing** pain: spig$_{h1}$
  - **amel.**: *Chin* graph petr-ra↓
    - **drawing** pain: *Chin*
    - **griping** pain: graph petr-ra$_{shn4•}$
    - **pressing** pain: *Chin*
- **sticking** pain: allox$_{sp1}$ bell-p$_{sp1}$ cob-n$_{sp1}$ hed$_{sp1}$ hist$_{sp1}$ mag-s$_{sp1}$ rauw$_{sp1}$ stroph-s$_{sp1}$ x-ray$_{sp1}$
- **stinging**: colch$_{k2}$ hyper$_{bg2}$ kali-s$_{fd4.de}$ laur mang$_{h2}$ melal-alt$_{gya4}$ nat-c$_{h2}$ nat-m *Phos* plb
- **stitching** pain: **Acon**$_{k*}$ aesc$_{k*}$ aeth *Agar*$_{k*}$ agath-a$_{nl2•}$ *Ail*$_{k*}$ all-s$_{k*}$ aloe *Alum*$_{k*}$ alum-sil$_{k2}$ alumn *Am-c*$_{k*}$ am-m$_{k*}$ ambr$_{b7.de*}$ *Anac*$_{k*}$ anan ang$_{b7.de*}$ anh$_{sp1}$ *Ant-c*$_{k*}$ *Ant-t*$_{k*}$ ap-g$_{bro1}$ *Apis*$_{k*}$ aq-mar$_{skp7•}$ arg-met$_{b7.de*}$ *Arg-n*$_{k*}$ arge-pl$_{rwt5•}$ *Arn*$_{k*}$ *Ars*$_{k*}$ ars-i$_{k2}$ *Asaf*$_{k*}$ asar$_{k*}$ *Asc-t*$_{bro1}$ aspar aster *Aur*$_{k*}$ aur-i$_{k2}$ *Aur-m* aur-s$_{k2}$ bad bamb-a$_{stb2.de•}$ bar-c$_{k*}$ bar-i$_{k2}$ bar-s$_{k2}$ *Bell*$_{k*}$ berb$_{k*}$ bism$_{b7.de*}$ **Borx**$_{k*}$ bov$_{k*}$ brom$_{k*}$ **Bry**$_{k*}$ bufo$_{k*}$ *Cact* cain calad$_{k*}$ **Calc**$_{k*}$ *Calc-p*$_{k*}$ calc-s calc-sil$_{k2}$ camph$_{k*}$ cann-i$_{k*}$ *Cann-s*$_{b7.de*}$ **Canth**$_{k*}$ *Caps*$_{k*}$ *Carb-an*$_{k*}$ *Carb-v*$_{k*}$ carbn-s *Card-m* cassia-s$_{cdd7•}$ *Caust*$_{k*}$ **Cham**$_{k*}$ *Chel*$_{k*}$ **Chin**$_{b7.de*}$ chinin-ar chinin-s cimic$_{bro1}$ cina$_{k*}$ cinnb cit-ac$_{rly4•}$ *Clem*$_{k*}$ cob-n$_{sp1}$ coc-c$_{k*}$ cocc$_{k*}$ coff$_{b7.de*}$

- **stitching** pain: ...
Colch k* *Coloc* k* *Con* k* corn k* croc k* crot-h crot-t k* cupr b7.de* cycl k* cystein-l rly4• dig k* *Dros* k* *Dulc* k* elaps k* elat hr1 ephe-si hsj1• euon *Eup-per* bg2 euphr b7.de* eupi k* falco-pe nl2• *Ferr* k* ferr-ar ferr-i ferr-p form bro1 galeoc-c-h gms1• gamb bg1 gels k* gnaph *Gran* k* *Graph* k* grat k* *Guaj* k* haem bro1 ham k* hep k* hydr-ac k* *Hydroph* rsj6• *Hyos* k* *Ign* k* inul bro1 *Iod* k* *Ip* irid-met srj5• jab k* jug-r k* kali-ar *Kali-bi* k* **Kali-c** k* *Kali-i* k* kali-m k2 kali-n k* **Kali-p** *Kali-s* kali-sil k2 kalm k* *Kreos* k* *Lach* k* *Lact* laur k* led k* *Lob-c* bro1 loxo-recl knl4• luf-op rsj5• *Lyc* k* m-ambo b7.de m-arct b7.de *Mag-c* k* mag-m b4.de* mag-s k* manc mang k* marb-w es1• med melal-alt gya4 mentho bro1 meny k* *Merc* k* **Merc-c** k* merc-i-f *Mez* k* mill k* moni rfm1• mosch k* *Mur-ac* k* myric ptk1 myrt-c c2* *Nat-ar* *Nat-c* k* **Nat-m** k* *Nat-n* k* nat-p nat-pyru rly4• nat-s k* *Nicc* k* *Nit-ac* k* **Nux-m** k* nux-v k* ol-an k* ol-j bro1* olnd k* ox-ac k* *Paeon* k* par k* pert-vc vk9 *Petr* k* petr-ra shn4• *Ph-ac* k* phel bro1 **Phos** k* phyt *Pieri-b* mlk9.de plan *Plat* k* plb k* polyg-h positr nl2• propl ub1• psor k* ptel c1 *Puls* k* **Ran-b** k* *Ran-s* k* raph k* rat rheum k* rhod bro1 rhus-r bro1 *Rhus-t* k* *Rhus-v* **Rumx** k* ruta k* sabad k* sabin b7.de* sal-fr sle1• samb *Sang* k* saroth sp1 *Sars* k* sec gk sel b7a.de **Seneg** k* *Sep* k* *Sil* k* sin-n k* sphing a1* **Spig** k* spong k* **Squil** k* *Stann* k* *Staph* k* *Stict* bro1 still *Stront-c* k* stry suis-pan rly4• *Sul-ac* k* **Sulph** k* sumb k* suprar rly4• *Tab* k* tarax k* ther k* *Thuj* k* tril-p br1* tritic-vg fd5.de tub c1* *Valer* k* vanil fd5.de verat k* *Verb* k* vinc k* viol-o b7a.de* viol-t k* *Zinc* k* zinc-p k2 zing k* [heroin sdj2]
  - **accompanied** by | **Mammae**; cancer in (See Cancer - mammae - accompanied - pain - stitching)
  - **boring** pain: meny h1 spong h1
  - **burning**: *All-c* alum h2 *Ars* bar-c *Carb-an* k* *Carbn-s* *Cina* *Crot-t* mur-ac k* sang ptk1
  - **downward**: agath-a nl2• alumn k* berb con
  - **forward**: agar
  - **inward**: berb borx k2
  - **itching**: calc h2
  - **outward**: arg-met b7.de* ars-s-f br1 *Asaf* k* bell bry b7.de* canth b7.de* carb-v b4.de* chin b7.de* colch b7.de* hyper mur-ac b4.de* nit-ac b4.de* sabad b7.de* *Spig* k* spong b7.de* thuj valer k*
  - **paroxysmal**: nat-m h2 tritic-vg fd5.de
  - **rhythmical**: am-m h2 *Calc* chin h1 cocc k*
  - **twitching**: calc h2
  - **up** and down: mang hr1
  - **upward**: gamb mang h2 mur-ac nat-c stann stront-c
  - **wandering** pain: acon carbn-s *Ferr* k* kali-c k2* **Puls** sang hr1 *Sulph* tub gk
- **stool**:
  - **after** | **agg.**: agar
  - **before**: spig b7.de*
  - **during** | **agg.**: spig b7.de*
- **stooping**:
  - **agg.**: alum ↓ am-c ars *Asc-t* ↓ card-m caust ↓ chel fago lyc mang ↓ merc merl mez nat-s nit-ac phos ↓ ran-b rhod *Seneg* sep ↓ staph ↓ zinc ↓
    - **cutting** pain: *Asc-t*
    - **pressing** pain: caust h2 *Ran-b* sep
    - **sore**: mang a1* phos h2 seneg
    - **stitching** pain: alum am-c k* ars k* card-m mang merc k* merl nit-ac h2 *Ran-b* staph a1 zinc
  - **amel.**: petr ↓ petr-ra ↓
    - **cramping**: petr h2
    - **griping** pain: petr-ra shn4•
- **straining**, lifting: alum ↓
  - **sore**: alum k1
- **stretching**:
  - **amel.**: stroph-s ↓
    - **gnawing** pain: stroph-s sp1
  - **arm**:
    - **agg.**: berb ↓ *Ran-b*
      - **tearing** pain: berb
- **stretching – arm**: ...
    - **amel.**: berb puls h1
- **suffocative** sensation; with: rauw ↓
  - **constricting** pain: rauw sp1
- **supper**:
  - **after**:
    - **agg.**: am-c ↓ lyc ↓
      - **stitching** pain: am-c h2 lyc h2
    - **amel.**: phos ↓
      - **sore**: phos
- **suppurative** deep in chest: *Phos* k* *Ran-b* bg2
- **swallowing** agg.: all-c alum *Calc-p*
- **synchronous** with pulse: iod ↓
  - **drawing** pain: iod h
- **talking**:
  - **after**: *Arg-met* ↓ *Calc* ↓ nat-m ↓
    - **pressing** pain: nat-m h2
    - **raw**; as if: *Arg-met* *Calc* k*
  - **agg.**: alum k2* am-c asc-t a1 **Borx** k* cann-s carb-an ↓ hed ↓ hep bro1 **Kali-c** kali-n lyc ↓ *Nat-m* prun puls ↓ rhus-t seneg ↓ *Stann* bro1 stram ↓ tab tub ↓
    - **excitedly**: *Nat-m* ↓ stann stram
      - **aching**: *Nat-m* k* stann stram k*
    - **needles**; as from: hed sp1
    - **pressing** pain: stram h1
    - **scraped**; as if: seneg ptk1*
    - **sore**: alum *Kali-c* lyc puls
    - **stitching** pain: borx cann-s carb-an rhus-t tub gk
- **tearing** pain: acon k2 aesc agath-a nl2• aloe *Am-c* b4a.de anac k* ant-t k* arg-met b7.de* aur h2 aur-m bamb-a stb2.de• bar-c bell k* berb borx b4a.de bry k* canth k* *Carb-v* k* carbn-h *Carbn-s* caust k* chel k2 cic bg2 *Clem* **Colch** k* con k* cub cycl k* *Dulc* k* elaps graph k* hura hyos ip b7.de* kali-bi k* *Kali-c* k* kali-i k* kali-n b4.de* kali-p kali-s fd4.de kali-sil k2 kreos bg2 led b7.de* merc k* merc-c bg2* nat-m k* **Nux-v** op b7.de* petr k* *Phos* k* psor k* *Puls* k* *Ran-b* rhus-t b7.de* rumx sang k* sil k* sol-t-ae a1 *Spig* k* stram b7.de* teucr b7.de* thuj k* valer k* *Zinc* k*
  - **paroxysmal**: kola stb3•
  - **wandering** pain: kali-c mrr1
- **temperature**, after change of: *Acon* ↓
  - **raw**; as if: *Acon* k*
- **thunderstorm**: rhod k2 spong fd4.de
  - **stitching** pain: rhod k2
- **torn** asunder; as if: *Euph* b4a.de rhus-t b7.de* *Spig* b7a.de
- **torn** loose; as if: ambr bg2 bry bg2 nux-v b7a.de* phos bg2 psor bg2
- **touch**:
  - **agg.**: am-c ↓ aq-mar ↓ arg-met ↓ arg-n bg1 **Arn** ↓ borx h2 bry ↓ calc h2 calc-p k2 canth ↓ cassia-s ↓ chel ↓ **Chin** ↓ cist ↓ coch c1 colch ↓ con ↓ crot-t ↓ dros *Kali-c* ↓ led br1* lyc ↓ mag-c ↓ mang ↓ med ↓ nat-c ↓ **Nat-m** bg1 *Nux-v* bg1 *Phos* podo ↓ psor ↓ *Ran-b* k* ruta ↓ sabin ↓ seneg k2 staph h1 stroph-s sp1 sulph h2 zinc ↓
    - **aching**: dros k*
    - **pressing**: mang h2 podo fd3.de• ruta h1
    - **sore**: am-c arg-met arg-n **Arn** k* borx a1 bry **Calc** k* calc-p canth cassia-s ccrh1• chel bg1 **Chin** k* cist colch con crot-t *Kali-c* k* *Led* lyc mag-c h2 med nat-c h2 nat-m nux-v phos h2 psor **Ran-b** k* *Seneg* zinc
    - **stitching** pain: aq-mar skp7• phos **Ran-b** k* sabin c1
  - **clothes** agg.; of: ozone ↓
    - **sore**: ozone sde2•
  - **spine** agg.; of: tarent bg1*
- **turning**:
  - **agg.**: alum h2 caps ↓ caust ↓ phos ↓ plb **Ran-b** k* ruta fd4.de spong fd4.de staph ↓ tub ↓
    - **pressing** pain: caps
    - **stitching** pain: caust phos **Ran-b** k* ruta fd4.de staph tub gk
  - **bed**; in:
    - **agg.**: alum ↓ caust irid-met ↓ kali-bi bg1 kreos bg1 **Ran-b** ↓ *Staph* a1 thuj

- **bed**; in – **agg.**: ...
  - **aching**: irid-met srj5•
  - **sore**: alum **Ran-b** k*
- **left**; to | **agg.**: kali-bi bg1

- **twisting** pain: carb-an h2* nit-ac h2* sulph bg2 tarax bg2
- **ulcerative** pain: ampe-qu bro1 *Arn* bro1 bry k* calc bro1 carb-an k* **Dros** bg2 eup-per bro1 kali-bi bg2 kreos k* *Lach* k* lyc bro1 mag-m k* merc k* phase bro1 **Phos** bg2 psor k* *Puls* k* *Ran-b* k* ran-s bro1 sang bro1 spig k* staph k* sulph
- **undulating** (See waves)
- **urination**:
  - **amel.**: lil-t bg1 spong fd4.de
  - **delayed**; if desire to urinate is: **Lil-t**
  - **during**:
    - **agg.**: clem ↓
      - **stitching** pain: clem b4a.de*
- **vexation** agg.: phos thuj ↓
  - **cramping**: thuj bg1
- **violent**: acal mtf11 psor jl2
- **waking**; on: acon-ac rly4• alum ↓ graph kali-bi merc-i-r mim-p rsj8• nit-ac ↓ petr-ra shn4• *Phos* seneg thuj tritic-vg fd5.de [heroin sdj2]
  - **night**: trios ↓
    - **griping** pain: trios rsj11•
  - **cramping**: alum h2 nit-ac h2
  - **sore**: merc-i-r
- **walking**:
  - **after**:
    - **agg.**: calc ↓
      - **raw**; as if: calc k*
  - **agg.**: agar allox ↓ am-c *Asaf* ↓ bell brom *Bry* bufo cact calc camph caps ↓ card-m caust ↓ cham chel cimic cinnb cocc colch coloc *Con* ↓ dig *Ferr* ↓ hep kali-i kali-n bg1 kali-p ↓ lact led ↓ loxo-recl ↓ lyss ↓ mag-s ↓ merc merc-i-r ↓ merl nat-m olnd ox-ac **Ran-b** k* rhus-t sars spig spong ↓ stann stront-c sul-ac sulph tarax tarent vanil fd5.de *Viol-t* zinc
    - **aching**: bell k* bufo *Cact* k* stront-c
    - **burning**: mag-s k*
    - **cramping**: *Ferr*
    - **drawing** pain: lact led h1
    - **dressing**, and: alum
    - **pressing** pain: caust k* vanil fd5.de
    - **sticking** pain: allox sp1
    - **stitching** pain: am-c *Asaf* caps a1 cinnb cocc coloc *Con* hep *Kali-i* kali-n h2 kali-p k2 loxo-recl knl4• lyss c1 merc-i-r olnd rhus-t spong
  - **air**; in open:
    - **after**:
      - **agg.**: sulph ↓
        - **burning**: sulph
        - **cutting** pain: sulph
    - **agg.**: am-m ↓ caust graph ↓ lyc *Merc* ↓ mez ↓ ran-b sulph zinc
      - **burning**: am-m h2
      - **cramping**: mez h2
      - **pressing** pain: graph h2
      - **stitching** pain: caust *Merc* *Ran-b* zinc
    - **amel.**: nat-m ↓ pall ↓ seneg k2
      - **sore**: nat-m
      - **stitching** pain: pall *Seneg*
  - **amel.**: alum ↓ *Chin* chlam-tr bcx2• dros mez nat-m ph-ac *Seneg* tritic-vg fd5.de
    - **boring** pain: alum k*
    - **cramping**: mez
    - **drawing** pain: *Chin*
    - **pressing** pain: *Chin* mez *Seneg* tritic-vg fd5.de
  - **rapidly**:
    - **agg.**: alum brom chin rhod seneg ↓ sulph vanil fd5.de
      - **cutting** pain: alum k*
      - **drawing** pain: seneg
      - **stitching** pain: brom chin sulph vanil fd5.de
- **walking – rapidly**: ...
    - **amel.**: lob bro1
  - **slowly** | **amel.**: borx
- **wandering** pain: acon bg2 agar bg2 *All-c* aloe bg2 ars-h bufo bg2 *Cact* *Ferr* kali-c k2 lyss *Ol-j* puls k2 *Seneg* k* sin-n *Tarent* tub gk
- **warm**:
  - **applications** | **amel.**: adam skp7• *Ars* bar-c h2 caust **Phos**
  - **drinks**:
    - **amel.**: aq-mar ↓ **Spig** mrr1
      - **stitching** pain: aq-mar skp7•
  - **food**:
    - **amel.**: chel k2 sulph ↓
      - **griping** pain: sulph
  - **room**:
    - **agg.**: mag-s sil *Sulph* ↓
      - **cramping**: *Sulph*
- **warm** in bed agg.; becoming: rhus-v
  - **stitching** pain: rhus-v k*
- **waves**; in: anac h2 dig *Dulc* k* glon bg2 spig k* teucr b7.de*
- **weather**:
  - **change** of weather: **Ran-b** k*
    - **stitching** pain: **Ran-b** k*
  - **wet**:
    - **agg.**: cassia-s ↓ *Cupr* cur ↓ *Kali-c* lac-d k2 med k2 **Nat-c** k* *Nat-s* ↓ *Ran-b* k* rhus-t bro1 *Sil* spig bro1
      - **pressing** pain: cassia-s ccrh1• *Cupr* *Kali-c* *Nat-s* *Sil*
      - **sore**: cur
- **wine** agg.: borx
- **winter** agg.: *Arg-met* *Kalm*
- **writing** agg.: carb-an ↓ mag-s ran-b rumx ↓ spig ↓
  - **pressing** pain: mag-s ran-b
  - **stitching** pain: carb-an rumx spig
- **yawning**:
  - **agg.**: aur ↓ bell *Borx* gal-ac c1 hep iod sne mag-c ↓ nat-s oci-sa sk4• phel sang
    - **sore**: gal-ac a1
    - **stitching** pain: aur k* bell *Borx* mag-c nat-s phel k*
  - **hindering** yawning: sphing ↓
    - **stitching** pain: sphing kk3.fr

▽ - **extending** to:

○ - **Abdomen**: berb ↓ stann ↓
    - **cutting** pain: berb
    - **digging** pain: stann h2
    - **Lower** part of abdomen: agath-a ↓ *Corn* ↓
      - **stitching** pain: agath-a nl2• *Corn*
  - **Across**: kali-c ↓ nept-m lsd2.fr
    - **drawing** pain: kali-c
  - **Arm**: *Aster* ↓ calc-ar k2 com ↓ positr nl2•
    - **left**: cact ↓ *Kalm* mrr1 spig ↓ tarent ↓
      - **stitching** pain: cact br1 spig k2 tarent
    - **drawing** pain: *Aster* com
  - **Axilla**: aur ↓ seneg ↓
    - **drawing** pain: aur h2 seneg
  - **Back**: acon ↓ agar ↓ am-c ↓ ambr ↓ *Anac* ↓ ang ↓ *Ant-c* ↓ *Apis* ↓ *Asaf* ↓ bell ↓ borx ↓ bov ↓ *Bry* ↓ calc ↓ *Canth* ↓ carb-v ↓ carbn-s ↓ *Card-m* ↓ caust ↓ *Chel* ↓ *Chen-a* ↓ chin ↓ cocc ↓ colch ↓ con ↓ *Corn* ↓ *Crot-c* ↓ crot-t ↓ cupr ↓ dulc ↓ ferr ↓ gamb ↓ glon ↓ hep ↓ kali-bi mrr1 *Kali-c* ↓ kali-i ↓ kali-n ↓ kali-sil ↓ lach ↓ lact ↓ laur ↓ lyc ↓ *Merc* ↓ mez ↓ *Myrt-c* ↓ nat-m ↓ nept-m lsd2.fr nit-ac ↓ ol-an ↓ ol-j ↓ ozone ↓ pall ↓ *Phel* ↓ phos ↓ *Phyt* ↓ plb ↓ rauw ↓ rhod ↓ rhus-t ↓ sabin ↓ sec ↓ *Seneg* ↓ *Sep* ↓ *Sil* ↓ spig ↓ staph ↓ sul-ac ↓ **Sulph** ↓ tab ↓ tarax ↓ thuj ↓ til ↓ vanil fd5.de
    - **right**: acon ↓ ars ↓ carb-v ↓ chel ↓ guaj ↓ merc-c ↓ merc-sul ↓ nit-ac ↓ nux-v ↓ phel ↓ phyt ↓ sep ↓

Chest

- **Back** – **right**: ...
  - **stitching** pain: acon bg2 ars bg2 carb-v bg2 chel bg2 guaj bg2 merc-c bg2 merc-sul bg2 nit-ac bg2 nux-v bg2 phel bg2 phyt bg2 sep bg2
  - **left**: bov↓ cinnb↓ com↓ gels↓ kali-p↓ lil-t↓ rhod↓ rhus-t↓ spig↓ sul-ac↓ ther↓ thuj↓
    - **stitching** pain: bov bg2 cinnb bg2 com bg2 gels bg2 kali-p bg2 lil-t bg2 rhod bg2 rhus-t bg2 spig bg2 sul-ac bg2 ther bg2 thuj bg2
  - **18 h**: laur↓
    - **stitching** pain: laur
  - **paroxysmal**: rauw sp1
  - **stitching** pain: acon b7.de* agar am-c bg2 ambr k* _Anac_ k* ang bg2 _Ant-c_ b7a.de _Apis_ k* _Asaf_ bell bg2 borx b4a.de bov k* _Bry_ k* calc k* _Canth_ k* carb-v k* carbn-s k2 _Card-m_ caust k* _Chel_ k* _Chen-a_ chin b7.de* cocc b7.de* colch k* con bg2 _Corn_ _Crot-c_ crot-t cupr bg2 dulc a1* ferr k* gamb glon hr1* hep _Kali-bi_ k* _Kali-c_ k* kali-i bg2 kali-n kali-sil k2 lach bg2 lact laur b7.de* lyc k* _Merc_ k* mez k* _Myrt-c_ b7a.de nat-m k* nept-m lsd2.fr nit-ac bg2 ol-an bg2 ol-j bg2 ozone sde2• pall _Phel_ bg2 phos bg2 _Phyt_ k* plb b7.de rhod k* rhus-t sabin b7.de* sec gk _Seneg_ bg2 _Sep_ _Sil_ k* spig b7.de* staph k2 sul-ac k* **Sulph** k* tab k* tarax b7.de* thuj bg2 til c1
  - **Ribs**; along:
    - **right**: hyper↓
      - **stitching** pain: hyper bg2
    - **left**: aml-ns↓ sil↓
      - **stitching** pain: aml-ns bg2 sil bg2
- **Back** and forth: apis↓
  - **drawing** pain: apis
- **Downward**: am-c bg1
  - **right**: borx bg2
- **Ear**:
  - **right**: bamb-a↓
    - **burning**: bamb-a stb2.de•
- **Face**: **Sulph**↓
  - **burning**: **Sulph** k*
- **Forward**: agar bg2
- **Front**: rauw↓
  - **paroxysmal**: rauw sp1
- **Groins**: plat↓
  - **drawing** pain: plat
- **Hand** | **left**: _Kalm_ mrr1
- **Heart**: sulph bg2
- **Liver**: _Calc-p_↓ ran-b↓
  - **cutting** pain: ran-b c1
  - **stitching** pain: _Calc-p_
- **Lower** jaw: apis↓
  - **drawing** pain: apis
- **Mouth**: ph-ac↓
  - **burning**: ph-ac h2
  - **coryza**; during: ph-ac↓
    - **burning**: ph-ac
- **Neck**; left: spig↓ zinc↓
  - **stitching** pain: spig k2 zinc
- **Scapula**: acon↓ _Bry_↓ _Chel_↓ _Ferr_↓ _Hep_↓ **Nat-m**↓ nux-v↓ ox-ac↓ phos↓ seneg↓ _Sulph_↓ vanil↓
  - **cutting** pain: **Nat-m**
  - **stinging**: seneg bg2
  - **stitching** pain: acon _Bry_ _Chel_ bg2 _Ferr_ _Hep_ nux-v bg2 ox-ac phos bg2 seneg _Sulph_ vanil fd5.de
- **Shoulder**: alum↓ aq-mar rbp6 bar-c↓ _Card-m_↓ _Sang_↓ spig↓ ther↓
  - **left**: aq-mar rbp6 kola stb3•
  - **stitching** pain: alum h2 bar-c _Card-m_ _Sang_ spig k2 ther
- **Shoulders**: ox-ac↓ _Verat_↓
  - **cutting** pain: ox-ac _Verat_
- **Side** to side: gnaph↓
  - **stitching** pain: gnaph

- **extending** to: ...
  - **Stomach**: caust↓ ox-ac↓
    - **stitching** pain: caust ox-ac
  - **Throat**: anac↓ _Ant-t_↓ apis bg2 bufo↓ calc bg2 calc-p↓ kali-n↓ mang-p↓ _Merc_↓ phos bg2 sabad↓ ther↓ thuj bg2
    - **burning**: _Ant-t_ bufo k2 calc-p kali-n mang-p rly4• _Merc_ sabad
    - **stitching** pain: anac calc ther
  - **Throat**-pit: thuj↓
    - **cutting** pain: thuj
  - **Through** chest: cann-i↓
    - **stitching** pain: cann-i c1
  - **Transverse**: nat-m↓ nit-ac↓
    - **stitching** pain: nat-m h2 nit-ac h2
  - **Umbilicus**: agar bg1 bry bg2* chel↓ mag-c bg1
    - **drawing** pain: chel
  - **Upward**: ars bg2 calc bg2 kali-c bg2 mur-ac bg2 squil bg2 thuj bg2
    - **right**: arn bg2 lach bg2 plat bg2 thuj bg2
    - **left**: am-m bg2 bov bg2 coc-c bg2 kali-c bg2 laur bg2 med bg2 sep bg2 squil bg2 stann bg2 zinc bg2

○ - **Anterior** part: **Apis**↓ berb↓ cann-s↓ _Canth_↓ card-m↓ carl↓ cartl-s↓ clem↓ colch↓ coloc↓ com↓ con↓ dulc↓ kali-bi↓ kali-n↓ lyc↓ **Merc**↓ mez↓ nit-ac↓ nux-m↓ sarr↓ sulph↓ ter↓ ther↓

- **midnight**: chel↓
  - **drawing** pain: chel
- **morning**: am-m↓ nit-ac↓
  - **pressing** pain: nit-ac h2
  - **stitching** pain: am-m k*
- **forenoon**: _Ran-b_↓
  - **perspiration**; during: ran-b↓
    - **stitching** pain: ran-b
  - **stitching** pain: _Ran-b_ k*
- **afternoon**: am-m↓ gamb↓
  - **stitching** pain: am-m k* gamb k*
- **evening**: gamb↓ nicc↓ zinc↓
  - **inspiration** agg.: kali-c↓
    - **stitching** pain: kali-c
  - **stitching** pain: gamb k* nicc k* zinc k*
- **night**: caust↓
  - **stitching** pain: caust k*
- **breathing** deep agg.: gamb↓
  - **stitching** pain: gamb k*
- **burning**: **Apis** kali-n k* sulph k*
- **cough** agg.; during: lyc↓ **Merc**↓
  - **stitching** pain: lyc **Merc** k*
- **cutting** pain: cartl-s rly4• colch k* coloc dulc k*
- **drawing** pain: berb card-m carl com dulc
- **inspiration** agg.: canth↓ _Card-m_↓ _Lyc_↓
  - **stitching** pain: canth k* _Card-m_ _Lyc_
- **scratching** agg.: cinnb↓
  - **burning**: cinnb k*
- **sitting**:
  - **amel.**: am-m↓
    - **stitching** pain: am-m k*
- **sneezing** agg.: _Merc_↓
  - **stitching** pain: _Merc_ k*
- **sore**: con merc nux-m sarr
- **standing** agg.: bov↓
  - **stitching** pain: bov k*
- **stitching** pain: cann-s _Canth_ k* card-m kali-n k* lyc k* **Merc** k* nit-ac k* ter ther
- **stooping** agg.: card-m↓ nit-ac↓
  - **stitching** pain: card-m nit-ac k*
- **tearing** pain: clem kali-bi k* mez k*
- **walking** agg.: card-m↓

- walking agg.: ...
  - stitching pain: card-m
- Aorta: adren bro1 stry bro1
- Axillae: agar↓ *Agn* k* alum↓ am-c↓ ang↓ ant-c↓ ant-t↓ arg-met↓ arg-n arn↓ **Ars**↓ asaf asar astac↓ aur↓ aur-m-n↓ bell k* berb↓ brach↓ brom↓ bry cact calc-act↓ calc-caust↓ calc-p↓ camph↓ canth↓ carb-an b4a.de carb-v k* *Caust*↓ cench k2 chel chin↓ cic h1 clem k* cocc↓ colch bg2 coloc↓ com↓ con k* *Crot-c* k* dios dros↓ dulc h2 elaps↓ form↓ graph k* grat↓ guaj↓ ham fd3.de• hep h2 hura↓ ind iod *Jug-c* c2* jug-r↓ kali-bi bg2 kali-c↓ kalm↓ kola stb3• lac-ac↓ lach↓ lact↓ lap-la↓ lat-m ptk1 laur↓ led↓ lil-t↓ *Lyc*↓ mag-c↓ mang↓ melal-alt↓ meny↓ merc-c↓ mez k2 nat-m↓ nat-s nit-ac k* nux-v↓ olnd↓ oxal-a↓ petr↓ phos↓ phys plb podo fd3.de• psor↓ puls↓ ran-s↓ rhus-t↓ ribo↓ ruta fd4.de sabin↓ samb↓ seneg sep↓ *Sil* k* spig↓ spong fd4.de stann↓ staph stront-c↓ sul-ac k* **Sulph**↓ symph fd3.de• teucr↓ thuj tritic-vg fd5.de tub-m jl2 vanil fd5.de verat k* viol-t↓ vip zinc↓
  - right: *Agn*↓ arg-met↓ carb-v↓ cocc↓ *Crot-c*↓ ham↓ kali-c↓ kali-p↓ laur↓ melal-alt↓ plut-n↓ ruta↓ sil↓ stann↓ staph↓ sul-ac↓ trios↓ vanil↓
    - burning: cocc h1 ham fd3.de• ruta trios rsj11•
    - cutting pain: *Crot-c* k* kali-c h2 plut-n srj7•
    - drawing pain: carb-v h2 kali-p fd1.de• vanil fd5.de
    - pressing pain: *Agn* carb-v h2 ruta fd4.de sil h2 staph h1
    - pulsating pain: trios rsj11•
    - stitching pain: arg-met h1 *Crot-c* k* laur melal-alt gya4 stann h2
    - ulcerative pain: sul-ac h2
    - extending to:
      - left: elaps
        - cutting pain: *Elaps*
  - left: calc↓ chel↓ cocc↓ colch rsj2• irid-met↓ led↓ lil-t↓ mang↓
    - drawing pain: lil-t bg2
    - pressing pain: chel h1 led
    - stitching pain: calc h2 cocc h1 irid-met srj5• mang a1
  - noon: bry↓
    - stitching pain: bry k*
  - evening: hura↓ rat↓ sep↓ stront-c↓ zinc↓
    - sore: sep
    - stitching pain: hura rat k* stront-c zinc k*
  - night: petr↓
    - stitching pain: petr h2
    - tearing pain: petr h2
  - aching: asaf k* bry k* chel dios k* ind phys k* ribo rly4• staph k* thuj k*
  - biting pain: berb bg2 nat-m h2 ruta h1
  - boils: petr↓
    - tearing pain: petr h2
  - boring pain: arg-met h1 berb bg2 plb k*
  - burning: am-c k* berb k* calc-p k* *Carb-v* k* caust k* coloc k* graph ptk1 jug-r k* kali-c k* kola stb3• laur b7.de lyc b4.de nat-m k* rhus-t b7.de sep k* spig k* thuj k* zinc k*
  - corrosive: agn b7.de* mez b4.de*
  - coryza; during: am-m b7a.de
  - cough agg.; during: sel rsj9•
  - cramping: com hura iod k*
  - cutting pain: ang h1* dios k* kali-c k* ruta h1 stann bg2 sul-ac k* thuj k*
  - digging pain: berb bg2
  - drawing pain: *Bell* k* cact chin h1 coloc com lil-t mang h2 nat-s seneg k* sil k* spong fd4.de tritic-vg fd5.de vanil fd5.de
    - paralyzed; as if: am-c
  - dull pain: lat-m bnm6•
  - lifting agg.: sul-ac↓
    - stitching pain: sul-ac h2
  - lifting arm: tritic-vg fd5.de tub c1
  - menses; before: *Calc*
  - motion:
    - agg.: stann↓
      - stitching pain: stann h2
- Axillae – motion: ...
    - amel.: dulc h1*
      - pulsating pain: dulc h2*
    - arms; of:
      - agg.: meny↓
        - stitching pain: meny h1
  - pinching pain: samb h1*
  - pressing pain: *Agn* ang h1 asaf bg2 asar h1* astac bry bg2 camph h1 carb-v chel bg2 chin h1 dros h1 led k* lyc mang h2 ruta fd4.de spong h1 staph bg2 teucr bg2
  - pulsating pain: dulc h2*
  - raising arm agg.: caps↓ kali-c↓ mag-c↓
    - sore: caps
    - stitching pain: kali-c h2 mag-c h2
    - tearing pain: kali-c k*
  - raw; as if: oxal-a rly4•
  - rest agg.: aur-m-n↓
    - stitching pain: aur-m-n k*
  - scar of an old abscess; in: thuj↓
    - cutting pain: thuj
  - sitting agg.: aur-m-n↓ chel↓ nat-s↓
    - stitching pain: aur-m-n chel k* nat-s k*
  - smarting: arg-n bg2 con b4.de*
  - sore: ars brach *Carb-an* b4a.de *Carb-v* k* dios form kali-c lac-ac *Mez* k* nux-v ran-s ribo rly4• sul-ac **Sulph** b4a.de zinc k*
  - sprained; as if: dros h1 mang h2
  - squeezed; as if: mang bg2
  - stitching pain: agar k* alum k* am-c bg2 ant-c h2 ant-t bg2 arg-met b7.de* arg-n arn b7.de* ars h2* asaf k* aur k* aur-m-n k* berb k* brom k* bry k* (non:calc slp) calc-act slp canth k* *Caust* k* chel b7.de* cocc bg2 con k* dros ptk1 elaps graph k* grat bg2 kali-bi k* kali-c k* kalm k* kola stb3• lach b7.de* lact k* lap-la sde8.de• laur k* led bg2 *Lyc* k* mag-c k* mang k* melal-alt gya4 meny b7.de* merc-c b4a.de mez k* nat-m h2* nat-s k* olnd k* petr h2 phos k* plb b7.de* puls b7.de* rhus-t b7.de* sil k* spig bg2 spong b7.de* stann h2* staph k* stront-c bg2 sul-ac bg2 *Sulph* k* teucr bg2 thuj k* verat k* viol-t b7.de* zinc k*
    - itching: stann h2 staph h1
  - tearing pain: alum k* arg-n k* **Ars** aur bell k* (non:calc slp) calc-caust a1* canth k* carb-v bg2 chel h1 chin h1* colch bg2 guaj bg2 kali-bi k* kali-c k* lach bg2 nat-m k* petr h2 psor sabin k* sulph bg2 thuj k* zinc k*
    - pulsating pain: lyc h2
  - ulcerative pain: sul-ac b4.de*
  - walking in open air agg.: ant-c↓
    - stitching pain: ant-c h2
  - wrenching: kali-bi bg2
  - ▽ extending to:
    - Below: thuj↓
      - drawing pain: thuj
    - Chest: canth↓ caust↓ cop↓ laur↓ mag-s↓ meny↓ zinc↓
      - stitching pain: canth k* caust h2 cop k* laur mag-s k* meny k* zinc h2
    - Down spine to lowest ribs: guaj↓
      - drawing pain: guaj
    - Elbow: verat↓
      - stitching pain: verat a1
    - Hand: arg-n a1
    - Mammae: caust↓
      - stitching pain: caust k*
    - Shoulder: phos↓
      - stitching pain: phos h2
    - Upper arm: led↓ squil↓
      - drawing pain: led
      - raising agg.: arn↓ rhus-t↓
        - drawing pain: arn rhus-t
      - stitching pain: squil h1

• **extending** to: ...
⁝ **Wrist**: elaps ↓
: **drawing** pain: elaps
○ • **Below**: canth ↓ *Caust* ↓ kali-c ↓ laur ↓ lyc ↓ mang ↓ mill ↓
⁝ **right**: plb ↓
: **stitching**: plb k*
⁝ **left**: canth ↓ euon ↓ mill ↓ petr ↓ stann ↓
: **stitching** pain: canth a1 euon k* mill a1 petr k* stann ptk1
⁝ **evening**: bell ↓
: **stitching**: bell k*
⁝ **pressing** pain: kali-c h2 lyc h2 mang h2
⁝ **standing** agg.: plb ↓
: **stitching**: plb k*
⁝ **stitching** pain: canth k* *Caust* k* kali-c h2 laur k* mang h2 mill a1
• **Glands** (= Axillary glands): aeth a1 am-c androc srj1• asar h1 **Bar-c** k* canth ↓ carb-an b4a.de clem b4a.de hep ↓ kali-c lat-m bnm6• lyc ↓ meny ↓ ozone sde2• plut-n srj7• prun rhus-g tmo3• rhus-t k* ruta ↓ sil ↓ sul-ac k* *Sulph* teucr ↓
⁝ **cutting** pain: aeth c1
⁝ **drawing** pain: sil h2
⁝ **sore**: teucr b7.de*
⁝ **stitching** pain: canth b7.de* hep k2 lyc meny b7.de*
⁝ **ulcerative** pain: ruta b7.de* teucr b7.de*
• **Muscles** | **right**: prim-v bro1
• **Region** of: anac ↓ aspar vh borx ↓ brom ↓ dros ↓ dulc ↓ gamb ↓ kali-bi meny olnd ↓ rhus-t ↓ sep ↓ spig ↓ squil ↓ tab ↓ thuj ↓ zinc
⁝ **right**: borx ↓ brom ↓ carb-v ↓ colch ↓ nat-c ↓
: **stitching** pain: borx brom carb-v colch k* nat-c
⁝ **left**: calc ↓ dig ↓ ruta ↓ sang ↓ zinc ↓
: **stitching** pain: calc k* dig k* ruta sang k* zinc
⁝ **morning**: ran-b
: **motion** agg.: ran-b
⁝ **afternoon**: nat-c ↓
: **15** h: bell ↓
. **stitching** pain: bell
: **sticking** pain: nat-c a1
⁝ **cough** agg.; during: dros ↓
: **stitching** pain: dros
⁝ **inspiration** agg.: ruta ↓
: **stitching** pain: ruta
⁝ **intermittent**: dulc
⁝ **lying** on painful side agg.: nat-c ↓
: **stitching** pain: nat-c k*
⁝ **motion** agg.: mang ↓
: **stitching** pain: mang k*
⁝ **pressing** pain: sep h2 squil h1 thuj h1
: **paroxysmal**: rhus-t h1 thuj h1
⁝ **pressure**:
: **amel.**: dros ↓
. **stitching** pain: dros k*
⁝ **pulsating** pain: squil h1 zinc
⁝ **raising** arm agg.: caps h1
⁝ **rubbing**:
: **amel.**: anac ↓
. **stitching** pain: anac h2
⁝ **sitting** agg.: spong ↓
: **stitching** pain: spong
⁝ **stitching** pain: anac h2 borx brom dros k* gamb k* olnd spig h1 tab k* thuj k*
: **intermitting**: thuj k*
: **inward**: thuj h1
⁝ **touch** agg.: caps h1 squil h1
⁝ **walking** agg.: nat-c ↓
: **stitching** pain: nat-c k*
⁝ **extending** to:
: **Arms**; down: jug-c mez k2 *Nat-ar* tax-br oss1•
: **Finger**; fourth: nat-ar

- **Axillae** – **Region** of – **extending** to: ...
: **Pectoral** muscles: *Brach*
- **Bifurcation** of trachea; rawness at:
• **speaking** and singing; when: *Arg-met* ↓
⁝ **raw**; as if: *Arg-met*
- **Bones**: *Ars* ↓ kali-bi ↓ naja ↓
• **broken**; as if: kali-bi bg2 naja bg2
• **stitching** pain: *Ars* b4a.de
- **Bones** and cartilages: arg-met bro1 arn br1 bell bro1 cham bro1 chin b7.de* *Cimic* bro1 guaj bro1 olnd bro1 plb bro1 *Ruta* bro1
- **Clavicles**: acon alumn am-c bg2 am-m apis asaf ↓ asar bg2 aur bg2 aur-m ↓ berb ↓ bism bg2 brom brucel ↓ bry ↓ calc-p caps cham k* chel ↓ chinin-s cina a1 cinnb coc-c ↓ crot-c k* dros dulc fd4.de ferr h1 fic-m gya1 gamb grat ↓ guaj ↓ hydr jatr-c kali-n lac-c ptk1 lach ↓ lachn ↓ led lyc mag-m k* manc ↓ mang mez bg2 nat-m bg1 nat-sil fd3.de• nit-s-d ↓ ol-an ↓ olib-sac wmh1 paeon ↓ pall ↓ phos ↓ phys ↓ pic-ac podo ↓ *Puls* k* rhod bg2 rhus-t rumx ruta fd4.de sabin ↓ sars bg2 stann ↓ still ↓ streptoc jl2 sulph ↓ sumb ↓ symph fd3.de• tarax ↓ tell k* tritic-vg fd5.de vanil fd5.de zinc
• **right**: brucel ↓ tarax ↓
⁝ **aching**: brucel sa3•
⁝ **boring** pain: tarax h1
• **left**:
⁝ **motion** agg.: coc-c ↓
: **sore**: coc-c
• **aching**: brucel sa3• dros k* jatr-c mag-m k* rhus-t k*
• **acute**: streptoc jl2
• **breathing** agg.: squil ↓
⁝ **stitching** pain: squil h1*
• **burning**: aur-m k* berb grat k* ruta fd4.de sulph
• **cough** agg.; during: apis k*
• **cutting** pain: calc-p k* ruta sabin c1
• **digging** pain: mang k*
• **drawing** pain: caps h1 dulc fd4.de led sars h2 stann tarax h1 tritic-vg fd5.de zinc
• **gnawing** pain: acon k* mang k*
• **inspiration** agg.: alumn ant-c dros mez
⁝ **aching**: dros
⁝ **stitching** pain: alumn k*
⁝ **waking** from a nightmare: rhus-t ↓
: **aching**: rhus-t
• **motion** of head agg.: am-m ↓
⁝ **stitching** pain: am-m k*
• **pressing** pain: asaf bg2 aur bg2 bism h1* led k* mag-m bg2 nit-s-d a1 podo fd3.de• puls k* sars h2 tritic-vg fd5.de zinc k*
• **rheumatic**: *Calc-p Colch*
• **sitting** agg.: cham
• **sore**: alumn am-m *Calc-p* coc-c lach bg2 lyc manc k* nat-m nat-sil fd3.de• phos phys still sumb symph fd3.de•
• **sticking** pain: guaj bg2 sars bg2
• **stitching** pain: alumn am-m k* berb k* bry k* chel k* guaj h2 kali-n h2 lachn k* lyc k* mez k* nat-m k* ol-an k* paeon pall phos h2 puls ptk1 sabin k* stann k* symph fd3.de• tarax h1 zinc
⁝ **intermittent**: sabin k*
⁝ **pulsating** pain: berb k*
⁝ **tearing** pain: am-m k*
⁝ **twitching**: chel k*
• **waking**; on: rhus-t sang
• **walking** agg.: paeon ↓
⁝ **stitching** pain: paeon
▽ • **extending** to:
⁝ **Fingers**:
: **Tips**: caps ↓
. **drawing** pain: caps h1
⁝ **Hand**: galla-q-r nl2•
⁝ **Teeth**: mag-m ↓

- **extending** to – **Teeth**: ...
  - **pressing** pain: mag-m h2
  - **Throat**: tritic-vg fd5.de tub c1
    - **Muscles** of: nat-m bg1
  - **Wrist**: *Calc-p*
- ○ **Above**: **Apis**↓ bad↓ *Con*↓
  - **right**: trios↓
    - **dull** pain: trios rsj11•
  - **cutting** pain: bad
  - **sore**: **Apis** *Con*
- **Below**: ail ant-c↓ arund *Aspar* aur-s↓ berb brom *Calc* *Calc-p* carb-ac chel cina↓ coc-c↓ coca↓ crat↓ dros dulc fd4.de *Ferr*↓ kali-c↓ lachn↓ lyc↓ naja nat-m↓ phos↓ plat↓ ptel puls bg2 rumx k2 ruta fd4.de sang↓ spig sulph tarent tritic-vg fd5.de ulm-c↓ vanil fd5.de zinc
  - **right**: alumn↓ **Ars**↓ bell↓ com *Dulc*↓ kali-c↓ *Lyc*↓ nat-m↓ ptel hr1 ulm-c↓
    - **drawing** pain: com
    - **sore**: ulm-c jsj8•
    - **stitching** pain: alumn **Ars** bell *Dulc* k* kali-c k* *Lyc* nat-m k* ulm-c jsj8•
  - **left**: chel↓ coc-c colch↓ *Con* crat br1 dulc fd4.de elaps gk kali-c↓ mez h2 myrt-c tl1 ruta fd4.de spig↓ *Sulph*↓ *Ther*↓ tub↓ vanil↓
    - **drawing** pain: coc-c vanil fd5.de
    - **pressing** pain: spig vml
    - **stitching** pain: chel colch k* kali-c h2 mez k* *Myrt-c* *Sulph* *Ther* tub c1
  - **morning**: nat-m↓ *Sang*
    - **stitching** pain: nat-m k*
    - **waking**; on: *Sang*
  - **noon**: coca↓
    - **stitching** pain: coca
  - **evening**: kali-c↓
    - **stitching** pain: kali-c h2
  - **night**:
    - **midnight**:
      - **after**:
        - **4** h: nat-m↓
          - **stitching** pain: nat-m
  - **aching**: *Ail* k* carb-ac k* coca dros k* naja sulph k*
  - **breathing** agg.: ant-c↓
    - **aching**: ant-c k*
  - **burning**: rumx k2 sang k*
  - **cough** agg.; during: lyc↓ tub c1
    - **stitching** pain: lyc k*
  - **cutting** pain: dulc k* kali-c h2
  - **drawing** pain: brom chel tritic-vg fd5.de vanil fd5.de zinc
  - **inspiration** agg.: cina↓ dros↓ lyc↓ mez h2 tritic-vg fd5.de
    - **aching**: dros mez
    - **stitching** pain: cina a1* lyc k*
  - **motion** agg.: lyc↓
    - **stitching** pain: lyc k*
  - **pressing** pain: ant-c h2 crat br1 plat h2 *Spig* k* zinc h2
  - **pressure**:
    - **agg.**: cina↓
      - **stitching** pain: cina
    - **amel.**: dulc↓
      - **cutting** pain: dulc k*
  - **raw**; as if: rumx bg2*
  - **sore**: coc-c *Ferr* phos **Puls** k* ulm-c jsj8•
  - **stitching** pain: *Ail* ant-c h2 arund k* aur-s k* chel k* cina *Dulc* k* lachn c1 sang spig k*
    - **itching**: spig h1
    - **pulsating** pain: lyc k*
    - **upward**: nat-m
  - **walking** agg.: bell↓
    - **stitching** pain: bell k*

- **Clavicles** – **Below**: ...
  - **extending** to:
    - **Deep** into chest: mez↓ ulm-c↓
      - **stitching** pain: mez k* ulm-c jsj8•
    - **Elbows**: kali-n↓
      - **stitching** pain: kali-n h2
    - **Scapula**: **Sulph**↓ ther↓
      - **inspiration** agg.: dros
        - **aching**: dros k*
      - **stitching** pain: **Sulph** ther
    - **Sternum**: *Ail*↓
      - **stitching** pain: *Ail*
  - **Region** of: agar↓ am-m↓ apis berb↓ brom↓ caps↓ cham↓ *Chel* coc-c ferr-m↓ kali-bi led *Lyc*↓ mang↓ plat stann symph↓ tell tritic-vg fd5.de zinc
    - **right**: berb↓ caust↓
      - **stitching** pain: berb k* caust k*
    - **left**: con↓ mang↓ meny↓ spig↓
      - **stitching** pain: mang k* meny k* spig k*
        - **downward** toward sternum: con
    - **cough** agg.; during: apis
    - **drawing** pain: coc-c led stann tritic-vg fd5.de zinc
    - **stitching** pain: berb k* mang k* symph fd3.de•
    - **tearing** pain: am-m k* brom k* caps k* cham k* *Lyc* k* stann k*
      - **fine**: agar k*
      - **paralyzed**; as if: ferr-m k*
- **Costal** cartilages: arg-met mtf11 *Arn*↓ bell↓ calc-p↓ cina↓ plb↓ psil↓ **Ran-b**↓ stann↓ staph↓
  - **morning**:
    - **bed** agg.; in: arg-met↓
      - **sore**: arg-met
  - **drawing** pain: stann
  - **expiration** agg.; during: bell↓
    - **burning**: bell k*
  - **pressing** pain: psil ft1
  - **sore**: *Arn* calc-p plb **Ran-b** staph
  - **stitching** pain: bell cina a1 psil ft1 staph h1
  - **stooping** agg.: staph↓
    - **pressing** pain: staph h1
  - ○ **Between**: staph↓
    - **stitching** pain: staph h1
  - **False** ribs; of: arg-met↓ *Arn*↓ bell↓ calc-p↓ grat↓ *Lyc*↓ merc-c↓ **Ran-b**↓ staph↓ sulph↓
    - **aching**: staph k*
    - **cutting** pain: arg-met
    - **gnawing** pain: bell k*
    - **inspiration** agg.: cimic↓
      - **cutting** pain: cimic
    - **sore**: arg-met *Arn* calc-p *Lyc* **Ran-b** k* staph sulph
    - **tearing** pain: grat k* merc-c k*
    - **Sternum**; near: cina↓ plat↓ sul-ac↓
      - **stitching** pain: cina plat sul-ac
  - **Fourth** ribs; of: psil↓
    - **stitching** pain: psil ft1
  - **Last** true ribs; of: ph-ac↓ sulph↓
    - **right**: ph-ac↓
      - **sore**: ph-ac
    - **sore**: ph-ac sulph
  - **Lower** ribs:
    - **stooping** agg.: staph↓
      - **stitching** pain: staph h1
  - **Third** | **left**: pix mtf11
- **Diaphragm**: acon↓ asaf bro1 bell↓ bism bro1 *Bry* bro1 cact bro1 *Chin*↓ cic↓ *Cimic* bro1* **Ip**↓ lyc↓ nat-m bro1 nux-m↓ nux-v bro1 olnd↓ sec bro1 spig bro1 *Stann* bro1 stict bro1 *Stry* bro1 tarax↓ verat bro1 verat-v↓ vib-t↓ viol-t↓ zinc↓ zinc-ox bro1

- **burning**: asaf bg2
- **constricting** pain: **Cact** mrr1
- **cramping**: cic h1 lyc bg2 nat-m h2* nux-v bg2 sec c2 stann h2* verat bg2 verat-v bg2 vib-t c2 zinc bg2
- **cutting** pain: cact c1
- **lying** on right side agg.: tarax ↓
  - ⋮ **stitching** pain: tarax h1
- **neuralgic**: bell bro1 stann ptk1
- **pinching** pain: bism h1
- **pressing** pain: bism h1 **Ip** nux-m bg2 viol-t b7a.de*
- **speaking**; on: ptel ↓
  - ⋮ **stitching** pain: ptel
- **stitching** pain: acon vh1 *Chin* b7a.de olnd b7.de* spig b7.de* tarax b7.de* viol-t b7.de*
- **tearing** pain: nux-m bg2
- **walking** agg.: bism ↓
  - ⋮ **pressing** pain: bism hr1

○ • **Region** of: agar ↓ asc-t c1 cench k2 echi fic-m gya1 hom-xyz c2 nux-m pert-vc vk9 ptel c1 ran-b k2 *Stann* c2 stram pd
  - ⋮ **forenoon**: nux-m
  - ⋮ **drawing** pain: agar
  - ⋮ **inspiration** agg.: nux-m
  - ⋮ **lifting**; after: borx hr1

- **External** chest: **Acon** ↓ agar ↓ alum ↓ am-c ↓ am-m ↓ ambr ↓ anac ↓ ang b7.de* ant-c b7.de* ant-t ↓ *Apis* bg2 arg-met ↓ arg-n ↓ *Arn* ↓ **Ars** ↓ asaf ↓ asar ↓ aur ↓ bar-c ↓ bell bg2 *Bism* ↓ *Borx* ↓ bov ↓ bry b7.de* cadm-s ↓ calad b7a.de calc ↓ *Camph* ↓ cann-s b7.de* canth ↓ caps b7.de* carb-v ↓ caust ↓ cham ↓ chel ↓ chin b7.de* *Cic* ↓ cina ↓ clem ↓ cocc ↓ colch ↓ con ↓ croc ↓ cupr b7.de* dig ↓ *Dros* ↓ *Dulc* b4.de* *Euph* ↓ ferr ↓ graph ↓ guaj ↓ hell ↓ hep ↓ hyos ↓ ign ↓ iod ↓ kali-bi bg2 kali-c ↓ kali-n ↓ kreos bg2 lach b7.de* laur ↓ led b7.de* *Lyc* ↓ *M-ambo* ↓ m-arct ↓ mag-c ↓ mag-m ↓ *Mang* ↓ meny ↓ merc ↓ merc-c ↓ mez b4.de* *Mosch* b7a.de *Mur-ac* ↓ nat-c ↓ nat-m b4.de* nit-ac ↓ nux-m ↓ **Nux-v** ↓ ol-an ↓ olnd b7.de* par ↓ ph-ac b4.de phos b4.de* phyt bg2 *Plat* ↓ plb ↓ puls b7.de* *Ran-b* b7.de* *Ran-s* b7a.de rheum ↓ rhod b4.de* rhus-t b7.de* rumx ↓ *Ruta* b7a.de sabad ↓ sabin b7.de* samb ↓ sars ↓ sel ↓ seneg b4.de* sep b4.de* *Sil* b4.de* *Spig* ↓ spong ↓ squil ↓ *Stann* b4a.de staph b7.de* stram ↓ stront-c b4.de* sul-ac b4.de* sulph b4.de* tarax ↓ teucr ↓ thuj ↓ valer ↓ verat b7.de* verb ↓ viol-t ↓ zinc ↓
  - **biting** pain: led b7a.de
  - **blow**; pain as from a: ang b7.de* ant-c b7a.de borx b4a.de *Cic* b7a.de dros b7.de* dulc b4.de* m-ambo b7.de mang b4.de* merc b4.de* mur-ac b4.de* nat-m b4.de* nux-m b7.de* olnd b7.de* *Plat* b4a.de sul-ac b4.de*
  - **boring** pain: acon bg2 rhus-t bg2 tarax b7.de*
  - **burning**: agar k* ambr k* apis b7a.de ars k* asaf b7.de* asar b7.de* bar-c k* *Bell* k* bism b7a.de bov k* calc b4a.de* canth b7.de* caps b7.de* cham b7a.de cic b7a.de colch b7.de* croc b7.de* dig k* dros b7.de* *Euph* k* ferr b7.de* iod bg2 kali-n k* laur b7.de* led b7a.de* *M-ambo* b7.de* m-arct b7.de mang b4a.de merc-c b4a.de *Mez* k* mosch b7a.de *Mur-ac* k* nat-c b4.de* nat-m k* nux-v b7.de* ph-ac k* phos b4.de* *Plat* k* puls b7.de* rheum b7.de* rhus-t b7.de* sel b7.de* *Seneg* k* stront-c k* sul-ac k* *Sulph* k* tarax b7.de* zinc k*
  - **burrowing**: led b7.de* olnd b7.de*
  - **clawing** pain: puls b7.de*
  - **compressed**; as if: arg-met bg2
  - **corrosive**: par b7.de* spong b7.de*
  - **cramping**: *Acon* b7.de* *Ang* b7a.de arg-met b7.de* calc b4.de* *Camph* b7a.de cham b7.de* cic b7a.de* cina b7.de* dig b4.de* dulc b4.de* mez b4.de* nit-ac b4.de* plat b4.de* sep b4.de* stram bg2 teucr b7.de* verat b7.de*
  - **cutting** pain: ang b7.de* cann-s b7.de* dig b4.de* dros b7.de* hell b7.de* kali-bi bg2 nat-c b4.de* staph b7.de* stram b7.de*
  - **drawing** pain: *Acon* b7.de* anac b4a.de asaf b7.de* *Borx* b4a.de bry cadm-s carb-v b4.de* cupr b7.de* dig b4.de* dulc b4.de* kali-bi bg2 kreos b7a.de lyc b4.de* mur-ac b4.de* nat-c b4.de* nux-v b7.de* puls b7.de* ran-s b7.de* rhus-t b7.de* sars b4.de* spig b7.de* stann b4.de* stront-c b4.de* tarax b7.de* zinc b4.de*

- **External** chest: ...
  - **dull** pain: olnd b7.de*
  - **gnawing** pain: acon bg2 arg-met b7.de* calc b4.de* mang b4.de* olnd b7.de* par b7.de* ruta b7.de* spong b7.de* stann bg2
  - **jerking** pain: merc b4.de* rhus-t b7.de* sil b4.de*
  - **paralyzed**; as if: nux-v b7.de*
  - **pecking**: ruta b7.de*
  - **pinching** pain: acon bg2 nux-v b7.de* phos b4.de* ran-s bg2 rhod b4.de* samb b7.de*
  - **pressing** pain: agar b4.de* alum b4.de* ambr b7.de* anac b4a.de ang b7.de* arg-met b7.de* arn b7.de* **Ars** b4a.de asaf b7.de* aur b4.de* *Bism* b7.de* bov b4.de* bry b7.de* camph b7.de* canth b7.de* carb-v b4a.de* chel b7.de* chin b7.de* cic bg2 cina b7.de* cocc b7.de* cupr b7.de* dig bg2 dros b7.de* dulc b4.de* euph b4a.de* ferr bg2 graph bg2 hyos b7.de* kali-bi bg2 kali-n b4.de* kreos b7a.de laur b7.de* led b7.de* *Lyc* b4a.de* mag-m b4.de* meny b7.de* mez b4.de* nux-v b7.de* olnd b7.de* plb b7.de* *Ran-b* b7.de* rheum b7.de* ruta b7.de* sabin b7.de* sars b4.de* seneg bg2 spig b7.de* squil b7.de* stann b4.de* staph b7.de* stront-c b4.de* *Sulph* b4.de* tarax b7.de* teucr b7.de* thuj bg2 valer b7.de* *Verat* b7.de* verb b7.de* zinc b4.de*
    - ⋮ **inward**: kreos b7a.de rhus-t b7.de*
  - **sore**: am-m b7.de* ambr b7a.de* ang b7a.de* *Apis* b7a.de arg-n bg2 *Arn* b7.de* ars bg2 bar-c b4.de* bell b4a.de bry b7.de* calad b7.de* caust b4a.de chin b7.de* cic b7a.de* ferr bg2 hep b4a.de ign b7.de* kali-bi bg2 kali-c bg2 lach b7a.de* led bg2 lyc b4a.de mag-c b4.de* mang b4.de* merc b4.de* mez b4.de* nat-c b4.de* nat-m b4.de* nit-ac b4.de* nux-v b7.de* ol-an bg2 ph-ac b4.de* *Phos* b4.de* *Ran-b* b7.de* rheum b7.de* rhod b4.de* rumx bg2 sep b4.de* sil b4a.de* spig b7.de* *Stann* b4a.de* staph b7.de* sulph b4.de* verat b7.de* zinc bg2
  - **sprained**; as if: arn b7.de* bell bg2 cocc b7.de*
  - **squeezed**; as if: ant-c b7.de* *Apis* b7a.de *Arn* b7.de* ran-b b7.de*
  - **stitching** pain: **Acon** bg2 am-c b4.de* am-m b7.de* ambr bg2 anac b4.de* ang b7.de* ant-c bg2 apis bg2 *Arn* b7.de* *Ars* b4a.de asaf b7.de* aur b4.de* bell b4.de* bism b7.de* borx bg2 bov b4.de* bry b7.de* calc b4.de* camph b7.de* cann-s b7.de* canth b7.de* caust b4.de* *Chin* b7.de* cina bg2 cocc b7.de* colch b7.de* con b4.de* croc b7.de* *Dros* b7.de* dulc b4.de* euph b4.de* graph b4a.de* guaj b4.de* hep b4.de* iod bg2 kali-bi bg2 kali-n b4.de* kreos b7a.de* laur b7.de* led bg2 lyc bg2 *M-ambo* b7.de* m-arct b7.de mag-c b4.de* mag-m b4.de* *Mang* b4.de* meny b7.de merc bg2 merc-c b4a.de mez bg2 mur-ac b4.de* nat-m b4.de* nit-ac b4.de* **Nux-v** b7.de* olnd b7.de* par b7.de* ph-ac b4.de* phos b4.de* plb b7.de* puls b7.de* ran-b b7.de* ran-s b7.de* rheum b7.de* rhod bg2 rhus-t b7.de* ruta b7.de* sabad b7.de* sabin b7.de* sars b4.de* seneg b4.de* sil b4.de* spig b7.de* spong b7.de* squil b7.de* stann b4.de* staph b7.de* stront-c b4.de* sul-ac b4.de* sulph b4.de* tarax b7.de* teucr b7.de* verat b7.de* verb b7.de* viol-t b7.de* zinc b4.de*
    - ⋮ **needles**; as from: anac bg2 caust bg2
  - **tearing** pain: acon bg2 am-c b4a.de* am-m b7a.de* ambr b7.de* ant-t b7.de* bar-c *Bry* b7.de* camph b7.de* carb-v b4a.de* chel b7.de* clem b4.de* colch b7.de* dulc b4.de* iod b4.de* kali-bi bg2 kali-c b4.de* lyc b4.de* merc b4.de* merc-c b4a.de nux-v b7.de* ran-b b7.de* rhod b4.de* sabin b7.de* *Spig* b7.de* teucr b7.de*
    - ⋮ **inward**: nat-m bg2
  - **ulcerative** pain: bry b7.de* puls b7.de*

- **Heart**: *(↗Angina)* abies-n bro1 *Abrot* **Acon** k* adon bro1* aesc *Agar* ail allox ↓ aln ↓ aloe bg2 alumn ↓ am-c ↓ ambr *Aml-ns* k* *Anac* ↓ anan ↓ ang ↓ ant-c bg2 ant-t b7a.de **Apis** k* apoc ↓ aq-mar rbp6 aran-ix sp1 *Arg-met* ↓ **Arg-n** k* arist-m c2 *Arn* k* **Ars** k* *Ars-i* ars-met ↓ ars-s-f ↓ *Asaf* k* asc-t aspar aster bro1 **Aur** aur-ar k2 aur-i k2 *Aur-m* aur-s ↓ bamb-a ↓ bapt ↓ bar-c ↓ bell k* *Bell-p* sp1 *Benz-ac* berb ↓ bomb-pr ↓ borx ↓ both fne1• both-ax ↓ bov bg2 brach ↓ *Brom* *Bry* k* bufo ↓ **Cact** k* cadm-met ↓ cadm-s ↓ calad ↓ *Calc* k* *Calc-ar* calc-f bro1 calc-i k2 calc-p bg2 *Camph* *Cann-i* cann-s b7.de* cann-xyz ↓ canth k* caps ↓ carb-ac ↓ carb-an ↓ carb-v ↓ carbn-s carc ↓ card-m carneg-g rwt1• caust k* **Cench** **Cere-b** k* cere-s c2* *Cham* k* *Chel* ↓ chin bg2 chinin-ar k2 chinin-s ↓ chlor cic bg2 *Cimic* k* *Cina* cinnb ↓ clem k* coc-c ↓ cod ↓ coff bro1 *Colch* k* coll ↓ *Coloc* ↓ colum-p ↓ com ↓ con k* conv bro1 corn corv-cor ↓ cot ↓ crat bg1* *Croc* ↓ *Crot-h* crot-t ↓ *Cupr* cupr-ar ↓ *Cycl* ↓ cypra-eg ↓ *Daph* k* des-ac rbp6 *Dig* k* digin ↓ dios bro1 dioxi ↓ elaps ↓ *Eup-per* ↓ euph ↓ euphr bg2 fago ferr ferr-i ferr-m ferr-p ↓ *Ferr-t* bro1 *Fl-ac* ↓ galla-q-r nl2• *Gels* ↓ *Glon* k* *Graph* grat ↓ guat sp1 *Haem* bro1 ham fd3.de• hed ↓ hell bg2 helo ↓ helo-s ↓

- **Heart**: ...
  Hep↓ hir↓ hist$_{sp1}$ *Hydr*↓ *Hydr-ac*$_{bro1}$ hydroph$_{rsj6•}$ hyos$_{b7a.de}$ hyper↓ iber$_{bro1}$ ign↓ ignis-alc$_{es2•}$ *Iod*$_{k*}$ iodof↓ ip$_{bg2}$ jab jac-c↓ **Kali-ar** *Kali-bi*$_{k*}$ *Kali-c*$_{k*}$ *Kali-chl* kali-cy↓ kali-i kali-m$_{k2}$ kali-n↓ kali-p kali-s$_{k2}$ **Kalm**$_{k*}$ kola$_{stb3•}$ *Kreos*↓ kurch$_{bnj1}$ lac-ac↓ lac-d lac-h↓ lac-leo↓ **Lach**$_{k*}$ lachn$_{c2}$ **Lact-v**↓ lap-la↓ *Lat-m*$_{k*}$ *Laur*$_{k*}$ led↓ lepi$_{bro1}$ lept↓ *Lil-t*$_{k*}$ **Lith-c**$_{k*}$ lith-m$_{c2}$ *Lob*$_{k*}$ lyc$_{bg2}$ *Lycps-v*$_{k*}$ *Lyss* m-arct↓ *Mag-c*↓ **Mag-m**↓ mag-p$_{br1}$ mag-s↓ magn-gr$_{bro1}$ manc↓ mand$_{sp1}$ med$_{bro1}$ mentho↓ meny$_{c2}$ *Merc* merc-c$_{k*}$ merc-i-f merc-i-r merc-sul$_{br1}$ mez$_{bg2}$ *Mur-ac*↓ myric↓ *Naja*$_{k*}$ nat-ar nat-c↓ *Nat-m*$_{k*}$ nat-n↓ nat-p nat-s↓ nit-ac↓ nux-m↓ nux-v$_{k*}$ oena ol-an↓ olib-sac↓ olnd onos$_{k*}$ *Op*↓ opun-s$_{a1}$ ovi-p$_{bro1}$ ox-ac$_{k*}$ ozone↓ *Paeon*$_{bro1}$ pall↓ par↓ paull$_{c2}$ **Petr**↓ ph-ac↓ *Phos*$_{k*}$ phyt$_{k*}$ pieri-b↓ pip-n$_{bro1}$ plac↓ *Plat*↓ plb$_{bg2*}$ plumbg↓ podo$_{c2}$ polyg-h↓ positr$_{nl2•}$ prim-vl↓ pseuts-m$_{oss1•}$ *Psor* ptel$_{bro1}$ **Puls**$_{k*}$ pyrog↓ pyrus↓ ran-b$_{k2}$ ran-s$_{k*}$ rauw$_{sp1}$ rhod **Rhus-t** rhus-v↓ ros-d↓ rumx$_{k*}$ ruta$_{b7.de*}$ sabad↓ sabin↓ *Samb* *Sang* saroth↓ scut↓ sec$_{bg2}$ seneg$_{k*}$ sep$_{bg2}$ sil↓ sin-n spect↓ sphing↓ **Spig**$_{k*}$ *Spong*$_{k*}$ stann$_{bg2}$ *Staph* still↓ stram↓ stront-c *Stroph-h*$_{bro1}$ stroph-s↓ suis-pan↓ sul-ac$_{bg2}$ sul-i$_{k2}$ sulph$_{bg2}$ suprar↓ symph↓ syph$_{bro1}$ *Tab*$_{k*}$ tarax *Tarent* tax↓ tell thal-xyz$_{srj8•}$ ther$_{k*}$ thuj$_{k*}$ thyr$_{bro1}$ *Trios*$_{rsj11•}$ tritic-vg↓ trom↓ tub$_{jl2}$ ust↓ valer↓ vanad↓ vanil$_{fd5.de}$ ven-m$_{rsj12•}$ verat$_{k*}$ verat-v$_{k*}$ verb$_{b7a.de}$ vesp vib↓ viol-o viol-t↓ vip x-ray$_{sp1}$ zinc$_{k*}$ zinc-p$_{k2}$ zinc-val$_{bro1}$ zing↓
  - **left**:
    - **extending** to | **right**: apis$_{bg2}$ kreos$_{bg2}$ phos$_{bg2}$ phyt$_{bg2}$ plb$_{bg2}$ zinc$_{bg2}$
  - **daytime**: mand↓
    - **pinching** pain: mand$_{sp1}$
  - **morning**: calc-p cund↓ dig ham↓ kola$_{stb3•}$ *Lith-c*↓ nat-m↓ podo↓ ruta$_{fd4.de}$ spong$_{fd4.de}$ tritic-vg$_{fd5.de}$ vanil$_{fd5.de}$
    - **bed** agg.; in: nat-m↓
      - **sore**: nat-m
    - **bending** | **over** the bed; on bending: *Lith-c*$_{k*}$
    - **chocolate**, after: raph$_{k*}$
    - **cutting** pain: cund
    - **pressing** pain: ham$_{fd3.de•}$ *Lith-c* nat-m$_{h2}$
    - **rising** | **after**:
      - **agg.**: nux-v↓ zinc↓
        - **stitching** pain: nux-v$_{k*}$ zinc$_{h2}$
      - **agg.**: con
    - **stitching** pain: podo$_{fd3.de•}$ spong$_{fd4.de}$ vanil$_{fd5.de}$
    - **waking** | **after**:
      - **agg.**: mez↓
        - **stitching** pain: mez$_{k*}$
      - **on**: kali-p$_{fd1.de•}$ *Tarent* vanil$_{fd5.de}$
  - **forenoon**: acon↓ bamb-a↓ coc-c↓ ruta$_{fd4.de}$ symph↓ thuj vanil$_{fd5.de}$
    - **pressing** pain: thuj$_{k*}$
    - **sore**: coc-c
    - **stitching** pain: acon$_{k*}$ bamb-a$_{stb2.de•}$ ruta$_{fd4.de}$ symph$_{fd3.de•}$
  - **noon**: agar↓ verat-v↓
    - **aching**: agar$_{k*}$
    - **burning**: agar$_{k*}$
    - **stitching** pain: verat-v$_{k*}$
  - **afternoon**: bamb-a↓ euphr ruta$_{fd4.de}$ sep↓ spong$_{fd4.de}$ vanil$_{fd5.de}$
    - **16** h: ars-met↓
      - **cutting** pain: ars-met
    - **stitching** pain: bamb-a$_{stb2.de•}$ sep$_{k*}$ spong$_{fd4.de}$
  - **evening**: aur$_{mrr1}$ bamb-a↓ cench↓ cinnb↓ dios↓ gink-b↓ kali-bi↓ kali-p$_{fd1.de•}$ lyss↓ mur-ac↓ nat-c↓ ph-ac$_{h2}$ podo↓ **Puls** raph rhus-t↓ ruta$_{fd4.de}$ spong$_{fd4.de}$ sulph thuj vanil↓ verb↓
    - **aching**: kali-bi$_{k*}$
    - **bed** agg.; in: kali-bi↓ *Nat-m*↓
      - **aching**: kali-bi
      - **pressing** pain: *Nat-m*
    - **cutting** pain: cinnb
    - **pressing** pain: **Puls** sulph$_{k*}$ thuj$_{k*}$
    - **sleep** agg.; on going to: mez↓
      - **stitching** pain: mez$_{k*}$
  - **evening**: ...
    - **stitching** pain: bamb-a$_{stb2.de•}$ cench$_{k2}$ dios$_{k*}$ gink-b$_{sbd1•}$ lyss mur-ac$_{h2}$ nat-c$_{k*}$ podo$_{fd3.de•}$ rhus-t ruta$_{fd4.de}$ spong$_{fd4.de}$ vanil$_{fd5.de}$ verb$_{k*}$
  - **night**: *Arg-n* aur-m↓ cann-i cench$_{k2}$ coc-c gink-b↓ iber↓ kola$_{stb3•}$ mag-m↓ mand$_{sp1}$ *Mez*↓ *Naja* nat-m nit-ac↓ spong$_{fd4.de}$ *Sulph*↓ syph$_{jl2}$ [tax$_{jsj7}$]
    - **midnight**:
      - **after**:
        - **2** h: carneg-g$_{rwt1•}$
        - **4-6** h: both-ax↓
          - **pressing** pain: both-ax$_{tsm2}$
        - **5** h:
          - **5-6** h: trios$_{rsj11•}$
            - **rising** | **amel.**: trios$_{rsj11•}$
    - **lying** down agg.; after: agar
    - **lying** on back agg.: asaf
      - **bursting** pain: asaf$_{k*}$
    - **pressing** pain: *Arg-n* cann-i$_{k*}$ coc-c
    - **sitting** up in bed:
      - **amel.**: asaf↓
        - **bursting** pain: asaf$_{k*}$
    - **stitching** pain: aur-m cench$_{k2}$ gink-b$_{sbd1•}$ iber$_{c1}$ mag-m$_{h2}$ *Mez* nit-ac$_{k*}$ *Sulph*
  - **night** when lying on the back, amel. by sitting up | **bursting** pain (See night - lying on back agg. - bursting; night - sitting - amel. - bursting)
  - **accompanied** by:
    - **numbness**:
      - **Arm** | **left** (See Heart; complaints - accompanied - upper - left - numbness)
    - **respiration**; difficult: *Arg-n* *Aur* *Cact*$_{k*}$ cimic dig$_{k2}$ kali-p$_{fd1.de•}$ kalm lac-d$_{k2}$ *Lat-m*$_{sne}$ psil$_{ft1}$ *Psor*$_{k*}$ sep *Spig* *Spong*$_{k*}$ *Tarent*
    - **weakness**:
      - **Arm** | **left** (See Heart; complaints - accompanied - upper - left - weakness)
    - **Abdomen**; distension of: mand$_{sp1}$
    - **Heart** disease; organic: *Ars-i*$_{bro1}$ *Cact*$_{bro1}$ calc-f$_{bro1}$ crat$_{bro1}$ kalm$_{bro1}$ nat-i$_{bro1}$ stront-i$_{bro1}$ tab$_{bro1}$
    - **Ovary** and difficult respiration; pain in left (See FEMALE - Pain - ovaries - accompanied - heart)
  - **aching**: acon$_{bg2}$ adon$_{bg1}$ aesc agar$_{bg2}$ ail ambr aml-ns arg-met$_{bg2}$ arn$_{nh6}$ asaf$_{bg2}$ aur-m aur-s$_{k*}$ bell$_{bg2*}$ bry$_{bg2}$ *Cact* calc$_{bg2*}$ carb-v$_{bg2}$ caust$_{bg2}$ colch$_{rsj2•}$ coloc$_{bg2}$ con crot-h$_{k*}$ cupr-ar$_{k*}$ cycl$_{bg2}$ *Dig*$_{k*}$ ferr-p$_{bg2}$ fl-ac$_{bg2}$ glon$_{k*}$ ignis-alc$_{es2•}$ kali-bi$_{k*}$ *Lach* led$_{bg2}$ lith-c$_{ptk1}$ *Lycps-v* *Merc*$_{k*}$ merc-i-r$_{k*}$ naja$_{bg2*}$ **Nat-m** *Nat-p* *Nux-v* *Phos*$_{k*}$ phyt$_{bg2}$ pyrog$_{bg2}$ pyrus rhus-t$_{bg2}$ rumx sang$_{bg2}$ seneg$_{k*}$ spig$_{bg2}$ spong$_{bg2*}$ stroph-h$_{ptk1}$ sulph$_{bg2}$ tab$_{ptk1}$ tarent$_{k*}$ verat-v$_{k*}$ vesp$_{k*}$ [spect$_{dfg1}$]
  - **alternating** with:
    - **rheumatism**: aur-m$_{k2}$ *Benz-ac* *Kalm*
    - **Limbs**; pain in: nat-p$_{tl1}$
    - **Spleen**; pain in: magn-gr$_{br1}$
    - **Teeth**; pain in: hist$_{sp1}$
    - **Toe**; pain in great: (↗*EXTREMITIES - Pain - toes - first - alternating - heart)* nat-p$_{k*}$
    - **Uterus**; pain in: *Lil-t*
  - **anus**; on wiping: apis$_{bg1}$
  - **ascending**:
    - **agg.**: aur$_{mrr1}$ *Crot-h*
    - **stairs**:
      - **agg.**: **Aur**↓ **Aur-m**↓
        - **pressing** pain: **Aur** **Aur-m**
  - **bending** double agg.: anac↓
    - **stitching** pain: anac$_{bg1}$
  - **bending** forward agg.: *Lil-t* **Lith-c**$_{k*}$
  - **bladder**, after pain in: lith-c
  - **blow**; pain as from a: *Cann-s*$_{b7a.de}$

Chest

- **boring** pain: aur bg2 aur-m k* *Cupr* k* rhod *Seneg* k* sep bg2 still a1
- **breathing**:
  - **agg.**: anac ↓ *Calc* ↓ crot-h graph ↓ mag-m ↓ rumx *Spig* ↓ *Staph* ↓
    - **pressing** pain: graph h2
    - **stitching** pain: anac k* *Calc* mag-m *Spig Staph*
  - **impossible**; almost: arg-n
- **broken**; as if | **break**; as if it would: bell bg2
- **burning**: acon bg2* agar bg2 arg-met b7.de arg-n bg2 arn *Ars* bg2* aur bg2* aur-m k* bamb-a stb2.de• bell bg2 bry ptk1 calc ptk1 carb-v k* cic bg2 colch bg2 cupr bg2* hydr k* hyos ptk1 kali-c k* kali-i k* kalm ptk1 lyss m-arct b7.de med *Op* k* ozone sde2• *Phos* ptk1 plat bg2 *Puls* k* rhus-t ptk1 rumx k* sulph ptk1 suprar rly4• syph ptk1 tarent k* ust verat bg2 verat-v bg2*
- **burrowing**: coc-c bg2
- **bursting** pain: aln vva1• am-c arg-n bg1 asaf k* cot br1 glon ptk1 ham fd3.de• lyss med phos ptk1 zinc ptk1
  - **obstruction**; as from: cot br1
- **catching**: cimic bg2 puls bg2
- **chest** and had not room enough; heart pressing against: lach ↓ ruta ↓
  - **pressing** pain: lach hr1* ruta fd4.de
- **chill**; during: *Calc*
- **chocolate** agg.: raph bg1
- **clawing** pain: hydr-ac bg2
- **coffee**; from abuse of: coff bro1
- **coition**; after: *Dig* k* positr nl2•
- **compressing** sides amel.: cot c1
- **convulsions**; before epileptic: *Calc-ar Lyc*
- **cough** agg.; during: agar bg1 am-c tl1 mag-m bg1 mez ↓ nat-m ↓ tarent
  - **stitching** pain: agar mez k* nat-m
- **cramping**: acon bg2 anan *Ars* k* *Bry* k* com bg2 cupr kali-bi k* *Kali-c* kali-p fd1.de• kola stb3• lac-h htj1• **Lach** k* **Lact-v** bg2 laur manc bg2 mez k* myric ptel k* ruta fd4.de sep tarent ther tl1 thuj vanil fd5.de vib tl1 zinc k*
- **cutting** pain: abies-n br1* abrot acon k* *Aesc* aml-ns bg2 anac bg2* apis k* apoc *Arg-n* **Ars** k* *Ars-i* ars-met ars-s-f k2 asc-t a1* aur k* aur-m k* aur-s k2 bov bg2 *Bry* k* bufo bg2 *Cact* k* cadm-met tpw6* calad bg2 calc bg1 calc-p bg2 cann-i bro1 caust bro1 cere-b bro1 chel *Colch* k* *Con* corv-cor bdg• *Croc* dig bro1 *Glon* k* iber bro1 *Iod* jac-c kali-bi bg2 *Kali-c* bg2* kali-i k* kali-n k* lac-ac *Lac-d* lepi br1 lith-c bro1 med k* *Naja* k* nux-m bg2 plb bg2 polyg-h bg2 sabin sep k* spig bg2* sul-i k2 **Sulph** k* syph k* tarent k* ther tritic-vg fd5.de tub jl2 verat bg2* zinc bg2
- **delivery**: *Cimic*
- **diarrhea** | **amel.**: mand bg*
- **digging** pain: bufo bg2
- **dragging**: iber bg2
- **drawing** pain: agar bg1 asaf bg2 aur bg2 aur-m bell b4a.de* calc b4a.de calc-ar bg2 cann-xyz bg2 *Canth* k* card-m cod croc bg2 *Ferr* k* ferr-m lyss c1 meny b7.de* naja gm1 nat-m b4a.de* nux-m bg2 olib-sac wmh1 olnd k* rhus-t bg2 **Spig** vanil fd5.de
  - **drawn** together; as if heart and ovary were: *Naja*
- **drinking**:
  - **after**:
    - **agg.**: chin ↓
      - **stitching** pain: chin k*
  - **hot** water | **amel.**: spig mrr1
  - **warm** water | **amel.**: spig br1
- **dull** pain: crot-h tl1 hir rsj4• tritic-vg fd5.de
- **eating**; after: aspar ↓ *Kali-bi* lil-t lyc manc nat-m stront-c
  - **pressing** pain: *Kali-bi Lil-t* k* lyc k*
  - **stitching** pain: aspar k*
- **emotions** agg.: phos bg1* thuj bg1
- **epistaxis**; with: ind bg1
- **eructations** | **amel.**: thuj bg1
- **excitement** agg.: *Cupr Dig* k* ham fd3.de• ruta fd4.de vanil fd5.de
- **exertion** agg.: *Arn* bro1 bry ↓ carb-an bro1 caust bro1 cer-s cere-s *Dig* k* *Lil-t Rhus-t* mrr1
  - **cramping**: bry
- **expiration**:
  - **agg.**: crot-t ↓ ign ↓ zinc ↓
    - **stitching** pain: crot-t k* ign k* zinc h2
  - **during** | **agg.**: phyt
- **fainting**, with pain in heart: arn k13 cact kr1* *Manc* kr1
- **faintness**; with: arn ↓
  - **stitching** pain: arn k*
- **fever**; during: *Cham* ↓
  - **pressing** pain: *Cham* b7a.de
- **followed** by | **Head**; pain in: merc-i-f ptk1
- **gnawing** pain: nat-m b4a.de*
- **grief**; from: *Gels* sne *Ign* sne lach k2
  - **sore**: *Gels Ign*
- **griping** pain: cact calc-ar k2 lil-t k2 ptel c1
- **hysterical**: zinc-val br1
- **inspiration**:
  - **agg.**: aesc ↓ agar bg1 anac bg1 *Calc-p* ↓ *Chel* ↓ crot-t ↓ galla-q-r nl2• laur ↓ mag-m ↓ nat-c ↓ plb bg1 positr ↓ ran-b k2 spig bg1* thres-a sze7• ulm-c ↓ vanil fd5.de
    - **stitching** pain: aesc anac *Calc-p Chel* crot-t laur mag-m h2 nat-c h2 plb positr nl2• ulm-c jsj8• vanil fd5.de
  - **deep**:
    - **agg.**: *Acon* ↓ aesc ↓ agar ↓ aur-m ↓ both-ax ↓ *Calc* ↓ con ↓ mez ↓ *Mur-ac* ↓ *Ran-b* ↓ *Sulph* ↓
      - **sticking** pain: both-ax tsm2
      - **stitching** pain: *Acon* aesc agar aur-m both-ax tsm2 *Calc* con h2 mez *Mur-ac Ran-b Sulph*
    - **amel.**: cann-i ↓
      - **stitching** pain: cann-i
- **jerking** pain: calc-ar carb-v con fl-ac
- **joint** to joint and then locates in heart; from: *Aur* ↓ crat ↓
  - **wandering** pain: *Aur* k* crat br1
- **loudly** spoken to, when: *Camph*
- **love**; from disappointed: dig c1
- **lying**:
  - **agg.**: agar *Aur* calam sa3• hydroph rsj6• kali-bi ↓ lil-t puls rumx ruta fd4.de **Spong** verb ↓
    - **pressing** pain: kali-bi ruta fd4.de
    - **stitching** pain: rumx verb
  - **amel.**: psor tl1
    - **stitching** pain: *Psor*
  - **back**; on:
    - **agg.**: asaf rumx *Sulph* ↓ ulm-c ↓
      - **sore**: ulm-c jsj8•
      - **stitching** pain: *Sulph*
    - **amel.**: *Cact* kola stb3• *Psor*
      - **stitching** pain: kola stb3•
  - **head** low; with the | **agg.**: **Spong**
  - **side**; on:
    - **agg.**: cench bg1
      - **left**:
        - **accompanied** by | **Head**; pain in (See HEAD - Pain - accompanied - heart)
    - **left**:
      - **agg.**: bar-c ↓ *Cact* camph ↓ colch *Crot-h* dig dios iber *Kali-ar* kali-c ↓ kola stb3• lac-del hrn2• *Lach* lyc ↓ med ↓ myric c1 *Naja* *Nat-m* phos k2* ran-b k2 **Spig** k* tell ulm-c ↓
        - **sore**: bar-c *Crot-h* kali-ar med ulm-c jsj8•
        - **stitching** pain: camph kali-c h2 kola stb3• lyc tell rsj10• ulm-c jsj8•
      - **amel.** | **can** only lie on left side: *Ars-met* rumx
      - **impossible**: kalm c1

- **lying – side**; on: ...
  - **right**:
    - **agg.**: alum bg1 arg-n lach bg1 lil-t rumx
    - **amel.**:
      - **can** only lie on right side: *Naja* **Spig**
        - **head** high; with the: **Spig** ↓
          - stitching pain: **Spig**
        - **stitching** pain: **Spig**
- **menses**:
  - **after** | **agg.**: *Lach Lith-c*
  - **before** | **agg.**: *Cact* lach lith-c spong
  - **during**:
    - **agg.**: *Arg-n Cact Con* lith-c *Puls*
      - **cutting** pain: *Con*
      - **painful** menses: **Con** crot-h ptk1
      - **pressing** pain: *Arg-n*
      - **stitching** pain: *Con*
  - **instead** of: cham ↓
    - **pressing** pain: cham k*
- **motion**:
  - **agg.**: aur-m ↓ both-ax ↓ *Bry* ↓ *Cact* cham ↓ con ↓ *Eup-per* ↓ kali-i lat-m sp1 lil-t med k2 phyt ran-b k2 spig br1* *Sulph* ↓
    - **cutting** pain: *Cact* med k2
    - **sore**: *Bry Eup-per*
    - **sticking** pain: both-ax tsm2
    - **stitching** pain: aur-m k* bry tl1 cham con h2 med k2 *Ran-b* **Spig** *Sulph* k*
    - **violent**: rauw ↓ stroph-s ↓
      - **sticking** pain: rauw sp1 stroph-s sp1
  - **amel.**: *Mag-m*
- **music** agg.; soft: thuj ↓
  - **cramping**: thuj k*
- **noise** agg.: agar
- **numbness** and lameness of left arm: *Rhus-t* ↓
  - **stitching** pain: *Rhus-t*
- **palpitations**:
  - **during**: *Acon* bro1 ars bro1 *Cact* bro1 caust bro1 cham bro1 *Coff* bro1 *Hydr-ac* bro1 laur bro1 mag-m bro1 nája bro1 plb *Spig* bro1 spong bro1
  - **with**: kali-c ↓
    - **burning**: kali-c br1*
- **paroxysmal**: cact k2 kola stb3• *Laur*
- **periodical**: *Spig* ↓
  - **stitching** pain: *Spig*
- **pinching** pain: kali-c h2* lac-leo hrn2• par b7.de* ph-ac h2* ran-s b7.de* suprar rly4•
- **pressing** pain: acon k* adon mtf11 agar k* ambr k* ant-t k* *Arg-n* k* *Arn* k* **Ars** k* *Asaf* k* **Aur** aur-ar k2 **Aur-m** bamb-a stb2.de• bell k* borx bg2 both-ax tsm2 bov k* brom bg2 *Bry* **Cact** k* *Calc* k* cann-i k* cann-s b7.de* canth b7.de* carb-an k* carb-v bg2 card-m caust bg2 *Cench* cham k* chin bg2 chinin-s coc-c k* colch k* coll con k* cycl k* dig bg2 *Eup-per* k* *Glon* k* *Graph* k* grat k* ham fd3.de• *Hydr-ac* k* hyos k* hyper k* iod k* kali-bi k* kali-c k* *Kalm* kola stb3• *Lac-d* **Lach** k* lap-la sde8.de• laur b7.de* led bg2 *Lil-t* k* lith-c k* lyc k* *Lycps-v* k* lyss m-arct b7.de manc mez bg2 nat-c k* *Nat-m* k* nat-n bg2 nat-s k* nux-m bg2 *Nux-v* k* ol-an olib-sac wmh1 olnd k* ozone sde2• pall petr k* *Phos* k* plat bg2 plb k* prim-vl c2 *Puls* k* *Rhus-t* k* rumx bg2 ruta fd4.de samb bg2 sang k* sec k* *Seneg* k* sep sil k* *Spig* k* *Spong* k* stram k* stront-c k* sulph bg2 symph fd3.de• *Tarent* thuj k* tritic-vg fd5.de tub jl2 vanad br1 vanil fd5.de verat k* vip k* zinc k* zing k* [tax jsj7]
  - **accompanied** by | **anxiety** (See MIND - Anxiety - heart; with)
  - **downward**: ars bg2 carb-v bg2
  - **inward**: acon vh1
  - **plug**; as from a: ran-s bg2 spig bg2
- **pressure**:
  - **agg.**: cact k2
  - **amel.**: aur-m ↓
    - **boring** pain: aur-m k*
- **pressure**: ...
  - **hand**; of:
    - **amel.**: aur-m ↓ bufo bg1 laur bg1 *Nat-m Puls* ↓
      - **pressing** pain: *Nat-m* k*
      - **stitching** pain: aur-m *Puls*
- **pricking**: aur bg2 ham bg2 manc bg2 verat-v bg2
- **pulsating** pain: arg-n camph clem *Glon* graph *Kali-c Lycps-v Nux-v* rumx sil spig tarent
- **pulsations**; during strong: coc-c ↓ *Crot-h* ↓
  - **sore**: coc-c *Crot-h*
- **radiating**: acon bg2 agar bg2 apis bg2 ars bg2 cimic bg2 dig bg2 *Glon* kalm bg2 lach bg2 *Lat-m* bg2 lil-t bg2 naja bg2 ox-ac bg2 phyt bg2 rhus-t bg2 spig bg2 tab bg2
- **raising** | **arm**:
  - **agg.**: bry ↓
    - **cramping**: bry
  - **arms** | **agg.**: bry bg1 dig pd
- **reading** aloud, while: *Calc* ↓ nat-m ↓
  - **stitching** pain: *Calc* nat-m k*
- **rest**:
  - **agg.**: rauw sp1
  - **amel.**: ox-ac ↓
    - **stitching** pain: ox-ac mrr1
- **rheumatic**: *(↗Heart; complaints - accompanied - rheumatic)* *Abrot* k* acon am-c anac ant-t apis *Arg-n* ars aspar br1* **Aur** aur-m aven br1 *Benz-ac Cact Cimic* k* cocc *Colch Crot-h* dig guaj k2 *Kali-ar Kali-c* k* *Kalm Lach Led* **Lith-c** k* *Lycps-v* **Naja** phyt *Puls Rhus-t* sacch *Sang Sep* **Spig** *Spong*
  - **accompanied** by | **constriction** of chest: asaf hr1*
- **riding** in a carriage agg.: carc fd2.de• cot c1 naja raph k* tritic-vg fd5.de
- **ringing** of a church bell: lyss ↓
  - **stitching** pain: lyss k*
- **rising** | **lying**; from | **agg.**: *Laur*
  - **sitting**; from | **agg.**: *Gels*
- **rubbing**:
  - **amel.**: mur-ac ↓
    - **stitching** pain: mur-ac h2
- **rubbing** against ribs; as if: cann-xyz bg2
- **scraped**; as if: bufo bg2
- **sitting**:
  - **agg.**: *Mag-m* mur-ac ↓ rhus-t ↓ spong fd4.de symph ↓
    - **stitching** pain: mur-ac a1 rhus-t spong fd4.de symph fd3.de•
  - **bent** forward:
    - **agg.**: viol-t ↓
      - **stitching** pain: viol-t
  - **erect** | **agg.**: acon bg3
- **sleep** agg.; during: aur-m ↓
  - **stitching** pain: aur-m
- **sneezing** agg.: mez ↓
  - **stitching** pain: mez k*
- **sore**: acon bg2* apis bg2* *Arn* bg2* ars bg2 bapt ptk1 bar-c k* bell bg2 *Cact* k* calc-ar camph bro1 cann-xyz bg2 *Cench Cimic* bg2* cinnb bg2 colch bg2 *Crot-h* k* dioxi rbp6 elaps bg2 *Fl-ac* k* *Gels* k* haem bg1* hyos bg2* ign bg2 kali-bi bg2* lach bg2* lap-la sde8.de• laur bg2* lept lil-t bg1 lith-c bg2* lycps-v bg2* *Mag-c* k* med *Naja* bro1 nat-m k* ol-an bg2 ox-ac k* puls samb bg2 saroth sp1 sec bg2* *Spig* k* sul-ac k* *Tab* bg2* thuj bg2
- **sprained**; as if: ant-t
- **squeezed**; as if: acon bg2* adon bro1 agar bg2 aml-ns bg2* *Arn* b7.de* ars bro1 borx b4a.de* brom bg2 bufo bg2 *Cact* bg2* cadm-s bro1 calc-ar bro1 cann-xyz bg2 carb-v bg2 *Caust* bg2 chin bg2 clem bg2 coc-c bro1 colch bro1 con bg2 dig bg2 hell bg2 hydr-ac bg2 iod b4a.de* iodof bro1 kali-c bg2* kalm bg2 lach bro1 laur bro1 *Lil-t* bg2* lycps-v bro1 lyss c1 mag-m bg2 mag-p bro1 magn-gr bro1 merc bg2 nat-m b4.de* nux-m bg2* ozone sde2• ph-ac b4a.de phos b4a.de *Plat* b4a.de ptel bro1 *Puls* b7a.de spig bg2* spong bro1 sulph bg2 tarent bg2 *Thyr* bro1 viol-t bg2

Chest

- **standing** agg.: aur-m-n carc ↓
  - **pressing** pain: aur-m-n k*
  - **stitching** pain: carc tpw2*
- **sticking** pain: allox sp1 both-ax tsm2 galla-q-r nl2• hed sp1 hist sp1 mag-s sp1 rauw sp1 stroph-s sp1 x-ray sp1
- **stimulants**; from abuse of: nux-v bro1 spig bro1
- **stinging**: aln vva1• *Apis* bg2 colch tl1 kali-s fd4.de lyss rumx bg2
- **stitching** pain: *Abrot* *Acon* k* aesc k* agar k* aloe bg2 alumn am-c k* *Anac* k* anan ang c1 **Apis** k* *Arg-met* k* *Arn* k* ars bro1 ars-met ars-s-f k2 asc-t k* aur k* aur-ar k2 aur-m k* aur-s k2 bamb-a stb2.de• bell k* benz-ac bg2 berb k* bomb-pr mlk9.de both-ax tsm2 brach **Bry** k* bufo *Cact* k* *Calc* k* calc-ar *Calc-p* k* camph k* cann-i k* cann-xyz bg2 *Canth* k* caps k* carb-ac k* carb-an bg2 carb-v k* carbn-s carc fd2.de• card-m **Caust** k* cench k2 cere-b bro1 *Cham* k* *Chel* k* chin k* chinin-ar cic bg2 *Cimic* k* *Clem* k* coc-c k* *Colch* k* *Coloc* k* con bg2 croc b7.de* crot-t k* *Cupr* k* *Cycl* k* cypra-eg sde6.de• daph k* dig k* digin a1 dios k* euph bg2 euphr k* gels k* *Glon* k* graph h2* *Ham* k* helo helo-s rwt2• *Hep* k* *Hydr* k* *Hydroph* rsj6• hyos k* iber k* ign k* iod bg2 iodof k* jac-c k* kali-bi k* *Kali-c* k* kali-cy a1 *Kali-i* k* kali-m k2 kali-n k* kali-p kali-s **Kalm** k* kola stb3• *Kreos* k* **Lach** k* lachn lap-la sde8.de• *Lat-m* bro1 *Laur* k* lepi br1 lil-t bro1 lith-c k* *Lyc* k* lycps-v k* *Lyss* m-arct b7.de mag-c k* **Mag-m** k* magn-gr bro1 manc k* med mentho bro1 meny k* merc-i-f k* merc-i-r k* mez b4.de* *Mur-ac* k* myric k* **Naja** k* nat-c b4.de* nat-m k* nat-n bg2 nit-ac k* nux-m b7.de* nux-v b7.de* op bg2 opun-s a1 (non:opun-v a1) ox-ac k* ozone sde2• paeon k* par k* **Petr** k* ph-ac k* phos phyt bro1 pieri-b mlk9.de plac rzf5• plat k* plb k* plumbg a1 podo bg2* positr nl2• **Psor** *Puls* k* *Ran-b* *Ran-s* k* *Rhus-t* k* rhus-v k* ros-d wla1 ruta fd4.de sabad bg2 sabin samb bg2 sang k* scut c1 sep k* sin-n k* sphing a1* **Spig** k* **Spong** k* **Staph** suis-pan rly4• sul-ac k* **Sulph** k* symph fd3.de• syph bro1 tab bg2* tarent k* *Tell* rsj10• thuj k* tritic-vg fd5.de trom valer k* vanil fd5.de verb k* viol-t k* vip k* *Zinc* k* zinc-p k2 [spect dfg1]
  - **burning**: anan *Mur-ac*
  - **needles**; as from: bufo bg2 cimic ptk1 colum-p sze2• lyss ptk1 manc ptk1
  - **outward**: clem k*
- **stooping** agg.: calc bg1 glon ↓ *Lil-t* *Lith-c* ↓ nat-m bg1 olnd
  - **sore**: *Lith-c*
  - **stitching** pain: glon k*
- **straightening** up difficult: mur-ac ↓
  - **stitching** pain: mur-ac h2
- **sudden**: mag-c ↓
  - **sore**: mag-c
- **sudden** appearing and sudden disappearing: ozone ↓
  - **pressing** pain: ozone sde2•
- **synchronous** with beat of heart: digin ↓ *Rhus-t* ↓ **Spig** ↓ zinc ↓
  - **stitching** pain●: (non:dig slp) digin a1* *Rhus-t* k* **Spig** k* zinc
- **talking** agg.: both-ax ↓ carb-an ↓
  - **sticking** pain: both-ax tsm2
  - **stitching** pain: carb-an h2
- **thinking** of the pain agg.: ox-ac ↓
  - **stitching** pain: ox-ac mrr1
- **tobacco**; from: kalm bro1 lil-t bro1 nux-v bro1 spig bro1 staph bro1 tab bro1
- **touching** spine: tarent k*
- **twisting** pain: *Lach* bro1 seneg bg2* tarent bg1*
  - **knot**; as if twisted into a: lob bg2 tab bg2 tarent bg2
- **urination**:
  - **after**:
    - **agg.**: lith-c bg2
    - **amel.**: *Lith-c* k* *Nat-m*
      - **pressing** pain: *Nat-m*
  - **before**: *Lith-c* k*
  - **during**: aspar *Lith-c* k*
    - **pressing** pain: lith-c k*
- **waking** | **after** | **agg.**: fago *Tarent*
  - **on**: both-ax ↓ fago ↓
    - **pressing** pain: both-ax tsm2
- **waking – on**: ...
  - **stitching** pain: fago k*
- **walking**:
  - **agg.**: acon ↓ arg-n *Cact* carc ↓ kali-i bg1 *Lyss* ↓ *Nat-m* ox-ac ozone ↓ ph-ac h2 *Ran-b* rhus-t seneg spig sulph
    - **pressing** pain: arg-n k* ozone sde2• seneg k*
    - **stitching** pain: acon k* carc fd2.de• *Kali-i* k* *Lyss* k* nat-m k*
  - **air** agg.; in open: carc ↓ nat-m ↓
    - **stitching** pain: carc fd2.de• nat-m
  - **amel.**: colch lap-la sde8.de• *Puls* rhus-t ↓
    - **pressing** pain: colch k* puls
    - **stitching** pain: puls rhus-t
- **wandering** pain: *Aur* dig bg1* *Kalm* led k13 *Puls*
- **wiping** arms agg.: apis ↓
  - **stitching** pain: apis bg1
- **yawning** agg.: merc-i-f
- ▽ **extending** to:
  - **right**: aloe bg2 apis bg2 arn bg2 helo bg2 lycps-v bg2 phyt bg2
  - **Abdomen**: lat-m ↓ ox-ac ↓
    - **left**: cact k2
    - **cramping**: lat-m br1
    - **stitching** pain: ox-ac mrr1
  - **Arm**: ox-ac ↓ ther ↓
    - **right**: helo-s rwt2• lil-t c1* phyt k* spig
    - **left**: acon mrr1 arn sne *Aur* sne *Cact* mrr1 cimic tl1 crot-h tl1 dig mrr1 lach mrr1 lat-m sp1* med hr1 *Naja* mrr1 *Rhus-t* mrr1 symph fd3.de• tarent tl1 ther tl1 visc bg3
    - **cutting** pain: ther c1
    - **stitching** pain: ox-ac mrr1
    - **Both** arms: acon bg2 am-m bg2 *Aur* sne cact bg2 cimic bg2 cinnb bg2 ham bg2 kalm bg2 lat-m bg3 nat-m bg2 sec k1 spig bg2* tab bg2 tarent bg2
  - **Axilla**: brom c1 ferr-i kali-n bg1 *Lat-m* k* lil-t bg1 mur-ac ↓
    - **left**: both-ax ↓ lat-m sp1
      - **pressing** pain: both-ax tsm2
    - **stitching** pain: mur-ac h2
    - **Back**; then: cact k2
      - **pressing** pain: cact k2
  - **Back**: agar ↓ aloe am-c bg2 anac bg2 *Ars-i* calc bg1 **Cench** *Crot-t* ferr-p bg2 glon k* *Kali-c* k* kali-i bg1 lac-h ↓ *Lil-t* lycps-v bg2 mur-ac ↓ *Naja* polyg-h bg2 rauw ↓ *Spig* **Sulph**
    - **cramping**: lac-h htj1•
    - **sticking** pain: rauw sp1
    - **stitching** pain: agar am-c *Anac* *Glon* *Kali-c* mur-ac h2
  - **Fingers**: lat-m br1
    - **left** hand; of: acon mrr1 *Cact* mrr1 rhus-t mrr1
  - **Front**: rauw ↓
    - **sticking** pain: rauw sp1
  - **Hand** | **left**: *Acon* am-m arn bg1 ars bg1 *Aster* *Aur* bar-c bg1 brom bg1 *Cact* k* chinin-s bg1 *Cimic* conv bg1 *Crot-h* cur bg1 *Dig* glon bg1 ham bg1 hydr bg1 iber c1 **Kalm** lach bg1 *Lat-m* lil-t bg1 med bg1* *Naja* k* *Nux-v* phos bg1 puls bg1 *Rhus-t* k* *Spig* *Tab* ther
  - **Head**: med bg1 spig bg1
  - **Leg** | **right**: alumn
  - **Lower** limbs: cham bg2
  - **Lung**; lower:
    - **right**: alumn ↓
      - **stitching** pain: alumn
  - **Nape** of neck and shoulder: *Naja* k* spig k2
  - **Ovary**: thyr bg1
  - **Scapula**: agar bg2 aloe bg2 aml-ns bg2 glon bg2 lil-t bg2 naja bg2 rumx bg2 spig bg2 thuj bg2
    - **right**: *Spig* kl
    - **left**: agar bg1 aloe am-n bg1 ars bg1 glon bg1 *Kali-c* ↓ kalm bg1 lach bg1 *Lil-t* *Naja* paeon bg1 rumx bg1 *Spig* bg1* spong fd4.de **Sulph** k ● tell ↓ thuj bg1
      - **stitching** pain: agar *Kali-c* *Kalm* paeon rumx **Sulph** tell rsj10•

- **extending** to – **Scapula**: ...
  - **Between**: *Sulph* bg2
  - **Shoulder**: ox-ac↓ spig k2 *Verat*
    - **right** shoulder and under right scapula; through chest to: chen-a c1
    - **left**: crot-h tl1 kola↓ lat-m c1* mand sp1 ther tl1
      - **cramping**: kola stb3•
      - **cutting** pain: ther c1
    - **stitching** pain: ox-ac mrr1
  - **Sternum**: *Spig* k*
  - **Stomach**: lac-h↓ lyc↓
    - **cramping**: lac-h htj1•
    - **stitching** pain: lyc
  - **Throat**: med hr1 *Naja* mrr1 [bar-s stj1]
  - **Upper** limbs:
    - **left**: *Acon*↓ arn↓ asper↓ bism↓ *Cact*↓ cimic↓ crot-h↓ *Kalm*↓ *Lat-m*↓ lepi↓ naja↓ *Ox-ac*↓ *Rhus-t*↓ *Spig*↓ tab↓
      - **stitching** pain: *Acon* bro1 arn bro1 asper bro1 bism bro1 *Cact* bro1 cimic bro1 crot-h bro1 *Kalm* bro1 *Lat-m* bro1 lepi bro1 naja bro1 *Ox-ac* bro1 *Rhus-t* bro1 *Spig* bro1 tab bro1
  - **Upward**: mag-p bg2 thyr bg1

○ • **Apex**: lil-t bro1* nat-m↓ streptoc jl2 ulm-c jsj8•
  - **sticking** pain: nat-m bg2
  - **stitching** pain: ulm-c jsj8•
  - **extending** to:
    - **Base**: med↓
      - **stitching** pain: med bro1

- **Base**: lob bro1
  - **extending** to:
    - **Apex** of heart: syph↓
      - **night**: syph↓
        - **stitching** pain: syph bro1
      - **cramping**: syph c1
- **Below**: lyc↓ ruta↓
  - **pressing** pain: lyc h2 ruta fd4.de
- **Muscles**: cupr bro1 hydr-ac bro1
- **Myocardium**: scarl jl2
  - **rheumatic**: psor jl2
- **Pericardium**:
  - **eating** agg.: ant-ar mtf11
  - **lying** down agg.: ant-ar mtf11
- **Region** of: acon↓ acon-ac↓ aesc↓ aeth *Agar*↓ am-c↓ am-caust am-m↓ aml-ns anac↓ arg-met↓ arg-n **Arn**↓ ars ars-met ars-s-f k2 **Arum-t** asaf asc-t↓ *Aur-m*↓ bamb-a↓ bell↓ *Benz-ac* both fne1• both-a rb3 both-ax↓ bov↓ brach *Brom*↓ bufo↓ calam sa3• calc↓ calc-ar k2 calc-p cann-i cann-s canth↓ carb-an↓ *Carb-v*↓ carbn-o *Carl*↓ *Caust*↓ cic a1 *Cimic* cinnb↓ clem↓ colch↓ con↓ crat br1 crot-t↓ dios elaps↓ eup-per↓ flor-p rsj3• *Graph* heroin↓ hir rsj4• hist↓ hydr-ac hyos↓ ignis-alc↓ *Iod*↓ jab kali-bi kali-c k* kali-s kola↓ lac-ac lac-h sk4• lach↓ **Lat-m** k* laur lil-t br1 lith-c mrr1 lob-s luf-op↓ *Lyc*↓ mag-c↓ meny↓ merc-c merc-i-f mez↓ mim-p rsj8• myric↓ *Naja Nat-m* onos ozone↓ pall c1 phos phyt plat↓ plb *Puls*↓ samb↓ sec sel rsj9• sin-n sol-ni sol-t-ae spig↓ *Spong* stann stict↓ sul-ac sulph syph↓ tab tax↓ tell thea ther br1 thuj tritic-vg fd5.de tub↓ tung-met bdx1• vanil fd5.de verat *Verat-v*↓ xan c1 zinc zinc-m
  - **morning**: dios fago nat-m spong fd4.de tritic-vg fd5.de
    - **rising** | **after**:
      - **agg.**: both-ax↓
        - **sticking** pain: both-ax tsm2
    - **agg.**: both-ax↓
      - **sticking** pain: both-ax tsm2
  - **forenoon**: fago vanil fd5.de
  - **afternoon**: fago spong fd4.de vanil fd5.de
  - **evening**: fago spong fd4.de sulph thuj
    - **18** h: hir↓
      - **dull** pain: hir rsj4•
    - **18**.45 h: calam sa3•
    - **amel.**: lac-h sk4•

- **Region** of – **evening**: ...
  - **bed** agg.; in: *Nat-m*
  - **accompanied** by:
    - **Upper** limbs:
      - **numbness**: lat-m sp1
      - **paralysis**: (↗*EXTREMITIES - Paralysis - upper limbs - pain in)* lat-m sp1
  - **acute**: aml-ns bov calc-p dios *Iod* mez
  - **ascending** agg.: rauw↓
    - **constricting** pain: rauw sp1
  - **beaten**; as if: ozone sde2•
  - **breathing**:
    - **arresting** breathing: bac↓ *Calc*↓ *Calc-p*↓ *Dios*↓
      - **cutting** pain: bac c1 *Calc Calc-p Dios*
    - **deep** | **agg.**: rumx
  - **burning**: acon k* aesc k* *Agar* k* arg-met *Ars* k* bell k* *Carb-v* k* *Carl* k* *Caust Cic* k* *Kali-c* k* plat k* *Puls* verat k* *Verat-v* k*
  - **chill**; during: cact bro1 tarent bro1
  - **constricting** pain: hist sp1 tub jl2
  - **cough** agg.; during: agar↓ elaps↓
    - **burning**: agar k*
    - **tearing** pain: elaps
  - **cutting** pain: acon-ac rly4• anac k* asc-t a1 aur-m *Brom Calc-p* k* cinnb *Dios* myric *Phos* spig syph jl2 tritic-vg fd5.de verat k* xan c1 [heroin sdj2]
  - **drawing** pain: calc h2 meny h1 tritic-vg fd5.de
  - **drinking** agg.; after: nat-m
  - **dull** pain: hist sp1
  - **exertion** agg.: both-ax↓
    - **slightest** exertion: both-ax↓
      - **sticking** pain: both-ax tsm2
    - **sticking** pain: both-ax tsm2
  - **fever**; during: spong b7.de
  - **fright**; after: bamb-a↓
    - **tearing** pain: bamb-a stb2.de•
  - **hiccough** agg.: agar↓
    - **burning**: agar k*
  - **inspiration**:
    - **agg.**: calam sa3• luf-op↓ nat-c a1 vanil fd5.de xan↓
      - **cutting** pain: luf-op rsj5• xan c1
    - **deep**:
      - **agg.**: both-ax↓ calc-p
        - **sticking** pain: both-ax tsm2
  - **lying** on left side agg.: tell c1
  - **pressing** pain: asaf tl1 cann-i tl1 hist sp1 spong fd4.de stict c1 tritic-vg fd5.de vanil fd5.de [tax jsj7]
  - **respiration**; -try
    - **quick** and difficult: nux-v
  - **sitting** | **bent** forward | **agg.**: hir rsj4•
    - **erect** | **amel.**: hir rsj4•
  - **sneezing** agg.: agar↓
    - **burning**: agar k*
  - **sore**: **Arn** *Aur-m* cimic k2 cinnb colch eup-per hyos *Lith-c* ozone sde2• samb sec tab thuj
  - **sprained**; as if: thuj h1
  - **standing** agg.: tung-met bdx1•
  - **sticking** pain: both-ax tsm2
  - **stitching** pain: ignis-alc es2• luf-op rsj5• sel rsj9• tritic-vg fd5.de vanil fd5.de [tax jsj7]
  - **swallowing** agg.: bamb-a↓
    - **tearing** pain: bamb-a stb2.de•
  - **tearing** pain: am-c bg2 am-m k* bamb-a stb2.de• bufo bg2 canth b7.de* carb-an bg2 clem k* colch b7.de* con bg2 crot-t elaps hyos k* kola stb3• lach bg1 **Lat-m** *Lyc* k* mag-c *Ther* thuj k*
    - **pulsating** pain: lyc h2
  - **waking**; on: kali-bi
  - **walking** agg.: both-ax↓
    - **sticking** pain: both-ax tsm2

- **Region** of: ...
  - **extending** to: *(↗Heart; complaints - accompanied - upper - left - pain)*
    - **Arm**:
      - **left**: am-m ↓ *Lat-m* ↓ med ↓ ozone ↓ rhus-t ↓ *Ther* ↓
        - **burning**: med$_{k2}$ ozone$_{sde2}$•
        - **tearing** pain: am-m *Lat-m* rhus-t *Ther*
    - **Back**: med ↓
      - **burning**: med$_{hr1}$
    - **Forearm**:
      - **left**: am-m ↓ cact ↓ rhus-t ↓
        - **tearing** pain: am-m$_{a1}$* cact$_{a1}$* rhus-t$_{a1}$*
    - **Nape** of neck: naja$_{c1}$
    - **Scapula**:
      - **left**: agar ↓ spig ↓ thuj ↓
        - **burning**: agar
        - **tearing** pain: spig$_{h1}$ thuj
    - **Shoulder** | **left**: naja$_{c1}$
    - **Upper** arm:
      - **left**: spig ↓
        - **tearing** pain: spig$_{h1}$
    - **Upper** limbs | **left**: *(↗Heart; complaints - accompanied - upper - left - pain)* **Lat-m** naja$_{c1}$
- **Spot**; in a small: kola$_{stb3}$•
- **Under** the heart: allox ↓
  - **sticking** pain: allox$_{sp1}$

- **Intercostal** region: acon ↓ aran ↓ arn ↓ ars ↓ ars-i ↓ asc-t ↓ aster ↓ bell ↓ brom ↓ bry ↓ chel ↓ cimic ↓ des-ac ↓ dulc ↓ gaul ↓ kalm ↓ mag-p ↓ mentho ↓ mez ↓ morg-g ↓ morph ↓ nept-m ↓ nux-v ↓ par ↓ phos ↓ puls ↓ **Ran-b** ↓ rhod ↓ samb ↓ *Sul-ac* ↓ syc ↓ vac ↓ verb ↓ zinc ↓
  - **right**: chel ↓
    - **motion** agg.: chel ↓
      - **neuralgic**: chel$_{mrr1}$
    - **neuralgic**: chel$_{mrr1}$
  - **herpes** zoster; after: ars ↓ mez ↓ ran-b ↓
    - **neuralgic**: ars$_{tl1}$ mez$_{tl1}$ ran-b$_{tl1}$
  - **neuralgic**: acon$_{bg2}$* aran$_{bg2}$* arn$_{bg2}$* ars$_{bg2}$* ars-i$_{bro1}$ asc-t$_{bg2}$* aster$_{bro1}$ bell$_{bg2}$* brom$_{bro1}$ bry$_{bg2}$* chel$_{bg2}$* cimic$_{bg2}$* des-ac$_{mtf11}$ dulc$_{mtf11}$ gaul$_{bro1}$ kalm$_{mrr1}$ mag-p$_{bg2}$* mentho$_{bro1}$ mez$_{bg2}$* morg-g$_{fmm1}$• morph$_{bro1}$ nept-m$_{lsd2.fr}$ nux-v$_{bg2}$* par$_{bg2}$* phos$_{bg2}$* puls$_{bg2}$* **Ran-b**$_{bg2}$* rhod$_{bg2}$* samb$_{bro1}$ syc$_{fmm1}$• vac$_{jl2}$ zinc$_{bg2}$*
  - **tearing** pain: *Sul-ac* verb$_{bg2}$
  - ○ **Lower** chest:
    - **left**: arg-met ↓ **Ran-b** ↓
      - **neuralgic**: arg-met$_{ptk1}$ **Ran-b**$_{mrr1}$
  - **Muscles**: abrot$_{bg2}$ acon$_{bg2}$* *[illegible]*$_{bro1}$ arist-m$_{bro1}$ arn$_{bg2}$* ars$_{bro1}$ ars-s-f ↓ asc-t$_{bg2}$* aza$_{bro1}$ borx$_{bro1}$* brass-n-o$_{srj5}$• *Bry*$_{bg2}$* caust$_{bro1}$ chel$_{bro1}$ chin$_{bg2}$* cimic$_{bg2}$* colch$_{bg2}$* dys$_{pte1}$*• echi$_{bro1}$ ferr$_{ptk1}$ ferr-p$_{ptk1}$ gaul$_{bro1}$ guaj$_{bg2}$* *Kali-c*$_{bro1}$ kalm$_{bg2}$ kreos ↓ lach$_{bg2}$* lil-t$_{bg2}$ med$_{mtf11}$ *Mez* ↓ morg-g$_{pte1}$* morg-p$_{pte1}$• nept-m$_{lsd2.fr}$ *Nux-v*$_{bg2}$* ol-j$_{bg2}$ ox-ac$_{bro1}$ *Phos*$_{bro1}$ puls$_{bg2}$* **Ran-b**$_{bg2}$* rham-cal$_{br1}$* rhod$_{bro1}$ rhus-r$_{bro1}$ rhus-t$_{bg2}$* rumx$_{bro1}$ sabad$_{bg2}$* sang$_{bg2}$ senec$_{bg2}$ seneg$_{bg2}$* sil$_{bg2}$ sin-n$_{bro1}$ sphing$_{c1}$* squil$_{bg2}$ sul-ac$_{bro1}$ sulph$_{bg2}$* syc$_{pte1}$* tab$_{bg2}$ tub-m$_{jl2}$ v-a-b$_{jl2}$ verat$_{bg2}$
    - **right**: asc-t$_{a2}$ card-m$_{bg2}$ chel$_{bg2}$ kali-c$_{bg2}$ merc$_{bg2}$ quas$_{br1}$
    - **left**: apis$_{bg2}$ arg-met$_{bg2}$ arg-n$_{bg2}$ bry$_{a1}$ nat-s$_{bg2}$ phos$_{bg2}$ rumx$_{bg2}$ stann$_{bg2}$ ther$_{bg2}$
    - **cutting** pain: ars-s-f$_{k2}$ asc-t$_{a1}$ borx kreos *Mez*
    - **rheumatic**: *Ran-b*$_{tl1}$
    - **riding** on horseback: sphing$_{a1}$*
    - **Spots**; in: pert-vc$_{vk9}$

- **Lower** part: *Agar* ↓ agn ↓ aloe ↓ alum ↓ am-m ↓ arg-met ↓ arn asaf ↓ asar ↓ bism bry ↓ *Cann-s* ↓ carb-ac ↓ cassia-s ↓ cench$_{k2}$ chel *Chin* choc ↓ cic ↓ coc-c ↓ croc dig ↓ euph ↓ fl-ac ↓ hell ↓ hep ↓ hyos ↓ kali-bi ↓ kali-c kali-p **Kalm** ↓ kreos ↓ lach lact ↓ laur ↓ lyc m-aust ↓ mag-c ↓ mang meph$_{a1}$ merc-c ↓ mosch ↓ *Naja* ↓ nat-ar ↓ nat-s ol-j *Ox-ac* ↓ phos ↓ plb ↓ **Puls**$_{k}$* ran-b$_{k2}$ rhus-t$_{k}$* ruta$_{fd4.de}$ sabad ↓ sal-fr ↓ sang ↓ seneg sep ↓ stann stry ↓ *Sulph* ↓ tarent teucr thuj ↓ tub$_{gk}$ valer vanil$_{fd5.de}$ verat viol-t ↓ zinc ↓

- **Lower** part: ...
  - **right**: *Ambr Chel*$_{k}$* *Chen-a* ↓ crot-t ↓ *Kali-c* med ↓ *Merc-c*$_{k}$* naja ph-ac$_{h2}$
    - **stitching** pain: *Chel Chen-a* crot-t$_{k}$* med
    - **extending** to:
      - **Axilla**: carb-an$_{bg1}$
      - **Liver**: med ↓
        - **stitching** pain: med$_{hr1}$
  - **left**: *Cact*$_{k}$* carb-v carbn-s caust ↓ cob ↓ colch *Kali-p*$_{k}$* lith-c med ↓ melal-alt$_{gya4}$ meph$_{a1}$ nat-m ↓ **Ox-ac Phos Ran-b**$_{mrr1}$ rhod ruta$_{fd4.de}$ sel ↓ squil ↓ tarent tub$_{gk}$ zinc ↓
    - **cutting** pain: squil$_{mrr1}$
    - **eating** | **amel.**: rhod
    - **pressing** pain: med$_{c1}$
    - **sore**: caust$_{h2}$ med$_{c1}$ nat-m$_{h2}$ zinc$_{h2}$
    - **stitching** pain: carbn-s cob **Ox-ac** sel$_{rsj9}$• tub$_{gk}$
  - **forenoon**: agar ↓
    - **stitching** pain: agar$_{k}$*
  - **noon**:
    - **12-17 h**: sel ↓
      - **stitching** pain: sel$_{rsj9}$•
  - **night**: ruta ↓
    - **pressing** pain: ruta$_{h1}$
    - **waking**; on: ruta ↓
      - **pressing** pain: ruta$_{h1}$*
  - **aching**: *Chin*$_{k}$* choc$_{srj3}$• croc$_{k}$* fl-ac kali-bi seneg$_{k}$* sep *Sulph*
  - **alternating** with | **Shoulder**; pain in: tub$_{gk}$
  - **burning**: chel$_{k}$* mag-c$_{h2}$ phos$_{k}$*
  - **cough** agg.; during: cassia-s ↓ kali-p$_{k2}$ meph$_{a1}$ tub$_{gk}$
    - **stitching** pain: cassia-s$_{ccrh1}$•
  - **cutting** pain: hell$_{h1}$ *Kali-c*$_{k}$* nat-ar$_{k2}$ *Ox-ac* stry
    - **dragging**: phos$_{k}$*
  - **drawing** pain: arg-met chel mang ruta$_{fd4.de}$ verat
  - **eating**; after: arg-n ↓
    - **aching**: arg-n
  - **expiration**:
    - **agg.**: verat$_{h1}$
    - **during**:
      - **agg.**: sel ↓
        - **stitching** pain: sel$_{rsj9}$•
  - **inspiration**:
    - **agg.**: *Sulph* ↓
      - **aching**: *Sulph*
    - **deep**:
      - **agg.**: carbn-s chel cob ↓ crot-t ↓ meph$_{a1}$ naja tub$_{gk}$
        - **stitching** pain: cob$_{k}$* crot-t$_{k}$* tub$_{gk}$
  - **lying**:
    - **amel.**: *Chel Chin* ↓
      - **aching**: *Chin*
    - **back**; on | **amel.**: ambr
    - **side**; on | **left** | **agg.**: **Phos** tub$_{gk}$
      - **painful** side | **amel.**: ambr$_{h1}$
  - **pressing** pain: *Agar*$_{k}$* agn$_{b7.de}$* alum$_{b4.de}$* arn$_{k}$* asaf$_{b7.de}$* asar$_{b7.de}$* bism$_{k}$* chin$_{k}$* cic$_{b7.de}$* croc$_{b7.de}$* dig$_{h2}$ hyos$_{b7.de}$* lact laur$_{b7.de}$* m-aust$_{b7.de}$ merc-c$_{b4a.de}$ phos$_{h2}$ plb$_{b7.de}$* ran-b$_{b7.de}$* rhus-t$_{bg2}$ ruta$_{b7.de}$* sabad$_{b7.de}$* *Seneg*$_{k}$* teucr$_{k}$* valer$_{k}$* viol-t$_{b7.de}$* zinc$_{k}$*
    - **asunder**: euph$_{h2}$
  - **pressure** agg.: meph$_{a1}$ ph-ac$_{h2}$
  - **respiration**: kali-bi ↓ lyc ↓ tub ↓
    - **stitching** pain: kali-bi$_{k}$* lyc$_{k}$* tub$_{gk}$
  - **sitting** agg.: *Chin* seneg
    - **aching**: *Chin*$_{k}$* seneg$_{k}$*
  - **sneezing** agg.: meph$_{a1}$ ruta$_{fd4.de}$
  - **sore**: am-m meph sal-fr$_{sle1}$•

- **squeezed**; as if: am-m bg2 carb-ac bg2 thuj bg2
- **stitching** pain: agar k* aloe *Arn* b7a.de bry *Cann-s* b7a.de cassia-s ccrh1• *Chel* k* coc-c k* hep **Kalm** k* kreos b7a.de lach k* mosch b7a.de *Naja* sang k* seneg k* sulph tub gk valer
- **touch** agg.: meph a1
- **walking**:
  - **agg.**: bism sep
    - **extending** transversely: bism
  - **amel.**: chin
    - **aching**: chin k*
- ▽ **extending** to:
  - **Abdomen**: *Chel* ↓ kali-c ↓ tub ↓
    - **cutting** pain: kali-c k*
    - **stitching** pain: *Chel* k* tub gk
  - **Back**: *Carbn-s* ↓
    - **stitching** pain: *Carbn-s*
  - **Shoulders**: sang ↓ tub ↓
    - **stitching** pain: sang k* tub gk

- **Lungs**: ail ↓ bufo ↓ calc-sil k2 canth ↓ caps ↓ celt ↓ clem a1 coca-c sk4• gal-ac br1 *Lyc* k* mosch ↓ ozone ↓ **Phos** podo fd3.de• psor ↓ rad-br ↓ rumx *Sulph* k* *Tub* k* vanil fd5.de zinc ↓
  - **right**: bry k* echi *Elaps* falco-pe nl2• gal-ac c1 kali-c tl1 *Mang* ↓ med ↓ pyrog pd rumx sulph vanil fd5.de
    - **adhering** to rib; as if lobe were: *Kali-c*
    - **coughing** and talking agg.: pyrog pd
    - **sore**: gal-ac a1 med hr1
    - **stitching** pain: *Mang* hr1
    - **extending** to | **Back**: chel mrr1
    - **Apex** and middle part: abies-c bro1 *Anis* bro1 *Ars* bro1 borx bro1 *Calc* bro1 com bro1 crot-t bro1 *Elaps* bro1 erio bro1 iodof bro1 *Phel* bro1 sang bro1 upa bro1
  - **left**: bamb-a ↓ falco-pe nl2• myrt-c gk **Phos** plut-n srj7• sulph k* tub tl1*
    - **evening**: *Sulph* k*
    - **breathing** agg.: asc-t br1
    - **cutting** pain: plut-n srj7•
    - **pressing** pain: bamb-a stb2.de•
    - **extending** to:
      - **right**: med ↓
        - **drawing** pain: med hr1
    - **Apex** and middle part: acon bro1 am-c bro1 *Anis* bro1 ant-s-aur bro1 crot-t bro1 *Lob-c* bro1 *Myrt-c* bro1 paeon bro1 phos bro1 *Pix* bro1 puls bro1 *Ran-b* bro1 rumx bro1 sil bro1 spig bro1 stann bro1 stict bro1 *Sulph* bro1 *Ther* bro1 tub bro1 ust bro1
  - **beaten**; as if: ozone sde2•
  - **burning**: canth tl1 caps gm1 phos tl1 rad-br sze8• sulph k2
    - **fire**; like: bufo ptk1
  - **cramping**: mosch zinc
  - **cutting** pain: celt a1
  - **drinking** cold water agg.: thuj ↓
    - **cramping**: thuj
  - **sore**: ail tl1 ozone sde2•
  - **standing**:
    - **agg.**: am-c ↓
      - **drawing** pain | **downward**: am-c h2
  - **sudden**: syc fmm1•
  - **tearing** pain: psor jl2
  - **waking** agg.; after: arum-t ↓
    - **cramping**: arum-t
  - ○ **Anterior** part: tub jl2
  - **Apex**: arum-t bg2 dol guaj ptk1 phos bg2 puls bg2* rumx bg2 ther bg2 tub c1* tub-a jl2 tub-m jl2
    - **right**: **Ars** k* bar-c bg2 cimic elaps bg2
      - **stitching** pain: **Ars**
      - **tearing** pain: elaps
      - **extending** to:
        - **Base**: cimic k*

- **Lungs – Apex – right – extending** to – **Base**: ... **stitching** pain: *Cimic*
    - **left**: anthraci ↓ calc-s *Con* guaj bg2 med c1 myric ptk1 sang hr1 sep ↓ sulph ↓ ther k* tub c1
      - **cutting** pain: sep tl1 sulph tl1
      - **stitching** pain: anthraci br1 ther br1
    - **inspiration** agg.: cimic
    - **extending** to:
      - **Arm**: tub c1
      - **Axilla**: tub c1
      - **Back**: tub nh
  - **Behind**: tub jl2
  - **Center** | **left**: plut-n srj7• rumx
  - **Lower** part: cench k2 tub gk
    - **right**: am-m bro1 berb bro1 bry bro1 cact bro1 card-m bro1 *Chel* bro1 dios bro1 kali-c bro1 lyc bro1 *Merc* bro1 syc fmm1• xan c1
    - **left**: agar bro1 ampe-qu bro1 asc-t br1* calc-p bro1 cimic bro1 *Lob-s* bro1 lyc bro1 myos-s bro1 nat-s bro1 *Ox-ac* k* **Phos** *Rumx* bro1 sil bro1 squil bro1 tub gk
      - **cutting** pain: ox-ac mrr1
    - **cough** agg.; during: guat sp1
  - **Nipple**; above | **left**: **Arum-t** k* **Sulph** k*
  - **Upper** part:
    - **extending** to:
      - **Neck**: gal-ac ↓
        - **aching**: gal-ac a1*
      - **Shoulder**:
        - **right**: gal-ac ↓
          - **aching**: gal-ac a1*
      - **Spine**: gal-ac ↓
        - **aching**: gal-ac a1*

- **Mammae**: acon bro1 aesc ↓ aeth ↓ agath-a nl2• aids nl2• all-s bro1 allox tpw4 aln vva1• aloe ↓ alum ↓ *Am-c* ↓ am-m ↓ ambr anan ↓ ant-c ↓ apis k* arg-n bro1 arn b7a.de *Ars* ↓ ars-i k2 arum-t ↓ *Asc-t* ↓ aster k* aur ↓ aur-s bro1 bamb-a stb2.de• bar-c ↓ bar-i ↓ **Bell** k* berb ↓ *Borx* *Bov* ↓ brom bro1 *Bry* k* *Bufo* cact calad *Calc* k* calc-i ↓ calc-p calc-sil ↓ *Cann-s* b7.de* canth *Carb-an* k* carb-v carbn-s ↓ cartl-s ↓ *Cham* k* *Chim* bro1 chinin-ar chinin-s ↓ chir-fl ↓ cic ↓ cimic k* clem k* *Colch* ↓ coli ↓ *Coloc* k* com ↓ **Con** k* cot bro1 croc bro1 *Crot-t* bro1 cycl dream-p ↓ *Dulc* euph ↓ eupi falco-pe nl2• ferr ↓ galeoc-c-h ↓ galla-q-r ↓ gels ↓ germ-met srj5• gink-b sbd1• granit-m es1• graph ↓ grat ↓ hell ↓ *Helon* ↓ *Hep* bro1 hippoc-k szs2 hura ↓ hydr k* hyper bro1 ind indg ↓ *Iod* ↓ irid-met ↓ kali-bi k* *Kali-c* ↓ kali-i ↓ kali-m ↓ kali-p fd1.de• kali-sil ↓ kola stb3• kreos lac-ac bro1* *Lac-c* k* lac-h ↓ lach bro1 *Lap-a* bro1 laur ↓ lavand-a ctl1• led ↓ lepi bro1 lil-t luna kg1• lyc med k* melal-alt gya4 **Merc** k* merl bro1 *Mez* ↓ mim-p rsj8• mosch murx k* naja bg2 nat-c ↓ nat-m bro1 nat-pyru ↓ nit-ac nux-m gk nux-v ↓ ol-an ↓ olnd ↓ onos bro1 orig c1 oxal-a ↓ pall bro1 pant-ac ↓ *Ph-ac* *Phel* k* *Phos* k* *Phyt* k* plat ↓ plb k* *Plb-i* bro1 plut-n ↓ polyg-h bro1 pot-e ↓ prun bro1 psor k* puls bro1 *Ran-s* ↓ rheum k* rhod ↓ *Rhus-t* ruta fd4.de sabal ↓ sabin ↓ sal-fr ↓ sang hr1* *Sec* ↓ sel ↓ *Sep* ↓ **Sil** k* spira ↓ spong ↓ stann stram stry ↓ *Sulph* sumb k* symph ↓ syph ↓ tab ↓ tarent-c ↓ thioc-ac ↓ thuj ↓ tritic-vg fd5.de tub mrr1 urol-h ↓ vanil fd5.de verat k* zinc k* zinc-p ↓ [*Merc-d* stj2]
  - **alternating** sides: lac-c mrr1
  - **right**: act-sp ↓ agath-a nl2• am-c h2 camph ↓ cench ↓ choc ↓ colch ↓ cot br1 cystein-l ↓ galeoc-c-h gms1• *Germ-met* ↓ gink-b sbd1• graph ↓ grat ↓ hep h1* *Ign* irid-met srj5• lavand-a ↓ melal-alt gya4 merc-c ↓ pall ↓ petr-ra ↓ **Phel** k* phos h2 podo fd3.de• psil ↓ rad-br ↓ sang k* sel rsj9• sep ↓ stry ↓ symph ↓ tritic-vg fd5.de zinc
    - **aching**: cot br1 zinc k*
    - **boring** pain: psil ft1
    - **cramping**: merc-c bg2
    - **cutting** pain: lavand-a ctl1•
    - **drawing** pain | **outward**: *Germ-met* srj5•
    - **menses**; during: irid-met srj5•
    - **pressing** pain: petr-ra shn4• phos h2 zinc
    - **sore**: rad-br c11
    - **stinging**: melal-alt gya4

- **right**: ...
  - **stitching** pain: act-sp bg1 agath-a nl2• cench k2 choc srj3• cystein-l rly4• galeoc-c-h gms1• graph sne grat k* lavand-a ctl1• pall br1 **Phel** podo fd3.de• sang k* sep h2 stry symph fd3.de•
    - **followed** by | **left**: choc srj3•
  - **tearing** pain: camph h1 colch sang a1
  - **And** under left nipple: cot ↓
    - **aching**: cot br1
- **left**: agath-a nl2• aln vva1• ambr ↓ androc srj1• arist-cl sp1 borx ↓ brom dgt1 chinin-ar com ↓ cot br1 croc br1 cypra-eg sde6.de• dulc fd4.de falco-pe nl2• gaba sa3• gels ↓ heroin ↓ irid-met ↓ kali-n ↓ lac-del hrn2• *Lach* *Lil-t* mosch myos-a rly4• nat-pyru ↓ ph-ac *Phel* ↓ **Phyt** mrr1 podo fd3.de• ptel c1 ruta fd4.de sacch-a gmj3 sang ↓ sel ↓ sil stry ↓ sumb ↓ symph ↓ vanil fd5.de [*Buteo-j* sej6]
  - **aching**: ambr h1 lil-t k* mosch k* nat-pyru rly4•
  - **burning**: chinin-ar symph fd3.de• [heroin sdj2]
  - **cough** agg.; during: *Con* mosch ptk1
  - **cramping**: lil-t bg2
  - **cutting** pain: agath-a nl2• com *Lach* *Lil-t* k* sel rsj9•
  - **eating**; after: rumx ptk1 stront-c ptk1
  - **jerking** pain | **drawn** backward by a string; as if: croc br1
  - **jumping**: croc ptk1
  - **menses**:
    - **before** | **agg.**: sacch-a gmj3
    - **between**: ust ptk1
    - **during**:
      - **agg.**: aln vva1• graph ptk1
        - **painful** menses: caust ptk1
  - **neuralgic**: sumb ptk1
  - **nurses** at the right side; when the child: *Borx* h2*
    - **drawing** pain: *Borx*
    - **stitching** pain: borx
  - **pressing** pain: ph-ac symph fd3.de•
  - **sore**: falco-pe nl2•
  - **stitching** pain: agath-a nl2• borx dulc fd4.de irid-met srj5• kali-n *Lach* lil-t *Phel* sne podo fd3.de• ruta fd4.de sang hr1 symph fd3.de• vanil fd5.de
    - **alternating** with | **Teeth**; pain in (See TEETH - Pain - alternating with - mamma)
    - **outward**: gels a1
  - **tearing** pain: chinin-ar *Phel* stry
  - **extending** to:
    - **Arm**, left: brom dgt1
    - **Body**; whole: **Phyt** mrr1
    - **Scapula**: lil-t ↓
      - **cutting** pain: lil-t k*
    - **Scapulae**: com ptk1
      - **Through**: cot br1
- **morning**: *Lil-t* plb ↓ ruta fd4.de sang ↓ zinc ↓
  - **stitching** pain: plb k* sang k* zinc k*
- **afternoon**: sang
- **evening**: agath-a nl2• *Con* *Lac-c*
- **night**: agath-a nl2• con sne graph sne petr-ra ↓
  - **pressing** pain: petr-ra shn4•
  - **stitching** pain: agath-a nl2• *Con* graph k*
  - **waking**; on: graph ↓
    - **stitching** pain: graph
- **abortion**; during: cimic ↓
  - **pricking**: cimic bro1
- **aching**: apis k* borx bg2 *Bov* bg2* con k* eupi k* lac-c bg1 lap-a br1 lil-t k* mosch k* nat-pyru rly4• stram k* zinc k*
- **ascending** and descending stairs: **Bell** ↓ calc ↓ carb-an ↓ *Con* ↓ **Lac-c** ↓ lyc ↓ *Nit-ac* ↓ phos ↓
  - **sore**: **Bell** calc carb-an *Con* **Lac-c** k* lyc *Nit-ac* phos
- **boring** pain: bufo ind indg k* plb spira a1
- **burning**: aesc k* ambr k* anan *Apis* k* *Ars* k* bell bry k* *Bufo* calc *Calc-p* k* carb-an chinin-ar *Cimic* k* com con k* *Hep* b4a.de indg iod lach lap-a br1 laur k* led *Lyc* k* *Mez* k* ol-an k* *Phos* k* *Phyt* sang sel sulph ptk1 symph fd3.de• tarent-c
  - **accompanied** by | **cancer** of mammae (See Cancer - mammae - accompanied - pain - burning)
- **children**; in: cham ↓
  - **infants**: cham ↓
    - **sore**: cham br1*
  - **sore**: cham vn
- **chill**; after: ign phyt k2
  - **sore**: phyt k2
- **cold**:
  - **bathing**:
    - **after**: sabal c1
    - **agg.**: sabal ↓
      - **sore**: sabal ptk1
- **cold** agg.; becoming: sep ↓
  - **stitching** pain: sep h2
- **contracting**: borx b4a.de* thuj b4a.de
- **cough** agg.; during: aids nl2• borx ↓ con sep ↓
  - **stitching** pain: borx con sep b4a.de
- **cramping**: bufo bg2 *Lil-t* plat ptk1 pot-e rly4•
- **cutting** pain: aeth c1* agath-a nl2• am-c aster bell borx bg2 bufo k* calc calc-p k* cham chinin-s *Colch* hura *Iod* lach lepi br1 lil-t k* olnd phyt plut-n srj7• sabin
  - **accompanied** by | **swelling**: aeth ptk1
- **delivery**; after: **Castor-eq** vh
- **descending**, on: bell calc carb-an *Hep* *Lac-c* lyc nit-ac phos
- **digging** pain: bufo bg2
- **drawing** pain: carb-v cham b7.de* kreos k* *Lil-t* plb stann sumb symph fd3.de• vanil fd5.de
  - **downward**: bufo bg2
  - **inward**: aster c1
- **empty**; when: *Borx*
  - **aching**: *Borx*
- **excitement** agg.: phyt k2
- **flow** of milk, on: *Kali-c* ↓
  - **stitching** pain: *Kali-c* k*
- **followed** by | **soreness**: conv a2 sang a1
- **gnawing** pain: bufo bg2*
- **griping** pain: borx b4a.de*
- **increasing** and decreasing gradually: plat ↓
  - **cramping**: plat
- **inspiration** agg.: con ↓ ger-i ↓ pall ↓
  - **stitching** pain: con ger-i rly4• pall
- **jar** agg.: bell k2* lac-c bro1*
- **lactation**; during: kali-c ↓
  - **tearing** pain: kali-c
- **leukorrhea**; during: *Bar-c* ↓
  - **tearing** pain: *Bar-c* b4a.de
- **lying**:
  - **agg.**: bell
  - **side**; on:
    - **left**:
      - **agg.**: lil-t ↓
        - **cutting** pain: lil-t k*
- **menopause**; during: sang hr1
  - **sore**: sang ptk1
- **menses**:
  - **after**:
    - **agg.**: *Lach* ↓
      - **sixteen** days: plut-n srj7•
      - **stitching** pain: *Lach*

- **menses**: ...
  - **amel.**: allox↓
    - **stitching** pain: allox sp1
  - **before**:
    - **agg.**●: aln↓ amp↓ *Bar-c* b4a.de bell b4a.de* **CALC** k ●* calc-i oss• calc-s oss• calc-sil oss• carb-v b4a.de carc oss*• cartl-s↓ chin sma chir-fl gya2 choc srj3• **CON** k ●* cycl↓ dream-p↓ *Foll* oss• helon↓ irid-met↓ kali-c **KALI-CHL** sne kali-m bg3* kali-s k2 kola sib3• lac-ac stj*• *Lac-c* k* lac-e hrn2• lutin bwa3 musca-d szs1 **Nat-m** ●* nat-sil fd3.de• nux-v ol-an↓ ozone sde2• *Phos* b4a.de phyt↓ pin-con oss2• *Puls*↓ sacch sst1• sacch-a gmj3 sang spong tub bg1* zinc b4a.de* [am-m stj1 ant-m stj2 aur-m stj2 bar-m stj1 beryl-m stj2 cadm-m stj2 calc-m stj1 *Chlor* stj2 chr-m stj2 cob-m stj2 cupr-m stj2 lith-m stj2 mag-lac stj2 mang-m stj2 merc-d stj2 mur-ac stj2 plb-m stj2 stront-m stj2 zinc-m stj2]
      - **sore**: aln vva1• amp rly4• *Calc* carc mrr1 cartl-s rly4• **Con** k* cycl bg1 dream-p sdj1• helon bg1 irid-met srj5• kali-chl sne kali-m bg1 kali-s *Lac-c* k* ol-an st phyt mrr1 *Puls* sang spong *Tub* k*
        - **accompanied** by | **swelling**: amp rly4• bry bro1 **Calc** bro1* canth bro1 carc mrr1 *Con* bro1* graph bro1 *Helon* bro1 kali-c bro1 lac-c bro1* mag-c bro1 merc bro1 *Murx* bro1 *Phyt* bro1 pot-e rly4• *Puls* bro1 sang bro1 tub mrr1
      - **tearing** pain: puls b7a.de
  - **between**: med↓
    - **sore**: med lp
  - **during**:
    - **agg.**: arge-pl↓ arum-t↓ berb↓ bry c1 cadm-met gm1 calc k* canth↓ *Con* k* dulc↓ graph↓ grat↓ *Helon*↓ hip-ac↓ indg↓ kali-c↓ kali-m bg3 lac-ac stj5• *Lac-c*↓ lutin bwa3 mag-c↓ *Merc* *Murx*↓ *Phel* *Phos* *Phyt* *Puls*↓ pyrid↓ sang k* thuj↓ *Tub* c1 *Tub-k* c1 *Zinc*↓
      - **burning**: indg
      - **painful** menses: canth↓ caust↓ sars↓
        - **sore**: canth ptk1 sars ptk1
        - **stitching** pain: caust ptk1
      - **sore**: arge-pl rwt5• arum-t k1 bry bro1 calc k* canth bro1 *Con* k* dulc graph bro1 *Helon* k* hip-ac sp1 kali-c bro1 *Lac-c* k* mag-c bro1 merc bro1 *Murx* bro1 *Phyt* k* *Puls* bro1 pyrid rly4• sang bro1 thuj *Zinc*
      - **stitching** pain: berb con b4a.de* grat
      - **stooping** agg.: grat↓
        - **stitching** pain: grat pd
      - **tearing** pain: calc
    - **beginning** of menses:
      - **agg.**: tub↓
        - **sore**: tub ptk1
  - **suppressed** menses; from: zinc
- **milk**; with: acet-ac br1 tritic-vg fd5.de
- **motion**:
  - **agg.**: mag-s sp1
  - **amel.**: ars↓
    - **burning**: ars ptk1
  - **arm**; of | **agg.**: hep h2*
- **nursing** the child:
  - **after**: borx a1* sabal c1
    - **stitching** pain: sabal c1
  - **between** the different times when the child is nursing: phel bro1
  - **when**: borx c1 **Crot-t** k ● lac-c c1* phyt c2* *Puls* **Sil** k* tritic-vg fd5.de
    - **agg.**: *Calc*↓ cham↓ **Sil**↓
      - **cramping**: cham ptk1
      - **cutting** pain: **Sil**
      - **stitching** pain: *Calc* k* **Sil**
      - **extending** to:
        - **Back**: colch↓
          - **cutting** pain: colch
    - **amel.**: phel↓
      - **aching**: phel ptk1*
    - **wandering** pains: *Puls*
- **periodical**: alum-sil gm1
- **pregnancy** agg.; during: *Bell* bro1 *Bry* bro1 *Calc-p*↓ *Con* c2 nux-m gk puls↓ **Sep** k ●
  - **burning**: *Calc-p*
  - **neuralgic**: *Con* bro1 puls bro1
  - **sore**: *Calc-p* k*
- **pressing** pain: ambr *Bell* k* carb-v carbn-s euph ph-ac k* puls b7.de* sabin b7.de* sang hr1 sulph symph fd3.de• tritic-vg fd5.de zinc
- **pressure**:
  - **agg.**: gaba sa3• plb plut-n srj7• sal-fr sle1• [tax jsj7]
  - **amel.**: borx c1 *Con*↓
    - **stitching** pain: *Con*
  - **hand**; of | **amel.**: borx c1 phyt c1
- **pulsating** synchronous with heartbeat: choc↓
  - **drawing** pain: choc srj3•
- **raising** arm agg.: bry sol-t-ae vml3•
- **rising** agg.: grat↓
  - **stitching** pain: grat k2
- **rubbing**:
  - **agg.**: con↓
    - **burning**: con h2
  - **amel.**:
    - **hard** rubbing: rad-br↓
      - **sore**: rad-br c11*
- **smarting**: con b4.de* thuj b4a.de
- **sneezing** agg.: hydr↓
  - **sore**: hydr ptk1
- **sore**: ambr ant-c apis *Arn* k* arum-t aur bg2 *Bell* k* *Bry* k* calad *Calc* k* calc-i k2 *Calc-p* k* carb-an cartl-s rly4• **Cham** k* chir-fl gya2 cic cimic bg2 clem bg2 coli rly4• *Con* k* dream-p sdj1• dulc falco-pe nl2• ferr a1 granit-m es1• graph k* grat bg2 hell *Helon* k* hep b4a.de *Iod* irid-met srj5• kali-m ptk1 **Lac-c** k* laur b7.de* lavand-a ctl1• lyc k* med k* *Merc* k* mosch *Murx* nat-m k* nit-ac onos k* oxal-a rly4• pant-ac rly4• phos k* *Phyt* k* pot-e rly4• psor jl2 *Puls* k* *Ran-s* rhod sabal bg3* sal-fr sle1• sang k* sep k* **Sil** k* symph syph k* tab k* thioc-ac rly4• *Zinc* zinc-p k2
  - **accompanied** by:
    - **leukorrhea**: dulc ptk1
    - **Axillary** glands; enlarged: lac-ac ptk1
- **stairs**; when ascending or descending: bell bg2 calc bg2 carb-an bg2 lac-c bg2 lyc bg2 nit-ac bg2 phos bg2
- **stepping** | **every** step; at●: *Con*
- **stinging**: *Apis* bg2 gels bg2 lap-a br1
- **stitching** pain: aeth k* agath-a nl2• allox tpw4 aloe bg2 alum k* am-c ambr k* anan **Apis** k* arg-n k* bar-c k* bar-i k2 bell k* berb k* *Borx* k* bov brom *Bry* k* *Calc* k* calc-i k2 calc-sil k2 **Carb-an** k* cimic k* clem a1 *Colch* b7a.de **Con** k* cycl k* dulc fd4.de ferr a1 galeoc-c-h gms1• galla-q-r nl2• graph k* grat k* hep b4a.de* hura c1 indg k* iod k* kali-bi k* *Kali-c* k* kali-i *Kali-p* kali-sil k2 kreos k* *Lach* lap-a laur k* *Lyc* melal-alt gya4 mez k* murx k* nat-c h2 *Nat-m* k* *Nit-ac* ptk1 nux-v b7.de* ol-an k* olnd *Phel* k* *Phos* k* *Phyt* k* plat plb k* polyg-h ptk1 psor k* *Puls* k* ran-s b7.de* rheum k* ruta fd4.de sabin sang k* *Sec* *Sep* k* **Sil** k* spong stry symph fd3.de• thuj b4a.de vanil fd5.de verat b7.de* zinc k*
  - **accompanied** by:
    - **cancer** of mammae (See Cancer - mammae - accompanied - pain - stitching)
    - **itching** of skin: aster mtf11
  - **downward**; from left nipple: *Asc-t*
  - **milk** would appear; as if: lac-h htj1• urol-h rwt•
  - **outward**: mez h2 ol-an
- **stooping** agg.: grat↓
  - **sore**: grat ptk1
- **tearing** pain: *Am-c* k* am-m bar-c k* *Bell* b4a.de *Bry* k* bufo *Carb-an* b4a.de carb-v k* cham b7.de* chinin-ar con h2 crot-t kali-c *Lil-t* bg2 phyt sne thuj b4a.de
- **touch** agg.: all-s vh1 am-c h2 aur-s c1 bell k2 con bg1 dream-p sdj1• gink-b sbd1• hep h2 nat-sil fd3.de• sal-fr sle1• sep bg1
- **turning** upper body quickly: arg-n hr1

- **ulcerative** pain: arg-n a1 **Calc** k* clem bg2 merc b4.de*
- **urination** agg.: clem↓
  - **sore**: clem ptk1
- **wandering** pains: *Puls*
- **yawning** agg.: mag-c↓
  - **sore**: mag-c ptk1
- ▽ **extending** to:
  - **Abdomen**: phel vml3•
  - **Back**: aster↓ colch↓ *Phel* plb stry↓
    - **boring** pain: plb
    - **pressure** agg.: plb↓
      - **boring** pain: plb
    - **stitching** pain: aster vh1* **Phel** k* stry
    - **tearing** pain: colch
  - **Ilium**: camph↓
    - **tearing** pain: camph h1
  - **Neck**: mur-ac bg1
  - **Outward**: cycl bg1 gels bg1 mez bg1 *Ol-an* bg1
  - **Scapula**: cot br1
  - **Shoulder**: sang tl1
    - **right**: sang a1
  - **Stomach**: sang a1
  - **Umbilicus**: agar bg1
- ○ **Above**: cyclosp sa3•
- **Between**: mez↓ ph-ac↓ sang↓
  - **burning**: mez h2 sang hr1
  - **stitching** pain: ph-ac h2
- **Heavy** mammae:
  - **supporting** mammae | **amel**.: *Bry* bro1 *Lac-c* bro1 phyt bro1
- **Lactiferous** tubes; along the: phel mtf11
  - **when** child nurses: *Phel*
- **Milk** breasts, in | **tearing** pain (See lactation - tearing)
- **Nipples**: *Agar*↓ *Alum*↓ am-c↓ ap-g↓ arg-n↓ **Arn**↓ *Ars*↓ arund↓ *Asaf*↓ asc-t↓ aur-s↓ **Bapt**↓ benz-ac↓ *Berb*↓ bism↓ *Borx*↓ bry↓ calc↓ *Calc-p* *Calen*↓ *Camph*↓ cann-i↓ cann-s↓ *Castm*↓ castor-eq↓ **Caust**↓ *Cham*↓ chel↓ chlam-tr↓ cic↓ cist↓ coc-c↓ cocc↓ colch↓ *Con*↓ crot-t k* cur dulc↓ *Eup-a*↓ falco-pe nl2• ferr-i **Fl-ac**↓ galeoc-c-h gms1• *Graph* k* *Ham*↓ helo↓ *Helon* hep↓ hydr↓ ign↓ kali-bi bg2 kali-s↓ kola stb3• *Lac-c* k* lach laps↓ *Lyc*↓ m-aust↓ mag-m↓ mang↓ med↓ melal-alt↓ *Merc*↓ *Merc-c* mez↓ mill↓ *Mur-ac*↓ musca-d szs1 nat-m↓ nat-sil↓ nit-ac k2 nux-v b7.de* oci↓ onos↓ orig↓ par↓ paraf↓ petr k2 *Phel* c2* phos↓ phyt c2 pieri-b↓ plan↓ plb↓ psor↓ *Puls*↓ pyrog↓ ran-b↓ ran-s↓ *Rat*↓ rauw↓ rheum h* rhus-t↓ ruta fd4.de sabin↓ sal-fr sle1• sang k* seneg↓ *Sep*↓ sil tl1 sulo-ac↓ sulph k* symph↓ tab↓ ter↓ thuj verat↓ verb↓ zinc
  - **right**: asc-t a1 *Borx*↓ chel↓ con↓ gink-b↓ grat↓ hydrog↓ mag-m↓ mang↓ mur-ac↓ neon srj5• phyt bg2 sal-fr sle1• sang↓ sumb↓ tub-d jl2 x-ray↓ zinc↓
    - **burning**: gink-b sbd1•
    - **drawing** pain: sumb
    - **sticking** pain: x-ray sp1
    - **stitching** pain: *Borx* chel con grat hydrog srj2• mag-m k* mang a1 mur-ac a1 sang zinc
    - **extending** to:
      - **left**: card-m↓
        - **stitching** pain: card-m
      - **Arm**; inner side of right: helo↓
        - **stitching** pain: helo c1
  - **left**: *Asc-t*↓ bapt↓ berb↓ crot-t↓ euon↓ falco-pe nl2• form↓ ran-b↓ rhus-t↓ sabin↓ senec↓ *Sil*↓ symph↓ tell↓ zinc↓
    - **burning**: senec ptk1 symph fd3.de•
    - **drawing** pain: crot-t euon tell a1* (non:til slp) zinc
    - **sore**: falco-pe nl2•
    - **stiffness** of left side of neck; with: asc-t↓
      - **cutting** pain | **downward**: asc-t c1
    - **stitching** pain: *Asc-t* bapt berb form ran-b rhus-t sabin k* *Sil*
      - **downward**: asc-t k13

- **Nipples – left**: ...
    - **extending** to:
      - **Scapula**: rhus-t↓
        - **stitching** pain: rhus-t
      - **Scapula**, left: spig↓
        - **cutting** pain: spig h1
      - **Upper** arm, left: spig↓
        - **cutting** pain: spig h1
  - **morning**: ran-b↓ rhus-t sulph↓
    - **drawing** pain: *Rhus-t*
    - **sore**: sulph
    - **stitching** pain: ran-b k* rhus-t k*
  - **evening**: con ferr-i
  - **biting** pain: caust b4a.de
  - **bitten** off; as if: tab bg2
  - **breathing** agg.: sulph
  - **burning**: *Agar* k* *Ars* bro1 arund br1* benz-ac k* castm bro1 cic k* con *Crot-t* bro1 *Graph* k* *Lyc* k* nat-sil fd3.de• onos bro1 orig bro1 petr bro1 phos psor *Puls* b7a.de* sang sep *Sil* k* **Sulph** k* symph fd3.de•
  - **cutting** pain: rauw tpw8*
  - **drawing** pain: crot-t k* kali-s fd4.de *Nux-v* b7a.de phyt bro1 puls bro1 sil bro1 zinc bg2
    - **string**; as if with a: crot-t mrr1 par mrr1 plb mrr1
  - **electric** shocks; like: bry b7.de*
  - **flatulence**; as from: rheum h
  - **inspiration** agg.: con↓ ign↓ par↓ verb↓
    - **stitching** pain: con k* ign k* par k* verb
  - **men**; in: musca-d szs1
  - **menses**:
    - **after**:
      - **agg.**: berb thuj↓
        - **cutting** pain: thuj
        - **pressing** pain: berb
        - **stitching** pain: thuj
    - **before** | **agg.**: [*Mag-lac* stj2]
    - **during**:
      - **agg.**: *Helon*↓
        - **sore**: *Helon* k*
  - **neuralgic**: plan ptk1
  - **nursing** the child:
    - **after**: sang↓ sulph↓
      - **burning**: sang sulph
    - **when**:
      - **agg.**: **Crot-t** k* *Merc-c* *Nux-v* phel mrr1* *Phyt*
        - **drawing** pain | **string**; as if with a: **Crot-t** k*
  - **nursing** women; in: borx mrr1
  - **pinching** pain: ran-s b7.de*
  - **pressing** pain: bism b7.de* mez b4.de* par b7.de*
  - **pulsating** pain: zinc h2
  - **radiating** over whole body: *Phyt* k*
  - **rising** agg.: ran-b tl1
  - **rubbing**:
    - **amel.**: melal-alt↓
      - **stitching** pain: melal-alt gya4
  - **sitting** agg.: nat-s↓
    - **stitching** pain: nat-s k*
  - **sore**: *Alum* ap-g bro1* arg-n **Arn** k* **Bapt** k* borx c2* calc b4.de* *Calc-p* *Calen* c2* *Castm* bro1 **Caust** k* *Cham* k* chlam-tr bcx2• cist bro1 colch *Con* bro1 **Crot-t** k* dulc *Eup-a* br1* falco-pe nl2• **Fl-ac** k* *Graph* k* *Ham* k* helo bg2 helon k* hep c2* hydr c2* kali-bi bg2 kola stb3• lac-c bg2* **Lach** k* laps c1* *Lyc* k* med k* *Merc* mill k* *Nit-ac* nux-v k* oci bro1 orig bro1 paraf bro1 *Phel* k* phos k* *Phyt* k* pieri-b mlk9.de pyrog ptk1 *Rat* bro1 rheum bg2 rhus-t sang k* seneg *Sep* *Sil* k* sulo-ac c2 *Sulph* k* zinc k*
    - **accompanied** by | **Bladder**; inflammation of: neon srj5•
  - **stinging**: bism castor-eq ign lyc mang mur-ac sabin sulph

- **Nipples**: ...
  - **stitching** pain: agar k* am-c *Asaf* asc-t c1 aur-s k2 bapt *Berb* bism k* *Borx* bry bg2 calc h2 *Camph* k* cann-i k* cann-s b7.de* castor-eq cham k* chel k* coc-c k* cocc b7.de* *Con* k* falco-pe nl2• galeoc-c-h gms1• ign k* *Kali-bi* k* lach k* *Lyc* k* m-aust b7.de mag-m mang k* melal-alt gya4 merc b4a.de *Mur-ac* k* nat-m ptk1 par b7.de* ran-b k* *Rheum* k* sabin k* sang *Sil* *Sulph* k* ter k* verat a1 verb zinc
    - **itching**: mang h2
    - **outward**: *Asaf*
  - **tearing** pain: bism b7.de* *Nux-v* b7a.de
  - **touch** of clothes agg.: calc ↓ cartl-s ↓ **Castor-eq** ↓ *Cham* ↓ *Con* ↓ *Crot-h* ↓ crot-t mrr1 helon ↓ irid-met ↓ oci ↓ petr ↓ phyt ↓ zinc ↓
    - **sore**: calc h2 cartl-s rly4• **Castor-eq** k* *Cham* bro1 *Con* k* *Crot-h* ptk1 **Crot-t** k* helon bro1* irid-met srj5• oci ptk1 petr k2 phyt bro1 zinc h2
  - **walking** agg.: con ↓
    - **stitching** pain: con k*
  - **weaning**: dulc ↓
    - **sore**: dulc
  - **extending** to:
    - **Back**: *Crot-t* bro1*
      - **drawing** pain: crot-t mrr1
    - **Body**; from nipple all over:
      - **nursing**; during: phyt ↓ puls ↓ sil ↓
        - **drawing** pain: phyt bro1 puls bro1 sil bro1
    - **Neck**: mur-ac ↓
      - **drawing** pain: mur-ac h2
    - **Outward**: berb ptk1 *Bry* ptk1 gels ptk1 kali-bi ptk1 lappa ptk1 lyc ptk1 mez ptk1 *Ol-an* ptk1 spig ptk1 stann ptk1
    - **Scapula**: com *Crot-t* *Rhus-t* x-ray ↓
      - **drawing** pain: rhus-t
      - **sticking** pain: x-ray sp1
  - **Above** | **left**: ran-b tl1
  - **Behind** left: berb ↓
    - **pressing** pain: berb
  - **Below**: agar ↓ mur-ac ↓
    - **right**: mur-ac ↓
      - **drawing** pain: mur-ac h2
    - **pregnancy** agg.; during: spig ↓
      - **stitching** pain: spig hr1
    - **stitching** pain: agar h2 mur-ac h2
  - **Beside** left nipple, towards the sternum: bism ↓
    - **pressing** pain: bism h1
  - **Lower** half:
    - **left**: cob-n ↓
      - **sticking** pain: cob-n sp1
  - **Region** of: bism ↓ borx ↓ caust ↓ chin ↓ spig ↓ verat ↓
    - **right**: pall ↓
      - **stitching** pain: pall c1*
    - **cough** agg.; during: borx ↓
      - **stitching** pain: borx hr1
    - **itching**; ending in: verat ↓
      - **stitching** pain: verat h1*
    - **sitting** erect:
      - **amel.**: spig ↓
        - **stitching** pain: spig h1
    - **stitching** pain: bism h1 borx caust h2 chin h1 spig h1 verat h1
    - **tearing** pain: bism h1
    - **walking**:
      - **16 h.**: cycl ↓
        - **stitching** pain: cycl a1
    - **extending** to:
      - **Back**: *Kali-i* ↓
        - **stitching** pain: *Kali-i*
      - **Umbilicus**: caust ↓
        - **stitching** pain: caust h2
  - **Under**: *Cimic* bg2
    - **right**: bell ↓ calc ↓ led ↓ mur-ac ↓ ozone ↓ stann ↓
      - **pressing** pain: bell h1 calc h2 led h1 mur-ac h2 stann h2
- **Nipples – Under – right**: ...
      - **sore**: ozone sde2•
    - **left**: cot c1 verb ↓
      - **aching**: cot br1
      - **pressing** pain: verb h
- **Opposite**; when child nurses pain in: *Borx* k*
- **Region** of: agath-a ↓ agn ↓ berb chel grat ↓ lac-ac nat-s ran-s rhus-t sil ↓ [heroin sdj2]
  - **left**: grat ↓ sil ↓
    - **stitching** pain: grat k* sil k*
  - **evening**: ran-s
  - **aching**: berb k* rhus-t k*
  - **hawking** up mucus agg.: nat-p
  - **pressing** pain: agn a1 chel nat-s
  - **sitting** bent forward agg.: rhus-t
    - **aching**: rhus-t
  - **stitching** pain: agath-a nl2• grat k* sil k*
  - **extending** to:
    - **Axilla** | **23** h: lac-ac kr1
  - **Under**: carb-v ↓ lach ↓ zinc ↓
    - **pressing** pain: carb-v h2 lach zinc
- **Skin**; below the: calc ↓ *Phos* ↓
  - **ulcerative** pain: calc b4a.de *Phos* b4a.de
- **Under**: am-c ↓ am-m ↓ brom ↓ bros-gau ↓ canth ↓ carb-v caust ↓ c e a n bg3 *Cimic* bg3* eup-per graph h2 heroin ↓ hyper ↓ kali-n ↓ kalm ↓ lach lil-t bg3 mag-c ↓ murx ↓ nat-c ↓ ol-an ↓ *Phel* ↓ phos ↓ plb ↓ *Puls* k* *Ran-b* k* raph c2* rob ↓ ruta fd4.de sang ↓ spong fd4.de succ-ac rly4• s u m b bg3* ust bro1 visc c1 zinc k*
  - **right**: aeth ↓ aloe ↓ bruc ↓ carb-an ↓ castm ↓ *Chel* ↓ cot br1 gamb ↓ hura *Kali-bi* ↓ kali-p ↓ lachn ↓ mag-c ↓ mag-m ↓ merc bg3 nicc ↓ *Phel* ↓ phos plb ↓ plut-n ↓ ptel ↓ spong fd4.de sulph ↓
    - **aching**: plut-n srj7•
    - **burning**: aeth k* phos k*
    - **cough** agg.; during: sulph ↓
      - **stitching** pain: sulph h2
    - **cutting** pain: *Chel* kali-p lachn c1
    - **menses**; during: am-m ↓
      - **stitching** pain: am-m
    - **stitching** pain: aloe bruc carb-an h2 castm chel k* gamb k* *Kali-bi* lachn c1 mag-m k* nicc k* *Phel* plb k* ptel c1 spong fd4.de sulph
      - **downward**: mag-c
    - **extending** to:
      - **Back**: *Kali-bi* ↓
        - **stitching** pain: *Kali-bi*
      - **Scapula**: plb ↓
        - **stitching** pain: plb
      - **Shoulder**: mag-c ↓
        - **stitching** pain: mag-c h2
  - **left**: aeth ↓ am-c ↓ ant-c ↓ arund ↓ *Aster* berb ↓ bros-gau mrc1 bry ↓ carb-v ↓ caul c1 *Caust* ↓ cimic com bg3 con irid-met ↓ *Kali-c* ↓ kali-n ↓ laur ↓ lil-t bg3 mag-c ↓ melal-alt gya4 mez ↓ mur-ac ↓ nat-c ↓ nicc ↓ ozone ↓ phel ↓ podo fd3.de• puls rumx ↓ ruta ↓ (non:samb bg3) stann ↓ sumb k* ust visc ↓ zinc ↓
    - **burning**: aeth a1 laur k* mur-ac h2* rumx k*
    - **cutting** pain: bry
    - **drawing** pain: stann h2
    - **menses**; during: caust ↓
      - **stitching** pain: caust h2
    - **rubbing**:
      - **amel.**: caust ↓
        - **stitching** pain: caust h2
    - **stitching** pain: aeth a1 am-c k* ant-c c1 arund k* berb k* bry carb-v *Caust* irid-met srj5• *Kali-c* kali-n h2 laur k* mag-c k* mez k* mur-ac nat-c h2 nicc ozone sde2• phel ruta fd4.de visc c1 zinc
      - **upward**: kali-c stann
    - **extending** to:
      - **Sternum**: mag-c ↓
        - **stitching** pain: mag-c h2

• **Under**: ...
⁝ **morning**: plb ↓
: **bed** agg.; in: plb ↓
. **stitching** pain: plb
: **rising**; after:
. **amel.**: plb ↓
stitching pain: plb
: **stitching** pain: plb k*
⁝ **afternoon**: kali-c ↓
: **13** h:
. **yawning** agg.: mag-c ↓
stitching pain: mag-c
: **14** h:
. **expiring**; on: sil ↓
stitching pain: sil
: **lifting**; after: kali-c ↓
. **stitching** pain: kali-c k*
: **sitting** agg.: mag-c ↓
. **stitching** pain: mag-c k*
: **stitching** pain: kali-c
: **walking**:
. **amel.**: carb-an ↓
stitching pain: carb-an
⁝ **night**: nit-ac ↓
: **stitching** pain: nit-ac h2*
⁝ **aching**: carb-v k* eup-per k*
⁝ **burning**: bros-gau mrc1 [heroin sdj2]
⁝ **cough** agg.; during: mosch sulph ↓
: **stitching** pain: sulph k*
⁝ **cutting** pain: rob
⁝ **inspiration** agg.: bry ↓ mag-c ↓
: **stitching** pain: bry mag-c
⁝ **lying** on left side agg.: phos h2
⁝ **menopause**; during (= climacteric): *Cimic* k*
⁝ **menses**; during: am-m ↓ caust ↓
: **stitching** pain: am-m caust k*
⁝ **pregnancy** agg.; during: *Cimic*
⁝ **rising** from sitting agg.: phos ↓
: **stitching** pain: phos k*
⁝ **sitting**:
: **agg.**: carb-an ↓ mag-c ↓
. **burning**: mag-c k*
. **stitching** pain: carb-an k*
: **bent** forward:
. **agg.**: am-m ↓
stitching pain: am-m k*
⁝ **sore**: am-c am-m caust sang ptk1
⁝ **stitching** pain: am-m brom canth k* hyper k* kali-n k* kalm k* lach k* mag-c k* murx nat-c k* ol-an k* *Phel* phos k* plb k* ruta fd4.de spong fd4.de zinc k*
⁝ **walking** agg.: kali-n ↓
: **stitching** pain: kali-n k*
⁝ **yawning** agg.: mag-c ↓
: **stitching** pain: mag-c k*
⁝ **extending** to:
: **Fingers**: aster
: **Scapulae**; left: com bg3
• **Upper** part:
⁝ **left**: visc ↓
: **stitching** pain: visc c1
- **Mammary** glands; male:
○ • **Nipples**:
⁝ **extending** to:
: **Scapula**: tell ↓
. **cutting** pain: tell k*
- **Mediastinum**: gaul mtf11

- **Middle** of chest: acon agar ↓ agath-a ↓ *Alum* am-c ↓ *Am-m* ↓ ant-c ↓ *Ars* ↓ asaf ↓ asar ↓ bell benz-ac ↓ bov ↓ *Bry* camph ↓ carb-ac ↓ carb-an ↓ carbn-s ↓ cassia-s ↓ castor-eq ↓ cham ↓ chin ↓ crot-c ↓ crot-h crot-t ↓ *Dros* ↓ gal-ac ↓ *Gamb Graph* grat ↓ gymno ↓ hyper ↓ ignis-alc es2• indg ↓ iod ↓ jug-c *Kali-c* ↓ *Kali-i* ↓ kali-n ↓ *Kreos* ↓ lact ↓ laur ↓ lith-c *Lyc* ↓ mag-c ↓ mag-s ↓ mand ↓ mez ↓ musca-d ↓ nat-m ↓ nat-pyru ↓ nux-v ↓ ol-an ↓ olnd ↓ ox-ac pall ↓ par ↓ ph-ac ↓ *Phos* plb ↓ positr ↓ puls ↓ ran-b ↓ raph ↓ rumx ↓ ruta fd4.de sabad ↓ samb ↓ sars seneg ↓ *Sep* ↓ *Spig* spong fd4.de squil ↓ sul-ac ↓ *Sulph* tell thuj ↓ tritic-vg fd5.de tub ↓ verat ↓ zinc ↓
• **afternoon**: *Am-m* crot-t ↓ mag-c ↓ mag-s ↓ spong fd4.de
⁝ **burning**: mag-s k*
⁝ **cutting** pain: mag-c k*
⁝ **pressing** pain: *Am-m* k*
⁝ **stitching** pain: crot-t k* mag-c h2 spong fd4.de
• **evening**: ran-b spong fd4.de
⁝ **pressing** pain: ran-b k*
• **aching**: crot-c crot-h gal-ac a1* lith-c sars k*
• **ascending** agg.: graph ↓
⁝ **stitching** pain: graph k*
• **bending** body forward agg.: pall ↓
⁝ **stitching** pain: pall k*
• **breakfast** agg.; after: verat ↓
⁝ **burning**: verat k*
• **burning**: agar k* *Ars* carbn-s cassia-s ccrh1• castor-eq *Dros* k* graph k* iod k* kali-n k* laur k* mag-s k* mez k* nat-pyru rly4• ol-an k* ph-ac k* sul-ac k* verat k*
• **cough**:
⁝ **after**: cina
⁝ **during**:
: **agg.**: cassia-s ↓ ph-ac ↓
. **burning**: cassia-s ccrh1•
. **pressing** pain: ph-ac h2
• **cutting** pain: mag-c h2*
• **dinner**; after: kali-n ↓
⁝ **stitching** pain: kali-n k*
• **drawing** pain | **downward**: kali-c h2
• **eating** agg.: alum spong fd4.de
• **expiration**:
⁝ **agg.**: ph-ac ↓
: **pressing** pain: ph-ac h2
⁝ **during**:
: **agg.**: cham ↓
. **stitching** pain: cham k*
• **inspiration**:
⁝ **after**: zinc ↓
: **stitching** pain: zinc h2
⁝ **agg.**: *Alum* ↓ graph ↓ *Kreos* ↓ sulph tub ↓ zinc ↓
: **burning**: graph k*
: **stitching** pain: *Alum* k* *Kreos* tub gk zinc k*
⁝ **amel.**: seneg ↓
: **stitching** pain: seneg k*
⁝ **deep** | **agg.**: thuj
• **menses**; during: kali-n ↓
⁝ **stitching** pain: kali-n
• **motion**:
⁝ **agg.**: equis-h nux-v ↓ seneg sulph tub ↓
: **stitching** pain: nux-v k* tub gk
⁝ **amel.**: seneg ↓
: **aching**: seneg k*
• **pressing** pain: agar k* agath-a nl2• *Alum* am-c h2 camph carb-an h2 crot-t k* *Gamb* k* gymno hyper k* iod h *Kali-c* k* lact k* laur k* lith-c ph-ac h2 *Phos* positr nl2• puls k* ran-b k* raph k* sabad k* sep *Spig* k* spong fd4.de tell k* thuj k* tritic-vg fd5.de
⁝ **load**; as from a: asaf carb-ac xyz61 samb
• **pressure**:
⁝ **agg.**: am-c ↓ ph-ac ↓

- **pressure – agg.**: ...
  - **aching**: am-c k*
  - **pressing** pain: ph-ac h2
  - **hand**; of | **amel.**: **Bry** kreos
- **radiating**: musca-d szs1
- **raising** arms agg.: sep
- **sitting** agg.: indg↓ pall↓ *Seneg* k*
  - **pressing** pain: seneg k*
  - **stitching** pain: indg pall k*
- **sore**: am-c h2 ignis-alc es2• *Sep*
- **stitching** pain: acon b7.de* agar k* alum k* *Am-m* k* ant-c b7.de* asar b7.de* benz-ac k* bov k* *Bry* b7.de* cham b7.de* chin b7.de* grat k* hyper k* indg iod k* *Kali-i* k* kali-n k* *Kreos* k* *Lyc* mag-c k* mand rsj7• nat-m k* nux-v k* olnd k* ox-ac pall k* par b7.de* phos k* plb b7.de* ran-b k2 rumx ruta fd4.de sars k* seneg k* *Sep* b4a.de spong fd4.de squil b7.de* tub gk zinc k*
- **stooping** agg.: ph-ac↓ zinc↓
  - **pressing** pain: ph-ac h2
  - **stitching** pain: zinc
- **stretching** the body: eupi↓
  - **stitching** pain: eupi k*
- **vexation**; after: ph-ac↓
  - **burning**: ph-ac k*
- **walking**:
  - **agg.**: kali-i↓ kali-n↓
    - **stitching** pain: kali-i k* kali-n
  - **air** agg.; in open: lyc
    - **pressing** pain: lyc k*
  - **amel.**: kali-i↓ tub↓
    - **stitching** pain: kali-i tub gk
- **writing** agg.: ran-b
- ▽ **extending** to:
  - **Abdomen**: berb↓ sulph↓
    - **cutting** pain: berb sulph
  - **Back**: *Crot-h*↓ ox-ac k2
    - **aching**: *Crot-h*
    - **motion** agg.: acon vh1
    - **stitching** pain: ox-ac
  - **Shoulder**: *Crot-h*
  - **Side**; right: cham↓
    - **stitching** pain: cham h1
  - **Throat**: **mez**↓
    - **burning**: mez k*

- **Muscles**: **calc**↓ cic↓ lat-m↓
  - **cough agg.**; during: hyos b7a.de
  - **cramping**: calc h2 cic h1 lat-m bnm6•
  - **rheumatic**: ran-b mtf11
  - ○ **Intercostal** region: lat-m↓
    - **cramping**: lat-m bnm6•
- **Pectoral muscles**: ant-c h2 berb↓ borx h2 *Bry* card-m↓ echi gels psa* kali-s fd4.de **merc** morg-g fmm1• nat-c↓ petr-ra shn4• phos h2 ran-b k2 rhus-t staph↓ **symph** fd3.de• [*Brach* stj]
  - **left**: nad rly4• ther↓
    - **pinching** pain: ther c1*
    - **stitching** pain: ther kr1
  - **drawing** pain: berb card-m nat-c a1
  - **sore**: borx hr1 staph a1
  - **tearing** pain: berb k*
  - ○ **Lower** part: mim-p skp7•
    - **cold** open air agg.: mim-p skp7•
    - **spreading** arms agg.: mim-p skp7•
    - **warm** bathing | **amel.**: mim-p skp7•
- **Pleura**: arn br1 bamb-a↓ borx tl1 bry tl1 *Caps* hr1 cimic br1* dros mtf11 guaj mrr1 *Kali-c* tl1 phos hr1* podo fd3.de• ran-b c1*
  - **right**: asc-t c1
- **Pleura**: ...
  - **accompanied** by:
    - **hoarse** voice: dros mtf11
    - **influenza**: asc-t br1* cimic mtf11
    - **laryngeal** catarrh: dros mtf11
  - **burning**: bamb-a stb2.de•
  - **eating** agg.: ant-ar mtf11
  - **intermittent**: dros mtf11
  - **lying** down agg.: ant-ar mtf11
  - **motion** agg.: acon vh1 bry tl1
    - **stitching** pain: bry tl1
  - **stitching** pain: bry tl1
  - **tubercular**: guaj mrr1
- **Posterior** part | **stitching** pain (See BACK - Pain - dorsal - stitching)
- **Precordial** region: *Acon* bro1 *Adon* bro1 *Adren* bro1 aesc bro1 agar bro1 am-c bro1 aml-ns bro1 apis bro1 *Ars* bro1 *Ars-i* bro1 aspar bro1 aur bro1 brom bro1 bry bro1 *Cact* bro1 calc bro1 calc-ar bro1 *Camph* bro1 carb-v bro1 cere-b bro1 cimic bro1 *Colch* bro1 coll bro1 cot bro1 *Crat* bro1 cupr bro1 *Dig* bro1 dios bro1 ferr bro1 glon bro1 haem bro1 *Hydr-ac* bro1 *Iber* bro1 ign bro1 *Iod* bro1 ip bro1 kalm bro1 lach bro1* lat-m bro1* laur bro1 *Lil-t* bro1 lith-c bro1 *Lycps-v* bro1 magn-gr bro1 med jl2 meny bro1 *Naja* bro1 nat-ar bro1 *Pneu* jl2 prim-v bro1 psor↓ *Puls* bro1 sapo bro1 *Spig* bro1 *Spong* bro1 streptoc↓ sulph tl1 syph↓ tab bro1 tarent tl1 *Thea* bro1 thyr bro1 toxo-g jl2 tub tl1 tub-d jl2 vac jl2* vanad bro1 verat-v bro1
  - **night**: syph↓
    - **cutting** pain: syph jl2
  - **cramping**: streptoc jl2
  - **cutting** pain: med jl2 syph jl2
  - **motion** agg.: med jl2
    - **cutting** pain: med jl2
    - **pricking**: med jl2
  - **physical** exertion; after: tub-d jl2
  - **pinching** pain: pneu jl2
  - **pressing** pain: lat-m bnm6•
  - **pricking**: psor jl2
  - **walking** agg.; after: tub-d jl2
  - ▽ **extending** to | **Hand** | **left**: med jl2
    - **Upper** limbs: brucel sa3•
- **Ribs**: agar↓ agath-a↓ aids↓ arg-met↓ aza br1 caps↓ carb-v↓ chin↓ cupr↓ fum↓ graph h2 kali-bi↓ kali-c↓ kali-s↓ lac-h↓ lac-leo↓ led↓ lyc↓ melal-alt gya4 nad rly4• naja↓ nat-c↓ oci-sa sk4• oxal-a↓ petr↓ ph-ac h2 plut-n srj7• podo↓ psor↓ sal-fr↓ sars↓ sep↓ stann↓ staph↓ stram↓ sulph h2 tritic-vg fd5.de verat h1
  - **right**: fic-m↓ irid-met↓ lac-leo↓ mur-ac↓ staph↓ tub-d jl2
    - **cramping**: fic-m gya1
    - **stitching** pain: irid-met srj5• lac-leo hrn2• mur-ac h2 staph h1
    - **extending** to | **left**: lac-del hrn2•
    - **Last** rib; under: chin↓ spect↓
      - **sore**: chin kr1 [spect dfg1]
  - **left**: agath-a↓ ampe-qu↓ irid-met↓ mur-ac↓ pant-ac↓ podo↓
    - **cutting** pain: pant-ac rly4•
    - **sore**: ampe-qu br1
    - **stitching** pain: agath-a nl2• irid-met srj5• mur-ac h2 podo fd3.de•
  - **broken**; as if: agar ptk1 caps ptk1 kali-bi bg1* naja ptk1 petr ptk1 psor ptk1 sep bg1 stram ptk1
  - **burning**: melal-alt gya4 ph-ac h2
  - **cough** agg.; during: arn↓ *Bry*↓
    - **sore**: arn b7.de* *Bry* b7a.de
  - **cramping**: petr h2
  - **cutting** pain: agath-a nl2• aids nl2• fum rly4• plut-n srj7• stann h2
  - **drawing** pain: cupr h2 stann h2
  - **inspiration** agg.: caps h1
  - **menses**; after: borx b4a.de

- **pleuritis**; after: abrot mtf11
- **pressing** pain: arg-met h1 cupr h2 stann h2
  - **button**; like a: lyc h2
- **rheumatic**: psor jl2
- **sore**: agath-a nl2• carb-v bg1* chin bg1 oxal-a rly4• ph-ac h2 sal-fr sle1•
- **sticking** pain: lac-h sk4•
- **stitching** pain: agath-a nl2• kali-c h2 kali-s fd4.de lac-leo hrn2• led h1 nat-c h2 podo fd3.de• sars h2 stann h2 staph tl1
- **stool**; before: petr ↓
  - **cramping**: petr bg2
- ▽ **extending** to:
  - **Sternum**: nat-c ↓
    - **stitching** pain: nat-c h2
- ○ **Anterior** part: nit-ac ↓ verat ↓
  - **pressing** pain: nit-ac h2 verat h1
  - **sore**: nit-ac h2
- **Between** ribs: *Borx* ↓ canth ↓ caps ↓ cina ↓ coc-c ↓ kreos ↓ mag-m ↓ *Mez* ↓ mur-ac ↓ nept-m lsd2.fr plat ↓ *Ran-b* mrr1 *Seneg* ↓ spig k2 spong fd4.de tarax ↓ teucr ↓
  - **right** then left: coc-c ↓
    - **stitching** pain: coc-c
  - **burning**: coc-c plat
  - **stitching** pain: *Borx* bg2 canth bg2 caps a1 cina a1 coc-c kreos k* mag-m k* *Mez* mur-ac bg2 *Ran-b* *Seneg* bg2 spig bg2* spong fd4.de tarax bg2 teucr bg2
  - **extending** to | **Heart**: lycps-v a3
- **Edges** of ribs: allox tpw3
- **False** ribs: agath-a ↓ calc ↓ caust ↓ *Chel* ↓ hep ↓ *Lyc* ↓ med ↓ meph ↓ nat-ar ↓ nat-m ↓ *Ph-ac* ↓ **Ran-b** ↓ samb ↓ **Sep** ↓ *Sulph* ↓ *Tarent* ↓
  - **right**: agar ↓ alum ↓ *Chel* ↓ lyc ↓ nept-m ↓ sep ↓
    - **drawing** pain: sep h2
    - **sore**: *Chel* lyc
    - **sticking** pain: agar
    - **stitching** pain: alum h2 nept-m lsd2.fr
  - **left**: agath-a ↓ bism ↓ cic ↓ med ↓ meny ↓ psor ↓ vac ↓
    - **breathing**; only on: nat-c ↓
      - **sticking** pain: nat-c a1
    - **pressing** pain: psor jl2
    - **sore**: agath-a nl2• med
    - **sticking** pain: cic h1
    - **stitching** pain: bism a1 meny h1 vac jl2
    - **extending** to:
      - **right**: mur-ac ↓
        - **stitching** pain: mur-ac h2
    - **Below**: narc-ps ↓
      - **aching**: narc-ps a1*
  - **cutting** pain: samb h1* sulph
  - **inspiration** agg.: *Arn* ↓ sulph ↓
    - **sore**: *Arn* sulph
  - **motion** agg.: *Arn* ↓ meph ↓
    - **sore**: *Arn* meph
  - **sore**: agath-a nl2• calc caust *Chel* hep *Lyc* med meph nat-ar nat-m *Ph-ac* **Ran-b** *Sulph* *Tarent*
  - **sticking** pain: **Sep**
- **Floating** | **left**: petr a1 ther br1
- **Fourth**:
  - **left**:
    - **stool**; before:
      - **during**; and: spig ↓
        - **sore**: spig h1
- **Joints**: chin ↓
  - **sore**: chin h1
- **Last** true rib:
  - **bending** forward agg.: cycl ↓
    - **stitching** pain: cycl h1
- **Lower**: aeth ↓ agath-a ↓ anac ↓ bamb-a ↓ bism ↓ chin ↓ hep ↓ kali-i ↓ kali-s ↓ lac-leo ↓ mag-m ↓ nat-c ↓ ozone ↓ plb ↓ rhus-t ↓ sep ↓ squil ↓ sulph ↓
  - **right**: aesc ↓ *Agar* ↓ bamb-a ↓ calc ↓ choc ↓ kali-c ↓ kali-n ↓ kali-s ↓ lac-leo ↓ mang ↓ merl ↓ nept-m ↓ positr ↓ verat ↓ zinc ↓
    - **pressing** pain: verat h1
    - **splinter**; as from a: *Agar* k*
    - **stitching** pain: aesc agar bamb-a stb2.de• calc choc srj3• kali-c kali-n h2 kali-s fd4.de lac-leo hrn2• mang h2 merl nept-m lsd2.fr positr nl2• verat zinc h2
  - **left**: *Agar* ↓ agath-a ↓ anac ↓ canth ↓ cean tl1 lyc ↓ melal-alt ↓ mur-ac ↓ **Ran-b** mrr1 sang ↓ sep ↓ sil ↓ tarax ↓ visc ↓ zinc ↓
    - **pressing** pain: lyc h2 melal-alt gya4 sep h2
    - **stitching** pain: *Agar* agath-a nl2• anac h2 canth mur-ac h2 *Ran-b* sang sil h2 tarax visc c1 zinc h2
    - **touch** agg.: sil h2
  - **morning**: bov ↓
    - **stitching** pain: bov
  - **afternoon**: canth ↓ stram ↓
    - **stitching** pain: canth stram
  - **evening**: mag-m ↓ zinc ↓
    - **stitching** pain: mag-m zinc h2
  - **night**: agath-a ↓
    - **inspiration** agg.: sil ↓
      - **stitching** pain: sil
    - **stitching** pain: agath-a nl2•
  - **aching**: lac-leo hrn2• ozone sde2•
  - **bending** and turning body agg.: ozone ↓
    - **aching**: ozone sde2•
  - **cough** agg.; during: bry ↓ kali-n ↓
    - **stitching** pain: bry kali-n h2
  - **inspiration** agg.: chin ↓
    - **stitching** pain: chin h1
  - **laughing** agg.: kali-n ↓
    - **stitching** pain: kali-n
  - **sitting** agg.: agar ↓ mag-c ↓
    - **stitching** pain: agar mag-c
  - **sneezing** agg.: castm ↓
    - **stitching** pain: castm
  - **stitching** pain: aeth a1 agath-a nl2• anac h2 bamb-a stb2.de• bism h1 chin hep kali-i kali-s fd4.de mag-m nat-c rhus-t h1* squil h1 sulph
    - **waves**; in: bamb-a stb2.de•
  - **tearing** pain: agath-a nl2• bism h1 kali-s fd4.de plb k* sep k*
  - **turning** agg.: plb ↓
    - **stitching** pain: plb
  - **walking** agg.: merc ↓
    - **stitching** pain: merc
  - **Spots**; in small: ozone ↓
    - **aching**: ozone sde2•
- **Seventh** rib:
  - **morning**:
    - 7.30 h: pert-vc ↓
      - **stitching** pain: pert-vc vk9
- **Short**:
  - **Below**: caps ↓ mur-ac ↓
    - **right**: bac ↓
      - **pinching** pain: bac jl2
    - **flatus**; passing:
      - **amel.**: mur-ac ↓
        - **pinching** pain: mur-ac a1
    - **pinching** pain: mur-ac a1
    - **pressing** pain: caps a1
- **Sixth**: bell ↓ ruta ↓
  - **morning**:
    - 7.30 h: pert-vc ↓
      - **stitching** pain: pert-vc vk9
  - **pressing** pain: bell h1 ruta h1

• **Third**: *Anis* br1
⁝ **accompanied** by | **cough**: anis br1
⁝ **Sternum**; near: anis br1
• **Under**: agath-a↓ cartl-s↓ chlam-tr↓ dig↓ mang-p↓ melal-alt gya4
⁝ **left** ribs; under: iris↓
: **cramping**: iris a1
⁝ **cramping**: agath-a nl2• cartl-s rly4• dig h2 mang-p rly4•
⁝ **stitching** pain: chlam-tr bcx2•

\- **Scapulae**; between: calc-act↓
• **stitching** pain | **outward**: (non:calc slp) calc-act slp

\- **Sides**: *Acon* adam skp7• aesc↓ agar agath-a nl2• ail↓ all-c↓ all-s alum alum-p k2 alum-sil k2 alumn am-c *Am-m*↓ *Ambr* anac ang *Apis*↓ arg-met *Arg-n* arn ars ars-i ars-s-f k2 *Asaf*↓ asar↓ asc-t aur aur-ar k2 aur-i k2 aur-m aur-s k2 bad *Bar-c*↓ bar-s↓ bell benz-ac↓ berb k* *Borx*↓ bov brom *Bry* k* cadm-s calad↓ *Calc* calc-p calc-s calc-sil k2* cann-s *Canth*↓ caps *Carb-v* *Carbn-s* **Card-m**↓ caust *Cean* c2 cedr *Cham*↓ *Chel* chin chinin-ar *Cimic* c2 cina↓ clem↓ *Cocc* colch *Coloc*↓ *Con* cop *Cor-r*↓ croc↓ crot-c↓ *Cupr* dig *Dios* c2 dulc elaps↓ euph↓ euphr falco-pe↓ ferr ferr-ar ferr-i ferr-p fl-ac gamb↓ gran↓ graph grat↓ *Guaj*↓ hura hydr-ac↓ hydrc hyos ign↓ indg↓ iod jug-c kali-ar kali-bi *Kali-c* *Kali-i*↓ kali-m k2 kali-n kali-p kali-sil↓ kalm lac-ac↓ *Lach*↓ lachn↓ lact laur led lil-t lob **Lyc** lycps-v mang↓ med *Meny* merc-i-f mez *Mosch*↓ mur-ac naja nat-ar↓ nat-c↓ *Nat-m* nat-p↓ *Nat-s*↓ nat-sil↓ nicc↓ nit-ac nux-m *Nux-v* ol-an↓ olnd↓ op *Ox-ac* c2 pall↓ par petr ph-ac↓ phos phys phyt pic-ac↓ plan plat↓ plb pop↓ positr↓ prun↓ *Puls* k* pyrog jl2 **Ran-b** raph rhus-t *Rumx* ruta fd4.de *Sabad*↓ sabin↓ sal-fr sle1• samb sars↓ *Sel*↓ seneg sep sil sphing↓ spig↓ *Spong* **Squil**↓ stann staph↓ stram stront-c↓ sul-ac sul-i k2 **Sulph** sumb symph↓ *Tab*↓ *Tarax*↓ thuj til tritic-vg fd5.de tub c1 tub-r jl2 *Valer*↓ vanil↓ verat verb↓ zinc zinc-p↓ [heroin sdj2]
• **both** sides: ran-b↓
⁝ **stitching** pain: ran-b ptk1
• **right**: abrot *Acon*↓ *Aesc* *Agar*↓ allox tpw3 alum↓ **Am-c**↓ am-m↓ ambr↓ *Anac*↓ ang↓ anis ant-c↓ apis↓ apoc↓ *Arg-met*↓ arn↓ ars arum-t↓ *Asaf* asar aspar↓ aur↓ aur-m↓ bar-c **Bell** benz-ac↓ bism blatta-o borx bov↓ brom *Bry* k* bufo↓ cact cain↓ calad↓ calc nh6 *Canth*↓ carb-an↓ *Carb-v*↓ card-m↓ cassia-s↓ *Caust* cench k2 cham **Chel** k* *Chen-a*↓ chim chin *Chinin-ar* chinin-s↓ choc↓ cimic cina↓ clem↓ coc-c↓ cocc colch coloc↓ com↓ con↓ cop↓ croc↓ crot-h cupr↓ cupr-act↓ dendr-pol sk4• dig digin↓ dirc↓ dulc↓ elaps equis-h↓ euon↓ euph↓ fago↓ falco-pe↓ ferr ferr-i ferr-p↓ fic-m↓ form graph↓ guare↓ gymno ham↓ hip-ac sp1 hydr hyos↓ ign↓ *Iod* irid-met↓ kali-bi tl1 **Kali-c**↓ *Kali-i*↓ kali-n↓ kali-s↓ kreos↓ lach↓ laur↓ lob-e c1 loxo-recl knl4• *Lyc*↓ m-aust↓ mag-c↓ mag-m↓ manc↓ mang↓ marb-w↓ melal-alt gya4 meny↓ merc↓ *Merc-c*↓ merc-i-f↓ *Mez*↓ mosch↓ mur-ac↓ murx↓ naja↓ nat-ar nat-c↓ *Nat-m*↓ nat-p↓ nat-s↓ nept-m↓ *Nit-ac*↓ oci-sa sp1 op↓ ozone↓ pall↓ par↓ petr-ra shn4• ph-ac↓ phos↓ phyt↓ plat↓ plb↓ positr↓ psil ft1 psor ptel pycnop-sa↓ *Ran-b*↓ ran-s↓ raph↓ rauw↓ rhus-t↓ rumx↓ ruta sabad↓ *Sang* k* *Sars*↓ sel sep *Sil*↓ *Spig*↓ spong fd4.de squil↓ stann↓ *Staph*↓ *Stront-c* sul-ac sul-i k2 sulph symph↓ tab↓ *Tarax*↓ tarent tep↓ teucr thuj trios rsj11• tritic-vg fd5.de trom urt-u↓ valer k2 verat verat-v viol-t↓ xan zinc h2 zing↓
⁝ **then** left: aur-m↓
: **tearing** pain: aur-m
⁝ **morning**: nit-ac↓
: **pressing** pain: nit-ac h2
⁝ **evening**: positr↓
: **stitching** pain: positr nl2•
⁝ **night**: nit-ac↓
: **stitching** pain: nit-ac h2
⁝ **aching**: bism k* caust k* chinin-ar choc srj3• (non:dig slp) digin a1* fago k* merc-i-f k*
⁝ **bending**:
: **body** | **left**; to:
agg.: petr↓
stitching pain: petr h2
. **right**; to:
agg.: staph↓
stitching pain: staph h1

\- **Sides – right – bending**: ...
: **left**; to:
. **agg.**: petr↓
cutting pain: petr h2
: **right**; to:
. **agg.**: cocc↓
drawing pain: cocc
⁝ **boring** pain: *Bism* colch k*
⁝ **breathing**:
: **agg.**: *Aesc*↓ ambr↓ ars↓ **Borx**↓ **Bry**↓ calc↓ chinin-s↓ *Cimic*↓ *Mez*↓ psor↓
. **sore**: *Aesc*
. **stitching** pain: aesc ambr ars h2 **Borx** k* **Bry** k* calc chinin-s *Cimic* *Mez* psor k*
: **deep**:
. **agg.**: psor↓
stitching pain: psor jl2
. **amel.**: tarax↓
stitching pain: tarax
⁝ **burning**: abrot k* alum k* ars k* asar *Bell* k* **Bry** k* carb-an coloc k* ham fd3.de• mur-ac h2 nat-c h2 nat-p raph k* rumx ruta h1 *Sang* sulph k* zinc
⁝ **cough** agg.; during: (↗cough) **Borx**↓ cann-s↓ cassia-s↓ chel↓ colch↓ hip-ac sp1 kali-s↓ lachn↓ sep↓ ziz↓
: **cutting** pain: colch lachn
: **sore**: kali-s tl1
: **stitching** pain: **Borx** cann-s cassia-s ccrh1• chel sep h2 ziz
⁝ **cramping**: marb-w es1•
⁝ **cutting** pain: agar aur h2 bell k* cain chinin-s colch con k* dirc c1 falco-pe nl2• guare k* iod lyc h2 pycnop-sa mrz1 rauw tpw8 sang sep stann k* thuj h1 trom k* xan c1
⁝ **dinner**; after: zinc↓
: **stitching** pain: zinc h2
⁝ **drawing** pain: asar *Bell* borx cench k2 cham cocc com (non:dig slp) digin slp kali-bi bg2 meny h1 mur-ac h2 ruta sang *Stront-c* sul-ac thuj
⁝ **dull** pain | **paroxysmal**: trios rsj11•
⁝ **expiration** agg.; during: oci-sa sp1
⁝ **gnawing** pain: ruta
⁝ **griping** pain: acon k* bov k* coloc h2 mag-m h2 mur-ac k* pycnop-sa mrz1 sulph k* verat k*
⁝ **inspiration** agg.: arg-met↓ carb-v↓ chlf br1 cycl↓ gink-b sbd1• graph↓ nit-ac↓ plat↓ sal-fr↓ sep↓ sil↓
: **stitching** pain: arg-met h1 carb-v h2 cycl a1 graph h2 nit-ac h2 plat h2 sal-fr sle1• sep h2 sil h2
⁝ **lying**:
: **back**; on:
. **agg.**: *Sulph*↓
stitching pain: *Sulph* k*
: **head** low; with the:
. **agg.**: kali-n↓
stitching pain: kali-n h2
: **side**; on | **left**:
agg.: calad↓ cench↓
stitching pain: calad cench k2
. **right**:
agg.: *Acon*↓ *Borx*↓ graph↓ *Kali-c*↓ kali-n↓ merc↓
stitching pain: *Acon* k* *Borx* graph h2 *Kali-c* kali-n h2 merc sne
⁝ **motion** agg.: gink-b sbd1•
⁝ **pressing** pain: acon vh1 *Anac* ang h1 ant-c h2 arg-met h1 ars h2 *Asaf* k* *Bell* k* bism h1 cact calc h2 *Carb-v* caust k* com con h2 cupr h2 kali-c h2 nit-ac h2 ph-ac h2 sep h2 squil tarax h1 tarent teucr k* thuj k* viol-t k* zinc h2
: **plug**; as from a: *Anac* lyc bg2
⁝ **pressure**:
: **agg.**: sul-ac↓
. **stitching** pain: sul-ac h2
: **amel.**: *Borx*↓ graph↓ nat-m↓
. **stitching** pain: *Borx* graph h2 nat-m h2

- **right**: ...
  - **raising** arms agg.: borx↓ nicc↓
    - **stitching** pain: borx nicc a1
  - **sitting** agg.: bry↓ mur-ac↓
    - **stitching** pain: bry mur-ac h2
  - **sneezing** or yawning: *Borx*↓
    - **stitching** pain: *Borx* k*
  - **sore**: *Aesc* am-m cassia-s ccrh1• *Caust* **Chel** con cupr-act elaps fic-m gya1 irid-met srj5• nat-ar nat-c hr1 ph-ac rhus-t sulph thuj h1 urt-u zinc h2
  - **squeezed**; as if: kali-bi bg2
  - **stitching** pain: abrot k* *Acon* b7.de* *Agar* k* alum b4.de* **Am-c** k* am-m k* ambr k* ant-c b7.de* apis k* apoc *Arg-met* k* arn b7.de* **Ars** k* arum-t *Asaf* b7.de* *Asar* k* aspar *Bell* k* benz-ac k* **Borx** k* *Brom* k* **Bry** k* bufo cain calad k* calc k* *Canth* k* carb-an b4.de* *Carb-v* k* card-m cassia-s ccrh1• caust b4.de* cench k2 cham k* **Chel** k* *Chen-a* *Chin* k* chinin-s choc srj3• cimic cina b7.de* clem b4.de* coc-c k* cocc b7.de* *Colch* k* coloc b4.de* con b4.de* cop k* croc k* dig b4.de* dulc b4.de* equis-h euon euph k* ferr k* ferr-p form k* graph b4.de* hyos b7.de* ign b7.de* iod b4.de* kali-bi **Kali-c** k* *Kali-i* kali-n h2* kali-s fd4.de kreos b7a.de lach bg2 laur b7.de* *Lyc* k* m-aust b7.de mag-c b4.de* mag-m k* manc mang k* meny k* merc k* *Merc-c* k* merc-i-f k* *Mez* k* mosch b7a.de mur-ac h2 murx naja nat-c k* *Nat-m* k* nat-s k* nept-m lsd2.fr *Nit-ac* k* op b7.de* ozone sde2• pall par b7.de* ph-ac b4.de* phos b4.de* phyt plat h2 plb b7.de* positr nl2• *Ran-b* k* ran-s k* rhus-t b7.de* ruta b7.de* sabad b7.de* sang k* *Sars* k* *Sep* k* *Sil* k* *Spig* b7.de* spong k* squil b7.de* stann b4.de* *Staph* k* sul-ac b4.de* *Sulph* k* symph fd3.de• tab k* *Tarax* b7.de* tep k* teucr b7.de* thuj b4.de* valer k2 verat k* verat-v viol-t b7.de* xan c1 *Zinc* k* zing k*
  - **stooping** agg.: **Am-c**↓
    - **stitching** pain: **Am-c**
  - **tearing** pain: arg-met h1 ars h2 aur-m k* *Bry* caust *Cocc* con h2 elaps iod h kali-c h2 kali-s fd4.de lyc plb sang sep zinc
  - **turning** body to right: zinc↓
    - **stitching** pain: zinc h2
  - **twisting** pain: rumx bg2
  - **walking** agg.: am-c↓ nat-m↓ sep↓
    - **stitching** pain: am-c h2 nat-m h2 sep h2
  - **extending** to:
    - **left**: acon↓ agar↓ allox tpw3 alum↓ calc↓ lachn hr1 petr bg2* puls bg2
      - **cutting** pain: petr h2
      - **stitching** pain: acon lp agar alum calc petr h2
    - **Abdomen**:
      - **left**: rhus-t↓
        - **stitching** pain: rhus-t h1
      - **And** left shoulder: dirc↓
        - **cutting** pain: dirc c1
    - **Back**: ambr↓ calc↓ choc↓ colch↓ merc↓ nit-ac↓ pall↓ sil↓
      - **stitching** pain: ambr calc choc srj3• colch merc nit-ac pall c1 sil
    - **Flank**: borx↓
      - **stitching** pain: borx a1
    - **Groin**:
      - **right**: borx↓
        - **stitching** pain: borx
    - **Jaw**: rauw↓
      - **cutting** pain: rauw tpw8*
    - **Kidneys**: sel kr1
    - **Liver**: kali-c↓
      - **pressing** pain: kali-c h2
    - **Scapula**: *Nit-ac*↓ phyt↓ **Sulph**↓ xan↓
      - **stitching** pain: *Nit-ac* phyt **Sulph** xan c1
    - **Scapulae**: ars bg1 guaj bg1 phos bg1 sulph bg1
      - **afternoon** | **16**-17 h: merc-sul vh
    - **Shoulder**: chinin-s↓ kreos bg1 lob bg1 phos bg1 phyt bg1 plb bg1 *Sang*
      - **cutting** pain: chinin-s c1

- **right – extending** to: ...
  - **Stomach**: sulph↓
    - **stitching** pain: sulph
  - **Upper** limbs: rauw↓
    - **right**: rauw↓
      - **cutting** pain: rauw tpw8
    - **cutting** pain: rauw sp1
  - **Apex** of right lung (See lungs - apex - **right**)
  - **Deep** in: chel↓
    - **nail**; as from a: chel ptk1
  - **Last** rib: *Ph-ac*↓
    - **sore**: *Ph-ac*
  - **Lower** part: aesc↓ alumn↓ *Chel*↓ *Chen-a*↓ **hyos**↓ *Kali-c*↓
    - **pressing** pain: hyos h1
    - **stitching** pain: aesc alumn *Chel* *Chen-a* ***Kali-c*** k*
    - **extending** to:
      - **Apex** of lung: acon↓
        - **stitching** pain: acon vh1
  - **Sixth** rib to cartilage; attachment of:
    - **extending** to | **Scapula**; through chest to inferior angle of right: chen-a hr1
  - **Spot**; in a: kali-bi tl1
  - **Upper** part: olib-sac↓
    - **stitching** pain: olib-sac wmh1
- **left**: **Acon**↓ adam skp7• *Aesc*↓ aeth↓ *Agar*↓ agath-a nl2• aids↓ all-c↓ aloe↓ *Alum*↓ alumn↓ *Am-c*↓ *Am-m*↓ *Ambr*↓ ammc↓ anac ang↓ ant-c↓ ant-t↓ *Apis* arg-met↓ *Arg-n* *Arn*↓ *Ars*↓ ars-h↓ arum-t arund asaf↓ asar↓ asc-c c1 *Asc-t*↓ aster aur bad↓ bamb-a↓ bapt a1* bar-c↓ bell↓ benz-ac berb borx↓ bov↓ brom *Bry*↓ cact k* calad↓ *Calc*↓ *Calc-p*↓ camph↓ *Cann-s*↓ canth↓ caps↓ carb-an *Carb-v*↓ carbn-s card-m *Carl*↓ cassia-s cdd7*• *Caust*↓ chel↓ *Chin*↓ *Chinin-s*↓ choc↓ cic *Cimic* k* *Cina*↓ cit-ac↓ clem cob-n sp1 cocc↓ colch k* *Coloc*↓ con↓ crat br1 *Croc*↓ *Crot-c*↓ crot-h↓ *Crot-t*↓ cupr↓ *Cur* cycl↓ *Dig*↓ digin↓ dulc echi↓ elaps↓ *Eup-per*↓ *Euph*↓ eupi↓ fago ferr ferr-ma↓ fl-ac fum↓ gal-ac↓ graph grat↓ guaj↓ ham↓ hell↓ hep hipp↓ hura↓ hydr↓ hydroph rsj6• hyper↓ ign ignis-alc↓ ind↓ iod↓ ip↓ iris a1 kali-ar↓ kali-bi *Kali-c*↓ *Kali-n*↓ kali-p↓ kola stb3• kreos↓ lac-c↓ lac-del↓ lac-h sk4• *Lach* k* lachn↓ lact↓ laur lepi↓ *Lil-t*↓ limest-b es1• loxo-recl knl4• *Lyc*↓ lyss↓ m-arct↓ *Mag-c*↓ mag-m↓ mag-p↓ malar↓ manc mang med↓ melal-alt gya4 meny↓ merc *Merc-c*↓ merc-i-f↓ mez mim-p rsj8• mosch↓ mur-ac myric *Myrt-c*↓ *Naja*↓ nat-c↓ **Nat-m** nat-p↓ *Nat-s* k* nat-sil fd3.de• *Nicc*↓ nit-ac↓ nux-v↓ oena↓ ol-j↓ olib-sac↓ olnd↓ *Ox-ac* pall par↓ *Petr*↓ petr-ra↓ ph-ac↓ **Phos** k* plan↓ *Plat*↓ plb↓ polyg-h psil↓ psor↓ puls↓ **Ran-b** k* *Ran-s*↓ rat↓ rhod rhus-t *Rumx* ruta fd4.de sabad↓ sabin↓ samb↓ sang↓ sars↓ sel rsj9• seneg *Sep*↓ sil sphing↓ *Spig* spong fd4.de squil↓ stann mtf11 staph stram↓ stront-c↓ sul-ac k2 *Sulph* sumb suprar↓ tarax↓ tarent *Teucr*↓ *Ther*↓ *Thuj*↓ trad a1* trios↓ trom↓ tub al* tung-met bdx1• upa↓ ust valer↓ vanil fd5.de verat verb↓ *Viol-t*↓ vip xan zinc zinc-p↓ zing↓ [heroin sdj2 spect dfg1]
  - **then** right: agar↓
    - **sore**: agar
  - **evening**: adam skp7• kali-n↓ mur-ac↓ nat-m↓ nit-ac↓ sul-ac↓ zinc↓
    - **stitching** pain: kali-n h2 mur-ac h2 nat-m h2 nit-ac h2 sul-ac h2 zinc h2
  - **aching**: *Apis* berb k* carb-an k* clem k* eup-per gal-ac a1 ham ignis-alc es2• iod kali-p mez k* oena petr-ra shn4• psil ft1 rhus-t k* *Rumx* *Seneg* sep sumb k* tarent zinc
  - **bending**:
    - **agg.**: adam skp7•
    - **forward**:
      - **amel.**: bamb-a↓
        - **stitching** pain: bamb-a stb2.de•
    - **left**; to:
      - **agg.**: calc↓
        - **stitching** pain: calc h2
  - **boring** pain: merc-i-f ph-ac h2* seneg k* spig h1

- **left**: ...
  - **breathing**:
    - **amel.**: nat-c ↓
      - **pressing** pain: nat-c a1
    - **deep** | **agg.**: adam skp7•
    - **hindering** breathing: cassia-s ↓
      - **pressing** pain: cassia-s ccrh1•
  - **bubble**; like a: lac-del hm2•
  - **burning**: all-c k* *Ars* bar-c k* *Carb-v* k* *Carbn-s* cycl k* *Euph* graph h2 grat ham fd3.de• ind laur k* malar jl2 mang h2 myrt-c nat-c k* ol-j ph-ac h2 **Phos** k* **Ran-b** k* **Rumx** sabad k* *Seneg* k* stront-c sul-ac k* zinc k*
  - **carrying** a weight: kali-n ↓
    - **stitching** pain: kali-n h2
  - **chill**; during: sil ↓
    - **stitching** pain: sil h2
  - **clawing** pain: seneg bg2
  - **cough** agg.; during: adam skp7• agar ↓ bell ↓ cassia-s ccrh1• caust ↓ crot-h ↓ germ-met srj5• iod ↓ irid-met ↓ kali-c ↓ nat-s tl1 nit-ac ↓ ox-ac ↓ sel ↓ sep ↓ sul-ac ↓ tub ↓
    - **cutting** pain: ox-ac
    - **stitching** pain: agar bell h1 caust h2 crot-h iod irid-met srj5• kali-c nit-ac h2 sel rsj9• sep h2 sul-ac h2 tub gk
  - **cramping**: agath-a nl2• arg-met h1 plat h2
  - **crushing**: anac bg2
  - **cutting** pain: *Agar* agath-a nl2• aids nl2• ars-h *Asc-t* aur h2 *Brom* *Calc* colch k* dulc fum rly1• iris a1 kali-c h2 lac-c lepi br1 *Lil-t* lyc k* manc **Nat-m** *Ox-ac* ph-ac h2 polyg-h k* psil ft1 rhod k* rumx spig h1 spong k* stann h2 staph h1 sumb tarent verat
  - **drawing** pain: anac brom cact calad *Calc* card-m cic clem dulc mang med nat-sil fd3.de• petr h2 phos ruta h1 stann h2 sul-ac h2 zinc h2
  - **dull** pain | **paroxysmal**: trios rsj11•
  - **expiration** agg.: nat-c ↓
    - **stitching** pain: nat-c a1
  - **gnawing** pain: arg-met h1 calc k* ruta h1* stann k*
  - **griping** pain: cina k* cupr bg2 graph k* petr-ra shn4• spong bg2 upa [heroin sdj2]
  - **inflammation** of the heart; with rheumatic: spig ↓
    - **sore**: spig br1
  - **inspiration** agg.: bamb-a ↓ calc ↓ calc-p ↓ cycl ↓ kali-n ↓ kola stb3• lyc ↓ mag-c ↓ nat-c ↓ nat-sil ↓ nit-ac ↓ ph-ac ↓ ruta ↓ sul-ac ↓ **Sulph** ↓ symph ↓ tub ↓
    - **stitching** pain: bamb-a stb2.de• calc h2 calc-p k* cycl a1 kali-n h2 kola stb3• lyc h2 mag-c nat-c a1 nat-sil fd3.de• nit-ac h2 ph-ac h2 ruta a1 sul-ac h2 **Sulph** symph fd3.de• tub gk
  - **laughing** agg.: adam skp7•
  - **lying**:
    - **agg.**: tub ↓
      - **stitching** pain: tub gk
    - **back**; on:
      - **agg.**: *Sulph* ↓
        - **stitching** pain: *Sulph*
    - **bed**; in:
      - **agg.**: nit-ac ↓
        - **stitching** pain: nit-ac h2
    - **side**; on:
      - **left**:
        - **agg.**: adam skp7• am-c ↓ camph ↓ kali-c ↓ *Lyc* ↓ *Phos* ↓ *Rumx* ↓ seneg ↓ sil ↓ *Stann* ↓
          - **burning**: seneg k*
          - **stitching** pain: am-c camph kali-c h2 *Lyc* *Phos* k* *Rumx* sil h2 *Stann* k*
      - **painful** side:
        - **agg.**: *Rumx* ↓
          - **sore**: *Rumx*
      - **right**:
        - **amel.**: adam skp7• **Phos** ↓
          - **stitching** pain: **Phos**
  - **lying down** agg.: hydroph rsj6•

- **left**: ...
  - **motion**:
    - **agg.**: calc ↓ *Sulph* ↓ tub ↓
      - **stitching** pain: calc h2 *Sulph* tub gk
    - **arm**; of:
      - **agg.**: zinc ↓
        - **stitching** pain: zinc h2
  - **pressing** pain: acon am-m h2 ambr h1 anac h2 ang h1 arg-met h1 aur bamb-a stb2.de• calad carb-v k* carbn-s cassia-s ccrh1• chel k* crat br1 crot-t cycl h1 dig digin a1 dulc k* ferr k* graph h2 hep k* ign k* kali-c h2 kali-p fd1.de• lyc h2 mag-m k* merc k* nat-c h2 nat-m h2 *Nat-s* nit-ac h2 nux-v pall petr h2 ph-ac h2 plat h2 psil ft1 ran-b k* sil k* spong k* staph k* sul-ac sulph k* tarent k* vanil fd5.de verat h1 zinc h2
    - **plug**; as from a: asar bg2
  - **rest** | **amel.**: adam skp7•
  - **rising** agg.: bamb-a ↓
    - **stitching** pain: bamb-a stb2.de•
  - **sitting** bent forward agg.: arg-met ↓
    - **pinching** pain: arg-met h1
    - **stitching** pain: arg-met h1
  - **sore**: *Am-m* *Arg-n* arum-t k2 arund bar-c calc calc-p chel *Eup-per* lac-c laur merc mur-ac nat-m phos psil ft1 ran-b *Rumx* stram zinc
  - **sprained**; as if: lyc h2
  - **standing** agg.: mag-c ↓
    - **stitching** pain: mag-c h2
  - **stitching** pain: **Acon** b7.de* *Aesc* aeth k* agar agath-a nl2• all-c aloe *Alum* k* alumn *Am-c* k* am-m k* ammc vh1 anac b4.de* ant-c k* ant-t k* *Apis* k* arg-met b7.de* *Arn* k* *Ars* asaf b7.de* bad k* bamb-a stb2.de• bar-c k* bell b4.de* berb k* borx k* bov k* *Bry* b7.de* calad k* *Calc* k* *Calc-p* k* camph k* *Cann-s* b7.de* canth b7.de* caps k* carb-v b4.de* carbn-s k2 *Carl* k* *Caust* k* chel k* *Chin* k* *Chinin-s* choc srj3• cic b7.de* *Cina* k* cit-ac rly4• clem k* cocc b7.de* colch b7.de* *Coloc* k* con b4.de* *Croc* k* *Crot-c* k* crot-h *Crot-t* k* cupr k* cycl k* dig b4.de* *Dulc* k* echi elaps *Euph* k* eupi k* fl-ac k* graph k* guaj k* ham fd3.de• hell k* *Hep* hipp k* hura hydr hyper k* *Ign* k* iod bg2 ip b7.de* kali-ar *Kali-c* k* *Kali-n* k* kola stb3• kreos b7a.de *Lach* k* lachn lact laur b7.de* loxo-recl knl4• *Lyc* k* lyss m-arct b7.de *Mag-c* k* mag-m k* *Mang* k* meny b7.de* *Merc* k* *Merc-c* b4a.de *Mez* k* mosch b7.de* mur-ac k* *Myrt-c* b7a.de *Naja* nat-c b4.de* *Nat-m* k* nat-p *Nat-s* k* nat-sil fd3.de• *Nicc* k* nit-ac b4a.de* olib-sac wmh1 olnd k* *Ox-ac* k* par b7.de* *Petr* bg2 ph-ac k* **Phos** k* plan *Plat* k* plb k* psor k* puls b7.de* *Ran-b* k* *Ran-s* k* rat rhus-t b7.de* **Rumx** k* ruta k* sabad k* sabin k* samb b7.de sang k* sars k* *Sel* b7a.de **Seneg** k* *Sep* k* sil h2 sphing a1 *Spig* k* spong k* squil b7.de* **Stann** k* staph k* *Sul-ac* k* **Sulph** k* suprar rly4• tarax k* tarent k* *Teucr* bg2 *Ther* *Thuj* k* trom tub gk *Ust* valer k* verat b7.de* verb b7.de* *Viol-t* b7.de* *Zinc* k* zinc-p k2 zing
    - **pulsating** pain: anac h2 verat h1
    - **upward**: bar-c
  - **stooping** agg.: stann ↓
    - **stitching** pain: stann h2
  - **sudden**: bamb-a ↓ kola stb3•
    - **stitching** pain: bamb-a stb2.de• kola stb3•
  - **tearing** pain: am-c *Ambr* anac berb cann-s *Carb-v* chel h1 *Dig* dulc h2* ferr-ma graph grat kali-c h2 mag-p bg2 sil k* spig h1 zinc
  - **walking** agg.: sul-ac ↓
    - **stitching** pain: sul-ac h2
  - **extending** to:
    - **right**: aesc bg2 apis bg2 arn ↓ asc-t ↓ calc bg2* carb-v k* *Caust* ↓ chel bg2 crot-h bg2 cycl ↓ graph k* ign bg1 kali-bi bg1 kreos bg2 lil-t bg1 nat-c bg2 rumx ↓
      - **aching**: carb-v graph
      - **inspiration** agg.: *Bry* ↓
        - **stitching** pain: *Bry*
      - **stitching** pain: aesc arn k2 asc-t c1 calc h2 *Caust* cycl hr1 *Kreos* nat-c rumx
    - **left**: asc-t ↓
      - **stitching** pain: asc-t k13
    - **Abdomen**: tub ↓
      - **stitching** pain: tub gk

- **left – extending** to: ...
  - **Arm**:
    - **left**: kola stb3•
      - **stitching** pain: kola stb3•
  - **Back**: am-c ↓ lyc ↓ sul-ac ↓ **Sulph** ↓ *Ther* ↓
    - **stitching** pain: am-c h2 lyc h2 sul-ac h2 **Sulph** *Ther*
  - **Elbow** | **right**: sel rsj9•
  - **Groin**: fl-ac k*
    - **burning**: fl-ac k*
    - **stitching** pain: fl-ac
  - **Hip**: cupr ↓
    - **stitching** pain: cupr
  - **Scapula**: caust ↓ kali-p ↓ *Lact* ↓ mag-c ↓ malar ↓ **Nat-m** ↓ **Sulph** ↓
    - **aching**: kali-p
    - **burning**: malar jl2
    - **cutting** pain: **Nat-m**
    - **stitching** pain: caust *Lact* mag-c h2 *Nat-m* **Sulph**
  - **Scapulae**: dulc fd4.de gels bg1 kali-c bg1 lil-t bg1 lyc bg1 mag-c bg1 pix bg1 rhod bg1 rhus-t bg1 sil bg1 spig bg1 sul-ac bg1 sulph bg1 ther bg1
  - **Shoulder**: asc-t ↓ calc-p ↓ ignis-alc es2• mag-c ↓ nat-m bg1 sang hr1 *Verat* k*
    - **stitching** pain: asc-t calc-p mag-c nat-m sang
  - **Throat**: calc ↓ sulph zinc bg1
    - **stitching** pain: calc
- **Apex** (See lungs - apex - left)
- **Fourth** rib | **Under**: xan c1
- **Heart**; under: samb ↓
  - **stitching** pain: samb bat1•
- **Lower** part: tub ↓
  - **bending** agg.: hir ↓
    - **cutting** pain: hir rsj4•
  - **motion** of arm agg.: caust ↓
    - **sprained**; as if: caust h2
  - **stitching** pain: tub gk
  - **walking**:
    - **amel**.: tub ↓
      - **stitching** pain: tub gk
  - **extending** to:
    - **Back**: carbn-s ↓
      - **cutting** pain: carbn-s k2
- **Upper** part: sep ↓ spig ↓ sul-ac ↓ tub ↓
  - **cough** agg.; during: tub ↓
    - **stitching** pain: tub gk
  - **inspiration** agg.: tub ↓
    - **stitching** pain: tub gk
  - **lying** agg.: tub ↓
    - **stitching** pain: tub gk
  - **motion** agg.: tub ↓
    - **stitching** pain: tub gk
  - **pressure**:
    - **amel**.: tub ↓
      - **stitching** pain: tub gk
  - **raising** arm agg.: tub ↓
    - **stitching** pain: tub gk
  - **sitting** bent forward agg.: kali-i ↓
    - **stitching** pain: kali-i
  - **sprained**; as if: spig h1
  - **stitching** pain: sul-ac h2 tub gk
  - **talking** agg.: tub ↓
    - **stitching** pain: tub gk
  - **tearing** pain: sep h2
  - **walking**:
    - **amel**.: tub ↓
      - **stitching** pain: tub gk

- **left – Upper** part: ...
  - **extending** to:
    - **Shoulders**: tub ↓
      - **stitching** pain: tub gk
- **morning**: bov brom ↓ bry chinin-s colch ↓ con elaps fago ferr ↓ fl-ac lil-t lyc mang ↓ merc merc-c nat-c ↓ nat-s nit-ac nux-v petr-ra shn4• puls *Ran-b* *Rumx* ↓ sang sars ↓ sel ↓ sep sulph sumb thuj
  - **aching**: fago k* nit-ac k*
  - **bed** agg.; in: colch petr-ra shn4• phel rumx sil
    - **pressing** pain: phel k* sil k*
  - **burning**: nat-c k*
  - **drawing** pain: lil-t nux-v sang
  - **inspiration** agg.: sumb ↓
    - **tearing** pain: sumb
  - **pressing** pain: thuj k*
  - **rising** agg.; after: ran-b ↓
    - **pressing** pain: ran-b
  - **sore**: ran-b
  - **stitching** pain: bov k* brom *Bry* k* colch k* con k* ferr k* lyc k* mang h2 merc-c k* nat-s k* nit-ac k* puls k* *Rumx* sang k* sars k* sel sep k* sulph k*
  - **tearing** pain: sumb
  - **Below** clavicle: crat ↓
    - **pressing** pain: crat br1
- **forenoon**: am-m bamb-a ↓ bov ↓ cham coloc nat-c ↓ ran-b
  - **11** h: cham ↓ hydr
    - **stitching** pain: cham
  - **pressing** pain: ran-b k*
  - **stitching** pain: am-m k* bamb-a stb2.de• bov cham k* coloc k* nat-c a1 *Ran-b*
- **noon**: naja rumx
  - **cutting** pain: rumx
  - **stitching** pain: naja
- **afternoon**: alum bar-c canth chel coloc form ham ↓ kali-bi led lyc nat-c ↓ nat-sil ↓ nicc sars ↓ seneg ↓
  - **13** h: nicc sars
    - **stitching** pain: sars
  - **14** h: elaps
    - **stitching** pain: elaps
  - **15** h: nat-m ol-an rumx ↓
    - **stitching** pain: nat-m ol-an rumx
  - **16** h: **Lyc** k*
  - **burning**: alum h2 bar-c k* ham fd3.de• seneg k*
  - **drawing** pain: alum nat-sil fd3.de•
  - **rising** from stooping agg.: nicc ↓
    - **stitching** pain: nicc k*
  - **stitching** pain: bar-c k* canth k* chel k* coloc k* kali-bi k* led k* lyc k* nat-c a1 nicc k* sars k*
  - **tearing** pain: nicc
- **evening**: bar-c calc caust ↓ cocc ↓ dig digin ↓ dios euph graph ↓ hyper kali-c ↓ kali-n ↓ lyc mag-s mang ↓ mez mur-ac nat-m nat-sil ↓ ran-b sars ↓ *Sel* ↓ *Seneg* spong fd4.de sulph thuj zinc
  - **20** h: kali-n
    - **pressing** pain: kali-n
  - **22** h: colch ↓
    - **boring** pain: colch
  - **aching**: sulph k*
  - **bed** agg.; in: calad ↓ nat-c nat-p ↓ nit-ac rhus-t *Rumx* ↓
    - **boring** pain: rhus-t
    - **burning**: nat-p *Rumx*
    - **stitching** pain: calad k* nat-c k* nit-ac k*
  - **breathing** deep:
    - **amel**.: colch ↓
      - **boring** pain: colch
  - **burning**: bar-c h2 *Seneg* k*
  - **chill**; during: tarent ↓
    - **sore**: tarent

- **evening**: ...
  - **cutting** pain: mang$_{h2}$
  - **drawing** pain: nat-sil$_{fd3.de}$• seneg
  - **entering** house from open air, on: mag-s↓
    - **stitching** pain: mag-s$_{k}$*
  - **lying** agg.: ant-c↓
    - **pressing** pain: ant-c$_{h2}$
  - **pressing** pain: caust$_{h2}$ dig digin$_{a1}$ euph$_{k}$* mang$_{h2}$ ran-b$_{k}$* zinc
  - **sitting** agg.: seneg↓
    - **pressing** pain: seneg$_{k}$*
  - **sore**: *Ran-b* seneg
  - **stitching** pain: bar-c$_{k}$* calc$_{k}$* cocc graph$_{h2}$ hyper$_{k}$* kali-n$_{k}$* lyc$_{k}$* mur-ac$_{k}$* nat-m ran-b$_{k}$* sars$_{h2}$ *Sel* seneg$_{k}$* sulph thuj$_{k}$* zinc$_{k}$*
  - **tearing** pain: kali-c$_{h2}$
- **night**: am-c *Caust*↓ *Chel* chin↓ con graph iod kali-c↓ **Lyc**↓ myris *Puls*↓ rumx sil↓ *Sulph*↓
  - **22** h: colch
  - **midnight**:
    - **after**:
      - **4** h: chel↓
        - **stitching** pain: chel
  - **aching**: iod
  - **air**, on going into open: am-m↓
    - **pressing** pain: am-m
  - **bed** agg.; in: merc-i-f↓
    - **aching**: merc-i-f
  - **pressing** pain: myris$_{c1}$
  - **stitching** pain: am-c$_{k}$* *Caust* chin$_{h1}$ **Con**$_{k}$* graph$_{k}$* kali-c$_{h2}$ **Lyc**$_{k}$* *Puls*$_{k}$* *Rumx* sil$_{h2}$ *Sulph*$_{k}$*
  - **waking**; on: graph↓
    - **stitching** pain: graph$_{k}$*
- **accompanied** by | **respiration**; complaints of: **Acon**$_{bg2}$ *Bell*$_{bg2}$ **Bry**$_{bg2}$ merc$_{bg2}$ sel$_{bg2}$ *Squil*$_{bg2}$
- **aching**: am-c$_{k}$* *Arg-n* bry$_{k}$* chin cop ferr$_{k}$* fl-ac$_{k}$* hydrc$_{k}$* kali-bi$_{k}$* lil-t$_{k}$* mur-ac$_{k}$* naja nux-m$_{k}$* op$_{k}$* pall phyt$_{k}$* rhus-t$_{k}$* seneg sep sulph
- **air**; in open:
  - **agg.**: am-m
  - **amel.**: nat-m
- **ascending**:
  - **agg.**: kali-bi↓
    - **aching**: kali-bi$_{k}$*
  - **stairs**:
    - **agg.**: borx↓ kali-bi staph *Sulph*↓
      - **stitching** pain: borx *Staph*$_{k}$* *Sulph*
      - **tearing** pain: kali-bi
- **bending**:
  - **agg.**: alum↓ nat-m↓
    - **sore**: alum nat-m$_{h2}$
  - **backward**:
    - **agg.**: rhod staph↓
      - **cutting** pain: rhod$_{k}$*
      - **stitching** pain: staph$_{h1}$
  - **forward**:
    - **agg.**: aloe alum alumn
      - **stitching** pain: aloe
    - **amel.**: chinin-s$_{c1}$
  - **right**; to | **agg.**: cocc
- **blood** entered forcibly; as if: zinc$_{h2}$
- **blowing** the nose agg.: sumb
  - **tearing** pain: sumb
- **boring** pain: colch$_{k}$* kali-c$_{k}$* merc-i-f$_{k}$* mur-ac$_{h2}$ plan$_{k}$* seneg$_{k}$* staph$_{h1}$
- **breathing**:
  - **agg.**: ars↓ bry↓ calc↓ caps↓ cic↓ graph↓ iod↓ lyc↓ meny↓ nat-c↓ nat-m$_{h2}$ phos↓ puls↓ zinc↓
- **breathing – agg.**: ...
  - **drawing** pain: puls$_{h1}$
  - **pressing** pain: ars$_{h2}$
  - **sore**: iod$_{h}$ nat-m$_{h2}$
  - **stitching** pain: calc$_{h2}$ caps$_{h1}$* cic$_{h1}$ graph$_{h2}$* lyc$_{h2}$* meny$_{h1}$* nat-c$_{h2}$* phos$_{h2}$* zinc$_{h2}$*
  - **tearing** pain: bry puls
  - **deep**:
    - **agg.**: *Acon*$_{k}$* all-c↓ aloe↓ *Ant-c* arg-met *Arn* ars↓ aur aur-s↓ *Bad*↓ bar-c borx **Bry**$_{k}$* bufo calc calc-p canth caps carb-an carb-v cham chel chin chinin-s clem↓ *Colch*↓ *Crot-c*↓ *Crot-h*↓ cycl *Elaps*↓ ferr ferr-p fl-ac form graph grat *Guaj*↓ **Kali-c**$_{k}$* *Kali-n* kali-sil$_{k2}$ lyc *Meny* *Mez* *Nicc*↓ nit-ac oena olnd↓ ph-ac phos phyt plat *Ran-b*↓ rhus-t rumx seneg *Sil* spig↓ spong stann sulph sumb thuj verat
      - **pressing** pain: arg-met$_{h1}$ **Kali-c** ph-ac spong$_{h1}$ thuj
      - **stitching** pain: *Acon*$_{k}$* all-c aloe ant-c$_{k}$* arg-met *Arn* ars$_{h2}$ aur$_{k}$* aur-s$_{k2}$ *Bad* bar-c$_{k}$* borx *Bry*$_{k}$* bufo *Calc*$_{k}$* calc-p$_{k}$* canth caps$_{k}$* carb-an$_{k}$* carb-v$_{k}$* cham *Chel* *Chin* chinin-s clem *Colch* *Crot-c*$_{k}$* *Crot-h*$_{a1}$ cycl *Elaps* fl-ac$_{k}$* form$_{k}$* graph$_{k}$* grat *Guaj* *Kali-c*$_{k}$* *Kali-n*$_{k}$* kali-sil$_{k2}$ lyc$_{k}$* *Meny*$_{k}$* *Mez*$_{k}$* *Nicc* nit-ac$_{k}$* olnd *Ph-ac* plat *Ran-b* rhus-t$_{k}$* **Rumx** seneg$_{k}$* *Sil* stann$_{k}$* *Sulph*$_{k}$* thuj verat$_{k}$*
      - **tearing** pain: spig$_{h1}$
- **burning**: *Agar* ail all-c$_{k}$* carb-v$_{k2}$ iod$_{h}$ kali-bi$_{k}$* prun rumx sabin$_{k}$* seneg$_{k}$*
  - **upward**: stront-c
- **chill**; during: *Acon*↓ bry↓ *Nux-v*↓ tarent↓
  - **sore**: tarent
  - **stitching** pain: *Acon*$_{b7.de}$ bry$_{b7.de}$* *Nux-v*$_{b7a.de}$
- **cold**:
  - **air** agg.: *Kali-c*↓
    - **stitching** pain: *Kali-c*
  - **water**:
    - **amel.**: borx↓
      - **stitching** pain: borx$_{h2}$
- **coryza**; during: acon↓
  - **stitching** pain: acon$_{b7a.de}$
- **cough** agg.; during: *(↗right - cough)* acon↓ am-m↓ ambr↓ ant-t↓ apis *Arn*$_{k}$* ars aur↓ *Bell* *Borx*↓ **Bry**$_{k}$* calc-s cann-s↓ caps carb-an↓ **Card-m**↓ caust *Chel* chin↓ clem↓ coff con crot-h↓ cur↓ dios↓ dulc↓ ferr↓ ferr-p↓ kali-bi↓ *Kali-c*↓ kali-n lact lyc **Merc**$_{k}$* nat-m↓ nat-s *Phos*$_{k}$* psor *Puls*$_{k}$* rhus-t rumx↓ sabad seneg *Sep* **Squil** *Stann*↓ stram sul-i↓ **Sulph** tarent tritic-vg$_{fd5.de}$ verat xan$_{c1}$ zinc
  - **morning**: cassia-s$_{ccrh1}$•
  - **evening**: cassia-s$_{ccrh1}$•
  - **cutting** pain: nat-m$_{h2}$
  - **drawing** pain: caps$_{h1}$
  - **pressing** pain: sul-i$_{k2}$
  - **stitching** pain: acon$_{k}$* am-m$_{bg2}$ ambr$_{bg2}$ ant-t *Arn*$_{k}$* *Ars*$_{k}$* aur$_{k}$* *Bell*$_{bg2}$ *Borx*$_{k}$* **Bry**$_{k}$* cann-s *Caps*$_{k}$* carb-an$_{b4a.de}$ **Card-m** caust$_{k}$* *Chel* chin$_{k}$* clem coff$_{k}$* *Con*$_{k}$* crot-h cur dios$_{bg2}$ dulc ferr$_{bg2}$ ferr-p kali-bi$_{bg2}$ *Kali-c*$_{k}$* kali-n$_{k}$* *Lyc*$_{k}$* **Merc**$_{k}$* nat-s$_{k}$* phos$_{k}$* *Puls*$_{k}$* rhus-t$_{k}$* rumx sabad$_{k}$* seneg$_{k}$* *Sep*$_{k}$* squil$_{k}$* *Stann* *Sulph*$_{k}$* verat$_{b7a.de}$* zinc$_{k}$*
- **cutting** pain: all-s ang arg-met aur$_{h2}$ cann-s$_{k2}$ cedr *Con*$_{k}$* dulc falco-pe$_{nl2}$• hura kali-c$_{k}$* kali-n$_{k}$* laur$_{k}$* nat-ar ph-ac$_{h2}$ plb sabin$_{c1}$ sumb$_{k}$*
  - **knife**; as with a: tab$_{bg2}$
  - **tearing** pain: stann$_{h2}$
- **digging** pain: mang$_{h2}$
- **dinner** | **after**:
  - **agg.**: agar↓ bry canth iod↓ nat-p rat zinc
    - **burning**: agar
    - **pressing** pain: iod$_{h}$
    - **stitching** pain: bry canth rat zinc
  - **during**:
    - **agg.**: sil↓

- **dinner – during – agg.**: ...
    - **stitching** pain: sil$_{h2}$
- **drawing** pain: agar aur-m berb borx$_{h2}$ bry cadm-s *Caps* chel cocc kali-bi led nat-sil$_{fd3.de}$• petr rhus-t$_{h1}$ sil$_{h2}$ spong$_{h1}$ thuj
- **eating**; after: arg-n brom caust rat ↓
    - **stitching** pain: caust$_{k*}$ rat
- **eructations**:
    - **after**: nit-ac ↓
        - **pressing** pain: nit-ac$_{h2}$
    - **amel.**: kali-c ↓ nux-v ↓ sep ↓
        - **pressing** pain: kali-c$_{h2}$ nux-v sep
- **excitement** agg.: phos
    - **stitching** pain: phos$_{k*}$
- **exertion** agg.: alum am-m$_{bg1}$ *Borx* ↓ calc$_{bg1}$ ferr
    - **stitching** pain: alum$_{k*}$ *Borx* ferr$_{k*}$
- **expectoration**; during: *Ang* ↓
    - **pressing** pain: *Ang*$_{k*}$
- **expiration**:
    - **agg.**: ant-c ↓ ars ↓ chin ↓ cina ↓ iod ↓ mang ↓ mur-ac ↓ sep ↓ sil ↓ spig ↓ stann ↓ staph ↓ zinc ↓
        - **burning**: mang$_{h2}$
        - **stitching** pain: ant-c ars$_{h2}$ chin$_{h1}$ cina iod$_{h}$ mang$_{h2}$ mur-ac$_{h2}$ sep$_{h2}$ sil$_{h2}$ spig$_{k*}$ stann$_{h2}$ staph$_{k*}$ zinc$_{k*}$
    - **during**:
        - **agg.**: ambr aur ↓ carb-v$_{h2}$ cina raph spig staph tarax ↓ zinc
            - **pressing** pain: ambr$_{k*}$ aur$_{h2}$ tarax$_{h1}$ zinc$_{h2}$
- **fever**; during: *Acon*$_{b7a.de}$ *Bry*$_{b7.de}$ kali-c$_{b4a.de}$ nux-v$_{b7.de}$
- **gnawing** pain: lil-t$_{k*}$ olnd
- **inspiration**:
    - **agg.**: acon aesc agar ↓ alum ↓ arn ars asc-c$_{c1}$ *Asc-t* ↓ aspar aur aur-ar$_{k2}$ aur-s$_{k2}$ *Bad* ↓ *Bar-c* ↓ benz-ac borx bov brom **Bry**$_{k*}$ *Calc* ↓ calc-s canth caps carb-v ↓ carbn-s caust cham **Chel**$_{k*}$ cimic$_{hr1}$ cocc colch con cycl ↓ ferr-ma ↓ graph ↓ grat iod ↓ *Kali-c*$_{k*}$ kali-n led lyc lyss ↓ meny ↓ *Merc-c* ↓ merl ↓ mez mur-ac ↓ nat-ar **Nat-m** ↓ nat-s nicc oena op phyt plat$_{h2}$ plb *Ran-b* **Rumx** sabad ↓ sang sel$_{kr1}$* sep sil spig spong ↓ **Squil**$_{k*}$ sul-ac ↓ **Sulph** ↓ sumb tarax thuj ↓ viol-t xan$_{c1}$
        - **burning**: lyss *Rumx*
        - **cutting** pain: *Asc-t* aur$_{h2}$ carbn-s$_{k2}$ con thuj$_{h1}$
        - **pressing** pain: arn$_{k*}$ con$_{k*}$ grat$_{k*}$ iod$_{h}$ kali-c$_{h2}$ meny$_{h1}$ mur-ac$_{h2}$ squil$_{h1}$
        - **sore**: nat-ar
        - **stitching** pain: *Acon*$_{k*}$ agar alum *Ars*$_{k*}$ aspar$_{k*}$ aur$_{k*}$ *Bad Bar-c Borx*$_{k*}$ bov$_{k*}$ **Bry**$_{k*}$ *Calc* canth$_{k*}$ carb-v$_{k*}$ caust$_{k*}$ cham *Chel* cocc$_{k*}$ colch$_{k*}$ con$_{k*}$ cycl$_{a1}$ graph$_{h2}$ iod$_{h}$ **Kali-c**$_{k*}$ kali-n$_{k*}$ led$_{k*}$ *Lyc*$_{k*}$ lyss meny$_{h1}$ *Merc-c* merl **Nat-m** nat-s nicc$_{k*}$ op$_{k*}$ plb$_{k*}$ *Ran-b* **Rumx** sabad sep$_{k*}$ sil$_{k*}$ *Spig*$_{k*}$ spong$_{h1}$ **Squil**$_{k*}$ sul-ac **Sulph**$_{k*}$ tarax$_{k*}$ viol-t$_{k*}$
        - **tearing** pain: ferr-ma lyc sang spig$_{h1}$
    - **deep**:
        - **agg.**: arg-met ↓ chinin-ar ↓ mez ↓ *Oena* ↓ ph-ac ↓ phyt ↓ spong ↓ sumb ↓ tab ↓
            - **aching**: chinin-ar mez *Oena* phyt
            - **cutting** pain: arg-met ph-ac$_{h2}$ spong$_{k*}$ sumb$_{k*}$ tab
- **jar**, on: plat$_{h2}$
- **laughing** agg.: acon **Bry**$_{k*}$ laur nicc plat$_{h2}$ psor
    - **stitching** pain: acon laur$_{k*}$ nicc$_{k*}$
- **leaning** on table: con ↓
    - **pressing** pain: con$_{h2}$
    - **stitching** pain: con$_{h2}$
- **leaning** over: hell
- **lifting** agg.: alum$_{h2}$ arn bar-c brom phos
    - **stitching** pain: bar-c$_{k*}$ phos$_{k*}$
- **lying**:
    - **agg.**: caps *Puls*$_{k*}$ ran-b *Rumx* seneg
        - **aching**: caps$_{k*}$
        - **burning**: *Rumx*
- **lying – agg.**: ...
    - **stitching** pain: *Puls*$_{k*}$ *Rumx Seneg*
    - **back**; on:
        - **agg.**: *Rumx* ↓ *Sulph* ↓
            - **burning**: *Rumx*
            - **stitching** pain: *Sulph*
        - **amel.**: adam$_{skp7}$• cimic$_{hr1}$ merc$_{sne}$ *Phos*$_{k*}$
    - **bed**; in:
        - **agg.**: calad ↓ calc con symph ↓
            - **pressing** pain: calad calc$_{k*}$ con$_{k*}$ symph$_{fd3.de}$•
    - **side**; on:
        - **left**:
            - **agg.**: am-c camph ↓ cench$_{k2}$ eup-per **Phos**$_{k*}$ *Puls* ↓ *Rumx* ↓ samb ↓ seneg ↓ *Stann* ↓
                - **aching**: eup-per
                - **burning**: *Phos*$_{k*}$ seneg
                - **sore**: *Puls Rumx*
                - **stitching** pain: am-c camph samb$_{xxb1}$ *Stann*$_{k*}$
            - **amel.**: *Rumx* ↓
                - **burning**: *Rumx*
                - **stitching** pain: *Rumx*
        - **painful** side:
            - **agg.**: *Bell* nat-c ↓ *Nux-v Ran-b Rumx* [heroin$_{sdj2}$]
                - **stitching** pain: nat-c$_{h2}$
            - **amel.**: *Ambr Bry* calad ↓ *Kali-c* pyrog$_{jl2}$
                - **stitching** pain: **Bry** calad
        - **right**:
            - **agg.**: lyc lycps-v phyt *Rumx* ↓ seneg ↓
                - **aching**: phyt
                - **burning**: *Rumx* seneg
                - **stitching** pain: lyc *Rumx*
            - **amel.**: cench$_{k2}$
- **menses**:
    - **after**:
        - **agg.**: borx ↓
            - **pressing** pain: borx$_{h2}$
    - **before**:
        - **agg.**: puls
            - **stitching** pain: puls$_{k*}$
    - **during**:
        - **agg.**: borx ↓ *Croc* ↓ phos puls$_{k*}$ sul-ac ↓
            - **stitching** pain: borx *Croc* phos$_{k*}$ sul-ac
- **mental** exertion agg.: cham
    - **stitching** pain: cham
- **motion**:
    - **after**:
        - **agg.**: calc ↓ viol-t ↓
            - **pressing** pain: calc viol-t
    - **agg.**: alum ↓ aster bad brom **Bry**$_{k*}$ calc caust ↓ **Chel** chin ↓ cimic$_{cp}$ clem$_{a1}$ gamb graph hell hyper lyc mang ↓ meny ↓ ox-ac ↓ petr-ra$_{shn4}$• phos psor pyrog$_{jl2}$ *Ran-b*$_{k*}$ **Rumx** ↓ sabad sars sulph viol-t zinc [heroin$_{sdj2}$]
        - **burning**: mang$_{h2}$
        - **stitching** pain: alum *Bad* **Bry**$_{k*}$ calc$_{h2}$ caust$_{h2}$ *Chel* chin$_{h1}$ gamb graph hyper lyc mang$_{h2}$ meny ox-ac phos *Ran-b* **Rumx** sabad sars *Sulph*
        - **tearing** pain: *Bry*
    - **amel.**: aur-m-n *Euph* ↓ indg ↓ *Kali-c* ↓ *Seneg* ↓ sep ↓
        - **burning**: *Euph Seneg*$_{k*}$
        - **drawing** pain: sep$_{h2}$
        - **stitching** pain: euph indg *Kali-c Seneg*
    - **arm**; of:
        - **agg.**: *Bry* ↓ dig ↓ led ↓ nat-m$_{h2}$
            - **burning**: *Bry*$_{k*}$
            - **pressing** pain: dig$_{h2}$
            - **stitching** pain: led$_{h1}$
            - **Opposite** side of chest; pain in: dig$_{h2}$

- **motion**: ...
  - **violent** motion:
    - **agg.**: alum ↓
      - **pressing** pain: alum h2
- **palpitations**; during: sep
- **paroxysmal**: *Ox-ac Phos*
- **pressing** pain: alum k* *Ambr* k* ang k* arg-met b7a.de arn k* aur aur-s k2 benz-ac calc-p k* carb-v h2 *Caust* k* chin k* con h2 *Cor-r* hyos iod k* *Kali-c* k* lact *Lyc* k* *Meny* k* mez k* mur-ac h2 nat-m k* par k* ph-ac h2 phos sars h2 sep k* sil h2 sul-ac sul-i k2 symph fd3.de• vanil fd5.de verb h
  - **finger**; as from a: phos h2
  - **flatulence**; as from: meny h1
  - **intermittent**: zinc h2
  - **outward**: *Asaf* cina h1* dulc h1 *Valer* zinc h2
  - **plug**; as from a: *Anac*
  - **pulsating** pain: asar h1 verat h1
- **pressure**:
  - **agg.**: brom dulc ↓ mag-m ↓ mang ↓ meny merc-i-f plat h2 sul-ac tarax
    - **burning**: mang h2
    - **sore**: mag-m h2
    - **stitching** pain: dulc a1 meny k* merc-i-f k* sul-ac k* tarax k*
  - **amel.**: adam skp7• borx *Bry* k* chin ↓ cimic dulc ↓ graph ↓ mag-c ↓ melal-alt gya4 petr-ra shn4• *Phos* k* thuj ↓ verb ↓
    - **cutting** pain: dulc h2 thuj h1
    - **stitching** pain: chin h1 graph h2 mag-c h2 verb h
- **raising** arm agg.: borx ↓ nicc ↓ ran-b ↓
  - **stitching** pain: borx nicc k* ran-b
- **reading** agg.: euph ↓
  - **stitching** pain: euph h2
- **respiration**: aesc **Bry** k* *Chel* kali-m k2 nat-m h2 *Puls*
- **riding** | **agg.**:
  - **wagon**; in a: dig *Rumx* ↓
    - **stitching** pain: dig *Rumx*
  - **horse**; a:
    - **agg.**: nat-c
      - **stitching** pain: nat-c
- **rising**:
  - **after**:
    - **amel.**: kali-c
      - **stitching** pain: kali-c
  - **agg.**: puls
  - **sitting**; from:
    - **agg.**: kali-c nat-c phos ↓
      - **stitching** pain: kali-c nat-c phos h2
  - **stooping**; from | **after** | **agg.**: nicc
    - **agg.**: kali-c ↓
      - **burning**: kali-c h2
      - **stitching** pain: kali-c h2
- **rubbing**:
  - **agg.**: mang ↓
    - **burning**: mang h2
  - **amel.**: sep ↓
    - **drawing** pain: sep h2
- **scratching**:
  - **amel.**: plat ↓
    - **stitching** pain: plat k*
- **screaming**, from: cupr ↓
  - **stitching** pain: cupr k*
- **sitting**:
  - **agg.**: am-m bry chin dig digin ↓ dulc ↓ euph ↓ graph h2 indg ↓ kali-c ↓ led ↓ mur-ac ↓ nat-s nat-sil ↓ nit-ac paeon ph-ac plan seneg spig spong fd4.de staph
    - **burning**: ph-ac h2 *Seneg*
    - **cutting** pain: ph-ac k*
    - **drawing** pain: chin h1 nat-sil fd3.de• nit-ac
- **sitting – agg.**: ...
  - **pressing** pain: chin k* graph h2 paeon k*
  - **stitching** pain: am-m bry chin (non:dig slp) digin slp dulc a1 euph h2 indg kali-c h2 led h1 mur-ac h2 nat-s *Seneg* spong staph
  - **amel.**: calad ↓
    - **pressing** pain: calad
  - **bent** forward:
    - **agg.**: agar ↓ am-c anac dulc ↓ rhus-t ↓ spong ↓
      - **pressing** pain: anac h2 dulc h2 rhus-t h1
      - **stitching** pain: agar h2 spong h1
      - **tearing** pain: anac
    - **amel.**: *Chel Ran-b*
  - **erect**:
    - **agg.**: dig
      - **tearing** pain: dig
- **sitting** up in bed agg.: am-c nicc ↓
  - **burning**: nicc
  - **stitching** pain: am-c
- **sleep**:
  - **before**: sulph ↓
    - **stitching** pain: sulph
  - **during**: cupr
    - **stitching** pain: cupr k*
  - **going** to sleep; before: sulph
- **sneezing**:
  - **after**: borx cina crot-h merc thuj
    - **stitching** pain: borx crot-h k* *Merc* k* thuj k*
  - **agg.**: acon ↓ borx ↓ grat ↓
    - **stitching** pain: acon bg2 borx bg2 grat bg2
- **sore**: acon bg2 agar alum am-c am-m arg-n *Arn* bar-s k2 calc *Carb-v Chin* **Con** iod kali-i lac-ac nit-ac h2 ph-ac phos *Puls Ran-b* rhus-t rumx seneg stram zinc h2
- **standing**:
  - **agg.**: calc euph ↓ *Nat-s* sars ↓ stann *Valer* ↓ zinc
    - **cutting** pain: stann k*
    - **pressing** pain: calc k* *Valer*
    - **stitching** pain: euph h2 *Nat-s* k* sars h2 zinc
  - **still**:
    - **amel.**: thuj ↓
      - **cutting** pain: thuj h1
- **stepping** agg.: plat h2
- **stitching** pain: *Acon* k* aesc k* agar k* *Alum* k* *Am-c* k* *Am-m* k* ang k* *Apis Arg-met* k* arg-n *Arn Ars* asaf aur k* aur-ar k2 aur-s k2 *Bad* k* *Bar-c* k* bell k* *Borx* **Bry** k* calad k* *Calc* k* calc-sil k2 cann-s b7a.de* *Canth* k* **Card-m Caust** cedr *Cham* k* *Chel* k* *Chin* k* clem k* cocc *Coloc* k* *Con* k* croc k* crot-c a1 *Cupr* k* dig h2 *Dulc* k* elaps falco-pe nl2• ferr-p fl-ac k* gamb gran k* graph k* *Guaj Hyos* k* ign k* indg *Kali-bi* k* **Kali-c** k* *Kali-i* k* kali-n k* *Kali-p Kalm Lach* k* lachn k* laur k* lil-t k* lyc k* mang h2 med *Meny* k* *Mosch* k* nat-c k* **Nat-m** k* nat-p *Nat-s* k* nicc k* nit-ac h2 nux-v k* ol-an k* op k* par k* petr ph-ac *Phos* k* pic-ac k* plat k* *Plb* k* positr nl2• *Puls* k* **Ran-b** k* rhus-t k* rumx *Sabad* b7a.de sal-fr sle1• samb k* sars k* *Sel Sep* k* sil k* sphing a1 spig k* *Spong* k* **Squil** k* stann k* staph k* sul-ac k* *Sulph* k* sumb *Tab* k* *Tarax* k* thuj k* tub gk verat k* verb h *Zinc* k* zinc-p k2 [pop dhh1]
  - **drawing** pain: mang h2 spong h1
  - **flatulence**; as from: nit-ac h2
  - **itching**: chin h1 dig h2 spig h1
  - **outward**: *Arg-n* asaf spong
  - **pulsating** pain: con h2 dulc a1 lyc h2
  - **tearing** pain: led h1 nat-m h2
  - **upward**: gamb mur-ac nat-c
    - **downward**; and: mang h2
- **stool** | **after**:
  - **amel.**: thuj ↓
    - **pressing** pain: thuj k*
  - **before**: calc-s

- **stooping**:
  - **after**:
    - **agg.**: nat-s
      - **stitching** pain: nat-s$_{k*}$
  - **agg.**: am-c lyc mang ↓ nit-ac sep
    - **sore**: nit-ac$_{h2}$
    - **stitching** pain: *Am-c*$_{k*}$ lyc$_{k*}$ mang nit-ac$_{h2}$
  - **amel.**: chin ↓ mag-c ↓
    - **stitching** pain: chin$_{h1}$ mag-c$_{h2}$
- **stretching**:
  - **agg.**: nit-ac ↓
    - **stitching** pain: nit-ac$_{h2}$
  - **amel.**: zinc ↓
    - **stitching** pain: zinc$_{h2}$
- **stretching** out: nit-ac ↓
  - **sore**: nit-ac$_{h2}$
- **synchronous** with pulse: dig ↓
  - **stitching** pain: dig$_{h2}$
- **talking** agg.: **Borx**$_{k*}$ *Kali-n* rhus-t tab
  - **stitching** pain: **Borx** *Kali-n*$_{k*}$ rhus-t$_{k*}$ tab$_{k*}$
- **tearing** pain: *Acon* aur-m$_{k*}$ berb bry cann-s *Carb-v*$_{k*}$ caust chel *Cocc* euph graph$_{k*}$ grat hydr-ac kali-bi kali-c$_{h2}$ kali-sil$_{k2}$ lact laur *Lyc*$_{k*}$ plb$_{k*}$ puls$_{k*}$ *Sel* sep sil$_{k*}$ sumb zinc
  - **cramping**: con$_{h2}$
- **touch** agg.: am-c ↓ calc ↓ carb-v ↓ chin ↓ **Con** ↓ crot-h ↓ iod ↓ kali-i ↓ lac-ac ↓ *Ph-ac* ↓ phos ↓ **Ran-b** ↓ *Rhus-t* ↓ sulph$_{h2}$ tarent ↓ verat ↓
  - **burning**: ph-ac$_{h2}$
  - **cutting** pain: ph-ac$_{h2}$
  - **pressing** pain: carb-v$_{h2}$
  - **sore**: am-c calc carb-v **Con** iod kali-i lac-ac *Ph-ac* **Ran-b** *Rhus-t* sulph tarent verat$_{h1}$
  - **stitching** pain: chin$_{h1}$ crot-h$_{k*}$ phos$_{h2}$
- **turning** | **chest**:
  - **agg.**: brom ↓
    - **aching**: brom$_{k*}$
  - **side**; to:
    - **left**: *Rumx* ↓
      - **sore**: *Rumx*
    - **right**: rumx
- **using** arms: ham ↓
  - **aching**: ham
- **vexation** agg.: nat-m ↓ phos
  - **stitching** pain: nat-m$_{h2}$ *Phos*$_{k*}$
- **waking**; on: *Arg-n* graph
  - **aching**: *Arg-n*
- **walking**:
  - **agg.**: agar am-c brom cact camph caps ↓ cham cocc colch dig merl nat-m olnd ox-ac **Ran-b**$_{k*}$ rhus-t sars seneg spig spong ↓ stann sul-ac sulph tarax tarent thuj ↓ viol-t zinc
    - **aching**: brom$_{k*}$
    - **cutting** pain: stann$_{k*}$ thuj$_{h1}$
    - **drawing** pain: cocc
    - **pressing** pain: cact
    - **stitching** pain: agar am-c *Brom*$_{k*}$ *Camph*$_{k*}$ caps$_{h1}$ cham$_{k*}$ cocc$_{k*}$ colch$_{k*}$ dig merl nat-m$_{k*}$ olnd$_{k*}$ ox-ac$_{k*}$ **Ran-b**$_{k*}$ rhus-t$_{k*}$ sars$_{k*}$ seneg$_{k*}$ spig$_{k*}$ spong$_{h1}$ stann sul-ac$_{k*}$ *Sulph* tarax$_{k*}$ tarent$_{k*}$ *Viol-t*$_{k*}$ zinc$_{k*}$
  - **air**; in open:
    - **agg.**: con ↓ euph ↓ sars ↓ stann ↓
      - **stitching** pain: con$_{h2}$ euph$_{h2}$ sars$_{h2}$ stann$_{h2}$
    - **amel.**: kali-n$_{h2*}$
      - **stitching** pain: kali-n$_{h2}$
  - **amel.**: euph ↓ nat-m
    - **pressing** pain: nat-m$_{k*}$
    - **stitching** pain: euph$_{h2}$
- **walking**: ...
  - **rapidly**:
    - **agg.**: ang ↓
      - **pressing** pain: ang$_{h1}$
- **warm** | **applications** | **amel.**: adam$_{skp7}$•
  - **room** | **agg.**: mag-s nat-m
- **warmth**:
  - **amel.**:
    - **heat** amel.: phos
      - **stitching** pain: *Phos*$_{k*}$
- **wine**:
  - **after**: borx ↓
    - **stitching** pain: borx
  - **agg.**: *Borx*
- **writing** agg.: fago *Rumx* ↓
  - **stitching** pain: *Rumx*
- **yawning** agg.: nat-s
  - **stitching** pain: nat-s$_{k*}$
- ▽ **extending** to:
  - **Abdomen**: chel ↓
    - **drawing** pain: chel
    - **Lower**: nit-ac ↓
      - **stitching** pain: nit-ac$_{h2}$
  - **Arms**, toward: brom ↓ nat-m ↓
    - **stitching** pain: brom nat-m
  - **Axilla**: card-m ↓ meny ↓ sil ↓
    - **drawing** pain: card-m meny$_{h1}$ sil
  - **Back**: alumn ↓ arum-t ↓ bov ↓ chel ↓ *Chen-a* ↓ guaj ↓ hep ↓ *Kali-c* ↓ kali-n ↓ lyc ↓ mez ↓ nit-ac ↓ ox-ac ↓ par ↓ sil ↓ zinc ↓
    - **burning**: zinc
    - **drawing** pain: chel zinc
    - **lying**:
      - **side**; on | **left**:
        - **agg.**: *Kali-c* ↓
          - **stitching** pain: *Kali-c*
        - **right**:
          - **amel.**: *Kali-c* ↓
            - **stitching** pain: *Kali-c*
    - **stitching** pain: alumn arum-t bov chel *Chen-a* guaj hep$_{h2}$ *Kali-c* kali-n lyc mez nit-ac$_{h2}$ ox-ac par sil
  - **Elbow**: sil ↓
    - **stitching** pain: sil
  - **Fingers**: com ↓
    - **drawing** pain: com
  - **Hypochondrium**: berb ↓
    - **stitching** pain: berb
  - **Hypogastrium**: stann ↓
    - **drawing** pain: stann$_{h2}$
  - **Neck**: caps ↓ mur-ac ↓
    - **drawing** pain: caps mur-ac$_{h2}$
  - **Precordial** region: chin ↓
    - **stitching** pain: chin
  - **Sacral** region: thuj ↓
    - **stitching** pain: thuj
  - **Scapula**: arum-t ↓ brom ↓ *Chel* ↓ *Chen-a* ↓ kali-p ↓ lact ↓ *Nat-m* ↓ seneg ↓ **Sulph** ↓
    - **aching**: kali-p$_{k2}$
    - **drawing** pain: brom
    - **stitching** pain: arum-t *Chel* *Chen-a* lact *Nat-m* seneg **Sulph**$_{k*}$
  - **Scapula**; left: spig ↓
    - **tearing** pain: spig$_{h1}$
  - **Shoulder**: cact ↓
    - **drawing** pain: cact
  - **Shoulders**: indg ↓ *Kali-c* ↓ laur ↓ nat-m ↓ *Sang* ↓
    - **sore**: laur
    - **stitching** pain: indg *Kali-c*$_{k*}$ nat-m *Sang*$_{k*}$

• **extending** to: ...
⁝ **Side**; other: apis bg2 calc bg2 cimic bg2 gnaph bg2 mang bg2 rumx bg2 thuj bg2
⁝ **Sternum**: laur↓
: **stitching** pain: laur
⁝ **Submaxillary** gland: *Calc*↓
: **drawing** pain: *Calc*
: **stitching** pain: calc
⁝ **Throat**: caps↓
: **drawing** pain: caps a1
⁝ **Upper** arm; left: spig↓
: **tearing** pain: spig h1

○ • **External** chest: nat-c↓ sul-ac↓ thuj↓
⁝ **burning**: nat-c sul-ac thuj
⁝ **Spots**; in: am-m↓
: **burning**: am-m

• **False** ribs: sulph↓ thuj↓
⁝ **burning**: sulph thuj

• **Lower** part: agath-a↓ am-c↓ carb-v↓ kali-n↓ led↓ nit-ac↓ ph-ac↓
⁝ **right**: aloe↓ bad↓ bry↓ *Cann-s*↓ *Canth*↓ carb-v↓ *Card-m*↓ **Chel**↓ *Chen-a*↓ dig↓ ferr-p↓ **Kali-c**↓ *Lach*↓ lyc↓ mag-c↓ mag-m↓ *Merc*↓ ph-ac↓ *Phos*↓ rumx↓ sep↓ sul-ac↓ *Thuj*↓ verat↓
: **cough** agg.; during: chin-b↓
. **stitching** pain: chin-b c1
: **stitching** pain: aloe bad bry k* *Cann-s* *Canth* k* carb-v k* *Card-m* **Chel** *Chen-a* dig ferr-p **Kali-c** *Lach* lyc mag-c h2 mag-m k* *Merc* ph-ac h2 *Phos* rumx sep sul-ac k* *Thuj* k* verat
⁝ **left**: aesc↓ agath-a↓ arg-met↓ berb↓ bov↓ *Calc-p*↓ canth↓ cham↓ *Colch*↓ eupi↓ gels↓ kali-c↓ *Lact*↓ mag-c↓ *Nat-s*↓ nit-ac↓ ox-ac↓ sabad↓ samb↓ squil↓ stry↓ tarax↓
: **stitching** pain: aesc k* agath-a nl2• arg-met berb k* bov k* *Calc-p* canth cham k* *Colch* eupi k* gels k* kali-c h2 *Lact* mag-c h2 *Nat-s* nit-ac h2 ox-ac sabad samb h1 squil stry tarax
: **urination**:
. **amel.**: aesc↓
stitching pain: aesc
⁝ **morning**: carb-an↓
: **stitching** pain: carb-an k*
⁝ **afternoon**: gels↓
: **stitching** pain: gels k*
⁝ **evening**: coc-c↓ dig↓ mag-c↓
: **stitching** pain: coc-c k* dig k* mag-c h2
⁝ **expiration** agg.; during: squil↓
: **stitching** pain: squil h1
⁝ **inspiration** agg.: ph-ac↓
: **stitching** pain: ph-ac h2
⁝ **menses**; at beginning of: kali-n↓
: **stitching** pain: kali-n
⁝ **motion** agg.: **Bry**↓ *Chel*↓
: **stitching** pain: **Bry** *Chel* k*
⁝ **sitting** agg.: ph-ac↓
: **stitching** pain: ph-ac h2
⁝ **standing** agg.: mag-c↓
: **stitching** pain: mag-c h2
⁝ **stitching** pain: agath-a nl2• am-c carb-v k* kali-n k* led k* ph-ac k*
: **flatulence**; as from: nit-ac h2
⁝ **stooping** agg.: mag-c↓
: **stitching** pain: mag-c h2
⁝ **walking**:
: **amel.**: ph-ac↓
. **stitching** pain: ph-ac k*

• **Side** lain on: caps↓
⁝ **pressing** pain: caps h1*

• **Side** to side: *Cimic*↓
⁝ **cutting** pain: *Cimic*

• **Upper** part: phos↓
⁝ **stitching** pain: phos h2

- **Skin**; below the: caust↓ *Dros*↓ mag-m↓ *Phos*↓ puls↓ **Ran-b**↓ verat↓
• **ulcerative** pain: caust bg2 *Dros* b7a.de mag-m bg2 *Phos* b4.de* puls b7a.de **Ran-b** b7.de* verat b7.de*

- **Spot**; in a: *Led*↓
• **burning**: *Led* k*

○ • **Sternum**; under: seneg bg2

- **Spots**; in: agar bg2 *Am-c*↓ *Am-m*↓ aral↓ arg-n br1 bufo bg2 hippoc-k szs2 *Led*↓ mang↓ mur-ac↓ nat-m bg2 ran-b↓ seneg↓ zinc↓
• **burning**: *Am-c* b4a.de *Am-m* k* aral vh1 *Led* mang mur-ac a1 ran-b br1 seneg k* zinc

- **Spots**; in small: oci-sa sk4• psor↓ ran-b k2
• **pressing** pain: psor bg2

- **Sternum**: acon↓ adam↓ aesc↓ aeth↓ agar agath-a↓ agn↓ aids↓ alum↓ am-c c2 anac↓ ang↓ *Ant-t*↓ apis arg-met↓ arizon-l↓ *Arn*↓ **Ars**↓ ars-h↓ ars-s-f↓ asaf astac↓ **Aur**↓ aur-ar k2 **Aur-m**↓ aur-s↓ aza br1 bamb-a stb2.de• bapt↓ *Bell* k* benz-ac↓ bism↓ borx bov↓ brom↓ *Bry* k* cact↓ calam sa3• *Calc*↓ calc-p calc-s camph↓ cann-xyz↓ *Canth*↓ caps carb-an carbn-s↓ *Carl*↓ cartl-s↓ **Caust**↓ cench↓ cham↓ chel↓ chin↓ chir-fl gya2 choc↓ cimic tl1 cina tl1 clem↓ cocc coloc↓ con cop↓ *Crot-c*↓ crot-h↓ crot-t↓ *Cycl*↓ *Dig*↓ dios br1 dros↓ dulc elat↓ euph↓ *Euphr*↓ eupi↓ falco-pe↓ *Ferr*↓ *Ferr-ar* fl-ac gamb↓ graph↓ gymno↓ ham↓ hell↓ hep↓ heroin↓ hir↓ hura hydr-ac↓ hydrog↓ ictod↓ ind↓ indg↓ inul↓ *Jug-c* kali-bi mrr1 kali-i *Kali-m*↓ kali-n↓ kali-p fd1.de• kali-s fd4.de kalm kola stb3• *Kreos* *Lac-ac*↓ lac-h↓ lac-lup↓ lac-v c2 lach lact↓ laur↓ led lipp↓ *Lyc*↓ lyss↓ mag-c↓ mag-m↓ mag-s↓ *Manc* mang↓ melal-alt↓ meny↓ *Merc*↓ merc-act↓ mez↓ morph mur-ac naja↓ nat-c↓ nat-m h2 nat-p tl1 nat-sil↓ nit-ac nit-s-d↓ olib-sac↓ *Olnd*↓ osm c2 ox-ac ozone↓ paeon c2 par↓ petr↓ ph-ac tl1 **Phos**↓ plb↓ pop↓ propr sa3• psor↓ ptel↓ *Puls* *Ran-b*↓ ran-s c2 rheum↓ rhus-t rhus-v↓ rumx↓ *Ruta* c2 sabin↓ sang↓ sars↓ scut↓ *Seneg*↓ sep↓ sil↓ spig↓ spong fd4.de squil↓ stann↓ staph↓ stram↓ stront-c c2 suis-pan rly4• sul-ac↓ *Sulph* k* symph↓ tab↓ tarax *Ter* *Thuj*↓ thyr↓ trios rsj11• tritic-vg fd5.de vanil fd5.de verat↓ verb↓ vinc↓ viol-t↓ zinc↓ zing [spect dfg1]

○ • **Left** of sternum; at: rheum↓
⁝ **burning**: rheum h

• **daytime**: *Calc-p*↓ nux-v↓
⁝ **stitching** pain: *Calc-p* nux-v

• **morning**: led↓ lyc↓ mang↓ nat-m↓ petr↓ sacch-a↓ sars↓ sulph↓ vanil↓
⁝ **pressing** pain: petr h2* sacch-a fd2.de• vanil fd5.de
⁝ **sore**: mang a1
⁝ **stitching** pain: led lyc nat-m sars sulph

• **afternoon**: borx h2 dulc↓ fl-ac ham↓ kali-i kali-p fd1.de• lyc↓ nat-m↓ nux-v↓ plb↓
⁝ **16** h: lyc↓
: **stitching** pain: lyc
⁝ **pressing** pain: fl-ac ham fd3.de• kali-i nat-m a1
⁝ **stitching** pain: dulc fd4.de lyc k* nux-v k* plb k*

• **evening**: acon↓ alum↓ bov↓ dulc↓ lyc↓ mag-c↓ mur-ac↓ sul-ac↓ symph↓
⁝ **bed** agg.; in: nat-c↓ sul-ac↓ thuj↓
: **stitching** pain: nat-c h2 sul-ac thuj
⁝ **inspiration** agg.: kali-c↓
: **stitching** pain: kali-c
⁝ **pressing** pain: alum h2* mur-ac h2
⁝ **sitting** agg.: mag-c↓
: **stitching** pain: mag-c
⁝ **stitching** pain: acon k* bov k* dulc fd4.de lyc mag-c k* sul-ac h2 symph fd3.de•

• **night**: am-c↓ chin petr↓
⁝ **midnight**:
: **after**: merc-c↓
. **tearing** pain: merc-c k*
⁝ **bed** agg.; in: ferr↓ ozone↓
: **stitching** pain: ferr k* ozone sde2•
⁝ **lying** down agg.: stram↓
: **cutting** pain: stram k*
⁝ **pressing** pain: am-c h2 petr h2

Chest

- **aching**: adam skp7• **Bry** cina a1
- **ascending**:
  - **agg.**: *Jug-c* ran-b ↓
    - **sore**: ran-b
  - **hills**:
    - **agg.**: ran-b ↓ rat ↓
      - **stitching** pain: ran-b rat k*
- **bending**:
  - **agg.**: tell rsj10•
  - **forward**:
    - **agg.**: dig ↓
      - **cramping**: dig h2
- **blow**; pain as from a | **door** had closed there; as if a: aids nl2•
- **breathing** deep agg.: agn a1* arg-met ↓ arn ↓ bamb-a ↓ bapt ↓ borx ↓ *Bry* ↓ caps ↓ carb-v ↓ *Caust* chin ↓ cina ↓ dulc ↓ hep ↓ lyc *Manc* ↓ nat-m psor rumx ↓ sil ↓ tell rsj10•
  - **pressing** pain: arg-met h1 borx h2
  - **stitching** pain: arg-met h1 arn bamb-a stb2.de• bapt borx h2 *Bry* k* caps carb-v **Caust** k* chin cina dulc fd4.de hep lyc *Manc* *Nat-m* k* psor rumx sil
- **burning**: aeth a1 agar h2 agath-a nl2• ars h2 asaf k2 bamb-a stb2.de• bov k* canth k* cham k* chel k* clem k* con h2 hura ind *Kali-bi* k* laur k* mag-s *Merc* mez k* mur-ac k* puls h1 sang sep k* stront-c sk4• sulph k* tarax h1 ter k* zinc k*
- **contracting**: dig h2 tritic-vg fd5.de
- **convulsive**: dig
- **coryza**; before: jug-c vml3•
- **cough**:
  - **after**: *Ferr* ↓
    - **burning**: *Ferr*
  - **during**:
    - **agg.**: am-c b4.de* ars bg2 bell k* beryl tpw5 **Bry** k* chel *Chin* k* con ↓ cor-r **Kali-bi** kali-c bg2 *Kali-i* kali-n *Kreos* mez b4.de* *Mur-ac* ↓ osm ox-ac petr b4a.de ph-ac *Phos* k* *Phyt* psor k* rumx *Sang* k* sep b4.de* sil b4.de* staph k* *Sulph* k* thuj
      - **sore**: *Mur-ac*
      - **stitching** pain: am-c *Ars* k* bell k* beryl tpw5 **Bry** k* con petr *Psor* k* sil sulph h2
  - **with**: chin ↓ *Kali-i* ↓ osm ↓ ox-ac ↓ *Phos* ↓ psor ↓
    - **tearing** pain: chin *Kali-i* osm ox-ac *Phos* psor
- **cramping**: cartl-s rly4• dig h2
- **cutting** pain: *Calc-p* elat hr1 manc mang a1 nat-c h2 petr phos rhus-v sep bg2 stram k* thuj bg2 verb
  - **knife** down sternum; like someone took a: lac-lup hrn2•
- **digging** pain: led k*
- **dinner**; after: borx ↓ phos ↓ sil ↓
  - **burning**: phos h2
  - **pressing** pain: borx h2
  - **stitching** pain: borx h2 sil h2
- **drawing** pain: dig h2 dulc nit-ac puls h1 spong fd4.de
- **drinking**:
  - **after**:
    - **agg.**: chin ↓ verat ↓
      - **pressing** pain: verat h1
      - **stitching** pain: chin h1
  - **agg.**: sep
  - **beer**: sep ↓
    - **burning**: sep
- **dull** pain: bapt a1 mang h2 melal-alt gya4
- **eating**:
  - **after**:
    - **agg.**: chin con hyos ↓ *Jug-c* verat ↓ zinc ↓
      - **pressing** pain: chin con h2 hyos h1 verat k* zinc
  - **agg.**: anac ↓
    - **pressing** pain: anac h2
- **eating**: ...
  - **while**:
    - **agg.**: zinc ↓
      - **stitching** pain: zinc
- **entering** room from open air: sul-ac ↓
  - **stitching** pain: sul-ac h2
- **eructations**:
  - **agg.**: kali-c ↓ mag-m ↓
    - **stitching** pain: kali-c h2 mag-m h2
  - **amel.**: petr ↓ phos ↓
    - **cramping**: phos
    - **pressing** pain: petr h2
- **exertion** agg.: *Caust* ↓
  - **stitching** pain: *Caust* k*
- **expiration**:
  - **agg.**: caust ↓
    - **stitching** pain: caust h2
  - **during**:
    - **agg.**: anac ↓ tarax ↓
      - **burning**: tarax h1
      - **pressing** pain: anac h2 tarax h1
- **flatus**; passing:
  - **amel.**: stram ↓
    - **cutting** pain: stram
- **gnawing** pain: par k*
- **griping** pain: bry bg2 puls h1
- **inspiration**:
  - **agg.**: agar ↓ borx ↓ bry caps chel dulc ↓ euph ↓ kali-p fd1.de• laur *Manc* ↓ *Nat-m* ↓ phos ↓ sil ↓ vanil ↓
    - **pressing** pain: agar h2 borx h2
    - **stitching** pain: dulc fd4.de euph h2 *Manc* *Nat-m* phos h2 sil h2 vanil fd5.de
  - **amel.**: nat-c ↓
    - **cutting** pain: nat-c h2
    - **sore**: nat-c h2
- **laughing** agg.: mur-ac ↓
  - **sore**: mur-ac h2
- **lifting** agg.: **Caust** ↓
  - **stitching** pain: **Caust** k*
- **lying** on left side agg.: visc c1
- **motion**:
  - **agg.**: arg-met ↓ *Bry* carb-an ↓ led nat-m ↓ ph-ac h2 ruta ↓
    - **pressing** pain: arg-met led nat-m h2
    - **stitching** pain: carb-an k* ruta
  - **amel.**: lyc ↓ nat-c ↓ phos ↓
    - **cutting** pain: nat-c h2
    - **sore**: nat-c h2
    - **stitching** pain: lyc phos h2
  - **head**; of | **agg.**: tarax h1
  - **jaw**; of lower | **agg.**: tarax h1
- **paroxysmal**: nat-m
- **pressing** pain: agar k* agath-a nl2• agn k* alum k* anac k* *Ant-t* arg-met k* arn h1 **Ars** k* ars-h hr1 asaf k* astac k* **Aur** k* aur-ar k2 **Aur-m** k* aur-s k2 bell h1 borx h2 bov k* brom k* *Bry* k* calc k* *Calc-p* k* camph h1 canth k* *Carl* a1 cench k2 chel k* cocc k* coloc h2 con k* cop k* crot-t k* *Cycl* k* dulc fd4.de *Euphr* k* eupi falco-pe nl2• *Ferr* k* gamb gymno ham fd3.de• hir skp7• ictod *Kali-m* kali-p fd1.de• kali-s fd4.de *Kalm* k* *Kreos* k* *Lac-ac* hr1 lac-h htj1• lact laur k* led k* lipp a1 lyss k* mag-m h2 meny h1* merc-act c2 mur-ac h2 nat-m nit-s-d a1 olib-sac wmh1 petr k* **Phos** k* ran-b k* rheum h rhus-t *Ruta* sabin c1 sars k* scut c1 *Seneg* k* sep h2 sil h2 staph h1 sulph k* tab k* thuj k* vanil fd5.de verat k* vinc a1 zinc k*
  - **regular** intermittent: verat h1
- **pressure**:
  - **agg.**: agath-a ↓ hir ↓ manc ph-ac [tax jsj7]
    - **burning**: agath-a nl2•

- **pressure – agg.**: ...
  - **pressing** pain: hir skp7•
  - **amel.**: chin ↓ kreos hr1*
    - **pressing** pain: chin h1
- **processus** xiphoideus | **pressing** pain (See xiphoid - pressing)
- **raising** arm agg.: chin
  - **pressing** pain: chin k*
- **raw**; as if: hell h1
- **respiration**: caps hep manc
- **rubbing**; after: led
- **scraped**; as if: led b7.de*
- **scratching** pain: mez h2
- **sitting**:
  - **agg.**: *Con* ↓ dulc ↓ euph ↓ *Indg* ↓ kali-i ↓ seneg ↓
    - **pressing** pain: euph h2 seneg
    - **stitching** pain: *Con* dulc h2* euph h2 *Indg* kali-i
  - **bent** forward:
    - **agg.**: chin kalm rhus-t
      - **pressing** pain: chin h1
      - **stitching** pain: *Rhus-t* k*
- **smoking** agg.; after: thuj
- **sneezing** agg.: bry ↓
  - **stitching** pain: bry
- **sore**: acon h1* adam skp7• arizon-l nl2• benz-ac borx hr1 bry *Calc-p* k* cann-xyz bg2 choc srj3• dros *Kreos* led k* mez mur-ac k* naja k* nat-c h2* nat-m h2* nat-sil fd3.de• *Osm* ph-ac k* psor bg2 ptel bg2* *Ran-b* k* rumx ruta c1 sabin k* sars staph h1 stront-c k* sul-ac sulph bg2 thyr bg1 zinc
- **sprained**; as if: rumx
- **squeezed**; as if: hydrog srj2•
- **standing** agg.: camph ↓ con ↓ euph ↓ plb ↓
  - **pressing** pain: camph h1 con h2 euph h2
  - **stitching** pain: euph h2 plb k*
- **stitching** pain: acon k* aesc aeth agar alum am-c k* ang b7a.de* arg-met k* *Arn* k* **Ars** k* ars-s-f k2 aur k* aur-ar k2 aur-s k2 bamb-a stb2.de• *Bell* b4.de* bism bov k* *Bry* k* cact *Calc* k* *Calc-p* *Canth* k* caps b7.de* carb-an carbn-s **Caust** k* cham chel chin b7.de* *Con* k* *Crot-c* crot-h cycl h1 *Dulc* k* euph b4a.de* ferr k* gamb graph k* hep k* hydr-ac hydrog srj2• indg k* inul br1 *Kali-bi* k* *Kali-i* k* kali-n kola stb3• lact laur k* *Lyc* k* mag-c k* mag-m *Manc* mang k* meny h1 mur-ac h2 nat-c h2 *Nat-m* k* nit-ac k* *Olnd* k* ox-ac k2 ozone sde2• petr b4a.de ph-ac k* *Phos* k* plb k* puls k* rheum *Rhus-t* k* ruta h1* sabin b7.de* sars k* *Seneg* sil spig b7.de* squil stann h2 staph stront-c sul-ac *Sulph* k* symph fd3.de• tab k* tarax k* *Thuj* k* vanil fd5.de vinc k* viol-t k* zinc k* [heroin sdj2 pop dhh1]
  - **downward**: chel squil
  - **itching**: staph h1
  - **upward**: *Ars* carbn-s
- **stooping** agg.: arg-met ↓ carb-v h2 dig h2 *Kalm* ph-ac h2 ran-b zinc ↓
  - **pressing** pain: arg-met *Kalm*
  - **stitching** pain: zinc
- **stretching** agg.: staph
- **swallowing** liquids agg.: kali-c ↓
  - **stitching** pain: kali-c h2
- **talking** agg.: alum ↓ mur-ac ↓ stram tax ↓
  - **pressing** pain: stram h1
  - **sore**: mur-ac h2 [tax jsj7]
  - **stitching** pain: alum
- **tearing** pain: aesc aur k* *Calc-p* k* *Dig* dulc h2* *Lyc* osm ox-ac k2 phos k* psor
- **touch** agg.: cann-s ↓ carb-v h2 cimx ↓ cop ↓ ignis-alc es2• mur-ac h2 ph-ac h2 psor ↓ *Ran-b* ↓ ruta ↓ staph h1 stront-c ↓ sul-ac ↓ sulph h2 tax ↓
  - **sore**: cann-s cimx cop ignis-alc es2• mur-ac ph-ac psor *Ran-b* ruta c1 stront-c sul-ac [tax jsj7]
  - **stitching** pain: sulph h2
- **twisting** pain: ph-ac ptk1
- **ulcerative** pain: staph h1
- **walking**:
  - **agg.**: alum ↓ arn ↓ *Caps* hr1 *Cic* ↓ cimic tl1 cinnb ↓ coc-c cocc ↓ hep ↓ *Jug-c* kali-s fd4.de mag-c ↓ psor ↓ sulph ↓
    - **pressing** pain: alum h2* arn h1 cic h1 coc-c sulph h2
    - **sore**: *Cic*
    - **stitching** pain: arn k* cinnb cocc c1 hep k* mag-c psor
  - **beginning** to walk: sulph ↓
    - **pressing** pain: sulph h2
- **writing** agg.: asaf ↓ cina ↓
  - **pinching** pain: cina a1
  - **pressing** pain: asaf k*
- **yawning** agg.: bell ↓ mur-ac ↓
  - **sore**: mur-ac h2
  - **stitching** pain: bell h1
- ▽ **extending** to:
  - **Arms**: ox-ac ↓
    - **tearing** pain: ox-ac k2
  - **Axilla**: kali-n ↓
    - **stitching** pain: kali-n
  - **Back**: chin ↓ *Con* ↓ dulc fd4.de *Kali-bi* *Kali-i* ↓ kali-s fd4.de lac-h htj1• laur ↓ ox-ac phyt
    - **stitching** pain: chin h1 *Con* dulc h2 **Kali-bi** *Kali-i* laur
  - **Elbow**: thuj ↓
    - **stitching** pain: thuj
  - **Lumbar** region: zinc ↓
    - **stitching** pain: zinc h2
  - **Scapula**: dulc fd4.de phos bg1
  - **Scapula**; right: elat ↓ phos ↓
    - **cutting** pain: elat hr1 phos
    - **stitching** pain: phos
  - **Shoulders**: *Kali-i* ↓ ox-ac ↓
    - **stitching** pain: *Kali-i* ox-ac k2
  - **Spine**: dulc ↓ elat ↓
    - **cutting** pain: dulc elat hr1
  - **Throat**: zinc bg1
- ○ **Above**: syph ↓
  - **pressing** pain: syph jl2
- **Behind**: acon ↓ *Agar* allox tpw4 alum ↓ ap-g bro1 *Arg-n* ars bro1 asc-t a1* aster bro1 aur bro1 aur-m k2 aza bro1 bamb-a ↓ *Bry* bro1 *Cact* camph ↓ carc tpw2* card-m bro1 *Caust* bro1 cham ↓ *Chel* k* chin ↓ *Cimx* con bro1 cystein-l ↓ *Dios* bro1 dream-p sdj1• dulc h1 *Eup-per* k* *Euphr* ↓ ferr ↓ fuma-ac ↓ iber c1 ind iod ↓ jug-r bro1 kali-bi kali-n bro1 kali-p ↓ kalm bro1 *Kreos* bro1 lac-h ↓ lact-v bro1 led ↓ lob mez ↓ mim-p rsj8• morph bro1 mur-ac ↓ nat-c ↓ nit-ac bro1 nit-s-d bro1 osm bro1 ox-ac k2 ph-ac bro1 phel bro1 *Phos* k* plac ↓ polys ↓ psor bro1 puls bro1 pyrid ↓ pyrog k2 *Ran-b* bro1 *Ran-s* c2* rhus-t ↓ *Rumx* k* ruta bro1* samb bro1 **Sang** k* sangin-n bro1 sel rsj9• *Seneg* sep bro1 *Sil* k* spig bro1 spong fd4.de sulph bro1 symph ↓ *Syph* tax ↓ ter tril-p bro1 vanil fd5.de zinc ↓
  - **right**: aq-mar skp7•
  - **morning**: nat-c ↓ vanil ↓
    - **pressing** pain: nat-c h2 vanil fd5.de
  - **evening**: stroph-s ↓
    - **aching**: stroph-s sp1
  - **night**: aur br1
    - **midnight**:
      - **before**:
        - **22**.15 h: aq-mar skp7•
          - **lasting** 15 minutes: aq-mar skp7•
  - **aching**: pyrog k2
  - **ascending** agg.: **Aur** ↓ **Aur-m** ↓ spig ↓
    - **crushing**: **Aur** **Aur-m** spig hr1
    - **pressing** pain: **Aur** **Aur-m**
  - **breathing**:
    - **agg.**: kali-c ↓
      - **pressing** pain: kali-c h2

- **Behind – breathing**: ...
  - **deep**:
    - **agg.**: allox↓ nat-c↓ olib-sac↓
      - **cramping**: allox sp1
      - **pressing** pain: nat-c h2 olib-sac wmh1
  - **burning**: *(↗under - burning)* bamb-a stb2.de• polys sk4• pyrid rly4• rhus-t hr1
  - **cough**:
    - **after**: *Euphr*↓ hep↓
      - **pressing** pain: *Euphr* hep
    - **during**:
      - **agg.**●: beryl sp1 **Bry** cadm-met sp1 carc mlr1• **Caust** *Chel* chin cina daph *Euphr* hep *Kali-bi* kali-n↓ osm *Phos* psor jl2 rumx *Sang* k* staph
        - **cutting** pain: kali-n
    - **with**: kali-n↓
      - **pressing** pain: kali-n c1
  - **cutting** pain: asc-t a1* fuma-ac rly4•
  - **drawing** pain: chin h1 kali-p fd1.de• spong fd4.de [tax jsj7]
  - **drinking** agg.: kali-c
  - **dull** pain: lac-h sk4•
  - **eructations** agg.: kali-c↓
    - **pressing** pain: kali-c h2
  - **food** had lodged, as if: all-c *Led*
  - **griping** pain: *Cact* led
  - **inspiration** agg.: allox tpw4 *Chel Kali-c Manc* sel rsj9• sil h2
  - **motion** agg.: bry↓ sel rsj9•
    - **pressing** pain: bry
  - **pressing** pain: acon alum h2 **Aur Aur-m** bamb-a stb2.de• camph h1 caust h2 cham h1 *Chel* k* dulc h2* *Euphr* ferr a1 kali-n c1 kali-p fd1.de• mez h2 nat-c h2 nit-s-d a1* ph-ac h2* *Phos* plac rzf5• pyrid rly4• rumx ruta fd4.de samb h1 spong fd4.de symph fd3.de• *Syph* k* ter vanil fd5.de
    - **intermittent**: dulc h2
  - **raw**; as if: iod h kali-n h2
  - **rheumatic**: merc br1
  - **running** agg.: stroph-s↓
    - **aching**: stroph-s sp1
  - **sitting**:
    - **agg.**: con↓
      - **pressing** pain: con k*
    - **erect**:
      - **amel.**: kalm
        - **pressing** pain: *Kalm*
  - **sore**: bry bg2
  - **squeezed**; as if: dulc h1
  - **stitching** pain: alum h2 cystein-l rly4• euphr h2 mur-ac h2 ruta fd4.de vanil fd5.de zinc h2
  - **swallowing** agg.: all-c cann-i↓ phos
    - **cutting** pain: cann-i k*
  - **walking** rapidly agg.: aur-m k2 **Seneg** stroph-s↓
    - **aching**: stroph-s sp1
  - **extending** to:
    - **Arms**: dios br1
      - **And** shoulders: ox-ac k2
    - **Axilla** | **right**: sel rsj9•
    - **Back**: ang c1 *Con* **Kali-bi** k* stict
    - **Sides**: rumx bg1 sulph bg1
      - **right**: sel rsj9•
- **Beside** sternum: gels↓
  - **burning**: gels psa
- **Border**:
  - **right**:
    - **morning**: kali-c↓
      - **pressing** pain: kali-c h2
- **Left** side; along the: bamb-a↓
  - **stitching** pain: bamb-a stb2.de•
- **Lower** part: *Cic*↓ kali-s fd4.de *Nit-ac*↓ rauw↓ thuj↓ vanil fd5.de
- **Lower** part: ...
  - **boring** pain: thuj h1
  - **cough**; from: am-c h2
  - **cramping**: rauw tpw8
  - **exertion** agg.: rauw↓
    - **cramping**: rauw tpw8*
  - **sore**: *Cic Nit-ac*
  - **extending** to:
    - **left**: psil↓
      - **sore**: psil ft1
  - **Under**: gels↓
    - **burning**: gels
- **Over** sternum: ven-m↓
  - **sore**: ven-m rsj12•
- **Spots**; in: anac bg1 carb-v h2 puls ruta sacch-a fd2.de•
- **Sternoclavicular** joint: til↓
  - **sore**: til c1
- **Sternocostal** joints: chin↓
  - **stitching** pain: chin h1
- **Tip** of: bamb-a stb2.de•
- **Under**: *Acon*↓ aloe bg2 anac↓ arag↓ *Ars*↓ *Asaf*↓ beryl↓ *Carb-v*↓ *Cham*↓ cina↓ clem↓ coc-c↓ con↓ cortico↓ cortiso↓ cund↓ dros↓ echi↓ *Eup-per*↓ ger-i↓ hippoc-k↓ kali-bi bg2 kola stb3• *Lach*↓ mag-s↓ manc↓ mang↓ mez↓ *Phos*↓ podo↓ psor↓ ran-s↓ **Rumx**↓ *Sang*↓ *Sangin-n*↓ seneg↓ sinus↓ staph↓
  - **aching**: manc ptk1 *Rumx* ptk1
  - **burning**: *(↗behind - burning)* *Acon Ars Asaf* beryl sp1 *Carb-v Cham* k* clem coc-c k* cund br1 echi ger-i rly4• hippoc-k szs2 *Lach* mag-s mang mez h2 *Phos* k* rumx k2 *Sang* k* *Sangin-n* br1 seneg
  - **cold** drinks:
    - **amel.**: hippoc-k↓
      - **burning**: hippoc-k szs2
  - **cough** agg.; during: am-c↓ **Bry**↓ chel↓ cina↓ iod↓ osm↓ psor↓ *Rumx*↓ staph↓
    - **sore**: am-c **Bry** chel cina iod osm psor k* *Rumx* staph h1
  - **digging** pain: cina h1*
  - **exertion** agg.: trios rsj11•
  - **inspiration** agg.: *Eup-per*↓
    - **sore**: *Eup-per*
  - **lodged**; as if food had: led ptk1 lyc ptk1
  - **motion** agg.: seneg↓
    - **burning**: seneg
  - **raw**; as if: kali-bi ptk1
  - **sore**: anac bg1 arag br1 con h2 *Eup-per* kola stb3• podo fd3.de• ran-s ptk1 **Rumx** sinus rly4• staph h1
  - **tearing** pain: cortico tpw7 cortiso sp1
  - **turning** body: *Eup-per*↓
    - **sore**: *Eup-per*
  - **ulcerative** pain: dros bg2 psor bg2*
  - **waking**; on: trios rsj11•
  - **warm** drinks agg.: ter↓
    - **burning**: ter c1
  - **extending** to:
    - **Clavicle**; left: phos↓
      - **burning**: phos h2
    - **Mouth**: cham↓
      - **burning**: cham h1
    - **Shoulder**:
      - **cough** agg.; during: *Kali-bi*↓
        - **burning**: *Kali-bi*
  - **Spot**; in a: anac↓
    - **sore**: anac h2
- **Upper** part: ars h2 beryl tpw5 plat↓ stann↓ sulph h2
  - **left**: phos↓ sep↓
    - **pressing** pain: phos h2 sep h2
  - **cough** agg.; during: beryl tpw5 sep h2 sil h2
    - **bending** head backward agg.: beryl↓

- **Upper** part – **cough** agg.; during – **bending** head backward agg.: ...
  - . **cutting** pain: beryl tpw5
  - : **cutting** pain: beryl tpw5
  - : **smoking** agg.: beryl ↓
    - . **cutting** pain: beryl tpw5
  - ⁝ **pressing** pain: plat h2 stann h2
- **Xiphoid** cartilage: stann ↓ sulph ↓ thuj ↓ vanil ↓
  - ⁝ **bursting** pain: thuj bg1
  - ⁝ **cough** agg.; during: kali-c ↓
    - : **pressing** pain: kali-c h2
  - ⁝ **inspiration** agg.: kali-c ↓
    - : **pressing** pain: kali-c h2
  - ⁝ **pressing** pain: vanil fd5.de
  - ⁝ **standing** agg.: spig ↓
    - : **pressing** pain: spig h1
  - ⁝ **stitching** pain: stann h2 sulph h2
  - ⁝ **stooping** agg.: carb-v ↓
    - : **pressing** pain: carb-v h2
  - ⁝ **swallowing** agg.: kali-c ↓
    - : **pressing** pain: kali-c h2

- **Upper** part: anac ↓ ang ↓ apis ↓ coc-c ↓ elaps ↓ kali-p fd1.de• merc-c ↓ plat ↓ sep ↓ spong fd4.de stann ↓ sulph ↓ vanil fd5.de
  - **left**: kali-p fd1.de• mang-p ↓ sel rsj9• sep ↓ spig h1 ther br1 vanil fd5.de
    - ⁝ **burning**: mang-p rly4• sep h2
    - ⁝ **pressing** pain: sep h2
    - ⁝ **sore**: sep h2
    - ⁝ **extending** to | **Shoulder**: anis tl1 myrt-c tl1 pix tl1 sulph tl1 ther tl1
  - **drawing** pain: sep h2 spong fd4.de
  - **fall**; as from a: sulph h2
  - **pressing** pain: ang vh1 plat h2 stann h2
  - **riding** agg.: graph h2
  - **sore**: apis bg1 coc-c bg1 elaps bg1 sulph h2*
  - **stitching** pain: anac b4a.de merc-c b4a.de
  - **touch** agg.: graph h2
  - **yawning** agg.: graph h2
- **Upper** part through apex of both lungs: elaps ↓ ind ↓
  - **cutting** pain: elaps ind
  - **walking**:
    - ⁝ **amel.**: elaps ↓
      - : **cutting** pain: elaps

PALPITATION of heart: *Abies-c* bro1 abrom-a bnj1 acetan c2 **Acon** k* acon-f a1 adam skp7• adon bro1* adren c2 aesc k* *Aeth* k* **Agar** k* agarin bro1 agn hr1 *Aids* nl2• alco a1 aloe k* alst c2 *Alum* k* alum-sil k2 alumn k* *Am-c* k* *Am-m* *Ambr* k* **Aml-ns** k* anac b2.de* androc bnm2• anemps br1 ang b2.de* anh sp1 ant-c k* *Ant-t* k* *Apis* k* apoc k* aran-ix sp1 *Arg-met* **Arg-n** k* arge-pl rwt5• arizon-l nl2• *Arn* k* **Ars** k* **Ars-i** k* art-v *Asaf* k* asar b2.de* asc-t k* aspar k* aster k* atra-r bnm3• atro a1 **Aur** k* aur-ar k2 aur-i k2 *Aur-m* k* aur-m-n k* aven c1* *Bad* k* *Bamb-a* stb2.de• bapt a1 *Bar-c* k* bar-i k2 *Bar-m* *Bell* k* bell-p sp1 benz-ac k* berb k* beryl tpw5* *Bism* k* bit-ar wht1• boerh-d zzc1• bond a1 borx k* *Bov* k* *Brom* k* *Bry* k* bufo k* but-ac sp1 buth-a sp1 **Cact** k* **Cadm-s** **Calc** k* *Calc-ar* k* calc-f sp1 calc-i k2 *Calc-p* k* calc-s *Camph* k* *Cann-i* k* *Cann-s* k* canth k* *Carb-an* k* *Carb-v* k* *Carbn-s* carc sp1* carl k* cassia-s ccrh1• *Caust* k* cean tl1 *Cedr* k* *Cham* k* *Chel* k* **Chin** k* *Chinin-ar* k* *Chinin-s* chlam-tr bcx2• chlol a1* cic bg2 cimic k* cit-ac rly4• cit-v a1* clem b2.de* cob-n sp1 coc-c k* *Coca* bro1 *Cocc* k* coff k* coff-t a1 coffin a1 **Colch** k* coli rly4• *Coll* coloc k* colocin a1 **Con** k* conv bro1 convo-s sp1 cop corn cortico sp1 crat bro1* croc b2.de* *Crot-c* k* *Crot-h* k* crot-t k* *Cupr* k* cupr-ar k* cupr-s a1 *Cycl* k* cypra-eg sde6.de• cystein-l rly4• cyt-l sp1 der a1 **Dig** k* digin a1* *Dios* diph jl2 diphtox jl2 dulc k* dys pte1*• *Elaps* ephe-si hsj1• epiph c2 eucal a1 *Eup-per* k* eup-pur a1* euphr bg2 eupi k* fago c2* falco-pe nl2• *Ferr* k* *Ferr-ar* *Ferr-i* *Ferr-p* k* flor-p rsj3• form k* galeoc-c-h gms1• galla-q-r nl2• gard-j vlr2• gast a1 *Gels* k* gink-b sbd1• gins a1 **Glon** k* gran a1 *Graph* k* grat k* *Guaj* k* guat sp1 haem a1 halo mtf11 ham k* hed sp1* hell k* helo-s bnm14• *Hep* k* hera a1 hist sp1 *Hydr* k* hydr-ac k* *Hydrog* srj2• *Hyos* k* hyper k* iber a1* *Ign* k* indg a1 **Iod** k* ip k* irid-met srj5• jab a1 *Kali-ar* k* *Kali-bi* k* kali-br hr1 **Kali-c** k* *Kali-chl* k* kali-cy a1 *Kali-fcy* k*

Palpiation of heart: ...
Kali-i k* *Kali-n* k* *Kali-p* *Kali-s* k* **Kalm** k* kiss a1 *Kola* br1* kreos k* *Lac-d* **Lach** k* lact lat-h bnm5• *Laur* k* *Lec* led k* lepi a1 *Lil-t* k* limen-b-c hrn2* lipp a1 lith-c bg2 *Lob* k* loxo-lae bnm12• luf-op rsj5• **Lyc** k* *Lycps-v* k* lyss m-ambo b2.de* m-arct b2.de m-aust b2.de* macro a1 *Mag-c* k* *Mag-m* k* mag-s sp1* malar jl2 *Manc* mand sp1 *Mang* k* mang-p rly4• *Med* melal-alt gya4 *Meli* k* meny b2.de* **Merc** k* *Merc-c* k* merc-cy a1* *Merl* k* mez k* *Mill* morb jl2 morg-g fmm1• morph a1* *Mosch* k* mucs-nas rly4• mur-ac k* murx mygal k* **Naja** k* **Nat-ar** **Nat-c** k* nat-i mtf11 **Nat-m** k* **Nat-p** k* *Nit-ac* k* nit-m-ac a1 nit-s-d a1 nitro-o a1 *Nux-m* k* **Nux-v** k* ol-j k* *Olib-sac* wmh1 *Olnd* k* *Op* k* oscilloc jl2 osm *Ox-ac* k* par k* pert jl2 petr k* petr-ra shn4• **Ph-ac** k* phasco-ci rbp2 *Phase* bro1 phase-xyz c2 **Phos** k* *Phys* k* pic-ac k* pieri-b mlk9.de pin-con oss2• pin-s a1* pip-n bg2 plac rzf5• plac-s rly4• *Plat* k* *Plb* k* plumbg a1 plut-n srj7• *Podo* k* positr nl2• pot-e rly4• *Prun* *Psor* k* **Puls** k* pycnop-sa mrz1 pyrog k2* ran-s b2.de* raph a1* rauw sp1 rein a1 rhod b2.de* rhus-g tmo3• rhus-r *Rhus-t* k* rhus-v a1 ribo rly4• ros-d wla1 rumx *Ruta* b2.de* sabad b2.de* sabin k* sacch-a fd2.de• sal-al blc1• sal-fr sle1• samb bg2 sang k* saroth sp1 *Sars* k* scarl jl2 *Sec* k* sel b2.de* seneg k* **Sep** k* *Sil* k* sol-t-ae a1 **Spig** k* spira a1 **Spong** k* squil k* stann staph k* *Stram* k* *Stront-c* k* stroph-h ptk1* stry k* stry-p br1 succ-ac rly4• suis-hep rly4• *Sul-ac* k* sul-i k* sulo-ac a1 **Sulph** k* sumb k* suprar rly4• **Tab** k* tarax k* tarent tell k* tep k* ter term-a bnj1 tetox pin2• thea k* *Ther* *Thuj* k* thyr br1* *Toxo-g* jl2 trach a1 tril-p trinit br1 tritic-vg fd5.de tub al* tub-a jl2 upa c2 urol-h rwt• v-a-b jl valer k* vanil fd5.de **Verat** k* *Verat-v* k* verb b2.de* vero-o rly4*• vesp k* viol-o b2.de* *Viol-t* k* visc sp1 wies a1 x-ray sp1 yohim c1* *Zinc* k* zinc-i ptk1 zinc-p k2 [bell-p-sp dcm1 calc-n stj1 heroin sdj2 spect dfg1]

- **daytime**: **Acon** k* *Iod* k* pneu jl2 rhus-t
- **morning**: agar k* alum k* bar-c *Carb-an* k* caust k* chel k* chinin-s coli rly4• dulc fd4.de fic-m gya1 *Hydr* k* ign bg2 kali-c k* kali-s fd4.de *Kalm* **Lach** lyc k* *Lycps-v* *Nat-m* nat-sil fd3.de• nux-v k* **Phos** k* podo k* *Rhus-t* ruta fd4.de sacch-a fd2.de• *Sarr* k* sep h2 **Spig** k* spong fd4.de sulph k* symph fd3.de• thuj tub c1* vanil fd5.de [heroin sdj2]
  - **7** h: sol-t-ae
  - **8** h: trios rsj11•
  - **bed** agg.; in: *Ign* k* kali-c k* *Rhus-t* ruta fd4.de spong fd4.de
  - **waking** | **after** | **suddenly**; waking: *Kali-bi*
    - ⁝ **on**: agar alum alum-p k2 *Carb-an* chinin-s coli rly4• hep kali-c h2* kali-p fd1.de• lac-h sk4• **Lach** *Nat-m* nux-v bro1* olib-sac wmh1 phos rhus-t *Sep* thuj
      - : **lie** with closed eyes; must: carb-an
- **forenoon**: cob-n sp1 dulc fd4.de kali-c h2 *Lach* nat-m k* olib-sac wmh1 podo fd3.de• ruta fd4.de sulph k* tritic-vg fd5.de
  - **9** h: chin
  - **11**.30 h: gaba sa3•
- **noon**: dig digin a1 mez k* sol-t-ae k* staph sulph k*
  - **eating**; before: mez k*
- **afternoon**: arg-n bell chel k* chinin-m c1 chinin-s colch k* crot-t k* dig digin a1 dulc fd4.de euphr k* form k* gels k* ham fd3.de• kali-s fd4.de *Lyc* lyss petr-ra shn4• ph... k* ruta fd4.de spong fd4.de suis-hep rly4• tell rsj10• tritic-vg fd5.de vanil fd5.de
  - **13** h: chel
  - **14**-18 h: carc tpw2*
  - **15**-17 h: agar
  - **17**-19 h: luf-op rsj5•
  - **17**-21 h: calam sa3•
- **evening**: *Agar* k* alum k* alum-p k2 ang bg2 arg-n k* brom k* bufo cact k* calc-ar k2 canth k* *Carb-an* k* carb-v k* *Carbn-s* carc fd2.de• *Caust* k* chel k* cycl k* dig k* dulc *Graph* *Hep* k* indg a1 kali-n bg2 kali-s fd4.de *Kalm* *Lec* *Lyc* k* *Lycps-v* *Manc* k* mez k* murx k* nat-c bg2 *Nat-m* nat-sil fd3.de• nit-ac bg2 olib-sac wmh1 par k* petr bg2 **Phos** k* ruta fd4.de sep k* sil k* spong fd4.de *Sulph* k* tab k* thuj tritic-vg fd5.de vanil fd5.de zinc bg2
  - **20** h: *Calc* vh
  - **bed** agg.; in: ang bg2* *Arg-n* bamb-a stb2.de• calc k* dulc fd4.de gink-b sbd1• kali-n k* **Lyc** k* mez sne nat-c h *Nat-m* *Nit-ac* k* ox-ac petr *Phos* k* ruta fd4.de sars h2 *Sep* k* streptoc pd *Sulph* k* vanil fd5.de
  - **eating**; after: tub k2
  - **lying** down agg.: dulc fd4.de nat-c h2 ruta fd4.de tritic-vg fd5.de vanil fd5.de
  - **sitting** agg.: petr h2

- **night**: agar k* aids nl2• alum am-c k* *Arg-met* **Arg-n** k* *Ars* k* ars-s-f k2 asaf k* aspar vh *Aur* k* aur-ar k2 aur-i k2 aur-s k2 bamb-a stb2.de• bar-c k* bar-i k2 bar-s k2 *Benz-ac* k* *Cact* k* **Calc** k* calc-ar k2 calc-i k2 *Calc-s* calc-sil k2 carb-ac c1 coc-c k* colch dig k* *Dulc* k* ferr ferr-ar **Ferr-i** ferr-p fic-m gya1 flav jl2 ham fd3.de• iber bro1 ign k* *Iod* kali-n k* kali-s fd4.de kola stb3• lach mrr1 lil-t bro1 limen-b-c mlk9.de loxo-recl knl4• *Lyc* k* macro c1 *Merc* k* merc-c k* morg-g pte1*• mur-ac k* nat-ar nat-c k* nat-m k* nit-ac k* *Ox-ac* k* petr *Phos* k* pitu-gl skp7• pot-e rly4• psor al2 **Puls** k* rhus-t bg2 saroth sp1 sep k* sil k* sol-t-ae k* *Spig* spong bg2* sul-i k2 *Sulph* k* *Tab* k* ter bg2 thea tritic-vg fd5.de tub c1* vanil fd5.de *Verat* zinc bg2
  - **midnight**: kali-n h2
    - **before** | **23**-3 h: *Colch*
    - **after**: ham fd3.de• nux-m c1 olib-sac wmh1 spig
      - **1**-2 h: **Spong**
      - **2** h: benz-ac *Kali-bi*
      - **3** h: am-c k2 **Ars** chin nit-ac h2
      - **4**-5 h: lyc k*
    - **wakes** up: bad k* benz-ac calc **Spong**
  - **bed** agg.; in: *Aur-m* mrr1 cact k* calc-ar k2 ferr *Iod* kali-n c1 kali-s fd4.de lil-t c olib-sac wmh1 *Ox-ac* k* *Ph-ac* **Puls** k* *Rhus-t* *Spig* **Sulph** k* vanil fd5.de
  - **eructations** | **amel**.: morg-g fmm1•
  - **flatus**; passing | **amel**.: morg-g fmm1•
  - **moving** about | **amel**.: morg-g fmm1•
  - **pressure** in pit of stomach: sulph k*
  - **waking**; on: *Aur-m* mrr1 limen-b-c hrn2• morg-g fmm1• nat-c h2
- **accompanied** by:
  - **anemia**: ars-i br1 stroph-h br1
  - **collapse**: am-c ptk1 beryl sp1 conv mtf11 naja mrr1
  - **expectoration**; bloody: acon bg2 ferr bg2 lycps-v bg2 mill bg2*
  - **faintness** (See GENERALS - Faintness - palpitations - during)
  - **heat**:
    - **flushes** of (See GENERALS - Heat - flushes - palpitation)
    - **internal**: acon bg2 benz-ac bg2 bov bg2 carb-v bg2 chin bg2 ign bg2 nit-ac bg2
  - **hemorrhoids**: coll mrr1
  - **indigestion**: *(↗indigestion - agg.)* abies-c bro1 *Abies-n* bro1 arg-n bro1 cact bro1 *Carb-v* bro1 *Chin* bro1 coca bro1 coff bro1 coll bro1 dios bro1 hydr-ac bro1 lyc bro1 nat-c gk nux-v a* prun-v bro1 puls a* sep bro1 spig bro1 tab bro1
  - **influenza**: iber bro1 leptos-ih jl2 saroth bro1
  - **masturbation** and seminal emissions | **young** people; in: bar-c br1
  - **menses**:
    - **absent**: ars-i br1
    - **irregular**: phys ptk1
  - **neuralgic** pain: lach ptk1
  - **numbness** of left arm and shoulder: rhus-t tl1
  - **oppression** (See Oppression - palpitations)
  - **perspiration**; cold: am-c bg2* cact bg2 calc bg2 carbn-o bg2 dig bg2 laur bg2 spig bg2 tab bg2 verat bg2
  - **relaxation**: *Acon* bg2 *Caust* bg2
  - **respiration**:
    - **complaints**: aur ptk1 kalm ptk1 merc-i-f ptk1 puls ptk1 sep bg2 spig ptk1 verat ptk1
    - **difficult** (See RESPIRATION - Difficult - palpitation)
  - **rush** of blood (See GENERALS - Orgasm - palpitation)
  - **thirst**: bov bg2
  - **urticaria**: bov ptk1
  - **vision**:
    - **dim**: puls bro1
    - **lost**: puls bg2

- **accompanied** by: ...
  - **weakness**; general (See GENERALS - Weakness - palpitation - with)
  - **yawning**: lyc bg2
  - ○ **Abdomen**:
    - **distension** of: abies-c kr1* but-ac sp1
    - **retraction** of: am-c bg2
  - **Anus**; fistula in: cact ptk1
  - **Back** | **pain** (See BACK - Pain - accompanied - palpitations)
  - **Chest**; congestion of (See Congestion - accompanied - palpitations)
  - **Ear**; noises in: coca bro1
  - **Face**:
    - **heat**: acon bg2 aml-ns bg2 *Arg-met* k* bell bg2 *Calc-ar* chin bg2 ferr bg2 *Glon* k* iber c1 kali-n h2* mag-m ptk1 op bg2 spong bg2
    - **pale**: ambr bg2*
    - **red**: agar bro1* aur bro1 bell bro1 cedr a1 *Chin* a1 elec al2 glon bro1 phos a1
  - **Female** genitalia; complaints of: cimic bro1 lil-t bro1
  - **Head**:
    - **complaints** (See HEAD - Complaints - accompanied - palpitation)
    - **congestion** to: sarr br1 scop ptk1
    - **pain** in: brom tl1 oscilloc jl2
    - **reverberates**: aur bro1 bell bro1 *Glon* bro1 spig bro1 spong bro1
  - **Hypochondrium**; sensation of fullness in: but-ac sp1
  - **Legs**; weakness of: beryl tpw5*
  - **Limbs**:
    - **pain** in: kalm sma lith-c sma
    - **trembling**: petr mtf11
  - **Mouth**; putrid odor in: spig br1*
  - **Stomach**:
    - **distension**: abies-c br1 asaf fr4 nat-n mtf11 prot mtf11
    - **heaviness**: upa bro1
    - **sinking**: cimic bro1
  - **Teeth**; complaints of: spig bg2
  - **Throat**; pulsating in: aran-ix sp1
  - **Upper** limbs; pain in: agar *Cact* *Calc* cimic
  - **Uterus** | **pain**; sore: conv br1*
  - **Valves**; complaints of the (See Heart; complaints - valves - accompanied - palpitations)
- **air** agg.; in open: ambr c1* caust k*
- **alternating** with:
  - **aphonia**: ox-ac k*
  - **cheerfulness** (See MIND - Cheerful - alternating - palpitation)
  - **hemorrhoids**: **Coll** k*
  - **mirth** (See MIND - Mirth - alternating - palpitation)
  - ○ **Head**; congestion to: glon bg2
  - **Lower** limbs; pain in: benz-ac
- **anemia**, with: ars bro1 *Chin* bro1 cycl bg2 dig bg2* eucal bg2 ferr bg2* *Ferr-r* bro1 hydr bg2 hyper bg2 kali-c bg2* kali-fcy bro1 nat-m bg2* ph-ac bg2* phos bro1 puls bg2* senec bg2 spig bro1 verat bro1
- **anger**: arn calc-ar bc falco-pe nl2• *Phos* sep k* staph
- **anticipation**; from: aur-m-n wbt2• *Dys* fmm1• ozone sde2•
- **anxiety**: *(↗MIND - Anxiety)*
  - **with**: *(↗MIND - Anxiety)* **Acon** k* aesc aeth bro1 agar k* aids nl2• alum k* alum-p k2 *Am-c* k* anac b2.de ang b2.de* ant-t k* *Apis* *Arg-met* *Arg-n* arn b2.de **Ars** k* asaf b2.de aspar k* **Aur** k* aur-ar k2 aur-i k2 *Aur-m* aur-m-n a1* aur-s k2 bar-c bar-s k2 bell b2.de* borx b2.de* *Bry* k* *Cact* k* **Calc** k* *Calc-p* k* calc-s *Camph* k* cann-s k* carb-v k* carbn-s *Caust* k* cench k2 cham b2.de* *Chel* k* **Chin** k* *Chinin-ar* coc-c bg2 *Cocc* k* *Coff* k* *Colch* k* coloc b2.de* convo-s sp1 *Croc* k* crot-c sk4• cupr k* cycl bg2 **Dig** k* *Dys* fmm1• elaps ephe-si hsj1• falco-pe nl2• *Ferr* k* ferr-ar ferr-p gels bg1 gink-b sbd1• *Graph* k* ham fd3.de• hell bg2 *Hep* hydrog srj2•

- **with**: ...
  Hyos k* ign b2.de* *Iod* ip kali-ar *Kali-c* k* *Kali-n* *Kali-p* kali-s *Kalm* k* *Lach* k* *Laur* k* led bg2 *Lil-t* k* lith-c *Lyc* k* m-ambo b2.de* m-arct b2.de m-aust b2.de mag-c b2.de* mag-m k2 melal-alt gya4 *Merc* k* merc-c b4a.de* mez h2 *Mosch* k* *Nat-ar* *Nat-c* k* **Nat-m** k* *Nat-p* *Nit-ac* k* nux-v k* oci-sa sk4• *Olnd* k* *Op* k* osm ox-ac bg1 parth vml3• petr b2.de petr-ra shn4• **Ph-ac** phase bro1 **Phos** k* *Plat* k* *Plb* k* *Psor* k* **Puls** k* ran-b bg2 *Rhus-t* k* ruta k* *Samb* sapo bro1 sars k* *Sec* k* seneg b2.de *Sep* k* sil b2.de* **Spig** k* *Spong* k* staph b2.de *Stram* sul-ac b2.de* **Sulph** k* suprar rly4• tab bg2 tax-br oss1• ther bg2 thuj k* tril-p c1 tritic-vg fd5.de valer b2.de *Verat* k* viol-o b2.de* *Viol-t* k* *Zinc* k* zinc-p k2
  - **evening**: sulph tl1
  - **fever**; before: acon b7a.de chin b7a.de puls b7a.de spig b7a.de
- **without**: ant-t b7.de* carb-an b4.de* ip b7.de* sul-ac b4.de* sulph b4.de* thuj b4.de* verat-v bg2 zinc b4.de*
  - **daytime**: sulph tl1
- **appearing**:
  - **suddenly**: aml-ns bg2 arg-met mrr1 *Bar-c* cann-s a1 cann-xyz bg2 fic-m gya1 glon bg2 graph bg2 kali-n bg2 lyc h2 *Mang* mosch ptk1 podo bg2 psil ft1* *Stry* k* sulph bg2 sumb bg2 tarent mrr1
    - **disappearing**; and | **gradually**: trios rsj11•
- **ascending** stairs agg.: ang arg-n **Ars** aspar *Aur-m* aur-s bar-m k2 bell k* berb beryl tpw5 bov *Bry* bufo *Cact* **Calc** k* calc-s cot c1 *Croc* crot-t dig ferr-i gaba sa3• glon k2 helon hydrog srj2• iber c1 *Iod* *Kali-p* kali-s fd4.de lavand-a ctl1• *Lyc* *Lycps-v* *Naja* *Nat-ar* *Nat-c* k* **Nat-m** nat-sil fd3.de• **Nit-ac** k* *Ph-ac* **Phos** plan c1 plat plb pneu jl2 *Puls* rauw tpw8 sabin spong **Sulph** k* tab ter thea *Thuj* k* verat
- **attention** is directed to anything, when: nat-c k*
- **audible**: aesc k* agar am-c k* androc srj1• **Ang** bg2 apis k* arn bg2 *Ars* k* ars-i ptk1 bamb-a stb2.de• bapt bg2* bell k* **Bism** bg2* bufo bg2 *Calc* camph k* carc tpw2* chin bg2 coca c1 *Cocc* bg2 colch *Cupr* bg2 *Dig* k* ferr-p bg2 glon k2 *Iod* k* kali-chl bg2 kalm k2 *Kola* stb3• lyc k* merc-c bg2 naja bg2* nat-m nat-p bg2 ozone sde2• pip-n bg2 plb bg2 plut-n srj7• puls bg2* pyrog k2 ruta fd4.de **Sabad** bg2* scroph-n c1 *Sec* bg2 sep k* sil bg2 spig k* spong fd4.de **Sulph** bg2* thuj k* verat-v br1 zinc bg2 zinc-p k2
  - **night**: am-c *Ars* colch
  - **lying** down agg.: carc gk6 cortico tpw7
- **back**:
  - **felt** in back: absin ptk1
    - **Scapulae**; between: choc srj3•
  - **pain** in the back; with: ruta fd4.de tub ptk1
- **bad** news: kali-p k2 spong fd4.de
- **bathing** | **agg.**: am-c bov pd*
- **beats**; six to ten: nat-m h2*
- **bed**; when going to: fago k* hir rsj4• kalm k2 nat-sil fd3.de• sol-t-ae k* upa k*
- **beer**; after: sumb k*
- **bending** | **backward** | **amel.**: arn dx1
  - **forward**:
    - **agg.**: kalm **Spig** k* vanil fd5.de
    - **must** bend forward: bell vh
- **breakfast** | **after** | **agg.**: phos k*
  - **amel.**: *Kali-c*
- **breathing** | **deep** | **amel.**: carb-v dulc fd4.de nat-sil fd3.de• vanil fd5.de
  - **holding** breath | **agg.**: cact c1* spig k*
- **bubbling**: bell gt1
- **burning** in heart, with (See Pain - heart - palpitations - with - burning)
- **burst** out of chest; as if heart would: *Arg-n* vh *Sulph* vh
- **chest**, felt in whole: conv a
- **children** who grow too fast; in: ph-ac c1*
- **chill**:
  - **after**: lil-t bg1
  - **before**: **Chin** k*
  - **during**: acon bg2 ars bg2 bov bg2 brom bg2 bry bg2 calc bg2 cann-xyz bg2 **Chin** b7a.de* chinin-s bro1 gels kali-c bg2 lil-t lyc bg2 *Merc* k* nat-m bg2* ph-ac k* phos k* puls bg2 rhus-t bg2 sars bg2 sep k* spig bg2 sulph k* thuj bg2
- **chilled**, from becoming: *Acon*
- **choking** in throat; with (See THROAT - Choking - palpitation)
- **chorea**, with: verat hr1
- **chronic** (= continuous): cact bg2 calc bg2* carb-v bg2* crat ptk1 hydr bg2 kalm bg2 mag-m bg2 phos bg2 sars bg2 stroph-h ptk1 sulph bg2* valer bg2
  - **nervous**: naja k2
- **closing** the eyes | **amel.**: carb-an ptk1
- **coffee** agg.: agarin bro1 bart k* cypra-eg sde6.de• dulc fd4.de **Nux-v** k* ox-ac k2 pin-con oss2•
- **coition**:
  - **after**: am-c k* crot-t bg2 *Dig* k* sec ptk1 *Sep* k*
  - **during**: agar ptk1 *Calc* k* crot-t *Lyc* k* *Ph-ac* k* **Phos** k* visc k*
- **cold**:
  - **amel.**: iod mrr1
  - **bathing** | **amel.**: *Iod* k*
- **coldness**; with: calc bg2 chin bg2 kali-chl bg2
  - ○ **Face**; of: *Camph* a
  - **Feet**; of: kali-chl c1
- **colic**; with: plb k*
- **colors**:
  - **red**:
    - **agg.** | **dark** red: nat-m vk4
- **company** agg.: plat
- **convulsions**:
  - **after**: kali-p st
  - **before**: *Cupr* k* *Glon* k*
    - **epileptic**: (↗*GENERALS - Convulsions - epileptic - aura - palpitation)* ars *Calc* *Calc-ar* cupr *Lach*
- **convulsive**: *Nux-v* k*
- **coryza**; during: anac ptk1
- **cough** agg.; during: agar agn hr1* am-c bg2 aml-ns gt1 arn b7.de* *Ars* b4a.de *Calc* k* calc-p *Carb-v* b4a.de cupr iber ptk1 kali-n k* lach bg2 *Nat-m* k* ol-j ptk1 psor *Puls* k* sec b7a.de stram k* *Sulph* k* tub a* x-ray sp1
- **digestion**; during●: (↗*eating - after - agg.)* **Lyc** melal-alt gya4 morg-g a *Sep* k*
- **dinner**; after: calc k* chin k* chinin-m c1 crot-t k* hep k* ign k* kali-p fd1.de• phos *Puls* k* sil k* stram sulph k* tub a
- **discharge** in women; after suppressed (See menses - suppressed)
- **drawing** up chest and throwing back right arm: ferr-ma k*
- **drinking** | **after** | **agg.**: benz-ac k* **Con** k* senec gt1 thuj bg2
  - **cold** water | **agg.**: thuj
- **eating**:
  - **after** | **agg.**: (↗*digestion)* *Abies-c* k* *Acon* k* alco a1 *All-s* vh1 alum alum-p k2 am-m aspar k* bad bg1 *Bov* k* bufo k* but-ac ah1* **Calc** k* calc-sil k2 *Camph* k* carb-ac a1 *Carb-an* k* *Carb-v* k* coc-c k* cop k* crot-t k* cub a1 cupr guat sp1* hep k* *Ign* k* kali-bi k2 kali-c lil-t bro1 **Lyc** k* manc k* melal-alt gya4 merc *Nat-c* k* *Nat-m* k* nat-p k* nat-sil k2 *Nit-ac* k* *Nux-v* k* phos k* plb psor **Puls** k* *Sep* k* sil k* spong fd4.de sulph k* thuj k* tub jl2
  - **amel.**: ign k2 nat-c k2 sep k2 sulph k2
  - **overeating** agg.; after: lyc mrr1
- **emissions** agg.; after: *Asaf* k* bar-c a sec bg2
- **emotions**; slight (See excitement)
- **epistaxis**; with: cact bg1 *Graph* k*
- **eructations**:
  - **amel.**: aur k* bar-c k* *Carb-v* k* morg-g pte1• mosch bg1*
  - **from**: agar k2 coloc h2
- **eruptions**; after suppressed: *Ars* *Calc* k*
- **exaltation**; after: *Coff*
- **excitement**; after: *Acon* bro1 alum am-val bro1 *Ambr* k* aml-ns vh anac bro1 **Arg-n** k* *Ars* k* *Ars-i* *Asaf* *Aur* *Aur-m* aur-s k2 *Bad* *Bell* bov pd brom k2* *Cact* k* calc k* *Calc-ar* k* calc-p tl1 carc fd2.de• cham bro1 *Chim* chinin-ar *Cocc* *Coff* k* *Crot-h* *Dig* dys fmm1• ferr gels bro1 glon k2 ham fd3.de• hydr-ac bro1 ign vn* iod bro1 *Kali-p* kali-sil k2 lac-d k2 lach bro1 lil-t k2 lith-c k* *Lycps-v* *Mosch* bro1 *Naja* nat-m *Nit-ac* k* nux-m bro1 *Nux-v* k* op bro1 ox-ac bg2 ozone sde2• *Ph-ac* **Phos** k* *Plat* k* pneu jl2 *Podo* *Puls* k* ruta fd4.de sal-al blc1• seneg *Sep* k* spong fd4.de stann bg2 staph bg2 stront-c bg2 tarent bro1
  - **sudden**: alumn *Cact* *Lach* *Nux-v*

Chest

- **exertion**:
  - **agg.**: alum bg2 am-c k* ambr k2 anac bg2 *Apoc* **Arg-met** **Arg-n** k* *Arn* **Ars** k* *Ars-i* ars-s-f k2 **Asaf** k* **Aur** aur-ar k2 aur-i k2 *Aur-m* aur-s k2 *Bar-c* bell bg2 *Bov* **Cact** **Calc** k* *Calc-ar* calc-sil k2 *Carb-an* carb-v carbn-s **Chin** k* chinin-ar **Chinin-s** cimic coca bg2 con bg2* conv a cortico tpw7* **Dig** ferr k2 ferr-i ferr-p gels a glon k2 gran k* *Graph* **Iod** k* *Kali-c* k* kali-i kali-sil k2 *Kalm* lac-d k2 **Lach** *Laur* k* **Lycps-v** macro a1 mag-s sp1 *Med* meny *Merc* k* **Naja** k* *Nat-ar* **Nat-m** k* *Nat-p* nat-sil fd3.de• *Nit-ac* k* *Ph-ac* **Phos** k* *Podo* k* prot jl2 **Psor** *Puls* *Rhus-t* k* sars k2 sil k* **Spig** k* *Spong* *Stann* k* **Staph** k* *Stram* sul-i k2 *Sulph* sumb thuj bg2 vesp [bell-p-sp dcm1 tax jsj7]
    - **least**; from the: ars ptk1 bell bro1 brom bro1 calc ptk1 calc-ar ptk1 chinin-s ptk1 cimic bro1 coca bro1 con ptk1 conv br1* dig bro1* *Iber* bro1 iod bro1* lil-t ptk1 med hr1 *Naja* mrr1 nat-m bro1 phos mrr1 prot jl2 rhus-t ptk1 sarcol-ac bro1 spig ptk1 stront-c sk4• sumb ptk1 thyr bro1*
    - **over**-exertion: coca br
    - **sudden**: *Arg-met* *Arg-n* rauw tpw8
    - **unusual**: *Arg-n* k* *Cact* chel k*
  - **amel.**: gels a kola stb3• mag-m k* sep a
  - **dinner** agg.; after: nit-ac k*
- **expanding** chest: lach gt1*
- **extra** systole: adon a aur a* cact a calc-ar bc con a conv ptk1 cortico mtf11 crat a dig a dys a* gels a hist mtf11 lac-h sze9• thyreotr mtf11 toxo-g jl2 visc a
- **face**, felt in: mur-ac h2*
- **fever**:
  - **before**: *Chin* b7a.de nux-v b7a.de puls b7a.de rhus-t b7a.de
  - **during** | **agg.**: *Acon* k* aesc agar k2 *Alum* b4a.de* aml-ns bg2 ant-t bg2 arn bg2 **Ars** k* aur bg2 bar-c bell bg2 bry bg2 calad bg2 **Calc** k* chin bg2 *Cocc* *Colch* b7a.de* crot-h k* cupr bg2 gels k2 hep bg2 *Ign* b7.de* iod bg2 lyc bg2 merc k* *Mur-ac* hr1 nat-m bg2 **Nit-ac** k* nux-v bg2 ph-ac b4.de* phos k* **Puls** k* *Rhus-t* b7.de* *Sars* k* *Sep* k* sil bg2 *Spig* b7a.de* spong bg2 sulph k* thuj bg2 viol-o bg2 zinc bg2
- **fistula**; with anal: cact ptk1
- **flatulence**:
  - **from**: abies-c br1 lyc k2 nat-m h2 spartin bwa3
  - **with**: abies-c a *Arg-n* bro1 cact bro1 carb-v a* coca bg* coll bg1* ham bg1* *Ing* sne *Nux-v* bro1 spong fd4.de
- **flatus**; from obstructed: arg-n a* coca a lyc a nux-v a
- **fright**; after: (↗*MIND - Ailments - fright; MIND - Ailments - mental shock)* **Acon** *Aur-m* cact *Coff* dig ptk1 *Nat-m* nux-m *Op* *Puls* stram tritic-vg fd5.de verat
- **goitre**, with: ars bg2 aur bg2 bad bg2 bell bg2 brom bg2 bufo ptk1 iod bg2 jab br1 *Nat-m* bg2 nit-ac bg2 phos bg2* spong bg2 thyr bg2
- **grief**; from: cact ptk1 *Dig* k* *Ign* bro1* *Nat-m* ptk1 nux-m *Op* k* *Ph-ac* k*
- **gurgling**: bell gt1
- **headache**:
  - **after**: cimic
  - **during**: aeth k* ant-t c1 arg-n bamb-a stb2.de• bell h1* bov bg2 brom k* bufo cact bro1 calc-ar ptk1 carbn-o a1 cot a1 hep h2 lith-c bro1 plb sil h2 *Spig* k* symph fd3.de•
- **hemorrhage**; during: tril-p a
- **hemorrhoids**; after suppressed: coll bro1
- **hold** left arm; must: aur hr1*
- **hunger**; during: *Kali-c* k*
- **hysteria**; during: bar-c *Cedr* *Gels* *Ing* sne kali-ar gk *Mosch* k* *Nat-m* *Nux-m* sumb ptk1 ther mrr1 valer a
- **indigestion** | **agg.**: *(↗accompanied - indigestion)* lyc mrr1 spartin bwa3
- **inspiration**:
  - **deep**:
    - **agg.**: asaf cact hr1 kalm petr-ra shn4• **Spig** k* tub c1*
    - **amel.**: arg-met ptk1 cann-xyz bg2 carb-v ptk1 dig bg2 ign bg2 mosch bg2
- **irregular**: *(↗GENERALS - Pulse - irregular)* alum k* androc bnm2• apoc br1 arg-n mrr1 **Ars** k* aur mrr1 aur-m k2* cact mrr1* *Chel* chir-fl bnm4• *Cocc* colch rsj2• conv br1 *Crat* br1 croc mrr1 *Dig* mrr1 glon mrr1 glycyr-g cte1• hir rsj4• ign mrr1 iod mrr1 kali-c k2 kalm mrr1 kola stb3• lach mrr1 lil-t mrr1 loxo-lae bnm12• *Lyc* vh lycps-v mrr1 *Mang* merc k* mosch mrr1 naja mrr1 **Nat-m** ●* nit-ac k* nux-v mrr1 olib-sac wmh1 *Ox-ac* k* ozone sde2* parathyr jl2 phos mrr1 ros-d wla1 *Sang* ser-ang br1 spartin bwa3 spig mrr1 spong mrr1 stram mrr1 streptoc jl2

- **irregular**: ... sulph mrr1 tarent mrr1 ther mrr1 toxo-g jl2 tritic-vg fd5.de tub jl2 vanil fd5.de visc c1 *Zinc* b4a.de [mag-s stj1]
  - **accompanied** by | **convulsions**; epileptic (See GENERALS - Convulsions - epileptic - during - palpitation)
  - **infectious** diseases; after: spartin-s br1
  - **influenza**; after: spartin-s br1
- **irritable** heart: anthraci jl2 ars a1* bar-c br1 cact c1 cere-b c1 coff-t hr1* diphtox jl2 ferr mrr1 hep c1 influ jl2 lil-t al1 med jl2 *Mucor* jl2 *Parathyr* jl2 pert jl2 prun br1 prun-v c2 scarl jl2 *Scut* br1 *Strept-ent* jl2 *Stroph-h* br1 *Toxo-g* jl2 tub-a jl2 tub-m jl2 *V-a-b* jl2 vac jl2
  - **tobacco**; from: dig br1 stroph-h br1
- **joy**; after: *Bad* k* *Coff* k* puls
- **kneeling** agg.: *Sep*
- **labor** pain; during: puls hr1
- **lachrymation**; with: am-c bg2*
- **laughing** agg.: iber ptk1
- **leaning**:
  - **backward** | **agg.**: *Chinin-ar* *Lach*
  - **forward** | **agg.**: ang c1
  - **forward** resting on arms agg.: sul-ac
- **loss** of fluid; from: arn bg2 chin bg2 ferr bg2* hyper bg2 kali-c bg2 nat-m bg2 olnd bg2 ph-ac bg2 phos bg2 plat bg2 stann bg2
- **lying**:
  - **agg.**: acon vh1 aran-ix sp1 ars a* asaf aur bg2 bamb-a stb2.de• *Benz-ac* k* *Cact* carc fd2.de• cench k2 chel coc-c crot-t k* cur cypra-eg sde6.de• dulc fd4.de ephe-si hsj1• *Ferr* *Glon* grat ham fd3.de• hir rsj4• iber vml3• kali-c a* kali-n k* kali-p fd1.de• kali-s fd4.de lac-h htj1• *Lach* k* lil-t bg2* lyc lycps-v k* mag-m bg2 mand rsj7• merc ptk1 nat-c **Nat-m** a* **Nux-v** k* olib-sac wmh1 *Ox-ac* k* petr-ra shn4• ph-ac **Puls** k* *Rhus-t* sep a* *Spig* k* spong k* **Sulph** k* thyr bro1* tritic-vg fd5.de vanil fd5.de viol-t
  - **amel.**: am-c vh arg-n k* *Colch* *Lach* *Laur* *Phos* *Psor*
  - **back**; on:
    - **agg.**: agar k2 ammc *Arg-met* *Ars* k* asaf aur k* *Cact* *Kali-n* k* *Lach* merc-i-f ptk1 pitu-a vml2• thyr bg1
    - **amel.**: gard-j vlr2• *Kalm* k* *Lil-t* k*
  - **dinner** agg.; after: crot-t lyc gk **NUX-V** k ●
  - **side**; on:
    - **agg.**: ang k* asar vh bar-c k* brom daph dulc fd4.de *Hydr* kali-s fd4.de *Lil-t* *Nat-c* k* nat-m k* nux-v bg2 *Phos* puls k* spong fd4.de tub viol-t k*
    - **left**:
      - **agg.**: agar k2 ammc ang bamb-a stb2.de• *Bar-c* k* bar-m bg2 brom k* bry **Cact** k* chin chinin-s cinnb bg1 clem daph c dig dulc fd4.de gard-j vlr2• gink-b sbd1• glon *Graph* k* hydrog srj2• *Kali-ar* kali-bi gk kali-c kali-p fd1.de• kali-s fd4.de *Kalm* k* *Lac-c* k* *Lach* k* *Lil-t* *Lyc* k* myric *Naja* k* *Nat-c* k* **Nat-m** k* nat-p **Phos** k* phys pitu-gl skp7• plb k* **Psor** k* **Puls** k* rhus-t c *Sarr* sep k* *Spig* k* *Tab* k* thea br* zinc-i ptk1
      - **amel.**: ign bg1* mag-m bg3*
    - **right**:
      - **agg.**: alum ptk1 *Alumn* k* *Arg-n* k* arge-pl rwt5• bad k* bamb-a stb2.de• brom bg1 kali-n k* kalm k2* lach bg1 *Lil-t* k* lycps-v bg2 mag-m bg2 plat k* spong
      - **amel.**: glon graph bg2* lac-c bro1 *Lach* k* nat-c ptk1 nat-m bg2* **Phos** k* **Psor** k* sabad bg1 *Tab* k*
  - **still** | **long** time; for a: alumn
- **lying** down agg.: arn bg2 lyc bg2 nux-v bg2 ox-ac bg2
- **masturbation**; after: calc bg2 cann-xyz bg2 *Dig* *Ferr* k* *Ph-ac* k* phos bg2 plat bg2 stann bg2
- **medicine**; after abuse of allopathic: com bg2 nux-v bg2 op bg2
- **menopause**: acon bg2 aml-ns bg2* *Calc-ar* br1* *Cimic* bro1 *Crot-h* ferr bg2* glon bg2* *Kali-br* hr1* **Lach** k* sep bg2* sumb ptk1 *Tab* tril-p bro1 valer a*
  - **obese** women; in: calc-ar br1
- **menses**:
  - **after** | **agg.**: agar k* alum-p k2 ars b4a.de *Ign* b7a.de iod k* lach bg2 lith-c bg2 *Nat-m* k* nit-ac plat bg2 seneg

- **before** | **agg**.: alum k* ambr bg2 *Cact* k* cimic bg2 crot-h bro1 *Cupr* k* eupi k* ign k* *Iod* k* *Kali-c* b4a.de lach bg2 laur bg2 lith-c bg2 lyc b4a.de *Nat-m* k* ph-ac b4a.de *Puls* b7a.de *Sep* k* **Spong** k* tril-p bg2 zinc
- **during**:
  - **agg**.: agar k* alum k* am-c bg2 *Arg-met* arg-n bg2* ars b4a.de aur aur-ar k2 aur-s k2 bell bg2 *Bov* k* bufo k* *Cact* k* cann-xyz bg2 carb-an bg2 chin b7a.de *Con* bg2 *Croc* k* crot-h bg2* cupr k* cycl bg2* graph bg2 *Ign* k* iod k* kali-n kola stb3• laur bg2 lil-t bg2 lith-c bg2 mang bg2 merl mosch bg2 nat-c bg2 *Nat-m* k* nat-p *Nit-ac* k* *Phos* k* phys bg2* plat bg2 puls bg2 rhus-t k* sep k* *Sil* k* *Spig* k* *Spong* bg2 sul-i k2 *Sulph* k* *Tab* k* thuj k* vib bg2
  - **amel**.: eupi k*
  - **beginning** of menses | **agg**.: cact bg2 iod b4.de* lyc b4a.de
- **suppressed** menses; from: *Acon* arn tl1 asaf hr1* bell *Cact* calc chin coff *Cycl* k* *Lil-t* *Lyc* merc nat-m nux-v phos *Puls* rhus-t k* sep *Verat*
  - **nervous** palpitation with small pulse: **Asaf** k1

- **mental** exertion agg.: *Ambr* aur-m k2 *Cact* *Calc-ar* k* cocc ptk1 cod *Ign* k* *Iod* kalm nat-c *Nux-v* *Plat* *Podo* *Staph* k* *Sulph*
  - **long** time; mental exertion for a: coca bro1
- **motion**:
  - **after**:
    - **agg**. | **rapid** motion: *Cocc* k* dulc fd4.de *Sil* *Spig*
  - **agg**.: acon agar k* *Am-c* *Apoc* *Arg-n* *Arn* ars k2 aspar k* *Aur* aur-ar k2 aur-i k2 aur-m ptk1 aur-s k* bell k* bov k* brom cact k* *Calc* **Cann-s** *Carb-v* k* *Carbn-s* chin k* *Cimic* *Cocc* *Con* **Dig** k* dirc c1 dulc fd4.de *Ferr* k* ferr-i ferr-p *Graph* k* *Hyos* iod k* jatr-c kali-n k* kali-p kalm *Lach* merc *Naja* k* *Nat-m* k* *Nit-ac* k* par bg2 **Phos** k* *Prun* **Psor** k* sabin *Sil* k* sol-t-ae k* **Spig** k* *Staph* k* *Stram* sul-i k2 sulph verat zinc-s k*
  - **amel**.: *Arg-met* *Arg-n* k* ferr bg1* gels bg1* gink-b sbd1• glon lob ptk1 *Mag-m* k* morg-g pte1• nux-m ptk1 par phos puls bg1 *Rhus-t* k*
    - **slow** motion: ferr puls
  - **arm**; of | **left** arm agg.; of: phos h2
  - **arms**; of | **agg**.: *Acon* arn-m borx bry camph chel *Dig* ferr led *Naja* *Puls* *Rhus-t* seneg *Spig* spong **Sulph** thuj
  - **beginning** of | **agg**.: cact
  - **legs**; of | **amel**.: gink-b sbd1•
  - **must** move: *Ferr* k*
  - **slightest** motion agg.: acon bro1 bell bro1 *Cact* bro1 *Calc-ar* bro1 calc-sil k2 *Carb-v* chin ptk1 cimic hr1* *Con* dig k* ferr bro1 iber k* kali-p pd *Lil-t* bro1 med *Merc* nat-m bro1 *Nit-ac* **Phos** **Spig** k* staph a1
- **motion** of fetus agg. | **first** movements: *Sulph* k*
- **mountain** climbing; from: coca br1
- **music**, when listening to: *Ambr* k* *Carb-an* bg2 carb-v kreos k2* *Staph* k* sulph
  - **hymns** in church: carb-an ptk1
- **nap**; during: calc h2
- **nausea**; with: agar bg2 arg-n bg2* bamb-a stb2.de• bov bg2 brom ptk1 *Nux-v* bg2 *Thuj* bg2
  - **faint**-like nausea, and causing her to become sick; with: arg-n k1
- **nervous** palpitation: acon bg2* adren bro1 ambr bg2 arg-n bg2 **Ars** ptk1 asaf bg2* atro bro1 aur bg2* bad bg2 brom bg2* cact bg2* calc ptk1 camph bg2 carb-v ptk1 cham bro1 chin bro1* cimic bg2 cocc bg2 coff bg2* com bg2 **Crat** ptk1 croc bg2 dig bg2* dys fmm1• elec mtf11 ferr bg2* gels bg2* *Glon* bro1 graph bg2* hydr-ac bro1 hyos bro1 *Iber* bro1 *Ign* bro1 kali-c bro1 kali-p bro1 lach bg2* lil-t bg2* lycps-v bg2* mag-m bg2 mag-p bro1 medul-os-si rly4• mosch bg2* mygal bg2 naja bro1* *Nat-m* ptk1 nux-m bg2 nux-v bg2* ol-an ptk1 ph-ac bg2* *Phos* bg2* pitu-p mtf11 plat bg2 prun-v bro1 **Puls** ptk1 rhus-t bg2 scut bro1 sep bg2* spig bg2* stram bg2 stront-c bg2 stroph-h ptk1 sulph ptk1 sumb bg2* *Tab* bro1 thuj ptk1 valer bg2* verat bg2* zinc bro1
  - **accompanied** by | **atrophy** (See GENERALS - Atrophy - accompanied - palpitations)
  - **pulse**; with small | **suppression** of discharge of women; from (See menses - suppressed - nervous)
- **noise** agg.: *(↗MIND - Sensitive - noise)*
  - **strange** noise; every: *(↗MIND - Sensitive - noise)* agar *Nat-c* k* **Nat-m** k* nat-p nat-s
  - **sudden**: petr-ra shn4•
- **old** people; in: | **maids**; old: bov br1*
- **opening** the eyes agg.: carb-an
- **pain**; during: acon bov bufo cimic dulc fd4.de glon hep ign kali-bi lach nit-ac k2 nux-v ruta fd4.de spig k* spong fd4.de tritic-vg fd5.de
- **painful**: agar h2 ferr bg2 gels bg2 ham bg2 hep bg2 *Ign* bg2 iod bg2 lach bg2 mag-m ptk1 spong ptk1 tritic-vg fd5.de zinc h2
- **paroxysmal**: *Acon* arg-met mrr1 ars k2 *Aur* bar-c ptk1 cann-xyz bg2* dulc fd4.de kali-c mtf11 *Lach* *Lyc* vh *Mag-p* mang ptk1 merc-i-f **Nat-m** ● nit-ac h2* *Nux-v* k* olnd bg2* phos h2* *Plb* psil ft1* *Puls* k* sec bg2 spig a1 sul-ac bg2 sulph bg2 ulm-c jsj8•
  - **six** to ten beats: nat-m h2
- **perceptible**; clearly: am-m bg2 *Bar-c* b4a.de* calc b4a.de* *Cycl* b7.de* dulc b4a.de* *Lyc* b4a.de* mur-ac b4a.de* pip-n bg2 plb b7.de* rhod b4a.de* rhus-t b7.de* sabin b7.de* spig b7a.de* verat b7.de*
- **periodical**: aesc benz-ac bg2 chel ptk1 colch thuj
  - **hour**, waking at night; every half: *Lyc*
- **perspiration**:
  - **during**: acon bg2 calc bg2 chin bg2 hep bg2 ign bg2 jab ptk1 lyc bg2 merc k* nux-v bg2 ph-ac bg2 phos bg2 *Rhus-t* bg2 sars bg2 **Sep** bg2 spig bg2 spong ptk1 sulph bg2 tab ptk1 thuj bg2 *Verat* ptk1
  - **foot**; after suppressed perspiration of: *Ars* *Sil*
- **preaching** agg.: naja ptk1
- **pregnancy** agg.; during: *Arg-met* k* *Con* *Laur* **Lil-t** k* **Nat-m** k ● **Sep** k ● sulph gt1
- **pressure** with the hand amel.: *Arg-n* k* moni rfm1•
- **puberty**; during: aur ptk1 aur-m-n a
- **raising** arms agg.: dig *Spig* *Sulph*
- **relaxation** with yawning, after: lyc h2
- **rest** agg.: mag-m bg2 phos bg2 rhus-t bg2 saroth sp1
- **rheumatic**: acon bg2 benz-ac bg2 bry bg2 colch bg2 dig bg2 kali-s bg2 *Kalm* bg2 *Lach* bg2 led bg2 lith-c bg2 puls bg2 rhod bg2 rhus-t bg2 spig bg2 spong bg2 verat bg2 verat-v bg2
- **riding** in a wagon: *Arg-n* aur nat-sil fd3.de• vanil fd5.de
  - **amel**.: *Nit-ac* *Rhus-t*
- **rising**:
  - **agg**.: cact bro1 con k* dulc fd4.de ferr-i ham fd3.de• kali-n h2 phos mrr1 sulph k*
  - **bed**; from | **agg**.: ars colch *Con* kali-s fd4.de *Lach* **Phos** sulph h2
  - **sitting**; from | **agg**.: brom *Cact* ferr-i *Lach* mag-m **Phos**
- **roused** suddenly; on being: chinin-s
- **sadness**:
  - **as** from: nux-m ptk1
  - **with** (See MIND - Sadness - palpitations)
- **sensation** of: glon bg2
- **sexual**:
  - **excesses**: sec ptk1
  - **excitement**: lil-t k2 *Ph-ac*
- **siesta**; after: staph bg2
- **sighing** | **amel**.: **Arg-met** k*
- **singing** in church, while: carb-an k*
- **sitting**:
  - **agg**.: agar anac bg2 *Ang* k* **Asaf** k* *Aspar* benz-ac *Carb-v* k* coloc dig bg2 dulc fd4.de *Ferr* ferr-p gins ham fd3.de• kali-s fd4.de *Lach* *Mag-m* k* nat-c h2* nat-sil fd3.de• petr bg2 phos h2* *Rhus-t* k* ribo rly4• *Sil* k* **Spig** k* spong fd4.de tere-la rly4• tritic-vg fd5.de
    - **eating**; after: *Phos* k*
  - **amel**.: cact ptk1 ham fd3.de• *Lach* k*
  - **bent** forward | **agg**.: ang dig kalm k* *Rhus-t* spig h1
  - **erect**:
    - **agg**.: acon bg2 bell bg2 brom bg2 bry bg2 con bg2 dig bg2 mag-m bg2 phos bg2 spig bg2
    - **amel**.: arn bg2 cact bg2 kali-n bg2 kalm nat-m bg2 spong bg2
  - **still** | **amel**.: iber vml3•
- **sitting** up in bed:
  - **agg**.: *Colch* *Phos*
  - **amel**.: *Ang* a1 asaf k* *Cact* *Lach*

Chest

- **sleep**:
  - **after** | **agg.**: lach k2 staph sne
  - **during**: aesc k2 alst bro1 am-c k* *Aur Calc Cann-i* k* ferr-i iber bro1 kali-bi kalm lach mrr1 *Merc Merc-c* k* *Nat-c* ph-ac bro1 *Sep* spong bro1 sulph k* zinc
  - **going** to sleep; on | **agg.**●: androc srj1• *Calc Carb-v* colch fuma-ac rly4• ham fd3.de• lach k2 *Nat-m* phos pitu-gl skp7• sil **Sulph** visc c1
- **soup**; warm: *Lach Phos Puls*
- **spasmodic**: *Iod* b4a.de merc-c b4a.de plb b7a.de *Sec* b7.de*
- **speak**, unable to: **Naja**
- **spices**; from: naja bg2
- **spoken** to; when: aur-m k2
  - **loss**; of his: gels hr1
- **standing** agg.: agar aur-m-n cact dig *Ferr* kali-n *Lach Nat-m* sil spong fd4.de tritic-vg fd5.de
  - **long** time; for a: alumn
- **starting** from sleep: cystein-l rly4• petr h2 ph-ac h2 tritic-vg fd5.de
- **stiff**, as if: aur-m ptk1
- **stool**:
  - **after** | **agg.**: *Agar* k* ant-t bg2 **Ars** k* caust k* **Con** k* crat ptk1 grat k*
  - **before**: ant-t bg2
  - **during** | **agg.**: *Ant-t* k* ars bg2 caust bg2 chinin-s bg2 con bg2 cycl k* ferr bg2 grat bg2 nit-ac k* petr *Sulph* k*
- **stooping** agg.: ang k* aur-m-n vml3• cact k* *Cann-s* iber vml3• lepi a1 *Nat-c* k* *Spig* k* sul-ac k* thuj a1 thyr al2* tritic-vg fd5.de
- **stop**, must: aur ptk1
- **strain** of the heart: *Arn* bro1 borx bro1 *Caust* bro1 coca bro1
- **stretching** out: phos h2 *Prot* jl2
- **sudden** (See appearing - suddenly)
- **suffocative** feeling, with: calc-ar ptk1
- **sun**, heat of agg.: coff ptk1
- **supper** agg.; after: cupr h2 *Lyc Ph-ac* **Puls** rumx sol-t-ae a1
- **supra** ventricular: rauw mtf11 thiop mtf11
- **surprise**; from a: *Coff* k* ferr bg2
- **swallowing** agg.: sol-t-ae
- **synchronous** with pulse | **not**: spig k2
- **talking** agg.: cortico tpw7* ham fd3.de• **Naja** k* (non:plat h2) *Puls* k* rumx
- **talking** in public; before: plat h2*
- **tea**; after: agarin bro1 chin bro1 lac-loxod-a hrn2•
  - **abuse** of tea; after: thea br1
- **thinking** about his wrongs agg.: iod k*
- **thinking** of it agg.: alumn k* *Arg-n* k* *Aur-m* bad bg1 *Bar-c* k* bar-m bg2 cact bg1 *Gels* k* ign bg1 *Lycps-v Ox-ac* k* sumb k*
- **thinking** of one's complaints agg.: alumn kr1
- **throat**; with choking in: nat-m ptk1 spong ptk1
- **thunderstorm**: *Nat-p* k* *Phos*
- **tobacco** from: acon agar bro1 *Agarin* bro1 agn br1* ars bro1 cact bro1 calad bro1 conv bg2* dig bro1 *Gels* bro1 iber c1 *Kalm* bro1 lycps-v bro1 *Nux-v* k* olib-sac wmh1 phos k* *Spig* bro1 spong staph bro1 *Stroph-h* bro1 tab bro1 thuj verat bro1
  - **young** men; in neurotic: agn br1
- **trembling** of hands; with: bov ptk1 thyr bg1
- **tremulous**: *Ars* aur-ar k2 bad a1 *Calc* canth bg2 cic hr1* *Cocc* lach bro1 lyc h2* *Mang Plb* staph h1 ulm-c jsj8•
- **tumultuous**, violent, vehement: abies-c bro1 absin bro1 acon k* aesc k* *Aeth* k* *Agar* k* alum alum-p k2 alumn *Am-c* k* ambr *Aml-ns* k* ammc bro1 anan vh1 androc srj1• *Ang* k* *Ant-c Apis* **Arg-n** k* *Ars* k* ars-i ars-s-f k2 asaf hr1* *Aur* k* aur-ar k2 aur-i k2 *Aur-m* aur-s k2 bamb-a stb2.de• bapt bar-c bar-i k2 bar-s k2 bell k* *Bism* bry k* cact br1* **Calc** k* *Calc-ar* camph bg2 cann-i cann-xyz bg2 carb-ac bro1 *Carb-v* k* *Carbn-s* carc hbh* cassia-s ccrh1• *Chel Chin* k* *Chinin-ar* choc srj3• cic a1 cimic bro1 coc-c *Coca* coff *Colch* k* *Con* k* conv br1* cop *Crat* ptk1 crot-c sk4• *Crot-t* cupr cupr-s *Cycl* **Dig** k* dulc a1 ephe bro1 falco-pe nl2• *Ferr-m* gala br1 gels bro1* **Glon** k* grat *Guaj* ham fd3.de• hell k* helo bro1 helo-s rwt2• hep hydrog srj2• hyos k* iber bro1 ignis-alc es2• **Iod** k* kali-ar **Kali-c** k* kali-chl *Kali-i* kali-m k2 *Kali-n* k* *Kali-p* kali-s *Kalm* k* *Kola* stb3• *Lach* k* lachn *Lil-t* bro1 *Lob Lycps-v* k* *Lyss M-aust* b7a.de mag-m a1 mag-p bg2 melal-alt gya4 merc bg2 morph mur-ac h2* *Naja* k* nat-ar nat-c k* **Nat-m** k* nat-sil fd3.de• neon srj5• *Nux-m Olnd* k* ox-ac *Phos* k* phys k* *Plat* k* *Plb* k* prun k* **Puls** k* pyrog bro1* rhus-t k* rumx ruta fd4.de sang a1 sec k* seneg k* **Sep** k* sil bg2 *Spig* k* *Spong* k* *Staph* stram k* stry *Sulph* k* sumb bg2 symph fd3.de• tab *Tarent* k* tell c1 thuj k* tritic-vg fd5.de vanil fd5.de *Verat* k* verat-v bro1* vesp viol-o k* *Viol-t* b7a.de visc bg2
  - **accompanied** by | **chorea** (= St. Vitus' dance of the heart): tarent tl1
  - **chest**; as if heart beat throughout the: conv br1 falco-pe nl2• nat-sil fd3.de• symph fd3.de•
  - **excitement** of mind; and: asaf k1
  - **heard** in back: absin br1
  - **jump** out of place; as if heart would: **Arg-n** vh1* kola stb3•
  - **sleep**; on falling asleep: sulph tl1
- **turning** | **bed**; in | **agg.**: cact hr1 *Dig Ferr-i Lach Lyc* k* *Manc Naja Phos* **Sulph** k*
  - **side**; to | **right**: alum k1
- **twitching**: am bg2 bell bg2 chin bg2 con bg2 nux-v bg2 plb bg2
- **unrequited** affections, from: *(↗MIND - Ailments - love)* *Cact Ign* **Nat-m** *Ph-ac*
- **urina** spastica, with (See urine - copious - hysteria)
- **urinary** complaints; with: aspar vh laur ptk1
- **urination** | **after** | **agg.**: androc srj1•
  - **amel.**: lith-c bg2
- **urine**:
  - **copious**, with: coff bro1*
    - **hysteria**; after an attack of: coff mh•
  - **scanty** with: apis c1*
- **uterine** complaints: conv bro1 lil-t bro1
- **vertigo**; with: adon bro1* aeth br1* aml-ns bg2 bell bro1 bov bg2 cact bro1* cocc ptk1 coron-v bro1 dig bro1 eucal bg2 iber bro1* *Kali-br* hr1 kali-s fd4.de lap-la sde8.de• nux-m bg2 plat h2* senec bg2 sep h2* sil h2 spig bro1* spong fd4.de sulph bg2 tritic-vg fd5.de tub al* vanil fd5.de
- **vexation** agg.: *(↗MIND - Ailments - reproaches)* acon agar k* *Aur-m* cham *Ign* iod **Lyc** k ● **Nux-v** k ● **Phos** k ● podo fd3.de• verat
- **violent** (See tumultuous)
- **visible**: agar bg2 androc srj1• ant-t k* *Ars* k* *Aur* aur-s k2 bell bg2 bov k* camph bg2 cann-s **Carb-v** k* *Carbn-s* carc mg1.de* chel coloc bg2 con k* dig bg2 dulc k* glon bg2* *Graph* k* hell bg2 iber c1* *Iod* k* kali-s fd4.de *Kalm* k* *Lach* k* mez bg2 mur-ac bg2 naja bg2* nat-m bg2 nat-s bg2 nit-ac bg2 petr h2 phyt bg2 plb bg2 *Puls* bg2* rhus-t b7.de* sec b7.de* sep ptk1 **Spig** k* *Staph Sulph* k* thuj k* *Verat* k*
  - **children**; in: kali-c mtf33
  - ○ **Apex** beat through clothing: mag-p ptk1
- **vomiting**; before: sang hr1
- **waking**; on: *(↗SLEEP - Waking - palpitation)* acon agar k* *Alum* k* alum-p k2 androc srj1• aran-sc *Ars Benz-ac Bufo Calc Cann-i* k* *Carb-an* k* chinin-s colch k* con k* cypra-eg sde6.de• dulc fd4.de eupi hep hydroph rsj6* ign ina-i mlk9.de kali-bi k* kali-c st kali-i kali-n h2 **Lach** k* macro c1 **Naja** k* nat-c h2 *Nat-m* nit-ac *Ox-ac* petr **Phos** k* plat rhus-t *Sep Sil* k* spong staph thuj k* trios rsj11• tritic-vg fd5.de zinc k* zinc-p k2
  - **lying** on left side; from: chinin-s
  - **menses**; before: alum
  - **startled** from a dream●: (non:dig slp) digin a1* eupi merc plut-n srj7• pot-e rly4• rad-br ptk2 **Rhus-t** k ● sil **Sulph** k ● tritic-vg fd5.de zinc h2
  - **suddenly**: adam skp7• anan chinin-s ptk1 con k* dios *Kali-bi Merc* sec k* trios rsj11•
- **walking**:
  - **agg.**: acon k* *Apoc* arg-n aur aur-ar k2 aur-i k2 **Aur-m** aur-s k2 brom k* *Cact* calc k* cassia-s ccrh1• chel dig glon k2 iber c1 *Iod Kali-i* lyc k* merc k* **Naja** nit-ac k* nit-s-d a1 pneu jl2 saroth sp1 seneg *Sep Staph* k*
  - **air** agg.; in open: ambr k* chel k* lyc *Nux-v* k* plat k* *Sep* k* sulph k* thuj
  - **amel.**: *Arg-n* arge-pl rwt5• glon *Mag-m Nux-m Rhus-t* spong fd4.de
  - **continued**:
    - **air**; in open | **amel.**: *Sep* k*
  - **eating** agg.; after: phos k*
  - **rapidly**:
    - **agg.**: **Aur-m** bufo euphr k* ferr ferr-p **Iod** kalm *Nat-m Ph-ac Phos Puls* **Sep** thuj tritic-vg fd5.de

- **rapidly**: ...
  - **amel.**: *Arg-n Sep*
- **slowly**:
  - **agg.**: *Nit-ac* k*
  - **amel.**: *Ferr Puls*
- **warm**:
  - **agg.**: iod mrr1
  - **bathing** | **agg.**: bamb-a stb2.de• *Iod Lach* spong fd4.de
  - **drinks**:
    - **agg.**: lach k2 plut-n srj7•
    - **amel.**: nux-m k*
  - **food** | **agg.**: plut-n srj7•
  - **room** | **agg.**: am-c bg2 *Lach* puls
- **warm** agg.; becoming: rhus-g tmo3•
- **washing** hands | **cold** water; in: *Tarent* k*
- **water**; as if in: bov hr1* sumb a1*
- **wave**-like, undulating: merc-c bg2 viol-t b7.de*
- **wine**: elaps gk flav jl2 *Naja Nux-v* [tax jsj7]
  - **except** port: iber c1
- **woman**, on seeing a: (↗*MIND - Homosexuality*) *Puls* k*
- **worms**; from: spig k*
- **writing** agg.: ferr-p k* nat-c k* upa k*

▽ - **extending** to:

○ • **Ear**: carc gk6*

- **Throat**: ephe-si hsj1• graph kalm k2 kola stb3• *Nat-m* ruta fd4.de *Spong* symph fd3.de• tritic-vg fd5.de [heroin sdj2]

○ - **Abdomen**; in: asaf bg2 bism bg2 bov bg2 calc bg2 carb-v bg2 coll bg2 nat-c bg2 nat-m bg2

- **Epigastrium**; in: med ptk1 olnd b7.de*

PARALYSIS: gels bro1

○ - **Diaphragm**: arg-n hr1 bell cact cimic con st* cupr mez mosch rhus-t sil stach c2

- **Heart**: acon k* *Ant-t* k* antip c2 ars k* ars-i *Bell* k* *Bufo* cann-i cann-s hr1 **Carb-v** k* chlol k* chlor cimic k* *Crot-h* k* *Cupr* k* *Dig* k* ergot c2 *Gels* k* *Hydr-ac* k* *Iod* k* jatr-u c2 **Lach** k* lob-p c2 *Merc-cy* hr1 **Naja** **Op** k* ox-ac k* *Phos* k* phys hr1 *Plb* k* sang k* sumb k* tub c1 verat k* verat-v k*
  - **sensation** of: *Anan* vh1
- **Internally** | **sensation** of: apis b7a.de nux-v bg2
- **Lung**: am-c bg2* *Am-m* k* *Ant-ar* bro1 **Ant-t** k* arg-met k2 *Arg-n* am bro1 *Ars* k* ars-i aur bg2 bac bro1 **Bar-c** k* bar-i k2 bufo bg2 *Calc* k* camph carb-ac br1 **Carb-v** k* **Chin** k* con br1 cupr k* cur bg2* dig bg2 diphtox bro1 dulc bro1 *Gels* k* graph bg2 grin bg2* hydr-ac k* *Iod* ip bro1* kali-cy mtf11 kali-i ptk1 **Lach** k* *Laur* k* lob bg2 lob-p c2* **Lyc** k* lyss c2* merc-cy br1* morph bro1 *Mosch* k* mur-ac bg2 naja br1 op k* *Phos* k* rhus-t bg2 samb senec solin c2 *Solin-act* c1* spartin bwa3 *Stann* verat bg2
  - **left**: asc-t a1
  - **accompanied** by | **croup**: *Ant-t* bg2 **Ars** bg2 mosch bg2
  - **catarrh**; from: **Ant-t** bg2 **Ars** bg2 *Camph* bg2 carb-v bg2 *Chin* bg2 dros bg2 graph bg2 hep bg2 *Ip* bg2 merc bg2 phos bg2 puls bg2 samb bg2 spong bg2 sulph bg2 verat bg2
  - **children**; in: **Acon** bg2 **Ant-t** bg2 bell bg2 cham bg2 hep bg2 ip bg2 lyss jl2 merc bg2 **Samb** bg2 sulph bg2
  - **congestion**; from: **Acon** bg2 ars bg2 aur bg2 *Bell* bg2 *Bry* bg2 cham bg2 **Chin** bg2 **Ip** bg2 nux-v bg2 op bg2 **Phos** bg2 **Samb** bg2 spong bg2 sulph bg2 **Verat-v** bg2
  - **old** people: *Ant-t Ars* k* aur bg2 **Bar-c** k* *Carb-v* k* **Chin** k* con bg2 **Lach** bg2 lyc k* *Op* k* phos k* verat bg2
  - **scarlatina**; during: *Calc* k*
  - **sensation** of: lob
    - **left**: med c1

PERICARDITIS (See Inflammation - heart - pericardium)

PERIODICITY: chel bg2 colch bg2 merc bg2

PERSPIRATION: agar k* anac k* ant-t k* **Arg-met** k* arn k* asar k* bamb-a stb2.de• bell k* ben **Bov** k* bufo bg2 **Calc** k* calc-p k2 calc-sil k2 canth k* *Cedr* k* *Chel* k* chin k* *Chlf* br1 cimx k* **Cocc** k* *Crot-c* k* dros k* dulc fd4.de **Euphr** k* galla-q-r nl2• ger-i rly4• glon k* graph k* haliae-lc srj5• hep k* ip k*

Perspiration: ...
Kali-n k* kali-s fd4.de ketogl-ac rly4• *Lyc* k* m-arct b7.de m-aust b7.de merc k* merc-c k* nat-m bg2 nit-ac k* olib-sac wmh1 op k* ozone sde2• *Petr* k* *Ph-ac* k* **Phos** k ●* plb k* puls bg2 rhus-t k* ruta fd4.de sabad k* sec k* **Sel** k* seneg k2 *Sep* k* sil k* spig k* spong fd4.de stann bro1 *Stry* k* tab thuj bg1 tritic-vg fd5.de vanil fd5.de verat k* [mag-s stj1]

- **daytime**: petr k*
- **morning**: bamb-a stb2.de• bov k* *Cocc* k* graph kali-n spong fd4.de vanil fd5.de
- **forenoon**: arg-n k*
- **afternoon** | **17**-21 h: chel dulc fd4.de
- **evening** | **walking** agg.: chin sabad
- **night**: agar k* anac k* arg-met arg-n a1 arum-i ptk2 bamb-a stb2.de• bar-c bell k* *Calc* k* cypra-eg sde6.de• dulc fd4.de kali-c bg1 kali-p fd1.de• kali-s fd4.de nit-ac k* *Sep* k* sil k* stann k* sulph bg1 tritic-vg fd5.de vanil fd5.de
  - **midnight**: (non:lyc kl) nat-m k* ph-ac h2
    - **after**: lyc h2*
      - **4** h: sep
      - **5-6** h: bov
  - **sleep**: euphr vanil fd5.de
  - **waking**; on: canth k* dulc fd4.de tritic-vg fd5.de
- **after** | **amel.**: ant-t b7.de* canth b7.de* cham b7.de* chel bg2 nux-v b7.de* puls b7.de* *Sulph* b4a.de
- **chilliness**; during: sep k*
- **coition**; after: agar k*
- **cold** agg.: agar k* *Camph* k* canth k* cocc k* hep k* lyc k* merc *Merc-c* b4a.de* petr k* seneg k2 *Sep* k* stann k*
- **fetid**: *Arn* bg2 graph bg2 hep bg2 **Lyc** bg2 *Phos* bg2 **Sel** bg2 *Sep* bg2
- **menses**; during: *Bell* k* kreos k*
- **offensive**: *Arn* carc fb* dulc fd4.de euphr k2 graph hep **Lyc** k* phos **Sel** *Sep*
- **oily**: *Arg-met*
- **profuse**: carc fb* ina-i mlk9.de tritic-vg fd5.de
  - **agg.**: bry bg2 **Chin** bg2 **Merc** bg2 samb bg2 *Sulph* bg2
- **red**: arn k*
- **walking** rapidly agg.: nit-ac h2

○ - **Abdomen** and chest; only on (↗*ABDOMEN - Perspiration - and*) arg-met h1 cocc h1 phos h2*

- **Axillae** (= Armpits): aids nl2• *All-c* k* aloe asar k* bacls-10 pte1*• *Bov* k* **Bry** k* cadm-s *Calc* k* caps b7.de* carb-ac k* carb-an k* *Carb-v* k* carbn-s carc fb* cass a1 cassia-s ccrh1• **Cedr** k* chel k* *Cur* k* cypra-eg sde6.de• **Dulc** k* dys fmm1• gink-b sbd1• gymno ham fd3.de• *Hep* k* *Hydr* hyos k* **Kali-c** k* kali-p *Kali-s* ketogl-ac rly4• lac-ac stj2*• *Lac-c* k* lach k* lappa st* laur k* lil-t k* lyc bro1 merc-c k* moni rfm1• *Nat-m* k* *Nit-ac* k* olib-sac wmh1 orot-ac rly4• osm bro1 ox-ac k* *Petr* k* petr-ra shn4• phos k* pieri-b mlk9.de podo fd3.de• prot jl2 psil ft1 **Rhod** k* ruta fd4.de sabad k* sanic **Sel** k* **Sep** k* **Sil** k* squil k* *Stry-p* bro1 sul-ac k* **Sulph** k* symph fd3.de• tab k* *Tell* k* *Thuj* k* tritic-vg fd5.de tub k* vanil fd5.de verat k* viol-t k* zinc k* [beryl stj2 cob-m stj2 mag-lac stj2 zirc-met stj2]
  - **right**: aq-mar skp7• lac-loxod-a hrn2•
  - **daytime**: dulc k*
  - **evening**: aids nl2• dulc fd4.de ruta fd4.de sabad k*
  - **night**: ruta fd4.de sacch-a fd2.de•
  - **acrid**: dulc fd4.de sanic
  - **brown**: *Lac-c* k* thuj
  - **chill**; during: tab bg2
  - **clammy**: *Stry-p* br1
  - **cold**:
    - **agg.**: lappa bg1* symph fd3.de• [nat-f stj2]
    - **air** agg.: bov
  - **coldness**; during: tab k*
  - **copious**: carc fd2.de• cassia-s ccrh1• kali-p fd1.de• petr h2 *Prot* jl2 *Sanic* k* sel k* thuj mtf33 tritic-vg fd5.de
  - **eats** holes in the linen: iod alj psor alj sep alj sil alj*
  - **fetid**: carb-v bg2 *Dulc* bg2 **Hep** bg2 kali-p bg2 lach bg2 merc-c bg2 *Nit-ac* bg2 osm bg2 phos bg2 *Rhod* bg2 *Sel* bg2 *Sep* bg2 *Sulph* bg2 tell bg2 thuj bg2
  - **frosty** deposit in the hair; with: sel bg3* thuj st
  - **garlic**, like: *Bov Kali-p* *Lach* k* osm ozone sde2• **Sulph** k* *Tell*

- **Axillae**: ...
  - **heat**; during: zinc h2
  - **musk**; like: con bg2
  - **offensive**●: *(↗EXTREMITIES - Odor; GENERALS - Odor of - offensive)* apis bov k* *Calc* bro1 carb-ac k* cass a1 con bg1 dulc k* gink-b sbd1• **Hep** k* *Hydr* *Kali-c* bro1 kali-p fd1.de• kali-s fd4.de* *Lac-c* k* *Lach* k* lappa ptk1 *Lyc* k* med ser merc-c nat-m ser nat-s ptk1 nat-sil fd3.de• **Nit-ac** k* *Nux-m* k* nux-v ser orot-ac rly4• osm k* **Petr** k* phos k* podo fd3.de• *Rhod* k* ruta fd4.de *Sel* *Sep* k* **Sil** k* *Stry-p* bro1 **Sulph** k* symph fd3.de• *Tell* k* thuj k* tritic-vg fd5.de tub c1 [tax jsj7]
    - **menses**:
      - **between**: sep k*
      - **during** | **agg.**: stram tell
  - **onions**; like: bov bg2*
  - **red**: arn *Carb-v* dulc **Lach** k* **Nux-m** k* nux-v thuj
  - **sour** smelling: asar k* ham fd3.de• ruta fd4.de sep mtf33
  - **strong**: apis bg2
  - **yellow**: lac-c
- **Mammae**: arg-met arn bov calc fic-m gya1 hep kali-n lyc plb rhus-t sel sep
  - **morning**: bov cocc graph kali-n
  - **night**: agar bar-c calc kali-c lyc sil stann sulph
  - ○ **Between**: [cob-m stj2]
    - **fetid**: *Nux-m*
  - **Under**: galla-q-r nl2•
- **Sternum**: **Graph** k* olib-sac wmh1 ruta fd4.de vanil fd5.de
  - **morning**: **Graph** k*

PETECHIAE: ars k* cop k* stram k*
- **purple**: ars k*
- **stellated**: stram k*

PHTHISIS pulmonalis (= pulmonary tuberculosis): *(↗GENERALS - Tuberculosis)* acal bro1 *Acet-ac* k* acon bro1 **Agar** k* agarin bro1 *All-s* br1* aloe c2* alumn k2 am-c b4a.de* am-m bg2* ant-ar c2* *Ant-i* bro1 ant-t k* arg-met c2* arg-n bg2 arn k2 *Ars* k* ars-br vh *Ars-i* k* ars-s-f k2 arum-t k2 atro bro1 aur b4a.de* aur-ar c2* aur-m c2 aur-m-n c2 bac c2* bac-t c2 bals-p c2* *Bapt* bro1 bar-c b4a.de *Bar-m* k* bell bg2* berb k2 beta br3* blatta-o c2* *Brom* k* bry b7.de* *Bufo* calad b7a.de (non:calag) **Calc** k* calc-ar bro1 calc-chln bro1 calc-hp bro1 *Calc-i* k2* **Calc-p** k* *Calc-s* calc-sil k2 calo br1* cann-s bro1 *Carb-an* k* *Carb-v* k* *Carbn-s* carc jl2 card-m k* caust tl1 cetr c2* chel tl1 *Chin* b7.de* chinin-ar k2* chlor k* cimic bro1* coc-c c2* cod bro1 *Con* k* corv-cor bdg• *Crot-h* bro1 cupr-ar bro1 cur c2 dig bg2 *Dros* k* *Dulc* k* *Elaps* k* erig vml3• erio c2* eupi c2 ferr b7.de* ferr-act bro1 ferr-ar k2* *Ferr-i* k* ferr-m mtf11 *Ferr-p* k* fl-ac k* form bro1 form-ac bro1 formal br1 gad c2 gal-ac c2* *Graph* k* *Guaj* k* guajol bwa3* ham k2* helx c2* **Hep** k* hippoz k* hydr bro1 hyos bg2 hyosin-hbr bro1 ichth c2* **Iod** k* iodof bro1 ip bro1* kalag bro1 kali-ar kali-bi k2* **Kali-c** k* *Kali-n* k* *Kali-p* **Kali-s** k* kali-sil k2* *Kreos* k* lac-ac bro1 *Lac-d* k* *Lach* k* lachn c2* laur b7.de* lec br1* led k* **Lyc** k* lycps-v c2 mag-c k2 malar mtf11 *Mang* b4a.de* mang-act bro1 *Med* k* *Merc* k* mill k* *Myos-s* bro1 *Myrt-c* k* naphtin c2* nat-ar nat-cac c2* *Nat-m* k* nat-p c2* nat-s c2* *Nat-sel* bro1 *Nit-ac* k* nux-m bg2 nux-v bg2* *Ol-j* k* ox-ac k* petr k* *Ph-ac* k* phel c2* **Phos** k* pilo bro1 pineal bro1 pix c2 *Plb* k* *Polyg-a* bro1 **Psor** k* ptel hr1 **Puls** k* pyrog c2* ran-b b7.de rumx c2* *Ruta* b7.de* sabal c2 salv c2* samb k* *Sang* k* sarr c1 sel b7a.de **Senec** k* *Seneg* k* *Sep* k* **Sil** k* silpho bro1 slag c2 spig b7.de **Spong** k* **Stann** k* stann-i c2* stict c2* still succ bro1 sul-ac k* sul-i k2 **Sulph** k* tarent-c k2 teucr-s c2* thea bro1 **Ther** k* thuj tl1 thyr c2 tril-p br1 **Tub** k* tub-a c2* tub-d al2 urea bro1 vanad bro1* verb c1 **Zinc** k* zinc-i c2 zinc-p k2 [mag-p stj1]
- **accompanied** by:
  - **ascarides**: ferr b7a.de
  - **coldness**: lachn br1
  - **cough**: acon b7a.de arn b7a.de sep b4a.de stann b4a.de
  - **diabetes**: *(↗Lungs; complaints of the - Accompanied - diabetes; GENERALS - Diabetes mellitus - Accompanied - respiration)* phos a2*
  - **diarrhea**: acet-ac bro1 arg-n bro1 arn bro1 *Ars* bro1 ars-i bro1 calc bro1 *Chin* bro1 *Coto* bro1 iod bro1 iodof bro1 *Ph-ac* bro1 *Phos* bro1 sil bro1
  - **dyspnea**: carb-v bro1 ip bro1 phos bro1

Phthisis pulmonalis – **accompanied** by: ...
  - **emaciation** (See GENERALS - Cachexia - tuberculosis)
  - **fever**; high: ars b4a.de bry b7a.de *Chin* b7a.de *Dros* b7a.de dulc b4a.de *Ferr* b7a.de *Laur* b7a.de nat-m b4a.de ph-ac b4a.de puls b7a.de stann b4a.de
  - **hemorrhage**: *(↗incipient - accompanied - arteries)* acal bro1 *Achil-m* bro1 *Acon* bro1 calc-ar bro1 ferr bro1 *Ferr-act* bro1 *Ferr-p* bro1 *Ham* bro1 helx gm1 *Ip* bro1 mill bro1 nit-ac bro1 nux-v bro1 *Phos* bro1 pilo-m bro1 solid br1 tril-p br1*
  - **indigestion**: ars bro1 calc bro1 carb-v bro1 *Cupr-ar* bro1 ferr-act bro1 ferr-ar bro1 gal-ac bro1 *Hydr* bro1 kreos bro1 *Nux-v* bro1 stry bro1 tub-a bro1
  - **jaundice**: ferr b7a.de puls b7a.de
  - **perspiration**: ars bg2 bry bg2 calc bg2 carb-v bg2 chin bg2 eupi bg2 ferr bg2 hep bg2 jab bro1 ph-ac bg2 phos bg2 samb bg2 sep bg2 sil bg2 stann bg2 sulph bg2
    - **night**: *Acet-ac* bro1 *Agar* bro1 ars bro1* ars-i bro1 atro bro1 bol-la br1 bry ptk1 calc ptk1 carb-v ptk1 chin bro1* erio br1* ferr ptk1 gal-ac bro1 hep bro1 *Jab* br1* kali-i bro1 lyc bro1 myos-s bro1 ph-ac bro1* phos bro1* pilo bro1 pilo-m bro1 *Salv* br1* samb bro1* sec bro1 sep ptk1 sil bro1* silpho bro1 stann bro1* sulph ptk1
  - **respiration**; asthmatic: meph ptk1
  - **vomiting**: kali-br bro1 kreos bro1*
    - **blood**: kali-br ptk1 kreos ptk1
  - ○ **Eyes**; inflammation of: puls b7a.de
  - **Heart**:
    - **complaints** of: puls b7a.de
    - **weakness** of (See Weakness - heart - accompanied - tuberculosis)
  - **Liver**; complaints of: chel bro1
  - **Mouth**; soreness in: lach bro1
  - **Tongue**:
    - **brown** discoloration: *Guaj* kr1*
    - **pale**: *Ferr* kr1*
    - **white** discoloration of the tongue: ars-i kr1*
- **acute**: ant-t bro1 *Ars* k* *Bry* k* calc bro1 calc-i bro1 *Chin* *Cimic* dros k* *Dulc* k* ferr k* ferr-act bro1 ferr-m bro1 **Ferr-p** k* *Hep* k* *Iod* bro1 *Kali-chl* kali-p *Kreos* lach k* laur k* led bg2 **Lyc** bg2 *Med* merc bg2 nat-m *Phos* k* pilo-m bro1 **Puls** k* *Sang* bro1 **Senec** **Sil** k* stann *Sulph* k* **Ther** k* tub bro1
  - **exacerbations** in all stages of: ferr-p pd *Kali-n* k*
  - **menses**; from suppressed: **Senec** k*
- **beginning** (See incipient)
- **catarrhal**: ars bg2 calc bg2 carb-v bg2 chin bg2 dig bg2 **Dulc** bg2 **Hep** bg2 *Lach* bg2 lyc bg2 *Merc* bg2 phos bg2 puls bg2 *Seneg* bg2 *Sep* bg2 sil bg2 **Stann** bg2 **Sulph** bg2 zinc bg2
- **chronic**: myos-a br1 sulo-ac mtf11
- **diarrhea**; from suppressed: ph-ac k2
- **discharges** | **suppressed**: bufo k2
- **epilepsy** | **suppressed**: bufo k2
- **exudative** state: *Am-c* b4a.de *Brom* b4a.de **Bry** b7a.de *Calc* b4a.de *Caust* b4a.de **Con** b4a.de *Hep* b4a.de *Iod* b4a.de *Kali-c* b4a.de *Kali-n* b4a.de *Kreos* b7a.de **Lyc** b4a.de *Merc* b4a.de *Petr* b4a.de *Phos* b4a.de puls b7a.de *Spong* b7a.de *Stann* b4a.de *Sulph* b4a.de
- **fibrosis**: *(↗Fibrosis)* bry bro1 calc bro1 sang bro1 *Sil* bro1 tub mtf11
- **fistula**; after operated anal: sil dp•
- **florida**: *Ferr* k* med nat-p *Puls* k* *Sang* k* **Ther** k*
- **hemorrhage**; after: *Chin* k* ferr-p c2
- **incipient**: acal br1* *Acet-ac* *Agar* k* *Ars-i* br1* *Bry* k* cact **Calc** k* calc-i bro1 **Calc-p** k* calc-sil mtf33 *Carb-v* k* *Dros* bro1 *Dulc* erig ptk2 *Ferr* k* ferr-p k* **Hep** k* iod bro1 **Kali-c** k* kali-i bro1 **Kali-p** *Lach* k* lachn br1* **Lyc** k* *Lycps-v* mang-act bro1 **Med** k* myrt-c br1* *Nat-s* k* ol-j bro1 petr **Phos** k* polyg-a bro1 **Psor** k* **Puls** k* *Rumx* *Sang* k* sec bro1 **Senec** k* **Sil** k* **Stann** succ bro1 *Sulph* k* *Ther* thuj tril-p bro1 **Tub** k* vanad bro1
  - **accompanied** by:
    - **Arteries**; hemorrhage from: *(↗accompanied - hemorrhage)* acal br1
    - **Tongue**; aphthae on: agar vk1 iod vk1 sulph vk1
  - **fever**; without: acal br1
  - ○ **Apex** of lungs: sulph mtf33
    - **left**: sulph mtf33

- **injury** to the chest, after: mill bro1* *Ruta* k*
- **last** stage: am-c k2 ars bry **Calc** k* **Carb-v** k* *Chin* k* *Dros* *Euon* kali-n **Lach** k* led lob k* **Lyc** k* *Phel* k* *Phos* k* *Psor* **Puls** k* *Pyrog* k* **Sang** k* *Seneg* **Tarent** k*
- **lying** on side agg.: calc
- **mercury**; after abuse of: calc bg2 *Carb-v* bg2 chin bg2 dulc bg2 *Guaj* bg2 **Hep** bg2 *Lach* bg2 lyc bg2 **Nit-ac** bg2 sil bg2 *Sulph* bg2
- **miners**, from coal dust: carbn-s nat-ar k2*
- **nervous**: bell b4a.de con b4a.de lyc b4a.de ph-ac b4a.de
- **nursing** mothers: *Kali-c* k*
- **old** people: *Nat-s* k* seneg mrr1
- **painful**: acon bro1 *Bry* bro1 calc bro1 cimic bro1 guaj bro1 *Kali-c* bro1 myrt-c bro1 phos bro1 pix bro1
- **pituitous**: *Aesc* k* **Ant-c** k* **Ant-t** k* ars b4a.de *Bar-m* bell b4a.de caust k* *Coc-c* dig b4a.de *Dulc* k* **Euon** k* *Ferr* **Ferr-p** k* **Hep** k* *Kali-c* k* **Kali-chl** k* **Kali-i** k* *Kreos* k* *Lach* **Lyc** k* **Med** *Merc* k* *Merc-c* mill k* *Nat-s* k* nit-ac b4a.de **Phos** k* **Psor** k* *Puls* k* **Sang** k* **Senec** k* *Seneg* k* sep b4a.de *Sil* **Stann** k* sul-ac b4a.de *Sulph* **Ther**
- **pressure** in intercostal muscles, from within outward, respiration agg.; with: **Asaf** hr1
- **progressive**: acon bg2 **Am-c** bg2 am bg2 ars bg2 bell bg2 *Calc* bg2 *Carb-v* bg2 dulc bg2 ferr bg2 **Hep** bg2 hyos bg2 *Kali-c* bg2 kali-n bg2 *Lyc* bg2 merc bg2 *Nit-ac* bg2 **Phos** bg2 **Spong** bg2 stann bg2 sul-ac bg2 **Sulph** bg2
- **purulent** and ulcerative: am-c bg2 am bg2 *Ars* k* *Ars-i* bell bg2 brom k* bry k* **Calc** k* *Carb-an* *Carb-v* k* *Carbn-s* chin k* con bg2 *Dros* k* dulc bg2* *Ferr* bg2* guaj k* *Hep* k* hyos k* **Iod** k* **Kali-c** k* *Kali-n* k* *Kali-p* kreos bg1 *Lach* k* laur bg2* led k* **Lyc** k* *Merc* k* nat-c bg2 nat-m k* *Nit-ac* k* *Nux-m* k* ph-ac bg2 **Phos** k* *Plb* *Psor* *Puls* k* rhus-t bg2 ruta samb bg2 sep k* *Sil* k* **Spong** bg2 stann k* *Sulph* k* zinc bg2
- **stone**-cutters: calc b4a.de* *Hep* bg2 lach bg2 lyc bg2* *Sil* k* sulph bg2
- **sycotic**: ars **Aur** *Aur-m* bar-c bry **Calc** k* *Carb-an* carb-v *Caust* cham chin *Dulc* *Ferr-p* *Lach* **Lyc** k* **Med** **Nat-s** k* **Nit-ac** k* *Phyt* *Puls* sep *Sil* staph sulph *Ther* **Thuj** k*
- **weather** agg.; cold wet: *Dulc*
- **young** people; in: fil br1
- ○ - **Bronchial** tubes: erio br1
- **Middle** lobes: phel br1

PICKING with fingers; sensation as if: | **External** chest: cic b7.de* phos b4.de*

PLEURALGIA (See Pain - pleura)

PLEURISY (See Inflammation - pleura)

PLEURODYNIA (See Pain - intercostal - muscles)

PLEUROPNEUMONIA (See Inflammation - lungs - pleuropneumonia)

PLUG; sensation of a: *(↗Pain - pressing - plug)* am-m ptk1 *Ambr* ptk1 anac k* aur k* cupr ptk1 *Kali-m* ptk1 *Phos* ptk1 *Ran-s* ptk1 stict ptk1 sulph ptk1 tarax ptk1 thlas ptk1 zinc ptk1
- ○ - **Intercostal** region: anac ptk1 aur ptk1 caust ptk1 cocc ptk1 *Lyc* ptk1 *Ran-s* ptk1 *Verat* ptk1

PNEUMONIA (See Inflammation - lungs)

PNEUMOTHORAX: *(↗Atelectasis)* acon-f mtf arn hr1* chlorpr jl1*
- **injuries**; after: arn hr1

POLLUTION; symptoms of heart and faintness are agg. after: asaf a1*

POLYPI: | **Heart**: calc bg2 lach bg2 staph bg2

PRESSURE:
- **abdomen**; on | **agg.**: *Cham* b7a.de
- **agg.**: am-m b7.de* ang b7.de* ant-c b7.de* asc-t bg2 *Bry* b7.de* **Chin** b7.de* *Cina* b7.de* *Dros* b7a.de ferr-p bg2 **Lach** bg2 meny b7.de* *Mosch* b7a.de nux-m b7.de* nux-v b7.de* olnd b7.de* plb bg2 ran-b b7.de* ran-s b7.de* ruta b7.de* seneg b4.de* spong b7.de* staph b7.de* sul-ac b4.de* *Sulph* b4a.de tarax b7.de* valer b7.de* viol-t b7.de*
  - **clothes** agg; of: benz-ac ptk1 con bg2
- **amel.**: am b7a.de* asaf b7.de* aur bg2 borx b4a.de* *Bry* b7.de* bufo bg2 caust ptk1 chin b7.de* cina b7.de* *Dros* b7.de* eup-per ptk1 ign b7.de* kreos b7a.de* meny b7.de* mosch b7a.de nat-m bg2 nat-s bg2* plb bg2 puls b7.de* sep bg2 verat b7.de* verb b7.de*

Pressure: ...
- **arms** against body agg.; of: psor bg2 spig bg2
- **hand**; of | **amel.**: *Cupr* b7a.de sep ptk1
- **spine** agg.; on: sec ptk1 tarent ptk1

PRICKLING: *(↗Tingling)* acon bg2 agar h2 bufo bg2 cadm-s bg2 calc h2 melal-alt gya4 petr-ra shn4• plat h2 seneg bg2
- ○ - **Axilla**; in: mez h2
- **Mammae**: arg-n bg2 cimic bg2
- **Thoracic** region: melal-alt gya4

PROTRUSION:
- **right** chest; stronger | **Ribs**: nat-m h2
- ○ - **Ribs**: *Spig* b7.de*
- **Sternum**: iris bg2

PULSATION: abrom-a bnj1 acon b7.de* agar k* alum b4.de* am-m k* anac b4.de* ars-h k* asaf k* *Aster* k* bapt bg2 *Bar-c* k* **Bell** k* bov b4.de* bry b7.de* *Cact* k* calad k* calc k* *Calc-p* k* calc-s k2 cann-s b7.de* *Caps* k* carb-v b4a.de* caust k* *Cham* b7.de* chel k* cinnb coc-c bg1 *Coff* b7.de* colch k* crot-t k* *Dig* k* dulc b4.de* fuma-ac rly4• glon bg2* graph k* hed sp1 hura *Hydr* k* ign k* iod h kali-bi bg2 *Kali-c* k* kali-n h2 kali-p kali-s fd4.de kreos bg2 lach k* lact k* lyc k* mag-m k* manc k* mang k* meny b7.de* merc k* nat-c k* nat-sil fd3.de• nux-m k* nux-v k* olnd b7.de* paeon k* par b7.de* *Phos* k* *Puls* k* ran-b b7.de* rumx sang bg2 **Seneg** k* *Sep* k* *Sil* k* *Spig* k* squil b7.de* stroph-s sp1 sulph k* thuj k* trom k* verat b7.de* visc sp1 *Zinc* k* [tax jsj7]
- **morning**: am-m k* *Cact* k* nat-sil fd3.de•
- **evening**:
  - **lying** | **after** | **agg.**: lyc
    - **bed**; in:
      - **after** | **agg.**: mang h2
  - ○ **Heart**; about: scut c1
- **night**: *Aster* k* nat-sil fd3.de• **Puls** k* sulph h2
  - **sleep**; interrupting: **Puls**
  - **waking**; on: **Sulph**
- **breathing**:
  - **holding** breath | **amel.**: sulph h2
- **cough** agg.; during: manc k*
- **eating**; after: am-m k* asaf k*
- **here** and there: coc-c bg1
- **lying** after eating agg.: asaf
- **lying** down agg.: galeoc-c-h gms1• meny h1
- **motion** agg.: *Glon* k* phos k*
- **standing** agg.: am-m k* nat-sil fd3.de•
- **talking** agg.: manc k*
- **trembling**: ars calc kreos *Nat-s* *Rhus-t* sabin *Spig* staph
- **waking**; on: galeoc-c-h gms1•
- **walking** rapidly agg.: nit-ac h2
- **wine** | **amel.**: nit-ac h2
- **writing** agg.: mag-s
- **yawning** agg.: calc bg2
- ○ - **Anterior** part: kali-n h2
- **Aorta**: plb k* sulph k* tarent k*
- **Axillae**: am-m k* cocc h1 dulc k* iod bg2 lyc bg2 puls bg2 spong k* zinc bg2
  - **right**:
    - **extending** to | **left**: lac-h htj1•
  - ▽ **extending** to arm: lac-h htj1•
- **Clavicles**; region of: berb bry k* *Kali-c* k* *Myrt-c* rhod k*
  - **night**: nit-ac h2
- **Costal** cartilages: plat k*
- **External** chest: am-m b7.de* bov b4.de* chin b7.de* nat-c b4.de* olnd b7.de* ran-b b7.de* sil b4a.de
- **Heart**: ars b4.de* bar-c b4.de* bov b4.de* calad b7.de* calc b4.de* clem bg2 colch bg2 crot-t bg2 fl-ac bg2 fuma-ac rly4• glon mrr1 graph b4a.de* hell b7.de* hydrog srj2• lyc b4.de* m-aust b7.de* melal-alt gya4 naja bg2 nux-v bg2 phos b4.de* plb bg2 rhus-t bg2 sec bg2 sep b4.de* sil b4.de* stroph-s sp1 sulph b4.de* term-a bnj1 zinc b4.de*
  - **morning** | **bed** agg.; in: graph h2
  - **ascending** agg.: stroph-s sp1
  - **radiating** from the heart: acon bg2 lil-t bg2

- **Heart**: ...
  - **shaking** the body: aloe bg2 alum bg2 ars bg2 bell bg2 bov bg2 glon bg2 nat-m bg2* rhus-t bg2 spig bg2 verat bg2
  - **waking**; on: galeoc-c-h gms1•
    - **awareness**; of: galeoc-c-h gms1•
▽ - **extending** to | **Head**: stroph-s sp1
○ - **About**, as if: galeoc-c-h gms1• scut rb2
- **Mammae**: *Bell* b4a.de borx k* cench k2 *Phos* b4a.de symph fd3.de•
○ - **Nipples**: zinc bg2
- **Ribs**: kali-c h2
○ - **False** ribs: puls
- **Sides**: nux-v bg2
  - **right**: asar ptk1 chel bg2 crot-t ptk1 dig h2* ign ptk1 ind ptk1 paeon ptk1 phos ptk1
    - **Lower** right side: phos h2
  - **left**: am-m h2* cann-xyz ptk1 gels ptk1 graph h2 meny h1* nat-c h2 sep h2 *Thuj* h1 zinc h2
    - **evening**: mag-c h2
    - **crackling**: sulph h2
- **Sternum**: ang h1 ars-met chin h1 *Lach* k* nat-c h2 *Sil* k* sulph k*
  - **right** side:
    - **extending** to | **Abdomen**; down: *Stict* c1*
○ - **Behind**: bell h1

PURPURA: kali-i k* phos k*

PURRING: *(↗Noises)* caust bg2* glon ptk1 **Spig** bg2*
○ - **Region** of heart:
  - **noise** in; purring: *(↗Noises)* *Glon* k* iod ptk1 pyrog k2* *Spig* ptk1 sulph bg2
  - **sensation** of; purring: caust bg3 pyrog bro1 *Spig* k*

QUIVERING (See Trembling)

RAISING ARMS agg.: *Acon* b7a.de anac bg2 ang bg2 ant-c b7.de* borx b4a.de bry b7.de* caps b7.de* chin b7.de* *Cupr* b7a.de ferr b7.de* kali-bi bg2 led b7.de* plb b7.de* puls bg2 ran-b b7.de* sulph b4a.de tarent bg2* tell ptk1 thuj b4.de*

RATTLING in (See RESPIRATION - Rattling)

RAWNESS, sternum (See Pain - sternum - raw)

READING:
- **agg.**: chin b7.de*
- **aloud** | **agg.**: cocc b7.de* nat-m bg2 *Puls* b7a.de

REDNESS (See Discoloration - redness)

RELAXED sensation: *Rhus-t* b7.de*

RESPIRATION: | **difficult** respiration agg.: *Nux-v* bg2

REST:
- **agg.**: arg-met b7.de* arn b7.de* bell b4.de* *Calc* b4a.de caps b7.de* cham b7.de* chin b7.de* cycl b7.de* *Euph* b4a.de ferr b7.de* *Kali-c* b4a.de m-aust b7.de meny b7.de* nat-m b4.de* par b7a.de ph-ac b4.de* puls b7.de* *Rhus-t* b7.de* ruta b7.de* samb b7.de* *Seneg* b4.de* *Sep* b4a.de stann b4.de*
- **amel.**: acon bg2 arn b7.de* *Bry* b7.de* chin b7.de* meny b7.de* nux-v b7.de* sabin b7.de* squil b7.de* staph b7.de* sul-ac b4.de*

RESTING, supporting:
- **arms** | **agg.**: arg-met b7.de*

RESTLESSNESS: bamb-a stb2.de• bell k* chin b7.de* fl-ac bg2 led b7.de* m-aust b7.de olib-sac wmh1 petr k* petr-ra shn4• seneg k* staph b7.de* thuj k* [buteo-j sej6]
- **accompanied** by | **nausea**: petr-ra shn4•
○ - **Heart**; about: anac k* arg-n bg2 *Ars* k* fl-ac bg2 kola stb3• lyss pyrid rly4•
  - **coryza**; during: anac b4a.de

RETRACTION of nipples: *(↗Inversion; Inversion - nipples)* ars-i pd aster vh *Aur-m-n* bro1 bell-p sne cadm-met sne* calc bro1 carb-an k* carc mlr1• caul bro1 cimic bro1 con k* croc bro1 crot-t bg2 cund k* *Epiph* bro1 ferr-i bro1 *Frax* bro1 graph ptk1 *Helon* bro1 hydr hr1* *Kali-br* bro1 lach hr1* lap-a bro1 *Lil-t* bro1 mel-c-s bro1 nat-hchls bro1 nat-s hr1* *Nux-m* k* phyt ptk1 podo bro1 **Sars** k* scir gm1 *Sec* bro1 *Sep* bro1 *Sil* k* thuj bg3* tub ptk1 ust bro1

REVOLVING; sensation as if the heart were: ant-t k*

RHEUMATIC complaints agg.; after: **Acon** bg2 *Ars* bg2 bell bg2 bry bg2 carb-v bg2 *Caust* bg2 *Cham* bg2 *Chin* bg2 coff bg2 *Hep* bg2 *Ign* bg2 *Lach* bg2 *Merc* bg2 nux-v bg2 phos bg2 **Puls** bg2 sil bg2 *Sulph* bg2

RHEUMATIC heart disease (See Pain - heart - rheumatic)

RIDING:
- **horse**; a: | **agg.**: graph b4.de* valer b7.de*

RIGHT side; heart seems to be on the: *Borx* b4a.de* ox-ac ptk1 *Phyt* ptk1

RISING:
- **after**:
  - **agg.**: am-m b7.de* nux-v b7.de* olnd b7.de* puls b7.de* *Ran-b* b7.de* rhus-t b7.de* spig b7.de*
  - **amel.**: alum bg2 canth b7.de* carb-an b4.de* dulc b4.de* glon bg2 mur-ac bg2 nux-v b7.de* puls b7.de* ran-b b7.de* rhus-t b7.de* stront-c b4.de*
- **agg.**: bell bg2 con bg2 kali-n bg2 sulph bg2
- **bed**; from | **agg.**: ant-c b7.de* ars bg2 calad b7.de* merc-c b4a.de plat b4.de* ran-b b7.de* stann b4.de* staph b7.de* *Verat* b7a.de
- **sitting**; from | **agg.**: brom bg2 calc-p bg2 kali-n b4.de* mag-m bg2 sil b4.de*
- **stooping**; from:
  - **agg.**: *Acon* b7.de* arg-met b7.de* *Bry* b7.de* calad b7.de* cann-s b7.de* cic b7.de* *Colch* b7a.de dig b4.de* ign b7.de* ran-b b7.de* stann b4.de* staph b7.de*
  - **amel.**: alum b4.de* ang b7.de* ars b4a.de asaf b7.de* bry b7a.de chin b7.de* dig b4.de* lach bg2 mang b4.de* olnd b7.de* puls b7.de* spig b7.de*

RISING; sensation of something: borx b4a.de phos bg2 stann bg2 thuj bg2
- **fever**; during: am-m bg2 merc bg2 *Nux-v* bg2 phos bg2
- **hot**; something: phos b4a.de plat b4a.de thuj b4a.de
○ - **Heart**: *(↗Heat - rising upward)* caust bg2 coloc ptk1 glon bg2 podo bg2* spong bg2* valer ptk1
○ - **Throat**; from heart to: *(↗Heat - rising upward)* caust ptk1 glon ptk1 phel vml3• phyt ptk1 podo ptk1 [tax jsj7]

RIVET or bullet; sensation of a: | **Lungs** | **left**: sulph ptk1
- **Mammae**; region of: lil-t k*

ROOM:
- **agg.**: bry b7.de* croc b7.de* laur b7.de* mag-p bg2 puls b7.de* *Rhod* b4.de* *Seneg* b4.de* spig b7.de* sul-ac b4.de* *Sulph* b4a.de verb b7.de*
- **amel.**: bry b7.de* cham b7.de* nux-v b7.de*

ROUGHNESS; sensation of: am-c bg2 ars bg2 calc bg2 carb-v bg2 kreos bg2 lyc bg2 merc bg2 sep bg2 sulph bg2 zinc bg2
- **coryza**; during: carb-v b4.de* kreos b7a.de nux-v b7a.de sulph b4.de*

RUBBING:
- **agg.**: phos bg2
- **amel.**: acon bg2 anac b4.de* calc b4.de* mur-ac bg2
○ - **Mammae**: *(↗Itching - mammae)* choc srj3•
- **Pleura** | **left**: tub jl2

RUMBLING: bros-gau mrc1 cocc b7.de* loxo-lae bnm12• nat-m bg2
- **audible**:
○ - **Sides** | **left**: cocc ptk1
- **cough** agg.; during: *Mur-ac* b4a.de
- **downward**: *Mur-ac* b4a.de
- **lying** down agg.: bros-gau mrc1

RUNNING agg.: borx b4a.de bry b7.de* cina b7.de* nux-v b7.de* plb bg2 seneg b4.de* *Sil* b4.de*

RUSH of blood (See Heat - flushes; Orgasm)

RUSHING in heart region: caust h2*

SADNESS felt in: arge-pl rwt5•
○ - **Heart**: calc bg2

SARCOIDOSIS pulmonalis: *(↗Fibrosis; GENERALS - Besnier-boeck-schaumann)* ars-br mtf *Ars-i* mtf *Beryl* mtf lyc mtf *Mang-s* mtf nat-ar mrr1* parathyr mtf pin-s mtf puls mtf tub mtf *Tub-m* mtf v-a-b mtf

SCLEROSIS of coronaries (See Arteriosclerosis)

SENILE heart (See Heart; complaints - old)

SENSITIVE: (↗*Pain - sore)* *Alum-sil* bro1 am-c b4a.de ang b7.de* ant-t bro1 *Apis* b7a.de aral bro1 *Arn* bro1 ars bro1 asc-t bg2* *Bry* bro1 calc bg2* calc-p bro1 calc-sil bro1 cann-s b7.de* canth b7.de* *Carb-v* bro1 *Caust* bro1 cimic bro1 cur bro1 *Eup-per* bro1 falco-pe nl2• ferr-p bro1 ham bro1 helon *Iod* bro1 kali-c bro1 med jl2 *Merc* bro1 mosch bg2 naja bg2 naphtin bro1 nat-c k* *Nat-s* bro1 nit-ac bro1 nux-v k* *Ol-j* bro1 *Phos* bro1 pop-cand bro1 puls bro1 *Ran-b* b7.de* ran-s b7.de* *Rumx* bro1 ruta bg2 sang bro1 seneg k* sep bro1 spong bro1 stann bro1 stront-c k* sulph k* zinc k*
- **cold** air; to: aesc tl1 *Ph-ac*

O · **Bronchial** tubes: all-s bro1 *Aral* bro1 bac bro1 calc-sil bro1 *Cham* bro1 chin bro1 *Cor-r* bro1 *Dulc* bro1 *Hep* bro1 iod bro1 kali-c bro1 mang-act bro1 *Merc* bro1 naja bro1 *Psor* bro1 *Sil* bro1 *Tub* bro1
- **touch**; slightest: ang c1

O - **Axillae**: kali-c b4a.de* nit-ac k* sul-ac k*
- **Internally**: *Ang* b7a.de *Calc* b4a.de chin bg2 nat-m bg2 seneg b4.de*
- **Lower** part: nat-c h2
- **Mammae** (See Pain - mammae - sore)

SEPARATED sensation: | **forcibly**; as if separated | **Lungs**: elaps ptk1*

O - **Mammae** separated from body plut-n srj7•

SHAKING of chest:
- **cough** agg.; during: aur bg1 bell bg1 bry bg1 calc-ar cench crot-h bg1 gels bg1 hyos kali-n bg1 *Lact* k* *Led* b7a.de lil-t bg1 mag-s k* mez bg1 phos bg1 plb bg1 rhus-t k*
- **shuddering**; with: mez h2*

SHIVERING: acon bg2 carb-an bg2 chin bg2 cina bg2 cocc bg2 *Dig* bg2 guaj bg2 hep bg2 kali-n bg2 **Meny** bg2 **Nux-v** bg2 ozone sde2• *Plat* bg2 ruta bg2 spig bg2 staph bg2

O - **Mammae** (See Chilliness - mammae)

SHOCKS: (↗*Jerks)* acon b7.de* alum ang k* ant-t arn k* calc k* cann-s k* cham b7a.de clem k* **Con** k* croc k* dulc k* *Graph* hep ind lat-m bnm6• led b7a.de* **Lyc** k* m-arct b7.de mang k* meny mez b4.de* mur-ac k* myrt-c nux-v ol-an olnd b7.de* *Plat* k* rhus-t k* ruta k* sec seneg b4.de* sep *Sulph* k* thuj bg2 zinc
- **cough**; with: con h2 **Lyc** k* *Seneg* k*
- **heart** beat, with the: calc k* nux-v bg1
  - **sleep** agg.; during: *Lach* spong

O - **Heart**; region of: acon bg2 *Agar* k* alum k* ang b7.de* ant-t b7.de* am b7.de* *Aur* b4a.de *Bufo* k* *Calc* k* cann-s b7.de* **Con** k* gels bg2 glon bg2* *Graph* k* hydrog srj2• lach *Lith-c* k* lyss mang k* nat-m bg2 *Nux-v* k* phos b4a.de phyt k* *Sep* b4a.de *Sulph* b4a.de tab bg2* *Zinc* k*
  - **chill**; during: calc nux-v
  - **dinner**; after: phos h2
  - **grief**; with: hydrog srj2•
  - **lying** agg.: *Agar*
  - **noise** agg.: *Agar* k* *Nux-v*
  - **sleep** agg.; during: *Lach*

▽ · **extending** to:
  ⁝ **Abdomen** and sacrum: nux-v
  ⁝ **Neck**; front of: graph
- **Sides**:
  - **left**: mang h2 sil h2 sulph h2
    ⁝ **Upper** part | **breathing** deep agg.: acon vh1

SHORT; sensation as if too: nux-v b7.de*

SHUDDERING: acon b7.de* agar ptk1 aur k*
- **right**: aur gels bg2
- **yawning** agg.: aur

O - **Mammae** (See Chilliness - mammae)

SICK FEELING; vague: acon bg2 arn b7.de* carb-v b4.de* spong b7.de*

O - **Heart**: cann-xyz bg2

SIDES: **Acon** bg2 am-c bg2 ang bg2 arg-met bg2 **Arn** bg2 brom bg2 **Bry** bg2 calc bg2 canth bg2 chin bg2 clem bg2 cocc bg2 con bg2 croc bg2 dulc bg2 grat bg2 hyos bg2 ign bg2 kreos bg2 lach bg2 meny bg2 *Merc* bg2 mosch bg2 nat-c bg2 nat-m bg2 nit-ac bg2 nux-v bg2 op bg2 par bg2 petr bg2 ph-ac bg2 **Phos** bg2 *Plat* bg2 plb bg2 **Puls** bg2 ran-b bg2 rhus-t bg2 sabad bg2 samb bg2 sars bg2 *Sil* bg2 **Squil** bg2 *Sulph* bg2 tarax bg2 zinc bg2

O - **Heart** seems to be on the right side (See Right)

SINGING agg.: am-c b4.de* carb-an b4a.de* carb-v b4a.de dros h1 *Puls* b7a.de stann b4.de* *Sulph* b4a.de

SINKING sensation: glon bg2 phos bg2

O - **Heart** (See Weakness - heart - about)

SITTING:
- **agg.**: acon bg2 agar bg2 am-c b4.de* am-m b7.de* anac b4.de* ang b7.de* ant-t b7.de* arg-met b7.de* ars b4.de* asaf b7.de* bell b4.de* calc b4.de* caps b7.de* carb-an b4.de* *Carb-v* b4.de* caust bg2 chel b7.de* chin b7.de* cina b7.de* colch bg2 coloc b4.de* cycl b7.de* dig bg2 dros b7.de* dulc b4.de* euph b4.de* ferr b7.de* led b7.de* mag-m b4.de* mang b4.de* meny b7.de* merc b4.de* mez b4.de* mur-ac b4.de* nat-c b4.de* petr bg2 **Phos** b4.de* puls b7.de* **Rhus-t** b7.de* ruta b7.de* sabad b7.de* sars b4.de* seneg b4.de* *Sep* b4a.de sil b4.de* spig b7.de* spong b7.de* stann b4.de* staph b7.de* sulph b4.de* tarax b7.de* teucr b7.de* thuj b4.de* valer b7.de* viol-t b7.de*
- **amel.**: acon bg2 alum b4.de* am-m b7.de* ang b7.de* bry b7.de* caps b7.de* colch bg2 glon bg2 nux-m b7.de* nux-v b7.de*
- **bent** forward | **agg.**: ang b7a.de arg-met b7.de* *Chin* b7.de* *Dig* b4a.de meny b7.de* rhod b4.de* *Rhus-t* b7.de* spig b7.de* spong b7.de*
- **erect**:
  - **agg.**: acon b7.de* nat-m b4.de* *Nit-ac* b4a.de
  - **amel.**: ang bg2 asaf bg2

SLEEP:
- **after**:
  - **agg.**: acon b7.de* ambr b7.de* bry b7.de* calc b4.de* chin b7.de* cocc b7.de* euphr b7.de* ign b7.de* kali-c b4a.de* m-ambo b7.de nux-m b7.de* nux-v b7.de* op b7.de* rheum b7.de* sabad b7.de* staph b7a.de*
  - **amel.**: nat-c b4.de*
- **during**: calc bg2 ph-ac bg2
- **falling** asleep; when | **agg.**: am-m b7.de* anac b4a.de ars b4a.de carb-v bg2 colch bg2 dig bg2 mez bg2 nux-m b7.de* phos bg2 ran-b b7.de* sulph b4.de*
- **siesta**:
  - **after** | **agg.**: staph b7a.de
- **starting** up from sleep agg.: nat-m bg2 ph-ac bg2

SMALL chest:
- **sensation** as if chest were too small: both-ax tsm2 ign k*

O - **Lung**; sensation of small right abies-c br1

SMALL mammae: cham b7.de* iod ptk1 lac-ac stj5• lyc ptk1 nux-m b7.de* onos ptk1 sabal ptk1 sulph ptk1
- **have** become smaller; mammae (See Atrophy - mammae)
- **one** mamma is smaller than the other: **Sabal** ptk1*

SMASHED; sensation in side of chest, as if ribs were: ph-ac h2

SMOKE in chest; as if: ars k* *Bar-c* k* brom bry merc ptk1 *Nat-ar*

SMOKED food; after: *Calc* b4a.de sil b4a.de

SMOKING agg.: cic b7.de* cycl b7.de* ign b7.de* phos bg2 seneg b4.de* spong b7.de* staph b7.de* thuj bg2

SNAPPING like breaking a thread: podo c1

SNEEZING:
- **agg.**: acon b7.de* agar bg2 ant-t b7.de* bell bg2 borx b4a.de* bry b7.de* caust ptk1 cina b7.de* dros b7a.de* grat bg2 hydr bg2 kali-bi bg2 merc b4.de* mez b4.de* phos bg2 *Rhus-t* b7a.de sec b7a.de seneg b4.de* sil b4.de* sulph b4a.de
- **amel.**: seneg bg2

SOFTNESS: | **sensation** of a soft substance | **Sternum**; under: brom bg2

O - **Mammae**; of: plut-n srj7• [heroin sdj2]

Chest

SOLDIER'S HEART (See Palpitation - irritable)

SOUNDS (See Murmurs; Noises)

SOUR food agg.: *Bell* bg2

SPASMODIC motion in: arn k*

SPASMS of: *(↗Pain - cramping)* acon k* aeth ptk1 alum bg2 ang k* arg-met b7.de* *Arg-n* k* *Ars* k* **Asaf** k* *Bell* k* bov b4.de* *Bry* b7.de* cact ptk1 *Calc* k* camph k* *Cann-s* k* *Carb-v* b4a.de *Caust* b4a.de* *Cham* k* chin k* *Cic* k* cina k* *Cocc* k* coff b7.de* *Colch* k* *Cupr* k* dig b4.de* *Elat* k* *Ferr* k* ferr-ar ferr-p *Gels* k* *Graph* k* *Hep* b4a.de *Hyos* k* *Ign* b7a.de* *Ip* k* *Kali-c* k* kali-n b4.de* kali-p *Lach* k* lact *Laur* k* led k* *Lyc* k* lycps-v bg2 mag-m b4.de* *Merc* k* merc-c b4a.de *Mez* k* *Mosch* k* nat-s k* nit-ac k* *Nux-m* b7.de* *Nux-v* k* *Op* k* ox-ac br1 petr b4.de* *Ph-ac* k* *Phos* k* plb k* *Puls* k* rad-br ptk1 *Rhus-t* b7a.de *Samb* k* *Sang* k* sars k* sec k* sep k* spig k* spong k* staph k* *Stram* k* stront-c b4.de* *Sulph* k* tab ptk1 tarent k* thuj b4.de* *Verat* k* *Vip* bg2* *Zinc* k* zinc-p k2

- **cold**; on becoming: mosch k2
- **colic**; with: *Cupr Sep* verat
- **compelling** him to bend forward: hyos k* ph-ac
- **cough** agg.; during: *(↗COUGH - Convulsions; COUGH - Convulsions - Chest)* agar am-c ars chlor cina k* cupr ferr b7a.de kali-c lach merc mosch k* samb bro1 sep *Sulph* k* verat b7a.de
- **exertion** agg.: ferr
- **frightening**: *Mosch* mrr1
- **heat** and congestion, with: puls k*
- **hysterical**: *(↗Pain - hysterical)* ars **Asaf** bell cic *Cocc* k* convo-s sp1 *Mosch* k* *Stram* k* zinc
- **menses** | **before** | **agg.**: bov k* *Cupr* b7.de *Lach* k* puls b7a.de
  - **during** | **agg.**: cham b7.de *Chin* k* *Cocc* *Coff* b7a.de *Cupr* b7a.de *Ign* b7a.de
- **respiration**; arresting: stram k*
- **walking** agg.: ferr

○ - **Bronchi**: ant-t bg2 ars bg2 asar bg2 bell bg2 calad bg2 camph bg2 canth bg2 cham bg2 chinin-s bg2 *Cocc* bg2 dros bg2 *Hell* bg2 hist sp1 **Ip** bg2 *Lach* bg2 lat-m sp1 laur bg2 *Mosch* bg2 nux-m bg2 nux-v bg2 ph-ac bg2 plb bg2 *Puls* bg2 rhus-t bg2 *Samb* bg2 sars bg2 sil bg2 spong bg2 verat bg2

- **Coronaries**: squil mtf
- **Diaphragm**: *(↗Constriction - diaphragm)* *Arg-n* hr1 asaf vh *Bell* k* *Chel* k* choc srj3• cic k* coch c1 cupr k* gels k* *Lob* k* *Mosch* k* oena k* ph-ac k* puls b7a.de stann bg2 staph k* stram k* *Stry-xyz* c2 verat hr1
- **External** chest: *Ang* b7a.de *Cic* b7.de* puls b7.de* *Stram* b7.de* verat b7.de*
- **Heart**: act-sp br1 *Agar* k* *Arg-met* calc *Cupr* k* *Gels* *Lach* k* mag-p nux-m b7.de* *Nux-v*
  - **chill**; during: calc nux-v
  - **lying** on back agg.: arg-met
- **Sides** | **left**: cina a1

SPOKEN to agg.; being: camph bg2

SPONGE in chest; sensation of a: bell bg2

SPOTS:

- **discoloration** (See Discoloration - spots)
- **itching** (See Itching - spots)

SQUATTING agg.: cadm-s ptk1

STAGNATION: *(↗GENERALS - Stagnated)*

- **blood** stagnated in chest; as if: *(↗GENERALS - Stagnated)* *Lob* k* seneg bg2
  - **chill**; during: ambr bg2
  - **cough** agg.; during: guaj b4a.de

○ - **Heart**; sensation of stagnation in lyc ptk1 sabad ptk1 zinc ptk1

STANDING:

- **agg.**: agar bg2 am-m b7a.de carb-an b4.de* con b4.de* euph b4.de* kali-n bg2 nat-m b4.de* sil bg2 stann b4.de* sulph b4.de* zinc b4.de*
- **amel.**: chin b7.de* cic b7.de* ruta b7.de* tarax b7.de*

STARTING UP of the trunk: nat-m bg2 nit-ac bg2 sep bg2 stram bg2 thuj bg2

STENOCARDIA (See Angina)

STENOSIS: | **Heart** | **Valves** (See Heart; complaints - valves - aortic - stenosis; Heart; complaints - valves - mitral - stenosis)

- **Lungs**: aspidin br1

STEPPING HARD agg.: seneg b4.de*

○ - **Ribs**: rat ptk1

STIFFNESS: bamb-a stb2.de• bapt hr1 ign bg2 lat-m bnm6• *Puls* b7.de* thuj bg2

○ - **Axillae**: bell bg2

- **Heart**: con bg2 ign bg2 puls bg2 thuj bg2

○ • **Region** of: *Rhus-t* hr1

- **Lungs** | **inspiration** agg.; deep: plut-n srj7•
- **Muscles**: acon vh1 lyc h2 puls h1

○ • **Pectoral** muscles:

⁝ **extending** to | **Biceps** and back: lac-h htj1•

- **Sternum**: con h2

STONE; sensation of a:

○ - **Inside**: caust mrr1

- **Sternum**: arg-n ptk1

STONECUTTERS; complaints of: calc b4a.de* lyc bg2* nat-c bg2 nit-ac bg2 ph-ac bg2 puls bg2* sil b4a.de* sulph bg2

- **accompanied** by | **weakness**: sil bro1

STOOL:

- **after** | **agg.**: ant-t b7a.de ars bg2 caust b4a.de* con bg2 sil b4.de*
- **before** | **agg.**: coloc bg2 spig b7.de*
- **during** | **agg.**: cycl bg2 spig b7.de* sulph bg2

STOOPING:

- **agg.**: acon b7.de* agar bg2 alum b4.de* am-c b4.de* am-m b7.de* ang b7.de* arg-met b7.de* arn b7.de* ars bg2 asaf b7.de* borx b4a.de bov b4.de* bry b7.de* cann-s b7.de* caps b7.de* carb-v b4.de* chin b7.de* cocc b7.de* coloc b4.de* cycl b7.de* dig b4.de* dros b7.de* ferr-p bg2 glon bg2 hell b7.de* ign b7.de* laur bg2 led bg2 lil-t bg2 lith-c bg2 mang b4.de* merc b4.de* mez bg2* nat-c b4.de* nit-ac b4.de* nux-v b7.de* olnd b7.de* ph-ac b4.de* phos b4.de* psor bg2 puls b7.de* ran-b b7.de* rhod b4.de* rhus-t b7.de* seneg b4.de* **Sil** b4.de* spig b7.de* spong b7.de* squil b7.de* stann b4.de* staph b7.de* sul-ac b4.de* valer b7.de* viol-t b7.de* zinc b4.de*
- **amel.**: ars b4a.de chin b7.de* *Hyos* b7a.de ign b7.de* *Nit-ac* b4a.de ran-b b7.de* sars b4a.de spig b7a.de valer b7.de*

STOPPED (See Ceases)

STRAIN:

○ - **Heart**:

- • **had** been strained; as if: ant-t st
- • **violent** exertion; strain of the heart from: *Arn* k* *Caust* *Nat-m* *Rhus-t*

STRETCHING:

- **agg.**: lyc bg2 staph b7.de*
- **amel.**: ferr-p bg2 puls b7.de*
- **sensation** of | **Heart**: aur bg2

SULPHUR agg.; abuse of: *Puls* b7a.de

SUN: | **exposure** to sun amel.: iod bg2

SUPPURATION of lungs (See Abscess)

SUSPENDED: | **Heart** was suspended from left ribs; as if: *(↗Thread)* kali-c k*

SWALLOWING agg.: all-c bg2 alum bg2 calc-p bg2 dios bg2 kali-bi bg2

SWELLING: ars h2 bell tl1 bry b7.de* cadm-s c1 calc k* cann-s b7.de* *Dulc* k* iod k* kali-bi c1 kali-chl kali-m kali-n b4.de* merc mez b4a.de nat-c k* pot-e rly4• rhus-t b7.de* ribo rly4• sep k* *Sil* k* *Sulph* k*

- **sensation** of: merc bg2

○ • **External** chest: phos b4a.de

- • **Internal**: bufo bg2
- • **Mammae**: benz-ac bg2 berb bg2 calc-p ptk1 lach bg2
  - ⁝ **Nipples**: onos bg2

○ - **Axillae**: bar-c bg2 bell b4.de* *Carb-an* b4a.de *Clem* b4.de* *Coloc* b4a.de hep b4.de* iod b4.de* *Kali-c* b4a.de lyc b4.de* merc-c b4a.de nat-c b4.de* nat-m b4.de* nit-ac b4.de* petr b4.de* phos b4.de* sep b4.de* *Sil* b4a.de sul-ac b4.de* **Sulph** b4.de* thuj b4a.de

- **scratching** after: nat-m h2

○ · **Glands** (= Axillary glands): aesc aeth am-c **Am-m** k* anan anth vh1 anthraci *Ars* ars-i k2 aster k* *Aur* aur-i k2 aur-s k2 **Bar-c** k* bar-i k2 bar-s k2 *Bell* brom cadm-s calc k* *Carb-an* carc mlr1• chim sne *Chin* b7a.de *Clem* *Coloc* *Con* k* crot-t tl1 cund sne haliae-lc srj5• ham fd3.de• **Hep** k* hydr sne *Iod* *Kali-bi* **Kali-c** kali-p kali-sil k2 **Lach** k* lap-la sde8.de• lat-m bnm6• *Lyc* k* **Merc** *Merc-i-r* moni rfm1• *Nat-c* *Nat-m* *Nat-s* **Nit-ac** k* petr *Ph-ac* k* **Phos** *Phyt* psor al2 *Puls* *Rhus-t* k* ribo rly4• sars sne *Sep* **Sil** k* sinus rly4• *Staph* k* sul-ac sul-i k2 *Sulph* k* symph fd3.de• tell c1 vesp br1

  - **right**: ham fd3.de• nat-m h2 trios rsj11•
  - **left**: haliae-lc srj5•
  - **accompanied** by:
    - **Mammae**:
      - **cancer** in (See Cancer - mammae - accompanied - axillary)
      - **pain** in: lac-ac ptk1
        - **sore** pain (See Pain - mammae - sore - accompanied - axillary)
    - **Upper** arm; sore pain in: vesp br1
  - **menses** | **after** | **agg.**: ozone sde2•
    - **before** | **agg.**: aur
  - **painful**: haliae-lc srj5•
  - **painless**: *Lach* symph fd3.de•
  - **sensation** of: benz-ac
  - **suppurative**: coloc h2 sep h2 sulph h2

- **Bones**: *Lach* b7a.de *Puls* b7a.de
- **Clavicles**: *Fl-ac* b4a.de phos
- **Heart**:
  - **sensation** as if: *(↗Enlarged - heart)* acon b7a.de* alum bg2 anac vh1 *Ang* bg2* arn bg2 ars bg2* *Asaf* bg2* aur bg2* bapt rb2 bell bg2* bov bg2 brom bg2 bufo bg2 cact bg2 camph b7a.de *Cann-s* b7a.de caps bg2 cench rb2 cent rb2 cic bg2 cimic bg2* *Colch* b7a.de conv bg2 dig bg2 eup-per bg2 glon bg2* grin bg2 iod bg2 *Kali-i* rb2 kalm bg2 **Lach** b7a.de* lil-t bg2 lycps-v bg2 *Med* rb2 naja bg2 phos b4a.de* phyt bg2 plb bg2* pyrog bg2* rhus-t bg2 rob rb2 ruta b7a.de sep ptk1 spig b7a.de* spong bg2 squil bg2 stront-c bg2 **Sulph** bg2* thea rb2 thlas bg1 verat-v bg2 zinc bg2
    - **burst**; progressive swelling as if heart would: spong bl2*
    - **lying** on left side amel.: ang hr1*
- **Mammae**: *(↗Hypertrophy - mammae)* aeth hr1* all-s bro1 anan bro1 apis k* arn k* ars-i asaf k* *Aster* bro1 aur-s k* bamb-a stb2.de• *Bell* k* bell-p bro1 brom k* *Bry* k* bufo k* *Calc* k* *Carb-an* k* castm bro1 *Cham* k* *Clem* k* *Con* k* *Crot-t* *Cupr* cur cycl k* *Dig* b4a.de dream-p sdj1• *Dulc* k* falco-pe nl2• ferr b7a.de graph k* helo bg2 *Helon* k* *Hep* k* hydrog srj2• irid-met srj5• kali-c mrr1 kali-i mrr1 lac-ac stj5• *Lac-c* k* lach-h sze9• *Lach* luna kg1• lyc k* lyss *Merc* k* merc-c k* merl c2* naja nat-c k* nat-m bg2 oci onos k* oxal-a rly4• pant-ac rly4• *Phos* k* *Phyt* k* pip-n c2 plb b7.de* psor k* **Puls** k* *Rhus-t* k* ruta b7.de* sabad bg2 sabin k* sal-fr sle1• samb **Sil** k* sol-a c2 sol-o c2* spig bg2 spong b7a.de* *Sulph* k* tarent k* tritic-vg fd5.de tub mrr1 urt-u bg2* vip k* *Zinc* [heroin sdj2 *Merc-d* stj2]
  - **alternating** sides: lac-c mrr1
  - **left**: cist bg2
    - **hard**, painful: cist ptk1
  - **accompanied** by:
    - **cancer** in mammae (See Cancer - mammae - accompanied - swelling)
    - **leukorrhea**: dulc ptk1
    - **Inguinal** glands; complaints of: oci ptk1
  - **blue**: *Apis* b7a.de
  - **children**; in: | **infants**: **Arn** bg2 bell bg2 bry bg2 *Cham* bg2 hep bg2 sil bg2
  - **cicatrices**: *(↗SKIN - Cicatrices)* *Graph* phyt **Sil**
  - **cold** bathing agg.: sabal ptk1

Swelling – Mammae: ...

  - **edematous**: arg-n bg2
  - **fever**:
    - **after**: arn b7a.de bry b7a.de puls b7a.de
    - **during** | **agg.**: apis bg2 bry bg2 *Calc* bg2 con bg2 lyc bg2 phos bg2 *Puls* b7a.de*
  - **hot**: *Bell* bry *Calc* k* *Merc* *Phos* k* phyt k2
  - **menopause**; during: sang ptk1
  - **menses**:
    - **after** | **agg.**: cycl k*
    - **before** | **agg.**: aln vva1• alum b4a.de amp rly4• bamb-a stb2.de• bell b4a.de bry k2 *Calc* k* carb-v b4a.de carc mrr1* cham b7a.de *Cocc* b7a.de con k* dream-p sdj1• granit-m es1• irid-met srj5• kali-c kali-s kola stb3• lac-ac stj*• *Lac-c* k* lac-f wza1• lac-h htj1• murx musca-d szs1 *Phos* b4a.de *Phyt* sne pot-e rly4• *Puls* b7a.de rhus-t b7a.de* sacch sst1• sal-al blc1• spong fd4.de *Tub* k* zinc b4a.de [am-m stj1 ant-m stj2 aur-m stj2 bar-m stj1 beryl-m stj2 cadm-m stj2 calc-m stj1 *Chlor* stj2 chr-m stj2 cob-m stj2 cupr-m stj2 *Kali-m* stj1 lith-m stj2 mang-m stj2 merc-d stj2 mur-ac stj2 plb-m stj2 stront-m stj2 zinc-m stj2]
    - **during** | **agg.**: arge-pl rwt5• bry bro1 calc k* canth bro1 *Cham* *Con* k* dulc graph bro1 helon k* kali-c bro1 lac-c k* mag-c bro1 merc bro1 *Murx* bro1 *Phyt* bro1 *Puls* bro1 *Sal-fr* sle1• sang bro1 thuj *Tub*
    - **instead** of: dulc ptk1 rat k*
  - **neuralgia** of uterus, with each attack of: nux-v
  - **nursing**: lac-ac stj5• puls h1
  - **painful**: arg-n bro1 *Aster* bro1 *Bell* bro1 *Bry* bro1 calc bro1 carb-an bro1 *Cham* bro1 clem bro1 *Con* bro1 dulc bro1 *Helon* bro1 *Hep* bro1 iod bro1 kali-m bro1 *Lac-c* bro1 lach bro1 *Med* bro1 merc bro1 onos bro1 *Phyt* bro1 plb bro1 rad-br bro1 sabal bro1 syph bro1
  - **perspiration**; during: bry bg2 calc bg2 cham bg2 *Puls* bg2 sil bg2
  - **secretion** of milk, with: *Asaf* k* *Cycl* k* *Tub* k* *Urt-u* a1
  - **touch**; sensitive to: all-s a1*
  - **weaning**, after: all-s ptk1 puls ptk1

○ · **Glands**: aeth tl1 calc h2* con tl1 oci br1 *Phyt* tl1

  - **Nipples**: calc b4a.de* *Cham* irid-met srj5• lac-ac stj5• *Lach* lyc k* *Merc* k* **Merc-c** k* orig st phos sil tl1 sulph
    - **right**: *Fl-ac* k* sulph
    - **morning**: fl-ac sulph
    - **menses**; before: lac-ac stj5•
    - **Glands** about nipples: merc-c b4a.de*

- **Pectoral** muscles: ran-b k2
- **Sternoclavicular** joint: til c1
- **Sternum**, lower part of: sacch

SWIMMING in water; as if the heart were: borx bov *Bufo* sumb

TACHYCARDIA (See Palpitation)

TALKING:

- **agg.**: alum ptk1 bell bg2 borx bg2 *Bry* b7.de* cann-s b7.de* canth b7.de* carb-an bg2 carb-v bg2 chel bg2 chin b7.de* cocc b7.de* ign b7.de* kali-c bg2 led b7.de* mur-ac bg2 nat-m bg2 plat bg2 puls b7.de* ran-b b7.de* rhus-t b7.de* spong bg2 *Stann* bg2 stram b7.de* **Sulph** bg2
- **loudly** agg.: alum b4a.de borx b4a.de *Calc* b4a.de *Carb-v* b4.de* chel bg2 *Hep* b4a.de kali-c b4.de* lyc b4a.de mur-ac b4.de* nat-m b4.de* *Ph-ac* b4a.de *Stann* b4.de* sul-ac b4a.de

TENDERNESS (See Pain - sore)

TENSION: *(↗Constriction)* acon bg2 agar b4.de* am-c bg2 am-m b7.de* arg-met b7.de* arg-n bg2 arn b7.de* ars b4.de* asaf bg2 *Bell* b4.de* brom bg2 bry b7.de* calc b4a.de* cann-s b7.de* carb-an bg2 *Caust* b4.de* cham b7.de* chin bg2 *Cic* b7.de* cinnb bg2 cocc b7.de* colch b7.de* con b4.de* dig b4.de* dulc b4.de* euph b4.de* ferr b7a.de* graph b4.de* hep bg2 ign b7.de* kali-bi bg2 kali-c bg2 kali-n b4.de* kreos bg2 lach bg2 lyc b4.de* mag-m b4a.de* merc bg2 mez b4.de* mosch b7a.de mur-ac b4.de* *Nat-m* b4.de* nat-s bg2 nux-v b7.de* olnd b7.de* op b7a.de* *Phos* b4.de* *Plat* bg2 *Puls* b7.de* rheum b7.de* *Rhod* b4.de* rhus-t b7.de* ruta b7.de* sabad b7.de* sabin b7.de* seneg b4.de* sep b4.de* sil bg2 spig b7.de* squil b7.de* *Stann* b4.de* staph b7.de* sul-ac b4.de* sulph b4.de* tarax b7.de* verat bg2 verb b7.de* viol-t bg2 *Zinc* b4.de*

- **cough** agg.; during: *(↗COUGH - Tension)* kali-n b4.de* phos b4.de* rhus-t b7.de* stann b4a.de sulph b4a.de

○ - **Axillae**: arg-n bg2 aur k* kali-p fd1.de• spig b7.de* teucr bg2 zinc bg2

- **Clavicles**: *Lyc* k* nat-m h2 *Zinc* k*
  - • **left**: zinc k*

○ • **Under**: calc-p ptk1 crat ptk1 *Lyc* rumx ptk1

- **External** chest: agar b4.de* am-m b7.de* am b7.de* asaf b7.de* calc b4a.de cham b7.de* chin b7.de* colch b7.de* dig b4.de* dros b7.de* dulc b4.de* euph b4.de* ferr b7.de* ign b7.de* iod b4.de* kali-bi bg2 kali-n b4.de* lyc b4a.de* mag-m b4.de* merc b4.de* mez b4.de* mosch b7a.de mur-ac b4.de* *Nat-c* b4a.de nat-m b4.de* nux-v b7.de* olnd b7.de* *Phos* b4.de* puls b7.de* rhod b4.de* rhus-t b7.de* sabin b7.de* sars b4a.de* spig b7.de* squil b7.de* *Stann* b4.de* stront-c b4.de* thuj b4.de* verb b7.de* *Zinc* b4a.de
- **Heart** and region of heart: ars bg2 bar-c bg2 bry bg2 *Cann-s* b7a.de* caust bg2 colch bg2 con bg2 ferr bg2 hyos bg2 kali-c bg2 kreos bg2 nat-m bg2 plat bg2 prun bg2 puls bg2 rhus-t bg2 sabin bg2 sec bg2 stann bg2 sulph bg2 thuj bg2 zinc bg2
- **Lower** part: puls bg2
- **Mammae**: *Bamb-a* stb2.de• *Bry* b7a.de cycl bg2 kola stb3• puls b7.de* spong fd4.de tritic-vg fd5.de vanil fd5.de
  - • **menses**; before: *Bamb-a* stb2.de• cupr sst3• kola stb3• ozone sde2• vanil fd5.de
- **Ribs** | **Lower**: agath-a nl2• sulph k*
- **Sides** | **night**: kali-c h2
- **Sternum**: sabin b7a.de
- **Upper** part: phos bg2 rhus-t bg2

THICKENING: | **Lungs**: bry bg2 hep bg2 iod bg2 kali-i bg2 lyc bg2 phos bg2 sulph bg2 tub bg2

THINKING agg.: ign bg2

THINKING of one's complaints agg.: bad bg2 bar-c bg2 *Carb-an* b4a.de lycps-v bg2 ox-ac bg2

THREAD; as if heart were hanging or swinging by a: *(↗Suspended - heart)* aur bg2* dig rb2* kali-c bg2* lach bg2* lil-t st* lyc st* nat-m bg2 nux-m bg2* tub rb2* zinc bg2

- **every** heart beat would tear it off; as if: lach gm1

THROBBING (See Pulsation)

THROMBOSIS:

○ - **Lungs** | **Artery**: aspidin br1

THROWING BACK:

- **shoulders** | **amel.**: calc ptk1

TICKLING in: bar-c bg2 bufo bg2 *Calc* cham k* cist k2 coc-c con k* graph h2 *Hydrog* srj2• ign k* *Iod* k* irid-met srj5• kali-bi bg2 kali-c h2 *Lach* k* merc k* mez k* mur-ac k* nux-m bg2 *Ph-ac* k* *Phos* k* positr nl2• puls *Rhus-t* k* **Rumx** k* sep k* *Stann* bg2 sul-ac k* suprar rly4• verat k* verb k* zinc k*

- **cough**; during (See COUGH - Tickling - chest)

○ - **Bronchi**; in: verat mtf33

- **Heart**: visc bg2
- **Mammae**: sabin bg2 sep bg2
- **Sides**:
  - • **right**: kali-c bg2
  - • **left**: chin bg2
- **Sternum**; behind: con tl1 sanic tl1 staph tl1

TIGHTNESS (See Constriction; Oppression)

TINGLING: *(↗Prickling)* acon agar b4.de* ars cadm-s calc b4a.de* choc srj3• colch falco-pe nl2• ignis-alc es2• plat b4.de* plb k* puls ran-b ran-s b7.de* *Rhus-t* k* seneg k* spong stann staphycoc rly4• tritic-vg fd5.de

- **swallowing** | **amel.**: moni rfm1•

○ - **Axillae**: mez b4.de*

- **Mammae** in: falco-pe nl2• melal-alt gya4 sabin k* sal-fr sle1•
  - • **left**: falco-pe nl2•

TOBACCO heart: apoc c2 cact br1* calad br1 conv br1 kalm ptk1 saroth br scop ptk1 scut c2

- **cigarettes**; especially: conv br1

TOUCH:

- **agg.**: acon b7.de* agn b7.de* *Alum* bg2 am-m b7.de* arg-met b7.de* arg-n bg2 *Am* b7.de* bar-c b4.de* borx b4a.de bry b7.de* *Calc* b4.de* canth b7.de* caps b7.de* carb-v b4.de* cham b7.de* chin b7.de* cocc b7.de* colch b7.de* cupr b7.de* dros b7.de* dulc b4.de* graph b4.de* *Hep* b4a.de iod b4a.de kali-bi bg2 kali-c bg2 **Lach** bg2 led b7.de* merc b4.de* nux-m b7.de* nux-v b7.de* par b7.de* ph-ac b4.de* phos b4.de* plb b7.de* puls b7.de* *Ran-b* b7.de* rhod b4.de* rhus-t b7.de* ruta b7.de* sabin b7.de* sars b4.de* seneg b4.de* sep bg2 spig b7.de* staph b7.de* stront-c b4.de* sulph b4.de* verat b7.de*

○ • **Sides** | **left**: *Nat-m* bg2

- **amel.**: mur-ac b4.de*
- **lungs** touched the back; as if: sulph bg2

TREMBLING: ambr apis *Arg-met* *Arg-n* *Ars* benz-ac k* both-ax tsm2 bov bros-gau mrc1 *Calc* calc-p k* *Camph* k* carb-an h2 *Carb-v* **Cic** *Cocc* dig k* falco-pe nl2• kali-c kali-n *Kalm* lac-c lachn lact k* lappa bg1* manc k* melal-alt gya4 merc b4.de* nat-p nicc phos positr nl2• ruta h1 sabin k* seneg k* **Spig** k* spong fd4.de *Staph* ther zinc h2

- **noon**, toward: spong fd4.de sulph k*
- **chilliness**; with: phos k*
- **cough**:
  - • **during**:
    - ⁝ **agg.**: rhus-t
    - ⁝ **amel.**: positr nl2•
- **dinner**; after: zinc k*
- **inspiration** agg.: ang h1
- **moving** the arms, on: *Spig*
  - • **raising** to head: spig hr1
- **painful**: benz-ac
- **sensation** of | **Heart**: *Bell* bg2 camph bg2 cina bg2 fl-ac bg2 nit-ac bg2 *Spig* bg2
- **weeping**; as from: stront-c

○ - **Axillae**: mang h2

- **Heart**: *(↗Fluttering)* absin aeth agar *Arg-met* *Arg-n* *Ars* k* *Ars-i* *Aur* aur-ar k2 aur-s k2 bad bell k* benz-ac bufo **Calc** k* calc-i k2 *Camph* k* chin ptk1 chinin-ar *Chinin-s* **Cic** k* cimic ptk1 cina k* cinnb *Cocc* k* colch b7a.de crot-h k* *Cupr* k* cupr-ar br1 **Dig** ptk1 *Glon* helo helo-s rwt2• *Iod* kali-n *Kalm* k* kreos b7a.de *Lach* lachn **Lil-t** k* lith-c melal-alt gya4 *Merc* merc-c b4a.de *Mosch* naja ptk1 *Nat-m* k* *Nat-p* nit-ac **Nux-m** k* nux-v ptk1 op *Phys* *Plat* k* *Rhus-t* k* *Sep* k* **Spig** k* *Staph* k* stram stroph-h ptk1 *Tab* *Tarent* k* thea *Ther* thuj b4a.de verat b7a.de
  - • **forenoon**: bell h1
  - • **evening**:
    - ⁝ **bed** agg.; in: anag cinnb
    - ⁝ **sitting** agg.: dig
  - • **night**: ambr sep h2
    - ⁝ **bed** agg.; in: thuj
  - • **ascending** stairs agg.: *Nat-p*
  - • **excitement**: lith-c hr1
  - • **lying**:
    - ⁝ **agg.**: iod
    - ⁝ **side**; on:
      - ⁝ **left** | **agg.**: *Camph* *Tab*
  - • **menses**; after: nat-p k*
  - • **paroxysmal**: nit-ac
  - • **pressure** agg.: kali-bi
  - • **sitting** agg.: iod k*
  - • **vertigo**; during: *Cocc* b7a.de
  - • **waking**; on: agar k* *Lach* *Merc* k*
- **Internally**: *Ambr* b7a.de* ang b7.de* apis bg2 cann-s b7.de* carb-an bg2 *Iod* b4a.de kali-c b4.de* lac-ac bg2 lac-c bg2 manc bg2 nat-s bg2 nicc bg2 phos b4.de* *Puls* b7a.de ruta b7.de* sabin b7.de* scroph-n bg2 seneg b4.de *Spig* b7a.de* stict bg2 stront-c bg2 sulph bg2 zinc bg2
- **Lungs**: sabin c1

TRICKLING in chest: thuj bg2

TRIFLES agg.: nat-c bg2

TUBERCULOSIS:

○ - **Bronchial** tubes: tub jl2

- **Lungs** (See Phthisis)

TUMORS:

○ - **Axillae**: ars-i k* *Bar-c* k* petr tell c2

• **encysted**: bar-c k*

- **Mammae**: aids nl2• ars-br vh ars-i c2* aster bro1* *Bell* bro1 berb-a bro1 brom c2* bry bro1 calc bro1 *Calc-f* bro1 calc-i c2* calen bro1 *Carb-an* k* cham bro1 chim c2* clem bro1 **Con** k* *Cund* k* ferr-i c2* gnaph bro1 *Graph* bro1 hecla c2* *Hydr* bro1 *Hyos* c2 iod bro1* kali-i *Lach* k* lap-a bro1 lyc bro1 merc tl1 merc-i-f c2* murx bro1 nit-ac bro1 osm c2 ph-ac c2 phel sne *Phos* k* *Phyt* k* plat sne *Plb-i* bro1 psor bro1 *Puls* bro1 sabin bro1 sang k* *Scir* bro1 *Scroph-n* br1* sec *Sil* k* skook c2 tep c2 thuj bro1 thyr br1* tub br1*

• **left**: *Calc-p* bg2

• **accompanied** by:

⁝ **perspiration**; hot: merc-i-f br1

⁝ **Stomach**; complaints of: merc-i-f br1

• **fibrocystic**: phos mrr1 phyt mrr1 puls mrr1 sil mrr1

• **fibroid**: *Thyr* br1

• **hard** scirrhus-like: con tl1

• **injury** from: arn pd

• **painful**: hydr sne phyt mrr1

- **Mammary** gland; male:

• **right**: thuj c1

• **left** | **walnut**; like a: bar-c pd calc-p

TURNING:

- **arms** agg.: spig b7.de*

- **around**; as if | **Heart**: aur bar-ox-suc rly4• *Cact* crot-h c1 lach c1* sol-t-ae rb2 stram tarent c1*

- **bed**; in:

• **agg.**: *Acon* b7.de* am-m b7.de* *Cann-s* b7.de* caps b7.de* carb-v b4.de* kreos b7a.de* lyc bg2 nux-v b7.de* ran-b b7.de* staph b7.de* sulph b4a.de*

• **amel.**: graph bg2

- **body** | **agg.**: euph b4.de* ran-b b7.de* rhod b4a.de

- **head** | **agg.**: bapt bg2

- **inside** out; as if turning | **Heart**: ars bg2

- **over**:

• **as if** | **Heart**: ant-t bg2 apis bg2* arn ptk1 aur bg2 bell bg2 *Cact* bg2* calc bg2 camph bg2 caust ptk1 crot-h bg2* lach bg2* laur bg2 lycps-v bg2 rhus-t ptk1 *Sep* ptk1 stram bg2 tab bg2* tarent bg2*

- **side**; to | **right**: spig b7.de*

- **something** were turning over; as if: cact *Camph* chim crot-h lach bg1 stram k*

TWITCHING: bamb-a stb2.de• calc h2 cic h1 falco-pe nl2• ham fd3.de• tritic-vg fd5.de

○ - **Heart**; region of: acon bg2 *Aesc* k* *Arg-met* k* *Arn* b7.de* camph ptk1 canth bg2 carb-v bg2 chin bg2 crot-t bg2 fl-ac bg2 ham fd3.de• helo c1 lil-t bg2* lith-c bg2 melal-alt gya4 *Mez* bg2 nat-m b4a.de* nux-v b7.de plb b7.de* stram bg2 thuj bg2 zinc bg2

• **lying** on back agg.: *Arg-met*

- **Internally**: cina b7.de* coloc b4.de* croc b7.de* crot-h bg2 dulc b4.de* ip b7.de* kali-c b4.de* lyc b4.de* *Mez* b4.de* nat-c b4.de* nat-m b4.de* nux-v b7.de* olnd bg2 plat bg2 puls bg2 sep b4.de* spig b7.de* squil b7.de* stann bg2 tarax bg2 valer b7.de*

- **Mammae**: sulph b4.de*

- **Muscles**; in: agar k* aloe bg2 anac k* ant-t bg2 ars bg2 asar b7.de* bry bg2 calc bg2 cann-xyz bg2 chel bg2 chin b7.de* cina hr1 coloc dros h1 dulc ham fd3.de• kali-c lat-m bnm6• lyc mez h2 nat-c k* nat-m k* olnd b7.de* plat b4.de* puls b7.de* seneg k* sep k* spig h1 stann k* stram b7.de* sulph bg2 symph fd3.de• tarax b7.de* tritic-vg fd5.de viol-t b7.de*

• **burning**: nat-c h2

ULCERS: *Ars* hep *Sulph*

○ - **Axillae**: borx k* *Carb-an* b4a.de con k2

- **External** chest: *Ars* b4.de* hep b4.de* *Lach* b7a.de *Mez* b4a.de *Sil* b4a.de *Sulph* b4.de*

- **Lungs**: **Calc** carb-v chin **Kali-c** k* kali-n *Led Lyc* mang k2 *Nit-ac* **Phos** puls ruta sep **Sil** stann *Sul-ac* sul-i k2 *Sulph Tub*

Ulcers: ...

- **Mammae**: alum sne alum-sil gm1 ars b4a.de ars-i sne ars-s-f k2 aster bro1 *Calc* calen bro1 clem k2* *Hep* k* hydr sne kreos bg2 *Merc* bg2* paeon c2* *Phos* k* **Phyt** k* **Sil** k* sulph thuj b4a.de

• **right**: *Com*

• **abscess**; at site of old: paeon gm1

• **accompanied** by | **cancer** of mammae (See Cancer - mammae - accompanied - ulcers)

• **cancerous**: ars-i br1 calc-sil k2* hydr sne scroph-n sne sil sne

• **scirrhous**, stinging, burning, odor of old cheese: **Hep** k*

• **serpiginous**: borx

○ • **Nipples**: anan bro1 *Arn* bro1 *Aur-s* bro1 *Calc* calc-ox bro1 calen bro1 carb-v bro1 *Castm* bro1 **Castor-eq** k* caust bro1 cham k* *Con* bro1 *Crot-t* bro1 *Cund* bro1 *Eup-a* bro1 gali bro1 ger bro1 *Graph* bro1 ham bro1 hep bro1 hipp bro1 *Merc* k* nit-ac bro1 *Paeon* bro1 *Phel* bro1 phos bro1 *Phyt* bro1 *Rat* bro1 sep bro1 *Sil* k* sulph k* thuj b4a.de

- **Sternum** and Clavicle, over: *Calc-p*

UNCOVERING: | **amel.**: ferr ptk1 sars ptk1

UNDULATION of heart; sensation of: *Benz-ac* k* *Spig* k*

UNEASINESS: | **Heart** and region of heart: acon bg2 anac bg2 chel bg2 dig bg2 fl-ac bg2 kali-bi bg2 mez bg2 naja bg2 stram bg2

URINATION:

- **amel.**: lil-t bg2 lith-c bg2 nat-ar bg2

- **delayed**; if desire to urinate is: lil-t ptk1

VAPOR in chest; sensation as if (See Smoke in)

VELVETY sensation in: ant-t k*

○ - **Lungs**: brom bg3*

VENESECTION agg.: *Chin* b7a.de *Squil* b7a.de

VESICLES (See Eruptions - vesicles)

VIBRATION: plut-n srj7•

- **sensation** as if: melal-alt gya4

○ • **Heart**: visc sp1

⁝ **fire**; as if nerves on: hydrog srj2•

VOMITING:

- **before** | **agg.**: *Cupr* b7.de*

- **during**: ars bg2 mosch b7a.de

- **green** | **amel.**: cocc ptk1

WAKING; on: agar bg2 alum bg2 am-m b7.de* ant-c b7.de* arn b7.de* cann-xyz bg2 carb-an bg2 colch bg2 con bg2 cycl bg2 dig b4.de* euphr b7.de* hep bg2 ign b7.de* kali-bi bg2 *Kali-c* b4a.de kreos bg2 mez bg2 nux-m b7.de* phos bg2 puls b7.de* ran-b b7.de* rhus-t b7.de* sabad b7.de* sec bg2 seneg b4.de* sep bg2 sil bg2 squil b7.de* staph bg2 zinc bg2

WALKING:

- **after** | **agg.**: puls b7.de* rhus-t b7.de* spig b7a.de valer b7.de*

- **agg.**: acon b7.de* am-c b4a.de arg-n bg2 arn b7.de* brom bg2 *Bry* b7.de* calc bg2 camph b7.de* caps b7.de* chin b7.de* cic b7.de* cocc b7.de* ferr b7.de* hep b4a.de ign b7.de* kali-bi bg2 led b7.de* lyc bg2 merc bg2 nat-m bg2 nit-ac b4a.de nux-v b7.de* olnd b7.de* phos bg2 phyt bg2 plat bg2 ran-b b7.de* rhus-t b7a.de ruta b7.de* sel b7a.de seneg bg2 spig b7.de* spong b7.de* squil b7.de* staph b7.de* *Sulph* b4a.de tarax b7.de* valer b7.de* verat b7.de* viol-t b7.de*

- **air**; in open | **after** | **agg.**: ferr b7.de* led b7.de* nux-v b7.de* *Rhus-t* b7.de* sabad b7.de* sulph bg2

• **agg.**: am-m b7.de* ambr b7a.de* bry b7.de* chel bg2 chin b7.de* coff b7.de* lyc bg2 m-arct b7.de mez bg2 nat-m bg2 nux-m b7.de* *Nux-v* b7.de* ran-b b7.de* rhus-t b7.de* sep bg2 spig b7.de* spong b7.de* staph b7.de* sulph bg2

- **amel.**: arg-n bg2 chin b7.de* cic b7.de* colch bg2 dros b7.de* ferr b7.de* glon bg2 mag-p bg2 mosch b7.de* phyt bg2 plb b7.de* puls b7.de* ran-b b7.de* rhus-t b7.de* ruta b7.de* sep bg2 staph b7.de* tarax b7.de* teucr b7.de*

- **beginning** to walk: ferr b7.de* ph-ac bg2 puls b7.de*

- **rapidly** | **agg.**: bell bg2 chin b7.de* euph bg2 seneg b4.de* *Sep* b4a.de spig b7.de* squil b7.de*

- **slowly**:

• **agg.**: nit-ac bg2

• **amel.**: borx bg2

WARM:
- **air**:
  - **agg.**: graph b4a.de *Sulph* b4a.de
  - **amel.**: *Carb-v* b4.de*
  - **wet** | **amel.**: sil bg2
- **amel.**: bar-c bg2 kali-bi bg2 meli bg2
- **applications**:
  - **agg.**: bar-c bg2
  - **amel.**: bar-c b4a.de phos ptk1
- **food** | **agg.**: *Carb-v* b4a.de euph b4.de*
- **room** | **agg.**: **Bry** bg2

WARM IN BED; after becoming: cham b7.de* led b7.de* m-arct b7.de puls b7.de* rhus-t b7.de*

WARMTH; sensation of (See Heat - sensation)

WARTS: carc az1.de• dulc fd4.de nit-ac b4a.de* thuj sne
- O - **Mammae**; on: castor-eq br1*
- O · **Mammae** | **Nipples**: morg-g fmm1• sep b4a.de thuj b4a.de
- **Sternum**; on: nit-ac k*

WASHING:
- **agg.**: *Thuj* b4a.de
- **amel.**: borx bg2

WATER, sensation of:
- **boiling** water was poured into chest; as if: **Acon**
- **cold** drops were falling into the water: hist vml3•
- **cold** water were falling from the heart; sensation as if drops of: cann-s cann-xyz ptk1
- **hot** water pouring from chest to abdomen: sang hr1
- O - **Heart** were in water; as if bov bg2 bufo bg2* der vml3• sumb bg2
- **In** chest; sensation of water: bov bg1 *Bufo* bg1 crot-c k* hep ptk1 ozone sde2• samb bg1
  - **hot** water in chest; as if: **Acon** cic *Hep* sang hr1
    - ⁝ **drops** of hot water: hep a1*
- O · **Bronchi**; in: ozone sde2•

WEAKNESS: acon k* adam srj5• agar bg2 ail aloe alum k* alum-sil k2 alumn k2 am-c k* am-m ammc **Ant-t** k* **Arg-met** k* *Arg-n Ars Ars-i* ars-s-f k2 asc-t aur-ar k2 bapt bell bg2 *Benz-ac* borx k* brom k* bufo bg2 cadm-s *Calc* k* calc-s calc-sil k2 canth k* **Carb-v** k* *Carbn-s* carl chin b7.de* chinin-ar coc-c cocc b7.de* con cycl *Dig* k* falco-pe nl2• gels bg2 ger-i rly4• *Hep* k* **Ign** bg2* iod k* kali-ar *Kali-c* k* kali-i kali-p kali-s kali-sil k2 kola stb3• lac-lup hrn2• lact **Laur** ptk1 manc mang k* merc bg2 nat-m b4.de* nat-s k* nit-ac k* nux-v b7.de* ol-j olib-sac wmh1 olnd k* *Ph-ac* k* *Phos* k* *Plat* k* *Psor* k* puls bg2 **Ran-s** k* raph rhus-t k* ruta k* *Sang* bg2 sel k2 **Seneg** k* *Sil* k* *Spong* k* **Stann** k* *Staph* k* *Sul-ac* k* sul-i k2 *Sulph* k* thuj til tub mrr1 zinc bg2
- **left** side: arg-met vh1
- **morning**:
  - **waking**; on: **Carb-v** k* dig
    - ⁝ **lasting** until 15 h: merc-i-r
- **evening**: ran-s
  - **lying** agg.: *Sulph*
- **bending** forward | **amel.**: nux-v
- **breathing** deep agg.: carb-v *Plat*
- **cough**:
  - **agg.**: carb-v k2 graph *Nit-ac* k* *Ph-ac* k* *Psor* k* *Rhus-t* b7.de* ruta k* sel c1 sep k* **Stann** k* thuj bg2
    - ⁝ **menses**; before: graph
  - **hindering** cough: *Stann* k*
- **eating**; while: carb-an
- **exertion** agg.; after: aloe alumn bro1 am-c bro1 *Arg-met* bro1 *Calc* bro1 canth bro1 *Carb-v* bro1 cocc bro1 *Dig* bro1 iod bro1 kali-c bro1 lob bro1 *Ph-ac* bro1 phos bro1 psor bro1 ran-s bro1 rhus-t bro1 ruta bro1 **Spong** k* **Stann** bro1* *Sulph* bro1
- **expectoration**; after: **Stann** k*
- **lying**:
  - **amel.**: alum
  - **side**; on | **agg.**: *Sulph* k*
- **menses**; before: spig b7a.de

Weakness: ...
- **paralytic**: arg-met k2
- **reading**:
  - **agg.**: sulph
  - **aloud** | **agg.**: cocc *Sulph*
- **singing** agg.: carb-v stann ptk1 sulph
  - **beginning** to sing: **Stann** k*
- **sitting** for a long time agg.: dig *Ph-ac* k*
- **speech**, impeding: *Calc* dig *Hep* ph-ac rhus-t *Stann* sul-ac *Sulph*
- **starting** from chest: seneg bg3*
- **sun**:
  - **agg.**: nat-m bg1
  - **walking** in the sun | **agg.**: nat-m h2
- **talking** agg.: arg-met k2* calc cench k2 *Ph-ac* k* rhus-t sil h2 **Stann** k* sul-ac *Sulph* k*
  - **loud**: calc gels kali-c h2 *Laur* **Sulph**
- **waking**; on: **Carb-v** k*
  - **amel.**: ph-ac ptk1
- **walking**:
  - **agg.**: *Lyss Rhus-t*
  - **air** agg.; in open: nat-m h2 *Rhus-t*
  - **amel.**: *Ph-ac*
  - **rapidly**:
    - ⁝ **agg.**: *Kali-c*
    - ⁝ **air**; in open: nat-m
- ▽ - **extending** to | **Body**; whole: seneg b4a.de*
- O - **Heart**: abies-c br1 acet-ac br1* acetan br1* acon bg2 *Adon* br1* adonin br1 adren bro1 aesc br1 *Am-c* bg2* *Am-caust* br1 *Am-m* bro1 androc bnm2• anh br1 ant-ar br1* ant-c bg1 *Ant-t* bg2* *Arn* bg2* ars bg2* ars-i bg2* asper ktp2 aur bro1 aur-m k2 benz-ac bg2 brom bg2 cact k2* *Calc* bg2* calc-ar br1* *Camph* bg2* carb-ac bro1 *Carb-v* bg2* chel k2 chin bro1 chinin-ar bro1 chlol br1 cocc k2 *Colch* bg2* conv br1* crat br1* croc bg2 *Crot-h* bg2* dig bg2* dios bro1 euon-a br1 euph bro1 ferr bro1 gala br1 gels k2 glon bg2 graph bg1 grin bro1 *Hell* bg2* helo bg2* helo-s bnm14• *Hydr-ac* bro1 iber bro1* kali-ar br1 kali-bi bg2* kali-br a1* *Kali-c* bg2* kali-chl br1 kali-cy br1 kali-fcy bg1* kali-m br1 kali-n br1 kali-p k2* kali-perm br1 kali-sil br1 kalm bro1 kola br1* kurch bnj1 *Lach* bg2* lil-t bro1* lob bg2 lycps-v bg2* merc bg2 merc-sul br1 morph bro1 mosch bro1 naja bg2* narc-ps br1 nat-m bg2 nit-ac bro1 nux-m bro1 nux-v bg2* olnd bg2* op bg2* parathyr jl2 parth gm1 petr h2* ph-ac k2 phase bro1 *Phos* bg2* phys br1 *Phyt* bg2 plb bro1 prun bro1 prun-v c2 psor br1* pyrog k2* rhus-t bg2* sang bg2* sarcol-ac bro1 saroth bro1 ser-ang br1* sol c1 spartin bwa3 spartin-s bwa2* spig bro1 squil k2* stroph-h br1* sumb bg2 tab bg2* thyr bro1 *Verat* bg2* vip bg2 zinc-i ptk1
  - **accompanied** by:
    - ⁝ **anemia** (See GENERALS - Anemia - accompanied - heart)
    - ⁝ **bronchiolitis**: ant-ar mtf11
    - ⁝ **constipation**: apoc bg2 cact bg2 dig bg2 kali-c bg2 lach bg2 lil-t bg2 naja bg2 nat-m bg2 phyt hr1* spig bro1
    - ⁝ **dropsy**: *(↗GENERALS - Dropsy - external - heart)* *Acetan* bro1 *Adon* bro1 *Apoc* bro1 *Ars* bro1 ars-i bro1 asc-c bro1 aspar br1 cact bro1 *Coffin* bro1 coll bro1 *Conv* bro1 *Dig* bro1 iber bro1 lach bro1 lycps-v bro1 olnd bro1 saroth bro1 ser-ang br1 squil bro1 *Stroph-h* bro1
    - ⁝ **metrorrhagia**: am-m bro1 dig bro1
    - ⁝ **obesity**: am-c br1
    - ⁝ **palpitations**: coca bro1 dig bro1
    - ⁝ **respiration**; difficult: *(↗Heart; complaints - accompanied - respiration; Heart; complaints - accompanied - respiration - difficult)* calc-ar br1
    - ⁝ **tuberculosis**: ars-i br1
    - ⁝ **vomiting**: ars bro1 camph bro1 *Dig* bro1
    - ⁝ **Face**; flushing heat of: lach gm1
    - ⁝ **Lungs** | **cancer**: | **dyspnea**: hydroq mtf11
      - ⁝ **complaints** of the: spartin bwa3
    - ⁝ **Spine**; flushes of heat up: lach gm1
  - **arteriosclerosis**, in: *(↗Arteriosclerosis)* cact br1
  - **cold** room, after walking in the hot sun agg.; after entering a: **Rhus-t** k*
  - **collapse**, as if she must fall; with sensation of: gala br1

- **Heart**: ...
  - **dyspnea**; with sinking, coldness and | **3** h; at: *Am-c* k1
  - **expectoration**; after: *Stann* bg2
  - **fever**; during: ars bg2 crot-h bg2 hydr-ac bg2 *Verat* bg2
  - **gradually**; increasing: hyos bg2
  - **infection**; after: crat mtf11
  - **influenza**; after: iber br1*
  - **menses**; after: am-c bg1 carb-an bg1
  - **nervous** and hysterical people; in: adren bro1 cact bro1 *Iber* bro1 ign bro1 *Lil-t* bro1 lith-c bro1 *Mosch* bro1 *Naja* bro1 pilo bro1 prun bro1 saroth bro1 spartin bwa3 *Spig* bro1 tab bro1 *Valer* bro1
  - **reading** aloud agg.: cocc bg2
  - **singing** agg.: carb-v bg2 *Sulph* bg2
  - **talking** agg.: **Calc** bg2 *Ph-ac* bg2 rhus-t bg2 *Stann* bg2 sul-ac bg2 **Sulph** bg2
  - **tendency**: cact mtf11
  - **walking** in open air agg.; after: rhus-t bg2
  - ○ **About** the heart; sensation of weakness: alum-p k2 ambr h1* arg-n bg2 ars bg2 *Ars-i* *Aur* *Aur-m* bell bg2 calc-ar k2 cann-xyz bg2 cham b7.de* cic b7.de* crat br1 dios br1 gard-j vlr2• gels *Helo-s* rwt2• hyper bg2 kali-bi bg1 kali-c h2 lach gm1 lat-m br1 lil-t bg2* lob *Merc* **Naja** nat-m bg1 **Nux-v** k* op bg2 petr h2 *Ph-ac* pyrog bg2* **Rhus-t** k ●* sang k* streptoc jl2 sulph bg1 sumb tarax bg2 thuj zinc bg2
    - **lying** on left side agg.: gard-j vlr2•
    - **tired** feeling (See about)
  - **Myocardium**: adon mtf11 arn ptk1 chinin-ar ptk1 conv mtf11 *Dig* br1 influ jl2* laur mtf11 sarcol-ac br1 spartin-s bwa2* stigm mtf11 streptoc mtf11 zinc-i ptk1
    - **fever**; during: eberth mtf11
    - **neurotic** persons; in: spartin-s bwa2
- **Lungs**: ail bro1 arum-t bro1 carb-v mrr1 phos k2
  - **accompanied** by | **cough**: ant-t tl1
- **Sternum**: zinc h2

WEATHER AGG.; WET: *Carb-v* b4.de* phyt bg2

WEEPING: | **amel.**: anac bg2

WEIGHT:
- **fall** from pit of chest to abdomen; seems to (See Falling - weight)
- **sensation** of weight on chest (See Oppression)

WET:
- **feet** | **agg.**: nux-m bg2

WHIRLING; sensation of: | **Heart**; about: ant-t b7.de* *Cact* k* *Iod* k* rhus-t

WHIRRING: | **Heart**: cycl bg2 phos bg2 plb bg2 spig bg2

WIND in chest; sensation of: sabin bg2

WINE:
- **agg.**: ant-c b7.de* borx k* nux-v b7.de* ran-b b7.de*
- **amel.**: *Acon* bg2

WOOD nailed between heart and lungs; sensation of: buth-a sp1

WRITING agg.: asaf b7.de* chin b7.de* cocc b7.de* nat-c bg2 valer b7.de*

YAWNING agg.: alum bg2 am-c bg2 aur b4.de* borx b4a.de* canth b7.de* croc b7.de* graph b4.de* hep b4a.de ign b7.de* mur-ac b4.de* nat-s ptk1 olnd bg2 phel bg2 phos bg2 stann b4.de sulph b4a.de*

AXILLA; complaints of (= Armpits): agn b2.de* am-c b2.de* am-m b2.de* anac b2.de* arg-met b2.de* arn b2.de* ars b2.de* asar b2.de* aur b2.de* bar-c b2.de* bell b2.de* borx b2.de* bov b2.de* bry b2.de* *Calc* b2.de* canth b2.de* caps b2.de* *Carb-an* b2.de* *Carb-v* b2.de* caust b2.de* chel b2.de* chin bg2 *Clem* b2.de* cocc b2.de* colch bg2 coloc b2.de* *Con* b2.de* cupr b2.de* dig b2.de* dulc b2.de* graph bg2 *Hep* b2.de* iod b2.de* kali-c b2.de* lach b2.de* laur b2.de* lyc b2.de* mag-c b2.de* mang b2.de* meny b2.de* merc b2.de* mez b2.de* nat-c b2.de* nat-m b2.de* nit-ac b2.de* olnd b2.de* petr b2.de* ph-ac b2.de* *Phos* b2.de* plb b2.de* puls b2.de* rhod b2.de* rhus-t b2.de* ruta b2.de* sabad b2.de* sel b2.de* seneg b2.de* *Sep* b2.de* *Sil* b2.de* spig b2.de* spong b2.de* squil b2.de* stann b2.de* staph b2.de* sul-ac b2.de* *Sulph* b2.de* teucr b2.de* thuj b2.de* valer b2.de* verat b2.de* viol-t b2.de* zinc b2.de* [fl-ac stj2 fl-pur stj2]
- **alternating** sides: colch ptk1
- **right**: agn bg2 *Arg-met* bg2 *Arg-n* bg2 am bg2 ars bg2 bar-c bg2 *Brach* bg2 brom bg2 bry bg2 carb-an bg2 carb-v bg2 cham bg2 clem bg2 gels bg2 gran bg2 grat bg2 guaj bg2 kali-c bg2 lach bg2 laur bg2 lyc bg2 mag-c bg2 *Mag-m* bg2 meny bg2 mez bg2 *Nit-ac* bg2 ph-ac bg2 ran-s bg2 *Raph* bg2 ruta bg2 sil bg2 staph bg2 **Sulph** bg2 **Thuj** bg2 verat bg2 viol-t bg2
- **left**: am-c bg2 am-m bg2 ant-t bg2 asaf bg2 asar bg2 cact bg2 calc bg2 chel bg2 coloc bg2 con bg2 cor-r bg2 **Dios** bg2 dros bg2 *Fago* bg2 *Form* bg2 lil-t bg2 *Mang* bg2 merc-c bg2 myric bg2 nat-s bg2 olnd bg2 plat bg2 prun bg2 sabin bg2 sang bg2 seneg bg2 *Sep* bg2 *Spig* bg2 *Spong* bg2 stann bg2 *Sul-ac* bg2 tell bg2 valer bg2 zinc bg2
- ▽ **extending** to | **Mammae**: caust bg2
- ○ **Glands**: acon-l bro1 am-c bg2 am-m bg2 arg-n bg2 ars bg2 asar bg2 *Aster* bro1 bar-c bg2* bell bg2* **Calc** bg2* *Carb-an* bg2* clem bg2 coloc bg2 *Con* bro1 cupr bg2 elaps bro1 graph bro1 **Hep** bg2* *Iod* bg2 jug-r bro1 kali-c bg2 *Lac-ac* bro1 lyc bg2 nat-m bg2 nat-s bro1 nit-ac bg2* ph-ac bg2 phos bg2 phyt bro1 raph bro1 rhus-t bro1 **Sil** bg2* *Staph* bg2 sul-ac bg2 *Sulph* bg2*
  - **alternating** sides: colch bg2

CARTILAGES; complaints of the: *Arg-met*

CLAVICLES; complaints of: | **Under**: *Calc-p* bg2

DIAPHRAGM; complaints of: apis bg2 asar bg2 asc-t bg2 bry bg2* cact bg2* cimic bg2* cupr ptk1 ign ptk1 nux-m bg2 nux-v bg2 ran-b bg2 sec bg2 spig bg2 stann bg2* stram bg2 stry ptk1 sulph bg2 verat bg2 verat-v bg2 zinc bg2
- **warm** bathing | **amel.**: lat-m bnm6•

HEART; complaints of the: abies-n vh1* **Acon** k* adon c2* alum b2.de* *Am-c* k* am-m bro1 ambr b2.de* aml-ns c2* ammc c2 anac b2.de* anemps br1 ang b2.de* ant-t b2.de* apis c2 apoc c2* arg-met c2 arg-n k2* *Arn* b2.de* *Ars* k* *Ars-i* k* asaf b2.de* asar b2.de* asc-t c2 aster c2 **Aur** k* aur-ar k2 aur-br c2 aur-i k2 **Aur-m** k* bacls-7 fmm1• *Bad* k* *Bar-c* b2.de* *Bell* b2.de* benz-ac k2* bism b2.de* borx b2.de* bov b2.de* *Brom* k* bry b2.de* bufo c2* **Cact** k* *Calc* k* calc-ar bro1* calc-f bro1 camph b2.de* cann-s b2.de* canth b2.de* carb-an b2.de* carb-v b2.de* *Caust* k* *Cench* k* cere-b c2 cham b2.de* chin b2.de* *Cimic* bg2* clem b2.de* coc-c c2 coca bro1 cocc b2.de* colch b2.de* *Coll* k* coloc b2.de* con b2.de* conv c2* coron-v bro1 cot c2* crat c2* croc b2.de* *Crot-c* mrr1 *Crot-h* k* *Cupr* k* cycl b2.de* *Dig* b2.de* digin c2* dirc c2 dros b2.de dulc b2.de* *Dys* fmm1• fago c2 ferr k* *Ferr-p* bro1* gels k* germ-met srj5• glon bg2* graph b2.de* grin c2* hell b2.de* hep b2.de* *Hydr* *Hydr-ac* bro1 hyos k* *Iber* c2* *Ign* b2.de* *Iod* k* iodof c2 ip b2.de* jab c2 kali-bi bg2* kali-c b2.de* *Kali-chl* bro1 kali-m c2 kali-n b2.de* *Kalm* k* kreos b2.de* lac-d c2 **Lach** k* *Laur* k* led k2 lepi c2* *Lil-t* k* **Lith-c** k* **Lob** k* *Lyc* b2.de* *Lycps-v* k* m-ambo b2.de m-arct b2.de m-aust b2.de mag-c b2.de* mag-m b2.de* magn-gr c2* mang b2.de* meny b2.de* *Merc* b2.de* merc-c bro1 mez b2.de* morg-g fmm1• *Mosch* k* mur-ac b2.de* myric c2 **Naja** k* nat-c b2.de* nat-i c2* *Nat-m* k* nit-ac b2.de* nux-m b2.de* *Nux-v* b2.de* olib-sac wmh1 olnd b2.de* op k* ox-ac k2* par b2.de* petr b2.de* ph-ac b2.de* *Phase* br1* phase-xyz c2 *Phos* k* phys c2 phyt c2 pilo bro1 plat b2.de* plb b2.de* polyg-pe c2 pop-cand c2 prot fmm1• prun c2* prun-p c2 *Psor* **Puls** k* pyrus c2 ran-s b2.de* rhod b2.de* rhus-t b2.de* rumx c2 ruta b2.de* sabin b2.de* sacch br1 sars b2.de* sec b2.de* seneg k* *Sep* b2.de* ser-ang br1 sil b2.de* spartin bwa3 spartin-s br1* **Spig** k* **Spong** k* squil br1* staph b2.de* stigm br1 stront-c b2.de* stroph-h c2* *Stry* bro1 sul-ac b2.de* sulph b2.de* sumb c2* tab ptk1 tarent ptk1 tax c2 thea br1 thuj b2.de* thyr bro1* tub c2 tub-m jl2 valer b2.de* *Verat* b2.de* verat-v c2* verb b2.de* viol-o b2.de* viol-t b2.de* *Zinc* b2.de* zinc-i ptk1 [bell-p-sp dcm1 *Ferr-n* stj2 *Lith-f* stj2 *Lith-i* stj2 *Lith-m* stj2 *Lith-met* stj2 *Lith-p* stj2 *Lith-s* stj2 *Mag-n* stj2 *Mang-act* stj2 *Mang-m* stj2 *Mang-n* stj2 *Mang-p* stj2 *Mang-s* stj2 *Mang-sil* stj2 *Nitro* stj2 *Zinc-n* stj2]
- **accompanied** by:
  - **ascites**: aur br1*
  - **collapse**: dig br1 naja mrr1
  - **constipation**: spig mrr1
  - **constricting** pain of the heart: *Cact* mrr1
  - **convulsions**; epileptic (See GENERALS - Convulsions - epileptic - during - heart)
  - **diplopia**: lach ptk1

- **dropsy** (See GENERALS - Dropsy - external - heart)
- **epistaxis**: cact bg2 dig bg2
- **faintness** (See GENERALS - Faintness - heart - disease)
- **goitre**; toxic (See EXTERNAL - Goitre - exophthalmic - accompanied - heart)
- **hemorrhage**: cact mrr1 crat ptk1 lycps-v ptk1
- **hemorrhoids**: cact bro1 coll bro1* dig bro1
- **hoarseness**: hydr-ac ptk1 nux-m ptk1 ox-ac ptk1*
- **hyperthyroidism**: flor-p jl1
- **indigestion**: abies-n br1
- **lachrymation**: am-c bg1* spong ptk1
- **menses**; complaints of: cact ptk1
- **perspiration**: spong ptk1
- **reaction**; lack of (See GENERALS - Reaction - lack - accompanied - heart)
- **respiration**: *(↗Weakness - heart - accompanied - respiration; RESPIRATION - Asthmatic - heart - complaints)*
  - **complaints** of: cact ptk1 carb-v ptk1 *Kalm* ptk1 spig ptk1 spong ptk1 stroph-h ptk1 sumb ptk1 tarent ptk1
  - **difficult**: *(↗Weakness - heart - accompanied - respiration; RESPIRATION - Asthmatic - heart - complaints)* acon bro1* *Acon-f* bro1 *Adon* bro1* *Adren* bro1 am-c k2* apis bro1 arn bro1 ars bro1 ars-i bro1 *Aspidin* br1 aur k2* aur-i k2 bism-met mtf11 buth-a mtf11 cact bro1* *Calc-ar* bro1 carb-v bro1* *Chinin-ar* bro1 cimic bro1 cinnb bg1 coll bro1 conv br1* crat gm1 dig k2* *Glon* bro1 *Iber* bro1 kali-n bro1 kali-p fd1.de• kalm bro1 lach bro1 **Laur** k* *Lycps-v* k* magn-gr bro1 naja k2* op bro1 ox-ac k2* *Queb* bro1 sarcol-ac br1* ser-ang br1 spig bro1 spong bro1 stroph-h bro1* stry-ar bro1 sumb bro1 **Tarent** thyr ptk1 visc bro1
- **rheumatic** complaints: *(↗Pain - heart - rheumatic)* *Lith-c* br1
- **sleeplessness** (See SLEEP - Sleeplessness - accompanied - heart)
- **tuberculosis** (See Phthisis - accompanied - heart - complaints)
- **uremia**: *Ser-ang* br1
- **urinary** complaints and difficult respiration (See BLADDER - Urinary - accompanied - heart)
- **urination**; urging for: dig ptk1
- **urine**:
  - **albuminous**: spartin bwa3
  - **scanty**: ser-ang br1 stigm br1 stroph-h br1
- **vertigo**: adon bg2 aml-ns bg2 eucal bg2 kali-c bg2* kalm bg2 lach bg2* lil-t bg2 naja bg2 ol-an bg2 phos bg2* plat bg2 *Spig* bg2 sulph bg2 verat bg2*
- **vision**; loss of: lach mtf33
- **weakness**: dig br1
- ○ **Abdomen**; complaints of: merc-i-f ptk1
- **Back**; complaints of: tab bg2
- **Elbows**; pain in: arn ptk1
- **Eyes**:
  - **closed**: spong ptk1
  - **complaints** of: am-c bg2 aur bg2 calc bg2 cann-xyz bg2 dig bg2 lach bg2 *Nat-m* bg2 phos bg2 puls bg2 sep bg2 spig bg2
- **Fingers**; numbness in: acon mrr1 *Cact* mrr1 iber hs1* ox-ac vwe rhus-t mrr1 spong tl1 thyr vml4*
- **Hand**:
  - **left**:
    - **numbness**: acon mrr1 *Cact* mrr1 rhus-t mrr1
    - **swelling**: *Cact* k*
- **Head**:
  - **complaints**: cact bg2* calc bg2 crot-h ptk1 dig bg2* glon ptk1 kalm bg2* lach ptk1 merc-i-f ptk1 naja bg2* phos bg2 spig bg2*
  - **pain**:
    - **Forehead**: naja br1
    - **Temples**: naja br1
- **Hip** pain: lith-c mrr1

- **accompanied** by: ...
  - **Hypochondria**; complaints of: agar bg2 aur bg2 cact bg2 calc bg2 card-m bg2 dig bg2 mag-m bg2 naja bg2 phos bg2 tab bg2
  - **Intestines**; cancer in (See ABDOMEN - Cancer - intestines - accompanied - heart)
  - **Kidneys**:
    - **complaints**: calc-ar mrr1 lycps-v mrr1 *Ser-ang* br1 squil mtf11
      - **dropsy**; and: squil mtf11
    - **inflammation**: adon bro1 ars bro1 *Coffin* bro1 *Dig* bro1 glon bro1 *Saroth* bro1 stroph-h bro1 verat-v bro1
  - **Liver**; complaints of the: agar ptk1 aur tl1* cact ptk1 calc ptk1 dig ptk1* mag-m ptk1 myric ptk1
  - **Lower** limbs | **swelling** of the: stigm br1
  - **Ovaries**; complaints of the: tarent mrr1
  - **Ovary** and difficult respiration; pain in left (See FEMALE - Pain - ovaries - accompanied - heart)
  - **Retina**; congestion of: cact bro1
  - **Skin**:
    - **coldness** of: dig br1
    - **discoloration**; yellow: dig br1
  - **Stomach** | **Epigastrium**; sinking sensation at: lepi br1
  - **Thyroid**; complaints of the: am-c mrr1 ars ptk1 bufo ptk1 cact ptk1 *Crot-h* ptk1 diphtox jl2 lach ptk1 lat-m ptk1 lyc mrr1 lycps-v ptk1 penic mtf11 phos ptk1 *Spong* ptk1 thyr ptk1
  - **Upper** limbs:
    - **right** | **complaints** of: ars ptk1 kalm ptk1 merc-i-f ptk1 merc-i-r ptk1
    - **left**:
      - **numbness**●: *(↗Hypertrophy - heart - numbness)* **Acon** k* **Cact** k* cimic dig k* *Glon* kalm *Lach* lat-m k* lepi br1 *Naja* k* ox-ac mrr1 phos **Rhus-t** k* *Spig* *Sumb*
      - **pain**: *(↗Pain - heart - region - extending; Pain - heart - region - extending - upper limbs - left)* acon agar aur **Cact** calc-ar chim *Cimic* *Crot-h* *Dig* ham fd3.de• iber **Kalm** *Lat-m* k* lepi br1 lyc med **Rhus-t** spig *Tab*
      - **weakness**: acon mrr1 dig mrr1
    - **numbness**: both-ax tsm2
- **alternating** with:
  - **aphonia**: ox-ac br1*
  - **drawing** pains: acon k*
  - **hemorrhoids**: coll ptk1*
  - **hoarseness**: ox-ac mrr1
  - **pains** in other parts: acon bg2 glon bg2
  - **rheumatic** complaints: benz-ac mrr1
  - **urine**; sediment in: benz-ac mrr1 colch mrr1
  - **voice**; lost (See aphonia)
  - ○ **Head**; complaints of: aml-ns ptk1 ferr bg2 glon bg2* nux-m ptk1 stroph-h ptk1 tab ptk1
  - **Joints**; pain in (See EXTREMITIES - Pain - joints - alternating with - heart)
  - **Uterus**; complaints of: conv bg2 lil-t ptk1
- **arteriosclerotic** (See Arteriosclerosis; GENERALS - Arteriosclerosis)
- **ascending** agg.: am-c tl1
- **blood** calcium disorders; after: parathyr mtf11
- **children**; in: ant-t mrr1
- **chill**; during: cact bro1
- **chronic**: crat br1
  - **accompanied** by:
    - **weakness**; general: ars mrr1 crat br1
      - **excessive**: crat br1
- **collapse** states; after: verat mtf11
- **congenital**: laur mrr1
- **contradict**; with disposition to (See MIND - Contradiction - disposition - heart)
- **degenerative**: *Bar-c* br1
  - **old** people; in: | **men**; old: bar-c br1

- **diarrhea**; from suppressed: abrot mtf33
- **edema**:
  - **with** (See GENERALS - Dropsy - external - heart)
  - **without**: *Ser-ang* br1
- **excitement**; slightest: coll tl1
- **followed** by | **hemorrhoids** (See RECTUM - Hemorrhoids - heart)
- **gout**; after: colch tl1
- **infectious** disease; after: naja mtf33
- **influenza**; after: adon br1
- **irritability**, with (See MIND - Irritability - heart)
- **liver** disorders; after: psor mtf11
- **menses** | **before** | **agg.**: *Cact* bro1 crot-h bro1 eupi bro1 lach bro1 *Lith-c* bro1 sep bro1 spong bro1
  - **during** | **agg.**: *Cact* bro1 crot-h bro1 eupi bro1 lach bro1 *Lith-c* bro1 sep bro1 spong bro1
- **mitral** regurgitation: adon vh1* *Apoc* vh1* cact mtf crat mtf gala mtf kali-c mtf laur br1* phos mtf33 psor mtf11 ser-ang mtf spong mtf stroph-h mtf
- **morphinism**; after: spartin-s br1
- **motion**; after slightest: maland mtf11
  - **amel.**: bell-p sp1
- **neuralgia**; with: spig br1
- **old** people; in: ars-i br1* bar-i mtf11 crat mtf11
- **overlifting** agg.: *Caust*
- **rheumatism**; after: *Acon* bg2* *Adon* br1* ars bg2 aur bg2* aven bro1 benz-ac bro1* bry bg2* cact bro1 *Caust* bg2* cimic bro1 colch bro1* crat br1 dig mrr1 gels ptk1 ign bro1 kal bro1 *Kalm* bg2* **Lach** bg2* led bro1* lith-c bro1 lycps-v bro1 naja bro1 nat-m tl1 phyt bro1 prop bro1 puls bg2 rham-cal br1 *Rhus-t* bro1 spig bg2* verat-v br1*
- **sadness**; with (See MIND - Sadness - heart)
- **sleep** | **after** | **agg.**: lach tl1
  - **during**: lach tl1
- **tea**; after abuse of: thea br1
- **thirst**; with: bufo bg2
- **thyroid** glands; after overactivity of (= thyrotoxicosis): dys mtf11 thyr mtf11
- **tricuspid** regurgitation: *Apoc* vh1* cact mtf crat mtf gala mtf kali-c mtf laur mtf psor mtf11 ser-ang mtf spong mtf stroph-h mtf
- **warm** room agg.: am-c tl1

▽ - **extending** to:

○ • **Axillae**: kali-n bg2* lat-m ptk1 seneg bg2 thyr ptk1
  - **Back** | **Ribs**; along: aml-ns bg2 sil bg2
  - **Downward**: syph bg2
  - **Head**: cinnb bg2 glon ptk1 lachn ptk1 lil-t bg2 lith-c ptk1 med ptk1 nux-m ptk1 phos ptk1 sep ptk1 spig ptk1 spong ptk1 stroph-h ptk1
  - **Scapulae** | **left**: *Agar* ptk1 aloe ptk1 cimic ptk1 *Kali-c* ptk1 *Kalm* ptk1 lach ptk1 laur ptk1 lil-t bg2* mez ptk1 *Naja* ptk1 rhus-t ptk1 rumx ptk1 **Spig** ptk1 sulph ptk1 tab ptk1 ther ptk1 thuj ptk1
  - **Sides**:
    - **right**: ox-ac bg2 **Phos** bg2
    - **left**: **Ars** bg2
  - **Throat**: asaf bg2 nat-c bg2 phel bg2 podo bg2 stann bg2 ter bg2 valer bg2
  - **Vertex**: tab bg2

○ - **Aorta**: aur bg3 crat br1 dig cda1
- **Apex** of heart: apis bg2* brom bg2 cact bg2 chinin-s bg2 cimic bg2 cycl bg2 kali-bi bg2 lil-t bg2* lycps-v bg2 sulph bg2*
- **Below**: absin bg2 apis bg2 calad bg2 chel bg2 cimic bg2 com bg2 croc bg2 euphr bg2 eupi bg2 hura bg2 nat-m bg2 *Phos* bg2 sang bg2 spig bg2 sulph bg2 thuj bg2 zinc bg2
- **Coronaries**: crat mtf11
- **Myocardium**: ars-i br1 bacls-7 mtf11 coenz-a mtf11 coxs mtf11 crat mtf11 phos mtf11 pitu-gl mtf11 sacch br1 spartin bwa3 staphycoc mtf11 sulph mtf11
  - **accompanied** by | **pericardial** damage: coxs mtf11
- **Pericardium**: acon bg2 ant-ar bg2 apis bg2 ars bg2 bry bg2 colch bg2 coxs mtf11 crat mtf11 kali-c bg2 kalm bg2 naja bg2 spig bg2 spong bg2 squil bg2
- **Region** of the heart: arg-n tl1 morg-g fmm1• staph tl1
  - **accompanied** by | **dropsy**: coll tl1

Heart; complaints of the: ...

- **Valves**: *(↗Exudation; Exudation - valves; Heart failure - accompanied - valves; Murmurs - cardiac; Murmurs - cardiac - valvular)* acon bro1 *Adon* bro1 apoc bro1 *Ars* bro1 *Ars-i* bro1 aur bro1* aur-br bro1* aur-i bro1 *Bar-c* ptk1 cact bro1* calc ptk1 calc-f bro1* camph bro1 colch k2 *Conv* bro1 *Crat* bro1 *Dig* bro1 ferr bro1 galan bro1 glon bro1* iod bro1* *Kali-c* ptk1 *Kalm* bro1* lach bro1* laur bro1* lith-c bro1 *Lycps-v* br1* naja k2* ox-ac bro1 phos bro1* plb bro1 *Puls* ptk1 rhus-t bro1* sang bro1 ser-ang bro1 spartin bwa3 spig bro1* spong bro1* stigm bro1 stroph-h br1* syph mtf11 tarent ptk1* thyr bro1* visc bro1 zinc-i ptk1
  - **accompanied** by:
    - **cough**; dry: phos mtf33
    - **palpitations**: kali-c mtf33
    - **rheumatic** pains: colch tl1 lith-c mrr1
    - **sexual** disturbances or diseases: visc br1
    - **Heart** failure (See Heart failure - accompanied - valves)
    - **Lungs**; hemorrhage of: cact ptk1 crat ptk1 *Lycps-v* br1*
  - **children**; in: naja mrr1

○ • **Aortic** valve: *(↗Murmurs - cardiac - valvular - aortic)* aur mtf33 kalm ptk1
    - **insufficiency**: adon vh1 cact vh1
    - **regurgitation**: adon mtf11
    - **stenosis**: adon vh1 naphthoq mtf11
  - **Mitral** valve: *(↗Murmurs - cardiac - valvular - mitral)* coll hl9 kali-c tl1 psor mtf11 stroph-s sp1
    - **insufficiency**: adon vh1 kali-c fr2 laur he1
    - **regurgitation**: *Apoc* br1* cact ptk1* dig btw2* laur ptk1 psor ptk1* stroph-h br1*
    - **stenosis**: adon vh1
  - **Tricuspid** valve | **regurgitation**: *Apoc* br1* cact ptk1 laur ptk1 psor ptk1* stroph-h ptk1
- **Ventricles**:
  - **left** | **acute**: acon-f mtf11

LUNGS; complaints of the: calc-p mtf33 parathyr jl2

- **right**: elaps tl1
  - **complaints**; from acute or chronic: sang tl1
- **left**: bac tl1 tub tl1
- **accompanied** by:
  - **collapse** (See GENERALS - Collapse - accompanied - lungs)
  - **diabetes**: *(↗Phthisis - accompanied - diabetes; GENERALS - Diabetes mellitus - Accompanied - respiration)* calc-p tl1*
  - **jaundice**: card-m ptk1 chel ptk1 hydr ptk1
  - **measles**: tub-a jl2*
  - **vision**; loss of: lach mtf33

○ • **Eyes**; complaints of: calc bg2 cann-xyz bg2 hep bg2 lach bg2 lyc bg2 nat-m bg2 phos bg2 sil bg2 sulph bg2
  - **Heart**; weakness of the (See Weakness - heart - accompanied - lungs - complaints)
  - **Liver**; complaints of: card-m ptk1 chel ptk1 hydr ptk1
- **chronic**: petr br1
- **eczema**; after suppressed: ars tl1
- **hopefulness**; with (See MIND - Hopeful - lungs)
- **nervous**: ol-an br1
- **old** people; in: *Bac* br1
- **smallpox**; after: acon bro1 *Ant-t* bro1 bry bro1 *Phos* bro1 sulph bro1 verat-v bro1

○ - **Apex** of lungs | **right**: *Borx* bg2 elaps bg2*
- **Base** | **left**: nat-s tl1
- **Central** third | **right**: sep tl1
- **Upper** third | **right**: ars tl1

MAMMAE; complaints of: acon b2.de* alum b2.de* am-c b2.de* ambr b2.de* *Apis* bg2 *Arn* b2.de* *Ars* b2.de* asaf b2.de* bar-c b2.de* *Bell* b2.de* borx b2.de* **Bry** b2.de* bufo br1 *Calc* b2.de* camph b2.de* cann-s b2.de* **Carb-an** b2.de* carb-v b2.de* caust b2.de* **Cham** b2.de* chim br1 *Clem* b2.de* cocc b2.de* coloc b2.de* **Con** b2.de* croc b2.de* cupr b2.de* dig b2.de* dulc b2.de* ferr b2.de* graph b2.de* guaj b2.de* *Hep* b2.de* hydr ptk1 iod b2.de* kali-c b2.de* kreos b2.de* lac-ac br1 lac-c ptk1 laur b2.de* lepi br1 lyc b2.de*

Mammae; complaints of: ...
mang b2.de* merc b2.de* mez b2.de* nat-c b2.de* nat-m b2.de* nit-ac b2.de* nux-m b2.de* nux-v b2.de* oci ptk1 op b2.de* orig br1 petr b2.de* ph-ac b2.de* phel ptk1 **Phos** b2.de* **Phyt** bg2* plb b2.de* *Puls* b2.de* ran-s b2.de* rheum b2.de* rhus-t b2.de* ruta b2.de* sabal ptk1 sabin b2.de* samb b2.de* scroph-n br1 sep b2.de* **Sil** b2.de* *Sulph* b2.de* thuj b2.de* urt-u ptk1 verat b2.de* zinc b2.de*

- **alternating** sides: puls ptk1
- **right**: apis bg2 bell bg2 borx bg2 carb-an bg2 con bg2 ign ptk1 kali-bi ptk1 murx bg2 phel bg2* sang bg2 **Sil** ptk1
  - ▽ • **extending** to | **Scapula**: merc ptk1
- **left**: borx ptk1 bov ptk1 calc bg2 cist bg2 fl-ac bg2 lach bg2 lil-t bg2* *Lyc* ptk1 *Phel* ptk1 sabad bg2
  - • **menses**; before: bung-fa mtf
  - ▽ • **extending** to:
    - ⁝ **Head**: glon ptk1
    - ⁝ **Upper** limbs; left: aster ptk1
- **alternating** with | **Teeth**; complaints of: kali-c ptk1
- **flat** (See Atrophy - mammae)
- **large** (See Hypertrophy - mammae)
- **menses**; before: bry bg3 bung-fa mtf calc bg2* chin bg2 *Con* bg2* cycl bg2 helo bg2 kali-c bg2 **Kali-m** bg3 kreos bg2 **Lac-c** bg2* lyc bg3 merc bg2 ol-an bg3 *Phyt* bg3 puls bg3 sal-fr sle1• sang bg2 spong bg2
- **sensitive** mammae (See Pain - mammae - sore)
- ▽ - **extending** to:
  - ○ • **Abdomen**: phel ptk1 sang ptk1
  - • **Arms**: lith-c ptk1
    - ⁝ **Inner** side: aster ptk1
  - • **Axilla**: brom ptk1
  - • **Backward**: **Crot-t** ptk1 laur ptk1 lil-t ptk1 til ptk1
    - ⁝ **left**: form ptk1
  - • **Fingers**: aster ptk1 lith-c ptk1
  - • **Forward**: ol-an bg2
  - • **Head**: lac-ac ptk1
  - • **Shoulder**:
    - ⁝ **left**: sang ptk1
    - ⁝ **Between**: phel ptk1
- ○ - **Behind**:
  - • **right**: am-m bg2 lob bg2
  - • **left**: ant-t bg2
- **Below**: *Phos* bg2
  - • **right**: carb-an ptk1 caust ptk1 chel ptk1 **Cimic** ptk1 *Graph* ptk1 laur ptk1 lil-t ptk1 merc-i-r ptk1 *Phos* ptk1 *Sulph* ptk1 ust ptk1
  - • **left**: apis ptk1 bry ptk1 *Cimic* bg2* con bg2 kali-c bg2 lach bg2 mez bg2 phos ptk1 sulph ptk1 thlas ptk1 *Ust* bg2* visc bg2
- **Nipples**: acon b2.de* agar b2.de* *Am* b2.de* bell b2.de* bism b2.de* bry b2.de* calc b2.de* camph b2.de* cann-s b2.de* carb-an b2.de* caust b2.de* *Cham* b2.de* cic b2.de* cocc b2.de* con b2.de* **Graph** b2.de* hep b2.de* ign b2.de* **Lyc** b2.de* m-arct b2.de m-aust b2.de mang b2.de* *Merc* b2.de* mez b2.de* mur-ac b2.de* nit-ac b2.de* nux-v b2.de* par b2.de* petr b2.de* phos b2.de* plb b2.de* **Puls** b2.de* ran-s b2.de* rat ptk1 rheum b2.de* rhus-t b2.de* sabad b2.de* sabin b2.de* sars b2.de* sep b2.de* sil b2.de* **Sulph** b2.de* thuj b2.de* zinc b2.de*
  - • **left**: nat-s ptk1 pyrog ptk1 rumx ptk1
  - ▽ • **extending** to:
    - ⁝ **Backward**: crot-t ptk1 phel ptk1
      - : **left**: sulph ptk1
    - ⁝ **Outward**: cycl bg2 gels bg2 mez bg2 *Ol-an* bg2
    - ⁝ **Scapula**: crot-t ptk1
  - ○ • **Under**:
    - ⁝ **left**: asc-t ptk1 rumx ptk1
      - : **accompanied** by | **palpitation**: asc-t ptk1

RESPIRATORY tract; complaints of: *Acal* br1 am-m br1 *Ant-t* br1 *Cann-s* br1 chlor br1 cop br1 dros br1 euph br1 ferr-p br1 iod br1 menth br1 phel br1 *Samb* br1 sang br1 spong br1 stann br1 still br1 verb br1 yohim br1 zing br1

- **accompanied** by | **measles**: *Ant-t* bro1 bell bro1 *Bry* bro1 calc bro1 chel bro1 ferr-p bro1 iod bro1 *Ip* bro1 kali-bi bro1 kali-c bro1 *Phos* bro1 rumx bro1 sil bro1 *Stict* bro1 sulph bro1 verat-v bro1 viol-o bro1

Respiratory tract; complaints of: ...

- **acute**: iod br1
- **alternating** with | **Joints**; pain in (See EXTREMITIES - Pain - joints - alternating with - respiratory)
- **catarrh**: osm-met br1
  - • **acute**: just br1
- **inflammation**: phos br1
- **irritation**: osm-met br1
- **obstruction**: ambro br1
- ○ - **Mucous** membranes am-c br1 squil br1

RIBS; complaints of:

- ▽ - **extending** to | **Upward**: apis ptk1
- ○ - **Along**: apis ptk1
- **Between**: acon bg2 aesc ptk1 aml-ns ptk1 am bg2 ars bg2 asc-t bg2 aster bg2 bell bg2 bry bg2* chel bg2 cimic bg2* mag-p bg2 mez bg2* nat-m bg2 nux-v bg2 par bg2 phos bg2 puls bg2 ran-b bg2* rhod bg2 rhus-t bg2 sil ptk1 spig bg2 tab bg2 verb bg2* zinc bg2
- **False** ribs: benz-ac ptk1
  - • **right**: berb ptk1
  - • **left**: arg-n ptk1
- **Fifth** rib and sternum:
  - • **right**: mag-c ptk1 thuj ptk1
  - • **left**: ox-ac ptk1
- **Lower** border: apis bg2 arg-n bg2 cimic bg2 nat-s bg2
- **Short** ribs (See false)
- **Under**: apis ptk1 chin ptk1 sulph ptk1 ter ptk1

STERNUM; complaints of: acon bg2 anac bg2 carb-v bg2 card-m bg2 cimic bg2 eup-per bg2 olnd bg2

- **alternating** with | **Throat**; pain in: tab bg2
- ▽ - **extending** to:
  - ○ • **Abdomen**: stict ptk1
  - • **Back**: kali-bi ptk1 kali-i ptk1 merc-sul ptk1
  - • **Spine**: con ptk1 stict ptk1
- ○ - **Under** sternum: am-c ptk1 aur ptk1 calc ptk1 *Caust* ptk1 cham ptk1 gels ptk1 iod ptk1 phos ptk1 rhus-t ptk1 *Rumx* ptk1 sang ptk1
  - ▽ • **extending** to | **Axilla**: kali-n ptk1

VALVULAR heart disorders (See Heart; complaints - valves)

MORNING: alum b4.de* am-c b4.de* ang b7.de* ant-c b7.de* ant-t b7.de* ars b4.de* aur b4a.de bell b4.de* borx b4a.de bov b4.de* bry b7.de* calad b7.de* calc b4.de* canth b7.de* cob bg2 cocc b7.de* dros b7.de* dulc b4.de* euph b4.de* hep b4.de* ign b7.de* kali-bi bg2 kali-c b4.de* kali-n b4.de* *M-ambo* b7.de* m-aust b7.de meny b7.de* nat-m b4.de* *Nux-v* b7.de* petr b4.de* *Ph-ac* b4a.de *Phos* b4a.de puls b7.de* ran-b b7.de* rhod b4.de* ruta bg2 sars b4.de* sel b7.de* sep b4.de* sil b4.de* staph b4.de* stront-c b4.de* sulph b4.de* thuj b4.de* valer b7.de* verat b7.de* zinc b4.de*

FORENOON: alum b4.de* am-m b7.de* ars b4.de* borx b4a.de mag-c b4.de* phos b4.de* sabad b7.de* staph b7.de* stront-c b4.de*

AFTERNOON: alum b4.de* am-c b4.de* am-m b7.de* ant-t b7.de* bov b4.de* bry b7.de* canth b7.de* chel b7.de* guaj b4.de* hyos b7.de* kali-bi bg2 kreos b7a.de lach b7.de* laur b7.de* mag-c b4.de* nat-m b4.de* nux-v b7.de* phos b4.de* plb b7.de* sabad b7.de* sep b4.de* stront-c b4.de*

EVENING: alum b4.de* ang b7.de* bar-c b4.de* bell b4.de* borx b4a.de bry b7.de* canth b7.de* carb-v b4.de* caust b4.de* cina b7.de* cocc b7.de* graph b4.de* *Guaj* b4a.de kali-bi bg2 kali-n b4.de* lach b7.de* laur b7.de* led b7.de* lyc b4.de* m-aust b7.de mag-c b4.de* meny b7.de* merc b4.de* mez b4.de* nat-m b4.de* nux-m b7.de* nux-v b7.de* petr b4.de* *Phos* b4a.de *Puls* b7.de* ran-b b7.de* rhus-t b7.de* sabad b7.de* sars b4.de* seneg b4.de* *Sep* b4.de* *Sil* b4a.de spig b7.de* *Stann* b4a.de stront-c b4.de* sulph b4.de* thuj b4.de* valer b7.de* verat b7.de*

NIGHT: abrot ptk1 am-c b4.de* *Am-m* b7.de* ang b7.de* apis b7a.de ars b4.de* aur b4.de* bell b4.de* bry b7.de* *Calc* b4.de* carb-an b4.de* carb-v b4.de* cham b7.de* chin b7.de* dulc b4a.de *Ferr* b7a.de guaj b4.de* hell b7a.de hep b4.de* kali-bi bg2 *Kali-n* b4a.de *Kreos* b7a.de *Lyc* b4.de* *Mag-c* b4a.de merc b4.de* mez b4.de* nat-c bg2 *Nat-m* b4a.de nit-ac b4.de* *Nux-v* b7.de* ph-ac b4.de* *Puls* b7.de* ruta b7.de* sel b7.de* staph b7.de* stront-c b4.de* tell bg2 zinc b4.de*
- **midnight** | **after**: sulph bg2

○ - **Lumbar** region: ferr ptk1

ABSCESS: asaf k* *Hep* k* iod k* lach mez k* *Ph-ac* k* *Sil* k* staph k* *Sulph* k* tarent k2 *Tarent-c*

○ - **Cervical** region: calc k2 *Lach* k* *Lyc* *Petr* k* ph-ac phos k2 psor k* sec sil k* sul-ac k2* *Tarent-c* k*
  - • **cicatrices**; old: *(↗SKIN - Cicatrices)* **Sil**
- **Coccyx**, just below: *(↗RECTUM - Abscess - below)* paeon tl1*
- **Lumbar** region: *Calc-p* k* **Sil** b4a.de staph c2
- **Psoas**: *(↗EXTREMITIES - Abscess - lower - psoas)* arn k* chin ptk1 *Cupr* k* *Ph-ac* k* *Sil* k* staph k* sulph ptk1 symph k* syph k*
- **Spine** | **Vertebrae**: lach bg2

ABSENT:

○ - **Vertebrae**: | **sensation** as if vertebrae are absent: mag-p ptk1

ADHERENT:

○ - **Dorsal** region | **Scapulae**: ran-b ptk1

AIR AGG.; DRAFT OF: calc-p bg2 caust sne nux-v b7.de* sumb ptk1

○ - **Cervical** region: *Calc-p* ptk1 hep ptk1 lach ptk1 merc ptk1 psor ptk1 sanic ptk1 *Sil* ptk1 stront-c ptk1
- **Dorsal** region | **Scapulae**; between: caust ptk1 hep ptk1
- **Nape**; on: *Hep* kali-ar k2 kola stb3• *Merc* sanic mtf33 *Sil*
- **Spine**: *Sumb* k*

ALIVE; sensation of something:

○ - **Dorsal** region: *Lach* b7a.de m-ambo b7.de

○ • **Scapulae**: croc b7.de* plb b7.de
  - ⁝ **right**: plb bg2

ANEMIA: | **Spinal** cord: agar bro1 *Plb* bro1 *Sec* bro1 stry-p bro1 tarent bro1

ANGER agg.: nux-v bg2

ANKYLOSING spondylarthritis: allox mtf11 carc mtf11 mand mtf11 med mtf11 sarcol-ac mtf11 tub-r jl2*

ANKYLOSIS: | **fibrous** ankylosis: tub-r mtf11

ANXIETY: | **Dorsal** region: *Ars* b4.de* carb-an bg2

ARCHING of the back (See Opisthotonos)

ASCENDING agg.: hura bg2 sanic bg2 sep bg2

ASLEEP; sensation as if: *(↗Numbness)*

○ - **Cervical** region: spig h1

○ • **Nape** of neck: rhus-t b7.de* spig b7.de*
- **Dorsal** region: con bg2 kreos bg2 merc b4.de* phos b4.de* *Sulph* b4a.de

○ • **Scapulae**: anac k* arg-met b7.de* calc bg2
- **Lumbar** region: berb bg2 phos h2

ATROPHY: | **Muscles** | **Long** muscles: thuj mtf33
- **Spine**: alum bg2 arg-n bg2 caust bg2 chin bg2 *Cocc* bg2 con bg2 indg bg2 mag-p bg2 nat-m bg2 ox-ac bg2 ph-ac bg2 *Phos* bg2 pic-ac bg2 plb bg2 sec bg2 sil bg2 *Staph* bg2 *Sulph* bg2

○ • **Muscles**: bov mtf calc mtf caust mtf cortiso mtf *Kali-hp* mtf **Kres** mtf mang mtf merc mtf plb mtf *Plb-act* mtf sec mtf stry mtf sulfa mtf *Syph* mtf thal mtf

BACKACHE (See Pain)

BALL; as if a:

○ - **Cervical** region | **Nape** of neck: bell bg2

BAND sensation (See Constriction)

BANDAGING: | **amel.**: tril-p bg2

BAR in the back; feeling as if a: ars k* lach k*

BENDING:
- **amel.**: meny b7.de* petr b4.de*
- **arms** | **backward** agg.: carb-v b4.de* caust b4.de* sanic bg2 sulph b4.de*
- **backward**:
  - • **agg.**: *Bar-c* b4a.de calc-p ptk1 chel bg2* cimic ptk1 con b4a.de fl-ac bg2 kali-c b4a.de nux-v bg2 plat b4.de* puls bg2 rhus-t bg2
  - • **amel.**: cycl bg2 ign ptk1 lach b7.de* nat-m bg2 petr bg2* puls b7.de* rhus-t b7.de* sabad b7.de* sabin b7.de* sil bg2
  - • **sensation** of:
    - ⁝ **Coccyx**: mag-p ptk1
    - ⁝ **Dorsal** region: mag-c bg2
- **body**:
  - • **agg.**: lach b7a.de sabin b7.de* staph b7.de*
  - • **backward** agg.: asaf b7.de* calc b4.de* chel b7.de* con b4.de* kali-c b4.de* *M-arct* b7.de* nux-v b7.de* puls b7.de* rhus-t b7.de*
  - • **forward** | **agg.**: asaf b7.de* chel b7.de* nux-v b7.de*
- **forward**:
  - • **agg.**: mang bg2 pic-ac ptk1
  - • **amel.**: caust bg2 kali-bi bg2 meny bg2 psor bg2 puls bg2 seneg bg2 sep bg2
- **head** | **backward** | **agg.**: caust b4.de* kali-c b4.de*
  - • **forward**:
    - ⁝ **agg.** | **Cervical** region: cimic ptk1 lyss ptk1 rad-br ptk1
- **inward**:
  - • **sensation** as if bent inward:
    - ⁝ **Dorsal** region | **Scapulae**: podo bg2

BIFIDA; spina (See Spina bifida)

BLOATING: | **Cervical** region: cact k2

BLOCKED; sensation as if: | **Spine**; base of (See Obstruction - spine)

BLOOD; extravasation of:

○ - **Lumbar** region: crot-h
- **Spinal** cord | **injuries**; from: *(↗Injuries - spine; EXTREMITIES - Paralysis - lower - injuries - spine)* acon mp1• *Arn* mp1• *Bell* mp1• lach mp1• nux-v mp1• sec mp1•

BLOW:
- **after** a hard blow; agg.: *Arn* b7.de*
- **sensation** as from a:
  - • **shock**; or sudden: bell ptk1 cic ptk1 *Sep* ptk1 stann ptk1

○ • **Cervical** region | **waking**; on: galla-q-r nl2•
  - • **Spine**: dig h2

BLOWING THE NOSE agg.: dig b4.de*

○ - **Cervical** region: kali-bi ptk1
- **Lumbar** region: calc-p ptk1 dig ptk1

Back

BLUISH:
- **right** side of back: vip
O - **Cervical** region | **Nape** of neck: ars *Lach* *Rhus-t*

BOARD; as if lying on a: bapt ptk1 sanic ptk1

BOILS (See Eruptions - boils)

BREATHING:
- **agg.**: *Acon* b7a.de alum bg2 *Am-m* b7a.de arg-met b7.de* arn b7.de* bry b7.de* calc bg2 *Caust* b4a.de croc b7.de* nux-v b7.de* spig b7.de*
O • **Dorsal** region | **Scapulae**: am-m ptk1
  • **Sacrum**: merc ptk1
- **deep**:
  • **agg.**: arg-met b7.de* carb-an b4.de* coloc ptk1 *Hep* b4a.de kali-n b4.de* spig bg2 sulph b4a.de verb b7.de*
    ⁝ **Cervical** region: chel ptk1
    ⁝ **Spine**: chel ptk1 ruta ptk1
  • **amel.**: *Lach* b7a.de meny b7.de*

BROWN (See Discoloration - brown)

BRUISES on spine (See Injuries)

BUBBLING sensation in: lyc ptk1 petros k* tarax k*
O - **Cervical** region: lyc ptk1
- **Coccyx**: aloe bg2 arg-met bg2 kali-c bg2 valer b7.de*
- **Dorsal** region: lyc b4.de* sep b4.de* squil b7.de* tarax b7a.de
O • **Scapulae**: asaf b7.de* berb kali-c bg2 lyc bg2* m-arct b7.de spig b7.de* squil b7.de* sulph bg2 *Tarax* k*
    ⁝ **right**: *Tarax*
    ⁝ **left**: spig
    ⁝ **Beneath**: lyc squil k*
- **Lumbar** region: ang b7.de berb bg2 lyc h2 sep h2
  • **lying** and rising from a seat agg.: berb

BUZZING sensation: | **Dorsal** region:
O • **Scapula**; under | **left**: kali-m ptk1
- **Lower** back: moni rfm1•

CALCAREOUS deposits: | **Spinal** cord: vario ptk1

CALCIFICATION of spine (See Caries; Curvature)

CANCER:
O - **Cervical** region: hydrc br1
- **Spine** | **metastasis**: tell mrr1

CARBUNCLES (See Eruptions - carbuncle)

CARIES of spine: *(↗Curvature)* ph-ac c2 *Sil* mrr1 syph c2*
O - **Dorsal** vertebrae: *Calc* b4a.de *Puls* b7a.de
- **Lumbar** vertebrae: *Sil*

CARRIED; being: | **amel.**: calc-p bg2

CAUDA EQUINA (See Compression)

CHEWING agg.: | **Cervical** region: form ptk1

CHILL; before: podo bg2

CHILLINESS (See Coldness)

CLOTHES: | **agg.** | **Cervical** region: caust ptk1
- **tight** | **agg.**: sep b4.de*

COCCYGODYNIA (See Pain - coccyx)

COITION:
- **after**: mag-m bg2 nit-ac bg2
- **agg.**: *Mag-m* b4a.de
O • **Spine**: nit-ac ptk1
- **during**: kali-bi bg2
  • **agg.**: cob ptk1 ferr ptk1 mag-m ptk1 nat-m ptk1 *Nit-ac* ptk1 sabal ptk1 staph ptk1 sulph ptk1
    ⁝ **Lumbar** region: cob ptk1

COLD:
- **air** agg.: bar-c b4a.de
- **applications** | **agg.**: *Calc* b4a.de *Phos* b4a.de *Rhus-t* b7.de* sabad b7a.de

COLD; AFTER TAKING A: *Arn* b7a.de bar-c bg2 cham b7.de* dulc b4a.de* nit-ac b4.de* *Nux-v* b7.de* puls b7.de* *Sep* b4a.de

COLD CLOTH; sensation of a (See Coldness - lumbar - cold; Coldness - sacral - wet; Coldness - spine - wet)

COLDNESS (= chilliness): *Abies-c* bro1 acon k* aesc agar allox sp1 alum k* alum-p k2 alumn k2 am-br am-c *Am-m* k* anac (non:anag slp) ang bg2* aphis apis k* *Arg-met* arn k* *Ars* k* ars-s-f k2 *Asaf* asar h1* aur aur-ar k2 aur-m-n aur-s k2 bamb-a stb2.de• bapt bar-c h2 *Bell* k* benz-ac k* berb k* beryl sp1 **Bol-la** k* borx h2* brom brucel sa3• *Bry* **Cact** k* calad *Calc* k* calc-s calc-sil k2 *Camph* k* *Canth* k* **Caps** k* carb-an carb-v k* carbn-s caust h2* cedr *Cham* chel chin k* chinin-ar k* chlf cic coc-c k* cocc k* coff k* colch k* com *Con* k* conv br1* croc k* *Crot-t* *Dig* k* dios *Dulc* k* elaps k* ephe-si hsj1• **Eup-per** k* **Eup-pur** k* euph h2 ferr ferr-ar ferr-p galla-q-r nl2• *Gels* k* gins k* grat guaj bg2 *Ham* hell k* helo c1 helo-s c1* hep k* hipp k* hydr hydrog srj2• *Hyos* k* hyper ign k* ip jatr-c kali-ar kali-bi k* kali-c kali-i kali-m k2 kali-n kali-p kali-s kali-sil k2 kalm kola stb3• kreos bg2 *Lac-d* **Lach** k* lachn lact laur k* *Led* k* *Lil-t* k* limest-b es1• *Lob* lyc k* mag-c mag-s bro1 mand rsj7• *Meny* k* merc k* merc-c merc-i-r *Mez* k* mosch bg2 mur-ac k* nat-ar **Nat-m** k* **Nat-s** k* *Nit-ac* nit-s-d nux-m bg2 *Nux-v* k* op k* ox-ac k* *Phos* phys pimp mtf11 plat podo fd3.de• **Puls** k* pyrog bro1 quas bro1 ran-b bg2 *Raph* k* *Rhus-t* k* rhus-v ruta k* sabad k* sang bg1 sanic sarr sars h2 *Sec* k* seneg sep k* **Sil** k* spig k* *Spong* k* squil bg2 *Stann* k* staph k* *Stram* k* stroph-s sp1 *Stry* k* **Sulph** k* sumb tarent thuj k* vac jl2 valer **Verat** k* [stront-m stj2 stront-met stj2]
- **one** side: croc bg2
- **right** side: arg-met bg2 caust bg2 hydr bg2 phos bg2 sulph bg2
- **left** side: canth bg2 galla-q-r nl2• plat bg2
- **morning**: arn k* asaf k* bry k* con k* ferr k* mez k* nit-s-d k* **Nux-v** k* sumb k*
  • **7** h: ferr
  • **8**.30-9 h: asaf
  • **menses**; after: kali-c
  • **rising** agg.: meny h1
  • **waking**; on: con k*
- **forenoon**: ang k* asaf berb k* cham k* con k* graph h2 hydr k* lyc k*
  • **9** h: mag-c h2
  • **10** h: con
  • **11** h: cham
    ⁝ **11-12** h: cimic hr1
  • **walking**:
    ⁝ **air** agg.; in open: hydr
    ⁝ **room** agg.; in a: ang
- **noon**: arg-n rhus-t k*
- **afternoon**: alum k* apis asaf k* carb-an h2 castm cic k* cimic k* *Cocc* fago k* guaj k* hyos k* lyc k* nat-ar rumx stram thuj k*
  • **14** h: cic nat-s
  • **15** h: *Apis* lyc
  • **16** h: mag-c
  • **17** h: nat-m h2
  • **stool** agg.; after: fago
- **evening**: alum h2 *Ars* k* bapt k* berb k* caps k* castm cimic k* *Cocc* k* coff *Dulc* k* graph h2 kali-c h2 kali-n h2 kreos k* *Lyc* k* *Mur-ac* k* nat-m k* nux-v k* podo fd3.de• **Puls** k* *Rhus-t* k* sang k* sep k* spong fd4.de *Stann* k* **Sulph** k* tab k* thuj k*
  • **18** h | **warm** room; in: lyc
  • **19** h: castm lyc
  • **21** h: castm kreos
  • **22** h: cench k2
  • **lying** down agg.; after: *Coff* *Lyc* nat-c h2 *Nux-v* sang
- **night**: androc srj1• *Ars* k* arum-t k* chin k* chinin-ar chinin-s coc-c k* dulc fd4.de kali-bi gk kali-s fd4.de lil-t k* lyc nat-ar nat-m k* *Puls* k* stront-c thuj k*
  • **bed** | **going** to bed | **when**: coc-c lil-t phos vh
    ⁝ **in** bed | **agg.**: calc bg1
- **accompanied** by:
  • **warmth** in the middle of the back and across the lower abdomen: coff a1

O • **Head**; coldness of (See HEAD - Coldness - accompanied - back)
• **Lumbar** region; weakness in (See GENERALS - Weakness - accompanied - lumbar)
- **air** agg.; in open: acon dulc neon srj5•
- **alternating** with heat (See Heat - alternating - cold)
- **cold**:
• **air** agg.: alum-sil k2 plut-n srj7• *Stront-c*
• **streak** running up and down spine: ptel c1
• **water** was spurted on; as if cold: alum-sil k2 alumn k2 caust croc br1 lyc *Phos* vh **Puls**
- **cold** air; as from: agar k2 benz-ac camph caust coff
▽ • **extending** from spine over body, like an epileptic aura: agar k*
- **dinner**; after: cedr k* cycl k*
- **draft** of cold agg.: allox sp1
- **dressing**, when: anth k*
- **eating** | **after** | **agg.**: crot-c k* sil staph h1
• **while** | **agg.**: raph
- **external**: coc-c k* dulc fd4.de lyc k*
- **fever** | **during** | **agg.**: aur-m-n c1 puls bro1
• **with**: cact br1
- **followed** by:
• **heat**: cimic hr1
• **suffocative** sensation: mag-p br1
- **headache**; during (See HEAD - Pain - accompanied - back - coldness)
- **ice**, as from: agar bg2* *Am-m* k* arg-n bg2 cocc k* phyt bg2 rhus-t bg2 stry bg2
• **painful**: psil ft1
O • **Cervical** region | **Nape** of neck: chel ptk1
- **icy** coldness running down back: *Vac* jl2 vario jl2
• **epilepsy**; before: *Ars*
- **itching**, ending in: *Am-m* k*
- **lying** down | **amel.**: castm kali-n k* sil k*
- **menses** | **after** | **agg.**: kali-c k*
• **during** | **agg.**: bell k* kreos k* ozone sde2•
- **motion** agg.: asaf k* *Eup-pur* phys k* sulph thuj k*
- **sitting** agg.: brom k*
- **sleep** | **siesta** agg.; after: cycl k*
- **spots**: agar k2
- **stool**:
• **after** | **agg.**: fago *Puls* sumb k*
• **before**: ars k*
• **during** | **agg.**: colch *Trom*
- **urination** | **after** | **agg.**: nat-m ser *Sars* k*
• **during**: caps bg2 nit-ac bg2 thuj bg2
- **waking**; on: dig digin a1
- **walking**:
• **agg.**: asaf k* hyos k* nit-s-d k* squil h1
• **air** agg.; in open: chin
• **warm** room; in a | **agg.**: squil h1
- **warm** stove, near: jug-c k*
• **amel.**: cocc h ham fd3.de• sulph h2
- **warmth** agg.: apis
- **waves**; in: rhus-t bg2
▽ - **extending** to:
O • **Abdomen**: cham h1 crot-t *Phos Sec Spig*
• **Arms**, into: gins verat k* [tax jsj7]
• **Body**, over whole: amyg bell *Lyc*
⁝ **evening** | **18**.30 h: lyc
• **Down** the back: (↗*CHILL - Descending; CHILL - Descending - Agg.)* abies-c acon **Agar** k* *All-c* alum arg-n ars asaf bar-c bell borx h2 brom bry canth ptk1 carl cedr chel cimic hr1 **Cina** vh *Cocc* coff *Colch* k* coloc sne conv br1 crot-t *Eup-per* k* *Eup-pur* glon helo c1 hep h2 *Hyper* iris kali-s fd4.de lac-c ptk1 lil-t k* *Lob* lyc mag-c mag-p c1 ol-an ol-j bg2

- **extending** to – **Down** the back: ...
ox-ac bg2 phos bg2* pic-ac podo fd3.de• **Puls** k* pyrus ruta sabad *Samb* sep *Sil* staph **Stram** k* stry valer ptk1 *Zinc*
⁝ **evening**: podo fd3.de•
: **21** h: all-c
⁝ **night** | **22** h: sep
⁝ **cold** water agg.:
: **poured** down; as if: abies-c c1 agar alum-sil k2 alumn anac ars lil-t *Lyc* **Puls** k* sabad stram vario zinc
: **trickling** down; as if: ars caps k* caust
⁝ **headache**; during: kali-s fd4.de mez h2
⁝ **motion** agg.: rumx
• **Feet**: croc
• **Genitals**: kola stb3•
• **Limbs**: eup-per k2 gins
• **Lower** limbs: acon ferr ham [tax jsj7]
• **Up** and down the back: abies-c bg2* aesc all-c aphis bapt k* bell bg2* caps bg2* eup-per bg2* **Eup-pur Gels** k* hell *Ip* k* lach mag-p br1 med puls ptk1 rumx bg2 ruta k* *Sulph* k*
⁝ **afternoon**: rumx
⁝ **followed** by | **suffocative** sensation: mag-p br1
• **Up** the back: *(↗CHILL - Ascending)* aesc am-m *Arg-n* k* ars bamb-a stb2.de• bar-c bol-la borx a1 *Calc-p* k* carb-an h2 choc srj3• *Cina Colch* con equis-h c1 *Eup-per Gels* hyos ip kali-bi kali-i kali-p **Lach** k* lil-t bg1 mag-c mag-p c1 merc-sul *Nat-s* ol-an *Ol-j* ptk1 ox-ac ptk1 phos phys plut-n srj7• *Puls* rhus-v ruta **Sulph** k* thuj h1 tub br1
⁝ **afternoon**:
: **14** h: nat-s
: **16** h: mag-c
⁝ **evening**: kali-p sulph h2
⁝ **eating**; after: *Arg-n* k*
⁝ **entering**; on:
: **cool** room: plut-n srj7•
: **open** air; from: *Arg-n* k*
⁝ **menses**; during: kreos
⁝ **motion** agg.: sulph thuj h1
⁝ **shivering**, after urinating, with: *Sars*
O - **Cervical** region: androc srj1• *Calc* calc-sil k2 cann-i k* carbn-s cass a1 chel k* chr-ac k* con bg1* *Dulc* k* fl-ac k* iris-foe kali-bi k2* kali-chl k* laur k* lyc k* nat-s k* op k* psil ft1 ran-s k* **Sil** k* *Spong* k* zinc k*
• **morning**: ran-s k*
• **evening**: dulc k* *Spong* k*
• **air**; sensitive to a draft of: *Hep Merc Sil*
• **creeping**: sil k*
• **sensation** of coldness: falco-ch sze4•
▽ • **extending** to:
⁝ **Occiput**: chel k* plut-n srj7•
⁝ **Sacrum** | **lying** down agg.: thuj
⁝ **Vertex**: *Sil* hr1
O • **Nape** of neck: *Calc* b4a.de sulph b4.de
• **Neck**: calc bg2 dulc bg2 kali-c bg2 phos bg2 sulph bg2 valer bg2
- **Dorsal** region: acon b7.de* agar k* alum b4.de* am-m b7a.de* **Anac** bg2 *Ang* b7.de* apis b7a.de* arg-met b7.de* arn b7.de* ars bg2 **Asaf** b7.de* asar b7.de* aur b4.de* bapt bg2 bar-c bg2 **Bell** b4.de* *Borx* b4a.de* bov b4a.de* calc b4.de* camph b7.de* **Canth** b7.de* *Caps* b7.de* carb-an bg2 carb-v b4.de* *Caust* b4.de* cham bg2 **Chel** b7.de* *Chin* b7.de* **Cocc** b7.de* *Coff* b7.de* **Colch** b7.de* con bg2 croc k* **Dig** b4.de* *Dulc* b4.de* eup-per bro1 gels bg2 glon bg2 *Graph* b4.de* guaj b4.de* hell b7.de* hep b4a.de* hydrog srj2• *Hyos* b7.de* ign b7.de* kali-c b4.de* kreos b7a.de* **Lach** b7.de* laur bg2 led b7.de* lyc b4.de* m-arct b7.de m-aust b7.de **Mag-c** b4.de* mang b4.de* **Meny** b7.de* merc b4.de* **Mez** b4.de* mosch bg2 mur-ac b4.de* nat-c b4.de **Nat-m** b4.de* nit-ac b4a.de* nux-m bg2 nux-v b7.de* op b7.de* par b7.de* ph-ac b4a.de* **Phos** b4.de* plat b4.de* plb bg1 puls b7.de* ran-b b7.de* *Rhus-t* b7.de* **Ruta** b7.de* **Sabad** b7.de* sabin b7.de* sars bg2 *Sec* b7.de* **Seneg** b4.de* *Sep* b4.de* *Sil* k* **Spig** b7.de* spong k* squil b7.de* **Stann** b4.de* staph b7.de* *Stram* b7.de* stront-c b4.de* *Sulph* b4.de* thuj k* valer bg2 vario bg2 verat b7.de* *Zinc* b4.de*
• **morning**: bamb-a stb2.de•

- **sensation** of: alum b4a.de *Am-m* b7a.de *Ars* b4a.de borx b4a.de carb-v b4.de* *Caust* b4a.de cocc b7.de coff b7.de con b4.de *Croc* b7.de* hyos b7.de ign b7a.de laur b7a.de meny b7.de* mez b4.de mosch b7a.de mur-ac b4.de *Puls* b7a.de ran-b b7.de *Rhus-t* b7a.de *Ruta* b7.de sabad b7.de sec b7.de* spong b7.de

○ • **Scapulae**: alum b4a.de* am-m bg2 androc srj1• aur b4a.de* bamb-a stb2.de• camph k* *Caust* b4a.de* chinin-s croc k* dios k* kreos b7a.de* phos phyt bg2 plat bg2 rhus-t k* sil bg2 stront-c bg2 viol-t bg2
  - **sensation** of: *Am-m* b7a.de m-aust b7.de viol-t b7.de
  - **Below**: agar k* camph ptk1
  - **Between**: abies-c k* acon bg2 agar k* *Am-c Am-m* k* *Arg-met* ars ptk1 aur k* bamb-a stb2.de• **Bol-la** cann-i k* **Caps** k* carl k* castm bro1 caust k* cham bg2 chel k* *Eup-per* k* helo bro1 helo-s rwt2• kreos bg2 lac-d lach bg2 *Lachn* k* led k* nat-c k* nat-m bg1 nat-s bg2 petr k* plut-n srj7• podo bg2 *Puls* k* pyrog bro1* *Rhus-t* k* sarr k* *Sep* k* *Sil* sulph tab k* tub br1* viol-t k* [spect dfg1]
    - **cold** water, as from: abies-c k* castm rb2 tub rb2
    - **cough**; with: *Am-m*
    - **fever**; during: rhus-t bg2
      - **intermittent**: rhus-t tl1
    - **ice**, like: agar am-m k* arg-met *Lachn* k* *Sep* ptk1
    - **ice**-cold hand; like an: sep h2
    - **wind**, as from: caust k* hep sulph
    - **extending** to | **Head**: plut-n srj7•
  - **Lower** margin: plat h2
- **Spine**: am-m cham haem iris-foe *Meny* k* plut-n srj7•
- **Vertebrae**:
  - **sensation** of: bac jl2
  - **wet**: bac jl2

- **Lumbar** region: agar bro1 asaf k* bapt bg1 beryl tpw5* *Bry* bg2* *Camph* k* cann-i k* canth k* *Carb-an* k* carb-v k* carbn-s cham k* chin k* cupr cupr-s a1* *Dulc* k* *Eup-per* bro1* **Eup-pur** k* gels bg2* hell k* hydrog srj2• **Hyos** bg2 kreos b7a.de* **Lach** k* laur bg2 led *Lyc* b4.de* med k* merc bg2 *Merc-c* b4a.de* nat-m k* nux-m k* ox-ac ph-ac b4a.de* plut-n srj7• podo k* psor bg1 *Puls* k* *Rhus-t* bg2* sabad bg2 sabin bg2 sanic ptk1* spong k* **Stront-c** b4.de* stroph-s sp1 *Sulph* k* *Sumb* k* tarent k* vario bg2 visc c1
  - **right** side: beryl tpw5 *Med*
  - **morning**: cham k* *Sumb* k*
  - **evening** | **sitting** agg.: canth
  - **night**: nat-m k* podo k*
    - **dinner**; during: hell k*
  - **accompanied** by weakness (See GENERALS - Weakness - accompanied - lumbar)
  - **air** agg. | **passed** over it; as if cold air: stann h2 *Sulph Sumb*
  - **air** agg.; draft of cold: tarent k*
  - **bending** forward; on: stroph-s sp1
  - **cold** cloth; as from a: lath ptk1 lyc bg2 *Sanic* vh *Tub* jl2
  - **cough**; with: *Carb-an* k*
  - **fanned**; as if: *Puls* vh
  - **fever**; during intermittent: rhus-t tl1
  - **icy** coldness: mang bg2 stry bg2
  - **lying** agg.: stroph-s sp1
  - **motion** agg.: podo k*
  - **sensation** of: *Bry* b7a.de canth b7a.de hell b7.de laur b7a.de *Rhus-t* b7a.de
  - **sitting** agg.: chin k* stroph-s sp1
  - **spots**; in: canth bg2
  - **standing** agg.: stroph-s sp1
  - **stool** | **after** | **agg.**: *Puls* k*
    - **before**: nux-m k*
  - **walking** agg.: *Camph* k* stroph-s sp1
  - **warm**:
    - **stove**:
      - **amel.**: hell k*
      - **not** amel.: plut-n srj7•
  - **water**; as from cold: vario bg2

Coldness – Lumbar region: ...

▽ • **extending** to:
    - **Abdomen** | **urination** agg.; after: sulph
- **Sacral** region: arg-met benz-ac k* calc-sil k2 *Dulc* hyos laur **Lyc** k ● ox-ac plut-n srj7• **Puls** k* *Sanic* k* stront-c sulph k*
  - **chill**; during: aesc asaf eup-pur *Puls* sulph k*
  - **icy** cold: arg-met ptk1 benz-ac ptk1 dulc ptk1
  - **menses**; during: *Puls*
  - **stool** agg.; during: ptel k*
  - **wet** cloth; as if from a: haliae-lc srj5• sanic ptk1* *Tub* jl2

▽ • **extending** to:
    - **Occiput**: gels hr1* ol-j pd
    - **Upward**: **Sulph**
- **Spine**: acon k* *Aesc* k* agar k* am-m bg2* ant-t bg2 arg-n bg1* atro k* bol-la bry k* canth k* caps ptk1 chlf k* cimic bro1 coc-c k* *Crot-c Crot-t* k* *Gels* k* gins k* glon bg1 helon ptk1 hydr bg2 *Hyos* k* jatr-c bg2 jug-c k* kali-n k* lachn ptk1 lept k* mag-p tl1 med ptk1 meny k* merc k* *Mez* k* mosch k* myric bg2 nux-v bg2 op k* petr ptk1 phys bg1 polyp-p bg2 rhus-t ptk1 ruta k* *Sanic* sec bg1* stry k* *Sumb* k* tab k* thuj k* trom k*
  - **stool** agg.; during: trom k*
  - **walking** agg.: gins k*
  - **waves**; in: *Abies-c* bro1 *Acon* bro1 *Aesc* bro1 *Ars* bro1 bol-la bro1 calen bro1 conv bro1 dulc bro1 echi bro1 frax bro1 *Gels* bro1 helo bro1 helo-s rwt2• *Mag-p* bro1 med bro1 raph bro1 stry bro1 tub bro1 *Zinc* bro1
    - **influenza**; during: gels tl1
  - **wet** cloth; as if from a: tub hr1*

▽ • **extending** to:
    - **Downward**: canth k* pic-ac tl1 *Ruta* stry k* thuj tl1
    - **Upward**: ange-s oss1• ox-ac ptk1
      - **fever**; during intermittent: rhus-t tl1

○ • **Marrow** of; in: helo bg2 helo-s rwt2• jatr-c bg2

COMFORTABLE position; cannot find a: | **Dorsal** region: bell bg2 phos bg2

COMPLAINTS of back: *Acon* b2.de agar b2.de* agn b2.de alum b2.de am-c b2.de am-m b2.de ambr b2.de anac b2.de *Ang* b2.de ant-c b2.de ant-t b2.de arg-met b2.de **Arn** b2.de **Ars** b2.de* asaf b2.de asar b2.de aur b2.de* bar-c b2.de **Bell** b2.de* bism b2.de borx b2.de bov b2.de bry b2.de **Calc** b2.de* camph b2.de cann-s b2.de canth b2.de caps b2.de carb-an b2.de *Carb-v* b2.de **Caust** b2.de cham b2.de chel b2.de *Chin* b2.de chinin-s ptk1 cic b2.de *Cimic* ptk1 cina b2.de **Cocc** b2.de* coff b2.de colch b2.de coloc b2.de con b2.de croc b2.de cupr b2.de cycl b2.de dig b2.de dros b2.de dulc b2.de euph b2.de euphr b2.de ferr b2.de gels ptk1 graph b2.de *Guaj* b2.de hell b2.de helodr-cal knl2• hep b2.de hyos b2.de hyper ptk1 ign b2.de iod b2.de ip b2.de *Kali-c* b2.de* kali-n b2.de kreos b2.de lach b2.de* laur b2.de led b2.de **Lyc** b2.de m-ambo b2.de m-arct b2.de m-aust b2.de mag-c b2.de mag-m b2.de mang b2.de meny b2.de *Merc* b2.de mez b2.de mosch b2.de mur-ac b2.de *Nat-c* b2.de **Nat-m** b2.de* nat-s ptk1 nit-ac b2.de nux-m b2.de **Nux-v** b2.de* olnd b2.de op b2.de par b2.de *Petr* b2.de ph-ac b2.de* phos b2.de* *Pic-ac* ptk1 plat b2.de plb b2.de **Puls** b2.de ran-b b2.de ran-s b2.de rheum b2.de rhod b2.de *Rhus-t* b2.de* *Ruta* b2.de sabad b2.de sabin b2.de samb b2.de sars b2.de sec b2.de* sel b2.de seneg b2.de **Sep** b2.de **Sil** b2.de* spig b2.de spong b2.de squil b2.de *Stann* b2.de staph b2.de stram b2.de stront-c b2.de sul-ac b2.de **Sulph** b2.de* tarax b2.de teucr b2.de thuj b2.de valer b2.de *Verat* b2.de verb b2.de viol-t b2.de *Zinc* b2.de*
- **alternating** sides: agar ptk1 bell ptk1 *Berb* ptk1 calc ptk1 calc-p ptk1 kali-bi ptk1 kalm ptk1
- **right** side: acon b7a.de* agar b4a.de* agn b7a.de* alum b4a.de* am-c b4a.de* *Am-m* b7a.de* ambr b7a.de* anac b4a.de* ang b7a.de* *Ant-c* b7a.de* *Ant-t* b7a.de* apis b7a.de *Arg-met* b7a.de* *Arn* b7a.de* *Ars* b4a.de* asaf b7a.de* *Asar* b7a.de* *Aur* b4a.de* bar-c b4a.de* bell b4a.de* *Borx* b4a.de* brom b4a.de *Bry* b7a.de* **Calc** b4a.de* cann-s b7a.de* *Canth* b7a.de* *Carb-an* b4a.de* carb-v b4a.de* *Caust* b4a.de* chel b7a.de* *Chin* b7a.de* **Cic** b7a.de* cina b7a.de* cocc b7a.de* *Colch* b7a.de* *Coloc* b4a.de* *Con* b4a.de* cupr b7a.de* dig b4a.de* dros b7a.de* dulc b4a.de* *Euph* b4a.de* **Fl-ac** b4a.de* *Guaj* b4a.de* hep b4a.de* *Iod* b4a.de* *Kali-c* b4a.de* *Laur* b7a.de* *Lyc* b4a.de* *M-arct* b7a.de* m-aust b7a.de* meny b7a.de* merc b4a.de* mez b4a.de* mill b7a.de mur-ac b4a.de* *Nat-m* b4a.de* nit-ac b4a.de* *Nux-v* b7a.de* *Olnd* b7a.de* petr b4a.de* *Phos* b4a.de* plat b4a.de* **Plb** b7a.de* *Ran-b* b7a.de* ran-s b7a.de* rhod b4a.de* *Rhus-t* b7a.de* ruta b7a.de* *Sabad* b7a.de* *Samb* b7a.de* sars b4a.de* *Sep* b4a.de* *Sil* b4a.de* spig b7a.de*

- **right** side: ...
spong b7a.de* stann b4a.de* staph b7a.de* sul-ac b4a.de* *Sulph* b4a.de* *Tarax* b7a.de* teucr b7a.de* thuj b4a.de* verb b7a.de* viol-t b7a.de* **Zinc** b4a.de*
  - **extending** to | **left** side: calc-p ptk1 cocc ptk1 kali-p ptk1 sulph ptk1 tell ptk1
- **left** side: *Acon* b7a.de* *Agar* b4a.de* agn b7a.de* *Alum* b4a.de* *Am-c* b4a.de* am-m b7a.de* ambr b7a.de* *Anac* b4a.de* ang b7a.de* ant-c b7a.de* ant-t b7a.de* *Apis* b7a.de arg-met b7a.de* *Ars* b4a.de* *Asaf* b7a.de* aur b4a.de* *Bar-c* b4a.de* bell b4a.de* *Bism* b7a.de* *Bry* b7a.de* calc b4a.de* cann-s b7a.de* canth b7a.de* carb-an b4a.de* *Carb-v* b4a.de* *Caust* b4a.de* chel b7a.de* *Chin* b7a.de* cina b7a.de* clem b4a.de *Cocc* b7a.de* colch b7a.de* *Coloc* b4a.de* con b4a.de* *Croc* b7a.de* *Cupr* b7a.de* *Dig* b4a.de* **Dros** b7a.de* *Dulc* b4a.de* euph b4a.de* *Ferr* b7a.de* fl-ac b4a.de glon ptk1 *Graph* b4a.de* guaj b4a.de* *Hell* b7a.de* *Hep* b4a.de* *Ign* b7a.de* iod b4a.de* *Kali-c* b4a.de* *Kali-n* b4a.de* *Kreos* b7a.de* laur b7a.de* *Led* b7a.de* lyc b4a.de* *M-ambo* b7a.de* *M-aust* b7a.de* *Mang* b4a.de* meny b7a.de* merc b4a.de* mez b4a.de* mill b7a.de *Mosch* b7a.de* mur-ac b4a.de* *Myrt-c* b7a.de *Nat-m* b4a.de* nit-ac b4a.de* nux-v b7a.de* olnd b7a.de* *Par* b7a.de* *Petr* b4a.de* *Ph-ac* b4a.de* phos b4a.de* plat b4a.de* plb b7a.de* psor b4a.de *Puls* b7a.de* ran-s b7a.de* *Rhod* b4a.de* *Rhus-t* b7a.de* *Ruta* b7a.de* sabad b7a.de* *Sabin* b7a.de* sars b4a.de* *Seneg* b4a.de* sep b4a.de* **Sil** b4a.de* *Spig* b7a.de* *Spong* b7a.de* *Squil* b7a.de* *Stann* b4a.de* *Staph* b7a.de* *Stront-c* b4a.de* sul-ac b4a.de* *Sulph* b4a.de* tarax b7a.de* *Teucr* b7a.de* *Thuj* b4a.de* *Valer* b7a.de* *Verat* b7a.de* verb b7a.de* viol-o fse1.de viol-t b7a.de zinc b4a.de*
  - **extending** to | **right** side: bell ptk1 cund ptk1 nat-c ptk1 ox-ac ptk1
- **accompanied** by:
○ - **Abdomen**:
  ⁝ **pain** | **cramping**: *Kali-c* b4a.de sars ptk1
  - **Heart**; complaints of (See CHEST - Heart; complaints - accompanied - back)
  - **Kidneys** | **complaints** of (See KIDNEYS - Complaints - accompanied - back - complaints)
  - **Stomach**; complaints of (See STOMACH - Complaints - accompanied - back - complaints)
- **spots**; in: agar ptk1 *Alum* ptk1 caust ptk1 chel ptk1 chin ptk1 kali-bi ptk1 *Lach* ptk1 nit-ac ptk1 ox-ac ptk1 ph-ac ptk1 *Phos* ptk1 plb ptk1 rhus-t ptk1 thuj ptk1 zinc ptk1
- **wandering**: berb ptk1 cimic ptk1 kali-bi ptk1

▽ - **extending** to:
○ - **Abdomen**: vario ptk1
  - **Chest**: arn ptk1 berb ptk1 camph ptk1 kali-n ptk1 laur ptk1 petr ptk1 samb ptk1 sars ptk1
    ⁝ **right**: acon ptk1 calc-p ptk1 kali-c ptk1 lyc ptk1 merc ptk1 sep ptk1
    ⁝ **left**: bar-c ptk1 *Bry* ptk1 mez ptk1 plat ptk1 zinc ptk1
  - **Downward**: agar ptk1 puls ptk1 stram ptk1
  - **Forward** | **left**: phos ptk1 sulph ptk1 zinc ptk1
  - **Genitals**: kreos ptk1 sulph ptk1
  - **Stomach**: berb ptk1 cupr ptk1
  - **Thighs**: berb ptk1 caust ptk1 cimic ptk1 hep ptk1 kali-c ptk1 vib ptk1
    ⁝ **stool** agg.: rhus-t ptk1
  - **Upward**: ars ptk1 gels ptk1 lach ptk1 lil-t ptk1 nit-ac ptk1 phos ptk1 rad-br ptk1 sulph ptk1 zinc-val ptk1
  - **Uterus**: sep ptk1 vib ptk1

○ - **Cervical** region (See Cervical)
- **Dorsal** region (See Dorsal)
- **Lumbar** region (See Lumbar)
- **Scapulae** (See Dorsal - scapulae)
- **Spinal** cord: acon bg2 ars bg2 bell bg2 bry bg2 calc bg2 carb-v bg2 caust bg2 chin bg2 **Cocc** bg2 dig bg2 *Dulc* bg2 ign bg2 lach bg2 lath br1 nat-c bg2 nat-m bg2 **Nux-v** bg2 ox-ac br1 ph-ac bg2 **Phos** bg2 puls bg2 rhus-t bg2 staph bg2 stry br1 *Sulph* bg2 verat bg2
○ - **Lower** part: gins br1
- **Spine** (See Spine)

COMPRESSION:

○ - **Coccyx**: bell bg2
- **Dorsal** region: aeth bg2 arg-n bg2 bry bg2 euphr bg2 kali-n bg2 led bg2 petr bg2
- **Lumbosacral** region: aeth ptk1 caust ptk1 thuj ptk1

CONCUSSION of spine: arn bro1* bell-p bro1 cic bro1* con bro1 **Hyper** k* phys bro1

○ - **Cervical** region: mez

CONGESTION:

○ - **Cervical** region: bell cact k2 carbn-h **Gels** glon *Kali-c*
- **Lumbar** region: acon bg2 gels bg2 nux-m bg2
- **Spine**: absin c2* *Acon* bro1 agar bro1 ail tl1 arn bro1 bell bro1 gels bro1* hyper bro1 *Nux-v* bro1 onos c2* oxyt br1* phos bro1 phys bro1 sec bro1 sil bro1 *Stry* bro1 tab bro1 verat-v c2*

CONSCIOUSNESS: | Bones; of: galeoc-c-h gms1•

CONSTRICTION or band: alum anac arg-n *Cham* chord-umb rly4• *Cocc* *Dulc* graph guaj h2 guar guare k* kali-c k* mang-p rly4• mez k* nit-ac puls ptk1 rhus-t

○ - **Cervical** region: acon bg2* agar *Aml-ns* bro1 apis asar k* *Bell* k* cench k2 chel k* dig bg2 dulc h2* fel bro1 *Glon* k* graph k2 helodr-cal knl2• iod bg2 *Lach* k* lyc bg2 *Nux-m* k* pyrog bro1 sep k* sphing kk3.fr spig bg2 spong ptk1 [bell-p-sp dcm1]
  - **cough** agg.; during: ip mrr1
▽ - **extending** to | **Diaphragm**: sphing kk3.fr
○ - **Nape** of neck: asar b7.de*
- **Dorsal** region: am-m b7.de* arg-n bg2 arn bg2 asaf b7.de* bry b7.de* canth b7.de* chord-umb rly4• con b4a.de graph b4.de* guaj b4.de* kali-c b4.de* kali-n b4.de* lyc b4.de* mez b4.de* nit-ac b4.de* nux-v b7.de* *Puls* b7.de* rhus-t b7.de* sabad b7a.de
○ - **Scapulae**: ang bg2 dulc fd4.de guaj bg2 kreos b7a.de* lach bg2 lyc bg2 mag-m nux-v b7.de* phos bg2 ran-s b7.de* rhus-t bg2 sep bg2 viol-t bg2
    ⁝ **Between** scapulae: kreos bg2 merc-cy bg2 phos bg2 rhus-t bg2
- **Lumbar** region: dulc fd4.de
  - **tight** band; as from a: arg-n bg2 arn bg2 cina k* mag-c bg1 petr-ra shn4• **Puls** k*
    ⁝ **eating**; after: cina a1
- **Spine**:
○ - **Lumbar** canal: agar mtf *Bry* mtf coloc mtf mag-p mtf rhus-t mtf sulph mtf tell mtf
  - **Vertebrae**: cham bg2

CONTRACTIONS (See Pain - drawing; Spasmodic; Spasms; Tension)

CONVULSIONS:

- **tetanic** | **Cervical** region | **Nape** of neck: op b7.de*
  - **Dorsal** region: ang b7.de* canth b7.de* cham b7.de* cic b7.de* *Ip* b7a.de nux-v b7.de* op b7.de* plb b7.de*

COUGH agg.: *Acon* b7.de* am-m bg2 arn b7.de* bell bg2* bry b7a.de* caps b7.de* chel bg2 *Chin* b7.de* cocc b7a.de *Graph* b4a.de kali-bi bg2* kali-i bg2 nat-m ptk1 nit-ac bg2 nux-v b7.de* psor bg2 puls b7.de* pyrog bg2 sep ptk1

○ - **Lumbar** region: acon ptk1 kali-bi ptk1 nit-ac ptk1
- **Sacrum**: bry ptk1 chel ptk1 tell ptk1

CRACKING: rhus-t mrr1

○ - **Cervical** region: *Agar* k* agn aloe alst bg1 anac aur-m-n bamb-a stb2.de• *Chel* k* chin chin-b c1 *Cocc* k* ham fd3.de• kali-s fd4.de limest-b es1• m-arct c1 melal-alt gya4 *Nat-c* k* nat-sil fd3.de• *Nicc* k* nit-ac nux-v ol-an *Petr* k* podo fd3.de• puls raph rhus-t mrr1 ruta fd4.de spong stann *Sulph* k* ther hr1 thuj k* tritic-vg fd5.de vanil fd5.de zing bg1 [spect dfg1]
  - **accompanied** by | **Head**; pain in: arge-pl rwt5•
  - **bending** head backward agg.: sulph h2
  - **motion** agg.: aloe bro1 *Cocc* bro1 *Nat-c* bro1 nicc bro1 ol-an bro1 thuj bro1
  - **rising** from stooping; on: nicc
  - **stooping** agg.: spong tritic-vg fd5.de
  - **turning** head agg.: lac-h htj1• ozone sde2•
○ - **Nape** of neck: anac b4a.de* nat-c bg2 nicc bg2 ol-an bg2 petr bg2 puls bg2 spong b7.de* sulph b4a.de* thuj bg2
  - **Vertebrae**: chel ptk1 cocc ptk1 ol-an ptk1
- **Dorsal** region: agar bg2 ham fd3.de• puls bg2 sabad b7.de* sec bg2 sep bg2 spong bg2 stann bg2 sulph bg2 zinc bg2
○ - **Scapulae**: anac b4a.de* cocc bg2 puls b7.de*
    ⁝ **morning**: puls h1
    ⁝ **lifting** arm; on: anac

Back

- **Dorsal** region – **Scapulae**: ...
  - ⁝ **motion** agg.: puls h1
- **Joints**: petr-ra shn4•
  - **impelled** to make them cracking; feels: petr-ra shn4•
- **Lumbar** region: limest-b es1• olib-sac wmh1 *Rhus-t* b7a.de sec bg2* sep bg2 sulph b4a.de* zinc b4.de*
  - **stooping** agg.: agar rhus-t
  - **walking** agg.: **Zinc** k*
  - ▽ **extending** to | **Anus**: sulph
- **Sacroiliac** symphyses: plac rzf5•
- **Sacrum**; across | **stooping** agg.: kali-bi rb2
- **Spine**: agar ptk1 petr bg2 sec bg2* sep bg2
  - **motion** agg.: *Agar* k* cocc irid-met srj5• kali-bi nat-sil fd3.de• puls sne sacch-a fd2.de• streptoc rly4•
  - ○ **Vertebrae**: nat-c ptk1 ol-an ptk1 sulph ptk1

CRAMP: (↗*Pain - cramping; Spasmodic*) arg-n ptk1 bell calc-p caust bg3* chin bg3* con h2 dulc fd4.de gels k2 iod kali-bi lat-m bnm6• led ptk1 lyc mag-m ptk1 mag-p ptk1 naja nux-v petr h2 plb verat h1

- **turning** body●: dros h1
- **walking** agg.: mag-m ptk1
- ○ **Muscles**: lat-m bnm6•

CRAWLING, as from insects (See Formication)

CREAKING noise: | **Dorsal** region: agn b7.de*

CURRENT; sensation of a:

- ○ **Dorsal** region | **burning**: m-ambo b7.de

CURVATURE of spine: (↗*Caries*) acon bg2 agar bg2 ant-c bg2 **Asaf** bg2* aur bg2* bar-c bg2* *Bar-m* bell b4a.de* bry bg2 **Calc** k* **Calc-f** k* calc-i mp1• *Calc-p* k* **Calc-s** k* *Carb-v* carbn-s caust bg2* cic bg2 clem bg2 coloc bg2 *Con* dros tl1* dulc bg2 ferr-i c2* hecla mp1• hep bg2* ip bg2 kali-c mrr1* lach bg2 *Lyc* k* *Merc* k* **Merc-c** k* mez bg2 nat-c mrr1 nat-m bg2 op **Ph-ac** k* *Phos* k* plb bg2 psor *Puls* k* rhus-t bg2* ruta bg2 sabin bg2 sep bg2* **Sil** k* staph bg2 **Sulph** k* syph c1* tarent ther bro1* thuj k* tub mrr1

- **left**; to the: calc-p mtf33
- **accompanied** by:
  - **Pott's** disease (See Tuberculosis - vertebrae - accompanied - curvature)
  - **respiration**; complaints of: acon ptk1 ant-c ptk1 asaf ptk1 aur ptk1 bar-c ptk1 bell ptk1 bry ptk1 calc ptk1 camph ptk1 cic ptk1 clem ptk1 coloc ptk1 dulc ptk1 hep ptk1 ip ptk1 rhus-t ptk1 ruta ptk1 sabin ptk1 sep ptk1 sil ptk1 staph ptk1 sulph ptk1 thuj ptk1
- **inwards**; sensation of curving: choc srj3•
- **lies** on back with knees drawn up: merc mtf33 **Merc-c** k*
- **pain** in spine: *Aesc* k* **Lyc** k* **Sil** k*
- **Scheuermann's** syndrome: v-a-b mtf11
- ○ **Cervical** region: *Calc* k* phos *Syph* k*
  - ○ **Vertebrae**: *Calc* b4a.de *Lyc* b4a.de *Puls* b7a.de
- **Dorsal** region: acon b7a.de asaf b7a.de aur b4a.de bar-c k* **Bell** b4a.de bufo *Calc* k* *Calc-s* *Cic* b7a.de *Con* ip b7a.de *Lyc* k* *Ph-ac* b4a.de *Phos* b4a.de plb k* *Puls* k* *Rhus-t* k* ruta b7a.de *Sep* b4a.de *Sil* k* *Staph* b7a.de *Sulph* k* *Syph* k* thuj k*
  - **right**; to: *Sil* b4a.de
- **Lateral** curve: sil k2
- **Lumbar** region: calc-s k2 graph bg2
- **Vertebrae**: **Calc** bg2 lyc bg2 phos k2 **Puls** bg2 **Rhus-t** bg2 **Sil** bg2 *Staph* bg2 **Sulph** bg2

DEGENERATION: | **Spinal** cord: pic-ac br1

DELIVERY; after: *Phos* b4a.de

- **difficult** delivery: nux-v b7a.de
- **forceps**; with | **Sacrum**: hyper ptk1
- ○ **Coccyx**: tarent ptk1
- **Sacrum**: hyper ptk1 nux-v ptk1 phos ptk1

DESCENDING agg.: berb bg2

DIARRHEA; during: | **agg.**: ferr b7.de* nux-v bg2 **Puls** bg2

DISCOLORATION:

- **bluish**:
  - ○ **Cervical** region: kali-i ptk1 sil ptk1 sul-i ptk1 sulph ptk1
    - ⁝ **Nape** of neck: pic-ac ptk1 sulph ptk1
- **brown**:
  - **spots**: sep thuj
  - ○ **Cervical** region: sanic ptk1
    - ⁝ **greasy**; skin brown and: apis *Lyc* *Petr* sep thuj
    - ⁝ **Nape** of neck: apis bg2 lyc bg2 *Thuj* b4a.de
  - **Dorsal** region | **spots**; in: *Sep* b4a.de
  - **Shoulders** | **spots**: ant-c (non:nat-c kl)
- **red** | **spots**:
  - ⁝ **Cervical** region | **Nape** of neck: carb-v b4.de* sep b4.de* stann b4.de*
  - ○ **Cervical** region: aml-ns *Bell* k* *Crot-h* k* *Graph* ptk1 iod lac-d merc phos ptk1 *Rhus-t* k* verat ptk1 vesp
    - ⁝ **swelling**; with: cic c1
- **spots** | **Cervical** region | **Nape** of neck: *Apis* b7a.de
  - **Dorsal** region: *Lach* b7a.de *Sep* bg2 zinc bg2
- **yellow** | **spots**:
  - ⁝ **Cervical** region | **Nape** of neck: iod b4.de*
  - ○ **Cervical** region | **Nape** of neck: *Lyc* b4a.de

DISCOMFORT; sensation of: choc srj3•

DISLOCATION; sensation of:

- ○ **Dorsal** region: ulm-c jsj8•
- **Lumbar** vertebra; last: sanic k* sarr bg1

DRAWING:

- **backward**:
  - ○ **Neck**; muscles of (See Spasmodic; Tension)
  - **Shoulders** | **amel.**: cycl b7.de*
- **inward** of affected part | **amel.**: sabin b7.de*
- **together** | **shoulders** agg.: cycl b7.de*
- **up**:
  - **lower** limbs | **agg.**: cinnb bg2

DRAWN TOGETHER; sensation as if:

- ○ **Dorsal** region | **Scapulae**: rhus-t bg2

DRINKING agg.: caps ptk1 chin b7.de*

DROPS; sensation of (See Trickling)

EATING:

- **after** | **agg.**: agar bg2 alum b4.de* ant-t b7.de* bell bg2 bry bg2 cham b7.de* chin b7.de* cina bg2 cob bg2 crot-c bg2 gels bg2 kali-bi bg2 kali-c bg2 nat-m bg2 nux-v b7.de* phos bg2 sil b4a.de
- **amel.**: kali-n ptk1
- **before** | **agg.**: am-c b4.de*
- **while**:
  - **agg.**: chin b7.de* kali-c ptk1
    - ⁝ **Spine**: kali-c ptk1

ECCHYMOSES: | **Dorsal** region | **sensation** of: nux-v b7.de*

- **Lumbar** region: merc-c vip

EJACULATION; after: bell bg2 ham bg2 sel bg2

ELONGATED; as if: | **Coccyx**: xan bg1*

EMACIATION: nux-v ptk1 plb ptk1 senec bg1 sulph k2 tab k* thuj ptk1

- ○ **Cervical** region: abrot bro1 *Calc* k* calc-p bro1* cench k2 iod k* *Lyc* k* mag-c ptk1 **Nat-m** k* phos k2 *Sanic* k* *Sars* k* senec bg1 sulph k2 verat bg1
- **Dorsal** region, scapular muscles: plb
- **Lumbar** region: plb k* sel k*

EMPROSTHOTONOS: bell k2 *Canth* k* *Ip* k* lach nux-m plut-n srj7•

ENERGY: | **rushing** up: dioxi rbp6

EPILEPTIC aura creeping down spine: *Lach* k*

ERUCTATIONS:

- **agg.**: *Phos* b4a.de sep bg2 zinc b4.de*

- **amel.**: alum b4.de* apis bg2 ars bg2 ign bg2 iod bg2 lyc bg2 nit-ac bg2 sep bg2* zinc bg2*

○ · **Dorsal** region | **Scapulae**; between: zinc ptk1

· **Spine**: zinc ptk1

ERUPTIONS: alum alum-sil k2 am-m ant-c ant-t arg-n arn *Ars* ars-s-f k2 bar-c bell berb bry calc calc-s cann-s *Carb-v* carbn-s carc sp1 *Caust* chin chinin-ar cina cist clem cocc con dulc euon fago gaert pte1*• gels psa granit-m es1• hep hip-ac sp1 *Jug-r* kali-p lach led luna kg1• *Lyc* mag-s sp1 *Merc* **Mez** nat-c k2 nat-m nat-ox rly4• *Nit-ac* ozone sde2• *Petr* ph-ac phos pin-con oss2• **Psor** puls-n ran-b k2 *Rhus-t* rhus-v rumx *Sep* k* *Sil* spong fd4.de squil staph stram suis-hep rly4• **Sulph** sumb tab thiam rly4• til tritic-vg fd5.de vanil fd5.de zinc

- **acne**: amph a1 carb-v k* carc mrr1* morg-p pte1• oxal-a rly4• positr nl2• ros-d wla1 rumx ptk1 sulph mrr1 tub-r vn*
  · **itching**: mag-s sp1
  ○ · **Cervical** region: amph jug-r lappa br1 pitu-a vml2•
- **biting**: bry
  ○ · **Cervical** region: cham h1
- **blisters**: | **Dorsal** region: caust bg2
- **blotches**: lach mez phos zinc
- **blue**: ran-b k2
- **boils**: aids nl2• cassia-s ccrh1• caust coloc *Crot-h* graph kali-bi **Kali-i** k* *Lach* mur-ac nat-ox rly4• ph-ac *Phyt* sanic **Sil** sne sul-ac sulph tarent k2 tarent-c *Thuj* zinc
  · **blood** boils: *Carb-an* k* *Caust* k* *Graph* k* hep iris kali-bi mur-ac h2 nat-m h2 sul-ac thuj k* zinc h2
  ⁝ **stinging** on touch: mur-ac h2
  · **groups**, in: berb
  ○ · **Cervical** region: androc srj1• *Calc* carb-an coloc crot-h cypr dig dream-p sdj1• *Graph* *Hep* indg **Kali-i** k* *Lach* morg-p pte1*• mur-ac nat-m *Nit-ac* *Petr* *Phos* plut-n srj7• *Psor* rhus-v sec **Sil** **Sulph** k* thuj ust
  ⁝ **right**: musca-d szs1
  ⁝ **Nape** of neck: **Apis** b7a.de *Arn* b7.de* *Euph* b4a.de pic-ac ptk1 *Rhus-t* b7a.de sil b4.de* sulph ptk1
  · **Dorsal** region: ars bg2 caust b4.de* fl-ac bg2 graph b4a.de* hep b4a.de* iris bg2 kali-bi bg2 lach bg2 mur-ac b4a.de* nat-m bg2 sec bg2 sul-ac b4a.de* sulph bg2 thuj b4a.de* zinc bg2
  ⁝ **Scapulae**: aids nl2• am-c am-m bg2 anthraci mrr1 bell k* led k* lyc *Nit-ac* petr-ra shn4• **Sil** sne zinc
  : **left**: aids nl2•
  : **Above**: anthraci mrr1
  ⁝ **Shoulders**; between: iod tarent-c zinc
  · **Lumbar** region: aeth a1 *Hep* psor rhus-t thuj k*
  · **Sacrum**: aeth thuj
- **burning**: am-m cist lyc h2 rhus-t
  · **scratching**; after: lac-d k2 til
- **carbuncle**: **Anthraci** ars *Crot-h* *Lach* *Sil* tarent k2
  ○ · **Cervical** region: *Anthraci* *Caust* crot-h *Hep* **Lach** k* morg-p pte1*• rhus-t **Sil** k* sulph
  · **Dorsal** region: *Hep* *Lach* tarent
- **crusts**: am graph nat-m
  ○ · **Cervical** region | **Nape** of neck: *Petr* b4a.de
- **dry** | **Cervical** region | **desquamating** in fine mealy scales: graph
  · **Coccyx**: nat-c h2
- **eczema**: am merc *Sil*
  ○ · **Cervical** region: anac aur-i k2 *Lyc* psor k* *Sil* ulm-c jsj8•
  ⁝ **Nape** of neck: caust bg2 *Lyc* bg2 *Petr* bg2 *Sep* bg2 sulph bg2
  · **Dorsal** region | **Shoulder**; between: carc mlr1•
- **edematous**:
  ○ · **Cervical** region | **right** side: pitu-gl skp7•
- **erythema**: (↗*SKIN - Eruptions - erythema*)
  ○ · **Cervical** region: chlol dig br1 gels hydrc a1 (non:hyos a1) morg-p pte1• rhus-v a1
- **fine**: con k* rhus-v k*
- **fish** scales, like: ars-i *Mez*
- **fleabites**, like: lap-la sde8.de• phys
- **fungous** growth on neck: thuj

Eruptions: ...
- **herpes**: all-s ars lach lyc h2 nat-c k* sep zinc
  ○ · **Cervical** region: ars carb-an caust clem *Con* dys fmm1• *Graph* hyos kali-n lac-d *Lyc* nat-m *Petr* psor *Sep* sulph syc bka1*•
  ⁝ **itching**: caust
  ⁝ **moist**: carb-an caust nat-m sep
  ⁝ **Nape** of neck: nat-m bro1 petr bro1
- **herpes** zoster: anthraq rly4• *Cist* *Lach* *Merc* *Ran-b* mrr1 rhus-t
  · **left**: lach mrr1
- **impetigo**: *Nat-m* *Petr* k*
- **itching**: amph a1 bar-c bar-m *Bry* calc cann-s carb-v cassia-s ccrh1• *Caust* cham con h2 lac-d k2 luna kg1• lyc medul-os-si rly4• *Mez* nat-m k2 ozone sde2• petr-ra shn4• puls rat rhus-t sep spong fd4.de squil staph tab thuj til viol-t wsf zinc
  · **evening**: fago
  ⁝ **and** night: *Sep*
  ⁝ **going** to bed; on: rumx
  · **air**; in open | **amel.**: cassia-s ccrh1•
  · **bathing** | **amel.**: cassia-s ccrh1•
  · **bed** agg.; in: cassia-s ccrh1•
  · **heat** of the sun agg.: cassia-s ccrh1•
  · **perspiration**: cassia-s ccrh1•
  · **scratching** agg.; after: mez
  · **spots**: zinc [tax jsj7]
  · **warm**; when: cocc k*
  ○ · **Cervical** region: mang hr1 morg-p pte1• ozone sde2• tell rsj10•
  ⁝ **menses**; before: carb-v h2
  · **Coccyx**: *Graph* led h1 nat-c h2
  · **Dorsal** region | **menses**; before: carb-v h2
  · **Lumbar** region: arund lyc
- **itch**-like: arg-n bar-c psor
- **maculae** (= syphilitic): syph
- **measly** spots: gels psa
  ○ · **Cervical** region: ars cop morph
- **miliaria** rubra: *Apis* k*
  ○ · **Cervical** region: **Sulph** k*
- **miliary**: ant-c ant-t bry caust **Chel** cocc hydrc nat-ar ph-ac prun psor sec sumb valer
  ○ · **Cervical** region | **Nape** of neck: ant-c bg2 caust b4.de* mez bg2 **Sec** bg2
  · **Dorsal** region: stram b7.de*
  ⁝ **Scapulae**: ant-c bg2 caust b4.de*
- **moist**: *Clem* nat-m psor
  ○ · **Coccyx**; on: *Arum-t* graph k* led k* nit-ac
  · **Sacrum**; on: graph led
- **nodules**:
  · **itching**: sil h2
  · **painless**:
  ⁝ **Cervical** region: *Graph* psor k*
  : **subcutaneous**: psor jl2
  . **chronic**: psor jl2
  · **red**: petr
- **painful**: led h1 luna kg1• lyc nicc-met sk4• spig succ-ac rly4• tritic-vg fd5.de
  · **spots**: luna kg1•
  · **touch**; to: cist hep luna kg1• ph-ac psor spig squil verb
- **patches**: calc kali-ar mez
  · **menses**; during: nux-m kr1
  · **red**:
  ⁝ **Cervical** region:
  : **heat**: cortiso tpw7
  : **scratching** agg.: cortiso tpw7
  : **washing** agg.: cortiso tpw7
- **pimples**: agar alum alum-p k2 arg-n am bell berb calc calc-sil k2 cann-s carb-v cham chel chlor cocc con crot-h dig dulc fd4.de ephe-si hsj1• fl-ac granit-m es1• hura hyper iod jug-r kali-bi *Kali-c* kali-p lac-e hm2• lach led lyc mag-m mag-s mang meph *Nat-m* nicc petr ph-ac positr nl2• psor *Puls* rhus-v

- **pimples**: ...
rumx sars *Sel* sil *Squil* staph streptoc rly4• tab tep til tritic-vg fd5.de vanil fd5.de vesp vip fkr4.de zinc
  - **evening**: cocc fl-ac ph-ac rumx
  - **itching**: arg-n asc-t calc cann-s carb-an carb-v h2 crot-t fl-ac hip-ac sp1 iod h led mag-m mill rat rhus-t sel
    - **evening** | **bed** agg.; in: nat-m h2
  - **red**: ph-ac h2
  - **scratching**; after: nat-c h2 psor
  - **sore**, pressing pain when touched: zinc
  - **suppurating**: chlor dulc fd4.de kali-bi
  - ○ **Cervical** region: agar alum berb borx h2 calc-sil k2 cann-s carb-an carb-v cinnb *Clem* crot-t dulc fd4.de *Gels* gins br1 hep hyos jug-r kali-bi kali-c kali-n lappa br1 lyc meph nat-ar nat-c h2 nat-m nicc pall petr ph-ac positr nl2• psor *Puls* rhus-t *Sil* *Staph* sul-ac *Sulph* thuj tritic-vg fd5.de trom verb zing
    - **burning**: am-c kali-n h2
    - **confluent**: tarent
    - **deep**-seated: til
    - **flattened**: rhus-t
    - **hard**: crot-t
    - **inflamed**: sulph
    - **itching**: bar-c h2 kali-c h2 puls h1 *Sil* *Staph*
    - **moist**: *Clem*
    - **painful** to touch: dulc fd4.de hep sulph
    - **scratching**; on: carb-an nat-c h2 nicc *Puls*
    - **suppurating**: calc-p dulc fd4.de nat-c
    - **extending** to | **Scalp**: clem
    - **Nape** of neck: arn bg2 bell bg2 carb-v bg2 hep bg2 kali-c bg2 kali-n bg2 lyc bg2 sil bg2 staph bg2
  - **Coccyx**: propr sa3•
  - **Dorsal** region: alum bg2 am-m *Apis* b7a.de berb bry b7.de* calc b4.de* *Carb-v* b4a.de *Cic* *Cist* cocc b7.de* dig b4.de* kali-bi bg2 led b7.de* oxal-a rly4• ph-ac b4.de* podo fd3.de• puls b7.de* sel b7.de* squil b7.de* stram b7.de* tritic-vg fd5.de vanil fd5.de
    - **Scapulae**: ant-c bar-c h2 berb com con crot-h mag-m merc mez h2 ph-ac h2 *Puls* rat squil vanil fd5.de
      - **left**: lach bg2
      - **Between**: positr nl2• zinc h2
    - **Shoulders**, between: gels lyc mag-m ph-ac rat squil
  - **Lumbar** region: ars-h calc chel chin clem kali-c nat-c nicc
    - **burning**: lyc
    - **inflamed**: sulph
    - **itching**: lyc tab
    - **oozing** when scratched: sulph
    - **painful**: lyc h2
    - **red** at night on scratching, morning amel.: apoc
    - **scratching**; after: chin nicc
- **prickly** heat (See miliaria)
- **psoriasis**, patches: calc kali-ar *Mez* positr nl2•
  - ○ **Cervical** region: petr-ra shn4• positr nl2•
- **purpura** | **Cervical** region: ars
- **pustules**: agar aur-m-n bell berb calc calc-sil k2 carc gk6* chin chlor clem crot-t dulc kali-bi kali-br *Lach* nat-c nat-m nicc-met sk4• petr positr nl2• rhod *Sep* *Sil* sulph
  - **black** points, with: kali-bi k*
  - **painful**: ant-t **Sil**
  - **sensitive**: nat-c
  - **smallpox**, like: ant-t sil
  - ○ **Cervical** region: ant-c aur bell calc-sil k2 kali-n morg-p pte1• nat-ar nat-c psor sars tab thuj zinc-act
    - **cowpox**; like: ant-t
    - **Nape** of neck: psor bg2 staph b7.de* zinc-s bg2
  - **Lumbar** region: calc chlor clem k* nat-c k*
  - **Spine**:
    - **painful**: sil tl1

- **pustules – Spine**: ...
    - **ulcers**; join to form: sil tl1
    - **variola**-like: sil tl1
- **rash**: *Calc* con merc mez psor stram tab
  - ○ **Cervical** region: ant-c bry caust **Chel** flor-p rsj3• mez nat-ar nat-c sec
    - **erysipelatous**: hydr
    - **itching**: calc *Mez*
    - **miliary**: nat-ar
    - **purple**: hyos
    - **red**: nat-ar
  - **Dorsal** region | **Scapulae** | **Between**: caust h2
    - **Shoulders**; between: carc sst•
  - **Lumbar** region: cham
- **red**: androc srj1• bell *Bry* calc **Chel** cocc fum rly1*• rhus-t spig spong fd4.de tab verb
  - ○ **Cervical** region: tell rsj10•
    - **left**: nat-s k2
- **scabs**, bloody: rhus-v
  - ○ **Cervical** region: ant-t
  - **Coccyx**: borx *Graph* *Sil*
  - **Sacral** region: *Sil*
- **scales**: am-m ars-i *Mez*
  - ○ **Cervical** region | **white**: graph nat-m k2 *Sil*
  - **Dorsal** region:
    - **Scapula** | **right**: am-m
- **smarting**: bry spig
- **sore** (See painful)
- **tetters** | **Cervical** region | **Nape** of neck: *Apis* b7a.de caust b4.de* graph b4a.de hyos b7.de* *Petr* b4a.de *Sulph* b4a.de *Thuj* b4a.de
  - **Dorsal** region:
    - **dry**: *Ars* b4a.de caust b4a.de nat-m b4a.de sep b4.de* zinc b4a.de
    - **Scapulae**: *Ars* b4a.de *Calc* b4a.de
- **tubercles**: am-c am-m caust iod mp1• lyc nicc squil
  - ○ **Cervical** region: ant-c carb-an caust nicc zinc
  - **Dorsal** region | **Shoulders**; between: mag-m h2
- **undressing** agg.: carc mg1.de*
- **urticaria**: apis atra-r bnm3• cann-s h1 choc srj3• lac-ac lach sulph
  - **scratching** agg.; after: lyc
  - ○ **Cervical** region: sil h2
    - **Nape** of neck: apis b7a.de*
  - **Dorsal** region: apis bg2
- **vesicles**: arn bry calc-caust caust h2 cist graph hura *Kali-c* *Lach* nat-c petr ran-b k2 rhus-t *Sep* wies
  - **evening**, itching when undressing: nat-c nat-s
  - **base**; on a red elevated: kali-bi
  - **painful**: caust h2
  - ○ **Cervical** region: calc-caust camph clem mag-c morg-p pte1• naja nat-hchls nat-m k2 nat-p petr zinc-s
  - **Dorsal** region:
    - **Scapulae**; on: am-c k* am-m ant-c *Ars* b4a.de caust cic k* lach vip
      - **painful** | **red**: cic h1
    - **Shoulders**; between: sep
      - **surrounded** by areola: crot-h
- **warm**; when: cocc k* stram
- ○ **Cervical** region: *Agar* ail k2 anac bro1 androc srj1• ant-c ant-s-aur ant-t am ptk1 ars bar-m bell berb bry calc-sil k2 caust cham chel *Clem* k* gaert pte1*• *Graph* *Hep* *Kali-bi* lap-la sde8.de• lappa br1 lyc k* mang mez k2 morg-p pte1*• musca-d szs1 nat-ar nat-m k* *Petr* k* petr-ra shn4• positr nl2• psor k* rhus-t sec sep k* **Sil** k* staph stram sul-ac h2 sul-i ptk1 sulph thuj
  - **blotches**: tell rsj10•
  - **itching**: pneu jl2 psor mrr1
  - **menses**; before: carb-v a1
  - **moist**: caust *Clem*
  - ○ **Margins** of hair: choc srj3• nat-m petr sul-ac mtf11 tritic-vg fd5.de

• **Nape** of neck: ant-c b7a.de *Ant-t* b7a.de *Apis* b7a.de arn bg2 bar-c b4.de* bell b4.de* borx b4a.de bry b7.de* calc bg2 carb-v bg2 caust b4.de* cham b7.de* clem b4a.de* hep b4.de* kali-c bg2 kali-n bg2 lyc b4.de* m-aust b7.de *Petr* b4a.de* *Puls* b7a.de sep b4.de* **Sil** b4.de* staph b7.de* sulph bg2
⁝ **menses**; before: carb-v b4a.de
- **Coccyx**: borx graph k* merc k*
- **Dorsal** region: alum bg2 bar-c b4.de* bell b4.de* calc b4.de* *Carb-v* b4a.de* *Caust* b4a.de dig bg2 fl-ac bg2 lach bg2 led bg2 mez bg2 nat-c bg2 nat-m b4.de* ph-ac b4a.de* puls bg2 sel bg2 *Sep* b4a.de* squil bg2 suis-hep rly4• zinc bg2
○ • **Scapulae**: alum b4a.de am-c bg2 ant-c b7a.de *Ars* b4a.de bell b4.de* bry b7.de* calc b4a.de caust b4a.de* cic bg2 cocc b7.de crot-h bg2 led bg2 lyc b4.de* merc b4.de* mez b4.de* ph-ac b4.de* *Phos* b4.de* puls b7.de* squil b7.de* thiam rly4•
⁝ **Between**: trios rsj11•
: **air**; in open | **amel.**: trios rsj11•
: **bed** agg.; in: trios rsj11•
: **itching**: trios rsj11•
: **warm** applications agg.: trios rsj11•
• **Shoulders**; between: carc mg1.de* gels psa positr nl2•
⁝ **menses**; before: carb-v b4a.de
⁝ **pustules**: vac jl2
⁝ **undressing** agg.: carc tpw2*
- **Lumbar** region: arund calc b4.de* nat-c bg2 rhus-t sep bg2 thuj b4.de*

ERYSIPELAS: *Apis* graph kali-i *Merc* ph-ac *Rhus-t*
○ - **Cervical** region: graph kali-i ph-ac
▽ • **extending** to | **Face**: rhus-t
- **Dorsal** region | **Shoulders**; across the: *Apis*
- **Lumbar** region: *Merc*

EXCITEMENT agg.: bar-c b4a.de*

EXCORIATION:
○ - **Cervical** region | **Nape** of neck: *Clem* b4a.de
- **Coccyx**: arum-t k2 led b7.de*
- **Dorsal** region: thuj bg2
- **Lumbar** region: nat-c ptk1

EXERTION:
- **agg.**: ferr bg2 kali-c b4.de* sulph b4a.de
○ • **Cervical** region: arg-n ptk1 *Calc* ptk1 lil-t ptk1 *Sep* ptk1
• **Lumbar** region: agar ptk1 calc-p ptk1 zinc-ar ptk1
- **mental**: *(↗Mental)*
• **agg.** | **Cervical** region: par ptk1 zinc ptk1

EXERTION OF THE EYES agg.: cina bg2

EXOSTOSIS: | **Sacrum**; on: rhus-t k*

EXPIRATION agg.: cina b7.de* colch bg2 spig b7.de*

FALL; after a: | **agg.**: arg-n bg2 *Arn* b7.de* **Hyper** bg2 *Kali-c* b4.de* nat-s bg2 sul-ac b4.de* xanth bg2

FALSE STEP; at a: | **agg.**: *Lyc* b4a.de *Phos* b4a.de podo bg2 sulph b4.de*

FATTY swelling cervical region (See Swelling - cervical - fatty)

FIBROSITIS (See Pain - rheumatic; Stiffness)

FISTULAE: *Calc-p Hep Ph-ac* **Phos Sil Sulph**
○ - **Dorsal** region: *Ant-c* b7a.de *Asaf* b7a.de merc b4a.de sil b4a.de *Sulph* b4a.de
○ • **Scapulae**: nit-ac b4a.de *Ph-ac* b4a.de *Sil* b4a.de

FLATULENCE agg.: carb-ac bg2

FLATUS; FROM OBSTRUCTED: am-m b7a.de

FLATUS; PASSING:
- **agg.**: sabad b7.de*
- **amel.**: berb ptk1 canth b7.de* kali-c bg2 phos bg2 pic-ac ptk1 ruta ptk1
○ • **Lumbar** region: *Lyc* ptk1 pic-ac ptk1 ruta ptk1

FLOWING sensation:
○ - **Dorsal** region | **Scapulae**: hep bg2*

FLUTTERING:
- **commencing** in sacrum and gradually rising to occiput: ol-j
○ - **Dorsal** region | **Shoulders**; between: *Cupr* k*
- **Lumbar** region: berb chim

FOREIGN BODY; sensation of a: | **Dorsal** region: lyc bg2

FORMICATION: **Acon** aesc *Agar* agn *All-c* alum h2 anac anan apoc arg-met *Arn Ars* ars-met arund asaf atra-r bnm3• atro bar-c bell berb bov cadm-met tpw6 carc tpw2* carl caust *Cham Cocc* con crot-h euon euon-a ptk1 graph lac-c ptk1 *Lach* lact mag-s manc merc-c nat-ar *Nat-c* nat-sil fd3.de• *Nux-v Osm* ox-ac pall *Ph-ac* **Phos** k* ran-s rat k* rhod sabad sars **Sec** k* sulph zinc-p k2
- **morning**: ars-met
- **afternoon**: asaf mag-s
- **evening**: *Lyc* mag-s osm
- **night**: bar-c bov zinc
- **cold** agg.: ars ptk1 lac-c ptk1
- **worms**; as from: staph rb2
▽ - **extending** to:
○ • **Back**; down the: carl
• **Fingers** and toes: sec
• **Limbs**: **Phos**
• **Up** and down: *Crot-h Lach* manc
○ - **Cervical** region: arund *Carl* dulc lac-c nux-v ptk1 phos plut-n srj7• sabin *Sec* k* spong
• **entering** a house; on: phos
○ • **Nape** of neck: dulc b4.de* sabin bg2
- **Coccyx**: borx bg2
- **Dorsal** region: acon b7.de* agar bg2 aloe bg2 alum bg2 anac b4a.de arg-met bg2 arn b7.de* asaf bg2 bar-c bg2 bell bg2 bov bg2 brom bg2 bry b7.de* caust b4a.de* chel bg2 con bg2 ferr bg2 graph b4a.de* hyper bg2 kali-i bg2 kalm bg2 lach bg2 laur bg2 lyc bg2 manc bg2 merc bg2 mez bg2 nat-c b4a.de* nat-m bg2 nat-sil fd3.de• nux-v bg2 ox-ac bg2 pall bg2 ph-ac b4a.de* phos bg2 phys bg2 plut-n srj7• ran-s b7.de* rat bg2 rhus-t b7.de* sabin b7.de* sars b4a.de* sec b7.de* sep b4a.de spong bg2 staph bg2 sulph b4a.de* thuj bg2 verat bg2 zinc bg2
• **ants**; as from: ran-s b7a.de
○ • **Scapulae**: *Anac* k* arg-met b7.de* fl-ac bg2 laur b7.de* m-arct b7.de mag-c bg2 mez b4.de* osm bg2 *Ph-ac* b4a.de sabad b7.de* sec bg2 sil thuj bg2 *Viol-t* b7.de* zinc
⁝ **right**: dulc bg2 hep ptk1 lach bg2
: **urination** agg.; during: hep h2
⁝ **left**: arg-met h1* euph bg2 med ptk1 mez bg2 sil bg2
⁝ **urination** agg.; during: hep b4a.de
• **Shoulders**, between the: carl laur viol-t
- **Lumbar** region: acon k* agar bg2 aloe bg2 alum bg2 alum-sil k2 arn bg2 ars arund asaf bg2 bar-c bg2 bell bg2 bov bg2 brom bg2 bry bg2 bufo-s canth caust bg2 chel bg2 con bg2 crot-t k* ferr bg2 graph b4a.de* hyper bg2 jatr-c bg2 kali-i bg2 kalm bg2 lach bg2 laur bg2 lyc bg2 manc bg2 meny k* merc bg2 merc-c k* mez bg2 nat-c b4.de* nat-m bg2 nux-v bg2 ox-ac bg2 pall bg2 ph-ac k* phos bg2 phys bg2 puls bg2 ran-s bg2 rat bg2 rhus-t bg2 sabin bg2 sars b4.de* sec bg2 sep bg2 spong bg2 stann k* staph bg2 sulph bg2 tarax k* thuj k* zinc bg2
• **paroxysms**: thuj
• **sitting** agg.: canth
▽ • **extending** to:
⁝ **Face**: arund
⁝ **Shoulders**: arund
- **Sacrum**: borx chin h1 crot-t graph ptk1 ph-ac sars
- **Spine**: **Acon** k* **Agar** k* arn h1* *Ars* k* arund con k* dream-p sdj1• kali-p *Lach* k* nat-c neon srj5• nux-m bg2 nux-v ptk1 ph-ac ptk1 phys br1 rhus-t h1 *Sal-ac* k* sec bg2 thuj bg2
○ • **Vertebrae**: acon bg2 arn bg2 con bg2

GLIDING; sensation of: | **Dorsal** region | **Vertebrae** over each other: *(↗Pain - spine - rubbing against)* ant-t ptk1 sanic bg2* *Sulph* bg2*
- **Lumbar** region | **Vertebrae** over each other: *(↗Pain - spine - rubbing against)* sanic ptk1

GOOSE FLESH: bapt a1

GREASY:
○ - **Cervical** region | **Nape** of neck: thuj b4a.de*

GRUMBLING, spine: sulph$_{h2}$

GURGLING: | **Lumbar** region: ang$_{bg2}$ lyc$_{bg2}$ sep$_{bg2}$

HAIR:

- **falling**: *(↗SKIN - Hair - falling)*
○ • **Cervical** region: *(↗SKIN - Hair - falling)* sul-ac$_{mtf11}$
- **graying** | **Cervical** region: sul-ac$_{mtf11}$
- **growth**: carc$_{gk}$ tub$_{gk}$
○ • **Spine**; along the | **children**; dark or long, fine hair on back of: **Tub**$_{mrr1}$

HANG DOWN of parts; letting:

- **arms** | **agg.**: ign$_{b7.de}$*

HARDNESS; sensation of: | **Lumbar** region: sep$_{bg2}$

HEAT: aesc aeth$_{a1}$ *Agar*$_{k}$* alum$_{ptk1}$ *Alumin* alumn *Apis* *Ars*$_{k}$* asaf aur bamb-a$_{stb2.de}$• bapt$_{ptk1}$ bar-c berb calc calc-s camph carb-an$_{ptk1}$ carb-v carl caust$_{h2}$ cham chin *Coff* con conch$_{fkr1}$* dig *Dulc* gels *Glon* hell helon hyos irid-met$_{srj5}$• laur *Led* lob-s *Lyc* mag-m$_{ptk1}$ mang$_{h2}$ *Med* melal-alt$_{gya4}$ meny *Merc* nat-c nat-m ol-an op par ph-ac **Phos**$_{k}$* *Pic-ac* plb podo$_{fd3.de}$• rhus-v sars sec$_{ptk1}$ *Sil*$_{k}$* sol-ni spig stann staph *Sulph*$_{k}$* *Sumb* vanil$_{fd5.de}$ verat *Zinc* zinc-p$_{k2}$

- **morning** | **waking**; on: con
- **forenoon**: hell
- **afternoon**: phos$_{h2}$
- **evening**: cham ph-ac$_{h2}$ phys verat$_{h1}$
- **alternating** with:
  • **cold** agg.: carl cham verat$_{k}$*
  • **shivering**: cham
- **eating**; after: staph
- **excitement**: pic-ac
- **exciting** news; while reading: *Gels*
- **flushes**: *Acon* bamb-a$_{stb2.de}$• bapt brom cic$_{a1}$ clem dig *Mang* merl spig$_{h1}$ **Sumb** tub$_{c1}$ vanil$_{fd5.de}$ yohim$_{c1}$*
  • **morning**: lil-t
  • **evening**: ph-ac sol-ni vanil$_{fd5.de}$
    ⁝ **stool** agg.; after: *Podo*
    ⁝ **supper** agg.; after: spig
    ⁝ **walking**, on continued: glon
  • **stool** | **after** | **agg.**: *Podo*
    ⁝ **during** | **agg.**: *Podo*
▽ • **extending** to:
    ⁝ **Body**: **Sumb**
      : **Directions**, in all: bapt$_{hr1}$
    ⁝ **Head**: pyrid$_{rly4}$• tub$_{c1}$
○ • **Cervical** region: aesc chlam-tr$_{bcx2}$• fl-ac hydr *Lach* *Med* **Phos** podo sarr
  • **Dorsal** region: acon$_{b7.de}$ staph$_{b7.de}$
  • **Lower** back: berb$_{bro1}$ staph$_{h1}$
  • **Lumbar** region: calc-p sumb
  • **Spine**, in: **Bol-la**
    ⁝ **accompanied** by | **Heart**; weakness of (See CHEST - Weakness - heart - accompanied - spine)
    ⁝ **warm** air streaming up spine into head: *Ars*$_{k}$* *Sumb*
    ⁝ **waves**; up in: *Lyc*
- **menses**; during: *Phos*
- **mental** exertion agg.: *Pic-ac* *Sil*
- **sitting** agg.: mang$_{h2}$ meny phos$_{h2}$ *Zinc*
- **streams** up: *Ars* *Lyc* *Verat*
- **sun** shining on it; as if: melal-alt$_{gya4}$
- **walking**:
  • **agg.**: verat
  • **air** agg.; in open: chin$_{h1}$ merc ph-ac sil$_{k}$* sol-ni
- **warm** bed agg.: pic-ac
- **wine** agg.: gins *Zinc*
▽ - **extending** to:
○ • **Down** back: calc-p$_{ptk1}$ coff con laur par phys sulph$_{k}$*

Heat – extending to: ...

  • **Up** the back: *Ars* bapt$_{ptk1}$ cann-i cocain$_{c1}$ hyos *Lyc* melal-alt$_{gya4}$ **Phos**$_{k}$* *Podo* sarr verat
    ⁝ **menses**; during: *Phos*
    ⁝ **stool** agg.; during: podo
    ⁝ **Down** the back; and: lac-d$_{k2}$
○ - **Cervical** region: aesc agar aml-ns bomb-chr$_{a1}$ cact$_{k2}$ *Calc* coloc com cycl fago *Fl-ac* *Glon* hydr kalm *Lach*$_{k}$* medul-os-si$_{rly4}$• merc$_{ptk1}$ merc-i-f *Nux-v* ol-an *Par* petr-ra$_{shn4}$• ph-ac$_{ptk1}$ phel *Phos* plut-n$_{srj7}$• positr$_{nl2}$• rhus-t samb$_{xxb1}$ sars *Sumb* tarent [bell-p-sp$_{dcm1}$]
  • **left**: lac-d$_{k2}$
  • **afternoon**: com
    ⁝ **cold** hands; with: sumb
  • **evening** | **19**-20 h: fl-ac
  • **sitting** agg.: dig
▽ • **extending** to:
    ⁝ **All** directions: rhus-t
    ⁝ **Down** back: glon *Par*
    ⁝ **Up**: calc *Fl-ac* *Glon* olib-sac$_{wmh1}$
○ • **Nape** of neck: cycl$_{b7.de}$ ign$_{b7.de}$* lach$_{b7.de}$* par$_{b7.de}$ phos$_{b4.de}$
- **Coccyx**: agar alum arn ars borx *Calc* carb-an carb-v caust chin colch graph hep ign laur led merc mur-ac ph-ac phos plat rhus-t spig staph sulph zinc
- **Dorsal** region: *Acon*$_{bg2}$ aeth$_{bg2}$ *Agar*$_{bg2}$ alum$_{b4.de}$* am-c$_{bg2}$ ambr$_{bg2}$ ang$_{bg2}$ ant-t$_{bg2}$ *Apis*$_{b7a.de}$* **Arn**$_{b7.de}$* **Ars**$_{bg2}$ asaf$_{bg2}$ bamb-a$_{stb2.de}$• *Bar-c*$_{bg2}$ *Bell*$_{bg2}$ bism$_{bg2}$ *Bry*$_{bg2}$ calc$_{bg2}$ *Canth*$_{bg2}$ *Carb-an*$_{bg2}$ **Carb-v**$_{bg2}$ **Caust**$_{bg2}$ cham$_{bg2}$ chel$_{bg2}$ chin$_{b7.de}$* chinin-s$_{bg2}$ cocc$_{bg2}$ coff$_{bg2}$ con$_{b4.de}$* **Dulc**$_{bg2}$ ferr$_{bg2}$ fl-ac$_{bg2}$ gels$_{bg2}$ helo$_{bg2}$ *Ign*$_{bg2}$ iod$_{bg2}$ *Kali-c*$_{bg2}$ lach$_{bg2}$ laur$_{bg2}$ **Lyc**$_{bg2}$ m-ambo$_{bg2}$ m-arct$_{b7.de}$ *M-aust*$_{b7.de}$* mag-m$_{bg2}$ **Mang**$_{bg2}$ melal-alt$_{gya4}$ **Meny**$_{b7.de}$* merc$_{k}$* mez$_{bg2}$ mur-ac$_{bg2}$ **Nat-c**$_{b4.de}$* nat-m$_{b4.de}$* nit-ac$_{bg2}$ **Nux-v**$_{bg2}$ olnd$_{bg2}$ ox-ac$_{bg2}$ **Par**$_{b7.de}$* *Ph-ac*$_{b4.de}$* *Phos*$_{k}$* **Pic-ac** plat$_{bg2}$ plb$_{bg2}$ **Puls**$_{b7a.de}$* rheum$_{bg2}$ *Rhus-t*$_{bg2}$ ruta$_{bg2}$ sabad$_{bg2}$ sel$_{bg2}$ seneg$_{bg2}$ **Sep**$_{bg2}$ *Sil*$_{bg2}$ **Spig**$_{b7.de}$* spong$_{bg2}$ **Stann**$_{bg2}$ staph$_{bg2}$ sul-ac$_{bg2}$ **Sulph**$_{bg2}$ tab$_{bg2}$ teucr$_{bg2}$ *Thuj*$_{bg2}$ *Verat*$_{b7.de}$* **Zinc**$_{bg2}$
  • **right** | **Liver** and kidneys; between: til$_{c1}$
  • **rising** upward; heat: ars$_{b4a.de}$
  • **sensation** of: bar-c$_{b4.de}$ carb-v$_{bg2}$ coff$_{b7.de}$* hyos$_{b7.de}$* laur$_{b7.de}$* meny$_{b7.de}$ spig$_{b7.de}$ staph$_{b7.de}$*
  • **spreads** to limbs: *Camph* melal-alt$_{gya4}$
▽ • **extending** to | **Cervical** region: bamb-a$_{stb2.de}$• melal-alt$_{gya4}$
○ • **Scapulae**: **Acon**$_{bg2}$ alum$_{bg2}$ *Ars*$_{bg2}$ asaf$_{bg2}$ *Bar-c*$_{bg2}$ bell$_{bg2}$ *Calc*$_{bg2}$ carb-v$_{bg2}$ *Chel*$_{k}$* chin$_{bg2}$ kali-c$_{bg2}$ lyc$_{bg2}$ *Merc*$_{bg2}$ mez$_{bg2}$ mur-ac$_{k}$* *Nat-c*$_{bg2}$ **Nux-v**$_{bg2}$ petr-ra$_{shn4}$• pip-n$_{bg2}$ *Plb*$_{bg2}$ **Puls**$_{b7.de}$* **Rhus-t**$_{bg2}$ sabin$_{bg2}$ **Sep**$_{bg2}$ *Sil*$_{bg2}$ spig$_{bg2}$ stann$_{bg2}$ staph$_{bg2}$ *Sulph*$_{bg2}$ tarax$_{bg2}$ *Thuj*$_{bg2}$ verat$_{bg2}$
    ⁝ **right**: *Caust*$_{bg2}$ lycps-v$_{bg2}$
      : **bathed** in hot water; as if: nat-s$_{c1}$
    ⁝ **left**: com$_{bg2}$ lach$_{bg2}$ *Nat-m*$_{bg2}$
    ⁝ **Between**: agar$_{bg2}$ arg-n *Ars*$_{bg2}$ bry$_{bg2}$ calc$_{bg2}$ carb-v$_{bg2}$ chel$_{bg2}$ ferr$_{bg2}$ glon$_{bg2}$* kali-c$_{h2}$ **Lyc**$_{k}$* mag-c$_{bg2}$ mag-m$_{bg2}$ merc$_{bg2}$ mur-ac$_{bg2}$ *Naja* *Phos*$_{k}$* *Pic-ac* plb$_{bg2}$ puls$_{h1}$* seneg$_{bg2}$ sulph$_{bg2}$ verat$_{bg2}$ zinc$_{bg2}$
- **Lumbar** region: *Acon*$_{bg2}$ act-sp$_{ptk1}$ alum$_{ptk1}$ *Apis*$_{bg2}$ arg-met$_{bg2}$ arn$_{bg2}$ **Ars**$_{bg2}$ ars-i arund asar$_{bg2}$ aur aur-s bapt bar-c$_{bg2}$ *Berb* *Borx*$_{bg2}$ *Bry*$_{bg2}$ bufo$_{bg2}$ calc$_{bg2}$ cann-xyz$_{ptk1}$ *Carb-an*$_{bg2}$ carb-v$_{bg2}$ **Caust**$_{bg2}$ cham$_{bg2}$ chin$_{bg2}$ cocc$_{bg2}$ colch graph$_{ptk1}$ helo$_{bg2}$ hura hyos *Ign*$_{bg2}$ *Kali-c*$_{bg2}$ kalm kreos$_{bg2}$ lac-c *Lyc*$_{bg2}$ mag-m$_{bg2}$ melal-alt$_{gya4}$ *Merc*$_{bg2}$ mur-ac$_{bg2}$ *Nat-m*$_{k}$* nit-ac *Nux-v*$_{k}$* *Ph-ac*$_{bg2}$ *Phos*$_{k}$* *Pic-ac* plb *Puls*$_{bg2}$ pyrid$_{rly4}$• raph **Rhus-t**$_{bg2}$ ruta$_{bg2}$ sabin$_{bg2}$ sarr sel sep$_{h2}$* *Sil*$_{bg2}$ stann$_{bg2}$ staph$_{bg2}$ sulph$_{k}$* tarax$_{bg2}$ thuj$_{k}$* verat$_{bg2}$
  • **air** agg.; in open: hyos
  • **breathing** deep agg.: sep
  • **eating**; after: sel
  • **externally**: clem
  • **hot** water flowing through lumbar vertebrae; as if: sumb$_{k}$*
  • **riding** in a carriage; after: hura
  • **sitting** agg.: colch hyos
  • **sleep**, after midday nap: sel

- **Lumbar** region: ...
  - **walking** in a room agg.: hyos
▽ · **extending** to:
    - ⁝ **Face**: arund
    - ⁝ **Rectum**: colch
- **Sacrum**: agar bg2 aloe bg2 alum bg2 arn bg2 **Ars** bg2 borx bg2 calc bg2 carb-an bg2 **Carb-v** bg2 **Caust** bg2 chin bg2 colch bg2 graph bg2 hep bg2 hydrog srj2• ign bg2 laur bg2 led bg2 *Merc* bg2 mur-ac bg2 *Ph-ac* bg2 **Phos** bg2 plat bg2 **Rhus-t** bg2 sars sep spig bg2 staph bg2 sulph k* zinc bg2
  - **radiating**: hydrog srj2•
- **Skin**; under the: bamb-a stb2.de•
- **Spine**: *Alum* *Ars* bamb-a stb2.de• bry cann-i carb-v coloc helo c1 helo-s c1* hyos *Lyc* *Med* *Nat-m* op *Phos* *Pic-ac* k* plb sarr *Sil* sin-n spig *Sumb* verat-v *Zinc*
  - **hot** water flowing in; as if: *Sumb*
  - **iron**; as from hot: *Alum* ptk1 bufo ptk1 camph ptk1
  - **spots**: *Phos*
▽ · **extending** to:
    - ⁝ **Head**: cann-i c1
      - ⁝ **warm** air was streaming upwards; as: *Ars* k* sarr c1 sumb ptk1
    - ⁝ **Upward**: *Ars* coca-c sk4• *Lyc* *Phos* *Podo* sarr
      - ⁝ **Neck** and ear; to: plut-n srj7•
○ · **Vertebrae**: carb-v bg2

HEAVINESS, weight: *Aesc* bro1 *Aloe* bro1 *Am-m* bro1 ambr anac bro1 androc srj1• ant-c bro1 arg-met arg-n arn bamb-a stb2.de• **Bar-c** k* bar-s k2 benz-ac bro1 *Berb* bro1 *Bov* k* carb-v **Cimic** k* colch k* coloc crot-c dioxi rbp6 equis-h *Eup-pur* bro1 euphr helon bro1* *Hydr* k* kali-c k* kali-chl kali-p *Kreos* bro1 lil-t k* mag-s mang nat-c *Nat-m* nat-p nat-s bro1 *Par* petr ph-ac *Phos* *Pic-ac* k* puls rhod *Rhus-t* sapin bg1 *Sep* k* spong fd4.de sulph

- **morning**: petr h2
  - **bed** agg.; in: ang c1 ant-t euphr pic-ac *Sep* sulph
  - **rising** agg.: ant-t euphr sulph h2
  - **waking**; on: phos h2 pic-ac *Sep*
- **forenoon**: sulph
  - **sitting** agg.: nat-c
- **night**: carb-v
- **lying** agg.: convo-s sp1 phos
- **motion** | **amel.**: nat-c hr1 rhod
- **rising** agg.: ant-t
- **stooping** agg.; after: bov ptk1
○ - **Cervical** region: *Agar* ang c1 apis bg1 asar bamb-a stb2.de• bit-ar wht1• *Calc-p* cann-i caps h1 carb-ac carbn-s bg1 cassia-s ccrh1• *Chel* falco-pe nl2• gels tl1 hippoc-k szs2 kali-c meny nux-v **Par** k* *Petr* petr-ra shn4• *Phos* plb **Rhus-t** k* sabin bg1 samb sep tab verat
  - **morning**: ang vh1 nux-v
  - **night**: convo-s sp1
  - **bending** forward agg.: cassia-s ccrh1•
  - **pressure** | **amel.**: cassia-s ccrh1•
  - **walking** agg.; after: *Rhus-t*
  - **weight** upon: coloc bg1 kali-c h2 nux-v bg1 **Par** *Phos* rhus-t tub bg1 vinc rb2
○ · **Muscles** (See cervical)
  - **Nape** of neck: apis bg2 chel bg2 kali-c bg2 meny b7a.de* *Nux-v* b7.de* *Par* b7a.de* petr b4.de* phos b4.de* *Rhus-t* b7.de* sabin b7.de* samb b7.de* tab bg2 verat bg2
- **Coccyx**: agar bg2 aloe bg2 ant-c k* *Ant-t* k* *Arg-n* k* berb bg2 bry bg2 carb-v bg2 *Chin* bg2 coc-c bg2 con bg2 *Sep* bg2
  - **sensation** as if a heavy weight were tugging at: *Ant-t*
  - **standing** | **amel.**: arg-n
  - **stool** agg.; during: arg-n
- **Dorsal** region: ambr b7.de* bell bg2 carb-v b4.de* carbn-s par b7a.de petr b4.de* phos b4.de* phyt sabin b7.de* sep b4.de* sil spong fd4.de sulph b4.de* til c1
○ · **Scapulae**: carbn-s bg2 kreos bg2 meny b7.de* phyt k* puls bg2 sil k*
    - ⁝ **bend** forward; compelling to: carbn-s rb2
    - ⁝ **Below**: puls h1

Heaviness, weight – **Dorsal** region – **Scapulae**: ...
    - ⁝ **Between**, as of a load: ang c1 calc ptk1 *Carbn-s* chin bg1* gran bg1* lach ptk1 lyss rb2 meny h1 *Nux-v* ptk1 phos bg2 rhus-t ptk1 sacch-a fd2.de• spong fd4.de tung-met bdx1•
  - **Vertebrae**: aloe bg2
- **Lumbar** region: agar bg2* allox tpw3 ammc vml3• *Ant-t* bg2* arg-met bg2 *Arg-n* k* arn *Bar-c* k* bov k* cadm-met tpw6 carb-ac chin bg2 **Cimic** k* colch k* coloc k* *Con* crot-c bg2* euphr bg2 gran bg2* *Hydr* *Kali-c* k* kali-p *Lil-t* k* mag-s mang bg1 *Merc* nat-c k* nux-m c1 *Ph-ac* *Phos* k* *Phyt* **Pic-ac** k* **Rhus-t** k* sabin b7.de* sep bg2* sulph bg2* syph
  - **night** | **midnight**: *Pic-ac*
  - **alternating** with | **Hip**; heaviness in (See EXTREMITIES - Heaviness - hip - alternating)
  - **inspiration** agg.: ammc vml3•
  - **lying** on left side amel.: *Coloc*
  - **menses** | **before** | **agg.**: bov
    - ⁝ **during** | **agg.**: *Cimic* *Kali-c*
  - **motion**:
    - ⁝ **agg.**: *Phos* *Pic-ac*
    - ⁝ **amel.**: nat-c
  - **sitting** agg.: nat-c h2
  - **turning** in bed agg.: *Corn*
  - **waking**; on: *Pic-ac*
▽ · **extending** to | **Thighs**: cimic ptk1
- **Sacral** region: agar bg2* *Aloe* bg2* ant-t mrr1 **Arg-n** k* bar-c h2* berb k* bry bg2* *Carb-v* bg2* **Chin** k* *Cimic* clem a1 coc-c bg2* *Con* k* dios *Ferr* *Helon* br1 hura mag-s *Phyt* pip-n bg1 podo fd3.de• *Rhus-t* *Sec* *Sep* k* spong fd4.de til c1 zing
  - **painful** | **sitting** for a long time agg.: allox sp1
  - **sitting** agg.: aloe *Arg-n* hura **Rhus-t** k*
  - **standing** | **amel.**: *Arg-n*
  - **stool** | **after** | **agg.**: bry bg2
    - ⁝ **during** | **agg.**: *Arg-n*
  - **walking** agg.: arg-n
- **Sacroiliac** region: aesc tl1
- **Vertebrae**: aloe bg2

HEMORRHAGE: | **Spinal** cord: acon bro1 *Arn* bro1 *Bell* bro1 lach bro1 nux-v bro1 sec bro1

HEMORRHOIDS: | **agg.** | **Sacrum**: abrot ptk1
- **protrusion** agg.; before: alum bg2

HICCOUGH agg.: teucr bg2

HYPERESTHESIA of skin: (↗*Sensitive - lumbar - skin)* merc petr plat tarent mp1•

IMMOBILE:
○ - **Dorsal** region | **Scapulae**: ran-b k2

INFLAMMATION:
○ - **Cellulitis**: am-c tl1
- **Cervical** region | **Vertebrae**: ph-ac ptk1
- **Glands**; cervical: aq-mar mtf11 *Calc* *Cist* mrr1 morg-p pte1*• rhus-t k2 streptoc mtf11 v-a-b mtf11
  - **accompanied** by | **scarlet** fever: ail bro1 am-c bro1 asim bro1 *Bell* bro1 *Carb-ac* bro1 crot-h bro1 hep bro1 lach bro1 merc bro1 *Merc-i-r* bro1 *Rhus-t* bro1
- **Joints**:
  - **accompanied** by:
    - ⁝ **crackling**: flav mtf11
    - ⁝ **herniated** disk: parat-b mtf11
  - **rheumatic**: flav mtf11
- **Lumbar** region: ars bg2 *Lath* bg2 merc bg2 *Rhus-t* bg2
- **Membranes** (= spinal meningitis): *(↗FEVER - Cerebrospinal)* abrot vh1 *Acon* k* **Apis** **Bell** k* *Bry* k* *Calc* *Cic* *Cimic* cocc crot-h cupr cyt-l br1 dulc echi br1 **Gels** helo-s c1 *Hyos* hyper *Ip* kali-i k* merc k* *Nat-m* *Nat-s* k* nux-v *Op* oreo br1 ox-ac k* *Plb* *Rhus-t* sec tub al verat-v k* *Zinc*
  - **accompanied** by | **Lower** limbs; weakness, numbness and coldness in: ox-ac mrr1

- **Membranes**: ...
  - **mercury**; after abuse of: *Kali-i*
  - **scarlet** fever or measles, eruptions do not develop; during: dulc
  - **suffocation**, warm room agg.: **Apis** op
  - **wet** agg.; getting: *Rhus-t* hr1
- **Nerves**: syc fmm1•
  - O **Cervical** region: syc fmm1•
  - **Dorsal** region | **Upper** dorsal roots: anan bro1
  - **Lumbosacral** plexus: berb bro1
- **Sacroiliac** symphyses: **Aesc** mrr1 morg-p pte1•
- **Sacrum**: des-ac rbp6
- **Spinal** cord (= myelitis): abrot vh1 acon k* ail vh1 alum bg2* alum-p k2 *Alumin Apis* arg-n br1* *Arn* bro1 *Ars* k* bar-m *Bell* k* bell-p bro1 *Benz-ac* bry bg2* calc k* camph canth k* carb-v bg2 caust k* cedr chel bro1 chin bg2 cic k* cocc k* colch coli jl2 con bro1 crot-h k* dig bg2 diphtox jl2 *Dulc* k* **Gels** k* hyos k* hyper k2* ign bg2 kali-i k* *Lach* k* lath br1* lyc merc k* naja bro1 nat-c bg2 nat-m k* *Nat-s* k* *Nux-v* k* **Op** k* ox-ac k* *Par* parathyr jl2 pert jl2 ph-ac bg2 **Phos** k* phys k* *Pic-ac* k* plb k* puls bg2 rhus-t k* sec k* sil k* staph bg2 staphycoc jl2 stram bro1 *Stry* bro1 sulph k* toxo-g jl2 verat bg2* zinc-p bg2*
  - **accompanied** by:
    - **convulsions**: pic-ac br1
    - **weakness**: *(↗GENERALS - Weakness - spinal)* pic-ac br1
  - **chronic**: *Ars* bro1 *Crot-h* bro1 lath bro1 *Ox-ac* bro1 *Plb* bro1 stry bro1 thal bro1
  - **eruptions** do not develop; when: bry dulc
  - **spasmodic**: arg-n bro1 ars bro1 chel bro1 merc bro1 verat bro1
  - O **Cervical** region: par rhus-t k2
  - **Dorsal** region: *Dulc* b4a.de
- **Spinal** cord and meninges (= meningomyelitis): agar bnf1.es apis qqh bell qqh hell qqh stram qqh tarent bnf1.es
- **Spine** | **Joints** of vertebrae: bacls-7 mtf11 cortico mtf11 des-ac mtf11 morg-p mtf11
- **Vertebrae** (= spondylitis): aesc mrr1 dys fmm1• eberth jl2 ph-ac ptk1 staphycoc jl2

INJURIES: *(↗GENERALS - Paralysis - Injuries)* arg-n bg2 *Arn* bg2 **Hyper** bg2 kali-c bg2 nat-s bg2 phys bg2 xanth bg2
- **after**:
  - **agg.** | **Lumbar** region: kali-c ptk1
- O **Cervical** region: **Arn** sne **Hyper** sne mez k* rhus-t mrr1*
- **Coccyx**●: bell-p ptk1 *Carb-an* k* caust sne gamb mrr1 **HYPER** k ●* kali-bi bg1 *Mez* k* ruta sne **Sil** k* symph tl1* thuj sne
- **Lumbar** region: *(↗Pain - lumbar - jar)*
  - **sensitive** to jar of walking; remains: *(↗Pain - lumbar - jar)* arn mp1• **Bry** mp1• *Thuj*
- **Spinal** cord | **bleeding** (See Blood - spinal - injuries)
- **Spine**: *(↗Blood - spinal - injuries; EXTREMITIES - Paralysis - lower - injuries - spine; GENERALS - Brown-séguard)* acon vh1 aesc mp1• *Apis Arn* k* bell-p ptk1* *Calc* calen mp1• caust sne cimic mrr1 *Con* k* dam mp1• **Hyper** k* ign c1 kali-c mp1• *Led* **Nat-s** k* *Nit-ac* k* *Rhus-t* k* *Ruta* k* *Sil* k* symph bro1* tell c1 *Thuj* zinc ptk1*
  - **after** injury, he lies on back, with head jerking backward: *Hyper* k*
  - **lifting** agg.: *Arn* mp1• borx mp1• **Calc** k* **Graph** mp1• **Lyc** mp1• *Nux-v* mp1• ph-ac mp1• **Rhus-t** k* *Ruta* mp1• sang mp1• *Sep* mp1•
  - **old** injuries: ign ptk1*
  - **railway** spine: bell-p c1* hyper kmy1
  - **shock** of spine (= concussion): *Arn* con k2* *Hyper* k* *Nit-ac*

INSENSIBILITY: | **Skin**; of: pop-cand br1

INSPIRATION agg.: acon b7.de* alum b4.de* ars b4.de* calc b4.de* caps b7.de* *Caust* b4a.de *Chin* b7.de* cina b7.de* coloc b4.de* *Con* b4a.de cycl b7.de* dulc b4.de* kali-bi bg2 kali-c b4.de* laur b7.de* led b7.de* lyc b4.de* merc b4.de* mez b4.de* ruta b7.de* sabin b7.de* sars b4.de* sep b4.de* spig b7.de* stann b4.de* sulph b4.de*

INSTABILITY: | **Sacrum**: *(↗Weakness - sacrum)* plac rzf5•

IRRITATION of spine (See Pain - spine - sore)

ITCHING: agar agath-a nl2• ail-s aloe *Alum* alum-p k2 am-m ang c1 **Ant-c** k* arg-met arn ars-i asc-t aur aur-s k2 *Bar-c* bar-s k2 benzol br1 calc calc-s calc-sil k2 carb-ac carb-v carbn-s **Caust** k* chel cist clem coc-c cocc corn cortiso tpw7 cystein-l rly4• daph dios dulc fd4.de fago falco-pe nl2• fl-ac glon *Graph* guaj ham fd3.de• hep hip-ac sp1 hura irid-met srj5• kali-bi *Kali-c* kali-n kali-p kali-sil k2 lac-ac lac-leo hrn2• lap-la sde8.de• *Lyc* mag-c mag-m mag-s med *Merc* merc-i-f **Mez** k* mill mur-ac *Nat-c* nat-m nat-p *Nat-s* nicc **Nit-ac** k* oci-sa sk4• ol-an osm pall ph-ac phos pieri-b mlk9.de plac-s rly4• *Positr* nl2• *Puls* raph *Rhus-t Ros-d* wla1 sal-fr sle1• *Sars* seneg *Sep Sil* spig spong **Sulph** k* symph fd3.de• tell ther *Thuj* trios rsj11• tritic-vg fd5.de tub-m zs vanil fd5.de ven-m rsj12• zinc zinc-p k2
- **morning**: asc-t falco-pe nl2• ham fd3.de• kali-c h2 lyc propr sa3•
  - **6-10 h**: kali-bi
  - **7 h**: pall rhus-t
  - **bed** agg.; in: rhus-t
- **forenoon**: fl-ac
- **afternoon**: fago oxal-a rly4• sars
- **evening**: con dulc fd4.de fago fl-ac ham fd3.de• kali-c h2 lyc mur-ac a1 olib-sac wmh1 rat spong fd4.de sulph thuj trios rsj11• vanil fd5.de
  - **bed** agg.; in: calc lac-h sk4• lyc merc nat-m propr sa3•
  - **undressing** agg.: cocc falco-pe nl2• hyper mag-m nat-c *Nat-s* osm puls
- **night**: agar ail apoc ars asc-t fl-ac ham fd3.de• *Mez* phos rhus-v spong fd4.de zinc h2
  - **lying** down agg.: mag-c
  - **warmth** of bed, in: nat-ar rhus-v sulph
- **burning**: agar alum berb *Calc* daph kali-c mag-c mez *Nux-v* raph
  - **morning** | **dressing**; while: nux-v
  - **evening** | **undressing**; while: nux-v
  - **night**: nux-v spong
  - **scratching** agg.; after: alum squil
  - **walking** in open air agg.: merc
- **cold** agg.; becoming: lyc spong
- **cold** air agg.: rhus-v
- **scratching**:
  - **amel.**: lac-leo hrn2• mag-c mag-m mez nat-c pall positr nl2• rat rhus-v
  - **changes** place after scratching: mez pall
  - **pain** after scratching: kali-c h2 nit-ac
  - **unchanged** by scratching: nat-c h2
- **spots**: luna kg1•
- **stinging**: alum anac am caust galeoc-c-h gms1• squil
  - **scratching** | **amel.**: anac
  - **sudden**:
    - **scratching** | **amel.**: ph-ac
- O **Cervical** region: agar agath-a nl2• agn **Alum** k* alum-sil k2 ammc anac *Ant-c* k* arg-n arizon-l nl2• ars bamb-a stb2.de• benz-ac *Berb* calc h2 carb-ac carb-v caust con h2 cycl flor-p rsj3• *Gels* grat hydr hydr-ac ign jug-c kali-bi kali-n lap-la sde8.de• laur lyc mag-c mag-m mang merc-i-f merc-i-r mez morph myric nat-ar nat-c **Nat-m** k* nat-p nicc nit-ac olib-sac wmh1 ox-ac pall pneu jl2 positr nl2• *Puls* rat *Rhus-t* rumx sars sep sil squil staph streptoc rly4• **Sulph** k* tarent tell rsj10• ther thuj trios rsj11• trom vanil fd5.de
  - **morning**: bamb-a stb2.de• fl-ac nat-m sulph ther
    - **rising** agg.; after: sulph
  - **evening**: calc carb-v fl-ac mag-c stront-c ther trom vanil fd5.de
    - **bed** agg.; in: calc sulph
    - **going** to bed; before: mag-m
    - **undressing** agg.: am-m hyper
  - **night**: ail hydr petr-ra shn4•
    - **bed**; in heat of: *Sulph*
  - **burning**: berb k* *Calc* k* *Kali-bi*
    - **scratching**; after: mag-c h2
  - **cold** | **amel.**: rhus-t k*
  - **menses**; during: mag-c
  - **scratching**; after: nat-m ozone sde2•

- **Cervical** region – **scratching**; after: ...
  - ⁝ **amel.**: mang$_{hr1}$
  - ⁝ **bleeds**, until it: mang$_{h2}$
  - ⁝ **changes** place after: sars
  - • **stinging**: carb-v$_{h2}$ rhus-t$_{h1}$
  - • **touch** agg.: psor
  - • **voluptuous**: mang$_{h2}$
  - • **walking** in open air agg.: nit-ac
  - • **warmth**:
    - ⁝ **agg.** | **heat** agg.: rhus-t$_{k}$*
  - ▽ • **extending** to | **All** directions: rhus-t
  - ○ • **Nape** of neck: agn$_{b7.de}$* alum$_{bg2}$ am-m$_{b7.de}$* bufo$_{bg2}$ carb-v$_{b4.de}$* caust$_{b4a.de}$ mez$_{b4a.de}$ nit-ac$_{b4.de}$* rhod$_{b4.de}$* rhus-t$_{b7.de}$* sep$_{b4.de}$* sil$_{b4.de}$* staph$_{b7.de}$* sulph$_{b4.de}$* ther$_{bg2}$
- **Coccyx**: agar$_{k}$* alum$_{k}$* am-c$_{h2}$* bar-c borx$_{k}$* *Bov*$_{k}$* canth$_{b7.de}$* carb-v$_{b4.de}$* chel$_{bg1}$ chin$_{b7.de}$* con dros$_{b7.de}$* fl-ac *Graph*$_{k}$* laur$_{bg2}$ led$_{b7.de}$* lyc par$_{b7.de}$* ph-ac$_{b4.de}$* plb$_{b7.de}$* propr$_{sa3}$• spig$_{k}$* verat$_{b7.de}$*
  - • **evening** | **bed** agg.; in: carb-v$_{h2}$
  - • **burning**: fl-ac
  - • **corrosive**: ph-ac$_{h2}$
  - • **menses**; during: dros graph ph-ac
  - • **warm** bed agg.: *Petr*
  - ▽ • **extending** to | **Upward**: petr$_{hr1}$
- **Dorsal** region: agar$_{b4.de}$* agn$_{b7.de}$* alum$_{b4.de}$* am-c$_{b4.de}$* am-m$_{b7a.de}$ *Ang*$_{b7a.de}$ ant-c$_{b7.de}$* *Ant-t*$_{bg2}$ arn$_{b7.de}$* bar-c$_{b4.de}$* calc$_{bg2}$ caust$_{b4.de}$* cocc$_{b7.de}$* graph$_{b4.de}$* guaj$_{b4.de}$* iod$_{bg2}$ irid-met$_{srj5}$• kali-c$_{b4.de}$* laur$_{b7.de}$* lyc$_{b4.de}$* m-aust$_{b7.de}$ mag-c$_{b4.de}$* mag-m$_{b4.de}$* mang$_{b4.de}$* merc$_{b4.de}$* merc-c$_{b4a.de}$ *Mez*$_{b4.de}$* mur-ac$_{b4.de}$* nat-c$_{b4.de}$* nat-m$_{b4.de}$* nat-s$_{bg2}$ nit-ac$_{b4.de}$* nux-v$_{b7.de}$* ph-ac$_{bg2}$ pic-ac$_{bg2}$ puls$_{b7.de}$* rhus-g$_{tmo3}$• sars$_{b4.de}$* sel$_{b7.de}$* seneg$_{b4.de}$* *Sep*$_{b4a.de}$ sil$_{b4.de}$* spig$_{bg2}$ spong$_{b7.de}$* sulph$_{b4.de}$* ther$_{bg2}$ thuj$_{b4.de}$* viol-t$_{b7.de}$* zinc$_{b4.de}$*
  - • **morning**: bamb-a$_{stb2.de}$•
  - ○ • **Scapulae**: alum$_{k}$* am-m$_{k}$* anac$_{bg2}$ arg-met$_{b7.de}$* arn$_{k}$* asaf$_{k}$* bar-c bell$_{b4.de}$* calc cann-s$_{b7.de}$* choc$_{srj3}$• com crot-h cund cystein-l$_{rly4}$• dios dulc$_{b4.de}$* form irid-met$_{srj5}$• laur$_{k}$* merc$_{k}$* merc-i-f mez$_{k}$* mosch$_{b7a.de}$ olnd$_{k}$* petr phel positr$_{nl2}$• rat ruta$_{k}$* seneg$_{k}$* sil$_{k}$* spig$_{k}$* stront-c$_{k}$* ther$_{k}$* thuj$_{bg2}$ viol-t$_{k}$* zinc$_{k}$*
    - ⁝ **right**: calc$_{bg2}$ fago$_{bg2}$ laur$_{bg2}$ mang$_{a1}$ merc$_{bg2}$ olnd$_{bg2}$ ozone$_{sde2}$• pall$_{bg2}$
    - ⁝ **left**: am-m$_{bg2}$ bar-c$_{bg2}$ caust$_{ptk1}$ fl-ac$_{bg1}$ grat$_{bg1}$ ham$_{bg1}$ phel$_{bg2}$ psil$_{ft1}$
    - ⁝ **rubbing**:
      - : **amel.**: grat
      - : **not** amel.: ozone$_{sde2}$•
    - ⁝ **spots**, in: fl-ac
    - ⁝ **Below**: hydrog$_{srj2}$•
    - ⁝ **Between**: all-s alum am-m arg-met calc$_{k}$* calc-s caust chinin-s choc$_{srj3}$• cortico$_{sp1}$ cortiso$_{tpw7}$ cystein-l$_{rly4}$• dios *Hipp* lap-la$_{sde8.de}$• laur mag-c mag-m mosch positr$_{nl2}$• rat ruta$_{h1}$ stront-c *Zinc*
      - : **evening**: dios mag-m zinc
      - : **night**: am-m cocc
        - . **undressing**; while: carc$_{gk6}$ sulph
      - : **scratching** | **agg.** | **after** scratching; burning: rat$_{k}$*
        - . **amel.**: mag-c
    - ⁝ **Border**; right outer: dulc$_{h1}$
  - • **Shoulders**; between: cortiso$_{tpw7}$ hipp$_{jl2}$
- **Lumbar** region: alum$_{h2}$ *Bar-c Berb* bufo-s carb-v$_{k}$* caust$_{k}$* chin$_{k}$* con dig fl-ac ham$_{fd3.de}$• hep iod$_{k}$* kali-bi kali-c$_{k}$* kali-n lach led lyc mag-c$_{k}$* *Mag-m Merc*$_{k}$* merc-c mez morph *Nat-m*$_{k}$* nicc ol-an phyt positr$_{nl2}$• psor *Puls Ros-d*$_{wla1}$ sul-i$_{k2}$ sulph$_{k}$* trios$_{rsj11}$•
  - • **evening**: trios$_{rsj11}$•
    - ⁝ **bed** agg.; in: nat-m$_{h2}$
  - • **burning**: alum$_{h2}$ *Berb*$_{a1}$ mag-c$_{h2}$
    - ⁝ **extending** to | **Abdomen** and thighs: nat-m
  - • **corrosive**: ph-ac$_{h2}$
  - • **scratch** it raw; must: *Bar-c*
- **Sacrum**: agar alum borx bov fl-ac graph laur led med merc par plb

Itching – Sacrum: ...
  - • **burning**: kali-c$_{h2}$
  - • **walking** agg.: merc
- **Spine**: sumb$_{ptk1}$

JAR agg.: *Graph*$_{ptk1}$ thuj$_{ptk1}$
- ○ - **Lumbar** region: thuj$_{ptk1}$ zinc-ar$_{ptk1}$
- **Spine**: *Bell*$_{ptk1}$ graph$_{ptk1}$ sil$_{ptk1}$ *Ther*$_{ptk1}$ thuj$_{ptk1}$

JERKING: petr$_{h2}$
- **left** side: agar$_{h2}$
- **night** | **sleep**; during: am-c$_{h2}$
- **work**; at manual: nit-ac$_{h2}$
- ○ - **Cervical** muscles: aeth$_{k}$* coloc$_{k}$* sep$_{k}$*
  - • **convulsions**; before: bufo$_{ptk1}$
  - • **sleep**; in: alum$_{k2}$
- **Coccyx**:
  - • **menses**; during: cic$_{ptk1}$
  - ▽ • **extending** to | **Bladder**: carb-an$_{h2}$
- **Dorsal** region:
  - • **pressure** on vertebrae; from: arn$_{a1}$
  - ○ • **Scapulae**: plat$_{b4.de}$* sep$_{b4.de}$*
- **Lumbar** region: sulph$_{h2}$
- **Sacral** region: chin$_{h1}$ petr$_{h2}$
- **Spine**: sabad$_{bg2}$

KYPHOSIS (See Curvature)

LAMENESS: abrot$_{br1}$* acon$_{bro1}$ aesc$_{bro1}$* agar$_{bro1}$ am-m$_{bro1}$ arn$_{k2}$ bell$_{bro1}$ *Berb*$_{bro1}$ *Bry*$_{bro1}$ calc$_{bro1}$ camph-mbr$_{bro1}$ *Caust*$_{bro1}$ *Cimic*$_{bro1}$ *Cupr-ar*$_{bro1}$ dios$_{bro1}$ dulc$_{bro1}$ get$_{bro1}$ gins$_{bro1}$ *Helon*$_{bro1}$ hyper$_{bro1}$ *Kali-c*$_{bro1}$ kali-p$_{bro1}$ kalm$_{bro1}$ lachn$_{bro1}$ led$_{bro1}$ lyc$_{bro1}$ nicot$_{bro1}$ phys$_{bro1}$ *Phyt*$_{bro1}$ rhus-t$_{bro1}$ ruta$_{bro1}$* sarcol-ac$_{bro1}$ *Sep*$_{bro1}$ spong$_{bro1}$ staph$_{bro1}$ *Stry*$_{bro1}$ sul-ac$_{bro1}$ *Sulph*$_{bro1}$ zing$_{bro1}$
- ○ - **Cervical**: *Bapt*$_{a1}$* nat-c$_{h2}$ par$_{a1}$ rad-br$_{c11}$ spig$_{h1}$
  - ○ • **Nape** of neck: zinc$_{ptk1}$
- **Lumbar**: berb$_{ptk1}$ cocc$_{bg2}$ coff$_{bg2}$ *Dulc*$_{bg2}$ gels$_{ptk1}$ kali-i$_{ptk1}$ lach$_{bg2}$* mag-m$_{bg2}$ **Nat-m**$_{bg2}$ ox-ac$_{ptk1}$ phos$_{h2}$* ran-s$_{bg2}$ *Rhus-t*$_{ptk1}$ sel$_{bg2}$ sil$_{bg2}$ sulph$_{ptk1}$ zinc$_{bg2}$
  - • **chill**; during: *Cocc*$_{bg2}$
- **Sacroiliac** region: aesc$_{tl1}$

LAUGHING agg.: *Camph*$_{ptk1}$ *Con*$_{b4a.de}$* phos$_{ptk1}$
- ○ - **Sacrum**: tell$_{ptk1}$

LEANING:
- **against** something:
  - • **agg.**: *Agar*$_{ptk1}$ hep$_{b4a.de}$ *Plb*$_{ptk1}$ *Ther*$_{ptk1}$
  - • **amel.**: carb-v$_{b4a.de}$ eupi$_{ptk1}$ kali-c$_{bg2}$ nat-m$_{bg2}$ sabad$_{b7.de}$* sarr$_{ptk1}$

LEUKORRHEA: | **agg.** | **Sacrum**: aesc$_{ptk1}$ psor$_{ptk1}$
- **amel.**:
  - ○ • **Lumbar** region: kreos$_{ptk1}$
  - • **Sacrum**: murx$_{ptk1}$

LIFTING a weight: | **agg.** (See Straining)

LOOKING upward agg.: | **Cervical** region: graph$_{ptk1}$

LOOSE sensation; as if: | **Vertebrae**: calc$_{ptk1}$

LUMBAGO (See Pain - lumbar)

LUMPS:
- **sensation** of a lump in: anac$_{ptk1}$ arn$_{k}$* bamb-a$_{stb2.de}$• berb$_{ptk1}$ *Carb-v*$_{ptk1}$ cinnb$_{ptk1}$ kali-s$_{fd4.de}$ phos$_{ptk1}$ sars$_{bg1}$
  - ○ • **Dorsal** region: arn$_{b7a.de}$
    - ⁝ **Scapulae**: am-m arn$_{bg2}$ calc$_{bg2}$ kreos$_{bg2}$ streptoc$_{rly4}$•
      - : **right**: ars$_{bg2}$ lach$_{bg2}$
      - : **left**: chen-v$_{bg2}$ phos$_{bg2}$ prun$_{bg2}$ rhus-t$_{bg2}$
      - : **Between**: arn$_{bg2}$ chin$_{bg1}$ lach$_{bg1}$ lyc$_{bg1}$ mag-s$_{bg2}$* nux-v$_{bg1}$ pall$_{bg1}$ phyt$_{bg1}$ plat$_{bg1}$ prun$_{bg1}$ rhus-t$_{bg1}$
  - • **Lumbar** region: carb-v$_{bg1}$
  - • **Sacral** region: bamb-a$_{stb2.de}$•

○ - **Cervical** region:

• **grit** under skin; small lumps like: plut-n srj7•

○ • **Nape** of neck: ant-c bg2 caust bg2 hep b4.de* nat-c b4a.de zinc bg2

- **Coccyx**: hep b4.de*
- **Dorsal** region: *Calc* b4a.de

○ • **Scapulae**: am-m b7.de* crot-h bg2 squil b7.de*

⁝ **left**: prun ptk1

⁝ **Between**: calc chin ptk1 lyc ptk1 mag-c ptk1 mag-s nux-v ptk1 rhus-t ptk1

LYING:
- **abdomen**; on | **amel.**: acet-ac ptk1 nit-ac ptk1 sel ptk1
- **agg.**: agar b4a.de* am-c b4.de* am-m b7.de* ant-t bg2 arg-met b7.de* aur b4.de* bell bg2 berb bg2 bry b7.de* carb-an bg2 cham bg2 chin b7.de* cic bg2 cocc b7.de* euph b4a.de ferr b7.de* gels bg2 hep b4.de* kali-n b4a.de kreos bg2 mag-c bg2 nat-c b4.de* nat-m b4.de* nat-s bg2 phos b4.de* puls b7.de* rhus-t bg2 sel b7.de* sil b4a.de sulph b4.de* tab bg2 tarax b7.de* zinc bg2

○ • **Sacrum**: berb ptk1

- **amel.**: asar b7.de* bry b7.de* cocc b7.de* guaj b4a.de kali-c bg2 kreos b7a.de *Nat-m* b4.de* nux-m bg2 nux-v b7.de* sep bg2

○ • **Sacrum**: agar ptk1

- **back**; on:

• **agg.**: aloe bg2 apis b7a.de *Bell* b4a.de bry b7.de* *Chin* b7a.de cimic bg2 coloc ptk1 dulc b4.de* euph b4a.de* ign b7.de* kali-n b4a.de* lyc bg2 nat-m bg2 puls bg2* rhus-t b7.de* stront-c b4.de* zinc bg2

• **amel.**: kali-c ptk1 nat-m ptk1 phos ptk1 *Ruta* b7a.de*

- **bed**; in | **agg.**: am-m b7.de* ang b7.de* carb-v b4.de* cina b7.de* cocc b7.de* euph b4a.de hep b4.de* ign b7.de* kali-n b4.de* m-ambo b7.de merc b4.de* nat-m b4.de* nux-v b7.de* petr b4.de* puls b7.de* rhod b4.de* rhus-t bg2 sep b4.de* staph b7.de* thuj b4.de* valer b7.de*
- **hard**; on something | **amel.**: kali-c ptk1 mag-m bg2 nat-m bg2* rhus-t b7a.de* sep bg2*
- **pillow**; on a | **amel.**: *Carb-v* ptk1 sep ptk1
- **side**; on:

• **agg.**: cina b7.de*

• **amel.**: kali-n b4a.de nat-c bg2

• **left** | **agg.**: kali-n bg2 ph-ac bg2 sep bg2

• **right**:

⁝ **agg.**: ars b4.de* cina b7.de* m-ambo b7.de sep bg2

⁝ **amel.**: nat-s bg2 ust bg2

LYING DOWN agg.; after: nux-v b7.de* *Phos* b4a.de

MANUAL LABOR:
- **agg.**: chel bg2 ferr b7.de
- **amel.**: nat-m a2

MASTURBATION agg.: abrot bg2 cob bg2 ph-ac bg2

MENSES:
- **absent** agg.: senec bg2
- **after** | **agg.**: berb bg2 borx bg2 calc-p bg2 *Kali-c* bg2 mag-c bg2 puls bg2 *Sep* bg2 ust bg2 verat bg2
- **amel.**: senec ptk1
- **before**:

• **agg.**: am-c bg2 asar bg2 bar-c bg2 berb bg2 brom bg2 *Calc* bg2 carb-v bg2 caul bg2 caust bg2 cimic bg2 *Cinnb* bg2 cocc bg2 dig bg2 hydr bg2 hyos b7.de* hyper bg2 kali-c bg2 kali-n bg2 kreos bg2 lach bg2 lyc bg2 *Mag-c* bg2 mag-m bg2 mosch b7.de* nat-m bg2 *Nit-ac* bg2 *Nux-m* b7.de* nux-v bg2 ol-an bg2 plat bg2 puls bg2 sabin bg2 sang bg2 senec bg2 sep bg2 *Spong* b7.de* sulph bg2 ust bg2 verat bg2 *Vib* bg2

⁝ **Lumbar** region: am-c bg2 *Bar-c* bg2 borx bg2 *Calc* bg2 caust bg2 con bg2 hyos bg2 kali-c bg2 mag-c bg2 mosch bg2 nit-ac bg2 nux-m bg2 phos bg2 spong bg2

⁝ **Nape** of neck: carb-v bg2 iod bg2 nat-c bg2 nit-ac bg2 nux-v bg2 sulph bg2

⁝ **Sacrum**: nux-m ptk1 sabin ptk1 spong ptk1

- **during**:

• **agg.**: acon bg2 agar bg2 aloe bg2 am-c b4.de* *Am-m* b7.de* ang bg2 arg-n bg2 ars bg2 asar bg2 bar-c bg2 **Bell** b4.de* *Berb* bg2 borx bg2 brom bg2 *Bry* b7.de* *Calc* bg2 calc-p bg2 camph bg2 cann-xyz bg2 canth bg2 carb-an bg2 carb-v bg2 castm bg2 **Caust** bg2* cham b7.de* chel bg2 cic bg2

Menses – during – agg.: ...

Cimic bg2 cinnb bg2 coc-c bg2 cocc bg2 *Croc* b7.de* cycl bg2 ferr bg2 ferr-p bg2 gran bg2 graph bg2 helo bg2 hydr bg2 ign bg2 iod bg2 **Kali-c** bg2 kali-i bg2 kali-n bg2 kalm bg2 kreos bg2 lac-c bg2 **Lach** bg2 lil-t bg2 *Lyc* bg2 mag-c bg2 mag-m bg2 mang bg2 med bg2 merc bg2 mosch bg2 nat-c bg2 nit-ac bg2 nux-m bg2 nux-v bg2 ol-an bg2 *Phos* bg2 prun bg2 *Puls* b7.de* rat bg2 sabin bg2 sang bg2 sars bg2 senec bg2 sep bg2 sil bg2 spong bg2 sulph bg2* tarent bg2 thuj bg2 ust bg2 verat bg2 zinc bg2

⁝ **Nape** of neck: berb bg2 *Calc* bg2 mag-c bg2 nat-m bg2 nit-ac bg2

• **amel.**: kali-bi bg2

• **beginning** of menses:

⁝ **agg.**: caust bg2 cic bg2 jab ptk1

⁝ **Lumbar** region: asar bg2 caust bg2 cham bg2 kali-p bg2 mag-c bg2 nit-ac bg2

⁝ **Sacrum**: asar ptk1

- **instead** of menses | **Sacrum**: spong ptk1
- **late** | **agg.**: phos b4.de*
- **suppressed** menses; from: *Puls* b7a.de

MENTAL EXERTION agg.: *(↗Exertion - mental)* cham ptk1 con ptk1 nat-c ptk1 *Pic-ac* ptk1

MERCURY moving up and down; sensation as from: | **Dorsal** region: phos bg2

MOISTURE:

○ - **Dorsal** region | **Scapulae**: lach bg2

MOLES: *(↗SKIN - Moles)* carc fb*

MOTION:
- **agg.**: aesc ptk1 agar ptk1 alum b4a.de* am-c b4.de* ambr b7.de* ang b7.de* apis b7a.de arg-met bg2 arn b7.de bufo bg2 calc bg2 canth b7.de* caps b7.de* carb-v b4.de* caust b4.de* cham b7a.de *Chin* b7.de* *Cimic* bg2 cina b7.de* cocc b7.de* colch b7.de* coloc b4.de* *Con* b4a.de dig b4.de* dros b7.de* *Dulc* b4a.de ferr b7.de* guaj b4.de* hell b7.de* hep b4.de* *Kali-bi* bg2 kali-c bg2* kreos b7a.de lach b7a.de led b7.de* lyc b4a.de m-aust b7.de* mang b4a.de mez b4.de* mur-ac ptk1 nat-c bg2 nit-ac b4.de* *Nux-v* b7.de* petr b4.de* *Phos* b4a.de psor bg2 puls b7.de* ran-b b7.de* rhus-t b7.de* ruta b7.de* samb b7a.de *Sars* b4a.de sel b7a.de seneg b4.de* squil b7.de* stann b4.de* stram b7.de* stront-c b4.de* sul-ac b4.de* sulph b4.de* thuj b4.de* *Verat* b7.de* zinc b4.de*
- **amel.**: aloe bg2 alum b4.de* am-m b7.de* ant-c b7a.de arg-met ptk1 arg-n ptk1 bar-c b4.de* bry b7.de* caust b4a.de chin b7.de* cina b7.de* coloc b4.de* *Dulc* ptk1 graph bg2 kali-bi bg2 kali-c b4.de* kali-n bg2 kreos b7a.de* mag-m b4.de* mez b4.de* nit-ac b4.de* olnd b7.de* ph-ac bg2* phos bg2 puls b7.de* rhod b4a.de rhus-t b7.de* sabad b7.de* staph b7.de* sul-ac b4.de* tab ptk1 vib bg2
- **arms**; of | **agg.**: ang bg2 apis b7a.de camph b7.de* chel b7.de* ferr b7a.de ign b7.de* ruta b7.de*
- **beginning** of | **agg.**: phos b4a.de sil b4.de* thuj b4.de*
- **body**; of | **agg.**: caust bg2
- **feet**; of | **agg.**: thuj bg2
- **fingers** agg.; of:

○ • **Dorsal** region | **Scapulae**: ran-b ptk1

- **hand** agg.; of | **Cervical** region: cimic ptk1
- **must** move | **without** amel.; but: lach ptk1 puls ptk1
- **slight**:

• **agg.** | **Coccyx**: tarent ptk1

MOUSE was running up the back; as if a: bry b7a.de *Sil* b4a.de *Sulph* k*

MOVEMENTS: | **clucking** movements | **left** side; on: ars h2

○ - **Sacral** region: cact bg2 cupr bg2 phos bg2

MURMURS:
- **respiratory**:

○ • **Scapula**; above the right | **rough** murmur: *(↗CHEST Murmurs)* tub jl2

NECK; pain in the (See Pain - cervical)

NECROSIS:

○ - **Vertebrae**: calc bro1 nat-m bro1 ph-ac bro1 sil bro1 stict bro1 syph bro1

○ • **Maxilla**; inferior: phos bro1

NODULES:

O - **Dorsal** region | **Shoulders**; between: mag-s ptk1

NUMBNESS: *(↗Asleep)* acon k* *Agar* k* bell bg1 berb k* bry bg3* calc *Calc-p* k* *Cocc* con bg1 cupr-ar dulc fd4.de helodr-cal knl2• kali-bi bg3* nat-sil fd3.de• nux-v ox-ac k* oxyt bro1* *Phos* bg1 phys plat bg3* pop-cand bg1 sec k* sep bg* sil k* vanil fd5.de

- **nap**; after: phos h2

O - **Cervical** region: berb bry bg1 castor-eq *Chel* k* dig hura hydrog srj2• merc-i-f par *Plat* k* rhus-t sacch-a fd2.de• tell vanil fd5.de xan c1

O · **Nape** of neck: dig bg2 merc-i-f bg2 petr bg2 plat b4.de* rhus-t b7.de* spig bg2 tell bg2

- **Coccyx**: berb **Plat** k*
  - · **menses**; during: plat
  - · **sitting** agg.: **Plat**
- **Dorsal** region: acon bg2 agar bg2 alum bg2 bell bg2 calc b4.de* lach bg2 ox-ac bg2 ph-ac bg2 phos bg2 plat b4a.de* sec b7a.de* thuj bg2

O · **Scapulae**: anac arg-met h1 bry ptk1 merc-i-f bg2

⁝ **right**: corian-s knl6•

⁝ **20** h: calc-caust c1

- **Lumbar** region: **Acon** k* apis ptk1 ars k* bell bg2 **Berb** k* bry bg2 calc bg2 carb-v k* cham bg2 dulc fd4.de frax bg1 gnaph bg2 graph bg1* **Kali-bi** bg2* lappa bg1* nux-m bg2 nux-v bg2 phos b4a.de* plat b4a.de* *Sil* k* spong k*
  - · **loss** of sensation: *Ars* bry con cupr-act kali-n zinc
    - ⁝ **morning** | **rising** agg.: *Nat-m*
    - ⁝ **evening**: alum mag-m
    - ⁝ **extending** to | **Lower** limbs: *Acon*
  - · **pain**; during (See Pain - lumbar - accompanied - numbness)
- **Part** lain on: calc
- **Sacrum**: berb *Calc-p* k* *Graph* k* ox-ac plat spong
  - · **sitting** agg.: plat

O · **Lower** limbs, and: *Calc-p* k* graph ptk1

- **Spine**:

▽ · **extending** to | **Downward**: phys ptk1

NURSING agg.; while: cham ptk1 crot-t ptk1 phos b4a.de puls ptk1 sulph ptk1

OBSTRUCTION; sensation of: | **Spine**; base of: plut-n srj7•

OPERATION; after: | **Lumbar** region: berb ptk1

OPISTHOTONOS: *(↗Spasmodic; Spasms; HEAD - Drawn; HEAD - Drawn - backward)* *Absin* k* acon k* agar amyg k* ang b2.de* ant-t bg2 apis *Ars* k* **Bell** k* berb both k* brach k* bry k* calc-p *Camph* k* *Canth* k* carb-an k* *Cham* k* *Chen-a* chin brm **Cic** k* cimic bg2 *Cina* k* clem b2.de* cocc b2.de* con b2.de* cor-r cori-r k* **Cupr** k* *Cupr-ar* k* dig k* dulc fd4.de glon k2 hydr-ac c1 **Hyos** k* hyper k* *Ign* k* iod bg2 *Ip* k* jasm a1 *Kali-br* hr1 *Lach* k* lat-m bnm6• led k* lyss hr1* med k* merc k2 *Morph* k* mygal mgm• nat-s k* *Nicot* bro1 nux-m a1* **Nux-v** k* oena k* **Op** k* petr k* phos k* *Phyt* k* *Plat* k* plb k* *Rhus-t* k* *Sec* k* *Stann* k* **Stram** k* **Stry** k* *Tab* k* ter k* *Verat-v* k* *Zinc* zinc-p k2

- **accompanied** by:
  - · **cholera** infantum (See RECTUM - Cholera - infantum - accompanied - opisthotonos)
  - · **convulsions**; tetanic (See GENERALS - Convulsions - tetanic - accompanied - opisthotonos)
  - · **vertigo** (See VERTIGO - Accompanied - opisthotonos)

O · **Abdomen**; cramping pain in (See ABDOMEN - Pain - cramping - accompanied - opisthotonos)

  - · **Masseter** muscles; cramping pain in the: cupr mtf11
- **coma**; with (See MIND - Coma - opisthotonos)
- **convulsions**; during epileptic: ars h2 *Cic* mrr1 stann h2
- **diarrhea** agg.; after: med ptk1 verat-v ptk1

OPPRESSION between scapulae: petr h2*

ORGASM:

O - **Neck**; nape of:

▽ · **extending** to:

⁝ **Forehead**; over top of head to:

⁝ **afternoon** | **motion** agg.: mang k*

OVERLIFTING (See Straining)

PAIN: abies-c oss4• abies-n abrom-a ks5 abrot bro1 acon k* adam skp7• **Aesc** k* *Aeth* *Agar* k* agath-a nl2• aids ↓ ail all-c ↓ all-s ↓ allox ↓ aloe **Alum** k* alum-p k2 alum-sil k2 *Alumn* am-c k* am-caust ↓ *Am-m* ambr ampe-qu ↓ anac anan *Androc* srj1• *Ang* k* anis ↓ ant-c ant-o ↓ ant-t k* *Apis* k* apoc ↓ aran *Arg-met* k* *Arg-n* k* arge-pl rwt5• arist-m br1 **Arn** k* ars ars-i ars-s-f ↓ arund ↓ asaf asar asc-t ↓ aster ↓ atp ↓ *Atro* *Aur* aur-m aur-s ↓ aza br1 bacls-7 pte1*• bad ↓ *Bamb-a* stb2.de• *Bapt* ↓ **Bar-c** k* bar-i ↓ bar-m ↓ bar-s k2 **Bell** k* bell-p ↓ bell-p-sp ↓ benz-ac k2 *Berb* k* beryl ↓ *Bism* *Bol-la* bond ↓ borx *Bov* ↓ brach brom brucel sa3• **Bry** k* but-ac ↓ buth-a ↓ cadm-met ↓ cain calad ↓ **Calc** k* calc-ar ↓ calc-caust c2 *Calc-f* ↓ calc-i ↓ calc-o-t ↓ **Calc-p** k* calc-s calc-sil k2 *Camph* *Cann-i* bro1 cann-s canth *Caps* carb-ac k* *Carb-an* *Carb-v* **Carbn-s** carc ↓ card-m *Cardios-h* rly4• *Carl* ↓ *Casc* ↓ cass a1 *Caul* k* *Caust* k* cench ↓ *Cham* k* *Chel* chen-a chin k* chinin-ar *Chinin-s* k* chir-fl ↓ chlor ↓ chord-umb rly4• chr-ac cic k* *Cimic* k* cina cinnb cit-ac ↓ clem cob k* coc-c k* *Cocc* k* cocc-s ↓ *Coff* ↓ *Colch* k* coli ↓ *Coloc* k* colum-p sze2• com ↓ *Con* conv ↓ cor-r corian-s knl6• corn ↓ corn-f ↓ cortiso ↓ cot ↓ crot-c sk4• *Crot-h* crot-t ↓ *Cub* cupr *Cupr-ar* ↓ cycl cypra-eg ↓ cystein-l rly4• daph ↓ des-ac ↓ dig ↓ digin ↓ dios *Dor* dream-p ↓ dros dulc k* dys pte1*• elaps elat ↓ eug ↓ euon ↓ **Eup-per** k* **Eup-pur** *Euph* euphr eupi br1 falco-pe ↓ *Ferr* k* ferr-ar ferr-i ↓ ferr-p fic-m gya1 fl-ac ↓ *Form* fuma-ac rly4• gad ↓ gaert pte1*• galeg c2 galeoc-c-h ↓ galla-q-r nl2• gamb k* gast ↓ *Gels* gent-l ↓ ger-i rly4• germ-met ↓ gins ↓ *Glon* ↓ glyc ↓ goss ↓ gran ↓ granit-m ↓ **Graph** k* grat *Gua* bro1 **Guaj** guare ↓ gymno haliae-lc srj5• ham bro1 hell helo ↓ helo-s ↓ *Helon* k* *Hep* hip-ac ↓ hippoc-k szs2 hom-xyz c2* hura br1 *Hydr* *Hydrog* srj2• hyos *Hyper* hyper-aet bta1• *Ign* ignis-alc ↓ ina-i mlk9.de ind k* inul c2 iod **Ip** *Ipom-p* irid-met srj5• iris ↓ jac-c ↓ junc-e c2 kali-ar *Kali-bi* k* kali-br ↓ **Kali-c** k* *Kali-i* kali-m k2* *Kali-n* kali-ox ↓ kali-p *Kali-s* kali-sil ↓ *Kalm* ketogl-ac ↓ kola ↓ kreos lac-ac ↓ **Lac-c** lac-d k2 lac-f ↓ lac-h htj1• lac-loxod-a ↓ *Lach* k* lachn ↓ lact lap-la sde8.de• lat-h ↓ lat-m bnm6• laur lavand-a ↓ *Led* lil-t k* lim ↓ lith-be ↓ lith-c lith-m ↓ *Lob* lob-s c2 loxo-lae bnm12• loxo-recl bnm10*• luf-op ↓ **Lyc** k* lycpr c2 lycps-v ↓ lyss mag-c *Mag-m* k* mag-p mag-s k* malar ↓ manc mand ↓ *Mang* ↓ mang-p ↓ *Med* k* melal-alt gya4 menis c2 mentho ↓ meph *Merc* k* *Merc-c* merc-i-f ↓ methyl br1 *Mez* k* mill ↓ mim-h ↓ mim-p skp7• mit ↓ mom-b bro1 morg-p pte1• *Morph* ↓ mosch ↓ mucs-nas rly4• **Mur-ac** *Murx* musca-d ↓ myric ↓ *Naja* nat-ar *Nat-c* k* **Nat-m** k* nat-ox rly4• nat-p nat-pyru rly4• **Nat-s** nat-sil ↓ neon srj5• nept-m ↓ nicc ↓ nicotam rly4• *Nit-ac* k* **Nux-m** **Nux-v** k* nymph c2 oena ol-an ol-j olib-sac wmh1 olnd ↓ op osm ↓ ost ↓ ox-ac k* ozone ↓ paeon ↓ pall **Par** paraf bro1 *Petr* k* petr-ra shn4• ph-ac k* **Phos** k* phys physala-p bnm7• phyt k* pic-ac br1* pieri-b mlk9.de pin-con oss2• pisc ↓ pitu-gl skp7• plac ↓ plac-s rly4• plat *Plb* plumbg ↓ pneu jl2 podo polyp-p ↓ polys sk4• positr ↓ prot pte1*• **Psor** k* ptel ↓ **Puls** k* puls-n ↓ pulx br1 *Rad-br* bro1 ran-a bro1 *Ran-b* k* ran-s ↓ raph ↓ rat rauw ↓ *Rhod* k* rhus-g ↓ *Rhus-r* **Rhus-t** k* rhus-v ↓ ribo rly4• rumx ↓ *Ruta* k* sabad sabal c2 sabin k* sal-fr ↓ *Samb* sang k* sanic ptk1 *Sarcol-ac* ↓ sarr k* sars scol ah1* *Sec* k* sel k* senec seneg **Sep** k* **Sil** k* sin-n ↓ sol c1 *Sol-ni* sol-t-ae ↓ solid ↓ *Spect* ↓ spig spong stann *Staph* k* staphycoc ↓ *Stel* bro1 *Still* ↓ stram streptoc ↓ *Stront-c* stroph-s ↓ stry bro1 suis-em ↓ suis-hep rly4• suis-pan ↓ *Sul-ac* sul-i ↓ **Sulph** k* suprar rly4• syc pte1*• symph ↓ tab c2 taosc iwa1• tarax tarent k* tax ↓ tell bro1* tep *Ter* c2 tere-la ↓ tetox pin2• teucr ↓ ther bro1 thioc-ac ↓ thuj thymol ↓ thyr c2 *Tril-p* ↓ trios c2* tritic-vg fd5.de *Tub* jl2 tung-met ↓ *Upa* bro1 uran-n br1 urol-h rwt• ust vac ↓ valer vanil fd5.de vario c2* verat verat-v ↓ verb ↓ *Vero-o* rly3• *Vib* ↓ viol-t vip ↓ visc ↓ wye bro1 x-ray ↓ xero bro1 yuc ↓ *Zinc* k* zinc-m ↓ zinc-p k2 zing [*Buteo-j* sej6 zirc-met stj2]

- **alternating** sides: bamb-a stb2.de• hydrog srj2•
- **right**: *Agath-a* ↓ arge-pl rwt5• asaf ↓ bad ↓ bar-c ↓ bell ↓ benz-ac ↓ blatta-a ↓ carb-v ↓ carc ↓ cupr ↓ dios ↓ fum ↓ kali-s ↓ lyc ↓ melal-alt gya4 merc-i-f ↓ pert-vc vk9 plat ↓ sep ↓ sil ↓ stann ↓ *Thuj* ↓ vanil ↓ [*Spect* dfg1]
  - · **aching**: asaf bar-c bell benz-ac blatta-a dios k* lyc merc-i-f
  - · **cutting** pain: fum rly1*•
  - · **digging** pain: *Agath-a* nl2• stann h2 *Thuj*
    - ⁝ **finger**; as from a: *Agath-a* nl2•
  - · **drawing** pain: bad carb-v carc fd2.de• cupr sep
  - · **pinching** pain: sil h2
  - · **pressing** pain: kali-s fd4.de lyc h2
  - · **sprained**; as if: bell h1
  - · **stitching** pain: plat h2 stann h2 vanil fd5.de

- **left**: aids nl2• aq-mar skp7• bism↓ carb-an↓ carb-v↓ cocc↓ con↓ cupr↓ dendr-pol sk4• dulc fd4.de galeoc-c-h gms1• hydroph rsj6• ina-i mlk9.de limen-b-c hrn2* lyc↓ mez↓ mur-ac↓ nat-m↓ olib-sac↓ petr↓ plat↓ rhod↓ ruta fd4.de spong fd4.de stann↓ stry↓ tarent↓ til↓ tritic-vg fd5.de
  - • **aching**: bism carb-an cocc galeoc-c-h gms1• mez tarent
  - • **burning**: galeoc-c-h gms1•
  - • **cramping**: olib-sac wmh1
  - • **cutting** pain: cupr stry
  - • **drawing** pain: carb-v h2 cupr h2 olib-sac wmh1 rhod til
  - • **pressing** pain: mur-ac h2 nat-m h2
  - • **sore**: galeoc-c-h gms1• petr h2 plat h2
  - • **sprained**; as if: con h2 lyc h2
  - • **stitching** pain: dulc fd4.de galeoc-c-h gms1• mur-ac h2 plat h2 stann h2
  - ▽ • **extending** to | **right**: bell bg1
- **daytime**: abrom-a ks5 agar↓ *Camph* nicc↓ tritic-vg fd5.de
  - • **stitching** pain: agar nicc
- **morning**: *Agar* k* all-s arge-pl rwt5• aur aur-s k2 berb k* borx bry k* calc-p canth caust h2 cimic cinnb conv bro1 crot-c sk4• dios dros dulc fd4.de equis-h eug euph eupi falco-pe nl2• galeoc-c-h↓ hep hydrog↓ ign kali-c k* kali-p↓ limest-b↓ mag-c↓ mag-m↓ mag-s mez↓ naja nat-m bro1 nat-p↓ nat-sil↓ *Nux-v* k* ox-ac↓ ozone↓ pant-ac rly4• pert-vc vk9 petr bro1 petr-ra shn4• phyt k* podo puls *Ran-b* rhod **Rhus-t** sne ruta k* sel bro1 spong fd4.de *Staph* bro1 stront-c stry↓ sulph h2 symph fd3.de• thuj tritic-vg fd5.de vanil fd5.de verat↓ zinc
  - • **aching**: berb dios k* equis-h eug k* euph eupi k* galeoc-c-h gms1• limest-b es1• mag-s phyt rhod k* thuj
  - • **bed** agg.; in: ang berb carb-v dulc fd4.de euph hep kali-n mag-s nat-m nit-ac *Petr* podo fd3.de• puls rat rhod *Ruta* sel rsj9• staph symph fd3.de• tritic-vg fd5.de vanil fd5.de
    - ⁝ **aching**: ang berb euph kali-n mag-s petr
    - ⁝ **drawing** pain: hep rhod
    - ⁝ **sore**: nat-m h2
    - ⁝ **stretching** agg.: plac rzf5•
  - • **bending** forward agg.:
    - ⁝ **bed**; in: puls↓
      - : **stitching** pain: puls
  - • **burning**: mag-m petr-ra shn4• vanil fd5.de zinc
  - • **coition**, by rest agg., by motion amel.; after: mag-m↓
    - ⁝ **burning**: mag-m
  - • **cutting** pain: all-s
  - • **drawing** pain: calc-p *Cimic* dulc fd4.de hep nat-sil fd3.de• ruta fd4.de zinc
  - • **lameness**: dios k*
  - • **motion**:
    - ⁝ **amel.**: am-m↓
      - : **sore**: am-m
  - • **pressing** pain: dulc fd4.de petr h2 ruta fd4.de verat h1
  - • **rising**:
    - ⁝ **after**:
      - : **agg.**: am-m↓ *Hep*↓
        - . **drawing** pain: *Hep*
        - . **tearing** pain: am-m
      - : **amel.**: nat-m↓ *Rat*↓
        - . **sore**: nat-m h2 *Rat*
    - ⁝ **agg.**: am-m calad caust cedr dream-p sdj1• graph *Hep Lyc Nat-m* nit-ac ran-b spong fd4.de stann sul-ac k2 sulph thuj vanil fd5.de verat
      - : **aching**: caust k* cedr k* graph k* hep k* ran-b k*
      - : **lameness**: nat-m
      - : **motion** amel.: rat↓
        - . **burning**: rat
      - : **sore**: am-m calad nat-m stann thuj
    - ⁝ **amel.**: adam skp7• *Lach* nat-c nat-m nit-ac
      - : **stitching** pain: nat-c h2
    - ⁝ **bed**; from:
      - : **after**:
        - . **amel.**: nat-m↓

Pain – morning – rising – bed; from – **after** – **amel.**: ...
pressing pain: nat-m

  - • **sore**: *Dros* kali-p fd1.de• ox-ac ozone sde2• symph fd3.de•
  - • **stitching** pain: borx bry hydrog srj2• nat-p spong fd4.de vanil fd5.de
  - • **tearing** pain: *Canth* kali-c mag-c h2 mez puls stry
  - • **waking**; on: aeth *Agar* apoc↓ arg-met berb calc-p cham chel chion sne dream-p sdj1• dulc fd4.de grat kali-bi kola stb3• lac-c *Lach* limen-b-c hrn2* mag-m mag-s myric nat-m nit-ac ozone↓ polys sk4• ptel ran-b ruta fd4.de spong fd4.de tung-met bdx1• urol-h rwt• vanil fd5.de x-ray sp1
    - ⁝ **aching**: berb cham k* ptel
    - ⁝ **pressing** pain: nit-ac h2
    - ⁝ **sore**: apoc a2* arg-met k* grat mag-m k* mag-s k* ozone sde2•
- **forenoon**: ars bamb-a↓ *Cham* equis-h kali-bi↓ kola stb3• myric↓ *Nat-m* nat-s ptel ruta fd4.de spong fd4.de tritic-vg fd5.de vanil fd5.de
  - • **10** h: am-m
    - ⁝ **aching**: am-m
  - • **11** h: pitu-gl skp7•
    - ⁝ **15** h; until: pitu-gl skp7•
  - • **aching**: equis-h myric a1 ptel k*
  - • **burning**: kali-bi
  - • **drawing** pain: ars bamb-a stb2.de•
  - • **pressing** pain: nat-m
  - • **stitching** pain: cham ruta fd4.de tritic-vg fd5.de
- **noon**: dios dulc fd4.de eupi rhus-t ruta fd4.de spong fd4.de
  - • **aching**: dios k* eupi k* rhus-t k*
  - • **burning**: rhus-t
- **afternoon**: abrot agar bov canth caust cham chel dream-p sdj1• dulc fd4.de equis-h gaba↓ glon hyos lyc↓ mag-c mag-m myric↓ nicc oci-sa sk4• ozone↓ pall plb ptel rumx ruta *Sep* spong fd4.de stry↓ tritic-vg fd5.de vanil fd5.de zinc zing
  - • **2.30** h: ozone↓
    - ⁝ **stitching** pain: ozone sde2•
  - • **17** h; after: abrom-a ks5
  - • **17.30** h: aq-mar skp7•
  - • **aching**: abrot k* agar cham k* chel k* equis-h gaba sa3• glon k* hyos k* myric a1 pall k* plb ptel k* rumx sep k* zing k*
  - • **stitching** pain: dulc fd4.de lyc nicc ozone sde2• plb ruta fd4.de spong fd4.de stry vanil fd5.de
- **evening**: acon agar alumn am-m sne aq-pet sne *Ars* ars-s-f k2 bar-c sne bart sne borx↓ brach sne bry sne *Calc-p* calc-s sne cann-s sne carb-v cham chel cist cocc coloc cupr-ar *Dios* sne dream-p sdj1• dulc fd4.de erig sne ferr sne ferr-i gels glon sne graph h2 ham fd3.de• hell sne helo sne hipp sne iris sne kali-ar kali-bi sne kali-n *Kali-s Kalm Lach* lact sne led lil-t luna sne *Lyc* lycps-v sne mag-c mag-m meny sne mez sne mur-ac sne myric sne *Naja* nat-ar nat-c↓ nat-m nat-s nit-ac nux-m sne nux-v ox-ac sne petr sne petr-ra shn4• phys pic-ac sne psor puls sne rad-br sne *Rhus-t* rumx sne ruta samars sne sarr seneg sne *Sep* sin-n spong fd4.de still sne stront-c sne stroph-h sne stry sne *Sulph* tanac sne ter thuj tritic-vg fd5.de valer sne vanil fd5.de vario sne vib sne vichy-g sne viol-o sne xan sne zing
  - • **21-0** h: usn↓
    - ⁝ **stitching** pain: usn a2
  - • **aching**: acon k* agar k* alumn *Ars* brach a1 cham cist ferr-i k* kali-s led lil-t k* phys sarr
  - • **bed** agg.; in: sulph↓
    - ⁝ **tearing** pain: sulph
  - • **cutting** pain: nat-m nat-s
  - • **drawing** pain: agar *Calc-p* carb-v chel *Lach* lyc nit-ac rhus-t ruta fd4.de
  - • **exertion**; after:
    - ⁝ **amel.**: ruta↓
      - : **aching**: ruta
  - • **lameness**: cupr-ar
  - • **lying** down agg.; after: thuj h1
  - • **sore**: petr-ra shn4• psor vanil fd5.de

- **stitching** pain: borx cham lach nat-c h2* rhus-t ruta fd4.de spong fd4.de stront-c vanil fd5.de
- **sunset** to sunrise; from: **Syph**

\- **night**: abrot ptk acon agar aloe k* *Am-m* ang apis arg-met *Arg-n* *Ars* ars-s-f k2 *Berb* bry calc k* calc-s calc-sil k2 carb-an carb-v carbn-s *Cham* chel cinnb crot-c sk4• dendr-pol sk4• *Dulc* *Ferr* ferr-act ferr-ar k2 ferr-i ferr-p hell *Helon* hep ign ina-i mlk9.de **Kali-c** sne kali-i kali-n *Kalm* *Kreos* lil-t loxo-recl knl4• lyc k* lycps-v ↓ *Mag-c* mag-m mag-s mang *Merc* k* **Merc-c** mez bro1 morg-p pte1*• *Naja* *Nat-ar* *Nat-c* *Nat-m* k* nat-p *Nat-s* *Nit-ac* *Nux-v* k* ph-ac phos phys phyt k2 plb podo puls ↓ rhod ruta fd4.de sars senec *Sil* spong fd4.de staph h1* **Sulph** syc pte1*• symph fd3.de• **Syph** k* tab tritic-vg fd5.de visc bro1

- **3-4 h**: **Nux-v** ↓
  - **sore**: **Nux-v**
- **midnight**: caust ↓
  - **before**: kalm
    - **23-0 h**: *Am-m* k*
      - **aching**: *Am-m*
  - **after**: mag-s
    - **3 h**: **Kali-c** kali-n nat-c tub jl2
      - **bed**; driving out of: **Kali-c**
      - **must** get up and walk: **Kali-c** ↓
        - **stitching** pain: **Kali-c**
      - **rising**:
        - **amel.**: nat-c ↓
          - **burning**: nat-c
    - **4 h**: ang bg1 *Nux-v* ruta staph bg1
      - **bed**; driving out of: *Nux-v*
      - **waking**; on: calc-p ↓ chel ↓
        - **drawing** pain: calc-p chel
    - **spasmodic** aching, when inspiring agg.: *Nit-ac* ↓
      - **aching**: *Nit-ac*
  - **cutting** pain: caust h2
  - **waking** him or her from sleep: *Chinin-s* nat-c
  - **waking**; on: nat-c ↓
    - **sore**: nat-c
- **aching**: agar k* aloe *Am-m* k* *Arg-n* k* berb helon lycps-v mag-c k* mag-m k* nat-c k* phys k* senec k* **Sulph** k*
- **bed**:
  - **driving** out of bed: **Kali-c** mrr1
  - **in** bed:
    - **agg.**: abrom-a ks5 loxo-recl knl4• *Nux-v* mrr1
      - **motion** amel.: mag-c ↓
        - **sore**: mag-c
- **burning**: dulc fd4.de helon *Ph-ac* spong fd4.de
- **drawing** pain: ars chel hep nat-m ruta fd4.de
- **jerking** pain: staph h1
- **menses**; during: am-m ↓
  - **aching**: am-m
- **motion**:
  - **must** move:
    - **side** to side; from: mag-s ↓
      - **tearing** pain: mag-s c1
- **sleep** agg.; after: am-m ↓
  - **aching**: am-m k*
- **sore**: *Am-m* *Berb* cham mag-c h2 mag-m *Nat-c*
- **stitching** pain: apis ars bry dulc nat-c nit-ac phos puls
- **tearing** pain: cinnb mag-s c1 nit-ac ph-ac rhod
- **turning** frequently amel.: nat-m ↓
  - **drawing** pain: nat-m

\- **abortion**; during threatening: caul c1* vib hr1*

\- **accompanied** by:

- **constipation** (See RECTUM - Constipation - accompanied - back)
- **heat**: limen-b-c hrn2•

\- **accompanied** by: ...

- **hemorrhoids** (See RECTUM - Hemorrhoids - accompanied - back)
- **leukorrhea** (See FEMALE - Leukorrhea - accompanied - back)
- **metrorrhagia** (See FEMALE - Metrorrhagia - accompanied - back)
- **nausea**: coloc k* nux-v ptk phys k* zing k*
- **palpitations**: tub ptk1
- **pollutions**; nightly: aur bro1 calc bro1 calc-p bro1 *Chin* bro1 **Cob** bro1* con bro1 cupr bro1 dam bro1 dig bro1 *Dios* bro1 ery-a bro1 form bro1 gels bro1 *Kali-c* bro1 lyc bro1 med bro1 nat-p bro1 *Nux-v* bro1 *Ph-ac* bro1 *Pic-ac* bro1 sars bro1 sel bro1 *Staph* bro1 *Sulph* bro1 zinc bro1
- **respiration**; impeded (See RESPIRATION - Impeded - pain - back)
- **salivation**: cinnm kr1*
- **urination**; painful (See BLADDER - Urination - dysuria - painful - accompanied - back)
- **urine**:
  - **bloody**: kali-bi ptk1
  - **burning**: ant-c ptk1
- **vomiting** (See STOMACH - Vomiting - accompanied - back)
- ○ **Abdomen**:
  - **pain**: neon srj5• sars ↓
    - **cramping**: sars ptk1
- **Head**:
  - **complaints** (See HEAD - Complaints - accompanied - back)
  - **pain** in (See HEAD - Pain - accompanied - back)
- **Kidneys**; congestion of (See KIDNEYS - Congestion - accompanied - back)
- **Stomach**; complaints of (See STOMACH - Complaints - accompanied - back - pain)
- **Testes**; pain in (See testes; MALE GENITALIA/SEX - Pain - testes - accompanied - back)
- **Uterus**:
  - **complaints** of (See FEMALE - Complaints - uterus - accompanied - back)
  - **pain** (See FEMALE - Pain - uterus - accompanied - back)

\- **aching**: abrot k* *Aesc* k* aeth k* agar k* agath-a nl2• aids nl2• ail k* all-s allox sp1 *Aloe* alum am-c am-caust a1 am-m ant-c k* apis apoc k* *Arg-n* *Ars* k* *Asaf* k* asc-t k* atp rly4• aur-m bamb-a stb2.de• *Bapt* k* bar-c k* bar-m k* bar-s k2 **Bell** k* benz-ac *Berb* k* *Bism* k* bol-la bond a1 brach a1 **Bry** cadm-met sp1 calad *Calc* k* calc-f calc-p k* calc-s calc-sil k2 *Cann-i* k* cann-s canth k* carb-ac k* *Carb-an* *Carbn-s* *Carl* a1 *Casc* cass a1 caul k* caust cham k* chel k* chinin-s cimic k* cinnb k* cit-ac rly4• *Cob* k* coc-c k* cocc colch k* coli rly4• com k* *Con* k* corn a1 cortiso sp1 cot a1* crot-t k* *Cupr-ar* k* des-ac rbp6 dig k* digin a1 dios k* elaps eug k* **Eup-per** k* **Eup-pur** euph a1 eupi k* falco-pe nl2• ferr ferr-ar ferr-i k* ferr-p galeoc-c-h gms1• gast a1 *Gels* gent-l a1 ger-i rly4• goss a1 gran a1 granit-m es1• **Graph** k* ham k* hell k* helon k* hippoc-k szs2 hyos k* hyper k* ind k* **Ip** iris jac-c a1 kali-ar *Kali-bi* k* *Kali-c* k* kali-m k2 kali-n k* kali-ox a1 *Kali-s* *Kalm* k* ketogl-ac rly4• kreos k* lac-ac k* lac-c lach k* lat-h bnm5• laur k* *Lil-t* k* lim a1 lith-m a1 lob lob-s a1 lyc lycps-v *Lyss* k* med menis a1 meph k* merc-i-f k* mez k* mit a1 *Morph* k* mucs-nas rly4• **Mur-ac** myric a1 nat-ar *Nat-c* k* **Nat-m** k* nat-ox rly4• *Nat-p* nit-ac **Nux-v** k* olnd op k* osm k* ost a1 ox-ac k* petr *Phos* k* phys k* phyt k2 *Pic-ac* k* plb k* plumbg a1 polyp-p a1 polys sk4• positr nl2• *Psor* k* ptel k* **Puls** k* **Ran-b** k* raph k* rauw sp1 rhod k* rhus-g a1 *Rhus-t* rhus-v k* ribo rly4• rumx *Ruta* sabin sal-fr sle1• samb a1 sang k* sarcol-ac sp1 *Sec* k* seneg k* **Sep** k* *Sil* k* sin-n k* sol-t-ae a1 stront-c stroph-s sp1 stry k* suis-pan rly4• sul-ac k* *Sulph* k* suprar rly4• taosc iwa1• tarent k* **Tell** k* *Ter* k* tere-la rly4• urol-h rwt• ust a1 vac a1 verat a1 verat-v a1 vip a1 yuc a1 zinc k2 zinc-m a1 zing a1 [bell-p-sp dcm1 *Buteo-j* sej6 *Spect* dfg1]

- **paroxysmal**: asaf k* phos

\- **acids**, after: *Lach*

- **air**; draft of:
  - **every**: calc-p k2* dulc fd4.de nat-sil fd3.de• *Nux-v* sumb bg1 verat
    - **drawing** pain: verat
- **air**; in open:
  - **agg.**: *Merc*↓ *Nux-v*↓
    - **aching**: *Nux-v* k*
    - **sore**: *Merc*
  - **amel.**: acon fic-m gya1 nux-v *Vib*
- **alternating** with:
  - **leukorrhea**: eupi pd
  - ○ **Abdomen**; pain in: vario br1
  - **Chest**; oppression of (See CHEST - Oppression - alternating - back)
  - **Head**; pain in (See HEAD - Pain - alternating - back)
- **apyrexia**, during: arn ars *Calc* caps cham chin cina ign *Nat-m* nit-ac nux-v petr samb sep sil spig stram thuj verat k*
- **arthritic**: *Calc-f* mrr1
  - **motion** | **amel.**: calc-f mrr1 rhus-t mrr1
  - ○ **Sacroiliac** symphyses: **Aesc** mrr1 morg-p fmm1•
  - **Spine**: morg-p fmm1•
- **ascending** stairs agg.: alum↓
  - **stitching** pain: alum
- **ascends** (See extending - upward)
- **bed**, confines him to: ars-s-f↓
  - **aching**: ars-s-f
- **bending**:
  - **agg.**: agar↓ arge-pl rwt5•
    - **broken**; as if: agar k2
  - **amel.**: petr↓
    - **drawing** pain: petr
  - **backward**:
    - **agg.**: arg-met bar-c *Calc* *Calc-p* *Chel* *Cimic* con dios dulc fd4.de eug sne hydrog srj2• kali-c lam mang plat puls sabin c1 sel stann
      - **drawing** pain: calc-p **Cimic**
      - **jerking** pain | **sticking**: chel
      - **tearing** pain: *Chel*
    - **amel.**: abrom-a ks5 acon aeth am-m bell cycl cypra-eg sde6.de• dulc fd4.de eupi fl-ac hura lach petr *Plb* hr1 puls rhus-t k* sabad sabin sil
      - **aching**: aeth k* eupi a1
      - **pulsating** pain: abrom-a ks5
      - **stitching** pain: abrom-a ks5
  - **forward**:
    - **agg.**: abrom-a ks5 cadm-met sp1 camph↓ dulc fd4.de ham fd3.de• nat-sil fd3.de• pert-vc vk9 petr-ra shn4• *Pic-ac* pieri-b mlk9.de ruta fd4.de sep bg1 spong fd4.de tritic-vg fd5.de vanil fd5.de
      - **pulsating** pain: abrom-a ks5
      - **stitching** pain: abrom-a ks5 vanil fd5.de
      - **tearing** pain: camph
    - **amel.**: chel des-ac rbp6 eug sne hydrog srj2• kali-c h2 lob bro1 meny nat-ar ph-ac *Plb* hr1 puls sang sec sep sulph fs thuj
    - **must** bend forward: *Caps* hr1
  - **head**:
    - **forward** | **agg.**: beryl sp1*
  - **left**; to | **agg.**: limen-b-c hrn2•
- **blow**; pain as from a: psor jl2 [tax jsj7]
- **boring** pain: *(↗digging)* acon agar *Agath-a* nl2• ang asaf bar-c *Bism* brom carb-ac cocc dulc fd4.de *Ham* kola stb3• laur *Lyc* mag-p nat-c psor ruta fd4.de thuj
  - **gimlet**; as with a: *Lyc*
- **break**; as if it would: *Aesc* k* aeth bro1 allox sp1 *Alumn* am-m bro1 **Bell** k* bry k2 calc-o-t bro1 *Camph* sne cann-i bro1 cham bro1 chel k* cocc cortiso tpw7* dulc bro1 *Eup-per* bro1 eupi bro1 falco-pe nl2• graph bro1 *Ham* bro1 kali-bi bro1 *Kali-c* kalm k* kola stb3• kreos k* *Nat-m* k* *Nux-v* ol-an bro1 ozone sde2• phos c1* pic-ac c1 plat bro1 *Puls* bro1 *Rhus-t* bro1 sanic bro1 *Sarcol-ac* bro1 seneg bro1 sil bro1 *Tril-p* bro1 vario
  - **accompanied** by | **hemorrhoids**: bell ptk1
- **break** open; as if bones would: *Sabin* mrr1
- **breathing**:
  - **agg.**: acon aesc alum alumn *Am-m* androc srj1• apis arn asar *Aur* aur-ar k2 aur-s k2 bell-p sp1 berb *Bry* sne calc cann-s carb-an carb-v carbn-s cham chel cinnb **Coloc** k* conv *Cop* cupr cupr-ar dig dulc inul kali-bi *Kali-c* kali-m k2 kali-n kali-p kali-s kalm led lob lyc↓ merc mur-ac nat-ar nat-c nat-m nat-p↓ nux-v par petr prun *Psor* ptel puls raph ruta sabin sal-fr sle1• sang k* sars seneg *Sep* spig spong fd4.de stann *Sulph* thuj tritic-vg fd5.de vanil fd5.de
    - **aching**: inul raph
    - **stitching** pain: am-m arn berb *Calc* lyc *Merc* nat-m nat-p petr hr1 psor k* spig hr1 *Sulph*
  - **arresting** breathing: cann-s↓
    - **aching**: cann-s
  - **deep**:
    - **agg.**: hippoc-k↓ nat-c↓ sars h2 vanil fd5.de
      - **aching**: hippoc-k szs2 nat-c
- **broken**; as if: agar arn k* *Bell* bg1* *Camph* sne chel c1 cina cocc bg1 conv corn-f br1 **Eup-per** k* ferr-i k2 ham bg3* ip k2 *Kali-c* k* lyc bg3* mag-c c1 mag-s pd* merc *Nat-m* k* *Nux-v* petr-ra shn4• **Phos** k* plat ruta senec ptk1 spong fd4.de verat
- **bruised** (See sore)
- **burning**: acon *Agar* agath-a nl2• alum bg3* alum-sil k2 alumn am-c ant-t apis arn **Ars** k* ars-s-f k2 asaf asar aur-m k* aur-s bamb-a stb2.de• bapt bg3 *Bar-c* bell berb k* *Bism* borx bry calc calc-f bro1 cann-i *Carb-an* k* carb-v carbn-s carl chel chr-ac clem coloc com cupr daph dulc galeoc-c-h gms1• *Glon* helo bro1 helo-s rwt2• helon k* hyper kali-ar k2 kali-bi *Kali-c* kali-i kali-m k2 kali-n *Kali-p* k* kali-s *Kalm* *Kreos* lac-d k2 *Lach* lachn lil-t lob *Lyc* k* lyss mag-c mag-m *Med* k* *Merc* mez mur-ac naja nat-sil fd3.de• nit-ac k* nux-m *Nux-v* olnd *Ph-ac* **Phos** k* *Pic-ac* k* rhus-t rumx ruta fd4.de sec bg3 sel seneg *Sep* k* *Sil* spong fd4.de streptoc rly4• **Sulph** ter bro1 *Thuj* tritic-vg fd5.de ust bro1 vanil fd5.de verat xero bro1 *Zinc* zinc-p k2 [spect dfg1]
  - **sparks**; as from: *(↗FEVER - Burning - sparks)* sulph mna
- **bursting** pain: malar jl2
- **carrying** | **agg.**:
  - **basket**; a: phos↓
    - **aching**: phos k*
  - **amel.**: galeoc-c-h gms1•
- **chill**:
  - **before**: **Aesc** aran *Ars* bry carb-v daph *Dios* *Eup-per* k* eup-pur *Ip* **Podo** rhus-t
    - **aching**: carb-v daph *Dios* **Eup-per** ip **Podo** rhus-t
  - **during**: ant-t apis *Arn* k* *Ars* k* ars-s-f k2 *Bell* k* **Bol-la** buth-a sp1 calc k* *Caps* k* carb-v carbn-s caust k* *Cham* k* chin k* chinin-ar **Chinin-s** cocc bg2 elat *Eup-per* k* gamb gels bg2* hep b4a.de* hyos k* ign k* *Ip* lac-ac lach k* lyc k* mosch myric *Nat-m* k* **Nux-v** k* phos k* podo k* *Puls* k* rhus-t bg2 sang sep k* sil bg2 sulph k* verat k* zinc zinc-p k2
    - **aching**: *Ant-t* *Eup-per* *Ip*
    - **drawing** pain: lyc h2 *Puls*
    - **sore**: cham h1
    - **extending** to | **Occiput** and vertex: **Puls**
  - **with**: caps↓ sil↓
    - **pressing** pain: sil h2
    - **tearing** pain: caps hr1 sil h2
- **clawing** pain: arg-n
- **coffee** agg.: *Cham*
  - **aching**: cham
- **coition**; after: cann-i k* cob bg1 kali-c bro1 mag-m bg2 merc↓ **Nit-ac** k* *Sabal*
  - **burning**: *Mag-m* k* merc ptk1
  - **men**; in: mag-m↓
    - **sore**: mag-m pd
- **cold**:
  - **agg.**: ran-b mrr1
  - **air**:
    - **agg.**: acon bro1 agar bacls-7 fmm1• bar-c *Bry* bro1 *Dulc* merc nit-ac *Nux-v* *Rhod* bro1 *Rhus-t* sabad sep sulph bro1 tritic-vg fd5.de
    - **amel.**: **Kali-s**

• **air – amel.**: ...
⁝ **aching**: kali-s
• **washing**:
⁝ **amel.**: vesp ↓
⁝ **aching**: vesp k*
- **cold**; after taking a: *Dulc* mag-p nit-ac sars
• **lameness**: **Dulc**
- **cold** agg.; after becoming: nit-ac ↓ sacch-a ↓
• **aching**: nit-ac sacch-a fd2.de•
- **cold**, during perspiration; on exposure to: *Dulc* ↓
• **stitching** pain: *Dulc*
- **compressed**; as if: con k* nat-pyru rly4• ruta fd4.de tritic-vg fd5.de
- **constant**: ribo rly4•
○ • **Lumbar** region:
⁝ **afternoon**: hip-ac sp1
⁝ **evening**: hip-ac sp1
• **Lumbosacral** region:
⁝ **standing** agg.: but-ac sp1
⁝ **extending** to | **Hips**: but-ac sp1
- **constricting** pain: bamb-a stb2.de•
- **constringing** (See contracting)
- **contracted**; as if: sal-fr sle1•
- **contracting**: *Bry* canth cham cocc dulc fd4.de *Graph* **Guaj** kali-c h2 kali-s fd4.de mag-m mez *Nux-v* ruta fd4.de sabad vanil fd5.de viol-t
- **convulsions**; with: acon
- **coryza**; during: kali-c b4.de*
- **cough** agg.; during: *Acon* *Am-c* am arund **Bell** bell-p ↓ **Bry** *Calc* calc-s *Caps* carb-an *Carb-v* ↓ chin chinin-s cocc cor-r dulc ↓ hydrog srj2• *Kali-bi* k* kali-c kali-n kreos *Merc* nat-c b4a.de nat-m k2 *Nit-ac* ph-ac phos puls pyrog ↓ rhus-t rumx seneg *Sep* stram sulph tell k* tub c1
• **aching**: am-c kali-n k* merc puls sep
• **stitching** pain: *Acon* k* am-c tl1 bell-p sp1 **Bry** *Caps* *Carb-v* b4a.de chin k* dulc fd4.de kali-bi kali-c *Merc* k* nit-ac puls k* pyrog k2 *Sep* k*
- **cramping**: *(↗Cramp; Spasmodic)* allox sp1 *Arg-n* bamb-a stb2.de• bell k* bry buth-a sp1 calad calc-o-t bro1 chin k* chir-fl bnm4• cimic bro1 coli rly4• *Coloc* bro1 con dulc fd4.de euph *Euphr* graph bro1 iris bro1 kali-s fd4.de lac-f wza1• lac-loxod-a hm2• lyc *Mag-p* k* mand rsj7• mez h2 nit-ac nux-v petr a1 scol ah1 sep k* tritic-vg fd5.de vanil fd5.de viol-t x-ray sp1
• **paroxysmal**: lyc h2
- **crossing** legs agg.: rhus-t bg1
- **cutting** pain: aesc tl1 agath-a nl2• ail *Alum* alum-p k2 *Arg-n* aur aur-m *Bell* berb mrr1 calc *Calc-p* canth caust *Coloc* *Con* cupr elaps *Eup-pur* fic-m gya1 *Gels* granit-m es1• graph guaj guare k* helon hydrog srj2• hyper ign ignis-alc es2• iod *Kali-bi* *Lith-c* mag-p mand rsj7• **Nat-m** *Nat-s* nux-v ozone sde2• petr plat sars seneg sep sil staph stry zinc bg1
• **upward**: *Coloc*
- **dampness** | **agg.**: bacls-7 fmm1•
- **delivery**:
• **after**: *Hyper* ↓ kali-c bro1
⁝ **aching**: *Hyper*
• **during**: bell ↓ *Caust* k* cocc coff **Gels** **Kali-c** k* *Nux-v* *Petr* **Puls** k* sabin mrr1
⁝ **break**; as if it would: bell bg2
- **descends**: acon *Aeth* alum am-c chel cimic cina cocc con cur elaps ferr-s *Glon* kali-bi *Kali-c* *Kalm* lil-t mag-c mang merc nat-m nat-s *Nux-m* nux-v ox-ac phys *Phyt* *Pic-ac* podo psor rat sang sep thuj ust zing
• **delivery**; during: *Nux-v*
- **diarrhea** agg.; after: bamb-a stb2.de•
• **cramping**: bamb-a stb2.de•
- **digging** pain: *(↗boring)* acon *Agath-a* nl2• *Dulc* sep k* *Thuj*
• **splinter**; as from a: agar
- **dinner**; after: agar cob indg phel phos rat ↓ sep sulph
• **aching**: agar k* cob k*
• **drawing** pain: rat
• **gnawing** pain: sep
- **dislocated**; as if:
• **accompanied** by | **respiration**; impeded (See RESPIRATION - Impeded - pain - back - dislocated)
- **dragging**: agar calc canth dream-p sdj1• kali-s fd4.de nat-p k2 tritic-vg fd5.de
- **drawing** pain: *Agar* *Alum* am-c ambr anac bro1 *Ang* ant-t arg-n *Ars* ars-s-f k2 aster aur bad *Bamb-a* stb2.de• bar-c bell bol-la *Bry* calc-p calc-s *Canth* *Caps* *Carb-an* *Carb-v* k* carc fd2.de• **Card-m** k* caust h2* *Cham* k* *Chel* *Chin* **Cimic** k* cina coc-c cocc *Colch* con crot-c crot-h crot-t cupr cycl dig dros dulc eupi *Graph* *Guaj* haliae-lc srj5• *Hep* *Hyper* ign kali-ar k2 kali-bi *Kali-c* k* kali-p kali-s kalm *Lach* lact *Lil-t* *Lyc* k* med k2 *Merc* mez mill mosch nat-ar nat-c *Nat-m* nat-p nat-sil fd3.de• **Nux-v** k* op ox-ac k2 ozone sde2• *Petr* *Phos* phyt k2 pic-ac psor *Puls* rat rhod rhus-r rhus-t k* ruta sabad *Sabin* bro1 sang seneg spong fd4.de stann stram k* *Stront-c* sul-ac *Sulph* k* ter teucr *Thuj* tritic-vg fd5.de valer vanil fd5.de verat viol-t zinc zinc-p k2 zing
• **downward**: ars h2 bry con h2 merc rhus-t a1
• **paroxysmal**: nat-c nit-ac h2
• **upward**: ars h2 lach nat-m
- **drinking** agg.: allox ↓ chin
• **cutting** pain: allox sp1
• **stitching** pain: chin
- **dull** pain: abies-n bro1 aesc bro1* *Agar* bro1 allox sp1 aloe bro1 am-m bro1 *Ant-t* bro1 apoc bro1 arg-met bro1 arg-n bro1 *Arn* bro1 bamb-a stb2.de• bapt bro1 bell-p bro1 *Berb* bro1 but-ac bro1* *Calc* bro1 *Calc-f* bro1 canth bro1 *Cimic* bro1 *Cob* bro1 *Cocc* bro1 cocc-s bro1 colch bro1* con bro1 conv bro1 cupr-ar bro1 dulc bro1* euon bro1 eupi bro1 ferr-p bro1 gels bro1 glyc bro1 *Helon* bro1 hip-ac sp1 hyper bro1 inul bro1 ipom-p bro1 *Kali-c* bro1 kali-i bro1 *Kalm* bro1 kreos bro1 lach bro1 lith-be bro1 *Lyc* bro1 lycpr bro1 morph bro1 *Nat-m* bro1 *Nux-v* bro1 ol-an bro1 *Ol-j* bro1 *Ox-ac* bro1 ozone sde2• pall bro1 petr bro1 ph-ac bro1 *Phyt* bro1 pic-ac bro1 pisc bro1 *Puls* bro1 *Pulx* bro1 rad-br bro1 *Rhus-t* bro1 ruta bro1* *Sabal* bro1 sabin bro1 senec bro1 *Sep* bro1 solid bro1 spong fd4.de *Staph* bro1 *Still* bro1 *Sulph* bro1 symph bro1 *Ter* bro1 tritic-vg fd5.de upa bro1 vanil fd5.de *Vib* bro1 visc bro1 zinc bro1
- **dysuria**, during: vesp ↓
• **aching**: vesp k*
- **eating**:
• **after**:
⁝ **agg.**: agar am-m b7a.de* ant-t bry cham cina *Daph* *Kali-c* k*
⁝ **aching**: agar ant-t
⁝ **tearing** pain: cham
• **agg.** | **erections**; after: (non:am-m a1)
• **amel.**: chel sne kali-n ph-ac sne
• **while**:
⁝ **agg.**: chin coc-c crot-c ↓
⁝ **aching**: crot-c k*
⁝ **stitching** pain: chin
- **electric** shock; as from an: *(↗Shocks - electric-like; Shocks - electric-like - spine)* kali-br mrr1
- **emissions** | **after**:
⁝ **agg.**: ant-c cob k* kali-br *Merc* ↓ ph-ac phos ↓ sars *Staph*
⁝ **aching**: ant-c cob kali-br ph-ac sars *Staph*
⁝ **burning**: *Merc* k* phos k*
• **amel.**: zinc bro1
- **erect** position:
• **amel.**: ozone ↓
⁝ **dull** pain: ozone sde2•
- **eructations**:
• **agg.**: zinc bg1
• **amel.**: nat-ox rly4• *Sep*
- **exertion** | **agg.** | **from**: *Agar* k* asaf berb bg1* bry k2 calc calc-p k* caust bg1 cocc bro1 crot-c sk4• dulc fd4.de ferr bg1 hyper bro1 kali-c bg1* kali-p bro1 lyc bg1 ox-ac k* ph-ac bg1 *Rhus-t* mrr1 ruta sec bg1 sep bg1 *Stry* sulph k* symph c1 vanil fd5.de verat bg1
• **amel.**: ruta *Sep*
- **falling** to pieces; as if lumbar region were: tril-p c1*
- **false** step; at a: podo *Sep* *Sulph* *Ther* *Thuj*
• **aching**: *Sulph*
- **fasting** agg.: kali-n

Back

- • **aching**: kali-n k*
- **fever**:
  - • **before**: arn b7a.de *Ars* b4a.de calc b4a.de cina b7a.de *Ip* b7a.de lach b7a.de nit-ac b4a.de *Nux-v* b7a.de puls b7a.de rhus-t b7a.de sabad b7a.de sep b4a.de sil b4a.de verat b7a.de
  - • **during**:
    - ⁝ **agg.**: acon bg2 alst ant-t bg2 apis bg2 *Arn* k* ars k* ars-s-f k2 *Bell* k* calc k* camph b7.de* *Caps* k* carb-v k* cassia-s ccrh1• caust k* chin k* chinin-s cocc k* eug *Eup-per* k* hyos ign k* ip bg2 kali-ar kali-c k* lach laur *Lyc* k* merc bg2 *Nat-m* k* nat-s **Nux-v** k* petr bg2 phos bg2 *Puls* k* *Rhus-t* k* *Sep* bg2 sil bg2 sulph k* verat bg2 zinc bg2 ziz
      - ⁝ **aching**: eug k* ziz k*
- **flatus**; passing | **amel.**: arg-n k2 berb canth bg1 coc-c kali-c bg1 nicc bg1 phos bg1 ruta vanil fd5.de
- **flatus**; with obstructed: calc h2
- **flesh** where loose; as if: lyc h2*
- **followed** by | **leukorrhea**: *(↗leukorrhea - with)* eupi br1
- **fullness** in abdomen; sensation of: bamb-a stb2.de•
- **gnawing** pain: agar *Alum* hell lil-t stry
- **gouty**: | **Dorsal** region: arn b7.de*
- **grasping** pain: phos h2
- **grief**; from: naja ↓
  - • **burning**: naja
- **griping** pain: con h2
  - • **paroxysmal**: lyc h2
- **hard** bed; as from a: bar-c h2
- **hemorrhoids**:
  - • **from**: aesc vh1
  - • **protrusion** of hemorrhoids; before: alum ↓
    - ⁝ **pressing** pain: alum h2
- **herpes** zoster, after: *Lach* ↓
  - • **stitching** pain: *(↗CHEST - Pain - herpes)* *Lach*
- **injuries**; after: calc *Con* **Hyper** *Kali-c* *Nat-s* nit-ac gk rhus-t k* sil gk *Thuj* vanil fd5.de [bell-p-sp dcm1]
- **inspiration** agg.: acon ↓ alum ↓ arn ↓ calc ↓ cham ↓ hippoc-k szs2 mez ↓ nat-c ↓ sars ↓ sulph ↓
  - • **stitching** pain: acon alum arn calc cham mez nat-c sars sulph
- **intermittent**: scol ah1 tetox pin2•
- **jar** agg.: *(↗spine - jar - agg.; stepping)* acon k* **Bell** berb k2* *Bry* bro1 *Carb-ac* *Carb-an* **Graph** hydrog srj2• kali-bi bro1 *Lob* bro1 mez bro1 petr h2 podo seneg *Sep* **Sil** k* sulph *Tell* bro1* *Ther* *Thuj*
- **jerking** pain: ang calc calc-p chin cinnb euph *Ferr* laur nat-c a1 nat-m petr ran-s sulph
- **kneeling**: | **after**:
  - ⁝ **agg.**: aids ↓
    - ⁝ **stitching** pain: aids nl2•
  - • **agg.**: aids ↓ euphr *Sep*
    - ⁝ **stitching** pain: aids nl2•
- **labor**-like: acon *Aloe* *Carb-v* *Cocc* *Coff* eup-pur ferr **Kali-c** *Kreos* *Lyc* *Nux-v* **Puls** **Sabin** sec *Sep*
- **lameness**: abrot *Aesc* agar b4a.de* *Alum* b4a.de asar b7.de* **Berb** k* *Cocc* b7.de* cupr-ar k* *Dios* k* *Dulc* k* ferr bg2 fl-ac helon hep b4a.de *Hyper* kali-br bg2 kali-c k* kali-n b4a.de kali-p lyss nat-c bg2 **Nat-m** k* *Nux-v* k* phos b4.de* phys plb puls-n rhus-t bg2 **Ruta** sel bg2 sil b4a.de* spig bg2 sulph bg2 verat b7a.de* zinc b4a.de* zing
  - • **sitting** a long time; as from | **lifting**; or as from: calc *Lyc* mur-ac olnd **Rhus-t** valer
- **lancinating**: agath-a nl2• alum bro1 ant-o asc-t bro1 *Berb* bro1 canth k2 colch bro1 *Coloc* k* con k2 dig h2* elaps kali-c kali-i kali-m bro1 lyc bro1 mim-h bro1 *Nat-s* *Nit-ac* nux-v bro1 ribo rly4• *Scol* bro1 sep bro1 sil bro1 stel bro1 *Stry* bro1
- **laughing** agg.: **Cann-i** phos plb tell
  - • **drawing** pain: phos
- **leaning**:
  - • **against** something:
    - ⁝ **amel.**: eupi ↓ zing ↓
      - ⁝ **aching**: eupi k* zing k*
- **leaning**: ...
  - • **backward**:
    - ⁝ **agg.**: kali-p ↓
      - ⁝ **stitching** pain: kali-p
  - • **chair**; against a:
    - ⁝ **agg.**: agar **Chinin-s** mrr1 hep h2 hyos k2 *Ther*
    - ⁝ **amel.**: eupi ferr sne lac-c sne sarr zing
  - • **side**; to | **agg.**: staph h1
- **leukorrhea**:
  - • **agg.**: agar *Ther*
  - • **amel.**: eupi k* sarr zing
  - • **with**: *(↗followed - leukorrhea)* *Aesc* bro1 eupi c1* gels hr1* graph bro1 *Helon* bro1 kali-bi bro1 kali-c c1 kali-n c1 kreos bro1 lyss c1 mag-s bro1 mur-ac tl1 *Murx* bro1 nat-hchls bro1 *Nat-m* bro1 ovi-p bro1 psor bro1 *Sep* b4a.de *Stann* bro1
- **lifting**:
  - • **after**: *Borx* ↓
    - ⁝ **stitching** pain: *Borx*
  - • **agg.**: *(↗overlifting)* anag arn mrr1 borx **Calc** calc-f c1 calc-p k2 calc-s k2 carb-an lp dream-p sdj1• **Graph** ham fd3.de• hura c1 **Lyc** med c1 nit-ac gk *Nux-v* ph-ac **Rhus-t** k* ruta gk sang *Sep* sulph bg1 tung-met bdx1• ulm-c jsj8• vanil fd5.de
    - ⁝ **stitching** pain: ph-ac rhus-t *Sep*
- **lying**:
  - • **abdomen**; on:
    - ⁝ **agg.**: arg-n bamb-a ↓ bell-p bg1 dulc ↓ symph fd3.de• tarax ↓ ust
      - ⁝ **aching**: bamb-a stb2.de•
      - ⁝ **stitching** pain: *Arg-n* dulc fd4.de tarax
    - ⁝ **amel.**: *Acet-ac* k* chel mag-c *Nit-ac* sel
      - ⁝ **aching**: nit-ac
  - • **agg.**: agar *Arn* bar-c h2 bell bro1 *Berb* k* beryl sp1 calc carb-an *Chin* coloc k* *Cur* daph dendr-pol sk4• dream-p sdj1• dulc bg1 euph *Ferr* galeoc-c-h gms1• hep *Ign* kali-c bg1 kali-i kali-n k* ketogl-ac ↓ *Kreos* lap-la rsp1 lob vh lyc mag-m mang bg1 naja nat-m nept-m lsd2.fr nicc-met sk4• nicc-s bro1 *Nux-v* k* pert-vc vk9 *Puls* *Rhus-t* k* ruta fd4.de samb bg1 spig spong fd4.de staph stroph-s ↓ tab tarax tritic-vg fd5.de vanil fd5.de vib
    - ⁝ **aching**: *Berb* *Cur*
    - ⁝ **burning**: kali-n h2 *Lyc*
    - ⁝ **sore**: hep ketogl-ac rly4• nat-m *Puls* stroph-s sp1
    - ⁝ **stitching** pain: galeoc-c-h gms1• *Kali-c* tarax h1
    - ⁝ **tearing** pain: ferr
  - • **amel.**: agar alum-sil k2 am-m mrr1 aq-mar skp7• arg-met mrr1 ars asar both-ax tsm2 bry cob dream-p sdj1• dulc fd4.de kali-c kali-m k2 kola stb3• *Nat-m* *Nux-v* petr-ra shn4• *Phos* plac-s rly4• *Psor* *Ruta* k* sars sep bro1 sil tritic-vg fd5.de urol-h rwt• vanil fd5.de
    - ⁝ **sore**: asar vanil fd5.de
  - • **back**; on:
    - ⁝ **agg.**: am-m ap-g apis ars ↓ bell berb bry carb-an *Chin* cina **Coloc** cur euph euphr guat sp1 hyos ign kali-n kali-p ↓ lyc mag-s nat-m nit-ac h2 prun psor puls ruta fd4.de sep spong fd4.de stann ↓ staph tell tritic-vg fd5.de zinc
      - ⁝ **aching**: carb-an nit-ac
      - ⁝ **broken**; as if: cina
      - ⁝ **burning**: ars
      - ⁝ **sore**: am-m bry hyos
      - ⁝ **stitching** pain: kali-p stann
    - ⁝ **amel.**: aesc bro1 ambr bufo cain br1 casc bg1 chin cob k* colch dulc fd4.de equis-h gnaph bro1 ign *Kali-c* lach **Nat-m** k* nux-v *Phos* puls *Rhus-t* k* **Ruta** k* sanic sep sil
      - ⁝ **aching**: equis-h *Nat-m*
  - • **hard**; on something:
    - ⁝ **amel.**: am-m bell eupi bro1 *Kali-c* lyc mag-m bg1 **Nat-m** k* puls *Rhus-t* k* sanic bg1 *Sep* k* stann
      - ⁝ **sore**: rhus-t k2
  - • **knees** and chest; on | **amel.**: petr-ra shn4•

- **pillow**; on a:
  - **agg.**: kali-n ↓
    - **pressing** pain: kali-n $_{h2}$
  - **amel.**●: *Carb-v* dulc $_{fd4.de}$ sep
    - **pressing** pain: *(↗lumbar - puts - pressing - plug)* *Carb-v*
- **side**; on:
  - **agg.**: cina des-ac $_{rbp6}$ dulc $_{fd4.de}$ ign *Nat-s* polys $_{sk4•}$ puls ruta $_{fd4.de}$ staph vanil $_{fd5.de}$
    - **broken**; as if: cina $_{h1}$
    - **sore**: ign
  - **amel.**: kali-n nat-c nat-s ↓ nux-v *Puls* zinc
    - **sore**: nat-s
  - **left** | **agg.**: dulc $_{fd4.de}$ ph-ac ruta $_{fd4.de}$ spong $_{fd4.de}$
  - **must** lie on side: nat-c $_{h2}$
  - **right**:
    - **agg.**: guat $_{sp1}$
    - **amel.**: kali-n nat-s ust

- **lying** still, when: colch ↓ nat-c ↓
  - **drawing** pain: colch nat-c
- **manual** labor agg.: kali-s $_{fd4.de}$ *Sulph* tritic-vg $_{fd5.de}$
- **massage** amel. (See rubbing - amel.)
- **masturbation**; after: nux-v $_{bro1}$ ph-ac $_{bro1}$ staph $_{bro1}$
- **menses**:
  - **after**:
    - **agg.**: berb borx calc-p kali-c mag-c puls verat
      - **aching**: berb $_{k*}$ *Kali-c* mag-c *Verat*
  - **amel.**: macro $_{c1}$ melal-alt $_{gya4}$
  - **before**:
    - **agg.**: acon am-c asar $_{k*}$ bar-c bar-s $_{k2}$ *Berb* borx brom *Calc* carb-an cartl-s $_{rly4•}$ *Caust* cinnb cocc dig eupi *Gels* granit-m ↓ *Hydr* hyos hyper **Kali-c** $_{k*}$ *Kali-n Kreos Lach Lyc Mag-c* mag-m nit-ac *Nux-m Nux-v* ol-an ozone ↓ petr-ra $_{shn4•}$ phos plat *Podo* **Puls** $_{k*}$ ruta sang sapin ↓ sep $_{mrr1}$ *Spong* $_{k*}$ urol-h $_{rwt•}$ *Ust Vib* zinc zinc-p $_{k2}$
      - **night**: *Berb* ↓
        - **sore**: *Berb*
      - **aching**: berb $_{k*}$ brom $_{k*}$ calc *Caust* eupi $_{k*}$ *Gels* granit-m $_{es1•}$ hyos hyper $_{k*}$ nux-v **Puls** sapin $_{a1}$ spong $_{k*}$
      - **burning**: kreos
      - **drawing** pain: hyos
      - **pressing** pain: nux-m podo
      - **sore**: ozone $_{sde2•}$
  - **during**:
    - **agg.**: abrom-a $_{ks5}$ acon agar aln $_{vva1•}$ aloe *Am-c* $_{k*}$ *Am-m* $_{k*}$ amp $_{rly4•}$ arg-n arn ars $_{k*}$ ars-i ars-s-f $_{k2}$ bar-c bar-s $_{k2}$ *Bell* $_{k*}$ *Berb* brom **Bry** *Calc* $_{k*}$ *Calc-p* calc-s calc-sil $_{k2}$ cann-i $_{c1*}$ carb-v $_{k*}$ carbn-s caul **Caust** $_{k*}$ cham *Chel* choc $_{srj3•}$ *Cimic Coc-c Con* ↓ croc crot-h dream-p ↓ eupi ferr ferr-ar ferr-i ferr-p granit-m ↓ *Graph* $_{k*}$ ham *Hell Hydr Ign* ignis-alc ↓ inul ↓ *Iod* kali-ar *Kali-c* $_{k*}$ kali-n *Kali-p* kali-s kali-sil $_{k2}$ *Kalm* kreos *Lac-c* lac-d *Lach* lachn *Lob Lyc* $_{k*}$ mag-c *Mag-m* $_{k*}$ mag-s mom-b $_{br1}$ nat-c nat-hchls ↓ nat-p nat-sil $_{fd3.de•}$ nicc *Nit-ac Nux-m* $_{k*}$ nux-v ol-an petr-ra $_{shn4•}$ *Phos* phys plac-s $_{rly4•}$ plat podo polys $_{sk4•}$ prun *Puls* $_{k*}$ rat rhus-t *Sabin* $_{k*}$ sang *Sars* sec senec seneg sep $_{k*}$ *Sil* **Sulph** suprar $_{rly4•}$ tarent *Thuj* tril-p $_{zr}$ tritic-vg $_{fd5.de}$ vib xan $_{k*}$ zinc zing [bor-pur $_{stj2}$]
      - **aching**: acon agar $_{k*}$ am-m $_{k*}$ *Bell* berb $_{k*}$ bry calc-p $_{k*}$ caul cimic crot-h $_{k*}$ dream-p $_{sdj1•}$ eupi $_{k*}$ ferr $_{k*}$ granit-m $_{es1•}$ graph $_{k*}$ inul $_{k*}$ *Kali-c* nat-c $_{k*}$ nat-hchls nat-p *Phos* phys $_{k*}$ rhus-t
      - **break**; as if it would: **Bell** *Nux-v Vib*
      - **broken**; as if: phos $_{k2}$
      - **cutting** pain: ars *Con* ignis-alc $_{es2•}$
      - **drawing** pain: nat-c $_{sne}$ *Sil* tritic-vg $_{fd5.de}$ zinc
      - **pressing** pain: agar *Nux-m* phys
      - **sore**: *Mag-m* phos *Thuj*
        - **bones**; as if in the: carb-v
      - **stitching** pain: ars $_{h2}$
      - **tearing** pain: agar am-c $_{h2}$ bell $_{h1}$ *Caust* phos **Sep**
        - **cramping**: bell

- **menses – during**: ...
  - **beginning** of menses | **agg.**: acon aloe *Asar* berb caust $_{k*}$ jab $_{ptk1}$ nit-ac thuj $_{b4a.de}$
  - **suppressed** menses; from: **Aesc** am-c apis *Bell Cocc* con $_{b4a.de}$ graph *Kali-c Nux-m* nux-v podo **Puls** $_{k*}$ sang senec ↓ *Sep Sil*
    - **aching**: **Aesc** *Kali-c Sep Sil*
    - **break**; as if it would: **Bell** *Nux-v* senec $_{vml3•}$
    - **drawing** pain: con $_{b4a.de*}$
- **menses** would come on; as if: apis calc calc-p cocc mosch puls $_{k2}$ *Vib*
- **mental** exertion agg.: cham con kali-c $_{gm1}$ nat-c *Pic-ac* $_{mrr1}$ sil ↓
  - **burning**: *Pic-ac* sil
- **motion**:
  - **agg.**: abrom-a $_{ks5}$ acon **Aesc Agar** alum alum-p $_{k2}$ alum-sil $_{k2}$ am-c am-m ↓ ang *Arn* asar **Bell** brom **Bry** bufo calc calc-p calc-s calc-sil $_{k2}$ caps *Carb-v* carbn-s *Caust* cham *Chel Chin* cimic cinnb *Cocc* **Colch** *Coloc Croc* crot-c $_{sk4•}$ cupr-s *Dig* dios dulc $_{fd4.de}$ equis-h eupi ferr ferr-p gent-l ↓ *Graph Guaj* $_{k*}$ hydrog $_{srj2•}$ hyper ↓ ign iris *Kali-bi* kali-i kali-s $_{fd4.de}$ *Kalm* lac-c $_{bro1}$ lach **Led** lob lyc mang mang-p $_{rly4•}$ meph *Merc* mez naja narz ↓ *Nat-c* nat-p nat-s nit-ac **Nux-v** ox-ac oxal-a ↓ *Petr* petr-ra $_{shn4•}$ phel *Phos Phyt Pic-ac* plan podo *Psor* ptel puls *Ran-b Rhus-t* $_{k*}$ ruta samb *Sars* sep sil stann stram streptoc $_{rly4•}$ stry ↓ sul-ac **Sulph** *Tarent* tell tritic-vg $_{fd5.de}$ vanil $_{fd5.de}$ visc ↓ *Zinc* zinc-p $_{k2}$
    - **aching**: *Aesc* $_{k*}$ agar $_{k*}$ am-c $_{k*}$ equis-h ferr $_{k*}$ gent-l $_{k*}$ narz $_{a1}$ ox-ac $_{k*}$ oxal-a $_{rly4•}$ *Petr* sil stry
    - **dragging**: agar
    - **drawing** pain: caps carb-v eupi sul-ac vanil $_{fd5.de}$
    - **jerking** pain: sulph $_{h2}$
    - **pressing** pain: *Zinc*
    - **sore**: chel chin merc ran-b stram
    - **stitching** pain: am-m **Bry** colch dig hyper $_{mrr1}$ lach lyc $_{h2}$ meph nit-ac $_{h2}$ phel phos *Rhus-t Sars* vanil $_{fd5.de}$
    - **sudden** motion: rhus-g $_{tmo3•}$
    - **tearing** pain: alum am-m *Caust* cinnb dig nit-ac visc $_{sp1}$
  - **amel.**: abies-c $_{oss4•}$ abrot $_{ptk}$ aesc aloe alum alum-p $_{k2}$ alumn ↓ am-c *Am-m* arg-n $_{bro1}$ arge-pl $_{rwt5•}$ bell $_{bro1}$ brucel ↓ bry calc-f calc-p caust $_{bro1}$ cina *Cob* $_{bro1}$ colch ↓ coloc cortiso ↓ cupr dios **Dulc** *Equis-h* $_{c1}$ ferr-m $_{bro1}$ fl-ac fuma-ac $_{rly4•}$ galeoc-c-h $_{gms1•}$ graph *Helon* $_{bro1}$ *Kali-c* kali-i ↓ kali-m $_{bro1}$ kali-n kali-p *Kali-s* kreos $_{k*}$ lach laur **Lyc** mag-c mag-m mang merc $_{bro1}$ morg-p $_{pte1*•}$ mur-ac ↓ nat-ar nat-c *Nat-s* nux-m nux-v $_{hbh}$ ox-ac petr ↓ petr-ra $_{shn4•}$ *Ph-ac* phos $_{k*}$ *Pic-ac* ↓ podo $_{fd3.de•}$ *Puls* $_{k*}$ rad-br $_{bro1}$ rat rauw ↓ *Rhod* **Rhus-t** $_{k*}$ ruta $_{fd4.de}$ samb *Sep* $_{k*}$ sin-n *Spig* spong $_{fd4.de}$ staph $_{k*}$ stront-c sulph $_{k*}$ syc $_{pte1*•}$ tritic-vg $_{fd5.de}$ ust vanil $_{fd5.de}$ vib *Zinc* $_{bro1}$
    - **aching**: graph $_{k*}$ rauw $_{sp1}$
    - **break**; as if it would: cortiso $_{tpw7}$
    - **burning**: mag-m *Pic-ac* rat
    - **drawing** pain: alum bry colch **Rhus-t** tritic-vg $_{fd5.de}$ vanil $_{fd5.de}$
    - **jerking** pain: petr
    - **sore**: *Am-m* **Kali-c** mag-c rat vanil $_{fd5.de}$
    - **stitching** pain: *Dulc* $_{k*}$ kali-i mur-ac staph
    - **tearing** pain: alumn dulc $_{k2}$
    - **wandering** pain: brucel $_{sa3•}$
  - **beginning** of:
    - **agg.**: bacls-7 $_{pte1*•}$ beryl $_{sp1}$ bry calc-f $_{c1}$ **Caps** *Carb-v* caust **Con Ferr** *Kali-p* **Lyc** morg-p $_{pte1*•}$ *Phos* **Puls** rauw ↓ **Rhus-t** sep sil syc $_{pte1*•}$ tab zinc
      - **aching**: rauw $_{sp1}$
  - **continued** motion | **amel.**: aesc $_{tl1}$ rhus-t $_{tl1}$
  - **gentle** motion:
    - **agg.**: rhus-g $_{tmo3•}$
    - **amel.**: bell *Calc-f* dulc $_{fd4.de}$ ferr *Kali-p* **Puls**
  - **head**; of:
    - **agg.**: acon ↓ bapt ↓ cupr-ar ↓ samb ↓ vanil ↓
      - **lameness**: bapt cupr-ar $_{k*}$
      - **stitching** pain: acon samb $_{xxb1}$ vanil $_{fd5.de}$
  - **must** move: ox-ac $_{bg1}$ *Puls* $_{sne}$ *Rhus-t* $_{mrr1}$ ruta $_{fd4.de}$
    - **constantly** in bed: phos *Puls* rhus-g $_{tmo3•}$ **Rhus-t**
    - **without** amel.; but: *Lach* **Puls** $_{k*}$

Back

- **shoulders**; of:
  - **agg.**: cocc↓
    - **aching**: cocc
- **music** agg.: ambr
- **nap**; after: phos↓
  - **sprained**; as if: phos h2
- **neuralgic**: mentho br1
- **noise** agg.: ars **Ther**
  - **running** water: *Lyss*
- **nursing** the child agg.; when: cham crot-t puls **Sil**
- **open** the mouth; on attempting to: stry↓
  - **jerking** pain: stry k*
- **overlifting** agg.: (↗*lifting - agg.*) bry k2 *Rhus-t* mrr1
- **ovulation**; during: granit-m↓
  - **aching**: granit-m es1•
- **palpitations**; with: ruta fd4.de tab ptk1
- **paralyzed**; as if: *Cocc* k* kali-p bro1 kali-s fd4.de kalm nat-m k* ran-s *Sabin* sil bro1 zinc
- **paroxysmal**: asaf kalm lyss nat-c pall phos
- **periodical**: *Ars* *Chinin-s* kali-s phos h2
- **perspiration**:
  - **during**: acon bg2 ant-t bg2 apis bg2 *Arn* bg2 **Ars** bg2 *Bell* bg2 **Calc** bg2 carb-v k* **Caust** bg2 *Chin* bg2 cocc bg2 ign bg2 kali-c bg2 *Lyc* bg2 **Merc** k* **Nat-m** bg2 **Nux-v** bg2 petr bg2 phos bg2 puls bg2 **Rhus-t** bg2 **Sep** bg2 sil bg2 **Sulph** bg2 thuj bg2 verat bg2 zinc bg2
  - **suppressed** perspiration; from: rhus-t k2
- **piercing**:
  - **accompanied** by | **nausea**: sphing c1*
- **pinching** pain: ger-i rly4• kali-n h2 lyc h2 nit-ac h2
- **pleuritis**; during | **pressing** pain (See CHEST - Inflammation - pleura - accompanied - back)
- **poking**, as if someone is (See boring)
- **pregnancy** agg.; during: aesc k2* arg-n hr1* cocc gsy1* kali-c bro1* nux-v vml4 phos↓ puls a2* sep tl1
  - **broken**; as if: phos k2
- **pressing** back against something hard amel.: **Sep**↓
  - **struck** with a hammer; as if: **Sep**
  - **tearing** pain | **sticking**: sep
- **pressing** pain: acon aeth *Agar* am-c ambr anac ant-c h2 apis arg-n arn aur aur-s k2 **Bell** berb borx calc calc-s calc-sil k2 caps carb-an carb-v carbn-s card-m caust *Chel* cocc con cycl cypra-eg sde6.de• *Dulc* elaps euph euphr fuma-ac rly4• graph hep h2 hyper *Kali-c* kali-m k2 kali-n kali-p kali-s fd4.de lach lap-la rsp1 led lyc mag-m melal-alt gya4 merc *Mur-ac* nat-m nat-s nept-m lsd2.fr nit-ac *Nux-m* ol-an pall petr *Phos* plat *Psor* puls rhod ruta fd4.de sabin *Samb* sars seneg *Sep* sil spong *Stann* staph sulph tarax *Thuj* tritic-vg fd5.de ust vanil fd5.de verat *Zinc* zinc-p k2
  - **bar**; as from a: ars lach
  - **downward**: lil-t br1 nit-ac h2
  - **plug**; as from a: *Aesc* bro1 *Agar* bro1 anac k2* aur-m bro1 benz-ac bro1 *Berb* bro1 *Carb-v* colch bro1 hyper bro1 lach nat-m bro1 *Nux-v* bro1 plat sep bro1 tell bro1
  - **pulsating** pain: sil
  - **upward**: puls h1
  - **vise**; as if in a: aeth br1 am-m gsy1
  - **weight**; as from a: anac c1*
- **pressure**:
  - **agg.**: acon aesc agar ang arn *Ars* bg1 berb k2 canth celt a1 chel chinin-s chord-umb rly4• **Cimic** bg1 cocc *Colch* coloc crot-t *Hep* lach nat-m↓ nux-m↓ phos plat plb polys sk4• ruta **Sil** bg1 sulph **Ther** bg1 thuj verb
    - **sore**: berb k2 nat-m k2 nux-m k2 sulph
  - **amel.**: aur camph carb-ac caust bro1 chord-umb rly4• cimic cortiso↓ *Dulc* fl-ac irid-met srj5• **Kali-c** k* led limen-b-c hrn2* mag-m meli bg1 *Nat-m* k* ozone sde2• ph-ac phos bg1 plb podo fd3.de• psor bg1 *Rhus-t* k* ruta sabad bg1 **Sep** k* spong fd4.de tril-p sne tritic-vg fd5.de vanil fd5.de verat vib zinc bg1
    - **aching**: **Kali-c** *Nat-m* *Sep*
    - **break**; as if it would: cortiso tpw7
- **pressure – amel.**: ...
    - **burrowing**: dulc h2
    - **sore**: vib
- **pulling** agg.: dios
- **pulsating** pain: abrom-a ks5 am-c arge-pl rwt5• ars h2 mez h2 musca-d szs1 ruta fd4.de sil tritic-vg fd5.de
- **pushed**; as if being: *Agath-a* nl2•
- **radiating**: ran-b k2
- **raising**:
  - **arm** agg.; right: thuj↓
    - **digging** pain: thuj
  - **arms**:
    - **agg.**: (↗*reaching*) *Graph* **Hyper**↓ nat-m bg1 [ang stj4]
      - **stitching** pain: **Hyper** mrr1
  - **thigh** | **sitting**; while: agar
- **reaching** up: (↗*raising - arms - agg.*) **Rhus-t**
- **reading** agg.: nat-c pic-ac mrr1
  - **drawing** pain: nat-c
- **rest**:
  - **agg.**: rauw↓
    - **aching**: rauw sp1
  - **amel.**: *Aesc* bro1 bacls-7 fmm1• colch bro1 nux-v bro1 pert-vc vk9 sil bro1 vanil fd5.de
- **rheumatic**: acon ambr anac ant-t arn↓ *Ars* asar aspar aur bacls-7 fmm1• bapt bar-c bell **Bry** *Calc* *Calc-p* calen *Carb-v* caul k2 cham *Chel* **Cimic** k* *Colch* com *Corn* cycl dros *Dulc* *Ferr* graph *Guaj* *Hep* ind↓ iod h *Kali-bi* kali-c↓ *Kali-i* k* lac-h sze9• lach lyc *Lycps-v* malar mtf11 *Med* k* mez morg-g pte1*• **Nux-v** ol-an petr *Phyt* plb↓ psil ft1 psor mtf11 *Puls* ran-b k* **Rhod** **Rhus-t** *Ruta* *Sang* squil stram stry↓ *Sulph* syc fmm1• syph k2* tarent k2 teucr thres-a sze7• ust valer verat zinc
  - **evening**: colch↓
    - **aching**: colch k*
  - **night**: gels↓
    - **aching**: gels k*
  - **aching**: arn k* ind k* kali-c k* plb k* stram k* stry k*
  - **motion** of head agg.: acon vh1
  - ○ **Dorsal** region: ambr b7.de* *Ant-c* b7.de* ant-t b7.de* bell b4.de* carb-v b4.de* cham b7a.de cycl b7a.de dros b7.de* gels bg2 guaj b4.de* *Puls* b7.de* ran-b b7a.de rhod b4a.de rhus-t b7.de* stram b7.de* sulph b4a.de teucr b7.de* verat b7.de* zinc b4a.de
    - **Scapulae**: ambr b7.de* asaf bg2 bell bg2 borx b4a.de camph b7.de* carb-v b4.de* caust bg2 dros b7.de* *Dulc* b4a.de graph b4.de* led bg2 lyc bg2 ol-an bg2 phyt bg2 ran-b b7.de* rhod b4.de* *Rhus-t* b7.de* staph b7.de* valer b7.de* verat b7.de*
      - **left**: sulph bg2
  - **Lumbar** region: *Ant-c* b7.de* **Bry** b7.de* dros b7.de*
  - **Muscles** | **Tendons**; and: arn br1
- **riding**:
  - **carriage**; in a:
    - **after**: **Nux-m**↓
      - **aching**: **Nux-m**
    - **agg.**: calc carb-ac fl-ac kali-c lac-c **Nux-m** *Petr* podo fd3.de• sep sulph ust
  - **horse**; a:
    - **agg.**: ars
      - **aching**: ars
  - **moped**; on a | **agg.**: pert-vc vk9
- **rising**:
  - **agg.**: ptel↓
    - **lameness**: ptel
  - **sitting**; from:
    - **after** | **long** time; after sitting for a: *Aesc* *Agar* am-c *Bell* *Berb* *Calc* *Phos* **Puls** **Rhus-t**
    - **agg.**: (↗*straightening*) aesc k* **Agar** alum alum-p k2 alum-sil k2 am-m a1 ant-c apis aran arg-n k* arge-pl rwt5• *Ars* bamb-a↓ bell↓ **Berb** k* bry *Calc* *Calc-s* calc-sil k2 cann-i *Canth* carb-an **Caust** k* chel sne con dulc fd4.de ferr ferr-p iris *Kali-bi* kali-p k* *Lach* bro1 *Led*

- **sitting**; from – **agg.**: ...
loxo-recl knl4• lyc **Merc** merl nat-s mrr1 nat-sil fd3.de• petr **Phos** *Psor* ↓ ptel **Puls** rhod **Rhus-t** ruta sep *Sil* k* spong fd4.de *Staph* **Sulph** k* tab tell k* thuj tritic-vg fd5.de tus-p *Zinc* zinc-p k2
  - **aching**: *Aesc* k* ars bell calc k* zinc k2
  - **cramping**: led ptk1
  - **sore**: apis *Psor* **Sulph**
  - **stitching** pain: bamb-a stb2.de• canth rhus-t
  - **amel.**: cob c1 kali-c bro1 ruta bro1 staph bro1
- **stooping**; from:
  - **agg.**: *Aesc* k* agar am-m *Berb* bism chel *Eupi* kali-bi lach *Lyc* med mur-ac *Nat-m* ph-ac *Phos* podo fd3.de• **Puls** *Rhus-t* sars *Sil* *Sulph* vanil fd5.de verat *Zinc*
    - **pressing** pain: verat h1
    - **stitching** pain: mur-ac *Rhus-t* vanil fd5.de
  - **long** time; for a: *Nat-m* **Puls**
    - **sore**: *Nat-m*

- **rubbing**:
  - **amel.**: aeth amp rly4• irid-met srj5• kali-n lach lil-t mang ↓ nat-m c1 nat-s **Phos** k* plb puls *Rhus-t* mrr1 thuj
    - **stitching** pain: mang h2
- **scratching**:
  - **after**: mag-c ↓
    - **burning**: mag-c
  - **amel.**: rhus-v ↓
    - **burning**: rhus-v
- **sewing**, while: iris sec
- **sexual** excesses; after: ars calc carb-v *Chin* *Nat-m* *Nat-p* **Nux-v** **Ph-ac** *Phos* *Puls* *Sep* **Staph** *Sulph* symph c1*
  - **drawing** pain: *Ars*
- **shivering**; during: **Arn** ↓ bell b4.de*
  - **sore**: **Arn**
- **shooting** (See stitching)
- **sitting**:
  - **after**: cupr-ar ↓ *Rhus-t* mrr1 syc pte1*•
    - **lameness**: cupr-ar
  - **agg.**: abrom-a ks5 **Agar** k* aloe alum bro1 alumn ↓ am-m k* ambr ang ↓ *Ant-t* k* apis **Arg-met** k* arg-n k* arge-pl rwt5• ars ↓ asaf asar aspar bar-c bar-s k2 *Bell* bro1 *Berb* k* beryl sp1 bism h1 bit-ar wht1• borx *Bry* *Calc* calc-f calc-sil k2 *Cann-i* k* carb-an *Carb-v* carbn-s *Caust* celt a1 cham chin chinin-s cimx cinnb ↓ cist cob k* cocc coff con cycl cypra-eg sde6.de• dig ↓ dream-p sdj1• dros dulc equis-h euphr ferr ferr-m bro1 ferr-p fl-ac galeoc-c-h gms1• helon hep hura hyos kali-bi *Kali-c* k* kali-i kali-m k2 kali-n kali-p k* kali-s kali-sil k2 kreos bro1 *Lac-c* bro1 *Lach* *Led* *Lyc* mag-c mag-m melal-alt gya4 meny merc k* mur-ac nat-ar nat-c nat-m nat-p *Nat-s* nat-sil fd3.de• nicc ↓ nit-ac ↓ *Nux-v* k* ol-an ox-ac pall *Par* *Ph-ac* phel *Phos* pic-ac plac-s rly4• plat ↓ plb ↓ plumbg ↓ podo *Prun* *Puls* k* *Rhod* **Rhus-t** k* *Ruta* sabad sal-fr ↓ **Sep** k* sil spong stann *Sulph* k* tab ter ther ↓ *Thuj* tritic-vg fd5.de tung-met bdx1• ust **Valer** vanil fd5.de **Zinc** k* zinc-p k2 [*Arg-p* stj2]
    - **aching**: berb bism borx cann-i cham k* cob k* cocc k* equis-h euphr k* helon melal-alt gya4 nat-c k* nux-v k* ox-ac pic-ac k* plb p l u m b g a1 podo puls **Sep** k* thuj k* **Zinc** k*
    - **burning**: ars asar borx kali-n h2 nat-sil fd3.de• spong fd4.de tritic-vg fd5.de **Zinc**
    - **cutting** pain: nat-s
    - **drawing** pain: *Bry* calc *Carb-v* lyc nat-c ph-ac h2 **Rhus-t** ruta fd4.de ter ther *Thuj* tritic-vg fd5.de vanil fd5.de
    - **dyspnea**, with: lyc
    - **pressing** pain: am-m gsy1 borx cocc kali-n h2 mur-ac a1 puls ruta fd4.de thuj h1 tritic-vg fd5.de vanil fd5.de
    - **sore**: asar *Calc* hep hyos kali-p fd1.de• nat-m ph-ac plat h2 *Ruta* sabad sal-fr sle1• thuj
    - **stitching** pain: ambr ang asar caust h2 *Chin* dulc galeoc-c-h gms1• kali-i kali-n kali-p k2 lyc mur-ac nat-c nicc par ph-ac ruta vanil fd5.de *Zinc*
    - **tearing** pain: alumn am-m *Berb* *Caust* cinnb dig ferr *Lyc* nit-ac spong

- **sitting**: ...
  - **amel.**: aeth bell bro1 borx caust dulc fd4.de mag-c meny mur-ac plb sars spong fd4.de staph stroph-s ↓ tritic-vg fd5.de vanil fd5.de
    - **pressing** pain: mur-ac
    - **sore**: stroph-s sp1
  - **bent** forward:
    - **agg.**: chel chinin-s kali-i laur nat-c nept-m lsd2.fr phos pic-ac ↓ ran-b sec sep spong fd4.de thuj
      - **aching**: sep k*
      - **sitting** erect amel.: chel ↓
        - **pressing** pain: chel
      - **stitching** pain: pic-ac
    - **must** sit bent forward: **Kali-c** **Sulph**
  - **erect**:
    - **agg.**: **Kali-c** petr-ra shn4• spong **Sulph**
    - **amel.**: fic-m gya1 pert-vc vk9 petr-ra shn4•
  - **feet** agg.; on his: cench k2
  - **long** time agg.; for a:
    - **after**: aloe asaf bamb-a ↓ berb *Calc* *Cupr-ar* lac-h sk4• lap-la sde8.de• *Led* lith-c lith-m ↓ pall ↓ *Ph-ac* *Phos* **Puls** *Rhod* *Rhus-t* k* ruta fd4.de spong fd4.de thuj tritic-vg fd5.de valer vanil fd5.de
      - **aching**: lith-m k* pall a1 phos k* **Puls**
      - **dull** pain: bamb-a stb2.de• vanil fd5.de
- **sitting** down agg.: cob ↓
  - **aching**: cob k*
- **sitting** up in bed agg.: abrom-a ks5
- **sleep**:
  - **during**:
    - **agg.**: abies-c oss4• am-c ↓ *Am-m* ars kalm lach puls vanil fd5.de zinc
      - **burning**: zinc h2
      - **drawing** pain: vanil fd5.de zinc
      - **jerking** pain: am-c
  - **going** to sleep; on | **agg.**: ham fd3.de• mag-m
  - **sound** sleep; after falling into a: *Am-m* kalm *Lach*
- **sneezing**:
  - **agg.**: arn arund hydrog srj2• *Sulph* **Tell** mrr1
    - **stitching** pain: arund
  - **before**: anag
- **sore** (= bruised, beaten): *Acon* k* aesc bro1 *Agar* k* **Alum** alum-p k2 alum-sil k2 alumn am-m ampe-qu br1 anac ang anis c1 ant-t bro1 *Apis* **Arn** k* *Ars* ars-i asar atp rly4• bar-c bro1 benz-ac k2 berb k* bry bro1 *Calc* calc-s calc-sil k2 camph h1 carb-ac carb-v carbn-s caust h2 *Cham* chin chord-umb rly4• cic *Cina* k* cinnb clem coc-c coli rly4• coloc *Con* conv cor-r corn dig *Dros* dulc k* **Eup-per** gins bro1 granit-m es1• graph bro1 grat *Ham* bro1 hep hip-ac sp1 hyos kali-ar **Kali-c** kali-n kali-p kali-s kali-sil k2 ketogl-ac rly4• kola stb3• lat-m bnm6• lyss mag-c *Mag-m* mag-s k* *Merc* k* mim-p rsj8• myric nat-ar *Nat-c* **Nat-m** k* nat-p *Nat-s* *Nux-m* **Nux-v** k* ox-ac petr-ra shn4• ph-ac bro1 **Phos** *Phyt* k* **Plat** podo fd3.de• *Psor* *Puls* *Ran-b* k* rat *Rhod* *Rhus-t* k* **Ruta** k* sabad *Sang* sep k2 sil bro1 sol-ni *Spig* *Stann* staphycoc rly4• stram stront-c stroph-s sp1 suis-em rly4• sul-ac **Sulph** k* symph fd3.de• tell bro1 tep ther *Thuj* trios rsj11• tritic-vg fd5.de vanil fd5.de verat vib *Zinc* zinc-p k2 [tax jsj7]
  - **accompanied** by | **Lumbar** region; weakness in: stroph-s sp1
  - **carrying** heavy things on back; as after: ozone sde2•
- **sprained**; as if: agar k* am-m h2 arg-n *Arn* *Bell* **Calc** con **Graph** kali-c h2 lyc mur-ac h2 nux-v olnd petr *Puls* rhod **Rhus-t** sep sulph
- **stabbed**; as if (See cutting)
- **stabbing** (See stitching)
- **standing**:
  - **agg.**: *Aesc* bro1 *Agar* agn asar bell bro1 berb both-ax tsm2 *Bry* *Calc* cann-i caps cocc coff *Con* dios bg1 dream-p sdj1• dulc fd4.de fuma-ac rly4• galeoc-c-h gms1• hep ign ind kali-bi kali-c kali-m bg1* kali-p *Kali-s* lil-t lith-c lyc meny merc mur-ac nat-m bg1 nat-sil ↓ nit-ac nux-v bro1 pert-vc vk9 petr *Ph-ac* *Phos* phys bg1 plan plb podo puls rumx *Ruta* sarcol-ac bro1 *Sep* k* spong stann ↓ stroph-s ↓ **Sulph** k* thuj tritic-vg fd5.de tus-p **Valer** vanil fd5.de verat vero-o rly4• zinc zinc-p k2
    - **aching**: lyc tus-p
    - **drawing** pain: caps con ign

• **agg.**: ...
⁝ **pressing** pain: mur-ac a1 nit-ac puls ruta fd4.de
⁝ **sore**: asar *Calc* hep stroph-s sp1 thuj
⁝ **stitching** pain: con nat-sil fd3.de• zinc
⁝ **tearing** pain: *Berb* bry stann
• **amel.**: aloe hr *Arg-n* k* *Bell* calc bg1 caust bro1 mur-ac sulph bro1 thuj bg1 tritic-vg fd5.de
⁝ **pressing** pain: mur-ac
⁝ **stitching** pain: calc
• **erect**:
⁝ **agg.** | **sitting**; after: *Thuj*
• **leaning** sideways agg.; and: thuj
- **steam** agg.; exposure to: kali-bi ↓
• **burning**: kali-bi
- **stepping** agg.: *(↗jar)* acon carb-ac carb-an podo c1 sep spong sul-ac ↓ *Sulph* *Ther* *Thuj*
• **drawing** pain: sul-ac h2
- **sticking** (See stitching)
- **stinging** (See stitching)
- **stitching** pain (= shooting): acon aesc k* **Agar** k* aids nl2• ail all-c all-s aloe k* *Alum* k* alum-p k2 alum-sil k2 alumn am-c am-m ambr anac apis k* arg-met arg-n arn arund asaf asar asc-t aur aur-m *Bamb-a* stb2.de• bar-c bar-i k2 bar-s k2 *Bell* bell-p sp1 **Berb** k* beryl sp1 borx h2 *Bov* brom **Bry** k* calad *Calc* calc-ar calc-i k2 calc-s cann-s carb-an carb-v carbn-s **Caust** cench k2 *Cham* chel *Chin* chord-umb rly4• *Cimic* cinnb cocc *Colch* coloc colum-p sze2• com *Con* corn cycl dig dros h1 *Dulc* elat eug euon ferr ferr-i ferr-p form galeoc-c-h gms1• gamb germ-met srj5• graph *Guaj* k* hell *Hep* hippoc-k szs2 hura hydrog srj2• hyos hyper k* *Ign* iod irid-met srj5• *Kali-bi* **Kali-c** k* kali-i kali-m k2 kali-n *Kali-p* **Kali-s** kalm kola stb3• *Kreos* *Lach* laur lavand-a ctl1• led lob-s luf-op rsj5• **Lyc** lyss mag-c mag-m *Mag-p* manc mang mang-p rly4• meph *Merc* k* merc-i-f *Mez* *Mur-ac* *Nat-c* nat-m k* nat-p nat-s bro1 nicc **Nit-ac** *Nux-v* olnd ox-ac bg1* paeon *Par* petr a1 phos *Phyt* plac rzf5• *Plat* plb positr nl2• psor k* *Puls* rat *Rhus-t* ruta fd4.de sabad sabin *Sanic* *Sars* sec *Sep* *Sil* *Spig* spong *Stann* staph stram stront-c suis-pan rly4• sul-ac sul-i k2 *Sulph* k* suprar rly4• tarax tell k* ther br1* thioc-ac rly4• **Thuj** thymol sp1 tritic-vg fd5.de tung-met bdx1• vanil fd5.de verat verb *Zinc* zinc-p k2
• **burning**: plat h2
• **cramping**: cina lyc h2 mag-c
• **digging** pain: stann h2
• **downward**: paeon
• **outward**: stann h2
• **paroxysmal**: lyc h2
• **pulsating** pain: chin h1 dulc kali-c samb xxb1
• **stinging**: *Apis* cham chlor galeoc-c-h gms1• rumx sulph vanil fd5.de *Zinc*
• **twitching**: stann h2
• **upward**: staph h1
- **stool**:
• **after**:
⁝ **agg.**: aesc aloe alum asaf bamb-a stb2.de• berb caps colch dig dros *Ferr* mag-m nat-m podo k* *Puls* rheum k* tab
: **aching**: rheum
: **drawing** pain: caps
⁝ **amel.**: nux-v ox-ac puls ruta fd4.de verat bg1
• **before**: agar ↓ bapt cic colch b7.de* ferr b7.de* kali-n *Nux-v* k* petr k* puls verat b7.de*
⁝ **broken**; as if: *Nux-v*
⁝ **burning**: agar bg2
⁝ **cramping**: petr bg2
⁝ **twisting** pain: verat h1
• **difficult**:
⁝ **during**: *Puls* ↓
: **aching**: *Puls* k*
: **pressing** pain: *Puls*

- **stool**: ...
• **during**:
⁝ **agg.**: *Aesc* bro1 alum bg2 apis *Ars* *Calc* b4a.de caps bro1 carb-an cic bg2 colch k* coloc cupr cycl *Dulc* ferr k* ferr-ar kali-i *Lyc* manc **Merc-c** b4a.de nicc nux-v k* phos plac-s rly4• *Podo* *Puls* k* rheum squil stront-c sulph tab zing
: **aching**: manc k*
: **cutting** pain: *Coloc*
: **drawing** pain: *Puls*
: **stitching** pain: *Coloc* nicc *Phos*
• **hard** stool:
⁝ **after** | **agg.**: ferr ptk1
• **urging** to:
⁝ **after**: **Tell** mrr1 zing
⁝ **during**: nux-v mrr1
⁝ **with**: zing ↓
: **drawing** pain: zing
- **stooping** | **after**:
⁝ **agg.**: **Aesc** ↓ agar ↓ chel ↓
: **aching**: **Aesc** k* agar k* chel k*
• **agg.**: *Aesc* k* **Agar** *Alum* alum-sil k2 amph a1 arn berb bro1 borx bov *Bry* bufo caj ↓ caps *Carb-v* *Cham* *Chel* clem *Cocc* con corn cycl sne daph des-ac rbp6 dig dios k* *Dulc* gua bro1 hep hura hyos irid-met srj5• kali-bi *Kali-c* kali-n kali-sil k2 lec ↓ lyc mang meny nat-m nux-v ol-an par petr-ra shn4• pic-ac plb puls rhod *Rhus-t* ruta sabin sars **Sep** *Sil* spong ↓ stront-c sul-ac *Sulph* k* tell k* thuj tritic-vg fd5.de vanil fd5.de verat *Zinc*
⁝ **aching**: *Agar* borx bov caps k* *Cham* kali-n k* *Sulph* k*
⁝ **drawing** pain: *Carb-v* sul-ac sulph tritic-vg fd5.de
: **upward**: sulph
⁝ **long** time; stooping for a: **NAT-M** k ●
⁝ **pressing** pain: borx sars h2 vanil fd5.de verat h1
⁝ **rising**; and on: verat ↓
: **broken**; as if: verat k*
⁝ **sore**: cham lec stront-c
⁝ **stitching** pain: caj *Rhus-t* sabin spong fd4.de vanil fd5.de verat zinc
⁝ **tearing** pain: bry *Chel*
- **stooping** a long time; as after: agar h2 bism h1 kreos bg sulph h2 thuj h1
- **straightening** up the back: *(↗rising - sitting - agg.)* aeth agar bufo calc *Cann-i* carb-ac chel *Kali-bi* kali-c lac-c kr1 lac-loxod-a hrn2• lach nat-c *Nat-m* nux-v petr-ra shn4• *Psor* *Sep* *Sulph* *Thuj*
• **amel.**: agar bg1 bov fl-ac bg1 laur nat-m bg1 nept-m lsd2.fr
• **cannot** straighten the back: alum hr1 calc-ar hr1 castn-v br1 *Hydr* hr1 lac-c hr1 lyc hr1
⁝ **walking** | **amel.**: hydr hr1
- **straining**; from: *(↗Straining)* aesc tl1 calc-p k2* calc-s k2*
- **stretching**:
• **amel.**: galeoc-c-h ↓ loxo-recl knl4•
⁝ **stitching** pain: galeoc-c-h gms1•
- **stretching** out: calc mag-c vanil fd5.de
- **striking** foot: *Sep* ↓
• **stitching** pain: *Sep* k*
- **struck** with a hammer; as if: **Sep**
- **stubbing** toe: *Sep* ↓
• **stitching** pain: *Sep*
- **sudden**: kali-br mrr1 vanil fd5.de
- **supper** agg.; after: sulph
• **aching**: sulph
- **suppurating**; as if: kreos bg2
- **swallowing** agg.: calc-p mrr1 *Caust* *Kali-c* nit-ac ↓ petr ↓ raph *Rhus-t*
• **aching**: kali-c raph k*
• **jerking** pain: petr
• **pressing** pain: nit-ac h2
- **talking**:
• **agg.**: cocc k* nat-c h2
⁝ **tearing** pain: cocc c1
• **impossible**: cann-i

- **tearing** pain: *Aesc* agar alum alum-sil$_{k2}$ alumn am-c am-m ant-c *Arn Ars* ars-s-f$_{k2}$ asar berb calc *Calc-p Canth Caps* carb-v carbn-s caust *Cham Chel Chin* chinin-ar$_{k2}$ *Cina* cinnb cocc colch cupr dros ferr ferr-ar ferr-p gad guaj kali-c kali-n kali-p kola$_{stb3•}$ led *Lyc Mang* merc mez **Nit-ac** *Nux-v* op petr *Ph-ac* **Phos** puls sabin$_{c1}$ sep *Sil Stann* stry sulph vanil$_{fd5.de}$ zinc zinc-p$_{k2}$
  - **cramping**: bell$_{h1}$
  - **drawing** pain: *Caps*$_{hr1}$ cham dulc$_{k2}$ nux-v op stram
  - **stitching** pain: stann$_{h2}$
  - **upward**: stann
- **throwing** shoulders backward:
  - **agg.**: ozone$_{sde2•}$
  - **amel.**: cycl
    - **drawing** pain: cycl
- **thrusting** (See lancinating)
- **thunderstorm**:
  - **before**: sulph$_{c1}$
  - **during** agg.: agar rhod
- **touch** agg.: calc↓ chel↓ lath$_{c1}$ merc↓ mur-ac↓ **Tell**$_{mrr1}$ vanil$_{fd5.de}$
  - **stitching** pain: calc merc mur-ac
  - **tearing** pain: chel
  - ▽ **extending** to | **Head**: tell$_{mrr1}$
- **turning**:
  - **agg.**: *Agar* alum-sil$_{k2}$ am-m bov *Bry* dios dulc$_{fd4.de}$ hep kali-bi kali-s$_{fd4.de}$ merc *Nux-v Sanic* sars sep sil spong$_{fd4.de}$ thuj tritic-vg$_{fd5.de}$ vanil$_{fd5.de}$ verat
    - **drawing** pain: *Bry* hep nux-v$_{k2}$ vanil$_{fd5.de}$
  - **amel.**: nat-m↓
    - **drawing** pain: nat-m
  - **bed**; in:
    - **agg.**: acon am-c$_{h2}$ *Bry* calad dulc$_{fd4.de}$ hep ign kali-bi kali-n loxo-recl$_{knl4•}$ mag-m merc nat-c *Nux-v*$_{k*}$ sep *Staph* sulph zinc
    - **amel.**: nat-m vanil$_{fd5.de}$
    - **must** sit up to turn over in bed: bry$_{ptk1}$ *Kali-c*$_{mrr1}$ kali-p **Nux-v**$_{k*}$ olib-sac$_{wmh1}$
      - **aching**: **Nux-v**
    - **must** turn: phos **Rhus-t**
  - **body**:
    - **agg.**: bov↓ *Nux-v*↓ sars↓ sep↓ thuj↓
      - **sore**: thuj
      - **stitching** pain: bov *Nux-v* sars sep
  - **body**; upper part of:
    - **agg.**: ozone↓
      - **cutting** pain: ozone$_{sde2•}$
  - **head**:
    - **agg.**: *Caust* ger-i$_{rly4•}$ lachn ruta$_{fd4.de}$ sanic spong$_{fd4.de}$ tritic-vg$_{fd5.de}$ vanil$_{fd5.de}$
      - **suddenly**: mag-m
- **twisting** pain: fuma-ac$_{rly4•}$
- **ulcerative** pain: kreos puls
- **unbearable**: phos$_{h2}$ tritic-vg$_{fd5.de}$
- **urination**:
  - **after**:
    - **agg.**: caust$_{k*}$ *Syph*
    - **amel.**: **Lyc**$_{k*}$ med$_{k*}$
  - **agg.**: hyper↓
    - **stitching** pain: hyper$_{mrr1}$
  - **amel.**: **Lyc**↓
    - **aching**: **Lyc**
  - **before**: bell↓ *Colch*$_{b7a.de}$ graph hep↓ *Lyc* nux-v$_{b7a.de}$ puls$_{b7a.de}$
    - **stitching** pain: bell$_{b4a.de}$ hep$_{b4a.de}$
  - **copious** | **amel.**: gink-b$_{sbd1•}$ **Lyc** *Med*
  - **desire** for; with (See urging - with)
  - **during**: *Ant-c Ip Kali-bi Nux-v*↓ phos *Puls*↓ *Sulph*
    - **drawing** pain: *Nux-v*$_{b7a.de}$ *Puls*$_{b7a.de}$
    - **scanty**: benz-ac$_{k2}$
- **urination**: ...
  - **urging** to urinate:
    - **with**: clem eupi *Lach* nat-s
      - **drawing** pain: *Lach*
- **urine**, on retaining: arn con *Nat-s* rhus-t
- **vertigo**; after: ign$_{hr1*}$
- **vexation**; after: nux-v
- **waking** | **after**:
  - **agg.**: grat↓ mag-s↓
    - **sore**: grat$_{a1}$ mag-s
  - **on**: abrot aesc arg-met arge-pl$_{rwt5•}$ bar-ox-suc$_{rly4•}$ berb calc-p chel dream-p$_{sdj1•}$ galeoc-c-h$_{gms1•}$ hep hydrog$_{srj2•}$ *Lach* mag-m mag-s myric positr↓ ptel puls puls-n↓ rhod tell$_{rsj10•}$ ven-m$_{rsj12•}$
    - **aching**: hep$_{k*}$ myric$_{k*}$ positr$_{nl2•}$ ptel$_{k*}$
    - **lameness**: abrot **Aesc** ptel puls-n
- **walking**:
  - **after**:
    - **agg.**: alum *Nat-c* petr-ra↓ *Phos* plat↓ stry zing↓
      - **aching**: *Nat-c* phos$_{k*}$ stry$_{k*}$
      - **broken**; as if: petr-ra$_{shn4•}$ plat
      - **lameness**: zing
  - **agg.**: abrom-a$_{ks5}$ **Aesc**$_{k*}$ *Agar* aloe$_{bro1}$ alum alum-p$_{k2}$ alum-sil$_{k2}$ am-c am-m amph$_{a1}$ *Ant-t*$_{bro1}$ arg-n arn *Asaf* bapt bell$_{k*}$ borx *Bry*$_{k*}$ calc↓ canth carb-an *Caust*$_{k*}$ cham *Chel*$_{k*}$ chin$_{bro1}$ *Cocc* coff *Colch*$_{bro1}$ coloc con dios euphr ferr ferr-p galeoc-c-h$_{gms1•}$ grat hep hyos hyper iris kali-bi$_{k*}$ **Kali-c**$_{k*}$ kali-m$_{k2}$ kali-p lac-ac$_{c1}$ lyc *Mag-m* meny mez$_{k*}$ mur-ac nat-ar nat-c nat-m$_{k2}$ nux-v$_{k*}$ ox-ac$_{bro1}$ paraf$_{bro1}$ petr$_{bro1}$ phos phyt$_{k*}$ plat podo *Psor* ran-a$_{bro1}$ **Ran-b**$_{k*}$ rhus-t *Ruta Sars* sep$_{k*}$ spig spong stront-c stroph-s↓ *Sulph*$_{k*}$ tab *Thuj* tritic-vg$_{fd5.de}$ vanil$_{fd5.de}$ verat zinc zing
    - **aching**: **Aesc**$_{k*}$ bapt$_{k*}$ borx cham euphr$_{k*}$ iris **Kali-c** lyc$_{k*}$ **Psor** sep$_{k*}$
    - **gnawing** pain: *Canth* stront-c
    - **pressing** pain: borx *Caust* mur-ac *Psor* vanil$_{fd5.de}$ zinc$_{h2}$
    - **prevents** walking: phos$_{h2}$
    - **sore**: hyos *Ruta* stroph-s$_{sp1}$ vanil$_{fd5.de}$
    - **stitching** pain: arn calc canth chel kali-p ran-b rhus-t sulph thuj zinc
    - **tearing** pain: canth *Chel* cocc$_{c1}$
  - **air**; in open:
    - **agg.**: arn↓ galeoc-c-h↓ kali-c↓ merc↓ nit-ac *Sil*↓ ter tritic-vg↓ *Zinc*
      - **burning**: arn galeoc-c-h$_{gms1•}$ kali-c *Sil*
      - **drawing** pain: ter tritic-vg$_{fd5.de}$
      - **pressing** pain: kali-c$_{h2}$
      - **sore**: merc *Zinc*
    - **amel.**: kali-n↓
      - **burning**: kali-n
  - **amel.**: am-c ant-c ap-g apoc↓ **Arg-met** *Arg-n* arn ars-met asar bar-c *Bell* beryl$_{sp1}$ bry calc-f cob **Dulc** equis-h$_{c1}$ ferr gamb *Kali-c*↓ kali-n kali-s kreos mag-s merc nat-ar nat-m *Nux-v Ph-ac* phos *Puls* **Rhus-t** *Ruta Sep* staph stront-c *Sulph*↓ tell thuj tritic-vg$_{fd5.de}$ tung-met↓ vib *Zinc* zinc-p$_{k2}$
    - **aching**: zinc$_{k2}$
    - **drawing** pain: bry **Rhus-t** *Sulph*
    - **pressing** pain: kali-n$_{h2}$ kali-s$_{fd4.de}$ puls ruta$_{fd4.de}$
    - **sore**: apoc$_{vh1}$ *Puls* thuj
    - **stitching** pain: *Kali-c* tung-met$_{bdx1•}$
  - **bent**:
    - **must** walk bent●: *(↗lumbar - walking - bent - must)* bamb-a↓ *Cann-i Kali-c* psor *Sep* spong$_{fd4.de}$ *Sulph* tritic-vg$_{fd5.de}$
      - **cramping**: bamb-a$_{stb2.de•}$
  - **must** walk: nux-v↓
    - **break**; as if it would: nux-v$_{k2}$
  - **rapidly** | **agg.**: sep$_{bg1}$
  - **slowly** | **amel.**: **Ferr**$_{k*}$ *Puls*
- **wandering** pain: ang chel cimic dros ham$_{fd3.de•}$ kali-bi$_{k2}$ *Kali-s* lac-c$_{mrr1}$ *Mag-p* puls$_{k2}$ sang$_{k*}$ sec senec tarent

- **warm**:
  - **applications**:
    - **agg.**: guaj k2 *Kali-s* bro1 puls bro1 sulph bro1
    - **amel.**: bacls-7 fmm1• calc-f caust cinnb dream-p sdj1• galeoc-c-h gms1• kola stb3• *Nux-v* phos mrr1 pin-con oss2• **Rhus-t** k* ruta fd4.de spong fd4.de
  - **bathing** | **amel.**: *Bamb-a* stb2.de• crot-c sk4• pert-vc vk9 *Rhus-t* mrr1 spong fd4.de
  - **bed**:
    - **agg.**: lil-t phyt k2 sulph
    - **amel.**: rhus-v ↓
      - **stitching** pain: rhus-v
  - **room**:
    - **agg.**: gels *Kali-s* k*
      - **aching**: kali-s
  - **stove**:
    - **amel.**: cinnb ↓
      - **tearing** pain: cinnb
- **warm** in bed agg.; becoming: sil ↓
  - **burning**: sil
- **weakness**; with: *Berb* ptk1 casc bg1 tritic-vg fd5.de
- **weather**:
  - **change** of weather | **cold** weather; to: **Calc-p** **Dulc** rhod *Rhus-t*
  - **cold** agg.: kali-i br1 ran-b mrr1
  - **wet** | **agg.**: **Calc** calc-p k2 **Dulc** k* kali-i br1 med k2 *Nux-m* *Phyt* k* ran-b mrr1 *Rhod* **Rhus-t** k* sep
- **wedge**; as from a: fic-m gya1
- **women**; in: helon br1
- **writing**:
  - **after**: mur-ac ↓
    - **sprained**; as if: mur-ac h2
  - **agg.**: dulc fd4.de kali-s fd4.de laur lyc mur-ac sep
  - **continued**; after: lyc mur-ac sep
    - **aching**: lyc k* mur-ac k* sep
- **yawning** agg.: calc-p plat
  - **drawing** pain: calc-p

▽ - **extending** to:

○ • **Abdomen**: caust ↓ cham nat-c ↓ ruta fd4.de sep ↓ spong fd4.de tritic-vg fd5.de vario ↓ visc ↓
    - **drawing** pain: caust h
    - **griping** pain: vario jl2
    - **neuralgic**: sep bro1 visc bro1
    - **sore**: caust k* nat-c h2
    - **tearing** pain: cham
  - **Anus**: nat-c bg1 phos bg1 rhus-t ↓
    - **drawing** pain: nat-c rhus-t a1
  - **Arm**; middle or left upper: nat-m ↓
    - **stitching** pain: nat-m
  - **Arms**: agath-a nl2• ars bg1 berb bg1 bomb-chr mlk9.de *Calc* calc-ar calc-f mrr1 carb-v ↓ flav ↓ nat-c ↓ phos bg1 ruta fd4.de vanil fd5.de
    - **drawing** pain: carb-v h2 nat-c h2
    - **neuralgic**: flav jl2
  - **Arms** and legs: calc-ar ↓
    - **stitching** pain: calc-ar
  - **Back**; down: berb ↓ *Cina* ↓ mag-c ↓ *Mang* ↓ nat-s ↓
    - **tearing** pain: berb *Cina* mag-c h2 *Mang* nat-s
  - **Chest**: agar ↓ borx ↓ hydrog srj2• *Kali-c* ↓ kali-p ↓ kali-s fd4.de mez ↓ nat-c ↓ psor ↓ ruta fd4.de sars ↓ spong fd4.de
    - **drawing** pain: agar gsy1
    - **stitching** pain: borx h2 *Kali-c* kali-p k2 mez h2 nat-c h2 psor jl2 sars
  - **Clavicle**: spig ↓
    - **stitching** pain: spig bro1
  - **Downward**: cocc bg1* phos bg1 sep br1
  - **Ears**: gels
  - **Elbow**: agath-a nl2•

- **extending** to: ...
  - **Esophagus**: agar ↓
    - **drawing** pain: agar gsy1
  - **Feet**: alum bg1 berb bg1 borx cob ptk1 dulc fd4.de ruta fd4.de sep spong fd4.de
  - **Front**: pert-vc vk9
  - **Groin**: *Sabin* spong fd4.de *Sulph* tritic-vg fd5.de
    - **walking** or rising from seat agg.: *Sulph* ↓
      - **drawing** pain: *Sulph*
  - **Groin** and thighs: *Sabin* ↓
    - **labor**-like: *Sabin*
  - **Head**: *Calc* k* carc ↓ *Chinin-s* gels mrr1 hell kalm mrr1 nat-m ox-ac k2 petr ↓ sang mrr1 sep sil k* tell ↓ tritic-vg fd5.de vanil fd5.de
    - **exertion** agg.; after: nat-m
      - **drawing** pain: nat-m
    - **pressing** pain: tell mrr1
    - **stepping**:
      - **every** step; at: sep
        - **stitching** pain: sep
    - **stitching** pain: carc fd2.de• kalm petr sep
    - **stool** agg.; during: *Phos* ↓
      - **stitching** pain: *Phos*
  - **Heart**; toward: nat-m
    - **jerking** pain: nat-m
  - **Heels**: colch dream-p sdj1• *Sep* spong fd4.de
  - **Hip**: malar ↓
    - **bursting** pain: malar jl2
  - **Hips**: *Bol-la* carc fd2.de• cimic *Lach* *Lyss* mosch *Nat-m* ↓ tetox pin2• urol-h rwt•
    - **right**: ozone sde2•
    - **drawing** pain: *Lach* mosch *Nat-m*
  - **Hypochondrium**:
    - **left**: lyc ↓
      - **sprained**; as if: lyc h2
    - **lying** or coughing, standing or sitting amel.; on: chinin-s ↓
      - **stitching** pain: chinin-s
  - **Knees**: arn hydrog srj2• *Kali-c*
    - **stitching** pain: arn
  - **Legs**: ars ↓ bell ↓ dulc ↓ lach ↓ *Phos* ↓ tritic-vg ↓
    - **drawing** pain: ars bell dulc k2 lach *Phos* tritic-vg fd5.de
  - **Limbs**: *Ars* ↓ *Chel* ↓ hyper ↓ **Phos** ↓
    - **stitching** pain: hyper k2
    - **tearing** pain: *Ars* *Chel* **Phos**
  - **Lower** limbs: agar agath-a nl2• ars bell bufo ↓ *Calc* *Calc-ar* camph carb-ac ↓ cham ↓ *Cimic* ↓ dream-p sdj1• helo-s rwt2• *Kali-c* lach lob-c *Phos* puls ↓ pycnop-sa mrz1 **Rhus-t** *Sabin* ↓ scol ah1 tetox pin2• tritic-vg fd5.de urol-h rwt• zinc bg1
    - **neuralgic**: bufo bro1 carb-ac bro1 cham bro1 *Cimic* bro1 puls bro1 *Sabin* bro1
  - **Lumbar** region: caust ↓
    - **drawing** pain: caust h
    - **sore**: caust k*
  - **Lumbar** region and abdomen: caust ↓
    - **drawing** pain: caust h2
    - **sore**: caust k*
  - **Lungs**: ozone ↓
    - **cutting** pain: ozone sde2•
  - **Nape** of neck | **evening**:
    - **lying** down agg.; after: nat-c
      - **sore**: nat-c
    - **walking** agg.: nat-s ↓
      - **tearing** pain: nat-s
  - **Nates**: mand ↓
    - **cramping**: mand rsj7•
    - **women**; in: thymol ↓

- **Nates – women**; in: ...
  - **stitching** pain: thymol sp1
- **Neck**: dulc fd4.de sang tritic-vg fd5.de
  - **drawing** pain: sang
  - **lying** down agg.; after: mag-m↓
    - **gnawing** pain: mag-m
- **Occiput**: *Gels Puls* vanil fd5.de
  - **Vertex** during chill; and: **Puls**
- **Occiput** and vertex:
  - **chill**; during: **Puls**↓
    - **drawing** pain: **Puls**
- **Pelvis**: *Eupi* spong fd4.de tritic-vg fd5.de
- **Pit** of stomach:
  - **sitting** agg.: nicc↓
    - **stitching** pain: nicc
- **Pubis**: bell↓ sabin c1*
  - **neuralgic**: bell bro1 sabin bro1
- **Ribs**: alum↓
  - **stitching** pain: alum
- **Sacrum**: bapt a1 calc-f k2 con gins↓ lyc h2 *Puls*↓ tep
  - **drawing** pain: con tep
  - **sore**: gins k*
  - **stitching** pain: lyc *Puls*
- **Scapula**: lyc↓ *Puls*↓
  - **stitching** pain: lyc *Puls*
- **Shoulder**: agath-a nl2• chel chin dulc fd4.de *Kalm* lyc spig↓ spong fd4.de vanil fd5.de
  - **right**: agath-a↓ alum↓ fic-m↓
    - **boring** pain: agath-a nl2•
    - **stitching** pain: alum fic-m gya1
  - **left**: choc↓
    - **stitching** pain: choc srj3•
  - **stitching** pain: spig bro1
- **Shoulders**: chel↓
  - **pressing** pain: chel
- **Shoulders** to loins on waking: ox-ac↓
  - **sore**: ox-ac k*
- **Side**; left:
  - **walking** agg.: spig↓
    - **stitching** pain: spig
- **Sternum**, into: laur↓
  - **stitching** pain: laur
- **Stomach**: **Cupr** lyc nicc nit-ac puls rhod thuj
  - **pressure** agg.: *Bell*
  - **sitting** agg.: bry nicc
- **Testes**: dulc fd4.de sulph
  - **walking** or rising from seat agg.: *Sulph*↓
    - **drawing** pain: *Sulph*
- **Thighs**: *Aesc*↓ agath-a nl2• aur-m↓ bapt↓ *Berb*↓ carb-ac↓ chin↓ cimic cocc↓ *Coloc*↓ cur↓ ham↓ *Helon*↓ *Kali-c* kali-m↓ lac-c↓ *Lyc* *Nux-v* ox-ac phyt↓ *Scol*↓ *Stel*↓ tell↓ xero↓
  - **tearing** pain: *Aesc* bro1 aur-m bro1 bapt bro1 *Berb* bro1 carb-ac bro1 chin cocc bro1 *Coloc* bro1 cur bro1 ham bro1 *Helon* bro1 kali-c bro1 kali-m bro1 lac-c bro1 *Ox-ac* bro1 phyt bro1 *Scol* bro1 *Stel* bro1 tell bro1 xero bro1
  - **Down**: agath-a nl2• *Cimic Nit-ac* ox-ac *Sep*
- **Upward**: agar *Alum* arn ars *Chinin-s* clem *Cocc Coloc* corn cycl dirc eup-pur **Gels** kalm kreos *Lach* led mag-m meny nat-m **Nit-ac** nux-m nux-v ox-ac *Petr* phos *Phyt* plb podo sep sil stann staph sulph ust
  - **constriction** of anus, with: *Coloc*
  - **delivery**; during: **Gels** *Petr*
  - **descends**, and: kali-c
  - **lying** down agg.; after: mag-m
  - **sitting** agg.: meny
  - **spreading** upwards like a fan: *Lach* k* nat-s ptk1

- extending to – **Upward**: ...
  - **stepping** | **every** step; at: sep
  - **stool** agg.; during: phos podo
  - **stooping** agg.: arn *Sil*
  - **twinges** up the back, drawing shoulders back amel.: cycl
- **Uterus**: helon↓ plat↓ sep↓
  - **cutting** pain: helon
  - **neuralgic**: plat bro1 sep bro1
- **Vertex**: rhus-t↓
  - **stitching** pain: rhus-t
- **Wrist**: agath-a nl2•

○ - **Cervical** region: abrot *Acon Aesc Aeth Agar* agn↓ aids↓ ail k* all-c all-s *Alum* k* alum-sil k2 alumn *Am-c* am-m ambr *Anac* androc↓ ang ant-c ant-s-aur↓ ant-t↓ *Apis* aq-mar skp7• arg-met arge-pl rwt5• arizon-l nl2• arn **Ars** *Ars-i* ars-s-f k2 arum-t asaf↓ *Asar Atro* aur↓ aur-m-n aur-s↓ *Bad*↓ *Bamb-a* stb2.de• bapt↓ bar-c bar-s k2 **Bell** benz-ac↓ berb beryl↓ bism↓ bit-ar wht1• bomb-chr↓ borx *Bov*↓ brach↓ *Bry* buth-a sp1 cact cadm-met↓ *Calc Calc-caust*↓ calc-f sp1* *Calc-p* k* calc-s calc-sil k2 *Camph* cann-i cann-s canth *Caps*↓ carb-ac carb-an *Carb-v* carbn-s carc↓ card-m carl↓ caul↓ **Caust** cench k2 *Chel Chin* chinin-ar *Chinin-s* chord-umb↓ **Cic** cimic k* cina↓ *Cinnb* cit-ac↓ clem coc-c *Cocc* cod colch coli↓ *Coloc* colum-p sze2• *Con* cortico tpw7* crat br1 crot-c crot-h crot-t↓ cund cupr k* cupr-ar cur cycl cypra-eg↓ cystein-l rly4• cyt-l sp1 *Daph* dendr-pol sk4• dig dios dioxi↓ dol dream-p sdj1• *Dros Dulc* echi elaps gk eup-per euph↓ falco-ch sze4• falco-pe nl2• fel br1 ferr ferr-ar ferr-ma br1 *Ferr-p* fic-m gya1 *Fl-ac* flav jl2 flor-p↓ *Form* gaba↓ gal-ac a1 gamb **Gels** germ-met srj5• gink-b sbd1• *Glon* **Graph** grat gua↓ *Guaj* ham k2 hed sp1 *Hell* helo-s bnm14• *Hep* hir↓ hist sp1 hydr↓ *Hydrog* srj2• *Ign* iod↓ *Ip* jac-c *Kali-ar Kali-bi* kali-c kali-cy kali-n *Kali-p* kali-s kali-sil k2 *Kalm* ketogl-ac↓ kola stb3• **Lac-c** lac-leo hm2• lac-loxod-a hm2• *Lach* lachn lact lap-la sde8.de• laur lavand-a ctl1• lec↓ led lepi br1 lil-t limen-b-c hm2* limest-b↓ luf-op↓ *Lyc Lyss* mag-c mag-m↓ *Mag-p* mag-s↓ mang↓ mang-p↓ marb-w↓ *Med* meny↓ meph *Merc* merc-i-f↓ *Merl*↓ *Mez* morg-p pte1• mosch mucs-nas rly4• musca-d↓ myos-a↓ myric naja nat-ar↓ *Nat-c*↓ nat-m *Nat-p*↓ nat-pyru↓ *Nat-s* nat-sil fd3.de• nept-m lsd2.fr nicc↓ nit-ac *Nux-m* nux-v ol-an olib-sac wmh1 olnd onos oreo br1 ox-ac ozone sde2• pall **Par** pert-vc vk9 petr petr-ra shn4• **Ph-ac** phel↓ *Phos* phys *Phyt* k* pic-ac k* pip-m pitu-gl skp7• plat↓ plb *Pneu* jl2 podo positr↓ psor k* ptel c1 *Puls* pycnop-sa mrz1 rad-br c11 *Ran-b* raph rat rheum↓ **Rhod** k* rhus-g tmo3• rhus-t k* *Rhus-v*↓ rumx ruta sabin sacch-a fd2.de• sal-al blc1• samb *Sang* sarr sars sel senec↓ sep *Sil* sol-ni↓ spig spong fd4.de stann staph stict↓ stram stront-c↓ stry suis-pan↓ sul-ac↓ sulph suprar↓ symph fd3.de• syph jl2 *Tab* taosc iwa1• tarax tarent tax↓ tep↓ ter thiam↓ thres-a sze7• thuj tritic-vg fd5.de tub c1 v-a-b jl2 vanil fd5.de vario verat *Verat-v*↓ vero-o rly4*• vesp viol-o↓ vip↓ x-ray sp1 xan c1 *Zinc* zinc-p k2 [*Buteo-j* sej6 heroin sdj2 pop dhh1 spect dfg1]
- **right**: apis↓ bamb-a↓ bung-fa mtf carc↓ colch↓ conch fkr1• cyclosp sa3• cystein-l rly4• dioxi↓ dulc fd4.de fic-m gya1 graph bg1 ham fd3.de• lac-leo↓ nux-v↓ olib-sac wmh1 pall c1 phyt mrr1 pitu-gl↓ plut-n↓ psil↓ sacch-a fd2.de• *Sang* mrr1 spong fd4.de sulph h2 symph fd3.de• trios rsj11• tritic-vg fd5.de visc c1 zinc↓
  - **burning**: colch rsj2•
  - **cramping**: olib-sac wmh1
  - **drawing** pain: bamb-a stb2.de• carc fd2.de• dulc h1 ham fd3.de• lac-leo hm2• nux-v bg1 plut-n srj7• sulph h2 symph fd3.de• zinc h2*
  - **sprained**; as if: dioxi rbp6
  - **stitching** pain: apis vh1
  - **tearing** pain: pitu-gl skp7• psil ft1
  - **turning** head agg.: carc tpw2* cinnb lac-h htj1• *Mez* ozone sde2•
  - **extending** to:
    - **left**: calc-p bg1
    - **Eye**: **Sang** mrr1
    - **Forehead**: **Sang** mrr1
- **left**: agar↓ aids↓ androc srj1• asar↓ bamb-a↓ bung-fa mtf carb-an bg1 cench k2 colch↓ *Con* cyclosp sa3• dulc fd4.de gink-b sbd1• ham fd3.de• hydrog srj2• kali-s fd4.de myos-a rly4• pert-vc vk9 podo fd3.de• propr sa3• rat↓ sel c1 spong fd4.de sulph↓ thres-a sze7• thuj h1 tritic-vg fd5.de vanil↓
  - **burning**: colch rsj2•
  - **drawing** pain: bamb-a stb2.de• dulc fd4.de
  - **followed** by | **right**: androc srj1• opun-s a1
  - **sore**: agar bg1 aids nl2•

Back

- **left**: ...
  - **sprained**; as if: asar h1 *Con* pert-vc vk9
  - **tearing** pain: rat sulph h2 vanil fd5.de
- **daytime** amel.: bamb-a stb2.de•
- **morning**: am-c↓ aml-ns↓ ant-c arg-met asaf bamb-a stb2.de• bar-c chel cimic↓ dendr-pol sk4• dulc fd4.de eupi falco-pe nl2• ferr-ma ferr-p gal-ac a1* ham fd3.de• kali-c kola stb3• limest-b↓ nat-c nat-sil fd3.de• *Nux-v* olib-sac↓ pall c1 *Rhod* ruta fd4.de sars h2 sel↓ sil spig spong fd4.de staph *Stram* sulph thuj tritic-vg fd5.de vanil fd5.de *Zinc*
  - **aching**: aml-ns falco-pe nl2• limest-b es1• thuj
  - **bed** agg.; in: stann↓
    - **stitching** pain: stann h2
  - **bending** head forward agg.: *Cimic*↓ tritic-vg↓
    - **drawing** pain: *Cimic* tritic-vg fd5.de
  - **burning**: am-c
  - **drawing** pain: ant-c cimic dulc fd4.de nux-v staph h1 tritic-vg fd5.de
  - **paralyzed**; as if: sel br1
  - **pressing** pain: dulc h1 limest-b es1• olib-sac wmh1 sil
  - **rising**:
    - **after**:
      - **agg.**: am-m↓
        - **sore**: am-m h2
    - **agg.**: calc-caust↓
      - **aching**: calc-caust
    - **amel.**: alum h2
  - **tearing** pain: kali-c *Stram*
  - **waking** | **after**:
    - **agg.**: arg-met↓ ph-ac↓
      - **sore**: arg-met ph-ac
    - **on**: aloe alum anac↓ ars asaf carc fd2.de• cyclosp sa3• falco-pe nl2• kali-bi kali-p fd1.de• kola stb3• lac-h htj1• plut-n↓ podo fd3.de• prot jl2 psor ruta fd4.de thuj vanil fd5.de verat
      - **aching**: ars falco-pe nl2•
      - **drawing** pain: aloe alum plut-n srj7• psor jl2
      - **pressing** pain: anac h2 asaf
- **forenoon**: agar bamb-a↓ kali-p fd1.de• spong fd4.de stry tritic-vg fd5.de
  - **10**.30 h: sal-al blc1•
  - **aching**: agar
  - **drawing** pain: bamb-a stb2.de•
- **noon**: ptel
- **afternoon**: bamb-a stb2.de• calc-p chel chinin-s dulc↓ fago↓ mag-c↓ mag-p nux-v olib-sac↓ ruta fd4.de stry↓ thuj tritic-vg fd5.de vanil fd5.de
  - **16** h: bamb-a stb2.de• *Chinin-s*
  - **17** h; until: pitu-gl↓
    - **tearing** pain: pitu-gl skp7•
  - **17-19** h: buth-a sp1
  - **burning**: fago
  - **drawing** pain: calc-p mag-c nux-v olib-sac wmh1 thuj tritic-vg fd5.de
  - **stitching** pain: dulc fd4.de stry
  - **tearing** pain: mag-c h2
- **evening**: alum ant-c↓ bov↓ brach coc-c↓ dios dulc fd4.de fl-ac form ham↓ *Kali-s* mag-c↓ mang↓ nat-c↓ nat-m nat-sil↓ *Nux-v* olib-sac↓ olnd ruta fd4.de sep↓ spong fd4.de staph↓ thuj tritic-vg fd5.de vanil fd5.de **Zinc**↓
  - **18**-4 h: guaj
  - **aching**: alum olnd **Zinc**
  - **bed** | **going** to bed | **when**: alum
    - **in** bed:
      - **agg.**: lyc↓
        - **stitching** pain: lyc
  - **burning**: mag-c
  - **cramping**: dulc fd4.de mang h2
  - **drawing** pain: ant-c h2 ham fd3.de• nat-m thuj tritic-vg fd5.de
  - **looking** upward agg.: form
  - **pressing** pain: fl-ac ham fd3.de• nat-sil fd3.de• olib-sac wmh1 sep h2
  - **sore**: sep h2
  - **stitching** pain: bov coc-c nat-c h2 ruta fd4.de staph a1 thuj vanil fd5.de
- **evening**: ...
  - **tearing** pain: *Nux-v*
- **night**: alum h2 bamb-a stb2.de• carb-an caust glon guaj ham fd3.de• *Kalm* lach mang↓ merc-c morg-p pte1*• nat-m↓ nat-s *Olnd* phyt mrr1 *Puls* rhod↓ ruta fd4.de sang sil h2 spong fd4.de stann sulph syph jl2 tritic-vg fd5.de *Zinc*
  - **midnight**: lach mag-s
    - **before**: sulph
      - **waking**; on: sulph↓
        - **tearing** pain: sulph
  - **digging** pain: mang
  - **pressing** pain: sulph h2
  - **stitching** pain: caust h2 kalm nat-m nat-s
  - **tearing** pain: rhod
- **accompanied** by:
  - **coryza**: ozone sde2•
  - **Dorsal** region; pain in: *Pneu* jl2
  - **Forehead**; pain: pneu jl2
  - **Head** | **pain** in (See HEAD - Pain - accompanied - neck - pain)
- **aching**: acon *Aesc* ambr bar-c bell bit-ar wht1• *Bry* ptk1 *Calc* *Calc-caust* cann-i carb-v chin ptk1 *Cimic* k* cit-ac rly4• colch rsj2• coli rly4• con dig dios falco-pe nl2• gaba sa3• **Gels** k* *Guaj* k* hell hydr ptk1 ign iod kali-p ptk1 kalm ptk1 ketogl-ac rly4• lac-leo hrn2• *Lach* ptk1 lachn ptk1 lil-t k* lyc ptk1 lyss ptk1 *Merl* mucs-nas rly4• myric naja nat-m onos ptk1 par ptk1 petr **Phyt** bg1* positr nl2• pycnop-sa mrz1 ran-b rhus-v sep sil ptk1 suis-pan rly4• suprar rly4• *Syph* thiam rly4• *Verat-v* k* vesp *Zinc*
- **air**; draft of:
  - **agg.**: calc-f sp1 **Calc-p** k* cimic dulc fd4.de podo fd3.de• **Rhus-t**
  - **slightest**: calc-p↓
    - **aching**: calc-p
- **air**; in open:
  - **agg.**: dulc fd4.de laur
    - **pressing** pain: *Laur*
  - **amel.**: fic-m gya1 psor k*
- **alternating** with:
  - **Forehead**, eminence frontal; pain in (See HEAD - Pain - forehead - eminence - alternating - cervical)
  - **Head**; pain in (See HEAD - Pain - alternating - cervical)
- **ascending** stairs agg.: ph-ac
  - **stitching** pain: ph-ac
- **bending** | **forward**:
  - **agg.**: cadm-met↓
    - **cramping**: cadm-met tpw6
  - **head**:
    - **agg.**: pert-vc vk9
    - **backward**:
      - **agg.**: *Bad*↓ bell chel cic cinnb cupr↓ cycl h1 dig↓ dulc fd4.de hep↓ kali-c kali-p fd1.de• lachn↓ laur lyc valer
        - **drawing** pain: cycl h1 dig h2 valer
        - **pressing** pain: bell cupr h2 dig h2 dulc fd4.de
        - **sore**: *Bad* cic hep
        - **sprained**; as if: lachn c1
      - **amel.**: cycl lac-c lac-leo↓ *Lyss* manc syph xan c1
        - **aching**: cycl lac-c lac-leo hrn2•
        - **pressing** pain: cycl h1
    - **forward**:
      - **agg.**: camph↓ cimic bg1 dulc fd4.de graph kali-p fd1.de• olib-sac wmh1 rad-br c11 rhus-t↓ stann tritic-vg fd5.de vanil fd5.de
        - **pressing** pain: rhus-t h1
        - **tearing** pain: camph h1
      - **amel.**: gels laur ruta fd4.de sanic
      - **must** bend head: *Laur*↓
        - **pressing** pain: *Laur*
    - **left** agg.; to: par
    - **right** agg.; to: sulph h2
- **blow**; pain as from a: cann-i a1 hydrog srj2• lach hr1* naja bg3*

- **blowing** the nose agg.: *Kali-bi*
- **boring** pain: bar-c *Mag-p* psor sulph h2
- **break**; as if it would: **Bell** *Chel* falco-pe nl2• form hir skp7•
- **breathing** deep agg.: *Chel*
- **broken**; as if: acon agar caust chel k* gels nux-v sabin thuj
- **burning**: alum-sil k2 am-c *Apis* *Ars* aur-m-n *Bar-c* bell beryl tpw5 bomb-chr a1 *Calc* carb-v *Caust* glon k2 grat gua bro1 kali-bi kali-n lach ptk1 lil-t lyc lyss mang-p rly4• *Med* **Merc** k* naja nat-c *Nat-s* nicc pall **Ph-ac** k* phel *Phos* *Rhus-t* spig k2 stront-c tab vesp [spect dfg1]
  - **itching**, sticking pain: *Calc*
  - **paroxysmal**: plb
  - **piercing** pain: apis
  - **stinging**: glon
- **cancer**; from: hydrc br1
- **chewing** agg.: zinc bg1
- **chill**; during: acon b7a.de ail ars-h buth-a sp1 nux-m c1
  - **tearing** pain: ars-h
- **cold**:
  - **agg.**: calc-f sp1 vero-o rly4*•
  - **air**:
    - **amel.**: aq-mar ↓
      - **tearing** pain: aq-mar skp7•
    - **wet**: nux-m *Ran-b*
      - **drawing** pain: *Nux-m*
  - **amel.**: ferr k2
- **cold** in open air; after taking a: phos
- **compressed**; as if: crot-h nat-pyru rly4• pip-m tritic-vg fd5.de
  - **fingers**; as if skin of neck were compressed between two: spong rb2
- **constricting** pain: dulc a1 *Ferr* *Glon* myos-a rly4• symph fd3.de•
- **cough** agg.; during: *Alum* *Bell* *Caps* lact **Sulph**
  - **aching**: *Bell*
  - **break**; as if it would: bell bg2
  - **pressing** pain: *Bell* *Caps*
  - **stitching** pain: alum h2
  - **tearing** pain: alum h2
- **cramping**: androc srj1• ant-c c1 ant-t vh1 arn *Asar* buth-a sp1 cadm-met tpw6 calc bg1 *Calc-p* k* **Cic** k* cimic k* coli rly4• dulc fd4.de gels hr1 glon mang h2 meny h1 naja ptk1 olib-sac wmh1 phyt ptk1 plat k* sel c1 *Spong* k* symph fd3.de• tritic-vg fd5.de verat-v ptk1 vip fkr4.de x-ray sp1 [tax jsj7]
  - **accompanied** by:
    - **Forehead | pain** (See HEAD - Pain - forehead - accompanied - cervical - pain - cramping)
- **crushed**, as if: marb-w es1•
- **cutting** pain: berb bg1 canth dig eup-per glon graph grat *Kali-bi* k* naja nat-sil fd3.de• samb k* stry thuj bg1
- **descending** stairs agg.: cadm-met ↓
  - **cramping**: cadm-met tpw6
- **digging** pain: mang *Thuj*
- **dinner**; after: con
- **dislocated**; as if: ang arn bg1 asar calc cinnb lachn vanil fd5.de
  - **separated**; as if: musca-d szs1
- **dragging**: *Gels* kali-s fd4.de pic-ac
- **drawing** pain: acon *Aesc* *Agar* ail all-s *Alum* *Am-c* ambr anac *Ang* ant-c apis asaf asar h1 aur aur-s k2 bad bamb-a stb2.de• bapt *Bell* berb borx *Bry* *Calc-p* camph cann-i cann-s canth carb-ac carb-an h2 *Carb-v* carbn-s carc fd2.de• carl caul **Chel** k* *Chin* cic **Cimic** k* clem coc-c cocc *Coloc* con crot-t cur dig dios dulc fd4.de *Ferr* fl-ac kali-bi kali-c *Kali-n* kali-sil k2 lac-leo hrn2• lact *Lil-t* *Lyc* lyss mang h2 med meny h1 *Merc* mosch *Nat-c* *Nat-m* *Nat-s* nicc nit-ac h2 *Nux-m* *Nux-v* olib-sac wmh1 pall *Petr* ph-ac phys plb psor k* *Puls* raph rat *Rhod* ruta sep sil spong fd4.de
- **drawing** pain: ...
stann *Staph* *Sulph* symph fd3.de• tep ter **Thuj** k* tritic-vg fd5.de vanil fd5.de viol-o zinc
  - **intermittent**: spig h1
  - **paralyzed**; as if: cocc staph h1
  - **paroxysmal**: sil
  - **rheumatic**: anac borx sep *Staph*
  - **upward**: ambr h1 calc cann-s *Petr* ter
- **drinking** cold drinks: hydrog srj2*•
- **dull** pain: olib-sac wmh1
- **eating**; after: cina ↓ *Nux-v* sep ↓ sulph ↓
  - **boring** pain: sulph h2
  - **cramping**: sep h2*
  - **tearing** pain: cina a1
- **entering** a room from open air; on: ran-b ↓
  - **aching**: ran-b
- **exertion** of arms agg.: ant-c ↓
  - **drawing** pain: ant-c h2
- **fever**; during: *Bry* b7a.de* *Rhus-t* b7a.de*
- **glands**, from swollen: graph h2 mur-ac a1
- **gnawing** pain: *Nat-s* k* *Thuj* k*
- **grasping** pain: nept-m lsd2.fr
  - **fist**; as from a: ozone sde2•
- **irritability**; with (See MIND - Irritability - pain - cervical)
- **jerking** pain: aeth aur caps h1 *Chin* tarax
- **lameness**: cycl h1
- **lancinating**: bell canth elaps
- **lifting** agg.: arg-n bg1 *Calc* bg1 lil-t bg1 sep bg1
- **lifting** the arm: *Ang* ↓
  - **dislocated**; as if: *Ang*
- **looking**:
  - **downward | agg.**: [pop dhh1]
  - **downward** or upward agg.: dioxi ↓
    - **sprained**; as if: dioxi rbp6
  - **upward | agg.**: form bg1 **Graph**
- **lying**:
  - **agg.**: caust ↓ dulc fd4.de *Glon* kali-i limest-b ↓ *Lyc* ruta fd4.de spong fd4.de
    - **pressing** pain: *Glon* limest-b es1• *Lyc*
    - **stitching** pain: caust h2 kali-i
    - **tearing** pain: *Lyc*
  - **amel.**: marb-w ↓
    - **pressing** pain: marb-w es1•
  - **back**; on:
    - **agg.**: cadm-met ↓ dulc ↓ graph lac-leo hrn2• spig
      - **cramping**: cadm-met tpw6
      - **pressing** pain: dulc h2*
    - **amel.**: kali-p fd1.de• lach k2
  - **side**; on:
    - **agg.**: dulc fd4.de graph bg1 lach k2
    - **painful** side | **amel.**: hydrog srj2•
    - **right | agg.**: ferr
- **lying** down agg.: lyc ↓
  - **sore**: lyc
- **manual** labor agg.: ant-c dulc fd4.de
  - **drawing** pain: ant-c
- **menses | before**:
  - **agg.**: nat-c nux-v sulph
    - **drawing** pain: *Nat-c* nux-v
  - **during**:
    - **agg.**: aids nl2• am-m ↓ bung-fa mtf *Calc* mag-c
      - **tearing** pain: am-m mag-c
- **mental** exertion agg.: par spig k2
  - **stitching** pain: spig k2

- **mental** exertion agg.: ...
  - **tearing** pain: spig k2
- **motion**:
  - **agg.**: acon↓ *Aesc*↓ alum↓ am-m↓ asaf↓ asar↓ *Bell*↓ bry↓ camph↓ caps↓ carb-v↓ *Coloc*↓ dig↓ glon↓ guaj↓ hyos↓ ign↓ kali-bi↓ merc↓ mez↓ nux-v↓ petr↓ *Rhus-t*↓ sars↓ spig↓ suis-pan↓ syph jl2 vanil↓ vario↓ verat↓ verat-v↓
    - **aching**: *Aesc* glon mez sars suis-pan rly4• verat-v
    - **drawing** pain: acon asaf *Bell* caps *Coloc* hyos *Rhus-t* vario
    - **pressing** pain: petr h2
    - **sore**: am-m h2 asar nux-v
    - **stitching** pain: alum bry gk camph h1 dig guaj merc sars spig k2 vanil fd5.de
    - **tearing** pain: carb-v dig ign kali-bi spig k2 verat
  - **amel.**: alum↓ aur-m-n morg-p pte1*• olib-sac↓ rhod mrr1 ruta fd4.de spig h1 *Sulph*↓ tritic-vg fd5.de v-a-b jl vanil fd5.de
    - **drawing** pain: alum tritic-vg fd5.de
    - **pressing** pain: olib-sac wmh1
    - **slow** motion: v-a-b jl2
    - **sore**: *Sulph*
  - **arms**; of | **agg.**: ang c1 tritic-vg fd5.de
  - **beginning** of | **agg.**: morg-p pte1*•
  - **circular** | **amel.**: dendr-pol sk4•
  - **continued** motion | **amel.**: v-a-b jl2
  - **head**; of:
    - **agg.**: (↗*turning; turning - head - agg.)* acon↓ *Aesc Agar Alum* alum-p k2 am-m asaf bad↓ *Bamb-a* stb2.de• bapt *Bell* brach *Bry* cann-s canth *Chel* chin cimic c1 *Cocc* colch *Coloc* cortico sp1 dig↓ *Dros* ferr c1 form gal-ac a1* glon *Hyper* ip kali-bi kali-c↓ *Kalm*↓ lap-la sde8.de• malar jl2 mang↓ merc merc-i-f↓ mez nat-c↓ nat-s nux-v plb↓ podo ptel c1 *Ran-b Rhus-t* sabad samb↓ sars spig k2 stram *Sulph Tarent* thuj↓ tritic-vg fd5.de vanil fd5.de verat-v
      - **burning**: nat-s plb
      - **cramping**: cimic hr1 mang h2
      - **digging** pain: thuj
      - **drawing** pain: nat-c h2 tritic-vg fd5.de
      - **pressing** pain: mez h2
      - **sore**: kali-c *Kalm* merc-i-f podo
      - **stitching** pain: acon am-m h2 bad dig samb h1 sars h2 thuj h1 vanil fd5.de
      - **tearing** pain: *Am-m* canth nat-c *Sulph*
    - **amel.**: colch↓
      - **burning**: colch rsj2•
    - **forward** and backward: cocc↓
      - **stitching** pain: cocc
    - **raising** head; or: chel↓
      - **riding** in a carriage:
        - **left** side: form↓
          - **broken**; as if | **break** in two; as if it would: form k*′
      - **broken**; as if: chel
    - **sideways**: *Agar* pert-vc vk9
  - **slight** motion | **agg.**: phyt mrr1
- **nervousness**; with (See MIND - Excitement - nervous - pain - cervical)
- **neuralgic**: bell bro1 bry bro1 chin bro1 chinin-s bro1 *Cimic* mrr1 hydr ptk1 nux-v bro1 puls bro1 zinc-p bro1
- **overlifting**, after: *Calc*
- **paralyzed**; as if: kali-s fd4.de nat-c h2 nat-m
- **paroxysmal**: anac guaj k2 *Kalm* nux-v sil *Stry*
- **periodical**: *Chinin-s* colch *Kali-s*
- **perspiration**:
  - **amel.**: thuj
  - **during**: *Acon* bg2 am-c bg2 graph bg2 mosch bg2 sabin bg2 sulph bg2
- **pinching** pain: sil h2 staph gk
- **position**; as from wrong: dulc h2 puls h1 thuj h1 zinc h2
- **pressing** pain: agar agn ambr *Anac* ant-s-aur *Ars* bamb-a stb2.de• *Bar-c* **Bell** k* benz-ac bism h1 bry canth *Carb-v* card-m *Chel Cocc Coloc* crot-t cupr cypra-eg sde6.de• dig dulc fd4.de *Elaps* euph h2 fic-m gya1 *Glon* graph grat guaj h2 ham fd3.de• ip h1 *Lach Laur* limest-b es1• lyc lyss marb-w es1• meny h1 merc mez h2 mosch *Nat-m Nat-s* nat-sil fd3.de• nit-ac ol-an olib-sac wmh1 **Par** k* petr h2 ph-ac **Phos** k* *Puls* rhus-t h1 samb sars sil spong *Staph* sulph h2 symph fd3.de• tarax thuj tritic-vg fd5.de
  - **bandaged**; as if: asar h1
  - **collar**; as from a tight: asar h1
  - **finger**; as from a: rheum h
  - **intermittent**: *Anac* k* dulc h2
  - **weight**; as from a: anac h2 caps h1 coloc **Par**
- **pressure**:
  - **amel.**: lac-leo hrn2• petr-ra shn4• *Prot* jl2 psor bg1 tritic-vg fd5.de xan c1 zinc bg1
    - **tearing** pain: zinc
- **pulsating** pain: bamb-a stb2.de• *Eup-per* lyss ruta fd4.de
- **raising**:
  - **arms** | **agg.**: *Ang* ant-c *Graph* tritic-vg fd5.de
  - **body**: caust bg1
    - **pillow**; from: x-ray sp1
  - **head** | **agg.**: ars chel senn
- **reading** agg.: nat-c
  - **drawing** pain: nat-c
- **rest**:
  - **amel.**: aq-mar↓
    - **tearing** pain: aq-mar skp7•
- **rheumatic**: acon ambr anac *Ant-c* ap-g br1 bacls-7 fmm1• bapt berb bism borx *Bry* calc *Calc-p* carbn-s caust **Cimic** k* *Colch Con* cycl *Dulc* dys pte1*• gels graph *Guaj* iod *Kali-i* br1 lachn br1 *Merc* mez morg-g pte1*• morg-p fmm1• nat-sil fd3.de• *Nux-v* prot fmm1• *Puls* **Ran-b** k* *Rhod* **Rhus-t** *Sang Sil Spig* squil h1 *Staph* stict k* *Sulph* tarent verat
- **riding** in a carriage agg.: form
- **rising**:
  - **agg.**: cadm-met↓
    - **cramping**: cadm-met tpw6
  - **bed**; from:
    - **agg.**: cinnb↓
      - **pressing** pain: cinnb
  - **stooping**; from:
    - **agg.**: nicc spig h1
      - **sprained**; as if: nicc
- **room** agg.: psor k*
- **scratching** agg.; after: mag-c↓
  - **burning**: mag-c
- **seminal** emission; on: glycyr-g cte1•
- **sitting**:
  - **agg.**: ant-c↓ aur-m kali-s fd4.de lyc↓ lyss nat-c↓ nux-v ruta fd4.de tritic-vg fd5.de
    - **drawing** pain: ant-c h2 aur-m nat-c nux-v tritic-vg fd5.de
    - **stitching** pain: lyc
  - **amel.**: rad-br c11 tarax↓
    - **stitching** pain: tarax h1
  - **bent** forward:
    - **agg.**: sulph↓
      - **stitching** pain: sulph
- **sleep**:
  - **amel.**: *Calc*↓
    - **burning**: *Calc*
  - **preventing** sleep: sil h2
- **sneezing** agg.: am-m arn lyc↓ mag-c
  - **cramping**: arn h1
  - **stitching** pain: am-m lyc mag-c
  - **tearing** pain: am-m

- **sore**: acon *Aesc* *Agar* aids nl2• ambr arg-met arn *Ars* ars-i arum-t k2 *Bad* bapt *Bell* borx hr1 bov brach calc-p *Carb-ac* caust chin h1 chord-umb rly4• cic cina k2 coloc cycl h1 dig dros dulc *Ferr* fl-ac *Gels* graph ham iod kali-bi *Kalm* *Lach* lec lyc merc-i-f naja nat-ar k2 nat-c *Nat-m* **Nat-s** k* *Nit-ac* nux-m nux-v petr-ra shn4• **Ph-ac** k* *Phos* phys podo psor puls ruta sabin sang sep **Sil** k* sol-ni stict ptk1 stram sulph tarent tep thiam rly4• *Thuj* *Zinc* zinc-p k2
  - **burning**: ph-ac
- **sprained**; as if: *Agar* *Ars* *Calc* cinnb *Con* dioxi rbp6 kali-n h2 lachn c1* lyc nat-m nicc *Ruta* sep *Sulph*
- **standing**:
  - **agg.**: tarax ↓
    - **stitching** pain: tarax h1
  - **erect** | **amel.**: rad-br c11
  - **still** | **agg.**: cham
- **stitching** pain: acon aeth agar alum alum-sil k2 ang arn aur bad bar-c bar-s k2 bell h1 *Bov* bry calc calc-sil k2 *Carb-an* carb-v carbn-s caust h2 cench k2 chel *Chin* cina a1 coc-c cocc con dig dulc fd4.de elaps ferr-p flor-p rsj3• germ-met srj5• graph h2 guaj ign kali-bi k2 kali-c lach lap-la rsp1 luf-op rsj5• lyc lyss mag-s merc nat-ar k2 nat-c h2 *Nat-m* k* *Nat-p* nat-s nat-sil fd3.de• nicc ozone sde2• ph-ac positr nl2• psor puls *Rhus-v* ruta fd4.de samb h1* *Sars* senec sep sil spig k2 spong *Stann* staph *Stry* suis-pan rly4• sul-ac h2* *Sulph* tarax thuj vanil fd5.de verat zinc
  - **downward**: hydrog srj2•
  - **itching**: stann h2
  - **pulsating** pain: cocc
  - **stinging**: *Apis* bar-c calc lyss phyt
  - **upward**: berb lyc
- **stool**; after:
  - **amel.**: asaf
    - **tearing** pain: asaf
- **stooping**:
  - **agg.**: agar ant-c berb borx ↓ canth gran graph kali-bi lac-ac manc nux-v ↓ par *Rhus-t* spig spong ↓ sulph
    - **drawing** pain: ant-c h2 berb borx c1 canth rhus-t spong fd4.de
    - **pressing** pain: canth
    - **sore**: nux-v
    - **stitching** pain: agar sulph
  - **impossible**: borx ↓
    - **drawing** pain: borx c1
- **stretching**:
  - **agg.**: nat-s ↓
    - **sore**: nat-s
  - **amel.**: aeth c1 sulph ↓
    - **stitching** pain: sulph
- **sudden**: nat-c ↓
  - **drawing** pain: nat-c h2
  - **tearing** pain: nat-c h2
- **sun** agg.: bit-ar ↓
  - **aching**: bit-ar wht1•
- **supper**; after:
  - **amel.**: lac-leo ↓ sep ↓
    - **aching**: lac-leo hrn2• sep
- **swallowing**:
  - **agg.**: calc-p k* colch ↓ nat-c h2 *Petr* ↓ sep ↓
    - **burning**: *Petr* k*
    - **cramping**: sep a2 (non:zinc hr1)
    - **pressing** pain: colch
  - **amel.**: *Spong* ↓
    - **stitching** pain: *Spong*
- **synchronous** with the pulse: cina ↓
  - **stitching** pain: cina h1*
- **talking** agg.: arn bg1 *Calc* sulph
  - **pressing** pain: sulph
  - **stitching** pain: *Calc*
- **tearing** pain: **Acon** aeth **Am-m** aq-mar skp7• arn asaf aur berb *Calc* calc-caust calc-sil k2 camph *Canth* *Caps* **Carb-v** carbn-s *Caust* chel *Chin* cic clem coc-c coloc con cupr dig gels *Glon* graph *Kali-c* kali-sil k2 kalm kola stb3• *Lach* laur led *Lyc* lyss mag-c mag-m meny h1 *Merc* nat-c *Nat-s* *Nux-v* olnd phos pitu-gl skp7• plb psor rat *Rhod* rhus-v sars sel sil *Spig* staph h1 stront-c sulph *Thuj* vanil fd5.de verat *Zinc* zinc-p k2
  - **jerking** pain: aur *Caps* rat
  - **paroxysmal**: nux-v
  - **upward**: berb canth *Lach*
- **thinking** agg.: spig ↓
  - **stitching** pain: spig k2
  - **tearing** pain: spig k2
- **throwing** head backward: glon ↓
  - **cramping**: glon kr1
- **touch**:
  - **agg.**: arizon-l nl2• chin cina ↓ nat-m ↓ *Nux-v* tell br1
    - **burning**: nat-m
    - **tearing** pain: cina a1
  - **amel.**: meny ↓
    - **cramping**: meny h1
- **turning**: *(↗motion - head - agg.)*
  - **bed**; in | **agg.**: ozone sde2•
  - **head**:
    - **agg.**: *(↗motion - head - agg.)* acon agar alum ↓ alumn a1 am-c am-m ant-c aur-s *Bamb-a* stb2.de• bell *Bry* *Calc* canth carbn-s carc fd2.de• chel chin h1 coloc cortico tpw7 dulc eup-per gal-ac a1* graph hyos lachn ↓ nat-m nat-s nat-sil ↓ ozone sde2• pert-vc ↓ plat *Ran-b* sanic sep spong stram tarent tritic-vg ↓ vanil ↓ verat
      - **dislocated**; as if: calc lachn
      - **drawing** pain: ant-c bamb-a stb2.de• chel hyos spong fd4.de tritic-vg fd5.de
      - **pressing** pain: canth *Coloc* *Nat-s*
      - **sprained**; as if: lachn c1 pert-vc vk9
      - **stitching** pain: alum nat-sil fd3.de• ozone sde2• vanil fd5.de verat
    - **left** agg.; to: *Alum* *Ant-c* bamb-a stb2.de• kali-p fd1.de• olib-sac wmh1 podo fd3.de• visc c1
      - **drawing** pain: *Ant-c*
    - **right** agg.; to: bamb-a stb2.de• dioxi ↓ lap-la rsp1 v-a-b jl2
      - **sprained**; as if: dioxi rbp6
- **twisting** and turning the head; on: calc ↓
  - **burnt**; sensation as if: calc k*
- **waking**; on: psor thuj
- **walking**:
  - **after**:
    - **agg.**: cur **Rhus-t** ↓
      - **pressing** pain | **weight**; as from a: **Rhus-t**
  - **agg.**: calc-p con dulc fd4.de ph-ac rat ↓ tab tritic-vg fd5.de
    - **drawing** pain: calc-p con tritic-vg fd5.de
    - **stitching** pain: ph-ac
    - **tearing** pain: rat
  - **air**; in open:
    - **agg.**: borx ↓ camph ↓ con ↓ meny ↓ sep ↓ tritic-vg ↓
      - **drawing** pain: borx hr1 camph h1 con tritic-vg fd5.de
      - **pressing** pain: meny h1 sep h2
    - **amel.**: sep ↓
      - **sore**: sep h2
  - **amel.**: mag-s ↓
    - **sore**: mag-s
  - **bent**:
    - **must** walk bent: cadm-met ↓
      - **cramping**: cadm-met tpw6
- **wandering** pain: **Lac-c**
- **warm**:
  - **applications**:
    - **agg.**: beryl ↓ morg-p fmm1•
      - **burning**: beryl tpw5

Back

- **warm – applications**: ...
  - **amel.**: cadm-met ↓
    - **cramping**: cadm-met tpw6
  - **room**:
    - **agg.**: caust ↓ *Kali-s* psor
      - **tearing** pain: caust h2
- **warmth**; external | **amel.**: bamb-a stb2.de• calc-f sp1 nat-sil fd3.de• *Rhus-t* spig k2 syph jl2
- **weather**:
  - **change** of weather: calc-f sp1 rhod mrr1
  - **cold** agg.: kali-i br1
  - **wet** | **agg.**: kali-i br1
  - **windy**: *Calc-p*
    - **drawing** pain: calc-p
- **writing** agg.: carb-an irid-met ↓ kali-s fd4.de zinc h2
  - **aching**: carb-an irid-met srj5• **Zinc**
- **yawning** agg.: arn h1 nat-c h2 nat-s
  - **cramping**: arn h1
  - **sore**: nat-s

▽ • **extending** to:
  - **Arm**: bry gk chel pd nat-m *Nux-v* taosc iwa1• vanil fd5.de
    - **left**: kalm *Lach* par vanil fd5.de
    - **And** fingers: ars sne *Kalm* nux-v par
  - **Arms**: colch ↓ plect ↓
    - **aching**: colch rsj2• plect
  - **Back**; down the: aeth k* am-c bamb-a stb2.de• bung-fa mtf chel cimic *Cocc* fic-m gya1 glon graph guaj *Kalm* lil-t mag-c *Med* ↓ nat-m phyt podo psor rat rhod ↓ sang sep stry tell br1 thuj verat xan br1
    - **burning**: *Med* k*
    - **stool** | **going** to; on: verat
    - **tearing** pain: mag-c rhod
  - **Brain**: ferr kalm *Par*
  - **Chest**: orot-ac ↓
    - **stitching** pain: orot-ac rly4•
  - **Clavicle**: nat-s ↓
    - **burning**: nat-s
    - **pressing** pain: nat-s
  - **Clavicles**: *Gels* nat-s
  - **Downward**: am-c ↓ asaf ↓ *Chel* ↓ coloc ↓ nat-c ↓ nux-v ↓ psor ↓ rat ↓ spong ↓ symph ↓
    - **drawing** pain: am-c asaf *Chel* coloc nat-c nux-v psor rat spong symph fd3.de•
    - **Arm**; left: pall ↓
      - **drawing** pain: pall c1
  - **Ear**: bov calc-p cann-s colch elaps ham fd3.de• lyss ruta fd4.de stry ↓ thuj
    - **drawing** pain: cann-s colch
    - **stitching** pain: bov stry thuj
    - **tearing** pain: thuj
    - **Behind**:
      - **right**: elaps spig gk
      - **left**: apis form bg1 limen-b-c hrn2*
  - **Elbow**: lyc ↓
    - **drawing** pain: lyc h2
  - **Epigastrium**: crot-c kali-c bg1 rat bg1 thuj bg1
    - **drawing** pain: crot-c
  - **Eye**: bamb-a stb2.de• gels lach bg1 ozone sde2• ph-ac bg1 pic-ac bg1 sel **Sil** sulph thea
    - **right**: bamb-a stb2.de• ozone sde2• **Sang** gsw2*
    - **left**: bamb-a stb2.de•
    - **stitching** pain: sel
  - **Face**: kola stb3•
  - **Finger**: colch ↓
    - **aching**: colch rsj2•
  - **Forehead**: chel ↓ *Chinin-s* vh daph **Gels** mrr1 gink-b sbd1• lyss ↓ mez ozone sde2• rat ruta fd4.de sars symph fd3.de• tub c1
    - **right**, to: merc-i-f bg1 **Sang** mrr1

- **extending** to – **Forehead**: ...
    - **aching** (See forehead)
    - **drawing** pain: lyss c1
    - **pressing** pain: chel bg1
    - **tearing** pain: rat sars
    - **walking** agg.: rat
  - **Head**: ambr ↓ apis bamb-a stb2.de• bung-fa mtf calc ↓ calc-p mrr1 *Carb-v* k* *Cimic* mrr1 *Ferr* fic-m gya1 gels mrr1 grat ↓ kalm mrr1 kola stb3• lap-la ↓ meny nat-sil ↓ ozone sde2• *Par* *Puls* sang hr1* **Sil** k* stront-c tritic-vg fd5.de vanil fd5.de
    - **left**: ozone sde2•
    - **drawing** pain: apis calc h2 *Carb-v* *Ferr*
    - **pressing** pain: ambr h1 grat nat-sil fd3.de•
    - **stitching** pain: kalm lap-la rsp1
    - **All** over: carb-v **Gels** grat kalm lachn c1 nat-s
    - **Through**: fl-ac
  - **Head** and shoulders: dios ↓ suprar ↓
    - **aching**: dios suprar rly4•
  - **Head** and shoulders; over: asar ↓
    - **dislocated**; as if: asar
  - **Jaws**: ang vh1
  - **Larynx** | **painful** to the touch: **Calc-p** vh
  - **Leg**; down back of left: sel c1
  - **Lumbar** region: stry ↓ tep ↓
    - **stitching** pain: stry tep
    - **stool**:
      - **going** to; on: verat ↓
        - **aching**: verat
  - **Nose**: kola stb3• lachn c1
  - **Occipital** region: aml-ns ↓
    - **aching**: aml-ns
  - **Occiput**: bung-fa mtf *Calc* ↓ calc-p caust tl1 chel *Cinnb* crat br1 cyt-l br1* dulc eup-per *Ferr* fic-m gya1 **Gels** gink-b sbd1• glon guaj ↓ hell kali-c kali-p fd1.de• kalm kola stb3• lat-m br1 lyc ↓ nat-c nat-m *Nat-s* olib-sac ↓ ozone sde2• *Petr* ↓ ph-ac ↓ *Phyt* pin-s ↓ **Sil** spig ↓ symph fd3.de• valer vanil fd5.de verat bg1
    - **right**: germ-met srj5•
    - **burning**: *Calc*
    - **drawing** pain: lyc h2 nat-m *Petr* ph-ac h2 pin-s spig h1 valer
    - **head** is bent back; when: cinnb
    - **irritability**; with: crat br1
    - **pressing** pain: chel bg1 guaj h2 nat-c nat-s olib-sac wmh1 ph-ac h2
    - **stitching** pain: cinnb k2 kali-c ph-ac h2
    - **tearing** pain: cyt-l br1
  - **Sacrum**: chel guaj lyc stry ↓
    - **stitching** pain: lyc stry
  - **Scapula**: ozone ↓
    - **stitching** pain: ozone sde2•
  - **Scapulae**: ant-c ↓ hydrog srj2• pitu-gl skp7• spong fd4.de
    - **right**: bamb-a stb2.de• spong fd4.de xan c1 [heroin sdj2]
    - **left**: pert-vc ↓
      - **sprained**; as if: pert-vc vk9
    - **drawing** pain: ant-c h2
  - **Shoulder**: alum ↓ am-m ↓ laur ↓ positr ↓ stry ↓ thuj ↓ til ↓
    - **right**: alum ↓
      - **lying** down; after:
        - **evening**: lyc ↓
          - **tearing** pain: lyc
      - **stitching** pain: alum
    - **stitching** pain: am-m laur positr nl2• stry thuj
    - **tearing** pain: alum am-m thuj til
  - **Shoulders**: alum borx calc-p camph carc ↓ caust *Chel* ↓ con ↓ crot-h daph dios dulc fd4.de falco-pe nl2• gels graph ham fd3.de• ina-i mlk9.de ip kali-n kali-p fd1.de• kalm lac-leo ↓ lach laur lyc ↓ mez mosch nat-m phyt plac rzf5• positr nl2• psor ↓ rhus-g tmo3• sang stry taosc iwa1• thuj *Verat-v* [spect dfg1]
    - **right**: *Acon* alum fic-m gya1 hydr kali-p fd1.de• lyc bg1 phos bg1 [spect dfg1]

- **extending** to – **Shoulders**: ...
  - **left**: borx bry bg1 dulc fd4.de podo fd3.de• ran-b
    - **walking** agg.: borx
  - **left** shoulder and scapula:
    - **walking** in open air agg.: borx ↓
      - **drawing** pain: borx k*
  - **evening** | **lying** down agg.; after: lyc
  - **aching**: *Verat-v*
  - **drawing** pain: borx camph carc fd2.de• *Chel* con h2 crot-h dulc fd4.de kali-n h2 lac-leo hrn2• lyc h2 mosch phyt psor jl2
  - **motion** agg.: equis-h
  - **pressing** pain: ip h1
  - **Between** shoulders; to: am-m *Apis* ip k2 phos k2 ran-b dp•
  - **Small** of back | **aching** (See lumbar)
  - **Sternum**: kali-bi bg1
  - **Teeth**: rhus-g tmo3•
  - **Temples**: fum rly1•
  - **Throat**: chin ruta fd4.de tritic-vg fd5.de
  - **Up** either side to top of head: *Lach* ↓
    - **tearing** pain: *Lach*
  - **Upward**: aml-ns bamb-a stb2.de• berb calc cann-s canth dios form **Gels** lach *Nat-s* *Petr* sang mrr1 sep **Sil** stram ter *Verat-v*
  - **Vertebra**, seventh: sep ↓
    - **pressing** pain: sep h2
  - **Vertex**: *Bell* berb calc calc-s ↓ carb-v caust *Chel* *Cimic* k* ferr fl-ac **Gels** *Glon* *Hell* *Kalm* lil-t bg1 puls rat ↓ rhus-r ↓ rhus-t *Sang* sep **Sil** *Stram* symph fd3.de• tritic-vg fd5.de verat-v
    - **cramping**: calc-s bg1
    - **stitching** pain: rhus-r *Sil*
    - **tearing** pain: rat
    - **Nape**, back and forth; to: *Chel*
  - **Wrist**: colch ↓
    - **aching**: colch rsj2•
  - **Wrists**: chel
- ○ **External**: arn ↓ aur-m-n ↓ *Calc* ↓ colch ↓ ign ↓ mez ↓
  - **burning**: arn aur-m-n k* *Calc* colch k* ign mez
- **Nape** of neck: *Acon* b7.de* adon ↓ aesc bro1 agar bg2 agn ↓ alum b4a.de *Am-c* b4.de* *Am-m* ↓ ambr ↓ aml-ns ↓ amp ↓ anac b4.de* ang ↓ *Ant-c* ↓ ant-t bg2 apis b7a.de arn ↓ ars ↓ asaf ↓ *Asar* ↓ bad ↓ bapt bg2 *Bar-c* ↓ bell bg2* *Berb* ↓ borx ↓ bov ↓ bry b7.de* bufo ↓ *Calc* ↓ calc-p ↓ camph ↓ cann-s b7.de* cann-xyz ↓ canth ↓ caps ↓ **Carb-v** ↓ *Caust* ↓ chel ↓ chin b7.de* chinin-ar bro1 *Cic* ↓ *Cimic* bro1 cina ↓ cinnb ↓ coca ↓ cocc ↓ colch ↓ coloc bro1 *Con* ↓ crot-t ↓ cupr ↓ cycl ↓ dig ↓ dios ↓ dulc b4.de* euph ↓ fago ↓ fel bro1 ferr b7a.de ferr-pic bro1 fl-ac ↓ form ↓ gard-j vlr2• *Gels* bro1 glon bg2 *Graph* b4.de* guaj ↓ ham fd3.de• hep ↓ hydr-ac ↓ hyos b7.de* hyper bro1 ign b7a.de iod ↓ ip b7.de* jug-c bro1 kali-bi bg2 kali-c b4.de* *Kali-n* b4a.de kali-p fd1.de• kali-perm ↓ lach bro1 *Lachn* ↓ laur ↓ led ↓ lyc bro1 m-ambo ↓ mag-c ↓ mag-m ↓ *Mag-p* ↓ mang ↓ meny b7.de* meph ↓ merc b4.de* merc-i-r ↓ mez b4.de* *Mosch* b7a.de musca-d szs1 myric bro1 nat-c ↓ nat-ch bro1* nat-m b4.de* nat-s bro1 nept-m ↓ nicc ↓ *Nux-m* ↓ nux-v b7.de* olnd ↓ par bro1 petr b4.de* ph-ac ↓ phos b4.de* phys ↓ **Phyt** bg2 pic-ac ↓ *Plat* ↓ plb ↓ pneu jl2 prun ↓ psor ↓ *Puls* ↓ rad-br sze8• ran-b ↓ rheum ↓ rhod b4.de* rhus-t b7a.de* ruta fd4.de sabad b7.de* *Sabin* b7a.de sal-fr ↓ samb ↓ sang ↓ sars b4.de* sep b4.de* sil ↓ spig b7.de* spong fd4.de stann b4.de* staph ↓ stram bg2 stront-c ↓ *Stry* ↓ sul-ac ↓ **Sulph** ↓ symph fd3.de• tab bg2 tarax ↓ thuj ↓ tritic-vg fd5.de vanil fd5.de verat b7a.de* verat-v ↓ vib-od bro1 viol-t ↓ x-ray bro1 xan ↓ zinc ↓ zinc-val bro1
  - **right**: gard-j ↓
    - **pressing** pain: gard-j vlr2•
    - **extending** to:
      - **Ear**:
        - **right**: gard-j ↓
          - **pressing** pain: gard-j vlr2•
  - **accompanied** by:
    - **respiration**; impeded (See RESPIRATION - Impeded - accompanied - neck)
    - **sneezing**: am-m bg2

- **Nape** of neck – **accompanied** by: ...
  - **Head**:
    - **complaints** (See HEAD - Complaints - accompanied - nape)
    - **pain** (See HEAD - Pain - accompanied - neck - pain - nape)
  - **Teeth**; pain in (See TEETH - Pain - accompanied - neck - pain)
  - **aching**: adon bro1 aesc bro1 ang bro1 bapt bro1 caust bro1 cocc ptk1 *Con* bro1 gels bro1* guaj bro1 *Par* bro1 ph-ac ptk1 pic-ac ptk1 rad-br bro1 stront-c ptk1 verat-v bro1 zinc bro1
  - **alternating** with | **Head**; pain in (See HEAD - Pain - alternating - neck)
  - **biting**: mag-c b4.de*
  - **blow**; pain as from a: bell bg2
  - **boring** pain: bar-c b4.de* cina bg2 coloc bg2 form bg2 mang bg2 merc bg2 psor bg2 sulph bg2 tarax bg2
  - **broken**; as if: bell bg2 chel bg2 graph bg2 thuj bg2
  - **burning**: am-c b4.de* apis b7a.de arn b7.de* *Bar-c* b4.de* calc b4.de* carb-v b4.de* colch b7.de* ign b7.de* merc b4.de* mez b4a.de ph-ac b4.de*
  - **clutching**: *Lyc* bg2
  - **cold**; as if from taking a: bry b7.de*
  - **contracting**: amp rly4• dulc fd4.de nept-m lsd2.fr nux-m sal-fr sle1•
  - **corrosive**: agn b7.de* nux-v b7.de*
  - **coryza**; during: *Am-m* b7a.de
  - **cough** agg.; during: alum b4a.de* bell b4.de* ferr bg2 merc b4a.de*
  - **cramping**: arn b7.de* *Asar* b7a.de bell bg2 calc-p bg2 *Cic* bg2 cimic bg2 glon bg2 hydr-ac bg2* kali-bi bg2 *Nux-v* bg2*
  - **cutting** pain: dig b4.de* graph b4a.de
  - **dislocated**; as if: agar b4.de* alum bg2 ambr bg2 ars bg2 asar b7.de* bell bro1 *Calc* b4a.de caust bro1 chel bg2 cinnb bg2 coca bg2 coloc bg2 dulc b4.de* fago bro1 kali-n bg2 *Lachn* bro1 lyc bg2 nat-c bg2 nat-m b4.de* nicc bg2 psor bg2 puls bg2 rhus-t b7a.de* sang bg2 sep b4.de* sulph bg2 thuj bg2 zinc bg2
  - **dragging**: coloc b4.de*
  - **drawing** pain: alum b4.de* am-c b4a.de am-m b7.de* ambr b7.de* ang b7.de* *Ant-c* b7.de* asaf b7.de* asar b7.de* bell b4.de* borx b4a.de calc b4a.de camph b7.de* cann-s b7.de* caps b7.de* *Carb-v* b4a.de chin b7.de* coloc b4.de* con b4.de* crot-t bg2 cycl b7.de* dig b4.de* hyos b7.de* kali-c b4.de* kali-n b4.de* *Lyc* b4.de* m-ambo b7.de meny b7.de* *Merc* b4.de* mosch b7.de* nat-c b4.de* nat-m bg2 nux-m b7.de* *Nux-v* b7.de* ph-ac b4.de* plb b7.de* psor bg2 *Puls* b7.de* *Rhod* b4.de* rhus-t b7.de* ruta b7.de* sep b4.de* staph b7.de* sulph b4.de* thuj b4.de* viol-t b7.de* zinc b4.de*
    - **alternating** with | **Chest**; constriction of (See CHEST - Constriction - alternating - drawing)
  - **exertion**; as if after: ant-t bg2 nat-m b4.de* rhus-t b7.de* zinc bg2
  - **flesh** where loose; as if: acon b7.de*
  - **grasping** pain: *Lyc* b4.de*
  - **menses** | **before** | **agg.**: coloc b4a.de sulph b4.de
    - **during** | **agg.**: sulph b4a.de
  - **paralyzed**; as if: asar b7.de* cina b7.de* cycl b7.de* meny b7.de* nat-c b4.de* nux-v b7.de* par b7.de* sil b4a.de spig b7.de* staph b7.de* verat b7.de*
  - **pinching** pain: alum b4a.de
  - **pressing** pain: agn b7.de* ambr b7.de* anac b4.de* asaf b7.de* asar b7.de* *Bar-c* b4.de* bell b4.de* bry b7.de* bufo bg2 carb-v b4.de* cocc b7.de* coloc b4.de* crot-t bg2 cupr b7a.de cycl b7.de* dig b4.de* dulc bg2 euph b4.de* gard-j vlr2• graph b4.de* lach b7.de* laur b7.de* lyc b4.de* meny b7.de* merc b4.de* mosch b7.de* *Nat-m* b4.de* petr bg2 ph-ac b4.de* phos b4.de* prun bg2 ran-b b7.de* rheum b7.de* rhus-t b7.de* *Sabin* b7a.de samb b7.de* sars b4a.de spong b7.de* stann bg2 staph b7.de* tarax b7.de* thuj b4.de*
    - **finger**; as from a: meph bg2
    - **outward**: bry bg2
    - **weight**; as from a: coloc bg2 nux-v b7.de* *Par* b7.de* phos bg2 rhus-t b7.de*

Back

- **Nape** of neck: ...
  - **rheumatic**: acon b7.de* ambr b7a.de anac b4.de* *Ant-c* b7a.de asaf b7.de* borx b4a.de* *Bry* b7a.de* calc-p bg2* carb-v b4a.de caust bro1 *Cimic* bro1 colch bro1 cycl b7.de* *Dulc* bro1 graph b4.de* guaj b4.de* iod b4.de* kali-i bro1 *Lachn* bro1 merc b4.de* mez b4.de* *Nux-v* b7.de* petr bro1 *Puls* b7.de* rad-br bro1 ran-b b7.de* *Rhod* b4.de* rhus-t b7.de* sang bro1 staph b7.de* stel bro1 *Stict* bro1 sulph b4a.de verat b7.de*
    - **motion**; only during: acon tl1
  - **sore**: agar b4a.de* aml-ns bro1 apis bg2 ars bg2 asar b7.de* bell bg2 bry b7.de* cann-xyz bg2 caust b4.de* chin b7.de* cimic bro1 coloc b4.de* cycl b7.de* dig bg2 fl-ac bg2 graph b4a.de hep b4a.de* iod bg2 kali-perm bro1 *Lach* bro1 lyc bg2 merc-i-r bg2 nat-m b4.de* nat-s bg2 nux-v b7.de* ph-ac b4.de* phys bg2 ruta bg2 sabin b7a.de sulph b4.de* tarax bro1 thuj b4.de* zinc bg2
  - **squeezing**: anac b4.de* arn bg2 *Plat* b4a.de sil b4.de* thuj b4.de*
  - **stitching** pain: acon b7.de* alum b4.de* *Am-m* b7a.de ang b7.de* apis b7a.de arn b7.de* *Bar-c* b4.de* bell b4.de* borx bg2 bov b4.de* bry b7a.de calc b4.de* camph b7.de* cann-s b7.de* carb-v b4a.de caust bg2 chin b7.de* cocc b7.de* dig bg2 graph b4.de* guaj b4.de* ign b7.de* laur b7.de* mag-c b4.de* merc b4.de* nat-c b4.de* par b7.de* ph-ac b4.de* puls b7.de* rhus-t b7.de* sars b4.de* sep b4.de* stann b4.de* staph b7.de* sul-ac bg2 sulph b4.de* tarax b7.de* viol-t b7.de* zinc b4a.de
  - **stool** agg.; during: acon ↓
    - **tearing** pain: acon b7a.de
  - **tearing** pain: acon bg2* alum b4a.de am-c bg2 am-m b7.de* ambr bg2 anac bg2 asaf b7.de* asar bro1 bad bro1 bar-c bro1 bell bro1 *Berb* bro1 *Bry* bro1 calc b4a.de camph b7.de* cann-xyz bg2 canth b7.de* **Carb-v** b4.de* *Caust* b4a.de chin b7a.de* chinin-ar bro1 colch bro1 coloc bg2 con b4a.de* dig bg2 ferr-pic bro1 graph b4.de* ign b7.de* kali-bi bg2 kali-c b4.de* laur b7.de* led b7.de* **Lyc** bg2 mag-c b4.de* mag-m b4.de* *Mag-p* bro1 meny b7.de* **Merc** b4a.de mez bg2 mosch bg2 nat-c b4.de* nat-m bg2 *Nux-m* b7a.de **Nux-v** b7.de* olnd b7.de* par b7.de* petr bg2 phos b4.de* plb b7.de* psor bg2 puls bg2 rhod b4a.de* rhus-t bg2 sars b4.de* sep bg2 sil b4.de* spig b7.de* staph bg2 stront-c b4.de* *Stry* bro1 **Sulph** b4.de* xan bro1 zinc b4a.de*
  - **twisting** pain: ang bg2 dios bg2 dulc bg2 sars bg2
  - **ulcerative** pain: puls b7.de*
  - **wedge**; as from a: cimic bg2
  - **wrong** position; as if from: dulc b4.de* lyc bg2 nux-v b7.de* psor bg2 puls b7.de* *Rhus-t* bg2 thuj bg2 zinc b4.de*
  - **extending** to:
    - **Forehead**: gink-b sbd1• ruta fd4.de
    - **Head**: ambr bg2 bar-c b4a.de calc b4a.de* canth bg2 carb-v bg2 caust b4a.de* gels bg2 guaj b4a.de* hell bg2 kali-c bg2 mang b4a.de* puls bg2 *Sang* bg2 sil b4a.de* valer bg2
    - **Temples**: gard-j vlr2•
- **Shoulder**; and right: gamb ↓
  - **cutting** pain: gamb
- **Spine**: hell ↓ *Lach* ↓ naja ↓
  - **night**: caust ↓
    - **tearing** pain: caust
  - **aching**: hell
  - **sore** (= spinal irritation): naja c2
  - **tearing** pain: *Lach*
- **Spots**; in: kali-br ↓
  - **burning**: kali-br
- **Spots**; in small: lyc ↓
  - **pressing** pain: lyc
- **Tendons**: am-m ↓
  - **drawing** pain: am-m h2
- **Vertebra**; between last cervical and first dorsal: staph ↓
  - **stitching** pain: staph h1
- **Vertebrae**: *Bar-c* b4a.de ham ↓ sabin ↓
  - **sore**: ham ptk1 sabin bg2
  - **Articulation** of last cervical and first dorsal vertebra:
    - **bending** neck forward; on: dig ↓
      - **sore**: dig a1*
  - **Fifth**: aspar vh

- **Cervical** region – **Vertebrae**: ...
  - **First**: nat-m ↓
    - **burning**: nat-m k1
  - **Fourth**: lac-d ↓
    - **pressing** pain: lac-d c1
  - **Seventh**: carb-ac ↓ *Chinin-s* ↓ con ↓ *Gels* ↓ sep ↓
    - **sore**: carb-ac *Chinin-s* a con k* *Gels* sep h2
  - **Sixth**: aspar vh
- **Coccyx**: acon ↓ aesc agar k* agn aloe ↓ alum k* alum-sil k2 am-c k* *Am-m* ambr ↓ ang ↓ ant-c ↓ ant-t bro1 **Apis** arg-met ↓ arg-n arn bro1 ars b4a.de ars-i ars-s-f k2 asaf bacls-10 fmm1• bell k* bell-p-sp ↓ berb ↓ borx k* bov k* *Bry* bro1 *Calc* *Calc-caust* bro1 *Calc-p* calc-s calc-sil k2 cann-i *Cann-s* cann-xyz bg2 *Canth* k* *Carb-an* k* *Carb-v* k* *Carbn-s* castm bro1 castor-eq k* **Caust** k* cench ↓ chin ↓ cic k* cimic k* *Cist* k* coc-c ↓ cocc ↓ colch coloc ↓ *Con* k* cor-r ↓ croc ↓ des-ac rbp6 dios dros ↓ ephe-si hsj1• *Euph* *Ferr-p* bro1 *Fl-ac* k* *Gamb* gins mtf11 graph k* grat k* hep hura ↓ *Hyper* k* ign k* iod k* *Kali-bi* k* *Kali-c* k* kali-i k* kali-m k2 *Kali-p* kali-sil k2 **Kreos** k* lac-c bro1 *Lach* k* lact laur bg2 led k* lil-t lith-c ↓ lob k* lyc ↓ *Mag-c* k* *Mag-p* bro1 manc ↓ *Med* k* meny ↓ *Merc* k* mez c1 mosch ↓ mur-ac k* musca-d szs1 nat-m nat-s ↓ nat-sil ↓ nicc ↓ *Nit-ac* nux-m ol-an ↓ oxal-a ↓ *Par* k* *Petr* k* petr-ra ↓ ph-ac k* phel ↓ *Phos* k* pic-ac plat plb k* puls ↓ *Rhus-t* k* *Ruta* sanic ↓ sel rsj9• *Sep* *Sil* k* spong fd4.de staph staphycoc ↓ sul-i k2 sulph k* suprar ↓ symph fd3.de• syph tarent k* tell ↓ tet bro1 *Thuj* k* trios rsj11• tritic-vg fd5.de ulm-c ↓ valer ↓ vanil fd5.de verat xan k* xanth bg2 **Zinc** k* zinc-p k2
  - **left**: med mtf11
  - **daytime**: des-ac rbp6
  - **morning** | **waking**; on: ars-s-f k2 *Kali-bi* staph mtf11
  - **evening**: alum *Apis* *Castor-eq* *Caust* graph *Kali-bi*
    - **burning**: apis
    - **drawing** pain: *Caust* graph
    - **pressing** pain: *Apis* kali-bi
  - **accompanied** by | **Soles** of the feet; sore pain in: thuj ptk1
  - **aching**: calc-p carb-v caust des-ac rbp6 *Fl-ac* hyper k2 *Kali-bi* oxal-a rly4• sulph xan *Zinc*
  - **appearing** gradually | **disappearing** gradually; and: coca-c sk4•
  - **biting**: aloe bg2 phel bg2
  - **blow**; pain as from a: kali-bi bg2 plat b4.de* ruta b7.de*
  - **boring** pain: arn b7.de* led bg2 manc bg2 nat-m bg2
  - **broken**; as if: cist lyc bg2 phos bg2 [bell-p-sp dcm1]
  - **burning**: apis *Ars* b4a.de canth carb-an b4.de* carb-v bg2 cist colch k* laur k* mur-ac k* *Phos* k* staph k* sulph h2
  - **burrowing**: arn b7.de*
  - **chronic**: carb-an ↓
    - **burning**: carb-an mrr1
  - **coition**; during: kali-bi k* kali-br ptk1
  - **corrosive**: agar b4.de* alum b4.de* canth b7.de* kali-c b4.de* kali-i bg2 ph-ac b4.de* phos bg2
  - **cramping**: *Bell* k* grat sil bg2 thuj bg2
  - **cutting** pain: arg-n bg2 canth hyper k2 kali-bi bg2 rhus-t bg2
  - **delivery**; after: hyper pd tarent
  - **digging** pain: arg-n bg2
  - **dislocated**; as if: agar hep b4a.de sulph k*
  - **drawing** pain: ant-c b7.de* *Ant-t* bro1 arg-n bg2 bry bg2 *Calc* carb-v k* **Caust** k* graph k* kreos k* lil-t mur-ac k* *Rhus-t* k* *Thuj* k*
    - **paroxysmal**: thuj
    - **upward**: mur-ac
  - **fall** | **after** a: bell-p bg3 **Hyper** *Mez* ruta bnt **Sil**
  - **fall**; as from a: aloe sne caust sne croc b7.de* kali-i k* nat-m sne ruta b7.de*
  - **fever**; during: agn bg2 arn bg2 *Ars* bg2 borx bg2 calc bg2 carb-v bg2 chin bg2 *Hep* bg2 ign bg2 merc bg2 ph-ac bg2 plat bg2 *Rhus-t* bg2 ruta bg2 sulph bg2
  - **gnawing** pain: agar alum k* *Gamb* *Kali-c* k* ph-ac
  - **injuries**:
    - **after**: *Carb-an* ↓ **Hyper** ↓ *Mez* ↓ **Sil** ↓ thuj ↓

- **injuries – after**: ...
  - **sore**: *Carb-an* **Hyper** k* *Mez* **Sil** thuj k2
  - **after** injuries; long: des-ac rbp6
- **jerking** pain: alum calc carb-an caust chin k* *Cic* k* rhus-t k* sulph k*
- **lancinating**: *Canth* petr-ra shn4• *Tarent*
- **leukorrhea**; with milky: **Kreos** kr1
- **lying**:
  - **agg.**: am-m ↓ *Carb-an* galeoc-c-h gms1•
    - **sore**: am-m gsy1 carb-an
  - **back**; on | **agg.**: bell h1 graph bg1
- **menses**:
  - **during**:
    - **agg.**: bell canth carb-an carb-v ↓ *Caust* cench k2 *Cic* k* *Cist* graph kali-c kreos merc mur-ac ↓ ph-ac pitu-a vml2• thuj zinc zinc-p k2
      - **aching**: zinc
      - **burning**: carb-v mur-ac
      - **cramping**: *Bell*
      - **drawing** pain: caust *Cic* graph kreos thuj
      - **gnawing** pain: kali-c
      - **jerking** pain: *Cic*
      - **sore**: bell carb-an caust cench k2 kreos
      - **stitching** pain: caust ph-ac
      - **tearing** pain: canth *Cic* merc
  - **instead** of: ars h2
  - **suppressed** menses; from: bell caust kali-c mag-c merc petr phos plat ruta thuj zinc
- **motion**:
  - **agg.**: *Caust* euph fl-ac kali-bi mez c1 *Phos* tarent
  - **hindering** motion: lach *Phos*
- **perspiration**; during: arn bg2 *Ars* bg2 borx bg2 *Calc* bg2 carb-v bg2 caust bg2 chin bg2 graph bg2 *Hep* bg2 ign bg2 *Merc* bg2 ph-ac bg2 **Rhus-t** bg2 *Sulph* bg2
- **pinching** pain: calc b4.de* zinc h2*
- **pressing** pain: acon bg2 agar bg2 aloe k* ambr bg2 ang bg2 apis k* berb bg2 calc calc-p cann-i *Cann-s* k* *Carb-an* *Carb-v* k* chin k* colch bg2 coloc bg2 hep k* hura bg2 iod h* kali-bi bg2 lith-c bg2 meny bg2 merc k* mosch bg2 nat-m bg2 nat-sil fd3.de• ol-an bg2 ph-ac k* phos k* puls bg2 ruta bg2 *Sep* k* spong bg2 symph fd3.de• tell bg2 thuj bg2 valer k* vanil fd5.de zinc k*
  - **plug**; as from a: cann-xyz bg2 carb-v bg2 cor-r bg2 lith-c bg2
- **pressure** | **abdomen**; on:
  - **amel.**: merc k*
    - **tearing** pain: *Merc* k*
  - **agg.**: *Arum-t* *Calc-p* *Carb-an* *Carb-v* *Euph* fl-ac *Kali-bi* mez c1 *Petr* phos k2 **Sil** tarent xan
    - **stitching** pain: *Sil*
- **pulling** upwards from tip of; sensation of: lil-t ↓
  - **drawing** pain: lil-t k*
- **riding** | **carriage**; in a | **agg.**: nux-m *Sil*
  - **long** carriage ride; as after a: **Sil**
- **rising**:
  - **sitting**; from:
    - **agg.**: *Caust* elaps gk *Euph* *Kali-bi* **Lach** **Sil** *Sulph*
      - **neuralgic**: lach bro1
      - **sore**: **Sulph**
      - **stitching** pain: **Sil**
    - **amel.**: kreos k*
      - **drawing** pain: kreos
    - **impossible**: bell
- **sitting** agg.: *Am-m* *Apis* arg-n bell bros-gau mrc1 *Carb-an* *Castor-eq* cench ↓ cist dros ↓ galeoc-c-h gms1• **Kali-bi** k* *Kreos* ↓ *Lach* led mez c1 *Par* *Petr* petr-ra shn4• plat rhus-t sel rsj9• **Sil** ↓ symph fd3.de• syph tarent thuj vanil fd5.de xan zinc
  - **aching**: petr plat
  - **burning**: *Apis* k* cist k*
  - **drawing** pain: *Kreos* *Thuj*
- **sitting** agg.: ...
  - **itching**, while: *Par* ↓
    - **stitching** pain: *Par*
  - **pressing** pain: *Apis* symph fd3.de• vanil fd5.de
  - **sore**: *Am-m* k* bros-gau mrc1 carb-an cench k2 *Cist* k* *Kali-bi* **Sil**
  - **stitching** pain: dros lach par k*
  - **tearing** pain: par k* rhus-t zinc
- **sitting** on something sharp; as if: *Lach* k*
- **sleep** agg.; during: *Am-m*
  - **sore**: *Am-m*
- **sore**: aloe bg2 alum k* *Am-m* k* *Arn* bro1 ars-s-f k2 calc-p *Carb-an* k* *Carb-v* k* **Caust** k* cench k2 *Cist* coc-c bg2 cocc bg2 *Euph* fl-ac hep b4.de* **Hyper** *Kali-bi* *Kali-i* lach merc bg2 *Mez* nat-m k* *Petr* phos k* *Rhus-t* bg2 *Ruta* k* sanic c2 **Sil** k* staphycoc rly4• **Sulph** k* thuj bg2 ulm-c jsj8• xan zinc-p k2
- **standing**:
  - **agg.**: verat
    - **stitching** pain: verat
  - **amel.**: arg-n bell tarent
  - **erect**:
    - **agg.**: thuj
    - **impossible**: thuj ↓
      - **drawing** pain: thuj h1
- **stitching** pain: agn k* aloe bg2 am-c k* ang b7.de* arg-met k* asaf b7.de* bry bg2 calc k* calc-p *Canth* k* carb-v b4.de* *Caust* colch k* dios dros b7.de* kali-c bg2 lact *Mag-c* mur-ac nat-m k* nat-s bg2 nicc *Par* k* ph-ac k* phel bg2 phos *Pic-ac* *Rhus-t* k* **Sil** suprar rly4• *Tarent* *Thuj* verat k* zinc k*
  - **itching**: dros ph-ac verat h1
  - **jerking** pain: carb-v rhus-t h1
  - **pulsating** pain: ign par
  - **startling**: calc-p (non:mur-ac hr1)
  - **stinging**: sil
- **stool**:
  - **after**:
    - **agg.**: euph ptk1 grat k* sulph
      - **aching**: sulph
      - **sprained**; as if: grat k*
  - **before**: sep ↓
    - **stitching** pain: sep
  - **during**:
    - **agg.**: phos ptk1 sulph ptk1
      - **stitching** pain: *Phos*
- **stooping** agg.: sulph
  - **sore**: sulph
- **stretching** | **amel.**: alum
- **sudden**: mag-c ↓
  - **cutting** pain: mag-c a1
- **tearing** pain: ant-c arn b7.de* *Bell* bro1 *Calc-caust* *Calc-p* k* *Canth* k* carb-v bg2 caust bg2 *Cic* k* graph bg2 kali-bi bro1 kreos bg2 *Mag-c* *Mag-p* bro1 *Merc* k* nat-s k* par b7.de* rhus-t bg2 *Sil* thuj bg2 zinc b4.de*
- **touch** agg.: alum alum-p k2 bell *Calc-p* *Carb-an* cist *Euph* fl-ac *Kali-bi* lach petr phos **Sil** xan
  - **burning**: *Carb-an* k* cist k*
  - **sore**: alum h2
- **ulcerative** pain: *Carb-an* *Phos* k*
- **urination**:
  - **before**: kali-bi k*
  - **during** | **agg.**: *Graph* k*
  - **impossible**: thuj ↓
    - **drawing** pain: thuj
- **violent**: kali-bi bg2
- **walking**:
  - **agg.**: bry *Kali-bi* sel rsj9• tritic-vg fd5.de
    - **drawing** pain | **sticking**: bry
  - **slowly** | **amel.**: bell petr-ra shn4•

▽ • **extending** to:
⁝ **Anus**: carb-v ↓ thuj ↓
: **stitching** pain: carb-v h2 thuj
⁝ **Back**; up: mur-ac ↓ *Phos* ↓ suprar ↓
: **stitching** pain: mur-ac *Phos* suprar rly4•
⁝ **Downward**: hyper k2
⁝ **Occiput**: ephe-si hsj1•
⁝ **Rectum** and vagina: ars-s-f k2 *Kreos*
: **drawing** pain: *Kreos*
⁝ **Sacrum**: ruta ↓
: **sore**: ruta
⁝ **Spine**:
: **upward**: caust sne hyper k2 mur-ac ↓ tritic-vg fd5.de
. **burning**: mur-ac
: **Vertex** during stool, drawing head backward; through spine to: *Phos* k*
⁝ **Thighs**: rhus-t bg3 *Thuj* ↓
: **drawing** pain: *Thuj*
⁝ **Urethra** | **urination** agg.; before: *Kali-bi*
○ • **Skin**; below the: colch ↓
⁝ **ulcerative** pain: colch b7.de*
- **Dorsal** region: abrot ↓ acon bg2 adon ↓ aesc *Agar* k* agath-a nl2• aloe bg2 alum b4.de* *Alumn* am-c b4.de* am-m ↓ ambr bg2 anac ↓ ang ↓ *Ant-c* ↓ *Ant-t* b7a.de apis k* arg-met arg-n ↓ arge-pl rwt5• arn bg2 ars b4.de* asaf k* asar ↓ asc-c ↓ atp ↓ aur k* aur-m aur-s k2 bad ↓ *Bamb-a* stb2.de• bar-c bg2 *Bell* k* benz-ac bg2 berb k* beryl ↓ bism bg2 bol-la ↓ borx ↓ bov b4.de* brom *Bry* k* *Cact* ↓ cadm-met sp1 calc k* calc-ar *Calc-p* camph ↓ cann-i cann-s b7.de* cann-xyz ↓ canth b7.de* caps b7.de* carb-an b4.de* **Carb-v** ↓ carc jl2 *Card-m* ↓ castm ↓ **Caust** b4a.de cham b7.de* *Chel* ↓ chin bg2 chord-umb ↓ cic ↓ *Cimic* k* cina ↓ cinnb ↓ cit-ac ↓ cob ↓ cocc k* *Colch* ↓ coloc con k2 cor-r ↓ cortiso sp1 crot-c ↓ cupr ↓ cycl ↓ daph dig ↓ dios dros ↓ dulc fd4.de equis-h ↓ euon ↓ euph ↓ *Euphr* ↓ ferr b7.de* ferr-i fl-ac bg2 flav jl2 gels bg2 *Gins* ↓ graph b4.de* guaj k* ham ↓ hell ↓ hep b4.de* hippoc-k szs2 hist sp1 hura hydrog srj2• hyos b7.de* *Hyper* ign b7.de* ignis-alc es2• ind iodof irid-met srj5• kali-bi bg2 kali-br ↓ *Kali-c* k* kali-n b4.de* kali-p *Kali-s* *Kalm* ketogl-ac ↓ kola stb3• **Kreos** b7a.de* lac-loxod-a hrn2• lach k* lap-la sde8.de• laur ↓ led k* lil-t lob lyc k* m-ambo b7.de m-arct b7.de m-aust ↓ mag-c b4.de* mag-m ↓ mag-s ↓ mang ↓ mang-p ↓ med ↓ medul-os-si ↓ meny ↓ meph bg2 *Merc* k* merc-c ↓ mez b4.de mosch ↓ mur-ac bg2 *Naja* k* nat-c k* *Nat-m* k* nat-p *Nat-s* nat-sil ↓ neon srj5• nicc ↓ nit-ac b4.de* nuph ↓ nux-m b7.de* nux-v b7a.de olnd bg2 onos op ↓ ox-ac bg2 oxal-a ↓ ozone sde2• pall ↓ par ↓ pert-vc vk9 petr k* petr-ra shn4• *Ph-ac* phel ↓ *Phos* k* phyt bg2 pic-ac plac ↓ plat bg2 plb bg2 pneu jl2 podo bg2* positr ↓ prun ↓ psor k* ptel c1 **Puls** b7.de* *Ran-b* k* rat ↓ rheum ↓ rhod b4a.de* rhus-g tmo3• rhus-t k* rob ↓ ruta k* sabad bg2 *Sabin* b7a.de sacch-a fd2.de• sacch-l ↓ samb ↓ sang sars bg2 sec b7.de* sel ↓ senec ↓ seneg k* *Sep* k* *Sil* b4.de* spig ↓ spong b7.de* stann staph k* stram k* streptoc ↓ stront-c ↓ stry ↓ sul-ac bg2 **Sulph** k* symph fd3.de• syph jl2 tab bg2 tarax ↓ tell ↓ tep ↓ teucr ↓ thuj bg2 tritic-vg fd5.de tub ↓ tub-r jl2 tung-met bdx1• urol-h ↓ vac jl2 *Valer* ↓ vanil fd5.de vario bg2 verat k* verb ↓ vero-o rly4• viol-t ↓ *Zinc* k* zinc-p k2 [buteo-j sej6]
• **one** side: *Guaj* ↓
⁝ **aching**: guaj bg2
⁝ **tearing** pain: *Guaj* b4a.de
• **right**: canth ↓
⁝ **pulsating** pain: canth bg2
• **left**: dulc ↓
⁝ **pulsating** pain: dulc bg2
• **morning**: calc-p ↓ cimic cp dulc fd4.de kali-s fd4.de ruta fd4.de sep h2 spong fd4.de symph fd3.de• tritic-vg fd5.de vanil fd5.de
⁝ **aching**: calc-p
⁝ **rising** agg.: *Brucel* sa3•
⁝ **waking**; on: calc-p ↓ ephe-si ↓ propr sa3•
: **sore**: calc-p ephe-si hsj1•
• **forenoon**:
⁝ **amel.**: ephe-si ↓
: **sore**: ephe-si hsj1•
• **noon**: bamb-a ↓
⁝ **constricting** pain: bamb-a stb2.de•

- **Dorsal** region: ...
• **afternoon**: calc-s ↓ erig ↓
⁝ **aching**: calc-s erig
• **evening**: calc-s ↓ erig ↓ mez ↓
⁝ **aching**: calc-s erig
⁝ **stitching** pain: mez h2
• **night**: ruta fd4.de syph jl2 zinc h2
• **night**, latter part of: calc-p ↓
⁝ **aching**: calc-p
• **accompanied** by:
⁝ **Cervical** region; pain in (See cervical - accompanied - dorsal)
⁝ **Kidneys**; pain in (See KIDNEYS - Pain - accompanied - dorsal)
• **aching**: aesc agath-a nl2• asc-c c1 bol-la calc *Calc-ar* *Cann-s* cit-ac rly4• ketogl-ac rly4• medul-os-si rly4• oxal-a rly4• pic-ac positr nl2• rhus-t tep urol-h rwt•
• **bending**:
⁝ **backward**:
: **agg.**: aur
: **amel.**: *Rhus-t* ↓
. **constricting** pain: *Rhus-t* a1
⁝ **body**:
: **backward** agg.: aur ↓
. **tearing** pain: aur
⁝ **forward**:
: **agg.**: cadm-met ↓ **Cimic** k* *Rhus-t* ↓ tritic-vg fd5.de vanil fd5.de
. **constricting** pain: *Rhus-t* k*
. **cramping**: cadm-met tpw6
⁝ **head**:
: **forward**:
. **agg.**: beryl ↓
stitching pain: beryl tpw5
• **biting**: m-aust b7.de
• **blow**; pain as from a: ang b7.de* *Arn* b7.de* chel bg2 cic b7.de* dig b4.de* plat b4.de* rhod b4.de* sep bg2 stann b4.de* staph b7.de*
• **boring** pain: acon b7a.de agar bg2 ang bg2 bism b7.de* brom bg2 cocc b7.de* hell bg2 laur bg2 mez bg2 phel bg2 psor bg2 **Sep** bg2 stann bg2 thuj b4.de*
• **break**; as if it would: *Lil-t*
• **breathing**:
⁝ **agg.**: irid-met ↓ plac ↓
: **stitching** pain: irid-met srj5• plac rzf5•
⁝ **arresting** breathing: berb ↓ *Sulph* ↓
: **stitching** pain: berb *Sulph*
⁝ **deep**:
: **agg.**: alum ↓ aur ↓ carb-an ↓ cinnb ↓ kali-n ↓ lac-h ↓ plac ↓ psor ↓ sabin ↓ spig ↓ *Sulph* ↓
. **stitching** pain: alum aur carb-an cinnb k2 kali-n lac-h htj1• plac rzf5• psor sabin spig *Sulph*
⁝ **hindering** breathing: apis berb *Bry* phys psor ruta fd4.de spong fd4.de sulph thuj
• **broken**; as if: alum bg2 ang bg2 *Chel* b7a.de cina b7.de* cocc b7.de* crot-c bg1 kreos bg2 lil-t bg1 lyc bg2 mag-s bg1 *Nat-m* bg2* *Phos* b4a.de plat bg2* psor bg2 verat b7.de*
• **burning**: acon bg2 agar bg2 agath-a nl2• alum b4a.de am-c b4.de* ant-t b7.de* apis b7a.de arn b7.de* *Ars* b4.de* asaf b7.de bar-c b4.de* bism b7.de* bry b7.de* *Cann-s* b7.de caps **Carb-an** b4.de* carb-v b4.de* cham b7.de chin b7a.de con b4a.de dios irid-met srj5• kali-c b4.de* kali-n b4.de kola stb3• lach b7a.de lyc b4.de* m-ambo b7.de m-arct b7.de mag-m b4.de* mang mang-p rly4• meny b7a.de merc b4a.de* mez b4.de mur-ac b4a.de* nat-c b4.de* nat-m b4a.de nit-ac b4.de* nux-v b7.de* olnd b7.de* par b7a.de ph-ac b4a.de phos b4.de plat b4.de *Puls* b7a.de rheum b7.de sel b7a.de senec bg2 seneg b4.de* *Sep* b4.de sil b4.de* spig b7a.de spong b7.de* stann b4.de sulph b4.de* *Thuj* b4.de* verat b7a.de *Zinc* k*

- **burrowing**: acon b7.de* dulc b4.de* kreos bg2 rhod b4.de* ruta b7.de* *Sep* b4a.de stann b4.de*
- **chill**; during: ail k2 *Chinin-s* sang
- **clawing** pain: arg-n bg2
- **clothes** agg.; tight: sep h2
- **cold**; as if from taking a: dig b4a.de *Valer* b7a.de
- **constricting** pain: bamb-a stb2.de•
- **contracting**: arn bg1 asaf bg2 bry b7a.de cham b7.de* dulc fd4.de ferr b7.de* *Graph* b4a.de guaj k* kali-bi bg2 kali-c bg2 kali-p fd1.de• mez b4a.de nux-v b7.de* op b7.de* viol-t b7a.de
- **corrosive**: m-aust b7.de spong b7.de*
- **cough** agg.; during: calc caps *Kali-bi* merc sil stram
  - **stitching** pain: caps **Merc**
- **cramping**: ang b7.de bell b4.de bry b7.de* cadm-met tpw6 caust b4.de *Cocc* b7.de con b4a.de dros b7.de euph b4a.de *Euphr* b7.de nit-ac b4.de petr b4.de phos b4.de *Plat* b4a.de *Sep* b4.de sil b4a.de tritic-vg fd5.de vanil fd5.de viol-t b7.de*
- **crushed**, as if: phos bg2 psor jl2
- **cutting** pain: agar agath-a nl2• alum b4.de* ang b7.de* arg-met b7.de* arn b7.de* ars bg2 asaf asc-c aur bg2 bov bg2 calc b4.de* calc-p bg2 canth b7.de* caust bg2 daph dig bg2 dulc b4.de* graph b4a.de hyper *Kali-bi* k* kali-n bg2 meny b7.de* nat-c b4.de* nat-m bg2 nat-s psor bg2 seneg b4a.de **Sep** b4a.de* sil b4.de* staph stry
- **delivery**; during: petr
  - **stitching** pain: petr
- **descending** stairs agg.: cadm-met ↓
  - **cramping**: cadm-met tpw6
- **digging** pain: acon bg2 *Agath-a* nl2• rhod bg2 thuj bg2
- **dislocated**; as if: agar b4a.de* ang bg2 *Arn* b7.de* bar-c bg2 bell b4.de* *Calc* b4.de* caps bg2 chel bg2 cinnb bg2 cocc b7.de* con bg2 hura bg2 kali-c b4.de* lyc bg2 m-aust b7a.de mur-ac b4.de* nux-v bg2 olnd bg2 petr b4.de* pic-ac bg2 rhod b4a.de *Rhus-t* b7.de* sulph b4.de* *Thuj* k* valer b7.de*
- **dragging**: nux-v b7.de* pic-ac bg2
- **drawing** pain: *Acon* b7.de* *Agath-a* nl2• alum k* *Am-c* b4a.de ambr b7.de* ant-t b7a.de* apis b7a.de arg-n bg2 *Ars* k* asaf b7.de* aur-m *Bamb-a* stb2.de• bell k* berb bg2 bry b7.de* calc b4.de* canth b7.de* caps b7.de* *Carb-v* b4.de* *Card-m* caust b4.de* cham b7.de* chin b7.de* **Cimic** cina b7.de* cocc b7.de* colch bg2 coloc *Con* b4a.de cycl b7.de* dig b4.de* dros b7.de* dulc bg2 **Guaj** k* hep b4.de* hyos b7.de* ind kali-bi bg2 *Kali-c* b4.de* kali-p fd1.de• *Lach* bg2 *Lyc* b4.de* med meny b7.de* *Merc* b4.de* mez b4.de* mosch b7.de* mur-ac h2 nat-c b4.de* nat-m b4.de* nit-ac k* nux-m bg2 nux-v b7.de* op b7.de* petr b4.de* ph-ac phos bg2 puls b7.de* rhod b4.de* rhus-t b7.de* ruta b7.de* sabad b7.de* sep b4.de* sil b4.de* spong fd4.de stann k* staph b7.de* *Stram* b7.de* stront-c b4.de* sul-ac b4.de* *Sulph* b4.de* teucr b7.de* thuj b4.de* tritic-vg fd5.de valer b7.de* vanil fd5.de verat b7.de* zinc b4.de*
  - **backward**: lil-t bg2
  - **downward**: ant-c b7a.de *Bry* b7a.de caps b7a.de meny b7a.de nux-v b7a.de staph b7a.de
  - **upward**: *Nux-v* b7a.de *Rhus-t* b7a.de spong b7a.de sulph bg2
- **dull** pain: abrot bg2 aesc bg2 aloe bg2 bism bg2 cob bg2 gels bg2 ham bg2 kali-br bg2 lil-t bg2 zinc bg2
- **exertion**:
  - **amel.**: calc-p ↓
    - **sore**: calc-p
- **exertion**; as if after: ant-t b7.de* *Apis* b7a.de bism b7.de* cocc b7.de* *Nat-m* bg2 phos bg2 sabad b7.de* sulph bg2
- **fall**; as from a: arn b7.de* ruta b7.de*
- **gnawing** pain: acon bg2 alum b4a.de *Bell* b4.de* berb bg2 hell b7.de* lil-t bg2 mag-m bg2 naja bg2 nat-c bg2 nux-v bg2 sep bg2 sulph bg2 tell bg2
- **hard** bed; as from a: bar-c b4.de*
- **inspiration**:
  - **agg.**: bry calc ↓ *Chel* cic ↓ dulc ↓ hippoc-k szs2 mur-ac ruta mrr1 tritic-vg fd5.de
    - **pressing** pain: mur-ac h2 tritic-vg fd5.de
    - **stitching**: calc cic a1 dulc a1
- **inspiration**: ...
  - **deep**:
    - **agg.**: sabin ↓ tub ↓
      - **stitching**: sabin tub gk
- **jar**; as if from a: *Arn* b7.de* petr b4.de* *Rhus-t* b7a.de
- **jerking** pain: agar bg2 am-c bg2 calc b4.de* *Cocc* b7a.de petr b4.de* staph b7.de* sulph b4.de*
- **labor**-like: cocc b7a.de hyos b7.de* *Sep* b4.de*
- **lameness**: *Arn* bg2 *Cocc* bg2 nux-m bg2 sabin bg2
- **lancinating**: agath-a nl2• bad *Gins* hura lap-la sde8.de• rob streptoc rly4•
  - **thrusts**; like: agath-a nl2• euon ran-b
- **lightening**-like: arg-n bg2
- **lying**:
  - **agg.**: lac-del hrn2•
  - **amel.**: bamb-a ↓ *Psor* ↓
    - **constricting** pain: bamb-a stb2.de•
    - **stitching** pain: *Psor*
  - **back**; on:
    - **agg.**: cadm-met ↓
      - **cramping**: cadm-met tpw6
- **lying** down agg.: beryl ↓
  - **stitching** pain: beryl tpw5
- **motion**:
  - **agg.**: agar bry cupr-ar lap-la rsp1 psor syph jl2 tub-r jl2 zinc
  - **amel.**: alum ↓ mez ↓ rhod k2 ruta fd4.de spong fd4.de tritic-vg fd5.de vanil fd5.de
    - **drawing** pain: alum mez h2 tritic-vg fd5.de
    - **stitching** pain: mez h2
  - **beginning** of:
    - **agg.**: beryl ↓
      - **stitching** pain: beryl tpw5
  - **head**; of | **agg.**: agar sang vanil fd5.de
- **needlework** or writing; from: ran-b ↓ *Sep* ↓
  - **burning**: ran-b *Sep*
- **overlifting**; as if from: calc b4a.de lyc b4a.de mur-ac b4a.de olnd b7.de* rhus-t b7.de* *Valer* b7a.de
- **paralyzed**; as if: *Cocc* b7.de nux-v b7.de* *Verat* b7a.de
- **pinching** pain: bell b4.de* cann-xyz bg2 kali-c h2* lyc bg2 nit-ac b4.de* sil b4a.de* stann b4.de* viol-t b7a.de zinc bg2
- **pressing** pain: acon bg2 agar bg2 aloe bg2 am-c bg2 am-m bg2 ambr b7a.de anac b4a.de *Ant-c* b7.de* apis b7a.de arg-met b7.de* *Arn* b7.de* asaf b7.de* asar h1 aur b4a.de bell b4.de* berb bg2 borx b4a.de* calc b4.de* cann-s b7.de* caps b7.de* carb-v b4.de* caust b4.de* chel b7.de* cocc b7.de* con k* cycl b7a.de *Dulc* b4.de* euph b4.de euphr b7.de* graph b4.de* ign b7.de* kali-bi bg2 kali-c k* kali-n b4.de* led b7.de* lyc b4.de* mag-m bg2 meny b7.de* merc b4.de* mur-ac k* nat-m b4a.de* nit-ac b4.de* nux-v b7.de* olnd b7.de* petr b4.de* phos b4.de* plat bg2 psor bg2 puls b7.de* rhod b4.de* rhus-t b7.de* ruta b7.de* sabin b7.de* samb b7.de* sars b4a.de* seneg b4a.de sep b4.de* sil bg2 spong b7.de* stann b4.de* staph b7.de* symph fd3.de• tarax b7.de* teucr b7.de* thuj b4.de* tritic-vg fd5.de vanil fd5.de verat b7.de* zinc b4.de*
  - **flatulence**; as from: zinc h2
  - **inward**: asaf bg2 laur bg2
  - **outward**: calc bg2 cann-s b7a.de *Cocc* b7a.de ruta b7.de* zinc bg2
  - **plug**; as from a: anac bg2 *Arn* b7.de* ars bg2 berb bg2 carb-v bg2 cinnb bg2 cor-r bg2 dig bg2 equis-h bg2 kreos bg2 lach b7.de* lob bg2 lyc bg2 mag-s bg2 phos bg2 plat b4.de* prun bg2
  - **stone**; as from a: coloc bg2 par bg2 sil bg2
  - **weight**; as from a: par b7.de*
- **pressure** agg.: stry-p ↓
  - **sore**: stry-p br1
- **rheumatic**: bamb-a stb2.de• **Cimic** *Dulc* *Rhus-t* ruta
- **riding** agg.: fl-ac ind podo fd3.de•
- **rising** agg.: cadm-met ↓
  - **cramping**: cadm-met tpw6

- **rubbing**:
  - **amel**.: phos↓
    - **tearing** pain: phos
- **rumbling**: alum bg2
- **sitting** agg.: *Arg-met* beryl↓ bry fl-ac kali-c kali-s fd4.de mang ph-ac *Phos* *Rhus-t*↓ symph fd3.de• tritic-vg fd5.de tub vanil fd5.de
  - **constricting** pain: *Rhus-t* k*
  - **drawing** pain: ph-ac
  - **stitching** pain: beryl tpw5
- **sitting** down agg.: arg-met↓ hura lach
  - **tearing** pain: arg-met hura
- **smarting**: alum bg2 graph b4a.de plat b4.de* staph b7.de* *Sul-ac* b4a.de *Zinc* b4a.de
- **sore**: *Acon* b7.de* agar b4a.de* aloe bg2 alum b4.de* am-m b7.de* *Apis* k* arn b7.de* ars b4.de* asar b7.de* atp rly4• bar-c bg2 calc b4a.de calc-p camph b7.de* carb-an b4.de* carb-v b4.de* caust b4.de* chin b7.de* chord-umb rly4• cimic bg2 cocc bg2 coloc b4.de* con b4.de* dig b4.de* dros b7.de* graph b4a.de hell b7.de* hydrog srj2• hyos b7.de* kali-c b4.de* kali-n bg2 ketogl-ac rly4• lach b7.de* *M-arct* b7.de* m-aust b7a.de mag-c b4a.de* mag-m b4.de* merc b4.de* nat-c b4.de* nat-m k* *Nat-s* nux-m b7a.de* **Nux-v** b7.de* pall ph-ac phos b4a.de* plat b4.de* plb psor bg2 ran-b b7.de* *Rhod* b4a.de *Ruta* b7.de* sabad b7.de* sec sep spig b7.de* stann k* staph b7.de* stram k* stront-c b4.de* sul-ac b4.de* sulph bg2 thuj b4.de* tritic-vg fd5.de vanil fd5.de **Verat** b7.de* zinc b4a.de* zinc-p k2
- **squeezing**: carb-v b4.de* kali-n b4.de* merc b4.de* nit-ac b4.de* zinc b4.de*
- **stepping** hard agg.: seneg
- **stitching** pain: acon b7.de* *Agar* alum b4.de* anac b4a.de ang b7.de* *Ant-c* b7.de* ant-t b7.de* apis b7a.de arg-met k* arn b7.de* *Asaf* k* aur b4.de* bell b4.de* beryl sp1 borx k* bov *Bry* k* *Cact* calc k* cann-s b7.de* canth caps b7.de* carb-v b4a.de* castm caust b4.de* cham b7.de* chel b7.de* chin k* chord-umb rly4• cina b7.de* cinnb k2 *Colch* k* *Con* b4.de* cupr b7.de* cycl b7.de* dig b4.de* dros k* *Dulc* b4.de* euph b4.de* fl-ac k* guaj b4a.de* ham fd3.de• hell b7.de* hep b4.de* hyos b7a.de ign b7.de* irid-met srj5• kali-bi k* kali-c k* kali-n kali-p kreos b7a.de *Lach* k* lap-la sde8.de• laur b7.de* led b7.de* lyc b4.de* m-arct b7.de m-aust b7.de mag-c b4.de* mag-m b4.de* mang k* merc b4.de* merc-c b4a.de mez b4.de* mosch b7.de* mur-ac b4.de* nat-c b4.de* nat-s nat-sil fd3.de• nicc nit-ac b4.de* olnd b7.de* par b7.de* **Petr** phos b4.de* plac rzf5• plat b4.de* plb b7.de* positr nl2• psor bg2 puls b7.de* ran-b k2 rat rhod bg2 rhus-t k* ruta b7.de* sabad k* sabin k* sars b4.de* sep b4.de* sil b4.de* spig b7.de* spong fd4.de stann b4.de* staph b7.de* stront-c k* sul-ac b4.de* sulph b4.de* tarax k* thuj b4.de* tritic-vg fd5.de tub gk valer b7.de* vanil fd5.de verat verb b7.de* *Zinc* k*
  - **burning**: stann h2
  - **needles**; as from: agar bg2 caust bg2
  - **radiating**: ran-b k2
- **stooping** a long time; as after: *Puls* b7.de*
- **stooping** agg.: arg-met↓ *Cocc*↓ meny↓ spong↓
  - **drawing** pain: meny h1 spong fd4.de
  - **stitching** pain: arg-met h1 *Cocc*
- **tearing** pain: adon bg2 agar bg2 am-c bg2 ambr bg2 anac b4a.de ant-c b7.de* **Ant-t** b7a.de ars b4.de* aur k* bell b4.de* berb k* brom *Bry* b7.de* *Calc* k* canth b7.de* caps b7.de* **Carb-v** b4.de* caust b4.de* cham b7.de* chel b7.de* chin b7.de* cina b7.de* cocc b7.de* colch b7.de* cupr bg2 dig bg2 dros b7.de* ferr b7.de* graph bg2 guaj b4.de* *Hep* bg2 hyos b7.de* ign b7.de* *Kali-c* k* kola stb3• *Lach* bg2 led b7.de* **Lyc** b4.de* mag-c bg2 mag-m b4a.de mang b4.de* merc b4.de* mez bg2 mosch bg2 nat-c bg2 **Nat-m** bg2 nit-ac b4.de* **Nux-v** b7.de* op b7.de* petr b4.de* ph-ac b4.de* plb b7.de* puls b7.de* ran-b bg2 rhod b4a.de* rhus-t b7.de* sabin b7.de* sel b7a.de *Sep* b4.de* sil b4.de* stann b4.de* stram b7.de* sul-ac bg2 **Sulph** b4.de* teucr bg2 valer bg2 zinc b4a.de*
  - **burning**: kali-c k*
- **turning** head agg.: *Bry* ind vanil fd5.de
- **twisting** pain: ang bg2 calc bg2 graph bg2 plb bg2 verat b7.de*
- **ulcerative** pain: arg-met b7.de* cic b7a.de kreos bg2 plat b4a.de
- **walking**:
  - **agg**.: *Agar* *Asaf*↓ bell *Cocc*↓ coloc galeoc-c-h gms1• nat-c *Psor* seneg *Sulph* vanil fd5.de
    - **stitching** pain: *Asaf* *Cocc* psor
  - **amel**.: beryl↓
    - **stitching** pain: beryl tpw5
  - **bent** | **must** walk bent: cann-i k2
- **warm** applications:
  - **amel**.: cadm-met↓ syph jl2
    - **cramping**: cadm-met tpw6
- **weather** agg.; cold wet: rhod k2
- **writing** agg.: mur-ac↓ petr↓
  - **aching**: mur-ac petr
- **zigzagging**: nuph bg2 sacch-l bg2
- ▽ **extending** to:
  - **Arms**: *Calc*↓ flav jl2 rhod k2 ruta fd4.de
    - **right**: agath-a nl2• bamb-a stb2.de• ruta fd4.de
    - **stitching** pain: *Calc*
    - **And** legs: *Calc*
  - **Body**; around the: vac jl2
  - **Chest**: ang bg2 bry bg2 kali-bi bg2 kali-c bg2 kali-n bg2 mez bg2 petr bg2 rhus-g tmo3• zinc bg2
  - **Hand**:
    - **right**: bamb-a stb2.de•
    - **Balls**: nept-m lsd2.fr
  - **Nipple**; left: *Asaf*
  - **Occiput**: *Cocc* ind kali-c↓ *Kalm* petr
    - **labor**; during: **Petr**↓
      - **stitching** pain: **Petr**
    - **stitching** pain: *Cocc* kali-c
  - **Pit** of stomach: rhod↓
    - **stitching** pain: rhod
  - **Ribs**: *Asaf*↓
    - **stitching** pain: *Asaf*
  - **Scapulae**: med k2
  - **Shoulders**: bamb-a stb2.de• *Galeoc-c-h* gms1• vanil fd5.de
  - **Sternum**: *Kali-bi* lac-c↓ laur
    - **cutting** pain: kali-bi lac-c
  - **Stomach**: arn bg2 bry dig bg2 glon bg2 hydr-ac bg2 ignis-alc es2• kali-c bg2 nicc bg2 polyg-h bg2 puls bg2 rat bg2 rhod stry bg2 sulph bg2 thuj bg2
    - **pressure** agg.: bell
  - **Thumb**; joint of: bamb-a stb2.de•
  - **Upward**: alum bg2 ars bg2 kali-bi bg2 nat-m bg2 nux-v bg2 phos bg2 plb bg2 sep bg2 sulph bg2
    - **Downward**; and: berb bg2
- ○ **Lower** part: allox↓
  - **break**; as if it would: allox tpw3*
- **Lower** vertebrae through chest: berb↓
  - **lancinating**: berb k*
- **Middle** part: beryl↓
  - **stitching** pain: beryl tpw5
- **Muscles**: syph jl2
- **Ribs**: bamb-a↓ kola stb3•
  - **drawing** pain: bamb-a stb2.de•
  - **inspiration** agg.: bamb-a↓
    - **drawing** pain: bamb-a stb2.de•
  - **tearing** pain: kola stb3•
  - **Below**:
    - **left**:
      - **extending** to:
        - **Sacroiliac** region; anterior: cortiso sp1*
          - **motion** | **amel**.: cortiso sp1*
          - **pressure** | **amel**.: cortiso sp1*

- **Scapulae**: acon aesc aeth agar↓ agath-a↓ aids↓ aloe↓ alum k* alum-p↓ alum-sil↓ alumn↓ am-c b4.de* *Am-m*↓ *Am-p* bro1 ambr↓ anac k* anag bro1 androc↓ ang↓ ant-c↓ ant-t↓ apis k* arg-met↓ arg-n↓ arge-pl↓ arn k* ars *Asaf* b7.de* asar↓ *Aspar* *Aur*↓ aur-m-n↓ a z a bro1 bamb-a stb2.de• bar-c bro1 bell k* bell-p-sp↓ berb bism↓ borx *Bov*↓ *Bry*↓ calad↓ *Calc* calc-ar k2 calc-p k* calc-sil k2 camph *Cann-i* bro1 cann-s↓ cann-xyz↓ canth↓ caps↓ *Carb-an*↓ *Carb-v* carbn-s↓ *Carl*↓ cassia-s cdd7*• caust cham **Chel** k* chen-a c2 *Chin* chinin-ar cic b7.de* *Cimic* cina k* cinnb↓ coc-c↓ cocc k* colch↓ *Coloc* con k* cor-r corn↓ croc↓ crot-c sk4• cund cupr b7.de* cycl↓ cypra-eg↓ cystein-l rly4• *Dig* dios↓ dulc fd4.de echi↓ elaps euph↓ *Fago* bro1 ferr↓ ferr-m↓ fl-ac↓ galeoc-c-h↓ gels↓ germ-met↓ glon↓ gran↓ graph k* grat↓ *Guaj*↓ h a m↓ hell hep k* hir↓ *Hydr* hyos↓ hyper↓ ign b7.de* ind↓ *Iod*↓ ip↓ *Jug-c* c2* jug-r bro1 kali-ar *Kali-bi*↓ *Kali-c* *Kali-chl* kali-m↓ kali-n↓ kali-p kali-s fd4.de kali-sil↓ kalm kola stb3• *Kreos* k* lac-c↓ lac-leo hrn2• lac-loxod-a hrn2• lach lachn↓ lact↓ lap-la↓ laur led lil-t lob lyc k* m-a m b o↓ m-aust↓ mag-c↓ *Mag-m*↓ manc↓ mang↓ med↓ menis bro1 meny merc k* merc-c↓ merc-i-f *Mez* morg-g fmm1• mosch↓ *Mur-ac*↓ *Myric* bro1 *Myrt-c*↓ naja nat-ar k* nat-c k* nat-m nat-s↓ nicc↓ nit-ac k* nux-m↓ *Nux-v* k* olnd↓ op↓ ox-ac↓ paeon↓ *Par*↓ petr↓ ph-ac *Phos*↓ *Phyt* k* pitu-gl↓ plat↓ plb podo↓ prun↓ psor↓ ptel↓ **Puls**↓ *Ran-b* k* ran-s rhod rhus-t rob↓ rumx ruta sabad↓ sabin↓ samb↓ sang *Sars*↓ seneg *Sep* k* sil spect↓ spig↓ spong *Squil*↓ *Stann*↓ staph↓ stram↓ stront-c↓ sul-ac↓ sulph k* syc fmm1• symph fd3.de• tab↓ tarax↓ *Tarent* **Tell** tep teucr↓ *Thuj*↓ tritic-vg fd5.de tub↓ *Valer* vanil fd5.de verat b7.de* verat-v verb↓ vesp viol-t↓ visc bro1 zinc zinc-p↓ [heroin sdj2]
  - **right**: abies-c bro1 acon↓ *Aesc* agath-a↓ *Ail* *All-c* am-m bro1 ambr anac aphis bro1 arn ars↓ *Asaf*↓ asc-t a1 bamb-a stb2.de• bar-c↓ bell↓ bism↓ borx↓ bry bro1 cain calen↓ cann-s↓ *Carb-v*↓ carc fd2.de• cassia-s↓ caust↓ **Chel** k* *Cic*↓ cocc↓ **Coloc** k* com↓ con crot-c↓ cund cycl↓ dulc↓ elat↓ ferr-m bro1 ferr-p bro1 fic-m gya1 ger-i↓ germ-met srj5• gink-b sbd1• *Gua* bro1 hyper↓ ichth bro1 iod↓ ipom-p bro1 jug-c k* kali-bi↓ *Kali-c* k* kali-p fd1.de• kali-s fd4.de kalm bro1 kola stb3• kreos↓ lac-leo hrn2• lac-lup hrn2• lachn↓ lap-la↓ laur↓ lob lyc lycps-v↓ lyss↓ mag-c bro1 mag-m↓ mag-p bg2 mand rsj7• meph↓ merc↓ merc-i-f↓ mez↓ morg-g pte1*• mur-ac↓ nat-c↓ nat-m↓ nat-s↓ nit-ac↓ ol-an↓ ozone sde2• pall bro1 petr hr1 petr-ra↓ phos↓ phyt bro1 plat↓ plb podo↓ polyg-h↓ puls-n bro1 ran-b k* ros-d wla1 ruta fd4.de samb↓ *Sang* bro1 sars↓ seneg↓ *Sep* *Sil*↓ spig↓ spong fd4.de staph↓ *Stict* bro1 stront-c bro1 sulph symph↓ tarax↓ tell trios↓ tritic-vg fd5.de *Urt-u* bro1 vanil↓ verat↓ zinc [heroin sdj2]
    - **night**:
      - **midnight**; after:
        - **4 h** | **waking**; on: *Chel*
    - **accompanied** by | **Wrist**; pain in left: asc-t a1
    - **aching**: ol-an ptk1
    - **alternating** pains: bry bg2
    - **anger**; after: coloc h2*
    - **bending** | **forward** | **agg**.: kali-p fd1.de• lob
      - **shoulders**:
        - **backward** | **amel**.: conv
    - **boring** pain: acon k* agath-a nl2• nat-c h2 ruta fd4.de sulph bg2
    - **breathing** agg.: *Aesc* *Chel* kali-c sars↓
      - **tearing** pain: kali-c sars h2
    - **burning**: agath-a nl2• asaf bg1 bar-c cann-s *Carb-v* caust com bg1 iod lachn laur *Lyc* lycps-v ptk1 mez bg1 nat-s bg1* plb seneg staph bg1 sulph verat k* zinc
    - **cough** agg.; during: sep↓
      - **stitching** pain: sep h2
    - **cramping**: chel lap-la rsp1 vanil fd5.de
    - **cutting** pain: asaf bg2 bell bg2 bry bg2 elat bg2 kali-bi bg2 nat-m bg2 polyg-h bg2
    - **dinner**; after: nat-c↓
      - **stitching** pain: nat-c h2
    - **drawing** pain: bamb-a stb2.de• **Coloc** k* con h2 lyc h2 nat-m h2 r u t a fd4.de sulph h2 tell tritic-vg fd5.de vanil fd5.de
    - **followed** by | **left**: kali-p tell
    - **inspiration** agg.: am-m↓ **Chel**↓ kali-c↓ sars↓ sep↓
      - **stitching** pain: am-m **Chel** kali-c sars h2 sep h2

- **Scapulae – right**: ...
    - **lying** agg.: *All-c* [com xyz62 graph xyz62 sulph xyz62]
    - **motion**:
      - **agg**.: calc petr
      - **arm**; of:
        - **agg**.: ail con ruta
        - **right** arm agg.; of: *Chel*
    - **neuralgic**: bamb-a stb2.de•
    - **pinching** pain: am-m h2 ger-i rly4•
    - **pressing** pain: bism h1 borx h2 carc fd2.de• cassia-s ccrh1• caust bg2 *Chel* lyc bg2 lyss mag-m h2* nat-c bg2 ruta h1* symph fd3.de• vanil fd5.de zinc bg2
      - **plug**; as from a: kreos bg2
    - **pulsating** pain: merc-i-f k*
    - **sitting** agg.: ant-c↓ puls↓
      - **pinching** pain: puls h1
      - **stitching** pain: ant-c vh1
    - **sitting** bent double; as from: anac k*
    - **sore**: anac bg2 arn bg2* ars calen bg2* caust h2* chel *Cic* crot-c bg1 cycl bg2 kali-c bg2* kreos ptk1 meph bg1 petr-ra shn4• plat bg2 podo bg2 spong bg2 zinc bg2
    - **stitching** pain: am-m *Asaf* bar-c h2 bry bg1 cic a1 cocc hr1 dulc a1 hyper bg2 *Kali-c* lap-la sde8.de• merc mur-ac a1 nat-c h2 nat-m bg2 nit-ac h2 phos podo fd3.de• ruta fd4.de samb *Sep* *Sil* spig h1 spong symph fd3.de• tarax trios rsj11• vanil fd5.de
    - **stooping** agg.: jug-c
    - **tearing** pain: anac dulc a1 *Kali-c* k* kola stb3• mag-m nat-m h2 plb k* sars h2 zinc k*
    - **ulcer**; as from an: cic h1
    - **walking** in open air:
      - **amel**.: sep↓
        - **stitching** pain: sep h2
    - **extending** to:
      - **left**: cocc↓
        - **stitching** pain: cocc
      - **Arm**: bamb-a stb2.de• ruta fd4.de
      - **Back**; down: sep↓
        - **stitching** pain: sep h2
      - **Breast**, near nipple: ang↓
        - **cutting** pain: ang hsa1*
      - **Cervical** region: androc srj1• fic-m gya1
      - **Chest**; front of: acon↓ ruta↓
        - **boring** pain: acon ruta fd4.de
      - **Chest**; through: kali-c↓ *Merc*↓
        - **stitching** pain: kali-c h2 *Merc*
      - **Finger**; first | **right**: bamb-a stb2.de•
      - **Hand**; right: plat↓
        - **drawing** pain: plat h2
      - **Neck**: hydrog srj2•
      - **Rib**; last false: sep↓
        - **stitching** pain: sep h2
      - **Shoulder**: *Chel* lac-leo hrn2* [spect dfg1]
      - **Sternum**: nat-c↓
        - **boring** pain: nat-c h2
    - **Between** spine and right scapula: bamb-a↓ zinc↓
      - **drawing** pain: bamb-a stb2.de•
      - **tearing** pain: zinc k*
    - **Edge** of, near spine: alumn *Card-m* *Chel* nat-c sang a1
    - **Inner** angle: samb↓
      - **stitching** pain: samb h1
    - **Outer** margin: cina↓ plat↓
      - **pressing** pain: plat h2
      - **sore**: plat h2
      - **stitching** pain: cina h1
  - **left**: *Acon* bro1 *Aesc* bro1 aeth bg2 agar k* aloe alum↓ am-m ambr anac ant-t bg2* aphis c1* arg-met↓ asaf *Aspar* bro1 aur↓ bar-c↓ berb↓ *Cact* calc↓ calc-f↓ carb-v card-m cham bro1 chel mrr1 colch k* coloc k* com↓ con corian-s knl6• cund cypra-eg↓ dig dios↓ dulc fd4.de

Back

· **Scapulae – left**: ...
echi↓ equis-h bg2 eup-pur bro1 euph↓ euphr↓ ferr bro1 fl-ac↓ galeoc-c-h gms1• *Gels* k* graph h2 grat↓ ham fd3.de• hell h1 heroin↓ hyper↓ kali-bi bg2 kali-c↓ kali-p↓ kola stb3• lac-h↓ lac-loxod-a hrn2• lap-la↓ led k* lil-t lob-s bro1 mang med↓ meny↓ merc↓ merc-c merc-i-f↓ mez↓ mill↓ morg-g pte1*• nat-c↓ nat-m↓ nat-p nat-sil fd3.de• nux-m bro1 *Onos* bro1 paeon↓ par↓ petr-ra↓ ph-ac↓ phos phyt pitu-gl↓ plat↓ podo fd3.de• polyg-h bg2 psil ft1 ptel ran-b↓ rhodi bro1 rhus-t↓ rumx↓ ruta fd4.de sabin bg2 sacch-a fd2.de• sal-al↓ samb↓ sang sep↓ sil↓ spig↓ spong fd4.de *Squil* stann↓ staph↓ stram bro1 sulph k* syc pte1*• symph fd3.de• tell↓ teucr↓ thuj trios↓ tritic-vg fd5.de tub tl1 verat-v bg2 zinc↓

: **evening**: alum↓
. **tearing** pain: alum k*

: **night**: bar-c↓
. **burning**: bar-c

: **bending** arms backward agg.: carb-v↓
. **tearing** pain: carb-v k*

: **boring** pain: aur bg1* berb bg2* dig k* hyper ptk1 meny k* mez ptk1 nat-c ptk1 paeon bg2 par bg1 ph-ac bg2* ruta bg2* spig h1* spong bg1

: **breathing** or coughing: dulc↓ sep↓
. **stitching** pain: dulc h2 sep

: **burning**: ambr bar-c card-m com echi bg1 euphr fl-ac galeoc-c-h gms1• lac-h htj1• med ptk1 nat-m sil teucr zinc
. **pricking** pain: fl-ac

: **cold**; after taking a: sep↓
. **tearing** pain: sep h2

: **cough** agg.; during: helo c1 *Myrt-c*↓
. **stitching** pain: *Myrt-c* b7a.de

: **cramping**: bar-c h2 lac-loxod-a hrn2• lap-la rsp1 nat-sil fd3.de•

: **cutting** pain: calc-f bg2 dios bg2 hell bg2 lil-t bg2 merc-i-f bg2 rumx bg2 samb bg2 spig bg2 tell bg2 thuj bg2

: **digging** pain: berb bg2

: **drawing** pain: asaf card-m con mez ptel sep *Squil* sulph bg2

: **itching** on place below and to right of it; and: pall↓
. **burning**: pall

: **lancinating**: sal-al blc1•

: **lowering** the shoulder; on: am-m↓
. **stitching** pain: am-m h2*

: **motion** agg.: dulc fd4.de hell h1

: **pinching** pain: euph h2

: **pressing** pain: nat-m bg2 plat bg2 rhus-t bg2
. **plug**; as from a: phos

: **pulsating** pain: bar-c bg2 kali-c bg2

: **rest** agg.: am-m↓ *Kalm*↓ manc↓ *Sep*↓ verb↓
. **stitching** pain: am-m *Kalm* manc *Sep* verb

: **riding** agg.: agar

: **rubbing** | **amel.**: cench k2

: **sitting** agg.: arg-met↓ mang↓ sulph↓
. **tearing** pain: arg-met h1 mang k* sulph

: **sore**: card-m coloc led bg2* merc bg2* petr-ra shn4• phyt ruta fd4.de

: **stitching** on left arm: sulph↓
. **stitching** pain: sulph h2

: **stitching** pain: am-m h2 ambr **Anac** bar-c calc h2 cypra-eg sde6.de• graph h2 grat kali-c h2 kali-p fd1.de• meny h1 mill pitu-gl skp7• ran-b bg2 sep h2 spig h1 *Sulph* zinc h2

: **tearing** pain: alum ambr **Anac** arg-met carb-v card-m mang k* sep k* stann h2 staph sne thuj k* trios rsj11• [heroin sdj2]

: **then** right: cund [bell xyz62 nat-c xyz62]

: **extending** to:
. **Heart**; below: med↓
boring pain: med hr1
. **Shoulder** and mammae: grat↓
stitching pain: grat
. **Throat**: zinc↓
stitching pain: zinc

· **Scapulae – left**: ...
: **Levator** anguli scapulae:
. **walking** and writing: agar↓
burning: agar
: **Spots**; in: galeoc-c-h gms1•
: **Superior** angle:
. **friction** amel.: *Alum*↓
burning: *Alum*
: **Tip** of: nat-c↓
. **boring** pain: nat-c k*

⁝ **morning**: bamb-a stb2.de• calc↓ **Chel** dulc fd4.de fic-m gya1 hyper↓ *Kali-c*↓ kali-p k* *Mez* nat-m nat-s ran-b↓ ruta fd4.de sil↓ tritic-vg fd5.de vanil fd5.de
: **bed** agg.; in: con↓ nat-m↓ nat-s↓
. **pressing** pain: nat-m nat-s
. **sore**: con h2 nat-m
: **pressing** pain: sil h2
: **stitching** pain: calc hyper ran-b
: **tearing** pain: *Kali-c* k*
: **walking** agg.: ran-b↓
. **stitching** pain: ran-b

⁝ **forenoon**:
: **9** h: calc↓
. **stitching** pain: calc

⁝ **afternoon**: mez↓ ruta↓ sep↓ thuj↓ vanil↓
: **stitching** pain: mez ruta fd4.de sep h2 thuj vanil fd5.de

⁝ **evening**: alum↓ canth↓ chel kali-n↓ kali-s fd4.de lyc nat-p nat-s k2 olnd↓ ran-b ruta fd4.de sep↓ spong fd4.de sulph↓ tritic-vg fd5.de
: **drawing** pain: chel lyc sulph h2
: **stitching** pain: canth kali-n ruta fd4.de sep h2
: **tearing** pain: alum k* olnd k*

⁝ **night**: kali-bi↓ nit-ac↓ puls↓ *Sulph*↓
: **midnight**:
. **after** | **4** h: *Chel*
: **bed** agg.; in: nat-m↓ *Sulph*↓
. **stitching** pain: nat-m *Sulph*
: **cramping**: nit-ac h2
: **stitching** pain: kali-bi puls *Sulph*

⁝ **accompanied** by | **respiration**; complaints of (See RESPIRATION - Complaints - accompanied - scapulae)

⁝ **aching**: aeth aids nl2• androc srj1• asaf calc-p *Chin* cor-r hell jug-c lil-t lyc merc-i-f mur-ac petr phyt verat-v [bell-p-sp dcm1 spect dfg1]

⁝ **air** agg.; in open: pitu-gl↓ seneg↓
: **stitching** pain: pitu-gl skp7• seneg

⁝ **bending**:
: **arms**:
. **agg.**: carb-v
leaning on it; when: sulph↓
stitching pain: sulph
stitching pain: carb-v
: **body**:
. **backward** agg.: aur sep
tearing pain: aur k* sep k*
: **head** and upper arm backward agg.: caust↓
. **pressing** pain: caust h2

⁝ **biting**: stront-c b4.de*

⁝ **blow**; pain as from a: agar bg2 anac b4.de* arn b7.de* asar b7.de* croc b7.de* dulc b4.de* kreos b7a.de verat b7.de*

⁝ **blowing** the nose agg.: hep↓
: **stitching** pain: hep

⁝ **boring** pain: acon k* agath-a nl2• aur-m-n calad bg2 corn dig laur bg2 mag-m h2* meny k* mez bg2 nat-c b4.de* paeon k* spig b7.de

⁝ **break**; as if it would: hir skp7• nat-m h2

⁝ **breathing**:
: **agg.**: acon↓ *Aesc* alumn calc guaj↓ sang
. **stitching** pain: acon guaj
: **deep**:
. **agg.**: hep↓

- **Scapulae – breathing – deep – agg.**: ...
    - **stitching** pain: hep$_{h2}$
  - **must** breath deeply: nat-m ↓ spong ↓
    - **drawing** pain: nat-m$_{h2}$ spong$_{fd4.de}$
    - **tearing** pain: nat-m$_{h2}$
  - **hindering** breathing: calc cann-s kali-n *Puls* ruta$_{fd4.de}$ spong$_{fd4.de}$ sulph
  - **broken**; as if: hell kreos merc-i-f ran-b sil
  - **burning**: *Acon*$_{b7.de}$ agath-a$_{nl2}$• alum$_{k}$* ambr$_{b7.de}$* *Ars*$_{b4a.de}$ asaf$_{b7.de}$ **Bar-c**$_{k}$* bry$_{b7.de}$* calc$_{b4a.de}$ cann-s$_{b7.de}$* *Carb-v*$_{k}$* carbn-s caust$_{k}$* chel$_{b7.de}$ cund echi$_{ptk1}$ ferr$_{b7.de}$ glon$_{tl1}$ iod$_{k}$* kali-c$_{k}$* lachn laur$_{k}$* lyc$_{k}$* mag-m$_{b4.de}$ mang med$_{ptk1}$ **Merc**$_{k}$* mez$_{k}$* mur-ac nat-c$_{k}$* nat-m$_{k}$* nux-v$_{k}$* phos$_{tl1}$ **Plb**$_{b7.de}$* **Puls**$_{b7.de}$* rob sabad$_{b7.de}$ sabin$_{b7a.de}$ seneg$_{k}$* *Sep*$_{k}$* *Sil*$_{k}$* spong$_{fd4.de}$ stann$_{k}$* staph$_{b7.de}$ sul-ac$_{k}$* sulph$_{k}$* teucr$_{b7.de}$* *Thuj*$_{b4a.de}$ verat$_{b7.de}$* *Zinc*$_{k}$*
  - **burrowing**: acon$_{b7.de}$* laur$_{bg2}$
  - **bursting** pain: seneg$_{bg2}$
  - **chill**; during: bell$_{bg2}$ chin$_{k}$* kreos$_{bg2}$ merc$_{bg2}$ nux-v$_{bg2}$ puls$_{bg2}$ ran-b$_{bg2}$ rhus-t$_{k}$* **Sep**$_{k}$* sulph ↓ tarax$_{bg2}$ zinc$_{bg2}$
    - **stitching** pain: bell$_{bg2}$ chin$_{bg2}$ merc$_{bg2}$ nux-v$_{bg2}$ puls$_{bg2}$ *Sep*$_{bg2}$ sulph$_{bg2}$ zinc$_{bg2}$
  - **cold** air agg.: cassia-s$_{ccrh1}$•
    - **pressing** pain: cassia-s$_{ccrh1}$•
  - **constricting** pain: bamb-a$_{stb2.de}$•
  - **contracting**: chin$_{b7.de}$* fl-ac$_{bg2}$ graph$_{b4.de}$* guaj$_{b4.de}$* *Rhus-t*$_{b7.de}$* viol-t$_{b7.de}$*
  - **cough** agg.; during: chin$_{c1}$ cor-r med ↓ *Merc* ↓ puls ↓ sep ↓ sil ↓ sulph
    - **stitching** pain: med *Merc*$_{b4.de}$* puls$_{bg2}$ sep$_{b4.de}$* sil$_{bg2}$ sulph$_{b4a.de}$*
  - **cramping**: ant-c$_{bg2}$ arn$_{bg2}$ bell$_{bg2}$ bry$_{bg2}$ chel$_{bg2}$ kali-c$_{bg2}$ kali-s$_{fd4.de}$ phos$_{bg2}$ vanil$_{fd5.de}$ viol-t$_{b7.de}$*
  - **cutting** pain: alum$_{b4a.de}$* alumn ang$_{b7.de}$* asaf$_{b7.de}$ calc$_{bg2}$ dios *Kreos*$_{b7a.de}$ lac-c$_{ptk1}$ lyc$_{bg2}$ med$_{ptk1}$ merc$_{bg2}$ merc-i-f myrt-c$_{b7a.de}$ rhus-t$_{k}$* samb$_{b7.de}$ spig$_{ptk1}$ sul-ac$_{b4.de}$* symph$_{fd3.de}$• thuj viol-t$_{b7.de}$*
  - **digging** pain: mang$_{bg2}$
  - **dislocated**; as if: aloe$_{bg2}$ *Am-m*$_{b7a.de}$ anac$_{bg2}$ bar-c$_{bg2}$ canth$_{b7.de}$* chel$_{bg2}$ chin$_{b7.de}$* coloc$_{b4.de}$* ign$_{bg2}$ kali-c$_{b4.de}$* mur-ac$_{b4.de}$* nux-v$_{bg2}$ petr$_{b4.de}$* plb$_{b7.de}$* rhod$_{b4a.de}$* *Rhus-t*$_{b7a.de}$ ruta$_{bg2}$ sep$_{bg2}$ stann$_{b4.de}$* sulph$_{b4.de}$*
  - **dragging**: verat$_{b7.de}$*
  - **drawing** pain: acon *Am-c*$_{b4a.de}$ ang$_{b7.de}$* ars$_{k}$* asaf$_{k}$* bell$_{b4.de}$* *Berb*$_{k}$* borx$_{k}$* *Calc*$_{k}$* camph$_{k}$* caps$_{b7.de}$* *Carl* *Caust*$_{k}$* cham$_{k}$* *Chel*$_{k}$* *Chin*$_{k}$* cimic cinnb$_{bg2}$ *Coloc*$_{k}$* con$_{k}$* dulc$_{b4.de}$* hep$_{k}$* ind kali-bi$_{bg2}$ kali-c$_{k}$* kali-n$_{k}$* kreos$_{b7a.de}$ lyc$_{k}$* mag-c$_{b4.de}$* med mez$_{k}$* mur-ac$_{k}$* naja$_{bg2}$ nat-c$_{b4.de}$* nat-m$_{b4.de}$* *Nux-v*$_{k}$* ph-ac$_{b4.de}$* plat$_{b4.de}$* puls$_{b7.de}$* ran-s$_{b7.de}$* rhod$_{k}$* rhus-t$_{b7.de}$* ruta$_{k}$* sars seneg$_{k}$* sep$_{k}$* sil$_{k}$* spong$_{fd4.de}$ *Squil*$_{k}$* stann$_{b4.de}$* staph$_{b7.de}$* *Sulph*$_{k}$* tell thuj tritic-vg$_{fd5.de}$ vanil$_{fd5.de}$
    - **paroxysmal**: sil$_{h2}$
    - **tearing** pain: stann$_{h2}$
    - **up** and down: chin$_{b7.de}$*
  - **dull** pain: apis$_{b7a.de}$ hell$_{b7.de}$*
  - **eating**; after: cina ↓
    - **tearing** pain: cina$_{a1}$
  - **eructations**:
    - **agg.**: zinc ↓
      - **stitching** pain: zinc
    - **amel.**: zinc ↓
      - **cutting** pain: zinc$_{ptk2}$
  - **fever**; during: *Ars*$_{bg2}$ bar-c$_{bg2}$ bell$_{bg2}$ *Chin*$_{bg2}$ kali-c$_{bg2}$ kreos$_{bg2}$ meny$_{bg2}$ *Merc*$_{bg2}$ nux-v$_{bg2}$ *Rhus-t*$_{bg2}$ **Sep**$_{bg2}$ sil$_{bg2}$ sulph$_{bg2}$ *Verat*$_{bg2}$ viol-t$_{bg2}$
    - **stitching** pain: sep$_{b4.de}$
  - **gnawing** pain: alum$_{k}$* nat-c$_{b4.de}$* ph-ac$_{k}$*
  - **grasping** pain: phos$_{b4.de}$*
  - **grasping** something agg.: berb$_{k}$*
  - **hang** down, arm: ign
  - **hawking**: caust ↓ hep ↓

- **Scapulae – hawking**: ...
    - **stitching** pain: caust$_{h2}$ hep$_{h2}$
  - **heat** of the sun:
    - **amel.**: cassia-s$_{ccrh1}$•
      - **pressing** pain: cassia-s$_{ccrh1}$•
  - **inspiration**:
    - **agg.**: chin ↓ dulc ferr-m ferr-ma ↓ kali-c ↓ mill ↓ sep tritic-vg$_{fd5.de}$
      - **stitching** pain: dulc ferr-ma kali-c mill sep
      - **tearing** pain: chin
    - **deep**:
      - **agg.**: acon ↓
        - **boring** pain: acon
  - **jerking** pain: calc-p
  - **lifting** agg.: iod ↓
    - **stitching** pain: iod$_{h}$
  - **lowering** the shoulder, on: am-m ↓
    - **stitching** pain: am-m
  - **lying**:
    - **agg.**: tub$_{tl1}$ vanil$_{fd5.de}$
    - **scapulae**; lying on:
      - **impossible**: nit-ac ↓
        - **stitching** pain: nit-ac$_{h2}$
    - **side**; on:
      - **left** | **agg.**: colch$_{rsj2}$•
  - **manual** labor: ferr ↓
    - **stitching** pain: ferr
  - **menses** | **after** | **agg.**: borx$_{b4a.de}$
    - **during**:
      - **agg.**: phos ↓ sil ↓
        - **drawing** pain: sil$_{b4a.de}$
        - **stitching** pain: phos
  - **motion**:
    - **agg.**: calc caps ↓ caust ↓ chin ↓ cina$_{h1}$ cocc ↓ colch$_{rsj2}$• dulc ↓ ferr ↓ hell *Ip* ↓ kali-c ↓ mag-m ↓ mez naja petr podo ↓ sulph ↓ tarent ↓ tub ↓
      - **cramping**: *Ip*
      - **drawing** pain: caps$_{h1}$
      - **pressing** pain: caust$_{h2}$ dulc$_{fd4.de}$ mag-m$_{h2}$
      - **sore**: chin cocc kali-c
      - **stitching** pain: ferr$_{c1}$ kali-c$_{h2}$ mez podo$_{fd3.de}$• sulph tarent tub$_{c1}$
    - **amel.**: am-m arge-pl$_{rwt5}$• carc$_{fd2.de}$• coloc ↓ paeon ↓ sabin samb ↓
      - **boring** pain: paeon$_{k}$*
      - **sore**: coloc
      - **stitching** pain: am-m samb
    - **arm**; of:
      - **agg.**: camph ↓ chel ign mag-m ↓
        - **pressing** pain: camph$_{h1}$ mag-m$_{h2}$
        - **tearing** pain: camph$_{h1}$
      - **right** arm agg.; of: caust ↓
        - **sore**: caust$_{h2}$
    - **arms**; of:
      - **agg.**: camph ↓
        - **stitching** pain: camph$_{h1}$
    - **head**; of:
      - **agg.**: ant-t cupr merc nat-s
        - **tearing** pain: nat-s
  - **nursing**, when: crot-t
  - **overlifting**; as if from: nux-v$_{b7.de}$* rhus-t$_{b7.de}$*
  - **paralyzed**; as if: apis$_{b7a.de}$ *Iod*$_{b4a.de}$ nat-c$_{b4.de}$* sabin$_{b7a.de}$
  - **perspiration**; during: am-m$_{bg2}$ *Ars*$_{bg2}$ bar-c$_{bg2}$ bell$_{bg2}$ *Calc*$_{bg2}$ caust$_{bg2}$ *Chin*$_{bg2}$ kali-c$_{bg2}$ *Merc*$_{bg2}$ nat-c$_{bg2}$ **Nux-v**$_{bg2}$ *Rhus-t*$_{bg2}$ **Sep**$_{bg2}$ sil$_{bg2}$ *Sulph*$_{bg2}$
  - **pinching** pain: am-m$_{b7.de}$* arn$_{bg2}$ bar-c$_{bg2}$ bell$_{b4.de}$* calc$_{b4.de}$* chel$_{b7.de}$* euph$_{bg2}$ kali-c$_{h2}$ meny$_{b7.de}$* merc$_{bg2}$ nit-ac$_{b4.de}$* puls$_{bg2}$ sulph$_{b4a.de}$ viol-t$_{b7.de}$*

Back

- **Scapulae**: ...
  - **pressing** pain: agar bg2 anac k* apis b7a.de arg-met k* arg-n arn k* asaf b7.de* aur-m-n bell k* bism b7.de* bry k* *Calc* k* camph b7.de* cann-xyz bg2 carb-an bg2 carb-v bg2 caust k* chel k* chin b7a.de* *Cocc* k* colch b7.de* con bg2 cor-r cupr bg2 cypra-eg sde6.de• dulc fd4.de elaps graph k* grat ind kali-c k* kalm kola stb3• lach k* laur k* led lyc k* m-ambo b7.de mag-m b4.de mez mur-ac b4.de* naja bg2 nat-c b4.de nat-m nat-s nit-ac nux-v k* ph-ac b4.de* phos bg2 phyt k* plat b4.de podo fd3.de• ran-b b7.de* ran-s k* rhod b4a.de rhus-t k* ruta k* sabin b7a.de* seneg k* sep k* sil b4.de* spong fd4.de stann b4.de* staph b7.de* stront-c b4.de* sulph bg2 tell teucr bg2 vanil fd5.de verat b7.de* zinc k*
    - **apart**; as if pressed: sil bg2
    - **plug**; as from a: *Chin* b7a.de phos b4.de* rhus-t b7.de*
  - **pressure**:
    - **agg.**: *Chin* sil h2
    - **amel.**: cassia-s ccrh1• mag-m ↓ petr-ra shn4• sep ↓
      - **pressing** pain: cassia-s ccrh1• mag-m h2
      - **stitching** pain: sep h2
  - **raising** arm to head impossible: lyc h2
  - **raw**; as if: coloc bg2 lach bg2 plat bg2 ran-b bg2
  - **rheumatic**: acon bro1 aesc alumn am-caust bro1 ambr asaf asc-t a1 *Berb* bro1 *Bry* k* calc carb-v chinin-s colch k* ferr-m k* *Ferr-p* bro1 graph guaj bro1 ham c2* hyos *Kali-c* bro1 kalm bro1 lac-ac bro1 *Led* bro1 lith-c bro1 *Lith-lac* bro1 lyc mag-s med bro1 *Mez* ol-an bro1 pall bro1 *Phyt* bro1 prim-o bro1 rad-br bro1 *Ran-b* k* rhod k* *Rhus-t* k* *Sang* bro1 stel bro1 *Stict* bro1 stront-c bro1 sulph bro1 syph bro1 urt-u bro1 valer viol-o bro1
  - **rising**:
    - **morning**: fic-m gya1 mand rsj7•
    - **amel.**: bamb-a stb2.de•
  - **rubbing**:
    - **amel.**: phos ↓
      - **tearing** pain: phos k*
  - **scraping**: nux-m bg2 rhod bg2
  - **sewing**, while: ran-b ↓
    - **burning**: ran-b k*
  - **shattered**; as if: chin bg2
  - **singing** agg.: stann bro1
  - **sitting**:
    - **agg.**: ant-c carc fd2.de• colch ↓ ind kola stb3• mang nat-s k2 sep ↓ tritic-vg fd5.de vanil fd5.de
      - **pressing** pain: carc fd2.de• ind
      - **stitching** pain: ant-c colch sep h2
      - **tearing** pain: mang k*
    - **bent** forward:
      - **agg.**: bov ↓ ph-ac ↓
        - **tearing** pain: bov ph-ac
  - **sore**: acon bg2 aloe bg2 am-m b7a.de* anac k* ant-t k* apis b7a.de* *Arn* ars k* bar-c k* berb calc-p k* cham bg2 chel k* chin b7.de* coloc b4.de* con crot-c bg2 dig bg2 dios gels bg2 gran bg2 graph k* ham ptk1 hell k* kali-c b4.de* *Kreos* k* lach bg2 led b7.de* lyc mag-m b4.de* meny b7.de* merc k* merc-i-f nat-m k* nux-v k* petr bg2 phos phyt bg2 plat b4.de* plb bg2 ran-b k* ruta fd4.de sil k* spong k* sulph b4.de* thuj k* verat k* vesp zinc k*
  - **speaking** loud: caust ↓
    - **stitching** pain: caust
  - **sprained**; as if: bar-c chel chin coloc kali-c mur-ac h2 nux-v petr k* sulph
  - **squeezing**: acon b7.de* anac b4.de* arn b7.de* asar b7.de* bar-c b4.de* bell b4.de* caust b4.de* chel bg2 ip b7.de* kali-c b4.de* merc bg2 puls b7.de* rhus-t b7a.de* verat b7.de* viol-t bg2
  - **stitching** pain: agar k* alum k* alum-p k2 alum-sil k2 alumn am-c h2* am-m k* ambr k* **Anac** k* ang b7.de* ant-c b7.de* arg-met b7.de* arge-pl rwt5• asaf b7.de* asar b7.de* aur bg2 *Bar-c* k* *Bell* k* berb *Bov* k* *Bry* k* *Calc* k* calc-sil k2 *Camph* k* cann-s k* canth b7.de* caps b7.de* *Carb-an* k* carb-v bg2 carbn-s *Caust* k* cham chel b7.de* chin k* cina b7.de* coc-c *Cocc* k* colch k* *Coloc* k* con b4.de* cupr b7.de* cycl b7.de* dig b4.de* *Dulc* k* ferr k* ferr-m germ-met srj5• graph k*

- **Scapulae – stitching** pain: ...
  grat bg2 *Guaj* k* hep k* hyos k* hyper k* ign b7.de* iod k* *Kali-bi* k* *Kali-c* k* kali-m k2 kali-n b4.de* kali-sil k2 kalm kreos k* lach k* lact lap-la sde8.de• laur k* lyc k* m-aust b7.de mag-c bg2* mag-m b4.de* manc mang b4.de* med meny k* merc k* merc-i-f mez b4.de* mosch b7.de* *Mur-ac* k* *Myrt-c* b7a.de *Nat-c* k* nat-m k* **Nit-ac** k* nux-v k* op ox-ac paeon *Par* k* *Phos* k* pitu-gl skp7• *Plb* k* prun puls k* *Ran-b* k* ruta b7.de* sabad b7.de* samb k* *Sars* k* seneg *Sep* k* sil k* spig k* spong k* *Stann* k* staph b7.de* stram *Sulph* k* tab tarax k* tarent *Thuj* k* tub c1 vanil fd5.de verb k* viol-t b7.de* *Zinc* k* zinc-p k2
    - **cramping**: ant-c h2
    - **sharp**: galeoc-c-h gms1•
    - **splinters**; as from: agar bg2
  - **stooping** agg.: cham sulph
    - **stitching** pain: sulph
  - **stretching**:
    - **amel.**: petr-ra ↓
      - **sore**: petr-ra shn4•
  - **swallowing** agg.: caust
    - **stitching** pain: caust
  - **tearing** pain: *Acon* k* agar bg2 *Alum* k* alum-p k2 am-m ambr bg2 *Anac* k* arg-met b7.de* ars b4a.de* asaf bg2 *Aur* k* bar-c b4.de* bell bg2 berb k* borx b4a.de* bov k* calc bg2 camph b7.de* canth b7.de* carb-v k* *Caust* k* cham bg2 chel k* chin k* cocc b7.de* coloc bg2 con bg2 cycl k* dig b4.de* dios k* dulc k* ferr b7.de* graph bg2 *Guaj* k* *Kali-c* k* kali-n k* lach k* laur b7.de* led k* *Lyc* bg2 *Mag-m* k* manc k* mang b4.de* meny b7.de* merc k* merc-c b4a.de mez k* mur-ac bg2 nat-c k* nat-m k* nat-s k* nicc k* nit-ac nux-v bg2 olnd b7.de* petr bg2 ph-ac k* phos k* plat bg2 plb k* psor k* ptel k* *Puls* b7a.de ran-s bg2 rhod b4a.de* rhus-t b7.de* ruta bg2 sars k* *Sep* k* sil b4a.de* squil bg2 stann k* *Sulph* k* thuj k* valer bg2 verat bg2 zinc k* zinc-p k2
    - **drawing** pain: (non:stann h2)
  - **touch** agg.: cina ↓
    - **tearing** pain: cina a1
  - **turning**:
    - **body**:
      - **agg.**: con ↓ ham fd3.de• vanil fd5.de
        - **sore**: con h2
      - **left**; to: am-m
        - **stitching** pain: am-m
    - **head**:
      - **agg.**: merc ↓
        - **sore**: merc k*
      - **left** agg.; to: caust ↓
        - **pressing** pain: caust h2
      - **right** agg.; to: caust ↓
        - **sore**: caust h2
  - **twisting** pain: bar-c bg2
  - **ulcerative** pain: cic b7.de* puls b7.de*
  - **waking**; on: colch rsj2• nicc ↓ rhod ↓
    - **drawing** pain: rhod
    - **tearing** pain: nicc k*
  - **walking**:
    - **agg.**: asaf coloc galeoc-c-h ↓ *Kali-p* nat-s nit-ac
      - **burning**: galeoc-c-h gms1•
      - **drawing** pain: asaf
      - **stitching** pain: coloc nit-ac
      - **tearing** pain: nat-s k* nit-ac h2
    - **amel.**: bar-c ↓
      - **burning**: bar-c
    - **rapidly**:
      - **agg.**: sep ↓
        - **stitching** pain: sep h2
    - **slowly**:
      - **amel.**: sep ↓
        - **stitching** pain: sep h2

- **Scapulae**: ...
  - **writing**:
    - **agg.**: carb-v ran-b↓ symph fd3.de•
      - **burning**: ran-b k*
    - **continued**; after: mur-ac
  - **yawning** agg.: nat-s↓
    - **sore**: nat-s
  - **extending** to:
    - **Arm**: aeth coc-c irid-met srj5•
      - **left**: psil ft1
      - **tearing** pain: coc-c k*
    - **Back**: stann↓ verat h1
      - **tearing** pain: stann h2
    - **Chest**: bar-c camph↓ kali-c rad-br bg1* sars sep symph fd3.de•
      - **stitching** pain: bar-c camph h1 kali-c sars sep
    - **Clavicle**: mag-m
      - **pressing** pain: mag-m h2*
    - **Downward**: chel↓
      - **sore**: chel
    - **Forward**: aml-ns bg2 arn bg2 borx bg2 camph bg2 caust bg2 chel bg2 dig bg2 dios bg2 grat bg2 kali-bi bg2 laur bg2 mang bg2 petr bg2 psor bg2 rat bg2 sars bg2 thuj bg2
      - **right**: acon bg2 ang bg2 kali-c bg2 lyc bg2 merc bg2 sep bg2
      - **left**: bar-c bg2 bry bg2 lac-c bg2 mez bg2 phos bg2 zinc bg2
    - **Head**: lyc bg1
    - **Heart**: thuj↓
      - **stitching** pain: thuj
    - **Lumbar** region: borx↓
      - **pressing** pain: borx h2
      - **riding** agg.: kali-c↓
        - **pressing** pain: kali-c
    - **Mammae**: grat↓
      - **stitching** pain: grat
    - **Neck**: mang↓
      - **drawing** pain: mang h2
    - **Occiput**: *Grat*↓ *Guaj*↓ **Petr**↓
      - **stitching** pain: *Grat* *Guaj* **Petr**
    - **Ribs**: asaf↓
      - **stitching** pain: asaf
    - **Sacrum**: calc-ar k2 coc-c↓
      - **pressing** pain: coc-c
    - **Shoulder**: stann↓
      - **tearing** pain: stann h2
    - **Shoulders**: spect↓
      - **right**: vanil fd5.de
      - **left**: kali-bi bg1
      - **aching**: [spect dfg1]
      - **Face**; and: ip k2 valer
    - **Sides**: anac↓
      - **tearing** pain: anac
    - **Sternum**: *Chel* kali-bi bg2
      - **pressing** pain: *Chel*
    - **Stomach**: borx
      - **pressing** pain: borx h2
    - **Upward**: calc bg2
  - **Angles** of: cadm-met sp1 cot br1 iod ruta↓
    - **stitching** pain: ruta
    - **Below**: ruta↓
      - **pressing** pain: ruta
      - **Inner** side; and: anac↓
        - **pressing** pain: anac h2
    - **Inner**: *Chel*↓
      - **left**: aphis c1* apoc vml3• carc tpw2* chel chr-ac cupr-ar bro1 *Ran-b* k* sang hr1 sanic
        - **bending** head backward agg.: sanic
        - **sitting** bent, needle work or typewriting: ran-b pd
        - **extending** to | **Chest**: aphis br1*

- **Scapulae – Angles** of – **Inner – left**: ...
  - **Edge** of, worse on breathing: *Sang*
  - **Margin** of: brom
  - **Upper** inner angle: **Rhus-t** mrr1
  - **cramping**: *Chel*
  - **Lower**: agath-a↓ alumn apis apoc↓ arn calc chel k* chen-a bro1 chinin-s↓ irid-met srj5• kali-bi kali-c bro1 kali-n↓ lach↓ led *Merc* bro1 mur-ac↓ podo bro1 rhus-t sulph
    - **morning**: sulph↓
      - **stitching** pain: sulph
    - **bending** backward:
      - **amel.**: lach↓
        - **stitching** pain: lach
    - **breathing**:
      - **agg.**: alumn chel clem
      - **deep**:
        - **agg.**: kali-n↓
          - **stitching** pain: kali-n h2
    - **burning**: agath-a nl2• sulph
    - **motion** | **amel.**: alumn
    - **raising** shoulders, when: rhus-t
    - **sitting** for a long time agg.: lach↓
      - **stitching** pain: lach
    - **stitching** pain: apoc chinin-s kali-bi kali-n h2 lach mur-ac h2 sulph
    - **extending** to:
      - **Chest**; through: chel↓
        - **stitching** pain: chel
  - **Upper**: alum↓ kali-bi kola stb3• vanil fd5.de
    - **burning**: alum
    - **stitching** pain: kola stb3•
- **Below**: agar↓ all-s↓ allox↓ aloe↓ alumn↓ anac↓ apis arn↓ arum-t↓ asaf asar↓ atp↓ aur↓ bad↓ bamb-a stb2.de• bell↓ bism↓ brom bry↓ **Calc** *Calc-p* cann-s↓ canth↓ card-m **Chel**↓ chen-v c2 cimic cimx↓ cist↓ cocc↓ con corn↓ cund↓ cupr↓ dig↓ dulc fd4.de *Elat* fic-m↓ fl-ac gels bg1 guaj↓ hell heroin↓ ind↓ *Jug-c*↓ kali-bi kali-c↓ kali-n kola stb3• *Kreos*↓ lach↓ lap-la↓ laur↓ led↓ lyc lyss↓ malar jl2 meny bg1 merc bg2 mez myric bg1 nat-ar↓ nat-c↓ nat-m↓ nat-s nat-sil fd3.de• nit-ac ol-j↓ olnd↓ ox-ac k2 par↓ petr-ra↓ ph-ac↓ *Phos*↓ phys↓ pic-ac↓ plb↓ podo bg2 psil↓ *Puls* pulx br1 *Ran-b* rhus-t rumx ruta fd4.de sabin↓ *Sil*↓ spong fd4.de stann staph↓ sul-i k2 *Sulph* tarent k2 ter↓ thuj↓ tritic-vg fd5.de ven-m rsj12• verat zinc↓ zing↓
  - **right**: *Abies-c* k* aesc agath-a↓ *All-c* asaf↓ aur↓ bad bamb-a stb2.de• bell↓ bry calc↓ cann-s↓ *Card-m* **Chel** k* **Chen-a** k* coloc↓ con conv cupr dig↓ elat↓ gink-b↓ *Guaj*↓ haliae-lc srj5• hydrog srj2• ind jug-c st kali-bi↓ kali-c↓ kali-n↓ kali-s fd4.de lac-c lach↓ lob↓ *Lycps-v* malar st* med nat-c↓ nat-m neon srj5• nux-v pall↓ pert-vc vk9 petr-ra↓ phos phys *Pic-ac* plut-n↓ *Podo* rhod rumx pd *Ruta* samb↓ sel rsj9• *Senec* *Seneg* hr1 sep↓ spong fd4.de staph↓ symph↓ tab↓ thuj↓ tritic-vg fd5.de vario st ven-m rsj12• zinc↓ [gels xyz62 heroin sdj2]
    - **forenoon**: sel rsj9•
    - **afternoon** | **16** h: bamb-a stb2.de•
    - **accompanied** by | **Face**; pale: chen-a hr1
    - **aching**: *Chel* ind petr-ra shn4• plut-n srj7•
    - **bending** forward agg.: lob
    - **breathing** deep agg.: *Guaj*↓
      - **stitching** pain: *Guaj*
    - **burning**: agath-a nl2• bry cann-s lob lycps-v ptk1 pall staph tab
    - **cough** agg.; during: seneg
    - **cutting** pain: asaf bg1 bell bg1 bry bg1 elat bg1 lach bg1
    - **drawing** pain: calc h2 sep h2
    - **face**; with pale (See accompanied - face)
    - **inspiration** agg.: coloc↓
      - **stitching** pain: coloc h2
    - **motion** agg.: gink-b↓ spong↓
      - **stitching** pain: gink-b sbd1• spong fd4.de
    - **pressing** pain: con h2 cupr h2 nat-c h2 nat-m h2 sep h2 staph h1 zinc h2
    - **pressure** | **amel.**: bapt hr1

· **Scapulae – Below – right**: ...
. . **raising** right arm agg.: flor-p rsj3•
. **sitting**:
after: *All-c* kali-s fd4.de
agg.: samb ↓
stitching pain: samb h1
. **stitching** pain: aur *Bad* **Chel** coloc h2 gink-b sbd1• *Guaj* kali-bi kali-c h2 kali-n h2 ruta fd4.de samb h1 spong fd4.de symph fd3.de• thuj zinc h2
pulsating pain: samb h1
. **tearing** pain: calc h2 dig k*
. **throwing** shoulders back: bad
stitching pain: *Bad*
. **extending** to | **Chest**; through: chen-a hr1
. **Spine**; near the: chen-a hr1

: **left**: aeth ↓ aids ↓ ail anac ↓ ant-t ↓ *Apis* arund bell ↓ bry *Cact* cann-i a1 carbn-s ↓ *Cench* chen-g nh1 chen-v *Cimic* corn *Crot-h* cund cupr ↓ cupr-ar daph dios ↓ dol echi ↓ **Gels** ham fd3.de• hydr hyper ↓ *Ind* kali-bi ↓ kali-p fd1.de• *Kreos* lac-ac ↓ *Lac-c* *Lach* lap-la ↓ led lob ↓ lyc ↓ med *Merc* mez ↓ *Naja* nat-c ↓ nat-m ↓ nat-sil ↓ nept-m lsd2.fr nit-ac ↓ ol-an ↓ *Ox-ac* par phyt psil ft1 *Psor* rumx ↓ sabin sang seneg *Sep* spong fd4.de sulph symph ↓ tab ↓ tarent thuj trios ↓ tritic-vg fd5.de verat-v ↓ xan zinc
. **aching**: aeth bg1 aids nl2• ant-t bg1 cench crot-h dios bg1 gels k2 kali-bi bg1 lach lob bg1 med naja nit-ac bg1 ol-an bg1 rumx bg1 sabin bg1 seneg bg1 verat-v bg1 xan bg1
. **breathing** deep agg.: kali-n ↓
stitching: kali-n h2
. **burning**: bry *Cund* echi ptk1 mez h2 tab
. **cough** agg.; during: *Stict* sulph ↓
stitching: sulph k*
. **cutting** pain: carbn-s daph hyper *Lac-c* lyc thuj
. **drawing** scapulae together: nat-m ↓
stitching: nat-m h2*
. **expiration** agg.: sep
. **inspiration** agg.: carbn-s ↓
cutting pain: carbn-s
. **lancinating**: nept-m lsd2.fr
followed by | **right**: psil ft1
. **lying** with shoulder on something hard amel.: agar kreos
. **motion** agg.: kali-p fd1.de• kreos *Psor*
. **pressing** pain: anac h2 bell h1 ind lap-la sde8.de• nat-c h2 nat-sil fd3.de• symph fd3.de• zinc
. **pressure** | **amel.**: kreos
. **rheumatic**: alumn
. **riding** in a carriage agg.: kreos phyt
evening: phyt
. **sitting**:
evening: seneg sulph
bent forward | **amel.**: merc
. **stitching** pain: anac k* carbn-s cupr k* kali-bi kali-p fd1.de• lac-ac mez h2 nat-c h2 nat-m h2 nat-sil fd3.de• nept-m lsd2.fr *Sulph* k* tarent
. **tearing** pain: trios rsj11•
. **extending** to:
Chest; into the: *Lyc* ↓
cutting pain: *Lyc*
Heart: bry ↓ staph ↓
stitching: bry staph

: **morning**: apis ox-ac ↓ ruta fd4.de
. **sore**: ox-ac

: **forenoon**:
. **11**.30 h: pert-vc vk9
lasting one hour: pert-vc vk9

: **afternoon**: cedr nat-sil fd3.de• ruta fd4.de
. **15** h: kreos ↓
stitching pain: kreos

: **evening**: aq-mar skp7• seneg ↓ *Sulph* ↓ tarent ↓
. **19** h: gels ↓

· **Scapulae – Below – evening – 19** h: ...
aching: gels
. **aching**: seneg *Sulph* tarent
: **night**: kali-bi tarent ↓
. **aching**: tarent
: **aching**: agar arn bell calc **Chel** cupr ind kali-bi kreos laur merc myric nat-m petr-ra shn4• phys rumx *Sulph* tarent
: **appearing** suddenly: pert-vc vk9
. **disappearing** gradually; and: pert-vc vk9
: **breathing** deep agg.: plb ↓
. **stitching** pain: plb
: **chill**; during: sang
: **cramping**: allox tpw3*
: **cutting** pain: asaf thuj
: **drawing** pain: asaf *Card-m* cimx cocc con mez nat-s nat-sil fd3.de• ph-ac h2 pulx br1 rhus-t ruta h1 spong fd4.de stann h2 sulph thuj tritic-vg fd5.de
: **expiration** agg.; during: *Sep* ↓
. **aching**: *Sep*
: **gnawing** pain: agar
: **inspiration** agg.: cupr ↓ guaj ↓
. **stitching** pain: cupr h2 guaj
: **lying**:
. **amel.**: stroph-s ↓
aching: stroph-s sp1
: **lying** down agg.: malar jl2
: **motion**:
. **agg.**: apis chel ↓ hell spong fd4.de stann tarent k2
aching: chel tarent
stitching pain: spong fd4.de tarent
. **amel.**: stroph-s ↓
aching: stroph-s sp1
. **arm**; of:
agg.: con ↓ led ↓
aching: led
pressing pain: con h2
. **arms**; of | **agg.**: con
: **neuralgic**: ter ptk1
: **pressing** pain: anac h2 apis brom **Calc** card-m chel con h2 ind lap-la sde8.de• lyc k* lyss nat-c k* nat-s phos k* rhus-t k* sabin a1 s t a n n h2 sulph tritic-vg fd5.de zinc k*
: **pressure**; hard | **amel.**: malar jl2
: **raising** arm agg.: con ↓
. **drawing** pain: con
: **rest** agg.: con sabin
: **rheumatic**: *Alumn* vh1
: **riding** agg.: phyt ↓
. **aching**: phyt
: **sewing**: ran-b
: **sitting** agg.: nept-m lsd2.fr psor samb ↓ seneg ↓ sep ↓ stroph-s ↓
. **aching**: seneg stroph-s sp1
. **drawing** pain: sep h2
. **pressing** pain: sep h2
. **stitching** pain: nept-m lsd2.fr samb
: **sore**: atp rly4• cist cund led nat-ar nat-c ol-j sul-i thuj tritic-vg fd5.de
. **burning**; between paroxysms of: plb
: **standing** agg.: cocc ↓
. **drawing** pain: cocc
: **stitching** pain: agar all-s aloe arum-t asar aur bad bism h1 bry calc cann-s canth **Chel** cimic corn cupr fic-m gya1 guaj *Jug-c* kali-bi kali-c kali-n *Kreos* lach lyc mez nat-c nat-m olnd par *Phos* pic-ac plb podo fd3.de• psil ft1 spong fd4.de stann h2 **Sulph** tarent thuj tritic-vg fd5.de zinc zing
: **stooping** agg.: asaf ↓ sulph ↓
. **stitching**: asaf sulph h2
: **tearing** pain: agar alumn aur h2 dig k* lyc k* *Sil* k* staph sne [h e r o i n sdj2]
: **turning** head agg.: nept-m lsd2.fr

- **Scapulae – Below**: ...
  - **walking** agg.: cocc↓ led↓ med↓ *Sil*↓
    - **aching**: led med
    - **drawing** pain: cocc
    - **tearing** pain: *Sil*
  - **wheezing**; with: ars↓
    - **sore**: ars
  - **writing** agg.: ran-b
  - **extending** to:
    - **Fingers**: cimx↓
      - **drawing** pain: cimx
    - **Lumbar** region: ox-ac k2
  - **Spine**; along: bamb-a stb2.de•
  - **Spot**; in a: pert-vc vk9
- **Between**: acon k* aesc k* aeth↓ *Agar* agath-a↓ ail↓ aloe↓ alum alum-sil k2 alumn↓ *Am-c* am-m ambr anac androc srj1• *Ang* ant-s-aur↓ apom bro1 arg-met↓ arg-n arn **Ars** k* ars-met↓ ars-s-f k2 arum-t asaf↓ asc-t a1* bamb-a↓ bar-c k* *Bell* berb bism bg2 bol-la borx↓ bov *Bry* k* calad **Calc** k* calc-ar↓ calc-caust↓ calc-p k* *Calc-s* calc-sil k2 camph k* cann-i bro1 cann-s↓ canth bg1 carb-ac↓ carb-an carb-v carbn-s carl↓ caust cham↓ *Chel* *Chen-a* bro1 *Chin* chinin-ar *Cimic* cimx↓ clem↓ cob coc-c *Cocc*↓ colch coloc com *Con* k* cop↓ corian-s knl6• crot-c↓ crot-t cupr cur cystein-l rly4• dig↓ dream-p↓ *Dros* dulc fd4.de echi elaps euon bro1 *Eup-per* eupi *Ferr* *Ferr-ar* ferr-p *Gins*↓ glon *Gran* bro1 *Graph* grat↓ gua bro1 *Guaj* k* ham↓ hell helo bg3 helon↓ *Hep* hippoc-k↓ hura hyper ind indg↓ ip jug-c bro1 *Kali-ar* *Kali-bi* k* kali-br kali-c k* kali-i bg2 kali-m k2 kali-n *Kali-p* kali-s kali-sil k2 *Kalm* *Kreos* lac-c lac-cp sk4• *Lach* lap-a laur led lil-t lob lyc k* lyss↓ *Mag-c*↓ mag-m mag-s k* mang↓ *Med* k* medul-os-si↓ meny merc merc-i-f kr1 mez↓ mill↓ mur-ac *Naja* k* *Nat-ar* k* nat-c nat-m nat-p **Nat-s** **Nit-ac** *Nux-m* *Nux-v* ol-an↓ ox-ac *Par* petr petr-ra shn4• *Ph-ac* *Phos* k* pic-ac↓ plat↓ plb *Podo* k* prun↓ psil↓ psor *Puls* rad-br bro1 ran-b ran-s↓ rhod *Rhus-t* k* *Rhus-v* rob↓ rumx↓ ruta sabad↓ sacch-a fd2.de• sars↓ senec↓ seneg *Sep* k* *Sil* sol-ni stann staph↓ stict stram↓ succ-ac↓ sul-ac↓ sulo-ac↓ *Sulph* k* symph↓ syph tab k* tell ter ther k* thlas bg1 *Thuj* tritic-vg fd5.de vanil fd5.de *Verat* viol-t↓ *Zinc* k* zinc-p k2 [heroin sdj2]
  - **right**:
    - **Spot**; in a: berb↓ chel↓
      - **sore**: berb ptk1 chel ptk1
  - **left** and spine: hydrog↓
    - **lifting**, working during menses and vexation agg.: *Phos*↓
      - **sore**: *Phos*
    - **pressure**, rest and warmth amel.: *Phos*↓
      - **sore**: *Phos*
    - **sore**: hydrog srj2•
  - **morning**: dulc fd4.de nat-c h2 podo psor↓ **Ran-b** ruta fd4.de staph h1
    - **aching**: staph
    - **bed** agg.; in: ang↓
      - **drawing** pain: ang
    - **stitching** pain: psor ran-b
    - **waking**; on: aeth anac↓ arg-n kali-bi ran-b
      - **pressing** pain: anac h2 arg-n k*
      - **tearing** pain: *Kali-bi*
  - **forenoon**: alum↓
    - **drawing** pain: alum
  - **afternoon**: alum bov↓ canth caust chel ruta
    - **13** h: chel↓
      - **burning**: chel
    - **16** h | **tearing** pain: (non:caust a1*)
    - **cutting** pain: bov
    - **drawing** pain: chel
    - **stitching** pain: bov
    - **tearing** pain: canth k* caust k*
  - **evening**: alumn sne bamb-a↓ bell cocc kali-c kali-n lac-c lyc nat-ar ruta fd4.de sulph thuj zing↓
    - **18** h: kali-n↓ zing↓

- **Scapulae – Between – evening – 18** h: ...
      - **drawing** pain: kali-n zing
    - **bed** agg.; in: ferr↓ thuj↓
      - **burning**: ferr
      - **stitching** pain: thuj
      - **tearing** pain: thuj
    - **cramping**: bamb-a stb2.de•
    - **drawing** pain: bell kali-n lyc zing
    - **stitching** pain: sulph
    - **tearing** pain: cocc k* sulph k*
  - **night**: carb-v↓ podo rhus-t sil tab
    - **midnight**:
      - **after**: mag-s
        - **tearing** pain: mag-s
    - **bed** agg.; in: ang↓
      - **stitching** pain: ang
    - **drawing** pain: rhus-t sil
    - **stitching** pain: carb-v
  - **aching**: *Aesc* ail arn arum-t *Bell* calad calc-ar calc-caust carb-ac ptk1 carb-an cimx bg1 clem dros dulc helon bg1* hippoc-k szs2 kali-p lac-c lob lyc bg1 medul-os-si rly4• merc naja *Nux-v* ox-ac phos plb ran-s rhod rhus-t k* rhus-v seneg *Sep* k* staph sulph bg1* tab thlas br1
    - **accompanied** by | **respiration**; impeded: calc ptk1
  - **air** agg.; in open: nat-c
    - **drawing** pain: nat-c
  - **beer**, agg.: phos
  - **bending**:
    - **backward**:
      - **agg.**: stann
      - **amel.**: sil
        - **drawing** pain: *Sil*
    - **forward**:
      - **agg.**: **Cimic**↓ kali-p fd1.de• lac-c nat-ar k2 vanil fd5.de
        - **drawing** pain: **Cimic** vanil fd5.de
      - **amel.**: nat-ar k*
  - **boring** pain: agath-a nl2• *Ph-ac* psor thuj
  - **breathing**:
    - **agg.**: acon↓ berb caps↓ carb-v↓ cop↓ *Guaj* kali-c↓ nat-ar k2 nit-ac nux-v prun psor↓ *Puls* stann
      - **stitching** pain: acon berb caps h1 carb-v cop *Guaj* kali-c nit-ac nux-v prun psor puls stann
    - **deep**:
      - **agg.**: acon↓ meny↓ nat-ar↓ prun↓
        - **stitching** pain: acon nat-ar prun
        - **tearing** pain: meny
  - **broken**; as if: crot-c ptk1 lil-t ptk1 *Mag-c* ptk1 nat-m ptk1 plat ptk1 sulo-ac c1 verat ptk1
  - **burning**: acon agath-a nl2• alum-sil k2 alumn *Ars* ptk1 ars-met bamb-a stb2.de• *Berb* bry calc h2 carbn-s k2 cur glon k* graph helon **Kali-bi** kali-br tl1 kali-c h2 **Lyc** k* mag-m *Med* k* merc *Nux-v* ox-ac ph-ac **Phos** k* pic-ac tl1 rob bg1* sabad senec *Sil* sul-ac h2 *Sulph* k* *Thuj* k* *Zinc*
    - **pulsating** pain: *Phos*
    - **stinging**, and: rumx sabad
  - **chill**; during: sang
  - **cold** air agg.: rhus-t tritic-vg fd5.de
  - **contracting**: chin h1 dulc fd4.de graph bg1 **Guaj** mag-m h2
  - **cough** agg.; during: calc dros k2 kali-bi↓ stram sul-ac
    - **aching**: calc kali-bi stram
    - **sore**: dros k2 sul-ac
  - **cramping**: bamb-a stb2.de• bell h1 dream-p sdj1• grat ptk1 ip **Phos** k* tritic-vg fd5.de verat ptk1
  - **cutting** pain: alum arn bov *Calc* canth bg1* *Hyper* kali-n meny **Nat-s** k* sul-ac h2 zinc ptk1
  - **dinner**; after: indg↓ phel↓
    - **stitching** pain: indg phel
  - **dragging**: naja

Back

- **Scapulae – Between**: ...
  - **drawing** pain: acon *Alum* am-c *Ars* bell borx bry **Calc** carb-an chel **Cimic** coloc *Dros* eupi graph grat **Guaj** *Hep* kali-bi kali-n lob *Lyc* mur-ac naja bg2 nat-c nat-m *Nat-s* nux-v *Ph-ac* *Phos* psor jl2 *Puls* *Rhus-t* ruta fd4.de sep *Sil* stann staph a1 stram h1 thuj tritic-vg fd5.de vanil fd5.de viol-t *Zinc* zinc-p k2
  - **drinking** agg.: rhus-t hr1
  - **eating** | **after** | **agg.**: *Arg-n* phel bg1
    - **agg.**: rhus-t hr1
  - **eructations**:
    - **before**: nit-ac ↓
      - **stitching** pain: nit-ac h2
    - **during**: sep ↓
      - **stitching** pain: sep
  - **expiration**:
    - **agg.**: sep ↓
      - **aching**: sep
    - **during** | **agg.**: raph sep
  - **gnawing** pain: nat-c
  - **inspiration** agg.: berb ↓ nat-ar nat-c ↓ puls ran-b ↓
    - **stitching** pain: berb nat-ar nat-c ran-b br1
  - **lacing** corsets, on: laur ↓
    - **stitching** pain: laur
  - **lancinating**: agath-a nl2• asc-t c1 canth bg1 *Gins*
  - **leaning** backward:
    - **amel.**: lac-c ↓
      - **aching**: lac-c
  - **lifting** agg.: stann h2
  - **lying**:
    - **agg.**: bry ↓ nat-m petr-ra shn4• ruta fd4.de
      - **sore**: nat-m
      - **stitching** pain: bry
    - **amel.**: ars brucel ↓
      - **aching**: brucel sa3•
      - **drawing** pain: *Ars*
    - **back**; on:
      - **agg.**: kali-n
        - **stitching** pain: *Kali-n*
    - **hard**; on something | **amel.**: petr-ra shn4• sanic pc
    - **side**; on | **left** | **agg.**: ph-ac
      - **right** | **amel.**: kali-n
  - **lying** down agg.: calc ↓ sulph ↓
    - **burning**: sulph
      - **itching** and stinging pain: calc
  - **menses**; during: *Am-c* sil
    - **drawing** pain: *Am-c* *Sil*
    - **pressing** pain: am-c
  - **mental** exertion agg.: helon ↓ *Pic-ac* ↓ *Sil* ↓
    - **burning**: helon *Pic-ac* *Sil*
  - **motion**:
    - **agg.**: ang ↓ arn ↓ bry *Calc* canth ↓ colch dros h1 ip kali-bi nux-v ox-ac petr plb ↓ podo puls ran-b ↓ rhod sil stann sulph vanil ↓ verat ↓
      - **burning** | **paroxysmal**: plb
      - **cramping**: ip ptk1
      - **drawing** pain: bry stann sulph vanil fd5.de
      - **pressing** pain: *Calc* k* stann h2
      - **stitching** pain: ang arn canth ip nux-v *Puls* ran-b br1 stann h2 verat
      - **tearing** pain: petr k*
    - **amel.**: calc ↓ kali-c laur mag-m ↓ mez ↓ nicc ↓ ph-ac ruta fd4.de sulph
      - **sore**: kali-c
      - **stitching** pain: calc mag-m mez nicc
    - **arm**; of:
      - **agg.**: carb-an ↓ sil ↓
        - **pressing** pain: carb-an h2 sil k*
    - **arms**; of | **agg.**: colch naja sil

- **Scapulae – Between – motion**: ...
    - **body**; of:
      - **agg.**: bry ↓
        - **stitching** pain: bry
    - **head**; of | **agg.**: kali-p fd1.de• nux-v vanil fd5.de
  - **paralyzed**; as if: nat-c h2
  - **pinching** pain: nit-ac h2
  - **pressing** pain: am-c k* ambr bg1* ant-s-aur *Arn* **Bell** k* bism bg2 bry k* **Calc** k* carb-an h2 carb-v k* *Chin* k* coc-c k* *Cocc* crot-t elaps graph k* hura indg k* kali-bi k* kali-br k* kali-c k* lach k* laur k* led k* lob lyss *Nux-v* petr k* psil ft1 psor ran-s bg2 ruta fd4.de sacch-a fd2.de• seneg sep k* sil k* stann h2 symph fd3.de• ter thuj k* vanil fd5.de
  - **pulsating** pain: merc-i-f *Phos* tab bg2
  - **respiration**; hindering: **Calc** ↓
    - **pressing** pain: **Calc**
  - **rest** agg.: *Calc* ↓
    - **cutting** pain: *Calc*
  - **rheumatic**: aspar calad dros h1 lob lycps-v mag-s *Rhus-t* *Rhus-v* sil h2 staph h1 verat
    - **pressing** pain: sil h2
  - **rising**:
    - **agg.**: carb-v vanil fd5.de
      - **pressing** pain: carb-v
    - **stooping**; from:
      - **after** | **agg.**: puls
  - **rubbing**:
    - **amel.**: carb-an ↓ phos ↓
      - **burning**: phos
      - **drawing** pain: carb-an
  - **scraping**: bry bg2
  - **scratching** agg.; after: mag-c ↓
    - **burning**: mag-c
  - **sitting**:
    - **agg.**: bell brucel ↓ bry calc-caust kali-c ↓ kali-p fd1.de• nat-m thuj ↓ tritic-vg fd5.de vanil fd5.de *Zinc* ↓
      - **aching**: brucel sa3•
      - **burning**: thuj *Zinc*
      - **pressing** pain: bell bry k* vanil fd5.de
      - **sore**: kali-p fd1.de• nat-m
      - **stitching** pain: kali-c h2 thuj h1 vanil fd5.de
    - **amel.**: cann-s ↓ chel ↓
      - **stitching** pain: cann-s chel
    - **bent** forward | **agg.**: bov ran-b k2
    - **erect**:
      - **agg.**: coloc ↓
        - **drawing** pain: coloc
      - **amel.**: bov
        - **cutting** pain: bov
        - **stitching** pain: *Bov*
  - **sleep**, waking from: kali-n ↓
    - **stitching** pain: kali-n h2
  - **sore**: *Acon* am-m ars bar-c chin k* cimic ptk1 crot-c dig *Gran* ham ptk1 *Hell* hyper ptk1 kali-bi bg1 kali-c kali-p fd1.de• lach lil-t bg1 mag-c bg1 mag-m mag-s *Meny* merc-i-f nat-m nux-v petr-ra shn4• *Phos* k* plat bg1 podo rhus-t sep ptk1 *Sil* succ-ac rly4• sulph ther tritic-vg fd5.de verat bg1
  - **sprained**; as if: am-m k* bell nux-v petr h2* sep h2 stann h2
  - **squeezing**: aloe bg2 verat bg2
  - **standing**:
    - **agg.**: nicc ↓ rumx
      - **aching**: rumx
      - **stitching** pain: nicc
    - **amel.**: brucel ↓
      - **aching**: brucel sa3•
  - **stepping** hard agg.: seneg ↓
    - **aching**: seneg

- **Scapulae – Between**: ...
  - **stitching** pain: acon aeth *Agar* aloe alum alum-sil k2 alumn ang arg-met h1 asaf asc-t *Berb* bov *Bry Calc Camph* cann-s carb-an carb-v carl cham chel chin *Coc-c Cocc Colch* coloc h2 con cop cupr dig dulc ferr guaj hep hura hyper indg kali-c kali-n kreos **Lac-c** k* lach laur lyc mag-m mag-s mang mez mill nat-ar nat-c **Nit-ac** k* nux-v ol-an *Par* **Petr** k* plb prun psor *Puls Ran-b* ruta h1 sars *Seneg* sep sil stann tab thuj vanil fd5.de verat
    - **outward**: calc h2
  - **stool**; before: verat h1
  - **stooping**: prun ↓
    - **agg.**: borx cham nit-ac ↓ nux-v petr-ra ↓ prun
      - **drawing** pain: borx nux-v
      - **sore**: cham nux-v petr-ra shn4•
      - **stitching** pain: nit-ac
      - **tearing** pain: borx
    - **pressing** pain | **plug** were forced inward; as if a: prun k*
  - **stooping** a long time; as after: puls h1
  - **summer** agg.: *Lyc* ↓
    - **burning**: *Lyc*
  - **swallowing** agg.: *Rhus-t* k*
  - **tearing** pain: agar k* anac k* bar-c k* *Berb* k* borx *Calc* k* calc-caust canth k* *Caust* k* cocc k* ferr k* kali-c k* kali-n k* *Lach* k* mag-m k* meny k* nat-c k* *Nat-s* k* petr k* psor k* puls rhus-t k* *Sil* k* thuj k* zinc k*
  - **turning** agg.: calad merc verat
    - **tearing** pain: verat k*
  - **turning** around: verat ↓
    - **stitching** pain: verat
  - **waking**; on: sil ↓ thuj ↓
    - **pressing** pain: sil h2 thuj k*
  - **walking**:
    - **agg.**: bell coc-c ↓ coloc ferr ↓ meny ↓ seneg
      - **aching**: bell
      - **drawing** pain: coloc
      - **pressing** pain: coc-c k*
      - **stitching** pain: coloc h2
      - **tearing** pain: ferr k* meny h1
    - **amel.**: brucel ↓ bry ferr puls
      - **aching**: brucel sa3•
      - **pressing** pain: bry k*
    - **bent**:
      - **must** walk bent: coloc ↓
        - **stitching** pain: coloc h2
  - **warm** agg.; becoming: lac-c ↓
    - **aching**: lac-c
  - **warmth** | **amel.**: *Rhus-t*
  - **weather** agg.; cold wet: *Nux-m*
  - **wine** agg.: ph-ac
  - **extending** to:
    - **Arms**; down: echi
    - **Back** of neck: dioxi rbp6 stict vanil fd5.de
    - **Back**; down the: kali-c ↓ merc ↓
      - **burning**: kali-c h2 merc
    - **Chest**: petr a1
    - **Downward**: kali-p fd1.de• *Verat*
    - **Epigastrium**: kali-c bg1 rat bg1 thuj bg1
    - **Hands**: sec ↓
      - **stitching** pain: sec a1
    - **Head** into temples; over: *Kalm* k*
    - **Lumbar** region: dros h1* ox-ac k*
    - **Nape**: *Nat-s* ↓
      - **burning**: *Nat-s*
    - **Sacrum**: *Zinc*
    - **Shoulders**: *Kalm* valer vanil fd5.de
      - **Face**; and: valer
    - **Spine**; down to: androc srj1•
    - **Sternum**: *Kali-bi* lac-c

- **Scapulae – Between – extending** to
    - **Stomach**: bry ↓
      - **stitching** pain: bry
  - **Deep** in scapulae: fl-ac bg2
  - **Lain** on: graph ↓
    - **sore**: graph h2
  - **Margins**: ran-b ↓
    - **left**: dulc ↓ zinc ↓
      - **stitching** pain: dulc k* zinc h2
    - **cutting** pain: ran-b ptk1
    - **Inner**: anac ↓ aur ↓ chel ↓ chin ↓ guaj ↓
      - **right**: asar ↓ *Card-m* ↓ chel ↓ guaj ↓ symph ↓
        - **blow**; pain as from a: asar h1
        - **cramping**: chel
        - **drawing** pain: *Card-m*
        - **stitching** pain: guaj h2 symph fd3.de•
      - **left**: ran-b ↓
        - **sore**: ran-b ptk1
      - **bending** | **backward**:
          - **agg.**: aur ↓
            - **tearing** pain: aur k*
        - **left**; to:
          - **agg.**: aur ↓
            - **tearing** pain: aur k*
      - **cramping**: chel
      - **pressing** pain: anac h2
      - **tearing** pain: aur chin h1 guaj h2
    - **Lower**: ant-c ↓ mur-ac ↓ nat-c ↓ plat ↓ ran-b ↓ seneg
      - **burning**: nat-c ran-b k*
      - **motion**:
        - **amel.**: nat-c ↓
          - **burning**: nat-c h2
      - **pressing** pain: ant-c h2 mur-ac h2 plat h2
      - **sewing**; from: ran-b ↓
        - **burning**: ran-b k*
      - **Inner**: allox sp1 alumn cic h1
    - **Outer**:
      - **right**: dulc ↓
        - **blow**; pain as from a: dulc h2*
  - **Spine**: agath-a ↓ ail ↓ arund ↓ calc ↓ phos ↓
    - **aching**: agath-a nl2• ail arund calc phos
    - **breathing** agg.: calc ↓
      - **aching**: calc
  - **Tips** of: alumn ↓ berb ↓ cimx ↓ mez ↓ plb ↓
    - **burning**: plb
    - **motion**:
      - **amel.**: alum ↓ alumn ↓
        - **tearing** pain: alum alumn k*
    - **sore**: cimx
    - **tearing** pain: alumn k* berb k* mez k*
  - **Upper** part: bar-c ↓ carb-v ↓ chel ↓ stann ↓
    - **burning**: bar-c carb-v chel stann h2
  - **Vertebrae**; near: asc-c ↓
    - **aching**: asc-c c1
- **Shoulders**:
  - **alternating** with | **Lower** chest; pain in (See CHEST - Pain - lower - alternating - shoulder)
  - **Between**: agath-a ↓ laur ↓ mag-m ↓ ph-ac ↓ thyr ↓ visc ↓
    - **aching**: visc c1
    - **boring** pain: agath-a nl2• laur mag-m h2 ph-ac
    - **bursting** pain: thyr bg1
    - **rest** agg.: laur ↓
      - **boring** pain: laur
  - **Joint**: staph tl1
    - **left**: cygn-ol sze3•

Back

- **Spine**: **Agar**↓ agath-a nl2• ail **Alum** am-c ang↓ arg-met↓ arn asaf **Bell**↓ *Berb*↓ borx↓ *Calc* *Chel* cina cinnb com crot-h↓ crot-t dig↓ euon↓ gins hell hura↓ *Kalm* lac-lup hrn2• lob *Lyc*↓ mag-m↓ merc↓ mez mur-ac↓ *Naja* nat-c↓ nat-m **Nat-s** *Nux-m* *Nux-v* par **Petr**↓ *Ph-ac* *Phos* psor raph↓ *Ruta* sabin seneg *Sep* **Sil** spig↓ stann staph↓ *Thuj* *Verat* verb↓ zinc
  - **boring** pain: *Lyc* mez naja phos psor
  - **cutting** pain: euon thuj
  - **fall**; as from a: *Ruta*
  - **inspiration**:
    - **agg**.: mur-ac↓
      - **pressing** pain: mur-ac
    - **deep** | **agg**.: alum
  - **motion** agg.: cocc
  - **pressing** on dorsal vertebra; jerking involuntary when: arn k*
  - **pressing** pain: ail asaf **Bell** gins mur-ac sabin sep staph h1 zinc
  - **sitting**:
    - **agg**.: *Ph-ac*
    - **bent** forward:
      - **agg**.: verb↓
        - **stitching** pain: verb h
  - **stitching** pain: **Agar** ang arg-met crot-h dig euon hura merc **Petr** raph ruta sabin spig h1 stann verb h
  - **stoop**, compelling to: **Cann-i**
  - **tearing** pain: *Berb* k* borx mag-m nat-c *Nat-s* psor *Sil* zinc
  - **touch**; to: calc h2
  - **extending** to:
    - **Sternum**: kali-bi↓ **Lac-c**↓
      - **stitching** pain: kali-bi **Lac-c**
  - **Between** scapula and spine: ars-met↓ *Graph*↓ lach↓ pic-ac↓ podo fd3.de• ran-b k* sep↓ *Sil*↓ vanil fd5.de
    - **right**: ozone sde2•
    - **morning** | **rising** agg.: *Brucel* sa3•
    - **burning**: ars-met *Graph* lach pic-ac sep *Sil*
- **Spots**; in: alum bg2 caust bg2 fl-ac bg2 galeoc-c-h gms1• kali-bi bg2 mag-m bg2 nit-ac bg2 ph-ac bg2 phos bg2 plb bg2 stram bg2 thuj bg2 zinc bg2
- **Upper** part: stann↓
  - **stitching** pain: stann h2
- **Vertebrae**: alum↓ chel↓ chinin-s bro1
  - **pressing** pain: alum bg2
  - **separated**; as if: chel bg2
  - **First**: nux-v↓
    - **sore**: nux-v hbh
  - **Near**: asc-c↓
    - **cutting** pain: asc-c c1
  - **Third**: cimic bg2 psor↓
    - **crushed**, as if: psor jl2

- **Hips**: brucel↓
  - **wandering** pain: brucel sa3•

- **Lumbar** region (= small of back): abies-n br1 abrot bg2 acon k* act-sp bro1 **Aesc** k* aeth *Agar* k* agar-ph↓ agath-a nl2• aids nl2• alet↓ all-c all-s allox sp1 aloe k* *Alum* k* alum-p k2 alum-sil k2 *Alumn*↓ am-c k* *Am-m* k* ambr aml-ns↓ *Anac*↓ anag anan androc srj1• ang k* ant-c k* ant-o↓ ant-s-aur↓ *Ant-t* bg2* anth↓ anthraq rly4• *Apis* apoc aq-pet↓ aran bg2 arb br1 **Arg-met** *Arg-n* k* arge-pl rwt5• arist-cl rbp3• *Arn* k* ars k* *Ars-h*↓ ars-i↓ ars-met ars-s-f k2 arum-t↓ arund asaf asar asc-t a1 aspar↓ aur k* aur-ar k2 aur-i↓ aur-m aur-s bad↓ *Bamb-a* stb2.de• *Bapt* bar-act br1 **Bar-c** k* bar-i↓ bar-ox-suc↓ bar-s↓ bell k* benz-ac↓ **Berb** k* beryl↓ bism↓ *Bit-ar* wht1• *Bol-la* borx k* both-ax↓ bov brach↓ brom brucel sa3• **Bry** k* bufo but-ac br1 cadm-met tpw6 cain calad↓ **Calc** k* *Calc-ar* calc-caust↓ calc-f k* calc-i↓ *Calc-p* k* calc-s calc-sil k2 camph cann-i cann-s cann-xyz↓ **Canth** k* caps k* *Carb-ac* k* *Carb-an* k* *Carb-v* k* *Carbn-s* k* carc↓ *Card-m* carl casc↓ cass a1 cassia-s ccrh1*• castn-v br1 *Caul* k* *Caust* k* cedr↓ cench k2 *Cham* k* cheir c1 chel k* **Chin** k* chinin-ar chinin-s mrr1 chir-fl↓ choc↓ chr-ac chr-o c2 cic a1 *Cimic* k* *Cimx* cina bro1 cinch↓ cinnb cinnm cit-ac↓ clem k* cob k* coc-c *Cocc* k* coff k* *Colch* k* coli jl2 *Coloc* k* colum-p sze2• com↓ *Con* k*

- **Lumbar** region: ...
conch fkr1.de conv br1 cop k* cor-r corn corv-cor↓ cot↓ croc crot-h crot-t cund cupr cupr-ar *Cur* cycl cypra-eg↓ des-ac rbp6 dig dios k* dioxi↓ diph-t-tpt jl2 dirc↓ *Dor*↓ dream-p sdj1• dros b7.de* **Dulc** k* *Echi* elaps elat↓ equis-h↓ erig↓ ery-a↓ **Eup-per** k* euph↓ eupi fago↓ *Ferr* k* ferr-ar ferr-i *Ferr-p* fic-m gya1 fl-ac form↓ franz↓ frax↓ fum rly1*• galeoc-c-h gms1• galla-q-r nl2• gamb *Gels* ger-i↓ gins c2* glon↓ gnaph bg2* gran↓ granit-m↓ **Graph** k* grat *Guaj* k* guare↓ gymno↓ *Ham* k* hell k* helo↓ *Helon* *Hep* k* hip-ac sp1 hipp↓ hura *Hydr* k* hydrang br1 hydrc hydrog srj2• *Hymos* bro1 hyos hyper ign k* ignis-alc es2• ind indg↓ iod iodof↓ *Ip* k* ipom-p bro1 irid-met srj5• iris jatr-c↓ jug-c kali-ar *Kali-bi* k* kali-br a1 *Kali-c* k* kali-chl↓ kali-cy↓ *Kali-i* k* kali-m k2 *Kali-n* k* kali-o bro1 kali-ox c2 *Kali-p* *Kali-s* kali-sil k2 kali-t↓ *Kalm* k* kola stb3• kreos k* *Lac-ac*↓ *Lac-c* *Lac-d* lac-e hrn2• lac-h sk4• *Lach* k* lachn↓ lact lap-la sde8.de• lat-m↓ lath c1* laur↓ lavand-a↓ lec **Led** k* lepi br1 *Lept*↓ lil-s↓ *Lil-t* lim↓ limen-b-c↓ lipp↓ lith-be bro1 lith-c↓ lob lob-s c2 loxo-recl knl4• luna kg1• lyc k* lycpr↓ lycps-v *Lyss* m-ambo b7.de *M-aust* b7a.de macro c2* mag-c k* *Mag-m* k* *Mag-p* mag-s k* maland jl2 malar jl2 manc↓ mand rsj7• mang med k* mela↓ melal-alt↓ meli *Meny* meph↓ merc k* *Merc-c*↓ merc-i-f↓ merl *Mez* k* mim-p↓ mit↓ morg-p pte1*• morph↓ *Mosch*↓ *Mur-ac* k* murx myos-a↓ myric↓ naja nat-ar *Nat-c* k* *Nat-m* k* nat-ox rly4• *Nat-p* nat-pyru rly4• *Nat-s* nat-sil fd3.de• neon srj5• nicc nicotam rly4• *Nit-ac* k* nit-m-ac↓ **Nux-m** k* **Nux-v** k* oci↓ ol-an ol-j k* olib-sac wmh1 onos *Op* k* orot-ac↓ osm ost c2 ox-ac k* oxal-a↓ ozone sde2• pall bg2 par↓ petr k* petr-ra↓ petros↓ *Ph-ac* **Phos** k* phys↓ physala-p bnm7• *Phyt* k* *Pic-ac* k* pimp c2* pin-con oss2• plac-s↓ plan *Plat* k* plb plumbg↓ plut-n↓ *Podo* polyp-p↓ positr nl2• *Propr* sa3• prun bg2 psil ft1 *Psor* k* ptel **Puls** k* puls-n↓ pycnop-sa↓ rad-br bro1 ran-a c2 ran-b k* *Ran-s* raph↓ rat rham-cal br1* rheum *Rhod* k* *Rhus-g* tmo3• **Rhus-t** k* rhus-v k* rob rumx↓ *Ruta* k* sabad b7.de* sabal c2* sabin k* sal-fr sle1• samb samb-c c2 sang sanic c2* sapin↓ sarcol-ac↓ sarr c2 sars b4.de* *Sec* k* sel b7.de* senec k* seneg↓ **Sep** k* *Sil* k* sin-n slag c2 sol-t-ae↓ *Spect*↓ spig↓ spira c2* spong b7.de* stann *Staph* k* stram streptoc↓ *Stront-c* k* *Stry* suis-em↓ suis-hep rly4• *Sul-ac* k* sul-i **Sulph** k* sumb↓ syc pte1*• symph↓ syph *Tab*↓ tanac↓ taosc iwa1• tarax tarent tax↓ tep↓ ter k* ther↓ thuj til↓ *Tril-p*↓ tritic-vg fd5.de trom↓ tus-p c2 ulm-c↓ urol-h rwt• ust↓ *Valer* k* vanil fd5.de **Vario** verat k* **Verat-v**↓ vib k* vip↓ visc c2 wist-s↓ xan↓ *Zinc* k* zinc-p k2 zing↓ ziz↓ [heroin sdj2]
  - **right**: aqui↓ borx↓ *Brucel* sa3• *Carb-ac*↓ carc mlr1• elat hr1 fic-m gya1 iris↓ kali-s fd4.de lac-leo hrn2• lac-lup hrn2• lavand-a↓ lyc↓ olib-sac↓ pert-vc vk9 petr-ra shn4• propr sa3• psil ft1 sep↓ sil h2 symph↓ tax↓ [heroin sdj2]
    - **aching**: lavand-a ctl1•
    - **boring** pain: *Carb-ac*
    - **cramping**: iris a1
    - **pressing** pain: aqui br1
    - **stitching** pain: borx h2 carc fd2.de• olib-sac wmh1 sep h2 symph fd3.de• [tax jsj7]
    - **tearing** pain: lyc h2
  - **left**: androc srj1• dulc↓ loxo-recl knl4• lyc↓ petr-ra shn4• pitu-gl skp7• ruta fd4.de spong↓ tritic-vg fd5.de zinc↓
    - **boring** pain: dulc bg2
    - **sore**: zinc h2
    - **stitching** pain: lyc h2 ruta fd4.de spong fd4.de
  - **22** h: carbn-s↓
    - **dislocated**; as if: carbn-s
  - **daytime**: agar bro1 ant-c↓ ox-ac↓
    - **aching**: ant-c k* ox-ac k*
    - **rest** agg.: am-c↓
      - **aching**: am-c
  - **morning**: alum aml-ns↓ ang *Arg-met*↓ arg-n borx bufo calc-p↓ carb-v *Carbn-s* chel *Cimic* cinnb↓ *Colch* cop↓ croc↓ dios dulc fd4.de *Eup-per* *Eup-pur* ham↓ *Hep* hipp↓ hura↓ ign↓ *Kali-bi*↓ kali-c kali-n↓ *Kali-p* lac-ac↓ lap-la sde8.de• limest-b↓ lyc↓ mag-m↓ mim-p rsj8• mit↓ mur-ac↓ naja nat-sil↓ nicc↓ **Nux-v** onos *Petr* petr-ra shn4• plan *Puls*↓ ran-b **Rhus-t**↓ sang sars↓ sel↓ senec sil↓ spong fd4.de stann↓ *Staph* k* stront-c *Stry* sulph↓ symph fd3.de• thuj↓ tritic-vg fd5.de vanil fd5.de zinc↓
    - **14** h, until: mag-c↓
      - **sore**: mag-c
    - **evening**, until: nat-s↓
      - **sore**: nat-s

- **morning**: ...
  - **evening**; and: kali-n↓
    - **pinching** pain: kali-n h2
  - **aching**: aml-ns bufo chel k* cimic k* cinnb k* cop k* croc k* *Dios* k* hura ign k* *Kali-bi* k* lac-ac k* lyc mag-m k* mit a1 mur-ac naja nicc k* **Nux-v** k* plan k* *Puls* k* ran-b k* **Rhus-t** k* sang k* sars *Senec* k* stann
  - **bed** agg.; in: *Agar*↓ aur↓ carbn-s chr-o↓ cocc form franz↓ hep *Nux-v* ozone↓ petr puls ruta staph tritic-vg fd5.de
    - **aching**: chr-o franz a1 *Nux-v*
    - **broken**; as if: (non:ang kl) *Staph*
    - **cutting** pain: ozone sde2•
    - **drawing** pain: hep nux-v
    - **pressing** pain: cocc tritic-vg fd5.de
    - **sore**: *Agar* aur *Nux-v* k* *Ruta*
    - **sprained**; as if: petr
  - **bending**:
    - **amel.**: plut-n srj7•
    - **forward**:
      - **agg.**: *(↗jar; stepping)* cocc puls
      - **bed**; in: puls↓
        - **stitching** pain: puls
    - **left**; to:
      - **agg.**: mang
        - **pressing** pain: mang
  - **burning**: vanil fd5.de zinc
  - **cutting** pain: petr
  - **drawing** pain: carbn-s dios hipp sulph thuj zinc
  - **exertion** agg.: ust↓
    - **dragging**: ust
  - **increasing** during the day: sanic mrr1
  - **lameness**: dios k* sel
  - **lancinating** | **iron**; as from hot: bufo
  - **motion**; after: petr↓
    - **cutting** pain: petr
  - **pressing** pain: ham fd3.de• kali-c limest-b es1• nat-sil fd3.de• symph fd3.de• tritic-vg fd5.de
  - **rising**:
    - **after**:
      - **agg.**: petr↓
        - **cutting** pain: petr
      - **amel.**: ang↓ cocc ferr ptk1 form kali-p nat-s↓ plut-n srj7• staph
        - **aching**: nat-s k*
        - **pressing** pain: ang h1 cocc form staph
    - **agg.**: aloe↓ arg-n↓ calc↓ *Calc-p*↓ cedr↓ chel↓ del↓ hipp↓ kali-c↓ limest-b es1• lyc↓ *Nat-m*↓ ox-ac↓ rat↓ sil↓ *Stry*↓ thuj↓ valer↓
      - **aching**: aloe calc k* cedr k* del a1 hipp k* lyc k* ox-ac
      - **lameness**: nat-m sil
      - **sore**: *Calc-p* kali-c k* *Nat-m* rat k* *Stry* thuj k* valer k*
      - **sprained**; as if: arg-n
      - **stitching** pain: chel
    - **amel.**: aur↓ nat-s↓ staph↓
      - **sore**: aur nat-s staph h1
    - **bed**; from | **after** | **agg.**: nat-s k2
      - **agg.**: arg-n *Calc* chel graph *Kali-c* *Lyc* nat-m petr rat *Sil* thuj valer
  - **sore**: alum *Arg-met* calc-p colch k* dios k* sil k*
  - **sprained**; as if: arg-n petr
  - **stitching** pain: borx kali-n h2 spong fd4.de vanil fd5.de
  - **stooping** agg.: petr↓
    - **cutting** pain: petr
  - **tearing** pain: stront-c
  - **waking**; on: apoc↓ arg-met↓ carbn-s↓ dioxi↓ erig↓ kali-n h2 mag-m h2 myric↓ op↓ plan↓ plut-n srj7• positr↓ propr sa3• sal-fr↓
    - **aching**: carbn-s erig k* op k* plan k* positr nl2• sal-fr sle1•
    - **dragging**: myric
    - **sore**: apoc a2 arg-met vh1 dioxi rbp6 kali-n h2
- **forenoon**: jug-c kali-n h2 nat-c↓ nat-sil fd3.de• stront-c sulph
- **forenoon**: ...
  - **9** h:
    - **amel.**: ruta↓
      - **tearing** pain: ruta
  - **10**.30 h: brucel sa3•
  - **11** h: lac-ac↓
    - **aching**: lac-ac
  - **11**.15 h: propr sa3•
  - **aching**: jug-c k* stront-c sulph k*
  - **sitting** agg.: jug-c↓ sulph↓
    - **aching**: jug-c k* sulph k*
  - **sore**: nat-c k*
- **noon**: lycps-v↓ sulph↓ thuj
  - **aching**: lycps-v
  - **drawing** pain: sulph thuj
- **afternoon**: bamb-a stb2.de• bry calc-f↓ canth↓ carbn-s cob↓ coc-c↓ coloc dios↓ dulc fd4.de erig↓ fago↓ hip-ac↓ hydrog↓ hyos jug-c↓ kali-c↓ kali-n h2 lycps-v↓ mag-c mag-m naja nicc ost↓ ozone↓ petr plb ptel↓ rhus-t↓ ruta↓ **Sep** stry↓ *Sulph*↓ vanil fd5.de
  - **14** h:
    - **sitting** agg.: hura↓
      - **aching**: hura
  - **15**-16 h: brucel sa3•
  - **16** h: mand↓ pitu-gl skp7•
    - **midnight** | **until**: pitu-gl skp7•
    - **dull** pain: mand rsj7•
  - **17** h: dios↓
    - **burning**: dios
  - **aching**: calc-f coc-c k* dios k* erig k* fago k* jug-c k* kali-c k* lycps-v ost a1 ptel k* rhus-t k* *Sep* k* stry
  - **amel.**: bamb-a↓
    - **drawing** pain: bamb-a stb2.de•
  - **burning**: mag-m ruta fd4.de
  - **cutting** pain: canth hydrog srj2• naja petr
  - **drawing** pain: bry carbn-s
  - **dull** pain: hip-ac sp1
  - **fever**; during: trom↓
    - **aching**: trom k*
  - **grinding**: hip-ac sp1
  - **inspiration** agg.; deep: sars↓
    - **aching**: sars
  - **motion** agg.: petr↓
    - **cutting** pain: petr
  - **sore**: cob mag-c h2 plb *Sulph* k*
  - **sprained**; as if: sep h2
  - **standing** agg.: plb↓
    - **tearing** pain: plb k*
  - **stitching** pain: coloc mag-c nicc ozone sde2• plb vanil fd5.de
  - **stooping** agg.: petr↓
    - **cutting** pain: petr
  - **tearing** pain: mag-m k*
- **evening**: alum apoc↓ bamb-a stb2.de• *Bar-c* k* bar-s k2 bart↓ bell h1 brucel sa3• cassia-s↓ caust↓ cob↓ coc-c↓ *Coloc* dios dirc↓ erig↓ ferr↓ ham↓ hip-ac↓ hura↓ ignis-alc es2• iris kali-n kali-s fd4.de kalm↓ lach led↓ lycps-v↓ mag-c mag-m meny murx↓ naja nat-c *Nat-s* nit-ac nux-m pic-ac podo↓ propr sa3• puls↓ ruta↓ sars↓ *Sep* sil h2 sin-n spong fd4.de stront-c stry↓ **Sulph** sumb↓ tanac↓ tritic-vg fd5.de vanil fd5.de zinc↓ zing
  - **19**.30 h:
    - **waking**; on: sep↓
      - **aching**: sep
      - **nap**; from a: sep
  - **21** h: hura↓
    - **lancinating**: hura
  - **aching**: alum k* apoc k* cob k* coc-c k* dios k* dirc k* erig k* ferr k* hura kalm k* lycps-v murx k* naja nux-m k* pic-ac k* stry sulph k* sumb k* tanac k*

Back

- **evening**: ....
  - **bed** agg.; in: alum ↓ *Kalm* ↓ sep ↓
    - **lameness**: *Kalm*
    - **sprained**; as if: sep h2
    - **stitching** pain: alum
    - **tearing** pain: alum
  - **burning**: mag-m ruta fd4.de
  - **constricting** pain: alum
  - **cramping**: dios iris led h1
  - **drawing** pain: *Bar-c* meny nit-ac ruta fd4.de stront-c sulph zing
  - **dull** pain: cassia-s ccrh1• hip-ac sp1
  - **grinding**: hip-ac sp1
  - **lameness**: alum h2 bart
  - **lying** down agg.; after: alum kalm mag-m naja ruta fd4.de sulph ↓
    - **burning**: sulph
    - **gnawing** pain: mag-m
  - **menstruation**, during: kali-n
  - **pressing** pain: ham fd3.de• kali-s fd4.de meny h1 puls h1 ruta fd4.de spong fd4.de vanil fd5.de zinc h2
  - **rest** agg.: nux-m ↓
    - **broken**; as if: nux-m
  - **sore**: caust k* cob k* *Coloc* kali-n h2 mag-c k* meny k* sars h2 stront-c *Sulph* k*
  - **stitching** pain: kali-n h2 lach nat-c pic-ac podo fd3.de• spong fd4.de stront-c vanil fd5.de zinc h2
- **night**: *Aesc* ↓ agar ↓ am-c **Am-m** ang ↓ aqui ↓ arg-n ↓ *Ars* bamb-a stb2.de• bar-c ↓ bit-ar wht1• borx ↓ bry cench k2 *Cham* *Chin* cinnb ↓ coc-c ↓ colch ↓ der ↓ eupi *Ferr* ferr-i fl-ac kali-n lac-ac lac-lup hrn2• laur *Lil-t* *Lyc* mag-c mag-m mag-s nat-pyru rly4• *Nat-s* nicc ↓ nit-ac ↓ *Nux-v* ↓ olib-sac wmh1 *Phos* ↓ podo propr sa3• rhus-t ruta ↓ sang ↓ sars senec ↓ *Sep* *Sil* spong fd4.de *Staph* k* *Sulph* tritic-vg fd5.de vanil fd5.de zinc
  - **midnight**:
    - **before**: laur rhus-t
      - **stitching** pain: laur rhus-t
    - **after**: **Am-m** ↓ bamb-a stb2.de• *Naja* ↓ **Sil** ↓ staph ↓ **Sulph** ↓
      - **1-4 h**: am-m
      - **2 h**: kali-n *Nat-s* ↓
        - **sore**: *Nat-s*
      - **3 h**: **Kali-c** ↓ kali-n ↓ *Nux-v* ↓
        - **bed**; driving out of: **Kali-c** kali-n
        - **burning**: *Kali-c*
        - **sore**: kali-n *Nux-v*
        - **stitching** pain: **Kali-c**
      - **4 h**: ang ↓ ruta ↓
        - **sore**: ang c1
        - **tearing** pain: ruta
        - **waking**; on: plut-n srj7• ptel hr1 staph
          - **pressing** pain: plut-n srj7• staph
      - **sore**: **Am-m** *Naja* **Sil** staph h1 **Sulph**
  - **aching**: *Aesc* agar k* arg-n coc-c k* der a1 fl-ac k* lyc k* mag-c k* mag-m k* nicc k* nit-ac k* *Nux-v* k* podo k* sang k* senec k* **Sep** k* sil k* sulph k* zinc
  - **bed**:
    - **driving** out of bed: mag-c h2
    - **going** to bed:
      - **when**: bapt ↓ sin-n ↓
        - **aching**: bapt sin-n
    - **in** bed:
      - **agg.**: **Am-m** bamb-a stb2.de• croc ↓ kalm kola stb3• lac-ac ↓ lil-t *Naja* nat-pyru rly4• puls zinc
        - **aching**: croc k* lac-ac k* naja
        - **gnawing** pain: lil-t
  - **broken**; as if: ferr-i *Mag-c*
  - **burning**: bar-c mag-m *Phos*
  - **cutting** pain: sulph h2
  - **drawing** pain: ars bry cinnb colch eupi ruta fd4.de sulph
  - **gnawing** pain: am-c
- **night**: ...
  - **lying** on left side agg.: bamb-a stb2.de•
  - **pressing** pain: aqui br1
  - **sleep** agg.; during: **Am-m**
  - **sore**: **Am-m** ang c1 **Sil** k* **Sulph**
  - **stitching** pain: ars borx h2 bry laur rhus-t
  - **tearing** pain: mag-m k* mag-s k*
  - **turning** in bed agg.: zinc ↓
    - **aching**: zinc
- **accompanied** by:
  - **diarrhea** (See RECTUM - Diarrhea - accompanied - back - pain - lumbar)
  - **dysentery** (See RECTUM - Dysentery - accompanied - back - pain - lumbar)
  - **flatulence**; obstructed: calc h2
  - **metrorrhagia** (See FEMALE - Metrorrhagia - accompanied - lumbar)
  - **numbness**: gnaph bro1
  - **perspiration**; cold, clammy: lath bro1
  - **positiveness** (See MIND - Positiveness - lumbar)
  - **respiration**; complaints of (See RESPIRATION - Complaints - accompanied - lumbar)
  - **sciatica**: *Rhus-t* bro1
  - **Abdomen**; complaints (See ABDOMEN - Complaints - accompanied - lumbar; ABDOMEN - Pain - accompanied - lumbar)
  - **Bladder**; pain in (See BLADDER - Pain - accompanied - lumbar)
  - **Head**; pain in (See HEAD - Pain - accompanied - back - pain - lumbar)
  - **Intestines**; pain in (See ABDOMEN - Pain - intestines - accompanied - lumbar)
  - **Lower** limbs; complaints of: ant-t bg2 berb bg2 bry bg2 cimic bg2 coloc bg2 ham bg2 kali-c bg2 lach bg2 nux-v bg2 phyt bg2 rhus-t bg2 sulph bg2 tell bg2
  - **Occiput**; pain in (See HEAD - Pain - occiput - accompanied - lumbago)
  - **Pelvis**; heaviness in: gnaph bro1
  - **Uterus**; pain in (See FEMALE - Pain - uterus - accompanied - lumbar)
- **aching**: acon k* **Aesc** k* aeth k* agar-ph a1 agath-a nl2• allox sp1 aloe alum k* am-c k* am-m k* aml-ns androc srj1• ant-t k* anth k* *Apis* apoc aq-pet a1 arg-n k* arge-pl rwt5• arn k* *Ars* k* *Ars-h* k* ars-met ars-s-f k2 arum-t k* asaf asar k* asc-t k* bad k* bapt k* *Bar-act* bar-c k* bar-ox-suc rly4• bar-s k2 bell k* **Berb** k* bit-ar wht1• bol-la brach k* *Brom* k* **Bry** k* bufo cadm-met sp1 **Calc** k* *Calc-ar* calc-f k* calc-p k* calc-sil k2 camph k* cann-s k* *Canth* k* *Carb-ac* k* carb-an k* *Carb-v* k* *Carbn-s* carl k* casc cass a1 caul k* *Caust* k* cham *Chel* k* *Chin* chinin-s cic *Cimic* k* cimx k* cinch a1 cinnb k* *Clem* cob k* *Coc-c* k* coff k* colch k* *Coloc* k* com k* con k* conv br1 cop a1 cot a1 crot-t k* cund a1 cupr cupr-ar k* cycl k* dig k* dios k* dirc a1 *Dor* k* **Dulc** k* equis-h erig a1 ery-a a1 eup-per k* fago a1 ferr a1 fic-m gya1 fl-ac form a1 franz a1 gamb a1 **Gels** k* glon k* gnaph k* gran a1 granit-m es1• *Graph* k* gymno ham k* hell *Helon* hep k* hipp k* *Hura* *Hydr* hyos k* *Hyper* ign k* *Ind* k* iodof k* irid-met srj5• iris jatr-c jug-c k* kali-bi k* kali-br k* *Kali-c* k* kali-chl k* kali-cy a1 kali-m k2 *Kali-n* k* kali-ox a1 *Kali-p* kali-sil k2 kali-t a1 *Kalm* k* *Kreos* k* *Lac-ac* k* lac-e hrn2• lach k* lepi a1 lept lil-s a1 *Lil-t* k* lim a1 limen-b-c hrn2• lipp a1 lob k* lyc k* lycpr a1 lyss k* mag-m k* mag-s k* mela a1 merc k* merc-i-f merl a1 mez k* mit a1 morph k* *Mur-ac* murx k* myric k* naja nat-ar nat-c k* nat-p nat-s k* nicc k* nit-ac k* nit-m-ac a1 nux-m k* **Nux-v** k* ol-an k* op k* osm k* ost a1 *Ox-ac* k* oxal-a rly4• petros k* *Phos* k* phys k* *Phyt* k* *Pic-ac* k* plan k* plb k* plumbg a1 plut-n srj7• *Podo* k* polyp-p a1 *Positr* nl2• prun k* *Psor* k* ptel k* *Puls* raph k* rhod k* rhus-g a1* rhus-t rhus-v a1 rumx sabin k* sal-fr sle1• samb k* sang k* sapin a1 sarcol-ac sp1 sarr k* *Sars* k* *Sec* k* *Senec* k* **Sep** k* *Sil* k* sol-t-ae a1 spira a1 *Staph* k* stram k* stront-c *Stry* k* *Sul-ac* k* **Sulph** k* sumb k* tab k* tanac a1 *Tarent* tep a1 thuj k* trom k* tus-p a1 ust k* verat k* vip k* *Zinc* k* zinc-p k2 zing k* ziz k* [*Spect* dfg1]

- **aching**: ...
  - **accompanied** by | **Stomach**; pain in (See STOMACH - Pain - accompanied - lumbar)
  - **alternating** with:
    - **Head**; pain in (See HEAD - Pain - alternating - lumbar - aching)
    - **Thighs**; pain in: am-c
  - **labor**-like: acon *Kreos* nux-v **Puls**
  - **paralyzed**; as if: carl k* *Cocc* k* kalm k* nat-m k* ran-s k* *Sabin* k* sel k* zinc k*
  - **wanting**; as if third vertebra were: *Psor*
- **air** agg.; draft of: med k2 nux-v
  - **broken**; as if: *Nux-v*
- **air** agg.; in open: agar bro1 lyc
  - **pressing** pain: lyc
- **alternating** with:
  - **anger** with himself (See MIND - Anger - himself - alternating - lumbar)
  - **discontentment** with himself (See MIND - Discontented - himself - alternating - lumbar)
  - **hemorrhoids**: *Aloe* k*
  - **Abdomen**; pinching in: kali-n h2
  - **Forehead**; pain in (See HEAD - Pain - forehead - alternating with - lumbar)
  - **Head**; pain in (See HEAD - Pain - alternating - lumbar)
  - **Thighs**; pain in: am-c
- **ascending** stairs agg.: alum carbn-s mand ↓ tus-p ↓
  - **aching**: tus-p k*
  - **drawing** pain: carbn-s
  - **dull** pain: mand rsj7•
  - **stitching** pain: alum
- **bandaging**: | **amel**.: tril-p hr1
- **bed**; when going to: naja ↓
  - **constricting** pain: naja
- **bending**:
  - **agg**.: mim-p rsj8•
  - **amel**.: acon ↓ am-m ↓ androc ↓ caust ↓ hura ↓ psor ↓
    - **aching**: androc srj1• caust k* psor k*
    - **drawing** pain: acon am-m hura
  - **backward**:
    - **agg**.: asaf ↓ bar-c cina con kali-c lac-leo hrn2• *Mang* nux-v ↓ plat puls rhus-t sabin sel streptoc ↓ thuj
      - **aching**: asaf k* con kali-c k* puls k* sabin k* sel k*
      - **broken**; as if: plat k*
      - **drawing** pain: bar-c sabin
      - **sore**: nux-v plat streptoc rly4•
    - **amel**.: acon am-m fl-ac hura puls h1 sabad sabin
      - **aching**: fl-ac puls k* sabad sabin k*
  - **body**:
    - **backward** agg.: rhus-t ↓
      - **pressing** pain: rhus-t h1
  - **forward**:
    - **agg**.: asaf ↓ chel ↓ stroph-s ↓
      - **aching**: asaf k*
      - **sore**: stroph-s sp1
      - **tearing** pain: chel
    - **amel**.: lavand-a ↓
      - **pressing** pain: lavand-a ctl1•
  - **left**; to:
    - **agg**.: plb
      - **stitching** pain: plb
- **biting**: m-aust b7.de
- **blow**; pain as from a: ant-t b7.de* arn b7.de* bit-ar wht1• dulc h1* kali-bi bg2 m-ambo b7.de nat-c b4.de* nux-m b7.de* ruta b7.de* sal-fr sle1• samb b7.de* sep bg2
- **blowing** the nose agg.: calc-p dig
- **blowing** the nose agg.: ...
  - **sore**: dig
- **boring** pain: acon b7.de* agar am-c bg2 asaf berb bg2 borx h2* bufo bg2 calad bg2 canth k* *Carb-ac* coc-c bg2 ign bg2 kreos bg2 ruta bg2
- **break**; as if it would: aloe arg-met **Bell** *Camph* sne chel *Ham* kali-p fd1.de• *Kreos* **Lyc** nat-m nux-v plat
- **breath**; takes away the: **Puls** ↓
  - **constricting** pain: **Puls**
- **breathing**:
  - **agg**.: alum am-c ammc k* arg-met ↓ both-ax ↓ carb-an carb-v coloc conch fkr1.de dulc ↓ kali-bi *Kali-c* merc prun *Sulph* vanil fd5.de
    - **drawing** pain: coloc vanil fd5.de
    - **stitching** pain: ammc arg-met h1 both-ax tsm2 carb-an dulc h2 *Merc* prun
    - **tearing** pain: *Kali-c*
  - **deep**:
    - **agg**.: arn asar aur cinnb ↓ conv cycl ↓ kali-n nat-m phel sang ↓ sars sep ↓ spong fd4.de vanil fd5.de
      - **burning**: sep
      - **sore**: conv sang k* vanil fd5.de
      - **stitching** pain: arn cinnb k2 cycl kali-n h2 nat-m phel spong fd4.de
  - **sitting**; while: dulc
- **broken**; as if: *Aesc* bg2* am-c bg2 am-m bg2 ang b7a.de* ant-t bg2 arg-met arn b7.de* *Ars* **Bell** b4a.de* bry *Camph* sne caps bg2 *Carb-an* k* *Cham* k* chel k* clem con cor-r eup-per bg2* ferr-i *Graph* k* *Ham* k* helo bg2 *Kali-c* k* kali-i bg2* kali-p fd1.de• kreos k* lil-t bg2 **Lyc** k* mag-c k* mag-m k* meli **Nat-m** k* *Nux-m* k* *Nux-v* b7.de* ox-ac **Phos** k* plan plat k* psor *Rhus-t* k* ruta bg2* senec bg2* *Sep* k* spong fd4.de staph k* sulph ulm-c jsj8•
  - **knocked** away; as if: arg-met k*
- **burning**: acon k* aesc aeth bg2* agar bg2 alum bg2* alumn am-c k* ant-s-aur apis b7a.de arg-met k* ars-i arund asar k* aur bamb-a stb2.de• bar-c k* bar-s k2 bell *Berb* k* borx k* carb-an b4a.de* carb-v bg2 cedr cham chel clem *Coloc* cupr guare k* helo bg2 *Helon* *Kali-c* kali-p kali-sil k2 *Kalm* kola stb3• *Kreos* k* lac-d *Lach* k* lachn lyc bg2 m-aust b7.de* mag-c k* *Mag-m* k* *Med* *Merc-c* mur-ac k* murx nat-c k* nat-p *Nit-ac* k* *Nux-v* *Ph-ac* k* *Phos* k* phyt bg2 pic-ac k* podo ptk1 *Ran-b* *Rhus-t* k* ruta fd4.de *Sep* k* sil spig h1 stann k* staph b7.de* sul-ac k* sulph k* **Ter** k* ther tl1 thuj k* vanil fd5.de verat zinc zinc-p k2 ziz k*
  - **deep**-seated: clem
  - **hot** iron were thrust through; as if a: alum bg2 bufo bg2 cann-xyz bg2
- **burrowing**: acon b7.de* dulc k* kreos k* rhod bg2 stann bg2
- **chill**:
  - **before**: **Aesc** *Eup-pur* **Podo**
  - **during**: alum bg2 arn bg2 ars k* bol-la ↓ bry bg2 *Calc* k* caust bg2 cocc bg2 gamb ↓ hep b4a.de* kali-c bg2 *Lach* b7a.de* *Lyc* b4a.de* myric ↓ nux-m b7.de* *Nux-v* k* ph-ac k* phos k* puls k* rhus-t k* sabad b7.de* sep k* sil k* sulph bg2 verat b7a.de*
    - **aching**: bol-la bro1 gamb k* myric k*
- **chronic**: aesc bro1 berb bro1 *Calc-f* bro1 *Rhus-t* bro1 sil bro1
- **clawing** pain: calc ign *Merc*
- **clutching**: graph bg2 merc bg2
- **coition**: agar k2 cann-i nit-ac
  - **after**: cann-i ↓ nit-ac ↓
    - **aching**: cann-i k*
    - **drawing** pain: nit-ac
- **cold**:
  - **agg**.: rhus-t tl1
  - **air** agg.: *Bar-c* *Nit-ac* sep
- **cold**; after taking a: **Dulc** k* *Nit-ac* plac rzf5• **Rhus-t**
  - **lameness**: **Dulc**
  - **sore**: **Dulc**
- **cold** agg.; becoming: bamb-a ↓
  - **stitching** pain: bamb-a stb2.de•

- **compressed**; as if: bell bov *Caust* ruta fd4.de stront-c *Thuj* tritic-vg fd5.de
- **constipation**; during: kali-bi ↓ tep ↓
  - **aching**: kali-bi tep
- **constricting** pain: am-c arund ger-i rly4• hell lach lyc meny *Puls* tanac
- **contracting**: ars bg2 bufo bg2 hell b7.de* *Kali-c* b4a.de mag-m k* meny b7.de* mez bg2 nux-v b7.de* puls b7.de* ruta b7.de* vanil fd5.de
- **corrosive**: alum b4.de* am-c b4.de* berb bg2 canth b7.de* equis-h bg2 lil-t bg2 mag-m b4.de* naja bg2 nicc bg2 ph-ac b4.de* phos b4.de* plb bg2 stront-c b4.de* sulph b4.de*
- **cough** agg.; during: *Acon* ↓ *Am-c* k* arn arund ↓ bell borx bry calc *Calc-s* caps carb-an ptk1 *Kali-bi* k* kali-n merc k* nit-ac k* ph-ac *Puls* k* pyrog bg2 *Rhus-t* ↓ sep sulph k* tell ↓
  - **aching**: arund k* kali-n k* merc k* tell
  - **broken**; as if: *Rhus-t*
  - **pressing** pain: kali-n h2
  - **stitching** pain: *Acon* k* am-c k* arn k* bell borx *Bry* caps merc *Nit-ac* k* puls pyrog sep sulph
- **cramping**: am-c h2 ant-c ptk1 *Bell* k* bry b7.de* *Calc* **Caust** k* cham bg2 **Chin** k* *Chinin-s* coc-c bg2 cocc b7.de* dios bg2 graph *Iris* k* lat-m bnm6• led bg2 lyc k* mag-m k* merc nux-v bg2 oci petr bg2 ph-ac k* *Plat* b4a.de plb bg2 podo fd3.de• rhus-t bg2 sil sulph bg2 thuj b4.de* vanil fd5.de
  - **paroxysmal**: plb
- **crushed**, as if: **Berb** k* **Chin** k* phos
- **cutting** pain: all-s *Alum* ang bg2 *Arg-n* k* arge-pl rwt5• *Arn* k* aur k* *Bell* k* calad calc-p cann-s cann-xyz bg2 canth k* *Chel* cit-ac rly4• dig k* *Dulc* k* *Eup-per* gels granit-m es1• hep k* hydrog srj2• *Ign* b7a.de ignis-alc es2• kali-bi k* *Kali-c* mag-c bg2 mag-m h2 mag-p bg2 mez k* nat-c k* *Nat-m* k* ozone sde2• petr k* phos bg2 plb bg2 psor k* puls bg2 rheum k* rhus-t bg2 sal-fr sle1• samb b7.de* senec stry *Sulph* k* thuj bg2 wist-s mfm zinc h2*
  - **outward**: ang
- **delivery**:
  - **after**: kali-c bg1
    - **difficult** delivery: *Nux-v* ↓
      - **lameness**: *Nux-v*
  - **during**: *Caust* ↓ kali-c ↓
    - **cutting** pain: kali-c
    - **sore**: *Caust*
- **digging** pain: arg-n k* berb k* bufo bg2 dulc ign bg2 kali-i bg2 ruta bg2
- **dinner**; after: phos k* sarcol-ac ↓ sulph k* zinc ↓
  - **aching**: phos k* sarcol-ac sp1 sulph k*
  - **stitching** pain: zinc h2
- **disappearing** slowly: brucel sa3•
- **dislocated**; as if: agar b4a.de* arg-n bg2 arn b7.de* bell bufo bg2 calc b4.de* canth b7.de* carc fd2.de• con dulc fd4.de eup-per bg2* ham fd3.de• hep b4.de* kali-bi bg2 lach bg2* lyc bg2 m-aust b7.de petr b4.de* puls b7.de* rhod b4.de* *Rhus-t* b7.de* sep b4.de* sulph b4.de*
- **dragging**: alet bg2 apis b7a.de arn bar-c k* calc bg2 coc-c colch k* *Con* ery-a *Ferr Ham* irid-met bg2* kali-chl kreos bg2 mag-c bg2 merl myric nux-v b7.de* phos *Pic-ac* k* plb k* **Sabin** *Sep* k* sul-ac bg2 xan c1 zinc bg2
  - **menses** would come on; as if: *Apis* sulph
- **drawing** pain: acon agar aloe am-c k* am-m ambr ang b7.de* *Arg-met* k* arg-n arn *Ars* k* ars-s-f k2 *Aur* bamb-a stb2.de• *Bar-c* k* bar-s k2 *Bell* k* benz-ac *Berb Bry Calc* k* calc-s calc-sil k2 **Caps** b7.de* *Carb-an* carb-v carbn-s card-m carl *Caust Cham* k* *Chel Chin* k* cinnb clem coc-c *Cocc* k* colch k* *Coloc Con* k* croc b7.de* cycl dig k* *Dulc* k* eupi hep k* hipp hura hyos ign k* indg *Kali-bi* k* *Kali-c* k* kali-m k2 kali-n kali-p kali-sil k2 kreos k* *Lach* k* *Led* k* *Lyc* m-aust b7.de mag-m meny b7.de* *Mez* k* *Mur-ac* nat-c h2 *Nat-m* k* nat-sil fd3.de• *Nit-ac Nux-v* k* **Ph-ac** k* *Plat* b4a.de plb psor *Puls Rhod* k* rhus-v ruta b7.de* **Sabin** k* samb b7.de* *Sep Sil* k* spong fd4.de staph b7.de* *Stram* k* *Stront-c* k* sul-ac k* *Sulph* k* ter *Thuj* k* tritic-vg fd5.de valer b7.de* vanil fd5.de verat k* *Zinc* k* zinc-p k2 zing
  - **cramping**: sil h2 sul-ac h2
  - **downward**: bar-c h2 caps h1 staph h1
- **drawing** pain: ...
  - **flatus**; as from obstructed: nat-c h2
  - **inward**: am-m h2
  - **jerking** pain: ph-ac h2
  - **paralyzed**; as if: cina a1
  - **paroxysmal**: ph-ac
- **drawing** up knees:
  - **amel.**: lavand-a ↓
    - **pressing** pain: lavand-a ctl1•
- **drawing** up the limbs agg.: arg-met
- **dull** pain: allox tpw3* borx b4a.de but-ac br1 cassia-s ccrh1• corv-cor bdg• dulc fd4.de ham bg2* hip-ac sp1 mand rsj7• mim-p rsj8• nat-sil fd3.de• phyt bg2 positr nl2• spong b7.de* suis-em rly4• symph fd3.de• tritic-vg fd5.de vanil fd5.de [tax jsj7]
- **eating** | **after**:
  - **agg.**: am-m b7a.de *Bry* cina kali-bi ↓ kali-c *Ran-b* ↓
    - **drawing** pain: bry
    - **stitching** pain: kali-bi *Ran-b*
  - **while**:
    - **agg.**: bry ↓ coc-c ↓
      - **aching**: coc-c k*
      - **pressing** pain: bry
- **elbows** and knees amel.; on: coloc ↓
  - **aching**: coloc
- **emissions** agg.; after: ham ↓
  - **aching**: ham k*
- **erect**, becoming: nat-m ↓
  - **aching**: nat-m k*
- **erections**:
  - **after**: mag-m h2
    - **violent** erections: mag-m ↓
      - **aching**: mag-m
- **exertion**:
  - **agg.**: *Agar* k* *Calc-p* con ↓ phys vanil fd5.de [heroin sdj2]
    - **broken**; as if: con
    - **dislocated**; as if: con
    - **lameness**: phys
  - **amel.**: galeoc-c-h gms1• rad-br ptk1
- **exertion**; as if after: *Ant-t* b7a.de hep b4a.de* kali-c b4.de* laur b7.de* meph bg2 merc b4a.de *Nux-m* b7a.de petr b4a.de* puls b7.de* sep bg2
- **expiration** agg.; during: spig ↓ *Sulph* ↓
  - **stitching** pain: spig h1 *Sulph*
- **fall**; as from a: arn b7.de* ruta b7.de*
- **false** step; at a: *(↗jar; stepping)* bell mrr1 carb-ac cocc podo thuj
  - **aching**: *(↗jar - aching; stepping - aching)* carb-ac podo k*
- **fatigue**; as from: aur h2 *Cina* a1 hep h2 kali-c h2 sep h2
- **fever**:
  - **after**: kreos b7a.de
  - **during** | **agg.**: *Acon* bg2 apis bg2 arn bg2 *Ars* bg2 bry bg2 **Calc** b4a.de* *Caust* bg2 *Cham* bg2 chin bg2 cocc bg2 *Ign* bg2 kali-c b4a.de* lyc bg2 merc bg2 *Nat-m* bg2 **Nux-v** bg2 phos bg2 **Puls** bg2 *Rhus-t* bg2 ruta bg2 **Sep** bg2 sil bg2 stront-c bg2 *Sulph* bg2
- **flatulence**:
  - **from**: sil ↓
    - **stitching** pain: sil
  - **with** (See accompanied - flatulence)
- **flatus**; from obstructed: coc-c ↓ *Kali-c* ↓ **Lyc** ↓
  - **pressing** pain: coc-c *Kali-c* **Lyc**
- **flatus**; passing | **after**:
  - **amel.**: coc-c ↓
    - **aching**: coc-c
  - **amel.**: am-m bar-c coc-c kali-c **Lyc** *Pic-ac Ruta*
- **flesh** where loose; as if: lyc h2 rhus-t b7.de*
- **followed** by:
  - **leukorrhea**: kreos b7a.de

- **followed** by: ...
  - **soreness**: conv$_{a2}$ sang$_{k*}$
- **gnawing** pain: alum *Alumn* am-c *Berb* canth hura lil-t mag-m nicc ph-ac *Phos* plb stront-c *Sulph*
- **grasping** pain: calc$_{b4.de*}$ *Cham*$_{b7.de*}$ graph$_{b4.de*}$ ign$_{b7.de*}$ kali-i$_{bg2}$ merc$_{b4.de*}$
- **griping** pain: arg-met$_{h1}$ graph$_{h2}$
- **hard** bed; as from a: merc$_{b4.de*}$
- **hemorrhoids**; during: aesc$_{bg1}$ bell$_{bg1}$ ham$_{bg1}$ nux-v$_{bg1}$
- **injuries**; after: **Agar**$_{sne}$ kali-c nat-s ↓
  - **lancinating**: nat-s
- **inspiration**:
  - **agg.**: alum ↓ aur ↓ **Coloc** ↓ conch$_{fkr1•}$ cycl ↓ spig ↓ spong ↓
    - **lancinating**: aur **Coloc**
    - **stitching** pain: alum aur *Coloc* cycl$_{h1}$ spig$_{h1}$ spong$_{fd4.de}$
  - **sitting** bent forward agg.: dulc ↓
    - **stitching** pain: dulc
- **jar** agg.: *(↗false; morning - bending - forward - agg.; stepping; walking - uneven; Injuries - lumbar; Injuries - lumbar - sensitive)* bell$_{mrr1}$ carb-ac cocc podo *Thuj*
  - **aching**: *(↗false - aching; stepping - aching)* carb-ac podo
- **jerking** pain: alum$_{k*}$ am-c asar$_{b7.de*}$ bry$_{b7.de*}$ chin$_{b7.de*}$ euph$_{b4.de*}$ ferr$_{b7.de*}$ m-ambo$_{b7.de}$ nux-v$_{b7.de*}$ petr$_{b4.de*}$ rhus-t$_{b7.de*}$
  - **stitching** pain: rhus-t$_{h1}$
- **kneeling** agg.: euphr ↓
  - **aching**: euphr$_{k*}$
- **labor**-like: acon$_{k*}$ bell$_{b4a.de}$ *Carb-an*$_{b4a.de}$ cham$_{b7.de*}$ chel$_{bg2}$ *Cocc*$_{b7a.de}$ croc$_{b7a.de}$ gels$_{bg2}$ ham$_{bg2}$ kali-c$_{b4a.de*}$ *Kreos*$_{k*}$ *Lil-t* *Mosch*$_{b7a.de}$ *Nux-v* onos$_{bg2}$ plat$_{b4a.de}$ **Puls**$_{k*}$ sabad$_{bg2}$ sabin$_{k*}$ sep$_{b4a.de}$ sulph$_{bg2}$
- **lameness**: *Aesc* agar$_{k*}$ alum$_{bg2}$ ang ars$_{bg2}$ berb$_{bg2}$ bry$_{bg2}$ *Caust* con$_{k*}$ cupr$_{bg2}$ *Cupr-ar*$_{k*}$ cur dios$_{k*}$ *Dulc* hep *Hyper* iris *Kali-c*$_{k*}$ kali-n$_{bg2}$ **Lach**$_{k*}$ *Lept* mag-m$_{bg2}$ *Nat-m*$_{k*}$ *Nux-v* **Phos** ptel puls-n **Rhus-t** *Ruta* sel sil zinc$_{bg2}$
  - **drawing** pain: cham$_{h1}$
- **lancinating**: anac anan asaf aur-s **Coloc** cupr *Elaps* ign *Kali-c* kali-m$_{k2}$ lac-c plac-s$_{rly4•}$ plb *Senec* **Verat-v**
  - **downward**: *Elaps*
  - **paroxysmal**: plb
  - **thrusts**, like: anan **Verat-v**
  - **upward**: *Coloc*
- **laughing** agg.: **Cann-i** *Con* *Phos* plb tell
  - **aching**: **Cann-i**$_{k*}$ tell
  - **stitching** pain: plb
- **leaning**:
  - **against** something:
    - **amel.**: zing ↓
      - **aching**: zing$_{k*}$
  - **chair**; against a:
    - **agg.**: plb ↓
      - **sore**: plb
  - **forward**:
    - **agg.**: hura lac-c
      - **drawing** pain: hura
  - **side**; to:
    - **agg.**: cina$_{a1}$
    - **amel.**: raph ↓
      - **aching**: raph
- **leukorrhea**:
  - **amel.**: kreos$_{bg1}$
  - **with** (See FEMALE - Leukorrhea - accompanied - lumbar) caust ↓ kali-n ↓ syph ↓
    - **sore**: caust$_{h2}$ kali-n$_{h2}$ syph$_{jl2}$
- **lifting** agg.: *Calc* calc-f$_{c1}$ *Calc-p* *Hura*$_{bg1*}$ kali-s$_{fd4.de}$ med nat-c ↓ nit-ac *Nux-v* ph-ac rhus-t$_{c1*}$ *Sang* sep *Staph* vanil$_{fd5.de}$
  - **jerking** pain: nat-c$_{h2}$
- **lifting** agg.: ...
  - **stitching** pain: nit-ac ph-ac sep$_{h2}$
- **lying**:
  - **abdomen**; on:
    - **agg.**: bamb-a ↓ gink-b$_{sbd1•}$ kali-s$_{fd4.de}$ symph$_{fd3.de•}$ tritic-vg$_{fd5.de}$
      - **stitching** pain: bamb-a$_{stb2.de•}$
    - **amel.**: chel malar$_{jl2}$ nit-ac sel
      - **can** only lie on abdomen: nit-ac ↓
        - **aching**: nit-ac
  - **agg.**: agar aml-ns ↓ androc ↓ *Arn* bell$_{bro1}$ **Berb**$_{k*}$ beryl ↓ bry *Calc* *Carb-an* cham colch ↓ daph$_{ptk2}$ ign kali-i kali-s$_{fd4.de}$ lac-d ↓ lap-la$_{rsp1}$ lavand-a$_{ctl1•}$ lyc$_{bg1}$ mag-m murx$_{bro1}$ nux-v ozone$_{sde2•}$ prun *Puls* **Rhus-t** ruta$_{k2}$ sil ↓ spong$_{fd4.de}$ tab tet ↓ tritic-vg$_{fd5.de}$ vib
    - **aching**: agar$_{k*}$ aml-ns androc$_{srj1•}$ mag-m$_{k*}$ *Nux-v* tab$_{k*}$ tet$_{a1}$
    - **broken**; as if: carb-an
    - **burning**: lac-d
    - **cutting** pain: *Arn*
    - **drawing** pain: carb-an colch
    - **lancinating**: berb$_{k*}$
    - **sore**: agar berb *Bry* cham puls **Rhus-t**
    - **stitching** pain: beryl$_{tpw5}$ sil$_{h2}$
    - **tearing** pain: berb
  - **amel.**: am-m$_{vh1}$ bamb-a ↓ bry cench$_{k2}$ *Cob* colch cop euon$_{bro1}$ hip-ac$_{sp1}$ kali-c kali-m$_{k2}$ *Nat-m* nux-v ozone$_{sde2•}$ ruta$_{k*}$ sars sep$_{bro1}$
    - **aching**: cob$_{k*}$
    - **drawing** pain: *Kali-c*
    - **stitching** pain: bamb-a$_{stb2.de•}$
    - **tearing** pain: *Bry* nux-v
  - **back**; on:
    - **agg.**: am-m ↓ *Ars* ↓ bamb-a$_{stb2.de•}$ bit-ar$_{wht1•}$ bry carb-an *Chin* *Coloc* ign irid-met$_{srj5•}$ kali-n *Lyc* mag-s malar$_{jl2}$ prun **Rhus-t** ruta$_{fd4.de}$ sep spong$_{fd4.de}$ symph$_{fd3.de•}$ tritic-vg$_{fd5.de}$ zinc
      - **aching**: ign lyc
      - **drawing** pain: **Coloc** sep
      - **lancinating**: **Coloc**
      - **menses**; at beginning of: bamb-a$_{stb2.de•}$
      - **sore**: am-m *Ars* *Bry* ign *Rhus-t*
      - **stitching** pain: *Coloc* prun
      - **tearing** pain: mag-s
    - **amel.**: ambr cob colch gink-b$_{sbd1•}$ *Kali-c* *Nat-m* ozone ↓ ruta$_{fd4.de}$
      - **cutting** pain: ozone$_{sde2•}$
      - **tearing** pain: ambr
  - **backward**; bent | **amel.**: cain
  - **bed**; in:
    - **agg.**: mand ↓
      - **dull** pain: mand$_{rsj7•}$
  - **face**; on the:
    - **amel.**: chel ↓
      - **stitching** pain: chel
  - **hard**; on something | **amel.**: **Nat-m** **Rhus-t**
  - **pillow**; on a | **amel.**: carb-v$_{bg1*}$
  - **quietly**:
    - **agg.**:
      - **motion** amel.: colch ↓
        - **drawing** pain: colch
  - **side**; on:
    - **agg.**: am-m ↓
      - **sore**: am-m
    - **amel.**: symph$_{fd3.de•}$ zinc
    - **left** | **agg.**: agar bamb-a$_{stb2.de•}$ ruta$_{fd4.de}$ spong$_{fd4.de}$ **Sulph**
    - **right**:
      - **agg.**: sep ↓
        - **stitching** pain: sep$_{h2}$
      - **amel.**: nat-s ↓
        - **can** only lie on right side: nat-s
        - **sore**: nat-s
- **lying** down:

Back

- **lying** down: ...
  - **amel.**: bamb-a ↓ ruta ↓
    - **stitching** pain: bamb-a stb2.de• ruta
- **masturbation**; from: nux-v bro1
- **menses**:
  - **after**:
    - **agg.**: berb borx b4a.de calc-p kali-n mag-c k* nux-m ↓ puls *Sep* ust
      - **aching**: berb k* calc-p kali-n puls
      - **dragging**: ust
      - **sore**: mag-c k*
      - **wood** were pressing from within out; as if a piece of: nux-m c1
  - **appearance**; on: *Caust* ↓
    - **tearing** pain: *Caust*
  - **before**:
    - **agg.**: acon am-c k* apis arum-d ↓ *Asar* bamb-a stb2.de• bar-c k* bar-s k2 berb brom k* *Bry* b7a.de *Calc* k* *Calc-p* canth carb-v b4a.de *Caul* caust k* cimic eupi ↓ *Ham* hyos k* iod kali-n k* kreos ↓ *Lyc* b4a.de *Mag-c* k* melal-alt ↓ mosch b7.de nat-m *Nit-ac* nux-m k* ol-an phos *Plat* b4a.de puls pulx br1 sabal c1 sabin sal-fr sle1• **Sep** *Spong* *Sulph* tril-p ust *Vib*
      - **aching**: am-c k* arum-d k* berb k* caust k* *Mag-c* melal-alt gya4 phos k* sal-fr sle1•
      - **burning**: kreos *Phos* b4.de*
      - **contracted**; as if: mag-c a1
      - **cutting** pain: *Ol-an*
      - **dragging**: canth
      - **drawing** pain: *Hyos*
      - **sitting** agg.: mag-c ↓
        - **dragging**: mag-c
      - **sitting**, walking amel.; while: mag-c ↓
        - **cutting** pain: mag-c
      - **sore**: mag-c h2 spong
      - **stitching** pain: *Nat-m*
      - **tearing** pain: eupi k*
  - **beginning**, at the: acon aloe *Asar* bamb-a stb2.de• berb *Caust* k* *Kali-s* **Lach** mag-c k* *Nit-ac* k* plut-n srj7• sabal c1 *Vib*
  - **delayed**: phos ↓ sul-ac ↓
    - **aching**: sul-ac k*
    - **burning**: phos h2
  - **during**:
    - **agg.**: acon agar agn hr1 aloe **Am-c** k* *Am-m* k* aqui ↓ arg-met *Arg-n* ars-i bar-c k* bar-s k2 *Bell* k* *Berb* borx b4a.de bov b4.de *Brom* *Bry* k* *Calc* k* calc-p k2 calc-s *Cann-i* canth b7.de *Carb-an* k* carb-v k* carbn-s carl castm ↓ caul *Caust* k* cench k2 *Cham* k* **Cimic** k* coc-c *Cocc* k* cop ↓ *Croc* b7.de cycl dream-p ↓ eupi ferr k* ferr-i *Ferr-p* gran ↓ *Graph* k* guare ↓ ham *Helon* hyos ign k* iod k* *Kali-c* k* kali-i kali-n k* *Kali-p* *Kali-s* *Kalm* kreos k* lac-ac **Lach** k* lachn laur b7.de *Lyc* k* *Mag-c* k* *Mag-m* k* mag-s k* mang med ↓ mom-b ↓ nat-c k* nat-p *Nicc* *Nit-ac* k* **Nux-m** k* *Nux-v* k* ozone sde2• *Phos* k* plat k* plb plut-n ↓ prun **Puls** k* rat sabin k* sars b4a.de sec b7.de senec sep stram b7.de sul-ac k* sul-i k2 **Sulph** k* *Tarent* *Thuj* tub c1 ust *Xan* zinc zinc-p k2 zing
      - **aching**: aloe *Am-m* k* berb k* castm caust *Coc-c* cop k* eupi k* gran a1 graph k* iod k* *Lach* lyc k* mag-c k* mag-m k* mom-b a1 nat-p k2 nit-ac k* plut-n srj7• prun k* rat k* **Sulph** k* tarent k* zing k*
      - **burning**: med phos
      - **contracting**: am-m
      - **cramping**: bell calc *Nux-v*
      - **cutting** pain: *Arg-n* caust helon zinc
      - **dragging**: dream-p sdj1• *Kali-c* sulph zinc
      - **drawing** pain: am-m calc carl cham mag-c sep
      - **labor**-like: agar am-m *Calc* *Cham* *Cimic* *Cycl* graph kreos *Lyc* *Nit-ac* **Puls** *Sulph*
      - **preceded** by tickling: graph h2
      - **pressing** pain: am-m aqui br1 *Carb-an* carb-v *Ferr-p* *Kali-c* *Lach* plat plb **Puls** **Sulph**
      - **sore**: am-c bar-c carb-v caust *Cimic* kali-i kali-n h2 mag-c mag-m mag-s thuj
      - **tearing** pain: *Caust* guare lachn
- **menses** – **during**: ...
  - **beginning** of menses:
    - **agg.**: acon ↓ aloe ↓ bamb-a ↓ berb ↓ nit-ac ↓ plut-n ↓
      - **aching**: acon aloe berb nit-ac plut-n srj7•
      - **drawing** pain: bamb-a stb2.de•
  - **instead** of: *Spong*
  - **suppressed** menses; from: con b4a.de kali-c *Nux-m* **Puls**
- **menses** would come on; as if: *Apis* *Calc-p*
  - **accompanied** by | **diarrhea** (See RECTUM - Diarrhea - accompanied - lumbar)
- **metrorrhagia**; during: bry b7a.de
- **mortification**; from: nux-v
- **motion**:
  - **after** | **agg.**: *Rhus-t*
  - **agg.**: acon **Aesc** *Agar* alum am-c ambr arg-met *Arn* asar bamb-a ↓ bell mrr1 beryl ↓ brom ↓ brucel sa3• **Bry** bufo ↓ calc calc-p canth caps *Caust* chel **Chin** cimic colch *Coloc* con ↓ conv croc cupr-ar ↓ dig ↓ dulc eup-per ↓ franz ↓ hydr ↓ hydrog srj2• ign iris kali-bi kali-c kali-i kali-n kali-p fd1.de• kalm lach lath bro1 lavand-a ↓ *Lyc* meph mez nat-c *Nat-s* nit-ac **Nux-v** *Ox-ac* ↓ ozone sde2• petr ↓ petr-ra shn4• phos phyt pic-ac plan plb podo propr sa3• *Psor* ptel *Puls* *Ran-b* **Rhus-t** *Sars* *Sep* spira ↓ stann sul-ac ↓ **Sulph** tep verat ↓ visc c1 zinc zinc-p k2 ziz
    - **aching**: **Aesc** k* alum k* am-c k* asar k* canth k* chel k* colch croc k* franz a1 hydr ign k* iris kali-bi k* kali-n lyc nit-ac k* *Ox-ac* *Phyt* k* *Pic-ac* plan k* podo k* *Psor* k* **Rhus-t** k* sars k* *Sep* k* spira a1 tep k* ziz k*
    - **broken**; as if: chel con kali-c *Rhus-t*
    - **cramping**: **Chin** plb
    - **crushed**, as if: **Chin**
    - **cutting** pain: kali-bi zinc
    - **drawing** pain: acon caps colch kali-n sul-ac h2
    - **jerking** pain: petr a1
    - **lameness**: cupr-ar k*
    - **lancinating**: plb
    - **pressing** pain: lavand-a ctl1• mez h2 **Psor**
      - **tighter** and tighter: lavand-a ctl1•
    - **sore**: arg-met bufo *Calc* **Chin** conv dig eup-per nux-v sul-ac verat h1
    - **sprained**; as if: caust kali-bi **Puls**
    - **stitching** pain: ambr arg-met h1 bamb-a stb2.de• beryl tpw5 chel **Coloc** dig h2 *Kali-bi* kalm lach meph mez h2 nat-c ptel
    - **sudden** motion: rumx ↓
      - **aching**: rumx
    - **tearing** pain: alum h2 brom *Bry* calc-p *Caust* k* croc k* dig h2 stann k* sulph k*
  - **amel.**: (↗*must*) aesc agar h2 alum am-c androc ↓ asaf ↓ aur ↓ bry calc calc-caust ↓ calc-f k* colch ↓ cupr dios *Dulc* ↓ ferr *Fl-ac* graph ignis-alc es2• indg ↓ kali-c kali-n kali-p *Kreos* limest-b ↓ nat-ar nat-c h2 nat-s nat-sil fd3.de• nux-m nux-v ox-ac ozone sde2• ph-ac phos plut-n srj7• podo positr ↓ propr sa3• puls rat *Rhod* k* **Rhus-t** k* *Ruta* sacch-a gmj3 *Staph* stront-c sulph h2 tritic-vg fd5.de valer k2 vanil fd5.de vib
    - **aching**: alum androc srj1• calc-caust calc-f kali-n kreos limest-b es1• nux-v k* positr nl2• rhod k* staph k* stront-c
    - **break**; as if it would: kreos
    - **broken**; as if: *Kreos* nux-m
    - **drawing** pain: am-c colch *Dulc* indg
    - **lameness**: dios k*
    - **lancinating**: *Nat-s*
    - **pressing** pain: limest-b es1•
    - **sore**: aur bry rat **Rhod** **Rhus-t** *Ruta*
    - **stitching** pain: asaf *Dulc* ox-ac ph-ac *Staph*
    - **tearing** pain: kali-c h2
  - **arms**; of | **agg.**: *Kreos*
  - **beginning** of:
    - **agg.**: androc ↓ dig ↓ *Led* ↓ tab ↓
      - **aching**: androc srj1• dig *Led* tab
    - **lying** down; after: anac bro1 con bro1 dig glyc bro1 *Rhus-t* bro1

- **motion – beginning** of – **lying** down; after: ...
  - **sore**: dig
- **feet**; of:
  - **agg.**: thuj bg1
  - **standing**; after:
    - **agg.**: thuj ↓
      - **cramping**: thuj
- **gentle** motion | **amel.**: prun
- **must** move: *(↗amel.)* mag-m h2 ox-ac bg1 *Puls* sne
  - **without** amel.; but: *Puls*
- **slight** motion | **agg.**: bufo ptk1 chin ptk1 lyc ptk1
- **must** lie down: sil ↓
  - **drawing** pain: sil h2
- **neuralgic**: aran bro1 bell bro1 clem bro1 coloc bro1 cupr-ar bro1 ham bro1 mag-p bro1 nux-v bro1
- **nursing** the child agg.; when: arn ↓ *Cham* ↓ *Puls* ↓
  - **cramping**: arn *Cham Puls*
- **overlifting**; as if from: acon bg2 caust b4a.de ferr b7.de* kali-bi bg2 rhus-t b7.de* staph b7.de*
- **paralyzed**; as if: acon b7.de* aesc bg2 agar b4.de* alum b4a.de* asar b7.de* aur b4a.de berb bg2 cham b7.de* cimic bg2 *Cocc* k* coff b7.de* dulc b4a.de* frax bg2 gels bg2 kali-i bg2 kalm lith-c bg2 m-aust b7.de nat-m k* nit-ac bg2 *Nux-v* b7a.de ox-ac bg2 ph-ac bg2 phos b4a.de* ran-s k* sabin k* sel k* *Sep* b4a.de sil b4.de* sulph bg2 *Verat* b7.de* zinc k*
- **penetrating**: alum bg2 bufo bg2 cann-xyz bg2 nat-m bg2
- **periodical**: ars
  - **aching**: ars k*
- **perspiration**; during: acon bg2 apis bg2 arn bg2 *Ars* bg2 bar-c bg2 bry bg2 **Calc** bg2 *Caust* bg2 *Cham* bg2 chin bg2 *Cocc* bg2 ign bg2 kali-c bg2 *Kreos* bg2 lyc bg2 mag-m bg2 *Merc* bg2 nat-m bg2 **Nux-v** bg2 phos bg2 puls bg2 **Rhus-t** bg2 sabin bg2 **Sep** bg2 sil bg2 *Sulph* bg2 thuj bg2 verat bg2
- **pinching** pain: sulph h2 zinc h2
- **pollutions**; after: ran-b b7.de*
- **position**; from lying in wrong: zinc ↓
  - **pressing** pain: zinc h2
- **pregnancy** agg.; during: arn ↓ *Bell* ↓ *Kali-c* ↓ lyss ↓ nux-v ↓ puls ↓ rhus-t ↓ valer mrr1
  - **burning**: rhus-t
  - **dragging**: arn bro1 *Bell* bro1 *Kali-c* bro1 nux-v bro1 puls bro1 rhus-t bro1
  - **sore**: lyss k*
- **pressing** pain: acon k* aeth agar all-c am-c bg2 am-m b7.de* ambr k* anag ang k* ant-t b7.de* apis b7a.de arg-met arge-pl rwt5• arn ars asaf k* aur aur-ar k2 aur-s k2 *Bell* k* berb borx k* bry k* *Calc* k* calc-p calc-s calc-sil k2 *Camph* cann-s b7.de* canth k* *Carb-an* k* *Carb-v* k* carbn-s **Caust** k* chel k* cina b7.de* clem coc-c cocc coff b7a.de* coloc con cycl cypra-eg sde6.de• *Dulc* bg2 elaps euph b4.de* graph k* ham fd3.de• hep b4.de* ign b7.de* iod b4.de* *Kali-c* k* *Kali-i* kali-m k2 kali-n b4.de* kali-s fd4.de kali-sil k2 kola stb3• lach k* *Led Lyc* k* m-aust b7.de* mag-m b4.de* melal-alt gya4 meny b7.de* merc bg2 merl mez b4.de* mosch b7.de* *Mur-ac* k* myos-a rly4• nat-m nat-sil fd3.de• *Nit-ac* k* *Nux-v* ol-an k* osm petr bg2 ph-ac b4.de* *Phos* k* *Plat Plb* k* prun bg2 **Psor** **Puls** k* ran-s rat rhod b4a.de* *Rhus-t* k* ruta b7.de* sabad bg2 **Sabin** k* samb k* seneg b4.de* sep k* sil k* *Spong* k* stann k* staph b7.de* *Stront-c* k* **Sulph** k* symph fd3.de• tarax k* thuj k* tritic-vg fd5.de valer bg2 vanil fd5.de verat b7.de* *Zinc* k* zinc-p k2
  - **inward**: am-m h2 kali-c bg2 ruta fd4.de
  - **menses** would come on; as if: *Apis Calc-p* plut-n srj7•
  - **outward**: am-m h2* calc bg2 cina bg2 dulc bg2 hydr bg2 kreos b7a.de nux-m bg2 ruta b7.de* tarax bg2
  - **paralyzed**; as if: cocc zinc h2
  - **plug**; as from a: anac bg2 cann-xyz bg2 carb-v bg2 cor-r bg2 equis-h bg2 hydr bg2 mosch bg2 rhod bg2
  - **squeezed** by hands; sensation as if internal organs were: lavand-a ctl1•
  - **thumb**, as by a: meny h1
  - **upward**: clem
  - **vise**; as if in a: aeth hr1 *Kali-i* zinc h2
  - **weight**; as from a: chin h1*
- **pressure**:
  - **agg.**: acon canth colch cycl *Graph* ↓ plat plb sulph ↓
    - **aching**: canth k* *Graph*
    - **pressing** pain: cycl
    - **sore**: plat sulph h2
    - **tearing** pain: acon k*
  - **amel.**: aesc arg-met aur carb-ac cassia-s ccrh1*• dig dulc fl-ac *Kali-c* ↓ led mag-m ↓ meli vml3• *Nat-m* ozone sde2• ph-ac plb *Rhus-t* ruta sabad *Sep* k* spong fd4.de symph fd3.de• vanil fd5.de verat ↓ *Vib*
    - **aching**: carb-ac k* dig a1 fl-ac
    - **cramping**: plb vanil fd5.de
    - **cutting** pain: dig *Dulc*
      - **deep** inside: *Dulc* k*
    - **drawing** pain: dig led ph-ac vanil fd5.de
    - **lancinating**: plb
    - **sore**: verat
    - **stitching** pain: arg-met aur dulc *Kali-c* mag-m h2 plb ruta
    - **tearing** pain: aur h2 mag-m h2 ph-ac h2
  - **deep**:
    - **amel.** | **cutting** pain: (non:dulc h1)
- **pressure** or rising, on: arg-met ↓
  - **burning**: arg-met
- **pulling** agg.: dios
  - **lameness**: dios k*
- **pulsating** pain: am-c mez nux-v h1
- **puts** pillow under it: *Carb-v* ↓
  - **pressing** pain | **plug**; like a: *(↗lying - pillow - amel. - pressing)* *Carb-v*
- **radiating**: cimic bg2 cob bg2 coc-c bg2 dios bg2 gels bg2 helo bg2 kali-c bg2 kreos bg2 lath bg2 nicc bg2 nux-v bg2 ox-ac bg2 plat bg2 sil bg2
- **raising** | **arms**:
    - **agg.**: *Elaps* ↓
      - **lancinating**: *Elaps*
  - **thigh**: agar ↓ aur
    - **jerking** pain: agar h2
    - **sitting**; while: agar k*
      - **stitching** pain: agar
- **raw**; as if: caust bg2 manc bg2 nat-c bg2
- **rest**:
  - **amel.**: lavand-a ↓ mim-p rsj8• sacch-a gmj3
    - **pressing** pain: lavand-a ctl1•
- **rheumatic**: acon *Ant-c* **Berb** **Bry** cact *Carb-an* **Cimic** *Colch Coloc Dulc Ferr* iod **Nux-v** *Phyt* rhod **Rhus-t** spong stram stry *Sulph* ter
- **riding** agg.: calc carb-ac ↓ sep
  - **aching**: calc k* carb-ac
- **rising**:
  - **after**:
    - **walk** agg.; and beginning to: tab ↓ zinc ↓
      - **aching**: tab zinc
  - **agg.**: aesc ↓ agar ↓ am-m ↓ ant-c ↓ *Ars* ↓ bar-c ↓ *Calc* ↓ calc-sil ↓ carb-an ↓ ferr ↓ iris ↓ lac-e ↓ led ↓ nat-m ↓ petr ↓ phos ↓ ptel ↓ puls ↓ rhus-t tl1 *Sil* ↓ *Sulph* ↓ thuj ↓ tritic-vg ↓ tus-p ↓ verat ↓ zinc ↓
    - **aching**: aesc k* agar k* am-m k* ant-c k* *Ars Calc* k* calc-sil k2 carb-an k* lac-e hrn2• led k* nat-m k* petr k* phos k* puls k* *Sil* k* sulph k* tus-p k* verat zinc k2
    - **drawing** pain: bar-c *Sulph* tritic-vg fd5.de
    - **lameness**: ptel
    - **sore**: ferr sulph thuj verat h1
    - **tearing** pain: iris
  - **amel.**: *Cob* ferr plut-n srj7• ptel *Ruta* sulph
    - **aching**: cob k* ferr k* ptel k* *Ruta* sulph k*
  - **bed**; from:
    - **agg.**: ant-t vh1
    - **before**: ant-t vh1
  - **sitting**; from:
    - **after** | **long** time; after sitting for a: am-c carb-an thuj

Back

- **rising – sitting**; from: ...
  - **agg.**: **Aesc** agar am-m ant-c arg-met↓ *Arg-n* ars bar-c bell↓ **Berb** *Brucel* sa3• **Calc** *Calc-s* calc-sil k2 canth carb-an **Caust** *Cham* *Cob* cycl hydr k* irid-met srj5• iris lac-e hrn2• *Lach* *Led* merl nat-m nat-sil fd3.de• *Petr* **Phos** ptel **Puls** **Rhus-t** sep *Sil* spong fd4.de *Staph* **Sulph** tab *Thuj* tritic-vg fd5.de tus-p verat zinc zinc-p k2
    - **burning**: arg-met bar-c berb
    - **cutting** pain: bell h1
    - **pressing** pain: nat-sil fd3.de• zinc h2*
    - **stitching** pain: canth
    - **tearing** pain: merl
  - **amel.**: cycl hr1
  - **squatting** agg.; from: ph-ac↓
    - **stitching** pain: ph-ac
  - **stooping**; from | **after** | **agg.**: am-m berb chel kali-bi *Lyc* mur-ac nat-m ph-ac *Phos* sulph hbh verat h1
    - **agg.**: berb↓ chel↓ *Lyc*↓ mur-ac↓ nat-m↓ ph-ac↓ *Sulph*↓ vanil↓ verat↓
      - **pressing** pain: chel h1*
      - **sore**: nat-m *Sulph* verat h1
      - **stitching** pain: *Lyc* mur-ac vanil fd5.de
      - **tearing** pain: berb chel ph-ac
- **rubbing**:
  - **amel.**: kali-c kali-n lil-t nat-s **Phos** plb
    - **gnawing** pain: *Phos*
    - **lancinating**: nat-s
    - **pressing** pain: kali-n h2
    - **stitching** pain: plb
- **rumbling**: alum bg2
- **scratching**: nat-c h2
- **screwed** together; as if: alum b4.de* stront-c b4.de* zinc b4.de*
- **separated**; as if: agar bg2 berb bg2 calc-p bg2 chel bg2 sulph bg2 *Tril-p* bg2 verat bg2
- **sewing**: iris *Lac-c*
  - **aching**: iris
- **shattered**; as if: am-m bg2
- **shivering**; during: nux-v b7.de
- **sitting**:
  - **agg.**: **Agar** k* ambr androc↓ ang **Arg-met** *Arg-n* asaf asar aur aur-s k2 bar-c **Berb** k* beryl↓ bit-ar wht1• borx *Brucel* sa3• *Bry* *Calc* calc-f calc-s canth carb-an *Carb-v* carbn-s caust cench k2 chinin-s *Cimx* *Cob* k* coff coloc dig dulc equis-h↓ euphr↓ *Ferr* hr1 gink-b sbd1• hep hura hyos ignis-alc es2• kali-c kali-i kali-m k2 kali-n kali-p kali-s led *Lyc* mag-c mag-m mag-s↓ melal-alt gya4 meli meny merc mur-ac nat-ar nat-c *Nat-m* nat-sil↓ nux-v ol-an ozone sde2• pall petr petr-ra shn4• ph-ac phel *Phos* propr sa3• *Prun* *Puls* *Rhod* **Rhus-t** *Ruta* sabad sil↓ spig↓ spong fd4.de stann stront-c suis-hep rly4• sul-ac *Sulph* tab *Thuj* tritic-vg fd5.de **Valer** k* vanil fd5.de *Zinc* zinc-p k2
    - **aching**: *Agar* androc srj1• carb-an k* caust k* chinin-s *Cob* k* equis-h hura lyc k* mag-c mag-m k* mur-ac nux-v k* ol-an k* pall *Phos* k* *Prun* k* puls k* rhod k* **Rhus-t** k* *Sulph* k* tab k*
    - **broken**; as if: meli
    - **burning**: asar borx h2
    - **cramping**: *Caust* vanil fd5.de
    - **cutting** pain: aur canth mag-c
    - **drawing** pain: ang calc *Caust* meny h1 ruta fd4.de stront-c sulph *Thuj* vanil fd5.de zinc h2
    - **pressing** pain: ang borx carb-v caust h2 coloc meny h1 mur-ac h2 nat-sil fd3.de• puls **Rhus-t** ruta fd4.de sulph h2
    - **sore**: agar berb bry kali-c mag-c h2 mag-s meny k* merc nat-m phel **Rhus-t** stront-c sul-ac
    - **sprained**; as if: hep melal-alt gya4 petr **Valer**
    - **stitching** pain: ambr ang arg-met asar bar-c beryl tpw5 dig dulc euphr kali-i kali-n lyc *Nat-c* ph-ac ruta sil h2 spig h1 stann vanil fd5.de *Zinc*
    - **tearing** pain: asaf berb bry kali-c *Lyc* nux-v
  - **amel.**: aeth borx caust lavand-a ctl1• mag-c meny ph-ac plb sal-fr sle1• sars spong fd4.de staph a1 tritic-vg fd5.de vanil fd5.de

- **sitting – amel.**: ...
    - **aching**: mag-c k* meny k*
    - **drawing** pain: aeth ph-ac staph h1
    - **sore**: caust
    - **stitching** pain: borx plb
    - **tearing** pain: ph-ac h2
  - **bent** forward:
    - **agg.**: beryl↓ cassia-s ccrh1*• chinin-s cocc kali-i *Lac-c* phos pic-ac puls ruta fd4.de spong fd4.de tritic-vg fd5.de vanil↓
      - **aching**: chinin-s phos k*
      - **sore**: *Kali-i*
      - **stitching** pain: beryl tpw5 pic-ac vanil fd5.de
    - **amel.**: chel nat-p fkr6.de puls h1 *Ran-b*
  - **erect**:
    - **agg.**: carb-ac conv des-ac rbp6 dulc fd4.de kali-bi kali-s fd4.de nat-c nat-m nat-p fkr6.de *Sulph* zing
      - **aching**: carb-ac k* kali-bi
      - **drawing** pain: zing
      - **sore**: conv
    - **amel.**: nat-m↓
      - **aching**: nat-m k*
  - **long** time agg.; for a | **after**: dulc fd4.de nat-sil fd3.de• *Phos* ruta fd4.de tritic-vg fd5.de vanil fd5.de
  - **walking**; after: ruta↓
    - **aching**: ruta
- **sitting** and standing, by walking amel.: *Ruta*↓
  - **digging** pain: *Ruta*
- **sitting** down agg.: zinc h2
- **sleep**:
  - **before**: nat-m
    - **agg.**: nat-m↓
      - **pressing** pain: nat-m
  - **during**:
    - **agg.**: zinc↓
      - **burning**: zinc
      - **drawing** pain: zinc h2
  - **going** to sleep; on | **agg.**: mag-m h2
- **sneezing** agg.: arund *Con* *Sulph*
  - **aching**: *Sulph* k*
  - **sprained**; as if: sulph h2
  - **stitching** pain: arund
- **snowstorm**, before a: ferr
- **sore**: acon k* aesc k* **Agar** k* *Alum* k* alum-sil k2 am-c k* *Am-m* k* ang k* ant-o anthraq rly4• apoc k* arg-met k* *Arg-n* k* **Arn** k* *Ars* k* ars-s-f k2 **Aur** k* aur-ar k2 aur-m aur-s k2 bamb-a stb2.de• bar-c k* bell **Berb** k* brom k* **Bry** k* calad k* calc b4.de* *Calc-p* *Caps* k* *Carb-ac* carb-an b4.de* carbn-s *Caust* k* *Cham* k* *Chel* **Chin** k* chir-fl gya2 *Cimic* *Cimx* k* *Cina* k* cinnb clem coc-c cocc k* *Colch* k* coli rly4• *Coloc* conv cor-r corn k* cupr-ar cur dig b4.de* dioxi rbp6 **Dulc** k* **Eup-per** *Ferr* k* ferr-ar gamb granit-m es1• *Graph* k* grat hell *Hep* k* hura hydrc ign b7.de* indg jatr-c kali-br kali-c b4.de* kali-i *Kali-n* k* kola stb3• kreos bg2 lac-c **Lach** bg2 lact lept *Lil-t* lith-c bg2 lob lyc lyss c1 m-ambo b7.de m-aust b7.de mag-c b4.de* *Mag-m* k* mag-s med *Meny* k* *Merc* k* *Naja* nat-c k* *Nat-m* k* *Nat-s* nit-ac bg2 *Nux-m* k* **Nux-v** k* orot-ac rly4• ox-ac phos k* phys pic-ac *Plat* k* plb ptel k* puls b7.de* *Ran-b* k* *Ran-s* k* **Rhod** k* **Rhus-t** k* *Ruta* k* sabad b7a.de sars b4.de* *Sil* stann h2 staph k* streptoc rly4• stront-c b4.de* stry suis-em rly4• *Sul-ac* k* sul-i **Sulph** k* *Tab* *Thuj* k* tritic-vg fd5.de valer b7.de* vanil fd5.de **Verat** b7.de* zinc b4a.de [tax jsj7]
  - **accompanied** by:
    - **positive** feeling (See MIND - Positiveness - lumbar)
    - **weakness**: stroph-s sp1
- **sprained**; as if: agar arg-met arg-n **Arn** **Calc** *Con* gamb *Lach* mur-ac ol-an petr-ra shn4• **Puls** *Rhod* **Rhus-t** *Sep* *Staph* sulph **Valer**
- **squeezing**: aeth bg2 arg-met b7.de* arn b7.de* bell bg2 bry bg2 caust b4a.de* *Chin* bg2 kali-i bg2 kali-n b4.de* plat bg2 ruta b7.de*
- **standing**: ph-ac↓

- **standing**: ...
  - **agg.**: agar berb both-ax$_{tsm2}$ *Bry* caps *Carb-an* coff *Con* *Ferr*$_{hr1}$ gink-b$_{sbd1•}$ *Kali-c* kali-m$_{k2}$ kali-s$_{fd4.de}$ led limest-b↓ *Lyc* mag-s↓ melal-alt↓ meny merc↓ mur-ac ped↓ ph-ac phos plan plb podo puls rhus-t↓ *Ruta* samb↓ sep spong$_{fd4.de}$ stry↓ suis-hep$_{rly4•}$ sul-ac *Sulph* tarax thuj tus-p **Valer**$_{k*}$ vanil$_{fd5.de}$ verat zinc$_{bg1}$ zing
    - **aching**: kali-c$_{k*}$ limest-b$_{es1•}$ meny$_{k*}$ mur-ac ped$_{a1}$ phos$_{k*}$ podo$_{k*}$ stry verat$_{k*}$
    - **broken**; as if: carb-an
    - **cramping**: merc
    - **drawing** pain: caps *Carb-an* con led ph-ac vanil$_{fd5.de}$
    - **lameness**: agar coff zing
    - **pressing** pain: melal-alt$_{gya4}$ mur-ac$_{h2}$ ph-ac$_{h2}$ puls rhus-t$_{h1}$ ruta$_{fd4.de}$ samb$_{h1}$ tarax verat$_{h1}$
    - **sore**: agar mag-s ruta$_{h1}$ sul-ac thuj zinc$_{h2}$ zing
    - **sprained**; as if: **Valer**
    - **stitching** pain: *Con* plb zinc$_{h2}$
    - **tearing** pain: berb bry ph-ac$_{k*}$
  - **amel.**: *Arg-n* berb↓ *Brucel*$_{sa3•}$ kreos meli tritic-vg$_{fd5.de}$
    - **aching**: *Arg-n*$_{k*}$
    - **broken**; as if: meli
    - **lancinating**: berb$_{k*}$
    - **tearing** pain: berb
  - **bent**:
    - **agg.**: sulph
      - **pressing** pain: sulph
  - **erect**:
    - **amel.**: petr↓
      - **cutting** pain: petr
    - **impossible**: agar$_{h2}$ *Bry* caust↓ cocc *Petr* phos *Sulph*
      - **pressing** pain: caust$_{h2}$
      - **sitting** for a long time; after: *Thuj*↓
        - **drawing** pain: *Thuj*
  - **leaning** sideways agg.; and: thuj
    - **stitching** pain: thuj
  - **tearing** pain | **alive**; as from something: ph-ac
- **stepping** agg.: (*↗false; jar; morning - bending - forward - agg.)* acon berb↓ carb-ac *Carb-an* spong *Sulph* *Thuj*↓
  - **aching**: (*↗false - aching; jar - aching)* acon$_{k*}$ carb-ac spong$_{k*}$
  - **pressing** pain: acon
  - **sore**: berb *Carb-an* *Thuj*
  - **sprained**; as if: *Sulph*
  - **stitching** pain: sulph
- **stitching** pain: **Acon**$_{k*}$ aeth **Agar**$_{k*}$ all-c aloe *Alum*$_{k*}$ alum-p$_{k2}$ am-c$_{k*}$ am-m ambr$_{k*}$ *Anac*$_{k*}$ androc$_{srj1•}$ ang$_{b7.de*}$ ant-s-aur apis$_{b7a.de}$ *Arg-met*$_{k*}$ arn$_{k*}$ arund *Asaf*$_{k*}$ asar$_{b7.de*}$ aspar *Aur*$_{k*}$ aur-ar$_{k2}$ aur-i$_{k2}$ aur-m aur-s$_{k2}$ bamb-a$_{stb2.de•}$ *Bar-c*$_{k*}$ bar-i$_{k2}$ bar-s$_{k2}$ *Bell*$_{k*}$ **Berb**$_{k*}$ beryl$_{tpw5*}$ borx$_{k*}$ both-ax$_{tsm2}$ bov **Bry**$_{k*}$ *Calc*$_{k*}$ calc-ar calc-caust calc-i$_{k2}$ *Calc-p* calc-s calc-sil$_{k2}$ cann-i canth$_{k*}$ caps carb-an$_{k*}$ carb-v$_{k*}$ carbn-s *Caust*$_{k*}$ cham *Chel*$_{k*}$ chin$_{k*}$ choc$_{srj3•}$ cimic$_{bg2}$ cina cinnb$_{k2}$ clem *Coc-c* *Cocc*$_{k*}$ *Colch*$_{k*}$ *Coloc*$_{k*}$ *Con*$_{k*}$ croc$_{b7.de*}$ cupr$_{k*}$ cycl dig$_{k*}$ dios dulc$_{k*}$ elat euph$_{b4.de*}$ eupi ferr$_{b7.de*}$ form gamb graph$_{k*}$ hep$_{k*}$ hyos *Hyper* ign$_{k*}$ indg iod$_{k*}$ irid-met$_{srj5•}$ jatr-c jug-c *Kali-bi*$_{k*}$ **Kali-c**$_{k*}$ *Kali-i* kali-n kali-p kali-sil$_{k2}$ kalm kreos lac-ac *Lach*$_{k*}$ laur$_{k*}$ *Led*$_{k*}$ *Lil-t* *Lyc*$_{k*}$ m-aust$_{b7.de}$ mag-c$_{k*}$ *Mag-m*$_{k*}$ *Mag-p* mang$_{b4.de*}$ *Merc*$_{k*}$ mosch mur-ac$_{b4.de*}$ *Nat-c*$_{k*}$ *Nat-m*$_{k*}$ nat-p *Nicc* *Nit-ac*$_{k*}$ *Nux-v*$_{k*}$ ol-an olib-sac$_{wmh1}$ ox-ac$_{bg2}$ ozone$_{sde2•}$ par *Ph-ac*$_{k*}$ *Phos*$_{k*}$ *Plat* *Plb*$_{k*}$ *Prun*$_{k*}$ *Puls*$_{k*}$ pycnop-sa$_{mrz1}$ *Ran-b* rat rhus-t$_{b7.de*}$ ruta$_{k*}$ sabin$_{b7.de*}$ sars *Sec* *Sep*$_{k*}$ *Sil*$_{k*}$ spig$_{k*}$ spong$_{k*}$ staph$_{k*}$ stram$_{k*}$ *Stront-c*$_{k*}$ *Stry* sul-i$_{k2}$ **Sulph**$_{k*}$ symph$_{fd3.de•}$ tarax$_{k*}$ tarent *Thuj*$_{k*}$ til vanil$_{fd5.de}$ verat$_{k*}$ *Zinc*$_{k*}$ zing
  - **accompanied** by | **respiration**; impeded (See RESPIRATION - Impeded - stitches - lumbar)
  - **burning**: mag-c$_{h2}$
  - **crawling**: lyc$_{h2}$
  - **downward**: aloe *Kali-c*
  - **fine**: acon$_{bg2}$ alum$_{bg2}$ hep$_{bg2}$ meny$_{bg2}$
  - **intermittent**: zinc$_{h2}$
  - **itching**: mag-c$_{h2}$
- **stitching** pain: ...
  - **jerking** pain: ph-ac$_{h2}$
  - **outward** around abdomen: **Berb**
  - **paroxysmal** (See sudden - stitching)
  - **radiating**: **Berb**
  - **stinging**: *Aur-m*
- **stool**:
  - **after**:
    - **agg.**: aesc alum$_{bg2}$ berb$_{bg2}$ *Carb-v*$_{k*}$ *Chin*↓ colch$_{k*}$ dig$_{k*}$ dros$_{k*}$ lipp↓ lyss mag-m$_{k*}$ melal-alt↓ nat-m plat$_{bg2}$ *Podo* puls$_{b7.de*}$ sil sulph$_{bg2}$ tab
      - **aching**: colch$_{k*}$ dros$_{k*}$ lipp$_{a1}$
      - **constricting** pain: tab
      - **drawing** pain: *Chin* mag-m
      - **pressing** pain: dig
      - **sore**: melal-alt$_{gya4}$ nat-m
    - **amel.**: cassia-s↓ coc-c↓ ox-ac ruta$_{fd4.de}$
      - **aching**: coc-c$_{k*}$
      - **dull** pain: cassia-s$_{ccrh1•}$
  - **amel.**: indg↓
    - **stitching** pain: indg
  - **before**: berb carb-v dulc$_{b4.de*}$ kali-n$_{h2}$ nat-c$_{k*}$ ox-ac↓ *Puls* sep$_{bg2}$ sulph$_{k*}$
    - **aching**: kali-n$_{k*}$ ox-ac
    - **cutting** pain: nat-c
    - **pressing** pain: berb *Carb-v*
  - **during**:
    - **agg.**: *Aesc*$_{bg2}$ agar am-m$_{bg2}$ *Arg-n* ars$_{b4.de*}$ *Carb-an*$_{k*}$ coloc grat kreos$_{b7a.de}$ lept$_{bg2}$ lyc$_{b4.de*}$ nicc↓ nux-v$_{b7a.de}$ ox-ac podo$_{bg2}$ rheum ruta$_{b7a.de}$ spong squil$_{k*}$ stann$_{b4.de*}$ stront-c$_{b4.de*}$ sulph tab$_{k*}$
      - **aching**: nicc$_{k*}$ squil$_{k*}$ sulph$_{k*}$ tab$_{k*}$
      - **broken**; as if: **Lyc**
      - **cutting** pain: rheum
      - **drawing** pain: stann$_{h2}$
      - **pressing** pain: spong
      - **stitching** pain: coloc nicc
    - **amel.**: indg
  - **hard** stool:
    - **amel.**: ox-ac↓
      - **aching**: ox-ac$_{k*}$
    - **during**: bry stront-c
      - **aching**: stront-c
      - **pressing** pain: bry
  - **soft** stool | **during**: nicc *Podo* rheum tab
  - **urging** to:
    - **during**: colch sin-a
      - **sprained**; as if: sin-a
    - **with**: kreos↓ **Nux-v**↓
      - **labor**-like: kreos **Nux-v**
- **stool**; as from urging for: rat
- **stooping**:
  - **after**:
    - **agg.**:
      - **long** time; stooping for a:
        - **work** in the garden: agar↓
          - **aching**: agar
  - **agg.**: *Aesc* *Agar* alum am-c am-caust↓ ang arn↓ ars aur-m↓ borx bry caj↓ *Cham* *Chel* clem colch con cur cycl des-ac$_{rbp6}$ dig dios *Dulc*$_{k*}$ *Echi* graph hep$_{h2}$ hura↓ hyos jug-c↓ kali-bi kali-n kali-s$_{fd4.de}$ kreos lac-ac lec↓ luf-op$_{rsj5•}$ lyc mag-m mang meny nat-ar nat-c nat-m nux-v ol-an ozone$_{sde2•}$ petr plb puls rhod ruta sabad sabin↓ samb↓ sars *Sil* spong$_{fd4.de}$ staph↓ **Sulph** *Thuj* tritic-vg$_{fd5.de}$ tus-p vanil$_{fd5.de}$ verat zinc
    - **aching**: *Aesc* alum am-caust cham con dig dios *Dulc* hura hyos jug-c kali-bi lyc mang meny nat-m plb puls rhod sabad sars *Sil* **Sulph** *Thuj* zinc
    - **break**; as if it would: **Chel**

- **stooping – agg.**: ...
  - **broken**; as if: clem mag-m
  - **cutting** pain: arn bg1 petr bg1 samb bg1
    - **upward**: arn
  - **drawing** pain: clem meny spong fd4.de staph h1 vanil fd5.de zinc h2
  - **lameness**: ang cur dios
  - **pressing** pain: borx chel h1 clem cycl meny h1 sabin sulph thuj h1 vanil fd5.de
  - **sore**: alum aur-m cham graph lec *Meny* nat-m nux-v *Sil* *Sulph* *Thuj* *Verat* h1
  - **sprained**; as if: ars ol-an
  - **stitching** pain: borx caj lac-ac puls ruta sabin spong fd4.de verat
  - **tearing** pain: *Bry* chel sabin
  - **amel.**: am-c↓ chel mag-c bg1 melal-alt↓ meny ph-ac puls sang sec bg1 tax↓
    - **aching**: chel melal-alt gya4 puls sang
    - **cramping**: am-c h2
    - **drawing** pain: mag-c h2 ph-ac
    - **stitching** pain: [tax jsj7]
    - **tearing** pain: ph-ac h2
- **stooping** a long time; as after: bism hr1 chin h1 **Dulc** graph h2 kreos b7a.de *Puls* b7.de* rhus-t b7.de*
- **stretched**; as if: chin b7.de*
- **stretching** agg.: *Calc* mag-c vanil fd5.de
  - **drawing** pain: mag-c
- **stretching** out: calc↓ mag-m↓
  - **broken**; as if: mag-m
  - **sprained**; as if: calc h2
- **sudden**: aeth↓ bamb-a↓ berb mrr1
  - **burning**:
    - **needles**; as from | **hot** needles: aeth bamb-a stb2.de•
  - **stitching** pain: bamb-a stb2.de•
- **support** | **amel.**: pert-vc vk9
- **swimming** | **amel.**: ozone sde2•
- **tearing** pain: acon k* *Aesc* *Agar* k* **Alum** k* alum-p k2 ambr k* ant-c arn k* *Ars* k* asaf b7.de* asar b7.de* aur b4.de* *Berb* k* brom *Bry* k* calc k* *Calc-p* canth k* carb-an bg2 *Carb-v* k* carbn-s carl k* *Caust* k* *Chel* k* chin k* cimic bg2 cina cinnb coc-c k* cocc k* *Colch* k* croc k* cupr dig k* dulc bg2 eupi k* *Ham* k* hura ign kali-bi bg2 *Kali-c* k* kali-p kreos bg2 led b7.de* lyc k* mag-c k* *Mag-m* k* mag-s k* merl k* *Mez* k* mur-ac k* nat-c k* *Nat-s* nit-ac bg2 nux-v k* ph-ac k* phos bg2 *Phyt* k* plb b7a.de* rat bg2 *Rhod* k* rhus-t k* ruta b7.de* sabin sep k* *Sil* bg2 spig k* *Spong* b7.de* *Stann* k* stram b7a.de stront-c k* *Sulph* b4a.de* thuj k* verat b7.de* zinc bg2 ziz bg2
  - **band**; as from a rubber: ozone sde2•
  - **jerking** pain: alum h2 chin h1
- **tickling**: kali-c h2
- **tormenting**: ant-t bg2 arn bg2 caps bg2 kali-c bg2 ptel bg2
- **torn** asunder; as if: sabin b7.de*
- **torn** loose; as if: kali-c bg2
- **touch**:
  - **agg.**: bry↓ calc↓ coli jl2 *Graph*↓ kali-c↓ phos↓ sep↓ sil h2
    - **aching**: bry k*
    - **broken**; as if: *Graph*
    - **sore**: graph h2 kali-c h2 phos h2 sep h2
    - **stitching** pain: calc h2
  - **amel.**: cycl↓ meny↓
    - **sore**: meny h1
    - **stitching** pain: cycl h1
- **turning**:
  - **agg.**: alum↓ bov **Bry** dulc fd4.de kali-bi kali-s fd4.de kola stb3• lac-leo hrn2• *Nux-v* sars sil spong fd4.de sulph thuj zinc
    - **cutting** pain: kali-bi
    - **sore**: alum sil *Thuj*
    - **suddenly**: mag-m↓
      - **aching**: mag-m k*
- **turning**: ...
  - **bed**; in:
    - **agg.**: borx↓ bry↓ kali-p fd1.de• lil-t↓ sacch-a fd2.de• staph h1
      - **drawing** pain: bry lil-t
      - **stitching** pain: borx h2*
    - **impossible**; almost: borx h2 **Bry** dios kali-n kali-p fd1.de• *Nux-v* *Zinc*
      - **lameness**: dios k*
    - **must** sit up to turn over in bed: **Nux-v**↓
      - **aching**: **Nux-v**
  - **body**:
    - **agg.**: alum borx↓ bov↓ mag-m *Nux-v* sars thuj
      - **drawing** pain: thuj
      - **pressing** pain: borx h2
      - **stitching** pain: bov nux-v sars
      - **walking**; when: hep
        - **sprained**; as if: hep
- **twisting** pain: bar-c bg2 colch bg2 graph h2* nux-v bg2 sulph bg2
- **ulcerative** pain: cann-s kreos nat-s prun
- **urination**:
  - **after**:
    - **agg.**: berb br1* sul-ac↓ syph
      - **drawing** pain: sul-ac
    - **amel.**: **Lyc** med
      - **aching**: **Lyc**
  - **before**: berb br1* graph *Nat-s*
    - **cutting** pain: graph
    - **dragging**: graph
    - **pressing** pain: graph
  - **during**: *Ant-c* b7a.de clem↓ phos sulph syph
    - **aching**: clem hr1 sulph
    - **agg.**: sulph↓
      - **dragging**: sulph
  - **retaining**: nat-s hr
  - **urging** to urinate:
    - **during**: lach bg2 nat-s raph
      - **aching**: raph k*
- **urine**, after a large flow of: caust↓
  - **aching**: caust k*
- **vertigo**; during: *Ambr* b7a.de
- **vexation**; after: nux-v
- **waking**; on: aesc bg1 aeth bg1 alum bg1 am-m b7.de* anac bg1 arg-n bg1 berb bg1 bit-ar wht1• bry calc-f bg1 calc-p bg1 carbn-s k2 *Card-m* chel bg1 colch erig bg1 ham bg1 hyper bg1 kali-bi bg1 kali-m bg1 kreos bg1 mag-m bg1 merc bg1 merc-i-f bg1 myric bg1 naja bg1 ox-ac bg1 plan bg1 psor bg1 ptel bg1 puls puls-n↓ ran-b b7.de* ruta b7.de* *Sep* sil bg1 spong bg1 staph b7.de* sulph bg1 verat bg1 zinc bg1
  - **drawing** pain: bry colch
  - **lameness**: puls-n
  - **sore**: berb
- **walking**:
  - **after**:
    - **agg.**: carb-an↓ con h2 nat-c h2 plat↓ puls↓ sep↓
      - **broken**; as if: carb-an plat k* sep
      - **pressing** pain: puls h1
    - **short** walk; after a: grat↓
      - **sore**: grat
  - **agg.**: acon↓ **Aesc** aeth *Agar* alum alum-p↓ am-c am-m apoc↓ arg-met arn asar↓ bapt↓ beryl↓ borx brach↓ *Bry* but-ac↓ canth *Carb-an* caust *Cham* chel *Cocc* coff colch↓ coloc con dios↓ ferr grat↓ hep hyos kali-bi↓ *Kali-c* *Kali-i* kali-n↓ *Kali-s* mag-c↓ mag-m h2 malar jl2 melal-alt↓ meny *Merc*↓ mez nat-ar nat-c k* nat-sil↓ nit-ac nux-v↓ ol-j onos ost↓ plat podo puls *Ran-b* ran-s rhus-v↓ ruta↓ sars **Sep** spong fd4.de stront-c stry↓ *Sulph* tab↓ *Thuj* tub c tus-p ust↓ vanil fd5.de verat *Zinc* zing↓

- **walking** – agg.: ...
  - **aching**: *Aesc*$_{k*}$ agar$_{k*}$ alum$_{k*}$ alum-p$_{k2}$ am-c$_{k*}$ am-m$_{k*}$ apoc bapt$_{k*}$ brach$_{k*}$ coff$_{k*}$ colch con$_{k*}$ dios$_{k*}$ grat$_{k*}$ hyos$_{k*}$ kali-bi$_{k*}$ mez$_{k*}$ nat-c$_{k*}$ ost$_{a1}$ podo$_{k*}$ rhus-v$_{k*}$ sep$_{k*}$ spong$_{k*}$ stry *Sulph*$_{k*}$ tab$_{k*}$ tus-p$_{k*}$ ust verat$_{k*}$ zinc$_{k*}$
  - **burning**: nux-v *Ran-b*
  - **cramping**: vanil$_{fd5.de}$
  - **cutting** pain: thuj
  - **drawing** pain: acon aeth arg-met *Carb-an* cocc sulph$_{h2}$ thuj vanil$_{fd5.de}$
  - **dull** pain: but-ac$_{br1}$
  - **gnawing** pain: stront-c
  - **lameness**: agar zing
  - **menses**; during: mag-m↓
    - **aching**: mag-m$_{k*}$
  - **pinching** pain: mag-c$_{h2}$
  - **pressing** pain: kali-n$_{h2}$ melal-alt$_{gya4}$ nat-sil$_{fd3.de}$• vanil$_{fd5.de}$
  - **sore**: alum caust hep hyos kali-c$_{h2}$ *Meny Thuj* vanil$_{fd5.de}$ zinc$_{h2}$ zing
  - **stitching** pain: arn beryl$_{tpw5}$ borx canth chel coloc ferr *Merc Ran-b* ran-s ruta sulph thuj *Zinc*
  - **tearing** pain: *Aesc*$_{k*}$ agar asar$_{h1}$ chel$_{h1}$ nux-v
  - **amel.**: am-c ant-c apoc **Arg-met** *Arg-n* ars-met asaf aur↓ bar-c↓ beryl↓ bry↓ cob dulc gamb gink-b$_{sbd1}$• kali-c$_{bg1}$ kali-n *Kali-p*↓ kali-s↓ kreos↓ mag-c mag-s↓ meli merc↓ mim-p$_{rsj8}$• nat-ar ozone$_{sde2}$• *Ph-ac* phel phos puls *Ruta* sabad **Sep** *Staph* sulph tab↓ thuj tritic-vg$_{fd5.de}$ valer$_{mrr1}$ vib *Zinc* zinc-p$_{k2}$
    - **aching**: ant-c$_{k*}$ *Arg-n*$_{k*}$ cob$_{k*}$ *Kali-p* kreos$_{k*}$ phos$_{k*}$ *Ruta* staph$_{k*}$ tab$_{k*}$ zinc$_{k2}$
    - **broken**; as if: meli
    - **burning**: bar-c
    - **burrowing**: dulc
    - **cramping**: merc
    - **drawing** pain: am-c ph-ac thuj
    - **gnawing** pain: am-c
    - **pressing** pain: am-c$_{h2}$ kali-n$_{h2}$ kali-s$_{fd4.de}$ puls ruta$_{fd4.de}$ sulph
    - **sore**: apoc aur bry mag-c$_{h2}$ mag-s phel puls ruta thuj
    - **sprained**; as if: staph
    - **stitching** pain: asaf beryl$_{tpw5}$ *Dulc* gamb *Kali-c Staph*
  - **beginning** to walk: zinc↓
    - **pressing** pain: zinc$_{h2}$
    - **standing** for a long time; after: thuj↓
      - **cramping**: thuj
  - **bent**:
    - **amel.**: melal-alt↓ *Sulph*↓
      - **aching**: melal-alt$_{gya4}$ *Sulph*$_{k*}$
    - **must** walk bent: ***(↗walking - bent - must)*** am-m gink-b$_{sbd1}$• kali-c sep$_{h2}$ spong$_{fd4.de}$ *Sulph*
  - **cane** pressed across the back amel.; with a: vib
  - **continued**:
    - **amel.**: zinc↓
      - **aching**: zinc$_{k*}$
  - **erect**:
    - **impossible**: arg-met↓ *Kali-c*↓ sep↓
      - **stitching** pain: arg-met *Kali-c* sep$_{h2}$
  - **rapidly**:
    - **agg.**: dros↓
      - **pinching** pain: dros$_{h1}$
  - **slowly**:
    - **amel.**: bell↓ **Ferr**$_{k*}$ *Puls*
      - **cramping**: bell$_{h1}$
      - **sore**: *Puls*
  - **uneven** ground agg.; on: ***(↗jar)*** podo *Thuj*
- **wandering** pain: brucel$_{sa3}$•
- **warm**:
  - **applications**:
    - **amel.**: arge-pl$_{rwt5}$• *Calc-f* caust hydrog$_{srj2}$• plac$_{rzf5}$• *Rhus-t*$_{k*}$ spong$_{fd4.de}$
- **warm – applications – amel.**: ...
    - **aching**: calc-f caust$_{k*}$ *Rhus-t*
  - **bathing**:
    - **amel.**: bamb-a↓
      - **drawing** pain: bamb-a$_{stb2.de}$•
  - **room**:
    - **entering** a warm room; when: gels↓
      - **aching**: gels
- **warm** in bed agg.; becoming: rhus-t$_{hr1}$
- **warmth**:
  - **amel.**: bamb-a↓ ozone↓ spong↓
    - **cutting** pain: ozone$_{sde2}$•
    - **drawing** pain: bamb-a$_{stb2.de}$•
    - **stitching** pain: bamb-a$_{stb2.de}$• spong$_{fd4.de}$
- **washing** agg.; after: aloe↓ aml-ns↓ calc-caust↓ equis-h↓ gamb↓ myric↓ *Podo*↓ ptel↓ *Sulph*↓
  - **aching**: aloe aml-ns calc-caust equis-h gamb myric *Podo* ptel *Sulph*
- **weather**:
  - **change** of weather: rhod$_{mrr1}$
  - **cold** agg.: allox$_{sp1}$
  - **wet**:
    - **agg.**: *Calc* **Dulc** *Ran-b* **Rhod** *Rhus-t*
      - **sore**: **Rhod Rhus-t**
    - **amel.**: allox$_{sp1}$
- **wet**; getting:
  - **after**: **Dulc**↓
    - **lameness**: **Dulc**
  - **agg.**: rhus-t$_{k2}$
- **writing** agg.: laur
- **yawning** agg.: am-m↓
  - **pressing** pain: am-m$_{h2}$
- ▽ **extending** to:
  - **Abdomen**: androc$_{srj1}$• bar-c$_{bg2}$ *Berb* bry$_{k*}$ cham cina$_{bg2}$ kali-c↓ kreos$_{k*}$ lac-lup$_{hrn2}$• lach$_{k*}$ lil-t$_{bg1}$ lyc$_{bg1}$ nat-c$_{bg2*}$ puls$_{bg1}$ *Ran-b*↓ ruta$_{h1}$ sabin$_{bg1}$ sep$_{bg1}$ spong$_{fd4.de}$ sulph$_{h2*}$ tritic-vg$_{fd5.de}$ vib$_{bg1}$
    - **sore**: bar-c$_{h2}$ nat-c$_{h2}$
    - **sprained**; as if: lach
    - **stitching** pain: kali-c$_{h2}$ puls *Ran-b*
    - **Around**: **Berb**
      - **Thighs**; and down: vib$_{bro1}$
    - **Ilium** to ovaries and uterus; over: vib
    - **Lower** part: ozone↓
      - **cutting** pain: ozone$_{sde2}$•
  - **Abdomen**; across: bar-c↓
    - **burning**: bar-c
  - **Abdomen**; walls of: cham↓
    - **drawing** pain: cham
  - **Arm**; to right upper and left lower: alum
  - **Arms**: rhod
  - **Arms**; into: carb-v↓ kali-bi↓
    - **drawing** pain: carb-v kali-bi
  - **Axilla**: canth↓
    - **stitching** pain: canth
  - **Back**: *Chel*↓
    - **cutting** pain: *Chel*
  - **Back**; up: ars dirc nat-ar nux-v
  - **Back**; up the: *Ars*↓ aspar↓ *Gels*↓ kali-c↓ *Lach*↓ led↓ nux-v↓
    - **drawing** pain: *Ars* aspar$_{bro1}$ *Gels*$_{bro1}$ kali-c$_{h2}$ *Lach* led nux-v
  - **Bladder** and groins: bell
    - **cramping**: bell
    - **pressing** pain: bell
  - **Body**:
    - **Around** the: acon caust cham *Cimic*
    - **Whole**; over the: berb$_{br1}$ mez
  - **Calves**: berb$_{k*}$ dulc$_{fd4.de}$ ozone$_{sde2}$• ph-ac$_{k*}$ tep$_{k*}$
    - **drawing** pain: tep

- **extending** to – **Calves**: ...
  - **short**; as if too: ozone sde2•
  - **Calves** and feet:
    - **motion** agg.: zinc↓
      - **cutting** pain: zinc
  - **Cervical** region: alum↓
    - **gnawing** pain: alum
  - **Chest**: kali-c↓ zinc↓
    - **left**: dulc fd4.de kali-c bg1
    - **stitching** pain: kali-c h2 zinc h2
  - **Coccyx**: carb-v equis-h hura ozone↓ sal-fr sle1•
    - **drawing** pain: carb-v
    - **lancinating**: hura
    - **pressing** pain: carb-v h2
    - **tearing** pain: ozone sde2•
  - **Downward**: cimic bg2 kali-bi bg2 *Kali-c* bg2
    - **stooping** agg.: staph
    - **Upward**; and: *Kali-c*
      - **walking** agg.: hep
  - **Epigastric** region: sulph h2
    - **night**: lyc
      - **cramping**: lyc
  - **Extremities**: *Ign*↓ *Kali-c*↓
    - **stitching** pain: *Ign* *Kali-c*
  - **Feet**: *Borx* dulc fd4.de kali-m bg1 lyc lyss olib-sac wmh1 sep still [kali-chl xyz62]
    - **lancinating**: kali-m k2
    - **pressing** pain: borx
  - **Genitals**: berb bg1 *Carl* dros erig sars h2
  - **Gluteal** muscles: *Aesc*↓ **Kali-c**↓
    - **labor**-like: **Kali-c**
    - **sprained**; as if: *Aesc*
  - **Gluteal** muscles and thighs: **Kali-c**
  - **Gluteal** regions and hips: **Kali-c**↓
    - **stitching** pain: **Kali-c**
  - **Groin**: **Sulph**↓
    - **right**: ran-b↓
      - **stitching** pain: ran-b
    - **evening**: lact↓
      - **drawing** pain: lact
    - **menses**; during: *Sulph*↓
      - **dragging**: *Sulph*
    - **pressing** pain: **Sulph**
    - **urination** agg.; after: sul-ac↓
      - **drawing** pain: sul-ac
    - **walking** agg.: coloc↓
      - **stitching** pain: coloc
  - **Groins**: *Bell* lac-d kr1 spong fd4.de *Sulph* tritic-vg fd5.de
    - **evening**: lact
    - **menses**; during: sulph
    - **Down** legs; and: plat
  - **Heart**: kali-c bg1
  - **Hips**: *Aesc* am-c *Am-m* *Bol-la* carb-v des-ac rbp6 *Ferr* hr1 gels kali-bi kali-s fd4.de *Lach* lap-la sde8.de• lyc↓ mosch *Nux-v* pall podo fd3.de• rhus-v↓ ruta k2 *Sep* *Sil* sulph bg1
    - **morning** | **rising** agg.: euphr thuj
    - **afternoon** and evening: sep↓
      - **sprained**; as if: sep
    - **cutting** pain: gels
    - **drawing** pain: lach rhus-v
    - **pressing** pain: lyc h2
    - **tearing** pain: carb-v
    - **Above** hip:
      - **sitting** and standing; on: **Valer**↓
        - **sprained**; as if: **Valer**
    - **And** legs:
      - **afternoon**: ars dios

- **extending** to – **Hips** – **And** legs: ...
      - **menses**; during: nit-ac
    - **Umbilical** region; over the hips, then to the:
      - **rubbing** | **amel.**: lil-t
  - **Hypochondrium**:
    - **morning** | **waking**; on: kali-n
  - **Kidneys**; region of: ozone sde2•
  - **Knee**: bamb-a↓ hydrog srj2• loxo-recl knl4• olib-sac wmh1 plb psor k* rhus-g tmo3• ruta h1 sulph h2
    - **stitching** pain: bamb-a stb2.de• psor
  - **Leg**:
    - **right**: mand↓
      - **dull** pain: mand rsj7•
  - **Legs**: am-c↓ cinnb↓ *Lach*↓ sep↓
    - **drawing** pain: am-c cinnb *Lach* sep
  - **Legs**; down: agar androc srj1• *Berb* *Borx* h2 carl coloc dios dulc k2 eupi↓ ign irid-met srj5• *Kali-bi*↓ **Kali-c** kali-m↓ kola stb3• lyc lyss nat-ar nit-ac ox-ac ozone↓ ph-ac pic-ac plat rhus-g tmo3• sep *Sil* stann stry tarent
    - **right**: propr sa3•
    - **motion** agg.: pic-ac
    - **short**; as if too: ozone sde2•
    - **stitching** pain: androc srj1• eupi *Kali-bi* kali-m k2 ox-ac *Sil* stry
    - **stool** agg.; during: agar grat
  - **Limbs** | **bending** backward and on raising the body; on: carl
  - **Linea** alba; in a circle to: caust↓
    - **tearing** pain: caust k*
  - **Liver**: *Lach*↓
    - **stitching** pain: *Lach*
  - **Loins** and pubes: *Vib*↓
    - **labor**-like: *Vib*
  - **Lower** limbs: berb↓ ham↓ hep↓ rhus-g tmo3•
    - **pressing** pain: berb ham fd3.de•
    - **sore**: berb hep
  - **Lung**; left: sep
    - **stitching** pain: sep
  - **Nape**: kali-bi bg1
  - **Nates**: dulc fd4.de **Kali-c** podo fd3.de• thuj
    - **3** h: **Kali-c**↓
      - **stitching** pain: **Kali-c**
    - **morning**:
      - **rising** agg.: thuj↓
        - **drawing** pain: thuj
  - **Occiput**: led↓
    - **tearing** pain: led
  - **Outward**: berb mrr1 tritic-vg fd5.de
  - **Patella** and back: tarent
  - **Pectoral** muscles and arms, after riding: brach
  - **Pelvis**: aloe androc srj1• *Arg-n*↓ aur-m↓ berb↓ cham↓ *Cimic*↓ eupi↓ ham↓ sil↓ spong fd4.de tep tritic-vg fd5.de *Vario*↓ visc↓
    - **drawing** pain: *Arg-n* bro1 aur-m bro1 berb bro1 cham bro1 *Cimic* bro1 eupi bro1 ham bro1 sil bro1 tep *Vario* bro1 visc bro1
    - **Posterior** part of pelvis and thighs: **Berb**
  - **Penis**: dros↓
    - **drawing** pain: dros
    - **stitching** pain: dros
  - **Perineum**: canth
  - **Pit** of stomach: nicc↓ rat↓ thuj↓
    - **stitching** pain: nicc rat thuj
  - **Pubes**: *Cycl*↓ *Sabin*↓
    - **labor**-like: *Cycl* hr1 *Sabin*
  - **Pubic** bone: **Sabin**↓ vib↓ xan↓
    - **drawing** pain: **Sabin** k* vib bro1 xan bro1
  - **Pubis**: mag-c **Sabin** k*
    - **cutting** pain: mag-c
  - **Pubis** and inguinal region: carl↓ kreos↓
    - **stitching** pain: carl kreos

- **extending** to: ...
  - **Rectum**: aloe calc coc-c lach$_{bg1}$ lyc nat-c$_{bg1}$ sulph$_{bg1}$ tritic-vg$_{fd5.de}$
    - **dragging**: calc
    - **drawing** pain: coc-c tritic-vg$_{fd5.de}$
    - **stitching** pain: lyc
  - **Rectum** and vagina:
    - **standing**:
      - **amel.**: kreos ↓
        - **constricting** pain: kreos
  - **Ribs**: caust ↓
    - **stitching** pain: caust
  - **Ribs** and ilium; between: *Teucr* ↓
    - **tearing** pain: *Teucr*
  - **Sacrum**: cimic *Nux-m*
    - **Coccyx**: sulph
    - **Thighs**; and: kali-bi
  - **Scapulae**: sulph
    - **right**: brucel$_{sa3}$• lyc$_{bg1}$ mag-m$_{bg1}$
  - **Short** ribs; below the: **Lyc** ↓
    - **pressing** pain: **Lyc**
  - **Shoulders**: ars carc ↓ indg lac-ac$_{kr1}$
    - **drawing** pain: *Ars* carc$_{fd2.de}$• indg
  - **Side** and shoulder; right: clem ↓
    - **burning**: clem
  - **Side**; into: nux-v ↓
    - **constricting** pain: nux-v
  - **Side**; toward the right: fic-m$_{gya1}$
    - **rising** from bending; after: ox-ac
  - **Spermatic** cords; down the | **ejaculation**; after: sars
  - **Spine** in zigzags to scapular region; along: euon ↓
    - **stitching** pain: euon
  - **Spine** to between scapulae; up the: ars ↓ phos ↓ sep ↓ sil ↓ thuj ↓
    - **burning**: ars phos sep sil thuj
  - **Stomach**: lyc$_{bg2}$ nicc nit-ac$_{k}$* puls$_{k}$* sulph$_{bg2}$* thuj
    - **drawing** pain: nit-ac puls
    - **stitching** pain: nicc
  - **Testes**: abrot erig ↓ sulph
    - **cough** agg.; during: osm
      - **pressing** pain: osm
    - **drawing** pain: erig
  - **Thighs**: agar am-m androc$_{srj1}$• ant-t$_{bg2}$ bell$_{bg2}$ **Berb** bry$_{bg2}$ carb-ac$_{k}$* carb-an$_{bg2}$ cham ↓ cinnb ↓ coloc dulc hep *Kali-bi*$_{k}$* *Kali-c*$_{k}$* kreos$_{k}$* lac-d$_{kr1}$ *Lyc*$_{k}$* nat-m$_{kl}$ nit-ac nux-v ox-ac$_{bg2}$ phyt$_{bg2}$ ruta$_{k2}$ sang$_{hr1}$ sep stann ↓ sulph$_{bg1}$ symph ↓ xanth$_{bg2}$
    - **right**: tell$_{bg2}$
    - **drawing** pain: agar berb cinnb *Dulc* kali-bi kreos ruta$_{fd4.de}$ stann$_{h2}$
    - **inspiration** agg.: carb-an nat-m
      - **stitching** pain: carb-an nat-m
    - **labor**; during: bell ↓
      - **drawing** pain: bell
    - **lameness**: cham$_{h1}$
    - **sore**: lyc
    - **stitching** pain: *Kali-bi* *Kali-c* nit-ac *Nux-v* symph$_{fd3.de}$•
    - **stool** agg.; during: kreos ↓ *Nux-v* ↓ stann
      - **drawing** pain: kreos$_{b7a.de}$ *Nux-v*$_{b7a.de}$ stann
    - **Posterior** portion of: **Berb**
  - **Toes**: eupi ↓
    - **stitching** pain: eupi
    - **tearing** pain: eupi
  - **Transversely**: cupr ↓ nat-m ↓ sulph ↓
    - **stitching** pain: cupr$_{h2}$ nat-m$_{h2}$ sulph$_{h2}$
  - **Umbilicus**: prun rhus-v
    - **stitching** pain: prun
  - **Upward**: acon$_{vh1}$ alum ars bell$_{mrr1}$ clem dirc kreos lach led nux-v puls$_{bg1}$ rad-br$_{c11}$ vanil$_{fd5.de}$
- **extending** to – **Upward**: ...
    - **fan**; like a: *Lach*
    - **sitting** agg.: meny
    - **stooping** agg.: arn *Sil*
  - **Urethra**: lach ↓
    - **stitching** pain: lach
  - **Uterus**: elaps helon *Nat-m*
    - **cutting** pain: helon
    - **stitching** pain: *Nat-m*
  - **Vagina**: kreos
    - **stitching** pain: kreos
- ○ **Flanks**: am-m ↓
  - **sprained**; as if: am-m$_{bg2}$
- **Hip**; above:
  - **motion** in bed agg.: lil-t ↓
    - **drawing** pain: lil-t
- **Hips**; above: agath-a ↓ ars ↓ bell ↓ carb-an ↓ castm ↓ caust ↓ dulc ↓ kali-bi ↓ staph ↓ thuj ↓
  - **left**: phos ↓
    - **stitching** pain: phos$_{h2}$
  - **aching**: agath-a$_{nl2}$• bell dulc kali-bi
  - **sore**: ars castm dulc staph
  - **stitching** pain: carb-an$_{h2}$ caust thuj
- **Ilium**: agar eupi form hell iris ruta$_{h1}$
  - **Attachment** of muscles: camph *Form* *Tarent*
  - **Between** ribs and ilium: caust ↓
    - **stitching** pain: caust
  - **Crest** of: carb-an ↓
    - **right**:
      - **morning**:
        - **sitting** down agg. but standing and walking amel.; on:
          - **extending** to | **Thigh**: staph
    - **pressing** pain: carb-an$_{h2}$
    - **sore**: carb-an$_{h2}$
- **Kidneys**; above: apis ↓ helon ↓ merc ↓ merc-c ↓ phyt ↓ solid ↓
  - **sore**: apis$_{bg1}$ helon$_{bg1}$ merc-c$_{bg1}$ phyt$_{bg1}$ solid$_{bg1}$ [merc$_{xyz62}$]
- **Kidneys**; over:
  - **left**: lavand-a ↓
    - **aching**: lavand-a$_{ctl1}$•
- **Muscles**: malar ↓
  - **dull** pain: malar$_{jl2}$
- **Ribs**:
  - **Last**: *Caust* ↓ merc ↓ ph-ac ↓ **Ran-b** ↓
    - **sore**: ph-ac **Ran-b**
    - **stitching** pain: *Caust* merc
  - **Last**; near: kali-bi ↓ lyss ↓
    - **burning**: kali-bi lyss
- **Skin**; below the: puls ↓
  - **ulcerative** pain: puls$_{b7.de}$*
- **Spine**: *Agath-a*$_{nl2}$• bell cact *Calc* *Calc-p* *Chel* con ↓ dulc$_{fd4.de}$ kali-i *Kalm* kreos phos ↓ plb psil$_{ft1}$ psor sabin sarr thuj vanil ↓ verb ↓
  - **right**: ozone$_{sde2}$•
  - **forenoon**: bry
  - **drawing** pain: con$_{h2}$ dulc$_{fd4.de}$
  - **motion** agg.: lyc
  - **stitching** pain: phos$_{h2}$ vanil$_{fd5.de}$ verb$_{h}$
  - **Spot**; in a small: ozone$_{sde2}$•
- **Spot**; in a: bar-c ↓ mang ↓ *Ph-ac* ↓ rhus-t ↓ zinc ↓
  - **burning**: bar-c mang$_{h2}$ *Ph-ac* rhus-t$_{h1}$ zinc
- **Vertebrae**: agar$_{bg2}$ am-m$_{bg2}$ arg-met$_{bg2}$ aur$_{bg2}$ berb ↓ bry$_{bg2}$ chel$_{bg2}$ dig$_{bg2}$ **Kreos**$_{bg2}$ mez$_{bg2}$ mur-ac$_{bg2}$ nux-m$_{bg2}$ ph-ac$_{bg2}$ phos$_{bg2}$ prun$_{bg2}$ puls$_{bg2}$ stann$_{bg2}$ thuj$_{bg2}$
  - **bending** backward after stooping; when: chel ↓
    - **tearing** pain | **torn** apart; as if: chel$_{h1}$*
  - **cutting** pain: dig$_{bg2}$
  - **gnawing** pain: ph-ac$_{bg2}$

- **Vertebrae**: ...
  - **pressing** pain: am-m bg2 aur bg2 chel bg2 puls bg2
  - **sitting** bent forward agg.: carb-v ↓
    - **pinching** pain: carb-v h2
  - **stitching** pain: arg-met bg2 aur bg2 bry bg2 mez bg2 phos bg2 prun bg2 thuj bg2
  - **tearing** pain: agar bg2 bry bg2 kreos bg2 mur-ac bg2 stann bg2
  - **ulcerative** pain: berb bg2 kreos bg2
  - **walking**:
    - **agg.**: chel ↓
      - **tearing** pain | **torn** apart; as if: chel h1*
  - **Fourth**: puls ↓
    - **pressing** pain: puls h1
  - **Last**: acon ↓ aesc ↓ cham ↓ *Nat-s* ↓ pic-ac ↓ plat ↓
    - **burning**: acon aesc cham pic-ac
    - **sore**: acon aesc cham *Nat-s* plat
- **Waist** line: calc ↓ mur-ac ↓ rumx ↓ sars ↓ sil ↓ tarent ↓
  - **aching**: calc mur-ac rumx sars sil tarent

- **Lumbosacral** region: acon tl1 **Aesc** k* agar k2 agath-a nl2• aids nl2• allox tpw3 androc ↓ ant-t mrr1 asc-t ↓ aspar ↓ carb-ac carb-an carbn-s *Cimic* k* cocc tl1 colch ↓ coloc dios ↓ dulc tl1* gels ↓ ger-i rly4• helon hura ↓ lil-t lyss jl2 med k2* melal-alt ↓ meli vml3• nat-sil fd3.de• **Onos** petr-ra shn4• *Phos* ↓ **Puls** rad-br c11 ruta fd4.de sacch-a fd2.de• sil sulph k2 syc pte1*• tub jl2 vario jl2 visc ↓
  - **morning**: carbn-s ign
  - **forenoon** | **11** h: pert-vc vk9
  - **night**: *Aesc* ↓ carb-ac
    - **aching**: *Aesc*
  - **aching**: **Aesc** agath-a nl2• aids nl2• androc srj1• asc-t aspar *Cimic* colch dios gels ger-i rly4• hura lil-t melal-alt gya4 **Onos** *Phos* sil visc c1
  - **alternating** with | **Head**; pain in (See HEAD - Pain - alternating - lumbosacral)
  - **bed** agg.; in: allox tpw3*
  - **coition**: agar k2
  - **cough** agg.; during: phos
  - **kneeling** agg.: allox tpw3*
  - **lying** | **back**; on | **amel.**: dulc fd4.de puls
    - **side**; on | **agg.**: puls
  - **menses**; during: tub c1
  - **pressure** agg.: tub jl2
  - **rising** agg.: allox tpw3*
  - **seminal** emission; on: glycyr-g cte1•
  - **standing** agg.: allox tpw3* but-ac ↓
    - **dull** pain: but-ac sp1
  - **standing** and walking; while: phos ↓
    - **lifting** too heavy a weight; as from: phos
  - **stooping** agg.: *Aesc* allox tpw3*
  - **turning** in bed agg.: sulph
  - **walking**:
    - **agg.**: tub c1
    - **amel.**: allox tpw3* rad-br c11
  - **weather** | **hot** | **amel.**: allox jl3
    - **wet** | **agg.**: allox tpw3*
  - **women**; in: thymol ↓
    - **stitching** pain: thymol sp1
  - ▽ **extending** to:
    - **Abdomen**: vario mtf11
    - **Hip**: but-ac ↓
      - **dull** pain: but-ac sp1
    - **Ilium** ending in cramp in uterus; over: sep vib
    - **Legs**; down the: allox tpw3* dulc fd4.de med k2 tub jl2
    - **Uterus**: helon
  - ○ **Spine**: haliae-lc ↓
    - **split**; as if: haliae-lc srj5•
- **Muscles**: chlorpr pin1• colch rsj2•

- **Muscles**: ...
  - **wet** applications: colch rsj2•
  - ○ **Psoas** muscles: *All-s* br1
- **Sacral** region: abrot absin acon act-sp **Aesc** k* **Agar** k* agath-a nl2• agn ↓ aids nl2• ail *All-c* ↓ all-s aloe k* *Alum* alum-p k2 alum-sil k2 am-c am-m ambr ↓ androc srj1• ang ant-c **Ant-t** k* ap-g vml3• *Apis* *Arg-met* arg-n arge-pl rwt5• arn *Ars* ars-i ars-s-f k2 asaf aster ↓ aur aur-ar k2 aur-i k2 aur-s k2 bad bamb-a stb2.de• *Bapt* *Bar-c* bar-i k2 bar-s k2 *Bell* **Berb** k* borx *Bry* calad **Calc** calc-i k2 *Calc-p* calc-s calc-sil ↓ cann-s ↓ cann-xyz ↓ canth *Caps* carb-ac *Carb-an* *Carb-v* carbn-dox knl3• carbn-s k* carc tpw2* caul *Caust* k* cench k2 cham chel *Chin* chinin-ar cic *Cimic* *Cimx* cina k* cinnb cob coc-c cocc k* coff colch *Coloc* com ↓ con cor-r croc cupr cupr-ar des-ac rbp6 dig *Dios* k* dioxi ↓ *Dulc* k* eup-per eup-pur ferr ferr-i fl-ac form gamb **Gels** glon *Graph* guare ↓ ham *Helon* *Hep* hydrog srj2• *Hyper* k* *Ign* k* iod jug-r ↓ kali-ar *Kali-bi* k* kali-br mrr1 *Kali-c* k* kali-i kali-m k2 kali-n *Kali-p* kali-s kali-sil k2 kola stb3• *Kreos* *Lac-c* *Lach* lachn ↓ lact lam lap-la sde8.de• *Laur* lec led *Lept* *Lil-t* limen-b-c ↓ lith-c k* *Lob* k* **Lyc** *Lyss* mag-c mag-m mag-s *Med* k* melal-alt gya4 meli meny *Merc* merl ↓ mez mosch **Mur-ac** murx naja nat-ar nat-c *Nat-m* k* nat-p *Nat-s* nicc ↓ **Nit-ac** k* **Nux-m** k* *Nux-v* k* ol-an ol-j k* olib-sac wmh1 **Onos** op ox-ac k* ozone sde2• pen c2 petr ph-ac ↓ phel *Phos* phys *Phyt* pic-ac pieri-b mlk9.de plan plat plb ↓ plut-n srj7• *Podo* positr nl2• *Psor* k* ptel **Puls** ran-b ran-s rhod k* *Rhus-r* *Rhus-t* k* *Ruta* *Sabad* ↓ sabin samb sang sanic mrr1 sarr sars *Sec* senec ↓ seneg **Sep** k* *Sil* spong squil ↓ staph staphycoc ↓ stram stront-c sul-ac sul-i k2 *Sulph* k* syph k2 tarax tarent ↓ **Tell** k* ter *Thuj* tritic-vg fd5.de tub jl2 ulm-c ↓ ust valer k* vanil fd5.de **Vario** verat visc ↓ xan k* zinc k* zinc-p k2 zing
  - **right** side: limen-b-c hrn2•
  - **daytime**: lil-t
  - **morning**: aids nl2• all-s ↓ ang calad dulc fd4.de ham fd3.de• ign kali-bi ↓ kali-n lac-c lil-t nat-m petr phos positr nl2• *Puls* sel spong fd4.de *Staph* sulph thuj tritic-vg fd5.de verat
    - **coition**; during: kali-bi
    - **cutting** pain: all-s
    - **drawing** pain: kali-bi lil-t
    - **increasing** during the day: sanic mrr1
    - **waking**; on: carb-v carbn-s dulc fd4.de *Kali-bi* positr nl2• ulm-c ↓
      - **pressing** pain: ulm-c jsj8•
  - **afternoon**: colch dulc fd4.de limen-b-c ↓ spong fd4.de
    - **16** h: lachn ↓
      - **burning**: lachn
    - **aching**: limen-b-c hrn2•
  - **evening**: agar bar-c dulc fd4.de ham fd3.de• lac-c led limen-b-c ↓ naja nit-ac olib-sac wmh1 petr h2 puls sep ter
    - **amel.**: lil-t
    - **drawing** pain: bar-c
    - **pressing** pain: limen-b-c hrn2* *Puls*
  - **night**: am-c ang arg-n cench k2 cham chin colch kali-bi k2 lach lyc mag-c mag-s nat-s nux-v *Puls* staph
    - **midnight**:
      - **after** | **1** h: staph
    - **bed**; driving out of: mag-c h2
    - **pressing** pain: ang
    - **waking** him frequently: colch
  - **accompanied** by:
    - **diarrhea** (See RECTUM - Diarrhea - accompanied - back - pain - sacral)
    - **dysentery** (See RECTUM - Dysentery - accompanied - back - pain - sacral)
    - **hemorrhoids** (See RECTUM - Hemorrhoids - accompanied - sacrum)
    - **pollutions**; nightly: **Cob** mrr1
  - **aching**: limen-b-c hrn2•
  - **afterpains**: sulph
  - **alternating** with | **Occiput**; aching in (See HEAD - Pain - occiput - alternating - sacrum)
  - **bending**:
    - **backward**:
      - **agg.**: bar-c con mang h2 plat *Puls* rhus-t

- **bending – backward – agg.**: ...
    - **cutting** pain: rhus-t
    - **drawing** pain: bar-c
  - **amel.**: lac-c puls
  - **forward**:
    - **agg.**: allox sp1 des-ac rbp6 pieri-b mlk9.de samb ↓
      - **cutting** pain: samb
    - **amel.**: sang tritic-vg fd5.de
- **blowing** the nose agg.: arg-n
- **boring** pain: acon calad dulc fd4.de kola stb3• led
- **breathing** agg.: berb carb-an carb-v **Merc** ruta sel spig sulph tarax
  - **stitching** pain: **Merc** spig
- **burning**: bamb-a stb2.de• borx *Carb-v* k* colch coloc *Ferr Helon* kreos ptk1 lachn mur-ac murx nat-c h2 ph-ac phos k* *Podo* k* rhus-t sabin sep sil staph h1 sulph tarent ter ptk1 thuj visc c1
  - **sticking** pain: mur-ac
- **chill**; during: ars gamb hyos **Nux-v** psor verat
- **coition**: *Agar* calc *Calc-p* kali-bi mrr1 *Kali-c* nat-c *Petr Phos* **Sep Sil** staph
- **cold**; after taking a: *Dulc* k* nit-ac
- **cough** agg.; during: am-c *Bry Chel* merc nit-ac sulph *Tell*
  - **stitching** pain: bry
- **cutting** pain: ail all-s alum arg-n bg2 *Bell Calc-p* dig gamb *Gels* guare k* helon kali-bi k* lob mag-m nat-c h2 nat-m nat-p nat-s rhus-t k* samb k* senec *Sulph*
- **delivery**; after: phos st
- **diarrhea**:
  - **during**: nux-v ↓
    - **drawing** pain: nux-v k2
  - **with** (See RECTUM - Diarrhea - accompanied - back - pain - sacral)
- **drawing** pain: acon *Am-c* ang h1 *Ant-c* arg-n aster bamb-a stb2.de• **Bar-c** bell *Chel Chin* cocc colch croc dig *Dios* dulc *Helon* hep ign kali-bi **Kali-c** kali-m k2 kali-sil k2 led lyc med k2 mur-ac nat-c nat-m **Nux-v** ruta fd4.de sabin samb sil spong stram sul-ac *Sulph* ter *Thuj* tritic-vg fd5.de valer verat zing
  - **flatus**; as from obstructed: nat-c h2
- **dull** pain: plut-n srj7• vanil fd5.de
- **dysentery**, with (See RECTUM - Dysentery - accompanied - back - pain - sacral)
- **emissions** agg.; after: *Graph*
- **exertion** agg.: agar dulc fd4.de rhus-t k2
- **fall**; as from a: ruta h1
- **falling**; from: kali-c
- **flatus**; from: agn hr1
- **flatus**; passing | **amel.**: *Pic-ac*
- **hard** bed; as from a: merc bg2
- **heat**; during: chin
- **hemorrhoids**; during: calc-f pd
- **instrumental** delivery, after: **Hyper**
- **jerking** pain: chin fl-ac
- **lameness**: **Aesc** *Calc-p* com dios a1 phos *Rhus-t* **Sil**
  - **lifting**; as from | **straining**; or as from: **Rhus-t** staph
- **laughing** agg.: *Tell*
- **leaning** against chair agg.: agar
  - **pressing** pain: agar
- **leukorrhea**; during: grat k2 psor tl1
- **lifting** agg.: anag bry *Calc* kali-s fd4.de nat-c h2 *Puls Rhus-t Sang* staph
- **lying**:
  - **agg.**: agar ap-g vh1* **Berb** chin dulc fd4.de galeoc-c-h gms1• kali-bi k2 naja nux-v puls tarax thuj uim-c ↓ zing
    - **compelled**: **Agar** calc-p cimx
    - **pressing** pain: *Berb*
- **lying – agg.**: ...
    - **sore**: ulm-c jsj8•
  - **amel.**: **Agar** kali-c kali-m k2 *Ruta* mrr1 tritic-vg fd5.de
  - **back**; on:
    - **agg.**: ap-g vh bapt bell *Ign* lyc puls *Tell*
      - **drawing** pain: bell
      - **still**; lying: **Rhus-t** ↓
        - **sore**: **Rhus-t**
    - **amel.**: *Agar* calc-p puls
    - **must** lie on the back: *Agar* ↓ calc-p ↓
      - **stitching** pain: *Agar* calc-p
  - **face**; on the | **amel.**: bapt
  - **forward**; with body bent | **amel.**: bry
  - **side**; on:
    - **agg.**: act-sp *Nat-s* puls
      - **sore**: act-sp *Nat-s*
    - **amel.**: *Puls*
      - **curled** up: des-ac rbp6
    - **right** | **agg.**: agar
- **menses**:
  - **before**:
    - **agg.**: am-c asar vh bar-c carb-an caust kali-n lac-h ↓ lach mag-c nux-m c1 nux-v puls sabal pd sep sne *Spong* ↓ *Vib*
      - **drawing** pain: lac-h htj1•
      - **sore**: *Spong*
  - **during**:
    - **agg.**: *Am-c Am-m Berb* borx calc calc-p k2 calc-s carb-v carbn-s *Caust* cench k2 cham cimic con ferr *Kali-c* kali-n *Kali-p* kreos lac-h ↓ laur k2 *Lob* lyc mag-c mag-m med ↓ *Nat-c* nat-p phos pitu-a vml2• prun *Puls* rat *Sabin* sang *Sars Senec Sulph* tritic-vg fd5.de vib mrr1 zinc zing [bell-p-sp dcm1]
      - **burning**: carb-v ferr med c1
      - **cutting** pain: *Senec*
      - **drawing** pain: cham con lac-h htj1• tritic-vg fd5.de zing
      - **pressing** pain: ferr
  - **scanty**: asc-c ↓
    - **pressing** pain: asc-c c1
  - **suppressed** menses; from: lob mrr1
- **motion**:
  - **agg.**: *Aesc Agar* ambr ↓ caust chel *Chin* coloc form hura kali-bi lil-t lyc phos phys phyt plan psor **Puls** sars sec tell k* tritic-vg fd5.de vanil fd5.de
    - **stitching** pain: ambr h1 coloc
  - **amel.**: aloe ang ap-g vml3• apoc vh1 coloc dulc fd4.de fl-ac kali-bi k2 kola stb3• *Lac-c Lyc* nat-c h2 **Nux-m** psor **Puls** rhod mrr1 **Rhus-t** spong fd4.de thuj tritic-vg fd5.de vanil fd5.de
    - **pressing** pain: aloe
    - **sore**: **Rhus-t**
    - **stitching** pain: kola stb3•
  - **arm**; of | **agg.**: chel
  - **gentle** motion | **amel.**: dulc fd4.de **Puls**
- **paralyzed**; as if: arg-n *Graph*
- **pinching** pain: aur bg2 caust b4a.de ph-ac b4.de* zinc bg2
- **pregnancy**:
  - **during**: **Kali-c** ↓
    - **agg.**: mag-c mrr1 puls a2 valer mrr1 xan c1
    - **stitching** pain: **Kali-c**
- **pressing** pain: acon agar *All-c* aloe ambr h1 ang arg-met *Berb* borx cann-s **Carb-an** *Carb-v* caust chel *Ferr* ham fd3.de• *Ign* iod h limen-b-c hrn2* *Lyss* mag-m a1 meny mosch mur-ac h2 **Nux-v** phyt bg1 podo fd3.de• *Puls* rhus-t bg1 ruta sabin samb *Sec* sep spong tarax thuj h1 tritic-vg fd5.de verat zinc
  - **blunt** instrument; as from a: mosch
  - **downward**: bell berb merl **Nux-v** sec *Sep*
  - **plug**; as from a: cann-xyz bg2 carb-v bg2 cor-r bg2 lith-c bg2
- **pressure**:
  - **amel.**: kali-c led mag-m *Nat-m* mrr1 *Sep* k*
    - **drawing** pain: led

- **raising** leg: bry vanil fd5.de
- **rheumatic**: ap-g br1 kali-bi kali-p mtf11 sulph zinc
- **riding** in a carriage agg.: lac-c **Nux-m** k*
- **rising**:
  - **amel.**: apoc vh1
  - **bed**; from | **amel.**: ap-g vml3•
  - **lying**; from | **impossible**: **Agar** sil
  - **sitting**; from:
    - **agg.**: **Aesc** k* ant-c bar-c **Calc** *Caust* con dulc fd4.de ferr *Kali-bi* kali-p dw1* *Lac-c* led k2 **Lyc** petr *Phos* psor *Puls* rhod **Sil** spong fd4.de *Staph* **Sulph** tell thuj verat zinc k2
      - **drawing** pain: *Bar-c Thuj*
      - **lameness**: phos **Sil** *Sulph*
  - **stooping**; from:
    - **agg.**: dulc fd4.de kali-s fd4.de *Lyc* mur-ac ↓ *Phos* sars verat
      - **stitching** pain: mur-ac h2
- **rock**; must: hydrog srj2•
- **rubbing**:
  - **amel.**: thuj ↓
    - **stitching** pain: thuj h1
- **separated**; as if: agar bg2 calc-p bg2 sulph bg2
- **sitting**:
  - **after**: aloe asaf bamb-a stb2.de• berb phos puls spong fd4.de tritic-vg fd5.do vanil fd5.de
  - **agg.**: aesc tl1 **Agar** k* aloe ang ant-t *Apis Arg-met Arg-n* asaf asar bar-c *Bell* **Berb** borx bufo calc k2 carb-an bg1 caust cist cob dulc fd4.de galeoc-c-h gms1• kali-bi k* *Kreos Lac-c Lyc* melal-alt gya4 meny merc nat-ar nat-c nat-s ol-an petr-ra shn4• phel phos k2 prun *Puls* **Rhus-t** ruta sabad sep k2 spig staph ↓ sulph k2 syph k2 tax ↓ ter *Thuj* tritic-vg fd5.de valer mrr1 vanil fd5.de
    - **burning**: borx
    - **drawing** pain: *Bell* ruta fd4.de staph h1 *Thuj*
    - **pressing** pain: agar aloe *Berb* tritic-vg fd5.de [tax jsj7]
    - **sore**: *Merc* **Rhus-t**
    - **stitching** pain: bar-c nat-s spig staph h1
  - **bent** forward | **must** sit bent forward: lyc
  - **erect** | **agg.**: des-ac rbp6
  - **still**:
    - **long** time agg.; for a: allox ↓ vanil ↓
      - **dull** pain: allox tpw3* vanil fd5.de
- **sneezing** agg.: arg-n
- **sore**: *Acon* k* aesc ptk1 *Agar* **Alum** alum-p k2 am-c *Am-m* androc srj1• ang arg-met *Arn* ars bapt *Berb Bry Calad* carbn-s *Caust* chin cina cinnb *Colch* coloc cor-r des-ac rbp6 dig dioxi rbp6 eup-per ferr *Fl-ac* gamb *Graph* *Hep* hyper ign kali-bi kali-i kreos lact *Lob* mag-c mag-m meny *Merc* nat-ar nat-c *Nat-m Nat-s Nux-m Nux-v* ox-ac phel *Phos* phyt *Plat* ran-b ran-s rhod **Rhus-t** *Ruta* k* *Sabad* sars *Sep* sil spong staph staphycoc rly4• stront-c *Sulph Tell* thuj ulm-c jsj8• *Verat*
  - **paralytic** pain in knees on rising from a seat (See sacrum - rising - sitting - after - sore - paralytic)
- **standing**:
  - **agg.**: *Agar* androc srj1• **Con** ham fd3.de• led *Lil-t Lith-c* merc *Phos* plan puls rhus-t spong valer mrr1 verat
    - **cutting** pain: rhus-t
    - **drawing** pain: led
    - **long** time; for a: limen-b-c ↓
      - **aching**: limen-b-c hrn2•
    - **stitching** pain: **Con** *Lith-c*
  - **amel.**: *(↗amel. - cutting)* arg-n bell melal-alt gya4 petr h2
    - **cutting** pain: *(↗amel.)* petr h2
    - **drawing** pain: bell
  - **erect**:
    - **impossible**: thuj ↓
      - **drawing** pain: thuj h1
- **startling**: mur-ac ↓
  - **stitching** pain: mur-ac hr1
- **stepping** agg.: acon ↓ spong ↓
  - **left** foot; with: spong
  - **pressing** pain: acon spong h1
- **stitching** pain: acon **Agar** agn aloe ambr ang arn ars asaf bar-c bell berb *Bry* calc *Calc-p* calc-s calc-sil k2 *Carb-an* carb-v chin h1 cocc coloc **Con** dulc hyper ign jug-r kali-bi kali-c kali-i kali-m k2 kali-n kali-sil k2 kola stb3• *Lith-c* lyc mag-c merc mur-ac nat-c nat-m k* nat-s nicc nit-ac ox-ac *Phos Phyt* plb puls ruta sil spong squil staph *Sulph* tarax tell thuj h1 vanil fd5.de verat *Zinc*
  - **burning**: mur-ac h2 thuj h1
  - **jerking** pain: thuj h1
- **stool**:
  - **after**:
    - **agg.**: aesc coloc ↓ *Podo* tab
      - **burning**: coloc
    - **amel.**: berb indg
      - **stitching** pain: indg
  - **before**: berb carb-v *Dios* kali-n nat-c sars zing
    - **drawing** pain: zing
  - **during**:
    - **agg.**: *Agar Arg-n* **Carb-an** coloc ↓ *Merc-c* **Nux-v** *Podo* k* sars *Tell*
      - **burning**: coloc bg2
  - **straining** at | **agg.**: *Agar Carb-an Tell*
  - **urging** to:
    - **with**: am-be lil-t *Merc-c* **Nux-v**
      - **pressing** pain: *Merc-c* **Nux-v**
- **stooping**:
  - **agg.**: **Aesc** k* aids nl2• arg-n hr1 borx bufo-s dulc mrr1* kali-bi tl1 lac-c lap-la sde8.de• lyc meny nat-ar ↓ ol-an plb puls sne rhod c1 ruta samb ↓ sars sulph *Tell* thuj tritic-vg fd5.de vanil fd5.de verat
    - **cutting** pain: samb
    - **sore**: nat-ar
  - **impossible**: aesc borx puls
- **stretching**:
  - **amel.**: alum
  - **leg** | **agg.**: bry
- **touch**:
  - **agg.**: colch lob vh
  - **clothes** agg.; of: *Lob* ↓
    - **sore**: *Lob*
- **turning** | **bed**; in | **agg.**: *Bry* dulc fd4.de *Nux-v Staph*
  - **left**; to | **amel.**: agar
- **twisting** pain: nux-v bg2
- **ulcerative** pain: *Puls*
- **urination**:
  - **before**: kali-bi mrr1
  - **during** | **agg.**: *Graph*
- **urine**; on retaining: *Nat-s*
- **walking**:
  - **after** | **agg.**: malar jl2 nat-c h2
  - **agg.**: acon **Aesc** k* *Agar* borx bry calad ↓ com ↓ dulc fd4.de form ham kali-bi *Kali-c* nat-ar k2 *Phos* sabad sars spong sulph tritic-vg fd5.de verat zinc
    - **lameness**: **Aesc** com
    - **pressing** pain: acon spong
    - **sore**: nat-ar
    - **stitching** pain: *Agar* calad
  - **air**; in open:
    - **agg.**: *Agar* ↓
      - **stitching** pain: *Agar*
    - **amel.**: ruta *Tell*
  - **amel.**: androc srj1• ang ap-g vh arg-met arg-n calc k2 cench k2 *Lyc* merc nat-ar petr-ra shn4• phos k2 psor rhus-t k2 sep k2 staph sulph k2 *Tell* thuj valer mrr1 zinc k2
    - **stitching** pain: staph

- walking – amel.: ...
  - rapidly:
    - agg.: bell ↓ *Bry* ↓
      - drawing pain: bell *Bry*
  - slowly:
    - amel.: bell dulc fd4.de kali-bi ↓ **Puls**
      - drawing pain: bell kali-bi
- warm bed agg.: *Coloc* ↓
  - burning: *Coloc*
- warmth:
  - amel.: sulph ↓
    - cutting pain: sulph
- weather:
  - change of weather: rhod mrr1
  - cold agg.: allox sp1
  - wet | agg.: allox sp1
- wood stretches across; as if a piece of: nux-m ptk1
- ▽ extending to:
  - Anus: asaf ↓
    - stitching pain: asaf
  - Coccyx | sitting agg.: kreos
  - Down legs: *Agar* agath-a nl2• arn bamb-a stb2.de• bapt a1 cimx *Coloc Graph Lac-c* lyc *Med Pic-ac* plat plb *Sep* tung-met bdx1•
    - delivery; after: phyt kr1*
    - stool agg.; after: rhus-t
    - Great toe: arn
  - Feet: ambr ↓ lyc spong fd4.de
    - drawing pain: ambr c1
  - Front: *Arg-met*
  - Gluteal region and hips: **Kali-c** ↓
    - stitching pain: **Kali-c**
  - Groin: plat *Sabin* **Sulph**
    - menses; during: arn plat bro1 puls bro1 *Sabin* sep bro1 **Sulph** vib bro1
    - Around pelvis: puls bro1 sep bro1
  - Hips: **Aesc** agath-a nl2• berb cimx coloc dulc fd4.de *Lac-c* pall phyt puls **Sep** ust
    - right hip: *Sulph*
    - Pelvis; and: arg-n vib mrr1
    - Thighs; and: *Cimic Lac-c Sep*
      - labor; during: *Cimic*
      - sitting agg.: thuj
  - Hips to feet; down outside of: coloc ↓ *Phyt* ↓
    - stitching pain: coloc *Phyt*
  - Ilium: thuj ↓
    - pressing pain: thuj h1
    - stitching pain: thuj h1
  - Lower extremities: agath-a nl2• *Cimic* cimx *Lac-c Lil-t Sep* tritic-vg fd5.de
  - Lumbar region: mur-ac ↓
    - drawing pain: mur-ac h2
  - Ovarian region: ust
  - Pubis: arg-met helon *Laur* mel-c-s br1 **Sabin** k* *Sulph*
    - Bone to another; from one: sabin c1*
  - Testis; from left side to left: thuj ↓
    - stitching pain: thuj
  - Thighs: agath-a nl2• arn berb *Cimic Coloc* dulc fd4.de kali-c kreos nux-v *Sec Sep Sulph Tell* tritic-vg fd5.de vib mrr1
    - right | pressing at stool or cough agg.: **Tell**
    - drawing pain: nux-v tritic-vg fd5.de
    - sitting agg.: dulc fd4.de thuj
  - Trochanter major: phys hbh
  - Uterus: *Cham* helon nat-m syph c1
- ○ Hips; and: ail ↓
  - cutting pain: ail
- Joints: des-ac rbp6 ozone sde2•

- Sacral region: ...
  - Spot; in a small | night: kali-bi tl1
- Sacroiliac region: allox ↓ com br1 cortiso ↓ mag-s ↓ vanil ↓
  - right: cortiso ↓
    - aching: cortiso tpw7*
  - morning: cortiso sp1
    - aching: cortiso tpw7
  - aching: allox tpw3* cortiso sp1
  - bending forward agg.: allox sp1
  - break; as if it would: cortiso tpw7
  - dull pain: allox tpw3* vanil fd5.de
  - half bent position; in: cortiso ↓
    - aching: cortiso sp1*
  - lying:
    - amel.: cortiso ↓
      - aching: cortiso tpw7*
  - menses; during: mag-s sp1
  - motion:
    - agg.: allox sp1
      - aching: allox tpw3
    - amel.: cortiso sp1
      - break; as if it would: cortiso tpw7
  - pressure of cushion | amel.: cortiso sp1
  - pulsating pain: mag-s sp1
  - sitting agg.: cortiso sp1
    - aching: cortiso tpw7*
    - break; as if it would: cortiso tpw7
  - standing:
    - amel.: cortiso ↓
      - aching: cortiso tpw7*
      - break; as if it would: cortiso tpw7
  - stooping:
    - agg.: allox ↓ cortiso ↓
      - morning: cortiso ↓
        - aching: cortiso tpw7
      - aching: cortiso tpw7
      - break; as if it would: cortiso tpw7
      - dull pain: allox tpw3
    - halfway agg.: cortiso ↓
      - aching: cortiso sp1*
  - walking agg.: allox sp1
    - aching: allox tpw3
- Sacroiliac symphyses: **Aesc** k* allox sp1 *Ant-t* apis *Arg-n* bamb-a stb2.de• *Bry* cadm-met tpw6 *Calc-p* cham tl1 *Cimic* coc-c ↓ *Coloc* conv br1 cortiso sp1 dios dulc fd4.de equis-h c1 ferr fuma-ac rly4• gels hep jug-c kali-s fd4.de kola stb3• loxo-recl knl4• mag-s sp1 nat-p ol-j ozone ↓ phos ↓ plb rhus-t rumx sabad spong sulph syc fmm1• tax-br oss1• tell hr1 *Thuj* tril-p ↓ ulm-c ↓ vanil fd5.de verat ↓ vip fkr4.de
  - right: fuma-ac rly4• ign dgt kali-s fd4.de nat-p ozone ↓ psil ft1
    - tearing pain: ozone sde2•
  - aching: **Aesc** *Coloc* jug-c *Sulph*
  - bandaging: | amel.: tril-p hr1
  - burning: rumx
  - cutting pain: nat-p
  - eating agg.: ulm-c ↓
    - sore: ulm-c jsj8•
  - electric shock; as from an: ulm-c jsj8•
  - menses; during: thuj ↓
    - sore: thuj
  - motion agg.; rapid: ozone ↓
    - tearing pain: ozone sde2•
  - running down leg | women; in: conv br1
  - separated; as if: calc-p tril-p hr1

- **sitting**:
  - **amel.**: ozone ↓
    - **tearing** pain: ozone sde2•
  - **impossible**: bamb-a stb2.de•
- **sore**: *Calc-p* coc-c hep rumx ulm-c jsj8• verat
- **standing** agg.: kali-s fd4.de spong h1
- **stitching** pain: phos vanil fd5.de
- **stooping** agg.: cadm-met tpw6
- **tearing** pain: *Bry* ozone sde2•

▽ - **extending** to:
  - **Down** region of sciatic nerves | **delivery**; during: *Cimic* k*
  - **Downward**: tax-br oss1•
  - **Foot**: bamb-a stb2.de•
  - **Groin**: *Thuj*
  - **Knee** | **Hollow** of: bamb-a stb2.de•
  - **Pelvic** region: ozone ↓
    - **tearing** pain: ozone sde2•

\- **Sacrum**: acon ↓ **Aesc** ↓ **Agar** ↓ agath-a ↓ alet ↓ allox ↓ aloe ↓ alum ↓ am-m ↓ amp ↓ androc ↓ ang ↓ arg-n ↓ arge-pl ↓ arn ↓ *Ars* ↓ asar ↓ atp ↓ aur ↓ aur-s ↓ *Bapt* ↓ *Bell* ↓ *Berb* ↓ borx ↓ *Bry* ↓ calad ↓ *Calc* ↓ *Calc-p* ↓ *Calc-s* ↓ calc-sil ↓ canth ↓ carb-an ↓ *Carb-v* ↓ carbn-s ↓ *Cham* ↓ chin ↓ *Cimic* ↓ *Coff* ↓ colch ↓ *Coloc* ↓ con ↓ croc ↓ cupr ↓ des-ac ↓ dulc ↓ eug ↓ eup-pur ↓ *Eupi* ↓ fl-ac ↓ **Gels** ↓ graph ↓ *Helon* ↓ hep ↓ *Ign* ↓ irid-met ↓ *Kali-bi* ↓ *Kali-c* ↓ kali-i ↓ kali-m ↓ kali-sil ↓ kreos ↓ lac-loxod-a ↓ *Lach* ↓ lil-t ↓ limen-b-c ↓ *Lyc* ↓ mag-m ↓ meli ↓ *Merc* ↓ *Mez* ↓ **Mur-ac** ↓ nat-m ↓ nux-m ↓ *Nux-v* ↓ ol-an ↓ ol-j ↓ op ↓ oxal-a ↓ ozone ↓ petr-ra ↓ phel ↓ *Phos* ↓ *Phyt* ↓ plat ↓ *Plb* ↓ ptel ↓ **Puls** ↓ rhod ↓ *Rhus-t* ↓ ruta ↓ sabin ↓ sal-fr ↓ samb ↓ *Sars* ↓ sec ↓ *Sep* ↓ *Sil* ↓ spong ↓ *Staph* ↓ stram ↓ *Sulph* ↓ thuj ↓ tritic-vg ↓ tub ↓ ulm-c ↓ ust ↓ vario ↓ verat ↓ *Zinc* ↓

- **morning**: ang ↓ atp ↓ calad ↓ kali-bi ↓ kali-n ↓ nat-m ↓ *Puls* ↓ sel ↓ *Staph* ↓ thuj ↓
  - **aching**: ang atp rly4• calad kali-bi k2 kali-n nat-m sel *Staph* thuj
  - **bed** agg.; in: petr ↓ staph ↓
    - **broken**; as if: staph
    - **sprained**; as if: petr h2
  - **labor**-like: *Puls*
- **evening**: canth ↓ led ↓ *Sep* ↓ ter ↓
  - **aching**: led *Sep* ter
  - **bed**; after going to: naja ↓
    - **gnawing** pain: naja
  - **gnawing** pain: canth
- **night**: arg-n ↓ kali-bi ↓
  - **aching**: arg-n kali-bi k2
  - **rising** and walking about; after:
    - **amel.**: ang ↓
      - **broken**; as if: ang
- **aching**: acon **Aesc** **Agar** agath-a nl2• alum amp rly4• androc srj1• arg-n arge-pl rwt5• atp rly4• aur aur-s k2 *Bapt* borx c1 calad *Calc* *Calc-p* *Calc-s* calc-sil k2 canth carb-an *Carb-v* carbn-s cham chin *Cimic* *Coff* colch con des-ac rbp6 eug eup-pur fl-ac **Gels** graph *Helon* hep *Ign* irid-met srj5• *Kali-bi* kali-c kali-m k2 kali-sil k2 *Lach* lil-t lyc *Merc* **Mur-ac** nat-m *Nux-v* ol-j op oxal-a rly4• *Phyt* ptel **Puls** *Rhus-t* sal-fr sle1• *Sep* *Sil* staph stram *Sulph* vario verat zinc k2
  - **flesh** were detached from bones; as if: acon kali-bi
- **biting**: aloe bg2 phel bg2
- **break**; as if it would: allox tpw3 aloe *Berb* k* cimic kali-c
- **broken**; as if: acon *Aesc* agar alum am-m ang arn *Ars* bry *Calc-p* *Eupi* graph hep lyc bg2 meli nux-m nux-v *Phos* k* plat rhus-t ruta sabin k2 *Staph* verat
- **burrowing**: calad
- **contracting**:
  - **accompanied** by | **leukorrhea** (See FEMALE - Leukorrhea - accompanied - sacrum - pain - contractive)
- **cough**; with: *Phos* ↓
  - **broken**; as if: *Phos*
- **cramping**: *Bell* lac-loxod-a hrn2• ptel c1 thuj tritic-vg fd5.de ulm-c jsj8•

\- **Sacrum**: ...
- **crushed**, as if: sil
- **digging** pain: arg-n bg2
- **dislocated**; as if: agar dulc fd4.de nux-v tub
- **dragging**: alet vh1 androc srj1• *Carb-v* helon k* *Sep* ust
- **fatigued**, weary; as if: des-ac rbp6
- **gnawing** pain: alum phos
- **labor**-like: *Cham* *Cimic* croc *Kali-c* kali-i kreos limen-b-c mlk9.de **Puls** *Sars* sec sep *Sulph*
- **lancinating**: cupr petr-ra shn4• *Plb* samb h1* *Zinc*
- **lying** | **abdomen**; on:
  - **agg.**: ulm-c ↓
    - **cramping**: ulm-c jsj8•
  - **agg.**: berb ↓
    - **break**; as if it would: berb k*
- **menses**; before: *Vib* ↓
  - **aching**: *Vib*
- **motion**:
  - **agg.**: *Aesc* ↓ *Colch* ↓
    - **aching**: *Aesc* *Colch*
  - **amel.**: kali-bi ↓
    - **aching**: kali-bi k2
- **pressure**:
  - **amel.**: allox ↓ colch ↓ mag-m ↓ *Sep* ↓
    - **aching**: colch *Sep*
    - **break**; as if it would: allox tpw3*
    - **tearing** pain: mag-m
- **rising**:
  - **sitting**; from:
    - **after**: *Verat* ↓
      - **sore** | **paralytic**: *Verat* k*
    - **agg.**: zinc ↓
      - **aching**: zinc k2
- **sitting**:
  - **agg.**: **Agar** ↓ berb ↓ borx ↓ petr ↓ spong ↓
    - **aching**: **Agar** borx c1
    - **break**; as if it would: berb k*
    - **sprained**; as if: petr h2
    - **tearing** pain: spong h1
  - **erect**:
    - **agg.**: lyc ↓
      - **tearing** pain: lyc
- **sprained**; as if: agar *Calc* lach ol-an k* rhod sulph
- **stooping** agg.: **Aesc** ↓ borx ↓ kali-bi ↓
  - **aching**: **Aesc** borx c1
  - **crushed**, as if: kali-bi tl1
- **stretching**:
  - **amel.**: alum ↓
    - **gnawing** pain: alum
- **tearing** pain: *Aesc* asar *Bry* *Coloc* helon *Lyc* mag-m *Mez* mur-ac ozone sde2• sabin k2 spong zinc h2
- **violent**: kali-bi bg2
- **walking**:
  - **agg.**: **Aesc** ↓ asar ↓ *Calc-p* ↓ *Colch* ↓
    - **aching**: **Aesc** *Colch*
    - **broken**; as if: *Calc-p*
    - **tearing** pain: asar
  - **amel.**: calc ↓ phos ↓ rhus-t ↓ sep ↓ sulph ↓ zinc ↓
    - **aching**: calc k2 phos k2 rhus-t k2 sep k2 sulph k2 zinc k2

▽ - **extending** to:
  - **Coccyx**: zinc ↓
    - **dragging**: zinc bg2
  - **Coccyx** and thighs: thuj ↓
    - **tearing** pain: thuj

· **extending** to: ...
⁝ **Lower** extremities: agath-a↓ atp↓ calc-ar↓ *Cimic*↓ *Lil-t*↓ polys↓ *Sep*↓
: **aching**: agath-a nl2• atp rly4• calc-ar *Cimic* *Lil-t* polys sk4• *Sep*
⁝ **Lumbar** region; toward: mur-ac↓
: **tearing** pain: mur-ac
⁝ **Nates**: helon↓
: **dragging**: helon ptk1
⁝ **Occiput**: led↓
: **tearing** pain: led
⁝ **Sciatic** nerve; down the: *Coloc*↓
: **tearing** pain: *Coloc*
⁝ **Thighs**: cham↓
: **labor**-like: cham h1
○ · **Coccyx**; and: nux-v↓
⁝ **dislocated**; as if: nux-v bg2
· **Hips**; and:
⁝ **walking** agg.: **Aesc**↓
: **tearing** pain: **Aesc**
· **Sacroiliac** symphyses: calc-p↓
⁝ **dislocated**; as if | **separated**; as if: calc-p k*
⁝ **walking**:
: **agg**.: *Calc-p*↓
. **dislocated**; as if | **separated**; as if: *Calc-p*

- **Spinal** cord: lact-v c2
- **Spine**: abrot bro1 acon k* adon bro1 aesc *Aeth* **Agar** k* agath-a↓ alum k2 alum-p k2 alum-sil k2 ambr↓ anac↓ *Ang* ant-c↓ ant-t↓ apis↓ aran *Arg-n* bro1 *Arn* ars *Asaf*↓ *Atro*↓ aur aur-ar k2 aur-s bapt↓ bar-s↓ *Bell* *Bell-p*↓ benz-ac *Berb* borx↓ brach cact k* *Calc*↓ calc-i↓ calc-p k2 calc-sil↓ camph cann-xyz bg2 *Caps* *Carb-ac*↓ carb-v carc fb card-m↓ caul↓ *Caust* cham↓ **Chel** chin chinin-ar **Chinin-s**↓ **Cimic** k* *Cina* cinch↓ cinnb cob *Cocc* colch coli↓ coloc colocin c2 *Con* conch↓ *Crot-c* k* crot-h↓ *Cupr*↓ cur cycl daph dios dulc fd4.de elaps eup-per↓ euph↓ ferr-i k2 franc br1 *Gels* k* glon **Graph**↓ *Gua*↓ ham↓ hell↓ helon↓ *Hep*↓ hura k* hyper k* ign iod↓ iodof irid-met srj5• jatr-c kali-act *Kali-ar*↓ kali-bi *Kali-c*↓ kali-fcy↓ kali-i↓ *Kali-p* kali-s fd4.de kali-sil k2 *Kalm* lac-ac *Lac-c*↓ lac-d k2 lac-h↓ *Lach* lachn↓ lact lact-v bro1 lat-m bnm6• *Lec*↓ led leptos-ih jl2 lil-t k2* lob-s c2* loxo-recl knl4• *Lyc*↓ lycps-v **Lyss**↓ mag-c mag-m mag-p↓ mang med menis c2* meph *Merc* merc-i-f↓ merc-i-r↓ methyl↓ mez k2 morph mosch mur-ac *Naja* *Nat-ar*↓ *Nat-c*↓ **Nat-m** **Nat-p**↓ nat-s k2 neon srj5• nicc↓ nicc-s bro1 nit-ac *Nux-m* k* *Nux-v* oena ol-j olnd *Ox-ac* bro1 par↓ paraf c2* *Petr* petr-ra shn4• *Ph-ac* **Phos** phys bro1 *Phyt*↓ *Pic-ac*↓ plan↓ *Plat*↓ plb plut-n↓ podo↓ polyg-h↓ *Puls*↓ querc-r svu1• ran-b *Rat*↓ *Rhus-t*↓ ribo rly4• **Ruta** sabad↓ samb↓ *Sang*↓ *Sars*↓ sec bro1 sep k2 **Sil** spig spong squil↓ staph stram↓ stry k* stry-p↓ sul-ac sulph sumb↓ symph fd3.de• syph k2 tab↓ tanac tarent k* *Tell* tep c2 ther bro1 thres-a sze7• thuj tritic-vg fd5.de tub↓ upa c2 valer↓ vanil fd5.de verat *Vib*↓ xan **Zinc** k* zinc-p k2 zinc-val↓
· **right**: kali-c↓ ozone↓
⁝ **burning**: kali-c ptk1
⁝ **dull** pain: ozone sde2•
· **morning**: agar↓ aur dulc fd4.de ephe-si↓ euphr kali-p fd1.de• mag-m↓ spong fd4.de vanil fd5.de
⁝ **rising** agg.; after: sulph
⁝ **sore**: agar ephe-si hsj1• mag-m h2
⁝ **waking**; on: euphr kali-p fd1.de•
: **stitching** pain: euphr
· **forenoon**:
⁝ **11**-14 h: ephe-si↓
: **stitching** pain: ephe-si hsj1•
· **afternoon**: stront-c
⁝ **walking** agg.: stront-c↓
: **drawing** pain: stront-c
· **evening**: mag-c↓ mez↓
⁝ **bed** agg.; in: kali-bi mag-m
: **drawing** pain: kali-bi
⁝ **stitching** pain: mag-c h2 mez
· **night**: *Ph-ac*↓

- **Spine** – **night**: ...
⁝ **midnight**:
: **after**: ant-s-aur
. **drawing** pain: ant-s-aur
⁝ **burning**: *Ph-ac*
⁝ **weakness** of extremities; with: arg-n
· **accompanied** by:
⁝ **appetite**; ravenous (See STOMACH - Appetite - ravenous - accompanied - spine)
⁝ **priapism**: pic-ac mrr1
⁝ **Uterus**; complaints of the: visc br1
· **aching**: **Agar** k* agath-a nl2• alum-sil br1 asaf k* calc-p k2 *Carb-v* k* *Chel* chinin-ar gels k2 lac-ac k* *Lac-c* k* *Lach* lycps-v lyss k* nat-m k2 *Nux-m* k* ol-j k* *Sil* k* stry-p br1 syph k2* **Tell** k* *Zinc* k*
⁝ **dull** sensation as from fullness of blood: phos k*
· **alternating** with:
⁝ **Stomach**; pain in: paraf br1
⁝ **Throat**; pain in:
: **accompanied** by | **Stomach**; pain in: paraf bro1
· **anger**; after: coloc k2*
· **bending**:
⁝ **backward**:
: **agg**.: *Calc* *Chel* dios mang peti
: **must** bend backward: bism↓
. **pressing** pain: bism hr1
· **breathing**:
⁝ **agg**.: dulc↓
: **stitching** pain: dulc h2*
⁝ **deep** | **agg**.: *Chel* led *Ruta*
· **broken**; as if: ham bg2
· **burning**: acon k* agar k* alum bg2* alum-sil k2* **Ars** k* *Asaf* k* bar-s k2 *Bell* k* cham cocc ptk1 *Gels* k* glon k* *Gua* bro1 helon k* kali-bi ptk1 kali-c bro1 kali-fcy bro1 kali-p bro1 *Kalm* **Lach** k* lachn k* *Lyc* k* mag-m *Med* k* mur-ac k2 *Nat-c* k* *Nat-p* nux-v bg2* *Ph-ac* k* **Phos** k* phys bg2* *Pic-ac* k* plb k* puls k* ran-b k2 **Sec** k* *Sep* k* stry-p br1* sulph bro1 tab ptk1 *Thuj* *Verat* k* *Zinc* k* zinc-p k2
⁝ **accompanied** by | **Head**; pain in: pic-ac bro1
⁝ **shooting** pain: acon
⁝ **stitching** pain: mag-m zinc
⁝ **upward**: plut-n srj7•
· **circle** from spine to abdomen; in a: acon↓
⁝ **cutting** pain: acon
· **coition**; after: nit-ac
⁝ **drawing** pain: nit-ac
· **cold** air agg.: ran-b k2
· **compressed**; as if: aeth bg2
· **convulsions**; after: acon
· **cough** agg.; during: **Bell** dulc fd4.de nat-m k2
· **cramping**: euph h2
· **cutting** pain: elaps ptk1 nat-s ptk1 polyg-h ptk1
· **digging** pain: kali-i
· **dinner**; after: *Agar* cob
· **drawing** pain: *Bell* berb *Caps* k* carb-v chin h1 chinin-ar **Cimic** *Cina* colch *Con* cycl daph mosch *Nat-m* nux-m bg2 nux-v k2 phys bg2 *Ruta* sulph *Thuj* vanil fd5.de verat *Zinc*
· **eating**; after: *Agar* *Kali-c*
· **exertion**; physical: pic-ac↓
⁝ **burning**: pic-ac k2
· **fall**; as from a: ruta h1
· **fever**; during: *Chinin-s*↓ *Cocc*↓
⁝ **sore**: *Chinin-s* k* *Cocc* k*
· **footsteps**: *Nux-v*↓ **Ther**↓
⁝ **sore**: *Nux-v* **Ther** k*
· **gnawing** pain: **Bell** mag-m

Back

- **hysterical**: *Kali-br* ↓
  - **sore**: *Kali-br* hr1
- **inspiration** agg.: chinin-s mrr1 led ↓
  - **pressing** pain: led
  - **stitching** pain: led h1
- **jar**:
  - **agg.**: (↗*jar)* acon alum-sil k2 **Bell Graph** podo *Sulph Ther Thuj*
  - **bed** agg.; jar of: **Bell** ↓ **Graph** ↓ *Lach* ↓ **Sil** ↓ **Ther** ↓ *Thuj* ↓
    - **aching**: **Bell Graph**
    - **sore**: **Bell** *Graph Lach* **Sil Ther** *Thuj*
- **leaning** against chair agg.: **Agar** ↓ plb ↓ **Ther** ↓
  - **sore**: **Agar** k* plb **Ther** k*
- **lying**:
  - **agg.**: *Lyc* ↓ vanil fd5.de
    - **burning**: *Lyc* k*
  - **amel.**: ephe-si ↓
    - **stitching** pain: ephe-si hsj1•
  - **back**; on:
    - **agg.**: mag-m ↓ *Nat-m* tritic-vg fd5.de
      - **sore**: mag-m h2
    - **amel.**:
      - **pressure**; with hard: *Nat-m* ↓
        - **sore**: *Nat-m*
  - **hard**; on something:
    - **amel.**: *Nat-m* ↓
      - **sore**: *Nat-m*
- **lying** down agg.: *Nat-m*
- **menses**; during: thuj ↓
  - **sore**: thuj
- **mental** exertion agg.: *Pic-ac* ↓ *Sil* ↓
  - **burning**: *Pic-ac* k* *Sil*
- **motion**:
  - **agg.**: aesc tl1 *Agar* dulc fd4.de hyper ↓ meph *Merc* ther ↓ vanil fd5.de
    - **sore**: ther k2
    - **stitching** pain: dulc fd4.de hyper mrr1 meph
  - **amel.**: euphr mag-m ↓ *Ph-ac* vanil fd5.de
    - **burning** | **stitching** pain: mag-m
  - **arms**; of | **agg.**: ang c1
- **neuralgic**: lac-h sze9• par bro1
- **noise** agg.: ars ther ↓
  - **sore**: ther k2
- **pinching** pain: ph-ac h2
- **pressing** pain: benz-ac led phos samb h1 sep h2 spong
  - **plug**; as from a: anac bg2
- **pressure**:
  - **agg.**: plat ↓ tarent ↓
    - **sore**: plat h2 tarent k2
  - **amel.**: verat
    - **pressing** pain: verat
  - **slight**:
    - **agg.**: stram ↓
      - **sore**: stram ptk1
- **pulsating** pain: agar bg2 *Lach* merc-i-f bg2 sumb bg2 thuj bg2
- **radiating**: sabad bg2
- **relieving** the headache: kali-p
- **rheumatic**: caul tl1 nat-s mrr1 puls k2
- **riding** in a carriage agg.: alum-sil k2
- **rubber**; as if made out of: conch fkr1•
- **rubbing**:
  - **amel.**: phos ↓
    - **burning**: phos
- **rubbing** against each other; as if vertebrae are: *(↗Gliding - dorsal - vertebrae; Gliding - lumbar - vertebrae)* ant-t ptk1
- **sewing** machine; from using a: agar ↓ *Cimic* ↓ *Nux-v* ↓ ran-b ↓
- **sewing** machine; from using a: ...
  - **sore**: agar bro1 *Cimic* bro1 *Nux-v* ran-b bro1
- **sexual** excesses; after: agar ↓ kali-p ↓ nat-m ↓
  - **sore**: agar bro1 kali-p bro1 nat-m bro1
- **shock**, on riding in a carriage; as from a: petr *Ther*
- **sitting**:
  - **agg.**: ephe-si ↓ helon kali-p ↓ kali-s fd4.de *Ph-ac Ruta* spong *Zinc* zinc-p k2
    - **aching**: helon
    - **burning**: kali-p fd1.de• **Zinc** k*
    - **sore**: ruta h1
    - **stitching** pain: ephe-si hsj1• ruta
  - **amel.**: mur-ac tritic-vg fd5.de
    - **pressing** pain: mur-ac
  - **erect**:
    - **agg.**: spong ↓
      - **pressing** pain: spong
- **sitting** and stooping, like a painful weakness; while: zinc ↓
  - **drawing** pain: zinc
- **small** place in: agar ↓
  - **burning**: agar k*
- **sore** (= spinal irritation): aesc **Agar** k* alum-p k2 alum-sil k2 ambr br1* *Ang* ant-c apis arg-n c2* *Arn* k* ars *Atro* k* bapt **Bell** k* *Bell-p* bro1 *Benz-ac* berb k* *Calc* calc-i k2 calc-p k2 calc-sil k2 *Carb-ac* card-m k2 caul k2 caust *Chel Chin* chinin-ar k* **Chinin-s** k* *Cimic* k* cinch c2 cob bro1 *Cocc* k* coli rly4• *Crot-c* crot-h *Cupr* k* *Dios* k* eup-per gels k* *Glon* **Graph** *Gua* br1* hell bg2 *Hep* k* hyper k* *Ign* c2* iod iodof *Kali-ar Kali-c* k* kali-i **Kali-p** k* *Lac-c* k* **Lach** *Lec* lil-t k* **Lyss** mag-m mag-p k2 *Med* k* merc-i-r methyl c2 *Naja* k* *Nat-ar Nat-c* **Nat-m** k* **Nat-p** *Nat-s* nicc **Nux-v** k* *Ol-j* k* ox-ac k* *Ph-ac* **Phos** k* phys k* *Phyt* k* pic-ac c2* plan *Plat* k* podo *Puls* k* *Ran-b* k* *Rat Rhus-t* **Ruta** k* sabad k* *Sang Sars* sec k* *Sep* k* **Sil** k* spig k* squil staph bro1 stram stry-p c2* sulph k* tanac *Tarent* k* *Tell* k* **Ther** k* *Thuj* tub bro1 valer k2 verat *Vib* **Zinc** k* zinc-val bro1
- **sprained**; as if: mag-m bg2
- **standing**:
  - **agg.**: ephe-si ↓ nit-ac *Ph-ac*
    - **stitching** pain: ephe-si hsj1• nit-ac
  - **amel.**: mur-ac tritic-vg fd5.de
    - **pressing** pain: mur-ac
- **stimulants**: *Zinc*
- **stitching** pain: **Agar** *Bell* **Berb** borx h2 calc-p k2 caps h1* chin h1 *Cocc* dulc elaps *Hyper* k* ign kali-bi led meph mez *Nit-ac* olnd *Petr Phos* phys bg2 ran-b k2 rat sabad bg2 spong fd4.de sul-ac tanac vanil fd5.de
  - **jerking** pain: ph-ac h2
  - **needles** in; as if icy: agar ptk1 cocc ptk1
  - **pulsating** pain: dulc
  - **upward**: cocc *Petr*
- **stool** agg., during: *Phos* k*
- **stooping**:
  - **agg.**: *Agar* daph ptk2 dulc fd4.de kali-s fd4.de sulph ↓ zinc
    - **drawing** pain | **upward**: sulph
- **stretching** out: med ↓
  - **sore**: med k*
- **swallowing** agg.: caust kali-c
  - **pressing** pain: kali-c
- **tearing** pain: acon k2 alum k2 aur-s k* berb calc-p k2 camph caps k* chel chin k* chinin-s *Cina* cocc k* **Hyper** mag-c k* *Mang* k* nat-m k* *Nat-s* nux-v k*
  - **downward**: *Cina* k* *Mang* nat-m
  - **drawing** pain: *Caps* hr1
- **thunderstorm**; before: *Agar* ↓ *Phos* ↓
  - **sore**: *Agar Phos*
- **touch** agg.: calc-sil ↓ chinin-s mrr1 lac-c tl1 tarent ↓ zinc-p ↓
  - **sore**: calc-sil k2 tarent k2* zinc-p k2
- **twitching**: cina ↓

- **twitching**: ...
  - **tearing** pain: cina h1
- **walking**:
  - **about**:
    - **amel.**: cina ↓ euphr ↓
      - **stitching** pain: cina h1* euphr
  - **agg.**: cocc tl1 kali-c tl1 *Mur-ac* nat-m k2 par *Ruta* sep stront-c verat
    - **pressing** pain: mur-ac verat h1
    - **sore**: *Ruta* verat h1
  - **air** agg.; in open: mur-ac ↓
    - **pressing** pain: mur-ac a1
  - **amel.**: *Ph-ac* sep tl1 zinc ↓ zinc-p k2
    - **burning**: zinc
- **warm** applications | **amel.**: dulc fd4.de mag-p k2

▽ • **extending** to:
  - **Abdomen**: meny ↓
    - **cutting** pain: meny h1
  - **Anterior** superior spinous process of left ilium: dros ↓
    - **tearing** pain: dros
  - **Chest**: ferr-i k2 stry-p br1
  - **Downward**: **Berb** cur cycl glon kalm k2 lil-t k2 mang nat-m phys ust
    - **throwing** shoulders forward agg., by throwing them backward amel.: cycl ↓
      - **drawing** pain: cycl
  - **Epigastrium**: nicc rat thuj
    - **stitching** pain: nicc rat thuj
  - **Ilium**; to anterior superior spinous process of left: dros ↓
    - **stitching** pain: dros k*
  - **Lower** extremities: agar
  - **Lumbar** region to region of bladder; down: **Berb** ↓
    - **stitching** pain: **Berb**
  - **Occiput**: *Phos* plb
    - **Coccyx** to occiput, drawing head backward; from: *Phos*
  - **Stomach**: *Thuj* ↓
    - **cutting** pain: *Thuj*
  - **Up** spine: agar ars bg1 caust mag-m nux-v petr phos sulph
    - **stooping** agg.: sulph

○ • **Articulations** of:
  - **motion** agg.: cocc ↓
    - **cutting** pain: cocc
- **Beside**: carb-v ↓
  - **pinching** pain: carb-v h2
- **Brain**; base of:
  - **extending** to:
    - **Coccyx**: lac-ac ↓ *Lac-c* ↓ rhus-t ↓
      - **aching**: lac-ac *Lac-c* k* rhus-t tl1
- **Cervical** region: adon ↓ *Aesc* ↓ *Ang* ↓ *Arn* ↓ carb-ac ↓ *Card-m* ↓ **Chinin-s** ↓ *Cimic* ↓ cinnb ↓ *Cocc* ↓ *Coloc* ↓ con ↓ dios ↓ *Gels* ↓ *Ham* ↓ *Hyper* ↓ *Lach* ↓ nat-ar ↓ *Nat-s* ↓ ox-ac ↓ **Par** ↓ plan ↓ stram ↓ **Sulph** ↓ *Tell* ↓
  - **sore**: adon mtf11 *Aesc* *Ang* *Arn* k* carb-ac *Card-m* **Chinin-s** *Cimic* cinnb *Cocc* *Coloc* con dios *Gels* *Ham* *Hyper* *Lach* nat-ar *Nat-s* ox-ac **Par** plan stram **Sulph** *Tell*
- **Dorsal** region: acon ↓ aesc ↓ *Agar* ↓ ail ↓ arn ↓ ars-met ↓ asaf ↓ *Bell* ↓ brach ↓ cact ↓ *Card-m* ↓ *Chel* ↓ **Chinin-s** ↓ *Cimic* ↓ *Cocc* ↓ colch ↓ *Coloc* ↓ *Cupr* ↓ gins ↓ *Graph* ↓ *Hell* ↓ hyper ↓ merc ↓ nux-v ↓ ph-ac ↓ **Phos** ↓ plb ↓ podo ↓ *Ruta* ↓ sec ↓ *Sil* ↓ **Tell** ↓ **Ther** ↓ *Zinc* ↓
  - **sore**: acon aesc *Agar* ail arn k* ars-met asaf *Bell* brach cact *Card-m* *Chel* **Chinin-s** *Cimic* *Cocc* colch *Coloc* *Cupr* gins *Graph* *Hell* hyper merc nux-v ph-ac **Phos** plb podo *Ruta* sec *Sil* **Tell** **Ther** *Zinc*
  - **First** vertebra:
    - **pressure** agg.; hard: choc ↓
      - **sore**: choc srj3•
- **Joints** of vertebrae: staph ↓
  - **drawing** pain: staph h1
- **Lower** part: ars ↓ chel ↓ lyc ↓ mag-c ↓
- **Lower** part: ...
  - **jerking** pain: mag-c h2
  - **pressing** pain | **fist**; as from a: lyc
  - **tearing** pain: ars k* chel mag-c h2
- **Lumbar** region: agar ↓ *Arg-n* ↓ bar-c ↓ bell ↓ *Chel* ↓ colch ↓ *Graph* ↓ hep ↓ *Lil-t* ↓ lyc ↓ mag-m ↓ med ↓ *Phos* ↓ pic-ac ↓ *Plat* ↓ tab ↓ **Thuj** ↓
  - **leaning** against chair agg.: plb ↓
    - **sore**: plb
  - **menses** agg.: thuj ↓
    - **sore**: thuj
  - **sore**: agar *Arg-n* bar-c bell *Chel* colch *Graph* hep h2 *Lil-t* lyc mag-m med *Phos* pic-ac *Plat* tab **Thuj**
  - **stepping** agg.: berb ↓ *Carb-an* ↓ **Thuj** ↓
    - **sore**: berb *Carb-an* **Thuj**
  - **Above**: *Zinc* ↓
    - **burning**: *Zinc*
- **Lumbosacral** region: nat-p ↓
  - **sore**: nat-p
- **Middle** of: cassia-s ↓ cina ↓ plat ↓
  - **bending** forward agg.: cassia-s ↓
    - **pressing** pain: cassia-s ccrh1•
  - **inspiration** agg.: cassia-s ↓
    - **pressing** pain: cassia-s ccrh1•
  - **jerking** pain: cina k*
  - **pressing** pain: cassia-s ccrh1•
    - **plug**; as from a: plat
  - **sitting**:
    - **amel.**: cassia-s ↓
      - **pressing** pain: cassia-s ccrh1•
  - **walking** agg.: cassia-s ↓
    - **pressing** pain: cassia-s ccrh1•
- **Sacral** region: am-c ↓ ang ↓ *Berb* ↓ *Colch* ↓ kali-bi ↓ *Lob* ↓ nat-ar ↓ rhus-t ↓ sarr ↓ *Sep* ↓ *Sil* ↓
  - **menses**; before: *Spong* ↓
    - **sore**: *Spong*
  - **sore**: am-c ang *Berb* *Colch* kali-bi *Lob* nat-ar rhus-t sarr *Sep* *Sil*
  - **stooping** agg.:
    - **walking**; and: nat-ar ↓
      - **sore**: nat-ar
- **Spots**; in: agar ↓ nit-ac ↓ *Phos* ↓
  - **burning**: agar nit-ac k2 *Phos*
- **Upper** part: cina ↓ gins ↓
  - **lancinating**: cina k* gins k*
  - **tearing** pain: cina
  - **extending** to:
    - **Sacrum**: gins ↓
      - **lancinating**: gins k*
- **Vertebrae**: acon bg2 agar bro1 agath-a ↓ alum ↓ ang bg2 ant-t ↓ arg-met bg2 arn bg2 asaf ↓ *Aur* bg2 *Bell* bg2 **Calc** bg2 cann-xyz bg2 carb-an ↓ carb-v bg2 chel bg2 chin bg2 chinin-s bg2 cimic ↓ cina bg2 cinnb ↓ cocc bg2 crot-t ↓ dros bg2 dulc bg2 euph ↓ graph bg2 hell bg2 ign bg2 kali-c bg2 kreos ↓ led bg2 lyc bg2 mang ↓ meny bg2 meph bg2 merc bg2 mosch bg2 mur-ac ↓ nat-m ↓ nit-ac bg2 nux-m bg2 nux-v bg2 petr bg2 ph-ac bg2 phos bg2 plat ↓ **Puls** bg2 **Rhus-t** bg2 *Ruta* bg2 sabad bg2 sabin bg2 samb bg2 sep bg2 **Sil** bg2 spong bg2 stann bg2 *Staph* bg2 stram ↓ sul-ac bg2 **Sulph** bg2 verb bg2 zinc bg2
  - **boring** pain: acon bg2
  - **burning**: ant-t bg2 asaf bg2 nat-m bg2 staph bg2
  - **cramping**: euph bg2
  - **cutting** pain: acon bg2
    - **stabbing**: agath-a nl2• bell
  - **digging** pain: acon bg2
  - **drawing** pain: cimic bg2 crot-t bg2
  - **gnawing** pain: bell bg2 hell bg2
  - **pinching** pain: bell bg2 meny bg2 ph-ac bg2

- **Vertebrae**: ...
  - ⁝ **pressing** pain: alum bg2 arn bg2 asaf bg2 bell bg2 calc bg2 cann-xyz bg2 carb-v bg2 crot-t bg2 dulc bg2 graph bg2 led bg2 nux-v bg2 plat bg2 sabin bg2 samb bg2 sep bg2 spong bg2 staph bg2 zinc bg2
  - ⁝ **sprained**; as if: bell bg2 cinnb bg2
  - ⁝ **tearing** pain: bell bg2 cina bg2 cocc bg2 dros bg2 ign bg2 kali-c bg2 lyc bg2 mang bg2 meny bg2 mosch bg2 mur-ac bg2 ruta bg2 stram bg2 sulph bg2 zinc bg2
  - ⁝ **ulcerative** pain: carb-an bg2 kreos bg2
  - ⁝ **Lower** vertebrae: *Alum* ↓
    - ⁝ **burning** | **hot** iron were thrust through; as if a: *Alum* k*
- **Whole**: ang ↓ cina ↓ *Elaps* ↓ mang ↓
  - ⁝ **cutting** pain: ang cina *Elaps* mang

- **Spot**; in a: ham fd3.de• hydrog srj2• nat-sil fd3.de• ozone sde2• petr-ra ↓ podo fd3.de• stram h1 sulph ↓
  - **sore**: petr-ra shn4• sulph h2
- **Spot**; in a small: sulph ↓
  - **gnawing** pain: sulph
- **Spots**; in: agar ↓ galeoc-c-h ↓ nit-ac ↓ *Ph-ac* ↓ **Phos** ↓ ran-b ↓ sulph ↓ thuj ↓ *Zinc* ↓
  - **boring** pain: thuj
  - **burning**: agar bro1 galeoc-c-h gms1• nit-ac *Ph-ac* **Phos** k* ran-b bro1 sulph bro1 *Zinc*
  - **pinching** pain: zinc h2
  - **pressing** pain: thuj h1

Trapezius muscles: *Burg-fa* mtf

- **turning** head | **left** agg.; to: bry

- **Vertebrae**: ang ↓ arg-met ↓ aur ↓ bell ↓ cann-xyz ↓ chel ↓ chin ↓ cic ↓ cina ↓ dig ↓ dulc ↓ grat ↓ hell ↓ ign ↓ led ↓ meny ↓ meph ↓ merc ↓ mosch ↓ nit-ac ↓ ph-ac ↓ phos ↓ rhod ↓ ruta ↓ sabin ↓ stann ↓ sul-ac ↓ verb ↓
  - **blow**; pain as from a: cic bg2 dig bg2 rhod bg2
  - **stitching** pain: ang bg2 arg-met bg2 aur bg2 bell bg2 cann-xyz bg2 chel bg2 chin bg2 cina bg2 dulc bg2 grat bg2 hell bg2 ign bg2 led bg2 meny bg2 meph bg2 merc bg2 mosch bg2 nit-ac bg2 ph-ac bg2 phos bg2 ruta bg2 sabin bg2 stann bg2 sul-ac bg2 verb bg2

PARALYSIS: *Cupr* k* *Gels* k* *Led* k*

- **sensation** of:
  - **leukorrhea**; during: con b4a.de
  - ○ **Cervical** region: cina h1 meny h1 spig h1 verat h1
    - ⁝ **Nape** of neck: cina bg2
  - **Lumbar** region: agar h2 cocc mrr1 con h2 mag-m h2* nat-m h2
    - ⁝ **menses** agg.: *Cocc* mrr1
  - **Sacrum**: kali-p mtf11 *Phos*
- ○ **Cervical** region: cocc bro1 lyc h2
  - **left**: lacer c1
- **Lumbar** region: agar b4a.de *Am* b7a.de aur b4a.de bar-c b4a.de carb-v b4a.de chel b7a.de *Chin* b7a.de *Cocc* b7.de* con b4a.de *Dulc* b4a.de *Hep* b4a.de *Ip* b7a.de kali-c b4a.de* *Lyc* b4a.de nat-m b4.de* **Nux-v** b7a.de petr b4a.de *Phos* b4a.de plb b7a.de* **Rhus-t** b7a.de ruta b7.de* sabad bg2 sabin b7.de sel b7.de* *Sep* b4a.de* sil b4.de* tarax b7a.de verat b7.de*
  - **exertion** agg.: nux-v ptk1
  - **fever**; during: *Cocc* b7a.de
- **Sacrum**: phos ptk1
- **Spine**: **Aesc** k* cocc bro1 con bro1 *Irid-met* bro1 phos k2 plb-i bro1 plect bro1 sec bro1 *Stry* bro1

PERSPIRATION: acon k* aloe sne **Anac** k* ars k* ars-s-f k2 bufo bg1 *Calc* k* calc-s calc-sil k2 camph k* casc k* caust k* **Chin** k* **Chinin-s** coff k* conch fkr1* dig digin a1 *Dulc* k* guaj k* haliae-lc srj5• hep k* hyos k* ip k* kali-bi k* kali-p fd1.de• kali-s fd4.de lac-c lach laur k* *Led* k* *Lyc* morph k* *Mur-ac* k* nat-c k* nat-p nat-sil fd3.de• nit-ac k* **Nux-v** k* par k* *Petr* k* petr-ra shn4• *Ph-ac* k* *Phos* k* *Puls* k* *Rhus-t* k* ruta fd4.de sabin **Sep** k* *Sil* k* spong fd4.de *Stann* stram k* **Sulph** k* tritic-vg fd5.de vanil fd5.de [bell-p-sp dcm1 cob-m stj2 mag-s stj1 mang xyz62 mosch xyz62]

- **daytime** | **rest** agg.: petr k*
- **morning**: chim chim-m k* morph a1 ruta fd4.de spong fd4.de
- **evening**: dulc fd4.de mur-ac h2
- **night**: anac ars k* calc k* coc-c k* coff k* dulc fd4.de guaj k* kali-p fd1.de• kali-s fd4.de lyc ozone sde2• phasco-ci rbp2 rhus-t h1* ruta fd4.de *Sep* k* sil h2

Perspiration – night: ...

- **midnight**; after: **Hep**
  - ⁝ **3** h: **Rhus-t**
  - ⁝ **4** h; waking at: petr
- **chill**; during: cann-s k*
- **cold**: acon k* chin k* colch k* cub k* morph a1 ph-ac *Sep* k* vanil fd5.de [bell-p-sp dcm1]
  - **coughing**; during and after: cub
- **eating**; after: card-m k* par k*
- **emissions** agg.; after: sil k*
- **menses** | **before** | **agg.**: *Nit-ac*
  - **during** | **agg.**: *Kreos* k*
- **motion** agg.: **Chin** k*
- **sleep** agg.; during: ruta fd4.de tab k*
- **stool** agg.; straining at: *Kali-bi* k*
- **waking**; on: hep k* ruta fd4.de spong fd4.de
- **walking**:
  - **agg.**: *Caust* lac-ac lach nat-c petr phos *Rhus-t* *Sep*
  - **rapidly** | **agg.**: nit-ac h2
- ○ **Cervical** region●: aids nl2• aloe sne *Anac* ant-t a1 ars k* arum-d a1 **CALC** k* calc-sil k2* cann-s k* cassia-s ccrh1• chel k* **Chin** k* dulc fd4.de elaps ferr fl-ac k* jab a1 kali-p fd1.de• lac-c hr1 lach ptk1 mag-c mang ptk1 med bg1* mosch *Nit-ac* k* nux-v k* **Ph-ac** k* phel k* pilo a1 ruta fd4.de sanic ptk1* *Sep* k* *Sil* spig spong fd4.de stann k* **Sulph** k* tet a1 tritic-vg fd5.de vanil fd5.de wies a1 [calc lac stj2 calc-met stj2]
  - **daytime**: ph-ac k*
  - **morning**: nux-v k* spong fd4.de stann h2 sulph h2 tritic-vg fd5.de
  - **evening**: fl-ac k*
  - **night**: aloe sne **Calc** k ●* dulc fd4.de rhus-t h1* **Sulph** k ● tet a1
  - **cold** | **Nape** of neck: con ptk1 *Sulph* bg2
  - **fever**; during: cassia-s ccrh1•
  - **menses**; before: *Nit-ac*
  - **motion**, least: **Chin** k*
  - **sleep**:
    - ⁝ **amel.**: samb k*
    - ⁝ **in**: **Calc** k* *Hyos* h1* *Lach* loxo-recl knl4• ph-ac k* *Phos* vh *Sanic* vh tritic-vg fd5.de
  - **walking** agg.: camph k* ruta fd4.de
  - ○ **Nape** of neck: *Anac* bg2 ars bg2 bell bro1 **Calc** bg2* *Chin* b7.de* ferr bg2 hell bg2 hyos bg2 m-ambo b7.de mag-c bg2 mang bg2 mosch bg2 nit-ac bg2 nux-v b7.de* **Ph-ac** b4a.de* phos bro1 puls bg2* rheum bro1 *Samb* bro1 *Sanic* bro1 *Sep* bg2 *Sil* bg2* spig bg2 stann bg2* stry bro1 **Sulph** b4.de* tub bg2 verat bro1
- **Dorsal** region: acon bg2 **Anac** b4a.de* ars bg2 bufo bg2 *Calc* b4a.de* caust bg2 **Chin** b7.de* coff b7.de* *Dulc* b4a.de* guaj b4.de* hep b4.de* *Ip* b7.de* lach bg2 led b7.de* *Lyc* b4.de* m-ambo b7.de *Mur-ac* b4a.de* nat-c bg2 nit-ac bg2 *Nux-v* b7.de* par b7.de* *Petr* b4.de* *Ph-ac* b4.de* phos b4.de* puls b7.de* rhus-t b7a.de* sabin b7a.de* **Sep** b4.de* sil bg2 stann b4.de* stram b7.de* sulph bg2
  - **cold**: acon b7.de chin b7.de
  - ○ **Scapulae**, between: syph dgt
- **Lumbar** region: asaf k* brass-n-o srj5• clem k* hyos k* naja ptk1 **Sil** k*
  - **night**: sil k*
  - **cold**: plan k*
  - **menses**; before: *Nit-ac* k*
- **Sacrum**: bufo bg2 *Coc-c* sne hyos sne plan k*
  - **cold**: plan k*

POLLUTION agg.: cob ptk1 ferr ptk1 mag-m ptk1 nat-m ptk1 *Nit-ac* ptk1 sabal ptk1 staph ptk1 sulph ptk1

POLYPUS: *Con*

POSITION agg.; any: bell bg2 calc bg2 hep bg2 ox-ac bg2 phos bg2 sil bg2

POTT'S DISEASE (See Tuberculosis - vertebrae)

PREGNANCY: | **during**: calc-p bg2 *Kali-c* b4a.de *Mosch* b7a.de *Nux-v* b7a.de **Puls** b7.de*

PRESSURE:
- **abdomen**; on | **amel.**: merc bg2
- **agg.**: *Agar* bg2* am bg2 ars bg2 bapt bg2 *Bell* ptk1 chinin-s bg2* **Cimic** bg2* ign bg2 lob bg2 lyc bg2 nux-v b7.de* phos bg2* phys bg2 *Plat* b4a.de ruta b7.de* sec bg2 **Sil** bg2 tell bg2 ter bg2 **Ther** bg2
  - ○ **Spine**: bell ptk1 lac-c ptk1 tarent ptk1
- **amel.**: aur b4.de* *Bry* ptk1 bufo bg2 cimic bg2 *Dulc* b4.de* **Kali-c** bg2* kreos bg2 led b7.de* mag-m bg2 *Nat-m* bg2* ph-ac b4.de* phos bg2 rhus-t b7a.de* *Ruta* b7.de* sabad bg2 sep bg2* verat b7.de* vib bg2
  - ○ **Dorsal** region | **Scapulae**: ol-an ptk1
  - **Lumbar** region: dulc ptk1 kali-c ptk1 nat-m ptk1 rhus-t ptk1 ruta ptk1 sep ptk1
  - **Spine**: verat ptk1
- **chest**; on | **agg.**: puls b7a.de*
- **external** (See Pressure)
- **left** side amel.; pressure on: dig bg2
- **right** side amel.; pressure on: dulc bg2

PRICKLING: acon k* aesc k* alum-sil k2 apis aur k* aur-m k* bamb-a stb2.de• lact ox-ac k* ran-s k* sol-t-ae k* tub c1 verat k* vichy-g a1
- **morning**: bamb-a stb2.de•
- **night**: taosc iwa1•
- **sleep** agg.; during: sol-t-ae k*
- ○ **Cervical** region: aids nl2• antip vh1 *Carb-an* k* choc srj3•
- **Dorsal** region: apis b7a.de ran-s b7a.de
  - ○ **Scapulae**: *Mez*
- **Lumbar** region: alum-sil k2
  - **exertion** agg.: alum-sil k2*
- **Sacral** region: mez ptk1

PROLAPSUS:
- ○ **Intervertebral** disk *(↗EXTREMITIES - Pain - Lower limbs - sciatic)* ambr mtf11 macro mtf11 med mtf11 prot mtf11 vario mtf11
  - **accompanied** by | **sexual** desire; diminished: ambr mtf11

PULLING agg.: dios ptk1

PULSATING: agar aloe ars asc-t k* **Bar-c** k* bell k* berb calc-ar calc-p cann-i cann-s carbn-s chin cimic cur daph dig br1 *Eup-per Eup-pur* ferr ferr-ar glon iod k* *Kali-c* lac-c *Lach* lyc k* **Nat-m** k* *Nit-ac Phos* k* puls pyrog pd ran-r c2 sep k* *Sil* k* sumb *Thuj* k*
- **alternating** with:
  - ○ **Back** | **pains** in: *Kali-c*
- **cough** agg.; during: *Nit-ac*
- **emotional** excitement, after: bar-c k*
- **express** an idea, when wishing to: raph k*
- **motion**:
  - **agg.**: phos
  - **amel.**: bar-c
- **sitting** agg.: calc-p cur thuj
- **stool** agg.; after: alum caps
- ○ **Cervical** region: aeth a1 **Apis** k* *Bell* ptk1 *Calc-p* chel con cur daph *Eup-per* ferr glon lyss manc nat-m *Nat-s Nit-ac* op k* *Phos* pyrog ptk1 raph rauw tpw8 *Sarr* br1 spig ptk1 staph sulph sumb **Verat-v** k*
  - **holding** head backward amel.: lyss manc
  - **lying** down agg.: plb
  - **menses** | **before** | **agg.**: *Nit-ac* k*
    - **during** | **agg.**: *Nit-ac* k* **Verat-v** k*
  - **motion** agg.: *Ferr*
  - **raising** head from stooping: kali-n h2*
  - **sitting** agg.: *Calc-p*
  - **writing** agg.: manc
  - ▽ **extending** to:
    - **Forehead**:
      - **moving** or stooping; on: ter
      - **And** occiput: chel
    - **Lumbar** region: cur
    - **Shoulder**: **Apis** con
  - ○ **Blood** vessels: bell tl1 pyrog tl1 spig tl1

Pulsating – Cervical region: ...
  - **Nape** of neck: **Bell** bg2 camph b7a.de cann-xyz bg2 con b4.de* ferr-p bg2 **Glon** bg2 kali-n bg2 laur bg2 manc bg2 nat-m bg2 op bg2 plb bg2 sulph bg2
  - **Vertebrae**: kali-n h2
- **Coccyx**: agar ign b7.de* ol-an bg2 par k*
- **Dorsal** region: ars bg2 **Bar-c** b4a.de* calc-p k* carbn-s chin b7.de* cur kali-c bg2 lyc b4.de* mez bg2 nat-m bg2 phos k* puls b7.de* ruta b7.de* sil b4.de* thuj b4.de*
  - ○ **Scapulae**: bar-c k* calc-p k* kali-bi bg2 kali-c k* kali-i bg2 merc k* mez bg2 nat-m bg2 ph-ac k* phos k* plan bg2 samb b7.de* sulph bg2 ter bg2 zinc k*
    - **left**: cench k2 mag-m ptk1 zinc
    - **rising** from stooping agg.: kali-n
    - **Between**: androc srj1• *Bar-c* k* hura kali-i k* merc-i-f *Phos* plan k* sulph ptk1 sumb k* ter k*
    - **Under** | **right**: cench k2 merc-i-f
  - **Spine**: dulc *Lach* **Phos**
- **Lumbar** region: alum bg2 am-c k* am-m bg2 ars bg2 **Bar-c** k* bar-s k2 *Bry* k* cann-s h1 *Caust* k* chel bg2 cimic colch k* *Coloc* k* graph k* hura ign b7.de* kali-c k* **Lac-c** k* lach k* med bg1 *Nat-m* k* *Nit-ac* k* nux-v b7.de* ruta k* **Sep** k* **Sil** k* sulph k* sumb k* thuj vib
  - **left**: cimic bg2
  - **evening** | **lying** down agg.; after: nat-m
  - **night**: ars k*
  - **alternating** with | **pain** in back: kali-c
  - **chill**; during: nux-v
  - **fever**: hura
  - **inspiration** agg.; deep: ben
  - **menses**; before: *Nit-ac*
  - **motion** | **amel.**: am-c bar-c
  - **pressure** | **amel.**: ruta h1
  - **sitting** agg.: colch k*
  - **stool** agg.; after: alum k*
  - ○ **Hips**; above: *Coloc*
- **Sacral** region: arge-pl rwt5• *Bar-c* berb caust graph hura bg1 ign kali-c lach **Nat-m** k* nit-ac nux-v ol-an sabin sars sep *Sil* tab
  - **evening**: tab
- **Spine**: agar arg-n ptk1 bar-c carbn-s cur **Lach** k* thuj
  - ○ **Vertebrae**: mez bg2 thuj bg2
- **Vertebrae**: sol-t-ae c2

PURRING: | **Dorsal** region: sulph bg2

QUIVERING:
- ○ **Cervical** region; in *Agn Ang*
- **Dorsal** region: ars bg2 asaf b7.de spig b7.de
  - ○ **Scapulae**: merc b4.de* sil b4.de* tarax bg2
    - **left**: kali-c bg2

RAISING of a part:
- **arms** agg.: anac b4a.de ang bg2 con b4.de* ferr b7.de* graph b4a.de* nat-m ptk1 rhus-t ptk1 sanic bg2*
- **thighs** agg. | **Lumbar** region: aur ptk1

RAWNESS (See Excoriation)

REDNESS (See Discoloration - red)

RELAXED sensation: | **Dorsal** region: *Ars* b4.de* tab bg2

REST:
- **agg.**: agar b4a.de **Alum** b4a.de am-c b4.de* am-m b7.de* bry b7a.de calc b4.de* cina b7.de* cocc b7.de* coloc b4.de* con b4.de* *Dulc* b4a.de euph b4.de* guaj b4a.de hep b4.de* kali-c b4.de* kali-n b4a.de kreos b7a.de m-ambo b7.de* m-aust b7.de* mang b4a.de *Meny* b7.de* nux-m b7.de* petr b4.de* *Puls* b7.de* rhod b4.de* *Rhus-t* b7.de* *Samb* b7.de* *Sel* b7a.de sep b4.de* sil b4.de* spig b7.de* staph b7.de* stront-c b4.de*
- **amel.**: am b7.de* bry b7.de* guaj b4.de* kali-c b4.de* nux-v b7.de* thuj b4.de*

RESTLESSNESS: carb-an h2 petr-ra shn4• thuj bg1
- ○ **Cervical** region: thuj h1
- **Dorsal** region: carb-an b4.de*
- **Lumbar** region: *Bar-c* k* *Calc-f* k* cedr chinin-s

Back

- **Lumbar** region: ...
  - **flatus**; passing | **amel.**: *Bar-c* k*

RIDING IN A CARRIAGE agg.: calc b4.de* calc-f ptk1 fl-ac bg2 kali-c b4.de* nux-m b7.de* petr b4.de* sil b4.de*
○ - **Coccyx**: nux-m ptk1
- **Sacrum**: nux-m ptk1

RISING:
- **after**:
  - **agg.**: carb-v bg2 ign b7.de* petr bg2 staph bg2
  - **amel.**: ang b7.de* ant-t b7.de* arg-met b7.de* chin b7.de* nux-v b7.de* puls b7.de* staph b7.de*
- **bed**; from | **agg.**: ant-t b7.de* bov b4.de* calad b7.de* calc b4a.de hep b4.de* ign b7.de* meny b7.de* nat-m b4.de* **Phos** b4a.de ran-b b7.de* sil b4.de* *Sul-ac* b4a.de thuj b4.de* valer b7.de*
- **sensation** as of something rising:
○ • **Dorsal** region | **Scapulae**: plb bg2
- **sitting**; from:
  - **agg.**: aesc bg2 agar bg2 aloe bg2 ant-c b7a.de *Arg-n* bg2 *Bar-c* b4a.de bell b4.de* *Calc* b4a.de calc-p bg2 canth b7.de* *Caust* b4.de* ferr b7.de* kali-bi bg2 lach b7.de* led b7.de* m-aust b7.de petr b4.de* phos b4.de* puls b7.de* sil b4a.de staph b7.de* *Sulph* b4.de* verat b7.de*
    ⋮ **Coccyx**: euph ptk1 *Lach* ptk1 *Sil* ptk1 sulph ptk1
  - **amel.** | **Coccyx**: kreos ptk1
- **stooping**; from:
  - **agg.**: am-m b7a.de* anac b4a.de asar b7.de* bell b4.de* *Bry* bg2 *Caust* b4a.de kali-bi bg2 laur b7.de* lyc bg2 nat-m b4.de* ph-ac b4.de* phos b4.de* puls b7.de* rhus-t b7.de* sars bg2 verat b7.de*
  - **amel.**: am-c b4.de* bov b4.de* chel b7.de* puls b7.de*

RUBBING: | **amel.**: alum b4.de* anac b4.de* kali-c bg2 mang b4.de* phos b4.de* plb b7.de* stann b4.de* thuj b4.de*

RUMBLING: hep h1*
○ - **Dorsal** region | **Scapulae**: rhus-t b7.de* tarax b7.de*

RUNNING (See Streaming)

SAGGING (See Curvature)

SCLEROSIS: | **Spinal** cord: arg-n br1 plb br1*

SCOLIOSIS (See Curvature)

SENSITIVE: *Tell* br1
- **draft**; to: ephe-si hsj1•
- **painful**:
○ • **Vertebrae**: | **Eminences**: phos bg2
- **pressure**; to: zinc mtf33
○ - **Cervical** region: cimic ptk
  - **pressure**; to | **slight**: lach mtf33
  - **touch** agg.: agar k2
○ • **Nape** of neck: nux-v b7.de*
- **Dorsal** region: **Agar** bg2 ang bg2 chin bg2 cimic bg2* mag-p bg2 nat-c b4.de* *Phos* bg2 squil bg2 tell bg2
  - **accompanied** by | **Kidneys**; inflammation of (See KIDNEYS - Inflammation - accompanied - back - sensitiveness - dorsal)
  - **touch** agg.: agar k2
○ • **Scapulae**: sulph bg2
  - **Spine**: stry-p bro1 tell bro1
- **Dorsolumbar** region | **touch** agg.: choc srj3•
- **Lumbar** region: agar bg2 cimic bg2 kali-c bg2 lil-t bg2 nat-m bg2 plb b7.de* zinc bg2
  - **hot** sponge; to: *Agar*
○ • **Skin**: *(↗Hyperesthesia)* mag-m h2 squil b7.de*
  ⋮ **left** side | **touch**; to: zinc h2
- **Sacral** region: galeoc-c-h gms1• lob bg2*
○ • **Spine**: lob bro1
- **Spine**: abrot bro1 acon bro1 agar bg2* apis bro1 arg-n bro1 *Ars* bro1 *Bell* bro1* bry bro1 *Chin* ptk1 *Chinin-ar* bro1 *Chinin-s* br1* cimic k2* *Cocc* bro1 crot-h bro1 cupr bg2 graph ptk1 *Hep* bro1 *Hyper* bro1* *Ign* bro1* kali-p bg2* *Lac-c* bro1

Sensitive – Spine: ...
Lach bro1* lob bro1 lyss ptk1 med bro1* menis bro1 nat-c k2 *Nat-m* bro1* nat-p ptk1 nux-v bg2* *Ox-ac* bro1 ph-ac bro1 *Phos* bro1* phys bro1* podo bro1 ran-b bro1 rhus-t bro1 ruta ptk1 sec bro1 senec-j bro1 sil bro1* stram ptk1 *Stry-p* bro1 sulph bro1 tarent bro1* tell bro1* *Ther* bro1* visc bro1 *Zinc* bro1*
  - **chill**; during: chinin-s bro1
  - **jar**; to: ther bro1
  - **noise**; to: ther bro1
  - **painful**: phys bg2
  - **pressure**; to: lac-c mtf33
    ⋮ **slight**: stram mtf33
  - **sitting** sideways | **amel.**: chinin-s bro1 ther bro1 zinc bro1
  - **touch**; to: **Chinin-s** mrr1 lac-c mtf33 tarent mtf33 zinc ptk2
- **Vertebrae**: chinin-s bg2 fl-ac bg2 hyper bg2 kreos bg2 *Phys* br1 zinc bg2
○ • **Between**: agar mp1• chinin-s bro1 nat-m bro1 ther br1*

SEXUAL excesses agg.: coloc bg2 kali-c bg2 nat-m bg2 ph-ac bg2 sil bg2 sulph bg2
○ - **Spine**: calc ptk1 croc ptk1 *Nux-v* ptk1 *Ph-ac* ptk1 *Sel* ptk1

SHIVERING: acon agar all-c anac androc bnm2• apis ars bar-act bell bol-la mtf11 borx brucel sa3• bry calc caps carb-v carl castm cham clem cocc coff *Colch* crot-t dig eup-per gamb gels guaj ign kali-bi kali-s fd4.de lach limest-b es1• lyc mag-c mag-m h2 mang k* meny *Mez* nat-m nicc osm phos positr nl2• puls rhus-t rumx ruta sabad sang sec seneg sep spong *Stann* staph stram stront-c *Sulph* thuj verat
- **morning**: apis cham meny staph
  - **bed** agg.; in: kali-c
  - **horrible** stories; as from: meny h1
  - **rising** agg.; after: staph
- **forenoon**: graph mag-c
- **afternoon**: carb-an h2 guaj h2 mag-c
- **evening**: apis bry canth caps cham cocc kali-s fd4.de mag-m mag-s nat-m h2 sang hr1 verat
  - **bed** agg.; in: sang
- **night**: carb-v kali-s fd4.de
  - **bed** agg.; in: raph
- **alternating** with | **heat** (See Heat - alternating - shivering)
- **fever**; during: *Coff* b7a.de
- **lying** down agg.: nat-c
- **stool** agg.; during: coloc trom
- **warm** | **room** | **agg.**: petr
  - **stove** | **amel.**: nicc
▽ - **extending** to:
○ • **Arms**: brucel sa3•
  - **Down** the back: agar all-c bry calc-caust chel *Colch* kali-s fd4.de mag-c rhus-v
  - **Fingers**: brucel sa3•
  - **Thighs**: brucel sa3•
  - **Up** the back: canth carb-an h2 dig puls rhus-v verb c1
○ - **Cervical** region: con h2
○ • **Nape** of neck: am-c b4a.de* bell bg2 caust b4.de* cham b7.de* con bg2 croc b7.de* *Graph* b4a.de* staph b7.de* valer b7.de*
- **Dorsal** region | **Scapulae**: *Bell* bg2 bry b7.de* *Nit-ac* bg2 ran-b b7.de* **Stront-c** bg2
- **Lumbar** region: asaf b7a.de* coff coff-t jatr-c lyc *Nit-ac* b4a.de* petr rhod b4a.de* stront-c bg2 visc c1
  - **stool** agg.; after: *Puls*
  - **warm** room agg.: petr
- **Spine**:
  - **accompanied** by | **hematuria**: nit-ac ptk1

SHOCKS:
- **left** side: plat h2
- **electric**-like: *(↗Pain - electric)*
○ • **Sacrum**; in: ulm-c jsj8•
  - **Spine**; along: *(↗Pain - electric)* agar ang calc-p vh cic corn
    ⋮ **extending** to | **Vertex**: lyc h2
○ - **Cervical** region: corn hydrog srj2• *Manc*

- **Cervical** region: ...
  - • **waking**; on: *Manc*
- **Dorsal** region: bell cic

○ • **Scapulae**, between: bell
  - ⁝ **left**: anac$_{h2}$
- **Flank** (See ABDOMEN - Shocks - sides - flank)
- **Lumbar** region: plat$_{h2}$
- **Sacrum**: cupr

SHORTENED (See Tension)

SHUDDERING (See Shivering)

SITTING:
- **after**: ambr$_{b7a.de}$ *Caust*$_{b4a.de}$ lach$_{b7.de*}$ led$_{b7.de*}$ *Phos*$_{b4a.de}$ puls$_{b7.de*}$ rhus-t$_{b7.de*}$
- **agg.**: agar$_{b4a.de*}$ aloe$_{bg2}$ am-c$_{b4.de*}$ am-m$_{b7.de*}$ ambr$_{b7.de*}$ ang$_{b7.de*}$ ant-c$_{b7.de*}$ ant-t$_{b7.de*}$ arg-met$_{b7.de*}$ arg-n$_{ptk1}$ asaf$_{b7.de*}$ asar$_{b7.de*}$ aur$_{b4.de*}$ bar-c$_{b4.de*}$ bell$_{b4.de*}$ berb$_{bg2}$ bism$_{b7.de*}$ borx$_{b4a.de}$ bry$_{b7.de*}$ calc$_{ptk1}$ canth$_{b7.de*}$ carb-v$_{b4.de*}$ *Caust*$_{b4.de*}$ chel$_{b7.de*}$ *Chin*$_{b7.de*}$ cob$_{bg2*}$ cocc$_{b7.de*}$ coff$_{b7.de*}$ cycl$_{b7.de*}$ dros$_{b7.de*}$ dulc$_{b4.de*}$ euph$_{b4.de*}$ euphr$_{b7.de*}$ ferr$_{b7.de*}$ fl-ac$_{bg2}$ graph$_{bg2}$ hep$_{b4.de*}$ *Kali-bi*$_{bg2}$ kali-c$_{b4.de*}$ kali-n$_{b4.de*}$ kreos$_{b7a.de}$ lyc$_{b4.de*}$ m-ambo$_{b7.de}$ m-arct$_{b7.de}$ mag-c$_{bg2}$ mang$_{b4.de*}$ *Meny*$_{b7.de*}$ merc$_{b4.de*}$ mur-ac$_{b4.de*}$ nat-c$_{b4.de*}$ nat-m$_{b4.de*}$ nux-v$_{b7.de*}$ olnd$_{b7.de*}$ par$_{b7.de*}$ *Petr*$_{b4.de*}$ ph-ac$_{b4.de*}$ phos$_{b4.de*}$ plat$_{b4.de*}$ *Puls*$_{b7.de*}$ rhod$_{b4.de*}$ *Rhus-t*$_{b7.de*}$ *Ruta*$_{b7.de*}$ sabad$_{b7.de*}$ samb$_{b7.de*}$ sanic$_{bg2}$ *Sel*$_{b7a.de}$ seneg$_{b4.de*}$ sep$_{b4.de*}$ sil$_{b4a.de}$ spong$_{b7.de*}$ stront-c$_{b4.de*}$ sul-ac$_{b4.de*}$ sulph$_{b4.de*}$ thuj$_{b4.de*}$ *Valer*$_{bg2*}$ *Zinc*$_{b4.de*}$

○ • **Coccyx**: am-m$_{ptk1}$ apis$_{ptk1}$ kali-bi$_{ptk1}$ par$_{ptk1}$ petr$_{ptk1}$
  - • **Lumbar** region: agar$_{ptk1}$ arg-met$_{ptk1}$ berb$_{ptk1}$ cob$_{ptk1}$ rhus-t$_{ptk1}$ valer$_{ptk1}$ zinc-ar$_{ptk1}$
  - • **Sacrum**: rhod$_{ptk1}$
  - • **Spine**: ph-ac$_{ptk1}$ ruta$_{ptk1}$ zinc$_{ptk1}$
- **amel.**: aesc$_{bg2}$ kali-bi$_{bg2}$ meny$_{b7.de*}$ merc$_{b4.de*}$ ph-ac$_{b4.de*}$ staph$_{b7.de*}$ sulph$_{b4.de*}$ thuj$_{b4.de*}$ verat$_{b7.de*}$

○ • **Spine**: mur-ac$_{ptk1}$
- **bent** forward:
  - • **agg.**: bov$_{b4.de*}$ chel$_{b7.de*}$ dulc$_{b4.de*}$ verb$_{b7.de*}$
    - ⁝ **Lumbar** region: kali-i$_{ptk1}$
  - • **amel.**: anac$_{b4a.de}$
    - ⁝ **Lumbar** region: ran-b$_{ptk1}$
- **cold** surface agg.; on a: dulc$_{bg2}$
- **cushion**; on a | **amel.**: xanth$_{bg2}$
- **erect**:
  - • **agg.**: *Alum*$_{b4a.de}$ des-ac$_{rbp6}$ kali-c$_{ptk1}$ lyc$_{b4.de*}$ spong$_{b7.de*}$ sulph$_{ptk1}$
    - ⁝ **Sacrum**: lyc$_{ptk1}$
  - • **amel.**: rhus-t$_{b7.de*}$
    - ⁝ **Cervical** region: rad-br$_{ptk1}$

SITTING DOWN agg.: valer$_{b7.de*}$ zinc$_{ptk1}$

○ - **Lumbar** region: zinc$_{ptk1}$

SITTING UP in bed: | **amel.**: lob$_{bg2}$

SLEEP:
- **after** | **agg.**: am-m$_{b7.de*}$ chin$_{b7.de*}$ lach$_{b7.de*}$
- **during**:
  - • **agg.**:
    - ⁝ **Coccyx**: am-m$_{ptk1}$
    - ⁝ **Lumbar** region: am-m$_{ptk1}$
- **falling** asleep agg.: mag-m$_{bg2}$

SNEEZING:
- **agg.**: ars$_{b4.de*}$ *Con*$_{b4a.de}$ mag-c$_{b4.de*}$ nux-v$_{b7.de*}$ *Phos*$_{b4a.de}$

○ • **Cervical** region: am-m$_{ptk1}$ arn$_{ptk1}$
  - • **Lumbar** region: con$_{ptk1}$ sulph$_{ptk1}$
- **amel.**: mag-m$_{bg2}$

○ • **Cervical** region: calc$_{ptk1}$

SOFTENING of cord: alum$_{bro1}$ alum-sil$_{bro1}$ arg-n$_{bro1}$ aur$_{bro1}$ *Aur-m*$_{bro1}$ bar-m$_{bro1}$ carbn-s$_{bro1}$ crot-h$_{k*}$ **Kali-p**$_{k*}$ *Lach*$_{b7a.de}$ merc naja$_{bro1}$ ox-ac$_{bro1}$ *Phos*$_{k*}$ phys$_{bro1}$ pic-ac$_{hr1*}$ plb$_{bro1}$ *Plb-i*$_{bro1}$ sec$_{hr1}$ *Sulph* zinc$_{bro1}$

SOLID; as if: | **Sacrum**: sep$_{ptk1}$

SPASMODIC drawing: *(↗Cramp; Opisthotonos; Pain - cramping; Spasmodic; Tension - cervical)*
- **sleep**; during: alum$_{k2}$

○ - **Body**; whole: ip$_{hr1*}$
- **Cervical** region: *(↗HEAD - Bending - head - backward; HEAD - Bending - Head - backward - must)* *Acon* alum ant-c *Apis* **Bell** calc camph cann-i cedr *Cham* chin **Cic** **Cimic**$_{k*}$ *Cina* *Cupr* eup-per *Gels* *Glon* *Hell* *Hep* hyos hyper *Ign* *Ip* kreos *Lyc* *Mez* mur-ac *Nat-m* *Nat-s* *Nux-v* **Op**$_{k*}$ *Phel* phyt$_{k2}$ pin-con$_{oss2•}$ plb$_{k2}$ samb stram *Tab* verat-v *Zinc*
  - • **afternoon**: mag-c$_{h2}$
  - • **evening**: ant-c
  - • **lying** agg.: ant-c
  - • **sleep**; during: alum
  - • **stool** agg.; during: phos$_{k2}$

○ • **Tendons** feel too short: hydrog$_{srj2•}$
- **Dorsal** region:
  - • **sensation** between shoulders while walking: calad
    - ⁝ **morning**: apis cham meny staph
- **Lumbar** region: bell$_{b4.de*}$ *Mag-m*$_{b4a.de}$ sil$_{b4.de*}$ sul-ac$_{b4.de*}$

SPASMS: *(↗Opisthotonos)* acon arge-pl$_{rwt5•}$ *Ars* *Calc-p* cic$_{k2}$ cimic$_{ptk1}$ *Crot-c* germ-met$_{srj5•}$ hydr-ac$_{ptk1}$ *Ign*$_{mrr3*}$ kali-c$_{h2}$ *Lach* *Mygal* *Nat-m* *Nat-s* *Nux-v* oena *Phys* *Rhus-t*$_{ptk1}$ ribo$_{rly4•}$ sec$_{ptk1}$ stram *Stry*$_{mrr1}$ syph tab
- **grief**; after: *Ign*$_{mrr1}$
- **hysteria**; with (See MIND - Hysteria - spasms - back)
- **nursing** the child agg.; when: arn *Cham* *Puls*
- **touch** agg.: acon

○ - **Cervical** region: arn$_{gsd1}$ cann-i$_{a1*}$ *Cic*$_{gsd1*}$ *Cimic*$_{mrr1}$ ign$_{gy3*}$ stram$_{a1}$ *Stry*$_{mrr1}$
  - • **hysteria**; with (See MIND - Hysteria - spasms - cervical)

○ • **Nape** of neck: ant-c$_{b7.de*}$ asar$_{b7a.de}$ nat-m$_{bg2}$ nux-v$_{bg2}$ spong$_{b7a.de}$
- **Dorsal** region: agar$_{bg2}$ *Ang*$_{b7.de*}$ arn$_{bg2}$ *Bell*$_{b4.de*}$ bry$_{bg2}$ caust$_{bg2}$ chel$_{bg2}$ *Cocc*$_{bg2}$ colch$_{bg2}$ con$_{b4a.de*}$ dros$_{bg2}$ *Euph*$_{b4.de*}$ ferr$_{b7.de*}$ iod$_{b4.de*}$ ip$_{bg2}$ lach$_{b7a.de*}$ laur$_{b7.de*}$ *Lyc*$_{b4.de*}$ mag-m$_{bg2}$ nat-c$_{b4a.de}$ nit-ac$_{bg2}$ nux-v$_{bg2}$ op$_{bg2}$ petr$_{bg2}$ phos$_{bg2}$ rhus-t$_{bg2}$ *Sep*$_{bg2}$ *Sil*$_{b4a.de}$ spong$_{bg2}$ thuj$_{bg2}$ viol-t$_{bg2}$

○ • **Scapulae**: ant-c$_{b7.de*}$ bry$_{b7.de*}$ chel$_{b7.de*}$ m-ambo$_{b7.de}$
- **Spinal** cord: pic-ac$_{ptk1}$
- **Spine**; along: *Cimic*$_{mrr1}$

SPINA BIFIDA: arn$_{k*}$ ars$_{k*}$ asaf$_{k*}$ bac$_{c2}$ bar-c$_{k*}$ bell$_{hr1}$ bry$_{bg2*}$ *Calc*$_{k*}$ calc-p$_{k*}$ *Calc-s* calen$_{hr1}$ cann-s$_{hr1}$ carb-v$_{k*}$ dulc$_{k*}$ eup-per$_{hr1}$ graph$_{k*}$ hep$_{k*}$ lach$_{k*}$ lyc$_{k*}$ merc$_{k*}$ mez$_{k*}$ nit-ac$_{k*}$ phos$_{k*}$ *Psor*$_{k*}$ ruta **Sil**$_{k*}$ staph$_{k*}$ sulph$_{k*}$ tub$_{bg2*}$

SPINAL IRRITATION (See Pain - spine - sore)

SPINAL MENINGITIS (See Inflammation - membranes)

SPONDYLITIS (See Inflammation - vertebrae)

SPONDYLOSIS (See Curvature)

SPOTS: calc cist lach *Lyc* sep spong sulph sumb zinc
- **brown** (See Discoloration - brown - spots)
- **red**: ant-c bell carb-v cist cocc lach sep stann vib vip

○ - **Cervical** region: *Carb-v* colch$_{rsj2•}$ hydroph$_{rsj6•}$ hyos petr
  - • **itching**: tell$_{rsj10•}$
  - • **red**: *Carb-v* cortiso$_{tpw7}$ luf-op$_{rsj5•}$ *Lyc* sep stann
    - ⁝ **left**: cortiso$_{tpw7}$
  - • **yellow**: iod
- **Dorsal** region | **Scapulae**; on: calc cist lach$_{k*}$ sumb
- **Lumbar** region: sep$_{bg2}$

SQUATTING: | **amel.**: *Acon*$_{b7a.de}$

STANDING:
- **agg.**: agar$_{b4.de*}$ am-c$_{b4.de*}$ arg-met$_{b7.de*}$ asar$_{b7.de*}$ bell$_{bg2}$ bry$_{b7.de*}$ caps$_{b7.de*}$ carb-an$_{bg2}$ caust$_{bg2}$ chin$_{b7.de*}$ cocc$_{b7.de*}$ coff$_{b7.de*}$ con$_{b4.de*}$ ferr$_{bg2}$ ferr-p$_{bg2}$ hep$_{b4.de*}$ ign$_{bg2}$ kali-c$_{bg2}$ led$_{b7.de*}$ lyc$_{bg2}$ m-ambo$_{b7.de}$ m-arct$_{b7.de}$ mag-s$_{bg2}$ merc$_{b4.de*}$ mur-ac$_{b4.de*}$ nit-ac$_{b4.de*}$ olnd$_{b7.de*}$

- **agg.**: ...
  Petr b4.de* ph-ac b4.de* phos bg2 podo bg2 puls b7.de* rhus-t b7.de* ruta bg2 samb b7.de* sep bg2 spig bg2 spong b7.de* stann b4.de* stry bg2 sul-ac b4.de* sulph bg2 tarax b7.de* thuj b4.de* *Valer* bg2 verat b7.de* zinc bg2
  - ○ • **Lumbar** region: con ptk1 psor ptk1 *Valer* ptk1 zinc ptk1 zinc-ar ptk1
  - • **Spine**: nit-ac ptk1 *Ph-ac* ptk1 zinc ptk1
- **amel.**: arg-n bg2* bell b4.de* berb bg2 calc b4.de* caust ptk1 dios bg2 kreos bg2 mill bg2 mur-ac b4.de* petr bg2 ruta b7.de* sulph ptk1 thuj b4.de*
  - ○ • **Cervical** region: rad-br ptk1
  - • **Coccyx**: arg-n ptk1 tarent ptk1
  - • **Spine**: mur-ac ptk1
- **bent** | **amel.**: *Nux-v* b7a.de
- **erect**:
  - • **agg.**: ign b7.de*
    - ⁝ **Sacrum**: petr ptk1

STENOSIS (See Constriction)

STEPPING:
- **agg.**: seneg bg2 spong b7.de*
- **hard** | **agg.**: seneg b4.de

STIFFNESS: abies-c oss4• acon k* aesc k* *Agar* k* agath-a nl2• allox sp1 *Alum* k* alum-p k2 alum-sil k2 *Am-m* *Anac* k* anan *Ang* *Apis* apoc k2 aran-ix sp1 arg-n *Ars* aur aur-m k* aur-s k2 *Bamb-a* stb2.de• *Bapt* k* *Bar-c* bar-s k2 *Bell* *Benz-ac* **Berb** k* *Bit-ar* wht1• bol-la *Bry* buth-a sp1 *Calc* calc-p k2 *Calc-s* k* calc-sil k2 caps h1 *Carb-an* *Carb-v* k* carbn-s cardios-h rly4• *Carl* k* caul k2 **Caust** k* cedr *Chel* k* *Cic* k* **Cimic** k* cocc k* colch rsj2• con cop k* corian-s knl6• cupr cupr-ar k* cystein-l rly4• dig k* dulc k2* falco-pe nl2• ferr a1 fum rly1*• galeoc-c-h gms1• gins k* *Guaj* haliae-lc srj5• helodr-cal knl2• *Helon* hippoc-k szs2 hydr *Ign* ind iris jac-c jac-g *Kali-ar* kali-bi *Kali-c* k* *Kali-p* *Kali-s* *Lach* **Led** k* limest-b es1• loxo-recl knl4• *Lyc* k* *Manc* med mucs-nas rly4• nad rly4• nat-ar nat-m k* nat-ox rly4• nat-pyru rly4• nat-s nicotam rly4• *Nit-ac* k* **Nux-v** k* ol-an olib-sac wmh1 olnd k* op k* *Petr* k* petr-ra shn4• *Phos* *Phyt* k* polyp-p a1 positr nl2• *Prun* k* *Puls* k* rauw tpw8* rheum rhod k2 rhus-g tmo3• **Rhus-t** k* rhus-v k* ribo rly4• ros-d wla1 ruta fd4.de sanic ptk1 sarcol-ac sp1 **Sep** k* **Sil** k* spong fd4.de *Staph* *Stram* k* *Stry* k* suis-em rly4• suis-hep rly4• sul-ac k* **Sulph** k* suprar rly4• syc fmm1• symph fd3.de• syph k2 tab tetox pin2• *Thuj* k* tritic-vg fd5.de tub vanil fd5.de verat vero-o rly4*• visc sp1 x-ray sp1 zinc zinc-p k2 zing [bell-p-sp dcm1 spect dfg1]
- **one** side: guaj ptk1
- **left** side: galeoc-c-h gms1•
- **morning**: ang calc h2 carb-v k* dulc fd4.de kali-s fd4.de nat-sil fd3.de• ox-ac k* petr-ra shn4• *Phyt* k* ruta fd4.de *Sep* stry k* sul-ac k* tritic-vg fd5.de *Zinc*
  - • **bed** agg.; in | **rising** amel.: anac
  - • **rising** agg.: bar-c calc-s *Carb-v* k* dulc fd4.de ferr-i ign mag-c h2 nat-sil fd3.de• staph sul-ac
  - • **waking**; on: bamb-a stb2.de• calc dulc fd4.de hydrog srj2• *Lach* *Led* melal-alt gya4 *Sep* ven-m rsj12•
- **noon**: dulc fd4.de valer
- **evening**: bar-c dios lyc petr symph fd3.de• vanil fd5.de
- **night**: *Lyc*
- **aerobic** | **not** amel.: fum rly1•
- **air**; from a draft of: **Rhus-t**
- **alternating** with | **Head**; heat in (See HEAD - Heat - alternating - back)
- **bed** agg.; in: allox sp1*
- **bending** | **backward** | **impossible**: stram ptk1
  - • **forward** | **agg.**: petr-ra shn4•
- **chill**; during: *Lyc* *Nat-s* *Tub*
- **cold** agg.; becoming: bamb-a stb2.de• calc-sil k2
- **cold**; taking a:
  - • **after**: dulc k2
  - • **as** from: sulph h2
- **cramping**: bamb-a stb2.de• *Nit-ac* k*
- **exertion** agg.; after: calc-sil k2 lyc k*
- **lying** | **abdomen**; on | **agg.**: ulm-c jsj8•
  - • **agg.**: puls ulm-c jsj8•
- **menses**; before: mosch ptk1 ozone sde2•
- **motion**:
  - • **agg.**: acon *Aesc* k* *Calc* *Cupr-ar* k* *Guaj* led h1

Stiffness – motion: ...
  - • **amel.**: allox sp1 bamb-a stb2.de• dulc k2 kali-p k2 rauw tpw8* **Rhus-t** sul-ac k*
  - • **beginning** of | **agg.**: *Aesc* anac con cupr-s ham fd3.de• ind irid-met srj5• *Lyc* med k2 rauw tpw8* **Rhus-t** sel rsj9• ulm-c jsj8•
  - ○ • **Shoulders**; of: cocc k* guaj
- **painful**: agath-a nl2• *Am-m* ars h2 *Bamb-a* stb2.de• *Calc* **Caust** k* dulc fd4.de falco-pe nl2• *Helon* kali-s fd4.de lat-m bnm6• *Manc* *Nit-ac* ozone sde2• podo fd3.de• *Puls* **Rhus-t** k* sanic ptk1 spong fd4.de vero-o rly4•
  - • **board**; as from a: ozone sde2•
- **perspiration**; after: calc-sil k2*
- **rest** agg.: rauw sp1
- **rising**:
  - • **agg.**: *Agar* k* *Bry* k* cham med k2 nat-sil fd3.de• spong fd4.de
  - • **sitting**; from | **agg.**: *Agar* am-m k* **Ambr** anac ang h1 *Bar-c* **Bell** berb bry carl **Caust** *Hydr* ind *Led* *Lyc* nat-sil fd3.de• *Petr* *Puls* **Rhus-t** *Sil* *Sulph*
  - • **stooping**; from | **agg.**: bamb-a stb2.de•
- **sitting**:
  - • **after**: am-m **Ambr** *Bar-c* *Bell* caust cham con cupr-ar k* dulc fd4.de ind kali-s fd4.de led petr-ra shn4• *Phos* **Rhus-t** k* *Sil* k* *Sulph* k*
  - • **agg.**: am-m a1
  - • **bent** forward | **amel.**: anac k*
- **standing**:
  - • **agg.**: stry k*
  - • **erect**:
    - ⁝ **agg.**: bry
    - ⁝ **impossible**: sil h2
- **stick**; like a: bamb-a stb2.de•
- **stool**:
  - • **after** | **agg.**: sep k*
  - • **agg.**: ferr ptk1
  - • **amel.**: asaf ptk1
- **stooping**:
  - • **after** | **agg.**: bov dulc fd4.de
  - • **agg.**: bamb-a stb2.de• *Berb* caps k* cic k* kali-c kali-s fd4.de spong fd4.de vanil fd5.de
  - • **impossible**: bamb-a stb2.de• borx ptk1 tritic-vg fd5.de
- **stooping**; as after prolonged: thuj h1
- **stretching**:
  - • **amel.**: allox sp1
  - • **not** amel.: fum rly1•
- **turning** in bed agg.: *Sulph* k*
- **walking**:
  - • **about** | **must** walk about for some time before he can straighten up: hydr spong fd4.de
  - • **agg.**: aur stry k*
  - • **amel.**: bry k* calc-s k* cop k* petr-ra shn4• **Rhus-t** sep *Sulph* k*
- **weather** agg., wet: *Phyt* **Rhus-t**
- **writing** agg.: laur k*
- ▽ **extending** to | **Upward**: ars ptk1
- ○ **Cervical** region: acon k* *Aesc* k* **Agar** k* agath-a nl2• allox tpw4* *Alum* k* alum-p k2 alum-sil k2 am-c k* *Am-m* k* **Anac** k* anan androc srj1• *Ang* *Ant-t* k* *Apis* apoc-a a1 **Arg-met** k* arge-pl rwt5• arizon-l nl2• *Ars* k* ars-s-f k2 arum-t k* asar aur k* *Aur-m-n* wbt2• bacls-7 fmm1• bad k* *Bamb-a* stb2.de• *Bapt* k* **Bar-c** k* bar-s k2 **Bell** k* berb k* *Bit-ar* wht1• brach k* *Brom* k* *Bry* k* buth-a sp1 calad **Calc** k* calc-caust c2* **Calc-f** mrr1 *Calc-p* k* calc-s k* calc-sil k2 camph cann-i *Canth* k* caps k* carb-ac k* carb-an k* *Carb-v* k* carbn-s caul **Caust** k* *Cedr* **Chel** k* *Chin* k* chinin-ar choc srj3• chr-o c2 **Cic** k* **Cimic** k* cinch a1 cinnb k2 *Cocc* colch k* *Coloc* com *Con* cor-r cupr sst3• cupr-act cupr-ar cycl k* cypra-eg sde6.de• cyt-l br1 dendr-pol sk4• des-ac rbp6 *Dig* k* *Dros* *Dulc* k* dys fmm1• elaps eup-pur k* **Euph** fago k* falco-ch sze4• falco-pe nl2• *Ferr* k* ferr-ar ferr-i ferr-p ferul a1 fic-m gya1 *Fl-ac* form k* galeoc-c-h gms1• *Gels* k* gent-c c2 get br1* *Glon* k* *Graph* k* *Guaj* ham fd3.de• **Hell** hell-f a1* helodr-cal knl2• *Hep* hippoc-k szs2 hura k* hyos k* hyper c2 **Ign** k* ina-i mlk9.de **Ind** k* irid-met srj5• itu c2 kali-ar k2 *Kali-bi* **Kali-c** k* *Kali-chl* *Kali-i* k* *Kali-n* k* kali-p *Kali-s* kali-sil k2 kalm k* *Lac-c* lac-cp sk4• lac-leo hm2• **Lach** k* **Lachn** k*

- **Cervical** region: ...
lat-m bnm6• laur k* *Led* limen-b-c hrn2* limest-b es1• loxo-recl knl4• **Lyc** k* *Lyss* **Mag-c** k* *Manc* *Mang* k* melal-alt gya4 meny *Merc* k* merc-i-f k* merc-i-r ptk1 *Mez* moni rfm1• morg-g fmm1• morg-p fmm1• morph k* mucs-nas rly4• mur-ac a1 myric nat-ar *Nat-c* k* *Nat-m* nat-ox rly4• nat-p nat-pyru rly4• *Nat-s* nat-sil fd3.de• nicotam rly4• **Nit-ac** k* **Nux-v** k* ol-an olib-sac wmh1 oxal-a rly4• pall k* pant-ac rly4• *Par* k* pert-vc vk9 *Petr* petr-ra shn4• ph-ac phasco-ci rbp2 *Phos* k* *Phys* k* *Phyt* k* pimp a1* plan a1* *Plat* plb k* plect a1* *Podo* *Positr* nl2• prot fmm1• *Psor* ptel c1 *Puls* *Pycnop-sa* mrz1 *Ran-b* ptk1* *Rat* *Rhod* k* rhodi br1* **Rhus-t** k* *Rhus-v* k* ribo rly4• ros-d wla1 ruta mrr1* sal-fr sle1• *Sang* sangin-n c2 sanguis-s hrn2• scroph-xyz c2 sec sel k* senec-j c1 *Sep* k* **Sil** k* sinus rly4• *Spig* k* *Spong* k* squil stann h2 *Staph* k* stict ptk1* stram k* *Stry* k* suis-hep rly4• sulfonam ks2 *Sulph* k* syc fmm1• symph fd3.de• *Syph* *Tab* k* taosc iwa1• *Tarent* k* tep k* tetox pin2• *Thuj* trif-p br1 tub ptk1 tung-met bdx1• vanil fd5.de vario al2 verat k* vichy-g a1* vinc c2 visc sp1 xan c1 *Zinc* zinc-p k2 zinc-val c2 zing k* [heroin sdj2 spect dfg1]
  - **one** side: coloc ptk1 guaj ptk1 stict ptk1
  - **right**: agar ptk1 bit-ar wht1• caust ptk1 *Chel* mrr1 des-ac rbp6 galla-q-r nl2• hydrog srj2• lac-lup hrn2• lachn hr1 nat-m ptk1 nicotam rly4• petr a1 phyt mrr1 plut-n srj7• pycnop-sa mrz1 spong fd4.de suis-hep rly4• [bell-p-sp dcm1]
  - **left**: agath-a nl2• bell ptk1 bit-ar wht1• carb-an bg1* chel ptk1 colch rsj2• coloc bg1* cupr sst3• des-ac rbp6 galeoc-c-h gms1• glon ptk1 guaj ptk1 kreos ptk1 lacer c1 lyc ptk1 nat-m bg1 nat-sil fd3.de• sanguis-s hrn2• spong fd4.de zinc h2
  - **morning**: alum h2 ang ars h2 asar bamb-a stb2.de• bell h1 bov k* *Brom* bufo *Calc* *Chel* dig digin a1 dulc fd4.de falco-pe nl2• ferr k* ham fd3.de• hell h1 *Kali-c* lyss manc *Rhod* ruta spig spong fd4.de *Sulph* verat a1 *Zinc* [arg-met stj1]
    - **rising**:
      - **agg.**: bov k* dulc fd4.de rhod
      - **amel.**: spig h1
    - **waking**; on: anac arg-met bamb-a stb2.de• *Calc* eupi k* falco-pe nl2• haliae-lc srj5• *Kali-c* manc *Phyt* k* plut-n srj7• pycnop-sa mrz1 *Rhod* sanguis-s hrn2•
  - **afternoon**: brom k* gaba sa3• nat-sil fd3.de• ptel k* spong fd4.de symph fd3.de• thuj
    - **waking**; on: bar-c
  - **evening**: acon am-m castm cimic k* meny nat-sil fd3.de• sel k* vanil fd5.de
    - **19** h: bamb-a stb2.de•
  - **night**: ars h2 *Dulc* gels kali-c **Phyt** k* senec-j c1
    - **3-4** h: spig h1
  - **accompanied** by:
    - **Head**:
      - **heaviness** in: bit-ar wht1•
      - **pain**: sil ptk1
    - **Shoulder**; stiffness in: bit-ar wht1•
    - **Spine**; complaints of: adon ptk1
    - **Teeth**:
      - **pain** (See TEETH - Pain - accompanied - neck - stiffness)
      - **sensitive**: bit-ar wht1•
  - **air** agg.; draft of: **Calc-p** k* *Caust* vh* *Cimic* ozone sde2• **Rhus-t**
  - **alternating** with | **Teeth**; pain in: mang h2
  - **bending** | **backward** | **agg.**: stram mtf33
    - **head**:
      - **forward** | **agg.**: kali-bi ptk1
  - **chill**; during: bell bg2 *Cic* b7.de* lyc bg2 merc bg2 sil bg2
  - **cold**; after taking a: bamb-a stb2.de• calc h2 *Dulc* k* *Guaj* *Nit-ac* **Rhus-t**
  - **coryza**; during: ars *Bell* dulc **Lach** k* lachn *Lyc* *Nux-v* *Rhus-t* sulph
  - **cough** agg.; during: ip mrr1
  - **dullness**; with (See MIND - Dullness - stiffness)
  - **eating**; after: *Nux-v*
  - **fever**; during: *Acon* b7a.de*
  - **headache**; during: (↗*HEAD - Pain - accompanied - neck - pain; HEAD - Pain - accompanied - neck - pain - nape; HEAD - Pain - accompanied - neck - stiffness - nape)* am-c ant-c arg-met bamb-a stb2.de• bar-c *Bell* *Calc* calc-ar kr1 caps carbn-s **Cimic** mrr1 crot-h cur cycl gels c1 *Glon* *Graph* *Ign* kali-c kali-n lac-c sne *Lach* mag-c merc-i-f mucs-nas rly4• mur-ac myric nat-c nat-m bg1 nept-m lsd2.fr ozone sde2• ph-ac phos bg1 sal-fr sle1• sang sep sil spig spong fd4.de tarent verat k* visc sp1 xan c1
    - **Forehead**; in: bamb-a stb2.de•
    - **Occiput**; in: graph spig vml
  - **intermittent**, during: *Cocc*
  - **ironing** agg.: bamb-a stb2.de•
  - **irritability**; from: *Rhus-t* mrr1
  - **lifting** agg.: **Calc** lyc **Rhus-t** sep h2
  - **lying** on back agg.: spig
  - **menses** | **before** | **agg.**: bamb-a stb2.de•
    - **during** | **agg.**: bamb-a stb2.de• *Calc*
  - **motion**:
    - **amel.**: allox tpw4 alum h2 caps h1 ph-ac h2 *Rhus-t* mrr1 [tax jsj7]
    - **slight** motion | **agg.**: phyt mrr1
    - **violent** motion | **amel.**: rat
  - **nut**; cracks like: bacls-7 fmm1•
  - **painful**: caps a1 chel mrr1 cimic ptk dulc fd4.de hell h1 nux-v b phos h2 sal-fr sle1• spong fd4.de
    - **motion**, only on: caps a1
  - **perspiration**; during: *Acon* bg2 bell bg2 *Calc* bg2 carb-v bg2 ign bg2 kali-c bg2 lyc bg2 nit-ac bg2 *Nux-v* bg2 puls bg2 *Rhus-t* bg2 *Sep* bg2 staph bg2 sulph bg2 thuj bg2
  - **rest** agg.: ph-ac rat *Rhod* *Rhus-t*
  - **rheumatic**: *Bell* tl1 caul c1 *Stict* br1
    - **draft**; from: bell tl1
    - **wet** head; from: bell tl1
  - **sleep** agg., during: *Alum*
  - **spot**; in a: pert-vc vk9
  - **stool** agg., after: *Chin* b7a.de *Puls*
  - **stooping** agg.: calc h2 nat-sil fd3.de•
  - **stretching** | **amel.**: sanguis-s hrn2• [tax jsj7]
  - **turning**:
    - **head**:
      - **agg.**: alum am-c *Am-m* aur *Bamb-a* stb2.de• bell h1 *Bry* calad *Calc* *Chel* *Coloc* *Dulc* kali-n lac-h htj1• ozone sde2• par pycnop-sa mrz1 rat sel kr1* spong h1 tarent
      - **left** agg.; to: alum kali-p fd1.de• lac-leo hrn2• spong fd4.de
      - **painful** side agg.; to: anac
      - **right** agg.; to: ozone sde2• pycnop-sa mrz1 sinus rly4• spong bg1
  - **waking**; on: anac choc srj3• des-ac rbp6 falco-pe nl2• graph h2 kali-c k* *Lach* limen-b-c hrn2* *Manc* melal-alt gya4 phys k* sanguis-s hrn2•
  - **walking** in open air agg.: bamb-a stb2.de• *Camph* *Lyc*
  - **warmth** | **amel.**: bamb-a stb2.de• *Rhus-t* mrr1
  - **washing**, from: *Dulc* **Rhus-t**
  - **weather**:
    - **change** of weather: bamb-a stb2.de•
    - **cold**:
      - **agg.**: acon vh
      - **wet** | **agg.**: *Rhus-t* mrr1
    - **stormy** | **agg.**: bamb-a stb2.de•
    - **wet** | **agg.**: bamb-a stb2.de• *Rhus-t* tl1*
  - **wind**, dry cold: caust vh
  - **yawning** agg.: cocc h1 nat-m k*
  - ▽ **extending** to:
    - **Arm**; down | **right**: sanguis-s hrn2•
    - **Downward**: anac ptk1
    - **Head**: bamb-a stb2.de• sal-fr sle1•
      - **right** side: bamb-a stb2.de•
    - **Kidneys**; region of: ozone sde2•

Back

- **extending** to: ...
  - **Nose**: lachn c1
  - **Occiput**: bit-ar wht1• *Rhus-t* mrr1
  - **Shoulder**: arizon-l nl2• pert-vc vk9 vanil fd5.de
  - **Temples**: spig ptk1
  - **Whole** back: des-ac rbp6
- ○ **Nape** of neck: *Acon* b7.de* agar bg2 alum b4.de* am-m b7.de* anac b4.de* ang b7.de* ant-t bro1 apis b7a.de arg-met b7.de* arg-n bg2 ars b4.de* *Aur* b4a.de **Bar-c** b4.de* **Bell** b4.de* bov b4.de* bry b7.de* bufo bg2 **Calc** b4.de* calc-caust bro1 calc-p bg2* camph b7.de* cann-xyz bg2 canth b7.de* caps b7.de* carb-an b4.de* **Carb-v** b4a.de* **Caust** b4.de* cham bro1 chel bro1 chin b7.de* *Cimic* bg2* cocc bg2* colch bg2* coloc b4.de* *Con* b4a.de dig b4.de* dros b7.de* dulc b4.de* ferr-p bro1 fl-ac bg2 form bg2 gels bro1 glon bg2 graph b4.de* guaj b4.de* hell b7.de* hyos b7.de* hyper bro1 ign b7.de* jug-c bro1 kali-bi bg2 **Kali-c** b4.de* kali-n b4.de* lac-c bro1 **Lach** b7.de* *Lachn* bro1 lat-m bnm6• laur bg2 **Lyc** b4.de* **Mag-c** b4.de* mang b4.de* med bro1 mentho bro1 meny b7.de* merc b4.de* merc-i-r bg2* mez b4.de* **Nat-c** b4.de* *Nat-m* b4.de* nicot bro1 **Nit-ac** b4.de* nux-v b7.de* petr b4.de* ph-ac b4.de* **Phos** b4.de* phyt bg2* pimp bro1 *Plat* b4.de* podo bg2 psor bg2 puls b7.de* rad-br bro1 rhod b4.de* rhodi bro1 *Rhus-t* b7.de* rhus-v bro1 ruta bg2 sars b4.de* sec b7.de* *Sel* b7a.de **Sep** b4.de* **Sil** b4.de* spig b7.de* spong b7.de* squil b7.de* stann b4.de* staph b7.de* stel bro1 **Stict** bg2* sulph b4.de* tab bg2 thuj b4.de* trif-p bro1 verat b7.de* vinc bro1 x-ray bro1 zinc b4.de*
  - **accompanied** by:
    - **Head**:
      - **complaints** of (See HEAD - Complaints - accompanied - nape - stiffness)
      - **pain** in (See HEAD - Pain - accompanied - neck - stiffness - nape)
    - **Teeth**; pain in (See TEETH - Pain - accompanied - neck - stiffness)
  - **overlifting**; from: calc b4a.de *Lyc* b4a.de
  - **sensation** as if: phys bg2
  - **spasmodic**: nat-c b4.de* zinc b4.de*
- **Coccyx**: petr h2*
- **Dorsal** region: acon b7.de* agar b4.de* agath-a nl2• alum bg2 am-m bg2 anac b4a.de* ang b7.de* apis bg2 ars b4.de* bamb-a stb2.de• bar-c b4.de* bell bg2 benz-ac bg2 berb bg2 bit-ar wht1• *Bov* b4.de* *Bry* b7a.de calc b4.de* caps b7.de* **Carb-v** bg2 **Caust** b4.de* cimic bg2 cina bg2 cocc bg2 dulc bg2* form bg2 galla-q-r nl2• gels bg2 guaj b4.de* kali-bi bg2 **Kali-c** b4.de* kali-i bg2 laur bg2 led b7.de* lyc bg2 nat-m b4.de* nat-pyru rly4• nit-ac b4.de* **Nux-v** b7.de* olnd b7a.de petr b4.de* phys bg2 phyt bg2 prun bg2 puls b7.de* pycnop-sa mrz1 rhus-t bg2 ruta fd4.de sel bg2 **Sep** b4.de* **Sil** b4.de* spong fd4.de sul-ac b4a.de* **Sulph** b4.de* thuj b4.de* urt-u bg2 vanil fd5.de *Verat* b7a.de zinc b4.de*
  - **one** side: guaj b4a.de
  - **left**: adon bg2
  - **night**: zinc h2
  - **inspiration** agg.: bit-ar wht1•
  - **motion** agg.: zinc h2
  - **standing** agg.: sarcol-ac sp1
  - ○ **Muscles**: syph jl2
  - **Scapulae**: agath-a nl2• androc srj1• cocc bro1 *Dulc* bro1 gran bro1 ind bro1 kali-s fd4.de nat-m h2 nat-pyru rly4• *Phyt* bro1 prim-v bro1 *Sang* bro1 senec-j bro1
    - **right**: agath-a nl2• allox tpw4
    - **left**: sulph bg2
    - **Below**:
      - **extending** to:
        - **Arm**: lac-h htj1•
        - **Chest**: lac-h htj1•
    - **Between**: allox tpw4* alum b4a.de* ang b7.de* bell b4.de* caust b4.de* cocc b7.de* *Kali-c* b4.de* led b7.de* nat-m bg2 phos bg2 sarcol-ac sp1 *Sep* b4a.de
- **Lumbar** region: abrom-a ks5 *Acon* b7.de* **Am-m** b7a.de* **Ambr** b7a.de* apis b7a.de ars b4.de* bamb-a stb2.de• **Bar-c** b4a.de* bell bg2 bit-ar wht1• *Bry* b7.de* carb-an b4a.de* carb-v b4.de* **Caust** b4.de* cystein-l rly4• dulc bg2* gels bg2 *Get* br1 guaj b4.de* ham fd3.de• ign b7.de* kali-bi bg2 kali-c b4.de* kali-s fd4.de **Lach** bg2* laur bg2 led bg2 limen-b-c hrn2* lyc b4.de* m-aust b7.de

Stiffness – Lumbar region: ...

nat-c b4.de* nat-m h2 nat-sil fd3.de• nit-ac bg2 nux-v b7a.de olib-sac wmh1 orot-ac rly4• oxal-a rly4• petr b4a.de* positr nl2• prun bg2 *Puls* b7.de* rheum b7.de* rhus-t b7.de* ros-d wla1 *Sel* b7a.de sep b4a.de* **Sil** b4a.de* staph b7.de* sulph b4a.de* suprar rly4• symph fd3.de• thuj b4a.de urt-u bg2 vanil fd5.de [bell-p-sp dcm1 heroin sdj2]

  - **left** side: abrom-a ks5
  - **morning**: mim-p rsj8• urol-h rwt•
  - **evening**: abrom-a ks5 petr h2
    - **lying** down | **amel.**: abrom-a ks5
  - **bending** forward agg.: abrom-a ks5
  - **motion**; from: abrom-a ks5 *Get* br1 visc c1
  - **painful**: dulc fd4.de ham fd3.de• kali-p fd1.de• kali-s fd4.de sep h2 suprar rly4•
  - **rising** from bed agg.: abrom-a ks5
  - **sitting** agg.: abrom-a ks5
  - **waking**; on: limen-b-c hrn2•
  - **walking** agg.: abrom-a ks5
  - **working**; from | **cold** water; in: abrom-a ks5
- **Lumbosacral** region: ambr bg1 anac bg1 arg-n bg1 ars bg1 **Bar-c** bg1 bell bg1 carb-an bg1 carb-v bg1 cham bg1 dios bg1 dulc fd4.de guaj bg1 ign bg1 kali-c bg1 nat-m bg1 nit-ac bg1 nux-v bg1 petr bg1 plut-n srj7• *Rhus-t* bg1 staph bg1 symph fd3.de• valer bg1
- **Sacral** region: acon k* agath-a nl2• aloe bg2 am-m apis k* arg-n bg2 *Bar-c* berb k* *Bry Caust* k* des-ac rbp6 dulc fd4.de *Lach* laur *Led Lyc* manc meph petr bg2 phos k2 prun puls rheum k* *Rhus-t* k* sil spong fd4.de *Sulph* thuj tritic-vg fd5.de
  - **morning**: dulc fd4.de thuj
  - **evening**: bar-act petr h2
  - **exertion** agg.; after: rhus-t k2
  - **lying** agg.: ulm-c jsj8•
  - **motion** agg.; beginning of: *Lach*
  - **rising** from sitting agg.: aloe hr phos k2 spong fd4.de
  - **sitting**; after: aloe hr ambr spong fd4.de
  - **standing** erect | **impossible**: rheum h
- **Spine** | **Vertebrae**: bar-c bg2 calc bg2 nit-ac bg2
- **Trapezius** muscle: bung-fa mtf

STOOL:
- **after**:
  - **agg.**: alum bg2 caps bg2 dros b7.de* puls b7.de*
  - **amel.**: adon bg2 asaf bg2 bell bg2 coc-c bg2 kali-bi bg2 ox-ac bg2 sulph bg2
    - **Cervical** region: asaf ptk1
- **before** | **agg.**: colch b7.de* ferr b7.de* nat-c bg2 nat-m bg2 verat b7.de*
- **during**:
  - **agg.**: *Carb-an* bg2 ferr b7.de* kreos bg2 *Puls* b7.de* rheum bg2
    - **Lumbar** region: bar-c ptk1 caps ptk1

STOOPING:
- **after**:
  - **agg.**:
    - **long** time; stooping for a: nat-m ptk1
      - **Lumbar** region: dulc ptk1
- **agg.**: *Aesc* bg2 agar b4.de* alum bg2 am-c b4.de* ang b7.de* ant-c b7a.de arg-met b7.de* arg-n bg2 arn bg2 aur b4.de* *Borx* b4a.de bov b4.de* bry b7.de* bufo bg2 caps b7.de* carb-v b4.de* *Caust* b4a.de chel b7.de* cina b7.de* clem bg2 cocc b7.de* con b4a.de graph b4a.de hep b4a.de kali-n b4.de* kreos b7a.de* *Lyc* b4.de* m-ambo b7.de m-aust b7.de *Meny* b7.de* mur-ac b4a.de nat-m b4.de* nux-v b7.de* par b7.de* petr bg2 phos b4.de* *Puls* b7.de* rhod b4.de* rhus-t b7.de* ruta b7a.de* sabin b7.de* samb b7.de* sars b4.de* sep bg2* staph b7.de* stront-c b4.de* sulph b4.de* thuj b4.de* *Verat* b7.de* verb b7.de* zinc b4.de*
  - ○ **Sacrum**: kali-bi ptk1
  - **Spine**: agar ptk1
- **amel.**: cann-xyz bg2 mag-c bg2 ph-ac b4.de* puls b7.de* *Sabin* b7a.de sec bg2

STRAINING; easily: *(↗Pain - straining)* ant-t ptk1 arge-pl rwt5• arn b7.de* borx k* **Calc** k* calc-p bg2 caust bg2 chin b7.de* cocc b7.de* **Graph** k* hydrog srj2• iod b4.de* **Lyc** k* *Mur-ac* b4a.de nat-c a1 nit-ac b4.de* *Nux-v* k* *Olnd* b7a.de ph-ac phos b4.de* pin-con oss2• **Rhus-t** k* sang k* *Sep Sil* b4a.de stann b4.de* sulph bg2
○ - **Cervical** region: calc ptk1
- **Lumbar** region: ant-t ptk1 med ptk1

STREAMING inside of right scapula: hep h2

STRENGTH; increased: mag-s sp1 ulm-c jsj8•

STRETCH lumbar region, desire to: dulc fd4.de sil h2

STRETCHING:
- **amel.**: alum b4.de* nat-m bg2 sabin b7.de*
- **arms** | **agg.**: sep b4.de* sulph b4.de*
- **limbs** | **agg.**: bell bg2 bry bg2 bufo bg2 lyc bg2 mag-c bg2 mag-m bg2 psor bg2

STRETCHING OUT:
- **morning**:
  - **8** h | **11** h; until: nat-m tl1

STRIKING foot against anything agg.: sep bg2

STUMBLING agg.: sep ptk1

SUN: | **amel.**: stront-c b4.de*

SUPPORTING the back: | **amel.**: nat-m bg2

SWALLOWING:
- **agg.**: caust bg2* kali-c bg2* nat-m bg2 petr b4.de* raph bg2 *Rhus-t* bg2* sep bg2
○ • **Cervical** region: calc-p ptk1 colch ptk1 zinc ptk1
• **Dorsal** region | **Scapulae**; between: kali-c ptk1 rhus-t ptk1
• **Spine**: caust ptk1
- **amel.** | **Cervical** region: spong ptk1

SWELLING: brass-n-o srj5• sel c1
- **painful**: puls h1 spong fd4.de
- **sensation** of:
○ • **Dorsal** region: berb bg2
⋮ **Scapulae**: mez bg2 sil bg2
• **Lumbar** region: berb bg2 bufo bg2 sil bg2
○ - **Cervical** region: nux-v h1 spong fd4.de
• **fatty**:
⋮ **extending** to | **Ear**; from ear to: am-m hr1*
○ • **Nape** of neck: agath-a nl2• ail vh1 apis ars bg2* *Bar-c* k* **Bell** bg2 berb bg1 calc b4a.de* carb-v bg1 der iod bro1 lach bg1 lyc bro1 phos bro1 puls k* sep sil bro1 spong fd4.de sumb tub c1
⋮ **cough**; from (See COUGH - Swelling - neck)
⋮ **fatty**: am-m ptk1
⋮ **sensation** of: sep b4.de*
⋮ **Cords** of neck; swelling of | **aching** pain in base of brain; with: med c1
⋮ **Glands**: *Am-c* bg2 aur mtf33 **Bar-c** k* bar-i k2* *Bar-m* mrr1 *Bell Calc* k* *Carb-v Cist* tl1* con k2* corian-s knl6• ferr c1 graph k2* *Hell* k* hep mrr1 hir rsj4• iod k* kali-p merc k2 mur-ac k* nat-p nit-ac k2 *Petr* k* phos k* *Sil* k* *Stann* bg2 staph sulph k* syc fmm1• syph k2* tub c1*
: **right**: bar-m mrr1 corian-s knl6•
: **accompanied** by | **Head**; complaints of (See HEAD - Complaints - accompanied - nape - glands)
• **Veins**: op bro1*
• **Vertebrae**: *Calc* b4a.de
⋮ **Seventh** cervical: calc h2
- **Coccyx**:
• **sensation** of: hep b4.de* syph c1*
○ • **Bone**: *Rhus-t* b7a.de
- **Dorsal** region: am-m berb bg2 **Calc** *Carb-an Kali-c* lyc sil spig spong **Staph** bg2
○ • **Bones**: *Ant-c* b7a.de *Calc* b4a.de *Puls* b7a.de sil b4a.de
• **Glands**: am-c bg2
• **Scapulae**: *Nat-m* b4a.de *Ph-ac* b4a.de sulph b4a.de

Swelling – Dorsal region – **Scapulae**: ...
⋮ **Bones**: dulc b4a.de rhus-t b7a.de *Staph* b7a.de *Sulph* b4a.de
• **Vertebrae**: *Calc* b4a.de *Sil* b4a.de
- **Lumbar** region: apis bg2 arn bg2 aur-m bg2 berb bg2 lyc h2* plb bg2 *Rhus-t* bg2 sil bg2 staph bg2
• **accompanied** by:
⋮ **Bladder**:
: **cutting** pain in | **urination** agg.; during: borx c1
○ • **Vertebrae**: sil b4a.de
- **Nape** of neck (See cervical - nape)
- **Spinal** cord | **dropsical**: *Calc* b4a.de *Sil* b4a.de
- **Spine** | **Lower** | **sensation** of: aur ptk1
• **Vertebrae**: **Puls** bg2 **Sil** bg2

SYRINGOMYELIA:
- **accompanied** by | **panaritium**; painless (See EXTREMITIES - Felon - painless - accompanied - syringomyelia)

TABES DORSALIS: **Alum** b4a.de am-m b7a.de ambr b7a.de anac b4a.de ang b7a.de arn b7a.de *Ars* b4a.de *Bar-c* b4a.de bell b4a.de *Bry* b7a.de **Calc** b4a.de camph b7a.de carb-an b4a.de *Carb-v* b4a.de *Caust* b4a.de cham b7a.de *Chin* b7a.de *Cocc* b7a.de *Con* b4a.de *Dig* b4a.de ferr b7a.de graph b4a.de hell b7a.de *Hep* b4a.de *Ign* b7a.de kali-c b4a.de laur b7a.de led b7a.de **Lyc** b4a.de nat-c b4a.de **Nat-m** b4a.de *Nux-m* b7a.de **Nux-v** b7a.de op b7a.de **Ph-ac** b4a.de *Phos* b4a.de plat b4a.de *Plb* b7a.de **Puls** b7a.de **Rhus-t** b7a.de *Ruta* b7a.de sars b4a.de *Sep* b4a.de *Sil* b4a.de **Stann** b4a.de *Staph* b7a.de **Stram** b7a.de stront-c b4a.de sul-ac b4a.de **Sulph** b4a.de thuj b4a.de *Valer* b7a.de verat b7a.de

TALKING agg.: cann-s b7a.de cocc b7.de*

TENSION: aeth *Agar* k* agath-a nl2• am-c h2 am-m aran-ix sp1 arg-n arge-pl rwt5• *Ars* aur ptk1 *Bamb-a* stb2.de• bar-c bar-s k2 berb bry carbn-s k2 carc fd2.de• coloc con dulc fd4.de falco-pe nl2• haliae-lc srj5• hep hyos ptk1 ign ignis-alc es2• kali-s fd4.de kali-sil k2 lac-leo hrn2• *Lil-t Lyc* k* med mez mosch nat-c nat-m nat-ox rly4• nux-v k2 ol-an olnd pieri-b mlk9.de pin-con oss2• *Puls* rat ruta fd4.de sal-fr sle1• sars sep spong fd4.de *Stry* mrr1 suis-em rly4• suis-hep rly4• *Sulph* k* tarax teucr thuj tritic-vg fd5.de tub br1 vanil fd5.de x-ray sp1 zinc
- **right** side: kali-s fd4.de sep
- **left**: kali-s fd4.de nat-m h2 sulph h2
- **forenoon**: bry lac-leo hrn2• ruta fd4.de spong fd4.de
- **night**: nat-c
• **turning** the body; on: hep
- **attempting** to straighten up; on: bell dulc fd4.de
• **amel.**: nat-c h2
- **dinner** | **after** | **agg.**: nat-c
• **before**: nicc
- **inspiration** agg.: lyc h2
- **lying** on other side agg.: sep
- **motion**:
• **agg.**: colch tritic-vg fd5.de
• **amel.**: am-m dulc fd4.de
• **arm**; of | **agg.**: sulph
• **body**; of:
⋮ **agg.** | **walking** in evening amel.: nat-c
- **painful**: bamb-a stb2.de• ruta fd4.de tritic-vg fd5.de vanil fd5.de
- **paroxysmal**: nat-c h2
- **sitting**:
• **agg.**: am-m nat-c ruta fd4.de tritic-vg fd5.de vanil fd5.de
• **bent** forward | **agg.**: nat-c h2* sulph
- **standing** agg.: ign spong fd4.de
▽ - **extending** to:
○ • **Anus** | **lying** and sitting; while: nat-c
• **Chest** | **stooping** agg.: chel
• **Neck**: lac-leo hrn2• laur
○ - **Cervical** region: *(↗Spasmodic)* agar agath-a nl2• aids nl2• aloe **Alum** k* am-m androc srj1• ant-c *Apis* arge-pl rwt5• aur *Bar-c* bar-s k2 **Bell** k* berb bism h1 bov *Bry* calc camph carb-an *Carb-v Carbn-s* carc fd2.de* *Caust* k* *Chel* chin c1 choc srj3• **Cic** k* **Cimic** k* cinnb colch con h2* cupr k* cygn-ol sze3• des-ac rbp6 dig dioxi rbp6 dulc elaps euph falco-pe nl2• fic-m gya1 *Gels* glon

Back

- **Cervical** region: ...
graph ham fd3.de• *Hell* *Hydrog* srj2• hyos hyper iod ip kali-c kali-s kola stb3• *Lac-c* lac-leo hm2• lap-la sde8.de• limen-b-c hm2* *Lyc* *Mag-s* mang h2 med mez mosch musca-d szs1 *Nat-c* *Nat-m* nat-ox rly4• *Nat-s* nat-sil fd3.de• nept-m lsd2.fr nicc nicot bro1 nit-ac *Nux-m* *Ol-an* olib-sac wmh1 par pieri-b mlk9.de pin-con oss2• *Plat* plb plut-n srj7• podo fd3.de• psor *Puls* *Rat* *Rhod* *Rhus-t* ruta fd4.de sal-fr sle1• sars sep k* sil *Spong* *Staph* *Stram* stront-c *Stry* bro1* suis-em rly4• suis-hep rly4• *Sulph* k* symph fd3 de• syph ptk1 thiam rly4• *Thuj* tritic-vg fd5.de *Tub* bg1* tung-met bdx1• vanil fd5.de verat verat-v *Zinc*
  - **right**: agath-a nl2• carc fd2.de• caust h2 fum rly1*• spong fd4.de zinc h2
  - **left**: agath-a nl2• cic a1 musca-d szs1 rat spong fd4.de tritic-vg fd5.de
  - **morning**: falco-pe nl2• ham fd3.de• kola stb3• mag-s ruta fd4.de sulph tritic-vg fd5.de
    - **rising** agg.: mag-s
    - **waking**; on: anac h2 falco-pe nl2•
  - **afternoon**: alum h2 vanil fd5.de
  - **evening**: am-m nat-m rat tritic-vg fd5.de
  - **night**:
    - **midnight**, before: *Sulph*
    - **lying** on side agg.: staph h1
  - **accompanied** by | **numbness**: plat ptk1
  - **cold**, damp air: *Nux-m*
  - **headache**; during: hydrog srj2• ruta fd4.de spong fd4.de
  - **lifting** agg.: sep h2
  - **menses**; before: iod *Nat-c* nux-v
  - **motion**:
    - **agg.**: bry camph h1 graph kali-c nat-c nicc *Rhus-t* sars tritic-vg fd5.de
    - **amel.**: con *Rhod* *Rhus-t*
    - **head**; of | **agg.**: nat-c h2 sulph h2 thuj h1
  - **rising** up quickly: caust h2
  - **sitting**:
    - **agg.**: kali-s fd4.de nat-c ruta fd4.de (non:sulph kl) vanil fd5.de
    - **bent** forward | **agg.**: sulph h2
  - **sleep** agg.; during: alum vanil fd5.de
  - **standing** agg.: rat
  - **stooping** agg.: am-c ant-c aur *Canth* kola stb3• lyc h2
  - **stretching** | **amel.**: sulph
  - **touch** agg.: mag-s a1*
  - **turning** head agg.: caust h2 mur-ac h2 podo fd3.de• spong suis-hep rly4• *Verat*
  - **waking**; on: aids nl2• anac psor
  - **walking**:
    - **agg.**: nat-c
    - **air** agg.; in open: *Lyc* meny h1
    - **amel.**: mag-s *Rhod* *Rhus-t* sulph
  - **warm**; becoming | **amel.**: mosch
  - **writing** agg.: kali-s fd4.de lyc
  - ▽ **extending** to:
    - **Eye**: sulph h2
    - **Shoulder**: agath-a nl2• carc fd2.de• falco-pe nl2• fic-m gya1 nat-sil fd3.de• sulph h2
      - **left**: kola stb3•
  - ○ **Nape** of neck: agar bg2 aloe bg2 alum b4.de* am-m b7.de* anac b4a.de ant-c b7a.de* apis b7a.de arn b7.de* aur b4.de* bar-c b4.de* bov b4.de* bry b7.de* calc b4.de* camph b7.de* canth b7.de* carb-an b4.de* *Caust* b4.de* chin b7a.de* cimic bg2 *Coloc* b4a.de *Con* b4.de* dig b4.de* euph b4.de* graph b4.de* hyos b7.de* ign ptk1 iod b4.de* ip b7.de* kali-c b4.de* lach b7.de* laur b7.de* mang b4.de* meny b7.de* mosch b7.de* *Nat-c* b4.de* nat-m bg2* nit-ac b4.de* par b7.de* plat b4.de* plb b7.de* *Puls* b7.de* *Rhod* b4a.de *Rhus-t* b7.de* sanic bg2 sars b4.de* sep b4.de* sil b4.de* *Spong* b7a.de staph b7.de* stront-c b4.de* sulph b4.de* *Thuj* b4.de* tub bg2* viol-o b7.de* viol-t b7.de* zinc b4.de*
  - **Vertebrae**: colum-p sze2•

- **Dorsal** region: agar bg2 agath-a nl2• *Am-c* b4a.de am-m b7.de* ambr bg2 ang b7.de* arg-n bg2 asaf b7.de* aur-m k* bell b4.de* berb bg2 bry b7.de* choc srj3• cimic bg2 *Coloc* b4a.de con b4.de* crot-c cypra-eg sde6.de• dulc fd4.de fic-m gya1 gels bg2 hep b4.de* kali-c bg2 kali-s fd4.de kola stb3• lac-leo hm2• lach b7a.de laur bg2 limen-b-c hm2* lyc k* mag-m bg2 mag-s mez b4.de* mosch b7.de* mur-ac h2* nat-c b4.de* **Nat-m** b4.de* olib-sac wmh1 olnd b7.de* ozone sde2• *Plat* b4a.de plut-n srj7• podo fd3.de• *Puls* b7a.de *Rhus-t* ruta fd4.de sacch-a fd2.de• sars b4a.de sep b4.de* spong fd4.de stront-c b4.de* sulph b4.de* tarax b7.de* teucr b7.de* vanil fd5.de *Zinc* k*
  - **left**: sep h2 spong fd4.de
  - **walking** | **amel.**: mag-s
  - ▽ **extending** to | **Chest**; across shoulders to: choc srj3•
  - ○ **Scapulae**: acon bg2 agath-a nl2• aids nl2• alum k* anac b4a.de ant-c b7a.de* *Bar-c* k* **Carb-an** k* caust h2* cic k* cimic bg2 colch k* *Coloc* k* con k* crot-h bg2 ferr b7.de* fic-m gya1 kali-c k* kreos b7a.de* lyc k* mag-m k* mang b4.de* merc k* merc-c k* *Mez* mur-ac k* nat-c k* *Nux-v* k* op k* ozone sde2• *Rhus-t* k* ruta fd4.de sacch-a fd2.de• sep k* sil k* stront-c b4.de* sulph k* zinc k*
    - **right**: agath-a nl2•
    - **evening**: sep
    - **motion** agg.: caust h2
    - **turning** head agg.: caust merc
    - **extending** to | **Neck**: fic-m gya1 mang h2
    - **Below**: agath-a nl2• con kali-c h2 kali-s fd4.de ozone sde2• zinc
      - **left**: kola stb3•
      - **painful**: ozone sde2•
      - **raising** arm agg.: con
      - **sitting** agg.: ozone sde2•
    - **Between**: agath-a nl2• alum h2 anac h2 ant-c h2 carb-an h2 *Colch* ferr fic-m gya1 *Hep* mag-m h2 mag-s c1 mur-ac h2 *Nat-c* nat-ox rly4• *Nux-v* ozone sde2• podo fd3.de• sep h2 spong fd4.de zinc
      - **excitement**; after: phos
      - **lying** agg.: sulph
      - **menses**; during: am-c h2
      - **motion** agg.: ozone sde2• sulph
      - **rubbing** | **amel.**: carb-an h2
      - **stooping** agg.: ant-c h2
      - **extending** to:
        - **Back**; down: mag-m h2
        - **Shoulder**: sulph h2

- **Lumbar** region: acon k* *Agar* am-c b4a.de* am-m ptk1 ambr ars bg1 aur-m *Bar-c* k* bar-s k2 **Berb** k* bov k* brom bry k* caps h1 carb-an bg2 carb-v k* carbn-s *Carl* caust k* *Chin* clem coc-c *Colch* cycl cypra-eg sde6.de• ign b7.de* lyc mag-c bg1 merl *Nat-m* nit-ac k* *Nux-v* k* *Phos* pieri-b mlk9.de *Plat* b4a.de positr nl2• *Puls* k* rheum ruta fd4.de sabin b7.de* samb b7.de* sars b4a.de* sep sil k* stront-c b4.de* *Sulph* k* tarax b7a.de thuj k* tritic-vg fd5.de verat *Zinc* k*
  - **morning** | **bed** agg.; in: sulph
  - **evening**: *Bar-c* ruta fd4.de
    - **standing** agg.: agar
    - **stepping** agg.: acon
  - **night**:
    - **midnight**; after | **4** h: sulph k*
  - **air** agg.; in open: lyc
  - **ascending** stairs agg.: carbn-s
  - **bending**:
    - **backward**:
      - **agg.**: bar-c h2
      - **amel.**: acon
  - **motion** agg.: brom sars h2
  - **rising** up: bar-c sulph
  - **sitting** agg.: zinc
  - **standing**:
    - **agg.**: agar lyc
    - **erect** | **agg.**: ign
  - **stool** agg.; after: berb plat
  - **stooping** agg.: bar-c h2 ruta fd4.de sabin **Sulph**

- **stretching** agg.: agar
- **touch** agg.: agar
- **walking** agg.: bry lyc

▽ · **extending** to:
  ⁝ **Hip**; left: sars h2
  ⁝ **Hypochondrium**; right: bar-c h2

- **Sacrum**: *Bar-c* bar-s k2 berb caps h1 caust des-ac rbp6 pieri-b mlk9.de puls samb h1 sars *Sulph* k* tarax *Zinc*
  - **evening**: bar-c
  - **ascending** agg.: carbn-s
  - **lying** agg.: *Berb*
  - **sitting** agg.: *Berb*

○ · **Coccyx**; and: sil bg2 thuj bg2
  - **Spine**: zinc h2
- **Spine**: agar ptk1 sulph ptk1
  - **bending** forward agg.: plut-n srj7•

○ · **Vertebrae**: cimic bg2 nat-c bg2 zinc bg2

TIGHT feeling: galeoc-c-h gms1• lavand-a ctl1• mag-c h2

TINGLING (See Formication)

TOUCH:

- **agg.**: *Agar* bg2 alum bg2 am-m b7a.de ars b4a.de* asar b7.de* bell bg2 berb bg2 bry bg2 carb-an b4.de* *Chin* b7.de* chinin-s bg2 *Cimic* bg2 cob bg2 colch b7.de* galeoc-c-h gms1• hyper bg2 kali-bi bg2 *Kali-c* bg2 kali-i bg2 kali-p bg2 lach bg2 lil-t bg2 mag-p bg2 merc b4.de* nat-m bg2 nicc bg2 *Nux-v* b7.de* phos b4.de* phys bg2 phyt bg2 plat b4.de* plb b7.de* rhus-t b7.de* sec bg2 sep b4.de* sil b4a.de* stram b7.de* stront-c b4.de* sulph bg2 tarent bg2 ther bg2 valer bg2 zinc bg2* ziz bg2

○ · **Cervical** region: lach ptk1
  - **Lumbar** region: cimic ptk1 lil-t ptk1
  - **Sacrum**: lob ptk1
- **amel.**: calc b4.de* cycl b7.de* meny b7.de* mur-ac b4.de*

TREMBLING: apis carb-v carc jl2 cimic *Cocc* k* eup-per iod h lil-t vanil fd5.de

- **morning**: apis
- **fever**; during: *Eup-per*
- **paroxysmal**: carb-v
- **sensation** of:
  - **pleasant**: coca-c sk4•

○ · **Lumbar** region: phos bg2

○ - **Cervical** region: nept-m lsd2.fr

○ · **Nape** of neck: carb-v bg2

- **Dorsal** region: apis bg2 cimic bg2 cocc b7.de* coff b7.de* eup-per bg2

○ · **Scapulae**: merc b4.de* *Sulph* k* tarax bg2
  ⁝ **forenoon**: sulph

- **Lumbar** region: benz-ac k* berb cimic k* merc nicc bg2 oci op bg2 phos bg2 thuj bg1
- **Spine**: lil-t ptk1

TRICKLING:

○ - **Dorsal** region: sumb bg2
- **Spine**; along: sumb br1*

TUBERCLES: | **Scapula**:

- **right** | **suppurative**; not: am-m
- **Spine**: puls ptk1 sil ptk1 spong ptk1

TUBERCULOSIS:

○ - **Spine**; of (See Tabes)
- **Vertebrae**; of (= Pott's disease): arg-met bro1 aur bro1* calc bro1 calc-i bro1 calc-p bro1* con bro1 get c2 iod bro1* kali-i bro1 merc-i-r bro1 ph-ac bro1* phos bro1* pyrog bro1 *Sil* bro1 stann ptk1* stict c2 still bro1 sulph bro1 syph bro1* tub bro1* vitr-an bro1
  - **accompanied** by | **curvature** of spine: get c2 kali-i c2 phos c2 *Pyrog* c2 stict c2
  - **lying** on back with knees drawn up: merc-c ptk1

TUMORS:

- **cysts**: *Phos* ptk1
- **pediculated** bluish as large as a cherry: *Con* k* thuj

Tumors: ...

- **sarcoma**: *Bar-c* k* calc-p bro1 *Cund* bro1 nit-ac bro1 sil bro1 thuj sne
- **steatoma**:

○ · **Cervical** region | **Nape** of neck: apis b7a.de bar-c b4.de* *Bell* b4a.de merc b4a.de *Merc-c* b4a.de mez b4a.de *Puls* b7.de

○ - **Cervical**: carb-v sne caust sne con mrr1
  - **accompanied** by | **cough**: cist tl1
  - **cystic**: brom ptk1
  - **fatty**: bacls-10 fmm1• **Bar-c** k* calc *Thuj* k*
  - **malignant**: calc-p k*

○ · **Glands**: dros tl1
  - **Nape** of neck | **fatty**: bar-c b4.de* calc b4.de*
- **Spine**: tarent ptk1*
- **Vertebra**: | **cysts**: lach ptk1* tarent ptk1*

TURNING:

- **bed**; in | **agg.**: *Acon* b7a.de borx b4a.de *Hep* b4a.de *Nux-v* b7.de* rhod b4a.de staph b7.de* sulph b4a.de*
- **body** | **agg.**: dros b7.de* guaj b4.de* hep b4.de* kali-bi bg2 nux-v b7.de* sanic ptk1 stann b4.de* staph b7.de* thuj b4.de* verat b7.de*
- **head**:
  - **agg.**: bell b4.de* bov b4.de* caust b4.de coloc b4.de* dros b7.de* dulc b4.de* nat-m b4.de* nux-v b7.de* sars b4.de*
    ⁝ **Cervical** region: *Bell* ptk1 bry ptk1
  - **left** agg.; to: caust bg2

TWITCHING: *Agar* agath-a nl2• alum calc carb-v h2 carc tpw2* chel jatr-c kali-bi kali-s fd4.de merc mez morph mygal nat-m nat-sil fd3.de• petr phys spig stry k* sulph vanil fd5.de *Zinc*

- **right**: agath-a nl2• calc melal-alt gya4 meny h1 nat-sil fd3.de•
- **left**: bapt a1 carb-v bg1
- **breathing** agg.: alum calc
- **electric** shocks; like: agar mrr1 *Ang* kali-s fd4.de *Nux-v*
- **lying** on back agg.: agar
- **opening** the mouth agg.: stry

○ - **Cervical** region: aeth agar bro1 arn bufo caust coloc mag-c h2 mag-m nat-m petr-ra shn4• ph-ac plut-n srj7• ran-b sep sulph tarax h1
  - **left**: plut-n srj7•
  - **raising** head agg.: ph-ac h2
  - **rest** agg.: ph-ac
  - **sensation** of: bism a1
  - **tearing**:
    ⁝ **extending** to:
      ⁝ **Vertex** | **walking** agg.: rat

▽ · **extending** to | **Down**: mag-c h2

○ · **Nape** of neck: ang b7a.de arg-met b7.de* asaf b7.de* caps b7.de* caust b4.de* chin b7a.de mag-c b4.de* nat-m b4.de* ph-ac b4.de* sep bg2 sulph b4.de* tarax b7.de*

- **Coccyx**: alum k* calc b4.de caust b4.de* chin b7.de *Cic* k* rhus-t b7.de
  - **menses**; during: *Cic*
  - **painful**: alum
- **Dorsal** region: agar b4.de* alum b4.de* ang b7.de* bry b7.de* carb-v b4.de* caust bg2 *Chin* b7a.de cina b7.de* laur b7.de* m-ambo b7.de mag-c bg2 meny b7.de* mez b4.de* mosch b7a.de nat-m b4.de* nit-ac stann b4.de* *Stry* tarax b7a.de
  - **manual** labor: nit-ac

○ · **Lower** dorsal region: ruta h1
  - **Scapulae**: asaf bg2 calc k* calc-p carc fd2.de• ham fd3.de• kali-bi bg2 lyc k* merc k* mez nat-c k* nat-m bg2 phos k* rhus-t k* sep k* spig b7.de* squil k* thuj k*
- **Lumbar** region: *Agar* k* agath-a nl2• *Alum* am-c bg2 calc k* caust bg2 chin b7.de* *Coloc* con k* crot-t dulc lach mag-c h2 melal-alt gya4 nat-c b4.de* petr puls b7.de* rat ruta b7.de* staph b7.de* sumb
  - **afternoon** | **13** h: mag-c
  - **evening**: agar
    ⁝ **bed** agg.; in: sulph
  - **lifting**; after: nat-c
  - **lying** agg.: bry

- **Lumbar** region: ...
  - **motion** agg.: petr
  - **pulsating**: con h2
  - **sitting** agg.: bry meny
  - **stooping** agg.: kali-c
  - **walking** agg.: rhus-t
  - ▽ **extending** to | **Rectum**: calc h2
- **Muscles**; of the: carc mg1.de*
- **Sacrum**: alum bg2 calc bg2 caust bg2 chin bg2 cic bg2 rhus-t bg2
  - **sitting** agg.: staph h1
- **Spine**: mang ptk1
  - ○ **Vertebrae**: bry bg2 ruta bg2

ULCERS: *Cist Merc-c*

- ○ **Cervical** region: sil
  - ○ **Nape** of neck: *Calc* b4a.de *Sil* b4.de*
- **Coccyx**: paeon k*
- **Dorsal** region: *Ant-c* b7a.de *Ars* b4a.de **Calc** b4a.de *Lyc* b4a.de *Sil* b4a.de
  - ○ **Scapulae**: kali-bi k* merc k*
- **Lumbar** region | **Bones**: **Sil** b4a.de
- **Sacrum**: *Arg-n Ars* crot-h *Paeon Zinc*
  - **burning** like fire: *Ars*

UNCOVERING:

- **amel.** | **Cervical** region: sars ptk1

UNDRESSING: | **after**: cocc b7.de*

UNEASINESS: | **Lumbar** region: bell bg2

URGING for stool agg.: | **Sacrum**: tell ptk1

URINATION:

- **after**:
  - **agg.**: caust ptk1 *Syph* ptk1
  - **amel.**: lyc bg2* med ptk1
    - ⁝ **Lumbar** region: nat-s ptk1
- **before** | **agg.**: graph ptk1 *Lyc* ptk1
- **during**: berb bg2 graph bg2 hep bg2 kali-bi bg2 puls bg2 rheum bg2 sulph bg2
  - **agg.**: ant-c ptk1 ip ptk1 kali-bi ptk1 sulph ptk1
    - ⁝ **Sacrum**: graph ptk1 sulph ptk1
  - ○ **Coccyx**: graph ptk1 kali-bi ptk1
- **retarded** agg.: graph ptk1 nat-s ptk1
- **retention** of urine agg.: crot-t bg2

VEXATION; after: nux-v b7.de

VIBRATION; sensation of: | **lying** agg.: streptoc mtf11

VOMITING:

- **after**: ars bg2
- **while**: fl-ac bg2 kali-c bg2 puls b7.de*

WAKING; on: am-m b7.de* ran-b b7.de* ruta b7.de* staph b7.de*

WALKING:

- **agg.**: **Aesc** bg2 agar b4.de* alum b4a.de am-c b4.de* am-m b7.de* ant-t bg2 arg-met b7.de* arn b7.de* asar b7.de* bell b4.de* bry b7.de* chel b7.de* cocc b7.de* coff b7.de* coloc b4.de* *Dulc* b4a.de euphr b7.de* ferr b7.de* graph bg2 hep b4.de* kali-bi bg2 kreos b7a.de m-arct b7.de meny b7.de* merc b4.de* mez b4.de* nux-v b7.de* olnd b7.de* *Petr* b4a.de phos b4.de* ran-b b7.de* rhus-t b7.de* ruta b7.de* sabad b7.de* *Sars* b4a.de sep b4.de* spig b7.de* spong b7.de* stront-c b4.de* **Sulph** b4.de* thuj b4.de* verat b7.de* zinc b4.de*
  - ○ **Lumbar** region: aesc ptk1 murx ptk1 psor ptk1 sep ptk1
  - **Spine**: graph ptk1 mur-ac ptk1 ruta ptk1 sulph ptk1
- **air**; in open:
  - **after** | **agg.**: nat-c b4.de* petr b4.de* plat b4.de* puls b7.de* rhus-t b7.de* ruta b7.de* verat b7.de*
  - **agg.**: arn b7.de* borx b4a.de calc b4.de* chin b7.de* ign b7.de* kali-c b4.de* merc b4.de* mur-ac b4.de* nat-m b4.de* nux-v b7.de* sil b4.de* verat b7.de*
  - **amel.**: sep b4.de*

Walking: ...

- **amel.**: am-c b4.de* ant-c b7a.de arg-n bg2 bell b4.de* coloc b4.de* dulc b4.de* kali-n b4.de* kreos bg2 mag-c bg2 merc b4.de* mur-ac b4.de* nat-c b4.de* nat-m b4.de* ph-ac b4.de* puls b7.de* rhus-t b7.de* ruta b7.de* sabad b7.de* *Sep* b4.de* staph b7.de* sulph b4.de* tab bg2 thuj b4.de* vib bg2 *Zinc* bg2
  - ○ **Lumbar** region: *Arg-met* ptk1 cob ptk1 rad-br ptk1 *Sep* ptk1
  - **Spine**: gels ptk1 hydr ptk1 ph-ac ptk1
- **bent** | **amel.**: *Nux-v* b7a.de
- **slowly** | **amel.**: bell bg2
- **uneven** ground agg.; on: podo bg2

WANTING; as if a vertebra was: ovi-p rb2

WARM:

- **agg.**: cinnb bg2 phos bg2 rhus-t bg2 sumb bg2
  - ○ **Vertebrae**: agar ptk1
- **air** steaming up spine into head; sensation of (See Heat - spine - extending - head - warm)
- **applications** | **amel.**: *Rhus-t* b7.de*
- **warm** from walking agg.; becoming: sil b4.de*

WARMTH; sensation of (See Heat)

WARTS: bar-c k2 nit-ac sil thuj k*

- **soft** | **Cervical** region: ant-c bro1
- ○ **Cervical** region: ant-c sne calc sne caust sne lyc sne nit-ac sep sne syph sne thuj
  - ○ **Nape** of neck: nit-ac bg2

WASHING agg.: carb-v b4.de* sulph bg2

WATER; sensation of:

- **boiling** water along the back; as if: ust ptk1
- **dripping** on | **Lumbar** region: med hr1

WAVELIKE sensation going up back: laur

WEAKNESS (= tired feeling): abrot k* *Aesc* k* *Aesc-g* bro1 aeth *Agar* allox tpw4 alum k2* alum-sil k2 alumn anan ant-t k* apis k* arg-n ptk1 arn bro1 **Ars** k* bac jl2 bamb-a stb2.de• bar-c k* berb k* *Brach* but-ac bro1 cain br1 **Calc** k* *Calc-p* c2* calc-s calc-sil k2 carb-ac carb-v carbn-s *Casc* castm castn-v br1 *Chin* c2* chinin-ar chord-umb rly4• *Cic* cimic cocc bg1* coloc con k2 cupr-ar cur dig br1 dulc fd4.de *Eup-per Gels* gins glyc bro1 **Graph** k* gua bro1 guaj helon k* hep hydr hydrog srj2• *Ign* c2* irid-met bro1* iris jac-c bro1 kali-c bg1* kali-cy kali-p k* *Lach* lob *Lyss* mand rsj7• med merc bro1 *Murx* naja k2 nat-ar **Nat-m** k* nat-p nit-ac **Nux-v** k* ol-j ox-ac k* pall petr k* **Ph-ac** k* *Phos* k* phys *Pic-ac* k* plb plut-n srj7• podo k* psor *Puls* pulx br1 pyrog k2* ran-b k2 raph *Rhus-t* sarr k* **Sel** k* **Sep** k* *Sil* k* staph bro1 sul-ac sul-i k2 **Sulph** k* tell ther tritic-vg fd5.de verat-v **Zinc** k*

- **left**: sulph h2
- **morning**: coloc dios kali-p fd1.de• ox-ac pall petr h2 sel k2 ther
  - **rising** agg.: nat-m
- **forenoon**: calc-s dulc fd4.de
- **afternoon**: dulc fd4.de stict c1
- **evening**: nat-p
- **night**: petr
- **abortion**; during: kali-c bro1
- **accompanied** by:
  - ○ **Ovaries** | **pain**: abrot ptk1
- **breathing** deep agg.: carb-v
- **coition**; after: calc k2 nat-p ptk1 sel mrr1
- **eating** agg.: *Nat-m*
- **ejaculation** agg.: nat-p mrr1 **Sel** k*
- **exertion** agg.: agar hr1 kali-c hr1 lach hr1 nat-m hr1 par hr1 sil hr1
- **leukorrhea**: con ptk1 graph k*
- **lying** down:
  - **agg.**: cic phos
  - **amel.**: *Casc Nat-m* nept-m lsd2.fr plut-n srj7•
- **manual** labor: *Lach* **Nat-m** *Sil*
- **mental** exertion; from: *Calc*
- **motion**:
  - **amel.**: ignis-alc es2•
  - **arms**; of | **agg.**: clem *Par Sil* sulph h2
- **piano**; playing: allox tpw4

- **riding** agg.: calc-s
- **sexual** excesses: agar *Calc* *Nat-m* **Nux-v** **Ph-ac** *Phos* **Sel**
- **sitting**:
  - **after**: *Sil*
  - **agg.**: agar allox tpw4 bar-c h2 **Calc** cic *Graph* kali-p k2 *Lyss* sul-ac k2 **Sulph** **Zinc** k*
  - **impossible**: pic-ac k2
- **sliding** down while sitting: calc k2 pic-ac k2 *Sulph* mrr1
- **standing** almost impossible: alum-sil k2 plut-n srj7• sul-ac
- **stool** agg.; after: sumb
- **typhoid** fever; after: **Sel**
- **walking**:
  - **after** | **agg.**: bapt petr tritic-vg fd5.de
  - **agg.**: *Graph* sabad sep **Sulph**
  - **amel.**: *Hydr* ignis-alc es2•
  - **snow** agg.; over: sanic c1
- **writing** agg.: lyc

○ - **Cervical** region: (↗*HEAD - Hold - up*) abrot bg1* acon *Aesc* *Aeth* ptk1 *Agar* aloe ant-t bg1* arg-n bg1 ars-met bapt hr1* *Cact* calc-p ptk1* caps h1 carc fd2.de• caul ptk1 chord-umb rly4• cimic **Cocc** k* *Gels* gins mtf11 *Glon* *Kali-c* kali-p k2 lac-d mtf11 *Lach* limest-b es1• malar jl2 mur-ac h2 nat-m ptk1 nit-ac nux-m c1 *Par* k* petr phos pic-ac *Plat* k* psil ft1 ptel c1 sanic pc* sep ptk1 *Sil* *Stann* staph sulph ptk1* tritic-vg fd5.de *Verat* k* verat-v bg1* viol-o *Zinc*

• - **accompanied** by:
  - **goose** flesh: psil ft1
  - **headache** (See HEAD - Pain - accompanied - cervical - weakness)
- **head** drops forward on chest: nux-m c1
- **manual** labor: *Agar* *Kali-c* *Lach* nit-ac *Sil* verat
- **motion** | **amel.**: petr-ra shn4•
- **writing** agg.: **Zinc**

○ - **Muscles**: op tl1
- **Nape** of neck: abrot bg2* acon b7.de* aesc bg2 aeth bro1 all-c bg2 ant-t b7.de* arn b7.de* ars bg2 bry b7.de* *Calc-p* bg2 caps bg2 carb-v bg2 caust bg2 cocc bg2 colch bro1 crot-h bg2 *Dig* b4a.de eup-pur bg2 fago bro1 gels bg2 glon bg2 *Kali-c* b4.de* lil-t bg2 lyc bg2 nat-m bg2 nit-ac b4.de* op bg2 par b7a.de* petr b4.de* phos b4.de* plat b4.de* *Sil* b4a.de* spig bg2 stann b4.de* staph b7a.de verat b7.de* viol-o b7.de* zinc bg2
  - **sensation** of: caps b7.de*

- **Coccyx**: petr bg2
- **Dorsal** region: aesc bg2 agar b4.de* *Apis* b7a.de arg-n bg2 arn b7.de* *Ars* bg2 calc-p bg2 carb-v bg2 *Cocc* bg2 dulc bg2 eup-per bg2 gels bg2 *Hep* b4a.de hydrog srj2• *Kali-c* b4a.de **Lach** b7a.de* lob bg2 nat-m b4a.de* nit-ac b4.de* nux-v b7a.de olnd b7a.de ox-ac bg2 petr b4.de* phos b4.de* **Pic-ac** bg2 psor bg2 rhus-t bg2 senec bg2 sep bg2 *Sil* b4a.de sulph b4a.de* tritic-vg fd5.de zinc b4a.de

○ - **Scapulae**: agar bg2 alum bg2 apis bg2 hura bg2 kali-bi bg2 nat-m bg2 sulph bg2 thlas bg2
  - **leaning** on something amel.: sarr
  - **stooping** | **amel.**: alumn
  - **Below**: sarr c1
  - **Between**: *Agar* k* alum ptk1 *Apis* ptk1 *Cocc* ptk1 kali-i ptk1 naja k2 *Nat-m* ptk1 petr-ra shn4• rad-br c11* raph ptk1 sarr k* sars ptk1 sul-ac ptk1 thlas ptk1

- **Lumbar** region: acon b7a.de *Aesc* k* *Agar* all-s *Alum* alum-p k2 alumn am-c ambr aml-ns vh1 *Arg-n* k* arn **Ars** k* ars-s-f k2 asar h1 aur k* aur-ar k2 aur-m aur-s k2 bamb-a stb2.de• bar-c k* bar-s k2 *Bell* k* benz-ac but-ac br1 **Calc** k* calc-p bg2 **Calc-s** k* calc-sil k2 camph carb-ac carbn-s carl caust bg2 chel cimic k* cimx *Cina* clem **Cocc** k* *Coloc* con cupr bg2 dios dulc bg2* *Eup-per* fum rly4• granit-m es1• *Graph* helo bg2 *Helon* *Hep* hura hydr hydrog srj2• ignis-alc es2• *Kali-bi* kali-br bg2 *Kali-c* k* kali-cy kali-i kali-p fd1.de• kali-s kali-sil k2 kreos bg2 *Lach* k* laur *Lec* *Led* lil-t *Lycps-v* lyss malar jl2 manc meph *Merc* k* merc-i-f morph *Mur-ac* *Murx* naja nat-c **Nat-m** k* nat-p nicc bg2 *Nux-m* k* nux-v k* *Nymph* *Ox-ac* k* *Pall* petr k* ph-ac bg2 *Phos* k* phyt **Pic-ac** k* plan *Psor* ptel **Puls** k* raph **Rhus-t** k* *Rhus-v* rumx *Ruta* sabin sanic *Sec* **Sel** k* senec k* **Sep** k* *Sil* k* spig bg2 stann bg2 sul-ac sul-i **Sulph** k* symph fd3.de• thuj tritic-vg fd5.de tub c1 *Zinc* k* zinc-p k2
  - **morning**: hura meph a1
    - **rising** agg.: nat-m h2

Weakness – Lumbar region: ...

  - **evening**: alum alumn *Coloc* hura petr h2 plut-n srj7•
  - **accompanied** by | **sore** pain (See Pain - sore - accompanied - lumbar)
  - **eating** agg.: nat-m
  - **ejaculation**; after: ham *Nat-p* phos k*
  - **exertion** agg.; after: phys plan
  - **fever**; during: hura
  - **learn** to walk; children do not: all-s k*
  - **leukorrhea**; during: *Con* **Graph**
  - **lying** | **abdomen**; on | **amel.**: malar jl2
    - **back**; on:
      - **agg.**: calc-s malar jl2 nat-p
      - **amel.**: nat-m
  - **menses** agg.: *Cocc* mrr1
  - **motion**:
    - **agg.**: pic-ac *Sulph*
    - **amel.**: ignis-alc es2•
  - **reaching** up agg.: zinc bg1
  - **riding** agg.: berb cere-b
  - **rising** from sitting agg.: phos h2
  - **sitting** agg.: alum canth ferr-p graph h2 helon hep iris-foe *Phos* symph fd3.de• thuj zinc
  - **standing** agg.: *Chel* *Cic* **Sulph** symph fd3.de•
  - **stooping** agg.: am-c h2 bamb-a stb2.de•
  - **urination** agg.; during: puls
    - **copious** urination: puls bg2
  - **walking**:
    - **after** | **agg.**: petr a1
    - **agg.**: brach but-ac br1 camph **Cocc** graph h2 malar jl2 petr sep h2 tritic-vg fd5.de *Zinc*
    - **beginning** to walk: *Zinc*

▽ - **extending** to | **Upward**: nux-m bg1

○ - **Waist**; below: bell bg2

- **Sacroiliac** symphyses: aesc k2 arg-n *Sep*
- **Sacrum**: (↗*Instability - sacrum*) agar bg2 ars bry bg2 calad bg2 carb-v bg2 coloc graph bg2 helo helo-s rwt2• *Helon* br1 kali-p mtf11 kalm lith-c merc nat-ar nat-m nux-m ozone sde2• petr k* *Phos* k* pic-ac plac rzf5• puls bg2 **Sep** k ●* sil k* sulph *Zinc*
  - **evening**: petr h2
  - **night**: *Lith-c*
  - **paralyzed**; as if: cocc mtf11
- **Spine**: *Aesc* bro1 *Alum-sil* br1* arg-n bro1 bar-c bro1 calc-p bg2* cocc bro1 *Con* bro1 irid-met br1 nat-m bg2* nux-m bg2 phos bg2* pic-ac bro1 sel bro1 sil bg2* *Stry* bro1 stry-p br1 zinc-pic bro1
  - **sitting** agg.: calc ptk1 sulph ptk1 zinc ptk1
  - **standing** impossible: sul-ac ptk1
  - **support** body; can not: ox-ac ptk1
  - **typhoid** fever; after: *Sel* ptk1

○ - **Vertebrae**: bar-c bg2 hep bg2

WEATHER:
- **cold**:
  - **wet** | **agg.**: *Nux-m* b7a.de
- **weather**; before stormy: agar bg2
- **wet** | **agg.**: *Rhod* b4.de* sars bg2

WET CLOTH; sensation of a (See Coldness - lumbar - cold; Coldness - sacral - wet; Coldness - spine - wet)

WHIPLASH (See Injuries)

WIND agg.: nat-c bg2

WIND was blowing; as if:
- **cool**, on back: asar rb2 chin rb2 culx rb2 ham fd3.de•

○ - **Dorsal** region | **Shoulders**; between: caust *Hep* sulph
- **Lumbar** region: sulph ptk1 *Sumb* k*

- **Neck**; on: olnd bg1

WORKING with hands: | **amel.**: nat-m b4.de*

WRINKLED: | **Cervical** region: iod mtf33 nat-m mtf33 sars ptk1

WRITING agg.: carb-v b4.de* lyc ptk1 mur-ac b4.de* sep ptk1
○ - **Cervical** region: carb-an ptk1 lyc ptk1 **Zinc** ptk1

YAWNING: | **after** | **agg.**: am-m b7.de* *Myrt-c* b7a.de
- **agg.**: calc-p ptk1 plat ptk1 sabad b7.de*
○ • **Cervical** region: cocc ptk1 nat-s ptk1

CERVICAL REGION; complaints of: acon ptk1 bar-c ptk1 *Calc* ptk1 cimic ptk1 gels ptk1 *Nux-v* ptk1 phyt ptk1 puls ptk1 rhus-t ptk1 sanic ptk1 sep ptk1 sil ptk1 staph ptk1 tub ptk1 [fl-pur stj2 lith-i stj2]
- **alternating** sides: calc-p ptk1 *Puls* ptk1

▽ - **extending** to:
○ • **Face**: kalm ptk1
• **Fingers**: par ptk1
• **Vertex**: kalm ptk1

○ - **Glands**: am-m ptk1 astac ptk1 bar-c ptk1 *Calc* ptk1 cist ptk1 graph ptk1 kali-c ptk1 lap-a ptk1 lyc ptk1 *Merc* ptk1 merc-i-f ptk1 rhus-t ptk1 *Sil* ptk1 *Sulph* ptk1 viol-t ptk1
• **accompanied** by | **rheumatic** complaints (See EXTREMITIES - Pain - rheumatic - accompanied - cervical - complaints)

- **Nape** of neck: acon b2.de* agar b2.de* agn b2.de* alum b2.de* *Am-c* b2.de* am-m b2.de* ambr b2.de* anac b2.de* ang b2.de* ant-c b2.de* ant-t b2.de* arg-met b2.de* arn b2.de* ars b2.de* asaf b2.de* asar b2.de* aur b2.de* **Bar-c** b2.de* **Bell** b2.de* borx b2.de* bov b2.de* bry b2.de* **Calc** b2.de* camph b2.de* cann-s b2.de* canth b2.de* caps b2.de* carb-an b2.de* *Carb-v* b2.de* *Caust* b2.de* cham b2.de* chin b2.de* *Cimic* bg2 cina b2.de* clem b2.de* cocc b2.de* colch b2.de* coloc b2.de* con b2.de* croc b2.de* cupr b2.de* cycl b2.de* dig b2.de* dros b2.de* dulc b2.de* euph b2.de* ferr b2.de* graph b2.de* guaj b2.de* hell b2.de* hep b2.de* hyos b2.de* ign b2.de* iod b2.de* ip b2.de* *Kali-c* b2.de* kali-n b2.de* *Lach* b2.de* laur b2.de* led b2.de* *Lyc* b2.de* m-ambo b2.de m-aust b2.de mag-c b2.de* mag-m b2.de* mang b2.de* meny b2.de* merc b2.de* mez b2.de mosch b2.de* *Nat-c* b2.de* **Nat-m** b2.de* *Nit-ac* b2.de* nux-m b2.de* **Nux-v** b2.de* olnd b2.de* op b2.de* par b2.de* *Petr* b2.de* ph-ac b2.de* *Phos* b2.de* *Phyt* bg2 plat b2.de* plb b2.de* *Puls* b2.de* ran-b b2.de* rheum b2.de* rhod b2.de* **Rhus-t** b2.de* ruta b2.de* sabad b2.de* sabin b2.de* samb b2.de* sars b2.de* sec b2.de* sel b2.de* **Sep** b2.de* **Sil** b2.de* spig b2.de* spong b2.de* squil b2.de* stann b2.de* staph b2.de* stront-c b2.de* **Sulph** b2.de* tarax b2.de* thuj b2.de* valer b2.de* verat b2.de* viol-o b2.de* viol-t b2.de* zinc b2.de*

▽ • **extending** to:
⁝ **Arms**: *Kalm* ptk1 *Lach* ptk1 nat-m ptk1 nux-v ptk1
⁝ **Downward**: acon bg2 ail bg2 bell bg2 carb-v bg2 chel bg2 dig bg2 kali-c bg2 kalm bg2 lyc bg2 mag-c bg2 nat-m bg2
⁝ **Eyes**: gels bg2 kalm bg2 lach bg2 ph-ac bg2 pic-ac bg2
⁝ **Face**: ol-an bg2 op bg2
⁝ **Head**: caust bg2 chel bg2 cimic bg2 crot-h bg2 gels bg2 glon bg2 kalm bg2 lach bg2 meny bg2 par bg2 sang bg2 sil bg2 stront-c bg2 verat bg2
⁝ **Shoulder**: lach bg2
⁝ **Teeth**: ol-an bg2
⁝ **Throat**: lach bg2
⁝ **Upward**: *Gels* bg2 glon bg2 kalm bg2 meny bg2 nat-m bg2 sang bg2 stront-c bg2
⁝ **Vertex**: lach bg2

○ • **Glands**: *Bar-c* b4a.de *Bell* b4a.de *Dulc* b4a.de *Iod* b4a.de petr b4a.de **Sil** b4a.de sulph b4a.de

- **Vertebrae**: acon bg2 anac bg2 arn bg2 calc bg2 carb-v bg2 *Con* bg2 dig bg2 guaj bg2 kali-n bg2 lach bg2 mang bg2 nat-c bg2 nit-ac bg2 nux-v bg2 puls bg2 sabin bg2 sep bg2 stann bg2 sulph bg2

COCCYX; complaints of: *Agar* b2.de *Agn* b2.de *Alum* b2.de am-c b2.de am-m b2.de ang b2.de ant-c b2.de *Apis* ptk1 arg-met b2.de *Arn* b2.de* asaf b2.de bell b2.de bell-p ptk1 *Borx* b2.de bov b2.de *Calc* b2.de cann-s b2.de *Canth* b2.de carb-an b2.de *Carb-v* b2.de *Caust* b2.de* *Chin* b2.de cic b2.de *Colch* b2.de croc b2.de dros b2.de **Graph** b2.de **Hep** b2.de *Hyper* ptk1 *Ign* b2.de iod b2.de kali-c b2.de *Kreos* ptk1 lach b2.de laur b2.de *Led* b2.de mag-c b2.de *Merc* b2.de mur-ac b2.de *Par* b2.de petr b2.de *Ph-ac* b2.de phos b2.de *Plat* b2.de plb b2.de

Coccyx; complaints of: ...
Rhus-t b2.de *Ruta* b2.de* sil b2.de* spig b2.de staph b2.de *Sulph* b2.de thuj b2.de valer b2.de verat b2.de zinc b2.de*

▽ - **extending** to:
○ • **Epigastrium**: puls bg2
• **Thighs**: rhus-t ptk1
• **Upward**:
⁝ **stool** | **after** | **agg.**: euph ptk1
: **during** | **agg.**: phos ptk1
⁝ **Arms**; to: hyper ptk1
⁝ **Downward**; and: kali-bi a3*
⁝ **Spine** to base of brain; along: phos k2*
• **Vagina**: kreos bg2

DORSAL REGION; complaints of: *Acon* bg2 agar bg2 agn bg2 alum bg2 am-c bg2 am-m bg2 ambr bg2 anac bg2 *Ang* bg2 ant-c bg2 ant-t bg2 arg-met bg2 **Arn** bg2 **Ars** bg2 asaf bg2 asar bg2 aur bg2 bapt bg2 bar-c bg2 **Bell** bg2 bism bg2 borx bg2 bov bg2 bry bg2 **Calc** bg2 camph bg2 cann-xyz bg2 canth bg2 caps bg2 carb-an bg2 *Carb-v* bg2 **Caust** bg2 cham bg2 chel bg2 *Chin* bg2 cic bg2 cimic bg2 cina bg2 **Cocc** bg2 coff bg2 colch bg2 coloc bg2 con bg2 croc bg2 cupr bg2 cycl bg2 dig bg2 dros bg2 dulc bg2 euph bg2 euphr bg2 ferr bg2 graph bg2 *Guaj* bg2 hell bg2 hep bg2 hyos bg2 ign bg2 iod bg2 ip bg2 *Kali-c* bg2 kali-n bg2 kreos bg2 lach bg2 laur bg2 led bg2 **Lyc** bg2 lycps-v bg2 mag-c bg2 mag-m bg2 mang bg2 meny bg2 *Merc* bg2 mez bg2 mosch bg2 mur-ac bg2 *Nat-c* bg2 **Nat-m** bg2 nit-ac bg2 nux-m bg2 **Nux-v** bg2 olnd bg2 op bg2 par bg2 *Petr* bg2 ph-ac bg2 phos bg2 *Phyt* bg2 plat bg2 plb bg2 **Puls** bg2 ran-b bg2 ran-s bg2 rheum bg2 rhod bg2 *Rhus-t* bg2 *Ruta* bg2 sabad bg2 sabin bg2 samb bg2 sars bg2 sec bg2 sel bg2 seneg bg2 **Sep** bg2 **Sil** bg2 spig bg2 spong bg2 squil bg2 *Stann* bg2 staph bg2 stront-c bg2 sul-ac bg2 **Sulph** bg2 tarax bg2 teucr bg2 thuj bg2 valer bg2 *Verat* bg2 verb bg2 viol-t bg2 *Zinc* bg2
- **alternating** sides: bell bg2
- **right**: acon bg2 agar bg2 alum bg2 am-c bg2 am-m bg2 ambr bg2 anac bg2 ang bg2 ant-c bg2 ant-t bg2 apis bg2 arg-met bg2 *Arn* bg2 *Ars* bg2 asaf bg2 asar bg2 aur bg2 bar-c bg2 bell bg2 borx bg2 bov bg2 *Bry* bg2 **Calc** bg2 cann-xyz bg2 *Canth* bg2 *Carb-an* bg2 carb-v bg2 caust bg2 *Chel* bg2 chin bg2 **Cic** bg2 cina bg2 cocc bg2 colch bg2 *Coloc* bg2 *Con* bg2 cupr bg2 dig bg2 dros bg2 dulc bg2 *Euph* bg2 **Fl-ac** bg2 *Guaj* bg2 hep bg2 iod bg2 kali-c bg2 *Laur* bg2 *Lyc* bg2 mag-p bg2 meny bg2 merc bg2 mez bg2 mur-ac bg2 *Nat-m* bg2 nit-ac bg2 *Nux-v* bg2 *Olnd* bg2 petr bg2 *Phos* bg2 plat bg2 *Plb* bg2 *Ran-b* bg2 ran-s bg2 rhod bg2 *Rhus-t* bg2 ruta bg2 sabad bg2 *Samb* bg2 sars bg2 sep bg2 sil bg2 spig bg2 spong bg2 stann bg2 staph bg2 sul-ac bg2 *Sulph* bg2 *Tarax* bg2 teucr bg2 thuj bg2 verb bg2 viol-t bg2 **Zinc** bg2
- **left**: *Acon* bg2 *Agar* bg2 agn bg2 *Alum* bg2 am-c bg2 am-m bg2 ambr bg2 *Anac* bg2 ang bg2 ant-c bg2 ant-t bg2 *Apis* bg2 arg-met bg2 ars bg2 asaf bg2 aur bg2 *Bar-c* bg2 bell bg2 *Bism* bg2 *Bry* bg2 calc bg2 cann-xyz bg2 canth bg2 carb-an bg2 carb-v bg2 *Caust* bg2 chel bg2 chen-v bg2 *Chin* bg2 cina bg2 cocc bg2 colch bg2 coloc bg2 con bg2 croc bg2 cupr bg2 dig bg2 **Dros** bg2 dulc bg2 euph bg2 ferr bg2 fl-ac bg2 **Glon** bg2 *Graph* bg2 guaj bg2 hell bg2 *Hep* bg2 *Ign* bg2 iod bg2 *Kali-bi* bg2 *Kali-c* bg2 kali-n bg2 kreos bg2 laur bg2 led bg2 lyc bg2 lycps-v bg2 *Mang* bg2 meny bg2 merc bg2 mez bg2 mosch bg2 mur-ac bg2 nat-m bg2 nit-ac bg2 *Nux-v* bg2 olnd bg2 *Par* bg2 petr bg2 ph-ac bg2 phos bg2 plat bg2 plb bg2 psor bg2 *Puls* bg2 ran-s bg2 rhod bg2 rhus-t bg2 *Ruta* bg2 sabad bg2 *Sabin* bg2 sars bg2 *Seneg* bg2 sep bg2 **Sil** bg2 spig bg2 *Spong* bg2 *Squil* bg2 *Stann* bg2 staph bg2 stront-c bg2 sul-ac bg2 *Sulph* bg2 tarax bg2 *Teucr* bg2 thuj bg2 *Valer* bg2 *Verat* bg2 verb bg2 viol-t bg2 zinc bg2

▽ - **extending** to:
○ • **Anus**: nat-c bg2
• **Downward**: ail bg2 coc-c bg2 dig bg2 nat-m bg2
• **Eyes**: chin bg2
• **Head**: puls bg2
• **Hypochondria**:
⁝ **right**: chel bg2 coc-c bg2 kali-n bg2 merc bg2
⁝ **left**: canth bg2 ign bg2 jatr-c bg2 kali-bi bg2 lyc bg2 phos bg2
• **Inguinal** region: bell bg2
• **Legs**: *Berb* bg2 cob bg2 helo bg2 lach bg2 sulph bg2
• **Occiput**: *Puls* bg2
• **Temples**: *Puls* bg2
• **Thighs**: berb bg2 cham bg2
• **Vertex**: ars bg2

○ - **Scapulae**: acon b2.de* agar b2.de* alum b2.de* *Am-c* b2.de* am-m b2.de* ambr b2.de* anac b2.de* ang b2.de* ant-c b2.de* arg-met b2.de* arn b2.de* ars b2.de* asaf b2.de* asar b2.de* aur b2.de* bar-c b2.de* bell b2.de* bism b2.de* borx b2.de* bov b2.de* bry b2.de* calc b2.de* camph b2.de* cann-s b2.de* canth b2.de* caps b2.de* carb-an b2.de* carb-v b2.de* **Caust** b2.de* cham b2.de* *Chel* b2.de* **Chin** b2.de* cic b2.de* cina b2.de* cocc b2.de* colch b2.de* coloc b2.de* con b2.de* croc b2.de* cupr b2.de* cycl b2.de* dig b2.de* dros b2.de* dulc b2.de* ferr b2.de* *Graph* b2.de* guaj b2.de* hell b2.de* hep b2.de* hyos b2.de* ign b2.de* iod b2.de* ip b2.de* *Kali-c* b2.de* *Kali-n* b2.de* **Kreos** b2.de* lach b2.de* laur b2.de* led b2.de* lyc b2.de* m-ambo b2.de m-arct b2.de m-aust b2.de mag-c b2.de* mag-m b2.de* mang b2.de* meny b2.de* *Merc* b2.de* mez b2.de* mosch b2.de* mur-ac b2.de* nat-c b2.de* nat-m b2.de* *Nit-ac* b2.de* *Nux-v* b2.de* olnd b2.de* op b2.de* par b2.de* petr b2.de* ph-ac b2.de* phos b2.de* plat b2.de* *Plb* b2.de* *Puls* b2.de* ran-b b2.de* ran-s b2.de* rhod b2.de* **Rhus-t** b2.de* ruta b2.de* sabad b2.de* sabin b2.de* samb b2.de* sars b2.de* seneg b2.de* **Sep** b2.de* sil b2.de* spig b2.de* spong b2.de* squil b2.de* *Stann* b2.de* staph b2.de* stront-c b2.de* sul-ac b2.de* sulph b2.de* tarax b2.de* tell ptk1 teucr b2.de* thuj b2.de* valer b2.de* verat b2.de* verb b2.de* *Viol-t* b2.de* zinc b2.de*

- **alternating** sides: plan bg2
- **right**: bry bg2* chel bg2* chen-a bg2 hydr bg2 jug-c bg2 kali-c bg2 ol-an ptk1 podo bg2* rumx ptk1 sang bg2 stict bg2
- **left**: chen-v bg2 cimic bg2* kalm bg2 lach bg2 lil-t bg2 phos bg2 ran-b bg2 sulph bg2 zinc-chr ptk1
  - **Angle**: bry bg2 chen-v bg2 cimic bg2
  - **Edge**; inner: ran-b bg2

▽ • **extending** to:
  - **Cervical** region | **Nape** of neck: nat-c bg2
  - **Chest**: petr bg2
  - **Elbow**: abrot bg2 berb bg2 coc-c bg2 lach bg2 lyc bg2 phos bg2 rhus-t bg2 sulph bg2
  - **Epigastrium**: bry bg2*
  - **Shoulder**:
    - **right**: stict bg2
    - **left**: kali-bi bg2
  - **Stomach**: bry bg2
  - **Upper** limbs: berb bg2 kali-bi bg2
    - **left**: kalm bg2

○ • **Beneath**: calc ptk1 *Gels* ptk1 merc ptk1 myric ptk1 squil ptk1
  - **right**: chel ptk1 coloc ptk1 podo ptk1 rumx ptk1
  - **left**: crat ptk1 gels ptk1

- **Between**: am-m ptk1 ars ptk1 calc ptk1 calc-p ptk1 caps ptk1 helon ptk1 nit-ac ptk1 phos ptk1 rhus-t ptk1 sep ptk1
  - **extending** to | **Heart**: bry ptk1 sulph ptk1
- **Region** of:
  - **extending** to | **Forward**: bry ptk1

- **Vertebrae**:

○ • **Last**: zinc ptk1
- **Upper**: kalm ptk1

LUMBAR REGION; complaints of:

acon b2.de* **Aesc** bg2* agar b2.de* aloe bg2 **Alum** b2.de* am-c b2.de* am-m b2.de* ambr b2.de* anac b2.de* ang b2.de* ant-c b2.de* **Ant-t** b2.de* arg-met b2.de* arg-n bg2 arn b2.de* ars b2.de* asaf b2.de* asar b2.de* aur b2.de* *Bar-c* b2.de* bell b2.de* **Berb** bg2* borx b2.de* bov b2.de* bry b2.de* calad b2.de* **Calc** b2.de* *Calc-p* bg2 cann-s b2.de* canth b2.de* caps b2.de* carb-an b2.de* carb-v b2.de* **Caust** b2.de* cham b2.de* chel b2.de* *Chin* b2.de* *Cimic* ptk1 cina b2.de* *Cocc* b2.de* coff b2.de* colch b2.de* coloc b2.de* con b2.de* croc b2.de* *Crot-h* bg2 cupr b2.de* dig b2.de* dros b2.de* dulc b2.de* eup-per ptk1 euph b2.de* ferr b2.de* graph b2.de* guaj b2.de* ham bg2 hell b2.de* hep b2.de* hyos b2.de* *Ign* b2.de* iod b2.de* ip b2.de* *Kali-bi* bg2 **Kali-c** b2.de* kali-n b2.de* **Kreos** b2.de* **Lach** b2.de* laur b2.de* led b2.de* *Lyc* b2.de* lycps-v bg2 m-ambo b2.de m-aust b2.de *Mag-c* b2.de* mag-m b2.de* mang b2.de* meny b2.de* *Merc* b2.de* mez b2.de* mosch b2.de* mur-ac b2.de* nat-c b2.de* nat-m b2.de* **Nit-ac** b2.de* *Nux-m* b2.de* **Nux-v** b2.de* op b2.de* *Petr* b2.de* ph-ac b2.de* phos b2.de* plat b2.de* plb b2.de* prun bg2 **Puls** b2.de* ran-b b2.de* ran-s b2.de* rheum b2.de* rhod b2.de* **Rhus-t** b2.de* *Ruta* b2.de* sabad b2.de* *Sabin* b2.de* samb b2.de* sang bg2 sanic ptk1 sars b2.de* sec b2.de* sel b2.de* seneg b2.de* **Sep** b2.de* *Sil* b2.de* solid ptk1 spig b2.de* spong b2.de* squil b2.de* stann b2.de* *Staph* b2.de* stram b2.de* stront-c b2.de* sul-ac b2.de* **Sulph** b2.de* tarax b2.de* thuj b2.de* tril-p bg2 valer b2.de* *Vario* ptk1 verat b2.de* *Zinc* b2.de* zinc-ar ptk1

- **accompanied** by | **Female** genitalia; complaints of (See FEMALE - Complaints - accompanied - lumbar)

▽ - **extending** to:

○ • **Cervical** region | **Nape** of neck: kali-bi bg2
- **Chest**: berb bg2* sulph bg2*
- **Epigastrium**: lyc bg2 puls bg2 sulph bg2
- **Forward**: *Berb* ptk1 cham ptk1 *Kali-c* ptk1 kreos ptk1 **Sabin** ptk1
- **Genitals**: gran bg2
- **Inguinal** region: kali-bi bg2 phos ptk1 sabin ptk1 vib ptk1
- **Legs**: cob bg2 kali-c ptk1
- **Lungs** | **left**: sep bg2
- **Pubes**: phos ptk1 sabin bg2* vib bg2*
- **Scapula** | **right**: nat-m bg2
- **Sternum**: kali-bi bg2
- **Stomach**: sulph ptk1
- **Urethra**: kali-bi bg2
- **Uterus**: nat-m ptk1
- **Vertex**: phos bg2

○ - **Vertebrae**: am-m bg2 aur bg2 kreos bg2* nux-m bg2 ph-ac bg2 phos bg2 prun bg2 stann bg2* zinc bg2*

SACRAL REGION; complaints of:

aesc ptk1 *Agar* bg2* *Agn* bg2 *Alum* bg2 am-c bg2 am-m bg2 ang bg2 ant-c bg2 arg-met bg2 *Arn* bg2 asaf bg2 bell bg2 *Borx* bg2 bov bg2 bufo bg2 *Calc* bg2 cann-xyz bg2 *Canth* bg2 carb-an bg2 *Carb-v* bg2 *Caust* bg2 *Chin* bg2 cic bg2 cimic bg2 cist bg2 *Colch* bg2 croc bg2 dros bg2 ferr-p bg2 gamb bg2 gels ptk1 **Graph** bg2* **Hep** bg2* hyper bg2* *Ign* bg2 iod bg2 kali-bi bg2 *Kali-c* bg2 kali-i bg2 kreos bg2 lach bg2 laur bg2 *Led* bg2 lob bg2 mag-c bg2 mag-p bg2 *Merc* bg2 mur-ac bg2* *Par* bg2 petr bg2 *Ph-ac* bg2 phos bg2 *Plat* bg2 plb bg2 puls ptk1 **Rhus-t** bg2* *Ruta* bg2 senec bg2 sep ptk1 sil bg2 spig bg2 staph bg2 *Sulph* bg2 tarent bg2 thuj bg2 valer bg2 verat bg2 zinc bg2

- **accompanied** by | **Genitals**; heaviness: lob ptk1

▽ - **extending** to:

○ • **Epigastrium**: puls bg2
- **Feet**: cob ptk1 kali-m ptk1
- **Rectum**: kreos bg2
- **Thigh**:
  - **right**: colch ptk1 tell ptk1
  - **left**: kali-c ptk1
- **Vagina**: kreos bg2

○ - **Sacroiliac** symphyses aesc bg2 alum bg2 am-m bg2 ant-t bg2 arg-n bg2 calc-p bg2 sil bg2 tril-p bg2

SPINE; complaints of:

Alum-sil br1 *Gua* br1 par ptk1 syph jl2 tell br1 ther ptk1 valer ptk1 vario ptk1 zinc br1

- **accompanied** by:
  - **constipation** (See RECTUM - Constipation - accompanied - spine)
  - **hiccough** (See STOMACH - Hiccough - accompanied - spine)
  - **neurological** complaints: *Arg-n* br1 mentho br1
- **neurasthenic**: cob br1
- **pollutions**; after: nux-v bg2 puls bg2
- **spots**; in: agar ptk1

▽ - **extending** to:

○ • **Downward**: cob ptk1 pic-ac ptk1 tab ptk1 tell ptk1
- **Feet**: cob ptk1
- **Occiput**: petr ptk1
- **Thighs**: rhod ptk1
- **Upward** | **Downward**; and: gels ptk1 phyt ptk1

○ - **Spinal** cord: agar ptk1 arg-n ptk1 chin ptk1 cocc ptk1 *Gels* ptk1 ign ptk1 **Lach** b7a.de med ptk1 **Nux-v** b7a.de* ox-ac ptk1 phos ptk1 pic-ac ptk1 plb ptk1 sec ptk1

DAYTIME: | **Lower** limbs: coloc bg2 dig bg2

MORNING:

○ - **Lower** limbs: acon b7.de* agn b7.de* alum b4.de* am-c b4.de* am-m b7.de* ambr b7.de* anac b4a.de ang b7.de* ant-t b7.de* arg-n bg2 arn b7.de* ars b4.de* aur b4a.de bar-c b4.de* borx b4a.de bov b4.de* bry b7.de* calc b4.de* camph b7.de* canth b7.de* caps b7.de* carb-an b4.de* *Carb-v* b4.de* caust b4.de* chin b7.de* con b4.de* dros b7.de* dulc b4.de* euph b4.de* ferr b7.de* form bg2 *Graph* b4.de* hep b4.de* *Ign* b7.de* kali-c b4.de* kali-n b4.de* *Kreos* b7a.de led b7.de* lyc b4.de* m-ambo b7.de m-arct b7.de m-aust b7.de mag-c b4.de* mag-m b4.de* merc b4.de* mez b4.de* nat-m b4.de* nit-ac b4.de* nux-m b7.de* **Nux-v** b7.de* petr b4.de* ph-ac b4.de* phos b4.de* plb b7.de* puls b7.de* ran-b b7.de* rheum b7.de* *Rhod* b4a.de *Rhus-t* b7.de* sabad b7.de* sabin b7.de* sars b4.de* sel b7.de* sep b4.de* sil b4.de* spig b7.de* spong b7.de* *Staph* b7.de* stront-c b4.de* sul-ac b4.de* sulph b4.de* tarax b7.de* teucr b7.de* thuj b4.de* valer b7.de* verat b7.de* viol-t b7.de*

- **Upper** limbs: alum b4.de* *Am-c* b4a.de* am-m b7.de* ambr b7.de* arn b7.de* ars bg2 aur b4.de* bar-c b4.de* bell b4.de* bov b4.de* bry bg2 *Calc* b4.de* canth b7.de* carb-an b4.de* carb-v b4.de* caust b4.de* cham b7.de* cina b7.de* clem b4.de* coff b7.de* croc b7.de* cupr b7a.de* dulc b4.de* ferr b7.de* hell b7.de* ign b7.de* iod b4.de* kali-c b4.de* kreos b7a.de* lyc b4.de* m-ambo b7.de m-aust b7.de mag-c b4.de* **Mag-m** b4.de* merc b4.de* merc-c b4a.de mez b4.de* nat-c b4.de* nat-m b4.de* nit-ac b4.de* nux-m b7.de* *Nux-v* b7.de* petr b4.de* phos b4.de* plb b7.de* puls b7.de* ran-b b7.de* ran-s b7.de* rhod b4.de* rhus-t b7.de* sep b4.de* sil b4.de* *Staph* b7.de* sulph b4.de* tab bg2 teucr b7.de* thuj b4.de* valer b7.de* *Verat* b7.de* verb b7.de* zinc b4.de*

FORENOON:

○ - **Lower** limbs: alum b4.de* am-c b4.de* am-m b7.de* borx b4a.de bov b4.de* cann-s b7.de* canth b7.de* carb-an b4.de* kali-c b4.de* kreos b7a.de merc b4.de* mur-ac b4.de* nat-c b4.de* nux-v b7.de* phos b4.de* plb b7.de* puls b7.de* ran-b b7.de* *Rhod* b4a.de rhus-t b7.de* *Sabad* b7.de* seneg b4.de* sep b4.de* sil b4.de* squil b7.de* staph b7.de* sulph b4.de* teucr b7.de* valer b7.de*

- **Upper** limbs: alum b4.de* am-c b4.de* ars b4.de* chel b7.de* fl-ac bg2 laur b7.de* mag-c b4.de* merc b4.de* ph-ac b4.de* phos b4.de* plb b7.de* *Sabad* b7.de* staph b7.de* zinc b4.de*

NOON: | **Lower** limbs: calc bg2

AFTERNOON:

○ - **Lower** limbs: agar b4.de* alum b4.de* am-c b4.de* am-m b7.de* ant-c b7.de* ant-t b7.de* ars b4.de* *Asaf* b7.de* bell b4.de* borx b4a.de bov b4.de* bry b7.de* calc b4.de* canth b7.de* carb-v b4.de* *Chel* b7.de* chin b7.de* cina b7.de* con b4.de* dros b7.de* graph b4.de* hyos b7.de* kali-c b4.de* kali-n b4.de* kreos b7a.de lach b7.de* laur b7.de* m-aust b7.de mag-c b4.de* mur-ac b4.de* nat-c b4.de* nux-m b7.de* nux-v b7.de* op b7.de* phos b4.de* plb b7.de* puls b7.de* ran-b b7.de* rhus-t b7.de* sars b4.de* sil b4a.de *Spig* b7.de* spong b7.de* *Stann* b4a.de sulph b4.de* teucr b7.de* valer b7.de* verat b7.de* viol-t b7.de* zinc b4.de*

- **Upper** limbs: alum b4.de* am-c b4.de* *Am-m* b7.de* ant-c b7.de* asaf b7.de* bov b4.de* calc-p bg2 canth b7.de* cham b7.de* chel b7.de* cocc b7.de* euphr b7.de* graph b4.de* kali-n b4.de* *Laur* b7.de* *Lyc* b4a.de mag-c b4.de* merc b4.de* nux-v b7.de* *Phos* b4.de* puls b7.de* sars b4.de* spig b7.de* stann b4a.de stront-c b4.de* sulph b4.de* teucr b7.de* valer b7.de* zinc b4.de*

EVENING:

○ - **Lower** limbs: acon b7.de* agn b7.de* alum b4.de* am-c b4.de* *Am-m* b7.de* ambr b7.de* ang b7.de* ant-c b7.de* *Ant-t* b7.de* apis b7a.de arg-met b7.de* *Arn* b7.de* *Asar* b7.de* bar-c b4.de* bell b4.de* bov b4.de* *Bry* b7.de* *Calc* b4.de* carb-an b4.de* carb-v b4.de* caust b4.de* cham b7.de* *Chin* b7.de* cocc b7.de* coff bg2 colch b7.de* coloc b4a.de con b4.de* croc b7.de* cycl b7.de* dig b4.de* dios bg2 dulc b4.de* euph b4.de* *Ferr* b7.de* gels bg2 *Graph* b4.de* hep b4.de* hyos b7.de* ign b7.de* iod b4.de* ip b7.de* kali-bi bg2 *Kali-c* b4.de* kali-n b4.de* kreos b7a.de* lach b7.de* laur b7.de* *Led* b7.de* lyc b4.de* m-ambo b7.de m-arct b7.de m-aust b7.de mag-c b4.de* mag-m b4.de* mang b4.de* meny b7.de* merc b4.de* merc-c b4a.de mez b4.de* nat-c b4.de* nat-m b4.de* nat-s bg2 *Nit-ac* b4a.de nux-v b7.de* par b7.de* petr b4.de* ph-ac b4.de* phos b4.de* plat b4.de* plb b7.de* **Puls** b7.de* **Ran-b** b7.de* *Ran-s* b7.de* rhod b4.de* **Rhus-t** b7.de* sabin b7.de* samb b7.de* sars b4.de* sel b7.de* seneg b4.de* *Sep* b4.de* **Sil** b4.de* spong b7.de* stann b4.de* *Staph* b7.de* stram b7.de* stront-c b4.de* sul-ac b4.de* sulph b4.de* thuj b4.de* *Valer* b7.de* *Zinc* b4.de*

- **Upper** limbs: acon b7.de* agn b7.de* alum bg2 am-c b4.de* am-m b7.de* ambr b7.de* anac b4.de* ang b7.de* ant-c b7.de* ant-t b7.de* arn b7.de* ars b4.de* asar b7.de* borx b4a.de* bov b4.de bry b7.de* calc b4.de* canth b7.de* caps b7.de* carb-an b4a.de carb-v bg2 caust b4a.de* chel b7.de* chin b7.de* colch b7.de*

Evening – Upper limbs: ...

con b4.de* dulc b4.de* ferr b7.de* hell b7.de* hyos b7.de* ign b7.de* ip b7.de* kali-bi bg2 kali-c b4.de* kali-n b4.de* kreos bg2 lach b7.de* laur bg2 *Led* b7.de* lith-c bg2 lyc b4.de* *M-ambo* b7.de m-arct b7.de m-aust b7.de mag-c b4.de* mag-m bg2 mang b4.de* meny b7.de* merc b4.de* mez b4.de* mosch b7.de* nat-c b4.de* nat-m b4.de* nit-ac bg2 nux-m b7.de* nux-v b7.de* par b7.de* petr bg2 phos b4.de* plb b7.de* **Puls** b7.de* ran-b b7.de* *Ran-s* b7.de* *Rhod* b4.de* **Rhus-t** b7.de* sabad b7.de* samb b7.de* sars b4.de* sep b4.de* sil b4.de* stann b4.de* staph b7.de* stront-c b4.de* sulph b4.de* teucr b7.de* thuj b4.de* *Valer* b7.de* zinc b4.de*

NIGHT:

- **midnight**:

• **before**:

⁝ **Lower** limbs: ang b7.de* bry b7.de* calad b7.de* carb-v b4.de* cham b7.de* ferr b7.de* ign b7.de* lach b7.de* **Led** b7.de* lyc b4.de* mag-c b4.de* nat-m b4.de* nux-v b7.de* *Puls* b7.de* ran-b b7.de* *Rhus-t* b7.de* sabad b7.de* sars b4.de* spig b7.de* spong b7.de* staph b7.de* stront-c b4.de* *Valer* b7.de*

⁝ **Upper** limbs: ang b7.de* cham b7.de* *Led* b7.de* *Puls* b7.de* rhus-t b7.de* valer b7.de*

• **after**:

⁝ **Lower** limbs: ambr b7.de* asaf b7.de* canth b7.de* caps b7.de* *Caust* b4a.de cham b7.de* ign b7.de* kali-n b4.de* merc b4.de* mez b4.de* *Nux-v* b7.de* *Ran-s* b7.de* rhus-t b7.de* sabad b7.de* samb b7.de* sars b4.de* stront-c b4.de*

⁝ **Upper** limbs: ambr b7.de* cham b7.de* *Dig* b4a.de **Merc** b4a.de *Nux-v* b7.de* ran-s b7.de*

- **amel.** | **Lower** limbs: nicc bg2

○ - **Ankles**: mag-m ptk1

- **Lower** limbs: alum b4.de* am-c b4.de* am-m b7.de* ambr b7.de* anac b4a.de ang b7.de* arn b7.de* *Ars* b4.de* aur b4.de* bar-c b4.de* *Bell* b4.de* *Brom* b4a.de *Bry* b7.de* bufo bg2 calad b7.de* calc b4.de* canth b7.de* carb-an b4.de* *Carb-v* b4.de* caust b4.de* **Cham** b7.de* *Chin* b7.de* cocc b7.de* colch b7.de* coloc b4a.de* con b4.de* croc b7.de* cycl b7.de* dig b4.de* *Dros* b7.de* dulc b4.de* euph b4.de* *Euphr* b7a.de ferr b7a.de* gels bg2 graph b4.de* hep b4.de* hyos b7.de* ign b7a.de* *Ip* b7a.de kali-bi bg2 *Kali-c* b4.de* kali-i bg2 kali-n b4.de* kalm bg2 kreos b7a.de lach b7a.de* *Led* b7.de* *Lyc* b4.de* m-arct b7.de mag-c b4.de* mag-m b4.de* *Mang* b4.de* **Merc** b4.de* *Merc-c* b4a.de mez bg2 mur-ac b4.de* nat-c b4.de* nit-ac b4.de* *Nux-v* b7.de* par b7.de* petr b4.de* *Ph-ac* b4a.de *Phos* b4.de* phyt bg2 plat b4.de* plb bg2 *Puls* b7.de* rhod b4.de* *Rhus-t* b7.de* ruta b7.de* sabad b7a.de sabin b7.de* sars b4.de* sec b7a.de sel b7.de* sep b4.de* *Sil* b4.de* spig b7.de* spong b7.de* stann b4.de* *Staph* b7a.de still bg2 stront-c b4.de* sulph b4.de* thuj b4.de* valer b7.de* visc bg2 zinc b4.de*

- **Shoulder** | **left**: phos ptk1

- **Upper** limbs: aloe bg2 alum b4.de* am-c b4.de* am-m b7a.de* ambr b7.de* anac b4.de* ant-c bg2 arg-n bg2 **Ars** b4.de* aur b4.de* *Bell* b4.de* *Bry* b7.de* *Calc* b4.de* canth b7.de* carb-v b4.de* caust b4a.de* cham b7.de* chin b7.de* coff bg2 croc b7.de* cupr bg2 dig b4.de* *Dros* b7a.de dulc b4a.de *Ferr* b7a.de ferr-p bg2 hep b4.de* hyos b7.de* *Ign* b7a.de* *Iod* b4a.de kali-bi bg2 kali-c bg2 kali-n b4.de* kalm bg2 *Lach* b7a.de **Lyc** b4.de* m-arct b7.de m-aust b7.de *Mag-c* b4.de* mag-m bg2 mang b4.de* *Merc* b4.de* merc-c b4a.de mur-ac b4a.de* nat-c bg2 nit-ac b4.de* nux-v b7.de* petr b4.de* ph-ac bg2 phos b4.de* puls b7.de* rheum b7.de* rhod b4.de* rhus-t b7.de* ruta b7.de* sabad bg2 sel b7.de* **Sep** b4.de* **Sil** b4.de* *Staph* b7a.de stront-c b4.de* sulph b4.de* thuj b4.de* valer b7.de* viol-t b7.de* zinc b4.de*

ABDUCTED:

- **lies** with limbs abducted: **Aeth** sne **CHAM** k ●* chir-fl brm4• hell ptk1 lac-c bg2 led bg2 plat bg2 *Psor* stram bg2 sulph

• **convulsions**; during: cupr nux-v

○ - **Fingers**, spasmodically *Glon* k* kali-cy c1 lac-c k* lyc bg2* med ptk1 *Olnd* b7a.de **Sec** k*

• **holding** things; while: agar tl1 apis tl1

- **Lower** limbs: colch k* graph bg2 led bg2 nux-v plat sil bg2 stry

• **adducted**; abducted then: lyc h2

• **spasmodically**: lyc b4a.de

• **standing** agg.: phos ptk1* pic-ac k* ter ptk1

• **walking** agg.: (↗ *Walking - gressus gallinaceous*) phos ptk1*

- **Toes**: *Apis* b7a.de sec b7a.de

• **spasmodically**: camph *Glon* k* sec gk

- **Upper** limbs: haliae-lc srj5• nat-c bg2
  - · **agg.** | **Shoulders**: chel ptk1

ABRADED; easily (See Excoriation)

ABSCESS:
O - **Ankle** joint: ang guaj *Ol-j* k* sil
- **Bones**: guaj k2
- **Elbows**: *(↗Suppuration - elbows)* crot-h k* petr a1
- **Feet**: *Merc* k* sil k* tarent
O · **Heels**: am-c ars k* lach
- **Fingers**: androc srj1• bufo gk *Fl-ac Hep* hydrog srj2• *Lach Mang*
  - · **recurrent** (See GENERALS - History - abscesses - fingers)
O · **Bend** of: merc bg2
  - · **Knuckles**: kali-bi bg2 *Sep* bg2
  - · **Nail**; around: hydrog srj2•
  - · **Tips**: phos k2
- **Forearms**: plb sil hr1
- **Hands**: anan k* lach k*
  - · **small**: dros bg2 *Sil* bg2
O · **Back** of hands: plb
  - · **Palm** of: ars k* crot-h bg1* cupr k* fl-ac k* sulph k* tarent-c ptk1
    - ⁝ **accompanied** by | **fever**; high: crot-h tl1
- **Hip** | **left**: stram k2*
- **Joints**: *(↗GENERALS - Abscesses - joints)* calc-p k* guaj k2 *Hep* k* *Merc* k* *Phos* k* *Sil* k* stram k2
- **Knees**: *Bell* k* *Calc* k* *Guaj* hep k* hippoz k* *Iod* k* *Merc* hr1 *Ol-j* k* **Sil** k* *Sulph* hr1 tax c2
  - · **gonarthrocace**: *Ars* k* **Calc** k* *Iod* k* **Sil** k*
- **Legs**: *Anan* hr1 both fne1• chin hr1 guaj k2 sulph k*
O · **Calves**: chin k*
- **Lower** limbs: *Anan* chin
  - · **psoas**: *(↗BACK - Abscess - psoas)* arn k* asaf k* chin k* *Cupr* k* hippoz hr1 *Ph-ac* k* *Sil* k* staph k* *Sulph* k* symph k* *Syph* k*
- **Nates**: carbn-o *Sulph* k* thuj tritic-vg fd5.de
- **Tendons**: *Mez* k*
- **Thighs**: calc k2 *Hep* k* lach k* psil ft1 **Sil** k* tarent k* tritic-vg fd5.de
- **Toes**: bufo gk *Canth* hr1 cocc
- **Upper** arms: agar k* **Lach** bg2
O · **Deltoid**: agar k*
- **Upper** limbs: anan k* sil
  - · **left**:
    - ⁝ **accompanied** by | **Tongue**; trembling of: sil kr1*
  - · **gangrenous**: anan
  - · **wounds**, after dissecting: *Ars* bufo gk *Lach* k* *Sil* k*

ACIDS agg.: | **Upper** limbs: lach bg2

ACROCYANOSIS: ser-a-c jl2 tub-d jl2 tub-m jl2

ACROMEGALY (See GENERALS - Acromegaly)

ADHESION of the fold of skin to growing nail (See Nails - growth - fold)

AGILITY (See GENERALS - Agility)

AIR:
- **draft** of air; sensitive to a | **Feet**: ars mtf ars-s-f mtf bell mtf *Calc* mtf *Calc-sil* mtf chinin-s mtf hep mtf mag-sil mtf maland mtf *Nat-sil* mtf nux-v mtf *Psor* mtf *Sil* mtf stram mtf thea mtf thuj mtf verat mtf zinc mtf
O - **Hand** | **warm** air; sensation of: vac jl2
- **Knees** | **warm** air through knees; sensation of: lach ptk1
- **Legs** | **warm** air; sensation of: sulph h2
- **Shoulders** | **Finger**; sensation as if air was passing down from shoulder to: *Fl-ac*
- **Wrist** | **warm** air; sensation of: vac jl2

AIR; DRAFT OF:
- **agg.** | **Lower** limbs: acon b7.de* bell bg2 caust bg2 chin b7.de* hep bg2 kali-c bg2 merc bg2 nux-v b7.de* sel b7.de* zinc bg2

AIR; IN OPEN:
- **agg.**:
O · **Lower** limbs: bry b7.de* cham b7.de* chel b7.de* *Cocc* b7.de* *Coff* b7.de* con b4.de* *Graph* b4a.de ign b7.de* ip b7.de* kreos b7a.de* laur b7.de* m-arct b7.de meny b7.de* **Nux-v** b7.de* phos b4.de* rhus-t b7.de* spig b7.de* staph b7.de*
  - · **Upper** limbs: bry b7.de* cham b7.de* *Cocc* b7.de* ign b7.de* laur b7.de* *Nux-v* b7.de* rhus-t b7.de* spig b7.de*
- **amel.**:
O · **Lower** limbs: mez bg2 puls bg2
  - · **Upper** limbs: mosch b7a.de

ALIVE; sensation of something: *(↗Mouse)* ign k* *Rhod* b4a.de
O - **Feet** | **Soles**: caust bg2
- **Legs**: anac b4.de* *Rhod* b4a.de sil k*
- **Lower** limbs: *(↗Mouse - lower; Rat - legs)* ars bg2
- **Shoulders**: berb k*
- **Thighs**: meny b7.de*
- **Upper** limbs: *(↗Mouse - upper; Rat - upper)* bell b4a.de berb bg2 cocc b7.de* croc b7.de* *Ign* k* mag-m b4.de* *Rhod* b4a.de sec b7.de* *Sulph* b4a.de
  - · **jumping** in arms: croc k*

AMPUTATED stump painful (See Pain - amputations)

ANALGESIA (See Insensibility; Numbness)

ANESTHESIA (See Numbness)

ANGER; after: | **Upper** limbs: *Coloc* b4a.de

ANKLE-DROP (See Paralysis - ankles)

ANKYLOSIS: kali-i ptk1 thiosin br1
O - **Elbows**: sil k*
- **Fingers**:
O · **Distal** joint: fl-ac
  - · **Proximal** joint: crot-h
- **Knees**: *Sil* hr1
- **Shoulders**: cupr ptk1

ANTHRAX: *Anthraci Ars* k* maland jl2 pyrog jl2 *Sec* staphycoc jl2

ANXIETY felt in: m-aust b7.de* puls a1 sep a1 tarent k2
O - **Hands**: sulph h2

ANXIOUS gait: nat-m b4.de*

APPETITE; ravenous:
- **agg.** | **Upper** limbs: olnd b7.de*

ARTHRITIC nodosities: abies-c oss4• abrot k* acon b2.de* agn k* alum k2 am-be br1* am-p c2* *Ant-c* k* ant-t k2 **Apis** arg-met k2 arn k* asper ktp2 *Aur* k* **Benz-ac** k* berb bro1 *Bry* k* *Cal-ren* bro1 **Calc** k* **Calc-f** k* *Calc-p Calc-s* caps k2 carb-an k* **Caul** bg2* *Caust* k* *Cic* k* cimic bro1 *Clem* cocc b2.de* *Colch* k* *Dig* k* *Elaps* elat bro1 eucal bro1 eup-per bro1 fago *Form* k* **Graph** k* *Guaj* k* *Hecla* bro1 hep k* iod k* kali-ar bro1 kali-br br1 kali-c mrr1 *Kali-i* k* kali-s *Kali-sil* bro1 lach b2.de* **Led** k* **Lith-c** k* **Lyc** k* mang med bro1 *Meny* k* *Merc* k* nat-lac c2* nat-m nat-uric bro1 nit-ac b2.de* nux-v k* pipe bro1 plb *Puls* k* ran-b *Rhod* k* *Rhus-t* k* ruta bro1 sabin k* sars k2 *Sil* k* *Staph* k* sul-ac *Sulph* k* tub-r vn ur-ac bro1 urea bro1 *Urt-u* x-ray sp1
- **painful**: **Led** k* nit-ac h2* *Sars* ptk1
- **painless**: ant-c tl1
- **pinching** and cracking on motion: **Led**

▽ - **extending** to:
O · **Heart**: colch tl1
  - · **Stomach**: colch tl1
O - **Condyles**; on: *Calc-p*
- **Elbows**: eup-per k2 mur-ac bg2
  - · **stiffness** of: lyc
O · **Above**: eup-per k2 mag-c
  - · **Olecranon**; on: still
- **Feet**: bufo eucal bro1 *Kali-i* **Led** *Nat-s* puls-n bro1 tarent-c bro1 *Zinc* bro1
- **Finger** joints●: *Aesc* agn k* *Am-p* br1* *Ant-c* **Apis** aur-s k2 ben bro1 **Benz-ac** k* berb k2 brom b4a.de* **Calc** k* *Calc-f* k* *Calc-p* calc-sil k2 carb-an bg2 carb-v bg2 *Caul* bro1 **Caust** k* cimic gk *Clem* k* *Colch* k* con bg2 *Dig* k* eup-per k2 **Graph** k* hep k* iod gk lach bg2 **Led** k* **Lith-c** k* **Lyc** k* med br1*

- **Finger** joints: ...
nat-m gk ox-ac petr bg2 puls gk ran-s *Rhod* k* sep bg2 *Sil* *Staph* k* stel bro1 sul-i k2 *Sulph* k* syc bka1• *Urt-u* zinc bg2 [kali-f stj1 mag-f stj1]
  - **stiffness**; with●: *Carb-an* *Graph* **Lyc**
- **Forearms**: am-c
- **Hands**: ant-c *Benz-ac* *Calc* carbn-s *Hep* *Led* k* plb
  - O **Back** of hands: am-p br1* eucal bro1 med bro1
- **Knees**: *Bufo* *Calc* caust tl1 *Led* *Nux-v* phyt k2
- **Lower** limbs: *Agn* b7a.de *Ant-c* b7.de* cic b7.de* meny b7a.de rhus-t b7.de* *Staph* b7.de*
- **Muscles**: olib-sac wmh1 syph xxb
- **Shoulders**: *Calc* crot-h bg2 *Kali-i* phos bg2
- **Skin** over joints; in: cal-ren c2 **Led**
- **Toes**: asaf caust *Graph* led k2 ran-s sabin sulph thuj k*
  - **fibrous** | **First** toe; of: *Rhod*
- **Upper** limbs: *Ant-c* b7.de* ars bg2 *Aur* b4a.de *Calc* b4.de* *Caust* b4a.de graph b4.de* *Led* b7a.de lyc b4.de* nit-ac b4.de* phos b4a.de *Staph* b7.de*
- **Wrists**: am-m bg2* *Benz-ac* *Brom* b4a.de *Calc* k* *Caust* b4a.de *Led* k* lith-c bg2 lyc k* mag-m a1 petr k* rhod k* ruta bro1 sabin bg2 *Staph* b7a.de
  - O **Dorsal** side: petr k*

ARTHRITIS (See GENERALS - Inflammation - joints)

ARTHRITIS DEFORMANS (See GENERALS - Inflammation - joints - deformans)

ARTHROSIS: am-p mtf11 flav jl2 mand mtf11 med jl2 stront-c mtf11 thyr mtf11 tub jl2 tub-r jl2 vac jl2
- **chronic**: mang-met mtf11 med jl2
- **painful**; very: quinhydr mtf11
- O **Hips**: calc mtf33 lyc mtf33 lyss jl2
- **Knees**: bac jl2* parathyr jl2
- **Scapulohumeral**: ser-a-c jl2

ASCENDING; when:
- **agg.**:
  - O **Lower** limbs: bry b7.de* caust b4.de* chin b7.de* hep b4.de* hyos b7.de* kali-c b4.de* nux-v b7.de* ran-b b7.de* sul-ac b4.de
  - **Upper** limbs: sul-ac bg2
- **stairs**:
  - **agg.** | **Lower** limbs: alum b4.de* arn b7.de* ars b4.de* asar b7.de* bar-c b4.de* bell b4.de* borx b4a.de bry b7.de* *Calc* b4a.de cann-s b7.de* carb-v b4.de* caust b4.de* chin b7.de* dig b4.de* dros b7.de* hyos b7.de* ign b7.de* m-aust b7.de mag-c b4.de* mur-ac b4.de* nat-m b4.de* nux-m b7.de* nux-v b7.de* phos b4.de* plat b4.de* plb b7.de* *Rhus-t* b7.de* ruta b7.de* sep b4.de* spig b7.de* stann b4.de* sulph b4.de* tarax b7.de* *Thuj* b4.de* verb b7.de*

ASLEEP (See Numbness; Tingling)

ATAXIA (See Incoordination)

ATHETOSIS: (↗*GENERALS - Chorea*) lath br1* stram mrr1 stry bro1* verat-v br1*

ATHLETE'S foot (See Eruptions - feet - fungus)

ATROPHY (See Emaciation)

AWKWARDNESS: (↗*Incoordination; MIND - Awkward*)
aeth k* **Agar** k* agath-a nl2• alum-sil k2* ambr anac androc srj1• **Apis** k* ara-maca sej7• arg-n br1* ars asaf k* asar aur-m-n wbt2• bar-c ptk1 bell bit-ar wht1• **Bov** k* bry bufo gk **Calc** k* calc-s calc-sil k2 camph k* cann-i sf *Caps* k* carb-v k2* cardios-h rly4• cartl-s rly4• *Caust* chin b7.de* choc srj3• cit-ac rly4• cocc *Con* k* cystein-l rly4• dig h2* dulc fd4.de euphr b7.de* gels k2 germ-met srj5• haliae-lc srj5• **Hell** k* hep *Hydrog* srj2• *Ign* k* **Ip** k* kali-bi k2 kali-c b4a.de* kali-chl c2 kali-s fd4.de lac-h sze9• lac-leo hrn2• lac-lup hrn2• **Lach** k* lat-m bnm6• levo jl3 limest-b es1• *Lol* j5.de loxo-recl knl4• lyc sf* mag-p k2 med k2 mez b4a.de* mosch sf musca-d szs1 nat-ar k2 *Nat-c* k* *Nat-m* k* nat-ox rly4• nat-s j5.de *Nux-v* k* op oxal-a rly4• ph-ac b4.de* phos h2* pieri-b mlk9.de plb positr nl2• *Puls* k* *Rheum* b7.de* *Rhus-g* tmo3• ruta b7.de* sabad b7.de* sabin sal-fr sle1• sars k* sep b4a.de* sil k* spong k* stann k* staph stram streptoc rly4• suis-em rly4• suis-pan rly4• sulph thuj k* tritic-vg fd5.de vanil fd5.de verat-v a1 vip [heroin sdj2]
- **children**; in: asaf ptk1 sil ptk1

Awkwardness: ...
- O **Fingers**: agar k* alumn k2 *Apis* asaf k* benz-ac k2 **Bov** *Calc* k* calc-s carbn-s dulc fd4.de graph *Hell* hyos kali-bi k2 kola stb3• nat-m k* *Nux-v* k* plb ptel k* sep *Sil*
  - O **Thumbs**; as if fingers were: **Phos**
- **Hands**: *Agar* k* *Apis* bit-ar wht1• **Bov** k* cann-s b7.de* carbn-s *Con* cystein-l rly4• dulc fd4.de gels k2 graph ham fd3.de• kali-n kola stb3• *Lach* k* *Manc* k* musca-d szs1 nat-sil fd3.de• *Phos* k* plb k* plut-n srj7• ptel k* rhus-v k* ruta fd4.de sep sil spong fd4.de suis-em rly4• symph fd3.de• tritic-vg fd5.de
  - **diverted** or talking, when: **Hell** k* nit-ac h2*
  - **drops** things: (↗*MIND - Awkward - drops*) abrot k* agar bg1* alumn androc srj1• **Apis** ara-maca sej7• aur-m-n wbt2• bamb-a stb2.de• bell bit-ar wht1• **Bov** k* bry choc srj3• cocc k2 *Con* cycl cypra-eg sde6.de• cystein-l rly4• dendr-pol sk4• dulc fd4.de falco-pe nl2• gins ham fd3.de• hell hydrog srj2• hyos kali-bi kola stb3• lac-h htj1• *Lach* k* limest-b es1• *Nat-m* nat-sil fd3.de• nux-v oxal-a rly4• ozone sde2• petr-ra shn4• plut-n srj7• ruta fd4.de sep k* sil h2 spong fd4.de *Stram* k* suis-em rly4• *Sulph* k* symph fd3.de• tritic-vg fd5.de vanil fd5.de [heroin sdj2 pop dhh1 tax jsj7]
    - **chorea**; from (See GENERALS - Chorea - accompanied - drops)
    - **reins**, when driving: abrot con a1 lyc
    - **Head**; during pain in: gink-b sbd1•
  - **menses** | **before** | **agg.**: lac-h htj1•
    - **during** | **agg.**: alumn
  - **missed**, taking hold of anything she wished; always: asaf hr1
- **Lower** limbs: (↗*Fall liability; Incoordination - lower; Tottering*)
Agar k* *Alum* alum-sil k2 bell bg2 bit-ar wht1• botul br1 bufo gk **Caust** *Con* dulc fd4.de gels kola stb3• musca-d szs1 *Nux-m* petr-ra shn4• ruta fd4.de sabad sec gk *Sil* spong fd4.de tritic-vg fd5.de *Verat*
  - **descending** stairs; missing steps when: *Stram* k*
  - **knocks** against things: ara-maca sej7• bamb-a stb2.de• caps choc srj3• *Colch* cypra-eg sde6.de• dulc fd4.de hyos j5.de ip k* irid-met srj5• kali-n h2* nat-m k* nux-v op ruta fd4.de sep gl1.fr• spong fd4.de tritic-vg fd5.de ulm-c jsj8• vanil fd5.de vip
    - **chill**; during: caps hr1
  - **stumbling** when walking: **Agar** k* alco a1 alum bg2 ambr bg2 ammc vml3• anac bg2 androc srj1• *Arg-n* bg2* ars a1 aur-s k2 *Bar-c* bg2* bell b4a.de* bit-ar wht1• both-ax tsm2 bufo br1 *Calc* cann-i a1 caps *Carl* a1 **Caust** k* chel a1 cocc bg2 *Colch* k* *Con* k* conch fkr1* cypra-eg sde6.de• dros bg2 dulc fd4.de falco-pe nl2• gels k* *Hyos* k* *Ign* k* iod **Ip** k* kali-br bg2* kali-p k2 *Lach* k* lact bg1 lil-t mag-c *Mag-p* med k2 mygal bg2 *Nat-c* h2* *Nat-m* nat-sil fd3.de• nux-v k* op k* petr-ra shn4• *Ph-ac* k* *Phos* k* positr nl2• ruta bg2* sabad k* sec bg2 sil spong fd4.de stann bg2 tritic-vg fd5.de ulm-c jsj8• verat k* zinc bg2*
    - **ascending** stairs agg.: ammc c1* both-ax tsm2 lac-h sze9• phys ptk1 tab ptk1
    - **descending** agg.: both-ax tsm2
    - **walk** on uneven ground; cannot: lil-t br1*
  - **trips** over things: ara-maca sej7•
- **Upper** limbs: apis bg2 bell bg2 cann-xyz bg2 lol bg2 manc bg2 mosch bg2

BALLISM (See Motion - involuntary)

BALLS in heels; sensation of: | **morning**: kreos k*

BANDAGED, sensation as if: (↗*Constriction*) anac k2 arund *Chin* k* hist vml3• nit-ac h2 pic-ac k2* **Plat** k*
- O **Ankles**: acon k* calc k* cham kr1* helo helo-s rwt2• petr k*
- **Elbows**: *Caust* k*
- **Feet**: mur-ac h2*
  - **iron**; as with: ferr
- **Hands**: nit-ac h2*
  - O **Bones** and joints: mang h2*
- **Knees**: *Anac* k* ars k* **Aur** k* caps fkm1• coloc k* *Graph* k* kali-c h2* mag-m k* *Nat-m* nit-ac nux-m plat **Sil** k* sulph zinc
  - **right**: graph k* mag-s
  - **rising** from a seat; when: caps fkm1•
  - **sitting** agg.: *Anac* ars h2* aur rb2 caps fkm1• graph
  - **walking**:
    - **agg.**: *Aur* k* caps fkm1• coloc k* graph k*

Extremities

- **Knees – walking**: ...
  - ⁝ **continued** | **amel.**: caps fkm1•
- **Legs**: acon rb2 ant-c cham rb2 chlor lyc nat-m k* petr pic-ac k* plat k2 stann sul-ac sulph
  - **evening**: ant-c h2* nat-m
  - ○ **Calves**: card-m lol ptk1 nat-p k* nit-ac h2*
  - **Knees**; below: til a1*
- **Lower** limbs: alumn anac arund rb2 aur rb2 benz-ac k* nat-m rb2 pic-ac k2 *Plat* til k*
  - **walking** agg.: til k*
  - ○ **Bones**: *Con* b4a.de nat-m bg2
  - **Joints**: nat-m h2*
- **Thighs**: acon nit-ac h2* *Plat* k* sulph
  - **walking** agg.: *Acon* tarent
- **Toes**: syph xxb
  - ○ **First**: *Plat*
    - ⁝ **Balls**: petr h2
- **Wrists**: manc bg2 mang bg2

BANDAGING:
- **agg.**: ovi-p br1
  - ○ **Upper** limbs: ovi-p bro1
- **amel.**: (↗*GENERALS - Binding; GENERALS - Binding up bandaging*) (non:*Arg-n* hr1) bry lp2* cyn-d jl1 lac-d ptk2* (non:*Mag-m* a1) pic-ac mp1* tril-p mta1*

BED; in:
- **agg.**:
  - ○ **Lower** limbs: sep bg2 sulph bg2
  - **Upper** limbs: hell bg2 ign bg2 **Iod** bg2 kali-c bg2 kali-n bg2 **Mag-m** bg2 petr bg2 sil bg2 stront-c bg2
- **amel.** | **Lower** limbs: am-m bg2

BEDSORES (See SKIN - Decubitus)

BENDING:
- **head**:
  - **agg.** | **Upper** limbs: nux-v b7.de* puls b7.de*
- **knees** | **agg.** | **Hollow** of knee: calc-p ptk1 chin ptk1 rhus-t ptk1
  - **involuntary** | **walking**; while: bry ptk1 cupr hr1*
- **lower** limbs:
  - **agg.**: alum bg2 am-c b4.de* ang b7.de* ant-c b7.de* bell b4.de* calc b4.de* camph b7.de* caust b4.de* chel b7.de* chin b7.de* cocc b7.de* coff b7.de* croc b7.de* graph b4.de* hep b4a.de ign b7a.de kali-bi bg2 led b7.de* m-ambo b7.de nit-ac b4.de* nux-v b7.de* olnd b7.de* par b7.de* puls b7.de* rhod b4.de* rhus-t b7.de* ruta b7.de* sel b7.de* spig b7.de* stann b4.de* tarax b7.de* thuj b4.de*
  - **amel.**: arg-met b7.de* *Calc* b4a.de caust bg2 cham b7.de* chin b7.de* *Coloc* bg2 guaj b4.de* kali-bi bg2 *Lyc* b4a.de puls b7.de* rhus-t b7.de* squil b7.de*
  - **backwards** | **agg.**: ant-c b7.de* caps b7.de* caust b4.de* cina b7.de* coff b7.de* m-aust b7.de puls b7.de* rhus-t b7.de*
  - **forwards** | **agg.**: coff b7a.de
  - **impossible**: ant-c bg2
- **thumbs** | **backward**: camph ptk1 lyc ptk1 merc ptk1
- **toes** | **walking**; while: bad ptk1 lyc ptk1
- **upper** limbs:
  - **agg.**: acon b7.de* agn b7.de* am-c b4a.de ang b7.de* ant-c b7.de* arg-met b7.de* arn b7.de* bell b4.de* bov b4.de* bry b7.de* calc b4a.de carb-an b4.de* carb-v b4.de* caust b4a.de chel b7.de* chin b7.de* cina b7.de* coff b7.de* con b4.de* croc b7.de* dros b7.de* dulc b4.de* graph b4a.de hep b4a.de iod b4.de* kali-bi bg2 m-ambo b7.de mag-c b4.de* merc b4.de* mez b4.de* mur-ac b4.de* nat-m b4.de* nit-ac b4.de* petr b4.de* ph-ac b4.de* puls b7.de* rhod b4a.de rhus-t b7.de* sabad b7.de* sel b7.de* seneg bg2 spong b7.de* stann b4.de* teucr b7.de* thuj b4.de* zinc b4.de*
  - **amel.**: arg-met b7.de* cham b7.de* chin b7.de* mang b4.de* mur-ac b4.de* puls b7.de*
  - **backwards**:
    - ⁝ **agg.**: anac b4.de* bov b4.de* calc b4.de* *Carb-v* b4a.de dros b7.de* dulc b4.de* *Ign* b7.de* kali-bi bg2 m-aust b7.de nat-m b4.de* plb bg2 *Puls* b7.de* sanic bg2 sep b4.de* sulph b4a.de teucr b7.de* thuj b4.de*

Bending – upper limbs **– backwards**.: ...
- ⁝ **amel.**: kali-c b4.de*
- **desire** irresistible to bend arm: **Ferr** k*
- **inwards**:
  - ⁝ **agg.**: am-m b7.de* *Ign* b7.de* staph b7.de* verat b7.de*
  - ⁝ **amel.**: am-m b7.de*

BENT (See Flexed)

BERGER's disease: sec mtf11

BITING nails (See MIND - Biting - nails)

BLOOD:
- **oozing** from fingernails: *Crot-h* k*
- **rush** of blood to: aesc mrr1 calc-s k2
  - ○ **Feet**: puls b7.de* rhus-t b7.de*
    - ⁝ **standing** agg.: graph
    - ⁝ **Heels**: gard-j vlr2•
      - ⁝ **sensation** of: gard-j vlr2•
        - . **motion** | **amel.**: gard-j vlr2•
  - **Fingers**: phos
    - ⁝ **hang** down agg.; letting arms: allox tpw4 phos
    - ⁝ **Nails**: apis st1 **Lach** bg2 *Op* ph-ac bg2 phos bg2
    - ⁝ **Tips**: rhus-t b7.de* valer b7.de*
  - **Hands**: elaps nat-s *Nux-m* ph-ac **Phos**
    - ⁝ **afternoon**: nat-s
    - ⁝ **hang** down agg.; letting arms: ph-ac phos h2 sul-ac h2
    - ⁝ **stomach**, from: phos
  - **Knees**: lact phel
    - ⁝ **13** h: phel
    - ⁝ **sitting** agg.: phel
    - ⁝ **standing** agg.: phel
  - **Legs**: lact meph nux-m phos *Prot* jl2 **Spong Sulph** tub-r jl2 *Zinc*
    - ⁝ **left**: nux-m
    - ⁝ **night** | **waking**; on: meph
    - ⁝ **stagnated**; as if blood: ruta fd4.de zinc h2*
    - ⁝ **Calf**, blood running sensation: dulc h2
    - ⁝ **Veins**, varicose: *Prot* jl2
      - ⁝ **menses**; before: arist-cl sp1
  - **Lower** limbs: *Acon* bg2 agn bg2 alum bg2 am-c bg2 am-m bg2 ambr bg2 anac bg2 ant-t bg2 *Apis* bg2 arg-met bg2* **Arn** bg2 asaf bg2 **Aur** k* *Bell* bg2 borx bg2 brom bg2 *Brucel* sa3• **Bry** bg2 calc k* cann-xyz bg2 carb-an bg2 **Carb-v** bg2 caust bg2 *Chin* bg2 cocc bg2 colch bg2 coloc bg2 con bg2 cupr bg2 cycl bg2 dulc bg2 elaps *Ferr* bg2 fl-ac bg2 *Graph* b4a.de* hell bg2 hep bg2 influ jl2* iod bg2 kali-c bg2 kali-n bg2 kreos bg2 *Lach* bg2 led bg2 **Lyc** bg2 mag-c bg2 mag-m bg2 meph ptk1 merc bg2 mur-ac bg2 nat-c bg2 *Nat-m* bg2 nit-ac bg2 *Nux-v* bg2 ol-an bg2 olnd bg2 op bg2 petr bg2 *Ph-ac* bg2 phel bg2* *Phos* bg2 plat bg2 plb bg2 **Puls** bg2 ran-b bg2 rhod bg2 **Rhus-t** bg2 ruta bg2 sabad bg2 *Sabin* bg2 sars bg2 sec bg2 **Sep** bg2 **Sil** bg2 spig bg2 spong bg2* stann bg2 staph bg2 stront-c bg2 sul-ac bg2 **Sulph** bg2* teucr bg2 *Thuj* bg2 thyr ptk1 zinc k*
  - **Toes** | **First**: led b7.de*
  - **Upper** limbs: *Acon* bg2 alum bg2 *Am-c* bg2 am-m bg2 *Apis* bg2 **Arn** bg2 bar-c bg2 bell bg2 borx bg2 bov bg2 brom bg2 *Bry* bg2 calc k* carb-v bg2 caust bg2 cham bg2 chel bg2 **Chin** bg2 cic bg2 cocc bg2 cycl bg2 dig bg2 dros bg2 dulc bg2 *Ferr* bg2 fl-ac bg2 hell bg2 hep bg2 ign bg2 iod bg2 kali-c bg2 lach bg2 laur bg2 *Lyc* bg2 m-aust b7.de mag-c bg2 *Meny* bg2 *Merc* bg2 merc-c bg2 mez bg2 mosch bg2 nit-ac bg2 *Nux-v* k* olnd bg2 op bg2 par bg2 *Ph-ac* b4.de* **Phos** b4.de* plat bg2 **Puls** bg2 rheum bg2 rhod k* **Rhus-t** bg2 ruta bg2 sabad bg2 sars bg2 sec bg2 sel bg2 **Sep** bg2 sil k* squil bg2 staph bg2 stront-c bg2 sul-ac bg2 **Sulph** k* tarax bg2 teucr bg2 *Thuj* bg2 valer bg2 verat bg2 zinc bg2
  - **Wrist**:
    - ⁝ **sensation** of: gard-j vlr2•
      - ⁝ **motion** | **amel.**: gard-j vlr2•
- **stagnated**; sensation as if blood:
  - ○ **Fingers**: croc b7a.de
  - **Lower** limbs: olnd b7.de*
  - **Thighs**: zinc b4a.de

- **stagnated**; sensation as if blood: ...
  - • **Upper** limbs: m-aust b7.de rhod b4.de*

BLOTCHES (See Eruptions - blotches)

BLOWING, as of wind issuing from toes: cupr k*

BLOWING NOSE agg.: | **Lower** limbs: *Bar-c* b4a.de

BOUND to the side; left arm feels as if: cimic k*

BREAK:

○ - **Thigh** would break; sensation as if ang h1
- **Upper** arm would break; sensation as if: samb h1

BREAKFAST:

- **after**:
  - • **agg.**:
    - ⁝ **Lower** limbs: cham b7.de* nux-v b7.de* par b7.de* plb b7.de*
    - ⁝ **Upper** limbs: cham b7.de* nux-v b7.de* plb b7.de*

BREATHING:

- **agg.**:
  ○ • **Lower** limbs: alum b4.de* cann-xyz bg2 *Caust* b4a.de nat-m b4.de* plat b4.de*
  - • **Upper** limbs: am-c bg2 bry b7.de* cann-xyz bg2 graph b4.de* kali-c b4.de* sulph b4.de*
- **amel.** | **Lower** limbs: asaf b7.de*
- **deep**:
  - • **agg.**: cann-xyz ptk1
    - ⁝ **Upper** limbs: cann-xyz ptk1
- **not** breathing; when:
  - • **agg.** | **Lower** limbs: clem b4.de*

BRITTLE: rad-br ptk1

- **sensation** of being | **Lower** limbs: calc bg2 thuj bg2

○ - **Nails** (See Nails - brittle)

BROKEN: | **Upper** arm; as if: bov bg1 *Cocc* bg1 cupr bg1 puls bg1 samb bg1 zinc bg1

BUBBLING sensation: mang h2 rheum

○ - **Elbows**: kreos k* mang k* rheum k* sil a1 spong k*
○ • **Bends** of elbow: bell b4.de* sil a1
- **Feet**: bell k* berb k* chel k* lach k* *Rheum* b7a.de squil b7.de*
- **Forearms**: spong k* zinc k*
○ • **Posterior** part: colch k*
- **Hips**: *Led* k*
- **Knees**: arg-met bell k* berb k* cot a1 nat-m k*
○ • **Hollow** of knees: rheum sil a1
  - ⁝ **extending** to | **Heel**: rheum ptk1
  - • **Patella**, in: asar k*
- **Legs**: ant-c k* am k* berb k* con k* rheum k* rhus-t k* spig b7.de* squil b7.de* sulph b4.de*
○ • **Calves**: berb a1 crot-h k* rheum spig k*
- **Lower** limbs: ant-c b7.de* asaf b7.de* asar b7.de* calc b4.de* rheum b7.de* *Sep* b4a.de squil b7.de*
▽ • **extending** to | **Downward**: bell h1* olnd h1* squil h1*
- **Nates**: ant-c k* zinc k*
  - • **standing** agg.: ant-c k*
- **Shoulders**: berb k* mang k* puls k* tarax k*
  - • **afternoon**: puls k*
  - • **chill**; during: *Tarax* b7.de*
- **Thighs**: berb k* cot a1 meny b7.de* olnd k* sil k* squil b7.de* viol-t b7.de*
- **Toe**; first | **left**: rheum h
- **Upper** arms: berb k* colch k* cupr k* nux-m k* petros k* squil k* zinc k*
  - • **right**: berb k*
  - • **left**: zinc k*
- **Upper** limbs: ambr b7.de* colch b7.de* kreos b7a.de *M-aust* b7.de* par b7.de* puls b7.de* rheum b7.de* rhus-t b7.de* spig b7.de* spong b7.de* squil b7.de* tarax b7.de* teucr b7.de*
  - • **left**: caust h2

BUCKLING; sensation of: | **Legs**: [heroin sdj2]

BUNIONS:

- **pressure** | **amel.**: graph ptk1

○ - **Feet**: agar bro1* am-c benz-ac bro1* graph bg1* hyper k* *Kali-chl* k* *Kali-i* bro1 lyc ptk1 paeon ptk1 ph-ac *Phos* plb rhod bro1* **Sil** k* sulph k2 verat-v bro1 zinc k*
  - • **frostbite**: | **after**: *Calc*
○ • **Soles**: calc
    - ⁝ **ulcerated**: *Calc*
- **Toes** | **First** toe: agar bro1 *Benz-ac* bro1 borx bro1 hyper bro1 iod bro1 kali-i bro1 *Rhod* bro1 sang bro1 sars bro1 *Sil* bro1 verat-v bro1

BURSAE: (*↗Inflammation - fingers - joints - bursitis; Inflammation - knees - bursae; GENERALS - Inflammation - bursae)* **ARN** k ● benz-ac bro1 calc-p cann-s kali-m c1* **NAT-M** k ● **Phyt** mrr1 psor al2 *Rhus-t* mrr1 *Ruta* bro1 **Sil** k* stann **Stict** syph xxb

- **cysts**: cann-s caust *Graph* iod kali-br psor al2 *Sil* *Sulph*

○ - **Shoulder** | **right**: **Sang** mrr1
- **Wrists**: ruta k* stann syph xxb
  - • **right**: stann

BUZZING sensation (See Vibration)

CALLOSITIES: **Ant-c** ptk1 bry ptk1 *Calc* ptk1 cist ptk1 *Graph* ptk1 ign ptk1 *Lyc* ptk1 phos ptk1* phyt ptk1 rad-br ptk1 rhus-t ptk1 **Sep** ptk1 **Sil** ptk1 sulph ptk1 symph ptk1

- **horny**: (*↗Hardness; Nails - horny; SKIN - Excrescences - horny)* **Graph** mrr1 ruta k2 tritic-vg fd5.de

○ - **Elbows**; on: *Graph* mrr1
- **Feet**: ant-c bg2 bar-c bg2 caust bg2 graph bg2 lyc bg2 ran-b bg2 rhus-t bg2 sep bg2 sil bg2 sulph bg2
○ • **Heels**; on: lyc bg2
    - ⁝ **inflamed**: plut-n srj7•
  - • **Soles**: anac-oc bro1 **Ant-c** k* *Ars* k* bar-c bg1* bry gk *Calc* graph ptk1 lyc bg1* nat-m gk phos sne plb ran-b bro1 sep ptk1 (non:sil bg2*) **Sulph** k ●* tub pd
    - ⁝ **tender**: *Alum* bar-c c1 lyc ser med *Nat-s* phos sne sil h2
    - ⁝ **Balls**: ant-c bg2
- **Hands**; on: *Am-c* ant-c bg2 borx h2 calc-f bg2 **Graph** k* kali-ar merc-i-r bg2 nat-m bg2 positr nl2• rhus-v sil k* **SULPH** k ●* thuj bg2
  - • **cracks**; with deep: cist k* graph
  - • **horny**: graph mtf33
  - • **wart**-like: borx bg2
- **Knees**; on: *Graph* mrr1
- **Lower** Limbs: *Graph* b4a.de **Sep** b4a.de *Sil* b4a.de
- **Nails**; under: ant-c k2*
- **Toes**; on: acet-ac bro1 ant-c k* ars bg calc bro1 cur bro1 *Ferr-pic* bro1 **Graph** k●* hyper bro1 lac-d sne lyc bro1 nit-ac bro1 *Ran-b* bro1 ran-s bro1 semp bro1 sep bro1 *Sil* bro1 sul-ac bro1
- **Upper** limbs: am-c b4a.de borx b4a.de *Graph* b4a.de *Sep* b4a.de sil b4a.de sulph b4a.de

CALLUS of fractured bones: | **excessive**: calc-p bg2 symph bg2

CANCER:

○ - **Bones**: merc-k-i gm1 methyl gm1 toxi gm1
  - • **osteosarcoma**: beryl mtf11 calc-f ptk1 euph gm1 graph hr1 *Hecla* c2* merc-k-i gm1 symph gm1 syph ptk1*
○ • **Fibula**: toxi gm1
  - • **Thighs** | **Femur**: methyl gm1
  - • **Tibia** | **right** | **osteosarcoma**: syph c1
    - ⁝ **osteosarcoma**: syph k* toxi gm1
  - • **Upper** arms: cadm-met gm1

CARBUNCLES: **Anthraci** *Arn* **Ars** *Hep* **Lach** **Sil** **Sulph** tarent-c

○ - **Forearms**: hep
- **Nates**: agar thuj
- **Thighs**: agar *Arn* asim *Hep*

CARIES of bone: (*↗Necrosis)* ang c1* *Ars* k* **Asaf** k* aur k* aur-s k2 *Calc* k* calc-f calc-p k* calc-sil k2 cist tl1 *Con* k* *Fl-ac* k* graph *Guaj* k* *Hep* k* **Lyc** k* **Merc** k* *Mez* k* **Nit-ac** k* *Ph-ac* k* *Phos* k* *Puls* ruta sec *Sep* **Sil** k* *Staph* k* *Sulph* k* *Ther*

○ - **Ankle** bones: asaf *Calc* *Guaj* k* plat-m *Puls* k* *Sil*
○ • **Internal** malleolus: *Sil*
- **Elbows**: *Sil* k*

- **Feet**: asaf k* calc Hecla Merc k* **Sil** k*
  - O • **Heels**: Calc-p k* plat-m Sil k*
- **Fibula**: **Sil**
- **Fingers**: Sil k*
- **Hands**, metacarpal bone: sil k*
- **Hip** (See Hip joint)
- **Joints**: aur-m k2 Nit-ac
- **Knees**: **Puls** b7a.de sil k*
- **Leg** | **sensation** as of caries: sep tl1
- **Legs**:
  - O • **Bones** | **Tibia**: Asaf Aur Calc dulc k2 Guaj k* Hecla kali-i Lach ph-ac Phos k* **Sil** k*
- **Lower** limbs: asaf b7.de* aur k* aur-m k* aur-m-n Calc k* caps b7a.de con b4.de* Euph b4a.de hep b4a.de Kreos b7a.de Lyc b4a.de merc b4a.de Mez k* Nit-ac k* ph-ac b4a.de Sep k* **Sil** k* staph b7.de* Sulph b4.de*
- **Shoulder** joint: sil
- **Thighs** | **Femur**: Calc calc-f st1 fl-ac k2 **Sil** Stront-c k*
- **Toes** | **left** big toe: **Sil**
- **Upper** arms | **Humerus**: Sil k*
- **Upper** limbs: Sil
- **Wrists**: Sil k*

CARPAL TUNNEL SYNDROME: arn mp1• bell-p mp1• brach mp1• brass-n-o srj5• calc vh calc-f mp1• calc-p vh* caust vh* form br1 guaj vh* hyper mp1• lach dgt lyc dsp1• **Med** dsp1• Nat-m dsp1• Nux-v dsp1• plb vh Puls dsp1• rhus-t dsp1*• ruta vh viol-o vh* zinc dsp1•
- **right**: Viol-o mrr1
- **left**: Guaj mrr1
- O - **Skin** retracted in lines; with caust vh plb vh ruta vh

CARRYING A WEIGHT agg.: | **Upper** limbs: ambr b7a.de

CATALEPSY: acon c1

CHAFED (See Excoriation)

CHANGING position:
- **amel.** | **Lower** limbs: Ars b4a.de ign bg2 iris bg2 kali-i bg2 psor bg2 staph bg2

CHAPPED hands: (↗Cracked - hands; Roughness - hands) Aesc allox tpw4 Alum k* alum-sil k2 am-c Anan apis Arn aur **Calc** k* calc-sil k2 **Calen** carb-ac castor-eq bro1 cench k2 cist bro1 **Graph** k* ham **Hep** k* hydr Kali-c kali-sil k2 kreos Lyc k* Mag-c k* Merc nat-ar bro1 Nat-c k* Nat-m **Petr** k* prim-o c2 psor k2 puls **Rhus-t Sars** k* **Sep** Sil Sulo-ac c2* **Sulph** Zinc
- **working** in water: alum ant-c **Calc** cham hep merc Rhus-t sars Sep **Sulph**
- O - **Fingers**: **Nat-m**
  - O • **Nails**; about the: **Nat-m**
  - • **Tips**: alum bg2* aur bg2 bar-c k* bell bg2 Graph bg2* merc bg2 nat-m bro1 olib-sac wmh1 Petr bg2* Ran-b bro1 Sanic bro1 sars bg2* sil bg2

CHILBLAINS: abrot k* acon bg2 **Agar** k* all-c k* aloe k* Alum alum-p k2 Alumn k* ambro c2 anac c1 ant-c b2.de* apis bro1 arist-cl sp1 Arn k* Ars k* asar b2.de* aur k* Bad k* Bell k* borx k* bry b2.de* bufo cadm-s k* calc c2* calc-s c2 Calen c2* camph b2.de* Canth bro1 carb-ac hr1 Carb-an k* Carb-v k* caust gk Cham k* chin k* cist mrr1 cocc b2.de* Colch b2.de* Cop k* cortico tpw7* Croc k* Crot-h hr1 crot-t bro1 Cycl k* ferr-p bro1 frag c2* ham c2* Hep b2.de* hyos k* ign b2.de* iod c2 kali-ar kali-c k* kali-chl k* kali-m c2 kali-p c2 kalm k* lach bg2* led bro1 Lyc k* m-arct b2.de* m-aust b2.de* mag-c b2.de* merc bro1 merc-i-r hr1 morg fmm1• morg-p pte1• Mur-ac k* **Nit-ac** k* nux-m b2.de* Nux-v k* op b2.de* **Petr** k* ph-ac k* Phos k* plan k* prot fmm1• **Puls** k* ran-b c1* rheum b2.de* rhus-t k* rhus-v c2 ruta b2.de* sec c2 sep k* sil bro1 stann k* staph k* sul-ac k* Sulph k* syc fmm1• tam c2* Ter bro1 Thuj k* Thyr c2* tub hr1* tub-m jl2 Verat-v c2* Zinc k*
- **air**; in open | **amel.**: borx br1
- **blue**: arn b2.de* bell b2.de* kali-c b2.de* kali-s tl1 puls b2.de*
- **burning**: sulph tl1
- **coldness** agg.: agar tl1
- **crawling**: arn b2.de* colch b2.de* nux-v b2.de* Rhus-t b2.de* sep b2.de*
- **cutting**: kali-c h2*
- **inflamed**: Ars k* bell b2.de* Carb-an hr1 cham k* hep b2.de* kali-c h2* lyc k* Nit-ac k* Nux-v phos b2.de* **Puls** k* rhus-t b2.de* staph k* Sulph k*
- **itching**: abrot br1* agar tl1 cortico tpw7 nux-v tl1 petr hr1* ruta tl1
  - • **warm** | **bed** | **agg.**: Cortico tpw7

Chilblains – itching – warm: ...
  - ⁝ **room** | **agg.**: cortico tpw7
- **moist**: petr hr1
- **painful**: agar tl1 arn k* Ars k* aur bell b2.de* chin b2.de* hep k* kali-c h2* lyc b2.de* mag-c b2.de* Nit-ac k* nux-v b2.de* Petr k* ph-ac k* phos k* Puls k* sep k*
- **pressing**: kali-c h2*
- **pulsating**: Nux-v k*
- **purple**: petr k2*
- **stitching**: kali-c h2*
- **unbroken**: Ter br1*
- **vesicular**: ant-c b2.de* bell b2.de* carb-an k* chin b2.de* cycl b2.de* mag-c k* Nit-ac k* phos k* **Rhus-t** k* sep k* sulph k*
- **warmth** agg. | **heat** agg.: puls hr1* syc bka1*•
- **weather** agg.; warm: frag br1
- O - **Feet**: abrot k* **Agar** k* Alumn k* am-c Anac k* ant-c k* aur aur-ar k2 bad k* Bell berb borx bry bufo cadm-s Carb-an k* carb-v k* Cham Chin colch Croc crot-h cycl k* hep k* hyos ign kali-chl k* kali-m k* kali-n Lyc Merc k* morg-p fmm1• mur-ac naja Nit-ac k* nux-m Nux-v Op k* **Petr** k* ph-ac Phos k* **Puls** k* ran-b k* rhus-t sep stann staph sul-ac Sulph k* syc pte1*• tam bro1 Thuj **Zinc** k* zinc-p k2
  - • **cracked**: merc nux-v petr
  - • **inflammation**: Lach k* merc nit-ac **Petr** k*
  - • **purple**: Lach Merc Puls k* Sulph k*
  - • **recent**, if: kali-p kr1
  - • **suppurating**: Lach k* Sil k* Sulph
  - • **swollen**: Merc k*
  - O • **Heels**: petr tl1
    - ⁝ **swollen** and red: petr
- **Fingers**: Agar b4.de* ars b4a.de berb borx b4a.de carb-an k* ign gk lyc k* nit-ac k* Nux-v Petr k* Phos b4.de* psor al2 Puls k* Stann b4.de* sul-ac k* Sulph k*
  - • **itching**: lyc h2* sulph k*
  - • **painful**: sul-ac k*
- **Hands**: abrom-a ks5 Agar k* aloe ars b4a.de borx b4a.de Bry b7a.de Carb-an b4a.de Croc k* gaert pte1*• Kali-chl k* lyc b4a.de Nit-ac k* nux-v b7a.de op k* **Petr** k* Phos b4.de **Puls** Stann k* sul-ac k* Sulph k* Zinc k*
  - • **itching**: **Puls** Zinc k*
  - • **swelling**: Zinc k*
  - • **weather** | **mild**: nit-ac h2 stann
  - • **winter** agg.: gaert pte1*•
- **Lower** limbs: Agar b4.de* am-c b4a.de ant-c b7a.de ars b4a.de asar b7.de aur b4.de bry b7.de Carb-an b4.de* Carb-v b4a.de cham b7.de chin b7.de cocc b7.de Croc b7a.de cycl b7.de hep b4a.de Hyos b7a.de ign b7.de kali-c b4.de m-aust b7.de* Nit-ac b4.de nux-v b7.de* op b7a.de petr b4.de* ph-ac b4a.de Phos b4.de Puls b7.de* rheum b7.de rhod b4.de rhus-t b7.de stann b4a.de staph b7a.de Sul-ac b4a.de Sulph b4a.de Thuj b4a.de Zinc b4a.de
- **Toes**: **Agar** k* Alum ambr c1 aur aur-ar k2 borx k* Carb-an k* Croc k* hydrog srj2• kali-c k* melal-alt gya4 nit-ac k* Nux-v **Petr** k* phos k* psor al2 **Puls** k* rhod k* sacch-a gmj3 sal-ac bro1 Thuj b4a.de
  - • **bluish**: kali-c h2*
  - O • **First** Toe | **cutting**: kali-c h2
- **Upper** limbs: Croc b7.de* cycl b7.de Hyos b7a.de m-arct b7.de m-aust b7a.de nux-v b7.de* op b7a.de Puls b7.de rhus-t b7.de* staph b7.de*

CHILL; during:
- **agg.** | **Lower** limbs: bry b7.de canth b7.de caps b7.de coff b7.de hell b7.de led b7.de Nux-v b7.de rhus-t b7.de sabad b7.de spig b7.de verat b7.de

CHILLINESS: agar k* Ars k* buth-a sp1 calc bro1 calc-s k2 cham k* chlor k* cimic k* coff k* cupr-n a1 ferr bro1 Gels k* Hyos k* lac-ac k* Nat-m k* nit-s-d hr1 Nux-v k* plb k* Psor k* puls h1* Rhus-t k* sec k* stram k* suprar rly4• vanil fd5.de
- O - **Elbows**: agar bg2
- **Feet**: acon bg2 **Agar** Am-c bg2 anac bg2 ant-c arg-met b7.de* ars h2* Bar-c bg2 Bell bg2* benz-ac bro1 Brom bg2 bry bufo bg2 canth bro1 cedr chel bg2 Chinin-ar bro1 coloc bg2 croc bg2 **Cupr** bg2 Dig bg2 Dros k* ign b7.de* kreos bg2 laur bg2 lyc bg2 m-arct b7.de Mag-c bg2 **Meny** bg2 merc bg2 mez bg2 nat-m bg2 neon srj5• Nit-ac nux-m bg2 par bg2 petr Phos puls bg2 ran-b bg2 Rhus-t k* **Sabad** bg2 samb b7.de* sep bg2 Sulph k* suprar rly4• thuj valer bg2 vanil fd5.de verat b7.de*

- **Feet**: ...
• **left**: stann$_{h2}$
• **extending** to | **Upward**: vesp$_{br1}$
• **motion**; after: calc
• **summer**: ant-c
- **Fingers**: acon$_{bg2}$ *Cupr*$_{bg2}$ dig$_{bg2}$ kali-c$_{bg2}$ kreos$_{bg2}$ mang$_{bg2}$ **Meny**$_{b7.de*}$ *Merc*$_{bg2}$ *Ph-ac*$_{bg2}$ ran-b$_{bg2}$ spig$_{bg2}$ sulph$_{bg2}$ thuj$_{bg2}$
○ • **Tips**: thuj$_{bg2}$
- **Forearms**: bry$_{bg2}$ caust$_{bg2}$ ign$_{bg2}$ nux-v$_{bg2}$ *Rhus-t*$_{bg2}$
- **Hands**: ambr$_{b7.de*}$ anac$_{b4.de*}$ *Bar-c*$_{b4.de*}$ *Bell*$_{bg2}$ chel$_{bg2}$ **Cupr**$_{bg2}$ *Dig*$_{bg2}$ dros$_{bg2}$ iod$_{bg2}$ kali-i$_{bg2}$ lach$_{bg2}$ meny$_{bg2}$ mosch$_{bg2}$ *Nat-m*$_{bg2}$ nux-v$_{b7.de*}$ phos$_{bg2}$ *Rhus-t*$_{bg2}$ **Sabad**$_{bg2}$ samb$_{b7.de*}$ spig$_{b7.de*}$ verat$_{bg2}$ zinc$_{bg2}$
- **Hips**: ham$_{k*}$
▽ • **extending** to | **Legs**: ham$_{bro1}$
- **Knees**: androc$_{srj1}$• benz-ac$_{bro1}$ bung-fa$_{mtf}$ carc$_{fd2.de}$• card-m$_{k*}$ caust$_{bg2}$ chim-m$_{hr1}$ *Chin*$_{b7.de*}$ *Chinin-ar*$_{bro1}$ *Coloc*$_{k*}$ ign$_{k*}$ lach$_{bg2}$ *Meny*$_{bg2}$ nit-ac$_{bg2}$ phos$_{bg2}$ *Puls*$_{bg2}$ sep$_{bg2}$ thuj$_{bg2}$
- **Legs**: ambr$_{bg2}$ androc$_{srj1}$• *Ars*$_{k*}$ bar-c$_{bg2}$ bell$_{bg2}$ bufo$_{bg2}$ **Chel**$_{bg2}$ chin$_{bg2}$ cinnb$_{k*}$ *Hep*$_{k*}$ kreos$_{b7a.de*}$ m-aust$_{b7.de}$ mosch$_{k*}$ par$_{k*}$ puls$_{b7.de*}$ rhod$_{k*}$ samb$_{k*}$ sep$_{k*}$ spong$_{k*}$
• **accompanied** by | **Sciatic** nerve; pain in (See Pain - lower limbs - sciatic - accompanied - chilliness)
• **sciatica**; in (See Pain - lower limbs - sciatic - accompanied - chilliness)
• **touch** agg.: chin$_{h1*}$
- **Lower** limbs: acon$_{bg2}$ agar$_{bg2}$ ambr$_{bg2}$ arg-met$_{bg2}$ arn$_{bg2}$ bapt$_{bg2}$ **Bell**$_{bg2}$ camph$_{bg2}$ caps$_{bg2}$ carb-an$_{bg2}$ carb-v$_{bg2}$ caust$_{h2*}$ chel$_{bg2}$ *Chin*$_{b7.de*}$ **Cic**$_{bg2}$ cocc$_{k*}$ coloc$_{bg2}$ *Croc*$_{bg2}$ cupr$_{bg2}$ dros$_{bg2}$ euph$_{bg2}$ hell$_{bg2}$ hep$_{b4a.de*}$ *Ign*$_{b7.de*}$ kreos$_{bg2}$ laur$_{bg2}$ led$_{bg2}$ lyc$_{bg2}$ m-arct$_{b7.de}$ meny$_{bg2*}$ *Merc*$_{bg2}$ merc-c$_{bg2}$ **Mez**$_{b4.de*}$ mosch$_{bg2}$ nat-c$_{bg2}$ nit-ac$_{bg2}$ nux-m$_{bg2}$ nux-v$_{b7.de*}$ olnd$_{bg2}$ par$_{k*}$ petr$_{bg2}$ plb$_{b7a.de*}$ *Puls*$_{b7.de*}$ ran-b$_{bg2}$ rhod$_{bg2}$ *Rhus-t*$_{b7.de*}$ **Sabad**$_{bg2}$ sabin$_{bg2}$ samb$_{bg2}$ sec$_{bg2}$ sep$_{k*}$ *Spig*$_{b7.de*}$ spong$_{bg2}$ sulph$_{bg2}$ valer$_{bg2}$ verat$_{bg2}$
• **sneezing** agg.: spig$_{h1*}$
⁝ **Anterior** part: thuj$_{bg2}$
- **Shoulders**: lept$_{k*}$
○ • **Between**: tub$_{ptk1}$
- **Thighs**: acon$_{k*}$ agar$_{bg2}$ arn$_{k*}$ ars-i$_{k*}$ bar-c$_{h2*}$ bell$_{bg2}$ *Bry*$_{bg2}$ caps$_{bg2}$ carc$_{fd2.de}$• chin$_{h1*}$ cic$_{h1*}$ hell$_{b7.de*}$ ign$_{bg2}$ lyc$_{bg2}$ merc$_{bg2}$ mosch$_{bg2}$ nit-ac$_{bg2}$ olnd$_{bg2}$ *Psor*$_{k*}$ puls$_{b7.de*}$ ran-b$_{b7.de*}$ rhod$_{bg2}$ samb$_{bg2}$ sars$_{h2*}$ sep$_{bg2}$ *Spong*$_{k*}$ **Stront-c**$_{bg2}$
- **Toes**: **Agar** asar borx bry$_{bg2}$ *Carb-an* *Carb-v* castor-eq *Croc* cycl op **Petr** phos *Puls* sulph thuj **Zinc**
○ • **Ball** of right big toe: ars-h
• **First** toe: nit-ac
- **Upper** arms: chel$_{k*}$ cocc$_{bg2}$ graph$_{bg2}$ *Ign*$_{b7.de*}$ m-aust$_{b7.de}$ **Mez**$_{bg2}$ ph-ac$_{bg2}$ puls$_{b7.de*}$ ran-b$_{b7.de*}$ rhus-t$_{b7.de}$
- **Upper** limbs: *Acon*$_{b7.de*}$ am-c$_{bg2}$ anac$_{bg2}$ astac$_{k*}$ bapt$_{bg2}$ bar-c$_{k*}$ *Bell*$_{k*}$ berb *Bry*$_{b7.de*}$ *Calc* cann-xyz$_{bg2}$ carb-ac *Caust*$_{k*}$ cham chel$_{bg2}$ chin$_{b7.de*}$ **Cic**$_{bg2}$ cinnb$_{k*}$ cocc$_{bg2}$ croc$_{b7.de*}$ cupr$_{bg2}$ dig$_{bg2}$ dulc$_{bg2}$ euphr$_{k*}$ graph$_{bg2}$ hell$_{bg2}$ hep$_{b4a.de*}$ ign$_{k*}$ kali-c$_{bg2}$ mang$_{bg2}$ merc$_{bg2}$ mez$_{k*}$ mosch$_{bg2}$ nat-m$_{bg2}$ **Nux-v**$_{b7.de*}$ petr$_{k*}$ ph-ac$_{bg2}$ *Plat*$_{k*}$ *Plb*$_{b7a.de*}$ *Puls*$_{k*}$ ran-b$_{bg2}$ raph$_{bro1}$ *Rhus-t*$_{bg2}$ ruta$_{bg2}$ **Sabad**$_{bg2}$ sars$_{h2*}$ sec$_{bg2}$ sep$_{bg2}$ sil$_{h2*}$ *Spig*$_{b7.de*}$ squil$_{b7.de*}$ staph$_{b7.de*}$ thuj$_{k*}$ *Verat*$_{b7.de*}$ zinc$_{k*}$
• **right**: phys plat
⁝ **air** agg.; in open: lyss
⁝ **extending** to | **Back** and legs: mez
• **left**: stann$_{h2*}$
• **afternoon**: sil$_{h2*}$
• **evening** | **lying** down agg.; after: *Nux-v*$_{k*}$
• **arms** away from the body amel.; holding the: spig$_{h1*}$
• **stool** agg.; after: plat$_{k*}$
• **walking** in open air agg.: chin$_{h1*}$
○ • **Anterior** surface: puls$_{h1*}$
• **Posterior** surface: raph$_{k*}$

CHOREA: **Agar**$_{k*}$ apis *Arg-n* *Ars* *Asaf* *Bell* *Calc* **Caust**$_{k*}$ *Cedr* *Cham* *Chel* chin *Chlol* *Cic* *Cimic*$_{k*}$ cocc$_{k*}$ coff con *Croc*$_{k*}$ *Cupr*$_{k*}$ dulc *Hyos* *Ign*$_{k*}$ iod ip kali-c *Lach* laur lyc lyss$_{mrr1}$ mag-p$_{br1}$ merc mez **Mygal**$_{k*}$ *Nat-m* nux-v *Op* plat puls rhod$_{k*}$ rhus-t$_{k*}$ sabin sec *Sep*$_{k*}$ sil stann staph$_{mrr1}$ *Stram*$_{k*}$ stront-c sulph syc$_{bka1}$• tanac **Tarent**$_{k*}$ verat-v zinc$_{k*}$ zinc-p$_{k2}$
- **night**: zinc$_{mrr1}$
- **coition** agg.: agar$_{mrr1}$ *Cedr*
- **fear**; from: *Calc* **Caust** *Ign*$_{k*}$ *Kali-br* *Laur* *Nat-m* *Stram* zinc
- **sleep** | **amel.**: *Agar*$_{vh}$ *Mygal*$_{vh}$
○ - **Crosswise**: agar$_{gt1}$ *Stram*$_{hr1}$
- **Feet**: *Zinc*$_{mrr1}$
- **Hands**: cina$_{ptk1*}$
- **Legs**: *Cocc*$_{k*}$ rhod$_{k*}$ stict$_{k*}$
• **left**: rhod$_{tl1}$
⁝ **storm**; at approach of: rhod$_{tl1}$
- **Lower** Limbs: *Zinc*$_{mrr1}$
- **Upper** limb:
• **left**: cimic$_{hr1}$
• **storm**; at approach of: rhod$_{tl1}$

CICATRICES: *(↗SKIN - Cicatrices)*
○ - **Fingers**: *Colch*$_{rsj2}$•
- **Hand**:
• **stinging** | **deep**: kali-bi

CLAUDICATIO INTERMITTTENS: *(↗Cramps - legs - walking; Limping; Pain - Legs - walking - agg.; Walking - Difficult)* lach$_{mrr1}$ lat-m$_{bnm6}$• plb$_{mrr1}$ prot$_{jl2}$ **Sec**$_{mrr1}$ [kali-n$_{stj1}$]

CLAWHAND: brass-n-o$_{srj5}$•

CLAW-LIKE fingernails: ars$_{k*}$ tub$_{xxb}$

CLENCHING:
○ - **Fingers**: *(↗Flexed - fingers)* acon$_{bg2}$ aeth$_{c1*}$ am-c$_{k*}$ ambr$_{bro1}$ anag$_{bro1}$ *Apis* arg-n$_{k*}$ *Ars*$_{k*}$ *Bell*$_{k*}$ bism$_{bro1}$ *Brach*$_{bro1}$ cann-s$_{bro1}$ caust$_{bro1}$ *Chin* chinin-ar *Cic*$_{k*}$ *Cina*$_{bro1}$ cocc$_{bg2*}$ colchin$_{bro1}$ *Coloc*$_{k*}$ **Cupr**$_{k*}$ *Cupr-act*$_{bro1}$ cycl$_{bro1}$ dios$_{bro1}$ *Glon*$_{k*}$ *Hell*$_{bro1}$ *Hydr-ac*$_{k*}$ *Hyos*$_{k*}$ ign$_{gk}$ *Ip*$_{k*}$ kali-bi$_{bro1}$ lach$_{k*}$ *Laur*$_{k*}$ lyc$_{k*}$ *Med* meny$_{k*}$ *Merc*$_{k*}$ *Nux-m* *Nux-v*$_{k*}$ *Oena*$_{k*}$ op$_{k*}$ par$_{k*}$ phos$_{k*}$ phyt$_{bg2}$ *Plat* ruta$_{bro1}$ sang$_{k*}$ sec$_{bro1*}$ sol-t$_{bro1}$ stann$_{bro1}$ stram$_{b7.de*}$ *Stry*$_{k*}$ sul-ac$_{b4a.de*}$ ter$_{k*}$
• **noon**: am-c$_{k*}$
• **accompanied** by | **Upper** limbs; stretching out of (See Stretching - upper - accompanied - fingers)
• **chill**, at beginning of: *Cimx*$_{k*}$
• **convulsive**: glon$_{k*}$ mag-p$_{k*}$ nux-m *Nux-v*
• **epileptic** convulsion: *Lach*$_{k*}$ lyc$_{h2*}$ *Mag-p*$_{k*}$ *Oena*
• **headache**; after: coloc$_{hr1}$
• **seizing** something, when: arg-met$_{h1}$ arg-n$_{k*}$ *Dros* stry
• **stretching** out arms: stry
- **Fists**: cupr$_{sst3*}$ hyos$_{mtf33}$
• **children**; in: hyos$_{mtf33}$
⁝ **newborns**: cham$_{mtf33}$
• **sleep**; during: adam$_{skp7}$•
- **Thumbs**: *Aeth*$_{k*}$ *Apis* ars$_{k*}$ art-v$_{k*}$ arum-t$_{k*}$ bell$_{k*}$ brach$_{k*}$ *Bufo* *Camph*$_{k*}$ *Caust*$_{k*}$ *Cham*$_{k*}$ *Cic*$_{k*}$ *Cocc*$_{k*}$ **Cupr**$_{k*}$ *Glon*$_{k*}$ hell$_{k*}$ hyos$_{k*}$ ign$_{k*}$ *Lach*$_{k*}$ mag-p$_{k*}$ **Merc**$_{k*}$ oena$_{k*}$ phyt$_{k*}$ **Plb**$_{a1}$ *Sec*$_{k*}$ sep$_{h2*}$ *Stann*$_{k*}$ staph stram$_{k*}$ sulph$_{k*}$ viol-t$_{k*}$
• **epilepsy**; in: aeth$_{c1*}$ *Bufo*$_{k*}$ *Caust* cham$_{k2}$ *Cic*$_{k*}$ cupr$_{mtf33}$ ign$_{gk}$ *Lach* **Plb**$_{a1}$ *Stann*$_{k*}$ staph sulph
⁝ **fright**; after: *Ign*
⁝ **falling** on head: *Cupr*
• **palms**; into: hell$_{ptk1}$
• **rheumatism**; during: kali-i$_{k*}$
• **sleep** agg.; during: viol-t$_{k*}$

CLOSED:
○ - **Fingers**: cupr$_{ptk1}$ lyc$_{k*}$ merc$_{ptk1}$ plb$_{ptk1}$ stry$_{k*}$
• **sleep**; during: hyos sul-ac
- **Thumbs**: cocc$_{k*}$ hyos$_{k*}$

CLOSING: | **Fingers** | **impossible**: *Caul* bg2
- **Hands** | **agg.**: chin b7.de*

CLOTH AROUND; TYING (See Bandaging)

CLUBBING of fingers: beryl sp1 laur br1*

CLUBFOOT: nux-v bro1* phos bro1 stry bro1

CLUCKING:
○ - **Arm**: ambr h1
- **Elbows**: mang h2
- **Feet**:
▽ · **extending** to | **Head**: calc h2
- **Knee**, sitting: bell h1
○ · **Hollow** of knee: asar h1
· **Outer** side of: arg-met h1
- **Legs** | **Bones** | **Tibia**: con h2
· **Calves**: sulph h2
⁝ **Outer** side of: rhus-t h1
- **Lower** limbs: bell h1
- **Shoulders**: mang h2
- **Thighs**: meny h1
- **Thumbs**: rhus-t h1

CLUMSINESS (See Awkwardness)

COBWEB on hands; sensation of: borx k*

COITION agg.: | **Lower** limbs: calc ptk1 coloc bg2 graph bg2 nat-m ptk1 sep bg2

COLD:
- **air**:
· **agg.**:
⁝ **Feet**: alum bg2
⁝ **Upper** limbs: acon b7.de* bry b7.de* cocc b7.de* ign b7.de* kali-bi bg2 nux-m b7.de* rhus-t b7.de* spong b7.de*
· **amel.** | **Upper** limbs: calc b4a.de *Thuj* b4a.de
· **blowing** on it; as if cold air was | **Lower** limbs: samb b7.de*
· **blowing** on part:
⁝ **Lower** limbs | **agg.**: nux-v b7.de* rhus-t b7.de*
- **applications**:
· **agg.** | **Lower** limbs: *Acon* b7.de* *Caust* b4.de* cham b7.de* *Coloc* b4a.de ign bg2 nux-m b7.de* *Rhus-t* b7.de* *Sabad* b7.de* sulph b4.de*
- **becoming**:
· **agg.**:
⁝ **Lower** limbs: arn b7.de* ars b4a.de* *Bry* b7a.de cham bg2 cocc b7.de* hep b4a.de *Lyc* b4a.de *Nit-ac* b4a.de nux-v b7.de* *Rhus-t* b7.de* sep b4.de*
⁝ **Upper** limbs: *Arn* b7.de* cocc b7.de* *Coloc* b4a.de *Kali-c* b4a.de lyc b4.de* nit-ac bg2 nux-v b7.de* **Rhus-t** b7.de* sil b4.de*
- **water**:
· **agg.** | **Upper** limbs: calc b4a.de* *Clem* b4a.de phos bg2 sul-ac b4.de* *Sulph* b4a.de

COLD; AFTER TAKING:
- **agg.**:
○ · **Lower** limbs: acon b7.de* am-c b4.de* bry b7.de* *Calc* b4.de* caust b4.de* cham b7.de* *Dulc* b4.de* nit-ac b4.de* *Nux-v* b7.de* petr b4.de* phos b4.de* sep b4.de* *Sulph* b4a.de
· **Upper** limbs: acon b7.de* bry b7.de* *Calc* b4a.de cham b7.de* *Dulc* b4a.de ign b7.de* *Nit-ac* b4a.de nux-v b7.de* *Sulph* b4a.de

COLDNESS: (↗*Raynaud's*) *Acon* k* adam srj5• aeth *Agar* k* *Agar-ph* bro1 agath-a nl2• agn k2 allox sp1 alum k* alumn k* ambr bg2* androc srj1• *Ant-c* **Ant-t** k* anthraci *Apis* k* aq-mar skp7• aran bg2 aran-ix sp1 *Arg-n* k* arist-cl sp1 **Ars** k* *Ars-h* k* *Ars-i* ars-s-f k2 atro k* *Aur-m* *Bamb-a* stb2.de• bell k* beryl sp1 bism k* *Bit-ar* wht1• both k* brom k2 bros-gau mrc1 bry k* bufo but-ac sp1 buth-a sp1 *Cact* **Calc** k* calc-hp bro1 *Calc-p* k* calc-s calc-sil k2 **Camph** k* cann-i k* cann-s k* *Canth* k* *Caps* k* carb-ac k* carb-an k* **Carb-v** k* *Carbn-h* *Carbn-s* cass a1 caust k* cedr *Cham* k* *Chel* k* chen-a k* chin k* chinin-ar chinin-s chord-umb rly4• *Cic* k* cina k2 cist mrr1 cob-n sp1 cocc k* cocc-s kr1* *Coff* coff-t a1 **Colch** k* *Coloc* k*

Coldness: ...
con k* convo-s sp1 crat br1* *Croc* *Crot-h* k* *Crot-t* k* **Cupr** k* cupr-ar k* cupr-m a1 cupr-n a1 cycl k* **Dig** k* dros *Dulc* k* echi *Eup-per* *Eup-pur* hr1 falco-pe nl2• *Ferr* k* ferr-ar *Ferr-p* galla-q-r nl2• *Gamb* *Gels* k* gins k* glon k* graph mrr1 haliae-lc srj5• *Ham* hed bro1 hell k* helo bg2* *Helo-s* rwt2• helon k* hep k* hydr-ac k* *Hydrog* srj2• *Hyos* k* ign bro1 *Iod* k* ip k* *Iris* jatr-c jug-r k* *Kali-bi* k* *Kali-br* k* *Kali-c* k* kali-chl k* kali-m k* kali-n k* *Kali-p* kali-s kali-sula a1* *Kalm* k* *Lach* *Laur* k* *Led* k* *Lept* lil-t k* lol bro1 lon-x br1* *Lyc* k* *Lycps-v* lyss k* m-ambo b7a.de manc k* mand sp1 *Med* meli bro1 *Merc* k* *Merc-c* k* *Mez* k* morph k* mucs-nas rly4• *Mur-ac* k* naja k* *Nat-c* k* *Nat-m* k* nat-ox rly4• nat-p nit-ac nux-m k* *Nux-v* k* olnd k* *Op* k* orot-ac rly4• *Ox-ac* k* paeon k* pall petr k* *Ph-ac* k* *Phos* k* phys k* *Phyt* k* *Pic-ac* k* plac-s rly4• plb k* positr nl2• *Puls* k* pyrog k2* quas bro1 raph k* *Rhus-t* k* ruta *Sabad* k* sabin k* sang bro1 sarr k* **Sec** k* sep bg2 *Sil* k* spig k* spong squil b7a.de stann k* **Stram** k* stront-c stroph-s sp1 stry k* sul-ac k* sulfon bro1 sulph k* syph jl2 *Tab* k* tarent ter tril-p bro1* tritic-vg fd5.de vanil fd5.de ven-m rsj12• **Verat** k* *Verat-v* k* verb k* vip k* visc sp1 *Zinc* k* zinc-p k2 [heroin sdj2]
- **one** side | **other** side hot: allox sp1
- **left**: carb-v h2* caust *Elaps*
- **daytime**: fl-ac k2 spig k*
- **morning**: anac k* bry k* calc-p k* carc fd2.de• con k* crot-h k* dulc fd4.de fl-ac k2 hep h2* lyc k* *Nux-v* k* ruta fd4.de spong fd4.de *Sulph* k* thuj k* tritic-vg fd5.de
- **forenoon**: dulc fd4.de spong fd4.de sulph h2*
- **afternoon**: ars k* chinin-s dulc fd4.de lyc k* ruta fd4.de spong fd4.de thuj k* tritic-vg fd5.de
- **evening**: ars k* calc-sil k2 chin k* jatr-c merc-cy k* nux-v k* phyt k* puls k* rhus-t k* spong fd4.de sulph k* tritic-vg fd5.de
· **stool** agg.; during: sulph k*
· **warm** room agg.: brom
- **night**: agath-a nl2• calc-sil k2 carb-v k* stram k* tritic-vg fd5.de
· **bed** agg.; in: agath-a nl2• carb-an k*
· **heat** of other side, with: *Puls* k*
- **accompanied** by:
· **nausea** (See STOMACH - Nausea - accompanied - extremities - coldness)
○ · **Head**:
⁝ **fullness** (See HEAD - Fullness - accompanied; HEAD - Fullness - accompanied - extremities)
⁝ **pain** (See HEAD - Pain - accompanied - extremities - cold)
- **agg.** | **Upper** limbs: agar bg2 am-c b4.de* cham b7.de* cist bg2 ign b7a.de kali-c b4.de* m-ambo b7.de* nat-m bg2 nit-ac b4.de* nux-m b7.de* **Rhus-t** b7.de* *Sabad* b7.de*
- **air** agg.; draft of: carc tpw2*
- **air** agg.; in open: chin
- **alternating** with:
· **heat**: bell helo-s rwt2• *Lyc* pyrid rly4• stram
⁝ **burning**: helo c1 helo-s c1
- **ascending** agg.: stroph-s sp1
- **children**; in: *Calc-p* br1
- **company** agg.: aur
- **convulsions**; with: aeth k* **Bell** k* *Bufo* hr *Cic* hell kr1* hydr-ac bro1 *Nicot* bro1 oena bro1
- **diarrhea**, with: **Ars** **Camph** *Carb-v* cop *Laur* nux-m podo *Sec* *Tab* **Verat**
- **during**:
· **agg.** | **Lower** limbs: puls b7.de
- **dyspnea**; with: gels hr1
- **excitement**: *Lach*
- **exertion** in open air agg.: plb
- **fever**; during: am-c bg2 apis bg2 *Arn* bg2 ars bg2 *Bell* bg2* bism a1 bry bg2 bufo bg2 calc bg2 camph bg2 carb-an carb-v bg2 chin bg2 colch bg2 dulc fd4.de *Eup-pur* hr1 ferr bg2* gels k2 kali-ar kali-br bg2 kali-sula a1 lach bg2 lyc bg2 mag-p bg2 meny bg2 op bg2 phyt bg2 pip-n bg2 plb bg2 sep spig bg2 **Stram** k* sulph bg2 verat bg2 verat-v bg2
- **followed** by:
· **heat**: pyrog jl2
· **pain**: pyrog jl2

- **headache**; with (See HEAD - Pain - accompanied - extremities - cold)
- **heat**; with:
  - ○ **Body**; of: chin *Colch* iod mrr1 nept-m lsd2.fr *Rhus-t*
  - **Face**; of: cham chin hell led k2 nept-m lsd2.fr
  - **Head**; of (See HEAD - Heat - coldness - extremities)
- **ice** in spots; like: **Agar** plut-n srj7•
- **icy** cold: calc tl1 lach mrr1
- **injuries**; after: **Bell-p** mrr1 led k2
- **menses**; during: arg-n k2 arn *Calc* cham k* lach k2 *Sec Sil* verat k2
- **mental** exertion agg.: *Lach*
- **motion** | **amel.**: *Acon* k* carc fd2.de•
- **pain**:
  - ○ **Abdomen**; with pain in: ars
  - **Back** and hips; with pain in: pall c1
- **painful**: syph hr1*
- **paralyzed** limbs: *Ars* caust cocc dulc *Graph Nux-v* **Rhus-t** zinc
- **rest** | **amel.**: stroph-s sp1
- **running** agg.: stroph-s sp1
- **sitting** agg.: kreos k*
- **spots**; in: camph mrr1
- **standing** agg.: stroph-s sp1
- **stool** agg.; during: ars bg2 puls b7a.de sec bg2 **Verat** bg2
- **waking**; on: carb-v k2
- **walking** agg. | **cold** air agg.: calc k2
- **warm** bed unendurable, yet: **Camph Led** *Mag-c Med* **Sec**

○ - **Ankles**: *Acon* k* agar k* berb k* calc-f ptk1 carc fd2.de• caust chin coca-c sk4• dream-p sdj1• ign bg1* lach mag-m ptk1 med bg1* rhus-t sne
  - **walking** in open air agg.: chin
  - ○ **Malleolus** in spots; inner: berb

- **Elbows**: *Agar* k* cedr k* dulc fd4.de gins k* graph iris-foe
  - ▽ **extending** to:
    - **Hand**: rhus-g tmo3•
      - **noon**; toward: cedr
  - ○ **Olecranon**: *Agar* k*

- **Feet**: abrot absin k* acet-ac k* *Acon* k* agar k* **Agn** hr1 allox tpw4 aloe k* alum k* alum-p k2 alum-sil k2 alumn k* *Am-br* k* *Am-c* k* am-m k* ambr k* *Anac* k* androc srj1• ang k* **Ant-c** k* **Ant-t** k* anth k* aphis **Apis** apoc k* a r a n - i x sp1 arg-met bg2 *Arg-n* k* arge-pl rwt5• *Arn* k* **Ars** k* **Ars-i** ars-s-f k2 ars-s-r hr1 asaf k* *Asar* k* asc-t k* atha a1 **Aur** k* aur-ar k2 aur-i k2 aur-s k2 bamb-a stb2.de• bapt k* *Bar-c* k* bar-i k2 bar-m bar-s k2 **Bell** k* benz-ac k* berb k* bit-ar wht1• both-ax tsm2 *Bov* k* brach k* **Brom** k* bros-gau mrc1 bry k* bufo k* but-ac sp1 *Cact* k* calad k* **Calc** k* calc-i k2 calc-p k* calc-s calc-sil k2 calen hr1 *Camph* k* cann-i k* cann-s k* *Canth* k* *Caps* k* *Carb-ac* k* *Carb-an* k* *Carb-v* k* carbn-o **Carbn-s** cass a1 *Caul* **Caust** k* cedr k* *Cham* k* *Chel* k* **Chin** k* *Chinin-ar* choc srj3• chr-ac a1* cic k* cimic k* *Cimx* k* *Cina* cinnb k* *Cist* k* cob-n sp1 *Cocc* k* coff k* *Coff-t* a1* *Colch* k* *Coloc* b4a.de* **Con** k* cot a1 crat *Croc* bg2* *Crot-c* k* crot-h k* *Crot-t* k* **Cupr** k* cupr-ar k* cupr-s a1* cycl bg2 cypra-eg sde6.de• daph k* **Dig** k* digin a1 dor k* **Dros** k* dulc bro1* *Elaps* k* ephe-si hsj1• eup-per k* *Eup-pur* hr1 euph b4a.de euph-c a1 euphr bg2 fago k* falco-pe nl2• **Ferr** k* ferr-ar **Ferr-i** ferr-p fl-ac k2 flor-p rsj3• form k* *Gels* k* *Glon* k* **Graph** k* *Hell* k* helo bro1 helo-s rwt2• *Hep* k* hipp k* hura hydrc k* *Hydrog* srj2• hydroph rsj6• hyos k* hyper k* iber k* ign k* ind k* **Iod** k* **Ip** k* iris **Kali-ar** k* kali-bi k* kali-br hr1 **Kali-c** k* kali-chl k* kali-i k* **Kali-m** k* **Kali-n** k* **Kali-p Kali-s** k* kali-sil k2 kiss a1 kola stb3• **Kreos** k* lac-ac k* lac-d k* lac-e hm2• lac-lup hm2• **Lach** k* lact k* lapa a1 laur k* lavand-a ctl1• led k* lil-t k* limest-b es1• **Lyc** k* *Lycps-v* m-aust b7.de mag-c k* mag-m k* mag-p bg2 mag-s k* malar jl2 manc k* mand rsj7• *Mang* k* *Med* k* **Meny** k* **Merc** k* *Merc-c* k* mez k* mim-p rsj8• moni rfm1• morph k* *Mur-ac* k* musca-d szs1 **Naja** narcot a1 *Nat-ar* k2* **Nat-c** k* **Nat-m** k* *Nat-n* bg2 nat-ox rly4• *Nat-p* k* *Nat-s* k* **Nit-ac** k* nitro-o a1 *Nux-m* k* *Nux-v* k* oena k* ol-an k* ol-j k* olib-sac wmh1 olnd k* op k* orot-ac rly4• *Ox-ac* k* pall k* **Par** k* peti a1 **Petr** k* **Ph-ac** k* **Phos** k* *Phyt* k* *Pic-ac* k* pieri-b mlk9.de pimp a1 pip-m k* plac-s rly4• plan k* plat k* *Plb* k* *Plut-n* srj7• *Podo* k* polyg-h bg2 polys sk4• positr nl2• *Psor* ptel k* **Puls** k* ran-b b7.de* raph k* **Rhod** k* rhus-g tmo3• *Rhus-t* k* rob k* rumx **Ruta** k* sabad k* *Sabin* k* sacch-a gmj3 *Samb* k* sang k* sanic tl1 *Sars* k* *Sec* bg2* sel b7a.de* **Sep** k* **Sil** k* spira a1 spong k* **Squil** k* *Stann* k* staph k* **Stram** k* *Stront-c* k* stry k* stry-p br1 sul-ac k* **Sulph** k* sumb k* tab k* *Tarent* k* tell k* **Thuj** k* thyr br1 trif-p a1* trios rsj11• tritic-vg fd5.de tub bg tus-p a1 valer bg2 vanad dx* vanil fd5.de *Verat* k* *Verat-v* k* verb k* vesp k* visc sp1 *Zinc* k* ziz a1*

- **Feet**: ...
  [ant-met stj2 cadm-met stj2 cupr-act stj2 cupr-f stj2 cupr-m stj2 cupr-p stj2 lac-mat sst4 *Mag-sil* stj2 moly-met stj2 *Nat-sil* stj2 *Nicc* stj1 *Nicc-met* stj2 niob-met stj2 rhodi stj2 rubd-met stj2 ruth-met stj2 spect dfg1 stront-m stj2 stront-met stj2 tax jsj7 techn stj2 yttr-met stj2 zirc-met stj2]
  - **right**: *(↗left; one; one - other)* aids nl2• ambr k* bar-c k* *Chel* k* con bg3* gink-b sbd1• ham fd3.de• hydrog srj2• *Lyc* k* nat-m bg1 olib-sac wmh1 pimp bg1* puls bg3* sabin bg3* *Sulph* k*
    - **heat** of left foot; with: allox tpw4 hydrog srj2•
    - **normal**; the other: lyc tl1
    - **walking** agg.: bar-c
  - **left**: *(↗one; one - other; right)* aeth bamb-a stb2.de• carb-v bg3 chin a1 euph h2* hydrc k* laur bg1 nat-n bg3 pip-m k* psor bg3 raph a1 r h u s - t bg3* ruta fd4.de stann bg1 sulph bg3 sumb k* *Tub*
  - **daytime**: chr-ac hr1 **Hep** mag-s k* nat-p k2 nit-ac phos k* *Sep Sil* k* s u l p h k*
    - **menses**; during: nat-p
  - **morning**: anac k* caps k* carc fd2.de• chel k* chin h1* coc-c k* graph k* hura lyc mag-m k* mang h2* merc k* nat-c h2* nat-sil fd3.de• nux-v k* **Sep** k* *Spig* stram k* **Sulph** hr1 sumb k* tritic-vg fd5.de
    - **5** h (See night - midnight - after - 5)
    - **7.30** h: ferr
    - **8** h: ferr hura meny
    - **bed** agg.; in: *Caps* b7a.de
  - **forenoon**: *Carb-an* k* chinin-s cop dulc fd4.de fago k* ham fd3.de• hura mez k* petr k* sep k* spong fd4.de tritic-vg fd5.de vanil fd5.de
    - **9**-15 h: *Carb-an*
    - **10** h: fago med
      - **10**-15 h: petr a1
    - **11** h:
      - **lying** down | **amel.**: *Sep*
    - **15** h; until: petr
  - **noon**: chinin-s chr-ac a1 kali-c h2* nit-ac k* spong fd4.de zing k*
    - **heat** and redness of the face; during: sep
    - **other** one burns; while the: hura
  - **afternoon**: bar-c chel k* chinin-s coca colch k* *Gels* k* kali-p fd1.de• mez k* nux-v k* sang k* *Sep* k* spong fd4.de squil k* *Sulph* k* zinc h2*
    - **13** h: chel
    - **14** h: chel lyc sars
    - **15** h: eup-pur lyc
    - **16** h: coff sang
      - **air**; in open | **amel.**: coff
    - **17** h: alum h2 graph
    - **hot** face, with: hura
  - **evening**: **Acon** k* aloe am-br k* *Am-c* k* androc srj1• ars k* bar-c h2* bell h1* **Calc** carb-an k* *Carb-v* k* carbn-s cham k* chel k* chin k* con k* dulc fd4.de graph k* ham fd3.de• hell k* *Ign* hr1 kali-p fd1.de• kali-s lyc k* mag-c k* mang k* nat-c h2* nat-n k* nat-sil fd3.de• nux-v k* ox-ac k* peti a1 petr k* ph-ac k* plan k* polys sk4• puls k* rhod k* **Sep** k* **Sil** k* spong fd4.de stront-c sulph k* til k* tritic-vg fd5.de vanil fd5.de verat k* *Zinc* k*
    - **18** h: cedr
    - **20** h: bar-c hep
    - **21** h: aloe kreos
    - **23** h (See night - midnight - before - 23)
    - **air** agg.; in open: mang k*
    - **bed**:
      - **in** bed:
        - **agg.**: aloe **Am-c** *Am-m* aur **Calc** carb-an *Carb-v* carbn-s carl chel dulc fd4.de *Ferr* ferr-p gink-b sbd1• **Graph** kali-ar *Kali-c* kali-s lyc meny h1* merc nat-c nit-ac nux-v par petr ph-ac *Phos* psor kl raph rhod rhus-t b7a.de* sars h2* senec kl **Sep Sil** staph k* sulph thuj tub bg* vanil fd5.de *Zinc*
        - **amel.**: sulph
  - **night**: aloe am-c am-m ant-c k* *Aur* bov k* bry calad **Calc** k* *Carb-v* *Carbn-s* chel com k* cop k* *Ferr* k* ferr-i ham fd3.de• iod k* kali-ar malar jl2 nat-sil fd3.de• nit-ac k* par k* petr k* *Phos* k* psor k* raph k* rhod k* ruta fd4.de sars k* sel rsj9• sep *Sil* sul-i k2 sulph k* thuj k* tritic-vg fd5.de vanil fd5.de verat k* *Zinc* k* zinc-p k2 [tax jsj7]

Extremities

- **night**: ...
  - **midnight**: calad
    - **before** | **23** h: fago
    - **after** | **5** h: hura
  - **bed** agg.; in: am-m *Aur* bamb-a stb2.de• **Calc** k* carb-v chel *Ferr* ham fd3.de• kali-bi gk nat-sil fd3.de• nit-ac petr phos plut-n srj7• psor bg1 raph k* rhod k* rhus-t bg1 sars bg1 sec gk sil sulph thuj k* tub c1 vanil fd5.de zinc
  - **waking**, and on: *Nit-ac* kl zinc kl
- **accompanied** by:
  - **burning**; internal (See Pain - feet - coldness - burning)
  - **heat** of extremities (See Heat - accompanied - feet)
  - **mental** symptoms (See MIND - Mental symptoms - accompanied - feet)
  - **vomiting** (See STOMACH - Vomiting - accompanied - feet - cold)
  - **Head**; complaints of (See HEAD - Complaints - accompanied - feet - cold)
- **alternating** with:
  - **heat**: alum k* fago a1
  - **Hands**; cold: aloe sep k* zing k*
  - **Legs**; pain in (See Pain - legs - alternating - feet)
- **anxiety**, during: cupr graph k* puls sulph k*
- **bed**:
  - **in** bed:
    - **agg.**: alum k* am-c ptk1 calc ptk1 *Ferr* k* graph ptk1 kali-c lach naja pd phos h2* psor ptk1 raph rhod k* sacch-a fd2.de• senec bg1* sep bg1* sil ptk1 thuj k* tritic-vg fd5.de tub ptk* vanil fd5.de zinc bg1
    - **amel.**: kali-s fd4.de mez h2*
- **breakfast** agg.; after: verat
  - **headache**; during: **Sep**
- **chill**, during (See icy - chill)
- **cholera**; during: *Kali-br* hr1 laur ptk1
- **clammy**: bar-c bro1 *Calc* bro1 laur bro1 *Sep* bro1 stry-p bro1
  - **injury** of back; after: nit-ac mrr1
- **cold**:
  - **air** blowing on it; as if cold: hydrog srj2•
  - **perspiration**; with: ars a1*
  - **Hands** and hot face; with cold (See hands - feet - face)
- **damp**: calc tl1
- **diarrhea**, with: dig k* *Lyc* nit-ac podo fd3.de• vanil fd5.de
- **dinner** | **after** | **agg.**: cann-i k* carb-v *Cor-r* hr1 phyt hr1 *Sulph* k*
  - **during** | **agg.**: sulph k*
- **dysentery**; cold feet to knee, in: aloe k1
- **eating** | **after** | **agg.**: aloe calc k* *Camph* k* caps k* cor-r a1
  - **while** | **agg.**: ign k* sulph h2*
- **emissions** agg.; after: aloe nux-v k*
- **excitement** agg.: crat br1 mag-c
- **exertion**; from: plb bg1
  - **least**: crat br1
- **fever**:
  - **before**: carb-v b4a.de sep b4a.de
  - **during** | **agg.**: *Agn* bg2 am-c k* **Ang** bg2 **Ant-c** bg2 antip vh1 apis kr1 *Arn* k* ars k* bapt bg2 bar-c k* bell bufo k* calad calc k* caps carb-an carb-v caust bg2 cedr hr1 chin k* chin-b hr1 **Cocc** bg2 *Colch* bg2 con bg2 gels c1 hell k* ign k* ip k* *Iris* kali-c kali-s **Kreos** bg2 *Lach* k* *Lyc* bg2 *Mag-c* b4a.de* meny k* naja bg2 nit-ac bg2* nux-v k* petr k* ph-ac bg2* phos bg2 ptel puls k* ran-b k* rhod k* **Ruta** bg2 *Sabad* hr1 **Sabin** bg2 samb k* *Sep* bg2 sil bg2* squil b7.de* stann *Stram* k* *Sulph* k* tarent ptk1* thuj bg2 tub pcr *Verat* b7a.de* *Zinc* h2*
- **headache**:
  - **after**: cupr h2*
- **headache**: ...
  - **during**: *Arg-n* k* ars aur aur-ar k2 *Bell* k* bufo cact *Calc* k* camph *Carb-v* k* carbn-s chin chr-ac coca cot a1* dirc k* *Ferr* k* ferr-p **Gels** k* lac-d k* lach k* laur mand mg **Meli** k* *Meny* k* *Naja* k* nat-m k* phos plat k* *Psor* k* sars k* **Sep** k* stram *Sulph* k* vario ptk1 verat bro1 verat-v k*
    - **menses**; after: *Ferr*
- **heat**; with:
  - **flushes** of heat: hydrog srj2•
  - **Abdomen**; of | **fever**; during: ip mtf33
  - **Body**: caps a1 samb mrr1 visc c1
    - **one** side of: ran-b
    - **sleep**; during: **Samb** k*
    - **Upper** part of: anac c1
  - **Face**; of (See FACE - Heat - cold - feet)
  - **Hands**; of (See Heat - hands - coldness - feet)
  - **Head**; of (See HEAD - Heat - coldness - feet)
  - **Thighs**; of: cocc hydrog srj2• thuj
- **house** amel.; in: mang
- **icy** cold: *Acon* hr1 agar k* alum h2* anac h2* androc srj1• ant-c h2* *Apis* ars h2* aur bamb-a stb2.de• bell k2 berb hr1 cact k* calad k* calc k2 **Camph** k* **Carb-v** k* cass a1 cedr k* cench k2 chin h1* chin-b c1 choc srj3• cob-n sp1 coloc hr1 **Crot-c** *Cupr* k* dor k* dulc fd4.de **Elaps** k* *Eup-per* k* ferr k2 *Gels* k* graph k* ham fd3.de• helo-s rwt2• *Hep* k* hydrog srj2• ip h1* kali-ar k2 kali-i c1 kali-n c1 kali-s fd4.de kola stb3• lac-d k2 **Lach** k* lact hr1 *Lyc* k* manc k* mang h2* marb-w es1• meny k* *Merc* *Merc-c* k* mez h2* nat-c h2* nat-p k* nat-sil fd3.de• nit-ac bg1 *Nux-m* k* par k* petr a1 **Phos** k* plb k2 polys sk4• *Psor* k* raph a1 rhod hr1 rhus-t h1* ruta fd4.de sabin bg1 samb k* sars k* **Sep** k* **Sil** k* squil k* stront-c bg1 *Sulph* k* tax-br oss1• tub xxb **Verat** k* zinc k* zinc-p k2
  - **accompanied** by:
    - **Head**; heat of (See HEAD - Heat - coldness - feet - icy)
    - **Soles**; burning: *Cupr*
  - **alternating** with heat: helo c1 helo-s c1
  - **bed** agg.; in: bell ptk1 ulm-c jsj8•
  - **chill**; during: agar bg2 alum bg2 am-c bg2 ant-c aur brom dgt1 cann-xyz bg2 *Carb-an* bg2 carb-v bg2 cench k2 chin b7a.de* cina bg2 crat br1 *Dros* b7a.de* *Eup-per* hr1 euph bg2 *Ferr* graph bg2 ham fd3.de• *Hep* bg2* kreos b7a.de* *Lyc* bg2* mang bg2 **Meny** k* merc bg2 mez bg2 nat-c bg2 nat-m bg2 nux-v bg2 *Petr* bg2 ph-ac bg2 *Phos* puls bg2 ruta fd4.de *Samb* b7a.de* sep stann bg2 teucr b7a.de* **Verat** *Zinc*
  - **cold air** | **amel.**: camph h1* led h1*
  - **followed** by | **heat** of right foot and leg: androc srj1•
  - **menses**; during: nat-p ptk1
  - **typhoid** fever; during: chinin-ar gm1
- **lying**:
  - **agg.**: tell
  - **amel.**: phos
- **menses**:
  - **after** | **agg.**: *Carb-v* *Chinin-s*
  - **before** | **agg.**: calc k* hyper k* *Lyc* k* *Nux-m*
  - **during** | **agg.**: *Arg-n* *Calc* k* cop k* *Crot-h* k* *Graph* k* nat-p *Nux-m* k* *Phos* k* sabin k* **Sil** k* tarent hr1
- **mental** exertion agg.: agar *Am-c* ambr *Anac* **Aur** bell **Calc** calc-p *Carb-v* *Caust* chin cocc *Cupr* gels kali-c *Lach* *Lyc* **Nat-c** *Nat-m* nit-ac **Nux-v** petr *Ph-ac* **Phos** psor **Puls** **Sep** **Sil**
- **motion** | **after** | **agg.**: *Cocc* colch rsj2•
  - **not** amel.: aran-ix sp1
- **one** cold: *(↗left; right)* chel ptk1 con ptk1
  - **fever**; during: *Lyc* bg2
  - **other** hot; the: *(↗left; right)* chel k* chin h1* con h2* dig k* hydrog srj2• ip k* kola stb3• lac-f c1 lach bg2 **Lyc** k* psor al *Puls* k* raph ptk tub bg2
    - **right**: bar-c bg2* chel bg2 lyc bg2* puls ptk1 sabin bg2*
    - **left**: carb-v bg2* naja bg2 nat-m bg2 psor bg2* rhus-t bg2 sulph bg2* tub ptk1

- **perspiration** of feet; suppressed: acon bg2 ant-c bg2 ant-t bg2 arn bg2 *Calc* bg2 *Caust* bg2 chin bg2 con k* graph bg2 ip bg2 lach bg2 **Lyc** bg2 nit-ac bg2 **Nux-v** bg2 phos bg2 puls bg2 *Rhus-t* bg2 **Samb** bg2 sel bg2 **Sep** bg2 *Sil* k* squil bg2 *Sulph* bg2 thuj bg2 verat bg2
- **pregnancy** agg.; during: *Lyc* k* rhus-t hr1 **Verat** k*
- **sensation** of: acon b7.de ars b4.de bell b4.de bros-gau mrc1 calc b4a.de chel b7.de laur b7.de m-aust b7.de merc b4.de nux-m b7.de verat b7.de
- **sitting**:
  - **agg.**: ars k* dulc fd4.de mez h2* puls h1* *Sep* k* symph fd3.de•
  - **amel.**: mang k*
- **sleep**; during: bell k2 bros-gau mrc1 samb zinc
  - **heat** of body; with: samb k*
- **spots**; in: agar mrr1
- **stool** | **after** | **agg.**: sulph k*
  - **during** | **agg.**: *Puls* b7a.de
- **sun** agg.; walking in the: *Lach*
- **supper** | **after** | **agg.**: lyc k*
  - **during**: ign
- **takes** cold through: con k* *Sil* k*
- **talking** agg.: am-c
- **urination** agg.; during: dig k*
- **vertigo**; during: sep h2*
- **vomiting**:
  - **after**: sin-a k*
  - **when** (See STOMACH - Vomiting - accompanied - feet - cold)
- **waking**; on: *Chel* puls h1* *Samb* verat k* zinc
- **walking**:
  - **after** | **agg.**: nit-ac k*
  - **agg.**: *Anac* k* *Aran* asaf k* carb-an h2* *Chin* k* mang k* mez k* plb ptk1 sil k*
  - **air** agg.; in open: *Anac* bar-c mang h2 plan plb
    - **rapidly**; walking: *Phos*
  - **amel.**: aloe
- **warm**:
  - **bathing**; after: lach k2
  - **foot**-bath:
    - **amel.** | **hot** foot-bath: glon
  - **room** | **agg.**: bamb-a stb2.de• hir rsj4• kali-br mez h2 rhod ptk ruta fd4.de tritic-vg fd5.de
  - **touch**; sensation of coldness, though warm to: *Sulph* k*
- **warmed**, cannot be: ars a1* spong fd4.de tritic-vg fd5.de
- **water**; as though in: carb-v bg2* chin bg1 form bg2* gels k* lyc bg2* mag-c h2* meny k* merc k* nat-m bg2 puls bg1 sabin bg2* sanic ptk1 **Sep** k* verat bg1
  - **cold** water running in foot; as if: verat h1
- **weather**; in hottest: *Asar*
- **wine** agg.: lyc k*
- **writing** agg.: chinin-s sep k*

▽ • **extending** to:
  - **Calves**: aloe crot-t k* kali-p fd1.de•
  - **Knees**: aeth k* aphis c1 chel k* ham fd3.de• ign k* kali-s fd4.de malar jl2 mang h2* *Meny* k* nat-m plut-n srj7•
  - **Upward**: helo-s br1* malar jl2

○ • **Back** of feet: graph k* mez a1
  - **walking** agg.: graph k*
- **Bones**: chin h1*
- **Hands**, and (See hands - feet)
- **Heels**: kali-p fd1.de• merc bg1* *Puls* b7a.de sang bg2* sep k*
  - **left**: psil ft1
    - **accompanied** by | **dysuria** (See BLADDER - Urination - dysuria - accompanied - heel)
  - **fever**; during: lyc dgt

- **Feet**: ...
  - **Soles**: acon k* ars k* card-m hr1 caust k* chel k* chinin-s colch k* *Coloc* k* dig h2* hyper k* kali-s fd4.de kola stb3• lach bg1 laur k* lith-c merc k* nat-sil fd3.de• *Nit-ac* k* nux-v k* phos bg1 *Puls* b7a.de rhod bg1 spong fd4.de *Sulph* k* symph fd3.de• thuj bg1 valer b7a.de
    - **morning**: chinin-s nat-sil fd3.de•
    - **evening** | **bed** agg.; in: *Aur* k* verat k*
    - **night**: nit-ac k*
      - **midnight**:
        - **after**:
          - **5 h** | **Face**; with hot: con
    - **air** agg.; in open: laur
    - **cold** air blowing on soles; as if: valer bg2 verat bg2
    - **fever**; during: colch b7a.de
    - **icy** cold: kali-s fd4.de *Nit-ac* k*
      - **bed** agg.; in: sulph ptk1
    - **menses**; during: *Calc Graph Nux-m Phos Sil* verat
    - **painful**: caust h2* spong fd4.de symph fd3.de•
    - **sensation** of coldness, although not cold: coloc k* valer b7.de
    - **warm** applications | **not** amel.: kola stb3•
    - **Heels**: sep
- **Fingers**: *Abrot* bg2* *Acon* k* act-sp k* adam skp7• *Agar* bg2* am-c bg2 ang k* *Ant-t* b7.de* apis k* asar bg2 bit-ar wht1• brass a1 buth-a sp1 calad k* *Calc* k* *Calc-p* k* *Carbn-s* caust k* *Cham* k* **Chel** k* chord-umb rly4• cic k* cocc k* colch k* coloc k* con k* crat br1 crot-h k* cupr mtf33 *Dig* k* dys fmm1• gels gins k* **Graph** k* *Hell* k* helo-s bnm14• hep bg2 hydr-ac k* **Kali-c** k* kali-p fd1.de• kreos bg2 *Lac-c* k* *Lac-d* lyc k* m-arct b7.de med k* *Meny* k* merc k* mosch k* mur-ac k* nit-ac bg2 ox-ac mrr1 par k* *Ph-ac* k* phos bg2 plan k* plb k* propl ub1• prot fmm1• ptel k* ran-b bg2 rat k* rhod k* *Rhus-t* rumx sacch-a fd2.de• samb xxb1 sars k* sec k* *Sep* k* spig bg2 spong fd4.de stann bg2 sulph k* sumb k* symph fd3.de• **Tarax** k* **Thuj** k* tritic-vg fd5.de tub-d jl2 tub-m jl2 vanil fd5.de verat k* vip k* [calc-f stj1]
  - **right**: ang h1* [bell-p-sp dcm1]
  - **left**: plut-n srj7• thuj h1*
  - **morning**: chinin-s rat k* spong fd4.de symph fd3.de•
  - **afternoon**, 14 h: plan tritic-vg fd5.de
  - **evening**: kali-p fd1.de• sulph symph fd3.de• thuj k*
  - **night**: *Mur-ac* k*
  - **accompanied** by | **Head**; complaints of (See HEAD - Complaints - accompanied - fingers - cold)
  - **alternating** with | **Head**; pain in (See HEAD - Pain - alternating - fingers)
  - **blue**, and: chel bro1 crat br1* cupr bro1 plut-n srj7• verat bro1
  - **chill**: *Apis Cact* crat br1 dig meny *Nat-m* nux-v par ph-ac *Rhus-t Sep* verat
  - **chorea**, during: laur ptk2
  - **excitement** agg.: crat br1
  - **exertion** agg.: crat br1
  - **fever**; during: ant-t bg2 cham bg2 tarax bg2 **Thuj** bg2
  - **heart** disease; in: laur ptk2
  - **perspiration**; during: ant-t bg2 cham bg2 *Chel* bg2 tarax bg2 thuj bg2
  - **sensation** of: bros-gau mrc1
  - **sitting** agg.: cham k*

▽ • **extending** to:
  - **Middle** of upper arms: graph k*
  - **Nape** of neck: coff k*
  - **Palms** and soles: dig k*

○ • **First**: chord-umb rly4• rhod k*
  - **Fourth**: lyc k*
  - **Joints**: chel k*
  - **Nails**; under: cann-s h1 falco-pe nl2•
  - **Second**: chord-umb rly4• mur-ac k* phos k* rhod k*
    - **left**: luf-op rsj5•
    - **Joints** of: agar k*
  - **Third**: rhod k* sulph k*

- **Third**: ...
  - **evening**: sulph k*
- **Tips**: abrot k* acon hr1 adam skp7• *Ant-t* k* *Arn* k* brom k* *Caps* k* carb-v k* *Carl* k* **Chel** k* cist k* coloc k* crot-c sk4• galla-q-r nl2• hell k* jatr-c lac-c ptk1 lac-d k* lob k* meny k* merc k* mur-ac k* ozone sde2• petr bg2* ph-ac k* ran-b k* sal-ac sars k* spig k* sulph k* sumb k* *Tarax* k* *Thuj* k* vanil fd5.de verat k2 *Zinc* k* zinc-p k2 [calc-f stj1]
  - **morning** | **rising** agg.; after: coloc k*
  - **accompanied** by | **Teeth**; pain in (See TEETH - Pain - accompanied - fingers - cold)
  - **air** agg.; in open: ph-ac
  - **chill**; during: acon hr1 mur-ac h2* ran-b k*
  - **heat**; during: *Caps* k*
  - **icy** cold: ant-t tl1* carb-v tl1 lac-d ptk1 marb-w es1• mez tl1 nux-m tl1 ozone sde2• verat tl1
  - **rest** of body is hot: thuj
  - **sensitive** to cold: sec k*
  - **writing**; after: carl k*
- **Toes**, and: carc fd2.de• crat br1 helo-s bnm14• kali-p fd1.de•

- **Forearms**: *Arg-n* arn bro1 ars k* *Brom* k* bry k* *Calc* k* carb-v bro1 caust k* *Cedr* k* con *Crot-c* **Graph** k* ham fd3.de• hydrc k* kali-chl k* med hr1* nat-c k2 nux-v k* **Phos** k* plb k* plut-n srj7• rhus-t k* verat-v k*
  - **right**: caust h2* kali-chl a1 med
  - **left**: malar jl2
  - **morning**: ham fd3.de• nux-v k*
    - **rising** agg.; after: nux-v
  - **deathly**: arn br1
  - **icy** cold: **Brom** k* nat-c k2 rhus-t k* thuj k*
  - **menses**; during: *Arg-n* k*
  - ▽ **extending** to:
    - **Fingers**: malar jl2
    - **Hand**: malar jl2

- **Hands**: abies-c k* acet-ac k* *Acon* k* *Agar* k* agath-a nl2• agn b7.de* allox tpw4 aloe alum k* alum-p k2 alum-sil k2 alumn k* am-c k* ambr k* amyg k* anac k* androc srj1• ang k* *Ant-t* k* anth k* *Apis* k* apoc k* aran hr1 *Arg-n* k* *Arn* k* **Ars** k* **Ars-i** ars-s-f k2 ars-s-r hr1 asaf k* asar k* atha a1 atro k* **Aur** k* aur-ar k2 aur-m-n k* aur-s k2 bamb-a stb2.de• *Bar-c* k* bar-i k2 *Bar-m* bar-s k2 bart a1 *Bell* k* benz-ac k* berb k* bit-ar wht1• *Bov* k* brach k* *Brom* k* bry k* *Cact* k* calad bg2 *Calc* k* **Calc-ar** k* calc-i k2 **Calc-p** k* calc-s calc-sil k2 calen a1* **Camph** k* cann-i k* cann-s k* canth b7.de* caps b7.de* *Carb-ac* k* *Carb-an* k* **Carb-v** k* carbn a1 *Carbn-o* bro1 *Carbn-s* cass a1 *Caust* k* *Cedr* k* cench k2 cham k* **Chel** k* **Chin** k* chin-b hr1* *Chinin-ar* *Chinin-s* choc srj3• chr-ac hr1 cic j* cimic k* *Cina* k* cinnb k* coca-c sk4• cocc k* coff k* coff-t a1* colch k* coloc k* com k* con k* conin a1 cop k* corn hr1 cot a1 crat br1 *Croc* k* *Crot-c* k* crot-h k* crot-t k* *Cupr* k* cupr-s k* **Cycl** k* cypra-eg sde6.de• *Dig* k* digin a1 dor k* *Dros* k* dulc fd4.de elaps ephe-si hsj1• *Eup-per* k* eup-pur k* euph k* euph-c a1 euphr k* fago k* **Ferr** k* ferr-ar **Ferr-i** **Ferr-p** fl-ac k2 galla-q-r nl2• gard-j vlr2• *Gels* k* gins k* glon k* **Graph** k* grat k* ham fd3.de• *Hell* k* helo-s rwt2• hep k* hura hydrc k* *Hydrog* srj2• hyos k* iber k* *Ign* k* ind k* indg k* inul k* **Iod** k* **Ip** k* iris jatr-c **Kali-ar** k* kali-bi k* **Kali-c** k* kali-cy a1 kali-i k* kali-m k2 kali-n k* **Kali-p** kali-s k* kali-sil k2 kreos k* lac-ac k* lac-d k* **Lach** k* lact k* laur k* *Led* k* lil-t k* limest-b es1• lob-s k* loxo-recl knl4• **Lyc** k* **Lycps-v** m-ambo b7.de m-arct b7.de mag-p bg2 mag-s k* manc k* *Mang* k* *Med* k* **Meny** k* **Merc** k* merc-c k* merc-i-r k* merc-sul k* *Mez* k* mim-p rsj8• morph k* mosch k* **Mur-ac** k* muru a1 naja k* narc-ps c1* narcot a1 nat-ar k2 **Nat-c** k* **Nat-m** k* nat-ox rly4• **Nat-p** nat-s *Nat-sil* stj2*• *Nit-ac* k* nit-s-d a1 **Nux-m** k* *Nux-v* k* oena k* ol-an k* **Olnd** k* *Op* k* orot-ac rly4• *Ox-ac* k* ozone sde2• *Pall* k* par b7a.de* peti a1 **Petr** k* **Ph-ac** k* *Phos* k* phys a1 *Phyt* k* pic-ac a1 pimp a1 pin-con oss2• plac-s rly4• plan a1 plat a1 *Plb* a1* plect a1 plumbg a1 polys sk4• positr nl2• *Propl* ub1• ptel a1* **Puls** k* *Pyrog* k* ran-b k* raph k* rhus-g tmo3• *Rhus-t* k* *Rob* k* rumx **Ruta** k* **Sabin** k* sacch-a gmj3 **Samb** k* *Sang* k* sars k* **Sec** k* *Sel* b7a.de* **Sep** k* sil k* spig k* spira a1 spong k* squil k* stann k* staph k* *Stram* k* stry k* sul-ac k* sul-i k2 **Sulph** k* *Sumb* k* symph fd3.de• *Tab* k* tarax k* tep k* teucr b7.de* ther k* *Thuj* k* thyr br1 trif-p a1* tritic-vg fd5.de vanad dx* vanil fd5.de **Verat** k* *Verat-v* k* verb k* vip k* *Zinc* k* zinc-p k2 ziz a1* [heroin sdj2 lac-mat sst4 mag-n stj2 *Mag-sil* stj2 nicc stj1 spect dfg1]
  - **alternating** sides: cocc b7a.de*

- **Hands**: ...
  - **right**: agath-a nl2• am-c a1 ant-t k* ars a1 *Calc* hr1 cann-i k* chel k* ferr k* *Gels* k* med k* mosch a1 pall k* plut-n srj7• sec k* spong fd4.de thuj a1
    - **then** left: med k*
    - **numbness** of left: ferr
    - **warmth** of left: lac-ac mez k* mosch
  - **left**: allox tpw4 ambr h1* carb-v bro1 chin h1* kali-m bg3 lat-m mrr1 nux-v bro1 thyr bg3* vip fkr4.de
    - **warmth** of the right hand; with: ros-d wla1
  - **daytime**: ars-met malar jl2 phos k*
  - **morning**: bell h1* carc fd2.de• chel k* chin k* cina coloc k* cycl k* dulc fd4.de fago k* gels k* lyc k* mang k* spong k* stram k* sumb k* tritic-vg fd5.de
    - **7**.30 h: ferr
    - **8** h: ferr
    - **8**.30 h: mez
    - **rising** agg.; after: coloc dulc fd4.de spong fd4.de
  - **forenoon**: calc k* calen a1 chin k* dulc fd4.de grat k* ham fd3.de• kali-s fd4.de mez k* nat-m k* spong fd4.de
    - **9** h: dros mez
    - **10** h: con fago ham fd3.de• led
  - **noon**: kali-c h2* ped a1 spong fd4.de vanil fd5.de zing k*
  - **afternoon**: alumn k* chinin-s dulc fd4.de gels k* nux-v k* spong fd4.de sulph k* tritic-vg fd5.de vanil fd5.de
    - **13** h: chel
    - **14**-15 h: chel
    - **15** h; after: eup-pur
    - **16** h: petr
    - **16**.30 h: mez
    - **17** h: *Rhus-t*
  - **evening**: *Acon* k* agar k* aloe alumn k* ambr k* ars k* aur k* bamb-a stb2.de• carb-an k* *Carb-v* k* carl k* chel k* chin k* colch k* coloc graph k* ham fd3.de• hep k* nat-c k* nat-sil fd3.de• ox-ac k* peti a1 phos k* polys sk4• spira a1 spong fd4.de sulph k* thuj k* tritic-vg fd5.de verat k*
    - **19** h: *Lyc* phos
    - **20** h: hep tarax
    - **air** agg.; in open: mang k*
    - **bed** agg.; in: aur carb-an colch k*
    - **heat**:
      - **after**: thuj k*
      - **during**: agar h2* sabad
  - **night**: *Aur* bry k* ferr-i k2 kali-p fd1.de• malar jl2 *Phos* k* sec a1 sep k* thuj vanil fd5.de
  - **abdomen**; with cutting and tearing in: *Ars* k*
  - **accompanied** by:
    - **thirstlessness** (See STOMACH - Thirstless - accompanied - hands)
    - **Head**; complaints of (See HEAD - Complaints - accompanied - hand - coldness)
  - **alternating** with:
    - **cold** feet: aloe sep zing
    - **heat**: bell cench k2 chin cimic cocc k* fago gels hr1 helo c1 helo-s c1 lil-t bg2 par k* positr nl2•
      - **Head**; of: nit-ac h2
  - **amel.**: puls k2
  - **blue**: agar mtf11 *Arg-n* ben-n borx h2 *Cact* *Camph* cocc con *Crot-h* crot-t elaps helo-s rwt2• inul lac-lup hrn2• morph *Nux-v* oena plb stram stry **Verat** hr1 zinc
  - **breakfast** agg.; after: verat k*
  - **chill**; during: agn b7a.de* ars h2* asar h1* aur bell h1* *Bry* b7a.de buth-a sp1 cact *Camph* canth *Carb-v* cedr cench k2 chel *Chin* b7a.de *Cimx* hr1 cina b7a.de colch con crat br1 dros b7a.de* gels c1 hep k* hyos h1* ip led h1* lyc k* mang h2* *Meny* k* **Mez** mur-ac h2* nat-c h2* *Nat-m* **Nux-v**

- **chill**; during: ...
olnd b7a.de *Op* k* petr k* **Phos** plb *Puls* hr1 samb k* **Sec** sep h2* spong h1* stann h2* staph h1* stram sulph h2* *Teucr* b7a.de thuj h1* **Verat**
- **cholera**; during: *Kali-br* hr1
- **clammy**: abies-c br1 positr nl2•
  - **injury** of back; after: nit-ac mrr1
- **cough** agg.; during: rumx k* *Sulph* k*
- **diarrhea**: apis brom dig **Phos** k*
- **dinner**; after: cann-i k*
- **eating**; after: aloe camph k* caps k* con k*
- **emissions** agg.; after: *Merc* k*
- **excitement** agg.: crat br1 lil-t
- **exertion**, least: crat br1
- **fever**; during: agar bg2 antip vh1 arn k* asaf aur bg2 bell bg2 camph bg2 canth caust bg2 con bg2 cycl k* dros h1* dulc fd4.de euphr k* gels c1 hell k* *Ign* b7.de* ip k* lyc bg2 *Meny* b7.de* mez bg2 naja bg2 nit-ac nux-v bg2 phos bg2 puls k* ran-b k* rhus-t bg2 **Ruta** bg2 sabad k* **Sabin** bg2 *Samb* b7.de* sel bg2 **Squil** b7.de* *Stram* bg2 sul-ac h2* sulph bg2 thuj bg2* verat bg2
- **headache**:
  - **after**: cupr h2*
  - **during**: ambr h1* ars a1 bell bro1 *Calc* bro1 carb-v h2* ferr bro1 lac-d c1* lach bro1 **Meli** hr1* *Meny* bro1 naja bro1 sars hr1 sep bro1 sulph bro1 vario ptk1 verat bro1 verat-v a1
- **heat**; with:
  - **Body**; of: ars-met puls a1* samb mrr1 tab bro1
    - **one** side: *Ran-b*
    - **Internal**: *Arn* hydrog srj2•
  - **Face**; of: agar **Arn** ars asaf camph h1 chin con cycl h1 euph graph h2 hyos ign nat-sil fd3.de• ruta sabin sil h2 spig h1 **Stram** sumb *Thuj* k*
  - **Feet**; of●: *Aloe Calc* k* coloc ph-ac *Sep* k*
  - **Fingers**; of: thuj h1
  - **Forehead**; of: ars asaf asar
  - **Head**; of (See HEAD - Heat - coldness - hands)
  - **Mouth** and throat; of: jatr-c c1
  - **Thighs**; of: thuj
- **icy**: *Acon* k* agar k* alum-sil k2 *Ambr* k* anac k* ant-t bg2 *Arg-n* k* ars k* asar aur aur-ar k2 bamb-a stb2.de• bell h1* buth-a sp1 *Cact* k* calc h2* *Camph* k* *Carb-v* k* cass a1 *Caust* k* cedr k* cench k2 chin h1* coloc k* dor hr1 dros hr1 dulc fd4.de *Eup-per* k* euphr bg2 ham fd3.de• helo c1 helo-s c1* hep h2* hydr-ac ptk1 hydrog srj2• ip h1* lach lyc k* *Manc* k* mang hr1 marb-w es1• *Meny* k* *Merc* hr1 merc-sul hr1* mez h2* *Nat-c* **Nux-m** k* *Nux-v* k* *Ph-ac* phos h2* *Plb* polys sk4• *Puls* hr1 sabin bg2 sanic sep h2* sil h2* spong fd4.de squil k* symph fd3.de• *Tab* hr1 tax-br oss1• thuj h1* thyr ptk1 vario hr1 **Verat** k*
  - **fever**; with: cact br1 thuj ptk1
- **lying** down:
  - **agg.**: kali-c
  - **amel.**: phos
- **menses**; during: aesc *Arg-n* ferr *Graph* k* kali-i *Phos* k* sabin k* sec sulph verat
  - **pain**; with: *Calc Graph Sabin*
- **mental** exertion agg.: lach *Ph-ac*
- **motion**; after: alumn k* *Cocc*
- **nausea**; during: gran k* kreos bg2 phos bg2 verat bg2
- **numb** and cold: chel hydrog srj2• *Lach Ox-ac*
- **old** people; in: bar-c k*
- **one** hand: acon bg2 ant-t b7a.de* *Chin* k* cocc b7a.de dig k* ferr ip b7a.de* lyc bg3* *Mosch* puls bg2* rhus-t bg3* sulph bg3* tab bg2
  - **colder** than the other: **Lyc** mrr1
  - **fingers** of other hot: thuj h1*
  - **hot**:
    - **and** pale, the other cold and red: mosch
    - **other** cold: ant-t b7a.de canth b7a.de chel mrr1 *Chin* k* cocc k* *Dig* k* *Ip* k* lyc mrr1 *Mosch* k* *Puls* k* *Tab*
  - **perspiration** of the other: ip k* mez mosch k*

- **Hands**: ...
  - **painful**: caust h2*
  - **perspiration**; during: arn bg2 bell bg2 *Camph* bg2 *Caust* bg2 cham bg2 chin k* dig k* fago k* ip bg2 *Lil-t* k* lyc bg2 merc-c k* mez bg2 nit-ac b4a.de* *Nux-v* bg2 phos bg2 *Rhus-t* bg2 **Samb** bg2 *Sel* bg2 *Sep* bg2 squil bg2 **Sulph** bg2 thuj bg2* *Verat* bg2
  - **reading** agg.: lyc k*
  - **rising** agg.; after: fago k*
  - **sacrum**; during pain in: hura
  - **sleep** agg.; during: ign k* merc k* samb k* vanil fd5.de
  - **smokers**, in: sec ptk1
  - **talking** agg.: am-c ph-ac k*
  - **uncovering**; on: mag-c ptk1
  - **urination** agg.; during: dig
    - **copious**: dig h2
  - **vertigo**; with: kola stb3• lap-la rsp1 merc k* sep b4a.de*
  - **vexation**; after: phos
  - **waking**; on: *Carb-v* ptk1 dig digin a1
  - **walking**:
    - **after** | **agg.**: alumn vh1
    - **agg.**: asaf camph chin
    - **air** agg.; in open: mang h2 phos plb
  - **warm** | **room** | **agg.**: hir rsj4• mez h2 *Nux-v* plan sep ptk1*
    - **touch**; sensation of coldness, yet warm to: phos h2
  - **water**; in:
    - **agg.**: con ptk1 lac-d ptk1 mag-c ptk1 mag-p ptk1 phos ptk1 tarent ptk1
    - **amel.**: fl-ac ptk1 gels ptk1 jatr-c ptk1
  - **weather**; even in hottest: *Asar* k*
  - **wine** agg.: verat k*
  - **wrap** them up; must: petr h2*
  - **writing**:
    - **after**: agar
    - **agg.**: chinin-s mez k*
  - ○ **Back** of hands: alum k2 anac chinin-s naja phos k* rhus-t k*
    - **afternoon**: chinin-s
    - **heat** of palms, with: anac k* coff *Ferr* hr1
  - **Feet**, and: carc fd2.de• crat br1 cupr sst3• ephe-si hsj1• gink-b sbd1• iod mtf33 kali-m ptk1 kali-s fd4.de nat-sil fd3.de• sacch-a fd2.de• samb mrr1 sanic ptk1 [heroin sdj2]
    - **chill**; during: agar b4a.de *Carb-an* b4a.de euph b4a.de hep b4a.de *Lyc* b4a.de *Nat-c* b4a.de *Nat-m* b4a.de *Petr* b4a.de ph-ac b4a.de stann b4a.de
    - **coryza**; during: anac b4a.de
    - **menses** | **during** | **agg.**: graph b4a.de *Verat* b7a.de
      - **suppressed** menses; from: *Verat* b7a.de
    - **Face**; with heat of: apis kr1 arn pd asaf pd **Bell** mrr1 cham pd chin c1 con a1 graph a1 stram bro1
  - **Palms**: *Acon* k* adam skp7• bung-fa mtf calc-sil k2 dig digin a1 hyos k* jatr-c med jl2 petr-ra shn4•
    - **accompanied** by | **Fingers**; convulsive movements of (See Convulsion - fingers - accompanied - hand - cold - palm)
- **Hips**: agar caust h2* gad gran ham hura malar jl2 merc merl mez morph tax ther valer
  - **right**: bell h1* bry kali-bi merl rhus-t
  - **left**: carb-v caust thuj
  - **forenoon** | **9 h**: ham
  - **icy** coldness: malar jl2
    - **followed** by | **fever**: malar jl2
    - **extending** to | **Body**; whole: malar jl2
  - **sensation** of: bell b4.de valer b7.de
- **Internal**: helo-s rwt2• rhus-t h1
- **Joints**: *Camph* k* cinnb k* *Nat-m* k* petr rhus-t sumb k*
  - **morning**: sumb k*
    - **bed** agg.; in: sumb k*

Extremities

- **air** agg.; in open: nat-m
- **Knees**: acon k* adam skp7• agath-a nl2• **Agn** k* alumn k2 ambr k* *Apis* k* **Ars** k* *Asar* k* aur k* *Benz-ac* k* calc bro1 calc-p k2 camph cann-s k* **Carb-v** k* carbn-o bg2 carbn-s carc fd2.de• *Card-m* cass a1 *Chin* k* *Chinin-ar* *Chinin-s* *Cimx* k* *Colch* k* coloc k* cop daph dig bg2 euphr k* ferr lp graph ham fd3.de• hydrog srj2• *Ign* k* kreos sne *Lach* k* m-arct b7.de meny bg2 *Merc* mez bg2 nat-c bro1 *Nat-m* k* *Nit-ac* k* petr k* **Phos** k* pin-con oss2• *Puls* k* raph k* rhod k* *Sec* *Sep* k* **Sil** k* stann k* sulph k* thuj bg2 vanil fd5.de *Verat* k*
  - **right**: ambr bg1 chel
  - **forenoon**: carc fd2.de• thuj
  - **evening**: agn euphr
    - **bed** agg.; in: ars h2 aur h2 phos tl1*
    - **waking**; on: euphr
  - **night**: **Carb-v** cop euphr **PHOS** k ● raph k* sep *Verat*
    - **bed** agg.; in: **Phos** k* sep
    - **waking**; on: euphr
  - **chill**; during: **Apis** **Carb-v** ign **Phos** sil
  - **fever**; during: **Agn** b7.de* ars bg2 *Puls* bg2 sep bg2
  - **hot** body; with: ars h2 visc c1
  - **lying** agg.: ars
  - **menses**; during: cop
  - **perspiration**; with cold: agn bg2 ars bg2* chin bg2 puls bg2 **Sep** bg2 *Sulph* bg2
  - **sensation** of: coloc b4.de dig b4.de m-aust b7.de phos b4.de verat b7.de
  - **spot**: petr h2*
  - **swollen** knee: *Led*
  - **waking**; on: carb-v k2
  - **walking** in open air agg.; after: sil
  - **warm**; sensation of coldness although: *Coloc* k*
  - **warmed**, cannot be: ars h1*
  - **water** poured over; as if cold: verat
  - **weather**; in hottest: *Asar*
  - **wind**, as from: benz-ac *Cimx*
  - ▽ **extending** to:
    - **Calf**: helo c1
    - **Foot**: rhus-g tmo3•
  - ○ **Hollow** of knees: agar ars-h
  - **Patella**: aur k* carc fd2.de• nat-m verat h1*
  - **Sides** | **Outer**: dig h2*
- **Legs**: acon k* agar agath-a nl2• aloe alum k* alum-p k2 alum-sil k2 alumn ambr k* ant-t anthraci aphis *Apis* *Arg-n* *Ars* k* ars-i ars-s-f k2 aur k* aur-ar k2 aur-i k2 aur-s k2 bar-c k* bar-i k2 bell k* benzol br1 berb bg2* bism bro1 brom bry *Calad* b7.de* **Calc** k* calc-i k2 calc-p k* calc-s calc-sil k2 *Camph* *Carb-an* k* **Carb-v** k* *Carbn-s* cassia-s ccrh1• *Caust* cedr *Cham* *Chel* k* *Chin* k* *Chinin-ar* *Chinin-s* cic cocc coff *Colch* k* com *Crot-c* crot-h bro1 *Cupr* **Dig** k* dios *Dulc* vh elaps euph euphr falco-pe nl2• *Ferr* gels k2 graph ham *Hep* hura hydrc *Hydrog* srj2• hyper ign k* iod kali-ar kali-i kreos bg2 lac-ac bro1 **Lac-c** k* **Lach** lact br1 lact-v bro1 *Laur* k* *Led* k* lyc k* mand rsj7• mang k* marb-w es1• *Med* *Meny* k* *Merc* k* mez k* mosch k* *Naja* *Nat-c* nat-m k* *Nat-p* *Nit-ac* k* *Nux-m* *Nux-v* *Op* *Ox-ac* k* oxyt bro1 *Petr* *Ph-ac* *Phos* pic-ac plan plat plb psor puls k* rhod bg2 **Rhus-t** k* ruta bg2* samb k* sang *Sec* *Sep* k* **Sil** k* spong **Stram** stront-c k* *Stry* sul-i k2 *Sulph* k* sumb *Tab* k* ther thuj k* tritic-vg fd5.de *Tub* valer bg2 **Verat** k* zinc bro1
  - **right**: ambr chel h1* *Elaps* hydrog srj2• mang h2* nit-ac bg1 ruta fd4.de sabin
    - **chill**; during: *Bry* chel elaps sabad *Sep*
    - **extending** to | **Knee**; up to: ambr k1 hydrog srj2•
  - **left**: chin h1* euph h2* *Hyper* ol-an sang tub
    - **evening** | **bed** agg.; in: tub k2
    - **chill**; during: carb-v caust thuj
  - **morning**: agath-a nl2• hep hura ruta fd4.de tritic-vg fd5.de
    - **7** h: hura
  - **noon**: dulc fd4.de nit-ac h2*
  - **afternoon**: aloe alumn nux-v
    - **16** h: chel sang
- **Legs – afternoon**: ...
    - **18** h: puls
  - **evening**: aloe chel colch euphr mang h2* puls sang *Sil* spong fd4.de sulph
    - **bed** agg.; in: aur h2 colch ph-ac **Sep** sil h2 tub
    - **waking**; on: euphr *Nit-ac*
  - **night**: agar aloe com kali-ar *Merc* spong fd4.de thuj verat
    - **amel.**: cassia-s ccrh1•
    - **snow** water; as from: verat
    - **waking**; on: nit-ac
  - **accompanied** by | **Spinal** meningitis (See BACK - Inflammation - membranes - accompanied - lower)
  - **air** | **blowing** on it; as if cold air: hydrog srj2•
  - **air** agg.; in open: ham
  - **burning** in thighs, with: tab
  - **coition**; after: *Graph* k*
  - **dinner**; after: cedr
  - **dressing**, when: anth k*
  - **fever**; during: carb-an *Eup-pur* meph sep **Stram**
  - **flushed** face: *Op*
  - **heat**; with:
    - **Body**; of: tab visc c1
    - **Face**; of: *Arn*
    - **Thigh**; of: plut-n srj7•
  - **icy**: *Apis* aur h2* **Calc** chel h1* chin-b c1 gels k2 kali-ar k2 nat-c k2 *Sep* *Sil* spong fd4.de *Tab*
  - **lying** agg.: chinin-s
  - **menses** | **before** | **agg.**: *Lyc*
    - **during** | **agg.**: arg-n bufo *Calc* lil-t *Sec* *Sil*
  - **perspiration**; with cold: *Ars* a1
  - **rest** | **amel.**: cassia-s ccrh1•
  - **sensation** of: ambr b7.de ars b4a.de bar-c b4.de bell b4.de calc b4a.de chel b7.de chin b7.de led b7.de mosch b7.de* puls b7.de *Rhod* b4a.de ruta b7.de *Samb* b7a.de stront-c b4.de valer b7.de
  - **sitting** agg.: camph hyper led mang h2*
  - **snow**, as from being in: verat
  - **spots**; in: morg-p fmm1•
  - **standing** agg.: nat-m samb
  - **sun** agg., walking in the: *Lach*
  - **uncovering** | **amel.**: *Camph* *Med* **Sec** *Tub*
  - **walking** agg.: *Nit-ac* plan
  - **warm** | **covers** | **not** amel.: ars a1*
    - **room** | **agg.**: acon meny **Sil**
  - **warmed**; cannot be: ars a
  - **wind**, as from: bar-c samb
  - **winter**: cassia-s ccrh1•
  - ▽ **extending** to:
    - **Body**; whole: malar jl2
    - **Thighs**: hydrog srj2•
  - ○ **Bones**:
    - **Tibia**: mosch h1* rhus-t b7.de* samb k*
      - **sensation** of: *Mosch* b7a.de
  - **Calves**: ars berb bufo chel con ptk1 hyper lach mang oxyt ptk2 rumx
    - **forenoon**: berb
    - **evening**: mang
      - **sitting**, rising amel.; coldness while: mang
    - **spots**; in: stront-c c1*
  - **Inner** side of leg: ruta h1
  - **Knee**; below | **warm** room; in: sil tl1
- **Lower** limbs: *Acon* bg2 *Aeth* agar k* apis k* *Ars* k* *Ars-i* asaf bamb-a stb2.de• bapt **Bell** k* *Bry* b7a.de* **Calad** k* calc k* calc-s calc-sil k2 camph bg2 carb-an h2* carb-v bg2* carbn-s *Caust* b4a.de* cham b7.de* *Chel* chin b7.de* cic k* cocc bro1 coff crot-c crot-t *Dig* k* dulc fd4.de euph bg2

- **Lower** limbs: ...
falco-pe nl2• ferr bg2 gels bg2 glon k2 hep bg2 hyos b7.de* *Ign* bg2 ip k* kali-bi bg2 kali-n b4a.de* kali-p fd1.de• kali-s fd4.de kreos bg2 **Lac-c** k* *Led* k* lyc k* malar jl2 mand rsj7• marb-w es1• melal-alt gya4 *Merc* bg2 merc-c b4a.de* *Mez* k* mosch mur-ac nat-c k* nat-m k* **Nit-ac** k* nux-v k* ol-an olnd b7a.de* **Op** k* *Ox-ac* k* par k* petr k* *Phos* k* plb k* positr nl2• **Puls** k* rhod k* rhus-t k* sabad b7.de* **Sabin** bg2 *Samb* bg2 sars h2* *Sec* k* *Sel* rsj9• **Sep** k* sil sinus rly4• spig bg2 spong k* *Stram* k* stront-c k* stry *Sulph* k* symph fd3.de• tab ptk1 tarent thlas bg1 *Thuj* b4.de* vanil fd5.de verat
  - **one** side: lach bg2 rhus-t bg2
  - **right**: echi c1 nit-ac h2* petr h2* *Sabin* bg2
  - **left**: agar h2* carb-v bg2 sulph h2*
  - **daytime**: nat-c k*
  - **morning**: con h2* symph fd3.de•
  - **forenoon**: dulc fd4.de rumx symph fd3.de•
    - ⁝ **bedtime**; until: sep
  - **noon**: nit-ac
    - ⁝ **bed** agg.; in: chel lyc sars
    - ⁝ **lifting** covers; when: lyc
  - **night**: agar h2* carb-v h2* *Lac-c* petr phos plut-n srj7•
    - ⁝ **waking**; on: *Nit-ac*
  - **accompanied** by:
    - ⁝ **rattling** and cold breath (See RESPIRATION - Rattling - accompanied - cold)
    - ⁝ **sciatica** (See Pain - lower limbs - sciatic - accompanied - coldness - limb)
    - ⁝ **Meninges** of spine; inflammation of (See BACK - Inflammation - membranes - accompanied - lower)
  - **alternating** with heat in head: sep
  - **bed** agg.; in: hydrog srj2•
  - **chorea**; during: laur ptk1
  - **clammy**: kali-n mrr1 laur ptk1
  - **icy** cold: apis calc ptk1 dulc fd4.de jatr-c ptk1 *Sep*
    - ⁝ **night** in bed: lil-t ptk1
    - ⁝ **spots**; in: agar berb
  - **menses**; during: bufo calc cham lil-t ozone sde2• *Sec* *Sil*
  - **nausea**; during: arg-n
  - **painful** limb: *Led* merc syph ptk1
  - **paralyzed** limb: *Ars* *Cocc* dulc graph *Nux-v* *Rhus-t*
  - **sensation** of: agar k* berb calc b4a.de camph b7.de carb-v k* caust k* chin b7.de* cic b7.de euph k* hep b4a.de ign b7a.de kreos b7a.de m-aust b7.de *Merc* k* mez k* nat-c k* petr k* rhod k* sabin b7.de *Sec* b7.de *Sep* b4a.de spong b7.de*
  - ○ **Affected** parts: calc bg2 ferr bg2 gels bg2 ign bg2 led bg2 mez bg2 nux-v bg2 puls bg2 rhus-t bg2
  - **Bones**, in: nit-ac bg1 sep bg1
    - ⁝ **Marrow**: aran bg2 chin bg2
  - **Sciatic** nerve:
    - ⁝ **left**:
      - ⁝ **accompanied** by | **dysuria** (See BLADDER - Urination - dysuria - accompanied - sciatic)
  - **Skin**: carb-v bg2 nux-m bg2
    - ⁝ **Under** skin: acon bg2 agar bg2 arg-met bg2 ip bg2 merc bg2
- **Nates**: agar k* beryl sp1 cench k2 daph k* hydr kali-s fd4.de ozone sde2•
  - **right**: beryl tpw5
  - **forenoon** | **11** h: hydr
  - **night** | **bed** agg.; in: *Cench*
  - **accompanied** by | **numbness** of nates: calc-p ptk1
  - **menses**; before: mang
  - ○ **Gluteal** region: agar beryl tpw5 calc
- **Painful** parts: led mez sil tritic-vg fd5.de
- **Shoulders**: arg-n k* arund hr1 aur k* bamb-a stb2.de• bry k* *Caust* k* cocc k* hell k* hydr k* hyper k* *Kali-bi* k* kali-c bg2 *Kreos* k* lyc k* phos k* rhus-t tl1 sep k* sil k* spig k* stry k* tep k* verat k* viol-o ptk1
- **Shoulders**: ...
  - **right**: granit-m es1•
    - ⁝ **accompanied** by | **Shoulder**; aching pain in right (See Pain - shoulders - right - aching - accompanied - coldness)
  - **morning**: aur k* sil k*
  - **forenoon**: bamb-a stb2.de•
  - **evening**:
    - ⁝ **21** h: hydr
    - ⁝ **supper** agg.; after: ran-b
  - **night** | **22** h: sep
  - **convulsions**; during epileptic: *Caust* k*
  - **eating**; after: arg-n k*
  - **fever**; during intermittent: rhus-t tl1
  - **warmth** | **not** amel.: bamb-a stb2.de•
  - ▽ **extending** to | **Lumbar** region: kreos
- **Thighs**: acon bro1 agar bg2 aloe alum bro1 am k* ars k* bar-c bell bg2 berb k* bism bro1 bry k* *Calad* b7.de* *Calc* k* calc-p bro1 camph k* **Caps** bg2 *Carb-an* bro1 *Carb-v* bro1 chin k* cic h1 cimic k* coc-c k* colch bro1 cop k* crot-h bro1 dulc fd4.de ham fd3.de• hell bg2 hura ign k* kali-bi k* lac-ac bro1 lact-v bro1 *Laur* bro1 lyc k* m-aust b7.de *Merc* k* mez bro1 mosch bg2 *Nat-m* bro1 nit-ac k* nux-v k* olnd bg2 op k* ox-ac bro1 oxyt bro1 phos puls k* ran-b k* rhod k* rhus-t bro1 sabad k* sars k* sep bro1 sil bro1 **Spong** k* *Sulph* k* symph fd3.de• *Tab* bro1 tax k* tep k* ther bg2 *Thuj* k* *Verat* bro1 zinc bro1
  - **right**: camph k* kali-bi bg1 ozone sde2•
  - **daytime**: lyc k* tax k*
  - **morning**: arn k* ham fd3.de• sulph h2* symph fd3.de• zinc-p k2
  - **afternoon**: lyc k*
  - **evening**: bry k* *Calc* k*
    - ⁝ **18** h: puls
    - ⁝ **rising** from sitting agg.: rhod k*
  - **night**: coc-c k* cop k* ign k* merc nux-v k*
  - **alternating** with heat (See Heat - alternating)
  - **chill**; during: *Thuj*
  - **cold** air blew on it, as if: camph
  - **colic**, during: *Calc* k*
  - **convulsions**; with: *Calc*
  - **eyes**; with staring of: cic c1
  - **fever**; during: calc bg2 *Ign* b7.de* nux-v bg2 **Spong** b7.de* sulph bg2 thuj bg2
    - ⁝ **intermittent**: rhus-t tl1
  - **heat**; during: spong h1*
  - **icy** cold, as if ice water poured down sciatic: acon k*
  - **menses**; after: colch ptk1 coll ptk1
  - **perspiration**; during: calad bg2 calc bg2 nux-v bg2 *Sulph* bg2 thuj bg2
  - **sensation** of: caps b7.de hell b7.de lyc b4.de m-aust b7.de mosch b7a.de olnd b7.de
  - **shaking** chill: *Thuj* k*
  - **sitting** agg.: chin k* dulc fd4.de ran-b k*
  - **standing** agg.: berb k*
  - ○ **Posterior** part: agar h2*
- **Thumbs**: mang bg2
  - ○ **Tips**: mang h2
- **Toes**: abrot ptk1 **Acon** k* agar bit-ar wht1• brass a1 brom b4a.de* *Calad* b7.de* card-m *Carl* k* chel k* chinin-s choc srj3• cinnb coff coff-t a1 con k* crat br1 daph k* dig k* dulc fd4.de *Ferr* k* gels helo-s bnm14• kali-p fd1.de• kali-s fd4.de lyc k* *Med* k* melal-alt gya4 meny nux-v k* ol-an k* ran-b bg2 ruta fd4.de *Sec* spira a1 streptoc rly4• *Sulph* k* symph fd3.de• tritic-vg fd5.de tub-d jl2 tub-m jl2 verat bg2
  - **morning**: chinin-s
  - **blue**, and: crat br1 sec gk
  - **exertion** agg.: crat br1
  - **fever**; during: dulc fd4.de lyc dgt
  - **icy**: carc fd2.de• *Ferr* kali-s fd4.de nat-sil fd3.de• symph fd3.de•
  - **sensation** of: acon b7.de ran-b b7.de

Extremities

- **sitting**:
  - **after**: *Carl* k*
  - **agg.**: bry
- **touch**; cold to: ant-t k*
- **walking** | **amel.**: bry
- ○ **Fingers**, and: carc fd2.de• crat br1 helo-s bnm14• kali-p fd1.de•
- **First** toe: ant-t k* brom k* iod k* ran-b k*
  - **Joints**: nat-m h2*
- **Third** toe: plut-n srj7•
- **Tips**: aloe meny bg2

- **Upper** arms: aq-mar skp7• *Am* b7a.de carbn-s k2 cass a1 coloc k* dulc fd4.de graph k* *Ign* k* kali-s fd4.de marb-w es1• mez nat-m k* ph-ac k* puls k* ran-b k* rhus-t k* spong fd4.de sulph k* sumb k* symph fd3.de• tep k*
  - **right**: sang a1
  - **burning**; with: graph k*
  - **dinner**; after: *Puls* k*
  - **eating**; after: coloc k*
  - **supper** agg.; after: ran-b k*
  - **wind** blew on them; as if: nat-m tep
- **Upper** limbs: acon k* am-c k* ambr bg2 amyg k* anac bg2 ant-t k* *Apis* b7a.de* aran bg2 *Am* bg2 ars k* arund k* asaf k* aster k* bar-act bar-c bg2 **Bell** k* berb k* bry k* *Calc* calc-i k2 *Camph* k* cann-xyz bg2 carb-v k* carbn-s cass a1 *Caust* k* cham b7.de* chel k* chin k* chinin-ar cic k* cimic k* cocc bg2 colch bg2 con croc bg2 crot-h k* dig k* *Dulc* k* euph bg2 euphr b7.de* falco-pe nl2• fl-ac k* gels hg2 *Graph* k* hell k* helo bg2 hep k* hyos b7.de* hyper k* ign k* iod k* ip k* kali-bi k* kali-c k* kali-chl k* kali-s kreos k* *Led* k* lyc k* m-arct b7.de m-aust b7.de mand rsj7• mang bg2 marb-w es1• melal-alt gya4 meny bg2 merc b4a.de* merc-c k* merl k* *Mez* k* mosch k* naja k* nat-c k* nat-m k* nux-v k* olnd b7a.de* *Op* k* ox-ac k* pall paull a1 petr bg2 ph-ac bg2 **Phos** k* *Plb* k* **Puls** k* ran-b bg2 raph bro1 *Rhus-t* k* ruta k* sabad b7.de* samb bg2 sars k* sec k* sep k* *Sil* k* sinus rly4• spig k* spong fd4.de squil bg2 staph k* stram b7.de* sul-i k2 sulph k* sumb k* tep k* thuj k* tritic-vg fd5.de verat k* vip k* zinc k* zinc-p k2
  - **right**: am-c k* ant-t k* berb k* chel k* dulc k* hell k* merl k* pall sang hr1
  - **left**: ars k* aster k* *Carb-v* k* fl-ac k* naja nux-m rhus-t k* sumb k*
  - **morning**: aur h2* caust k* chel k* dulc k* hep k* spong fd4.de staph h1*
  - **forenoon**: berb k*
  - **afternoon**: euphr h2* nux-v k* sil k*
    - **14** h: euphr
    - **17** h: chel
  - **evening**: nux-v k* tritic-vg fd5.de
    - **lying** down agg.; after: nux-v k*
  - **night**: am-c k*
    - **midnight**:
      - **after**:
        - **1** h: mang
        - **menses**; before: mang
  - **accompanied** by | **sciatica** (See Pain - lower limbs - sciatic - accompanied - arms)
  - **chill**; during: bell dig hell mez
  - **cold** air agg.: kali-c lyss
    - **blew** upon left arm; as if: aster k*
    - **passing** down the fingers; as if: fl-ac
  - **cough** agg.; during: ars calc ferr *Hep* kali-c *Rhus-t* rumx sil
  - **diarrhea**; during: phos ptk1*
  - **eating**; after: ars camph h1
  - **eyes**; with staring of: cic c1
  - **fever**; after: sil
  - **lying** on back agg.: ign k*
  - **menses** | **before** | **agg.**: mang k*
    - **during** | **agg.**: mang
  - **pain**; during: chel fl-ac k*
  - **paralyzed** arm: am-c *Dulc* k* *Rhus-t*
  - **raising** them: verat k*

Coldness – Upper limbs: ...

  - **rest** agg.: *Dulc* k*
  - **rheumatism**; during: *Sang* k*
  - **sensation** of: bry b7.de* cann-s b7.de *Caust* b4.de* chel b7.de cic b7.de *Cocc* b7.de* dig b4.de dulc b4.de graph b4.de hell b7.de ign b7a.de m-ambo b7.de m-arct b7.de m-aust b7.de mang b4.de mez b4.de mosch b7.de ph-ac b4.de puls b7.de ran-b b7.de *Rhus-t* b7.de* ruta b7.de *Sec* b7.de sep b4.de thuj b4a.de verat b7.de
  - **sitting** agg.: chin k*
  - **stiffness** and numbness, with: aster k* sulph
  - **thrill** down the arm; a cold: *Lyss* k*
  - **walking**:
    - **warm** room agg.: squil
    - **air**; in open:
      - **after** | **agg.**: sil h2
  - **water**, as if dashed with cold: mez k*
  - **wind**, as from cold: aster k*
  - ○ **Internally**: raph br1 ruta h1
- **Wrists**: calc-f ptk1 *Gels* k* rhus-t k* sang k* sulph lp
  - **puerperal** fever: puls k*

COMPLAINTS of extremities: cic tl1 lact-v br1

- **alternating** with:
  - ○ **Eye**; complaints of (See EYE - Complaints - alternating with - extremities)
  - **Head**; complaint of (See HEAD - Complaints - alternating - extremities)
- ○ **Ankle** (See Ankles)
- **Hands** (See Hands)
- **Knee** (See Knees; complaints)
- **Leg** (See Legs)
- **Lower** limbs (See Lower)
- **Nates**: graph ptk1 ph-ac ptk1 staph ptk1 sulph ptk1
- **Shoulder** (See Shoulders)
- **Thigh** (See Thighs)
- **Thumbs** (See Thumbs)
- **Toes** (See Toes)
- **Upper** limbs:
  - ○ **Bones** (See Upper limbs - bones)
  - **Forearms** | **Ulnar** nerve; along: aran ptk1 hyper ptk1 kalm ptk1 podo ptk1 rhus-t ptk1 tub ptk1

COMPRESSION: led k* nat-s k*

- **amel.** | **Lower** limbs: acon b7.de*
- ○ **Ankles**: chlf k* led k* nat-m k* nat-s sep k* thuj
  - **walking** in open air agg.; after: sep
- **Elbows**: chlf k* chlor nat-s k*
  - **evening**: nat-s k*
- **Feet**: ang k* cimic k*
  - ○ **Heels**: alum k*
- **Forearms**: led k* nat-s k*
  - **left**: led k* nat-s k*
- **Hips**: tarent
- **Joints**: coloc k* merc
- **Knees**: aur k* led k* nat-m k* nat-s k* plat spig k*
  - **walking** agg.: spig k*
- **Legs**: arg-n k* coloc a1 led k* nat-s k*
  - ○ **Calves**: jatr-c led sol-ni
- **Thighs**: led a1 *Plat* sabad k* stront-c
  - **motion**:
    - **agg.**: sabad k*
    - **continued** motion | **amel.**: sabad k*
- **Toes** | **First**: plat
- **Upper** arms: am-m k* brom k* led k* nat-s k*
- **Wrists**: led k* nat-s k*

CONCRETIONS in joints; calcareous (See Arthritic)

CONGESTED (See Blood - rush)

CONSCIOUSNESS:

○ - **Hip** | **strange** feeling: arizon-l nl2•

CONSTRICTION: *(↗Bandaged)* alumn k* ars-i k2 arund cact k2 carbn-s *Chin* k* con kola stb3• *Lyc* k* nit-ac pic-ac k2 plat k2 rhus-t suis-pan rly4• vanil fd5.de
- **bandage**; as by: cact k2
- **intolerance** of: sec mrr1
- **tape**; as by: cact k2

○ - **Ankles**: acon am-m b7.de* cham ferr b7.de* graph k* helo helo-s rwt2• nat-m b4.de* nit-ac b4.de* petr b4.de* *Plat* stront-c b4.de*
  - . **band**; as if from a: acon b7.de* *Anac* b4a.de *Aur* b4a.de calc b4a.de* graph b4.de nat-m b4.de* nit-ac b4.de* petr b4.de* stann b4.de*
  - . **string**; as if tied with a: acon am-br
- **Bones**: con h2* symph fd3.de•
- **Elbows**: agar caust lach mang mang-p rly4• nux-v bg2 peti k* petr rat sep
  - . **left**: agar
  - . **morning**: peti k* petr
  - . **cord**; as with a: rat

○ . **Bends** of elbow: elaps k* rat k*
  - ⁝ **bending** agg.: rat k*
- **Feet**: alum bg2 am-m b7.de* anac k* *Caust* b4a.de graph nat-m nit-ac k* nux-v b7.de* *Petr* plb b7.de* rhus-t b7.de* sec b7.de* stront-c k*
  - . **right**: aloe bg2 visc c1
  - . **band**; as if from a: graph b4.de* petr b4.de* stann bg2
- **Fingers**: aeth carb-an croc dros elaps lach nux-v phos sep spong
  - . **periodical**: *Phos*

○ . **Nails**, cramping under: elaps k*
- **Forearms**: cupr gins
  - . **right**: cupr
  - . **left**: iris a1
  - . **vise**, as in a: brom
  - . **walking** in open air agg.: mez
- **Hands**: cocc *Cupr* nux-v prun
- **Hips**: anac k* anag ang cimic bg2 cina b7.de* *Coloc* eug lyc k* olnd b7.de* polyg-h bg2

○ . **Joints**: meny b7.de*
- **Joints**: *Anac* *Aur* cact k2 calc carb-an *Coloc* ferr **Graph** *Lyc* **Nat-m** **Nit-ac** *Petr* sil *Stront-c*
- **Knees**: alumn k2 *Anac* k* aur bg2 ferr b7.de* graph bg2 mosch b7a.de nat-m k* *Nit-ac* k* *Plat* ruta b7.de* sil k* spig b7.de* squil b7.de* sulph vac jl2 zinc k*
  - . **afternoon**: nit-ac h2*
  - . **evening**: sulph h2*
  - . **band**; as if from a: anac b4.de* ars bg2 aur b4.de* coloc b4.de* graph b4.de* kali-c bg2 mag-m bg2 nat-m b4.de* nit-ac b4.de* nux-m b7.de* sil b4.de* sulph b4.de* zinc b4.de*

○ . **Bends** of knees: nit-ac h2
  - ⁝ **band**; as if from a: chin b7.de*
- **Legs**: am-m b7.de* *Anac* ang b7.de* ars k* benz-ac caust bg2 **Chin** cocc b7.de* ferr-p bg2 gels bg2 guaj k* kreos b7a.de *Lyc* k* manc nit-ac k* nux-v b7.de* petr k* *Plat* sec mrr1 stann k* sul-ac k* *Sulph* k*
  - . **band**; as if from a: ant-c b7.de* ars b4.de* chin b7.de* cocc b7.de* lyc bg2 nat-m bg2 nit-ac b4.de* petr b4.de* phos bg2 stann b4.de* sul-ac b4.de* sulph b4.de*
  - . **cold** | **amel.**: sec mrr1
  - . **garter**; as with a: alumn ant-c card-m **Chin** *Cocc* *Manc* raph
  - . **painful**: ant-c
- **Lower** limbs: alum k* alumn am-br k* am-c b4a.de *Anac* k* ars k* carb-an k* carbn-s *Caust* b4a.de chin k* cocc b7.de* graph k* **Lyc** k* mur-ac k* par b7.de* petr k* *Phos* k* *Plat* k* rhus-t b7.de* sec mrr1 stront-c k* sul-ac k* sulph k*
  - . **band**; as from a: chin ptk1

○ . **Joints**: carb-an b4.de* coloc b4.de* graph b4.de*
- **Nates**: plat thuj
- **Shoulders**: agar bov *Cact* k* cina h1 nit-ac plat h2* positr nl2• sep h2* suis-pan rly4•

Constriction – Shoulders: ...
  - . **left**: agar positr nl2•
  - . **band** around shoulder; as from a: sabad b7.de*
- **Thighs**: acon anac k* asar b7.de* carb-v k* cocc b7.de* granit-m es1• kola stb3• lyc manc med c1 mur-ac k* nit-ac k* **Plat** rhus-t b7.de* ruta b7.de* sul-ac k* sulph k* symph fd3.de•
  - . **right**: arizon-l nl2•
  - . **left**: iris a1
  - . **band**; as by a: *Coloc* nit-ac h2 sulph
  - . **bandage**; as from a tightly drawn: acon k* anac b4a.de lyc bg2 merc bg2 nit-ac b4.de* olnd b7.de* **Plat** k* *Puls* b7a.de sul-ac b4.de* sulph b4.de*
  - . **sitting** agg.: *Plat*
  - . **string**; as by a: am-br lyc manc
  - . **walking** agg.: lyc olnd
- **Toes**: graph b4.de* nux-v b7.de* rhus-t b7.de*
  - . **band**; as if from a: plat b4.de*

○ . **First**: *Plat*
  - ⁝ **Ball**: graph h2*
- **Upper** arms: alumn am-m bg2 bism brom bg2 colch rsj2• iris bg2 lach bg2 led bg2 manc mez k* phys plat h2* sec bg2 staphycoc rly4• vanil fd5.de
  - . **right**: *Alumn*
  - . **left**: iris a1

○ . **Elbow**; above the: phys
  - . **Shoulder**; near: alumn
- **Upper** limbs: alumn brom *Chin* coloc kola stb3• nit-ac *Nux-m* k* raph
  - . **right**: cupr
  - . **left**: cimic bg1
  - . **bandage**; as from a: *Con* b4a.de *Plat* b4a.de
  - . **hair** pin; as from a: kola stb3•
  - . **spasmodic** while writing: sul-ac

○ . **Bones**: con
- **Wrists**: *Cocc* manc sil

○ . **Tendons** of: carb-v ign lach

CONTORTIONS of limbs (= drawing limbs into bent position): acon b2.de* alum b2.de* am-m b2.de* ambr b2.de* anac b2.de* ang bg2 ant-c b2.de* ant-t b2.de* arg-met b2.de* arn b2.de* ars bg2 asaf bg2 **Bell** b2.de* bism b2.de* bry bg2 **Calc** b2.de* camph bg2 canth bg2 carb-an b2.de* carb-v b2.de* caust b2.de* *Cham* b2.de* chel b2.de* chin b2.de* cic b7.de* cina b2.de* cocc b2.de* coff b2.de* colch b2.de* coloc b2.de* con b2.de* *Cupr* b2.de* cycl b2.de* dig b2.de* dros b2.de* dulc bg2 euph b2.de* ferr b2.de* **Graph** b2.de* guaj b2.de* hell bg2 hep b2.de* *Hyos* b2.de* kali-c b2.de* kali-n b2.de* laur b2.de* **Lyc** b2.de* m-aust b2.de mag-m b2.de* meny b2.de* merc b2.de* nat-c b2.de* *Nat-m* b2.de* nit-ac b2.de* nux-v b2.de* *Op* bg2 petr bg2 phos b2.de* **Plat** b2.de* plb b2.de* puls bg2 ran-b bg2 rheum bg2 rhus-t b2.de* ruta b2.de* sabad b2.de* sabin b2.de* sars b2.de* **Sec** b2.de* sep b2.de* sil b2.de* spig b2.de* spong b2.de* stann b2.de* **Stram** b2.de* sul-ac b2.de* sulph b2.de* verat b2.de*
- **coryza**; during: phos b4.de*

CONTRACTION of muscles and tendons: *(↗Shortened; GENERALS - Shortened)* abrot br1* acon acon-c am-caust vh1 ambr bg2 androc srj1• ant-c c1 *Ant-t* br1 arg-met mrr1 *Ars* atra-r bnm3• *Bar-c* *Bell* bry **Calc** cann-s mrr1 canth carb-v carbn-s **Caust** k* cedr cimx c2 **Coloc** k* con *Crot-c* *Crot-h* *Cupr* ferr ferr-m **Graph** *Guaj* k* hydr-ac hydrc hyos br1 jatr-c kali-ar *Kali-i* **Lyc** *Merc* mez bg2* mill mur-ac *Nat-c* *Nat-m* nat-p mrr1 *Nux-v* k* oena olib-sac wmh1 olnd bg2 op ph-ac h2 *Phos* k* plb k* psor al2 *Ruta* **Sec** *Sep* k* *Sil* spong fd4.de still stram sulph symph fd3.de• syph thal-xyz srj8• vib [am-c stj1 am-m stj1 am-p stj1 am-s stj1]
- **right**: crot-c tl1
- **left**: rhus-t h1
- **morning**: am-m h2
- **night**: plb
- **accompanied** by | **formication**: sol-ni br1
- **chill**; during: caps b7a.de **Cimx** par b7a.de
- **cold**; after taking a: guaj k2
- **hysterical**: bell bro1 *Cocc* bro1 *Cupr* bro1 hyos bro1 *Ign* bro1 lyc bro1 merc bro1 nux-v bro1 sec k2 stram bro1 valer k2 zinc k2*

Extremities

- **involuntary**: *Op* mp1•
- **painful**: cocc br1
  - **abdomen**; after cramping pain in: abrot bro1
- **paralysis** of extensor muscles; from: *Ars* k* chen-a ptk1 olnd ptk1 **Plb** sec ptk1 valer ptk1
- **periodical**: *Sec*
- **rheumatic**: caust tl1
- **sensation** of: am-m k2 dulc fd4.de ruta fd4.de
- **slow**: stram
- **stiff** during exacerbation of pains: guaj h2 *Phos*
- **sudden**: sec

○ - **Ankle** tendons: *Caust* b4a.de hep b4a.de ign b7a.de nux-v b7.de* ran-b b7.de* ruta fd4.de sep b4a.de* spig b7.de* sul-ac b4a.de
- **Elbows**: *Ang* b7a.de ars glon *Graph* b4a.de kreos b7a.de lyc k* nux-v k* rat c1 *Sep* b4a.de tep
  - **flexed**, as if tendons were contracted: *Apis Caust*

○ - **Bends** of elbow: *Caust* k* elaps graph h2 *Puls* sars sulph
- **Feet**: acon alum h2* *Cann-s* cann-xyz bg2 carb-an *Caust* ferr-s guare ind merc-c nat-c nat-m plat ruta tl1 *Sec* sep zinc h2
  - **left**: cycl
  - **alternating** with hand (See hands - alternating)
  - **cramping**: *Nat-m* phos
  - **spasmodic**: acon bism

○ - **Bones**: staph h1
  - **Heels**: am-m h2 *Colch* k* (non:coloc kl*) led sep
    - **convulsive**:
      - **evening** | **bed** agg.; in: am-m k*
  - **Soles**: berb *Caust* mtf33 cham irid-met vml3• nux-v plb b7a.de rhus-t spig h1 sulph h2 *Syph* k* verat h1 zinc h2
- **Fingers**: aeth k* alum k* am-c k* ambr anac k* *Ant-t Apis* k* arg-met *Arg-n Ars* k* bell benz-ac mrr1 *Calc* k* calc-sil k2 cann-s k* caps b7.de* carb-v carbn-s **Caust** k* chel chin cina k* cocc k* coff k* colch k* crot-t *Cupr* k* cycl k* *Dros Ferr* ferr-ar ferr-p gins *Graph* k* hedy a1* hyos kali-bi k2 kali-cy kali-i lyc mag-s mang k* med *Merc* k* morph *Nat-c* k* nux-v k* oena op ox-ac par ph-ac phos k* *Plat* plb k* prot fmm1• rat c1 rhod rhus-t ruta sabad k* sabin sal-fr sle1• *Sec* k* sel sep k* *Sil* spig stann k* sulph tarent tell
  - **morning**: phos
  - **afternoon**: morph
  - **accompanied** by:
    - **Forearm**; weakness of | **paralytic** (See Weakness - forearms - paralytic - accompanied - fingers)
  - **chill**; before: *Cimx*
  - **cholera**: cupr
  - **convulsions**; during intervals of: sec k*
  - **cramping**: calc h2 cycl ptk1
  - **epilepsy**: *Lach Mag-p Merc*
  - **grasping** something agg.: arg-n *Dros* stry
    - **after**: graph h2
  - **hysterical**: zinc ptk1*
  - **lying** on that side, while: crot-t
  - **periodical**: *Phos*
  - **spasmodic**: *Anac* arg-n a1 *Bell Calc* caust *Cic* k* *Cina* colch *Dros* gels c1 *Glon Hydr-ac Ip* kali-c *Lach Laur* **Mag-p** k* med meny mosch phos phyt *Sec* syc pte1• ter
  - **vomiting** blood, after: ars
  - **yawning** agg.: crot-t nux-v

○ - **Adductors**: arg-n
  - **First**: alum caps h1 cycl graph
  - **Fourth**: prot jl2 sabad sulph symph fd3.de•
  - **Joints**: iod b4a.de
  - **Muscles** | **Flexor** muscles: *Ars Caust* k* cimx *Sil* spig h1
  - **Second**: cina sil
  - **Third**: *Benz-ac* vh plut-n srj7• sabad
- **Forearms**: bell bg2 bism b7.de* calc k* calc-ar *Caust* k* cina k* cocc bg2 coloc con k* hydrc *Meny* mez k* nat-c k* nat-p k2 plb ran-b bg2* rheum k* rhod k* sep k* spong bg2 stann k* verat
- **Forearms**: ...
  - **walking** agg.: viol-t
  - **writing** agg.: nat-p k2

○ - **Muscles** | **Flexor** muscles: arn h1
  - **Wrist**; near the: caust h2 sil
- **Hands**: acon b7.de* aloe bg2 *Anac* k* ars aur k* bell calc calc-sil k2 cann-s k* carb-v carbn-s *Caust* cina k* cinnb cocc b7.de* colch coloc k* euphr ferr-s hydr-ac kali-bi k* lyc k* mag-s merc merc-c k* mur-ac k* *Nat-c* hr1 *Nux-v* k* op ph-ac phos plb bg2 prot jl2 ran-b b7.de* ruta fd4.de sabin b7.de* *Sec* k* *Sil* k* sol-ni spong fd4.de *Stann* k* sulph symph fd3.de• tab valer k2 zinc k*
  - **alternating** with feet: stram k*
  - **Dupuytren's** contraction: bar-c a benz-ac a calc-f a *Caust* a *Gels* c1 *Guaj* a lappa c1 lyc a nat-m a nat-p a* *Plb* prot xyz60 ruta spong fd4.de sulph a tub-r jl2*
  - **grasping** involuntarily things taken hold of: ambr dros k* sulph k*
  - **paroxysmal**: cann-s cina phos
  - **spasmodic**: bism hr1
  - **tearing**: sulph

▽ - **extending** to | **Forearm**; over: coloc

○ - **Palm** of: anac h2 bry gk carb-an *Caust* k* graph ptk1 guaj ptk1 nat-m ptk1 nux-v *Plb* mrr1 prot pte1* ruta fd4.de sabad stann stry tub-r vn* *Verat* k*
  - **Tendons** of: carb-v *Caust* lach (non:sulph kl) tub-r vn*
    - **Flexor**: am-m sne lach sne *Lyc* sne plan sne *Plb* psil ft1 ruta k2 sulph h2*
- **Hips**: am-m k* carb-v coloc euph meny
- **Joints**: abrot bro1 am-m bro1* *Anac Aur* brass-n-o srj5• *Caust* k* *Cimx* bro1 *Colch* coloc bro1 *Form* k* *Graph Guaj* bro1 kali-i bro1 *Merc Nat-m* k* *Nit-ac* petr sec stront-c *Tell* bro1 [am-c stj1 am-p stj1 am-s stj1]
- **Knee**, hollow of: *Am-m* k* anac b4a.de ang h1* *Arn* b7.de* ars k* aur b4a.de *Bar-c* b4a.de bell berb *Bry* b7a.de calc h2 calc-p bg2 carb-an carb-v **Caust** k* *Cimx* k* coloc k* con k* cupr b7a.de dig b4a.de dros b7a.de euphr ferr *Graph* k* **Guaj** k* hyos b7a.de ign b7a.de kreos k* lach k* led k* m-ambo b7.de mag-c b4.de* med merc k* *Mez* k* mosch b7a.de *Nat-c* k* **Nat-m** k* nat-p k2 nat-s nit-ac nux-v k* ol-an k* ox-ac petr phos k* rheum b7a.de *Rhus-t* k* rhus-v ruta samb k* sars h2 stann b4a.de *Staph* k* *Sulph* syph *Tell* k* verat k*
  - **bending** agg.: rhus-t h1
  - **chill**; during: *Cimx*
  - **lying**:
    - **agg.**: staph h1
    - **back**; on | **agg.**: nat-s
  - **rising** from feet: ruta h1* staph h1* sulph h2
  - **walking** agg.: am-m h2 carb-an h2 phos h2
- **Legs**: alum bg2 am-c **Am-m** apoc *Aster* bad bov b4a.de cann-i canth caust bg2 cedr *Cic* ferr kali-c bg2 merc-c mez nat-c bg2 *Nat-m* nux-v ox-ac *Phyt* puls sil bg2 sulph symph fd3.de• syph k2*
  - **left**: lycps-v bg2
  - **evening**: cedr
    - **walking** agg.: ferr
  - **accompanied** by | **Sciatic** nerve; pain in (See Pain - lower limbs - sciatic - accompanied - contraction)
  - **painful**: syph jl2
  - **sciatica**, in (See Pain - lower limbs - sciatic - accompanied - contraction)

○ - **Calves**: agar agn arg-n ars *Bov* calc-p caps *Caust* guaj h2 irid-met vml3• jatr-c led med nat-c nat-m puls sars h2 sil sulph h2
    - **cramping**: ferr
    - **spasmodic**: (↗*Cramps - legs - calves)* ars bart merc sil
    - **walking** agg.: agar alum h2 kali-n h2 *Lyc* nat-m h2 sil h2 sulph h2
  - **Tendo** Achillis: acon k* *Calc Cann-s Carb-an* k* cimic k* *Colch* euphr *Graph Kali-c* plan bg2 *Sep* zinc k*
- **Lower** limbs: aesc am-c h2 **Am-m** k* ambr k* anac h2 *Ars* aster *Bar-c* k* bism bov bg2 canth **Caust** k* *Coloc* k* croc b7a.de *Guaj* hydr-ac kreos b7a.de *Lach* b7a.de merc bg2 nat-c k* nat-m k* nux-v k* olnd ph-ac *Phos* k* plb b7.de* puls *Rhus-t* sabin b7.de* sec sep bg2 sil stry sulph bg2 tarent tell zinc k*
  - **left**: lycps-v bg2
  - **evening**: olnd

- **menses**; during: phos
- **rising** agg.: olnd
- **standing** agg.: bar-c h2

- **Nates**: rhus-t
- **Shoulders**: brom elaps kali-c k* *Mag-c* k* nit-ac bg2 plb rhod k* sul-ac b4a.de
  - **morning**: mag-c
    - **extending** to | **Back**: mag-c
  - **convulsive**: cit-v
  - **sudden**: alum
  - ▽ **extending** to:
    - **Back**: mag-c
    - **Hand**: elaps
- **Skin**: cupr
- **Thighs**: am-c b4.de* ambr k* asar *Bar-c* b4a.de berb calc bg2 carb-v *Caust* b4a.de cham coloc b4.de* euph b4.de* *Graph* b4a.de guaj b4.de* hyos bg2 mag-c *Mez* b4a.de ol-an plat puls *Rhus-t* k* ruta sabin symph fd3.de•
  - **abscess**, after: *Lach*
  - **chill**; during: cimx
  - **drawn** together; as if: cann-s k*
  - **menses** | **after** | **agg.**: nat-p
    - **before** | **agg.**: cham
  - **sitting** down, when: sabin
  - **spasmodic**: asar
  - **walking** agg.: carb-an **Nux-v** k* pall *Rhus-t*
  - ○ **Bends** of thighs: agar carb-an *Caust Rhus-t*
    - **walking** agg.: *Rhus-t* thuj
  - **Hamstrings**: *Acon* agar am-c h2 *Am-m* k* *Ambr* ant-c ant-t asar *Bar-c Calc-p* caps fkm1• carb-an **Caust** k* *Cimx* k* coloc bro1 graph k* **Guaj** k* kali-ar lach bro1 led *Lyc* lyss med k* nat-c **Nat-m** k* nat-p *Nit-ac* **Nux-v** phos *Phyt* puls *Rhus-t Ruta* k* samb sulph k*
  - **Lower** part of thigh: sul-ac h2
- **Thumbs**: anac bg2 colch *Hell* merc bg2 sec staph
  - **right**: cycl
- **Toes**: anan vh1 androc srj ars asaf crot-c *Ferr* ferr-ar gamb gels guare jatr-c kali-n mag-s merc paeon phyt plat *Sec*
  - **night**: merc
    - **sitting** agg.: kali-n
  - **cramping**: cham h1 nux-v rhus-t h1
  - **drawn**:
    - **down**: *Ars* chel phyt
    - **up**: *(↗Drawn - upward)* apis *Camph* ferr-s *Lach* sec
  - **sitting** agg.: kali-n
  - **walking** agg.: hyos
  - **yawning** agg.: nux-v
  - ○ **Muscles** | **Flexor** muscles: ruta k2
- **Upper** arms: asar b7.de* bism b7.de* calc k* *Nat-m* k* rhod k* stram k* sulph k* symph fd3.de•
  - ○ **Muscles**:
    - **Flexor** muscles: crot-h ruta k2 sil syph hr1*
      - **sensation** as if contracted: cimx br1
  - **Tendons**: **Caust** k*
- **Upper** limbs: agar all-s ant-t *Ars* asar bg2 atro bell *Calc* cann-i carbn-s ferr *Hydr-ac Ip Lyc* merc merc-c nit-ac bg2 nux-v k* olnd k* op ox-ac phos plb ran-b rhod k* *Rhus-t* k* sec sul-ac bg2 tab valer k2
  - **drink**, on attempting to: atro
  - **paralysis**, during: carbn-s
  - **spasmodic**: ant-c vh1 *Ip* tab
  - **writing** agg.: sul-ac h2
  - ○ **Extensor** muscles when writing: nat-p
- **Wrists**: bell-p ptk1 ferr-s sne jatr-c
  - **right**: glon bg2
  - **shortening** of tendons: carb-v *Caust*

CONVULSION: *(↗Cramps)* absin k* *Acon* k* aesc k* *Agar* k* ant-c k* ant-t aran k* *Ars* k* ars-i k2 *Art-v* aster atro k* *Bell* k* bism brom *Bufo* k* *Calc Camph* cann-s mrr1 canth k* *Carb-ac* carbn-h carbn-o carbn-s k2 *Caust Cham* k* chinin-ar *Chlf Chlor* **Cic** k* **Cina** *Cocc* k* *Con* convo-s sp1 cori-m a1 *Crot-c* **Cupr** cupr-ar k* *Cupr-s Dig* dol c1 glon *Hydr-ac* k* **Hyos** k* *Hyper* ign gk *Ip* jatr-c kali-cy a1 kali-i *Lach* lat-h bnm5• *Lyc Merc-c Merc-cy* k* morph k* *Mosch* k* naja gm1 *Nux-m* **Nux-v** k* *Oena* k* olnd k* **Op** k* ox-ac pegan-ha tpi1• phos k* phys mrr1 *Picro* vh *Plb* k* *Puls* ran-s k* sabad k* sabin c1 santin *Sec* k* *Sil* **Stram** k* **Stry** k* tab k* tarent k* thea valer *Verat* verat-v

- **one** side: dulc hr1 elaps plb
  - **other** side paralyzed: apis *Art-v* hell *Stram*
- **right**: chen-a
- **left**: *Ip*
  - **paralyzed** side; of: *Art-v*
- **morning**: squil
- **alternately** extended and flexed: bell k2 (non:carb-ac kl) carbn-o kl *Cic Cupr* lyc nux-v *Sec Tab*
- **alternating** with | **trembling** of body: nux-v
- **alternation** of single muscles: bell k*
- **chill**; during: *Lach* merc nux-v
- **clonic**: *Ars* atro k* bell k2 brom k* carb-ac carbn-o coc-c cocc k* cupr cupr-s dol c1 ign nux-m op k* phos k* *Picro* vh *Plb* **Sec** *Stram* **Stry** sul-ac
- **coffee** agg.: stram k*
- **coition**; during: bufo
- **cough** agg.; during: cina mrr1 *Cupr* dros k2
- **diarrhea**; during: sulph mtf33
- **eating**; while: plb k*
- **hiccough**; after: *(↗GENERALS - Convulsions - epileptic - after - hiccough; STOMACH - Hiccough - accompanied - convulsions)* bell k* cupr hr1*
- **interrupted** by painful shocks: stry k*
- **menses** | **before** | **agg.**: puls
  - **during** | **agg.**: nux-m tarent
- **motion** agg.: cocc nux-v k*
- **stretching** limb amel.: sec
- **tetanic**: ang vh *Ars* hydr-ac k* *Hyper* mag-p br1 mill
- **tonic**: bell k2 carbn-o cic hr1 plb *Sec* k*
- **vertigo** on rising from a chair; convulsion after: nux-v
- **vinegar** amel.: stram k*
- ○ **Feet**: bar-m bism ptk1 *Calc* camph cina mrr1 *Cupr* iod *Merc-c Nat-m Nux-v* op phos k* plb k2 *Sec* stram verat ptk1 *Zinc*
  - **left**: cina bro1
  - **night**: iod
  - **menses**; during: hyos
  - **tetanic**: *Camph Nux-v*
  - **tonic**: phos k* verat bg2*
  - **touch** agg.: *Nux-v*
  - ▽ **extending** to | **Knees**: stram
- **Fingers**: agar bg1* am-c arn ars *Bell* bry b7a.de *Calc* camph bg1 cann-s cham k* **Chel** k* *Cic* k* cina b7a.de clem cocc coff *Cupr* k* dros ferr hell *Ign* k* iod ip kali-n lach lyc merc-c mosch nat-m nux-v phos plb rheum bg1 rhus-t b7a.de santin *Sec* k* spig bg1 stann staph k* sulph tab verat k*
  - **accompanied** by:
    - **Hand** | **cold** | **Palm**: diosm br1
      - **heat** | **Palm**: diosm br1
  - **epilepsy**; during (See GENERALS - Convulsions - epileptic - during - fingers)
  - **stretching** them: staph h1*
  - **tonic**: ars k*
  - ○ **First**: cycl k*
- **Forearms**: aphis (non:apis a1) chen-a k* sec k* zinc k* zinc-m a1
  - **tetanic**: zinc k* zinc-m a1
  - ○ **Flexor** muscles of: carbn-o cham k*
  - **Radial** side: merc k*
- **Hands**: acon k* ambr anac apis a1 arum-t bar-m *Bell* k* bism calc *Camph* k* cann-s carb-v carbn-s caust cic tl1 cina mrr1 coloc cupr b7a.de dros graph *Iod* k* kali-bi kali-i k* *Merc* mosch nat-m paeon plat plb k* rheum b7a.de *Sec* k* *Stram* k* *Stry* k* sul-ac tab verat b7a.de* *Zinc* k* zinc-m a1

- **Hands**: ...
  - **clonic**: *Stry* k*
  - **menses**; during: hyos k*
  - **taking** hold of something: ambr *Dros* stry sulph
  - **tetanic**: camph zinc k* zinc-m a1
  - **writing** agg.: sil hr1
○ • **Feet**; and: cupr-act bro1 ign bro1
  - **Palms**: scroph-n bg2
- **Hips**: phos
- **Knees**: ars h2* berb
- **Legs**: acet-ac ant-t ars cann-i card-m k* cupr-s *Jatr-c* kali-i lat-m bnm6• *Merc-c* podo sep k* stram k* stry tab k* tarent k* tell k*
  - **right**: acet-ac podo stram
  - **tetanic**:
    ⁝ **extending** to | **Body**; over: strych-g c1*
○ • **Calves**: berb k* cupr k* ferr-m
- **Lower** limbs: alco a1 ars k* atra-r bnm3• cann-i k* cham b7.de* *Cic Cina* k* cocc *Crot-c Cupr* k* gamb k* hydr-ac k* *Hyos* k* *Ign* k* *Ip* k* *Lach Lyss* meny b7a.de* *Merc-c* k* mosch k* nux-v k* *Op* k* phos k* *Plb* k* sacch-a fd2.de• sec k* spong k* *Squil* k* *Stram* k* **Stry** k* tab k*
  - **right**: sep h2*
  - **night**: plb
    ⁝ **1-4 h**: tab
  - **alternately** flexed and extended: *Cic Cupr* lyc nux-v tab
  - **alternating** with | **Upper** limbs (See upper - alternating - lower)
  - **clonic**: coc-c k* cocc k* *Plb* sep k*
  - **painful**: stry k*
  - **spasmodically** adducted: lath c1 lyc *Merc*
  - **tonic**: phos k* plb
▽ • **extending** to | **Upper** limbs: phos
- **Muscles**:
○ • **Extensor** muscles: **Cina**
  - **Flexor** muscles: *Bell*
- **Nates**: bar-c calc nux-v sep
- **Thighs**: ars dig podo
- **Thumbs**: aesc arum-t *Bell* k* *Cocc* k* *Cupr* k* cycl k* nat-m plb a1
- **Toes**: **Chel** k* *Cupr* k* *Sec* k* zinc ptk1
  - **ascending** stairs agg.: hyos ptk1
  - **epilepsy**; during (See GENERALS - Convulsions - epileptic - during - fingers)
  - **walking** agg.: hyos ptk1
○ • **First**: apis
  - **Joints**: sec bg2
- **Upper** limbs: acon k* agar k* agar-ph a1 am-c k* apis a1* ars k* arum-t atra-r bnm3• **Bell** k* bry k* camph k* cann-i k* carb-ac c1 caust k* *Cham* k* chinin-ar *Cic* k* cina b7a.de *Cocc* k* croc b7.de* *Crot-c* cupr k* cupr-s k* hydr-ac k* hyos k* *Ign* k* *Iod* k* *Ip* k* jatr-c kali-bi bg2 kali-i k* linu-c a1 lyc lyss m-ambo b7.de meny *Merc-c* k* nat-m nit-ac b4a.de *Op* k* phos k* *Plat* plb k* rheum b7a.de ruta sabad k* samb b7.de* *Sec* k* *Sil* squil k* staph b7.de* *Stram* k* **Stry** k* sul-ac k* sul-i k2 *Sulph* k* tab k* thal-xyz srj8• verat k* verat-v
  - **one** side: sabad
  - **right**: am-c tl1
    ⁝ **extending** to | **left**: visc
  - **left**: caust k*
  - **night**: bell k* nux-v sulph
    ⁝ **1-4 h**: tab
  - **alternating** with | **Lower** limbs; convulsion of: *Hyos* stram
  - **clonic**: cocc a1 cupr-s k* stry k* sul-ac k*
    ⁝ **attempting** to use them; on: plb
  - **drawing** limb:
    ⁝ **backward**: *Am-c* k*
    ⁝ **hither** and thither: nit-ac h2*
  - **epileptic** | **starting**; from: *Sulph* k*
  - **miscarriage**, after: ruta

Convulsion – Upper limbs: ...
  - **more** than legs: camph k* glon tl1 *Stram*
  - **prosopalgia**, in: plat
  - **rotation**, convulsive: (↗*Motion - upper limbs - rotation*) *Camph* k*
  - **tetanic**: anthraci camph k* cann-s k* mosch b7.de* stram b7a.de verat bg2
  - **working** hard with hands amel.: agar
▽ • **extending** to:
    ⁝ **up** and down after exertion: caust
    ⁝ **Finger**: acon
    ⁝ **Trunk**: agar-ph k*
- **Wrist**, 8-11 h: *Nat-m*

CORNS: *Acet-ac* k* *Agar* k* alum-p k2 *Am-c* k* ambr b2.de* anac b2.de* anac-oc c2 **Ant-c** k* arg-met b2.de* *Arn* k* *Bar-c* k* *Borx* k* bov k* *Brom* b4a.de *Bry* k* bufo bg2 **Calc** k •* calc-caust c2 *Calc-s* calc-sil k2 camph b2.de* *Carb-an* k* carb-v b2.de* *Caust* k* cench k2 chin chin-b c2 cist ptk1 cocc b2.de* coloc con b2.de* *Cur* k* ferr-pic c2 *Graph* k* *Hep* k* *Hydr* c2 hyper c2 *Ign* k* iod b2.de* kali-ar k2 kali-c b2.de* kali-n b2.de* kiss c2 **LYC** k •* lyss m-ambo b2.de* m-arct b2.de* m-aust b2.de* med c2 nat-c k* *Nat-m* k* nit-ac k* *Nux-v* k* ozone sde2• petr k* *Ph-ac* k* *Phos* k* phyt ptk1 pimp c2 plb k2 *Psor* k* puls b2.de* rad-br ptk1 ran-b b2.de* *Ran-s* k* rhod k* **Rhus-t** k •* rumx c2 ruta b2.de* sal-ac c1* sang k2 semp ptk2 **SEP** k •* **Sil** k* spig b2.de* spong fd4.de staph k* sul-ac b2.de* *Sulph* k* symph ptk1 ter thuj b2.de* verat b2.de* wies c2
- **aching**: ant-c lyc sep sil sul-ac h2* sulph
- **boring**: borx b2.de* calc k* caust k* hep b2.de* kali-c b2.de* kiss a1 nat-c k* *Nat-m* k* phos k* puls b2.de* *Ran-s* k* rhod b2.de* *Sep* k* *Sil* k* spig b2.de* thuj k*
- **burning**: *Agar Alum* am-c k* *Ant-c Arg-met* k* bar-c k* bar-s k2 borx b2.de* *Bry* k* *Calc* k* *Calc-s* carb-v k* caust k* cench k2 graph k* *Hep* k* **Ign** k* kali-c b2.de* lipp a1 lith-c *Lyc* k* m-ambo b2.de* meph k* nat-c b2.de* *Nat-m* nit-ac h2* *Nux-v* k* *Petr* k* *Ph-ac* k* phos k* pimp a1 psor al2 puls b2.de* *Ran-b* k* *Ran-s* k* *Rhus-t* k* sal-ac tl1 sang k2 **Sep** k* sil k* spig b2.de* staph b2.de* *Sulph* k* thuj k*
  - **night**: nat-m h2*
- **drawing** pain: lyc h2* nat-c h2* sep h2*
  - **night**: sep h2*
- **horny**: (↗*SKIN - Excrescences - horny*) *Ant-c* k* graph ran-b k* sulph k*
- **inflamed**: *Ant-c* borx b2.de* calc k* hep b2.de* *Lyc* k* *Nit-ac* b2.de* phos b2.de* *Puls* k* rhus-t b2.de* *Sep* k* **Sil** k* *Staph* k* **Sulph** k*
- **jerking**: anac b2.de* cocc b2.de* dios m-ambo b2.de* m-arct b2.de nux-v b2.de* phos k* puls b2.de* rhus-t b2.de* **Sep** k* sul-ac k* *Sulph* k*
- **painful**: *Agar* k* alum k* alum-p k2 am-c b2.de* ambr k* *Ant-c* arn k* asc-t a1 aster *Bar-c* k* bar-s k2 borx a1 bov k* *Brom* b4a.de bry k* bufo bg2 calad calc k* *Calc-s* calc-sil k2 camph b2.de* carb-an b2.de* carb-v b2.de* carl a1 caust cench k2 chin-b c1 fl-ac a1 gran a1 ham a1 *Hep* k* ign k* *Iod* kali-ar k2 kali-c k* kiss a1 lach lith-c *Lyc* k* lyss c2 m-ambo b2.de* *M-arct* b2.de* mag-m a1 med c1 meph k* nat-c b2.de* nat-m k* neon srj5• *Nit-ac* k* nux-v k* paeon a1 petr b2.de* phos k* phyt a1 psor al2 puls k* ran-b b2.de* ran-s k* raph a1 rhus-t k* sang a1 sep k* sil k* spig k* spong fd4.de staph b2.de* sul-ac b2.de* sul-i k2 **Sulph** k* thuj b2.de* verat b2.de*
  - **boils**; like: nux-v b7.de
  - **excoriated**; as if: ambr c1
  - **touch** agg.: asc-t a1 bry kali-c spong fd4.de
  - **ulcerated**, as if: am-c borx
- **pinching**: bar-c k*
- **pressing**: agar k* anac b2.de* *Ant-c* k* arg-met b2.de* bov k* *Bry* k* calc k* *Calc-s* carb-v k* *Caust* k* graph k* ign b2.de* iod k* **Lyc** k* m-ambo b7.de m-arct b2.de* m-aust b2.de* ph-ac k* phos b2.de* ruta b2.de* *Sep* k* sil k* staph b2.de* **Sulph** k* verat b2.de*
- **pulsating**: calc k* ham a1 kali-c k* *Lyc* k* sep k* sil k* sulph k*
- **shooting**: *Bov* k* hep c1 **Nat-m** k*
  - **weather**; during rainy: borx c1
- **sore**: aesc k* *Agar* k* ambr k* ant-c k* *Arn* k* *Bar-c* bar-s k2 *Bry* k* *Calc* k* *Calc-s* calc-sil k2 *Camph* k* **Carb-an** k* caust b2.de* fl-ac k* *Graph* k* *Hep* k* **Ign** k* kali-c b2.de* lith-c **Lyc** k* m-ambo b2.de* m-arct b2.de* med nat-c nat-m b2.de* nat-p nit-ac a1 *Nux-v* k* petr ph-ac b2.de* phos k* *Puls* k* *Ran-b* k* ran-s *Rhus-t* k* sal-ac tl1 *Sep* k* **Sil** k* *Spig* staph b2.de* sul-ac b2.de* *Sulph* k* thuj verat k*

- **stinging**: *Agar* k* **Alum** k* alum-p k2 am-c k* ant-c k* arg-met b2.de* arn b2.de* ars h2* arum-t bg2 *Bar-c* k* bar-s k2 borx k* *Bov* k* **Bry** k* calad k* **Calc** k* **Calc-s** k* calc-sil k2 carb-ac bg2 carb-an k* carb-v h2* caust k* chel a1 cic a1 cocc b2.de* con b4a.de graph b2.de* hep k* ign k* kali-c k* kali-n b2.de* kiss a1 *Lyc* k* m-ambo b2.de* m-arct b2.de mag-m **Nat-c** k* **Nat-m** k* nat-p *Nit-ac* b2.de* *Petr* k* ph-ac k* *Phos* k* ptel *Puls* k* ran-b k2 *Ran-s* k* *Rhod* k* **Rhus-t** k* rumx sel bg2* *Sep* k* *Sil* k* spig b2.de* staph k* sul-ac k* **Sulph** k* *Thuj* k* verat k*
  - **night**: ars h2* bart a1 nat-m h2* rhod a1 sulph h2*
  - **walking** agg.: phos h2*
  - **weather**; in rainy: borx h2
- **suppurating**: thuj bg1
- **tearing**: alum bg2 am-c k* arn k* ars h2* *Bry* k* calc k* calc-s caust b2.de* cocc k* ign b2.de* kali-c k* **Lyc** k* mag-m h2* nat-c b2.de* nux-v b2.de* rhus-t b2.de* *Sep* k* **Sil** k* sul-ac k* **Sulph** k* thuj
  - **night**: ars h2*
- **warm** bed agg.: sulph k2
- **yellow**: ferr-pic br1

○ - **Ankles**: ign b7.de* m-ambo b7.de*
- **Feet**:

○ · **Heels**: arn b7.de* lyc bg2 *Phos* k*
  - **Soles**: *Ant-c* b7a.de maland mtf11 morg-p mtf11 psor mtf11
    - ⁝ **horny**: (↗*SKIN - Excrescences - horny)* **Ant-c** *Ars* *Calc* kali-ar phos sne sil
- **Toes | Balls**: *Ant-c* b7.de* calad b7a.de ran-s b7.de*

CORRUGATED nails (See Nails - corrugated)

COUGH agg.:

○ - **Lower** limbs: borx b4a.de caps b7.de* caust b4a.de* nat-s bg2 nux-v bg2 phos bg2 *Rhus-t* b7.de* sep bg2 tell bg2
- **Shoulders**: dig ptk1 ferr ptk1 lach ptk1
  - **right**: pyrog ptk1
  - **left**: rumx ptk1
- **Upper** limbs: acon b7.de* alum bg2 ant-t b7.de* caps b7.de* dig b4.de* *Puls* b7.de*

COVER hands:
- **aversion** to: (↗*Uncover inclination)* mag-c bg1*
- **desire** to: ign k* syph xxb

COVERS: | **agg.** | **Upper** limbs: cham b7.de* mag-c bg2 *Verat* b7.de*
- **amel.** | **Upper** limbs: nux-v b7.de* rhus-t b7.de*

COXITIS (See Inflammation - hips - joints)

CRACKED skin: allox sp1 cortico sp1 cortiso sp1 rauw sp1 tritic-vg fd5.de *X-ray* sp1
- **frostbite**; from: nit-ac b4.de*

○ - **Feet**: anan vh1 aur sne *Aur-m* com *Hep* k* **Lyc** sne maland jl2 merc sne morg-p fmm1• **Sars** k* *Sep* sne sil mrr1 staph sne sulph syc fmm1• symph fd3.de• thuj mrr1 tritic-vg fd5.de
  - **cold** weather; during: maland jl2
  - **washing**; from: maland jl2

○ · **Heels**: acon sne ars bg1 arund br1 aur sne bov sne coc-c bg1 fic-m gya1 *Graph* bg2 kali-c sne kali-p bg1 lach ser *Lyc* k* med ser merc sne morg-p pte1*• rauw tpw8* *Sep* sne staph sne sulph sne syc pte1*• til ban1• wies a1
    - ⁝ **deep**: til ban1•
  - **Soles**: ars k* merc-c bg1* petr-ra shn4• *Sars* mrr1 symph fd3.de• tritic-vg fd5.de wies a1
- **Fingers**: *Alum* b4.de* am-m apis b7a.de arn b7.de* **Ars** b4a.de arund br1 *Aur* b4.de* aur-m-n wbt2• bar-c k* bar-s k2 **Calc** k* calc-sil k2 *Caust* bg2 chord-umb rly4• *Cist* k* cortico sp1 *Cycl* b7.de* *Fl-ac* b4a.de* *Graph* b4a.de* *Hep* k* ign sne *Jug-c* mrr1 kali-bi gk kali-c k* kreos b7a.de* mag-c k* mang b4a.de* *Merc* k* morg-p pte1• nat-c b4.de* nat-m b4.de* *Nit-ac* bg2* ozone sde2• **Petr** k* phos rhus-t b7.de* *Ruta* b7.de* sanguis-s hm2• sanic ptk1 **Sars** k* *Sep* b4a.de sil k* spong fd4.de staph sne **Sulph** b4.de* ulm-c jsj8• *X-ray* sp1 zinc k*
  - **winter** agg.: *Petr* tl1

○ · **Base** of fingers, at: sulph h2
  - **Between**: *Ars* *Aur-m* *Graph* morg-p pte1*• sulph x-ray sp1 zinc k*
  - **First**: ign sne mang-p rly4• plac rzf5• sil staph sne
  - **Joints**: chord-umb rly4• *Graph* kali-c sne mang k* merc phos k* *Sanic* k* spong fd4.de *Sulph* k*

Cracked – Fingers – Joints: ...
    - ⁝ **ulcerate**; that: *Merc*
  - **Knuckles**: bacls-7 fmm1• morg-p fmm1•
  - **Nails**:
    - ⁝ **Around**: amp rly4• **Ant-c** ars graph mtf33 lach bg3 *Nat-m* k* ruta fd4.de *Sil* symph fd3.de•
    - ⁝ **Corners** of: lach ptk2
    - ⁝ **Under**: graph mtf33
      - ⁝ **bleeding**: graph mtf33
  - **Tips**: alum bg2 am-m ptk1 ant-c vh aur bg2 *Aur-m* bacls-7 pte1*• bar-c k* bell bg2* cist mrr1 dys fmm1• **Graph** k* ign sne med ptk1* merc bg2* nat-m bg1* **Petr** k* ran-b ptk1 sars bg2* sil bg2* sulph sne syc pte1* x-ray sp1
    - ⁝ **bleeding**: ulm-c jsj8•
- **Hands**: (↗*Chapped)* *Aesc* allox sp1 **Alum** k* *Am-c* anan ant-c *Anthraci* k* apis b7a.de arn k* **Ars** b4a.de *Aur* k* *Aur-m* aur-s k2 bacls-7 fmm1• bar-c k* bar-s k2 **Calc** k* calc-f st1 calc-s k2 calc-sil k2 carb-v mrr1 *Carbn-s* castor-eq br1 *Caust* bg2 cench *Cist* k* cortico sp1 cycl k* dulc fd4.de dys pte1*• *Fl-ac* b4a.de **Graph** k* *Hep* k* hydroph rsj6• *Jug-c* mrr1 kali-c k* kali-s kreos k* *Lach* k* *Lyc* *Mag-c* k* maland k* mang b4a.de* *Merc* k* morg-p fmm1• *Nat-c* k* *Nat-m* k* **Nit-ac** k* ozone sde2• **Petr** k* phos *Psor* *Puls* *Rhus-t* k* rhus-v ruta k* *Sanic* k* **Sars** k* sec *Sep* k* **Sil** k* **Sulph** k* *X-ray* sp1 **Zinc** k*
  - **burning**: *Petr* sars zinc
  - **cold** agg.; becoming: petr tl1 sanic zinc
  - **deep** and bleeding: alum cist mrr1 hep br *Merc* **Nit-ac** k* **Petr** sanic *Sars*
  - **itching**: merc *Petr*
  - **painful**: graph bg2 merc bg2 **Petr** bg2 *Sulph* bg2
  - **wetting**, from: alum ant-c **Calc** calc-s k2 *Cist* dulc fd4.de kali-c maland jl2 nit-ac petr k2 *Puls* *Rhus-t* rhus-v sars **Sep** **Sulph** zinc
  - **winter** agg.●: alum **Calc** k* calc-s k2 *Cist* k* graph gk maland jl2 *Merc* k* **Petr** *Psor* *Sanic* **Sep** **Sulph** k*

○ · **Back** of hands: cist bg2 cortiso tpw7* dulc fd4.de graph gk kreos bg2 *Merc* morg-p pte1• mur-ac h2* nat-c k* petr k* *Rhus-t* k* *Sanic* k* **SEP** k●
    - ⁝ **warm** applications agg.: cortiso tpw7
  - **Palms**: alum bg2 anthraci mrr1 bacls-7 pte1*• calc-f bro1* *Cist* k* dys pte1• graph bg2 kreos bg2* merc-c ptk1 *Merc-i-r* k* morg-p pte1• *Petr* k* ran-b bro1* *Rhus-t* b7a.de* sulph k*
    - ⁝ **deep**: **Petr** mrr1
    - ⁝ **moist**: merc-i-r ptk1
    - ⁝ **Balls**: hep
- **Hips**: puls bg2
- **Joints**; bends of: bacls-7 pte1• **Graph** hippoz mang hr1 morg-p pte1• *Nit-ac* mrr1 psor bl1
- **Lower** limbs: *Alum* k* *Aur* k* *Aur-m* bar-c k* *Calc* k* chin b7.de* coff b7.de* croc b7.de* *Cycl* b7.de* **Hep** k* lach *Mang* b4a.de merc k* nat-c k* nat-m k* petr k* plat b4.de* puls b7.de ruta b7.de* sabin b7a.de sars b4.de* *Sulph* k* valer b7.de* verat b7.de* *Zinc* k*
- **Shoulders**: arn bg2 petr valer bg2
- **Thumbs**: benz-ac dgt1 morg-p pte1*• sars k* spong fd4.de symph fd3.de•
  - **right**: cortico sp1*

○ · **Bend** of thumb joint: mang h2
- **Toes**: lach b7.de* petr-ra shn4• sabad ptk1 sars ptk1

○ · **Between**: aur-m carb-an eug k* *Graph* k* hydrog srj2• *Lach* k* **Nat-m** k● *Petr* bro1 psor bg1 sabad bro1* *Sars* k* **Sil** k*
    - ⁝ **deep**: *Hydr*
    - ⁝ **itching** violently: maland jl2 **Nat-m** k●
  - **Under**: dulc fd4.de fic-m gya1 hydrog srj2• sabad k*
- **Upper** limbs: apis b7a.de cund bg2 **Graph** bg2 kali-ar kali-c bg2 kreos bg2 phos bg2 sil k*
- **Wrists**: kali-ar **Sulph** bg2 syc pte1•

CRACKING in joints: acon k* agar agn b2.de* am-c k* anac k* *Ang* k* *Ant-c* k* ant-t b2.de* arn sne bar-c b2.de* benz-ac bg1* brom bry b2.de* calad k* *Calc* k* calc-f c2* *Camph* k* cann-xyz ptk1 **Caps** k* carb-an k* carbn-s card-b c2 carl caul caust b2.de* *Cham* k* chin k* chlf cic b2.de* clem *Cocc* k* coff ptk1 coloc b2.de* con b2.de* croc k* dulc fd4.de euphr b2.de* *Ferr* k* gins graph bg1 guare haliae-lc srj5• hep b2.de* ign b2.de* ip b2.de* irid-met srj5• *Kali-bi* k* *Kali-c* k* kali-m c2* kali-n b2.de* *Kali-s* ketogl-ac rly4• lac-cp vml2• **Led** k* *Lyc* k* lyss m-ambo b2.de* m-arct b2.de* m-aust b2.de* mand rsj7• med c1 meny b2.de*

Extremities

Cracking in joints: ...
Merc k* mez b2.de* *Nat-c* k* *Nat-m* k* nat-p k* nat-pyru rly4• *Nat-s* k* **Nit-ac** k* *Nux-m* sne *Nux-v* k* ozone sde2• **Petr** k* *Phos* k* plb k* psor al2 puls b2.de* ran-b b2.de* raph rheum ptk1 **Rhus-t** k* ruta ptk1* *Sabad* k* sabin b2.de* sacch-a fd2.de• sars b2.de* sel b2.de* seneg b2.de* *Sep* spong b2.de* stann b2.de* *Sulph* k* *Thuj* k* tritic-vg fd5.de tub xxb vanil fd5.de verat b2.de* x-ray mtf11 *Zinc* b2.de*

- **morning**: brom ruta fd4.de sacch-a fd2.de•
  - **rising** agg.; after: brom
- **bending** agg.: dulc fd4.de lyc h2 ruta fd4.de spong fd4.de
- **convulsions**; during: acon
- **motion** agg.: acon bro1 ang bro1 *Benz-ac* bro1 calc-f bro1 camph bro1 *Caust* bro1 cocc bro1 gins bro1 *Graph* bro1 kali-bi bro1 kali-m bro1 led bro1 nat-m bro1 *Nat-p* bro1 *Nit-ac* bro1 *Petr* bro1 thuj bro1 zinc bro1
- **stretching** them; when: thuj mtf33
- **turning** agg.: caul
- **walking**:
  - **agg.**: am-c bry caul cocc vanil fd5.de
  - **air** agg.; in open: ruta ptk1
- **warm** bed agg.: led br1
- ○ **Ankles**: am-c ant-c aster *Camph* k* **Canth** k* *Caps* b7a.de carbn-s caust k* euphr b7.de* hep k* kali-bi kali-s fd4.de *Led* b7a.de mag-s *Nit-ac* k* nux-v petr k* ph-ac k* ruta fd4.de sars b4.de* *Sep* sulph k* thuj k*
  - **right**: mand rsj7•
  - **evening**: am-c fic-m gya1
  - **bending** agg.: ant-c
    - **side** to side; from: caust
  - **false** step; at a: caust
  - **stepping** agg.: euphr h2 ruta fd4.de
  - **stretching** agg.: ant-c thuj
  - **walking** agg.: carbn-s kali-s fd4.de *Nit-ac* nux-v sulph
- **Elbows**: am-c k* ant-c k* brom *Caps* b7a.de cartl-s rly4• cinnb con k* dios kali-s fd4.de *Kalm* k* *Led* b7a.de m-arct b7.de med c1 merc k* mur-ac nat-m k* *Petr* b4a.de sulph k* tep thuj k* zinc zing
  - **right**: mand rsj7•
  - **afternoon**: kalm
  - **stretching** out: kali-s fd4.de thuj
- **Feet**: caust petr ph-ac ruta fd4.de sars sulph thuj vanil fd5.de
- **Finger** joints: alum-p k2 ars-met bar-c b4.de* benz-ac k2 caps k* *Carb-an* des-ac rbp6 hep bg2 kali-n k* *Led* b7a.de m-ambo b7.de meph bg2 merc *Nux-v* bg2 petr-ra shn4• seneg b4.de* sulph teucr bg2 vanil fd5.de
  - **closing** the hands: ars-met
  - **feels** impelled to make them crack: meph petr-ra shn4•
  - ○ **Distal** joint: hydr phos
  - **Knuckles**: bacls-7 fmm1•
- **Hands**: plut-n srj7• ruta fd4.de sep h2
  - ○ **Back** of hands | **Tendons** of: kali-m k2
- **Hips**: aloe anac k* *Bry* b7a.de *Camph* k* *Caps* b7a.de *Cocc* k* coloc b4a.de *Croc* k* dulc fd4.de glon *Led* b7a.de nat-m *Nit-ac* b4a.de ozone sde2• *Petr* b4a.de plut-n srj7• *Rhus-t* b7a.de
  - **right**: mand rsj7•
  - **morning** | **rising** agg.: aloe
  - **walking** agg.: plut-n srj7•
- **Knees**: acon k* alum k* am-c k* *Ars* aster *Benz-ac* bry calad k* *Calc* *Camph* k* caps k* **Caust** k* *Cham* k* *Cocc* k* *Con* k* cop *Croc* k* dulc fd4.de flav jl2 gins glon haliae-lc srj5• hura ign k* kali-p fd1.de• kali-s fd4.de ketogl-ac rly4• lach lap-la sde8.de• *Led* k* *Lyc* b4a.de m-aust b7.de* mag-m bg2 mag-s *Mez* nat-ar nat-m k* nat-pyru rly4• nat-s hr1 nept-m lsd2.fr nit-ac k* *Nux-v* k* petr k* podo *Puls* k* ran-b b7.de* raph ruta fd4.de sel k* *Sep* **Sulph** k* tab tep thuj k* vanil fd5.de verat k*
  - **right**: mez
  - **left**: aster calad dulc fd4.de nept-m lsd2.fr podo fd3.de•
  - **ascending** stairs agg.: hura
  - **cartilage** slipped; as if: petr
  - **descending** stairs agg.: **Caust** hura
  - **flexing**, when: calad nat-ar ruta fd4.de sel vanil fd5.de

Cracking in joints – **Knees**: ...
  - **lying** down agg.: sel
  - **motion** agg.: nept-m lsd2.fr
  - **painless**: acon ketogl-ac rly4•
  - **stretching** agg.: con h2 cop kali-s fd4.de mag-s ran-b rhus-t thuj
  - **walking** agg.: alum *Ars* *Benz-ac* bro1 bry calad *Calc* **Caust** k* cocc br1* croc bro1 dios bro1 glon hura led mag-s nat-ar bro1 nat-m nit-ac nux-v k* podo c1 tab vanil fd5.de
  - ▽ **extending** to | **Limb**: nat-ar
  - ○ **Patella**: con ran-b
- **Lower** limbs, joints of: *Benz-ac* brach bry *Camph* carc fd2.de• caust *Cham* cocc con dream-p sdj1• led *Merc* b4a.de nux-v petr puls ran-b sel *Sep* tab thuj
  - **stepping** agg.: euphr mag-s
  - **stooping** agg.: croc
  - **walking** agg.: bry
- **Shoulders**: aloe anac k* ant-t k* bar-c k* brach *Calc* k* *Caps* b7a.de carbn-s chinin-s bg2 *Cic* k* cinnb *Croc* k* ferr k* gins *Kali-c* k* kali-s fd4.de *Led* b7a.de merc k* mez k* nat-ar nat-m nat-sil fd3.de• ozone sde2• *Petr* b4a.de phos k* *Rhus-t* b7a.de sabad k* sars k* spong fd4.de thuj k* tritic-vg fd5.de
  - **right**: carbn-s lac-lup hrn2• sars h2 tritic-vg fd5.de
  - **morning**: aloe
  - **night** | **bed** agg.; in: mez
  - **elevation** of arm: bamb-a stb2.de• *Kali-c* kali-s fd4.de nat-ar
    - **crack**; as if would: mur-ac h2*
  - **stretching** out: sabad
- **Thumbs**: bar-c h2 kali-n h2 nux-v plut-n srj7•
- **Toes**: ant-c b7.de* *Caps* b7a.de kali-s fd4.de *Led* b7a.de podo fd3.de• vanil fd5.de
  - ○ **First**: ant-c h2
- **Upper** limbs, joints of: anac b4.de* ant-t bar-c b4.de* benz-ac brach chinin-s *Croc* kali-bi kali-c b4.de* merc k* mur-ac *Nit-ac* b4a.de *Petr* b4a.de phos b4.de* sep h2 thuj k*
  - **leaning** on arm; when: thuj
- **Wrists**: ant-c b7.de* *Am* k* *Caps* b7a.de cartl-s rly4• cic k* *Con* k* kali-bi kali-s fd4.de *Led* b7a.de merc k* ox-ac ozone sde2• phos podo fd3.de• rhus-t b7a.de ruta fd4.de sel k* symph fd3.de• tep
  - **evening**: con
  - **and** tearing in hands at night: sel
  - **stretching** out: kali-s fd4.de sel

CRAMPS: *(↗Convulsion; Pain - cramping)* allox sp1 ambr ptk1 anan *Ars* k* ars-s-f k2 atro k* **Bell** k* bufo buth-a sp1 *Calc* k* calc-s camph k* carbn-o carbn-s card-m k2 cartl-s rly4• *Caust* cedr chin k2 cic k2 cimic ptk1 *Cocc* colch **Coloc** *Con* *Crot-c* crot-h **Cupr** *Dios* dros k2 *Dulc* k* eup-per ferr *Graph* *Hell* *Hyos* ign k* jatr-c kali-bi k* *Kali-c* kali-m k2 kali-p kali-s kiss a1 kola stb3• lim a1 **Lyc** mag-p mrr1 **Merc** merc-c k* merc-sul k* *Mur-ac* nat-f sp1 nat-m k* *Nit-ac* nux-v k* olnd k* op k* ox-ac pegan-ha tpi1• *Petr* k* phos k* phys br1* *Phyt* k* **Plat** *Plb* k* ran-b ptk1 *Rhus-t* ribo rly4• *Rob* ruta fd4.de sarcol-ac sp1 *Sec* k* sel k* **Sep** *Sil* spong fd4.de staph k* stroph-s sp1 suis-em rly4• **Sulph** *Tab* tarent k* tritic-vg fd5.de vanil fd5.de *Verat* k* vip ptk1 *Zinc* k* zinc-s k*

- **right**: elaps ribo rly4•
- **morning**: dulc fd4.de sulph
- **afternoon**: dulc fd4.de sulph
- **night**: merc
- **accompanied** by | **diarrhea** (See RECTUM - Diarrhea - accompanied - extremities)
- **ascending** agg.: stroph-s sp1
- **children**; in: chin mtf11
- **chill**; during: cupr *Sil*
- **coition**; during: *Cupr* mrr1
- **cold** air agg.: bufo
- **cough**:
  - **after**: dros k2
  - **with**: dros mtf33
- **dancers**: prot mtf11
- **delivery**; during: plat k2
- **ejaculation**: bufo
- **exertion** agg.; after: mag-p k* sacch-a fd2.de•

- **intermittent**: phyt k*
- **menses**: cimic k2
  - **suppressed** menses; from: *Cupr* b7a.de
- **motion** agg.: nux-v k* tritic-vg fd5.de
- **pregnancy**: *Cupr Verat* vib
- **pressure** agg.: zinc zinc-s a1
- **sleep** agg.: *Cupr* mrr1
- **stool**:
  - **before**: cupr bg2
  - **during** | **agg.**: ant-t bg2 ars bg2 bell k* colch bg2 *Cupr* bg2 merc-c bg2 plat bg2 sec bg2 verat bg2
- **sudden**: cortiso gse

○ - **Ankles**: agar k* am-m b7.de* ars b4.de* calc b4a.de calc-p k* carl k* cina bg2 cupr k* dulc b4.de* euph b4.de* euphr bg2 gels bg2 iod b4.de* mag-m b4.de* meny b7.de* mez b4.de* *Plat* k* rhus-t b7.de* rumx ptk1 sec b7.de* sel k* staph b7.de* sul-ac b4.de* sulph bg2 thuj bg2 zinc-i ptk1
  - **right** inner ankle | **night** | **waking**; on: dulc h2
    - **walking** | **amel.**: dulc h2
  - **left**: nat-m bg2
  - **evening**: sel k*
    - **lying** agg.: sel
  - **night**: iod h*
    - **waking**; on: dulc h1
    - **walking** | **amel.**: dulc h1*
  - **pressing** foot to floor | **amel.**: zinc-i ptk1
  - **sensation** as if extremities were going to sleep; with: *Plat*

▽ • **extending** to:
    - **Calf**: cupr
    - **Heel**; over: agar k*
    - **Toes**: nat-c h2*
- **Buttocks** (See nates)
- **Elbows**: chel b7.de* kalm bg2 kreos b7a.de* rhus-t b7.de* sabad bg2 sec b7.de* verb b7.de*
- **Feet**: *Acon Agar* agar-ph a1 allox sp1 alum b4.de* am-c k* am-m b7.de* anac b4.de* *Ang* k* arg-cy arg-met k* ars k* ars-i k2 ars-s-f k2 *Asc-t* bar-c b4.de* **Bell** k* berb bism k* bry k* calad b7.de* *Calc* k* calc-i k2 calc-p k* calc-sil k2 *Camph* k* carb-v b4.de* **Carbn-s** card-m k2 **Caust** k* cham tl1 chin b7.de* cho bro1 coca-c sk4• *Colch* k* *Coloc* **Cupr** k* dig digin a1 dulc fd4.de euph b4.de* ferr k* ferr-ar ferr-i ferr-p form k* frax br1* gels k* gnaph k* graph k* hep k* hipp a1 hippoz mtf11 hyper k* ign b7.de* iod k* *Jatr-c* k* *Lac-c* k* lach k* lachn k* lil-t k* *Lyc* k* m-aust b7.de mag-c b4.de* mag-m manc k* meph k* merc bg2 *Merc-c* b4a.de mosch k2 *Nat-c* k* nat-f sp1 *Nat-m* k* nat-p nept-m lsd2.fr nux-m nux-v k* olnd k* ox-ac k* ozone sde2• *Petr* k* *Ph-ac* k* phos k* phys k* plat plb k* pneu mtf11 podo c1 prot jl2 ran-b k* *Rhus-t* ribo rly4• rumx ptk1 sanic k* *Sec* k* *Sep* k* *Sil* k* spig k* *Stram* k* stry k* sul-ac k* sul-i k2 *Sulph* k* til k* tritic-vg fd5.de valer k2* verat k* verat-v k* verb k* zinc k* zinc-p k2
  - **alternating** sides: nept-m lsd2.fr
  - **right**: crot-c sk4• dulc fd4.de ferr a1 gels psa* mand rsj7• nat-c h2* polys sk4• stry a1 tritic-vg fd5.de
  - **left**: hyper a1 lachn hr1 melal-alt gya4 meph a1 nat-m h2* ozone sde2• petr-ra shn4• til a1 zinc a1
  - **daytime**: ox-ac k* *Petr* k* *Sep*
  - **forenoon** | **9** h: lachn
  - **evening**: tritic-vg fd5.de
    - **21** h: lyc
    - **drawing** up limbs, on: ferr k*
    - **walking** agg.: verat
  - **night**: calc mrr1 form k* lachn k* lyc k* nat-c k* sanic valer k2
  - **alternating** with:
    - **vision**; dim (See VISION - Dim - alternating - cramps)
    - **Hands**; cramps in (See hands - alternating - feet)
  - **bed** agg.; in: bry k* calc mrr1 gnaph k* sanic
  - **chill**; during: *Cupr* elat nux-v
  - **cholera**; during: **Cupr** sec **Sulph** lp **Verat**
  - **coition**, on attempting: *Cupr*
  - **exertion** agg.; after: petr-ra shn4•

- **Feet**: ...
  - **menses**; during: lachn sulph wies a1*
  - **motion** agg.: calc k* ph-ac k*
    - **first** motion after resting: plb
  - **sitting** agg.: euph k*
  - **sleep** | **going** to sleep; on | **agg.**: hyper
    - **preventing** sleep: valer ptk
  - **standing** agg.: euph
  - **stretching** agg.: calc mrr1 caust k* verat k*
  - **walking**:
    - **agg.**: sil
    - **amel.**: ozone sde2•
    - **difficult**: card-m k2
  - **warmth** | **amel.**: ozone sde2•

▽ • **extending** to:
    - **Ankles**: ozone sde2•
    - **Legs**: ozone sde2•

○ • **Back** of feet: anac bg1* bry bg2 camph b7.de* com k* gels bg2 lach ptk1 plb k* puls bg2 ran-b k* rhus-t bg2 rhus-v k* verat-v bg1*
    - **walking** agg.: ran-b
  - **Border** of foot; inner | **bending** foot inward: nat-c h2 sep h2
  - **Heels**: alum bg1 *Anac* k* ang b7.de* ant-c b7.de* bry k* cann-s h1* caust bg2* crot-c k* eug led k* (non:mag-c k*) nept-m lsd2.fr podo fd3.de• sel k* sep h2*
    - **left**: nept-m lsd2.fr
    - **morning** | **bed** agg.; in: mag-c h2*
  - **Inside** of: crot-t k* ozone sde2•
  - **Outside** of: nicc k* ozone sde2• polys sk4•
    - **sitting** during menses: nicc k*
  - **Soles**: acon k* *Agar* k* alum b4.de* *Alumn Am-c* k* anac b4.de* ang k* *Apoc* apoc-a vh arn b7.de* ars k* ars-s-f k2 bar-c k* bell k* berb k* bry k* cact k* calad k* **Calc** k* calc-act a1 calc-sil k2 **Carb-v** k* **Carbn-s** card-m **Caust** k* cham chel k* coff k* *Colch* k* com k* crot-t k* *Cupr* bg2* *Elat* eug k* euph b4.de* *Ferr* k* ferr-ar form k* gent-c k* graph bg1 *Hep* k* hipp k* kali-c kali-p lob a1 m-aust b7.de* med merc b4.de* mur-ac b4.de* nat-ar nat-c h2 nat-m k* nept-m lsd2.fr *Nit-ac* nit-m-ac a1 nux-v k* olnd k* orig a1 ozone sde2• *Petr* k* *Phos* k* plat b4.de* plb k* rhus-t ribo rly4• ruta k* sang sanic bg1 sec k* sel k* sep k* **Sil** k* stann k* staph k* *Stront-c* k* *Stry* k* **Sulph** k* *Syph* tarent k* thuj k* til k* *Verat* k* verat-v ptk1 *Verb* k* zing k*
    - **right**: carbn-s a1 nept-m lsd2.fr stann bg1
    - **left**: calc bg1* thuj bg1
    - **daytime**: nux-v k*
      - **attempting** to rise; on: nux-v
    - **evening**: hipp k* nat-m k* zing k*
      - **19** h: nat-ar
      - **lying** down agg.; after: *Carb-v* k*
    - **night**: *Agar* k* bry a1 calad k* calc k* cupr br1 eug br1 med melal-alt gya4 *Nit-ac Nux-v Petr* k* **Sulph** zing br1
      - **midnight**:
        - **after** | **3** h: ferr form
      - **cholera**; during: **Sulph**
      - **drawing** up limbs: kali-c k* nux-v k*
      - **lying** agg.: sel k*
      - **lying** down agg.: bry
      - **rising** agg.: plat
    - **bed** | **in** bed | **agg.**: bell carb-v sep thuj k*
      - **putting** foot out of bed (See putting - bed)
    - **colic**, preceding: plb k*
    - **crossing** feet; on: alum ptk
    - **dancing**, when: bar-c
    - **drawing** on boot: *Calc*
    - **fever**; during intermittent: elat
    - **flexing** thigh: bell h1*
    - **hanging** foot down, on: berb k*
    - **menses**; during: sulph

Extremities

- **Soles**: ...
  - **motion** agg.: eug k* petr
  - **pregnancy** agg.; during: **Calc** k*
  - **putting** out foot; on: chel coff k*
    - **bed**; out of: chel
  - **riding** in a carriage agg.: thuj
  - **sitting** agg.: bry hipp stann
  - **smoking** agg.: calad
  - **standing** agg.: verb
  - **stepping** agg.: chel sulph
  - **stretching** agg.: caust k*
  - **walking**:
    - **after** | **agg**.: calc k*
    - **agg**.: *Bar-c* petr *Sil* k* *Sulph* k* vib
    - **air** agg.; in open: carb-v
    - **amel**.: calc h2 nit-m-ac a1 *Verb*
  - **Side** lain on; on the: staph

- **Fingers**: acon bg2 agar b4.de* am-c b4.de* am-m b7.de* ambr br1 anac k* *Ang* b7a.de arg-n bg2 *Arn* k* ars k* asaf b7.de* aur b4.de* bell bg2 bry b7.de* buth-a sp1 calc k* cann-s b7.de* *Carb-v* k* card-m **Chel** k* cina b7.de* cocc b7.de* coff b7a.de* coloc b4a.de com con k* croc bg2 *Cupr* k* *Cupr-ar* cycl k* der k* dig bg2 dios br1 dros b7.de* dulc k* euph k* euphr b7.de* ferr k* gels k2 graph k* hipp jl2 hippoz mtf11 hyper k* ign k* kali-c k* kali-n b4a.de* *Lach* b7a.de* lil-t k* lyc k* mag-c k* mag-m b4.de* *Mag-p* mrr1 mang bg2 meny b7.de* **Merc** k* mosch b7.de* mur-ac b4.de* nat-c bg2 *Nat-m* k* nux-v k* olnd b7.de* ph-ac b4.de* phos b4.de* plat b4.de* plb k* rhus-t bg2 ribo rly4• ruta b7a.de sabad k* **Sec** bg2* sep b4.de* sil b4a.de spong b7.de* *Stann* k* staph b7.de* stront-c b4.de* *Sulph* k* tab k* tril-p k* v-a-b mtf11 valer b7.de* verat k* verb b7.de*
  - **morning**: orig a1 tab k*
  - **evening**: ars hipp jl2 orig a1
  - **night** | **midnight** | **bed** agg.; in: nux-v
    - **bed** agg.; in: ars
  - **begin** in: cupr bg1
  - **cholera**, with: *Colch* **Cupr** sec **Verat**
  - **cold** air agg.: am-c h2*
  - **cutting** with scissors: con k*
  - **delivery**; during: **Cupr** **Dios**
  - **motion** agg.: merc k*
  - **periodical**: *Phos* k*
  - **pick** up a small object, on attempting to: *Stann* k*
  - **playing**:
    - **piano**: *Mag-p* k*
    - **violin**: *Mag-p* k*
  - **sewing**: arn b7a.de euphr b7a.de kali-c **Lach** b7a.de *Sec* b7a.de
  - **shoemaking**: *Stann* k*
  - **stretching** them: ars
  - **writing** agg.: *(↗writing; Pain - fingers - writing)* arg-met ptk1 arn ptk1 brach k* caust bg1 cycl k* dros k2* gels ptk1 *Mag-p* k* pic-ac ptk1 prot jl2 *Sil* b4a.de **Stann** k* sul-ac br1* tril-p **Zinc** b4a.de
  - ○ **First**: anac h2* cycl k* graph h2* kali-chl k* nat-p k* ozone sde2• pana a1 sulph h2*
    - **writing** agg.: *Cycl*
  - **Fourth**: calc h2* cocc k* com k* nept-m lsd2.fr peti a1 *Sulph*
    - **writing** agg.: cocc
  - **Joints**: euphr h2* mag-c h2* plat h2* ribo rly4•
    - **Metacarpophalangeal** joints: anac h2
    - **Proximal** joints: ars h2 calc h2
  - **Second**: am-m k* caust h2* cina a1 hura lil-t k* plb k* *Sulph*
  - **Third**: arg-n a1 ars a1 hura ribo rly4• sep k* *Sulph* k*
    - **evening**: sep k* *Sulph* k*
    - **extending** to | **Elbow**: sep sulph
  - **Tips**: ars h2* vinc a1

- **Forearms**: acon b7.de* agath-a nl2• am-c anac k* ang b7.de* arn k* asaf b7.de* berb k* *Calc* k* calc-p k* cina k* coloc k* con b4.de* corn ferr-ma gels br1 graph h2* kali-i kola stb3• kreos b7a.de lyc k* meny b7.de* merc b4.de* mosch b7.de* mur-ac k* nat-c h2 par b7.de* ph-ac k* plat k* plb k* *Rhod* b4.de* ruta k* sep k* spong b7.de* stann b4.de* stront-c b4.de*

- **Forearms**: ...
  - **left**: anac bg1 coloc bg1 meny bg1 plat bg1 ruta bg1
  - **morning**: calc
  - **afternoon**: lyc k*
  - **night** | **bed** agg.; in: anac k*
  - **elbow**; resting: plat
  - **flexing**: arn k* mur-ac k*
  - **motion** agg.: kali-i plb
  - **walking** agg.: sep
  - **writing** agg.: cycl mrr1 gels c1
  - ▽ **extending** to | **Fingers**: cycl mrr1
  - ○ **Anterior** part: berb k* plat k* plb k*
  - **Muscles**:
    - **Extensor** muscles: merc
    - **Flexor** muscles: chinin-s
  - **Sides** | **Outer**: nat-c h2*

- **Hands**: acon k* aeth k* *Agar* am-m b7.de* ambr k* anac k* ang b7.de* anthraci ptk1 arg-met b7.de* ars k* asaf b7.de* aur b4.de* bamb-a stb2.de• **Bell** k* bism k* **Calc** k* calc-s k* calc-sil k2 cann-s b7.de* carb-v k* caust k* chin b7.de* cina k* cocc k* *Coloc* k* *Cupr* k* dios k* dulc k* euph b4.de* euphr k* ferr-ar ferr-ma *Graph* k* hep jatr-c *Kali-bi* *Kali-c* kali-sil k2 kiss a1 kreos b7a.de lac-e hrn2• lact k* lepi a1 lyc k* mag-p k* mang k* meny b7.de* merc k* merc-c k* merc-i-f k* mosch b7.de* mur-ac k* naja *Nat-m* k* nat-p k* nept-m lsd2.fr nit-ac k* nux-v b7.de* olnd k* paull a1 *Ph-ac* b4a.de *Phys* plat k* plb k* prun bg2 puls pyrog ptk1 ruta k* sabad k* sec k* sil k* spig b7.de* spong b7.de* stann b4.de* stram k* stront-c b4.de* stry k* sul-ac k* sulph k* tab thuj b4.de* tritic-vg fd5.de valer k2* verb b7.de* zing a1
  - **right**: acon k* agath-a nl2• gent-l a1 lyc bg1 merc-i-f k* merc-i-r plb k* sabad k* tritic-vg fd5.de
  - **left**: calc k* euphr k* kola stb3• merc bg1* nat-p k* olnd bg1 sulph k*
  - **morning**: *Calc* peti a1
  - **afternoon**: calc-s k* dios k* mucs-nas rly4•
    - **15** h: dios
  - **evening**: lyc k*
    - **21** h: lyc
  - **night**: *Calc* k* valer k2
    - **bed** agg.; in: plb k*
  - **alternating** with:
    - **vision**; dim (See VISION - Dim - alternating - cramps)
    - **Feet**; cramps in: stram
  - **cholera**: **Cupr** *Sec* verat a1
  - **closing** the hand agg.: chin k*
  - **exertion** agg.: plat k* sec *Sil* k*
  - **extending** agg.: plb k*
  - **flexing**, after: merc k*
  - **grasping** something agg.: ambr k* **Dros** k* graph lyc k* nept-m lsd2.fr nit-ac k* plat k* stann k* thlas bg1 tritic-vg fd5.de
    - **stone**; a cold: nat-m k*
  - **motion**:
    - **agg**.: ars k* gent-l a1 merc k* sec
    - **amel**.: acon k*
  - **playing**:
    - **piano**: bamb-a stb2.de•
    - **violin**: bamb-a stb2.de•
  - **rest**; after: plb k*
  - **sleep**, prevent: valer pd*
  - **typing**; when: bamb-a stb2.de•
  - **writing** agg.: *(↗Pain - hands - writing - agg.)* *Alum-sil* ambr bro1 *Anac* *Arg-met* bro1 *Arg-n* bro1 bamb-a stb2.de• brach bro1 *Caust* bro1 *Cimic* bro1 cupr bro1 *Cycl* k* dros k2* euph k* gels k* graph bro1 hep bro1 kali-p mtf11 **Mag-p** k* *Nat-p* k* phos h2* pic-ac plat prot jl2 ran-b c1 ruta bro1 salol c1 sil k* stann k2* sul-ac br1* sulph bro1 tril-p c1
  - ○ **Back** of hands: mag-c ptk1 verat ptk1
    - **night** | **bed** agg.; in: anac

· **Bones**; metacarpal: aur h2
· **Hands**:
⋮ **Palms**: coloc k* crot-h bg2 *Cupr* bro1 mur-ac k* naja k* nept-m lsd2.fr nux-v bg2 paull a1 sabin bg2* scroph-n bro1 scroph-xyz c2 spig h1* stann h2* stry k* zing k*
⋮ **motion** | **amel.**: mur-ac a1
· **Palms** | **Balls**: plat k*
· **Transversely** across: ruta
· **Ulnar** side: anac h2* cocc k* nept-m lsd2.fr puls

- **Hips**: agn a1 *Ang* k* arg-met aur bell k* cann-s k* carb-an h2* carb-v caust cimic k* coloc k* cop k* cur hep b4a.de jug-c k* kali-c b4.de* led ptk1 nat-m k* *Ph-ac* k* *Phos* plat b4.de* ruta k* *Sep* k* sul-ac k* valer
· **right**: sul-ac k*
· **left**: anthraq rly4• jug-c
· **night**: jug-c k* sep h2*
· **delivery**; during: *Cimic*
· **eating** agg.: ph-ac
· **menses**; during: form k*
· **sitting** agg.: ph-ac
· **walking** agg.: carb-an h2* nat-m a1 sep h2*
○ · **Gluteal** muscles: agar k* bell k* gels k* hyos k* *Hyper* k*
· **Joints**: bar-c b4.de* form bg2 kali-c b4.de* nat-m bg2 ph-ac bg2 *Plat* b4a.de sep bg2 sulph b4.de*

- **Joints**: *Anac* ang aur *Bell Bry* **Calc** k* camph canth caust cic cocc hist jl3 *Hyos Ign* lach laur merc op *Par* ph-ac k* **Plat** k* plb rhus-t *Sec Stram Sulph* k* verat

- **Knees**: anac b4.de* ang k* arg-met arn k* arund k* bell b4.de* berb bry k* cadm-s *Calc* k* cann-s b7.de* carb-an k* carb-v caust b4.de* chin b7.de* *Coloc* k* crot-t k* dios k* hep k* hyper k* kali-n b4.de* lach k* led k* lyc b4a.de olnd b7.de* par b7.de* petr k* phos b4a.de *Plat* b4a.de plb k* ruta b7.de* sel b7.de* sulph k* tab k* ter ptk1 yuc a1 *Zinc* k*
· **alternating** sides: sulph
· **morning**: dios k*
· **afternoon** | **15** h: dios
· **night**: bry k*
⋮ **midnight**:
⋮ **before** | **22**-23 h: sulph
· **drawing** on boot: calc
· **motion** | **amel.**: arg-met h1
· **sitting**:
⋮ **agg.**: bell a1 bry k* paeon k*
⋮ **long** time agg.; for a | **after**: chin
· **standing** agg.: ang
· **waking**; on: lach k*
· **walking** agg.: ang carb-an chin petr
○ · **Above**: arg-met h1 mand rsj7•
· **Hollow** of knees: ang bg2 bell k* berb *Calc* k* cann-s caust kali-n lyc k* paeon petr phos bg2* phys plb k* sulph k*
⋮ **left**: mag-p bg2
⋮ **stamping** foot: berb
⋮ **stretching** leg agg.: *Calc* k*
· **Patellae**: calc bg2 hep bg1 kali-bi bg2

- **Legs**: abrot bro1 acet-ac k* acon b7.de* aesc-g bro1 agar k* agar-ph a1 alum k* am-br bro1 am-c k* am-m b7.de* ambr k* amph a1 anac b4.de* anag ang k* ant-t b7.de* arg-met b7.de* arn b7.de* *Ars* k* ars-i k2 arum-t k* arund k* atra-r bnm3• bacls-7 fmm1• bapt bg2* bar-c k* bell k* blatta-o *Bov* k* bry k* bufo k* *Calc* k* calc-p bg2 camph k* cann-s b7.de* canth tl1 carb-ac bro1 *Carb-an* k* *Carb-v* k* *Carbn-s* caust k* **Cham** k* chin b7.de* chlor k* cho bro1 cimic bro1 *Cimx* bro1 cina k* cit-v k* coca-c sk4• cocc b7.de* coff b7.de* *Colch* k* **Coloc** k* con b4.de* crot-h k* **Cupr** k* *Cupr-ar* bro1 dig dios k* dulc b4.de* elat hr1 eug euphr b7.de* eupi bro1 falco-pe nl2• *Ferr* k* ferr-p gels k* glon k* graph k* hep b4a.de* *Hyos* b7.de* hyper bro1 *Ign* b7.de* iod k* *Ip* b7a.de irid-met bro1 *Jatr-c* k* kali-bi k* kali-c b4.de* **Kali-chl** kali-m k2 kali-n b4.de* kali-ox a1 lac-e hrn2• lach k* lact lat-m bnm6• lath br1* led b7.de* lil-t k* lol bro1 lyc k* m-ambo b7.de m-aust b7.de mag-c b4.de* mag-m b4.de* *Mag-p* k* manc k* med bro1 *Meny* b7.de* merc b4.de* merc-c k* mez b4.de* mosch b7a.de nat-c k* *Nat-m* *Nit-ac* k* nux-m b7.de* **Nux-v** b7.de* olnd k* orig a1 ox-ac bro1 petr k* petr-ra shn4• *Ph-ac* phos b4.de* pin-s bro1 plat k* plb k* podo k* prot pte1*• *Puls* k* *Rhod* b4.de* *Rhus-t* k* ruta b7.de* sarcol-ac bro1 sars k* sec k* sel b7.de* *Sep* b4.de* *Sil* b4.de* sol-t bro1 spig b7.de* spong b7.de* stann b4.de* *Staph* b7.de* stront-c b4a.de stry k* suis-em rly4• sul-i k2 **Sulph** k* tab thuj b4a.de tritic-vg fd5.de tub-r jl ust bro1 vanil fd5.de verat k* verat-v k* verb k* vib bg2 vip bro1 zinc bg2 zinc-s k*
· **left**: luf-op rsj5• mag-c bg2 nat-m bg2 podo bg2
· **daytime**: *Ferr-m* ox-ac k*
· **morning**: ars h2* arum-t k* crot-h k* dulc fd4.de orig a1
⋮ **bed** agg.; in: zinc h2
⋮ **waking**; on: arum-t
· **forenoon** | **bed** agg.; in: rhus-t
· **evening**: orig k* sep k*
⋮ **21** h: lyc
⋮ **bed** agg.; in: nit-ac h2
⋮ **lying** down agg.; after: *Puls*
⋮ **walking** agg.: ferr a1
· **night**: ambr bacls-7 pte1*• carb-an k* carb-v merc merc-d k* nat-m k* pall sinus rly4• *Sulph*
⋮ **midnight**; after | **4**-5 h: bufo
· **bed** agg.; in: cupr-ar br1 dios k* nux-v k* plb *Puls* rhus-t k*
⋮ **left**: colch rsj2•
· **chill**; during: cupr elat *Nux-v*
· **cold** agg.: lath br1
· **cough** agg.; during: dros
· **delivery**; during: bell hr1 cupr mag-p nux-v yl1
· **drawing** up leg agg.: zinc h2*
· **exertion** agg.: alum k* **Sec** mrr1
· **extension**, on: *Calc* k* plb k*
· **lifting** agg.: calc iod
· **lying** agg.: am-c
· **menses**; during: *Gels Graph*
· **motion** agg.: tritic-vg fd5.de verat-v k*
· **pregnancy** agg.; during: *Gels* ham *Vib* k*
· **pressure**:
⋮ **amel.**: ox-ac k* rhus-t k*
⋮ **flexors** agg.; upon: lyc
· **sitting**:
⋮ **agg.**: calc bg1 iod h*
⋮ **amel.**: cina
· **sleep**; on going to: hyper
· **stool** agg.; during: colch cupr sec bg1 *Sulph* verat
· **stretching** out the foot: *Sulph*
· **urinate**, on attempting to: *Pareir* k*
· **walking** agg.: (↗ *Claudicatio*) arag br1 beryl tpw5 carb-ac br1 *Carb-an Carb-v* cina dulc a1 gels hep h2 **Sec** mrr1
○ · **Bones**:
⋮ **Tibia**: agar bg2* am-c b4a.de* ars bg2* calc bg2* carb-an bg1 caust bg2* con bg1 merc bg1 mosch bg2* nat-m bg2* petr bg2* sars bg2*
⋮ **Region** of: *Am-c* arag br1 calc h2 carb-ac br1 carb-an h2 coloc h2
. **walking** agg.: carb-ac br1
. **extending** to | **Toes**: sars h2
· **Calves**: (↗ *Contraction - legs - calves - spasmodic*) *Acon* k* *Agar* k* agar-ph a1 aids nl2* allox sp1 *Alum* k* alum-p k2 alum-sil k2 alumn am-c k* *Ambr* k* amp rly4• *Anac* k* anag ang bg2* ant-t k* anthraq rly4• arg-met k* **Arg-n** k* arn bg2 *Ars* k* ars-s-f k2 aspar k* bapt k* bar-c k* bar-s k2 bell k* berb k* bov k* bry k* bufo k* cadm-s **Calc** k* *Calc-p* k* calc-s calc-sil k2 *Camph* k* cann-i k* cann-s b7a.de* carb-ac k* carb-an k* carb-v k* carbn-s card-m carl k* *Caust* k* **Cham** k* chel k* chin k* chinin-ar cimic ptk cina bg2 clem k* cocc k* coff k* *Colch* k* **Coloc** k* *Con* k* conin a1 *Crot-h* k* **Cupr** k* cypra-eg sde6.de• des-ac mtf11 dig k* dulc k* elaps euphr k* eupi k* falco-pe nl2• *Ferr* k* ferr-ar ferr-m ferr-p gins k* *Gnaph* k* **Graph** k* guaj k* **Hep** k* hydrc k* hyos k* ign k* *Iris* jatr-c k*

Extremities

- **Calves**: ...
kali-ar kali-bi k* kali-br k* *Kali-c* k* kali-i k* kali-n bg2 kali-p kali-sil k2 kiss a1 kola stb3• kreos b7a.de lac-ac k* lach k* lachn lact k* lath c1 led k* limest-b es1• lob luf-op rsj5• **Lyc** k* lyss k* *Mag-c* k* *Mag-m* k* *Mag-p* k* manc k* *Med Meny* bg2 merc k* merc-c k* mez bg2 nat-ar *Nat-c* k* nat-f sp1 *Nat-m* k* nat-p nept-m lsd2.fr *Nit-ac* k* nux-m k* *Nux-v* k* oena olib-sac wmh1 olnd k* *Petr* k* petr-ra shn4• *Ph-ac Phos* k* pitu-gl skp7• plat bg2* **Plb** k* podo c1* puls k* *Rhod* bg2 *Rhus-t* k* rhus-v k* ruta bg2* sang k* sarcol-ac sp1 sars k* **Sec** k* *Sel* k* *Sep* k* **Sil** k* sin-n k* sinus rly4• sol-ni sol-t a1 spig k* stann k* staph k* stront-c ptk1 stroph-s sp1 stry k* suis-em rly4• **Sulph** k* tab tarent k* thuj k* tril-p c1 tritic-vg fd5.de tub mtf11 ust mtf11 valer k2 *Verat* k* *Verat-v* k* verb bg2 vib bg2* vip ptk1 *Zinc* k* zinc-i ptk1 zinc-p k2
  - **right**: acon bg1 agar k* amp rly4• bros-gau mrc1 dulc fd4.de kali-c lachn a1 lyss merc bg1 nept-m lsd2.fr ozone sde2• petr-ra shn4• plut-n srj7• podo fd3.de• trios rsj11• tritic-vg fd5.de trom ulm-c jsj8•
  - **left**: agar bg1* arg-n bg1 aspar bg1 berb bg1 bros-gau mrc1 bry bg1 coloc bg1 dulc fd4.de kali-n bg1 lyc bg1 mag-c bg2 mag-s bg1 nat-m bg2* petr-ra shn4• ph-ac bg1 phos bg1 podo bg2 ruta fd4.de sang bg1 spig bg1 sulph bg1 v-a-b mtf11 zinc bg1 [tax jsj7]
    - **bed** agg.; in: phys ptk ruta fd4.de
    - **turning** in bed agg.: phys ptk1
  - **daytime**: graph k* *Petr* k*
    - **sitting** bent forward agg.: *Lyc*
  - **morning**: bry k* carb-an k* dulc fd4.de lach k* nit-ac k* podo fd3.de•
    - **bed** agg.; in: bov k* cartl-s rly4• *Caust* k* graph k* hep k* ign k* lac-ac k* lach k* lachn a1 nat-c h2* nit-ac podo fd3.de• sil k* *Sulph* k*
    - **rising** agg.: dulc fd4.de ferr lac-ac
    - **stretching** leg agg.: carl a1 nat-c h2*
    - **waking**; on: lob k*
  - **forenoon**: nat-m k* sulph k*
  - **afternoon**: alum h2* ant-t k* dulc fd4.de elaps hyos h1*
  - **evening**: kali-n k* mag-c k* nux-v k* sel k* sil h2* sulph k*
    - **bed** agg.; in: *Ars* bell h1* mag-c k* nit-ac h2* *Puls*
    - **sleep** agg.; on going to: berb k* nux-m
  - **night**: *Ambr* k* anac k* androc srj1• arg-n k* ars k* berb k* bry k* **Calc** k* calc-f jl carb-an k* carb-v caust k* cham bg1 coca cocc k* dig digin a1 *Eupi* k* *Ferr Ferr-m Graph* k* *Kali-c* k* led h1* **Lyc** k* lyss *Mag-c* k* *Mag-m* k* med *Nit-ac* k* nux-m *Nux-v* peti a1 petr k* plb k* rhus-t h1 rhus-v k* ruta fd4.de sars k* *Sec* gk sep k* stann k* suis-em rly4• **Sulph** k* zinc k*
    - **midnight** | **after**: petr-ra shn4• *Rhus-t* h1*
    - **bending** feet agg.: chin
  - **accompanied** by:
    - **Abdomen**:
      - **complaints** (See ABDOMEN - Complaints - accompanied - calves)
      - **pain** in (See ABDOMEN - Pain - accompanied - calves)
    - **Foot** soles; cramps in: stront-c ptk1
  - **air** agg.; draft of: petr-ra shn4•
  - **ascending** agg.: berb k* conin c1 stroph-s sp1
  - **bed** agg.; in: allox tpw4* androc srj1• ars k* bov k* **Calc Carbn-s** *Caust* k* cupr-ar br1 *Eupi Ferr Ferr-m* graph k* hep k* ign k* *Kali-c* lac-ac k* lach a1 lachn mag-c k* mang-p rly4• nux-v k* phys k* **Rhus-t** k* ruta fd4.de *Sec* gk sep sil k* **Sulph** k*
    - **flexing** thigh, on: nux-v k*
    - **turning** over (See turning in)
  - **bending**:
    - **knee**:
      - **agg.**: cocc k* hep k* ign
      - **amel.**: calc h2* cham h1* rhus-t h1*
    - **thigh** | **agg.**: bell h1*
  - **carrying** a weight: graph h2
  - **chill**; during: puls b7a.de
  - **cholera**; during: *Ant-t Camph Colch* **Cupr** *Jatr-c Kali-p Mag-p* sec a1 **Sulph Verat**
  - **coition**:
    - **after**: coloc k* tritic-vg fd5.de

- **Calves – coition**: ...
    - **attempting**; on: *Cupr*
    - **during**: cupr k* *Graph* k*
  - **colic**; with: coloc ptk1 plb ptk1 sec a1
  - **coryza**; during: anac b4a.de
  - **crossing** legs agg.: alum k* valer ptk1
  - **dancing**: *Sulph*
  - **delivery**; during: nux-v
  - **descending**, on: coca
  - **diarrhea**, with: jatr-c kr1 sec a1
  - **drawing** off boots: conin c1
  - **drawing** up knee: coff
  - **drawing** up leg agg.: kali-c nit-ac
  - **dysentery**; during: merc-c ptk1
  - **exertion** agg.; after: sil h2*
  - **fear** agg.: lach bg1*
  - **flat**; muscles become: jatr-c hr1*
  - **flexing** leg, on: cocc coff k* kali-c k* nux-v k*
  - **lifting** the foot: agar k*
  - **lying**:
    - **agg.**: bry k* led k* mag-c sel
    - **amel.**: anac
    - **Side** lain on: staph
  - **menses** | **before** | **agg.**: *Phos* vib bg3*
    - **during** | **agg.**: cupr phos verat wies a1*
  - **mortification**; from: *Coloc*
  - **motion**:
    - **agg.**: bapt k* bufo calc k* coca hyos ign k* lyc k* nux-m k* tritic-vg fd5.de
      - **lying** agg.: nux-m
    - **amel.**: androc srj1• arg-met bry k* ferr k* rhus-t k*
    - **feet**; of | **agg.**: cham h1
  - **pregnancy** agg.; during: cham bro1 *Cupr* bro1 mag-p bro1 nux-v bro1 **Sep** k • *Verat* bro1 vib sf*
  - **pressing** foot to floor | **amel.**: cupr bg1 cupr-ar ptk1 ign bg1 nux-m bg1 zinc-i ptk1
  - **pulling** on boots agg.: *Calc* conin a1 nit-ac h2*
  - **rest** | **amel.**: stroph-s sp1
  - **rising** | **bed**; from | **agg.**: ferr mag-c
    - **sitting**; from | **agg.**: alum *Anac*
  - **running** agg.: stroph-s sp1
  - **sitting**:
    - **agg.**: aids nl2• dulc fd4.de ign lyc olnd plat **Rhus-t**
    - **walking**; after: plat **Rhus-t**
  - **sleep**:
    - **before**: *Nux-m*
    - **during** | **agg.**: ant-t k* graph inul k* *Kali-c* nat-m petr-ra shn4• tep k*
  - **standing**:
    - **agg.**: euphr k* ferr k* nat-m k* stroph-s sp1
      - **long** time; for a: euphr k*
    - **amel.**: cupr-ar ptk1
    - **toes** agg.; on: alum h2
  - **stepping** agg.: *Sulph* k*
  - **stool** | **after** | **agg.**: med c1 ox-ac trom
    - **during** | **agg.**: apis ptk1 podo c1* sec ptk1 verat ptk1
  - **stretching**:
    - **agg.**:
      - **bed** agg.; in: **CALC** k •* carl cham cupr tl1 lyss nat-c pin-s *Sulph* k*
      - **waking**; on: aspar
      - **walking** agg.: phos
    - **foot** | **agg.**: chin nit-ac thuj
    - **leg**:
      - **agg.**: bar-c bufo **CALC** k • carl **Lyc** k • nat-c h2 nept-m lsd2.fr **Nux-v** k • **Sep** k • **Sulph** k •
      - **amel.**: bell h1 *Cupr* ptk1

- Calves: ...
  - tailors: anac bro1* anag bro1 mag-p bro1*
  - **taking** off boots: conin c1
  - **thinking** about it: spong staph
  - **turning** foot while sitting: nat-m k*
  - **turning** in bed agg.: mag-c k* zinc h2
  - **waking**; on: (↗*SLEEP - Waking - cramps - calves*) graph kl lob kl ruta fd4.de staph kl tritic-vg fd5.de verat-v kl
  - **walking**:
    - **after** | **agg.**: carb-an k* plat **RHUS-T** k ●
    - **agg.**: agar k* am-c k* **Anac** k* arg-met arg-n k* ars k* berb k* **Calc-p** k* cann-s k* cinnb ptk1 coca dulc k* ign k* kali-n h2* lact k* lyc k* mag-m k* nat-m k* nit-ac pitu-gl skp7• puls k* sul-ac k* **Sulph** k*
    - **amel.**: verat ptk1
  - **warm** room | **amel.**: petr-ra shn4•
  - **extending** to | **Heel**: valer ptk1
- **Tendo** Achillis: arist-m a1 *Calc Caust* k* dios a1 petr h2*
  - **night** | **bed** agg.; in: *Caust*

- **Lower** limbs: agar bg2 alum bg2 ambr k* ang b7.de* ant-c b7.de* ant-t k* arg-n bg2 ars k* ars-i k2 bar-c b4.de* bell b4.de* bism b7.de* bov b4.de* bufo bg2 cain *Calc* k* calc-sil k2 *Camph* bg2 cedr k* cham ptk1 cimic cina k* **Coloc** k* crot-h **Cupr** k* cupr-ar a1 dros b7.de* elaps eup-per *Euphr* b7a.de *Ferr Ferr-m* gels bg2 graph k* hep b4a.de hyos k* iod *Ip* b7a.de jatr-c kali-bi k* kali-m ptk1 kali-n b4.de* kali-s k* kola stb3• kreos b7a.de lac-c bg2 lac-h sk4• lat-m bnm6• med ptk1 meny b7a.de* merc-c b4a.de merc-n k* merc-ns merc-pr-r mur-ac k* nit-ac b4.de* oena k* ph-ac k* phos k* phyt k* pic-ac k* *Plat* b4a.de plb k* *Rhus-t* b7a.de sacch-a fd2.de• sec k* sep sil k* spong b7a.de* stram b7.de* stront-c ptk1 *Sulph* ptk1 tarent k* tritic-vg fd5.de valer k2 vanil fd5.de *Verat* b7a.de vip k* zinc zinc-m a1 zinc-p k2
  - **right**: bufo
  - **left**: kola stb3• propr sa3•
  - **morning**: bov bry kola stb3• nit-ac tritic-vg fd5.de
  - **afternoon** | **14** h: propr sa3•
  - **evening**: jatr-c sil
  - **night**: *Ambr* ars bry calad carb-v eug *Eup-per* iod ip lachn lyc mag-c mag-m nit-ac nux-v *Rhus-t* sec sep staph sulph
  - **bending** foot forward: coff
  - **coition**; during: ign dgt
  - **colic**; with: coloc
  - **crossing** legs agg.: alum
  - **descending** stairs agg.: arg-met
  - **drawing** on boot: *Calc*
  - **lifting** legs, when: coff
  - **sitting** agg.: olnd paeon *Rhus-t*
  - **standing** agg.: euph euphr
  - **stepping** out, when: alum k*
  - **walking** | **after** | **agg.**: nit-ac
    - **agg.**: am-c carb-v *Lyc* nit-ac rhus-t sep
      - **sitting**; after: nit-ac h2
  - ▽ **extending** to | **Leg**: bar-c *Calc*
  - ○ **Bones**: nat-c bg2 nat-m bg2 sulph bg2

- **Nates**: bamb-a stb2.de• bell k* bry cann-s k* caust k* *Cycl* b7a.de graph k* hyos b7.de* kola stb3• mang b4.de* nept-m lsd2.fr ph-ac b4.de* plat b4.de* rhus-t k* *Sep* verat b7.de*
  - **night** | **bed** agg.; in: *Sep*
  - **standing** agg.: bamb-a stb2.de• rhus-t
  - **stooping** agg.: bell h1 cann-s
  - **stretching** out limbs: sep h2*

- **Shoulders**: cimic k* elaps k* lil-t k* lyc bg2 *Naja* bg2* *Plat* k* [sol-ecl cky1]
  - **evening**: orig a1
    - **18** h: elaps
  - **pressure**; hard | **amel.**: [sol-ecl cky1]
  - ▽ **extending** to | **Hand**: elaps

- **Thighs**: abrot bro1 aesc-g bro1 *Agar* k* agn b7.de* alum a1 am-br bro1 *Am-m* bro1 ambr k* anac b4.de* ang b7.de* ant-c b7.de* ant-t bg2* *Arg-met* k* arn b7.de* *Ars* k* ars-i k2 *Asar* k* aur bg2 bamb-a stb2.de• bapt bro1 bar-c bro1 bell k* brach k* bry b7.de* calc bro1* *Camph* bg2* cann-s k* carb-ac bro1 carb-an k* carb-v k* *Carbn-s Caust* bro1 chel bg1* chin b7.de* cho bro1 cimic bro1 *Cimx* bro1 cina k* *Cocc* bro1 colch b7.de* **Coloc** k* con b4.de* crot-h k* cupr bg2* *Cupr-ar* bro1 cycl k* dig k* digin a1 dulc fd4.de eupi bro1 *Ferr* k* ferr-ar ferr-p gels a1* ham fd3.de• hep k* *Hyos* k* hyper bro1 iod k* ip irid-met bro1 jatr-c bro1 kali-ar *Kali-bi* k* *Kali-c* k* kali-m k2 kali-p kola stb3• lac-loxod-a hrn2• lath bro1 lol bro1 *Lyc* k* lyss mag-m b4.de* *Mag-p* bro1 mang k* med bro1 meny b7.de* merc b4.de* merc-c bg2* mosch b7.de* mur-ac k* nad rly4• naja k* nit-ac bg2* nux-v bg2* ol-an ox-ac bro1 *Petr* k* ph-ac pin-s bro1 *Plat* k* plb k* podo c1 *Puls* k* ran-b k* rhus-t k* ribo rly4• ruta k* sabin samb b7.de* sarcol-ac bro1 *Sec* k* *Sep* k* *Sil* bro1 sol-t bro1 stry k* sul-i k2 **Sulph** k* tarent k* tep k* ter thuj b4.de* tritic-vg fd5.de ust bro1 valer k* vanil fd5.de verat k* *Verb* k* vip bro1 wies a1 zinc-s bro1
  - **right**: calam sa3• dulc fd4.de sulph k* tarent k* tritic-vg fd5.de
  - **left**: anthraq rly4• cina dulc fd4.de ham fd3.de• luf-op rsj5• rhus-t k* zinc-i bg1 [tax jsj7]
    - **walking** agg.: luf-op rsj5•
  - **daytime**: petr
  - **afternoon**: calam sa3•
  - **evening**: bell k*
    - **bed** agg.; in: *Ars*
  - **night**: *Ambr* calam sa3• calc mrr1 carb-an k* ham fd3.de• hep k* *Ip* kali-c
  - **ascending** stairs agg.: carb-v
  - **bed** agg.; in: calc mrr1 mur-ac h2*
  - **dancing**; while: kola stb3•
  - **flexing** leg: plat h2*
  - **intermittent**: plat h2*
  - **menses**; during: wies k*
  - **pulsating**: plat h2*
  - **raising** thigh: carb-v h2* hep h2*
  - **sitting** agg.: iod mag-m ptk1 meny ptk1 plat
  - **sleep** | **during** | **agg.**: *Kali-c*
    - **going** to sleep; on | **agg.**: tep
  - **stretching** agg.: calc mrr1
  - **walking**:
    - **agg.**: agn a1 carb-v h2 *Sep* tritic-vg fd5.de
    - **air** agg.; in open: *Verb*
  - ○ **Anterior** part | **menses**; before: dict ptk1 xan ptk1
  - **Inner** side: gels bg2* kali-bi bg2* nat-c sne nicotam rly4• plat h2* sep h2* tritic-vg fd5.de
    - **extending** to | **Foot**: calam sa3•
  - **Outer** side: ant-c h2* carb-v a1
  - **Posterior** part: ang a1 cann-s a1 dios a1 plat h2*

- **Thumbs**: agar k* aml-ns anac h2* anag hr1 asaf k* conin c1 mang k* nat-m k* plat h2* podo fd3.de• valer k*
  - **holding** objects: graph h2*
  - **playing** piano: zinc h2*
  - **twitching**, with: valer k*
  - **writing** agg.: agar h2 aml-ns bell h1 brach *Cycl* mur-ac h2*
    - **accompanied** by | **Finger**; contraction of first: cycl ptk1
  - ○ **Adductor** muscles: merc h1
  - **Extensor** muscles: zinc h2

- **Toes**: allox tpw4 *Am-c* k* am k* *Ars* k* *Asaf* bar-c k* *Bar-m* k* beryl tpw5 **Calc** k* calc-sil k2 cann-s k* carb-an k* carb-v b4a.de carbn-h carbn-s **Caust** k* *Cham Chel* coc-c k* *Crot-h Cupr* k* cupr-act ptk1 *Cupr-ar* dig digin a1 dios br1 *Ferr* k* ferr-p gels graph b4.de* *Hep* k* hura hyos b7.de* ign b7.de* *Kali-c* k* lil-t k* *Lyc* k* m-ambo b7.de* m-aust b7.de merc b4a.de mosch k* nat-c k* nat-m b4.de* nicc k* *Nux-v* k* ol-an k* ox-ac bg1 petr b4.de* *Ph-ac* phos k* phyt plat k* plb k* psor k* rhus-t *Ruta* b7.de* sang *Sec* k* sep k* sil k* stry k* sulph k* tab k* tarent k* thuj b4.de* v-a-b jl verat ptk1 verat-v zinc-chr ptk1
  - **right**: chlam-tr bcx2• coc-c bg1*
  - **morning** | **bed** agg.; in: nicc
  - **afternoon** | **17** h: lil-t

Extremities

- **evening**: petr h2* ruta fd4.de
  - **bed** agg.; in: ars
- **night**: calc k* coc-c k* form a1 kiss a1
  - **midnight** | **bed** agg.; in: nux-v
  - **bed** agg.; in: *Ars* merc-i-f
- **alternating** with:
  - **menses**; painful: dios ptk1
  - **Glottis**; spasm of: *Asaf*
- **bed** agg.; in: allox tpw4*
- **delivery**; during: cupr
- **lying** agg.: coc-c bg1
- **menses**; during: sulph k*
- **pregnancy** agg.; during: *Calc* k*
- **stretching** out foot: bar-c h2* psor k* sulph k*
- ○ **Back** of: merc bg1 ox-ac bg1
- **Fifth**: coc-c k*
  - **night**: coc-c k*
    - **lying**; on: coc-c
- **First**: calc-p coloc k* gamb k* kali-c k* nux-v k* plat h2* psor k* sil k* tarent k*
  - **night** | **lying** down agg.: chin-b kr1
  - **bed** agg.; in: gamb k*
  - **stretching** out foot; on: psor
  - **walking** agg.: gamb *Sil*
- **Fourth**: coc-c k*
  - **night**: coc-c k*
    - **lying**; on: coc-c
- **Joints**: cham b7.de* nux-v b7.de*
- **Muscles** | **Flexor** muscles: dios
- **Second**: sep k*
- **Third**: coc-c k* iod
  - **night**: coc-c k*
    - **lying**; on: coc-c

- **Upper** arms: agar arg-met k* asaf b7.de* bell k* cina b7.de* com k* jatr-c kr1 kali-bi k* lact a1 lil-t k* lyc mag-c h2* meny b7.de* mur-ac k* olnd b7.de* petr k* *Ph-ac* rhus-t ruta b7.de* spong fd4.de sulph k* valer k*
  - **exertion** agg.: mur-ac k*
  - **holding** something in hand; on: petr h2 rhus-t valer
  - **motion** agg.: petr h2
  - **raising** arm agg.: arg-met
  - **writing** agg.: valer ptk1
  - ○ **Biceps**: ruta valer k*
  - **Deltoid**: petr h2* urt-u a1
  - **Inner** side: sulph k*
- **Upper** limbs: agar k* alum k* **Am-c** k* *Ang* b7a.de ant-t ars k* ars-i k2 atra-r bnm3• *Bell* k* bism b7.de* bry b7a.de* bufo cact **Calc** k* *Camph* b7a.de* *Cann-s* b7.de* caps k* carb-v k* carbn-s caust k* chin bg2 cimic k* *Cina* b7a.de cit-v k* coff bg2 **Coloc** k* crot-c k* cupr k* dios k* dros b7.de* eupi k* fl-ac k* graph k* guaj bg2 guare k* hell b7a.de hura hyper k* iod k* ip b7.de* *Jatr-c* kali-i k* kali-n b4.de* kali-s k* lac-h sk4• lach k* lyc k* lyss m-ambo b7.de m-arct b7.de mag-m bg2 *Meny* b7a.de merc k* *Merc-c* b4a.de mosch b7a.de mur-ac b4.de* *Nat-m* nux-v k* olnd b7a.de* **Ph-ac** lp phos k* plat b4a.de* plb k* rhod bg2 sabad b7a.de sec k* *Sil* b4.de* spong fd4.de sul-ac b4a.de* sulph k* *Tab* tril-p valer *Verat* b7.de*
  - **right**: am-c bg1 bufo carb-v bg1 fl-ac bg1 hura bg1 merc bg1
  - **left**: alum bg1 bell bg1 cact caps h1* cit-v bg1 corn bg1 hyper bg1
  - **morning**: fl-ac k*
  - **evening**: spong fd4.de
    - **21** h: lyc
  - **night**: cit-v a1
    - **midnight** | **before** | **waking**; on: caust k*
      - **after**: sulph
  - ○ **Joints**: *Anac* b4a.de *Aur* b4a.de bov b4a.de *Plat* b4a.de
- **Wrists**: aml-ns anac bov bg2 calc-p k* cina cit-v k* com k* euphr k* hura nat-p k* *Ph-ac* plb staph k* sulph

Cramps – Wrists: ...
  - **right**: hura staph k*
  - **left**: sulph k*
  - **coldness** in part: plb
  - **motion** agg.: calc-p k*
  - **stretched** out; when arm is: cina
  - **writing** agg.: aml-ns *Arg-met* bro1 arn bro1 bell bro1 bell-p bro1 brach *Caust* bro1 *Con* bro1 *Cupr* bro1 cycl bro1 ferr-i bro1 *Gels* bro1 *Mag-p* bro1 nux-v bro1 pic-ac bro1 ran-b bro1 *Ruta* bro1 sec bro1 sil bro1 *Stann* bro1 staph bro1 *Stry* bro1 sul-ac bro1 viol-o bro1 zinc bro1

CRAWLING, creeping (See Formication)

CREAKING (See Cracking)

CREEPING (See Formication)

CREPITATION in joints (See Cracking)

CRIPPLED: | **poliomyelitis**; after: calc-p gm1 calc-s gm1 nat-ar gm1

CRIPPLED nails (See Nails - stunted)

CROSSED: | **sensation** as if:
- ○ **Fingers**: bell bg2 carb-v bg2* graph bg2*
  - **Tips**: staph bg2
- ○ - **Lower** limbs: gels ptk1 lil-t ptk1 murx ptk1 rhod ptk1 *Sep* ptk1 thuj ptk1
  - **walking** agg.: lath k*

CROSSING: | **amel.**; crossing extremities | **Lower** limbs: gels bg2 nux-v bg2 rhod bg2 sep bg2 thuj bg2 vib bg2 zinc bg2
- ○ - **Legs**: *(↗GENERALS - Crossing; GENERALS - Crossing of)*
  - **agg.**: agar b4.de* alum b4a.de* ang b7.de* arn b7.de* asaf b7.de* aur b4.de* bell b4.de* dig b4.de* kali-n b4.de* laur b7.de* mur-ac b4.de* nux-v b7.de* phos b4.de* plat b4.de* rheum b7.de* rhus-t b7.de* squil b7.de* valer b7.de* verb b7.de*
    - **Thighs**: agar ptk1
  - **amel.**: ant-t ptk1 lil-t ptk1 murx ptk1 rhod ptk1 sep bg1* *Thuj* bg1* zinc hr
  - **impossible**: *Lath* k*
    - **sitting** agg.: lath br1
  - **unconsciously**: cench k2
  - **uncross** them when lying or sitting; cannot: bell ptk1 ther ptk1

CURVATURE of bones: *(↗Curving; Deformed)* am-c b2.de* **Asaf** b2.de *Bell* b2.de calc b2.de* cic b2.de ferr b2.de hep b2.de* iod b2.de* ip b2.de kali-c mtf33 *Lyc* b2.de **Merc** b2.de mez b2.de *Nit-ac* b2.de petr b2.de ph-ac b2.de *Phos* b2.de plb b2.de *Puls* b2.de rhod b2.de ruta b2.de *Sep* b2.de **Sil** b2.de staph b2.de *Sulph* b2.de symph tl1 syph mtf33

CURVED fingernails (See Nails - curved)

CURVING and bowing: *(↗Curvature)* ambr b7a.de ant-t b7a.de bac jl2 *Calc* k* calc-f bnf1.es *Calc-p* k* carb-an b4a.de caust b4a.de chin b7a.de cina b7a.de colch b7a.de *Coloc* b4a.de con b4a.de cupr bnf1.es euph b4a.de *Graph* b4a.de *Guaj* b4a.de *Hyos* b7a.de kali-c b4a.de lyc k* m-aust b7a.de mang bnf1.es meny b7a.de merc b4a.de merc-c b4a.de nat-m bnf1.es* *Phos* b4a.de plb b7a.de rhus-t b7a.de *Sec* b7a.de *Sil* k* stram b7a.de sulph b4a.de syph k2* zinc bnf1.es
- ○ - **Foot**:
  - ○ **Sole** | **contraction** of flexors; from: ruta tl1
- **Legs**: *Ph-ac* b4a.de *Staph* b7a.de *Sulph* b4a.de
  - **straightening** impossible: cic bro1
- **Toes**: graph bro1

CUSHIONS; as if walking on: ulm-c jsj8•

CUTTING with shears agg.: con bg2

DARKNESS agg.: | **Lower** limbs: zinc bg2

DEADNESS (See Numbness)

DEFORMED: *(↗Curvature)*
- ○ - **Bones** (See Curvature)
- **Fingers**: ambr bg2 anac bg2 arg-met bg2 *Calc* bg2 caust bg2 cina bg2 cocc bg2 coff bg2 colch bg2 ferr bg2 *Graph* bg2 lyc bg2 nux-v bg2 phos bg2 plat bg2 **Ruta** bg2 sec bg2 sil bg2

- **Fingers**: ...
○ · **Joints**: kali-c ptk1 lyc ptk1 med jl2
- **Hands**: anac bg2 caust tl1 *Lach* bg2 med tl1 **Merc** bg2 nux-v bg2 sec bg2
○ · **Back** of hands: plb a1
· **Joints** (See GENERALS - Inflammation - joints - deformans)
- **Joints**: kali-c mtf33
- **Nails** (See Nails - distorted)
- **Upper** limbs: ant-c bg2 lyc bg2 sec bg2

DESCENDING:
- **stairs**:
· **agg.** | **Lower** limbs: am-m b7.de* arg-met b7.de* ars bg2 bar-c b4.de* bell b4.de* bry b7.de* canth b7.de* coff b7.de* kali-bi bg2 lyc b4.de* mang bg2 nit-ac b4.de* plb b7.de* rhod b4a.de ruta b7.de* sabin b7.de* stann b4.de* sulph b4.de* verat b7.de* verb b7.de*

DESQUAMATION (See Eruptions - desquamating)

DETACHED (See Separated)

DIRTY:
○ - **Hands**: allox sp1
- **Nails** | **Fingernails**: but-ac sp1

DISCOLORATION: (↗*Raynaud's*)
- **blackness**: ars tarent k* vip k*
- **blotches**: berb cimx cocc hura lac-e hm2•
· **red**: lach sulph k*
- **blue**: agar apis arg-n k2 beryl sp1 bism bol-la both-a rb3 **Carb-v** *Crot-c* cyt-l a1 *Dig* dros k2 kali-ar *Lach* laur br1 lyss *Merc* naja k2 nat-f sp1 nat-m k2 *Op* oxyum-sc mcp1• rob sulfa sp1 thymol sp1 tub-a jl2 verat k2* zinc-m a1
· **chill**; during: nat-m k2
· **dark** | **menses**; during: verat k2
· **menses**; during: verat tl1
· **pressure** agg.: both-a rb3
○ · **Hands**:
⁝ **chill**; during: apis b7a.de nux-v b7a.de
⁝ **fever**; during: am-c bg2 apis bg2 calc bg2 camph bg2 *Cupr* bg2 samb bg2 **Verat** bg2
· **Lower** limbs: bufo bg2
- **dark** colored: vip k*
- **ecchymoses** (See Ecchymoses)
- **gray**; dirty: sec k2
- **greenish** yellow: vip k*
- **lead** colored: sec
- **lividity**: agar bapt chlol k* ox-ac k* phos k* sul-ac k*
· **spots**, in: bapt k* vip k*
⁝ **alternating** with | **redness** (See redness - alternating - livid)
· **yellowish**: vip k*
- **marbled**: berb *Thuj*
- **mottled**: *Ars* k* **Lach** zinc-m a1
- **paleness**: glon k2 hydr-ac k* naja ox-ac k* rob k* sec k*
- **purple**: apis *Verat-v* zinc k* zinc-m a1
· **spots**; in: apis *Lach*
- **redness**: *Bell* k* carbn-o merc-n k* merc-ns sep k* stram vip k*
· **alternating** with | **livid** spots: chlol
· **blotches**: dream-p sdj1• lach sulph k*
· **disappearing** on pressure: chinin-s kali-br k* verat-v
· **spots**, in: cadm-s elaps lach vip k*
⁝ **bluish** red: vip k*
⁝ **burning**: berb ph-ac h2* sulph tab
⁝ **itching**: berb cocc mrr1 euph zinc
⁝ **night** | **bed** agg.; in: cocc mrr1
⁝ **swollen**: plb
⁝ **washing** agg.; after: sulph
- **white** | **spots**: (↗*SKIN - Discoloration - white - spots*) ozone sde2•
- **yellowish**: crot-h tl1 phos k*
· **spots**, in: vip k*

Discoloration: ...
○ - **Ankle**:
· **blue** spots: *Sul-ac* sulph h2*
· **chronic**: stront-c mtf11
· **cyanosis**: ser-a-c jl2
· **dark**, spreading up the limb: naja
· **purple**: arn k* *Lach* k*
⁝ **spots**: **Sul-ac**
· **redness**: apis ars-h calc k* *Cham* k* lac-ac *Lach* lyc k* mang b4.de* mim-h a1 pall c1 rhus-t k* rhus-v a1 stann b4.de* sul-ac k*
⁝ **left**: mim-h a1*
⁝ **spots**, in: calc k* cortiso tpw7 lyc b4.de* **Sul-ac** k*
⁝ **left**: cortiso tpw7*
⁝ **afternoon**: lyc
⁝ **streaks**: ferr-ma k*
· **sensation**: limen-b-c hrn2•
· **tetter**: all-s k*
· **white** in spots: *Calc* k*
- **Elbow**:
· **brown** spots: cadm-s *Lach* *Petr* b4a.de sep k*
· **red**: *Ant-c* b7a.de
⁝ **spots**: *Phos* k*
· **spots**: calc *Sep* k* vip
- **Feet**:
· **redness** | **Joints**: lyc mang stann
- **Fingers**: act-sp k* sec a1
· **black**: sec k* vip k*
· **blue**: *Agar* bg2* alum-sil k2 ars-s-f k2 ben-n *Carb-v* bg2* caust *Cocc* corn crat br1 *Crot-h* *Cupr* k* dig k2 ham fd3.de• laur bg2 nat-m nux-m nux-v op k* ox-ac bg2* *Petr* k* ruta fd4.de *Sec* b7.de* *Sil* vip k*
⁝ **morning**: petr k*
⁝ **chill**; during: ars k2 sec gk
⁝ **cold**, and: crat br1 ox-ac mrr1 sec gk
⁝ **excitement** agg.: crat br1
⁝ **exertion** agg.: crat br1
⁝ **Toes**, and: crat br1
· **bronze** | **Tip**: tub c1
· **brown**:
⁝ **spots**: ant-t chlam-tr bcx2•
⁝ **right**: chlam-tr bcx2•
⁝ **Nails**; pigmentation around: naphtin bro1
· **freckles**: ferr
· **greenish**: colch k*
· **livid**: brass a1 chinin-s ox-ac k*
· **pale**: both-ax tsm2 calc k2 cic bg2 *Kreos* bg2* lach bg2 sec bg2 verat b7.de*
⁝ **accompanied** by | **Head**; complaints of (See HEAD - Complaints - accompanied - fingers - pale)
· **redness**: **Acon** bg2 *Agar* k* apis apoc arg-n arist-cl sp1 arum-i arum-t benz-ac berb *Borx* k* cann-i k* *Cit-v* k* cortiso sp1 fl-ac k* graph k* kali-bi k* lach laur bg2 *Lyc* k* mag-c bg2 mur-ac bg2* *Nux-v* k* plb ran-b bg2 rhod bg2 sil spong fd4.de sulph k* ther k* *Thuj* k* tritic-vg fd5.de vanil fd5.de zinc
⁝ **right**: abrom-a ks5
⁝ **evening**: sulph k*
⁝ **blotches**: arg-n
⁝ **burnt**; as if: plut-n srj7• tritic-vg fd5.de
⁝ **chilblains**; like: borx c1
⁝ **cold** air; from: borx a1
⁝ **dark** red | **marbled**: nat-m b4.de*
⁝ **frostbitten**, as if: borx a1 lyc h2*
⁝ **points**: lach k*
⁝ **spots**: agar k2 benz-ac k* card-b a1 cor-r k* lach bg2 ph-ac h2* plb k* spong fd4.de zinc k*
⁝ **stripes**: apis
⁝ **Nails**; around: ozone sde2•

Extremities

- **spots**: ant-t bg2 *Con* k* corn ferr bg2 lyc mang k* *Nat-m* k* *Ph-ac* k* *Plb* k* sabad bg2
- **violet**: stry k*
- **white**: gins helo-s bnm14• lach k* vip k*
  - **coldness**; during: *(↗Raynaud's)* gins
  - **spots**: ozone sde2•
- **yellow**: ant-t k* *Chel* k* con k* elaps ign b7.de* ph-ac k* sabad k* *Sil* b4a.de
  - **spots**; in: ant-t k* bism con k* elaps lyc b4a.de petr b4.de* sabad k*
- ○ **Back**:
  - **red**: cortiso tpw7*
    - **chilblains**; after: berb hr1
  - **Ring**; under wedding: cob-n sp1
- **First**:
  - **black**: phos k*
    - **spots**: apis rhus-t k*
  - **redness**:
    - **blotches**: arg-n
    - **Back** of: arg-n
- **Fourth** | **redness**: lyc
- **Joints**: cann-s *Cham* chel cinnb *Lyc* pall spong sulph
  - **red**: *Cham* b7a.de **Lyc** bg2 spong bg2 sulph bg2
- **Nails**: ant-c k* ars k* ars-br vh graph mur-ac b4.de nit-ac k* thuj k*
  - **black**: *Ars* k* *Graph* k* *Lept* vh *Nat-m* vh
    - **Around**: **Nat-m** vh
  - **blood** settles under nails: apis
  - **blueness**: acon k* aesc k* agar am-c h2* apis apoc *Arg-n* arn *Ars* asaf aur k* aur-ar k2 aur-s k2 cact *Camph* *Carb-v* k* carbn-s *Chel* k* *Chin* k* chinin-ar *Chinin-s* chlf k* cic cocc k* colch k* con k* *Cupr* *Dig* k* *Dros* k* eup-pur *Ferr* ferr-ar ferr-p gels k* gins k* *Graph* ip lyc h2* manc k* merc k* merc-sul *Mez* mur-ac k* *Nat-m* k* *Nit-ac* k* nit-s-d c1 **Nux-v** k* op k* *Ox-ac* *Petr* k* ph-ac k* *Phos* plb k* rhus-t k* rhus-v a1 samb xxb1 sang sars k* sep *Sil* k* *Sulph* k* sumb k* tarent *Thuj* k* **Verat** *Verat-v*
    - **accompanied** by | **Abdomen**; pain in (See ABDOMEN - Pain - cramping - accompanied - nails)
    - **chill**; during: apis arn **Ars** ars-s-f k2 *Asaf* *Carb-v* k* carbn-s *Chel* *Chin* *Chinin-s* *Cocc* con k* *Dros* eup-per bro1 *Eup-pur* k* *Ferr* hr1 ip kali-ar meny bro1 mez mur-ac h2* **Nat-m** k* **Nux-v** k* petr ph-ac psor al2 **Rhus-t** sulph thuj verat k*
    - **fever**; during: ip bg2 laur bg2 nux-v bg2 **Sil** hr1
    - **menses**; during: *Arg-n* *Thuj*
    - **perspiration**; during: *Chel* bg2 chin bg2 cocc bg2 dig bg2 nat-m bg2 *Nit-ac* bg2 sil bg2
  - **dark**: morph k* ox-ac k*
  - **gray**: merc-c k* *Sil* k*
  - **livid**: ars k* *Colch* op k* *Ox-ac* k* sul-ac k*
  - **Mees'** lines (See white - stripes)
  - **purple**: androc srj1• apis ars k* op k* samb sec k* stram k*
  - **red**: ars k* crot-c k* lith-c
    - **black**; then: *Ars* k*
    - **Root**: cortiso tpw7* upa br1*
  - **white**: cupr k* nit-ac sil h2* spong fd4.de
    - **spots**: *Alum* k* ars k* calc k2 ina-i mlk9.de **Nit-ac** k* ozone sde2• ph-ac podo fd3.de• sep k* **Sil** k* spig bg2 spong fd4.de **Sulph** k* thal dx thuj bg2 tritic-vg fd5.de tub k* [tax jsj7]
    - **stripes** (= broad band shaped stripes): thal-xyz srj8•
  - **yellow**: am-c ambr aur bell bry canth carb-v cham chin **Con** k* ferr ign lyc *Merc* *Nit-ac* *Nux-v* op plb **Sep** **Sil** k* spig *Sulph*
- **Second**:
  - **redness**:
    - **Joints**; of | **Middle**: ars-h k*
- **Third**:
  - **marbled** | **Nail**; near: nat-m h2
- **Tips**:
  - **black**: sol-ni
  - **blue**: agar apis bg2 borx colch crot-c op ozone sde2• phos tub-d jl2 tub-m jl2

- **Fingers – Tips – blue**: ...
    - **evening**: phos
    - **cold** agg.; becoming: ozone sde2•
  - **brown**: tub ptk1*
  - **redness**: acon ptk1 berb k* calc fago mur-ac k* ozone sde2• thuj hr1
    - **chilblains**; after: berb k*
  - **white**: alum der fl-ac
  - **yellow** in spots: elaps

- **Foot**:
  - **blackness**: ant-c tl1 crot-h sol-ni vip k*
  - **blueness**: *Arg-n* arn borx dros elaps kali-br *Kali-c* lach led limest-b es1• *Mur-ac* oena k* oxyurn-sc mcp1• phos k* puls rhus-t sars k2 sep stram k* tub gk verat vip k*
    - **spots**; in: kreos sulph
  - **livid**: merc-c k* ox-ac k* stram k*
  - **pale**: **Apis** chin ph-ac
  - **purple**: led tl1 op k* sec k*
    - **spots**; in: apis led tl1 sec k2
  - **redness**: agar k* apis arg-met bg2 *Arn* b7.de* ars b4.de* aur b4a.de **Bry** b7.de* calc k* carb-v k* *Carbn-s* *Chin* b7a.de graph k* hyos k* lach k* nat-c k* ped a1 phos k* *Puls* k* rhus-t sars k* sep *Sil* k* stann k* thuj k* urt-u tl1 vesp k* vip zinc k*
    - **evening**: apis
    - **menses**; during: puls k2
    - **spots**; in: *Acon* b7.de* apis ars k* bry chin k* elaps *Lach* led k* lyc mang phyt squil b7.de* thuj k*
      - **burning**: ars h2
  - **sensation**: limen-b-c hrn2•
  - **spots**: ang bg2 cimic bg2 led ptk1 phos h2*
    - **white**: apis morg-p fmm1•
  - **white**: marb-w es1•
  - **yellow**-grayish: vip k*
  - ○ **Back** of:
    - **blue**: vip k*
    - **marbled**: *Caust* thuj
    - **redness**: *Rhus-t* k* thuj k*
      - **morning** | **8** h: *Rhus-t*
      - **spots**: carbn-o puls k* thuj k*
  - **Ball** of:
    - **redness**: rhus-t
      - **spots**: rhus-t b7.de*
  - **Heel**:
    - **purplish**: puls k*
    - **redness**: ant-c *Petr* k* raph a1 *Thuj* b4a.de
  - **Sole** of:
    - **blue**: med k2
      - **spots**: kali-p
    - **redness**: bry k* kali-c k* phos k* *Puls*
      - **spots**; in: *Ars*
    - **spots**: ars bg2
    - **white** spots: nat-m k*
      - **bleached**; as if: bar-c plb

- **Forearm**:
  - **blotches**: cimx hura *Tell* rsj10•
  - **blue**: apis arg-n bism k* plat *Samb* b7.de* sep sulph k2
  - **bluish** spots: **Sul-ac** k*
  - **brown**: petr-ra shn4•
  - **dark**: acon ant-c *Ars* caust com sep
  - **lividity**: *Ars* vesp vip k*
  - **mottled**: *Crot-h* k* **Lach** spong fd4.de
  - **purple** spots: *Kali-c* kali-p
  - **redness**: anac k* *Apis* arn bell colch k* hura kreos mang rhus-t k* spong fd4.de
    - **right**: osteo-a jl2
    - **dark** red | **marbled**: thuj b4a.de

- **redness**: ...
  - **spots**; in: agn b7.de* *Ars* berb borx chel *Euph* k* kali-n h2 mag-m h2 *Merc* k* olnd rhus-v spong fd4.de sulph k* tarent tax thuj k* vesp
  - **streaks**: anthraci euph b4a.de*
    - **itching** on touch: euph h2* kali-n h2*
  - **touch** agg.: mim-p rsj8•
- **spots**: carbn-o mang mill nat-m
  - **left**: mim-p rsj8• sel rsj9•
- **white** spots: *Berb* ozone sde2•

○ • **Back** | **dark** brown spots: guat sp1

- **Hand**:
- **black**: sol-ni spira a1 sul-ac k* tarent k* vip k*
  - **dots**, in: petr k*
  - **spots**, in: sol-ni
- **blotches**: ars k* sep k*
  - **itching**: sep k* *Tell* rsj10•
- **blueness**●: acon k* aesc agar k* am-c k* aml-ns bro1 *Ant-c* *Ant-t* k* *Apis* k* *Arg-n* k* **Arn** k* *Ars* k* bar-c k* ben-n borx k* both-ax tsm2 *Brom* *Cact* *Calc* b4a.de *Camph* k* *Carb-an* k* *Carb-v* k* *Chinin-ar* *Cocc* k* con k* *Crot-h* k* crot-t k* cupr k* *Dig* k* dros elaps k* helo helo-s rwt2• inul k* *Kali-c* k* **Lach** k* *Laur* k* merc-c bg2 morph k* naja bg2 *Nit-ac* bro1 **Nux-v** k* oena k* olnd bro1 op bg2 ox-ac bg2 oxyurn-sc mcp1• ph-ac k* phos *Plb* k* puls rhus-t samb k* sec b7.de* *Spong* k* *Stram* k* stront-c bro1 stry k* tab thuj bg2 tub hr* *Verat* k* *Verat-v* vip bg2 *Zinc* k* zinc-p k2
  - **morning**: spong k*
  - **night**: phos samb k*
    - **waking** agg.; after: samb
  - **chill**; during: acon bg2 am-c bg2 apis b7a.de* *Camph* cocc b7.de* dros h1* nux-v k* ph-ac h2* sec bg2 *Spong* k* stram **Verat** k* zinc bg2
  - **cold** | **washing** agg.; after: am-c
  - **coldness**; with: androc srj1• *Nux-v* sep
  - **convulsions**; with: *Aesc*
  - **hanging** down, when: both-ax tsm2 sep
  - **marbled**: cupr
  - **perspiration**; during: am-c bg2 apis bg2 bar-c bg2 *Calc* bg2 camph bg2 **Samb** bg2 *Verat* bg2
  - **spots**: nit-ac k* ped a1
    - **old** people; in: bar-c
  - **winter** agg.: cupr
- **brown** | **spots**: nat-c b4a.de
- **brownish** red: arg-n k* sul-ac k* sulph k*
  - **afternoon**: sulph k*
  - **spots**: arg-n k* nat-m
  - **streaks**: sul-ac k*
- **copper** colored spots: nit-ac k*
- **dirty**: psor k2*
- **greenish**: crot-h k*
- **lividity**: amyg a1 **Ars** k* merc k* merc-c a1 morph k* naja nux-v k* op k* ox-ac k* plb k* stram k* stry k*
  - **spots**: lyc
- **mottled**: amyg a1 crot-h a1 **Lach** naja
- **paleness**: *Ars* bell both-ax tsm2 *Calc* k* *Camph* k* cedr k* con k* ign k* *Ip* ph-ac k2 *Plb* *Sang* *Sec* spig h1* zinc
- **purple**: apis kali-p *Lach* naja op k* *Phos* rhus-t sec k* sep ptk1* thuj k* vip k*
  - **chilliness**; during: thuj
  - **spots**: *Kali-c*
- **redness**●: **Agar** k* all-c bg2 **Apis** k* bar-c k* *Bell* k* berb borx bg2 bry k* carb-an k* cench k2 chin-b c1* coca-c sk4• cypra-eg sde6.de• dulc bg2 *Fl-ac* k* hep k* merc-c b4a.de mez nat-m nat-s nux-v k* ped a1 phos k* pieri-b mlk9.de plan puls ran-b bg2 rhus-t sabad b7.de* sang hr1 seneg sep h2* spira a1 staph k* stram k* sulph k* sumb k* vesp k*
  - **right**: staph h1*
  - **left**: cocc h1*

- **Hand** – **redness**: ...
  - **spots**: agar k2 all-s k* alum ant-t b7.de* apis b7a.de* *Bell* k* berb *Cor-r* dros b7.de* elaps kali-i lach m-ambo b7a.de mag-m mang merc k* nat-c k* nat-m *Ph-ac* pitu-gl skp7• puls b7.de* sabad k* sep k* squil b7.de* stann k* sulph bg2 tab zinc k*
    - **hot**; but not: puls a1
- **sensation**: limen-b-c hrn2•
- **spots**: ant-t bg2 bell bg2 dros bg2 ferr bg2 iod bg2 kali-c bg2 nat-c bg2 nat-m bg2 **Nit-ac** bg2 sabad bg2 sep bg2 stann bg2 zinc bg2
- **white** | **spots**: ozone sde2•
- **yellowness**: canth k* *Chel* k* cupr-ar k* elaps ign k* *Lyc* *Sil* k* spig k* spira a1
  - **accompanied** by | **Abdomen**; complaints of (See ABDOMEN - Complaints - accompanied - hands)
  - **dark**: aran k*
  - **greenish**: cupr-ar k*
  - **spots**, in: elaps med

○ • **Back** of:
  - **blotches**: apis arg-n k*
    - **itching**: cit-v k*
    - **red**: arg-n k* brass a1 cit-v k* cortiso sp1
    - **stinging**: apis
  - **blueness**: carbn-o plb k*
    - **spots**: sars sec
  - **brown**: *Iod* k* *Thuj* k*
    - **bruised**; as if: *Nat-m*
    - **spots**●: cop k* guat jl3 *Lach* lyc kl *Nat-m* k* petr sep st sulph
      - **dark**: guat sp1
  - **petechiae**: berb k*
  - **purpura** hemorrhagia: *Lach* *Phos*
  - **redness**: aur-s k* berb brom cic cimic k* *Crot-h* dulc h2* ferr k* mur-ac k* ped a1 spong fd4.de sul-ac k* sulph sumb vip
    - **morning**: ped a1 sulph k*
    - **afternoon**: cimic k*
    - **evening**: cimic k* sulph k*
      - **air** agg.; in open: dulc
    - **nettles**, as from: nat-s k*
      - **warm** from walking, when: dulc h2
    - **spots**: *Agar* bell k* calc k* cic k* cop k* dros h1* hura nat-c k* osm k* pitu-gl skp7• spong fd4.de stann k* sulph k*
      - **dusky**: berb k*
      - **itching**: brom k* dros h1*
      - **white**: *Berb* *Calc* nat-c nit-ac
    - **streaks**, in: vip k*
  - **yellow** in spots: cop k* crot-c med jl2
- **Hypothenar** eminences:
  - **red** | **bright** red: acon bro1
- **Palm**:
  - **brown** spots: iod nat-c thuj
  - **mottled**: apis bg2 fl-ac bg2
  - **red** spots: apis k* cor-r a1 fl-ac bg2 sep h2*
    - **Between** first finger and thumb: iod h
  - **redness**: aeth dgt1 *Eos* br1 fl-ac k* olib-sac wmh1
  - **yellow**: *Chel* k* sep bro1*

- **Hips**:
- **blackness**: crot-h k*
- **redness**: lac-ac ph-ac rhus-t vip k*
  - **spots**; in: lac-ac rhus-t k*
    - **hot**: rhus-t h1
  - **stripes**; in:
    - **extending** to | **Umbilicus**: ph-ac

- **Joints**:
- **pale**: led tl1 sal-ac tl1
- **redness**: apis mrr1 bell k2* *Cocc* colch k* dulc k2 ferr-p tl1 *Form* mrr1 kali-bi k2 *Kalm* *Merc* **Puls** **Rhus-t** *Verat-v*
  - **rheumatic** joints; about painful: caps vml1.nl colch tl1 stict mrr1

- **Knee**:
  - **blue** spots: kola$_{stb3}$•
  - **brown** spots; dark | **Posterior** part: phos$_{kl}$
  - **dark** in spots, anterior part: (non:phos$_{kl}$)
  - **redness**: cypra-eg$_{sde6.de}$• eos$_{br1}$ lac-ac$_{k}$* lachn$_{k}$* petr$_{k}$*
    - **spots**; in: iod$_{b4a.de}$ lyc$_{k}$* petr$_{k}$* rhus-t$_{b7.de}$*
    - **Anterior** part: merc nat-m
    - **Hollow**: sil$_{bg2}$
    - **Posterior** part: am-c kreos
  - ○ **Patella**:
    - **ascending** stairs agg.: (non:cann-s$_{k}$*)
    - **red** streaks: ph-ac$_{h2}$
- **Leg**:
  - **black**: iod$_{k}$* vip$_{k}$*
    - **spots**; in: vip
  - **blood** specks: phos
  - **blotches**: lac-ac$_{k}$* led$_{ptk1}$ *Nat-c* phos
  - **blue**: ambr$_{k}$* *Anthraci* arg-n *Carb-an* *Carbn-s* con elaps kali-br$_{k}$* lath$_{br1}$ lyc$_{k}$* morg$_{fmm1}$• mur-ac$_{k}$* **Nux-v**$_{k}$* ox-ac$_{k}$* plb sars$_{k2}$ sulph$_{k2}$ vip$_{ptk1}$
    - **left** | **menses**; during: ambr
    - **adolescents**: morg$_{fmm1}$•
    - **menses**; during: ambr$_{b7.de}$*
    - **spots**: phos$_{h2}$* *Sars*$_{k}$* *Sul-ac*
      - **indurated**: *Sars*$_{k}$*
    - **women**; in: morg$_{fmm1}$•
  - **brown**: thuj$_{b4a.de}$
    - **bluish**: *Anthraci* vip$_{k}$*
    - **spots**: *Petr*$_{k}$* thuj$_{k}$*
  - **crusts**: mez
  - **cyanosis**: con$_{k}$* elaps
  - **dark** | **hang** down; when letting limb: hydr-ac
  - **marbled**: **Caust**
  - **mottled**: con$_{k}$* led
  - **purple**: led *Petr*$_{hr1}$ vesp$_{k}$*
    - **spots**: **Apis** *Crot-h* sec$_{k2}$
  - **purpura**: kali-i$_{k}$* *Lach* **Phos** *Sec* ter$_{hr1}$
  - **reddish**: aeth$_{k}$* am-c arist-m$_{a1}$ arn arund$_{k}$* *Bry*$_{b7a.de}$ *Chin*$_{b7a.de}$ con cop$_{k}$* elaps hydr-ac$_{k}$* kali-bi$_{k}$* kali-br$_{k}$* *Lach* luf-op$_{rsj5}$• lyc$_{k}$* merc$_{k}$* *Nat-c*$_{k}$* phos$_{k}$* puls$_{k}$* rhus-t$_{k}$* rhus-v$_{k}$* sil$_{b4.de}$* sulph$_{k}$* thuj$_{k}$*
    - **evening**: arist-m$_{a1}$ fago$_{k}$*
    - **spots**: *Acon*$_{b7.de}$* *Calc*$_{k}$* caust$_{b4.de}$* con$_{k}$* dulc$_{k}$* graph$_{k}$* guare$_{k}$* kali-br$_{k}$* kali-n$_{k}$* lyc$_{k}$* mag-c$_{b4a.de}$ merc$_{k}$* sars$_{k}$* sil$_{k}$* sul-ac$_{k}$* sulph$_{bro1}$ zinc
      - **evening**: trios$_{rsj11}$•
      - **night**: trios$_{rsj11}$•
      - **burning**: lyc$_{h2}$* ph-ac trios$_{rsj11}$•
      - **covered** with crusts; becomes: *Zinc*
      - **insect** bites; as from: carbn-dox$_{knl3}$• lyc$_{h2}$
      - **itching**: trios$_{rsj11}$•
    - **walking** agg.: nux-v$_{k}$*
  - **spots**: *Calc*$_{k}$* *Chel* con *Lyc* *Phos* *Stann* *Zinc*
  - **white** spots: calc$_{k}$*
  - **yellow** spots: carl graph$_{b4a.de}$ hydrc$_{k}$* stann$_{k}$* vip$_{k}$*
  - ○ **Calf**:
    - **blotches**: petr$_{k}$*
    - **blue** spots: dros$_{tl1}$ kali-p
    - **redness** in spots: cench$_{k2}$ *Con* graph$_{k}$* kali-br$_{k}$* lach sars$_{h2}$*
      - **motion** impossible; making: *Con*$_{b4.de}$*
    - **spots**: chel$_{h1}$* con graph *Sars*
    - **yellow** spots: kali-br$_{k}$*
  - **Tibia**:
    - **coppery** spots: nit-ac$_{ptk1}$
    - **spots**: ambr ant-c$_{k}$* *Caust* kali-n *Lach* mag-c *Phos* sec$_{k2}$ *Sil* sul-ac
- **Lower** limbs:
  - **black**: ant-c$_{b7.de}$*
    - **spots**; painful: nux-v$_{k}$*
  - **blotches**: ant-c crot-t lach nat-c sulph
  - **bluish**: *Apis*$_{b7a.de}$ arn$_{b7a.de}$* bism$_{k}$* carb-an$_{bg2}$ carb-v$_{bg2}$ cupr$_{k}$* *Ox-ac* puls$_{bg2}$ sec$_{k}$* verat$_{k}$*
    - **left**: ambr$_{bg1}$
    - **spots**: am-c ant-c$_{k}$* *Arn*$_{b7.de}$* con kreos$_{b7a.de}$ lach mosch$_{b7a.de}$ phos sars$_{k2}$ **Sul-ac** *Sulph*
  - **brownish**: arg-n$_{k}$* thuj$_{bg2}$
  - **burnt**; as if: *Nat-c*$_{bg2}$
  - **dark**: *Mur-ac*$_{hr1}$
  - **dusky**: carb-v$_{k2}$
  - **greenish**: vip$_{k}$*
    - **yellow** as from a bruise: con
  - **livid**: kali-act kali-ar$_{k}$* morph$_{k}$*
  - **marbled**: **Caust**$_{k}$* lyc thuj$_{k}$*
  - **purple** in spots: borx ptel$_{k}$*
  - **purpura** hemorrhagia: kali-i$_{mp1}$• *Lach*$_{k}$* **Phos**$_{k}$* *Sec*$_{k}$* *Sul-ac*$_{mp1}$• ter$_{k}$*
  - **redness**: petr plb$_{k}$* ptel sep stram$_{k}$* *Sulph*$_{b4.de}$* vip$_{k}$*
    - **spots**; in: ars$_{k}$* bry$_{b7.de}$* *Calc*$_{k}$* *Caust*$_{k}$* chin$_{b7.de}$* con$_{k}$* *Graph*$_{k}$* kali-i kali-n$_{b4.de}$* *Lach* lyc$_{k}$* merc$_{k}$* mez$_{k}$* petr$_{k}$* ph-ac$_{k}$* sil$_{k}$* *Sul-ac*$_{k}$* *Sulph*$_{k}$*
    - **Inner** side of: petr$_{k}$*
  - **spots**: ant-c bry flor-p$_{rsj3}$• hyos kali-br kali-n nat-c sulph
  - **yellow**: kali-br$_{k}$* vip$_{k}$*
    - **spots**: ambr$_{b7.de}$* *Arn*$_{b7.de}$*
    - **stripes**; in: vip
- **Nails**: ant-c$_{b2.de}$* ars$_{b2.de}$* *Caust*$_{bg2}$ ferr$_{bg2}$ *Graph*$_{b2.de}$* mur-ac$_{b2.de}$* *Nit-ac*$_{b2.de}$* sil$_{bg2}$ sulph$_{b2.de}$* thuj$_{bg2}$
  - **black**: crot-h$_{bg2}$ graph$_{bg2}$
  - **blue** | **accompanied** by | **Abdomen**; complaints of (See ABDOMEN - Complaints - accompanied - nails)
    - **chill**; during: am-c$_{bg2}$ ars$_{bg2}$ *Aur*$_{b4a.de}$* chel$_{bg2}$ chin$_{bg2}$ *Cocc*$_{b7a.de}$* dig$_{bg2}$ dros$_{b7.de}$* nat-m$_{bg2}$ *Nux-v*$_{b7.de}$* petr$_{b4a.de}$* puls$_{b7a.de}$ sil$_{bg2}$
  - **yellow**: ambr$_{b2.de}$* ant-c$_{b2.de}$* ars$_{b2.de}$* aur$_{b2.de}$* bell$_{b2.de}$* bry$_{b2.de}$* calc$_{b2.de}$* canth$_{b2.de}$* carb-v$_{b2.de}$* caust$_{b2.de}$* cham$_{b2.de}$* chel$_{b2.de}$* chin$_{b2.de}$* **Con**$_{b2.de}$* ferr$_{b2.de}$* hep$_{b2.de}$* ign$_{b2.de}$* lyc$_{b2.de}$* *Merc*$_{b2.de}$* *Nit-ac*$_{b2.de}$* *Nux-v*$_{b2.de}$* op$_{b2.de}$* plb$_{b2.de}$* puls$_{b2.de}$* **Sep**$_{b2.de}$* *Sil*$_{b2.de}$* spig$_{b2.de}$* *Sulph*$_{b2.de}$*
- **Nates**:
  - **redness**: cann-s carb-v$_{ptk1}$ cham$_{ptk1}$ hyos$_{k}$* lap-la$_{sde8.de}$• med$_{jl2}$ sang$_{k2}$ sulph$_{ptk1}$
    - **newborns**: med$_{jl2}$
    - **spots**; in: mag-c$_{ptk1}$
  - **spots**; in: cann-s mag-c
- **Shoulders**: am-m$_{sne}$ rhus-t$_{sne}$
  - **blackness** in spots: vip$_{k}$*
  - **brown** liver spots: ant-c$_{b7.de}$*
  - **mottled**: berb$_{k}$*
  - **redness**: berb chin$_{k}$* chinin-s ferr-p$_{k2}$ lac-c lach$_{k}$* merc-d$_{a1}$ osteo-a$_{jl2}$ ph-ac puls-n tab$_{k}$*
    - **right**: osteo-a$_{jl2}$
  - **spots**: berb ph-ac *Sul-ac* tab
  - **yellow** spots: ant-c$_{k}$*
- **Thigh**:
  - **blotches**: lac-ac$_{k}$*
  - **blue**: anthraci bism$_{k}$* both$_{k}$* kreos$_{k}$*
    - **marks**: arn$_{k}$*
    - **spots**: ant-c$_{k}$* *Arn* ars-s-f$_{k2}$ kreos morph$_{k}$* mosch$_{k}$* vip$_{k}$*
  - **brownish**:
    - **spots**: cann-s$_{k}$* *Mez* nat-s
    - **Inside** thigh: *Thuj*$_{k}$*

- **cyanosis**: ars
- **greenish**: kali-n$_{k*}$
- **livid**: anthraci arn$_{k*}$
- **marbled**: **Caust**
- **redness**: anac$_{k*}$ bell$_{k*}$ *Bry*$_{b7a.de}$ chin$_{b7.de*}$ kali-c nat-m puls rhus-t$_{k*}$ sil thuj
  - **night**: rhus-v$_{k*}$
  - **spots**: bell$_{k*}$ calc$_{k*}$ caps$_{k*}$ crot-t cycl$_{k*}$ *Graph*$_{k*}$ hir$_{rsj4}$• med merc$_{k*}$ petr$_{k*}$ plan$_{k*}$ rhod$_{k*}$ rhus-t$_{k*}$ sulph$_{k*}$
    - **burning**: ferr-ma$_{a1}$ ph-ac$_{k*}$
    - **itching**: graph$_{h2*}$ nat-m$_{k*}$ psil$_{ft1}$
      - **scratched**; when: med
  - **Between** thighs (See thigh; MALE GENITALIA/SEX - Discoloration - red - thighs)
- **spots**: am-c ant-c cann-i cycl flor-p$_{rsj3}$• *Graph* mur-ac rhod
- **white**, in spots: calc ozone$_{sde2}$•
- **yellow**:
  - **marks**: arn$_{k*}$
  - **spots**: stann$_{bg2}$

- **Thumbs**:
  - **black**: vip$_{k*}$
  - **brownish**: sulph$_{k*}$
  - **dark**: cic$_{k*}$
  - **purple**: plut-n$_{srj7}$•
  - **red**: cimic$_{k*}$ lach$_{k*}$ trach$_{a1}$ vesp$_{k*}$
    - **spots**: canth$_{bg2}$ lyc$_{h2}$ mang$_{h2}$
      - **right**: chlam-tr$_{bcx2}$•
  - **white**: vip$_{k*}$
    - **spots**; in: sulph
  - **yellow**: sulph$_{k*}$

- **Toes**: carb-v$_{k2}$ *Sec*$_{k*}$
  - **blackness**: crot-h$_{k*}$ melal-alt$_{gya4}$ phos *Sec* sol-ni
  - **blue**: crot-t$_{bg2}$ ham$_{fd3.de}$• sars$_{k2}$ sec$_{ptk1*}$
    - **and** cold: crat$_{br1}$
    - **chill**; during: ars$_{k2}$
    - **excitement** agg.: crat$_{br1}$
    - **exertion** agg.: crat$_{br1}$
    - **Fingers**, and: crat$_{br1}$
  - **redness**: *Agar*$_{k*}$ *Alum*$_{k*}$ *Am-c*$_{k*}$ apis arn$_{b7.de*}$ aster$_{k*}$ aur$_{k*}$ *Aur-m*$_{k*}$ berb$_{k*}$ borx$_{k*}$ *Carb-v*$_{k*}$ hydrog$_{srj2}$• nat-m$_{k*}$ nit-ac *Nux-v* phos$_{k*}$ *Sabin*$_{b7.de*}$ sep$_{k*}$ staph$_{b7.de*}$ thuj$_{k*}$ tub$_{c1}$ zinc$_{k*}$
    - **shining**: thuj$_{k*}$
    - **wet** agg.; after getting feet: nit-ac$_{k*}$
  - **violet**-colored: stry$_{k*}$
  - **white** | **perspiration**; from: graph$_{ptk1}$
  - ○ **Between** toes | **white** bleached: bar-c plb
  - **Fifth** | **redness** | **morning**: lyc
    - **spots**; in: staph
  - **First**:
    - **blackness**: iod$_{k*}$
    - **redness**: alum$_{k*}$ *Am-c*$_{k*}$ arn aster *Benz-ac* bry$_{k*}$ coc-c$_{k*}$ eup-per *Nat-m* *Nit-ac*$_{k*}$ sabin$_{k*}$ tub$_{c1}$
      - **spots**; in: nat-c
  - **Nails**: apis *Ars*$_{k*}$ camph dig *Graph*$_{k*}$ lac-e$_{hrn2}$• mur-ac$_{b4.de}$ *Nit-ac* *Ox-ac* sep$_{sne}$ *Sil*
    - **black**: lac-e$_{hrn2}$•
    - **blueness**: apis bart$_{a1}$ dig$_{br1}$
      - **accompanied** by | **Abdomen**; pain in (See ABDOMEN - Pain - cramping - accompanied - nails)
    - **gray**: merc-c$_{b4a.de}$
    - **purple**: androc$_{srj1}$•
    - **red** | **Root**: upa$_{br1}$
    - **yellow**: con$_{b4a.de*}$
  - **Third** | **blue**: plut-n$_{srj7}$•

- **Toes**: ...
  - **Tips**:
    - **blueness**: op$_{k*}$ tub-d$_{jl2}$ tub-m$_{jl2}$
    - **redness**: chin$_{bg2}$ mur-ac$_{k*}$ sep$_{h2*}$ thuj$_{k*}$

- **Upper** arm:
  - **blue** spots: plat$_{k*}$
  - **red** spots: plat$_{b4.de*}$ rhus-t$_{b7.de*}$ sulph$_{b4.de*}$
  - **redness**: anac dulc$_{bg2}$
  - **spots**: plat$_{bg2}$ rhus-t$_{bg2}$

- **Upper** limbs: lac-e$_{hrn2}$•
  - **black**: lac-e$_{hrn2}$• vesp
    - **spots**; in: vip
  - **blotches**: chlol$_{k*}$ rhus-v$_{k*}$
  - **blue**: *Apis* arg-n bism$_{k*}$ *Cupr*$_{b7.de*}$ elaps lac-e$_{hrn2}$• mez$_{bg2}$ morph$_{k*}$ sec$_{b7.de*}$ sep$_{bg2}$ sil$_{bg2}$ sulph *Verat*$_{b7.de*}$
    - **asthma**; with: *Kali-c*
    - **hang** down agg.; letting arms: sep
    - **reddish**: vip$_{k*}$
    - **spots**; both in: **Sul-ac**$_{k*}$
  - **brown** spots: ant-c$_{b7.de*}$ guare$_{k*}$ guat$_{jl3}$ *Lyc* *Petr* thuj
    - **dark** brown | **Back** of arms: guat$_{sp1}$
  - **copper** colored spots: *Nit-ac*
  - **cyanotic** (See blue)
  - **gray**: caul$_{bg2}$
  - **liver** spots: ant-c$_{k*}$ ferr$_{bg2}$ guare$_{k*}$ lyc$_{k*}$ *Merc* *Mez*
    - **dark**; becoming: *Mez*
    - **itching**: lyc
  - **livid**: agar-ph$_{k*}$ amyg$_{k*}$ *Ars*$_{k*}$ crot-h$_{k*}$ *Lyc* naja ox-ac$_{k*}$ vip$_{k*}$ zinc-m$_{k*}$
    - **spots**: *Hell* lyc
  - **marbled** spots: berb
  - **mottled**: amyg$_{k*}$ *Lach* naja nat-m puls$_{bg2}$
  - **orange** colored: (non:cinnb$_{a4}$) crot-h$_{k*}$ (non:kali-i$_{a4}$) (non:rhus-t$_{a4}$) sil$_{k*}$ (non:vip$_{a4}$)
  - **petechiae**: berb cop$_{k*}$ cupr$_{k*}$ phos phys$_{k*}$
  - **purple**: naja vesp$_{k*}$
    - **spots**; in: ars
  - **purpura** hemorrhagia: *Lach*$_{k*}$ *Phos*$_{k*}$ *Sec*$_{k*}$ *Sul-ac*$_{k*}$ ter$_{k*}$
  - **redness**: acon$_{k*}$ ant-c apis arg-met$_{bg2}$ arn$_{k*}$ ars *Bell*$_{k*}$ bry$_{k*}$ chinin-s chlol cit-v$_{k*}$ cupr hydr-ac$_{k*}$ jac-c$_{k*}$ jug-c$_{k*}$ *Kali-bi*$_{k*}$ merc merc-c rhus-v$_{k*}$ **Ruta**$_{k*}$ sabad$_{bg2}$ stram$_{k*}$ sulph tritic-vg$_{fd5.de}$ vac$_{jl2}$ vesp$_{k*}$ vip$_{k*}$
    - **left**: vac$_{jl2}$
    - **evening**: fago$_{k*}$
    - **blisters**; around: [bell-p-sp$_{dcm1}$]
    - **drinking** warm drinks: phos
    - **scarlatina**; as in: am-c$_{b4a.de}$ **Bell**$_{b4a.de*}$ *Euph*$_{b4a.de}$ lach$_{bg2}$
    - **spots**: apis$_{k*}$ aster berb bry$_{k*}$ cop$_{k*}$ *Cupr*$_{k*}$ dulc elaps *Graph*$_{k*}$ hir$_{rsj4}$• kali-bi$_{k*}$ kali-i lac-ac$_{a1}$ *Lach*$_{k*}$ led$_{k*}$ mag-m$_{b4.de*}$ merc$_{k*}$ mez$_{b4.de*}$ nat-c$_{b4.de*}$ oena$_{k*}$ ph-ac$_{b4.de*}$ *Phos*$_{k*}$ phyt plat *Rhus-t*$_{k*}$ sabad$_{k*}$ sep$_{k*}$ spira$_{a1}$ stann$_{b4.de*}$ stram$_{b7.de*}$ *Sulph*$_{k*}$ *Thuj*
      - **burning**: sulph$_{h2*}$
      - **washing** with soap; after: **Sulph**$_{●*}$
    - **streaks**: apis euph helo-s$_{bnm14}$• sabad$_{b7.de*}$
  - **spots**: am-c ant-c berb bry$_{k*}$ crot-h$_{k*}$ cupr$_{bg2}$ lach$_{bg2}$ led nat-m$_{bg2}$ oena$_{k*}$ petr$_{bg2}$ sabad$_{bg2}$ sulph$_{bg2}$ tep$_{k*}$ vip$_{k*}$
  - **white**: berb kreos$_{bg2}$
    - **accompanied** by | **Head**; pain in (See HEAD - Pain - accompanied - arms)
    - **spots**; in: apis$_{k*}$
  - **yellow**:
    - **rings**: nat-c
    - **spots**; in: petr$_{k*}$ vip

- **Wrist**:
  - **right** | **red** patch: beryl$_{tpw5}$

Extremities

- **left** | **red** spots: trios rsj11•
- **brown** spots: *Petr* k*
- **redness**: apis cub k* mag-c bg2 merc bg2
  - **right**: osteo-a jl2
  - **spots**: zinc b4.de*
- **sensation**: limen-b-c hrn2•
- **spots**: am-c bg2 dros kali-c k* mag-m bg2 *Merc* k* *Petr* k* sul-ac bg2 thuj bg2

DISLOCATED feeling (See Pain - dislocated)

DISLOCATION: *(↗Sprains; GENERALS - Injuries - dislocation)* drym-cor jsx1.fr oxal-c jsx1.fr rham-pr bta1•

○ - **Ankles**: bry nat-c nux-v phos mtf33 psor jl2* ruta sulph tritic-vg fd5.de
- **left**: kali-bi

- **Elbows**: ferr-p ptk1 psor jl2
- **Hip**; spontaneous dislocation of: bell bry k* **Calc** *Calc-f* c1 **Caust** *Coloc* k* lyc *Nat-m* b4a.de puls *Rhus-t* k* ruta tl1 sulph k* *Thuj* k* zinc
  - **pain**; from: carb-an dros kali-i nit-ac
  - **sitting** down agg.: ip
  - **walking** agg.: thuj mtf33
- **Knees**:

○ • **Patella**: cann-s b7.de* gels
  - **going** up stairs, when: cann-s k* cann-xyz ptk1

- **Shoulders**: thuj h1*
- **Thumbs**: acon bg2 cupr bg2 laur hg? nux-v bg2 verat bg2
- **Upper** limbs: *Rhus-t* b7a.de *Ruta* b7a.de

DISLOCATION; EASY (= spontaneous): ars ptk1 *Calc* ptk1 carb-an ptk1 chel ptk1 graph ptk1 lyc ptk1 nat-c ptk1 phos ptk1 prun ptk1 rhus-t ptk1 ruta ptk1 sep ptk1

- **lameness** | **after**: rheum ptk1

○ - **Ankles**: agn b7.de* bufo bg2 carb-an b4.de* *M-aust* b7.de* **Nat-c** b4.de* *Nat-m* b4.de* nit-ac b4.de* nux-v b7.de* phos b4.de* **Ruta** b7a.de thuj b4a.de

- **Finger** joints: *(↗Give - fingers)* *Am-c* b4a.de bell bg2* hep b4a.de* teucr bg2*
- **Knees**: cann-s b7a.de nux-v b7.de*
- **Toes**; joints of: carb-an b4.de* lyc b4.de* thuj b4a.de

DISORDERED STOMACH:

- **agg.** | **Lower** limbs: bry b7.de* *Puls* b7.de* staph b7.de*

DISTENSION (See Fullness; Swelling)

DISTORTED nails (See Nails - distorted)

DRAGGING: *(↗Paralysis)* con naja *Sulph*

- **walking** agg.: naja rhus-t bg2

○ - **Feet**: ars bg2 bell bg2 borx bg2 cann-xyz bg2 con bg2 plb bg2 staph bg2 ulm-c jsj8•
- **left** | **vertigo**; after: cypr c1
- **walking** agg.: caust mrr1 *Mygal* bro1 nux-v bro1* tab bro1

- **Legs**: bar-c con merc *Nux-v* *Op* **Phos** plb *Sec*
  - **walking** agg.: atro *Bell* bg1 con lach ptk1 lath ptk1 merc *Mygal* ptk1 naja ptk1 *Nux-v* k* *Op* phos ptk1 *Plb* rhus-t ptk1 *Sec* tab ptk1 ter

DRAWING up:

○ - **Ankle** | **agg.**: kali-bi bg2

- **Extremities**:
  - **agg.**: *Agar* k* alum k* am-m k* *Anac* k* *Ant-t* k* asar k* bell k* borx k* bry carb-an b2.de* **Carb-v** k* cham k* chel k* chin k* coff k* coloc dig k* dros k* dulc k* ferr k* *Guaj* k* hep k* ign k* kali-c k* mag-c k* merc bg2 mez k* mur-ac k* nat-m k* nux-m b2.de* nux-v k* olnd k* par k* petr k* plat k* **Puls** k* rheum k* rhod k* **Rhus-t** k* sabad k* sabin k* **Sec** k* stann k* staph k* thuj k* verb k* zinc k*
  - **amel.**: abies-c c1* acon agar *Alum* k* *Am-c* k* am-m k* anac k* ang b2.de* *Ant-c* k* arg-met k* arn k* aur k* *Bar-c* k* bar-m bell k* bov k* *Bry* k* **Calc** k* calc-s cann-s k* caps k* *Carb-v* k* caust k* cham k* *Chin* k* cina k* clem k* colch coloc sf1.de con k* croc k* crot-h bg dig k* dros k* dulc k* ferr k* gnaph c1 graph k* guaj k* *Hell* *Hep* k* ign k* *Kali-c* k* kali-i lac-c lach bg laur k* lyc b2.de m-aust b2.de *Mang* k* meny k* *Merc* k* **Merc-c** mur-ac k* *Nat-m* k* nux-v k* petr k* phos k* plat k* plb k* *Puls* k*

Drawing up – **Extremities** – **amel.**: ...
Ran-b rheum k* *Rhus-t* k* *Ruta* k* sabin k* sel k* **Sep** k* sil bg spig k* spong k* stann k* staph k* **Sulph** k* **Thuj** k* valer k* verat k*

- **Knee**:
  - **agg.**: bell b4.de* hep b4a.de kali-c b4a.de plat b4.de*
  - **involuntary** | **walking** agg.: ign ptk1
  - **spread** apart; and | **lying** on back agg.: plat ptk1
- **Lower** limbs: arg-n ptk1
  - **agg.**: acon b7a.de *Bry* b7a.de coff b7.de* nux-v b7.de* olnd b7.de* rheum b7.de* sabin b7.de* verb b7.de*
  - **amel.**: anac b4.de* carb-v b4.de* cham b7.de* chin b7.de* *Coloc* bg2 crot-h bg2 guaj b4.de hep bg2 lach bg2 lyc b4a.de mang b4.de* meny b7.de* sep bg2 sil bg2
  - **changing** position; when: hell hr1
- **Shoulders** | **agg.**: calc ptk1

DRAWN: *(↗Flexed)*

- **apart** (See Abducted; Clenching; Flexed)
- **backward**:
  - **sensation** as if | **Lower** limbs: cycl bg2 par bg2

○ • **Legs**: bufo plb
  - **agg.**: mosch b7.de*
  - **sensation** as if: androc srj1•
  - **sitting** agg.: spong
  - **thigh**, on the: canth op plb
    - **attempting** to walk: spong
- **Shoulders**: hyos b7a.de

- **downward** | **Toes**: ars bg2* colch bg2* cupr bg2* hyos bg2* plb bg2
- **flat**:

○ • **Legs** | **Calves**: ars bg2 jatr-c bg2

- **inward**:

○ • **Fingers**: *Ant-t* vh1
  - **right** | **sudden**: cina mtf33
- **Lower** limbs: acon k*
- **Thumbs**: *Aeth* ant-t h *Apis* ars art-v arum-t *Bell* brach *Bufo* *Camph* *Caust* *Cham* *Cic* *Cocc* **Cupr** k* *Glon* hell hyos ign *Lach* mag-m k* mag-p merc oena phyt plut-n srj7• *Sec* stann staph stram sulph viol-t
  - **convulsions**; during: cupr tl1 mag-p tl1
  - **fever**; during: bell bg2 sulph bg2 *Viol-t* b7.de*
- **Toes**: ant-c bg2 *Ant-t* vh1 colch bg2 graph h2* mag-m h2 petr h2* sars h2
- **Upper** limbs: kali-n bg2 nit-ac h2

- **knots**; drawn in | **Legs**: ars bg2
- **out** of shape | **Fingers**: zinc k2
- **outward**:

○ • **Finger**; first | **left**: dig h2
- **Hand**:
  - **left** | **playing** the piano; while: merl k*
- **Upper** limbs: [*Buteo-j* sej6]

- **together**: ars k* lyc
  - **spasmodically**: lyc merc

○ • **Fingers**: phos ptk1
- **Hips**: coloc ptk1 polyg-h ptk1
- **Shoulders**: rhus-t bg2
- **Upper** limbs: caust bg2 phos bg2

- **upward**: *(↗Contraction - toes - drawn - up)* acon agar am-c amyg *Arg-n* *Ars* carb-an *Carb-v* k* caust *Cham* crot-h cupr *Hell* *Hep* *Hyos* jatr-c *Merc* *Nat-m* nux-v op k* ox-ac *Phos* *Phyt* plat *Plb* k* pyrus sec stann stry sul-ac tab zinc
  - **morning**: plat
    - **waking**; on: plat
  - **evening**: carb-an
    - **standing** agg.: carb-an
  - **night**: merc h1* stann
    - **waking**; on: stann
  - **abdomen**, on: arg-n *Ars* carb-v k* cham *Cina* *Cupr* *Hyos* jatr-c lat-m bnm6• *Merc-c* *Mur-ac* ox-ac *Plb* *Verat* zinc

- **upward – abdomen**, on: ...
  ⁝ **necrosis** of femur; in: *Sil*
  • **alternating** with extension: carbn-o *Cic Cupr Lyc* nux-v sec tab
  • **change** of position, every: *Hell*
  • **chill**; during: *Caps* cimx
  • **convulsively**: *Arg-n Cupr Hyos* nux-v *Plb* tab
  • **involuntarily**: carb-v *Ign*
  • **motion** agg.: tab
  • **periodical**: *Sec*
  • **sleep**; during (See SLEEP - Position - limbs - drawn)
  • **stepping** agg.: caust
  • **walking** agg.: am-c ign *Plb* spong
O • **Lower** limbs: ars bg2 carb-v bg2 *Coloc* bg2 cupr bg2 lach bg2 phos bg2
  • **Toes**: ars bg2 camph ptk1 cic ptk1 ferr bg2 lach bg2*
  • **Upper** limbs: ign bg2

DREAMS agg.; during: | **Lower** limbs: zinc b4.de*

DROPPING, wrist: plb k*
- **lead** poisoning; from: plb tl1

DROPS falling in lower limbs; sensation of: bell h1*

DROPS things (See Awkwardness - hands - drops)

DROPSY (See Swelling)

DRYNESS: chord-umb rly4• falco-pe nl2• mand rsj7• tritic-vg fd5.de
O - **Feet**: ars k* chel k* fic-m gya1 gua bg1 manc (non:phos kl) ptel sacch sst1• sep k* sil *Sulph* ptk1 tritic-vg fd5.de
O • **Back**: cortiso tpw7
  • **Soles**: bism k* falco-pe nl2• hipp jl2 manc k* petr-ra shn4• phos h2* tritic-vg fd5.de
- **Fingers**: aeth bro1 anac h2* anag k* ant-t bg2 chord-umb rly4• dulc fd4.de falco-pe nl2• *Fl-ac* bg2 ham fd3.de• mim-p rsj8*• nat-m k* petr-ra shn4• puls k* *Sil* k* spong fd4.de zinc-p k2
  • **afternoon**: *Sil*
  • **evening**: puls k*
O • **Back**: abrom-a ks5 cortiso tpw7
  • **Between**: morg-p pte1•
  • **Joints**: chord-umb rly4• psor tl1
  ⁝ **sensation** of: anac bg2 ant-t bg2 *Puls* b7.de* *Sil* bg2
  • **Nails** | **About**: graph bro1 mim-p rsj8• nat-m k* petr bro1 sacch sst1• *Sil*
  • **Tips**: ant-t k* dulc fd4.de ham fd3.de• *Sil* k* spong fd4.de
- **Hands**: acet-ac k* acon-ac rly4• aesc k* aeth k* all-c k* allox tpw4* **Anac** k* anag k* *Ars* k* atro k* bapt bg2 **Bar-c** k* bar-s k2 bell k* brass a1 *Calc-p* k* cann-s chel k* cimic k* clem k* cortico tpw7* cortiso tpw7* crot-h dream-p sdj1• dulc fd4.de dys pte1*• fago k* falco-pe nl2• ferr bg2 gad a1 gua bg1 ham k* *Hep* k* hydroph rsj6• iris lach k* lap-la sde8.de• lob **Lyc** k* mand rsj7• mim-p rsj8• morg-p fmm1• narc-ps a1 *Nat-c* k* *Nat-m* k* nat-sil fd3.de• ol-j k* op ozone sde2• *Ph-ac* k* phos k* pip-m a1 plb k* plut-n srj7• polyp-p a1 ptel puls rhod *Rhus-t* rhus-v k* sabad k* sacch sst1• spong fd4.de *Sul-ac* k* **Sulph** k* sumb k* symph fd3.de• tell rsj10• *Thuj* k* *Zinc* k* zinc-p k2
  • **morning**: fago a1 zinc h2*
  • **forenoon**: sabad k*
  ⁝ **10** h: gels
  • **afternoon**: fago k* gels k*
  • **night**: til k*
  • **heat**; during: sabad b7.de
  • **parchment**; like: *Anac* **Bar-c** crot-h *Sulph*
O • **Back** of hands: alum k2 cortiso tpw7* morg-p pte1•
  ⁝ **sun** agg.: cortiso tpw7
  • **Palms**: ars ptk1 bad k* bar-c bg2 bell k* bism k* cham bg2* chinin-ar k2 crot-h bg2 diph ptk1 dys pte1• ferr-p a1 flav jl2 gels bg2* haem k* ham bg2* hep bg2 kali-bi bg2* laur k* *Lyc* k* morg-p pte1• nat-c bg2 *Nux-m* ptk1 petr-ra shn4• pip-m k* polyp-p a1 rhus-t bg2* rhus-v k* sabad sang k2 sars mrr1 sulph bg2* tax k* thuj bg2
  ⁝ **crusts**: sel ptk1
- **Joints**: canth k* croc ferr k2 lyc k* m-arct bg **Nux-v** k* ph-ac **Puls** k*

Dryness: ...
- **Knees**:
O • **Joints**: ars-met nux-v k*
  ⁝ **sensation** of: benz-ac bufo bg2
- **Lower** limbs: agar lact bg1 luf-op rsj5• mand rsj7• op k* phos b4a.de plut-n srj7• podo fd3.de• sep b4a.de sil b4a.de spong fd4.de tritic-vg fd5.de
O • **Joints** | **sensation** of: benz-ac bg2 canth b7.de* croc b7.de* *Nux-v* b7.de*
- **Toes** | **Nails**: sacch sst1• *Sil Thuj*
- **Upper** limbs:
O • **Joints** | **sensation** of: canth b7.de*

DUPUYTREN'S contraction (See Contraction - hands - dupuytren's)

EATING:
- **after**:
  • **agg.**:
  ⁝ **Lower** limbs: ant-c b7.de* arn b7.de* bell b4.de* *Bry* b7.de* cann-s b7.de* canth b7.de* caps b7.de* *Cham* b7.de* chel b7.de* *Chin* b7.de* cina b7.de* *Cocc* b7.de* dros b7.de* *Ferr* b7.de* *Ign* b7.de* kali-bi bg2 kali-c b4a.de* kali-n b4.de* m-aust b7.de mag-c b4.de* *Nux-v* b7.de* op b7.de* *Puls* b7.de* ran-b b7.de* rhus-t b7.de* *Ruta* b7.de* sil b4a.de staph b7.de* tarax b7.de* verat b7.de*
  ⁝ **Upper** limbs: ant-c b7.de ant-t bg2 bism b7a.de bry b7.de* canth b7.de* cham b7.de* chel b7.de* chin b7.de* *Cocc* b7.de* con bg2 ferr b7.de* ign b7.de* nux-v b7.de* puls b7.de* ruta b7.de*
- **before**:
  • **agg.** | **Upper** limbs: olnd b7.de* sabad b7.de*
- **while**:
  • **agg.**: clem ptk1 ind ptk1
  ⁝ **Lower** limbs: *Cocc* b7.de* ign b7.de* nux-v b7.de* ph-ac b4a.de puls b7.de*
  ⁝ **Upper** limbs: bism b7.de* canth b7.de* *Cocc* b7.de* kali-bi bg2 olnd b7.de* puls b7.de* stram b7.de*
  • **amel.**: nat-c ptk1

ECCHYMOSES: carb-v mrr1 ham mrr1 helo-s bnm14• lach mrr1 led mrr1 merc-c petr-ra shn4• *Sec* **Sul-ac** *Tarent Vip*
- **eight** hours after itching: allox sp1
O - **Fingers**: coca
O • **Tips**: allox sp1
- **Legs**: crot-h zinc b4a.de
  • **hot** bath; after: allox sp1
- **Lower** limbs: agav-a bg3 phos solid bg3 *Sul-ac*
- **Nails**; under: helo-s bnm14•
- **Upper** arms: vip
- **Upper** limbs: vip
  • **sensation** of: chin b7.de* par b7.de* *Sul-ac* b4a.de

EDEMA (See Swelling)

EJACULATION agg.: | **Lower** limbs: bell bg2

ELECTRICAL current; sensation of an: *(↗Shocks)* agar ail anh sp1 bamb-a stb2.de• bol-la dor gels hist sp1* hydrog srj2• nicotam rly4• plac-s rly4• x-ray sp1
O - **Feet**: gels
- **Fingers**:
  • **right** hand: coca-c sk4•
  • **touching** things; on: *Alum* k*
- **Hands**: gels ptel vml3•
  • **right**: x-ray sp1
- **Legs**: anh sp1 bamb-a stb2.de• bol-la dor hydrog srj2•
  • **night**: bamb-a stb2.de•
- **Nates**: bamb-a stb2.de•
- **Upper** limbs: bol-la dor gels loxo-recl knl4• nicotam rly4• plac-s rly4• plut-n srj7•

ELEVATION:
- **agg.**; elevation of extremities | **Lower** limbs: kali-c bg2 phyt bg2 sep bg2

Extremities

- **amel.**; elevation of extremities | **Lower** limbs: bar-c bg2* *Carb-v* bg2 con bg2 dios bg2 gran bg2 graph ptk1 ham bg2* phyt bg2 sep bg2*
- **sensation** of | **Lower** limbs: ph-ac bg2 podo bg2

○ - **Feet** | **sitting** agg.: cench k2
- **Shoulders**: *(↗Raised - shoulders)* merc bg2 sep h2*
  - **left** | **sensation** as if higher then right shoulder: hell ptk1 merc ptk1

ELONGATION (See Longer)

EMACIATION: *(↗Withered; GENERALS - Atrophy - muscles)* acet-ac br1 alum-sil k2 ars bar-c k2 bell bg2 *Calc* k* carb-v k2 carbn-s cina bg2 clem cupr bg2 iod k2 lyc bg2 nit-ac phos k2 phyt **Plb** k* ruta fd4.de *Sec* sil bg2* staph sne stront-c **Sulph** k*
- **left** side: cupr bg2 sil bg2 sulph bg2
- **accompanied** by | **Mesenteric** glands; disease of (See ABDOMEN - Complaints - mesenteric - accompanied - extremities)
- **diseased** limb: *Ars* bry carb-v dulc *Graph* **Led** *Mez* nat-m nit-ac ph-ac phos **Plb** k* **Puls** *Sec* sel *Sep* sil
- **malnutrition**; from: abrot tl1
- **paralyzed** limb: *Kali-p* nux-v **Plb** k* *Sec* *Sep*

○ - **Feet**: *Ars* carb-v k2 **Caust** k* chin iod h* nat-m plb sel bro1
- **Fingers**: lach ruta fd4.de *Sil* k* thuj

○ • **First**: lach thuj
  - **Tips**: ars thal dx
- **Forearms**: *Phos* **Plb** k*
- **Hands**: ars k* chin cupr k* graph k* mez b4a.de ph-ac bg2 *Phos* k* **Plb** k* **Sel** k* sil b4a.de
  - **left**: *Sil* b4a.de
- **Hips**: calc

○ • **Gluteal** muscles: lath plb
- **Legs**: *Abrot* k* acet-ac bro1 *Am-m* bro1 *Apis* *Arg-n* bro1 benz-ac berb *Bov* *Calc* *Caps* cench k2 chin iod bro1 kali-i bro1 *Lath* bro1 nit-ac **Nux-v** pin-s bro1 **Rhus-v** sanic bro1 sarr sel k* syph thuj tub bro1

○ • **Calves**: sel
- **Lower** limbs: *Abrot* k* am-m *Apis* arg-met *Arg-n* k* *Ars* k* bar-c k2 berb k* bry b7a.de* *Calc* k* carb-v b4a.de* caust bg2 chin dig b4a.de dulc k* *Ign* b7a.de lath led b7a.de mez b4a.de nat-m k* nit-ac k* nux-v b7a.de* ph-ac k* pin-s c2* *Plb* k* rhus-t ptk1 *Sanic* sec b7a.de sel k* thal dx
  - **painful** limb: *Ol-j* **Plb** k ● thal dx
- **Nates**: bar-m *Lach* *Lath* k* nat-m sacch
  - **children**; in: | **infants**: nat-m ptk1
- **Shoulders**: *Plb* k* sumb
- **Thighs**: *Abrot* bro1 acet-ac bro1 bar-m *Calc* k* cench k2 kali-i bro1 *Lath* bro1 *Nit-ac* k* pin-s bro1 plb sacch *Sel* k*
- **Thumbs**: thuj

○ • **Balls**: **Plb** ●*
- **Upper** arms: *Nit-ac* k* plb

○ • **Inner** side: plb
- **Upper** limbs: ars carb-an chin cupr graph *Iod* k* *Lyc* k* **Plb** k* sel syph thuj
  - **right**: carb-an cupr *Plb* thuj
  - **accompanied** by | **Lower** limbs; dropsy of (See Swelling - lower - accompanied - upper)
  - **vaccination**; after: maland thuj
- **Wrists**: **Plb** sel bg2

EMOTIONS agg.:

○ - **Lower** limbs: *Nat-m* bg2
- **Upper** limbs: *Nat-m* bg2

EMPTINESS; sensation of: | **Legs** | **Calves**: nat-m bg2
- **Upper** limbs: coff b7.de* *Op* b7.de*

ENLARGEMENT:
- **children**; in: sacch br1
- **osteo**-arthropathy; hypertrophic pneumonic: thuj st
- **sensation** of: alum ant-c k* cann-i k2* carb-v k2 sep

○ • **Bones**: mez k2
  - **Feet**: **Apis** k* *Coloc* k* daph mang
    - ⁝ **walking** in open air agg.; after: mang
  - **Fingers**: benz-ac calad positr nl2•

Enlargement – sensation of – **Fingers**: ...
  - ⁝ **touching** something: *Caust*
  - **Hands**: ang bg1 aran k* bapt bell bg1 *Brucel* sa3• cact ptk1 cann-i caust bro1 chel bg1 clem cocc bg1* *Cupr* gins bro1 hyos ptk1 kali-n k* laur bg1 mang bg1 mez bg1 nux-m tl1 *Op* bg1 ptel rhus-t bg1
    - ⁝ **walking** in open air agg.; after: mang h2
  - **Knees**: alum merc ptk1
  - **Legs**: cedr k* falco-pe nl2• nux-m *Plat* sep
  - **Lower** limbs: merc bg2 ph-ac bg2 phel bg2
  - **Toes**: apis k* *Laur* k*
  - **Upper** limbs: *Cupr* hyos kali-n b4.de* *Lyc* manc ptel sep verat

○ - **Hands**; veins of: cic c1
- **Joints**; of (See Arthritic)
- **Nates**: am-m ptk1
- **Toes**: *Laur*

EPILEPTIC aura:

○ - **Arm**: calc *Lach* *Sulph*
- **Feet**:

○ • **Heels**:
    - ⁝ **extending** to | **Occiput**: *Stram*

EROSIVE GNAWING:

○ - **Arms** and hands: plat h2
- **Axilla**: agn c1 mez h2*
- **Toes**:
  - **accompanied** by | **urticaria**: sulph bro1
- **Upper** limbs: hell h1* led h1* rhus-t h1* ruta h1 spong h1* verat h1*

ERUCTATIONS:
- **amel.** | **Lower** limbs: mag-c bg2 *Puls* bg2* sep b4.de*

ERUPTIONS: *(↗Irritation)* agar alumn *Am-c* am-m anac *Apis* **Ars** ars-s-f k2 arund *Bar-c* bar-m bell bov brom *Bry* **Calc** calc-p calc-s canth carb-v carbn-o carbn-s **Caust** chel chin chinin-ar k2 chinin-s chlor cimic cob con cop crot-c crot-t cupr cupr-ar dulc fd4.de elaps euph fago fl-ac *Graph* guare hep iod jug-r *Kali-ar* kali-bi kali-br **Kali-c** kali-m k2 kali-p kali-s *Kreos* lach led **Lyc** mag-s manc **Merc** **Mez** mur-ac murx nat-ar k2 nat-c **Nat-m** nat-ox rly4• nat-p nat-pyru rly4• *Nit-ac* nux-v oena oxal-a rly4• petr petr-ra shn4• ph-ac phos pip-m plan plut-n srj7• podo *Psor* *Puls* **Rhus-t** rhus-v ribo rly4• *Rumx* ruta sabad sars sec sel **Sep** **Sil** spong fd4.de staph stram stront-c suis-hep rly4• **Sulph** tab tarax tep *Thuj* til tritic-vg fd5.de vanil fd5.de
- **acne**: cortico tpw7*
- **black**: *Ars* *Sec*
- **bleeding**: *Calc*
  - **scratching**; after: alum h2 cupr-ar
- **blisters**: *Ars* carb-v k2 dulc fd4.de falco-pe nl2• plut-n srj7•
  - **blood** blisters:
    - ⁝ **gangrenous**; becoming: *Sec*
    - ⁝ **Arm**-pit: [bell-p-sp dcm1]
  - **blue**: ran-b tl1
- **blotches**: ant-c aur berb carb-v cimx cocc hura lach merc mur-ac nat-c nat-m sars sulph zinc
- **boils**: all-c alum-sil k2 am-c apoc ars ars-s-f k2 aur-m *Bell* *Brom* calc carbn-s clem cob dream-p sdj1• elaps graph guare **Hep** hyos iris kali-bi kali-n *Lyc* mang-p rly4• *Merc* mez nat-m nit-ac nux-v petr ph-ac psor rat *Rhus-t* rhus-v sec sep stram **Sulph** thuj tritic-vg fd5.de
- **burning**: **Ars** bov carb-v k2 dulc fd4.de fago falco-pe nl2• lac-ac **Merc** nux-v **Rhus-t** til
  - **scratching**; after: staph til
- **confluent**: *Cop* phos rhus-v
- **cracked**: phos
- **desquamating**: agar aloe sne *Am-c* am-m am *Ars* ars-s-f k2 bar-c calc chinin-s choc srj3• *Crot-t* dulc fd4.de elaps ferr hydr kreos merc **Mez** petr-ra shn4• rhus-v ruta fd4.de sanguis-s hm2• sep sulph thuj
- **dry**: bry falco-pe nl2• ger-i rly4• merc mim-p rsj8• tarent k2 tritic-vg fd5.de vanil fd5.de
- **eczema**: *Anil* am *Ars* ars-i k2 ger-i rly4• graph k2 kali-br merc positr nl2• *Psor* tarent k2
- **elevations**: alumn anac aur cic cop crot-h crot-t cupr cupr-ar dros genist gent-c kali-br merc nat-m nit-ac petr plan plb puls spong fd4.de sul-ac thuj tritic-vg fd5.de urt-u

- **erythematous**: *(↗SKIN - Eruptions - erythema)* ars thuj
- **exuding**: *(↗moist)* carb-v k2 crot-h cupr hell *Kali-s* *Merc* *Nat-m* rhus-v sol-ni
  - **water**:
    - **bloody**: carb-v k2
    - **thin**: crot-h tarent-c
    - **yellow**: cupr hell hydrog srj2• *Rhus-v* sol-ni
- **fleabites**, like: sec
- **gritty**: nat-m
- **groups**: nat-m
- **hard**: bov tritic-vg fd5.de
- **herpes**: alum borx caust com *Con* cupr *Dulc* *Graph* led *Lyc* manc k* mang merc mur-ac *Nat-m* nicc nux-v petr psor sars sec sep staph thuj k* zinc
- **hot**: fago
- **impetigo**: carbn-s k2
- **indurations** after eruptions: kali-br
- **itching**: agar androc srj1• arg-n *Bov* bry calc cortiso gse fago genist gent-c ger-i rly4• lac-ac lac-e hm2• *Lac-h* sk4• lach led luna kg1• mag-s merc moni rfm1• nat-m nux-v phos puls *Rhus-t* ros-d wla1 rumx ruta fd4.de sep sil sulph tarax til tritic-vg fd5.de urt-u vanil fd5.de [spect dfg1]
  - **immersing** hands in water agg.: rhus-t hr1
  - **without**: alum-sil k4 luna kg1•
- **itch**-like: ars bry *Sulph* tarent k2
- **knots**, reddish, hard: kali-bi k*
- **measles**, like: arge-pl rwt5• cop rhus-t
- **moist**: *(↗exuding)* bry *Merc* nat-m
- **nodules**: olib-sac wmh1 petr sep
- **painful**: **Arn** bar-s k2 bov falco-pe nl2• hep lach-h sk4• merc tritic-vg fd5.de
- **patches**: ail k2 *Carb-v* iris jug-c phos *Puls* *Sars* thuj viol-t
- **petechiae**: *Ars* aur-m berb
- **pimples**: acon agar am-c am-m anac ant-c ant-t arg-n arn **Ars** ars-s-f k2 asc-t bar-c bar-m bar-s k2 bell berb bov **Bry** bufo calc *Calc-p* *Calc-s* cann-s carb-an carbn-s castm **Caust** chel chinin-s cit-v k* clem cob com *Con* crot-c cund sne cupr-ar dulc fd4.de elaps fago falco-pe nl2• *Fl-ac* *Graph* hura iris iris-foe jatr-c kali-ar kali-br *Kali-c* kali-chl kali-m k2 kali-p kali-s kreos lac-ac *Lach* *Lyc* mag-c mag-m mang *Merc* mez morph mur-ac *Nat-m* *Nat-s* nicc ol-an k* op osm ph-ac plan plat psor puls rat **Rhus-t** rhus-v rumx ruta fd4.de sabad sars sel **Sep** spig spong fd4.de stann staph stront-c *Sulph* tab tarax thuj til valer vanil fd5.de *Verat* zinc zinc-p k2 [spect dfg1]
- **pustules**: aids nl2• am-c anac ant-c arg-n ars ars-s-f k2 asc-t bry chel chlor cocc cop crot-c cupr cupr-ar dulc fd4.de elaps fl-ac hyos iris jug-c kali-bi kali-br lach lyc merc mez positr nl2• rhod *Rhus-t* rhus-v ros-d wla1 rumx ruta sars sil squil staph stram **Sulph** tab tarent thal-xyz srj8• thuj tritic-vg fd5.de vac verat
- **rash**: aids nl2• alum alum-sil k2 ant-t *Apis* ars bell bry calad *Chlol* cop cupr daph *Dig* form kali-ar led mez nat-m nux-v *Petr* phyt **Puls** rheum *Rhus-t* sep sil sul-i *Sulph* tep thal-xyz srj8• *Vesp* zinc
  - **accompanied** by | **spots**:
    - **Hands** | **Back** of hands: cortiso tpw7
    - **Joints**; pain in (See Pain - joints - accompanied - rash)
- **red**: bell bov chlol crot-c gins jug-r kali-bi mag-s merc nat-m rhus-v spong fd4.de tritic-vg fd5.de valer vanil fd5.de
- **roseola**, after abuse of mercury: *Kali-i*
- **rough**: rhus-v
- **scabs**: arn ars cit-v k* iris-foe kali-br **Kali-s** *Mez* mur-ac phos plb podo rhus-t rhus-v **Sil** staph sul-ac zinc
- **scales**: arn *Ars-i* calc-s k2 *Kali-s* *Merc* *Mez* nat-ar k2 phos pip-m rhus-t rhus-v sec sulph tritic-vg fd5.de vanil fd5.de zinc
- **scurfs**, brownish: am-m bar-m cinnb merc
- **tubercles**: ant-c caust crot-h nat-c
- **urticaria**: acon ant-c *Apis* *Bell* berb *Calc* chinin-s **Chlol** *Cop* dulc hydrc hyper indg kali-br kali-i lac-leo sk4• *Lach* lyc merc *Nat-m* *Rhus-t* *Rhus-v* *Sulph* tarax *Urt-u*
  - **warm** applications agg.: cassia-s ccrh1•
- **varicella**, like: *Ant-t* syc bka1*•
- **vesicles**: acon am-m anac **Ant-c** **Ant-t** arg-n arn **Ars** ars-i ars-s-f k2 bell bov brom bufo calad *Calc* calc-p calc-s cann-s canth *Carb-v* carbn-o *Caust* chin chlor cit-v k* clem crot-h cupr cupr-ar daph *Dulc* elaps fl-ac graph hep hura indg iod iris kali-ar kali-bi kali-chl kali-i kali-m k2 kali-s *Lach* lachn mag-c manc mang *Merc* mez nat-ar k2 nat-c **Nat-m** nat-p nit-ac ph-ac **Phos** **Ran-b** rhus-r **Rhus-t** **Rhus-v** ruta sabad sars sec sel sil sol-ni spong sul-i k2 *Sulph* tritic-vg fd5.de vanil fd5.de verat vip zinc zinc-p k2

- **vesicles**: ...
  - **white**: agar
- ○ - **Ankles**: cact *Calc* k* calc-p *Chel* k* graph bg1 nat-m bg1 nat-p ptk1 osm petr bg1 *Psor* k* puls rhus-v sel sep stront-c sulph bg1 tep
  - **boils**: merc
  - **dry**: cact
  - **eczema**: *Chel* nat-p k* *Psor* k* syc bka1•
    - **itching**: nat-p tl1
    - **varicose**: syc fmm1•
  - **herpes**: cact cycl *Kreos* nat-c *Nat-m* *Petr* sulph
  - **moist**: chel
  - **patches**: *Calc*
    - **red** | **bed** | **going** into: cortiso tpw7
      - **heat**: cortiso tpw7
  - **pimples**: calc-p *Hell* b7a.de nat-p bg2 sel b7.de* sep k* stront-c k* sulph b4.de*
  - **pustules**: cupr-ar *Lach*
  - **rash**: cortiso tpw7 osm tep
  - **red**: calc chel sars
  - **spots**: puls k*
  - **tetters**: cycl b7a.de hell b7a.de *Kreos* b7a.de nat-c b4a.de nat-m b4a.de petr b4a.de *Staph* b7a.de sulph b4a.de
  - **urticaria**: *Nat-m*
  - **vesicles**: aster rhus-v sel
- ○ **Malleolus**: *Cact*
    - **Medial**; on | **red** points: bung-fa mtf
- **Areola**, red: nat-m olib-sac wmh1
- **Elbows**: am-m bg2 ant-t bg2 aster bell bg2 berb *Brom* cact cupr dulc bg2 hep hyos bg2 iris *Kali-s* kreos lach k* merc k* *Phos* k* *Psor* sabin k* sel rsj9• *Sep* *Staph* k* sulph k* syph ptk1* tep thuj tritic-vg fd5.de zinc k*
  - **blister**: crot-h
    - **black**: ars
  - **desquamation**: sulph
  - **eczema**: brom calc bg2 cupr bg2 lac-ac stj5• merc bg2 phos bg2 sep bg2 staph bg2 thuj bg2
  - **elevations**: merc
    - **itchy** and scaly: merc
  - **herpes**: borx cact **Cupr** hep *Kreos* *Phos* k* psor *Sep* k* *Staph* k* *Thuj* k*
    - **ringworm** (See ringworm)
  - **itching**: merc nat-c ptk1 pitu-gl skp7• *Sep* staph h1* syph ptk1*
  - **miliary**: zinc bg2
  - **nodules**: eupi mur-ac
  - **painful**: merc
  - **pimples**: ant-c k* asc-t berb bry k* calad b7.de* *Dulc* k* *Hyos* k* kali-n lach merc k* nat-c ol-an k* sabin k* sep *Staph* k* sulph tarax thuj k*
    - **biting**: kali-n
    - **burning**: kali-n
    - **inflamed** base; on: tarax
  - **psoriasis**, patches: falco-pe nl2• *Iris* kali-ar *Kali-s* morg-g pte1• *Phos*
  - **pustules**: eup-per hep jug-c jug-r k* lach mang-p rly4• sulph bg2 tritic-vg fd5.de
    - **itching**: hep tritic-vg fd5.de
    - **yellow**: jug-c jug-r k*
  - **rash**: calad *Mez* sulph
  - **red**: cinnb rhus-t tritic-vg fd5.de
  - **ringworm**: cupr k* tub c1
  - **scales**: calc jug-r *Kali-s* merc *Sep* *Staph* sulph tritic-vg fd5.de
  - **scurfy**: *Sep* bg2
  - **suppurating**: sulph
  - **tetters**: cupr b7a.de *Kreos* b7a.de sep b4.de staph b7a.de
  - **tubercle**: am-c caust mag-c mur-ac
  - **urticaria**: aran
  - **vesicles**: *Ars* calad nat-p sulph k*

- **vesicles**: ...
  - **black**: *Ars*
  - **suppurating**: sulph
  - **white**: sulph
  - **yellow**: sulph
- ○ **Bends** of elbow●: am-m bry calad calc *Cupr* *Graph* k* *Hep* merc *Mez* k* moni rfm1• nat-c **Nat-m** k ● podo fd3.de• *Psor* k* **Sep** k ●* staph sulph
  - **crusts**: *Cupr* *Mez* **Psor**
    - **thick**: sep ptk1
  - **dry**: *Mez*
  - **eczema**: *Cupr* *Graph* kali-ar vg *Mez* moni jl2* nat-c mrr1 **Psor** sulph gk
  - **exudation**: sulph
  - **fissures**: *Kali-ar*
  - **herpes**: cupr graph kreos **Nat-m** sep thuj
  - **itching**: limest-b es1• sulph h2* zinc h2*
    - **evening**: cupr h2*
    - **corrosive**: ant-c h2*
  - **painful**: am-m ant-c dros dulc hura lachn nat-c ol-an phos rhus-t sep
  - **pimples**: am-m h2* ant-c dulc h1* hura hyos lac-h sk4• nat-c h2* ol-an k* phos *Sep* thuj
    - **morning**: dulc h1*
    - **evening** | **warm** room; in: dulc h1
  - **pustules**: asc-t a1 sulph
  - **rash**: calad *Hep* sep zinc
  - **red**: *Cor-r* rhus-t
  - **scabies**: bry merc
  - **scratching** agg.; after: nat-c h2*
  - **vesicles**: *Calc* *Nat-c* rhus-v sulph
    - **red**: *Nat-c*
  - **yellow**, scaly: cupr ptk1
- **Olecranon**: berb k*
  - **dry**, furfuraceous: aster k* sep
  - **pimples**: berb k*

\- **Feet**: *Anan* *Ars* k* aster bar-c bism bro1 bov *Calc* k* carbn-o *Caust* chinin-s con cop k* croc crot-c dulc bg1 elaps k* genist glycyr-g cte1• graph bg2* ketogl-ac rly4• lac-del hm2• lach med *Mez* k* *Petr* bro1 phos plac-s rly4• *Rhus-t* k* rhus-v samars gm1 sanguis-s hm2• sec k* sep stram sulph k* zinc bg2

- **black**: *Ars* *Sec*
- **bleeding**: *Calc*
- **blisters**; infected: ¦ **walking** agg.: arist-cl sp1
- **blotches**: ant-c jug-r kreos lyc podo fd3.de• sep sulph
- **boils**: anan calc k* led lyc h2* sars sil **Stram** k*
- **burning**: bov mez
- **confluent**: cop rhus-v
- **coppery** spots: *Graph*
- **desquamation**: agar bg1 ars bg2* berb bg1 chin bg2* chinin-s dulc k* **Manc** bg2* merc bg1 **Mez** petr-ra shn4• sanguis-s hm2• sulph bg2* thlas bg2 thuj bg1
- **dry**: *Mez*
- **eczema**: moni jl2 petr-ra shn4•
- **elevation**: cop
- **flea** bite, like: sec k*
- **fungus**: graph ptk1 sanic ptk1 tub mrr1
- **hard**: bov *Lach*
- **herpes**: **Alum** *Mez* *Nat-m* *Petr* **Sulph**
- **itching**: androc srj1• aster bov calc con lac-h sk4• *Mez* sep sil
  - **biting**: *Calc*
  - **burning**: bov *Mez*
- **miliary**: ars
- **nodes**: *Ang*
- **painful**: lyc phos spig sulph
- **papules**:
  - **left**: beryl tpw5
  - **itching**: beryl tpw5

\- **Feet – papules – itching**: ...

- **bed** agg.; in: beryl tpw5
- **scratching**; when: beryl tpw5
- **warm** applications agg.: beryl tpw5

- **pimples**: ars bar-c bov bry k* *Carbn-s* con k* crot-c cupr *Hell* b7a.de led mosch ph-ac b4a.de sec b7.de* sel sep k* stront-c b4.de* sulph zinc
- **pustules**: *Calc* *Con* *Merc* *Rhus-t* sep
- **rash**: bov bry cortiso tpw7
- **red**: androc srj1• bov crot-c ketogl-ac rly4• lac-h sk4•
- **scabs**: *Calc* rhus-v *Sil*
- **scaly**: rhus-v
- **scurf**: *Sil*
- **tetters**: alum b4.de* lyc b4a.de *Thuj* b4a.de
- **tubercles**: carb-an rhus-t
- **urticaria**: *Calc* sulph
- **vesicles**: *Ars* k* aster carbn-o *Caust* k* *Con* elaps *Graph* lach *Manc* nat-c ptk1 nit-ac *Phos* rhus-v *Sec* sel sep sulph tarax vinc vip zinc
  - **black**: **Ars** nat-m
  - **phagedenic**: *Con* *Sel* *Sulph* *Zinc*
  - **rubbing** agg.: caust
  - **suppurating**: *Con* *Graph* *Nat-c* *Sel* *Sil*
  - **watery**: rhus-v
  - **white**: *Cycl* *Graph* *Lach* sulph
- ○ **Back** of feet: aster bov carbn-o *Caust* cortiso tpw7 lach led med merc petr *Psor* puls sars tarax thuj zinc
  - **right**: sal-al blc1•
    - **herpes**: sal-al blc1•
    - **painful**: sal-al blc1•
    - **ulcerative**: sal-al blc1•
    - **vesicles**: sal-al blc1•
  - **bed** | **agg.**: cortiso tpw7
  - **eczema**: merc *Psor*
  - **elevations**: petr puls thuj
  - **impetigo**: *Carbn-s*
  - **itching**: aster *Calc* carb-an h2* lach led h1* *Psor* sep h2* tarax
  - **nodules**: carb-an h2* petr
  - **painful**: bov psor
  - **papular**: anthraco br1
  - **pimples**: carb-an bg2 *Caust* led k* mosch k* sep h2*
  - **pustules**: calc con sars sep
  - **rash**: cortiso tpw7
  - **scaly**: psor
  - **sun** agg.: cortiso tpw7
  - **tetters**: caust b4a.de hep b4a.de lyc b4a.de sep b4a.de sil b4a.de
  - **vesicles**: aster bov carbn-o cassia-s ccrh1• lach moni jl2 tetox pin2• zinc
    - **noon** | **amel.**: cassia-s ccrh1•
    - **night**: cassia-s ccrh1•
    - **cold applications** | **amel.**: cassia-s ccrh1•
    - **itching**: aster sep h2* tarax h1*
    - **scratching** agg.: cassia-s ccrh1•
    - **ulcerative**: zinc
    - **warm** applications agg.: cassia-s ccrh1•
  - **warm** applications agg.: cortiso tpw7
- **Ball**, nodule: zinc h2
- **Heel**:
  - **blisters**: calc *Caust* k* graph k* *Lach* led *Nat-c* k* nat-m *Petr* *Phos* plut-n srj7• sep *Sil* squil bro1
    - **rubbing**; from slight: lam br1
  - **boils**: calc lach
  - **desquamating**: elaps
  - **itching**: caust h2* sil h2*
  - **pustules**: *Nat-c*
    - **black** ulcerating: nat-c a1
  - **ulcerated**: lam br1 nat-c

- **Sole** of: anan androc srj1• ars bell bry bufo chinin-s con dulc fd4.de elaps kali-bi manc med gk nat-m nat-s gk pip-m sulph
  - **blisters**: all-c bro1 ars k* bell bg2 bufo bg1* calc k* dulc fd4.de gaert pte1*• kali-bi bg2 manc bg2 nat-c bg2 nat-m bg2 plut-n srj7• sulph bg2
    - **night**: gaert pte1*•
    - **itching**: gaert fmm1•
    - **rubbing** agg.; slight: lam br1
  - **boils**: kreos b7a.de rat k*
  - **chicken** pox: dys fmm1•
  - **desquamating**: ars chinin-s elaps kali-p fd1.de• *Manc* k* psil ft1* sulph
  - **herpetic**: morg-g fmm1•
  - **pimples**: con
  - **psoriasis**: cor-r br1 *Phos*
  - **scales**: kali-p fd1.de• pip-m
  - **urticaria**: propr sa3•
  - **vesicles**: *Ars* k* bell k* *Bufo* *Calc* k* kali-ar k2 kali-bi k* *Kali-c* *Manc* k* med gk merc ptk1 nat-c bg2* nat-m k* nat-s ptk1 sulph k*
    - **bloody** serum: nat-m
    - **corroding**, eating: *Ars* sulph
    - **fetid** water, with: *Ars*
    - **spreading**: **Ars** *Calc*
    - **ulcerating**: **Ars** *Calc* psor sulph
    - **yellow** fluid, with: *Ars* *Bufo*

- **Fingers**: aln bro1 anac bg2* ant-c bg2 arn ars *Barbit* bro1 bell bg2 borx *Bov* bro1 canth caust k* choc srj3• *Cist* **Clem** bg2 cupr k* cycl k* dulc fd4.de fl-ac graph k* grat bg2 hep k* *Kali-s* kreos bg2 *Lach* k* lim bro1 *Lob-e* bro1 lyc bg2 merc bg2 mez mur-ac k* nat-c bg2* nat-m bg2 nat-s k2 nit-ac bg2* petr k2* ph-ac k* plb bg2 prim-f bro1 puls bg2 ran-b k* rhus-t k* rhus-v ruta fd4.de sars k* sel bro1 sep sil k* spig k* spong fd4.de sulph tab tarax k* ther bg2 thuj vanil fd5.de verat bg2 zinc bg2
  - **blotches**: ant-c arg-n ars berb caust cocc con lach led nat-c rhus-t verat
  - **boils**: calc k* cassia-s ccrh1• *Lach* psor tl1 sil
  - **burning**: caust h2* ran-b
  - **copper**-colored spots: cor-r
  - **desquamation**●: agar am-m ptk1 bar-c k* chlol hr1 dulc fd4.de elaps k* *Graph* merc k* *Mez* nat-m bg2 petr-ra shn4• plut-n srj7• *Rhus-v* ruta fd4.de sabad k* *Sep* still *Sulph* k*
  - **dry**: anag psor trios rsj11*•
  - **eczema**: ambr bg2 borx br1 *Calc* vh caust bg2 cypra-eg sde6.de• *Graph* bg2 *Lyc* k* merc bg2 **Nit-ac** bg2 ran-b bg2 sep bg2 sil staph thuj bg2
    - **accompanied** by | **falling** out of nails: borx br1*
    - **painful**: arn
  - **elevated** spots: syph
  - **excrescences**: ars thuj
    - **greenish**: ars
    - **wart**-like: thuj
  - **herpes**: ambr caust *Cist* **Graph** *Kreos* merc nit-ac psor ran-b thuj zinc
  - **itching**: caust h2* ran-b
  - **moist**: nat-s k2
  - **painful** nodules: *Calc*
  - **pemphigus**: (↗*SKIN - Eruptions - pemphigus)* lyc
  - **phagedenic** blisters: calc dream-p sdj1• *Graph* hep kali-c *Mag-c* nit-ac ran-b sil sulph
  - **pimples**: acon bg2 agn b7.de* anac ant-c k* arn k* ars bar-c k* berb brom tl1 bry b7.de canth k* carb-ac cycl k* elaps graph k* *Kali-c* lach b7.de* laur b7.de* *Lyc* k* mez k* mur-ac k* *Nat-c* b4a.de par b7.de* *Ph-ac* k* plb b7.de* puls b7.de* *Ran-b* b7a.de *Rhus-t* b7.de* sars k* sep b4a.de sil b4a.de *Spig* k* squil b7.de* tab tarax k* *Ther* *Zinc* k*
    - **red**: bros-gau mrc1 ph-ac h2* verat a1
  - **pocks**: sil bg2
  - **psoriasis**: graph k2 lyc teucr
  - **pustules**: aln br1 anac k* bar-c k* borx k* cassia-s ccrh1• cinnb cocc cupr k* hydrog srj2• kali-bi k* mag-c bg2 plb bg2 positr nl2• puls bg2 rhus-t sang sars k* sil bg2 spig k* zinc k*

- **Fingers – pustules**: ...
    - **crusts**; forming offensive: aln br1
  - **rash**: cortiso tpw7 hydr sil thal-xyz srj8•
  - **scabs**: aln br1 anag cit-v k* kali-bi lyc mur-ac rhus-v thuj
  - **scales**, white: lyc *Sep*
  - **tetters**: *Alum* b4a.de ambr b7.de* *Caust* b4.de* graph b4a.de *Kreos* b7a.de merc b4.de *Ran-b* b7.de*
  - **tubercles**: berb caust *Con* hydrc *Lach* *Led* lyc nat-c rhus-t verat zinc
  - **urticaria**: hep thuj k* urt-u
    - **cold**; on becoming: thuj
  - **vesicles**: apis b7a.de bell k* *Borx* k* calc calc-sil k2 *Cit-v* k* *Clem* k* cupr k* cupr-ar cycl fl-ac k* *Graph* k* hell b7.de* hep k* *Kali-c* *Kali-s* lach k* mag-c k* mang k* *Mez* k* *Nat-c* k* *Nat-m* k* nat-s *Nit-ac* petr k2 *Ph-ac* phos *Plb* prot jl2 *Puls* *Ran-b* k* *Rhus-t* k* rhus-v k* *Sars* sec b7.de* *Sel* *Sep* k* *Sil* k* *Sulph* k* vanil fd5.de
    - **bluish**: *Ran-b*
    - **burning**: ran-b
    - **frostbite**; after: graph b4a.de *Hep* b4a.de *Kali-c* b4a.de *Mag-c* b4.de* *Nit-ac* b4.de* sil b4a.de
    - **itching**: lach bg2 prot jl2 ran-b sabad bg2 sars h2 sil h2
    - **spreading**: **Clem** bg2 graph bg2 kali-c bg2 mag-c bg2 nit-ac bg2 sil bg2 sulph bg2
    - **ulcers**, becoming: calc dream-p sdj1• graph kali-c mag-c nit-ac petr k2 ran-b sil
  - ○ **Back** of fingers: cortiso tpw7 mur-ac h2
    - **bed** | **agg.**: cortiso tpw7
    - **sun** agg.: cortiso tpw7
    - **warm** applications agg.: cortiso tpw7
  - **Between** the fingers (See hands - between the)
  - **First**: agar *Calc* kali-c mag-c nat-c pieri-b mlk9.de ruta fd4.de sil symph fd3.de•
    - **pimples**: anac h2* sulph
    - **psoriasis**: anag teucr
    - **pustules**: anac h2*
    - **tubercles**: lyc h2*
    - **vesicles**: *Calc* kali-c mag-c nat-c sil sulph
      - **burning**: nat-c h2*
      - **cold** washing; after: (non:nat-c kl)
      - **corroding**: mag-c h2*
      - **discharging** water: kali-c
      - **phagedenic**: *Calc*
      - **washing** | **amel.**: nat-c kl
    - **wart**-like: lyc h2
  - **Fourth** finger: cycl falco-pe nl2•
    - **vesicles**: graph kali-c h2* nat-m h2*
      - **itching**: nit-ac h2*
  - **Joints**: cycl k* hell bg2 hep bg2 hydr *Mez* nat-c k2 **Psor**
    - **boils**: calc bg2 psor tl1
    - **dry**: **Psor** k*
    - **pimples**: cycl b7a.de
    - **scurfy**: anac bg2
    - **ulcers**, itching: *Mez*
    - **vesicles** | **corroding**: hep bg2
  - **Nails**, about: eug graph bro1 merc psor bro1* sel stann-m bro1 tub xxb
    - **crusts**: *Ars*
    - **desquamation**: chlol cortico tpw7 petr-ra shn4• *Sabad* b7a.de sel b7.de*
    - **psoriasis**: graph bro1 *Sep* bro1
    - **pustules**: bell h1*
      - **extending** to | **Wrist**; over hand to: *Kali-bi*
    - **ulcers**: *Ars*
    - **vesicles**: ail *Nat-c*
    - **winter**: psor jl2
  - **Palmar** surface | **desquamation**: psil ft1
  - **Second** finger, psoriasis: anag
  - **Sides**: *Mez* sabad tarax h1* tax tub dgt

- **Third** finger: cycl dream-p sdj1• plut-n srj7•
- **Tips**: ars bar-c *Cist* cupr elaps *Nat-c* psor
  - **blisters**: ail bg2* alum cupr k*
  - **cracked**: ran-b br1
  - **desquamation**●: agar b4a.de all-c dgt bar-c k* elaps k* manc bg2 merc b4a.de nat-m mrr1 ph-ac k* phos k* sabad b7.de* sulph b4a.de thea bg2
  - **eczema**: cupr bg2 *Graph* bg2 nat-c mrr1 petr bg2 sanic bg2
  - **pimple**: elaps
  - **pustules**: *Hep* bg2 lach bg2 *Nat-c* bg2 ph-ac bg2 *Psor* sep bg2
  - **vesicles**: ail *Ars Cupr Nat-c* k*
    - **filled** with blood: **Ars**

- **Forearms**: acon-ac rly4• agar bg2 *Alum* am-c bg2 am-m bg2 ant-t ars bov bg2 bry calad *Carb-an* k* *Caust* k* cinnb con cupr dream-p sdj1• granit-m es1• *Graph* kali-n bg2 lac-e hrn2• lach bg2 laur bg2 *Lyc* bg2 mag-c bg2 mag-s mang *Merc Mez* mur-ac bg2 phos rhod bg2 rhus-t ribo rly4• sabad bg2 sel sil bg2 spong k* staph bg2 sulph bg2 symph fd3.de• *Tarax* tritic-vg fd5.de vanil fd5.de zinc k*
  - **boils**: **Brom** b4a.de *Calc* k* carb-v cassia-s ccrh1• cob *Iod Lach* lyc k* mag-m *Nat-s* petr k* sil k* tritic-vg fd5.de
  - **crusts**: *Mez* petr hr1
  - **desquamation**, bran-like: agar h2* lac-e hrn2• merc bg2 stront-c bg2
  - **eczema**: *Alum* bg2 aur-i k2 *Con* bg2 *Graph* mang bg2 *Merc* k* *Mez* moni jl2 nat-m bg2 nux-v bg2 *Sil* sulph bg2 thuj
  - **excoriated**: rhus-t
  - **herpes**: *Alum Con* mag-s mang **Merc** nat-m sulph
  - **itching**: carb-an h2* choc srj3• kali-n h2* lac-leo sk4• mang h2* *Mez* streptoc rly4• tritic-vg fd5.de vanil fd5.de
  - **miliary**: bry bg2 merc-c bg2 sel bg2
    - **moist**: alum bg2 cupr bg2
  - **moist**: *Alum Merc Mez* rhus-t
  - **nodules**:
    - **red** itching: nat-m h2
    - **Flexors**; on: hippoz
  - **pimples**: *Alum* b4a.de am-c am-m k* amph a1 ant-t k* ars asc-t bell k* borx bry k* calad k* calc-p canth b4a.de *Carbn-s Caust* cit-v k* fago gamb hep b4a.de iod *Kali-bi* k* kali-br a1 kali-n lach laur lyc k* mag-c mag-i a4 *Mag-s* mang merc k* nat-m *Nat-s* ol-an osm ph-ac rat rhod k* sabad k* sars sel b7.de* *Sep* b4a.de sil b4a.de spong b7a.de staph b7.de* *Sulph Tax* thuj k* valer *Zinc* k*
    - **morning**: mang
    - **afternoon**: mag-c
    - **evening**: am-c fago
    - **alternating** with asthma (See RESPIRATION - Asthmatic - alternating - forearm - pimples)
    - **burning**: am-c calad mang nat-s
    - **itching**: am-c h2* am-m calad carbn-s caust gamb lyc mag-c h2* nat-s sabad staph h1* sulph *Zinc*
      - **daytime**: zinc h2*
    - **menses**; during: sulph
    - **scratching** agg.; after: am-m kali-n h2* mag-c h2* mang a1
      - **oozing**: kali-n
    - **washing**, from: mag-c
  - **psoriasis**: *Rhus-t*
  - **purulent** discharge: rhus-t
  - **pustules**: anac ant-t *Calc* cassia-s ccrh1• cop lyc h2* phos bg2 rhod rhus-t *Staph* k* tarent
    - **painful**: tarent
  - **rash**: am-c ant-t bry calad merc mez rheum ribo rly4• sel
    - **alternating** with asthma (See RESPIRATION - Asthmatic - alternating - forearm - rash)
  - **raw**: petr rhus-t
  - **red**: lac-h sk4• petr ph-ac h2* ribo rly4• sel rsj9• spong fd4.de symph fd3.de• tritic-vg fd5.de vanil fd5.de
  - **rupia**: kali-i
  - **scales**: alum merc petr

- **Forearms – scales**: ...
    - **whitish**: *Merc*
      - **cheese**, smelling like: *Calc*
    - **yellow**: rhus-t
  - **scratching** | **after** | **lumps**; raised: granit-m es1•
    - **agg.**: mang *Mez*
  - **spots**; dry red: spong fd4.de tritic-vg fd5.de vanil fd5.de
    - **itching**; violent: granit-m es1•
  - **stitching** on touch: petr h2*
  - **sun**; from exposure to: **Sulph** vh
  - **tetters**: alum b4.de* *Calc* b4a.de *Con* b4.de graph b4a.de hep b4a.de lyc b4a.de mang b4a.de merc b4.de nat-m b4.de nux-v b7.de sulph b4.de*
  - **tubercle**: *Agar* am-c jug-r kali-n lach mur-ac ph-ac
    - **scratching**; after: agar h2
  - **urticaria**: am-c calad cassia-s ccrh1• chin clem dream-p sdj1• lac-e hrn2• lyc *Nat-m* sil
    - **morning**: chin
    - **evening**: lyc
    - **heat**; during: calad
    - **scratching** agg.; after: calad calc chin sulfonam ks2
  - **vesicles**: anac ant-t arn ars calad carbn-o caust chin cit-v k* hura kola stb3• merc k* nat-sil fd3.de• petr phos k* podo fd3.de• rhus-r rhus-t rhus-v sars sil k* spong k* *Staph* sulph
    - **burning**: sil
    - **itching**: nat-sil fd3.de• sil h2*
    - **scratching** agg.; after: sars
    - **stinging**: rhus-t
    - **transparent**: rhus-t
    - **white**: calad

- **Hands**: agar bg2 alum k* am-m k* anag k* ant-c bg2 ant-t ars k* bar-m borx bro1 bov bg2 carb-an bg2 **Carb-v** k* *Cic* cist k* *Clem* cocc com con cop dig bg2 dulc falco-pe nl2• **Graph** *Hep* k* ip bg2 kali-c bg2 *Kali-s* kalm kreos k* *Lach* **Lyc** k* mag-c bg2 med *Merc* k* *Mez* k* *Mur-ac* k* nat-c *Nat-m Nat-s Nit-ac* k* oena ped bro1 *Petr* phos pieri-b mlk9.de pix c2* psor puls *Rhus-t* k* rhus-v ruta sanguis-s hrn2• sanic *Sars* sel k* sep *Spig* bg2 spong fd4.de *Staph* still suis-hep rly4• *Sul-ac* k* *Sulph* k* tarax bg2 tritic-vg fd5.de urol-h rwt• vanil fd5.de zinc k*
  - **left**: ven-m rsj12•
  - **black**: *Sec*
  - **bleeding**: *Alum Lyc Merc Petr*
  - **blister**-like: ran-b tl1
    - **manual** labor; from: arist-cl sp1
  - **blotches**: arg-n ars carb-an indg kali-chl merc rhus-t rhus-v sep spig stann sulph urt-u
  - **boils**: *Calc* k* calc-s bg2 coloc iris lach led *Lyc* k* *Psor*
    - **small**: iris
  - **brown**: nat-m
  - **burning**: bacls-7 fmm1• bufo cic tl1 nit-ac h2* rhus-t
    - **scratching**; after: *Mez* **Staph**
    - **touch** agg.: canth **Cic**
  - **circinate**: bacls-7 fmm1•
  - **confluent**: cic cop genist phos
  - **cracked**: *Alum Lyc Merc Petr*
  - **crusty**: *Anthraci* **Graph** *Petr Sanic*
  - **desquamation**: all-s alum k* am-c k* am-m k* anac bg2 ars bg2 bar-c k* calc b4a.de cic bg2 crot-c sk4• dulc fd4.de ferr k* *Graph* hep bg2 kreos bg2 laur k* merc k* mez nat-m k* petr-ra shn4• *Ph-ac* k* phos k* rhus-t k* ruta bg2 sanguis-s hrn2• *Sep* k* sulph k*
  - **dry**: anag k* bov lyc merc *Petr* mrr1 *Psor*
  - **eczema**: abies-c oss4• ambr bg2 anag bro1 ars aur-m-n wbt2• bar-c bro1 berb bro1* borx br1 *Bov* bg2* calc bro1* *Canth* carb-v mrr1 carc gk6 clem cob-n sp1 cor-r bg2* cortiso sp1 **Dulc** bg2 **Graph** k* *Hep* bro1 hyper bro1 ip bg2 *Jug-c* k* kreos bro1 lyc k* maland bro1 *Merc* k* *Mez* moni jl2 musca-d szs1 nat-c bg2* nat-m bg2 *Nit-ac Petr* bro1* phos *Pix* bro1 plb bro1 rhus-v bro1 sabal c1 sanic bro1 sars bg2 sel bro1 sep bg2* *Sil* staph bg2 still bro1 thuj bg2 verat bg2 **Zinc** bg2*

- **eczema**: ...
  - **itching**: carc gk6
- **elevated**: bar-m **Cic** kali-c lach merc nat-m nit-ac rhus-v sul-ac urt-u
- **exudation**, yellow: *Rhus-v*
- **fine**: **Carb-v**
- **furfuraceous**: *Alum*
- **hard**: am-m bov led ph-ac rhus-t spig
- **herpes**: *Borx Bov Calc* cist k* *Con* **Dulc** k* *Graph* kreos *Lim* bro1 lith-c bro1 merc *Mez Nat-c* nat-m nit-ac bro1 ran-b sars sep *Staph* verat **Zinc**
- **itching**: anag mrr1 androc srj1• ars h2* **Carb-v** k* cist k2 cob-n sp1 daph *Graph* ignis-alc es2• jug-r *Mez* mur-ac h2* nit-ac h2* phos pieri-b mlk9.de plut-n srj7• psor sanic sep h2* staph succ-ac rly4• sulph k2 tritic-vg fd5.de urt-u zinc
  - **midnight**, after: sul-ac h2*
- **itch**-like: *Anan Psor Sep*
- **menses**; during: dulc br1
- **millet** seed-like: bar-m k* dig bg2 led bg2
- **moist**: cist k2 *Clem* kali-c kali-s mang merc *Mez* morg-p fmm1• *Petr* ran-s rhus-t
- **nodules**: *Petr* sep
- **papular**: anthraco br1
- **pemphigus**: **Sep** bg2
- **pimples**: acon *Agar* am-c am-m b7a.de anac ant-c k* *Apis* b7a.de arg-n ars k* bell *Bov* bry *Canth* k* *Carb-v* k* carbn-s chinin-s *Cic* k* cupr-ar dig k* elaps hep k* iod kali-ar kali-bi bg2 kali-chl *Kreos* k* lac-ac *Lach* b7a.de *Lyc* k* m-ambo b7a.de merc k* mur-ac k* nit-ac k* ol-an op oxal-a rly4• pieri-b mlk9.de psor *Ran-b* b7a.de *Rhus-t* k* rhus-v sarr sec b7.de* *Sel* k* *Sep* b4a.de spig b7.de* squil b7.de* staph b7.de* sul-ac b4a.de *Sulph Tarax* k* vanil fd5.de *Zinc* k*
  - **burning**: bov cic hr1 rhus-t
  - **greenish**: cupr-ar
  - **hard**: bov *Rhus-t* rhus-v
  - **itching**: acon am-c bov hep h2* kreos *Lyc* sel sulph tarax h1* [spect dfg1]
    - **periodically**: sulph
    - **warm** in bed, when becoming: mur-ac
  - **red**: acon anac ars bov sulph til [spect dfg1]
  - **scurfs**, forming: mur-ac
  - **stinging**: acon
  - **suppurating**: anac elaps
- **psoriasis** diffusa: *Ars Calc* carc dtp *Clem Graph Kali-bi Lyc* mez **Petr** *Rhus-t* sars k2 sel c1 *Sulph*
- **purple**: *Petr* thal-xyz srj8•
- **pustules**: *Anac* ars bg2 asc-t *Carbn-s* chel cic fl-ac *Kali-bi* k* *Merc* nat-m phos *Psor* rhus-t k* rhus-v ruta sanic sars *Sep* sil k* squil staph sul-ac bg2 **Sulph** thal-xyz srj8•
  - **confluent**: anac rhus-v
  - **itching**: asc-t squil **Sulph**
  - **itch**-like: ruta *Sulph*
  - **purulent**: anac sars
  - **red**, evening: **Sulph**
  - **swelling**: *Rhus-t* k*
  - **watery**: rhus-t k*
- **rash**: *Agar* bry *Carb-v* corian-s knl6• cortiso tpw7 cupr dig kali-ar led **Lyc** phyt rhus-t stram thal-xyz srj8• verat
- **rawness**: *Petr* k* *Sulph*
  - **watery** oozing; with constant: petr tl1
- **red**: androc srj1• bell berb bov canth carb-an cic cycl jug-r lap-la sde8.de• lyc *Merc Ran-s* spig spong sul-ac sulph verat
- **scales**: anac anag hr1 *Anthraci* arn bacls-7 fmm1• *Clem Graph* hep k* *Merc* mur-ac *Petr Psor* rauw sp1 sars sec *Sep* sulph k2 tritic-vg fd5.de
  - **white**: *Graph Sep*
  - **winter** agg.; in: *Petr Sep*
- **scurfy**: sars k* sep k*
- **sloughing**: *Ars* k* kali-bi k*
- **small**: *Vac* jl2
- **spots**, in: *Apis*
  - **red**: spong fd4.de zinc bg1
  - **whitish**: nat-m ozone sde2•
- **tetters**: alum b4a.de ambr b7.de bov b4.de* *Calc* b4a.de *Con* b4a.de *Dulc* b4.de* graph b4a.de ip b7.de *Kreos* b7a.de lyc b4a.de merc b4.de *Nat-c* b4.de* nat-m b4.de petr b4a.de sars b4a.de sep b4a.de staph b7.de* *Thuj* b4a.de verat b7.de* zinc b4.de*
- **tubercles**: ars carb-an hydrc kali-chl *Merc* nit-ac rhus-t rhus-v sep spig stram
- **urticaria**: apis berb bufo *Carb-v Hep* hyper nat-c *Nat-m* nat-s *Sars* **Sulph** *Urt-u* ven-m rsj12•
  - **morning**: chin
  - **red** after rubbing: nat-m h2*
  - **vesicular**: **Hep** bg2 stann bg2 sulph bg2
- **vesicles**: am-m b7.de* *Anag* k* anan ant-c k* aran arg-n bg2 arn ars bell b4.de* *Borx* k* bov k* bufo bg2 canth b7.de* **Carb-ac** carbn-s caust k* chin clem k* cocc k* com hell hep k* kali-ar kali-bi kali-c k* kali-i *Kali-s* kali-sil k2 kreos ptk1 lac-ac *Lach* k* m-ambo b7.de mag-c k* mag-m *Merc* k* merl mez k* morg-g pte1*• *Nat-m* k* *Nat-s Petr* ph-ac b4a.de phos k* plan *Psor* ptel *Ran-b Rhus-t* k* *Rhus-v* ruta sanic sars k* sec *Sel* k* *Sep* k* *Sil* k* spig spong fd4.de *Squil* k* *Sulph* k* ter tritic-vg fd5.de verat-v ptk1 vip
  - **black**: *Sec*
  - **burning**: *Canth* rhus-v
  - **confluent**: ruta
  - **corroding**: clem k* *Graph* kali-c mag-c k* nat-m bg2 nit-ac *Sep* bg2 sil k*
  - **crops**, in: *Anag* k*
  - **denuded** spots, on: nat-m
  - **elevated** base: kali-bi
  - **gangrenous**: sec bg2
  - **hard**: lach
  - **healing**, new vesicles appear after: *Anag* k*
  - **inflamed**: *Rhus-t*
  - **itching**: anag hr1 **Carb-ac** lach bg2 nat-m h2* sel bg2 sep h2* tritic-vg fd5.de
  - **patches**: rhus-t
  - **phagedenic**: graph kali-c *Mag-c Nit-ac* sil
  - **spots**, in: cic
  - **stinging**: mag-c h2*
  - **watery**: anag *Ars Nat-c Psor* rhus-t ruta
  - **white**, with red areola: sanic uran-n
  - **yellowish**: rhus-v *Sulph*
  - **Areola**, red: bov ruta
- **weather**, cold: sep
- **weepy** (See moist)
- ○ **Back** of hands: berb bov chel cortiso tpw7 cupr graph gk jug-r kali-chl k* *Kali-s* kreos k* *Merc Mez* k* mur-ac k* nat-c k* petr ptk1 phos pix bg3* puls bg3* sanic *Sep* spong fd4.de **Sulph** k*
  - **bed | agg.**: cortiso tpw7
  - **boils**: calc
  - **confluent**: cop
  - **copper** colored: psor
  - **cracks**: *Merc*
  - **crusts**, yellow: *Merc Mez*
  - **desquamating**: am-m ars-i bg2 bar-c calc *Graph* merc
  - **eczema**: borx bg2 bov bg2* cortiso sp1 cypra-eg sde6.de* *Graph Jug-c* kreos br1 *Merc* **Mez** mur-ac ptk1* nat-c k* phos *Sep* syc pte1*•
    - **itching**; with: syc fmm1•
  - **elevations**: anac dros plb sul-ac
  - **excrescences**; wart-like: **Thuj**
  - **herpes**: *Carbn-s Graph* lyc nat-c petr sep thuj
  - **itching**: am-m cic a1 *Merc Mez* petr-ra shn4• sanic **Sulph** tarax h1* [bell-p-sp dcm1]
    - **night**: *Merc*
  - **measles**, like: cop
  - **moist**: bov kreos *Mez*

Extremities

- **Back of hands**: ...
  - **patches**; round: cortiso sp1
  - **pemphigus**: *(↗SKIN - Eruptions - pemphigus)* sep
  - **petechiae**: berb
  - **pimples**: acon **Agar** am-m ars b4a.de calc b4a.de calc-p canth carb-v *Carbn-s* cic kali-chl *Lyc* b4a.de mur-ac b4a.de* propr sa3• *Sep* b4a.de sil b4a.de sulph b4a.de* tarax h1* zinc
    - **itching**: am-m zinc
  - **psoriasis**, chronic: *Ars* aur bar-c **Graph** hep *Lyc Maland* **Petr** *Phos* phyt *Rhus-t* sars *Sulph*
  - **pustules**: anac cimic helo-s rwt2• sanic *Sil* sulph syc bka1•
    - **burning**: syc bka1*•
    - **itching**: syc bka1•
  - **rash**: cortiso tpw7 *Dig*
  - **red**: helo-s rwt2• jug-r nat-c h2 sul-ac h2*
    - **patches**: calc cortiso tpw7 flor-p rsj3•
      - **bed** | **going** into: cortiso tpw7
      - **heat**: pitu-gl skp7•
    - **spots**: bell h1* plut-n srj7• spong fd4.de
  - **scabs**: mur-ac plb *Sep* sul-ac sulph
  - **scaly** tetter: lyc sars *Sep* sulph
  - **spots**, red (See red - spots)
  - **sun** agg.: cortiso tpw7
  - **syphilitic** psoriasis: *Ars* aur *Merc* phos
  - **tetters**: *Alum* b4a.de **Bov** b4a.de *Calc* b4a.de *Kreos* b7a.de *Lach* b7a.de *Mez* b4a.de *Nat-c* b4a.de *Petr* b4a.de *Sep* b4a.de sil b4a.de *Sulph* b4a.de **Thuj** b4a.de
  - **tubercles**, white, itching: carb-an h2*
  - **urticaria**: acon apis berb cop hyper indg *Sulph* thuj k*
    - **cool**; when hands become: thuj
  - **vesicles**: anac arg-n brom cadm-met tpw6 *Calc Canth* cic *Graph* indg kali-chl k* *Kali-s Mez* ozone sde2• phos psor **Rhus-t** rhus-v sol-ni s p o n g fd4.de **Sulph** zinc
    - **burning**: mez
    - **cold**; after taking a: zinc
    - **discharging**:
      - **acrid** fluid: sol-ni
      - **yellowish** fluid: sol-ni
    - **itching**: cic kali-chl **Mez** ozone sde2• phos sulph h2*
      - **night**: phos h2*
      - **warm** room; entering: ozone sde2•
    - **moist**: mez
    - **red**: psor
    - **spots**, in: rhus-t
    - **swelling**: cadm-met tpw6
    - **watery**: calc rhus-v
    - **yellow**: arg-n k*
  - **warm** applications agg.: cortiso tpw7
  - **weather** agg.; cold: **Sep** k ●
- **Between** first and second fingers: cic
- **Between** thumb and first finger: bruc iod h*
  - **blood** boil: ars h2*
  - **desquamation**: am-m k*
  - **dry**: verat h1
  - **herpes**: ambr
  - **itching**: ambr h1*
  - **pimples**: agar arn bry canth ham sulph thuj
    - **burning** on touch: canth
    - **itching**: ars sulph
  - **tubercle**: *Ars*
  - **vesicles**: grat *Nat-s* **Sulph** verat a1
- **Between** second and third fingers: **Sulph** k ●
  - **vesicles**: *Sulph* k*
- **Between** the fingers: *Canth* carbn-s *Graph* k* hell lach lyc nit-ac olnd phos *Psor* k* puls rhus-v sep sul-ac *Sulph*
  - **blisters**: dys pte1•
  - **burning**: nit-ac h2*
- **Between** the fingers: ...
  - **chicken** pox: dys fmm1•
  - **desquamation**: am-m k* ferr b7a.de laur b7.de*
  - **eczema**: moni jl2 tell rsj10•
  - **herpes**: ambr graph merc *Nit-ac* k*
  - **itching**: ambr c1 ars h2* bry bg1 canth lyc mag-c h2* moni jl2 nit-ac h2* **Psor Sulph**
    - **midnight**; after: sul-ac h2
  - **moist**: *Graph*
  - **pimples**: ars graph b4a.de lyc mag-c h2* mez b4a.de ph-ac puls k* *Sep* b4a.de sul-ac b4a.de sulph bg2
  - **pustules**: caps rhus-t
  - **scaly**: laur
  - **tetters**: ambr b7a.de graph b4a.de *Nit-ac* b4a.de
  - **urticaria**: hyper merc
  - **vesicles**: anag *Apis* ars h2* *Calc Canth* carbn-s k2 *Hell* k* iod laur k* mag-c h2* moni jl2 *Nat-m* olnd phos **Psor** *Puls* rhus-t k* rhus-v ruta *Sel* k* **Sulph**
    - **burning**: canth
    - **itching**: canth **Phos** ●* *Psor* **SULPH** k ●
      - **warm** bed agg.: *Rhus-v* vh
      - **washing** agg.: *Rhus-v* vh
- **Between** third and fourth fingers: mag-c
  - **pimples**: canth
  - **vesicles**: hell h1 mag-c
- **Palms**: anag k* androc srj1• arn aur borx bg2 crot-h dulc fd4.de *Graph* kali-c morg-p fmm1• *Nat-s* ran-b k2* sel br1 *Sep Sulph* tritic-vg fd5.de
  - **blisters**: bufo k* canth bg2 kali-c bg2 kreos bg2 mag-c bg2 nat-m bg2 ran-b k*
  - **chapped**: ran-b br1
  - **copper**-colored spots: cor-r
  - **cracked**: ran-b br1
  - **crusty**: anthraci mrr1
  - **desquamation** of: am-c k* arn k* brucel sa3• bry sys calc-f bg2 chinin-s cor-r bg2 dulc fd4.de elaps bg3* **Graph** bg2* hydr merc bg2 p e t r - r a shn4• psil ft1* **Rhus-t** ●* sabad sel bg2 **Sep** k ●* **Sulph** k ●*
  - **discharge**, thin watery: crot-h *Nat-s*
  - **dry** eruptions: anag bro1 *Ars* bro1 trios rsj1• x-ray bro1
  - **dry** tetter: *Caust Nat-s Sel Sulph*
  - **eczema**: sulph ptk1 vario ptk1
  - **elevated** red blotches: *Fl-ac*
  - **herpes**: *Aur Kreos* psor ran-b *Sep*
  - **pemphigus**: bufo mtf11
  - **pimples**: nat-s *Petr* b4a.de psor *Sep* b4a.de spig thuj
    - **hard** itching, discharging stony concretion: thuj k*
  - **psoriasis**: aur calc k* *Clem* cor-r br1* crot-h k* graph k* hep k* kali-s k* *Lyc* k* *Med* c1* *Merc* mez bg1 *Mur-ac Nat-s* petr k* **Phos** k* *Psor* sars *Sel* k* sil sul-ac *Sulph* x-ray alj
    - **itching** and burning: petr hr1
  - **pustules**: *Lach*
  - **rash**: form
  - **raw**: *Nat-s*
  - **red** spots: apis
  - **scales**: hep *Lyc Nat-s* petr pip-m rhus-t sabad sars *Sel* sep *Sulph* tritic-vg fd5.de
  - **scurfy** tetters: cinnb *Lyc Nat-s* sulph
  - **smooth** spots: cor-r
  - **syphilitic** psoriasis: *Ars Ars-i* aur *Merc* phos *Sel*
  - **tetter**: *Am-m* b7a.de *Kreos* b7a.de ran-b b7a.de* **Rhus-t** b7a.de
  - **urticaria**: rhus-v stram h1*
  - **vesicles**: anag bg1 *Anthraci* k* bufo k* canth caust cob-n sp1 *Kali-c* k* kreos ptk1 mag-c *Merc* k* ran-b rhus-t rhus-v ruta tritic-vg fd5.de
    - **grouped**: anag ser*
    - **itching**: caust h2* *Kali-c* rhus-t tritic-vg fd5.de
      - **warm** bed agg.: *Rhus-v* vh
      - **washing** agg.: *Rhus-v* vh
    - **large**: anthraci
    - **scratching** agg.; after: mag-c h2*

- **Palms – vesicles**: ...
    - **transparent**: merc
    - **watery**: bell h1*
    - **yellow**: anthraci bufo rhus-t rhus-v
  - **Balls**: ant-c h2 mez
- **Ulnar** side of:
  - **boils**: coloc
  - **vesicles**: ant-c lach sel

- **Hips**: chord-umb rly4• ger-i rly4• *Nat-c* nat-pyru rly4• nicc osm sel c1
  - **boils**: alum k* am-c bar-c graph k* hep k* jug-r lyc *Nit-ac* k* *Ph-ac* k* **Phos** b4a.de rat sabin *Sulph* b4a.de
    - **right**: cassia-s ccrh1•
  - **desquamation**: rhus-v bg2
  - **herpes**: *Nat-c* nicc *Sep*
  - **pimples**: ant-c b7a.de cann-s b7.de* cham b7.de* clem b4.de* graph b4.de* hyper laur b7.de* *Lyc* b4a.de merc b4.de* nat-c b4.de* sel b7a.de thuj b4a.de
  - **pustules** | **right**: cassia-s ccrh1•
  - **tubercles**: rat rhus-t
  - **vesicular**: calc

- **Joints**: aeth ant-c *Apis* *Ars-i* ptk1 borx ptk1 calc-p clem ptk1 dulc ptk1 *Graph* ptk1 hura kreos ptk1 *Merc* k* *Nat-m* nat-p phos k* **Psor** k* *Ran-b* ptk1 **Rhus-t** sep k* sulph ptk1 thyr ptk1 ust
  - **desquamation**: phos
  - **eczema**: led phos
  - **herpes**: dulc *Kreos* psor tl1 staph
  - **itching**: phos
  - **pimples**: *Calc-p* sep
  - **scabs**: *Staph*
  - **tetters**: calc b4.de* *Graph* b4a.de *Merc* b4a.de
  - **urticaria**: clem verat
  - **vesicles**: nat-c ptk1 nat-p phos **Rhus-t**
  - **winter**: *Merc* *Phos* *Psor* k* *Rhus-t*
  - ○ **Bends** of: carc cd caust **Graph** *Hep* led *Nat-c* **Nat-m** k ●* nit-ac gk *Psor* k* puls gk **Sep** ● staph sulph gk tub al
    - **eczema**: *Aeth* bro1 am-c k* aur-m-n wbt2• caust bro1 cupr bg2 **Graph** k* hep bro1 kali-ar bro1 led lyc bro1 mang-act bro1 merc *Nat-m* bro1 psor bro1 *Sep* k* *Sulph* k*
    - **itching**: sep h2*
    - **pimples**: sep h2*

- **Knees**: anac ant-c arn ars canth carb-v *Dulc* iod kreos bg1 *Lac-c* lach led ptk1 merc *Nat-m* nat-p *Nux-v* petr bg1 ph-ac phos *Psor* rhus-t sabad samb sars sep *Thuj*
  - **blebs**: *Anthraci*
  - **blotches**: ant-c sulph
  - **boils**: am-c *Calc* cassia-s ccrh1• *Nat-m* k* *Nux-v* k* *Sep* b4a.de
  - **burning**: nux-v
  - **copper**-colored: stram
  - **crusty**: *Psor* sil
  - **eczema** rubrum: anil arn rhus-t
  - **gritty**: nat-m
  - **herpes**: ars carb-v k* *Dulc* *Graph* k* kreos merc nat-c **Nat-m** *Petr* k* phos *Sulph*
  - **itching**: anac h2* hep h2* nat-m nux-v ph-ac h2* thuj h1* zinc h2*
  - **knots**; reddish hard: psil ft1
  - **painful**: arn
  - **pimples**: anac b4a.de ant-c k* bry k* canth b7.de* hep hura kali-c b4.de* lach b7a.de merc b4a.de nicc nux-v b7.de* ph-ac k* puls sars sep k* sulph *Thuj* k* zinc k*
  - **psoriasis**: *Iris* morg-g pte1• *Phos*
  - **pustules**: cassia-s ccrh1• *Iris* *Phos* thuj a
  - **rash**: *Iod* *Led* nux-v sep ter zinc
  - **red** spot: petr h2*
  - **scaly**: *Hydr*

- **Knees**: ...
  - **tetters**: *Carb-v* b4a.de *Dulc* b4a.de *Nat-c* b4.de* *Nat-m* b4.de* *Petr* b4.de* phos b4a.de *Sulph* b4.de*
  - **urticaria**: zinc
  - **varicella**, like: thuj h1*
  - **vesicles**: ant-c arn carb-v *Caust* iod iris nat-p phos rhus-t sabad sars sep
    - **greenish**: iod
    - **itching**: carb-v
    - **scratching**; after: sars sep
    - **stinging**: *Rhus-t*
    - **varioloid**: ant-c
  - ○ **Hollow** of knees ●: **Ars** *Bov* bry calc *Carbn-s* chin dulc **Graph** *Hep* kali-c kreos bg1 led *Merc* k* *Mez* mrr1 *Nat-m* petr phos *Psor* k* puls gk sars sep sulph gk tep thuj bg1 tub gk zinc
    - **burning**: *Merc*
    - **crusty**: *Bov*
    - **dry**: bry *Psor*
    - **eczema**: *Graph* lac-ac stj5• moni jl2 sulph gk
    - **herpes**: **Ars** calc *Con* **Graph** k* *Hep* bro1 kreos led nat-c **Nat-m** k* *Petr* phos *Psor* *Sep* bro1 *Sulph* xero bro1
    - **itching**: agar **Ars** k* bry led *Psor* zinc
    - **moist**: *Graph* **Merc** **Sep**
    - **pimples**: bry b7.de* led b7.de* propr sa3• puls b7.de* sep
    - **pustules**: bry *Carbn-s* *Cinnb*
    - **rash**: *Hep* sep zinc
    - **rawness**: ambr
    - **red**: merc nat-m
    - **scabies**: ars bry merc
    - **scabs**: puls
    - **sore**: merc
    - **spots**: petr
    - **tetters**: ars b4a.de* calc b4.de* **Graph** b4a.de kreos b7a.de *Merc* b4a.de *Nat-c* b4.de* *Nat-m* b4.de* petr b4a.de* phos b4a.de sep b4a.de *Sulph* b4.de* *Thuj* b4a.de
    - **urticaria**: *Zinc*
    - **vesicles**: chin iod phos puls sars sep

- **Legs**: agar k* alum alum-p k2 am-m ars arund bov bry calc k* *Caust* chinin-s chlor chrysar bro1 cupr cupr-ar daph dream-p sdj1• fago gins bro1 *Graph* bro1 kali-ar kali-bi kali-br kali-c k* lach k* mag-c bro1 merc mez muru a1 murx *Nat-c* k* *Nat-m* nit-ac k* *Petr* k* petr-ra shn4• ph-ac *Podo* puls k* *Rhus-t* ribo rly4• rumx *Sec* sep k* staph k* stram sulph k* symph fd3.de• thuj tritic-vg fd5.de vanil fd5.de zinc
  - **bleeding** after scratching: *Cupr-ar*
  - **blisters**, black: *Ars*
  - **blotches**: ant-c arg-n aur carb-v cocc hura jug-r kreos lac-ac merc nat-c petr phos podo fd3.de• rhod thuj
  - **boils**: *Anan* *Anthraci* *Ars* k* *Calc* castor-eq gaert pte1*• kreos b7a.de *Mag-c* k* *Nit-ac* k* nux-v **Petr** k* **Rhus-t** k* *Sil* k*
    - **blood** boils: mag-c
  - **burning**: aur h2* calc h2* lac-ac petr hr1 *Rhus-t*
  - **copper** colored spots: graph
  - **denuded** spots: calc
  - **desquamating**: agar *Carb-an* kali-s k2 mag-c h2* merc *Sulph* thuj
  - **dry**: calc-p clem *Dol* vanil fd5.de
  - **eczema**: *Apis* **Ars** carb-v **Graph** k* kali-br *Lach* led *Lyc* *Merc* *Nat-m* **Petr** k* *Rhus-t* *Sars* **Sulph**
  - **elevations**: aur cupr kali-br
    - **spots**: *Syph*
  - **erythema** nodosum: morg-p fmm1•
  - **excoriations**: *Graph* *Tarent-c*
  - **groups**, in: nat-m
  - **herpes**: ars calc calc-p com *Graph* kali-c *Lach* lyc lyss mag-c merc nat-m *Petr* sars *Sep* staph *Zinc*
    - **circinate**: syc fmm1•

Extremities

- **itching**: arund aur h2* *Calc* carb-v lac-ac luna kg1• petr hr1 psor puls *Rhus-t* rumx sulph gk
  - **corrosive** on touch: nat-m h2*
- **leprous** spots: *Graph* *Nat-c*
- **moist**: apis bry *Calc* *Graph* *Kali-br* hr1 *Merc* *Petr* *Rhus-t* symph fd3.de• tarent-c
- **nodules**: agar *Merc*
  - **subcutaneous**: psor jl2
    - **long** time; persisting: psor jl2
- **painful**: kali-br a1 luna kg1•
  - **spots**: luna kg1•
- **patches**, large as the hand: caust
- **petechiae**: am-m phos
- **pimples**: agar am-c arg-met k* arn arum-t bell bov k* bry b7.de* calc b4.de* chinin-s con b4.de* elaps fl-ac hura iris-fl kali-bi kali-chl merc k* morph *Nat-m* k* nicc petr b4a.de ph-ac b4.de* *Puls* k* rhus-t b7.de* ribo rly4• sars *Sep* k* sil b4.de* staph k* stront-c sul-ac thuj k* tritic-vg fd5.de vanil fd5.de verat
  - **bleeding** easily: agar
  - **burning**: arg-met h1 puls h1* staph h1*
  - **itching**: allox tpw3 asc-t bell elaps kali-bi petr a1 sep staph h1* stront-c ziz
  - **moist**: puls
  - **red**: iris-fl kali-chl rumx
  - **scratching** agg.; after: agar h2* mang a1 nat-c h2*
  - **white**: agar h2* staph
- **psoriasis**: kali-ar morg-g pte1• **Phos**
- **pustules**: arg-n ars *Dulc* *Kali-bi* kali-br *Lach* mez *Psor* rumx staph stram **Sulph** *Thuj* k*
  - **right**: aq-mar skp7•
  - **itching**: *Arg-n* asc-t
  - **vaccination**; after: sulph
- **rash**: aids nl2• calc cortiso tpw7 daph hyos *Nat-m* sil
  - **irritating**: luf-op rsj5•
- **red**: aids nl2• bell kali-bi mag-c h2* merc sulph
  - **patches**: aids nl2• *Calc* podo fd3.de• sil sul-ac
- **scabs**: arn calc-p iris-fl kali-br *Lach* **Nit-ac** petr hr1 ph-ac podo *Sep* staph **Sulph** zinc
- **scales** in spots: *Merc* syph k2 zinc
- **scurfy**: ars calc *Kali-bi* sabin sep staph vanil fd5.de zinc
- **sore** (See painful)
- **spots** during menses; painful: *Petr*
- **tetters**: *Caust* b4a.de *Clem* b4a.de cycl b7a.de graph b4a.de *Kreos* b7a.de *Lyc* b4.de* merc b4a.de *Mez* b4a.de plb b7.de* *Rhus-t* b7a.de *Sars* b4a.de sep b4a.de sil b4a.de staph b7.de* sulph b4a.de *Zinc* b4.de*
- **tubercles**: ant-c caust crot-h nat-c petr
  - **ulcerate**: *Nat-c*
- **urticaria**: *Calc* *Chlor* cypra-eg sde6.de• dream-p sdj1• marb-w es1• rhus-t sulfonam ks2 **Sulph**
- **varicella**, like: ant-t
- **vesicles**: *Ant-c* bov **Caust** com dulc hyos kali-bi *Kali-c* mang petr a1 *Psor* **Rhus-t** *Sec* staph stram *Sulph* vip
- **white**: agar
  - **spots**: *Calc* symph fd3.de•
- ○ **Bones**:
  - **Tibia**: germ-met srj5• vanil fd5.de
    - **papular**: anthraco br1 sul-ac h2*
    - **vesicles**, watery: bell h1*
- **Calves**: aids nl2• apis bell caust kali-ar k* mag-c petr phyt sars sep *Sil* thuj trios rsj11•
  - **bed** agg.; in: trios rsj11•
  - **blotches**: aids nl2• aur carb-v lach merc petr phos thuj
  - **boils**: bell **Sil** k*
  - **desquamation**: mag-c trios rsj11•
  - **dry**: trios rsj11•
  - **eczema**: *Graph*

- **Legs – Calves**: ...
  - **elevated**: mag-c
  - **herpes**: cycl *Lyc* sars
  - **itching**: carb-v h2* petr h2* ph-ac h2* sars h2* sep h2* sil thuj h1* trios rsj11• zinc h2*
  - **lumps**: nit-ac
  - **nodes**, white: thuj
  - **pimples**: agar arg-n asc-t bov bry elaps hura kali-bi lach nat-c ph-ac puls rumx sabin sars *Sep* staph zinc
    - **ulcers**, becoming: ph-ac
  - **pustules**: kali-bi kali-br
  - **rash**: aids nl2• *Calc* hyos h1* nat-m h2* sil h2* trios rsj11•
  - **red**: hyos h1* mag-c trios rsj11•
    - **spots**: *Con* *Lyc* phyt
  - **scabs**: kali-br
  - **smooth**: mag-c
  - **stitching**: sep h2*
  - **tubercles**: petr
  - **urticaria**: carb-v
  - **vesicles**: caust sars sep

- **Lower** limbs: agar am-c am-m anac b4a.de *Ant-c* apis arn **Ars** arund *Bar-c* bar-m bell k* *Bov* bry **Calc** *Calc-p* calc-sil k2 *Carb-v* carbn-o **Caust** chel chin chinin-ar chinin-s chlor *Clem* k* con k* cop crot-c *Crot-t* cupr cupr-ar dulc elaps *Euph* k* fago *Graph* k* iod jug-r *Kali-ar* kali-bi k* kali-br *Kali-c* k* *Kali-s* kreos lach led *Lyc* k* mag-c manc mang k* *Merc* k* mez b4.de* murx nat-c k* nat-m k* nat-p nit-ac nux-v **Petr** k* ph-ac k* phos phyt plan **Psor** *Puls* **Rhus-t** *Rhus-v* rumx ruta sabad sars sec sel **Sep** k* **Sil** k* staph stram stront-c **Sulph** tarax tep thal-xyz srj8• thuj k* til tritic-vg fd5.de vanil fd5.de vero-o rly4*•
  - **black**: sec
  - **bleeding** after scratching: calc cupr
  - **blotches**: ant-c lach nat-c sulph
    - **dark**, purple: agav-a br1
  - **boils**: all-c am-c apoc *Ars* aur-m bell carbn-s clem **Hep** hyos kali-bi nat-m nit-ac nux-v petr ph-ac phos *Rhus-t* rhus-v sec k* sep sil stram *Sulph* thuj
  - **burn**; spots like a: lach
  - **burning**: bov fago lac-ac *Merc* nux-v til
    - **scratching** agg.; after: til
  - **cold** bathing | **amel.**: *Lyc*
  - **confluent**: cop rhus-v
  - **desquamation**: agar ars calc-p chinin-s crot-t *Dulc* b4a.de elaps kreos mag-c merc sulph thuj
  - **dry**: bry falco-pe nl2•
  - **eating** agg.: nux-v *Sulph*
  - **eczema**: *Anil* apis arn ars *Bov* chel chrysar bwa3 jug-r kali-br merc *Petr* *Psor* *Rhus-t*
  - **elevations**: aur cop cupr kali-br mag-c petr puls thuj tritic-vg fd5.de
  - **fleabites**: sec
  - **gangrenous**: hyos k*
  - **gritty**: nat-m
  - **groups**, in: nat-m
  - **hard**: aur bov
  - **herpes**: *Alum* **Bov** caust clem com **Graph** kali-c lach led **Lyc** **Merc** mur-ac **Nat-m** nicc *Petr* sars *Sep* sil staph **Tell** zinc
  - **hot**: chel fago
  - **itching**: *Agar* anac arg-n bov bry *Calc* calc-sil k2 caust chrysar bwa3 daph dulc fago jug-r *Kali-c* lac-ac lach led mang marb-w es1• *Merc* mur-ac *Nat-c* **Nat-m** nat-p nicc *Nux-v* petr puls rhus-t rumx sel **Sep** *Sil* **Staph** sulph tarax til
  - **itch**-like: ars bry chel squil b7.de* sulph
  - **knots**, reddish, hard: kali-bi
  - **lumpy**: petr ther thuj
  - **miliary**: alum ars bov daph merc nux-v sil sulph
  - **moist**: *Bov* bry chel kreos merc nat-m
  - **nodules**: petr ther thuj

- **painful**: arn bov
- **papules**: lach lachn merc nux-v ph-ac rhus-t sel sep thuj
  - **roseolous** papules without fever or itching: cub$_{c1}$
- **petechiae**: agav-a$_{br1}$ am-m apis$_{ptk1}$ ars kali-i led$_{ptk1}$ solid$_{br1*}$
- **phagedenic**: ars nux-v sulph
- **pimples**: agar am-c am-m ant-c arg-n arn asc-t bar-c$_{k*}$ bell berb bov$_{k*}$ bry$_{k*}$ calc$_{k*}$ calc-sil$_{k2}$ cann-s castm chel chinin-s clem$_{k*}$ con$_{k*}$ crot-c elaps fago fl-ac *Graph*$_{k*}$ hura hyos$_{b7.de*}$ iris iris-fl kali-bi kali-br kali-c kali-chl *Kali-s* kali-sil$_{k2}$ mag-c$_{k*}$ mang$_{k*}$ merc$_{k*}$ *Merc-c*$_{b4a.de}$ mez$_{k*}$ morph nat-m$_{k*}$ nat-p nicc petr$_{k*}$ ph-ac$_{k*}$ *Puls* rhus-t$_{b7.de*}$ rumx *Sars*$_{k*}$ sep$_{k*}$ sil stann$_{k*}$ staph$_{k*}$ stront-c sulph thea thuj til tritic-vg$_{fd5.de}$ vanil$_{fd5.de}$ verat zinc
  - **bleeding**: agar thea
  - **burning**: mang
    - **scratching** agg.: staph
  - **flat**: ant-c plan
  - **hard**: plan
  - **indolent**: chel
  - **itching**: asc-t bell elaps *Hep* kali-bi mang *Petr* *Ph-ac* sel *Sep* stann staph sulph
    - **scratching** agg.; after: mag-c
  - **painful**: bry thea tritic-vg$_{fd5.de}$
  - **red**: asc-t chel clem graph kali-c sars sulph thea til
  - **white**: plan
  - **yellow**: ant-c
- **pustules**: aids$_{nl2\bullet}$ am-c ars bry clem crot-c cupr-ar dulc hyos jug-c kali-bi kali-br lyc mez rhus-t rumx sars stram thal-xyz$_{srj8\bullet}$ thuj tritic-vg$_{fd5.de}$ verat
  - **black**: *Ars* nat-c sec
  - **burn**: mez$_{k*}$
  - **groups**: hyos
  - **itching**: cassia-s$_{ccrh1\bullet}$
    - **heat**: cassia-s$_{ccrh1\bullet}$
    - **scratching** agg.: cassia-s$_{ccrh1\bullet}$
    - **uncovering** agg.: cassia-s$_{ccrh1\bullet}$
  - **red**: lyc mez
    - **areola**: ant-c
  - **suppurating**: con thuj
- **rash**: alum$_{h2*}$ bry mez nat-m nux-v rhus-t sep tep zinc
  - **itching**: alum$_{h2*}$
- **red**: bell bov chel crot-c kali-bi mag-c merc nat-m rhus-v tritic-vg$_{fd5.de}$
- **rough**: rhus-v
- **scabs**: arn ars bell$_{h1*}$ *Bov* calc iris-fl *Kali-br* *Lach* mez podo rhus-v *Sabin* *Sil* staph zinc
  - **elevated**, white: mez
- **scales**: calc-p clem kali-ar *Kali-s* pip-m rhus-v
  - **spots**, in: *Merc* zinc
  - **spring**; in: lach$_{hr1}$
- **scurfs**: bar-m *Merc* *Petr*
  - **spots**, in: *Merc*
- **smooth**: mag-c
- **sore**: merc
- **stinging**: ant-c nux-v petr sabin
- **tetters**: **Bov**$_{b4.de*}$ caust$_{b4.de*}$ *Clem*$_{b4a.de}$ **Graph**$_{b4.de*}$ *Lyc*$_{b4.de*}$ mag-c$_{b4.de*}$ merc$_{b4.de*}$ mur-ac$_{b4a.de}$ nat-m$_{b4.de*}$ *Petr*$_{b4.de*}$ sep$_{b4.de*}$ sil$_{b4.de*}$ zinc$_{b4a.de}$
- **tubercles**: syph$_{k2}$
- **ulcerating**: ph-ac sel$_{c1}$
- **urticaria**: *Apis* *Aur*$_{b4a.de}$ *Calc* **Chlol** clem kali-i marb-w$_{es1\bullet}$ merc plan sulph zinc
  - **scratching** agg.; after: clem spig$_{h1}$ zinc
- **varicella**, like: ant-t
- **vesicles**: acon am-c$_{k*}$ *Ant-c*$_{k*}$ apis arn **Ars**$_{k*}$ aster aur$_{b4a.de}$ bell$_{k*}$ *Bov*$_{k*}$ *Bufo* *Calc*$_{k*}$ cann-s carb-v carbn-o **Caust**$_{k*}$ chin clem$_{k*}$ cupr elaps galla-q-r$_{nl2\bullet}$ *Graph*$_{k*}$ hyos$_{k*}$ iod kali-ar kali-bi lach$_{k*}$ lachn manc

\- **Lower** limbs – **vesicles**: ...
Nat-c$_{k*}$ **Nat-m** nat-p **Nit-ac** olnd$_{b7.de*}$ *Petr*$_{k*}$ ph-ac phos **Rhus-t**$_{k*}$ rhus-v sabad$_{k*}$ sars sec sel$_{k*}$ *Sep*$_{k*}$ *Sil* **Sulph**$_{k*}$ tarax$_{b7.de*}$ tell$_{c1}$ verat zinc

  - **bloody** serum: *Nat-m*
  - **burning**: verat
  - **corroding**: borx caust graph sep sil sulph
  - **itching**: *Calc* carb-v cassia-s$_{ccrh1\bullet}$
    - **heat**: cassia-s$_{ccrh1\bullet}$
    - **scratching** agg.: cassia-s$_{ccrh1\bullet}$
    - **uncovering** agg.: cassia-s$_{ccrh1\bullet}$
  - **red**: *Calc*
  - **scratching** agg.; after: sars sep
  - **spreading**: nit-ac *Rhus-t*
  - **stinging**: *Rhus-t*
  - **ulcerating**: sulph zinc
  - **varioloid**: ant-c
  - **water**, with fetid: ars
  - **weather** agg.; cold: dulc
  - **white**: mez thuj
    - **red** borders; with: corn-s
  - **yellow** fluid: ars bufo
  - **Joints**: carb-v$_{bg2}$ sabad$_{bg2}$
- **white**: agar

\- **Nates**: ant-c borx canth caust glycyr-g$_{cte1\bullet}$ *Graph* mez *Nat-c* nat-m nux-v oxal-a$_{rly4\bullet}$ pot-e$_{rly4\bullet}$ sars$_{mrr1}$ sel symph$_{fd3.de\bullet}$ thuj *Til* tritic-vg$_{fd5.de}$ vanil$_{fd5.de}$

- **blotches**: ant-c bry sars symph$_{fd3.de\bullet}$
- **boils**: acon$_{bg1}$ agar alum alum-p$_{k2}$ am-c aur-m bar-c bart borx$_{h2}$ cadm-s calad graph *Hep*$_{k*}$ indg *Lyc* nit-ac *Ph-ac*$_{k*}$ phasco-ci$_{rbp2}$ phos plb psor *Rat* sabin sars$_{k*}$ sec sep *Sil* *Sulph* thuj tritic-vg$_{fd5.de}$
  - **blood** boils: aur-m hep$_{h2*}$ lyc$_{h2*}$
- **circumscribed**: *Med*$_{mrr1}$
- **dry**: nat-c$_{h2*}$
- **elevations**: mez
- **erythematous**: *Med*$_{mrr1}$
  - **infants**; in (See RECTUM - Eruptions - anus - rash - children - newborns)
- **excoriation**: *Rhus-t* thuj
- **herpes**: borx caust kreos *Nat-c*$_{k*}$ nicc
- **itching**: calc-p caust graph mag-m$_{h2*}$ *Nat-c*$_{h2}$ thuj til
- **knots**: ther
- **leprous** spots, annular: *Graph*
- **painful**: graph
- **papules**: cub$_{c1}$
  - **roseolous** papules without fever or itching: cub$_{c1}$
- **pimples**: ant-c ars-h bar-c berb calc canth chel cob$_{k*}$ graph ham hura kali-n lyc mag-c mang meph merc mez$_{h2*}$ nat-p nux-v *Petr* plan rhus-t sel sulph thuj *Til* vanil$_{fd5.de}$
  - **right**: mim-p$_{rsj8\bullet}$
  - **left**: lachn$_{c1}$
  - **itching**: kali-n lyc mag-c$_{h2*}$ mag-m$_{a1}$ thuj$_{h1*}$ *Til*
  - **painful**: ham lyc$_{h2*}$ mang$_{a1}$ sulph
  - **scratching** agg.; after: mag-c$_{h2*}$
  - **watery**: lachn$_{c1}$
- **pustules**: ant-c calc grat hyos jug-c ph-ac ros-d$_{wla1}$
- **red**: mag-m$_{h2*}$
- **scabs**: chel *Graph* psor
- **scratching** agg.; after: kali-n$_{h2*}$
- **scurfy**: calc-p symph$_{fd3.de\bullet}$
  - **tubercles**: hep mag-m$_{h2}$ mang phos
- **tetters**: borx$_{b4a.de}$ nat-c$_{b4a.de}$
- **urticaria**: hydr lyc
- **vesicles**: borx cann-s carb-an crot-t iris olnd ph-ac rhus-t
  - **corroding**: borx

○ • **Between** nates: olnd oxal-a rly4• vanil fd5.de
⁝ **moisture**: arum-t thuj
⁝ **pimples**: sulph vanil fd5.de
⁝ **pustules**: phos
⁝ **rash** in children, newborns; red: **Med** vh*
⁝ **rawness** (See Excoriation - nates)
⁝ **Upper** part of: hep

- **Shoulders**: alum bg2 alumn am-m bg2 ant-c bg2 ars k* berb bg2 choc srj3• cocc bg2 dulc fd4.de ham fd3.de• kali-c bg2 kali-n bg2 mag-c bg2 nux-v k* sep k* vanil fd5.de zinc bg2
  - **left** | **pustules**: *Vac* jl2
  - **acne**: morg-p pte1• tub-r jl2
  - **black** pores: *Dros*
  - **boils**: am-c k* am-m k* anthraci mrr1 bell dream-p sdj1• graph b4a.de hydr *Kali-n* k* lyc b4.de* nit-ac ph-ac k* *Sil* b4a.de sulph zinc b4.de*
    ⁝ **blood** boils, large: *Calc* jug-r lyc zinc
  - **desquamation**: *Ferr* merc
  - **eczema**: petr
  - **elevations**: alumn
  - **herpes**: kali-ar
  - **itching**: marb-w es1• *Trios* rsj11•
    ⁝ **air**; in open | **amel.**: trios rsj11•
    ⁝ **bed** agg.; in: trios rsj11•
    ⁝ **warm** applications agg.: trios rsj11•
  - **papular**: anthraco br1
  - **pimples**: *Ant-c* k* berb chel *Cist* cob cocc com des-ac rbp6 dulc fd4.de fl-ac hura jug-r kali-c kali-chl kali-n h2* mag-c mag-m mim-p rsj8• puls sulph tab vanil fd5.de zinc
    ⁝ **bleeding** when scratched: cob mosch
    ⁝ **boils**, like: zinc
    ⁝ **burning**: mag-m
    ⁝ ⁝ **scratching**; after: kali-c h2
    ⁝ **indolent**: chel
    ⁝ **itching**: allox tpw3 choc srj3• hura mag-m
    ⁝ ⁝ **scratching**; after: kali-c h2 mag-c h2
    ⁝ **painful**: kali-chl thea
    ⁝ **red**: ant-c h2* chel com hura jug-r kali-chl
    ⁝ **stitching**: kali-n h2*
  - **pustules**: alum bg2 ant-c *Calc* kali-bi kali-br rhod
  - **rash**: berb *Calc* puls tep
  - **red**: marb-w es1•
  - **scabs**: ars
  - **spots**: marb-w es1•
  - **tubercles**: crot-h kali-chl phos rhus-t
  - **urticaria**: lach
  - **vesicles**: am-m k* ant-c k* chlor crot-h lach mag-c mang medus br1 *Merc* rhus-t vip
    ⁝ **burning**: am-m
    ⁝ **scratching**; after: mag-c mang

○ • **Back** of the shoulder | **boils**: anthraci mrr1

- **Thighs**: agar alum bg2 arge-pl rwt5• ars aster bar-m *Calc* k* chinin-s choc srj3• chrysar bro1 crot-t cund sne cystein-l rly4• dulc fd4.de fago falco-pe nl2• gins bro1 *Graph* k* kali-ar kali-bi kali-c kali-sil k2 kreos mag-c bro1 merc morg-g pte1*• *Nat-c* nat-m nit-ac nux-v osm petr k* phos plan positr nl2• *Psor* rad-br mrr1 *Rhus-t* rhus-v *Sil* staph sulph k* thuj *Til* tritic-vg fd5.de vanil fd5.de
  - **blisters**:
    ⁝ **black**: *Anthraci*
    ⁝ **scratching**; after: lach
  - **blotches**: aur carb-v crot-h merc rhod zinc
  - **blue** spots: *Arn*
  - **boils**: acon bg1 agar all-s alum alum-p k2 am-c k* androc srj1• apoc k* aur bg2 aur-m *Bell* k* *Calc* calc-sil k2 carbn-s *Clem* k* *Cocc* k* *Hep* k* *Hyos* k* *Ign* k* kali-bi k* *Lach* *Lyc* mag-c k* *Nit-ac* k* *Nux-v* k* *Petr* k* petr-ra shn4• ph-ac k* phos k* plb puls bg1 rhus-t bg2 rhus-v *Sep* k* **Sil** k* *Spong* b7a.de *Sulph* b4a.de thuj k*

- **Thighs – boils**: ...
    ⁝ **right**: calc hell kali-bi kali-c rhus-v
    ⁝ **left**: ven-m rsj12•
  - **burning**: fago lac-leo sk4• plut-n srj7• til
    ⁝ **scratching** agg.; after: til
  - **circinate**: syc fmm1•
  - **copper** colored spots: *Mez*
    ⁝ **menses**; during: mez kr1
  - **crusts**: anac *Clem* graph *Ph-ac*
  - **desquamation**: chinin-s crot-t kreos sulph
  - **eczema**: bros-gau mrc1 graph k2 petr *Rhus-t*
    ⁝ **warmth** agg. | **heat** agg.: bros-gau mrc1
  - **elevated**: plan tritic-vg fd5.de
  - **herpes**: *Clem* *Graph* k* kali-c *Lyc* **Merc** mur-ac nat-c k2* **Nat-m** k* nit-ac petr k* sars *Sep* staph zinc
  - **hot**: fago
  - **itching**: agar alum h2* *Carb-v* cassia-s ccrh1• fago kali-c hr1 lac-leo sk4• mag-m h2* merc nat-m petr h2* positr nl2• sep sulph gk *Til*
    ⁝ **rubbing** gently | **amel.**: cassia-s ccrh1•
    ⁝ **washing** with cold water: cassia-s ccrh1•
  - **knots**: nat-c h2*
    ⁝ **reddish**, hard: kali-bi
  - **menses**; during: kali-c b4.de* sil b4.de
  - **miliary** | **menses**; during: nux-v b7.de
  - **moist**: *Crot-t* graph k2 merc nat-m
  - **petechiae**: *Ars*
  - **pimples**: agar ant-c k* asc-t bar-m berb bov bry k* calc k* cann-s k* canth b7.de* castm *Caust* b4a.de chel k* choc srj3• clem k* cocc k* cystein-l rly4• elaps fago fl-ac graph k* hyos b7.de* *Kali-c* k* *Kali-chl* kali-cy *Lach* lyc mag-c *Mang* k* meph *Merc* k* *Mez* *Nat-m* k* nux-v b7.de* *Petr* k* *Phos* plan rhod b4.de* *Rhus-t* b7.de* rumx sacch-a fd2.de• sars *Sel* k* *Spong* b7a.de *Stann* k* staph k* streptoc rly4• *Sulph* thea *Thuj* k* *Til* tritic-vg fd5.de vanil fd5.de zinc k*
    ⁝ **biting**: agar h2*
    ⁝ **burning**: mang
    ⁝ ⁝ **morning** | **evening**; and: mang
    ⁝ ⁝ **scratching** agg.: agar h2 *Staph* *Til*
    ⁝ **flat**: ant-c plan
    ⁝ **indolent**: chel
    ⁝ **itching**: asc-t chel h1* mag-m a1 nat-m h2* stann staph sulph zinc [spect dfg1]
    ⁝ ⁝ **morning**: mang
    ⁝ ⁝ **evening**: mang sulph
    ⁝ ⁝ **scratching** agg.; after: mag-c
    ⁝ **painful**: bry thea tritic-vg fd5.de
    ⁝ ⁝ **touch** agg.: phos h2
    ⁝ **red**: asc-t chel clem graph kali-c lac-h htj1• mag-m a1 sars sulph thea *Til*
    ⁝ ⁝ **areola**; with: nat-m h2
    ⁝ **sore** from scratching: mang h2* nat-m h2*
    ⁝ **white**: lac-h htj1• plan
  - **pustules**: am-c *Ant-c* dulc grat *Hyos* *Jug-c* lach lyc mez nat-sil fd3.de• petr-ra shn4• staph stram *Thuj* tritic-vg fd5.de verat
    ⁝ **burn**: mez
    ⁝ **groups**, in: hyos
    ⁝ **points** depressed; with: verat
    ⁝ **red**: lyc mez
    ⁝ **yellow**: *Ant-c*
  - **rash**: bry caust cub merc mez nat-m *Nux-v* ol-an osm *Petr* rhus-t **Sulph** ter
    ⁝ **brownish**: mez
    ⁝ **burning** during menses: nux-v a1
    ⁝ **gnawing** after scratching: mez
    ⁝ **itching**:
    ⁝ ⁝ **burning** during menses: rhus-v
    ⁝ ⁝ **scratching** agg.; after: mez

- **red**: falco-pe nl2• mag-m h2* merc musca-d szs1 rhus-v tritic-vg fd5.de
  - **patches**: calc cycl gt1 plut-n srj7•
- **ringworm**: cassia-s ccrh1•
- **rough**: kreos rhus-v
- **scaly**: mez
- **scurfs**: bar-m merc *Mez*
  - **spots**, in: *Merc*
- **tetters**: *Clem* b4a.de *Graph* b4.de* *Kreos* b7a.de merc b4.de* nat-m b4a.de petr b4.de* *Rhus-t* b7a.de staph b7.de* *Zinc* b4.de*
- **tubercles**: mag-m h2* *Nat-c*
- **urticaria**: all-c caust h2* clem iod lac-leo sk4• merc sulph h2* *Zinc*
  - **itching**: caust h2* dulc h2* sulph gk
  - **scratching**; after: clem *Zinc*
- **vesicles**: ant-c aster cann-s caust clem *Crot-t* *Kali-c* lach nat-c olnd petr a1 podo fd3.de• sars sel sulph verat vip
  - **areola**, red: psil ft1 sulph
  - **black**: *Anthraci*
  - **burning**: verat
  - **itching**: aster clem psil ft1
  - **scratching** agg.; after: sars
  - **stitching**: psil ft1
  - **ulcers**, become: aster
  - **white** with red border: cann-s
- ○ **Areola**, red: nat-m
- **Back** of thigh: lac-leo sk4•
- **Between**: bros-gau mrc1 *Carb-v* hep kali-c h2* nat-m nat-s *Petr* puls sel
  - **pimples**: *Caust* b4a.de petr b4a.de sel b7a.de
  - **tetters**: *Nat-c* b4a.de *Nat-m* b4a.de petr b4a.de
- **Ham**, roughness: kreos
- **Inside**: aids nl2• alum bg2 gels psa *Graph* mrr1 kreos bg2 plut-n srj7• sil bg2
  - **menses**; during: kali-c h2 nux-v kr1 sil k*
    - **itching**: mur-ac a1
    - **pimples**: sulph h2

\- **Thumbs**: choc srj3• dulc fd4.de hep ruta fd4.de sanic tritic-vg fd5.de vanil fd5.de

- **blisters**: hep k* ignis-alc es2• lach bg2 *Nat-c* bg2 nit-ac bg2 ph-ac bg2 sep bg2
- **boils**: hep kali-n k*
- **desquamating**: petr-ra shn4•
- **fissures** | **right**: cortico tpw7
- **pemphigus**: (↗*SKIN - Eruptions - pemphigus*) lyc
- **pimples**: ant-c k* berb *Kali-c* k* lach bg2 *Lyc* k* *Ther* k* vanil fd5.de
  - **itching**: kali-c h2*
  - **Beside** the ball of: berb ther
- **pustules**: cic sanic
- **tubercle**: *Ars* caust h2*
- **vesicles**: *Hep* *Lach* k* mang h2* mez *Nat-c* k* nat-s nit-ac *Ph-ac* ruta fd4.de *Sep*
  - **Ball**: ph-ac h2
- **Tip** of: ail
  - **vesicles**: ail nit-ac

\- **Toes**: am-c k* borx br1 cocc b7.de* crot-c cupr cupr-ar graph kali-bi lach led med nat-c nit-ac ph-ac k* rhus-v ruta *Sil* *Sulph* zinc

- **blisters**: ars graph bg2* lach bg2 nit-ac k* ph-ac k* plb k2 rhus-t bg2 ruta bg2 sec bg2 sel c1* symph fd3.de• zinc bg2
- **blotches**: ant-c lach sulph zinc
- **desquamating**: petr-ra shn4•
- **eczema**:
  - **accompanied** by | **falling** out of nails: borx br1*
- **herpes**: alum
- **pemphigus**: *Ars* bro1 graph bro1 petr bro1 sep bro1
- **pimples**: am-c borx k* sulph zinc
- **pustules**: crot-c cupr-ar cycl graph kali-ar kali-br ph-ac

\- **Toes**: ...

- **scabs**: med c1 **Sil**
- **sore** to touch: androc srj1• zinc h2*
- **spikey** (See Excrescences - horny - toes - spikes)
- **tetters**: alum b4.de* graph b4a.de lach bg2 petr bg2
- **vesicles**: *Caust* cupr graph k* ham fd3.de• *Lach* k* *Nat-c* nit-ac k* *Petr* ph-ac k* rhus-t bg2 rhus-v ruta bg2 sec bg2* *Sel* *Sulph* zinc k*
  - **frostbite**; after: mag-c b4.de nit-ac b4.de
  - **phagedenic**: **Ars** b4a.de caust b4a.de *Graph* b4a.de mag-c b4a.de nat-c b4a.de *Petr* b4a.de *Sep* b4a.de sil b4a.de *Sulph* b4a.de
  - **spreading**: graph *Nit-ac* petr h2*
  - **watery**: rhus-v
  - **white**: graph
- **wheals**: sulph bro1
- ○ **Between**: alum k* bamb-a stb2.de• bros-gau mrc1 bry gk *Petr* k* psor bg1 rhus-t bg2 sil mrr1 sulph bg2 thuj mrr1
  - **desquamating**: bamb-a stb2.de•
  - **eczema**: moni jl2
  - **fungus**: sil mrr1
  - **herpes**: alum graph
  - **itching**: moni jl2
  - **painful**: sulph h2*
  - **pimples**: mosch nat-c b4a.de sulph k*
  - **rash**: rhus-t
  - **scabs**: psor bg1
  - **soreness**: berb carb-an *Graph* lyc merc-i-r mez nat-c ph-ac ran-b
  - **vesicles**: hell k* moni jl2 sil
    - **walking** agg.: sil
  - **white**: sulph h2*
- **Nails**; around: psor jl2
  - **winter**: psor jl2
- **Tips**:
  - **blisters**: nat-c ptk1
  - **vesicles**: nat-c h2*

\- **Upper** arms: anac bg2 ant-t carb-v bg2 cinnb dulc bg2* grat kali-c bg2 lach bg2 laur bg2 led k* merc nux-v petr-ra shn4• sep k* spong fd4.de staph sne tritic-vg fd5.de vanil fd5.de

- **blotches**: sacch-a fd2.de• sep h2* vanil fd5.de
  - **scaling** off: berb
- **boils**: aloe *Bar-c* k* **Brom** b4a.de carb-v k* coloc *Crot-h* iod jug-r mez *Sil* k* *Zinc* k*
- **crawling**: lach
- **crusts**: anac
- **eczema**: grat bg2 kali-c bg2 mang bg2 nat-m bg2 sulph bg2 syc fmm1•
- **herpes**: kali-c mang nat-m sulph
- **itching**: mag-s mim-p rsj8• olib-sac wmh1 petr-ra shn4• sep h2* tritic-vg fd5.de
- **miliary**: ant-c bg2
- **pimples**: anac ant-c k* ant-t k* arn carb-v k* dulc iod *Kali-c* k* lach *Laur* k* led b7a.de mang mim-p rsj8• mosch sep k* spong fd4.de sulph tax til tritic-vg fd5.de valer
  - **bleeding**, after scratching: mosch
  - **itching**: carb-v h2* kali-c h2*
- **pustules**: anac k* dulc fd4.de merc
- **rash**: ant-c bry germ-met srj5• mez rheum tell rsj10•
- **scaly** white: ars-i k1 mim-p rsj8•
- **tetters**: *Caust* b4a.de *Graph* b4a.de kali-c b4.de mang b4.de nat-m b4.de sulph b4.de
- **tubercles**: ars caust cocc dulc mang
- **urticaria**: sulfonam ks2
- **vesicles**: aran sep h2*

\- **Upper** limbs: agar alum alumn *Ant-c* ant-t arn **Ars** arund bro1 brom bry **Caust** k* chel cimic cinnb cob com con cop crot-h cupr elaps euph fl-ac graph guare hep jug-r kali-ar kali-br lach **Lyc** mag-s merc **Mez** moni rfm1• mur-ac nat-c **Nat-m** nit-ac nux-v oena petr ph-ac k* phos *Psor* **Rhus-t** *Rhus-v* rumx

Extremities

- **Upper** limbs: ...
  ruta fd4.de sars **Sep** **Sil** **Sulph** k* tab thuj til tritic-vg fd5.de valer vanil fd5.de vero-o rly4*• vip zinc
  - **black**: sec
  - **bleeding**: [bell-p-sp dcm1]
    - ⁝ **scratching**; after: cupr-ar
  - **blotches**: cimx hura mur-ac nat-m tritic-vg fd5.de vanil fd5.de
  - **boils**: aloe am-c ars bar-c k* *Bell* *Brom* k* *Calc* calc-sil k2 carb-an carb-v cob coloc elaps gaert fmm1• graph guare iod iris *Kali-n* *Lyc* mag-m *Mez* **Petr** k* ph-ac **Rhus-t** *Sil* sulph syph tritic-vg fd5.de *Zinc*
    - ⁝ **right**: osteo-a jl2
  - **bran**-like: *Borx*
  - **burning**: con merc *Nat-c* **Rhus-t** spig
    - ⁝ **scratching**; after: sil staph
  - **chickenpox**; like: led
  - **clusters**: rhus-t
  - **confluent**: cop phos
  - **cracked**: phos
  - **crawling**: lach
  - **crusts** (See scabs)
  - **desquamating**: agar k* *Am-c* k* am-m arn bar-c calc chinin-s crot-t ferr hydr led *Merc* **Mez** **Rhus-t** *Rhus-v* sep *Sulph*
    - ⁝ **thick** whitish scales: crot-t
  - **dry**: dol ger-i rly4• hyper merc **Psor**
  - **eczema**: bougv gm1 **Bov** bg2 calc bg2 *Canth* caust bg2 *Con* bg2 **Dulc** bg2 ger-i rly4• graph k* hell h1* kali-c bg2 *Merc* k* mez moni jl2* nat-c bg2 nat-m bg2 petr tl1 phos k* *Psor* k* sep bg2 *Sil* k* trichom mtf11
    - ⁝ **discharging** | **salt** rheum: *Lyc* b4a.de
  - **elevations**: alumn anac carb-v cic crot-h crot-t dros graph hep kali-br kreos merc mez bg2 nat-m k* nit-ac plb staph bg2 sul-ac urt-u
    - ⁝ **bleeding** after scratching: cupr-ar
    - ⁝ **shiny**: crot-t
    - ⁝ **spots**: syph k*
    - ⁝ **whitish**: crot-t
    - ⁝ **Tips** become white and scaly: merc
  - **erythematous**: (↗*urticaria; SKIN - Eruptions - erythema)* bor-ac c1
  - **excoriation**: arn ruta sul-ac
  - **excrescences**: *Ars* *Lach* *Thuj*
  - **exuding** water:
    - ⁝ **thin**: crot-h
    - ⁝ **yellow**: cupr hell *Rhus-t* sol-ni
  - **granulations** (See elevations)
  - **hard**: caust mez sep sil tritic-vg fd5.de
  - **herpes**: alum borx **Bov** calc caust *Con* cupr dol *Dulc* *Graph* kali-c kreos *Lyc* mag-s *Manc* *Mang* **Merc** *Nat-c* *Nat-m* k* nux-v *Phos* *Psor* sars sec *Sep* *Sil*
    - ⁝ **circinate**: syc fmm1•
    - ⁝ **crusty**: con thuj
    - ⁝ **furfuraceous**: merc phos
    - ⁝ **Joints**, on the: *Calc* merc
  - **itching**: agar anag ant-c ant-t berb bov calad cann-s h1* carb-an carb-v *Caust* cupr dulc ger-i rly4• *Jug-c* kali-c kali-chl kali-i kreos lach *Laur* *Led* lyc mag-c mag-s mang *Merc* *Mez* nat-m nat-s nux-v phos psor *Puls* **Rhus-t** **Sep** spig *Sulph* tab til tritic-vg fd5.de urt-u vanil fd5.de zinc
  - **itch**-like: alum berb graph *Lach* k* merc nit-ac phos rhus-t k* sabad b7a.de sars sel k* *Sep* squil b7.de* *Sulph*
  - **leprous**: *Meph* *Phos*
  - **lumps**: phos
    - ⁝ **bluish**, oozing and scabbing; hard: *Calc-p*
  - **measles**, like: cop rhus-v
  - **menses**; during: dulc br1
  - **miliary**: alum ant-t k* borx bg2 bry calad b7.de* cop merc nux-v k* rhus-v sel k* sulph k* valer b7.de*
    - ⁝ **scratching**; after: kali-c h2
  - **moist**: alum bov con kreos rhus-t
    - ⁝ **purulent** discharge: lyc rhus-t
  - **nodules**: hippoz petr sep
  - **painful**: ars kali-c lyc merc petr
  - **papules**: *Crot-h* *Kali-bi*
    - ⁝ **roseolous** papules without fever or itching: cub c1
  - **pemphigus**: *(↗SKIN - Eruptions - pemphigus)* sep ter
  - **petechiae**: berb
  - **pimples**: acon *Agar* k* am-c am-m anac k* ant-c b7a.de* ant-t k* arg-n arn **Ars** k* arum-t asc-t bar-c k* bell k* berb bov k* brom tl1 bry k* bufo-s *Calc-p* calc-s k* cann-s canth k* *Carb-an* *Carb-v* k* carbn-s **Caust** k* chel chin k* chinin-s cob com crot-c cupr-ar dulc k* elaps *Fl-ac* hura *Iod* k* jatr-c kali-ar kali-bi k* kali-c k* kali-chl kali-n k* kreos lac-ac lach k* lyc k* mag-c k* mag-m mang merc k* merc-c b4a.de mez k* mur-ac k* nat-m bg2 nat-s nit-ac k* nux-v b7.de* ol-an k* op osm ph-ac k* plat psor puls k* rat rheum b7.de* **Rhus-t** k* rhus-v ruta fd4.de sabad sars sel **Sep** k* spig staph *Sulph* k* tab tarax thuj til tritic-vg fd5.de valer k* *Zinc* k*
    - ⁝ **bleeding**, when scratched: cob tritic-vg fd5.de
    - ⁝ **burning**: agar h2* am-c bov mag-m nat-s *Rhus-t*
      - ⁝ **scratching** agg.; after: canth carb-an
    - ⁝ **disappear** from scratching: mag-c h2*
    - ⁝ **hard**: arg-n bov calc-s k* rhus-t rhus-v valer
    - ⁝ **head**; with a black depressed: calc-s k*
    - ⁝ **indolent**: chel
    - ⁝ **inflamed**: calc-s k*
    - ⁝ **itching**: acon agar h2* am-c am-m asc-t bar-c cann-s carb-an carbn-s caust hura iod h* kreos lyc mag-c *Mag-m* *Merc* sabad sel sulph ziz
    - ⁝ **menses**; during: sulph
    - ⁝ **painful**: kali-chl thea
    - ⁝ **red**: acon anac ars bov chel com elaps hura iod h* kali-chl mag-s rhus-t sulph til tritic-vg fd5.de
    - ⁝ **sensitive**: *Calc-s* k*
    - ⁝ **stinging**: acon arg-n
    - ⁝ **white**: til valer
      - ⁝ **scratching**; after: kali-c h2
  - **psoriasis**: *Iris* kali-ar *Kali-s* rhus-t sil
  - **pustules**: anac ant-c k* arg-n *Ars* arund asc-t bell h1* borx calc chel chlor cocc cop crot-h cupr elaps fl-ac iris jug-c *Kali-bi* k* *Kali-br* *Merc* *Mez* *Nat-m* phos *Psor* *Rhod* *Rhus-t* k* rhus-v ruta sars sec *Sep* *Sil* spig squil *Staph* still **Sulph** tab tarent thal-xyz srj8•
    - ⁝ **black**: anthraci *Ars* lach sec
    - ⁝ **ecthyma**, like: phos k*
    - ⁝ **hair** in centre, with a: kali-bi k* kali-br
    - ⁝ **heal** very slowly: *Psor*
    - ⁝ **inflamed** halo, with: chlor rhus-v sep
    - ⁝ **large**: sep
    - ⁝ **point**:
      - ⁝ **dark** in centre: kali-bi
      - ⁝ **red**: crot-t k* mez h2*
  - **rash**: alum ant-t bell berb bry calad chlol cupr daph dig elaps form kali-ar led mag-p *Merc* *Mez* nux-v phyt *Puls* rheum *Rhus-t* sec *Sep* *Sil* stram *Sul-i* *Sulph* tep thal-xyz srj8•
    - ⁝ **alternating** with asthma (See RESPIRATION - Asthmatic - alternating - upper)
    - ⁝ **brownish**: mez
    - ⁝ **itching**: alum caust nux-v rheum sep sul-i
    - ⁝ **red**: mez stram
  - **red**: am-c ant-c arg-met cycl dulc gins jug-r mag-c mag-s *Merc* *Mez* nat-m phos sep *Staph* *Sulph* valer vanil fd5.de
    - ⁝ **scarlet** fever, like: cocc
  - **scabs**: *Alum* k* am-m *Ars* *Calc* cit-v k* *Jug-c* *Jug-r* *Mez* mur-ac k* phos plb podo *Rhus-t* rhus-v *Sep* k* *Staph* sul-ac *Sulph*
    - ⁝ **itching**: sep
    - ⁝ **moist**: alum staph
    - ⁝ **serum**, of: rhus-t rhus-v k*
    - ⁝ **white**: mez

- **scabs**: ...
  - **yellowish** brown: rhus-t
- **scales**: agar anthraci arn **Ars** berb cupr *Fl-ac Iris Kali-s Merc Phos* pip-m puls *Rhus-t* sec *Sil Sulph*
  - **fall** off on scratching: sulph
  - **spots**; in: merc
- **scurfs**, brownish: am-m cinnb
- **smarting**: anag hyper urt-u
- **stinging**: mag-c puls
- **tetters**: bov$_{b4.de*}$ calc$_{b4.de}$ caust$_{b4.de}$ con$_{b4.de*}$ *Dulc*$_{b4a.de}$ graph$_{b4.de*}$ hell$_{b7.de}$ kali-c$_{b4.de}$ *Kreos*$_{b7a.de}$ mang$_{b4a.de}$ merc$_{b4.de*}$ nat-c$_{b4.de}$ *Nat-m*$_{b4.de*}$ phos$_{b4.de*}$ sep$_{b4.de}$ sil$_{b4.de*}$
- **tubercles**: ars crot-h *Nat-c* phyt rhus-t
  - **painful**: ars
  - **ulcerate**: *Nat-c*
- **urticaria**: *(↗erythematous)* acon ant-c *Apis* berb calad cann-s$_{h1*}$ *Carb-v* chinin-s *Chlol* cop dulc$_{h2*}$ hep hydrc hyper indg kali-i lach lyc merc morg-g$_{pte1*•}$ *Nat-c Nat-m* nat-s *Phos* rhus-v **Sulph** thuj *Urt-u*
  - **red** after rubbing: nat-m$_{h2*}$
  - **white**: nat-m$_{h2*}$
- **variola**: led$_{b7.de*}$ rhus-t$_{b7a.de}$ sec$_{b7.de*}$
  - **black**: *Ars*$_{b4a.de}$
- **vesicles**: am-m$_{k*}$ anac anag *Ant-c*$_{k*}$ *Ant-t* arn *Ars* asc-t bell bov$_{k*}$ brom bruc bufo calad calc calc-p calc-sil$_{k2}$ canth caust chin chlor cinnb cit-v$_{k*}$ com *Crot-h* cupr-ar cycl$_{k*}$ daph dulc elaps fl-ac hipp hura indg iod iris *Kali-ar* kali-bi *Kali-c*$_{k*}$ kali-chl *Kali-i Lach Mag-c* mang medus$_{br1}$ *Merc* merc-c$_{k*}$ mez$_{k*}$ *Nat-c*$_{k*}$ *Nat-m*$_{k*}$ phos psor *Puls*$_{k*}$ *Ran-b*$_{k*}$ **Rhus-t**$_{k*}$ *Rhus-v* ruta sars$_{k*}$ **Sep**$_{k*}$ *Sil* sol-ni *Spong*$_{k*}$ *Staph Sulph*$_{k*}$ tell$_{c1}$ ter vip
  - **black**: *Ars*
  - **cold**:
    - **air** agg.: dulc
    - **water** | **agg.**: clem
  - **discharging** acrid serum: rhus-t
  - **itching**: daph nat-m$_{h2*}$
  - **periodical**:
    - **week** | **four** to six weeks; every: *Sulph*
  - **phagedenic**: clem$_{b4a.de}$
  - **putrid**: *Ars*
  - **red**, small: *Nat-m*
  - **rubbing**; after: ant-c$_{h2*}$
  - **scratching** agg.; after: *Calc*
  - **shooting** pain: mag-c
  - **ulcers**, change into: calc
- **wheals**: nat-m$_{bg2}$
- **white**: agar kali-c kali-chl merc nat-m
- **yellowish**: hell$_{h1*}$
- ○ **Joints**:
  - **eczema**: sep$_{bg2}$
  - **pimples**: *Ant-c*$_{b7a.de}$ bry$_{b7.de*}$
  - **tetters**: calc$_{b4.de}$ *Kreos*$_{b7a.de}$ merc$_{b4.de*}$ *Staph*$_{b7a.de}$

\- **Wrists**: am-m *Ant-c* ant-t apis ars$_{k*}$ *Ars-i Calc* caust cimic$_{k*}$ crot-h dros euph$_{k*}$ hep$_{k*}$ ip$_{bg2}$ led merc$_{k*}$ *Mez*$_{k*}$ moni$_{rfm1•}$ olnd petr-ra$_{shn4•}$ *Psor*$_{k*}$ *Rhus-t*$_{k*}$ ribo$_{rly4•}$ ruta$_{fd4.de}$ sulph$_{k*}$ tarax$_{k*}$

- **blisters**, forming scabs: am-m
- **blotches**: aur-m carb-v cocc
- **boils**: allox$_{tpw3}$ *Iod* osteo-a$_{jl2}$ sanic$_{k*}$
- **burning**: merc
- **crusts**: am-m$_{k*}$ *Mez* rhus-t
- **desquamating**: am-m$_{gsy1}$ rhus-v
- **dry**: merc *Psor*
- **eczema**: *Jug-c* lac-ac$_{stj5•}$ *Mez* moni$_{rfm1•}$ *Psor*$_{k*}$
- **elevations**: merc
- **fissures**: *Kali-ar*
- **herpes**: ip merc *Psor*$_{k*}$

\- **Wrists**: ...

- **itching**: merc *Mez Psor*$_{k*}$ rhus-t sars$_{h2*}$ stann$_{h2*}$
  - **night**: sars$_{h2*}$
- **itch**-like: ant-t olnd *Psor*$_{k*}$ *Sulph*
- **metal** contacts; where: morg-g$_{fmm1•}$
- **miliary**: led$_{bg2}$
- **pemphigus**: *(↗SKIN - Eruptions - pemphigus)* sep
- **pimples**: am-m$_{b7a.de*}$ *Ant-t*$_{k*}$ arg-n arn asc-t bar-c$_{k*}$ bry$_{k*}$ bufo-s calc-p carb-an crot-c cycl elaps *Hell*$_{b7a.de}$ hep$_{bg2}$ hura jatr-c led$_{b7.de*}$ mag-c merc$_{bg2}$ op plan psor$_{k*}$ **Rhus-t**$_{k*}$ *Rhus-v* sep staph sulph tarax ziz
  - **burning**, after scratching: carb-an
  - **exuding** water: hura psor rhus-v$_{k*}$
    - **pressure** agg.: mag-c
  - **hard** base: arg-n$_{k*}$
  - **itching**: allox$_{tpw3}$ bar-c carb-an hep$_{h2*}$ mag-c mang$_{a1}$ ziz
  - **sore**: sep
  - **stinging**: arg-n
  - **washing** agg.: allox$_{tpw3}$
- **pustules**: *Ant-c* arg-n cocc *Crot-h* elaps iris sep sulph
  - **confluent**: rhus-v
  - **hard**: cocc
  - **itching**: asc-t$_{a1}$ cocc
  - **pustular** tumors: cupr-ar
  - **red**: lyc
    - **areola**: cocc
- **rash**: calad elaps hydr led ribo$_{rly4•}$
  - **burning** after scratching: calad
  - **itching**: calad led
- **scabs** (See crusts)
- **scales**: ars-i merc rhus-t
- **scurf**: sars$_{h2*}$
  - **brownish**: am-m
- **spots**: *Apis Calc* dros jac-c *Merc* ribo$_{rly4•}$
- **tubercles**: am-c am-m$_{h2*}$ crot-h mag-c
  - **itching**: mag-c$_{h2*}$
- **urticaria**: hep$_{h2*}$ stann$_{h2*}$
- **vesicles**: am-m$_{k*}$ bufo calad calc-p *Crot-h* hep$_{k*}$ iris kali-i merc *Mez* nat-m prot$_{jl2}$ *Rhus-t*$_{k*}$ rhus-v ruta$_{fd4.de}$ sars$_{h2*}$ *Sulph*$_{k*}$
  - **burning**: am-m bufo *Mez* sars$_{h2*}$
    - **scratched**; when: am-m
  - **erysipelatous**: rhus-t rhus-v
  - **hard** base: am-m
  - **itching**: am-m bufo calc-p kali-i nat-m prot$_{jl2}$ ruta$_{fd4.de}$ sars$_{h2*}$
  - **scratching** agg.; after: nat-m$_{h2*}$
  - **scurfy** from scratching: am-m
  - **symmetrical**: sep$_{hr1}$
  - **water**; containing limpid: rhus-t
  - **white**: calad
  - **yellow**: rhus-t *Sulph*
- ○ **Anterior** surface: bry
  - **elevations**: anac
  - **pimples**: mang
  - **pustules**: anac
  - **vesicles**: rhus-t
- **Dorsal** side: helo-s$_{rwt2•}$
  - **painless**: helo-s$_{rwt2•}$
  - **pimples**: calc-p cimic *Mez*
  - **vesicles**: rhus-v
- **Radial** side:
  - **pimples**: ant-c
  - **vesicles**: ant-c$_{h2*}$ merc nat-m sars

ERYSIPELAS (See Inflammation - erysipelatous)

EXCORIATION:
O - **Feet**: all-c ptk1
O · **Heels**: all-c bg1
· **Joints**: ars bg2
· **Soles**: sil h2
- **Fingers**: **Graph** bg2 laur bg2
O · **Between**: *Ars* b4a.de graph b4a.de*
- **Hands**: ruta bg2 sul-ac bg2 sulph bg2
- **Joints**; bends of: bell *Caust* **Graph** lyc *Mang Ol-an Petr Sep* squil *Sulph*
- **Knee**, bend of: *Ambr* k* bry bg2 nit-ac bg2 **Sep** k*
- **Legs**: lach
O · **Tibia**; over: bism bro1
- **Nates**: puls b7.de* sel b7.de*
O · **Between**●: arg-met ars-s-f k2 arum-t bufo calc bg2 carbn-s **Graph** k* nat-m k* *Nit-ac* k* puls *Sep* k* sulph
⁝ **walking** agg.: graph mtf33
- **Thighs** | **menses**; before: sep b4a.de
- **Thighs** between: aeth agn b7.de* *Am-c* k* *Ambr* anan ars k* ars-s-f k2 aur bg2 bar-c k* bufo *Calc* k* carb-v bg2 carbn-s **Caust** k* cham ptk *Chin* k* chinin-ar coff b7.de* con bg2 goss *Graph* k* **Hep** k* iod h* kali-ar **Kali-c** k* **Kreos** k* *Lyc* k* *Mang* b4a.de meph bg2 **Merc** k* nat-ar k2 *Nat-c* k* nat-m k* *Nit-ac* k* ol-an bg2 *Petr* k* phos h2* rhod k* sang k2 sel b7.de* **Sep** k* squil *Sul-ac* k* **Sulph** k* thuj bg2 zinc
· **left**: lyc h2
· **dentition**; during: caust ptk
· **leukorrhea**; from (See FEMALE - Leukorrhea - acrid)
· **menses**; during (See FEMALE - Menses - acrid)
· **riding** agg.: carb-an bg2 ruta bg1
· **walking** agg.: aeth hr1* **GRAPH** k ●* ruta sul-ac **Sulph** k ●
- **Toes**; between: (↗*Perspiration - toes - between - rawness)* aur-m bamb-a stb2.de• berb carb-an clem k* coff b7a.de *Fl-ac* gink-b sbd1• *Graph* k* hell b7a.de hydrog srj2• *Iod* b4a.de lach **Lyc** k ●* mang k* merc-i-f mez *Nat-c* k* **Nat-m** k ●* nat-ox rly4• nat-sil fd3.de• nit-ac k* ph-ac k* ran-b k* **Sep** k ●* **Sil** k* sulph ser syph zinc k*
· **walking** agg.: carb-an h2 graph mtf33

EXCRESCENCES: ars thuj
- **fungous**:
O · **Elbows**: chel b7a.de
· **Knees**: *Ant-c* b7a.de arn b7a.de *Ars* b4a.de con b4a.de *Iod* b4a.de *Led* b7a.de *Puls* b7a.de *Sil* b4a.de **Spong** b7a.de *Sulph* b4a.de *Zinc* b4a.de
· **Upper** limbs: *Ars* b4a.de
- **horny**: (↗*SKIN - Excrescences - horny)* ruta fd4.de thuj tritic-vg fd5.de
O · **Feet** | **Soles**: **Ant-c** k* *Graph*
· **Fingers** | **Tips**: *Ant-c* bro1 pop-cand br1*
· **Hands** | **cracked** at base: thuj
· **Nails**; under: *Ant-c* k* graph k*
· **Toes**: *Ant-c* b7a.de ruta fd4.de
⁝ **spikes**; with: androc srj1•
O - **Fingers**: ant-c k2
- **Hands**: lach

EXERTION; physical:
- **agg.**:
O · **Lower** limbs: am-m b7.de* ant-c b7.de* *Arn* b7.de* asaf b7.de* borx b4a.de *Bry* b7a.de cann-s b7a.de caust b4.de* cocc b7.de* con b4.de* croc b7.de* gels bg2 hep b4a.de ign b7a.de *Lyc* b4a.de *Nat-m* b4a.de nux-v b7.de* *Phos* b4a.de *Rhod* b4a.de **Rhus-t** b7.de* ruta b7.de* *Sil* b4.de* spong b7.de* verat b7.de*
· **Upper** limbs: agar b4.de *Alum* b4a.de am-m b7.de arn b7.de bry b7.de *Caust* b4.de* cina b7.de cocc b7.de croc b7.de graph b4.de hell b7.de hep b4.de *Kali-c* b4.de* kali-n b4.de lach b7a.de merc b4.de mur-ac b4.de *Nux-v* b7.de *Phos* b4a.de plat b4.de puls b7.de *Rhus-t* b7.de* *Ruta* b7a.de sabad b7.de sabin b7.de *Sep* b4.de *Sil* b4.de spong b7.de **Stann** b4.de* verat b7.de
- **amel.**:
O · **Lower** limbs: ign b7.de* nat-m b4.de*

Exertion; physical – **amel.**: ...
· **Upper** limbs: sil b4a.de

EXFOLIATION of nails (See Nails - exfoliation)

EXOSTOSIS: (↗*Nodes; Nodules; GENERALS - Exostosis)* aur aur-m calc k2 **Calc-f** k* dulc hecla sne* mez nat-sil fd3.de• ph-ac rhus-t ruta k2* **Sil** staph k2 sulph syph xxb
O - **Feet**: hecla mtf11
O · **Heels**: conch mtf11
- **Fingers**: *Calc-f* k* *Hecla* bro1 nat-sil fd3.de• sil k2
- **Forearms**: *Dulc* k*
- **Joints**: sil k2
- **Knees** | **Patella**: calc-f
- **Legs**:
O · **Bones** | **Tibia**: *Ang Aur Aur-m* bad calc-f *Calc-p Cinnb Dulc Hecla* merc merc-c ptk1 **Nit-ac** k* phos c1 *Phyt* rhus-t sars
- **Toes**: sil k2
- **Wrists**: choc srj3• mag-m h2 ruta k2*

EXPANSION (See Enlargement)

EXTEND THE ARMS, desire to: am-c bell sabad tab verb

EXTENDED: verat h1
- **involuntarily**: petr h2
O - **Upper** limbs: ben-n *Chin* dig nux-v sep *Stram* stry
· **alternating** with | **flexed** upper limbs (See Flexed - upper - alternating - extended)
· **involuntarily**: petr h2
· **paroxysms**; during: *Cic* **Cina** stry
· **rigidly**: merc
· **take** hold of something; as if he had intended to: dulc k* phos k*

EXTENSION: (↗*Stretching)*
O - **Feet**: phyt plat plb gk
- **Fingers**:
· **difficult**: arn *Ars Camph* carbn-s *Coloc* cupr *Cupr-ar* hyos merc mosch plat plb stram syph tab
· **impossible**: prot fmm1•
- **Legs**:
· **agg.** | **Knee**; hollow of: carb-an ptk1 *Rhus-t* ptk1
· **difficult**: carbn-o dig h2* pic-ac stry
· **impossible**: con plb
⁝ **sitting** agg.: *Lath* k*
· **necessary**: sul-ac
· **paroxysm**:
⁝ **before**: bufo
⁝ **during**: nux-v stry
· **spasmodic**: bufo cina
⁝ **waking**; on: **Bell**
- **Thumbs** | **spasmodic**: bell bg2 *Camph* bg2

FALL: | **as** if she would: sabin c1

FALL, liability to: (↗*Awkwardness - lower; GENERALS - Fall; tendency; VERTIGO - Fall tendency)* ars b4.de* **Bell** b4a.de calc b4.de* *Caust* k* cic b7.de* cocc k2 colch b7.de dros b7.de hydr-ac bg2 *Hyos* b7.de* ign b7.de* iod k* ip bg2 lyc bg2 mag-c k* mur-ac h2* nat-c b4a.de* nat-m bg2 nit-ac b4.de* nux-v k* ph-ac k* phos k* psor al1 stram b7.de*
- **children**; in: caust mtf33 psor al1
- **fever**; during: (↗*VERTIGO - Fall tendency - fever)* chinin-s c1
- **forward** | **walking** backward; when: mang-act bro1
- **walking** agg.: mag-c bro1

FALLING OFF; sensation of:
O - **Legs** | **Calves**: rumx bg2 tab bg2

FALLING OUT of nails (See Nails - falling)

FALSE STEP; from a:
- **agg.** | **Lower** limbs: ars b4.de* *Bry* b7.de* caust b4.de* led b7.de* *Lyc* b4a.de ph-ac b4a.de* phos b4.de* puls b7.de* spig b7.de* valer b7.de*

FANNED; wants hands and feet: *Med* k*

FATTY degeneration: | **Muscles**: phos k2

FEAR felt in feet: ruta pd spong a1

FEATHER BED (= quilt filled with feathers):
- **agg.**:
○ • **Lower** limbs: *Coloc* b4a.de lyc b4.de* *Mang* b4a.de *Merc* b4a.de sulph b4.de*
• **Upper** limbs: lyc b4.de* *Merc* b4a.de

FELON (= Panaritium; Whitlow): *All-c* k* alum k* **Am-c** k* *Am-m* ammc c2 *Anac* antho bg2 **Anthraci** k* **Apis** k* arn *Ars* bg2* asaf bar-c k* bell bro1 *Benz-ac* berb bor-ac mtf bov k* *Bry* bro1 *Bufo* k* *Calc* calc-f bro1 calc-s bro1 calc-sil k2 calen bro1 *Caust* chin *Cist* k* con crot-h bro1 cur **Dios** k* eug ferr ferr-p tl1 **Fl-ac** k* gins **Hep** k* *Hyper* k* **Iod** k ● *Iris* k* kali-c kali-sil k2 kalm kola stb3• *Lach* k* lap-la sde8.de• led k* *Lyc* k* m-arct c2 *Merc* k* **Myris** c1* *Nat-c* *Nat-hchls* *Nat-m* *Nat-s* k* **Nit-ac** k* ol-myr bro1 ozone sde2• par k* petr phos bro1 *Phyt* plb psor al2* puls pyrog jl2 *Rhus-t* k* *Sang* *Sep* **SIL** k ●* staphycoc jl2 **Sulph** k ●* syph ptk1 **Tarent-c** k* teucr **Thuj** ptk1 thyr bg2 tritic-vg fd5.de wies a1 [heroin sdj2]
- **air**; in open | **amel.**: nat-s k2
- **burning**: **Anthraci** con h2
- **chronic**: dios ptk1 hep ptk1 sil ptk1
- **cold** | **applications** | **amel.**: *Apis* *Fl-ac* *Led* **Nat-s** **Puls**
  • **water** | **amel.**: apis ptk1 fl-ac ptk1 led ptk1 *Nat-s* ptk1 *Puls* ptk1
- **deep**-seated: bry calc ptk1 hep lyc merc-c ptk1 rhus-t *Sil* ptk1 sulph ptk1
- **delivery**:
  • **after**: all-c bro1*
  • **during**: all-c gsy1
- **gangrenous**: *Ars* *Lach*
- **hangnails**, from: lyc *Nat-m* sulph
- **injuries**; after: *Led* k*
- **itching**: **Apis**
- **malignant**: anthraci bro1 *Ars* bro1 carb-ac bro1 *Lach* bro1
  • **burning**; with: *Anthraci* *Ars* **Tarent-c**
- **maltreated**: *Hep* phos *Sil* stram *Sulph*
- **onychia** (See root)
- **painless**:
  • **accompanied** by | **syringomyelia**: aur bro1 *Aur-m* bro1 bar-m bro1 lach bro1 *Sec* bro1 sil bro1 thuj bro1
- **panaritium** (See Felon)
- **paronychia** (See nail)
- **periodical** | **winter**; every: **Hep**
- **predisposition** to (See recurrent)
- **prick** with a needle under the nail, from: all-c bov *Led* sulph
- **pulp**; inflammation of (See root)
- **pulsating**: con h2* sep h2*
- **purple**: *Lach*
- **recurrent**: bufo gk dios bro1 hep bro1 sil bro1
- **runaround** (See nail - runaround)
- **sensation** of felon, without pus: iris pd
- **sloughing**, with: **Anthraci** *Ars* *Carb-ac* *Euph* *Lach*
- **splinters**:
  • **from**: *Bar-c* k* hep iod lach *Led* nit-ac petr sil sulph
  • **sensation** of: hep k2 nit-ac
- **stinging** pain: **Apis** **Lach** sep **Sil**
- **sulfur**, after abuse of: apis
- **suppurative** stage: *Calc* calc-s c1 **Hep** kola stb3• **Sil**
- **ulcerative** pain: con h2*
- **whitlow** (See Felon)

○ - **Bone**:
  • **caries**: asaf aur fl-ac *Lach* lyc merc mez ph-ac **Sil** sulph
    ⁝ **offensive** pus; with: fl-ac
  • **deep**-seated pain, warm bed agg.: sep
- **Hands** | **Palms**: lach *Sil* sulph
- **Lymphatics**, inflamed: all-c *Bufo* *Hep* *Lach* rhus-t
- **Nail**; beginning in (= Paronychia): alum bro1 apis mrr1 arist-cl mtf11 bacls-10 pte1*• bacls-7 fmm1• bufo bro1* calc-s bro1 *Dios* bro1 graph bro1 hep bro1* led mrr1 *Nat-s* bro1 nit-ac tl1* par petr *Phyt* plb puls *Rhus-t* sep **Sil** k* *Sulph* k* syc pte1*• thuj mrr1
  • **burning**, aggressive: tarent-c mrr1

Felon – **Nail**; beginning in: ...
  • **chronic**: asaf mtf11
  • **cold** water | **amel.**: apis gsd1
  • **runaround**: all-c alum *Apis* bov bufo *Caust* con crot-t dios k* eug ferr *Fl-ac* graph *Hep* kola stb3• lach *Merc* *Nat-hchls* *Nat-m* *Nat-s* par phos plb puls ran-b rhus-t ruta *Sang* sep *Sil* sulph syph
    ⁝ **vaccination**; after: **Thuj**
    ⁝ **Lymphatics**, inflamed: all-c hep lach op rhus-t sin-n
  • **syphilitic**: syph jl2
  • **warmth** agg.: apis mrr1
○ • **Fingers**: bacls-7 fmm1•
- **Periosteum**: *Am-c* asaf calc calc-p canth dios *Fl-ac* mez phos sep **Sil** sulph
- **Root** of nail; at: (↗*Suppuration - fingers - nails)* arn bro1 calen bro1 caust *Fl-ac* bro1 graph k* hep k2 phos bro1 psor bro1 sang hr1 sars bro1 sil bro1 upa bro1
  • **vaccinations**; from: thuj tl1
- **Tendons** affected: graph *Hep* lach *Led* *Merc* nat-s *Nit-ac* ran-b rhus-t **Sil** sulph
- **Thumbs**: all-c k* am-m borx *Bufo* eug fl-ac gran *Hep* k* kali-c kali-i nux-v k* op ozone sde2• sep k* *Sil* sul-ac *Sulph* k*
○ • **Palmar** surface of: hep k*
- **Toes** | **First** toe: caust ptk1
- **Under** nail: alum caust coc-c sulph

FEVER: | **before**:
  • **agg.** | **Lower** limbs: chin b7.de cina b7.de rhus-t b7.de spong b7.de
- **during**:
  • **agg.** | **Lower** limbs: bry b7.de canth b7.de *Chin* b7.de hell b7.de *Nux-v* b7.de pyrog ptk1 *Rhus-t* b7.de* tub ptk1

FIBROSITIS (See Pain - muscles - rheumatic)

FILTHY (See Dirty)

FISTULOUS openings: fl-ac k2 mez k2
○ - **Ankles**: *Calc-p* k*
- **Hands** | **Palms**: ars
- **Hips**: *Calc* *Carb-v* *Caust* **Lach** *Ph-ac* **Phos** *Sil*
- **Joints**: *Calc* hep ol-j **Phos** **Sil** *Sulph*
- **Knees**: *Iod*
- **Legs**: ruta
- **Thighs**: *Calc*

FLAT FOOT: abrot bg2 calc bg2 calc-p bg2* chin bg2 ferr-act bg2 guaj bg2 nat-c bg2 ph-ac bg2 phos bg2 sep bg2 stront-c bg2 sulph bg2
○ - **Toes**; flat: am-c bg2 caust bg2 con bg2 nat-c bg2 ol-an bg2 valer bg2 zinc bg2

FLATUS; discharge of: | **agg.** | **Lower** limbs: carb-v b4.de*
- **amel.** | **Lower** limbs: canth b7.de* carb-v bg2

FLEXED: (↗*Drawn)* acon ars carbn-h carbn-o colch sec
- **convulsions**; during: colch hydr-ac *Hyos* phos plb
○ - **Ankles**: chel b7a.de pin-s mtf11 rhus-t b7.de* sec b7.de* stram b7a.de
- **Elbows**: *Ant-c* b7a.de
- **Feet** | **Soles**: anac j5.de *Nux-v* j5.de *Plb* j5.de
- **Fingers**: (↗*Clenching - fingers)* acon b7.de* aeth hr1* alum b4.de* ambr k* anac b4.de* ant-t b7.de* arg-met b7a.de* *Ars* k* *Bell* b4a.de bism b7.de* bufo bg2 *Calc* b4a.de* carb-v b4a.de caust k* chin b7.de* *Cina* b7.de* cocc b7a.de* coff b7.de* colch k* coloc b4.de **Cupr** k* cycl b7.de* dros b7.de* ferr b7.de* *Graph* b4.de* *Hyos* kali-c b4a.de* kali-i j5.de lyc b4.de* m-arct j5.de meny b7.de* **Merc** k* nat-c b4a.de nat-m b4.de* nux-m nux-v k* *Phos* k* *Plat* k* **Plb** *Rat* j5.de rhus-t b7.de* *Ruta* b7a.de* sabad b7a.de sabin b7a.de sec k* sep b4.de* *Sil* j5.de spig b7.de* stann b4.de* *Stram* sul-ac b4.de* *Verat* b7a.de
  • **extending** the arm agg.: plat h2*
  • **extension** and flexion alternately, jerking: kali-c h2
○ • **First**: sep h2
  • **Phalanx**: plb a1
- **Hands**: anac j5.de m-arct j5.de *Merc* j5.de
○ • **Palms**: nux-v j5.de
- **Knees**: am-m b7.de* brass-n-o srj5• carb-an b4.de* chin b7.de* dig b4.de* guaj b4a.de* lyc k* m-arct j5.de merc b4.de* sulph k*
  • **convulsions**; during tetanic: stram

- **Leg** upon thigh: bufo guaj k2 *Hyos* lat-m bnm6• *Op* *Plb* vip j5.de*
  - • **cannot** allow one leg to be bent in the morning in bed: *Zinc*
  - • **painfully**: nux-v
  - • **walk**; when he tries to: *Plb* spong h1
- **Lower** limbs: hep j5.de sec j5.de
  - • **shortening** of tendons; as if from: *Con* b4.de*
  - ○ • **Joints**: ant-c bg2 ant-t b7.de *Calc* b4a.de carb-an b4a.de *Caust* b4a.de chin b7.de* *Ferr* b7a.de *Graph* b4a.de *Guaj* b4a.de hep b4.de* *Hyos* b7.de* *Lyc* b4a.de m-aust b7.de merc b4.de* merc-c b4a.de sec b7.de* *Sil* b4.de* spong b7.de* stram b7a.de *Verat* b7a.de
- **Thigh** upon abdomen: arg-n *Ars* carb-v cham *Cina* *Cupr* hydr-ac *Hyos* lat-m bnm6• *Merc-c* *Mur-ac* ox-ac *Plb* verat zinc
  - • **accompanied** by | **Abdomen**; pain in: *(↗ABDOMEN - Pain - flexing)* catar br1
  - • **convulsions**; during: stram
  - • **lying** on back agg.: stram ptk1
  - • **walk**; when he tries to: *Plb*
- **Thumbs**: lat-m bnm6•
  - • **extending** and flexing into palms: acon bg2 *Bell* bg2 *Cham* bg2 cocc bg2 *Cupr* bg2 *Hyos* bg2 *Ign* bg2 olnd bg2 rhus-t bg2 viol-t bg2
  - • **perspiration**; during: *Bell* bg2 *Cham* bg2 hyos bg2 ign bg2 stann bg2 stram bg2 viol-t bg2
- **Toes**: anac b4.de* ant-t b7.de* am b7.de* *Ars* k* bism b7.de* calc b4a.de carb-v j5.de cham b7.de* chel b7.de* colch euph b4.de* ferr b7.de* *Graph* b4a.de* *Hyos* k* kali-c b4a.de* kali-n b4a.de* lyc b4.de* mag-m b4.de* merc b4.de* *Nux-v* b7.de* *Paeon* j5.de plat b4.de* plb b7.de* rhus-t b7.de* sars b4.de* sec b7.de* sulph b4.de*
- **Upper** limbs: acon alum b4.de* anac b4.de* ars *Calc* b4a.de carbn-o caust b4.de* coff b7.de* *Ferr* b7a.de graph b4.de* *Guaj* b4a.de hydr-ac kali-c b4.de* laur b7.de* lyc b4.de* morph nux-v b7a.de plb sec b7.de* stann b4.de* stry tax
  - • **left**: caust
  - • **agg.**: hyos b7.de* spong b7.de* teucr b7.de* valer b7.de*
  - • **alternating** with:
    - ⁝ **extended** upper limbs: carbn-o *Cic* k* *Cupr* k* hyos **Lyc** k* nux-v *Plb* sec *Tab* k*
      - ⁝ **periodical** | **week**; every: lyc
      - ⁝ **sitting** agg.: nit-ac
  - • **backward**: acon lyc
  - • **sleep** agg.; during: *Ant-t*
  - • **spasmodically**: *Caust* hydr-ac nux-m nux-v plb stry
  - ○ • **Bones** | **sensation** as if drawn bent: am-c b4.de am-m bg2
  - • **Chest**, over: lat-m bnm6• morph olnd tab
    - ⁝ **sleep** agg.; during: sang hr1
  - • **Elbow**, at: lyc
- **Wrists**: androc bnm2• cina b7a.de *Plb* sang sne

FLEXIBLE:

○ - **Hands**:
  - • **accompanied** by | **Fingers**; slender: syph jl2

FLOATING in the air; as if (See Lightness)

FLUTTERING:

○ - **Shoulders**; between cupr ptk1
- **Thighs**: cench
- **Upper** arm while resting it on the table; in: phyt k*

FOREIGN body; as of a:

○ - **Fingers**: bell bg2
- **Foot** | **shoe**; in: bamb-a stb2.de•

FORMICATION: *Acon* k* *Agar* k* *Alum* alum-sil k2* alumn k2 *Arg-n* ars k* ars-h k* ars-s-f k2 aur b4a.de *Bamb-a* stb2.de• bar-act br1 *Bar-c* bros-gau mrc1 cact cadm-s k2 calc-p ptk1 *Camph* k* caps carb-ac k* carbn-s carl k* caust coloc k2 crot-c hep k* hipp hydr-ac k* *Ign* k* kali-ar kali-c kali-sil k2 lach k* *Laur* **Lyc** k* mag-c h2* *Mez* nat-ar k2 nux-m c1 *Nux-v* **Ph-ac** k* *Phos* k* pic-ac k2 plb k* psor k* *Puls* k* *Rhod* k* **Rhus-t** k* sabad k* **Sec** k* sil b4a.de stram k* stront-c ptk1 stry k* sulph b4a.de **Tarent** k* teucr k* tritic-vg fd5.de tub c1 vanil fd5.de verat verin a1 *Zinc* k*
- **right**: agar hipp sacch-a fd2.de• vanil fd5.de
- **left**: sulph h2*

Formication: ...
- **morning** | **bed** agg.; in: teucr k*
- **evening**: graph h2* mag-c h2*
  - • **bed** agg.; in: sulph h2
- **accompanied** by | **contraction** of extremities (See Contraction - accompanied - formication)
- **alternating** with | **numbness** (See Numbness - alternating with - formication)
- **convulsions**; after: stry k*
- **fever**; during: *Acon* bg2 am bg2 colch bg2 plat bg2 **Rhus-t** bg2 sec bg2 *Sep* bg2 spig bg2 stram bg2
- **menses**; during: *Graph* k*
- **neuralgia**; in: acon mtf11
- **paralysis**; during: **Phos**
- **perspiration**; during: *Acon* bg2 *Am* bg2 **Ars** bg2 colch bg2 plat bg2 **Rhus-t** bg2 sec bg2 *Sep* bg2 sil bg2 stram bg2
- **sitting** agg.: kali-c k* teucr k* vanil fd5.de
- **sleep**; disturbing (See SLEEP - Waking - formication)
- **stool** agg.; after: sec bg2
- **waking**; on: *Puls*
  - ○ • **Side** lain on; in: *Puls*
- **walking** agg.: graph
- **weather** agg.; rough: rhod k*

○ - **Ankles**: agar a1 ars-i meph nuph a1 pall k* rhus-v k* sacch-a fd2.de•
  - ▽ • **extending** to:
    - ⁝ **Os** calcis: rhus-v k*
    - ⁝ **Toes**: petr-ra shn4•
- **Elbows**: canth bg2 merc bg2
- **Feet**: acon aeth **Agar** k* alum k* alum-p k2 am-c k* ambr b7.de* ang k* ant-c ant-t a1 apis k* am k* ars k* ars-h ars-i k* arund k* bell k* borx canth k* caps k* carb-an k* carbn-s carc fd2.de• carl k* *Caust* k* chel k* chin b7.de* cic k* clem k* colch b7.de* coloc k* con k* croc k* *Crot-c* k* dulc k* euph k* graph k* guaj k* hep k* hyper k* ign k* jatr-c kali-bi bg2 kali-c k* kali-n k* kreos k* laur b7.de* lyc k* mag-c k* manc k* mang k* mez k* nat-ar k2 *Nat-c* k* *Nat-m* k* nat-p nux-v k* op k* par k* petr-ra shn4• phos k* plat bg2 plb k* puls b7.de* *Rhod* k* *Rhus-t* k* rhus-v k* sal-ac c1 sars k* **Sec** k* *Sep* k* spong k* *Stann* k* stram stront-c k* *Sulph* k* tarax tax k* tritic-vg fd5.de zinc k* zinc-p k2
  - • **right**: mang bg1 nat-c bg1
  - • **morning**: carb-an h2* *Hyper* k* nat-c k*
    - ⁝ **bed** agg.; in: *Rhus-t*
    - ⁝ **stepping** agg.: puls
  - • **night**: phos k* sulph h2* tritic-vg fd5.de
  - • **chill**; during: canth k*
  - • **heat**; after: *Sulph* k*
  - • **raising** foot agg.: sars h2*
  - • **sitting** agg.: carl tritic-vg fd5.de
  - • **standing** agg.: ant-t a1 mang k* sep k* tritic-vg fd5.de
  - • **stepping** agg.: sars h2*
  - • **walking** in open air | **amel.**: borx zinc
  - ▽ • **extending** to:
    - ⁝ **Body**: caps nat-m
    - ⁝ **Upward**: bell h1 stann h2 tritic-vg fd5.de
    - ⁝ **Uterus**; from feet up legs to: tarent rb2
  - ○ • **Back** of feet: agar a1 am-c a1 cic a1 mag-c h2* zinc h2*
  - • **Heels**: agar k* am-c bell k* caust k* ferr-ma k* *Graph* k* lyc bg2 nat-c k* par k* phos k* stront-c k* *Sulph* k* zing k*
    - ⁝ **morning** | **bed** agg.; in: *Graph*
    - ⁝ **evening** | **bed** agg.; in: nat-c h2
    - ⁝ **sticking**: *Sulph* k*
    - ⁝ **extending** to | **Toes**: bell h1*
  - • **Sole** of: agar k* *Alum* b4a.de am-c bell k* berb k* calc-p k* **Caust** k* cic k* clem b4a.de* *Coloc* k* con k* croc b7.de* fl-ac k* hep k* hura kali-c k* kola stb3• laur k* m-ambo b7.de mag-m k* nat-m k* nit-s-d a1 pic-ac k* plb k* puls b7.de* raph sep k* spig b7.de* spong k* staph k* sulph h2* thuj h1* tritic-vg fd5.de vip k* zinc zing
    - ⁝ **evening**: zing k*
      - ⁝ **sitting** agg.: zing

- **Sole** of: ...
  - ⁝ **rest** agg.: sep k*
  - ⁝ **rubbing** | **amel**.: sulph h2*
  - ⁝ **sitting** agg.: mag-m k* staph k* zing a1
  - ⁝ **standing** agg.: plb k* zing k*
  - ⁝ **stepping** agg.: con h2
  - ⁝ **walking** agg.: (non:con k*) plb k* spong k* zing a1
- **Fingers**: **Acon** k* aeth k* agar k* alum k* am-m b7a.de* ambr b7.de* apis b7a.de ars k* arum-i ptk2 brom k* *Calc* k* cann-s b7.de* *Caust* k* cina b7.de* colch k* croc b7.de* gins k* graph k* hep k* kali-c k* kreos k* lach k* laur bg2 **Lyc** k* m-arct b7.de m-aust b7.de* *Mag-c* k* mag-m bg2 *Mag-s* mez k* mur-ac k* *Nat-c* k* *Nat-m* k* nit-ac k* op k* paeon k* phos k* plat k* plb k* psor k* ran-b k* *Rhod* k* *Rhus-t* k* sabad b7.de* sacch-a fd2.de• samb k* **Sec** b7.de* sep k* *Sil* k* spig b7a.de staph k* sul-ac k* sulph b4a.de* teucr b7.de* *Thuj* k* verat k* verb b7.de*
  - · **morning** | **in** bed: psor k*
  - · **evening**: alum k* ars k* colch k*
  - · **anxiety**:
    - ⁝ **as** from: (non:verat kl)
    - ⁝ **from**: verat kl
  - · **fever**; before: rhus-t b7a.de
  - · **writing** agg.: *Acon*
  - ○ · **Back** of fingers: bar-act ran-b
  - · **Between**: alum bg2
  - · **First**: croc mag-s phos psil ft1 tab
    - ⁝ **Tips**: graph nat-m thuj h1*
  - · **Fourth**: agar *Aran* bamb-a stb2.de• mag-s phos rhod
    - ⁝ **Tips**: sep h2* sul-ac h2*
  - · **Joints**: sulph h2
  - · **Nails**; under: lach bg2
  - · **Second**: acon caust h2* mag-s mez sul-ac h2* tab
    - ⁝ **Tips**: kali-c thuj h1*
  - · **Third**: *Aran* caust mag-s sulph tab
    - ⁝ **Tips**: thuj h1*
  - · **Tips**: acon b7.de* **Am-m** k* cann-s *Colch* b7a.de croc b7.de* cupr k* cypra-eg sde6.de• glon graph hep k* kreos b7a.de m-ambo b7.de m-arct b7.de m-aust b7.de mag-m h2* mag-s k* morph **Nat-m** k* *Nat-s* plat rhus-t b7.de* **Sec** k* sep k* spig k* stry sulph k* tep *Thuj* k* verat b7.de*
    - ⁝ **right**: nat-m bg2
    - ⁝ **afternoon**: *Am-m*
    - ⁝ **evening**: nat-c
- **Forearms**: acon alum am k* bry bg2 *Calc* b4a.de carb-an carbn-s *Caust* k* chin chlor con k* ign bg2 lach merc k* plb puls b7.de* sacch-a fd2.de• *Sec* k*
- **Gluteal** muscles: agar tl1
- **Hands**: **Acon** agn apis ptk1 am k* ars k* ars-h arund atro bar-c k* bry k* calad ptk1 canth carb-an ptk1 carbn-s caust k* chel cocc ptk1 croc b7.de* cupr dulc form ptk1 *Graph* guare *Hyos* k* *Hyper* k* kali-n k* kreos k* lac-ac lach k* laur b7.de* lyc k* mez k* mur-ac b4a.de nux-v k* op k* par b7.de* ph-ac phos k* *Plat* k* puls b7.de* *Rhod* k* *Ruta* b7a.de* **Sec** k* seneg k* sep b4a.de spig k* stram b7a.de stront-c ptk1 *Sulph* k* thuj k* tritic-vg fd5.de vanil fd5.de verat k* visc c1
  - · **right**: hipp jl2 nat-c h2 sacch-a fd2.de• vanil fd5.de
  - · **left**: cact k2 flor-p rsj3•
  - · **morning**: bamb-a stb2.de• *Hyper* nat-c sacch-a fd2.de•
  - · **evening**: lac-ac nat-c h2 ph-ac h2
  - · **night**: ars
  - · **chill**; during: canth
  - · **menses**; during: *Graph*
  - · **pressing** them, on: spig h1
  - · **spider**; as if from a: visc tl1*
  - · **water**, after putting them in: *Sulph*
  - · **yawning** in open air, while: *Phos*
  - ○ · **Back** of hands: bar-act a1 borx bg1 nat-m bg1 ozone sde2• visc bg1
    - ⁝ **left**: ozone sde2•
    - ⁝ **spider** were crawling over it; as if large: ozone sde2•
- **Hands**: ...
  - · **Palms**: bar-c berb ol-an par psil ft1 seneg spig tritic-vg fd5.de vanil fd5.de vip
    - ⁝ **right**: ol-an bg2
  - · **Ulnar** side of: agar
    - ⁝ **writing**; after: agar
- **Hips**: ang b7.de*
- **Joints**: am carl ip sec
- **Knees**: *Acon* b7a.de apis carb-an bg1 chin bg1 crot-t k* cycl k* gent-l k* kali-c k* merc bg1 rat k* rhus-t k* zinc k*
  - · **right** knee; under skin of: rat rb2
  - ○ · **Hollow** of knees: chin bg1
- **Legs**: agar k* alum k* amyg k* ant-c b7.de* apis k* arg-met b7.de* *Arg-n* *Am* ars aster bar-c k* bell b4.de* bov k* calc k* *Calc-p* k* caps k* carbn-o carbn-s caust k* cic b7.de* graph k* guaj k* helo-s rwt2• *Hep* hydrog srj2• ip b7.de* jatr-c *Kali-c* k* kreos k* lac-ac k* lach lil-t k* m-ambo b7.de morph k* naja nicc k* **Nux-v** k* op k* pall *Ph-ac* k* phos pic-ac *Plat* puls k* *Rhod* k* rhus-t b7.de* sabin b7a.de **Sec** k* **Sep** k* spig b7.de* stann k* staph k* stram k* sul-ac k* sulph *Tab* tarent tax k* thal dx verat k* *Zinc* k*
  - · **right**: bit-ar wht1•
  - · **evening**: lac-ac k* *Plat* sep h2*
    - ⁝ **walking** agg.: graph k*
  - · **night** | **bed** agg., in: *Zinc*
  - · **rising** from sitting agg.: sulph h2
  - · **sitting** agg.: guaj h2* ol-an k* *Plat*
    - ⁝ **motion** | **amel**.: gink-b sbd1•
  - ▽ · **extending** to | **Upward**: bell h1
  - ○ · **Bones** | **Tibia**: sacch-a fd2.de• sul-ac h2*
  - · **Calves**: agar k* alum k* ant-c k* bar-c k* castm caust k* *Cham* k* coloc k* ip k* lach k* nux-v k* onos plb k* rhus-t bg2 rhus-v sang *Sec* mrr1 sol-ni spig k* sul-ac k* sulph verat bg2 zinc k*
    - ⁝ **evening**: alum
    - ⁝ **chill**; during: am-c b4.de
    - ⁝ **fever**; during: am-c b4.de
    - ⁝ **sitting** agg.: bar-c
    - ⁝ **standing** agg.: verat
    - ⁝ **walking**:
      - ⁚ **agg**.: sul-ac
      - ⁚ **air**; in open:
        - . **after** | **agg**.: nux-v
- **Lower** limbs: acon b7.de* aeth k* alum tl1 apis bg2 am k* *Ars* k* aster k* bov k* **Calc** k* *Calc-p* caps k* caust k* euphr graph k* *Guaj* b4a.de *Helo* helo-s rwt2• hep k* hyper a1 kali-c b4.de* kreos b7a.de lachn lyc bg2 nit-ac k* nux-v ptk1 op k* orni c *Phos* b4a.de *Plat* k* podo fd3.de• rhod k* rhus-t b7a.de* rumx sabad k* **Sec** k* *Sep* k* stann b4a.de staph bg2 stry k* sulph k* teucr b7.de* *Verat* b7a.de
  - · **evening** | **bed** agg.; in: sulph
  - · **night** | **bed** agg.; in: helo helo-s rwt2• orni c
  - · **accompanied** by | **sciatica** (See Pain - lower limbs - sciatic - accompanied - formication)
  - · **crossing** legs agg.: plat h2*
  - · **menses**; during: graph *Puls*
  - · **paralyzed** limb: *Nux-v*
  - · **riding** agg.: *Calc-p* rumx
  - · **sitting**:
    - ⁝ **after**: *Calc-p* sep k*
    - ⁝ **agg**.: cic h1* kali-c h2 plat h2
  - · **standing** agg.: hep h2*
  - · **walking** agg.: hep h2*
  - ○ · **Bones**: aeth a1 *Guaj*
- **Nates**: agar tl1 ang h1* ars k*
- **Paralyzed** parts: rhus-t h1*
- **Shoulders**: ars-h arund berb k* caust k* chinin-s cocc k* fl-ac k* lac-c k* lach bg2 lyc mag-c mez bg2 osm sarr sec bg2 thuj urt-u k*
  - · **morning**: *Mag-c*
  - · **evening** | **bed** agg., in: osm thuj

• **urination** agg.; during: hep

- **Thighs**: acon k* arg-met b7.de* ars k* caust cic b7.de* euph k* gins a1 *Guaj* k* hep b4a.de hydr-ac k* hydrog srj2• ip bg1 kreos bg1 m-ambo b7.de merc b4.de* *Nat-c* k* nit-ac k* *Pall* k* phos k* **Sec** k* sep spig k* staph k* stram sul-ac k*
  • **heat**; with: hydrog srj2•
  • **numb** while sitting: hep k*
  • **sitting** agg.: guaj h2

▽ • **extending** to:
  ⁝ **Abdomen**: ars k*
  ⁝ **Toes**: guaj h2* sep k*

- **Thumbs**: alum k* ambr bg2 chel k* cina bg2 mez nat-c h2* phos k* plat bg2 plb k* rhod k* sabad bg2 teucr bg2 zinc k*

○ • **Flexor** side of: plat h2*
  • **Proximal** joint: cina h1
  • **Tips**: am-m cina nat-c h2* nat-m

- **Toes**: agar k* alum k* am-c k* *Am-m* k* ars k* asaf b7.de* berb k* *Brom* b4a.de carc fd2.de• caust k* chel k* chin b7.de* cic k* colch k* con k* euph euphr k* guaj k* hep k* jatr-c kali-c k* lach k* lyc k* m-arct b7.de mag-c k* mag-m k* mez b4a.de nat-c k* nat-m nept-m lsd2.fr nicc k* phos k* plat k* plb k* puls b7.de* ran-s k* *Rhod* k* *Sec* k* sep k* spig b7.de* staph b7.de* stram sulph k* thuj k* verat b7.de* zinc k* zing k*
  • **evening**: ars k* colch a1 lyc k* puls k*
    ⁝ **walking** agg.: lyc k*
  • **night**: hep h2* nicc k*
  • **freezing**, as after: caust h2*

○ • **Balls**: colch b7.de*
  • **Fifth**: crot-t k* phos k*
  • **First**: alum k* ars h2 brom k* *Caust* k* chin k* gins k* jatr-c phos k* plat k* plb k* zinc a1
    ⁝ **afternoon**: nit-ac
      ⁝ **17** h: castm
    ⁝ **night**: brom k* mez k*
    ⁝ **freezing**, as after: alum k*
    ⁝ **twitching**, with: crot-t k*
    ⁝ **waking**; on: brom
    ⁝ **Balls**: am-c a1 caust k*
  • **Plantar**: mag-c h2 phos h2 staph h1
  • **Second**: nat-c h2
  • **Tips**: acon k* agar k* **Am-m** k* colch nit-s-d a1 spig h1 sulph h2 thuj ptk1

- **Upper** arms: cic a1 lach bg2 sep k* thuj k*
  • **left**: flor-p rsj3•

- **Upper** limbs: **Acon** k* *Alum* k* alum-p k2 am-c bg2 apis k* arn k* arum-t arund atro bamb-a stb2.de• *Bell* k* bry b7.de* cact cann-s b7a.de caps k* carbn-s caust k* cham bg2 chin cic *Cocc* k* con croc b7.de* *Graph* k* guare *Hep* ign b7.de* kali-n k* lach k* m-ambo b7a.de m-aust b7.de* *Mag-c* b4a.de nat-c nat-m k* nat-p nux-m op b7.de* pall phos k* plat k* plb *Rhod* k* *Rhus-t* rhus-v rumx sabad b7a.de sarr **Sec** k* stry sulph k* teucr b7.de* urt-u *Verat* b7a.de vip
  • **right**: nat-c h2*
  • **left**: nat-m h2*
  • **daytime**: *Arg-n*
  • **evening**: nat-c
    ⁝ **bed** agg.; in: *Sulph*
    ⁝ **walking** agg.: *Graph*
  • **night**:
    ⁝ **midnight**; before | **waking**; on: caust
  • **lying** down agg.: rumx
  • **mercury**; after abuse of: hep
  • **warm** bed agg.: rhod

○ • **Bones**: cham b7.de* rhus-t b7.de*

- **Wrists**: calc h2* caust h2* galla-q-r nl2•
  • **flies**; as if from: galla-q-r nl2•

FRACTURES: (↗*GENERALS - Injuries - bones)* arn mrr1 **Bry** mrr1 *Calc* st1 **Calc-p** tl1* *Calen* st1 eup-per mrr1 **Ruta** tl1* *Sil* st1 **Symph** tl1* [bell-p-sp dcm1]

- **open** fractures: *Calen* st1

Fractures – **open** fractures: ...
  • **suppuration**; with: **Arn** st1

○ - **Ankles**: phos ptk1

- **Legs**:

○ • **Bones**:
    ⁝ **Tibia**: anthraci hr1
      ⁝ **open** fracture: *Anthraci* hr1*

FREEZING:

- **complaints** from freezing (See Chilblains)
- **easily**: zinc h2

FRIGHT; after:

- **agg.**:

○ • **Lower** limbs: ign b7.de* spong b7.de*
  • **Upper** limbs: phos b4.de*

FROSTBITE:

○ - **Lower** limbs: *Agar* b4a.de borx b4a.de *Carb-v* b4a.de *Nit-ac* b4a.de **Phos** b4a.de

- **Upper** limbs: borx b4a.de

FROZEN sensation:

○ - **Feet**: alum bg1 pic-ac k* prot pte1*• puls k*
  • **cold** weather | **agg.**: prot fmm1•

- **Lower** limbs: ol-an bg2

FULLNESS: (↗*Swelling)* aesc k2 apoc k2 *Aur* aur-m nux-m phos k* *Puls* rhus-t h1* sul-i k2

- **heart** disease; in: arn br1

○ - **Feet**: aesc naja k2 rhus-v sumb
  • **menses**; during: aesc al

○ • **Soles**: apis b7a.de
    ⁝ **network** of veins as if marbled: caust lyc thuj
  • **Veins** of: *Ant-t* ars *Carb-v* sul-ac sumb

- **Forearms** | **Veins** of: nux-v bg2 puls bg2 rhod bg2
- **Hands**: aesc k2 *Ars* b4a.de brom k* *Caust* k* crot-h bg2 fl-ac k* kali-n b4a.de naja k2 nat-s k* *Nux-m* k* puls sumb k*
  • **afternoon** | **knitting**; while: nat-s
  • **evening**: nux-m k*
  • **menses**; during: aesc al
  • **taking** hold of anything: *Caust* k*

○ • **Palms**: ars
    ⁝ **night**: ars
  • **Veins** of: (↗*Swelling - hands - veins)* acon bg2 aloe bg2 alum k* alumn am-c k* arn k* bar-c k* bell bg2 bry bg2 calc k* castm caust bg2 cham bg1 **Chel** k* *Chin* k* chin-b c1 *Cic* k* crot-t bg2 cycl bg2* fl-ac bg2 ham fd3.de• ind laur k* lyc bg2 manc bg2 *Meny* bg2 merc bg2 merl c1 mez bg2 mosch bg2 nat-m bg2 nux-v k* olnd k* op k* ph-ac bg2 *Phos* k* plb bg2* **Puls** k* rheum k* rhod k* rhus-t k* ruta k* sars bg2 sel bg2 sep bg2 sil bg2 staph bg2 stict c1 stront-c bg2 sul-ac sulph k* sumb *Thuj* k* **Vip**
    ⁝ **afternoon**: alum k*
    ⁝ **evening**: alum k*
    ⁝ **chill**; during: am-c bg2 **Chel** *Meny* *Phos* bg2 thuj bg2
    ⁝ **cold** washing agg.; after: *Am-c* k*
    ⁝ **fever**; during: chin hyos *Led* meny
    ⁝ **perspiration**; during: am-c bg2 bar-c bg2 phos bg2 *Sulph* bg2 thuj bg2

- **Hips**: borx h2
- **Joints**: cinnb k* ham k*
  • **sensation** of: mang h2
- **Legs**: bell clem com k* ham k* merc bg1 mez nat-c osm k* ph-ac pic-ac staph h1* vip ptk1
  • **fever**; during: **Chinin-s** k*
  • **hanging** down, when: *Carb-v*
  • **menses**; during: ambr

○ • **Joints**: *Ham*
  • **Veins**: *Calc* *Carb-v* *Chinin-s* ham fd3.de• puls stict c1 sulph *Vip*

- **Shoulders**: bry k*
- **Upper** limbs: alumn k* verat k*

○ • **Veins** of: stict c1

- **Veins**: arg-n$_{k2}$ aur$_{k2}$ phos$_{k2}$

FUNGUS HAEMATODES: (↗*SKIN - Excrescences - fungus haematodes*) *Phos* sang
○ - **Fingers**: *Phos*
- **Thighs**: *Phos*

FUZZINESS, sensation of: dulc$_{fd4.de}$ hyper$_{k*}$ **Sec**$_{k*}$
○ - **Feet**: ars$_{k*}$ hyper$_{k*}$
  • **morning**: *Hyper*$_{k*}$
○ • **Soles**: plut-n$_{srj7}$•
- **Fingers**: ars$_{k*}$ colch$_{k*}$ dulc$_{fd4.de}$ sec$_{ptk1}$ tab$_{ptk1}$
- **Hands**: hell$_{k*}$ *Hyper*$_{k*}$ merc$_{k*}$ olib-sac$_{wmh1}$
  • **morning**: hyper$_{k*}$
- **Thumbs**: olib-sac$_{wmh1}$
- **Upper** limbs | **right**: phyt$_{ptk1}$

GANGLION: (↗*Nodules; GENERALS - Tumors - ganglion; SKIN - Ganglia*) bov$_{c2}$ carc$_{mlr1}$• ferr-ma$_{c2}$ kali-i$_{sne}$ ph-ac$_{c2}$ plb-xyz$_{c2}$ *Ruta*$_{c2*}$ sil$_{c2}$ sulph$_{c2}$ thuj$_{c2}$
○ - **Feet**:
○ • **Back** of feet: *Bry*$_{b7a.de}$ plb$_{b7.de*}$
  • **Soles** | **right**: bufo-s
- **Hands**: *Am-c*$_{bg2}$ bacls-7$_{fmm1}$• phos$_{bg2}$ rhod$_{bg2}$ **Sil**$_{bg2}$
  • **right**: bacls-7$_{pte1}$•
○ • **Back** of hands: am-c$_{k*}$ arn$_{sne}$ ozone$_{sde2}$• *Ph-ac* plb *Sil* zinc
  • **Palms**: ruta
- **Instep**, on the: ferr-m
- **Upper** limbs: *Am-c*$_{b4.de*}$ *Ph-ac*$_{b4.de*}$ *Phos*$_{b4.de*}$ *Plb*$_{b7.de*}$ *Sil*$_{b4.de*}$ *Zinc*$_{b4a.de}$
- **Wrist**, on: am-c aur-m benz-ac$_{c1*}$ *Calc* calc-f$_{bro1*}$ carb-v lach$_{pd}$ mag-m$_{h2}$ phos$_{bro1}$ rhus-t$_{c1*}$ ruta$_{c1*}$ *Sil*$_{k*}$ sulph thuj$_{c1*}$

GANGRENE: **Ars** *Carb-an* *Carb-v* *Chin* *Crot-h* helo$_{c1}$ helo-s$_{c1*}$ **Lach** med$_{c1}$ *Phos* *Plb* **Sec**$_{k*}$ verat verat-v$_{a1}$ vip$_{k*}$
- **diabetic**: (↗*GENERALS - Diabetes mellitus - accompanied - gangrene*) carb-ac$_{bg3*}$ con$_{bg3*}$ lach$_{bg3*}$ lyc$_{pcr}$ sec$_{a1}$ solid$_{bg3*}$
- **spots**, in: vip$_{k*}$
- **swellings**, like: anthraci
- **threatened** with blue parts: both$_{fne1}$•
○ - **Feet**: ant-c$_{k*}$ ant-t$_{k*}$ *Ars* calen *Lach* lol$_{a1}$ merc$_{k*}$ ric$_{a1}$ **Sec**$_{k*}$ vip$_{k*}$
  • **burning**, tearing pain: **Sec**
  • **cold** agg.: *Sec*$_{k*}$
  • **diabetic**: lyc$_{pcr}$
- **Fingers**: plb$_{k2}$ *Sec*$_{k*}$
- **Hands**: *Ars*$_{k*}$ *Lach* *Sec*$_{k*}$
- **Knees**: phos
- **Legs**: *Anthraci* both$_{fne1}$• crot-h$_{k*}$ iod *Sec*$_{k*}$
- **Lower** limbs: anthraci *Ars* crot-h lach phos$_{k2}$ sec
  • **cold** agg.: *Ars*$_{b4a.de}$
- **Shoulders**: *Crot-h*$_{k*}$
- **Thighs**: crot-h$_{k*}$ *Sec*$_{k*}$
- **Toes**: both$_{fne1}$• crot-h cupr iod$_{k*}$ lach plb$_{k2}$ **Sec**$_{k*}$
  • **old** people; in: *Carb-an* *Carb-v* cupr *Ph-ac* **SEC**$_{k}$ ●
- **Upper** limbs: **Ars**$_{k*}$ *Crot-h*$_{k*}$ ran-b$_{bg2*}$ ran-fl$_{bro1}$ *Sec*$_{k*}$
  • **cold** agg.: *Sec*$_{k*}$

GENU VALGUM (See Knees; position - inward)

GENU VARUM (See Knees; position - outward)

GIVE WAY:
○ - **Ankles**: *Carb-an*$_{b4a.de}$ *Nat-c*$_{b4a.de}$ sulph$_{b4a.de}$
- **Fingers**: (↗*Dislocation; easy - finger*) bell$_{b4a.de}$ *Carb-an*$_{b4a.de}$ hep$_{b4.de*}$ m-ambo$_{b7.de}$ nux-v$_{b7.de*}$ *Teucr*$_{b7.de*}$
- **Knees**: cann-s$_{b7a.de}$
  • **accompanied** by | **Head** pain: glon$_{tl1}$
  • **vertigo**; during: *Coloc*$_{b4a.de}$
- **Lower** limbs: acon$_{b7.de*}$ arg-met$_{b7.de*}$ arn$_{b7.de*}$ *Ars*$_{b4.de*}$ aur$_{b4.de*}$ bell$_{b4.de*}$ bry$_{b7.de*}$ camph$_{b7.de*}$ cann-s$_{b7a.de}$ carb-an$_{b4.de*}$ chel$_{b7.de*}$ chin$_{b7.de*}$ *Cic*$_{b7a.de}$ clem$_{b4.de*}$ cocc$_{b7.de*}$ coff$_{b7.de*}$ colch$_{b7.de*}$ cupr$_{b7.de*}$ hep$_{b4a.de}$ ign$_{b7.de*}$ kali-c$_{b4.de*}$ kreos$_{b7a.de}$ *Lyc*$_{b4.de*}$ m-aust$_{b7.de*}$

Give way – **Lower** limbs: ...
merc$_{b4.de*}$ *Nit-ac*$_{b4a.de}$ *Nux-v*$_{b7.de*}$ plat$_{b4.de*}$ puls$_{b7.de*}$ rhod$_{b4a.de}$ *Ruta*$_{b7.de*}$ sabad$_{b7.de*}$ stann$_{b4.de*}$ staph$_{b7.de*}$ stram$_{b7.de*}$ *Sulph*$_{b4.de*}$ thuj$_{b4a.de}$ viol-t$_{b7.de*}$
- **Toes**: *Carb-an*$_{b4a.de}$ lyc$_{b4a.de}$

GLISTENING: | **Toes**: sabin$_{ptk1}$

GLOW from foot to head; sensation of: *Visc*$_{k*}$

GOOSE FLESH: (↗*SKIN - Goose*) acon sec symph$_{fd3.de}$• tritic-vg$_{fd5.de}$
○ - **Forearms**: ign ran-b tritic-vg$_{fd5.de}$
- **Legs**: calc lac-h$_{htj1}$• nat-ox$_{rly4}$• rhod staph
- **Lower** limbs: bapt chinin-ar rhod
- **Thighs**: aur calc ign spig staph
- **Upper** arms: (non:ham$_{slp}$) lam$_{a1*}$ sulph tritic-vg$_{fd5.de}$
- **Upper** limbs: chinin-s merl phel phos sanic spig stann tritic-vg$_{fd5.de}$

GOUT (See Arthritic; Pain - joints - gouty)

GRASPING something:
- **agg.**:
○ • **Upper** limbs: acon$_{b7.de}$ *Am-c*$_{b4a.de}$ am-m$_{b7.de}$ arg-met$_{b7.de}$ arn$_{b7.de*}$ bell$_{b4.de}$ bov$_{b4.de*}$ bry$_{b7.de}$ calc$_{b4.de*}$ *Cann-s*$_{b7.de}$ *Carb-v*$_{b4a.de}$ *Caust*$_{b4.de*}$ cham$_{b7.de*}$ chin$_{b7.de*}$ dros$_{b7.de*}$ graph$_{bg2}$ kali-c$_{b4.de}$ kali-n$_{b4.de}$ laur$_{b7.de}$ led$_{b7a.de*}$ lyc$_{b4a.de}$ merc$_{b4.de*}$ nat-c$_{b4.de*}$ nit-ac$_{bg2}$ nux-m$_{b7.de}$ nux-v$_{b7.de}$ op$_{b7.de*}$ *Phos*$_{b4a.de}$ plat$_{b4a.de*}$ *Puls*$_{b7.de}$ rhus-t$_{b7.de}$ sabad$_{b7.de}$ sec$_{b7.de}$ *Sil*$_{b4.de}$ spig$_{b7.de}$ verat$_{b7.de*}$
  • **Wrists**: ferr-p$_{ptk1}$
- **amel.** | **Upper** limbs: lith-c$_{ptk1}$ spig$_{b7.de*}$
- **cold**; something:
  • **agg.** | **Upper** limbs: nat-m$_{b4.de}$
- **firmly**:
  • **agg.** | **Upper** limbs: coff$_{b7a.de}$ lyc$_{bg2}$ phos$_{bg2}$ *Rhus-t*$_{b7a.de}$ spig$_{b7.de*}$

GRESSUS (See Walking - gressus equinus)

GROWING PAINS (See GENERALS - Pain - growing)

GROWTH of nails (See Nails - growth)

GURGLING (See Bubbling)

HAIR:
- **abnormal** growth of hair: carc$_{mlr1}$•
○ • **Legs**: carc$_{mlr1}$•
  • **Upper** limbs: carc$_{mlr1}$• med$_{ptk1*}$
- **sensation** of a hair:
○ • **Fingers**: fl-ac$_{bg2*}$ nat-m$_{bg2}$
  • **Upper** limbs: aloe$_{bg2}$ nat-m$_{bg2}$ visc$_{bg2}$
    ⁝ **bristling**: aloe$_{bg2}$

HANG DOWN, letting:
○ - **Limbs**:
  • **agg.**: *Alum* *Am-c* ang$_{bg}$ bar-c$_{bg}$ bell$_{bg}$ berb **Calc** *Carb-v* *Caust* cina con$_{bg}$ dig hep ign lyc m-aust$_{c1}$ nat-m nux-v ox-ac par ph-ac phos phyt plat plb *Puls* ran-s ruta *Sabin* sil$_{bg}$ stann stront-c$_{bg*}$ sul-ac sulph thuj tub$_{gk}$ valer **VIP**
  • **amel.**: acon am-m anac ant-c arg-met arg-n *Arn* asar *Bar-c* *Bell* berb$_{bg1}$ borx *Bry* calc$_{bg*}$ camph caps **Carb-v**$_{ptk1}$ caust chin cic cina *Cocc* coff colch coloc **Con**$_{k*}$ cupr dros euph ferr graph hep ign *Iris* *Kali-c* kreos *Lach* *Led* lyc *Mag-c* *Mag-m* mang$_{bg1}$ merc *Mez* nat-c nat-m nit-ac nux-v olnd *Petr* phos plb puls$_{k*}$ ran-b ran-s$_{ptk1}$ rat$_{bg1}$ *Rhus-t* ruta *Sep*$_{ptk1}$ *Sil* stann sul-ac sulph teucr$_{k*}$ thuj verat verb *Vip*$_{ptk1}$
- **Lower** limbs:
  • **agg.**: calc$_{b4a.de*}$ dig$_{b4.de}$ hep$_{b4a.de}$ lath$_{bro1}$ m-aust$_{b7.de}$ puls$_{b7.de}$ sulph$_{b4a.de}$
  • **amel.**: asar$_{b7.de*}$ bell$_{b4.de*}$ con$_{bg2}$ *Rhus-t*$_{b7a.de}$ teucr$_{b7.de*}$ verat$_{bg2}$
- **Shoulder** | **amel.**: phos$_{ptk1}$
- **Upper** limbs: colch$_{bg2}$ glon$_{bg2}$

Extremities

- **Upper** limbs: ...
  - **agg.**: alum b4a.de* *Am-c* b4a.de ang b7.de* caust b4a.de cina b7.de* ign b7.de* *Lyc* b4a.de m-aust b7.de nat-m b4a.de* nux-v b7.de* par b7.de* ph-ac b4.de* phos b4.de* plat b4.de* puls b7.de* ruta b7.de* *Sabin* b7.de* stront-c b4.de* sul-ac b4.de* thuj b4a.de* valer b7.de*
  - **amel.**: *Acon* k* anac arn b7.de* asar b7.de* *Bar-c* k* borx bry caps chin **Con** k* cupr *Ferr* k* graph lac-d lach *Led* k* lyc k* mag-m bg2* phos k* plb ran-b *Rhus-t* k* *Sang* ptk1 sil ptk1 *Sulph* k* teucr b7.de* thuj

HANGING on upper arm; something heavy is (See Heaviness - upper arms - something)

HANGNAILS (See Nails - hangnails)

HARDNESS: *(↗Callosities - horny; Induration)* rad-br ptk1

○ - **Feet**:
○ · **Soles**; skin of: **Ars**
  ⋮ **without** sensation: ars k1
- **Fingernails** (See Nails - hardness - fingernails)
- **Hands**:
○ · **Skin**: am-c k* choc srj3• **Graph** k* petr k2* rhus-v **Sulph** k*
  ⋮ **rough**; and: nat-m bg2
  · **Tissue**: petr tl1
- **Legs** | **Calves**: ars h2*
- **Upper** arm; muscles of: mag-c h2* petr bg2 vanil fd5.de

HEAT: *(↗Pain - burning)* agar *Aids* nl2• aloe k2 bapt k* brom k* bufo carb-ac k* carb-an bg2 cic a1 cupr dulc fd4.de fl-ac k2 *Guaj* k* kali-s fd4.de lil-t k* nat-m h2* physala-p bnm7• psil ft1 puls bg2 ribo rly4• ruta fd4.de sec k2 sep bg2 stann *Sulph* k* tritic-vg fd5.de vanil fd5.de verat *Zinc*

- **one** side | **other** side cold; when (See Coldness - one - other)
- **evening**: fl-ac k2 vanil fd5.de
  · **21**.30 h: bung-fa mtf
- **night**: arn k* dulc fd4.de morg-p fmm1• podo fd3.de•
  · **bed** agg.; in: dulc fd4.de fago *Led*
- **accompanied** by | **Feet**; coldness of: bapt a1*
- **alternating** with cold: bell k* helo-s rwt2• *Lyc* stram k*
- **chilliness** over back, during: gins k*
- **creeping**: kali-s fd4.de op k*
- **during**:
  · **agg.** | **Lower** limbs: caps b7.de chin b7.de puls b7.de rhus-t b7.de
- **eruptions**; before: nat-m h2*
- **paralyzed** limb: *Alum* phos
- **uncovering** | **must** uncover: *(↗Uncover inclination)* agar aur-s wbt2• glon bg1
- **warmth** of bed intolerable: agar *Led*

○ - **Ankles**: ang k* apis bg2 bry bg2 calc bg2 **Caust** bg2 cycl h1* dream-p sdj1• euph b4.de* hyos k* *Kali-bi* k* *Kali-c* bg2 kreos bg2 laur k* lyc k* *Merc* bg2 mez bg2 nat-c bg2* nat-m bg2 nit-ac bg2 osm k* petr bg2 phos bg2 rat **Rhus-t** bg2 ruta bg2 *Sep* bg2 sil bg2 spig bg2 stront-c bg2 **Sulph** b4a.de* tarax bg2 verat bg2
- **Elbows**: alum k* am-m bg2 arg-met k* arund asaf bg2 berb carb-an bg2 carb-v bg2 *Caust* bg2 dulc bg2 graph bg2 kali-c h2* kali-n bg2 laur bg2 merc bg2 nat-c bg2 ph-ac bg2 phos bg2 *Plat* bg2 **Rhus-t** bg2 sep k* *Stann* bg2 staph bg2 stront-c bg2 **Sulph** bg2 teucr bg2 thuj bg2
- **Feet**: acon k* agar k* alum bg2 am-c bg2 anac bg2 ang k* *Apis* k* arg-met bg2 arn k* ars k* ars-h ars-s-f k2 arund k* aster bamb-a stb2.de* bell b4.de* bov bg2 brom k* **Bry** b7.de* bufo k* cadm-met tpw6 calad calc k* calc-sil k2 camph k* carb-an k* carb-v k* carbn-s *Caust* k* **Cham** k* cimic k* cina b7.de* *Cocc* k* coff k* coloc k* conch fkr1* crot-h k* cub k* dulc bg2* ferr-i mrr1 *Fl-ac* mrr1 gink-b sbd1• *Glon* graph bg2* ham fd3.de• helo-s rwt2• hep bg2 hydrog srj2• hyos k* ign k* kali-ar *Kali-bi* k* *Kali-c* bg2 kali-chl k* kali-i k* kali-m k2 kali-s fd4.de ketogl-ac rly4• kola stb3• *Lac-c* mrr1 lach k* laur k* led k* luf-op rsj5• *Lyc* k* mag-c mrr1 mag-m b4.de* malar jl2 *Med* bg2 merc k* mez k* mill k* morph k* mur-ac b4.de* nat-c k* nat-m k* nat-p *Nat-s* nit-ac k* *Nux-v* k* ox-ac k2 oxal-a rly4• par k* *Petr* k* ph-ac k* phos k* phyt k* pieri-b mlk9.de plut-n srj7• polyg-h bg2 psil ft1 *Psor* k* ptel k* **Puls** k* rheum k* rhus-t k* rhus-v k* ribo rly4• *Ruta* k* sabin k2 sang bg2* sars b4.de* *Sec* k* *Sep* k* *Sil* k* sphing kk3.fr spig k* spong k* **Squil** b7a.de* stann k* staph k* stram bg2 stront-c b4.de* **Sulph** k* sumb k* symph fd3.de• tarax bg2 thres-a sze7• til k* tritic-vg fd5.de tung-met bdx1• vanil fd5.de vip k* zinc k* zinc-p k2 [beryl-m stj2 heroin sdj2]
  · **one** foot, coldness of the other: chel dig hydrog srj2• ip **LYC** k ●* **Puls** k ●* sulph cr

Heat – Feet – one foot, coldness of the other: ...
  ⋮ **right** cold | **left** warm: allox tpw4 chel c1 neon srj5•
  ⋮ **left** cold | **right** warm: lyc c1 morg-g pte1*•
· **right**: mez bg1 pip-m bg1
· **left**: allox tpw4 ang bg1 carb-v bg1 cham bg1 coloc bg1 dulc fd4.de get bg1 lyc bg1 ruta fd4.de
· **midnight**:
  ⋮ **before**: mag-m
  ⋮ **after**: calad
    ⋮ **3** h: clem
    ⋮ **3-5** h: hyper
· **morning**: apis dulc fd4.de nat-s *Nux-v* k* ptel k* tritic-vg fd5.de
· **forenoon** | **11** h: bamb-a stb2.de•
· **afternoon**: gels k* hura tritic-vg fd5.de
· **evening**: alum k* bell k* bry k* carbn-s caust k* ham fd3.de• kali-c h2* kali-s fd4.de *Led* k* mag-m *Nat-s* nit-ac k* nux-m k* *Sil* spong fd4.de tritic-vg fd5.de vanil fd5.de
  ⋮ **20** h: nicc
  ⋮ **cold** hand, with: aloe
  ⋮ **lying** down agg.; after: stront-c
· **night**: bamb-a stb2.de• calc *Cham* mrr1 dulc fd4.de *Ign* k* kali-s fd4.de mag-m k2 malar jl2 morg-g pte1*• morg-p pte1*• *Nat-s* ph-ac k* ptel gk sacch sst1• *Sang* mrr1 *Sep* k* *Sil* k* spong fd4.de staph k* **Sulph** k* symph fd3.de• tritic-vg fd5.de vanil fd5.de
  ⋮ **bed** agg.; in: dulc fd4.de *Sil* spong fd4.de tritic-vg fd5.de vanil fd5.de
    ⋮ **walking** in open air agg.; after: *Alum*
  ⋮ **lying** on back agg.: ign k*
  ⋮ **uncovering** foot: *(↗Uncover inclination - feet)* **Cham** mrr1 *Fl-ac* mrr1 sacch sst1• tritic-vg fd5.de vanil fd5.de
· **accompanied** by | **perspiration**: sel rsj9•
· **alternately** hot and cold: *Gels* k* graph polyg-h ptk1 sec sulph k2
· **bed** agg.; in: calc carc fd2.de• fago k* helo c1 helo-s c1* hep hura ketogl-ac rly4• merc mez k* nat-p sne *Sang* *Sil* k* stront-c **Sulph** vanil fd5.de
· **burning**: *(↗Pain - burning; Pain - feet - burning)* *Agar* apoc-a vh ars aster bamb-a stb2.de• calc cham cocc eup-per k2 fl-ac *Graph* helo c1 helo-s c1* kali-ar kali-c kola stb3• *Lyc* mag-m k2 **Med** *Nat-s* **Ph-ac** phyt plan **Puls** sabin k2 *Sang* sanic **Sec** *Sep* stann **Sulph** vesp ptk2 *Zinc*
  ⋮ **spots**: bamb-a stb2.de•
  ⋮ **summer**: vesp ptk2
  ⋮ **uncovers** them●: *(↗Pain - feet - uncovers - burning; Uncover inclination - feet)* agar aloe k2 apoc-a vh ars zf calc k2 calc-caust k2 *Cham* k* clem a1 fl-ac k2 helo c1 helo-s c1* kali-i zf kola stb3• lyc zf mag-c mag-m vh **Med** k* nat-m zf nat-s zf *Phos* vh **Puls** sabin k2 *Sang* *Sanic* **Sec** gk sil zf staph zf **Sulph**
· **children**; in: *Med* mrr1 vanil fd5.de
· **chill**; during: acon bg2 agar h2* ars bg2 calc bg2 cann-s k* gels bg2 laur bg2 lyc bg2 nat-c b4a.de* nit-ac h2* puls bg2 rat k* *Spong* k* sul-ac bg2 sulph bg2
· **cold**:
  ⋮ **body**; with coldness of: arn bro1 *Calad*
  ⋮ **hands**; with coldness of: *Aloe* *Calc* coloc ph-ac *Sep* k*
  ⋮ **perspiration** of hands: hura
  ⋮ **touch**; yet cold to: bamb-a stb2.de• **Sec** br
· **coryza**; during: nux-v b7.de*
· **dinner**; after: calen phos k*
· **dry** heat: bell k* crot-t br1 phos k*
· **eating**; after: calen
· **fever**; during: aza bro1
· **fire** were forcing to head; as if: zinc
· **flushes**: colch k* ribo rly4• stann k* **SULPH** k ● trios rsj11•
· **freezing**, as after: bamb-a stb2.de• kali-c h2*
· **lying** on back agg.: ign k*
· **menses**; during | **beginning** of menses: kola stb3•

- **perspiration**:
  - **cold** perspiration; after: hura
  - **during**: acon bg2 bry bg2 led bg2 *Nux-v* bg2 *Phos* bg2 puls bg2 squil bg2 staph bg2 sulph bg2
- **pricking**: rhus-v
- **sleep**; on going to: alum
- **standing** in hot water; as if: bry bg2
- **tingling**: berb k* merc k* sumb k*
- **uncovering** foot: *(↗Pain - feet - uncovers - burning; Uncover inclination - feet)* bros-gau mrc1 calc mrr1 *Cham* bg2* ferr-i mrr1 *Fl-ac* bg2 graph mrr1 mag-c mrr1 mag-m h2* *Med* bg2 nat-m sne psor bg2 *Puls* mrr1 ribo rly4• *Sang* mrr1 sanic bg2 sec mrr1 *Staph* gk* sulph h2* tritic-vg fd5.de vanil fd5.de
- **walking** agg.; after: carl k* puls k*
- ○ **Back** of feet: agar bg2 alum bg2 ant-t bg2 asaf bg2 *Bry* bg2 calc k* camph bg2 canth bg2 **Caust** bg2 *Chin* bg2 coloc k* cupr-s k* hep bg2 *Ign* bg2 lyc bg2 mag-m bg2 mur-ac bg2 nat-c bg2 nux-v bg2 plb k* *Puls* k* rhus-t k* sil bg2 spig bg2 stram bg2 sulph bg2 *Tarax* bg2 thuj h1*
  - **sudden**: calc k*
- **Heels**: arn bg2 **Caust** bg2 cycl bg2 graph bg2 hell bg2 **Ign** bg2 kali-bi kali-n bg2 led bg2 *Nat-c* bg2 *Puls* bg2 rheum bg2 *Rhus-t* bg2 sabin bg2 *Sep* bg2 sil bg2 spong k* **Stann** bg2 stront-c bg2 sul-ac bg2 *Sulph* bg2 *Thuj* bg2 verat bg2 viol-t bg2 zinc bg2
  - **left**: psil ft1
- **Soles**: ail k2 aloe k2 alum bg2 am-m k* **Ambr** bg2 *Anac* bg2 apoc apoc-a vh *Ars* bg2 ars-s-f asar bg2 bell k* berb k* bry bg2 *Calc* k* *Canth* bg2* carb-v k* carbn-s *Carl* k* *Caust* bg2 *Cham* k* chel b7.de* clem k* coc-c k* *Cocc* corh br1 cub k* *Cupr* bg2 dulc eup-per k* *Ferr* k* ferr-p fl-ac k* *Glycyr-g* cte1• *Graph* k* ham fd3.de• helo-s rwt2• hep bg2 kali-n k* kali-s fd4.de* ketogl-ac rly4• kreos b7a.de* *Lach* k* *Led* bg2 *Lil-t* k* lith-c **LYC** k ●* m-ambo b7.de mag-m bg2 *Manc* mang k* med merc bg2 mur-ac k* *Nat-c* k* nat-m k* nit-ac nux-m *Nux-v* k* ol-an bg2 olnd bg2 ox-ac *Petr* k* *Ph-ac* k* *Phos* k* plb k* psor k* *Puls* k* rhus-t bg2 ruta b7.de* sabad bg2 sacch-a fd2.de• samb k* *Sang* k* *Sanic* sars k* *Sep* k* *Sil* k* spig squil bg2 stann k* staph bg2* stram stront-c bg2 **Sulph** k* *Tarax* bg2 *Thyr* vh tritic-vg fd5.de vanil fd5.de verat verb bg2 viol-t bg2 zinc k*
  - **right**: fl-ac bg1 nat-c bg1 tung-met bdx1•
  - **morning**: eup-per k* tritic-vg fd5.de
    - **bed** agg.; in: bamb-a stb2.de• mag-m k2 nux-v
  - **forenoon**: nat-c k*
  - **afternoon** | **sitting** agg.: lyc k*
  - **evening**: ham fd3.de• kali-s fd4.de **Lach** petr a1 *Phos* *Sang* tritic-vg fd5.de ulm-c jsj8• vanil fd5.de zinc k*
    - **18** h: bamb-a stb2.de•
    - **lying** down agg.; after: am-m nux-v *Sulph*
    - **wine**; after: psor k*
  - **night**: bar-c bg3* fl-ac **Lach** petr thyr vh tritic-vg fd5.de vanil fd5.de
  - **accompanied** by | **cough** agg.; during: nat-c b4.de*
  - **burning**: bamb-a stb2.de• kali-s fd4.de
  - **chill**; after: sulph h2*
  - **fever**; during: aesc canth corh br1 cupr *Ferr* graph *Lach* **Sulph**
  - **fire**; as from: nat-m bg2
  - **flushes**, in: cub k*
  - **menopause**; during: *Sang* hr1
  - **menses**; during: carb-v cham *Petr* k* *Sulph*
  - **motion** | **amel.**: sars h2*
  - **sitting**:
    - **after**: coc-c k* cocc
    - **agg.**: mur-ac a1
  - **uncovers them**●: *Calc* **Cham** cur fl-ac mag-m vh *Petr* *Phos* vh **Puls** *Sang* *Sanic* **Sulph** vanil fd5.de
- **Fingers**: *Agar* bg2 alum bg2 am-c bg2 *Am-m* bg2 apis k* asaf bg2 asar bg2 *Aza* br1 borx k* calc bg2 *Caust* bg2 cina bg2 coloc bg2 con bg2 croc bg2 dig bg2 euph bg2 fago k* graph bg2 *Kali-c* bg2 *Lach* bg2 lact k* laur bg2 **Lyc** bg2 mag-c k* mag-m bg2 mang h2* merc bg2 mez bg2 *Mosch* bg2 mur-ac bg2 nat-c bg2 nit-ac bg2 *Olnd* bg2 par k* petr bg2 ph-ac bg2 phos bg2 plat bg2 *Puls* bg2 ran-b bg2 ran-s bg2 rhod bg2 rhus-t k* sabad bg2 sabin bg2 sec bg2 sep bg2 **Sil** bg2 *Spig* bg2

- **Fingers**: ...
  staph bg2 sul-ac bg2 **Sulph** bg2 tarax bg2 *Teucr* bg2 ther bg2 thuj k* vanil fd5.de verat bg2 zinc bg2
  - **alternately** hot and cold as if dead: par
  - **chill**; during: agar bg2 mag-c bg2 rhus-t bg2 *Sabad* bg2 sil bg2 sulph bg2 thuj bg2
  - **perspiration**; during: sabad bg2 *Thuj* bg2
  - **sensation** of: lyc h2*
  - ○ **Flexor** surfaces: zinc bg2
  - **Nails**: hura
    - **Around**: graph mtf33
    - **Under**: caust bg2 graph mtf33
  - **Tips**: *Am-m* bg2 ant-t bg2 apis bg2 canth bg2 caust bg2 *Croc* bg2 daph fago fl-ac bg2 hura kali-c bg2 laur bg2 mur-ac bg2 nat-c nit-ac bg2 *Olnd* bg2 phos bg2 rhod **Sabad** b7.de* sec bg2 **Sil** bg2 spig bg2 staph bg2 sul-ac bg2 sulph bg2 **Teucr** bg2 **Thuj** bg2 vinc bg2
- **Forearms**: agar bg2 am-c bg2 am-m bg2 anac k* apis am bg2 asaf bg2 aur-m-n k* bry k* *Calc* bg2 caps bg2 carb-an bg2 carb-v bg2 **Caust** bg2 dig bg2 euph bg2 *Graph* bg2 kali-bi bg2 laur bg2 **Led** b7a.de* *Lyc* bg2 mag-m bg2 **Merc** bg2 mosch bg2 mur-ac bg2 nit-ac k* olnd bg2 ph-ac bg2 ran-s bg2 *Rhus-t* k* *Staph* bg2 *Sulph* bg2 tarax bg2 tarent k* thuj bg2 zinc bg2
  - ○ **Anterior** part, sensation of: lyc
  - **Posterior** part: bell k*
- **Hands**: acon k* aesc k* **Agar** k* aloe alum k* alum-p k2 alum-sil k2 alumn k* *Am-c* b4a.de* anac k* ang bg2 *Ant-t* k* apis k* arg-n k* ars b4a.de* ars-i arum-d k* arund k* asaf asar bg2* aza br1 bapt bg2 *Bar-c* k* bar-i k2 bar-m bar-s k2 **Bell** k* berb k* bol-la borx k* brom k* **Bry** b7.de* bufo k* cadm-s calad k* calc k* calc-i k2 calc-s calc-sil k2 camph k* cann-s k* *Canth* bg2 caps k* carb-an k* *Carb-v* k* carbn-s castm cench k2 *Cham* k* **Chel** k* chin chinin-ar chinin-s chlor k* cina k* clem k* coca-c sk4• cocc k* coff colch k* com k* corn k* croc k* crot-t k* cub k* cur *Cycl* k* daph k* dig k* dros k* dulc k* eup-per euphr k* fago k* falco-pe nl2• ferr k* ferr-i ferr-ma k* ferr-p *Fl-ac* k* form k* gad k* galla-q-r nl2• gamb gels k* *Glon* gran k* *Graph* k* grat k* *Guaj* k* ham k* **Hell** b7.de* hep k* hura hydr k* hyos k* ign k* *Iod* k* iris *Kali-bi* k* *Kali-c* k* kali-m k2 kali-n k* *Kali-p* kali-s kali-sil k2 ketogl-ac rly4• kreos k* lac-ac **Lach** k* lact laur k* **Led** k* *Lil-t* k* **Lyc** k* m-aust b7.de *Mag-c* k* mang k* med bro1* merc k* merl k* mez k* mill k* morph k* mosch bg2 mur-ac k* murx k* **Nat-c** k* nat-m k* nat-ox rly4• nat-p nat-s k* nicc **Nit-ac** k* **Nux-m** k* *Nux-v* k* ol-an k* ol-j bro1 **Op** k* ox-ac k* *Petr* k* *Ph-ac* k* phel k* **Phos** k* phys k* pin-con oss2• pip-m k* *Plan* k* plat bg2 positr nl2• psil ft1 *Psor* ptel k* **Puls** k* ran-b bg2 raph k* rat k* rheum k* **Rhod** k* rhus-t k* rhus-v k* ruta *Sabad* k* sabin bg2* sang k* sarr sars k* **Sec** bg2* **Sep** k* sil k* sol-t-ae k* *Spig* k* spong k* **Squil** b7.de* *Stann* k* **Staph** k* stront-c k* sul-i k2 **Sulph** k* sumb k* tab k* **Tarax** k* til k* tritic-vg fd5.de tub xxb vanil fd5.de verat k* zinc k* [beryl-m stj2 calc-f stj1 heroin sdj2]
  - **one** hand: brom bg2 **Dig** bg2 mez ptk1 mosch bg2 **Puls** bg2
    - **coldness** of the other: ant-t b7a.de canth b7a.de cham b7a.de chin k* cocc k* *Dig* k* hep bg1 *Ip* k* lyc bg3* mez bg3* mosch k* *Puls* k* tab k*
  - **right**: aids nl2• allox tpw4 arum-d bg1 chin bg1 cocc bg1 euphr bg1 galla-q-r nl2• gamb bg1 mang bg1 *Puls* bg1 staph h1*
    - **accompanied** by | **cold** left: allox tpw4
  - **left**: aesc bg1 alum bg1 arg-n bg1 carb-an bg1 com bg1 **Nit-ac** bg2 stann h2*
  - **morning**: alumn k* bamb-a stb2.de• calc k* chinin-s cycl k* fago k* hura kali-c h2* nux-m k* *Nux-v* k* sulph k* tritic-vg fd5.de
    - **8** h: fago
    - **coldness**; during: calc k* fago k* nux-m k* nux-v k* sulph k*
    - **writing** agg.: chinin-s
  - **forenoon**, 10 h: fago gels pip-m
  - **noon**: mag-c k*
  - **afternoon**: *Apis* berb k* cench k2 fago k* gels k*
    - **14** h: lyc
    - **15** h:
      - **15**-17 h: sulph
      - **cold** sweat; during: hura
    - **16** h: fago
    - **17** h: petr

Extremities

- **evening**: aloe alum h2* asaf k* bell k* cann-s k* carb-an k* dros k* euphr k* ferr k* ham fd3.de• kali-c h2* lac-ac k* *Led* k* *Lyc* k* murx k* nat-m k* nux-m k* nux-v k* petr h2* rhus-t k* sars sep k* *Stann* sulph
  - **18** h: asaf
  - **19** h: cocc
  - **20** h: nicc
  - **21** h: sarr
  - **air** agg.; in open: carb-an k*
  - **bed** agg.; in: kali-c h2*
  - **burning**: petr h2*
  - **chilliness**; during: asaf k*
  - **lying** | **after** | **agg.**: carb-v k*
    - **agg.**: asar sulph k*
  - **reading** agg.: ferr-p k*
  - **shivering**; during: *Sulph* k*
- **night**: arg-n k* *Calc* k* com k* *Ign* k* morg-p pte1• nit-ac h2* psil ft1 sang hr1 sil staph k* sulph til k*
  - **midnight**:
    - **after**:
      - **1**.30 h: chinin-s
      - **2**-5 h: ign
      - **3** h: clem
  - **bed** agg.; in: *Sil* k*
    - **cold** feet; with: *Sulph*
    - **walking** in open air agg.; after: alum
  - **cold** legs and feet, with: com k*
- **accompanied** by:
  - **emaciation** (See GENERALS - Emaciation - accompanied - hands)
  - **Head**; heat of (See HEAD - Heat - accompanied - hands)
- **air**; in open | **amel.**: phos verat
- **alternating** with:
  - **coldness**: cench k2 chin bg1 cocc positr nl2• sec
  - **shivering**: phos h2
- **anxiety**; with: carb-v lyc h2* phos
- **burning**: *Med* hr1
- **chill**:
  - **after**: sep k* sulph h2*
  - **during**: acon bg2 agar h2* alum k* *Apis* k* asar bg2 cadm-s k* carb-v bg2 *Chin* *Cina* k* coff k* dros bg2 kali-c h2* kreos bg2 lyc bg2 mez h2* *Nat-c* k* nat-s k* nux-v k* ph-ac k* phos k* puls k* rat k* *Sabad* b7a.de* sep bg2 spong k* *Stann* b4a.de* thuj bg2
- **chilliness**; during: alum k* coff k*
- **cold**:
  - **after**: sep k*
  - **agg.**: caps ptk1
  - **and** pale, the other hot: *(↗Pain - hands - one - other - burning)* aids nl2• mosch
- **coldness**:
  - **left** arm, of: sep
  - **Face**, of: cench k2 cina k* nat-c
  - **Feet**, of●: acon allox tpw4 aloe k2 calad com fl-ac ptk1 galla-q-r nl2• mur-ac h2 *Nux-m* *Sep* k*
    - **or** hot feet and cold hands: **Sep** k*
  - **Fingers**; of | **Tips**: [calc-f stj1]
- **coryza**; during: nux-v b7.de*
- **cough** agg.; during: ant-t b7.de* nat-c b4.de*
- **covers** | **agg.** (= intolerance of): phos bg2
- **dry**: bell h1* [heroin sdj2]
- **eating**; hot and burning after: lyc k* phos k* sulph k*
- **excitement** agg.: graph phos sep
- **fever**; during: aza bro1 nux-v b7.de puls b7.de zinc h2*
- **flushes**, in: calc h2* colch k* hydr k* pip-m k* **Sulph**
  - **beginning** in hands: *Phos*
- **fright**; after: calc

- **Hands**: ...
  - **internal** heat: spig h1*
  - **lying** on back agg.: ign k*
  - **menses**; during: carb-v petr k* sec
  - **perspiration**, during cold: acon bg2 *Calc* bg2 hell bg2 hura lyc bg2 **Nux-v** bg2 op bg2 phos bg2 **Sep** bg2 squil bg2 staph bg2
  - **shivering**; during: ign k*
  - **sitting** agg.: calc k*
  - **sleep**; on going to: alum
  - **sneezing**, caused by: senn c1
  - **stitching** pain, during: gamb k*
  - **stool** agg.; during: hep
  - **sudden**: ferr-m ferr-ma k* glon k*
  - **talking** agg.: graph k*
  - **vomiting**; after: verat k*
  - **waking**; on: hydrog srj2•
  - **weather**, even in cold and rainy: chin-b c1 rhod ptk1
  - **writing** agg.: chinin-s mez k*
  - ○ **Back** of hands: act-sp bg2 agar bg2 all-c all-s k* alum bg2 ang k* *Apis* k* aur bg2 bry bg2 calc bg2 chel k* cycl b7.de* dulc bg2 fl-ac bg2 ham fd3.de• kreos bg2 laur bg2 med k2 **Nat-c** k* nat-m bg2 nat-s bg2 nux-v k* **Rhus-t** k* samb bg2 sep k* sulph k* thuj k*
  - **Palms**: **Acon** k* ail k2 alum h2* am-m k* anac k* aphis br1* *Apis* b7a.de* arg-n k* ars h2* ars-met **Asar** k* *Aza* br1 bad k* berb k* *Borx* k* **Bry** k* *Calc* calc-sil k2 canth b7a.de* carb-an carb-v k* carbn-o carbn-s chel b7.de* chin b7a.de* chinin-ar coff k* colch k* com k* corh br1 crot-h k* crot-t bg2 cub k* diosm br1 diph ptk1 dulc bg2 *Eup-per* *Ferr* k* ferr-p *Fl-ac* k* *Gels* k* glycyr-g cte1• graph bg2* ham k* hep k* hydr k* ind k* **Ip** k* iris kola stb3• kreos k* lac-c lac-h sk4• **Lach** k* laur k* *Lil-t* k* *Lyc* k* m-ambo b7.de mag-c bg2 mag-m *Med* k* merc k* mez bg2 **Mur-ac** k* naja nat-c h2* nat-m bg2 nit-ac k* *Nux-v* k* ol-an k* ol-j k* *Petr* k* ph-ac k* **Phos** k* puls b7.de* *Ran-b* bg2 ran-s bg2 raph k* rheum k* rhus-t bg2* rhus-v k* *Samb* k* sang k2* *Sel* bg2 *Sep* k* sil **Spig** b7.de* *Stann* k* **Sulph** k* sumb k* tab k* tarent k* tax k* til k* tub-a jl2 vanil fd5.de verat k* zinc k* zinc-p k2 zing k*
    - **morning**: carb-an k* sil k*
      - **bed** agg.; in: nux-v
    - **forenoon**: calc h2* fl-ac k*
    - **afternoon**: arg-n k* gels k* stann *Sulph* *Zinc* k*
      - **17** h: chel lil-t til
    - **evening**: acon k* cench k2 iod mag-m k* vanil fd5.de
      - **lying** down agg.; after: am-m nux-v
    - **night**: **Lach** nit-ac h2* *Ol-j* k*
    - **accompanied** by:
      - **Fingers**; convulsive movements of (See Convulsion - fingers - accompanied - hand - heat - palm)
      - **Head**; heat in (See HEAD - Heat - accompanied - palms)
    - **chill**:
      - **after**: sulph h2*
      - **during**: ferr bro1
    - **coldness**:
      - **after**: asar k* merc k* sulph k*
      - **Backs** of hands; with coldness of the: anac coff
    - **dry** heat: ars-met chinin-ar corh br1 ferr-p k* gad k* gels ptel k*
    - **flushes**: cub k* phys ptk1
    - **menopause**; during: sang hr1*
    - **menses**; during: carb-v *Petr*
    - **sitting** agg.: ferr-p
    - **spreads** from: chel k*
    - **walking** in open air agg.; after: lyc
    - **Balls**: carb-v k*
    - **Ulnar** side of hand: laur
- **Hips**: ang bg2 ant-c bg2 arg-met bg2 am bg2 bar-c bg2 **Bell** bg2 berb bro1 **Bry** bg2 *Calc* bg2 *Carb-v* bg2 **Caust** bg2 *Chel* k* chin bg2 cic bg2 cocc bg2 coloc bg2 dulc bg2 euph bg2 ferr bg2 hell bg2 ign bg2 *Kali-c* bg2 kreos bg2 led bg2 **Lyc** bg2 *Merc* bg2 mez bg2 *Nat-c* bg2 nat-m bg2 nit-ac bg2 *Nux-v* bg2 ph-ac bg2

- **Hips**: ...
phos k* puls bg2 rhus-t k* ruta bg2 *Sep* bg2 sil bg2 *Stann* bg2 *Stront-c* bg2 **Sulph** bg2 thuj bg2 valer b7.de* verat bg2 zinc h2*
- **Joints**: bell k2* *Cimic Form* mrr1 guaj k* guare kali-bi k2 kali-s fd4.de *Kalm* **Led** k* sal-ac c1* *Stict* k*
- **Knees**: aids nl2• anac bg2 ant-t bg2 apis bg2 apoc apoc-a a1 arg-met bg2 *Ars* bg2 arund k* *Asaf* bg2 aur-m k* *Bar-c* bg2 *Bar-m* brom bg2 bry k* bung-fa mtf calc bg2 camph k* cann-xyz bg2 *Carb-v* bg2 **Caust** bg2 *Chin* bg2 cina k* coc-c k* colch k* dros b7.de* hyos k* ign k* iod bg2 kali-c h2* kali-n bg2 kali-s fd4.de *Lach* led bg2 *Lyc* k* meny k* *Merc* bg2 mur-ac bg2 nat-c bg2 nat-m bg2 nat-sil fd3.de• nit-ac bg2 **Nux-v** bg2 ol-j k* olnd bg2 *Petr* bg2 ph-ac bg2 phos k* plat bg2 *Puls* bg2 **Rhus-t** bg2 sabad bg2 sal-fr sle1• *Sars Sep* bg2 spig bg2 **Stann** bg2 *Staph* bg2 *Stront-c* bg2 sul-ac bg2 sulph k* **Tarax** bg2 thuj bg2 tritic-vg fd5.de ven-m rsj12• verat k* zinc bg2
  - **left**: aids nl2• sal-fr sle1•
  - **morning**: sulph k*
    - **sitting** agg.: sulph k*
  - **night**: aids nl2• coc-c k*
  - **accompanied** by:
    - **coryza** (See NOSE - Coryza - accompanied - knees)
    - **Nose**; cold: ign tl1*
  - **hot** air blew through, as if: *Lach*
  - ○ **Hollow** of knees: dros k*
  - **Patella**: bufo bg2 nat-m bg2
- **Legs**: acon k* agar bg2 aids nl2• anac bg2 ang bg2 ant-c bg2 apoc apoc-a a1 ars k* **Asaf** bg2 bapt berb k* *Borx* k* bov k* *Bry* bg2 bufo bg2 calc k* *Calc-p* cann-xyz bg2 caust bg2 chel bg2 chin bg2 cic k* coff b7.de* *Crot-c* crot-h k* crot-t cycl k* dig bg2 graph k* guaj k* *Ham* hyos k* ign bg2 iod k* kali-br k* *Kali-c* bg2 lach bg2 lil-t k* *Lyc* k* *Mag-c* bg2 mang k* meny bg2 *Meph* k* merc bg2 mez k* nat-c bg2 *Nat-s* k* nit-ac k* nux-v bg2 ox-ac k* oxal-a rly4• ph-ac k* phos bg2 podo fd3.de• *Puls* bg2 ran-s bg2 **Rhus-t** bg2 ribo rly4• sabad bg2 **Sep** bg2 *Sil* bg2 spig k* stann bg2 staph k* stront-c bg2 sulph k* **Tarax** bg2 *Verat* k* zinc bg2
  - **right**: *Sulph* bg2
  - **left**: cycl h1* ham fd3.de•
  - **morning**: nat-s plat
  - **afternoon**, 15 h: gels
  - **evening**: cycl k* *Nat-s* k*
    - **20** h: sulph
  - **night**: aids nl2• lath c1 *Meph* k*
    - **bed**; after going to: aids nl2• fago
    - **waking** from rush of blood to lower legs: meph br1
  - **agreeable**: neon srj5•
  - **alternately** hot and cold: *Verat*
  - **flushes**: cob k* ribo rly4•
  - **sensation** of a warm hand on leg: agar h2
  - **sitting** agg.: berb k*
  - **uncovers** them: crot-c ribo rly4• [bell-p-sp dcm1]
  - **walking** agg.; after: rhus-t
  - ○ **Bones** | **Tibia**: agar bg2 ang bg2 ars bg2 asaf bg2 bell bg2 calc bg2 *Cycl* bg2 kali-c bg2 lach bg2 **Merc** bg2 *Mez* bg2 nux-v bg2 **Phos** bg2 *Puls* bg2 rhus-t bg2 sep bg2 tarax bg2 thuj bg2 zinc bg2
  - **Calves**: alum bg2 **Ars** bg2 asaf bg2 *Bry* bg2 calc bg2 graph bg2 ign bg2 *Lyc* bg2 nat-c bg2 nit-ac bg2 *Nux-v* bg2 puls bg2 **Rhus-t** bg2 *Sep* bg2 sil bg2 spig bg2 **Stann** bg2 *Staph* bg2 **Sulph** bg2 tarax bg2 thuj bg2 verat bg2 zinc bg2
  - **Internal**: staph h1*
  - **Sides** | **Inner**: mang h2*
- **Lower** limbs: acon k* aids nl2• alum bg2 *Ars* bg2 bapt k* bar-c bg2 *Borx* bg2 bry k* bufo bg2 **Calc** b4a.de* carb-an bg2 carb-v bg2 caust bg2 chin bg2 cina bg2 coloc k* dulc fd4.de eupi k* fl-ac bg2 graph bg2 guaj bg2 *Kali-c* bg2 *Lach* bg2 laur bg2 **Led** b7a.de* lil-t k* **Lyc** bg2 mag-c bg2 mag-m bg2 mang k* merc bg2 *Mez* k* morph k* nat-c bg2 nat-m k* nit-ac k* nux-v bg2 olnd bg2 op k* *Ph-ac* bg2 phos bg2 phys k* plat k* puls bg2 rhus-t bg2 ruta bg2 sep bg2 *Sil* bg2 sol-t-ae k* spig k* stann bg2 **Staph** bg2 stram k* stront-c bg2 sulph b4.de* thres-a sze7• thuj bg2 *Vac* jl2 verat k* zinc bg2
  - **left**: aids nl2•
  - **night**: acon bapt a1 dulc fd4.de plat

- **Lower** limbs – **night**: ...
    - **midnight**:
      - **after**: nit-ac h2
        - **1** h: mang
    - **cold** during daytime; but: lath ptk1
    - **waking**; on: coloc spig
  - **bed** agg.; in: eupi a1
  - **chilliness**, after: nit-ac k*
  - **dry**: sulph h2*
  - **here** and there: graph h2*
  - **sensation** of: agar b4.de* borx b4a.de bry b7.de calc b4.de cina b7.de coff b7.de* cycl b7.de* *Lach* b7a.de laur b7.de m-arct b7.de m-aust b7.de *Mez* k* nux-m b7.de* olnd b7.de rhus-t b7.de* ruta b7.de staph b7.de thuj b4.de* [pop dhh1]
    - **accompanied** by | **heaviness** of lower limbs (See Heaviness - lower - accompanied - heat)
  - **wind** or wire darting through; sensation of hot: dig ptk1
  - ○ **Joints**: eupi
- **Nates**: caust bg2 colch ptk1 *Graph* bg2 kali-c bg2 **Lyc** bg2 merc bg2 mez bg2 *Ph-ac* bg2 *Phos* bg2 *Rhus-t* bg2 sep bg2 **Staph** bg2 *Sulph* bg2 thuj bg2 zinc bg2
  - **right**: psil ft1
- **Shoulders**: **Acon** bg2 aesc am-m bg2 bell bg2 brom *Bry* bg2 calc bg2 *Carb-v* bg2 cocc bg2 ferr bg2 graph bg2 *Ign* bg2 *Kali-c* bg2 lyc bg2 mag-c bg2 mag-m bg2 meny bg2 merc bg2 mez bg2 mur-ac bg2 nat-c bg2 nux-v k* par bg2 ph-ac bg2 *Phos* bg2 plat bg2 plb bg2 *Puls* bg2 **Rhus-t** bg2 sars h2* *Sep* bg2 spig bg2 spong k* *Staph* bg2 stront-c bg2 **Sulph** bg2 thuj bg2 ulm-c jsj8• urt-u k* zinc bg2
  - **right**: cob ptm1•
  - **left**: ulm-c jsj8•
    - **accompanied** by | **Ear**; heat in | **left** (See EAR - Heat - left - accompanied - shoulder - left)
      - **Face**; heat in | **left** (See FACE - Heat - left - accompanied - shoulder - left)
  - ○ **Acromion**: phos
- **Thighs**: all-c am bg2 asaf bg2 berb bro1 borx k* bov bg2 carb-an bg2 *Carb-v* bg2 carbn-o caust b4.de* **Chin** bg2 clem k* coc-c k* cocc bg2 colch bg2 dros k* dulc bg2 euph bg2 graph bg2 guaj bg2 kali-c laur bg2 lyc bg2 meny bg2 **Merc** bg2 merc-c bg2 *Mez* bg2 mur-ac bg2 murx nit-ac k* *Nux-v* bg2 olnd bg2 ph-ac bg2 phos bg2 plb bg2 plut-n srj7• podo c1 rhod bg2 rhus-t k* ruta bg2 sabin bg2 *Sep* bg2 *Spig* bg2 stann h2* staph k* sul-ac bg2 sulph k* *Thuj* b4a.de* viol-t bg2 vip fkr4.de zinc h2*
  - **night**: nit-ac k*
  - **alternating** with coldness: nit-ac h2*
  - **cold**:
    - **Back**, with: *Sulph* k*
    - **Hands** and feet, with: **Thuj** k*
  - **creeping**: chin k*
  - **dry**: *Sulph* k*
  - **formication**; with (See Formication - thighs - heat)
  - **pregnancy** agg.; during: podo
  - **prickling**: orot-ac rly4• osm k*
  - **sitting**; after: graph
  - **stool** agg.; after: *Lyc* trom
  - ○ **Internal**: chin h1* staph h1*
  - **Upper** part: bung-fa mtf
- **Thumbs**: graph bg2 lach bg2 laur bg2 merc bg2 nux-v bg2 olnd bg2 ox-ac k2 phos k* sars bg2 staph bg2 zinc k*
- **Toes**: *Agar* bg2 *Alum* bg2 am-c bg2 *Ant-c* bg2 apis k* **Arn** bg2 asaf k* aster k* aza br1 bamb-a stb2.de* berb k* borx k* calad bg2 calc bg2 carb-an bg2 *Carb-v* bg2 **Caust** bg2 cimic bg2 coc-c k* con bg2 cycl k* dulc bg2 graph bg2 hura kali-bi k* *Kali-c* bg2 kreos bg2 lach k* lyc bg2 mag-m k* merc bg2 mez bg2 mosch bg2 mur-ac bg2 nat-c bg2 nit-ac bg2 **Nux-v** bg2 olnd bg2 par bg2 **Ph-ac** bg2 phos bg2 plat bg2 *Puls* bg2 *Ran-s* bg2 rhus-t bg2 ruta bg2 sabin bg2 sec gk sep bg2 sil bg2 **Staph** bg2 **Sulph** bg2 **Tarax** bg2 *Thuj* bg2 viol-t bg2 zinc k*
  - **afternoon**: asaf
  - **night**: coc-c k*

- **burning**: borx sec gk
- **cold** feet, with: apis sec gk
- **crawling**: berb k*

○ • **Fifth**: bamb-a stb2.de•

- **First**: am-c k* aster *Nit-ac* k* rhus-t k*
  - ⁝ **Balls**: am-c k* carb-an h2* *Nit-ac* a1
- **Tips**: am-m bg2 ant-t bg2 arn bg2 chin bg2 **Kali-c** bg2 *Mur-ac* bg2 nat-m bg2 olnd bg2 puls bg2 *Sep* bg2 sil bg2 *Thuj* bg2 zinc bg2
  - ⁝ **shooting** to head like electric sparks; heat: sep k*

- **Upper** arms: acon bg2 *Agar* bg2 alum bg2 am-c bg2 arg-met bg2 *Ars* bg2 *Asaf* bg2 bell bg2 *Borx* bg2 *Bry* bg2 calc-p carb-v bg2 caust bg2 cic k* **Cocc** bg2 colch bg2 coloc bg2 dig bg2 dulc bg2 *Ferr* bg2 graph bg2 *Ign* bg2 kali-c bg2 mang bg2 mez bg2 mur-ac bg2 nat-m k* nux-v bg2 olnd bg2 ph-ac bg2 phos bg2 *Sep* bg2 valer bg2 zinc bg2
- **Upper** limbs: aesc k* alum k* alumn k* am-c bg2 arund k* aur k* calc-p bg2 cann-i k* chin k* cic con dulc fd4.de falco-pe nl2• graph k* guare k* *Lach* lil-t k* lyc k* melal-alt gya4 mez h2* *Nat-m* k* nux-v ol-an k* par k* *Phos* phys k* rhus-t k* ruta h1* spong stram tarent k* verat k* vip k* zinc
  - **right**: melal-alt gya4
  - **left**: rhus-t h1*
    - ⁝ **extending** to | **right**: germ-met srj5•
  - **morning**: alumn k* dulc fd4.de
  - **night**: dulc fd4.de *Lach* phos
  - **burning** heat: guare urt-u
  - **flushes**: caps nux-v rhod sil
  - **pregnancy** agg.; during: zing bro1
  - **prickly**: apis lach a1
  - **sensation** of: acon bg2 *Agar* bg2 agn b7.de* alum bg2 am-c bg2 ang b7.de ant-c bg2 apis bg2 asaf bg2 borx bg2 bov bg2 **Bry** b7.de* bufo bg2 calc bg2 carb-an bg2 **Carb-v** bg2 *Caust* bg2 cocc bg2 coloc bg2 con bg2 croc bg2 cupr bg2 cycl b7.de* dig bg2 euph bg2 *Graph* b4.de* **Kali-c** bg2 *Lach* bg2 laur bg2 led bg2 lyc bg2 m-aust b7.de mag-m bg2 mang bg2 merc bg2 mez bg2 mosch bg2 **Mur-ac** bg2 nat-c bg2 nit-ac b4.de* nux-m b7.de* nux-v b7.de* olnd bg2 petr bg2 **Ph-ac** bg2 **Phos** bg2 plat bg2 **Puls** bg2 ran-b bg2 ran-s bg2 rheum b7.de rhod b4.de* **Rhus-t** b7.de* ruta b7.de* sabad bg2 sabin bg2 *Sep* bg2 sil bg2 spig b7.de* spong bg2 **Stann** bg2 *Staph* b7.de* sul-ac bg2 **Sulph** bg2 tarax bg2 teucr bg2 verat bg2 *Zinc* bg2
  - **sun** shining on it; as if: melal-alt gya4
  - **water** were running through; as if hot: *Rhus-t* k*

○ • **Bones**: bufo bg2

  - **Externally**: mez k* *Petr* k* rhus-v ruta stram k*
  - **Joints** | **sensation** of: *Sulph* b4a.de
- **Wrists**: **Acon** bg2 agar bg2 alum bg2 *Am-c* bg2 *Anac* bg2 ang h1* ant-t bg2 **Apis** bg2 arg-met bg2 ars bg2 arund k* asar bg2 bapt bg2 bar-c bg2 bell bg2 borx bg2 bov bg2 **Bry** bg2 bufo bg2 **Calc** bg2 camph bg2 cann-s bg2 *Canth* bg2 caps bg2 carb-an bg2 **Carb-v** bg2 *Caust* bg2 cham bg2 cina bg2 *Cocc* bg2 colch k* croc bg2 **Cycl** bg2 dulc bg2 *Ferr* bg2 graph bg2 guaj bg2 **Hell** bg2 hep k* hydr k* *Ign* bg2 ina-i mlk9.de iod bg2 *Kali-c* bg2 kreos bg2 lac-ac k* **Lach** bg2 *Laur* bg2 **Led** bg2 **Lyc** bg2 mag-c bg2 mang bg2 merc bg2 mez bg2 mosch bg2 mur-ac bg2 **Nat-c** bg2 nat-m bg2 nit-ac k* **Nux-m** bg2 *Nux-v* bg2 **Op** bg2 *Petr* bg2 *Ph-ac* bg2 **Phos** bg2 plat bg2 **Puls** bg2 ran-b bg2 **Rheum** bg2 **Rhod** bg2 **Rhus-t** k* ruta bg2 *Sabad* bg2 *Sabin* bg2 sars bg2 **Sec** bg2 **Sep** bg2 sil bg2 **Spig** bg2 spong bg2 **Squil** bg2 **Stann** bg2 **Staph** bg2 *Stront-c* bg2 **Sulph** k* **Tarax** bg2 thuj bg2 verat bg2 zinc bg2

HEATED; from becoming: zinc ptk1

○ - **Lower** limbs: acon b7.de* alum bg2 bry b7.de* ign b7.de* nux-v b7.de* zinc b4.de*

- **Upper** limbs: acon b7.de* bry b7.de* ign b7.de* nux-v b7.de* *Zinc* b4a.de

HEAVINESS: acon k* adam srj5• aesc *Agar* k* aids nl2• ail allox sp1 *Aloe* *Alum* k* alum-sil k2* alumn k2 am-c am-p br1 ambr k* ammc amyg anac k* androc srj1• ant-c k* ant-t k* *Apis* k* aran-ix sp1 **Arg-met** *Arg-n* arist-cl sp1 *Arn* k* **Ars** k* *Ars-i* asaf k* atro aur-ar k2 aur-i k2 *Bamb-a* stb2.de• bar-c k* bar-i k2 bar-m bell b4.de* benzol br1 bit-ar wht1• bros-gau mrc1 **Bry** bufo cact bg1 cadm-met tpw6* calad *Calc* k* calc-i k2 calc-p calc-sil k2 camph k* cann-i cann-s k* canth b7.de caps k* carb-an *Carb-v* k* *Carbn-s* carc sp1 cartl-s rly4• *Caust* *Cham* k* **Chel** *Chin* k* chinin-ar choc srj3• cimic *Clem* cob-n sp1 cocc b7.de coff k* *Coloc* k* **Con** k* convo-s sp1 cor-r croc b7a.de *Crot-h* crot-t *Cupr* cycl dig k* dulc k* eupi ferr ferr-ar ferr-i ferr-p fic-m gya1

Heaviness: ...
Gels k* gins glon gran *Graph* k* haliae-lc srj5• **Hell** k* helodr-cal knl2• hep k* hipp hippoc-k szs2 hist sp1 hyos hyper *Ign* b7.de* iod k* ip irid-met srj5• *Kali-ar* kali-bi *Kali-c* k* **Kali-p** kali-s k2 kalm ketogl-ac rly4• kreos k* lac-lup hrn2• lach lact lap-la sde8.de• led k* *Lyc* *Lyss* m-ambo b7.de *M-arct* b7.de* m-aust b7.de mag-c b4.de* manc mand rsj7• marb-w es1• **Merc** k* *Merc-c* k* merc-i-f *Mez* k* morph *Mosch* b7a.de nat-ar k2 nat-c b4.de* *Nat-m* nat-p k2 nat-pyru rly4• nit-ac k* **Nux-v** k* *Olib-sac* wmh1 *Onos* op k* osm paeon pall br1 par k* petr k* **Ph-ac** k* **Phos** k* phys *Pic-ac* pin-s plb k* positr nl2• psil ft1 *Puls* k* ran-b b7.de rauw sp1 *Rheum* b7.de* rhod b4.de ruta k* *Sabad* k* sabin sal-fr sle1• *Sec* k* sel *Sep* k* *Sil* k* spig k* spong fd4.de squil b7.de stann k* *Staph* b7a.de* stram k* stront-c b4.de stroph-s sp1 sul-i k2 *Sulph* k* suprar rly4• taosc iwa1• tep ter ther thuj k* tritic-vg fd5.de trom ulm-c jsj8• valer k2 vanil fd5.de verat visc sp1 zinc k* zinc-p k2 zing [bell-p-sp dcm1 heroin sdj2]

- **left**: anac h2* carb-v h2*
- **daytime**: sabad a1 sulph k*
- **morning**: calad carb-an k* carc fd2.de• caust k* cob-n sp1 dulc fd4.de iod h* nat-m *Nit-ac* k* pall spong fd4.de tritic-vg fd5.de *Zinc*
  - **6** h: pic-ac
  - **bed** agg.; in: dulc h2* nat-m k* *Nit-ac* k* phos k* spong fd4.de *Zinc*
  - **rising** | **after** | **amel**.: lyc nat-m
    - ⁝ **agg**.: phos k*
  - **waking**; on: bamb-a stb2.de• bar-c carc fd2.de• clem k* kali-p fd1.de• lyc nat-m phos k* pic-ac a1 sacch-a fd2.de• spong fd4.de *Sulph* k* verat k* *Zinc*
  - **walking** agg.: nux-v k* pic-ac
- **forenoon**: caust k* cham k* grat k* phos h2* *Sabad* k* stront-c
- **noon** | **walking** agg.: dig
- **afternoon**: mag-m k* spong fd4.de
  - **15** h: cadm-met tpw6 plan
  - **16** h: pic-ac
- **evening**: am-c ammc k* par k* phos k* *Sabad* k* spong fd4.de tritic-vg fd5.de
  - **21** h: cocc
- **night**: carb-v k* caust k* petr k* sep spong fd4.de
  - **midnight**:
    - ⁝ **after** | **3** h | **waking**; on: mez
    - ⁝ **4** h: lyc
- **accompanied** by:
  - **rheumatic** complaints (See GENERALS - Pain - rheumatic - accompanied - extremities)

○ • **Head**; complaints of (See HEAD - Complaints - accompanied - extremities - heaviness)

- **ascending** stairs agg.: clem k* lyc
- **breakfast** agg.; after: ther k* verat
- **chill**:
  - **before**: ther k*
  - **during**: *Bell* bg2 chin bg2 *Cina* bg2 coc-c k* **Hell** b7.de* **Kreos** bg2 merc bg2 nat-m bg2 nux-v bg2 phos bg2 puls bg2 rhus-t bg2 sabad bg2 sep h2* spig bg2 stann bg2 sulph bg2 verat bg2
- **coition**; after: bufo
- **dinner**; after: ant-c k* sulph k*
- **ejaculation**; after: ph-ac puls k* staph b7.de*
- **exertion** agg.: *Lach*
- **fever**; during●: apis bg2 *Bell* bg2 **Calc** k* **Gels** hell bg2 merc bg2 **Nux-v** k* **Rhus-t** k* stann bg2 staph bg2 sulph k*
- **lead**; as if: cob-n sp1
- **lying**:
  - **amel**.: granit-m es1•
  - **side**; on:
    - ⁝ **left** | **agg**.: merc-i-f
- **menses**:
  - **before** | **agg**.: bar-c k* cimic bg2 com con k* kali-c bg2 *Lyc* k* merc k* nat-m bg2 nit-ac zinc
  - **during** | **agg**.: cocc graph b4a.de kali-c b4.de mag-m b4.de nat-m k* ph-ac b4a.de sulph b4.de* zinc b4a.de
  - **suppressed** menses; from: graph b4a.de*
- **mental** exertion agg.: *Ph-ac*

- **motion**:
  - **agg.**: *Lach* mez k* sabad a1
  - **amel.**: caps cham k* sacch-a fd2.de•
- **nervous** persons; in (See MIND - Excitement - nervous - extremities)
- **painful**: agar h2* spong fd4.de
- **paralytic**: dulc fd4.de plb
- **perspiration**; during: apis bg2 *Bell* bg2 **Calc** bg2 hell bg2 merc bg2 **Nux-v** bg2 **Rhus-t** bg2 staph bg2 stram bg2 *Sulph* bg2
- **playing** piano, after: anac
- **pregnancy** agg.; during: *Calc-p*
- **rest** agg.: caps h1*
- **rising**:
  - **amel.**: merc nat-m
  - **sitting**; from | **agg.**: carb-v
- **sexual** excesses: *Puls*
- **sitting** agg.: caps h1* ruta h1
- **spasms** | **before**: plb bg1
- **storm**; during: *Phos*
- **waking**; on: cham k* irid-met srj5• sacch-a fd2.de• sep h2* staph b7.de* tep k*
- **walking**:
  - **agg.**: acon k* anac h2* *Calc* lac-e hrn2• paeon k* **Pic-ac** k*
  - **air**; in open:
    - **agg.**: lyc sil zinc
    - **amel.**: carb-v h2

○ - **Ankles**: alum h2* ant-c ptk1 caust h2* crot-t bg1* cupr k* kali-c h2* kali-p fd1.de• led bg1* nat-m h2* nit-ac h2* plut-n srj7• sec ptk1 sil h2* sulph h2* vanil fd5.de
  - **painful**: cupr ptk1
- **Elbows**: am-c h2* cer-s a1 chinin-ar k* cic a1 coll a1 con k* led a1 phos h2* plb a1 samb k* sars h2* zinc bg2
  - **left**: plut-n srj7•
- **Feet**: acon k* *Agar* k* *Agn* k* **Alum** k* alum-sil k2 am-c anac k* ant-c k* ant-t b7a.de apis k* aran *Arn* k* **Ars** k* *Ars-i* k* ars-s-f k2 *Aur* aur-ar k2 aur-s k2 bar-c k* *Bell* k* berb k* borx k* *Bov* k* bry k* cadm-met tpw6 cadm-s *Calc* k* calc-ar calc-i k2 calc-sil k2 cann-i k* cann-s k* canth k* carb-ac k* *Carb-v* k* carbn-s carl k* cartl-s rly4• caust k* cham h1* chin h1* clem k* coca *Cocc* colch k* coloc k* croc k* crot-h k* crot-t bg2 *Cupr* bg2 *Cycl* k* eup-per ferr ferr-ar ferr-i gamb k* *Graph* k* ham fd3.de• hell k* *Ign* k* ind iod k* *Kali-ar* *Kali-c* k* kali-n h2* kali-p kali-sil k2 ketogl-ac rly4• kreos k* lac-h sk4• lach *Led* k* lyc k* **Mag-c** k* mag-m k* manc bg2 mang k* merc k* nat-ar k2 *Nat-c* k* **Nat-m** k* nat-p nat-s k* nicc k* nit-ac k* nux-v k* *Ol-an* k* op k* *Petr* k* **Phos** k* **Pic-ac** k* *Plat* plb k* **Puls** k* *Rhod* b4a.de* rhus-t b7.de* rhus-v k* ruta ptk1* *Sabad* k* sabin k* *Sars* sec bg2 **Sep** k* *Sil* spong k* stann staph b7.de* stram k* sul-ac k* sul-i k2 **Sulph** k* tab k* tep k* thuj k* tritic-vg fd5.de ulm-c jsj8• vanil fd5.de verat k* verb k* xan zinc k*
  - **right**: *Agn* k*
  - **left**: cypr c1 ruta fd4.de
    - **vertigo**; after: cypr c1
  - **morning**: apis carl k* spong fd4.de
    - **bed** agg.; in: mag-m k* *Nat-m* sep sulph k*
    - **waking**; on: nat-s k*
  - **forenoon**: bry k* coloc k*
  - **afternoon**: lyc nux-v k* tritic-vg fd5.de
    - **sitting** agg.: lyc k*
    - **walking** agg.: lyc k*
  - **evening**: am-c apis borx mag-c h2* mang nat-m k* plat h2* ruta fd4.de spong fd4.de thuj k* tritic-vg fd5.de
    - **18** h: mang
    - **undressing** agg.: *Apis*
    - **walking** agg.: lyc
  - **night**: apis carb-an h2* caust k* nit-ac h2*
    - **bed** agg.; in: caust k*
  - **ascending** stairs agg.: borx h2 cann-s k* lyc mag-c k*
  - **bending** them: led h1*
  - **chilliness**; during: hell k*

- **Feet**: ...
  - **dinner**; after: *Carb-v* k*
  - **eating**; after: bry cann-s k* carb-v b4a.de op k*
  - **fever**; during: canth b7.de
  - **lead**; like filled with: nat-m tl1
  - **lying** agg.: led h1* spong fd4.de
  - **menses** | **before** | **agg.**: bar-c cycl lyc zinc
    - **during**:
      - **agg.**: colch nat-m k* sars h2* *Sulph* zinc
      - **amel.**: **Cycl** k*
  - **motion** | **amel.**: nicc k* zinc
  - **rising** after a meal, when: bry a1*
  - **sadness**; with (See MIND - Sadness - heaviness - feet)
  - **sitting** agg.: alum anac k* led h1* **Mag-c** *Plat* **Rhus-t** k* tritic-vg fd5.de
  - **standing** agg.: ham fd3.de• kali-n h2* *Nat-m* k* phos k*
  - **stepping** agg.: nit-ac h2*
  - **vexation**; after: nat-m h2*
  - **walking**:
    - **after** | **agg.**: alum *Arn* cann-s caust k* *Con* murx *Rhus-t* ruta
    - **agg.**: cann-i k* kali-n h2* kreos k* lyc h2* manc k* nat-c hr1 phos k* plb k* *Sep* k* *Sulph* k* vanil fd5.de verat k*
    - **air** agg.; in open: nit-ac h2
    - **amel.**: ars-i led h1* **Mag-c** k* *Nat-m* k* *Sulph* k*
    - **Foot**, bones of: staph h1

○ - **Soles**: bry bg2 ph-ac bg2
    - **walking** agg.: ph-ac h2 thuj h1
- **Fingers**: acon bg2 berb coll a1 hipp a1 m-arct b7.de* par k* phos k* *Plb* k* rhus-v stroph-h ptk1 valer b7.de*

○ - **Tips**: phos bg2 plb bg2* stroph-h ptk1
- **Forearms**: acon k* aeth k* alum k* am-m k* anac k* ant-s-aur bg1 aran k* **Arg-n** k* aur k* berb k* cann-i k* caust h2* coll a1 cot br1 *Croc* k* cur bg1 ham fd3.de• kali-n h2* ketogl-ac rly4• laur k* lyc k* m-arct b7.de m-aust b7.de *Mur-ac* k* myric bg1 nat-m h2* nux-v ph-ac k* plb a1 ruta fd4.de sabad k* sabin bg2* spig k* spong k* stroph-h ptk1 sulph k* symph fd3.de• *Tell* k* teucr k* thuj k*
  - **right**: lyc bg2
  - **left**: tell bg1 teucr bg2
  - **forenoon**: lyc k* ruta fd4.de
  - **night**, 22 h: tell
  - **coition**; after: sabin k*
  - **rest** agg.: aur k*
  - **sore**, and: cot br1
  - **waking**; on: aran k*

○ - **Elbow**; from pain in bend of: ulm-c jsj8•
- **Hands**: acet-ac acon k* aesc k* *Alum* k* alum-sil k2 am-c k* ang k* *Ars* k* *Bar-c* **Bell** k* *Bov* k* *Brucel* sa3• bry k* cann-s k* *Caust* k* chel k* coll a1 cycl k* ham fd3.de• hipp a1 hippoc-k szs2 iris *Kali-n* k* kali-p fd1.de• *Lyc* k* m-arct b7a.de manc nat-m k* nicc k* ol-an orot-ac rly4• ox-ac k* *Ph-ac* k* **Phos** k* phyt k* pic-ac plac rzf5• plb k* puls k* rhod k* ruta fd4.de sacch-a fd2.de• sars sil spira a1 spong stann sul-ac k* tell a1 teucr tritic-vg fd5.de *Zinc* k*
  - **right**: bov cann-s k* ruta fd4.de sulph h2* [bell-p-sp dcm1]
  - **evening**: ham fd3.de• lyc k*
  - **night**: kali-n tritic-vg fd5.de
  - **hang** down; letting arms:
    - **agg.**: sul-ac h2
    - **amel.**: goss bg1
  - **menses** | **before** | **agg.**: bar-c kreos zinc
    - **during** | **agg.**: zinc h2*
  - **motion** | **amel.**: cann-s nicc k*
  - **warm** bed agg.: goss
  - **writing** agg.: caps *Caust* *Chel* lyc k*
- **Hips**: agar all-c *Alum* androc srj1• ant-t k* arg-n bg2 ars-met *Con* kali-c h2* kreos mag-m h2* mag-s k* mucs-nas rly4• nat-ar nat-m a1 (non:nat-s k) ph-ac k* sars h2*

- **alternating** with:
  - **Loins**; heaviness in (See lumbar)
  - **Lumbar** region; heaviness in: mag-s c1
- **walking** | **amel.**: ph-ac

- **Joints**: *Cham* *Chin* k* *Mez* nit-ac h2* olib-sac wmh1 *Ph-ac* plb k* sabad a1 *Staph*
  - **morning**: carb-v h2*
- **Knees**: act-sp anac apis asar berb camph cann-s caust chel bg2 *Chin* b7.de* clem a1 cocc h1* coloc bg2 *Con* k* euphr h2* graph h2* hydrog srj2• *Hyos* kali-n h2* lach (non:lec kl) *Led* kl lyc h2* mag-c b4.de* mag-m h2* merc nat-m k* nat-pyru rly4• nit-ac **Nux-m** nux-v ptk1 ox-ac phos b4.de* *Plat* plb b7.de* podo c1 puls k* rhus-t k* ruta k* sanic sars spong k* *Stann* k* staph sulph k* symph fd3.de• tritic-vg fd5.de ven-m rsj12• verat k*
  - **right**: kali-bi bg1 symph fd3.de•
  - **left**: phos h2*
  - **morning** | **bed** agg.; in: sulph h2*
  - **afternoon**: mag-c h2* ruta fd4.de
  - **ascending** stairs agg.: caust h2 dig h2 hyos
  - **menses**; during: sars h2*
  - **rest** agg., during: **Nux-m**
  - **rising** from sitting agg.; after: berb puls h1*
  - **sitting** agg.: camph k* mag-c h2*
  - **walking**:
    - **after** | **agg.**: berb calc-s ruta h1
    - **agg.**: mag-c h2
    - **amel.**: kali-n h2* ruta h1
- ○ **Hollow** of knees: rhus-t bg2
- **Legs**: acon a1 adam srj5• *Aeth* *Agar* k* allox tpw4* **Alum** k* am-c k* am-m *Ambr* k* anac b4.de* ang k* ant-t *Arg-n* ars k* arum-t asar *Bell* k* berb k* brach brom bg2 *Bry* k* bufo cact k* cain *Calc* k* *Calc-p* calc-sil k2 *Camph* k* **Cann-i** k* cann-s *Carb-ac* *Carb-v* *Carbn-s* *Caust* k* *Cham* *Chel* *Chin* cimic bro1 *Cimx* clem k* cob ptm1• *Colch* *Coloc* k* con bro1 convo-s sp1 corian-s knl6• cot br1 croc crot-t cupr h2* dig k* dros b7.de euphr b7.de* falco-pe nl2• *Ferr* k* ferr-p flor-p rsj3• *Gels* k* gins bro1 *Graph* k* *Gua* bro1 ham fd3.de• hell bro1 hep b4a.de* hippoc-k szs2 hydroph rsj6• ind *Ip* b7.de *Kali-bi* k* *Kali-c* k* kali-n kali-sil k2 kreos b7a.de lac-ac stj5• lach k* lact laur b7.de led b7.de* limest-b es1• lyc h2* *Lyss* k* m-arct b7.de *Mag-m* k* *Med* k* *Merc* k* nat-ar *Nat-c* *Nat-m* k* nat-p k* nit-ac h2* **Nux-m** *Nux-v* k* olib-sac wmh1 *Onos* ozone sde2• pall bro1 *Petr* *Phos* k* *Phyt* *Pic-ac* k* plat *Plb* positr nl2• propr sa3• *Puls* k* querc-r svu1• **Rhus-t** k* ruta k* sarr sars sec k* sep h2* *Sil* spig b7.de spong k* stann k* staph b7.de stront-c sulfon bro1 *Sulph* k* tarax h1* *Tarent* k* teucr b7.de thuj k* tritic-vg fd5.de tub-r jl2 *Vac* jl2 valer k* vanil fd5.de verat k* verb k* vib-od bro1 zinc k* [sol-ecl cky1]
  - **left**: ruta fd4.de thuj h1*
  - **daytime**; by: puls tl1 rhus-t tl1 verat tl1
  - **morning**: ars h2* falco-pe nl2• ruta fd4.de spong fd4.de tritic-vg fd5.de vanil fd5.de [sol-ecl cky1]
    - **waking**; on: adam srj5• falco-pe nl2• *Pneu* jl2 positr nl2•
  - **forenoon**: ham fd3.de• puls h1*
  - **afternoon**: nat-c h2* spong fd4.de
  - **evening**: alum am-c k* *Apis* ham fd3.de• puls h1* ruta fd4.de (non:uran-met k) uran-n
  - **night**: *Caust* k* hydrog srj2• kali-c h2* spong fd4.de
  - **accompanied** by:
    - **Head**; complaints of (See HEAD - Complaints - accompanied - leg - heaviness)
    - **Teeth**; pain in (See TEETH - Pain - accompanied - legs)
  - **ascending** stairs agg.: hep h2 med hr1 **Nat-m** *Phos*
  - **band**; as from a: ozone sde2•
  - **chill**; before: *Cimx*
  - **crossing** legs agg.: bell h1* stann h2* verb h*
  - **eating**; after: arn dros h1*
  - **exertion** agg.: **Gels** pic-ac k*
  - **influenza**; during: gels tl1

- **Legs**: ...
  - **menses**:
    - **amel.**: arist-cl sp1
    - **before** | **agg.**: anthraq rly4• *Lyc* pneu jl2 sulph zr
    - **during** | **agg.**: *Calc-p* nicc *Sars*
  - **painful**: plat h2*
  - **rest** agg.: nit-ac h2*
  - **rising** from sitting agg.: puls h1
  - **sadness**; with (See MIND - Sadness - heaviness - legs)
  - **sitting** agg.: **Alum** ham fd3.de• *Mag-m* plat h2* rhus-t h1* spig h1* thuj h1* tritic-vg fd5.de
  - **sore**; and: cot br1
  - **standing**:
    - **agg.**: alum h2* cortiso tpw7 samb h1* stroph-s sp1
    - **impossible**: rhus-t a1
  - **walking**:
    - **after** | **agg.**: kali-n h2* nit-ac h2*
    - **agg.**: alum h2* bell h1* coloc h2* med bro1 *Nat-c* ozone sde2• rhus-t h1* stann *Sulph*
    - **amel.**: kali-n h2* nit-ac h2* rhus-t h1* sec
  - ▽ **extending** to:
    - **Upward**: ozone sde2•
      - **Downward**; then: ozone sde2•
  - ○ **Bones**:
    - **Tibia**: dig h2* kali-n h2* ruta fd4.de spong h1*
      - **walking** rapidly agg.: spong h1
  - **Calves**: acon a1 agar k* *Aloe* *Arg-n* ars-i berb k* cham k* euphr k* hydrog srj2• kali-c h2* ketogl-ac rly4• lyss mag-m h2* plat h2* rhus-t k* sacch-a fd2.de• sep stann h2* staph h1* sulph
- **Lower** limbs: acet-ac acon k* *Agar* k* aids nl2• all-s aloe k* **Alum** k* alum-p k2 alum-sil k2 alumn am-c k* am-m ambr k* anac k* androc srj1• ang b7.de* ant-c b7a.de ant-t k* apis b7a.de *Aran* **Arg-met** *Arg-n* k* arge-pl rwt5• arist-cl sp1 *Arn* *Ars* k* ars-s-f k2 asaf asar bamb-a stb2.de• bar-c bar-s k2 *Bell* k* **Berb** k* bit-ar wht1• borx b4a.de both fne1• bov brom bros-gau mrc1 bry k* bufo bg2 cact cadm-met tpw6* cain calam sa3• **Calc** k* calc-ar calc-p calc-s *Camph* k* **Cann-i** *Cann-s* b7.de* canth b7.de* caps *Carb-ac* **Carb-v** k* *Carbn-s* carc fd2.de• cartl-s rly4• castm caust k* cham k* *Chel* k* chin k* chinin-ar choc srj3• cic *Cimx* clem k* coc-c **Cocc** colch *Coloc* k* **Con** convo-s sp1 cor-r cot br1 crot-h dig dios *Dulc* k* elec al2 eupi falco-pe nl2• ferr-i fic-m gya1 fl-ac k* **Gels** k* ger-i rly4• gins k* granit-m es1• *Graph* k* guaj h2* *Ham* *Hell* k* *Hep* k* *Ign* k* ignis-alc es2• ind indg iod k* ip h1* *Kali-ar* kali-bi k* *Kali-c* k* kali-n **Kali-p** kali-s kali-sil k2 kola stb3• kreos k* lac-e hrn2• **Lach** laur *Lec* led k* limest-b es1• luf-op rsj5• luna kg1• *Lyc* k* lyss m-arct b7.de *Mag-m* k* *Med* k* *Merc* k* *Merc-c* *Merc-i-f* *Mez* k* murx nat-ar **Nat-c** k* *Nat-m* k* nat-p nat-s nat-sil fd3.de• *Nit-ac* k* *Nux-m* k* *Nux-v* k* olib-sac wmh1 *Onos* op k* osm ozone sde2• *Petr* k* *Ph-ac* k* *Phos* k* phyt **Pic-ac** k* *Plat* plb k* podo fd3.de• *Positr* nl2• psil ft1 ptel *Puls* k* pycnop-sa mrz1 rad-br bg1 rat rhod k* **Rhus-t** k* *Ruta* k* *Sabad* k* sacch-a fd2.de• sanic sars h2* sec k* senec *Seneg* *Sep* k* **Sil** k* sin-a k* spig k* spirae a1 spong *Stann* k* staph k* stram h1* stry sul-ac k* sulfonam ks2 **Sulph** k* symph fd3.de• taosc iwa1• *Tarent* *Thuj* k* til tritic-vg fd5.de ulm-c jsj8• vanil fd5.de verat k* verb k* vip fkr4.de visc bg2 xan *Zinc* k* [heroin sdj2 pop dhh1]
  - **right**: *Brucel* sa3• sacch-a fd2.de• thuj bg1
  - **left**: carb-v bg1
  - **daytime**: cassia-s ccrh1• *Puls*
  - **morning**: ambr ars calc h2* card-m falco-pe nl2• ham fd3.de• kreos lec mur-ac h2* nat-sil fd3.de• phos h2* *Sil* spong fd4.de sulph k* tritic-vg fd5.de verat
    - **bed** agg.; in: caust mag-m nat-sil fd3.de• spong fd4.de sulph k* zinc h2
    - **waking**; on: calc h2* falco-pe nl2• ozone sde2• phos k* plut-n srj7• spong fd4.de sumb
  - **forenoon**: *Merc* puls
    - **11** h: zing
  - **afternoon**: **Arg-n** bamb-a stb2.de• bry fago kali-s fd4.de nux-v k* phyt k* spirae a1 tritic-vg fd5.de zinc k*
    - **15** h: plan
    - **16** h: kali-cy

- **evening**: alum k* am-c bamb-a stb2.de• carc fd2.de• clem k* *Coloc* fago ham fd3.de• indg c1 kali-n h2* kali-s fd4.de nat-m k* nicc op ruta fd4.de sal-fr sle1• spong fd4.de thuj tritic-vg fd5.de
  - **18** h: op
  - **21** h: pic-ac
  - **bed** agg.; in: indg spong fd4.de
- **night**: carb-an h2* carb-v caust h2* fic-m gya1 lac-e hrn2• petr h2* *Sulph* thuj tritic-vg fd5.de vanil fd5.de
  - **midnight**; after: crot-t
  - **amel.**: cassia-s ccrh1•
  - **bed** agg.; in: sulph tritic-vg fd5.de vanil fd5.de
- **accompanied** by | **heat**; sensation of: bamb-a stb2.de•
- **air** agg.; in open: graph
- **ascending** stairs agg.: bamb-a stb2.de• bry ham fd3.de• kola stb3• lyc *Med* k* *Nat-m* ptk1 phos h2* ruta fd4.de stann h2 thuj verb
- **beaten**; with heaviness as if: **Berb** hr1*
- **constipation**: tep
- **descending** stairs agg.: med hr1 verb h
- **dinner**; after: kali-n h2* sulph k*
- **exertion** agg.; after: **Con Gels** k* **Lach Pic-ac** k* **Rhus-t**
- **fatigue**, as from: aphis arg-n calc h2* *Hydrog* srj2• kreos lact luf-op rsj5• mag-m merc-i-f mosch murx nat-s psor puls ruta sulph
- **fever**; during: alum bg2 *Calc* bg2 canth bg2 *Chin* bg2 ign bg2 *Nat-m* bg2 *Nux-v* bg2 *Puls* bg2 sep bg2 stann bg2 sulph bg2 thuj bg2
- **lead**; as from: ozone sde2•
- **lying** agg.: nit-ac h2* ruta c1 spong fd4.de tritic-vg fd5.de vanil fd5.de
- **menses**:
  - **after** | **agg.**: nat-m h2*
  - **before** | **agg.**: bar-c b4.de* *Carl Con Graph Kali-c* b4a.de lach *Lyc* k* phel thuj b4a.de
  - **during** | **agg.**: *Am-c* calc-p cocc *Graph* kali-n nicc nit-ac *Sep* sulph *Zinc* k*
  - **suppressed** menses; from: *Graph* nat-m nux-v phos rhus-t ruta verat
- **mortification**; from: puls
- **motion**:
  - **agg.**: **Lach** spong fd4.de
  - **amel.**: cassia-s ccrh1• mag-c h2* nat-m nit-ac plut-n srj7•
- **painful**: bov ptk1
- **periodical**: *Aran*
- **perspiration**; during: bell bg2 *Calc* bg2 canth bg2 *Chin* bg2 hell bg2 ign bg2 mez bg2 nat-c bg2 nat-m bg2 **Nux-v** bg2 phos bg2 *Puls* bg2 *Rhus-t* bg2 *Sep* bg2 stann bg2 **Sulph** bg2 thuj bg2
- **riding**, during: rumx
- **rising** from sitting agg.: mag-c h2* vanil fd5.de
- **sitting** agg.: **Alum** k* cassia-s ccrh1• croc mag-c h2* mag-m nat-c k* nit-ac plat sars spig stann k*
- **sleep** agg.; after: *Sep*
- **sore**, and: cot br1
- **standing** agg.: bry stann h2* sulph valer
- **stretching** leg | **amel.**: anac h2
- **vexation**; after: lyc nux-v k*
- **walking**:
  - **after**:
    - **agg.**: anac h2* **Arg-met** kali-bi kali-n kali-p fd1.de• murx ruta sil h2* stann h2* *Sulph*
    - **amel.**: cassia-s ccrh1• nit-ac h2* rat rhod
  - **agg.**: acon a1 anac arn bamb-a stb2.de• bell **Berb** bry *Calc* **Cann-i Carb-v** carc fd2.de• chin h1* chinin-s **Con** crot-t dulc fd4.de **Gels** hep kali-c h2* **Lach** *Lec* lyc *Mag-m Med* k* mucs-nas rly4• nat-sil fd3.de• petr phos k* pip-m puls rhod rhus-t ruta fd4.de sars spig h1* spong fd4.de *Stann* k* *Sulph* k* thuj tritic-vg fd5.de zinc
  - **air** agg.; in open: lyc h2 sil h2
  - **beginning** to walk: zinc h2
- **Bones**: sulph h2

\- Lower limbs – **Bones**: ...
  - **sitting** agg.: sulph h2
- **Joints**: calc h2* nit-ac h2* ph-ac h2* tritic-vg fd5.de

\- **Shoulders**: acon b7.de* anac bg2* arn b7.de* bros-gau mrc1 bry bg2 cann-xyz bg2 carb-an k* *Carbn-s* bg2* chin bg1* con bg2 *Ferr* hep k* hipp a1 kali-c bg2* kali-n h2* kreos bg2 lach bg2* led bg2* limest-b es1• lyss c1 mag-m h2* *Nat-m* nat-s *Nux-m* par phos h2* phyt bg2 pieri-b mlk9.de pin-con oss2• plb bg2* *Puls* k* *Rhus-t* bg2* sal-al blc1• spong fd4.de stann bg2 staph bg2* sulph k* taosc iwa1• thuj zinc k*
- **right**: kali-m bg1
  - **Under**: kali-m ptk1
- **left**: plut-n srj7•
- **coat** is too heavy; as if: bamb-a stb2.de•
- **motion** agg.: led a1 mur-ac h2*
- **waking**; on: zinc

\- **Thighs**: agar k* agath-a nl2• *Agn* aloe bg2 *Alum* bro1 am-c androc srj1• **Ang** k* aran k* *Arn* ars asar h1* *Bell* k* *Brucel* sa3• *Bry* k* *Calc* k* camph h1* cann-i bro1 cassia-s ccrh1• caust h2* cham *Chin* k* cic b7.de* cimic bro1 con bro1 croc crot-t *Dulc* k* fic-m gya1 gins bro1 graph h2* *Gua* bro1 *Guaj* hell h1* *Ip Kali-c* lach laur bg1 *Lyc* k* lyss mag-c h2* mag-m h2* mand rsj7• med bro1 *Merc* k* murx nat-m bg2* nat-s nux-v k* pall bro1 petr k* ph-ac h2* phos h2* *Pic-ac* bro1 *Puls* rat bg1 rheum *Rhod* k* *Sars* k* *Sep* k* spong fd4.de squil h1* *Stann* k* staph b7.de* stict bg2 sulfon bro1 *Sulph* bro1 symph fd3.de• *Thuj* k* verb k* vib-od bro1 zinc k*
- **right**: fic-m gya1 rat
- **morning**: *Calc* dulc fd4.de ham fd3.de• kali-c h2* spong fd4.de
- **night**: kali-c h2* sep h2*
  - **midnight**; after: crot-t
- **ascending** stairs agg.: asar h1 mand rsj7•
- **cold** air agg.: cassia-s ccrh1•
- **exertion**; violent:
  - **agg.**: carc jl2
  - **amel.**: carc sp1
- **lying** agg.: staph h1*
- **menses** | **before** | **agg.**: bell brom carb-an cocc kali-n h2* nux-m
  - **during** | **agg.**: *Am-c* carb-an *Castm* cub *Graph* nit-ac *Sars*
- **motion**; continued | **amel.**: cassia-s ccrh1•
- **paralytic**: dulc fd4.de kali-c h2* kali-n h2* symph fd3.de•
- **paroxysmal**: thuj h1*
- **pressure** | **amel.**: cassia-s ccrh1•
- **rising** from sitting agg.: cassia-s ccrh1•
- **sitting** agg.: kali-c h2* kali-n h2* mag-c h2* rat sars h2* symph fd3.de•
- **stool** agg.; after: lyc h2*
- **walking** | **after** | **agg.**: ang h1*
  - **agg.**: bell h1 cic h1 mag-c h2 petr a1* sars h2 zinc h2

\- **Toes**: apis b7a.de valer b7.de*

\- **Upper** arms: alum ptk1 brucel sa3• carb-v b4.de* cocc bg2 colch rsj2• cot br1 guaj h2* kali-s fd4.de kreos bg2 lat-m ptk1 led b7.de* m-arct b7.de mez b4.de* phos h2* plb a1 spig b7.de* spira a1 stann h2* sulph h2* teucr b7.de*
- **right**: brucel sa3•
- **left**: propr sa3• sulfonam ks2
- **night**: sep h2*
- **raising** them: cic hr1
- **something** heavy is hanging on the upper arm; sensation as if: sulph h2*
- **sore**, and: cot br1

\- **Upper** limbs: abrom-a ks5 acon k* aesc k* *Agar* aloe *Alum* k* alum-p k2 alum-sil k2 *Am-c* k* *Am-m* k* anac k* *Ang* k* ant-c ant-s-aur bg1 *Ant-t* k* *Apis* aran-ix sp1 **Arg-n** k* arn k* ars-h *Ars-met* arund k* aster aur aur-ar k2 bar-c k* bar-s k2 *Bell* k* benz-ac berb k* bism bit-ar wht1• brach *Brucel* sa3• bry k* bufo k* cact k* cadm-s *Calc* k* camph k* cann-i k* *Carb-ac* k* carb-an k* carb-v k* carbn-s cardios-h rly4• cartl-s rly4• **Caust** k* chel k* cic k* cimic bro1 cinnb k* cocc k* colch k* **Con** k* cor-r corn cot br1 croc k* crot-h k* crot-t k* *Cur* k* cycl k* cypra-eg sde6.de• dig k* dulc k* elec al2 falco-pe nl2• *Ferr* k* ferr-p fl-ac **Gels** k* ger-i rly4• *Glon* k* granit-m es1• *Ham* k* hep h2* hippoc-k szs2

- **Upper** limbs: ...
hura hydroph rsj6• kali-i kali-n bg2 **Kali-p** k* *Lach* k* *Lat-m* bro1 laur k* *Lec* led k* limest-b es1• *Lyc* k* lyss *M-arct* b7.de* m-aust b7.de* mag-c h2* manc *Merc* k* *Merc-c* *Mez* k* mosch bg2 mur-ac k* *Nat-c* k* **Nat-m** k* nat-p k* nat-s k* nat-sil fd3.de• nit-ac h2* *Nux-m* k* nux-v k* olib-sac wmh1 *Onos* op k* par k* petr k* *Ph-ac* phasco-ci rbp2 *Phos* k* phys *Pic-ac* k* pin-con oss2• pip-m k* plan k* plat k* **Plb** k* positr nl2• **Puls** k* rad-br bg1 rhod k* rhus-t *Sabad* k* sarr sep k* *Sil* k* sol-ni sphing a1 spig k* spong *Stann* k* staph b7.de* *Stram* k* stroph-h ptk1 sul-ac k* *Sulph* k* *Sumb* k* suprar rly4• symph fd3.de• taosc iwa1• *Tarent* k* tep k* tere-la rly4• teucr k* thuj k* til k* tritic-vg fd5.de valer k* verat k* zinc zing k* [bell-p-sp dcm1 sol-ecl cky1]
  - **right**: abrom-a ks5 aloe bg2 *Am-c* k* **Am-m** k* anac h2* androc srj1• *Apis* *Caust* k* *Fl-ac* k* mag-c h2* merc-i-f bg2 nat-c h2* nat-p bg2 par bg2 paraf ah1 *Phos* bg2* pic-ac bg2 rhod sulph bg2 ven-m rsj12•
  - **left**: arg-n arund k* bar-c k* both-ax tsm2 *Calc* camph k* cann-xyz bg2 carb-ac bg2 carb-v k* conin c1 *Dig* k* kali-i bg2 led a1 mand rsj7• merc bg2 merc-i-f plat h2* spig h1* spong fd4.de thuj h1*
  - **daytime**: sulph k*
  - **morning**: ant-s-aur ham fd3.de• *Iod* nat-sil fd3.de• spong fd4.de *Sulph* tritic-vg fd5.de [sol-ecl cky1]
    - **waking**; on: fl-ac k* *Iod* nat-sil fd3.de•
    - **washing** agg.: *Phos* k*
    - **writing** agg.: phos k*
  - **forenoon**, 11 h: zing
  - **noon**: sulph k*
  - **afternoon**: nux-v k* tritic-vg fd5.de
    - **15 h**: plan
  - **evening**: *Am-m* ham fd3.de• mur-ac h2* spong fd4.de tritic-vg fd5.de
  - **night**: *Merc* stann k*
  - **accompanied** by | **stiffness** (See Stiffness - upper limbs - accompanied - heaviness)
  - **ascending** stairs agg.: *Nux-v*
  - **bed** agg.; in: staph k* til k* tritic-vg fd5.de
  - **chill**; during: cina b7a.de kreos b7a.de
  - **dinner**; after: plect k*
  - **emissions** agg.; after: staph k*
  - **exertion** agg.: *Phos* *Pic-ac* *Stann* tritic-vg fd5.de
  - **hanging** down, while: ang h1* valer
  - **menses**; during suppressed: graph
  - **motion**:
    - **agg.**: carb-v k* grat k* nat-c *Stann* k*
    - **amel.**: *Apis* camph led k* *Rhod* k*
  - **numbness**; with: *Ambr* *Apis* *Bufo* cham croc fl-ac graph kali-c lyc mag-m *Nux-v* puls *Sep* sil
  - **playing** piano agg.: (↗*Playing - piano*) *Cur* *Gels* merc-i-f
  - **pressure** | **amel.**: abrom-a ks5
  - **raising** them; on: cic cocc mag-c h2 merc mur-ac phos taosc iwa1•
    - **right** arm: limest-b es1•
  - **sore**, and: cot br1
  - **sudden**: carc gk6*
  - **walking** agg.: abrom-a ks5 anac k* ang k* spig h1*
  - **washing** agg.: phos k*
  - **writing** agg.: caps *Carb-v* *Caust* ferr-i fl-ac kali-c mez phos k* spig
  - ○ **Bones**: mez bg2 sulph bg2
- **Wrists**: hipp a1 led a1 plb a1 sacch-a fd2.de• spong fd4.de sul-ac h2* symph fd3.de•
  - **right**: limest-b es1•

HEMIBALLISM (See Motion - involuntary - one side)

HEMORRHAGE:
- **after**:
  - **agg.** | **Lower** limbs: sec bg2
- **easily**: helo-s bnm14•
  - ○ **Upper** limbs: **Alum** bg2

Hemorrhage: ...
- **sensation** of:
  - ○ **Feet** | **Soles**: led b7a.de

HIP DYSPLASIA (See Hip joint)

HIP JOINT disease: (↗*Pain - hips; Suppuration - hips*) acon c1* am-c anac *Ang* apis *Arg-met* k* arn *Ars* k* ars-i k* *Asaf* asar *Aur* aur-i k2 aur-s k2 *Bell* *Bry* **Calc** k* calc-hs bro1 calc-i bro1 **Calc-p** k* *Calc-s* calc-sil k2 *Canth* *Caps* carb-ac *Carb-v* carbn-s carc xxb **Card-m** *Caust* k* *Cham* **Chin** k* chinin-ar cist k* colch **Coloc** k* dig dros tl ferr bro1 ferr-p bro1 *Fl-ac* k* get c2 graph hecla *Hep* k* hippoz k* hydr hyper bro1 iod k* iris **Kali-c** k* *Kali-i* k* *Kali-p* **Kali-s** kali-sil k2 lac-c *Lach* *Lyc* k* lyss mtf11 *Merc* k* merc-i-r bro1 *Nat-m* **NAT-S** k* *Nit-ac* *Nux-v* *Ol-j* *Petr* **Ph-ac** k* *Phos* k* *Phyt* *Puls* k* *Rhus-t* k* sep **Sil** k* staph k* still c2* **Stram** *Sulph* k* **Tub** k*
- **right**: **Led** *Phyt*
- **left**: *Nat-s* mrr1 *Stram*

HOLDING parts together: | **agg.** | **Lower** limbs: ign b7a.de*
- ○ **Upper** limbs:
  - **right** | **palpitations**; during: aur ptk1

HOOP (See Bandaged)

HORNY excrescences (See Excrescences - horny)

HORRIPILATION (See Goose)

HOUSEMAID'S knee (See Inflammation - knees - bursae)

HUMMING (See Vibration)

HYGROMA PATELLAE: arn bro1* calc-p bro1 *Iod* bro1

HYPERESTHESIA (See Sensitive)

HYPERTROPHY (See Thick)

INCOORDINATION: (↗*Awkwardness; Tottering; GENERALS - Locomotor*) *Agar* k* **Alum** k* alum-p k2 alum-sil k2 alumin-m br1 anh br1* apis k2 arag br1* *Arg-n* k* ars astra-e mp4* astra-m br1 aur-s c1 bar-c ptk1 bell k* botul br1 bufo br1 *Calc* cann-i a2 carbn-s cartl-s rly4• *Caust* k* chlol *Cimic* ptk1 cit-ac rly4• coca *Cocc* k* **Con** k* crot-c crot-h sne *Cupr* cypra-eg sde6.de• echi ptk1 ferr ptk1 *Fl-ac* *Gels* k* germ-met srj5• glon ptk1 *Graph* k* *Hell* k* *Helo* k* helo-s c1* hyos ptk1 ign bro1* irid-met srj5• ix bnm8• *Kali-br* k* kali-p ptk1 lac-h sze9• *Lach* k* lat-h bnm5• lat-m bnm6• lavand-a ctl1• *Lil-t* k* mag-m a1 mang mrr1* merc k* merc-n c1 naja nat-c k2 nat-s hr1 nux-m *Nux-v* k* *Onos* k* op mtf33 oxyt ptk2 pedclr br1 *Ph-ac* *Phos* k* phys br1* physala-p bnm7• pic-ac k2 pieri-b mlk9.de plat ptk1 *Plb* k* psil ft1 *Rhus-t* ptk1 sec k* *Sil* spartin bwa3 *Stram* k* streptoc rly4• sulfon br1* *Sulph* k* syph jl2 ter tl1 tub ser verat mtf33 visc sp1 *Zinc* k* [tax jsj7]
- **accompanied** by:
  - **vertigo** (See VERTIGO - Accompanied - staggering)
  - ○ **Head**; complaints (See HEAD - Complaints - accompanied - incoordination)
- **eating** | **amel.**: nat-c k2
- **excitement**; after: gels k2
- **rising** from siting: calc-p tl1
- **walking** agg.: alum bro1 arag bro1 arg-n bro1 aster bro1 *Bar-m* bro1 bell bro1 cocc bro1 *Gels* bro1 ix bnm8• kali-br bro1 med bro1 onos bro1 oxyt bro1 ph-ac bro1 *Phys* bro1 pic-ac bro1 plb bro1 sec bro1 sil bro1 trion bro1 *Zinc* bro1
- ○ **Lower** limbs: (↗*Awkwardness - lower; Tottering; Unsteadiness - lower; Walking - infirm; GENERALS - Locomotor; VERTIGO - Accompanied - staggering*) *Alum* bell bufo br1 cann-i a1 chlol crot-c cupr bg2 lath bg2 mang-act br1 *Nux-m* k* nux-v bg2 *Onos* oxyt br1 *Phos* k* *Plb* *Sil* *Sulph* tarent mtf33 zinc bg2
- **Upper** limbs: bell cupr *Gels* *Merc* *Onos* plb
  - **walking** agg.: hyos

INDENTED:
- **pressure**; on:
  - ○ **Feet**: led tl1
  - **Legs**: led tl1
- **pressure** with fingers; from | **Upper** limbs: borx bg2 merc bg2

INDURATION: (↗*Hardness*)
- ○ **Bones** | **Periosteum**: ruta k2

- **Feet**:
  - ○ **Heels**: aur lyc k*
  - **Soles**: *Ant-c* b7.de* **Ars**
- **Fingers**: ant-t bg2 caust crot-h graph k* med petr k2 phyt
  - ○ **Tendons** of: carb-an **CAUST** k •* gels c1
- **Forearms**: *Sil*
  - **spots**: carb-an bg2
  - ○ **Cellular** tissue: **Sil** bg2
- **Hands**: ars dulc fd4.de *Sulph*
  - ○ **Palms**: *Cist* **Lyc** k •
    - **Tendons**: *Plb* mrr1 sulph h2*
- **Legs**: graph *Mag-c* sulph
- **Nates**: ph-ac thuj k*
- **Tendons**: *Caust* mrr1
- **Upper** limbs: *Caust* b4a.de mag-c petr tab

INFILTRATION with bloody serum:
- ○ **Lower** limbs: dig k*
- **Nates**: vip k*

INFLAMMATION: ars-s-f k2 calc-sil k2 *Lach* k* merc-n k* merc-ns rhus-t k2 sec bg1 sulph bg1 tritic-vg fd5.de vip k*
- **night**: allox sp1 merc k2
- **erysipelatous**: anan **Lach** rhus-t hr1 streptoc jl2 sulph k2 vip
- ○ **Ankles**: apoc k2 arn k* ars-s-f k2 kali-c h2* **Led** mrr1 *Mang* k* morg-p pte1• phyt stann b4.de*
  - **erysipelatous**: *Lach Rhus-t* tep k*
  - ○ **Joints**: dros tl1 dys fmm1•
  - **Skin**: morg-p fmm1•
- **Bones**: *Asaf Aur Calc* **Fl-ac** mang hr1 **Merc** *Mez* **Ph-ac** *Rhus-t* **Sil**
  - ○ **Periosteum**: asaf k2 aur tl1 puls mtf33 *Staph* hr1*
- **Elbows**: ant-c k* lac-ac lach sal-ac tl2 sil
  - **erysipelatous**: anan vh1 ars lach sulph
  - ○ **Ligaments**: ant-c bg2
  - **Tendon**: ant-c ptk1
- **Feet**: acon k* arn k* *Ars* k* ars-s-f k2 borx k* **Bry** calc k* calen *Carb-an* k* carc fb *Com* dulc hydrog srj2• kali-bi k* **Led** mrr1 lyc b4a.de *Merc* k* mygal *Phos* k* *Puls* k* *Rhus-v* k* sars b4.de* sil k* **Sulph** thuj b4.de* zinc k*
  - **dark** red: rhus-v k* sil
  - **erysipelatous**: *Apis Arn* k* borx h2 *Bry* dulc nux-v puls k* *Rhus-t* k* sil sulph
    - **dancing**; after: berb borx h2
    - **desquamating**: dulc
    - **spots**, in: apis
  - ○ **Back** of feet: calc mag-c morg-p pte1• puls k* thuj k*
    - **Skin**: morg-p fmm1•
  - **Bone**: dys fmm1• sarr
  - **Heels**: ant-c sabin
    - **erysipelatous**: *Ant-c* b7a.de
    - **rheumatic**: sabin
    - **Inner** side: morg-p pte1•
      - **Skin**: morg-p fmm1•
  - **Joints**: caul tl1 dros tl1
  - **Periosteum**: *Aur-m* dys pte1• guaj
  - **Soles**: *Puls*
    - **fasciitis**; plantar: phyt mrr1
- **Fingers**: *(↗Spina)* **Am-c** k* apis apoc k2 ars-s-f k2 calc-s con k* *Cupr Hep* hydrog srj2• kali-c k* lyc k* *Mag-c* k* mang k* nat-m k* nit-ac k* puls k* ran-b k* *Sil* syc pte1• tarent k* tritic-vg fd5.de
  - **erysipelatous**: carb-ac c1 *Lyc* b4.de* *Mag-c* b4a.de rhod k* rhus-t k* spong b7.de* sulph k* thuj k*
  - ○ **Bones**: *Staph*
    - **Periosteum**: **Led**
  - **Joints**: *Benz-ac* bro1 berb bro1 *Bry* bro1 **Caul** mrr1 *Caust* mrr1 des-ac rbp6 fl-ac bro1 kali-c k2 *Lyc* k* med bro1 *Nat-p* bro1 pip-m bro1 positr nl2• prim-o bro1 puls bro1 *Rhus-t* bro1 staph bro1 *Stel* bro1 syc pte1*• [heroin sdj2]
    - **bursitis**: *(↗knees - bursae; Bursae; GENERALS - Inflammation - bursae)* Ruta

Inflammation – Fingers – Joints: ...
- **gouty**: stel br1
- **painful**: syc bka1•
- **rheumatic**: des-ac rbp6
- **warm** water | **amel.**: syc bka1•
- **weather**; warm | **amel.**: syc bka1•
- **Middle**: lyc h2*
  - **Nails**: *Calen* c2 kali-c moni jl2
    - **Around**: con k* hell h1* kola stb3• moni jl2 *Nat-m Nat-s* ph-ac k* sil c1 tritic-vg fd5.de
    - **Roots**: *Hep* kali-c h2* *Stict*
    - **Under**: sil c1
  - **Tips**: *Thuj*
    - **erysipelatous**: *Thuj* b4.de*
- **Forearms**: *Ars* lyc k* *Rhus-t* k*
  - **erysipelatous**: anan ant-c k* apis *Bell* b4a.de bufo carb-ac c1 *Kali-c* **Lach** *Lyc* b4a.de merc k* petr k* rhus-t b7.de*
  - ○ **Periosteum** of: *Aur*
- **Hands**: anac k* *Anthraci* arn k* ars k* ars-s-f k2 *Bry* k* bufo carc fb cocc crot-c mre1.fr *Crot-h* cupr k* dys pte1• ferr hep *Kalm Lach Lyc M-arct* b7a.de manc k* nat-m bg2 ran-b b7.de* *Rhus-t* k* *Sil* sulph vesp
  - **callosities**: *Phos*
  - **dark** red: anthraci *Lyc* rhus-t
  - **erysipelatous**: *Bell* b4a.de carb-ac c1 graph k* hep b4.de* *Lach* ran-b b7.de* *Rhus-t* k* ruta b7.de*
  - ○ **Joints**: caul tl1 **Caust** mrr1
  - **Palms**: bry dys pte1• syc pte1*•
  - **Skin**: prot fmm1•
    - **Back** of the hand: prot jl2
- **Hips**:
  - ○ **Joints** (= coxitis): apis arg-met bg2* bacls-7 fmm1• calc mtf11* caust bg2 kali-c br1 *Lith-c* mrr1 lyc mtf33 med mtf11 medul-os-si mtf11 phos k2 *Puls* mrr1 tub mtf33
    - **left**: bacls-7 fmm1• *Nat-s* mrr1
    - **synovitis**: mez mtf11
- **Joints**: *(↗Pain - rheumatic; GENERALS - Inflammation - joints)* abrot sf* **Acon** k* agn c1 am-be sf am-caust sf am-m sf am-p sf* *Ang* k* ant-c sf *Ant-t* hr1* **Apis** apoc k2 aran mg aran-ix mg arb a1* arist-cl sp1* *Arn* ars sf ars-s-f k2 asar sf *Aur* k* *Aur-m-n* wbt2• bar-c sf **Bell** *Benz-ac* sf* berb sf* **Bry** k* cact k2 *Calc* calc-p sf calc-sil k2 *Cardios-h* rly4• caul sf *Caust* k* cham c* chin sf* *Chinin-s* mrr1 cimic bro1 clem sf *Colch* hr1* coloc sf conch a1 cortiso sp1 crot-h sf cycl sf dulc k2 eup-per k2* euphr mg ferr sf* *Ferr-p* k* form sf* *Form-ac* sf* *Gaul* sf gins sf gnaph bro1 graph mrr1 *Guaj* k* hed mg hep sf hip-ac mtf11 hyper k* ichth c ign mrr1 *Iod* k* kali-ar k2 *Kali-bi* bro1* *Kali-c* kali-chl sf *Kali-i* k* kali-s mrr1 *Kalm* k* *Kreos* k* *Lac-ac* k* lach k* **Led** k* lil-t bro1 *Lith-be* sf lith-c k* lith-sal sf *Lyc* mand mg *Mang* k* mang-act bro1 meny k* *Merc* k* mez sf morg-g mtf11 *Nat-m* k* *Nat-s* k* nat-sil bro1 nit-ac bro1 nux-m mrr1 pall sne parat-b mtf11 parathyr mtf11 ph-ac sf phos sf *Phyt* k* plb mrr1 *Psor* k* *Puls* k* pyrog sf rad-br sf* ran-b sf* *Rhod* k* *Rhus-t* k* *Ruta* k* sabad sf sabin k* sal-ac sf* sang sf *Sars* k* *Sep* k* **Sil** k* solid bro1 spong sf *Stel* sf* stict sf* sul-i mg sul-ter bro1 *Sulph* k* syph hr1* tarax sf thuj sf tub sf* tub-r mtf11 urt-u sf valer mrr1 verat sf verat-v viol-t bro1 visc mg
  - **evening**: acon k* merc k2
  - **night**: acon k* **Iod** k* kalm mrr1 *Lac-ac* hr1 mang k* *Rhod*
  - **accompanied** by:
    - **erythema** nodosum: **Chinin-s** mrr1
    - **Lung**; cancer of (See CHEST - Cancer - lung - accompanied - joints)
    - **Uterus**; complaints of (See FEMALE - Complaints - uterus - accompanied - arthritis)
  - **chronic**: allox mtf11 *Am-p* bro1 ant-c bro1 arb bro1 arn bro1 *Ars* bro1 *Benz-ac* bro1 *Berb* bro1 cal-ren bro1 calc bro1 calc-f bro1 calc-p bro1 caul bro1 *Caust* bro1 *Chin* bro1 *Cimic* bro1 colch bro1 colchin bro1 ferr-i bro1 ferr-pic bro1 *Guaj* bro1 hep bro1 *Iod* bro1 *Kali-br* bro1 *Kali-i* bro1 lac-ac bro1 l e d bro1 lyc bro1 *Merc* bro1 merc-c bro1 nat-br bro1 nat-p bro1 nat-s bro1 osteo-a mtf11 phyt bro1 *Pipe* bro1 *Puls* bro1 rad-br bro1 *Rhus-t* bro1 *Ruta* bro1 sabin bro1 sal-ac bro1 sep bro1 sil bro1 staph bro1 *Stel* bro1 *Sul-ter* bro1 s u l p h bro1 thyr bro1 tub bro1

Extremities

- **Joints**: ...
  - • **erratic**: p-benzq mtf11
  - • **erysipelatous**: *Bry* k* rhod
  - • **gonorrhea**; after suppressed (See Pain - joints - rheumatic - gonorrhea)
  - • **infectious**: osteo-a mtf11
  - • **psoriatic**: *(↗SKIN - Eruptions - psoriasis)* sulph mrr1
  - • **sudden**: *Kalm* mrr1
  - • **synovitis**: *Acon* bro1 ant-t c1* apis k* arn bro1 bell k* berb bro1 bry k* calc k* calc-f ptk1 canth bro1 caust k* ferr-p k* fl-ac bro1 *Hep* bro1 iod k* kali-c k* kali-i k* led k* lyc k* merc k* myris c1 phyt k* puls k* rhus-t k* ruta bro1 *Sabin* bro1 sep k* sil k* slag bro1 stict bro1 sulph k* verat-v k*
  - • **warmth** agg. | **heat** agg.: guaj led sulph mrr1
  - ○ • **Small** joints: lith-c mrr1 streptoc jl2
- **Knees**: *Acon* bro1 *Agn* b7a.de *Apis* k* *Arn* k* ars-s-f k2 bar-c bg2 *Bar-m* k* bell bg2* *Benz-ac* k* berb bg2 **Bry** k* *Calc* canth bro1 *Chin* b7.de* cist bro1 *Cocc* k* colch bg2 eup-per k2 *Fl-ac Guaj* hell bro1 *Hep* bro1 *Iod* k* kali-c bro1 *Kali-i* bro1* kalm bg2* lac-ac *Led* k* lyc bg1 merc bg1 nat-p tl1 nat-s bg2 *Nux-v* k* petr bg2 *Phos* k* phyt *Psor* **Puls** k* *Rhus-t* k* ruta bro1 sal-ac tl2 *Sars* sil k* *Slag* bro1 stict bro1* *Sulph* k* tub verat-v bg2
  - • **chronic**: ant-t bro1 *Benz-ac* bro1 berb bro1 *Calc-f* bro1 calc-p bro1 hep bro1 *Iod* bro1 *Kali-i* bro1 *Merc* bro1 phyt bro1 rhus-t bro1 ruta bro1 *Sil* bro1 tub bro1
  - • **erysipelatous**: nux-v **Rhus-t** sulph
  - • **gonorrhea**; suppressed: *Med* sil
  - • **hygroma** (See bursae)
  - • **synovitis**: mez mtf11
  - ○ • **Below** knees: allox sp1
  - • **Bursae**: *(↗fingers - joints - bursitis; Bursae; GENERALS - Inflammation - bursae)* *Apis* c2* arn c2 bry mld4 calc-f mld4 hep mld4 *Kali-i* c2 kali-m br1 nat-m ptk1 *Rhus-t* c2 ruta tl1* sil c2* slag c2 *Stict* c2* syc pte1*•
  - • **Hollow** of | **menses**; before: *Puls* b7a.de
  - • **Joints**: bry mtf11 conv mtf11 gins mtf11 *Morg* fmm1• morg-g fmm1• parathyr jl2 stict mtf11
    - ⁝ **purulent**: parathyr jl2
    - ⁝ **weather** agg.; wet: erig mtf11
- **Legs**: *Acon* k* ars-s-f k2 aur b4a.de *Borx* k* bov *Calc* k* com lyc b4a.de nat-c k* phos b4.de* *Puls* b7.de* sil b4.de* sulph k* zinc b4a.de
  - • **dancing**; after: *Borx* k*
  - • **epistaxis**; with: borx
  - • **erysipelatous**: anan **Apis** arn k* ars *Bell* b4a.de *Borx* k* *Bufo Calc* k* *Dulc* b4a.de *Graph* b4a.de *Hep* k* *Hydr Kali-c* b4a.de **Lach** lyc merc k* *Nat-c* k* *Puls Rhus-t Sil Sulph* k* *Ter Thuj* b4a.de zinc k*
  - ○ • **Bones**:
    - ⁝ **Tibia**: ang c1 *Asaf Aur* aur-m k2 *Calc Guaj* hecla kali-i lach **Ph-ac** **Phos** sabad b7a.de **Sil** *Still* stront-c
      - ⁝ **Nerve**: pareir bro1
  - • **Periosteum**: **Asaf** *Aur Kali-bi* **Led** *Merc Ph-ac* **Phos** sil still *Sulph*
  - • **Tendo** Achillis: *Sep Zinc*
- **Ligaments**: bry k2 sil mtf33
- **Lower** limbs:
  - • **erysipelatous**: *Borx* hr1 *Sulph* k*
  - ○ • **Psoas** muscles: *Calc*
    - ⁝ **suppuration** seems impending, also if pelvic bones are involved; if: asaf k1
  - • **Sciatic** nerve: aesc bro1
    - ⁝ **right**: mand sp1
  - • **Veins** (See GENERALS - Inflammation - blood - veins)
- **Lymphatics**: *Bufo* mrr1* cupr st iod st lach st mygal st
  - • **elephantiasis** arabum: myris c1
  - ○ • **Arm**; of: **Bufo** cupr h2
  - • **Forearms**: sulph mrr1
- **Pulp** of nails (See Felon - root)
- **Shoulders**: ferr-p k2
  - • **periarthritis** humeroscapularis: apis mtf11 guaj mtf11 med jl2

Inflammation: ...

- **Tendons** (= tendinitis): *(↗GENERALS - Inflammation - tendons)* ant-c c1 aur-m-n wbt2• bry mrr1 kali-chl c kali-m c1 lil-t mrr1 penic mtf11 **Phyt** mrr1 *Rhod* **Rhus-t** k •* sil mtf33
- **Thighs**: nat-c k* rhus-t k* *Sil* k*
  - • **erysipelatous**: sulph bro1
  - ○ • **Femur**, periosteum of: *Aur Mez Phyt*
  - • **Inner** side: allox sp1
- **Thumbs**: nat-c h2* positr nl2• sars h2*
- **Toes**: am-c k* apoc k2 berb borx br1 carb-an k* caust hell b7a.de hydrog srj2• lach *Nit-ac* k* ph-ac phos k* *Puls* k* *Sabad* b7a.de *Sabin* b7a.de sep k* sil ptk1 sulph k* tarent k* teucr k* *Thuj* k* zinc k*
  - • **erysipelatous**: **Apis**
  - • **frostbitten**: *Agar*
    - ⁝ **as** if: borx h2
  - • **wet** agg.; after getting feet: nit-ac k*
  - ○ • **Balls**: borx br1
  - • **First** toe: *Am-c* positr nl2• ran-s ptk1 sulph h2*
    - ⁝ **Ball**: phos h2
  - • **Joints**: am-c bro1 *Benz-ac* bro1 borx bro1 both bro1 carb-v bro1 *Caul* mrr1 *Colch* bro1 daph bro1 kali-c k2 *Led* bro1 *Rhod* bro1 teucr bro1
  - • **Nails**: sabad bro1
    - ⁝ **Around**: moni jl2 sil c1
    - ⁝ **Under**: sabad br1* sil c1
- **Upper** arm | **erysipelatous**: bell k* euph b4.de* petr k* rhus-t b7.de* sep b4a.de *Sil* b4a.de
- **Upper** limbs: *Ant-c* b7a.de* arg-met ars-s-f k2 crot-h k* cupr k* kali-bi k* kali-i k* lach k* merc petr k* ran-b k* *Rhus-t* k* rhus-v k* sep
  - • **erysipelatous**: am-c *Apis* arn *Ars* bell bufo *Carb-ac* form *Hippoz* *Kali-c* kalm **Lach** petr k* *Ph-ac* **Rhus-t** k* rhus-v scol a1*
    - ⁝ **burning**: petr h2*
  - • **phlegmonous**: rhus-t rhus-v k*
  - • **spots**, in: merc-c k*
  - ○ • **Joints**: *Agn* b7a.de
  - • **Nerves**: morg-g fmm1• morg-p fmm1•
    - ⁝ **night**: morg-p fmm1•
- **Wrists**: abrot tl1 euph k* rhus-t k* syc pte1*•
  - • **painful**: syc bka1•
  - • **warm** water | **amel.**: syc bka1•
  - • **weather**; warm | **amel.**: syc bka1•
  - ○ • **Skin**: syc fmm1•

INFLUENZA; after: | **Lower** limbs: gels bg2

INGROWING NAILS (See Nails - ingrowing)

INJURIES: *(↗Paralysis - lower - injuries; GENERALS - Injuries)*

- **after** | **Upper** limbs: **Arn** b7.de* lach b7.de* puls b7.de* **Rhus-t** b7.de* *Ruta* b7.de*
- **bites** (See GENERALS - Wounds - bites)
- **penetrating**: hyper tl1 led tl1
- **surgical**: [bell-p-sp dcm1]
- ○ - **Ankles**: *Arn Calc* des-ac rbp6 pieri-b mlk9.de *Rhus-t Ruta Stront-c* k*
- **Elbow** | **tennis** elbow: *(↗GENERALS - Injuries - tennis)* agar st ambr st* arn mtf bry mtf calc-f mtf *Rhus-t* st symph bg
- **Fingers**: bufo br1 falco-pe nl2• *Hyper* br1* spong fd4.de
  - • **accompanied** by:
    - ⁝ **pain**:
      - ⁝ **aching**: led k2
      - ⁝ **extending** to | **Arm**; in streaks up the: *(↗Pain - fingers - extending - upward)* bufo br1
      - ⁝ **shooting**: hyper k2
  - • **amputated** stump painful●: *(↗Pain - amputations; GENERALS - Pain - amputation)* *All-c* k2 ph-ac hr1 phos *Staph*
  - • **cuts**: ina-i mlk9.de
  - • **dissecting** wounds●: *Apis* **Ars** hydrog srj2• **Lach** sil sne

- **Fingers**: ...
  - **painful**:
    - ⁝ **aching** pain: led k2
    - ⁝ **shooting** pain: hyper k2
  - ○ **Nails**, of●: hydrog srj2• hyper k* *Led*
    - ⁝ **lacerations**●: **Hyper**
    - ⁝ **splinter** of glass: *Sil*
    - ⁝ **Matrix** (See root)
    - ⁝ **Root** of nail: hyper bro1
  - **Tips**, crushed and lacerated: arist-cl sp1 *Carb-ac* st dulc fd4.de **Hyper** k* *Led* *Ruta* st spong fd4.de
- **Foot**:
  - **contusion**: prot jl2
  - ○ **Heel**: *Psor* jl2
  - **Sole** | **painful**: hyper bro1
- **Hand**:
  - **contusion**●: *Arn* spong fd4.de
  - **fracture** with laceration●: *Hyper*
  - **lacerations**: **Calen** hyper spong fd4.de
  - **sprain**●: **Arn** *Bell-p* st1 *Calc* *Rhus-t* *Ruta*
  - ○ **Palm** | **painful**: hyper bro1
- **Hips**: con *Rhus-t* sil tarent
- **Joints**: arn k2 bry k2 rhus-t mrr1 [bell-p-sp dcm1]
- **Legs** | **Tendo** Achillis: taosc iwa1• [irid-met stj]
- **Nerves**: (↗*GENERALS - Injuries - nerves*) hyper tl1 [bell-p-sp dcm1]
  - **sentient**: hyper k2
- **Shoulders**: *Ferr-m* *Rhus-t* zinc
  - **rheumatic** lameness, with: *Ferr-m*
  - **straining**, after: *Rhus-t*
- **Soft** parts: arn tl1 hyper tl1
- **Tendons**: symph mtf11
- **Thigh**:
  - **contusion**:
    - ⁝ **right**: bros-gau mrc1
    - ⁝ **bending** the body forward | **agg.**: bros-gau mrc1
    - ⁝ **Posterior** part: bros-gau mrc1
- **Thumbs**: petr-ra shn4•
  - **bite** of a cat: *Lach* *Led*
- **Toes**: *Hyper* br1
  - **lacerated**: hyper k2
  - ○ **Nails**: *Hyper* br1
- **Upper** limbs: lyc bg2 zinc bg2
- **Wrists**●: *Arn* *Bry* mp1• *Calc* *Hyper* mp1• *Rhus-t* *Ruta* sil spong fd4.de *Stront-c*

INSECURE: visc sp1
- **walking** (See Incoordination - lower)

INSENSIBILITY: (↗*Numbness*)
- ○ **Feet**: bell bg2 nat-m bg2
  - **touch** and stitches; to: acon vh1 ant-c h2*
  - ○ **Soles**: ars bg2 chel bg2 sec bg2
- **Fingers**: caust bg2 colch bg2 ferr bg2 kali-c bg2 *Kreos* bg2 *Phos* bg2 sec bg2
  - **heat** of stove; to: *Plb* thuj
  - ○ **Tips**: ang b7.de* ant-t b7.de* ars bg2 cann-s b7.de* cham b7.de* coff b7.de* colch b7a.de cupr b7a.de ferr b7.de* kreos b7a.de m-aust b7.de mag-m bg2 *Sec* b7a.de spong b7.de* stann bg2 **Staph** b7.de*
    - ⁝ **pricking** and pinching; to: pop-cand a2*
- **Forearm**:
  - **heat** of stove, to: *Plb* thuj
  - **pain**, to: kreos *Plb*
  - **touch**; to | **left**: chin-b hr1 nux-v hr1*
- **Hands**: acon vh1 stram h1*
  - **burning**, to: *Plb* k*
  - **pain**, to: kreos plb
  - **pricking**, to: plb k*

Insensibility: ...
- **Lower** limbs: am-m b7.de* ambr b7.de* ant-c b7.de* arn b7.de ars b4.de* asar b7.de* aur b4.de* bry b7.de* *Carb-v* b4.de* chel b7.de* con b4a.de* *Kreos* b7a.de **Lyc** b4.de* merc-c bg2 *Olnd* b7.de* op b7.de* ph-ac bg2 puls b7.de* sec b7.de* thuj bg2
- **Upper** limbs: acon b7.de* *Alum* b4a.de ambr b7a.de ang b7.de* ant-t b7.de* ars b4.de* aur b4.de* *Bell* b4.de* bry b7.de* caust b4.de* cocc b7.de* colch b7.de* *Con* b4a.de ferr b7.de* kali-c b4.de* kali-n b4.de* *Lyc* b4.de* m-aust b7.de mag-m b4.de* musca-d szs1 nat-m b4.de* *Nux-v* b7a.de *Olnd* b7.de* plat b4a.de puls b7.de* *Rhus-t* b7.de* *Sec* b7.de* spong b7.de* stann b4.de* staph b7.de* stram b7.de* stront-c b4.de* sulph b4.de* verb b7.de* zinc b4.de*

INSPIRATION:
- **agg.**:
  - ○ **Lower** limbs: alum bg2 plat bg2 sabin b7.de*
  - **Upper** limbs: agn b7.de*

INTERTRIGO (See Excoriation)

INVERSION:
- ○ **Feet**: cic ptk1 nux-v k* sec k*
- **Knees**: nat-c bg2 stann bg2
- **Lower** limbs: cic bg2* merc bg2* *Nux-v* bg2* petr bg2* **Psor** bg2* sec bg2*
- **Upper** limbs: bell bg2 laur bg2

IRRITATION of skin: (↗*Eruptions*)
- ○ **Fingers**:
  - ○ **Nails**; under: (↗*Pain - fingers - nails - under*) am-br br1
    - ⁝ **biting** nails | **amel.**: am-br br1*
- **Hands**:
  - ○ **Back** of hands: cortiso tpw7*
    - ⁝ **sun** agg.: cortiso tpw7
- **Knees**:
  - ○ **Side**: allox tpw4
    - ⁝ **night**: allox tpw4
    - ⁝ **warm** bathing agg.: allox tpw4
- **Legs** | **Knees**; below: allox tpw4
- **Thighs** | **warmth** agg. | **heat** agg.: allox tpw4
  - ○ **Inner** side: allox tpw4

ISCHIAS (See Pain - lower limbs - sciatic)

ITCHING: abrot k* **Agar** k* aloe *Alum* alum-sil k2 alumn am-c k* am-m ambr anac ant-c ant-t apis arn *Ars* k* ars-i ars-s-f k2 arund br1* asc-t aster aur aur-ar k2 aur-i k2 bar-c bar-i k2 bar-m bar-s k2 bell berb *Bism* bov k* brach bry *Calc* calc-i *Calc-s* calc-sil k2 cann-s canth carb-ac carb-v carbn-s cassia-s ccrh1• *Caust* chel chin chinin-ar choc srj3• chord-umb rly4• cimic cinnb clem coc-c cocc coli rly4• coloc com k* con k* corn cupr cycl cystein-l rly4• dig dios dulc fago k* gran graph grat ham k* hura ign indg k* iod jug-c jug-r *Kali-ar* kali-bi kali-br k* kali-c k* kali-i kali-n kali-p kali-s kola stb3• lac-ac k* lach lachn laur led luf-op rsj5• lyc k* mag-c mag-m mag-s malar jl2 mand rsj7• mang merc k* merc-i-f mez mill mur-ac nat-ar nat-c nat-m nat-p k* **Nat-s** nicc nicc-met sk4• nicotam rly4• nit-ac *Nux-v* k* ol-an olnd op osm paeon k* pall k* petr-ra shn4• ph-ac *Phos* k* phyt plac-s rly4• plat *Plb* prun prun-v bro1 *Psor* puls ran-b *Rhus-t* rhus-v rumx ruta sabad sal-fr sle1• sars sel *Sep* *Sil* *Spig* spong **Sulph** tarent **Tell** thuj til *Trios* rsj11• tritic-vg fd5.de urol-h rwt• valer bro1 vanil fd5.de ven-m rsj12• verat zinc k* zinc-p k2 [*Buteo-j* sej6 *Spect* dfg1]
- **left**: dream-p sdj1• sulph h2*
- **morning** | **rising** agg.: *Rumx*
- **forenoon**: com k* dulc fd4.de
- **noon**: cassia-s ccrh1•
- **afternoon**: fago k* spong fd4.de
- **evening**: alum-p k2 com k* daph k* dulc fd4.de ruta fd4.de spong fd4.de tell rsj10• vanil fd5.de
  - **bed** agg.; in: sulph h2* vanil fd5.de
- **night**: cassia-s ccrh1•
  - **bed** agg.; in: rumx
- **air**; in open | **amel.**: cassia-s ccrh1•
- **bathing** | **amel.**: cassia-s ccrh1•
- **bed** agg.; in: cassia-s ccrh1• fago k* lyc k* nux-v k* rumx
- **burning** on scratching: lach nat-p phos rumx sabad sabin **Sulph**
- **coition**; after: agar
- **cold** applications | **amel.**: cassia-s ccrh1• tritic-vg fd5.de

Extremities

- **eruptions** (See Eruptions - itching)
- **heat** of the sun agg.: cassia-s ccrh1•
- **paralyzed** limb: phos
- **perspiration**: cassia-s ccrh1•
- **rest** agg.: psor jl2
- **scratching**:
  - **agg.**: *Alum* alum-p k2 ars ars-s-f k2 *Bism* cassia-s ccrh1• corn ham *Led* petr ph-ac rhus-v spong fd4.de streptoc rly4• stront-c **Sulph** thioc-ac rly4•
  - **amel.**: alum ant-t bov camph cann-i chel chin coloc cypra-eg sde6.de• graph *Jug-c* *Kali-c* laur led *Mag-c* mag-m malar jl2 *Mang* merc mill **Nat-c** nat-s nicc ol-an olnd pall ph-ac ruta fd4.de spong fd4.de tarax *Thuj* tritic-vg fd5.de vanil fd5.de
- **symmetrical**: rhus-g tmo3•
- **undressing** agg.: cassia-s ccrh1• *Nat-s* k* rumx
- **warm** | **applications** | **agg.**: cassia-s ccrh1•
  - **bed** | **agg.**: cortico sp1* sulph k2
- ○ **Ankles**: acon bg2 agar h2* agath-a nl2• ambr b7.de* ant-c b7.de* apis k* aur b4a.de* berb k* borx h2 bov k* bros-gau mrc1 cact k* calc k* carb-ac k* *Chel* k* cocc k* com k* cycl b7.de* dig b4.de* dios k* galla-q-r nl2• ham fd3.de• hep k* ign b7.de* ina-i mlk9.de jug-c k* kali-c k* kali-p fd1.de• *Lach* k* **Led** k* lith-c k* lyc k* *Mez* b4.de* mur-ac b4.de* *Nat-p* k* nat-sil fd3.de• olnd k* osm k* pall k* ped a1 ph-ac b4.de* puls bro1 ran-b k* rhus-t k* rhus-v k* ruta fd4.de *Sel* k* sep k* spong fd4.de stann b4.de* staph b7.de* sulph k* symph fd3.de• thea urol-h rwt• vinc viol-t b7.de*
  - **left**: bros-gau mrc1 mim-p rsj8•
  - **morning**: sep k*
    - **bed** agg.; in: kali-c k*
  - **evening**: rhus-v k* *Sel* sep k* spong fd4.de sulph k*
  - **night**: ham fd3.de• hep k* spong fd4.de
  - **biting**: berb k*
  - **burning**: berb k* calc h2* *Lith-c* petr h2* staph h1*
    - **sleep**; when falling asleep: mur-ac h2
  - **corrosive**: dig h2*
  - **red** from scratching: ph-ac h2* ruta fd4.de
  - **scratching** agg.: *Led* k*
  - **spots**: galla-q-r nl2• vinc
  - **sticking**: berb k*
  - **tingling**: com k*
  - **walking** agg.: aur h2* cocc k* dios k*
  - **warmth**:
    - **agg.**: **Led** rhus-v k*
    - **amel.**: cocc k*
  - ○ **Below**: ant-c h2*
  - **Inner**: spong fd4.de tarax h1*
    - **right**: staph h1*
  - **Malleoli**, around: arist-m br1 borx a1
    - **Externally**: petr a1 staph a1
  - **Sides** | **Outer**: petr h2* ruta fd4.de spong fd4.de
- **Elbows**: agar k* alum k* am-m bg2 arg-met k* berb calc-i k* canth bg2 caust k* coloc b4.de* crot-h k* cycl k* dol br1* dulc bg2 fago k* hep b4a.de* ign k* indg k* kali-n k* lach bg2 lachn k* laur k* mang med *Merc* k* merc-i-f mur-ac k* **Nat-c** k* nat-p ol-an k* olnd bg2 pall k* petr k* petr-ra shn4• phos k* psor k* puls bg2 rhus-t b7.de* rhus-v k* sabad b7.de* sacch-a fd2.de• sel rsj9• *Sep* k* spig bg2 spong fd4.de *Sulph* k* trios rsj11• tritic-vg fd5.de vanil fd5.de
  - **left**: psor jl2
  - **evening**: *Sulph* k*
  - **rubbing** | **amel.**: ol-an k*
  - **scratching** | **amel.**: mang a1 ol-an k* vanil fd5.de
  - ○ **Bends** of elbow: am-m b7.de* canth k* carbn-s cupr cypra-eg sde6.de• *Hep* k* kali-p fd1.de• laur k* nat-c k* nit-ac k* ol-an olnd a1 petr k* phos h2* podo fd3.de• psor rumx sel bro1 **Sep** k* spig h1* spong fd4.de sulph k* symph fd3.de• ter k*
    - **afternoon**: spong fd4.de sulph k*
    - **evening**: cupr k* spong fd4.de sulph h2*
  - **Olecranon**: agar k* ars-met mag-m k* nit-ac k* olnd k* phos bg2 puls k* sep h2* spig b7.de*
- **Extensor** surface: coc-c k*
- **Feet**: *Agar* k* alum k* am-c k* am-m bro1 anac k* ant-s-aur c1* apis k* *Ars* k* arum-t asaf b7.de* aur k* aur-ar k2 *Bell* k* *Berb* k* bism k* *Bov* k* bry k* *Calc* k* cann-i a1 cann-s cann-xyz bg2 canth k* *Caust* k* cer-s a1 cham k* *Chel* k* *Cocc* k* coloc k* con k* corn k* crot-c k* dios k* dream-p sdj1• dulc fago k* graph b4.de* hep a1 hip-ac sp1 hipp a1 hura k* hydrog srj2• *Ign* k* ina-i mlk9.de jug-r k* kali-ar kali-c k* kali-n a1 *Lach* k* laur b7.de* **Led** k* lyc k* m-aust b7.de mag-c k* magn-gr bro1 maias-l hm2• mang b4.de* merc-i-f k* moni rfm1• mur-ac k* nat-m k* nat-p k* nat-s bro1 nat-sil fd3.de• nit-ac k* nux-v k* ol-an k* pant-ac rly4• phyt k* pic-ac bg2* pieri-b mlk9.de psor k* puls k* ran-s k* rhod b4.de* *Rhus-t* k* rhus-v k* ruta b7.de* sabad k* sal-fr sle1• sars k* *Sel* k* **Sep** k* *Sil* b4.de* spong k* stann b4.de* stram k* stroph-h ptk1 sul-i **Sulph** k* tarent k* *Tell* k* thuj k* tritic-vg fd5.de vanil fd5.de verat k* verat-v viol-t b7.de* *Zinc* k* [sol-ecl cky1 spect dfg1]
  - **right**: coli rly4•
  - **morning**: arge-pl rwt5•
  - **afternoon**: fago k*
  - **evening**: corn a1 dream-p sdj1• kali-c k* nux-v k* sel k* vanil fd5.de zinc k*
  - **night**: *Apis* canth k* dulc fd4.de **Led** *Lith-c* puls h1* *Rhus-t* sabad k*
    - **midnight**, before: puls k*
  - **bed** agg.; in: *Apis* **Led** k* merc-i-f k* *Puls* bro1 rhus-t bro1 *Sulph* tub c1 zinc
  - **biting**: bell k* berb k* spong k* tritic-vg fd5.de
  - **burning**: berb k* stram
  - **cold** agg.; becoming: tarent k*
  - **cold** bathing | **amel.**: [sol-ecl cky1]
  - **frozen**; as if: **Agar (non:**kali-c kl)
    - **had** been frozen; as if it: caust h2 kali-c h2*
  - **motion** | **amel.**: psor k* rhus-v spig
  - **rubbing** agg.: corn k*
  - **scratching**:
    - **agg.**: bism corn k* *Led* k* *Puls* bro1 rhus-t bro1
    - **amel.**: cann-i k*
  - **sticking**: berb k* lach k* puls h1* zinc
  - **tickling**: bry k*
  - **walking** agg.; after: alum spong fd4.de
  - **warming** up agg.: rhus-v k*
  - ○ **Back** of feet: agar k* alum k* anac k* apis k* asaf k* bell k* berb k* *Bism* k* bros-gau mrc1 calc k* **Caust** k* chel k* coloc h2* dig k* hep k* ign b7.de* lac-h sk4• lach k* **Led** k* mag-m k* mosch b7a.de nat-c h2* nat-m k* nat-s k* nat-sil fd3.de• nit-ac k* olnd a1 ped a1 podo fd3.de• puls k* ran-s k* *Rhus-t* k* sars k* spig k* stann k* stram bg2 *Tarax* k* thuj k*
    - **left**: adam skp7• bros-gau mrc1
    - **morning** | **bed** agg.; in: *Puls*
    - **evening**: nat-s k*
      - **undressing**: apis *Nat-s* k*
    - **night**: dig k*
    - **biting**: berb k*
    - **burning**: berb k*
    - **corrosive**: agar h2*
    - **scratching**:
      - **agg.**: berb k* *Bism* k* *Led* k*
      - **amel.**: mag-m k* nat-s k* tarax k*
    - **sticking**: berb k* mur-ac h2*
    - **warm** bed agg.: apis **Led** k* merc-i-f sulph zinc
  - **Heels**: berb k* bov k* calc h2* card-m *Caust* k* cham k* fl-ac k* ign b7.de* lach k* lob k* lyc med ptk1 mur-ac h2* nat-c k* nat-m bg2 nicc k* olnd k* *Ph-ac* k* *Phos* k* puls h1* ran-s b7.de* rat sabin k* sel b7.de* staph k* tarent bg1 vanil fd5.de verat k* viol-t b7.de*
    - **right**: carbn-dox knl3•
    - **left**: mag-p bg2 melal-alt gya4 nicc k*
    - **rubbing** | **amel.**: mur-ac h2*
    - **scratching** | **amel.**: caust h2*
    - **warm** bed agg.: caust
  - **Joints**: aur k* calc dig kali-c *Mez* mur-ac ph-ac stann

- **Outer** side of: grat k* merc-i-f k* sars k* spong fd4.de
  - **stinging**: merc-i-f k*
- **Sides**: nicc-met sk4•
  - **Inner**: *Ambr* bov k* bufo caust bg2 laur k*
- **Sole** of: *Agar* k* *Alum* k* alum-sil k2 *Am-c* k* am-m k* *Ambr* k* ammc anan bro1 ant-t b7.de* anth bro1* arge-pl rwt5• aur k* bell bg2 *Berb* k* bov k* brach k* cadm-met tpw6 *Calc-s* k* cann-i k* caust k* cer-s a1 cere-b a1 cham k* *Chel* k* chin b7.de* cimic bg1* con k* crot-c k* cupr k* dros b7.de* dulc fd4.de elaps euph k* ferr-ma gins k* graph k* ham fd3.de• *Hep* k* *Hydr* bro1 *Hydrc* k* ind bro1 kali-n k* *Kali-p* kreos k* lith-c mang h2* med k* merc-i-f k* mur-ac k* nat-c k* nat-m k* nat-s bro1 ol-an k* olnd b7.de* ped a1 petr k2 phos k* *Propr* sa3• psil ft1 psor k* ran-s k* rat k* rheum h* rhus-t bg2 sabin b7.de* sal-fr sle1• sars k* sel k* sep h2* *Sil* k* spig b7.de* spong fd4.de stry k* *Sulph* k* tarax b7.de* tarent ptk1 *Trios* rsj11• tritic-vg fd5.de vanil fd5.de *Zinc* k*
  - **right**: maias-l hrn2• ulm-c jsj8•
  - **left**: ulm-c jsj8•
  - **afternoon**, 14 h: ol-an
  - **evening**: am-c k* am-m k* phos k* sel k* *Trios* rsj11•
  - **night**: dulc fd4.de sal-fr sle1• sars h2* *Zinc* k*
  - **bed** agg.; in: *Trios* rsj11•
  - **biting**: berb k* tritic-vg fd5.de
  - **burning**: berb k* kali-n k* petr k2 psor ptk1
    - **scratching** agg.; after: am-c
  - **eruptions**; without: alum-sil k4
  - **motion** | **amel.**: mur-ac k* olnd k* sars h2*
  - **prickling**: crot-t k*
  - **pulsating**: flor-p rsj3•
    - **left** foot: flor-p rsj3•
  - **scratching** | **amel.**: chin k*
  - **sitting** agg.: chin k*
  - **sticking**: berb k*
  - **tickling**: alum k* euph k* kali-n k* mang a1
  - **voluptuous**: rat k*
    - **scratching** agg.; after: sil
  - **walking** agg.: chin k* mur-ac k* **Sulph** k*
  - **warm** applications agg.: trios rsj11•
  - **wine** agg.: psor k*

\- **Fingers**: *Agar* k* agath-a nl2• *Alum* k* alum-sil k2 am-c k* am-m bg2 ambr bg2 **Anac** k* anag mtf11 ant-c bg2 apis k* am b7.de* ars k* ars-h arum-d k* arum-i a1 arum-t k2 asc-t aur k* berb k* borx bg2 calad k* calc k* camph b7.de* cann-s k* canth b7.de* carb-an h2* carb-v k* *Caust* k* cent a1 chel b7.de* chord-umb rly4• cit-v k* coc-c k* cocc bg2 *Con* k* crot-h bg2 cycl b7.de* cystein-l rly4• euph k* grat bg2 ham fd3.de• hep k* ign bg2 jatr-c jug-r k* lach k* lact k* laur bg2 lith-c bg2 lol bg2 lyc k* m-arct b7.de mag-c k* mang k* merc k* mez k* nat-c k* nat-m k* nux-v k* olnd b7.de* ox-ac paull a1 petr k* ph-ac bg2 phos k* plan k* plat k* plb bg2 podo fd3.de• prun k* *Psor* bg2* puls k* ran-b k* ran-s bg2 *Rhod* k* rhus-v k* ruta fd4.de sabad b7a.de sel k* sil k* spig bg2 spong fd4.de staph b7.de* stry k* *Sul-ac* k* **Sulph** k* tarent k* ther bg2 thuj *Trios* vml3• tritic-vg fd5.de **Urt-u** k* vanil fd5.de verat b7.de* verb bg2 zinc k*

- **afternoon**: coc-c k* jug-r k* spong fd4.de
- **evening**: calad podo fd3.de• spong fd4.de sulph k*
  - **bed** agg.; in: nat-m k*
- **bed**; when going to: nux-v
- **burning**: calc a1 euph h2*
- **cool**, when: thuj k*
- **frozen**, as if they had been: *Agar* spig h1*
  - **formerly**: lyc h2*
- **lying** agg.: calad k*
- **scratching** agg.: alum h2* ars k* arum-d
- **smoking** agg.: calad
- **warm** room agg.: nux-v k*
- ○ **Back** of fingers: ars k* berb borx b4a.de carb-an k* caust h2* **Con** k* merc-i-r k* nat-m k* sars k* sulph k*
- **Basis** of fingers | **left**: lavand-a ctl1•

\- **Fingers**: ...

- **Between**: alum bg2 anac bg2 aur bg2 brom bg2 chord-umb rly4• hep bro1 med hr1 morg-p pte1*• ph-ac bro1 *Psor* bro1 scroph-n c1 sel bro1 sep bro1 tritic-vg fd5.de
- **First**: agar k* agath-a nl2• anac k* calc carb-an k* caust k* crot-h k* fl-ac k* hell hura lach k* lyc h2* nat-c h2 nat-m k* ozone sde2• ped a1 petr-ra shn4• plat h2* podo fd3.de• sil symph fd3.de• teucr k* tritic-vg fd5.de
  - **evening**: fl-ac k*
  - **spot**; small: ozone sde2•
  - **Joints**:
    - **Distal**: nat-c h2* petr k* viol-t a1
    - **Middle**: euph h2* manc k* nat-m h2*
    - **Proximal**: berb k* fl-ac k* verat k* verat-v a1
  - **Phalanx**; middle and distal: lyc h2*
  - **Tip**: am-m k* nat-m k*
    - **morning**: am-m k*
    - **scratching** does not amel.: am-m k*
- **Fourth** finger: anac h2* arizon-l nl2• asc-t k* con k* cystein-l rly4• lach k* lyc k* ol-an k* peti a1 podo fd3.de• spong fd4.de tritic-vg fd5.de
  - **night**: sulph k*
- **Joints**: alum apis *Borx* bry *Camph* k* caust h2* hydr k* nux-v k* petr k* sal-fr sle1• sel c1*
  - **Back** of: *Borx*
- **Nails**:
  - **Around**: *Hep* merc k*
  - **Root**: upa br1*
  - **Under**: sep h2*
- **Second**: ars k* ars-h chel k* crot-h k* crot-t k* cystein-l rly4• gran k* kali-n k* lith-c nat-m k* olnd k* ph-ac k* rhod k* teucr k* vanil fd5.de verat k* verb k*
  - **Basis** of finger | **left**: lavand-a ctl1•
- **Third** fingers: asc-t crot-h crot-t lith-c *Rhod* ruta fd4.de sal-fr sle1• teucr ther
- **Tips**: am-m b7.de* ambr k* ant-c b7.de* hep b4a.de nat-m bg2 plat k* prun k* sars bg2 spig k* *Sul-ac* k*

\- **Forearms**: *Agar* k* am-c k* am-m k* anac k* arge-pl rwt5• berb k* bol-la borx bov k* *Carb-an* k* carb-v h2* carbn-s caust k* chinin-s choc srj3• cit-v k* clem k* colch k* con h2* cop k* dulc k* euph k* gels hura hyos b7.de* kali-bi k* kali-c bg2 kali-n k* kola stb3• *Lac-leo* sk4• laur k* mag-c k* mag-m k* mag-s k* mang merc bg2 merc-i-f k* mez k* mill a1 mur-ac k* myric k* ol-an k* ped a1 peti a1 petr-ra shn4• psor *Puls* k* ran-b b7.de* rat k* rhus-g tmo3• *Rhus-t* k* rhus-v ros-d wla1 rumx sars k* spig k* spong fd4.de streptoc rly4• stront-c k* sulph k* symph fd3.de• tax k* til k* tritic-vg fd5.de urol-h rwt• vanil fd5.de verb k* wies a1

- **right**: sulfonam ks2 ulm-c jsj8• vanil fd5.de
- **left**: mim-p rsj8• olib-sac wmh1
- **morning**: am-m k* mag-c k* peti a1 tax k*
- **noon**: cassia-s ccrh1•
- **evening**: am-m k* ped a1 vanil fd5.de
  - **bed** agg.; in: sars
  - **undressing**: mag-c h2*
- **night**: am-m k* anac k* asc-t k* cassia-s ccrh1• *Mez* psil ft1
  - **amel.**: tax k*
- **burning**: agar k* calad carb-v h2* euph h2* *Kali-bi*
- **cold** applications | **amel.**: cassia-s ccrh1•
- **corrosive**: ars h2*
- **lying** down agg.; after: kali-bi k*
- **red** spot on scratching: mag-c h2* ros-d wla1 tritic-vg fd5.de
- **rubbing**; after: sulph h2*
- **scratching** | **amel.**: choc srj3• dulc h1 mag-c k* mill k* ol-an k* tritic-vg fd5.de
- **spots**, in: kali-n k* lac-del hrn2•
- **voluptuous**: merc k*
- **warm** applications agg.: cassia-s ccrh1•
- **washing** agg.: mag-c h2*
- ○ **Anterior** part: am-c k* am-m berb k* bov k* carb-an k* mag-c k* ol-an k* sars k* symph fd3.de•

- **Posterior** part: ulm-c jsj8•

\- **Hands**: **Agar** k* agath-a nl2• aloe *Alum* k* alum-p k2 alum-sil k2 am-m bg2 ambr **Anac** k* anag mrr1* ant-s-aur *Anthraci* apis arg-met ars k* asc-t k* aur k* aur-m a1 bar-c k* *Berb* k* bomb-pr a1 borx bg2 *Bov* k* bry k* calc k* *Camph* cann-s k* canth k* *Carb-an* k* *Carb-v* k* carbn-s carneg-g rwt1• *Caust* k* chinin-s cina b7.de* *Cit-v* k* clem bro1 cocc b7.de* colch k* cortico tpw7 dig bg2 dios k* dulc fd4.de euph bg2 fago k* fl-ac k* glon k* gran graph k* haliae-lc srj5• ham k* *Hep* k* ip bg2 jug-r k* kali-ar kali-bi k* *Kali-c* k* *Kali-s* kali-sil k2 kreos k* *Lach* k* *Lyc* k* med *Merc* k* merc-c b4a.de mur-ac k* *Nat-m* h2* *Nit-ac* k* ol-an k* osm k* paull a1 *Petr* petr-ra shn4• *Ph-ac* k* *Phos* k* phyt k* pieri-b mlk9.de pin-con oss2• pip-m bro1 plan k* plat k* plb b7.de* *Psor* k* ran-b k* *Rhus-t* k* rhus-v k* ruta sabad k* sars k* sel k* *Sep* k* sil spig bg2 spong fd4.de stann k* staph bg2 **Sulph** k* tarax k* tell br1* trios rsj11• tritic-vg fd5.de urol-h rwt• vanil fd5.de verat b7.de* zinc k* [spect dfg1]

- **morning**:
  - **rising** agg.: rhus-v sulph
  - **waking**; on: ham *Sulph*
- **evening**: dulc fd4.de spong fd4.de *Sulph* k*
  - **22** h: mag-c k*
  - **bed** agg.; in: phos k*
  - **lying** down agg.; after: ph-ac k*
- **night**: canth k* *Lith-c* ruta sabad k*
  - **midnight**: rhus-t k*
    - **lying** down agg.; after: kali-bi k*
- **biting**: berb k*
- **burning**: **Agar** apis arg-met *Kali-bi* kali-c h2* nat-m h2*
- **chilblains**, as from: **Agar** arg-met *Cit-v* *Puls*
- **crawling**: berb k*
- **hot** water amel.: *Rhus-t* rhus-v k*
- **motion** | **amel.**: sars k*
- **nettles**, as from: *Arum-dru* a1* nat-m h2* nit-ac k* urt-u
- **rising** from bed agg.: rhus-t sulph k*
- **rubbing** | **after** | **agg.**: *Nat-m* k* nit-ac h2*
  - **amel.**: berb k* ham k* nit-ac h2*
- **scratching**:
  - **agg.**: ars k* fago a1 ham k* *Ph-ac* rhus-v a1 **Sulph**
  - **amel.**: alum k* anac camph merc ol-an spong fd4.de
- **sticking**: berb k* lach k* merc-i-f merc-i-r k*
- **touch** agg.: psor k*
- **warm** | **applications** | **agg.**: *Cortico* tpw7
  - **bed** | **agg.**: cortico sp1
- **water**, on immersing in: rhus-v k*

○ • **Back** of hands: **Agar** alum k* anag apis k* ars-i k* borx k* calc k* *Camph* k* carb-an k* caust k* cent a1 *Cimic* k* cina k* com k* *Dig* k* *Euph* k* eupi k* fago k* flor-p rsj3• franz a1 gran k* indg k* jug-r k* kola stb3• lac-c bg2 lap-la sde8.de• lepi a1 limest-b es1• merc k* merc-i-r k* mez k* morg-p pte1• nat-c k* nat-s ol-an k* *Ph-ac* k* phos plat k* ptel k* *Puls* k* rhus-v k* rosm lgb1 rumx *Scroph-n* c1 spira a1 spong fd4.de stann k* **Sulph** k* thioc-ac rly4• tritic-vg fd5.de vanil fd5.de

  - **forenoon**: *Sulph* k*
  - **afternoon**: cimic k*
  - **evening**: cimic k* merl k* spong fd4.de **Sulph** k* vanil fd5.de
  - **night**: dig k* phos k* sulph k*
    - **rubbing**; after: rhus-v k*
  - **burning**: stann k*
  - **corroding**: merc k*
  - **flea** bites, as from: borx h2 nat-c k*
  - **scratching**:
    - **agg.**: ph-ac k*
    - **amel.**: alum camph k* merc k* ol-an k* plat h2*
  - **spots**: sulph k*
  - **stinging**: ars-i k* camph h1* phos k*
  - **warmth** agg.: *Sulph* k*

\- **Hands**: ...

- **Between** fingers: alum k* anac k* antip vh aur k* brom k* camph b7.de* carb-v carbn-s caust k* cycl k* grat kreos b7a.de lach b7.de* mag-c h2* merc bg2 nat-s k* *Ph-ac* plb b7.de* *Psor* k* *Puls* k* ran-s b7.de* rhod k* rhus-t bg2 rhus-v k* sabad bg2 scroph-n c1 sel k* **Sulph** k*
  - **morning**: **Sulph** k*
    - **waking**; on: rhus-v k* sulph k*
  - **evening**: ran-s k*
  - **night**: anac h2*
  - **First**:
    - **Thumb**; and: *Agar* k* ambr k* aur k* grat k* hura iod jatr-c kreos k* plb k* sumb k*
      - **night**: *Agar* k*
- **Palms**: agar k* alum k* ambr k* **Anac** k* anag mrr1 ant-s-aur bro1 ant-t a1 apis k* arg-met h1 arg-n arge-pl rwt5• ars aur aur-ar k2 *Benz-ac* k* berb k* calc *Camph* k* carb-v k* *Caust* k* chel k* cinnb k* com k* con k* crot-h dios k* dulc fd4.de fago bro1* form k* gink-b sbd1• *Gran* k* graph grat k* *Hep* k* hydr k* ind k* jatr-c *Kali-c* k* *Kali-p* kali-sil k2 kreos bg2* lac-c bg2 lac-del hrn2• lim bro1 lyc k* mag-c k* mag-s k* mang k* merc k* morg-p pte1• *Mur-ac* k* nat-m k* ol-an k* peti a1 petr k* phys k* pitu-gl skp7• podo fd3.de• psil ft1 ran-b k* rhodi br1 *Rhus-t* k* *Rhus-v* k* ruta b7.de* *Sel* k* sil k* spig k* spong b7.de* staph k* stram stry k* **Sulph** k* syc pte1*• symph fd3.de• ther *Trios* vml3• tritic-vg fd5.de tub bro1* tub-a br1 vanil fd5.de
  - **left**: aq-mar skp7• cench k2
  - **midnight**: rhus-t k*
  - **morning**: arge-pl rwt5• mag-c k* ol-an k* petr-ra shn4•
  - **afternoon**: form k* nat-m k* tet a1
  - **evening**: dios k* dulc fd4.de mag-c k* mang h2* ol-an k* podo fd3.de• sulph k* symph fd3.de• ther
  - **night**: **Acon** **Anac** k* carb-v k* dulc fd4.de hydr k* syc pte1*•
  - **burning**: agar k* aur-m petr k2 ran-b k* spig k*
    - **rubbing**; after: **Sulph**
  - **detergent** agg.: syc bka1•
  - **excitement** agg.: syc bka1•
  - **flour** agg.: syc bka1•
  - **jaundice**; in: ran-b ptk1
  - **licking** amel.: mang h2*
  - **periodical**, at intervals of ten or twelve hours: rhus-v
  - **rubbing** | **amel.**: anac a1 **Anag** mag-s k* ol-an a1
  - **scratching**:
    - **agg.**: mang h2
    - **amel.**: ant-t a1 chel k* graph k* grat a1 mag-c k* mang k* ol-an k* ulm-c jsj8•
  - **stinging**: ran-b k* ruta h1
  - **walking** about | **amel.**: com k*
  - **warmth** agg. | **heat** agg.: syc bka1•
  - **washing** agg.; after: rhus-v k*
  - **Balls**: con k* graph k* *Sep* k*
    - **spots**, in: *Sep* k*
  - **Fingers**; near root of: kali-c lyc

\- **Hips**: agar alum k* am-m b7a.de aur k* *Bov* k* bry k* caust k* chel dig k* dios k* iod b4.de* kali-n b4.de* lach k* led k* mag-c k* mag-m k* merc nat-c k* nat-m k* nat-p k* nicc k* osm k* ph-ac k* phos k* puls k* sars k* *Sep* k* stront-c b4.de* sulph k* zinc k*

- **morning**: alumn k*
  - **cool** agg.; becoming: dios
- **noon**: nicc k*
- **evening**: mag-m k* nicc k* zinc k*
  - **lying** down, before: mag-m
- **burning**: chel h1*
  - **scratching**; after: mag-c
- **corrosive**: led k*
- **spots**, in: osm k*
- **standing** agg.: mag-c
- **stinging**: dios k* led h1*
- **walking** agg.: chel k*

- **warm** in bed: *Sulph* k*
- ○ **Gluteal** region: coloc k* fl-ac k* mur-ac k* ph-ac k* tarax k*
- **Joints**: chel b7.de* led b7.de*
- **Tuber** ischiadicum: agar h2

- **Joints**: apis clem k* colch gk lith-c bg2 merc k* nat-p k* nux-v k* pin-s a1* sel bg2* sep k* *Spig* til a1 zinc k*
- ○ **Bends** of: hep bro1 nit-ac *Ph-ac* k* *Psor* bro1 sel k* sep h2* zinc

- **Knees**: acon agath-a nl2• ambr k* ant-c h2* ars-met asaf b7.de* asc-t aster aur k* berb k* bov k* bry k* calc-i k* *Caust* k* cinnb k* cob *Coloc* k* *Con* b4a.de dol br1* *Eos* br1 fago k* galeoc-c-h gms1• hep k* hura ign k* *Iod* b4a.de kali-c k* kali-n k* kali-p fd1.de• kalm k* lach k* lachn k* lith-c lyc k* mag-m k* *Mang* k* merc-i-f k* *Mez* k* mur-ac k* nat-c k* nat-m k* nat-p nit-ac k* petr phos k* plac-s rly4• *Psor* k* puls ptk1 ran-b b7.de* rhus-t sars k* sel rsj9• **Sulph** tetox pin2• thuj k* vanil fd5.de viol-t b7.de* *Zinc* k* [temp elm1]
  - **morning** | **6** h: lac-h sk4•
  - **evening**: *Mang* k* zinc k*
  - **night**: cinnb k*
  - **burning**:
    - ⋮ **scratching** agg.; after: nat-c h2*
    - ⋮ **sleep**; when falling asleep: mur-ac
  - **painful** after scratching: rhus-t h1
  - **scratching** | **amel.**: bov k* mag-m k* mang a1
  - **sitting** agg.: fago k*
  - **stinging**: merc-i-f k*
  - ○ **Back** of (See bend)
  - **Bend** of: agath-a nl2• am-m b7a.de ars bov k* bry b7.de* caust k* chin b7.de* cocc b7.de* coloc h2* *Con* k* galeoc-c-h gms1• lyc b4a.de* mang k* *Mez* b4a.de* *Nat-c* k* nat-m k* nit-ac h2* nux-v b7.de* phos h2* plac-s rly4• *Psor* rat k* rhus-t b7.de* *Sars* k* *Sep* k* spong k* **Sulph** k* vanil fd5.de verat a1 **Zinc** k*
    - ⋮ **right**: cortico tpw7
      - ⋮ **warm** applications agg.: cortico sp1
    - ⋮ **left**: plac-s rly4•
    - ⋮ **evening**: rat rhus-t h1* sars h2* *Zinc* k*
    - ⋮ **night**: mang h2*
    - ⋮ **biting**: lyc h2*
    - ⋮ **burning**: chin h1* lyc h2*
      - ⋮ **scratching**; after: coloc h2 rat
    - ⋮ **warm** | **bed** | **agg.**: *Cortico* tpw7
      - ⋮ **room** | **agg.**: *Cortico* tpw7
  - **Patella**: aloe asaf k* bufo caust k* hydr melal-alt gya4 nit-ac k* phos k* samb k* sars k* viol-t b7.de*
    - ⋮ **left**: bufo bg2
  - **Tendons**: rhus-t h1*

- **Legs**: **Agar** k* allox sp1 aloe *Alum* k* am-m b7a.de ambr b7.de* anac ant-c b7.de* ant-t arund k* asaf b7.de* asc-t aster bell k* bell-p bro1 berb k* bism k* bov bro1 brom bry b7.de* bufo cact **Calc** k* calc-sil k2 **Caust** k* chel k* chord-umb rly4• *Chrysar* br1 coc-c k* cocc b7.de* coloc k* con k* corn k* cortico tpw7* crot-h cupr-ar k* cypra-eg sde6.de• dulc k* euph k* *Fago* bro1 flor-p rsj3• galeoc-c-h gms1• ham fd3.de• hip-ac sp1 hura iod k* iris-fl jug-r k* kali-bi k* kali-c k* kali-n k* kali-p kali-sil k2 kola stb3• lach laur k* luf-op rsj5• *Lyc* k* merc k* **Mez** k* mosch b7.de* nat-c k* nat-m k* nat-sil fd3.de• nicc k* nicotam rly4• nit-ac bro1 nux-v k* op b7.de* osm k* pall *Petr* *Phos* k* phyt k* podo fd3.de• positr nl2• *Rhus-t* ros-d wla1 rumx k* sabad k* sabin b7.de* sars k* seneg k* sep gk **Sil** k* spig b7.de* spong fd4.de staph k* stel bro1 stram stront-c k* sulfonam ks2 **Sulph** k* tarax b7.de* tarent k* thuj trios rsj11• tritic-vg fd5.de ven-m rsj12• verat k* zinc k* [sol-ecl cky1 spect dfg1]
  - **left**: trios rsj11•
  - **morning**: nat-sil fd3.de• propr sa3• sabad k* spong fd4.de
    - ⋮ **walking** agg.; after: sulph
  - **afternoon**: coc-c k* fago k*
  - **evening**: agar h2* fago k* kali-c k* kali-n k* olib-sac wmh1 rumx sel rsj9• spong fd4.de sulph k* trios rsj11•
    - ⋮ **18** h: aster
    - ⋮ **20** h: con
    - ⋮ **bed** agg.; in: ambr h1* ros-d wla1 staph h1*
    - ⋮ **lying** agg.; after: ambr h1

- **Legs**: ...
  - **night**: cupr-ar k* hura *Mez* k* nat-m k* phyt k* positr nl2• **Rhus-t** k* rumx spong fd4.de sulfonam ks2 **Sulph** k* tritic-vg fd5.de
  - **air** agg.; in open: aster
  - **atmosphere**, exposure to: still k*
  - **bed** agg.; in: carbn-s *Cupr-ar* k* sulfonam ks2 sulph
  - **burning**: agar h2* calc h2* kali-c h2*
  - **cold** bathing | **amel.**: [sol-ecl cky1]
  - **cold**; when: dios k*
  - **corrosive**: bism bufo dig h2* euph h2* ph-ac h2*
    - ⋮ **menses**; during: inul
  - **eruptions**; without: galeoc-c-h gms1•
  - **followed** by | **ecchymoses**: allox sp1
  - **insect** bites; as of: aids nl2• carbn-dox knl3• luna kg1•
  - **paroxysms**: corn k*
  - **rubbing**:
    - ⋮ **agg.**: corn k*
    - ⋮ **amel.**: cupr-ar k*
  - **scratching** | **amel.**: laur olib-sac wmh1 podo fd3.de• spong fd4.de
  - **sleep**; before: petr-ra shn4•
  - **spots**: calc k* luna kg1•
  - **touch**:
    - ⋮ **agg.**: nat-m k* propr sa3•
    - ⋮ **feet** agg.; of: **Kali-c**
  - **undressing** agg.: agar cact cupr-ar k* dios k* *Rumx* sel rsj9•
  - **waking**; on: propr sa3• *Sulph* k* tritic-vg fd5.de
  - **warm** applications agg.: *Cortico* tpw7 trios rsj11•
  - ○ **Calves**: aloe alum k* berb k* cact calc carb-ac k* carbn-s **Caust** k* chel k* chord-umb rly4• cinnb cocc crot-c k* cycl k* euphr k* graph *Hep* hura ip k* kali-bi k* kola stb3• laur k* lyc k* mag-c k* mag-m k* *Mang* k* merc-c b4a.de mez k* mur-ac h2* nat-c k* nat-m k* *Nit-ac* ol-an k* paeon k* phos k* phyt k* rhus-g tmo3• rhus-t b7.de* rumx sabad sabin b7.de* *Sars* k* sul-i *Sulph* symph fd3.de• tarax ther k* thuj k* verat k* verat-v viol-t b7.de* zinc
    - ⋮ **morning**: cycl h1* rumx sars k*
    - ⋮ **evening**: cycl k* daph euphr h2* sars k*
      - ⋮ **lying** down agg.: tarax k*
      - ⋮ **walking** agg.: euphr h2*
    - ⋮ **night**: rumx symph fd3.de• *Zinc* k*
      - ⋮ **waking**; on: rhus-g tmo3•
      - ⋮ **walking** agg.: (non:cocc h1*)
    - ⋮ **bleeding** after scratching: cycl h1* mez h2*
    - ⋮ **burning**: berb k* mez k*
      - ⋮ **scratching** agg.; after: cycl h1* sars h2*
    - ⋮ **rubbing** | **amel.**: paeon k*
    - ⋮ **scratching** | **amel.**: laur k* mag-c k* mag-m k* nat-c k*
    - ⋮ **spots**, in: graph k* sars k*
    - ⋮ **standing** agg.: verat
    - ⋮ **undressing**: cact k*
    - ⋮ **voluptuous**: euphr k* *Mang*
    - ⋮ **walking** agg.: cocc k*
  - **Tendo** Achillis: staph h1*
  - **Tibia**, over: agn b7.de* alum k2 ant-c h2* asaf b7.de* aster bism k* cact *Calc* k* chel k* choc srj3• cocc k* crot-t grat hep k* kali-c k* kali-n h2* lach k* mag-m h2* *Mang* k* *Nit-ac* *Ph-ac* k* phos k* plb k* plut-n srj7• *Rumx* sars k* sep k* spig h1* spong fd4.de staph b7.de* stront-c symph fd3.de• tritic-vg fd5.de
    - ⋮ **right**: olib-sac wmh1

- **Lower** limbs: **Agar** k* aloe *Alum* alum-p k2 alum-sil k2 alumn *Am-c* k* am-m k* *Ambr* anac *Ant-c* ant-s-aur ant-t **Apis** aq-mar rbp6 arge-pl rwt5• am **Ars** ars-i arund asaf asc-t aster aur aur-ar k2 aur-i k2 aur-s k2 *Bar-c* bar-s k2 bell berb *Bism* *Bov* brach bry bufo cact *Calc* k* calc-i cann-i cann-s canth carb-ac **Carb-v** carbn-s cassia-s cdd7*• **Caust** k* cham **Chel** chin chinin-ar cinnb clem coc-c k* *Cocc* coli rly4• coloc com k* con k* corn crot-c cupr cycl dig dios dulc elaps euphr fago k* gins gran **Graph** grat ham fd3.de• hep hura ign iod *Ip* b7a.de

Extremities

- **Lower limbs**: ...
iris-foe$_{k*}$ jug-c jug-r kali-ar kali-bi kali-c$_{k*}$ kali-i kali-n kali-p kali-sil$_{k2}$ kalm lach$_{k*}$ lachn lact laur led$_{k*}$ lith-c **Lyc**$_{k*}$ mag-c$_{k*}$ mag-m mag-s mand$_{rsj7}$• mang **Merc**$_{k*}$ merc-i-f **Mez**$_{k*}$ mur-ac nat-ar nat-c$_{k*}$ **Nat-m**$_{k*}$ nat-p *Nat-s* nicc nicc-met$_{sk4}$• *Nit-ac* nux-v ol-an *Olnd* osm paeon pall *Petr* ph-ac *Phos*$_{k*}$ phyt pin-con$_{oss2}$• plat plb prun **Psor** **Puls** ran-b ran-s **Rhus-t**$_{k*}$ rhus-v$_{k*}$ rumx ruta sabad sacch-a$_{fd2.de}$• sars$_{k*}$ sec$_{k*}$ sel seneg **Sep** **Sil**$_{k*}$ *Spig* **Spong** stann **Staph** stram stront-c$_{k*}$ stry sul-i$_{k2}$ **Sulph**$_{k*}$ tab taosc$_{iwa1}$• tarax **Tarent** *Tell* thea ther *Thuj*$_{k*}$ til tritic-vg$_{fd5.de}$ vanil$_{fd5.de}$ verat$_{k*}$ *Zinc*$_{k*}$ [heroin$_{sdj2}$ tax$_{jsj7}$]
  - **right**: sulfonam$_{ks2}$
  - **daytime**: calc ind
  - **morning**: alumn ant-c nat-c rumx sabad sars sep sulph
  - **noon**: nicc
  - **afternoon**: coc-c fago nat-c
    - ⋮ **13** h: ars-s-f$_{k2}$
    - ⋮ **14** h: ol-an
    - ⋮ **17** h: fago
  - **evening**: alum am-m aster clem cycl fago$_{k*}$ ind kali-c kali-n lyc mag-c mag-m mang merc$_{k*}$ mez$_{k*}$ nat-m$_{k*}$ *Nat-s* nicc nit-ac$_{k*}$ nux-v phos podo$_{fd3.de}$• rhus-v rumx sars sel sep stront-c sulph tarax tell thuj$_{k*}$ zinc
    - ⋮ **18** h: aster fago
    - ⋮ **20** h: con
    - ⋮ **22** h: plan
  - **night**: am-m$_{k*}$ bar-c bros-gau$_{mrc1}$ canth cinnb cocc cupr-ar dig hep hura merc-i-f *Mez* nat-m phos$_{k*}$ phyt **Rhus-t** rhus-v rumx sabad sulfonam$_{ks2}$ *Sulph* til zinc
    - ⋮ **midnight**: puls
  - **air** agg.; in open: alum aster rumx still
  - **bed** agg.; in: cupr-ar kali-c lyc merc-i-f nux-v *Puls* rhus-t$_{k2}$ sil staph tarax til zinc
  - **biting**: alum bell *Berb* spig spong
  - **boil**, at the site of a previous: graph
  - **burning**: *Agar* alum anac apis *Berb* calc dulc hep kali-n led lith-c mez mur-ac nat-c nit-ac$_{h2*}$ nux-v paeon rhus-t sars
    - ⋮ **scratching** agg.; after: mag-c
    - ⋮ **sleep**; when falling asleep: mur-ac
    - ⋮ **spots**, in: rhus-t
  - **chilly**, on becoming: rhus-t
  - **cold** agg.; becoming: dios tarent
  - **corrosive**: ars bufo chel euph led tax
  - **creeping**: ars
  - **dinner**; after: laur mag-c
  - **dressing**; while: nux-v
  - **eruptions**; without: alum-sil$_{k4}$
  - **frozen**, as if: kali-c
  - **heat**; after: *Rhus-v* **Sulph**
  - **menses**; during: inul
  - **motion** | **amel.**: mur-ac olnd psor spig
  - **pain**; during: fl-ac
  - **paroxysms**: corn
  - **prickling**: crot-t
  - **rubbing**:
    - ⋮ **agg.**: corn
    - ⋮ **amel.**: cupr paeon
  - **scratching**:
    - ⋮ **agg.**: *Alum* *Bism* corn *Led*
    - ⋮ **amel.**: alum bov bros-gau$_{mrc1}$ cann-i chin kali-c laur led mag-c mag-m nat-c nat-s nicc olnd pall tarax thuj vanil$_{fd5.de}$
    - ⋮ **must** scratch until raw: psor$_{k2}$
  - **sitting** agg.: asaf chin fago
  - **sleep** agg.; on going to: mag-m mur-ac sep
  - **spots**, in: calc graph osm phos sars
  - **standing** agg.: mang verat
  - **sticking**: ant-c *Berb* calc caust graph lach plat rhus-t staph zinc

- **Lower limbs – sticking**: ...
    - ⋮ **spots**, in: calc
  - **stinging**: dios merc-i-f
  - **tickling**: alum bry cocc coloc euph ign kali-n lach pall
  - **tingling**: com
  - **touch** agg.: nat-m
  - **undressing** agg.: agar apis cact cupr cupr-ar dios fago ham$_{k*}$ jug-r mag-c **Nat-s**$_{k*}$ *Rumx* still
  - **varicose**: graph
  - **voluptuous**: euphr rat *Sulph*
  - **waking**; on: sulph
  - **walking** | **after** | **agg.**: alum
    - ⋮ **agg.**: asaf chel chin cocc dios mur-ac nux-v sulph
  - **warm** bed agg.: *Agar* *Alum* led *Sulph*
  - **warmth**:
    - ⋮ **agg.**: rhus-v
    - ⋮ **amel.**: cocc
  - **wine** agg.: psor
  - ○ **Bones**: cycl$_{b7.de*}$
- **Nates**: *Am-c*$_{k*}$ ant-t asc-t$_{k*}$ bar-c$_{k*}$ calc$_{k*}$ *Calc-p* carb-ac$_{k*}$ *Caust*$_{k*}$ cham$_{k*}$ con$_{k*}$ cypra-eg$_{sde6.de}$• dulc$_{k*}$ gran$_{k*}$ kali-c$_{k*}$ kola$_{stb3}$• laur$_{b7.de*}$ lyc$_{k*}$ *Mag-c*$_{k*}$ mag-m$_{k*}$ mez$_{k*}$ mur-ac$_{a1}$ olnd$_{k*}$ *Petr* ph-ac$_{b4a.de}$ prun$_{k*}$ ruta$_{fd4.de}$ sars$_{b4.de*}$ sel$_{k*}$ *Sil*$_{k*}$ staph$_{k*}$ stront-c$_{k*}$ **Sulph** symph$_{fd3.de}$• tarax$_{b7.de*}$ ther$_{k*}$ thuj$_{k*}$ vanil$_{fd5.de}$ zinc$_{k*}$
  - **morning** | **rising** agg.: nat-c
  - **evening**: ruta$_{fd4.de}$ sars$_{k*}$ vanil$_{fd5.de}$
    - ⋮ **bed** agg.; in: lyc$_{k*}$ staph$_{h1*}$
    - ⋮ **undressing**: mag-c$_{k*}$
  - **night**: con$_{h2*}$ petr
    - ⋮ **bed** agg.; in: merc-i-f$_{k*}$
  - **air** agg.; in open: rumx
  - **bed** agg.; in: rumx
  - **burning**: am-c
  - **cold** | **applications** | **agg.**: stront-c$_{sk4}$•
    - ⋮ **water** | **amel.**: petr
  - **corrosive**: sulph$_{h2*}$
  - **dinner**; after: laur$_{k*}$
  - **scratching**:
    - ⋮ **agg.**: petr
    - ⋮ **amel.**: kali-i$_{k*}$ olnd$_{k*}$ thuj$_{k*}$
  - ○ **Between**: alum *Bar-c* con$_{k*}$ kali-c$_{h2*}$ ruta$_{fd4.de}$
- **Shoulders**: alumn$_{k*}$ am-c$_{k*}$ arge-pl$_{rwt5}$• ars$_{k*}$ bamb-a$_{stb2.de}$• bar-c$_{k*}$ berb$_{k*}$ bov$_{k*}$ brom carb-ac$_{k*}$ carbn-s$_{k2}$ caust$_{k*}$ cent$_{a1}$ cob$_{k*}$ coloc$_{k*}$ cund$_{k*}$ cycl$_{k*}$ dios$_{k*}$ dol$_{br1}$ fl-ac$_{k*}$ *Gels* hep ign$_{b7.de*}$ jug-c$_{k*}$ kali-bi$_{k*}$ kali-br$_{k*}$ kali-c$_{k*}$ mag-c$_{k*}$ mag-m$_{k*}$ mang$_{k*}$ mez$_{k*}$ *Mill*$_{k*}$ myric$_{k*}$ nat-c$_{k*}$ nicc$_{k*}$ op$_{k*}$ osm pall podo$_{fd3.de}$• puls sars$_{k*}$ stront-c$_{k*}$ sulph$_{k*}$ symph$_{fd3.de}$• ther thuj$_{k*}$ *Urt-u*$_{k*}$
  - **left**: bamb-a$_{stb2.de}$•
  - **morning**: fl-ac
    - ⋮ **dressing**; while: mag-c$_{h2*}$ mag-m$_{k*}$
  - **forenoon**: mag-c$_{k*}$
  - **afternoon**: bamb-a$_{stb2.de}$• fl-ac$_{k*}$ mag-c$_{k*}$
    - ⋮ **14** h: ol-an
    - ⋮ **menses**; during: mag-c$_{k*}$
  - **evening**: fl-ac hura osm symph$_{fd3.de}$•
    - ⋮ **lying** down agg.: mur-ac$_{k*}$ osm
    - ⋮ **sleep**; before going to: mag-c$_{k*}$
  - **alternating** with | **pain** (See Pain - shoulders - alternating with - itching)
  - **burning**: mez$_{k*}$
  - **menses**; during: mag-c
  - **scratching**:
    - ⋮ **agg.**: stront-c
    - ⋮ **amel.**: bov$_{k*}$ ol-an$_{k*}$

- **Thighs**: agar k* agath-a nl2• *Alum* k* alum-sil k2 am-c b4.de* am-m b7a.de anac b4.de* androc srj1• ang b7.de* ant-c k* aq-mar skp7• *Ars* k* ars-h ars-s-f k2 asc-t k* aster k* **Bar-c** k* *Bar-m* bar-s k2 bell-p bro1 berb k* bov b4.de* bry k* **Calc** k* calc-sil k2 canth b7.de* carb-ac k* *Carb-v* k* carbn-s *Caust* k* chin k* chord-umb rly4• *Chrysar* br1 cic b7.de* cinnb k* clem k* cocc b7.de* con k* corn k* crot-c k* crot-t cystein-l rly4• dig b4.de* dios k* dulc b4.de* *Euph* k* euphr b7.de* fago k* gran *Guaj* k* ham fd3.de• ina-i mlk9.de kali-c k* *Kali-i* k* kali-n h2* kali-p fd1.de• kali-sil k2 lac-del hm2• lach k* lachn k* laur b7.de* led b7.de* lith-c lyc k* lyss m-arct b7.de m-aust b7.de mag-m b4.de* merc k* mosch b7.de* mur-ac k* nat-c b4.de* nat-m k* nit-ac k* nux-v k* olnd b7.de* osm ozone sde2• pall k* petr k* phos k* plb k* plut-n srj7• ran-b k* ran-s b7.de* rhod b4.de* rhus-v k* ros-d wla1 *Rumx* bro1 samb b7.de* *Sars* k* sep k* sil k* *Spig* k* spong k* stann k* staph b7.de* stel bro1 stront-c k* **Sulph** k* symph fd3.de• tab k* tarax b7.de* thea *Thuj* k* til trios rsj11• tritic-vg fd5.de vanil fd5.de viol-t b7.de* *Zinc* k* [heroin sdj2]
  - **left**: cortiso tpw7
  - **daytime**: calc
  - **morning** | **dressing**; while: mag-c h2 nux-v
  - **afternoon**: nat-c k*
    - **17** h: dios fago
  - **evening**: anac h2* *Ant-c* k* aster bamb-a stb2.de• fago k* lyc k* oci-sa sk4• spong fd4.de stront-c *Zinc* k*
    - **air** agg.; in open: aster
    - **bed** agg.; in: nux-v k* sil k* zinc k*
    - **sleep**; before going to: mag-c h2* spong fd4.de
  - **night**: *Bar-c* dulc h2* ina-i mlk9.de led h1* nit-ac h2* rhus-v spong fd4.de **Sulph** til vanil fd5.de zinc
    - **undressing**: nux-v
  - **air** agg.; in open: aster
  - **biting**: alum k* berb k* chel h1* lyc spig k*
  - **boil**, at site of a previous: graph
  - **burning**: agar *Alum* anac k* apis *Bar-c* berb k* calc k* cic h1* dulc k* led k* mang h2* nux-v k* rhus-t k* sars k*
    - **scratching** agg.; after: mag-m h2* phos h2* samb h1*
    - **spots**, in: rhus-t k*
  - **chilly**, becoming: dios k*
  - **corrosive**: agar h2* ars k* chel k* dig h2* euph k* led k* ph-ac h2* tarax k*
  - **crawling**: sulph h2*
  - **eruptions**; without: alum-sil k4
  - **exertion** agg.: cortiso tpw7
  - **itch**-like: ol-an k*
  - **nodules** after scratching: mag-m h2*
  - **pain**; during: fl-ac k*
  - **painful** after scratching: euphr h2*
  - **rubbing** | **amel.**: anac h2* ang h1*
  - **scratching**:
    - **agg.**: ars mag-m h2
    - **amel.**: *Alum* k* cic h1* cortiso tpw7 led k* pall k* sep h2* spig h1* ulm-c jsj8• vanil fd5.de
    - **not** amel.: mag-m h2* nit-ac h2*
  - **sleep** agg.; on going to: sep k*
  - **spots**: phos k*
  - **sticking**: ant-c k* berb k* calc k* caust k* graph h2* rhus-t k* stann h2*
    - **spots**, in: calc k*
  - **tickling**: cocc coloc k* kali-n k* lach k* pall
  - **walking** agg.: euphr h2* nux-v k*
  - **warm** bed agg.: *Alum* bar-c *Caust* cortiso tpw7 *Sulph*
  - ○ **Anterior** side: ulm-c jsj8•
  - **Bend** of thighs: aq-mar skp7•
  - **Between**: agath-a nl2• ars k* *Carb-v* k* *Caust* b4a.de cinnb cocc b7.de* *Kali-c* k* kreos b7a.de nat-m k* nit-ac k* petr k* rhod k* stann k* sulph k* viol-t b7.de*
    - **menses**; during: kali-c b4.de*

- **Thighs**: ...
  - **Genitalia**; near: ars h2 bamb-a stb2.de• bar-c *Carb-v* caust *Graph* kali-c h2 lyc h2 mag-m h2 rhus-t sabin
  - **Inguinal** region; near (See genitalia)
  - **Inner** side: agath-a nl2• alum h2* androc srj1• antip vh1 *Cinnb* k* ham fd3.de• mang h2* pieri-b mlk9.de samb h1* sil h2* sulph h2* symph fd3.de• vanil fd5.de
  - **Outer** side: mag-m h2* nit-ac h2* stann h2* zinc h2*
- **Thumbs**: ant-c bg2 aur-m carb-v h2* chel k* cimic k* cocc bg2 con k* grat bg2 kali-n k* lach k* mez k* olib-sac wmh1 olnd k* plb bg2 sep k* spong bg2 staph bg2 symph fd3.de• vanil fd5.de vesp k*
  - **left** | **Nail**; under: bros-gau mrc1
  - **evening**: cimic k*
  - **burning**: aur-m mang h2*
  - **nettles**, like: lach k*
  - **scratching** | **amel.**: chel k* olnd k* vanil fd5.de
  - **tickling**: kali-n k*
  - ○ **Balls**: *Agar* k* aloe cocc h1* gamb k* manc k* nat-c h2* spong k* verat k*
  - **Nails**; under: bros-gau mrc1 sep h2*
  - **Tips**: ambr hr1 ant-c h2*
- **Toes**: *Agar* k* aids nl2• *Alum* k* am-c k* am-m b7.de* *Ambr* k* *Arg-met* arn k* ars k* ars-s-f k2 arum-t k2 bamb-a stb2.de• *Berb* k* bry k* *Carb-an* k* caust k* chel k* *Clem* k* *Colch* *Cycl* k* euphr b7.de* *Graph* k* ham fd3.de• *Hep* k* ind k* iod k* jatr-c kali-c bro1 ketogl-ac rly4• lach k* lact k* m-arct b7.de m-aust b7.de *Mag-c* k* mag-s k* maland bro1* *Merc* k* merc-c b4a.de *Mez* k* mosch b7a.de mur-ac k* nat-c nat-m k* nat-s k* nit-ac nux-v k* paeon k* ph-ac phos k* plat *Puls* k* ran-s b7.de* rheum b7.de* rhod k* rhus-v ruta sabad b7a.de sep k* sil sinus rly4• spig b7.de* spong b7.de* *Staph* k* *Stront-c* k* **Sulph** k* symph fd3.de• tarax b7.de* thuj k* tritic-vg fd5.de vanil fd5.de verat *Zinc* k* [*Buteo-j* sej6]
  - **daytime**: ind k*
  - **morning**: arge-pl rwt5• vanil fd5.de
    - **falling** asleep: mur-ac k*
    - **waking**; on: spong h1*
  - **evening**: *Alum* k* ind k* merc k* nat-s k* nit-ac phos k* vanil fd5.de zinc
    - **lying** down agg.; after: *Clem* k*
    - **scratching** agg.; after: *Alum*
    - **undressing**: nat-s
  - **night**: bamb-a stb2.de• hep h2* puls h1* sal-fr sle1•
  - **air** agg.; in open: alum k*
  - **biting**: berb k*
  - **burning**: arg-met k2 berb k* hep k* ind mur-ac nat-c paeon k* staph h1*
  - **cold** | **amel.**: ina-i mlk9.de
  - **dinner**; after: mag-c k*
  - **frozen**, as if: borx a1
  - **frozen**, toes that had been: **Agar** **Alum** carb-an h2* nat-c nux-v k* paeon *Puls* k* *Sil* staph sulph k* zinc
  - **scratch** until they bleed, must: *Arg-met*
  - **scratching**:
    - **agg.**: *Alum* *Arg-met* ina-i mlk9.de sal-fr sle1• *Zinc*
    - **not** amel.: arge-pl rwt5• bamb-a stb2.de•
  - **sticking**: berb k* graph plat puls h1* staph
  - **undressing**: *Nat-s* k*
  - **voluptuous**: spong h1* thuj k*
  - **walking** agg.; after: alum
  - **warm**; when: alumn a1 tritic-vg fd5.de
  - **warmth** agg. | **heat** agg.: ina-i mlk9.de rhus-v k*
  - ○ **Around** toe | **left**: aq-mar skp7•
  - **Balls**: cann-s b7.de* rhus-t b7.de* spig b7.de* viol-t b7.de*
  - **Between**: bamb-a stb2.de• cycl k* graph k* hippoc-k szs2 jatr-c k* ketogl-ac rly4• mang med merc k* mosch k* *Nat-m* *Nat-s* k* nat-sil fd3.de• sal-fr sle1• thuj k* tritic-vg fd5.de vanil fd5.de
  - **Fifth**: aids nl2• bamb-a stb2.de• borx ham fd3.de• nicc k* rheum h staph k*
    - **afternoon** | **16** h: ol-an

Extremities

- **Fifth**: ...
  - **evening**: staph k*
  - **scratching** | **amel.**: nicc k*
  - **Balls**: borx puls h1*
- **First**: alum k* am-c k* ant-c h2* ars k* cycl k* graph k* *Kali-c* merc-i-f k* nat-c k* nit-ac k* plat k* ruta staph k* verat k* *Zinc*
  - **evening**: nit-ac k* zinc h2*
  - **burning**: nat-c k*
  - **creeping**: ars k*
  - **freezing**, after: am-c zinc
  - **sticking**: graph k* plat k* rhus-t h1* staph k* zinc h2*
  - **Balls**: am-c k* brach a1 mur-ac h2* *Nat-s* rhus-t h1* zinc h2*
  - **Distal** joint: caust h2 sep h2
  - **Tips**: am-m k* ambr h1* kali-c k* sep h2*
- **Fourth**: aids nl2• hydrog srj2• nicc k* tarax h1*
  - **scratching** | **amel.**: nicc k*
- **Nails**:
  - **Roots** of nails: upa br1
  - **Under**: sil h2*
- **Second** | **Balls**: puls h1
- **Third**: aids nl2• cench k2 nicc k*
  - **scratching** | **amel.**: nicc k*
- **Under**: kali-c h2* phos h2*

\- **Upper** arms: acon k* anac anag am k* berb k* bov k* bry k* canth carb-v bg2 carbn-s chel k* coc-c k* cocc k* dig bg2 dulc k* euph k* flor-p rsj3• kali-bi k* kali-i k* kali-n k* lach k* laur k* led k* lyc k* m-arct b7.de m-aust b7.de mang k* mez k* mosch b7a.de *Nux-v* k* olnd k* pall petr-ra shn4• ph-ac k* phos podo fd3.de• *Psor* ran-b b7.de* ran-s b7.de* rhus-g tmo3• ruta k* sep k* spong k* stront-c k* sulfonam ks2 *Tell* rsj10• thuj k* tritic-vg fd5.de vanil fd5.de

- **right**: vult-gr sze5•
- **morning** | **dressing**; while: nux-v
- **evening** | **undressing**; while: nux-v k*
- **burning**: berb k* dulc k* nux-v k*
- **coldness**; during: spong
- **corrosive**: led k*
- **crawling**: thuj k*
- **motion** agg.: anac x h2*
- **scratching**:
  - **agg.**: stront-c
  - **amel.**: chel led k* *Mang* k* pall [tax jsj7]
- **spots**: berb k* [tax jsj7]
- **stinging**: euph h2* led h1* ran-s k*
- ○ **Biceps**: | **right**: psor jl2
- **Inner** side: acon k* bov k* carb-v h2* kali-i k*
- **Outer** part: mang k* ruta fd4.de
  - **scratching** | **amel.**: chel k* mang k*
- **Posterior** part: tax k*

\- **Upper** limbs: *Agar* k* aloe alum k* alum-p k2 alum-sil k2 alumn am-c k* am-m ambr amyg-p anac k* ang k* ant-c k* ant-t k* anthraci apis k* arg-met k* am k* ars k* ars-i arund br1* asc-t aur k* aur-m aur-s k2 bar-c bar-s k2 benz-ac borx **Bov** k* bry k* calad calc k* calc-i calc-p camph cann-s canth k* carb-ac k* carb-an k* carb-v k* carbn-s **Caust** k* chel k* chin k* chinin-s cimic cina cinnb cit-v k* cob coc-c cocc k* colch coloc com con k* cop com cortico tpw7 cupr bg2 cupr-ar a1 cycl cystein-l rly4• dig dios dulc euph eupi fago k* fl-ac k* form k* galeoc-c-h gms1• gels glon gran graph k* grat k* ham k* hell b7.de* hep hura hydr hydr-ac k* ign ind iod k* *Ip* b7a.de jatr-c jug-c k* jug-r k* kali-bi k* kali-br kali-c k* kali-i k* kali-n k* kali-p kali-sil k2 lach k* lachn lact laur led k* lyc k* *Lyss* mag-c k* mag-m k* mag-s manc mang k* merc k* merc-i-f merc-i-r mez k* mill morph mur-ac myric nat-ar nat-c k* nat-m k* nat-p nat-s nat-sil fd3.de• nicc nit-ac *Nux-v* k* ol-an olnd op k* osm pall k* petr ph-ac phos k* phys phyt pip-m bro1 plan plat k* plb podo k* prun psor k* ptel puls k* ran-b ran-s b7.de* rat rhod rhodi br1* *Rhus-t* k* rhus-v k* rumx ruta k* sabad sal-fr sle1• sars k* sel k* *Sep* k* *Sil* k* sin-a sol-ni spig spong staph k* streptoc rly4• stront-c stry k* sul-i k2* **Sulph** k* tarent k* tax k* **Tell** k* teucr *Thuj* k* til tritic-vg fd5.de *Urt-u* k* vanil fd5.de ven-m rsj12• verat k* verb k* vesp zinc [spect dfg1]

- **left**: psor jl2 trios rsj11•
- **daytime**: calc k*

\- **Upper** limbs: ...

- **morning**: am-m ham hell h1* mag-c ol-an rhus-v sulph tax
  - **dressing**; while: mag-m nux-v rhus-t *Sulph*
  - **washing** agg.: bov
- **forenoon**: mag-c sulph
- **afternoon**: aloe cimic coc-c fl-ac form jug-r mag-c nat-m sulph
  - **14** h: ol-an
  - **menses**; during: mag-c
- **evening**: am-m bov k* calc-p chin k* cimic dios fago k* fl-ac hura mag-c merl nat-sil fd3.de• ol-an sin-a k* spong fd4.de *Sulph* k* thuj k* vanil fd5.de
  - **21** h: asc-t calc-p hydr
  - **bed** agg.; in: hell h1* nat-sil fd3.de• vanil fd5.de
- **night**: agar k* am-m anac ars k* asc-t k* canth carb-v chin h1* cupr k* cupr-ar a1 dig hydr kali-br k* merc phos k* rhus-v ruta sabad sulph *Thuj* k* til k* ven-m rsj12•
  - **midnight**: rhus-t
    - **before** | **22** h: mag-c
- **bed** agg.; in: *Alum* cinnb k* cupr-ar k* kali-bi kali-br mag-c mur-ac nat-m ph-ac phos rhus-v sars spong fd4.de **Sulph** k* **Tell** k*
- **biting**: *Berb*
- **burning**: *Agar* k* berb calc h2* cupr h2* dulc hir rsj4• mez nux-v ran-b spig stann
- **cool**, when: thuj k*
- **corrosive**: chel k* hell k* led merc ruta h1
- **crawling**: berb thuj k*
- **erosive** gnawing (See corrosive)
- **eruptions**:
  - **suppressed** eruptions; after: *Hep*
  - **without**: alum-sil k4 galeoc-c-h gms1•
- **flea** bites, as from: nat-c tab k* thuj a1
- **here** and there: ph-ac a1 plat k*
- **hot** water amel.: *Rhus-t* rhus-v
- **lying** down agg; after: calad
- **menses**; during: mag-c
- **mercury**; after abuse of: *Hep*
- **motion**:
  - **agg.**: crot-t k*
  - **amel.**: com sars
- **nettles**, as from: lach nit-ac **Urt-u**
- **rubbing**:
  - **agg.**: crot-t k* *Nat-m* k* rhus-v
  - **amel.**: ang k* berb cupr-ar k* ham mag-s ol-an vanil fd5.de
- **scratching**:
  - **agg.**: ars cupr-ar a1 ham ph-ac k* rhus-v k* sal-fr sle1• stront-c **Sulph**
  - **amel.**: alum k* ant-t bov camph chel coloc k* graph jug-c k* led mag-c mang merc ol-an olnd ph-ac k* tritic-vg fd5.de vanil fd5.de
  - **must** scratch until raw: psor k2
- **sitting** in church: com k*
- **spots**: berb cop k* kali-bi kali-n merc k* nat-m k* psor sulph
- **sticking**: berb caust k* lach merc-i-f
- **stinging**: ars-i phos ran-b ran-s
- **sudden**: ph-ac a1 phos
- **tickling**: kali-n staph
- **touch** agg.: crot-t k* psor
- **undressing** agg.: crot-t k* cupr-ar k* kali-br mur-ac nux-v ph-ac
- **voluptuous**: merc *Sulph*
- **warm** room agg.: nux-v
- **warmth** agg.: chin h1* *Cortico* tpw7 sulph
- **water**, immersing in: rhus-v k*
- ○ **Joints**: merc sep zinc

\- **Wrists**: agar k* alum k* am-m bg2 *Anac* k* apis arg-met b7.de* ars k* asc-t k* aur k* bar-c k* berb k* bism b7.de* calc-p k* cimic k* cinnb cypra-eg sde6.de• dios k* hep k* hydr k* ign k* kali-bi k* kali-c k* kali-i k* kali-n b4.de* led b7.de*

- **Wrists**: ...
mag-c k* manc k* mez k* nat-sil fd3.de• ped a1 plat k* podo fd3.de• psor k* rhus-t k* rhus-v k* sars k* sel b7.de* spong fd4.de staph gk *Sulph* k* symph fd3.de• vanil fd5.de zinc k* [heroin sdj2]
  - **left**: mim-p rsj8•
  - **afternoon**: sulph k*
  - **evening**: calc-p k* cimic k* *Sulph* k* vanil fd5.de
    - **21** h: calc-p nat-sil fd3.de•
  - **night**: asc-t k* hydr k* vanil fd5.de
  - **biting**: berb k*
  - **scratching**:
    - **agg.**: **Sulph** k*
    - **amel.**: ulm-c jsj8•
  - **spots**, in: kali-bi k* psor k*
  - ○ **Dorsal** side: cimic k* con pitu-gl skp7• symph fd3.de•
    - **right**: pitu-gl skp7•
    - **violent** (See dorsal)
  - **Inner** side: nat-m k* nept-m lsd2.fr plat h2* plb k* scroph-n c1 upa k* verat k*
  - **Outer** side: anac h2* ulm-c jsj8•
  - **Palmar** side: arg-met h1 com k* con k* mag-c k* mang rhus-v k* sars k* sel k*

JERKING: *(↗Twitching)* acon aesc *Agar* *Alum* k* alum-p k2 alum-sil k2 *Am-m* *Ambr* *Anac* k* *Apis* arg-met *Arg-n* *Ars* k* aster hr1 *Bar-m* bell cadm-s calc-sil k2 cann-i card-m k2 *Caust* k* **Cham** k* chel *Chin* k* **Cic** k* cimic **Cina** cocc k2 colch crot-h k* *Cupr* k* dulc a1 eucal hr1 gal-ac a1* *Glon* k* graph helo-s rwt2• hist sp1 **Hyos** k* hyper k* *Ign* k* iod ip bg1 *Kali-i* k* *Kali-n* kali-p k2 kali-s *Lach* bg1 lat-m bnm6• *Lil-t* *Lyc* k* mag-c bg1 **Merc** k* mur-ac nat-c *Nat-m* nux-m onos op k* phos phys ptk1 phyt **Plb** k* pycnop-sa mrz1 sec k* *Sep* k* sil k* *Stram* k* sul-i k2 sulph sumb k* tab mrr1 *Tarent* k* *Valer* k* verat k* *Visc* k* *Zinc* k*

- **one** side | **sleep**; during: ant-t ptk1 sulph ptk1
- **one** side, other side paralyzed: apis art-v bell *Stram*
- **right**: ars bg1 calc bg1 sep
- **left** side paralyzed, right side convulsed: art-v k*
- **evening**: graph
  - **bed** agg.; in: kali-n
- **night**: *Ambr* dig k2 hep c1 *Kali-i* k* mag-c bg1 phos sec k* sep staph h1 sulph hr1 *Visc* k* zinc mrr1
- **alternately** of flexors and extensors: *Plb*
- **cold** agg.; becoming: cimic k2
- **cough** agg.; during: arg-n bg2 stram ptk1
- **emotions**; from: cimic k2
- **falling** asleep: *Agar* *Alum* arg-met **Ars** k* cham hr1 cob k* *Gels* hyper **Ign** k* **Kali-c** *Nat-ar* nat-m nux-v k2 *Phys* k* *Sel* sil *Sulph* k* *Thuj*
- **lying**:
  - **agg.**: *Anac*
  - **back**; on | **agg.**: calc-p
  - **side**; on | **agg.**: onos
- **menses**: cimic k2
- **motion**:
  - **agg.**: sep
  - **amel.**: *Merc* *Thuj* valer k* zinc
- **one** leg and one arm: apis apoc k* *Bry* bro1 hell k* mygal bro1 stram zinc bro1
- **painful**: am-m hr1 cupr h2* plat hr1 sec k* *Verat* hr1
- **periodical**: bar-m
- **pressure**; from: cimic k2
- **sleep**:
  - **amel.**: agar k2
  - **during** | **agg.**: *Ail* cann-i cann-s cina tl1 colch *Cupr* gard-j vlr2• *Kali-c* k* *Lyc* merc-c nat-c nux-v k2 phos puls sep k2 *Sil* sulph mtf33 **Zinc**
  - **going** to sleep; on | **agg.**: ign tl1
- **touch** agg. | **children**; in: kali-c mtf33
- **walking** | **amel.**: valer
- ○ - **Ankles**: *Calc* k* spig h1 stann h2*
- **Bones**: cham h1*

Jerking: ...
- **Elbows**: agn a1 aloe bg2 nat-m k* stram k* zinc
  - **motion** | **amel.**: agn a1
- **Feet**: anac k* ars k* *Bar-c* k* bar-m k* *Cic* cina cupr mtf33 *Graph* k* hyos k* ip *Kali-bi* *Kali-br* lyc k* nat-c nat-s nux-v phos h2* puls k* *Sep* sil h2* staph bg2 **Stram** sul-ac k*
  - **accompanied** by | **Teeth**; pain in (See TEETH - Pain - accompanied - feet)
  - **sleep** | **during** | **agg.**: nat-c phos sep
    - **going** to, on: *Bell* *Kali-c* phos h2 *Zinc*
  - **spasm**, in: *Cina* k*
  - **standing** agg.:
    - **walking** | **amel.**: verat a1
  - **violent**: cina br1
  - ○ **Back** of feet: anac h2*
  - **Heels**: mag-m bg2
  - **Sole** of: crot-t ferr-ma kali-n c1
- **Fingers**: aloe bg2 cadm-s *Calc* k* caust ptk1 **Cic** k* **Cina** k* *Cocc* k* cycl ptk1 dulc a1 *Merc* k* *Merc-c* mez h2* *Nat-c* k* nit-ac h2* *Op* rheum ptk1 stann ptk1 stram k* sulph ptk1
  - **epilepsy**: **Cic** k*
  - **gastric** fever: stram k*
  - **painful**: cocc
  - **sleep** agg.; during: sul-ac ptk1
  - **writing** agg.: *Caust* bro1 cina bro1 cycl bro1 kali-c bro1 stann k* sul-ac bro1*
  - ▽ **extending** to | **Arms**; both | **chorea**; in: *Cupr*
    - **Shoulder**: *Ars*
  - ○ **Fourth**: com k* meny
  - **Joints**: carbn-s *Nat-c* hr1
    - **rheumatic**: carbn-s des-ac rbp6
  - **Second**: stann h2*
  - **Tips**: staph bg2
- **Forearms**: caps **Cic** *Cupr* hyper *Ign* k* jal staph
  - **evening**: *Ign* k*
- **Hands**: bar-m k* brom *Cina* *Cocc* k* *Coff* k* *Cupr* k* *Graph* hyos k* jug-r kali-bi bg2 *Merc* k* nat-c k* *Nat-m* nux-v pall k* ran-b sec k* **Stram** k*
  - **convulsive**: bar-m k* cina br1 merc
    - **right** hand: colchin c1
  - **electric** shocks: jug-r
  - **exertion** agg.: *Merc*
  - **going** to sleep, on: nat-c
  - **grasping** something agg.: nat-c
  - **violent**: cina br1
- **Hips**: *Ars* k* cann-s k* graph mag-c *Pall* k* *Puls* k* valer
  - **accompanied** by | **Sciatic** nerve; pain in (See Pain - lower limbs - sciatic - accompanied - hip)
  - **sciatica**, in (See Pain - lower limbs - sciatic - accompanied - hip)
  - ○ **Joints**: bell nux-v puls sulph
- **Knees**: anac c1 *Arg-n* *Ars* benzol br1 colch lat-m bnm6• meny *Mez* k* **Puls** k* spig k* staph a1 stram k* *Sul-ac* sulph ptk1 verat a1
  - **sitting** agg.: mez
  - **sleep**; in first: ars h2
  - **upward**:
    - **cough** agg.; during: ther
    - **sitting** agg.: *Ars* lyc *Meny*
  - ○ **Patella**: spig h1
- **Legs**: *Agar* k* anac c1 *Arg-n* ars carb-v con bg2 dig k* helo-s rwt2• hyper *Kali-i* lyc med c1 *Meny* k* nat-c k* *Phos* k* plat k* rhus-t bg2 sep sil k* sul-ac k* tab c2
  - **afternoon**: ars
  - **drawing** pain, after: phos h2*
  - **falling** asleep: *Ars* hyper **Kali-c** nat-c sep
  - **lying** on back agg.: nat-s

Extremities

- **Legs**: ...
  - **motion** | **amel.**: carb-v k*
  - **sitting** agg.: ars carb-v *Meny* k*
  - **sleep** agg.; during: cinnb
  - **walking** agg.: phos h2*
  - ○ **Calves**: anac c1 *Graph* mag-m a1 **Op** k* rhus-t h1 tarax
    - **touch** | **amel.**: tarax c1
  - **Knees**; below: anac h2
  - **Tendo** Achillis, evening: rat
- **Lower** limbs: *Agar* k* *Alum* alum-p k2 am-c ambr anac ant-t k* apoc *Arg-met* *Arg-n* *Ars* ars-s-f k2 asaf bar-c bar-s k2 berb calc bg1 carb-v *Carbn-s* chel chinin-s **Cic** k* **Cina** cinnb cocc coff crot-h k* *Cupr* k* *Gels* k* *Glon* k* guare k* helo helo-s rwt2• hep *Ign* k* ip bg1 *Kali-c* k* kali-i kali-sil k2 lach ptk1 *Lil-t* *Lyc* k* mag-c *Manc* k* meny k* merc *Mygal* k* *Nat-ar* *Nat-c* k* *Nat-m* k* nit-ac **Nux-v** k* onos *Op* k* ph-ac *Phos* *Plat* puls sep sil squil stann **Stram** k* stront-c *Sul-ac* **Sulph** k* *Tarent* tax-br oss1• thuj *Verat* k* **Zinc** k* zinc-p k2
  - **right**: meny k* mez sep zinc k*
    - **sitting** still agg.: plut-n srj7•
    - **sleep**; when falling asleep: *Arg-met*
    - **stranger** enters the room; when a: zinc
  - **left**: acon vh1 cod kali-br bg1 kali-i sne lach bg1 mag-c nat-c h2* nit-ac puls bg1 sep h2*
  - **forenoon**: sep h2*
  - **afternoon**: *Ars*
  - **evening**: am-c cinnb hep mag-c
  - **night**: *Arg-n* *Phos*
  - **cough** agg.; during: stram ptk1
    - **sitting** agg.: *Stram* k*
  - **hang** down; must let leg: *Verat*
  - **lying**:
    - **agg.**: alum am-c anac arg-n meny ptk1 *Verat*
    - **back**; on | **agg.**: nat-s
  - **motion**:
    - **agg.**: mang
    - **amel.**: hep *Thuj* valer k*
  - **pain** in thigh, from: lyc h2*
  - **painful**: hep lyc ptk1 *Meny* k*
  - **sitting** agg.: *Ars* lyc *Meny* k* sep h2*
  - **sleep** | **during** | **agg.**: *Ant-t* k* *Arg-n* cann-i c1 cinnb con cupr *Kali-c* k* *Lyc* k* mag-c nat-c *Nat-m* k* nit-ac ph-ac *Phos* *Sulph* k* **Zinc** k* zinc-p k2
    - **going** to sleep; on:
      - **agg.**: *Agar* *Anac* *Arg-met* bapt hr1 cham hyper **Kali-c** mag-c nat-c h2 *Nat-m* *Sulph* tax-br oss1• *Thuj* *Zinc*
        - **one** leg is jerked up: sulph
  - **sleeplessness**; during: thuj
  - **standing** agg.: mygal k*
  - **stepping** out, on: coff k* rhus-t
  - **stitches** in first toe, from: sil h2*
  - **upward**: ant-t bg2 arg-n bg2 bell bg2 calc bg1 coloc bg2 glon bg2 hep bg2 kali-c bg2 lach bg2* lyc bg2 meny bg2 mygal bg2 stram bg2 zinc bg2
- **Nates** | **jerking** up: cupr ptk1
- **Paralyzed** parts: arg-n merc *Nux-v* *Phos* *Sec* *Stry*
- **Shoulders**: alum k* ars k* *Lyc* puls k* sil k* spig sul-ac bg2 zinc
  - **right**: petr a1
  - **sudden**: alum k*
- **Side**:
  - **lain** on: cimic
  - **not** lain on: onos
- **Tendons**: cham h1* *Ign* hr1 *Kali-i* hr1
- **Thighs**: anac c1 *Arg-n* caps k* chin bg2 kali-bi k* *Kali-c* k* *Kali-i* k* lach k* lact laur lyc *Meny* k* nat-c nat-m nux-v k* phos k* plat k* rhus-t k* sabad bg2 sep stram k*
  - **right**: lyc *Meny* k* sil bg2
    - **drawing** up leg or standing amel.: *Meny* k*

Jerking – **Thighs**: ...
  - **evening**: kali-bi
  - **sitting** agg.: meny k*
  - **walking** agg.: sep
  - ○ **Posterior** part: manc phos h2*
    - **walking** agg.: phos h2*
- **Thumbs**: aeth a1
- **Toes**: **Agar** k* anac *Arg-n* hr1 berb k* *Calc* k* calc-p k* *Merc* k* nat-c a1
- **Upper** arms: anac ant-c h2* dulc a1 kali-bi k* *Lyc* meny nat-m nit-ac ph-ac
  - **right**: am-c kali-n ran-b
  - **left**: cupr h2*
  - **evening**: kali-bi
  - **painful**: cic hr1 mang a1
- **Upper** limbs: aesc *Agar* bro1 *Alum* k* amyg k* *Anac* ant-c br1* aran k* *Arg-n* ars asaf k* aur aur-m *Bar-m* k* bell k* berb k* camph k* cham chel **Cic** k* **Cina** k* cocc k* coff k* crot-h k* *Cupr* k* dulc *Graph* k* *Hyos* k* hyper k* *Ign* k* inul k* *Ip* k* kali-br k* kali-c lact-v bro1 *Lil-t* *Lyc* k* meny k* mez mygal k* nat-c nit-ac onos op bro1 plat *Puls* k* ran-b k* sil k* *Stann* k* **Stram** k* stront-c *Stry* sul-ac **Sulph** k* *Tarent* k* *Thlas* bro1 *Thuj* k* valer k* verat k* verat-v k* *Zinc*
  - **right**: aesc sep
    - **and** fingers: mez h2
  - **left**: acon vh1 androc srj1• *Cic* k* cimic ptk1 kali-i sne stann h2*
  - **daytime**: *Thuj* k*
  - **evening**: graph sil
  - **night**: am-c h2* bar-m k* graph k* lyc
  - **backward**: alum mez bg1
  - **cold** air agg.: sulph k*
  - **motion** of arm, on: dulc h2*
  - **paralyzed** arm: arg-n *Merc* *Nux-v* phos sec
  - **sideways**: arg-n ptk1
  - **sleep** | **during** | **agg.**: arg-met vh1 ip *Lyc* nat-c
    - **falling** asleep | **when**: *(↗Twitching - upper limbs - evening - sleep)* alum arg-met vh graph hyper k* kali-c lyc bg1 sil stront-c *Stry*
  - **talking** agg.: cic h1*
  - **towards** each other: ip ptk1
  - **upward**: arg-n ptk1 cic ptk1 cina ptk1 sabad ptk1 stram ptk1 sulph ptk1
  - **warm** room | **amel.**: sulph k*
  - **wind** agg.; cold: sulph hr1
- **Wrists**: anac arund k* chin bg2 pall k* rhus-t a1 thlas bg2
  - **right**: nat-c a1 pall k* *Rhus-t* a1 verat a1
  - **painful**: pall k*
  - **sudden**: pall k*

JUMPING: | **gait**: bufo bg2 verat-v tl1

JUMPING, sensation of something alive in arms (See Alive - upper - jumping)

KNEELING:
- **agg.** | **Lower** limbs: cocc b7.de* sep b4.de*

KNITTING:
- **agg.**:
  - ○ **Elbows**: mag-c ptk1
  - **Upper** limbs: kali-c b4.de* mag-c b4.de*
  - **Wrists**: kali-c ptk1
- **amel.** | **Upper** limbs: lyc b4.de*

KNOBBY: | **Fingers** | **Tips**: *Laur* k*
- **Toes** tips: laur br1

KNOCK KNEE (See Knees; position - inward)

KNOCKED together: agar k* *Con*
- ○ **Feet**: *Cann-s*
- **Knees**: agar arg-met *Arg-n* k* bry *Caust* k* chel clem coff *Colch* k* *Con* k* *Glon* k* nux-v
  - **fright**; after: cinnb

- **Knees**: ...
  - **walking** agg.: arg-n ptk1 caust ptk1 colch ptk1 con ptk1 glon ptk1 **Lath** bro1* *Phos* bg2 zinc ptk1
- **Toes**: *Asaf* plat

KNOCKING against things:
- **agg**.: cupr b7a.de

○ • **Lower** limbs: carb-v bg2 *Caust* b4a.de

LAMENESS: abrot k* acet-ac k2 aesc bg2 *Agar* k* agarin bro1 aloe k* *Am-m* b7.de* anac bg2 *Apis* arn k2 *Ars* k* *Aster* k* bell b4.de berb k2 bov k* bry k* calc b4a.de *Calc-p* bro1 cann-i k* carb-v b4a.de* *Carl* k* *Caust* k* *Cham* k* chel k* *Chin* k* cina b7a.de **Cinnb** k* *Cocc* k* **Colch** k* *Con* k* cupr k* dios br1 *Dros* k* dulc fd4.de *Eucal* bro1 *Ferr* b7a.de *Form* k* gins bro1 grat bg2 ip bro1 kali-bi k2 kali-br bg2 kali-chl k* kali-n k* kali-p bro1 kreos k* *Lith-c* bro1 lol bg2 med k2 **Merc** k* mez b4a.de nat-ar k2 nat-c k* nux-v bg2 pic-ac k2 plb b7.de *Puls* b7.de *Rhod* b4.de *Rhus-t* k* *Ruta* *Sil* k* *Spong* k* stram k* stront-c b4.de thuj b4a.de trios bro1 uran-n bg2 valer b7a.de verat k* xero bro1 *Zinc* k* [spect dfg1]
- **left** arm and foot after fright: stann
- **morning** | **waking**; on: abrot nat-c *Zinc*
- **evening**: sil h2*
- **night**: *Cham* k* ruta fd4.de
- **accompanied** by:
  - **urination**; complaints of (See BLADDER - Urination - complaints - accompanied - extremities)
  - ○ **Abdomen**; complaints of (See ABDOMEN - Complaints - accompanied - extremities - lameness)
- **fever**; during: *Arn* bg2 **Ars** bg2 *Bell* bg2 cina bg2 cocc bg2 cycl bg2 *Ign* bg2 *Nux-v* b7.de* *Ph-ac* bg2 puls bg2 rhus-t b7.de **Sabad** b7a.de* sabin bg2
- **intermittent**: influ jl2*
- **move**; beginning to: rhus-t k2
- **perspiration**:
  - **during**: *Acon* bg2 arn bg2 **Ars** bg2 bell bg2 cina bg2 cocc bg2 cycl bg2 *Ign* bg2 *Nux-v* bg2 ph-ac bg2 puls bg2 *Sabad* bg2 sabin bg2
  - **suppressed** perspiration; from: calc-sil k2
- ○ **Ankles**: abrot aesc k* am-br a1 *Arn* bry caps k* cedr k* com k* des-ac rbp6 dios k* fl-ac k* lath br1 laur k* lil-t k* lyss k* plb k* **Ruta** k*
  - **morning**: dios k* hipp a1 plb k*
    - **rising** agg.; after: caps k*
  - **evening** | **walking** agg.: fl-ac
  - **sitting** agg.: *Nat-m* k*
  - **sprain**, after: des-ac rbp6 *Rhus-t* **Ruta**
  - **sudden**: com k*
  - **walking**:
    - **agg**.: des-ac rbp6 *Nat-m* k*
    - **air** agg.; in open: com
- **Elbows**: *All-c* dios k* dulc k* hydr k* iris merc-i-f k* mez petr sars h2
  - **morning**: dios k*
- **Feet**: abrot k* am-br k* *Aur* bell k* *Colch* com k* fl-ac k* hydrog srj2• hyper k* lath a1 merc-i-f k* nat-m *Rhus-t* sil k* thuj k* tub k*
  - **afternoon**: thuj k*
  - **pregnancy** agg.; during: sil k*
  - ○ **Sole** of: (non:cupr slp) cupr-act slp kali-p k* ulm-c jsj8•
    - **evening**: ulm-c jsj8•
- **Fingers**: bov k* *Calc* k* carb-v hipp a1 hyper k* kali-c kali-m ptk1 merc-i-f a1 prot fmm1• *Sep* k*
  - ○ **Second**: cimic k* rhus-t k*
  - **Third**: bry k*
    - **writing**; after: bry k*
- **Forearms**: agar aids nl2• bell berb k* *Caust* cere-b a1 colch k* dulc k* fl-ac k* merc-i-f k* myric k* nat-m *Sil* stront-c sulph thuj k*
  - ○ **Wrist**; near: cere-b a1 myric k*
- **Hands**: abrot k* acet-ac k* agar k* ars k* *Caust* ptk1 *Cupr* k* fl-ac k* hipp a1 *Kali-bi* k* mez ptk1 nat-m nat-s k* phos rhus-t k* *Sil* k* stront-c sulph k* tab k* tub mtf33 *Zinc* k*
  - **10** h: abrot
  - **convulsions**; before: kali-bi hr1
  - **exertion** agg.; after: mez ptk1 *Sil* k*
  - **raising** a cup or glass: tub mtf33

Lameness – Hands: ...
  - **sudden**: cann-s k*
  - **writing** agg.: mez ptk1 *Sil* k* tub mtf33
- **Hips**: abrot k* ammc arn ars-n bry k* cham bg1 cocc k* dios k* dros bg2 dulc a1 fl-ac k* ph-ac a1 pot-e rly4• rhus-t k* sars h2 zing k*
  - **left**: am-m *Fl-ac* k*
  - **afternoon**, 14 h: dios
  - **bathing**, while: ars-met
  - **rising** from sitting agg.; after: ars-met
  - **stepping** agg.: euph h2
  - **walking**:
    - **agg**.: dios k* euph k*
    - **amel**.: ars-met
- **Joints**: (↗*Pain - joints - rheumatic*) abrot k* all-c bro1 arn k2 berb k2 brom cinnb **Rhus-t** k* **Ruta** k* *Sil* sulph bro1
  - **chill**; during: *Rhus-t* *Tub*
  - **fever**; during: *Rhus-t* *Tub*
  - **perspiration**; from suppressed: rhus-t k2
  - **sprain**, after: calc **Rhus-t** **Ruta**
  - **waking** agg.; after: hydrog srj2• nat-c k*
- **Knees**: abrot *All-c* k* ars aur *Bar-c* k* berb k* bry *Calc* k* calc-s k* caps carb-v cinnb cocc k* com k* dios k* fl-ac *Kali-c* lath br1 merc rheum sep *Spong* k* *Sulph* k*
  - **right**: com k* lyss spong k*
  - **left**: *Calc* k* calc-s k* [tax jsj7]
  - **morning**: abrot caps dios lyss k*
  - **descending** agg.: sulph h2
  - **kneeling** agg.: ars-h k*
  - **rising** from sitting agg.; after: *Berb* k*
  - **sitting** agg.: kali-c h2
  - **walking** | **after** | **agg**.: carb-v h2
    - **agg**.: bry cinnb lac-h htj1• merc merc-sul c1
- **Legs**: carb-v h2 hep h2 kali-bi bg1 kali-br hr1
  - **exercise**; as from: cob-n sp1
  - **urination** agg.; during: lyc bg2
  - ○ **Calves**: ars-i k* pic-ac k*
- **Lower** limbs: acon bg2 aesc-g agar tl1 alum bg2 apis arn ars k* *Bell* berb k* calc-p k* carb-v caust k* cocc bg2 **Colch** dig dulc fd4.de fl-ac gels bg2 hydrog srj2• iod kali-bi bg1 lyc k* **Nat-m** k* ox-ac k* ph-ac *Phos* k* *Plb* k* prot fmm1• *Rhus-t* k* ruta fd4.de sep sil k* stann **Sulph** zinc
  - **right**: sil h2
  - **morning**: nat-m k* *Sil*
    - **waking**; on: hydrog srj2•
  - **afternoon**: myric k*
  - **evening**: *Lyc* k*
  - **chill**; during: ign *Lyc* *Rhus-t* *Tub*
  - **fever**; during: *Rhus-t* *Tub*
  - **intermittent**: prot pte1*•
  - **menses** | **before** | **agg**.: nit-ac
    - **during** | **agg**.: mag-m phos
  - **perspiration**; from suppressed: **Colch** k* **Rhus-t**
  - **rising** from sitting agg.: sil h2
  - **walking**:
    - **agg**.: ammc bell calc carb-an *Colch* coloc dros eup-per kali-i lyc k* nit-ac puls *Rhus-t* ruta fd4.de zinc
    - **amel**.: sil h2
- **Muscles** | **Flexor** muscles: calc-p k*
- **Shoulders**: abrot k* aesc k* *All-c* ambr bism k* bry k* cann-i a1 carb-ac k* cer-s a1 cimic k* cinnb a1 coc-c k* dios k* *Fl-ac* k* kali-i k* *Lach* k* laur k* *Merc-i-f* k* *Nat-m* k* phyt k* psor k* *Rhus-t* k* sep k* til a1 zing k*
  - **right**: merc-i-f k*
  - **morning** | **waking**; on: abrot calc-ar
  - **evening** | **heated**; when: coc-c
  - **night** | **waking**; on: coc-c

Extremities

- **Shoulders**: ...
  - **raising** arm agg.: bry k*
  - **smoking** agg.: carb-ac k*
  - **walking** agg.: carb-ac k*
  - **writing** agg.: merc-i-f
- **Thighs**: aloe *Ars* k* *Ars-met* aur bar-c *Calc* k* *Carb-v* card-m k* caust *Chin* k* cinnb k* cocc k* dirc a1 dros k* hep h2 hyper *Iris* *Kali-c* lyss k* *Merc* nux-v puls k* sarr k* sil h2 *Stann* sulph k* *Zinc*
  - **right**: sil h2
  - **ascending** stairs agg.: bar-c
  - **flatus**; from: carb-v h2
  - **menses**; during: *Carb-an* k*
  - **motion** | **amel**.: cocc
  - **walking**:
    - **agg**.: bar-c cinnb zinc
    - **air** agg.; in open: nux-v
- **Thumbs**: calc-s k* kali-c h2* laur bg2 mez bg2 nit-ac bg2 phos bg2 rhod bg2 sabad bg2
- **Toes**: *Aur* ruta bg1
- **Upper** arms: abrot k* act-sp *Agar* k* bell bry k* colch k* com k* iris pieri-b mlk9.de plat h2 plect a1 puls-n thuj k* zing k*
  - **left**: agar k*
  - **raising** it, on: bry k*
  - **riding** agg.: abrot k*
  - **writing** agg.: agar k*

▽ - **extending** to | **Neck**; back of: iris

- **Upper** limbs: abrot k* *Acon* bro1 *Agar* k* alum am-c bro1 ars k* bapt bro1 **Bell** k* berb bism bov k* *Brom* **Calc** k* calc-p cann-i bro1 carb-v k* carl k* *Caust* k* *Cinnb* k* *Cocc* com *Cycl* dig *Dulc* *Ferr* *Fl-ac* k* glon k* graph hyper kali-c k* kreos lat-m bnm6• lyc *Mag-c* merc-i-f k* mez nat-s k* ol-an par bro1 *Phyt* plb *Psor* *Rhus-t* *Rhus-v* bro1 *Sep* **Sil** k* stann sul-ac thuj k* tub mtf33 verat k* ziz bro1
  - **right**: acet-ac **Ferr** k* fl-ac k* kali-c h2 merc-i-f k* nit-ac h2 ozone sde2• **Sang** k* sulph h2
  - **left**: agar k* brom gt1* hyper kali-c h2 lach merc-i-f a1 *Rhus-t*
  - **morning**: fl-ac k*
    - **waking**; on: abrot k*
  - **forenoon**: *Fl-ac* k*
  - **afternoon**: agar k*
  - **night**, 22 h: fl-ac
  - **beaten**, as if: anthraci kr1 plat h2 verat k*
  - **exertion** agg.; slight: sil h2
  - **lying** on it: fl-ac
  - **neuralgia**, after: ars k*
  - **raising** | **arm** | **agg**.: syph
    - **cup** or glass; a: tub mtf33
  - **rheumatic**: *Calc-p* carb-v k* **Rhus-t**
  - **spot**, in: plat h2
  - **waking**; on: abrot k*
  - **walking** agg.: dig digin a1
  - **weather** agg.; cold wet: **Rhus-t**
  - **writing**:
    - **after**: *Agar* fl-ac *Merc-i-f* k*
    - **agg**.: tub mtf33
- **Wrists**: acet-ac k* all-c asar k* calc-p k* cimic k* com k* dios k* hipp a1 *Kali-c* k* lac-c lept a1 lyss k* *Merc* mez nux-v plb k* rhus-t **Ruta** sil k*
  - **morning**: plb k* sil k* tanac a1
  - **bruised**, as if: calc-p k* **Ruta**
  - **sprain**, after: hipp jl2 **Rhus-t** **Ruta**

LANGUOR (See Heaviness)

LARGE (See Enlargement)

LASSITUDE (See Heaviness)

LAUGHING agg.:

○ - **Lower** limbs: tell bg2
- **Upper** limbs: carb-v b4a.de*

LICKING part with tongue:

- **amel**. | **Upper** limbs: mang b4.de*

LIFTING:

- **high** when walking (See Walking - lifting)
- **weight**; lifting a:
  - **agg**.:
    - **Elbows**: cham ptk1
    - **Lower** limbs: *Caust* b4a.de graph b4.de* iod b4.de* ph-ac b4.de*
    - **Upper** limbs: alum bg2 caust b4.de* ruta bg2 sep b4.de*
  - **amel**. | **Upper** limbs: spig ptk1

○ - **Lower** limbs:
  - **impossible** | **lying**; when: lath c1*

LIGHTNESS, sensation of: *(↗MIND - Delusions - light [=low - is)* agar1*]• *Asar* k* calc-ar hr1* camph b7a.de* cann-i carl chin k* *Coff* k* dig gins hyos k* ign b7a.de *Ip* b7a.de lact br1 m-aust b2.de* nat-m k* nux-m k* nux-v b2.de* *Op* k* **Ph-ac** rhus-t k* spig k* stict k* *Stram* k* thuj k*

- **chill**; during: spig b7.de
- **in** spite of much walking or a bad night: gins c1

○ - **Lower** limbs: acon ptk1 bell bg2 *Ign* b7a.de manc bg2 *Op* b7.de* *Ph-ac* k* spig ptk1 stict k* zinc-i ptk1
  - **walking** agg.; after: valer k*

○ - **Legs**: helodr-cal knl2•
- **Single** limbs: **Cann-i** mrr1
- **Upper** limbs: helodr-cal knl2• ph-ac ptk1

LIMPING: *(↗Claudicatio; Walking - difficult)* abrot bg2 acon b7.de* ant-c bg2 bell b4.de* calc bg2 carb-an b4a.de *Caust* bg2* coloc bg2* dros b7.de* dulc bg2* hep bg2 hydrog srj2• kali-bi bg2 kali-c bg2* kali-i bg2 lyc bg2 merc bg2 nit-ac b4.de* phos b4.de* rhus-t ptk1 sabin b7.de* sec mrr1 sep b4.de* sulph bg2 syph bg2 tab bg2*

- **intermittent**: prot fmm1•
- **pain** in knee; from: spig h1

LIPOMA: petr tl1

○ - **Thighs**: bar-c tl1 petr tl1

LOCOMOTOR ATAXIA (See GENERALS - Locomotor)

LONGER:

- **sensation** as if: ulm-c jsj8•

○ - **Lower** limbs: alum bg2 aster bg2 carb-an bg2 coloc b4a.de* kali-c ptk1 kreos b7a.de* lac-c bg2 phos bg2 rhus-t b7a.de* sulph b4a.de* thuj b4a.de*
    - **standing** agg.: kreos ptk1
  - **Upper** limbs:
    - **right** | **body**; as if right arm longer then: cupr ptk1

○ - **Fingers**: kali-n h2 phos mrr1* [tax jsj7]
  - **sensation** of elongation: tab bg2
- **Legs**: *Kali-c* kreos k* stram k* thuj k*
  - **sensation** as if: alum bg1 aster bg1 coloc bg1 kreos ptk1 lac-c bg1 phos bg1 rhus-t bg1 sulph bg1 tab bg1
    - **night** | **lying** down agg.: carb-an phos k13
- **Toes** seem: kola stb3• thuj bg1

LOOSE; as if flesh were: mez bg2 staph h1 *Thuj* k* visc bg2

○ - **Foot** | **left**: arg-met h1
- **Lower** limbs: kreos b7a.de led b7.de* mosch b7a.de nux-v b7.de* rhus-t b7.de*
- **Shoulders**: croc bg2 kali-bi bg2 staph bg2
- **Thighs**: nat-c h2
- **Upper** limbs: **Bry** bg2 *Dros* b7.de* ign b7a.de* rhus-t b7.de* staph b7.de* sulph b4a.de thuj b4.de*

LOOSENESS:
- **sensation** of looseness:
  - ○ • **Ankles**: arg-met b7.de*
  - • **Bones**: nat-m bg2
  - • **Hips**: apis bg2 calc bg2 lyss c1 staph bg2 thuj bg2
  - • **Joints**: agar bg2 arg-met bg2 arg-n bg2 bov ptk1 bry bg2 bufo bg2 calc-p bg2 caps bg2 caust bg2 chel bg2* croc dulc bg2 falco-pe nl2• fl-ac bg2 kali-bi bg2 m-ambo b2.de* med ptk1 nat-c bg2 nat-m bg2 ph-ac bg2* phos bg2 phyt bg2 positr nl2• *Psor* bg2* **Stram** k* sulph bg2 thuj ptk1 wildb c1
    - ⁝ **Small** joints: carb-an bg2 nat-c bg2
  - • **Knee** joints: phos b4.de*
  - • **Shoulders** | **Joints**: *Croc* b7a.de
- ○ - **Fingernails**; of (See Nails - exfoliation)

LOSS of nails (See Nails - falling)

LUMPS (See Nodules)

LUPUS of one elbow: hep

LYING:
- **affected** part; on:
  - • **agg.**:
    - ⁝ **Lower** limbs: am-c b4.de* ars bg2 carb-an b4.de* carb-v b4.de* chin b7.de* dros b7.de* hep b4.de* ign b7.de* kali-bi bg2 kali-i bg2 mur-ac b4.de* rhod b4.de* rhus-t b7.de* sabad b7a.de sep b4.de* sil b4.de* staph b7.de* tell bg2
    - ⁝ **Upper** limbs: am-c b4.de* **Ambr** b7.de* anac b4.de* ars b4.de* *Bar-c* b4.de* calc b4.de* croc b7.de* dros b7.de* graph b4.de* hep b4a.de* ign b7.de* *Iod* b4a.de kali-c b4.de* mag-c b4.de* mag-m b4.de* petr b4.de* rheum b7.de* rhod b4a.de rhus-t b7.de* **Sil** b4.de* sulph b4.de* *Thuj* b4a.de
- **after**:
  - • **agg.** | **Lower** limbs: acon b7.de* calad b7.de* caps b7.de* sel b7.de*
- **agg.**: kali-c ptk1
  - ○ • **Legs**:
    - ⁝ **Bones** | **Tibia**: puls ptk1
  - • **Lower** limbs: am-c b4.de* asaf b7.de* bry b7.de* calc b4.de* carb-v b4.de* caust b4.de* cham b7.de* chin b7.de* dros b7.de* *Ferr* b7.de* gnaph bg2 ign b7.de* kali-bi bg2 led b7.de* lyc b4.de* merc b4.de* nux-m b7.de* nux-v b7.de* olnd b7.de* petr b4.de* plb b7.de* *Puls* b7.de* *Rhus-t* b7.de* ruta b7.de* sel b7.de* sep b4.de* *Sil* b4.de* spong b7.de* staph b7.de* viol-t b7.de*
- **amel.**:
  - ○ • **Knees**: merc bg2
  - • **Lower** limbs: am-m bg2 bar-c b4.de* *Bry* b7.de* canth b7.de* *Gnaph* bg2 kali-n b4.de* nux-m b7.de* *Nux-v* b7.de* olnd b7.de* par b7.de* sabad b7.de*
- **arms** stretched out; with | **Upper** limbs: *Alum* b4a.de
- **arms** under head agg.; with: olnd b7.de* staph b7.de*
- **back**; on:
  - • **agg.**:
    - ⁝ **Lower** limbs: nux-v b7.de* sep bg2
    - ⁝ **Upper** limbs: cham b7.de* kali-n bg2 nux-v b7.de*
  - • **amel.**:
    - ⁝ **Lower** limbs: bry b7.de* ign b7.de*
    - ⁝ **Upper** limbs: *Bry* b7.de* *Ign* b7.de* puls b7.de*
- **bed**; in:
  - • **agg.**:
    - ⁝ **Lower** limbs: alum b4.de* *Am-c* b4a.de am-m b7.de* ambr b7.de* ant-t b7.de* arg-met b7.de* arn b7.de* ars b4.de* asar b7.de* aur b4.de* *Bell* b4.de* bov b4.de* bry b7.de* canth b7.de* carb-an b4.de* carb-v b4.de* caust b4.de* *Cham* b7.de* clem b4.de* colch b7.de* coloc b4a.de con b4.de* dros b7.de* *Ferr* b7.de* **Graph** b4.de* hell b7.de* hep b4.de* ign b7.de* *Kali-c* b4.de* kali-n b4.de* led b7.de* lyc b4.de* m-ambo b7.de m-arct b7.de m-aust b7.de mag-c b4.de* mag-m b4.de* merc b4.de* mez b4.de* mur-ac b4.de* nat-c b4.de* *Nat-m* b4a.de nit-ac b4a.de *Nux-v* b7.de* *Par* b7a.de petr b4.de* ph-ac b4.de* phos b4.de* plat b4.de* **Puls** b7.de* ran-b b7.de* rhod b4.de* **Rhus-t** b7.de* ruta b7.de* sabad b7.de* sabin b7.de samb b7.de* sel b7.de* seneg b4.de* *Sep* b4.de* sil b4.de* spong b7.de* staph b7.de* *Stront-c* b4.de* sulph b4.de* teucr b7.de* thuj b4.de* *Valer* b7.de* viol-t b7.de*

Lying – bed; in – **agg.**: ...
- ⁝ **Upper** limbs: alum b4.de* am-c b4.de* am-m b7.de* ambr b7.de* arn b7.de* ars b4.de* asaf b7.de* asar b7.de* aur b4.de* bar-c b4.de* *Bry* b7.de* *Calc* b4.de* carb-an b4.de* *Cham* b7.de* chin b7.de* con b4.de* croc b7.de* dulc b4.de* euph b4.de* ferr b7.de* hell b7.de* ign b7.de* *Iod* b4a.de kali-c b4.de* led b7.de* *Lyc* b4.de* m-ambo b7.de m-arct b7.de m-aust b7.de *Mag-c* b4.de* *Mag-m* b4a.de mang b4.de* merc b4.de* mez b4.de* mosch b7.de* nat-c b4.de* nat-m b4.de* nit-ac b4.de* nux-v b7.de* olnd b7.de* petr b4.de* phos b4.de* *Puls* b7.de* *Rhod* b4.de* *Rhus-t* b7.de* ruta b7.de* sep b4.de* *Sil* b4.de* spig b7.de* spong b7.de* staph b7.de* stront-c b4.de* sul-ac b4.de* sulph b4.de* teucr b7.de* valer b7.de* zinc b4.de*
- • **amel.** | **Upper** limbs: am-m b7.de* bry b7.de* canth b7.de* *Nux-v* b7.de* *Olnd* b7.de* sep b4.de*

- **side**; on:
  - • **side** lain on | **agg.** | **Upper** limbs: ars b4.de* hep b4.de* *Ign* b7.de* mang b4.de* nux-v b7.de* puls b7.de* rheum b7.de* rhus-t b7.de* *Sil* b4.de* *Thuj* b4a.de
    - ⁝ **amel.** | **Upper** limbs: carb-an b4.de*
  - • **side** not lain on | **Upper** limbs: carb-an b4.de cham b7.de ign b7.de* kali-bi bg2 m-aust b7.de nux-v b7.de *Sep* b4a.de
  - • **painful** side:
    - ⁝ **agg.**:
      - ⁝ **Lower** limbs: *Nux-v* b7.de* sabad b7a.de
      - ⁝ **Upper** limbs: ign b7.de* *Nux-v* b7.de* spong b7.de*
    - ⁝ **amel.**:
      - ⁝ **Lower** limbs: ambr b7.de* arn b7.de* bry b7.de* carb-v b4.de* *Caust* b4a.de cham b7.de* ign b7.de* puls b7.de*
      - ⁝ **Upper** limbs: ambr b7.de* arn b7.de* bry b7.de* cham b7.de* *Ign* b7.de* kali-c b4.de* lyc b4.de* m-aust b7.de nux-v b7.de* *Puls* b7.de*
  - • **painless** side:
    - ⁝ **agg.**:
      - ⁝ **Lower** limbs: *Bry* b7.de* *Caust* b4a.de cham b7.de* *Ign* b7.de* m-aust b7.de *Sep* b4a.de
      - ⁝ **Upper** limbs: bry b7.de* cham b7.de* fl-ac bg2 ign b7.de* mag-m bg2 nux-v b7.de* puls b7.de*
    - ⁝ **amel.** | **Lower** limbs: am-c b4.de* ign b7.de* m-aust b7.de mag-m b4.de* *Nux-v* b7.de*
  - • **unusual** side:
    - ⁝ **agg.** | **Upper** limbs: carb-an bg2 cham bg2 ign bg2 nux-v bg2 puls bg2 rheum bg2 rhus-t bg2

LYING DOWN:
- **after**:
  - • **agg.** | **Upper** limbs: ang b7.de* hep bg2 ign b7.de* ip b7.de* m-ambo b7.de m-arct b7.de mosch b7.de* nux-v b7.de* *Puls* b7.de* rhus-t b7.de* sabad b7.de*
- **agg.** | **Lower** limbs: ang b7.de* ign b7.de* ip b7.de* m-ambo b7.de nux-v b7.de* par b7.de* *Puls* b7.de* ran-b b7.de* rhus-t b7.de* sabad b7.de* samb b7.de* staph b7.de* teucr b7.de*
- **amel.**:
  - ○ • **Lower** limbs: *Am-m* b7.de* *Nux-v* b7.de* puls b7.de*
  - • **Upper** limbs: *Am-m* b7.de* *Nux-v* b7.de* olnd b7.de* spig b7.de*
- **before**:
  - • **agg.**:
    - ⁝ **Lower** limbs: nux-v b7.de* ran-b b7.de*
    - ⁝ **Upper** limbs: nux-v b7.de* ran-b b7.de*

MENSES:
- **after**: calc-p bg2 kreos bg2 nat-p bg2
  - • **agg.**:
    - ⁝ **Lower** limbs: calc-p bg2 kreos bg2
    - ⁝ **Upper** limbs: graph bg2
- **before**:
  - • **agg.**:
    - ⁝ **Hips**: calc bg2 cimic bg2 lach bg2 sars bg2 ust bg2
    - ⁝ **Lower** limbs: aesc bg2 bar-c bg2 *Calc* bg2 caul bg2 cham b7.de* cimic bg2 coloc b4a.de* con bg2 cycl bg2 gels bg2 hyos b7.de* hyper bg2 kali-c bg2 kali-p bg2 lac-c bg2 lach bg2 **Lyc** bg2 mag-m b4.de* merc bg2

Extremities

- **before – agg.** – **Lower** limbs: ...
  nit-ac bg2 phos bg2 sars b4.de* staph bg2 sulph bg2 ust bg2 vib bg2 *Zinc* bg2
  ⁝ **Nates**: mang bg2
  ⁝ **Thighs**: carb-an bg2 *Cham* bg2 hyos bg2 mag-m bg2
  ⁝ **Upper** limbs: ang bg2 bar-c bg2 *Coloc* b4a.de kali-c bg2 kreos bg2 lyc b4.de* nit-ac b4.de* puls b7.de* sep b4.de* sil b4.de*
- **during**:
  - **agg.**:
    ⁝ **Lower** limbs: aesc bg2 agar bg2 agn bg2 aloe bg2 alum bg2 am-c bg2 *Ambr* b7.de* apis bg2 arn bg2 ars bg2 asar bg2 bell bg2 berb bg2 bov b4.de* *Bry* b7.de* bufo bg2 *Calc* bg2 calc-p bg2 cann-xyz bg2 canth bg2 *Carb-an* b4.de* carb-v bg2 castm bg2 caul bg2 caust bg2 cham b7.de* *Cimic* bg2 cocc bg2 coff bg2 colch bg2 con bg2 croc bg2 crot-h bg2 cupr bg2 cycl bg2 ferr bg2 gels bg2 glon bg2 **Graph** bg2 ham bg2 hyos bg2 iod bg2 *Kali-c* b4.de* kali-i bg2 *Kali-n* bg2 kalm bg2 lach bg2 lil-t bg2 lyc b4.de* *Mag-c* bg2 mag-m b4.de* mosch bg2 nat-c bg2 nat-m bg2 nat-s bg2 *Nit-ac* bg2 nux-m b7.de* *Nux-v* b7.de* ol-an bg2 *Petr* bg2 phel bg2 *Phos* bg2 *Puls* b7.de* rhod bg2 rhus-t bg2 sars b4.de* sec b7.de* sep bg2 *Sil* bg2 spong b7.de* *Stram* b7.de* sul-ac bg2 **Sulph** bg2 thuj bg2 verat b7.de* vib bg2 **Zinc** bg2
    ⁝ **Shoulders**: fl-ac ptk1 sang ptk1 ust ptk1
    ⁝ **Thighs**: mag-m ptk1 meny ptk1 xan ptk1
    ⁝ **Upper** limbs: *Agar* bg2 alum bg2 am-c b4.de* am-m b7.de* arn bg2 ars bg2 bell b4.de* berb bg2 bry b7.de* calc bg2 canth bg2 carb-v bg2 c h a m b7.de* coff bg2 con bg2 croc bg2 crot-h bg2 elaps bg2 **Graph** b4.de* hyos bg2 kali-c b4.de* kali-n bg2 lob bg2 lyc b4.de* mag-c b4.de* mag-m b4.de* merc bg2 nat-c bg2 nat-m bg2 nit-ac b4.de* *Nux-m* b7.de* *Nux-v* b7.de* ol-an bg2 petr b4.de* phos b4.de* puls b7.de* rhod bg2 rhus-t bg2 sec bg2 sep bg2 sil bg2 spong bg2 stram b7.de* sul-ac bg2 s u l p h bg2 verat b7.de* zinc b4.de*
    ⁝ **Wrist**: nat-p ptk1
  - **beginning** of; at the: lyc bg2 nit-ac bg2 sep bg2 sil bg2
    ⁝ **agg.** | **Lower** limbs: ars bg2
    ⁝ **amel.** | **Lower** limbs: cycl bg2

MENTAL EXERTION agg.: | **Upper** limbs: borx b4a.de

MERCURY; after abuse of:
- **agg.** | **Lower** limbs: stront-c b4.de*

METASTASIS: apat mtf11

MILK LEG (= phlebitis): *(↗GENERALS - Inflammation - blood - veins) Acon* c2* *All-c* k* ant-c k* apis k* *Arn* k* *Ars* k* **Bell** k ●* *Bism* c2* both st1 **Bry** k* *Bufo* k* **CALC** k ●* calc-f bg2 carbn-s *Cham* *Chin* k* crot-h k* d i g bg2 euph bg2 graph k* *Ham* k* helo-s bnm14• hep k* hippoz c2 *Iod* k* *Kali-c* k* kreos bg2 **LACH** k ●* *Led* **Lyc** k ●* merc k* *Nat-s* k* nux-v k* parathyr jl2 **Puls** k ●* rhod k* **RHUS-T** k ●* *Sabin* bg2 **Sep** k ●* *Sil* k* **Sulph** k ●* urt-u c2* verat vip bg2*
- **left**: parathyr jl2
- **contractions**, with: *Sil* k*
- **delivery**; after: acon bg2 all-c ptk1 *Arn* bg2 ars bg2 *Bell* bg2 calc bg2 iod bg2 lach bg2 nux-v bg2 puls bg2 **Rhus-t** bg2 sil bg2 sulph bg2

MISSING steps (See Awkwardness - lower - descending)

MOISTURE:

○ - **Knees** | **Hollow** of knees: graph bg2

MOTION: *Bell* nux-v sars stram
- **after**:
  - **agg.**:
    ⁝ **Lower** limbs: arn b7.de* croc b7.de* iod b4.de* puls b7.de* *Zinc* b4a.de
    ⁝ **Upper** limbs: hyos b7.de* *Kali-c* b4a.de puls b7.de* *Zinc* b4a.de
- **agg.**:
  ○ - **Knee** | **Hollow**: nat-c ptk1 plb ptk1
  - **Lower** limbs: acon b7.de* agn b7.de* *Ambr* b7a.de ang b7.de* ant-t bg2 arg-met b7.de* *Arn* b7.de* ars b4.de* asar b7.de* bar-c b4.de* bell b4.de* **Bry** b7.de* bufo bg2 calc b4.de* camph b7.de* cann-s b7.de* canth b7.de* caps b7.de* *Caust* b4a.de cham bg2 chel b7.de* *Chin* b7.de* cocc b7.de* c o l c h b7.de* coloc b4.de* dig b4.de* dros b7.de* euph b7.de* graph bg2 *Guaj* b4a.de hep b4a.de* hyos b7.de* ign b7.de* iod b4.de* ip b7.de* kali-bi bg2 kali-c b4.de* kalm bg2 *Kreos* b7a.de laur b7.de* *Led* b7.de* lyc b4.de* m-aust b7.de* mag-c b4.de* *Merc* b4.de* nat-c b4.de* nux-m b7.de* *Nux-v* b7.de* par bg2 petr b4.de* ph-ac b4.de* phos b4.de* phyt bg2 *Puls* b7.de* ran-b b7.de* rheum b7.de* rhus-t b7.de* ruta b7.de* sabad bg2 sabin b7a.de* *Sars* b4a.de sel b7.de* sep b4.de* sil b4.de* spig b7.de* spong bg2 squil b7.de* staph b7.de* s u l p h b4.de* tarax bg2 teucr b7.de* thuj b4.de* verat b7.de*
  - **Upper** limbs: *Acon* b7.de* agar b4.de* agn b7.de* alum bg2 am-c b4.de* am-m b7.de* anac b4.de* ang b7.de* ant-t b7.de* arg-met b7.de* *Arn* b7.de* *Bell* b4.de* bov b4.de* **Bry** b7.de* bufo bg2 *Calc* b4a.de cann-s b7a.de caps b7.de* carb-v b4.de* caust b4.de* chel b7.de* *Chin* b7.de* cic b7.de* c o c c b7.de* colch b7.de* coloc b4.de* croc b7.de* dig ptk1 dros b7.de* euph b4.de* *Guaj* b4a.de hep b4.de* hyos b7.de* ign b7.de* kali-bi bg2 kali-c b4.de* kalm bg2 led b7.de* lyc b4.de* m-arct b7.de mag-c b4.de* m a g - m b4.de* mag-p bg2 merc b4.de* mez b4.de* mur-ac b4.de* nat-c b4.de* *Nat-m* b4.de* nit-ac b4.de* *Nux-v* b7.de* ph-ac b4.de* phos b4.de* plat b4.de* puls b7.de* ran-b b7.de* *Rheum* b7a.de rhod b4.de* rhus-t ptk1 ruta b7.de* sabad b7.de* sabin b7.de* sars b4.de* *Sep* b4.de* sil b4.de* spig b7.de* spong b7.de* squil b7.de* stann b4.de* **Staph** b7.de* sulph b4.de* verat b7.de*
- **agility**, great: coca a1 form c1 *Stram* [tax jsj7]
- **air**; in open:
  - **agg.** | **Lower** limbs: phyt bg2
- **amel.**: ars ptk1 *Rhus-t* ptk1 *Zinc* ptk1
  ○ - **Heels**: gard-j vlr2•
  - **Lower** limbs: *Agar* b4a.de am-m b7.de* anac b4.de* ang b7.de* arg-met b7.de* arn bg2 ars b4.de* asaf b7.de* aur b4.de* bar-c b4.de* *Bell* b4.de* bism b7.de* *Bry* b7.de* calc b4.de* *Caps* b7.de* *Caust* b4a.de *Cham* b7.de* chin b7.de* cina b7.de* con b4.de* croc b7.de* cycl b7.de* *Dros* b7.de* dulc b4.de* euph b4.de* ferr b7a.de* gels bg2 guaj b4.de* hyos b7.de* kali-c b4.de* kali-p bg2 lach bg2 laur b7.de* lyc b4a.de* mag-c b4.de* mag-m b4.de* mang b4.de* *Meny* b7.de* merc-c b4a.de mosch b7a.de* mur-ac b4.de* nat-c b4.de* nat-m bg2 *Nux-v* bg2 olnd b7.de* ph-ac b4.de* plat b4.de* plb b7.de* *Puls* b7.de* *Rhus-t* b7.de* ruta b7.de* sil b4.de* spig b7.de* spong b7.de* stann b4.de* stront-c b4.de* sulph b4.de* teucr b7.de* valer b7.de* verb b7.de* viol-t b7.de* zinc-val bg2
  - **Upper** limbs: acon b7.de* alum b4.de* *Am-m* b7.de* anac b4.de* ang b7.de* arg-met b7.de* asaf b7.de* aur b4.de* bism b7.de* calc b4.de* c h a m b7.de* chin b7.de* cina b7.de* cocc b7.de* con b4.de* cycl b7.de* d r o s b7.de* dulc b4.de* euph b4.de* *Ferr* b7a.de ferr-p bg2 hyos b7.de* ign b7.de* kali-bi bg2 *Lyc* b4.de* mang b4.de* meny b7.de* merc b4.de* m o s c h b7.de* mur-ac b4.de* nat-m b4.de* ph-ac b4.de* phos b4.de* plat b4.de* psor bg2 puls b7.de* rhod b4.de* rhus-t b7.de* ruta b7.de* *Sabad* b7.de* sars b4.de* sep b4.de* stann b4.de* staph b7.de* stront-c b4.de* *Thuj* b4a.de valer b7.de* *Verat* b7.de* verb b7.de* viol-t b7.de*
- **athetosis** (See Athetosis)
- **backward** motion of arm agg. | **Upper** limbs: ign bg2
- **beginning** of:
  - **agg.**:
    ⁝ **Lower** limbs: asar b7.de* bry b7.de* calc b4.de* caps b7.de* carb-v b4.de* caust b4.de* chin b7.de* cocc b7.de* *Con* b4a.de dros b7.de* *Ferr* b7.de* mag-c b4.de* nit-ac b4.de* petr b4.de* plat b4.de* *Puls* b7.de* rhod b4.de* *Rhus-t* b7.de* thuj b4.de*
    ⁝ **Upper** limbs: *Caps* b7a.de cupr b7.de* ferr b7.de* puls b7.de* rhus-t b7.de*
- **bizarre**: hyos mrr1
- **circular**, spiral: stram br1
- **constant**: *Ars* k* *Bell* tarent k2
  - **convulsions**, between: *Arg-n*
  - **sleep**, during: **Caust**
- **continued**:
  - **amel.**:
    ⁝ **Lower** limbs: caps b7.de* chin b7.de* cina b7.de* dros b7.de* *Ferr* b7.de* *Puls* b7.de* ran-b bg2 sabad b7.de* *Samb* b7.de*
    ⁝ **Upper** limbs: caps b7.de* dros b7.de* ferr b7.de* puls b7.de* sabad b7.de* samb b7.de*
- **control** of, lost: *Bell* chinin-s *Gels* k* merc-c op *Stram*
- **convulsive**: absin acon **Agar** agar-ph *Arg-n* aster aur-m **Bell** k* calc-p cann-i carbn-s *Caust* *Chlor* cocc k* colch *Con* b4.de crot-h *Cupr* k* kali-c lyc *Merc-c* k* mygal **Op** k* phos *Plb* rhus-t *Santin* *Sec* **Stram** sul-ac verat *Zinc* k* *Ziz*

- **morning** | **waking**; on: rhus-t h1
- **alternating** with trembling of body: arn
- **lying**:
  - **back**; on: calc-p
  - **side** amel.; on: calc-p
- **motion**, on: cocc k*
- **now** in upper, now in lower: hyos
- **sneezing**: phos h2
- **use**, on attempting to: cocc k* **Pic-ac** k*

- **difficult**: acon anac ars atro aur h2 *Camph* k* carb-ac chel *Con* *Cupr* cycl dulc gels hydr-ac lyc phys br1 *Pic-ac* stront-c
  - **walking**, after: gels
- **distortion**: phos h2
- **false** move:
  - **agg.** | **Lower** limbs: ars b4.de*
- **graceful**: stram br1* [neon stj2]
- **head**; of:
  - **agg.** | **Upper** limbs: cupr b7.de*
- **involuntary**: (↗*MIND - Gestures)* acon b2.de agar alum k* atra-r bnm3• aur b2.de bell k* calc camph b2.de canth b2.de caust b2.de* cham b2.de chin b2.de *Cocc* b2.de colch b2.de con b2.de *Crot-c* *Cupr* k* *Hell* k* **Hyos** b2.de *Ign* b2.de kali-c b2.de *Lach* b2.de lyc b2.de m-ambo b2.de m-arct b2.de meny b2.de *Merc* *Mosch* b2.de nat-m nux-m b2.de op k* phos plb b2.de* pyrog ptk rhus-t b2.de samb b2.de sep b2.de spig b2.de staph b2.de *Stram* k* thal-xyz srj8• verat b2.de zinc mrr1
  - **one** side: *Alum* calc h2 hell mrr1
  - **one** arm and leg: *Apoc* *Cocc* k* *Hell*
  - **paralyzed** limb: arg-n merc phos
  - **peculiar** to daily duties: bell
  - **stool**, after: carb-v h2
  - **thinking** of movements: aur h2
  - ○ **Knee** | **Patella**: nept-m lsd2.fr
  - **Lower** limbs | **right**: cocc ptk1
- **irregular**: *Agar* k* *Bell* **Hyos** kali-br lach merc mtf33 *Plb* *Sec* stram **Tarent**
- **loss** of power of: *Apis* ars *Bell* canth carbn-h cocc hydr-ac lath lyc naja oena op sars sec *Stram* stry *Tarent* thal-xyz srj8•
  - **morning** | **waking**; on: sil zinc
- **ludicrous**: zinc k*
- **oscillatory**: acon zinc
- **rhythmic**: hyos mrr1 stram ptk2*
- **sleep**, during: acon b7.de* ant-t b7a.de bry bg2 camph b7a.de *Caust* k* hyos b7.de* kali-c b4.de* m-aust b7.de nat-c b4.de* puls b7.de* rheum b7.de* rhus-t b7.de* sep b4.de *Stram* b7.de* *Sulph* b4a.de viol-t b7.de*
- **slow** motion: bit-ar wht1• merc-n merc-ns verat h1
- **throwing** about of limbs: *Bell* b4.de* cina b7.de *Hyos* b7.de meny b7.de *Merc-c* b4a.de *Puls* b7a.de *Stram* b7.de
- **upward** then forcibly thrown downward: **Bell** k*
- **violent** motion:
  - **amel.** | **Deltoid**: phys ptk1
- **waving**: cyt-l bg1
  - **arm** and leg; left | **sighing**; with: bry

○ - **Feet**:
  - **left** | **spasmodic**: cina ptk1
  - **amel.** | **Lower** limbs: med bg2
  - **angular**: merc mtf33
  - **constant** motion: (↗*Restlessness - feet)* ars mtf33 indol br1 *Lach* zinc k2*
  - **convulsive**: op plb *Zinc*
  - **difficult**: nat-m
  - **disordered**: merc k2
  - **downward**, as if stamping: cina
  - **forward** | **agg.**: hyos b7.de* *Rhus-t* b7a.de
  - **incoordination**: merc mtf33
  - **involuntary**: atra-r bnm3• cina mtf33
  - **nervous**, in bed: *Zinc*

- **Fingers**: agar fl-ac kali-br ptk1 *Lach* mosch ptk1 ox-ac *Stram* tarent
  - **agg.**: acon bg2 *Asaf* b7.de* bry bg2 camph b7.de* caust bg2 chin b7.de* cic b7.de* dros bg2 hep bg2 hyos bg2 ign bg2 m-ambo b7.de rhod bg2 spig b7.de* staph bg2 verat bg2
  - **automatic**: zinc
  - **constant**: (↗*Restlessness - fingers)* indol br1 kali-br *Stram* sulph
  - **convulsive**: *Cham* bg2 ign bg2 kali-c bg2 lyc bg2 nux-v bg2 staph bg2
  - **counting** with fingers; as if he were: mosch
  - **difficult**: calc ptk1 plb rob tarent vip
    - **afternoon**: mag-s
  - **impossible**: ars bg2 merc bg2
  - **irregular**: *Cupr*
  - **sleep**, during: ars h2 ign b7.de* puls b7.de* rheum b7a.de
  - ○ **First** finger | **spasmodic**: con ign
- **Forearm**:
  - **difficult**: chel con merc
  - **impaired**: ars clem
- **Hands**: (↗*MIND - Gestures - hands)*
  - **agg.**: ant-t bg2 *Bry* b7a.de chin b7.de* led bg2 meny b7.de* merc bg2 nat-c bg2 rhod bg2 sabad b7.de* sil bg2 staph b7.de* sulph bg2
  - **angular**: merc mtf33
  - **automatic**: *Acon* k* cann-i coca *Kali-i* nux-v k* zinc k*
    - **head**, to: apoc bro1 bry bro1 hell bro1 nux-v ptk1 plb zinc bro1
    - **strikes** his face; he: acon
  - **clutching**: *Hyos* k*
  - **convulsive**: apis bell *Kali-c* k* *Nat-m* *Op* plb k* *Zinc*
  - **diminished** power of: carbn-s con *Plb*
  - **disordered**: merc k2
  - **face**, toward: stry
  - **hasty**: *Bell*
  - **head**; toward: acon vh1
  - **incoordination**: atra-r bnm3• *Bell* *Cupr* *Cypr* *Gels* merc k* plb puls
  - **playing** with: *Mur-ac* k*
  - **sleep** during: ars h2
  - **write**, power of direction impaired; when trying to: aesc ter
- **Knees**:
  - **difficult**: dios
  - **impossible**: *Chel*
  - **involuntary**, to and fro: thuj
- **Legs**: caust
  - **night** | **sleep**; in: *Caust*
  - **automatic**: hell
    - **one**, of: hell
  - **awkward**: con
  - **constant**: **Zinc** mrr1
  - **convulsive**: acet-ac agar *Caust* merc-c *Mygal* op plb sul-ac
  - **difficult**: camph chel kali-n nat-m ox-ac pic-ac **Plb**
  - **downward**, on sneezing: spig
  - **dread** of: ham
  - **extend** or cross legs when sitting; cannot (See Crossing - legs - impossible; Extension - legs - impossible)
  - **involuntary**: bry k* crot-c hell bro1 lyc bro1 *Mygal* bro1 stict tarent bro1
    - **night**: *Stict*
    - **forward** | **walking**; while: merc bro1
    - **resting** on floor; when: aq-mar skp7•
  - **sensation** as if | **Skin**; under: plut-n srj7•
  - **wavelike**: sep
- **Lower** limbs: orot-ac rly4•
  - **agg.**: am-c b4a.de ars b4.de* camph b7.de* cham b7.de* chel b7.de* chin b7.de* cocc b7.de* croc b7.de* hep b4.de* ign b7.de* iod b4.de* mang b4a.de meny b7.de* *Merc* b4a.de nat-c b4.de* petr b4.de* puls b7.de*

- **agg.**: ...
rhus-t b7.de* ruta b7.de* sabad b7.de* sabin b7.de* staph b7.de* sulph b4.de* thuj b4a.de zinc b4.de*
- **amel.**: acon b7.de* am-m b7.de* arn b7.de* cham b7.de* cina b7.de* croc b7.de* dulc b4.de* merc-c b4a.de mosch b7.de* ph-ac b4.de* puls b7.de* rhod b4.de* squil b7.de* viol-t b7.de*
- **chorea** like: agar *Arg-n* coff *Mygal*
- **constant**: tarent k2
- **control**, loss of: alum cann-i chlor *Gels* glon hydrog srj2• *Plb* stram
- **convulsive**: *Merc-c* *Mygal* nat-m hr1 *Plb* stram
- **difficult**: camph b7.de* cann-s b7.de* carb-v b4.de* carbn-s mur-ac b4.de* *Plb* rhus-t b7.de* sabad b7.de* sep b4.de* sil b4.de*
  ⁝ **lifting** when lying (See Lifting - lower - impossible - lying)
- **forward** | **agg.**: euph b4a.de *Lyc* b4a.de
- **impossible**: ox-ac ptk1
- **involuntary**: acon bg2 bell bg2 cocc b7.de* *Hyos* b7.de* lach bg2 meny b7a.de merc op b7.de* rhus-t bg2 stram k* sulph bg2 verat b7.de* zinc bg2 zinc-val bg2
  ⁝ **pain**; with: cocc h1
- **slow**: merc
- **throwing** about: cina b7.de* meny b7.de* merc bg2 stram b7.de*

- **Shoulder**:
- **difficult**: tub-r jl2
- **impossible**: thuj bg2
- **limited**: tub-r jl2

- **Thigh**, involuntary: bry bro1 hell bro1 lyc bro1 *Mygal* bro1 op tarent bro1
- **Thumb** | **convulsive**: calc calc-p coc-c cocc k* con crot-c
- **Toes**: fl-ac
- **involuntary**: op
- **restricted**: ars

- **Upper** arm, difficult: coc-c
- **Upper** limbs:
- **one** side: *Alum* apis bell *Hell*
  ⁝ **constant**: bry ptk1
- **right** | **involuntarily**: cocc ptk1
- **agg.**: anac b4.de* ang b7.de* asar b7.de* *Bry* b7a.de calc bg2 *Cann-s* b7a.de caust b4.de* *Cham* b7a.de chel b7.de* chin b7.de* cocc b7.de* coff b7.de* con b4.de* croc b7.de* cycl b7.de* dig b4.de* dros bg2 dulc bg2 ign b7.de* kali-c b4.de* *Led* b7a.de mag-c b4.de* meny b7.de* *Merc* bg2 nat-m b4.de nat-n bg2 nit-ac bg2 nux-m b7.de* nux-v b7a.de petr bg2 ph-ac bg2 plat b4.de* *Puls* b7.de* *Rhus-t* b7.de* sabad b7.de* sabin b7.de* sars b4.de* sil bg2 stann bg2 *Staph* b7.de* sulph bg2 verb b7.de*
- **agitated**, lower limbs quiet: stram k*
- **amel.**: acon b7.de* agn b7.de* calc b4.de* cham b7.de* puls b7.de* rhus-t b7.de* samb b7.de* squil b7.de*
- **automatic**: *Cocc* *Hell* k* op
- **backward** and forward: morph op ptk1
- **beating** with one, grasping with the other: *Stram* k*
- **behind** him agg.: ferr ptk1 ign ptk1 kali-bi ptk1 puls ptk1 *Sanic* ptk1 *Sep* ptk1 teucr ptk1
- **circular**, spiral: stram hr1
- **clutching**: hyos ptk1
- **constant**: *Bell* tarent k2
- **convulsive**: anan vh1 apis *Arg-n* aur-m *Bell* k* camph bg2 *Caust* k* cocc bg2 con *Ign* bg2 *Merc-c* mez *Mygal* k* *Op* k* plb k* sabad bg2 squil bg2 *Stram* k* sul-ac tab zinc-s
- **difficult**: alum k2 ars aur k* cinnb clem con eupi glon merc stann ter thuj
  ⁝ **walking** in open air, while: anac
- **dry**, as if joints were: thuj
- **face**, toward: stry
- **fiddling**, as if: clem k*
- **forward**:
  ⁝ **over** chest during clonic cramp: atro
  ⁝ **violently**; thrown forward: ip

Motion – Upper limbs: ...
- **graceful**: stram hr1
- **hurried**: *Agar* k* *Bell*
- **idiotic** manner: merc
- **involuntarily**: *Cocc* k* hell hyos b7.de* ign b7.de* m-ambo b7.de mosch b7a.de nat-m bg2 op k* samb b7.de* staph b7.de* stram b7.de*
- **irregular**: *Agar* k* *Bell* merc tab tarent k*
  ⁝ **left** arm: *Cimic* k*
- **nervous**: rhus-t ptk1
- **rotation**: *(↗Convulsion - upper - rotation)* alum bg2 camph bg2 graph bg2
  ⁝ **right** arm: calc bg2
- **side** to side, from: cupr-ar k*
- **stretching**, upward: alum h2
- **throwing** about: hyos b7.de* *Sabad* b7a.de *Samb* b7a.de stram b7.de*
- **turning**: alum h2*
- **up** and down: cupr-ar k*
  ⁝ **slowly**: ars
- **upward** and outward: *Arg-n* k*
- **wild**: kali-br hr1*

- **Wrist**:
- **difficult**: rhod tep
- **impossible**: tep

MOTIONLESS; holding limb:
- **agg.** | **upper** limbs: coff b7.de* plb a1

MOUSE running up limbs; sensation of a: *(↗Alive; Rat)*
arn b2.de* aur b2.de* **Bell** b2.de* bry b7a.de *Calc* k* cimic tl1 ign bg2 nit-ac b2.de* rhod b2.de* sep k* *Sil* k* stram bg2 *Sulph* k*

○ - **Lower** limbs: *(↗Alive - lower; Rat - legs)* bell b4a.de *Calc* b4a.de *Sep* k* **Sulph** k*
- **epilepsy**; during (See GENERALS - Convulsions - epileptic - during - mouse)
- **running** down: lyss

- **Upper** limbs: *(↗Alive - upper; Rat - upper)* arn b7a.de **Bell** k* *Calc* k* caust b4a.de *Ign* b7a.de *Sulph* k*
- **epilepsy**; before (See GENERALS - Convulsions - epileptic - aura - mouse)
- **running** down: caust h2

NECROSIS: *(↗Caries; GENERALS - Necrosis)*

○ - **Ankles** | **Tarsus**: plat-m bro1
- **Hip**:
○ • **Joint** | **avascular**: *(↗GENERALS - Necrosis - bone - avascular)* nat-s mtf
- **Legs**:
○ • **Bones** | **Tibia**: asaf bro1 carb-ac bro1 hep bro1 lach bro1 nit-ac bro1 phos bro1 sal-ac c1

NERVOUS feeling (See Restlessness)

NETWORK of blood vessels:
- **marbled**; red as if | **Lower** limbs: caust b4.de* lyc b4.de* thuj bg2

NODES: *(↗Exostosis)* *Agar* ars calc-f c2 carb-an caust form c2 *Kali-bi* c2 *Kali-i* c2 lyc mag-c *Mez* mur-ac nat-m nit-ac ph-ac sil k* still c2 zinc
- **red** | **Thighs**: musca-d szs1
- **syphilitic**:
○ • **Legs**: asaf bg2 carb-an bg2 cinnb bg2 cist bg2 cor-r bg2 iod bg2 kali-bi bg2 kali-i bg2 merc-i-r bg2 nit-ac bg2
  ⁝ **Bones** | **Tibia**: calc-f ptk1 cinnb ptk1 nit-ac tl1 sul-i ptk1

○ - **Nates**; on: ther ptk1

NODOSITIES (See Arthritic)

NODULES: *(↗Exostosis; Ganglion)*
- **injuries**; after: ruta k2

○ - **Ankles**: agath-a nl2•
- **Elbows**: caust b4.de mur-ac b4.de*
- **left**: agath-a nl2•

- **Feet**: colch bg2 sel b7.de*
- **Fingers**: (↗*Spina*) agn b7.de* anac b4.de* cocc b7.de* lach b7.de* led b7.de* lyc b4.de* mag-c b4.de* morg-p fmm1• rhus-t b7.de* staph b7.de* syc bka1*• verat b7.de*

○ • **First** | **Flexor** surface: con h2
- **Forearms**: calc mez b4.de* mur-ac nat-m b4.de* zinc b4.de*
- **Hands**: ars b4.de* cocc b7.de* nat-m b4.de* nit-ac b4.de* *Spig* b7a.de stram b7.de* sul-ac b4.de*

○ • **Palms**: caust ptk1 ruta ptk1
- **Joints**: form ptk1

○ • **About** joints: form ptk1 ruta br1
 • **In** joints: acet-ac br1
- **Knees**: chin h1
- **Legs**: sel b7.de*

○ • **Calves**: merc k* nit-ac k*
- **Lower** limbs: *Agar* k* am-m b7.de* ant-c b7.de* *Aur* b4a.de carb-an k* carb-v k* *Caust* k* chin b7.de* dulc k* hep k* kali-c k* mag-m k* mang k* meny b7a.de merc k* mez k* *Nat-c* b4a.de petr k* rhod k* stront-c k* thuj k*
 • **pressing** and tearing: kali-c h2

○ • **Joints**: apis b7a.de led b7.de*
- **Muscles**: hippoz jl2 syph k2*

○ • **Upper** limbs: hippoz jl2
- **Shoulders**: *Calc* b4a.de *Sil* b4a.de
- **Thighs**: chin b7.de* lach b7.de* staph b7.de*

○ • **Femur**: aesc tl1 ferr tl1
- **Upper** arms: ars b4.de* *Bar-c* b4a.de nat-m b4.de* puls b7.de* zinc b4.de*
- **Upper** limbs: agar b4.de* ant-c b7.de* ant-t b7a.de ars b4.de* *Brom* b4a.de calc b4a.de carb-an b4.de* caust b4.de* cocc b7.de* dulc b4.de* hippoz bro1 lyc b4.de* mag-c b4.de* mag-m b4.de* mang b4.de* merc b4.de* mez b4.de* mur-ac b4.de* nat-m b4.de* nit-ac b4.de ph-ac b4.de* sil b4.de* spig b7a.de stann b4.de* staph b7.de* sulph b4a.de valer b7a.de zinc b4.de*

○ • **Joints**: apis b7a.de led b7.de
- **Wrists**: stann b4.de

NOISE; rough:

○ - **Shoulder** blades; above
 • **right**: tub jl2

NUMBNESS: (↗*Insensibility; Tingling*) abrot absin bro1 *Acon* k* **Agar** k* agath-a nl2• aids nl2• ail allox sp1 aloe bg2 *Alum* k* alum-p k2 alum-sil k2* alumn k2* am-c b4.de* *Ambr* k* anac b4.de* *Ant-t* k* *Apis* k* apoc k2 aran bro1 **Arg-met** k* **Arg-n** k* arist-cl sp1 *Arn* k* *Ars* ars-h ars-i k2 aster atra-r bnm3• atro *Aur* k* aur-ar k2 aur-s k2 aven br1* *Bamb-a* stb2.de• bar-c bro1 bar-m bell berb k2 brass-n-o srj5• bry k* bufo *Calc* k* calc-f sp1 *Calc-p* k* *Calc-s* calc-sil k2 camph k* cann-i cann-s canth caps b7.de* *Carb-ac* carb-an k* **Carb-v** k* carbn-o **Carbn-s** k* carc sp1* *Carl* caust k* cedr *Cham* k* chel *Chin* k* *Chinin-ar* chinin-s chord-umb rly4• cic k* cimic k2 **Cocc** k* coloc k2 *Con* k* convo-s sp1 *Croc* b7.de* *Crot-c* *Crot-h* cupr cupr-ar dig bg2 dros bg2 *Dulc* k* echi ptk1 eup-pur euphr bg2 fago falco-pe nl2• *Fl-ac* k* galeoc-c-h gms1• **Gels** k* germ-met srj5• **Graph** k* **Guaj** k* ham helo bro1 *Helo-s* rwt2• hep bg2 hippoc-k szs2 hist sp1 hyos k* *Hyper* k* ign k* iod *Ip* b7.de* *Kali-ar* *Kali-br* hr1 kali-c k* kali-n bg2* kali-p *Kali-s* kalm k* *Kreos* lac-leo hrn2• **Lach** bg2 lact lat-m sp1 laur *Led* k* *Lon-x* bro1 **Lyc** k* lycpr bro1 *M-ambo* b7.de* m-arct b7.de m-aust b7.de mag-m k2* mand sp1 *Merc* k* mez k* *Morph* bro1 muru a1 musca-d szs1 naja *Nat-m* k* nat-p nat-s neon srj5• nit-ac k* **Nux-m** k* *Nux-v* k* oena *Onos* k* **Op** k* **Ox-ac** k* paeon *Petr* k* ph-ac b4.de* **Phos** k •* phys physala-p bnm7• *Pic-ac* bro1 plat k* *Plb* k* *Psor* k* *Puls* k* *Pycnop-sa* mrz1 pyrog k2* rheum b7.de* *Rhod* k* **Rhus-t** k* ruta fd4.de sarcol-ac sp1 sarr **Sec** k* **Sep** k •* *Sil* k* spig bg2 spong fd4.de *Stram* k* sul-i k2 sulfa sp1 *Sulph* k* tab *Tarent* tax ter teucr b7a.de* *Thal* bro1 thea thuj k* tritic-vg fd5.de valer vanil fd5.de verat k* vip visc c1 xan *Zinc* k* zinc-p k2 [*Buteo-j* sej6]

- **one** side: caust b4.de* **Cocc** b7.de* *Ph-ac* b4a.de
 • **paralyzed**; other side: cocc
- **left**: alum h2 bufo hr1 carbn-o a1 caust cupr-ar dios med st mez h2 prot gsc puls ptk1 *Sumb*
- **daytime**: lyc k*
- **morning**: *Ambr* ox-ac k* peti a1 ruta fd4.de spong fd4.de stront-c sk4• vanil fd5.de *Zinc*
 • **waking**; on: aids nl2• aur bufo calc-p k* coca-c sk4• ruta fd4.de vanil fd5.de *Zinc*
- **forenoon** | **10** h: ant-t
- **afternoon**: ham k* ruta fd4.de vanil fd5.de

Numbness – afternoon: ...
 • **16** h: puls
- **evening**: dulc k* graph h2 peti a1 vanil fd5.de
 • **paralytic**: valer
 • **perspiration**, after: tax
 • **remaining** in one position; on: fago
- **night**: bov bg1 croc k* graph k* kali-c k* lyc k* ph-ac h2 vanil fd5.de
 • **waking**; on: mez h2 thuj k*
- **alternating** arms and legs: *Phos*
- **alternating** with | **formication**: hist sp1
- **chill**; during: carb-v bg2 cocc bg2 lyc bg2 merc bg2 *Nux-v* b7.de* phos bg2 rhus-t k* sil bg2
- **cold** agg.; becoming: sumb
- **delivery**; during: cupr hr1
- **epileptic** convulsions; during: bufo hr1
- **exaltation**; with: mag-p k2 nat-m
- **excitement**: | **during**: mag-m vh
- **exertion** agg.: alum h2 *Sep* k*
- **headache**; before: nat-m mrr1
- **heat**; during: apis k* *Bell* bg2 calc bg2 cann-xyz bg2 carb-v k* cham bg2 chin bg2 cocc k* croc bg2 graph bg2 *Hyos* bg2 ign bg2 kali-c k* **Lyc** k* merc bg2 nat-m k* *Nux-v* k* **Op** bg2 petr bg2 **Ph-ac** bg2 *Phos* bg2 *Puls* k* rhod bg2 rhus-t k* sep bg2 sil bg2 stann bg2 stram bg2 sulph bg2 *Thuj* bg2 verat bg2
- **hysterical**: gels hr1
 • **spasm**; with: gels lp
- **lying**:
 • **agg.**: aloe *Aur* aur-s k2 *Carb-v* *Chin* kali-c *Sulph* *Verat* **Zinc**
  : **eating**; after: aloe
  : **labor**; after normal: *Sep*
 • **still** | **agg.**: *Graph*
 • **them** agg.; on: alumn vh1 am-c arn bar-c bry bufo *Calc* carb-an **Carb-v** *Chin* glon *Kali-c* lyc mez phel *Puls* pycnop-sa mrz1 rheum rhod **Rhus-t** *Sil* *Sumb*
- **manual** labor (See exertion)
- **menses**; during: *Graph* k*
- **mental** exertion; after: plat k2
- **migratory**: *Cocc* raph ptk2
- **motion** | **amel.**: am-c anac aur vanil fd5.de
- **pain**; after: acon bg3
- **paralyzed**; as if: aven br1 spong fd4.de
- **perspiration**; during: apis bg2 *Calc* bg2 carb-an bg2 carb-v bg2 *Cham* bg2 chin bg2 cocc bg2 graph bg2 ign bg2 kali-c bg2 **Lyc** bg2 **Merc** bg2 nat-m bg2 **Nux-v** bg2 petr bg2 phos bg2 puls bg2 rhod bg2 *Rhus-t* bg2 sep bg2 *Sil* bg2 sulph bg2 *Thuj* bg2 verat bg2
- **pressure**; from: alum k2 ambr k2
- **rest** agg.: aur-ar k2
- **sensation** of: acon mrr1
- **sitting** agg.: am-c cham k* cop k* *Graph* k* lact k* lyc a1 *Mur-ac* hr1 spong fd4.de sulph k* teucr hr1
- **sleep** agg.; during: bufo a1 lac-leo hrn2• nat-m h2 urol-h rwt•
- **spasms** | **before**: plb bg1
- **stool** | **after** | **agg.**: sec bg2
 • **during** | **agg.**: sec bg2
- **waking**; on: aids nl2• *Aur* aur-s k2 bry k* bufo chord-umb rly4• erig mez k* puls k* thuj
- **walking** in open air agg.: alum convo-s sp1 *Graph* k*
- **warmth** agg.: sec k*

○ - **Ankles**: agath-a nl2• caust k* crot-c sk4• glon k* hep k* *Lac-c* k* nat-m k* par b7.de* rhus-t k* sulph k* thuj b4.de*
 • **night**: *Sulph* k*
 • **swelling**; with in rheumatism: lac-c kr1

○ • **Malleolus** | **pain**; with: caust kr1
- **Distal** parts: phys mrr1
- **Elbows**: (↗*Tingling - elbows*) all-c k* bell bg2 caust bg2 cinnb k* dig k* dios k* graph h2* jatr-c kali-bi bg2 kali-n kola stb3• kreos k* nat-s bg2* phasco-ci rbp2 phos k* pip-m k* puls bg2* sulph b4.de* symph fd3.de•
 • **evening** | **lying** down agg.: phos
 • **motion** agg.: all-c k*

Extremities

▽ · **extending** to:
⁝ **Fingers**; tips of: jatr-c
⁝ **Wrists**: phasco-ci rbp2

O · **Bends** of elbow: hura plb sulph
· **Lain** on: graph h2

- **Feet**: abrot k* acet-ac k* *Acon* k* aeth br1* agar aids nl2• *Alum* k* alum-p k2 alum-sil k2 alumn k* am-c k* am-m k* ambr k* ammc vh1 ang k* ant-c k* ant-t k* *Apis* k* *Arg-met* k* **Arg-n** k* am k* **Ars** k* ars-h k* ars-i k* ars-s-f k2 arund k* asaf k* asar k* atra-r bnm3• *Bapt* k* bar-c b4.de* bell k* bry k* cact k* cadm-met gm1 *Calc* k* calc-p k* calc-s *Camph* k* cann-i k* *Carb-an* k* *Carb-v* k* carbn-o *Carbn-s* k* *Caust* k* cench k2 cham k* cic b7.de* cinnb k* clem b4a.de cob bro1 coca **Cocc** k* cod hr1* *Coff* b7.de* colch k* *Coloc* k* **Con** k* croc k* cub k* cupr k* des-ac rbp6 dig digin a1 dios k* euph k* euphr k* fago k* falco-pe nl2• ferr k* ferr-ar ferr-i ferr-p fic-m gya1 fl-ac k2 *Form* bg2* gels k2* glon k* **Graph** k* grat k* ham bg2 hell k* helon k* hipp jl2 hyper k* ign k* iod *Kali-ar* kali-bi bg2 kali-c k* kali-n k* kali-p kali-s kali-sil k2 kola stb3• lach lact br1 lact-v bro1 lat-h bnm5• lat-m bnm6• laur k* **Lyc** k* m-aust b7.de mag-m k* mag-s k* mang k* marb-w es1• merc bg2 merc-c k* mez k* mill k* morg-p pte1*• musca-d szs1 nat-ar nat-c k* nat-m k* nat-p nept-m lsd2.fr *Nit-ac* k* **Nux-v** k* *Olnd* b7.de* onos bro1* op k* **Ph-ac** k* **Phos** k* phys k* pic-ac k* *Plat* k* *Plb* k* prot pte1* psor k* *Puls* k* pyrog k2* rhod k* rhus-t k* ruta fd4.de sabad k* *Sec* k* sep k* sil k* sphing k* spig k* spong fd4.de stann b4.de* stram k* stront-c b4.de* strych-g br1 sul-ac k* sulph k* sumb k* symph fd3.de• tetox pin2• thal-xyz srj8• *Thuj* k* trios rsj11• tung-met bdx1• ulm-c bro1 upa k* vanil fd5.de verat b7.de* verat-v k* viol-o bro1 vip k* zinc k* zinc-p k2
· **right**: alum k* am-c bg2* ant-c k* ant-t bg1 ars k* bar-c bg1 camph ptk1 *Kali-bi* bg3* laur bg1 lyc bg1 mang k* nux-m bg1 petr bg1 podo fd3.de• rhus-t bg1* ruta fd4.de sep k* symph fd3.de• vanil fd5.de zinc
⁝ **then** left: coloc mill
· **left**: bapt bg1* des-ac rbp6 *Glon* k* graph bg3* kali-c bg3* lac-c hr1 med ptk1 nat-c bg1 *Nat-m* k* nept-m lsd2.fr olib-sac wmh1 ph-ac phos bg1* psor ptk1 puls hr1 *Thuj* k* vanil fd5.de xan c1
⁝ **then** right: coloc bg1* mill k*
⁝ **walking**, only while: ph-ac
· **daytime**: *Carb-an*
· **morning**: aids nl2• alum dios nux-v k* ruta fd4.de sil k*
⁝ **bed** | **in** bed | **agg.**: alum calc-p mag-s k* ruta fd4.de
⁝ **waking**; in bed on: aids nl2•
· **forenoon**: am-m k* nat-c k* vanil fd5.de
· **afternoon**: fago k* mang k* mez k* phos vanil fd5.de
⁝ **14** h: mang
⁝ **16**-20 h | **chill**; with: lyc
· **evening**: *Calc* k* phos puls k* zinc k*
⁝ **bed** agg.; in: carb-an
· **night**: am-m k* bry k* *Ferr* k* lyc k* mag-m k* zinc
⁝ **bed** agg.; in: alumn *Calc* k*
· **accompanied** by | **diabetes** (See GENERALS - Diabetes mellitus - accompanied - feet)
· **alternating** with numbness of hands: **Cocc** k*
· **ascending** stairs agg.: nat-m
· **chill**; with: bufo bg2 calc bg2 cedr *Cimx* k* ferr *Lyc* k* nux-m **Puls** k* sep stann stram
· **crossing** legs agg.: allox tpw4 laur k* **Phos** k ● spong fd4.de
· **diarrhea** agg.; after: merc-sul c1
· **dinner** | **after** | **agg.**: *Kali-c* k* mill k*
⁝ **during** | **agg.**: kali-c k*
· **eating**; after: **Kali-c** k*
· **excitement** agg.: sulph
· **fever**; during: ant-c bg2 *Calc* bg2 con bg2 nux-v bg2 sec bg2 *Sulph* bg2
· **lying** agg.: caust k* ruta fd4.de sulph k*
· **menses**; before: hyper
· **motion**:
⁝ **agg.**: bapt
⁝ **amel.**: helm c1 helon mtf mill c1 vanil fd5.de
· **painful**: mag-m a1 puls tritic-vg fd5.de
· **perspiration**; during: bell bg2 *Calc* bg2 graph bg2 *Sulph* bg2

- **Feet**: ...
· **pressing** on the spine, when: *Phos*
· **riding**:
⁝ **agg.**: *Calc-p*
⁝ **cold** wind; in: ham
· **shivering**; during: *Lyc* b4a.de
· **sitting** agg.: allox tpw4 am-c k* *Ant-t* k* bry gk cadm-met gm1 *Calc* calc-p k* calc-sil k2 cann-s k* caust k* cham k* coloc k* euph k* graph k* grat k* helon k* jug-c k* laur k* lyc k* mill nat-c k* nept-m lsd2.fr *Phos* *Plat* k* *Puls* rhod k* sep k* spong fd4.de sul-ac k* symph fd3.de•
· **standing** agg.: mang k* merc merc-sul k* nept-m lsd2.fr *Sec* vanil fd5.de
· **stooping** agg.: coloc k*
· **stretching** out: cham k*
· **vomiting**; when (See STOMACH - Vomiting - accompanied - feet - numbness)
· **walking**:
⁝ **after** | **agg.**: rhod k*
⁝ **agg.**: ant-c k* graph ph-ac k* *Sec* vanil fd5.de
⁝ **air**; in open | **amel.**: *Thuj*
· **weather** agg.; cold: prot jl2

▽ · **extending** to | **Legs**: lat-h bnm5•

O · **Back** of feet: graph k* ham fd3.de• thuj k*
⁝ **walking** in open air agg.: graph
· **Heels**: *Alum* k* alum-sil k2 arg-met k* ars-s-f k2 caust k* chel con k* graph ign k* lyc k* nux-v k* rhus-t k* sep k* stict bg1 *Stram* k* stront-c bg2 thuj k*
⁝ **morning** | **rising** agg.: stram
⁝ **sitting** agg.: *Con* k*
⁝ **stepping** agg.: *Alum* k* arg-met caust k* rhus-t k*
· **Joints**: cann-i k* nat-m bg2
⁝ **right**: colch rsj2•
· **Outside** of: ars-s-f k2 ruta fd4.de
· **Sole** of: *Alum* alumn *Ars* k* bry k* *Cann-i* k* cann-xyz bg2 cham k* chel k* **Cocc** k* cupr eupi k* fl-ac helo c1 helo-s c1* hydrog srj2• kali-s fd4.de lac-h htj1• lat-m bnm6• laur k* lim bro1 merc-sul nat-c *Nux-v* k* olnd k* *Phos* bg2* plb k* puls k* raph k* rhus-t b7.de* sapin bg1 *Sec* k* sep k* sulph k* symph fd3.de• syph k* thuj k* ulm-c jsj8• xan bg1 zinc k*
⁝ **left**: cann-i k* symph fd3.de•
⁝ **evening**: sulph k*
⁝ **night**: cham k*
⁝ **needles**, as if walking on: eupi c1
⁝ **sitting** agg.: **Cocc** k* laur a1 thuj k*
⁝ **standing** agg.: puls k* *Sec*
⁝ **walking**:
⁝ **agg.**: cham k* helo c1 helo-s c1* hydrog srj2• olnd k* *Sec*
⁝ **amel.**: puls k* zinc k*
⁝ **extending** to | **Thighs**: ars k*
⁝ **Hollow** of foot: bry merc-sul

- **Fingers**: abrot k* *Acon* k* act-sp k* aesc bro1 agar k* aids nl2• ail k* allox tpw4 alum k* alum-sil k2 am-c k* am-m k* ambr b7.de* *Aml-ns* k* anac k* androc srj1• ang b7.de* ant-t k* *Apis* k* aran bg2* arist-cl sp1 *Ars* k* *Ars-i* aster k* atro k* *Bar-c* k* bar-i k2 bar-m bar-s k2 bell bry k* bufo **Calc** k* calc-f sp1 calc-i k* calc-sil k2 cann-s b7.de* *Carb-an* k* carbn-o *Carbn-s* k* carc fd2.de• *Carl* *Caust* k* cham k* chel b7a.de* chir-fl gya2 chlf hr1 *Cic* k* *Cimic* *Cimx* k* cina b7.de* *Cocain* bro1 cocc k2 coff k* colch k* *Con* k* cop bg2 croc b7.de* crot-h k* cub k* *Cupr* k* **Dig** k* dios dulc fd4.de euph k* euphr k* falco-pe nl2• *Ferr* k* ferr-ar *Ferr-i* ferr-p fl-ac gels k2 gins k* **Graph** k* *Hep* k* hipp jl2 hydrc k* *Iod* k* *Kali-ar* kali-c k* *Kali-chl* k* kali-n kali-sil k2 kola stb3• *Kreos* k* lach k* lath bro1 lil-t k* lipp a1 **Lyc** k* m-arct b7.de m-aust b7.de mag-m k* mag-p bro1 mag-s bro1 merc k* merc-c merc-i-f k* morph k* mosch k* *Mur-ac* k* nat-m k* nat-p k* nit-ac k* nux-m nux-v k* ol-an k* olnd op b7.de* *Ox-ac* bro1 paeon k* *Par* k* petr-ra shn4• ph-ac k* **Phos** k* **Plat** k* *Plb* k* podo k* pop-cand bro1 prop bro1 prot jl2* psor bg2 ptel k* puls k* rhod k* **Rhus-t** k* ruta fd4.de sabin b7.de* sarcol-ac bro1 sarr sars k* **Sec** k* *Sep* k* *Sil* k* sinus rly4• spong k* stann k* staph k* stram k* stront-c k* sul-ac b4.de* sul-i k2 *Sulph* k* syc pte1*• symph fd3.de• ter k* thal bro1* *Thuj* k* thyr ptk1 tritic-vg fd5.de upa bro1 verat k* verb b7.de* zinc k*
· **one** side: cact ph-ac

- **right**: cann-i hr1 hydrc k* hydrog srj2• lac-h sk4• *Lil-t* hr1 nat-p k* *Plat* hr1 sep sulph bg1 thuj bg1
- **left**: kola stb3•
  - **accompanied** by | **Heart** disease (See CHEST - Heart; complaints - accompanied - fingers)
  - **extending** to:
    - **Chest** | **left** side: rhus-g tmo3•
- **morning**: aids nl2• am-c caust k* cham k* dios k* *Ferr* kreos lyc h2 merc phos k* puls rhus-t k* *Sulph* k*
  - **bed** agg.; in: puls k*
  - **rising** agg.: stram k* zinc h2
  - **waking**; on: aids nl2• galla-q-r nl2• *Phos* mrr1
- **forenoon**: fl-ac k* sulph k*
- **evening**: lipp a1 sep k* ter k*
  - **lying** down agg.: mag-m
- **night**: am-c carc fd2.de• kali-n h2 *Mur-ac* k* ozone sde2• puls k*
  - **midnight**:
    - **after** | **4-5** h: lac-h sk4•
- **accompanied** by:
  - **Heart** disease (See CHEST - Heart; complaints - accompanied - fingers)
  - **Stomach**; pain in (See STOMACH - Pain - accompanied - fingers)
- **air**, cold: nit-ac k*
- **carrying** load on arm: carl k*
- **chest** complaints: *Carb-an*
- **chill**; during: acon bg2 am-c bg2 am-m bg2 calc bg2 cedr chel bg2 *Cimx* cupr bg2 ferr hep bg2 lyc bg2 mur-ac bg2 ph-ac h2 puls bg2 rhus-t hr1 sec bg2 **Sep** k* stann k* sulph bg2 thuj k* verat bg2
- **convulsions**; between: *Sec*
- **eating**; after: *Con*
- **epilepsy**; during: cupr k*
- **fever**:
  - **before** an attack of intermittent: nux-v b7a.de puls k*
  - **during** | **agg.**: am-c bg2 ant-t bg2 *Calc* bg2 chel bg2 hep bg2 puls bg2 *Sec* bg2 sep bg2 sulph bg2 thuj k*
- **grasping** something agg.: acon k* am-c calc
- **headache**; during: podo c1
- **perspiration**; during: am-m bg2 ant-t bg2 *Ars* bg2 *Calc* bg2 *Cham* bg2 chel bg2 hep bg2 nux-v k* puls bg2 **Sulph** bg2 thuj bg2 *Verat* bg2
- **playing** piano, while: dulc fd4.de sulph k*
- **sitting** agg.: *Cham* k*
- **writing**; after: carl

▽ - **extending** to | **Upward**: *Ars* iber c1 moni rfm1•

○ - **First**: agar k* apis bar-c h2 calc h2 *Caust* k* euphr k* ham fd3.de• hura kreos lac-h sk4• lyc k* nat-m k* *Par* k* phos k* rhod k* *Rhus-t* k*
  - **left** hand: anac nat-m rhus-t symph fd3.de• thuj h1
  - **morning**: lyc nat-m k* *Rhus-t* k*
  - **chill**; during: ph-ac h2
  - **extending** to | **Arm**; up radial side of: anac carb-an phos
  - **Side** of: ph-ac h2
  - **Tip** of: graph k* ham fd3.de• kali-s fkr2.de spong k* thuj h1
- **Fourth** finger: aids nl2• alum k* anac k* *Aran* k* arg-n k* calad k* calc-s k* coca com k* con bg2 dig h2 dios k* eupi k* ign gk inul k* lipp a1 lyc k* med k* nat-c k* nat-m k* nat-sil fd3.de• op k* ozone sde2• *Plat* k* rhus-g tmo3• sars sinus rly4• sulph k* sumb thuj k*
  - **right**: carc fd2.de• inul k* lipp a1
  - **left**: calad hr1 dios k* ignis-alc es2• podo fd3.de• sumb thuj k* *Vac* jl2
  - **morning**: calc-s k* lyc k* nat-sil fd3.de•
    - **waking**; on: aids nl2• lyc
  - **afternoon**: calc-s k* nicc k*
  - **evening**: lipp a1 sulph k*
    - **bed** agg.; in: sulph k*
  - **night**: carc fd2.de• nat-c h2
  - **rising** | **amel.**: nat-c h2

- **Fingers – Fourth** finger: ...
  - **rubbing** | **amel.**: lipp a1 nat-c k*
  - **sitting**; after: alum k*
  - **waking**; on: coca lyc k*
  - **writing** agg.: com k*
  - **extending** to | **Wrist**: rhus-g tmo3•
  - **Tip** of: choc srj3• plb k*
- **Joints**: anac bg2 euphr h2* *Lach* bg2 **Lyc** bg2
- **Second**: bamb-a stb2.de• calc carbn-o dig k* dulc fd4.de euphr k* gamb k* ham fd3.de• hydrog srj2• lac-h sk4• lipp a1 lyc k* mur-ac k* nat-m k* nat-sil fd3.de• phos k* rat k* rhus-t k* ruta fd4.de
  - **left**: luf-op rsj5•
  - **morning**: bamb-a stb2.de• lyc k* nat-m k* rhus-t k*
  - **night**: mur-ac k*
  - **air**; cold: phos
  - **Tip** | **left**: thuj h1
- **Third** finger: aids nl2• alum h2 anac k* ang h1* *Aran* k* arg-n k* bamb-a stb2.de• calc k* carbn-o com k* con bg2 dig h2 dulc fd4.de eupi k* ign gk lipp a1 lyc k* nat-m k* nicc k* op k* phys k* rat k* rhus-g tmo3• sabad k* sars k* sulph k* sumb thuj k*
  - **right**: lipp a1 rat k*
  - **left**: dios bg2 dulc fd4.de podo fd3.de• sumb thuj k*
  - **morning**: aids nl2• lyc k*
    - **waking**; on: aids nl2• bamb-a stb2.de• lyc k*
  - **afternoon**: dulc fd4.de nicc k*
  - **evening**: lipp a1
    - **19** h: phys
    - **bed** agg.; in: sulph
  - **night**: nat-c h2
    - **rising** | **amel.**: nat-c h2
  - **sitting**; after: alum h2*
  - **writing** agg.: com k*
  - **extending** to | **Wrist**: rhus-g tmo3•
  - **Tip** of: thuj h1
- **Tips**: acon bg2 act-sp bg2 ant-t k* *Apis* k* arg-met ptk1 arg-n k* ars k* bamb-a stb2.de• cann-s k* cann-xyz bg2 carb-an k* carb-v bg1 carbn-s *Caust* chel k* cupr sst3• dulc fd4.de *Fl-ac* b4a.de graph k* ham fd3.de• hydrog srj2• iber a1* kali-bi bg2 kali-c k* kali-p k* *Kreos* b7a.de *Lach* k* lath br1 lyc bg2 mag-m k* mag-p bg2* mez k* mur-ac k* nat-m ptk1 ox-ac k2 ph-ac k* **Phos** k* plb bg2 rhus-t k2 ruta fd4.de sal-fr sle1• *Sec* k* *Spong* k* stann k* *Staph* k* sulph ptk1 sumb k* syph bg1 tab k* tell k* thuj k*
  - **left** | **lying** on left side agg.: iber c1
  - **morning**: kali-c k* *Lach* k*
  - **chill**; during: mur-ac h2 stann k*
  - **heart**; with pain in: iber c1
  - **rubbing** | **amel.**: mag-m h2*
  - **stretching** hands, on: tell k*
  - **wet**; after getting: rhus-t
  - **whooping** cough; during: *Spong* k*

- **Forearms**: (↗*Tingling - forearms)* **Acon** aesc k* agar agath-a nl2• ail aloe alum k* am-m k* ars-met bapt k* berb k* both-ax tsm2 caps bg2 carb-an carb-v *Carbn-s* cedr k* *Cham* chin k* chinin-ar cinnb k* *Cocc* k* coloc k* com k* *Crot-c Cupr* cypra-eg sde6.de• dios k* euphr k* *Fl-ac* k* *Gels Glon* **Graph** k* helo helo-s rwt2• hydrc k* hydrog srj2• *Kali-c* k* kali-n k* lavand-a ctl1• *Lyc* k* lyss mag-m k* med k* merc k* merc-sul morg-p pte1• *Nat-m* k* *Nit-ac* k* nux-v k* *Op* k* *Pall* k* *Plb* k* *Psor* puls k* rheum k* rhus-t k* sec k* sep stront-c k* *Sulph* k* tell k* thuj k* zinc
  - **right**: *Am-m* k* bell bg2 *Chin* coloc k* euphr k* hep *Nit-ac* k* sulph k*
  - **left**: **Acon** alum k* *Bapt* a1 cinnb k* dios hr1 fl-ac k* ignis-alc es2• kali-c k* med k* onos
  - **morning**: mag-m k* nux-v k*
    - **rising** agg.; after: mag-m nux-v
    - **waking**; on: kali-c k*
  - **forenoon**: fl-ac k* zinc zing k*
  - **afternoon**, 17 h: phys
  - **night**: arg-n nh rhus-t k* sulph h2

- **night**: ...
  - **midnight**, after:
    - **5** h: fl-ac
      - **lying** on right side agg.: fl-ac
  - **midnight**, before | **22** h: tell
- **bending** agg.: chin k*
- **edematous**: chel
- **grasping** something agg.: **Cham** k*
- **hangs** down, when: berb k*
- **lying**:
  - **agg.**: puls k*
  - **side**; on:
    - **left** | **agg.**: sulph h2
  - **table** agg.; lying on | **writing**; when: lyc
- **motion** | **amel.**: *Cinnb* k* puls k*
- **painful**: com k* euphr h2
- **raising** arm agg.: *Puls* sep
- **rubbing** | **amel.**: sulph h2
- **sitting** agg.: fl-ac merc k*
- ▽ **extending** to:
  - **Finger**: pall k*
    - **Fourth** finger; tip of: cinnb
- ○ **Anterior** part: aloe cham fl-ac k*
- **Lain** on: aesc vh1
- **Posterior** part: berb k* caj k* peti a1 plb k*
- **Radial** side: fl-ac k*
- **Ulnar** side: rheum h

\- **Hands**: abrot k* *Acon* k* aesc aeth br1 agar k* aids nl2• allox tpw4 aloe alum k* alum-sil k2 am-c k* ambr k* androc srj1• *Apis* k* arg-n k* arist-cl sp1 *Ars* k* ars-h k* ars-i k2 ars-s-r hr1 asaf k* asc-t k* aster k* atra-r bnm3• atro k* bapt k* bar-c k* bell k* borx k* both-ax tsm2 bov bg2 bry k* bufo cact cadm-met gm1 cadm-s k2 *Calc* k* calc-f sp1 calc-i k* calc-p k* calc-s k* calc-sil k2 *Camph* cann-i bro1 cann-s k* carb-ac k* **Carb-an** k* *Carb-v* k* carbn-o *Carbn-s* k* cassia-s ccrh1• *Caust* k* cedr k* cench k2 cham b7.de* chel k* chord-umb rly4• cimic *Coca* coca-c sk4• **Cocc** k* cod a1* *Colch* k* com k* *Con* k* croc k* **Crot-c** cub k* *Cupr* k* cycl k* cypra-eg sde6.de• cyt-l bro1 dios k* *Dulc* elaps euphr k* eupi k* falco-pe nl2• *Ferr* k* ferr-ar ferr-p k* *Fl-ac* k* form bg2 *Gels* gins k* glon tl1 **Graph** k* guare k* ham fd3.de• hell k* helo helo-s rwt2• hep h2 hipp jl2 hippoc-k szs2 hydrc *Hyos* k* *Hyper* k* iber bro1 ign b7.de* *Kali-ar* k* **Kali-c** k* kali-cy gm1 **Kali-n** k* kali-p *Kali-s* kali-sil k2 lac-leo hrn2• *Lach* k* lil-t bro1 loxo-recl knl4• luf-op rsj5• **Lyc** k* lyss k* m-arct b7.de m-aust b7.de mag-c b4.de* mag-p bro1 manc k* mand sp1 med merc k* merc-c k* merc-i-f k* merc-sul k* *Mez* k* moni rfm1• naja nat-c b4.de* *Nat-m* k* nept-m lsd2.fr *Nit-ac* k* nux-m k* *Nux-v* k* *Onos* *Op* k* ox-ac k* par b7.de* **Phos** k* phys k* pic-ac k* pin-con oss2• plat k2 *Plb* k* *Psor* ptel k* *Puls* k* pyrog k* raph k* rhod b4.de* ros-d wla1 *Ruta* b7a.de* sarr k* *Sec* k* sep k* *Sil* k* sinus rly4• *Spig* k* squil b7.de* stram k* stront-c k* stry k* strych-g br1 sulph k* sumb k* tela bro1 tetox pin2• thal-xyz srj8• *Thuj* k* trios rsj11• tung-met bdx1• vanil fd5.de verat b7.de* verat-v k* vip *Zinc* k* zinc-p k2 [buteo-j sej6]

- **alternating** sides: **Cocc** k* echi ptk1
- **right**: alum bg1 am-c k* asc-t k* cann-s k* cycl k* elaps *Ferr-p* hr1 *Gels* k* graph k* *Hep* k* hydrog srj2• kali-p lac-e hrn2• lil-t lyss k* merc k* nat-m nat-p k2 nat-sil fd3.de• nept-m lsd2.fr nit-ac k* phos h2* rhus-t hr1 rumx bg2 sil h2 spig thuj vanil fd5.de [bell-p-sp dcm1]
  - **then** left: *Cocc* k*
- **left**: acon k* agar bg1 aloe k* asc-t a1 aster k* *Bapt* a1 cact carb-an h2 coca-c sk4• con h2 *Crot-h* k* dig dios k* euphr ferr k* fl-ac k* *Glon* *Graph* k* *Lac-c* k* *Lach* k* *Lat-m* k* med k* merc-sul mez k* naja nat-c h2 *Nit-ac* phys hr1 phyt podo fd3.de* *Rhus-t* k* sars hr1 stry vanil fd5.de
  - **accompanied** by | **Heart** disease (See CHEST - Heart; complaints - accompanied - hand)
  - **cold**; with right hand: *Ferr*
  - **menses**; during: *Graph*
- **daytime**: apis *Zinc*
- **morning**: aids nl2• *Carb-an* k* fl-ac k* ham fd3.de• *Kali-c* k* mag-c h2 *Nit-ac* k* *Phos* k* prot pte1* sil *Spig* *Thuj* vanil fd5.de
  - **7** h: dios

\- **Hands** – **morning**: ...

- **bed** agg.; in: *Carb-an* k* fl-ac lyc k* nat-c h2 nit-ac k* *Phos* k*
- **waking**; on: aids nl2• alum calc-p *Ferr* *Kali-c* k* *Phos* k* vanil fd5.de *Zinc* k*
- **washing** agg.: *Carb-v* k*

- **afternoon**: mez vanil fd5.de
- **evening**: borx nux-m k*
- **night**●: agar h2 ambr ars-i bg1 bry k* carb-v k* ham fd3.de• kali-n h2 lyc k* mag-m k* merc-pr-r bg1 pall k* prot pte1* sep k* **Sil** k* vanil fd5.de
  - **midnight**, after:
    - **4** h: nat-c
    - **5** h: fl-ac
  - **grasping** something agg.: sep k*
  - **lain** on: am-c k* petr k*
  - **sleep** agg.; during: croc k* lac-leo hrn2•
- **accompanied** by:
  - **nausea** (See STOMACH - Nausea - accompanied - hand - numb)
  - **Heart** disease (See CHEST - Heart; complaints - accompanied - hand)
- **air**, cold: lyc
- **alternating** with numbness of feet (See feet - alternating)
- **carrying** anything: ambr sep h2*
- **chill**; during: *Apis* k* *Bry* bg2* calc bg2 *Cimx* k* dros bg2 ferr guare k* *Lyc* k* mur-ac b4a.de* nux-m nux-v k* petr bg2 ph-ac k* **Puls** k* sec k* **Sep** k* stann k*
- **eating**; after: con b4a.de* lyc k*
- **excitement** agg.: *Sulph*
- **exertion** agg.: ruta
- **fever**; during: calc bg2 nux-v bg2 sec bg2 *Sep* b4.de* zinc bg2
- **grasping** something:
  - **agg.**●: *Calc* k* *Cham* k* cocc ptk1 sep k*
  - **amel.**: spig k*
- **heat** in stomach, with: con h2
- **lain** on: aesc vh1 am-c ambr graph *Kali-c* petr vanil fd5.de
- **lying**:
  - **agg.**: ambr mag-c nat-m petr-ra shn4• puls h1
  - **hard**; on something | **agg.**: nat-m
- **menses**; during: *Graph* k* kali-n sec
- **motion**:
  - **agg.**: bapt k*
  - **amel.**: am-c k* *Apis* cann-s k* carb-an k* *Ferr* nat-m puls h1 spig k* stront-c
- **one** hand numb, the other asleep: *Phos*
- **painful**: euphr h2 mag-m h2*
- **paralytic**: nit-ac
- **perspiration**; during: *Calc* bg2 lyc bg2 *Nux-v* bg2 puls bg2 sep bg2 thuj bg2 zinc bg2
- **pocket**, on putting hand into: nat-m k*
- **prosopalgia**, side of: cocc hr1
- **resting** hand on anything agg.: nit-ac k*
- **resting** head on hand agg.: squil k* vanil fd5.de
- **riding** in a carriage agg.: form k*
- **sewing**, while: *Crot-h* k*
- **shivering**; during: stann b4a.de
- **sitting** agg.: am-c k* cadm-met gm1 graph k* merc k*
- **sleep**; during: petr-ra shn4•
- **talking** agg.: lyc k*
- **using**, on: graph k*
- **waking**; on: alum k* calc-p chord-umb rly4• form k* hippoc-k szs2 manc k* mez ros-d wla1
- **walking** agg.: rhod k*
- **water**, after emersion in: carb-v sulph k*

- **wet**; getting:
  - **agg.**: *Rhus-t* k*
  - **amel.**: spig k*
- **writing** agg.: agar k* *Zinc* k*
- ▽ **extending** to | **Arm**: agar aster k* dios k* fl-ac k*
- ○ **Back** of hands: caj k* lam k* laur med phos k*
- **Palms**: acon k* bry k* con h2 kali-c a1 lob-s k* op k* phos k* plb k2 psor k* stram syph
  - **morning**: psor k*
- **Radial** nerve, distribution of: ph-ac k*
- **Ulnar** side: aran c1* dig h2 plb k*
  - **writing**; after: agar

- **Hips**: agar k* *Apis* ars-met bapt k* calc k* rhus-t k* sep bg1 staph k*
  - ▽ **extending** to:
    - **Abdomen** | **standing** agg.: staph k* sulph
- **Joints**: alum k* con ip k* *Led* k* *Lyc* k* plat k* puls k* rhus-t k2
  - **cold** and wet; after exposure to: *Rhus-t*
  - **rheumatism**; during: acon bro1 cham bro1 kreos tl1 led bro1 puls *Rhus-t* bro1
- **Knees**: alum k* calc k* carb-v k* caust k* chin b7.de* cinnb k* clem a1 *Coloc* k* fl-ac k* graph k* kali-c k* lach meli bro1* merc-i-f bg1* nat-p bg2* nept-m lsd2.fr onos petr bg2 phys bg1 *Plat* k* sep b4.de* sulph bg2* thuj
  - **left**: nept-m lsd2.fr
  - **morning**: caust k*
    - **sitting** agg.: sulph
  - **evening** | **stooping** agg.: *Coloc* k*
  - **night**: graph
  - **driving**; while: nept-m lsd2.fr
  - **sitting**:
    - **after**: alum
    - **amel.**: bar-c ptk1
  - **sleep** agg.; during: graph
  - **walking** rapidly agg.: kali-c k*
  - ▽ **extending** to:
    - **Scrotum**: bar-c br1*
      - **sitting** down | **amel.**: bar-c bro1
    - **Toes**: nept-m lsd2.fr
  - ○ **Hollow** of knee: onos k*
- **Legs**: acet-ac *Acon* k* agar k* ail k* aloe *Alum* k* alum-p k2 alum-sil k2 alumn k* *Am-c* k* am-m k* ambr k* anac k* anan ang k* *Ant-c* ant-t k* *Apis* k* *Aran* k* *Arg-met* k* *Arg-n* k* arn *Ars* k* ars-i asaf b7.de* asar k* aster atro k* bapt k* bell k* borx k* bov k* bry b7.de* bufo cact k* *Calc* k* calc-f sp1 calc-i k2 *Calc-p* k* camph k* canth k* *Carb-an* k* carb-v k* *Carbn-s* carc fd2.de• *Caust* k* cedr k* cham k* chin k* chinin-ar chlol a1 cic b7.de* coca-c sk4• *Cocc* k* *Coloc* k* **Con** k* *Crot-h* k* cupr k* cupr-ar a1* dig b4.de* dios k* dulc k* eup-per k* *Eup-pur* k* euph b4.de* euphr bg2 fago k* falco-pe nl2• ferr k* ferr-ar ferr-i ferr-p glon k* gnaph bg2 **Graph** k* *Ham* k* hep b4a.de hydrog srj2• hydroph rsj6• *Hyper* k* ign k* iod k* ip b7.de* *Kali-c* k* kali-p kali-sil k2 kalm bg2 lac-c k* lach k* lact k* laur k* led tl1 **Lyc** k* m-arct b7.de m-aust b7.de mag-m k* med k* meph a1 *Merc* k* *Merc-c* k* mez k* morg-p fmm1• nat-c k2 *Nat-m* k* nit-ac k* nux-m k* **Nux-v** k* *Onos* k* *Op* k* *Ox-ac* k* peti a1 *Phos* k* *Phys* k* *Phyt* k* pic-ac k* **Plat** k* plb k* prot fmm1• *Psor* k* *Puls* k* rhod k* **Rhus-t** k* rumx ruta fd4.de samb k* sec k* **Sil** k* spong b7.de* stram k* sul-i k2 sulph k* tab k* *Tarent* k* thuj k* vanil fd5.de verat-v k* vip k* zinc k*
  - **one** side and pain in the other: sil k*
  - **right**: alum h2* alumn k* apis bg1 cedr bg1 dios k* eup-per eup-pur k* kali-c k* lac-c k* lyss k* sabad k* tarent k* vanil fd5.de zinc k*
    - **then** left: spong k*
  - **left**: *Arg-n* k* asar borx cann-i k* carc fd2.de• *Crot-h* k* *Crot-t* dios k* fl-ac k* ham fd3.de• hep bg1 *Hyper* k* lac-c *Lil-t* lyc bg1 med k* mim-p rsj8• nicc k* olib-sac wmh1 onos *Phos* puls k* pycnop-sa mrz1 ruta fd4.de sep stram k* thlas bg1 vanil fd5.de
    - **lying** | **back**; on | **agg.**: nicc
      - **side**; on:
        - **left** | **agg.**: *Phos*
  - **daytime**: *Carb-an* k*

- **Legs**: ...
  - **morning**: *Ambr* aq-mar skp7• caust k* dios k* ham fd3.de• hep k* nicc k* ruta fd4.de spong fd4.de
    - **bed** agg.; in: *Ambr* hep k* lac-del hrn2• nicc k*
  - **noon**: spong k*
    - **sleep** agg.; after: spong
  - **afternoon**: bov k* fago k* nicc k* vanil fd5.de
  - **evening**: *Calc* k* dios k* hyper k* merc-c k* *Plat* k* vanil fd5.de
    - **lying** on it; while: alum
    - **sitting** agg.: *Calc* dios graph *Plat*
  - **night**: alum k* *Am-c* k* kali-c k* merc k* nit-ac k* phos k* zinc k*
    - **bed**; when going to: psor k*
  - **accompanied** by | **spinal** meningitis (See BACK - Inflammation - membranes - accompanied - lower)
  - **air**; in open | **amel.**: pic-ac
  - **bed** agg.; in: lac-del hrn2• plat k* zinc
  - **chill**; during: eup-pur *Nux-v*
  - **convulsions**; before: plb
  - **crossing**, while●: *Agar* allox tpw3* carb-an k* *Crot-h* k* laur phos k* sep spong fd4.de
  - **diarrhea** agg.; after: merc-sul c1
  - **driving** a car; while: falco-pe nl2•
  - **excitement** agg.: *Sulph*
  - **gouty**: *Acon* k*
  - **lain** on: am-c k*
  - **lying**:
    - **agg.**: aloe bell k* phos k* sumb k*
    - **leg** agg.; on: alumn
  - **menses**; during: **Puls** k*
  - **motion** agg.: lac-del hrn2• laur k*
  - **rising**:
    - **agg.**: puls (non:sulph kl)
    - **sitting**; from | **agg.**: *Puls*
  - **rubbing** | **amel.**: lac-del hrn2• stram k*
  - **sitting**:
    - **after**: **Acon** k* *Graph* k* lyss k* spong fd4.de
    - **agg.**: acon bg1 agar k* am-c k* am-m k* *Ant-c* k* bad k* brom bg1 *Calc* k* calc-sil k2 chin c1 con k* *Crot-h* hr1 grat k* ign k* lyc k* nicc k* nux-v k* petr a1 *Phos* k* *Plat* k* *Puls* k* spong fd4.de sul-ac k*
  - **sleep** agg.; after: *Spong* k*
  - **squatting**: | **agg.**: aq-mar skp7•
  - **standing** agg.: am-c k* nux-v k*
  - **stretched**, when: cham k*
  - **walking**:
    - **agg.**: *Coloc* petr a1 *Rhus-t* *Sep* thuj
      - **sitting**; after: nux-v spong fd4.de
    - **amel.**: aq-mar skp7• lac-del hrn2•
  - **weather** agg.; cold: apis
  - ▽ **extending** to | **Thighs**: hydrog srj2•
  - ○ **Calves**: acon k* aq-mar skp7• ars k* ars-s-r hr1 berb k* *Bry* k* cham k* coll a1 *Coloc* k* dulc k* falco-pe nl2• graph lach k* nux-v k* phos k* plat ptk1 *Sec* mrr1 sil k* trios bg1 vanil fd5.de verat bg2 verat-v k*
    - **morning**: aq-mar skp7•
    - **afternoon**: dulc k*
    - **evening**: dulc k*
    - **squatting**: aq-mar skp7•
    - **walking** | **amel.**: aq-mar skp7•
  - **Tibia**, about: kalm k* vanil fd5.de
- **Lower** limbs: acet-ac acon k* agar k* ail aloe bg2 *Alum* k* alum-p k2 alum-sil k2 alumn am-c b4.de* *Ambr* k* androc bnm2• ang b7.de* ant-c k* ant-t *Apis* k* *Arg-met* k* *Arg-n* arn b7.de* ars k* ars-i ars-s-f k2 asaf b7.de* asar bg2 aster aur k* aur-ar k2 aur-s k2 *Bar-c* bg2 bell bg2 berb k* bov k* bufo k* **Calc** k* calc-i k2 *Calc-p* k* calc-s camph b7.de* cann-i k* *Canth* k* *Carb-an* k* *Carb-v* k* carbn-s cardios-h rly4• caust k* cham b7.de* *Chel* k* chin k* chinin-ar *Chinin-s*

- **Lower** limbs: ...
cic k* cimic cocc k* colch k* coloc b4a.de* *Con* k* croc k* crot-h bg2 cupr k* cupr-ar k* der a1 des-ac rbp6 dulc b4.de* euph k* euphr k* falco-pe nl2• ferr b7.de* fl-ac **Gnaph** bg2 **Graph** k* guaj b4.de* guare k* ham fd3.de• hyper bg2 ign iod k* kali-ar k* *Kali-bi* bg2* *Kali-br* **Kali-c** k* kali-n k* kali-p *Kali-s* kali-sil k2 kreos k* lac-c lact lat-m led k* *Lyc* k* lyss m-ambo b7.de m-arct b7.de mang b4.de* med k2 *Merc* k* merc-c k* mez k* morg-p pte1• morph k* mosch k* musca-d szs1 naja nat-m k* nat-s nit-ac bg2 nux-m k* *Nux-v* k* olnd k* *Onos* k* o p k* ox-ac k* *Petr* k* ph-ac k* *Phos* k* *Pic-ac* k* pin-con oss2• plan ptk1 plat k* **Plb** k* psil ft1 psor **Puls** k* rheum k* *Rhod* k* *Rhus-t* k* ruta fd4.de samb bg2 *Sec* k* *Sep* k* sil k* *Spong* k* squil k* sul-ac k* sulph k* **Tarent** k* ter k* teucr k* thuj k* thyr ptk1 tritic-vg fd5.de vanil fd5.de *Verat* b7.de* vip k*
  - **right**: alumn k* cedr ptk1 dulc fd4.de eup-per ptk1 **Kali-c** k* nux-m ptk1 sil h2 sul-ac h2 sulph h2 zinc ptk1
    - **accompanied** by | **left** arm; numbness of (See upper limbs - left - accompanied - right)
  - **left**: cupr-ar des-ac rbp6 dulc fd4.de ham fd3.de• kreos lac-c med bg1 *Meny* vh nat-m h2* phos h2* psor bg1 ruta fd4.de sep sulph h2 thlas bg1
    - **accompanied** by | **right** arm; numbness of (See upper limbs - right - accompanied - leg)
  - **morning**: ham fd3.de• phos k*
    - **bed** agg.; in: *Aur Sulph* k* teucr k*
  - **afternoon** | **sitting** agg.: teucr
  - **evening**: dulc fd4.de mez k* sil k* sulph k*
    - **bed** agg.; in: dulc fd4.de hydrog srj2•
    - **sitting** agg.: sil k*
  - **night**: alum k* *Calc-p* k* graph h2 ph-ac h2
  - **accompanied** by | **Meninges** of spine; inflammation of (See BACK - Inflammation - membranes - accompanied - lower)
  - **alternating** with:
    - **pain** (See Pain - lower limbs - alternating with - numbness)
    - **sciatica** (See Pain - lower limbs - sciatic - alternating with - numbness)
  - **ascending** stairs agg.: nux-m k*
  - **chill**; during: con
  - **crossing** the legs, when: agar k* alum ptk1* ambr k2 ang *Carb-an Crot-h* fl-ac kali-c ptk1 laur plat h2 psor al2 rad-br bg1 rheum sabad sne sep squil k*
  - **eating**; after: kali-c
  - **exertion**; cramping numbness during: alum
  - **gouty** limbs: *Acon*
  - **kneeling**, after: op opun-s a1 (non:opun-v a1)
  - **lain** on: alumn am-c bufo *Carb-an* ozone sde2• *Rhus-t*
  - **lying** agg.: aur kali-c h2* sulph k* tritic-vg fd5.de
  - **menses** | **before** | **agg.**: ang podo sne
    - **during** | **agg.**: carb-an sne hyos b7a.de *Kali-n* **Puls** k* *Sec*
  - **pain**; after: cocc
  - **rest**; after: op opun-s a1 (non:opun-v a1)
  - **riding** agg.: *Calc-p* k*
  - **sitting**:
    - **after**: sep k*
    - **agg.**: *Ant-c Ant-t* calc *Calc-p* k* calc-sil k2 chin k* con crot-h euph k* euphr *Graph* kali-c k* lyc h2 lyss nux-v k* ph-ac k* plat h2 ros-d wla1 sep k* sil sulph teucr tritic-vg fd5.de
  - **sleep** | **siesta**; during: *Nat-m*
  - **standing** agg.: sep k*
    - **long** time; for a: puls ptk1
  - **stool** agg.; after: trios k*
  - **walking** agg.: *Alum* k* **Kali-n** k* *Plb Rhus-t* k* *Sep* k* *Thuj*
  - ▽ **extending** to | **Waist**-line: *Calc-p*
  - ○ **Bones**: graph bg2 kalm bg2
  - **Joints**: mosch k*
  - **Side** of affected ovary: apis gsy1
- **Nates**: allox tpw3* *Alum* h2* *Calc-p* k* caust bg2 dig k* moni rfm1• plb k* raph k* spong k* sulph k*

- **Nates**: ...
  - **accompanied** by | **coldness** of nates (See Coldness - nates - accompanied - numbness)
  - **rising** after sitting; on: calc-p
  - **sitting** agg.: *Alum* k* *Calc-p* k* dig k* guaj *Sulph* k*
- **Paralyzed** parts: phys br1
- **Shoulders**: (↗*Tingling - shoulders)* acon bg2 alumn k* bell bg2 caust bg2 cocc k2 ferr b7.de* fl-ac bg2 kali-bi bg2 merc k* ox-ac k* plb k* *Puls* k* sep k* *Urt-u* k* zinc k*
  - **right**: cassia-s ccrh1•
  - **left**: merc-i-f a1* rhus-t tl1 xan hr1*
  - **morning**: zinc k*
  - **night**: sep k*
  - ▽ **extending** to:
    - **Fingers** | **Tips**: ox-ac k2*
- **Side** not lain on: fl-ac k*
- **Thighs**: acon k* allox sp1 aloe bg2 *Ars* k* asar k* aster k* berb k* bry bg2* cadm-s *Calc* k* canth k* carb-v k* carbn-s carc mg1.de* chel k* chin b7.de* cic k* colch b7.de* *Con* k* crot-h bg2 dig k* euph k* euphr *Ferr* k* *Fl-ac* k* glon k* **Graph** k* guaj k* hep b4a.de ign b7.de* iod k* kali-bi bg2 *Kreos* k* *Lac-d* k* m-aust b7.de *Med* meny b7.de* merc k* nit-ac bg2 nux-m k* nux-v oci k* ox-ac k* phos bro1 plat k* *Plb* k* podo samb bg2 sec k* *Spong* k* tep k* thuj b4.de* trios rsj11• vanil fd5.de
  - **right**: allox tpw3 bry bg1 calc-f bg1 fl-ac bg1 nicc-met sk4• vanil fd5.de
  - **left**: bamb-a stb2.de• lyc bg1 med phos k*
    - **sitting** agg.: bamb-a stb2.de•
  - **afternoon**: bamb-a stb2.de• vanil fd5.de
  - **evening** | **crossing** legs; when: fl-ac k*
  - **night**: plb
  - **crossing** legs agg.: fl-ac k* nux-m k*
  - **eating** agg.: ferr bg1
  - **exertion**:
    - **agg.**: carc sp1
    - **amel.**: carc mg1.de*
  - **heat**; during: ferr bg2 graph bg2 spong k*
  - **lain** on, one: tell k*
  - **lying** agg.: merc k*
  - **menses**; before: podo
  - **motion** | **beginning** of | **agg.**: allox tpw3*
    - **continued** motion | **amel.**: allox tpw3
  - **paralytic**: acon k*
  - **rising** from sitting agg.: chin k* sulph k*
  - **sitting** agg.: allox tpw3* graph k* merc k* puls k* sil k* thuj k* trios rsj11• vanil fd5.de
    - **eating**; after: ign
  - **sleep**, short: (non:carc jl2)
    - **amel.**: carc mg1.de*
  - **standing** agg.: chin k*
  - **walking** agg.: carb-v k*
  - ▽ **extending** to:
    - **Foot**: con k*
    - **Knee**: allox tpw3*
  - ○ **Anterior**: chel k* *Lac-d* plan plat k* plb bg1 sec bg1
  - **Outer** side: caj k* lac-d *Plb* stram a1
- **Thumbs**: alum k* calad k* cann-i k* *Caust* k* cina bg2 dulc fd4.de euphr k* hura kali-c k* nat-m k* op k* plat k* plb k* stront-c k* stry k* tung-met bdx1• verb k* zinc bg2
  - **right**: cann-i c1 lac-e hrn2• ox-ac plb k* plut-n srj7•
  - **left**: alum k* calad gard-j vlr2• nat-m k*
  - **morning**: kali-c h2 nat-m k* plat h2
  - **afternoon**: alum k* ham fd3.de•
  - **painful**: *Caust*
  - ○ **Balls**: coll a1 gamb k* lam a1
  - **Nails**; under: colch bg2

- **Proximal** joint: cina h1
- **Tip** of: cina ham fd3.de• hydrog srj2• phos k* zinc k*

\- **Toes**: abrot ptk1 *Acon* k* aids nl2• allox tpw4 alum-sil k2 apis k* **Arn** b7.de* *Ars* k* benz-ac *Calc* k* camph carb-v k2 *Caust* *Cham* k* *Chel* k* colch b7.de* *Con* k* crot-h cub cycl k* fago glon **Graph** k* lach bg1 lyc k* m-aust b7.de nat-m bro1* *Nat-s* bg2* nept-m lsd2.fr nux-v b7.de* ozone sde2• ph-ac k* *Phos* k* plb k* podo fd3.de• puls k* pycnop-sa mrz1 sabad b7.de* **Sec** k* sil bro1 sulph bro1 thal bro1* thuj

- **right**: ozone sde2• petr-ra shn4•
- **morning**: aids nl2• lyc
  - **waking**; on: aids nl2•
- **prickling**; hot: acon k*
- **walking** agg.: *Acon* *Caust* cycl ph-ac

▽ • **extending** to:
  - **Other** parts: thal ptk1
  - **Upward**: *Ars* thal dx

○ • **Balls**: puls b7.de*
- **First**: ars ptk1 calc ptk1 cham k* nat-c nat-s k* nux-v petr-ra shn4• rad-br bg1
  - **morning**: nat-s
    - **sitting** agg.: nat-s
  - **afternoon**: nat-c
- **Tips**: acon phos bg2 tab
  - **beginning** in: tab

\- **Upper** arms: *(↗Tingling - upper arms)* am-c k* bry k* cact ptk1 carb-ac carbn-s croc k* fl-ac k* hura inul a1 kali-c h2* kali-s fd4.de lat-m ptk1 mag-m ptk1 merc k* morg-p pte1• plat k*

- **left**: mim-p rsj8•
- **morning** | **bed** agg.; in: merc
- **sitting** agg.: merc k*

○ • **Deltoid**: plb k*

\- **Upper** limbs: *(↗Tingling - upper limbs)* abrom-a ks5 abrot k* **Acon** k* aesc k* *Aeth* k* agar bg2 ail k* allox sp1 *Alum* k* alum-p k2 alum-sil k2 *Alumn* am-c k* am-m k* *Ambr* k* amyg k* anac b4.de androc srj1• **Apis** k* aran k* arg-met arg-n br1 ars k* ars-i ars-s-f k2 aster bro1 aur k* aur-ar k2 bapt bg2 *Bar-c* k* bar-i k2 bar-s k2 bell k* berb k* borx h2 both k* *Bufo* *Cact* k* calc b4.de* calc-p k* cann-i k* canth k* caps h1 *Carb-an* b4.de* *Carb-v* k* carbn-o **Carbn-s** k* castor-eq caust cedr k* *Cham* k* chel k* chinin-ar chr-ac k* cic k* cimic k* cinnb k* **Cocc** k* cod k* colch k* *Con* k* *Croc* k* *Crot-c* k* *Cupr* k* cupr-ar k* *Cur* k* dig b4.de* dios k* dros b7.de *Dulc* k* euph b4a.de euphr k* fago k* falco-pe nl2• *Fl-ac* k* *Gels* glon k* **Graph** k* *Guaj* b4a.de hell k* helo helo-s rwt2• helodr-cal knl2• *Hep* k* hippoc-k szs2 hura hydroph rsj6• hyos b7.de* hyper bg2 iber bro1 *Ign* b7.de* iod k* kali-ar kali-bi k* *Kali-c* k* kali-m ptk1 **Kali-n** k* kali-p *Kali-s* kali-sil k2 kreos lac-c k* *Lach* k* lat-m bro1* led k* lepi a1* lil-t bro1 **Lyc** k* lyss k* m-ambo b7.de m-arct b7.de m-aust b7.de *Mag-m* k* magn-gr bro1 med k* meph k* merc k* merc-c k* merc-i-f k* morg-p fmm1• nat-m k* nat-p k* nat-s nit-ac k* *Nux-v* k* ol-j k* *Olnd* b7a.de *Onos* **Ox-ac** k* *Pall* k* par bro1 petr k* *Phos* k* phys k* **Plat** k* *Plb* k* psil ft1 *Psor* k* *Puls* k* pyrog k2 *Rhod* k* **Rhus-t** k* sanguis-s hrn2• sarr k* *Sec* k* *Sep* k* sil k* *Spig* k* stann stront-c k* *Sulph* k* sumb k* tarent k2 tep k* teucr b7.de *Thuj* k* tritic-vg fd5.de tub jl2 tung-met bdx1• urt-u k* vanil fd5.de verat k* vip k* xan k* **Zinc** k*

- **alternating** sides: ozone sde2•
- **right**: *(↗Tingling - upper limbs - right)* am-c am-m ars k* bamb-a stb2.de• bell bg2 calc bg1 cann-xyz bg2 carb-an h2* carneg-g rwt1• castor-eq chel k* chin bg1 fum rly4• graph bg2* *Hep* k* kali-bi k* **Kali-c** bg2 kali-n h2 kali-p bg1 kali-s fd4.de lach k* *Lil-t* k* *Lyc* k* lyss mag-m k* mand rsj7• merc bg2 merc-i-f k* mur-ac ptk1 nat-p k* nit-ac h2 paraf ah1 phos h2* phys k* phyt bro1* sanguis-s hrn2• scop ptk1 *Sil* k* thuj vanil fd5.de *Verat* bg2
  - **accompanied** by:
    - **Eye**:
      - **left** | **pain** over left eye; neuralgic: mur-ac ptk1
    - **Leg**; numbness of left: ars kali-c k*
  - **aphasia**; with (See MIND - Aphasia - upper - numbness - right)
  - **heart** disease; in: lil-t

\- **Upper** limbs – **right**: ...
  - **lying**:
    - **side**; on | **left** | **agg.**: *Mag-m*
      - **right** | **agg.**: *Am-c* *Ars* *Carb-v* fl-ac kali-p fd1.de• petr *Spig* vanil fd5.de
  - **extending** to:
    - **left**: zinc-ar ptk1 zinc-i ptk1
    - **Hand**: mand rsj7•

- **left**: *(↗Tingling - upper limbs - left)* *Acon* k* aesc k* ail k* alum bg1 ambr k* anac k* androc srj1*• apis k* *Bar-c* k* bufo **Cact** k* calc bg1 calc-p bg2 cham k* cinnb k* cupr-ar k* dig bg2* glon k* *Graph* kali-c h2 kali-n h2 kalm k* kreos lac-c k* *Lach* k* lat-m mag-s bg2* *Med* k* melal-alt gya4 meph a1 mill k* muru a1 naja k* nat-m h2* nicc bg2 nux-v k* pall bg2 petr k* *Phos* k* psor bg1 puls bro1 pycnop-sa mrz1 rhod k* rhus-t bg1* spig ptk1 sulph bg1* sumb k* tarax k* tarent k* thlas bg1 vanil fd5.de xan k*
  - **accompanied** by:
    - **right** leg; numbness of: *Tarent* k*
    - **Heart** disease (See CHEST - Heart; complaints - accompanied - upper - left - numbness)
  - **lying** on it; from: cact *Nat-m* vanil fd5.de
  - **paralysis** of whole left side; with: bapt hr1
  - **sleep** agg.; during: lac-del hrn2•
- **daytime**: ambr anac
  - **rest** agg.: ambr
- **morning**: am-c h2 crot-h k* fl-ac k* mag-m k* nux-v peti a1 phos k* psor k* puls vanil fd5.de zinc
  - **bed** agg.; in: *Kali-c*
    - **waking** agg.; after: mag-s br1
  - **lying**:
    - **arm** agg.; on: arg-met
    - **Arm** under head; with: ph-ac
  - **pain** in region of heart: pall k*
  - **waking**; on: aur calad fl-ac kali-c h2 *Mag-m* mag-s musca-d szs1 nit-ac psor teucr vanil fd5.de zinc
- **forenoon**: fl-ac k* mill k* zing k*
  - **10** h: zing
- **afternoon**: alum-sil k2 calc-p k* carl k* nicc k* teucr k*
- **evening**: borx h2 bry k* lyss merc-c k* phos k* plb k*
  - **19** h: *Phys*
  - **20** h: cinnb
  - **lying** down agg.; mag-m h2
- **night**: abrom-a ks5 am-c h2 *Ambr* k* arg-n tl1 carb-v k* cham sne cop k* *Croc* k* hep k* hyper k* *Ign* k* kali-c k* kali-n h2 lap-la sde8.de• *Lyc* mag-m k* merc k* nit-ac k* *Nux-v* k* ozone sde2• *Pall* k* petr k* ph-ac k* phos k* puls sep h2 sil vanil fd5.de
  - **midnight**, before | **22** h: fl-ac
  - **lying** on it: cop k* hep k* petr k*
  - **sleep** agg.; during: bros-gau mrc1 croc k*
- **accompanied** by:
  - **Heart**:
    - **disease** (See CHEST - Heart; complaints - accompanied - upper - left - numbness)
    - **pain** (See CHEST - Pain - heart - region - accompanied - upper - numbness)
- **bed** | **going** to bed | **when**: psor
  - **in** bed | **agg.**: androc srj1• carb-an *Ign* k* mag-m phos k*
- **carrying** anything, when: *Ambr* k*
- **clothes** too tight; as if: paraf ah1
- **cold** agg.; becoming: sumb
- **colic**; with: aran k*
- **convulsions**; between epileptic: cupr
- **covers**, under: sep k*
- **eating** | **after** | **agg.**: cocc k* *Kali-c*
  - **while** | **agg.**: cocc k*

Extremities

- **exertion**:
  - **after**:
    - **agg.**: sulph h2
    - **violent** exertion: *Kali-c*
  - **agg.** | **cramping**: alum
- **fever**; during intermittent: agar k* am-m k* ars-s-r k* cocc k* merc-sul k* zinc
- **grasping** anything firmly: am-c h2 **Cham** k* chin cocc k*
- **hanging** down, when: berb k* kali-s fd4.de
- **holding** anything in hands: *Apis* k* com k* puls h1
- **laying** arm on table: bar-c k*
- **leaning** on it: ambr c1 hep petr sil sumb k*
- **lying**:
  - **agg.**: abrom-a ks5 aur merc rumx sulph k* tritic-vg fd5.de
  - **arm** agg.; not lying on: fl-ac ptk1 mag-m ptk1
  - **arm** agg.; on●: *Ambr* arg-met ars bamb-a stb2.de• *Bar-c* bufo *Calc* calc-sil k2 carb-an *Carb-v* k* cop *Graph* hep ign *Kali-c* k* kali-p fd1.de• *Lach* *Nat-m* k* pall petr *Phos* **Puls** k* **Rhus-t** k* sep *Sil* *Spig* staph gk sulph bg1 sumb vanil fd5.de
  - **back**; on | **agg.**: kali-n h2
- **measles**; during: zinc k*
- **menses**; during: graph kali-n sec
- **motion**:
  - **agg.**: plb k* ruta
  - **amel.**: *Ambr* *Apis* aur dros merc k* mim-h c1 phos h2 rumx sep k* sulph
- **pain** in arm, with: kali-n h2 phos h2
- **raising** them: allox tpw3* kali-s fd4.de lyc h2
  - **upright**: *Puls* sep
    - **amel.**: ars k* puls ptk1
- **resting** head on arm agg.: ph-ac h2 *Phos* k* *Rhus-t* k* sep k*
- **resting** on arm agg.: ambr carb-an fl-ac k* *Sil* hr1
- **riding** in a carriage agg.: form k*
- **scratching** agg.; after: sulph
- **sitting** agg.: alum k2 *Graph* k* lyc nicc k* *Teucr* k* tritic-vg fd5.de
- **sleep** | **siesta**; during: graph k*
- **using** it: *Puls* k* *Spig*
- **weather**, cold: *Kali-c* *Sumb*
- **working** agg.: phos bg1
- **writing** agg.: cere-b k* *Merc-i-f* k* spig k*
- ▽ **extending** to | **Thumb**: sumb
- ○ **Anterior** part: plan
- **Bones**: cham bg2
- **Side** not lain on: fl-ac mag-m

- **Wrists**: acon k* agath-a nl2• bov k* carb-v k* com k* croc b7.de* fil hr1 hipp jl2 hura ign bg2* kali-n k* lyc bg2 *Plb* k* **Zinc** k*
  - **right**: *Viol-o* mrr1
  - **morning** | **bed** agg.; in: hipp jl2
  - **measles**; during: **Zinc**
  - ▽ **extending** to:
    - **Fingers**: viol-o mrr1
    - **Hand**: viol-o mrr1

NURSING; while:

- **agg.** | **Lower** limbs: *Phos* b4a.de

ODOR of feet offensive, without perspiration: *(↗CHEST - Perspiration - axilla - offensive; GENERALS - Odor of; GENERALS - Odor of - offensive)* arge-pl rwt5• bar-c b4.de* fl-ac mrr1 *Graph* k* *Kali-c* b4a.de *Lyc* mrr1 *Nit-ac* b4a.de phos b4a.de sep k* *Sil* k* sulph b4a.de thuj b4a.de* zinc b4.de*

ONYCHIA (See Felon - root)

ONYCHOPHAGY (See MIND - Biting - nails)

OOZING from edematous legs: *Graph* k* hep sne **Lyc** k* tarent-c k*

ORGASM (See Blood - rush)

OSTEOPOROSIS: *(↗GENERALS - Osteoporosis)* cortiso mtf11 dys mtf11 mucor mtf11 [*Bor-pur* stj2]

- **injury**; after an: cortiso mtf11

○ - **Thighs**: [*Stront-m* stj2 *Stront-met* stj2]

OVERLIFTING agg.: | **Lower** limbs: am b7.de* chin b7.de* rhus-t b7.de* *Ruta* b7a.de

OWN; as if legs were not his: *Agar* *Bapt* op sumb

PAIN: *Abrot* k* absin br1 *Acon* *Act-sp*↓ *Aesc* aeth k* **Agar** k* agath-a↓ *Agn*↓ aids↓ *All-c*↓ all-s k* allox↓ *Aloe*↓ *Alum* alum-p↓ alum-sil k2* alumn am-c **Am-m**↓ ambr h1 ammc↓ ampe-qu↓ anac anan↓ *Androc* srj1• ang↓ *Ant-c*↓ ant-t anthraci antip↓ aphis↓ *Apis* apoc apoc-a↓ aq-mar↓ arg-met arg-n↓ arist-m br1 *Arn* **Ars** k* ars-h k* ars-i ars-s-f↓ arund↓ asaf asar↓ asc-t aster atp↓ *Aur* aur-ar k2 aur-i k2 aur-m↓ aur-m-n↓ aur-s k2 aza br1 *Bad*↓ *Bamb-a* stb2.de• *Bapt* bar-act↓ bar-c bar-s k2 **Bell** k* bell-p↓ bell-p-sp↓ benz-ac↓ berb beryl↓ bism↓ *Bol-la* both k* bov↓ bran↓ brass-n-o srj5• bros-gau↓ **Bry** k* bufo↓ but-ac br1 *Buteo-j*↓ cact cadm-met↓ *Calc* calc-f↓ calc-i k2 calc-p calc-s calc-sil↓ camph↓ cann-i cann-s↓ canth k* caps *Carb-ac*↓ carb-an carb-v carbn-h carbn-o carbn-s carc↓ card-m↓ *Cardios-h* rly4• *Carl* carneg-g rwt1• cartl-s↓ *Caul* **Caust** cedr *Cham* **Chel** *Chin* k* chinin-ar *Chinin-s*↓ chlor↓ chord-umb↓ cic↓ cimic k* *Cina* cinch↓ cinnb k* *Cist*↓ cit-v↓ *Clem*↓ cob↓ coc-c↓ coca cocc coff **Colch** k* coli↓ *Coloc* con cop *Corn*↓ corn-f↓ cortiso sp1 croc↓ crot-h k* crot-t k* cupr k* *Cur*↓ cycl↓ cystein-l rly4• cyt-l sp1 *Daph*↓ des-ac↓ dig digin a1 dios *Dros* k* *Dulc* k* echi↓ elaps *Elat*↓ eucal↓ **Eup-per** eup-pur k* euph k* eupi↓ eys↓ fago k* falco-pe↓ *Ferr* k* ferr-ar ferr-i k2 ferr-p↓ fic-m gya1 fl-ac↓ form k* galla-q-r↓ *Gels* ger-i↓ gink-b↓ gins↓ glon *Graph* *Guaj* guare↓ haliae-lc↓ ham hedeo↓ *Hell* hep heroin↓ hip-ac↓ hippoc-k↓ hippoz↓ hist↓ hydr k* hydrc↓ hydrog↓ hydroph rsj6• hyos k* hyper↓ ign ind k* indg k* *Ip* iris jal↓ jatr-c jug-c **Kali-ar** *Kali-bi* kali-br↓ *Kali-c* k* *Kali-i* kali-m k2 kali-n kali-p **Kali-s** kali-sil↓ **Kalm** k* ketogl-ac↓ kiss↓ kola↓ *Kreos* k* lac-ac **Lac-c**↓ lac-del hrn2• lach k* lachn↓ lact k* lam↓ lat-m↓ *Laur*↓ *Lec*↓ led k* lepi lil-t↓ limen-b-c↓ limest-b↓ lith-c **Lyc** k* lycps-v *Lyss* *Mag-c*↓ *Mag-m*↓ *Mag-p* mag-s↓ magn-gr↓ manc↓ mand↓ **Mang**↓ marb-w↓ **Med** melal-alt↓ meny↓ meph k* **Merc** k* *Merc-c* k* merc-d↓ merc-i-f k* merc-i-r merl k* mez **Mill**↓ *Mim-p*↓ mosch k2 mucs-nas rly4• *Mur-ac* myric↓ naja *Nat-ar* *Nat-c* nat-f sp1 nat-hchls↓ nat-m nat-ox rly4• *Nat-p* nat-s k2 neon↓ nicc-met↓ nicotam rly4• *Nit-ac* **Nit-s-d**↓ *Nux-m*↓ **Nux-v** oci-sa↓ *Ol-an*↓ olib-sac↓ olnd↓ op osm ox-ac k* oxal-a↓ ozone↓ paeon↓ pall↓ par↓ petr↓ petr-ra shn4• *Ph-ac* *Phos* k* phys k* physala-p bnm7• **Phyt** k* *Pic-ac*↓ pieri-b mlk9.de plac-s↓ plan plat **Plb** k* plect↓ plut-n↓ podo polys↓ pop↓ *Positr*↓ pot-e↓ psor ptel k* **Puls** puls-n↓ pyrog k2* quas↓ rad-br c11 ran-a↓ ran-s↓ raph↓ rauw↓ **Rhod** **Rhus-t** rhus-v↓ ribo rly4• *Ros-d*↓ *Ruta* sabad sabin sacch-a fd2.de• sal-fr↓ *Samb*↓ *Sang* k* sarcol-ac↓ *Sars* *Sec* k* sel senec↓ sep k* sil k* sinus↓ sol-ni solid br1 **Spig**↓ **Spong**↓ squil k* *Stann*↓ staph k* *Stel*↓ *Still*↓ stram k* stront-c stroph-s↓ *Stry* k* suis-em↓ suis-hep↓ suis-pan↓ sul-ac **Sulph** k* sumb suprar↓ symph↓ *Syph*↓ tab k* tanac↓ taosc iwa1• tarax↓ tarent k* tax k* tell *Thal*↓ thal-xyz↓ thea↓ ther↓ thuj thyr↓ til↓ tril-p↓ tritic-vg fd5.de tub jl2 tub-m jl2 tub-r↓ *Tung-met*↓ *Valer* vanil fd5.de vario jl2 **Verat** *Verat-v*↓ verin↓ vero-o↓ vinc↓ vip k* x-ray↓ xan↓ zinc zinc-p k2 zinc-s a1 zing↓ [uva stj]

- **one** side: ambr↓ **Ars**↓
  - **tearing** pain: ambr c1 **Ars**
- **alternating** sides: bamb-a stb2.de• **Lac-c** k*
- **right**: *(↗right side)* caust↓ *Form* sne guat sp1 **Lyc** sne
  - **sore**: caust h2
  - **then** left: bell br1 *Form* sne **Lyc** br1 mez br1 sang br1 sulph br1
- **right** side; whole: *(↗right)*
  - **neuralgic**:
    - **accompanied** by | **suppression** of urine (See KIDNEYS - Suppression - accompanied - neuralgic)
- **left**: *Aesc*↓ cocc↓ dulc fd4.de galeoc-c-h gms1• mez↓ nat-ar hr1 olib-sac wmh1 *Sumb*↓
  - **aching**: *Sumb* k*
  - **drawing** pain: cocc h1 mez h2
  - **shooting** pain: aesc
  - **stitching** pain: *Aesc*

- **then** right: *Colch* k* elaps kali-c kola stb3• *Kreos* **Lach** naja nit-m-ac phyt *Plan* rhus-t
- ○ **Arm** and leg: form ↓
  - **tearing** pain: form k*
- **Arm** and right thigh: agar ↓
  - **tearing** pain: agar h2
- **daytime**: sulph ↓
  - **sore**: sulph
- **morning**: acon ↓ acon-l ↓ aesc ↓ androc srj1• apoc ↓ arg-n *Aur* ↓ calc-p carneg-g ↓ cinnb k* clem cob-n sp1 dulc fd4.de hep ↓ heroin ↓ kali-bi lyc meph ↓ **Nux-v** ↓ phos **RHUS-T** sne ruta fd4.de spong fd4.de sulph tritic-vg fd5.de
  - **6** h: ptel ↓
    - **sore**: ptel
  - **7** h: myric ↓
    - **aching**: myric
  - **aching**: carneg-g rwt1• [heroin sdj2]
  - **bed** agg.; in: *Aur* ↓ *Nat-hchls* ↓ *Nux-v* **Puls** k* *Rhus-t* *Staph* ↓ *Zinc* ↓
    - **sore**: *Aur* *Rhus-t* *Staph* *Zinc*
    - **stitching** pain: *Nat-hchls*
  - **burning**: dulc fd4.de phos k* spong fd4.de tritic-vg fd5.de
  - **drawing** pain: acon acon-l a1 calc-p k*
  - **rising** | **after**:
    - **agg.**: carb-v ↓ *Nat-m* ↓ sulph ↓
      - **sore**: carb-v h2 *Nat-m* sulph
    - **amel.**: *Aur* ↓
      - **sore**: *Aur*
  - **shooting** pain: kali-bi
  - **sore**: aesc apoc arg-n *Aur* clem **Nux-v** sulph
  - **stitching** pain: *Kali-bi* phos k* ruta fd4.de spong fd4.de tritic-vg fd5.de
  - **tearing** pain: hep lyc k* meph k* spong fd4.de
  - **toward**: *Ars* bov *Kali-c* *Nux-v* rhus-t thuj
  - **waking**; on: aesc arg-n k2 aur carb-v ↓ *Hep* *Nux-v* ↓ op k* petr-ra ↓ *Puls* sulph tell zinc
    - **aching**: petr-ra shn4•
    - **drawing** pain: *Aur* *Hep* *Nux-v*
    - **sore**: zinc h2
    - **tearing** pain: carb-v *Hep*
- **forenoon**: am-c dulc fd4.de mag-m merc nat-ar plan k* spong fd4.de tritic-vg ↓
  - **aching**: am-c k* nat-ar
  - **drawing** pain: merc tritic-vg fd5.de
  - **sore**: mag-m
- **noon**: bry dulc fd4.de sulph
  - **until** midnight: bell mag-s rhus-t
  - **sore**: sulph
- **afternoon**: aq-pet ↓ calc cina cob ↓ dulc ↓ gels ↓ glon k* kali-c lyc k* lycps-v nit-ac pall ↓ plan ↓ ptel ruta fd4.de spong fd4.de staph thuj tritic-vg fd5.de
  - **13** h: aq-mar ↓
    - **shooting** pain: aq-mar skp7•
  - **13**.30 h: pert-vc ↓
    - **stitching** pain: pert-vc vk9
  - **14**.30-21 h: aq-mar ↓
    - **severe**: aq-mar skp7•
  - **16** h: elaps ↓
    - **stitching** pain: elaps
  - **aching**: aq-pet a1 nit-ac k* ptel k*
  - **burning**: dulc fd4.de gels k* tritic-vg fd5.de
  - **drawing** pain: calc k* lyc k* ruta fd4.de
  - **sleep** agg.; after: con ↓
    - **sore**: con h2
  - **sore**: cina cob kali-c pall *Staph* thuj
  - **stitching** pain: plan k* ruta fd4.de spong fd4.de
- **evening**: am-c am-m br1 apoc k* *Ars* ars-s-f k2 *Bell* cact k* calc calc-p cob-n sp1 colch coloc ↓ dulc k2 *Ferr* ↓ ferr-i ↓ *Kali-s* *Kalm* *Led* mag-s par ↓ petr ph-ac plan **Plb** k* *Puls* *Rhus-t* ruta fd4.de sacch-a fd2.de• sil ↓ sol-ni spong fd4.de sul-ac ↓ sulph tritic-vg fd5.de
  - **18** h: **Rhus-t** ↓
    - **drawing** pain: **Rhus-t**
  - **21** h: mag-s ↓
    - **drawing** pain: mag-s
  - **bed** agg.; in: carb-v ↓ con ↓ *Ferr* ↓
    - **burning**: carb-v k*
    - **tearing** pain: con k* *Ferr*
  - **drawing** pain: calc-p k* coloc k* led mag-s k* ph-ac k* *Puls* rhus-t k* ruta fd4.de spong fd4.de **Sulph** k* tritic-vg fd5.de
  - **lying** down | **after** | **agg.**: *Ars* tritic-vg fd5.de
    - **agg.**: petr ↓
      - **sore**: petr
  - **sitting** agg.: am-m ↓
    - **tearing** pain: am-m
  - **sleep**; before: sulph ↓
    - **stitching** pain: sulph
  - **sore**: am-c ferr-i petr sil h2
  - **stitching** pain: *Ars* calc k* *Dulc* *Led* par plan k* plb ruta fd4.de sil k* spong fd4.de tritic-vg fd5.de
  - **tearing** pain: *Ars* *Dulc* *Ferr* mag-s *Puls* ruta fd4.de sul-ac k* sulph
- **night**: acon *Agar* alum alum-p k2 alum-sil k2 am-c k* androc srj1• am *Ars* ars-s-f k2 *Asaf* *Aur* aur-ar k2 bell ↓ beryl ↓ bry calc carb-v **Cham** cinnb cit-v ↓ dulc eupi ↓ *Ferr* *Fl-ac* gels k* graph *Hep* kali-bi *Kali-c* *Kali-i* kali-m k2 kali-s tl1 kalm *Lach* led k2 lyc **Merc** *Merc-i-f* merc-sul k* *Mez* nat-m *Nit-ac* *Nux-v* phos *Phyt* **Plb** k* podo *Puls* k* *Rhod* *Rhus-t* ruta fd4.de sabin sacch-a ↓ *Sars* *Sil* ↓ spong fd4.de *Sulph* k* syph thuj tritic-vg fd5.de *Tub* ↓ vanil ↓
  - **2-3** h: **Kali-c** ↓
    - **stitching** pain: **Kali-c**
  - **midnight**: sulph
    - **before**: bry
    - **after**: **Ars** ars-s-f k2 gels *Merc* *Sars* *Sulph* *Thuj*
      - **0-6** h: aq-mar skp7•
        - **lightning**-like: aq-mar skp7•
      - **2-3** h: **Kali-c**
      - **4** h: gels *Lyc* ↓
        - **sore**: *Lyc*
  - **aching**: am-c k* *Aur* *Merc* *Nux-v* podo k*
  - **bed**: stroph-s sp1
    - **driving** out of bed: aur k2 aur-m-n wbt2• **Cham** *Ferr* k* **Merc** syph k2
      - **tearing** pain: *Cham* *Ferr* *Merc*
  - **burning**: dulc fd4.de kali-c spong fd4.de vanil fd5.de
  - **cramping**: phos
  - **crampy**: phos
  - **drawing** pain: bell k* calc k* **Carb-v** k* *Cham* cit-v k* graph h2 hep *Lyc* merc k* *Nux-v* *Puls* *Rhod* **Rhus-t** k* sabin
  - **gnawing** pain: nit-ac
  - **motion** | **must** move: syph xxb
  - **sleep** agg.; after: cycl ↓
    - **sore**: cycl
  - **sore**: nat-m *Nux-v* sacch-a fd2.de•
  - **stitching** pain: beryl tpw5 *Dulc* *Ferr* *Hep* *Sil* tritic-vg fd5.de
  - **sunset** to sunrise; from: syph k2
  - **tearing** pain: *Calc* carb-v *Cham* *Dulc* eupi k* *Ferr* *Hep* *Lyc* nux-v *Puls* *Rhod* **Rhus-t** sabin sars k* *Tub*
- **accompanied** by:
  - **coryza**: **Acon** bg2 ars bg2 bell bg2 *Bry* bg2 chin bg2 **Gels** bg2 hep bg2 merc bg2 nat-m bg2 **Puls** bg2 *Sep* bg2 sulph bg2
  - **cough**: caps b7.de*

Extremities

○ • **Abdomen** | **complaints** of (See ABDOMEN - Complaints - accompanied - extremities - pain)
• **Head**; complaints of (See HEAD - Complaints - accompanied - extremities - pain)

- **aching**: aesc bro1 **Agar** agath-a nl2• all-c bro1 allox sp1 alum-sil k2 am-c k* androc srj1• *Ant-c* apis bro1 apoc *Arn* k* *Ars* k* *Aur* aza br1* *Bapt* k* *Bell* bov *Bry* k* but-ac sp1 calc bro1 *Calc-p* k* calc-sil k2 cann-i k* *Carb-v* k* carc sp1* *Carl* k* caust bro1 *Cham* chin k* chinin-ar chord-umb rly4• *Cimic* k* *Cocc* *Con* bro1 cupr *Cur* k* cycl bro1 cystein-l rly4• dulc fd4.de echi bro1 eucal bro1 **Eup-per** k* fago k* ferr k* ferr-ar *Gels* k* ger-i rly4• glon haliae-lc srj5• ham k* hedeo bro1 hell k* hippoc-k szs2 *Hydr* hydrc **Ip** jal br1 jug-c k* *Kalm* bro1 ketogl-ac rly4• lac-ac a1 lac-c lach k* lec br1 led k* *Lyc* lyss melal-alt gya4 *Merc* k* merc-c k* mez k* mosch *Mur-ac* myric bro1 naja nat-ar *Nat-m* nit-ac k* **Nux-v** oci-sa sp1 osm k* oxal-a rly4• ozone sde2• petr-ra shn4• *Phyt* plb k* podo k* polys sk4• *Positr* nl2• pot-e rly4• ptel k* *Puls* *Pyrog* k* quas bro1 *Rad-br* bro1 ran-s bro1 *Rhod* bro1 **Rhus-t** k* *Samb* sec bro1 sil bro1 staph k* *Stel* bro1 still k* stram k* stront-c stroph-s sp1 stry bro1 suis-em rly4• suis-pan rly4• sumb k* suprar rly4• *Syph* tell c1 thyr bro1 *Tub* tub-m vn* *Tung-met* bdx1• vanil fd5.de *Verat* x-ray sp1 zinc k* [bell-p-sp dcm1 heroin sdj2]
  • **cold**; as from: nit-ac
  • **wandering** pain: chinin-ar k2
- **air**; draft of:
  • **agg.**: ant-c mtf bufo mtf calc-p mrr1 **Caust** mtf con mtf daph mtf graph mtf *Kalm* mtf phos mtf *Rhus-t* mtf
  • **warm** draft agg.; even a: *Sel*
- **air**; in open:
  • **agg.**: plut-n srj7•
  • **amel.**: **Kali-s** k* petr-ra shn4• **Puls** k* sabin
    ⁝ **drawing** pain: sabin
- **alternately** in arms and legs: merc-i-r
- **alternating** with:
  • **chill**: *Hell* b7a.de
  • **chill** and heat: brom
  • **delirium** (See MIND - Delirium - alternating - limbs)
  • **eruptions**: crot-t st staph st
○ • **Face**; pain in (See FACE - Pain - alternating with - limbs)
  • **Head**; pain in (See HEAD - Pain - alternating - limbs)
- **amputations**; after: (↗*Injuries - fingers - amputated; GENERALS - Pain - amputation)* acon br1* all-c a1* am-m hr1* arn ptk1 asaf br1* bell br1 cupr br1 hell br1 *Hyper* hr1* ign br1 kalm hr1 med hr1* ph-ac hr1* ran-b hr1 spig br1 staph mrr1 symph c2* verat br1
- **appearing** and disappearing:
  • **gradually**: *Stann*
  • **suddenly**: kali-bi mrr1
- **ascending** stairs agg.: *Calc* dulc fd4.de phos tritic-vg fd5.de
  • **sore**: phos
- **bathing** | **after**: mand rsj7•
- **beaten**; as if: (↗*sore)* arn br1 ham fd3.de•
- **bed** agg.; in: carb-v↓ carl↓ fago↓ led↓ **Merc**↓
  • **aching**: carl k* **Merc**
  • **burning**: carb-v fago k* led k*
- **bed**, in contact with: **Arn**↓ aur↓ bapt↓ kali-p↓ merc-ns↓ *Nux-v*↓ pyrog↓ *Rhus-t*↓
  • **sore**: **Arn** aur bapt gk kali-p fd1.de• merc-ns *Nux-v* pyrog k2* *Rhus-t*
- **beer**; after: bamb-a stb2.de•
- **beginning** with a jerk: *Cocc*↓
  • **drawing** pain: *Cocc*
- **blow**; pain as from a: ruta tl1
- **boring** pain: bamb-a stb2.de• *Carb-v* cocc c1 coloc dulc fd4.de *Mez* plan k* ruta fd4.de
- **broken**; as if: aeth k* agar k2 carl k* **Cocc** k* **Eup-per** k* *Ip* nat-m k2 plb k* raph k* ther k2 tril-p
- **bruised** (See sore)
- **burning**: (↗*Heat; Heat - feet - burning)* abrot agar k2 aloe k2 alum-sil k2 anac k* *Ars* k* arund br1 asaf tl1 bamb-a stb2.de• *Bell* k* cadm-met tpw6* calc-f sp1 cann-i k* carb-an k* *Carb-v* k* carbn-s k2 cartl-s rly4• cham k2 chin k* chinin-ar k2 cocc k* coloc dros tl1 dulc fd4.de eys sp1 hip-ac sp1 hist sp1 *Kali-ar*

- **burning**: ...
kali-br k* kali-c k* kali-p kali-s fd4.de kreos k* lat-m mtf11 laur k* led k* marb-w es1• nit-ac k* *Ph-ac* phos k* plac-s rly4• plan k* plat k* plb k* pot-e rly4• rauw sp1 ruta fd4.de sec k2 spong fd4.de staph k* syph jl2 tarent k2 tritic-vg fd5.de vanil fd5.de vip k* zinc mrr1
  • **accompanied** by | **lungs**; inflammation of (See CHEST - Inflammation - lungs - accompanied - extremities)
  • **wandering** pain: plat k*
- **chill**:
  • **after**: puls↓
    ⁝ **drawing** pain: puls
  • **before**: **Arn** *Calc* *Carb-v* *Cina* **Eup-per** lyc nux-v *Plb*↓ rhus-t tub k2
    ⁝ **boring** pain: *Carb-v*
    ⁝ **drawing** pain: tub k2
    ⁝ **stitching** pain: calc *Plb* rhus-t
    ⁝ **tearing** pain: carb-v
  • **during**: *Acon* b7a.de allox sp1 ang aran k* arn **Ars** k* ars-s-f k2 asaf aur aur-ar k2 *Bapt*↓ bar-c k* bell b4a.de bol-la bro1 borx b4a.de **Bov** bry k* *Calc* calc-s canch bro1 canth b7.de *Caps* k* carbn-s caust chin bro1 *Chinin-s* k* *Cimx* *Cina* *Cocc* coff b7.de **Coloc** k* cycl **Dulc** **Eup-per** k* *Eup-pur* k* *Euph* *Ferr* form formal bro1 *Gels* k* *Graph* hell k* *Hep* k* *Ign* k* **Ip** *Kali-ar* *Kali-c* **Kali-n** *Kali-s* kali-sil k2 kreos b7a.de lach k* led k* **Lyc** k* merc b4.de **Mez** mur-ac *Nat-ar* nat-c nat-m k* nat-s k2 **Nux-v** k* *Op* petr *Ph-ac* phel bro1 phos b4.de plb *Psor* **Puls** k* **Pyrog** ran-b **Rhus-t** k* sabad k* **Sep** k* sil squil stram sulph k* **Tub** verat b7.de xan
    ⁝ **aching**: aran arn ars **Eup-per** k* *Ip* nat-m *Nux-v* **Pyrog** *Rhus-t* sabad tub
    ⁝ **drawing** pain: *Ars* k* ferr hell h1 lyc h2 *Merc* *Nux-v* ph-ac h2 *Puls* **Rhus-t** tub k2
    ⁝ **sore**: *Arn* *Bapt* bell b4a.de eup-per gk *Nux-v* *Rhus-t* *Tub*
    ⁝ **stitching** pain: *Ars* *Hep* lyc psor *Rhus-t*
    ⁝ **tearing** pain: **Ars** **Bell** *Caps* *Ferr* graph hell k* *Hep* *Kali-c* kali-s led k* **Lyc** *Nux-v* ph-ac phos *Puls* k* **Rhus-t** *Sabad* sulph *Tub*
- **chronic**: *Stront-c*↓
  • **sprained**; as if: *Stront-c* kr1*
- **coffee**: | **amel.**: arg-met
- **coition**; after: **Sil** tub
  • **aching**: tub
  • **sore**: **Sil** k*
- **cold**:
  • **agg.**: bry mrr1 *Calc* mrr1 calc-p mrr1 *Ferr* sne kali-bi k2
  • **air** agg.: **Ars** daph k* kali-ar *Kalm* kola stb3• rhus-t mtf *Sel* *Tarent*
    ⁝ **shooting** pain: daph br1
  • **applications**:
    ⁝ **agg.**: agar bg1 nux-m sne
    ⁝ **amel.**: ang c1 apis bell mrr1 *Guaj* *Lac-c* **Led** plut-n srj7• **Puls** k* sabin hr1 **Sec** syph mrr1 thuj tritic-vg fd5.de tub gk
  • **drinks**:
    ⁝ **agg.**: *Cocc*↓
      ⁝ **tearing** pain: *Cocc*
  • **exposure** to:
    ⁝ **agg.**: phos↓ spong↓
      ⁝ **burning**: phos k2 spong fd4.de
  • **food**:
    ⁝ **agg.**: *Cocc*↓
      ⁝ **tearing** pain: *Cocc*
  • **food** and drink | **tearing** pain (See drinks - agg. - tearing; food - agg. - tearing)
  • **water**:
    ⁝ **agg.**: ant-c *Ars* *Form* sne *Phos* *Rhus-t* *Tarent*
    ⁝ **amel.**: *Puls*
  • **wet**: *Calc* mrr1
○ • **Paralyzed** parts: agar↓
    ⁝ **stitching** pain: agar
- **cold**; after taking a: *Dulc*↓ guaj k2 nit-ac↓ sel↓ zing↓

 • **drawing** pain: nit-ac h2 zing k*
 • **tearing** pain: *Dulc* *Guaj* sel
- **cold**; becoming:
 • **agg.**: **Ars** bar-c k2 bry *Calc* chin k2 colch k2 graph *Kalm* **Nux-v** *Ph-ac* *Phos* *Puls* *Ran-b* **Rhus-t** tarent
  ⁝ **night**: chin k2
  ⁝ **sore**: *Ph-ac*
  ⁝ **tearing** pain: *Phos*
 • **amel.**: merc k2 verat k2
- **coldness**; during: gins↓ graph↓ *Puls*↓ ther↓
 • **drawing** pain: graph k* *Puls* ther k2
 • **sore**: gins
- **convulsions**:
 • **after**: plb k*
 • **before**: ars↓
  ⁝ **drawing** pain: ars k*
- **coryza**; during: calc b4.de* caust b4.de* hep b4a.de ip b7.de* **Merc** b4a.de nit-ac↓ *Nux-v* b7a.de sep b4a.de
 • **tearing** pain: nit-ac h2
- **cough**:
 • **agg.**: tell bg1
 • **during**:
  ⁝ **agg.**: *Caps* hr1
   : **cutting** pain: caps
   : **shooting** pain: caps
   : **stitching** pain: caps
- **cramping**: *(↗Cramps)* abrot bro1 agar h2 alumn bro1 ant-t bro1 antip bro1 *Asaf* bro1 calc bro1 canth bro1 carb-v h2 carbn-s bro1 chin h1 *Cocc* bro1 *Coloc* bro1 croc bro1 *Cupr* bro1 dulc fd4.de falco-pe nl2• galla-q-r nl2• gins bro1 hippoc-k szs2 hippoz mtf11 lac-del hm2• mag-p bro1 meny bro1 olib-sac wmh1 *Plat* bro1 psor mtf11 ruta fd4.de sarcol-ac mtf11 sec bro1 sil bro1 spong fd4.de *Stry* bro1 sul-ac h2 symph fd3.de• vanil fd5.de verat bro1 [*Buteo-j* sej6]
- **crural** neuralgia (See thighs - crural)
- **crushed**; as if: aids nl2•
- **cutting** pain: apis cina ger-i rly4• kali-s fd4.de vanil fd5.de
- **darting** (See stitching)
- **delivery**; after: caul sma rhod
- **digging** (See boring)
- **dinner**; after: nit-ac↓
 • **sore**: nit-ac h2
- **dislocated**; as if: *(↗sprained; Sprains)* *Bar-c* bg limen-b-c mlk9.de
- **dragging**: ruta fd4.de
- **drawing** pain: acon k* aeth a1 agar k* *Alum* k* alum-p k2 *Am-c* am-m k2 anac k* ang ant-t k* *Arg-met* *Ars* k* asaf aur k* aur-ar k2 aur-m aur-s k2 *Bamb-a* stb2.de• *Bapt* bar-c bell *Bry* k* calc calc-p k* calc-s camph bro1 cann-s canth k* caps carb-an **Carb-v** k* *Carbn-s* card-m k2 carl k* *Caul* caust k* cham k* *Chel* k* *Chin* chinin-ar cic k2 cimic k* cinch a1 cit-v k* *Cocc* k* colch k* *Coloc* k* con k* *Cupr* dig h2 *Dulc* ferr *Graph* k* guaj k2 *Hep* k* hyos k* hyper k* ign mrr1 ip k* jatr-c kali-ar *Kali-bi* k* *Kali-c* k* kali-n k* kali-p kali-s kali-sil k2 lach k* lact k* *Led* k* *Lyc* k* mag-m mag-s med meph a1 *Merc* k* *Mez* k* mill naja *Nat-m* k* nat-p **Nit-ac** k* **Nit-s-d** bg nux-m *Nux-v* petr ph-ac phos k* phyt k2 *Plat* plb k* *Puls* k* *Rhod* k* **Rhus-t** k* rhus-v ruta fd4.de sabad k* *Sec* k* sep k* sil k* spong stram **Sulph** k* ther k2 *Thuj* k* tritic-vg fd5.de tub k2 *Valer* vanil fd5.de verat k* zinc k* zinc-p k2 zing
 • **cramping**: asaf *Graph* kali-n petr *Plat* sil h2
 • **downward**: lyc
 • **paralyzed**; as if: *Aur* *Cocc* *Hep* kali-p k2 *Mag-m* mez h2 *Nux-v* **Rhus-t** sabad
 • **paroxysmal**: *Cocc*
 • **upward**: mag-c h2
 • **wandering** pain: caust k* *Chin* *Cocc* *Colch* jatr-c kali-n puls h1 *Sulph* k*
- **drinking**:
 • **agg.**: **Crot-c**
 • **water | amel.**: sal-al blc1•
- **dull** pain: bamb-a stb2.de• dulc fd4.de kali-s fd4.de ruta fd4.de tritic-vg fd5.de vanil fd5.de
- **eating | after**:
  ⁝ **agg.**: bry *Cocc*↓ *Indg* kali-bi sep
   : **tearing** pain: *Cocc*
 • **amel.**: nat-c
- **electric** shock; as from an: arg-met mrr1
- **epistaxis**; during: nat-c bg1
- **erratic**: *Caul*↓ daph↓ iris↓ kali-bi↓ *Kali-s*↓ kalm↓ *Lac-c*↓ magn-gr↓ *Mang-act*↓ phyt↓ *Puls*↓ rhod↓ sal-ac↓ *Stel*↓
 • **shooting** pain: *Caul* bro1 daph br1 iris bro1 kali-bi bro1 *Kali-s* bro1 kalm bro1 *Lac-c* bro1 magn-gr bro1 *Mang-act* bro1 phyt bro1 *Puls* bro1 rhod bro1 sal-ac bro1 *Stel* bro1
- **eructations | amel.**: carb-v k2
- **eruption**, after: *Dulc*↓
 • **stitching** pain: *Dulc*
- **excitement**: alum-sil k2
- **exercise**; as after violent: aesc
- **exertion**:
 • **after**:
  ⁝ **agg.**: *Agar*↓ cimic↓ **Rhus-t**↓ sacch-a↓ streptoc↓ zinc↓
   : **sore**: *Agar* cimic **Rhus-t** sacch-a fd2.de• streptoc rly4•
   : **tearing** pain: zinc k*
  ⁝ **slight** exertion: *Agar* alum ambr tsm1 ang c1 bar-c berb calc k* **Caust** cimic con gels ign kali-c kali-n mag-c nat-c *Nat-m* phos *Rhus-t* *Ruta* sabin *Sep* sil stann sul-ac sulph zinc
 • **amel.**: galeoc-c-h gms1•
  ⁝ **air**; in open: plan↓
   : **stitching** pain: plan k*
- **exertion**; as after: petr-ra shn4•
- **extensor** muscles:
 • **sitting** agg.: verat↓
  ⁝ **tearing** pain: verat h1
- **feather** bed agg.: sulph↓
 • **drawing** pain: sulph h2
 • **tearing** pain: sulph k*
- **fever**:
 • **after**: sabad b7a.de
 • **before**: *Arn* b7a.de **Ars**↓ *Bry* b7a.de calc↓ *Carb-v*↓ cina b7a.de ign b7a.de lach b7a.de puls b7a.de rhus-t b7a.de sulph↓
  ⁝ **tearing** pain: **Ars** b4a.de calc b4a.de *Carb-v* b4a.de sulph b4a.de
 • **during**:
  ⁝ **agg.**: *Acon* b7a.de* alum bg2 *Ant-c* b7a.de* apis bg2 *Arn* k* ars k* bell k* **Bry** k* *Calc* k* caps b7.de* carb-v b4.de* caust bg2 cedr↓ cham bg2 *Chin* k* *Cimic* sne *Cocc*↓ *Colch* b7a.de* cypra-eg sde6.de• dulc bg2 elat c1 **Eup-per** k* *Ferr* k* *Gels* k* gink-b sbd1• *Hell* b7.de* **Ign** b7a.de* kali-c bg2 kali-n b4a.de *Lyc* b4.de* mag-c↓ mang k2 *Merc* *Mosch*↓ mur-ac k2 nat-m nat-s k2 **Nux-v** k* petr-ra shn4• phos k* polio mtf11 psor↓ ptel k* puls k* *Pyrog* *Rhod* k* *Rhus-t* k* *Ruta*↓ sec sep k* sil bg2 *Spig*↓ sulph k* tarax b7a.de* thuj bg2 tub valer verat b7a.de* *Zinc* bg2
   : **aching**: ars mrr1 eup-per mrr1 puls *Pyrog* k* *Rhus-t* k* *Tub*
   : **sore**: *Arn* bg2 *Ars* bg2 *Bell* bg2 bry bg2 calc bg2 **Chin** bg2 *Cocc* bg2 ign bg2 mag-c bg2 *Mosch* bg2 **Nat-m** bg2 **Nux-v** bg2 phos bg2 **Puls** bg2 **Rhod** b4a.de* *Ruta* bg2 sep bg2 sil bg2 *Spig* bg2 sulph bg2 thuj bg2 valer bg2 *Verat* bg2
   : **stitching** pain: *Dulc* psor **Rhus-t** sulph
   : **tearing** pain: ars b4.de **Calc** k* **Carb-v** cedr bro1 **Chin** k* *Dulc* *Ferr* *Kali-c* **Lyc** k* *Nux-v* k* phos *Puls* *Rhus-t* k* *Sep* k* *Sil* *Sulph* **Tub**
- **fright** agg.: merc
 • **sore**: merc
- **gnawing** pain: *Ars* cocc dros eup-per eup-pur k* lach k* merc nit-ac symph fd3.de•
- **growing** pains (See GENERALS - Pain - growing)
- **headache**; during: dulc fd4.de gels hr1* sang bro1
- **heart** disease; in: arn↓
 • **sore**: arn br1
- **heat**; during: arn↓ ars↓ bell↓ **Chin**↓ dulc↓ mang↓ *Nat-m*↓ *Nux-v*↓ phos↓ **Puls**↓ pyrog↓ *Rhod*↓ sulph↓ *Tub*↓
 • **sore**: arn ars bell **Chin** dulc k2 mang k2 *Nat-m* *Nux-v* phos **Puls** pyrog k2 *Rhod* sulph h2 *Tub*

Extremities

- **heated**, after being: zinc↓
  - **tearing** pain: zinc k*
- **heated**; from becoming: zinc↓
  - **stitching** pain: zinc k*
- **influenza**: | **after** | **pain** remaining: lycpr br1*
  - **during**●: *Acon* **Bry** *Caust Chel* **Eup-per** *Euph Gels* gink-b sbd1• naja petr-ra shn4•
- **influenza**; as from: ozone sde2•
- **injuries**:
  - **after**: hyper↓
    - **shooting** pain | **upward**: hyper k2
  - **after** injuries; long: gink-b sbd1• phasco-ci rbp2
- **jerking** pain: am-m **Carbn-s** cimic tl1 *Puls* sulph h2
- **kneeling** agg.: ozone↓
  - **stitching** pain: ozone sde2•
- **lacerating** (See tearing)
- **lancinating** (See cutting; stitching)
- **loss** of fluids: *Ph-ac*↓
  - **burning**: *Ph-ac*
- **lying**:
  - **agg.**: *Ars* aur-s k2 bry dulc fd4.de iod lyc *Merc* nux-v rhus-t tritic-vg fd5.de verat
    - **drawing** pain: **Rhus-t** k* tritic-vg fd5.de
    - **sore**: lyc *Nux-v*
    - **Side** lain on: dros *Graph* **Kali-c Nux-m** nux-v rhus-t tl1 sep
  - **amel.**: **Am-m**↓
    - **tearing** pain: **Am-m** k*
  - **back**; on:
    - **agg.**: *Rhus-t*↓
      - **tearing** pain: *Rhus-t* hr1
  - **side**; on:
    - **painful** side:
      - **agg.**: **Ars**↓
        - **tearing** pain: **Ars**
  - ○ **Side** lain on: **Arn**↓ graph↓ nux-m↓ **Ruta**↓
    - **sore**: **Arn** k* graph nux-m tl1 **Ruta**
  - **Side** not lain on: *Rhus-t*↓
    - **sore**: *Rhus-t*
- **lying** down agg.: beryl↓
  - **stitching** pain: beryl tpw5
- **lying** upon the limbs, while: dros↓
  - **aching**: dros k*
- **menses**:
  - **before**:
    - **agg.**: alum bg2 *Berb*↓ cimic bg2 con bg2 gels hr1 mag-c bg2* nit-ac bg2* ol-an bg2* phos↓
      - **sore**: nit-ac h2 phos
      - **tearing** pain: *Berb* k*
  - **during**:
    - **agg.**: am-c b4.de *Bell* berb k* bry k* *Carb-v*↓ castm *Cimic* con *Graph* k* kali-c b4.de kali-n *Kalm* lyc b4.de mag-m b4.de nit-ac k* nux-m k* nux-v k* petr b4.de phos k* rhod b4.de sep k* spong stram k* sul-ac b4.de verat k*
      - **burning**: *Carb-v*
      - **drawing** pain: con **Nux-m** k* *Spong* stram k*
      - **scanty** menses: carb-v↓
        - **sore**: carb-v
      - **sore**: cimic k2 nit-ac phos sep verat b7a.de
      - **stitching** pain: *Graph*
      - **tearing** pain: sul-ac k*
    - **amel.**: hip-ac br1
    - **beginning** of menses | **agg.**: lyc b4.de nit-ac b4.de sep b4.de sil b4.de
  - **suppressed** menses; from: dig↓
    - **tearing** pain: dig
- **mental** exertion agg.: colch kali-c gm1
- **motion**:
  - **agg.**: aesc agar↓ alum-sil k2 androc↓ bamb-a↓ berb k* **Bry** k* calc-p cann-s↓ caps carb-an↓ chin cina a1 cinnb k2 *Cocc* **Colch** *Coloc* croc↓ cypra-eg sde6.de• dulc *Euphr* ger-i rly4• graph↓ *Guaj Ham*↓ hyos↓ kali-bi k2 *Kalm* lac-c k2 lacer c1 lach↓ *Led* k* med k2 merc-c naja nat-ar↓ *Nat-m Nux-m Nux-v* olib-sac wmh1 *Ox-ac Phyt Plb Ran-b* ruta↓ sabad↓ sabin c1 *Sil* squil stel mrr1 streptoc rly4• thuj↓ vanil fd5.de verat↓ zinc
    - **drawing** pain: cann-s caps k* *Led* naja *Nux-v* sabad thuj k* verat k*
    - **sore**: aesc agar androc srj1• bamb-a stb2.de• *Bry* carb-an chin croc graph h2 *Ham* lach nat-ar k2 *Nux-v* streptoc rly4•
    - **stitching** pain: *Guaj* hyos *Plb* ruta fd4.de
    - **tearing** pain: guaj h2 naja plb k*
  - **amel.**: agar alum mrr1 am-c↓ ang c1 *Arg-met* arist-cl sp1 *Ars*↓ *Aur* carc↓ cham chin *Con* dig *Dulc Euph*↓ *Ferr* ignis-alc↓ *Kali-c* kali-i k2 kali-p k* **Kali-s** lach led↓ *Lyc Med* meph↓ merc *Mur-ac Nat-s* nux-m↓ *Phos*↓ pot-e rly4• psor k* **Puls** k* **Pyrog** k* *Rat* **Rhod Rhus-t** k* *Ruta* sep *Stel*↓ *Sulph*↓ thuj tritic-vg fd5.de *Tub Valer* k* vanil fd5.de *Zinc*
    - **aching**: am-c k* carc tpw2 ferr k2 ignis-alc es2• *Mur-ac Puls* pyrog mrr1 **Rhus-t** thuj k2 *Tub*
    - **drawing** pain: *Arg-met* ferr kali-p k2 led *Lyc* k* meph a1 nux-m *Rhod* **Rhus-t** thuj k* tritic-vg fd5.de tub k2 **Valer**
    - **pressing** pain: rhus-t k2
    - **slow** motion: *Ferr*↓ **Puls**↓
      - **tearing** pain: *Ferr* **Puls**
    - **sore**: aur pyrog k2 **Rhus-t** *Tub*
    - **stitching** pain: agar k2 alum *Arg-met Ferr Kali-c* **Kali-s** *Phos* k* psor **Rhus-t** *Stel Tub Valer*
    - **tearing** pain: **Agar** k* *Arg-met Ars Cham Euph Ferr* kali-p k2 kali-s k2 *Lyc* mur-ac psor k* *Puls Rhod* **Rhus-t** sep k* *Sulph* thuj k* *Tub*
  - **beginning** of:
    - **agg.**: agar beryl↓ caps carb-v *Caust* **Ferr** fl-ac galeoc-c-h gms1• graph *Kali-p* lach *Led* **Lyc** *Med* nit-ac osteo-a jl2 petr *Ph-ac* **Phos** plb psor **Puls** k* pyrog rhod **Rhus-t** ruta *Sil* valer
      - **shooting** pain: agar
      - **stitching** pain: beryl tpw5
      - **tearing** pain: agar
  - **continued** motion:
    - **agg.**: nat-ar↓
      - **sore**: nat-ar hr1*
    - **amel.**: agar **Cham** osteo-a jl2 *Puls* mrr1 **Rhus-t** stel mrr1 tub tl1
      - **shooting** pain: agar
      - **sore**: (non:nat-ar k2) **Rhus-t**
      - **stitching** pain: agar
  - **downward** motion agg.: borx k2
  - **slightest** motion agg.: *Bry* mrr1
- **neuralgic**: absin bro1 *Acon* bro1 alum bro1 arg-met mrr1 **Ars** k* bell bro1 bran bro1 cann-s *Carbn-s* bro1 caul bro1 *Cham* k* chel k* colch *Coloc* k* *Corn* corn-f br1 daph bro1 dulc fd4.de elat bro1 eucal bro1 *Gels* k* guaj bro1 hydrog srj2• kali-c bro1 kalm bro1 *Lyc* k* *Mag-p* k* magn-gr bro1 *Mim-p* bro1 nat-ar nicc-met sk4• nit-ac bro1 *Ox-ac* bro1 pall br1 phos bro1 phyt bro1 *Plb* k* polys sk4• *Puls Rhod* bro1 rhus-t bro1 ribo rly4• sars bro1 sil bro1 stry bro1 *Tarent* thal-xyz srj8• xan c2
- **noise** agg.: cocc **Coff** *Nux-v*
  - **shooting** pain: cocc
  - **stitching** pain: cocc
- **overexertion**, after: arn↓
  - **sore**: arn br1
- **palpitations**, with (See CHEST - Palpitation - accompanied - limbs - pain)
- **paralyzed**; as if: ambr c1 ang vh *Aur* aur-m-n wbt2• cina h1* colch bro1* dulc fd4.de ferr k2 fl-ac ham fd3.de• kali-s fd4.de *Mag-m* meph a1 *Merc-c Nux-v Phyt* bro1 rhod k2 *Rhus-t* k* ruta fd4.de sabad **Staph** sne *Thal* bro1 thuj verat-v bro1 verin bro1 xan bro1
- **paroxysmal**: **Carbn-s** caul *Caust Cocc Mag-p* **Nux-v** phos **Plb** k* **Puls** *Sec*
- **periodical**: *Gels*↓ kali-bi k2 lyc↓
  - **tearing** pain: *Gels* lyc k*

- **perspiration**:
  - **amel**.: *Acon* sne *Ars* ars-h sne *Bry* k* cham sne clem sne *Eup-per* sne gels hr1* lyc sne nat-m k2 *Nux-v Rhus-t* sne sal-ac sne stroph-h sne syph sne tarent sne thuj k* visc sne
  - **during**: acon bg2 alum bg2 ant-c bg2 *Ant-t* b7a.de* apis bg2 arn bg2 *Ars* bg2 bell bg2 *Bry* bg2 **Calc** bg2 caps bg2 carb-v bg2 caust bg2 *Cham* bg2 *Chin* bg2 cocc ↓ colch bg2 dulc bg2 ferr bg2 *Hell* bg2 *Hep* ↓ *Ign* bg2 kali-c bg2 kali-n bg2 **Lyc** bg2 mag-c ↓ **Merc** bg2 *Merc-c* bg2 mosch ↓ *Nat-m* ↓ **Nux-v** b7.de* ph-ac ↓ phos bg2 puls bg2 *Rhod* bg2 **Rhus-t** bg2 ruta ↓ sabad bg2 **Sep** bg2 sil bg2 spig ↓ **Sulph** bg2 tarax bg2 thuj bg2 valer ↓ verat bg2 zinc bg2
    - ⁝ **sore**: *Arn* bg2 ars bg2 bell bg2 bry bg2 calc bg2 **Chin** bg2 cocc bg2 *Hep* bg2 ign bg2 mag-c bg2 merc bg2 mosch bg2 *Nat-m* bg2 **Nux-v** bg2 ph-ac bg2 phos bg2 *Puls* bg2 **Rhod** bg2 rhus-t bg2 ruta bg2 *Sep* bg2 sil bg2 spig bg2 *Sulph* bg2 thuj bg2 valer bg2 verat bg2
    - ⁝ **tearing** pain: *Merc* b4a.de *Merc-c* b4a.de *Sulph* b4a.de
  - **suppressed** perspiration; from: rhus-t k2
- **piercing** (See stitching)
- **pinching** pain: carb-an k* pot-e rly4• rhod ruta fd4.de
- **pressing** pain: agar k* alum-sil k2 aq-mar skp7• arund *Asaf* bar-c bell *Carb-v* card-m k2 chin dig digin a1 dros k* dulc fd4.de *Gels* guare k* kali-c k* kali-s fd4.de *Led* *Nat-m* nux-m k* olnd k* petr k* phyt rhus-t k2 ruta spig spong fd4.de thuj k* tritic-vg fd5.de vanil fd5.de
  - **constricting** pain: arund *Chin* k* ham fd3.de•
  - **cramping**: dros
  - **drawing** pain: sulph h2 thuj k*
  - **finger**; as from a: carb-an h2
  - **wandering** pain: agar k* kali-c nux-m k*
- **pressure**:
  - **agg**.: ang c1 cina cocc dulc ↓ galeoc-c-h gms1• merc phos ↓ *Plb* **Staph** sne tritic-vg fd5.de
    - ⁝ **sore**: *Cina* dulc k2
    - ⁝ **stitching** pain: phos k* plb
    - ⁝ **tearing** pain: merc k* plb k*
  - **amel**.: aq-mar skp7• *Ars* bry chin k2 dulc ↓ *Form* sne *Mag-p* oci-sa ↓ *Plb* k* puls sne rauw sp1
    - ⁝ **aching**: oci-sa sp1
    - ⁝ **stitching** pain: ars dulc fd4.de plb
  - **slight** | **agg**.: galeoc-c-h gms1•
- **pulsating** pain: bamb-a stb2.de• bell des-ac rbp6 dulc fd4.de **Kali-c** kali-s fd4.de kola stb3• lac-del hm2• ruta fd4.de suis-pan rly4• symph fd3.de• tritic-vg fd5.de vanil fd5.de
- **putting** limb out of bed; when: merc ↓
  - **tearing** pain: merc
- **radiating**: berb mrr1
- **rest**:
  - **agg**.: arg-met hr1 arum-dru a1 psor jl2
  - **amel**.: eup-per ↓
    - ⁝ **sore**: eup-per gk
- **rheumatic**: *(↗joints - rheumatic; Inflammation - joints; GENERALS - Inflammation - joints; GENERALS - Pain - rheumatic; GENERALS - Pain - rheumatic - joints)* *Abrot* k* *Acon* k* act-sp k* *Aesc* *Agar* k* aids nl2• alf br1 all-s c2 aln c2 alst-s mtf11 alum mrr1 alumn am-be c2 am-caust c2 am-m ambro c2 anac c2 anag c2* ang c1* anis c2 *Ant-c* tl1 *Ant-t* k* anthraco c2 *Apis* k* apoc k2 arb c1* *Arg-met* k* **Arn** k* **Ars** k* *Ars-i* k* asaf k2 asc-c c2 asc-t c2 aspar bro1 *Aur* k* aur-ar k2 aur-i k2 aur-m k2 **Aur-m-n** **Bad** k* bapt bar-act br1 *Bell* k* bell-p c2* **Benz-ac** k* *Berb* c2 bit-ar wht1• bov c2 bran bro1 **Bry** k* *Cact* k* caj c2 *Calc* k* calc-caust c2 *Calc-p* k* *Calc-s* *Camph* k* cann-s *Caps* k* *Carb-ac* *Carb-v* *Carbn-s* k* carc br1* card-m k* carl c2 cas-s c1* *Caul* k* **Caust** k* cedr k* **Cham** k* chamae hsa1 **Chel** k* *Chin* k* *Chinin-ar* *Chinin-s* c2 chr-o c2 *Cimic* k* cinnb c2 cit-l c2 clem k* coca c2 cocc c2 coch c2 **Colch** k* coll c2 *Coloc* k* convo-d c2 *Corn* cot c2 *Crot-c* *Crot-h* k* *Crot-t* k* cub c2 cupr cupre-au c2 cycl c2 daph c2 *Dig* dios c2 dirc c2 dovy-r bta1• *Dulc* k* elaps elat c2 elec c1* eucal c2* eup-per k* eup-pur c2 euph k* fago c2 fel c2 *Ferr* k* *Ferr-ar* ferr-i k2 ferr-m c2 ferr-ma c2 ferr-p k* **Form** k* franc c2 frax-e ah1 galv c2 gamb mrr1 gast c2 gaul c2* *Gels* k* gins c2 glon c2 gnaph c2 grat gua c2 *Guaj* k* gunn-p bta1• *Ham* k* hedy c1 hell helon c2 *Hep* k* hydrc hyper c2 ichth c2 ictod c2 *Ign* *Iod* c2* irid-met c2* iris c2 junc-e c2 *Kali-ar* *Kali-bi* k* *Kali-c* k* kali-chl

- **rheumatic**: ...
kali-cy c2 kali-fcy c2 **Kali-i** k* kali-m c2* kali-n c2 kali-p *Kali-s* k* kali-sil k2 **Kalm** k* kreos c2 *Lac-ac* k* *Lac-c* k* lac-d k2 lac-v c2 *Lach* lappa c2 lath c2 led k* lepi c2 lil-t br1 linu-c c2 lith-c c2 lith-lac c2 **Lyc** k* lycpr c2 m-ambo c2 *Macro* c2 *Mag-c* mag-p mag-s magn-gr c2 malar c2 mand sp1 mang c2 mang-m c2 **Med** k* meli vml3• meph *Merc* k* merc-i-f merc-i-r k* merc-sul merl c2 meth-sal br1* methyl c2 *Mez* k* mill mim-h c2 mur-ac naja k2 **Nat-ar** nat-c c2* nat-lac c2 nat-p c2* nat-s k2 nat-sal c2 *Nit-ac* nux-m k* *Nux-v* k* *Nyct* c1* ol-an ol-j c2 olnd c2 oxyt c2 pall petan-v bta1• *Petr* k* *Ph-ac* k* *Phos* k* **Phyt** k* pin-s c2 pip-m c2 plan ↓ plat k* plect c2 polyp-p c2 prun-v bro1 psil ft1 *Psor* ptel c1* **Puls** k* puls-n c2 pyre-p c2 pyrog k2 pyrus c2 rad-br bro1* ran-a c2 *Ran-b* k* rheum c2 **Rhod** k* **Rhus-t** k* rumx c2* *Ruta* k* sabad c2 sabin c1* sacch c2 sacch-a fd2.de• *Sal-ac* k* *Sal-mo* c1* *Salol* c1* **Sang** k* sanic c2* sapin c2 **Sars** k* scroph-xyz c2 sec *Sep* *Sil* k* skook c2 solid c2 spig k* spong c2 squil stann staph c2 *Stel* k* stict k* *Still* c2 stry-xyz c2 strych-h bta1• sul-ac c2 sul-i k2 **Sulph** k* syc fmm1• *Syph* k* tarax c2 *Tarent* k* tax c2 tep c2 ter teucr k* thuj k* til c2 tub mrr1 ur-ac c2 urt-u c2* *Valer* k* vanad dx *Verat* k* vichy-g c2 viol-o c2 viol-t k* wies c2 wildb c2 x-ray sp1 zinc k* zinc-p k2 [calc-m stj1 uva stj]
  - **right**:
    - ⁝ **extending** to | **left**: bell-p sma dulc k2 **Lyc**
  - **left**:
    - ⁝ **extending** to | **right**: **Lach** naja *Rhus-t*
  - **night**: abrot mrr1 *Acon* bro1 alum mrr1 arn bro1 aur mtf33 cham bro1 *Cimic* bro1 *Colch* bro1 eucal bro1 *Kali-i* bro1 kali-m bro1 kalm bro1 lac-ac bro1 led bro1* *Merc* bro1 mez k2 phyt bro1 *Puls* bro1 rhod bro1 rhus-t bro1 sang tl1 sars bro1 sil bro1 *Sulph* bro1
    - ⁝ **bed**; driving out of: **Cham** k* *Ferr* lac-c led **Merc** sulph *Verat*
  - **accompanied** by:
    - ⁝ **diabetes** (See GENERALS - Diabetes mellitus - accompanied - rheumatic)
    - ⁝ **eczema**: *(↗joints - accompanied - rash; joints - gouty - accompanied - eczema; GENERALS - Inflammation - joints - accompanied - skin)* alum bro1 arb br1* lac-ac bro1 *Rhus-t* bro1 ur-ac bro1 urea bro1
    - ⁝ **menses**; painful (See FEMALE - Menses - painful - accompanied - rheumatic)
    - ⁝ **respiratory** complaints (See RESPIRATION - Asthmatic - accompanied - rheumatic)
    - ⁝ **restlessness**: *Acon* bro1 bit-ar wht1• caust bro1 cimic bro1 puls bro1 *Rhus-t* bro1
    - ⁝ **salivation**: *Dulc* kr1*
    - ⁝ **urine**; offensive: benz-ac mrr1 colch mrr1
    - ⁝ **Cervical** glands | **complaints**: phyt mrr1
    - ⁝ **Colon**; inflammation of: podo mrr1
    - ⁝ **Heart**; complaints of the | **Valves** (See CHEST - Heart; complaints - valves - accompanied - rheumatic)
    - ⁝ **Parotid** glands | **complaints** of: phyt mrr1
    - ⁝ **Soles**; extreme tenderness of (See feet - soles - sore - accompanied - rheumatism)
    - ⁝ **Tongue**:
      - ⁝ **cracked**: *Lyc* kr1*
      - ⁝ **dryness** of tongue: *Dulc* kr1*
  - **acute**: **Acon** *Ant-c* *Ars* asc-c aur tl1 aur-m k2 *Bell* k* **Bry** cact k2 calc-s caul *Cham* *Chel* chin chinin-s cimic **Colch** k* *Dulc* ferr-p tl1 glon *Guaj* mrr1 ign *Kali-bi* *Kalm* *Lac-c* *Lach* led tl1 **Merc** *Nux-v* phyt k2 *Puls* rad-br mrr1 *Rhod* **Rhus-t** k* sal-ac sang spig vml *Sulph* c2 tub tl1* verat verat-v tl1
  - **alternating** with: kali-bi ptk1 lappa ptk1 urt-u ptk1
    - ⁝ **catarrh**: kali-bi tl1
    - ⁝ **chorea** (See GENERALS - Chorea - alternating)
    - ⁝ **diarrhea**: abrot br1* cimic dulc k* gnaph br1* *Kali-bi* k*
    - ⁝ **dysentery** (See RECTUM - Dysentery - alternating - rheumatism)
    - ⁝ **dyspnea**: *(↗RESPIRATION - Asthmatic - alternating - pain)* guaj
    - ⁝ **eruptions**: abrot mtf33 crot-t kalm k2 staph urt-u bro1
    - ⁝ **gastric** complaints: **Kali-bi** k*

Extremities

- **alternating** with: ...
  - **hemoptysis** (See EXPECTORATION - Bloody - alternating - rheumatism)
  - **hemorrhoids**: *Abrot* k* (non:calli-h) coll ptk2
  - **mental** symptoms: cimic ptk1*
  - **urine**; sediment in: benz-ac mrr1 colch mrr1
  - **urticaria**: *Urt-u* k*
  - **Chest** affection: led
  - **Head**; pain in (See HEAD - Pain - alternating - rheumatism)
  - **Heart**; pain in (See CHEST - Pain - heart - alternating - rheumatism)
  - **Kidneys**; pain in (See KIDNEYS - Pain - alternating - rheumatism)
  - **Nose**; catarrh of: kali-bi k2
  - **Pulmonary** complaints: (↗*RESPIRATION - Asthmatic - alternating - pain)* **Kali-bi** k*
- **bathing** | **agg.**: caust mrr1
- **boring** pain: plan k*
- **catarrhal** symptoms: cist tl1
  - **before**: stict br1
    - **or** after: stict c1
- **children**; in: abrot mtf33 nat-p tl1*
- **chronic**: bell tl1 led tl1 petr tl1 rauw mtf11 rhod tl1 **Rhus-t** mrr1 tub-d jl2
- **cold**:
  - **amel.**: am-c ptk1 *Guaj* k* kali-i mrr1 kali-s mrr1 *Lac-c* k* **Led** k* **Puls** k* rad-br mrr **Sec** k* sulph mrr
  - **bathing**:
    - **amel.** | **feet**; of: *Led* bro1 sec bro1
  - **drinks**:
    - **agg.** | **overheated**; when: bry k2
- **cold**; after taking a: acon arn *Bry* calc *Calc-p Coloc Dulc* gels *Guaj* med k2 *Merc Nit-ac* ph-ac *Rhus-t* sulph
- **cold**; becoming | **after** | **head**: bell k2
  - **agg.**: arg-met k2 bar-c k2 bell-p sp1 caust mrr1 colch k2 nat-ar k2 nux-v mrr1 *Ph-ac* **Rhus-t** rumx k2
- **comes** and goes: colch tl1
- **deforming** (See GENERALS - Inflammation - joints - deformans)
- **diarrhea**:
  - **during** | **chronic**: kali-bi gk *Nat-s*
  - **following** diarrhea; rheumatism (See RECTUM - Diarrhea - followed - rheumatism)
  - **suppressed** diarrhea; from: *Abrot* k*
- **dyspnea**, with: ars-s-f mrr
- **eruptions**; after acute: dulc
  - **suppressed**: mez
- **exertion** agg.; after: caust mrr1
- **gonorrhea**, after suppressed: *(↗joints - rheumatic - gonorrhea; URETHRA - Discharge - gonorrheal)* benz-ac k2 calc-p k2 *Clem* con *Cop* crot-h daph k* gels hr1 irisin br1 jac-c c2 kalm *Lyc* **Med** k* *Phyt* k* *Puls* k* *Sars* k* *Sep Sulph* k* **Thuj** k*
- **hemorrhoids**; suppressed: *Abrot*
- **injured** parts: *Caust*
- **loquacity**; with (See MIND - Loquacity - rheumatic)
- **massage** | **amel.**: bell-p sp1
- **menses**: cimic k2
- **mercury**; after abuse of: arg-met arn asaf *Bell* calc *Carb-v Cham* **Chin Guaj Hep** *Kali-i Lach* lyc mez *Nit-ac* ph-ac *Phyt* podo puls rhod **Sars** *Sulph* valer
- **motion**:
  - **amel.**: fic-m gya1
    - **violent** motion: bell-p sp1
  - **continued** motion | **amel.**: agar tl1 bry k2 med mtf11 stel mrr1
- **nervous** persons; in: viol-o bro1

- **rheumatic**: ...
  - **overheating** and exertion; from: *Zinc*
  - **perspiration**:
    - **amel.**: acon vh1
    - **with**: *Calc* bro1 **Form** hep bro1 lac-ac bro1 **Merc** k* rham-cal bro1 sal-ac bro1 *Sulph Til* k*
  - **pressing** pain: *Merc*
  - **radiation** therapy; after: rad-br mrr1
  - **rest** agg.: agar tl1 euph bro1 puls bro1 rhod bro1 *Rhus-t* bro1
  - **sitting** agg.: agar tl1
  - **spring**: *Colch*
  - **stiffness**; with: **Led** mrr1
    - **cold** | **amel.**: **Led** mrr1
  - **syphilitic**: *Benz-ac Fl-ac Guaj* bro1 hecla bro1 hep bro1 kali-bi k* **Kali-i** k* kalm *Merc* k* *Nit-ac* nit-m-ac bro1 *Phyt* k* still bro1
  - **tearing** pain: *Act-sp* br1 am-m *Colch Guaj Puls* **Rhus-t** *Sulph*
  - **tonsillitis**, after (See THROAT - Inflammation - tonsils - followed - rheumatism)
  - **warm**:
    - **agg.**: cham bro1 kali-m bro1 *Led* bro1 *Merc* bro1 phyt mrr1 *Puls* bro1
    - **bed** | **agg.**: *Led* mrr1
  - **weather**:
    - **change** of weather: chel k2
    - **cold**:
      - **agg.**: arg-met k2 ars ars-s-f k2 **Bry** calc k2 **Calc-p** k* *Camph* br1 carb-v *Caust* tl1 cimic k2 *Colch Dulc Kali-bi Kalm* med k2 nit-ac *Nux-v Ph-ac Phos* phyt mrr1 *Puls* ran-b k2 *Rhod* **Rhus-t** sul-ac *Tub*
      - **wet** | **agg.**: abrot mrr1 arg-met k2 arn bro1 ars bro1 *Calc-p* bro1 cimic bro1 colch bro1* *Dulc* bro1 influ mp4• kali-i bro1 *Merc* bro1 nat-s bro1 nux-m bro1 phyt bro1* ran-b bro1 *Rhod* bro1 *Rhus-t* bro1 ruta mrr1 sars bro1 verat bro1
    - **dry** | **agg.**: caust tl1*
    - **warm**:
      - **agg.**: **Colch** *Kali-bi* k*
      - **first** warm days: bry
  - **wind** agg.; cold: acon k2
  - ▽ **extending** to:
    - **Brain**: bell bro1 op bro1
    - **Downward**: cact bro1 *Kalm* bro1
    - **Lower** limbs: *Kali-c*
    - **Upward**: arn br1 *Kalm* **Led** k*
  - ○ **Covered** by flesh; in places least: sang k*
- **riding** agg.: bry
- **rising** | **after**:
  - **amel.**: naja ↓ *Nux-v* ↓
    - **sore**: naja *Nux-v*
  - **agg.**: ant-t ↓
    - **sore**: ant-t
- **rubbing**:
  - **amel.**: canth ↓ *Phos* ↓ *Plb* ↓
    - **shooting** pain: plb mrr1
    - **stitching** pain: *Plb*
    - **tearing** pain: canth *Phos* plb mrr1
- **scraping** pain: bry **Chin** coloc kali-s fd4.de **Ph-ac** plb k2 **Rhus-t** *Sabad* spong fd4.de
- **scratching** agg.; after: kreos ↓
  - **burning**: kreos k*
- **screwing** pain: carb-an h2
- **sharp**: haliae-lc srj5• neon srj5•
- **shivering**; during: *Ars* ↓ bell ↓ *Ign* b7a.de
  - **sore**: bell b4.de*
  - **tearing** pain: *Ars* b4a.de
- **shooting** pain: *(↗stitching)* *Acon Aesc Agar* agath-a nl2• arg-n k2 aur bufo *Calc Con* cystein-l rly4• dulc fd4.de *Hep* iris *Kali-bi Merc* plan plb mrr1 ruta fd4.de sinus rly4• spig spong fd4.de xan

- **cramping**: plat

\- **sitting**:

- **agg.**: **Agar**↓ **Am-m**↓ **Arg-met** hr1* asaf↓ bry↓ cina↓ coloc↓ dulc fd4.de galeoc-c-h gms1• ignis-alc↓ kali-s k2 kalm k2 led↓ plan↓ *Pyrog* ruta fd4.de sabad↓ spong fd4.de tritic-vg fd5.de tub k2 **Valer** k* zinc↓
  - **aching**: ignis-alc es2•
  - **drawing** pain: coloc k* led spong fd4.de **Valer**
  - **sore**: asaf bry pyrog k2 sabad
  - **stitching** pain: plan k* zinc k*
  - **tearing** pain: **Agar** **Am-m** k* zinc k*
    - **wandering** pain: cina a1
- **walking**; after: *Ruta*↓
  - **sore**: *Ruta*

\- **sleep**:

- **after**:
  - **agg.**: *Agar* *Arg-n*↓ *Lach* merc-c op ptel↓
    - **sore**: *Arg-n* ptel
- **during** | **agg.**: *Ars*
- **going** to, on: *Kali-c*

\- **smarting**: symph fd3.de•

\- **sneezing** agg.: caps↓ tell bg1

- **cutting** pain: caps
- **shooting** pain: caps
- **stitching** pain: caps

\- **sore**: *(↗beaten)* abrot *Acon* aesc *Agar* agath-a nl2• aids nl2• *All-c* *Alum* alum-p k2 alum-sil k2 alumn am-c ambr hr1 ammc ampe-qu br1 anac androc srj1• ang c1 anthraci aphis c1 *Apis* apoc *Arg-met* arg-n **Arn** k* ars ars-s-f k2 asar h1 aster atp rly4• *Aur* aur-m-n aur-s k2 *Bad* bamb-a stb2.de• **Bapt** *Bar-c* bar-s k2 **Bell** bell-p sp1 beryl sp1 bov brass-n-o srj5• *Bry* bufo *Calc* calc-sil k2 camph caps hr1 *Carb-ac* *Carb-an* **Carb-v** **Carbn-s** cartl-s rly4• *Caust* cham **Chel** *Chin* *Chinin-s* chlor chord-umb rly4• **Cimic** k* cinnb k2 *Cist* *Clem* cob cocc *Colch* coli rly4• *Con* cupr *Daph* *Dros* k* dulc elaps elat **Eup-per** ferr ferr-ar ferr-i ferr-p *Gels* ger-i rly4• gins graph *Ham* hell *Hep* hip-ac sp1 hyper **Ip** kali-bi kali-br kali-c kali-n kali-p kali-sil k2 *Kalm* kola stb3• *Kreos* *Lac-ac* *Lac-c* *Lach* lact *Lec* *Led* k* lil-t limest-b es1• *Lyc* *Lyss* mag-c mag-s manc mand sp1 **Mang** med k2 *Merc* k* merc-i-f mez mim-p rsj8• nat-ar nat-c **Nat-m** nat-p **Nit-ac** **Nux-v** oxal-a rly4• ozone sde2• petr *Ph-ac* k* *Phos* *Phyt* *Pic-ac* plac-s rly4• plb podo fd3.de• *Puls* pyrog k2* ran-s rhod k2 **Rhus-t** rhus-v ribo rly4• **Ruta** k* sacch-a fd2.de• sal-fr sle1• sars sec sel **Sil** sol-ni **Spong** *Stann* **Staph** stroph-s sp1 suis-hep rly4• suis-pan rly4• sul-ac **Sulph** tarax *Thuj* til *Tub* tung-met bdx1• valer *Zinc* zinc-p k2

- **accompanied** by | **Head**; pain in (See HEAD - Pain - accompanied - extremities - sore)
- **walk**; as after a long: ozone sde2•

\- **sprained**; as if: *(↗dislocated; Sprains)* *Agn* st1 *Aloe* hr *Am-c* st1 androc srj1• **Arn** br1* asaf st1 bell-p br1* bros-gau mrc1 calc bro1 *Carb-an* st1 carb-v k* *Chin* bro1 **Led** st1 **Mill** st1 oxal-a rly4• petr-ra shn4• rhod **Rhus-t** k* **Ruta** bro1*

\- **standing** agg.: allox↓ alum↓ sulph↓

- **dragging**: allox sp1
- **sore**: alum sulph

\- **stitching** pain: *(↗shooting)* abrot k* *Acon* *Aesc* aeth a1 *Agar* k* aids nl2• *Alum* alum-p k2 am-m k2 anan androc srj1• ant-t *Apis* *Arg-met* arn k* *Ars* k* ars-s-f k2 asar aur aur-ar k2 *Bamb-a* stb2.de• bar-c bell benz-ac k* *Berb* beryl tpw5 bov *Bry* *Calc* k* calc-i k2 calc-s calc-sil k2 cann-i k* carb-v *Carbn-s* carl k* caust cham k2 chin chinin-ar k2 cimic k* cina cocc *Colch* coloc k* *Con* cystein-l rly4• dros *Dulc* *Elat* eucal a1 eup-per k2 falco-pe nl2• *Ferr* ferr-ar ferr-i ferr-p *Gels* *Guaj* *Hep* *Hydroph* rsj6• hyper k2 *Iris* *Kali-ar* *Kali-bi* **Kali-c** k* *Kali-i* kali-n kali-p **Kali-s** kali-sil k2 kalm k* kola stb3• *Laur* *Lyc* k* mag-p br1 med k2 *Merc* merc-c k* merl k* nat-hchls *Nat-p* *Nat-s* *Nit-ac* **Nit-s-d** bg paeon k* par petr-ra shn4• ph-ac k* phos k* phyt k* pieri-b mlk9.de plan k* *Plb* *Psor* *Puls* k* rhod k* **Rhus-t** k* *Ros-d* wla1 ruta fd4.de sec k* senec *Sep* sil k* *Spig* spong fd4.de staph k* *Stel* suis-hep rly4• suis-pan rly4• *Sulph* symph fd3.de• tanac a1 *Tarent* thea thuj tritic-vg fd5.de tub k2 tung-met bdx1• **Valer** vanil fd5.de vero-o rly4*• xan zinc k* zinc-p k2 zing k* [pop dhh1]

- **burning**: **Ars** aur bar-act br1 spig
- **cramping**: cimic *Cina* plat
- **drawing** pain: mur-ac h2 *Puls* k*

\- **stitching** pain: ...

- **inward**: phyt
- **jerking** pain: **Carbn-s**
- **needles**; as from: pic-ac br1 plb bg1
- **paroxysmal**: gels ph-ac
- **splinters**; as from: carc fd2.de• hydrog srj2• kali-s fd4.de *Nit-ac*
- **tearing** pain: *Ars* *Carbn-s* coloc *Sec*
- **upward**: hyper k2
- **wandering** pain: arg-met arn k* aur cimic mrr1 ferr kali-n *Kali-s* kalm k* lyc k* merl k* psor *Puls* *Stel* tanac a1

\- **stomach** complaints; with: nat-s hr

\- **stool** agg.; during: *Acon* b7a.de am-m b7a.de* *Cham* b7a.de rhod↓ rhus-t bg2 tell bg1

- **tearing** pain: rhod b4a.de rhus-t bg2

\- **stretching**:

- **amel.**: allox↓ helo-s rwt2• nit-ac↓ ruta↓
  - **dragging**: allox sp1
  - **drawing** pain: nit-ac k* ruta fd4.de

\- **stretching** out limbs, on: cham↓ hipp↓

- **tearing** pain: cham hipp k*

\- **sudden**: *Berb*↓ carbn-s↓ tritic-vg↓ tub-m jl2 vanil↓

- **stitching** pain: *Berb* mrr1 tritic-vg fd5.de vanil fd5.de
- **tearing** pain: carbn-s

\- **tearing** pain: **Acon** k* *Act-sp* br1 aesc k2 **Agar** k* alum *Am-c* *Am-m* *Ambr* anac ant-c ant-t *Arg-met* arg-n k2 *Arn* k* *Ars* k* ars-s-f k2 asar **Aur** aur-ar k2 aur-i k2 aur-m aur-s k2 *Bar-c* bar-s k2 bell k* benz-ac k* *Berb* k* bism bov *Bry* k* cact *Calc* k* calc-s calc-sil k2 canth *Caps* *Carb-v* *Carbn-s* *Carl* k* *Caust* k* cedr *Cham* k* *Chel* **Chin** k* *Chinin-ar* *Cina* coc-c k* *Cocc* *Colch* *Coloc* *Con* k* crot-h k* *Cupr* *Dulc* eup-per k2 *Euph* eupi k* *Ferr* form *Gels* *Graph* k* *Guaj* hell k* hyos k* iris kali-ar kali-bi k* *Kali-c* *Kali-i* *Kali-n* k* kali-p kali-s kali-sil k2 kalm k* kiss a1 **Lach** k* lachn k* lam k* laur led *Lyc* k* *Lyss* *Mag-c* *Mag-m* mag-s k* meph k* **Merc** k* *Merc-c* k* merc-d a1 merl k* mill mur-ac naja nat-ar *Nat-c* k* nat-p **Nat-s** neon srj5• *Nit-ac* k* *Nux-v* k* *Ol-an* osm paeon k* *Ph-ac* *Phos* k* plb k* plect a1 *Psor* k* *Puls* k* **Rhod** **Rhus-t** ruta sabin sars k* *Sec* k* sel k* sep k* sil **Spig** spong fd4.de squil sul-ac k* sulph symph fd3.de• *Tab* tarent k2 thuj k* tritic-vg fd5.de **Tub** tub-r jl* vanil fd5.de vinc k* *Zinc* k* zinc-p k2

- **alternating** with | **Teeth**; pain in (See TEETH - Pain - alternating with - limbs)
- **burning**: *Ars* dig c1 merl k*
- **cramping**: nat-c h2 ruta h1
- **downward**: rhus-t k2 *Sulph*
- **jerking** pain: asar h1 **Chin** paeon
- **paralyzed**; as if: **Cham** *Chin* **Colch** kali-p k2 *Mag-m* *Phos* *Plb*
- **paroxysmal**: anac paeon **Plb** k*
- **twitching**: *Am-m* cact k* chin k* ph-ac h2
- **wandering** pain: **Am-m** k* arg-met *Carbn-s* *Caust* k* cham k* *Colch* con h2 *Ferr* *Kali-bi* k* kali-s k2 laur k* lyc k* *Merc* k* nat-s k* *Puls* rhod k*

\- **thinking** about: ox-ac

\- **throbbing** (See pulsating)

\- **thunderstorm**:

- **agg.**: hyper k2 **Med** *Nat-c* psor al2 **Rhod** tub k2
- **during**: *Nat-c*↓
  - **tearing** pain: *Nat-c*

\- **torn** asunder; as if: nat-c

\- **tossing** about in bed amel.: cham↓

- **tearing** pain: cham k*

\- **touch** agg.: act-sp mrr1 **Chel** *Chin* k* *Cimic* sne cina a1 cocc graph↓ lac-h sk4• mez k2 oxal-a↓ sabin c1 **Staph** sne stel mrr1 tarent k2 vip

- **changing** place on touch: *Sang*
- **sore**: graph h2 oxal-a rly4•
- **tearing** pain: *Chin* k*

\- **twinging**: berb mrr1

\- **ulcer** is present or has healed; limb on which an: graph↓

- **sore**: graph h2

\- **ulcerative** pain: agar

Extremities

- **undulating** (See waves)
- **vertigo**; during: gels psa
- **waking**; on: aesc↓ *Bar-c*↓ naja↓ oxal-a↓ ptel↓ puls↓ sulph↓ tell↓ *Zinc*↓
  - **aching**: ptel bg1 puls tell k*
  - **pressing** pain: *Bar-c*
  - **sore**: aesc naja oxal-a rly4• sulph *Zinc*
- **walking**:
  - **after**:
    - **agg.**: raph rhod rhus-t *Ruta* symph↓ tritic-vg fd5.de
      - **sore**: raph rhod **Ruta** symph fd3.de•
  - **agg.**: apoc↓ aur-s k2 coff coloc↓ dulc fd4.de ger-i rly4• lyc merc olib-sac wmh1 op ruta streptoc rly4• symph↓ thiam rly4• tritic-vg fd5.de verat↓
    - **aching**: op k*
    - **drawing** pain: coloc k* verat k*
    - **sore**: apoc symph fd3.de•
  - **air**; in open | **after**:
    - **agg.**: *Chin*↓
      - **pressing** pain: *Chin*
    - **amel.**: clem↓ kali-s↓
      - **sore**: clem
      - **tearing** pain: kali-s k2
  - **amel.**: *Agar* *Alum*↓ *Arg-met* *Ars* *Aur*↓ *Cham* chin *Ferr* *Kali-c*↓ kali-i *Kali-s* *Lyc* *Merc* nat-ar nat-s k2 phos pop↓ psor↓ *Puls* **Pyrog**↓ *Rhod* **Rhus-t** ruta sacch-a↓ seneg tritic-vg fd5.de tub k2 *Valer* *Verat*
    - **aching**: nat-ar **Pyrog** **Rhus-t** *Tub*
    - **drawing** pain: *Lyc* tub k2 **Valer** verat k*
    - **sore**: agar *Aur* ruta
    - **stitching** pain: *Alum* *Ars* *Kali-c* *Kali-s* *Phos* k* psor *Rhus-t* sacch-a fd2.de• [pop dhh1]
- **wandering**, shifting pain: (↗*GENERALS - Pain - wandering*) acon aesc k2 agar alum-sil k2 **Am-m** apoc-a bro1 *Am* ars k* ars-s-f k2 asaf aur mrr1* aur-ar k2 bamb-a stb2.de• bapt k* bell berb k2 bry *Calc-p* k* **Carbn-s** *Caul* k* *Caust* cedr cham chinin-ar cimic bro1 cinnb colch k* coloc ferr-p c1 form gels c1 gink-b sbd1• ign *Kali-bi* k* kali-n **Kali-s** k* *Kalm* k* kola stb3• lac-ac k* **Lac-c** k* laur *Lyc* *Mag-p* mang bro1 merc-i-r *Merl* mosch k* nat-ar nat-s nit-s-d a1 *Nux-m* k* nux-v *Phyt* k* plat sne *Plb* k* plut-n srj7• **Puls** k* puls-n bro1 ran-a a1 *Rhod* k* sabin sang hr1 sars sep *Sil* stel bro1* *Still* sulph k* *Tarent* tax a1 *Tub* k* tub-m jl2 valer *Verat-v*
- **warm**:
  - **applications**:
    - **agg.**: ant-t apis *Bry* *Guaj* iod kali-i kali-s k2* lac-c k2 lat-m bnm6• phyt mrr1 ptel *Puls* k* **Sec** sep stel *Sulph* thuj
    - **amel.**: aesc agar am-c ant-c aq-mar skp7• arg-met **Ars** ars-s-f k2 *Bry* cact calc-p k2 carc mlr1• *Caust* cham chin *Colch* k* *Coloc* ferr k2 *Graph* kali-ar k2 **Kali-bi** *Kali-c* **Kali-p** k* kali-sil k2 kalm lac-d k2 *Lyc* **Mag-p** merc *Nux-v* k* *Ph-ac* phos k2 phyt k2 podo c1 pyrog rhod k2 **Rhus-t** **Sil** *Sulph* syph c1* tub k2
      - **aching**: carc mg1.de
      - **stitching** pain: agar k2
  - **bed**:
    - **agg.**: apis *Aur* sne *Carb-v*↓ ferr sne kali-m k2 *Lac-c* *Led* mag-c c1 **Merc** mez k2 phyt stel *Sulph* syph k2* *Verat*
      - **drawing** pain: sulph
      - **stitching** pain: *Carb-v* *Led* stel
      - **tearing** pain: sulph
    - **amel.**: am-c k2 **Ars** ars-s-f k2 *Kali-bi* lyc k2 *Nux-v* *Ph-ac* *Pyrog* **Rhus-t**
  - **room**:
    - **agg.**: plan↓ stel↓
      - **stitching** pain: plan k* stel
- **warmth**:
  - **amel.**: aesc↓ agar↓ cham↓ kali-p↓ *Lyc*↓ *Nux-v*↓ **Rhus-t**↓ ther↓
    - **drawing** pain: cham kali-p k2 *Nux-v* *Rhus-t* ther k2
    - **sore**: *Nux-v* **Rhus-t**
    - **tearing** pain: aesc k2 agar k2 *Lyc*
- **waves**; in: *Bamb-a* stb2.de• dulc fd4.de
- **weather**:
  - **change** of weather: *Calc-p* carbn-s↓ chel k2 cinnb k2 dulc fd4.de *Gels*↓ nat-c k2 psor al2 **Rhod** *Sil* tub k2
    - **stitching** pain: carbn-s k2
    - **tearing** pain: *Gels*
  - **cold**:
    - **agg.**: bros-gau↓ nit-ac↓
      - **sprained**; as if: bros-gau mrc1
      - **stitching** pain: nit-ac k2
    - **wet**:
      - **agg.**: calc-sil↓ cimic↓
        - **aching**: calc-sil k2
        - **stitching** pain: cimic mrr1
  - **warm**:
    - **amel.**: *Colch*↓
      - **tearing** pain: *Colch*
  - **wet**:
    - **agg.**: am-c ant-c *Arg-met* ars-s-f k2 bell borx bros-gau↓ bry **Calc** calc-sil k2 carb-v caust cimic k2 **Colch** con *Dulc* elaps gk gels↓ hep lyc **Merc** nat-s *Nit-ac* nux-m *Phyt* **Puls** **Rhod** **Rhus-t** ruta *Sars* *Sep* *Sil* sulph *Tub* **Verat**
      - **drawing** pain: gels psa
      - **sprained**; as if: bros-gau mrc1
      - **tearing** pain: *Dulc* lyc *Rhod* *Rhus-t*
- **wet**; after getting: *Dulc*↓ **Rhus-t**↓
  - **tearing** pain: *Dulc* **Rhus-t**
- **wine** agg.: led mez zinc
  - **drawing** pain: *Led* mez
  - **sour**: *Ant-c*

▽ - **extending** to:

- ○ **Body**; whole: chel↓
  - **burning**: chel tl1
- **Feet**: mag-s↓ ph-ac↓
  - **burning**: ph-ac ptk1
  - **tearing** pain: mag-s
- **Head**: carb-v↓
  - **tearing** pain: carb-v h2

○ - **Ankles**: abrom-a↓ abrot k* acon k* act-sp mrr1 agar agn↓ aids↓ *All-c* all-s↓ aloe↓ alum k* alum-sil↓ alumn am-c bro1 am-m↓ ambr b7.de* ammc↓ **Anac**↓ androc↓ *Ang* b7a.de ant-c *Ant-t* apis↓ apoc↓ aq-mar↓ *Arg-met*↓ arg-n↓ arge-pl↓ *Am* ars ars-i↓ asaf↓ asar↓ asc-t aster *Aur*↓ aur-m-n↓ bamb-a stb2.de• bapt bar-act↓ bar-c↓ bell benz-ac berb bism↓ bit-ar wht1• *Bol-la* bov brom↓ bry bufo↓ but-ac br1* cact *Calc*↓ *Calc-p*↓ calc-sil↓ camph↓ cann-i cann-s↓ caps↓ carb-ac↓ *Carb-an* carb-v↓ carbn-s↓ carc fd2.de• castor-eq↓ *Caul* *Caust* k* *Cham* *Chel* *Chin*↓ chinin-ar↓ chinin-s↓ chlor↓ choc↓ cic↓ cinnb↓ clem↓ coca↓ cocc↓ coff↓ colch *Coloc*↓ com br1 con↓ conv↓ *Cop* croc br1 crot-t↓ cupr↓ cycl↓ des-ac rbp6 dig↓ digin↓ dios dream-p sdj1• dros k* dulc fd4.de dys pte1*• erig↓ euon bro1 eup-per↓ euph↓ falco-pe nl2• ferr k* ferr-ar ferr-p fl-ac↓ form gels gins↓ gran↓ graph grat↓ *Guaj* ham↓ *Hell*↓ hep↓ heroin↓ hyos↓ ign↓ indg↓ inul br1 iodof↓ jatr-c jug-c↓ kali-bi↓ **Kali-c**↓ kali-n k* kali-p↓ kali-s fd4.de kali-sil↓ *Kalm* kola stb3• kreos↓ *Lac-ac* lac-c lac-d k2 lach↓ lach lact↓ lappa bro1 lath bro1 laur↓ **Led** k* lil-t limen-b-c↓ *Lith-c* lith-m↓ lob-s *Lyc* lyss m-ambo↓ m-aust↓ mag-c↓ mag-m↓ manc↓ mang↓ mang-m c2 med merc merc-i-f↓ *Mez* mosch↓ mucs-nas rly4• naja↓ nat-ar↓ nat-c↓ nat-m k* nat-p nat-s nat-sil↓ nit-ac↓ nit-s-d↓ nux-v↓ ol-an↓ olnd↓ osm ox-ac↓ par↓ petr↓ ph-ac *Phos* k* *Phyt* plan↓ plat plb podo polys sk4• prop c2 propr sa3• *Prun*↓ psor↓ ptel↓ puls puls-n↓ ran-b k* ran-s↓ rat↓ *Rheum* b7a.de rhod↓ rhus-g↓ **Rhus-t**↓ rhus-v rumx ruta k2 sabin↓ sacch-a↓ *Sal-ac* sal-fr↓ samb↓ sang↓ sars↓ sel↓ seneg k* sep sil bro1 sin-n spig spong stann↓ staph↓ stict stram↓ stront-c b4.de* stry suis-pan↓ sul-ac↓ sul-i↓ sulph symph fd3.de• tab↓ taosc iwa1• tarax↓ tell↓ tep↓ tet bro1 *Teucr*↓ thuj til↓ tritic-vg fd5.de trom↓ tub c1 tung-met↓ valer k* vanil fd5.de ven-m↓ verat verat-v↓ verb bro1 viol-t↓ *Visc* bro1 xan zinc

- **right**: agar↓ bit-ar↓ cann-i a1 dream-p sdj1• dros↓ fic-m gya1 kali-n↓ kali-s fd4.de nat-m↓ osm↓ podo fd3.de• rat↓ rhus-g↓ ruta fd4.de samb↓ spong fd4.de vanil fd5.de ven-m↓
  - **aching**: rhus-g tmo3•

- **right**: ...
  - **cramping**: ven-m rsj12•
  - **pinching** pain: osm
  - **shooting** pain: bit-ar wht1•
  - **tearing** pain: agar dros kali-n h2 nat-m h2 rat samb h1*
- **left**: asc-t↓ bit-ar wht1• cann-i a1 caul a1 des-ac rbp6 dream-p sdj1• erig mtf11 gels psa kali-i↓ plut-n↓ propr sa3• ruta fd4.de spong fd4.de vanil fd5.de
  - **followed** by | **right**: bamb-a stb2.de•
  - **gnawing** pain: kali-i bg2
  - **sprained**; as if: asc-t a1 dream-p sdj1• plut-n srj7•
- **daytime**: mang-m↓
  - **drawing** pain: mang-m
  - **pressing** pain: mang-m k*
- **morning**: all-c alumn ang↓ carb-ac carbn-s dios dream-p sdj1• ham fd3.de• *Led* lyc↓ mag-c↓ mez nit-s-d↓ plb↓ puls↓ ruta fd4.de sep sulph symph↓ tritic-vg fd5.de vanil fd5.de
  - **aching**: carb-ac
  - **bed** agg.; in: carbn-s↓ symph↓
    - **broken**; as if: carbn-s symph fd3.de•
  - **boring** pain: mez
  - **drawing** pain: lyc sulph vanil fd5.de
  - **motion** of feet agg.: puls↓
    - **tearing** pain: puls h1
  - **pressing** pain: ang h1 *Led* nit-s-d a1
  - **rising**:
    - **after**:
      - **agg.**: rheum↓
        - **sprained**; as if: rheum h
      - **walking** about; and:
        - **agg.**: camph↓
          - **sprained**; as if: camph k*
    - **agg.**: dig↓ nat-s↓ nit-ac↓
      - **sprained**; as if: dig nat-s nit-ac
    - **bed**; from:
      - **agg.**: abrom-a↓
        - **dull** pain: abrom-a ks5
  - **sore**: mag-c symph fd3.de•
  - **sprained**; as if: plb
  - **standing** agg.: coca↓
    - **sprained**; as if: coca
  - **stepping**:
    - **every** step; at: graph↓ psor↓
      - **stitching** pain: graph psor
  - **tearing** pain: puls
  - **waking**; on: mez↓ nat-s↓ sulph↓
    - **left**: bit-ar wht1•
    - **boring** pain: mez
    - **drawing** pain: sulph
    - **gnawing** pain: sulph k*
    - **pressing** pain: mez k*
    - **tearing** pain: nat-s
  - **walking**:
    - **agg.**: alumn ang↓ dream-p sdj1• ign↓ mez nux-v↓ plb psor ruta fd4.de
      - **drawing** pain: ang
      - **sprained**; as if: ign nux-v plb psor
    - **amel.**: sulph
    - **impossible**: dig↓ nat-s↓
      - **sprained**; as if: dig nat-s
- **forenoon**: cham↓ chinin-s↓ kali-c↓
  - **drawing** pain: cham kali-c h2
  - **stitching** pain: chinin-s
- **noon**: con↓ kali-bi↓
  - **evening**; until: con↓
    - **tearing** pain: con
  - **tearing** pain: con kali-bi
- **afternoon**: carbn-s↓ con↓ dios ham↓ hyos↓ indg↓ petr-ra shn4• ptel↓ rhus-v spong fd4.de trom↓ *Valer*↓ vanil fd5.de verat
  - **15** h: lyc tab tax
  - **16**.30 h: sal-al blc1•
  - **17** h: lyc↓
    - **tearing** pain: lyc
  - **17-20** h: ven-m rsj12•
  - **drawing** pain: ham fd3.de• indg ptel vanil fd5.de
  - **sore**: hyos *Valer*
  - **tearing** pain: carbn-s con trom
- **evening**: crot-t↓ dios fl-ac↓ gran↓ indg↓ kali-c↓ led lyc↓ merc↓ nat-c nat-s plan ptel↓ ruta fd4.de spong fd4.de stram↓ stront-c↓ sulph↓ vanil fd5.de
  - **bed** agg.; in: lyc↓ samb↓ zinc↓
    - **stitching** pain: lyc zinc
    - **tearing** pain: samb h1*
  - **burning**: sulph
  - **drawing** pain: fl-ac indg kali-c h2 lyc nat-s ptel stram h1 sulph vanil fd5.de
  - **lying** agg.: nat-s plan
  - **lying** down | **after**:
    - **agg.**: nat-s↓
      - **pressing** pain: nat-s
    - **agg.**: plan↓
      - **boring** pain: plan
  - **pressing** pain: crot-t k* nat-s k*
  - **sprained**; as if: gran
  - **stitching** pain: merc stront-c
  - **walking** agg.: fl-ac↓ verat↓
    - **drawing** pain: fl-ac
    - **sprained**; as if: verat
- **night**: cham↓ des-ac rbp6 kali-s fd4.de nat-m↓ phos↓ ruta fd4.de *Sulph* vanil fd5.de
  - **23**-7 h: sulph
  - **midnight**: stront-c↓
    - **after** | **2** h: agar
    - **motion** agg.: *Led*↓
      - **pressing** pain: *Led*
    - **tearing** pain: stront-c
    - **waking**; on: ambr↓ coloc↓
      - **pressing** pain: ambr
      - **tearing** pain: coloc
  - **drawing** pain: cham nat-m vanil fd5.de
  - **lying** agg.: dros↓
    - **stitching** pain: dros
  - **pressing** pain: ruta fd4.de
  - **standing** agg.: coca↓
    - **sprained**; as if: coca
  - **tearing** pain: phos h2
  - **waking**; on: kali-c↓ *Lyc*↓ nat-m↓
    - **drawing** pain: kali-c h2 nat-m
    - **tearing** pain: kali-c h2 *Lyc* nat-m
- **aching**: *Agar* cann-i carb-ac castor-eq coloc con conv br1 cycl mrr1 dios hell jug-c *Lac-d* laur *Led* naja nat-p ox-ac plan *Podo* ptel puls-n *Rhus-t* rhus-v sep sin-n stront-c stry suis-pan rly4• sul-i tab zinc [heroin sdj2]
- **ascending**:
  - **agg.**: carbn-s↓
    - **stitching** pain: carbn-s k2
  - **stairs** | **agg.**: alumn *Plb* valer k2
- **bed**; before going to: ammc↓
  - **tearing** pain: ammc
- **bending** from side to side agg.: caust↓
  - **sprained**; as if: caust
- **boring** pain: agar am-c ang k* apis aur aur-m-n bufo che! clem coloc graph grat hell k* led *Mez* nat-s plan spig b7.de*
- **broken**; as if: ang bg2 bov b4.de* calc k* carbn-s caust k* hep k* mez b4.de* symph fd3.de•

Extremities

- **burning**: agar ang$_{b7.de}$ aur$_{b4a.de}$ berb *Bry*$_{b7a.de}$ calc$_{b4.de}$ euph$_{k*}$ kali-bi$_{k2}$ kola$_{stb3}$• kreos$_{k*}$ laur manc nat-c$_{k*}$ nit-ac$_{h2}$ petr$_{b4.de}$ plat *Puls* *Rhus-t*$_{b7a.de}$ sulph$_{k*}$ symph$_{fd3.de}$• vanil$_{fd5.de}$ verat$_{b7.de*}$ *Zinc*
- **chill**; during: podo$_{br*}$
- **cold**:
  - **amel.**: bit-ar$_{wht1}$•
  - **washing**:
    - **amel.**: cann-s ↓
      - **stitching** pain: cann-s
- **crushed**; as if: caust$_{h2}$
- **cutting** pain: arg-met$_{k*}$ benz-ac *Coloc* eup-per hyos$_{b7.de*}$ iodof lyss merc$_{bg2}$ merc-i-f nux-v$_{bg2}$ rhus-t sang stry tell tep
- **dinner**; after: indg ↓
  - **pressing** pain: indg$_{k*}$
- **dislocated**; as if: aids$_{nl2}$• anac$_{b4.de*}$ ang$_{b7.de*}$ ant-c$_{b7.de*}$ arn$_{b7.de*}$ ars$_{b4.de*}$ bar-c$_{b4.de*}$ *Bry*$_{k*}$ bufo$_{bg2}$ calc$_{b4.de*}$ calc-p camph$_{b7.de*}$ carb-v$_{b4a.de}$ *Caust*$_{b4.de*}$ chel$_{b7.de*}$ cocc$_{b7.de*}$ cycl$_{b7.de*}$ dig$_{b4.de*}$ dros$_{b7.de*}$ graph$_{b4.de*}$ hell$_{b7.de*}$ hep$_{b4a.de}$ ign$_{b7.de*}$ kali-bi$_{k*}$ led$_{b7.de*}$ limen-b-c$_{hrn2*}$ lyc$_{b4.de*}$ m-ambo$_{b7.de}$ m-aust$_{b7.de}$ merc$_{b4.de*}$ mez$_{b4.de*}$ mosch$_{b7a.de}$ nat-m$_{b4.de*}$ nux-v$_{b7.de*}$ ph-ac$_{b4.de*}$ phos$_{b4.de*}$ plat$_{b4.de*}$ prun$_{bro1}$ puls$_{b7.de*}$ rheum$_{b7.de*}$ rhod$_{b4a.de}$ **Rhus-t**$_{b7.de*}$ ruta$_{b7a.de*}$ sep$_{b4.de*}$ sil$_{b4.de*}$ sulph$_{b4.de*}$ valer$_{b7.de*}$ verat$_{b7.de*}$ verat-v **Zinc**$_{b4.de*}$
- **dorsiflexion**: bit-ar$_{wht1}$•
- **dragging**: mez$_{b4.de*}$
- **drawing** pain: abrot *Agar* alum$_{k*}$ alum-sil$_{k2}$ am-c$_{b4.de*}$ ambr$_{b7.de*}$ anac$_{b4.de*}$ ang$_{k*}$ arg-met *Arn*$_{b7.de*}$ *Ars* aster aur-m-n bapt bism$_{b7.de*}$ bov$_{b4.de*}$ cact camph cann-s$_{k*}$ *Caul* caust$_{k*}$ cham chel coloc com croc$_{b7.de*}$ cupr dig dios dulc$_{b4.de*}$ erig fl-ac ham$_{fd3.de}$• indg kali-bi kali-c kali-sil$_{k2}$ kreos$_{k*}$ *Led* lyc m-aust$_{b7.de*}$ mang-m med merc$_{b4.de*}$ mez naja nat-m nat-s nit-ac nux-v$_{b7.de*}$ par$_{b7.de*}$ ptel puls-n rhod rhus-t$_{k*}$ rhus-v sil spig$_{k*}$ spong staph stram stront-c$_{k*}$ sulph symph$_{fd3.de}$• tarax$_{k*}$ thuj$_{k*}$ **Valer**$_{k*}$ vanil$_{fd5.de}$ verat$_{b7.de*}$ zinc
  - **cramping**: arg-met sulph
  - **paralyzed**; as if: phos$_{h2}$
  - **paroxysmal**: coloc
  - **tearing** pain: clem kali-bi spong tarax
  - **upward**: ars fl-ac guaj$_{h2}$ ham$_{fd3.de}$• kreos phos$_{h2}$ rhus-v spong$_{h1}$
- **dull** pain: abrom-a$_{ks5}$ ven-m$_{rsj12}$•
- **edema**, with: *Stront-c* ↓
  - **sprained**; as if: *Stront-c*$_{vh}$
- **exertion** agg.; after: valer$_{k2}$
- **exertion**; as after: *Alum*$_{b4a.de}$ arg-met$_{b7.de*}$ caust$_{b4.de*}$ croc$_{b7.de*}$ mang$_{b4a.de}$ nux-v$_{b7.de*}$
- **false** step; at a: caust chel coloc **Led**
  - **sprained**; as if: caust
- **flexion**: chinin-s ↓
  - **sprained**; as if: chinin-s
- **gnawing** pain: berb$_{k*}$ graph$_{k*}$ laur$_{k*}$ nat-m$_{bg2}$ ran-s$_{b7.de*}$ sars sulph$_{k*}$
- **gonorrhea**; after suppressed: *Med* thuj
- **gouty**: abrot$_{dgt1}$ ambr$_{b7.de*}$ arn$_{b7.de*}$ *Bry*$_{b7a.de}$ **Led** petr stel$_{mtf11}$ verat$_{b7a.de}$
  - **left**: psor$_{bg2}$
- **inflamed**: abrot ↓
  - **sprained**; as if: abrot$_{tl1}$
- **jar** agg.: lil-t *Valer* ↓
  - **sore**: *Valer*
- **lying**:
  - **agg.**: ars ↓ aur-m-n ↓ sep ↓
    - **drawing** pain: aur-m-n
    - **tearing** pain: ars sep$_{h2}$
  - **amel.**: sil ↓
    - **tearing** pain: sil
  - **bed**; in:
    - **agg.**: aloe ↓
- **lying – bed**; in – **agg.**: ...
  - **sprained**; as if: aloe
- **menses**; after: nat-p
  - **aching**: nat-p
- **motion**:
  - **agg.**: *Arn* ars ↓ bar-c ↓ bit-ar$_{wht1}$• bol-la bry$_{k*}$ bufo *Cham* *Chel* cocc des-ac$_{rbp6}$ fl-ac ↓ *Guaj* kali-bi ↓ *Kalm* kreos ↓ lac-c ↓ *Led* lil-t mand$_{rsj7}$• mez ↓ nat-s ↓ staph ↓ sulph vanil$_{fd5.de}$ zinc
    - **boring** pain: bufo mez
    - **drawing** pain: fl-ac staph
    - **pressing** pain: lac-c *Led* nat-s$_{k*}$ staph$_{a1}$
    - **shooting** pain: bufo
    - **sprained**; as if: cocc zinc
    - **stitching** pain: bar-c bufo kreos
    - **tearing** pain: ars$_{h2}$ kali-bi
  - **amel.**: arg-met ↓ aur-m-n bism ↓ bit-ar ↓ *Cham* ↓ dios dros ↓ indg ↓ mez ↓ nat-s plan **Rhus-t** ↓ sulph ↓ valer ven-m$_{rsj12}$•
    - **aching**: plan **Rhus-t**
    - **drawing** pain: arg-met bism$_{h1}$ indg *Valer*
    - **pressing** pain: aur-m-n$_{k*}$ indg$_{k*}$ nat-s$_{k*}$
    - **sore**: mez
    - **sprained**; as if: bit-ar$_{wht1}$•
    - **stitching** pain: *Cham*
    - **tearing** pain: arg-met cham dros **Rhus-t** sulph
- **paralyzed**; as if: caps$_{b7.de*}$ caust croc$_{b7.de*}$ *Dros*$_{b7.de*}$ mez$_{b4.de*}$ nat-m$_{b4.de*}$ nat-p par$_{k*}$ ph-ac$_{k*}$ phos$_{b4.de*}$ plb$_{k*}$ seneg$_{b4a.de}$
- **paroxysmal**: bamb-a$_{stb2.de}$• coloc hep sil
- **pinching** pain: sulph$_{h2}$
- **pressing** pain: *Agar*$_{k*}$ all-c$_{k*}$ ambr$_{k*}$ ang$_{b7.de*}$ arg-n$_{k*}$ aur$_{k*}$ aur-m-n$_{k*}$ berb brom$_{k*}$ camph$_{k*}$ *Chel*$_{k*}$ clem$_{k*}$ coloc$_{k*}$ crot-t$_{k*}$ cycl$_{b7.de*}$ dig$_{k*}$ digin$_{a1}$ dulc$_{fd4.de}$ gins$_{k*}$ graph$_{b4.de*}$ hell$_{k*}$ ign$_{k*}$ indg$_{k*}$ kali-p$_{fd1.de}$• kola$_{stb3}$• kreos$_{b7a.de}$ lac-c *Led*$_{k*}$ m-aust$_{b7.de}$ mang-m$_{k*}$ merc$_{b4.de*}$ mez$_{k*}$ nat-m$_{k*}$ nat-s$_{k*}$ nat-sil$_{fd3.de}$• nit-ac nit-s-d$_{a1}$ ruta$_{fd4.de}$ seneg$_{k*}$ sep$_{k*}$ spig$_{k*}$ spong$_{fd4.de}$ stront-c$_{b4.de*}$ sul-ac$_{k*}$ vanil$_{fd5.de}$ verat$_{k*}$ verb$_{k*}$ viol-t$_{b7.de*}$
  - **cramping**: verb
  - **paroxysmal**: coloc$_{k*}$ indg
- **pulsating** pain: lith-m propr$_{sa3}$• *Ruta*
- **rheumatic**: abrot$_{bro1}$ *Act-sp*$_{bro1}$ am-c bacls-7$_{pte1*}$• bapt cact calc-p$_{k2}$ *Caul*$_{bro1}$ caust$_{bro1}$ *Chel* chinin-s clem colch$_{k*}$ corv-cor$_{bdg}$• gnaph gua$_{bro1}$ *Guaj*$_{k*}$ ham$_{fd3.de}$• *Kalm* *Lac-c* *Led*$_{bro1}$ *Lyc* mang-act$_{bro1}$ mang-m$_{bro1}$ med$_{bro1}$ *Ol-j* plan *Prop*$_{bro1}$ *Puls*$_{bro1}$ rad-br$_{bro1}$ *Rhod*$_{bro1}$ *Ruta*$_{bro1}$ sacch-a$_{fd2.de}$• sang sil$_{bro1}$ stel$_{bro1*}$ stict stram ↓ sulph$_{bro1}$ syph urt-u$_{k*}$ *Verat-v* viol-o zinc
  - **boring** pain: plan
  - **drawing** pain: stram
- **rising** agg.; after: coloc ↓
  - **drawing** pain: coloc
- **room**:
  - **amel.**: graph ↓
    - **sprained**; as if: graph
- **rotating**: lac-h ↓
  - **sore**: lac-h$_{htj1}$•
- **rubbing**:
  - **agg.**: sulph ↓
    - **burning**: sulph
  - **amel.**: zinc ↓
    - **tearing** pain: zinc$_{h2}$
- **running** agg.: berb ↓ mez vanil$_{fd5.de}$
  - **stitching** pain: berb
- **running** upstairs: **Valer** ↓
  - **sprained**; as if: **Valer**
- **shooting** pain: *Acon* apis aur berb bufo *Calc-p* choc$_{srj3}$• *Ferr-p* naja nux-v osm sep trom xan
  - **upward**: aur bit-ar$_{wht1}$• guaj nux-v

- **sitting**:
  - **agg.**: agar↓ am-m↓ ang↓ arg-met↓ arg-n aur-m-n bry *Caust* chel↓ coloc↓ con↓ dig↓ gins↓ grat↓ ham fd3.de• indg↓ kali-n↓ led nat-s phys↓ plut-n↓ **Rhus-t**↓ sep↓ stann↓ symph fd3.de• teucr↓ **Valer** vanil fd5.de verat↓
    - **aching**: bry chel phys **Rhus-t**
    - **boring** pain: agar coloc grat led
    - **drawing** pain: ang h1 caust dig indg kl (non:jug-r kl) nat-s **Valer** verat h1
    - **pressing** pain: agar h2 arg-n k* aur-m-n k* chel h1 coloc k* led k* nat-s k*
    - **sore**: arg-met h1 gins
    - **sprained**; as if: plut-n srj7•
    - **tearing** pain: agar h2 am-m arg-met coloc con h2 kali-n h2 sep h2 stann h2 teucr
  - **amel.**: cycl↓
    - **aching**: cycl
    - **sprained**; as if: cycl
- **sore**: agar agn am-m k* aq-mar skp7• arg-met b7.de* arn k2 ars bell bg2 berb calc b4.de* cann-s cham chlor cinnb clem con dig h2 falco-pe nl2• hep h2 hyos k* lac-h htj1• mag-c k* med k2 *Mez* k* nat-m plat rhus-v ruta sacch-a fd2.de• sel spig symph fd3.de• thuj k2 valer k*
- **sprained**; as if: agar all-s aloe **Anac** ang ant-c h2 **Arn** k* ars asc-t bar-c *Calc* calc-sil k2 camph k* carb-v h2 caust chel chin h1 chinin-s coca cocc cycl des-ac rbp6 dig dream-p sdj1• dros eup-per fl-ac gran graph hell hep ign kali-bi kali-n laur **Led** lyc *Merc* mosch nat-m nat-s nit-ac nux-v ph-ac *Phos* plat plb *Prun* k* psor puls rhus-g tmo3• **Rhus-t Ruta** sep h2 *Sil* *Stront-c* k* sulph h2 tep thuj *Valer* verat zinc
  - **paroxysmal**: hep
- **standing**:
  - **agg.**: anac↓ aur-m-n↓ berb↓ camph↓ chinin-s↓ cycl kali-n↓ led mag-c↓ *Mez*↓ rat↓ rhus-v spig↓ stront-c *Sulph* **Valer** vanil fd5.de
    - **aching**: cycl stront-c
    - **boring** pain: aur-m-n *Mez*
    - **drawing** pain: anac h2 camph kali-n h2 spig
    - **pressing** pain: spig k*
    - **sore**: mag-c h2 mez valer
    - **sprained**; as if: chinin-s cycl sulph **Valér**
    - **stitching** pain: berb
    - **tearing** pain: kali-n h2 rat
  - **amel.**: cycl a1
- **stepping** agg.: alum↓ borx h2 bry graph↓ kali-c↓ **Led** mag-c↓ *Mez* nat-m nat-s↓ psor↓ rhus-t ruta fd4.de sil tritic-vg fd5.de vanil fd5.de
  - **drawing** pain: kali-c nat-s
  - **left** foot; with: **Anac**↓
    - **sprained**; as if: **Anac** k*
  - **pressing** pain: borx h2
  - **sore**: mag-c h2 nat-m h2
  - **stitching** pain: alum graph kali-c psor tritic-vg fd5.de
- **stitching** pain: abrot *Acon* agar k* agn b7.de* *Alum* k* ambr androc srj1• ang k* ant-c k* apis apoc arg-n arge-pl rwt5• arn k* ars b4.de* ars-i asaf b7.de* asar k* aur bapt bar-c berb *Bov* k* bufo *Calc* calc-p calc-sil k2 cann-s carb-v carbn-s caust k* cham chel chinin-s clem coff colch coloc con b4.de* crot-t dios dros k* ferr-p form gins gran graph guaj k* ham *Hell* k* hep k* ign indg kali-c k* kali-s fd4.de kali-sil k2 kreos k* lach led k* *Lith-c* lyc k* m-aust b7.de mang k* merc k* mosch k* naja nat-c k* nat-m k* nux-v k* ol-an olnd b7.de* osm petr phos psor puls k* rhod k* *Rhus-t* k* *Ruta* sal-fr sle1• sang sep sil k* spig k* stann b4.de* staph stront-c k* sulph k* symph fd3.de• tarax b7.de* thuj k* tritic-vg fd5.de trom tung-met bdx1• vanil fd5.de verat b7.de* verb viol-t xan zinc k*
  - **outward**: lith-c mosch
  - **tearing** pain: caust symph fd3.de•
  - **upward**: aur caust h2 guaj mang h2 nux-v
- **stool** agg.; during: verb↓
  - **stitching** pain: verb c1
- **stooping** agg.: cycl↓
  - **sprained**; as if: cycl
- **stretching**:
  - **agg.**: dig↓
    - **sprained**; as if: dig
  - **amel.**: bit-ar wht1•
- **sudden**: indg↓ valer↓ ven-m↓
  - **cramping**: ven-m rsj12•
  - **sore**: valer
  - **stitching** pain: indg
- **tearing** pain: *Acon* k* *Agar* k* alum k* alum-sil k2 am-c k* am-m ambr ammc *Arg-met* k* arg-n a1 *Arn* k* *Ars* k* *Aur* b4a.de bar-act a1 **Bell** berb bism calc *Calc-p* camph carb-an carbn-s caust bg2 cham *Chin* chinin-ar cic b7.de* clem *Colch* k* coloc k* con k* *Dros* k* dulc b4.de* euph k* gins *Guaj* hell hep b4.de* indg kali-bi **Kali-c** k* kali-n kali-sil k2 lac-c lact led k* *Lyc* m-aust b7.de mag-m b4.de* mang-m merc b4a.de mez nat-ar nat-c nat-m b4.de* *Nat-s* nux-v b7.de* par b7.de* puls k* ran-b b7.de* rat rhod b4.de* **Rhus-t** k* rumx ruta bg2 sabin samb k* *Sep* b4a.de sil spong k* stann k* staph stront-c k* sulph symph fd3.de• tarax b7.de* tep *Teucr* k* thuj tritic-vg fd5.de trom *Zinc* k*
  - **constricting** pain: stront-c
  - **cramping**: kali-c h2
  - **drawing** pain: dulc h1
  - **paralyzed**; as if: dros h1 til
  - **pulsating** pain: ol-an
  - **upward**: **Bell** caust h2 con h2 samb h1*
  - **wandering** pain: lact
- **touch** agg.: ars des-ac rbp6 graph h2 kali-n h2 lyc mur-ac↓ nat-m plat↓ sep
  - **sore**: ars h2 mur-ac h2 nat-m plat h2
- **travelling**; after: aq-mar↓
  - **sore**: aq-mar skp7•
- **ulcerative** pain: am-m b7.de* hep b4a.de *Kali-n* b4.de* **Nat-m** b4.de* ruta b7.de*
- **waking**; on: ambr mez
  - **pressing** pain: ambr mez
- **walking**:
  - **after**:
    - **agg.**: *Rhus-t*↓ sep↓ suis-pan↓
      - **aching**: *Rhus-t* suis-pan rly4•
      - **pressing** pain: sep h2
  - **agg.**: agar↓ alumn am-m↓ ambr h1 ang↓ aster berb↓ bit-ar wht1• bry bung-fa mtf calc-p camph↓ carc fd2.de• caust chel coloc↓ cycl des-ac rbp6 *Dros* erig mtf11 fl-ac gins↓ hep↓ kali-n *Kalm* *Lach*↓ *Led* lith-c lyc↓ mag-c↓ merc↓ mez nat-m↓ nat-s↓ nit-ac nit-s-d↓ petr-ra↓ *Phos* plan↓ psor↓ puls rhus-v ruta spong fd4.de stront-c stry sulph vanil fd5.de
    - **aching**: calc-p cycl stront-c
    - **boring** pain: coloc *Mez*
    - **broken**; as if: caust k* hep k*
    - **burning**: agar
    - **cutting** pain: cycl a1
    - **drawing** pain: ang h1 coloc erig
    - **pressing** pain: ang h1 camph k* coloc k* gins k* merc h1 nat-s k* nit-s-d a1
    - **sore**: am-m mag-c mez nat-m
    - **sprained**; as if: caust cycl *Dros* fl-ac petr-ra shn4• *Phos* psor puls sulph
    - **stitching** pain: agar berb *Lach* lyc sulph
    - **tearing** pain: camph *Dros* plan puls h1
  - **air** agg.; in open: benz-ac↓ graph↓ iodof↓
    - **cutting** pain: benz-ac iodof
    - **sprained**; as if: graph
  - **amel.**: arg-met↓ *Bell*↓ ph-ac *Rhus-t* sulph teucr↓ **Valer**
    - **drawing** pain: arg-met **Valer**
    - **sprained**; as if: **Valer**
    - **tearing** pain: *Bell* teucr
  - **beginning** to walk:
    - **continued** walking amel.: plut-n↓

Extremities

• **walking – beginning** to walk – **continued** walking amel.: ...
. **sprained**; as if: plut-n srj7•
⁝ **continued**:
: **amel.**: mag-c ↓
. **sore**: mag-c
• **warm** feet amel.: kali-c ↓
⁝ **tearing** pain: kali-c h2
• **warmth**:
⁝ **agg.**: *Guaj* lac-c **Led Puls**
⁝ **amel.**: am-c ↓ ars ↓ chel
: **tearing** pain: am-c ars
▽ • **extending** to:
⁝ **Calf**: con ↓ thuj ↓
: **drawing** pain: thuj h1
: **stitching** pain: con h2
⁝ **Foot**: hell ↓ kreos ↓
: **stitching** pain: hell kreos
⁝ **Heels**: agar ↓ sal-fr ↓
: **burning**: agar
: **shooting** pain: agar
: **stitching** pain: agar sal-fr sle1•
⁝ **Knee**: ars ↓ *Guaj* ↓ kreos ↓ lyc ↓ spong ↓
: **drawing** pain: lyc h2
: **shooting** pain: guaj
: **stitching** pain: guaj
: **tearing** pain: ars *Guaj* kreos spong
⁝ **Outward**: *Lith-c*
⁝ **Soles**: stann
⁝ **Tendo** Achillis: taosc iwa1•
⁝ **Tibia**: ph-ac ↓ tritic-vg ↓
: **stitching** pain: ph-ac h2 tritic-vg fd5.de
⁝ **Toes**: am-c ↓ graph ↓ hell ↓ kali-p fd1.de• kreos ↓ lil-t stann ↓
: **stitching** pain: graph h2 hell kreos
: **tearing** pain: am-c h2 hell stann h2
⁝ **Toes**; over the soles to the: kreos ↓
: **burning**: kreos
⁝ **Upward**: bell but-ac br1 carc fd2.de• ferr nat-s phos plb puls tritic-vg fd5.de
○ • **Above**: arge-pl ↓ meny ↓ nit-ac ↓
⁝ **burning**: meny h1 nit-ac bg1
⁝ **stitching** pain: arge-pl rwt5• meny h1
• **Anterior** part: acon agar ↓ berb calc-p chel merc-i-f ↓ rumx ↓ ruta
⁝ **boring** pain: chel merc-i-f
⁝ **burning**: berb
⁝ **gnawing** pain: berb k*
⁝ **pulsating** pain: ruta
⁝ **rheumatic**: acon
⁝ **stitching** pain: berb
⁝ **tearing** pain: agar berb rumx
• **Below**: mur-ac ↓ zinc ↓
⁝ **pressing** pain: zinc h2
⁝ **sore**: mur-ac h2
• **Bones**: aur ↓ *Bism* ↓ cupr ↓ graph ↓ *Led* ↓ *Mez* ↓ puls ↓ ruta ↓ sabin ↓ staph ↓
⁝ **boring** pain: *Mez*
⁝ **burning**: ruta
⁝ **gnawing** pain: graph k*
⁝ **pressing** pain: *Bism* cupr *Led* k* sabin staph
⁝ **stitching** pain: aur puls
• **Inner** malleolus: *Arg-met* ↓
⁝ **sore**: *Arg-met*
• **Malleolus**: alum ↓ am-c ↓ ambr ↓ arn ↓ bapt ↓ berb ↓ bry calc chinin-s ↓ cic ↓ coloc graph ↓ grat ↓ iod ↓ kali-c ↓ lach ↓ mez ↓ nat-m ↓ nit-ac ↓ par ↓ phos ↓ plb sil ↓ spong ↓ sulph valer ↓ verat-v
⁝ **aching**: chinin-s graph
⁝ **boring** pain: cic mez

• **Malleolus**: ...
⁝ **stitching** pain: bapt berb iod kali-c lach nit-ac phos valer
⁝ **tearing** pain: alum am-c ambr arn berb cic a1 grat mez nat-m par phos sil spong
⁝ **Inner**: *Agar* ↓ arg-met ↓ berb bov chel coc-c ↓ coff ↓ dulc ↓ hura indg ↓ kali-bi laur ↓ led ↓ mez nat-m ↓ puls ↓ rhus-t ↓ spig ↓ sulph ↓ tarax ↓ verat-v verb ↓ zinc ↓
: **right**: tarent
: **evening**:
. **bed** agg.; in: led ↓
boring pain: led
: **aching**: berb mez verat-v
: **boring** pain: led sulph
: **burning**: berb laur spig h1 zinc
: **sitting** agg.: berb ↓ par ↓ tarax ↓
. **stitching** pain: berb par tarax
: **stitching** pain: berb chel coc-c coff indg nat-m rhus-t spig h1 tarax h1 verb c1
: **tearing** pain: *Agar* arg-met berb dulc a1 puls zinc
: **walking** agg.: puls ↓
. **stitching** pain: puls
: **Behind**: rheum ↓
. **burning**: rheum h
⁝ **Outer**: agar ↓ am-c apis ↓ arg-met ↓ arg-n ↓ arn ↓ *Bov* ↓ bry ↓ canth ↓ carb-ac chinin-s ↓ cic clem ↓ con ↓ dios ↓ dulc ↓ kali-n ↓ lach laur mag-m ↓ mang ↓ nat-c ↓ par ↓ rhod ↓ samb ↓ sars ↓ sil ↓ stront-c ↓ sulph ↓ thuj valer ↓ zinc ↓
: **morning**:
. **bed** agg.; in: arg-n ↓
boring pain: arg-n
: **aching**: cic laur
: **drawing** pain: am-c h2 kali-n h2
: **motion**:
. **amel.**: bism ↓
drawing pain: bism a1
: **sitting** agg.: agar ↓ arg-met ↓
. **stitching** pain: agar h2 arg-met h1 (non:arg-n kl)
: **sore**: valer
: **stitching** pain: agar h2 apis arg-met arg-n *Bov* bry chinin-s clem dios mang sars sil h2 sulph thuj
. **burning**: thuj h1
: **tearing** pain: arn canth con h2 dulc a1 kali-n mag-m nat-c h2 par rhod samb h1* stront-c zinc
: **walking** agg.: arg-met *Mang* ↓ sulph ↓
. **stitching** pain: *Mang* k* sulph
: **Behind**: meny ↓
. **gnawing** pain: meny h1
: **Below** outer ankle:
. **walking** agg.: nat-c ↓
stitching pain: nat-c h2
• **Outer**: mez ↓
⁝ **cramping**: mez h2
⁝ **walking**:
: **amel.**: euph ↓
. **cramping**: euph h2
• **Sides**:
⁝ **Inner**: ang berb ↓ com dios dulc ↓ hyper kali-s ↓ lob-s merc mez ↓ ph-ac ↓ ruta fd4.de symph fd3.de• thuj ↓ trom vanil fd5.de
: **stitching** pain: berb kali-s fd4.de ph-ac h2 symph fd3.de•
: **tearing** pain: dulc h2 mez h2 thuj
⁝ **Outer**: abrot all-c ↓ ang ↓ arg-n berb ↓ bism ↓ caust ↓ des-ac rbp6 dulc ↓ fl-ac ham fd3.de• kali-n ↓ meny ↓ merl ↓ nat-c ↓ podo fd3.de• rat ↓ rhus-t spong fd4.de symph fd3.de• thuj ↓ tritic-vg fd5.de vanil fd5.de verat
: **evening**: fl-ac
: **boring** pain: arg-n
: **burning**: all-c ang kali-n h2
: **cutting** pain: meny h1

- **Sides – Outer**: ...
  - **standing** agg.: ruta↓
    - **burning**: ruta
  - **tearing** pain: berb bism caust h2 dulc h2 kali-n merl nat-c h2 rat thuj
  - **walking** agg.: rhus-t
  - **extending** to:
    - **Tendo** Achillis: bism↓
      - **tearing** pain: bism a1
- **Top**: *Puls*↓
  - **burning**: *Puls*

- **Bones**: agar k2 *Alum*↓ am-c↓ anac↓ androc↓ ang c1 aran bro1 *Arg-met Arn Ars* ars-s-f k2 **Asaf** k* *Aur* k* bamb-a stb2.de• *Calc Calc-p* k* *Carb-an*↓ carb-v caust *Cham* chin choc srj3• chord-umb↓ cinnb *Cocc Colch* coloc↓ *Con Crot-h*↓ *Cupr Dros* tl1 **Eup-per** k* falco-pe↓ *Ferr Fl-ac* form↓ gels k* graph *Guaj Hep* iod *Ip* k* *Kali-bi* bro1 kali-c *Kali-i* k* kali-s fd4.de lach *Led Lyc Lyss*↓ mag-m bro1 mag-s mang mang-act bro1 meph↓ **Merc** k* *Merc-i-f* mez k* mur-ac nat-c↓ nat-m nat-ox rly4• **Nit-ac Nux-v** ozone sde2• **Ph-ac** k* *Phos* phyt k2* plut-n srj7• positr nl2• pot-e rly4• **Puls Pyrog** *Ran-s* bro1 *Rhod Rhus-t* rhus-v bro1 **Ruta** k* sacch-a↓ sal-fr↓ *Sang* bro1 *Sars* k* *Sep* sphing↓ spig↓ spong fd4.de *Staph* k* *Still* bro1 stront-c bro1 sul-i k2 *Sulph* symph↓ *Syph* mrr1 tarent k2 ther thuj↓ trios bro1 *Tub*↓ vanil fd5.de verat↓
  - **morning**:
    - **bed** agg.; in: **Nux-v**↓
      - **sore**: **Nux-v**
  - **night**: kali-i mrr1 mang↓ nit-ac mtf33 phyt mrr1 syph mrr1
    - **burrowing**: mang h2
  - **aching**: am-c tl1 calc-p k2 chord-umb rly4• **Eup-per** k* falco-pe nl2• form **Ip** *Lyss Mur-ac* nit-ac plut-n srj7• positr nl2• pyrog k2 sal-fr sle1• sphing kk3.fr tarent k2 *Tub* k*
  - **air**; in open | **amel.**: *Mang* hr1
  - **boring** pain: arg-met aur k2 calc-p k2 *Carb-an* b4a.de *Carb-v* caust bg2 mang k* phos sulph bg2 thuj b4a.de
  - **burrowing**: carb-an bg2 nat-c bg2 thuj bg2
  - **chill**; during: *Arn*↓ *Ars*↓ arum-t↓ chin↓ **Eup-per**↓ *Ferr*↓ **Ip**↓ mag-c↓ mur-ac↓ nat-m↓ *Puls*↓ *Pyrog*↓ *Rhus-t*↓
    - **aching**: *Arn Ars* arum-t k2 chin **Eup-per** k* *Ferr* **Ip** mag-c mur-ac nat-m *Puls Pyrog Rhus-t*
  - **deep** in: plut-n srj7•
  - **drawing** pain: cham *Chin Cocc* gels kali-c led merc *Mez* puls h1 sulph tub k2
  - **fractures**; in old: bamb-a stb2.de• symph mtf11
  - **pressing** pain: *Alum* coloc kali-c sacch-a fd2.de• symph fd3.de•
  - **sawing**; as if: syph ptk2 tarent ptk2
  - **scraping** pain: **Ph-ac** spig h1
  - **sitting** agg.: am-m↓
    - **sore**: am-m
  - **sore**: anac androc srj1• arg-met chord-umb rly4• *Crot-h* **Eup-per** graph h2 **Ip** *Kali-bi Lyss Mang* meph bg2* nat-c bg2 *Nit-ac* **Nux-v** rhus-t k2 ruta c1* sulph symph fd3.de• tub k2* verat
    - **paralyzed**; as if: *Calc*
  - **tearing** pain: agar h2 arg-met bg2 cham h1 cocc c1 spig h1
  - ○ **Condyles**: agar↓
    - **stitching** pain: agar
  - **Long** bones: agar↓ bry↓ *Calc*↓ *Led*↓ sabin↓
    - **drawing** pain: bry a1 *Led* k* sabin hr1
    - **sore**: agar h2 *Calc*
    - **Middle** of long bones: bufo *Phyt* tub↓ *Zinc*↓
      - **tearing** pain: tub k2 *Zinc*
  - **Metatarsal** (See feet - bones - metatarsal)
  - **Periosteum**: bry↓ *Mez*↓ nit-ac↓ ph-ac↓ *Rhod*↓
    - **drawing** pain: nit-ac h2
    - **tearing** pain: bry *Mez* ph-ac *Rhod*

- **Elbows**: abrot k* acon k* aesc k2 agar agath-a↓ agn all-c↓ all-s k* aloe k* *Alum* k* alum-p k2 alum-sil k2 *Alumn* am-c am-m↓ ambr tsm1 ammc↓ ampe-qu br1 androc↓ ang↓ ant-c k* ant-t k* apis↓ aq-mar skp7• arg-met k* arg-n↓ *Arn*↓ ars bro1 ars-h ars-i ars-s-f↓ arund↓ *Asaf*↓ aster k* aur aur-ar↓ aur-i k2 aur-m↓ aur-m-n↓ aur-s k2 bapt bar-c↓ *Bell*↓ *Berb*↓ beryl↓ both-ax tsm2 **Bov**↓ brom↓ *Bry* k* bufo↓ bufo-s↓ cact↓ calc k* calc-i↓ calc-p k* calc-s calc-sil↓ camph↓ cann-i canth↓ caps↓ carb-an↓ *Carb-v* b4a.de carbn-s cartl-s rly4• cass a1 castor-eq caul↓ *Caust* k* cedr k* cer-s a1 cham k* chel chin *Chinin-ar*↓ chr-ac a1 cic cimic k* cina↓ cinnb bro1 clem coc-c↓ cocc↓ colch bro1 *Coloc* k* com↓ con↓ cop↓ *Corn* croc↓ crot-c k* crot-h crot-t↓ cupr k* cur↓ cycl k* des-ac↓ dig k* digin↓ dios k* dros↓ dulc k* elaps erig vml3• euphr↓ eupi↓ fago k* falco-pe nl2• ferr k* ferr-ar ferr-i *Ferr-m* bro1 fl-ac k* foen a1* form k* fum↓ galeoc-c-h↓ gels k* ger-i↓ gink-b sbd1• gins↓ glon graph↓ grat k* gua bro1 *Guaj* k* guare↓ gymno↓ ham fd3.de• hell↓ hep k* hir↓ hura↓ hydr↓ hydrog↓ hyos k* hyper k* ind↓ indg↓ *Iod* k* iris jac-c k* jug-c k* kali-ar k* *Kali-bi* k* kali-c k* kali-i↓ kali-m k2 kali-n k* kali-p↓ kali-s fd4.de kali-sil↓ kalm k* kola stb3• kreos↓ *Lac-ac* k* lac-h htj1• lach k* lachn k* lact↓ lap-la sde8.de• laur k* *Led*↓ lept k* lob k* *Lyc* k* lycpr bro1 lyss m-ambo↓ mag-c k* mag-m↓ mag-s manc k* mang k* med↓ *Menis* bro1 meny↓ merc k* merc-i-f k* mez k* *Mur-ac*↓ naja↓ nat-ar nat-c nat-m↓ nat-p↓ nat-s k* nat-sil fd3.de• nicc↓ nicc-met sk4• nit-ac↓ nit-s-d a1 nux-m nux-v ol-j bro1 osm par↓ peti a1 petr k* ph-ac k* phel↓ phos k* phys k* phyt pip-m k* plan k* plat k* plb k* podo fd3.de• prun psor↓ puls k* ran-b ran-s↓ raph↓ rat↓ rhod↓ *Rhus-t* k* rhus-v k* ribo↓ rumx ruta sabad↓ sabin↓ sacch-a↓ sal-fr↓ samb↓ *Sars*↓ sec↓ seneg k* sep k* *Sil Spig*↓ spong *Stann*↓ staph↓ still a1 *Stront-c*↓ stry k* sul-ac k* sul-i k2 sulph k* symph fd3.de• tab↓ taosc iwa1• tarax↓ tarent k* tax↓ tell k* tep k* ter k* ther↓ thuj k* til↓ tong↓ tritic-vg fd5.de trom↓ ust↓ valer k* vanil fd5.de verat k* verb↓ viol-o↓ viol-t↓ *Visc* bro1 xan k* zinc zinc-o c2*
  - **right**: arg-n↓ asc-t a1 aur↓ bapt hr1 beryl↓ brucel sa3• canth↓ clem↓ coloc↓ crot-c sk4• dulc fd4.de falco-pe nl2• foen-an↓ gels↓ ham fd3.de• kali-s fd4.de marb-w↓ phasco-ci rbp2 phos↓ sal-al↓ samb bat1• sulph↓ symph fd3.de• tritic-vg fd5.de tub k2 zinc↓
    - **aching**: marb-w es1•
    - **boring** pain: aur bg2 clem bg2
    - **drawing** pain: canth phos h2 sulph h2
    - **dull** pain: sal-al blc1•
    - **sore**: beryl tpw5
    - **sprained**; as if: gels c1
    - **stitching** pain: falco-pe nl2• foen-an a1 symph fd3.de• tritic-vg fd5.de
    - **tearing** pain: arg-n coloc phos h2 zinc
  - **left**: agar↓ both-ax tsm2 cartl-s↓ cass a1 crot-t↓ falco-pe nl2• ferr↓ flor-p↓ gels c1* gink-b sbd1• ham↓ *Iod*↓ kali-bi↓ kali-p↓ kali-s fd4.de ketogl-ac↓ limest-b↓ mag-p↓ mang↓ nat-m↓ phos↓ plut-n↓ psil↓ psor↓ ruta fd4.de symph↓ tax↓ tritic-vg fd5.de vanil↓ xan c1*
    - **then** right: *Calc-p*↓
      - **stitching** pain: *Calc-p*
    - **aching**: flor-p rsj3•
    - **boring** pain: crot-t bg2
    - **drawing** pain: agar kali-p fd1.de• psor jl2 ruta fd4.de
    - **dull** pain: ketogl-ac rly4• xan c1
    - **heart** complaints; during: arn br1
    - **pressing** pain: plut-n srj7•
    - **shooting** pain: mag-p bg2 nat-m bg2
    - **sore**: agar cartl-s rly4• phos h2
    - **sprained**; as if: psil ft1
    - **stitching** pain: ferr a1 ham fd3.de• kali-bi limest-b es1• mang a1 symph fd3.de• [tax jsj7]
    - **tearing** pain: agar *Iod* symph fd3.de• vanil fd5.de
    - **extending** to:
      - **right**: *Calc-p*↓
        - **shooting** pain: *Calc-p*
  - **morning**: bov↓ brach k* carb-v↓ dios k* dulc fd4.de ham fd3.de• kali-s fd4.de lyc nat-sil fd3.de• puls↓ ran-b ruta fd4.de sep k* sumb thuj trom↓ *Zinc*↓
    - **6 h**: dios
    - **7.30 h**: ozone↓
      - **stitching** pain: ozone sde2•
    - **8 h**: ham↓ mag-c↓ trom↓

Extremities

- **morning** – **8** h: ...
  - **stitching** pain: ham fd3.de• mag-c trom
  - **aching**: sumb
  - **bed** agg.; in: *Carb-v*↓ sumb↓
    - **aching**: sumb
    - **sore**: *Carb-v*
  - **drawing** pain: carb-v h2 lyc k* thuj k*
  - **motion** agg.: puls↓
    - **sore**: puls
  - **shooting** pain: trom
  - **sore**: carb-v ham fd3.de• puls
  - **tearing** pain: bov lyc *Zinc*
  - **waking**; on: des-ac↓
    - **aching**: des-ac rbp6
- **forenoon**: abrot k* alum↓ cham↓ dios k* plan k* spong fd4.de thuj↓ vanil fd5.de
  - **9** h: ham↓ sulph↓
    - **burning**: ham fd3.de• sulph
  - **10** h:
    - **knitting**; while: mag-c↓
      - **tearing** pain: mag-c
  - **sitting**:
    - **amel**.: indg↓
      - **tearing** pain: indg
  - **sore**: thuj
  - **stitching** pain: cham
  - **tearing** pain: alum
- **noon**: arg-met cedr k* cham↓ crot-t↓ lyc↓ tarent↓
  - **boring** pain: crot-t
  - **shooting** pain: tarent
  - **stitching** pain: cham lyc tarent
- **afternoon**: com↓ kali-n↓ kali-s↓ naja↓ spong fd4.de sulph k* vanil fd5.de
  - **13** h: grat↓
    - **tearing** pain: grat
  - **15** h: gels↓
    - **drawing** pain: gels
  - **16** h: dios
  - **17** h: stry
  - **drawing** pain: sulph k*
  - **shooting** pain: naja
  - **stitching** pain: com kali-n kali-s fd4.de naja vanil fd5.de
- **evening**: alum↓ am-c↓ arg-met↓ bov↓ carb-an↓ castor-eq cop dios k* dulc k* eupi↓ fl-ac ham fd3.de• jac-c k* lyc↓ mag-m↓ merc↓ mez↓ psor↓ rat↓ ruta↓ spong fd4.de *Still*↓ stront-c↓ thuj↓ tritic-vg fd5.de zinc↓
  - **17**-22 h: chel↓
    - **stitching** pain: chel
  - **19** h: chinin-s dios
  - **21** h: calc-p lyc
  - **aching**: fl-ac *Still*
  - **bed** agg.; in: mag-c↓ *Nat-c*↓
    - **drawing** pain: mag-c *Nat-c* k*
  - **burning**: arg-met carb-an k* ham fd3.de•
  - **lying** agg.: nat-c k* phos k*
    - **drawing** pain: *Nat-c* k*
  - **pressing** pain: cop k*
  - **pulling** the door: bell chinin-s
  - **sore**: am-c still
  - **stitching** pain: bov eupi lyc mag-m ruta fd4.de thuj tritic-vg fd5.de zinc
  - **tearing** pain: alum lyc merc mez h2 psor rat stront-c
  - **twinging**: carb-an k*
- **night**: am-c↓ aq-mar↓ **Ars**↓ dig k* falco-pe nl2• gels k* kali-n merc-i-f k* *Phos* sep↓ ter k* tritic-vg fd5.de
  - **23** h until morning: *Sulph*
  - **bed** agg.; in: ars↓
- **night** – **bed** agg.; in: ...
  - **tearing** pain: ars
  - **burning**: sep
  - **drawing** pain: *Ars Phos*
  - **putting** arm out of bed; from: am-c
  - **shooting** pain: aq-mar skp7•
  - **sore**: merc-i-f
  - **tearing** pain: am-c **Ars** *Phos*
- **accompanied** by:
  - **Heart**; complaints of the (See CHEST - Heart; complaints - accompanied - elbows)
  - **Upper** limbs; weakness in (See Weakness - upper limbs - accompanied - elbow)
- **aching**: aesc agath-a nl2• ang asaf both-ax tsm2 caul coc-c des-ac rbp6 dios fl-ac galeoc-c-h gms1• gels ger-i rly4• glon gymno ham hydr led merc-i-f ol-j phos *Podo* ribo rly4• rumx ruta sal-fr sle1• sep thuj ust xan
  - **alternating** with | **Knees**; pain in: dios
- **air** agg.; draft of: gels c1
- **air** agg.; in open: lact↓
  - **tearing** pain: lact
- **air**-condition:
  - **agg.**: aq-mar↓
    - **shooting** pain: aq-mar skp7•
- **alternating** with:
  - **Knees**; pain in: dios
  - **Shoulder**; pain in: kalm
- **bed**; after going to: dios k*
- **bending**:
  - **agg.**: chel↓ dulc↓
    - **drawing** pain: chel dulc k*
    - **sore**: dulc
  - **arms**:
    - **agg.**: all-s k* chel dulc k* ham fd3.de• mag-c k* mez↓ mur-ac puls k* rat↓ ruta fd4.de spong↓ stann sma stront-c↓ tritic-vg fd5.de
      - **tearing** pain: mez h2 puls rat k* spong stront-c
- **blow**; pain as from a: ang b7.de* bar-c bg2 caust b4.de* hep b4.de* ruta b7.de*
- **boring** pain: alum k* am-c k* aur bufo caust bg2 clem crot-t dulc k* mez k* nat-s k* nux-m k* nux-v k* phos bg2 ran-s bg2 spong thuj k*
- **broken**; as if: *Bry* k* coc-c k* phos k* symph fd3.de•
- **burning**: agar alum k* *Arg-met* k* arund k* asaf k* bell k* berb k* calc-p k* carb-an k* carb-v k* cartl-s rly4• coc-c colch coloc k* ham fd3.de• kali-n k* m-ambo b7.de merc k* mur-ac k* ph-ac k* phos k* *Plat* k* rhus-t b7.de sep *Stann* b4a.de sulph k* symph fd3.de• ter k* tong a1
- **burnt**; sensation as if: bell h1
- **carrying** a weight; after: *Cham* symph fd3.de•
- **chill**; during: ang hell↓ **Podo**
  - **stitching** pain: hell
- **cold** air agg.: aq-mar↓
  - **shooting** pain: aq-mar skp7•
- **cramping**: des-ac rbp6 fum rly1*• verb
- **cutting** pain: **Alum** bg2* bell bg2 caust cedr k* con bg2 graph h2 hep hir rsj4• hydr k* manc med mur-ac bg2 ph-ac k* plb bg1 puls bg2 tell
  - **paralyzed**; as if: graph h2
- **dislocated**; as if: alum bg2 *Ambr* b7a.de *Arn* b7.de* lach bg2 mang bg2 puls b7a.de **Rhus-t** b7.de*
- **drawing** pain: acon k* agar aloe k* ambr b7a.de* *Arg-met* k* **Ars** k* aur-m aur-m-n *Bell* k* berb *Bry* canth k* carb-v carbn-s caul caust cham k* chel chin b7.de* coc-c coloc com con dig dios dulc k* elaps euphr graph grat hell kali-bi *Kali-c* k* kali-n k* kali-sil k2 lach lact led lyc *Mang* mez k* *Mur-ac* k* *Nat-c* k* nat-s nux-v b7.de* petr ph-ac k* phos h2 rhod *Rhus-t* k* rhus-v ruta sabad k* sec seneg k* sil stann staph stront-c k* *Sulph* k* tab thuj valer b7.de* vanil fd5.de verat b7.de* viol-o k* zinc k*
  - **cramping**: *Rhus-t*
  - **downward**: kali-bi lach mez sec seneg thuj
  - **paralyzed**; as if: bell h1 cham h1 graph k*

- **drawing** pain: ...
  - **upward**: kali-n h2 stann
- **extending** the arm agg.: lyc↓ ruta↓
  - **drawing** pain: ruta
  - **tearing** pain: lyc
- **fist**, making: sulph↓
  - **sore**: sulph h2
- **gnawing** pain: dulc k* indg k* mag-c k* phos k* puls bg2 ran-s k* rumx bg2 stront-c k*
- **gout**: ars-h caust k* kali-i
- **hang** down; letting arms:
  - **agg.**: ang↓
    - **pressing** pain: ang h1
  - **amel.**: rat↓
    - **tearing** pain: rat
- **jerking** pain: rhus-t k*
  - **downward**: sulph h2
- **knitting**, while: mag-c↓
  - **tearing** pain: mag-c
- **leaning** on elbow: camph
  - **pressing** pain: camph k*
- **lifting** agg.: sulph↓
  - **sore**: sulph
- **lying**:
  - **agg.**: carb-an kreos nat-c phos
  - **side**; on | **left**:
    - **agg.**: *Phos*↓
      - **tearing** pain: *Phos*
  - **painless** side:
    - **agg.**: nux-v
      - **boring** pain: nux-v
- **motion**:
  - **agg.**: agn ambr tsm1 **Bry** k* *Calc-s* *Carbn-s* chin↓ clem↓ *Coloc*↓ cycl↓ dulc fd4.de graph↓ *Guaj* hydr↓ kali-bi kali-s↓ led lyc↓ mag-c↓ mand rsj7• med↓ plb prun↓ rhus-t↓ ruta fd4.de sil↓ spong fd4.de staph↓ streptoc↓ sulph thuj↓ ust vanil fd5.de
    - **aching**: hydr prun
    - **cutting** pain: med
    - **drawing** pain: **Bry** k* *Coloc* k* rhus-t k* sil staph k*
    - **pressing** pain: agn k* dulc fd4.de led k* sulph k*
    - **sore**: clem cycl h1 streptoc rly4•
    - **stitching** pain: kali-s fd4.de mag-c med hr1 ruta fd4.de spong vanil fd5.de
    - **tearing** pain: chin graph lyc sil thuj
  - **amel.**: am-m↓ *Arg-met* *Aur-m-n* bell-p sp1* bism carb-v↓ castm↓ cocc↓ dulc k* graph↓ *Lyc* mez ol-an↓ ran-a↓ **Rhus-t** **Sulph**↓ ust↓ vanil fd5.de
    - **aching**: ol-an ust
    - **boring** pain: dulc
    - **drawing** pain: carb-v h2 dulc k* graph mez ran-a a1 *Rhus-t*
    - **pressing** pain: aur-m-n k* bism mez k*
    - **sore**: aur-m-n
    - **stitching** pain: arg-met vanil fd5.de
    - **tearing** pain: am-m aur-m-n castm cocc h1 *Lyc* **Rhus-t** **Sulph** vanil fd5.de
  - **arm**; of:
    - **agg.**: ang↓
      - **sore**: ang h1
- **pain** in side, with: fl-ac k*
- **paralyzed**; as if: ambr b7a.de ang b7a.de* arg-met b7.de bell b4.de* *Bry* caps b7.de* cham k* cina b7.de* cocc b7.de* graph k* lyss mez b4.de* prun k* sabin b7.de* samb b7.de* sars bg2 staph b7.de* stront-c b4.de* valer b7.de*
- **paroxysmal**: kreos rat
- **pinching** pain: bufo-s merc-i-f k* prun k*
- **pressing** pain: acon k* agar k* agn k* alum bg2 ang k* arg-met b7.de* aur-m-n k* camph k* *Caust* clem k* coc-c coloc k* cop k* dig k* digin a1 dulc fd4.de gins k* graph k* hell k* hep k* hyos b7.de* indg k* iod k* *Led* k* lyc h2* mang h2 mez k* nat-s k* nit-s-d a1 nux-v b7.de* podo fd3.de• rat ruta k* sabad b7.de sabin bg2 sacch-a fd2.de• *Sars* k* spong k* symph fd3.de• ter k* tong a1 verat k* verb h* zinc k*
  - **paralyzed**; as if: graph h2
  - **prickling** pain: verat k*
- **pressing** together: nat-s bg2
- **pressure**:
  - **amel.**: aq-mar↓ gink-b sbd1•
    - **shooting** pain: aq-mar skp7•
- **pronation**, on: sars sma
- **pulsating** pain: des-ac rbp6
- **raising** arm agg.: graph↓ ozone↓ rat↓
  - **stitching** pain: ozone sde2•
  - **tearing** pain: graph rat
- **rash**; disappearance of: *Lept*
- **rest** agg.: aq-mar↓
  - **shooting** pain: aq-mar skp7•
- **resting** on arm: ang↓
  - **sore**: ang h1
- **rheumatic**: acon k* aesc k2 ammc k* ant-t k* ars k* bacls-7 pte1*• bapt *Bry* calc k* carbn-s caust↓ *Colch* coloc cupr euphr↓ *Ferr* form gnaph mtf11 grat guaj k* ham fd3.de• hydr hyos mtf11 hyper k* iris *Kali-bi* k* kali-m k2 kalm k* lach k* lob k* *Lyc*↓ mag-s mez nat-ar *Nat-c* nicc prun ran-b **Rhus-t**↓ rhus-v k* sal-ac k* sep k* syc pte1* tub k2 ust zinc k*
  - **right**: ambr mtf11 morg-g fmm1•
  - **left**: lavand-a ctl1• tab mtf11
  - **drawing** pain: caust euphr k* mez *Rhus-t* zinc k*
  - **pressing** pain: zinc k*
  - **tearing** pain: *Ars* *Calc* *Lyc* **Rhus-t**
- **riding**; after: verat k*
- **rubbing**:
  - **amel.**: phos↓ vanil↓ *Zinc*↓
    - **tearing** pain: phos h2 vanil fd5.de *Zinc*
- **scraping** pain: coc-c
- **shooting** pain: acon agath-a nl2• aq-mar skp7• bell *Calc-p* galeoc-c-h gms1• naja plb tarent tep trom
  - **alternating** with | **Shoulder**; shooting in (See shoulders - shooting - alternating - elbow)
- **sitting** agg.: gins↓ phos plect↓ *Rhus-t*↓ ruta fd4.de sulph↓
  - **drawing** pain: plect a1 *Rhus-t* sulph k*
  - **gnawing** pain: phos
  - **pressing** pain: gins k*
- **sleep**:
  - **siesta**:
    - **after**:
      - **agg.**: graph↓
        - **pressing** pain: graph k*
- **sore**: agar all-c alumn am-c ang k* asaf aur-m-n bar-c beryl tpw5 bov k* brom calc-p camph carb-an bg2 *Carb-v* caust k* cedr cic bg2 cinnb clem colch con crot-c sk4• *Crot-h* bg2 cycl dros k* dulc k* ham fd3.de• hep ind iod lach led mag-s merc-i-f nat-s *Ol-j* phos k* plat h2* puls k* ruta k* stann bg2 sul-ac k* *Sulph* k* symph fd3.de• tell ter thuj k* valer b7.de* verat k* zinc
  - **strained**; as if: beryl tpw5
- **sour** food agg.: aq-mar↓
  - **shooting** pain: aq-mar skp7•
- **splinter**; as from a | **glass**; of: hydrog srj2*
- **sprained**; as if: *Ambr* cur ferr-m gels lach mang nicc puls tab tell
- **squeezed**; as if: aur bg2 chel bg2 dros b7.de* kreos bg2 plat bg2 rhus-t bg2 *Ruta* b7a.de spong bg2 verb bg2
- **stiffness**; with: am-c bg2 ang bg2 *Kali-c* bg2 *Lyc* bg2 sep bg2

- **stitching** pain: acon k* agar aloe alum k* alum-p k2 alum-sil k2 am-c k* ammc androc srj1• apis k* *Arg-met Asaf* k* aster bell k* berb bov k* brom *Bry* k* calc *Calc-p* calc-s calc-sil k2 caps k* carb-an bg2 carbn-s k2 caust cedr cham chel chin b7.de* coc-c cocc b7.de* colch coloc b4.de* com con k* cupr dulc fd4.de euphr a1 eupi falco-pe nl2• graph grat k* guare ham fd3.de• hell k* hep hura hydr indg iris kali-bi k* kali-c k* kali-n k* kali-s fd4.de kalm kola stb3• kreos b7a.de laur k* lyc k* mag-c k* mag-m k* meny b7.de* *Merc* k* mez mur-ac k* naja nat-m bg2 nux-m b7.de* phos k* phys plb ran-s b7.de* raph rhod k* ruta fd4.de sabin b7.de* sars k* *Sep* sil *Spig* k* spong k* stry symph fd3.de• tab tarax k* tep ter ther *Thuj* k* tritic-vg fd5.de trom valer b7.de* vanil fd5.de viol-t k* zinc k* [tax jsj7]
  - **burning**: *Arg-met*
  - **downward**: acon bov caps cupr *Guaj* thuj
  - **stinging**: arg-met berb sil
- **straightening** out the arm in front of him: am-c
- **stretching** | **arm**:
  - **agg.**: hep k* kali-c mez ↓ puls k* ruta symph fd3.de•
    - **pressing** pain: ruta
    - **stitching** pain: mez
  - **limbs**:
    - **agg.**: mand ↓
      - **cramping**: mand rsj7•
- **taking** hold of something: **Calc** ↓
  - **tearing** pain: **Calc**
- **tearing** pain: acon k* agar k* *Alum* k* alum-p k2 alum-sil k2 am-c k* am-m ambr k* ant-t h7.de* arg-met arg-n **Ars** k* ars-h *Ars-l* ars-s-f k2 **Aur** k* aur-ar k2 aur-m-n bar-c k* bell bg2 *Berb* **Bov** k* bry k* cact *Calc* calc-i k2 calc-sil k2 canth b7.de* caps bg2 carb-an bg2 *Carbn-s* *Caust* k* chin k* *Chinin-ar* cina k* clem coc-c cocc b7.de* colch k* coloc con k* croc k* cycl *Erig* bg2 euphr k* graph *Grat* k* hyper indg **Iod** k* **Kali-ar** kali-bi k* **Kali-c** k* kali-i *Kali-n* k* kali-p kali-sil k2 kalm *Lachn* lact laur b7.de* led k* **Lyc** k* mag-c k* mag-m k* mag-s *Merc* k* *Mez* k* mur-ac k* nat-c k* nat-p *Nat-s* nicc nit-ac k* nux-m b7.de* par k* ph-ac k* phel *Phos* k* psor puls k* ran-b b7.de* rat **Rhus-t** k* rhus-v ruta k* sabin bg2 sars k* sep sil k* spong k* stann bg2 staph bg2 *Stront-c* k* sul-i k2 **Sulph** k* symph fd3.de• tab tarax bg2 tell tep thuj til valer b7.de* vanil fd5.de verb k* *Zinc* k*
  - **alternating** with | **Shoulder**; tearing in (See shoulders - tearing - alternating - elbow)
  - **cramping**: aur h2
  - **downward**: am-c berb colch kali-bi kalm lyc merc nat-c nicc nit-ac rhus-t rhus-v ruta sulph h2 thuj til zinc h2
  - **twitching**: rhus-t h1
  - **upward**: sulph h2 zinc h2
- **tendon** snapped from place, as if: sars sma
- **tomatoes**:
  - **agg.**: aq-mar ↓
    - **shooting** pain: aq-mar skp7•
- **touch** agg.: ambr calc-p cycl ↓ dros ↓ dulc k* gink-b sbd1• hyos k* mang a1 ph-ac k* sil ↓ staph a1
  - **drawing** pain: sil
  - **sore**: cycl h1 dros h1 dulc h2
- **turning** agg.: tab ↓
  - **drawing** pain: tab k*
- **twinging**: carb-an k*
- **ulcerative** pain: carb-an bg2 cic b7.de* *Crot-h* bg2 dros b7.de* plat bg2 stann bg2 sul-ac bg2
- **walking**:
  - **after**:
    - **agg.**: acon ↓ acon-c a1 tell ↓ valer k*
      - **pressing** pain: acon k*
      - **sore**: tell
  - **agg.**: ang ↓ bell ↓ crot-c ↓ merc ↓
    - **cutting** pain: bell
    - **pressing** pain: ang h1
    - **sore**: crot-c sk4•
    - **stitching** pain: merc
- **walking**: ...
  - **air** agg.; in open: anac ↓ con ↓
    - **pressing** pain: anac
    - **tearing** pain: con
  - **amel.**: gins ↓
    - **pressing** pain: gins
- **wandering** pain: cact
- **warm** applications:
  - **amel.**: aq-mar ↓
    - **shooting** pain: aq-mar skp7•
- **warmth**:
  - **agg.**: *Guaj*
  - **amel.**: bell-p sp1* *Caust* **Rhus-t** symph fd3.de•
    - **pressing** pain: *Caust*
    - **tearing** pain: caust **Rhus-t**
- **weather** agg.; wet: erig vml3•
  - **aching**: erig
- **wind** agg.: carb-v ↓
  - **drawing** pain: carb-v k*
- **yawning**; with: mang ↓
  - **dislocated**; as if: mang h2

▽ • **extending** to:
  - **Axilla**: **Ars** ↓
    - **drawing** pain: **Ars**
    - **tearing** pain: *Ars*
  - **Finger**:
    - **Fourth**: aesc arund ham fd3.de• jatr-c kali-p fd1.de• lyc phyt puls seneg
    - **Tip**: aq-mar skp7•
  - **Fingers**: am-c ↓ am-m ↓ bov ↓ cupr ↓ kalm ↓ nat-c ↓ plb ↓ puls ↓ thuj ↓
    - **shooting** pain: plb thuj
    - **stitching** pain: bov cupr thuj
    - **tearing** pain: am-c am-m kalm nat-c puls thuj
  - **Forearm**: aur-m-n ↓ dios ↓ led ↓ verb ↓ xan ↓
    - **aching**: dios xan
    - **pressing** pain: aur-m-n verb h
    - **sore**: led
  - **Forearm**; middle of: mag-c ↓
    - **tearing** pain: mag-c h2
  - **Hand**: am-c ↓ berb ↓ camph ↓ carc fd2.de• kali-bi k* lach k* merc ↓ nicc phos ↓ tarent k* xan ↓
    - **dull** pain: xan c1
    - **pressing** pain: camph h1
    - **tearing** pain: am-c berb kali-bi merc phos h2
  - **Shoulder**: colch ↓ cycl k* indg ↓ lachn ↓ phos rhus-v ↓ ruta fd4.de still k* symph fd3.de• xan ↓
    - **boring** pain: phos
    - **dull** pain: xan c1
    - **gnawing** pain: phos
    - **stitching** pain: colch indg
    - **tearing** pain: lachn phos rhus-v
  - **Wrist**: acon ↓ ars k* **Calc** ↓ colch ↓ dulc ↓ guaj kali-n k* ketogl-ac ↓ lyc ↓ melal-alt gya4 nicc ↓ nit-ac ↓ pert-vc ↓ peti a1 phyt prun rhus-t sulph ↓ vanil fd5.de
    - **drawing** pain: dulc h2 guaj h2 rhus-t sulph h2
    - **dull** pain: ketogl-ac rly4•
    - **shooting** pain: acon *Guaj*
    - **stitching** pain: acon *Guaj* pert-vc vk9
    - **tearing** pain: **Calc** colch guaj h2 lyc nicc nit-ac **Rhus-t**

○ • **About** the: gels ↓
  - **aching**: gels
- **Above**: *Calc* ↓ *Caust* ↓
  - **pressing** pain: *Calc* b4a.de *Caust* b4.de*
- **Above**; just:
  - **bending** arms agg.: caps ↓

- **Above**; just – **bending** arms agg.: ...
  - **sore**: caps fkm1•
- **Bends** of elbow: alumn anac k* arg-met asaf↓ aur-m-n k* bar-c↓ canth↓ carb-an k* caust k* chel chin↓ cina clem k* coc-c↓ cocc k* coloc↓ con↓ gels k* glon graph k* grat↓ ham fd3.de• hell↓ hep hura hyos k* iod k* **Kali-c**↓ kali-n↓ laur↓ led↓ lyc k* merc-i-f k* mur-ac↓ nat-c k* nat-s↓ olnd↓ plb k* *Puls* k* *Rat*↓ rhus-v↓ sep↓ spig k* still k* sulph↓ tarent↓ tep↓ teucr↓ thuj k* tritic-vg fd5.de valer k* verat k* zinc↓
  - **right**: canth↓ merc-i-f↓ rat↓
    - **stitching** pain: merc-i-f rat
    - **tearing** pain: canth
  - **morning**: alum k* kali-c↓ lyc k* merc-i-f k*
    - **stitching** pain: kali-c
  - **aching**: arg-met clem k*
  - **boring** pain: led k*
  - **burning**: kali-n k* laur k* led k* rat k* rhus-v k* sulph k* tep k* teucr k*
  - **chill**; before: rat↓
    - **stitching** pain: rat
  - **cutting** pain: con k* mur-ac k*
  - **drawing** pain: arg-met *Caust* chin h1 hell kali-n k* *Puls Rat* thuj k* valer k* verat k*
  - **extending** the arm:
    - **agg.**: hep↓
      - **sore**: hep
    - **amel.**: rat↓
      - **drawing** pain: rat
  - **flexion**, on: mur-ac↓
    - **cutting** pain: mur-ac
  - **hang** down agg.; letting arms: still k*
  - **motion**:
    - **agg.**: hura plb k* *Puls* k*
    - **amel.**: coc-c k*
  - **paralyzed**; as if: cina k* cocc k*
  - **paroxysmal**: plb k*
  - **pressing** pain: anac k* arg-met h1 aur-m-n k* carb-an h2 clem h2 hyos k* iod k* rat sep h2
  - **pressure**:
    - **amel.**: arg-met
      - **aching**: arg-met
  - **rest** agg.: coc-c↓ coloc↓
    - **stitching** pain: coc-c coloc
  - **sore**: caust valer zinc
  - **stitching** pain: asaf coc-c coloc grat kali-c led merc-i-f nat-c rat *Spig* tarent tritic-vg fd5.de
  - **stretching**:
    - **arm**:
      - **agg.**: alumn **Caust** k* clem graph *Hep Puls* thuj
        - **aching**: clem k*
        - **tearing** pain: hep
      - **amel.**: rat↓
        - **pressing** pain: rat
    - **upper** arm: clem↓
      - **pressing** pain: clem h2*
  - **tearing** pain: bar-c canth k* **Kali-c** k* laur k* nat-s k* olnd k* rat sep h2 zinc k*
  - **touch** agg.: nat-c k*
  - **walking** agg.: aur-m-n↓ gels k*
    - **pressing** pain: aur-m-n k*
  - **writing**:
    - **after**: gels k*
    - **agg.**: valer↓
      - **drawing** pain: valer
      - **sore**: valer
  - **extending** to:
    - **Fingers**: hura
      - **First** finger: psil ft1
    - **Palm**: carb-an k*

- **Elbows** – **Bends** of elbow – **extending** to: ...
    - **Shoulder**: plb k*
    - **Tip** of elbow: grat↓
      - **stitching** pain: grat
- **Bones**: sil↓
  - **drawing** pain: sil k*
- **Condyles**: ant-t↓ arg-met↓ arg-mur↓ brom↓ coc-c↓ indg↓ mang↓ merc↓ sabin↓
  - **drawing** pain: arg-met arg-mur a1 coc-c k*
  - **stitching** pain: ant-t brom indg mang a1 merc sabin
- **Olecranon**: agar↓ alum k* am-c arg-met↓ arg-n↓ bov↓ bry↓ calc↓ carb-an k* caust k* chel↓ chinin-ar coc-c↓ hep k* kali-n k* lact↓ lyc↓ mur-ac↓ nat-c↓ nat-m↓ ph-ac↓ raph c2 rhod k* sep↓ spig↓ spong k* stann↓ valer↓ verat k*
  - **night**: sep↓
    - **stitching** pain: sep k*
  - **aching**: spong k*
  - **bending** arms agg.: bry↓ stann↓
    - **sore**: stann
    - **stitching** pain: bry
  - **boring** pain: alum k* am-c caust k*
  - **burning**: chel k* ph-ac k*
  - **drawing** pain: carb-an k* lact k*
  - **motion** agg.: hep k*
    - **aching**: hep k*
  - **pressing** pain: hep h2
  - **rest** agg.: agar↓ arg-n↓
    - **stitching** pain: arg-n k*
    - **tearing** pain: agar k*
  - **sore**: carb-an h2 hep h2 stann
  - **stitching** pain: agar k* arg-met arg-n k* bry k* calc k* coc-c k* mur-ac k* nat-m k* sep k* spig k* spong k*
  - **tearing** pain: bov k* lyc k* mur-ac h2 nat-c k* valer k*
  - **extending** to:
    - **Bend** of elbow: nat-c↓
      - **tearing** pain: nat-c h2
- **Posterior** surface: laur↓ mag-c↓ sabad↓ thuj↓
  - **motion**:
    - **amel.**: sabad↓
      - **stitching** pain: sabad k*
  - **stitching** pain: laur k* sabad k* thuj k*
  - **tearing** pain: mag-c k*
- **Spot**; in a small: ozone↓
  - **stitching** pain: ozone sde2•
- **Spots**; in: galeoc-c-h↓
  - **shooting** pain: galeoc-c-h gms1•

- **Externally**: carb-an↓
  - **burning**: carb-an k*
- **Feet**: abrot acon↓ act-sp mrr1 aesc↓ agar k* agn b7a.de ail all-c↓ all-s↓ allox↓ aloe *Alum* alum-p k2 alum-sil k2 alumn *Am-c* bro1 am-m k* ambr ammc↓ *Anac* anag anders↓ androc↓ ang↓ ant-c ant-t k* *Apis* aq-mar↓ *Arg-met*↓ arg-n↓ *Arn Ars* ars-h ars-i ars-s-f↓ arum-d↓ arum-t arund asaf asc-t aster *Aur* aur-ar↓ *Aur-m* aur-m-n↓ aur-s↓ aza↓ bacls-7 pte1*• bamb-a stb2.de• bapt↓ bar-c↓ bar-s k2 bell berb bism blatta-o borx↓ *Bov*↓ bran↓ *Brom* c2* *Bry*↓ bufo↓ cadm-met↓ cain↓ *Calc Calc-caust* bro1 calc-f↓ *Calc-p*↓ calc-s calc-sil k2 calo c2 *Camph*↓ *Cann-s* cann-xyz↓ *Canth*↓ caps↓ carb-ac carb-an↓ *Carb-v* carbn-o *Carbn-s*↓ *Caul* k* *Caust* k* cedr↓ *Cham*↓ **Chel**↓ *Chin* chinin-ar↓ *Chinin-s*↓ choc↓ cimic↓ *Cina*↓ cinnb↓ clem↓ cob coc-c↓ cocc coff colch k* *Coloc* colocin↓ com↓ con cop↓ corn↓ croc↓ crot-c crot-h crot-t *Cupr Cur*↓ *Cycl* bro1 cypra-eg↓ daph↓ des-ac↓ *Dig* dios dirc dor↓ dros↓ *Dulc* eug↓ euon↓ eup-per euph↓ euphr↓ fago ferr k* ferr-ar ferr-i ferr-ma↓ *Ferr-p*↓ *Fl-ac*↓ galeoc-c-h↓ gels ger-i↓ *Graph* bro1 *Guaj* gymno↓ ham fd3.de• hell helo↓ *Hep*↓ hip-ac↓ hipp↓ hir↓ hura hyos b7.de* hyper↓ ign↓ indg↓ inul br1 iod ip↓ iris↓ jal↓ jatr-c kali-ar↓ kali-bi bg2 **Kali-c**↓ kali-i bro1 *Kali-n*↓ kali-p↓ kali-s fd4.de kali-sil↓ kalm ketogl-ac rly4• kreos↓ lac-ac↓ lac-d↓ lac-leo↓ *Lach* lachn↓ lat-m↓ laur↓ *Led* k* lil-t↓ *Lith-c Lyc* m-aust b7a.de *Mag-c*↓ mag-m↓ mag-p↓ manc↓

- **Feet**: ...
mang↓ *Mang-act* bro1 *Mang-m*↓ **Med**↓ meli↓ meny↓ meph↓ *Merc* merc-c merc-i-f *Merc-i-r*↓ merl↓ *Mez* mill mosch mur-ac myric↓ naja↓ nat-ar k* nat-c *Nat-m* nat-p↓ *Nat-s* nat-sil↓ neon↓ nit-ac k* nux-m *Nux-v* *Ol-an*↓ ol-j↓ olnd↓ op↓ osm ox-ac↓ oxal-a↓ ozone↓ pant-ac↓ par↓ *Petr* petr-ra↓ *Ph-ac* bro1 *Phel*↓ phos *Phyt* k* pic-ac↓ pip-m plac-s↓ plan plat *Plb* plect↓ plut-n↓ pneu↓ podo polyg-h polyp-p↓ positr↓ prot↓ prun↓ psil ft1 psor ptel↓ puls ran-b c1* *Ran-s*↓ raph↓ *Rat*↓ rauw↓ rheum↓ *Rhod* **Rhus-t** k* rhus-v rumx *Ruta* k* sabin k* sal-fr↓ samb↓ sang sanic↓ sars sec sel senec↓ sep bro1 *Sil* k* sol-ni spig spong squil↓ stann *Staph* still↓ stram stront-c b4.de* stry suis-pan↓ *Sul-ac*↓ sul-i k2 sulph k* syc fmm1• symph↓ *Syph* tab↓ tanac↓ tarax↓ tarent tax-br oss1• tep↓ ter tere-la↓ tet bro1 teucr thal-xyz srj8• *Thuj* k* til↓ trios↓ tritic-vg fd5.de trom↓ tub↓ upa bro1 urol-h↓ urt-u tl1 ust valer k2* vanil fd5.de *Verat* verat-v verb↓ vesp↓ vinc↓ viol-t↓ vip↓ wies xan↓ zinc k* zinc-p↓ zing↓
  - **alternating** sides: *Lac-c* nat-p
  - **right**: aids nl2• bapt↓ *Chel*↓ cypr hr1 dulc fd4.de iris↓ kalm lith-c mand rsj7• mez↓ myos-a↓ nit-ac↓ plut-n srj7• *Rat*↓ sal-al blc1• sep↓ sulph↓ tere-la↓ vanil fd5.de visc↓
    - **aching**: visc c1
    - **burning**: mez bg1 sulph bg1 tere-la rly4•
    - **cramping**: mand rsj7•
    - **drawing** pain: bapt a1 *Chel* dulc fd4.de
    - **shooting** pain: iris a1
    - **sore**: myos-a rly4• sal-al blc1•
    - **stitching** pain | **needles**; as from: sal-al blc1•
    - **tearing** pain: nit-ac h2 *Rat* sep h2 sulph h2
  - **left**: ail androc srj1• ars↓ asc-t a1 borx↓ cham↓ coloc↓ crot-h des-ac↓ dulc fd4.de ephe-si↓ ferr-i↓ hura↓ hyper kali-p↓ kali-s↓ kola stb3• melal-alt↓ mur-ac murx nat-m↓ puls↓ ruta fd4.de sang sanic↓ stroph-s↓ trios↓ vanil fd5.de
    - **burning**: borx bg1 cham bg1 coloc bg1 des-ac rbp6 dulc fd4.de hura bg1 kali-p fd1.de• sang bg1
    - **cramping**: melal-alt gya4 trios rsj11•
    - **cutting** pain: trios rsj11•
    - **drawing** pain: ars h2 ferr-i k2 nat-m h2
    - **paralyzed**; as if: hyper
    - **shooting** pain: stroph-s sp1
    - **sore**: kola stb3•
    - **sprained**; as if: hyper sanic
    - **stitching** pain: asc-t a1 dulc fd4.de ephe-si hsj1• kali-p fd1.de• kali-s fd4.de
      - **followed** by | **right**: psil ft1
    - **tearing** pain: ars h2 nat-m h2 puls h1
    - **walking** agg.: mag-c ptk1 nat-m↓
      - **cramping**: nat-m h2
    - **Metatarsus** | **motion**:
      - **amel.**: hydrog↓
        - **twinging**: hydrog srj2•
      - **waking**; on: hydrog↓
        - **twinging**: hydrog srj2•
  - **23 h**:
    - **lying** on the other side: com↓
      - **drawing** pain: com
  - **morning**: ang↓ ars↓ *Brucel* sa3• cench k2 dios dulc fd4.de kali-bi↓ nit-ac↓ ph-ac↓ **Rhus-t** ruta fd4.de spong fd4.de sulph tritic-vg fd5.de vanil fd5.de
    - **8 h** until afternoon: coloc
    - **bed** agg.; in: hep↓ *Nat-s*↓
      - **burning**: hep k* *Nat-s*
    - **drawing** pain: ang k* ars h2 kali-bi k* ph-ac h2 tritic-vg fd5.de
    - **lying**:
      - **amel.**: mag-c↓
        - **sore**: mag-c
    - **rising** agg.: **Rhus-t** vanil fd5.de
    - **sprained**; as if: **Rhus-t**
    - **stepping** agg.: puls↓
      - **sore**: puls

- **Feet – morning**: ...
    - **tearing** pain: ars h2 nit-ac h2
    - **waking**; on: dulc fd4.de mag-c↓ nat-s↓ *Sulph* tarent thuj↓ tritic-vg fd5.de
      - **sore**: mag-c nat-s
      - **stitching** pain: thuj
  - **forenoon**:
    - **10 h**: sil↓
      - **stitching** pain: sil
    - **11 h**: hura
  - **noon**: am-c↓ arund hura↓
    - **burning**: am-c k* hura
    - **left** one burning while the other is cold: hura↓
      - **burning**: hura
  - **afternoon**: com↓ dulc fd4.de gard-j vlr2• ham↓ kali-bi↓ lith-c mez phos ptel↓ rhus-v ruta fd4.de spong fd4.de vanil fd5.de
    - **aching**: ptel
    - **drawing** pain: com vanil fd5.de
    - **sore**: phos
    - **stitching** pain: dulc fd4.de ham fd3.de• mez k* ruta fd4.de
    - **tearing** pain: kali-bi
  - **evening**: acon all-c *Arn*↓ ars-h bamb-a stb2.de• calc↓ caust↓ dulc fd4.de ferr-m fl-ac graph↓ ham fd3.de• hipp↓ lach↓ led lyc mag-c *Nat-s*↓ nat-sil↓ ph-ac↓ phos puls ruta fd4.de sang↓ sil spong fd4.de sulph tritic-vg fd5.de vanil fd5.de
    - **bed** agg.; in: ars↓ calc↓ hep↓ merc↓ stront-c↓ **Sulph**↓ tritic-vg↓
      - **burning**: calc hep merc stront-c **Sulph** tritic-vg fd5.de
      - **drawing** pain: ars k* hep h2
    - **burning**: calc k* dulc fd4.de *Nat-s* nat-sil fd3.de• ruta fd4.de sang k* *Sulph* k* tritic-vg fd5.de
    - **cramping**: hipp jl2
    - **drawing** pain: caust k* dulc fd4.de ph-ac h2 ruta fd4.de
    - **pressing** pain: dulc fd4.de fl-ac lach led ruta fd4.de
    - **sore**: *Arn* mag-c h2
    - **tearing** pain: graph lach
    - **walking** agg.: agar↓
      - **drawing** pain: agar
  - **night**: agar↓ *Ars*↓ ars-met↓ calc↓ caul cham coloc↓ dulc fd4.de hep↓ kali-c lac-c↓ lyc *Merc*↓ *Mez* *Nat-c*↓ phos plb↓ rhod↓ ruta fd4.de *Sep*↓ sil spong stront-c **Sulph**↓ syc pte1*• *Syph* tritic-vg fd5.de vanil fd5.de verat
    - **bed** agg.; in: nat-p↓ **Sulph**↓
      - **burning**: nat-p k* **Sulph**
      - **menses**; during: nat-p↓
        - **burning**: nat-p k*
    - **burning**: ars-met coloc dulc fd4.de lac-c *Nat-c* ruta fd4.de *Sep* k* sil k* spong fd4.de **Sulph** k* tritic-vg fd5.de
    - **drawing** pain: agar k* calc k*
    - **sitting** agg.: olnd↓
      - **aching**: olnd
    - **sleep** agg.; during: ars-met↓
      - **burning**: ars-met
    - **sore**: plb *Sulph*
    - **stitching** pain: dulc fd4.de phos k* ruta fd4.de sulph h2 vanil fd5.de
    - **tearing** pain: *Ars* hep *Merc* phos rhod *Sulph*
    - **waking**; on: bar-c↓
      - **aching**: bar-c
  - **accompanied** by | **sciatica** (See lower limbs - sciatic - accompanied - foot)
  - **aching**: agar bro1 allox sp1 *Am-m* bro1 ang arn bro1 aza bro1 bov brom bro1 bry calc caust clem *Coloc* *Cur* dios dros bro1 euon bro1 fago galeoc-c-h gms1• ger-i rly4• gymno ham hir rsj4• *Kali-c* kalm lac-ac lat-m bnm6• laur bro1 led bro1 mez nit-ac olnd oxal-a rly4• petr phos phyt k* prun bro1 ptel *Rhus-t* bro1 sal-fr sle1• staph h1 still suis-pan rly4• *Sulph* vanil fd5.de verat k* vip
  - **air** agg.; in open: **Caust**↓
    - **drawing** pain: **Caust**

- **air** agg.; in open: ...
  - ⁝ **tearing** pain: *Caust*
- **arthritic**: arg-n ↓
  - ⁝ **drawing** pain: arg-n k*
- **ascending** agg.: **Led** mag-c
  - ⁝ **sore**: mag-c h2
- **bathing**: petr ↓
  - ⁝ **sore**: petr hr1
- **bending** agg.: coff sel
- **blow**; pain as from a: hell b7.de* ign b7.de* nux-m b7.de*
- **boring** pain: aesc ang *Bell* k* bufo *Caust* cocc coloc b4.de* con bg2 merc mur-ac *Ran-s* k* spig b7.de* sulph *Zinc* k*
- **broken**; as if: hep bg1* kali-bi k* kali-c k* lac-d psor symph fd3.de• zinc bg2*
- **burning**: (↗*Heat - feet - burning*) agar k* alum b4a.de alum-sil k2 *Am-c* k* anac k* anders zzc1• ant-c k* apis k* arg-met b7.de *Arn* k* *Ars* k* ars-s-f k2 aster aur-m aza bro1 *Bell* b4a.de *Berb* borx b4a.de* bov b4.de bran bro1 bry cadm-met sp1 *Calc* k* calc-f sp1 *Calc-s* k* cann-s caps carb-v b4.de *Carbn-s* *Caust* k* cham k* chel chin chinin-ar *Cocc* k* coloc colocin c2 con corn k* croc des-ac rbp6 dulc k* eup-per fago *Graph* k* ham fd3.de• helo bro1 *Hep* k* hip-ac sp1 hyos ign b7.de kali-ar *Kali-c* k* kali-i kali-p *Kali-s* kreos *Lach* k* lachn laur b7.de led k* lil-t *Lyc* k* mag-m b4.de **Med** k* *Merc* k* merl *Mez* k* mur-ac b4.de nat-ar *Nat-c* k* *Nat-m* k* *Nat-s* nat-sil fd3.de• neon srj5• *Nit-ac* k* nux-v b7.de ox-ac petr k* *Ph-ac* k* *Phos* k* phyt plan *Puls* k* rat rauw sp1 rhus-t rhus-v ruta b7.de* sabin k2 sang sanic mrr1 sars b4a.de *Sec* k* *Sep* k* *Sil* k* *Spig* k* spong fd4.de squil k* *Stann* k* *Staph* *Stram* k* stront-c k* **Sulph** k* tarax k* tere-la rly4• thal-xyz srj8• thuj trios rsj11• tritic-vg fd5.de vesp *Zinc* k* zinc-p k2 zing
  - ⁝ **corrosive**: ruta tl1 sulph tl1
- **burrowing**: *Asaf* b7.de* bell b4.de* merc b4.de* mur-ac b4.de* nux-m b7.de* *Rhod* b4.de* spig b7.de*
- **chilblains**; as from: aq-mar rbp6 berb borx caust cham nux-v
- **chill**:
  - ⁝ **after**: *Cham* ↓
    - ⁝ **tearing** pain: *Cham*
  - ⁝ **during**: *Chinin-s* ↓ cupr *Eup-per* ↓
    - ⁝ **cutting** pain: *Chinin-s*
    - ⁝ **stitching** pain: *Eup-per*
- **coffee** amel.; after: calo
- **cold**:
  - ⁝ **air**:
    - ⁝ **amel.**: med ↓
      - . **burning**: med jl2
- **coldness**; with external: *Lach* ↓
  - ⁝ **burning**: *Lach* b7a.de
- **contracting**: chin h1 kali-s fd4.de ruta fd4.de
- **covered** in bed agg.; on being: cham ↓
  - ⁝ **tearing** pain: cham
- **cramping**: hipp jl2 pneu jl2
- **cutting** pain: abrot bro1 *Act-sp* bro1 alum k* ambr k* apis bro1 ars k* bamb-a stb2.de• bufo bg2 calc k* cedr bro1 *Chinin-s* coloc k* dulc k* ger-i rly4• led bro1 lyc k* mag-m k* meny b7.de* mur-ac k* *Nat-c* k* osm pant-ac rly4• plat k* plut-n srj7• sep bro1 thuj k* urol-h rwt•
  - ⁝ **transversely** across: plat
- **dinner**; after: cain ↓ carbn-s
  - ⁝ **tearing** pain: cain
- **drawing** pain: agar k* alum k* am-c ammc k* *Anac* k* ang k* arg-met b7.de* arn k* *Ars* k* asaf *Aur* k* aur-ar k2 aur-m-n k* aur-s k2 bapt k* bar-c k* bell k* bism b7.de* borx bov k* bry k* calc k* camph k* cann-s k* canth carb-v k* carbn-s *Caul* k* *Caust* k* **Chel** chin k* chinin-ar chinin-s clem k* coc-c k* cocc k* colch b7.de* *Coloc* k* con k* cupr k* dig k* dios k* dros k* dulc fd4.de ferr k* ferr-i fl-ac k* ham k* hep k* hyper k* ign b7.de* indg kali-ar kali-bi k* kali-c k* kali-sil k2 kreos b7a.de* lach k* led k* *Lyc* k* *Mag-c* k* mang k* merc k* *Mez* k* mur-ac k* naja nat-c k* nat-m nat-p k* nat-s nit-ac k* nux-v k* *Ol-an* olnd k* petr k* ph-ac k* plb k* plect a1 polyp-p a1 **Puls** k* ran-b rat *Rhod* k* **Rhus-t** rhus-v k* ruta fd4.de sars k* sec k* sil k* sol-ni spong k* stann k* staph b7.de* stram b7.de* *Stront-c* k* *Sulph* k* symph fd3.de• tanac a1 tarax k* thuj k* tritic-vg fd5.de tub jl2 valer k2 vanil fd5.de verat k* vinc k* zinc k*
  - ⁝ **burning**: tarax
  - ⁝ **cramping**: arg-met chin h1 hyper nat-m h2 ph-ac
  - ⁝ **cutting** pain: bell k*
  - ⁝ **fatigue**, as from: kali-c h2
  - ⁝ **paralyzed**; as if: acon k* aur **Rhus-t** k*
  - ⁝ **paroxysmal**: coc-c k* nat-m k* ph-ac k*
  - ⁝ **pinching** pain: kali-c k*
  - ⁝ **tearing**, dragging: ars bov k*
  - ⁝ **upward**: dros led h1 nit-ac *Sil* *Spong* sulph
- **dull** pain: tritic-vg fd5.de
- **eating**; after: graph ↓
  - ⁝ **pressing** pain: graph
  - ⁝ **sore**: graph
  - ⁝ **stitching** pain: graph k*
- **excoriation**, in: phos ↓
  - ⁝ **stitching** pain: phos h2
- **exertion**:
  - ⁝ **agg.**: bar-c caust phos **Rhus-t**
  - ⁝ **amel.**: dios ↓
    - ⁝ **aching**: dios
- **exertion**; as after: alum b4a.de bar-c b4.de* *Cann-s* b7a.de led b7.de* olnd b7.de* phos b4.de*
- **fever**; during: apis ↓ nux-v b7a.de puls b7a.de
  - ⁝ **burning**: apis b7a.de
- **foot**-bath, after: calc-caust c1
- **gnawing** pain: meny b7.de* ran-s b7.de*
- **gouty**: graph ↓ *Led* k* lyc mrr1 nat-p mrr1 *Nat-s* urt-u tl1
  - ⁝ **right**: *Lyc* mrr1
  - ⁝ **left**: psor jl2
  - ⁝ **tearing** pain: graph h2
- **heat**: ran-a k*
- **jerking** pain: acon bg2 agar bg2 anac b4.de ars b4.de bar-c b4.de berb bg2 cham bg2 euphr bg2 hyos h1 kali-n mag-m bg2 petr a1 rat rhus-t bg2 rumx bg2 sec bg2 spig b7a.de stann b4a.de* staph bg2 sul-ac b4.de teucr bg2 valer bg2 zinc bg2
- **jumping** to knee: asaf ↓
  - ⁝ **pressing** pain: asaf
- **lifting** agg.: berb
- **lying** in bed agg.: *Cur* ↓
  - ⁝ **aching**: *Cur*
- **menopause**; during: sang ↓
  - ⁝ **burning**: sang
- **menses** | **before** | **agg.**: am-m bro1
  - ⁝ **during**:
    - ⁝ **agg.**: *Am-c* b4a.de am-m k* ars k* carb-v ↓ mag-c k*
      - . **burning**: carb-v b4a.de
      - . **tearing** pain: am-m
- **motion**:
  - ⁝ **agg.**: acon ars h2* aur-m k2 bar-c ↓ bry bufo calc ↓ caust cench k2 *Cham* ↓ chin ↓ coff *Guaj* *Led* nat-c ↓ nit-ac ↓ ph-ac bg1 puls sel staph ↓ sulph ↓ thuj tritic-vg fd5.de vanil fd5.de
    - ⁝ **boring** pain: bufo
    - ⁝ **cramping**: ph-ac h2
    - ⁝ **drawing** pain: nit-ac h2 vanil fd5.de
    - ⁝ **pressing** pain: staph h1
    - ⁝ **stitching** pain: bar-c bufo calc chin sulph
    - ⁝ **tearing** pain: bar-c *Cham* nat-c a1
  - ⁝ **amel.**: abrot calo cur dios guaj ↓ *Kali-c* ↓ *Kali-s* ↓ *Lyc* ↓ psor *Rhod* **Rhus-t** *Verat* verb ↓
    - ⁝ **stitching** pain: guaj *Kali-c* *Kali-s* *Lyc* *Rhus-t* verb c1

Extremities

- **motion**: ...
  - **toes**; of:
    - **agg.**: nat-c ↓
      - **tearing** pain: nat-c h2
- **paralyzed**: am-m k*
- **paralyzed**; as if: acon ang k* aur b4.de* cham k* *Chin* k* eug kalm mag-m b4.de* nat-m k* ol-an olnd k* par k* phos b4.de* *Plb* k* puls b7.de* **Rhus-t** tab
- **paroxysmal**: sec tritic-vg fd5.de
- **perspiration**:
  - **cold**:
    - **Soles**:
      - **amel.**: med ↓
        - **burning**: med jl2
  - **from**: graph ↓ **Lyc** ↓
    - **sore**: graph **Lyc**
  - **with**: *Sil* ↓
    - **burning**: *Sil*
- **pinching** pain: chin h1 hyos k* ip k* sulph h2
  - **narrow** shoes; as from: cypra-eg sde6.de•
- **placing** foot on floor: tarent ↓
  - **stitching** pain: tarent
- **pregnancy** agg.; during: phos ↓
  - **tearing** pain: phos
- **pressing** pain: *Alum* k* anac k* ang k* arg-n arn b7.de* asaf k* aur k* aur-m-n *Bell* k* bism b7.de* brom bry b7.de* caust k* cinnb cupr b7.de* cycl b7.de* dig dulc fd4.de fl-ac graph k* kali-n kali-s fd4.de lach *Led* k* lil-t lyc k* *Mang-m* mez mur-ac k* naja nat-s nux-v b7.de* olnd k* petr b4.de* *Ph-ac* k* *Plat* k* ruta fd4.de sabin b7.de* *Sars* k* spig b7.de* spong fd4.de *Stann* k* staph b7.de* stront-c k* *Sul-ac* k* thuj vanil fd5.de verat a1 verb k* viol-t b7.de*
  - **blunt** instrument; as from a: ang dulc fd4.de
  - **drawing** pain: bry staph h1
  - **inward**: lach
  - **outward**: lil-t
  - **tensive**: stront-c
  - **tight** shoes; as if from: nux-v b7.de*
- **pressure**:
  - **agg.**: cina ↓
    - **sore**: cina
  - **boot** agg.; pressure of: *Brucel* sa3• coloc bg1 nux-v bg1 vanil fd5.de
- **pressure**, like: *Cina* ↓
  - **stitching** pain: *Cina*
- **pulsating** pain: bell bg2 bufo bg2 cann-xyz bg2 ketogl-ac rly4• suis-pan rly4•
- **rest** agg.: verb ↓
  - **stitching** pain: verb c1
- **rheumatic**: *Act-sp* bro1 ant-c apis bro1 *Aur* berb bro1 calc k* *Caul* bro1 *Caust* k* colch k* crot-t ↓ cupr sst3• ferr-i franc br1 gaert pte1*• graph bro1 *Guaj* **Hep** kali-i br1 *Lach* **Led** k* lith-c k* mag-m mang-act bro1 *Merc* merc-i-r myric bro1 nat-s *Nit-ac* phos *Phyt* k* plb *Puls* bro1 ran-b bro1 *Rhod* *Rhus-t* bro1 *Ruta* k* sars stram stry zinc
  - **tearing** pain: crot-t *Graph* puls
- **riding** in a carriage, stitches from inside outward, when: *Berb* ↓
  - **stitching** pain: *Berb* k1
- **rising** agg.; after: bry ↓
  - **drawing** pain: bry k*
- **rubbing**:
  - **amel.**: zinc ↓
    - **tearing** pain: zinc h2
- **shooting** pain: arg-met aster bell daph ferr iris **Kali-c** ruta fd4.de spong fd4.de tarent xan
  - **sticking** ending in electric shocks: daph
- **shop**; girls working in a: squil ↓
  - **sore**: squil bro1*
- **sitting**:
  - **agg.**: alum *Arg-met* ↓ asaf ↓ aur-m-n carb-v ↓ chin ↓ coloc ↓ dig dulc fd4.de ham fd3.de• manc ↓ nat-c **Rhus-t** ruta fd4.de spong fd4.de stann h2 tarax valer vanil fd5.de
    - **drawing** pain: aur-m-n carb-v k* chin h1 coloc k* **Rhus-t** k* spong fd4.de valer k2 vanil fd5.de
    - **pressing** pain: aur-m-n spong fd4.de tarax
    - **sore**: *Arg-met*
    - **stitching** pain: asaf manc k*
  - **amel.**: stront-c bg1 tarax ↓
    - **drawing** pain: tarax
- **smarting**: ph-ac h2
- **sore**: agar bro1 all-c bro1* alumn ang b7.de* *Ant-c* c2* ant-t *Arg-met* arn k* arund bar-c k* bell k* berb borx bg2 bry k* calc calc-s carb-ac carb-an carb-v caust bro1 cham chin k* *Cina* clem cocc b7.de* com *Cycl* bro1 ferr ger-i rly4• *Graph* hyos jal bro1 kali-ar kali-bi k* kali-n lac-leo hrn2• laur k* led c2* lil-t **Lyc** k* mag-c mag-m k* mag-p br1 med bro1 merc *Mez* nat-c nat-m nat-s nux-v bg2 ol-j op petr bro1 ph-ac k* phos k* phyt bro1 plac-s rly4• plb puls k* ran-b rumx k* **Ruta** k* sars b4a.de* sep **Sil** k* suis-pan rly4• sul-ac b4.de* sulph thuj k* urol-h rwt• valer bro1 zinc k*
  - **paralyzed**, as if: ph-ac
  - **pebbles**; as if stepping on: hep bro1 lyc bro1
- **sprained**; as if: ang **Arn** ars bar-c berb *Bry* calc *Camph* carb-v carbn-s caust cop crot-t *Cycl* dros ferr-ma *Hep* hyper *Kalm* kreos merc nat-m nux-v petr-ra shn4• phos prot jl2 prun k* puls **Rhus-t** sanic sil sulph til valer zinc
- **squeezed**; as if: ang b7a.de* arg-met b7a.de camph b7a.de cimic bg2 olnd b7a.de verb b7a.de
- **standing** agg.: agn ↓ ang ↓ chin eup-per ger-i ↓ nat-m ↓ *Puls* rhus-v ruta fd4.de sil ↓ squil ptk1 tarax vanil fd5.de
  - **drawing** pain: chin tarax
  - **sore**: ang ger-i rly4• **Ruta**
  - **stitching** pain: agn nat-m k* *Puls* k* sil k*
- **stepping** agg.: ambr bg1 ars ↓ bell ↓ *Berb* ↓ bry calc-p ↓ carb-v ↓ caust cench k2 dulc fd4.de kali-p fd1.de• *Nat-m* ↓ positr nl2• **Ruta** tarent ↓ thuj tritic-vg fd5.de vanil fd5.de
  - **stitching** pain: ars bell h1 *Berb* k* calc-p *Nat-m* k* ruta fd4.de tarent
    - **followed** by | **numbness**: berb hr1
  - **tearing** pain: carb-v h2
- **stitching** pain: abrot br1 acon agar k* agn k* ail *Alum* k* am-c k* ambr k* *Anac* k* androc srj1• ant-c apis arg-met arg-n arn k* ars k* arum-d asaf k* aster aur k* aur-ar k2 aur-s k2 *Bamb-a* stb2.de• bar-c k* *Bell* k* berb *Bov* bry k* calc k* *Calc-p* calc-sil k2 *Canth* carb-an k* *Carb-v* k* carbn-s caust cham chel k* chin k* chinin-ar cina cocc b7.de* coff b7.de* coloc con cupr dig k* dor dulc fd4.de eup-per euph k* fago *Ferr-p* *Fl-ac* *Graph* k* *Guaj* ham fd3.de• *Hell* hep k* hura hyos hyper ign b7.de* iris kali-ar **Kali-c** k* **Kali-s** kali-sil k2 *Kalm* lyc k* mag-c k* mag-m k* manc mang meli meph *Merc* k* mez **Mur-ac** k* *Nat-c* k* nat-m k* nat-s *Nit-ac* k* *Nux-v* ol-an olnd k* ozone sde2• par k* petr k* ph-ac k* *Phel* phos k* pic-ac positr nl2• puls k* ran-b k* ran-s k* raph rheum b7.de* rhod k* rhus-t k* rhus-v ruta k* samb *Sars* k* senec *Sep* k* *Sil* k* spig spong fd4.de stann k* stront-c k* stry sul-ac k* *Sulph* k* symph fd3.de• tarax tarent *Thuj* k* tritic-vg fd5.de vanil fd5.de verb h* viol-t k* vip xan zinc k* zing
  - **asleep**; as if: lyc k*
  - **burning**: bufo coloc rhus-t *Sulph* zinc h2
  - **cramping**: cina
  - **followed** by | **numbness**: *Berb* k13
  - **rhythmical**: nat-m
  - **shocks**, ending in: daph
  - **tearing** pain: guaj sil k*
  - **twitching**: carbn-s *Cina*
  - **upward**: bar-c *Plb* ruta xan
- **storm**; during: caust ↓
  - **tearing** pain: caust
- **tearing** pain: *Agar* k* agn k* all-s alum k* alum-p k2 alum-sil k2 am-c k* am-m k* ambr k* ammc ang b7.de* ant-c *Arg-met* k* arn k* **Ars** k* ars-s-f k2 aur b4.de* bar-c *Bell* k* berb *Bism* k* borx b4a.de* bov k* bry cain *Calc* k*

- **tearing** pain: ...
  calc-sil k2 *Camph* k* canth b7.de* carb-an b4.de* carb-v carbn-s **Caust** k* *Cham* k* chel tl1 *Chin* k* chinin-ar chinin-s cocc k* *Colch* k* *Coloc* k* con b4.de* crot-t *Dulc* k* *Ferr* b7.de* *Graph* k* hep k* hyper kali-ar kali-bi k* *Kali-c* k* *Kali-n* k* kali-p kali-sil k2 *Kalm* lach laur b7.de* *Lyc* k* mag-c b4.de* mag-m b4.de* *Merc* k* *Merc-i-r* merl *Mez* k* mur-ac b4.de* nat-ar *Nat-c* k* *Nat-m* k* nat-p **Nat-s** nit-ac k* nux-v b7.de* ol-an par b7.de* petr b4.de* ph-ac b4.de* *Phos* k* plat b4.de* *Puls* *Rat* *Rhod* k* sabin c1 sars k* sec sep k* *Sil* k* spig k* spong k* *Stann* k* staph b7.de* *Stront-c* k* sul-ac k* *Sulph* k* tep *Ter* thuj trom verat k* *Zinc* k*
  - **alternating** with:
    - **paralyzed** feeling: hyper k*
    - **stiffness**: ars h2
  - **drawing** pain: ars bov kali-c h2 stann h2 zinc h2
  - **jerking** pain: chin h1
  - **stitch**-like: bry
  - **wandering** pain: merl
- **touch** agg.: acon borx bry chin ferr-ma
  - **burning**: borx
  - **tearing** pain: *Chin*
- **ulcerative** pain: am-c b4a.de am-m h2* bar-c b4.de* berb bro1 bry k* caust graph b4.de* hep kreos b7a.de lyc *Mag-c* myric bg2 **Nat-m** nat-s *Ph-ac* bro1 puls bro1 *Ran-b* bro1 sulph b4.de* zinc b4.de*
- **uncovering** agg.: stront-c
- **uncovers**: androc ↓ cham ↓ ham ↓ sanic ↓ sulph ↓
  - **burning**: (↗*Heat - feet - burning - uncovers; Heat - feet - uncovering; Uncover inclination - feet)* androc srj1• cham mtf33 ham fd3.de• sanic mrr1 sulph h2*
- **vomiting**; when (See STOMACH - Vomiting - accompanied - feet - pain)
  - **cramping** (See STOMACH - Vomiting - accompanied - feet - cramp)
- **waking**; on: abrot ephe-si ↓ sep
  - **burning**: ephe-si hsj1•
- **walking**:
  - **after**:
    - **agg.**: kali-c ↓ puls ↓
      - **burning**: kali-c k* puls h1
      - **stitching** pain: kali-c k*
  - **agg.**: agn alumn ↓ am-m h2 ambr ang ant-c mrr1 ant-t ars-h bamb-a stb2.de• bar-c bell ↓ *Brucel* sa3• carb-an ↓ carbn-s caust cham ↓ chr-met dx clem coloc crot-h dulc fd4.de ferr *Guaj* lac-leo ↓ lap-la sde8.de• lith-c mag-c nat-c nat-m h2 nit-ac petr phyt plb podo fd3.de• puls rhus-v ruta fd4.de sabad **Sil** ↓ spong fd4.de stroph-s ↓ stry sulph syc fmm1• tarent ↓ tax thuj ↓ tritic-vg fd5.de vanil fd5.de
    - **aching**: phyt stry
    - **bones** of one's legs; sensation as if walking on the: cham tl1* cypra-eg sde6.de•
    - **burning**: carb-an k* *Nat-c* k* nat-m k* phyt
    - **cutting** pain: thuj h1
    - **drawing** pain: bar-c k* clem k* coloc crot-h ferr c1 nit-ac k* petr k*
    - **pressing** pain: ang h1
    - **shooting** pain: bell nat-c h2 stroph-s sp1 tarent
    - **sore**: alumn cham lac-leo hrn2• **Ruta** **Sil**
    - **stitching** pain: nat-m h2 ruta fd4.de tarent tritic-vg fd5.de
    - **tearing** pain: agn *Sil*
  - **air**; in open:
    - **after** | **agg.**: dulc fd4.de *Rhus-t*
    - **agg.**: bell ↓ lyc ↓
      - **stitching** pain: bell lyc
    - **amel.**: nat-m ↓
      - **stitching** pain: nat-m
  - **amel.**: am-m ↓ arg-met ↓ *Bell* ↓ bor-ac vh1 *Coloc* ↓ dig *Puls* **Rhus-t** sep ↓ vanil fd5.de *Verat*
    - **pressing** pain: *Coloc*
    - **sore**: arg-met sep
    - **tearing** pain: am-m *Bell*
- **walking – amel.**: ...
  - **carefully**:
    - **must** walk carefully: ars ↓
      - **drawing** pain: ars h2
  - **uneven** ground agg.; on: hyos bg1
- **wandering** pain: ars-h choc srj3• coloc iris *Puls*
- **warm**:
  - **applications** | **agg.**: aur-m k2 *Guaj*
  - **bathing** | **amel.**: cench k2
  - **bed**:
    - **agg.**: agar ↓ aur-m k2 calc ↓ *Mag-c* merc ↓ stront-c ↓ **Sulph** ↓ verat
      - **burning**: agar k* calc merc stront-c **Sulph**
    - **amel.**: *Am-c* ↓ **Caust** k* *Cham* ↓ **Rhus-t** ↓
      - **drawing** pain: **Caust** **Rhus-t**
      - **tearing** pain: *Am-c* *Caust* *Cham*
- **weather**:
  - **change** of weather: vip ↓
    - **stitching** pain: vip
    - **tearing** pain: vip
  - **wet** | **agg.**: *Dulc* *Rhod* *Rhus-t*
- **weight** on foot, on bearing: calo k*
- **wet**; after getting: *Dulc* ↓
  - **tearing** pain: *Dulc*
- **writing** agg.: coloc ↓
  - **pressing** pain: coloc

▽ • **extending** to:
  - **Ankle**: ozone ↓
    - **stitching** pain: ozone sde2•
  - **Back**: nit-ac ↓
    - **drawing** pain: nit-ac
  - **Ball** of: lyc ↓ mez ↓ plat ↓ sulph ↓ zinc ↓
    - **stitching** pain: lyc h2 mez h2 plat h2 sulph h2 zinc h2
  - **Body**: *Plb* tritic-vg fd5.de
  - **Calves**: dros dulc fd4.de melal-alt ↓
    - **cramping**: melal-alt gya4
    - **drawing** pain: dros dulc fd4.de
  - **Hips**: nit-ac ↓ *Nux-v* sulph ↓
    - **aching**: nit-ac
    - **drawing** pain: sulph
  - **Knee**: bar-c ↓ bell ↓ bry ↓ xan ↓
    - **stitching** pain: bell h1 xan
    - **tearing** pain: bar-c bry
  - **Knees**: dirc guaj k2 kali-p fd1.de• nit-ac ↓ sil ↓ xan bg1
    - **drawing** pain: nit-ac sil
    - **shooting** pain: xan
  - **Shoulders**: bell ↓
    - **drawing** pain: bell h1
  - **Thighs**: caust ↓
    - **tearing** pain: caust
  - **Tibia**: bamb-a stb2.de• nat-m
  - **Toes**: chel graph ↓ kali-bi ↓ kali-c ↓ urol-h ↓
    - **cutting** pain: urol-h rwt•
    - **tearing** pain: graph h2 kali-bi kali-c
  - **Upward**: dirc dros ferr-i **Led** k* nat-m nit-ac nux-v *Plb* *Sil* sulph

○ • **Back** of feet: acon ↓ aesc aeth ↓ agar alum *Anac* ↓ ang ↓ ant-t ↓ *Arg-met* ↓ arg-n ↓ *Arn* ↓ ars ↓ asaf aster ↓ aur aur-m-n ↓ bamb-a ↓ bapt ↓ bar-c ↓ berb ↓ brom ↓ *Brucel* sa3• *Bry* ↓ cain ↓ calc ↓ *Camph* ↓ canth ↓ carb-an ↓ card-m *Caust* b4a.de cer-s ↓ chel chin ↓ cic ↓ cocc ↓ colch ↓ coloc com ↓ *Con* ↓ *Cop* cupr ↓ cycl ↓ dig ↓ digin ↓ dulc fd4.de eup-per ferr ferr-i ferr-m ↓ ger-i ↓ gins ↓ graph ↓ guaj ham ↓ hell hep ↓ ign ↓ indg ↓ jatr-c ↓ kali-bi ↓ kali-c ↓ kali-i ↓ kali-n ↓ kola stb3• lach k* laur ↓ *Led* ↓ lil-t lyc ↓ mag-m ↓ manc ↓ mang ↓ merc ↓ merc-c ↓ merc-i-f merl ↓ mez mur-ac ↓ *Nat-c* ↓ nat-m ↓ nat-s nat-sil fd3.de• nit-s-d ↓ nux-m nux-v ↓ olnd ↓ par ↓ *Phyt* plan plat ↓ plb podo ↓ puls *Ran-b* b7a.de ran-s ↓ rat ↓ rheum ↓ rhus-t ↓ rhus-v ↓ ruta fd4.de sabin ↓ sang sars ↓ sep ↓ sil sol-ni ↓ spig ↓ stram ↓ stroph-s ↓ suis-pan ↓

Extremities

• **Back** of feet: ...
sul-ac↓ *Sulph*↓ symph fd3.de• syph tab↓ *Tarax* thuj↓ tritic-vg fd5.de tung-met↓ valer↓ vanil fd5.de xan zinc↓ zing↓
: **right**: kola stb3• rat↓
: : **tearing** pain: kola stb3• rat
: **left**: adam skp7• ger-i↓ kali-i↓ xan↓
: : **dull** pain: xan c1
: : **scratching**; after: adam skp7•
: : **sore**: ger-i rly4• kali-i
: **morning**:
: : **bed** agg.; in: hep↓
. **burning**: hep
: **forenoon**: ars↓
: : **tearing** pain: ars
: **noon**: bamb-a↓
: : **burning**: bamb-a stb2.de•
: **afternoon**: com↓
: : **drawing** pain: com k*
: **evening**: agar ferr ferr-i k2 kali-n↓ led nat-c↓ ruta fd4.de symph fd3.de• vanil fd5.de
: : **22** h: arg-n↓
. **pressing** pain: arg-n
: : **bed** agg.; in: con↓ nat-s↓
. **tearing** pain: con nat-s
: : **burning**: agar
: : **drawing** pain: nat-c h2
: : **pressing** pain: led
: : **tearing** pain: kali-n h2
: : **walking** agg.: agar
: **night**: syph k2
: **aching**: asaf chel *Coloc* ger-i rly4• jatr-c lil-t merc-i-f mez suis-pan rly4• xan
: **appearing** suddenly:
: : **disappearing** suddenly; and: bamb-a↓
. **drawing** pain: bamb-a stb2.de•
: **arthritic**: sil↓
: : **tearing** pain: sil
: **boring** pain: aesc aur aur-m-n coloc lil-t mez nat-s
: **burning**: agar alum h2 ant-t b7a.de bamb-a stb2.de• bapt berb calc canth k* chin k* dulc fd4.de hep k* ign k* led b7a.de lyc h2 mag-m manc nux-v b7a.de olnd b7a.de **Puls** k* rhus-t k* sil spig k* stram k* *Sulph* symph fd3.de• tarax k* thuj tritic-vg fd5.de
: **clucking**: chel h1
: **drawing** pain: arg-met arg-n a1 asaf k* aster bamb-a stb2.de• *Bry* camph k* *Caust* cer-s a1 chel k* chin k* cic a1 colch b7.de* coloc con k* cycl b7.de* dig digin a1 ferr ferr-i k2 gins k* ham indg k* jatr-c kali-bi k* led k* mang h2 mur-ac h2 nat-c h2 nat-s k* nit-s-d a1 nux-v k* ran-b k* rhus-v k* sars k* tarax k* tritic-vg fd5.de zing k*
: : **cramping**: arg-met
: : **pulsating** pain: arg-met
: **lying** agg.: ars↓
: : **tearing** pain: ars
: **menses**; during: lyss
: **motion**:
: : **agg.**: ang↓ *Camph*↓ cop nat-sil fd3.de• plb↓ sulph↓ vanil fd5.de
. **drawing** pain: camph
. **pinching** pain: *Camph* k*
. **stitching** pain: sulph h2
. **tearing** pain: ang plb
: : **amel.**: mang↓
. **drawing** pain: mang h2
: **pinching** pain: *Camph* k* par k* sulph h2 thuj k*
: **pressing** pain: acon bg2 ang k* arg-n k* aur-m-n brom k* bry bg2 cain caust k* coloc bg2 cycl bg2 ferr-m hell k* jatr-c *Led* k* mur-ac h2 *Nat-c* k* olnd b7.de* plat b4a.de* ran-b b7.de* sul-ac b4a.de* symph fd3.de• tarax k* thuj k* vanil fd5.de
: : **drawing** pain: bry
: : **pinching** pain: thuj

• **Back** of feet – **pressing** pain: ...
: **tearing** pain: camph
: **tremulous**: plat k*
: **rheumatic**: chin ferr ferr-i ol-j rhus-t syph vesp
: **rubbing**:
: : **amel.**: nat-c↓
. **drawing** pain: nat-c h2
: **sitting** agg.: asaf bell↓ cycl↓ mur-ac↓ nat-s↓ *Tarax* vanil fd5.de
: : **aching**: asaf
: : **drawing** pain: cycl h1 mur-ac h2
: : **pressing** pain: cycl *Tarax*
: : **stitching** pain: bell h1 mur-ac a1
: : **tearing** pain: nat-s
: **sleep** agg.; during: asar↓
: : **stitching** pain: asar h1
: **sore**: carb-an chin cocc com eup-per indg kali-i laur mag-m h2 sil stroph-s sp1 thuj h1
: **sprained**; as if: bar-c
: **standing**:
: : **agg.**: chin↓ cic↓ mur-ac↓ nat-c↓ tarax↓
. **drawing** pain: chin k* mur-ac h2 nat-c h2 tarax k*
. **tearing** pain: cic a1
: : **amel.**: cycl↓
. **pressing** pain: cycl a1
: **standing** and sitting: mur-ac↓
: : **stitching** pain: mur-ac h2
: **stepping** agg.: nux-m
: **stitching** pain: acon bg2 agar b4a.de* *Anac* k* ang b7.de* arg-n bg2 asaf b7.de* aur h2* bamb-a stb2.de• berb ptk1 chin h1 coloc h2* guaj b4a.de* hep b4a.de* kali-c b4a.de* lyc b4a.de* merc-c b4a.de mur-ac bg2* nat-m bg2 nux-v b7a.de par b7.de* podo c1 *Puls* k* ran-b b7.de* ran-s b7.de* rheum h* rhus-t b7.de* ruta k* sep b4a.de* spig b7.de* sulph h2* symph fd3.de• tarax b7.de* tung-met bdx1• vanil fd5.de zinc h2
: **stretching** agg.: bry
: **tearing** pain: aeth ang k* *Arg-met* k* *Arn* k* ars k* berb bry k* *Camph* k* canth k* caust k* cic a1 colch k* coloc k* *Con* k* cupr k* graph k* ign k* jatr-c kali-bi k* kali-c k* kali-n h2 kola stb3• led k* lyc mag-m h2 merc merl mez k* nat-c h2 *Nat-s* k* plat k* plb k* *Puls* k* rat rheum h* sabin k* sil k* sol-ni spig k* sulph k* symph fd3.de• tab k* thuj valer bg2 zinc k*
: : **cramping**: nat-c h2
: : **drawing** pain: berb merl
: : **paroxysmal**: plb
: : **sticking** pain: berb
: : **twitching**: cupr h2 spig tab
: : **upward**: *Camph*
: **touch** agg.: puls sabin↓
: : **tearing** pain: sabin
: **ulcerative** pain: nat-c bg2 puls b7.de*
: **walking**:
: : **agg.**: agar arg-met pd bry calc cic↓ coloc mag-m↓ plb↓ ruta fd4.de
. **boring** pain: coloc
. **drawing** pain: coloc k*
. **tearing** pain: cic a1 mag-m h2 plb
: : **air**; in open:
. **agg.**: acon↓
pressing pain: acon
writing agg.: coloc↓
pressing pain: coloc
. **amel.**: coloc↓
pressing pain: coloc
: : **amel.**: arg-met↓ zinc↓
. **drawing** pain: arg-met
. **tearing** pain: zinc
: : **stone** pavement agg.; on a: sep↓
. **stitching** pain: sep h2

- **Back** of feet: ...
  - **warm**:
    - **bed**:
      - **agg.**: plb↓
        - **tearing** pain: plb
      - **amel.**: **Caust**
  - **extending** to:
    - **Ankle**: adam$_{skp7}$•
    - **Heels**: puls↓
      - **tearing** pain: puls
    - **Pelvis**: ferr-i
    - **Thighs**: *Camph*↓
      - **pinching** pain: *Camph*$_{k*}$
      - **tearing** pain: *Camph*
    - **Toes**: kali-c↓ mag-m↓ merl↓ syph
      - **tearing** pain: kali-c mag-m$_{h2}$ merl
  - **Bones**: bism↓ cupr↓ dig↓ mez↓ staph↓ symph↓
    - **pressing** pain: bism$_{k*}$ cupr$_{h2}$ dig mez staph$_{h1}$ symph$_{fd3.de}$•
  - **Outer** part of: ang↓ arn↓
    - **drawing** pain: ang$_{h1}$ arn
- **Balls**: arn↓
  - **cramping**: arn$_{bg2}$
- **Between** toes: *Nat-c*↓
  - **burning**: *Nat-c*
- **Bones**: acon agar *Alum* arg-met↓ ars *Asaf* aur$_{k*}$ bell bism *Carb-v* *Chin*$_{k*}$ cocc *Cupr* dulc$_{fd4.de}$ graph↓ hyper↓ kali-n↓ lach led *Merc* mez nit-ac phos↓ plat$_{k*}$ puls↓ rhod↓ *Ruta*$_{k*}$ *Sabin* spig stann *Staph*$_{k*}$ symph$_{fd3.de}$• *Syph*$_{bg1}$ teucr ther↓ vanil$_{fd5.de}$ verat zinc
  - **morning**: led↓
    - **boring** pain: led
  - **boring** pain: *Bism* led mez
  - **burning**: *Ruta* symph$_{fd3.de}$•
  - **drawing** pain: cupr$_{b7a.de*}$ rhod$_{b4a.de}$ staph$_{b7a.de}$
  - **gnawing** pain: graph$_{b4.de*}$
  - **pressing** pain: *Bism*$_{b7a.de}$ cupr$_{b7a.de}$ kali-n$_{b4.de*}$ sabin$_{b7a.de}$ staph$_{b7.de*}$ verat$_{b7.de*}$
  - **sore**: hyper$_{bg1}$ phos$_{bg1}$ puls$_{bg1}$ ther$_{bg1}$
  - **squeezed**; as if: plat$_{bg2}$
  - **tearing** pain: arg-met$_{h1}$ carb-v$_{h2}$ chin$_{h1}$ spig$_{h1}$ staph$_{h1}$ symph$_{fd3.de}$•
  - **walking** agg.: mez↓
    - **boring** pain: mez
  - **Metatarsal** bones: gard-j↓ plat↓ sabin↓ syc$_{fmm1}$•
    - **cramping**: plat$_{h2}$
    - **pressing** pain: gard-j$_{vlr2}$•
    - **shooting** pain: sabin$_{br1}$
    - **walking** agg.: caul$_{a1}$
- **Heels**: acon act-sp↓ aeth↓ agar$_{k*}$ agn↓ *All-c*↓ alum am-c *Am-m*$_{k*}$ ambr$_{b7.de*}$ anac↓ anag ang↓ *Ant-c*↓ aran$_{k*}$ arg-met$_{b7.de*}$ *Arg-n*↓ arist-cl↓ arist-m$_{br1}$ arn↓ ars ars-h arund↓ aur aur-ar$_{k2}$ aur-m-n↓ bad$_{c1}$ bamb-a$_{stb2.de}$• bapt bar-c↓ bell↓ berb bism↓ borx bros-gau↓ bry↓ *Calc*$_{k*}$ *Calc-caust*$_{c2}$ calc-p calc-sil↓ cann-s↓ cann-xyz↓ caps *Carb-an* carbn-s↓ carl↓ *Cassia-s*$_{zzc1}$• castor-eq *Caust*↓ cedr cham *Chel* chin↓ cic↓ *Cimic*↓ cina↓ cinnb clem$_{k*}$ cocc↓ colch$_{gk}$ *Coloc* con$_{gk}$ crot-h cycl$_{c2*}$ dios dros↓ dulc$_{fd4.de}$ eup-per eup-pur↓ euph euphr↓ eupi↓ fago↓ *Ferr*$_{k*}$ *Ferr-ar* ferr-ma↓ fl-ac gard-j$_{vlr2}$• graph haliae-lc↓ hell hep↓ heroin↓ ign indg↓ jatr-c$_{kr1*}$ kali-ar↓ kali-bi$_{k2}$ kali-c *Kali-i* *Kali-n*↓ kali-p$_{fd1.de}$• kali-s↓ kali-sil↓ kreos↓ lac-c$_{bg1}$ lac-d$_{k2}$ lap-la$_{sde8.de}$• laur↓ led lyc lyss m-ambo↓ m-arct↓ mag-c↓ mag-m↓ *Manc*↓ mang$_{k*}$ *Med*$_{ptk1*}$ meny↓ meph merc↓ merc-i-f merl↓ mez↓ morg-p$_{pte1*}$• mur-ac↓ *Nat-c* nat-m nat-p↓ nat-s nit-ac↓ nit-s-d↓ nux-m↓ nux-v↓ ol-an↓ olnd↓ osm par↓ *Petr*$_{k*}$ ph-ac↓ phos phyt$_{k*}$ *Plat*↓ plb↓ *Plut-n*↓ polyg-h↓ ptel↓ **Puls**$_{k*}$ ran-b ran-s raph$_{k*}$ rheum↓ **Rhod**$_{k*}$ *Rhus-t* rhus-v ruta sabin$_{c2*}$ sacch-a↓ sang sars↓ sep *Sil*↓ spong *Stann*↓ staph↓ stront-c↓ stry↓ sul-ac↓ sulph symph$_{fd3.de}$• tart-ac$_{c2*}$ tep↓ *Ter*↓ teucr↓ thuj tritic-vg$_{fd5.de}$ trom↓ tub↓ upa$_{k*}$ *Valer*$_{k*}$ vanil$_{fd5.de}$ verat viol-t↓ vip↓ xan *Zinc*$_{k*}$ zinc-p$_{k2}$ zing

- **Heels**: ...
  - **right**: agar↓ *Am-m* ars-h bad$_{c1}$ bamb-a↓ chel↓ dulc$_{fd4.de}$ euph↓ gard-j↓ hydrog↓ kali-p$_{fd1.de}$• kali-s↓ lyss nat-m↓ olib-sac↓ sulph↓ tritic-vg$_{fd5.de}$ valer
    - **aching**: gard-j$_{vlr2}$•
    - **burning**: olib-sac$_{wmh1}$
    - **gnawing** pain: nat-m$_{bg2}$
    - **shooting** pain: hydrog$_{srj2}$•
    - **sore**: euph
    - **stitching** pain: agar bamb-a$_{stb2.de}$• chel dulc$_{fd4.de}$ kali-s$_{fd4.de}$ sulph
    - **walking** agg.: gink-b$_{sbd1}$• tritic-vg$_{fd5.de}$
  - **left**: bry dulc$_{fd4.de}$ kali-p↓ myric↓ nat-m↓ nicc↓ olib-sac$_{wmh1}$ plut-n↓ psil↓ puls↓ ruta$_{fd4.de}$ spong$_{fd4.de}$ symph$_{fd3.de}$• thuj↓ tritic-vg$_{fd5.de}$ vanil$_{fd5.de}$ xan
    - **burning**: psil$_{ft1}$
    - **gnawing** pain: xan$_{bg1}$
    - **sore**: myric$_{c1}$ plut-n$_{srj7}$• puls
    - **stitching** pain: kali-p$_{fd1.de}$• nat-m$_{sne}$ nicc thuj
  - **morning**: am-c bamb-a↓ dulc$_{fd4.de}$ eupi↓ ign↓ petr↓ *Rhus-t*↓ sacch-a$_{fd2.de}$• sul-ac↓
    - **bed** agg.; in: am-m↓ anac↓ bry↓ fago↓ *Graph*↓ puls↓ sang↓
      - **burning**: fago *Graph*
      - **stitching** pain: bry puls sang
      - **tearing** pain: am-m anac
    - **burning**: eupi
    - **stitching** pain: bamb-a$_{stb2.de}$• dulc$_{fd4.de}$ eupi ign *Rhus-t*
    - **tearing** pain: petr sul-ac
    - **waking**; on: am-c ars petr↓ sacch-a$_{fd2.de}$• sul-ac↓
      - **tearing** pain: petr sul-ac
  - **afternoon**: clem nat-m↓ *Ran-b*↓ ruta$_{fd4.de}$ tritic-vg$_{fd5.de}$ vanil$_{fd5.de}$
    - **sitting** agg.: nat-s↓
      - **stitching** pain: nat-s
    - **standing** agg.: nat-s↓
      - **tearing** pain: nat-s
    - **stitching** pain: nat-m *Ran-b*
  - **evening**: am-m ang↓ dulc$_{fd4.de}$ kali-s↓ merc↓ *Nat-c* **Puls** ruta$_{fd4.de}$ sep↓ spong$_{fd4.de}$ symph$_{fd3.de}$• thuj↓ tritic-vg$_{fd5.de}$ zinc
    - **21** h:
      - **spinning**; while: nat-s↓
        - **tearing** pain: nat-s
    - **bed** agg.; in: acon↓ lyc↓ mag-c↓ nit-ac↓ stann↓ sulph↓
      - **drawing** pain: acon lyc sulph$_{h2}$
      - **stitching** pain: mag-c$_{h2}$ nit-ac$_{h2}$
      - **tearing** pain: mag-c$_{h2}$ stann$_{h2}$
    - **boring** pain: **Puls**
    - **sitting** agg.: stront-c↓
      - **tearing** pain: stront-c
    - **stitching** pain: ang$_{h1}$ kali-s$_{fd4.de}$ merc sep$_{h2}$ thuj
  - **night**: *Am-m* calc↓ euphr↓ kali-p↓ ruta$_{fd4.de}$ sacch-a$_{fd2.de}$• sep↓ spong$_{fd4.de}$ vanil$_{fd5.de}$
    - **midnight**:
      - **after**:
        - **3** h: *Am-m*
          - **tearing** pain: am-m
    - **bed** agg.; in: *Am-m* kali-n↓ sacch-a$_{fd2.de}$•
      - **burning**: kali-n
      - **stitching** pain: am-m
      - **tearing** pain: am-m
    - **burning**: ruta$_{fd4.de}$
    - **stitching** pain: am-m$_{h2}$ calc euphr kali-p$_{fd1.de}$• ruta$_{fd4.de}$ sep
    - **tearing** pain: am-m
  - **aching**: agar calc-p carbn-s carl ferr kali-c phyt puls spong zinc [heroin$_{sdj2}$]
    - **intermittent**: sabin$_{c1}$
  - **ascending** stairs agg.: carbn-s
  - **bed** agg.; in: anac↓
    - **tearing** pain: anac

- **Heels**: ...
  - **boring** pain: act-sp bg1 agar aran k* aur aur-m-n led **Puls** k* *Zinc*
  - **burning**: ant-c c1 arg-met arund carl *Cycl* k* eupi fago *Graph* k* hell b7a.de *Ign* k* *Kali-n* led b7a.de m-ambo b7.de* puls raph rheum b7.de rhus-t k* ruta fd4.de sabin b7a.de sep spong b7a.de *Stann* b4a.de sul-ac tep verat k* viol-t b7.de vip zinc
  - **burnt**; sensation as if: *Plut-n* srj7•
  - **cutting** pain: am-c bros-gau mrc1 crot-h bg1 eup-per kali-p fd1.de• mag-m k* nat-s puls k* sulph k*
  - **drawing** pain: acon bg1 anac k* ang k* *Ant-c* k* aur k* aur-m-n k* bell bg1 berb cann-s k* carb-an h2 chin k* con k* crot-h bg1 indg bg1 kreos b7a.de* led lyc k* merc k* nit-s-d bg1* par k* *Plat* k* ptel k* rhus-t k* sep k* sulph k* thuj k* tub jl2
    - **cramping**: plat h2
  - **elevating** feet:
    - **amel.**: phyt
      - **aching**: phyt
  - **excoriated**; as if: borx c1
  - **frozen** previously: carl ↓
    - **aching**: carl
  - **gnawing** pain: ran-s b7.de*
  - **gouty**: calc colch gk kali-i led bg2 lyc med jl2 meph sabin
  - **griping**: graph h2
  - **motion**:
    - **agg.**: *Cassia-s* zzc1• dros ↓ kreos ↓
      - **stitching** pain: kreos
      - **tearing** pain: dros
    - **amel.**: spong ↓
      - **stitching** pain: spong
  - **nails** under the skin; like: *Rhus-t*
  - **paralyzed**; as if: caust puls
  - **pinching** pain: alum *Chel* k* nat-c h2* osm a1 ran-b a1* raph a1
  - **pressing** pain: alum k* anac h2* ang k* bamb-a stb2.de• bell a1 cann-xyz bg2 carbn-s eup-pur graph h2* hell b7.de* hep b4a.de* kali-c h2 kali-p fd1.de• lac-d k2 m-arct b7.de petr b4a.de* ran-b b7.de* ruta b7.de* sacch-a fd2.de• spong k* stann h2* symph fd3.de•
    - **tearing** pain: stann h2
    - **vise**; as if in a: alum
  - **pressure**:
    - **amel.**: bell ↓
      - **pressing** pain: bell a1
    - **slightest** | **agg.**: bad c1 *Brucel* sa3•
  - **pulsating** pain: *Nat-c*
  - **putting** it down, when: graph ↓
    - **stitching** pain: graph
  - **rest** agg.: valer k2
  - **resting** with boot off | **amel.**: raph valer
  - **rheumatic**: anan bapt colch gk *Kali-i* br1 mang k* meph phyt **Rhod** sabin
  - **rising**:
    - **amel.**: bry ↓ puls ↓
      - **stitching** pain: bry puls
    - **sitting**; from | **agg.**: graph
  - **rubbing**:
    - **amel.**: *Am-m* nat-s ↓
      - **stitching** pain: am-m nat-s
      - **tearing** pain: am-m h2 nat-s
  - **sciatic** | **left**: med jl2
  - **scratching**, while: sars ↓
    - **stitching** pain: sars
  - **shooting** pain: ant-c c1 con ptk1 puls bg2* sabin br1* sil bg2 spong fd4.de trom
  - **sitting** agg.: agar ↓ ang ↓ berb ↓ cann-s ↓ chin ↓ cic ↓ cina ↓ cycl mrr1 dulc fd4.de indg ↓ kali-i ↓ mur-ac ↓ *Rhus-t* ↓ ruta fd4.de sep ↓ sil ↓ spong fd4.de symph fd3.de• **Valer** k*
    - **drawing** pain: cann-s k* chin h1 indg k*
    - **sore**: cycl mrr1

- **Heels – sitting** agg.: ...
    - **stitching** pain: agar h2 ang h1 berb cic cina *Rhus-t* ruta sep h2 sil spong **Valer**
    - **tearing** pain: cina kali-i mur-ac h2
  - **sleep** agg.; on going to: aur ↓
    - **drawing** pain: aur k*
  - **sore**: agar *All-c* ptk1 am-m k* arg-met h1 ars bg2 bell berb borx k* calc-p caps k* carl caust *Cimic* k* cocc k* *Cycl* k* fago jatr-c kali-bi k* lac-c ptk1 **Led** k* mag-m *Mang* nux-m nux-v ph-ac k* polyg-h ptk1 ran-b sep symph fd3.de• teucr valer bg2* zinc
    - **paroxysmal**: caps h1
  - **spasmodic**: arist-cl mtf11
  - **spinning**; while: mur-ac ↓
    - **tearing** pain: mur-ac h2
  - **splinter**; as from a: *Petr* *Rhus-t* ruta fd4.de sulph
  - **sprained**; as if: euph b4a.de laur br1 led bg1
  - **squeezed**; as if: alum bg2 led b7a.de
  - **standing**:
    - **after**: berb ↓
      - **drawing** pain: berb
    - **agg.**: agar k* am-c androc srj1• berb caust mtf33 cham colch gk con ↓ cycl hr1* kali-i ↓ mang ↓ psor ↓ ran-b ↓ *Rhus-t* ↓ sil ↓ spong ↓ symph fd3.de• zing ptk1
      - **sore**: agar berb cycl mrr1 mang
      - **stitching** pain: berb con psor al2 ran-b *Rhus-t* sil spong
      - **tearing** pain: berb kali-i
  - **standing** long, after: zing ↓
    - **aching**: zing
  - **stepping** agg.: agar ↓ arg-met ↓ ars ↓ bell ↓ berb ↓ bros-gau ↓ con ↓ *Nit-ac* ↓ ph-ac ↓ *Rhus-t* ↓ ruta ↓ sep ↓ stann ↓ zinc ↓
    - **burning**: bros-gau mrc1 con h2 zinc h2
    - **pressing** pain: stann h2
    - **sore**: agar arg-met h1 bell ph-ac h2 zinc k2
    - **stitching** pain: ars h2 bros-gau mrc1 *Nit-ac* *Rhus-t* ruta fd4.de sep
    - **tearing** pain: berb sep h2
  - **stitching** pain: aeth agar k* agn b7.de* am-c k* am-m k* ambr k* ang k* ars k* arund bad bamb-a stb2.de• bar-c k* berb bros-gau mrc1 bry k* calc k* calc-sil k2 carl chel k* chin b7.de* cic k* cina k* con k* dulc fd4.de eup-per euphr k* eupi ferr-ma *Graph* k* haliae-lc srj5• hep k* ign k* kali-ar kali-c k* kali-n k* kali-s fd4.de kali-sil k2 kreos k* lyc k* m-ambo b7.de m-arct b7.de mag-c k* *Manc* meny k* merc k* nat-c k* nat-m k* nat-p *Nat-s* k* nit-ac k* nux-v k* ol-an olnd k* *Petr* k* ph-ac k* *Puls* k* *Ran-b* k* ran-s b7.de* rhod k* *Rhus-t* k* ruta k* *Sabin* k* sang sars k* *Sep* k* *Sil* k* spong k* stront-c b4a.de stry sulph k* thuj k* trom **Valer** k* zinc k*
    - **boring** pain: *Puls*
    - **burning**: agar puls h1 sep sul-ac
    - **cutting** pain: berb eupi lyc h2
    - **darting** pain: rhod
    - **itching**: berb nat-m
    - **nail**; as from a: bros-gau mrc1
    - **needles**; as from: lyc bg2
    - **outward**: sabin c1
    - **paroxysmal**: sep spong
    - **prickling** pain: carl
    - **pulsating** pain: *Ran-b*
    - **rhythmical**: carl
    - **shooting** pain: eupi
    - **splinter**: mang nat-c nit-ac *Petr* k* ph-ac sulph h2
    - **stinging**: bad berb kali-s fd4.de sep
    - **tearing** pain: sil
    - **tingling** pain: berb
    - **upward**: agar spong
  - **sudden**: caust ↓
    - **tearing** pain: caust h2

- **Heels**: ...
  - **tearing** pain: aeth am-c **Am-m** k* anac k* ang bg2 *Arg-met* k* *Arg-n* arn k* *Ars* k* bapt berb bism k* calc-caust caps k* carb-an h2 caust h2* chin b7.de* cina k* *Colch* k* dros b7.de* euph bg2 graph k* ign b7.de* kali-i kreos led k* *Lyc* m-ambo b7.de m-arct b7.de merc bg2 merl mez k* mur-ac h2 nat-s k* par k* petr k* phyt plb b7.de* sep k* *Sil* k* stann bg2 staph stront-c bg2 sul-ac k* sulph k* *Ter* viol-t b7.de* zinc k*
    - **cramping**, when limbs are crossed: ang
    - **paroxysmal**: caps
    - **sticking** pain: merl staph h1
    - **torn** out; as if: stann k*
    - **twitching**: am-c h2 mag-c h2 merl
    - **upward**: plb sulph
  - **treading** agg.: sep ↓
    - **tearing** pain: sep
  - **ulcerative** pain: am-c *Am-m* k* berb carb-an *Caust* cycl bg2 graph kali-bi bg2 *Kali-i* laur k* nat-c bg1 *Nat-s Zinc*
  - **walking**:
    - **after**:
      - **agg.**: berb ↓ spong ↓
        - **stitching** pain: berb spong
    - **agg.**: acon agar am-c am-m ↓ ambr *Ars* bell ↓ berb *Caust* cinnb colch gk con ↓ *Cycl* ↓ dros ↓ dulc fd4.de euph fago ↓ jatr-c kali-bi kali-p fd1.de• *Led* ↓ lyc lyss ↓ mang ↓ nat-s ↓ nit-ac nux-v ↓ ph-ac ↓ plut-n ↓ puls ↓ raph sacch-a fd2.de• sep ↓ spong symph fd3.de• thuj ↓ tritic-vg fd5.de vanil fd5.de *Zinc*
      - **aching**: spong
      - **burning**: cycl h1 zinc h2
      - **drawing** pain: berb led
      - **sore**: am-m bell caust *Cycl* euph fago jatr-c *Kali-bi Led* lyss mang nux-v ph-ac plut-n srj7• puls sep
      - **stitching** pain: berb con nat-s thuj
      - **tearing** pain: berb dros nat-s
    - **air** agg.; in open: *Cycl* ↓
      - **sore**: *Cycl* hr1
    - **amel.**: cycl ptk1* laur k* sacch-a fd2.de• sulph ↓ **Valer** k*
      - **sore**: cycl mrr1
      - **tearing** pain: sacch-a fd2.de• sulph
    - **beginning** to walk: puls sacch-a fd2.de•
  - **warmth** | **amel.**: stram
  - **weather**:
    - **cold** agg.: kali-i br1
    - **wet** | **agg.**: kali-i br1
  - **wine** agg.: **Zinc** k*
    - **boring** pain: **Zinc**
  - **extending** to:
    - **Foot**:
      - **Back** of: sars ↓
        - **stitching** pain: sars h2
      - **Hands**:
        - **Palms**:
          - **Balls**: aeth ↓
            - **stitching** pain: aeth
    - **Leg**: polys sk4•
    - **Nates**: merc ↓
      - **tearing** pain: merc h1
    - **Thigh**: ars ↓ ferr ↓
      - **aching**: ferr
      - **stitching** pain: ars h2
    - **Tongue**: vip ↓
      - **burning**: vip
  - **Bones**: berb caps coloc crot-h dulc fd4.de ign ruta fd4.de symph fd3.de•
  - **Metatarsal** joint | **right**: gard-j vlr2•
  - **Periosteum**: coloc ↓
    - **tearing** pain: coloc h2
- **Joints**: *Agar* ↓ am-c ↓ ambr *Anac* ↓ ang ↓ *Arn* ↓ ars ↓ arum-t ↓ asaf ↓ aster aur ↓ bell bov ↓ *Bry* bufo ↓ *Calc Carb-v* ↓ carbn-s ↓ caust ↓ cedr
- **Joints**: ...
  clem coloc con crot-t ↓ cupr ↓ cycl ↓ dulc fd4.de euph ↓ graph *Guaj* hell kali-bi ↓ *Kali-c* kali-p ↓ kalm ↓ led ↓ limen-b-c ↓ lyss ↓ merc ↓ mez morg-p pte1*• mosch ↓ nat-m nat-s nat-sil fd3.de• ol-an ↓ osm ph-ac *Phos* ran-b ↓ rhus-t ↓ sep ↓ sil ↓ *Staph* stront-c symph fd3.de• tarent thuj ↓ valer k2 verat
  - **right**: colch rsj2• cycl ↓ eupi ↓ syph ↓
    - **dislocated**; as if: cycl tl1 eupi c1 syph rb2
  - **aching**: clem *Kali-c* phos
  - **blow**; pain as from a: nat-m bg2 ol-an bg2
  - **boring** pain: coloc *Hell*
  - **burning**: carbn-s k2
  - **dislocated**; as if: ang b7.de* *Arn* b7.de* ars b4.de arum-t aur b4a.de bell k* bry b7.de* bufo bg2 calc bg2 *Carb-v* b4.de* crot-t bg2 cupr b7a.de cycl b7.de* euph b4.de* kalm bg2 limen-b-c hrn2* nat-m b4.de* ran-b b7.de* rhus-t bg2 sil bg2
  - **drawing** pain: am-c *Anac* ang k* ars k* bov caust dulc kali-p fd1.de• merc mosch k* stront-c thuj k* valer k2
  - **motion**:
    - **agg.**: led ↓
      - **pressing** pain: led h1
    - **amel.**: kali-c ↓
      - **pressing** pain: kali-c
  - **pressing** pain: *Agar* ang asaf aur coloc graph hell kali-c led lyss merc *Mez* nat-m nat-s sep stront-c
  - **pulsating** pain: nat-m bg2 ol-an bg2
  - **squeezed**; as if: caust bg2 kali-bi bg2 sep bg2
  - **walking** agg.: cycl ↓ mez ↓
    - **boring** pain: mez
    - **dislocated**; as if: cycl h1
  - **wandering** pain: coloc
- **Os** calcis: aran ptk1 cinnb ptk1
  - **boring** pain: aran bro1
  - **motion**; continued:
    - **amel.**: aran ↓
      - **boring** pain: aran
- **Periosteum**: *Coloc* ↓
  - **aching**: *Coloc*
- **Sides**: arg-met
  - **boring** pain: arg-met
  - **Inner**: caust ↓ chin ↓ cina ↓ colch ↓ dig ↓ **Kali-c** ↓ *Led* ↓ phos ↓
    - **drawing** pain: chin h1 dig h2
    - **pressing** pain: *Led*
    - **tearing** pain: caust h2 cina colch **Kali-c** phos h2
  - **Outer**: am-m ↓ ambr ↓ ang ↓ bism ↓ caust dulc fd4.de graph ↓ hep ↓ stann ↓ zinc
    - **pressing** pain: ang h1 bism h1 dulc fd4.de
    - **sore**: hep h2
    - **tearing** pain: am-m ambr h1 bism h1 graph stann h2 *Zinc*
- **Soles**: *Abrom-a* ↓ aesc ↓ aeth ↓ agar agn ↓ ail ↓ all-s ↓ aloe bg2 alum k* alum-p k2 *Alum-sil* ↓ *Alumn* ↓ am-c ambr b7a.de ammc ↓ anac k* anag ang b7.de* *Ant-c* tl1 ant-t ↓ aphis ↓ apis bg2 *Apoc-a* bro1 aq-mar ↓ *Arg-met* ↓ arg-n ↓ arn ↓ *Ars* k* ars-s-f ↓ ars-s-r ↓ arum-d ↓ arum-t ↓ arund ↓ asaf ↓ asar ↓ asc-t ↓ aster ↓ aur ↓ aur-ar ↓ aur-m ↓ aur-m-n ↓ *Bamb-a* stb2.de• bar-c *Bell* ↓ berb borx bro1 bov k* brach ↓ bry cact cadm-met ↓ calc calc-caust ↓ calc-f ↓ calc-p ↓ *Calc-s* ↓ calc-sil ↓ camph ↓ cann-i br1* *Canth* carb-an ↓ carb-v *Carbn-s* ↓ **Caust** k* cephd-i ↓ *Cham* ↓ chel ↓ chin bg1 cic ↓ clem ↓ coc-c ↓ *Cocc* ↓ *Colch* ↓ coloc tl1 com ↓ con ↓ cop ↓ corh ↓ croc k* crot-h ↓ *Crot-t* cub ↓ cupr *Cycl* ↓ cypra-eg sde6.de• daph ↓ dig ↓ dios dros ↓ dulc fd4.de elaps ↓ *Eos* ↓ eup-per ↓ eupi ↓ fago ↓ ferr br1* fic-m gya1 *Fl-ac* ↓ gamb ↓ gels gent-l ↓ graph *Gua* bro1 guare ↓ ham ↓ hell ↓ *Hep* ↓ hir ↓ hura ↓ hydr ↓ hydrog ↓ hyos ign b7a.de iris-foe ↓ jal ↓ jatr-c ↓ kali-ar ↓ kali-bi ↓ *Kali-c* ptk1 kali-i bro1 kali-m ↓ kali-n ↓ kali-p ptk1 *Kali-s* ↓ kali-sil ↓ *Kalm* ↓ ketogl-ac rly4• kola stb3• *Kreos* b7a.de *Lac-c* ↓ lac-e hrn2* *Lach* ↓ *Lachn* ↓ lact ↓ lat-m ↓ *Led* k* *Lil-t* ↓ lim bro1 lith-c lob-s ↓ *Lyc* k* lyss m-aust ↓ mag-c ↓ *Mag-m* ↓ mag-s ↓ *Manc* ↓ *Mang* ↓ mang-act ↓ med k2* meny ↓ merc merc-i-f merc-i-r merl ↓ mez *Mur-ac* c2* musca-d ↓ myos-a ↓ myric ↓ nat-ar ↓ nat-c bro1 nat-m ↓ nat-p nat-s k2 nat-sil fd3.de• nicc ↓ nit-ac ↓ *Nux-m* ↓ *Nux-v* ↓ ol-an ↓ olib-sac ↓ olnd ↓ ox-ac ↓

Extremities

- **Soles**: ...
  oxal-a↓ par↓ pareir *Petr* k* petr-ra shn4• ph-ac bro1 phel↓ *Phos* phyt mrr1 pip-m plac-s↓ plat plb k* plut-n↓ podo↓ propr sa3• psil↓ psor↓ puls k* pycnop-sa↓ ran-s raph↓ rauw↓ rheum↓ rhus-t b7a.de* rhus-v↓ ruta fd4.de sabad b7.de* sabin↓ sacch-a↓ *Sang*↓ *Sanic*↓ sars↓ sec sep↓ *Sil* spect↓ spig↓ spong fd4.de squil↓ *Stann* staph↓ *Still* streptoc↓ stront-c↓ stry↓ succ-ac↓ suis-pan↓ sul-ac↓ sul-i ptk1 sulph sumb↓ syc pte1*• symph fd3.de• syph ptk1 tab↓ *Tarax*↓ tarent↓ tep↓ *Ter*↓ thal-xyz↓ thuj k2* tritic-vg fd5.de upa↓ valer↓ vanil fd5.de verb bro1 viol-t↓ zinc zinc-ar ptk1 zinc-p↓
  - **right**: bros-gau↓ camph↓ crot-h↓ crot-t↓ fl-ac↓ kali-p↓ led↓ sil↓ tarax↓
    - **burning**: bros-gau mrc1 camph bg1* crot-h bg1* crot-t bg1* fl-ac bg1* led bg1* sil bg1* tarax bg1*
    - **stitching** pain: kali-p fd1.de•
      - **followed** by | **left**: bamb-a stb2.de•
  - **left**: am-c↓ bamb-a↓ borx↓ bov↓ olib-sac↓ ruta↓
    - **burning**: am-c bg1 bov bg1 ruta fd4.de [borx xyz62]
    - **cutting** pain: bamb-a stb2.de•
    - **stitching** pain: olib-sac wmh1
  - **midnight**: sars↓
    - **tearing** pain: sars
  - **morning**: alum↓ dios hydr↓ nat-sil fd3.de• nux-m↓ ph-ac↓ phyt↓ ruta fd4.de tritic-vg fd5.de vanil fd5.de zinc
    - **aching**: dios hydr
    - **bed** agg.; in: hep↓ psor↓ sulph↓ tritic-vg↓
      - **burning**: hep tritic-vg fd5.de
      - **drawing** pain: sulph
      - **sore**: psor
    - **boring** pain: nux-m
    - **burning**: ph-ac phyt tritic-vg fd5.de zinc
    - **rising** | **after**:
      - **agg.**: plb↓ sep↓
        - **sore**: plb sep sne
      - **bed**; from:
        - **agg.**: fl-ac↓ med↓ nicc↓
          - **stitching** pain: fl-ac med hr1 nicc
    - **stepping** agg.: spig↓
      - **sore**: spig h1
    - **stitching** pain: alum h2
  - **forenoon**: nat-c↓
    - **tearing** pain: nat-c
  - **afternoon**: bamb-a↓ crot-t gels↓ kali-n↓ *Nat-c*↓ nat-sil↓ nux-v↓ ol-an↓ ruta fd4.de spong fd4.de
    - **16** h: plan
    - **agg.**: cupr↓ *Eug*↓ zing↓
      - **cramping**: cupr bro1 *Eug* bro1 zing bro1
    - **burning**: gels nat-sil fd3.de• ol-an
    - **lying** agg.: nux-v↓
      - **tearing** pain: nux-v
    - **stitching** pain: bamb-a stb2.de• *Nat-c* ruta fd4.de
    - **tearing** pain: kali-n nux-v
  - **evening**: alum↓ berb com↓ dig↓ dulc fd4.de ham↓ **Lach**↓ lyc↓ mag-m merc↓ nat-c↓ nat-sil↓ petr-ra shn4• ph-ac↓ *Phos*↓ *Rhus-t*↓ ruta fd4.de sil spong fd4.de sulph↓ tritic-vg fd5.de vanil fd5.de zinc↓
    - **18** h; until: sil↓
      - **tearing** pain: sil k*
    - **bed** agg.; in: ant-c↓
      - **stitching** pain: ant-c h2
    - **burning**: berb dulc fd4.de ham fd3.de• **Lach** lyc mag-m merc nat-c nat-sil fd3.de• ph-ac h2 *Phos* ruta fd4.de sulph h2 tritic-vg fd5.de zinc
    - **drawing** pain: com k* dulc fd4.de ham fd3.de• ruta fd4.de
    - **scratching** agg.; after: am-c↓
      - **burning**: am-c
    - **stitching** pain: alum h2 dig dulc fd4.de ph-ac h2 *Rhus-t* ruta fd4.de spong fd4.de sulph
    - **tearing** pain: mag-m sil sulph

- **Soles**: ...
  - **night**: aloe↓ bar-c↓ *Calc*↓ **Cham**↓ dulc fd4.de fl-ac↓ kali-n↓ **Lach**↓ lyc↓ mag-m↓ merc-i-f↓ nat-s↓ petr↓ *Ph-ac*↓ *Sang*↓ sil sulph vanil fd5.de
    - **22**.30 h: hura↓
      - **stitching** pain: hura
    - **bed**; before going to: sulph↓
      - **shooting** pain: sulph
    - **boring** pain: merc-i-f
    - **burning**: aloe bar-c *Calc* **Cham** dulc fd4.de fl-ac **Lach** lyc mag-m nat-s petr *Ph-ac* *Sang* sil **Sulph**
    - **cutting** pain: sulph
    - **putting** them to the ground: mur-ac↓
      - **burning**: mur-ac
    - **sore**: bar-c
    - **stitching** pain: dulc fd4.de
    - **tearing** pain: kali-n h2
    - **Palms** and soles: *Lach*↓
      - **burning**: *Lach*
  - **accompanied** by | **Foot**; swelling of: sabad ptk1
  - **aching**: asaf caust croc dios hydr kali-c lim bro1 oxal-a rly4• puls bro1 *Rhus-t* stry succ-ac rly4• sul-i sumb vanil fd5.de viol-t
  - **ascending** stairs agg.: bros-gau↓
    - **burning**: bros-gau mrc1
  - **bed**:
    - **in** bed:
      - **agg.**: canth↓ **Cham**↓ helo-s↓ hep↓ mag-m↓ *Ph-ac*↓ *Plb*↓ *Sang*↓ **Sulph**↓ tritic-vg↓
        - **burning**: canth **Cham** k* helo-s rwt2• hep mag-m k2 *Ph-ac* *Plb* *Sang* **Sulph** k* tritic-vg fd5.de
      - **amel.**: nat-c↓
        - **burning**: nat-c k*
        - **sticking** out; not amel. by: hydrog↓
          - **burning**: hydrog srj2•
  - **biting**: ant-t bg2 bell bg2 plat bg2
  - **boring** pain: bell mez nux-m ran-s tarax k*
  - **burning**: *Abrom-a* zzc1• aesc ail all-s aloe alum k* alum-p k2 alum-sil k2 am-c *Ambr* k* *Anac* k* apoc-a bro1* ars k* ars-s-f ars-s-r arum-d arund bro1 aur-m bar-c bell k* berb bov cadm-met sp1 **Calc** k* calc-f sp1 *Calc-s* k* calc-sil k2 *Canth* k* *Carb-v* k* *Carbn-s* *Caust* k* cephd-i zzc1• *Cham* k* chel clem coc-c *Cocc* *Coloc* con h2 cop corh br1 croc k* crot-h crot-t *Cupr* k* dulc *Eos* br1 eup-per ferr bro1 fl-ac *Graph* k* guare ham fd3.de• hep k* hir skp7• hydrog srj2• ign bro1 jal kali-ar kali-bi kali-c kali-m k2 kali-n kali-p *Kali-s* kali-sil k2 kola stb3• kreos k* lac-c *Lach* k* *Lachn* k* lat-m bnm6• *Led* b7.de *Lil-t* lim bro1 **Lyc** k* mag-c *Mag-m* k* *Manc* *Mang* k* mang-act bro1 med k* merc k* merl mur-ac myric nat-ar *Nat-c* k* nat-m nat-p *Nat-s* nat-sil fd3.de• nicc bro1 nux-v k* olib-sac wmh1 olnd b7a.de ox-ac petr k* *Ph-ac* k* *Phos* phyt *Plb* podo fd3.de• propr sa3• psor al2* *Puls* k* pycnop-sa mrz1 rauw tpw8* rhus-t b7a.de ruta b7a.de* sabad b7a.de sacch-a fd2.de• *Sang* k* sanic k* sec sep k* *Sil* k* squil k* stann staph b7a.de *Sul-i* k* **Sulph** k* tab tarax k* tarent k2 tep thal-xyz srj8• tritic-vg fd5.de viol-t b7a.de *Zinc* k* zinc-p k2
  - **burnt**; sensation as if: plut-n srj7•
  - **chill**; during: ars↓
    - **burning**: ars b4a.de
  - **cold**:
    - **touch**; to: sec↓ *Sulph*↓
      - **burning**: sec gk *Sulph* k*
    - **water**:
      - **amel.**: hir↓
        - **burning**: hir skp7•
  - **convulsions**: ars
  - **convulsive**: bar-c
  - **cramping**: agar bro1 am-c bro1 apoc-a bro1 bar-c h2 carb-v bro1 *Colch* bro1 *Cupr* bro1 med bro1 mur-ac a1 *Nux-v* bro1 stann h2 stront-c bro1 sulph bro1 verb bro1 zinc bro1
  - **cutting** pain: alum k* ars k* calc h2 coloc dios dulc k* elaps mur-ac ol-an plb bg2 sil k* streptoc rly4• sulph k*

- **Soles**: ...
  - **drawing** pain: *Alumn* ammc k* *Anac* k* aphis asc-t aster k* aur bg2 aur-m-n k* bar-c k* *Bell* cact caust k* cham k* cic k* colch k* coloc k* com k* con k* crot-h cupr k* dulc fd4.de ham fd3.de• *Hep* k* hyos k* ign k* *Kali-p* kreos b7a.de led k* mag-c k* mez bg2 nit-ac h2 nux-v k* ruta fd4.de sacch-a fd2.de• sars k* sil k* spong bg2* sulph k*
    - **alternating** with | **Calf**; drawing pain in (See legs - calves - drawing pain - alternating - foot)
    - **cramping**: cact
  - **eating**; after: sil ↓
    - **burning**: sil
  - **exertion**:
    - **amel.**: plb ↓
      - **sore**: plb
  - **fever**; during: ars ↓ corh ↓
    - **burning**: ars b4a.de corh br1
  - **griping**: kali-n h2
  - **lightning**-like: daph thal-xyz srj8•
  - **lying** agg.: hydrog ↓
    - **burning**: hydrog srj2•
  - **menopause**; during: sang ↓ *Sulph* ↓
    - **burning**: sang bro1 *Sulph* bro1
  - **menses** | **before**:
    - **agg.**: carb-v ↓
      - **burning**: carb-v bro1
    - **during**:
      - **agg.**: carb-v ↓ cassia-s ↓ kali-n ↓ petr ↓ raph ↓
        - **burning**: carb-v k* cassia-s ccrh1• petr
        - **stitching** pain: raph
        - **tearing** pain: kali-n h2
  - **motion**:
    - **agg.**: led ↓ plb ↓ spig ↓
      - **pressing** pain: led
      - **stitching** pain: spig
      - **tearing** pain: plb
    - **amel.**: aloe coloc hyos ↓ olnd ↓ psor ↓ puls sabin ↓
      - **stitching** pain: olnd
      - **tearing** pain: coloc hyos psor sabin
  - **paralyzed**; as if: par
  - **pecking**: phos h2
  - **perspiration**: **Nit-ac** ↓
    - **stitching** pain: **Nit-ac** k*
  - **pinching** pain: bry k* upa k*
  - **pressing** pain: anac h2 aur k* bell h1 camph k* graph b4a.de* hell b7.de* jatr-c kali-s fd4.de led k* nat-c bg2 nux-m k* olnd k* ph-ac k* plat k* rhus-t k* ruta b7.de* sabad k* sabin b7.de* sars h2* stann b4a.de* staph b7.de* tarax b7.de* vanil fd5.de verb b7.de* viol-t b7.de*
    - **burning**: led h1
    - **cramping**: nat-c
    - **paroxysmal**: ph-ac
    - **pea**; as if walking on a hard: nux-m hr1
    - **pinching** pain: ph-ac
  - **pressure**:
    - **agg.**: plb ↓
      - **tearing** pain: plb
    - **amel.**: alum mtf bell mtf petr-ra shn4• plb mtf
      - **pressing** pain: bell h1
      - **tearing** pain: plb
  - **putting** foot to ground agg.: mur-ac ↓
    - **burning**: mur-ac h2
  - **rest** agg.: staph ↓
    - **pressing** pain: staph h1
  - **rheumatic**: aphis calc jatr-c ↓ *Kali-i* br1 med phyt mrr1 sil k2
    - **drawing** pain: jatr-c
  - **rising**:
    - **agg.**: sulph
    - **sitting**; from | **agg.**: graph

- **Soles**: ...
  - **rubbing**:
    - **amel.**: alum ↓ ant-c ↓ gamb ↓ kali-n ↓ plb ↓ pycnop-sa ↓ sulph ↓ vanil ↓
      - **burning**: kali-n h2 pycnop-sa mrz1
      - **stitching** pain: alum ant-c h2 gamb kali-n vanil fd5.de
      - **tearing** pain: plb sulph
  - **scratched**; as if | **saw**; by a: zinc h2
  - **scratching**: (non:zinc h2)
  - **shooting** pain: agar alum bell borx c1 calc-p daph plb ruta fd4.de sulph
    - **splinters**; as from: *Agar*
  - **sick** headache, with: *Sang* ↓
    - **burning**: *Sang*
  - **sitting** agg.: agar ↓ anac ↓ ang ↓ asaf carb-v ↓ dros ↓ elaps ↓ hell ↓ hydrog ↓ jatr-c ↓ lac-leo ↓ lyc ↓ merl ↓ mur-ac ↓ nat-s ↓ phos ↓ plat ↓ sacch-a ↓ sars ↓ sep ↓ spig ↓ spong fd4.de stann ↓ symph ↓ tarax ↓ thuj ↓
    - **aching**: asaf
    - **burning**: anac carb-v hydrog srj2• lyc mur-ac sacch-a fd2.de• tarax h1
    - **cutting** pain: elaps
    - **pressing** pain: hell h1 plat sars h2 stann h2 tarax h1
    - **sore**: lac-leo hrn2• thuj
    - **stitching** pain: dros jatr-c mur-ac a1 sars sep spig tarax
    - **tearing** pain: agar h2 ang h1 merl mur-ac h2 nat-s phos h2 symph fd3.de•
  - **sore**: aesc bro1 **Alum** k* *Alum-sil* k4 alumn ambr **Ant-c** k* aq-mar skp7• *Arg-met* arn bro1 arum-t aster **Bar-c** k* bell bg1 berb brach calc k* canth *Carbn-s* caust cham k* *Coloc* crot-h fago bg1 graph k* hep *Ign* kali-c k* *Lac-c* lact **Led** k* lil-t lyc k* **Med** k* merc musca-d szs1 myos-a rly4• **Nat-c** k* nit-ac bro1 *Nux-m* k* nux-v oxal-a rly4• *Petr* bro1 ph-ac bro1 phos plac-s rly4• plb k* plut-n srj7• psor k* *Puls* k* rhus-v *Ruta* bro1 sabad *Sanic* bro1 sars sep sne *Sil* k* stann suis-pan rly4• sul-ac k* sul-i k* sulph syph thuj k* zinc ptk1 [spect dfg1]
    - **accompanied** by:
      - **rheumatism**: ant-c tl1
      - **Coccyx**; pain in (See BACK - Pain - coccyx - accompanied - soles)
    - **inflamed**; as if: nit-ac
    - **jerking** pain: sul-ac h2
  - **spikes**, as if stepping on: *Cann-i* k* ruta fd4.de
  - **spinning**; while: mur-ac ↓
    - **tearing** pain: mur-ac h2
  - **splinter**; as from a: agar ruta fd4.de
  - **sprained**; as if: cham cupr *Cycl* k* mur-ac
  - **standing**:
    - **after**: carb-v ↓ merc ↓ sul-i ↓
      - **burning**: carb-v merc sul-i
    - **agg.**: anac androc srj1• berb croc dulc fd4.de ruta fd4.de sabad ↓ sul-i k* symph fd3.de• syph vanil fd5.de zinc-ar ptk1
      - **aching**: croc sul-i
      - **pressing** pain: sabad
      - **sore**: sul-i
      - **stitching** pain: berb vanil fd5.de
    - **amel.**: euph mur-ac ↓
      - **stitching** pain: mur-ac a1
  - **stepping** agg.: *Alum* ars-h berb brom bry *Cann-i* *Canth* dulc fd4.de kali-c ↓ mez ↓ nat-c nicc ↓ nit-ac ↓ puls ruta ↓ spig ↓ staph ↓ sulph *Zinc*
    - **drawing** pain: mez ruta fd4.de
    - **pressing** pain: kali-c h2
    - **stitching** pain: berb c1 bry nat-c h2 nicc nit-ac h2 ruta fd4.de spig h1 staph sulph
  - **stitching** pain: aeth *Agar* k* agn k* ail alum k* alum-p k2 alum-sil k2 ang k* ant-c k* arn k* ars k* arum-t asar k* bamb-a stb2.de• bell k* berb **Borx** k* bry k* calc calc-caust calc-p calc-sil k2 camph k* carb-an k* chin k* cic k* clem k* coc-c cocc k* coloc con k* crot-h cub daph dig k* dros k* dulc fd4.de elaps eup-per eupi *Fl-ac* gamb gent-l graph k* hura

Extremities

• **Soles – stitching** pain: ...
Ign k* iris-foe jatr-c kali-n k* kali-p fd1.de• kali-s fd4.de *Kalm* kreos b7a.de led k* lob-s lyc k* m-aust b7.de mag-m k* mag-s meny k* *Nat-c* k* nat-m h2 nat-p nat-s k* nicc nit-ac k* nux-v k* ol-an olnd k* par k* ph-ac k* phos k* plb k* psil ft1 psor al2 *Puls* k* ran-s b7.de* raph rheum k* *Rhus-t* k* rhus-v ruta fd4.de sabin k* sars k* sep k* sil k* spig k* spong fd4.de stry sulph k* tarax k* thuj k* tritic-vg fd5.de vanil fd5.de
: **burning**: alum berb *Fl-ac* ph-ac h2
: **corrosive**: plat h2
: **crawling**: arn berb mag-m
: **itching**: dros spig h1 tarax
: **jerking** pain: ph-ac h2
: **needles**; as from: bamb-a stb2.de• kali-s fd4.de tritic-vg fd5.de vanil fd5.de
: **outward**: *Tarax* thuj
: **prickling** pain: ant-c bell h1 sep
: **pulsating** pain: berb clem con h2
: **splinter**; as from a: agar kali-s fd4.de ruta fd4.de
: **tearing** pain: chin phos
: **twitching**: bamb-a stb2.de• dig nat-s ph-ac
⁝ **stone** pavements agg.: *Ant-c* ↓
: **sore**: *Ant-c*
⁝ **sudden**: ang ↓ cic ↓
: **tearing** pain: ang cic
⁝ **summer** agg.: vesp ↓
: **burning**: vesp
⁝ **swellings**; with longitudinal: *Plb* ↓
: **sore**: *Plb* b7a.de
⁝ **tearing** pain: agar k* agn b7.de* *Alumn* am-c k* ammc ang h1* *Arg-met* k* *Ars* aur aur-ar k2 aur-m-n bell k* berb calc k* calc-sil k2 chin b7.de* cic k* *Colch* k* coloc k* con k* crot-t cupr k* graph k* hep k* hyos k* **Kali-c** k* kali-n k* kali-sil k2 mag-m k* *Merc-i-r* merl mez h2 mur-ac h2 nat-c k* *Nat-s* k* nux-v b7.de* olnd par k* phos k* plb k* psor k* puls k* sabin bg2 sars bg2 sep sil k* stront-c bg2 sulph bg2 symph fd3.de• *Ter* valer k* zinc k*
: **burning**: sabin
: **constriction**: stront-c
: **drawing** pain: colch
: **lightning**-like: phel
: **paroxysmal**: plb
: **sticking** pain: zinc
: **twitching**: cupr h2 kali-n
⁝ **tired**; when: zinc-ar ↓
: **aching**: zinc-ar ptk1
⁝ **touch** agg.: crot-t puls sep ↓
: **stitching** pain: sep
⁝ **travelling**; after: aq-mar ↓
: **sore**: aq-mar skp7•
⁝ **ulcerative** pain: aloe bg2 alum bg2 ambr ant-c bg2 arg-n bg2 bar-c *Calc* k* *Canth* k* graph hep bg2 *Ign* b7.de* kali-c bg2 kali-n bg2 kreos led bg2 lyc k* mag-m bg2 *Med* bg2 merc bg2 *Nat-s* nit-ac bg2 nux-v bg2 phos k* plb bg2 *Puls* k* sabad bg2 sars bg2 *Sil* bg2 spig b7.de* stann bg2 *Sulph* k* thuj zinc k*
⁝ **uncovering** agg.: *Sanic* ↓
: **burning**: *Sanic* mrr1
⁝ **waking**; on: hydrog ↓
: **sore**: hydrog srj2•
⁝ **walking**: bry ↓ eupi ↓ nat-c ↓ *Rhus-t* ↓
. **after**:
. **agg.**: ant-c ↓
stitching pain: ant-c h2
: **agg.**: agar ↓ aloe k* alum alumn ↓ ambr androc srj1• ant-c k* *Arg-met* ↓ *Ars* ars-h arum-t ↓ bamb-a stb2.de• bar-c bell ↓ berb bry cact calc ↓ *Cann-i* canth carb-v carbn-s ↓ caust k* cham ↓ chr-ac ↓ coc-c cocc ↓ *Con* ↓ cupr ↓ ephe-si hsj1• eup-per ↓ eupi ↓ gels gent-l ↓ graph bro1 **Hep** ↓ hydrc ign kali-c lac-c ↓ *Led* lyc k* med meny ↓ merc merl ↓ *Mez* ↓ mur-ac bro1 nat-c nat-sil fd3.de• *Nit-ac* ↓

• **Soles – walking – agg.**: ...
nux-v ↓ olnd par *Petr* bro1 ph-ac bro1 phos plb plut-n ↓ puls rhus-t k* ruta fd4.de sabad ↓ sep ↓ sil spong fd4.de squil ↓ *Staph* ↓ sulph syc bka1• thuj ↓ tritic-vg fd5.de vanil fd5.de viol-t *Zinc*
. **aching**: kali-c *Rhus-t* viol-t
. **burning**: carb-v coc-c graph kali-c lyc *Nat-c* k* **Sulph**
. **drawing** pain: cupr kl
. **pavement**; on: aloe ptk1
. **pressing** pain: kali-c h2 led
. **shooting** pain: agar bell plb
. **sitting** long; after: **Sulph** ↓
burning: **Sulph**
. **sore**: *Aloe* **Alum** alumn ambr **Ant-c** *Arg-met* *Ars* arum-t *Bar-c* calc *Canth* carb-v carbn-s cham chr-ac *Con* eup-per graph **Hep** lac-c **Led** **Lyc** **Med** *Mez* *Nat-c* *Nit-ac* nux-v phos plut-n srj7• *Puls* **Ruta** sabad *Sil* squil *Staph* sulph thuj *Zinc*
. **stitching** pain: agar bell cocc con eupi gent-l k* meny h1 plb *Rhus-t* sep h2 tritic-vg fd5.de
. **tearing** pain: agar bell berb con graph merl
: **air** agg.; in open: hep ↓
. **burning**: hep
: **amel.**: bar-c ↓ cycl ↓ lac-leo ↓ mur-ac ↓ ol-an ↓ *Verb* ↓
. **burning**: ol-an
. **drawing** pain: (non:cupr kl)
. **pressing** pain: *Verb*
. **sore**: bar-c lac-leo hrn2•
. **sprained**; as if: cycl a1
. **stitching** pain: mur-ac a1
: **stitching** pain | **needles**; as if walking on: bry ptk1 eupi ptk1 nat-c ptk1 *Rhus-t* k*
⁝ **wandering** pain: psor
⁝ **warm** bed agg.: plb ↓
: **tearing** pain: plb
⁝ **warmth**:
: **amel.**: plb ↓
. **sore**: plb
⁝ **weather**:
: **cold** agg.: kali-i br1
: **wet** | **agg.**: kali-i br1
⁝ **extending** to:
: **Back**: puls ↓
. **tearing** pain: puls
: **Calves**: puls ↓
. **stitching** pain: puls h1
: **First** toe: *Crot-t* merc-i-f ph-ac ↓
. **pressing** pain: ph-ac
: **Hips**: cann-i c1 plb ↓
. **shooting** pain: plb
. **stitching** pain: plb
: **Inner** side: cupr ↓ mur-ac ↓
. **pressing** pain: cupr h2 mur-ac h2
: **Knees**: kali-p nat-s ↓
. **burning**: nat-s hr
: **Knees**; above: puls ↓ sil ↓
. **tearing** pain: puls sil
: **Lumbar** region: plb
: **Thighs**: ars ↓ led ↓ spong ↓
. **cutting** pain: ars
. **drawing** pain: spong k*
. **pressing** pain: led
: **Toes**: aur-m-n ↓ caust ↓ fic-m gya1 jatr-c ↓ sep
. **drawing** pain: aur-m-n k* caust h2 jatr-c
⁝ **Balls**: am-c ↓ *Ars* ↓ aur-m-n ↓ berb ↓ cina ↓ cypra-eg sde6.de• hell ↓ kali-n ↓ kali-s ↓ lyc ↓ med ↓ mez ↓ nat-c ↓ ph-ac ↓ ran-s ↓ squil ↓ tritic-vg ↓
: **night**: plat ↓
. **tearing** pain: plat h2

- **Soles – Balls**: ...
  - **boring** pain: ran-s
  - **burning**: mez h2 squil h1
  - **gnawing** pain: ran-s k*
  - **sore**: *Ars* b4a.de berb bg2 med ptk1 nat-c h2 ph-ac b4a.de
  - **stitching** pain: am-c k* aur-m-n k* berb bg2 cina h1* kali-s fd4.de tritic-vg fd5.de
  - **tearing** pain: hell h1 kali-n h2 lyc h2
  - **Hollow**: anag bamb-a ↓ cham dulc fd4.de fic-m ↓ lith-c mur-ac myric psil ft1 rhus-t ruta fd4.de sacch-a fd2.de• sanic vanil fd5.de
    - **aching**: fic-m gya1 rhus-t
    - **cutting** pain: bamb-a stb2.de• mur-ac
    - **stitching** pain: bamb-a stb2.de• ruta fd4.de vanil fd5.de
  - **Inner** margins: kali-s ↓ mur-ac ↓
    - **stitching** pain: kali-s fd4.de mur-ac h2
  - **Outer** margins: ars ↓ rheum ↓
    - **stitching** pain: ars k* rheum h
- **Spots**; in: arn ↓
  - **drawing** pain: arn k*
- **Transversely** across: mag-m bg2

- **Fingers**: abies-c oss4• abrot bro1 *Acon* k* act-sp mrr1 aesc ↓ agar k* agn ↓ aloe ↓ alum alum-p ↓ alum-sil k2 alumn am-c *Am-m* ↓ *Ambr* ↓ aml-ns ↓ *Anac* ↓ anag ↓ anan ↓ ang b7.de* ant-c ant-t ↓ apis k* *Arg-met* ↓ arg-n ↓ **Arn** ↓ ars k* ars-h ↓ ars-i ↓ ars-s-f ↓ arum-dru ↓ arund k* asaf ↓ asar ↓ *Aur* ↓ aur-ar ↓ aur-i k2 aur-m-n ↓ aur-s ↓ aza bro1 bamb-a ↓ bapt ↓ bar-c *Bell* ↓ bell-p-sp ↓ benz-ac k* *Berb* ↓ *Bism* ↓ bol-la borx ↓ bov ↓ brach ↓ *Brom* ↓ bry k* cact *Calc* calc-p k* calc-s calc-sil k2 *Camph* ↓ cann-i ↓ canth ↓ caps ↓ *Carb-an* **Carb-v** ↓ *Carbn-s* ↓ cardios-h ↓ carl ↓ cassia-s ccrh1• **Caul** k* caust k* cedr ↓ cham ↓ chel ↓ *Chin* ↓ *Chinin-ar* ↓ chinin-s choc ↓ **Cic** ↓ cina ↓ cist k* *Cit-v* ↓ clem k* cocc ↓ coff ↓ *Colch* *Coloc* ↓ com ↓ con ↓ croc ↓ crot-h k* crot-t ↓ cupr ↓ cycl ↓ daph ↓ *Dig* ↓ digin ↓ *Dios* k* *Dros* ↓ dulc fd4.de elaps ↓ elat k* euph ↓ *Euphr* ↓ fago ↓ fic-m ↓ fl-ac ↓ gamb ↓ ger-i ↓ gink-b sbd1• gins ↓ gran ↓ **Graph** ↓ grat *Guaj* gymno ↓ ham ↓ hedy ↓ hell ↓ helo-s bnm14• *Hep* hipp ↓ hydr hydrog ↓ hyos ↓ ign ↓ ind ↓ indg ↓ iod ↓ iodof k* iris jug-r ↓ kali-ar ↓ kali-bi k* kali-c kali-m ↓ *Kali-n* ↓ kali-p ↓ kali-s fd4.de kali-sil k2 kalm k* kola stb3• kreos ↓ lach k* lact k* laur k* led b7.de* lil-t k* lith-c a1 lob-s ↓ lyc k* m-ambo ↓ m-arct ↓ m-aust ↓ *Mag-c* ↓ *Mag-m* ↓ *Mag-s* ↓ manc ↓ mand rsj7• mang melal-alt gya4 *Meny* ↓ *Merc* ↓ merc-c ↓ mez k* moni ↓ morg-g pte1*• mosch k* mur-ac ↓ *Nat-ar* *Nat-c* ↓ *Nat-m* ↓ nat-ox ↓ nat-p ↓ nat-s nat-sil fd3.de• nicc nicc-s ↓ *Nit-ac* k* nit-s-d ↓ nux-m nux-v ↓ ol-an ↓ olnd k* orot-ac ↓ ox-ac pall ↓ **Par** ↓ pe... *Ph-ac* ↓ **Phos** ↓ *Phyt* plat *Plb* k* podo ↓ positr nl2• prun ↓ psor ↓ ptel ↓ *Puls* ↓ puls-n ↓ ran-b ↓ *Ran-s* ↓ raph k* rat ↓ rheum ↓ **Rhod** k* *Rhus-t* k* rhus-v ↓ ribo rly4• ruta fd4.de sabad ↓ sabin ↓ sacch-a ↓ samb ↓ santin ↓ *Sars* k* sec bro1 sep *Sil* spig spong fd4.de *Stann* ↓ *Staph* ↓ staphycoc ↓ *Stront-c* ↓ *Stry* k* *Sul-ac* ↓ sulph k* symph ↓ tab ↓ tarax ↓ tarent k* tell k* tep ↓ teucr ↓ ther ↓ thuj k* tritic-vg fd5.de trom ↓ tung-met ↓ upa urt-u k* ust ↓ v-a-b ↓ valer ↓ vanil fd5.de verat k* verb ↓ viol-t ↓ vip k* xan ↓ *Zinc* ↓ zinc-p ↓
  - **right**: arum-dru ↓ *Bism* ↓ chel ↓ crot-c sk4• dulc fd4.de fic-m gya1 melal-alt gya4 spong fd4.de symph fd3.de• trios rsj11• tritic-vg fd5.de vanil fd5.de viol-o bg1
    - **stitching** pain | **splinter**; as from a: arum-dru a1
    - **tearing** pain: *Bism* chel vanil fd5.de
  - **left**: elat ↓ ph-ac ↓ ruta ↓ xan ↓
    - **morning**: merc-i-r ↓
      - **sore**: merc-i-r
    - **cramping**: ph-ac h2
    - **delivery**; during: dios ↓
      - **cramping**: dios mrr1
    - **stitching** pain: elat hr1 ruta fd4.de xan c1
  - **morning**: coloc k* crot-h k* dios ↓ dulc fd4.de hell ↓ kali-c k* merc-i-r k* mez ↓ nat-s ↓ ruta ↓ tritic-vg fd5.de
    - **7 h**: dios ↓
      - **stitching** pain: dios
    - **aching**: merc-i-r
    - **drawing** pain: kali-c k*
    - **motion** agg.; beginning of: *Rhus-t*
    - **rising** agg.; after: coloc k*
    - **stitching** pain: dios mez ruta fd4.de

- **Fingers – morning**: ...
    - **tearing** pain: hell h1 mez nat-s
    - **waking**; on: crot-c sk4•
  - **forenoon**: ars ↓ dulc fd4.de fago ↓ kali-s ↓ sulph ↓ thuj k* tritic-vg ↓ trom ↓ vanil fd5.de
    - **burning**: dulc fd4.de fago
    - **drawing** pain: kali-s fd4.de thuj k* tritic-vg fd5.de vanil fd5.de
    - **stitching** pain: trom
    - **tearing** pain: ars sulph
  - **afternoon**: dulc ↓ ruta ↓ sulph ↓ thuj ↓
    - **drawing** pain: sulph k*
    - **stitching** pain: dulc fd4.de ruta fd4.de thuj
  - **evening**: alum ↓ ang ↓ brom ↓ carb-v ↓ colch ↓ dulc fd4.de hipp ↓ lyc k* *Rhus-t* a1 stront-c ↓ sulph k* thuj ↓ tritic-vg fd5.de vanil fd5.de zinc ↓
    - **18 h**: lyc ↓
      - **tearing** pain: lyc
    - **20 h**:
      - **spinning**; while: am-m ↓
        - **tearing** pain: am-m
    - **bed** agg.; in: asar ↓ lyc ↓
      - **drawing** pain: asar k*
      - **tearing** pain: lyc
    - **burning**: alum dulc fd4.de
    - **cramping**: hipp jl2
    - **drawing** pain: lyc k* sulph k* vanil fd5.de
    - **moving** them; when: sulph ↓
      - **tearing** pain: sulph
    - **pinching** pain: colch k*
    - **sleep**; before going to: ambr ↓ sulph ↓
      - **tearing** pain: ambr a1 sulph
    - **stitching** pain: ang thuj
    - **tearing** pain: brom carb-v lyc stront-c zinc h2
    - **writing** agg.: calc-p k*
  - **night**: borx dulc fd4.de kali-n *Mag-s* *Merc* ozone sde2• phos ↓ puls k* ruta ↓ sulph tritic-vg fd5.de
    - **bed** agg.; in: mag-s ↓ phos ↓ puls ↓
      - **tearing** pain: mag-s phos puls h1
    - **drawing** pain: *Merc* phos puls h1 ruta fd4.de
  - **abscess**; in: hydrog ↓
    - **stitching** pain | **splinter**; as from a: hydrog srj2•
  - **accompanied** by | **Teeth**; pain in (See TEETH - Pain - accompanied - fingers - pain)
  - **aching**: abrot ang apis *Aza* br1 bry cic dios euphr fic-m gya1 ger-i rly4• gymno ham hell kalm lob-s mez nat-ox rly4• orot-ac rly4• positr nl2• rhus-t ribo rly4•
  - **arthritic**: ant-c tl1
  - **biting**: sars b4.de*
  - **biting** nails | **amel.**: am-br bg1
  - **blow**; pain as from a: ruta b7.de*
  - **boring** pain: carb-v k* cocc k* daph hell k* lach k* mag-c k* mez k* ran-s k*
  - **breath**, with each: am-c ↓
    - **stitching** pain: am-c
  - **burning**: *Agar* k* alum k* am-m b7.de anan apis k* ars asaf k* asar b7.de *Aza* bro1 bamb-a stb2.de• *Berb* borx k* calc carb-v carl caust k* cina b7.de coff coloc k* con k* croc k* dig k* dulc fd4.de fago fl-ac gamb gins bro1 gran graph kali-ar *Kali-c* k* *Laur* b7.de* lyc mag-c b4a.de* merc k* mez k* mosch k* mur-ac b4a.de* *Nat-c* k* nicc nit-ac k* nux-v *Olnd* k* par b7a.de petr plat k* ran-s b7.de rhod *Rhus-t* b7.de* rhus-v ruta fd4.de sars bro1 sec *Sil* k* spig b7.de staph k* sul-ac k* *Sulph* k* tarax b7.de tep teucr k* ther thuj b4a.de tritic-vg fd5.de vanil fd5.de verat b7.de vip
    - **frostbitten**; as if: agar borx hr1 lyc
  - **burnt**; sensation as if: nat-c bg2 prun bg2 sil b4a.de*
  - **burrowing**: ol-an bg2
  - **chill**; during: nux-v
  - **closed**; when: nat-s vanil fd5.de verat

- **cold**:
  - **agg.**: stram
  - **air** agg.: agar am-c ↓
    - **stitching** pain: am-c
  - **amel.**: caust *Lac-c*
  - **applications** | **agg.**: cassia-s ccrh1•
  - **washing**:
    - **agg.**: ol-an ↓
      - **tearing** pain: ol-an
    - **amel.**: led ↓ puls ↓
      - **tearing** pain: led puls
- **coldness**; during: gins ↓
  - **stitching** pain: gins
- **contracting**: hedy a1*
- **convulsions**; during: santin ↓
  - **gnawing** pain: santin
- **cramping**: acon tl1 hipp jl2 lil-t meny h1 nat-p tl1 v-a-b jl2
- **creeping**: acon
- **cut** off; as if: mosch b7a.de
- **cutting** pain: bell bg2 con bg2 mang bg2 mur-ac bg2 petr bg2 stann bg2 staphycoc rly4•
- **dislocated**; as if: acon b7.de* alum b4.de* *Ambr* b7a.de ang bg2 bar-c b4.de* bell b4.de* camph b7.de* cham b7.de* graph b4a.de ign b7.de* kali-n b4.de* kreos b7a.de m-ambo b7.de m-arct b7.de m-aust b7.de mag-c b4.de* *Nat-m* b4.de* nux-m b7.de* olnd b7.de* petr b4.de* phos b4.de* puls b7.de* rhod b4a.de* spig b7.de* stann b4.de* sulph b4.de* verat b7.de*
- **drawing** pain: acon k* agar k* alum bg2 am-c k* ambr k* ang k* **Ant-c** k* ant-t k* apis b7a.de arg-met b7.de* arg-n a1 arn k* ars k* asar k* aur k* aur-m-n k* bar-c k* *Bell* k* bry k* cact k* *Camph* canth b7.de* caps bg2 carb-an h2* *Carb-v* k* carbn-s *Caul* k* *Caust* k* cham b7.de* chel b7.de* chin b7.de* cic a1 cina k* *Cit-v* k* clem k* cocc b7.de* coff b7.de* colch b7.de* *Coloc* k* com con k* dig k* digin a1 dios k* *Dros* bg2 ham hell k* hep k* hyos b7.de* indg k* kali-c k* kali-s fd4.de kali-sil k2 kreos b7a.de led b7.de* lyc k* m-arct b7.de m-aust b7.de mag-s k* mang k* merc k* mez k* mosch k* mur-ac k* nat-c k* nat-s k* nit-ac k* nit-s-d a1 nux-m k* nux-v k* olnd b7.de* par b7.de* *Petr* k* ph-ac b4a.de plat k* plb k* prun bg2 ptel bg2 *Puls* b7.de* puls-n **Rhus-t** k* rhus-v k* ruta b7a.de* sabad b7.de* sabin b7.de* sacch-a fd2.de• sep k* *Sil* k* stann k* staph k* *Stront-c* k* sulph k* teucr b7.de* thuj k* tritic-vg fd5.de valer b7.de* vanil fd5.de verb b7.de* zinc k*
  - **cramping**: zinc h2
  - **jerking** pain: sulph h2
  - **paralyzed**; as if: bell h1 *Sil*
  - **paroxysmal**: lyc h2 sacch-a fd2.de•
  - **tearing** pain: carb-an h2
- **excoriating**: ambr bg2 kali-c bg2 petr bg2
- **exertion** agg.: bry
- **festering**: bry bg2 ol-an bg2
- **gnawing** pain: alum b4.de* berb cina k* mag-c k* merc bg2 olnd ph-ac phos bg2 *Ran-s* b7.de* santin stront-c k*
- **grasping** something | **amel.**: lith-c
- **injuries**; after: | **long** after the injury: gink-b sbd1•
- **jerking** pain: acon bg2 aloe bg2 *Am-c* ars *Chin* k* cic b7.de* con bg2 kali-bi bg2 m-aust b7.de meny k* mez nit-ac bg2 ph-ac ran-s k* rheum k* sil a1 spig b7.de* stann bg2 staph k* sulph bg2
- **lying** on left side agg.: *Phos* ↓
  - **tearing** pain: *Phos*
- **massage** | **amel.**: cassia-s ccrh1•
- **menses** | **after** | **amel.**: *Caul* vh
  - **during**:
    - **agg.**: am-m ↓ sulph ↓
      - **cramping**: am-m b7.de sulph b4.de
- **motion**:
  - **agg.**: bry tl1 cassia-s ccrh1• *Guaj* hep hyos ↓ kali-c led ↓ nit-ac rhus-t ruta fd4.de sabad bcn stann ↓ vanil fd5.de
    - **drawing** pain: hyos h1 ruta fd4.de
- **motion – agg.**: ...
    - **pressing** pain: hyos h1
    - **stitching** pain: bry tl1 vanil fd5.de
    - **tearing** pain: led stann
  - **amel.**: am-m ↓ dulc fd4.de fic-m gya1 lith-c ruta ↓ tritic-vg fd5.de vanil fd5.de
    - **sore**: ruta
    - **stitching** pain: am-m
- **paralyzed**; as if: acon b7.de* asar b7a.de aur b4a.de bell b4.de* benz-ac *Bism* b7a.de *Brom* b4a.de *Carb-v* b4a.de *Caust* b4a.de *Chin* b7a.de cina b7.de* cocc b7.de* cycl b7.de* dig b4.de* hell b7.de* kali-c b4.de* kreos b7a.de meny b7a.de mez b4.de* mosch b7.de* par b7.de* rhod b4a.de* rhus-t b7a.de sabad b7.de* sabin b7.de* sil k* spig b7.de* staph b7.de* verb b7.de*
- **paroxysmal**: agar ang calc *Euphr Meny* mur-ac olnd ph-ac plat rat ruta sil verb
- **pecking**: aur b4.de* mez b4a.de verb b7.de*
- **pinching** pain: am-c k* caust k* colch k* euphr k* olnd h1* stront-c
- **pressing** pain: acon b7.de* *Agar* agn b7.de* *Anac* ang k* arg-met k* asaf k* bell k* bism b7.de* bry k* colch b7.de* coloc k* con k* cycl k* dig digin a1 euph k* euphr h2 graph bg2 hell k* hyos b7.de* *Led* k* **Lyc** merc k* *Mez* k* mur-ac *Nat-s* k* nit-s-d a1 nux-v k* olnd k* ph-ac k* phos *Plat* k* prun bg2 psor al2 ran-s b7.de* rhod k* ruta k* sabad b7.de* sabin k* sacch-a fd2.de• *Sars* k* sep spig b7.de* spong b7.de* stann k* staph k* sulph k* symph fd3.de• tarax k* teucr b7.de* tritic-vg fd5.de verb k* viol-t b7.de* zinc k* [bell-p-sp dcm1]
  - **crushed**; as if bones were: olnd
- **pressure** | **amel.**: dulc fd4.de kali-bi k2 lith-c
- **pulsating** pain: aml-ns bro1 anag borx bro1
- **raw**; as if: **Graph** bg2
- **rest** | **amel.**: cassia-s ccrh1•
- **rheumatic**: *Act-sp* bro1 alumn *Ant-c* bro1 bapt benz-ac k2 berb bro1 *Calc* *Caul* k* caust tl1 clem k* **Colch** k* des-ac rbp6 fago bro1 gran bro1 graph bro1 grat gua bro1 ham fd3.de• hyper bro1 kali-bi k2 kali-s fd4.de lappa bro1 led bro1* lith-c bro1 lyc bro1 med bro1 nicc paeon bro1 *Phyt* psil ft1 puls bro1 ran-s bro1 *Rhus-t* bro1 ruta fd4.de sabad bcn sacch-a fd2.de• sal-ac c1 scarl jl2 ust
  - **menopause**; during: sal-ac c1
  - **syphilitic**: *Nit-ac*
- **rising** from sitting agg.: carb-v ↓
  - **stitching** pain: carb-v
- **rubbing** fingers; on: arum-dru ↓
  - **stitching** pain | **stinging**: arum-dru a1
- **shooting** pain: agar choc srj3• ind nicc-s phyt sabin c1 tep trom
- **sitting** agg.: aur-m-n ↓ **Rhus-t** ↓
  - **drawing** pain: aur-m-n k* **Rhus-t**
- **sleep** agg.; during: rheum ↓
  - **drawing** pain: rheum
- **sore**: alum am-c k* apis arg-n bg1 brach bry camph cina b7.de* com croc crot-h bg2 fl-ac bg1 kali-c bg1 **Led** mez k* nat-c bg2 nat-m k* nat-sil fd3.de• nit-ac k* petr k* rhus-t ruta sacch-a fd2.de• sec sep spig b7.de* sulph k* tung-met bdx1•
- **sprained**; as if: aloe graph kali-n nat-m phos puls sulph
- **squeezed**; as if: caust b4.de* cina bg2 cupr bg2 dulc b4a.de fl-ac bg2 hep b4a.de kali-n b4.de* olnd b7a.de *Plat* b4a.de prun bg2 ruta b7.de* verb b7.de*
- **stitching** pain: abrot bg2* aesc agar agn k* alum bg2 am-c k* *Am-m* k* ambr k* *Anac* k* *Apis* arn k* ars k* arund asaf b7.de* bamb-a stb2.de• bapt bar-c k* bell b4a.de* berb bov k* brom bry k* *Calc* k* calc-sil k2 cann-i caps bg2 carb-an k* *Carb-v* k* carbn-s cardios-h rly4• *Caust* k* **Cic** cina b7.de* cocc b7.de* colch b7.de* con k* croc b7.de* cycl bg2 daph *Dig* k* dios dros b7.de* dulc fd4.de elaps fl-ac k* graph k* grat bg2 hep k* ind jug-r **Kali-c** k* kali-s fd4.de kali-sil k2 kalm **Lach** bg2 laur b7.de* lil-t lyc k* *Mag-m* k* mag-s mang meny b7.de* merc k* *Mez* k* moni rfm1• mur-ac k* nat-ar k2 nat-c b4.de* *Nat-m* k* nat-p *Nat-s* nit-ac k* nux-v b7.de* olnd b7.de* pall par k* petr k* ph-ac k* phos k* phyt plat k* plb podo fd3.de• ran-b b7.de* ran-s k* rheum b7.de* *Rhod* k* *Rhus-t* k* ruta fd4.de sabad k* sabin k* *Sars* k* sep k* sil k* spig b7.de* *Stann* k* staph k* *Sul-ac* k*

- **stitching** pain: ...
  sulph k* tab tarax b7.de* tarent tep teucr b7.de* *Thuj* k* tritic-vg fd5.de trom tung-met bdx1• valer b7.de* vanil fd5.de verb k* viol-t k* vip xan zinc k*
  - **burning**: caust iod
  - **itching**: arum-dru a1
  - **jerking** pain: *Carbn-s*
  - **paroxysmal**: ust verb
  - **splinter**; as from a: **Arn** arum-dru a1 *Bell* k* carb-v colch hep hydrog srj2• kali-s fd4.de lach **Nit-ac** k* petr puls ran-s sil k* sulph k*
  - **stinging**: ambr *Apis* arund kali-s fd4.de sil tritic-vg fd5.de
- **stretching** them apart: am-c vanil fd5.de
- **tearing** pain: *Acon* k* *Act-sp* bro1 *Agar* k* agn alum k* alum-p k2 alum-sil k2 am-c k* *Am-m* k* *Ambr* k* anac k* apis *Arg-met* k* arn *Ars* k* ars-i ars-s-f k2 asaf k* *Aur* k* aur-ar k2 aur-s k2 bar-c k* *Bell* k* berb bism k* bov b4.de* brom bry k* cact calc k* calc-p calc-sil k2 canth b7.de* carb-an k* **Carb-v** k* *Carbn-s Caul* bro1 **Caust** k* cedr bro1 chel k* *Chin* k* *Chinin-ar* clem k* cocc b7.de* coff k* *Colch* k* *Coloc* crot-t cupr k* cycl b7.de* daph *Dig* k* dios dros bg2 gran graph k* grat bg2 guaj k* hell k* ign k* iod k* kali-ar kali-bi k* *Kali-c* k* kali-m k2 *Kali-n* k* kali-p kali-s fd4.de kali-sil k2 kola stb3• kreos k* *Lach* bg2 laur b7.de* *Led* k* *Lyc* k* *Mag-c* k* mag-m k* *Mag-s* manc *Mang* k* meny *Merc* k* merc-c k* *Mez* k* mur-ac k* nat-c k* nat-m k* nat-p *Nat-s* nicc *Nit-ac* bg2 ol-an olnd k* **Par** b7.de* petr bg2 *Ph-ac* k* **Phos** k* plb k* psor puls k* ran-b b7.de* rheum b7.de* rhod k* *Rhus-t* k* ruta k* sabad k* sabin k* samb *Sars* k* sep k* *Sil* k* spig b7.de* *Stann* k* *Staph* k* *Stront-c* k* sul-ac k* **Sulph** k* tarax bg2 tep teucr k* thuj k* vanil fd5.de **Verat** bg2 verb k* *Zinc* k* zinc-p k2
  - **jerking** pain: chin h1 dig h2 zinc h2
  - **paralyzed**; as if: dig meny
  - **pressing** pain: stann h2
  - **pulsating** pain: spig h1
  - **torn** off; as if: nat-m bg2
  - **twitching**: am-m h2 staph h1
- **touch** agg.: *Chin* ↓
  - **tearing** pain: *Chin*
- **twinging**: berb k2 rhus-t k*
- **ulcerative** pain: am-m k* berb bry bg2 carb-v bg2 caust bg2 graph bg2 kali-c bg2 kreos b7a.de par bg2 plat bg2 sars k* **Sil** k* *Sulph*
- **variola**, in: *Thuj*
- **vibrating**: berb
- **waking**; on: sabad k*
- **walking** agg.; after: croc
- **wandering** pain: ars-h iris nat-ar
- **warm** water, putting hands in: *Caust Phos* k*
- **warmth** | **amel**.: agar *Ars Bry Calc* cassia-s ccrh1• **Hep** lyc rhus-t stram
- **wetting** with warm water, after: phos ↓
  - **drawing** pain: phos k*
- **writing** agg.: *(↗Cramps - fingers - writing)* acon bapt ↓ bry calc-p cist k* cycl tl1* fago ↓ iris melal-alt gya4 mur-ac nat-s ↓ ozone sde2• prot jl2 sacch-a fd2.de• stann mrr1
  - **aching**: fago
  - **stitching** pain: bapt *Bry*
  - **tearing** pain: nat-s

▽ • **extending** to:
  - **Arm**: alum ↓ merc ↓
    - **tearing** pain: alum merc
  - **Body**: hyper tl1
    - **Side**; corresponding: helo-s bnm14•
  - **Chest**, elbow, shoulder and wrist: vip ↓
    - **tearing** pain: vip
  - **Elbow**: brass-n-o srj5• eupi ↓ nat-m plat k* *Plb* k*
    - **drawing** pain: eupi k* nat-m plat k*
  - **Nails**; below: all-s ↓
    - **tearing** pain: all-s vh1
  - **Shoulder**: brass-n-o srj5• nux-m *Plb Propr* sa3•
    - **drawing** pain: nux-m
  - **Tips**: berb ↓

- **extending** to – **Tips**: ...
    - **stitching** pain: berb
  - **Upper** limbs: helo-s bnm14•
  - **Upward** from injured finger: *(↗upward; Injuries - fingers - accompanied - pain - extending - arm)* bufo br1 hydrog srj2•
  - **Wrist**: mag-c ↓ vip ↓
    - **tearing** pain: mag-c vip

○ • **Back** of fingers: abrom-a ↓ berb ↓ brom ↓ carb-an ↓ caust ↓ cocc ↓ hell ↓ lach ↓ nat-c ↓ ran-s ↓ rhus-t ↓ sabad ↓ sars ↓ sil ↓ zinc ↓
  - **boring** pain: lach
  - **burning**: abrom-a ks5 brom k* cocc k* ran-s k* sil k*
  - **stitching** pain: caust sabad
  - **tearing** pain: berb carb-an h2 hell h1 nat-c sars h2 zinc
  - **twinging**: rhus-t k*
- **Balls**: *Sulph* ↓
  - **burning**: *Sulph* k*
- **Between**: morg-p ↓
  - **evening**: *Rhus-t*
  - **burning**: morg-p pte1*•
- **Bones**: alum k* apis ars k* aur-m-n ↓ crot-h k* dios k* fl-ac bg2 kali-bi k2 mez k* ph-ac ↓ ran-s ↓ **Sil** verat k* viol-o ↓
  - **boring** pain: aur-m-n ran-s
  - **gnawing** pain: ran-s k*
  - **grasping**, when: verat k*
  - **pressing** pain: viol-o ptk1
  - **tearing** pain: ph-ac h2
- **Externally**: ars ↓ fl-ac ↓
  - **burning**: ars fl-ac
- **First** (= index finger): abrot ↓ acon k* aeth ↓ *Agar* ↓ alum ↓ am-m ↓ ambr ↓ ammc k* anac ↓ arund ↓ bamb-a ↓ bapt ↓ bar-c ↓ bell ↓ berb ↓ *Bism* ↓ calc ↓ camph ↓ caps ↓ carb-ac ↓ carb-v ↓ card-m ↓ *Caust* ↓ cham chel k* chin cocc k* com ↓ con croc ↓ crot-h k* des-ac ↓ dig ↓ dulc fd4.de ephe-si ↓ ferr-ma ↓ *Fl-ac* k* gamb ↓ ham fd3.de• heroin ↓ hura hydr k* ind indg k* iod ↓ iris jug-r k* kali-bi ↓ *Kali-c* ↓ kali-i ↓ kali-n k* kali-s ↓ kalm k* lac-lup hrn2• lachn ↓ lil-t k* lyc k* lyss mag-c ↓ mag-m k* mang med meny ↓ merc ↓ merc-i-f k* nat-ar nat-c ↓ nat-m ↓ nat-p k* nat-s ↓ nat-sil fd3.de• nicc ↓ olnd ↓ pall k* par ↓ petr ↓ phos ↓ plan k* plat ↓ psil ft1 ran-b ↓ ran-s ↓ rhod ↓ rhus-v ↓ ribo ↓ ruta fd4.de sabad ↓ sacch-a ↓ sep ↓ **Sil** spig k* spong fd4.de stann ↓ sulph ↓ symph ↓ tarax ↓ tarent ↓ thuj til ↓ tritic-vg fd5.de vanil fd5.de verb ↓ zinc ↓
  - **right**: arum-dru ↓
    - **pulled** forcibly; sensation as if: arum-dru a1
  - **morning**: dulc ↓ lyc ↓
    - **stitching** pain: dulc fd4.de lyc
  - **forenoon**: thuj
    - **11** h: thuj ↓
      - **drawing** pain: thuj
    - **drawing** pain: thuj k*
  - **afternoon**:
    - **17** h: thuj ↓
      - **stitching** pain: thuj
    - **spinning**; while: nat-s ↓
      - **tearing** pain: nat-s
  - **evening**: agar ↓ anac ↓ dios ↓ kalm k* mag-c ↓ mang rhus-v ↓ ruta fd4.de sabad ↓ tritic-vg fd5.de verb ↓
    - **20** h: hura ↓
      - **stitching** pain: hura
    - **aching**: dios rhus-v
    - **bed** agg.; in: kali-bi ↓ mez ↓ rhod ↓
      - **drawing** pain: kali-bi k*
      - **stitching** pain: rhod
      - **tearing** pain: mez
    - **drawing** pain: anac k* mang sabad verb
    - **tearing** pain: agar k* mag-c
  - **night**: kali-n ↓
    - **tearing** pain: kali-n h2

Extremities

- **First**: ...
  - **aching**: abrot carb-ac com des-ac rbp6 fl-ac rhus-v ribo rly4• sabad stann
  - **and** crawling: *Agar* ↓
    - **burning**: *Agar*
  - **appearing** suddenly:
    - **disappearing** suddenly; and: bamb-a ↓
      - **stitching** pain: bamb-a stb2.de•
  - **broken**; as if: cham k*
  - **burning**: acon *Agar* alum arund berb card-m chel ephe-si hsj1• ferr-ma hura *Kali-c* nat-c h2 olnd sil [heroin sdj2]
  - **contracting**: caps a1
  - **cramping**: mag-m h2 mang h2
  - **cut** with a sharp instrument; as if slightly: mag-c h2 nat-m h2
  - **cutting** pain: mang h2
  - **drawing** pain: acon k* agar k* alum k* anac k* bar-c h2 calc h2 carb-v k* caust k* chel k* chin h1 dig k* kali-bi k* mang k* par k* petr k* plat k* sabad k* sulph k* symph fd3.de• thuj k* tritic-vg fd5.de vanil fd5.de verb k*
    - **cramping**: plat h2
    - **jerking** pain: plat h2
    - **paralyzed**; as if: agar bar-c h2 chel a1 sabad k* verb k*
    - **upward**: chin k* sulph sne
  - **extending** it: am-m ↓
    - **tearing** pain: am-m
  - **gnawing** pain: kali-bi k* phos ran-s k*
  - **motion** agg.: sabad ↓ verb ↓
    - **aching**: sabad
    - **stitching** pain: verb
  - **paralyzed**; as if: agar *Caust* crot-h k* mang h2 plan k* sabad verb
  - **pressing** pain: chel k* nat-s k* ruta fd4.de tarax zinc h2
  - **rheumatic**: *Hydr*
  - **scratching**: (non:mag-c h2) (non:nat-m h2)
  - **shooting** pain: nat-p stann tarent
  - **sprained**; as if: alum cham lachn c1 spig h1 stann
  - **stitching** pain: aeth agar ambr bamb-a stb2.de• bapt berb calc camph carb-v cham chel croc dig dulc fd4.de hura kali-c kali-s fd4.de kalm lyc lyss merc nat-m nat-p par phos rhod sabad sacch-a fd2.de• *Sil* stann symph fd3.de• tarent thuj tritic-vg fd5.de vanil fd5.de verb
    - **outward**: meny
    - **thistle**; as from a: aeth
  - **tearing** pain: agar k* am-m ambr bell *Bism* calc caust chel dig h2 gamb iod kali-bi kali-c h2 kali-i kali-n lyc mang h2 nat-c nat-m nicc par ran-b rhod sabad sep h2 til
    - **paralyzed**; as if: dig h2
    - **splinter**; as from a: agar
    - **twitching**: dig h2 mag-m h2
  - **ulcerative** pain: **Sil**
  - **writing** agg.: ran-b ↓
    - **tearing** pain: ran-b
  - **extending** to:
    - **Elbow**: kalm ↓
      - **tearing** pain: kalm
    - **Forearm**: nat-m ↓
      - **tearing** pain: nat-m h2
  - **Back** of fingers: acon ↓ berb ↓ grat ↓ nat-m ↓ par ↓ rhus-t ↓
    - **burning**: acon berb
    - **stitching** pain: grat nat-m par rhus-t
    - **tearing** pain: grat
  - **Balls**: calc-p k* kreos k*
    - **aching**: calc-p k*
  - **Bones**: ran-s ↓ symph ↓
    - **gnawing** pain: ran-s k* symph fd3.de•
  - **Extensor** muscle: nit-ac ↓
    - **drawing** pain: nit-ac h2
  - **Externally**: chel ↓
    - **burning**: chel

- **First**: ...
  - **Joints**: acon k* **Act-sp** ambr ↓ arg-n k* **Bell** ↓ berb k* bov ↓ calc ↓ carb-v ↓ caul caust ↓ chel ↓ *Coloc* crot-h ↓ dulc fd4.de heroin ↓ kali-c ↓ kali-p ↓ lac-ac ↓ nat-m k* nat-p k* nat-s k* nux-v ↓ phys k* rhus-t ruta ↓ spong k* sumb ↓ symph ↓ tritic-vg fd5.de vanil fd5.de verat-v viol-o zinc
    - **afternoon**: lyc ↓
      - **tearing** pain: lyc
      - **weather**; during rough: rhod ↓
        - **tearing** pain: rhod
    - **evening**: agar ↓ am-m ↓ nat-m ↓
      - **stitching** pain: nat-m
      - **tearing** pain: agar k* am-m
    - **aching**: phys spong sumb
    - **boring** pain: nat-s k*
    - **burning**: [heroin sdj2]
    - **drawing** pain: ruta vanil fd5.de
    - **pressing** pain: nat-s k*
    - **sore**: caust crot-h lac-ac
    - **stitching** pain: bov calc dulc fd4.de kali-p fd1.de• nat-m nat-s symph fd3.de• tritic-vg fd5.de
    - **tearing** pain: ambr **Bell** berb calc carb-v caust kali-c nat-m nux-v
      - **paralyzed**; as if: bell h1 chel h1
    - **working**: bov ↓
      - **stitching** pain: bov
    - **Distal**: agn ↓ am-m ↓ ambr ↓ bell ↓ berb ↓ cham ↓ gamb ↓ hura ↓ lyc ↓ nat-c ↓ nux-v ↓ petr ↓ stann ↓ sulph ↓ sumb ↓
      - **aching**: sumb
      - **burning**: berb nat-c
      - **drawing** pain: stann h2
      - **pressing** pain: bell h1
      - **stitching** pain: agn (non:bar-c kl) cham gamb hura lyc petr sulph
      - **tearing** pain: am-m ambr bell h1 (non:carb-v kl) nux-v
    - **Middle**: agar ↓ arg-n ↓ arn ↓ **Bell** ↓ berb k* calc ↓ camph ↓ carb-v ↓ indg ↓ kali-c ↓ lyc ↓ nat-m ↓ nat-sil fd3.de• rhod k* rhus-t k* staph ↓ symph ↓ tritic-vg fd5.de ust ↓ vanil fd5.de zinc ↓
      - **aching**: zinc
      - **boring** pain: carb-v
      - **burning**: berb
      - **drawing** pain: arg-n k* berb k* calc k* camph k* lyc k* staph h1 symph fd3.de• tritic-vg fd5.de ust k* vanil fd5.de
      - **stitching** pain: arn carb-v indg kali-c tritic-vg fd5.de
      - **tearing** pain: agar k* **Bell** calc carb-v h2 kali-c nat-m
    - **Proximal**: agar ↓ am-m ↓ arg-met ↓ aur-m-n ↓ bapt ↓ berb ↓ bry k* calc k* carb-ac ↓ carb-v ↓ chel ↓ euon ↓ fl-ac ↓ ham k* jatr-c lyc ↓ mag-c ↓ mag-m ↓ mang k* merc-c ↓ nat-m ↓ puls k* rhus-t k* spig ↓ stann ↓ tritic-vg ↓ vanil fd5.de
      - **aching**: am-m nat-m
      - **boring** pain: aur-m-n
      - **burning**: berb fl-ac
      - **drawing** pain: arg-met h1 euon k* vanil fd5.de
      - **motion**:
        - **amel.**: stann ↓
          - **tearing** pain: stann h2
      - **pressure**:
        - **amel.**: mag-m ↓
          - **tearing** pain: mag-m h2
      - **stitching** pain: agar bapt berb carb-ac mag-c tritic-vg fd5.de
      - **tearing** pain: berb calc carb-v h2 chel h1 lyc mag-m h2 merc-c spig h1 stann h2
  - **Nails**: am-m ↓ berb k* coc-c ↓ colch ↓ con k* kali-c k* puls k* ran-b k* sep ↓ **Sil** thuj ↓
    - **afternoon**: am-m ↓
      - **tearing** pain: am-m
    - **stitching** pain: coc-c sep thuj
    - **tearing** pain: am-m colch con kali-c sep
    - **Under** nail:
      - **cold** water agg.: sul-ac ↓
        - **tearing** pain: sul-ac h2

- **First**: ...
  - **Phalanges**:
    - **Distal**: mosch k* sacch-a fd2.de• vanil fd5.de
    - **Middle**: staph k* vanil fd5.de
    - **Proximal**: nat-sil fd3.de• osm plat k*
  - **Sides**: berb ↓ plb ↓
    - **tearing** pain: berb k* plb k*
    - **Inner**: mez ↓
      - **tearing** pain: mez h2
    - **Outer**: merc ↓
      - **tearing** pain: merc
  - **Skin**: berb ↓ camph ↓ carb-v ↓ nat-m ↓
    - **stitching** pain: berb camph carb-v nat-m
  - **Tendons**: nat-m ↓
    - **tearing** pain: nat-m
  - **Tips**: aeth ↓ bamb-a ↓ berb k* kali-c ↓ kali-s ↓ nat-c ↓ nat-m k* nat-s ↓ olnd ↓ sulph ↓ teucr k* tritic-vg fd5.de zinc k*
    - **aching**: teucr
    - **burning**: kali-c olnd
    - **grasping** something agg.: *Rhus-t* ↓
      - **stitching** pain: *Rhus-t*
    - **stitching** pain: aeth a1 bamb-a stb2.de• berb kali-s fd4.de nat-c nat-s sulph zinc
    - **tearing** pain: kali-c nat-m zinc
    - **touch** agg.: mur-ac ↓
      - **stitching** pain: mur-ac a1
- **Fourth**: agar ↓ all-c k* aloe am-m ↓ anac ↓ arg-met ↓ arg-n ↓ arn ↓ ars ↓ asaf ↓ aur ↓ aur-m-n ↓ bar-c ↓ bell ↓ berb ↓ bism ↓ brom ↓ bry ↓ cact ↓ calad ↓ canth k* caps ↓ carb-v ↓ carbn-s ↓ *Caust* ↓ cham ↓ chel k* chinin-s ↓ cinnb k* coc-c ↓ coca colch ↓ coloc k* com ↓ con k* cycl ↓ dios k* gels k* hell ↓ hydrog srj2• hyos k* inul ↓ kali-c ↓ kali-n ↓ kali-p ↓ kalm k* laur ↓ led ↓ lith-c lyc ↓ mag-c ↓ merc ↓ merc-i-f ↓ mez ↓ naja nat-c ↓ nat-m ↓ nat-p k* nat-s ↓ nit-ac ↓ nux-m ↓ ozone sde2• ph-ac ↓ phos ↓ phyt k* psil ft1 rhod k* rhodi a1 rhus-t k* rosm ↓ ruta fd4.de sacch-a ↓ sang ↓ sil ↓ spig ↓ stann ↓ stry k* sulph ↓ symph fd3.de• tab ↓ tarax ↓ tarent k* ther ↓ thuj ↓ tritic-vg fd5.de verb ↓ zinc ↓
  - **left**: chin ↓ *Vac* ↓
    - **burning**: *Vac* jl2
    - **jerking** pain: chin h1
  - **morning**: nat-ar nux-m k*
    - **rising** agg.: kali-bi ↓
      - **drawing** pain: kali-bi
  - **forenoon**: sulph ↓
    - **tearing** pain: sulph
  - **afternoon**: calc-p k* canth ↓ chinin-s indg ↓
    - **tearing** pain: canth indg
  - **evening**: ambr ↓ arn ↓
    - **drawing** pain: arn k*
    - **tearing** pain: ambr arn
  - **night**: nat-c ↓
    - **rising**:
      - **amel.**: nat-c ↓
        - **tearing** pain: nat-c h2
    - **tearing** pain: nat-c h2
  - **aching**: arn
  - **bending**:
    - **amel.**: ph-ac ↓
      - **pressing** pain: ph-ac h2
  - **burning**: spig stann tarax ther kr1 tritic-vg fd5.de
  - **cutting** pain: bell h1
  - **drawing** pain: arn k* bry k* calad k* chel k* com k* kali-n k* nat-s k* ph-ac h2 phos k* sacch-a fd2.de• sil k* sulph k* thuj k*
    - **cramping**: phos h2
  - **flexing** amel.: ph-ac ↓
    - **drawing** pain: ph-ac k*
  - **motion**:
    - **agg.**: carb-v ↓ sars ↓
      - **drawing** pain: sars h2

- **Fourth – motion – agg.**: ...
      - **tearing** pain: carb-v sars h2
    - **amel.**: cina ↓ kali-c ↓ thuj ↓
      - **cramping**: cina a1
      - **drawing** pain: thuj k*
      - **tearing** pain: kali-c h2
    - **hand**; of:
      - **agg.**: spig ↓
        - **pressing** pain: spig h1
  - **pressing** pain: arg-n k* aur k* aur-m-n a1 led k* nat-s k* ph-ac h2 ruta h1 tarax thuj h1
  - **rest** agg.: aur ↓
    - **pressing** pain: aur k*
  - **rheumatic**: hell ↓ tell k*
    - **tearing** pain: hell
  - **sitting** agg.: arg-n ↓
    - **pressing** pain: arg-n k*
  - **sitting**, reading: com k*
  - **sore**: chinin-s nit-ac h2 verb
  - **sprained**; as if: lyc h2 nux-m phos h2
  - **stitching** pain: asaf berb brom cact caps carbn-s *Caust* cham hydrog srj2• kali-c kali-p fd1.de• laur led merc-i-f nat-m phyt rosm lgb1 ruta fd4.de sang sil symph fd3.de• tarax verb zinc
  - **tearing** pain: agar k* am-m anac arg-met h1 ars h2 bar-c h2 bell h1 bism brom canth carb-v h2 chel coc-c colch cycl h1 inul kali-c h2 laur mag-c merc mez nat-c nit-ac phos h2 sulph tab thuj
    - **jerking** pain: agar h2
    - **paralyzed**; as if: hell h1
  - **using** fingers: tarent k*
  - **walking** agg.: nat-s ↓
    - **pressing** pain: nat-s k*
  - **writing** agg.: ozone sde2•
  - **Back** of fingers: mag-c ↓
    - **tearing** pain: mag-c
  - **Balls**: berb ↓ caps ↓ mur-ac ↓ stann ↓ staph ↓ sulph ↓
    - **cramping**: staph h1
    - **cutting** pain: stann h2
    - **pinching** pain: sulph h2
    - **pressing** pain: staph h1 sulph h2
    - **stitching** pain: berb caps
    - **tearing** pain: mur-ac
  - **Bones**: sars ↓
    - **drawing** pain: sars h2
    - **tearing** pain: sars h2
  - **Joints**: aeth k* agar ↓ aloe ant-c k* arg-met arn ↓ aur k* bry ↓ calc k* carb-v ↓ caust ↓ chinin-s ↓ colch crot-h gamb ↓ ham fd3.de• kalm k* lach k* lyc k* melal-alt ↓ mur-ac k* nat-p k* nat-s ↓ rhod k* ruta ↓ sabad k* sabin ↓ sars ↓ symph ↓ teucr k*
    - **night**: ruta ↓
      - **drawing** pain: ruta
    - **aching**: arn gamb melal-alt gya4
    - **bending** fingers agg.: ham fd3.de• mur-ac
    - **drawing** pain: caust k* ruta
    - **pressing** pain: ruta h1
    - **rheumatic**: hyper k* *Lach* k*
    - **sore**: chinin-s
    - **stitching** pain: aloe bry sars symph fd3.de•
    - **tearing** pain: agar k* arg-met aur calc carb-v h2 kalm lyc k* nat-s sabin teucr
    - **Distal**: aeth ↓ aloe arg-met ↓ aur ↓ hyper k* kalm ↓ lyc ↓ sabin ↓ teucr ↓
      - **tearing** pain: aeth arg-met aur kalm lyc sabin teucr
    - **Metacarpal**: melal-alt gya4
    - **Middle**: agar ↓ brom ↓ bufo ↓ calc ↓ iod ↓ mur-ac ↓ rhod k* sabin ↓ sulph ↓
      - **sore**: sulph h2
      - **stitching** pain: brom bufo
      - **tearing** pain: agar calc iod h mur-ac sabin

Extremities

- **Fourth – Joints – Middle**: ...
  - **extending** to:
    - **Metacarpal** bone: mur-ac↓
      - **tearing** pain: mur-ac a1
  - **Proximal**: agar↓ aloe↓ anac↓ *Benz-ac*↓ calc k* lach k* lyc↓ merc-i-f↓ propr sa3• sabad↓ sabin↓ teucr k*
    - **burning**: sabad
    - **stitching** pain: aloe anac merc-i-f
    - **tearing** pain: agar k* *Benz-ac* calc lyc k* sabin
  - **Sides**:
    - **Inner**: fl-ac↓ mill↓
      - **burning**: fl-ac mill
    - **Outer**: apis↓ prun↓
      - **burning**: apis prun
  - **Tips**: am-m↓ ambr k* anthraci↓ apis↓ arg-n↓ arn↓ aur-m-n↓ carb-v k* fl-ac↓ kali-c k* merl↓ myric k* nat-ar nat-c k* spig k* sul-ac↓ symph fd3.de• zinc k*
    - **burning**: apis aur-m-n fl-ac kali-c sul-ac
    - **drawing** pain: kali-c h2
    - **pressing** pain: spig h1
    - **stitching** pain: am-m arg-n aur-m-n fl-ac merl k*
    - **tearing** pain: ambr h1 anthraci arn carb-v kali-c nat-c spig zinc
- **Joints**: *Acon*↓ *Agar*↓ agn↓ aloe↓ alum↓ am-c↓ am-m↓ *Ambr*↓ aml-ns↓ anac↓ ang↓ **Ant-c** apis↓ arg-met↓ arn↓ ars k* arund asaf↓ *Asar*↓ aur k* aur-i k2 aur-m-n↓ aur-s↓ bapt↓ *Bar-c*↓ bell↓ benz-ac k* berb↓ bism↓ bov↓ bros-gau mrc1 bry k* bufo↓ *Calc* calc-p calc-sil k2 camph↓ cann-i↓ carb-v carbn-s↓ **Caul** k* **Caust** cham↓ chel↓ chin↓ cina↓ cist k* clem↓ cocc↓ *Colch* k* coloc com↓ con↓ crot-c sk4• crot-h↓ daph↓ dig↓ dios↓ dulc fd4.de euon↓ euphr↓ ferr-ma↓ fic-m gya1 fl-ac k* ger-i↓ graph bro1 grat↓ *Guaj* guat sp1 ham fd3.de• *Hell*↓ hydr-ac hyos↓ hyper↓ ign↓ indg↓ iod↓ iris kali-bi k* kali-c k2 kali-n kali-s fd4.de kali-sil↓ kiss↓ kola stb3• kreos↓ lac-ac k* lac-h↓ lachn↓ laur↓ led k* lith-c lyc bro1 m-ambo↓ m-aust↓ mag-c↓ mag-m↓ manc mang↓ meny↓ merc↓ merc-c↓ mez morg-p pte1*• mosch↓ mur-ac↓ nat-m↓ nat-s k* nat-sil fd3.de• nit-ac↓ nit-s-d↓ nux-m↓ nux-v↓ olib-sac↓ olnd↓ onos ox-ac paeon↓ par↓ petr-ra shn4• ph-ac↓ phos physala-p bnm7• phyt↓ pin-con oss2• plan↓ plat↓ polyg-h psor al2 puls↓ pycnop-sa mrz1 pyrus rheum↓ rhod k* *Rhus-t*↓ ribo↓ ruta fd4.de sabad↓ sabin↓ sacch-a fd2.de• samb↓ *Sars*↓ seneg↓ sep sil k* spig↓ spong fd4.de stann↓ staph stict↓ still k* stront-c↓ sul-ac k2 sulfonam ks2 sulph k* symph fd3.de• *Tarent* k* tax↓ tell↓ tep↓ teucr↓ thuj↓ tritic-vg fd5.de trom↓ upa k* ust↓ vanil fd5.de verb↓ vinc↓ zinc↓
  - **right**: mag-c↓
    - **dislocated**; as if: mag-c bg1
  - **forenoon**: ars↓ mag-c↓ sulph↓ trom↓
    - **shooting** pain: trom
    - **tearing** pain: ars mag-c sulph
  - **evening**: *Calc* dulc fd4.de ham fd3.de• lyc↓ staph stront-c↓
    - **drawing** pain: staph k*
    - **tearing** pain: lyc stront-c
  - **night**:
    - **bed** agg.; in: *Phos*↓
      - **tearing** pain: *Phos*
  - **aching**: bry cann-i coloc com ger-i rly4• kali-bi led ribo rly4• tax k*
  - **boring** pain: aur aur-m-n carb-v k* coloc daph hell k* mez nat-s
  - **burning**: apis k* bufo cann-i carb-v caust dulc fd4.de mang a1 olib-sac wmh1 spig b7.de tritic-vg fd5.de vinc
  - **cutting** pain: bapt dios bg1 mur-ac ph-ac
  - **dislocated**; as if: acon bg2 alum bg2 am-c bg2 ang bg2 camph bg2 fl-ac bg2 *Graph* bg2 ign bg2 kali-n bg2 kiss rb2 laur bg2 lyc bg2 m-ambo b7.de mag-c h2* nat-m bg2 nux-m bg2 phos k* rhod bg2 stann bg2 sulph bg2
  - **drawing** pain: aloe k* am-c b4.de* aml-ns anac b4a.de ang b7.de* **Ant-c** k* asaf k* *Asar* b7a.de aur k* *Bar-c* k* bell b4.de* bov b4.de* carb-v **Caust** k* chel b7.de* cist k* *Coloc* k* euon k* hyos k* kali-c b4a.de kali-s fd4.de m-aust b7.de* nat-s k* olnd b7.de* ph-ac k* phos plan k* plat k* rhod k* *Rhus-t* ruta b7.de* seneg k* sep k* sil k* spig b7.de* spong b7.de* stann k* staph k* sulph k* tep k* teucr b7a.de ust k* vanil fd5.de
- **Joints – drawing** pain: ...
  - **paralyzed**; as if: staph h1
  - **gouty**: berb k2 *Calc* k* calc-p k2 *Hep* k* **Lyc** k* ruta fd4.de sabin bg2 stel br1 *Sulph*
  - **gouty** nodosities; in: agn↓
    - **tearing** pain: agn
  - **jerking** pain: anac nat-m rhus-t k*
  - **motion**:
    - **agg.**: *Led*↓ ruta↓ staph↓
      - **drawing** pain: ruta fd4.de staph h1
      - **tearing** pain: *Led*
    - **amel.**: coloc↓ **Rhus-t**↓ vanil↓
      - **drawing** pain: coloc **Rhus-t** vanil fd5.de
      - **pressing** pain: coloc
    - **passive** motion | **agg.**: ang ars k* dulc fd4.de ruta fd4.de sep
  - **paralyzed**; as if: acon bg2 ambr bg2 arg-met *Aur* b4a.de bar-c bg2 bell b4.de* bry bg2 carb-v bg2 cina bg2 cocc bg2 crot-h bg2 dig bg2 hell bg2 kreos bg2 laur bg2 mang bg2 par b7a.de* rhod bg2 sabin bg2 sil bg2 spig bg2 verb b7a.de*
  - **paroxysmal**: anac kali-n mag-c
  - **pressing** pain: arg-met k* arn asaf k* coloc k* con k* graph bg2 hell k* laur bg2 merc bg2 mez k* nat-s k* nit-s-d a1 ph-ac bg2 ruta bg2 *Sars* spong h1* stann staph bg2 tritic-vg fd5.de zinc bg2
  - **pulsating** pain: polyg-h
  - **rheumatic**: *Act-sp* *Aesc* alumn k* ant-c c1 *Calc* **Caul** k* *Colch* *Coloc* ferr k* fic-m gya1 *Glon* *Gran* k* *Guaj* *Kali-bi* lac-ac lach lith-c *Manc* plan k* *Podo* psil ft1 tell teucr x-ray mtf11
    - **afternoon**: chinin-s
    - **goes** to heart: nat-p
  - **rising** agg.; after: asaf↓
    - **tearing** pain: asaf
  - **shooting** pain: *Acon* caust h2 phyt tep trom
  - **short**; as if tendons were too: nux-v k*
  - **sleep**; before going to: sulph↓
    - **tearing** pain: sulph
  - **sore**: alum benz-ac bg2 bry carb-v bg2 caul caust bg2 iod kali-c k2 lac-ac lyc nat-m nat-sil fd3.de• nit-ac bg2 sabin bg2 sep spig bg2 sulph
  - **squeezed**; as if: anac bg2 euphr bg2 mag-c bg2 mang bg2 olnd bg2 ph-ac bg2 sulph bg2
  - **stitching** pain: *Acon* agn b7.de* aloe k* am-m k* arn b7.de* asaf aur-m-n bar-c k* bov bg2 calc camph k* *Carb-v* k* carbn-s cham colch bg2 con k* ferr-ma grat bg2 *Hell* k* hyper ign b7.de* indg iod kali-bi bg2 kali-s fd4.de laur bg2 mag-c bg2 mang k* meny b7.de* mosch k* nat-m k* nit-ac k* paeon ph-ac k* phyt plat k* rhus-t b7.de* ruta fd4.de sabin bg2 sars k* *Sep* k* spig k* spong b7.de* stann k* staph b7.de* stict sul-ac k* *Sulph* k* tell rsj10• tep thuj trom verb bg2 zinc
  - **tearing** pain: acon *Agar* k* agn k* am-c am-m h2* *Ambr* b7a.de anac bg2 ant-c bg2 arg-met k* ars bg2 asaf k* **Aur** k* aur-s k2 berb bism bg2 bry k* calc k* calc-sil k2 carb-v k* carbn-s chin bg2 cist clem k* colch k* *Coloc* k* dig k* graph bg2 hell k* ign b7.de* kali-bi k* kali-c k* kali-n k* kali-s fd4.de kali-sil k2 lac-h sze9• lachn led k* **Lyc** k* m-ambo b7.de mag-c k* mag-m bg2 merc k* merc-c k* mur-ac bg2 nat-m bg2 ph-ac h2 phos k* psor k* puls k* rheum k* *Rhus-t* k* ruta b7.de* sabad bg2 sabin k* samb k* sars k* sep bg2 **Sil** k* spig b7.de* stann staph tl1 stront-c k* sul-ac bg2 *Sulph* k* teucr k* thuj k* verb bg2 zinc k*
    - **alternating** with | **Head**; pain in (See HEAD - Pain - alternating - fingers - joints)
    - **cramping**: kali-n h2
    - **paralyzed**; as if: dig
    - **pressing** pain: stann h2
    - **twitching**: ph-ac h2
  - **ulcerative** pain: kali-c bg2
  - **waking**; on: *Calc* tritic-vg fd5.de
  - **wandering**: coloc k* polyg-h psor k* sulph k*
  - **weather** agg., cold: calc-p k2
  - **extending** to:
    - **Shoulder**: *Ars*↓
      - **tearing** pain: *Ars*
    - **Upward**: brom k*

- **Joints – extending** to: ...
  - **Wrist**, into: mag-c ↓
    - **tearing** pain: mag-c
  - **Between** metacarpophalangeal joints: mez ↓
    - **tearing** pain: mez h2
  - **Distal**: alum ↓ ang k* aur ↓ bism ↓ carb-v ↓ sep k*
    - **motion** agg.: ang k* sep k*
    - **sore**: alum sep
    - **tearing** pain: (non:agar a1) aur k* bism k* carb-v (non:lyc a1) (non:mag-c a1) (non:zinc a1)
  - **Metacarpophalangeal**: ruta ↓ spig ↓ tritic-vg ↓
    - **jerking** pain: spig h1
    - **pressing** pain: ruta h1 tritic-vg fd5.de
    - **Between** second and third finger: rosm lgb1
  - **Middle**: brom ↓ carb-v ↓ caul ↓ jac-c k* jac-g lil-t k* ruta ↓ sabin ↓ staph ↓
    - **closing** hand agg.: caul ↓
      - **cutting** pain: caul a1
    - **cutting** pain: caul
    - **drawing** pain: ruta h1
    - **pressing** pain: ruta h1
    - **tearing** pain: brom a1* carb-v k* sabin staph h1
  - **Proximal**: agar ↓ aloe ↓ alum ↓ arund k* aur ↓ brom ↓ calc ↓ card-m ↓ com ↓ croc ↓ iris kali-bi ↓ kali-c ↓ kali-i ↓ kalm ↓ lyc ↓ mag-c ↓ nat-m ↓ ol-an ↓ ph-ac ↓ polyg-h ↓ ruta ↓ staph ↓ symph fd3.de• tax ↓ tritic-vg fd5.de upa k* vanil fd5.de zinc ↓
    - **left**: gink-b sbd1•
    - **evening**: iris kali-i ↓
      - **tearing** pain: kali-i k*
    - **aching**: tax k*
    - **dislocation**; as from: alum ruta
    - **drawing** pain: card-m com k* croc k* kali-c k* ol-an ph-ac k* staph k* vanil fd5.de
    - **gnawing** pain: kalm k*
    - **motion**:
      - **agg.**: staph ↓
        - **drawing** pain: staph k*
      - **amel.**: com ↓
        - **drawing** pain: com k*
    - **pulsating** pain: polyg-h
    - **rheumatic**: arg-n card-m ↓ ferr k* plan k*
      - **drawing** pain: card-m
    - **sprained**; as if: nat-m
    - **stitching** pain: aloe calc com kali-bi
    - **tearing** pain: agar k* aur h1 brom k* kali-i k* lyc k* mag-c k* zinc k*
    - **wandering** pain: polyg-h
- **Muscles**:
  - **Extensor** muscles: hep ↓ puls ↓
    - **drawing** pain: hep h2
    - **tearing** pain: hep h2 puls h1
  - **Flexor** muscles: aster
- **Nails**: *All-c* ↓ alum ant-c k* berb ↓ calc ↓ *Calc-p* *Caust* colch *Graph* hep kola stb3• lach ↓ lappa ↓ m-aust ↓ merc mosch ↓ myris k* naja nat-m nat-s ↓ *Nit-ac* nux-v *Petr* k* puls ran-b ↓ raph k* rhus-t ↓ sars ↓ sep ↓ **Sil** squil sulph teucr
  - **boring** pain: colch
  - **burrowing**: caust bg2
  - **cutting** pain: petr ptk1 sars ptk1
  - **gnawing** pain: alum ptk1 berb ptk1 lach ptk1 lappa ptk1
  - **jerking** pain: alum b2.de* calc b2.de* caust b2.de* *Graph* b2.de* m-aust b2.de mosch b2.de* nat-m b2.de* nit-ac b2.de* nux-v b2.de* *Puls* b2.de* rhus-t b2.de* sep b2.de* sil b2.de* sulph b2.de*
  - **neuralgic**: *All-c* bro1 alum bro1 colch bro1
  - **sore**: *Petr*
  - **touch** agg.: caust petr k*
  - **ulcerative** pain: *Calc-p* k* m-aust b7.de nat-s **Puls** k* ran-b b7.de
  - **Around**: con ↓ hydrog srj2• lith-c merc ↓
    - **burning**: con
- **Nails – Around**: ...
    - **shooting** pain: lith-c merc
    - **stitching** pain: lith-c merc
  - **Roots**: *All-c* bro1 berb bro1 bism bro1 calc *Calc-p* k* myris bro1 sang k*
  - **Under**: *(↗Irritation - fingers - nails)* **Alum** k* ant-c bell ↓ berb bism calc ↓ calc-p carb-v bg2 caust k* coc-c ↓ colch ↓ con ↓ elaps *Eos* ↓ fl-ac bg2 **Graph** bg2 hep bg2 kali-c bg2 kali-n ↓ led ↓ merc bg2 naja nat-m ↓ *Nat-s* *Nit-ac* *Petr* ↓ plat ↓ puls ↓ ran-b raph k* sars *Sep* c2 *Sil* k* *Sulph* symph ↓
    - **aching**: caust
    - **burning**: calc *Caust* elaps *Eos* br1 kali-c merc nit-ac *Sars* k*
    - **cutting** pain: sars ptk2
    - **gnawing** pain: **Alum** k* sars bro1 sep bro1
    - **horny** growths, from: *Ant-c* *Graph*
    - **neuralgic**: berb bro1*
    - **pressing** pain: caust h2 symph fd3.de•
    - **pressure** agg.: sars
    - **shooting** pain: caust
    - **sore**: caust h2 kali-n h2
    - **splinters**; as from: *(↗Nails - under - splinter)* bell calc-p bg2* carb-v coc-c bg2* colch b2.de* *Fl-ac* k* *Hep* k* nat-m bg2 **Nit-ac** k* *Petr* k* plat k* ran-b k* *Sil* k* *Sulph* k*
    - **stitching** pain: calc caust con graph led a1 nat-m nat-s puls sil sulph
      - **splinter**; as from a: led bg2 nit-ac
    - **tearing** pain: *Bism* calc-p fl-ac kali-c kali-n naja
    - **touch** agg.: caust
- **Palmar** surface of fingers: **Rhus-t** ↓
  - **stitching** pain: **Rhus-t**
- **Periosteum**: **Led** ↓
  - **deep**-seated: am-c ↓
    - **sore**: am-c tl1
  - **sore**: **Led**
- **Phalanges**:
  - **Distal**: beryl ↓ nat-m ↓
    - **sore**: beryl tpw5 nat-m h2
- **Second**: agar ↓ all-c k* alum k* am-m ↓ ang ↓ apis ↓ arn ↓ ars ↓ aur-m ↓ bamb-a stb2.de• bapt *Bism* ↓ calc ↓ calc-p ↓ cann-s ↓ carb-an ↓ carb-v ↓ carbn-s caust ↓ chel ↓ chin ↓ cinnb k* cocc ↓ coloc ↓ crot-h k* crot-t ↓ cupr ↓ cycl ↓ dios ↓ dulc fd4.de euphr ↓ fic-m gya1 form ↓ gamb ↓ gard-j vlr2• ham fd3.de• hell ↓ hura iod ↓ iris kali-bi ↓ *Kali-c* ↓ kali-i ↓ kali-n ↓ kali-s fd4.de kola stb3• lach ↓ lact k* lap-la sde8.de• lith-c lyc k* mag-c ↓ mag-m ↓ mang ↓ med merc ↓ mez ↓ myric k* nat-c k* nat-p k* nat-s ↓ nux-m olnd ↓ osm k* ox-ac ↓ par ↓ phos ↓ pip-m ↓ plb ↓ ran-s k* rhus-t ↓ rhus-v ruta fd4.de sabad ↓ sil k* stann ↓ sul-ac ↓ sulph sumb ↓ tarax ↓ thuj ↓ til ↓ tritic-vg fd5.de upa vanil fd5.de verat k* zinc ↓
  - **left**: sel ↓ sulph ↓
    - **jerking** pain | **burning** pain: sulph h2
    - **shooting** pain: sel rsj9•
  - **morning**:
    - **bed** agg.; in: rhus-t ↓
      - **aching**: rhus-t
  - **afternoon**: nat-s ↓ sulph ↓
    - **15** h: caust ↓
      - **tearing** pain: caust
    - **17** h: thuj ↓
      - **stitching** pain: thuj
    - **drawing** pain: sulph k*
    - **spinning**; while: nat-s ↓
      - **tearing** pain: nat-s
    - **tearing** pain: nat-s
  - **evening**: bamb-a ↓ kali-i ↓ lyc ↓
    - **bed** agg.; in: ars ↓
      - **drawing** pain: ars
    - **stitching** pain: bamb-a stb2.de• lyc
    - **tearing** pain: kali-i
  - **night**: lyc ↓

Extremities

- **Second – night**: ...
  - **tearing** pain: lyc k*
  - **aching**: phos pip-m rhus-t
  - **burning**: apis bamb-a stb2.de• coloc *Kali-c* mez sul-ac vanil fd5.de
  - **clenching**; when: bamb-a stb2.de•
  - **cramping**: dulc h2 mang h2
  - **dinner**; after: aur-m ↓
    - **tearing** pain: aur-m
  - **drawing** pain: am-m k* ars k* bamb-a stb2.de• calc h2 carb-v k* chel k* chin k* cocc k* crot-t k* mang k* par k* stann k* sulph k* thuj k* zinc h2
    - **cramping**: stann h2
    - **jerking** pain: stann h2
  - **feather** covering, under: lyc ↓
    - **tearing** pain: lyc k*
  - **gouty**: bamb-a ↓
    - **drawing** pain: bamb-a stb2.de•
  - **motion** agg.: alum k* ham fd3.de• kali-s fd4.de vanil fd5.de verat k*
  - **pressing** pain: nat-s k* tarax
  - **rheumatic**: bapt hr1
  - **shooting** pain: cinnb nat-p sumb
  - **sore**: cann-s dios kali-c h2
  - **sprained**; as if: mag-c h2
  - **stitching** pain: arn bamb-a stb2.de• calc carb-an chel cinnb cupr dios dulc fd4.de euphr gamb kali-bi kali-c lach lyc merc nat-p olnd ox-ac ruta fd4.de sil sul-ac sulph sumb thuj vanil fd5.de verat
  - **tearing** pain: agar k* am-m ang h1 aur-m *Bism* calc calc-p carb-v h2 caust cycl form hell h1 iod kali-i kali-n kola stb3• lyc k* mag-m mang h2 merc nat-s plb ruta h1 sabad *Sil* sulph til vanil fd5.de
    - **twitching**: mag-m h2
  - **uncovering**:
    - **amel.**: lyc ↓
      - **tearing** pain: lyc h2
  - **Back** of fingers: mang ↓ nat-c ↓
    - **burning**: nat-c
    - **tearing** pain: mang a1
  - **Balls**: psil ft1
  - **Joints**: agar ↓ arg-met ↓ bell ↓ berb ↓ brom ↓ carb-ac k* carb-an ↓ iris kali-s fd4.de laur ↓ lyc ↓ mag-m ↓ merl ↓ morg-p pte1• nat-ar nat-m k* nat-s ↓ par ↓ puls-n sil ↓ spong ↓ stann k* sumb ↓ upa ↓ vanil fd5.de verat-v k*
    - **drawing** pain: arg-met bell k* upa k*
    - **pressing** pain: nat-s k* spong
    - **shooting** pain: sumb
    - **sore**: agar carb-an
    - **tearing** pain: agar berb brom k* laur lyc mag-m merl par sil
    - **Distal**: am-m ↓ ant-t k* arg-met ↓ arn ↓ bell k* carb-v ↓ crot-h k* iris
      - **boring** pain: carb-v
      - **drawing** pain: carb-v h2
      - **stitching** pain: ant-t arn carb-v
      - **tearing** pain: am-m arg-met
    - **Metacarpus**: lap-la sde8.de•
    - **Middle**: berb ↓ brom ↓ carb-ac k* ephe-si hsj1• hell ↓ kali-c ↓ kali-s fd4.de mag-m ↓ ruta ↓ sep ↓ sil ↓ stann k* stict k* thuj ↓ vanil fd5.de verat verat-v k*
      - **left**: ephe-si hsj1•
      - **boring** pain: hell
      - **stitching** pain: sep thuj vanil fd5.de
      - **tearing** pain: berb brom k* hell h1 kali-c h2 mag-m ruta h1 sil
    - **Proximal**: berb ↓ carb-v ↓ cina ↓ lachn ↓ laur ↓ lyc ↓ mang ↓ merl ↓ nat-m k* puls vanil fd5.de
      - **burning**: berb carb-v cina h1
      - **stitching** pain: carb-v mang
      - **tearing** pain: berb lachn c1 laur lyc merl
  - **Nails**: ambr ↓ kali-c ↓ teucr ↓ vanil ↓
    - **burning**: kali-c vanil fd5.de
    - **tearing** pain: ambr teucr
    - **Under**: lyc ↓
- **Second – Nails – Under**: ...
      - **tearing** pain: lyc h2
  - **Phalanges**:
    - **Distal**: gard-j vlr2• mez ↓ zinc ↓
      - **boring** pain: mez
      - **tearing** pain: mez h2 zinc h2
    - **Middle**: nicc ↓ ph-ac ↓ ruta ↓
      - **tearing** pain: nicc ph-ac ruta h1
    - **Proximal**: ph-ac ↓
      - **tearing** pain: ph-ac
  - **Sides**:
    - **Inner**: mez ↓
      - **tearing** pain: mez h2
    - **Outer**: berb ↓ merl ↓
      - **burning**: berb
      - **tearing** pain: merl
  - **Spots**; in: sul-ac ↓
    - **burning**: sul-ac
  - **Tendons**: merl ↓ sil ↓
    - **bending** agg.: sil ↓
      - **tearing** pain: sil
    - **tearing** pain: merl sil
  - **Tips**: arn ↓ castm ↓ lyc merl mez ↓ par ruta ↓ stann ↓ vanil fd5.de viol-o ↓ zinc
    - **21** h: castm ↓
      - **stitching** pain: castm
    - **stitching** pain: arn castm lyc merl a1 mez ruta fd4.de stann viol-o
    - **tearing** pain: lyc merl zinc
- **Sides**: sars ↓
  - **burning**: sars
  - **Inner**: zinc ↓
    - **burning**: zinc k*
- **Tendons**, flexor (See muscles - flexor)
- **Third**: agar ↓ all-c k* aloe ↓ ant-c ↓ arg-n ↓ *Arn Bism* ↓ brom ↓ *Calc* ↓ camph ↓ cann-s ↓ carb-v ↓ carbn-s ↓ caust ↓ cina ↓ colch crot-h k* cycl ↓ gard-j vlr2• *Gymno* hura ↓ kali-bi ↓ kali-c ↓ kali-i ↓ kreos ↓ lac-loxod-a hrn2• led lil-t k* mag-m ↓ mang ↓ merl ↓ naja nat-c ↓ ol-an ↓ osm ↓ phos ↓ phyt ↓ pip-m k* plut-n srj7• rat ↓ ribo rly4• ruta fd4.de sabad ↓ stann ↓ *Sulph* ↓ tarax ↓ thuj k* til ↓ trom ↓ vanil fd5.de viol-t ↓ zinc ↓
  - **right**: colch rsj2•
  - **left**: lac-loxod-a hrn2• thres-a sze7•
  - **forenoon**: sulph ↓
    - **tearing** pain: sulph
  - **evening**: ambr ↓ kali-i ↓
    - **tearing** pain: ambr kali-i
  - **night**: nat-c ↓
    - **rising**:
      - **amel.**: nat-c ↓
        - **tearing** pain: nat-c h2
    - **tearing** pain: nat-c h2
  - **aching**: *Arn* led naja pip-m
  - **burning**: osm tarax
  - **coldness**; during: crot-h k*
  - **cramping**: mang h2
  - **drawing** pain: *Calc* k* cina kali-bi k* kreos k* rat stann k* sulph k* zinc h2
  - **motion**:
    - **amel.**: viol-t ↓
      - **stitching** pain: viol-t
  - **rest** agg.: cina ↓ rat ↓
    - **drawing** pain: cina rat
  - **rheumatic**: thuj k*
  - **shooting** pain: crot-h trom
  - **sore**: ruta
  - **sprained**; as if: phos h2

- **Third**: ...
  - **stitching** pain: ant-c arg-n cann-s carbn-s caust crot-h hura kali-c nat-c phyt ruta fd4.de thuj trom viol-t
  - **tearing** pain: agar k* aloe *Bism* brom calc camph carb-v cycl kali-i mag-m merl ol-an sabad *Sulph* til
    - **jerking** pain: agar h2
  - **Joints**: arg-met ↓ *Calc* carb-v ↓ lac-loxod-a hrn2• merc-c mur-ac ↓ op rhus-t k* ribo rly4• ruta fd4.de sil ↓ stann k* tarent k* teucr ↓ thuj k* upa ↓ vanil fd5.de verat-v k*
    - **left**: mand rsj7•
    - **9 h**: sil ↓
      - **stitching** pain: sil
    - **night**: ruta ↓
      - **drawing** pain: ruta h1
    - **drawing** pain: arg-met mur-ac h2 ruta h1 upa k*
    - **rheumatic**: sang k* thuj k*
    - **stitching** pain: ruta fd4.de sil
    - **tearing** pain: calc carb-v h2 merc-c op teucr thuj
    - **Distal**: teucr ↓
      - **tearing** pain: teucr
    - **Middle**: calc ↓ nat-p ↓ op ↓ sil ↓ sulph ↓ thuj ↓
      - **9 h**: sil ↓
        - **burning**: sil
      - **burning**: nat-p sil
      - **sore**: sulph h2
      - **tearing** pain: calc op thuj
      - **extending** to:
        - **Proximal** joint: mur-ac ↓
          - **tearing** pain: mur-ac h2
    - **Proximal**: *Benz-ac* ↓ berb ↓ carb-v ↓
      - **burning**: berb carb-v
      - **tearing** pain: *Benz-ac*
  - **Metacarpal**: lyss verat-v
  - **Nail**, on inner border of: osm ↓
    - **burning**: osm
  - **Nails**: nat-m k*
    - **Behind**: sulph ↓
      - **tearing** pain: sulph h2
  - **Phalanges**:
    - **Distal**: colch ↓ gard-j vlr2• plan zinc ↓
      - **tearing** pain: colch zinc h2
    - **Middle**: chel k* rhus-t stann
      - **left**: mand rsj7•
      - **motion** agg.: mand rsj7•
    - **Proximal**: *Arn* k*
      - **tearing** pain: arn
  - **Sides**:
    - **Inner**: glon k*
    - **Outer**: thuj ↓
      - **pressing** pain: thuj h1
  - **Tips**: arn ↓ cham k* nat-ar
    - **tearing** pain: arn
- **Tips**: abrot ↓ allox ↓ alum ↓ am-c ↓ am-m bro1 ambr ↓ anthraci ↓ apis ↓ arn ↓ *Ars* ↓ arund ↓ aur-m-n ↓ bamb-a ↓ bell ↓ berb *Bism* ↓ borx bro1 bufo-s ↓ calc ptk1 calc-p ↓ canth ↓ carb-an ↓ carc ↓ caust chel bro1 chin ↓ cist k* coc-c ↓ colch k* com ↓ con ↓ corn ↓ croc ↓ crot-c ↓ cupr ↓ dros ↓ elat ↓ fago ↓ gins ↓ graph ↓ hyos ↓ hyper k* kali-c bro1* kreos ↓ lac-c ptk1 *Lach* ↓ laur ↓ led ↓ lept ↓ luf-op ↓ m-ambo ↓ m-arct ↓ mag-c ↓ mag-m ↓ mag-s ↓ med ↓ merc ↓ merc-i-f k* merl ↓ mez ↓ mur-ac ↓ nat-c ↓ nat-m ↓ nat-s k2 nicc ↓ olib-sac ↓ olnd ↓ osm ↓ paeon k* **Petr** ↓ phyt ↓ puls ↓ *Ran-s* ↓ **Rhus-t** ↓ ruta fd4.de sabad ↓ sabin ↓ sal-fr sle1• *Sars* sec k* sep ↓ *Sil* k* spig ↓ *Stann* ↓ *Staph* ↓ stry k* sulph k* tab ↓ teucr bro1 *Thuj* ↓ verb ↓ viol-o ↓ vip ↓ zinc ↓
  - **right**: mag-c ↓
    - **dislocated**; as if: mag-c bg1
  - **morning**: sulph k*
    - **rising** agg.; after: mag-c ↓
      - **tearing** pain: mag-c

- **Fingers – Tips**: ...
  - **evening**: **Am-m** ↓ caust merc-i-f k*
    - **shooting** pain: *Am-m*
    - **stitching** pain: *Am-m*
    - **tearing** pain: **Am-m**
  - **night**: bamb-a ↓ mag-s ↓ *Sulph* ↓
    - **shooting** pain: *Sulph*
    - **stitching** pain: bamb-a stb2.de• *Sulph*
    - **tearing** pain: mag-s
  - **aching**: com phyt k*
  - **boring** pain: sulph
  - **burning**: am-m anthraci apis k* bell canth b7.de* caust con corn bg1 croc k* crot-c gins laur b7.de luf-op rsj5• m-ambo b7.de mag-m med ptk1 mur-ac nat-m ptk1 nat-s olib-sac wmh1 olnd b7.de sabad k* *Sars* *Sil* k* *Sulph* tab *Teucr* b7.de*
  - **bursting**; sensation as if: caust bg2*
  - **chill**; during: bell ↓
    - **shooting** pain: bell
    - **stitching** pain: bell
  - **crushed**; as if: caust bg2
  - **cutting** pain: ars bg2 hyper k* petr k*
  - **drawing** pain: am-c k* *Ars* k* kreos k* petr k* zinc k*
  - **festering**: alum bg2 nat-c bg2 nat-m bg2 sars bg2
  - **fever**; during: elat ↓
    - **shooting** pain: elat c1
  - **fine**: staph bg2
  - **gnawing** pain: berb bg1 fago k* nat-m bg2
  - **grasping** something agg.: **Rhus-t** ↓
    - **stitching** pain: **Rhus-t**
  - **hang** down agg.: sulph ↓
    - **stitching** pain: sulph
  - **playing** piano: *Gels*
  - **pressure** agg.: chel ↓
    - **tearing** pain: chel
  - **rubbing**:
    - **amel.**: mag-m ↓
      - **stitching** pain: mag-m a1
  - **shooting** pain: *Am-m* bell berb elat lept *Sulph*
  - **sore**: allox tpw4 calc-p nat-c *Sars* sulph bg1
  - **stitching** pain: abrot alum am-c **Am-m** k* ambr k* apis b7a.de* arund aur-m-n bamb-a stb2.de• bell k* berb bufo-s carb-an carc fd2.de• chin k* coc-c con k* dros b7.de* elat graph hyos *Lach* laur b7.de* led lept m-ambo b7.de m-arct b7.de mag-m merc merl a1 mez k* mur-ac k* nat-m bg2 nat-s bg2 nicc olnd b7.de* osm **Petr** phyt bg2 puls *Ran-s* b7.de* **Rhus-t** sabad b7.de* sabin b7.de* sec k* sep b4.de* spig k* *Stann* k* staph b7.de* **Sulph** *Thuj* k* verb b7.de* viol-o b7.de* vip
    - **frostbitten**; as if: spig
    - **splinters**; as from: nat-m bg2
  - **tearing** pain: **Am-m** k* ambr arn *Ars* k* bell bg2 berb *Bism* k* calc caust k* chel colch b7.de* cupr k* mag-c mag-s spig b7.de* *Staph* k* teucr b7.de* zinc k*
  - **ulcerative** pain: **Sil**
  - **walking** in open air agg.: *Am-m* ↓
    - **stitching** pain: *Am-m*
  - **extending** to:
    - **Arm**: *Ars* ↓ fago ↓ zinc ↓
      - **drawing** pain: *Ars* zinc
      - **stitching** pain: fago
    - **Hand**: am-c ↓
      - **drawing** pain: am-c
    - **Shoulder**: *Ars* ↓ gels
      - **tearing** pain: *Ars*
- **Flexors**: ptel ↓
  - **aching**: ptel

- **Forearms**: acon k* _Aesc_ k* aeth↓ agar k* agath-a nl2• agn↓ ail↓ all-c k* aloe↓ alum k* alum-p↓ alum-sil k2 am-c k* am-m k* _Ambr_↓ anac bro1 anag ang↓ _Ant-c_↓ ant-t↓ apis apoc k* arg-met↓ _Arg-n_ k* **Arn**↓ ars k* ars-i ars-met↓ ars-s-f↓ arum-d k* asaf k* asar↓ asc-t k* aur k* aur-ar k2 aur-m↓ aur-m-n k* aur-s k2 bamb-a↓ bapt k* bar-act↓ bar-c k* bar-s k2 _Bell_↓ benz-ac↓ berb k* beryl↓ bism k* borx _Bov_↓ brom↓ bry k* bufo↓ cact↓ calad k* calc k* _Calc-p_↓ calc-sil k2 camph↓ canth↓ caps↓ _Carb-ac_↓ _Carb-an_↓ _Carb-v_ k* _Carbn-s_↓ **Card-m**↓ cartl-s rly4• castm↓ castor-eq caul k* **Caust**↓ cedr k* _Cham_ k* chel k* chin k* chinin-s↓ chlor↓ choc↓ **Cic**↓ cimic k* _Cina_↓ cinnb bro1 cist↓ _Clem_↓ coc-c↓ coca cocc k* **Colch** k* coli↓ coloc k* com↓ con↓ cor-r k* corn-f↓ cot↓ croc k* crot-t↓ cupr k* _Cycl_ k* cypra-eg sde6.de• cystein-l↓ _Dig_↓ dios k* dros↓ dulc fd4.de elat↓ _Eup-per_ bro1 euph k* euphr↓ _Eupi_↓ ferr↓ ferr-m bro1 ferr-ma↓ ferr-pic bro1 fl-ac k* form↓ gels k* gins↓ gran↓ _Graph_↓ _Grat_↓ gua bro1 _Guaj_↓ gymno↓ ham↓ hell k* hep↓ hura hyos↓ hyper k* ina-i mlk9.de ind↓ indg↓ iod k* iris↓ jatr-c↓ kali-bi k* kali-c bro1 kali-chl k* kali-i↓ **Kali-n**↓ kali-p↓ kali-s fd4.de kali-sil↓ _Kalm_ bro1 kerose a4 ketogl-ac↓ kreos↓ lach k* lact↓ laur↓ led k* lil-t lyc↓ lyss↓ m-ambo↓ m-arct↓ mag-c↓ _Mag-m_↓ _Mag-p_ mag-s↓ mang k* med medul-os-si↓ _Meny_↓ merc k* merc-i-f k* merc-i-r↓ _Merl_↓ _Mez_ k* morg-p pte1• mosch↓ _Mur-ac_↓ murx k* myric↓ nat-ar↓ nat-c↓ nat-m k* nat-p↓ **Nat-s**↓ _Nicc_↓ nicotam rly4• _Nit-ac_ k* nit-s-d↓ nux-m↓ _Nux-v_↓ ol-an↓ _Olnd_↓ op↓ osm↓ ox-ac↓ pall↓ par↓ pert-vc↓ petr↓ ph-ac k* phel↓ _Phos_↓ phys k* phyt k* plan k* plat k* plb k* _Podo_ polyp-p↓ positr↓ prun k* psil↓ puls k* _Ran-b_↓ _Ran-s_↓ raph↓ rat↓ rheum↓ **Rhod** k* _Rhus-t_ k* _Rhus-v_↓ ruta fd4.de sabad↓ sabin k* sal-ac↓ samb↓ sars k* senec↓ seneg↓ sep bro1 sil k* sphing a1* spig k* spong k* stann bro1 _Staph_ k* still k* stram↓ stront-c sul-ac↓ sulph k* symph↓ tab↓ tarax↓ tarent k* tell↓ tep k* teucr k* thuj k* til↓ tong↓ tritic-vg fd5.de trom k* tung-met↓ upa _Urt-u_↓ _Valer_↓ vanil fd5.de _Verat_↓ verat-v k* verb k* viol-t↓ vip↓ _Zinc_↓ zinc-p↓ zing↓
  - **right**: ant-c↓ aq-mar skp7• arg-met↓ asc-t a1 aur↓ bamb-a↓ _Bism_↓ canth↓ carneg-g↓ cench k2 coloc↓ _Cycl_ k* dulc fd4.de ferr-ma↓ kali-s fd4.de mag-c↓ mand↓ _Merc-i-f_ spong fd4.de symph↓ vanil fd5.de
    - **then** left: arg-met↓
      - **tearing** pain: arg-met
    - **and** left knee: asc-t a1
    - **burning**: carneg-g rwt1•
    - **cutting** pain: mand rsj7•
    - **drawing** pain: ant-c coloc ferr-ma mag-c symph fd3.de•
    - **pressing** pain: _Cycl_
    - **sore**: _Cycl_ merc-i-f
    - **stitching** pain: bamb-a stb2.de• dulc fd4.de mag-c spong fd4.de symph fd3.de• vanil fd5.de
    - **tearing** pain: arg-met k* aur k* _Bism_ k* canth
    - **Posterior** part: psil ft1
  - **left**: aesc↓ agar _Asaf_↓ asc-t a1 beryl tpw5 camph↓ _Carb-ac_↓ _Carb-v_↓ carbn-s↓ cartl-s rly4• chel↓ clem↓ coloc↓ galeoc-c-h gms1• kali-c↓ kreos↓ led↓ _Med_ nat-m↓ nit-ac↓ pall↓ plut-n srj7• rat↓ rhus-v↓ ruta↓ sal-ac c1 sil↓ symph fd3.de• thuj↓ vanil fd5.de
    - **aching**: _Carb-ac_
    - **drawing** pain: _Agar_ chel k* clem bg1 kali-c h2* kreos bg1 led bg1 pall bg1 rhus-v bg1 ruta fd4.de sil bg1 thuj bg1
    - **followed** by | **right**: psil ft1
    - **jerking** pain: sil h2
    - **pressing** pain: carbn-s k2
    - **sore**: nat-m h2
    - **stitching** pain: aesc
    - **tearing** pain: _Asaf_ camph _Carb-v_ coloc nit-ac h2 rat sil h2
  - **daytime**: plb k* sulph k*
  - **morning**: alum↓ ars k* bar-c k* bry k* chinin-s coloc k* dios k* eupi↓ kali-bi _Lyc_ k* mez↓ nat-ar phos↓ thuj k* vanil fd5.de
    - **aching**: nat-ar
    - **drawing** pain: bry k* eupi lyc k* thuj vanil fd5.de
    - **pressing** pain: bry k*
    - **stitching** pain: mez
    - **tearing** pain: alum mez k* phos
    - **waking**; on: alum k* cact↓ ham↓ kali-bi
      - **drawing** pain: alum
      - **stitching** pain: ham fd3.de• kali-bi
  - **morning – waking**; on: ...
    - **tearing** pain: alum cact
  - **forenoon**: agar↓ dulc fd4.de led↓ mag-c↓ ol-an↓ sil spong fd4.de trom k* verat-v
    - **11** h: mag-s↓
      - **tearing** pain: mag-s
    - **aching**: trom
    - **drawing** pain: sil
    - **sore**: led
    - **stitching** pain: dulc fd4.de mag-c
    - **tearing** pain: agar ol-an
  - **noon**: cedr k* trom k*
    - **eating**; before: senec↓
      - **stitching** pain: senec
  - **afternoon**: agar dulc fd4.de ind↓ lycps-v↓ nat-s k* nicc↓ ruta fd4.de sulph k* thuj k* tritic-vg fd5.de
    - **13**.30 h: pert-vc↓
      - **stitching** pain: pert-vc vk9
    - **16** h: sulph↓
      - **aching**: sulph
    - **aching**: lycps-v nat-s
    - **drawing** pain: ind ruta fd4.de sulph k* thuj k*
    - **driving**:
      - **agg.**: thuj↓
        - **tearing** pain: thuj
    - **tearing** pain: _Nat-s_ nicc thuj k*
  - **evening**: all-c k* alum am-c brom↓ bufo↓ calc-s castor-eq com↓ dios↓ fl-ac k* ham↓ kali-c↓ mand↓ nat-s↓ op↓ rhod↓ sang a1 spong fd4.de stront-c sulph k* thuj↓ tritic-vg fd5.de vanil fd5.de
    - **20** h: phys
    - **aching**: com dios
    - **bed** | **going** to bed:
      - **after**: phyt↓
        - **aching**: phyt
      - **in** bed:
        - **agg.**: mosch↓
          - **drawing** pain: mosch
    - **cutting** pain: mand rsj7•
    - **drawing** pain: alum k* bufo kali-c h2 op k* sulph k* vanil fd5.de
    - **gnawing** pain: stront-c
    - **pinching** pain: fl-ac k*
    - **pressing** pain: fl-ac k*
    - **stitching** pain: fl-ac ham fd3.de• thuj
    - **tearing** pain: alum brom nat-s op k* rhod
  - **night**: agar aloe alum↓ _Arg-n_ choc srj3• cycl↓ graph↓ _Lyc_ _Mez_ plan _Zinc_↓
    - **23** h: com↓ trom
      - **aching**: com
    - **aching**: aloe
    - **bed** agg.; in: _Ars_↓ kali-n↓ _Merc_↓ _Rhod_↓
      - **tearing** pain: _Ars_ kali-n h2 _Merc_ _Rhod_ k*
    - **boring** pain: arg-n
    - **burning**: graph _Zinc_
    - **lying** on it: graph↓
      - **burning**: graph
    - **sore**: cycl
    - **stitching** pain: alum
  - **aching**: agar aloe bell _Calc-p_ _Carb-ac_ carb-an carbn-s cartl-s rly4• chlor cic cinnb cocc coli rly4• com dios elat **Eup-per** fl-ac hell hyos jatr-c _Merc_ _Merc-i-f_ merc-i-r nux-m phys phyt _Rhus-t_ sabad _Sabin_ sep sil spig sulph tarent trom k* verat-v
    - **intermittent**: trom k*
    - **outward**: nux-v
  - **air** agg.; in open: pall↓
    - **drawing** pain: pall
  - **appearing** suddenly:
    - **disappearing** suddenly; and: pert-vc↓

- **appearing** suddenly – **disappearing** suddenly; and: ...
  - **stitching** pain: pert-vc vk9
- **bed** agg.; in: aloe am-c am-m k* *Mez* sulph k*
  - **pressing** pain: am-m k*
- **bending** | **arms**:
  - **agg.**: chin cina ↓ sabad k*
    - **aching**: sabad
    - **pressing** pain: cina a1
  - **fingers**:
    - **agg.**: asaf ↓
      - **tearing** pain: asaf k*
- **blow**; pain as from a: bov b4.de* cic b7.de*
- **boring** pain: am-c arg-n asaf k* aur aur-m-n bov k* calc caust bg2 cina a1 coloc dulc k* hell hep k* led mez nat-c k* *Ph-ac* k* plan plb k* ran-s k* spig b7.de* spong bg2 thuj
- **broken**; as if: arn k* calc-p k* cupr k*
- **burning**: *Agar* k* agath-a nl2• alum am-c k* am-m k* arn b7.de asaf k* aur aur-m aur-m-n bell *Berb* borx bov bry b7a.de calad carb-an carb-v carbn-s card-m *Caust* k* chel con dulc fd4.de euph b4.de *Graph* k* ham fd3.de• *Kali-bi* laur *Led* b7a.de lyc mag-m mang merc k* mez mosch mur-ac k* nat-m nat-s ol-an olnd b7.de osm ph-ac k* phos plb prun ran-s k* rat rhus-t k* rhus-v *Spong* staph stram *Sulph* k* tarax k* tarent *Thuj* k* *Urt-u* vip zinc k* zinc-p k2
- **burrowing**: cina bg2 croc bg2 rhus-t bg2
- **coition**; on flexing after: sabin ↓
  - **sore**: sabin
- **cold**; when: phos ↓
  - **tearing** pain: phos k*
- **contracting**: mez h2
- **cramping**: con h2 meny h1 mur-ac h2 nat-c h2 spong h1
- **crushed**; as if: guaj ptk1 gymno ptk1
- **cutting** pain: ars-met bism *Bov* mosch mur-ac *Teucr*
- **dislocated**; as if: cocc b7.de* led b7.de* nat-c b4.de*
- **drawing** pain: acon k* *Agar* k* aloe alum k* alum-p k2 alum-sil k2 am-c am-m k* ambr k* anac k* ang k* *Ant-c* k* apis b7a.de arg-met arg-n arn b7.de* ars asaf k* bar-c k* bell k* berb brom bry k* bufo calad b7.de* **Calc** k* calc-p calc-sil k2 canth k* *Carb-v* k* carbn-s **Card-m** k* **Caust** k* cham k* *Chel* k* chin k* cimic cina k* cist *Clem* k* coc-c coloc k* com k* con k* croc k* crot-t k* cupr *Cycl* k* cypra-eg sde6.de• dig bg2 dios k* *Dulc* k* euph k* ferr bg2 ferr-ma k* fl-ac k* gels k* gins gran graph hell k* hep k* ind kali-bi k* kali-c k* kali-chl k* kali-n bg2 kali-sil k2 kalm kreos k* laur led k* lyc k* m-ambo b7.de mag-c k* *Mag-p* mang k* *Meny* k* merc-i-f *Mez* k* mosch k* mur-ac k* nat-c k* nat-m k* nat-p nat-s nit-ac k* *Nux-v* k* olnd b7.de* op k* osm pall k* petr phos k* *Phyt* *Plat* polyp-p a1 *Puls* k* ran-s k* *Rhod* k* **Rhus-t** k* *Rhus-v* k* ruta k* samb b7.de* seneg k* *Sep* k* sil k* spong k* stann k* staph k* *Sulph* k* symph fd3.de• tarax k* tell k* teucr b7.de* *Thuj* k* *Valer* k* vanil fd5.de *Verat* zinc k* zinc-p k2 zing
  - **alternating** with | **pressure**: gins k*
  - **cramping**: anac ang arg-met h1 calc-p cina graph h2 kalm laur lyc *Meny* mur-ac nat-c plat *Rhod* zinc
  - **downward**: am-m ant-c calc cham chel clem cocc com cupr ind kali-c kreos nat-m phos *Rhod* sulph thuj
  - **intermittent**: croc k* lyc k* nat-c h2
  - **paralyzed**; as if: ant-c k* arg-n ferr-ma kali-c h2 mosch nit-ac k* petr h2 ran-s k* *Rhus-v*
  - **plaster**; as from a: nat-c h2
  - **upward**: anac ars brom
- **exertion** | **after**:
  - **agg.**: berb ↓
    - **drawing** pain: berb
  - **agg.**: berb ↓ tab ↓
    - **drawing** pain: berb
    - **stitching** pain: tab
- **exertion**; as after: ang bg2 merc b4.de* nat-m bg2 nux-v bg2 par bg2
- **extending** the arm agg.: cina ↓ mang ↓
  - **drawing** pain: cina mang a1
- **flexing** arm: dulc ↓ mur-ac ↓
- **flexing** arm: ...
  - **drawing** pain: dulc h2 mur-ac
- **gnawing** pain: bry k* gels bg2 *Graph* k* kali-n bg2 stront-c bg2
- **grasping** something agg.: *Calc* ↓ chel choc srj3• lach prun ↓
  - **pressing** pain: prun k*
  - **tearing** pain: *Calc*
- **hang** down agg.; letting arms: berb k* hydrog srj2* nat-m k* stront-c ↓ zinc
  - **tearing** pain: stront-c
- **headache**; during: verat ↓
  - **drawing** pain: verat
- **jerking** pain: arg-met bg2 caps b7.de* dulc bg2 led sil spig b7.de*
  - **paralyzed**; as if: cina a1
- **leaning** on it: carbn-s ↓
  - **pressing** pain: carbn-s k2
- **lying** agg.: am-m ↓ aur-m-n laur ↓
  - **drawing** pain: laur
  - **pressing** pain: am-m k* aur-m-n k*
- **lying** on table: ph-ac ↓
  - **sore**: ph-ac
- **motion**:
  - **agg.**: acon ↓ anac k* *Calc* carb-v ↓ chel croc galeoc-c-h gms1• led nit-ac ↓ rhus-t k* sabad ↓ sabin k* sal-ac c1 spig ↓ *Staph* thuj ↓ zinc ↓
    - **aching**: sabad *Sabin*
    - **burning**: thuj
    - **drawing** pain: carb-v k* staph h1
    - **pressing** pain: anac k* led k* *Staph*
    - **shooting** pain: acon
    - **sore**: nit-ac zinc
    - **sprained**; as if: galeoc-c-h gms1•
    - **stitching** pain: acon spig
    - **tearing** pain: carb-v h2
  - **amel.**: *Agar* ↓ alum am-m ↓ *Arg-met* ↓ aur-m-n k* bar-c *Bism* calc ↓ camph cina ↓ cocc con ↓ dulc ↓ *Lyc* ↓ mag-c ↓ mosch ↓ *Rhod* ↓ **Rhus-t** sars ↓ sphing a1 spig k* stront-c sulph ↓ thuj ↓ *Valer* ↓
    - **aching**: **Rhus-t** spig
    - **drawing** pain: alum am-m h2 *Arg-met* calc k* cina con dulc a1 mag-c k* mosch k* **Rhus-t** thuj
    - **pressing** pain: am-m aur-m-n k* *Bism* k* camph k* cocc k*
    - **sore**: aur-m-n
    - **tearing** pain: *Agar* k* am-m arg-met bism cina cocc *Lyc* *Rhod* *Rhus-t* sars sulph h2 *Valer*
    - **violent** motion: am-m ↓
      - **tearing** pain: am-m
  - **arm**; of:
    - **agg.**: staph ↓
      - **tearing** pain: staph h1
  - **fingers** agg.; of: asaf
    - **tearing** pain: asaf
  - **hand**; of:
    - **agg.**: staph ↓
      - **tearing** pain: staph h1
- **neuralgic**: chinin-s corn-f br1 iod k*
- **paralyzed**; as if: acon b7a.de* aeth alum b4.de* ambr b7a.de ant-c b7.de* bar-c k* berb bism b7.de* bov b4a.de caps h1 caust k* *Cham* cina bg2 cocc b7.de* **Colch** cycl b7.de* dig b4.de* dros b7.de* dulc bg2 ferr bg2 graph k* kali-c b4.de* **Kali-n** bg2 kreos bg2 *Med* meny b7.de* mosch b7.de* nat-m b4.de* nit-ac bg2 nux-v b7.de* petr b4.de* ph-ac k* phos b4.de* plat b4.de* ran-s b7.de* rhod bg2 ruta b7.de* sabin b7.de* sars b4.de* seneg b4.de* sil k* stann b4.de* *Staph* k* stront-c b4.de* sulph k*
- **paroxysmal**: ang arg-met berb calc choc srj3• ferr kreos mosch mur-ac *Ph-ac* plat plb ruta verb
- **periodical**: cist ↓ gran ↓
  - **drawing** pain: cist gran k*
- **pinching** pain: calad dig bg2 dulc k* fl-ac k* mang k* nat-m k* osm ph-ac k* spig staph h1 sulph k*

Extremities

- **pressing** pain: agar k* am-m k* ambr bg2 *Anac* k* ant-c k* arg-met k* asaf k* **Aur** k* aur-m-n k* *Bell* k* berb k* bism k* brom bry k* calc k* camph k* cina b7.de* clem k* cocc k* coloc k* con k* crot-t *Cycl* k* dig k* ferr-ma k* fl-ac k* gins k* graph k* hell k* hep k* hyper k* indg k* jatr-c laur bg2 *Led* k* lil-t lyc k* m-arct b7.de **Mang** k* meny k* *Merc* *Merl* k* mez k* mosch k* mur-ac nat-s k* nit-s-d a1 nux-v b7.de* *Olnd* k* osm ph-ac k* *Plat* k* prun k* puls k* rhod ruta k* sabad b7.de* sabin k* *Sars* k* sep k* sil a1 spig b7.de* spong b7.de* stann k* *Staph* k* stront-c symph fd3.de• tarax k* tong a1 *Verat* k* verb k*
  - **cramping**: *Anac* arg-met h1 meny h1 plat h2
  - **paralyzed**; as if: bell h1 bism h1 *Cycl* graph k* ruta h1 staph
  - **paroxysmal**: arg-met
- **pressure**:
  - **agg.**: bell ↓ beryl tpw5 nat-m ↓
    - **burning**: bell
    - **sore**: nat-m h2
  - **amel.**: mag-m ↓ mang ↓ sulph ↓
    - **pinching** pain: mang k*
    - **tearing** pain: mag-m h2 sulph
- **pulsating** pain: dulc fd4.de ketogl-ac rly4• lyss merc-i-f symph fd3.de•
- **raw**; as if: cic bg2 hep bg2 rhus-t bg2
- **rest**:
  - **agg.**: spig ↓
    - **pinching** pain: spig
  - **amel.**: beryl tpw5
- **rheumatic**: *Aesc* agar asc-t bapt chel k* chinin-s *Colch* corv-cor bdg• form *Hydr* hyos k* iris lyc ↓ lycps-v merc k* merc-i-f k* merc-i-r a1 *Nit-ac* *Phyt* k* *Podo* psil ft1 *Rhus-t* sang a1 stry k*
  - **drawing** pain: chel k* chinin-s lyc *Phyt* k* **Rhus-t**
- **riding** agg.: bry ↓
  - **drawing** pain: bry
- **rubbing**:
  - **amel.**: chin ↓ ol-an ↓ phos ↓
    - **burning**: ol-an
    - **tearing** pain: chin h1 phos h2
- **scraping** pain: anac h2 bry kali-s fd4.de
- **scratching** agg.; after: borx ↓ caust ↓ clem ↓ laur ↓ sulph ↓
  - **burning**: borx caust clem laur sulph
- **shooting** pain: *Acon* aur-m k2 bell cystein-l rly4• form ham medul-os-si rly4• plb sabin c1 still thuj trom
- **sitting** agg.: aur-m-n k* cina ↓ led k* nat-s ↓ **Rhus-t** ↓ sabin ↓ thuj ↓
  - **aching**: led **Rhus-t**
  - **boring** pain: led
  - **pressing** pain: aur-m-n k*
  - **stitching** pain: sabin thuj
  - **tearing** pain: cina nat-s
- **sleep**:
  - **siesta**:
    - **after**:
      - **agg.**: graph ↓
        - **pressing** pain: graph h2
- **sore**: acon ail aloe **Arn** ars-met aur-m-n bamb-a stb2.de• bar-act beryl tpw5 *Calc* calc-p camph canth k* carb-an **Caust** cedr chel *Cic* coca com con k* cot br1 croc k* crot-t cupr *Cycl* dig **Eup-per** ham hep hura iod kali-bi led lyc merc merc-i-f merc-i-r mur-ac k* nit-ac ol-an *Ph-ac* k* phos plan positr nl2• prun *Rhus-t* k* ruta k* sabin sal-ac sil sul-ac sulph symph fd3.de• thuj *Zinc* k*
  - **strained**; as if: beryl tpw5
- **sprained**; as if: aur-m led h1 nat-c tab
- **squeezed**; as if: *Cic* b7a.de dros b7.de* hep bg2 mur-ac bg2 olnd b7a.de sul-ac bg2
- **stitching** pain: *Acon* k* aesc aeth agn b7.de* alum k* anac k* ang b7.de* ant-c k* apis arg-met k* arn b7.de* asaf k* asar aur-m bamb-a stb2.de• bapt bell k* benz-ac *Berb* borx *Bov* k* **Bry** b7.de* bufo calc k* camph k* canth b7.de* caps bg2 *Carb-an* k* carbn-s *Caust* k* cham chel **Cic** k* clem k* cocc b7.de* coloc cupr cycl k* *Dig* k* dios dros b7.de* dulc fd4.de euphr b7.de* *Eupi* fl-ac form graph *Guaj* k* ham hyos b7.de* iris kali-i kalm lyc k* m-arct b7.de mag-c k* mag-m mang b4.de* meny bg2 merc k* mez k* mosch b7.de* myric nat-ar k2 nat-c k* nit-ac bg2 olnd b7.de* ox-ac pert-vc vk9 *Ph-ac* k* plb psil ft1 *Ran-b* k* *Ran-s* k* raph rhod k* rhus-t bg2 sabad k* sabin k* *Sars* k* senec *Sil* spig k* *Spong* k* staph k* still stram k* stront-c k* sul-ac symph fd3.de• tab tarax k* teucr b7.de* *Thuj* k* trom tung-met bdx1• viol-t k* *Zinc*
  - **acute**: berb castm merc ph-ac
  - **burning**: *Berb* spig
  - **downward**: chel *Ran-s* sars
  - **drawing** pain: clem
  - **fine**: stram tarax
  - **upward**: asaf podo fd3.de• zinc
- **styloid** process of ulna: asaf ↓
  - **scraping** pain: asaf
- **tearing** pain: *Acon* k* *Aesc* aeth *Agar* k* *Alum* k* alum-p k2 alum-sil k2 am-c k* am-m k* *Ambr* k* anac h2* ant-t b7.de* arg-met k* *Ars* ars-s-f k2 asaf k* aur k* aur-m bar-c k* bell k* *Berb* *Bism* k* borx bov k* brom *Bry* k* cact **Calc** k* calc-p calc-sil k2 camph k* canth k* **Carb-v** k* *Carbn-s* **Caust** k* *Cham* chel *Chin* k* cic k* *Cina* k* cinnb clem cocc k* *Colch* k* *Coloc* crot-t cupr k* cycl k* *Dig* k* dulc k* *Graph* k* *Grat* k* *Guaj* k* hell hyos *Hyper* indg *Kali-bi* k* **Kali-c** k* kali-chl kali-n kali-p kali-sil k2 kalm lach k* lact laur k* led lyc k* mag-c k* *Mag-m* k* mag-s mang k* meny *Merc* k* *Merl* *Mez* k* *Mur-ac* k* myric nat-c k* nat-m k* **Nat-s** *Nicc* *Nit-ac* k* ol-an op par k* ph-ac phel *Phos* k* plb *Puls* k* ran-b k* rat rheum k* *Rhod* k* *Rhus-t* k* ruta k* sabin k* *Sars* k* sep k* *Sil* stann k* staph k* *Stront-c* k* *Sulph* k* symph fd3.de• tab tarax k* tep teucr k* *Thuj* k* til *Valer* k* verb k* *Zinc* k* zinc-p k2
  - **cramping**: calc h2 cina gran ruta
  - **jerking** pain: mur-ac h2
  - **paralyzed**; as if: *Bism* cocc *Colch* kali-n h2 nat-m phos sars h2 sil h2 stann
  - **paroxysmal**: arg-met aur *Calc* cocc mur-ac a1
  - **pinching** pain: dulc h1
  - **twitching**: cupr h2 dulc h2
  - **upward**: mur-ac h2 thuj h1
- **touch**:
  - **agg.**: anac ↓ beryl tpw5 chin ↓ cupr nit-ac ↓ sabin k* sal-ac c1 *Staph* zinc ↓
    - **aching**: *Sabin*
    - **pressing** pain: anac h2 staph h1
    - **sore**: nit-ac h2 zinc h2
    - **stitching** pain: cupr
    - **tearing** pain: chin h1 nit-ac
  - **amel.**: bism meny k* *Staph* ↓
    - **pressing** pain: *Bism* k* meny *Staph*
- **turning** arm: zinc ↓
  - **sore**: zinc
- **twinging**: chinin-s mang
- **ulcerative** pain: stront-c bg2
- **waking**; on: agar lycps-v
  - **aching**: lycps-v
- **walking** agg.: calc ↓
  - **pressing** pain: calc h2
- **wandering**: nat-ar
- **warm** | **applications**:
  - **amel.**: *Chel* *Chin* *Dulc* ferr gran *Kali-c* kalm lyc *Nit-ac* **Nux-v** **Rhus-t** *Sil* *Zinc*
    - **drawing** pain: *Chel* *Chin* *Dulc* ferr gran *Kali-c* kalm lyc *Nit-ac* **Nux-v** **Rhus-t** sil *Zinc*
  - **stove**:
    - **amel.**: cinnb ↓
      - **tearing** pain: cinnb
- **washing** agg.; after: lyc ↓
  - **tearing** pain: lyc h2
- **weather** agg.; wet: *Rhod* ↓

- **weather** agg.: ...
  - : **tearing** pain: *Rhod*
- **writing** agg.: acon am-m↓ anac$_{k*}$ berb↓ cic↓ cinnb↓ *Cycl*$_{k*}$ fago fl-ac lyc↓ **Mag-p** *Merc-i-f* ox-ac↓ ran-b$_{sma}$ thuj↓
  - : **aching**: anac
  - : **drawing** pain: **Mag-p**
  - : **pressing** pain: am-m anac *Cycl*
  - : **stitching** pain: berb lyc ox-ac thuj
  - : **tearing** pain: cic cinnb *Ran-b*$_{k*}$

▽ • **extending** to:
  - : **Elbow**: agath-a$_{nl2}$• spig
  - : **Finger**: asc-t cocc con *Cycl* puls rhod$_{sma}$
    - : **Fourth** finger: agar kreos
    - : **Tip**: aq-mar$_{skp7}$•
  - : **Fingers**: agar↓ alum↓ am-m↓ carb-v↓ clem↓ con↓ *Cycl*↓ eupi↓ ind↓ iod↓ kreos↓ mur-ac↓ nat-c↓ phos↓ plb↓ sars↓ still↓ stram↓ thuj↓
    - : **cramping**: cycl$_{mrr1}$
    - : **drawing** pain: agar am-m carb-v$_{h2}$ clem ind kreos mur-ac$_{h2}$ phos sars$_{h2}$
    - : **pressing** pain: con$_{k*}$ *Cycl*$_{k*}$
    - : **shooting** pain: plb still thuj
    - : **sore**: iod
    - : **stitching** pain: eupi plb still thuj
    - : **tearing** pain: alum$_{h2}$ carb-v$_{h2}$ mur-ac$_{a1}$ nat-c$_{h2}$ sars$_{h2}$
    - : **twinging**: stram$_{k*}$
    - : **Fourth** finger: *Cist*↓
      - . **drawing** pain: *Cist*
    - : **Joints**: *Coloc*↓
      - . **tearing** pain: *Coloc*
    - : **Third**: rat↓
      - . **tearing** pain: rat
    - : **Tips**: alum↓ asaf↓ aur-m↓ sep↓
      - . **tearing** pain: alum asaf aur-m sep
  - : **Hand**: *Agar*↓ alum↓ am-m↓ *Berb*↓ *Carb-v*↓ caust↓ cham↓ cocc↓ coloc↓ elat↓ fl-ac↓ grat↓ kali-c↓ lyc↓ mag-c↓ mag-m↓ mur-ac↓ nit-ac↓ psil$_{ft1}$ rat↓ trom↓ zinc↓
    - : **aching**: elat fl-ac nit-ac trom
    - : **drawing** pain: alum$_{h2}$ carb-v$_{h2}$ cocc kali-c lyc mag-c
    - : **tearing** pain: *Agar* alum am-m *Berb* *Carb-v* caust cham coloc grat lyc mag-m mur-ac rat zinc
  - : **Palm**: chel↓ *Meny*↓
    - : **drawing** pain: chel *Meny*
  - : **Thumb**: agar croc cupr↓ mag-m↓
    - : **drawing** pain: cupr
    - : **tearing** pain: mag-m$_{h2}$
  - : **Wrist**: alum↓ bar-c↓ *Calc*↓ carb-v↓ cham↓ guaj↓ kali-n↓ vanil↓
    - : **drawing** pain: carb-v$_{h2}$ cham vanil$_{fd5.de}$
    - : **tearing** pain: alum$_{h2}$ bar-c *Calc* guaj$_{h2}$ kali-n$_{h2}$

○ • **Anterior** part: agar↓ aloe↓ am-c↓ ant-c↓ arg-met↓ asaf$_{k*}$ berb↓ calad↓ carb-v↓ chel↓ gels *Hep*↓ meny↓ nat-s↓ ol-an↓ plb$_{k*}$ sars↓ sphing$_{kk3.fr}$ spong tarent thuj↓
  - : **morning**: thuj↓
    - : **drawing** pain: thuj$_{k*}$
  - : **boring** pain: asaf plb spong
  - : **burning**: agar am-c berb calad chel ol-an plb
  - : **drawing** pain: aloe ant-c$_{h2}$ arg-met asaf$_{k*}$ berb$_{k*}$ carb-v$_{k*}$ *Hep* meny$_{k*}$ nat-s$_{k*}$ sars$_{h2}$ thuj$_{k*}$
- **Bones**: acon↓ *Arg-n*↓ arn↓ asaf↓ bar-c↓ bism↓ calad↓ canth↓ carb-v↓ caust↓ chin↓ *Graph*↓ kali-bi↓ led↓ *Merc-i-f*↓ nat-c↓ nat-m↓ *Ph-ac*↓ puls↓ *Rhus-t*↓ sabin↓ sulph↓ symph↓ vanil↓ zinc↓
  - : **left**: merc-i-f↓
    - : **drawing** pain: merc-i-f$_{k*}$
  - : **boring** pain: nat-c *Ph-ac* *Rhus-t*$_{a1}$
  - : **drawing** pain: acon$_{k*}$ *Arg-n*$_{k*}$ arn$_{k*}$ bar-c calad$_{k*}$ canth$_{k*}$ carb-v$_{h2}$ chin kali-bi$_{k*}$ led$_{k*}$ *Merc-i-f*$_{k*}$ puls$_{h1}$ sabin symph$_{fd3.de}$• vanil$_{fd5.de}$ zinc
  - : **gnawing** pain: *Graph*$_{k*}$
- **Bones**: ...
  - : **scraping** pain: asaf$_{bg2}$
  - : **sore**: bism$_{a1}$ nat-m$_{h2}$
  - : **tearing** pain: bar-c$_{h2}$ carb-v$_{h2}$ caust$_{h2}$ ph-ac$_{h2}$ puls$_{h1}$ sulph$_{h2}$ zinc$_{h2}$
  - : **Between**: calad
  - : **Radius**: agar↓ all-c$_{k*}$ arg-met↓ bapt↓ berb↓ bism↓ calc↓ camph↓ carb-v↓ caust↓ chin↓ euph↓ fl-ac$_{k*}$ gymno indg↓ jac-c$_{a1}$ kali-bi↓ *Lyc* mang↓ *Mez*$_{k*}$ nat-c nat-m osm$_{k*}$ phos↓ rhus-t$_{k*}$ sabin$_{k*}$ samb↓ sil↓ sulph↓ thuj↓ verat-v$_{k*}$ *Zinc*↓
    - : **aching**: *Sabin*
    - : **broken**; as if: gymno$_{k*}$
    - : **drawing** pain: carb-v$_{h2}$ euph indg$_{k*}$ samb$_{k*}$ sulph$_{k*}$ thuj$_{k*}$
    - : **hang** down agg.; letting arms: nat-m osm
    - : **pressing** pain: camph$_{h1}$ phos$_{h2}$
    - : **sore**: bism$_{h1}$ phos *Rhus-t* sil
    - : **stitching** pain: bapt
    - : **styloid** process: kali-c↓ kali-n↓ merl↓ ol-an↓
      - . **tearing** pain: kali-c$_{k*}$ kali-n$_{k*}$ merl$_{a1}$ ol-an$_{a1}$
    - : **tearing** pain: agar arg-met berb$_{k*}$ calc camph carb-v$_{k*}$ caust chin$_{h1}$ kali-bi mang$_{h2}$ *Zinc*
    - : **Elbow**; below: staph↓
      - . **drawing** pain: staph
    - : **Head** of: fl-ac$_{k*}$ hyper$_{a1}$ verat-v$_{a1}$
    - : **Periosteum**: cycl$_{k*}$ *Merc* *Mez*$_{k*}$ phos$_{k*}$
  - : **Ulna**: acon↓ *Agar*↓ aran↓ *Arg-n*$_{k*}$ ars↓ bism↓ brach↓ bry↓ calc calc-s$_{k*}$ *Caust*$_{k*}$ cham$_{k*}$ chin$_{k*}$ cocc↓ cupr↓ *Cycl*↓ dig↓ dulc↓ euph↓ ferr↓ form$_{k*}$ hyper↓ kali-bi↓ kali-chl↓ kali-n↓ kalm↓ kreos↓ lyc↓ lycps-v↓ mez↓ nat-m↓ oxyt↓ phel↓ phyt↓ plat$_{k*}$ *Podo* puls↓ *Rhus-t*$_{a1}$ ruta↓ sars↓ spong$_{fd4.de}$ stront-c↓ tub$_{c1}$ verat-v$_{k*}$ verb↓ *Zinc*↓
    - : **aching**: verat-v
    - : **boring** pain: arg-n
    - : **dislocated**; as if: cocc$_{h1}$
    - : **drawing** pain: chin *Cycl* dulc$_{k*}$ euph$_{k*}$ kreos$_{k*}$ lyc$_{k*}$ nat-m$_{k*}$ phyt$_{k*}$
    - : **gnawing** pain: kali-n$_{h2}$ stront-c
    - : **neuralgic**: acon$_{bg2}$ aran$_{bg2}$ ferr$_{bg2}$ hyper$_{bg2*}$ kalm$_{bg2*}$ lycps-v$_{bro1}$ oxyt$_{bro1}$ puls$_{bg2}$ rhus-t$_{bg2*}$
    - : **pinching** pain: dig$_{h2}$
    - : **pressing** pain: sars$_{h2}$
    - : **sore**: ars bism$_{h1}$ brach$_{bro1}$ ruta
    - : **tearing** pain: *Agar*$_{k*}$ bry$_{k*}$ caust chin$_{k*}$ cupr$_{k*}$ kali-bi$_{k*}$ kali-chl$_{k*}$ lyc mez$_{k*}$ phel$_{a1}$ sars$_{k*}$ verb$_{k*}$ *Zinc*
    - : **Elbow**; near: mez↓ phel↓ sil↓
      - . **sore**: mez
      - . **tearing** pain: phel$_{k*}$ sil$_{k*}$
    - : **Lower** part:
      - . **rheumatic**: bapt$_{hr1}$
      - . **writing** agg.: chinin-s$_{mp1}$•
    - : **Middle** of:
      - . **forenoon**: thuj↓
        - **tearing** pain: thuj
      - . **writing** agg.: thuj↓
        - **tearing** pain: thuj
    - : **Posterior** part: dig↓ thuj↓
      - . **tearing** pain: dig thuj
    - : **Wrist**; near: *Calc*↓ melal-alt↓
      - . **sore**: *Calc* melal-alt$_{gya4}$
- **Elbow**; near: arn↓ bell↓ carb-v↓ caust↓ com↓ eupi↓ hell↓ meny↓ mur-ac↓ ol-an↓ sars↓ staph↓ sulph↓ thuj↓ zinc↓
  - : **cutting** pain: bell mur-ac
  - : **drawing** pain: carb-v$_{h2}$ com$_{a1}$ eupi$_{k*}$ hell$_{k*}$ staph sulph$_{k*}$
  - : **stitching** pain: arn eupi meny ol-an thuj
  - : **tearing** pain: carb-v$_{h2}$ caust$_{h2}$ sars$_{h2}$ zinc$_{h2}$
- **Extensor** surface: agar↓ mang↓ spong↓
  - : **stitching** pain: agar mang$_{a1}$ spong$_{fd4.de}$
- **Externally**: aur-m-n↓ con↓ mur-ac↓

- **Externally**: ...
  - **burning**: aur-m-n con mur-ac
- **Flexors**: *Colch* ↓ plat ↓ tarent ↓
  - **pressing** pain: plat h2
  - **stitching** pain: tarent
  - **tearing** pain: *Colch*
- **Lower** part:
  - **right**: mand ↓
    - **dull** pain: mand rsj7•
  - **rheumatic**: bapt hr1
  - **writing** agg.: chinin-s
- **Muscles**:
  - **Extensor** muscles: cic ↓ coloc k* hep k* mur-ac k* sil stram ↓
    - **cutting** pain: mur-ac
    - **drawing** pain: hep k* mur-ac k*
    - **tearing** pain: cic a1 hep h2 mur-ac
    - **twinging**: stram k*
  - **Flexor** muscles: arn k* *Calc* com ↓ gels k* *Hep* ↓ nux-v k*
    - **drawing** pain: com k* *Hep* k*
    - **Radial** side: chinin-ar chinin-s
- **Nerves**:
  - **Ulnar**: oxyt ptk2 visc sp1
    - **right**: xan c1
- **Posterior** part: acon ↓ bar-act ↓ berb k* chinin-s ↓ con ↓ dulc ↓ euph ↓ mang ↓ merc-i-f ↓ ol-an ↓ osm ↓ petr ↓ prun ↓ ruta fd4.de
  - **forenoon**: chinin-s ↓
    - **aching**: chinin-s
  - **aching**: berb chinin-s
  - **burning**: berb dulc fd4.de euph ol-an osm prun
  - **drawing** pain: acon k* mang k* petr k* ruta fd4.de
  - **pinching** pain: berb k* merc-i-f k*
  - **pressing** pain: petr h2
  - **sore**: bar-act a1 con
- **Radial** side: agar k* berb a1 **Card-m** ↓ fl-ac merc k* pall ↓ rhus-t k* *Thuj* ↓
  - **morning**: merc k*
  - **drawing** pain: **Card-m** pall a1 *Thuj*
- **Sides**:
  - **Inner**: camph ↓ mag-m ↓ mang ↓ nat-m ↓ phos ↓ sars ↓ tarax ↓ thuj ↓ zinc ↓
    - **pressing** pain: camph h1 mang h2 tarax h1
    - **tearing** pain: camph h1 mag-m h2 nat-m h2 phos h2 sars h2 thuj h1 zinc h2
  - **Outer**: nit-ac ↓ osm ↓ symph ↓ thuj ↓
    - **right**: osm ↓
      - **burning**: osm
    - **burning**: osm
    - **sore**: nit-ac h2
    - **tearing** pain: symph fd3.de• thuj h1
- **Spots**; in: am-c ↓ graph ↓ ran-s ↓ sulph ↓
  - **burning**: am-c graph sulph
    - **stinging**: ran-s
- **Tendons**: *Calc* caust ↓ chel k* chin k* chinin-s coc-c ↓ hep ↓ kali-m c1 kali-n ↓ mag-s ↓ nat-c ↓ podo fd3.de• sil k* tab ↓
  - **drawing** pain: hep k* nat-c k*
  - **tearing** pain: *Calc* caust k* coc-c k* kali-n k* mag-s k* tab k*
- **Ulnar** side: arn ↓ aster ↓ berb ↓ cham ↓ chinin-s ↓ con ↓ hyper ↓ ox-ac ↓ psil ↓ thuj ↓
  - **afternoon**:
    - **writing** agg.: chinin-s ↓
      - **drawing** pain: chinin-s
  - **drawing** pain: arn k* aster cham chinin-s
  - **pressing** pain: hyper pd
  - **stitching** pain: berb cham chinin-s con ox-ac psil ft1 thuj
- **Upper** side: nat-c ↓
  - **drawing** pain: nat-c h2

- **Forearms**: ...
  - **Wrist**; near: agar ↓ ant-c ↓ asc-t k* bell ↓ bov ↓ *Calc* caust ↓ cham k* com k* dros ↓ galeoc-c-h ↓ indg ↓ kali-bi ↓ mag-m ↓ melal-alt ↓ mez k* olnd k* rhus-v ↓ sep ↓ spira a1 *Teucr* ↓ zinc ↓ zing k*
    - **burning**: agar bov caust kali-bi rhus-v zinc
    - **cutting** pain: bell h1 dros *Teucr*
    - **drawing** pain: ant-c h2 indg k* mez k* olnd k* zing k*
    - **sprained**; as if: *Calc* galeoc-c-h gms1• melal-alt gya4
    - **tearing** pain: mag-m h2 mez h2 sep h2
- **Hands**: abrot acon *Act-sp* aesc aeth ↓ agar k* agn ↓ aids ↓ *All-c* ↓ aloe ↓ alum ↓ alum-p ↓ alum-sil k2 alumn *Am-c* ↓ am-m **Ambr** ↓ ammc ↓ anac k* anag anders ↓ ang ↓ ant-t ↓ apis arg-met ↓ arg-n ↓ *Arn* ↓ ars ars-h ↓ ars-s-f ↓ arum-d arum-dru ↓ arund ↓ asaf ↓ asar ↓ *Aur* ↓ aur-m ↓ bamb-a stb2.de• bapt ↓ bar-c bar-s k2 bell benz-ac berb ↓ *Bism* ↓ bol-la borx ↓ bov ↓ brom *Bry* ↓ cadm-s ↓ cain ↓ *Calc* *Calc-p* ↓ *Calc-s* ↓ calc-sil ↓ calo c2 camph ↓ cann-s ↓ cann-xyz ↓ canth ↓ *Caps* ↓ carb-ac ↓ *Carb-an* ↓ carb-v carbn-s card-m ↓ carl ↓ caul **Caust** ↓ cedr ↓ cench ↓ cham chel ↓ *Chin* ↓ chinin-ar ↓ chinin-s ↓ choc ↓ cic *Cina* ↓ cist clem cocc *Colch* coll ↓ *Coloc* ↓ com con ↓ corn ↓ corv-cor ↓ croc ↓ crot-c crot-h cupr cupr-ar ↓ cycl ↓ daph ↓ *Dig* dios dros ↓ dulc fd4.de dys pte1*• elaps ↓ ery-a euph ↓ euphr fago ferr ferr-ar ferr-m ↓ fic-m ↓ fl-ac form ↓ gamb ↓ gels gent-l ger-i ↓ gins ↓ glon ↓ gran ↓ *Graph* ↓ grat *Guaj* guat sp1 gymno ham ↓ *Hell* ↓ *Hep* hura hyos ↓ hyper ↓ ign ↓ ina-i ↓ indg ↓ iodof *Iris* ↓ jug-r ↓ kali-ar ↓ kali-bi k* **Kali-c** ↓ kali-m ↓ *Kali-n* ↓ kali-p ↓ kali-s fd4.de kali-sil ↓ kalm kola stb3• kreos lac-ac ↓ lach lact ↓ lappa ↓ laur ↓ led k* lil-t lith-c lyc m-ambo ↓ m-arct ↓ mag-c ↓ *Mag-m* ↓ mag-s sp1 manc ↓ *Mang* ↓ **Med** ↓ *Meny* ↓ *Merc* ↓ merc-c ↓ *Merc-i-f* merc-i-r merl ↓ *Mez* k* morg-p pte1*• mosch mur-ac ↓ naja nat-c nat-m ↓ nat-n ↓ nat-p ↓ nat-s nat-sil fd3.de• nept-m lsd2.fr nicc ↓ nicc-s ↓ *Nit-ac* ↓ nux-m ↓ nux-v b7.de* *Ol-an* ↓ ol-j ↓ olnd ↓ *Op* ↓ ox-ac ↓ pall ↓ par ↓ *Petr* ↓ ph-ac ↓ phos phys phyt pic-ac ↓ *Plat* ↓ plb k* plut-n ↓ positr ↓ propr sa3• prot fmm1• prun ↓ ptel puls k* rad-br ↓ ran-b k2 ran-s *Rat* ↓ rheum ↓ *Rhod* ↓ **Rhus-t** k* rhus-v rumx ruta k* sabad ↓ sabin samb ↓ sang sars *Sec* ↓ sel b7a.de seneg ↓ *Sep* ↓ *Sil* ↓ sinus ↓ sol-ni sol-t-ae ↓ spect ↓ spig ↓ spong fd4.de *Squil* ↓ *Stann* ↓ *Staph* streptoc ↓ *Stront-c* ↓ stry suis-pan ↓ sul-ac ↓ *Sulph* symph ↓ tab taosc iwa1• tarent tell tep ↓ ter ↓ teucr ↓ thal-xyz ↓ thres-a sze7• thuj ↓ tritic-vg fd5.de ust vac jl2 valer ↓ vanil fd5.de verat ↓ *Verb* ↓ vesp vib ↓ viol-o ↓ vip ↓ *Zinc* ↓ zinc-p ↓ [*Buteo-j* sej6 uva stj]
  - **one** side hot and pale:
    - **other** cold and red: mez ↓ mosch ↓
      - **burning**: (↗*Heat - hands - cold - and)* mez c1 mosch
  - **alternating** sides: caust ↓
    - **tearing** pain: caust
  - **right**: asc-t a1 bros-gau ↓ canth ↓ dulc fd4.de fago ↓ fic-m gya1 hydrog ↓ mand rsj7• phos ↓ rat ↓ sel ↓ spong fd4.de symph fd3.de• vanil fd5.de
    - **burning**: bros-gau mrc1 fago bg1 phos bg1 sel rsj9• symph fd3.de•
    - **light** playing over it; as from: hydrog srj2•
    - **tearing** pain: canth rat
  - **left**: asc-t a1 dulc fd4.de fic-m gya1 fl-ac ↓ flor-p ↓ galla-q-r nl2• melal-alt gya4 nat-m ↓ nit-ac ↓ ph-ac ↓ phos ↓ rhus-t ↓ trios rsj11• vanil fd5.de zinc ↓
    - **accompanied** by | **Right** knee; pain in (See knees - right - accompanied - left)
    - **burning**: fl-ac bg1 nat-m bg1 rhus-t bg1 zinc bg1
    - **drawing** pain: flor-p rsj3•
    - **tearing** pain: nit-ac h2 ph-ac h2 phos h2
  - **morning**: ars ↓ *Brucel* sa3• calc carb-v ↓ dios dulc fd4.de kali-bi lyc nat-c petr ↓ ph-ac sacch-a fd2.de• sang spong fd4.de sulph ↓ tritic-vg fd5.de
    - **aching**: dios
    - **bed** agg.; in: petr ↓
      - **stitching** pain: petr a1
    - **burning**: dulc fd4.de petr spong fd4.de sulph tritic-vg fd5.de
    - **drawing** pain: ars h2 dios k* kali-bi k* lyc k* ph-ac
    - **lying**:
      - **amel.**: mag-c ↓
        - **sore**: mag-c h2
    - **tearing** pain: ars h2 carb-v
    - **waking**; on: agar dulc ↓ fic-m gya1 mag-c ↓ petr ↓ sacch-a fd2.de• thuj ↓

- **morning** – **waking**; on: ...
    - **burning**: dulc fd4.de petr
    - **sore**: mag-c h2
    - **stitching** pain: thuj
- **forenoon**: dios dulc fd4.de fago hura nat-s ↓ ruta ↓ spong fd4.de thuj ↓
    - **burning**: fago nat-s
    - **other** is cold; while the: fago ↓
        - **burning**: fago
    - **stitching** pain: ruta fd4.de thuj
    - **tearing** pain: thuj
    - **writing** on a cold table, from: fago
- **noon**: am-c ↓ mag-c ↓ thuj ↓
    - **burning**: am-c mag-c
    - **tearing** pain: thuj
- **afternoon**: cham ↓ cist fago ↓ kali-bi ↓ phos ↓ rumx vanil fd5.de
    - **13** h:
        - **sitting** agg.: lycps-v ↓
            - **aching**: lycps-v
    - **14** h: laur ↓
        - **burning**: laur
        - **tearing** pain: laur
    - **burning**: cham fago phos
    - **tearing** pain: kali-bi
- **evening**: abrot acon *Alum* ↓ arge-pl rwt5• brom ↓ cedr ↓ cist dios dulc fd4.de graph ↓ kali-n ↓ lac-ac ↓ led lyc ↓ mag-m ↓ nat-c ↓ nat-s nit-ac ph-ac phos ↓ ptel **Puls** ↓ rhod ↓ ruta ↓ *Sel* ↓ spong fd4.de **Sulph** ↓ thuj ↓ tritic-vg fd5.de vanil fd5.de
    - **aching**: led
    - **bed** agg.; in: mag-m ↓ plat ↓
        - **stitching** pain: mag-m plat
        - **tearing** pain: mag-m
    - **burning**: cedr dulc fd4.de phos **Puls Sulph**
    - **drawing** pain: nat-s nit-ac k* ph-ac ptel k* ruta fd4.de tritic-vg fd5.de vanil fd5.de
    - **stitching** pain: arge-pl rwt5• lac-ac mag-m rhod
    - **tearing** pain: *Alum* brom graph kali-n led lyc nat-c rhod *Sel* thuj
- **night**: am-c dios lac-c ↓ lyc ↓ merc ↓ merc-i-f pall ↓ phos prot ↓ sel spong fd4.de sulph symph fd3.de• vanil fd5.de
    - **midnight**:
        - **before**:
            - **22** h: cham ↓
                - **stitching** pain: cham
    - **aching**: dios
    - **bed** agg.; in: phos ↓
        - **tearing** pain: phos
    - **burning**: lac-c pall prot pte1* spong fd4.de vanil fd5.de
    - **tearing** pain: lyc h2* merc *Sel*
- **aching**: aesc ang asaf calc-p choc srj3• croc dios euphr ger-i rly4• ham kalm led mez nit-ac ptel streptoc rly4• [spect dfg1]
- **alternating** with | **Head**; complaints of: hell
- **asleep**, falling: nit-ac ↓
    - **drawing** pain: nit-ac h2
- **bed**:
    - **in** bed:
        - **agg.**: iodof merc-i-f
        - **only** in bed: *Lyc* ↓
            - **tearing** pain: *Lyc* k*
- **biting**: nat-m b4.de* zinc b4.de*
- **blow**; pain as from a: arn b7.de* stann b4.de*
- **boring** pain: bism cina b7.de* daph hep b4.de* *Nat-c* k* pall ran-s k* spig b7.de*
- **breath**, with each: am-c ↓
    - **stitching** pain: am-c
- **broken**; as if: borx bg1
- **burning**: *Acon* b7.de* **Agar** k* am-c k* anac k* anders zzc1• ant-t apis k* arg-met arg-n *Ars* ars-h ars-s-f k2 arund asar b7.de aur-m berb bry k* *Calc* k* *Calc-s* calc-sil k2 cann-s canth *Caps* carb-v k* *Carbn-s* cedr cench k2 cham chel k* cocc bro1 con corn daph dulc fd4.de elaps fago *Fl-ac* graph *Hell* b7.de hep hura hyos jug-r kali-ar kali-bi kali-c k* *Kali-s* lach k* laur k* led lil-t lyc k* mag-c k* **Med** k* merc mez morg-p fmm1• nat-c nat-m k* nat-p nat-s nit-ac k* nux-m k* nux-v k* ol-j bro1 *Op* b7.de ox-ac pall k* *Petr* k* ph-ac k* *Phos* k* plat k* prot fmm1• *Puls* rad-br sze8• ran-s rhod k* *Rhus-t* k* rhus-v sabin b7.de* sang bro1* sars k* *Sec* b7.de sei *Sep* k* sil bro1 sol-t-ae *Spong* k* *Squil* b7.de *Stann* k* *Staph* b7.de stront-c k* **Sulph** k* symph fd3.de• thal-xyz srj8• thuj tritic-vg fd5.de vanil fd5.de zinc k*
    - **internal** heat: ph-ac
    - **nettles**; as from: arum-dru a1 carl nat-m
- **bursting**; sensation as if: vib bg2
- **chill**; during: nux-v *Spong* ↓
    - **burning**: *Spong*
- **closing** the hand agg.: (non:calli-h kl) (non:calo k*) caul kl chin ↓ dios med merc sacch-a fd2.de•
    - **drawing** pain: chin k*
    - **pressing** pain: merc k*
- **cold**:
    - **amel.**: guaj lac-c *Led Puls*
    - **applications**:
        - **amel.**: anders ↓
            - **burning**: anders zzc1•
    - **numb**; or cold and: *Lyc* ↓
        - **burning**: *Lyc*
    - **washing** agg.: *Caps* ↓
        - **burning**: *Caps*
    - **water**:
        - **amel.**: apis ↓
            - **stitching** pain: apis
- **corrosive**: *Lyc* b4a.de plat b4.de*
- **cramping**: anac gsy1 dulc fd4.de euph h2 mang h2
- **cutting** pain: aids nl2• *All-c* bro1 ambr c1 corv-cor bdg• lappa bro1 mur-ac *Nat-c* k* sel bro1 stann stry sulph bro1 ust
- **dinner**; after: kali-bi ↓
    - **drawing** pain: kali-bi k*
- **drawing** pain: acon b7.de* aesc agar k* agn k* aloe am-c k* ambr b7a.de* anac k* ang k* ant-t b7.de* apis b7a.de arg-met k* arg-n k* asaf asar b7.de* aur bell bg2 bry k* calc k* calc-sil k2 cann-s canth k* caps b7.de* carb-an k* carb-v k* carbn-s k* card-m **Caust** k* cham k* chel k* chin k* chinin-s *Cina* k* cist *Clem* k* coloc k* dios k* euph k* *Euphr* k* gent-l a1 grat k* ham k* hell b7.de* hyos bg2 ign b7.de* ina-i mlk9.de kali-bi k* kali-c k* kali-sil k2 kreos b7a.de led lyc k* m-arct b7.de mag-c k* mag-m k* mang b4a.de* meny b7.de* merc k* mez k* mosch b7.de* mur-ac k* nat-c k* nat-p k* nat-s k* *Nit-ac* k* nux-v b7.de* ol-an k* par b7.de* petr k* ph-ac k* phos k* plat k* plb b7.de* prun bg2 ptel k* ran-s b7.de* *Rhod* k* **Rhus-t** k* ruta b7a.de* sabin b7.de* samb b7a.de sec k* seneg b4.de* *Sil* k* spig b7.de* squil b7.de* stann k* staph k* *Stront-c* k* *Sulph* k* tell k* teucr b7.de* thuj k* tritic-vg fd5.de valer b7.de* vanil fd5.de viol-o b7.de* zinc k*
    - **cold**; as from taking a: cham k*
    - **cramping**: anac ang arg-met aur cann-s chin *Cina* euphr grat lact lyc mosch ph-ac *Plat Sil*
    - **grasping** pain: chin h1
    - **inward**: mag-c mag-s k* nux-v k* sec k*
    - **jerking** pain: plat k*
    - **paralyzed**; as if: cham h1 mez k* nit-ac k* sil
    - **paroxysmal**: cann-s lyc
    - **shocks**; like: phyt k*
    - **upward**: nux-v
- **eating**; after: sulph ↓
    - **burning**: sulph
- **eczema**, in: *Merc* ↓
    - **burning**: *Merc*

- **epileptic** fit, before | **left** hand: *Calc-ar*
- **exertion**:
  - **amel.**: dios ↓
    - **aching**: dios
- **exertion**; as after: ars$_{bg2}$ crot-h$_{bg2}$ grat$_{bg2}$ sulph$_{bg2}$
- **feather** covering, under: lyc ↓
  - **tearing** pain: lyc$_{k}$*
- **fever**; during: hura ↓
  - **burning**: hura
- **foot**-bath, after: calc-caust$_{c1}$
- **gnawing** pain: bar-c berb cadm-s gran laur merc plat
- **gouty**: *Carbn-s* gins lyc
- **grasping** something agg.: get kali-c *Nat-s* nept-m$_{lsd2.fr}$
- **hang** down; letting arms:
  - **amel.**: arn ↓
    - **tearing** pain: arn
- **heat**; during: apis ↓ nux-v ↓ sec ↓
  - **burning**: apis$_{b7a.de}$ nux-v$_{b7.de}$ sec$_{a1}$
- **holding** anything: coff dulc$_{fd4.de}$ guaj phos sep sil vanil$_{fd5.de}$
- **jerking** pain: canth$_{bg2}$ *Chin*$_{k}$* mez nat-c nat-n puls sep$_{bg2}$ sul-ac$_{bg2}$ valer$_{b7.de}$*
- **lying** on left side agg.: *Phos* ↓
  - **tearing** pain: *Phos*
- **menses** | **before**:
  - **agg.**: carb-v ↓
    - **burning**: carb-v$_{bro1}$
  - **during**:
    - **agg.**: carb-v ↓ sec ↓
      - **burning**: carb-v$_{k}$* sec
- **motion**:
  - **agg.**: am-m ↓ bapt caps form galeoc-c-h$_{gms1}$• gent-l *Guaj* laur led ↓ mag-s$_{sp1}$ meny plb puls sep sil ↓ staph ↓ trios$_{rsj11}$• vanil$_{fd5.de}$ verb ↓ vip ↓
    - **drawing** pain: caps$_{k}$* meny$_{k}$*
    - **pressing** pain: led$_{h1}$ staph$_{h1}$ verb$_{h}$
    - **sore**: (↗*turning - sore)* sil
    - **stitching** pain: am-m vip
  - **amel.**: acon ↓ com dios dulc$_{fd4.de}$ *Rhus-t* ↓
    - **shooting** pain: acon
    - **stitching** pain: acon *Rhus-t*
- **paralyzed**; as if: acon$_{b7a.de}$* *Act-sp* agar agn$_{b7.de}$* am-m$_{b7.de}$* ambr$_{b7a.de}$* ang$_{b7a.de}$ ant-t$_{bg2}$ bar-c$_{b4.de}$* bell$_{b4.de}$* bism$_{b7.de}$* cann-s$_{b7.de}$* carb-v$_{bg2}$ caust$_{b4.de}$* cham$_{k}$* chel$_{b7.de}$* *Chin*$_{b7a.de}$ crot-h$_{bg2}$ cupr$_{bg2}$ cycl$_{b7.de}$* dig$_{b4.de}$* fl-ac$_{bg2}$ ham$_{fd3.de}$• ign$_{bg2}$ kali-n$_{bg2}$ kreos$_{b7a.de}$* meny$_{b7a.de}$ merc$_{b4.de}$* mez$_{k}$* nat-m$_{bg2}$ nit-ac nux-v$_{b7.de}$* phos$_{bg2}$ sabin$_{b7.de}$* sel sil$_{b4.de}$* staph$_{b7a.de}$ stront-c$_{b4a.de}$ tab ter$_{bg2}$ zinc$_{bg2}$
- **paroxysmal**: ang arg-n calc cina coloc euph *Euphr* ferr-m lyc mang *Meny* merc ph-ac plat ruta sec sil tab verb
- **piano**; while playing: merl ↓
  - **drawing** pain | **outward**: merl$_{k}$*
- **pinching** pain: bar-c$_{k}$* euphr$_{k}$* ol-an ph-ac$_{h2}$
- **playing** piano: merc ruta$_{fd4.de}$
- **pressing** pain: anac$_{k}$* ang$_{k}$* arg-met$_{k}$* arg-n$_{k}$* arn$_{k}$* asaf$_{k}$* aur bell$_{k}$* bism$_{b7.de}$* bry$_{k}$* carb-v$_{k}$* clem$_{k}$* coloc$_{k}$* cupr$_{k}$* cycl$_{k}$* dulc fl-ac$_{k}$* hell$_{k}$* hep$_{k}$* hyos$_{bg2}$ kali-c$_{k}$* kali-p$_{fd1.de}$• *Lach*$_{k}$* *Led*$_{k}$* lil-t$_{k}$* m-arct$_{b7.de}$ *Mang* meny$_{b7.de}$* *Merc*$_{k}$* *Mez*$_{k}$* mur-ac nat-m nat-s$_{k}$* nit-ac$_{bg2}$ olnd$_{k}$* ph-ac$_{k}$* *Plat* plb$_{k}$* puls$_{k}$* ran-s$_{b7.de}$* rhod$_{k}$* ruta$_{k}$* sars$_{k}$* sil stann$_{k}$* staph$_{k}$* teucr$_{b7.de}$* thuj$_{k}$* tritic-vg$_{fd5.de}$ verb$_{k}$* zinc$_{k}$*
  - **asunder**: *Led*$_{k}$*
  - **inward**: lach$_{k}$*
  - **outward**: lil-t$_{k}$*
- **pressure** agg.: chel ↓ kali-bi$_{k2}$ vanil$_{fd5.de}$
  - **tearing** pain: chel
- **pulsating** pain: am-m carb-v dulc$_{fd4.de}$ gels rhus-t suis-pan$_{rly4}$• sulph
- **rheumatic**: act-sp aesc alumn ambr$_{bro1}$ ammc ant-t ↓ asc-t bapt berb$_{bro1}$ **Caul**$_{k}$* caust$_{bro1}$* chel$_{bro1}$ *Clem* **Colch** com corv-cor$_{bdg}$• cupr$_{sst3}$• ery-a euphr gaert$_{pte1}$*• *Graph* ↓ *Guaj*$_{k}$* hyos$_{mtf11}$ *Lac-c* lach led$_{bro1}$ lyc lycpr$_{bro1}$ med *Merc-i-f* morg-p$_{fmm1}$• phyt prot$_{jl2}$ psil$_{ft1}$ ptel *Puls*$_{k}$* rad-br$_{c11}$ **Rhus-t**$_{k}$* *Ruta*$_{bro1}$ sal-ac$_{c1}$ sang$_{k}$* scarl$_{jl2}$ streptoc$_{jl2}$ *Stry* syc$_{bka1}$• ust *Viol-o* zinc zing ↓ [uva$_{stj}$]
  - **drawing** pain: ant-t$_{k}$* euphr$_{k}$* puls **Rhus-t** zing$_{k}$*
  - **menopause**; during: sal-ac$_{c1}$
  - **tearing** pain: ammc chel *Graph* puls
  - **thunderstorm**; in: *Rhod*$_{tl1}$
  - **warm** water | **amel.**: syc$_{bka1}$•
  - **weather**; dry | **amel.**: syc$_{bka1}$•
- **riding** in a carriage agg.: zinc ↓
  - **tearing** pain: zinc
- **rubbing**:
  - **amel.**: kali-n ↓ laur ↓
    - **tearing** pain: kali-n laur
- **running** agg.: agar
- **shocks** in heart, during: glon ↓
  - **stitching** pain: glon
- **shooting** pain: acon apis calc-s dulc$_{fd4.de}$ form iris$_{c1}$ nicc-s pic-ac spong$_{fd4.de}$ sulph
- **sitting** agg.: nat-s ↓
  - **tearing** pain: nat-s
- **sore**: abrot arg-n$_{bg1}$ *Arn*$_{k}$* ars bell bism calc$_{bg2}$ calc-p carb-an$_{bg2}$ carb-v$_{k}$* cina$_{bg2}$ crot-h cupr-ar dros$_{b7.de}$* ferr ger-i$_{rly4}$• ham$_{fd3.de}$• *Hep* *Kali-bi*$_{k}$* lil-t mag-c mez$_{k}$* nat-c nat-m$_{k}$* nicc$_{k}$* *Nit-ac*$_{bg2}$ olnd ph-ac phos$_{k}$* positr$_{nl2}$• **Rhus-t**$_{bg2}$ rhus-v *Ruta*$_{k}$* sars$_{b4a.de}$* sil$_{k}$* sinus$_{rly4}$• sulph verat$_{bro1}$ vip
  - **paralyzed**, as if: ph-ac
- **sprained**: nit-ac ↓
  - **drawing** pain: nit-ac$_{k}$*
- **sprained**; as if: acon *Am-c* ambr anac$_{h2}$ *Arn* bar-c bov *Bry* **Calc** *Carb-an* carb-v *Caust* dios hep kali-n kalm nit-ac$_{h2}$ phos plut-n$_{srj7}$• prun puls rhod *Rhus-t* *Ruta* sabin seneg sil sulph thuj verb zinc
- **squeezed**; as if: acon$_{bg2}$ **Ambr**$_{bg2}$ arg-met$_{bg2}$ ars$_{bg2}$ aur$_{bg2}$ **Calc**$_{bg2}$ cann-xyz$_{bg2}$ chin$_{bg2}$ cina$_{bg2}$ dros$_{b7.de}$* euph$_{bg2}$ euphr$_{bg2}$ *Graph*$_{bg2}$ kali-n$_{bg2}$ laur$_{bg2}$ lyc$_{bg2}$ mang$_{bg2}$ merc$_{bg2}$ mosch$_{bg2}$ nat-m$_{bg2}$ olnd$_{b7a.de}$ plat$_{bg2}$ ruta$_{bg2}$ sabad$_{bg2}$ spig$_{bg2}$ stann$_{bg2}$ thuj$_{bg2}$ verb$_{bg2}$ zinc$_{bg2}$
- **steam**, from: kali-bi ↓
  - **burning**: kali-bi
- **stitching** pain: acon$_{k}$* aesc aeth$_{a1}$ am-c$_{k}$* am-m$_{k}$* ambr$_{k}$* anac$_{k}$* ang$_{k}$* apis$_{k}$* arn$_{k}$* ars$_{k}$* arum-d arund asaf$_{k}$* aur$_{bg2}$ bamb-a$_{stb2.de}$• bapt bar-c *Bell*$_{k}$* berb borx$_{bg2}$ bov$_{k}$* bry$_{k}$* cain *Calc*$_{b4a.de}$ calc-s camph cann-s$_{b7.de}$* canth$_{bg2}$ caps$_{k}$* carb-ac *Carb-an*$_{k}$* carb-v carbn-s *Caust*$_{k}$* cham chel$_{k}$* chin$_{k}$* *Cina*$_{k}$* clem$_{bg2}$ colch$_{b7.de}$* *Coloc* con cycl dios dulc$_{bg2}$* euphr ferr fic-m$_{gya1}$ form gins glon graph$_{k}$* guaj$_{k}$* hell$_{k}$* hyper ign$_{k}$* *Kali-c*$_{k}$* kali-n$_{bg2}$ kali-sil$_{k2}$ *Kalm* kreos$_{b7a.de}$* lac-ac lach$_{k}$* laur$_{bg2}$ led$_{k}$* lil-t$_{k}$* lyc$_{k}$* m-ambo$_{b7.de}$ m-arct$_{b7.de}$ mag-c$_{k}$* *Mag-m*$_{k}$* mag-s manc meny$_{b7.de}$* merc-c$_{b4a.de}$ mez$_{k}$* mosch$_{k}$* mur-ac$_{k}$* nat-m$_{k}$* *Nat-s* nit-ac$_{k}$* nux-v$_{k}$* ol-an par$_{k}$* petr$_{k}$* ph-ac$_{k}$* phos$_{k}$* phyt$_{bg2}$ pic-ac plat *Plb*$_{k}$* positr$_{nl2}$• puls *Ran-b*$_{k}$* ran-s$_{b7.de}$* rhod$_{b4.de}$* *Rhus-t*$_{k}$* ruta$_{fd4.de}$ sabad samb *Sars*$_{k}$* seneg$_{k}$* sep$_{k}$* sil *Spong* squil$_{b7.de}$* stann$_{k}$* staph$_{k}$* suis-pan$_{rly4}$• *Sulph*$_{k}$* tab thuj *Verb*$_{k}$* vip *Zinc*$_{k}$* zinc-p$_{k2}$
  - **acute**: dulc$_{fd4.de}$ merc-i-f
  - **burning**: gamb rhod sulph
  - **fine**: arn arund clem led nat-m
  - **itching**: nat-m
  - **pricking** pain: plat
  - **shifting**: euphr$_{k}$*
  - **stinging**: aesc ambr led merc sulph
  - **tearing** pain: zinc
  - **twitching**: *Cina* lyc mez
  - **wandering** pain: con plat

- **subcutaneous**: par↓
  - **stitching** pain | **splinters**; as from: par
- **tearing** pain: *Acon* aeth a1 *Agar* k* alum k* alum-p k2 alum-sil k2 am-c k* am-m k* *Ambr* k* ammc anac k* arg-met k* arn k* ars k* asaf b7.de* *Aur* k* bapt bar-c k* *Bell* k* berb *Bism* k* borx b4a.de* bov bg2 brom calc k* *Calc-p* calc-sil k2 canth k* carb-an k* *Carb-v* k* carbn-s **Caust** k* chel k* *Chin* k* chinin-ar chinin-s *Cina* k* *Colch* k* coll *Coloc* cupr k* dig k* dros b7.de* dulc k* euph k* *Graph* k* *Grat* bg2 indg kali-ar kali-bi k* **Kali-c** k* kali-m k2 *Kali-n* k* kali-p kali-sil k2 kalm kola stb3• kreos lach k* laur k* led k* *Lyc* k* *Mag-m* k* mag-s *Mang* k* meny k* merc k* merc-c b4a.de merl *Mez* k* mur-ac k* nat-c k* nat-m k* **Nat-s** *Nit-ac* k* *Ol-an* par b7.de* *Petr* k* ph-ac k* *Phos* k* plat k* plb k* puls ran-b b7.de* *Rat* rheum k* *Rhod* k* rhus-t k* ruta k* sabad b7.de* sabin b7.de* sars k* sec *Sel* k* sep k* *Sil* k* spig b7.de* *Stann* k* staph k* stront-c k* *Sulph* k* tab tep teucr k* thuj verb k* *Zinc* k* zinc-p k2
  - **burning**: merl
  - **jerking** pain: chin h1
  - **paroxysmal**: rhod thuj
  - **pressing** pain: stann h2
  - **sticking** pain: zinc
  - **twitching**: cupr h2 rat stann
  - **wandering** pain: berb stann
  - **waves**; in: mez
- **touch** agg.: *Chin*↓ cupr↓ lyc↓ myric myris nit-ac staph↓ *Sulph*
  - **pressing** pain: cupr h2 staph h1
  - **stitching** pain: lyc
  - **tearing** pain: *Chin* nit-ac h2
- **touching** hair on hand; on: ign↓
  - **stitching** pain | **splinters**; as from: ign k*
- **turning** hand agg.: bamb-a↓
  - **sore**: (↗*motion - agg. - sore)* bamb-a stb2.de•
- **uncovering**:
  - **hands** | **agg.** | **fever**; during: *Nux-v* stram
    - **amel.**: lyc↓
      - **tearing** pain: lyc h2
- **waking**; on: nit-ac
  - **drawing** pain: nit-ac k*
- **walking**:
  - **agg.**: nat-s↓
    - **pressing** pain: nat-s k*
  - **air** agg.; in open: am-m↓
    - **stitching** pain: am-m
- **wandering** pain: ars-h choc srj3• ham fd3.de• *Iris* tell
- **warm** from fast walking: dulc↓
  - **burning**: dulc
- **warmth** agg.; external: bry caust *Guaj* lac-c led *Puls*
- **washing** | **after**:
  - **agg.**: aesc↓
    - **stitching** pain: aesc
  - **agg.**: alum iod merc sulph
- **weather** agg.; wet: *Rhus-t*
- **wet**; after getting feet cold and: phos↓
  - **burning**: phos
- **wetting** with warm water, after: *Phos*↓
  - **drawing** pain: *Phos* k*
- **writing**:
  - **after**: thuj↓
    - **drawing** pain: thuj h1
  - **agg.**: (↗*Cramps - hands - writing)* acon agar ant-c ars-i bamb-a↓ bar-c cinnb *Coloc*↓ cycl mrr1 euph fl-ac kali-c kola stb3• **Mag-p** melal-alt gya4 meny *Merc-i-f* nat-sil fd3.de• prot jl2 sabin samb *Sil* stann mrr1 sul-ac thuj valer zinc
    - **drawing** pain: euph meny *Sil*
    - **sore**: bamb-a stb2.de•
    - **stitching** pain: *Coloc*
    - **tearing** pain: kola stb3•

▽ • **extending** to:
  - **Arm**: nat-s↓
    - **drawing** pain: nat-s
  - **Arm** on moving it; into: hep↓
    - **sore**: hep
  - **Back**; into: caust↓
    - **tearing** pain: caust
  - **Elbow**: ang↓ *Caust*↓ cer-s↓ cere-s↓ dros↓ kola stb3• phyt↓ plac↓ sep↓ tab↓
    - **aching**: cer-s cere-s
    - **drawing** pain: phyt plac rzf5• sep h2 tab
    - **sore**: dros h1
    - **stitching** pain: ang *Caust*
    - **tearing** pain: kola stb3•
  - **Fingers**: canth↓ cina↓ colch↓ elat↓ euphr↓ gels↓ kali-c↓ lyc↓ nat-s↓ petr↓ taosc iwa1•
    - **aching**: elat
    - **drawing** pain: canth colch nat-s
    - **stitching** pain: cina euphr gels petr
    - **tearing** pain: kali-c lyc
    - **Third** (= Ring finger): elaps↓
      - **drawing** pain: elaps
  - **Larynx** and back to hand: euphr↓
    - **stitching** pain: euphr
  - **Shoulder**: fl-ac ham lat-m sinus↓ vanil fd5.de vesp
    - **aching**: sinus rly4•
    - **tearing** pain: lat-m
  - **Upper** arm: *Ars*↓ canth↓ lach↓ lat-m↓
    - **stitching** pain: canth
    - **tearing** pain: *Ars* lach lat-m

○ • **Back** of hands: aeth↓ agar↓ alum-sil↓ am-c am-m↓ amp↓ *Anac*↓ ang↓ apis↓ arg-met arg-n arn asaf↓ asar aur-m↓ bamb-a stb2.de• bar-c berb *Brucel* sa3• bry↓ *Calc*↓ carb-v carl↓ caust↓ chel↓ chin↓ cic↓ con↓ cop↓ cycl dulc fd4.de euphr↓ ferr *Ferr-i*↓ fl-ac↓ graph↓ ham hep hura↓ ille↓ jatr-c↓ kali-bi kali-c kali-n↓ kali-p↓ laur↓ lyc↓ melal-alt gya4 merc *Merc-c*↓ merc-i-f mez↓ morg-p↓ nat-c nat-s↓ nux-v↓ ol-an↓ phys rhus-v↓ ruta fd4.de stann↓ staph↓ suis-pan↓ *Sulph*↓ symph fd3.de• tarent thuj↓ vanil fd5.de verb viol-o↓ zinc↓ zing
  - **right**: gink-b sbd1• psil ft1
  - **morning**: ham↓ sulph↓
    - **burning**: ham fd3.de• sulph
  - **afternoon**: nat-s↓
    - **burning**: nat-s
  - **evening**: ang↓ dulc↓ ham↓ **Sulph**↓
    - **burning**: dulc fd4.de ham fd3.de• **Sulph**
    - **pressing** pain: ang k*
    - **rheumatic**: ang↓
      - **pressing** pain: ang k*
  - **night**: am-c
    - **midnight**:
      - **after**: hep↓
        - **aching**: hep
  - **aching**: amp rly4• arg-n carb-v cycl h1 hep kali-c merc verb
  - **boring** pain: hep
  - **burning**: agar alum-sil k2 apis k* aur-m berb bry *Calc* carl cop dulc fl-ac ham fd3.de• laur morg-p pte1• nat-s nux-v k* rhus-v *Sulph* thuj b4a.de
    - **nettles**; as from: carl
  - **cold** washing agg.: bros-gau mrc1
  - **cramping**: stann h2
  - **drawing** pain: *Anac* arg-met asaf k* chel k* chin h1 cic a1 *Ferr-i* jatr-c kali-bi k* kali-p fd1.de• lyc k* staph k* vanil fd5.de viol-o zing k*
    - **cramping**: anac arg-met
  - **motion** agg.: staph↓
    - **drawing** pain: staph h1
  - **pinching** pain: chel h1 euphr k* ol-an

Extremities

- **Back** of hands: ...
  - **pressing** pain: anac h2 ang k* arg-met arg-n k* arn k* asaf k* berb carb-v h2 cycl k* ham fd3.de• ille c1 kali-c h2 staph h1 verb h
  - **pressure** agg.: ille ↓
    - **pressing** pain: ille c1
  - **rheumatic**: zing ↓
    - **drawing** pain: zing k*
  - **shooting** pain: berb dulc fd4.de ferr
  - **sore**: bamb-a stb2.de• carb-v con bg1 graph ham fd3.de• hep hura *Ruta*
  - **sprained**; as if: am-m h2 bar-c h2
  - **stitching** pain: berb ferr *Merc-c* b4a.de suis-pan rly4•
  - **tearing** pain: aeth a1 anac h2 caust h2 chel h1 kali-c h2 kali-n h2 mez h2 sulph h2 verb h zinc h2
  - **warm** from walking: dulc ↓
    - **burning**: dulc
  - **extending** to | **Shoulder**: ham
  - **Spots**; in: cop ↓ fl-ac ↓
    - **burning**: cop fl-ac
- **Balls**: nept-m ↓
  - **aching**: nept-m lsd2.fr
- **Between** fingers: alum ↓ *Ars* ↓ carbn-s ↓ cycl ↓ graph ↓ led ↓ nat-ar ↓ puls ↓ rhus-v ↓ thuj ↓
  - **burning**: alum rhus-v
  - **pressing** pain: led k* puls k* thuj k*
  - **sore**: *Ars* graph nat-ar bro1
  - **stitching** pain: carbn-s cycl puls
  - **tearing** pain: alum cycl
  - **First**:
    - **Second**; and: ran-s ↓
      - **stitching** pain: ran-s
    - **Thumb**; and: agar ↓ alum ↓ berb ↓ iod ↓ *Kali-c* ↓ lyc ↓ ol-an ↓ ran-b ↓ rat ↓ rhus-t ↓ sulph ↓
      - **burning**: alum berb iod k* rhus-t sulph
      - **drawing** pain: agar k*
      - **stitching** pain: ol-an
      - **tearing** pain: agar *Kali-c* lyc ran-b rat
      - **writing** agg.: *Ran-b* ↓
        - **tearing** pain: *Ran-b*
  - **Second**:
    - **Third**; and: nat-c ↓ nat-s ↓ phel ↓
      - **tearing** pain: nat-c h2 nat-s phel
  - **Third**:
    - **Fourth**; and: aeth ↓
      - **tearing** pain: aeth
- **Between** wrist and knuckle of thumb: lyc ↓
  - **tearing** pain: lyc
- **Bones**: agar ↓ anac ↓ arg-met ↓ ars ↓ aur ↓ *Bism* ↓ carb-v ↓ caust ↓ chel ↓ chin ↓ cupr ↓ dig ↓ graph ↓ kali-c ↓ mang ↓ nat-c ↓ ph-ac ↓ phos ↓ sars ↓ stann ↓ staph ↓ suis-pan ↓ vanil fd5.de zinc ↓
  - **cramping**: aur h2
  - **cutting** pain: anac h2
  - **drawing** pain: agar h2 ars h2 carb-v h2 mang h2 nat-c h2
  - **jerking** pain: anac chin
  - **pressing** pain: arg-met h1 aur h2 sars h2 staph h1
  - **stitching** pain: suis-pan rly4•
  - **tearing** pain: arg-met h1 ars h2 aur h2 *Bism* h1* caust h2 chel h1 chin h1 cupr h2 dig h2 graph h2 kali-c h2 nat-c h2 ph-ac h2 phos h2 stann h2 zinc h2
  - **Metacarpal**: iod ↓
    - **sore**: iod h
    - **First** finger: iod ↓
      - **sore**: iod h
      - **tearing** pain: iod h
    - **Fourth** finger: bapt hr1 kali-p ↓ verb ↓
      - **sore**: kali-p fd1.de• verb h*
- **Hollow** of: acon ↓ cann-s ↓ caps ↓
  - **jerking** pain: caps a1
- **Hollow** of: ...
  - **stitching** pain: acon cann-s
    - **pulsating** pain: acon
- **Hypothenar**:
  - **right** | **rheumatic**: psil ft1
- **Joints**: act-sp mrr1 alumn ↓ am-m ↓ *Ambr* ↓ **Anac** ang ↓ *Arg-met* ↓ arge-pl rwt5• *Arn* ↓ ars ↓ asaf ↓ aur-m-n ↓ bamb-a stb2.de• bar-c ↓ bell *Bry* ↓ cadm-s ↓ caust ↓ chel ↓ clem coloc con fic-m gya1 hell ↓ hep ↓ hir ↓ indg ↓ kali-c kalm *Lac-c* lach limen-b-c ↓ *Mang* ↓ nat-c ↓ nat-p ↓ nat-s phos phys plb *Puls* rauw ↓ rhus-t ↓ ruta fd4.de sars ↓ *Sep* ↓ *Spig* ↓ squil ↓ sulph ↓ thuj
  - **left**: bamb-a stb2.de• get ↓
    - **dislocated**; as if: get a1*
    - **stitching** pain: bamb-a stb2.de•
  - **evening**: nat-c ↓ sulph ↓
    - **burning**: nat-c
    - **tearing** pain: sulph
  - **night**: *Phos* ↓
    - **tearing** pain: *Phos*
  - **aching**: clem fic-m gya1 *Kali-c* phys
  - **boring** pain: coloc
  - **burning**: nat-c rauw tpw8*
  - **carrying** things: bamb-a stb2.de•
  - **closing** hands; when: caul ↓
    - **cutting** pain: caul c1*
  - **cutting** pain: hir rsj4•
  - **dislocated**; as if: am-m b7.de* *Ambr* b7a.de anac b4a.de *Arn* b7a.de bar-c b4.de* *Bry* b7a.de caust b4a.de* con b4a.de hep b4.de* limen-b-c hrn2* puls b7a.de rhus-t b7.de*
  - **drawing** pain: **Anac** ang k* ars k* aur-m-n chel k* clem k* coloc k* *Mang* k* nat-p nat-s k* phos thuj k*
  - **gouty**: pin-s plb ruta fd4.de
  - **grasping** something; when: bamb-a ↓
    - **stitching** pain: bamb-a stb2.de•
  - **motion**:
    - **agg.**: bamb-a ↓ sulph ↓
      - **sprained**; as if: bamb-a stb2.de•
      - **tearing** pain: sulph
    - **amel.**: kali-c ↓
      - **pressing** pain: kali-c
  - **pressing** pain: ang k* asaf k* coloc k* hell k* kali-c
  - **rest** agg.: aur-m-n ↓
    - **drawing** pain: aur-m-n
  - **sore**: alumn *Arg-met* asaf
  - **stitching** pain: bamb-a stb2.de• bry rauw tpw8 ruta fd4.de sars *Sep* *Spig* squil
  - **tearing** pain: cadm-s *Coloc* indg lach rauw tpw8 spig sulph
    - **pulsating** pain: spig h1
  - **waking**; on: asaf ↓ lach
    - **pressing** pain: asaf k*
  - **Metacarpal** joints | **rheumatic**: caul tl1
- **Muscles**:
  - **Extensor** muscles: merl ↓
    - **tearing** pain: merl
- **Palms**: *Abrom-a* ↓ aesc ↓ aids nl2• ail ↓ all-s ↓ aloe ↓ am-m ↓ anac k* anis ↓ apis ↓ aq-mar skp7• ars ↓ asaf ↓ asc-t aur-m aza bro1 bamb-a ↓ bapt ↓ bell ↓ berb bol-la ↓ borx ↓ calad ↓ calc calc-f ↓ *Calc-s* ↓ *Canth* ↓ carb-an ↓ *Carb-v* ↓ carbn-s ↓ *Caust* ↓ cephd-i ↓ chel ↓ chin ↓ clem ↓ *Coloc* ↓ *Con* ↓ cop ↓ corh ↓ crot-c crot-h k* dulc fd4.de dys pte1• eupi ↓ ferr ↓ ferr-p ↓ fl-ac ↓ form ↓ gad ↓ gamb ↓ ger-i ↓ graph ↓ ham ↓ hir ↓ ille inul ↓ *Ip* ↓ kali-act ↓ kali-s fd4.de kalm ↓ lac-c ↓ *Lach* ↓ *Lachn* ↓ laur ↓ led lil-t ↓ lim ↓ *Lyc* ↓ mag-c ↓ malar ↓ mang ↓ *Med* ↓ merc ↓ merc-i-f mez morg-p ↓ mur-ac ↓ *Nat-ar* nat-c ↓ nat-m ↓ nat-ox ↓ nat-s nicc ↓ nit-ac ↓ ol-j ↓ olib-sac ↓ olnd ↓ ox-ac ↓ par ↓ *Petr* ↓ ph-ac ↓ *Phos* ↓ phys ↓ phyt plb ↓ prim-v ↓ psil ft1 puls-n ↓ *Ran-s* ↓ *Rhus-t* rumx ↓ ruta fd4.de sabad ↓ sabin *Samb* ↓ *Sang* ↓ sanic ↓ sars ↓ sec ↓ *Sel* ↓ seneg ↓ *Sep* ↓ spig ↓ spong fd4.de **Stann** ↓ staph ↓ stront-c ↓ stry

- **Palms**: ...
  Sulph↓ symph fd3.de• taosc iwa1• tarent tep↓ thuj↓ trif-p bro1 tritic-vg fd5.de upa↓ vanil fd5.de verb↓ zinc↓ zing↓
  - **right**: asc-t a1 symph fd3.de•
  - **left**: cench k2 graph↓ hir↓ kali-s fd4.de ran-s↓ rhus-t↓
    - **burning**: graph bg1 hir skp7• rhus-t bg1
    - **gnawing** pain: ran-s ptk1
    - **inability** to double fingers; with: inul↓
      - **tearing** pain: inul br1
  - **morning**:
    - **bed** agg.; in: calc↓ symph↓
      - **stitching** pain: calc symph fd3.de•
  - **afternoon** | **15** h: aq-mar skp7•
  - **evening**: borx↓ calad↓ **Lach**↓ lyc↓ nat-s ran-s↓ rumx↓ ruta fd4.de stront-c↓ thuj↓ tritic-vg fd5.de upa↓
    - **21** h: aq-mar skp7•
    - **22** h: sulph↓
      - **stitching** pain: sulph
    - **burning**: **Lach** rumx upa k*
    - **drawing** pain: nat-s k* ruta fd4.de tritic-vg fd5.de
    - **gnawing** pain: ran-s k*
    - **stitching** pain: borx calad lyc thuj
    - **tearing** pain: stront-c
  - **night**: **Lach**↓ spong↓
    - **midnight**: malar↓ rhus-t↓
      - **before**:
        - **22** h: sulph↓
          - **shooting** pain: sulph
      - **burning**: malar jl2 rhus-t
      - **stitching** pain: rhus-t
    - **and** soles: *Lach*↓
      - **burning**: *Lach*
    - **burning**: **Lach** spong fd4.de
  - **aching**: *Aza* br1 merc-i-f nat-ox rly4• nat-s
  - **biting**: *Sel* b7a.de
  - **boring** pain: mez
  - **burning**: *Abrom-a* zzc1• aesc ail all-s k* anac b4a.de apis k* ars *Aza* bro1 bol-la bro1 *Calc* k* calc-f sp1 *Calc-s* *Canth* k* *Carb-v* carbn-s cephd-i zzc1• chel k* chin b7.de cop corh br1 ferr bro1 ferr-p bro1 fl-ac form k* gad bro1 graph k* ham k* hir skp7• *Ip* lac-c *Lach* k* *Lachn* k* laur b7.de lil-t lim bro1 *Lyc* k* mag-c k* malar jl2 *Med* merc k* mez k* morg-p pte1• mur-ac nat-c k* nat-m k* ol-j bg1* olib-sac wmh1 ox-ac *Petr* k* *Phos* k* phys k* prim-v bro1 puls-n bro1 rhus-t k* rumx sabad *Samb* b7a.de *Sang* k* sanic sars sec k* *Sep* k* spong fd4.de **Stann** k* **Sulph** k* tarent k* tep k* tritic-vg fd5.de upa k*
    - **stinging**: borx
  - **cold** water:
    - **amel**.: apis↓ hir↓
      - **burning**: hir skp7•
      - **stitching** pain: apis
  - **cramping**: coloc h2
  - **cutting** bread: *Calc*
  - **cutting** pain: aids nl2•
  - **drawing** pain: aloe k* aur-m *Caust* chin k* *Coloc* led k* nat-s k* *Rhus-t* k* ruta fd4.de sabin k* tritic-vg fd5.de vanil fd5.de zinc h2 zing k*
  - **fever**; during: corh↓
    - **burning**: corh br1
  - **gnawing** pain: kalm k* *Ran-s* k*
  - **menopause**; during: sang↓ *Sulph*↓
    - **burning**: sang bro1 *Sulph* bro1
  - **menses**; during: carb-v↓ cassia-s↓ petr↓
    - **burning**: carb-v cassia-s ccrh1• petr
  - **motion** agg.: anac
  - **pinching** pain: mang k* spong h1
  - **pressing** pain: asaf k* olnd k* plb k*
  - **pulsating** pain: berb merc-i-f
  - **rubbing**; after: **Sulph**↓
    - **burning**: **Sulph** k*

- **Palms**: ...
  - **shooting** pain: sulph
  - **sore**: am-m aq-mar skp7• ars k* ger-i rly4• nat-c nat-s k2 rhus-t ptk1
  - **stitching** pain: apis bamb-a stb2.de• berb borx k* calad carb-an caust clem *Con* eupi gamb kali-act lyc mag-c nat-ar k2 nat-m nat-s nicc nit-ac par ph-ac rhus-t sel seneg sep staph **Sulph** symph fd3.de• thuj verb
    - **acute**: gamb
    - **crawling**: anis
    - **drawing** pain: ph-ac
    - **tearing** pain: verb
    - **tingling** pain: staph
  - **tearing** pain: anis bapt bell berb calc carb-v caust inul lyc mang h2 spig stront-c sulph thuj zinc
  - **warm** bathing; after: nat-c↓
    - **burning**: nat-c
  - **extending** to:
    - **Back** of forearm: gamb↓
      - **stitching** pain | **tingling** pain: gamb
    - **Elbow**: eupi↓
      - **stitching** pain | **tingling** pain: eupi
    - **Fingers**: *Caust*↓ sabin
      - **drawing** pain: *Caust* sabin k*
    - **Forearm**: stront-c↓ sulph↓
      - **tearing** pain: stront-c sulph k*
  - **Balls**: anac↓ aur aur-m↓ carb-an↓ cham↓ cupr↓ kali-n↓ mag-m↓ mang↓ nat-c nept-m lsd2.fr ran-s↓ sil↓ sulph↓ zinc↓
    - **evening**:
      - **bed** agg.; in: mag-m↓
        - **stitching** pain: (non:mag-c kl) mag-m a1*
        - **tearing** pain: mag-m
    - **burning**: zinc k*
    - **drawing** pain: aur-m k* nat-c k*
    - **gnawing** pain: kali-n h2
    - **grasping** something agg.: nept-m lsd2.fr
    - **pressing** pain: cupr h2 zinc k*
    - **shooting** pain: sulph
    - **stitching** pain: carb-an cham cupr mag-m ran-s sil sulph
    - **tearing** pain: anac h2 kali-n h2 mag-m mang h2 sil
    - **writing** agg.: nat-c
      - **drawing** pain: nat-c
  - **Between** first finger and thumb: zinc↓
    - **tearing** pain: zinc
  - **Hypothenar**:
    - **left**: psil↓
      - **stitching** pain: psil ft1
  - **Middle** of hands: bamb-a↓
    - **stitching** pain: bamb-a stb2.de•
  - **Radial** side: canth↓ caust↓ kali-bi↓ ol-an↓ phos↓ sulph↓
    - **burning**: phos
    - **tearing** pain: canth caust kali-bi ol-an sulph
      - **bone**; as if in: caust
      - **flesh** would be torn from bone; as if: ol-an
    - **extending** to:
      - **Finger**: sulph↓
        - **tearing** pain: sulph
  - **Ulnar** side: sep↓
    - **burning**: sep
- **Radial** side of: cham↓ phos↓
  - **stitching** pain: cham phos
- **Spots**; in: arg-n↓ arn↓ cop↓ fl-ac↓ mang↓
  - **burning**: arg-n a1 cop fl-ac mang
  - **drawing** pain: arn k*
- **Tendons**: spig↓ taosc iwa1•
  - **drawing** pain: spig k*
  - **Extensor** tendons: ferr-i↓ led↓ nat-c↓
    - **drawing** pain: ferr-i k* led h1 nat-c h2

- **Ulnar** side: anac↓ arn↓ arum-d berb↓ bism↓ carb-an↓ castm↓ caust mrr1 led↓ lyc↓ merc-i-f↓ mill↓ mur-ac↓ nat-m↓ nat-s↓ nicc positr↓ rhod↓ rhus-t sep stann↓ tarent↓
  - **right**: aq-mar skp7•
  - **night**: nicc
  - **drawing** pain: anac h2 arn carb-an h2 sep k*
  - **jerking** pain: arn
  - **motion**:
    - **amel.**: nicc↓
      - **tearing** pain: nicc
  - **pressing** pain: led k* nat-s k* stann h2
  - **sore**: carb-an h2
  - **stitching** pain: berb carb-an merc-i-f mill positr nl2• tarent
  - **tearing** pain: arn berb bism h1 castm lyc mur-ac h2 nat-m h2 nicc rhod sep
    - **paroxysmal**: rhod
  - **writing** agg.: nicc↓
    - **tearing** pain: nicc
  - **extending** to:
    - **Elbow**: aq-mar skp7• sep↓
      - **tearing** pain: sep
    - **Fourth** finger: rhod↓
      - **tearing** pain: rhod
    - **Index** finger: sulph↓
      - **gnawing** pain: sulph
    - **Wrist**: lyc↓
      - **tearing** pain: lyc

- **Hips**: *(↗Hip joint)* abrot k* *Acon* k* act-sp k* *Aesc* k* aeth↓ *Agar* k* agn↓ aids nl2• ail k* all-c↓ *All-s* br1* alum alum-p↓ alum-sil↓ am-c am-m k* ambr b7a.de* ammc anac↓ *Anag* anan↓ *Ang*↓ *Ant-c*↓ ant-t apis k* apoc↓ *Arg-met* k* *Arg-n* hr1 arge-pl rwt5• *Arn* k* **Ars** k* *Ars-i* arum-t arund↓ asaf b7a.de* asar k* asc-t aster k* *Aur* k* aur-i k2 aur-m↓ aur-m-n↓ aur-s k2 bacls-7 fmm1• bad k* *Bamb-a* stb2.de• bapt k* *Bar-c* k* bar-i k2 bar-s k2 *Bell* k* bell-p-sp↓ benz-ac k* *Berb* k* bov k* brom k* brucel sa3• *Bry* k* **Calc** k* *Calc-p* k* *Calc-s* calc-sil k2 camph↓ cann-i k* cann-s↓ cann-xyz↓ *Canth* k* *Caps*↓ carb-ac k* *Carb-an* k* *Carb-v*↓ carbn-s carc↓ **Card-m** cardios-h↓ cassia-s↓ castm↓ *Caust* k* cham k* **Chel** k* chin↓ *Chinin-ar*↓ cic↓ *Cimic* cimx *Cina*↓ cinnb k* cist bro1 clem k* cob↓ coc-c↓ coca↓ cocc k* coff **Colch** k* coli gmj1 **Coloc** k* con k* cop k* croc↓ crot-c↓ crot-h↓ *Crot-t* cupr cur↓ cycl b7a.de cypra-eg↓ des-ac↓ dig k* dios k* dros k* dulc tl1* elaps gk elat bro1 euon eup-per↓ **Eup-pur**↓ *Euph* k* euphr↓ fago *Ferr* k* ferr-ar↓ *Ferr-i* ferr-ma↓ ferr-p↓ *Fl-ac* k* form k* gaert pte1*• gamb↓ gels k* ger-i↓ gins↓ glyc bro1 gran k* graph b4a.de* grat gua bro1 haliae-lc srj5• ham k* *Hell*↓ helon **Hep** k* hura *Hydr* hyos b7.de* hyper k* *Ign*↓ ina-i mlk9.de *Indg* *Iod* ip↓ irid-met↓ *Iris*↓ jug-c *Kali-ar* *Kali-bi* k* *Kali-c* k* *Kali-i* k* kali-n k* *Kali-p* *Kali-s* kali-sil k2 *Kalm* k* kola stb3• *Kreos* k* lac-c *Lac-d* lac-h sk4• *Lach* k* lap-la↓ lat-m↓ *Laur*↓ **Led** k* *Lil-t* k* lim bro1 lina↓ lith-c lob-s k* loxo-recl bnm10• *Lyc* k* *Lyss* m-ambo↓ m-arct↓ m-aust↓ mag-c k* mag-m bro1 mag-s k* manc↓ mang↓ mang-p↓ *Med* k* melal-alt gya4 meny↓ meph↓ *Merc* k* *Merc-c*↓ merc-i-f k* merc-i-r k* mez k* mosch↓ mur-ac↓ *Murx* k* musca-d↓ naja↓ nat-ar *Nat-c*↓ *Nat-hchls* nat-m k* nat-p↓ nat-pyru↓ *Nat-s* k* nat-sil fd3.de• nept-m lsd2.fr nicc↓ nit-ac k2 nit-s-d↓ nux-m k* nux-v b7.de* ol-an↓ olnd b7.de* osm↓ ox-ac k* ozone↓ pall k* pant-ac↓ par↓ petr bg2 *Ph-ac* *Phos* k* phys *Phyt* pieri-b mlk9.de pimp↓ plat plb k* plumbg k* plut-n srj7• podo polyg-h↓ positr↓ prun k* psor ptel k* **Puls** k* rad-br bro1 ran-b↓ raph↓ *Rat*↓ rhod k* **Rhus-t** k* rhus-v ruta k* sabad k* sabin k* sal-al blc1• samb↓ sang sanic↓ sarr↓ *Sars* scol ah1 seneg k* *Sep* k* **Sil** k* sin-n k* sol-ni bro1 sol-t-ae↓ *Spect*↓ spig↓ spong fd4.de stann k* staph k* still↓ **Stram** k* *Stront-c*↓ succ-ac↓ sul-i k2 *Sulph* k* suprar↓ symph fd3.de• *Syph*↓ tab↓ tarent k* tax k* tell k* tep↓ ter tere-la↓ teucr↓ ther↓ *Thuj* k* til k* tong c2* *Tril-p*↓ tritic-vg fd5.de trom k* tub al* ust *Valer* k* vanil fd5.de ven-m rsj12• *Verat* k* verat-v k* *Vero-o* rly3• visc↓ xan k* zinc bg2 zinc-p↓ zing [heroin sdj2]
  - **alternating** sides: haliae-lc srj5• **Lac-c** uva c1 verat
    - **shooting** pain: uva c1
  - **right**: aesc *Agar* k* agn↓ ail tl1 alum androc srj1• ant-t bro1 ara-maca sej7• arg-met↓ arge-pl rwt5• *Asar*↓ asc-t a1* bacls-7 pte1*• bamb-a stb2.de• bar-c brass-n-o srj5• calam sa3• carb-an k* carneg-g↓ *Chel* bro1 coc-c↓ coli↓ *Coloc*↓ con↓ corn daph dulc fd4.de ephe-si hsj1• fl-ac↓ graph bro1 ham fd3.de• indg kali-bi *Kali-c* k* kali-s fd4.de kola stb3• lac-c lachn↓ lap-la sde8.de• **Led** k* lil-t k* lim bro1 *Lyc*↓ **Lyss** k* *Mag-m*↓ mang↓ merc-c↓ merc-i-r mez *Murx* *Nat-c*↓ nat-m↓ nat-s k2* nat-sil fd3.de• nit-ac↓ nux-m bro1 olib-sac wmh1 osteo-a jl2 ozone sde2• pall k* phos plut-n srj7• propr sa3• ptel c1 rhod↓ ruta fd4.de sabad↓ samb bat1• sel rsj9• sep spong fd4.de stram bro1 sulph↓ symph↓ ter↓ ther↓ thuj↓ tritic-vg fd5.de vanil fd5.de vero-o rly4*• [*Buteo-j* sej6 heroin sdj2 spect dfg1]
    - **aching**: carneg-g rwt1• ozone sde2•
    - **cutting** pain: agn kali-c bg1
    - **dislocated**; as if: agar bg2 con bg2 nat-m bg1 sulph bg1 thuj bg2* [spect dfg1]
    - **drawing** pain: bamb-a stb2.de• *Chel* dulc fd4.de kali-bi lil-t nit-ac sep h2 symph fd3.de• ther
    - **pressing** pain: arg-met h1 *Asar* k* *Kali-bi* *Led* k* **Lyss** nat-c h2 nit-ac k* sabad *Sep* k* symph fd3.de•
      - **held** tight; as if: phos h2
    - **rising** from sitting agg.: chel↓
      - **shooting** pain: chel
      - **stitching** pain: chel
    - **shooting** pain: chel sabad spong fd4.de sulph
    - **sore**: coli rly4• lil-t nat-c h2* *Sep*
    - **sprained**; as if: pall rhod
    - **stepping** with left leg: arg-met↓
      - **pressing** pain: arg-met h1
    - **stitching** pain: androc srj1• chel *Coloc* fl-ac ham fd3.de• kali-s fd4.de kola stb3• lil-t *Lyc* mang a1 merc-c nat-m bg2 nat-sil fd3.de• ptel c1 sabad sep sulph symph fd3.de•
    - **tearing** pain: agar agn coc-c daph lachn *Mag-m* *Nat-c* ozone sde2• ter
    - **walking** agg.: lac-e hrn2•
    - **extending** to:
      - **left** hip: kali-s fd4.de lith-c
      - **Back**: apoc↓
        - **neuralgic**: apoc vh1
      - **Thigh**: dulc fd4.de lil-t x-ray sp1
      - **Toes**: gins c1
    - **Spot**; in a | **air** agg.; in open: vip-l-f a1
  - **left**: *Acon* aeth↓ agn aids nl2• *Am-m* k* ant-c k* apis bg1 arg-n ars-met asc-t a1 bacls-7 fmm1• bar-act↓ benz-ac brom k* **Carb-an**↓ carneg-g↓ **Caust** chel↓ cic↓ cocc colch rsj2• coli↓ coloc bro1 *Con*↓ dulc fd4.de erig br1 eup-per fic-m gya1 gels psa ham fd3.de• hell↓ hura↓ hydroph rsj6• ignis-alc↓ irid-met bro1 iris c1 kali-i↓ kali-s fd4.de kola stb3• *Kreos*↓ laur lepi↓ lyc mag-c↓ med↓ nat-m↓ nat-pyru↓ *Nat-s* k* nat-sil fd3.de• nept-m lsd2.fr olib-sac↓ onos ovi-p c2* pall k* podo c1 propr sa3• psil ft1 puls↓ rumx↓ ruta fd4.de sacch-a fd2.de• sang k* *Sanic* sars↓ sep↓ sol-ni bro1 spong fd4.de stann↓ *Stram* k* sulph symph↓ ulm-c jsj8• vac↓ vero-o rly4*• xan k* [heroin sdj2 tax jsj7]
    - **aching**: carneg-g rwt1• ignis-alc es2•
    - **burning**: [heroin sdj2]
    - **cutting** pain: kali-i lepi br1
    - **dislocated**; as if: caust bg2* chel bg2 dulc bg2* hura bg2 irid-met vml3• iris c1* *Kreos* laur bg2* nat-pyru rly4• pall bg2 sulph
    - **drawing** pain: *Acon* aeth *Am-m* **Ant-c** dulc fd4.de ruta fd4.de stann h2 *Sulph*
    - **lying** on right side, when: bell *Cham*
    - **neuralgic**: bar-act bg2
    - **pressing** pain: acon cocc coloc k* hell k* lyc h2 puls h1 symph fd3.de•
      - **ball**; as from a: *Con*
    - **shooting** pain: nat-s bg2
    - **sore**: aids nl2• apis bg2 coli rly4• nat-m h2
    - **sprained**; as if: caust bg2 laur lyc h2 nat-m h2
    - **stitching** pain: am-m **Carb-an** cic cocc med c1 nat-s olib-sac wmh1 rumx bg1 sars bg1 sep spong fd4.de stram
    - **tearing** pain: acon lyc h2 mag-c vac jl2
    - **extending** to:
      - **Knee**: lepi↓
        - **cutting** pain: lepi br1
  - **daytime**: dulc fd4.de kali-bi k* lyss

- **morning**: aesc agar$_{k*}$ aids↓ alum↓ am-c *Ars*↓ aster bry↓ colch↓ coloc$_{k*}$ dios$_{k*}$ dulc$_{fd4.de}$ ferr-ma fl-ac$_{k*}$ ham$_{fd3.de}$• kali-n↓ lyc *Mag-m*↓ rat↓ **Rhus-t** ruta$_{fd4.de}$ sabin staph stront-c symph$_{fd3.de}$• tritic-vg$_{fd5.de}$ vanil$_{fd5.de}$
  - **aching**: aesc
  - **bed** agg.; in: agar↓ dulc$_{fd4.de}$ *Puls* vanil$_{fd5.de}$
    - **pressing** pain: agar$_{k*}$
  - **drawing** pain: ars$_{h2}$ colch dulc$_{fd4.de}$ stront-c tritic-vg$_{fd5.de}$
  - **rising**:
    - **after**:
      - **agg.**: agar↓ fl-ac↓
        - **sore**: agar fl-ac
    - **agg.**: nat-m↓ sabin↓ *Sulph*↓
      - **stitching** pain: nat-m sabin$_{c1}$ *Sulph*
    - **amel.**: phos
      - **aching**: phos
  - **sore**: agar aids$_{nl2}$• alum ars$_{h2}$ bry fl-ac rat
  - **sprained**; as if: ars$_{h2}$ kali-n lyc
  - **tearing** pain: *Ars* *Mag-m* stront-c tritic-vg$_{fd5.de}$
  - **waking**; on: am-c kali-n$_{k*}$ mag-m↓ *Med* propr$_{sa3}$• symph$_{fd3.de}$•
    - **sore**: mag-m
- **forenoon**: am-m↓ dulc$_{fd4.de}$ equis-h nat-c↓ prun puls↓ ruta$_{fd4.de}$ spong$_{fd4.de}$ sulph↓
  - **drawing** pain: dulc$_{fd4.de}$ ruta$_{fd4.de}$ sulph
  - **menses**; during: nat-c↓
    - **sore**: nat-c
  - **pressing** pain: puls$_{h1}$
  - **sore**: am-m equis-h
  - **tearing** pain: nat-c
- **noon**: nicc↓
  - **burning**: nicc$_{k*}$
  - **scratching** agg.; after: nicc↓
    - **burning**: nicc
- **afternoon**: abrot$_{k*}$ agar brucel$_{sa3}$• canth↓ chel$_{k*}$ dulc$_{fd4.de}$ kali-n↓ mag-m↓ merc-c↓ naja spong$_{fd4.de}$ sulph$_{k*}$
  - **13** h: hura
  - **15** h: *Lach*
    - **15**-16.30 h: propr$_{sa3}$•
  - **16** h: ptel↓
    - **lasting** all night: mag-c↓
      - **tearing** pain: mag-c
    - **stitching** pain: ptel
  - **17**-20 h: ven-m$_{rsj12}$•
  - **burning**: mag-m$_{k*}$
  - **drawing** pain: chel dulc$_{fd4.de}$ sulph
  - **motion** of right arm towards left agg.: plb↓
    - **stitching** pain: plb
  - **stitching** pain: canth merc-c spong$_{fd4.de}$
  - **tearing** pain: kali-n mag-m
- **evening**: agar ant-c aster cham↓ con↓ dios$_{k*}$ dulc↓ fago$_{k*}$ *Ferr* *Kali-bi* kali-n↓ mag-m↓ mag-s↓ merc-i-r nat-sil$_{fd3.de}$• nicc↓ ran-b↓ ruta$_{fd4.de}$ *Sulph*↓ tab↓ *Tarent*$_{k*}$ ther tritic-vg$_{fd5.de}$ valer
  - **19** h: form↓
    - **shooting** pain: form
  - **21** h: erig
  - **aching**: dios
  - **bed** | **going** to bed:
    - **after**: *Ferr*↓ lyc↓ *Mag-m*↓ nat-c↓
      - **tearing** pain: *Ferr* lyc *Mag-m* nat-c
    - **in** bed:
      - **agg.**: ant-t↓ *Sep*↓
        - **stitching** pain: ant-t *Sep*
  - **burning**: mag-m$_{k*}$ nicc$_{k*}$
  - **drawing** pain: *Ant-c* dulc$_{fd4.de}$ ran-b ruta$_{fd4.de}$ ther
  - **lying** down agg.; after: mag-m↓
    - **burning**: mag-m
  - **scratching** agg.; after: mag-m↓ nicc↓
- **evening – scratching** agg; after.: ...
    - **burning**: mag-m nicc
  - **shooting** pain: *Ferr Sulph*
  - **sprained**; as if: cham con merc-i-r
  - **stitching** pain: nat-sil$_{fd3.de}$• sulph tab
  - **tearing** pain: kali-n mag-m mag-s sulph$_{h2}$
  - **walking** agg.: ant-c calc↓ con$_{k*}$ crot-h erig$_{k*}$ ran-b$_{k*}$
    - **drawing** pain: ant-c calc$_{h2}$ crot-h ran-b
- **night**: agar↓ *Am-m*↓ arn↓ ars↓ bell$_{k*}$ cham *Coloc* dulc$_{fd4.de}$ euph ferr ferr-ma kali-bi *Kali-c* *Kali-i* kali-s$_{fd4.de}$ lach **Lyc**↓ mag-c↓ mag-m↓ merc nat-m↓ nat-s petr$_{k*}$ prun$_{k*}$ *Rhus-t* *Sep*↓ sin-n$_{k*}$ *Sulph* syph tarent$_{k*}$
  - **midnight**:
    - **before**: *Ferr* prun
    - **after**:
      - **4** h: *Coloc*↓
        - **boring** pain: *Coloc*
      - **5** h: verat
  - **bed** agg.; in: dulc$_{fd4.de}$ form↓ hyper *Phos*
    - **sore**: form phos
  - **before** falling asleep: *Sulph*↓
    - **shooting** pain: *Sulph*
  - **boring** pain: *Kali-i*
  - **burning**: bell *Euph* mag-m$_{k*}$
  - **drawing** pain: *Coloc*
  - **gnawing** pain: *Kali-i*
  - **lying** on it: *Caust*↓ kali-bi↓
    - **sore**: *Caust* kali-bi
  - **sore**: ars$_{h2}$ nat-m
  - **sprained**; as if: ars$_{h2}$
  - **stitching** pain: *Am-m* **Lyc** *Merc* *Sep* sulph
  - **tearing** pain: agar$_{h2}$ arn mag-c mag-m *Merc* nat-s$_{k2}$ sep$_{h2}$ syph$_{k2}$
  - **waking**; on: puls-n↓
    - **aching**: puls-n
- **accompanied** by:
  - **diarrhea**: elat$_{br1}$
  - **Heart**; complaints of the (See CHEST - Heart; complaints - accompanied - hip)
- **aching**: aesc ail arge-pl$_{rwt5}$• bapt bry carb-ac carb-an *Caust* coli$_{rly4}$• dios eup-per gamb ham lat-m$_{bnm6}$• lyss mang-p$_{rly4}$• med melal-alt$_{gya4}$ merc-i-f mosch *Phos* *Phyt* plut-n$_{srj7}$• positr$_{nl2}$• puls *Rhus-t* staph still succ-ac$_{rly4}$• suprar$_{rly4}$• tab tarent tere-la$_{rly4}$• [bell-p-sp$_{dcm1}$ heroin$_{sdj2}$ *Spect*$_{dfg1}$]
- **afterpains**: *Sil*
- **alternating** with | **Shoulder**; pain in (See shoulders - alternating with - hip)
- **ascending** stairs agg.: bry carbn-s↓ nat-s ph-ac↓ *Plb* podo rhus-t ruta$_{fd4.de}$ thuj verb [heroin$_{sdj2}$]
  - **sore**: ph-ac
  - **stitching** pain: carbn-s$_{k2}$ ph-ac
- **backwards**; from before: sep↓
  - **pressing** pain | **tearing** pain: sep
- **bandage**; tight:
  - **amel.**: tril-p↓
    - **falling** in pieces; as if: tril-p$_{zr}$
- **bandaging**:
  - **amel.**: tril-p↓
    - **broken**; as if | **falling** apart; as if pelvis were: tril-p$_{hr1}$
- **bed**; when going to: fl-ac
- **bending**:
  - **body**:
    - **backward** agg.: caps *Puls*
      - **drawing** pain: *Caps*
  - **legs**:
    - **backward** agg.: ant-c↓
      - **drawing** pain: ant-c

- **bending**: ...
  - **painful** side; to:
    - **agg.**: mag-c ↓
      - **sore**: mag-c h2
  - **right**; to | **agg.**: *Rhus-t*
- **blow**; pain as from a: cina b7.de* ruta b7.de* stann bg2
- **boring** pain: acon bg2 ang bg2 arn k* cina b7.de* *Coloc* kali-i *Kreos* k* lil-t merc bg2 *Mez* rhod ruta bg2*
- **breathing**:
  - **agg.**: alum ↓
    - **tearing** pain: alum
  - **deep**:
    - **agg.**: nat-m ↓
      - **sprained**; as if: nat-m
- **broken**; as if: pimp a1 zing k*
  - **falling** apart; as if pelvis were: aesc bro1 *Tril-p* bro1
- **burning**: acon bg2 arn bg2 *Ars* k* arund k* aur-m-n k* bell k* berb *Carb-v* k* caust bg2 chel b7.de cic b7.de cur *Euph* k* gels k* hell k* ign bg2 iod *Kali-c* kali-n k* kreos lap-la sde8.de• lith-c mag-m k* nicc k* ozone sde2• rhus-t k* ruta b7.de tarent k* valer k* vanil fd5.de visc bg2 *Zinc*
  - **itching** pain: lith-c
  - **prickling** pain: caust h2
- **burrowing**: arn b7.de* ruta b7.de*
- **carrying**, when: caps ↓
  - **stitching** pain: caps
- **chill**; during: ail k2 arn k* calc k* lyc k* nux-v k* rhus-t k* sep k*
  - **sore**: **Arn**
  - **stitching** pain: ail hr1
- **coryza**; during: sep ↓
  - **drawing** pain: sep
- **cough** agg.; during: arg-met ars b4.de* bell k* *Caps* b7a.de **Caust** k* kali-bi bg2 rhus-t k* sulph k* *Valer* verat b7a.de
  - **pressing** pain: *Caust*
  - **shooting** pain: caps
  - **stitching** pain: bell sulph
  - **tearing** pain: *Caps*
- **cramping**: bar-c h2 meny h1
- **crossing** legs agg.: all-s k*
- **cutting** pain: agn alum k* berb *Bry* k* calc k* *Coloc* b4a.de dig k* dios bg1 dulc bg2 gamb gins graph *Ign* kali-bi lyc mur-ac k* nat-s pant-ac rly4• *Phyt* tell
- **delivery**:
  - **after**: **Hyper**
    - **instrumental**: hyper
  - **during**: *Cimic*
    - **pressing** pain: *Cimic*
- **dinner**; after: kali-bi ↓
  - **aching**: kali-bi
- **dislocated**; as if: agar k* am-c bg2 *Am-m* b7a.de anac b4a.de ang b7.de* arn b7.de* bamb-a stb2.de• bar-c b4a.de bell b4.de* bry b7a.de* *Calc* b4a.de *Caust* k* con b4.de* dulc b4a.de euph b4.de* fl-ac bg2 hep b4a.de* *Ign* k* ip irid-met vml3• iris bg2 kreos b7a.de* laur lina rb2 m-ambo b7.de mag-m h2* merc mosch *Nat-m* b4.de* nat-pyru rly4• nit-ac b4a.de nux-v b7.de* olnd b7.de* osm bg2 pall petr b4.de* phos b4.de* psor k* **Puls** k* rhod b4.de* rhus-t b7a.de* sanic bg2* seneg b4.de* stann b4.de* sulph k* thuj zinc bg2
- **drawing** back the leg: ferr-ma ↓
  - **drawing** pain: ferr-ma
- **drawing** pain: acon k* aeth am-c am-m ang b7.de* *Ant-c* k* ant-t b7.de* arg-met k* *Arg-n* arge-pl rwt5• *Arn* *Ars* k* asar k* aster aur bamb-a stb2.de• bapt benz-ac bry *Calc* k* calc-p camph b7.de* *Caps* *Carb-an* *Carb-v* k* *Carbn-s* caust k* cham **Chel** chin k* cina b7.de* cinnb coc-c *Cocc* k* colch k* *Coloc* *Con* k* crot-h cycl b7.de* *Dig* k* *Dulc* k* ferr-ma gels hell *Hep* *Kali-bi* k* kreos b7a.de *Led* lil-t lyc m-aust b7.de mang k* meph naja nat-c k* *Nat-m* k* nat-p *Nit-ac* nux-v k2 par petr ph-ac k* *Phyt* plat plb **Puls** k* ran-b k* rhod k* *Rhus-t* k* ruta *Sep* k* sil h2 spig k* stann k*
- **drawing** pain: ...
  Stront-c k* *Sulph* k* symph fd3.de• ter ther *Thuj* til tritic-vg fd5.de vanil fd5.de verat **Zinc** k*
  - **alternating** with | **Shoulder** (See shoulders - drawing - alternating - hips)
  - **burning**: til
  - **cramping**: aur *Coloc* plat samb xxb1 verat
  - **downward**: aeth am-c bamb-a stb2.de• cann-s *Carb-an* *Carb-v* carbn-s cinnb crot-h kali-bi lil-t nat-m nit-ac h2 *Puls* *Rhus-t* sep ther thuj
  - **inward**: thuj
  - **paroxysmal**: arg-n k* cocc coloc zing
  - **sticking** pain: arg-n k* clem symph fd3.de•
  - **twitching**: colch sil h2
  - **wandering** pain: bry
- **driving** a car: brucel sa3•
- **dull** pain: ven-m rsj12•
- **eating** | **after** | **agg.**: *Indg*
  - **while** | **agg.**: ph-ac
- **exertion** agg.; after: **Calc** **Rhus-t**
- **exertion**; as after: cina b7.de*
- **falling** in pieces; as if: tril-p c1*
- **fever**; during: *Arn* b7.de* bell bg2 lyc bg2 nat-m bg2 puls bg2 *Rhus-t* bg2 *Sep* bg2
- **flexing** leg amel.: kali-bi
- **gnawing** pain: am-c k* *Am-m* k* benz-ac k* *Elat* k* **Eup-pur** k* *Kali-i* k* pall k*
- **gouty**: am-p bg2 bell coloc bg2 *Led* *Nit-ac* petr k* *Sil* b4.de*
- **increasing** and decreasing gradually: sep ↓
  - **pressing** pain: sep h2
- **inspiration** agg.: alum ↓ sabin ↓
  - **stitching** pain: alum sabin c1
- **jerking** of limbs: *Lyc*
- **jerking** pain: bry bg2 colch b7.de* graph b4.de* kali-bi k* kali-c bg2 *Lyc* mag-m **Mez** *Puls* sil *Sulph* k*
- **laughing** agg.: arg-met
- **limping** gait; causes: *Acon* b7.de *Apis* b7a.de* arn b7a.de ars b4a.de bell b4.de* *Calc* b4a.de caust b4a.de coloc b4.de* dros b7a.de hep b4a.de lyc b4.de* *Merc* b4a.de petr b4a.de *Phos* b4a.de puls b7a.de *Rhus-t* b7.de* *Sep* b4a.de sil b4a.de *Staph* b7.de sulph b4a.de thuj b4a.de zinc b4.de*
- **lying**:
  - **after** | **agg.**: acon
  - **agg.**: coloc ferr ↓ kali-i kali-s fd4.de mag-m ↓ murx nat-c ↓ plb staph ↓ symph fd3.de• tritic-vg ↓ *Valer* vanil fd5.de
    - **drawing** pain: tritic-vg fd5.de
    - **sore**: staph
    - **tearing** pain: ferr mag-m nat-c
  - **amel.**: androc srj1• plut-n srj7•
    - **aching**: plut-n srj7•
  - **leg** drawn up; with:
    - **amel.**: *Coloc* ↓
      - **drawing** pain: *Coloc*
  - **side**; on:
    - **agg.**: prun **Rhus-t**
    - **left**:
      - **agg.**: cassia-s ↓
        - **tearing** pain: cassia-s ccrh1•
    - **painful** side:
      - **agg.**: ars-met bapt *Caust* ↓ cop ↓ dros gk kali-bi nat-m ↓ rhod **RHUS-T** k ● sep ↓ staph ↓ vanil fd5.de verat-v
        - **sore**: *Caust* cop kali-bi nat-m sep staph gk
      - **amel.**: bell *Coloc* ferr-ma
        - **drawing** pain: ferr-ma
    - **painless** side:
      - **agg.**: bell cham
      - **amel.**: mag-m ↓
        - **tearing** pain: mag-m

- **lying – side**; on: ...
  - **right**:
    - **agg.**: sabad ↓
      - **pressing** pain: sabad k*
    - **amel.**: cassia-s ↓
      - **tearing** pain: cassia-s ccrh1•
- **menses** | **before**:
  - **agg.**: aesc k2 calc *Cimic Coloc* b4a.de *Kali-c* ↓ lach sars thuj ust
    - **aching**: lach
    - **burning**: *Kali-c*
    - **sore**: calc *Lach*
  - **during**:
    - **agg.**: *Calc* cop k* *Graph* k* *Mag-m* ↓ med ↓ *Nat-c* ↓ nit-ac ↓ sep tarent k*
      - **burning**: med
      - **drawing** pain: nit-ac h2
      - **sore**: *Mag-m Nat-c*
      - **tearing** pain: nat-c
- **motion**:
  - **agg.**: acon agar agn all-s k* ang ↓ ant-t bg1 *Arg-met* ↓ arge-pl rwt5• brucel sa3• *Calc* ↓ *Carbn-s* card-m k2 cassia-s ↓ cob ↓ *Coloc* croc ↓ euph fl-ac gels helon *Iod* ↓ kali-bi *Kali-c* ↓ *Kalm Lac-c Led* lyc ↓ mag-c mand rsj7• merc merc-c ↓ nat-ar ↓ *Nat-s Nux-v* petr ↓ ph-ac ↓ ruta fd4.de sanic sep ↓ sil ↓ stront-c sk4• *Sulph* zinc
    - **cutting** pain: lyc
    - **drawing** pain: *Acon* gels ruta fd4.de sep
    - **pressing** pain: *Led*
    - **sore**: *Arg-met* cob croc fl-ac *Kali-c* ph-ac h2 sulph h2
    - **sprained**; as if: ang h1 *Euph* lyc h2 petr sulph h2
    - **stitching** pain: agn calc *Coloc Merc* merc-c nat-ar *Sulph*
    - **tearing** pain: acon *Calc* cassia-s ccrh1• *Coloc Iod Merc* sil
  - **amel.**: agn ↓ alum ↓ am-m bg1 arg-met brucel sa3• caust ↓ *Euph* ↓ ferr *Gels* kali-c ↓ kali-n ↓ kali-s fd4.de lap-la sde8.de• laur ↓ lil-t *Lyc* k* melal-alt gya4 *Meny* ↓ *Merc-c* ↓ nat-ar nat-c ↓ *Puls Rhus-t* ruta ↓ sabad ↓ stel ↓ sulph ↓ ther ↓ *Valer* ven-m rsj12•
    - **burning**: kali-c h2
    - **drawing** pain: *Arg-met* lil-t **Rhus-t** ther
    - **pressing** pain: puls h1
    - **shooting** pain: sulph
    - **stitching** pain: caust laur *Meny Merc-c* nat-c ruta fd4.de sabad stel
    - **tearing** pain: agn alum *Euph Ferr* kali-n nat-c h2 **Rhus-t**
  - **bed** agg.; in: *Agar* nat-s ruta fd4.de valer
  - **beginning** of:
    - **agg.**: bamb-a stb2.de• *Caust* con *Ferr* ham fd3.de• *Lyc* k* nit-ac ↓ *Ph-ac Puls Rhus-t* sabin sal-al blc1• *Sep* ↓
      - **drawing** pain: nit-ac
      - **sore**: *Sep*
  - **body**; of:
    - **sideways** agg.: sulph ↓
      - **sitting**; while: euph ↓
        - **sore**: euph h2
      - **sore**: sulph
  - **impossible**: sil ↓
    - **drawing** pain: sil h2
- **neuralgic**: lyc bg2 rhus-t bg2
- **ovarian** complaints: *Nat-hchls*
- **paralyzed**; as if: acon k* agar bg2 am-m k* ang bg2 arg-met k* arg-n bg2 asar b7.de* *Aur* k* *Bell* k* caust bg2 cham chel k* cina b7.de* cocc k* dros k* dulc bg2 euon euph b4.de* led k* lyc m-aust b7.de nat-m b4.de* phos bg2 plb k* rhus-t bg2 sol-ni sulph b4.de* zinc bg2
- **paroxysmal**: *Bell* k* bov k* caust cocc k* coloc k* zing
- **periodical**: *Merc* ↓
  - **stitching** pain: *Merc*
- **perspiration**; during: acon bg2 *Arn* bg2 ars bg2 bell bg2 *Calc* bg2 *Caust* bg2 cham bg2 hep bg2 merc bg2 nux-v bg2 puls bg2 **Rhus-t** bg2 ruta bg2 *Sep* bg2 staph bg2 *Sulph* bg2
- **pinching** pain: aeth a1 caust b4.de* cocc b7.de* dros bg2 dulc h1 kali-c h2 laur b7.de* led h1 mag-c b4.de* mosch b7.de* zinc h2
- **pressing** pain: acon k* aesc k2 agar k* am-m bg2 ambr b7.de* arg-met asar k* aur-m-n k* berb bry bg2 calc bg2 cann-xyz bg2 carb-v b4.de* caust k* chin b7.de* *Cimic* cocc b7.de* colch b7.de* *Coloc* k* crot-c k* crot-t cypra-eg sde6.de• *Euph* k* ferr-ma hell k* hep iod b4.de* kali-bi kali-c bg2 *Led* k* lyc k* lyss c1 mez k* mosch k* nat-c k* nat-m bg2 nat-s k* nit-ac nit-s-d a1 nux-v b7.de* petr k* phos b4.de* *Puls* k* rhod b4.de* **Rhus-t** ruta b7.de* sabad k* sabin b7.de* sars b4.de* *Sep* k* *Stann* k* staph b7.de* symph fd3.de• teucr bg2 *Zinc* k*
  - **paralyzed**; as if: cocc
  - **paroxysmal**: cocc coloc k*
  - **tearing** pain: led h1
- **pressure**:
  - **agg.**: alum ↓ alumn ↓ cassia-s ↓ caust ↓ *Cina* ↓ ozone sde2• stront-c sk4•
    - **sore**: alum h2 alumn caust *Cina*
    - **tearing** pain: cassia-s ccrh1•
  - **amel.**: *Am-m* ↓ *Bry* ↓ *Merc-i-f* ↓ sulph ↓
    - **drawing** pain: *Bry*
    - **stitching** pain: *Am-m* sulph
    - **tearing** pain: *Merc-i-f*
- **pulsating** pain: am-c bg2 dulc fd4.de musca-d szs1 podo fd3.de• polyg-h ptel k* staph bg2
- **radiating**: *Coloc* bg2
- **rest**:
  - **agg.**: kali-n ↓
    - **burning**: kali-n
    - **only** during rest: nat-s ↓
      - **pinching** pain: nat-s
  - **amel.**: brucel sa3•
- **rheumatic**: abrot k* *Acon* all-s k* ant-t k* arn k* cact *Calc* ↓ *Carb-ac Carbn-s* chel k2 **Colch** cupr sst3• form k* graph ↓ hydr k* *Kali-bi* k* *Kalm Lac-c Led Lyc* mag-s maland mtf11 mand rsj7• *Med* meph k* merc-i-f merc-i-r k* nat-m *Nit-ac* ph-ac *Phos Phyt* plb podo k* *Puls Rhod* ↓ **Rhus-t** k* sabad sang k* sin-n k* stann stram sulph tarent k* *Valer* verat-v zinc
  - **right**: calad carb-ac erig nux-m *Sep*
    - **and** left shoulder: **Led**
  - **left**: *Acon* lyc sang *Sanic Stram*
    - **and** right shoulder: *Ferr*
  - **drawing** pain: lyc meph *Rhod Rhus-t*
  - **stitching** pain: chel *Lyc*
  - **tearing** pain: *Acon Calc* graph *Kalm Rhus-t*
  - **walking** agg.: mand rsj7•
- **rising**:
  - **agg.**: aesc kali-s fd4.de sarr tritic-vg fd5.de
  - **sitting**; from:
    - **agg.**: agar anac ↓ *Aur* card-m chel con kali-bi ↓ kali-n led lyc nat-c *Nat-s* nit-ac ↓ ph-ac *Rhus-t* sang ↓ sep ↓ tarent ↓
      - **drawing** pain: nit-ac
      - **pressing** pain: nit-ac h2
      - **sore**: anac kali-bi nat-c sang a1 sep h2 tarent
      - **sprained**; as if: anac h2
      - **stitching** pain: chel
- **rotating** the leg inwards, on: *Coloc*
- **rubbing**:
  - **amel.**: nat-s ↓ ol-an ↓ phos ↓
    - **pressing** pain: nat-s
    - **stitching** pain: phos
    - **tearing** pain: ol-an
- **scratching**:
  - **agg.**: led ↓
    - **stitching** pain | **itching**: led
- **screwing** pain: sulph h2

Extremities

- **shooting** pain: ail **Ars** bell bry *Calc* calc-p *Chel* cimic$_{bg2}$ cinnb coloc$_{tl1}$ *Ferr* form lach merc-c$_{bg2}$ mez$_{bg2}$ phyt$_{bg2}$ sabad sabin$_{c1}$ spong$_{fd4.de}$ *Sulph* thuj
- **sitting**:
  - **agg.**: am-m ↓ arn asar aur-m-n ↓ brass-n-o$_{srj5}$• calc ↓ **Carb-an** ↓ caust$_{k*}$ chin eup-per$_{k*}$ euph ↓ ham$_{fd3.de}$• ip ↓ kali-bi ↓ kali-c ↓ *Kali-i* ↓ lap-la$_{sde8.de}$• laur ↓ mang ↓ melal-alt$_{gya4}$ mur-ac ↓ nat-sil$_{fd3.de}$• par ↓ petr$_{k*}$ ph-ac *Rhus-t* ruta$_{fd4.de}$ sabad ↓ sacch-a$_{fd2.de}$• sang ↓ sel$_{rsj9}$• spong$_{fd4.de}$ staph sulph$_{k*}$ tarent$_{k2}$ ther tritic-vg$_{fd5.de}$ vanil$_{fd5.de}$ verat ↓
    - **aching**: eup-per melal-alt$_{gya4}$ *Rhus-t* sabad staph verat
    - **cutting** pain: calc mur-ac$_{h2}$
    - **dislocated**; as if: ip
    - **drawing** pain: caust chin **Rhus-t** ruta$_{fd4.de}$ ther
    - **extended** thigh, with: *Arn* ↓
      - **drawing** pain: *Arn*
    - **gnawing** pain: am-m
    - **griping**: mur-ac$_{a1}$
    - **only** while sitting: mur-ac ↓
      - **pinching** pain: mur-ac$_{h2}$
    - **pressing** pain: arn aur-m-n$_{k*}$ caust$_{h2}$ petr$_{k*}$ staph$_{h1}$
    - **sore**: kali-bi mang$_{h2}$ sang sulph
    - **stitching** pain: **Carb-an** euph kali-c *Kali-i* laur spong$_{fd4.de}$
    - **tearing** pain: am-m caust euph kali-c par ph-ac
  - **amel.**: aur cassia-s ↓ plut-n$_{srj7}$• tarent$_{k*}$
    - **aching**: plut-n$_{srj7}$•
    - **sore**: tarent
    - **tearing** pain: cassia-s$_{ccrh1}$•
- **sitting** down agg.: nat-s
- **sleep** agg.; after: acon *Lach*
- **sneezing** agg.: arg-met *Kali-c* ↓
  - **sore**: *Kali-c*
  - **sprained**; as if: arg-met
- **sore**: abrot *Acon*$_{k*}$ aesc agar$_{k*}$ aids$_{nl2}$• all-c alum$_{k*}$ am-c$_{k*}$ am-m anac$_{k*}$ apis *Arg-met* *Arn*$_{k*}$ ars$_{h2}$ bamb-a$_{stb2.de}$• bov bry$_{k*}$ carb-ac carb-an carc$_{fd2.de}$• *Caust*$_{k*}$ chin$_{b7.de*}$ *Cina* cob coff$_{b7.de*}$ coli$_{rly4}$• cop croc crot-h des-ac$_{rbp6}$ dulc$_{h2*}$ *Ferr*$_{k*}$ fl-ac$_{k*}$ form gins hura kali-bi *Kali-c* kali-n$_{bg2}$ kali-sil$_{k2}$ kola$_{stb3}$• kreos *Laur* lil-t mag-c$_{bg2}$ mag-m$_{k*}$ manc mang$_{k*}$ meny$_{bg2}$ *Nat-c*$_{k*}$ nat-m$_{k*}$ **Ph-ac**$_{k*}$ phyt puls **Ruta**$_{k*}$ sars seneg$_{b4.de*}$ **Sep** *Sil* *Staph* *Sulph*$_{k*}$ tarent tell thuj$_{k*}$ visc$_{ptk1}$ zinc$_{k*}$ zing
  - **downward**: aesc
- **spasmodic**: lyss$_{jl2}$
- **sprained**; as if: *Aesc*$_{bro1}$ am-m$_{k*}$ *Arg-met* *Arn* ars$_{h2}$ bamb-a$_{stb2.de}$• bar-c *Calc* *Calc-p*$_{bro1}$ *Caust*$_{k*}$ cham chin *Coloc*$_{bro1}$ con *Euph* hep *Ign* ip kali-n laur$_{k*}$ lyc merc-i-r mez *Nat-m*$_{k*}$ nit-ac nux-v petr *Phos* psor *Puls*$_{k*}$ *Rhod* **Rhus-t**$_{k*}$ rhus-v sarr$_{bro1}$ seneg sol-t-ae stann *Sulph* tell
  - **paroxysmal**: caust
- **squeezed**; as if: *Ang*$_{b7a.de}$ bar-c$_{bg2}$ caust$_{bg2}$ coloc$_{bg2}$ ruta$_{b7a.de}$
- **standing**:
  - **agg.**: androc$_{srj1}$• arge-pl$_{rwt5}$• *Coloc* ↓ kali-c ↓ *Kali-i* ↓ kali-n ↓ kali-s ↓ laur ↓ *Led* plut-n$_{srj7}$• *Rhus-t* ↓ tarent ↓ *Valer* verat ↓
    - **aching**: plut-n$_{srj7}$•
    - **drawing** pain: valer$_{k2}$ verat
    - **sore**: tarent
    - **stitching** pain: kali-c *Kali-i* kali-n kali-s$_{fd4.de}$ laur
    - **tearing** pain: *Coloc* *Rhus-t*
  - **amel.**: chin ↓ nat-sil$_{fd3.de}$• staph
    - **drawing** pain: chin$_{h1}$
- **stepping** agg.: arg-met ↓ arg-n asar *Caust* dulc ↓ kali-c psor ↓ **Rhus-t** sabin sulph ↓
  - **dislocated**; as if: *Caust* dulc$_{a1}$ psor sulph
  - **pressing** pain: arg-met$_{h1}$ **Rhus-t**
  - **sprained**; as if: arg-met$_{k*}$ arg-n
- **stitching** pain: acon aeth *Agar*$_{k*}$ agn ail **Alum**$_{k*}$ alum-p$_{k2}$ alum-sil$_{k2}$ am-c$_{bg2}$ am-m$_{k*}$ ammc anan ang$_{b7.de*}$ ant-t$_{k*}$ *Apis* apoc arg-met arg-n$_{bg2}$ arge-pl$_{rwt5}$• **Ars**$_{k*}$ asaf$_{b7.de*}$ aster bacls-7$_{fmm1}$• bar-c *Bell*$_{k*}$ *Berb* *Bry*$_{k*}$ *Calc*$_{k*}$ calc-p calc-sil$_{k2}$ cann-xyz$_{bg2}$ canth$_{k*}$ caps **Carb-an**$_{k*}$ *Carbn-s* cardios-h$_{rly4}$• castm *Caust*$_{k*}$ cham *Chel*$_{k*}$ chin *Chinin-ar* cic$_{k*}$ *Cina* cinnb clem$_{k*}$ coca cocc colch$_{k*}$ *Coloc*$_{k*}$ con$_{k*}$ crot-h cupr dros$_{b7.de*}$ dulc$_{k*}$ euon euph$_{k*}$ euphr *Ferr*$_{k*}$ ferr-ar ferr-p *Fl-ac* form ger-i$_{rly4}$• gran graph grat ham *Hell*$_{k*}$ hep$_{bg2}$ hyos$_{k*}$ ign$_{k*}$ *Kali-bi*$_{k*}$ *Kali-c*$_{k*}$ *Kali-i* kali-n kali-s$_{fd4.de}$ *Kalm* kola$_{stb3}$• kreos$_{k*}$ lac-c *Lach*$_{bg2}$ laur$_{k*}$ led$_{k*}$ lil-t$_{k*}$ *Lyc*$_{k*}$ m-arct$_{b7.de}$ *Mag-c*$_{k*}$ mag-m manc mang$_{k*}$ meny$_{k*}$ *Merc*$_{k*}$ *Merc-c*$_{k*}$ mez nat-ar nat-c$_{k*}$ *Nat-m*$_{k*}$ nat-p *Nat-s*$_{k*}$ nat-sil$_{fd3.de}$• *Nit-ac*$_{k*}$ nux-v olnd$_{b7.de*}$ ox-ac par ph-ac$_{k*}$ phos$_{k*}$ phyt **Plb**$_{k*}$ ptel puls$_{b7.de*}$ raph *Rhus-t*$_{k*}$ ruta$_{fd4.de}$ sabad sabin$_{k*}$ *Sep*$_{k*}$ *Sil*$_{k*}$ sol-ni spong$_{bg2*}$ sulph$_{k*}$ symph$_{fd3.de}$• tab tell teucr$_{k*}$ thuj$_{k*}$ valer$_{bg2}$ verat-v *Zinc*$_{k*}$ zinc-p$_{k2}$ [tax$_{jsj7}$]
  - **acute**: caust
  - **backward**: laur
  - **burning**: cic$_{h1}$ mag-c
  - **cramping**: cina
  - **downward**: aeth aster *Bry* calc-p cinnb colch ferr *Kalm* **Plb** *Sil* *Sulph*
  - **itching**: led mag-c
  - **outward**: merc-c
  - **paroxysmal**: alum castm nat-c par
  - **pulsating** pain: arg-met
  - **tearing** pain: colch ph-ac
  - **twitching**: cina
- **stool** agg.; during: cinnb ↓ kreos$_{b7a.de}$ nux-v$_{bg1}$ pall tell$_{bg1}$
  - **pressing** pain: pall
  - **stitching** pain: cinnb
- **stooping** agg.: agar calc ↓ card-m coloc gent-l lyc *Nat-s* sil *Thuj* ↓
  - **aching**: gent-l
  - **sore**: *Sil*
  - **stitching** pain: calc *Thuj*
- **stretching** out limb, on: brucel$_{sa3}$• ruta
  - **amel.**: sel$_{rsj9}$•
- **sudden**: bar-c ↓ lyc olib-sac ↓
  - **sprained**; as if: lyc
  - **stitching** pain: bar-c olib-sac$_{wmh1}$
- **tearing** pain: *Acon* aesc agar$_{k*}$ all-s alum$_{k*}$ alum-p$_{k2}$ alum-sil$_{k2}$ am-m$_{k*}$ ambr$_{k*}$ ant-t$_{b7.de*}$ *Arn*$_{k*}$ *Ars*$_{k*}$ aur-m bar-c$_{b4.de*}$ bell$_{k2}$ *Berb* bry *Calc*$_{k*}$ calc-p cann-s$_{k*}$ *Canth* *Caps* *Carb-v*$_{k*}$ cassia-s$_{ccrh1}$• *Caust* cham$_{bg1}$ chin$_{b7.de*}$ cina$_{k*}$ clem colch$_{k*}$ *Coloc* cycl$_{b7.de*}$ dios dulc$_{k*}$ elat$_{hr1}$ *Euph*$_{k*}$ *Ferr* ferr-i ferr-p gamb graph$_{k*}$ hep$_{k*}$ *Iod*$_{k*}$ iris *Kali-ar* kali-bi **Kali-c**$_{k*}$ *Kali-n*$_{k*}$ *Kali-p* kali-sil$_{k2}$ *Kalm*$_{k*}$ lach led *Lyc*$_{k*}$ mag-c **Mag-m**$_{k*}$ mag-s merc merc-c$_{k*}$ merc-i-f *Mez*$_{k*}$ *Nat-c*$_{k*}$ nat-p nicc **Nux-v**$_{b7.de*}$ ol-an par$_{k*}$ ph-ac phos$_{b4a.de}$ plb$_{bg2}$ *Puls*$_{bg2}$ *Rat* rhod *Rhus-t*$_{k*}$ sabad$_{b7.de*}$ sabin$_{k*}$ samb$_{b7.de*}$ *Sep*$_{k*}$ *Sil* stann$_{k*}$ stram stront-c$_{bg2}$ sulph$_{bg2}$ *Syph* tab tax ter teucr$_{b7.de*}$ thuj tritic-vg$_{fd5.de}$ *Zinc*$_{k*}$ zinc-p$_{k2}$
  - **alternating** with | **Upper** arm; tearing in right: bry$_{k*}$
  - **downward**: *Alum* am-m bell$_{k2}$ caust *Coloc* *Kalm* led lyc mag-m mag-s *Rat* tep
  - **drawing** pain: acon ars aur-m dulc kali-bi kreos ter zinc$_{h2}$
  - **paroxysmal**: *Alum* carb-v *Coloc*
  - **pressing** pain: ambr$_{h1}$ zinc
  - **pulsating** pain: *Merc*
- **thinking** about the pains: *Ox-ac*
- **touch** agg.: *Bell*$_{k*}$ bry ↓ *Caps* ↓ des-ac ↓ ruta *Sulph*$_{k*}$
  - **drawing** pain: *Caps*
  - **sore**: des-ac$_{rbp6}$ ruta$_{h1}$ sulph$_{h2}$
  - **stitching** pain: bry
- **turning** in bed agg.: am-c *Nat-s*$_{k*}$
- **ulcerative** pain: coloc$_{bg1}$ kali-n$_{bg2}$ ph-ac$_{bg1}$ sulph$_{bg1}$
- **urination**:
  - **before**: *Dulc* ↓ kreos$_{bg2}$
    - **burning**: *Dulc*$_{b4.de*}$
  - **during** | **agg.**: berb$_{k*}$

- **vexation** agg.: *Coloc*
- **waking**; on: hep↓
  - **aching**: hep
- **walking**:
  - **after**:
    - **agg.**: malar$_{jl2}$ tell$_{k*}$
      - **sprained**; as if: tell
    - **amel.**: am-c
  - **agg.**: acon↓ aesc$_{k2}$ agar alum↓ *Am-m* ammc androc$_{srj1•}$ ant-c arg-met arg-n ars-h asaf↓ asar asc-t$_{a1}$ *Aur* berb↓ bry↓ calc carb-an carb-v caust↓ cocc↓ *Coloc* con cop↓ dros dulc↓ euph euphr↓ fic-m$_{gya1}$ gran↓ ham *Hep* *Hydr* iris kali-bi$_{k2}$ kali-s$_{fd4.de}$ lac-c lac-leo↓ *Led* lyc mag-m↓ mang↓ *Med* merc↓ mez nat-c↓ nat-s pall *Ph-ac* plut-n$_{srj7•}$ podo$_{fd3.de•}$ psor ran-b↓ rhod *Rhus-t*↓ rumx ruta$_{fd4.de}$ samb↓ sang↓ sep *Sil*↓ sol-mm↓ stann staph *Sulph* tarent↓ tell↓ tritic-vg$_{fd5.de}$
    - **aching**: fic-m$_{gya1}$ ham plut-n$_{srj7•}$ staph
    - **dislocated**; as if: bry$_{rb2}$
    - **drawing** pain: *Am-m* *Ant-c* asaf asar bry calc *Carb-v* caust$_{h2}$ coloc *Hep* ran-b *Sulph*
    - **pinching** pain: lac-leo$_{hrn2•}$
    - **pressing** pain: acon aesc$_{k2}$ asar$_{h1}$ caust$_{h2}$ coloc staph$_{a1}$
    - **sore**: alum bry caust cop hep$_{c1}$ kali-bi mag-m sang$_{a1}$ tarent tell
    - **sprained**; as if: arg-met calc con lyc mez rhod stann
    - **stitching** pain: arg-met berb calc cocc *Coloc* dulc$_{a1}$ euphr gran ham mang$_{a1}$ merc nat-c *Nat-s* sol-mm
    - **tearing** pain: *Aesc* caust *Coloc* mag-m *Rhus-t* samb *Sil* sulph$_{h2}$
  - **air**; in open:
    - **agg.**: bar-c cham↓ hep↓ mez↓
      - **sprained**; as if: cham hep mez
    - **amel.**: *Acon* lyc
  - **amel.**: agar↓ am-c androc$_{srj1•}$ bell↓ chin↓ cinnb↓ *Ferr* kali-bi *Kali-i*↓ **Kali-s** **Lyc** nat-c↓ nat-sil$_{fd3.de•}$ plb↓ podo$_{fd3.de•}$ **Puls** *Rhus-t* sep↓ stront-c↓ ther↓ *Valer*
    - **drawing** pain: chin cinnb *Rhus-t* ther
    - **shooting** pain: *Ferr*
    - **sore**: agar nat-c$_{h2}$ sep
    - **stitching** pain: *Ferr* *Kali-i* plb
    - **tearing** pain: bell$_{k2}$ *Ferr* stront-c
  - **beginning** to walk: nit-ac↓ ph-ac↓
    - **pressing** pain: nit-ac$_{h2}$
    - **sore**: ph-ac
    - **stitching** pain: ph-ac
  - **bent**:
    - **agg.**: *Bry*↓
      - **stitching** pain: *Bry*
  - **slowly**:
    - **amel.**: *Sep*↓
      - **stitching** pain: *Sep*
- **wandering** pain: *Colch* *Iris* med
- **warm** | **applications** | **amel.**: androc$_{srj1•}$ *Rhus-t*$_{k*}$ staph
  - **bed**:
    - **agg.**: **Merc**↓
      - **tearing** pain: **Merc**
- **warmth**:
  - **agg.**: still↓
    - **stitching** pain: still
  - **amel.**: *Coloc*↓
    - **stitching** pain: *Coloc*
- **weather**:
  - **change** of weather: chel$_{k2}$
  - **wet** | **agg.**: lap-la$_{sde8.de•}$ *Phyt* *Rhus-t* *Sil*
- **yawning** agg.: arg-met
- ▽ **extending** to:
  - **right** side: stann↓
    - **drawing** pain: stann$_{h2}$

- **extending** to: ...
  - **Abdomen**: chel↓ coca↓ gins↓
    - **cutting** pain: gins
    - **shooting** pain: chel
    - **stitching** pain: chel coca
  - **Ankles**: aesc↓ calc↓ led↓ manc↓ merc-i-r↓ plan↓
    - **aching**: aesc merc-i-r plan
    - **pressing** pain: led$_{h1}$
    - **sore**: manc
    - **tearing** pain: calc$_{h2}$
  - **Back**: fago lyc$_{bg1}$ rhus-t symph$_{fd3.de•}$ tritic-vg$_{fd5.de}$
  - **Calf**: thuj↓
    - **shooting** pain: thuj
  - **Chest**: phos↓
    - **stitching** pain: phos
  - **Downward**: am-c bar-c dulc$_{fd4.de}$ *Indg* kali-i$_{k2}$ **Kalm** *Med* merc-i-r plan rhus-t sang$_{hr1}$ scol$_{ah1}$ spong$_{fd4.de}$ vanil$_{fd5.de}$
  - **Femur**; down: *Sulph*↓
    - **shooting** pain: *Sulph*
  - **Foot**: ara-maca$_{sej7•}$ berb bry↓ cact *Caps*↓ fago$_{k*}$ kalm$_{k2}$ lach lyc mag-p mag-s↓ sep↓ sulph↓ thuj↓
    - **cough** agg.; during: caps↓
      - **tearing** pain: caps$_{a1*}$
    - **drawing** pain: thuj
    - **shooting** pain: *Caps* lach sulph
    - **stitching** pain: bry *Caps* sulph
    - **tearing** pain: caps$_{k*}$ *Kalm*$_{k*}$ lyc$_{k*}$ mag-s sep$_{k*}$
  - **Genitals**: eupi↓
    - **stitching** pain: eupi
  - **Groin**: aids$_{nl2•}$ dulc↓ ox-ac↓ phys symph$_{fd3.de•}$
    - **dragging** | **pressed** out; as if everything would be: ox-ac
    - **stitching** pain: dulc$_{a1}$
  - **Heel**: ars-met arund↓ *Kali-i*
    - **burning**: arund
    - **stitching** pain: *Kali-i*
  - **Hip**; from hip to: cimic$_{a1}$ thuj ust
  - **Hypogastrium**: zinc↓
    - **tearing** pain: zinc$_{h2}$
  - **Ilium** to ilium: lil-t↓
    - **stitching** pain: lil-t
  - **Knee**: abrot↓ arg-n bar-c brucel$_{sa3•}$ *Bry*↓ canth↓ caps carb-ac colch↓ coloc *Hydr* *Kali-bi* *Kali-c* *Kali-i*↓ *Kalm* lach *Lyc*↓ *Mag-m*↓ *Med* mez↓ nat-ar↓ *Nat-s* nux-m *Nux-v*↓ *Ph-ac* **Plb**↓ puls *Rat*↓ rhus-t rhus-v *Sep* sil↓ vanil$_{fd5.de}$ xan
    - **cough** agg.; during: *Caps*↓
      - **tearing** pain: *Caps*
    - **cutting** pain: nat-s$_{k2}$
    - **drawing** pain: arg-n$_{a1}$ rhus-t$_{h1}$
    - **shooting** pain: *Caps* *Nux-v*
    - **sore**: abrot
    - **stitching** pain: *Bry* caps colch *Coloc* *Kali-c* *Kali-i* mez nat-ar **Plb**
    - **tearing** pain: canth *Caps* colch *Coloc* *Kali-c* *Lyc* *Mag-m* nat-s$_{k2}$ *Rat* *Rhus-t* sil
    - **Hollow** of knee: bamb-a$_{stb2.de•}$
  - **Leg**: colch↓
    - **shooting** pain | **tearing**: colch$_{k*}$
  - **Leg**, in front of: dios *Phyt*
  - **Liver** region: grat
  - **Lumbar** region: alum↓ lyc↓ tritic-vg↓
    - **sprained**; as if: lyc
    - **stitching** pain: alum
    - **tearing** pain: alum tritic-vg$_{fd5.de}$
  - **Sacrum**: ant-c *Carb-v*↓ lyss stann↓ tritic-vg$_{fd5.de}$
    - **drawing** pain: ant-c stann$_{h2}$ tritic-vg$_{fd5.de}$
    - **pressing** pain: carb-v$_{h2}$
    - **tearing** pain: *Carb-v* tritic-vg$_{fd5.de}$
  - **Sciatic** nerve; down to: calc↓ carb-an↓ *Coloc*↓ lyc↓

- **extending** to – **Sciatic** nerve; down to: ...
  - **aching**: carb-an
  - **tearing** pain: calc *Coloc* lyc
  - **Shoulder**: mag-c ↓
    - **burning**: mag-c h2
    - **sore**: mag-c h2
  - **Stomach**: bry ↓
    - **tearing** pain: bry
  - **Testes**: staph
  - **Thigh**: am-m carb-ac c1 kali-s fd4.de kreos lil-t ruta fd4.de tritic-vg fd5.de vanil fd5.de
  - **Tibia**: ferr ↓
    - **stitching** pain: ferr
  - **Toes**: *Kalm* nat-ar nicc ↓
    - **tearing** pain: nicc
  - **Umbilicus**: hedy ↓
    - **tearing** pain: hedy a1*
- ○ **Above**: con ↓ sep ↓
  - **pressing** pain: con h2 sep h2
  - **tearing** pain: sep h2
- **Bones** | **Deep** in: plut-n srj7•
- **Externally**: aur-m-n ↓ carb-v ↓
  - **burning**: aur-m-n k* carb-v k*
- **Gluteal** muscles: agar ↓ arg-met ↓ asaf ↓ aur ↓ camph ↓ cham ↓ chinin-s ↓ coc-c ↓ con ↓ cot ↓ cycl ↓ euph ↓ euphr ↓ gels ↓ ham ↓ meny ↓ merc ↓ mosch ↓ *Puls* ↓ seneg ↓ staph ↓ *Sulph* ↓ tab ↓ tep ↓ verat ↓ viol-t ↓ zinc ↓
  - **right**: euphr ↓ psil ↓
    - **burning**: euphr k*
    - **stitching** pain: psil ft1
  - **boring** pain: merc k* staph k*
  - **burning**: agar k* euphr k*
  - **drawing** pain: camph k* cycl k* gels k* mosch k* *Sulph* k* verat k*
  - **sore**: arg-met euph ham *Puls* seneg zinc
  - **stitching** pain: asaf k* aur k* cham k* chinin-s con k* cot a1 gels a1 meny k* staph k* tab k* viol-t k*
  - **tearing** pain: agar k* coc-c k* tep a1
- **Gluteal** region: cact ↓ cimic ↓ eup-per k* euph a1 euphr k* hura iod ↓ kalm k* laur k* lepi k* med mez ↓ nit-ac k* puls k* rhus-t k* sol-t-ae k* spig k* tab k*
  - **right**: hydrog srj2•
    - **pressure** agg.: hydrog srj2•
  - **pressing** pain: cact k* cimic k* iod h mez k*
  - **sitting**; after: laur k* puls k*
  - **walking** agg.: spig k* tab k*
- **Joints**: acon ↓ agn ↓ all-c ↓ aloe ↓ alum ↓ am-c b4.de* *Am-m* ↓ anac b4a.de ang ↓ ant-c b7.de* ant-t ↓ arg-met b7a.de arn ↓ *Ars* ↓ asaf ↓ asar b7.de* aur ↓ *Bar-c* ↓ *Bell* ↓ *Bry* ↓ calc ↓ *Canth* ↓ caps ↓ *Carb-an* b4a.de carb-v ↓ caust b4a.de cham b7.de* chel ↓ chin ↓ cimic ↓ cocc b7.de* colch ↓ *Coloc* ↓ con ↓ croc ↓ dros b7a.de* dulc ↓ *Euph* ↓ *Euphr* ↓ *Ferr* ↓ graph ↓ hell ↓ hep b4a.de *Ign* ↓ ip ↓ iris ↓ kali-bi ↓ kali-c ↓ kali-n ↓ kreos ↓ led b7.de* lyc ↓ m-arct ↓ m-aust ↓ mag-c ↓ mag-m ↓ meny ↓ merc ↓ *Merc-c* ↓ mez ↓ mosch ↓ *Nat-m* ↓ nit-ac ↓ nux-v b7a.de par b7.de* petr ↓ ph-ac ↓ phos b4.de* plb ↓ puls b7.de* *Rheum* b7a.de *Rhod* ↓ **Rhus-t** b7.de* ruta ↓ sabad ↓ *Sabin* ↓ samb ↓ seneg b4.de* *Sep* ↓ sil ↓ stann ↓ staph ↓ stront-c ↓ sulph ↓ verat ↓
  - **daytime**: sulph ↓
    - **shooting** pain: sulph
  - **morning**: *Sulph* ↓
    - **shooting** pain: *Sulph*
  - **evening**:
    - **bed** agg.; in: *Ferr* ↓
      - **shooting** pain: *Ferr*
  - **night**: sulph ↓
    - **shooting** pain: sulph

– **Hips** – **Joints**: ...
  - **burning**: bell b4.de chel b7.de hell b7.de* iris kali-n nux-v k* rhus-t b7.de*
    - **tearing** pain: kali-n
  - **cutting** pain: calc b4.de* *Ign* b7a.de kali-bi bg2 lyc bg2
  - **dislocated**; as if: agn b7.de* *Am-m* b7a.de ang b7.de* arn b7.de* *Bar-c* b4a.de *Bry* b7.de* calc b4.de* caust b4.de* cham b7.de* chin b7.de* dulc b4a.de *Euph* b4a.de ip b7a.de kreos b7a.de led b7a.de mosch b7a.de *Nat-m* b4a.de nit-ac b4a.de nux-v b7.de* *Phos* b4a.de puls b7.de* *Rhod* b4a.de *Rhus-t* b7.de* sulph b4.de*
  - **drawing** pain: ang b7.de* *Ant-c* b7.de* arn b7.de* asaf b7.de* calc b4.de* caps b7.de* carb-v b4a.de chin b7.de* con b4a.de dulc b4.de* hell b7.de* hep b4a.de led b7.de* mosch b7a.de nat-m b4a.de petr b4.de* plb b7.de* *Rhus-t* b7.de* sil b4.de* stann b4a.de stront-c b4.de*
  - **jerking** pain: *Bell* b4.de* bry b7.de* *Coloc* b4a.de graph b4.de* sulph b4.de*
  - **nail**; as from a: aloe bg2
  - **paralyzed**; as if: acon b7a.de arg-met b7.de* asar b7.de* aur b4a.de chel b7a.de dros b7.de* hell b7.de* lyc b4.de* m-aust b7.de plb b7.de* seneg b4a.de *Sep* b4a.de stann b4.de* verat b7.de*
  - **pressing** pain: acon bg2 agn b7.de* ang b7.de* arg-met b7.de* arn b7.de* asar bg2 caust b4.de* coloc bg2 hell b7.de* led b7.de* merc-c b4a.de mez bg2 nit-ac b4.de* petr bg2 puls b7.de* rhus-t b7.de* sabad b7a.de sep b4.de* staph b7.de*
  - **shooting** pain: colch *Ferr* sulph
  - **sore**: acon b7.de* all-c bg2 *Am-c* b4a.de croc b7.de* dulc b4a.de ferr b7.de* m-arct b7.de m-aust b7.de par b7.de* ph-ac b4.de* ruta b7a.de sep b4.de* sulph b4a.de
  - **squeezed**; as if | **clamps**; as if from: *Coloc* b4a.de
  - **stitching** pain: agn b7.de* alum b4a.de* *Am-m* b7a.de ant-t b7.de* arg-met b7.de* *Ars* b4a.de asaf b7.de* bar-c b4.de* *Bell* b4.de* calc b4.de* caust b4.de* *Cham* b7a.de cocc b7.de* coloc b4a.de dulc b4a.de *Euphr* b7a.de *Ferr* b7.de* hell b7.de* ign b7.de* kali-c b4.de* lyc b4.de* mag-c b4.de* mag-m b4.de* meny b7.de* merc b4.de* *Merc-c* b4a.de nat-m bg2 nux-v b7.de* par b7.de* *Phos* b4a.de rhod b4a.de *Rhus-t* b7.de* *Sabin* b7a.de
  - **tearing** pain: agn b7.de* alum b4a.de* *Am-m* b7a.de ars b4a.de asaf b7.de* bar-c b4.de* calc b4.de* *Canth* b7a.de caust b4.de* cimic bg2 colch b7.de* euph b4.de* *Ferr* b7.de* hep b4a.de kali-c b4.de* kali-n b4.de* *Led* b7a.de lyc b4.de* mag-c b4.de* mag-m b4.de* merc b4.de* *Merc-c* b4a.de par b7.de* *Rhus-t* b7a.de samb b7.de* stront-c b4.de*
  - **torn** off; as if: hep b4a.de
- **Muscles**: lat-m bnm6•
- **Nerve**; external sciatic:
  - **left**: malar ↓
    - **dull** pain: malar jl2
- **Spots**; in: rhus-t ↓ til ↓
  - **burning**: rhus-t k*
  - **drawing** pain: til
- **Trochanter**: cic a1* verat-v k13
  - **extending** to:
    - **Knee**; hollow of: pall ↓
      - **shooting** pain: pall hr1*
  - **walking** agg.: cina h1
- **Tubera** ischiadica: hep ↓ symph ↓
  - **sprained**; as if: hep h2* symph fd3.de•

– **Ischium**:
- **right**: lachn ↓
  - **tearing** pain: lachn c1

– **Joints**: *(↗GENERALS - Inflammation - joints; GENERALS - Pain - joints)* abies-c oss4• abrot k2* acon k* *Acon-c* a1 *Act-sp* ↓ aesc k* agar agar-ph a1 *Agn* ↓ all-c k* aloe ↓ *Alum* k* alum-p k2 alum-sil k2 alumn hr1 am-c bro1 am-m bro1 am-p mtf11 *Ambr* ↓ anac ↓ anag ↓ androc ↓ ang ↓ anh sp1 ant-s-aur ↓ *Ant-t* ↓ anthraq ↓ *Apis* *Apoc* k* *Apoc-a* a1 aran k* arb ↓ **Arg-met** k* arg-n mtf11 arist-cl sp1 **Arn** k* *Ars* k* *Ars-i* ars-s-f k2 arthr-u mtf11 *Arum-t* ↓ asaf k* asar ↓ asc-t k* aster k* atp ↓ aur k* aur-ar k2 aur-i k2 *Aur-m-n* wbt2• aur-s k2 bar-act ↓ bar-c k* bar-i k2 bar-m bg2 bar-s ↓ *Bell* k* bell-p sp1 benz-ac k2 berb bg2 *Bol-la* borra-o oss1• *Bov* ↓ **Bry** k* bufo ↓ cact ↓ cadm-met gm1 cadm-s ↓ caj k* calad ↓ *Calc* k* *Calc-f* mrr1 calc-i k2 **Calc-p** k* calc-s k* calc-sil ↓ *Camph* ↓ cann-i k* *Caps* k* carb-ac k* carb-an k* *Carb-v* ↓

- **Joints**: ...
Carbn-s *Carl*↓ cartl-s rly4• casc hr1 cassia-s zzc1• *Caul*↓ *Caust* k* cedr k* *Cham* k* chel mrr1 chel-g↓ *Chin* k* chinin-ar *Chinin-s*↓ chlor↓ choc↓ cimic mrr1 *Cimx* *Cinnb* k* cist k* *Cit-v* hr1 clem↓ cob↓ coc-c↓ *Coca*↓ *Cocc* *Coch* hr1 coff↓ *Colch* k* coli jl2 *Coloc* com br1 con k* conch↓ convo-s sp1 cop k* *Cor-r*↓ cot br1 croc k* *Crot-h*↓ crot-t k* cupr sst3• cycl k* daph k* dig k* dios k* dros bro1* *Dulc* k* erig↓ euon bro1 **Euph**↓ eys sp1 *Ferr* k* *Ferr-ar* ferr-i *Ferr-p* form↓ galeoc-c-h↓ gast↓ gels k* gink-b↓ *Gins*↓ *Graph*↓ grat↓ *Guaj* k* guare↓ hell k* *Hep*↓ hera↓ hippoz hr1 hist sp1 hydr k* hydrc k* *Hyos*↓ *Hyper*↓ ign ind↓ indg↓ *Iod* k* ip k* iris jac-c k* jatr-c *Kali-bi* k* *Kali-c* k* *Kali-i*↓ kali-n kali-p kali-s k2 kali-sil k2 *Kalm* k* kreos bro1 *Lac-ac* k* *Lac-c* k* *Lach*↓ lappa bro1 lat-h bnm5• lat-m bnm6• lath↓ lavand-a ctl1• **Led** k* *Lith-c*↓ loxo-recl bnm10• luna kg1• *Lyc* k* lyss k* mag-c↓ mag-f jl3 *Mag-m*↓ magn-gr↓ maias-l hm2• mal-ac↓ mand sp1* *Mang* k* mang-act bro1 marb-w es1• med tl1 *Meny*↓ *Merc* k* *Merc-c*↓ mez k* mill↓ morph k* mosch↓ *Mur-ac*↓ musca-d szs1 *Nat-ar* k* *Nat-c*↓ nat-f jl3 nat-m k* nat-n↓ nat-p↓ *Nat-s* k* nit-ac nit-s-d↓ *Nux-m*↓ **Nux-v** k* ol-an olib-sac wmh1 olnd↓ pant-ac↓ par penic mtf11 petr k2 *Ph-ac* k* *Phos* k* phys↓ physala-p bnm7• *Phyt* k* pic-ac↓ *Plan*↓ *Plat*↓ **Plb** k* plect↓ plut-n srj7• positr nl2• *Prun*↓ psil ft1 ptel↓ **Puls** k* pyrus↓ rad-br mrr1 *Ran-b* mrr1 ran-s k* raph k* *Rheum* *Rhod* k* **Rhus-t** k* ribo rly4• rumx k2 *Ruta* k* sabad k* *Sabin* k* sal-ac tl2 sal-fr↓ *Salol*↓ *Sang* *Sars*↓ sec↓ sel k* senec k* *Seneg*↓ *Sep*↓ *Sil* k* sol-ni sol-t-ae k* **Spect**↓ **Spig**↓ spong fd4.de squil↓ *Stann*↓ *Staph* k* stict↓ *Stram*↓ **Stront-c**↓ stroph-s jl3 sul-ac k* *Sulph* k* symph fd3.de• syph k2* **Tarax**↓ tarent k2 tax-br oss1• tep↓ ter k* teucr↓ thal-xyz↓ thala jl3 thuj k* tritic-vg fd5.de trom↓ tub k2 tub-r vn* v-a-b jl **Valer**↓ vanil fd5.de *Verat*↓ verat-v k* vesp↓ viol-o↓ zinc bro1 zinc-p↓
  - **alternating** sides: *Lac-c* mang
  - **right**: *Chel* mrr1
  - **left**: cain↓ olib-sac wmh1
    - **dislocated**; as if: cain
  - **morning**: *Aur* caps↓ caust cham↓ cob↓ coch hr1 dios k* dulc fd4.de nit-ac↓ **Nux-v** k* **Ph-ac**↓ pyrus↓ rhod mrr1 **RHUS-T** sne staph tritic-vg fd5.de verat↓ viol-o
    - **bed** agg.; in: anac↓ androc↓ **Aur** carb-v↓ *Chin* coff↓ **Nux-v** **Puls** k* *Rhus-t*↓
      - **sore**: anac androc srj1• aur carb-v chin coff **Nux-v** *Rhus-t*
    - **drawing** pain: cham k*
    - **rising** | **after**:
      - **agg.**: phos↓
        - **drawing** pain: phos
      - **agg.**: caps↓
        - **broken**; as if: caps h1
    - **sore**: aur caps h1 cob nit-ac **Ph-ac** pyrus verat
    - **waking**; on: abrot↓ **Rhus-t** mrr1 sol-ni verat verat-v a1
      - **sore**: abrot
  - **forenoon**: ars k* aur↓ caust sabad k*
    - **sitting** agg.: ars k*
    - **sore**: aur
  - **afternoon**: dig k* ruta fd4.de
    - **sleep** agg.; after: dig k*
  - **evening**: acon↓ all-c vh1 cham↓ hydr k* kali-s mrr1 *Kalm* k* lac-ac *Led* *Merc*↓ nat-c nat-s↓ par↓ *Puls*↓ sacch-a fd2.de• stront-c teucr k* tritic-vg fd5.de
    - **19** h: cham↓
      - **sore**: cham
    - **drawing** pain: nat-c k* nat-s k* *Puls*
    - **eruptions**, during the: *Merc*↓
      - **tearing** pain: *Merc*
    - **sore**: cham
    - **stitching** pain: acon k* par k*
    - **tearing** pain: *Merc* nat-c h2 stront-c
  - **night**: act-sp vh1 *Carb-an* k* cedr **Cham** mrr1 *Con*↓ dios k* dulc fd4.de gels hell k* **Iod** k* *Kali-bi* *Kali-i*↓ kalm mrr1 lac-ac *Led* *Mang* k* **Merc** k* nat-c plb k* rad-br mrr1 *Rhod* **Rhus-t** mrr1 ruta fd4.de sil spig↓ stront-c *Sulph* k* tritic-vg fd5.de tub mrr1
    - **midnight**:
      - **before**:
        - **22** h: cedr
  - **night – midnight – before – 22** h: ...
        - **22-6** h: *Rhus-t*
      - **after**: nux-v
        - **2** h: puls gk
    - **amel.**: *Ars* *Mag-p* *Plb*
    - **bed** agg.; in: **Cham** mrr1 hell↓ *Hep*↓ *Led*↓ **Merc**↓ nat-c↓ **Rhus-t** mrr1
      - **tearing** pain: hell *Hep* *Led* **Merc** nat-c h2
    - **restlessness**; with: tub mrr1
    - **rubbing** | **amel.**: merc mtf33
    - **sore**: *Con* spig
    - **stitching** pain: cedr *Kali-i* sil
  - **accompanied** by:
    - **abortion** (See FEMALE - Abortion - accompanied - joint)
    - **menses**:
      - **absent** (See FEMALE - Menses - absent - accompanied - joint)
      - **painful** (See FEMALE - Menses - painful - accompanied - joint)
    - **rash**: *(↗gouty - accompanied - eczema; rheumatic - accompanied - eczema; GENERALS - Inflammation - joints - accompanied - skin)* Form mrr1
  - **aching**: aesc all-c anthraq rly4• atp rly4• bol-la carb-an *Carl* *Chinin-s* choc srj3• clem cot br1 dios br1 erig galeoc-c-h gms1• *Gels* kali-c *Kalm* lat-m bnm6• lavand-a ctl1• led luna kg1• merc mosch phos ptel pyrus rhod rhus-t sal-fr sle1• [**Spect** dfg1]
  - **acute**: bry mtf11 ferr-p mtf11 mal-ac mtf11 rhod mtf11
  - **air**; in open:
    - **agg.**: kali-i k2 *Phyt* *Rhus-t* k*
    - **amel.**: iod k2
  - **alternating** with:
    - **colic**: plb
    - **respiratory** complaints: **Kali-bi** mrr1
    - **urine**; offensive: benz-ac mrr1
    - **Eye** inflammation: bry k2
    - **Foot**; perspiration of: merc k2 sil k2
    - **Forehead**; pain in (See HEAD - Pain - forehead - alternating with - joints - pain)
    - **Head**; pain in (See HEAD - Pain - alternating - joints - pain)
    - **Heart** symptoms: abrot k2* aur k2 aur-m k2 kalm k2 led k2 nat-p ptk1
    - **Limbs**; pain in: bry
    - **Occiput**; pain in (See HEAD - Pain - occiput - alternating - joints)
    - **Skin** complaints: staph ptk1
    - **Stomach**; complaints of the: **Kali-bi** mrr1
    - **Uterus**; hemorrhage of: sabin
  - **amenorrhea**: *Lach*
  - **appearing** and disappearing | **suddenly**: kali-bi mrr1
  - **bed** agg.; in: calc-p k* hell *Kalm* k* *Led* stront-c *Sulph*
  - **bending** agg.: *Cocc* coff↓ psor al2 *Ran-a* k* *Ran-b* *Ruta*
    - **sore**: coff
  - **boring** pain: arg-met bell a1 clem k* colch ptk1 coloc conch fkr1* mang *Rhod* ruta fd4.de thuj
  - **broken**; as if: carb-an k* par k*
  - **burning**: abrot k* ant-t k* apis bro1 ars bro1* bell k2* *Carb-v* *Caust* bro1 colch bro1* guaj mrr1 guare k* hist jl3 ign j5.de kali-c *Mang* k* mang-act bro1 merc bro1 *Nat-c* nat-n *Nit-ac* k* olib-sac wmh1 *Plat* *Rhus-t* bro1 sabin k13 sulph bro1 thuj k* zinc
  - **caries**: *Aur-m*↓
    - **boring** pain: aur-m
    - **gnawing** pain: *Aur-m*
  - **chill**:
    - **before**: *Calc*↓
      - **drawing** pain: calc
      - **stitching** pain: *Calc*

Extremities

- **chill**: ...
  - **during**: bol-la bro1 *Calc* ↓ cann-i ↓ chin bro1 **Cimx** *Ferr Hell* k* *Hep* ↓ led ↓ lyc ↓ nat-ar k2 nux-v ↓ ph-ac b4a.de phos ↓ podo mrr1 **Rhus-t** ↓
    - **aching**: cann-i
    - **drawing** pain: **Cimx**
    - **stitching** pain: *Calc* **Hell** k*
    - **tearing** pain: *Cimx Hep* led lyc nux-v phos **Rhus-t**
- **chronic**: *Am-p* bro1 ant-c bro1 anthraco bro1 benz-ac bro1 berb bro1 *Bry* bro1 calc bro1 *Calc-caust* bro1 carbn-s bro1 caul bro1 *Caust* bro1 cimic bro1 colch bro1 *Dulc* bro1 euon bro1 ferr bro1 guaj bro1 hep bro1 iod bro1 kali-bi bro1 kali-c bro1 *Kali-i* bro1 led bro1 *Lith-c* bro1 lyc bro1 med bro1 merc bro1 mez bro1 *Ol-j* bro1 petr bro1 phyt bro1 *Puls* bro1 rhod bro1 *Rhus-t* bro1 ruta bro1 sil bro1 *Stel* bro1 still bro1 streptoc mtf11 sul-ter bro1 *Sulph* bro1 tax bro1
  - **causeless**: rhod mtf11
- **coition** | **amel.**: bamb-a stb2.de•
- **cold**:
  - **air** | **amel.**: rad-br mrr1
  - **applications**:
    - **amel.**: bell mrr1 guaj mrr1 kali-i mrr1 kali-s mrr1 lac-c mrr1 led mrr1 puls mrr1 sabin ↓ sulph mrr1
      - **wandering**, shifting pain: sabin c1
  - **exposure** to | **after**: arg-met k2 *Calc* **Calc-p** cimic mrr1 con **Dulc** kali-c mrr1 *Kalm Ph-ac* **Rhus-t** rumx k2* sil mrr1
  - **wet**: arn mrr1
- **cold**; after taking a: *Calc-p* caps caust ↓ guaj k2 *Mang Nux-m* **Rhus-t**
  - **stitching** pain: caust k*
- **cold**; becoming | **after** | **head**: bell k2
  - **agg.**: *Ph-ac* ↓
    - **sore**: *Ph-ac*
- **cough** agg.; during: caps k2
  - **stitching** pain: caps k2
- **cough** amel. when pain increases: coloc
- **cutting** pain: acon bro1 bry bro1 cadm-s *Caul* bro1 cimic bro1 guare k* hyos k* kalm bro1 *Sabad* k* vesp k*
- **descending**, on: *Arg-met* ↓
  - **sore**: *Arg-met*
- **dislocated**; as if: agar agn c1* anac *Arn Bar-c* bg caps k* *Ign* kali-i med c1 merc nit-ac phos puls k* stram sulph symph fd3.de•
- **drawing** pain: acon k* aloe bro1 am-c h2* am-m bro1 ant-s-aur ant-t k* apoc-a bro1 arg-met bar-act a1 *Bry* k* calc h2* *Carl* k* caust bro1 cham k* chin bro1 *Cimx* k* *Cist* k* clem k* coc-c k* *Colch* bro1 coloc *Gins* bro1 graph j5.de hep j5.de hyos k* kali-bi kali-c j5.de *Led* lyc k* mez k* nat-c nat-m k* nat-p k2 nat-s k* nit-ac k* nit-s-d a1 *Nux-m* k* *Par* phos k* plat *Puls* k* rhod k* *Rhus-t* bro1 sabad j5.de sabin j5.de sec k* sep j5.de **Staph** j5.de sulph h2* tep
  - **cramping**: *Par Plat*
  - **paralyzed**; as if: cham k* nat-m k* staph h1
  - **sticking** pain: calc k*
  - **tearing** pain: act-sp vh1 coloc k*
  - **wandering** pain: acon k* cham k*
- **dull** pain: pant-ac rly4•
- **eating**; after: *Bry*
- **epistaxis**; after: agar ↓
  - **sore**: agar
- **exertion** | **after** | **agg.**: act-sp mrr1 androc srj1• *Calc* **Rhus-t** mrr1 ruta mrr1 sabin
  - **agg.**: calc ↓ calc-caust ↓
    - **stitching** pain: calc k*
    - **tearing** pain | **drawing**: calc-caust
- **fatigued**; as if: dig staph tl1
- **fever**; during: *Calc* ↓ caust ↓ *Hell* ↓ lyc ↓ merc ↓ ph-ac ↓ phos ↓ **Rhus-t** ↓ sil ↓ *Sulph* ↓ thuj ↓ *Tub* ↓
  - **stitching** pain: *Hell* merc **Rhus-t** sil thuj
  - **tearing** pain: *Calc* caust *Hell* lyc merc ph-ac phos **Rhus-t** *Sulph Tub*
  - **Not** lain on; in limbs: nux-v ↓
- **fever**; during – **Not** lain on; in limbs: ...
  - **tearing** pain: nux-v
- **flexed**; when | **extension**; after full: cocc k2
- **gnawing** pain: *Dros* k* mag-c mang **Ran-s** zinc
- **gouty**: *Abrot* k* *Acon* bro1 adren br1 aesc k2 agar **Agn** k* *Alum* am-be c2* am-c am-m am-p c2 ambr ambro c2 anac anag k* ant-c k* ant-t k2 anthraco c2 *Apis* k* apoc-a vh1 arb c1* **Arg-met Arn** k* *Ars* k* ars-h *Ars-i Asaf* asar asper ktp2 aur aur-ar k2 aur-i k2 aur-m bro1 aur-m-n bro1 *Bapt* k* *Bar-c* bar-i k2 **Bell** k* bell-p c2 *Benz-ac* k* berb k2* bism borx bov **Bry** k* *Bufo* cact k2 caj c2* cal-ren c2 **Calc** k* calc-f k2 calc-i k2 **Calc-p** k* **Calc-s** k* canth caps k2 carb-an carb-v *Carbn-s* k* carl c2* **Caust** k* cedr c2 cham k* *Chel Chim Chin* k* *Chinin-ar* chinin-s br1* chr-o c2 *Cinnb* k* *Cocc* k* **Colch** k* *Colchin* bro1 *Coloc* k* *Cupr* c2* daph c2* dros *Dulc* k* eucal c2 eup-per k* *Ferr* k* ferr-ar ferr-i ferr-p ferr-pic bro1 *Form* k* frag br1 gast c2 gent-l c2 get br1 gnaph c2 *Graph* grat c2 *Guaj* k* hell *Hep* k* hera c2* hydrc c2 *Hyos Ign* ins br1 *Iod* k* irid-met c2* jab bro1 jal c2 *Kali-ar* k* kali-bi c2* **Kali-c** k* *Kali-i* k* kali-n kali-p kali-sil k2 *Kalm* k* kiss c2 lappa c2 *Laur* **Led** k* lith-be mtf11 lith-c c2* **Lyc** k* lycpr c2 lysd c2 m-ambo b7.de **Mag-c** k* mag-m mag-p k2* malar c2 *Mang* k* mang-act br1* med hr1* meny **Merc** k* *Mez Nat-ar Nat-c* nat-lac c2* *Nat-m* k* nat-ox-act mtf11 nat-p k* *Nat-s* k* nat-sal bro1 nit-ac k* nux-m k* **Nux-v** k* ol-j k* *Ox-ac* c2* pancr c2* petr k* *Ph-ac* k* *Phos* k* *Phyt* k* pin-s c2 pipe c2 plat c2 *Plb* k* plb-xyz c2 prim-v br1 **Psor** k* *Puls* k* pyrus c2 querc bro1 querc-r c2 querc-r-g-s br1 rad-br c11* *Ran-b* k* ran-s k* *Rhod* k* **Rhus-t** k* ruta **Sabin** k* sacch-l c2 *Sal-ac* k* samb *Sang Sars* k* sec **Sep** *Sil* k* solid c2 spig k* **Spong** k* squil *Stann* **Staph** stel c2* stram *Stront-c* sul-ac sul-i k2 **Sulph** k* tarax tax c2* tep c2 thlas mtf11 *Thuj* k* ur-ac c2* urea c2 *Urt-u* c2* valer verat k* verb vichy-g c2 viol-o viol-t k* *Visc* br1 wies c2 wildb c2 zinc
  - **left**:
    - **extending** to | **right**: *Colch*
  - **accompanied** by:
    - **cracking**: | **motion** agg.: caust mtf11 cocc mtf11
    - **deposits**: am-be br1 rhod mtf11
    - **eczema**: (*↗accompanied - rash; rheumatic - accompanied - eczema; GENERALS - Inflammation - joints - accompanied - skin)* alum bro1 arb br1* lac-ac bro1 *Rhus-t* bro1 ur-ac bro1 urea br1*
    - **indigestion**: ant-t bro1 chin bro1 *Colch* bro1 nux-m bro1 thuj bro1
    - **rheumatism**: abrot mtf11 lith-c mtf11 nat-m mtf11 ran-b mtf11
    - **urine**; albuminous (See URINE - Albuminous - accompanied - gout)
    - **Abdomen** | **complaints** of (See ABDOMEN - Complaints - accompanied - gout)
    - **Head**; complaints of: arn bg2 bell bg2 bry bg2 caps bg2 caust bg2 *Coloc* bg2 ign bg2 ip bg2 *Nux-v* bg2 puls bg2 sabin bg2 sep bg2 verat bg2
    - **Stomach**; pain in (See STOMACH - Pain - accompanied - gout)
  - **acute**: colch ptk1 form br1 sabin ptk1 urt-u ptk1
  - **alternating** with:
    - **anxiety** (See MIND - Anxiety - alternating - joints - gouty)
    - **asthma**: sulph
    - **diarrhea**: ant-c k2
    - **Forehead**; pain in (See HEAD - Pain - forehead - alternating with - joints - gouty)
    - **Head**; pain in (See HEAD - Pain - alternating - joints - gouty)
  - **chronic**: am-p br1 berb br1 chin br1 colch br1 euon-a br1 form br1 kali-br br1 kali-c tl1 lyc br1 nat-s br1 plb br1
  - **debilitated** men: *Staph* k*
  - **gastric** symptoms, with (See STOMACH - Complaints - accompanied - gout)
  - **increase** as cough diminishes: coloc
  - **jar** agg.: bell k2
  - **motion**:
    - **agg.**: form br1
    - **slightest** motion agg.: *Colch* mrr1
  - **neuralgic**: form br1
  - **pressure** | **amel.**: form br1

- **gouty**: ...
  - **suppressed**: *Abrot* br1
  - **swelling**, without: abrot dgt1
  - **warm** room agg.: sabin br1
  - **weather**; change of: bry k2
  - **wine** agg.; sour: ant-c k2
- **grasped**, when: cina h1
- **holding** them long in wrong position: staph ↓
  - **drawing** pain: staph h1
- **jar** agg.: arn mrr1 bell tl2* bry mrr1 sal-ac tl2
- **jerking** pain: mang nat-c plat sul-ac verat
- **lying**:
  - **agg.**: aur ↓ chin k* mand rsj7• *Nux-v* ↓ ruta
    - **sore**: aur *Nux-v*
  - **side**; on:
    - **left**:
      - **agg.**: phos
        - **tearing** pain: phos
    - **painful** side:
      - **amel.**: *Nux-v* ↓ *Rhus-t* ↓
        - **sore**: *Nux-v Rhus-t*
    - **right** | **agg.**: merc
- **menses**:
  - **after** | **amel.**: caul mrr1
  - **before** | **agg.**: caul mrr1
  - **during**:
    - **agg.**: cimic ↓
      - **sore**: cimic k2
- **motion**:
  - **agg.**: acon *Act-sp* ↓ agar ↓ *Ant-t* k* *Arg-met* ↓ *Arn* k* bell k2* **Bry** k* *Calc* ↓ caps k* *Cham* k* chin ↓ cina h1 *Cocc* **Colch** k* croc k* cycl k* ferr-p form br1 *Guaj Hyos* ↓ *Kali-bi Kalm* k* *Lac-ac Lac-c* k* **Led** k* lyc k* *Mang* k* nux-v k* olib-sac wmh1 par k* petr k2 phos k* *Phyt* plb k* rheum *Ruta* sal-ac tl2 sal-al blc1• sars ↓ staph h1 tritic-vg fd5.de
    - **broken**; as if: par k*
    - **drawing** pain: *Act-sp* vh1
    - **pressing** pain: led k*
    - **rapid** motion: phos ↓
      - **sprained**; as if: phos h2
    - **sore**: agar *Arg-met Arn Calc* chin h1 nux-v petr k2 staph a1
    - **stitching** pain: *Bry* k* *Hyos* ruta fd4.de sars k*
    - **tearing** pain: hyos h1 led
  - **amel.**: *Arg-met* **Aur** aur-s wbt2• calc-f mrr1 caps k* cedr chel chin coch a1* *Coloc* ↓ **Con** ↓ dros *Dulc* hr1 *Ferr* fic-m gya1 *Kali-c* ↓ kali-i k2* kali-p k2 nat-s k* olib-sac wmh1 *Phos* k* rad-br mrr1 *Rhod* k* **Rhus-t** k* ros-d wla1 ruta mrr1* sacch-a fd2.de• sulph teucr k* tub mrr1 tub-r vs* valer mrr1 vanil fd5.de
    - **drawing** pain: coloc phos k*
    - **pressing** pain: *Kali-c*
    - **sore**: caps h1 *Chin* coloc **Con Rhus-t Tub**
    - **stitching** pain: dros k* *Rhus-t* k* ruta fd4.de
    - **tearing** pain: *Coloc*
  - **slight** motion | **agg.**: colch mrr1 *Form* mrr1 guaj mrr1
- **nap**; after: dig ↓
  - **sore**: dig h2
- **numbness**; with: *Lyc*
- **paralyzed**; as if: am-c apis arg-met **Arn** k* asar **Aur** bov *Calc* **Caps** *Carb-v* caust bro1 *Chin* **Colch** *Croc Dros* **Euph** kali-c lath bro1 *Led* k* *Mez* nat-c *Par* phos bro1 *Plb Puls Rhus-t Sabin* k* sars *Seneg* **Staph** stram **Valer**
- **peg** were driven in; sensation as if a: bufo br1
- **perspiration**; from suppressed: rhus-t k2
- **pinching** pain: kreos meny
- **pressing** pain: agn *Alum* k* calc k* carb-an h2 chin k* clem coloc k* *Kali-c* k* *Led* k* lyc h2* nat-s k* nit-ac j5.de nit-s-d a1 par k*
  - **tearing** pain: led
- **pressure**:
  - **agg.**: act-sp vh1 fic-m gya1 zinc ↓
    - **stitching** pain: zinc k*
  - **amel.**: bry form k*
  - **hard** | **amel.**: chin vml
- **rest** | **amel.**: sal-al blc1•
- **rheumatic**: *(↗rheumatic; Lameness - joints; GENERALS - Inflammation - joints; GENERALS - Pain - rheumatic - joints)* abrom-a ks5 abrot k* *Acon* k* act-sp k* aesc k2 agar bro1 agn k* all-c k* am-be bro1 am-c mtf11 am-caust bro1 ant-c mtf11 *Ant-t* k* *Apis* bro1 apoc k* arg-met *Arn* k* ars k* ars-i *Ars-s-f* k* asc-c c1 asc-t k* **Aur** k* aur-m k2 bacls-10 fmm1• bacls-7 fmm1• bar-act br1 *Bell* k* *Benz-ac* k* berb k* **Bry** k* *Cact* k* caj oss• *Calc* k* **Calc-p** k* *Calc-s* camph bro1 cann-s k* carbn-s k2* carc mlr1• *Casc* bro1 caul k* **Caust** k* cedr *Cham* k* *Chel* k* *Chim* k* chin bro1 *Chinin-s* k* chlf k* *Cimic* k* clem k* *Cocc* k* **Colch** k* *Colchin* bro1 *Coloc* k* corv-cor bdg• dig br1* dios bro1 dros tl1 *Dulc* k* *Eup-per* bro1 euphr k2 fago mtf11 *Ferr* k* ferr-i **Ferr-p** k* ferr-pic c2 fic-m gya1 flav jl2 **Form** k* form-ac mtf11 franc bro1 gaul bro1 gels k* germ-met srj5• gins bro1 gonotox jl2 *Guaj* k* ham k* *Hep* k* hymos bro1 ign k* indg **Iod** k* **Kali-bi** k* kali-c k* *Kali-chl* k* *Kali-i* k* kali-m k2* kali-p k2 *Kali-s* k* *Kalm* k* kreos *Lac-ac* k* *Lac-c Lach* k* lap-la sde8.de• *Led* k* lith-be mtf11 **Lyc** k* macro bro1 mag-p tl1 mand mtf11 *Mang* k* meli vml3• *Merc* k* meth-sal bro1 mez mtf11 morg fmm1• nat-lac bro1 *Nat-m* k* nat-p k* nat-pyru mtf11 *Nat-s* nat-sal bro1 *Nux-v* k* nyct bro1 ol-j k* *Olib-sac* wmh1 ox-ac k* petr k2* *Phos* k* *Phyt* k* pic-ac pin-s bro1 *Prop* bro1 prot fmm1• psor al2 *Puls* k* *Rad-met* bro1 ran-b k* *Rham-cal* bro1 rheum *Rhod* k* **Rhus-t** k* rumx k2 *Ruta* k* sabin k* *Sal-ac* k* salol bro1 *Sang* k* sec k* senec k* sep **Spig** k* spong *Staph* k* *Stel* bro1 stict k* still bro1 streptoc ↓ stront-c k* stry bro1 sul-i k2 *Sulph* k* syph bro1 *Ter* k* teucr k* thuj k* til bro1 vac mtf11 verat br* *Verat-v* k* *Viol-o* bro1 viol-t k*
  - **accompanied** by | **deformities** and contractions: *Caust* tl1
  - **acute**: streptoc mtf11
  - **alternating** with | **Eye**; inflammation of (See EYE - Inflammation - alternating - joints)
  - **chronic**: caust mtf11 iod tl1 kali-bi mtf11 mag-p mtf11 nat-s tl1 phyt tl1 ran-b mtf11 sep tl1
  - **gonorrhea**; after suppressed: *(↗rheumatic - gonorrhea)* *Acon* bro1 *Arg-met* bro1 arg-n bro1 arn bro1 bry bro1 caust bro1 cimic bro1 clem k* con cop k* *Daph* bro1 gels bro1 guaj bro1 iod bro1 *Irisin* bro1 jac-c bro1 kali-bi bro1 kali-i bro1 kalm bro1 lyc **Med** k* merc k* nat-s bro1 phyt k* psor *Puls* bro1 rhus-t bro1 *Sars* bro1 sulph bro1 **Thuj** k*
  - **menopause**; beginning at: caul tl1 cimic tl1
  - **periodical**: caul tl1
  - **storm**; before: meli hr1
  - **weather**:
    - **change** of weather: meli hr1
    - **rainy**: meli hr1
  - **extending** to:
    - **Lower** limbs; from upper to: *Kalm*
    - **Upward** to more proximal joints: arn bro1 **Led** bro1*
  - **Large** joints: *Acon* bro1 arb bro1 arg-met bro1 asc-c bro1 *Bry* bro1 dros bro1 *Merc* bro1 mim-h bro1 rhus-t bro1 stict bro1 verat-v bro1
  - **Small** joints: *Act-sp* bro1 benz-ac bro1 bry bro1 *Caul* bro1 *Colch* bro1 kali-bi bro1 lac-ac bro1 *Led* bro1 lith-c bro1 lith-lac bro1 *Puls* bro1 rhod bro1 ruta bro1 *Sabin* bro1 viol-o bro1
- **rising**:
  - **agg.**: cassia-s zzc1• tub mrr1
  - **amel.**: aur ↓ coff ↓ *Nux-v* ↓
    - **sore**: aur coff *Nux-v*
  - **sitting**; from:
    - **agg.**: *Rhus-t* ↓
      - **stitching** pain: *Rhus-t*
- **scraping** pain: bry *Sabad*
- **shooting** pain: *Camph* **Caust** sne *Hep* plan tep trom verat
  - **electric** shocks; as from: verat
- **sitting**:
  - **agg.**: coloc ↓ mand rsj7•
    - **drawing** pain: coloc
    - **sore**: coloc

Extremities

- **sitting**: ...
  - **amel.**: sal-al blc1•
- **sleep** agg.; during: sul-ac k*
- **sore**: abrot *Agar* *Alum* alum-p k2 alumn anac ang *Apis* apoc **Arg-met** k* **Arn** k* atp rly4• **Aur** k* bar-s k2 *Bell* bell-p sp1 berb k2 *Bov* bufo calad *Calc* carb-an *Carb-v* *Carbn-s* *Caust* *Cham* chel chel-g homp• **Chin** chlor *Cist* clem cob coff colch k2 coloc *Con* *Crot-h* cupr *Dig* *Dros* *Ferr* guaj k2 hyos *Hyper* kali-i *Lac-c* lappa ptk1 *Led* *Lith-c* mang k2 *Mez* *Mur-ac* *Nat-m* nat-n nat-p *Nit-ac* **Nux-v** par petr k2 **Ph-ac** phos phys pic-ac plb positr nl2• **Puls** k* **Rhus-t** *Ruta* *Salol* c1 *Sep* *Spig* squil *Sulph* k* symph fd3.de• tub *Verat* viol-o zinc
  - **paralyzed**; as if: *Arn* *Calc*
- **sprained**; as if: agar agn alum am-c *Ambr* arg-met *Arg-n* **Arn** k* ars *Arum-t* bar-c bell *Bry* *Calc* *Calc-p* caps carb-ac *Carb-an* carb-v *Caust* cham chel chin h1 cocc *Con* *Cor-r* dig ferr fl-ac *Graph* *Ign* kali-c *Kali-n* kali-sil k2 *Lach* **Led** *Lyc* mag-c *Merc* mez *Nat-m* nux-v par *Petr* **Phos** *Prun* **Puls** ran-b *Rhod* **Rhus-t** *Ruta* sabin k* sars *Sep* sil *Spig* spong *Stann* staph **Sulph** thuj valer verat
- **standing** agg.: calc-sil k2
- **stitching** pain: abrot k2 acon k* agar k* *Agn* aloe androc srj1• *Apis* k* arist-cl sp1 *Arn* k* *Asaf* *Bar-c* k* *Bell* benz-ac bro1 *Bov* **Bry** k* **Calc** k* calc-sil k2 *Camph* *Carbn-s* carl k* *Caust* k* cedr cham k* chin bro1 *Cimic* bro1 clem k* *Cocc* *Colch* k* *Con* conch fkr1* dig *Dros* k* gast a1 *Graph* *Guaj* k* **Hell** k* *Hep* k* *Hyos* *Ign* ind indg a1 kali-bi bg2 **Kali-c** k* *Kali-i* k* *Kali-n* kali-p *Kali-s* kali-sil k2 *Kalm* bro1 *Kreos* k* lac-ac k* *Led* k* lith-c bro1 *Mag-m* magn-gr bro1 **Mang** k* *Meny* **Merc** k* *Merc-c* mill nat-c j5.de *Nat-m* k* nit-s-d a1 nux-v j5.de par k* ph-ac bro1 *Phos* k* phys *Plan* plect a1 *Puls* k* ran-b k2 *Rhod* **Rhus-t** k* ruta fd4.de **Sabin** *Sars* k* *Sep* **Sil** k* **Spig** *Spong* *Stann* *Staph* stict *Stront-c* stroph-s sp1 *Sul-ac* **Sulph** k* symph fd3.de• **Tarax** k* **Thuj** k* tritic-vg fd5.de trom verat verat-v bro1 **Zinc** k*
  - **burning**: ign k*
  - **drawing** pain: puls k*
  - **pulsating** pain: led
  - **shocks**, like: verat
  - **tearing** pain: *Calc* k* camph k* sabin k*
  - **transversely**: **Zinc**
  - **twitching**: carbn-s
  - **wandering** pain: acon k* cedr symph fd3.de•
- **swelling**, without: arg-met vh1 berb dgt1 iod
- **tearing** pain: *Acon* *Act-sp* br1 *Agn* aloe am-c *Ambr* ant-s-aur ant-t k* apis **Arg-met** arist-cl sp1 arn j5.de* *Ars* *Ars-i* *Aur* aur-ar k2 aur-s k2 **Bell** k* *Bov* *Bry* cact k* *Calc* k* calc-i k2 *Camph* k* carbn-s k2 *Carl* **Caust** k* *Chin* k* cist k* *Colch* k* *Coloc* *Con* *Dros* ferr ptk1 *Graph* grat k* **Guaj** k* *Hell* ptk1 *Hep* ptk1 hera j5.de *Hyos* *Iod* *Kali-bi* k* **Kali-c** *Kali-n* kali-s kali-sil k2 kreos lach j5.de *Led* **Lyc** **Merc** k* nat-c nat-m nat-p *Nat-s* k* *Nit-ac* k* nit-s-d a1 *Nux-v* olnd ptk1 petr *Ph-ac* *Phos* *Plat* **Puls** k* rhod **Rhus-t** k* *Sabin* *Sars* k* sec j5.de* *Sep* *Sil* spig *Staph* *Stram* **Stront-c** k* **Sulph** tep teucr thuj k* *Tub* **Zinc** zinc-p k2
  - **downward**: *Sulph*
  - **jerking** pain: acon caust **Chin** **Rhus-t** sulph
  - **paralyzed**; as if: **Bell** chin cocc dig **Staph**
  - **sticking** pain: **Led** k* *Zinc*
  - **twitching**: led
  - **wandering** pain: *Camph* *Kali-bi*
- **touch** agg.: act-sp vh1 bry ↓ chin mrr1 cocc dulc ↓ fic-m gya1 *Mang* petr k2 *Rhus-t* ↓ spig vml
  - **sore**: dulc h2 petr k2
  - **stitching** pain: bry k* *Rhus-t* hr1
- **tubercular** family history: bov tl1 caust tl1 dros tl1 tub tl1
- **urination**:
  - **copious** amel.: benz-ac k2
  - **scanty**: benz-ac k2
- **waking**:
  - **after**:
    - **agg.**: nat-c ↓
      - **drawing** pain: nat-c k*
    - **amel.**: sul-ac
- **walking**:
  - **after**:
    - **agg.**: bry k* caj k* calc-p k* cann-i k* caps k* carb-ac k* carbn-s cedr k* cinnb k* cist k* crot-t k* dios k* *Ferr* k* gels k* jac-c k* kali-bi k* lac-ac k* *Led* k* lyss k* merc k* nat-m k* nat-s k* nit-ac ↓ *Nux-v* k* olnd k* phys k* phyt k* plb k* raph k* rhus-t k* ruta sel k* sol-t-ae k* sulph k*
      - **sprained**; as if: nit-ac h2
  - **agg.**: ang ↓ caps hr1 nat-s k* *Ran-b*
    - **drawing** pain: ang k*
    - **hamstrings** shortened; as if: am-m bro1 caust bro1 cimx bro1
  - **amel.**: **Cham** mrr1 rhod mrr1
- **wandering**, shifting pain: aesc k2 anag k* *Ant-t* k* arb br1 *Ars* **Aur** k* berb k2* *Calc-p* *Camph* cedr chel choc srj3• *Cinnb* k* *Coca* *Cocc* *Colch* k* ferr-p k2 form k* gink-b sbd1• hell k* *Hyper* k* *Iris* **Kali-bi** k* *Kali-s* k* *Kalm* lac-ac k* **Lac-c** *Lach* k* *Mang* k* *Merc-c* k* nat-ar nat-s nux-m mrr1 phyt **Puls** k* *Rhod* sabin k* thal-xyz srj8• tub k2*
- **warm** | **bed** | **agg.**: calc lac-c **Led** *Plb* rad-br mrr1 *Sabin* *Sulph*
  - **room**:
    - **agg.**: *Sabin* ↓
      - **tearing** pain: *Sabin*
- **warmth**:
  - **agg.**: borra-o oss1• caust cedr *Guaj* iod k2 kali-i mrr1 kali-s mrr1 *Lac-c* k* **Led** mand rsj7• merc sne **Puls** sabin pfa sulph mrr1
    - **tearing** pain: *Led*
  - **amel.**: aesc k2 arg-met k2 **Ars** *Bry* k* calc-f mrr1 *Caust* kali-p k2 *Lyc* *Nux-v* phos k2* rhod k2* *Rhus-t* k* ruta mrr1 sal-ac c1 *Sulph* tub mrr1
- **weakness**; from: act-sp mrr1
- **weather**:
  - **change** of weather: ran-b mrr1 *Rhod* mrr1
  - **cold**:
    - **agg.**: **Calc** **Calc-p** **Dulc** nux-m c1 *Ph-ac* **Rhus-t** mrr1
    - **wet** | **agg.**: ant-t arg-met k2 arn mrr1 calc k2 cimic k2 **Colch** dulc mrr1 elaps gk gink-b sbd1• kali-c mrr1 mang k2 meli vml3• ran-b mrr1 **Rhus-t** mrr1 ruta mrr1 sil mrr1 tub mrr1
  - **dry** | **amel.**: **Rhus-t** mrr1
  - **warm** | **agg.**: kali-bi mrr1
  - **wet** | **agg.**: cimic tl1 gink-b sbd1• nux-m ptk rhod mrr1 **Rhus-t** mrr1
  - **windy** and stormy: *Rhod* mrr1 **Rhus-t** mrr1
- **weight**; on bearing: rauw sp1
- **wet** | **getting**: dulc mrr1
- **wine** agg.: *Led*
  - **drawing** pain: *Led* k*
  - **sour** wine: **Ant-c**
- **winter**: calc-p *Kalm*
- **wrong** position; lying in: staph
- ▽ **extending** to:
  - **Bones**; into: cham ↓
    - **stitching** pain: cham k*
  - **Bones**; into long: *Caust* ↓
    - **tearing** pain: *Caust*
  - **Downward**: *Kalm* mrr1
    - **wandering**, shifting pain: *Kalm* mrr1
- ○ **Side** not lain on: nux-v
- **Small** joints: act-sp br1* colch tl1 dros tl1 fic-m gya1 led br1 med tl1*
  - **menses**; after | **amel.**: *Caul* vh

\- **Knees**: abies-c oss4• abrot *Acon* *Aesc* aeth ↓ agar agath-a ↓ agn ↓ aids nl2• *All-c* aloe **Alum** ↓ alum-p ↓ *Alum-sil* ↓ alumn am-c am-m ↓ ambr ↓ ammc ↓ *Anac* b4a.de anag androc ↓ *Ang* k* ant-c k* *Ant-t* k* anthraq ↓ *Apis* k* apoc *Arg-met* b7a.de *Arg-n* ↓ *Arn* *Ars* ars-h ↓ *Ars-i* ars-s-f k2 arund ↓ asaf asar ↓ asc-t aster atra-r skp7*• **Aur** aur-ar k2 aur-i ↓ aur-m ↓ aur-m-n aur-s ↓ bad *Bamb-a* stb2.de• bapt bar-act ↓ *Bar-c* bar-i k2 bar-m ↓ bar-s k2 *Bell* k* **Benz-ac** k* berb k* *Bol-la* borx ↓ bov ↓ brach ↓ brom bry k* bufo ↓ cact cadm-s ↓ cain caj calad k* **Calc** k* calc-f gm1 calc-i k2 *Calc-p* *Calc-s* calc-sil k2 *Camph* ↓ cann-i a1* cann-s k* cann-xyz ↓ *Canth* k* caps k* carb-ac carb-an carb-v carbn-s card-b ↓ card-m cartl-s ↓ cassia-s ccrh1*• castm ↓ *Caul* ↓ **Caust** k* cedr cham k* **Chel** *Chin* k* chinin-ar k2 chinin-s ↓ chord-umb ↓

- **Knees**: ...
chr-met dx cic ↓ *Cimx* cina ↓ *Cinnb* cist clem cob ↓ coc-c ↓ *Cocc* cod coff ↓ colch coli ↓ *Coloc* *Com* *Con* *Cop* corian-s ↓ corn ↓ cortico tpw7 croc ↓ crot-c k* crot-h ↓ crot-t ↓ cupr k* cupr-ar ↓ cycl ↓ daph des-ac rbp6 dig digin ↓ dios k* dream-p sdj1• dros ↓ dulc fd4.de dys pte1*• elaps k* erig *Eug* ↓ euon euph ↓ euphr b7a.de fago ↓ ferr k* ferr-ar ferr-ma ↓ *Ferr-p* ↓ fic-m ↓ fl-ac form galeoc-c-h ↓ gamb gard-j ↓ *Gels* gent-l ↓ ger-i ↓ germ-met srj5• gink-b sbd1• gins ↓ glon gran ↓ **Graph** ↓ grat ↓ *Guaj* guare guat sp1 gymno ↓ ham hell *Hep* ↓ hipp ↓ hura hydr hyos ↓ hyper *Ign* ↓ ina-i mlk9.de indg *Iod* k* iodof a1 ip ↓ iris ↓ jac-c jatr-c ↓ jug-c jug-r ↓ kali-ar kali-bi k* **Kali-c** kali-chl kali-i k* kali-m ↓ *Kali-n* ↓ kali-p *Kali-s* kali-sil k2 *Kalm* k* ketogl-ac ↓ kola stb3• kreos bro1 *Lac-ac* *Lac-c* lac-e ↓ *Lach* lachn ↓ lact ↓ lap-la ↓ lappa bro1 lat-m ↓ lath ↓ laur ↓ **Led** k* lil-t lith-c ↓ lob lob-s ↓ lol ↓ loxo-recl bnm10• *Lyc* lycps-v ↓ lyss *M-ambo* ↓ m-arct ↓ *M-aust* ↓ mag-c mag-m bro1 mag-s ↓ malar jl2 manc ↓ *Mang* ↓ mang-m ↓ med meli k* meny ↓ *Meph* ↓ *Merc* k* merc-c ↓ merc-i-f merc-i-r merl ↓ *Mez* k* mill ↓ moni rfm1• morg-g pte1• morg-p pte1*• mosch k* mur-ac bro1 murx musca-d ↓ myric ↓ *Myrt-c* naja ↓ nat-ar *Nat-c* ↓ *Nat-m* nat-p *Nat-s* nat-sil fd3.de• nept-m ↓ nicc ↓ nit-ac k* nit-s-d ↓ nux-m ↓ *Nux-v* oci-sa sk4• ol-an ↓ ol-j olib-sac wmh1 olnd ↓ op osm ↓ ox-ac ozone ↓ paeon ↓ par ↓ petr ph-ac ↓ *Phos* k* phys *Phyt* pic-ac *Pieri-b* mlk9.de pip-m plan ↓ *Plat* *Plb* k* plect ↓ podo polyp-p ↓ positr ↓ pot-e ↓ prun ↓ psil ft1 *Psor* ptel ↓ *Puls* k* puls-n ↓ *Pyrog* pyrus ↓ querc-r svu1• rad-br mrr1 ran-a ↓ ran-b ↓ ran-s ↓ rat ↓ rheum b7.de* *Rhod* **Rhus-t** *Rhus-v* ribo ↓ rob ↓ rumx ruta sabad b7.de* sabin ↓ sacch-a ↓ sal-ac tl1 sal-fr ↓ *Salol* ↓ samb ↓ sanic sarr ↓ *Sars* sec ↓ seneg k* sep sil spect ↓ *Spig* ↓ spong fd4.de *Stann* ↓ *Staph* ↓ stel bg1 *Stict* *Stram* ↓ streptoc ↓ *Stront-c* k* stry suis-hep ↓ sul-ac k* sul-i k2 *Sulph* k* sumb symph fd3.de• syph tab ↓ *Tanac* ↓ taosc iwa1• tarax ↓ tarent tax tax-br oss1• tell ↓ tep ↓ teucr ↓ thal-xyz ↓ thuj til ↓ tong ↓ tritic-vg fd5.de trom ↓ tub al* upa ↓ urt-u ↓ vac jl2 valer k* vanil fd5.de ven-m ↓ **Verat** verat-v *Verb* k* viol-t ↓ vip ↓ xan xero bro1 zinc k* zinc-p ↓ [heroin sdj2]

- **alternating** sides: ars ↓ bry ↓ coloc ↓ cycl ↓ mag-m ↓ puls ↓
  - **aching**: cycl
  - **drawing** pain: bry coloc puls
  - **sore**: cycl
  - **tearing** pain: ars mag-m puls
- **right**: agar aids nl2• anthraq rly4• aq-mar skp7• arg-met ↓ bit-ar wht1• calc ↓ cassia-s ccrh1• *Chin* cimic bg1 *Coloc* ↓ corian-s ↓ dream-p sdj1• dulc fd4.de elat hr1 fic-m gya1 fl-ac gard-j vlr2• gink-b sbd1• grin vh kali-n ↓ kali-s fd4.de kola stb3• lac-lup hrn2• lachn ↓ limen-b-c hrn2* lyc k2 meli meny ↓ nat-c ↓ nat-sil fd3.de• nux-m ↓ oci-sa sk4• olib-sac wmh1 oxal-a ↓ petr-ra shn4• *Puls* vh rat ↓ ruta fd4.de sacch-a ↓ spig ↓ spong fd4.de *Sulph* bg1* symph fd3.de• trios rsj11• tub c1 vanil fd5.de ven-m rsj12• *Verb* xan ↓ zinc ↓
  - **accompanied** by | **left** hand; pain in: *Agar*
  - **alternating** with | **Temple**; pain in right (See HEAD - Pain - temples - right - alternating - knee)
  - **boring** pain: meny bg2
  - **dislocated**; as if: aids nl2•
  - **dull** pain: xan c1
  - **followed** by | **left** knee: benz-ac calc-p hr1 iris a1
  - **hang** down agg.; letting legs: *Psor* vh
  - **motion** agg.: bit-ar wht1• chel tl1
  - **rest** | **amel.**: bit-ar wht1•
  - **sore**: corian-s knl6• oxal-a rly4• petr-ra shn4•
  - **sprained**; as if: arg-met calc h2 fic-m gya1 nat-c h2 nux-m sulph h2
  - **stitching** pain: kola stb3•
  - **swinging** legs; on: bit-ar wht1•
  - **tearing** pain: agar *Coloc* kali-n h2 lachn a1 rat sacch-a fd2.de• spig zinc
  - **walking** | **amel.**: kali-s fd4.de limen-b-c hrn2• psil ft1
  - **extending** to | **Ankle** | **right**: cassia-s ccrh1•
    - **Toes**: elat hr1
- **left**: aids ↓ apis bg1* arg-met ↓ ars ↓ asc-t a1 aster aur ↓ bac jl2 *Bamb-a* stb2.de• bapt benz-ac berb dgt1* brom bung-fa mtf calad ↓ carb-ac cassia-s ↓ caul a1 caust ↓ chin chir-fl gya2 coloc ↓ *Con* ↓ des-ac rbp6 diaz sa3• dulc fd4.de fic-m gya1 flor-p rsj3• galeoc-c-h ↓ gard-j vlr2• gent-l ↓ ham fd3.de• helia ptk2 *Kali-i* ↓ kali-p ↓ kali-s fd4.de kalm kola stb3• lac-h htj1• lac-lup hrn2• lach ↓ lachn ↓ limest-b ↓ luf-op rsj5• melal-alt ↓ nat-m ↓ nat-sil fd3.de• nept-m ↓ oci-sa sk4• olib-sac wmh1 ozone sde2• pall petr-ra shn4• phos ↓ *Plat* podo fd3.de•

- **left**: ...
Psor ↓ rhus-g tmo3• rhus-t ↓ ruta fd4.de sacch-a ↓ samb bat1• sel rsj9• sil ↓ spig ↓ spong fd4.de sulph ↓ symph ↓ tarax ↓ tritic-vg fd5.de vanil fd5.de xan c1 zinc ↓ [heroin sdj2 tax jsj7]
  - **morning**: bung-fa mtf
  - **night**: bung-fa mtf
  - **aching**: galeoc-c-h gms1•
  - **boring** pain: aur bro1 bamb-a stb2.de• caust bro1 coloc bro1 rhus-t bro1 spig bro1 tarax bro1
  - **cutting** pain: petr-ra shn4• sel rsj9•
  - **drawing** pain: dulc fd4.de kali-p fd1.de• nat-m h2 ruta fd4.de sacch-a fd2.de• sil h2 spong fd4.de
  - **dull** pain: kali-s fd4.de xan c1
  - **followed** by | **right**: androc srj1• *Calc-p* petr-ra shn4• psil ft1 sel rsj9•
  - **increasing** and decreasing: gard-j vlr2•
  - **paralyzed**; as if: lach
  - **pressing** pain: gard-j vlr2•
  - **shooting** pain: cassia-s ccrh1•
  - **sore**: aids nl2• *Con* limest-b es1• phos h2 plat h2
  - **sprained**; as if: ars h2 gent-l a1 sulph h2
  - **stitching** pain: asc-t a1 bamb-a stb2.de• dulc fd4.de melal-alt gya4 nept-m lsd2.fr ruta fd4.de sacch-a fd2.de• spong fd4.de symph fd3.de• vanil fd5.de
  - **tearing** pain: arg-met vh1 calad *Kali-i* lachn *Psor* k* sulph zinc h2
  - **Lateral** side: bung-fa mtf [phos stj2]
- **morning**: abrot ant-t asc-t bamb-a ↓ bry calc carb-ac cod ↓ coloc dios dulc fd4.de graph ↓ ham fd3.de• hyper ign ↓ kali-bi kali-s ↓ *Lach* lyc ↓ mez nat-ar nat-c ↓ *Nux-v* ozone ↓ phos plect ↓ ruta fd4.de sep spong fd4.de *Staph* ↓ stront-c ↓ sulph ↓ sumb symph fd3.de• tritic-vg fd5.de vanil fd5.de zinc ↓
  - **4-8 h**: ign ↓
    - **stitching** pain: ign
  - **aching**: bry carb-ac dios sumb
  - **bed** agg.; in: aur ↓ graph ↓ merl ↓ nux-v ↓ sumb ↓
    - **aching**: sumb
    - **drawing** pain: nux-v k*
    - **sore**: aur graph nux-v
    - **tearing** pain: merl
  - **burning**: phos tritic-vg fd5.de
  - **dislocated**; as if: ozone sde2•
  - **drawing** pain: dios k* kali-bi nux-v k* plect a1
  - **motion** agg.: ign ↓
    - **stitching** pain: ign
  - **rising**:
    - **after**:
      - **agg.**: agar h2 arg-met ↓ kali-bi ↓ kali-s ↓ phos ↓ rhod ↓ *Staph* ↓
        - **drawing** pain: kali-bi k*
        - **sprained**; as if: arg-met
        - **stitching** pain: kali-s fd4.de phos rhod *Staph*
      - **amel.**: aur ↓ graph ↓
        - **sore**: aur graph h2
    - **agg.**: (non:agar kl) asc-t ↓ diaz sa3• fic-m gya1 kali-bi lac-e ↓ led lyc h2 ozone ↓ *Rhus-t* symph fd3.de•
      - **dislocated**; as if: ozone sde2•
      - **sore**: lac-e hrn2•
      - **tearing** pain: asc-t
  - **sitting** agg.: nat-c ↓
    - **stitching** pain: nat-c
  - **sore**: graph nux-v zinc
  - **sprained**; as if: cod sulph h2
  - **stitching** pain: bamb-a stb2.de• calc ign kali-s fd4.de lyc nat-c ruta fd4.de spong fd4.de *Staph*
  - **tearing** pain: lyc stront-c zinc
  - **walking** agg.: bry ↓ fic-m ↓ *Lach* ↓ nat-c ↓
    - **aching**: bry fic-m gya1 *Lach*
    - **stitching** pain: nat-c

Extremities

- **forenoon**: bamb-a↓ bov↓ calc↓ coloc dios dulc fd4.de jug-c merc-i-r ruta fd4.de spong fd4.de thuj tritic-vg fd5.de vanil fd5.de
  - **9** h: trom
  - **drawing** pain: coloc k* tritic-vg fd5.de
  - **stitching** pain: bamb-a stb2.de• bov calc ruta fd4.de
  - **walking** agg.: nat-c↓
    - **sprained**; as if: nat-c
- **noon**: arund cinnb dios dulc fd4.de *Sulph*↓
  - **aching**: dios
  - **riding** agg.: calc↓
    - **stitching** pain: calc
  - **tearing** pain: *Sulph*
- **afternoon**: abrot aids nl2• alum↓ ammc↓ arund carbn-s↓ cycl↓ dios dulc fd4.de erig ham fd3.de• lyc↓ lycps-v mag-c *Nat-m* nicc↓ phyt plect↓ ptel↓ rumx ruta fd4.de sep spong fd4.de stront-c↓ sulph tritic-vg fd5.de vanil fd5.de
  - **13** h: sars↓
    - **tearing** pain: sars
  - **14** h: sars↓
    - **tearing** pain: sars
  - **15** h: sulph↓
    - **tearing** pain: sulph
  - **16** h: fago↓
    - **tearing** pain: fago
    - **walking** agg.: pip-m↓
      - **stitching** pain: pip-m
  - **17** h: chin↓
    - **tearing** pain: chin
  - **17-20** h: ven-m rsj12•
  - **aching**: dios lycps-v
  - **burning**: lyc
  - **drawing** pain: ammc k* cycl k* (non:dios a4) ham fd3.de• lyc k* plect a1 ptel k* sep k* stront-c sulph k* tritic-vg fd5.de
  - **sleep** agg.; after: cycl↓
    - **drawing** pain: cycl k*
  - **tearing** pain: alum carbn-s lyc nicc
- **evening**: abrot↓ aeth↓ agath-a↓ *Alum*↓ *Am-m*↓ ammc↓ ant-t↓ calc↓ carb-an castor-eq caust↓ cham↓ cist cob coloc cycl dios dulc erig fl-ac↓ kali-bi↓ kali-c↓ *Kali-i*↓ kali-n↓ lach↓ *Led* lyc lycps-v mag-c↓ murx nat-c↓ nat-m↓ nat-s↓ petr↓ phos↓ plan plb↓ *Puls*↓ *Rhod* ruta fd4.de sep↓ spong fd4.de stront-c↓ *Sulph*↓ thuj↓ tritic-vg↓ vanil fd5.de zinc
  - **19** h: lyc↓
    - **drawing** pain: lyc
  - **21** h: dios↓ ptel↓
    - **drawing** pain: dios a4
    - **stitching** pain: ptel
  - **aching**: agath-a nl2• cob cycl dios erig *Led* lycps-v
  - **bed** agg.; in: ant-t↓ calad colch thuj↓
    - **sore**: thuj
    - **stitching** pain: ant-t
  - **boring** pain: coloc zinc
  - **drawing** pain: cham h1 dulc fd4.de nat-c h2 nat-m h2 ruta fd4.de sep h2 sulph h2 tritic-vg fd5.de
  - **lying** | **after**:
    - **agg.**: alum↓ *Nat-s*↓
      - **tearing** pain: alum *Nat-s*
    - **agg.**: petr↓ spong↓
      - **stitching** pain: petr a1 spong
  - **pressing** pain: coloc k* fl-ac k* led k* nat-s k*
  - **sitting** agg.: *Led*↓ nat-s↓
    - **pressing** pain: *Led* nat-s k*
  - **sore**: abrot dios lach
  - **sprained**; as if: petr h2 sulph h2
  - **stitching** pain: aeth *Alum* *Am-m* ant-t calc dulc fd4.de kali-c lyc plb spong stront-c thuj
- **evening**: ...
  - **tearing** pain: alum ammc caust h2 *Cist* coloc kali-bi kali-c kali-n led **Lyc** mag-c h2 petr phos *Puls* *Sulph*
  - **walking**:
    - **amel.**: *Coloc*↓
      - **tearing** pain: *Coloc*
- **night**: arge-pl rwt5• bell↓ cact caj *Calc*↓ *Calc-i*↓ calc-p *Camph*↓ carb-an↓ castm coc-c dios dulc fd4.de ferr-p↓ form↓ gels **Graph**↓ *Kali-bi* *Kali-i* lach *Lyc* *Merc* mez *Nat-m* *Petr* phos↓ phyt plb gk polyp-p↓ *Puls*↓ *Rhod* ruta fd4.de sacch-a↓ spong fd4.de *Sulph* tub c1 vanil fd5.de zinc
  - **22** h: chel↓
    - **stitching** pain: chel
  - **23-7** h: *Sulph*
  - **midnight**: stront-c↓
    - **tearing** pain: stront-c
  - **aching**: coc-c *Kali-bi* vanil fd5.de
  - **bed** agg.; in: carb-an↓ *Merc*↓ nat-c↓ nat-s↓ nit-ac↓ *Puls*↓ rhod↓ **Sulph**↓
    - **tearing** pain: carb-an *Merc* nat-c nat-s nit-ac *Puls* rhod **Sulph**
  - **boring** pain: *Calc-i* calc-p
  - **cutting** pain: form
  - **drawing** pain: polyp-p a1 ruta fd4.de spong k* sulph zinc k*
  - **gnawing** pain: *Kali-i* *Nat-m*
  - **shooting** pain: ferr-p k2 *Kali-bi*
  - **sore**: **Graph** puls h1 sacch-a fd2.de•
  - **stitching** pain: bell *Calc* *Camph* carb-an *Kali-bi* merc sne phos vanil fd5.de
  - **stretching** agg.: calc-p↓
    - **boring** pain: calc-p
  - **tearing** pain: carb-an *Kali-i* **Lyc** *Puls*
  - **waking**; on: led↓
    - **pressing** pain: led k*
- **aching**: *Aesc* agath-a nl2• anac bro1 androc srj1• apoc asc-t bell brom bry calc calc-p cann-i carb-ac chel chord-umb rly4• cic clem cob coli rly4• com con bro1 cop corn dios dulc h1 *Eug* fago fl-ac galeoc-c-h gms1• gamb ger-i rly4• glon hell *Hydr* jatr-c lach lat-m bnm6• led k* lil-t lob-s lyc lyss mang-m med meli bro1 *Merc* mez *Mur-ac* nat-m nux-v *Ol-j* k* op osm petr phys *Podo* positr nl2• ptel puls-n pyrus **Rhus-t** rhus-v ribo rly4• sal-fr sle1• *Stram* stront-c syph tab upa vanil fd5.de verat-v xan zinc [heroin sdj2 spect dfg1]
  - **wandering** pain: clem
- **air**; in open:
  - **agg.**: **Caust** phos↓ *Phyt*
    - **drawing** pain: **Caust**
    - **tearing** pain: **Caust** phos h2
  - **amel.**: pic-ac sumb
- **alternating** with:
  - **Elbow**; pain in: dios k*
  - **Forehead**; heat and pressure on: hell
- **appearing** suddenly: bamb-a↓ lyc↓ sal-ac↓
  - **disappearing** suddenly; and: bamb-a↓
    - **stitching** pain: bamb-a stb2.de•
  - **stitching** pain: bamb-a stb2.de• lyc sal-ac c1
- **arthritic**: sep↓
  - **drawing** pain: sep k*
- **ascending**:
  - **agg.**: alum↓
    - **drawing** pain: alum h2
  - **stairs**:
    - **agg.**: agar *Alum* arn *Bad* bar-c gk bell bry↓ cann-s *Carb-v* colch cortico↓ dios dulc fd4.de elaps gk lac-e↓ lith-c mur-ac↓ nat-sil fd3.de• nux-m oci-sa sk4• phos bg1 pieri-b mlk9.de *Plb* sulph↓ symph fd3.de• tritic-vg fd5.de vanil fd5.de
      - **broken**; as if: colch
      - **burning**: sulph
      - **cutting** pain: cortico tpw7

- **ascending – stairs – agg.**: ...
  - . **shooting** pain: agar
  - . **sore**: lac-e hrn2• mur-ac
  - . **sprained**; as if: nux-m
  - . **stitching** pain: agar bar-c bry sulph symph fd3.de•
- **bed** | **going** to bed:
  - : **before**: ammc ↓
    - . **tearing** pain: ammc
  - : **in** bed:
    - : **agg.**: rhod ↓ **Suiph** ↓ thuj ↓
      - . **drawing** pain: rhod k*
      - . **stitching** pain: thuj
      - . **tearing** pain: **Sulph**
- **bending**:
  - : **agg.**: anac ↓ aspar ↓ bung-fa mtf canth carb-an ↓ cham ↓ hell ↓ malar jl2 mur-ac ↓ oci-sa sk4• phys ruta fd4.de *Spig* spong fd4.de stann sulph ↓ tab ↓ tarax ↓
    - : **drawing** pain: anac k* spong fd4.de
    - : **pressing** pain: spong fd4.de tarax h1
    - : **sore**: aspar carb-an hell spig sulph
    - : **stitching** pain: cham mur-ac ruta fd4.de tab
  - : **amel.**: ferr
- **blow**; pain as from a: arn b7.de* mez b4.de* plat b4.de* sul-ac b4.de*
- **boring** pain: agar k* alum k* am-c k* aur k* *Aur-m-n* bamb-a stb2.de• bufo calc-p k* canth k* *Caust* k* chel k* coloc k* crot-t grat k* *Hell* k* indg k* mag-c k* meny b7.de mez k* nat-c k* nat-p k* nat-s k* plan k* ran-s k* ruta fd4.de sep k* zinc k*
  - : **wandering** pain: nat-s
- **breakfast**; during: gels psa
- **broken**; as if: bry bg2 chel k* colch k* cupr k* dros k* hep k* kali-c bg2 lyc k* merc k* sep b4a.de
- **burning**: am-c anac ant-t b7.de apis k* *Arg-met* **Ars** b4a.de arund asaf k* bar-c bell berb brom k* bry k* cann-s k* carb-v k* **Chel** k* chin b7.de fl-ac *Iod* b4a.de kali-n k* ketogl-ac rly4• lach lachn lyc k* *M-ambo* b7a.de *Mur-ac* k* nat-s k2 nit-ac k* petr k* ph-ac phos k* plat k* plb *Rhus-t* ruta fd4.de sabad k* stann k* stront-c k* sul-ac k* sulph k* tab tarax k* tarent tep thuj k* tritic-vg fd5.de
  - : **stinging**: bell
- **burrowing**: hell b7.de* *Mang* b4a.de *Rhod* b4a.de spig b7.de* zinc b4.de*
- **chill**:
  - : **before**: chinin-s ↓
    - : **sore**: chinin-s
  - : **during**: agar ars-h caust bg2 chin k* chinin-s ↓ *Cimx Cocc* hell bg2* *Nat-m Nat-s Nux-v* k* phos ↓ podo k* puls k* pyrog k2 rhus-t k* sabad ↓ sep k* sulph k*
    - : **aching**: *Nat-m* nux-v *Rhus-t*
    - : **sore**: chinin-s phos
    - : **stitching** pain: *Hell* b7.de sabad b7a.de
- **cold**:
  - : **amel.**: kali-i mrr1 *Led* plb *Puls*
  - : **exposure** to | **agg.**: *Calc-p Kalm Sep*
- **cold** agg.; becoming: *Calc* ↓ *Kali-c* ↓ *Lyc* ↓ *Merc* ↓ phos ↓ **Rhus-t** ↓ sep ↓ *Sil* ↓
  - : **tearing** pain: *Calc Kali-c Lyc Merc* phos **Rhus-t** sep *Sil*
- **convulsive**: nux-v
- **cough** agg.; during: bry caps *Nit-ac* b4a.de
  - : **shooting** pain: nit-ac
  - : **stitching** pain: nit-ac
- **cramping**: anac bro1 bell h1 caps bro1 chin h1 lath bro1 paeon bro1 petr h2 *Puls* bro1 sil bro1 symph fd3.de• *Verb* bro1 xan c1
- **crossing** legs agg.: anag ang ↓ mur-ac ↓ petr podo fd3.de•
  - : **drawing** pain: (non:anag kl) ang kl
  - : **tearing** pain: mur-ac
- **cut** with a sharp instrument; as if slightly: kali-c h2
- **cutting** pain: *Acon* k* ant-t bg1 arg-met k* arg-n bg1 bar-c k* bufo bg2* *Calc* calc-p canth b7.de* corian-s knl6• cortico tpw7 form graph k* *Ign* b7a.de kali-bi k* kali-s fd4.de manc mez musca-d szs1 nat-p nux-v bg2 plat sep b4.de* stry *Sul-ac* tax thuj bg1 verat k*
- **descending** stairs agg.: arg-met *Bad* bar-c gk cann-s cortico ↓ eupi kali-s fd4.de melal-alt gya4 merc nit-ac olib-sac wmh1 ozone ↓ pieri-b mlk9.de **Rhus-t** k ● ruta fd4.de sal-fr ↓ staph gk sulph ↓ symph fd3.de• vanil fd5.de ven-m rsj12• verat
  - : **cutting** pain: cortico tpw7
  - : **shooting** pain: sal-fr sle1•
  - : **sore**: sulph verat
  - : **sprained**; as if: nit-ac
  - : **stitching** pain: ozone sde2•
- **dinner** | **after**:
  - : **agg.**: mag-c ↓ phos ↓ sep ↓
    - . **tearing** pain: mag-c h2 phos sep
  - : **amel.**: phos ↓
    - : **tearing** pain: phos
- **dislocated**; as if: agar b4.de* agn b7.de* aids nl2• am-c b4.de* *Arg-met Arn* ars bg2 bufo bg2 calad b7.de* calc b4.de* *Caust* b4.de* chin b7.de* gels graph b4.de* *Ign* ip b7.de* kali-bi bg2 kali-c b4.de* kali-n b4.de* kreos b7a.de meny b7.de* merc nat-c b4.de* nat-m b4.de* nit-ac b4.de* nux-m b7.de* ozone sde2• petr b4.de* phos b4.de* pip-m plat b4.de* plb b7.de* puls b7.de* rhod b4.de* *Rhus-t* b7.de* spig b7.de* staph b7.de* sulph b4a.de thuj
- **dragging**: petr b4.de*
- **drawing** pain: *Acon* k* *Agar* k* agn b7.de* aloe k* *Alum* k* alum-p k2 alum-sil k2 am-c k* ambr k* ammc k* *Anac* k* ang k* ant-c k* ant-t b7.de* arg-met k* arg-n k* ars k* ars-i asaf b7.de* asar k* aster aur k* aur-ar k2 aur-i k2 aur-m-n k* aur-s k2 bapt benz-ac k* **Bry** k* cact k* *Calc* k* calc-sil k2 camph b7.de* cann-i k* canth b7.de* *Caps* carb-v k* carbn-s card-m *Caul* k* **Caust** k* cham k* *Chel* k* *Chin* k* *Chinin-ar* cist k* clem k* cocc k* coff b7a.de coloc k* com k* croc k* crot-h k* cupr k* cupr-ar k* cycl k* dig k* dios k* dulc fd4.de gran k* graph k* grat k* *Guaj* k* hell k* hep k* *Ign* b7a.de indg k* iod k* jug-r k* kali-ar kali-bi k* kali-c k* kali-m k2 kali-n k* kali-p kali-s kali-sil k2 kreos b7a.de lach k* *Led* k* *Lyc* k* *M-ambo* b7a.de *M-aust* b7.de mag-c k* mag-m k* med meny b7.de* merc-c mez k* mur-ac k* naja nat-ar nat-c k* *Nat-m* k* nat-p *Nat-s* k* nit-ac k* nit-s-d a1 nux-v k* ol-an k* olnd k* osm *Ox-ac* par k* petr a1 ph-ac k* *Phos* k* plat k* plb b7.de* polyp-p a1 ptel k* **Puls** k* ran-b b7.de* rat rheum b7.de* *Rhod* k* *Rhus-t* k* rhus-v k* ruta fd4.de sabad k* sabin k* sacch-a fd2.de• sars bg2 sec k* sep k* sil k* spig k* spong k* stann k* staph k* *Stront-c* k* sul-i k2 sulph k* *Tanac* b7a.de tarax b7.de* thuj k* tritic-vg fd5.de vanil fd5.de verat k* *Zinc* k* zinc-p k2
  - : **boring** pain: mez k*
  - : **cramping**: arg-n k* lyc olnd phos h2 sulph
  - : **downward**: cham kali-n lach mag-c nat-s ph-ac rhus-v sec
  - : **ending** with a jerk: nit-ac h2
  - : **jerking** pain: stann h2
  - : **paralyzed**; as if: chel k* gran a1 mag-m h2 nat-m k* plect a1 staph k*
  - : **paroxysmal**: coloc k* croc lyc phos
  - : **stitching** pain: nat-c k* nat-m h2 sil k* symph fd3.de•
  - : **tearing** pain: bry clem k* ol-an k*
  - : **twitching**: stann k*
  - : **upward**: indg kali-c nit-ac
- **drawing** up legs | **amel.**: cham
- **dull** pain: cassia-s ccrh1• ruta fd4.de ven-m rsj12• [tax jsj7]
- **eating**; after: bry ↓
  - : **tearing** pain: bry
- **eruptions**; after suppressed: *Sep*
- **exertion** agg.; after: caust con dulc graph *Mag-c* nat-c pieri-b mlk9.de ruta fd4.de sacch-a fd2.de• zinc
- **exertion**; as after: anac b4a.de ant-t b7.de* arg-met b7.de* *Cann-s* b7a.de caust b4.de* con b4.de* croc b7.de* dig b4.de* dulc b4.de* graph b4.de* hep b4a.de ip b7.de* laur b7.de* mag-c b4.de* nat-c b4.de* nux-v b7.de* verat b7.de* zinc b4.de*
- **extending** limb: *(↗extending limb - amel.; stretching - agg.; stretching - amel.; stretching - desire)* chel ferr *Kali-c*

Extremities

- **extending** limb: ...
  - **amel.**: *(↗extending limb; stretching - agg.; stretching - amel.; stretching - desire)* ferr
- **fall**; after a: stict c1
- **fever**; during: **Calc** bg2 chin bg2 *Lyc* bg2 **Nat-m** bg2 nux-v bg2 petr bg2 *Puls* bg2 rhus-t bg2 *Sep* bg2 sulph bg2 thuj bg2
- **fire**, when near: sumb k*
  - **aching**: sumb k*
- **flexing** limb (See bending - agg.)
- **gnawing** pain: benz-ac k* kali-i k* *Merc* *Nat-m* nux-v h1* ran-s k* rhus-t hr1 zinc k*
- **gouty** (= gonagra): *Ant-c*↓ **Benz-ac** **Calc** caust tl1 chin b7a.de con b4.de* crot-h↓ *Eup-per* *Guaj* *Lach* *Led* k* *Nux-v* petr h2 plb gk sep↓ verat b7.de*
  - **drawing** pain: *Ant-c* crot-h k* sep h2
- **grasping** pain: cann-xyz ptk1 nux-m tl1
- **heat**; during: lach↓
  - **sprained**; as if: lach
- **jerking** pain: aloe bg2 alum bg2 *Am-c* *Anac* *Chin* coloc b4a.de m-aust b7.de* petr h2 puls b7.de* spig b7.de* spong b7.de* sul-ac b4.de* verat b7a.de
- **kneeling** agg.: *Bar-c* *Bar-m*↓ ruta fd4.de tarent ptk2
  - **shooting** pain: *Bar-c*
  - **stitching** pain: bar-c *Bar-m* ruta fd4.de
- **lying**:
  - **agg.**: *Agar*↓ bamb-a stb2.de• calad carb-an con↓ *Kali-i* lil-t merc↓ petr↓ vanil fd5.de
    - **boring** pain: bamb-a stb2.de•
    - **broken**; as if: merc k*
    - **drawing** pain: *Agar* k* vanil fd5.de
    - **sprained**; as if: petr h2
    - **tearing** pain: con h2
  - **amel.**: atra-r bnm3• caj psil ft1 ruta fd4.de sulph
  - **side**; on | **painful** side:
    - **agg.**: nat-m↓
      - **sore**: nat-m
    - **right** | **agg.**: verat-v
- **lying** down:
  - **after**:
    - **agg.**: lil-t↓
      - **aching**: lil-t
    - **amel.**: cassia-s↓ sulph↓
      - **tearing** pain: cassia-s ccrh1• sulph
  - **amel.**: *Sulph*↓
    - **sprained**; as if: *Sulph*
- **menses**; during: cop mag-c b4.de* zinc↓
  - **drawing** pain: zinc
  - **sore**: mag-c
- **motion**:
  - **agg.**: aids nl2• *Arg-met*↓ ars↓ asar↓ berb bol-la **Bry** bufo cact *Carbn-s* cassia-s↓ cham↓ **Chel** *Chin*↓ *Cocc* *Coloc*↓ dulc fd4.de *Elaps*↓ *Ferr-p*↓ *Guaj* hep↓ ign iod↓ iris kali-bi *Kali-c*↓ *Kalm* kola stb3• lac-ac lac-c lap-la sde8.de• *Led* lycps-v↓ mand rsj7• merc merc-c↓ nat-ar nux-m↓ petr plan *Plb* puls↓ rheum ruta fd4.de sel↓ spong fd4.de staph *Sulph*↓ trios rsj11• vanil fd5.de verat [heroin sdj2]
    - **aching**: lycps-v
    - **boring** pain: bufo
    - **cutting** pain: sel rsj9•
    - **drawing** pain: coloc k* iod h staph k*
    - **pressing** pain: hep lac-c *Led* k* *Sulph* k* vanil fd5.de
    - **shooting** pain: bufo *Coloc* *Ferr-p*
    - **sore**: *Arg-met* chin *Kali-c* puls h1 verat h1
    - **sprained**; as if: arg-met nux-m
    - **stitching** pain: *Bry* bufo cham coloc *Elaps* ferr-p led merc-c plb ruta fd4.de spong *Staph* k* *Sulph*
    - **tearing** pain: ars asar cassia-s ccrh1• *Chin* kali-bi **Led** *Merc* plb
- **motion**: ...
  - **amel.**: agar androc srj1• arg-met↓ asar↓ aur-m-n↓ bar-c↓ *Bell*↓ calc camph↓ carb-ac↓ cassia-s↓ *Cham*↓ colch com↓ cycl dios dulc fd4.de indg *Jac-g* *Kali-c*↓ kali-i mrr1 kali-n↓ kola stb3• lap-la↓ lob **Lyc** merc-c↓ mez *Mur-ac*↓ nat-s nept-m↓ olib-sac wmh1 phos↓ pic-ac psor↓ **Puls** ran-a↓ ran-b *Rat*↓ *Rhod* *Rhus-t* ruta fd4.de sep *Sil*↓ spong fd4.de *Stict* stroph-s sp1 sulph tab↓ vanil fd5.de ven-m rsj12• *Verat* viol-t↓
    - **aching**: *Agar* bar-c cycl dios *Mur-ac* **Rhus-t**
    - **boring** pain: ruta fd4.de sep
    - **drawing** pain: agar arg-met *Rhod* k* *Rhus-t* vanil fd5.de
    - **pressing** pain: arg-met aur-m-n k* com k* cycl h1 kali-c mez k* ran-a a1 tab k*
    - **sore**: carb-ac cycl *Puls* sulph
    - **stitching** pain: *Calc* camph *Cham* *Kali-c* lap-la sde8.de• merc-c nept-m lsd2.fr phos ruta fd4.de spong fd4.de viol-t
    - **tearing** pain: *Agar* asar *Bell* cassia-s ccrh1• kali-n psor *Rat* **Rhus-t** *Sil*
  - **backward** and forward:
    - **amel.**: plb↓
      - **stitching** pain: plb
  - **beginning** of:
    - **agg.**: bac jl2 bung-fa mtf calc bg1 cassia-s ccrh1*• dulc fd4.de *Led* nat-ar↓ *Puls* *Rhus-t* ruta fd4.de verat
      - **sore**: nat-ar
  - **continued** motion | **amel.**: bac jl2 cassia-s ccrh1*• *Equis-h* c1 *Jac-c* *Jac-g* ruta fd4.de vanil fd5.de
- **neuralgic**: bell iodof a1 lac-ac nat-ar symph br1 tarax ptk1 thal-xyz srj8•
- **paralyzed**; as if: all-c anac k* arg-met ars b4a.de aur b4.de* *Bar-c* b4a.de berb caps b7.de* carb-v k* chel chin k* cocc colch coloc k* con b4.de* croc b7.de* crot-h *Euon* fago kali-c k* lol bg2 mag-m k* mosch k* nat-m b4.de* nux-v b7.de* petr b4.de* phos b4a.de phys plb k* puls k* ruta k* *Sabad* b7.de* seneg b4a.de stann bg2 staph b7.de* sulph k* valer b7.de* verat k*
- **paroxysmal**: bamb-a stb2.de• bell nux-v *Plb*
- **periodical**: sec↓
  - **drawing** pain: sec
- **perspiration**; during: bar-c bg2 bry bg2 **Calc** bg2 caust bg2 chin bg2 ferr bg2 **Hell** bg2 led bg2 lyc bg2 *Merc* bg2 nat-m bg2 *Nux-v* bg2 phos bg2 puls bg2 **Rhus-t** bg2 **Sep** bg2 stann bg2 staph bg2 **Sulph** bg2 thuj bg2 verat bg2
- **pinching** pain: ang h1 card-b a1 merc-i-f k* pot-e rly4• ruta fd4.de sil k*
- **pressing** pain: agn b7.de* alum k* *Anac* k* ang k* arg-met k* arg-n k* asaf k* *Aur* k* aur-m-n k* bar-act a1 bar-c b4.de* bell b4.de* borx brom k* cadm-s calad *Calc* k* *Camph* k* caps b7.de* carb-v h2 chel k* cic k* clem k* colch b7.de* coloc k* com k* cop k* cupr k* cycl k* dig k* digin a1 dulc b4.de* fl-ac k* gins k* ham fd3.de• hell k* hep b4.de* jatr-c kali-c k* kali-s fd4.de kreos b7a.de lac-c **Led** k* m-arct b7.de m-aust b7.de *Mag-m* mang-m k* mez k* mur-ac b4a.de* nat-m b4.de* nat-s k* nit-ac h2 nit-s-d a1 ox-ac k* plat b4.de* rheum k* sabad b7.de* sabin b7.de* sars k* **Sil** spig h1 spong b7.de* stann k* staph b7.de* stront-c k* **Sulph** k* symph fd3.de• tab k* tarax b7.de* *Thuj* k* tritic-vg fd5.de vanil fd5.de verb
  - **constricting** pain: *Anac* *Aur* cann-s k* **Sil**
  - **downward**: mang-m k*
  - **drawing** pain: camph h1 nat-s k*
  - **paroxysmal**: coloc
  - **tearing** pain: led k*
  - **twisted**; as if: clem k*
  - **wavering**: dulc h2
- **pressure**:
  - **agg.**: cassia-s↓ caust↓ chel↓ cortico↓ hell↓ oci-sa sk4• ol-j petr-ra↓ plb↓ ran-b spig↓
    - **cutting** pain: cortico tpw7
    - **shooting** pain: cassia-s ccrh1•
    - **sore**: caust chel hell petr-ra shn4•
    - **tearing** pain: plb spig
  - **amel.**: acon-c ars atra-r skp7*• bung-fa mtf cassia-s ccrh1• kali-s fd4.de mez↓ plb↓ ruta fd4.de
    - **pressing** pain: mez h2

- **pressure – amel.**: ...
  - **tearing** pain: plb
- **pulsating** pain: calad calc symph$_{fd3.de}$• tarent
- **putting** foot upon the floor: aur↓
  - **drawing** pain: aur
- **raising** limb while sitting, on: phos↓
  - **sore**: phos
- **rheumatic**: *Acon*$_{k*}$ *Agar* aml-ns ammc apoc arg-met$_{bro1}$ *Ars* ars-h asar↓ asc-t aur bacls-7$_{pte1}$• bapt *Benz-ac*$_{k*}$ *Berb*$_{k*}$ bol-la brom **Bry**$_{k*}$ cact **Calc** *Calc-p* *Caust* chel↓ *Chin*$_{bro1}$ *Cimic* *Cinnb* *Clem* *Cocc* con cop$_{k*}$ corv-cor$_{bdg}$• daph$_{br1*}$ dios$_{bro1}$ *Dulc*$_{bro1}$ elaps$_{bro1}$ ferr-p form gels graph *Guaj*$_{k*}$ ham$_{fd3.de}$• hydr hyper iod↓ iris jac-c$_{bro1}$ *Jac-g* jug-r *Kali-bi* **Kali-c**$_{k*}$ *Kali-i*$_{bro1}$ *Kalm* lac-ac$_{k*}$ *Lac-c* *Lach* *Led*$_{k*}$ *Lyc* *Mang-act*$_{bro1}$ *Med* meli$_{bro1}$ *Merc*$_{bro1}$ merc-i-r mez$_{k*}$ nat-m nat-p$_{bro1}$ nicc *Nux-v* ol-j *Petr* *Phos* *Phyt* plb ptel *Puls*$_{bro1}$ puls-n$_{k*}$ rad-br$_{bro1}$ ran-b$_{k2}$ *Rhod* **Rhus-t** sabin$_{bro1}$ sal-ac sanic sep *Stict*$_{k*}$ stry syc$_{pte1*}$ *Thuj* trom *Verat-v* visc$_{bro1}$ zinc
  - **right**: cinnb gels$_{hr1}$ grin$_{vh}$ jac-g kali-bi led lob nicc olib-sac$_{wmh1}$ phos *Phyt*
    - **hang** down agg.; letting legs: *Psor*$_{vh}$
  - **left**: bacls-10$_{pte1*}$• bapt *Berb* *Glon* helia$_{c1*}$ *Phyt*
  - **coldness | amel.**: led$_{tl1}$
  - **drawing** pain: iod$_{k*}$ mez$_{h2}$ *Rhus-t* *Zinc*
  - **stitching** pain: acon asar chel **Kali-c** *Lach*
  - **tearing** pain: ars-h asar hyper *Lach* **Rhus-t**
- **riding** a bicycle: cortico↓
  - **cutting** pain: cortico$_{tpw7}$
- **rising**:
  - **after**:
    - **agg.**: coloc↓
      - **drawing** pain: coloc$_{k*}$
    - **amel.**: aur↓ graph↓
      - **sore**: aur graph
  - **agg.**: ars↓ diaz$_{sa3}$• kali-c↓
    - **sprained**; as if: ars$_{h2}$ kali-c
  - **kneeling**; from: *Spig*
  - **sitting**; from:
    - **after**:
      - **agg.**: *Verat*↓
        - **sore | paralytic**: *Verat*$_{k*}$
    - **agg.**: agar↓ ars↓ asc-t berb$_{k*}$ bov↓ *Brucel*$_{sa3}$• calc↓ carb-v cassia-s$_{ccrh1}$• caust↓ chin↓ cocc↓ fago kali-c lap-la$_{sde8.de}$• mez mur-ac↓ nat-sil$_{fd3.de}$• *Nux-v* **Rhus-t** rumx ruta$_{fd4.de}$ sep↓ **Sulph** *Verat*
      - **drawing** pain: chin$_{h1}$ cocc sep
      - **long** time; sitting for a: kali-bi↓
        - **sprained**; as if: kali-bi
      - **sore**: ars *Berb* sulph verat$_{h1}$
      - **stitching** pain: agar bov rhus-t
      - **tearing** pain: calc$_{h2}$ caust mur-ac
    - **amel.**: phos↓ sil↓
      - **sore**: phos
      - **tearing** pain: sil$_{h2}$
- **rubbing**:
  - **amel.**: canth↓ castm cedr nept-m↓ ol-an↓ *Phos* plb↓ sul-ac↓ tarent *Zinc*↓
    - **stitching** pain: nept-m$_{lsd2.fr}$
    - **tearing** pain: canth castm ol-an *Phos* plb sul-ac$_{h2}$ *Zinc*
- **scraping** pain: aids$_{nl2}$• samb
- **scratching**: (non:kali-c$_{h2}$)
- **shooting** pain: *Acon*$_{k*}$ agar ant-c$_{c1}$ apis ars$_{bg2}$ *Bar-c* brach bufo *Coloc* *Ferr-p* *Iod* *Kali-bi* led$_{bg2}$ lyss **Nit-ac**$_{k*}$ podo rhus-t$_{k*}$ sal-fr$_{sle1}$• sulph$_{k*}$ tep trom
  - **side** to side, from: rhus-t
- **sitting**:
  - **after**: bell berb con dig kali-s$_{fd4.de}$ nit-ac nux-v **Rhus-t** sep spong$_{fd4.de}$ tritic-vg$_{fd5.de}$ zinc
- **sitting**: ...
  - **agg.**: *Agar* alum↓ am-c↓ *Am-m*↓ *Anac*↓ ang↓ *Arg-met*↓ ars↓ asaf asc-t aur-m-n bar-act↓ bar-c↓ bell bry↓ calc camph carb-v castor-eq chin↓ cist coloc con↓ crot-h cycl↓ dig↓ dulc$_{fd4.de}$ euph↓ gins↓ graph grat↓ ham$_{fd3.de}$• indg jatr-c↓ kali-c↓ kali-s$_{fd4.de}$ lach led mag-m↓ merc↓ merl↓ mez *Mur-ac*↓ *Nat-m*↓ nat-s nit-s-d↓ oci-sa$_{sk4}$• ozone$_{sde2}$• phys plect↓ podo$_{fd3.de}$• puls↓ ran-a↓ *Rat*↓ **Rhus-t** ruta$_{fd4.de}$ sabad↓ sep↓ *Sil*↓ spong$_{fd4.de}$ stann↓ staph↓ stroph-s$_{sp1}$ symph$_{fd3.de}$• thuj↓ tritic-vg$_{fd5.de}$ verat↓ verb↓ [heroin$_{sdj2}$]
    - **aching**: agar bar-c led **Rhus-t**
    - **boring** pain: agar *Aur-m-n* coloc grat indg mez
    - **drawing** pain: *Agar* anac$_{h2}$ chin$_{k*}$ coloc$_{k*}$ cycl$_{k*}$ dig$_{k*}$ lach$_{k*}$ led$_{k*}$ mez$_{k*}$ *Nat-m*$_{k*}$ plect$_{a1}$ **Rhus-t** spong$_{fd4.de}$ staph$_{h1}$ tritic-vg$_{fd5.de}$ verat$_{k*}$
    - **pressing** pain: *Anac* arg-met$_{h1}$ asaf$_{k*}$ *Aur-m-n*$_{k*}$ bar-act$_{a1}$ camph$_{k*}$ coloc$_{k*}$ gins$_{k*}$ ham$_{fd3.de}$• led$_{k*}$ mez$_{k*}$ nat-s$_{k*}$ nit-s-d$_{a1}$ ran-a$_{k*}$ tritic-vg$_{fd5.de}$ verb
    - **sore**: ang arg-met ars asaf bry coloc jatr-c sabad sep
    - **sprained**; as if: am-c calc$_{h2}$
    - **stitching** pain: alum *Am-m* asaf aur-m-n *Calc* euph indg merc *Rhus-t* stann staph
      - **shifting**: asaf
    - **tearing** pain: *Agar* *Arg-met* bar-c con dulc kali-c led mag-m merl *Mur-ac* puls *Rat* sep$_{h2}$ *Sil* stann$_{h2}$ thuj
  - **amel.**: cassia-s↓ chin↓ kali-c↓ mur-ac↓ rat↓ sil↓ zinc↓
    - **drawing** pain: chin$_{k*}$ kali-c
    - **shooting** pain: cassia-s$_{ccrh1}$•
    - **sore**: zinc
    - **stitching** pain: mur-ac rat sil
    - **tearing** pain: zinc
- **sleep**; preventing: caust↓ lyc↓
  - **tearing** pain: caust$_{h2}$ lyc$_{h2}$
- **sneezing** agg.: *Kali-c*↓
  - **sore**: *Kali-c*
- **sore**: acon aesc aids$_{nl2}$• ambr ang$_{k*}$ anthraq$_{rly4}$• *Arg-met*$_{k*}$ **Ars**$_{k*}$ ars-h asaf asar *Aur*$_{k*}$ bar-c berb$_{k*}$ brach *Bry*$_{k*}$ bufo$_{k*}$ calc calc-p camph$_{k*}$ canth carb-ac carb-an cartl-s$_{rly4}$• caust$_{k*}$ chel *Chin*$_{k*}$ chinin-s chord-umb$_{rly4}$• cic$_{k*}$ cist coloc *Con*$_{k*}$ cupr cycl$_{k*}$ elaps **Graph**$_{k*}$ ham hell *Hep*$_{k*}$ hura hyos jatr-c *Kali-ar* kali-bi *Kali-c* kali-p lac-ac lac-c lac-e$_{hrn2}$• lach **Led**$_{k*}$ lyc m-ambo$_{b7.de}$ mag-c *Meph* mez$_{k*}$ mur-ac$_{k*}$ myric nat-c nat-m nat-p nat-s nat-sil$_{fd3.de}$• *Nux-v*$_{k*}$ ol-an *Ol-j* petr$_{k*}$ phos$_{k*}$ *Plat*$_{k*}$ plb *Puls*$_{k*}$ rhod rhus-v rumx ruta sabad sacch-a$_{fd2.de}$• *Salol*$_{c1}$ sarr$_{k*}$ sep$_{k*}$ spig$_{k*}$ *Stann*$_{k*}$ staph$_{k*}$ streptoc$_{rly4}$• suis-hep$_{rly4}$• sulph$_{k*}$ tarent tax tell thuj urt-u verat$_{k*}$ zinc$_{k*}$
  - **paroxysmal**: plb
- **sprained**: *Arn*↓ petr↓
  - **stitching** pain: *Arn* petr
- **sprained**; as if: agar am-c arg-met ars$_{h2}$ calc *Calc-p* carbn-s caust chin$_{h1}$ cod con elaps$_{k*}$ fic-m$_{gya1}$ gent-l$_{k*}$ graph hipp *Ign* kali-bi kreos *Lach* *Lyc* meny$_{h1}$ nat-m nit-ac phos prun rhod **Rhus-t** rob$_{bg2}$ sars spig sulph
- **squatting**, when: calc chir-fl$_{gya2}$
- **squeezed**; as if: arg-met$_{b7a.de}$ bry$_{b7a.de}$ led$_{b7a.de}$
- **standing**:
  - **agg.**: aeth↓ *Agar*↓ alumn ang↓ arg-met berb↓ calc carb-an carb-v↓ cassia-s↓ chin↓ cupr↓ cycl↓ dulc$_{fd4.de}$ hell↓ iod kali-s↓ lach mag-c↓ malar$_{jl2}$ nit-ac↓ nux-v plb↓ podo rat↓ rhus-t↓ rumx↓ ruta$_{fd4.de}$ sars↓ stann↓ stront-c *Sulph* symph$_{fd3.de}$• valer verat↓ verb↓
    - **aching**: stront-c
    - **drawing** pain: ang$_{k*}$ *Calc* carb-v$_{k*}$ chin$_{k*}$ cupr$_{k*}$ cycl$_{k*}$ stann$_{k*}$ verat$_{k*}$
    - **pressing** pain: verb
    - **shooting** pain: nit-ac sulph
    - **stitching** pain: aeth hell kali-s$_{fd4.de}$ nit-ac plb rat rhus-t rumx sulph
    - **tearing** pain: *Agar* berb cassia-s$_{ccrh1}$• mag-c sars$_{h2}$ sulph$_{h2}$

Extremities

- **standing**: ...
  - **air** agg.; in open: con ↓
    - **sore**: con
  - **amel.**: chin ↓ sil ↓
    - **drawing** pain: chin k*
    - **tearing** pain: sil
  - **sitting** agg.; after: rhus-t ↓
    - **stitching** pain: rhus-t
- **starting** on falling asleep, from stitches: merc ↓
  - **stitching** pain: merc
- **stepping**:
  - **agg.**: aur ↓ caust con plat ↓ sacch-a ↓ sulph ↓ verb ↓
    - **drawing** pain: aur h2
    - **sprained**; as if: plat h2 sulph h2
    - **stitching** pain: verb
    - **tearing** pain: caust h2 sacch-a fd2.de•
  - **hard**:
    - **agg.**: calc ↓
      - **aching**: calc bg1
- **stirred** up inside; as if being all: gard-j vlr2•
- **stitching** pain: acon aeth *Agar* agn b7.de* aloe k* **Alum** k* alum-p k2 alum-sil k2 am-m k* ammc anac androc srj1• ang b7.de* ant-c k* ant-t k* *Apis* k* apoc *Arg-met* k* arn k* ars k* ars-i arund asaf k* asar b7.de* asc-t aur aur-ar k2 aur-m aur-m-n *Bamb-a* stb2.de• bapt *Bar-c* k* bar-i k2 bar-m bar-s k2 **Bell** k* berb bov k* brach *Bry* k* bufo *Calc* k* calc-i k2 *Calc-s* calc-sil k2 camph b7.de* canth k* *Carb-an* k* carbn-s caust k* cedr cham chel k* chin k* chinin-ar cina k* cinnb clem coc-c cocc k* *Coloc* k* con k* dulc fd4.de *Elaps* euph k* euphr k* ferr-ma ferr-p gran graph k* grat *Guaj* k* gymno ham *Hell* k* hep k* hura hydr hyper ign k* indg *Iod* k* iris *Kali-ar* **Kali-c** k* kali-chl kali-m k2 kali-n kali-p *Kali-s* kali-sil k2 *Kalm* kola stb3• lac-ac lac-c lach lap-la sde8.de• laur k* *Led* k* lith-c lyc lyss m-aust b7.de mag-c mag-m k* manc mang k* med meny k* *Merc* k* merc-c mez k* mur-ac k* myric nat-ar nat-c k* *Nat-m* k* nat-p nat-s nat-sil fd3.de• nept-m lsd2.fr **Nit-ac** k* nux-v k* ol-an olnd ozone sde2• par b7.de* *Petr* k* ph-ac k* *Phos* k* phys phyt *Pieri-b* mlk9.de pip-m plb k* podo ptel *Puls* k* rat rheum k* rhod k* *Rhus-t* k* ruta fd4.de sabad k* sacch-a fd2.de• sal-ac c1 sanic *Sars* k* *Sep* k* *Sil* k* spig k* spong k* *Stann* k* *Staph* k* stict stront-c k* stry suis-hep rly4• sul-ac k* sul-i k2 **Sulph** k* symph fd3.de• tab tarax k* tep *Thuj* k* trom valer k* vanil fd5.de verat k* verb k* viol-t k* vip zinc k* [tax jsj7]
  - **boring** pain: hell
  - **burning**: apis *Arg-met* lith-c mur-ac *Staph* sul-ac
  - **drawing**; after: guaj k* *Staph*
  - **itching**: viol-t
  - **outward**: cham
  - **paroxysmal**: bamb-a stb2.de• phos
  - **shifting**: cham lyc
  - **shooting** pain: berb
  - **smarting**: sep
  - **sore**: bry
  - **tearing** pain: berb bry *Calc* lyc merc
  - **transversely**: rhus-t
  - **twitching**: euphr
- **stool** agg.; after: dios
- **stooping** agg.; after: anac croc graph kali-s fd4.de plan
- **stretching**:
  - **agg.**: *(↗amel.; desire; extending limb; extending limb - amel.)* ant-c bov ↓ calc-p caust ↓ laur ↓ med vanil fd5.de
    - **boring** pain: calc-p
    - **drawing** pain: caust k* vanil fd5.de
    - **stitching** pain: bov laur med vanil fd5.de
  - **amel.**: *(↗agg.; desire; extending limb; extending limb - amel.)* anac ↓ dros dulc fd4.de kali-s fd4.de mur-ac ↓ ruta fd4.de vanil fd5.de
    - **drawing** pain: anac k* ruta fd4.de vanil fd5.de
    - **stitching** pain: mur-ac k*
  - **desire** to stretch: *(↗agg.; amel.; extending limb; extending limb - amel.)* meli vh*
- **stretching** out: petr ↓
  - **tearing** pain: petr h2
- **sudden**: lyc ↓ nat-s ↓ op ↓
  - **pressing** pain: nat-s k*
  - **sprained**; as if: lyc
  - **stitching** pain (See appearing - stitching)
  - **tearing** pain: lyc op
- **supper** agg.; after: sep ↓
  - **tearing** pain: sep
- **supporting** body with knee: ph-ac ↓
  - **drawing** pain: ph-ac h2
- **swelling**: lach ↓
  - **drawing** pain: lach k*
- **tearing** pain: *Acon* k* *Agar* k* **Alum** k* alum-p k2 *Alum-sil* k4 am-c k* am-m k* ambr k* ammc arg-met k* *Arg-n* *Arn* k* ars b4.de* ars-h asar asc-t aur-m **Bar-c** k* bar-i k2 *Bell* k* *Berb* *Brom* b4a.de bry k* *Calc* k* calc-i k2 calc-sil k2 camph k* cann-i cann-xyz bg2 canth k* carb-an k* carb-v carbn-s cassia-s ccrh1• *Caust* k* cham chel tl1 *Chin* k* *Cist* *Clem* k* coc-c cocc k* *Colch* k* coloc k* con k* crot-t dios dulc k* euph k* fl-ac gran k* grat guaj hep k* hyper ign *Indg* iod k* iris jatr-c kali-bi k* **Kali-c** k* kali-i k* kali-m k2 *Kali-n* k* kali-p kali-sil k2 kreos b7a.de* *Lach* lachn lact laur k* **Led** k* **Lyc** k* lyss m-arct b7.de m-aust b7.de mag-c k* *Mag-m* k* mag-s mang k* *Merc* k* merl mez k* mill *Mur-ac* k* *Nat-c* k* nat-m k* nat-p *Nat-s* nicc nit-ac k* nux-v b7.de* op par k* petr k* *Phos* k* *Plb* k* psor **Puls** k* ran-b b7.de* rat *Rhod* k* **Rhus-t** k* sabad b7.de* sacch-a fd2.de• *Sars* k* *Sep* k* *Sil* k* *Spig* k* *Stann* k* stict bro1 *Stront-c* k* sul-ac k* sul-i k2 *Sulph* k* tarax b7.de* teucr thuj til tong bro1 *Valer* b7.de* verat-v bro1 vip **Zinc** k* zinc-p k2
  - **alternating** with | **stiffness**: *Ars*
  - **boring** pain: agar h2 canth
  - **downward**: **Alum** *Bar-c* bry canth chin h1 *Lyc* merl nat-c nat-s op phos h2 thuj
  - **drawing** pain: arg-n caust h2 cham h1 stann h2 *Sulph* thuj
  - **jerking** pain: puls h1
  - **paralyzed**; as if: *Chin*
  - **paroxysmal**: castm
  - **stitch**-like: alum calc sil
  - **torn** off; as if: phos
  - **torn** open; as if: calad mag-c
  - **twitching**: brom kali-i kreos plb
  - **upward**: caust *Chin* dulc fago fl-ac mez mur-ac nat-c nicc nit-ac phos spig stann h2 stront-c sulph zinc
  - **wandering** pain: lact
- **thinking** of it agg.: ox-ac
- **thunderstorm**; during: med ↓
  - **stitching** pain: med
- **touch** agg.: acon ant-c ↓ *Arn* ↓ ars ↓ *Chin* cot ↓ hyper oci-sa sk4• spig ↓ staph ↓ tab ↓
  - **pressing** pain: staph h1
  - **sore**: ars h2 spig h1
  - **stitching** pain: ant-c *Arn* cot br1 tab
  - **tearing** pain: *Chin*
- **turning**:
  - **leg** agg.: am-c ↓
    - **sprained**; as if: am-c
  - **limb** agg.: am-c calc verat-v
- **ulcerative** pain: caust b4.de* rhod b4a.de
- **waking**; on: agar ↓ diaz sa3• zinc
  - **drawing** pain: agar k*
- **walking**:
  - **after**:
    - **agg.**: acon ↓ alum berb clem ↓ cycl dulc fd4.de hydr kali-n mosch nit-ac ↓ phys *Rhus-t* ruta fd4.de spong fd4.de tell ↓ tritic-vg fd5.de valer
      - **pressing** pain: acon k*
      - **sore**: *Berb* tell
      - **sprained**; as if: tell
      - **tearing** pain: clem nit-ac

- **walking – after**: ...
  - **amel.**: grat↓ plect↓
    - **drawing** pain: grat$_{k*}$ plect$_{a1}$
  - **agg.**: agar↓ aloe↓ *Am-m*↓ ammc anac ang↓ ant-t *Arg-met*↓ arg-n asaf asc-t *Aur* aur-m-n bar-act↓ *Berb* *Bry* bufo↓ bung-fa$_{mtf}$ *Calc*↓ calc-caust↓ *Calc-p* camph↓ caps carb-an↓ cassia-s↓ caust **Chel** chin↓ *Cinnb* cist clem cocc↓ *Coloc* conch↓ cop↓ cortico$_{tpw7}$ crot-h *Cupr*↓ cycl dig dios dros dulc$_{fd4.de}$ euph euphr↓ flor-p$_{rsj3}$• form gard-j$_{vlr2}$• gels graph↓ grat *Guaj* hydr ip↓ iris jac-g jatr-c kali-bi *Kali-c* kali-s$_{fd4.de}$ *Lac-ac* *Lach* lachn↓ **Led** lil-t lyc↓ *Mag-c* *Med* merc merc-i-r merc-sul$_{c1}$ mez mur-ac↓ *Mygal* nat-c nat-m nat-s nit-ac olib-sac↓ petr petr-ra$_{shn4}$• ph-ac↓ phos↓ phys plan podo$_{fd3.de}$• positr$_{nl2}$• rheum↓ ruta$_{fd4.de}$ sal-fr$_{sle1}$• sep↓ *Spig*↓ spong$_{fd4.de}$ staph stram↓ stront-c *Sulph*↓ symph$_{fd3.de}$• thiam↓ thuj tritic-vg$_{fd5.de}$ *Valer*↓ vanil$_{fd5.de}$ verat↓ verb vip zinc↓
    - **aching**: *Hydr* nat-m positr$_{nl2}$• stront-c
    - **boring** pain: mez
    - **broken**; as if: dros$_{k*}$
    - **burning**: stram tritic-vg$_{fd5.de}$
    - **cutting** pain: *Calc-p* cortico$_{tpw7}$ kali-s$_{fd4.de}$ thiam$_{rly4}$•
    - **drawing** pain: anac$_{h2}$ ang$_{k*}$ aur *Calc* chin$_{h1}$ clem coloc$_{k*}$ *Cupr*$_{k*}$ dulc$_{fd4.de}$ kali-c *Led* ph-ac$_{h2}$ phos$_{k*}$ ruta$_{fd4.de}$ sep$_{k*}$ spig$_{k*}$ staph$_{k*}$ tritic-vg$_{fd5.de}$ verat$_{k*}$
    - **pressing** pain: anac$_{k*}$ arg-n$_{k*}$ asaf$_{k*}$ cop$_{k*}$ cycl$_{k*}$ *Led* nat-s$_{k*}$ spong$_{fd4.de}$
    - **shooting** pain: cassia-s$_{ccrh1}$• *Coloc* sulph
    - **sore**: *Arg-met* *Bry* *Calc-p* carb-an cycl dios mag-c$_{h2}$ mur-ac nat-s thuj zinc
    - **sprained**; as if: agar *Calc-p* graph ip lyc nat-c$_{h2}$ nat-m petr$_{h2}$ spig$_{h1}$ *Sulph*
    - **stitching** pain: agar aloe am-m aur-m-n *Bry* bufo *Calc* calc-caust caust cinnb cocc coloc conch$_{fkr1.de}$ euphr kali-s$_{fd4.de}$ lach *Led* lyc merc mur-ac olib-sac$_{wmh1}$ petr rheum ruta$_{fd4.de}$ spig sulph thuj *Valer*
    - **tearing** pain: *Am-m* asc-t bar-act$_{a1}$ berb calc camph grat lachn **Led** merc nit-ac *Spig* stront-c *Sulph* zinc
  - **air**; in open:
    - **agg.**: con↓ dulc↓ hell↓ merc↓ sulph↓
      - **shooting** pain: sulph
      - **sore**: con
      - **stitching** pain: hell merc sulph
      - **tearing** pain: dulc
    - **amel.**: *Alum*↓
      - **stitching** pain: *Alum*
  - **amel.**: *Agar* alum↓ ars↓ bac$_{jl2}$ bar-c↓ bell↓ chin↓ coloc↓ dulc$_{fd4.de}$ grat *Indg*↓ *Kali-c*↓ kali-n↓ *Kali-s* limen-b-c$_{mlk9.de}$ **Lyc** mur-ac↓ nat-c nat-m↓ nat-s phos↓ *Puls* *Pyrog* *Rhod* **Rhus-t**↓ ruta$_{fd4.de}$ sulph *Valer* *Verat*
    - **boring** pain: indg$_{br1*}$
    - **burning**: phos
    - **drawing** pain: *Agar* chin$_{k*}$ *Lyc* **Puls** **Rhod** **Rhus-t**
    - **sore**: ars *Puls*
    - **stitching** pain: alum *Kali-c* nat-m phos *Rhus-t*
    - **tearing** pain: *Agar* alum bar-c bell coloc grat *Indg* kali-n$_{h2}$ mur-ac **Puls** **Rhus-t** sulph$_{h2}$
  - **cold** air; in:
    - **amel.**: sumb↓
      - **aching**: sumb
  - **continued** | **air**; in open | **amel.**: sumb
    - **amel.**: bac$_{jl2}$ calc$_{bg1}$ dios
  - **level** ground; on:
    - **amel.**: nit-ac↓
      - **sprained**; as if: nit-ac
- **wandering**, shifting pain: clem dios iris kali-bi *Kalm* lil-t lycps-v nat-s osm psil$_{ft1}$ *Puls* ran-a tarent
  - **from** one to the other: dios **Lac-c**
- **warm** bed agg.: **Caust**↓ dios **Led** *Lyc*↓ **Merc**↓ mosch *Petr* plb *Puls* *Sulph*
  - **drawing** pain: **Caust** *Lyc*
- **warm** bed agg.: ...
  - **tearing** pain: *Led* **Merc** plb
- **warm** covering, from: bry↓ *Elaps*↓
  - **stitching** pain: bry$_{k*}$ *Elaps*
- **warmth**:
  - **agg.**: *Guaj* kali-i$_{mrr1}$ **Led**
  - **amel.**: androc$_{srj1}$• canth **Caust**↓ gink-b$_{sbd1}$• oci-sa$_{sk4}$•
    - **tearing** pain: **Caust**
- **waves**; in: bamb-a$_{stb2.de}$•
- **weather**:
  - **change** of weather: vip↓
    - **stitching** pain: vip
    - **tearing** pain: vip
  - **wet** | **agg.**: *Calc* *Phyt* *Rhus-t*
- **wine** agg.: benz-ac↓ zinc↓
  - **drawing** pain: benz-ac$_{k*}$ zinc
- **wrapping** warm amel.: nat-c↓
  - **tearing** pain: nat-c$_{h2}$
- **yawning** agg.: sars↓
  - **tearing** pain: sars
- ▽ **extending** to:
  - **Ankle**: bry↓ caust↓ cham↓ indg↓ rhus-t↓ vanil↓
    - **drawing** pain: rhus-t$_{h1}$ vanil$_{fd5.de}$
    - **tearing** pain: bry caust$_{h2}$ cham$_{h1}$ indg rhus-t$_{h1}$
  - **Body**; all: cassia-s↓
    - **tearing** pain: cassia-s$_{ccrh1}$•
  - **Crest** of ilium: sulph↓
    - **tearing** pain: sulph
  - **Downward**: kali-p kola$_{stb3}$• *Phos* rhus-t ruta$_{fd4.de}$ vanil$_{fd5.de}$
  - **Feet**: *Phos* *Tarent*
  - **Fibula**: bapt$_{hr1}$
  - **Foot**: kali-n↓ lyc↓ nat-c↓ phos↓ sil↓ sulph↓
    - **drawing** pain: kali-n nat-c$_{h2}$ phos$_{h2}$
    - **tearing** pain: lyc$_{h2}$ sil$_{h2}$ sulph$_{h2}$
    - **Sole** of: bamb-a↓
      - **stitching** pain: bamb-a$_{stb2.de}$•
  - **Groin**: rhus-t
  - **Hip**: caust↓ lach *Led* lyc↓ mur-ac↓ nit-ac↓ puls↓ ruta$_{fd4.de}$ sol-ni symph$_{fd3.de}$• tarent
    - **stitching** pain: *Lach* lyc ruta$_{fd4.de}$
    - **tearing** pain: caust mur-ac nit-ac puls
  - **Instep**: elat
  - **Leg**: arg-n↓ ferr-p↓ mez↓
    - **stitching** pain: ferr-p mez
    - **tearing** pain: arg-n$_{a1}$
  - **Leg**, up the: dios rhus-t vanil$_{fd5.de}$
  - **Lumbar** region: fago↓ stront-c↓
    - **tearing** pain: fago stront-c
  - **Soles**: mag-c↓ plb
    - **drawing** pain: mag-c
  - **Thigh**: chin↓ kali-n↓ mag-c↓ nicc↓
    - **sprained**; as if: kali-n
    - **tearing** pain: chin mag-c$_{h2}$ nicc
  - **Tibia**: indg spong$_{fd4.de}$ symph$_{fd3.de}$•
  - **Toes**: *Alum*↓ bamb-a↓ caust↓ sulph↓ valer
    - **stitching** pain: bamb-a$_{stb2.de}$•
    - **tearing** pain: *Alum* caust$_{h2}$ sulph$_{h2}$
- ○ **Above**: ambr↓ ulm-c↓
  - **right**: visc↓
    - **stitching** pain: visc$_{c1}$
  - **sore**: ulm-c$_{jsj8}$•
  - **sprained**; as if: ambr$_{h1*}$
- **Around**: ars-s-f$_{br1}$
- **Behind**: corian-s↓
  - **cramping**: corian-s$_{knl6}$•

- **Below**: verat tl1
- **Bends** of knees: ozone ↓
  - **left**: ozone ↓
    - **stitching** pain: ozone sde2•
  - **stitching** pain: ozone sde2•
- **Front**:
  - **ascending** stairs agg.: cortico ↓
    - **cutting** pain: cortico sp1
  - **bending** agg.: cortico ↓
    - **cutting** pain: cortico sp1
  - **pressure** agg.: cortico ↓
    - **cutting** pain: cortico sp1
  - **riding** a bicycle: cortico ↓
    - **cutting** pain: cortico sp1
  - **walking** agg.: cortico ↓
    - **cutting** pain: cortico sp1
- **Hollow** of knees (= popliteus): agar agath-a ↓ agn ↓ *Alum* am-c ↓ ambr ↓ ammc vml3• anag androc ↓ ang ↓ arg-met arizon-l ↓ ars ars-h *Bar-c* ↓ bell ↓ berb brom *Bry* ↓ calc calc-caust ↓ calc-p cann-s ↓ cann-xyz ↓ canth ↓ carb-an carbn-s card-m castor-eq caust bro1* chel chin coc-c ↓ colch coloc ↓ con cortiso ↓ cupr cupr-ar ↓ *Cycl* ↓ dios dros dulc fd4.de fago fl-ac gard-j vlr2• gels graph grat ↓ gymno ham ↓ hep hydrog srj2• indg ↓ *Iod* ↓ ip jatr-c kali-bi kali-c ↓ kali-chl bg1 kali-n ↓ kali-p ↓ kalm ketogl-ac ↓ lac-c *Led* ↓ lith-c ↓ lyc bro1* mag-c manc mang meny ↓ merc-i-f ↓ merl ↓ mez ↓ mill ↓ mosch ↓ *Mur-ac* ↓ nat-ar *Nat-c* k* nat-m nat-s ↓ nat-sil fd3.de• *Nit-ac* nit-s-d ↓ *Nux-v* ↓ ol-an ↓ olnd op ox-ac par petr ↓ ph-ac ↓ phel ↓ phos ↓ phys bro1* *Phyt* ↓ plat ↓ *Plb* polys sk4• prun ↓ rad-br ptk1 rad-met bro1 rat ↓ rauw tpw8* rheum ↓ rhod ↓ rhus-t rhus-v rumx ruta fd4.de sars ↓ sep ↓ spong fd4.de stann ↓ staph ↓ sul-ac ↓ *Sulph* ↓ symph fd3.de• tab ↓ *Tarax* ↓ thuj ↓ *Valer* ↓ vanil fd5.de verat ↓ *Zinc* ↓
  - **right**: berb gard-j vlr2• hydrog srj2• nat-sil fd3.de• plb ↓ sacch-a fd2.de• spong fd4.de ulm-c ↓
    - **drawing** pain: plb bg2
    - **pressing** pain: gard-j vlr2•
    - **stitching** pain: ulm-c jsj8•
    - **walking** | **amel.**: psil ft1
  - **left**: ars-h dulc fd4.de gard-j vlr2• nat-p ruta fd4.de spong fd4.de symph fd3.de•
    - **accompanied** by | **dysuria**: *Agar*
  - **morning**: zinc ↓
    - **sore**: zinc h2
    - **tearing** pain: zinc
  - **afternoon**:
    - **walking** agg.: bry ↓
      - **stitching** pain: bry
  - **evening**: cortico ↓ lyc ↓
    - **bed** agg.; in: asar ↓ cortiso ↓
      - **drawing** pain: asar h1 cortiso tpw7
    - **drawing** pain: cortico sp1
    - **tearing** pain: lyc h2
  - **night**: alum gard-j vlr2• lyc ↓ mur-ac ↓ nit-ac ↓ phos ↓ spong fd4.de
    - **bed** agg.; in: bell ↓ chin ↓ *Sep* ↓
      - **burning**: bell chin k* *Sep*
    - **stitching** pain: lyc nit-ac
    - **tearing** pain: mur-ac h2 phos
  - **aching**: agath-a nl2• androc srj1• arg-met berb brom hep ip mez ptk1 plb polys sk4• rumx
  - **ascending** agg.: alum ↓
    - **drawing** pain: alum k*
  - **bending** knee agg.: calc-p castor-eq chin rhus-t spong fd4.de
    - **drawing** pain: *Rhus-t* k* spong fd4.de
    - **pressing** pain: spong h1
  - **burning**: am-c k* ars-h *Bar-c* berb k* castor-eq *Chel* grat k* ham fd3.de• indg *Iod* ketogl-ac rly4• lith-c petr k* sul-ac k* sulph thuj k*
    - **sore**: bar-c
  - **chill**; during: *Lyc* ↓
    - **stitching** pain: *Lyc*

- **Hollow** of knees: ...
  - **cold** agg.; hands becoming: am-c ↓
    - **burning**: am-c k*
  - **cutting** pain: sep k* thuj bg1
  - **drawing** pain: agn k* alum k* ang bg2 *Arg-met* k* *Bry* calc-p cann-s k* cann-xyz bg2 canth k* carb-an k* carbn-s *Caust* chin k* cortiso tpw7 *Cycl* k* graph ham fd3.de• kali-p fd1.de• *Led* lyc k* mag-c k* meny k* mosch k* mur-ac *Nat-m* k* nat-s k* nit-s-d a1 *Nux-v* ol-an k* ph-ac phel k* *Phyt* rhod k* *Rhus-t* k* ruta fd4.de spong fd4.de stann k* staph k* symph fd3.de• thuj verat k* zinc
    - **downward**: agar mosch phel stann symph fd3.de•
    - **jerking** pain: chin h1
    - **tearing** pain: nat-m k*
    - **trembling**: staph k*
  - **hot**: sulph ↓
    - **stitching** pain: sulph k*
  - **lying** down agg.: cortiso ↓ staph ↓
    - **drawing** pain: cortiso tpw7* staph k*
  - **motion**:
    - **agg.**: agn ↓ coloc ↓ hep ↓ *Nat-c* *Plb*
      - **pressing** pain: hep h2
      - **stitching** pain: agn coloc
    - **amel.**: nat-s ↓ staph ↓
      - **drawing** pain: nat-s k* staph
  - **paralyzed**; as if: con
  - **pinching** pain: bell h1 prun a1
  - **pressing** pain: alum k* arg-met h1 bell h1 brom chin k* gard-j vlr2• plat k* spong fd4.de *Sulph* k*
    - **alternating** with | **Axilla**; pressing in: spong h1
    - **cramping**: sulph
    - **downward**: rheum h *Sulph* k*
    - **drawing** pain: spong h1
    - **jerking** pain: spong h1
  - **pressure**:
    - **amel.**: arg-met ↓
      - **drawing** pain: arg-met
  - **pulsating** pain: coloc bg2 olnd
  - **rising** from sitting agg.: ars-h chin ↓ mur-ac ↓ *Nux-v* ↓ rat ↓ *Rhus-t* ↓
    - **burning**: chin h1
    - **drawing** pain: *Nux-v* *Rhus-t*
    - **stitching** pain: rat
    - **tearing** pain: mur-ac h2
  - **shooting** pain: agn arizon-l nl2• bell cupr-ar sulph
  - **sitting**:
    - **agg.**: arizon-l ↓ bar-c ↓ berb grat ↓ ham fd3.de• mang ↓ meny ↓ mur-ac ↓ nat-s ↓ plat ↓ spong fd4.de stann ↓ sulph ↓ tarax ↓
      - **burning**: bar-c grat k*
      - **drawing** pain: meny h1 mur-ac nat-s k*
      - **pressing** pain: plat k* sulph k*
      - **shooting** pain: arizon-l nl2• sulph
      - **stitching** pain: mang stann sulph
      - **tearing** pain: mur-ac tarax
    - **amel.**: *Valer* ↓ *Zinc* ↓
      - **tearing** pain: *Valer* *Zinc*
    - **crossed** legs; with:
      - **agg.**: *Lyc* ↓
        - **drawing** pain: *Lyc*
  - **sore**: ambr kali-n manc mez plb stann zinc h2
  - **standing** agg.: agn ↓ berb ↓ cortiso ↓ cycl a1 graph meny ↓ par rumx stroph-s ↓ verat ↓
    - **aching**: rumx stroph-s sp1
    - **drawing** pain: cortiso tpw7* cycl graph meny h1 verat h1
    - **shooting** pain: agn
    - **short**; as if tendons were too: graph
    - **stitching** pain: agn berb

- **Hollow** of knees: ...
  - **stitching** pain: agar agn ammc bell berb *Bry* carb-an carbn-s chel coc-c coloc cupr-ar mang merc-i-f mill nat-m ol-an plb rat sep stann sul-ac sulph symph fd3.de• tab thuj
  - **stretch**; inclination to: hydrog srj2•
  - **synchronous** with pulse: chin ↓
    - **drawing** pain: chin h1
  - **tearing** pain: ars berb calc calc-caust dulc fd4.de iod kali-c kali-n lyc h2 mag-c merl mez h2 *Mur-ac* nat-m ph-ac phos plb sars h2 symph fd3.de• *Tarax Valer Zinc*
    - **drawing** pain: ars
  - **walking**:
    - **agg.**: alum ↓ ars berb ↓ *Bry* ↓ carb-an ↓ card-m *Caust* chel colch fago gard-j vlr2• gels graph ↓ kali-n ↓ lac-h sk4• mag-c mang ↓ nat-ar nat-c k2 nat-m ↓ *Nux-v Phyt* ↓ rhod *Rhus-t* ruta ↓ spong fd4.de *Zinc* ↓
      - **drawing** pain: *Caust* graph mag-c k* nat-m *Nux-v Phyt* rhod k* ruta fd4.de spong fd4.de zinc
      - **pressing** pain: alum k* spong
      - **sore**: zinc h2
      - **stitching** pain: berb *Bry* carb-an mang
      - **tearing** pain: berb kali-n k* *Zinc*
    - **amel.**: grat ↓
      - **burning**: grat k*
    - **beginning** to walk: *Nit-ac*
  - **warm**; when: chin ↓
    - **burning**: chin k*
  - **extending** to:
    - **Calf**: mosch ↓ stann ↓ zinc ↓
      - **drawing** pain: mosch stann
      - **tearing** pain: zinc h2
    - **Downward**: *Alum* mang merl
    - **Heel**: *Alum*
    - **Hip**: mur-ac ↓
      - **tearing** pain: mur-ac h2
    - **Leg**: (non:carb-an st) (non:rhus-t st)
    - **Leg**; down back of: *Bar-c* ↓
      - **burning**: *Bar-c*
    - **Tendo** Achillis: kali-bi
    - **Thigh**: cortiso ↓ mag-c ↓ mez ↓ ph-ac ↓ verat ↓
      - **drawing** pain: cortiso tpw7* verat
      - **tearing** pain: mag-c mez h2 ph-ac
    - **Toes**: *Cycl* ↓
      - **drawing** pain: *Cycl* hr1
  - **Outer** side: ham ↓ staph ↓ tarax ↓
    - **drawing** pain: ham fd3.de• tarax h1
    - **pressing** pain: staph h1 tarax h1
  - **Tendons**: asar ↓ chin ↓
    - **drawing** pain: asar h1 chin h1
    - **Outer**: spong ↓
      - **pressing** pain: spong h1
- **Inner** side | **walking** agg.: cortico sp1
- **Joints**: bufo ↓ nat-m ↓
  - **nail**; as from a: nat-m bg2
  - **pulsating** pain: bufo bg2
- **Patella**: acon ↓ alum b4a.de am-c aml-ns *Arg-met* ↓ arn ↓ ars-h asaf bamb-a ↓ bar-c ↓ *Bar-m* ↓ bar-ox-suc ↓ bell berb bry cact calc k* *Camph* ↓ *Cann-s* ↓ *Carb-ac* carb-v ↓ caust ↓ cham ↓ chel chin ↓ chord-umb ↓ cina ↓ clem coc-c cocc ↓ *Colch* ↓ coli ↓ con ↓ crot-h ↓ cupr-ar ↓ cycl ↓ cyclosp sa3• dulc fd4.de ery-a ↓ fic-m ↓ gels ↓ goss ↓ graph ↓ ham fd3.de• hell ↓ kali-n kali-p ↓ kali-s fd4.de kalm kreos lac-ac lachn ↓ led manc ↓ melal-alt ↓ merl ↓ nat-c nat-m ↓ nicc ↓ *Nit-ac* petr ↓ ph-ac ↓ phos ↓ plect ↓ podo ↓ psor rhus-t ribo ↓ ruta fd4.de samb ↓ sarr sil ↓ spig ↓ staph ↓ stram stront-c ↓ *Sulph* ↓ symph fd3.de• taosc iwa1• tarax ↓ tep ↓ thlas bg1 thuj ↓ valer vanil fd5.de zinc
  - **right**: bamb-a ↓ bapt hr1 lachn ↓ nicc ↓ ulm-c jsj8•
    - **stitching** pain: bamb-a stb2.de• nicc
    - **tearing** pain: lachn a1

- **Patella**: ...
  - **left**: olib-sac ↓
    - **stitching** pain: olib-sac wmh1
  - **forenoon**: nat-c
    - **boring** pain: nat-c
  - **afternoon**: nicc ↓
    - **stitching** pain: nicc
  - **evening**: coc-c dulc fd4.de ruta fd4.de ulm-c jsj8• zinc
  - **night**: bamb-a ↓ caust ↓ zinc
    - **stitching** pain: bamb-a stb2.de•
    - **tearing** pain: caust
  - **aching**: acon calc chord-umb rly4• coc-c coli rly4• fic-m gya1 ribo rly4• tep
  - **ascending** stairs agg.: thuj ↓
    - **stitching** pain: thuj
  - **bending** knee agg.: hell ↓ nit-ac pyrog
    - **sore**: hell nit-ac h2
  - **boring** pain: am-c kreos led nat-c
  - **broken**; as if: bry k* con k*
  - **burning**: bar-c lachn c1 tarax thuj h1
  - **descending** stairs agg.: nit-ac ↓
    - **sore**: nit-ac
  - **dinner**; after: phos ↓
    - **tearing** pain: phos
  - **dislocated**; as if: arn b7a.de calc b4a.de *Cann-s* b7a.de gels ptk1 kali-n b4a.de nit-ac b4a.de *Rhus-t* b7a.de
  - **drawing** pain: berb k* calc h2 caust k* crot-h k* cycl k* goss a1 plect a1
  - **gouty**: crot-h ↓
    - **drawing** pain: crot-h k*
  - **jerking** pain: alum h2
  - **kneeling** agg.: *Bar-m* ↓ ruta ↓
    - **stitching** pain: *Bar-m* ruta fd4.de
  - **motion**:
    - **agg.**: aml-ns berb ↓ coc-c ery-a ph-ac ↓ staph ↓
      - **stitching** pain: ph-ac staph
      - **tearing** pain: berb
    - **amel.**: psor viol-t ↓
      - **stitching** pain: viol-t
      - **tearing** pain: psor
  - **paralyzed**; as if: kali-n
  - **pressing** pain: acon bg2 alum k* bell h1 calc h2 coc-c led k* podo fd3.de• *Sulph* k* vanil fd5.de
  - **pressure** agg.: coc-c
  - **rheumatic**: clem fic-m gya1
  - **rising**:
    - **sitting**; from | **after**:
      - **agg.**: carb-v ↓ ham ↓
        - **stitching** pain: carb-v ham fd3.de•
      - **agg.**: calc
  - **rubbing**:
    - **amel.**: manc ↓ phos ↓
      - **stitching** pain: manc
      - **tearing** pain: phos
  - **running** agg.: ulm-c jsj8•
  - **scraping** pain: samb
  - **shooting** pain: bell carb-v bg1 cupr-ar
  - **sitting**:
    - **agg.**: bell calc camph ↓ con ↓ kali-s fd4.de merl ↓ spig ↓
      - **stitching** pain: camph merl spig
      - **tearing** pain: con merl
    - **amel.**: arg-met ↓
      - **sore**: arg-met
  - **sore**: acon alum *Arg-met* bar-ox-suc rly4• bry *Carb-ac* chin chord-umb rly4• ery-a hell kali-p fd1.de• *Led* k* nit-ac petr sil
  - **sprained**; as if: calc h2 cycl a1 kali-n h2 nit-ac h2
  - **stepping** up or down: thlas bg1

Extremities

- **Patella**: ...
  - **stinging**: lachn$_{c1}$
  - **stitching** pain: bamb-a$_{stb2.de}$• *Bar-m* bell *Camph* carb-v cham cina coc-c cupr-ar dulc$_{fd4.de}$ graph ham$_{fd3.de}$• kali-s$_{fd4.de}$ kreos lac-ac lachn melal-alt$_{gya4}$ nat-m nicc ph-ac ruta$_{fd4.de}$ staph thuj
    - **burning**: asaf lachn
    - **drawing** pain: calc
    - **electric** sparks, like: coc-c melal-alt$_{gya4}$
    - **needles**; as from: manc$_{bg2}$
    - **tearing** pain: arg-met
    - **tensive**: spig
  - **tearing** pain: **Alum**$_{k*}$ arg-met$_{h1}$ berb carb-v$_{bg2}$ caust$_{k*}$ clem$_{k*}$ cocc$_{bg2}$ *Colch* con kali-p$_{fd1.de}$• kreos$_{k*}$ lachn merl phos$_{k*}$ psor$_{k*}$ staph$_{h1}$ stront-c$_{k*}$ *Sulph*$_{k*}$ zinc
    - **drawing** pain: cocc merl
    - **jerking** pain: chin$_{h1}$
  - **ulcerative** pain: asaf
  - **waking**; on: clem ↓
    - **tearing** pain: clem
  - **walking**:
    - **agg.**: acon arg-met ↓ berb calc ↓ coc-c coloc ↓ crot-h ↓ led *Nit-ac*$_{k*}$ petr-ra ↓
      - **drawing** pain: crot-h$_{k*}$
      - **sore**: arg-met *Led* nit-ac petr-ra$_{shn4}$•
      - **stitching** pain: calc coloc
    - **amel.**: sulph ↓
      - **tearing** pain: sulph$_{h2}$
    - **continued**:
      - **amel.**: coloc ↓
        - **stitching** pain: coloc
    - **level** ground; on:
      - **amel.**: nit-ac ↓
        - **sore**: nit-ac
  - **wandering** pain: psor
  - **extending** to:
    - **Back**: tarent
    - **Hip**: calc ↓
      - **stitching** pain: calc
    - **Leg**; into: berb ↓
      - **drawing** pain: berb$_{k*}$
  - **Below**: arg-n ↓ calc-act ↓ streptoc ↓ zinc ↓
    - **boring** pain: arg-n$_{a1}$
    - **sore**: calc-act$_{h1}$ streptoc$_{rly4}$• zinc$_{h2}$
  - **Tendon**: *Chel* ham$_{fd3.de}$• *Zinc*
    - **walking** agg.: *Zinc*
- **Side**; lateral | **cutting** pain (See sides - outer - cutting)
- **Sides**: puls ↓
  - **sore**: puls$_{h1}$
  - **Inner**: alum ↓ bamb-a ↓ bar-c ↓ berb ↓ bry ↓ calc ↓ canth ↓ cham ↓ cinnb ↓ euph ↓ ham ↓ laur ↓ meny ↓ nat-m ↓ ol-an ↓ ran-b ↓ sars ↓ stann ↓ staph ↓ zinc ↓
    - **morning**: ammc ↓
      - **stitching** pain: ammc
    - **dinner**; after: grat ↓
      - **stitching** pain: grat
    - **motion**:
      - **amel.**: zinc ↓
        - **stitching** pain: zinc
    - **sitting** agg.: euph ↓ plb ↓
      - **stitching** pain: euph plb
    - **standing** agg.: thuj ↓
      - **stitching** pain: thuj
    - **stepping**:
      - **every** step; at: phos ↓
        - **stitching** pain: phos
    - **stitching** pain: bamb-a$_{stb2.de}$• bar-c berb bry canth cham cinnb euph ham$_{fd3.de}$• laur meny sars staph zinc

\- **Knees – Sides – Inner – stitching** pain: ...
      - **nails**; as from: nat-m
    - **tearing** pain: alum bar-c calc ol-an ran-b stann$_{h2}$
    - **walking**:
      - **agg.**: ran-b ↓ rhus-t ↓
        - **stitching** pain: rhus-t
        - **tearing** pain: ran-b
      - **amel.**: bar-c ↓
        - **tearing** pain: bar-c
    - **extending** to:
      - **Toes**:
        - **First**: carbn-s ↓
          - **stitching** pain: carbn-s
  - **Outer**: ant-c ↓ canth ↓ caust ↓ cham ↓ cortico ↓ hep ↓ hyper ↓ iod ↓ kali-i ↓ kali-n ↓ merl ↓ nicc ↓ sabad ↓ spig ↓ stann ↓ staph ↓ symph ↓ tarax ↓ thuj ↓
    - **ascending** stairs agg.: cortico ↓
      - **cutting** pain: cortico$_{sp1}$
    - **cutting** pain: cortico$_{tpw7}$
    - **extension**; extreme: cortico ↓
      - **cutting** pain: cortico$_{sp1}$
    - **flexion**; extreme: cortico ↓
      - **cutting** pain: cortico$_{sp1}$
    - **pressure** agg.: cortico ↓
      - **cutting** pain: cortico$_{sp1}$
    - **riding** a bicycle: cortico ↓
      - **cutting** pain: cortico$_{sp1}$
    - **sitting** agg.: kali-i ↓ sabad ↓
      - **stitching** pain: sabad
      - **tearing** pain: kali-i
    - **standing** agg.: nicc ↓ stann ↓
      - **stitching** pain: nicc stann
    - **stitching** pain: ant-c cham nicc sabad stann staph symph$_{fd3.de}$• tarax thuj
      - **burning**: merl staph
    - **tearing** pain: canth caust hep hyper iod kali-i kali-n spig$_{h1}$
    - **touch** agg.: staph ↓
      - **stitching** pain: staph
    - **walking** agg.: cham ↓ cocc ↓ cortico ↓ nit-ac ↓ staph ↓
      - **cutting** pain: cortico$_{sp1}$
      - **stitching** pain: cham cocc nit-ac staph
- **Tendons**: ant-t ↓ berb ↓ con ↓ euphr ↓ merl ↓ nat-m ↓ ph-ac ↓ phos ↓ raph ↓ *Rhus-t* ↓ samb ↓ sep ↓
  - **evening**: ant-t ↓
    - **stitching** pain: ant-t
  - **motion** agg.: ph-ac ↓ *Rhus-t* ↓
    - **stitching** pain: ph-ac *Rhus-t*
  - **rising** from sitting agg.: *Rhus-t* ↓
    - **stitching** pain: *Rhus-t*
  - **sore**: sep$_{h2}$
  - **standing** agg.: berb ↓
    - **stitching** pain: berb
  - **stitching** pain: ant-t berb con euphr merl nat-m ph-ac phos raph *Rhus-t* samb
  - **touch** agg.: *Rhus-t* ↓
    - **stitching** pain: *Rhus-t*
  - **walking**:
    - **agg.**: ant-t ↓ berb ↓ euphr ↓
      - **stitching** pain: ant-t berb euphr
    - **air** agg.; in open: con ↓
      - **stitching** pain: con

\- **Legs**: abrot acet-ac acon$_{b7a.de}$ *Aesc* aeth ↓ **Agar**$_{k*}$ agath-a ↓ agn ↓ aids ↓ allox ↓ *Alum* alum-p$_{k2}$ alum-sil$_{k2}$ alumn ↓ am-c am-m *Ambr* ↓ *Anac* anag ↓ *Ang* ↓ anis$_{bro1}$ ant-c ↓ ant-t ↓ anthraq ↓ ap-g ↓ *Apis* ↓ *Apoc* aran$_{bro1}$ arg-met ↓ *Arg-n* ↓ *Arn* *Ars* ars-h ↓ ars-s-f$_{k2}$ arund ↓ *Asaf* ↓ asar ↓ asc-t aster ↓ atra-r$_{bnm3}$• atro ↓ *Aur* ↓ aur-ar ↓ aur-m ↓ bad bamb-a$_{stb2.de}$• bapt bar-act ↓ bar-c bar-i ↓ bar-s$_{k2}$ **Bell**$_{k*}$ bell-p ↓ benz-ac berb bism ↓ blatta-o bol-la ↓ borx ↓ bov brach ↓ brom ↓ *Bry* ↓ but-ac ↓ cadm-met$_{tpw6}$ cadm-s ↓

- **Legs**: ...
calad ↓ calc bg3 calc-f ↓ calc-p calc-sil ↓ camph ↓ cann-i bro1 cann-s ↓ canth ↓ *Caps* k* *Carb-ac* ↓ *Carb-an* c2* carb-v carbn-s k* carc jl2* card-m ↓ cardios-h ↓ carl ↓ castor-eq ↓ caul *Caust* cench ↓ cham k* chel bro1 *Chin* ↓ chinin-ar ↓ chinin-s ↓ chir-fl ↓ chlol ↓ chlor ↓ choc ↓ chord-umb ↓ cic bro1 cimic ↓ *Cimx* cina cinnb cist ↓ clem ↓ cob ↓ coc-c cocc *Coff* colch coloc com ↓ *Con* ↓ conv ↓ cot ↓ croc b7.de* crot-c crot-h ↓ crot-t ↓ cupr b7.de* *Cycl* ↓ cystein-l ↓ dig ↓ digin ↓ dios k* dirc ↓ dros b7.de* *Dulc* echi ↓ eug ↓ *Eup-per* euph bro1 euphr ↓ eys ↓ fago falco-pe ↓ ferr bro1 ferr-act ↓ ferr-i ↓ ferr-m ↓ ferr-s ↓ fl-ac form gamb ↓ *Gels* k* glon *Gnaph* bro1 goss ↓ *Graph* ↓ grat ↓ **Guaj** guare ↓ gymno ham ↓ hell helo bro1 helo-s rwt2• *Hep* ↓ heroin ↓ hip-ac ↓ hipp ↓ hippoc-k ↓ hir rsj4• hura ↓ *Hydr* hyos ↓ *Hyper* ↓ ign b7a.de ina-i ↓ ind ↓ indg k* *Iod* k* **Ip** ↓ irid-met bro1 jac-c jac-g jug-r ↓ kali-ar *Kali-bi* k* kali-br ↓ *Kali-c* k* *Kali-i* kali-m ↓ *Kali-n* kali-p ↓ **Kali-s** kali-sil ↓ *Kalm* k* *Kreos* *Lac-ac* ↓ lac-c ↓ lac-h sk4• lac-leo sk4• **Lach** k* lachn ↓ lact ↓ lat-h bnm5• lat-m bnm6• laur ↓ *Led* lil-t ↓ *Lob* ↓ loxo-recl bnm10• luf-op ↓ *Lyc* k* lycpr ↓ lycps-v lyss m-ambo ↓ m-arct ↓ m-aust ↓ mag-c mag-m bro1 mag-p ↓ mag-s malar jl2 manc mand rsj7• *Mang* ↓ mang-act bro1 mang-o bro1 med ↓ medul-os-si rly4• melal-alt gya4 menis bro1 *Meny* ↓ meph ↓ *Merc* merc-c merc-i-f merl *Mez* k* mill ↓ morg-p ↓ mosch ↓ *Mur-ac* ↓ murx k* naja nat-ar nat-c nat-m nat-p nat-s bro1 nicc ↓ nit-ac k* nit-s-d ↓ *Nux-m* *Nux-v* ol-an ↓ ol-j ↓ olnd ↓ op osm ↓ ozone ↓ pall ↓ par ↓ *Petr* petr-ra ↓ ph-ac k* phasco-ci rbp2 *Phos* k* phys *Phyt* pic-ac bro1 plac-s ↓ plan ↓ *Plat* *Plb* k* plect ↓ plut-n ↓ pneu jl2 podo polys ↓ propr sa3• prun ↓ psil ↓ psor ↓ ptel ↓ *Puls* k* *Pyrog* ran-b ↓ ran-s ↓ raph ↓ rat ↓ rauw ↓ rheum ↓ **Rhod** k* **Rhus-t** k* *Rhus-v* ribo ↓ rumx ruta fd4.de sabad ↓ sabin bro1 samb ↓ *Sang* sarcol-ac ↓ sarr *Sars* ↓ sec ↓ sel ↓ senec ↓ *Sep* sil bg3* sin-n ↓ sol-t-ae ↓ spect ↓ *Spig* ↓ spong fd4.de squil ↓ *Stann* *Staph* still ↓ stram ↓ stront-c ↓ stroph-s ↓ *Stry* suis-em ↓ suis-pan ↓ sul-ac ↓ sul-i ↓ *Sulph* sumb ↓ symph fd3.de• *Syph* tab ↓ *Tarax* ↓ tarent tax ↓ tep ↓ ter tere-la ↓ teucr thal-xyz ↓ thuj til ↓ tong bro1 trif-p bro1 tritic-vg fd5.de *Tub* tub-r ↓ tung-met ↓ ulm-c ↓ *Vac* jl2 valer vanil fd5.de *Vario* ↓ *Verat* verat-v ↓ verb ↓ vib bro1 viol-t ↓ *Vip* bro1 visc ↓ x-ray ↓ xan *Zinc* ↓ zinc-p k2

- **right**: abrom-a ks5 *Agar* ↓ benz-ac bov *Brucel* sa3• *Chel* ↓ hydrog ↓ iod ↓ kali-p ↓ limest-b ↓ melal-alt gya4 nat-c hr1 nat-m ↓ olib-sac wmh1 pert-vc vk9 petr-ra shn4• rat ↓ spong fd4.de stict ↓ sulfa sp1 trios rsj11• tritic-vg fd5.de vanil fd5.de visc c1
  - **aching**: limest-b es1• melal-alt gya4
  - **burning**: *Agar* k*
  - **drawing** pain: *Agar* *Chel* kali-p fd1.de• nat-m h2
  - **shooting** pain: iod
    - **downward**: hydrog srj2•
  - **stitching** pain: petr-ra shn4• stict tritic-vg fd5.de vanil fd5.de
  - **tearing** pain: petr-ra shn4• rat tritic-vg fd5.de
- **left**: cassia-s ↓ colch rsj2• dirc a1 dulc fd4.de hir skp7• mand rsj7• medul-os-si rly4• mim-p ↓ nat-c polys ↓ propr sa3• v-a-b ↓ vanil fd5.de
  - **aching**: mand rsj7• polys sk4•
  - **cramping**: mim-p rsj8• v-a-b jl2
  - **lying**:
    - **side**; on:
      - **left** | **agg.**: hir skp7•
  - **tearing** pain: cassia-s ccrh1•
  - **extending** to | **Downward**: dirc a1
  - **Lateral** side: ulm-c ↓
    - **waves**; in: ulm-c jsj8•
- **daytime**: murx
- **morning**: aesc agar ambr ↓ ang ↓ aran ↓ ars ↓ aur dios dulc fd4.de *Eup-pur* indg ↓ lach led nat-s ↓ polys sk4• prun ↓ rhod stront-c ↓ *Sulph* symph ↓ tritic-vg fd5.de vanil fd5.de verat a1
  - **8** h: lach ↓
    - **aching**: lach
  - **9** h | **amel.**: hir skp7•
  - **aching**: agar aur
  - **bed** agg.; in: **Caust** ↓ ferr ↓ psor sulph ↓
    - **sore**: **Caust** ferr
    - **tearing** pain: sulph k*
  - **boring** pain: aran
  - **burning**: agar k* nat-s sulph k* tritic-vg fd5.de
  - **clawing**: stront-c k*
  - **cramping**: ars h2
- **morning**: ...
  - **drawing** pain: ang k* ars k* indg k* *Sulph* tritic-vg fd5.de vanil fd5.de
  - **exertion** agg.; after: sulph ↓
    - **burning**: sulph
  - **pressing** pain: led k* tritic-vg fd5.de
  - **rising** agg.; after: plb ↓
    - **sore**: plb
  - **sore**: prun a1 symph fd3.de•
  - **tearing** pain: ambr dulc sulph k*
  - **waking**; on: aur kali-n ↓ kali-p symph ↓ vanil fd5.de
    - **aching**: aur
    - **sore**: kali-n symph fd3.de•
- **forenoon**: mand sp1 ptel ↓ sil ↓
  - **aching**: ptel
  - **tearing** pain: sil
- **noon**: com ↓ sulph ↓
  - **aching**: com
  - **tearing** pain: sulph k*
- **afternoon**: alumn ↓ *Coff* dulc fd4.de elaps erig ↓ indg ↓ led ↓ lyc ↓ lycps-v nicc ↓ nux-m nux-v ↓ podo ptel rumx ruta ↓ sep spong fd4.de sulph ↓ vanil fd5.de
  - **14**-17 h: sil ↓
    - **tearing** pain: sil
  - **16**.30 h: sal-al blc1•
  - **aching**: erig lycps-v ptel sep
  - **drawing** pain: elaps ruta fd4.de vanil fd5.de
  - **sitting** agg.: alumn ↓ sulph ↓
    - **burning**: sulph k*
    - **stitching** pain: alumn
  - **stitching** pain: lyc
  - **tearing** pain: alumn indg led nicc k* nux-v sulph
  - **walking** agg.: nicc ↓
    - **tearing** pain: nicc k*
- **evening**: agar ↓ alum ↓ ant-c ↓ arg-met ↓ ars bar-c ↓ bry ↓ caust cham ↓ chel cinnb crot-h cycl ↓ dulc fd4.de erig ↓ *Ferr* ↓ fl-ac hir skp7• kali-bi ↓ kali-i ↓ kali-n kalm lac-ac ↓ lach ↓ led ↓ lyc lyss ↓ mag-c ↓ mag-m ↓ merc-c nat-c ↓ *Nat-s* ↓ nicc ↓ *Phos* plan **Puls** rat ↓ ruta ↓ sang ↓ seneg ↓ *Sil* ↓ spong fd4.de staph *Still* ↓ *Sulph* uran-n ↓ vanil fd5.de zinc ↓
  - **18** h: elaps ptel
    - **18**-19 h: rauw tpw8
  - **19** h: nat-ar
  - **22** h: fago ↓
    - **aching**: fago
  - **aching**: erig *Still* *(non:*uran-met k*)* uran-n
  - **bed** agg.; in: alum *Ferr* ↓ puls ↓ staph
    - **shooting** pain: *Ferr*
    - **sore**: puls h1
    - **stitching** pain: alum *Ferr*
  - **burning**: agar k* *Nat-s* sang k* seneg k* sulph k*
  - **drawing** pain: ant-c k* arg-met bar-c k* caust k* cham k* cycl h1 fl-ac k* lyc k* mag-c h2 nat-c h2 phos k* **Puls** k* rat ruta fd4.de *Sil* k* *Sulph* zinc k*
  - **pressing** pain: lach k*
  - **sitting** agg.: nat-s ↓
    - **pressing** pain: nat-s k*
  - **sore**: alum bry lyss mag-m
  - **stitching** pain: *Ferr* lac-ac lyc ruta fd4.de vanil fd5.de
  - **tearing** pain: alum k* caust kali-bi kali-i kali-n led *Lyc* k* nicc k* *Sulph* k*
  - **walking** agg.: hir skp7•
- **night**: abrom-a ks5 **Agar** *Alum* ↓ am-m anac ↓ anag ↓ aur pd aur-m k2 *Bar-c* carb-an ↓ caust cham ↓ *Coff* croc *Ferr* ↓ gels ↓ kali-bi *Kali-c* *Kali-i* kali-p ↓ lac-h sk4• lyc med br1 **Merc** mez mur-ac **Nit-ac** nux-v ↓ *Petr* petr-ra shn4• *Ph-ac* *Phos* **Phyt** *Plb* *Rhus-t* sec sep ↓ spong suis-em ↓ *Sulph* syc pte1*• symph ↓ **Syph** thuj tritic-vg ↓ *Tub* ↓ verat ↓
  - **midnight**: lyc ↓

Extremities

- **night** – **midnight**: ...
  - **before**:
    - **22** h: form ↓
      - **tearing** pain: form
    - **23** h: com ↓ mill ↓
      - **drawing** pain: com mill
  - **after** | **5** h: kali-p
  - **tearing** pain: lyc
  - **aching**: caust med suis-em rly4•
  - **amel.**: *Puls*
  - **ascending** stairs agg.: *Ars* ↓ thuj ↓
    - **broken**; as if: *Ars* thuj
  - **bed** agg.; in: *Phos* syph k2
  - **broken**; as if: *Merc* symph fd3.de•
  - **burning**: sep
  - **drawing** pain: anac carb-an k* cham k* kali-c h2 kali-p fd1.de• *Lyc* k* ph-ac h2 phos k* syph jl2 thuj k* tritic-vg fd5.de *Tub* verat k*
  - **preventing** sleep: ange-s ↓
    - **aching**: ange-s oss1•
  - **sore**: gels *Merc* *Mez* nux-v sulph
  - **tearing** pain: *Alum* am-m h2 anag *Ferr* kali-c h2 *Lyc* k* *Merc* **Nit-ac** sulph k*
  - **waking** and turning in bed; on: carb-an ↓
    - **broken**; as if: carb-an
- **accompanied** by | **Head**; complaints of (See HEAD - Complaints - accompanied - leg - pain)
- **aching**: aesc agar agath-a nl2• aids nl2• allox sp1 alum alum-p k2 alum-sil k2 anac arg-n bro1 *Arn* bro1 *Ars* aur aur-ar k2 bapt k* bol-la *Bry* but-ac sp1 calc bro1 *Carb-ac* *Carb-an* carc sp1 chel chir-fl gya2 chlol cimic bro1 cocc bro1 *Colch* bro1 com conv br1 dios k* *Eup-per* k* fago ferr-s fl-ac gamb *Gels* bro1 guaj bro1 ham **Ip** *Kali-c* *Kali-i* kali-sil k2 *Lac-ac* **Lach** lat-m bnm6• laur k* *Led* lil-t k* luf-op rsj5• lycpr bro1 mag-c bro1 med k* melal-alt gya4 *Merc* merc-i-f morg-p pte1• *Mur-ac* **Ph-ac** k* phos *Phyt* polys sk4• ptel puls **Pyrog** k* **Rhus-t** k* rumx sabin bro1 sarcol-ac bro1 sep k* sil sin-n staph bro1 still stroph-s sp1 suis-em rly4• suis-pan rly4• sul-i sumb syph tere-la rly4• **Tub** tung-met bdx1• ulm-c bro1 vac *Vario* bro1 verat-v x-ray sp1 zinc [spect dfg1]
  - **corns**; as from: asc-t k*
  - **wandering** pain: chinin-ar
- **air**; in open:
  - **agg.**: **Caust** ↓ con ↓ graph ↓
    - **drawing** pain: *Caust* k* graph k*
    - **tearing** pain: **Caust** k* con h2
  - **amel.**: *Mez* ↓
    - **drawing** pain: *Mez*
- **alternating** with:
  - **Feet**; cold: rhus-t
  - **Head**; heaviness of: hell
- **arthritic**: sil ↓
  - **tearing** pain: sil k*
- **ascending** stairs agg.: bad dulc fd4.de nat-m ↓
  - **sore**: bad nat-m
- **bed** agg.; in: ign ↓ *Lyc* ↓
  - **drawing** pain: ign k* *Lyc*
- **bending** | **backward**:
  - **agg.**: clem ↓
    - **drawing** pain: clem k*
  - **knee** | **amel.**: cadm-met tpw6
- **blow**; pain as from a: agar b4.de* anac b4.de* arn b7.de* euph b4.de* hep b4.de* mez b4.de* plat b4.de*
- **blowing** the nose agg.: graph ↓
  - **stitching** pain: graph
- **boring** pain: aeth *Anac* k* aran arn b7.de* ars bov caust hell *Ign* merc k* merc-i-f mez *Nux-m* phos rhod sil stann staph b7.de* sulph k*
- **broken**; as if: ang b7.de* carb-an k* graph k* hep bg1 nat-s bg2 symph fd3.de• thuj vac valer c1 *Verat* k*
  - **would** break; as if it: thuj rb2
- **burning**: *Agar* k* alum k* anac k* ang b7.de ant-c b7.de *Apis* arg-met b7.de **Ars** k* arund bro1 *Asaf* k* bapt bar-c bro1 bell k* berb k* borx k* bov k* cadm-met sp1 calc k* calc-f sp1 cann-s b7.de castor-eq caust k* chel k* chin b7.de chir-fl gya2 coc-c k* con crot-c mre1.fr crot-h k* dig k* dros tl1 dulc fd4.de eys sp1 guaj b4a.de hip-ac sp1 hyos k* jug-r k* *Kali-bi* k* kali-br k* *Kali-c* k* *Led* k* lyc k* m-ambo b7.de m-arct b7.de *Mag-c* b4a.de mang h2 meny b7.de merc-c k* merl k* mez k* nat-c k* *Nat-s* k* nux-v b7.de pall k* *Petr* *Ph-ac* b4a.de *Pic-ac* plac-s rly4• prun k* psil ft1 puls b7.de ran-s b7.de rauw sp1 rhus-t k* sabad b7a.de sec mrr1 *Sep* k* spig b7.de staph b7.de* still bro1 stront-c k* *Sulph* k* tarax k* tarent k* tep k* thuj tritic-vg fd5.de verat b7.de *Zinc* k*
  - **sparks**; as from: anac
- **burrowing**: arn b7.de* bov b4.de* cina b7.de* *Rhod* b4.de* spig b7.de* stann b4.de*
- **bursting**; sensation as if: caust bg2 ham bg2 lac-c bg2 merc bg2 sep bg2 staph bg2 *Vip* bg2
- **chill**:
  - **before**: *Eup-per* eup-pur *Nux-v* ↓ *Puls*
    - **aching**: *Eup-per* puls
    - **drawing** pain: *Nux-v* k*
  - **during**: *Ars* k* calc bg2 *Cimx* **Eup-per** ↓ *Ferr* ↓ kali-n ↓ lyc k* *Nat-m* nux-v ↓ *Puls* k* **Pyrog** **Rhus-t** ↓ sep k* *Spong* *Sulph* ↓ tub
    - **aching**: **Eup-per** *Nat-m* nux-v **Rhus-t** *Tub*
    - **drawing** pain: *Puls* *Rhus-t* *Tub*
    - **stitching** pain: ferr lyc
    - **tearing** pain: *Ars* *Ferr* kali-n h2 *Rhus-t* *Sulph* *Tub*
- **cold**:
  - **air** agg.: ars *Kalm* *Rhus-t* tub
  - **amel.**: sec ↓
    - **burning**: sec mrr1
  - **applications** | **amel.**: *Led* *Puls* *Syph* thuj
- **cold**; after taking a: *Iod*
- **cold** agg.; becoming: *Agar* *Dulc* *Kalm* ph-ac *Phos* *Rhus-t* *Tub*
  - **drawing** pain: *Phos*
- **contracting**: anthraq rly4• sul-ac h2
- **cough** | **during** | **agg.**: bell caps *Nux-v* *Sulph*
  - **with**: *Carb-an* ↓
    - **aching**: *Carb-an*
- **cramping**: cardios-h rly4• falco-pe nl2• hep h2 hippoc-k szs2 meny h1 nit-ac h2 ruta fd4.de spong fd4.de sul-ac h2 tub jl2 tub-r jl2
- **crossing** legs agg.: anag kali-n ↓ nux-v ↓ phos *Rhus-t*
  - **bed** agg.; in: *Phos* ↓
    - **drawing** pain: *Phos*
  - **drawing** pain: kali-n h2
  - **stitching** pain: nux-v phos
- **crural** neuralgia (See thighs - crural)
- **cry** out, causes him to: sep
- **cutting** pain: agar *Anac* ars-h bell k* calc k* coloc k* con dros b7.de* gamb guare ign b7.de* lyc b4a.de mur-ac k* ph-ac k* *Plat* *Rhus-t* *Thuj* k*
  - **paroxysmal**: thuj
- **diarrhea**: manc
- **dinner** | **after**:
    - **agg.**: agar ↓
      - **burning**: agar k*
  - **agg.**: sulph
- **dislocated**; as if: alum bg2 calc b4.de* meny b7.de*
- **drawing** pain: acon k* *Agar* k* agn b7.de* *Alum* k* am-c k* *Am-m* *Anac* k* ang b7.de* ant-c k* arg-met arg-n arn b7.de* *Ars* k* asaf k* *Bapt* k* *Bar-c* k* bar-s k2 *Bell* k* bism b7.de* borx *Bry* k* calad b7.de* *Calc* k* calc-sil k2 camph canth b7.de* caps b7.de* carb-an k* carb-v k* carbn-s *Caul* k* *Caust* k* cham k* **Chel** k* chin k* cic k* cina cist clem coloc k* con k* croc b7.de* crot-h k* *Cycl* k* dig k* digin a1 dros b7.de* dulc k* euph a1 euphr b7.de* *Ferr* k* ferr-m k* fl-ac k* *Gels* goss k* graph k* *Guaj* k* ham k* hell k* *Hep* k* hyos ign b7.de* indg a1 iod jug-r a1 kali-bi k* *Kali-c* k* kali-m k2 kali-n k* kali-p kali-s kali-sil k2 kreos k* lach k* lact *Led* k* *Lyc* k* m-ambo b7.de m-aust b7.de *Mag-c* k* mang k* *Meny* k* meph a1 *Merc* k* merc-c *Mez* k* mosch k* mur-ac k* nat-c k* *Nat-m* k*

- **drawing** pain: ...
  Nat-s k* nit-ac nit-s-d a1 nux-m b7.de* *Nux-v* k* ol-an k* olnd k* par b7.de* petr ph-ac k* phos k* phyt k* plat k* **Puls** k* ran-b b7.de* ran-s b7.de* rat k* *Rhod* k* **Rhus-t** k* *Rhus-v* k* ruta fd4.de sabad k* sabin b7a.de sars k* *Sep* k* *Sil* k* sol-t-ae k* spig b7.de* spong k* squil k* stann k* staph k* stront-c k* stry k* sulph k* symph fd3.de• *Tarax* k* thuj k* til k* tritic-vg fd5.de *Tub* k* valer b7.de* vanil fd5.de viol-t k* zinc k* zinc-p k2
  - **burning**: rat
  - **cramping**: anac h2 caust chin cina dulc h2 graph hep h2 *Meny* mosch nat-c nat-m h2 petr ph-ac h2 rhod
  - **downward**: anac h2 bism h1 calc dulc h2 kali-c lach lyc bg1 mag-c mag-m meph a1 rhod sil h2 spig thuj h1
  - **jerking** pain: cic a1 thuj h1
  - **paralyzed**; as if: acon k* agn k* arg-met bell k* chel hep hyos k* kali-c h2 meny nat-m k* nit-ac *Phos* plect a1 *Rhus-v* ruta h1
  - **paroxysmal**: merc k* ph-ac k* thuj k*
  - **upward**: carb-an h2 lach lact meny h1 nat-m h2 nit-ac
- **drawing** up limb amel.: cinnb ↓
  - **drawing** pain: cinnb
- **dull** pain: vanil fd5.de [tax jsj7]
- **eating**:
  - **after** | **agg.**: *Kali-c*
  - **amel.**: *Nat-c* ↓
    - **stitching** pain: *Nat-c*
  - **while**:
    - **agg.**: ph-ac
      - **tearing** pain: ph-ac k*
- **elevation** of feet amel.: bar-c dios
- **ending** in jerking: *Sil* ↓
  - **drawing** pain: *Sil*
- **exertion** | **after** | **agg.**: ign a1* (non:ing a1) *Nat-m* sul-ac
  - **agg.**: lycps-v
- **exertion**; as after: apis b7a.de arg-met b7.de* coloc b4.de* mosch b7.de* olnd b7.de* puls b7.de* sul-ac b4.de*
- **fatigue**, after: clem ↓
  - **sore**: clem
- **fever** | **during**:
  - **agg.**: puls ↓ *Pyrog* ↓ **Rhus-t** ↓ **Tub** ↓
    - **aching**: puls *Pyrog* **Rhus-t Tub**
  - **with**: alum-sil k2 **Am-c** bg2 calc bg2 *Lyc* bg2 *Puls* k* pyrog k2 ran-a ran-s **Rhus-t** sep bg2 sil bg2 *Spong* staph bg2
- **flexing**, on: medul-os-si rly4• plan
  - **foot**: bad
- **gnawing** pain: alum k* ars k* *Aur* k* aur-ar k2 bell brom k* choc srj3• euph b4.de* *Kali-i* k* laur b7.de* nat-c k* nit-ac phys k* stront-c tarax k* zinc bg2
- **gouty**: anan *Apis Bry* psor sars
- **growing** pains: *(↗GENERALS - Pain - growing)* agar k2* ap-g lmj asaf ih1.de *Aur* lmj bell k* *Calc* lmj calc-f lmj calc-p k2* cench lmj cimic k* dros lmj *Eup-per* ferr-act lmj fl-ac ggd **Guaj** hep lmj hipp lmj kali-p dm* m-aust st1 mag-p dm* mang dm* *Merc* lmj morg-p pte1• nat-p lmj nit-ac lmj ol-j lmj **Ph-ac** k* **Phos** lmj plan ggd sulph lmj *Syph* lmj
- **hang** down agg.; letting arms: bar-c graph ↓ hep *Puls* spong fd4.de
  - **burning**: graph h2
- **jerking** pain: agar bg2 alum bg2 am-c anac k* ars bg2 bell bg2 bov bg2 camph bg2 cinnb clem bg2 dig bg2 dros bg2 euphr bg2 *Ip* bg2 kali-bi bg2 kali-c bg2 laur bg2 led bg2 mez nat-m bg2 nit-ac phos k* plat b4.de* *Puls* bg2 rat *Rhus-t* k* ruta bg2 sep b4a.de* spig bg2 spong bg2 stann bg2 staph bg2 sul-ac b4.de teucr bg2 valer bg2 *Verat* bg2
- **labor**-like: carb-v
- **lying**:
  - **agg.**: *Alum* ↓ am-m ↓ calc *Kali-i* mand sp1 ruta fd4.de vanil fd5.de
    - **drawing** pain: am-m gsy1
    - **tearing** pain: *Alum*
  - **quietly** | **amel.**: sulfonam ks2
- **lying**: ...
  - **side**; on:
    - **left**:
      - **agg.**: com ↓
        - **aching**: com
- **lying** down agg.: alum ↓ calc ↓ stront-c ↓
  - **clawing**: stront-c a1
  - **sore**: alum calc
- **menses** | **after**:
  - **agg.**: calc-p
    - **aching**: calc-p
  - **during**:
    - **agg.**: abrom-a ks5 *Ambr Bell* bov carb-an cham ↓ con mag-m ↓ petr ↓ raph ↓ spong stram ↓
      - **aching**: ambr
      - **drawing** pain: *Con* spong k*
      - **pressing** pain: ambr b7.de* carb-an k*
      - **sore**: petr
      - **stitching** pain: raph
      - **tearing** pain: cham b7.de mag-m k* spong b7.de stram b7.de
- **motion**:
  - **agg.**: acon alum berb *Bufo* ↓ *Carbn-s Colch* coloc ↓ con ↓ dig ↓ *Gels* ↓ *Guaj* iod kali-br *Kalm* laur merc merc-i-r ↓ nux-v op *Puls* ↓ sars ↓ *Staph Tarax* vanil fd5.de
    - **aching**: dig laur merc-i-r
    - **cutting** pain: con
    - **drawing** pain: *Gels* iod k* vanil fd5.de
    - **rapid** motion: carc mg1.de*
    - **sore**: *Bufo* dig nux-v *Puls*
    - **stitching** pain: coloc merc sars
  - **amel.**: *Agar Alum* ↓ arg-met ↓ **Bell** ↓ coloc dios *Dulc* ferr ↓ *Gels* indg *Iod* ↓ *Kali-c* ↓ *Kali-p* **Kali-s** kalm ↓ lac-h sk4• *Lyc* ↓ *Mur-ac* ↓ nit-ac ph-ac ↓ plan **Puls** *Pyrog Rat* ↓ *Rhod* **Rhus-t** sil ↓ *Tarax* ↓ *Tub* visc c1
    - **aching**: dios *Mur-ac* puls **Rhus-t**
    - **drawing** pain: *Iod* ph-ac **Puls Rhod Rhus-t** *Tarax*
    - **stitching** pain: alum *Kali-c Kali-s Lyc Rhus-t Tub*
    - **tearing** pain: agar *Alum* arg-met **Bell** ferr kalm *Rat Rhod* **Rhus-t** sil *Tarax Tub*
  - **gentle** motion | **amel.**: carc mg1.de*
- **neuralgic**: ars dirc kalm nat-ar thal-xyz srj8•
- **numbness** in the other; with: sil
  - **tearing** pain: *Sil*
- **paralyzed**; as if: acon k* *Agar* agn b7.de* am-c k* ang b7.de* bar-c bell b4.de* carb-v b4.de* cham chel chin k* cina b7.de* cocc k* cycl b7.de* eug ign b7.de* kali-bi bg2 kali-c b4.de* kali-n k* m-aust b7.de mag-m b4.de* meny b7.de* mez b4.de* mosch k* nat-m k* *Nit-ac* nux-v b7.de* petr b4.de* *Phos* k* puls b7.de* ruta k* staph b7.de* stront-c sul-ac sulph
- **paroxysmal**: cocc *Gels* plb *Rhod* **Rhus-t** sul-ac thuj
- **perspiration**; during: acon bg2 *Am-c* bg2 bell bg2 bry bg2 **Calc** bg2 graph bg2 ign bg2 *Lyc* bg2 merc bg2 mez bg2 nux-v bg2 ph-ac bg2 puls bg2 **Sep** bg2 sil bg2 staph bg2 *Sulph* bg2
- **pinching** pain: (non:hyos kl) nux-m k* ph-ac h2 sabad k* sil k* valer b7.de*
  - **stitching** pain: hyos h1
- **pregnancy** agg.; during: verat ↓
  - **tearing** pain: verat
- **pressing** pain: *Agar* k* agn b7.de* *Anac* k* ang k* arg-met arn b7.de* asaf b7.de* aur k* *Bell* k* calc b4.de* camph k* carb-an k* carb-v h2 carl k* caust b4.de* chel chin b7.de* cic k* clem k* coloc b4.de* con b4.de* cupr b7.de* cycl b7.de* euph k* hell k* ign b7.de* indg k* kali-c k* kalm k* lach k* *Led* k* lil-t k* m-arct b7.de m-aust b7.de *Mang* k* meny b7.de* mez b4.de* mur-ac b4.de* nat-c k* nat-s k* nux-m b7.de* nux-v b7.de* olnd b7.de* *Ph-ac* k* ran-s k* rheum b7.de* rhus-t b7.de* ruta b7.de* sabad b7.de* sabin b7.de* sars k* sep b4.de* spong fd4.de *Stann* k* staph b7.de* symph fd3.de• tarax b7.de* teucr k* thuj k* tritic-vg fd5.de valer b7.de* verat k* verb k* viol-t b7.de* zinc k*
  - **drawing** pain: agar k* anac h2

Extremities

- **pressing** with hands amel.: puls ↓
  - **sore**: puls$_{h1}$
- **pressure**:
  - **amel.**: abrom-a$_{ks5}$ cassia-s ↓ rauw$_{tpw8}$ sulfonam$_{ks2}$
    - **tearing** pain: cassia-s$_{ccrh1}$•
- **resting** feet on floor while sitting: *Ars* ↓
  - **drawing** pain: *Ars*
- **rheumatic**: agar$_{bg2}$ am-c ambr ↓ aml-ns anac anan ang ↓ asaf asc-t$_{a1}$ *Bell* berb$_{k*}$ bov$_{bg2}$ *Bry*$_{bro1}$ *Cact* *Calc* ↓ carb-v$_{k*}$ *Carbn-s* carc$_{tpw2*}$ card-m caust$_{bg2}$ chel$_{bro1}$ cimic clem colch$_{bro1}$ com croc$_{bg2}$ daph$_{bro1}$ *Dulc*$_{k*}$ *Elaps* franc$_{br1}$ graph ↓ *Guaj* ham hyper iod *Kali-c*$_{k*}$ kali-n *Kalm* kreos$_{bg2}$ *Lach*$_{k*}$ *Led*$_{k*}$ *Lith-c* *Lyc*$_{k*}$ lycps-v lyss mag-m mand$_{rsj7}$• *Med* meph$_{a1}$ merc$_{bro1}$ mez nat-m nat-s$_{bg2}$ *Nit-ac* pall petr ph-ac phos *Phyt*$_{k*}$ puls$_{bg2}$ *Rhod* *Rhus-t*$_{k*}$ rumx sang$_{bro1}$ sep$_{k*}$ stel$_{bro1}$ still$_{bg2}$ stront-c stry teucr$_{bg2}$ ust valer$_{bro1}$ *Verat* zinc$_{k*}$
  - **right**: *Kalm* lach ruta ven-m$_{rsj12}$• viol-t
  - **left**: elaps mag-s zinc
  - **evening**: mand$_{rsj7}$•
  - **drawing** pain: ang$_{k*}$ carb-v$_{k*}$ cimic$_{k*}$ elaps iod$_{k*}$ lyc mez$_{h2}$ *Phos*
  - **extending** feet: meph$_{a1}$
  - **gonorrhea**, after: **Med** *Sars*
  - **pressing** pain: anac$_{k*}$
  - **tearing** pain: ambr$_{k*}$ *Calc* **Caust** colch graph$_{k*}$ *Kalm* *Lyc* *Merc* nit-ac petr$_{k*}$ rhod **Rhus-t** *Zinc*
- **riding**:
  - **agg.**: lyc ↓
    - **drawing** pain: lyc$_{k*}$
  - **carriage**; in a:
    - **agg.**: nat-m ↓
      - **stitching** pain: nat-m
- **rise** from seat; must: ph-ac ↓
  - **drawing** pain: ph-ac$_{h2}$
- **rising**:
  - **after**:
    - **agg.**: coloc ↓
      - **drawing** pain: coloc
    - **amel.**: ferr ↓
      - **sore**: ferr
  - **agg.**: agar carb-an ↓ plan puls sulph ↓ tritic-vg$_{fd5.de}$
    - **burning**: sulph$_{k*}$ tritic-vg$_{fd5.de}$
    - **stitching** pain: carb-an
  - **sitting**; from:
    - **agg.**: rat ↓
      - **drawing** pain: rat
- **rubbing**:
  - **amel.**: phos ↓
    - **tearing** pain: phos
- **rubbing** of trousers: cot ↓
  - **stitching** pain: cot$_{br1}$
- **scratching** agg.: chel ↓ corn ↓ iris-foe ↓ seneg ↓ sulph ↓
  - **burning**: chel$_{h1}$ corn$_{k*}$ iris-foe seneg$_{k*}$ sulph$_{k*}$
- **shivering**; during: ars ↓
  - **tearing** pain: ars$_{b4.de}$
- **shooting** pain: *Acon* aesc aeth anac bell cann-i *Con* cystein-l$_{rly4}$• *Ferr* *Gels* guaj *Hyper* iod lat-h$_{bnm5}$• naja *Rhus-t* *Sil* [heroin$_{sdj2}$]
  - **paroxysmal**: *Gels*
  - **upward**: *Guaj* xan
- **sitting**:
  - **agg.**: abrom-a$_{ks5}$ agar *Alum* ↓ am-c ↓ am-m anac ↓ ant-c ↓ arg-met arg-n ars bar-c ↓ brom bry ↓ carb-v caust chin ↓ cina ↓ clem coloc ↓ crot-h cycl ↓ dig ↓ digin ↓ dios *Dulc* euph ↓ gink-b$_{sbd1}$• *Indg* ↓ iod ↓ **Kali-s** led lob medul-os-si$_{rly4}$• meny ↓ mez ↓ mosch nat-m nat-s ph-ac ↓ phos ↓ *Pyrog* *Rhod* **Rhus-t** ↓ ruta$_{fd4.de}$ sep ↓ sil ↓ stann ↓ staph ↓ **Sulph** ↓ *Tarax* ↓ tritic-vg$_{fd5.de}$ valer$_{k2}$
    - **aching**: agar brom led **Rhus-t**
- **sitting – agg.**: ...
    - **drawing** pain: agar$_{k*}$ am-c am-m$_{h2}$ anac$_{h2}$ ant-c$_{h2}$ arg-n$_{k*}$ *Ars*$_{k*}$ bar-c$_{h2}$ caust chin coloc$_{k*}$ cycl$_{k*}$ dig digin$_{a1}$ iod led$_{k*}$ meny mez$_{k*}$ rhus-t$_{h1}$ ruta$_{fd4.de}$ stann$_{h2}$ *Tarax*$_{k*}$ valer$_{k2}$
    - **hang** down agg.; letting legs: *Ars* ↓
      - **drawing** pain: *Ars*
    - **pressing** pain: agar$_{h2}$ anac$_{k*}$ arg-met nat-s$_{k*}$ tritic-vg$_{fd5.de}$
    - **sore**: bry ruta sep
    - **stitching** pain: euph phos
    - **tearing** pain: agar *Alum*$_{k*}$ am-c$_{h2}$ caust$_{h2}$ cina euph *Indg* ph-ac sil stann$_{k*}$ staph **Sulph**$_{k*}$ **Valer**
  - **amel.**: cina ↓ *Puls*
    - **drawing** pain: cina
- **sleep**:
  - **after** | **amel.**: plan
  - **falling** asleep:
    - **when**: *Lach* ↓
      - **stitching** pain: *Lach*
  - **going** to, on: kali-c *Kalm* *Lach*
  - **preventing** sleep: visc$_{c1}$
- **sore**: acon agar$_{k*}$ alum$_{k*}$ alum-p$_{k2}$ alum-sil$_{k2}$ alumn am-m ang$_{k*}$ apis asar$_{k*}$ aur-m bad **Bell**$_{k*}$ *Berb* brach bry$_{k*}$ *Calc*$_{k*}$ canth$_{k*}$ carb-ac carb-an carbn-s card-m castor-eq **Caust**$_{k*}$ chel chin$_{k*}$ chlor chord-umb$_{rly4}$• cic cimic clem coff$_{k*}$ *Coloc* con$_{k*}$ cot$_{br1}$ croc$_{k*}$ dig$_{k*}$ **Eup-per** ferr$_{k*}$ ferr-i gels graph *Guaj*$_{k*}$ hura hyos$_{k*}$ ina-i$_{mlk9.de}$ iod **Kali-c** kali-n kali-p kali-sil$_{k2}$ *Led* lyc lyss m-ambo$_{b7.de}$ m-aust$_{b7.de}$ mag-c$_{k*}$ mag-m$_{k*}$ med$_{k2}$ merc$_{k*}$ *Mez*$_{k*}$ nat-ar *Nat-c* nat-m nat-p nat-s *Nit-ac* nux-m$_{k*}$ osm petr$_{k*}$ *Ph-ac*$_{k*}$ phos$_{k*}$ *Phyt* pic-ac plb$_{k*}$ prun psor$_{k*}$ *Puls*$_{k*}$ *Rhus-t*$_{k*}$ ribo$_{rly4}$• **Ruta** *Sep*$_{k*}$ sil$_{k*}$ stann$_{k*}$ suis-pan$_{rly4}$• *Sulph*$_{k*}$ symph$_{fd3.de}$• tarent tep thuj$_{k*}$ valer$_{k*}$ zinc$_{k*}$
  - **alternating** with | **Arms**; bruised sensation of: cic$_{k*}$
  - **numb**: bad
- **spots**:
  - **formerly** ulcerated: petr ↓
    - **pressing** pain: petr$_{k*}$
- **sprained**; as if: agar am-c ars$_{h2}$
- **squeezed**; as if: *Ang*$_{b7a.de}$ bry$_{b7a.de}$ camph$_{b7a.de}$ olnd$_{b7a.de}$ verb$_{b7a.de}$
- **standing**:
  - **agg.**: *Agar* alumn ↓ arg-met ↓ berb caust ↓ coloc ↓ dig ↓ *Kali-bi* lac-leo$_{sk4}$• mez nat-s phos ↓ podo ruta$_{fd4.de}$ sil ↓ spong$_{fd4.de}$ tarax ↓
    - **boring** pain: coloc
    - **cutting** pain: arg-met
    - **drawing** pain: caust$_{h2}$ mez$_{k*}$ nat-s$_{k*}$ ruta$_{fd4.de}$ tarax$_{k*}$
    - **gnawing** pain: tarax$_{k*}$
    - **sore**: alumn dig$_{h2}$
    - **stitching** pain: phos sil tarax
    - **Bones**: dros ↓
      - **gnawing** pain: dros$_{h1}$
  - **amel.**: cina ↓
    - **drawing** pain: cina
- **stitching** pain: acon aesc aeth *Agar*$_{k*}$ agn$_{k*}$ *Alum*$_{k*}$ alum-p$_{k2}$ alumn am-c$_{k*}$ am-m$_{b7.de*}$ *Anac*$_{k*}$ ang$_{b7.de*}$ ant-c$_{k*}$ *Apis* arg-met$_{b7.de*}$ arn$_{b7.de*}$ ars *Asaf*$_{b7.de*}$ aster atro *Bell*$_{k*}$ berb bov$_{k*}$ *Bry*$_{k*}$ *Calc*$_{k*}$ cann-i caps$_{k*}$ *Carb-an*$_{k*}$ carb-v carbn-s *Caust*$_{k*}$ cham chel$_{k*}$ *Chin*$_{k*}$ cina$_{b7.de*}$ clem$_{k*}$ cob coc-c *Cocc* *Coloc*$_{k*}$ *Con* cycl$_{b7.de*}$ dig$_{k*}$ dros$_{b7.de*}$ dulc$_{k*}$ echi *Euph*$_{k*}$ euphr$_{k*}$ *Ferr* *Gels* glon *Graph*$_{k*}$ grat *Guaj*$_{k*}$ hell$_{k*}$ hyos$_{b7.de*}$ *Hyper* ign$_{b7.de*}$ ind jug-r kali-c$_{k*}$ *Kali-i* kali-m$_{k2}$ kali-s kali-sil$_{k2}$ *Kalm* lac-ac lach led *Lyc* m-ambo$_{b7.de}$ m-arct$_{b7.de}$ m-aust$_{b7.de}$ *Meny*$_{b7.de*}$ *Merc*$_{k*}$ merc-c *Mez* mosch *Mur-ac*$_{k*}$ naja nat-ar nat-c$_{k*}$ nat-m nit-ac *Nux-v*$_{k*}$ pall par$_{b7.de*}$ petr petr-ra$_{shn4}$• ph-ac$_{k*}$ phos pic-ac *Plat*$_{k*}$ *Plb*$_{k*}$ plut-n$_{srj7}$• puls$_{b7.de*}$ ran-s$_{k*}$ raph rheum$_{k*}$ *Rhus-t*$_{k*}$ rhus-v ruta$_{b7.de*}$ sabin$_{b7.de*}$ samb$_{k*}$ sars$_{k*}$ sec senec *Sep*$_{k*}$ **Sil**$_{k*}$ *Spig*$_{b7.de*}$ spong$_{b7.de*}$ staph$_{k*}$ stram$_{k*}$ sulph$_{k*}$ tarax$_{k*}$ tarent teucr$_{b7.de*}$ *Thuj*$_{k*}$ tritic-vg$_{fd5.de}$ *Tub* valer$_{b7.de*}$ vanil$_{fd5.de}$ verb viol-t$_{k*}$ vip zinc
  - **downward**: chel *Kalm* *Sil*
  - **jerking** pain: *Carbn-s*

- **stitching** pain: ...
  - **paroxysmal**: *Gels*
  - **pulsating** pain: coc-c
  - **upward**: *Guaj* xan
- **stool**:
  - **amel.**: hir skp7•
  - **during**:
    - **agg.**: rhus-t ↓
      - **stitching** pain: rhus-t
- **stooping** agg.: plan
- **stretching**:
  - **amel.**: ozone ↓
    - **tearing** pain: ozone sde2•
  - **leg**:
    - **agg.**: berb ↓
      - **burning**: berb
- **stretching** out: ars dros plan ruta
- **talking** agg.: ol-an ↓
  - **drawing** pain: ol-an k*
- **tearing** pain: *Acon* agar k* agn k* **Alum** k* alum-p k2 *Alum-sil* k4 am-c b4.de* *Am-m* b7a.de* *Ambr* k* anac b4.de* anag ant-c b7.de* ant-t b7.de* arg-met *Arg-n* arn b7.de* *Ars* k* ars-s-f k2 asaf k* aur-m bapt bro1 bar-act bro1 bar-c k* bar-i k2 **Bell** k* bell-p bro1 berb k* borx k* bov b4.de* brom bry k* cadm-s *Calc* k* calc-p calc-sil k2 camph k* canth b7.de* caps *Carb-an* k* *Carb-v* k* carbn-s **Caust** k* *Cham* k* chel k* chin k* chinin-ar chinin-s *Cic* cina *Cinnb* cob bro1 colch k* *Coloc* k* con k* croc k* crot-t cupr k* cycl k* *Dios* bro1 *Dulc* k* *Euph* k* *Ferr* *Graph* k* *Guaj* k* hell hep k* *Hyper* k* *Ign* k* *Indg* iod k* ip kali-ar kali-bi k* *Kali-c* k* *Kali-i* *Kali-n* k* kali-p kali-s kali-sil k2 *Kalm* k* kreos b7a.de lach k* lachn lact laur b7.de* *Led* *Lob* *Lyc* k* m-arct b7.de m-aust b7.de mag-c k* *Mag-m* k* mang b4.de* *Merc* k* merc-c b4a.de merl *Mez* k* mill mur-ac b4.de* nat-ar nat-c k* nat-m nat-p **Nat-s** nicc k* *Nit-ac* k* nux-v k* ol-an k* olnd b7.de* op ozone sde2• pall par b7.de* petr ph-ac k* phos k* plb b7.de* *Puls* k* rat *Rhod* k* **Rhus-t** k* sabad k* sabin b7.de* samb k* *Sars* k* sel *Sep* k* *Sil* k* spong k* *Stann* k* *Staph* k* sul-i k2 **Sulph** k* tab *Tarax* k* teucr k* thuj k* til tritic-vg fd5.de valer b7.de* verat k* verb k* visc bro1 *Zinc* k* zinc-p k2
  - **burning**: bell k*
  - **convulsive**: (non:lyc kl)
  - **cramping**: stann h2
  - **downward**: agar agn ars aur-m *Bar-c* calc-p carb-an h2 caust *Cham* chel *Lyc* nicc nux-v thuj verb *Zinc*
  - **jerking** pain: lyc h2*
  - **paralyzed**; as if: agar bell h1 *Cham* til k*
  - **paroxysmal**: aur-m
  - **pulsating** pain: arg-met
  - **upward**: **Bell** caust h2 con h2 guaj h2 lach sulph
  - **wandering** pain: lact k* rhod
- **touch**:
  - **agg.**: acon borx chir-fl ↓ con ↓ galeoc-c-h gms1• med k2 puls
    - **burning**: borx kl (non:bov kl) chir-fl gya2 con
    - **sore**: con h2
  - **each** other agg.; touching: galeoc-c-h gms1•
  - **sheets** agg.; of: galeoc-c-h gms1•
  - **slightest** touch agg.: galeoc-c-h gms1•
- **ulcerative** pain: *Kreos* k* *Nux-v* b7a.de osm puls k*
- **unbearable**: dros tl1
- **uncovering**:
  - **amel.**: *Sulph* ↓
    - **tearing** pain: *Sulph*
- **urinating**, during: *Nat-c* ↓
  - **sore**: *Nat-c*
- **vexation**; after: sep
- **waking**; on: abrot aur kali-p
- **walking**:
  - **after**:
    - **agg.**: alum a1 guaj ↓ **Ruta** ↓ spong fd4.de sulfonam ↓
- **walking – after – agg.**: ...
      - **aching**: sulfonam ks2
      - **sore**: guaj **Ruta**
  - **agg.**: (↗*Claudicatio*) *Aesc* ↓ am-c ↓ am-m anac ↓ ang ↓ aur-m ↓ bar-c berb ↓ *Brucel* sa3• bry canth ↓ carb-an chel chlor ↓ cina ↓ coloc ↓ con ↓ cupr-ar dulc fd4.de fago ferr *Gels* ↓ graph ↓ *Guaj* hep hyos ↓ ign mag-s nat-p nat-s ↓ nux-v petr ph-ac ↓ phyt puls ruta fd4.de sabad ↓ *Sil* ↓ sol-ni ↓ stann ↓ stront-c ↓ **Sulph** ↓ tab tarax ↓ tritic-vg fd5.de
    - **aching**: bry cupr-ar phyt
    - **cramping**: cina a1
    - **drawing** pain: anac k* ang k* coloc k* *Gels* hep h2 hyos k* nat-s k* *Nux-v* ruta fd4.de stront-c tarax h1
    - **jerking** pain: petr a1
    - **pinching** pain: sabad
    - **pressing** pain: anac k*
    - **sore**: *Aesc* aur-m berb canth carb-an chlor coloc con h2 ferr graph ph-ac h2 sol-ni
    - **sprained**; as if: am-c
    - **stitching** pain: *Sulph* tritic-vg fd5.de
    - **tearing** pain: bar-c *Sil* stann **Sulph** tritic-vg fd5.de
  - **air**; in open:
    - **agg.**: cina ↓ euph ↓ *Lyc* ↓
      - **drawing** pain: cina *Lyc*
      - **tearing** pain: euph h2
    - **amel.**: cina ↓
      - **tearing** pain: cina
  - **amel.**: abrom-a ks5 *Agar* *Alum* ↓ am-c am-m ↓ arg-met ↓ asaf ↓ *Bar-c* ↓ **Bell** ↓ *Dulc* *Euph* ↓ *Ferr* ↓ grat ↓ hir skp7• *Indg* *Kali-c* ↓ kali-n **Kali-s** **Lyc** ph-ac ↓ *Puls* pyrog k2 **Rhod** ↓ **Rhus-t** ruta fd4.de sep ↓ syph ↓ *Tub* *Valer* **Verat**
    - **aching**: kali-n pyrog k2 **Rhus-t**
    - **drawing** pain: agar am-m h2 *Lyc* ph-ac *Puls* **Rhod** **Rhus-t** sep k* syph jl2 *Tub* valer k2
    - **pressing** pain: sep h2
    - **stitching** pain: agar *Kali-c* *Kali-s* lyc *Rhus-t* *Tub*
    - **tearing** pain: agar *Alum* arg-met asaf *Bar-c* **Bell** *Euph* *Ferr* grat *Indg* kali-n h2 **Lyc** **Rhus-t** *Tub* **Valer**
  - **bent**:
    - **amel.**: am-m ↓
      - **drawing** pain: am-m gsy1
- **warm**:
  - **applications**:
    - **agg.**: cassia-s ↓
      - **tearing** pain: cassia-s ccrh1•
  - **bed**:
    - **agg.**: *Guaj* *Lyc* ↓ **Merc** mez petr plb psor sep ↓ sil ↓ staph *Sulph* **Syph** **Verat**
      - **burning**: sep
      - **drawing** pain: *Lyc*
      - **tearing** pain: **Merc** plb sil *Sulph*
    - **amel.**: agar carc gk6 **Caust** ↓ *Cham* ↓ **Lyc** ↓ *Merc* mez pyrog k2 *Tub* ↓
      - **tearing** pain: *Agar* **Caust** *Cham* **Lyc** *Tub*
  - **clothing**:
    - **amel.**: agar ↓ ars ↓ **Lyc** ↓
      - **tearing** pain: agar ars **Lyc**
- **warmth**:
  - **amel.**: agar am-c ars carc mg1.de* **Caust** ↓ cist bg1 mand rsj7• **Nux-v** *Ph-ac* *Pyrog* *Tub*
    - **drawing** pain: **Caust**
- **wavelike** downwards: cocc k*
- **weather**:
  - **change** of weather: lach bg1
  - **cold** agg.: allox sp1
  - **wet**:
    - **agg.**: *Dulc* *Rhus-t* **Verat**
    - **amel.**: allox sp1

Extremities

- **wet**, getting: *Rhus-t*
- ▽ **extending** to:
  - **Ankle**: kali-bi ptel
  - **Downward**: pert-vc$_{vk9}$
  - **Feet**: bism↓ kalm pic-ac ptel *Rhod* still
    - **drawing** pain: bism$_{h1*}$
  - **Genitals**: staph$_{hr1}$
  - **Heel**: cic↓ kalm↓ sep↓
    - **aching**: kalm
    - **drawing** pain: cic$_{a1}$ sep$_{h2}$
  - **Hips**: melal-alt$_{gya4}$ nit-ac nux-v
    - **aching**: melal-alt$_{gya4}$ nit-ac
  - **Knee**: nit-ac↓
    - **drawing** pain: nit-ac$_{h2}$
  - **Toes**: agar↓ **Alum**↓ calc↓ kali-n nux-v↓ *Rhod* sep↓ zinc↓
    - **aching**: kali-n
    - **drawing** pain: agar calc rhod sep
    - **tearing** pain: **Alum** nux-v zinc
- ○ **Anterior** part | **left**: gard-j$_{vlr2}$•
- **Bones**: **Agar** alum-sil$_{k2}$ am-c↓ ang$_{bg2}$ **Ars**↓ *Asaf*↓ berb$_{bg2}$ carb-v↓ chin↓ cocc$_{k2}$ dios *Dulc* *Guaj* ip$_{mrr1}$ *Kali-bi*$_{k*}$ kali-c↓ *Kali-i* kali-n↓ *Led* *Lyc* *Merc* *Mez* nit-ac↓ nux-m↓ nux-v **Ph-ac**↓ *Phyt* **Rhus-t**↓ ribo↓ ruta$_{fd4.de}$ sabad↓ sil↓ symph↓ **Syph** thuj$_{bg2}$ tritic-vg$_{fd5.de}$ vanil$_{fd5.de}$ viol-t↓ zinc↓
  - **right**: asc-t$_{a1}$
  - **evening**: am-c↓
    - **scraping** pain: am-c
  - **drawing** pain: kali-c$_{h2}$ nit-ac$_{h2}$ ruta$_{fd4.de}$ zinc$_{h2}$
  - **pressing** pain: ars$_{b4.de*}$ kali-n$_{b4.de*}$ merc$_{b4.de*}$ sabad$_{b7.de*}$ sil$_{b4.de*}$ symph$_{fd3.de}$• viol-t$_{b7.de*}$ zinc$_{b4.de*}$
  - **scraping** pain: am-c **Ars** *Asaf* led **Ph-ac** **Rhus-t**
  - **smashed** to pieces; as if: nux-m$_{c1*}$ tritic-vg$_{fd5.de}$
  - **sore**: chin$_{h1}$ ribo$_{rly4}$• symph$_{fd3.de}$•
  - **tearing** pain: carb-v$_{h2}$ kali-c$_{h2}$
  - **twitch** up the legs; must: am-c↓
    - **scraping** pain: am-c
  - **walking**:
    - **amel.**: am-c↓
      - **scraping** pain: am-c
  - **Tibia**: acon↓ **Agar** alum↓ alum-sil↓ am-c↓ am-m↓ ambr↓ anac anag ang↓ *Ant-c*↓ aq-mar$_{rbp6}$ arag$_{bro1}$ arg-met arg-n↓ arn↓ ars$_{k*}$ ars-s-f$_{k2}$ *Asaf*$_{bg3*}$ *Asar*↓ asc-c↓ *Aur* *Aur-m*↓ *Aur-m-n* bad$_{k*}$ bamb-a$_{stb2.de}$• bapt bar-c bell↓ berb bov↓ brom↓ *Bry*↓ bufo↓ calc *Calc-p* carb-ac$_{k*}$ *Carb-an*$_{k*}$ carb-v carc$_{fd2.de}$• card-m *Castor-eq*$_{k*}$ caust cham↓ chel↓ *Chin*↓ chinin-ar↓ cina *Clem* coff↓ *Colch*↓ *Coloc*↓ com↓ con↓ crot-h↓ cupr$_{sst3}$• cycl↓ dig↓ *Dulc*$_{k*}$ ephe-si↓ euph↓ fago↓ ferr$_{br1*}$ ferr-i fl-ac↓ gamb↓ gels$_{hr1}$ graph↓ grat↓ guaj$_{k2}$ hydrog↓ hyos↓ hyper ign↓ indg↓ *Iod* kali-ar *Kali-bi*$_{k*}$ **Kali-c**↓ *Kali-i* kali-n↓ kali-s$_{k2}$ kalm lac-del↓ **Lach**$_{k*}$ lachn↓ laur↓ *Led* lyc↓ *Mag-c*↓ mag-s↓ mang$_{k*}$ mang-o$_{c2*}$ meny↓ *Merc* merl↓ *Mez*$_{k*}$ mill↓ mosch↓ mur-ac↓ muru↓ nat-c↓ nat-m nat-s↓ *Nit-ac*$_{k*}$ nit-s-d$_{c2}$ *Nux-m* nux-v↓ ozone$_{sde2}$• petr↓ petr-ra↓ *Ph-ac* *Phos*$_{k*}$ phys↓ *Phyt*$_{k*}$ pic-ac pieri-b↓ plut-n$_{srj7}$• psor↓ *Puls* pycnop-sa↓ ran-a↓ rat↓ *Rhod*↓ **Rhus-t** ruta$_{fd4.de}$ sabad↓ sabin↓ sacch-a↓ samb↓ sarr sars↓ sep$_{k*}$ sil spig↓ spong$_{fd4.de}$ stann staph$_{k*}$ still$_{bg3*}$ stry↓ sul-i$_{ptk1}$ **Sulph**↓ symph$_{fd3.de}$• syph$_{c2*}$ tarax↓ tarent thuj trom$_{c2}$ tus-p$_{c2}$ vac$_{jl2}$ vanil$_{fd5.de}$ verat visc$_{c1}$ zinc
    - **right**: agar↓ alum↓ arg-met↓ asc-t$_{a1}$ bamb-a↓ castor-eq$_{br1}$ dulc$_{fd4.de}$ ferr-i$_{k2}$ hydrog↓ kali-p↓ kali-s$_{fd4.de}$ lachn↓ rat↓ spong$_{fd4.de}$ staph↓
      - **burning**: bamb-a$_{stb2.de}$•
      - **stitching** pain: alum bamb-a$_{stb2.de}$• hydrog$_{srj2}$• kali-p$_{fd1.de}$• kali-s$_{fd4.de}$ staph$_{hr1}$
      - **tearing** pain: agar arg-met kali-s$_{fd4.de}$ lachn$_{hr1}$ rat
    - **left**: asc-c↓ aur↓ aur-m-n↓ bit-ar$_{wht1}$• bov↓ ephe-si$_{hsj1}$• kali-s↓ ozone$_{sde2}$• plut-n$_{srj7}$• vanil$_{fd5.de}$ visc↓
      - **boring** pain: asc-c aur-m-n
      - **stitching** pain: aur bov kali-s$_{fd4.de}$ visc$_{c1}$
      - **extending** to | **right**: ozone$_{sde2}$•

- **Bones – Tibia**: ...
  - **daytime**: clem↓
    - **aching**: clem
  - **morning**: *Agar* clem↓ dulc$_{fd4.de}$ kali-bi↓ kali-n↓ kali-s$_{fd4.de}$ lycps-v↓ phos↓ ruta$_{fd4.de}$ vanil$_{fd5.de}$
    - **aching**: lycps-v
    - **bed** agg.; in: psor↓
      - **sore**: psor
    - **boring** pain: clem
    - **drawing** pain: kali-bi$_{k*}$
    - **tearing** pain: dulc$_{a1}$ kali-n$_{h2}$ phos$_{h2}$
    - **waking**; while: psor$_{jl2}$
  - **forenoon**: agar↓ trom↓
    - **aching**: agar
    - **boring** pain: trom
  - **noon**: *Agar*↓
    - **drawing** pain: *Agar*$_{k*}$
  - **afternoon**: bamb-a↓
    - **sitting** agg.: agar↓
      - **aching**: agar
      - **drawing** pain: agar$_{k*}$
    - **stitching** pain: bamb-a$_{stb2.de}$•
  - **evening**: alum↓ ang↓ carc$_{fd2.de}$• chin↓ dulc$_{fd4.de}$ grat↓ kali-i↓ kali-n↓ kali-s↓ *Led* nat-c↓ ruta$_{fd4.de}$ spong$_{fd4.de}$ *Sulph*↓ thuj↓
    - **18** h: arg-met↓
      - **drawing** pain: arg-met
    - **19** h: sulph↓
      - **drawing** pain: sulph
    - **21** h: thuj↓
      - **drawing** pain: thuj
    - **bed** agg.; in: alum↓ con↓ lyc↓ mez↓
      - **stitching** pain: alum
      - **tearing** pain: con lyc$_{h2}$ mez$_{h2}$
    - **boring** pain: grat nat-c
    - **drawing** pain: ang$_{k*}$ chin$_{k*}$ dulc$_{fd4.de}$ *Sulph*$_{k*}$ thuj$_{k*}$
    - **sore**: alum
    - **tearing** pain: kali-i kali-n kali-s$_{fd4.de}$ led *Sulph*
  - **night**: agar↓ asaf$_{tl1}$ *Aur* carb-an↓ *Caust*↓ dros$_{tl1}$ hep↓ *Kali-i* kali-s$_{fd4.de}$ kalm$_{k2}$ **Merc**↓ mez$_{mrr1}$ nit-ac↓ nux-v↓ *Ph-ac* *Phyt*$_{k*}$ **Rhus-t** *Syph*$_{jl2}$ vanil$_{fd5.de}$
    - **bed** agg.; in: *Aur* carb-an *Merc* *Mez* psor **Rhus-t**
      - **sore**: *Merc* *Mez*
    - **boring** pain: **Aur** **Merc** *Mez*
    - **burning**: *Caust* mez$_{a1}$ *Ph-ac*
    - **sore**: *Mez* nit-ac nux-v
    - **tearing** pain: agar carb-an caust hep kali-s$_{fd4.de}$ kalm$_{k2}$ *Ph-ac*
  - **accompanied** by:
    - **Occiput**; pain in (See HEAD - Pain - occiput - accompanied - tibia)
    - **Throat**; pain in: lach$_{ptk1}$
  - **aching**: agar anac berb bufo *Carb-ac* chinin-ar clem com fago fl-ac gamb hydrog$_{srj2}$• ign **Lach** mez nat-m nit-ac **Ph-ac** plut-n$_{srj7}$• pycnop-sa$_{mrz1}$ sep sil stry
  - **appearing** suddenly:
    - **disappearing** suddenly; and: bamb-a↓
      - **burning**: bamb-a$_{stb2.de}$•
      - **stitching** pain: bamb-a$_{stb2.de}$•
  - **bending** knee agg.: rhus-t↓
    - **pressing** pain: rhus-t$_{h1}$
  - **boring** pain: anac ars asc-c **Aur** *Aur-m-n* brom chel cina *Clem* coloc grat led mang$_{k*}$ **Merc** *Mez* nat-c nit-s-d$_{c1}$ trom
  - **broken**; as if: agar$_{k2}$ vac$_{jl2}$
  - **burning**: agar$_{k*}$ ang$_{h1}$ arg-met$_{h1}$ arn bamb-a$_{stb2.de}$• bry *Caust* *Kali-bi* lach$_{k*}$ *Mag-c*$_{k*}$ mang$_{a1}$ mez$_{a1}$ ph-ac rhus-t$_{h1}$ sabad$_{k*}$ symph$_{fd3.de}$• tarax$_{h1}$ verat$_{h1}$ **Zinc**$_{k*}$
  - **burrowing**: spig$_{h1}$
  - **bursting**; sensation as if: muru$_{a1}$
  - **cramping**: lac-del$_{hrn2}$•

· **Bones – Tibia**: ...

: **crossing** legs agg.: **Rhus-t**

: **cutting** pain: calc h2 carb-ac mag-c

: **descending** a mountain: bar-c ↓

. **drawing** pain: bar-c

: **drawing** pain: acon k* *Agar* k* **Anac** k* ang k* *Ant-c* *Arg-met* arg-n a1 ars k* asaf k* aur-m-n k* bar-c bell h1 brom k* bry calc k* *Calc-p* carb-an k* carb-v caust chel k* *Chin* k* clem k* *Coloc* k* crot-h k* dig k* dulc fd4.de ephe-si hsj1• graph k* hyper indg k* kali-ar kali-bi k* *Kali-c* kali-n k* kali-s fd4.de *Led* k* mag-s k* *Mang* k* *Merc* k* mez h2 mill k* mosch nat-s k* nit-ac nit-s-d a1 nux-v petr k* *Puls* k* ran-a k* *Rhus-t* sabin sars sil k* *Staph* k* sulph k* symph fd3.de• vanil fd5.de zinc k*

. **burning**: nat-c h2

. **cramping**: nat-c h2 petr h2

. **downward**: nat-c h2 zinc h2

. **jerking** pain: carb-an

. **paralyzed**; as if: petr h2

. **upward**: sars h2

: **drawing** up toes: puls ↓

. **sore**: puls h1

: **elevating** leg amel.: aur bar-c

: **extending** the leg; when: aur

: **gnawing** pain: berb a1 carb-ac c1 *Carb-an* carc fd2.de• *Kali-i* laur a1 nit-ac phys a1

: **growing** pains: mang mrr1

: **jerking** pain: meny h1

: **menses**; during: kali-c ↓ *Sep* ↓ *Sil* ↓

. **tearing** pain: kali-c *Sep* k* *Sil*

: **motion**:

. **agg.**: berb cycl ↓ sep ↓

pressing pain: cycl h1

sore: sep h2

tearing pain: cycl h1

. **amel.**: *Agar* arg-met arg-n ↓ ars-s-f k2 aur-m-n *Dulc* *Mang* ↓ psor *Rhod* ↓ *Rhus-t* **Valer** ↓ verat

drawing pain: arg-n **Aur-m-n** k* *Mang* **Valer**

tearing pain: arg-met *Rhod*

: **neuralgic**: mez tl1

: **paralyzed**; as if: card-m

: **pinching** pain: mez h2 sil h2

: **pressing** pain: agar h2 ang h1 asaf k* aur k* bell k* brom k* calc h2 carb-an k* caust k* coloc h2 cycl h1 kali-n kalm k* led k* meny h1 *Merc* mez nat-c h2 petr h2 ph-ac k* puls k* sacch-a fd2.de• sep h2 sil stann k* staph thuj h1 zinc

. **pulsating** pain: stann h2

: **pressure** agg.: asc-t a1

: **pulsating** pain: arg-met carc fd2.de• kali-s fd4.de

: **rheumatic**: rumx k* zinc ↓

. **drawing** pain: zinc k*

: **short** duration: ozone sde2•

: **sitting**:

. **agg.**: *Agar* anac *Aur-m-n* ↓ chin ↓ coloc ↓ con ↓ cycl ↓ euph ↓ grat ↓ led ↓ mang ↓ mez ↓ mur-ac ↓ nat-c ↓ nit-s-d ↓ sep ↓ staph ↓ **Valer** ↓

aching: agar anac

boring pain: agar *Aur-m-n* mez nat-c h2

drawing pain: *Agar* chin k* coloc k* cycl h1 mang h2 nit-s-d a1 staph k* **Valer**

pressing pain: chin h1 coloc h2 con h2 cycl h1 staph h1

sore: sep h2

tearing pain: euph grat led mang mur-ac

. **amel.**: cycl ↓ mang ↓ mur-ac ↓

drawing pain: cycl h1 mang h2

tearing pain: mur-ac h2

: **sleep**; preventing: polyp-p br1

· **Bones – Tibia**: ...

: **sore**: agar alum alum-sil k2 asaf *Asar* *Aur* *Aur-m* *Calc* calc-p k2 carb-an caust coff con graph hyos iod h *Kali-bi* kali-c *Kali-s* mag-c *Mang* *Mez* nat-m *Nit-ac* nux-v petr **Phos** psor *Puls* *Rhus-t* **Ruta** sep *Sil* symph fd3.de• *Syph* k* thuj

: **standing** agg.: agar ↓ agn ↓ alum ↓ aur-m-n mag-c ↓ mang ↓ rat

. **aching**: agn

. **drawing** pain: agar mang k*

. **pressing** pain: agn a1

. **sore**: alum mag-c mang h2

: **stitching** pain: alum am-m *Ant-c* aur bamb-a stb2.de• berb bov bry cham chel *Chin* guaj hyper kali-c kali-i kali-s fd4.de led mez petr-ra shn4• pieri-b mlk9.de puls k* rhus-t samb staph tl1 **Sulph** thuj vanil fd5.de *Zinc*

: **stretching** leg agg.: aur ptk1 chin ↓ con ↓

. **drawing** pain: chin h1

. **pressing** pain: aur k* chin h1 con h2

: **tearing** pain: agar alum am-c ambr *Arg-met* arg-n *Ars* k* bell berb *Bry* carb-an *Caust* *Colch* con cycl h1 dulc euph *Ferr* graph grat guaj *Kali-bi* **Kali-c** *Kali-i* kali-n kali-s fd4.de kalm k2 lachn *Led* lyc merl mur-ac nat-c nat-s **Nit-ac** petr-ra shn4• *Ph-ac* k* *Phos* *Puls* rat *Rhod* sars h2 sep k* *Sil* spong staph *Sulph* thuj verat h1 *Zinc*

. **cramping**: con h2

. **downward**: guaj h2 kali-n h2 sars h2 verat h1 zinc h2

. **paralyzed**; as if: mez h2

. **rhythmical**: phos h2

. **twitching**: lyc h2

: **touch** agg.: nit-ac ↓

. **sore**: nit-ac mtf33

: **walking**:

. **agg.**: alum ↓ ang ↓ bry calc ↓ carb-an carc fd2.de• clem coc-c con ↓ crot-h ↓ cycl ↓ ephe-si hsj1• ign lac-del ↓ mag-c ↓ merc merl mez nat-m nat-s *Nux-m* petr phos rhod ruta fd4.de stry sulph ↓ symph fd3.de• thuj ↓

aching: clem ign stry

boring pain: mez nat-s

cramping: lac-del hrn2•

drawing pain: ang h1 crot-h k* cycl h1 symph fd3.de• thuj k*

pressing pain: calc h2 carb-an k* cycl h1

sore: alum h2 carb-an mag-c

tearing pain: con sulph thuj

. **amel.**: **Agar** asaf ↓ aur-m-n bar-c ↓ chin ↓ cycl ↓ *Dulc* *Mang* ↓ nat-c ↓ *Ph-ac* ↓ *Tub* **Valer** ↓ verat

boring pain: *Aur-m-n* nat-c h2

drawing pain: *Agar* *Aur-m-n* bar-c chin cycl h1 *Mang* **Valer**

pressing pain: asaf *Ph-ac*

. **cold** air; in | **agg.**: ephe-si hsj1•

: **weather** agg.; wet: *Dulc* mez *Phyt* *Verat*

: **extending** to:

. **Ankle**: brom ↓

drawing pain: brom k*

. **Feet**: mag-m ↓ sulph ↓

drawing pain: mag-m h2 sulph k*

. **Toes**:

First: nat-c ↓

tearing pain: nat-c h2

: **Edges**: ephe-si ↓

. **drawing** pain: ephe-si hsj1•

: **Spot**; in a: *Mag-c* ↓

. **burning**: *Mag-c* k*

: **Spots**; in: ambr k*

: **Upper** part, in front of tibia: psil ft1

· **Calves**: acon ↓ *Aesc* ↓ agar agn ↓ aids ↓ allox tpw3 aloe ↓ alum bg3 *Alum-sil* ↓ am-c ↓ am-m b7a.de ambr b7a.de *Anac* androc srj1• ang ↓ ant-c ↓ ant-t anthraq rly4• aq-mar ↓ *Arg-met* ↓ arg-n *Am* *Ars* ars-i ↓ arund asaf ↓ aster ↓ aur ↓ aur-m ↓ aur-m-n ↓ bamb-a ↓ bapt ↓ bell ↓ bell-p sp1 benz-ac berb ↓ bism ↓ borx *Bry* ↓ but-ac ↓ *Cact* cain ↓ **Calc** k* calc-f sp1 calc-p calc-sil k2 camph ↓ cann-i br1 canth caps b7a.de **Carb-an** ↓ carb-v ↓ carbn-s ↓ carc ↓ cassia-s ccrh1• castm ↓ caul ↓

- **Calves**: ...
Caust↓ cham chel chim↓ chin↓ chir-fl↓ chlol↓ chlorpr pin1• chord-umb↓ cic cina↓ cist↓ clem↓ coc-c↓ coca↓ cocc↓ colch *Coloc*↓ con↓ croc↓ crot-h↓ cupr cycl↓ cystein-l↓ dig digin↓ dios↓ dros↓ dulc fd4.de *Elaps* ephe-si↓ eug **Eup-per**↓ euph↓ *Euphr*↓ eupi fago↓ falco-pe↓ *Ferr*↓ ferr-i↓ fl-ac↓ galla-q-r↓ gamb↓ *Gels* germ-met srj5• gins↓ glon granit-m↓ graph bg3 grat↓ *Guaj*↓ ham↓ hell hir skp7• hyos↓ hyper ign k* *Indg*↓ iod jatr-c↓ jug-c *Kali-bi* kali-br *Kali-c*↓ kali-i↓ kali-m↓ kali-n↓ *Kali-p*↓ kali-s↓ kali-sil↓ kalm kola stb3• lac-ac↓ lac-del↓ lach lat-m↓ laur↓ *Led*↓ limest-b↓ lipp↓ lith-c lob↓ lyc k* lycps-v↓ lyss↓ mag-c mag-m↓ manc↓ mang↓ mang-p↓ med↓ melal-alt gya4 meny↓ merc↓ merc-c merc-cy *Merc-i-r* mez mosch↓ mur-ac↓ myris↓ nat-ar↓ nat-c↓ nat-m↓ nat-p **Nat-s**↓ nit-ac bg3 nit-s-d↓ *Nux-m*↓ *Nux-v* k* olib-sac↓ olnd↓ ox-ac par↓ petr-ra shn4• ph-ac↓ phel↓ phos pic-ac pieri-b↓ pip-m plac-s↓ plat↓ plb plut-n↓ prot pte1* ptel↓ *Puls* puls-n↓ pyrus↓ quas↓ rad-br c11 ran-b↓ ran-s↓ raph↓ rat↓ *Rhus-t* rhus-v↓ ribo↓ rumx↓ ruta fd4.de sabad sabin↓ sang sars↓ sec sel sep bg3 sil sin-n *Spig*↓ spong fd4.de stann bg3 staph bg3 stroph-s↓ stry suis-em↓ sul-ac k* sul-i k2 sulfonam↓ sulph symph fd3.de• tab↓ tarax↓ tarent *Ter* teucr↓ thuj tritic-vg fd5.de tub c1 tung-met bdx1• ulm-c↓ upa valer bg3 vanil fd5.de verat verat-v verb↓ viol-t↓ visc↓ xan *Zinc*↓
  - **right**: *Agar*↓ *Caust*↓ chir-fl↓ gels a1 kali-s↓ rat↓ trios rsj11• tritic-vg↓ xan c1
    - **burning**: *Agar* chir-fl gya2
    - **drawing** pain: *Agar* gels psa kali-s fd4.de
    - **shooting** pain: gels a1
    - **tearing** pain: agar *Caust* rat tritic-vg fd5.de
  - **left**: *Buteo-j*↓ carneg-g↓ cassia-s↓ dulc fd4.de gels a1 ham↓ lavand-a↓ mang-p↓ plac-s↓ ruta↓ symph↓ ven-m↓
    - **aching**: carneg-g rwt1• lavand-a ctl1•
    - **burning**: plac-s rly4•
    - **cramping**: carneg-g rwt1• mang-p rly4• ven-m rsj12• [*Buteo-j* sej6]
    - **drawing** pain: dulc fd4.de gels psa ham fd3.de• ruta fd4.de symph fd3.de•
    - **tearing** pain: cassia-s ccrh1•
  - **morning**: calc-p tritic-vg fd5.de vanil fd5.de
    - **descending** stairs agg.: rhus-t
    - **waking**; on: gard-j vlr2• gels lycps-v↓ plut-n srj7•
      - **aching**: lycps-v
  - **afternoon**: agar↓ carc↓ castm↓ dulc fd4.de grat↓ mag-c↓ nat-c↓ rhus-t ruta fd4.de spong fd4.de **Valer**↓ vanil fd5.de
    - **16** h:
      - **laying** right limb across the left; when: *Valer*↓
        - **tearing** pain: *Valer*
      - **lying** on back with leg flexed: nat-m
    - **17** h: castm↓ valer↓
      - **tearing** pain: castm valer
    - **drawing** pain: agar h2 castm vanil fd5.de
    - **stitching** pain: carc fd2.de• grat
    - **tearing** pain: mag-c nat-c **Valer** k*
  - **evening**: alum am-m↓ bamb-a↓ calc dulc fd4.de ferr-i↓ ham↓ mag-m↓ nat-s↓ nux-v *Puls* ran-b↓ rat↓ ruta fd4.de spong fd4.de stann↓ staph sulph↓ verat
    - **bed** agg.; in: anac↓ mag-m↓ sil↓ staph
      - **sore**: mag-m
      - **tearing** pain: anac c1 sil
    - **boring** pain: sulph
    - **burning**: alum h2 sulph h2
    - **drawing** pain: alum bamb-a stb2.de• calc k* dulc fd4.de ham fd3.de• *Puls* rat k* ruta fd4.de verat k*
    - **shooting** pain: sulph
    - **sitting** with knees bent: coca
    - **sore**: ferr-i stann
    - **stitching** pain: dulc fd4.de ruta fd4.de sulph
    - **tearing** pain: am-m mag-m nat-s ran-b sulph
  - **night**: anac androc srj1• arg-n ars↓ bros-gau mrc1 calc oss• cham *Gels* graph↓ hir skp7• lyc mur-ac↓ nux-v pic-ac sabad sulph symph fd3.de• tritic-vg↓

- **Calves – night**: ...
    - **drawing** pain: ars h2 graph h2 tritic-vg fd5.de
    - **sore**: *Gels*
    - **tearing** pain: mur-ac sabad
  - **aching**: aids nl2• allox tpw3* androc srj1• ang anthraq rly4• ars berb but-ac sp1 chir-fl gya2 chlol eup-per fago *Gels* granit-m es1• jatr-c *Kali-bi* lat-m bnm6• led lycps-v lyss merc mur-ac petr-ra shn4• plut-n srj7• ptel *Puls* sep sin-n stroph-s sp1 suis-em rly4• sulfonam ks2 tarax teucr
    - **accompanied** by | **numbness**: lappa ptk1
  - **ascending** stairs agg.: arg-n rhus-t sulph
    - **drawing** pain: arg-n k*
  - **bathing**; after: pip-m
  - **bed** agg.; in: am-m↓ ven-m↓
    - **cramping**: ven-m rsj12•
    - **tearing** pain: am-m
  - **bending** feet agg.: calc
  - **bent**; when legs are: chel↓
    - **stitching** pain: chel k*
  - **blow**; pain as from a: nux-m c1
  - **boring** pain: coloc *Cupr* mez sulph
  - **burning**: agar alum am-c aur dig dulc fd4.de eupi ham fd3.de• mang h2 mez plac-s rly4• plb ran-s rhus-t sars sulph tarax h1 tarent tritic-vg fd5.de visc c1 zinc h2
  - **burrowing**: spig h1
  - **chill**:
    - **during**: *Ars* thuj
      - **drawing** pain: *Ars* thuj k*
    - **with**: sil↓
      - **tearing** pain: sil h2
  - **clawing**: mang h2
  - **cold** applications agg.: trios rsj11•
  - **cough** agg.; during: *Nux-v*
  - **cramping**: cupr h2 falco-pe nl2• galla-q-r nl2• lac-del hrn2• led h1 olib-sac wmh1 ribo rly4• ruta fd4.de visc sp1
  - **crossing** legs agg.: dig valer
    - **tearing** pain: valer k2
  - **cutting** pain: alum h2* *Chel* coloc h2 dros h1* mur-ac bg2 ph-ac h2 stry *Thuj*
  - **deep** in: glon
  - **descending** stairs agg.: *Arg-met* puls-n tritic-vg fd5.de
    - **drawing** pain: arg-met
  - **dinner**; after: canth↓ grat↓
    - **stitching** pain: grat
    - **tearing** pain: canth
  - **drawing** on boots, when: graph↓
    - **stitching** pain: graph
  - **drawing** pain: acon k* agar agn *Alum* k* *Anac* ang k* ant-c h2 ant-t *Arg-met* *Arg-n* k* *Ars* asaf k* aster aur-m-n k* bamb-a stb2.de• bapt k* berb k* bism h1 bry k* cain calc k* *Calc-p* k* camph k* *Cann-i* k* caps **Carb-an** carbn-s castm caul caust k* chel k* *Cic* cist coc-c k* cocc colch k* coloc k* con k* *Cupr* k* dios k* dulc h1 eupi k* fl-ac k* gels k* gins k* graph k* *Guaj* ham fd3.de• hell k* hyper k* *Kali-bi* kali-i k* kali-n *Kali-p* kali-s fd4.de *Led* lipp a1 lyc manc med meny h1 *Mez* k* nat-ar nat-c nat-s k* nit-ac h2 nit-s-d a1 nux-m k* *Nux-v* plat *Puls* k* pyrus quas a1 rat k* *Rhus-t* rhus-v k* rumx ruta fd4.de sabin k* sang sec **Sil** spig k* stann h2 *Sulph* k* symph fd3.de• tab thuj k* tritic-vg fd5.de upa vanil fd5.de verat k* viol-t k* zinc k*
    - **alternating** with:
      - **pressure**: gins k*
      - **Foot**; drawing in sole of: sulph
    - **cramping**: **Anac** ang arg-met *Carb-an* coloc graph h2 manc plat *Sil* sulph
    - **downward**: agar h2 alum bism h1 chel coc-c fl-ac sang thuj zinc
    - **griping** pain: sulph k*
    - **paralyzed**; as if: *Nux-v*
    - **paroxysmal**: ant-t k* cist k* coc-c k* graph k* thuj k*
    - **pressing** pain: bry k* gins k* nat-c k*
    - **tearing** pain: calc k* kali-n

- **Calves – drawing** pain: ...
    - **twitching**: mez$_{h2}$
    - **upwards** to back: manc
  - **drawing** up feet amel.: cham
  - **eating**; after: bry↓ clem↓
    - **sore**: clem
    - **tearing** pain: bry
  - **exertion**; as after: aloe$_{bg2}$
  - **fever**; before: hyos↓ puls↓
    - **drawing** pain: hyos$_{b7a.de}$ puls$_{b7a.de}$
  - **flashes** of: xan
  - **gnawing** pain: euph$_{k*}$
  - **griping**: led$_{h1}$ mang$_{h2}$
  - **jerking** pain: cupr$_{h2}$
  - **lying**:
    - **agg.**: berb↓ kali-p↓ puls↓
      - **pinching** pain: berb$_{k*}$
      - **stitching** pain: kali-p$_{fd1.de}$• puls
    - **amel.**: stroph-s↓
      - **aching**: stroph-s$_{sp1}$
    - **legs**; with crossed:
      - **agg.**: *Valer*↓
        - **tearing** pain: *Valer*$_{k*}$
      - **amel.**: sulfonam↓
        - **aching**: sulfonam$_{ks2}$
    - **side**; on | **left**:
        - **agg.**: cassia-s↓
          - **tearing** pain: cassia-s$_{ccrh1}$•
      - **right**:
        - **amel.**: cassia-s↓
          - **tearing** pain: cassia-s$_{ccrh1}$•
  - **lying** down:
    - **amel.**: nux-m↓ ruta↓
      - **drawing** pain: nux-m$_{k*}$ ruta$_{fd4.de}$
  - **menses**; during: berb mag-m↓
    - **sore**: mag-m$_{h2}$
  - **motion**:
    - **agg.**: berb↓ bry$_{k*}$ calc↓ cassia-s↓ cocc↓ nat-c↓ *Nux-v* plb↓ plut-n↓ rumx
      - **aching**: plut-n$_{srj7}$• rumx
      - **drawing** pain: cocc
      - **pinching** pain: nat-c$_{h2}$
      - **stitching** pain: berb calc
      - **tearing** pain: berb cassia-s$_{ccrh1}$• plb
    - **amel.**: agar am-c ars-i cupr dulc↓ indg↓ *Rat*↓ *Rhus-t* sabad↓ staph$_{a1}$ stroph-s↓ sulph↓ *Valer*↓ visc↓
      - **aching**: stroph-s$_{sp1}$ visc$_{c1}$
      - **burning**: visc$_{c1}$
      - **tearing** pain: dulc$_{h1}$ indg *Rat* sabad sulph *Valer*
    - **feet** and toes agg.; of: caust↓
      - **tearing** pain: caust$_{h2}$
    - **feet**; of | **agg.**: cham
  - **pinching** pain: ant-c$_{h2}$ dig digin$_{a1}$ hyos$_{k*}$ mang$_{k*}$ myris$_{k*}$ nat-c$_{k*}$ ph-ac$_{k*}$ stann$_{h2}$ thuj$_{k*}$
    - **cramping**: ph-ac$_{h2}$
  - **pressing** pain: agar$_{k*}$ *Anac* ars$_{h2}$ calc$_{h2}$ cic$_{a1}$ *Led* mur-ac$_{h2}$ sep$_{h2}$ spong$_{fd4.de}$ stann$_{h2}$ staph$_{h1}$ tarax$_{h1}$ tritic-vg$_{fd5.de}$ verat$_{h1}$
    - **cramping**: anac$_{h2}$ verat$_{h1}$ verb$_{h}$
  - **pressure**:
    - **agg.**: cassia-s↓
      - **tearing** pain: cassia-s$_{ccrh1}$•
    - **amel.**: cassia-s$_{ccrh1}$• eupi plb↓
      - **stitching** pain: plb
      - **tearing** pain: plb
  - **pulling** on boots agg.: graph↓
    - **shooting** pain: graph$_{k*}$
  - **pulsating** pain: allox$_{sp1}$

- **Calves**: ...
  - **rheumatic**: ant-t jal lach lycps-v plb puls sal-ac$_{mtf11}$
  - **rising**:
    - **agg.**: graph↓ tritic-vg↓
      - **drawing** pain: graph$_{k*}$ tritic-vg$_{fd5.de}$
    - **bed**; from | **immediately** after: nat-p tritic-vg$_{fd5.de}$
  - **room**:
    - **amel.**: grat↓
      - **stitching** pain: grat
  - **rubbing** | **after**:
    - **agg.**: thuj↓
      - **stitching** pain: thuj
    - **amel.**: castm↓ nat-s↓ ph-ac↓
      - **pinching** pain: ph-ac$_{h2}$
      - **tearing** pain: castm nat-s
  - **scratching**: (non:dulc$_{h1}$)
  - **shooting** pain: alum bell *Calc-p* cystein-l$_{rly4}$• *Lyc Plb* sulph tarent
  - **sitting**:
    - **agg.**: agar am-m↓ ars↓ asaf↓ berb↓ bros-gau$_{mrc1}$ castm↓ cina↓ coloc↓ *Dros*↓ euph↓ ham↓ indg↓ jatr-c↓ kali-i↓ mang↓ mur-ac↓ puls rat↓ *Rhus-t*↓ ruta$_{fd4.de}$ stroph-s↓ sul-ac sulph **Valer**↓
      - **aching**: stroph-s$_{sp1}$
      - **burning**: mang$_{a1}$
      - **cutting** pain: mur-ac$_{h2}$
      - **drawing** pain: castm coloc kali-i mur-ac$_{a1}$ puls ruta$_{fd4.de}$ sulph
      - **pinching** pain: asaf$_{k*}$ berb$_{k*}$
      - **sore**: jatr-c
      - **stitching** pain: am-m asaf *Dros* ham$_{fd3.de}$• mang *Rhus-t*
      - **tearing** pain: agar am-m ars cina coloc euph indg mur-ac rat sulph **Valer**
      - **twinging**: **Valer**
    - **amel.**: cassia-s↓ tarax↓
      - **stitching** pain: tarax
      - **tearing** pain: cassia-s$_{ccrh1}$•
    - **walking**; after: plat↓
      - **drawing** pain: plat$_{h2}$
  - **sore**: *Aesc* alum$_{k*}$ ant-c$_{h2}$ ant-t anthraq$_{rly4}$• aq-mar$_{skp7}$• arn ars-i berb *Bry* caust *Chel* chim chord-umb$_{rly4}$• clem coca croc crot-h ephe-si$_{hsi1}$• **Eup-per**$_{k*}$ fago *Ferr* ferr-i *Gels*$_{k*}$ ham$_{fd3.de}$• jatr-c *Kali-c* lac-ac limest-b$_{es1}$• mag-m mang-p$_{rly4}$• merc-cy mez$_{h2}$ mosch nat-m$_{k*}$ *Nux-m* nux-v olib-sac$_{wmh1}$ pic-ac plb puls-n rhus-t sep$_{h2}$ stann staph$_{ptk1}$ symph$_{fd3.de}$•
    - **paralyzed**; as if: mag-m$_{h2}$ ulm-c$_{jsj8}$•
  - **spasmodic**: raph
  - **sprained**; as if: graph$_{h2}$
  - **squeezed**; as if: *Euphr*$_{b7a.de}$ led$_{b7a.de}$
  - **standing** agg.: arg-n$_{a1}$ arn arund berb↓ bros-gau$_{mrc1}$ coloc↓ euph↓ euphr *Ign*↓ iris kali-i↓ mag-m↓ nat-s↓ nux-m ruta$_{fd4.de}$ spong$_{fd4.de}$ sulph↓
    - **drawing** pain: arn$_{k*}$ nat-s nux-m$_{k*}$ ruta$_{fd4.de}$
    - **tearing** pain: berb coloc euph *Ign* kali-i mag-m$_{h2}$ sulph
  - **stepping**:
    - **agg.**: dulc↓ sil↓ tritic-vg↓
      - **stitching** pain: dulc$_{fd4.de}$ sil tritic-vg$_{fd5.de}$
    - **every** step; at: rhus-t$_{a1}$
  - **stitching** pain: *Agar* aloe *Alum* alum-sil$_{k2}$ am-c am-m ang arg-n asaf bell berb bry$_{k*}$ calc *Calc-p* calc-sil$_{k2}$ camph carb-v carc$_{fd2.de}$• caust chel clem coc-c coloc con cycl$_{h1*}$ dros dulc eupi gamb *Graph* grat *Guaj* hell *Indg* jatr-c kali-n kali-p$_{fd1.de}$• led *Lyc* meny merc nat-p nux-v petr-ra$_{shn4}$• ph-ac pieri-b$_{mlk9.de}$ *Plb* puls *Rhus-t* ruta$_{fd4.de}$ sars sil *Spig* spong *Staph Sulph* tarax$_{k*}$ *Tarent* thuj tritic-vg$_{fd5.de}$ upa vanil$_{fd5.de}$
    - **downward**: chel eupi ph-ac *Sulph*
    - **outward**: berb
    - **paroxysmal**: caust plb
    - **tearing** pain: calc
    - **upward**: *Guaj* xan

- **Calves – stitching** pain: ...
  - **wandering** pain: berb
  - **stretching**:
    - **agg.**: graph ↓
      - **drawing** pain: graph h2
    - **amel.**: calc-f sp1
  - **tearing** pain: agar *Alum* *Alum-sil* k4 am-m ambr anac c1 arn ars aur-m berb bry calc *Calc-p* calc-sil k2 canth carb-v carbn-s castm *Caust* chin cic cina colch *Coloc* croc euph *Ign* *Indg* kali-bi kali-c kali-i kali-m k2 kali-n kali-sil k2 laur led lob mag-c mag-m mang merc mez mur-ac nat-c nat-m **Nat-s** olnd par petr-ra shn4• phel plb ran-b raph rat sabad sil staph k* sulph tab teucr tritic-vg fd5.de *Valer* k* *Zinc*
    - **cramping**: ran-b
    - **downward**: arn carb-v caust dulc a1 mag-m phel sulph zinc
    - **drawing** pain: calc kali-n
    - **lacerating**: plb tritic-vg fd5.de
    - **paroxysmal**: ambr aur-m plb
    - **pressing** pain: berb
    - **pulsating** pain: **Valer** k*
    - **sticking** pain: staph
    - **twitching**: am-m zinc h2
    - **upward**: arn mag-m
  - **tensive**: berb cupr
  - **touch** agg.: ant-c ↓ *Calc*
    - **sore**: ant-c h2
  - **ulcerative** pain: agar
  - **uncovering** | **amel.**: calc-f sp1
  - **vertigo**; during: *Ambr* b7a.de
  - **walking**:
    - **after**:
      - **agg.**: am-m cinnb dulc fd4.de *Rhus-t* spong fd4.de
        - **stitching** pain: am-m
    - **agg.**: alum anac arg-n a1 *Ars* arund *Brucel* sa3• **Calc** cann-i ↓ canth ↓ caps *Carb-an* *Chel* ↓ dulc fd4.de gard-j vlr2• grat ↓ gymno ign iris jatr-c lyc mur-ac myric ↓ nat-c ↓ nat-p ↓ nit-ac bg1 *Nux-v* olnd ↓ onos petr ↓ plb ↓ puls ran-b ↓ rhus-t a1* sacch-a ↓ *Sil* ↓ spig spong ↓ staph ↓ sulph *Thuj* ↓ tritic-vg fd5.de ulm-c ↓ verat-v viol-t ↓ zinc
      - **aching**: myric
      - **cutting** pain: *Thuj*
      - **drawing** pain: alum *Anac* cann-i k* **Carb-an** k* *Lyc* nat-c *Nux-v* *Sil* spig k* verat-v k* viol-t k*
      - **sore**: alum *Chel* petr hr1 staph h1 ulm-c jsj8•
      - **stitching** pain: arg-n (non:chin kl) grat nat-p sacch-a fd2.de• spong staph tritic-vg fd5.de
      - **tearing** pain: canth *Ign* olnd plb ran-b tritic-vg fd5.de
    - **air** agg.; in open: fago ↓ merc ↓ mez ↓ nat-c ↓
      - **aching**: fago
      - **burning**: mez
      - **cutting** pain: nat-c hr1
      - **stitching** pain: merc
    - **amel.**: agar ↓ arg-met ↓ *Dros* ↓ kali-i ↓ *Rhus-t* ↓ sulph ↓ **Valer** ↓
      - **drawing** pain: agar arg-met sulph h2
      - **stitching** pain: *Dros* k* *Rhus-t*
      - **tearing** pain: agar kali-i **Valer**
  - **warm** | **applications**:
    - **amel.**: ars ↓
      - **tearing** pain: ars h2
    - **bed**:
      - **agg.**: plb ↓
        - **tearing** pain: plb
      - **amel.**: caust tl1 *Nux-v* plb ↓ upa ↓
        - **stitching** pain: plb upa
  - **extending** to:
    - **Heel**: *Coloc* ↓ mag-m ↓ sang ↓
      - **drawing** pain: sang
      - **tearing** pain: *Coloc* mag-m h2
    - **Knees**: chel ↓

- **Calves – extending** to – **Knees**: ...
      - **drawing** pain: chel
      - **Hollow** of knees: nat-s ↓ rhus-t ↓
        - **drawing** pain: rhus-t
        - **tearing** pain: nat-s
    - **Tendo** Achillis: fl-ac ↓
      - **drawing** pain: fl-ac
    - **Thighs**: chel ↓ kali-s ↓ ruta ↓
      - **drawing** pain: chel kali-s fd4.de ruta fd4.de
    - **Tibia**; down: led
    - **Toes**: sulph ↓
      - **tearing** pain: sulph
  - **Above**: sep ↓
    - **tearing** pain: sep h2
  - **Below**: lyc ↓ sep ↓
    - **tearing** pain: lyc h2 sep h2
  - **Internally**: dulc ↓
    - **cut** with a sharp instrument; as if slightly: dulc h1
  - **Middle** of calves: nit-ac ↓
    - **drawing** pain: nit-ac h2
- **Knees**; below: *Chel* ↓ cina ↓ cupr ↓ ph-ac ↓
  - **pressing** pain: *Chel* cupr h2 ph-ac h2
  - **stitching** pain: cina h1*
  - **tearing** pain: cupr h2
- **Muscles**: lat-m bnm6•
  - **right**: mand ↓
    - **dull** pain: mand rsj7•
  - **morning**: mand rsj7•
  - **rest** agg.: mand rsj7•
  - **walking** agg.: gard-j vlr2•
  - **Tibia**; of: calc ↓
    - **sprained**; as if: calc h2
- **Near** inner ankle: meny ↓
  - **sprained**; as if: meny h1
- **Periosteum**: chin ↓ hyper ↓
  - **shooting** pain: hyper
  - **sore**: chin h1
- **Shins** (See bones - tibia)
- **Sides**:
  - **Inner**: sulph ↓
    - **sore**: sulph h2
- **Spots**; in: sil ↓
  - **sore**: sil
- **Tendo** Achillis: acon ↓ aesc *Alum* ↓ am-c ↓ anac bg3 ang ↓ arist-m c2* aur ↓ aur-m-n bell ↓ benz-ac k* berb bit-ar wht1• bry calad *Calc* calc-caust bro1 camph ↓ *Cann-s* carb-ac *Carb-an* caust bro1 chel ↓ cic ↓ cimic k* *Cinnb* coc-c *Colch* euphr k* graph ↓ hep ↓ ign k* ina-i mlk9.de *Irid-met* vml3• *Kali-bi* k* *Kali-c* ↓ ketogl-ac ↓ kreos ↓ laur *Led* *Lyc* b4a.de mag-c ↓ med bro1 *Merc* k* merl mez ↓ mill mur-ac k* myric c2 nat-ar bro1 nat-m ↓ nat-s osteo-a jl2 petr-ra shn4• rat rhod rhus-t ruta bro1* sep bg3 sil ↓ sul-ac ↓ *Sulph* ↓ symph fd3.de• tarent k2 ter bro1 tet c2 thuj k* upa c2* valer bg3* vanil fd5.de *Zinc*
  - **morning**: sulph
  - **evening**: *Alum* ↓ carb-an ↓ ruta ↓
    - **drawing** pain: carb-an ruta fd4.de
    - **tearing** pain: *Alum*
  - **night**: mur-ac
  - **aching**: *Cimic* petr-ra shn4•
  - **ascending** stairs agg.: rhus-t vanil fd5.de
  - **boring** pain: aur-m-n bell h1
  - **drawing** pain: acon bg2 aesc alum k* ang bg2 benz-ac berb k* *Calc* cann-s k2 *Carb-an* chel graph k* *Kali-bi* ketogl-ac rly4• lyc mag-c mur-ac k* nat-m k* nat-s k* ruta fd4.de sulph k* thuj valer bg2* vanil fd5.de *Zinc* k*
  - **exertion** agg.: *Ign*
    - **tearing** pain: *Ign*
  - **hangs** down; when leg: berb ↓

- **Tendo** Achillis – **hangs** down; when leg: ...
  - **stitching** pain: berb
  - **insertion**, at the: bism ↓ colch ↓
    - **tearing** pain: bism h1 colch
  - **lying**:
    - **amel.**: *Mur-ac* hr1
    - **bed**; in:
      - **agg.**: hep ↓
        - **tearing** pain: hep h2
  - **motion**:
    - **amel.**: alum ↓ **Valer** ↓
      - **drawing** pain: alum k* **Valer** k*
  - **rest** agg.: alum ↓ aur ↓
    - **drawing** pain: alum h2
    - **stitching** pain: aur
  - **rheumatic**: bry cimic
  - **shooting** pain: tarent k2
  - **sitting** agg.: *Mur-ac* hr1
  - **sore**: *Aesc* k* *Bry* carb-ac *Cimic* k* coc-c k* mill
  - **sprained**; as if: kreos k*
  - **standing** agg.: benz-ac berb rat ↓
    - **tearing** pain: rat
  - **stitching** pain: am-c aur berb camph cimic hep mur-ac k* nat-m rhus-t sil sul-ac *Sulph* b4a.de tarent thuj
  - **tearing** pain: *Alum* k* bell berb *Calc* k* *Caust* k* cic *Colch* hep b4a.de* *Ign* *Kali-c* mez k* nat-s rat thuj k* *Zinc* k*
    - **upward**: rat
  - **walking**:
    - **after** | **agg.**: cinnb coc-c merc
    - **agg.**: berb bry cimic *Cinnb* coc-c cocc tl1 *Ign* mur-ac ↓ petr-ra shn4• rhod ptk1 symph fd3.de• vanil fd5.de [irid-met stj]
      - **drawing** pain: mur-ac h2 vanil fd5.de
      - **stepping** on the toes; when: kali-bi
      - **tearing** pain: *Ign*
    - **continued** | **amel.**: *Kali-bi Rhod Rhus-t* valer k2
    - **rapidly**:
      - **agg.**: mag-c ↓ thuj ↓
        - **drawing** pain: mag-c thuj
- **Tendons**: nat-s ↓ phys ↓ pyrus ↓ ruta ↓
  - **drawing** pain: nat-s k* phys k* pyrus ruta fd4.de
  - **walking** agg.: chinin-s
- **Veins**: cham ↓
  - **tearing** pain: cham h1
  - **Saphenous**: calc-f jl3
    - **motion** agg.: calc-f sp1

– **Lower** limbs: abrot *Acon* ↓ act-sp ↓ aesc k* aeth ↓ **Agar** *Agn* ↓ aids ↓ ail ↓ aloe ↓ alum bg3 alum-p ↓ alum-sil k2 alumn am-c b4.de* *Am-m* ↓ ambr ↓ *Anac* k* androc ↓ *Ang* ↓ ant-c ant-t ↓ *Apis* aran ↓ *Arg-met Arg-n* ↓ arge-pl ↓ arn k* *Ars* k* *Ars-h* k* ars-i ars-s-f k2 asaf ↓ asar ↓ aster ↓ *Aur* k* *Aur-m* ↓ aur-s k2 bad k* *Bamb-a* stb2.de• bapt bg2 bar-act ↓ bar-c b4.de* bar-s k2 *Bell* bell-p-sp ↓ benz-ac ↓ berb k* *Bism* ↓ *Bol-la* borx ↓ *Bov* k* *Brucel* sa3• *Bry* bufo ↓ cact cadm-s ↓ cain ↓ calad ↓ *Calc* k* *Calc-ar* ↓ *Calc-p* k* *Calc-s* calc-sil k2 camph ↓ cann-s ↓ canth ↓ *Caps* ↓ carb-ac carb-an ↓ *Carb-v* k* carbn-s carc hbh* cassia-s cdd7*• castor-eq ↓ *Caul* ↓ *Caust* cedr k* *Cham* *Chel* k* *Chin* chinin-ar chinin-s ↓ chlor ↓ *Cic* ↓ cimic *Cina* ↓ cinnb ↓ cist ↓ clem ↓ cob ↓ *Cocc* ↓ coff b7.de* *Colch* ↓ *Coloc* k* con k* cot ↓ croc ↓ crot-h ↓ crot-t ↓ cupr k* cycl ↓ dig k* dios ↓ dream-p ↓ dros ↓ dulc b4.de* echi elaps erio a1 **Eup-per** ↓ *Euph* ↓ *Euphr* ↓ eupi ↓ falco-pe ↓ *Ferr* ferr-ar ferr-i ↓ fl-ac ↓ form ↓ galla-q-r nl2• *Gels* k* granit-m ↓ graph k* *Grat* ↓ *Guaj* ham k* hedy a1* hell helo-s ↓ helon ↓ **Hep** ↓ heroin ↓ hipp ↓ hyos ↓ hyper ↓ *Ign* ↓ *Indg* inul br1 iod b4.de* *Ip* ↓ *Iris* ↓ kali-ar kali-bi bg2 kali-c bg3 *Kali-i* ↓ kali-n k* kali-p kali-s fd4.de kali-sil ↓ *Kalm* k* ketogl-ac rly4• kola stb3• kreos ↓ *Lac-c* lac-h sk4• lac-lup hrn2• lacer a1 lach k* lat-m bnm6• laur ↓ lavand-a ↓ led bg3 *Lil-t* k* *Lith-c* *Lyc* k* m-ambo ↓ m-arct ↓ *M-aust* ↓ mag-c b4.de* *Mag-m* ↓ *Mag-p* mag-s ↓ *Manc* ↓ mand ↓ mang mrr1 *Med* melal-alt gya4 meny ↓ *Merc* k* merc-c merc-i-f k* merc-i-r k* *Mez* k* mit a1 mosch ↓ mucs-nas rly4• mur-ac b4.de* myric k* nat-ar *Nat-c* k* *Nat-m* k* *Nat-p* ↓ **Nat-s** ↓ nat-sil fd3.de• nicc ↓ *Nit-ac* k* nit-s-d a1 nux-m ↓ *Nux-v* k* olib-sac ↓ olnd b7.de* op ↓ orot-ac ↓

– **Lower** limbs: ...
ox-ac k2 par ↓ *Petr* k* petr-ra shn4• ph-ac *Phos* k* *Phys* k* *Phyt* pic-ac k* pip-m ↓ pitu-gl skp7• plan k* *Plat* **Plb** k* plumbg k* podo ↓ polyg-h ↓ positr ↓ pot-e ↓ propr sa3• prun psil ↓ psor ptel k* *Puls* k* pycnop-sa ↓ rad-br mrr1 *Ran-b* *Ran-s* ↓ rat ↓ rauw tpw8 rhod k* rhus-g tmo3• **Rhus-t** k* *Rhus-v* ↓ rumx ↓ ruta k2 sabad ↓ sabin ↓ sacch-a fd2.de• sang k* sanic ↓ sarr ↓ sars k* sec k* seneg *Sep* k* *Sil* k* sol-ecl ↓ sol-ni spect ↓ spig ↓ spong fd4.de *Squil* ↓ **Stann** k* *Staph* ↓ stram ↓ stront-c k* suis-pan ↓ *Sul-ac* ↓ sul-i ↓ sulfonam ↓ *Sulph* k* symph ↓ syph k2 *Tarax* tarent tell ↓ ter k* tetox pin2• teucr ↓ thal a1 thuj k2 tritic-vg fd5.de tub k2 tung-met ↓ ulm-c ↓ uran-n ↓ *Vac* ↓ *Valer* k* vanil fd5.de vario ↓ *Verat* ↓ verb ↓ vib ↓ vip k* visc ↓ xan k* *Zinc* k* zinc-p k2

- **alternating** sides: cic ↓
  - **sore**: cic a1
- **right**: ang ↓ *Chel* ↓ lac-lup hrn2• nit-ac ↓ olib-sac wmh1 phos ↓ spong ↓ sulph ↓ symph ↓
  - **night**:
    - **extending** to:
      - **Toes**: gins ↓
        - **boring** pain: gins br1
  - **cramping**: lac-lup hrn2• sulph h2
  - **drawing** pain: *Chel* nit-ac h2 phos h2 spong fd4.de symph fd3.de•
  - **sore**: ang h1
  - **tearing** pain: sulph h2
- **left**: bamb-a ↓ bar-act ↓ *Bar-c* ↓ *Carb-v* ↓ con ↓ lavand-a ↓ lyc ↓ nat-m ↓ petr ↓ phos ↓ propr sa3• ruta ↓ sil ↓ suis-pan ↓ verat-v bg2
  - **aching**: suis-pan rly4•
  - **cramping**: lavand-a ctl1• propr sa3•
  - **drawing** pain: bamb-a stb2.de• bar-act br1 *Bar-c* *Carb-v* con h2 nat-m h2 petr h2 ruta fd4.de
  - **pressing** pain: phos h2
  - **tearing** pain: con h2 lyc h2 sil h2
  - **extending** to:
    - **right**: ambr ↓
      - **tearing** pain: ambr
- **daytime**: phos plumbg k*
- **morning**: anac carb-an ↓ caust ham fd3.de• hep ↓ *Ph-ac* ↓ phos k* sang k* sil spong fd4.de stann k* stront-c ↓ tritic-vg fd5.de
  - **amel.**: aur colch merc mez nux-v syph
  - **bed** agg.; in: ant-t bov bry nit-ac spong fd4.de sulph
    - **drawing** pain: *Sulph*
  - **rising** | **after**:
    - **agg.**: kali-bi ↓
      - **drawing** pain: kali-bi
    - **agg.**: nux-v ↓ **Rhus-t** stann k*
      - **sore**: nux-v stann h2
  - **sore**: carb-an *Caust Ph-ac*
  - **tearing** pain: hep stront-c
  - **waking**; on: androc ↓ aur plut-n ↓ tritic-vg fd5.de
    - **aching**: androc srj1• aur plut-n srj7•
- **forenoon**: nat-s ↓ ptel ↓
  - **9** h: phys
  - **sore**: nat-s ptel
- **noon**: agar ↓
  - **burning**: agar
- **afternoon**: bell myric ↓ sang
  - **13** h: propr sa3•
  - **16** h: *Coloc*
  - **sore**: myric
- **evening**: alum ↓ ambr *Ars* ↓ calc caust ↓ ferr-ma kali-c **Kali-s** *Led Lyc* mag-s ↓ mez k* nat-c ↓ *Nat-m* nat-s nit-ac plan k* plumbg k* puls sep sil still ↓ stront-c sulph ↓ tritic-vg fd5.de zinc k*
  - **18**-19 h: rauw sp1
  - **aching**: still
  - **bed** agg.; in: carb-an carb-v ↓ *Ferr* ↓ ferr-ma *Kali-s* phos puls ↓ sulph
    - **drawing** pain: carb-v h2 puls k2 *Sulph*
    - **tearing** pain: *Ferr Sulph*

- **evening**: ...
  - **drawing** pain: caust h2 *Nat-m* nit-ac **Puls** sil stront-c sulph zinc
  - **motion**:
    - **amel.**: stront-c ↓
      - **drawing** pain: stront-c
  - **pinching** pain: mez k*
  - **pressing** pain: nit-ac h2
  - **sore**: sulph
  - **stitching** pain: *Ars* nat-m
  - **tearing** pain: alum mag-s nat-c
  - **walking** agg.: sulph ↓
    - **tearing** pain: sulph
- **night**: alum k* alumn ambr anac ↓ arn k* *Ars* bamb-a stb2.de• *Bell Bry* carb-an carb-v cham *Cic* ↓ coloc ery-a fago ↓ *Ferr* graph hep iod kali-c kali-n ↓ kali-p ↓ *Lac-c Lyc* mag-c *Mag-p* mag-s mang *Med* **Merc** *Mez Nat-c Nat-m* **Nit-ac** k* *Nux-v Phos* **Phyt** propr sa3• *Rhod* ↓ **Rhus-t** ruta fd4.de sang sep staph stront-c sk4• *Sulph* ter *Tub* ↓ vanil fd5.de *Verat* ↓ zinc ↓
  - **midnight**:
    - **before**: **Ferr** prun
      - **22** h: plan
      - **23-7** h: *Sulph*
    - **after**: *Ars* nux-v
      - **3-5** h: *Kali-c* sep
      - **4** h: coloc
        - **tearing** pain: coloc
  - **aching**: med k*
  - **bed** agg.; in: kali-c ↓ **Merc** *Mez* ruta fd4.de *Sulph Verat*
    - **burning**: kali-c
  - **burning**: fago
  - **drawing** pain: *Nat-c* nat-m phos h2 *Tub* vanil fd5.de zinc h2
  - **lying** upon it; when: **Ars** ↓
    - **tearing** pain: **Ars**
  - **pressing** pain: kali-n h2
  - **putting** feet out of bed amel.: sulph ↓
    - **tearing** pain: sulph
  - **sore**: kali-p fd1.de• phos
  - **stitching** pain: *Merc*
  - **tearing** pain: alum anac *Ars Cic* kali-c h2 lyc h2 *Merc* **Nit-ac** *Rhod Verat*
- **aching**: aesc agar k2 aids nl2• androc srj1• arge-pl rwt5• ars-i bg1* aur *Calc-p Cimic* cob **Eup-per** k* falco-pe nl2• **Gels** k* granit-m es1• guaj ptk1 helo-s rwt2• helon ptk1 lavand-a ctl1• lil-t ptk1 *Med* k* melal-alt gya4 merc merc-i-f mucs-nas rly4• nat-ar nit-ac bg1* nit-s-d bg1 orot-ac rly4• *Phyt* ptk1 pic-ac ptk1 polyg-h ptk1 positr nl2• ptel pycnop-sa mrz1 **Rhus-t** k* rumx sep bg1 suis-pan rly4• sul-ac ptk1 sul-i ptk1 sulfonam ks2 tell bg1 *Tub* vac bg1 vario bg1* [bell-p-sp dcm1 heroin sdj2 sol-ecl cky1 spect dfg1]
- **air** agg.; in open: caust tl1 *Cocc* graph *Mag-p*
  - **tearing** pain: **Caust**
- **alternating** with:
  - **numbness**: gnaph bg2
  - **palpitations** (See CHEST - Palpitation - alternating - lower)
  - **Eye**; complaints of: kreos
  - **Stomach**; pain in (See STOMACH - Pain - alternating - limbs)
  - **Upper** limbs; pain in (See upper limbs - alternating with - lower)
- **ascending** stairs agg.: arge-pl rwt5• nat-m ↓ stann ↓
  - **sore**: nat-m h2 stann
- **bathing**: sulph
- **blow**; pain as from a: arn b7.de* *Bell* b4a.de cina b7.de* kreos b7a.de m-ambo b7.de m-aust b7.de mosch b7a.de nux-m b7.de* plat b4.de* puls b7.de* ruta b7.de*
- **boring** pain: act-sp aeth am-m apis aran ars bg2 cadm-s canth k* cocc b7.de* coloc dios bg2 *Ign* kali-bi *Merc* ran-b k* ran-s k* *Rhod*
- **broken**; as if: agar k2 ars k* bell bg2 borx bg2 bufo bg2 calc bg2 kali-bi bg2 lyc b4.de* mag-m b4.de* mez b4.de* ph-ac b4.de* phos b4.de* pip-m a1 **Ruta** sep b4a.de sulph bg2 thuj bg2 vac jl2 zinc b4.de*
- **burning**: agar alum k* anac *Apis* ars k* bapt bar-c k* borx b4a.de bufo *Calc* b4a.de carb-v k* castor-eq caust k* chin k* chinin-ar coloc b4a.de crot-h ptk1 dream-p sdj1• dulc gels *Kali-c* k* lach led k* *Lyc* k* m-ambo b7.de mag-c k* mag-m k* mang k* nat-c k* nat-s ptk1 nit-ac olib-sac wmh1 ph-ac k* *Phos* k* pic-ac ptk1 plat k* plb k2 pot-e rly4• prun ptel puls k* *Rhus-t* ruta sec mrr1 *Sil* k* *Stann* b4a.de sulph b4a.de thuj k* *Vac* jl2 *Zinc* k* zinc-p k2
- **burnt**; sensation as if: am-c bg2 caust b4.de* lach bg2 zinc bg2
- **burrowing**: arn bg2 ruta bg2
- **carrying** a weight; while: rauw sp1
- **chill**:
  - **before**: *Nux-v*
  - **during**: acon bg2 am-c bg2 arn k* **Ars** k* bar-c bg2 bell bg2 bry k* calc bg2 canth bg2 caps k* caust bg2 cham bg2 **Chin** k* coff bg2 coloc bg2 *Ferr* guaj bg2 hell bg2 *Ign* bg2 kali-n bg2 kreos bg2 lach bg2 led k* lyc k* mez k* nat-m k* nat-s k2 **Nux-v** k* phos k* *Puls* k* **Pyrog** rhod bg2 *Rhus-t* k* sabad bg2 *Seneg* bg2 sep k* spig bg2 spong bg2 sulph k* tarax bg2 tarent k2 thuj k* *Tub* ↓ verat bg2
    - **aching**: nat-s k2 nux-v **Rhus-t** tarent k2
    - **stitching** pain: ferr *Tub*
    - **tearing** pain: *Ars* **Rhus-t**
- **clawing**: valer a2
- **cold**:
  - **amel.**: *Apis Coff Guaj Lac-c* **Led** ozone sde2• **Puls Sec** syph k2
    - **burning**: sec mrr1
  - **exposure** to:
    - **agg.**: *Calc-p* ↓ *Phos* ↓ rhus-t ↓
      - **drawing** pain: *Calc-p Phos* rhus-t k2
- **cold** agg.; becoming: *Agar Ars* bry calc *Dulc* graph *Kalm* **Nux-v** ph-ac *Phos* **Rhus-t** spong fd4.de *Tarent Tub*
  - **tearing** pain: *Phos Rhus-t*
- **corrosive**: agn b7.de* *Lyc* b4a.de nux-v b7.de* plat b4a.de ruta b7a.de spig b7.de* spong b7.de* staph b7.de* tarax b7.de*
- **cough** agg.; during: *Caps* ↓
  - **tearing** pain: *Caps*
- **crossing** limbs in bed: aur bg1 phos k*
- **crural** neuralgia (See thighs - crural)
- **cutting** pain: alum k* bell k* bufo bg2 calc k* coloc b4.de* dros k* dulc k* *Graph* k* ign lyc k* mag-m k* mur-ac k* *Nat-c* k* sep k* sil k* stann k* sul-ac k* *Vac* jl2
- **dancing** amel.: *Sep* k*
  - **sore**: sep
- **dislocated**; as if: am-c b4.de* calc b4.de* *Carb-v* b4.de* *Caust* b4.de* con b4.de* iris bg2 kali-bi bg2 kali-c b4.de* mag-m b4.de* merc mez b4.de* *Nat-m* b4.de* petr b4.de* phos b4.de* sarr stann b4.de* thuj b4.de*
- **dragging**: carb-ac bg2 spig bg2
- **drawing** pain: *Acon* k* *Agar Alum* k* am-c am-m k* ambr c1 anac k* *Ang* k* ant-c k* ant-t k* apis b7a.de *Arg-met Arg-n Arn* b7.de* ars k* ars-i bamb-a stb2.de• *Bapt* **Bar-c** k* bar-s k2 bell b4.de* berb k* *Bry* k* calc k* calc-p caps b7.de* **Carb-v** k* carbn-s *Caust* k* *Cham* k* **Chel** k* chin cina k* cinnb cist clem k* cocc b7.de* colch b7.de* coloc bg2 *Con* k* dig k* dros b7.de* *Dulc* k* *Ferr* k* ferr-i *Gels* k* **Graph** k* grat **Hep** k* hyos b7.de* hyper a1 *Iod* k* kali-ar kali-bi k* *Kali-c* k* kali-i bg2 kali-n k* kali-sil k2 kreos k* lach k* led k* *Lyc* k* m-ambo b7.de *M-aust* b7a.de mag-c k* mand rsj7• mang b4.de* *Merc* k* mez k* *Mur-ac* b4a.de nat-ar *Nat-c* k* *Nat-m* k* *Nit-ac* k* *Nux-v* k* par k* petr k* ph-ac k* *Phos* pic-ac plat k* *Puls* k* ran-s b7.de* rat *Rhod* b4a.de **Rhus-t** k* rhus-v ruta fd4.de sars h2 *Sep* k* *Sil* k* spong fd4.de stann k* *Stront-c* k* *Sul-ac* b4a.de sul-i k2 *Sulph* k* symph fd3.de• tarent k2 thuj k* tritic-vg fd5.de *Tub Valer* k* vanil fd5.de verat k* *Zinc* k*
  - **cramping**: *Arg-n* chin gels graph *Hep* iod merc-i-f nat-m h2 phos *Sulph*
  - **downward**: chel gels graph h2 nat-m h2 nit-ac *Puls* sil
  - **followed** by | **jerking** pain: *Sil*
  - **paralyzed**; as if: carb-ac c1 **Carb-v** *Chel* k* mez par

- **drawing** pain: ...
  - **paroxysmal**: nat-m
  - **upward**: sep h2
- **eating** | **after** | **agg.**: *Indg* kali-c
  - **while**:
    - **agg.**: ph-ac ↓
      - **tearing** pain: ph-ac
- **electric** shock; as from an: arg-met mrr1
- **ending** in jerking: *Sil*
- **eructations** | **amel.**: thuj bg1
- **excitement**: alum-sil k2*
- **exertion**:
  - **agg.**: alum androc srj1• bar-c **Calc** *Caust* ign phos **Rhus-t** stann
  - **amel.** | **violent** exertion: carc sp1
- **exertion**; as after: aloe bg2 alum b4.de* bar-c b4.de* calc b4.de* cann-s b7.de* croc b7.de* gels bg2 ip b7.de* mosch b7.de* nux-m b7.de* nux-v b7.de* olnd b7.de* phos b4.de* *Puls* b7.de* *Ruta* b7a.de stann b4.de* verat b7.de*
- **fatigue**; as from: petr-ra shn4•
- **feather** beds: *Asaf* k*
- **fever** | **during**:
  - **agg.**: acon bg2 agn bg2 am-c bg2 ant-c bg2 arn bg2 **Ars** b4a.de* bell bg2 *Calc* bg2 canth bg2 **Caps** b7a.de* **Carb-v** b4a.de* caust bg2 chin bg2 colch bg2 ferr bg2 ign bg2 ip bg2 kali-n b4a.de* *Lyc* bg2 mag-c bg2 mag-m bg2 nat-m bg2 nat-s k2 *Nux-v* bg2 phos bg2 pitu-gl skp7• *Puls* bg2 rhod bg2 rhus-t bg2 samb bg2 *Sep* bg2 spong bg2 *Sulph* bg2 thuj bg2 verat bg2
    - **aching**: nat-s k2 *Puls* **Rhus-t**
  - **with**: kali-n ↓
    - **drawing** pain: kali-n h2
- **flatus**; from obstructed: carb-v ↓
  - **tearing** pain: carb-v h2
- **flexing** limb, on: cocc br1 nux-v k* tritic-vg fd5.de
  - **halfway**: rauw sp1
- **gnawing** pain: alum h2 *Ars* k* *Bell* k* berb bg2 lyc nit-ac par bg2 plat ran-s k* ruta
- **gouty**: *Bry* led tl1
  - **extending** to | **Upward**: led tl1
- **grasping** pain: ign b7.de* led b7.de* stront-c b4.de*
- **growing** pains (See GENERALS - Pain - growing)
- **hang** down amel.; letting limb: bell **Con** verat
- **hanging** over side of bed amel.: verat ↓
  - **tearing** pain: verat k*
- **hard** bed; as if from a: arn b7.de*
- **heat**; during: calc-s k2
- **increasing** and decreasing gradually: zinc bg2
- **jerking** pain: anac b4.de* ant-c bg2 ant-t b7.de arg-n bg2 ars b4.de* **Bell** bg2 bufo bg2 calc b4.de* *Caust* bg2 chin bg2 cic b7.de* *Cimic* bg2 colch b7.de* coloc bg2 *Cupr* bg2 *Euphr* b7a.de hep bg2 kreos b7a.de lach bg2 lyc bg2 mag-c b4.de* meny b7a.de merc b4.de* op b7a.de petr bg2 ph-ac b4.de* *Phos* b4.de* *Phys* bg2 *Sep* b4a.de sil bg2 spig b7a.de stann b4.de* stram b7.de* sul-ac b4.de* *Sulph* b4.de* *Tarent* bg2 *Valer* k* *Zinc* b4.de*
- **kneeling**, after: aids ↓ op ↓
  - **stitching** pain: aids nl2• op
- **labor** like: aloe dream-p sdj1•
- **lain** on; limb: graph ↓
  - **sore**: graph h2
- **lightning**-like: coloc bg2
- **lying**:
  - **amel.**: am-m *Dios* ham k*
  - **side**; on:
    - **painful** side:
      - **agg.**: **Ars** ↓
        - **tearing** pain: **Ars**
- **lying** down agg.: sulfonam ↓
  - **aching**: sulfonam ks2
- **menses** | **before**:
  - **agg.**: berb *Caul* gels bg1 lach nit-ac nux-m bg1 nux-v phos k* sep k* syph vib
    - **aching**: caul ptk1
    - **drawing** pain: phos sep
    - **sore**: caul
  - **during**:
    - **agg.**: am-c ↓ *Am-m* ↓ ambr bell *Berb* ↓ bry calc-p ↓ caul *Cham* cimic ↓ con cycl dream-p ↓ graph ham kali-n k* mag-m ↓ mosch nit-ac ↓ nux-m nux-v petr ↓ phos *Puls* ↓ rhus-t sec sep spong stram sul-ac ↓ verat
      - **aching**: calc-p caul cimic dream-p sdj1•
      - **drawing** pain: am-c b4a.de *Am-m* b7a.de ambr b7a.de con k* nit-ac h2 nux-m petr b4.de phos b4.de* *Puls* b7a.de rhus-t sep k* *Spong* k* stram b7a.de
      - **sore**: caul mag-m h2 nit-ac sep
      - **tearing** pain: *Bell* *Berb* bry cham con rhus-t sep sul-ac
- **motion**:
  - **after**:
    - **agg.**: calc-p ↓
      - **aching**: calc-p
  - **agg.**: acon alum alum-sil k2 *Apis* ars ↓ berb **Bry** calc ↓ calc-p k* carbn-s carc sp1* cocc *Gels* ↓ *Guaj* kali-p *Kalm* ↓ kreos *Lac-c* *Led* mang *Merc* nat-s *Nux-v* olib-sac wmh1 *Phos* *Phyt* *Plb* k* puls *Ran-b* spong fd4.de sulph vanil fd5.de
    - **drawing** pain: *Gels*
    - **must** move; but: thal dx
    - **sore**: calc h2
    - **tearing** pain: alum ars h2 *Bry* *Kalm*
  - **amel.**: *Agar* *Arg-met* *Arg-n* ↓ *Ars* ↓ *Aur-m-n* *Bell* *Calc* calc-p caps carc sp1 *Coloc* cupr euph **Ferr** gels *Indg* iod ↓ *Kali-bi* *Kali-c* ↓ kali-p **Kali-s** **Lyc** melal-alt gya4 *Merc* merc-i-f ↓ merc-i-r k* *Mur-ac* *Nat-s* *Ph-ac* *Plan* plut-n ↓ **Puls** *Rat* **Rhod** **Rhus-t** ruta *Sep* stel ↓ stront-c sulph *Tarax* tritic-vg fd5.de **Tub** *Valer* vanil ↓ *Zinc*
    - **aching**: agar k2 plut-n srj7• *Puls* **Rhus-t**
    - **drawing** pain: *Arg-n* ferr iod lyc h2 merc-i-f **Rhus-t** sep h2 stront-c *Tub* **Valer** vanil fd5.de
    - **stitching** pain: arg-met *Kali-c* *Kali-s* stel
    - **tearing** pain: agar h2 *Arg-met* *Ars* bell k2 euph *Puls* *Rhod* **Rhus-t** sep h2 *Tarax* valer zinc
  - **beginning** of | **agg.**: calc carb-v *Caust* *Ferr* gels indg *Kali-p* **Lyc** mag-c nit-ac *Petr* *Plat* *Rhod* **Rhus-t** thuj
- **nail**; as from a: anac bg2 bufo bg2 coloc bg2 hyper bg2
- **neuralgic**: arg-met mrr1 bamb-a stb2.de• cupr k* ferr nat-ar plb k* ter k* thal dx xan c1
- **paralyzed**; as if: *Acon* b7a.de aeth c1 agar *Am-m* k* bar-c b4a.de carb-v k* caust b4.de* *Cham* k* chel k* *Chin* k* cimic cina k* *Cocc* k* colch b7.de* croc b7.de* dig k* *Euphr* b7a.de *Hep* b4a.de hyos b7.de* ign b7.de* iris bg2 kali-bi bg2 kreos b7a.de led b7.de* *Lyc* b4a.de *M-aust* b7a.de mang b4.de* mez k* *Nat-m* k* nux-v b7.de* olnd b7.de* par b7.de* ph-ac b4a.de phos b4.de* podo prun k* puls b7a.de rhus-t b7.de* ruta fd4.de sabad b7.de* *Sars* b4a.de *Sec* b7a.de *Seneg* k* *Sep* k* *Sil* k* *Stann* k* stront-c k* sul-ac b4.de* *Sulph* k* thuj b4a.de uran-n bg2 *Verat* k*
- **paroxysmal**: *Ars* **Bell** *Caust* chinin-s *Coff* *Coloc* *Gels* k* *Ign* *Kali-i* *Lyc* *Mag-p* nat-m k* **Plb** k* **Rhus-t** *Tarent* *Tub*
- **periodical**: *Ars* lyc lyss rhus-t
- **perspiration**:
  - **amel.**: *Gels*
  - **during**: am-c bg2 **Ant-t** bg2 *Arn* bg2 **Ars** bg2 bar-c bg2 bell bg2 bov bg2 bry bg2 *Calc* bg2 canth bg2 carb-v bg2 caust bg2 *Chin* bg2 *Hell* bg2 ign bg2 *Kali-n* bg2 led bg2 *Lyc* bg2 **Merc** bg2 *Merc-c* bg2 **Nat-m** bg2 **Nux-v** bg2 op bg2 *Ph-ac* bg2 *Phos* bg2 puls bg2 *Rhod* bg2 **Rhus-t** bg2 ruta bg2 **Sabad** bg2 **Sep** bg2 sil bg2 **Sulph** bg2 *Tarax* bg2 thuj bg2 verat bg2
  - **suppressed** perspiration; from: rhus-t k2
    - **drawing** pain: rhus-t k2

- **pinching** pain: anac k* ant-c b7.de* arn b7.de* bell *Calc* k* carb-an h2 carb-v caust b4.de* chin b7.de* dros b7.de dulc b4.de* graph hyos b7.de* iod ip b7.de* kali-c led b7.de* mang b4.de* meny b7.de* mez k* mur-ac b4.de* *Nat-c* k* nit-ac par b7.de* ph-ac phos sabad b7.de* sep sil k* stann b4.de* sul-ac b4.de* sulph k* thuj b4.de* zinc
- **plug**; as from a: agar bg2 anac bg2
- **pregnancy** agg.; during: ham ↓
  - **aching**: ham ptk1
- **pressing** pain: ambr bg2 anac b4.de* *Ang* b7a.de *Arg-met* arn bg2 asaf k* caust b4.de* cic k* cimic k* cycl k* dros k* iod b4.de* kalm led k* lyc bg2 mez k* *Nat-m* b4a.de nat-s nit-s-d a1 *Olnd* k* ph-ac k* *Plat* b4a.de ran-s k* *Rhod* k* rhus-t bg2 ruta k* *Sars* k* spong fd4.de *Stann* k* *Staph* k* *Sul-ac* b4a.de sulph k* *Verat* k* zinc k*
  - **cramping**: dros
  - **downward**: nit-ac h2 rhod k*
  - **drawing** pain: ran-s k*
  - **dull** pain: phyt bg2 puls bg2
  - **grasping** pain: *Stront-c*
  - **outward**: dulc bg2
- **pressure**:
  - **agg.**: ham k2 *Phos* plb
  - **amel.**: *Ars* **Mag-p** rauw tpw8 ruta fd4.de tritic-vg fd5.de
- **raising** | **foot**, pain preventing flexion: berb
- **rest**; after: op ↓
  - **stitching** pain: op
- **rheumatic**: ambr b7.de* anac b4.de* ang b7.de* ant-c k* ant-t k* *Apis* arg-met *Arn* b7a.de asaf b7.de* *Bry* b7.de* cact cadm-s calc-s *Carb-v* k* *Carbn-s* *Caust* cimic *Clem* colch coloc cycl b7.de* euph b4.de* gels bg2 graph k* *Guaj* ham fd3.de• hydr k2 iod b4.de* kali-bi bg2 *Kali-c* kali-n *Kalm* *Lac-c* lact **Led** k* *Lith-c* mang meph merc-c k* mez b4.de* nat-m k* nit-ac *Ph-ac* k* *Phos* *Phyt* plb *Puls* b7.de* *Rhod* k* rhus-r *Rhus-t* sabad b7.de* sabin b7.de* sal-ac c1 sang k* *Sep* stann stront-c sul-ac *Verat* k* *Zinc* k*
  - **alternating** sides: *Lac-c*
  - **night**: sal-ac c1
  - **burning**: apis
  - **drawing** pain: iod *Zinc*
  - **leaves** lower and goes to upper limbs: *Led* k*
  - **perspiration**; from suppressed: sal-ac c1
  - **warm** applications | **amel.**: ignis-alc es2•
  - **extending** to | **Upward**: led tl1
- **riding** agg.: rumx ↓
  - **aching**: rumx
- **rising**:
  - **sitting**; from:
    - **agg.**: cycl ↓ *Eup-per* ↓ mag-c ↓ **Ruta** ↓
      - **broken**; as if: **Ruta**
      - **sore**: cycl h1 *Eup-per*
      - **stitching** pain: mag-c
    - **amel.**: mag-c ↓
      - **tearing** pain: mag-c
- **rubbing** of trousers: cot ↓
  - **stitching** pain: cot br1
- **scraping** pain: am-c bg2 chin b7.de* puls b7a.de *Rhus-t* b7a.de sabad b7a.de
- **scratching**, from: prun ↓
  - **stitching** pain: prun
- **shooting** pain: aesc aeth *Alum* **Bell** *Coloc* gels *Lach* mag-s nat-c h2 *Nux-v* phos **Plb**
  - **burning**: fl-ac bg2
  - **downward**: aesc anac **Plb**
  - **upward**: ulm-c jsj8•
- **sitting**:
  - **agg.**: *Agar* k* *Alum* ↓ am-m ant-c apis ↓ **Arg-met** *Arg-n* ↓ arn ↓ *Aur-m-n* **Bell** ↓ calc cham chin cob croc dulc fd4.de ham k* *Indg* iod ip ↓ lac-h sk4• led **Lyc** mag-m nit-ac k* olnd paeon ph-ac plat ruta fd4.de sacch-a fd2.de• *Sep* spong fd4.de staph sulph tritic-vg fd5.de *Valer* verat
    - **drawing** pain: *Arg-n* chin iod **Valer**

- **sitting** – **agg.**: ...
    - **pressing** pain: *Arg-met*
    - **sore**: apis
    - **sprained**; as if: ip
    - **tearing** pain: agar *Alum* arn **Bell** ph-ac valer
  - **low** agg., sitting: sulph ↓
    - **tearing** pain: sulph h2
- **sore**: aesc agar alum k* alum-p k2 alum-sil k2 alumn anac b4.de* ang b7.de* ant-t k* apis k* *Arn* k* *Ars* b4a.de asaf b7.de* asar k* aster aur b4.de* *Bell* k* *Berb* bov b4.de* bry b7.de* bufo *Calc* k* camph b7.de* canth b7.de* carb-an k* *Carb-v* k* carbn-s cassia-s ccrh1• caul **Caust** k* *Chel* chin b7.de* clem b4.de* *Cocc* coff b7.de* *Con* cot br1 croc b7.de* crot-t cupr k* cycl b7.de* dig b4.de* dulc b4.de* **Eup-per** k* euph b4.de* ferr-i form gels ptk1 graph k* ham k* hell b7.de* ign b7.de* ip b7a.de kali-bi kali-c b4.de* kali-sil k2 kreos b7a.de laur b7.de* *Led* k* lyc b4.de* m-arct b7.de mag-c k* mag-m k* manc mang k* merc mez b4.de* mur-ac b4.de* myric *Nat-c* k* nat-m k* nat-p nat-s *Nit-ac* k* nux-m b7.de* *Nux-v* k* par b7.de* *Ph-ac* k* *Phos* k* pic-ac plat b4.de* plb ptel puls k* ran-b b7.de* *Rhod* b4.de* **Rhus-t** k* *Rhus-v* **Ruta** k* sabin b7a.de* sang bg2 sanic sec b7a.de *Sep* k* sil k* spig k* spong k* *Stann* k* staph b7.de* suis-pan rly4• *Sulph* k* thuj b4.de* valer k* verat k* zinc k*
  - **paralyzed**; as if: calc h2
  - **paroxysmal**: plb
- **sprained**; as if: *Arn* berb carb-v caust hipp jl2 nat-m olnd puls rhus-t thuj h1
- **squeezed**; as if: acon b7.de* anac b4.de* ang bg2 ant-c b7.de* arg-met b7.de* *Arn* b7.de* bell b4.de* calad b7.de* calc b4.de* carb-v b4.de* *Cina* b7a.de clem b4.de* colch b7.de* *Coloc* b4a.de euph b4.de* graph b4.de* ign b7.de* iod b4.de* kali-c b4.de* kali-n b4.de* led b7.de* *Lyc* b4a.de mez b4.de* mosch b7.de* nat-c b4.de* nit-ac b4.de* nux-m b7.de* olnd b7.de* ph-ac b4.de* phos b4.de* plat b4.de* *Ruta* b7.de* sep b4.de* sil b4.de* sulph b4.de* valer b7.de* visc bg2 zinc b4.de*
- **standing**:
  - **agg.**: aesc k* *Agar* alum ↓ alumn ↓ ham k2 phyt ptel k* rauw tpw8* stann k* sulph ↓ *Valer*
    - **aching**: aesc
    - **drawing** pain: valer k2
    - **sore**: alum alumn
    - **tearing** pain: sulph
  - **erect**:
    - **agg.**: agar bry graph puls
    - **amel.**: bell
- **stepping** hard agg.: merc ↓
  - **stitching** pain: merc k*
- **stepping** out: berb
- **stitching** pain: aesc aeth *Agar* aids nl2• ail alum k* alum-p k2 am-m bg2 apis *Arg-met* arg-n bg2 ars k* ars-h asar aur b4.de* bamb-a stb2.de• bar-c k* **Bell** bov k* bry k* cain calc k* calc-p k2 caps b7.de* carb-v k* carbn-s castor-eq caust k* chel b7.de* chin b7.de* chinin-ar k2 chlor cic cinnb *Cocc* k* coff bg2 colch b7.de* coloc k* con k* *Dig* b4a.de dros k* dulc k* euphr k* *Ferr* k* gels *Grat* *Guaj* b4a.de kali-ar *Kali-c* k* *Kali-n* b4a.de *Kali-s* kalm kreos k* led *Lyc* k* *Mag-c* k* *Manc* mang k* *Merc* k* merc-c k* mur-ac k* nat-c k* nat-m k* *Nat-p* nit-ac k* nux-v k* op ph-ac k* phos k* phyt **Plb** prun *Puls* *Ran-s* b7a.de **Rhus-t** k* *Sars* k* *Sep* k* *Sil* *Stann* k* staph *Sulph* k* symph fd3.de• *Tarent* *Thuj* k* tub tung-met bdx1• *Vac* jl2 zinc k* zinc-p k2
  - **burning**: thuj
  - **downward**: aesc anac *Kali-c* *Sil*
  - **ice-cold** needles; as from: agar
  - **needles**; as from: ars bg2 caust bg2 cocc bg2 lach bg2 rhus-t bg2
  - **paroxysmal**: *Gels*
  - **splinters**; as from: *Nit-ac*
  - **upward**: bar-c med k2
- **stool**:
  - **after** | **agg.**: agar k2
  - **before**: bapt
  - **during**:
    - **agg.**: coloc *Nux-v* *Rhus-t* *Tell*

- **stool – during – agg.**: ...
  - **shooting** pain: rhus-t
  - **stitching** pain: *Rhus-t*
  - **tearing** pain: *Rhus-t*$_{k*}$
- **storm**; during: caust↓
  - **drawing** pain: caust$_{h2*}$
  - **tearing** pain: caust$_{k*}$
- **stretch** leg, must: sulph↓
  - **tearing** pain: sulph$_{h2}$
- **stretching**:
  - **amel.**: act-sp↓
    - **boring** pain: act-sp
- **stunning**, stupefying: olnd$_{b7.de*}$
- **sudden**: acon↓ arg-n↓ ars↓ cimic↓ coff↓ **Coloc**↓ eup-per↓ *Iris*↓ kali-c↓ kali-i↓ mag-p↓ *Nux-v*↓ plb↓ puls↓ rhus-t↓ sil↓ ulm-c↓ verat↓
  - **shooting** pain: acon$_{bg2}$ arg-n$_{bg2}$ ars$_{bg2}$ cimic$_{bg2}$ coff$_{bg2}$ **Coloc**$_{bg2}$ eup-per$_{bg2}$ *Iris*$_{bg2}$ kali-c$_{bg2}$ kali-i$_{bg2}$ mag-p$_{bg2}$ *Nux-v*$_{bg2}$ plb$_{bg2}$ puls$_{bg2}$ rhus-t$_{bg2}$ sil$_{bg2}$ ulm-c$_{jsj8•}$ verat$_{bg2}$
- **tearing** pain: *Acon*$_{k*}$ aeth *Agar*$_{k*}$ agn$_{k*}$ **Alum**$_{k*}$ alum-p$_{k2}$ alum-sil$_{k2}$ am-m$_{b7.de*}$ ambr$_{k*}$ anac$_{k*}$ ant-c$_{k*}$ ant-t *Arg-met* arn$_{k*}$ **Ars**$_{k*}$ asar$_{b7.de*}$ *Aur-m* bar-c$_{k*}$ *Bell*$_{k*}$ berb *Bism*$_{b7a.de}$ **Bry**$_{b7a.de}$ *Calc*$_{k*}$ *Calc-ar* calc-p$_{k2}$ canth$_{k*}$ *Caps*$_{k*}$ carb-an$_{b4.de*}$ carb-v$_{k*}$ carbn-s **Caust**$_{k*}$ *Cham*$_{k*}$ *Chel*$_{b7a.de}$ *Chin*$_{k*}$ *Chinin-ar* *Cic* cina$_{k*}$ cocc$_{b7.de*}$ *Colch*$_{k*}$ **Coloc**$_{k*}$ *Con* dulc$_{k*}$ *Euph*$_{b4a.de}$ eupi *Ferr* gels$_{k2}$ *Graph*$_{k*}$ *Guaj*$_{b4a.de}$ hep$_{k*}$ *Ign*$_{k*}$ *Indg* iod$_{b4.de*}$ *Ip*$_{b7a.de}$ **Kali-ar** *Kali-bi*$_{k*}$ **Kali-c**$_{k*}$ kali-n$_{k*}$ kali-p *Kali-s*$_{k*}$ **Kalm**$_{k*}$ kola$_{stb3•}$ kreos$_{k*}$ lach led$_{b7.de*}$ **Lyc**$_{k*}$ m-ambo$_{b7.de}$ mag-c$_{k*}$ *Mag-m*$_{k*}$ mag-s *Mang*$_{b4a.de}$ merc$_{k*}$ mez$_{k*}$ *Mur-ac*$_{b4a.de}$ nat-ar *Nat-c*$_{k*}$ nat-m$_{b4.de*}$ nat-p **Nat-s** nicc **Nit-ac**$_{k*}$ nux-m nux-v$_{k*}$ par$_{k*}$ ph-ac phos$_{k*}$ **Plb**$_{k*}$ *Puls*$_{k*}$ rhod$_{k*}$ **Rhus-t**$_{k*}$ ruta$_{k2}$ sars$_{k*}$ sec$_{b7a.de}$ sep *Sil*$_{k*}$ *Squil*$_{b7a.de}$ stann$_{k*}$ *Stront-c*$_{k*}$ *Sul-ac*$_{b4a.de}$ *Sulph*$_{k*}$ *Tarax* teucr$_{k*}$ thuj *Tub* *Vac*$_{jl2}$ valer *Verat*$_{k*}$ verb *Zinc*$_{k*}$ zinc-p$_{k2}$
  - **downward**: acon$_{b7a.de}$ *Agar*$_{b4a.de}$ *Agn*$_{b7a.de}$ *Alum*$_{b4a.de}$ anac$_{b4a.de}$ ant-c$_{b7a.de}$ ant-t$_{b7a.de}$ *Ars* aur$_{b4a.de}$ bar-act$_{a1}$ *Bar-c*$_{k*}$ bell$_{k2}$ bism$_{b7a.de}$ canth$_{b7a.de}$ caps$_{b7a.de}$ *Carb-v*$_{b4a.de}$ caust$_{b4a.de}$ *Cham* chel$_{b7a.de}$ *Chin*$_{b7a.de}$ *Cic* colch$_{b7a.de}$ croc$_{b7a.de}$ dulc$_{b4a.de}$ euphr$_{b7a.de}$ eupi ferr$_{b7a.de}$ *Graph*$_{b4a.de}$ kali-c$_{b4a.de}$ *Kalm* laur$_{b7a.de}$ *Lyc*$_{b4a.de}$ *M-aust*$_{b7a.de}$ mag-c$_{b4a.de}$ mag-s *Merc*$_{b4a.de}$ mez$_{b4a.de}$ **Mur-ac**$_{b4a.de}$ nat-c$_{b4a.de*}$ nat-m$_{b4a.de}$ *Nux-v*$_{b7a.de}$ ph-ac$_{b4a.de}$ phos$_{b4a.de}$ puls$_{b7a.de}$ rhod$_{b4a.de}$ *Rhus-t*$_{b7a.de}$ sabin$_{b7a.de}$ sars$_{b4a.de}$ *Sep*$_{b4a.de}$ sil$_{b4a.de}$ spig$_{b7a.de}$ stann$_{b4a.de}$ *Sulph*$_{k*}$ thuj$_{b4a.de}$ valer$_{k*}$ verat$_{k*}$ verb$_{k*}$
  - **paralyzed**; as if: *Cham*
  - **paroxysmal**: sulph$_{h2}$
  - **upward**: *Acon*$_{b7a.de}$ **Anac**$_{b4a.de}$ *Arn*$_{b7a.de}$ *Ars*$_{b4a.de}$ *Bell*$_{k*}$ bov$_{b4a.de}$ calc$_{b4a.de}$ carb-v$_{b4a.de}$ *Caust*$_{b4a.de}$ chin$_{b7a.de}$ clem$_{b4a.de}$ con$_{b4a.de}$ *Dulc*$_{b4a.de}$ euphr$_{b7a.de}$ meny$_{b7a.de}$ merc$_{b4a.de}$ nat-c$_{b4a.de*}$ *Nit-ac*$_{b4a.de}$ *Nux-v* phos$_{b4a.de}$ *Puls*$_{b7a.de}$ rhod$_{b4a.de}$ rhus-t$_{b7a.de}$ sars$_{b4a.de}$ sep$_{k*}$ spig$_{b7a.de}$ spong$_{b7a.de}$ stront-c$_{k*}$ thuj$_{b4a.de}$ valer$_{b7a.de}$
- **thinking** about it agg.: sabad$_{b7.de*}$ staph$_{b7.de*}$
- **torn** asunder; as if: calc$_{b4.de*}$ carb-v$_{b4.de*}$ sep$_{b4.de*}$ teucr$_{b7.de*}$
- **touch**:
  - **agg.**: *Bell* berb *Bry* *Chin* cot↓ guaj merc↓ mez *Nit-ac*↓ nux-v plat puls ruta sulph
    - **stitching** pain: cot$_{br1}$ merc *Nit-ac*
    - **tearing** pain: *Chin*
  - **ankle** agg.; even slightest touch of: des-ac$_{rbp6}$
- **ulcerative** pain: benz-ac caust$_{b4.de*}$ nat-m$_{b4.de*}$ phos$_{b4a.de}$ sep$_{b4.de*}$ zinc$_{b4.de*}$
- **undressing**: nat-s
  - **agg.**: mez↓
    - **burning**: mez
- **vexation**; after: sep spong$_{fd4.de}$
- **walking**:
  - **after**:
    - **agg.**: agar↓ anac↓ *Berb*↓ **Ruta**↓ spong↓
- **walking – after – agg.**: ...
  - **drawing** pain: anac$_{h2}$
  - **pressing** pain: anac$_{h2}$ spong$_{fd4.de}$
  - **sore**: agar *Berb* **Ruta**
  - **agg.**: aesc↓ am-c↓ am-m ambr anac ant-c arg-n↓ arn asaf$_{k*}$ berb bry calc-p cann-i$_{k2}$ *Chel*↓ *Coloc*$_{k*}$ cypra-eg$_{sde6.de•}$ gels ham$_{k2}$ hep hyos lac-h$_{sk4•}$ led lyc merc$_{k*}$ nept-m↓ nicc↓ nit-ac nux-m *Nux-v* ol-an petr *Phos* *Phyt* plb$_{k*}$ *Ran-b* sep$_{k*}$ *Sil*↓ spong$_{fd4.de}$ stann stram stront-c↓ *Sulph*$_{k*}$ tab tarent$_{k*}$ thuj vanil$_{fd5.de}$ viol-t
    - **aching**: merc nux-m
    - **chilliness**; during: sep↓
      - **stitching** pain: sep
    - **drawing** pain: asaf coloc *Gels* *Hep*
    - **pressing** pain: arg-n$_{a1}$ asaf
    - **sore**: aesc *Chel*
    - **sprained**; as if: am-c$_{h2}$
    - **stitching** pain: nept-m$_{lsd2.fr}$
    - **tearing** pain: nicc sep *Sil* stront-c sulph$_{h2}$
  - **air**; in open:
    - **after**:
      - **agg.**: phos *Sulph*↓
        - **sore**: *Sulph*
    - **amel.**: *Agar* am-c *Am-m* *Arg-met* *Ars* bar-c↓ *Bell* calc-s$_{k2}$ chin *Cocc*↓ dig *Dulc* **Ferr** *Indg* **Kali-c**↓ *Kali-i* kali-n↓ *Kali-s* **Lyc** nat-s$_{k2}$ *Puls* **Pyrog** **Rhus-t** ruta$_{fd4.de}$ *Seneg* sep *Stel*↓ sulph↓ tritic-vg$_{fd5.de}$ *Tub* *Valer* vanil$_{fd5.de}$ *Verat*
      - **aching**: nat-s$_{k2}$ *Tub*
      - **drawing** pain: *Lyc* **Rhus-t** *Tub* **Valer** vanil$_{fd5.de}$
      - **gnawing** pain: **Bell**$_{k*}$
      - **pressing** pain: kali-n$_{h2}$
      - **shooting** pain: **Bell**
      - **stitching** pain: arg-met ars **Bell** *Cocc* **Kali-c** **Kali-s** *Lyc* **Puls** **Rhus-t** *Stel* *Tub*
      - **tearing** pain: bar-c$_{h2}$ **Bell** *Ferr* *Lyc* **Rhus-t** sulph *Valer* verat
  - **rapidly** | **amel.**: cassia-s$_{ccrh1•}$
- **wandering** pain: aesc ars-h bell$_{bg2}$ *Caul* *Iris* *Kali-bi* *Kalm* *Lac-c* *Lach* mag-p psil$_{ft1}$ *Sang* vib
- **warm**:
  - **applications**:
    - **agg.**: hell **Lac-c** *Led* *Puls* verat zinc
    - **amel.**: agar$_{k2}$ *Ars* *Bar-c* *Caust* *Cham*↓ graph *Lyc* nat-c ph-ac *Phos* stront-c sulph
      - **aching**: agar$_{k2}$
      - **tearing** pain: *Caust* *Cham*
  - **bed**:
    - **agg.**: coloc *Ferr* *Guaj* led **Merc** plb *Sulph* syph **Verat**
      - **tearing** pain: *Sulph*
    - **amel.**: *Agar* *Ars* bell carc$_{sp1*}$ caust *Dulc* **Lyc** *Mag-p* **Nux-v** *Ph-ac* *Phos* **Pyrog** **Rhus-t**
      - **shooting** pain: *Mag-p*
- **warmth**:
  - **amel.**: **Caust**↓ *Coloc*↓ **Lyc**↓ *Rhus-t*↓
    - **tearing** pain: **Caust** *Coloc* **Lyc** *Rhus-t*
- **waves**; in: anac$_{bg2}$ arn$_{b7.de*}$ asaf$_{b7.de*}$ bamb-a$_{stb2.de•}$ cocc$_{b7.de*}$ mez$_{bg2}$ olnd$_{b7.de*}$ plat$_{bg2}$ rhod$_{bg2}$ sep$_{bg2}$
- **weakness**; with: plb$_{k*}$
- **weather**:
  - **change** of weather: *Berb* *Kali-bi* lach *Ran-b* *Rhod*
  - **wet**:
    - **agg.**: borx *Calc-p*↓ *Dulc*↓ *Ran-b* *Rhod* *Rhus-t* ruta *Ter* **Verat**
      - **aching**: *Calc-p*
      - **drawing** pain: rhus-t$_{k2}$
      - **tearing** pain: *Dulc* *Rhod* *Rhus-t*
  - **windy**: lach

Extremities

▽ • **extending** to:

⁝ **Downward**: aeth aloe am-c am-m *Apis* arg-n ars bar-c bell k2 berb bry *Calc* cann-s caps carb-an *Carb-v* card-m caust cham cocc coloc crot-h dios elat eup-pur ferr gnaph guaj hyper ind iris kali-ar kali-bi kali-c *Kali-i* kali-p **Kalm** lac-c **Lach** lyc mag-p medul-os-si rly4• mur-ac nat-m nit-ac nux-m *Nux-v* ph-ac *Phyt Plb* puls *Rhus-t* ruta sep spong fd4.de staph still *Sulph* tell ther thuj verat zinc

⁝ **Foot**: alum ptk1 *Apis* caps ptk1 *Colch* lach lyc ptk1 merc-i-f phyt puls ptk1 rhus-t ptk1 sang spong fd4.de zinc

⁝ **Head**: thuj ↓

: **drawing** pain: thuj

⁝ **Heart**; region of: alum-sil k2 benz-ac tl1 nat-p tl1

⁝ **Outward**: caust bg2

⁝ **Shoulder**: bell ↓

: **drawing** pain: bell h1

⁝ **Temple**: alum-sil k2

⁝ **Toes**; to tips of: calc ↓

: **drawing** pain: calc h2

⁝ **Upward**: acon k* agar alum-sil k2 caust bg2 cimic eup-per bg2 eup-pur guaj kali-p lach **Led** k* melal-alt gya4 *Nux-v Phyt Plb* podo puls bg2 rhus-t ruta stront-c bg2 thal-xyz srj8• verat zinc k*

○ • **Bones**: **Agar** k* alum b4.de* am-m ↓ anac ↓ ang ↓ aran arg-met ↓ ars ↓ asaf ↓ aur bg2 bar-c bg2 *Bell* ↓ *Bism* ↓ bond a1 borx ↓ bry ↓ calc ↓ calc-p a1 cann-s ↓ canth bg2 carb-v k* caust ↓ cham ↓ chel ↓ chin k* cocc ↓ coloc k* con k* cupr ↓ dros b7.de* eup-per ↓ euph bg2 graph b4.de* guaj k* *Hep* ↓ *Iod* ↓ **Ip** kali-bi k* kali-c k* *Kali-n* ↓ lach bg2 laur ↓ *Led* ↓ lil-s a1 lyc k* mag-c ↓ mag-m k* mag-s ↓ *Mang* ↓ *Merc* k* *Merc-c* ↓ mez k* mur-ac b4.de* nat-c ↓ nit-ac b4.de* nux-m ↓ olnd k* petr ph-ac ↓ phos b4.de* puls b7.de* *Rhod* rumx ↓ ruta b7.de* sabad ↓ sabin samb ↓ sars b4.de* sep b4.de* sil b4.de* staph ↓ still ↓ stront-c ↓ *Sulph* k* teucr ↓ ther ↓ thuj ↓ tub k2 valer vanil fd5.de verat ↓ viol-t ↓ zinc k*

⁝ **aching**: lyc mag-m *Mez* nit-ac bg1 ph-ac phos *Puls* rumx still bg1 zinc

⁝ **blow**; pain as from a: caust bg2

⁝ **boring** pain: aur b4a.de *Carb-v* chel bg2 coloc kali-bi nat-c k* rhod k*

⁝ **broken**; as if: graph bg2 kali-bi bg2 puls bg2 ruta b7.de* verat b7.de* zinc bg2

⁝ **burning**: euph *Ruta* b7.de

⁝ **cutting** pain: bell bg2

⁝ **drawing** pain: anac k* bar-c k* bry b7.de* calc k* cann-s b7.de* caust h2* *Chin* k* *Con* k* cupr b7a.de graph k* *Hep* b4a.de ip b7.de* kali-bi bg2 *Kali-c* k* led bg2 mag-c k* merc-c b4a.de nit-ac b4a.de olnd b7.de* ph-ac b4a.de phos b4a.de *Puls* b7a.de *Rhod* k* sabad b7.de* sabin sep k* staph b7a.de **Valer** k* zinc k*

⁝ **gnawing** pain: am-m bg2 canth b7.de* dros b7.de* kali-bi bg2

⁝ **paralyzed**; as if: led b7.de* petr b4.de* zinc b4.de*

⁝ **pressing** pain: cocc b7.de* con k* *Guaj* k* kali-c k* kali-n k*

: **outward**: cham bg2 eup-per bg2

⁝ **sore**: agar b4.de* aur b4.de* calc b4.de* cann-s b7.de* chin b7.de* graph b4.de* *Hep* b4a.de kali-bi bg2 *Led* k* mag-c b4.de* *Mang Mez* bg2 *Nit-ac* nux-m bg2 petr b4.de* phos b4.de* puls b7.de* *Ruta* b7.de* sep b4.de* valer b7.de*

⁝ **squeezed**; as if: petr b4.de*

⁝ **stitching** pain: ars k* *Bell* k* carb-v k* caust k* chin b7.de* *Dros* b7.de* graph k* *Iod* k* lyc k* *Merc* k* nit-ac k* puls b7a.de samb b7.de* *Sep* b4a.de sil k* stront-c k* valer b7.de* viol-t b7.de* zinc k*

⁝ **tearing** pain: **Agar** k* am-m k* ang b7.de* arg-met k* ars k* asaf b7.de* aur k* bar-c k* *Bism* b7a.de borx b4a.de carb-v k* chin k* kali-bi bg2 *Kali-c* k* *Kali-n* k* laur b7.de* lyc k* mag-c k* mag-s *Merc* k* *Merc-c* b4a.de mez k* **Nit-ac** phos k* *Rhod* k* ruta bg2 sabin b7a.de* staph b7.de* stront-c k* teucr k* thuj verat b7.de* *Zinc* k*

⁝ **ulcerative** pain: phos bg2 puls b7.de* ther bg2

⁝ **walking** agg.: mag-m

⁝ **extending** to:

: **First** toes: ars ↓

. **stitching** pain | **periosteum**; as if in: ars a1

. **tearing** pain | **periosteum**; as if in: ars h1*

• **Deep**: bar-act bg2

• **Flexors**: plb ↓

⁝ **cramping**: plb bg2

• **Inner** side: petr k* plb ↓

⁝ **sore**: petr

⁝ **stitching** pain: plb

• **Joints**: acon ↓ agar ↓ allox sp1 alum b4.de* am-c b4.de* ambr ang ↓ *Arg-met* ↓ arn *Ars* k* aur ↓ bacls-7 pte1• bar-act ↓ *Bar-c* k* *Bell* ↓ berb ↓ bov b4.de* bry bufo ↓ cadm-s ↓ calc b4.de* calc-f sp1 carb-v ↓ carc sp1 chel k* chin ↓ cimic colch ↓ coloc ↓ con b4.de* cortico sp1 cycl ↓ *Dig* k* dros ↓ dulc ↓ euph ↓ euphr ↓ ferr-i ↓ *Guaj* guat sp1 ham ↓ *Hep* ↓ hip-ac sp1 hyos ↓ *Iod* b4a.de kali-bi ↓ kali-c bg3 kali-n b4.de* *Kalm Led* lil-t ↓ *Lyc* mag-c b4.de* mand sp1 *Mang* k* *Merc* ↓ merc-c ↓ mez b4.de* mosch ↓ *Mur-ac* ↓ naja ↓ nat-c ↓ nat-m bg3 nat-s ↓ nux-v ↓ petr ↓ ph-ac a1 phos k* *Phyt* psil ft1 *Puls* rad-br mrr1 rauw sp1 rhod *Rhus-t* ruta ↓ sabin saroth sp1 sarr ↓ *Sars* ↓ seneg b4.de* *Sep* k* *Sil* k* spig ↓ stront-c stroph-s sp1 sul-ac k* sulfa sp1 *Sulph* k* tarax ↓ *Teucr* ↓ thuj ↓ x-ray sp1 *Zinc* ↓

⁝ **evening**: coloc ↓

: **boring** pain: coloc

⁝ **aching**: ferr-i

⁝ **boring** pain: alum k* coloc con bg2 lil-t bg2 mag-c k* *Zinc* k*

⁝ **burning**: bar-c k* *Merc* b4a.de nat-c k* phos k* stront-c k*

⁝ **bursting**; sensation as if: ham bg2

⁝ **cutting** pain: hyos b7.de*

⁝ **descending** agg.: arg-met ↓

: **sore**: arg-met

⁝ **drawing** pain: am-c bg2 berb bg2 chel cycl bg2 hyos b7.de* kali-bi bg2 led bg2 lyc k* *Merc* b4a.de nat-s bg2 petr b4.de* *Rhod* k* sep k* sil bg2 stront-c k* sulph bg2

⁝ **gnawing** pain: am-c b4.de* zinc b4.de*

⁝ **paralyzed**; as if: bar-c b4a.de euph b4.de* lyc b4.de* *Sars* b4a.de *Seneg* b4a.de sep b4.de*

⁝ **pressing** pain: bar-c k* naja sep k* stront-c k*

⁝ **sore**: agar k* *Arg-met* k* aur b4a.de calc k* chin b7.de* *Dig* k* merc-c b4a.de *Mur-ac* b4a.de nat-c k* ph-ac ruta b7.de* sarr sep k*

⁝ **squeezed**; as if: ang b7.de* bell b4.de* carb-v b4a.de mez b4.de* petr b4.de* rhod b4.de* sep b4.de* sulph b4.de*

⁝ **stitching** pain: acon bar-c bell bg2 cadm-s calc k* colch dros b7.de* dulc k* euphr b7.de* *Hep* b4a.de hyos b7.de* *Kali-c* b4a.de *Kali-n* b4a.de mag-c k* *Mang* b4a.de merc k* nux-v petr k* phos k* rhus-t b7.de* sep b4.de* *Sil* k* spig k* stront-c k* *Sul-ac* b4a.de tarax b7.de* thuj k*

⁝ **tearing** pain: bar-act a1 *Bell* k* bufo bg2 calc k* hyos b7.de* *Iod* b4a.de kali-bi bg2 kali-c k* *Kali-n* b4a.de *Led* b7a.de lyc b4.de* merc k* mosch b7a.de *Sars* b4a.de sep b4a.de *Stront-c* k* *Sulph* b4a.de *Teucr* k* zinc k*

⁝ **walking** agg.: coloc ↓

: **boring** pain: coloc

⁝ **Spots**; in: *Mang* ↓

: **burning**: *Mang*

• **Muscles**: psil ↓ thal-xyz srj8•

⁝ **stitching** pain: psil ft1

• **Periosteum**: ph-ac b4.de* phyt bg2 rhod ↓

⁝ **night**: rhod ↓

: **drawing** pain: rhod

⁝ **drawing** pain: rhod

⁝ **motion**:

: **amel.**: rhod ↓

. **drawing** pain: rhod

⁝ **weather** agg.; wet: rhod ↓

: **drawing** pain: rhod

• **Posterior** part: *Helon* ↓ **Pic-ac** ↓

⁝ **aching**: *Helon* **Pic-ac**

⁝ **burning**: *Helon* **Pic-ac**

• **Sciatic** nerve: (*↗sciatic - shooting; BACK - Prolapsus - Intervertebral)* abrot tl1 acetan bro1 acon k* **Aesc** mrr1 agar k* aids nl2• *Am-m* k* anac ↓ anan k* ang k* ant-ar c2 apis ↓ apoc bro1 *Arg-n* k* *Arn* k* *Ars* k* ars-met c2* ars-s-f k2* ars-s-r c2* asar k* auran hr1 *Bamb-a* stb2.de• bar-c *Bell* k* bell-p ↓ berb k* **Bry** k* **Bufo** k* *Cact* ↓ *Calc* k* calc-f mrr1 *Calc-p* calc-s k2 calc-sil k2 canth bg2 caps k* carb-ac ↓ carbn-o c2* *Carbn-s* k* carc tpw2* card-m k* cardios-h rly4• carl c2 caul ↓ *Caust* k*

- **Sciatic** nerve: ...
  cerv c2 *Cham* k* chel chim chin bro1* chinin-s cho hsa1 *Cimic* k* cinnb c2 cist k* cit-v hr1 coc-c k* cocc *Coff* k* colch ↓ **Coloc** k* con ↓ corn-f ↓ cot br1* cupr ↓ cur k* daph ↓ der a1 *Dios* k* dros k* *Elaps* *Elat* k* eup-pur k* euph k* *Ferr* k* *Ferr-ar* ferr-p fl-ac flav jl2* form-ac mtf11 gaert pte1*• gaul c2* *Gels* k* gins c2* glon c2* *Gnaph* k* *Graph* k* *Guaj* k* hep k* hip-ac sp1 hydr c2 hymos bro1 hyper k* *Ign* k* *Indg* k* inul c2 **Iris** k* *Kali-ar* *Kali-bi* k* kali-br mrr1 kali-c k* kali-cy br1 **Kali-i** k* *Kali-p* k* kali-s bg2* kali-sil k2 kalm k2 kola stb3• kreos ↓ lac-ac k* *Lac-c* k* lac-d k* lac-h mtf11 *Lach* k* lachn k* lap-la sde8.de• *Led* k* lob-s c2 lol br1 *Lyc* k* lyss k* mag-c ↓ **Mag-p** k* mag-s sp1 malar jl2 mand sp1 med c2* *Meny* k* merc k* methyl br1 mez k* morph ↓ muru a1 nat-ar *Nat-m* k* *Nat-s* k* nept-m lsd2.fr nit-ac k* *Nux-m* k* **Nux-v** k* *Nyct* c1* oena c2 *Ol-j* k* ox-ac ↓ pall k* paraf ↓ passi c2 *Petr* k* ph-ac k* *Phos* *Phyt* k* plan k* plat ↓ *Plb* k* plb-xyz c2 *Podo* k* polyg-h bro1 polyg-pe c2 prot pte1* psor k* *Puls* k* puls-n c2 pyrus c2 rad-br mrr1 *Ran-b* k* **Rhus-t** k* *Ruta* k* sabin bg2 sacch-l c2 sal-ac k* sal-fr sle1• *Sal-mo* c1* sang ↓ saroth sp1* sel ptk1 senec c2 *Sep* k* sil k* sol-t-ae c2 solid c2 spig bg2 spong fd4.de *Stann* ↓ *Staph* k* *Still* k* stram k* stront-c c2 stry bro1 succ-ac mtf11 sul-ac ↓ *Sulph* k* syph c2* **Tell** k* tep c2 ter k* thal bg2 thala mtf11 thein bro1 thuj c2* tritic-vg fd5.de trom c2 upa c2 *Valer* k* *Verat* k* *Verb* ↓ visc c1* x-ray sp1 xan k* xanth bg2 *Zinc* k* zinc-p k2 zinc-s mtf11 zinc-val bro1 [am-c stj1 am-p stj1 am-s stj1 arg-met stj1 chr-met stj1 kali-m stj1 kali-n stj1 vanad stj1]
  - **alternating** sides: **Lac-c** k*
  - **right**: bamb-a stb2.de• bell bg2* carbn-s chel k* chinin-s *Coloc* k* *Dios* k* germ-met srj5• *Gnaph* bro1* graph bg2* *Kali-c* mrr1 kali-cy gm1 kali-i bg2 kali-s fd4.de *Kalm* bro1 lac-ac c1 lac-h htj1• *Lach* k* **Lyc** k ●* mag-p bro1* mand sp1 morph bro1 nept-m lsd2.fr olib-sac wmh1 *Phyt* k* plan puls bro1 ran-b bro1 rhus-t bg1 *Ruta* sne sep spong fd4.de sul-ac bro1 *Tell* k*
  - **left**: acon bro1 aids nl2• *Am-m* k* arag br1* aran-ix a *Ars* bro1 bamb-a stb2.de• *Bapt-c* c1 caust a* cedr bro1 cham a cimic k* colch bro1 coloc bg2* des-ac rbp6 elat eup-per bg2 eup-pur k* flav jl2 germ-met srj5• graph gk *Hyper* a ign a iris k* *Kali-bi* k* *Kali-c* kali-i vh kola stb3• lach k* led bg2* lyss a* mag-c bro1 mand rsj7• med a* meny bg1* *Mez* bro1 morph bro1 nat-s a nux-v bro1 **Phos** k ● psor a puls bg2* rhus-t a* sal-ac c1 sal-fr sle1• sel bg1* *Spig* bro1 staph sne still a stram a sulph bg2* sumb bro1 tell thuj k* upa a visc a
    - **accompanied** by | **dysuria**: *Agar*
    - **extending** to:
      - **Downward**: elat ↓ iris ↓ sal-fr ↓
        - **shooting** pain: elat c1 iris c1 sal-fr sle1•
    - **burning**: sal-ac c1
  - **daytime**: coloc sep
    - **amel.**: ruta ptk1
  - **morning**: acon bro1 arg-n ars bamb-a stb2.de• *Bry* k* chinin-s bro1 kali-bi lac-d k2 nux-v k* spong fd4.de staph sulph tritic-vg fd5.de
    - **9-16 h**: verb bro1
    - **early** | **amel.**: syph bro1
  - **forenoon**: ruta fd4.de sep
  - **noon**: bamb-a stb2.de• coloc k* nat-m k* sulph bro1
  - **afternoon**: am-m bell bry chel coff k* indg k* kali-bi nux-v
  - **evening**: am-m bry k* chel coloc ferr hyper indg k* iris kali-bi *Kali-i* led meny mez pall k* *Phos* *Puls* k* staph sne valer
  - **night**: acon bro1 arg-n *Ars* k* bamb-a stb2.de• bell k* cham k* cimic bro1 coff k* *Coloc* k* ferr k* *Ferr-ar* gels k* gins bro1 gnaph hyper ign bro1 indg kali-bi kali-c hr1 *Kali-i* k* led *Mag-p* bro1 mag-s sp1 *Merc* k* *Mez* k* nux-v k* pall k* phyt k* plat bro1 plb *Puls* k* *Rhus-t* k* ruta bro1 sal-ac c1* sep staph *Syph* k* tell k* verat zinc
    - **midnight**: ars bro1 bell bro1 ferr mez bro1 *Nux-m* sulph bro1
      - **before**: ferr led
      - **after**: *Ars* rhus-t
        - **4 h**: coloc
    - **amel.**: staph
  - **accompanied** by:
    - **chilliness** in legs: bamb-a stb2.de• *Nux-v*
    - **coldness**:
      - **face**; of: bamb-a stb2.de•

- **Sciatic** nerve – **accompanied** by – **coldness**: ...
      - **general**; in (See GENERALS - Heat - lack - accompanied - sciatica)
      - **limb**; of painful: glon br1 *Led* merc sil
    - **congestion** (See GENERALS - Congestion - blood - accompanied - sciatica)
    - **contraction** of muscles and tendons: am-m bro1 *Bell* bro1 gels bro1 mag-p bro1 *Nux-v* bro1 plat bro1 plb bro1 zinc bro1
      - **Legs**; of: *Nux-v*
    - **diabetes** mellitus: kreos mtf11
    - **faintness** (See GENERALS - Faintness - pain - sciatic)
    - **formication**: gnaph ptk1
    - **hemorrhoids**: **Aesc** mrr1
    - **lachrymation**: chel bro1 mez bro1 *Puls* bro1 rhus-t bro1
    - **nausea**: bamb-a stb2.de•
    - **numbness**●: acon bro1* agar bro1 ars bro1 caust bro1* cham bro1* **Coloc** k ●* glon bro1 *Gnaph* k* graph bro1* *Kalm* bro1 lac-c bro1 led bro1 lith-c bro1 merc bro1 mez bro1 nux-v **Phyt** k ●* *Plat* bro1 plb mrr1 **Rhus-t** k ●* sep bro1 spig bro1
    - **perspiration**: spig bro1
    - **pollutions**; nightly: **Cob** mrr1
    - **salivation**: mez bro1
    - **sensitiveness**: *Bell* bro1 coff bro1 ign bro1 kali-i bro1 ter bro1
    - **trembling** lower limbs: bamb-a stb2.de•
    - **weakness**: *Ars* bro1 chin bro1 colch bro1 gels bro1 grat ptk1 kalm bro1 *Verat* bro1
    - **Arms**; coldness, swelling and paralysis of: verat bro1
    - **Cervical** region; stiffness of: mez bro1
    - **Face**:
      - **pale** discoloration: spig bro1
      - **red** discoloration: acon bro1 *Bell* bro1 cham bro1 verb bro1
    - **Foot**; pain in: mag-p ptk1
    - **Heart**; anxiety in region of (See CHEST - Anxiety - heart - accompanied - sciatica)
    - **Hip**; jerking: *Kali-bi*
    - **Pneumogastric** nerve; complaints of: arn bro1
    - **Skin**; pinching pain in: sul-ac bro1
    - **Spine**:
      - **pain**: petr ptk1
      - **sensitive**: lac-c bro1 nat-m bro1 phos bro1 sil bro1 sulph bro1 tell bro1
    - **Stomach**; complaints of: verat bro1 verb bro1
  - **air**; in open | **amel.**: **Kali-i** mez **Puls** thuj
  - **alternating** with:
    - **cough**: staph ptk1
    - **numbness**: *Gnaph* k*
    - **Other** parts; pain in: ign bro1
  - **appearing** | **gradually**:
    - **disappearing**; and | **gradually**: arg-n bro1 plat bro1 *Stann* bro1 sulph bro1 verat bro1
    - **suddenly**:
      - **disappearing**; and | **suddenly**: *Bell* bro1 carb-ac bro1 chr-ac bro1 coloc bro1 kali-bi bro1 *Mag-p* bro1 ovi-p bro1 oxyt bro1
  - **ascending** agg.: acon agar bamb-a stb2.de• *Led* ptk1 nux-v ptk1 podo ruta k*
  - **atrophy**, with: *Calc* ptk1 caust ptk1 glon br1 *Ol-j* k* **Plb** k ●*
  - **bed** agg.; in: hyper kali-bi *Kali-i* lyc ruta k* sep
  - **beginning** at ankle: ars cimic plat
  - **bending**:
    - **backward**:
      - **agg.**: caps k*
      - **amel.**: dios bro1
    - **forward**:
      - **agg.**: thuj
      - **amel.**: coloc bro1
    - **leg**:
      - **agg.**: [arg-met stj1]

- **Sciatic** nerve – **bending** – **leg**: ...
  - **amel.**: *Ars* k* coloc k* gnaph ptk1 graph vh guaj *Kali-bi* k* *Kali-i* k* puls bg1 tell *Valer* k*
- **blowing** the nose agg.: graph bg1*
- **brown** spots on the skin: *Sep* k*
- **burning**: *Ars* bufo gels lach lyc *Phos* ran-b k2 rhus-t ruta
- **burning**; with: acon bro1 all-c bro1 anthraci bro1 apis bro1 ars k* bufo caps bro1 coloc gels k* *Gnaph* mp1• lach k* lyc k* *Phos* *Rhus-t* k* ruta sal-ac bro1 spig bro1
- **chronic**: am-m bg2 *Ars* bro1 calc bro1 gels bg2 kali-i bro1 lyc bg2* nat-m bg2 phos bro1 plb bg2* ran-b br1* *Rhus-t* bro1 sulph bg2* visc bg2 zinc bro1
- **closing** the eyes | **amel.**: bry bro1
- **cold**:
  - **agg.**: *Ars* k* asar bell bro1 caps bro1 caust chin bro1 coloc k* gnaph sne kali-bi bro1 *Mag-p* k* mez k2 pall k* *Phos* *Ran-b* **Rhus-t** k* ruta bro1 sil
  - **amel.**: ars bro1 puls bro1
  - **applications** | **agg.**: *Ars* *Bry* k* *Mag-p* *Nux-v* *Phos* **Rhus-t** ruta
  - **water** | **agg.**: *Calc* **Rhus-t** sulph
  - **wet** places; from exposure to cold: *Ars* *Nat-s* *Rhus-t*
- **cold**; after taking a: carbn-s k2
- **coldness** of painful limb; with (See accompanied - coldness - limb)
- **cough** agg.; during: *Caps* k* caust k* gnaph sne kali-i sne sep k* *Tell* k*
- **cramping**: am-m bro1 *Cact* bro1 caul bro1 cimic bro1 *Coloc* bro1 con bro1 cupr bro1 gnaph bro1 iris bro1 *Mag-p* bro1 nux-v bro1 plat bro1 plb bro1 stann bro1 sulph bro1 thuj bro1 *Verb* bro1
- **deep** pain: kali-bi ptk1 ruta ptk1
- **descending** agg.: am-m k* des-ac rbp6 ruta k*
- **discharge** from ear, with: visc ptk1
- **drawing** pain: *Cham* bro1 chin bro1 coloc bro1 ph-ac bro1 phos bro1 *Puls* bro1 spig bro1 *Stann* bro1 sulph bro1 verb bro1
- **eruptions**; after suppressed: mez k*
- **extending** from | **Vertebrae**: nat-m ptk1 sil ptk1
- **flexing** leg | **abdomen** amel.; on: **Coloc** k●* glon ptk1 gnaph bro1*
- **griping**: cact bro1
- **hang** down agg.: valer k*
- **hang** over sides of bed, letting leg: *Verat* k*
- **increasing** and decreasing suddenly: **Bell** berb mrr1 **Kali-bi** k* *Mag-p* sel ptk1 sulph
- **influenza** after: iris c1
- **injuries**; after: *Arn* k* *Hyper* k* *Ruta* mp1•
- **intermittent**: *Ars* bro1 *Chin* bro1 chinin-s bro1 *Coloc* bro1 cupr bro1 *Ign* bro1 mag-p bro1 nux-v bro1 *Spig* bro1 sulph bro1
- **jar** agg.: bamb-a stb2.de• **Bell** k* caps bro1 *Nux-m* k* *Spig* bro1 *Tell* k*
- **jerking** muscles, with: kali-c ptk1
- **kneeling** down, pressing head firmly against floor: | **amel.**: sang bro1
- **laughing** agg.: *Tell* k*
- **lifted**; when: nux-v
- **lying**:
  - **agg.**: am-m bro1 coloc ferr gnaph k* kali-bi hr1 *Kali-i* k* meny *Nat-m* k* ruta k* sep tell k* valer
    - **stretched** out; with limb: cham
  - **amel.**: **Am-m** k* bar-c *Bry* k* *Cob* mrr1 *Dios* k* lach k* *Ruta* mrr1
  - **back**; on:
    - **agg.**: kali-i rhus-t
    - **amel.**: *Phos* k*
  - **must** lie down: indg c1
  - **side**; on:
    - **left** | **agg.**: kali-c *Phos*
    - **painful** side:
      - **agg.●**: bamb-a stb2.de• coloc bro1 dros *Kali-c* **Kali-i** k* lac-h htj1• **Lyc** k* nux-v *Phos* **Rhus-t** sep *Tell*
      - **amel.**: **Bry** *Coloc* k*

- **Siatic** nerve – **lying** – **side**; on: ...
  - **right**:
    - **agg.**: rhus-t
    - **amel.**: *Phos* k*
- **maddening** pain: *Acon* bro1 arg-n bro1 ars bro1 *Bell* bro1 carb-ac bro1 *Cham* bro1 chin bro1 coff bro1 colch bro1 *Coloc* bro1 kreos bro1 *Mag-p* bro1 morph bro1 nux-v bro1 ox-ac bro1 *Spig* bro1 verat bro1
- **mechanical** treatment amel.: aesc tl1
- **mental** exertion agg.: kalm bro1 mag-p k*
- **motion**: *(↗motion - must)*
  - **agg.**: acon k* ars bro1 bell bro1* **Bry** k* calc card-m k2 chel chin bro1 *Cocc* *Coff* k* colch bro1 *Coloc* k* *Dios* k* eup-pur k* gels k* gnaph k* *Guaj* indg c1 *Iris* *Kali-c* lac-c lach k* led mag-p k* merc mez nux-m k* nux-v k* pall k* *Phos* *Phyt* k* plb puls k* *Ran-b* k* sep *Spig* bro1 *Staph* k* syph tritic-vg fd5.de *Verb* bro1
  - **amel.**: *(↗must)* acon agar aids nl2• am-m bro1 *Arg-met* *Ars* bro1 caps cham coc-c *Dios* bro1 *Dulc* *Euph* k* **Ferr** k* gels k* *Ign* bro1 indg k* *Kali-bi* k* *Kali-i* k* *Kali-p* k* kreos lac-c k* *Lyc* k* mag-c bro1 mag-s sp1 mand sp1 meny merc-i-f kr1 nat-s ox-ac bro1 *Puls* k* rhod **Rhus-t** k* *Ruta* sep k* sil sulph k* syph gk ter k* tritic-vg fd5.de valer k*
    - **slow** motion: aids nl2• *Ferr* kali-p *Puls* syph gk
  - **beginning** of | **agg.**: *Gels* lac-c bro1 **Rhus-t** k* ruta thuj
  - **continued** motion:
    - **agg.**: coloc
    - **amel.**: med k2
  - **must** move: *(↗amel.; motion)* bry ptk1 caust ptk1 lyc ptk1 mag-c ptk1 *Rhus-t* ptk1 valer ptk1 zinc-val ptk1
- **nervousness**; with (See MIND - Excitement - nervous - pain - sciatic)
- **numbness**; with (See accompanied - numbness)
- **overheated**, from being: zinc
- **pain** in spine and all over, with: *Petr* k*
- **periodical**: *Aran* bro1 *Ars* bro1 *Cedr* bro1 *Chinin-s* k* chr-ac bro1 kali-bi bro1 *Lyc* lyss k* *Nicc-s* bro1 nux-v bro1 ox-ac bro1 parth bro1 *Rhus-t* k* sal-ac bro1 *Spig* bro1 sulph bro1 toxi bro1 *Verb* bro1
  - **every** 4 days: *Lyc*
  - **regular** intervals: carbn-s
- **plug**; as from a: anac bro1
- **pregnancy**:
  - **during**:
    - **agg.**: gels mp1• lach mrr1 valer a*
    - **amel.**: sep ptk1
- **pressure**:
  - **agg.**: ars bro1 *Coloc* k* dros gels bro1 *Kali-bi* k* kali-c k* *Kali-i* k* *Lyc* k* phyt plb k* *Podo* hr1 *Rhus-t* ptk1 staph sne verb bro1 zinc bro1
  - **amel.**: ars k* bell bro1 *Bry* bro1 coff k* coloc k* **Mag-p** k* meny k* *Mez* bro1 nux-v bro1 phyt plb bro1 *Rhus-t* ruta fd4.de spig bro1 tritic-vg fd5.de
- **pulsating**: coloc *Ign* hr1 lac-ac k*
- **raising** the leg: *(↗standing - leg - amel.)* bamb-a stb2.de•
- **rest**:
  - **agg.**: *Kali-i* mrr1 mag-s sp1
  - **amel.**: am-m bro1 bry bro1 dios bro1 kreos bro1 *Mag-p* bro1 nux-v bro1
- **restlessness**; with (See MIND - Restlessness - pain, from - sciatic)
- **rheumatic**: acon bro1 bry bro1 *Cimic* bro1 guaj bro1 hymos bro1 led bro1 *Rhus-t* bro1
- **riding** on a streetcar agg.: bamb-a stb2.de• coc-c bg1
- **rising** from sitting agg.: aesc mp1• cham chel bg1 coloc ferr kali-p lach *Lyss* *Nat-s* k* rhus-t k* ruta sep staph sulph *Tell* lp thuj
- **rubbing** | **amel.**: acon bro1
- **shooting** pain: *(↗sciatic)* acon ptk1 *Coloc* ptk1 hyper tl1 iris ptk1 mag-c ptk1
- **sitting**:
  - **agg.**: agar mp1• **Am-m** k* apoc bg1 ars bro1 bell ptk1 berb *Bry* k* *Cob* mrr1 coloc dios ferr hyper ptk1 ind ptk1 indg k* iris kali-bi k* kali-i k* lach lept ptk1 **Lyc** k* lyss mag-c bro1 *Meny* merc *Rhus-t* bro1 ruta sep spong fd4.de staph tritic-vg fd5.de *Valer* k* [*Arg-met* stj1]
    - **long** time agg.; for a: hyper ptk1

- **Sciatic** nerve – **sitting**: ...
  - **amel.**: bell bro1 gnaph k* guaj kali-i lac-h htj1• nept-m lsd2.fr
    - **leg** straight out on a chair; with: germ-met srj5•
  - **chair**; in a | **amel.**: gnaph ptk1
  - **sleep** agg.; after: **Lach** led *Tell* lp
  - **sneezing** agg.: ferr bg1* kali-i sne sep k* *Tell* k* verb bro1
  - **sore**: apis bro1 arn bro1 bell-p bro1 corn-f bro1 phyt bro1 ruta bro1
  - **splinter**; as from a: ign bro1 rhus-t bro1
  - **spraining** agg.: tell ptk1
  - **standing**:
    - **agg.**: *Aesc* agar bar-c bell bro1 ferr germ-met srj5• gnaph sne kali-bi k* kali-i k* lach bg1 nept-m lsd2.fr nux-v k* *Sulph Valer* k*
    - **amel.**: bell k* mag-p k* meny staph k* tell ptk1
    - **leg** raised on a chair; with:
      - **agg.**: valer nh
      - **amel.**: (↗*raising)* valer nh*
  - **stepping** agg.: asar bar-c gnaph k* nux-m sulph bg1
  - **stitching** pain: acon bro1 *Bell* bro1 cact bro1 caust bro1 cimic bro1 coloc bro1 daph bro1 gels bro1 mag-c bro1 *Mag-p* bro1 *Nux-v* bro1 phyt bro1 plb bro1 *Stry* bro1 sul-ac bro1 *Verat* bro1 *Verb* bro1 xan bro1 zinc-p bro1
  - **stool**:
    - **after** | **agg.**: nux-v bg2
    - **agg.**: rhus-t ptk1
    - **before**: kali-bi bg1
    - **during** | **agg.**: nux-v bg2 tell bg2
    - **straining** at | **agg.**: *Nux-v* plat bg1 *Rhus-t Sep Tell* k*
  - **stooping** agg.: agar k* card-m dros kali-i sne nat-s spig bro1 *Tell* k* tritic-vg fd5.de
  - **stretching**:
    - **leg**:
      - **agg.**: arn berb calc-s k2 *Caps* cham germ-met srj5• guaj *Valer* k*
      - **amel.**: cupr bg1 dulc bg1 ferr bg1 hep bg1
  - **summer**:
    - **agg.**: xan ptk1
    - **amel.**: ign ptk1
    - **winter**; with cough in: staph k*
  - **syphilitic**: *Kali-i* bro1 merc-c bro1 phyt bro1
  - **talking** agg.: verb bro1
  - **tearing** pain: aesc bro1 arg-n bro1 *Ars* bro1 *Bell* bro1 bry bro1 caust bro1 *Cham* bro1 chin bro1 *Coloc* bro1 dios bro1 gels bro1 gnaph bro1 ign bro1 kalm bro1 *Mag-p* bro1 mez bro1 nux-v bro1 paraf bro1 phos bro1 phyt bro1 puls bro1 rhus-t bro1 ruta k2* sang bro1 *Spig* bro1 ter bro1
  - **temperature**; change of: verb bro1
  - **tonic** contractions, chronic: *Nat-m* tell
  - **torpor**; with (See MIND - Torpor - pain - sciatic)
  - **touch**:
    - **agg.**: ars bro1 bell k* berb bry bro1 caps **Chin** bro1* **Chinin-s** k* cocc coff ptk1 *Coloc* k* ferr gels guaj *Kali-c* **Lach** k* *Led Mag-p* k* mez k* *Nux-v* bro1 plb bro1* *Spig* bro1 sulph tell mrr1 verat visc ptk1
    - **slight** touch agg.: lach mrr1
  - **touching** or closing teeth agg.: verb bro1
  - **turn** over on the well side before he can rise from bed: *Kali-c*
  - **turning** in bed agg.: coloc sne *Nat-s* k*
  - **uncovering** limb: *Mag-p* k* **Sil** ptk1
  - **urination** | **amel.**: tell k*
  - **uterine** complaints; from: (non:bell bro1) bell-p ptk1 ferr bro1* gnaph ptk1 graph bro1 merc bro1* puls bro1* sep bro1* sulph bro1*
  - **vexation** agg.: coloc spong fd4.de
  - **walking**:
    - **agg.**: bamb-a stb2.de• bar-c berb *Chinin-s* coff *Coloc* gnaph sne ign iris a1 lach *Led* nat-ar nat-s nept-m lsd2.fr psor spong fd4.de staph sne *Sulph* zinc
    - **amel.**: agar am-m k* ars bg1* caps *Coc-c Dios* bro1 **Ferr** *Ign* bro1 indg *Kali-bi* k* *Kali-i* k* kali-p kali-s fd4.de lac-h htj1• **Lyc** k* mag-c bro1 ox-ac bro1 ph-ac *Puls* bro1 **Rhus-t** k* ruta sep k* sulph bro1 syph tell sne tritic-vg fd5.de *Valer* k*

- **Lower** limbs – **Sciatic** nerve – **walking**: ...
  - **bent** | **must** walk bent: bamb-a stb2.de•
  - **must** walk: ars bg1* kali-i sne sep bg1* sulph bg1*
  - **wandering** pain: ant-ar c1
  - **warm**:
    - **bed**:
      - **agg.**: *Coloc* k* led *Merc*
      - **amel.**: *Ars* caust kali-bi k2 **Lyc** *Mag-p Nux-v Phos Sil*
    - **room** | **agg.**: **Puls** k*
  - **warmth**:
    - **agg.**: cham bro1 ferr ptk1 *Guaj* k* **Led** k* merc ptk1 mez bro1 plb bro1 *Puls* bro1 verat visc ptk1 xan bro1 zinc
      - **heat** agg.: *Led* verat zinc
    - **amel.**: aids nl2• **Ars** k* bell k* caust *Coloc* k* gnaph sne kali-c *Kali-p* **Lyc** k* **Mag-p** k* mand sp1* morph bro1 nat-m *Nux-v* k* pall k* *Phos* k* **Rhus-t** k* *Sil* staph thuj
  - **weather**:
    - **change** of weather: *Kali-bi* lach
    - **cold**:
      - **wet** | **agg.**: ran-b mrr1
    - **warm** | **agg.**: kali-bi xan br1
    - **wet**:
      - **agg.**: mez k2 *Phyt* ran-b k* **Rhus-t** ruta
      - **amel.**: asar
  - **wet**; after getting: *Dulc* ptk1 *Rhus-t* ptk1
  - **wind**; before a heavy: berb
  - **winter** agg.: ign k*
  - **yawning** agg.: zinc bg1*
  - **extending** to:
    - **Chest**: corn-f bro1
    - **Downward**: carbn-s vh *Coloc* ↓ dios br1 lac-h htj1• lach ↓ *Ruta* ↓ spong fd4.de
      - **shooting** pain: *Coloc* lach *Ruta*
    - **Extremities**: coloc bro1 gnaph bro1 graph bro1 kalm bro1 pall bro1
    - **Face**: arund bro1
    - **Knee**: bamb-a stb2.de• coloc k* elat k* ind ptk1 *Kali-bi* lp *Lach* k* plan k*
      - **Hip** to knee; from: coloc elat *Lach* plan
    - **Pelvis**: arund bro1
    - **Shoulder**: arund bro1 germ-met srj5•
      - **Outward**: berb mrr1
    - **Thigh** | **Posterior** part: berb mrr1
    - **Upward**: bell bg1 dulc bg1 hep bg1 kalm bro1 mag-c bg1 phos bg1 ran-b bg1
  - **Foot** sole: ars bg2 calc bg2 *Kali-c* bg2 mag-p ptk1 merc bg2
  - **Heel**, becomes localized in●: anan k* **Sep** k ●*
  - **Hip** to knee (See extending to - knee - hip)
  - **Spots**; in: ign bro1 kali-bi bro1 lil-t bro1 ox-ac bro1
  - **Thighs**: mand rsj7•
    - **sitting** agg.: mand rsj7•
- **Skin**: bell ↓ *Mang* hr1 nux-v ↓ ran-s ↓
  - **biting**: bell bg2 nux-v b7.de* ran-s b7.de*
- **Skin**; below: am-c ↓ anac ↓ asaf ↓ aur ↓ *Bry* ↓ calc ↓ euph ↓ graph ↓ hep ↓ kali-c ↓ kreos ↓ led ↓ phos ↓ puls ↓ sulph ↓ valer ↓
  - **ulcerative** pain: am-c b4.de* anac b4.de* asaf b7.de* aur b4.de* *Bry* b7.de* calc b4.de* euph b4.de* graph b4.de* hep b4.de* kali-c b4.de* kreos b7a.de led b7.de* phos b4.de* puls b7.de* sulph b4.de* valer b7.de*
- **Spots**; in: chel ↓ lyc ↓ mag-c ↓ ph-ac ↓
  - **burning**: chel b7.de* lyc k* mag-c k* ph-ac k*
- **Transverse**: zinc bg2

- **Lower** limbs, legs and feet:
  - ▽ **extending** to:
    - **Abdomen**: thal-xyz srj8•
    - **Anterior** chest: thal-xyz srj8•
- **Muscles**: chir-fl ↓ convo-s sp1 dig ↓ luna ↓ positr ↓ ruta ↓ tub-m jl2
  - **evening**: luf-op ↓
    - **aching**: luf-op rsj5•

- **aching**: chir-fl bnm4• dulc fd4.de luna kg1• positr nl2• ruta fd4.de
- **rheumatic**: bacls-10 mtf11 bacls-7 mtf11 calc mrr1 caul tl1 *Cimic* tl1* gaert mtf11 morg-g mtf11 morg-p mtf11 osteo-a mtf11 rhus-t tl1
- **stitching** pain: dig c1

○ • **Attachment** of muscles: phyt rhod ruta fd4.de
- **Extensor** muscles: calc-p ↓ luna ↓
  - **aching**: calc-p luna kg1•
- **Flexor** muscles: anac arn carbn-s caust cic colch rsj2• dros gels kalm kola stb3• mand rsj7• merc mez op *Phos* plan plb rhus-t sep
  - **morning**: caust
  - **forenoon**: caust
  - **boring** pain: plan
  - **exertion** agg.: gels
  - **gnawing** pain: merc
  - **motion** agg.: mand rsj7• nux-v
  - **pressing** pain: arn cic *Dros*
  - **rheumatic**: merc-i-r
  - **waking**; on: sep
- **Joints**; near: hyos ↓
  - **drawing** pain: hyos h1
- **Knee**; above:
  - **right**: chlam-tr ↓
    - **sore**: chlam-tr bcx2•
  - **waking**; on: chlam-tr ↓
    - **sore**: chlam-tr bcx2•

- **Nails**: alum ↓ am-m k* ant-c k* apis ↓ bell k* berb ↓ *Calc* ↓ calc-p ↓ *Caust* k* chin ↓ colch ↓ con ↓ elaps ↓ *Fl-ac* ↓ *Graph* k* *Hep* k* kali-c k* m-ambo b2.de* *M-aust* b2.de *Merc* k* mez ↓ mosch ↓ mur-ac ↓ nat-m k* *Nit-ac* k* *Nux-v* k* par k* *Petr* plat ↓ puls k* ran-b k* rhus-t k* ruta ↓ sabad k* sars ↓ sep k* *Sil* k* *Squil* k* stann sul-ac ↓ sulph k* teucr b2.de* thuj ↓ vinc ↓ zinc
  - **burning**: alum ant-c apis gsd1 calc caust k* con bg2 elaps bg2 **Graph** hep merc nat-m nit-ac bg2 nux-v puls sars bg2* *Sep* sulph vinc bg2
  - **pressing** pain: m-ambo b2.de*
  - **sore**: alum b2.de* ant-c b2.de* calc b2.de* caust b2.de* **Graph** b2.de* hep b2.de* m-ambo b2.de* m-aust b2.de* merc b2.de* mez bg2 nat-m b2.de* nux-v b2.de* puls b2.de* *Sep* b2.de* sulph b2.de*
  - **stitching** pain: alum *Calc* caust *Graph* mosch *Nat-m* nit-ac k* nux-v *Puls* rhus-t sep sil sulph
  - **tearing** pain: colch *Fl-ac* hep *Nit-ac* petr plat ran-b *Sil* *Sulph*
  - **ulcerative** pain: *Am-m* b2.de* bell b2.de* berb bg2 calc-p bg2 caust b2.de* chin b2.de* **Graph** b2.de* hep b2.de* kali-c b2.de* m-ambo b2.de* m-aust b2.de* merc b2.de* mosch b2.de* mur-ac b2.de* *Nat-m* b2.de* nux-v b2.de* **Puls** b2.de* ran-b b2.de* *Rhus-t* b2.de* ruta b2.de* *Sep* b2.de* *Sil* b2.de* sul-ac b2.de* sulph b2.de* thuj b2.de*

  ○ • **Edges**: calc-p bg1 rad-br bg1
  - **Roots**: sulph ↓
    - **burning**: sulph bro1
  - **Sides**: calc-p ↓
    - **burning**: calc-p ptk2
  - **Under**: bism ↓ calc-p ↓ coc-c ↓ fl-ac ↓
    - **splinter**; as from a: (↗*fingers - nails - under - splinters*) calc-p ptk1 coc-c ptk1 fl-ac ptk1
    - **tearing** pain: bism ptk2

- **Nates**: agar k* aloe ↓ *Alum* ↓ ambr ↓ *Anac* ↓ ant-c ↓ arg-met ↓ *Ars* ↓ aur-m ↓ *Bamb-a* stb2.de• *Bar-c* ↓ berb ↓ bit-ar wht1• bry k* *Calc* k* calc-p k* *Camph* ↓ carbn-o ↓ card-m ↓ caust k* cham ↓ *Chin* ↓ cina cist k* coca colch ↓ coloc k* croc b7.de* crot-t ↓ cupr k* cypra-eg ↓ dig ↓ dros ↓ dulc fd4.de eup-per euph k* euphr ↓ *Guaj* ↓ *Hep* b4a.de hura ↓ iod irid-met ↓ kali-bi k* kali-c kali-n ↓ kali-s fd4.de kalm k* lap-la rsp1 lat-m bnm6• laur ↓ lyc ↓ mag-m ↓ mag-s ↓ mang ↓ med k2 merc k* merl ↓ mez k* mill k* mur-ac ↓ nat-c ↓ nat-m ↓ nept-m ↓ nit-ac k* nux-v ↓ ol-an ↓ ozone sde2• par ↓ ph-ac ↓ *Phos* pieri-b mlk9.de plb k* podo ↓ prun ↓ *Puls* *Rhus-t* ↓ ruta fd4.de sanic ↓ sars ↓ sel ↓ sep sil ↓ spong fd4.de staph k* stront-c ↓ **Sulph** k* symph ↓ tarent k* thuj k2 tritic-vg fd5.de vanil fd5.de ven-m rsj12• zinc ↓
  - **right**: bamb-a ↓ chlam-tr ↓ kali-p ↓ kali-s ↓ ozone ↓ *Rhus-t* ↓ sep ↓ tritic-vg ↓ visc ↓
    - **drawing** pain: kali-p fd1.de• *Rhus-t* sep h2 tritic-vg fd5.de
    - **dull** pain: chlam-tr bcx2•

- **Nates – right**: ...
    - **shooting** pain: ozone sde2•
    - **stitching** pain: bamb-a stb2.de• kali-s fd4.de visc c1
    - **tearing** pain: ozone sde2•
  - **left**: agar ↓ bamb-a stb2.de• colch rsj2• *Cycl* ↓ dulc fd4.de germ-met srj5• kali-s fd4.de loxo-recl knl4• mand ↓ ozone ↓ ph-ac ↓ psil ft1 spong fd4.de
    - **cutting** pain: mand rsj7•
    - **drawing** pain: agar h2 bamb-a stb2.de• *Cycl* hr1 dulc fd4.de ph-ac
    - **stitching** pain: ozone sde2•
  - **morning**: dulc fd4.de kali-p k2 kali-s fd4.de mill k*
    - **6** h until night: tarent
  - **forenoon**: alum ↓ mill ↓
    - **cutting** pain: alum
    - **pressing** pain: mill k*
    - **tearing** pain: mill
  - **afternoon**: ozone ↓ vanil fd5.de
    - **15**.30 h: ol-an ↓
      - **stitching** pain: ol-an
    - **17** h | **air** agg.; in open: coca
    - **tearing** pain: ozone sde2•
  - **evening**: mill k* nat-c ↓ ruta fd4.de spong fd4.de
    - **bed** agg.; in: staph ↓
      - **stitching** pain: staph
    - **lying** down agg.; after: sulph ↓
      - **burning**: sulph
    - **tearing** pain: nat-c h2
  - **night**: dulc fd4.de
    - **riding** in a carriage agg.: nit-ac
    - **sitting**; after: staph k*
  - **accompanied** by | **stiffness** all over body: bit-ar wht1•
  - **aching**: bry *Calc* calc-p cupr staph
  - **boring** pain: cina coloc merc k* staph h1
  - **burning**: bar-c bry calc-p coloc lyc mag-m mang **Merc** k* mez sep stront-c sulph
  - **cutting** pain: alum k*
  - **dinner**; during: laur ↓
    - **stitching** pain: laur
  - **drawing** pain: agar aloe bamb-a stb2.de• bar-c berb bry calc *Camph* *Chin* crot-t cupr dig h2 dulc fd4.de mang mez nat-m nit-ac ph-ac *Rhus-t* ruta fd4.de sep h2 sil spong fd4.de tritic-vg fd5.de zinc
    - **cramping**: calc h2 mang ph-ac h2
  - **gnawing** pain:
    - **corrosive** itching: staph h1
    - **dogs**; as if gnawed by: hura
  - **hindering** labor: *Kali-c*
  - **lying** on back agg.: kali-p k2
  - **menses**; during: cench k2
    - **sore**: cench k2
  - **motion**:
    - **agg.**: bamb-a ↓ bit-ar wht1• hydrog ↓
      - **drawing** pain: bamb-a stb2.de•
      - **sore**: hydrog srj2•
    - **amel.**: kali-n ↓
      - **tearing** pain: kali-n
  - **periodically**: *Bar-c* ↓
    - **tearing** pain: *Bar-c*
  - **pinching** pain: kali-c h2 sulph h2
  - **pressing** pain: chin a1 cupr h2 cypra-eg sde6.de• iod k* lyc h2 mill k* podo fd3.de• sars h2 sep k* tritic-vg fd5.de zinc h2
    - **plug**; as from a: *Anac*
    - **pulsating** pain: chin h1
  - **pressure**:
    - **agg.**: hydrog srj2• mill k* podo fd3.de•

- **pressure**: ...
  - **amel.**: bamb-a↓ mang↓ *Rhus-t*↓
    - **drawing** pain: bamb-a stb2.de• mang a1 *Rhus-t*
- **raising** left leg agg.: ozone sde2•
- **rising**:
  - **agg.**: dros↓
    - **tearing** pain: dros
  - **amel.**: agar↓
    - **tearing** pain: agar
  - **sitting**; from:
    - **agg.**: mang↓
      - **drawing** pain: mang h2
  - **stooping**; from | **agg.**: bamb-a stb2.de•
- **scratching**:
  - **agg.**: prun↓
    - **stitching** pain: prun
  - **amel.**: staph↓
    - **stitching** pain: staph
- **shooting** pain: carbn-o ozone sde2• spong fd4.de symph fd3.de•
- **sitting**:
  - **after**: agar↓ puls↓
    - **sore**: agar h2 puls h1
  - **agg.**: agar↓ alum↓ calc-p↓ caust↓ cench↓ chin k* chlam-tr↓ cina cycl dulc fd4.de guaj↓ **Hep** mang↓ *Phos* sel↓ sep stann↓ *Staph* sulph tritic-vg fd5.de vanil fd5.de
    - **boring** pain: cina staph h1
    - **burning**: mang
    - **drawing** pain: *Chin Cycl* k* dulc fd4.de
    - **dull** pain: chlam-tr bcx2•
    - **pressing** pain: chin h1* phos h2 stann h2
    - **sore**: agar caust cench k2 *Hep* phos h2 sel sep
    - **stitching** pain: alum calc-p guaj mang a1
  - **amel.**: mag-m↓ mang↓ nat-c↓
    - **drawing** pain: mang
    - **tearing** pain: mag-m nat-c h2
- **sore**: agar arg-met *Ars* k* calc-p card-m caust cist *Hep* lyc k* mag-m mag-s merc nat-m nit-ac nux-v phos bg2 *Puls* sanic sel sulph thuj k2 zinc
- **standing**:
  - **agg.**: berb↓ chin↓ mang↓ nat-c↓ verat↓
    - **drawing** pain: chin mang verat a1
    - **stitching** pain: berb
    - **tearing** pain: nat-c
  - **amel.**: chlam-tr↓ *Cycl*↓
    - **drawing** pain: *Cycl* k*
    - **dull** pain: chlam-tr bcx2•
- **stitching** pain: *Alum* ant-c bamb-a stb2.de• bar-c berb *Calc* **Calc-p** k* carbn-o cham dulc euphr *Guaj* k* irid-met srj5• kali-s fd4.de laur merc ol-an ozone sde2• par plb prun ruta fd4.de staph sulph symph fd3.de•
  - **itching**: mur-ac a1
- **sudden** appearing and sudden disappearing: ozone↓
  - **shooting** pain: ozone sde2•
  - **tearing** pain: ozone sde2•
- **tearing** pain: agar ambr *Bar-c* berb chin h1 cina colch dros kali-c kali-n kali-s fd4.de lyc mag-m merl mez mill nat-c nept-m lsd2.fr ozone sde2• symph fd3.de• thuj zinc
  - **crawling**: kali-c h2
  - **downward**: aur-m *Bar-c* symph fd3.de• thuj
- **touch** agg.: sulph↓
  - **sore**: sulph h2
- **ulcerative** pain: calc phos *Puls*
- **waking**; on: agar↓
  - **drawing** pain: agar h2
  - **tearing** pain: agar h2
- **walking** agg.: agn a1 bamb-a↓ berb↓ dulc fd4.de mag-m↓ mag-s↓ *Mez* mill↓ ph-ac↓ tritic-vg fd5.de
  - **drawing** pain: bamb-a stb2.de• ph-ac tritic-vg fd5.de

- **Nates – walking agg.**: ...
  - **pressing** pain: mill k*
  - **sore**: mag-s
  - **tearing** pain: berb mag-m
- **wine** agg.: zinc↓
  - **drawing** pain: zinc
- ▽ **extending** to:
  - **Anus**: colch↓
    - **tearing** pain: colch
  - **Feet**: bamb-a stb2.de• nit-ac↓
    - **drawing** pain: nit-ac
  - **Hip**: staph bro1
  - **Hips** and groins: nat-m↓
    - **tearing** pain: nat-m h2
  - **Knee**: bamb-a stb2.de• kali-s fd4.de
  - **Lower** limb: mand↓
    - **cutting** pain: mand rsj7•
    - **motion** agg.: mand↓
      - **cutting** pain: mand rsj7•
  - **Thigh**: bamb-a↓ dulc↓
    - **drawing** pain: bamb-a stb2.de• dulc fd4.de
- ○ **Between**: ambr↓ arg-met↓ caust↓ graph↓ sep↓ sulph↓ thuj↓
  - **burning**: arg-met sep thuj k*
  - **riding** a horse; after: *Carb-an*↓ *Sulph*↓
    - **sore**: *Carb-an* b4a.de *Sulph* b4a.de
  - **sore**: caust bg2 graph tl1 sulph h2
  - **tearing** pain: ambr
- **Inner** side: sep↓
  - **tearing** pain: sep h2
- **Spot**; in a small: bamb-a stb2.de•
- **Spots**; in small: **Calc-p**↓
  - **stitching** pain: **Calc-p**
- **Tubera** ischiadica: aur↓ bamb-a stb2.de•
  - **pinching** pain: aur h2

- **Paralyzed** parts●: *Agar* arn *Ars* bell calc *Caust* **Cham**↓ cina *Cocc* crot-t *Kali-n* *Lat-m* nux-v● k2 *Phos* *Plb* rhus-t↓ sil sulph
  - **drawing** pain: *Cocc*
  - **sore**: plb
  - **stitching** pain: ars nux-v
    - **hot**: **Ars**
  - **tearing** pain: arn *Ars* bell calc caust **Cham** *Cocc* crot-t *Kali-n* lat-m *Nux-v* *Phos* *Plb* rhus-t sil
- **Scapulohumeral** region: syph jl2
  - **left**: psor↓
    - **cramping**: psor jl2
  - **evening**: psor↓
    - **cramping**: psor jl2
  - **rest** agg.: psor↓
    - **cramping**: psor jl2
- **Sciatica** (See lower limbs - sciatic)
- **Shoulders**: abies-c oss4• abrot acon k* acon-ac↓ adam↓ aesc aeth↓ *Agar* agath-a nl2• agn↓ ail↓ all-c aloe↓ *Alum* k* alum-p↓ alum-sil k2 alumn am-c am-m am-p br1* *Ambr*↓ aml-ns↓ ammc *Anac*↓ anag k* ant-t↓ apis k* *Arg-met* *Arg-n*↓ arge-pl rwt5• arn k* *Ars* ars-i↓ ars-s-f↓ arum-t↓ asaf↓ asar b7.de* asc-t aspar astac↓ aster atp↓ aur aur-ar k2 aur-i↓ aur-m aur-m-n↓ aur-s k2 aza br1* bad bamb-a stb2.de• bapt bar-c k* bar-s k2 **Bell**↓ bell-p-sp↓ *Berb* bism↓ borx↓ *Bov*↓ brach↓ brom bros-gau mrc1 *Brucel* sa3• *Bry* k* *Cact* *Calad* *Calc* calc-i↓ *Calc-p* *Calc-s* calc-sil k2 camph↓ *Cann-i* bro1 cann-s b7.de* canth↓ caps↓ carb-ac carb-an↓ carb-v *Carbn-s* carc gk6 card-m casc a1 *Caust* cham **Chel** k* chin chinin-ar chinin-s *Cic*↓ *Cimic* cimx cina↓ *Cist* clem↓ cob-n sp1 coc-c coca↓ cocc bro1 *Colch* coloc com con bro1 conch↓ cop cor-r↓ corv-cor↓ cot↓ *Croc*↓ *Crot-c* k* *Crot-h* crot-t↓ cupr cur↓ cycl↓ cystein-l↓ daph des-ac rbp6 dig digin↓ dios dirc dros *Dulc* *Echi* elaps↓ elat↓ *Euon*↓ eup-per eup-pur↓ euph↓ euphr↓ fago k* falco-pe nl2• **Ferr** k* *Ferr-ar* *Ferr-i*↓ **Ferr-m** *Ferr-p* fl-ac form↓ *Gamb*↓ gels gent-c↓ ger-i↓ gins glon *Gran*↓ granit-m es1• *Graph* k* grat↓ guaj guat sp1 *Ham* hell *Hep* k* hir↓

Extremities

- **Shoulders**: ...
hura hydr↓ *Hydrog* srj2• hyper *Ign* ind indg↓ inul↓ *Iod* iodof a1 *Iris* jatr-c jug-c jug-r bro1 kali-ar *Kali-bi* k* kali-c k* *Kali-i* kali-m↓ *Kali-n* kali-p kali-s fd4.de kali-sil k2 *Kalm* k* ketogl-ac↓ kola stb3• kreos k* lac-ac k* lac-c lac-e hrn2• *Lach* lachn lact↓ lap-la sde8.de• lat-m bnm6• laur lec *Led* k* lil-t lith-c↓ lob k* lob-s↓ loxo-recl knl4• *Lyc* k* lyss m-ambo↓ *Mag-c* k* *Mag-m* mag-s↓ manc↓ mand rsj7• mang *Med* k* melal-alt gya4 menis bro1 meny↓ *Merc* merc-c merc-i-f merc-sul *Mez* k* mill↓ mim-p rsj8*• morg-p pte1*• mosch mur-ac musca-d↓ myos-a↓ *Myric* bro1 myrt-c naja *Nat-ar* k* *Nat-c* k* nat-f sp1 nat-m nat-p↓ nat-s nat-sil↓ nicc↓ nit-ac k* nit-s-d↓ nux-m *Nux-v* ol-an olib-sac↓ olnd ox-ac↓ pall par↓ pert-vc↓ petr↓ ph-ac phasco-ci rbp2 phel↓ *Phos* phys *Phyt* pic-ac↓ pin-con oss2• pip-m↓ plan *Plat*↓ *Plb* plect↓ plut-n srj7• *Podo*↓ positr↓ pot-e↓ propr sa3• prun psil↓ psor ptel *Puls* k* *Ran-b* k* ran-s↓ raph *Rat*↓ *Rhod* **Rhus-t** ros-d↓ rumx ruta fd4.de sabad↓ sabin c1 sacch-a↓ sal-al blc1• sal-fr↓ salol c1 **Sang** k* sanic mrr1 sarcol-ac↓ sarr↓ sars sec↓ senec↓ sep k* *Ser-a-c* jl2 sil sin-n↓ spig k2 spong fd4.de squil↓ stann↓ *Staph* staphycoc↓ stram streptoc↓ stront-c stry suis-pan↓ sul-ac↓ sul-i↓ **Sulph** k* sumb↓ symph fd3.de• tab taosc iwa1• tarax↓ tarent tep↓ ter↓ teucr↓ thiam↓ *Thuj* tril-p tritic-vg fd5.de trom tub↓ tub-r jl2 urt-g a1 ust↓ *Valer*↓ vanil fd5.de verat k* verat-v↓ verb↓ vesp viol-t↓ vip visc bro1 zinc zinc-p k2 [ang stj4 *Ferr-lac* stj2 *Ferr-n* stj2 heroin sdj2]
  - **alternating** sides: des-ac rbp6 **Lac-c** lyc bg3 mag-m↓
    - **drawing** pain: mag-m h2
  - **right**: abrom-a ks5 agar↓ agath-a nl2• agn↓ am-c↓ am-m ammc apis arg-met↓ arg-n↓ asaf↓ asc-t a1 bamb-a stb2.de• berb bism↓ bov↓ brom↓ brucel sa3• cact↓ **Calc** k ● carb-ac c1 carb-v carbn-s↓ carc↓ card-m k2 casc a1 *Caust*↓ **Chel** k* chen-a hr1 cimic cimx *Coc-c*↓ colch rsj2• *Coloc* con↓ *Crot-c* cypra-eg sde6.de• ephe-si hsj1• euph↓ ferr bg3* **Ferr-m** k* ferr-p k2* fl-ac fum rly1*• galeoc-c-h↓ gels↓ gink-b sbd1• ham↓ helia↓ ignis-alc↓ inul br1 iris kali-c↓ *Kalm* kola stb3• lac-e hrn2• lac-lup hrn2• lact lap-la rsp1* laur↓ lavand-a ctl1• *Led Lept* limest-b↓ lob luf-op↓ **Lyc** k ● lyss mag-c k* mag-m b4a.de mand rsj7• mang↓ marb-w↓ med melal-alt gya4 merc↓ *Merc-i-f*↓ musca-d szs1 nat-c b4a.de *Nat-m*↓ nat-p k2 nat-sil fd3.de• *Nit-ac* olib-sac wmh1 osteo-a jl2 ozone sde2• pall ph-ac↓ phos↓ *Phyt* plect c2 plut-n srj7• positr↓ propr sa3• prun↓ psil ft1 psor↓ puls-n c2 pyrog pd **Ran-b**↓ *Rat*↓ rhod↓ ruta fd4.de sabin↓ sal-al↓ **Sang** k* sanic mrr1 sel↓ sep b4a.de sil↓ spong fd4.de stann↓ staph↓ stront-c↓ *Sulph*↓ tax↓ thuj trios↓ tritic-vg fd5.de urt-u c2 vanil fd5.de visc c1 vult-gr↓ xan c1 zinc↓ [spect dfg1]
    - **accompanied** by:
      - **Knee**; pain in left: asc-t a1
      - **Leg**; pain in left: asc-t a1
    - **aching**: galeoc-c-h gms1• mand rsj7•
      - **accompanied** by | **coldness** of the shoulder: granit-m es1•
    - **boring** pain: arg-met arg-n ferr k2 rhod b4a.de ruta fd4.de
    - **burning**: am-m *Carb-v* k* marb-w es1• stront-c b4a.de *Sulph* b4a.de [tax jsj7]
    - **cough** agg.; during: borx↓
      - **stitching** pain: borx
    - **cutting** pain: caust bg1 ignis-alc es2• luf-op rsj5• sulph
    - **dislocated**; as if: agn b7a.de sabin b7a.de staph b7a.de
    - **drawing** pain: agar b4a.de am-c k* am-m k* carb-v k* caust b4a.de coc-c con b4a.de euph k* ferr-p *Lyc* k* merc b4a.de nat-c h2 *Nat-m* b4a.de nat-sil fd3.de• rhod b4a.de sep h2 sulph b4a.de thuj k* vanil fd5.de
    - **dull** pain: bamb-a stb2.de• sal-al blc1• sel rsj9•
    - **followed** by | **left** shoulder; pain in: am-m *Apis* bad *Ferr* bg3 ferr-p bg3 jatr-c lac-c lob *Lyc* lyss propr sa3•
    - **ice**; as if covered by: psil vml3•
    - **lying** on painful side agg.: bamb-a stb2.de•
    - **motion** agg.: marb-w↓
      - **burning**: marb-w es1•
    - **pressing** pain: apis bamb-a stb2.de• calc b4a.de casc a1 kali-c b4a.de laur ph-ac h2 prun sil b4a.de* vanil fd5.de
    - **pulsating** pain: trios rsj11•
    - **putting** arm behind back impossible: marb-w↓
      - **burning**: marb-w es1•
    - **shooting** pain: asc-t c1 gels a1 iris
    - **sore**: coloc ferr b7a.de ferr-p k2 *Merc-i-f* ozone sde2• positr nl2• psor
  - **right**: ...
    - **stitching** pain: *Apis* asaf b7a.de brom calc b4a.de carb-v k* carbn-s carc fd2.de• caust *Chel* k* colch ferr b7a.de ham fd3.de• iris kola stb3• lap-la rsp1 limest-b es1• merc-i-f pall plut-n srj7• **Ran-b** ruta fd4.de stront-c b4a.de sulph b4a.de thuj b4a.de vult-gr sze5• [helia stj7]
    - **tearing** pain: agar agn b7a.de am-c arg-met bism b7a.de* bov b4a.de cact carb-v k* *Caust* b4a.de *Coc-c* ferr b7a.de* *Ferr-p* kali-c b4a.de led b7a.de lyc b4a.de mag-c h2 mag-m mang a1 nat-m b4a.de phos b4a.de *Rat* stann b4a.de stront-c b4a.de *Sulph* b4a.de vanil fd5.de zinc b4a.de
    - **extending** to:
      - **Chest**; through: chen-a hr1 lac-lup hrn2•
      - **Hand**: bamb-a stb2.de•
      - **Wrist**: musca-d szs1
  - **left**: *Agar* agn↓ alum-p k2 alumn ammc anac↓ androc↓ aq-mar skp7• arg-met *Arg-n* hr1 asaf↓ asc-t a1 aspar vh asper ktp2 atp↓ aur↓ bamb-a stb2.de• *Bell*↓ brucel sa3• cassia-s↓ chel mrr1 cic↓ cinnb colch↓ conch fkr1.de crot-c↓ crot-h tl1 cyclosp sa3• dendr-pol sk4• des-ac rbp6 dulc fd4.de ephe-si hsj1• ferr↓ galeoc-c-h↓ graph k2 guaj ham fd3.de• hydrog↓ ind *Iod* iodof a1 kali-c↓ *Kali-i*↓ kali-m k2 kali-s fd4.de *Kalm* kola stb3• lavand-a↓ **Led** mag-c bg3 mag-m↓ mand rsj7• mang-m med c1 merc-c muru a1 nat-c↓ nat-m nat-p↓ nat-sil fd3.de• nux-m bg3* olib-sac wmh1 ozone sde2• pert-vc↓ *Ph-ac Phos*↓ plut-n↓ positr nl2• psor↓ rhodi ptk2 **Rhus-t** k ●* ros-d↓ ruta fd4.de sal-fr sle1• **Sang** bg3 sel↓ spong fd4.de staph↓ sul-ac↓ **SULPH** k ●* symph fd3.de• tax↓ tell rsj10• ther tl1 tril-p c1 trios↓ tritic-vg fd5.de tub al vanil fd5.de verat↓ viol-t↓ [*Buteo-j* sej6 heroin sdj2 pop dhh1 spect dfg1]
    - **then** right: aeth↓
      - **drawing** pain: aeth
    - **accompanied** by:
      - **Forearm**; pain in right: asc-t a1
      - **Hip**; pain in right: **Led** k* nux-m
    - **aching**: colch rsj2• hydrog srj2• lavand-a ctl1• positr nl2•
    - **boring** pain: aur ph-ac
    - **burning**: hydrog srj2• sel rsj9•
    - **cough** agg.; during: *Ferr* rhus-t sulph↓
      - **stitching** pain: sulph
    - **cutting** pain: crot-c sk4•
    - **drawing** pain: nat-p tritic-vg fd5.de vanil fd5.de
    - **dull** pain: trios rsj11•
    - **electric** shock; as from an: hydrog srj2•
    - **lying** on painless side agg.: nat-m
    - **motion** agg.: asc-t↓ ephe-si↓
      - **shooting** pain: asc-t a1
      - **stitching** pain: ephe-si hsj1•
    - **pinching** pain: cassia-s ccrh1•
    - **pressing** pain: anac h2 bamb-a stb2.de• bell nux-m hr1 plut-n srj7• staph h1 sul-ac h2 tritic-vg fd5.de
      - **followed** by | **right**: bamb-a stb2.de•
    - **shooting** pain: galeoc-c-h gms1• hydrog srj2•
    - **sore**: atp rly4• ind kali-c h2 *Kali-i* mag-c h2 pert-vc vk9 positr nl2• sulph
    - **sprained**; as if: conch fkr1•
    - **stitching** pain: agn hr1 androc srj1• asaf b7a.de *Bell Graph* ham fd3.de• iodof a1 kali-s fd4.de med olib-sac wmh1 ros-d wla1 staph b7a.de verat b7a.de viol-t b7a.de [tax jsj7]
    - **tearing** pain: alumn cassia-s ccrh1• cic ferr graph nat-c h2 *Phos* psor jl2 spong fd4.de vanil fd5.de
    - **wedge**; sensation of a: mag-m h2
    - **extending** to:
      - **right**: asc-t *Calc-p* lach lyc bg3 *Med* naja [heroin sdj2]
      - **Arm**: colch↓
        - **aching**: colch rsj2•
      - **Downward**: asper ktp2
      - **Elbow** | **left**: brucel sa3•
      - **Finger**: colch↓
        - **aching**: colch rsj2•
      - **Hand**:
        - **evening**: luna↓
          - **aching**: luna kg1•
      - **Hypochondrium** | **left**: bamb-a stb2.de•

- **left – extending** to: ...
  - **Neck**: sal-fr sle1•
  - **Wrist**: colch ↓
    - **aching**: colch rsj2•
- **morning**: arg-met arg-n ars bry ↓ carb-an ↓ carb-v ↓ *Caust* colch ↓ coloc ↓ dios gels ↓ hura ↓ hyper ↓ kali-c ↓ kali-n ↓ kalm lyc ↓ mag-c ↓ naja ↓ nat-m ↓ ol-an *Phos* phys ↓ ran-b rhod ↓ ruta fd4.de *Sep* ↓ sil ↓ spong fd4.de staph ↓ sumb tritic-vg fd5.de trom ↓ vanil fd5.de
  - **6** h: bry ↓
    - **tearing** pain: bry
  - **bed** agg.; in: am-m ↓ mez *Nat-m* ↓ ol-an rhod ↓ staph sulph ↓ sumb ↓
    - **aching**: sumb
    - **boring** pain: mez
    - **drawing** pain: *Nat-m* staph
    - **shooting** pain: sulph
    - **stitching** pain: sulph
    - **tearing** pain: am-m rhod sulph
  - **boring** pain: arg-met arg-n
  - **cough** agg.; during: carb-an ↓
    - **stitching** pain: carb-an
  - **drawing** pain: carb-v h2 dios hyper kali-c naja rhod *Sep* staph
  - **eating**; after: gels ↓
    - **stitching** pain: gels
  - **motion** of arm agg.: puls ↓
    - **stitching** pain: puls
  - **pressing** pain: *Phos* k* staph h1 tritic-vg fd5.de
  - **rising** agg.: cupr ↓ kalm phos ran-b
    - **sore**: cupr
  - **shooting** pain: phys trom
  - **sore**: kali-n
  - **stitching** pain: carb-an carb-v colch gels hura lyc nat-m phys sil trom
  - **tearing** pain: bry coloc lyc mag-c h2
  - **waking**; on: abrot ↓ calc-s ↓ *Carb-v* ↓ chel ↓ coca ↓ coloc ↓ dioxi ↓ fl-ac kali-bi kali-c kalm melal-alt gya4 *Nat-m* ↓ propr sa3• puls ↓ sulph ↓ vanil fd5.de verat a1
    - **aching**: coca
    - **drawing** pain: coloc kali-c *Nat-m*
    - **sore**: abrot calc-s chel dioxi rbp6 fl-ac
    - **tearing** pain: *Carb-v* puls sulph verat
- **forenoon**: cham dios dulc fd4.de hyper *Lyc* mag-c ↓ spong fd4.de sulph ↓ tritic-vg fd5.de vanil fd5.de
  - **9** h | **evening**; until: lyc
  - **10** h: kalm sil ↓
    - **stitching** pain: sil
  - **11** h: lac-ac
  - **cutting** pain: sulph
  - **drawing** pain: cham lyc
  - **tearing** pain: mag-c
  - **walking** agg.: sulph ↓
    - **cutting** pain: sulph
- **forenoon**, 10 h: kalm ↓ tritic-vg ↓
  - **pressing** pain: kalm tritic-vg fd5.de
- **noon**: bamb-a stb2.de• dulc fd4.de phyt ↓ vanil fd5.de
  - **aching**: phyt
  - **eating**; before: senec ↓
    - **stitching** pain: senec
- **afternoon**: canth ↓ cham chel coloc ↓ cupr dios euphr ↓ ham ↓ indg ↓ kali-n ↓ kali-s ↓ kreos ↓ mag-c mag-s ↓ nicc ↓ pert-vc vk9 psor ↓ ruta fd4.de stront-c ↓ tritic-vg fd5.de vanil fd5.de
  - **13** h: dios ↓
    - **aching**: dios
  - **13**.30 h: chel ↓
    - **aching**: chel
  - **14** h: hyper ↓ laur ↓
    - **stitching** pain: hyper laur
- **afternoon**: ...
  - **14**.30 h: pert-vc vk9
  - **16** h: arg-n ↓ indg ↓ *Lyc* ↓ ptel ↓ trios ↓
    - **boring** pain: arg-n
    - **pulsating** pain: trios rsj11•
    - **stitching** pain: indg ptel
    - **tearing** pain: indg *Lyc*
  - **17** h: arg-met ↓ mag-c ↓ sulph ↓
    - **tearing** pain: arg-met mag-c sulph
  - **aching**: coloc dios
  - **raising** arm agg.: nicc ↓
    - **tearing** pain: nicc
  - **stitching** pain: canth chel euphr ham fd3.de• indg kali-s fd4.de kreos mag-c nicc stront-c
  - **tearing** pain: chel kali-n mag-s psor vanil fd5.de
- **evening**: abrom-a ks5 alumn ↓ am-c ↓ *Ambr* ↓ calc-s ↓ chel cist dios ↓ dulc fd4.de fl-ac kali-n ↓ kali-s fd4.de lach ↓ led lyc mag-c merc ↓ *Mez* mur-ac ↓ nat-m ↓ nat-s pall propr sa3• psor ↓ puls rhod ↓ ruta fd4.de sang sep ↓ spong fd4.de still ↓ stry sulph ↓ symph ↓ tritic-vg fd5.de vanil fd5.de zinc ↓
  - **18** h | **walking** agg.: rhus-t
  - **19** h: dios stry
  - **aching**: mez still
  - **bed** agg.; in: kali-s fd4.de nat-m ↓ nux-v rhod ↓ sil ↓ tritic-vg fd5.de zinc ↓
    - **tearing** pain: nat-m rhod sil zinc
  - **bending** forward agg.: carb-ac ↓
    - **aching**: carb-ac
  - **burning**: alumn dios sep sulph
  - **drawing** pain: ambr chel lach lyc nat-m nat-s tritic-vg fd5.de
  - **lying** down agg.; after: sulph ↓
    - **burning**: sulph
  - **pressing** pain: chel k* fl-ac k* nat-s k* spong fd4.de symph fd3.de• tritic-vg fd5.de vanil fd5.de
  - **shooting** pain: sulph
  - **sitting** agg.: mez ↓ *Rhus-t* ↓
    - **pressing** pain: mez k* *Rhus-t*
  - **sore**: am-c calc-s mag-c h2
  - **sprained**; as if: *Ambr*
  - **stitching** pain: calc-s fl-ac lyc merc mur-ac puls sulph
  - **tearing** pain: kali-n lyc mez psor rhod zinc
  - **walking** agg.: rhus-t ↓
    - **burning**: rhus-t
- **night**: abrot acon ↓ alum ↓ bell calc castm *Caust* coloc ↓ cop ↓ *Crot-t* ↓ dig ferr k2 graph ↓ *Kali-bi* kali-c *Kali-n* lyc ↓ mag-c *Merc* *Phos* phyt ↓ plut-n ↓ puls ↓ **Sang** sep sil spira ↓ spong fd4.de stict sulph tep ↓ thuj ↓ tritic-vg fd5.de vanil fd5.de zing ↓
  - **midnight**: ammc ↓ castm ↓
    - **after**:
      - **2-8** h: *Ph-ac*
      - **4** h: fago ↓ rhus-t hr1
        - **aching**: fago
      - **5-6** h: fago
      - **2-5** h: kali-n ↓
        - **tearing** pain: kali-n
    - **tearing** pain: ammc castm
  - **aching**: sil
  - **bed** | **going** to bed:
    - **before**: am-m ↓
      - **tearing** pain: am-m
    - **in** bed:
      - **agg.**: bar-c ↓ coloc ↓ naja *Phos* ↓ *Sang* k*
        - **drawing** pain: coloc
        - **tearing** pain: bar-c coloc *Phos*
  - **before** falling asleep: sulph ↓
    - **shooting** pain: sulph
  - **burning**: puls
  - **drawing** pain: acon coloc thuj tritic-vg fd5.de zing

Extremities

- **night**: ...
  - **gnawing** pain: sulph k*
  - **lying** on it, while: sulph
  - **lying** on side agg.: acon ↓ merc-i-f ↓
    - **sore**: acon merc-i-f
  - **pressing** pain: cop k* sep k* spira a1 spong fd4.de tritic-vg fd5.de vanil fd5.de
  - **sore**: *Sulph*
  - **sprained**; as if: sep
  - **stitching** pain: alum graph phyt plut-n srj7• *Sulph*
  - **tearing** pain: bell coloc *Crot-t* graph kali-bi kali-n h2 lyc h2 *Merc Sulph* tep
  - **turning** in bed agg.: **Sang**
  - **warm** bed agg.: caust ↓ *Merc* ↓ thuj ↓
    - **tearing** pain: caust *Merc* thuj
  - **warm** wrapping amel.: sil
- **abducting** arm agg.: *Chel* plut-n srj7•
- **aching**: abrot acon acon-ac rly4• aesc agar ail arg-met arge-pl rwt5• asaf borx *Brucel* sa3• *Calc* calc-p calc-sil k2 cann-i carb-ac c1 carb-an carc tpw2* *Caust* chel coca coloc crot-t cur cystein-l rly4• dios ferr-i ger-i rly4• granit-m es1• hura hydr jatr-c jug-c kali-bi kali-p ketogl-ac rly4• lac-c lach lat-m bnm6• laur led lil-t lob-s lyss merc-i-f mez mosch musca-d szs1 myos-a rly4• myric naja *Nat-m Nit-ac* pip-m plan prun sal-fr sle1• sep sil sin-n *Staph* staphycoc rly4• suis-pan rly4• sumb teucr trom ust verat verat-v zinc [bell-p-sp dcm1]
- **air**; in open:
  - **agg.**: lact ↓ nat-c ↓
    - **drawing** pain: nat-c
    - **tearing** pain: lact
  - **amel.**: calc-s ↓
    - **sore**: calc-s
- **alternating** with:
  - **itching**: arge-pl rwt5•
  - **Elbow**; pain in (See elbows - alternating - shoulder)
  - **Face**; pain in (See FACE - Pain - alternating with - shoulder)
  - **Head**; pain in (See HEAD - Pain - alternating - shoulder)
  - **Hip**; pain in: kalm
- **appearing** suddenly: pert-vc vk9
  - **disappearing** suddenly: pert-vc vk9
- **bed**: musca-d szs1
  - **in** bed:
    - **agg.**: aur-m ↓ coloc ↓ fago ↓ lyc ↓ nat-m ↓ positr ↓ staph ↓ sumb ↓
      - **aching**: fago positr nl2• sumb
      - **drawing** pain: aur-m coloc lyc nat-m staph
- **bending**:
  - **arms**:
    - **agg.**: crot-h ↓ laur ↓
      - **aching**: laur
      - **sore**: crot-h
    - **forward** agg.: ign ↓
      - **cutting** pain: ign
  - **head** | **agg.**: puls
- **blow**; pain as from a: colch b7.de*
- **boring** pain: arg-met k* arg-n aur aur-m-n coloc dulc fd4.de *Ferr* hell *Mez* k* nat-s ph-ac phos k* plb bg2 *Rhod* k* ruta fd4.de
- **breakfast** agg.; after: gels ↓
  - **shooting** pain: gels
- **breathing**:
  - **agg.**: berb ↓ bry crot-c sk4• nit-ac ↓ stann ↓ sulph
    - **stitching** pain: berb nit-ac stann
  - **deep**:
    - **agg.**: *Chel* ↓
      - **aching**: *Chel*
- **broken**; as if: *Chel* k* *Cocc* k* mag-m bg2 nat-m k* symph fd3.de•
- **burning**: adam skp7• alumn am-m k* ant-t *Ars* aur-m-n berb *Carb-v* k* carbn-s k* clem cocc dios graph grat *Iris* kali-bi kali-c kali-s fd4.de mag-m mang meny b7.de merc mur-ac olib-sac wmh1 par k* ph-ac k* *Phos* k* plb b7.de pot-e rly4• puls *Rhus-t* k* sep k* spong k* stront-c k* sulph symph fd3.de• tab tep urt-g a1
- **burrowing**: bar-c bg2 mez bg2 nat-m bg2
- **chill**; during: *Hell* ↓
  - **stitching** pain: *Hell*
- **chilliness**; with: lept sma
- **chilly**, when: nit-ac ↓
  - **stitching** pain: nit-ac
- **cold**:
  - **air**:
    - **agg.**: mim-p skp7•
    - **amel.**: thuj
      - **tearing** pain: thuj
- **cold** agg.; becoming: *Calc Calc-p Chel Dulc* **Hep** *Kali-c Lyc* ↓ *Merc* **Nux-v** *Phos Psor Rhod* **Rhus-t Sil** *Sulph*
  - **aching**: sil
  - **tearing** pain: **Hep** *Lyc* **Nux-v** *Phos* **Rhus-t** *Sil Sulph*
  - **uncovering**; when: sil ↓
    - **pressing** pain: sil h2
- **cough** agg.; during: am-c ars borx ↓ *Bry* carb-an ↓ chin k* dig k* *Ferr* hyper ↓ *Lach* merc ↓ *Phos Puls* k* pyrog pd rhus-t rumx sma sang *Sep* ↓ sulph b4a.de* thuj verat ↓ xan
  - **pressing** pain: dig
  - **stitching** pain: borx carb-an hyper merc puls *Sep* sulph verat
- **cutting** pain: anac *Bell* caust bg2 colch *Coloc* corv-cor bdg• crot-c sk4• *Dig* dios bg1 eup-per eup-pur hir rsj4• kali-bi bg2 manc merc-i-f sil streptoc rly4• sul-ac k* sulph k* thuj verat k*
  - **stabbing** from within out: bell
- **dinner**; after: asc-t calc ↓ mez phos phys sep ↓ zinc ↓
  - **boring** pain: mez phos
  - **drawing** pain: sep h2
  - **sprained**; as if: sep h2
  - **stitching** pain: calc phos zinc
  - **tearing** pain: phos sep h2
- **dislocated**; as if: agar agn b7.de* alum b4a.de* ambr b7.de* anac h2 ant-t k* *Arn* b7.de* ars bg2 asar b7.de* *Bov* b4a.de *Bry* b7.de* caps k* caust k* conch fkr1.de cor-r *Croc* k* dros b7.de* fl-ac hep b4a.de* *Ign* k* kali-s fd4.de lyc bg2 m-ambo b7.de* *Mag-c* k* mag-m merc k* mez mur-ac b4a.de* myrt-c nat-m b4.de* nat-sil fd3.de• nicc nit-ac b4a.de olnd b7a.de* petr b4.de* phos b4.de* psil ft1 puls b7.de* rhod b4.de* **Rhus-t** k* ruta b7.de* sabin b7.de* *Sep* k* spig b7.de* stann b4a.de* *Staph* b7.de* sulph k* ter rb1 thuj b4.de*
- **drawing** pain: *Acon* aeth agar am-c am-m ambr anac anag ang apis k* *Arg-met Arg-n* arn k* ars k* asaf b7.de* aur-m aur-m-n bapt berb k* borx k* brom *Bry* camph canth carb-an bg2 *Carb-v* k* carbn-s caust k* cham k* chel k* cimx clem coc-c colch k* coloc k* crot-h cupr dios dros k* dulc elaps euph k* ferr-m ferr-p gent-c gins glon hell hep k* ign iod *Iris* jatr-c kali-bi k* *Kali-c* k* kali-sil k2 kreos k* lact led lil-t *Lyc* m-ambo b7.de *Mag-m* mang k* mez k* mosch b7a.de* naja nat-c k* *Nat-m* nat-p nat-s nat-sil fd3.de• nux-v k* ol-an pall petr k* ph-ac *Phos* phys *Plat* k* plb bg2 psor jl2 *Puls* k* ran-s k* *Rhod* k* rhus-t ros-d wla1 sabad sang sanic *Sep* k* sil stann staph *Sulph* k* tab teucr k* thuj tritic-vg fd5.de tub jl2 vanil fd5.de verat zinc k*
  - **alternating** with:
    - **Fauces**; scraping in: sulph
    - **Hips**: bry k*
  - **cramping**: *Plat*
  - **paralyzed**; as if: chel k* kali-bi *Phos* staph thuj
  - **paroxysmal**: lyc
  - **thread**; as from a: plat h2
- **dull** pain: urt-g a1
- **eructations**:
  - **amel.**: mag-c ↓ sep bg1
    - **sore**: mag-c h2

- **eructations** – **amel**.: ...
  - **tearing** pain: sep$_{h2}$
- **exertion** agg.: pic-ac ↓
  - **sore**: pic-ac
- **exertion**; as after: mez$_{bg2}$ mur-ac$_{bg2}$ nat-m$_{bg2}$
- **expiration** agg.; during: caust ↓
  - **stitching** pain: caust
- **extending** the arm agg.: anag ↓
  - **drawing** pain: anag
- **gnawing** pain: am-c$_{k*}$ cot$_{a1}$ nicc$_{k*}$ plect$_{a1}$ sulph$_{k*}$ urt-g$_{a1}$
- **griping**: *Ign*$_{bg2}$
- **hang** down; letting arms:
  - **agg**.: mez nux-v ruta thuj
    - **tearing** pain: thuj
  - **amel**.: mag-m ↓ *Phos*
    - **tearing** pain: mag-m$_{h2*}$
- **holding** anything firmly with hand: bry
- **house**, on going into: bry ↓
  - **tearing** pain: bry
- **inspiration** agg.: agn ↓ berb ↓ hyper ↓ kali-c ↓
  - **pressing** pain: kali-c$_{h2}$
  - **stitching** pain: berb hyper
  - **tearing** pain: agn
- **jerking** pain: alum$_{bg2}$ arn ars *Bell*$_{bg2}$ chin$_{bg2}$ colch$_{b7.de*}$ fl-ac mez mosch *Puls*$_{k*}$ sil tarax$_{k*}$
  - **downward**: sulph$_{h2}$
- **knitting**, while: kali-c ↓
  - **tearing** pain: kali-c
- **lain** on: dros ↓ *Ign* ↓ *Lach* ↓
  - **sore**: dros$_{h1}$ *Ign Lach*
- **lifting** agg.: abies-c$_{oss4}$• coloc *Ferr* ind nat-m ↓ *Sang* sep stann staph
  - **pressing** pain: coloc ind sep$_{h2}$ staph
  - **sore**: nat-m$_{h2}$
- **lying**:
  - **agg**.: coc-c ↓ *Lyc* ↓ **Rhus-t** ↓ stann ↓
    - **drawing** pain: stann
    - **sore**: *Lyc*
    - **sprained**; as if: coc-c
    - **stitching** pain: **Rhus-t**
  - **arm** under head agg.; with: staph ↓
    - **drawing** pain: staph$_{h1}$
  - **back**; on | **amel**.: bamb-a$_{stb2.de}$•
  - **bed**; in | **agg**.: musca-d$_{szs1}$
  - **quietly** | **amel**.: sang
  - **side**; on:
    - **agg**.: musca-d$_{szs1}$ rhus-t ↓
      - **shooting** pain: rhus-t
    - **left**:
      - **agg**.: cassia-s ↓
        - **tearing** pain: cassia-s$_{ccrh1}$•
      - **amel**.: nux-v ↓
        - **tearing** pain: nux-v
    - **painful** side:
      - **agg**.: ferr$_{sma}$ kali-s$_{fd4.de}$ *Lach* nat-m nux-v *Ph-ac* positr$_{nl2}$• *Rhod* **Sang**$_{vh*}$ sulph ↓ *Thuj* tritic-vg$_{fd5.de}$ vanil$_{fd5.de}$ zinc ↓
        - **aching**: nat-m
        - **boring** pain: ph-ac
        - **drawing** pain: thuj
        - **stitching** pain: sulph
        - **tearing** pain: thuj zinc
      - **amel**.: coc-c kali-bi *Lyc* nux-v puls
        - **tearing** pain: lyc puls
    - **right**:
      - **amel**.: cassia-s ↓
        - **tearing** pain: cassia-s$_{ccrh1}$•
- **lying** down agg.: cassia-s ↓
  - **pinching** pain: cassia-s$_{ccrh1}$•
- **menses**:
  - **before** | **agg**.: sep$_{b4a.de}$
  - **during**:
    - **agg**.: mag-c
      - **dislocated**; as if: mag-c$_{b4.de*}$
  - **instead** of: ars ↓
    - **stitching** pain: ars
- **motion**:
  - **agg**.: abies-c$_{oss4}$• agn ↓ am-m ↓ asc-t berb ↓ brucel$_{sa3}$• *Bry* calc-sil ↓ *Camph* ↓ carb-v cassia-s ↓ caust chel crot-c$_{sk4}$• echi fago *Ferr Ferr-m* ↓ ferr-p *Graph* ↓ *Guaj* ign ↓ irid-met ↓ iris kali-bi kali-i kali-n kalm kola$_{stb3}$• lac-ac *Led* luf-op ↓ mag-c ↓ *Mag-m*$_{k*}$ mand$_{rsj7}$• med$_{k2}$ *Merc* ↓ mez ↓ mur-ac$_{a1}$ nat-c ↓ nat-m ozone$_{sde2}$• *Phos* propr$_{sa3}$• *Ran-b* sang$_{a1}$ sil ↓ spong$_{fd4.de}$ stann ↓ *Staph* sulph ↓ tell$_{rsj10}$• vanil$_{fd5.de}$ verat ↓
    - **aching**: calc-sil$_{k2}$ mand$_{rsj7}$•
    - **boring** pain: *Ferr* phos
    - **cutting** pain: luf-op$_{rsj5}$•
    - **drawing** pain: caust ferr-p *Iris* mag-m staph
    - **pressing** pain: staph$_{h1}$
    - **sprained**; as if: mag-c$_{h2}$
    - **stitching** pain: carb-v ign irid-met$_{srj5}$• *Iris* kola$_{stb3}$• staph sulph
    - **tearing** pain: agn am-m$_{h2}$ berb *Camph* carb-v cassia-s$_{ccrh1}$• chel *Ferr-m* ferr-p *Graph Led* mag-m *Merc* mez nat-c sil stann sulph verat
  - **amel**.: alumn am-m ↓ arg-met aur-m ↓ bapt calc carb-an ↓ carb-v ↓ carc ↓ cham *Cocc* ↓ colch dios dros euph **Ferr** *Ferr-p* ign ↓ iod ↓ *Kali-c* ↓ kali-p *Lyc* mag-m$_{a1}$ mag-s ↓ med ↓ mez mur-ac nat-c ↓ nicc ↓ *Ph-ac* psor ↓ **Rhus-t** ruta ↓ *Sep* ser-a-c$_{jl2}$ stann sulph ↓ thuj ↓ verb
    - **aching**: calc carc$_{tpw2*}$ kali-p verb
    - **boring** pain: mez
    - **drawing** pain: am-m *Arg-met* aur-m$_{k2}$ carb-v$_{h2}$ cocc ign *Rhus-t* sep thuj
    - **pressing** pain: verb$_{h}$
    - **slow** motion: *Ferr* ↓ *Ferr-m* ↓ *Ferr-p* ↓ *Puls* ↓
      - **tearing** pain: *Ferr Ferr-m Ferr-p Puls*
    - **sore**: kali-c$_{h2}$
    - **sprained**; as if: arg-met mur-ac nicc stann$_{h2}$
    - **stitching** pain: *Cocc* iod *Kali-c* med **Rhus-t** ruta$_{fd4.de}$
    - **tearing** pain: arg-met carb-an cocc *Ferr* ferr-p kali-c$_{h2}$ lyc mag-s nat-c psor **Rhus-t** sulph thuj verb$_{h}$
  - **arm**; of:
    - **agg**.: *Arg-met* ↓ asar bell calc cann-s carc ↓ caust chel croc crot-c$_{sk4}$• cystein-l ↓ dig ↓ dros ↓ fago ↓ *Ferr Ham* ↓ ign ↓ *Iris Kali-bi* kali-c kali-n kreos lac-ac *Lach Led* mag-c med merc mur-ac nat-ar nat-m ↓ olnd petr phyt puls *Rhod* **Rhus-t** ↓ ruta *Sang* sanic ↓ sars ↓ sep spig$_{k2}$ spong$_{fd4.de}$ *Staph* ↓ stram ↓ sulph ↓ vesp ↓
      - **aching**: calc croc cystein-l$_{rly4}$• nat-ar
      - **drawing** pain: carc$_{fd2.de}$• staph$_{h1}$
      - **pressing** pain: chel dig$_{h2}$ kali-bi led
      - **sore**: *Arg-met* cann-s dros fago *Ham* ign kali-c mag-c$_{h2}$ nat-m sanic sars stram sulph$_{h2}$
      - **sprained**; as if: asar mag-c$_{h2}$ petr ruta sep *Staph* vesp
      - **stitching** pain: *Puls* **Rhus-t** staph
    - **amel**.: calc ↓ *Lyc* ↓ sulph ↓
      - **pressing** pain: calc
      - **sore**: *Lyc* sulph$_{h2}$
    - **backward** agg.: berb dros *Ign Kali-bi* laur puls sep zinc
  - **beginning** of:
    - **agg**.: ephe-si$_{hsj1}$• ind ↓
      - **aching**: ind
  - **head**; of:
    - **side** to side; from: cupr ↓
      - **stitching** pain: cupr
  - **shoulders**; of | **amel**.: ph-ac

- **out** than natural; as if the shoulder were standing farther: kali-n↓
  - **dislocated**; as if: kali-n h2*
- **paralyzed**; as if: ambr b7.de* asaf b7.de* asar *Berb* brom carb-v bg2 *Caust* k* *Chel* chin b7.de* euph b4a.de *Ferr* k* ham fd3.de• ind kali-bi k* kali-i kali-n laur k* lyc k* lyss mag-c bg2 mang mez mur-ac k* *Nat-m* k* *Nux-v* k* ph-ac phos podo fd3.de• prun puls b7a.de *Rhod* k* rhus-t b7.de* sep b4a.de stann k* staph k* stront-c valer k* verat b7a.de
- **paroxysmal**: ind lyc *Puls* sarr
- **perspiration**:
  - **amel.**: thuj
  - **during**: nux-v b7.de
- **pinching** pain: cina h1 colch k* kali-c h2 mez h2 ph-ac h2 puls a1 rhod bg2 sep h2 sulph h2*
- **placing** arm behind back impossible: *Ferr*↓
  - **sore**: *Ferr*
- **placing** arm over head: thuj↓
  - **tearing** pain: thuj
- **plug**; as from a: mag-m bg2
- **pressing** arm down: mag-m↓
  - **tearing** pain: mag-m h2
- **pressing** pain: acon k* agath-a nl2• aloe am-c k* am-m k* ammc k* *Anac* k* ang k* *Arg-met* k* arg-n k* arn b7.de* arum-t asar b7.de* astac a1 aur-m-n k* bamb-a stb2.de• *Bell* k* bism h1 borx bov k* brom k* *Bry* k* calc k* camph k* cann-s b7.de* carb-an k* card-m casc a1 **Caust** k* chel k* clem k* colch b7.de* coloc k* cop cor-r crot-t dig k* digin a1 fl-ac k* *Hell* k* hep b4a.de hydr hyper ind k* kali-bi k* kali-c k* kali-m k2 kali-n k* kali-p kalm k* kreos b7a.de* lach k* *Laur* k* **Led** k* *Lyc* k* mag-c k* mag-m k* merc k* mez k* mur-ac k* *Nat-c* k* nat-m nat-p *Nat-s* k* *Nit-ac* k* nit-s-d a1 nux-m olib-sac wmh1 olnd k* petr k* ph-ac k* phos k* plat b4.de* prun k* puls k* *Ran-b* k* *Rhus-t* k* sabad k* sabin bg2 **Sep** k* sil k* spong fd4.de stann k* *Staph* k* stront-c k* sul-ac bg2 **Sulph** k* symph fd3.de• teucr b7.de* thuj k* tritic-vg fd5.de valer b7.de* vanil fd5.de verat k* verb k* zinc k*
  - **downward**: carb-an bg2 nux-v bg2 staph bg2
  - **intermittent**: sul-ac h2
  - **tearing** pain: *Led* zinc k*
  - **tremulous**: sul-ac h2
- **pressure**:
  - **agg.**: cassia-s↓ crot-h↓
    - **drawing** pain: crot-h
    - **tearing** pain: cassia-s ccrh1•
  - **amel.**: cassia-s↓ coc-c nat-c [heroin sdj2]
    - **pinching** pain: cassia-s ccrh1•
    - **pressing** pain: nat-c k*
- **pulsating** pain: *Led* mur-ac ph-ac thuj
- **putting** the arm behind him agg.: **Ferr** k* *Rhus-t* k* **Sanic** k*
- **raising**:
  - **arm**:
    - **agg.**: abies-c oss4• agar↓ *Alum* alumn↓ *Bar-c* k* *Bry* calc carb-ac hr1* card-m chel cic↓ cocc coloc↓ cystein-l↓ dros *Ferr* gran↓ hep *Ign* *Iris* *Kali-bi* kali-n kreos lac-c *Led* lyc mag-c mag-m nat-c nat-m *Nit-ac* ozone sde2• petr *Phos* phyt plut-n srj7• prun puls *Rhus-t* **Sang** k* *Sanic* sars↓ sep sul-ac *Sulph* syph taosc iwa1• thuj tub↓ vanil fd5.de visc c1 zinc [ang stj4]
      - **aching**: coloc cystein-l rly4•
      - **pressing** pain: kali-bi sep h2
      - **sore**: dros h1 gran nat-m
      - **sprained**; as if: **Alum** alumn mag-c h2 petr h2 phos *Sulph*
      - **stitching** pain: agar cic *Iris* *Led* mag-m sars sul-ac tub gk
    - **amel.**: ph-ac ruta↓
      - **sprained**; as if: ruta h1
    - **impossible**: **Ferr**↓ *Ferr-m*↓ mag-m↓
      - **tearing** pain: **Ferr** k* *Ferr-m* mag-m h2
  - **arms**:
    - **agg.**: anag↓ bry↓ calc↓ coc-c↓ cocc↓ *Iris*↓ mag-m↓ sanic↓ zinc↓
- **raising – arms – agg.**: ...
      - **drawing** pain: anag bry calc coc-c cocc *Iris* mag-m sanic zinc h2
    - **eating**; after: cocc↓
      - **drawing** pain: cocc
- **rest** agg.: abrom-a ks5
- **resting** arm on table: sep↓
  - **sprained**; as if: sep h2
- **rheumatic**: abies-c oss4• acon k* agar alumn am-caust bro1 am-m ammc ant-t apis ars aur aur-ar k2 bacls-7 pte1* bapt *Berb* k* brom *Bry* k* *Cact* *Calc* *Calc-p* carb-ac carb-v carbn-s card-m *Caust* cham mtf11 *Chel* *Chim* *Chin* chinin-s *Cimic* **Colch** k* coloc crot-c cupr sst3• dig *Dulc* dys pte1* ery-a fago **Ferr** *Ferr-i* *Ferr-m* k* *Ferr-p* k* *Fl-ac* form gaert pte1* granit-m↓ graph grat *Guaj* k* *Ham* k* ign ind *Iod* *Iris* jatr-c jug-c *Kali-bi* *Kali-c* k* *Kali-i* kali-m k2 *Kali-n* *Kalm* k* *Lac-ac* k* *Lac-c* lach *Led* k* lith-c bro1 *Lith-lac* bro1 *Lyc* lyss mag-c k* *Mag-m* k* mand rsj7• mang **Med** k* *Merc* merc-i-f morg-g mtf11 morg-p pte1* naja *Nat-ar* *Nat-c* *Nat-m* nat-p nat-sil fd3.de• nit-ac nux-m nux-v ol-an k* olib-sac wmh1 olnd pall k* ph-ac *Phos* phys↓ *Phyt* k* plan prim-o bro1 ptel c1 *Puls* rad-br bro1 ran-b k* **Rhod** k* rhodi ptk2 **Rhus-t** k* sabin sacch-a fd2.de• *Sang* k* *Sanic* k* *Staph* stel bro1 stict k* stram stront-c k* stry **Sulph** k* syc pte1* symph fd3.de• syph k2* *Thuj* trom urt-u bro1 ust viol-o bro1 wildb c2 zinc
  - **right**: colum-p sze2• morg-g fmm1• sang tl1
  - **left**: *Aspar* br1 rhodi br1
  - **night**: gaert fmm1•
  - **aching**: *Caust* nat-ar plan
  - **drawing** pain: agar h2 carb-v chel a1 lyc naja phys
  - **rising** agg.: luf-op rsj5•
  - **sore**: granit-m es1•
  - **tearing** pain: *Bry* *Ferr* *Ferr-m* ferr-p grat kali-bi nat-m nux-m puls **Rhus-t**
  - **walking** agg.: mand rsj7•
  - **extending** to:
    - **Back**: luf-op rsj5•
    - **Downward**: rhodi br1
    - **Fingers**: mang hr1
    - **Neck**: lac-ac luf-op rsj5• nat-sil fd3.de•
  - **Muscular** and tendinous tissue: arn br1
- **riding** agg.: cund *Rhus-t*
- **rising** | **after**:
  - **agg.**: cocc↓ coloc↓ thuj↓
    - **drawing** pain: cocc coloc thuj
  - **bed**; from:
    - **amel.**: kali-n↓
      - **tearing** pain: kali-n h2
- **rubbing**:
  - **amel.**: carb-an↓ laur↓
    - **tearing** pain: carb-an h2 laur
- **scratching**: (non:meny h1)
  - **after**: kali-c↓
    - **burning**: kali-c
- **shooting** pain: agath-a nl2• ail alum alumn asc-t bell *Calc* calc-p crot-t hr1 elat *Ferr* form iris lith-c phys ptel *Rhus-t* sulph trom
  - **alternating** with | **Elbow**; shooting in: tep
  - **downward**: *Ferr*
- **sitting**:
  - **agg.**: aur↓ coloc↓ led↓ merc↓ ox-ac↓
    - **boring** pain: aur
    - **burning**: merc
    - **drawing** pain: coloc led
    - **sore**: coloc
    - **stitching** pain: ox-ac
  - **long** time agg.; for a | **after**: all-c aur coloc led propr sa3• rhod
  - **still**:
    - **amel.**: cassia-s↓
      - **tearing** pain: cassia-s ccrh1•
- **sleep**; before: sulph↓

- **sleep**; before: ...
  - **stitching** pain: sulph
- **sleeping** after: acon ↓
  - **sore**: acon
- **sore**: abrot acon k* aesc alum k* am-c k* aml-ns arg-met arn k* atp rly4• aur k* bapt berb brach brom calc-p calc-s camph cann-s k* chel *Chin Cic* cina k2 cocc k* coloc *Con* k* cop crot-c crot-h cupr *Dros* elaps fago *Ferr* k* fl-ac gels *Gran* granit-m es1• ham hep *Ign* k* ind iod *Kali-c* kali-i kali-n laur *Led Lyc* lyss m-ambo b7.de mag-c k* merc-i-f mez mur-ac nat-c nat-m nit-ac **Nux-v** olib-sac wmh1 pert-vc vk9 phos pic-ac plat *Podo* positr nl2• psor ruta sacch-a fd2.de• sanic sarr sep k* spig b7.de* staph stram k* stry sul-i k2 sulph thiam rly4• thuj k* verat k*
  - **paralyzed**; as if: *Led* mag-c
  - **paroxysmal**: crot-h
- **spasmodic**: verat-v bg2
- **sprained**; as if: agar **Alum** k* *Ambr* arg-met arn asar berb bry caust coc-c croc cycl hep *Ign* lyc mag-c mang merc mur-ac *Nat-m* nicc pall petr phos puls rhod **Rhus-t** k* ruta *Sabin* k* sep spig stann h2 *Staph Sulph* ter thiam rly4• thuj
  - **paralyzed**; as if: stann h2
- **squeezed**; as if: acon b7.de* *Cic* b7a.de colch bg2 kali-c bg2 mez bg2 ph-ac bg2 sep bg2
- **standing** erect agg.: arn ↓
  - **drawing** pain: arn
- **stitching** pain: acon k* aesc *Agar* k* agn b7.de* ail **Alum** k* alum-sil k2 alumn am-c am-m bro1 ambr k* ammc anac bg2 ang ars ars-i asaf k* asar k* asc-t aur k* aur-ar k2 aur-i k2 aur-s k2 **Bell** k* berb borx k* brom *Bry* k* **Calc** k* calc-i k2 calc-p calc-s calc-sil k2 camph canth k* carb-an *Carb-v* k* **Carbn-s** caust k* cham *Chel Chin* chinin-ar *Cic* k* cina k* clem *Cocc* colch k* crot-h crot-t cupr k* dig dulc elat euphr **Ferr** ferr-ar *Ferr-i* ferr-p form glon *Graph* k* grat k* *Guaj* k* ham fd3.de• hell hura hydr hyper k* indg inul iod iodof a1 *Iris Kali-c* k* kali-n kali-p kali-s fd4.de kali-sil k2 kola stb3• kreos k* lach k* *Laur* k* *Led* k* lith-c lob *Lyc* k* mag-c k* mag-m k* med *Merc* mez k* mill mosch b7a.de* mur-ac k* nat-c k* nat-m nat-p nat-s nicc nit-ac k* nux-m *Nux-v* ox-ac pall petr *Phos* k* phys phyt plat k* plb k* ptel puls k* **Ran-b** k* ran-s k* raph *Rhus-t* k* ruta sabad sarcol-ac sp1 sars k* senec *Sil* k* squil k* stann k* *Staph* k* stront-c k* stry sul-ac k* sulph k* tab tep *Thuj* k* trom *Valer* k* verat verb viol-t zinc k* zinc-p k2
  - **accompanied** by | **Mammae**; cancer of (See CHEST - Cancer - mammae - accompanied - uterus)
  - **burning**: graph plb stann
  - **downward**: *Aesc* vh1 carbn-s caust *Ferr Kreos Rhus-t* sabad sil squil sulph
  - **tearing** pain: asar caust mosch petr
- **stool** agg.; during: acon ↓
  - **tearing** pain: acon b7a.de
- **stooping** agg.: borx ↓
  - **drawing** pain: borx
  - **tearing** pain: borx
- **sun**; in the: adam ↓
  - **burning**: adam skp7•
- **swallowing** food agg.: *Rhus-t*
- **tearing** pain: acon k* aesc agar agn k* *Alum* k* alum-p k2 alum-sil k2 alumn am-c k* *Am-m* k* *Ambr* k* ant-t bg2 apis b7a.de arg-met k* arge-pl rwt5• *Ars* k* ars-s-f k2 asar b7.de* aur-m bar-c *Bell* k* *Berb* bism borx k* *Bov Bry* cact calc k* calc-p k* calc-sil k2 cann-s k* canth b7.de* carb-an *Carb-v* k* carbn-s caust cham chel *Chin* k* chinin-ar cic cist coc-c cocc colch k* coloc crot-t cupr bg2 dulc k* *Euon* **Ferr** k* ferr-ar *Ferr-m Ferr-p Gamb Graph* k* grat hell hep k* *Hyper* inul iod h* kali-ar kali-bi k* **Kali-c** k* kali-i kali-m k2 *Kali-n* k* kali-p kali-sil k2 kalm kreos bg2 lach k* lachn *Laur* k* *Led* k* **Lyc** k* *Lyss Mag-c* k* *Mag-m* k* mag-s *Mang* k* *Merc* k* merc-c *Mez* mosch k* mur-ac k* nat-c k* *Nat-m* k* nat-p *Nat-s* nicc nux-m nux-v k* par k* ph-ac phel *Phos* k* plb psor *Puls Rat Rhod* k* *Rhus-t* k* sabin b7.de* sang sars k* sec sep k* sil k* spong fd4.de stann k* *Staph* k* *Stront-c* k* sul-ac k* **Sulph** k* tep *Thuj* k* vanil fd5.de verat verb k* **Zinc** k* zinc-p k2
  - **alternating** with:
    - **pulsation**: bar-c
- **tearing** pain – **alternating** with: ...
  - **Elbow**; tearing pain in: tep
  - **drawing** pain: alum borx h2* coc-c dulc
  - **jerking** pain: am-c h2 *Chin* sulph
  - **paralyzed**; as if: agar carb-v chin h1 *Ferr Ferr-m* kali-n rhod stann h2
  - **pulsating** pain: sil
  - **torn** off; as if: mez bg2
- **thinking** of it agg.: bapt
- **thunderstorm**; before: *Rhod*
- **torn** off; as if: *Sep* b4a.de
- **touch** agg.: acon bry *Chin* ↓ ferr-p k2 kali-c ↓ mang mur-ac ↓
  - **sore**: ferr-p k2 kali-c h2
  - **tearing** pain: *Chin* ferr-p k2 mur-ac
- **turning**:
  - **bed**; in:
    - **agg.**: nat-sil fd3.de• *Sang* k*
    - **amel.**: nux-v
- **ulcerative** pain: berb thuj
- **uncovering** the part: nat-m ↓
  - **drawing** pain: nat-m
- **vexation**; after: *Coloc*
- **waiting**: merc-i-f ↓
  - **sore**: merc-i-f
- **waking**; on: abrot acon ↓ brucel sa3• chel ↓ falco-pe nl2• fl-ac ↓ fum rly4• nux-v ↓ ozone sde2• rumx zinc
  - **pressing** pain: zinc k*
  - **sore**: acon chel fl-ac nux-v
- **walking**:
  - **agg.**: arg-met aur-m-n brom carb-ac ↓ dig ↓ hydr kali-n lac-ac ↓ *Led* ↓ mez ↓ nat-s pall phos staph ↓ sulph
    - **aching**: arg-met brom
    - **boring** pain: mez
    - **pressing** pain: aur-m-n k* hydr k* *Led* nat-s k* staph h1 sulph k*
    - **shooting** pain: lac-ac
    - **sitting**; after: ran-b ↓
      - **pressing** pain: ran-b
    - **sore**: arg-met carb-ac
    - **stitching** pain: dig lac-ac
  - **air**; in open:
    - **after**:
      - **agg.**: pall ↓
        - **drawing** pain: pall
    - **agg.**: brom ↓
      - **drawing** pain: brom
    - **amel.**: euph ↓
      - **drawing** pain: euph
  - **amel.**: arg-met ↓ calc-s euph *Rhod* **Rhus-t** thuj ↓
    - **sprained**; as if: arg-met
    - **stitching** pain: **Rhus-t** thuj
  - **slowly**:
    - **amel.**: *Ferr Ferr-m* ↓
      - **tearing** pain: *Ferr Ferr-m*
- **wandering** pain: cact hyper *Kali-s Phyt* senec
- **warm**:
  - **applications**:
    - **agg.**: *Guaj*
    - **amel.**: echi *Ferr* **Hep** lac-h htj1• *Lyc* **Rhus-t** *Sil* spig k2 *Thuj*
  - **bathing** | **amel.**: mim-p skp7•
  - **bed**:
    - **agg.**: aur-m ↓ caust ↓ *Ferr* ↓ *Sulph* ↓ thuj
      - **drawing** pain: aur-m k2
      - **stitching** pain: *Sulph*
      - **tearing** pain: caust *Ferr Thuj*

- **warmth** | **agg.**:
  - **heat** agg.: rhus-t↓
    - **shooting** pain: rhus-t
  - **amel.**: carc↓ graph↓
    - **aching**: carc$_{tpw2*}$
    - **heat** amel.: ferr↓
      - **boring** pain: ferr
    - **tearing** pain: graph$_{h2}$
- **weather**:
  - **change** of weather: chel$_{k2}$
  - **cold**:
    - **wet**:
      - **agg.**: carbn-s↓ **Rhus-t**↓
        - **stitching** pain: carbn-s
        - **tearing** pain: **Rhus-t**
  - **wet** | **agg.**: **Dulc** *Phyt* *Ran-b* **Rhus-t** verat$_{hr1}$
- **wedge**; sensation of a: mag-m$_{b4.de*}$
- **weight** of bed clothes: *Ferr*↓
  - **boring** pain: *Ferr*
- **wind** agg.: carb-v↓
  - **drawing** pain: carb-v$_{h2}$
- **wine** agg.: *Ph-ac*
- **writing** agg.: fl-ac *Merc-i-f* sep↓ *Valer*
  - **sprained**; as if: sep$_{h2}$
- **yawning** agg.: mag-c↓
  - **sore**: mag-c

▽ • **extending** to:
  - **Arm**: ars bapt brom bry calc-p↓ chel↓ cimx coc-c↓ colch$_{rsj2•}$ ferr$_{sma}$ galeoc-c-h↓ glon ind lach↓ *Lyss*↓ mag-m↓ mang↓ nat-c↓ nat-m↓ ol-an↓ puls↓ rat↓ rhodi$_{ptk2}$ stront-c↓ sulph↓
    - **left**: colch$_{rsj2•}$
    - **aching**: brom
    - **burning**: mag-m$_{h2}$ nat-m$_{h1}$ puls sulph
    - **drawing** pain: bry chel cimx mang$_{h2}$
    - **shooting** pain: galeoc-c-h$_{gms1•}$
    - **tearing** pain: ars calc-p coc-c ferr lach *Lyss* mag-m$_{h2}$ mang nat-c ol-an rat stront-c sulph
  - **Back**: ars dios ruta$_{fd4.de}$ vanil$_{fd5.de}$ verat↓
    - **stitching** pain: verat$_{a1}$
  - **Cervical** muscles: cham↓ chel↓
    - **stitching** pain: cham chel
  - **Cervical** region: ozone$_{sde2•}$
  - **Chest**: am-c↓ camph$_{sma}$ kali-bi$_{bg1}$ mag-c↓ pall↓ sars sulph$_{bg1}$ vanil$_{fd5.de}$
    - **stitching** pain: *Camph* pall$_{c1}$ *Sulph*
    - **tearing** pain: am-c mag-c$_{h2}$
  - **Clavicle**: arg-met↓ mag-c↓ par↓ sars↓
    - **tearing** pain: arg-met$_{h1}$ mag-c par sars
  - **Deltoid** muscle: bol-la chel ferr-p$_{k2}$
  - **Deltoid** region: zinc↓
    - **drawing** pain: zinc$_{h2}$
  - **Ear**: kali-i$_{bg1}$
    - **tearing** pain: kali-i$_{bg1}$
  - **Elbow**: abrot ars↓ carb-ac↓ *Crot-c*↓ cupr-ar cupre-au$_{c1}$ dulc$_{fd4.de}$ ferr *Ferr-m*↓ fl-ac ind *Kalm*$_{mrr1}$ kola$_{stb3•}$ mag-c↓ nat-c↓ petr phos plb sars↓ sil↓
    - **aching**: abrot plb
    - **boring** pain: ferr
    - **drawing** pain: carb-ac petr$_{k*}$
    - **pressing** pain: sil$_{h2}$
    - **tearing** pain: ars *Crot-c* *Ferr-m* mag-c$_{h2}$ nat-c sars
  - **Fingers**: adam$_{skp7•}$ apis *Calc-p* chin↓ *Cocc* elat fago$_{ptk1*}$ ferr fl-ac$_{k*}$ hydrog↓ kali-n↓ kalm$_{k2}$ *Kreos*↓ *Lachn*↓ lat-m$_{sma}$ lyss↓ mag-m↓ med$_{a1}$ naja nat-c↓ nux-v par↓ rhus-t thuj zinc↓
    - **aching**: elat hydrog$_{srj2•}$
    - **stitching** pain: *Kreos* *Rhus-t*
  - **extending** to – **Fingers**: ...
    - **tearing** pain: chin$_{h1}$ kali-n$_{c1}$ *Lachn* lyss mag-m nat-c$_{h2}$ par thuj zinc
    - **Fourth**: nat-c↓
      - **tearing** pain: nat-c$_{h2}$
    - **Joints** of: mag-c↓
      - **tearing** pain: mag-c$_{h2}$
    - **Tips**: apis↓ chel↓ elaps↓ ferr↓ *Nux-v*↓ *Rhus-t*↓
      - **boring** pain: ferr
      - **drawing** pain: apis chel elaps *Nux-v* *Rhus-t*
  - **Hand**: *Arn* caust↓ chinin-s colch$_{rsj2•}$ glon jatr-c *Kalm*$_{mrr1}$ lat-m lyc↓ *Mag-m*$_{k*}$ plat↓ sang$_{mrr1}$ sarr↓ sil↓ tril-p$_{c1}$ [arg-met$_{stj1}$]
    - **drawing** pain: lyc plat$_{h2}$
    - **pressing** pain: sil$_{h2}$
    - **sore**: sarr
    - **stitching** pain: caust
    - **Back** of: *Crot-t*↓
      - **tearing** pain: *Crot-t*
    - **Palms**: mag-m↓
      - **tearing** pain: mag-m$_{h2*}$
  - **Head**: ind kali-n↓ nat-m↓ olib-sac$_{wmh1}$ sang$_{mrr1}$ verat$_{a1}$
    - **drawing** pain: nat-m$_{h2}$
    - **tearing** pain: kali-n$_{h2}$
  - **Hip**: mag-m↓
    - **burning**: mag-m
  - **Lung**; back of: dios↓
    - **drawing** pain: dios$_{k*}$
  - **Neck**: agath-a$_{nl2•}$ anag apis arg-met↓ berb↓ lac-ac nat-sil↓ sal-fr$_{sle1•}$ sang$_{k2*}$
    - **drawing** pain: anag nat-sil$_{fd3.de•}$
    - **tearing** pain: arg-met berb
    - **And** occiput: arg-met$_{bg1}$ berb$_{bg1}$ crot-h$_{bg1}$ elaps$_{bg1}$ eup-per$_{bg1}$ mang$_{bg1}$ meny$_{bg1}$ phos$_{bg1}$ thuj$_{bg1}$ verat$_{bg1}$
    - **Nape** of: *Agath-a*↓ anag↓ apis↓ tritic-vg↓
      - **drawing** pain: *Agath-a*$_{nl2•}$ anag apis tritic-vg$_{fd5.de}$
  - **Occiput**: berb↓
    - **tearing** pain: berb
  - **Scapula**: mag-c↓ mag-m↓
    - **tearing** pain: mag-c mag-m
  - **Side**, down: fago$_{k*}$ vanil$_{fd5.de}$
  - **Spine**: gels↓
    - **shooting** pain: gels$_{c1}$
  - **Thighs**: nux-v↓
    - **drawing** pain: nux-v
  - **Upper** arm:
    - **Bone**: sulph↓
      - **tearing** pain: sulph$_{h2}$
    - **Middle** of: mag-c↓
      - **tearing** pain: mag-c$_{h2}$
  - **Upper** limbs: psil$_{ft1}$
  - **Wrist**: *Aesc*↓ brach↓ chel *Cimic* *Guaj* kali-n↓ *Kalm*$_{mrr1}$ lyc mag-c↓ *Puls* rat↓ verat↓
    - **drawing** pain: chel *Puls*
    - **sore**: brach verat
    - **sprained**; as if: puls
    - **stitching** pain: *Aesc*$_{vh1}$
    - **tearing** pain: kali-n$_{h2}$ mag-c rat

○ • **Acromion**: berb↓ cham mez↓
  - **burning**: mez
  - **stitching** pain | **burning**: berb
- **Beneath**: **Ail**↓ lyc↓ sulph↓
  - **burning**: **Ail** lyc sulph
- **Between**: beryl↓
  - **burning**: beryl$_{tpw5}$
  - **warm** applications agg.: beryl↓
    - **burning**: beryl$_{tpw5}$
- **Clavicle** joins shoulder; where: des-ac$_{rbp6}$

- **Deltoid**:
  - **right**: _Ferr_ ↓
    - **pinching** pain: _Ferr_
- **Joints**: acon b7.de* agar ↓ agn ↓ am-c ↓ am-m ↓ _Ambr_ ↓ ant-t ↓ arg-met ↓ arn ↓ asaf ↓ bism ↓ bov ↓ **Bry** ↓ calc b4.de* canth ↓ carb-v ↓ _Caust_ ↓ cham ↓ chel ↓ _Cic_ ↓ cocc ↓ _Coloc_ ↓ croc b7.de* crot-h ↓ cupr ↓ dig b4.de* dros ↓ euph ↓ _Ferr_ ↓ graph ↓ hell ↓ hep ↓ ign b7.de* iod ↓ kali-c ↓ _Kreos_ ↓ lach ↓ laur ↓ led ↓ lyc ↓ m-arct ↓ mag-m b4.de* mang ↓ **Merc** ↓ mez ↓ nat-c b4.de* nat-m b4.de* _Nit-ac_ ↓ nux-m ↓ nux-v b7.de* ox-ac ↓ petr b4.de* ph-ac ↓ phos b4.de* prun ↓ puls ↓ ran-b ↓ rhod b4.de* rhus-t ↓ sabin ↓ _Sars_ ↓ sep ↓ sil ↓ spig ↓ stann ↓ **Staph** ↓ stront-c ↓ sul-ac ↓ sulph b4a.de tep ↓ thuj ↓ valer ↓ _Verat_ ↓ verb ↓ viol-t ↓ _Zinc_ ↓
  - **right**: sep ↓ sil ↓
    - **jerking** pain: sil b4a.de
    - **squeezed**; as if: sep b4a.de
  - **blow**; pain as from a: cic b7.de*
  - **drawing** pain: am-c b4.de* am-m b7.de* ambr b7a.de asaf b7.de* calc bg2 canth b7.de* carb-v b4.de* caust bg2 cham b7.de* cocc b7.de* hep b4a.de ign b7.de* kali-c b4a.de mag-m b4.de* mang b4a.de nat-c b4a.de nat-m b4.de* ph-ac b4.de* rhod b4.de* sabin b7a.de sep b4.de* _Staph_ b7.de* _Sulph_ b4a.de _Zinc_ b4a.de
  - **paralyzed**; as if: ambr b7.de* arn b7a.de euph b4.de* _Ferr_ b7a.de lyc bg2 mez bg2 nat-m bg2 nux-v b7.de* ph-ac b4a.de* prun bg2 puls b7.de* sabin b7a.de* sars bg2 stann bg2 staph b7.de* valer b7.de*
  - **pressing** pain: agn b7.de* arg-met bg2 bism b7.de* bry bg2 calc b4.de* _Caust_ bg2 dros b7.de* kali-c b4.de* laur bg2 led b7.de* mez b4.de* _Nit-ac_ b4a.de sabin b7.de* sep bg2 stann b4a.de **Staph** b7.de* valer bg2
  - **shooting** pain: am-c ferr ox-ac tep
  - **sore**: cic k* _Coloc_ b4a.de* crot-h bg2 cupr dros b7.de* ferr b7.de* ign k* kali-c b4.de* lyc bg2 m-arct b7.de nat-c bg2 nat-m b4.de* _Nux-v_ k* spig b7.de* sulph bg2 _Verat_ b7a.de
  - **squeezed**; as if: acon bg2 _Cic_ b7a.de dros b7.de* kali-c bg2 puls bg2
  - **stitching** pain: asaf b7.de* **Bry** b7.de* calc b4.de* caust b4.de* chel b7.de* cocc b7.de* crot-h bg2 ferr b7.de* graph b4.de* hell b7.de* ign b7.de* iod b4.de* _Kreos_ b7a.de laur b7.de* led b7a.de* lyc b4a.de mag-m b4.de* merc b4.de* nux-m b7.de* phos b4a.de puls b7.de* _Sars_ b4a.de sil bg2 staph b7.de* stront-c b4.de* sul-ac b4.de* sulph b4a.de* thuj b4.de* verat b7.de* verb bg2 viol-t b7.de* zinc b4a.de
  - **tearing** pain: agar bg2 agn b7.de* am-c b4.de* am-m b7a.de* _Ambr_ b7.de* ant-t bg2 arg-met b7.de* asaf bg2 bism b7.de* bov b4.de* _Bry_ b7.de* calc b4.de* canth bg2 carb-v b4.de* caust b4.de* cocc b7.de* ferr b7.de* graph bg2 ign b7.de* kali-c b4.de* lach bg2 led b7.de* lyc bg2 mag-m b4.de* mang bg2 **Merc** b4.de* mez bg2 nat-c bg2 nat-m b4.de* nux-v bg2 ph-ac bg2 phos b4.de* puls b7.de* ran-b b7.de* rhod bg2 rhus-t b7.de* sabin b7.de* sep bg2 stann bg2 staph bg2 stront-c b4.de* **Sulph** b4a.de* thuj bg2 zinc b4.de*
  - **extending** to:
    - **Arm**: calc-p ↓ ferr ↓
      - **shooting** pain: calc-p ferr
- **Ligaments**: nux-v ↓
  - **tearing** pain | **torn** loose; as if: nux-v bg2
- **Posterior** part: nat-m ↓
  - **tearing** pain: nat-m h2
- **Side** lain on: rhod zinc ↓
  - **tearing** pain: zinc
- **Side** not lain on: kali-bi
  - **tearing** pain: kali-bi
- **Spots**; in: agar ↓ kali-bi ↓ mang ↓ _Phos_ ↓ ran-b ↓ _Sulph_ ↓
  - **burning**: agar bro1 kali-bi mang _Phos_ bro1 ran-b bro1 _Sulph_ bro1
- **Top** of shoulders: _Carb-v_ ↓
  - **burning**: _Carb-v_
- **Under**:
  - **right**: kali-c ↓
    - **sore**: kali-c
  - **left**: kali-i ↓
    - **sore**: kali-i

- **Sole** of foot:
  - **stepping** agg.: con ↓
    - **crawling**: con h2
- **Spots**; in: agar ↓ hist ↓ **Kali-bi** ↓ nat-sil ↓ plan ↓ rhus-t ↓ sacch-a ↓ symph ↓
  - **burning**: agar k2 hist vml• nat-sil fd3.de• plan k*
  - **sore**: **Kali-bi**
  - **stitching** pain: rhus-t k* sacch-a fd2.de• symph fd3.de•
- **Spots**; in small | **touch** agg.: ign tl1
- **Tendons**: anac ant-c c1 bry ↓ calc-p cham ↓ **Kali-c** ↓ ketogl-ac rly4• lac-leo hm2• nat-sil fd3.de• pot-e rly4• _Rhod_ k* _Rhus-t_ _Ruta_ ↓
  - **drawing** pain: cham h1
  - **expansion** of: agar k* thuj
  - **sore**: bry _Calc-p_ _Ruta_ mrr1
  - **stitching** pain: **Kali-c**
  - **tearing** pain: cham h1
  - ○ **Attachments** of tendons: _Phyt_ k* _Rhod_ _Rhus-t_
- **Thighs**: abrot **Acon** ↓ act-sp ↓ aesc aeth ↓ _Agar_ k* agn ↓ aids ↓ all-c ↓ aloe _Alum_ k* alum-p k2 alum-sil k2 alumn am-c _Am-m_ ↓ ambr ↓ ammc _Anac_ k* androc ↓ ang ↓ anis c2* ant-c ↓ ant-t apis aran bro1 arg-met _Arg-n_ ↓ arn k* _Ars_ k* ars-h ars-i ars-s-f ↓ arum-d ↓ arum-t arund ↓ asaf ↓ asar b7.de* asc-t aspar ↓ aster aur aur-ar ↓ _Aur-m_ aur-m-n ↓ aur-s ↓ bamb-a stb2.de• _Bapt_ ↓ bar-act ↓ bar-c bar-i k2 bar-m bar-s k2 _Bell_ bell-p ↓ benz-ac _Berb_ beryl tpw5 bism ↓ bol-la ↓ borx ↓ _Bov_ ↓ brach bros-gau mrc1 brucel sa3• _Bry_ k* _Cact_ calc calc-i k2 calc-p calc-s calc-sil k2 calo ↓ camph cann-i k* cann-s ↓ canth ↓ _Caps_ k* carb-ac carb-an bro1 _Carb-v_ _Carbn-s_ k* carc jl2 carl cass a1 cassia-s ↓ _Castm_ k* _Caul_ ↓ **Caust** ↓ cham k* chel k* chim ↓ _Chin_ k* _Chinin-ar_ ↓ _Chinin-s_ cic bro1 _Cimic_ _Cimx_ _Cina_ ↓ cinnb ↓ _Cist_ _Clem_ ↓ cob coc-c ↓ cocc coff colch _Coloc_ com con ↓ cot ↓ croc b7.de* crot-c ↓ crot-h ↓ crot-t ↓ cupr cupr-ar _Cycl_ ↓ daph dendr-pol sk4• dig dios k* dros k* _Dulc_ k* echi _Elat_ ↓ ephe-si ↓ eug euon ↓ _Eup-per_ ↓ euph k* euphr eupi ↓ eys ↓ ferr k* ferr-ar ferr-i ferr-ma ↓ ferr-p fl-ac flor-p ↓ form furf-i ↓ _Gels_ k* _Gnaph_ bro1 granit-m ↓ _Graph_ ↓ grat ↓ _Guaj_ _Ham_ ↓ hell helo bro1 helo-s rwt2• _Hep_ k* heroin ↓ hippoc-k ↓ hura hydr hyos ↓ _Hyper_ _Ign_ ↓ ina-i mlk9.de _Ind_ ↓ _Indg_ k* inul ↓ iod k* _Ip_ ↓ irid-met bro1 iris jal jug-c kali-ar _Kali-bi_ k* _Kali-c_ k* kali-chl ↓ _Kali-i_ kali-m ↓ kali-n kali-p ↓ kali-s fd4.de kali-sil k2 _Kalm_ k* ketogl-ac ↓ kola stb3• kreos b7a.de lac-ac lach k* lachn ↓ lact ↓ lat-m ↓ laur lavand-a ↓ lec ↓ _Led_ lil-t lith-c _Lyc_ lycpr ↓ lyss ↓ m-arct ↓ m-aust b7.de mag-c mag-m k* mag-s _Manc_ ↓ mand ↓ _Mang_ ↓ mang-act bro1 mang-m ↓ mang-o bro1 mang-p ↓ _Med_ k* menis bro1 meny meph ↓ _Merc_ k* merc-c ↓ merc-i-f _Merl_ ↓ _Mez_ k* mosch mur-ac muru a1 _Murx_ k* myric naja _Nat-ar_ _Nat-c_ ↓ _Nat-m_ nat-ox ↓ nat-p ↓ nat-s bro1 nicc ↓ nicc-met ↓ _Nit-ac_ k* nuph ↓ nux-m _Nux-v_ ↓ _Ol-an_ ↓ _Olnd_ ↓ op ox-ac ↓ _Pall_ ↓ par ↓ _Petr_ petr-ra shn4• _Ph-ac_ k* phasco-ci rbp2 phel ↓ phos k* phys _Phyt_ pic-ac k* pieri-b mlk9.de pitu-gl ↓ _Plat_ ↓ **Plb** k* plut-n srj7• podo pot-e ↓ propr ↓ prun ↓ psor ↓ _Ptel_ ↓ puls k* **Pyrog** k* _Ran-b_ ↓ ran-s ↓ _Rat_ ↓ _Rheum_ ↓ _Rhod_ ↓ _Rhus-t_ k* rhus-v ↓ ruta fd4.de sabad b7a.de sabin k* sacch-a ↓ sal-fr ↓ _Samb_ ↓ sang ↓ sanic ↓ sarcol-ac ↓ sarr _Sars_ sec ↓ sel ↓ seneg ↓ _Sep_ sil k* _Spig_ b7a.de spong squil ↓ stann _Staph_ k* stict ↓ still ↓ stram k* stront-c stry suis-pan ↓ sul-ac sul-i k2 sulfonam ↓ _Sulph_ symph fd3.de• syph tab ↓ _Tarax_ ↓ tarent tax ↓ tep ↓ ter ↓ teucr ↓ thal-xyz ↓ _Thuj_ til ↓ tong bro1 trif-p bro1 trios ↓ tritic-vg fd5.de trom _Tub_ ↓ ulm-c ↓ valer k2 vanil fd5.de _Vario_ ↓ verat k* verat-v ↓ _Verb_ vib bro1 viol-t ↓ _Vip_ bro1 visc ↓ x-ray ↓ xan zinc zinc-p k2 zing ↓
  - **right**: abrom-a ks5 agar _Am-m_ ↓ ars-s-f k2 asc-t a1 bros-gau mrc1 calc ↓ _Camph_ ↓ cass a1 _Chel_ ↓ cist clem ↓ _Coloc_ k* dulc fd4.de gard-j vlr2• kali-c kali-s fd4.de kalm lavand-a ↓ lith-c nat-m ↓ nicc-met sk4• petr-ra shn4• _Phyt_ ↓ plut-n srj7• psil ft1 ruta ↓ samb ↓ sang hr1 sep ↓ spong fd4.de stram symph fd3.de• tritic-vg fd5.de vanil fd5.de visc ↓
    - **drawing** pain: _Camph_ _Chel_ k* lavand-a ctl1• nat-m h2 samb xxb1
    - **sitting** agg.: aeth a1
    - **sore**: calc bg1 _Camph_
    - **stitching** pain: visc c1
    - **tearing** pain: _Am-m_ clem kali-s fd4.de _Phyt_ ruta fd4.de sep h2 symph fd3.de•
    - **touch** agg.: sal-al blc1•
    - **extending** to | **Knee**: sal-al blc1•
    - **Spots**; in: sal-al ↓
      - **sore**: sal-al blc1•

- **left**: aids↓ *Am-m*↓ asc-t a1 bamb-a stb2.de• bry↓ colch↓ dulc fd4.de gels psa granit-m↓ ham fd3.de• hura iris kali-i↓ kali-s↓ lac-cp sk4• mag-m↓ nicc-met sk4• olib-sac↓ pitu-gl skp7• *Rhus-t* sep↓ spong fd4.de symph fd3.de• tritic-vg fd5.de vanil fd5.de xan c1
  - **accompanied** by | **Elbow** | **right**: asc-t a1
    - **Shoulder** | **right**: asc-t a1
  - **aching**: colch rsj2•
  - **clawing**: bry a1*
  - **cramping**: aids nl2• granit-m es1•
  - **cutting** pain: gels psa
  - **drawing** pain: olib-sac wmh1
  - **motion** agg.: aids↓
    - **cramping**: aids nl2•
  - **sitting** agg.: ang vh1
  - **tearing** pain: *Am-m* kali-i kali-s fd4.de mag-m h2 sep symph fd3.de•
- **9** h: trom↓
  - **wandering**, shifting pain: trom
- **daytime**: kali-c mag-c
- **morning**: am-c aur caust con↓ dios graph↓ ham fd3.de• kali-n↓ lyc↓ nat-c↓ ran-b↓ rhod↓ spong fd4.de sulph sumb tritic-vg fd5.de vanil↓ viol-t
  - **bed** agg.; in: **Caust**↓ sumb↓
    - **aching**: sumb
    - **sore**: **Caust**
  - **drawing** pain: kali-n *Sulph*
  - **pressing** pain: con h2
  - **rising** | **after**:
    - **agg.**: bar-c↓ valer↓
      - **sore**: valer
      - **tearing** pain: bar-c
    - **agg.**: ars *Lac-d* nat-m↓
      - **stitching** pain: nat-m
  - **sitting** agg.: nat-c↓
    - **stitching** pain: nat-c
  - **sore**: lyc nat-c h2 *Sulph* viol-t
  - **stitching** pain: vanil fd5.de
  - **tearing** pain: graph ran-b rhod sulph
  - **waking**; on: aids↓ kali-n↓ spong fd4.de sulph
    - **cramping**: aids nl2•
    - **sore**: kali-n h2 *Sulph*
- **forenoon**: bry↓ jug-c spong fd4.de
  - **9** h: trom
  - **stitching** pain: bry
- **noon**: dulc↓ form↓ stry
  - **shooting** pain: form
  - **stitching** pain: dulc fd4.de form
  - **walking** agg.; after: phys
- **afternoon**: agar coff graph↓ lyc lycps-v↓ nat-c↓ ozone↓ *Ran-b*↓ sep spong fd4.de sulph tritic-vg fd5.de
  - **aching**: lycps-v
  - **drawing** pain: agar lyc *Ran-b* sep sulph
  - **menses**; during: nux-v↓
    - **tearing** pain: nux-v
  - **sleep** agg.; after: nux-v↓
    - **tearing** pain: nux-v
  - **tearing** pain: *Coff* graph nat-c ozone sde2•
  - **walking** agg.: hyper↓ nat-c↓ nat-s↓ valer↓
    - **sore**: hyper nat-s valer
    - **stitching** pain: nat-c
- **evening**: agar am-c↓ am-m↓ asc-t aur colch dios dulc fd4.de ferr graph↓ hyper kali-c lyc↓ mag-m↓ meny↓ murx nat-c↓ nit-ac pitu-gl skp7• **Puls** ran-b↓ rat↓ ruta↓ spong fd4.de stront-c↓ stry sulph thuj tritic-vg fd5.de zinc zinc-p↓
  - **16**-20.30 h: rhus-t
  - **19** h: gels↓
    - **aching**: gels
  - **bed** agg.; in: carb-v↓ colch↓ kali-c↓ mag-c↓ mag-m↓ *Sulph*↓
- **evening – bed** agg.; in: ...
    - **drawing** pain: carb-v colch kali-c *Sulph*
    - **sore**: mag-c mag-m a1
    - **tearing** pain: mag-m h2
  - **drawing** pain: colch kali-c meny h1 nit-ac **Puls** rat *Sulph* thuj *Zinc* zinc-p k2
  - **lying** down agg.; after: dulc fd4.de sep
  - **neuralgic**: pitu-gl skp7•
  - **scraping** pain: am-c
  - **sitting** agg.: meny↓ stront-c
    - **sore**: meny h1
  - **sleep** agg.; after: cycl↓
    - **aching**: cycl
    - **drawing** pain: cycl
  - **sore**: kali-c h2 mag-m h2
  - **tearing** pain: am-m colch graph kali-c h2 lyc nat-c ran-b ruta fd4.de stront-c
  - **walking** agg.: *Sulph*↓
    - **drawing** pain: *Sulph*
- **night**: ars↓ aur calc↓ cham cinnb coff dros euph ferr kali-bi kali-c↓ kali-p↓ lach mag-s mand↓ *Merc* *Mez* nat-m↓ nit-ac↓ nux-v **Puls**↓ ruta↓ sep stry sulph syph k2 tritic-vg fd5.de
  - **midnight**:
    - **after**: merc↓
      - **drawing** pain: merc
  - **aching**: cinnb *Kali-bi* sulph
  - **bed**:
    - **in** bed:
      - **agg.**: *Alum*↓ carb-an↓ carb-v↓ coff↓ colch↓ *Euph*↓ *Ferr*↓ graph↓ kali-c↓ puls↓ sulph↓ *Syph*↓ zinc↓
        - **burning**: carb-v *Euph* graph h2
        - **stitching** pain: *Ferr* graph zinc
        - **tearing** pain: *Alum* carb-an h2 coff colch kali-c h2 puls sulph *Syph*
      - **amel.**: *Kali-c*↓ *Staph*↓ tax↓
        - **stitching** pain: *Kali-c* *Staph*
        - **tearing** pain: tax
  - **drawing** pain: ars kali-c mand rsj7• nat-m **Puls**
  - **falling** asleep, before: sulph↓
    - **shooting** pain: sulph
  - **pressing** pain: ruta sulph h2
  - **shooting** pain: kali-bi
  - **sleep** agg.; during: sep
  - **sore**: aur h2 kali-p fd1.de• sep h2 sulph h2
  - **stitching** pain: ars calc *Cinnb* coff kali-bi nat-m nit-ac tritic-vg fd5.de
  - **Side** lain on: *Caust*↓
    - **sore**: *Caust*
- **abducting** agg.: caps↓
  - **dislocated**; as if: caps h1
  - **sprained**; as if: caps h1*
- **accompanied** by | **Abdomen**; cramping pain in (See ABDOMEN - Pain - cramping - accompanied - thighs)
- **aching**: agar anac arg-n bro1 *Arn* bro1 *Bapt* bro1 bol-la calc bro1 calc-p carc sp1* caust chim cimic bro1 cinnb cob cocc bro1 *Colch* bro1 cot br1 daph dios bro1 *Eup-per* bro1 furf-i sna1 *Gels* bro1 granit-m es1• guaj bro1 ham hep *Ip* kali-i *Lach* lat-m bnm6• laur bro1 lavand-a ctl1• lil-t bro1 lycpr bro1 mag-c bro1 mand rsj7• med k2* merc-i-f mur-ac nat-ar nat-p *Ph-ac* bro1 phyt plut-n srj7• pot-e rly4• *Pyrog* k* **Rhus-t** sabad sabin bro1 sarcol-ac bro1 sep k* spig staph bro1 still stry suis-pan rly4• sulfonam ks2 *Thuj* *Tub* ulm-c bro1 *Vario* bro1 verat-v x-ray sp1
  - **accompanied** by | **Back**; aching pain in: cot br1
  - **downward**: caps nat-ar phys
  - **paralyzed**, as if: verat
- **air** agg.; in open: ant-t **Caust**
  - **drawing** pain: **Caust**
  - **tearing** pain: *Caust*
- **alternately** right then left: sulph↓

- **alternately** right then left: ...
  - **drawing** pain: sulph
- **alternating** with:
  - **Arms**; convulsive pain in: sil
  - **Chest**, pressure in: sang hr1*
  - **Lumbar** region; pain in (See BACK - Pain - lumbar - alternating - thighs)
- **amputation** of thigh; after: asaf ↓
  - **neuralgic**: asaf hr1
- **arthritic**: asc-t
- **ascending**:
  - **agg.**: *Bar-c* ↓ hyos ↓ kali-bi ↓ kali-c ↓ lyc ↓
    - **drawing** pain: *Bar-c* hyos kali-bi kali-c lyc
  - **stairs**:
    - **agg.**: aspar vh bar-c calc ↓ kali-c kola stb3• *Ph-ac* ↓ podo ↓ sep
      - **aching**: sep
      - **sore**: calc *Ph-ac* podo fd3.de•
- **bed** agg.; in: iodof lach ↓ ruta fd4.de zinc ↓
  - **stitching** pain: lach zinc
- **bending**:
  - **knee**:
    - **agg.**: *Puls* ↓
      - **sore**: *Puls*
    - **amel.**: ars
- **bent**; when knees are: lyc ↓
  - **tearing** pain: lyc
- **blow**; pain as from a: am-c b4.de* *Ars* b4a.de bov b4.de* caust b4.de* cina b7.de* euph b4.de* hep b4.de* kali-c b4.de* nat-m b4.de* phos b4a.de sep b4a.de sulph b4.de*
- **boring** pain: act-sp agar ang k* *Apis* arn b7.de* carb-an hell ign led merc k* merc-i-f mez nat-p ran-b k* rhus-t k* sabad spig k* spong k* staph k* tarax k*
- **break**; as if it would: thuj
- **broken**; as if: am-c bg1 anis borx h2 calc bg2 cocc k* coloc bg2 cupr b7a.de dros k* hyos b7.de* kali-c bg2 nat-c h2 nit-ac nux-v plat k* plb bg2 puls k* pyrog k2 ruta b7.de* *Sulph* k* tep k* *Tub* k* valer verat k*
- **burning**: agar alum am-c androc srj1• *Apis* arg-met *Ars* k* arund k* asaf b7.de aur-m-n bar-c bro1 *Berb* borx k* bov k* carb-an k* carb-v k* carbn-s caust b4a.de *Chin* b7.de* clem cocc b7.de coloc con crot-c crot-t dulc k* eup-per *Euph* k* eys sp1 graph b4.de grat ham fd3.de• kali-c bro1 kali-i lachn laur k* led bro1 *Lyc* k* *Manc* meny b7.de merc k* merc-c b4a.de *Mez* k* mur-ac k* nat-c nat-ox rly4• nux-v b7.de olnd k* ph-ac k* *Phos* k* plb k* psor rhod k* rhus-t k* ruta b7.de sabin b7.de spig b7.de staph b7.de still bro1 sul-ac k* *Sulph* k* tab thuj b4a.de til tritic-vg fd5.de viol-t b7.de *Zinc* zinc-p k2
  - **band** around: borx
  - **cold**, yet they are: ph-ac
  - **needles**; as from | **hot** needles: nicc-met sk4•
- **burrowing**: arn b7.de* asar b7.de* caps b7.de*
- **chill**:
  - **before**: *Nux-v* ↓
    - **drawing** pain: *Nux-v*
  - **during**: ars k* **Borx** k* chin k* *Cimx Dulc* eup-per ↓ euph b4a.de* ferr ↓ guaj bg2 lach bg2 nat-m k* puls **Pyrog** sep ↓
    - **drawing** pain: ferr *Puls* sep h2
    - **sore**: *Ars* eup-per
- **clawing**: bry k*
- **coition**; after: nit-ac
  - **drawing** pain: nit-ac
- **cold** air agg.: cassia-s ↓ *Kalm* ↓ *Rhus-t* ↓
  - **dull** pain: cassia-s ccrh1•
  - **tearing** pain: *Kalm Rhus-t*
- **contracting**: dulc fd4.de spong fd4.de sul-ac h2
- **coryza**; during: sep ↓
  - **drawing** pain: sep k*
- **cough** agg.; during: borx ↓ *Caps* b7a.de
- **cough** agg.; during: ...
  - **burning**: borx b4a.de*
  - **pressing** pain: caps
  - **extending** to | **Knee**: *Caps*
- **cramping**: aids nl2• cycl tl1 hippoc-k szs2 lat-m bnm6• ph-ac h2 propr sa3• sul-ac h2 symph fd3.de• trios rsj11• vanil fd5.de
- **crossing** legs agg.: *Agar* aur beryl tpw5 dig *Rhus-t* ↓ ruta fd4.de
  - **cutting** pain: dig
  - **drawing** pain: agar *Rhus-t*
  - **tearing** pain: agar
- **cutting** pain: ant-t asar bg2 *Aur-m Bell* k* bov bg2 *Bry* b7.de* *Calc* dig k* dros b7.de* gels graph bg1 *Ign* b7a.de plb bg2 ruta fd4.de sal-fr sle1• stann k* *Stry Sul-ac* k* sulph bg2 vanil fd5.de
- **descending**, on: **Sabin**
- **dinner** | **after**:
  - **agg.**: carbn-s sep ↓ sulph
    - **drawing** pain: sulph
    - **tearing** pain: sep sulph
  - **during**:
    - **agg.**: sulph ↓
      - **drawing** pain: sulph
- **dislocated**; as if: ambr b7.de* aspar vh caps b7.de* euph b4.de* led b7.de* mez b4.de* nat-m b4.de* rhus-t b7.de* stann b4.de* staph b7.de*
- **drawing** pain: acon *Agar* k* agn *Alum* k* alum-p k2 alum-sil k2 am-c ambr *Anac* k* ang k* ant-c k* ant-t b7.de* apis arg-met b7.de* *Arg-n Arn* k* ars ars-i asaf k* asar asc-t aster aur k* bar-c k* bar-m bar-s k2 *Bell* k* berb bry k* calc-p *Camph* k* cann-s b7.de* canth k* caps b7.de* carb-ac carb-an k* *Carb-v* k* *Carbn-s Caul Caust* k* cham k* **Chel** k* *Chin* k* *Chinin-ar* cic hr1 cina b7.de* cinnb *Clem* k* coc-c cocc colch k* *Coloc* k* con k* cupr k* *Cycl* k* dig k* *Dulc* k* euon euphr b7.de* eupi *Ferr* ferr-ar ferr-i flor-p rsj3• *Gels* graph h2 grat *Guaj* k* *Hep* k* hyos k* ind iod k* ip b7.de* kali-bi k* **Kali-c** k* kali-chl kali-m k2 kali-n kali-p kali-sil k2 kreos k* lach led k* *Lyc* m-arct b7.de m-aust b7.de mag-c k* mang b4a.de mang-m meny k* *Merc* k* merc-c *Mez* k* mosch b7a.de mur-ac k* nat-ar nat-c *Nat-m* k* nat-s *Nit-ac* k* *Nux-m* k* *Nux-v* k* *Ol-an* olnd b7.de* par b7.de* phos k* *Plat* k* plb **Puls** k* *Ran-b* k* rat *Rhod* k* **Rhus-t** k* rhus-v ruta k* sabad k* sabin k* samb k* sars k* *Sep* k* *Sil* spig k* spong k* squil k* *Stann* k* staph k* *Stram* k* sul-i k2 **Sulph** k* symph fd3.de• tab ter *Thuj* k* tub k2 valer k* verat b7.de* verb k* viol-t k* *Zinc* k* zinc-p k2 zing
  - **backward**: sulph
    - **and** forth: phos
  - **burning**: rat
  - **cramping**: anac arg-n ars aur h2 carb-v chin *Cycl* dig h2 *Gels* iod kali-n h2 lyc *Meny* mur-ac h2 plat rhus-v ruta h1 samb h1 *Sep Sulph* thuj valer verat *Verb*
  - **downward**: *Agar* anac apis asaf bar-c bell bry *Calc-p* carb-v h2 coc-c coloc kreos merc mez h2 mur-ac nux-v *Ran-b* sil
  - **menses** would come on; as if: bry
  - **outward**: bell
  - **paralyzed**; as if: agar bell chel a1 cocc colch dulc h1 *Hep* hyos h1 **Kali-c** *Nux-v* staph ter
  - **paroxysmal**: arg-n ars grat nat-m *Rhod* sep squil
  - **sprained**: carb-v
  - **sticking** pain: am-c h2 hyos
  - **tearing** pain: *Acon Anac Chin* clem *Coloc Dulc Guaj* merc nux-v **Rhus-t** spig stann tep thuj
  - **upward**: graph h2
  - **wandering** pain: dulc mez nux-m rhus-v
  - **wavelike**: mez
- **drawing** up leg:
  - **amel.**: mag-m ↓
    - **stitching** pain: mag-m
- **drawing** up legs:
  - **amel.**: *Caust* ↓ cinnb guaj ↓ rhus-t
    - **drawing** pain: *Caust* cinnb guaj *Rhus-t*
    - **pressing** pain: guaj h2
- **drawn** up, when: sabin ↓
  - **sore**: sabin

Extremities

- **driving**: asc-t
- **dull** pain: bamb-a stb2.de• cassia-s ccrh1•
- **eating**; after: dros↓
  - **tearing** pain: dros
- **emissions** agg.; after: *Agar*
- **exertion**:
  - **agg.**: am-c anac *Caust* kali-c *Nat-c* ol-an↓
    - **sore**: ol-an
    - **violent** exertion: carc↓
      - **aching**: carc sp1
  - **amel.**:
    - **violent** exertion: carc↓
      - **aching**: carc mg1.de*
- **exertion**; as after: am-c b4.de* anac b4.de* camph b7.de* caust b4.de* kali-c b4.de* nat-c b4.de* *Rheum* b7a.de
- **extending** limb amel.: agar↓
  - **drawing** pain: agar
- **fever**; during: arn bg2 **Ars** bg2 carb-v bg2 chin bg2 *Ip*↓ merc bg2 **Nat-m** bg2 nux-v bg2 ozone↓ pyrog↓ sep bg2 staph bg2 *Thuj* bg2 **Tub**↓
  - **aching**: *Ip* pyrog **Tub**
  - **drawing** pain: nat-m b4a.de
  - **sore**: ars b4.de
  - **tearing** pain: ozone sde2•
- **flying**: trom
- **gnawing** pain: ars bg2 benz-ac k* berb k* *Elat* hr1 kali-bi kali-i kreos k* nux-v h1* par k* ran-s b7.de* stront-c stry
- **grasping** it, on: merc↓
  - **sore**: merc
- **jar** agg.: valer↓
  - **sore**: valer
- **jar**; as if from a: am-c b4.de*
- **jerking** pain: ang caps b7.de chin b7.de cinnb *Gels* led mag-m h2 mang mez nat-c nux-v b7.de petr a1 phos b4.de plat b4.de puls rat *Rhus-t* k* sabad b7.de *Sep* b4a.de sil valer
- **lying**:
  - **agg.**: *Alum*↓ am-c clem↓ puls↓ ruta fd4.de sil↓ spong fd4.de staph↓ tritic-vg fd5.de vanil fd5.de
    - **sore**: sil staph
    - **stitching** pain: puls
    - **tearing** pain: *Alum* clem
  - **amel.**: *Phyt*↓
    - **tearing** pain: *Phyt*
  - **thigh**; on:
    - **agg.**: *Caust*↓ kali-bi↓
      - **sore**: *Caust* kali-bi
    - **amel.**: carb-v↓
      - **drawing** pain: carb-v
- **menses**:
  - **after**:
    - **agg.**: *Con*↓
      - **tearing** pain: *Con* b4a.de
  - **before**:
    - **agg.**: *Bry* b7a.de cham k* crot-h hyos b7.de mag-m spong staph↓ vib
      - **drawing** pain: cham spong *Vib*
      - **stitching** pain: staph
  - **during**:
    - **agg.**: am-c k* *Berb* bov k* *Carb-an* k* carl castm caul↓ *Cham* cimic con k* *Crot-h* kali-c↓ *Kali-i* kali-n *Kalm* lac-c lyc↓ *Mag-m* k* *Nit-ac* nux-v *Petr*↓ petr-ra shn4• *Puls* k* *Sars* k* spong b7.de stram b7.de *Xan*
      - **burning**: sars b4a.de
      - **cutting** pain: stram
      - **drawing** pain: caul mrr1 *Cham* con h2 *Puls* spong *Stram*
      - **pressing** pain: *Carb-an* kali-i lyc nux-v
      - **sore**: *Am-c* bov *Nit-ac*
      - **tearing** pain: carb-an kali-c nux-v *Petr*
- **motion**:
  - **agg.**: abrom-a ks5 aids↓ arg-met↓ aur↓ *Berb* bry↓ calc↓ cocc coff colch *Coloc*↓ dig gels *Guaj* iod iris↓ *Kalm*↓ kola stb3• kreos↓ lyc↓ merc nat-ar↓ nat-m nux-v↓ olib-sac↓ ozone↓ petr k* ph-ac↓ phos↓ plb sanic sec↓ sep sil spig *Staph* staphycoc↓ vanil fd5.de
    - **aching**: dig staphycoc rly4•
    - **cramping**: aids nl2•
    - **cutting** pain: calc
    - **drawing** pain: iod nat-m olib-sac wmh1
    - **sore**: arg-met cocc c1 dig lyc h2 nux-v phos
    - **stitching** pain: coff *Coloc* iris kreos merc nat-ar ph-ac plb staph vanil fd5.de
    - **tearing** pain: aur berb bry calc coff *Coloc* *Kalm* *Merc* ozone sde2• *Plb* sec
  - **amel.**: aeth *Agar* *Alum*↓ arg-met↓ arg-n↓ brucel sa3• caps cham coc-c↓ con *Dulc* *Euph*↓ eupi↓ **Ferr** hyos ind↓ *Indg* iod↓ *Kali-c*↓ *Kali-s*↓ kreos *Lyc* merc-i-f mosch mur-ac↓ **Puls** *Rat*↓ *Rhod* **Rhus-t** sabin sep↓ spig↓ *Sulph*↓ tub↓ valer k2 vanil fd5.de zinc↓ zinc-p↓
    - **aching**: mur-ac **Rhus-t** tub
    - **drawing** pain: arg-n con *Dulc* *Ferr* hyos iod **Puls** **Rhod** **Rhus-t** zinc-p k2
    - **pressing** pain: eupi k* ind spig h1
    - **sore**: caps
    - **stitching** pain: alum arg-met *Kali-c* *Kali-s* *Rhus-t*
    - **tearing** pain: *Alum* coc-c *Dulc* *Euph* merc-i-f mur-ac *Rat* *Rhod* **Rhus-t** sep *Sulph* *Valer* zinc
- **neuralgic**: carbn-s k2 *Phyt* pitu-gl skp7• plb thal-xyz srj8•
- **numbness**; with: agar↓ hep↓ rhod↓
  - **tearing** pain: agar hep h2 rhod
- **paralyzed**; as if: aeth agar k* am-m k* ang b7.de* arg-met b7.de* ars k* asaf b7.de* asar b7.de* bell k* bry *Carb-v* k* cham k* chel chin k* *Cina* k* cocc k* colch k* dios dros b7.de* dulc b4.de* *Ferr* k* ferr-ar *Guaj* k* *Kali-c* k* kali-i laur led b7.de* m-aust b7.de merc b4.de* mez b4.de* mosch b7.de* nit-ac nux-v k* plb b7.de* puls b7.de* rhus-t b7.de* sabin b7.de* sep b4.de* sil stann b4.de* staph k* stront-c k* sul-ac tep verat k* verb b7.de* zinc k*
- **paroxysmal**: *Anac* *Aur-m* bell dulc fd4.de *Kali-i* nit-ac *Plb* *Rhod* sul-ac
- **perspiration**:
  - **amel.**: *Gels*↓
    - **sore**: *Gels*
  - **during**: arn bg2 *Ars* bg2 chin bg2 *Merc* bg2 mez bg2 **Nat-m** bg2 nux-v bg2 rhus-t bg2 *Sep* bg2 staph bg2 thuj bg2
- **pinching** pain: anac h2 arn a1 asaf a1 berb a1 colch k* dros h1 dulc k* *Led* mag-m k* mang h2 meny a1 mosch a1 ol-an a1 ph-ac k* prun k* sul-ac k* zinc h2
- **plug**; as from a: agar b4.de* anac bg2
- **pressing** pain: acon k* *Agar* k* all-c k* *Aloe* k* alum bg2 *Anac* k* ang k* arn k* asar k* bell b4.de* bism b7.de* camph k* cann-s b7.de* caps k* caust h2 chel k* chin b7.de* cocc b7.de* coloc k* con crot-t k* cupr k* cycl b7.de* dig b4.de* dros k* eupi k* *Guaj* k* hell k* ign k* ind kali-c k* *Kali-i* kali-p kali-sil k2 ketogl-ac rly4• *Led* k* m-arct b7.de m-aust b7.de merc k* mez k* mosch b7.de* *Mur-ac* k* nat-s k* nit-ac b4.de* nux-v *Olnd* k* *Ph-ac* k* phyt prun puls b7.de* rhus-t b7.de* *Ruta* k* sabin k* *Sars* k* sil k* spig b7.de* spong b7.de* *Stann* k* sul-ac k* symph fd3.de• tarax b7.de* tarent teucr b7.de* thuj k* valer b7.de* verat k* verb k*
  - **bandaged**; as if: tarent
  - **cramping**: anac h2 rhus-t h1 verat h1
  - **deep**-seated: ign k* merc k*
  - **dragging** down: con merc k*
  - **outward**: aloe
  - **paroxysmal**: **Acon** **Anac**
  - **plug**; as with a: *Agar* **Anac**
  - **pulsating** pain: stann k*
  - **rhythmical**: **Anac** k*
  - **shooting** pain: mur-ac h2 sabin k*
  - **sticking** pain: olnd k* sul-ac h2
- **pressure**:
  - **agg.**: beryl tpw5 spig↓
    - **pressing** pain: spig h1

- **pressure**: ...
  - **amel.**: coff↓ dulc↓ nuph↓ plb↓
    - **stitching** pain: dulc nuph plb
    - **tearing** pain: coff
- **pulsating** pain: bry caust$_{bg2}$ com ol-an$_{k*}$ tarent
- **raising**:
  - **leg**: carb-v cocc tritic-vg$_{fd5.de}$
  - **thigh**:
    - **sitting**; while: cocc↓
      - **sore**: cocc
- **rest**:
  - **amel.**: sulfonam↓
    - **aching**: sulfonam$_{ks2}$
- **rheumatic**: agar ang↓ ant-t *Arg-n* *Ars* asc-t bacls-10$_{pte1•}$ bapt bell berb$_{bro1}$ *Bry*$_{bro1}$ *Carb-v* carbn-s cass$_{a1}$ chel$_{bro1}$ colch$_{bro1}$ daph$_{br1*}$ dulc$_{k*}$ granit-m↓ *Guaj* ham$_{fd3.de•}$ hydr iod kali-bi *Kali-c* lach led$_{bro1}$ lyc mag-s mand$_{rsj7•}$ meph$_{a1}$ merc$_{k*}$ mez naja ph-ac *Phyt*$_{bro1}$ plb **Rhod**↓ *Rhus-t*$_{bro1}$ sabin salol$_{c1}$ sang$_{k*}$ sanic sep *Stann* stel$_{bro1}$ stry valer$_{bro1}$ verat↓ *Zinc*
  - **evening**: mand$_{rsj7•}$
  - **aching**: granit-m$_{es1•}$
  - **drawing** pain: agar$_{h2}$ ang carb-v iod meph **Rhod** **Rhus-t** sep$_{h2}$ verat *Zinc*
  - **stitching** pain: bapt
- **riding**; after: nat-m↓
  - **tearing** pain: nat-m
- **rising**:
  - **agg.**: arn carbn-s cham chin *Ferr* lycps-v *Rhus-t* symph$_{fd3.de•}$
    - **aching**: lycps-v
  - **amel.**: carb-an↓ caust↓ kali-c↓ mag-c↓ sil↓
    - **tearing** pain: carb-an$_{h2}$ caust kali-c mag-c sil$_{h2}$
  - **bed**; from:
    - **agg.**: gins↓ nat-c↓
      - **sore**: gins$_{c1}$
      - **stitching** pain: nat-c
  - **sitting**; from:
    - **agg.**: ang↓ cham chel$_{bg1}$ chin↓ cic↓ *Ferr* graph↓ nit-ac ph-ac rat↓ rhus-t↓ thuj vanil$_{fd5.de}$
      - **burning**: chin$_{h1}$
      - **drawing** pain: ang$_{h1}$ chin graph$_{h2}$ rat rhus-t$_{h1}$ thuj
      - **pressing** pain: ang$_{h1}$
      - **tearing** pain: cic thuj
    - **amel.**: aur↓
      - **drawing** pain: aur$_{h2}$
- **rubbing**:
  - **agg.**: sulph↓
    - **burning**: sulph
  - **amel.**: aeth$_{a1}$ am-c↓ anac↓ mosch↓ phos↓ sul-ac↓ tarent
    - **burning**: phos$_{h2}$
    - **sore**: am-c
    - **stitching** pain: anac mosch
    - **tearing** pain: sul-ac
- **rubbing** of trousers: cot↓
  - **stitching** pain: cot$_{br1}$
- **scar**, in an old: lach
- **scraping** pain: am-c caust$_{bg2}$ *Chin* grat
- **scratched**; as if: staph$_{h1}$
- **scratching**: (non:staph$_{h1}$)
  - **after**: euphr$_{k*}$ grat↓ mag-m↓ mang↓ plan↓ (non:symph$_{fd3.de}$)
    - **burning**: grat mag-m$_{h2}$ plan
    - **sore**: mang$_{h2}$
  - **agg.**: caust↓
    - **tearing** pain: caust$_{h2}$
  - **amel.**: alum↓
    - **burning**: alum
- **shaking** limb: merc-i-f
- **shivering**; during: borx↓
  - **tearing** pain: borx$_{b4a.de}$
- **shooting** pain: acon aesc *Alum* anac *Apis* **Ars** ars-i arum-d aur-m **Bell** *Calc-p* cinnb form iris kali-bi *Kali-c* lec myric naja sal-fr$_{sle1•}$ sep sil spong$_{fd4.de}$ stram sulph tarent trom
  - **downward**: aesc apis aur-m calc-p form kali-bi *Kali-c* lec sep
- **sitting**:
  - **agg.**: *Agar* *Alum*↓ am-c **Am-m**↓ anac anis↓ arg-n↓ arn asaf↓ aur↓ **Bell**↓ calc↓ carb-an↓ chin↓ cist clem↓ coloc *Con*↓ dig↓ dulc$_{a1}$ euph↓ *Ferr* grat↓ *Guaj* ham$_{fd3.de•}$ *Hep* ign↓ ind iod↓ ip↓ kali-bi kali-c↓ kali-i *Kali-s* kreos↓ *Lach* led lil-t **Lyc** mag-c↓ mag-m mang↓ mang-m↓ meny↓ mill mur-ac nat-c↓ ph-ac↓ phos↓ *Phyt*↓ plat↓ **Pyrog** ran-b↓ *Rat*↓ *Rhod* **Rhus-t**↓ ruta sars↓ sep sil↓ *Spig*↓ spong$_{fd4.de}$ squil↓ stann↓ stront-c *Sulph* thuj tritic-vg$_{fd5.de}$ valer$_{k2}$ vanil$_{fd5.de}$ verat↓ verb zinc↓ zinc-p↓
    - **boring** pain: agar
    - **broken**; as if: anis verat$_{a1}$
    - **burning**: asaf grat phos$_{h2}$ tritic-vg$_{fd5.de}$
    - **cutting** pain: bell vanil$_{fd5.de}$
    - **dislocated**; as if: ip$_{ptk1}$
    - **drawing** pain: am-c anac$_{h2}$ arg-n aur$_{h2}$ chin dig dulc$_{h2}$ iod led mang-m meny mur-ac plat ran-b **Rhod** **Rhus-t** spig$_{h1}$ squil *Sulph* *Thuj* valer$_{k2}$ verb$_{h}$ zinc-p$_{k2}$
    - **pressing** pain: coloc$_{k*}$ *Guaj* ind led mang$_{h2}$ mur-ac$_{k*}$ rhus-t$_{h1}$ sars$_{h2}$ spig$_{h1}$ verb$_{h}$
    - **shooting** pain: bell
    - **sore**: chin ign kali-c kreos meny sil sulph
    - **stitching** pain: **Bell** *Con* *Dulc* kali-c *Kali-i* mur-ac nat-c ph-ac *Spig* vanil$_{fd5.de}$
    - **tearing** pain: agar *Alum* **Am-m** asaf bell$_{h1}$ calc$_{h2}$ carb-an$_{h2}$ clem coloc *Dulc* euph hep kali-c **Lyc** mag-c mur-ac ph-ac *Phyt* *Rat* ruta$_{fd4.de}$ *Spig* stann$_{h2}$ zinc$_{h2}$
  - **amel.**: aur kali-bi↓ nit-ac↓ rhus-t↓ sulfonam↓ sulph↓
    - **aching**: sulfonam$_{ks2}$
    - **drawing** pain: aur kali-bi nit-ac$_{h2}$ rhus-t$_{h1}$ sulph
    - **pressing** pain: aur$_{h2}$
    - **tearing** pain: aur nit-ac$_{h2}$
  - **walking**; after: hydr
- **sitting** down agg.: bov↓ nit-ac↓
  - **drawing** pain: nit-ac$_{h2}$
  - **stitching** pain: bov
  - **tearing** pain: nit-ac$_{h2}$
- **sleep**:
  - **after**:
    - **agg.**: acon *Lach* ph-ac↓
      - **sore**: ph-ac$_{h2}$
      - **stitching** pain: **Lach**
    - **amel.**: sep
  - **before**: *Sulph*↓
    - **stitching** pain: *Sulph*
  - **during**:
    - **agg.**: bar-c sep
      - **sore**: sep$_{h2}$
  - **short** sleep:
    - **amel.**: carc$_{jl2}$
      - **aching**: carc$_{sp1*}$
  - **siesta**:
    - **during**: phos↓
      - **drawing** pain: phos$_{h2}$
- **smarting**: lyc$_{h2}$
- **sore**: *Acon*$_{k*}$ all-c *Am-c*$_{k*}$ am-m anac$_{h2}$ androc$_{srj1•}$ ang$_{k*}$ arg-met *Arn* ars asar$_{h1}$ aur$_{k*}$ bapt bar-c$_{k*}$ **Bell** berb bry$_{k*}$ *Calc*$_{k*}$ *Calc-p* calo *Camph*$_{k*}$ caps$_{k*}$ carb-an carbn-s **Caust**$_{k*}$ cham$_{k*}$ *Chel* chin$_{k*}$ clem *Cocc*$_{k*}$ *Coff*$_{k*}$ crot-c$_{sk4•}$ crot-h dig dulc ephe-si$_{hsj1•}$ ferr-i fl-ac gels graph$_{k*}$ grat *Guaj*$_{k*}$ *Ham* *Hep*$_{k*}$ hyper ign$_{b7.de*}$ ina-i$_{mlk9.de}$ iod kali-bi kali-c$_{k*}$ kali-n kali-p$_{fd1.de•}$ kola$_{stb3•}$ lach lact laur *Led*$_{k*}$ *Lyc* lyss m-arct$_{b7.de}$ mag-c$_{k*}$ *Mag-m*$_{k*}$ mand$_{sp1}$ mang$_{k*}$ mang-p$_{rly4•}$ *Meny*$_{k*}$ *Merc*$_{k*}$ merc-i-f mez$_{k*}$ mosch murx nat-ar *Nat-c*$_{k*}$ nat-m$_{bg2}$

Extremities

- **sore**: ...
nat-s nicc *Nit-ac* k* *Nux-v* k* ol-an olnd *Ph-ac* k* phos k* *Plat* k* plb podo fd3.de• *Puls* k* **Rhus-t** k* **Ruta** k* sabad b7.de* sabin k* sacch-a fd2.de• sang sanic seneg k* *Sep* k* *Sil* spig k* squil k* staph k* sul-i k2 *Sulph* k* symph fd3.de• tab tarax b7.de* *Thuj* k* valer k* viol-t k* zinc k*
  - **paroxysmal**: sul-ac
  - **skating** too long; as from: crot-h
- **sprained**; as if: am-c caps k* laur bro1 led h1 stann h2 staph h1
- **squeezed**; as if: cycl b7a.de ran-b b7a.de ruta b7a.de sabad b7a.de valer b7a.de verat b7a.de
- **standing**:
  - **agg.**: aur berb calc carb-an ↓ euph ↓ euphr ↓ grat ↓ kali-c ↓ mag-s mez ↓ nat-c ↓ ph-ac ↓ *Phyt* ↓ ran-b ↓ rhus-t ↓ stann ↓ sulfonam ks2 syph valer vanil fd5.de verat viol-t ↓ *Zinc*
    - **broken**; as if: valer
    - **burning**: ph-ac k*
    - **drawing** pain: kali-c rhus-t h1 verat h1 viol-t
    - **sore**: grat kali-c h2
    - **stitching** pain: calc carb-an euphr rhus-t stann
    - **tearing** pain: carb-an euph h2 kali-c h2 mez nat-c *Phyt* ran-b
  - **amel.**: anis ↓ euph
    - **broken**; as if: anis
- **stepping** agg.: arg-n ↓ asar *Calc* ↓ nuph vml3• petr plat ↓
  - **drawing** pain: plat h2
  - **pressing** pain: arg-n a1
  - **stitching** pain: *Calc*
- **stepping** forward agg.: nit-ac ↓
  - **sore**: nit-ac h2
- **stinging**: calc bg1
- **stitching** pain: acon k* aesc **Agar** k* agn k* *Alum* ammc *Anac* k* ang k* apis *Arg-met* arn b7.de* **Ars** k* ars-i arund asaf k* asar k* aster *Aur-m* bar-c k* **Bell** k* berb *Bov* k* *Bry* k* calc k* *Calc-p* cann-s b7.de* caps b7.de* *Carb-an* k* carb-v carbn-s carc fd2.de• caust cham chel k* chin k* chinin-ar chinin-s cinnb cocc b7.de* coff *Coloc* k* con k* dig k* dros k* dulc k* euphr b7.de* eupi *Ferr* k* ferr-ar ferr-ma form gels graph k* *Guaj* k* hell hyos b7.de* *Ign* b7a.de *Ind* inul ip iris kali-bi bg2 *Kali-c* *Kali-i* *Kali-s* kali-sil k2 *Kalm* kreos lach laur k* led b7.de* lith-c lyc k* m-arct b7.de m-aust b7.de mag-c k* mag-m manc *Mang* k* *Meny* b7.de* meph *Merc* k* merc-c b4a.de merl mez k* *Mur-ac* k* myric naja nat-ar *Nat-c* k* nat-m nat-p nit-ac k* nuph nux-m b7.de* *Nux-v* k* olnd k* ox-ac *Pall* par b7.de* ph-ac k* *Phos* k* phyt plb k* *Ptel* puls b7.de* rat rhod *Rhus-t* k* *Sabad* k* sabin b7.de* *Samb* k* *Sars* k* *Sep* k* *Sil* k* *Spig* k* spong k* squil k* *Stann* k* staph k* stict stram stront-c k* sulph k* tab *Tarax* k* *Tarent* teucr b7.de* *Thuj* k* tritic-vg fd5.de trom vanil fd5.de viol-t b7.de* *Zinc* k* zinc-p k2 [heroin sdj2]
  - **burning**: **Ars** arund berb carb-an graph iris mur-ac olnd sulph
  - **downward**: aesc apis *Ars* *Aur-m* *Bry* calc-p carb-v cinnb coloc *Kali-c* *Kali-i* *Kalm* mur-ac *Nux-v* pall *Sil* staph
  - **drawing** pain: sabad k* thuj
  - **electric**: agar k*
  - **itching**: samb xxb1 *Spig* *Staph*
  - **outward**: berb rhus-t
  - **tearing** pain: hell kali-c kali-i ph-ac sep zinc
  - **transverse**: **Zinc**
  - **twitching**: ang carbn-s mag-m mang h2 sabad stann stram
  - **upward**: *Lach*
  - **wandering** pain: graph
- **stool**:
  - **after**:
    - **agg.**: *Lyc* b4a.de
      - **pressing** pain: *Lyc*
  - **during**:
    - **agg.**: alum b4a.de coloc ↓ *Rhus-t*
      - **drawing** pain | **downward**: coloc bg2
  - **straining** at | **after**: sep
- **stooping** agg.: sulph ↓
  - **drawing** pain: sulph
- **stretching**:
  - **agg.**: caps ↓ **Ruta** ↓
    - **sore**: caps **Ruta**
  - **leg**:
    - **agg.**: ang ↓ *Ars* *Caps* cham cimx ruta
      - **pressing** pain: ang h1
    - **amel.**: agar dros *Ferr*
  - **limb**:
    - **amel.**: agar ↓ ozone ↓
      - **tearing** pain: agar ozone sde2•
  - **limb** and turning from side to side | **amel.**: merc-i-f **Rhod** **Rhus-t**
  - **limbs**:
    - **agg.** | **sprained**; as if: (non:caps h1)
- **sudden**: chinin-s ↓ sep ↓ tritic-vg ↓ vanil ↓
  - **shooting** pain: sep
  - **stitching** pain: chinin-s sep tritic-vg fd5.de vanil fd5.de
- **supper** agg.; after: sep ↓
  - **tearing** pain: sep
- **synchronous** with pulse: *Anac* ↓
  - **stitching** pain: *Anac*
- **tearing** pain: *Agar* k* aloe **Alum** k* alum-p k2 alum-sil k2 *Am-c* *Am-m* k* anac h2 ang b7.de* ant-t b7.de* arn b7.de* **Ars** k* ars-s-f k2 asaf k* asar k* aur k* aur-ar k2 *Aur-m* aur-s k2 bapt bro1 bar-act bro1 *Bar-c* k* *Bell* k* bell-p bro1 benz-ac berb borx k* bry k* *Calc* calc-sil k2 *Camph* k* canth k* caps k* *Carb-an* k* carb-v k* carbn-s *Caust* k* cham k* chel k* *Chin* k* *Chinin-ar* *Cic* k* cina k* cinnb *Clem* k* cob bro1 coc-c cocc bg1 coff *Colch* k* *Coloc* k* con k* cycl *Dios* bro1 dros b7.de* *Dulc* k* elat hr1 *Euph* k* ferr k* *Ferr-ar* *Graph* k* grat *Guaj* k* hep k* hyper k* *Kali-ar* kali-bi k* *Kali-c* k* *Kali-i* kali-m k2 kali-s kali-sil k2 *Kalm* k* lach laur led **Lyc** k* lyss m-arct b7.de mag-c k* mag-m mag-s mang *Merc* k* *Merl* *Mez* k* mur-ac k* nat-ar *Nat-c* k* *Nat-m* k* **Nat-s** nicc nit-ac k* nux-v k* ol-an par k* petr k* *Ph-ac* k* phel phos k* *Phyt* plat b4.de* **Plb** k* prun puls k* ran-b b7.de* *Rat* rhod *Rhus-t* k* ruta fd4.de sabad sabin k* *Sars* k* sec sel b7.de* sep k* *Sil* k* *Spig* k* *Stann* k* *Stront-c* k* sul-ac *Sulph* k* symph fd3.de• *Syph* tax tep ter teucr b7.de* thuj trom *Valer* k* viol-t b7.de* visc bro1 *Zinc* k* zinc-p k2
  - **burning**: merl
  - **cramping**: nat-c h2
  - **downward**: agar am-m ant-t *Aur-m* canth carb-v caust cham *Cic* kali-i *Kalm* lach led lyc h2 mag-c nat-c h2 ph-ac **Plb** *Rhus-t* sec sil symph fd3.de• tep thuj
  - **drawing** pain: *Acon* agar h2 *Anac* *Ars* carb-an *Chin* clem *Coloc* dulc merc nux-v **Rhus-t** spig stann tep thuj
  - **intermittent**: nat-c h2
  - **jerking** pain: chin h1 mag-c h2 *Rhus-t*
  - **paralyzed**; as if: bell h1 caust h2 lyc h2 mez sep h2
  - **paroxysmal**: alum carb-v carbn-s *Chin* coff *Coloc* **Plb**
  - **pulsating** pain: caust lyc h2 phos sec sil
  - **smarting**: graph lyc
  - **sticking** pain: coloc dulc iod lyc mag-c h2 mur-ac sep
  - **twitching**: asaf bell h1 *Chin* guaj h2 mag-c nicc stront-c
  - **up** and down: borx hr1
  - **upward**: colch nux-v *Valer* zinc
- **touch**:
  - **agg.**: abrom-a ks5 androc ↓ aur borx ↓ *Chin* ↓ nicc-met ↓ nux-v phos ↓
    - **burning**: androc srj1• borx h2 nicc-met sk4• phos
    - **tearing** pain: *Chin*
  - **amel.**: am-c ↓ lyc ↓ mang ↓ nat-c ↓ ruta ↓ sep ↓ sulph ↓ tarax ↓
    - **sore**: am-c h2 lyc h2 mang h2 nat-c h2 ruta h1 sep h2 sulph h2 tarax h1
- **turning** in bed agg.: kali-n ↓
  - **sore**: kali-n h2
- **twinging**: mang a1
- **twitching**: *Coloc* phos
- **ulcerative** pain: arg-met kali-c nit-ac b4.de* puls b7.de* sep k* staph zinc bg2
- **urination** | **pressing** to urinate; when: carb-an pareir

- **walking**:
  - **after**:
    - **agg.**: *Arn*↓ calc↓ *Camph*↓ clem↓ crot-h↓ mag-c↓ meny↓ merc↓ ph-ac↓ *Ruta*↓ symph↓
      - **drawing** pain: camph$_{h1}$
      - **sore**: *Arn* calc *Camph* crot-h mag-c meny merc ph-ac *Ruta* symph$_{fd3.de}$•
      - **tearing** pain: clem
  - **agg.**: agar agn↓ am-c↓ *Am-m* ang↓ *Arn Ars* asar aur bar-c↓ *Berb* beryl$_{tpw5}$ brach calc↓ calc-p carb-v↓ *Carbn-s*↓ cham chel↓ chin cic↓ cist clem↓ coc-c↓ cocc↓ *Coff*↓ *Coloc*$_{k^*}$ con↓ crot-c↓ dios *Dros* dulc↓ euph gels↓ *Guaj* hyos↓ ind↓ kali-bi↓ kali-c *Kali-i*↓ kreos↓ led lyc↓ mag-c↓ mag-s *Med* meny mur-ac↓ nat-ar nat-c↓ nat-m nat-s↓ *Nit-ac*↓ nux-m *Nux-v*↓ olnd↓ ph-ac pitu-gl↓ plan↓ plat plb↓ *Pyrog* ran-b↓ sabad↓ sabin samb↓ sep↓ *Sil*↓ *Spig* squil↓ stann *Staph*$_{k^*}$ sulph tarent tritic-vg$_{fd5.de}$ vanil$_{fd5.de}$ *Verb*↓ *Viol-t*↓
    - **aching**: calc-p meny staph
    - **burning**: coloc (non:ph-ac$_{h2}$)
    - **drawing** pain: agn ang asar berb carb-v *Carbn-s* clem **Coloc** con gels hyos$_{h1}$ ind kali-bi kreos nat-m *Nux-v* plan plat samb$_{xxb1}$ squil *Sulph Verb Viol-t*
    - **neuralgic**: pitu-gl$_{skp7}$•
    - **pressing** pain: aur$_{h2}$ cic$_{a1}$ *Led* meny$_{h1}$
    - **sitting**; after: agar↓ cocc↓
      - **drawing** pain: agar$_{h2}$
      - **sore**: cocc
    - **sore**: am-c$_{h2}$ arn calc$_{h2}$ chel crot-c$_{sk4}$• *Guaj* mag-c nat-c nat-s olnd ph-ac *Sil* spig staph$_{a1}$
    - **sprained**; as if: stann$_{h2}$
    - **stitching** pain: berb calc carb-v coc-c cocc$_{k^*}$ con kali-c *Kali-i* lyc mur-ac$_{a1}$ nat-c plb sabad sep sil *Spig* staph
    - **tearing** pain: agar ars aur bar-c$_{h2}$ cic *Coff* con dulc lyc$_{h2}$ mur-ac$_{h2}$ *Nit-ac* ran-b sep
  - **air**; in open | **after**:
    - **agg.**: guaj↓
      - **sore**: guaj
    - **agg.**: verb↓
      - **cramping**: verb$_{h}$
  - **amel.**: *Agar Alum*↓ *Arg-met*↓ bar-c↓ *Bell* caps↓ coc-c↓ *Dulc* euph↓ *Ferr Indg Kali-c*↓ **Kali-s** lach↓ **Lyc** *Merc* mur-ac↓ ph-ac↓ phos↓ *Puls* rat↓ **Rhod Rhus-t** ruta$_{fd4.de}$ *Sulph*↓ syph↓ valer$_{k2}$ vanil$_{fd5.de}$ zinc-p↓
    - **burning**: ph-ac$_{h2^*}$
    - **drawing** pain: bar-c$_{k^*}$ dulc$_{h2}$ *Lyc*$_{k^*}$ phos$_{k^*}$ **Rhus-t**$_{k^*}$ *Sulph*$_{k^*}$ *Valer* zinc-p$_{k2}$
    - **shooting** pain: sulph
    - **sore**: **Bell** caps
    - **stitching** pain: *Agar* alum *Arg-met Dulc Ferr Kali-c Kali-s* lach *Rhus-t* sulph vanil$_{fd5.de}$
    - **tearing** pain: *Alum* coc-c *Dulc* euph **Lyc** mur-ac rat *Rhod* **Rhus-t** sulph syph *Valer*
  - **beginning** to walk: ferr↓ ph-ac↓ **Rhus-t**↓
    - **sore**: ph-ac **Rhus-t**
    - **stitching** pain: ferr ph-ac
  - **bent**:
    - **agg.**: *Bry*↓
      - **stitching** pain: *Bry*
  - **rapidly**:
    - **after**: staph↓
      - **sore**: staph
- **wandering**, shifting pain: fl-ac hydr *Iris Kali-bi* trom
- **warm**:
  - **bed**:
    - **agg.**: kali-c↓ kali-m↓ *Lyc*↓ *Merc*↓ *Nat-m*↓ **Puls**↓
      - **drawing** pain: kali-c *Lyc Merc Nat-m* **Puls**
      - **tearing** pain: kali-c$_{h2}$ kali-m$_{k2}$ merc
    - **amel.**: **Caust**↓ *Lyc*↓
      - **drawing** pain: **Caust** *Lyc*
- **warmth**:
  - **amel.**: bar-c↓ *Caust*↓ **Lyc**↓
    - **tearing** pain: bar-c *Caust* **Lyc**
- **waves**; in: anac$_{b4.de}$ mez$_{b4.de}$ plat$_{b4.de}$ rhod$_{b4.de}$ sep$_{b4.de}$
- **weather**:
  - **change** of weather: berb
  - **cold**:
    - **wet**:
      - **agg.**: **Calc-p**↓
        - **sore**: **Calc-p**
  - **wet** | **agg.**: kali-c
- **wind**; before a heavy: berb

▽ • **extending** to:
  - **Ankles**: apis↓ ars↓ arund↓ nat-ar
    - **burning**: apis arund
    - **tearing** pain: ars$_{h2}$
  - **Calf**: chel↓ flor-p↓ valer↓
    - **drawing** pain: flor-p$_{rsj3}$•
    - **sore**: chel valer
  - **Chest**: caust↓ puls
    - **stitching** pain: caust
  - **Down** thigh:
    - **cough** agg.; during: caps
    - **stool** agg.; during: *Rhus-t*
    - **urinate**; during effort to: pareir
  - **Downward**: *Aur-m* dulc$_{fd4.de}$ *Guaj Kali-c Kalm Murx Nit-ac* ruta$_{fd4.de}$ sars spong$_{fd4.de}$ vanil$_{fd5.de}$
    - **menses**; during: berb kali-i *Nit-ac* xan
    - **Feet** | **Heels**: bros-gau$_{mrc1}$ *Lac-d*
  - **Foot**: anac↓ asaf↓ *Sil*↓
    - **drawing** pain: asaf *Sil*
    - **shooting** pain: anac$_{gsy1}$
  - **Foot**; sole of: kreos↓
    - **stitching** pain: kreos
  - **Heel**: flor-p↓
    - **drawing** pain: flor-p$_{rsj3}$•
  - **Hip**: bry↓ graph↓ ruta↓ valer$_{k2}$
    - **drawing** pain: bry ruta$_{h1}$
    - **tearing** pain: graph$_{h2}$
  - **Knee**: *Agar*↓ ars↓ *Aur-m* coloc↓ dulc$_{fd4.de}$ grat↓ *Guaj* indg$_{c1}$ nat-c↓ nat-m↓ spong$_{fd4.de}$ sulph↓ symph$_{fd3.de}$• tritic-vg$_{fd5.de}$
    - **cough** agg.; during: caps↓
      - **aching**: caps
      - **pressing** pain: caps$_{a1}$
    - **drawing** pain: *Agar* coloc grat guaj$_{h2}$ nat-m$_{h2}$
    - **tearing** pain: ars$_{h2}$ dulc$_{h1}$ guaj$_{h2}$ nat-c$_{h2}$ sulph$_{h2}$
  - **Lumbar** region: kali-n↓
    - **sore**: kali-n$_{h2}$
  - **Penis**: clem↓
    - **drawing** pain: clem
      - **twitching**: clem$_{k^*}$
  - **Sacral** region: olib-sac↓ ruta↓
    - **drawing** pain: olib-sac$_{wmh1}$ ruta$_{h1}$
  - **Sole**: kreos↓
    - **drawing** pain: kreos
  - **Toes**: *Apis*↓ *Gels*↓ sep↓
    - **drawing** pain: apis *Gels*
    - **shooting** pain: *Apis* sep
    - **stitching** pain: *Apis*
  - **Upward**: puls sabin

○ • **Anterior** part: agar↓ all-c am-m↓ ambr↓ ant-c↓ arg-met↓ arg-n↓ ars$_{k^*}$ *Aur-m* bar-c↓ bell↓ berb$_{k^*}$ bry$_{k^*}$ carl$_{k^*}$ cham↓ chel↓ chin↓ clem$_{a1}$ *Coff* con↓ cupr cupr-ar$_{k^*}$ dig$_{k^*}$ dream-p$_{sdj1}$• dulc↓ euph↓ hell *Hep*↓ *Hyper*$_{k^*}$ kali-bi↓ kali-s↓ kalm$_{k^*}$ laur↓ led$_{k^*}$ *Lil-t*$_{k^*}$ lyc↓ lyss mag-c↓ mang↓ med$_{jl2}$ *Meny*↓ mosch↓ mur-ac↓ naja nat-ar↓ nat-c↓ nat-m↓ nat-s nux-v↓ pic-ac$_{k^*}$ *Plb*$_{k^*}$ *Puls*$_{k^*}$ rat↓ *Rhus-t*$_{k^*}$ **Ruta**↓

Extremities

- **Anterior** part: ...
sabad↓ sabin↓ samb↓ sanic spong$_{fd4.de}$ staph stram↓ sulph$_{k}$* syph *Thuj* tritic-vg$_{fd5.de}$ ulm-c↓ vanil$_{fd5.de}$ *Vib*↓ zinc↓
  - **morning**: ars$_{k}$* tritic-vg$_{fd5.de}$
  - **evening**: *Sulph*↓
    - **drawing** pain: sulph
    - **sore**: *Sulph*
  - **aching**: ambr$_{a1}$ cupr dig hell nat-ar nat-s pic-ac
  - **burning**: chin$_{h1}$ tritic-vg$_{fd5.de}$
  - **drawing** pain: agar ant-c arg-met arg-n bar-c bry dig dulc kali-bi lyc *Meny* rat samb$_{h1}$ staph$_{h1}$ stram *Sulph Vib*
    - **cramping**: meny
    - **paralyzed**; as if: dulc
  - **gnawing** pain: berb$_{k}$*
  - **menses**; before: *Vib*↓
    - **drawing** pain: *Vib*
  - **motion**; violent:
    - **amel.**: cina↓
      - **tearing** pain: cina$_{a1}$
  - **pressing** pain: bell$_{h1}$ dig$_{h2}$ lyc$_{h2}$ mang$_{h2}$
  - **pressure** agg.: *Sulph*↓ zinc↓
    - **sore**: *Sulph* zinc$_{h2}$
  - **sitting** agg.: bapt↓
    - **sore**: bapt$_{a1}$
  - **sore**: arg-met cham *Hep* laur *Lyss* nat-c$_{h2}$ nux-v plb **Ruta** sabin$_{k}$* *Sulph* ulm-c$_{jsj8}$• zinc
  - **standing** agg.: cina↓
    - **cramping**: cina$_{a1}$
  - **stitching** pain: agar$_{bg2}$ chel$_{bg2}$ mosch$_{bg2}$ nat-m$_{bg2}$ plb$_{bg2}$ puls$_{bg2}$ sabad$_{bg2}$
  - **tearing** pain: am-m$_{h2}$ ars$_{h2}$ bar-c$_{h2}$ chin$_{h1}$ *Coff* con$_{h2}$ euph$_{h2}$ kali-s$_{fd4.de}$ mag-c$_{h2}$ mur-ac$_{h2}$ **Plb**
  - **walking**:
    - **agg.**: euph nat-c↓ olnd↓ spig↓ staph
      - **sore**: nat-c$_{h2}$ olnd spig$_{h1}$
    - **air** agg.; in open: con↓
      - **cramping**: con$_{h2}$
    - **amel.**: bar-c↓ *Sulph*↓
      - **drawing** pain: bar-c *Sulph*
  - **extending** to:
    - **Ankle**: nat-ar↓
      - **aching**: nat-ar
    - **Knee**: agar↓ bar-c↓
      - **drawing** pain: agar bar-c
  - **Inguinal** region; near: aids$_{nl2}$• dream-p$_{sdj1}$• euph ozone$_{sde2}$• *Rhus-t* spong$_{fd4.de}$ vanil$_{fd5.de}$
    - **pressing** pain: rhus-t$_{k}$*
    - **tearing** pain: ozone$_{sde2}$•
  - **Lower** part: agar anac$_{k}$* *Calc-p Lyc* mag-c$_{k}$* *Thuj*$_{k}$* *Tub*
    - **aching**: lyc *Thuj* tub
  - **Upper** part: tarax↓
    - **sore**: tarax$_{h1}$
- **Back** of thighs: choc↓ ind↓ *Kali-c*↓ visc↓
  - **shooting** pain: choc$_{srj3}$• ind *Kali-c* visc$_{c1}$
- **Bends** of thighs: am-c↓ ang↓ ant-t↓ arg-met↓ bar-c↓ berb↓ bov↓ cann-s↓ caust↓ chin↓ dig↓ euph↓ gamb↓ graph↓ grat↓ laur↓ mag-m↓ mang↓ merl↓ nat-c↓ nat-m↓ nat-s↓ rhus-t↓ ruta↓ sars↓ sil↓ spong↓ thuj↓
  - **evening**: nat-s↓
    - **burning**: nat-s
    - **sore**: nat-s
  - **burning**: bar-c mag-m$_{h2}$ mang$_{h2}$ nat-c$_{h2}$ nat-s
  - **drawing** pain: ang$_{h1}$ arg-met$_{h1}$ chin gamb graph merl nat-m thuj
  - **menses** | **before**:
    - **agg.**: sars↓
      - **sore**: sars

- **Bends** of thighs – **menses**: ...
  - **during**:
    - **agg.**: bov↓
      - **sore**: bov
  - **pressing** pain: am-c$_{k}$* ang$_{h1}$ bar-c dig$_{k}$* rhus-t ruta
  - **sitting** agg.: bar-c↓
    - **burning**: bar-c
  - **sore**: berb bov dig laur mang nat-s sars
  - **sprained**; as if: euph$_{h2}$
  - **stitching** pain: cann-s caust dig gamb grat sil spong
  - **tearing** pain: ant-t gamb
  - **walking** agg.: dig↓ nat-s↓ spong↓
    - **burning**: nat-s
    - **sore**: nat-s

[illegible] graph↓ hep↓ kali-c↓
[illegible] ↓
[illegible] p$_{bg2}$ kali-c lyc *Nat-c*

- **Bo**[illegible] agar am-c *Am-m*↓ ang↓ aur bell↓ borx↓ bry *Calc*↓ cann-i canth↓ carb-an↓ con↓ dros *Euph*$_{k}$* fl-ac graph↓ guaj$_{ptk1}$ *Indg* ip$_{k}$* kali-bi *Led* lyc↓ mag-c↓ mang↓ meny↓ merc↓ *Merc-i-r*↓ *Mez* mur-ac↓ naja nat-m nat-s nit-ac phos plut-n$_{srj7}$• psil↓ puls ruta$_{ptk1}$ sabin↓ sarr$_{c2}$ sep *Sil*↓ stann↓ stront-c↓ sulph↓ symph↓ tep↓ thuj tritic-vg$_{fd5.de}$ vanil$_{fd5.de}$ verat zinc
  - **left**: plut-n$_{srj7}$•
  - **forenoon**: verat
  - **evening** | **lying** down agg.; after: ip verat
  - **night**: aur dros *Mez* symph$_{fd3.de}$• tritic-vg$_{fd5.de}$
    - **sleep** agg.; during: dros
    - **stretching** leg | **amel.**: dros
  - **aching**: bry fl-ac **Ip** *Merc-i-r* phos plut-n$_{srj7}$• tep
  - **boring** pain: carb-an kali-bi led mez phos
  - **crossing** legs agg.: aur
  - **gnawing** pain: am-m$_{b7.de}$* bell$_{k}$* canth$_{a1}$ dros$_{h1}$ led$_{k}$* lyc$_{b4a.de}$ mang$_{b4a.de}$ nit-ac phos$_{b4a.de}$ stront-c$_{k}$*
    - **bone** marrow; as if in: bell$_{mp1}$• stront-c$_{hr1}$*
  - **pressing** pain: con$_{h2}$ guaj$_{k}$* *Led* merc$_{k}$* nat-s
  - **shivering**; during: borx$_{b4a.de}$
  - **sitting** agg.: sep symph$_{fd3.de}$•
  - **sore**: bry *Calc* graph mag-c$_{h2}$ meny *Mez* nit-ac phos **Puls Ruta** sabin *Sil* sulph symph$_{fd3.de}$•
  - **stitching** pain: psil$_{ft1}$ tritic-vg$_{fd5.de}$
  - **tearing** pain: *Am-m* ang$_{h1}$ borx$_{hr1}$ mur-ac *Nit-ac* stann$_{h2}$ sulph$_{h2}$ symph$_{fd3.de}$• thuj *Zinc*
- **Crural** nerves: *Apis* ars coff gels$_{c1}$ **Gnaph** iodof$_{a1}$ podo$_{hr1}$ *Staph*$_{k}$* xan$_{k}$*
  - **boring** pain: *Apis*
  - **shooting** pain: apis podo$_{hr1}$
  - **stitching** pain: *Apis* ars *Coff Staph*$_{k}$*
  - **Anterior**: am-m$_{bro1}$ coff$_{bro1}$ *Coloc*$_{bro1}$ gels$_{c1}$* gnaph$_{c1}$* *Lim*$_{bro1}$ lycpr$_{bro1}$ nat-ar$_{bro1}$ oena$_{bro1}$ sanic$_{c1}$ spig$_{bro1}$ *Staph*$_{bro1}$ sulph$_{bro1}$ *Xan*$_{bro1}$
- **Femur**: alumn↓ asar↓ bar-c↓ berb↓ carb-an↓ *Chin*↓ cob↓ colch↓ coloc↓ graph↓ guaj↓ ip↓ kali-bi↓ meny↓ merc-c↓ mez↓ nat-m↓ sabin↓ sep↓
  - **drawing** pain: alumn asar bar-c berb carb-an$_{h2}$ *Chin* cob colch coloc graph guaj$_{h2}$ ip$_{h1}$ kali-bi meny merc-c mez$_{h2}$ nat-m sabin sep
- **Genitalia**; near: **Graph**↓ *Merc*↓ plut-n↓ rhod↓
  - **sore**: **Graph** *Merc* rhod
  - **stitching** pain: plut-n$_{srj7}$•
  - **Female**: borx↓ kreos↓ laur↓ sulph↓
    - **burning**: borx kreos laur sulph
    - **sore**: kreos
  - **Male**: bar-c↓ caust↓ *Crot-t*↓ ferr-ma↓ nat-m↓ nit-ac↓ rhus-t↓
    - **burning**: bar-c crot-t ferr-ma rhus-t$_{h1}$
    - **sore**: caust *Crot-t* nat-m nit-ac
    - **stitching** pain: nat-m

- **Groin**; near (See inguinal)
- **Hamstrings**: *Am-m* carbn-dox$_{knl3}$•
- **Inguinal** region; near | **stitching** pain (See genitalia - stitching)
- **Inner** side: agar↓ aids$_{nl2}$• aloe am-c *Am-m*↓ anac↓ ant-c↓ arn↓ ars-h asaf↓ bar-c↓ bell↓ berb↓ bry↓ calc↓ calc-p *Camph*↓ caps↓ carbn-s↓ cass$_{a1}$ caul↓ chel↓ chin↓ cic↓ cocc↓ *Coloc*↓ dig↓ ephe-si↓ fl-ac↓ gels↓ kali-bi↓ kali-c↓ lac-ac↓ *Lachn*↓ laur↓ *Lyc*↓ mag-m↓ mang↓ meny↓ merl↓ mez↓ mosch↓ nat-ar nat-m↓ nat-p↓ nat-s nit-ac↓ ol-an$_{k*}$ par↓ phel↓ plb↓ podo$_{hr1}$ ran-b↓ ruta$_{fd4.de}$ sabad↓ sabin$_{k*}$ sang sars$_{k*}$ sil$_{k*}$ spig↓ spong$_{k*}$ stann↓ *Staph*↓ sul-ac↓ sulph$_{k*}$ symph↓ tarax thuj↓ tritic-vg$_{fd5.de}$ vanil$_{fd5.de}$ verb$_{k*}$ zinc↓
  - **left**: caul↓ nicotam↓
    - **cramping**: nicotam$_{rly4}$•
    - **drawing** pain: caul$_{a1}$
  - **forenoon**: sulph↓
    - **drawing** pain: sulph
  - **afternoon**: *Coloc*↓ stry↓ sulph↓
    - **drawing** pain: *Coloc* sulph
    - **stitching** pain: stry
  - **evening**: agar↓ bry↓ kali-bi↓ sulph↓
    - **burning**: agar bry
    - **drawing** pain: kali-bi
    - **sore**: sulph$_{h2}$
  - **alternating** with | **Chest**; heat of (See CHEST - Heat - alternating - pain)
  - **ascending** stairs agg.: nat-p↓
    - **sore**: nat-p
  - **burning**: agar bry cocc *Lachn* *Lyc* mez sars sulph
  - **cramping**: mag-m$_{h2}$
  - **drawing** pain: am-c ant-c asaf berb caul chel chin *Coloc* dig ephe-si$_{hsj1}$• gels kali-bi nat-p nit-ac par ran-b sil stann sulph thuj zinc
    - **pressing** pain: stann$_{h2}$
    - **tearing** pain: berb
  - **leaning** to left:
    - **amel.**: phel↓
      - **sore**: phel
  - **menses**; during: phel↓ sars↓
    - **burning**: sars
    - **sore**: phel
  - **pinching** pain: mag-m$_{k*}$ mang$_{h2}$ meny$_{h1*}$ sul-ac$_{k*}$
  - **pressing** pain: anac$_{k*}$ calc$_{h2}$ mosch$_{k*}$ nit-ac$_{h2}$ sars$_{k*}$ spong$_{k*}$ stann$_{h2}$ sul-ac$_{h2}$ tarax$_{k*}$
    - **backward**: spong$_{k*}$
  - **pressure** agg.: laur↓
    - **stitching** pain: laur
  - **riding** a horse; after: spig↓
    - **sore**: spig$_{h1}$
  - **rubbing**:
    - **after**:
      - **agg.**: samb↓
        - **burning**: samb
      - **amel.**: sulph↓
        - **burning**: sulph$_{h2}$
  - **sitting** agg.: calc↓ dig↓ ran-b↓ tarax↓
    - **drawing** pain: dig ran-b
    - **pressing** pain: calc$_{h2}$
    - **stitching** pain: calc tarax
  - **sore**: bell$_{h1}$ *Camph* cocc fl-ac mez nat-p phel spig staph$_{h1}$ thuj$_{h1}$
  - **stepping** agg.: berb↓
    - **stitching** pain: berb
  - **stitching** pain: arn bar-c calc carbn-s chel cocc lac-ac laur mang$_{a1}$ nat-m sabin spong stann *Staph* sulph verb
    - **twitching**: sabad$_{k*}$
  - **sudden**: mosch↓
- **Inner side – sudden**: ...
    - **pressing** pain: mosch$_{k*}$
  - **tearing** pain: *Am-m* berb$_{k*}$ calc$_{h2}$ caps$_{k*}$ cic$_{a1}$ kali-bi$_{k*}$ kali-c$_{k*}$ merl$_{k*}$ plb$_{k*}$ sulph$_{k*}$ symph$_{fd3.de}$• zinc$_{k*}$
  - **touch** agg.: cocc↓ *Lyc*↓
    - **burning**: *Lyc*
    - **stitching** pain: cocc
  - **turning** in a circle to left; on: cocc↓
    - **sore**: cocc
  - **walking**:
    - **agg.**: agar↓ *Lyc*↓
      - **burning**: agar *Lyc*
    - **rapidly**:
      - **agg.**: mez↓
        - **sore**: mez
  - **extending** to | **Chest**: puls
  - **Knees**; above: alumn ammc calc-p cann-i chel cina dig fl-ac kreos lil-t puls stry sul-ac
  - **Upper** part: rhus-t↓ ruta↓
    - **burning**: ruta$_{h1}$
    - **pressing** pain: rhus-t$_{h1}$
    - **sprained**; as if: rhus-t$_{h1}$
- **Knees**; above: aloe↓ alum↓ am-c↓ arn↓ asaf↓ **Bell**↓ berb↓ carb-an↓ castm↓ caust↓ cham↓ chel↓ colch↓ cupr↓ dulc↓ ferr↓ grat↓ guaj↓ hep↓ indg↓ kali-c↓ kali-i↓ kali-n↓ kreos↓ led↓ lyc↓ mag-c↓ mag-m↓ mand↓ mang↓ meny↓ mez↓ myric↓ nat-m↓ *Nit-ac*↓ nux-v↓ ol-an↓ olnd↓ *Ph-ac* plat↓ puls↓ *Rhus-t*↓ ruta↓ sars↓ sil↓ spong↓ staph↓ sul-ac$_{c1}$ teucr↓ thuj tong↓ tritic-vg$_{fd5.de}$ *Tub* **Zinc**↓
  - **right**: bit-ar↓ psil↓ visc↓
    - **stitching** pain: bit-ar$_{wht1}$• psil$_{ft1}$ visc$_{c1}$
  - **morning**:
    - **bed** agg.; in: aphis↓ hep↓
      - **tearing** pain: aphis$_{c1}$ hep$_{k*}$
  - **evening**: colch↓ *Mang*↓ nux-v↓ sars↓
    - **bed** agg.; in: colch↓ mag-m↓
      - **tearing** pain: colch$_{k*}$ mag-m$_{h2*}$
    - **stitching** pain: *Mang* nux-v
    - **tearing** pain: colch$_{k*}$ (non:mag-m$_{kl}$) sars$_{h2}$
  - **night**: mag-m↓ sars↓ sil↓
    - **tearing** pain: mag-m$_{k*}$ sars$_{h2}$ sil$_{k*}$
  - **back** and forth: sil↓
    - **tearing** pain: sil$_{k*}$
  - **cramping**: mand$_{rsj7}$• thuj$_{h1}$
  - **drawing** pain: am-c caust$_{h2}$ chel$_{a1}$ kali-n$_{h2}$ led mez myric nat-m plat sars$_{h2}$ thuj
    - **jerking** pain: plat$_{h2}$
  - **jerking** pain: mang$_{a1}$
  - **shooting** pain: mang$_{h2}$
  - **sitting** agg.: **Bell**↓ nat-m↓ phos↓ spong↓ thuj↓
    - **drawing** pain: nat-m thuj
    - **stitching** pain: **Bell** phos spong
  - **sore**: cupr$_{h2}$ kali-c$_{h2}$ lyc$_{h2}$ nit-ac$_{h2}$ sul-ac$_{h2}$
  - **standing** agg.: plb↓
    - **tearing** pain: plb$_{k*}$
  - **stitching** pain: arn asaf **Bell** berb cham ferr grat guaj kreos led mang meny nux-v olnd ruta sars spong staph tritic-vg$_{fd5.de}$ *Zinc*
    - **paroxysmal**: alum
    - **pulsating** pain: spong
    - **transverse**: **Zinc**
  - **stretching** limbs agg.: mand↓
    - **cramping**: mand$_{rsj7}$•
  - **tearing** pain: aloe alum$_{k*}$ carb-an$_{k*}$ castm colch$_{k*}$ hep$_{k*}$ indg$_{c1}$ kali-c$_{k*}$ kali-i$_{k*}$ kreos$_{k*}$ led$_{k*}$ mag-c$_{k*}$ mag-m$_{k*}$ mang$_{k*}$ mez$_{k*}$ *Nit-ac* ol-an$_{k*}$ puls$_{k*}$ *Rhus-t*$_{k*}$ sars$_{h2}$ sil$_{k*}$ teucr$_{k*}$ tong$_{a1}$
    - **drawing** pain: dulc$_{h2}$ kreos$_{k*}$
    - **paroxysmal**: alum$_{k*}$
    - **twitching**: *Rhus-t*$_{k*}$

Extremities

- **Knees**; above: ...
  - **walking**:
    - **agg.**: mez ↓
      - **tearing** pain: mez$_{k*}$
    - **air** agg.; in open: sars ↓
      - **stitching** pain: sars
  - **extending** to:
    - **Ankles**: indg ↓
      - **tearing** pain: indg$_{c1}$
- **Lower** part: bism ↓ hell ↓ nit-ac ↓ ph-ac ↓ sars ↓ spig ↓ spong ↓ thuj ↓ *Tub* ↓ verb ↓
  - **pressing** pain: bism$_{k*}$ hell$_{k*}$ nit-ac$_{h2}$ ph-ac$_{k*}$ sars$_{h2}$ spig$_{h1}$ spong$_{h1}$ thuj$_{k*}$ *Tub* verb$_{h}$
  - **Posterior** part: asar ↓ petr ↓ sars ↓
    - **pressing** pain: asar$_{h1}$ petr$_{h2}$ sars$_{h2}$
- **Middle**: aeth ant-c ↓ ars asar bar-c ↓ bry ↓ *Calc* ↓ chel chin cocc graph ↓ guaj ↓ hep ↓ ille ↓ *Indg* kali-bi ↓ kali-i lach laur ↓ mag-m mez ↓ murx nat-c ↓ nat-s ↓ nicc ↓ ph-ac ↓ phos ↓ plat ↓ plb ↓ ruta ↓ sabin ↓ staph sulph thuj ↓ valer ↓ verb ↓
  - **afternoon**:
    - **sitting** agg.: nicc ↓
      - **sore**: nicc
  - **evening**: *Kali-i* murx
    - **bed** agg.; in: mag-m ↓
      - **sore**: mag-m
    - **sitting** agg.: kali-i ↓
      - **gnawing** pain: kali-i$_{k*}$
  - **aching**: asar chin cocc lach
  - **ascending** stairs agg.: *Calc* ↓
    - **sore**: *Calc*
  - **broken**; as if: ille$_{c1}$
  - **drawing** pain: guaj$_{h2}$ kali-bi mez staph$_{h1}$ sulph thuj verb$_{h}$
  - **menses** | **before** | **agg.**: mag-m
    - **during**:
      - **agg.**: am-c ↓ indg ↓
        - **sore**: am-c indg
  - **pulsating** pain: bry
  - **rest** agg.: thuj ↓
    - **drawing** pain: thuj
  - **sitting** agg.: kali-i nicc ↓ plat ↓
    - **sore**: nicc plat
  - **snap** on stepping; as if tendon would: plb
  - **sore**: ant-c bar-c bry *Calc* chel cocc graph hep kali-bi laur mag-m nat-c$_{h2}$ nat-s nicc ph-ac phos plat ruta$_{h1}$ sabin thuj valer
  - **standing** agg.: valer ↓
    - **sore**: valer
  - **touch** agg.: kali-c ↓
    - **sore**: kali-c$_{h2}$
  - **walking**:
    - **agg.**: staph
    - **air** agg.; in open: thuj ↓
      - **sore**: thuj
    - **beginning** to walk: ph-ac ↓
      - **sore**: ph-ac
  - **Anterior** part of: cob **Sabin** sulph
    - **rest** agg.: sulph
    - **walking** agg.: **Sabin**
  - **Internal** part of: lil-t ol-an sulph verat
  - **Posterior** part of: am-br dios laur
- **Muscles**: lat-m$_{bnm6•}$
- **Outer** side: agar am-m anac ↓ anag ang ↓ arg-mur ↓ asaf ↓ aster ↓ aur ↓ bar-c ↓ bell ↓ berb ↓ carb-an ↓ carb-v ↓ caust ↓ cham ↓ chinin-s cic ↓ cocc ↓ coloc ↓ com cycl ↓ euph ↓ fl-ac helo-s$_{rwt2•}$ iris-foe ↓ kali-n ↓ kreos led ↓ lil-t lyc ↓ mang ↓ meny ↓ merc-i-f mez ↓ mur-ac ↓ nat-ar ↓ nat-c ↓ olnd ↓ op ↓ ph-ac ↓ *Phyt* ran-b ↓ rhod ↓ *Rhus-t* ↓ ruta$_{fd4.de}$ sars ↓ spig ↓ spong$_{fd4.de}$ stann ↓ still ↓ sul-ac ↓ sulph ↓ symph ↓ ter ↓ thuj ↓ tritic-vg$_{fd5.de}$ *Valer* ↓ vanil$_{fd5.de}$ zinc ↓

- **Outer** side: ...
  - **evening**: cham ↓
    - **stitching** pain: cham
  - **aching**: nat-ar still
  - **burning**: zinc$_{h2}$
  - **crossing** legs agg.: stann ↓
    - **drawing** pain: stann$_{h2}$
  - **drawing** pain: agar anac ang$_{h1}$ arg-mur aster berb carb-v cic coloc led meny$_{h1}$ op stann$_{h2}$ ter thuj valer zinc
    - **pressing** pain: stann$_{h2}$
  - **gnawing** pain: kreos$_{k*}$
  - **motion**:
    - **amel.**: rhod ↓
      - **stitching** pain: rhod
  - **pressing** pain: anac$_{h2}$ ang$_{h1}$ olnd$_{k*}$ ph-ac$_{h2}$ ruta$_{h1}$ spig$_{h1}$ sul-ac$_{h2}$ symph$_{fd3.de•}$
  - **sitting**:
    - **agg.**: bell ↓ cocc ↓ kreos ↓ mur-ac ↓
      - **gnawing** pain: kreos
      - **stitching** pain: bell cocc mur-ac
    - **amel.**: mang ↓
      - **stitching** pain: mang
  - **sore**: anac$_{h2}$ aur$_{h2}$ meny$_{h1}$ sulph$_{h2}$ zinc$_{h2}$
  - **stitching** pain: asaf bar-c bell cham cocc iris-foe mang mur-ac rhod vanil$_{fd5.de}$
    - **pulsating** pain: cocc
  - **tearing** pain: *Am-m*$_{k*}$ anac$_{h2}$ berb$_{k*}$ carb-an$_{k*}$ caust$_{k*}$ cycl$_{k*}$ euph$_{h2}$ kali-n$_{k*}$ led$_{k*}$ lyc$_{h2}$ mez$_{h2}$ nat-c$_{h2}$ ph-ac$_{h2}$ *Phyt* ran-b$_{k*}$ *Rhus-t*$_{k*}$ sars$_{h2}$ spig$_{h1}$ *Valer*$_{k*}$ zinc$_{k*}$
  - **walking** agg.: mang ↓ mur-ac ↓
    - **stitching** pain: mang mur-ac
  - **extending** to:
    - **Foot**: still ↓
      - **aching**: still
- **Periosteum**: led ↓ spig ↓
  - **pressing** pain: spig$_{h1}$
  - **sore**: led$_{h1}$
  - **tearing** pain: spig$_{h1}$
- **Posterior** part: *Agar Am-m* ang ↓ ant-c ↓ *Ars* asar ↓ bell ↓ berb ↓ bros-gau$_{mrc1}$ bry ↓ calc ↓ camph canth ↓ caps carb-ac cham chin ↓ con ↓ *Cycl* ↓ dig ↓ dios dros dulc ↓ euphr ↓ eupi ↓ fl-ac ↓ graph ↓ ham$_{fd3.de•}$ *Hep* ign ↓ ind *Indg* ↓ iris ↓ *Kali-bi* ↓ *Kali-c* ↓ *Kali-i* ↓ kali-s ↓ ketogl-ac ↓ lach *Lam* ↓ laur ↓ led lyc ↓ mag-m ↓ mang ↓ merc-i-f ↓ mez naja *Nat-m* ↓ nit-ac nuph ↓ nux-m par ↓ petr ↓ ph-ac ↓ phos ↓ ptel ↓ ran-b ↓ rat ↓ ruta$_{fd4.de}$ sacch-a ↓ *Sel* ↓ sep sil ↓ spong$_{fd4.de}$ staph ↓ *Sulph* symph ↓ tritic-vg$_{fd5.de}$ vanil$_{fd5.de}$ visc ↓ zinc ↓
  - **evening**: calc ↓
    - **drawing** pain: calc
    - **lying**:
      - **after**:
        - **agg.**: phos ↓
          - **tearing** pain | **rhythmical**: phos$_{k*}$
    - **yawning** agg.: zinc ↓
      - **stitching** pain: zinc
  - **aching**: carb-ac dros ind led mez naja ptel$_{k*}$
  - **burning**: agar ham$_{fd3.de•}$ mag-m$_{h2}$ mez$_{h2}$ ph-ac staph$_{h1}$ tritic-vg$_{fd5.de}$
  - **clawing**: con$_{h2}$
  - **cramping**: ang$_{h1}$ cycl$_{h1*}$
  - **crossing** limb: rat ↓
    - **tearing** pain: rat$_{k*}$
  - **drawing** pain: *Agar Am-m* ant-c asar bry calc *Cycl* dig$_{h2}$ dulc$_{h2}$ led lyc *Nat-m* ran-b symph$_{fd3.de•}$ zinc
  - **gnawing** pain: berb$_{k*}$ par$_{k*}$
  - **lying** agg.: asar ↓
    - **drawing** pain: asar
  - **motion**:
    - **amel.**: caps ↓

- **Posterior** part – **motion** – **amel.**: ...
  - . **drawing** pain: caps h1
  - . **stitching** pain: caps a1
  - ⁝ **pressing** pain: dros ind ketogl-ac rly4• *Led* k* petr a1 zinc h2
  - ⁝ **relaxing** the muscles amel.: *Ars*
  - ⁝ **sitting** agg.: *Am-m* cina↓ con↓ dig↓ ind↓ led↓ spong fd4.de vanil fd5.de
    - : **boring** pain: cina a1
    - : **drawing** pain: *Am-m* dig h2 led
    - : **pressing** pain: ind
    - : **stitching** pain: con
  - ⁝ **sore**: chin fl-ac ign *Indg* mang mez h2 phos h2 **Ruta** sacch-a fd2.de• symph fd3.de• zinc h2
  - ⁝ **standing** agg.: euphr↓
    - : **stitching** pain: euphr
  - ⁝ **stitching** pain: canth caps a1 con dulc a1 euphr iris *Kali-bi* *Kali-c* *Kali-i* laur merc-i-f nuph sil staph visc c1 zinc
    - : **pulsating** pain: berb
  - ⁝ **stooping** agg.: dros↓
    - : **pressing** pain: dros
  - ⁝ **tearing** pain: agar h2 bell h1 canth k* dulc h2 eupi graph k* hep kali-bi k* kali-c h2 kali-i k* kali-s fd4.de *Lam* mag-m h2 phos k* rat k* *Sel* k* symph fd3.de•
  - ⁝ **walking**:
    - : **agg.**: *Agar*↓ am-m↓ *Ran-b*↓ samb↓
      - . **drawing** pain: *Agar* am-m *Ran-b* samb h1
    - : **air** agg.; in open: con↓
      - . **stitching** pain: con
    - : **amel.**: dig↓ zinc↓
      - . **drawing** pain: dig h2 zinc
      - . **pressing** pain: zinc h2
  - ⁝ **extending** to:
    - : **Leg** | **right**: hip-ac sp1
- **Spot**; in a: nicc-met↓
  - ⁝ **burning**: nicc-met sk4•
- **Spots**; in: mang nicc-met sk4•
  - ⁝ **right**: sal-al blc1•
- **Upper** part: aeth↓ arg-met↓ arn↓ carb-an↓ carb-v↓ cham↓ colch↓ euph↓ euphr↓ kali-c↓ kali-i↓ lyc↓ mez↓ mosch↓ *Plat*↓ plut-n↓ puls↓ samb↓ sil↓ spong↓ thuj↓
  - ⁝ **drawing** pain: arg-met h1 carb-an euph h2 mez h2 mosch *Plat* samb xxb1 thuj
    - : **upward**: euphr h2
  - ⁝ **stitching** pain: aeth carb-v cham kali-i mez plut-n srj7• sil spong thuj
    - : **upward**: cham
  - ⁝ **tearing** pain: arn k* colch k* kali-c k* lyc k* mez k* puls thuj k*

- Thumbs: acon↓ aeth↓ agar k* alum↓ am-c am-m↓ ambr↓ anac br1* anag k* arg-met↓ arg-mur↓ *Arn*↓ ars↓ arum-d↓ arum-t↓ arund↓ asaf↓ asar↓ astac↓ aster k* aur↓ bamb-a↓ bapt↓ bar-c↓ berb↓ bov↓ brach↓ brom↓ bry k* calc↓ calc-p k* calc-s k* camph↓ carb-v↓ *Carbn-s*↓ cassia-s ccrh1• *Caust*↓ cham k* chel k* chin chinin-s cina↓ cinnb k* clem↓ coc-c k* colch↓ *Coloc*↓ con conin a1 corv-cor↓ cupr↓ dios k* dulc k* elat↓ ephe-si↓ ferr k* ferr-ma↓ fl-ac↓ gran↓ graph↓ grat↓ *Guaj*↓ ham fd3.de• hell↓ *Hep*↓ heroin↓ hura↓ hyper↓ ign↓ indg↓ iod↓ jac-c kali-bi k* kali-c↓ kali-i↓ kali-n↓ kali-s↓ kola stb3• **Kreos** k* lach↓ lachn↓ lap-la sde8.de• laur k* led k* lith-c↓ lob-s↓ lyc↓ lycps-v↓ m-arct↓ m-aust↓ mag-c↓ mag-m k* *Manc* br1* mang↓ mang-m k* meny↓ merc k* merc-i-f k* mez↓ morg-g pte1*• mosch↓ mur-ac↓ nat-c k* nat-m↓ nat-s↓ nat-sil fd3.de• nicc↓ nit-ac↓ nit-s-d↓ nux-v↓ ol-an↓ olnd↓ ox-ac k2* pall k* par↓ petr↓ ph-ac↓ phel↓ phos k* pieri-b mlk9.de plat↓ plb↓ positr↓ prun↓ puls↓ ran-b↓ rat↓ rheum↓ rhod↓ rhus-v↓ rumx ruta fd4.de sabad↓ sabin↓ sang k* sars↓ seneg↓ sep↓ sil↓ sinus rly4• spig↓ *Spong* k* stann↓ *Staph*↓ stram↓ stront-c↓ stry k* sul-ac↓ sulph↓ symph↓ tab↓ tarent k* teucr↓ thuj↓ tritic-vg fd5.de valer↓ vanil fd5.de verb↓ vesp↓ vip k* *Zinc*↓

- **alternating** sides: rat↓
  - ⁝ **tearing** pain: rat
- **right**: *Brucel* sa3• coloc↓ dulc fd4.de ephe-si hsj1• fic-m↓ gels↓ guaj k2 lap-la sde8.de• limest-b↓ ol-an k* ox-ac k2 positr↓ psil ft1 *Spong* k* tritic-vg fd5.de vanil fd5.de

- Thumbs – right: ...
  - ⁝ **drawing** pain: coloc tl1
  - ⁝ **pressing** pain:
    - : **followed** by | **left**: bamb-a stb2.de•
  - ⁝ **shooting** pain: gels psa
  - ⁝ **sore**: limest-b es1• positr nl2•
  - ⁝ **stitching** pain: dulc fd4.de fic-m gya1 guaj
- **left**: am-c↓ anag borx↓ bov↓ hydroph rsj6• kali-c↓ **Kreos** k* lith-c↓ luf-op rsj5• lyc↓ merc-i-f k* olib-sac↓ ox-ac↓ ozone sde2• spong fd4.de [spect dfg1]
  - ⁝ **cold** agg.; becoming: am-c↓
    - : **sore**: am-c
  - ⁝ **sore**: am-c kreos
  - ⁝ **sprained**; as if: *Kreos*
  - ⁝ **stitching** pain: lith-c olib-sac wmh1 ox-ac
  - ⁝ **tearing** pain: borx h2 bov kali-c h2 lyc h2
- **21 h**: dios↓
  - ⁝ **aching**: dios
- **morning**: ars↓ ham↓
  - ⁝ **bed** agg.; in: ars↓ stram↓
    - : **stitching** pain: ars stram
  - ⁝ **rising** agg.; after: mag-m
  - ⁝ **stitching** pain: ars ham fd3.de•
- **afternoon**: agar↓ calc-s k* ham fd3.de• lyc↓ sulph k*
  - ⁝ **burning**: agar
  - ⁝ **drawing** pain: sulph k*
  - ⁝ **stitching** pain: lyc
- **evening**: dios k* hyper↓ mag-c↓ stry k* tarent k* thuj k*
  - ⁝ **drawing** pain: thuj k*
  - ⁝ **tearing** pain: hyper mag-c
- **night**: bamb-a↓ kali-n↓ sars↓
  - ⁝ **burning**: sars
  - ⁝ **pressing** pain: bamb-a stb2.de•
  - ⁝ **tearing** pain: kali-n h2
- **aching**: calc-p chel chin laur positr nl2• sang k* [heroin sdj2]
- **adduction**, on: con conin a1 spong fd4.de
- **boring** pain: *Led* mag-c bg2 ol-an k*
- **broken**; as if: cham
- **burning**: agar arum-t arund berb chel dulc fd4.de ephe-si hsj1• gran graph ham fd3.de• *Hep* lach lap-la sde8.de• laur m-arct m-aust merc nux-v ol-an olnd sars staph symph fd3.de• vesp zinc
  - ⁝ **tearing** pain: agar
- **cold** applications agg.: cassia-s ccrh1•
- **cramping**: mang h2
- **crushed**; as if: cina bg2 plat bg2
- **cutting** pain: con h2 corv-cor bdg• merc-i-f stry zinc bg2
- **drawing** pain: acon k* alum k* ambr k* anac *Arn* k* bry k* chin h1 *Coloc* con k* indg k* kali-bi k* kali-s fd4.de nat-c h2 nat-m k* nat-s k* nat-sil fd3.de• ol-an hr1 par k* puls k* rhus-v k* spong stann h2 sulph k* thuj k*
  - ⁝ **cramping**: anac dulc h1 meny h1
  - ⁝ **paralyzed**; as if: mosch k* nit-ac h2 sabad k*
  - ⁝ **paroxysmal**: ferr-ma k* thuj k*
- **exertion** agg.: sulph↓
  - ⁝ **drawing** pain: sulph k*
- **gnawing** pain: kali-bi k* mag-c h2* olnd k*
- **grasping** pain: am-c bg2
- **grasping** something agg.: phos↓
  - ⁝ **sprained**; as if: phos
- **griping**: am-c h2
- **jerking** of arms: cocc↓
  - ⁝ **drawing** pain: cocc
- **jerking** pain: am-c h2 sabad bg2

Extremities

- **lifting** agg.: ruta
- **massage** | **amel.**: cassia-s ccrh1•
- **motion**:
  - **agg.**: *Brucel* sa3• cassia-s ccrh1• cham coc-c k* *Coloc*↓ ferr k* kali-bi k* ozone sde2• phos ruta fd4.de symph fd3.de•
    - **drawing** pain: *Coloc*
    - **sprained**; as if: phos h2
  - **amel.**: jac-c jac-g nat-c↓ thuj↓
    - **drawing** pain: nat-c h2 thuj k*
- **paralyzed**; as if: acon k* *Caust* laur k* prun k* rhod k*
- **paroxysmal**: agar prun k*
- **pinching** pain: bry k* kali-i k* kali-n h2 mang k* meny h1* prun bg2
- **pressing** pain: arg-met h1 bamb-a stb2.de• colch bg2 grat bg2 hell k* laur bg2 nat-s k* nit-s-d a1 phos sars bg2 verb k*
- **pressure**:
  - **amel.**: mag-c↓ tarent k*
    - **stitching** pain: mag-c tarent
- **pulsating** pain: fl-ac k* merc-i-f
- **raw**; as if: mez bg2 spong bg2
- **rest** | **amel.**: cassia-s ccrh1•
- **rheumatic**: bacls-7 pte1*• bapt hr1 corv-cor bdg• jac-c jac-g morg-p pte1*• olib-sac wmh1
- **scratching**, from: olnd↓
  - **gnawing** pain: olnd k*
- **shooting** pain: arum-d dulc sang
- **sore**: am-c k* brach coc-c cupr h2 kreos positr nl2• vip
- **sprained**; as if: calc-p camph h1* cham graph ptk1 kali-n **Kreos** lachn nat-m phos prun k* rhod
- **squeezed**; as if: anac bg2 asar bg2 kali-n bg2 merc bg2 mur-ac bg2 plat bg2 sil bg2 spong bg2 valer bg2 verb bg2
- **stitching** pain: agar ambr k* anac bg2 ars asaf asar bg2 bapt berb bry carbn-s cham colch k* dulc elat graph bg2 grat bg2 *Guaj* k* hura ign bg2 kali-n bg2 laur bg2 lith-c lob-s lyc lycps-v mag-c mang a1 meny k* merc k* mez bg2 nat-c bg2 nat-m k* nat-s nux-v bg2 pall petr bg2 ph-ac bg2 ran-b rheum bg2 sabad k* sabin bg2 sang sars bg2 sil k* spong bg2 *Staph* k* stram sulph tab tarent thuj verb bg2 *Zinc* k*
  - **alternating** with | **Toe**; stitches in first: sulph
  - **burning**: stram
  - **drawing** pain: bry
  - **intermitting**: berb
  - **itching**: *Staph*
  - **jerking** pain: *Carbn-s*
  - **needles**; as from: staph tl1 zinc
  - **twitching**: nat-s
- **sudden**: coc-c↓ ol-an↓ olib-sac↓ ran-b↓
  - **drawing** pain: coc-c k* ol-an k*
  - **stitching** pain: olib-sac wmh1
  - **tearing** pain: ran-b
- **tearing** pain: aeth a1 agar k* alum bg2 am-c k* am-m ambr h1* anac k* arg-met h1 arg-mur asar bg2 astac aur h2 bar-c bg2 berb bov k* brom calc k* carb-v k* clem k* colch bg2 coloc bg2 graph bg2 grat bg2 hyper indg iod bg2 kali-bi k* kali-c kali-i kali-n k* laur k* led bg2 lyc k* mag-c k* mag-m k* mang h2 nat-c bg2 nat-m k* nat-s nat-sil fd3.de• nicc nit-ac bg2 par k* phel phos plb k* rat rheum k* rhod k* sabad bg2 seneg bg2 sep bg2 sil k* spig k* stann bg2 *Staph* k* stront-c bg2 sul-ac k* sulph k* teucr bg2 zinc k*
  - **burning**: agar k*
  - **drawing** pain: anac clem mag-m zinc
  - **paroxysmal**: nat-m
  - **torn** out; as if it would be: kali-i
  - **twitching**: brom rat staph h1 sul-ac
- **twitching**: acon k*
- **using** it: phos↓
  - **aching**: phos
- **warm** applications | **amel.**: cassia-s ccrh1•
- **writing**:
  - **agg.**: ox-ac↓ prun↓ ran-b↓ sabad↓ thuj k*
    - **drawing** pain: thuj k*
    - **sprained**; as if: prun
    - **stitching** pain: ox-ac sabad
      - **tingling**: sabad
    - **tearing** pain: ran-b

▽
- **extending** to:
  - **Arm**, up the: ars↓ chin↓ colch↓ kali-s↓ spong↓ zinc↓
    - **drawing** pain: ars chin colch kali-s fd4.de spong zinc
  - **Back** of hand: asaf↓
    - **stitching** pain: asaf
  - **Chest**: sul-ac↓
    - **tearing** pain: sul-ac h2
  - **Elbow**: anac↓ calc-s k*
    - **tearing** pain: anac
  - **Hand**: xan c1
  - **Shoulder**: aster k* psil ft1
  - **Tip**; toward:
    - **sitting** agg.: nat-s↓
      - **tearing** pain: nat-s
  - **Wrist**: nat-c↓
    - **drawing** pain: nat-c h2

○
- **Balls**: aeth↓ agn↓ am-m↓ anac↓ ang↓ arn k* berb↓ bism↓ bry k* calc-p k* carb-an↓ carb-v↓ cina↓ cupr↓ dig↓ dros↓ dulc↓ elat↓ euph↓ gamb↓ graph↓ ham fd3.de• hura↓ kali-c↓ kola stb3• lach k* laur↓ lith-c↓ lyc↓ manc↓ meny↓ merl↓ nux-v↓ ox-ac k* petr↓ ph-ac↓ plb podo↓ ran-b↓ sang k* *Sil*↓ *Spong* k* staph↓ tarent↓ teucr↓ verat↓ xan
  - **right**: des-ac↓ sang hr1
    - **aching**: des-ac rbp6 sang
  - **evening**: chinin-s
    - **writing** agg.: ox-ac↓
      - **stitching** pain: ox-ac
  - **burning**: laur lith-c nux-v
  - **cramping**: dulc h2 spong h1
  - **drawing** pain: cupr dulc h2* *Spong*
  - **motion**:
    - **amel.**: staph↓
      - **tearing** pain: staph h1
  - **pressing** pain: agn a1 ang h1 euph h2 meny k*
  - **shooting** pain: tarent
  - **sore**: arn cina h1* hura ran-b
  - **stitching** pain: aeth a1 am-m anac berb carb-an carb-v dig elat hr1 gamb graph hura lith-c manc ox-ac petr ph-ac podo fd3.de• *Sil* tarent verat
    - **stung**; as if: hura
  - **tearing** pain: am-m anac berb bism dros gamb kali-c lyc merl ph-ac h2 ran-b *Sil* staph teucr
  - **writing** agg.: mang↓ mur-ac a1
    - **cramping**: mang h2 mur-ac a1
  - **extending** to:
    - **Back** of head and neck: plb k*
    - **Forearm**: spong
- **Between** first finger and thumb: agar↓ rat↓
  - **tearing** pain: agar h2 rat
- **Bones**: carb-v↓ chel↓ sul-ac↓
  - **tearing** pain: carb-v h2 chel h1 sul-ac h2
- **Joints**: acon↓ aloe↓ am-c↓ am-m↓ ambr k* ang↓ arg-n↓ asaf k* aur↓ aur-i k2 aur-m↓ aur-m-n↓ benz-ac↓ berb k* calc↓ calc-p↓ camph↓ castm↓ caust↓ cench k2 cham↓ chel↓ chin↓ clem↓ colch↓ con↓ cupr↓ cypra-eg sde6.de• dios k* dulc fd4.de erig *Graph*↓ ham fd3.de• hed mtf indg↓ iod↓ kali-bi↓ kali-c k* kali-i k* kali-n k* laur↓ *Led*↓ *Lyc*↓ *M-ambo*↓ m-aust↓ mang↓ mang-m k* merc↓ merc-c↓ mez↓ nat-m k* nat-s↓ nat-sil fd3.de• osm k* petr k* phos↓ podo fd3.de• prun↓ puls↓ rhod↓ ruta fd4.de sacch-a fd2.de• sil a1 spig↓

· **Joints**: ...
sul-ac k* *Sulph* k* symph fd3.de• tell ↓ thuj ↓ tritic-vg fd5.de vanil fd5.de verat k* zinc ↓
: **left**: kreos ↓
: **dislocated**; as if: kreos bg2
: **morning**: mez ↓
: **pressing** pain: mez k*
: **evening**: nat-s ↓
: **pressing** pain: nat-s k*
: **aching**: asaf berb osm
: **bending** impossible: lyc ↓
: **tearing** pain: lyc h2
: **burning**: dulc fd4.de mang a1 spig
: **cramping**: sil h2
: **dislocated**; as if: acon b7a.de calc-p camph b7a.de* cham b7a.de con bg2 cupr *Graph* b4a.de* kali-n b4a.de* laur bg2* *M-ambo* b7a.de m-aust b7a.de nat-m b4a.de* petr b4a.de* phos b4a.de* prun bg2 puls b7a.de* sulph b4a.de* symph fd3.de• verat b7a.de*
: **drawing** pain: aloe ang h1 chel k* nat-s k* sacch-a fd2.de•
: **gouty**: carb-v k* lyc
: **motion**:
: **amel.**: led ↓
. **tearing** pain: led h1
: **pressing** pain: asaf k* aur k* graph h2 indg k* *Led* k* mez k* nat-s k*
: **pulsating** pain: caust k* nat-m k*
: **rest** agg.: aur ↓
: **pressing** pain: aur k*
: **rheumatic**: ambr k* caul *Graph* k* olib-sac wmh1
: **splinter**; as from a: colch
: **sprained**; as if: ang h1 calc-p camph h1* con h2 cupr h2 graph h2 kali-n nat-m h2 petr h2 phos h2 rhod spig h1 sulph verat h1
: **stitching** pain: clem dulc fd4.de ham fd3.de• symph fd3.de• thuj
: **tearing** pain: am-c h2 am-m arg-n a1 aur aur-m aur-m-n benz-ac calc castm chel chin cupr graph h2 iod kali-bi *Led Lyc* merc merc-c nat-m nat-s nat-sil fd3.de• **Sil** sul-ac sulph tell thuj zinc
: **paralyzed**; as if: chel
: **paroxysmal**: lyc
: **writing** agg.: grat ↓
: **tearing** pain: grat
: **extending** to | **Shoulder**: aster
: **Carpometacarpal**: verb ↓
: **sprained**; as if: verb h
: **Distal**: am-m ↓ bar-c ↓ chel ↓ gran ↓ ign ↓ laur ↓ nat-c ↓ spong ↓ thuj ↓
: **drawing** pain: bar-c k* chel a1 nat-c a1 thuj a1
: **sore**: spong h1
: **stitching** pain: am-m bar-c gran ign laur nat-c spong thuj
: **Metacarpophalangeal**: ham ↓ spig ↓
: **left**: phos ↓
. **sore**: phos
: **sore**: ham fd3.de• spig h1
: **Proximal**: agn ↓ bar-c ↓ bry ↓ cham ↓ colch ↓ coloc ↓ grat ↓ ign ↓ kali-p ↓ led ↓ nat-m ↓ nit-ac ↓ psil ft1 sacch-a ↓ sars ↓ spig ↓ thuj ↓ til ↓ zinc ↓
: **asleep**, falling: nit-ac ↓
. **drawing** pain: nit-ac h2
: **waking**; on: nit-ac ↓
. **drawing** pain: nit-ac h2
: **drawing** pain: colch k* coloc k* nit-ac k* sacch-a fd2.de• spig k* thuj k*
: **stitching** pain: agn bry cham grat ign kali-p fd1.de• led nat-m sars thuj til
: **tearing** pain: bar-c h2 zinc h2

· **Nails**: am-m ↓ nat-s ↓
: **ulcerative** pain: am-m nat-s
: **Roots** of nails: fl-ac ↓ nat-c ↓
: **stitching** pain: fl-ac nat-c h2

- **Thumbs – Nails**: ...
: **Under**: am-m ↓ bapt ↓ bar-c ↓ berb bg1 bism bg1 carb-v ↓ coc-c ↓ fl-ac ↓ *Graph* ↓ hura ↓ kali-c ↓ led ↓ mez ↓ nat-m ↓ positr ↓ spong fd4.de *Thuj* ↓ *Zinc* ↓
: **night**:
. **bed** agg.; in: sulph ↓
tearing pain: sulph
: **drawing** pain: bar-c a1 nat-m
: **sore**: mez h2 positr nl2•
: **splinter**; as from a: hura c1* positr nl2•
: **stitching** pain: am-m bapt coc-c *Graph* led a2 *Thuj Zinc*
: **tearing** pain: bar-c h2 carb-v fl-ac kali-c zinc
. **upward**: berb

· **Phalanges**:
: **Distal**: aur ↓
: **tearing** pain: aur h2
: **Proximal**: sep ↓
: **tearing** pain: sep h2

· **Sides**: mang ↓
: **tearing** pain: mang
: **Inner**: asaf ↓ kali-i ↓
: **pressing** pain: asaf k*
: **tearing** pain: kali-i
: **Outer**: mang ↓
: **tearing** pain: mang

· **Spots**; in: lach ↓
: **burning**: lach

· **Tips**: agar ↓ am-m ↓ ambr ↓ bar-c ↓ berb ↓ borx ↓ calc-p ↓ carb-v k* con ↓ croc ↓ dulc ↓ graph ↓ gymno ↓ lach ↓ lyc k* mag-s ↓ mez ↓ mur-ac ↓ nat-m k* nat-s ↓ olnd ↓ phel ↓ phyt ↓ sabad ↓ sep ↓ sil ↓ spong fd4.de *Staph* ↓ sulph teucr ↓ vip ↓ zinc k*
: **right**: vip-l-f ↓
: **sore**: vip-l-f a1
: **evening**:
: **sitting** agg.: am-m ↓
. **stitching** pain: am-m
: **walking** agg.: merc-c ↓
. **stitching** pain: merc-c
: **boring** pain: nat-m bg2
: **burning**: con croc dulc fd4.de gymno lach mur-ac olnd sil sulph teucr
: **dinner**; after: mag-s ↓
: **stitching** pain: mag-s
: **drawing** pain: zinc
: **gnawing** pain: nat-m k*
: **pulsating** pain: borx
: **shooting** pain: phyt
: **sore**: calc-p vip
: **stitching** pain: agar am-m ambr bar-c berb calc-p graph mag-s mez nat-m nat-s phyt sabad sep staph vip *Zinc*
: **taking** hold of anything agg.: mez ↓
: **stitching** pain: mez
: **tearing** pain: ambr h1 carb-v lyc phel *Staph* zinc
: **burning**: carb-v
: **waking**; on: nat-m ↓
: **stitching** pain: nat-m

- **Toes**: *Acon* ↓ *Act-sp* ↓ aesc ↓ *Agar* ↓ agn b7a.de aids ↓ ail ↓ *Alum* ↓ alum-p ↓ alum-sil ↓ am-c ↓ am-m ambr ↓ *Anac* ↓ androc srj1• ang ↓ ant-c ↓ ant-t ↓ **Apis** ↓ *Arg-met* ↓ arg-n ↓ arge-pl rwt5• *Arn* ↓ *Ars* ↓ arum-d ↓ arund ↓ *Asaf* ↓ asar ↓ asc-t ↓ aster *Aur* aur-ar ↓ *Aur-m* ↓ *Aur-m-n* ↓ aur-s ↓ aza ↓ bamb-a ↓ bar-c ↓ *Benz-ac* berb bism ↓ *Borx* ↓ bov ↓ brom bry ↓ bufo-s ↓ cact ↓ cadm-met ↓ cadm-s ↓ calad ↓ *Calc* k* calc-p calc-sil k2 camph b7a.de cann-i ↓ *Canth* ↓ caps ↓ carb-an ↓ *Carb-v* ↓ *Carbn-s* ↓ carl ↓ *Caul Caust* k* chel *Chin* ↓ cic ↓ *Cina* ↓ cist ↓ clem ↓ coc-c ↓ coca-c ↓ cocc coff ↓ colch tl1 *Coloc Con* ↓ croc ↓ crot-h crot-t ↓ cupr ↓ *Cupr-act* ↓ cycl b7a.de cystein-l ↓ daph ↓ dig digin ↓ *Dios* ↓ dros ↓ dulc *Elat* ↓ euon ↓ fago ↓ ferr ferr-ma ↓ *Ferr-p* ↓ fic-m ↓ fl-ac ↓ flor-p ↓ gels ↓ ger-i ↓ gins ↓ *Graph* ↓ guare ↓ ham ↓ hell helo-s bnm14• *Hep* ↓ hura hyos ↓ *Hyper* ↓ ind ↓ indg ↓ iod jatr-c ↓

- **Toes**: ...
kali-bi k* **Kali-c** ↓ kali-i kali-n ↓ kali-p kali-s fd4.de kali-sil ↓ *Kalm* ↓ kola stb3• kreos ↓ lac-del ↓ lach lact lat-m ↓ laur ↓ led tl1 lil-t *Lith-c* *Lyc* m-arct ↓ m-aust ↓ mag-c ↓ mag-m ↓ mag-s ↓ med ↓ merc merl ↓ mez mosch ↓ mur-ac ↓ naja nat-ar ↓ *Nat-c* ↓ nat-m nat-p ↓ nat-s ↓ neon ↓ nicc ↓ **Nit-ac** ↓ **Nit-s-d** ↓ nux-v ol-an ↓ olnd ↓ oxal-a ↓ paeon ↓ *Pall* ↓ par ↓ petr ↓ *Ph-ac* ↓ *Phos* *Phyt* k* pip-m *Plat* plb polyp-p ↓ positr nl2• psor ↓ puls k* puls-n ↓ pyrus ↓ ran-b k2 *Ran-s* ↓ *Rat* ↓ rheum ↓ **Rhod** k* rhus-t rhus-v ↓ ros-d ↓ rumx ruta fd4.de sabad sabin ↓ sang sars ↓ sec sel sep *Sil* sphing kk3.fr spig kk3.fr spong fd4.de stann ↓ *Staph* ↓ *Stict* *Stront-c* ↓ stry suis-pan ↓ sul-ac ↓ *Sulph* symph fd3.de• *Syph* *Tarax* ↓ tarent tell tep ↓ teucr ↓ thuj tritic-vg fd5.de valer b7.de* vanil fd5.de *Verat* ↓ verb ↓ vinc ↓ viol-t ↓ visc ↓ *Zinc* zinc-p ↓
  - **right**: aur ↓ carb-v ↓ cench k2 daph br1 fic-m gya1 gard-j vlr2• lac-del hrn2• lyc ↓ mez ↓ nicc ↓ stront-c ↓
    - **tearing** pain: aur bg2 carb-v bg2 lyc bg2 mez bg2 nicc bg2 stront-c bg2
  - **left**: *Agn* ↓ aids nl2• caul a1 cic ↓ jatr-c ↓ mag-c ↓ mag-s ↓ neon ↓ ruta fd4.de spig ↓
    - **burning**: neon srj5•
    - **cramping**: aids nl2•
    - **stitching** pain: aids nl2•
    - **tearing** pain: *Agn* cic bg2 jatr-c bg2 mag-c h2 mag-s bg2 spig h1
  - **daytime**: ind ↓
    - **burning**: ind
  - **noon**:
    - **bending** body:
      - **left** agg.; to: thuj ↓
        - **stitching** pain: thuj
  - **afternoon**: coloc ↓ dulc ↓ gard-j vlr2• ham ↓ mez ↓ spong ↓ tritic-vg ↓
    - **pressing** pain: coloc
    - **stitching** pain: dulc fd4.de ham fd3.de• mez spong fd4.de tritic-vg fd5.de
  - **evening**: aids ↓ **Am-m** ↓ androc srj1• cist coloc ↓ dulc fd4.de kola stb3• lyc ↓ nat-s ↓ ruta ↓ spong fd4.de symph fd3.de• tritic-vg ↓ urol-h ↓ vanil fd5.de
    - **18** h: arg-met ↓
      - **tearing** pain: arg-met
    - **20** h: am-m ↓
      - **tearing** pain: am-m
    - **bed** agg.; in: asar ↓ con ↓
      - **drawing** pain: asar k* con k*
    - **drawing** pain: nat-s k*
    - **sleep**; when falling asleep: merl ↓
      - **stitching** pain: merl
    - **sprained**; as if: coloc
    - **stitching** pain: aids nl2• cist dulc fd4.de lyc nat-s ruta fd4.de spong fd4.de tritic-vg fd5.de urol-h rwt•
    - **tearing** pain: **Am-m** lyc
  - **night**: *Am-c* androc srj1• coc-c fic-m gya1 kali-c kola stb3• led merc merc-i-f nat-c *Nux-v* ↓ plat ruta ↓ sulph ↓ symph fd3.de• *Syph* vanil fd5.de
    - **amel.**: nicc ↓
      - **tearing** pain: nicc
    - **burning**: plat
    - **sleep**; during: led ↓
      - **cutting** pain: led
      - **lying** on back agg.: sep ↓
        - **cutting** pain: sep
    - **stitching** pain: *Nux-v* ruta fd4.de
    - **tearing** pain: plat sulph
  - **aching**: arn aza br1 carl coc-c cupr dios euon fic-m gya1 flor-p rsj3• g e r - i rly4• ham hell lat-m bnm6• led mez mosch phos puls-n pyrus sulph
    - **pulsating** pain: arn
  - **annually**: tarent
  - **ascending** stairs agg.: coloc ↓
    - **sprained**; as if: coloc
  - **bed**:
    - **in** bed:
      - **agg.**: agar ↓
  - **bed – in** bed – **agg.**: ...
        - **stitching** pain: agar
      - **amel.**: am-m ↓
        - **tearing** pain: am-m
  - **bending** | **body**:
    - **left**; to:
      - **agg.**: thuj ↓
        - **stitching** pain: thuj
    - **feet**:
      - **agg.**: hipp ↓
        - **sore**: hipp
  - **blow**; pain as from a: mez b4.de* ruta b7.de*
  - **boring** pain: aesc chin b7.de* coloc merc k* mez *Ran-s* k* sabin b7.de*
  - **broken**; as if: cocc k* lach bg1*
  - **burning**: aesc *Agar* k* alum k* ant-c k* **Apis** k* arn k* ars arund *Asaf* k* aur aur-ar k2 *Aur-m* *Berb* *Borx* k* cadm-met sp1 calad k* calc k* carb-an k* caust *Con* k* dulc k* *Ferr-p* fl-ac *Hep* ind *Kali-c* k* kali-p kreos b7a.de lith-c *Lyc* mag-m b4a.de merc k* mez k* mosch k* mur-ac k* nat-c k* neon srj5• nit-ac k* nux-v k* olnd b7.de paeon par b7.de ph-ac k* phos plat k* positr nl2• *Puls* ran-s b7.de *Ruta* b7.de* sabin k* sars bro1 sec *Staph* k* symph fd3.de• *Tarax* k* thuj vanil fd5.de viol-t b7.de zinc b4a.de
    - **intermittent**: dulc h2
    - **paroxysmal**: *Tarax*
    - **stitching** pain: dulc h2
  - **burnt**; sensation as if: nat-c bg2
  - **burrowing**: agar b4.de* *Rhod* b4a.de
  - **chill**; during: lyc ↓ merc bg2 sulph bg2 thuj bg2
    - **stitching** pain: lyc
  - **cold**:
    - **amel.**: aster ↓
      - **stitching** pain: aster
  - **cold** feet, with: apis ↓ sec ↓
    - **burning**: apis sec a1
  - **cramping**: aids nl2• calc tl1 cupr bro1 *Cupr-act* bro1 dig bro1 *Dios* bro1 hyos bro1 lac-del hrn2• lyc bro1 rhus-t bro1 sec bro1 sep bro1 sulph bro1 visc sp1
  - **crushed**; as if: hyper bro1
  - **cut** off; as if: mosch b7a.de
  - **cutting** pain: acon bg2 alum b4.de* ant-c b7.de* aur bg2 aur-m calc carb-an h2* cina k* coloc dios k* ger-i rly4• kali-c bg2 led k* paeon ph-ac k* puls k* sep k* *Sil* k*
  - **decreasing** gradually: am-m ↓
    - **stitching** pain: am-m
  - **delivery**; during: dios ↓
    - **cramping**: dios mrr1
  - **dislocated**; as if: am-c b4a.de *Arn* b7.de* aur b4.de* crot-t bg2 *Hep* b4a.de kali-c b4.de* mosch b7a.de petr b4.de* syph *Zinc* b4.de*
  - **drawing** pain: agar k* am-c bg2 anac k* ang k* ant-c b7.de* arg-n k* a r s bg2 asaf k* asar b7.de* asc-t aster k* *Aur* k* *Aur-m-n* k* bar-c k* berb k* cact k* *Camph* *Caul* k* caust k* chel k* cic b7.de* clem k* cocc k* colch k* coloc k* con k* cycl b7.de* dig k* digin a1 gels psa ham hell k* indg k* led k* lyc bg2 m-aust b7.de mag-m k* mez k* nat-c k* nat-m bg2 nat-s k* nit-s-d bg* ol-an par b7.de* plat k* plb b7.de* polyp-p a1 rat rhus-t b7.de* rhus-v k* ruta k* sabin bg2* sars k* *Sep* k* sil k* stront-c k* sulph bg2 *Thuj* k* valer b7.de* vanil fd5.de vinc k* zinc bg2
    - **cramping**: *Anac* plat vinc
    - **paralyzed**; as if: aur
    - **shifting**: arg-n k*
    - **tearing** pain: carb-an k* clem k* sulph zinc
    - **upward**: anac k* caust k* dig digin a1 *Thuj* k*
  - **fever**; during: elat ↓
    - **shooting** pain: elat c1
  - **frostbitten**, as if: borx ↓
    - **burning**: borx h2
  - **frozen** previously: agar ↓ carl ↓ phos
    - **aching**: carl

- **frozen** previously: ...
  - **burning**: agar carl phos h2
  - **pressing** pain: phos h2
- **gnawing** pain: benz-ac k* hyper k* kali-c k* ran-s b7.de*
- **gouty**: *Benz-ac* ↓ *Graph* ↓
  - **tearing** pain: *Benz-ac Graph*
- **hot** | **stitching** pain (See warm - stitching)
- **increasing** gradually: am-m ↓
  - **stitching** pain: am-m
- **jerking** pain: *Am-m* anac b4.de* cic h1 mez par puls b7.de* ran-s sabin b7.de*
- **jumping**: cycl ↓
  - **sore**: cycl
- **menses**; during: sulph ↓
  - **cramping**: sulph b4.de
- **motion**:
  - **agg.**: am-c nept-m ↓ nux-v ↓ plb ↓ symph fd3.de• thuj
    - **cramping**: nept-m lsd2.fr
    - **stitching** pain: nux-v
    - **tearing** pain: plb
  - **amel.**: agar ↓ anac ↓ cocc ↓ coloc ↓ lyc ↓ psor ↓
    - **drawing** pain: lyc k*
    - **pressing** pain: coloc
    - **stitching** pain: agar cocc
    - **tearing** pain: anac h2 cocc psor
- **paralyzed**; as if: aur k* *Chin* k*
- **pecking**: plat h2
- **perspiration**; from: bar-c ↓ graph ↓ iod ↓ lyc ↓ nit-ac ↓ *Petr* ↓ sanic ↓ sep ↓ *Sil* ↓ zinc ↓
  - **sore**: bar-c bro1* graph k* iod bro1 lyc bro1 nit-ac bro1 *Petr* bro1 sanic bro1 sep *Sil* bro1 zinc bro1*
- **pinching** pain: am-m b7.de* bar-c k* kali-bi bg2 puls k* sul-ac h2
  - **twitching**: sul-ac h2
- **pressing** pain: ang arg-met b7.de* asaf b7.de* bism b7.de* borx b4a.de brom camph caust k* chel clem *Colch* k* coloc cupr h2 cycl b7.de* gins graph k* guare hell kali-s fd4.de led b7.de* mez mosch b7.de* nat-s nux-v b7.de* olnd k* ph-ac k* puls b7.de* rhus-t b7.de* staph b7.de* viol-t b7.de*
  - **alternating** with | **drawing** pain: gins
  - **crushed**; as if: olnd
- **pressure** agg.: *Cina* ↓
  - **sore**: *Cina*
- **pulsating** pain: kali-bi bg2 mur-ac a1 ph-ac bg2
- **rheumatic**: *Act-sp* bro1 apoc-a bro1 arg-met asc-t a1 **Aur** *Benz-ac* bro1 borx bro1 both bro1 *Caul* bro1 caust bro1 *Colch* bro1 corv-cor bdg• daph bro1 *Gnaph* bro1 *Graph* ↓ hyper bro1 kali-c k* *Led* bro1 *Lith-c* bro1 nit-ac bro1 paeon bro1 ph-ac bro1 *Puls* bro1 sabin bro1 *Sil* bro1 stict stront-c *Teucr*
  - **tearing** pain: *Graph*
  - **Tip**: am-m bro1 *Hyper* bro1 kali-c bro1 *Sil* bro1 syph bro1
- **rising** agg.; after: asaf ↓
  - **tearing** pain: asaf
- **rubbing**:
  - **amel.**: laur ↓ nicc ↓ phos ↓
    - **tearing** pain: laur nicc phos
- **shooting** pain: *Acon* agar ambr c1 apis aster calc-p daph dulc *Elat* kali-bi bg2 med
- **sitting** agg.: *Am-m* ↓ *Aur-m-n* ↓ berb ↓ calc ↓ dig phos ↓
  - **drawing** pain: *Aur-m-n* k*
  - **stitching** pain: aur-m-n calc
  - **tearing** pain: *Am-m* berb phos
- **sleep** agg.; during: led
- **sore**: *Ars* aster aur k* bar-c bro1 berb brom bro1 calc *Canth* caust *Cina* coca-c sk4• coff *Coloc* cycl daph graph lyc mur-ac a1 nat-ar bro1 nat-c *Nat-m* **Nit-ac** oxal-a rly4• ph-ac k* plat ran-b ruta sep sulph thuj h1 zinc
  - **burning**: lyc
- **sore**: ...
  - **ulcerated**; as if: ph-ac
- **sprained**: crot-t ↓
  - **tearing** pain: crot-t
- **sprained**; as if: am-c berb bry bg1 coloc zinc
- **standing** agg.: *Agar* ↓ am-m ↓ anac ↓ ars calc nat-m stann ↓ *Verat* ↓
  - **stitching** pain: *Agar* calc *Verat*
  - **tearing** pain: am-m anac h2 stann h2
- **stepping** agg.: *Borx* a1* (non:bov kl) bry lap-la sde8.de* led thuj
  - **pressing** pain: borx h2
- **stitching** pain: *Acon* *Agar* k* agn b7.de* aids nl2• ail *Alum* k* alum-p k2 alum-sil k2 am-c k* *Am-m* k* ang ant-t k* apis arg-n arn k* arum-d arund *Asaf* b7.de* aster aur k* *Aur-m-n* aur-s k2 bamb-a stb2.de• bar-c k* *Berb* bov k* bry k* bufo-s cadm-s *Calc* k* calc-p calc-sil k2 cann-i caps b7.de* *Carb-v* k* *Carbn-s* *Caust* k* chel cina cist cocc colch b7.de* *Coloc* crot-t cycl cystein-l rly4• dros b7.de* dulc k* elat fago ferr-ma graph k* ham fd3.de• *Hell* k* *Hep* k* hyper kali-bi kali-c k* kali-n b4.de* kali-s fd4.de kali-sil k2 *Kalm* kola stb3• kreos b7a.de lach laur b7.de* led k* *Lyc* m-arct b7.de mag-c k* mag-s med merc k* merl mez k* mosch b7a.de *Nat-c* b4a.de nat-m k* nat-s **Nit-ac** k* **Nit-s-d** bg *Nux-v* olnd k* *Pall* par k* petr ph-ac k* phos k* plat k* plb *Puls* k* ran-b k* *Ran-s* k* rheum b7.de* rhus-t k* ros-d wla1 ruta fd4.de sabad k* sabin k* *Sil* k* spig b7.de* spong fd4.de *Stict* stry suis-pan rly4• sul-ac k* *Sulph* k* tarax k* tarent thuj k* tritic-vg fd5.de *Verat* k* verb k* zinc k*
  - **biting** pain: *Hyper*
  - **burning**: arund chel
  - **cramping**: calc cina sil
  - **itching**: ran-s spig h1
  - **jerking** pain: carbn-s
  - **needles**; as from: calc ham fd3.de• kali-s fd4.de petr h2
  - **outward**: berb bg1
  - **paroxysmal**: calc
  - **smarting**: nat-m
  - **sprained**: crot-t k*
  - **stinging**: kali-s fd4.de *Verat*
  - **tearing** pain: tarax
  - **twitching**: berb carbn-s *Cina* merl
  - **upward**: lach *Nux-v* pall
- **stool** agg.; during: nux-v ↓
  - **stitching** pain: nux-v
- **stretching** out foot; on: bar-c ↓
  - **pinching** pain: bar-c
- **stubbing**; when: colch lp*
- **sudden**: kola stb3•
- **tearing** pain: *Acon* *Act-sp* bro1 agar k* *Agn* alum b4.de* am-c k* *Am-m* k* ambr b7.de* *Anac* k* ant-c b7.de* *Arg-met* k* arn b7.de* asaf k* aur k* aur-s k2 bar-c b4.de* *Benz-ac* k* berb k* bism k* brom bro1 bry k* calc k* calc-sil k2 camph k* canth b7.de* carb-an k* *Carb-v* k* carbn-s *Caul* bro1 *Caust* k* *Chin* k* cic cocc k* *Colch* k* *Coloc* con k* croc crot-t k* dios k* *Graph* k* hell k* hep b4.de* indg jatr-c kali-bi bg2 **Kali-c** k* kali-n b4.de* kali-sil k2 laur k* *Led* k* lyc k* m-arct b7.de mag-c b4.de* mag-m k* mag-s merl mez k* mur-ac b4.de* *Nat-c* k* nat-m k* nat-p nat-s k* nicc ol-an pall bro1 par k* *Ph-ac* b4a.de phos k* *Plat* k* plb k* psor k* puls b7.de* *Rat* ruta b7.de* sars b4.de* sep k* sil k* spig b7.de* *Stront-c* k* sulph k* syph bro1 tarax b7.de* tarent k* tep teucr k* thuj k* valer k* zinc k* zinc-p k2
  - **cramping**: *Anac*
  - **drawing** pain: carb-an clem sulph zinc
  - **jerking** pain: chin h1
  - **paroxysmal**: plb
  - **smarting**: merl
  - **sticking** pain: zinc
  - **twitching**: chin
  - **upward**: anac h2 stann h2
- **touch** agg.: androc srj1• *Chin* ph-ac
  - **tearing** pain: *Chin*
- **twinging**: berb k2

Extremities

- **ulcerative** pain: berb carb-an carb-v caust k* *Kali-i* kola stb3• nat-c nat-m b4.de* ph-ac k* phos bg2 plat b4.de* sil valer zinc k*
- **waking**; on: nat-s ↓
  - **tearing** pain: nat-s
- **walking**:
  - **agg.**: agn am-c ant-c arn ↓ ars aur-m ↓ aur-m-n ↓ bry camph carb-v ↓ carbn-s ↓ caust crot-t ↓ cycl ↓ dros ↓ hydrog ↓ *Kali-c* kali-s ↓ lyc mag-c ↓ mez nat-m nat-s ↓ phos plb ↓ positr nl2• ran-b ↓ ruta fd4.de sil thuj vanil fd5.de zinc ↓
    - **aching**: mez phos
    - **burning**: phos
    - **cutting** pain: aur-m
    - **drawing** pain: aur-m-n k*
    - **pressing** pain: mez h2 phos h2 sil h2
    - **sore**: cycl h1 hydrog srj2• lyc zinc
    - **stitching** pain: arn carbn-s crot-t k* dros h1 kali-s fd4.de *Lyc* ran-b ruta fd4.de
    - **tearing** pain: *Agn Camph* carb-v crot-t mag-c h2 nat-s plb
  - **amel.**: calc ↓
    - **stitching** pain: calc
- **wandering** pain: clem
- **warm**: *Acon* ↓
  - **bed**:
    - **agg.**: nux-v ↓ plb ↓
      - **burning**: nux-v
      - **tearing** pain: plb
  - **stitching** pain: *Acon*
- **wet** agg.; after getting feet: nit-ac ↓
  - **burning**: nit-ac

▽ • **extending** to:
  - **Ankle**: brass-n-o srj5•
  - **Body**: hyper tl1
    - **Side**; corresponding: helo-s bnm14•
  - **Foot**: anac bg2 helo-s bnm14•
  - **Hip**: *Nux-v Pall*
    - **shooting** pain: nux-v *Pall*
    - **stitching** pain: *Nux-v* pall
  - **Instep**: anac ↓
    - **cramping**: anac gsy1
  - **Knee**: brass-n-o srj5•
  - **Lower** limb: helo-s bnm14•
  - **Root** of foot: iod ↓
    - **cramping**: iod h
  - **Sole**; hollow of: psil ↓
    - **stitching** pain: psil ft1
  - **Thigh**: caust bg2
  - **Tips**: caps ↓
    - **stitching** pain: caps a1

○ • **All** toes: kali-c ↓ petr ↓ ran-b ↓ *Zinc* ↓
  - **dislocated**; as if: kali-c b4a.de petr b4a.de ran-b b7a.de *Zinc* b4a.de
- **Balls**: alum ↓ am-c ambr ↓ ant-c ↓ ant-t ↓ *Bry* ↓ calc-p ↓ cann-s ↓ cina ↓ coff ↓ colch ↓ daph ↓ dros ↓ gels psa hell ↓ hep ↓ *Kali-c* ↓ lach ↓ laur ↓ led b7.de* lyc ↓ med ptk1 mur-ac ↓ nat-p k2 par ↓ ph-ac ↓ plat ↓ puls ↓ ran-s ↓ rhus-t ↓ sabin ↓ sil ↓ spig ↓ *Squil* ↓ sulph ↓ symph fd3.de• tab valer ↓
  - **left**: cann-i ↓
    - **stitching** pain: cann-i c1
  - **aching**: sulph
  - **burning**: ant-c b7.de* *Bry* b7.de *Kali-c* b4a.de laur b7.de *Squil* b7.de*
  - **dislocated**; as if: *Am-c* b4a.de
  - **drawing** pain: am-c bg2 cann-s b7.de*
  - **frozen**; formerly: plat ↓
    - **sore**: plat h2
  - **shooting** pain: alum calc-p daph
  - **sore**: med c1 ph-ac sil
- **Balls**: ...
  - **stitching** pain: alum ambr b7.de* ant-c b7.de* ant-t b7a.de *Bry* b7.de* calc-p cann-s b7.de* cina b7.de* coff b7a.de colch b7.de* daph dros h1* hep bg2 *Kali-c* b4a.de lyc b4a.de mur-ac a1 par bg2 puls bg2 ran-s b7.de* rhus-t b7.de* sabin b7.de* spig b7.de*
  - **tearing** pain: colch b7.de* dros b7.de* hell b7.de* plat h2 valer bg2
  - **ulcerative** pain: lach bg2 lyc bg2 rhus-t b7.de*
  - **walking** agg.: am-c *Ars* ↓ caust ↓ ph-ac ↓ plat ↓ sil ↓
    - **sore**: *Ars* caust ph-ac plat h2 sil
- **Between**: berb ↓ carb-an ↓ *Fl-ac* ↓ *Graph* ↓ lyc ↓ merc-i-r ↓ mez ↓ *Nat-c* ↓ *Nat-m* ↓ ph-ac ↓ ran-b ↓ sil ↓ **Zinc** ↓
  - **sore**: berb carb-an *Fl-ac Graph* lyc merc-i-r mez *Nat-c Nat-m* k* ph-ac ran-b sil tl1 **Zinc**
- **Bones**: cycl ↓ mez sep symph fd3.de• vanil fd5.de
  - **pressing** pain: cycl b7.de*
- **Fifth**: agar ↓ aloe am-m ↓ anag androc ↓ apis ↓ arn ↓ ars ↓ asaf asar asc-t blatta-o bry ↓ calc ↓ cann-s ↓ carb-an ↓ caust ↓ chel con cycl ↓ dios ↓ dream-p ↓ ferr-ma ↓ fl-ac graph ↓ hep ↓ hura kali-bi ↓ kali-p ↓ kali-s ↓ *Led* ↓ lith-c lyc ↓ lyss ↓ mag-c ↓ mag-m ↓ meph ↓ merc-i-f mez ↓ mosch ↓ mur-ac ↓ nat-s ↓ olnd ↓ paeon ↓ ph-ac ↓ rheum ↓ rumx ruta fd4.de sep ↓ spong fd4.de staph symph ↓ ther thuj ↓ til ↓ tritic-vg fd5.de zinc ↓
  - **right**: opun-s a1 psil ft1 tritic-vg fd5.de
  - **left**: asc-t a1 spong fd4.de
  - **morning**: anag lyc ↓
    - **stitching** pain: lyc h2
  - **evening**: zinc ↓
    - **tearing** pain: zinc
  - **aching**: dios
  - **boring** pain: dios
  - **burning**: androc srj1• ars carb-an meph staph symph fd3.de• til
  - **chilblains**; as from: aloe
  - **drawing** pain: cycl h1
  - **pinching** pain: mosch k* ph-ac h2
  - **pressing** pain: cycl h1 ferr-ma *Led* nat-s olnd paeon ph-ac ther
  - **shoes**; could not wear: androc srj1•
  - **sore**: agar bry dream-p sdj1• mur-ac staph
  - **standing** agg.: am-m ↓
    - **stitching** pain: am-m
  - **stitching** pain: agar h2 am-m apis asaf calc cann-s chel con hep h2 hura kali-p fd1.de• kali-s fd4.de lyc ph-ac rheum h ruta thuj tritic-vg fd5.de
    - **cramping**: ruta h1
    - **frostbitten**; as if: lyc h2
    - **pulsating** pain: con ruta fd4.de
  - **tearing** pain: arn caust graph kali-bi lyss mag-c mag-m mez nat-s sep thuj zinc
  - **walking** agg.: am-m ↓ nat-c ↓ ther ↓
    - **afternoon** | **burning**: (non:nat-c kl)
    - **burning**: nat-c kl
    - **pressing** pain: ther hr1
    - **stitching** pain: am-m
  - **Balls**: nit-ac puls ↓ ruta fd4.de
    - **burning**: puls h1
    - **stitching** pain: puls h1 ruta fd4.de
    - **walking** agg.: nit-ac
  - **Joints**: coloc ↓
    - **aching**: coloc
- **First**: aesc ↓ agar ↓ agn ↓ *All-c* aloe ↓ alum ↓ alumn ↓ *Am-c* k* *Am-m* ↓ ammc anac ↓ anag *Ant-c* ↓ arg-met ↓ *Arn* ↓ ars bro1 asaf aster *Aur Aur-m* ↓ aur-m-n ↓ bamb-a ↓ bapt bar-c bro1 *Benz-ac Berb* borx ↓ both bov ↓ brom ↓ bry calc bro1 calc-p calc-sil ↓ *Cann-i* ↓ caps ↓ carb-ac carb-an ↓ carb-v carbn-s ↓ carl ↓ castm ↓ *Caust* ↓ chel ↓ chin cic ↓ *Cimic Cist* ↓ clem ↓ coc-c ↓ cocc ↓ *Colch* coloc com ↓ con ↓ conv ↓ crot-t ↓ cycl ↓ daph ↓ dios *Dulc* elat k* *Eup-per* k* euphr ↓ ferr-ma ↓ form ↓ gamb ↓ ger-i ↓ gins ↓ gnaph *Graph* hell *Hep* ↓ hura hyper ↓ ind indg ↓ *Iod* jal br1 jatr-c ↓ jug-r ↓ kali-bi ↓ kali-c bro1 kali-i ↓ kali-n ↓ kali-s fd4.de kali-sil ↓ *Kalm* ↓ kola stb3• lac-ac lach ↓ lachn ↓ lap-la sde8.de• laur ↓ **Led** k* luf-op rsj5• *Lyc* mag-c ↓ mag-m ↓ mag-s ↓

- **First**: ...
mang meph merc↓ merc-i-f merc-i-r merl↓ mez mosch↓ mur-ac↓ *Nat-c*↓ nat-m↓ nat-p nat-s nat-sil↓ *Nit-ac*↓ nit-s-d↓ *Nux-m*↓ ol-an↓ olib-sac wmh1 par↓ ph-ac phos phys *Phyt* *Pip-m* plat *Plb* k* positr nl2• prim-v bro1 puls rad-br c11 *Ran-s* rat↓ *Rhod* rhus-t↓ ros-d↓ ruta fd4.de sabin sang↓ sars↓ sep bro1 *Sil* k* sphing↓ spong fd4.de stry↓ sul-ac↓ sulph syc fmm1• symph fd3.de• tarax↓ tarent tep↓ thal-xyz↓ thuj gk tritic-vg↓ tub c1 tung-met bdx1• ulm-c↓ vanil fd5.de verat↓ viol-t↓ *Zinc*
  - **right**: alumn↓ ant-c↓ bamb-a↓ benz-ac↓ both br1 *Buteo-j*↓ cic↓ *Cimic*↓ *Cist*↓ coca-c↓ con↓ dendr-pol sk4• dulc fd4.de gink-b sbd1• iris↓ kali-s fd4.de lachn↓ lyc↓ mag-c↓ mag-m↓ mur-ac↓ nit-s-d↓ olib-sac↓ phos↓ *Ran-s*↓ ruta↓ sacch-a↓ sil↓ spong↓ symph↓ verat↓ *Zinc*↓
    - **boring** pain: *Ran-s*
    - **burning**: ant-c *Cimic* con olib-sac wmh1 *Ran-s* sacch-a fd2.de• verat
    - **cramping**: [*Buteo-j* sej6]
    - **cutting** pain: iris a1
    - **followed** by | **left**: *Dulc* *Pip-m* *Ran-s*
    - **sore**: coca-c sk4•
    - **stitching** pain: alumn bamb-a stb2.de• benz-ac *Cist* dulc fd4.de kali-s fd4.de lyc nit-s-d bg phos h2 *Ran-s* ruta fd4.de sacch-a fd2.de• spong fd4.de
    - **tearing** pain: cic k* lachn hr1 mag-c h2 mag-m h2 mur-ac h2 sil h2 symph fd3.de• *Zinc* k*
  - **left**: aesc↓ agn↓ alum↓ *Am-c* apoc-a↓ carc fd2.de• coc-c↓ colch tl1 dulc fd4.de *Eup-per* kali-p↓ kali-s↓ kalm↓ kola stb3• lachn↓ lap-la sde8.de• led↓ luf-op rsj5• mand rsj7• *Mang* hr1 nat-sil↓ phos↓ rat↓ ruta fd4.de spong↓ symph fd3.de• tub c1 ulm-c↓ vanil↓ visc↓
    - **burning**: aesc apoc-a vh1 lachn vanil fd5.de
    - **stitching** pain: agn alum carc fd2.de• coc-c dulc fd4.de kali-p fd1.de• kali-s fd4.de kalm kola stb3• led nat-sil fd3.de• phos h2 spong fd4.de visc c1
      - **needles**; as from: ulm-c jsj8•
    - **tearing** pain: coc-c rat symph fd3.de•
  - **morning**: alum↓ anag dulc fd4.de jug-r↓ **Led** lyc merc-i-r sulph↓
    - **7** h: ozone↓
      - **stitching** pain: ozone sde2•
    - **bed** agg.; in: ars↓ jug-r↓ ozone↓
      - **burning**: ars
      - **sprained**; as if: jug-r
      - **stitching** pain: ars ozone sde2•
    - **boring** pain: **Led**
    - **cutting** pain: alum sulph
    - **sprained**; as if: jug-r
    - **walking** agg.: *Led*
  - **forenoon**: nat-c↓
    - **11** h: sil↓
      - **tearing** pain: sil
    - **tearing** pain: nat-c
  - **noon**: pip-m
  - **afternoon**: am-m↓
    - **14** h: ol-an↓
      - **tearing** pain: ol-an
    - **tearing** pain: am-m
  - **evening**: alumn↓ *Cist*↓ com↓ dulc fd4.de euphr↓ ind↓ kali-s↓ lyc↓ mag-c↓ nat-m↓ nat-s phos↓ ruta fd4.de sars↓ sil↓ spong fd4.de stry thuj↓ tritic-vg↓
    - **bed** agg.; in: *Am-c* mag-m↓
      - **tearing** pain: mag-m
    - **boring** pain: ind
    - **drawing** pain: com k* thuj k*
    - **lying** down, before: mag-s↓
      - **tearing** pain: mag-s
    - **motion** agg. | **stitching** pain: (non:phos kl)
    - **stitching** pain: alumn *Cist* dulc fd4.de euphr kali-s fd4.de lyc mag-c h2 nat-m phos ruta fd4.de spong fd4.de tritic-vg fd5.de
    - **tearing** pain: sars sil

- **First**: ...
  - **night**: aloe↓ alum↓ *Benz-ac* form↓ kali-i↓ kali-n↓ kali-p↓ *Mang* k* *Plb* sacch-a↓
    - **bed** agg.; in: thuj↓
      - **stitching** pain: thuj
    - **burning**: form sacch-a fd2.de•
    - **sprained**; as if: aloe
    - **stitching** pain: alum form kali-n h2 kali-p fd1.de• sacch-a fd2.de•
    - **tearing** pain: kali-i
  - **aching**: calc carb-ac coc-c conv br1 ger-i rly4• graph *Kali-c* mag-c phys tung-met bdx1•
  - **alternating** with | **Heart**; pain in: *(↗CHEST - Pain - heart - alternating - toe)* nat-p
  - **bed** agg.; in: aloe↓ jug-r↓
    - **sprained**; as if: aloe jug-r
  - **boring** pain: agar aur-m-n ind **Led** *Nux-m* *Ran-s* *Sil* symph fd3.de•
  - **burning**: aesc am-c ant-c ars benz-ac borx *Cimic* *Colch* con form lachn ph-ac plat h2 *Ran-s* ruta h1 thal-xyz srj8• vanil fd5.de verat viol-t k*
    - **frostbitten**; as if: zinc h2
    - **pressing** pain: viol-t k*
  - **burnt**; sensation as if: caust h2
  - **cold applications** | **amel.**: sabin
  - **cutting** pain: alum ant-c aster bg2 aur-m-n con ger-i rly4• ph-ac h2 sang sphing kk3.fr stry sulph
    - **jerking** pain: ph-ac h2
    - **rhythmical**: ant-c
  - **dinner**; after: mag-s↓
    - **stitching** pain: mag-s
  - **dislocated**; as if: *Am-c* b4a.de arn b7a.de aur b4a.de
  - **drawing** pain: agar h2 *Ant-c* k* aur bry k* caust k* chel k* colch k* coloc k* com k* con k* cycl k* jatr-c kali-bi nat-m k* nat-sil fd3.de• plat k* plb k* rhus-t k* sars k* sep h2 sulph k* *Thuj* k* vanil fd5.de
    - **cramping**: plat
    - **paralyzed**; as if: aur
    - **upward**: bry k*
  - **frostbitten**; as if: bry phos
  - **gnawing** pain: kali-c h2 *Ran-s* k* symph fd3.de•
  - **gouty**: ant-c↓ benz-ac↓
    - **tearing** pain: ant-c benz-ac
  - **hiccoughs**, from: ph-ac
  - **hot**: thuj↓
    - **stitching** pain: thuj
  - **increasing** and decreasing gradually: am-m↓
    - **stitching** pain: am-m k*
  - **jerking** pain: agar
  - **lightning**-like: daph thal-xyz srj8•
  - **long**: arn↓ caust↓
    - **stitching** pain: arn k* caust k*
  - **lying** | **amel.**: puls
  - **lying** down agg.; after: *Nux-m*↓
    - **boring** pain: *Nux-m*
  - **motion**:
    - **agg.**: aster caust↓ chin mosch↓ phos↓ sabin
      - **drawing** pain: caust k*
      - **sprained**; as if: mosch
      - **stitching** pain: phos h2
    - **amel.**: bapt hr1 cocc↓ dros↓ ind plb↓
      - **drawing** pain: plb k*
      - **tearing** pain: cocc dros plb
  - **neuralgic**: phyt thal-xyz srj8•
  - **pinching** pain: meph
  - **pressing** pain: arg-met h1 borx h2 carb-ac coloc cycl gins graph h2 jatr-c kali-s fd4.de lap-la sde8.de• **Led** *Nat-s* *Plat* rhus-t h1 sep sulph
    - **bandaged**; as if tightly: *Plat*
  - **pressure** agg.: *Hep*↓ nat-s↓ ruta↓
    - **stitching** pain: *Hep* nat-s
    - **tearing** pain: ruta

Extremities

- **First**: ...
  - **pulsative**: asaf ketogl-ac rly4•
  - **rest** agg.: ind↓
    - **boring** pain: ind
  - **rheumatic**: am-be bro1 apoc arn bro1 bapt hr1 *Benz-ac* bro1 borx bro1 both bro1 cinnb *Colch* bro1 conv bro1 crot-t gnaph bro1 hyper↓ kali-c bro1 *Led* k* ol-an rhod bro1 sabin sil bro1
    - **right**: *Benz-ac* bry cist lac-c
    - **left**: agn *Led*
    - **stitching** pain: hyper
    - **tearing** pain: crot-t
  - **rubbing**:
    - **amel.**: nat-c↓
      - **tearing** pain: nat-c h2
  - **shooting** pain: alum daph pip-m sulph tarent
  - **sitting** agg.: agar↓ *Am-m*↓ *Con*↓ graph↓ mag-m↓ nat-m↓ par↓ sabin↓ sil↓ symph↓
    - **drawing** pain: agar h2
    - **stitching** pain: *Con* graph nat-m sabin sil h2 symph fd3.de•
    - **tearing** pain: agar *Am-m* con h2 mag-m h2 par
  - **sore**: alum *Arn* *Bry* clem h2 ger-i rly4• *Nat-c* *Sulph*
  - **spinning**; while: mur-ac↓
    - **tearing** pain: mur-ac h2
  - **sprained**; as if: aloe *Arn* jug-r lyc mez mosch sil
  - **stamping** amel.: caps↓
    - **stitching** pain: caps
  - **standing** agg.: *Am-m*↓ con↓ nat-m↓ rhus-t↓ sil↓
    - **stitching** pain: am-m nat-m h2 rhus-t h1 sil
    - **tearing** pain: *Am-m* con nat-m
  - **stepping** agg.: alum↓ asaf↓ *Aur-m*↓ berb↓ borx↓ sil↓
    - **cutting** pain: alum h2
    - **pressing** pain: borx h2
    - **stitching** pain: asaf *Aur-m* berb
    - **ulcerative** pain: sil
  - **stitching** pain: agar agn alum alumn am-c am-m ammc arn ars *Asaf* aster *Aur-m* bamb-a stb2.de• bar-c *Benz-ac* k* *Berb* bov bry calc calc-sil k2 *Cann-i* caps carb-v carl castm *Caust* chel *Cist* coloc crot-t daph dulc fd4.de euphr ferr-ma form gamb gins graph *Hep* hura hyper jatr-c *Kali-c* kali-n kali-s fd4.de kali-sil k2 *Kalm* kola stb3• lach laur *Led* *Lyc* mag-c mag-s merl nat-m nat-s nit-ac nit-s-d bg ph-ac phos pip-m puls h1 *Ran-s* k* rat rhus-t ros-d wla1 ruta fd4.de sabin sang sep h2 *Sil* sphing kk3.fr spong fd4.de sul-ac sulph symph fd3.de• tarax tarent thuj tritic-vg fd5.de verat zinc
    - **alternating** with | **Thumb**; stitching in (See thumbs - stitching - alternating - toe)
    - **boring** pain: sabin
    - **burning**: alum berb *Caust* k* mag-c plat h2 tarax h1
    - **crawling**: berb plat h2
    - **cutting** pain: sil
    - **drawing** pain: bry
    - **fine**: am-m h2* caust k* kali-c led mag-s rhus-t sulph
    - **frostbitten**; as if: *Nit-ac* zinc h2
    - **needles**; as from: ulm-c jsj8•
    - **paroxysmal**: lyc
    - **prickling** pain: sul-ac h2 zinc
    - **pulsating** pain: berb hep
    - **splinters**; as from: agar coc-c
    - **tearing** pain: am-c symph fd3.de•
    - **tickling** like electric shocks: sabin
    - **twitching**: berb hell h1 kali-n
    - **upward**: benz-ac *Hep*
  - **sudden**: bry coc-c↓ lyc↓ nat-m↓ nat-s↓ sacch-a↓
    - **drawing** pain: coc-c k*
    - **sprained**; as if: lyc
    - **stitching** pain: lyc nat-m nat-s sacch-a fd2.de•

- **First**: ...
  - **tearing** pain: agar am-c *Am-m* anac *Ant-c* arg-met h1 aur-m bar-c *Benz-ac* calc calc-sil k2 carb-an carbn-s caust cic coc-c cocc con crot-t dulc graph hep indg kali-bi *Kali-c* kali-i kali-n kali-sil k2 lachn lyc mag-c mag-m mag-s merc merl mez mur-ac nat-c nat-m ol-an par plat plb rat ruta sang sars sep *Sil* *Sulph* symph fd3.de• tarent tep thuj *Zinc*
    - **burning**: con rat ruta h1
    - **drawing** pain: agar h2 kali-bi mez sars h2
    - **paroxysmal**: merc
    - **pulsating** pain: dulc
    - **sticking** pain: berb symph fd3.de• zinc
    - **twitching**: am-m h2 brom
    - **ulcerative** pain: ol-an k* plat
  - **touch** agg.: arg-met↓ chin lyc bg1 *Mang* k* nux-v bg1 ph-ac h2* plb hr1 sabin tarent bg1
    - **cutting** pain: ph-ac h2
    - **tearing** pain: arg-met
  - **ulcerative** pain: am-c caust nat-c ol-an k* zinc
  - **walking** agg.: alum↓ alumn↓ am-m↓ aur↓ aur-m↓ borx↓ brach↓ bry↓ calc-p↓ chin↓ con↓ euphr↓ hep↓ kali-s↓ **Led**↓ mag-m↓ nat-m↓ phos↓ pip-m↓ **Sil**↓ tarax↓
    - **burning**: borx brach
    - **cutting** pain: alum aur-m
    - **stitching** pain: alumn am-m euphr kali-s fd4.de nat-m h2 phos tarax
    - **tearing** pain: con hep mag-m nat-m
    - **ulcerative** pain: aur bry calc-p chin **Led** pip-m **Sil**
  - **warm** bed agg.: *Am-c*
  - **weather** agg.; wet: am-c
  - **extending** to:
    - **Ankles**: bov↓
      - **stitching** pain: bov
    - **Chest**: rhus-t↓
      - **stitching** pain: rhus-t k*
    - **Heel**: alum↓ nat-c↓
      - **cutting** pain: alum
      - **tearing** pain: nat-c
    - **Hip**: *Hep*↓
      - **stitching** pain: *Hep*
    - **Knee**: merc↓
      - **tearing** pain: merc
- **Balls**: agar↓ alum↓ am-c ambr ant-c↓ borx↓ *Bry* *Cann-i*↓ *Caust*↓ *Colch* k* con↓ dros↓ *Kali-c*↓ **Led** lyc↓ mag-m↓ mur-ac↓ petr↓ ph-ac↓ phos↓ pic-ac↓ plb gk rhus-t↓ tab visc↓ zinc↓
  - **burning**: ant-c *Caust* *Kali-c* zinc h2
  - **drawing** pain: am-c h2 petr h2
  - **pressing** pain: borx h2 *Caust* lyc h2 petr h2
  - **sore**: **Led** lyc pic-ac
  - **stitching** pain: alum am-c ambr h1 *Cann-i* *Caust* k* *Kali-c* h2 mag-m h2* mur-ac h2 ph-ac h2 phos h2 rhus-t h1 visc c1 zinc h2
  - **tearing** pain: agar h2 caust h2 con h2 dros h1 petr h2 ph-ac h2
  - **walking** agg.: lyc↓
    - **sore**: lyc h2
- **Extensor** muscle: nat-c↓
  - **tearing** pain: nat-c h2
- **Joints**: *Apoc* *Arn*↓ asaf↓ aster aur↓ *Benz-ac* berb↓ bry↓ calc↓ *Cann-i* carb-v *Caust* choc↓ *Cimic*↓ coff *Coloc*↓ dulc *Eup-per* ger-i↓ ind *Iris* kali-bi↓ kali-p↓ kola stb3• **Led** lob-s↓ nat-m↓ nat-s ph-ac↓ phos plb gk prun rat↓ rhod↓ ruta fd4.de sabin sang sep↓ sil spong fd4.de *Stann*↓ *Sulph*↓ syc bka1• symph↓ tritic-vg↓ upa vanil fd5.de
  - **afternoon**: sulph↓
    - **drawing** pain: sulph
  - **aching**: *Cann-i* choc srj3• cimic ger-i rly4• nat-s
  - **boring** pain: ind nat-s
  - **burning**: *Cimic* ph-ac
  - **drawing** pain: led k* nat-s k* *Sulph* k* vanil fd5.de

- **First – Joints**: ...
  - **gouty**: acon b7.de* agar b4a.de am-c b4a.de*•ambr k* ammc apis bg2 apoc-a vh *Arn* k* ars k* asaf k* aster bell bg2 *Benz-ac* *Bry* k* calc *Calc-p* canth bg2 carb-v b4a.de* *Caust* k* *Cimic* con b4a.de* *Dulc* elat eup-per k2 *Gnaph* k* graph b4a.de* guaj b4a.de* hep b4a.de kalm **Led** k* **Lyc** k* m-ambo b7.de mosch b7.de* *Nux-v* b7.de* olnd b7.de* par b7.de* ph-ac b4a.de* phos plat plb gk ran-b b7.de* ran-s b7.de* ruta fd4.de *Sabin* k* sep b4a.de* *Sil* k* squil b7.de* staph b7.de* sul-ac b4a.de sulph k* *Tarax* b7.de* thuj b4a.de* *Verat* b7.de* zinc
    - **left**: ammc apoc-a vh ruta fd4.de
  - **pressing** pain: asaf *Caust* *Coloc* **Led** nat-s rhod
  - **shooting** pain: *Cann-i* kali-bi *Stann*
  - **sore**: aur h2 bry ger-i rly4• lob-s nat-m h2
  - **sprained**; as if: *Arn* prun rat
  - **stitching** pain: *Benz-ac* berb calc h2 *Cann-i* kali-bi kali-p fd1.de• *Led* nat-m h2 nat-s sep h2 sil spong fd4.de stann symph fd3.de• tritic-vg fd5.de
  - **extending** to:
    - **Limbs**; up: cimic ↓
      - **aching**: cimic
  - **Proximal**: con ↓
    - **tearing** pain: con h2
- **Nails**: agar ↓ coc-c ↓ colch ↓ *Graph* ↓ hep ↓ kali-c ↓ kola ↓ lyc ↓ **Nit-ac** ↓ *Sil* ↓ sulph ↓ teucr ↓ *Thuj* ↓
  - **night**:
    - **bed** agg.; in: sulph ↓
      - **shooting** pain: sulph
  - **flesh**; as if nail would enter in: colch *Graph* kali-c teucr
  - **inflamed**; as if: lyc *Sil*
  - **shooting** pain: sulph
  - **splinter**; as from a: agar **Nit-ac**
  - **stitching** pain: coc-c kola stb3• *Sil* sulph *Thuj*
  - **tearing** pain: colch hep *Thuj*
  - **torn** out; as if nail would be: thuj
  - **Along** the side of the toe nail: lavand-a ctl1•
  - **Roots** of nails: calc-p ↓
    - **aching**: calc-p
  - **Under**: *Agar* cain ↓ calc ↓ caust ↓ coc-c ↓ iod ↓ nat-sil ↓ **Nit-ac** *Sil* spong fd4.de *Sulph* vanil fd5.de zinc ↓
    - **left**: coloc ↓ lachn ↓
      - **burning**: lachn c1
      - **tearing** pain: coloc h2
    - **burning**: calc h2 *Nit-ac* vanil fd5.de
    - **pressing** pain: calc h2
    - **stitching** pain: cain caust k* coc-c iod h nat-sil fd3.de•
    - **tearing** pain: iod h zinc h2
- **Tips**: arn ↓ asaf aur-m-n ↓ bar-c ↓ berb bism ↓ bry ↓ calc carl ↓ caust ↓ coc-c ↓ colch ↓ *Con* ↓ **Kali-c** ↓ kali-s ↓ *Led* ↓ mez ↓ nat-s ↓ olnd ↓ par ↓ *Ran-s* ↓ sars ↓ sep ↓ spong fd4.de stann ↓ staph ↓ sulph ↓ zinc ↓
  - **burning**: calc con mez h2 olnd staph h1
  - **drawing** pain: bar-c k*
  - **pressing** pain: bism h1 kali-s fd4.de
  - **shooting** pain: stann
  - **sitting** agg.: *Con* ↓
    - **stitching** pain: *Con*
  - **sore**: zinc
  - **stitching** pain: aur-m-n bar-c h2 bry carl coc-c colch *Con* kali-c h2 *Led* mez nat-s olnd par *Ran-s* sep spong fd4.de stann staph h1 sulph zinc
    - **burning**: sep
    - **pulsating** pain: mez h2 spong fd4.de zinc
  - **tearing** pain: arn bar-c bism caust **Kali-c** sars h2 zinc h2
- **Fourth**: agar ↓ asc-t berb ↓ brom calc-s carb-v ↓ chel colch ↓ dios dros ↓ fl-ac form gamb ↓ mag-c ↓ merc-i-f mez ↓ mur-ac nat-s ↓ ph-ac ↓ ran-b ↓ rhus-t ↓ tarax ↓ thuj ↓
  - **left**: asc-t a1
  - **drawing** pain: colch k* tarax h1
- **Fourth**: ...
  - **pinching** pain: ph-ac h2
  - **pressing** pain: ph-ac
  - **pulsating** pain: mur-ac
  - **sore**: dios
  - **sprained**; as if: berb
  - **stitching** pain: agar berb chel dros h1 mez nat-s ran-b rhus-t thuj
    - **twinging**, drawing: berb
  - **tearing** pain: carb-v gamb mag-c
  - **extending** to | **Hip**: gard-j vlr2•
- **Joints**: agn ↓ all-s ↓ ambr arg-met ↓ *Arn* asaf ↓ *Aur* ↓ berb ↓ bry ↓ *Camph* ↓ *Cann-i* ↓ *Caust* ↓ *Colch* coloc ↓ con fic-m gya1 graph ham ↓ kali-c k2 kali-s fd4.de *Led* nat-s ↓ nat-sil fd3.de• plb positr nl2• puls ↓ rhod mrr1 ruta fd4.de *Sabin* sang sil ↓ spong fd4.de stront-c ↓ *Sulph* symph fd3.de• teucr ↓ tritic-vg ↓ upa vanil fd5.de verat ↓
  - **left**: cann-i ↓
    - **shooting** pain: cann-i c1
  - **burning**: berb
  - **drawing** pain: aur k* berb k* sabin k* sil k* verat k*
  - **gouty**: ambr b7.de* arn asaf calc k2 calc-p k2 *Caust* *Dulc* graph k* kali-bi bg2 lyc mrr1 *Mang* hr1 nat-p mrr1 plb gk positr nl2• ran-s ruta fd4.de *Sabin* spong fd4.de staph gk sulph thuj
    - **right**: *Lyc* mrr1
  - **pressing** pain: coloc con led h1 nat-s
  - **shooting** pain: *Cann-i*
  - **sore**: *Camph* kali-c k2 puls
  - **sprained**; as if: all-s bry
  - **stepping** agg.: borx
  - **stitching** pain: asaf berb cann-i ham fd3.de• kali-s fd4.de led bg2 ruta fd4.de spong fd4.de tritic-vg fd5.de
  - **tearing** pain: agn b7.de* arg-met b7a.de *Aur* b4a.de *Caust* bg2 kali-c b4a.de sabin b7.de* stront-c b4a.de teucr b7.de*
  - **walking** agg.: petr ↓
    - **sprained**; as if: petr h2
  - **weather** agg.; cold: calc-p k2
  - **Small** joints: caul
- **Nails**: ant-c bro1 ars-h ↓ *Camph* ↓ *Carb-v* ↓ caust coc-c ↓ *Fl-ac* bro1 *Graph* hep bro1 hura m-ambo ↓ m-aust b7a.de merc-sul mosch ↓ nit-ac bro1 nux-v ↓ sars ↓ *Sil* ↓ *Sulph* ↓ syc pte1*• *Teucr* k* thuj ↓
  - **jerking** pain: mosch b7a.de
  - **pressing** pain: m-ambo b7.de sars h2
  - **sore**: m-ambo b7.de m-aust b7.de*
  - **splinter**; as from a: ars-h coc-c *Nit-ac* *Sil* *Sulph*
  - **tearing** pain: *Camph* *Carb-v* caust graph hep hura thuj
  - **ulcerative** pain: m-ambo b7.de mosch b7a.de nux-v b7.de
  - **walking** agg.: camph
    - **tearing** pain: *Camph*
  - **Roots** of nails: *Asaf* ↓ nat-m ↓
    - **burning**: *Asaf* k*
    - **stitching** pain: nat-m a1
  - **Under**: ant-c ↓ camph b7a.de carb-v bg2 caust k* *Eos* ↓ eup-per fl-ac bg2 **Graph** bg2 hep k* kali-c bg2 merc k* nat-sil fd3.de• *Sep* c2 *Sil* k* teucr ↓ thuj
    - **burning**: *Eos* br1
    - **cutting** pain: sil h2
    - **fever**; during intermittent: eup-per
    - **splinter**; as from a: fl-ac bro1
    - **ulcerative** pain: ant-c bro1 graph bro1 teucr bro1
- **Second**: berb bry canth ↓ carb-v ↓ caust ↓ cham ↓ colch ↓ coloc dros ↓ dulc fd4.de fl-ac ham ↓ kali-i ↓ kali-n ↓ *Led* ↓ lyc ↓ mur-ac nat-s plb ↓ rat ↓ ruta fd4.de sacch-a ↓ spig ↓
  - **right**: zinc ↓
    - **tearing** pain: zinc h2
  - **drawing** pain: caust k* colch k* plb k*
  - **stitching** pain: canth cham dros h1 dulc fd4.de ham fd3.de• kali-n h2 *Led* sacch-a fd2.de• spig
  - **tearing** pain: canth carb-v dulc kali-i lyc plb rat
    - **pulsating** pain: dulc

Extremities

- **Second**: ...
  - **Balls**: puls↓
    - **burning**: puls h1
    - **stitching** pain: puls h1
  - **Joints**: berb↓ stront-c↓
    - **tearing** pain: berb stront-c
  - **Nails**: bamb-a↓
    - **stitching** pain: bamb-a stb2.de•
- **Spots**; in: ph-ac↓
  - **sore**: ph-ac
- **Third**: agar↓ aloe ambr↓ asaf↓ berb bry↓ carb-v↓ chel colch↓ dros↓ fl-ac form kali-s↓ kola stb3• *Led*↓ lyc↓ mag-m mez↓ mur-ac nat-s↓ rat↓ ruta fd4.de sacch-a↓ sal-fr↓ sep↓ spong fd4.de sulph↓ thuj
  - **morning**: mag-m
  - **drawing** pain: colch k* sacch-a fd2.de•
  - **pulsating** pain: mur-ac
  - **sore**: mez h2
  - **stitching** pain: agar asaf chel dros kali-s fd4.de *Led* nat-s sacch-a fd2.de• sal-fr sle1• sep spong fd4.de sulph
  - **tearing** pain: ambr bry carb-v lyc mez rat
  - **ulcerative** pain: berb
  - **Nail**; under: ars-h↓
    - **splinter**; as from a: ars-h
- **Tips**: am-c↓ *Am-m* b7a.de aur↓ aur-m-n↓ bamb-a↓ berb↓ *Camph*↓ caps↓ caust↓ chin↓ con↓ dig↓ fl-ac↓ kali-c ptk1 led↓ merc↓ merl↓ mez↓ mosch↓ *Mur-ac*↓ nat-s↓ nit-s-d↓ olnd↓ puls↓ ran-b↓ sars↓ stry↓ sulph↓ zinc ptk1
  - **morning**: bamb-a↓
    - **stitching** pain: bamb-a stb2.de•
  - **evening**: am-m↓ puls↓ ran-b↓
    - **shooting** pain: am-m
    - **sore**: ran-b
    - **stitching** pain: am-m puls ran-b
  - **aching**: zinc ptk1
  - **burning**: *Mur-ac* k* sars
  - **crushed**; as if: caust bg2
  - **lying** agg.: sulph↓
    - **stitching** pain: sulph
  - **pressing** pain: led mosch
  - **shooting** pain: *Am-m* aur bg2
  - **sitting** agg.: aur-m-n↓ sulph↓
    - **stitching** pain: aur-m-n sulph
  - **sleep**; when falling asleep: merl↓
    - **stitching** pain: merl
  - **sore**: con h2 zinc bg1
  - **stitching** pain: am-c k* am-m k* aur-m-n bamb-a stb2.de• berb caps k* chin k* dig fl-ac k* kali-c merc merl k* mez k* nat-s k* nit-s-d bg olnd b7.de* puls k* ran-b bg2* stry sulph k*
    - **boring** pain: chin h1
    - **outward**: caps h1
  - **tearing** pain: **Am-m** k* *Camph*
  - **walking** in open air agg.: am-m↓
    - **stitching** pain: am-m
- **Toenails** agg.; touching: lac-del↓
  - **pulsating** pain: lac-del hrn2•
- **Under**: alum↓ con↓ symph↓
  - **burning**: alum h2 con h2 symph fd3.de•

- **Upper arms**: abrot acon↓ act-sp↓ aesc↓ agar b4.de* *Agn*↓ all-c↓ allox↓ aloe↓ *Alum*↓ alum-p↓ alum-sil↓ alumn am-c↓ *Am-m*↓ ambr↓ ammc↓ **Anac** anag androc srj1• ang ant-c ant-t↓ anthraq↓ apis k* aran arg-met arg-n arn↓ **Ars**↓ ars-h ars-i ars-met arum-t↓ asaf asar↓ aspar aster↓ aur aur-ar↓ aur-m↓ aur-m-n↓ aur-s k2 bamb-a stb2.de• *Bar-c* k* **Bell** berb bism↓ borx↓ bov brach bry k* bufo↓ cact calam sa3• calc calc-act↓ calc-p↓ calc-sil k2 camph↓ cann-s↓ canth caps↓ carb-ac↓ carb-an↓ *Carb-v*↓ *Carbn-s*↓ card-m cass a1 castm↓ caust gm1 cedr↓ cham chel chim *Chin* chinin-ar↓ chinin-s cic cimic↓ *Cina*↓ cinnb clem coc-c↓ *Cocc* b7a.de coff↓ colch coloc↓ com↓ con↓ conch↓ corn-f↓ corv-cor↓ cot↓ croc↓ crot-h crot-t cupr↓ *Cycl* cypra-eg sde6.de• cystein-l↓ dig↓ dros b7.de* dulc elaps↓ euon **Eup-per**↓ euph euphr↓ eupi *Ferr* ferr-ar↓ ferr-i ferr-ma↓ ferr-p k2 fic-m gya1 fl-ac form gaba↓ galeoc-c-h↓ gels gins↓ granit-m↓ graph↓ *Grat*↓ *Guaj*↓ ham hell↓ *Hep*↓ hipp↓ hura↓ hyos↓ hyper↓ ign k* ina-i mlk9.de ind↓ *Indg*↓ *Iod* iodof a1 ip↓ iris jal jatr-c↓ *Kali-ar*↓ kali-bi *Kali-c* *Kali-n*↓ kali-p kali-s fd4.de kali-sil↓ *Kalm* kreos↓ lac-c↓ lach lachn↓ lact↓ lat-h bnm5• laur↓ led k* lil-t lob↓ lyc *Lyss*↓ m-aust↓ mag-c *Mag-m*↓ *Mag-p* mag-s↓ manc↓ *Mang* medul-os-si↓ melal-alt↓ meny↓ *Merc*↓ merc-i-f merc-i-r↓ merl↓ mez k* morg-p pte1• mosch mur-ac murx musca-d↓ myric↓ nat-ar nat-c nat-m nat-p↓ **Nat-s**↓ nat-sil fd3.de• nicc↓ nit-ac nit-s-d↓ nux-m *Nux-v*↓ ol-an↓ olnd↓ osm ox-ac↓ ozone↓ paeon par↓ petr↓ petr-ra↓ *Ph-ac*↓ phel↓ phos phyt plan↓ *Plat*↓ plb plumbg podo fd3.de• pot-e↓ propr sa3• psor↓ *Puls* k* pyrid↓ *Ran-b*↓ ran-s↓ *Rat*↓ rheum↓ *Rhod* *Rhus-t* rhus-v↓ rumx↓ ruta fd4.de sabad sabin sacch-a↓ sal-fr↓ samb↓ *Sang* sanic↓ sarr *Sars*↓ sec↓ *Sep*↓ sil sin-n↓ spect↓ spig↓ spong fd4.de squil↓ **Stann**↓ *Staph* stram↓ stront-c↓ stry sul-ac↓ sul-i↓ sulph sumb symph↓ tarax tarent tep ter↓ teucr↓ ther↓ thuj tritic-vg fd5.de urt-u *Valer*↓ vanil fd5.de *Verat* verat-v vesp ptk2 vinc↓ xan zinc b4.de* zinc-p↓ [heroin sdj2]
  - **right**: acon↓ arg-met↓ arg-n↓ bamb-a↓ **Bell**↓ canth carc↓ cassia-s ccrh1• *Caust*↓ cinnb↓ coc-c↓ *Cocc*↓ coloc↓ conch↓ crot-h *Cycl* dulc↓ eupi ferr-i k2 ferr-p k2 fl-ac fum rly1• galeoc-c-h↓ ign↓ kali-p↓ melal-alt gya4 merc-i-f↓ ozone sde2• petr↓ podo fd3.de• *Ran-b*↓ sil↓ staph↓ symph↓ tax↓ tritic-vg fd5.de
    - **aching**: galeoc-c-h gms1•
    - **boring** pain: bamb-a stb2.de• merc-i-f
    - **drawing** pain: arg-met arg-n k* **Bell** carc fd2.de• *Caust* coloc k* ferr-p kali-p fd1.de• staph h1 symph fd3.de•
    - **gnawing** pain: canth k*
    - **jerking** pain: sil h2
    - **pressing** pain: cassia-s ccrh1• *Cycl* dulc fd4.de ozone sde2• symph fd3.de•
    - **shooting** pain: acon bg1
    - **sore**: cinnb [tax jsj7]
    - **stitching** pain: caust *Cocc* conch fkr1* tritic-vg fd5.de
    - **tearing** pain: canth coc-c eupi ign petr h2 *Ran-b*
    - **Humerus**: bry↓ gels↓ phyt↓
      - **aching**: bry ptk1 gels ptk1 phyt ptk1
  - **left**: *Agar*↓ alum↓ *Am-m*↓ *Arg-n* hr1 *Asaf*↓ aur↓ bamb-a stb2.de• bov↓ carbn-s↓ cartl-s rly4• cass a1 caust↓ cina↓ colch↓ coloc↓ dulc fd4.de *Ferr*↓ flor-p↓ hydrog↓ kali-s fd4.de kola stb3• marb-w es1• melal-alt gya4 mez↓ nat-sil fd3.de• nux-m hr1 ozone↓ petr-ra↓ puls↓ rhus-g↓ **RHUS-T** k ● ruta↓ spong fd4.de sulph↓ symph↓ tarax↓ tritic-vg fd5.de ven-m↓ xan↓
    - **aching**: hydrog srj2• melal-alt gya4
    - **burning**: hydrog srj2•
    - **cramping**: cina tl1
    - **cutting** pain: colch rsj2•
    - **drawing** pain: *Agar* alum coloc dulc fd4.de flor-p rsj3• ruta fd4.de
    - **dull** pain: colch rsj2• ven-m rsj12•
    - **gnawing** pain: *Ferr*
    - **pressing** pain: *Asaf* carbn-s kali-s fd4.de symph fd3.de• tarax h1
    - **shooting** pain: mez bg1 rhus-t bg1
    - **sore**: ozone sde2• sulph h2
    - **stinging**: rhus-g tmo3•
    - **stitching** pain: kali-s fd4.de petr-ra shn4• *Rhus-t* h1 xan c1
    - **tearing** pain: agar *Am-m* aur h2 bov caust puls
    - **warm** applications:
      - **amel.**: flor-p↓
        - **drawing** pain: flor-p rsj3•
    - **extending** to:
      - **First** finger: psil ft1
      - **Forearm**: psil ft1
  - **daytime**: coloc↓
    - **drawing** pain: coloc k*
  - **morning**: ambr↓ ars-i bov↓ chel con↓ dulc fd4.de euph eupi↓ fl-ac↓ ham↓ kali-s↓ lyc mag-s↓ mez rhus-t spong fd4.de sulph↓ vanil↓ zinc↓
    - **6 h**: bry↓
      - **tearing** pain: bry

- **morning**: ...
  - **bed** agg.; in: euph↓
    - **aching**: euph
    - **pressing** pain: euph$_{h2}$
  - **boring** pain: mez
  - **drawing** pain: lyc$_{k*}$ vanil$_{fd5.de}$
  - **pressing** pain: con$_{h2}$ fl-ac kali-s$_{fd4.de}$ mez$_{k*}$
  - **rising** agg.; after: dulc
  - **sore**: bov ham
  - **stitching** pain: zinc
  - **tearing** pain: ambr$_{a1}$ eupi mag-s spong$_{fd4.de}$ sulph$_{k*}$
  - **waking**; on: agar↓ ars-s-r euph↓ kali-c↓ melal-alt↓ mez spong$_{fd4.de}$
    - **boring** pain: mez
    - **drawing** pain: agar kali-c
    - **pressing** pain: euph mez$_{k*}$
    - **shooting** pain: melal-alt$_{gya4}$
- **forenoon**: agar alum↓ bov chel↓ com dulc↓ symph↓
  - **11** h: bry↓
    - **tearing** pain: bry
  - **aching**: com
  - **drawing** pain: agar com dulc$_{fd4.de}$
  - **tearing** pain: agar alum chel symph$_{fd3.de•}$
- **noon**: nicc↓ sulph
  - **lying** down agg.; after: *Rhus-t*
  - **tearing** pain: nicc
- **afternoon**: abrot bov↓ canth↓ dulc$_{fd4.de}$ fl-ac form↓ nat-s↓ phos ruta$_{fd4.de}$ stry thuj↓ vanil↓
  - **13** h | **riding** agg.: hydr
  - **14** h: **Rhus-t**
  - **15** h: dios phos **Rhus-t** sarr
  - **stitching** pain: form vanil$_{fd5.de}$
  - **tearing** pain: bov canth nat-s thuj
- **evening**: agar↓ alum↓ anac bamb-a$_{stb2.de•}$ calc↓ chin chinin-s↓ clem↓ colch com↓ con↓ elaps↓ fic-m$_{gya1}$ kali-bi kali-c↓ kali-p↓ lyc↓ ox-ac sars↓ spong$_{fd4.de}$ stry sulph tritic-vg$_{fd5.de}$ zinc zing↓
  - **aching**: anac ox-ac
  - **amel.**: nat-s↓
    - **stitching** pain: nat-s
    - **tearing** pain: nat-s$_{k*}$
  - **bed** agg.; in: dulc fic-m$_{gya1}$ led lyc↓ staph↓
    - **drawing** pain: led lyc staph$_{h1}$
    - **pressing** pain: staph$_{h1}$
  - **drawing** pain: com$_{k*}$ kali-bi$_{k*}$ kali-p$_{fd1.de•}$ sulph$_{k*}$ zinc zing$_{k*}$
  - **lying** down:
    - **amel.**: am-m↓
      - **tearing** pain: am-m
  - **pressing** pain: anac$_{h2}$
  - **shooting** pain: sulph
  - **sitting** agg.: anac↓
    - **aching**: anac
  - **sore**: stry
  - **stitching** pain: calc elaps stry sulph
  - **tearing** pain: agar alum clem con$_{k*}$ kali-c lyc$_{k*}$ sars sulph$_{k*}$
  - **twinging**: chinin-s
  - **walking** in open air agg.: anac↓
    - **aching**: anac
- **night**: am-m↓ androc$_{srj1•}$ ars$_{k*}$ *Cact* cass$_{a1}$ *Castm* caust↓ cham crot-t dros$_{ptk}$ *Ferr* kola$_{stb3•}$ mang *Merc* nat-m nux-v *Phyt* puls ruta$_{fd4.de}$ *Sang* sep↓ stry sulph tritic-vg$_{fd5.de}$ vanil↓
  - **midnight**: sulph↓
    - **before**:
      - **23** h: am-m↓
        - **tearing** pain: am-m
    - **after**: carb-an↓
      - **3** h: nat-c↓
        - **tearing** pain: nat-c$_{h2}$
- **night – midnight – after**: ...
      - **4** h: rhus-t$_{hr1}$ verat
      - **tearing** pain: carb-an
    - **drawing** pain: sulph
  - **bed** agg.; in: arg-n↓ trios↓
    - **burning**: arg-n trios$_{rsj11•}$
  - **boring** pain: mang
  - **drawing** pain: *Ars*
  - **gnawing** pain: mang$_{h2}$
  - **lying** on upper arm agg.: nat-m
  - **sleep** agg.; during: sep
  - **sore**: sep$_{h2}$
  - **stitching** pain: caust vanil$_{fd5.de}$
  - **tearing** pain: am-m$_{h2}$ caust$_{h2}$
  - **warm** bed agg.: caust↓
    - **tearing** pain: caust$_{h2}$
  - **Side** not lain on: kali-bi↓ puls↓
    - **tearing** pain: kali-bi puls
- **aching**: abrot allox$_{sp1}$ anac arg-met arg-n calc cass$_{a1}$ chinin-ar$_{k2}$ cinnb com cupr **Eup-per** gaba$_{sa3•}$ galeoc-c-h$_{gms1•}$ gels kali-n kali-p led lob merc-i-r mez musca-d$_{szs1}$ paeon pot-e$_{rly4•}$ pyrid$_{rly4•}$ **Rhus-t** rumx sabad sabin stram tep vesp zinc [spect$_{dfg1}$]
- **air** agg.; draft of: ant-c↓
  - **drawing** pain: ant-c$_{h2}$
- **air**; in open:
  - **agg.**: calc↓
    - **tearing** pain: calc
  - **amel.**: sulph↓
    - **tearing** pain: sulph
- **ascending** stairs agg.: *Calc*↓
  - **sore**: *Calc*
- **bed** agg.; in: caust↓ con↓ dulc led *Lyc*↓ mag-s↓ *Rhus-t* spong$_{fd4.de}$ sulph↓ til↓
  - **tearing** pain: caust$_{k*}$ con$_{k*}$ *Lyc* mag-s spong$_{fd4.de}$ sulph$_{k*}$ til$_{k*}$
- **bending**:
  - **arms**:
    - **agg.**: anac↓ ant-c
      - **cutting** pain: anac
    - **backward** agg.: **Rhus-t** ulm-c$_{jsj8•}$
- **bent** agg.; while: rat↓
  - **tearing** pain: rat
- **biting**: canth$_{b7.de*}$ zinc$_{b4.de*}$
- **blow**; pain as from a: *Anac*$_{k*}$ bar-c$_{b4.de*}$ cina$_{b7.de*}$ cycl$_{b7.de*}$ hell$_{b7.de*}$ kreos$_{b7a.de}$ plat$_{b4.de*}$
- **boring** pain: act-sp$_{bg1}$ arg-met$_{b7.de*}$ asaf$_{b7.de*}$ aur aur-m-n bamb-a$_{stb2.de•}$ canth$_{k*}$ *Cina*$_{k*}$ *Mang*$_{k*}$ merc-i-f mez plb$_{b7.de*}$ rhus-t$_{b7.de*}$
- **break**; as if it would: borx cinnb
- **broken**; as if: cocc$_{k*}$ cupr$_{k*}$ samb$_{k*}$ sulph
- **burning**: *Agar*$_{k*}$ alum$_{k*}$ am-c$_{k*}$ arg-met$_{b7.de}$ arg-n arn asar$_{b7.de}$ berb borx$_{k*}$ carb-v$_{k*}$ carbn-s caust colch$_{k*}$ coloc$_{k*}$ dig$_{k*}$ dulc$_{k*}$ graph$_{k*}$ hura kali-bi kali-c$_{k*}$ kali-s$_{fd4.de}$ mang$_{k*}$ mur-ac$_{k*}$ nat-c nat-m$_{k*}$ nat-s nux-v$_{b7.de}$ ph-ac$_{k*}$ rhus-t sep$_{k*}$ sulph symph$_{fd3.de•}$ ther$_{ptk1}$ thuj tritic-vg$_{fd5.de}$ zinc$_{k*}$
  - **downward**: all-c
  - **externally**: fl-ac
- **burrowing**: cocc$_{bg2}$ mang$_{bg2}$ nat-m$_{h2*}$ stann$_{bg2}$
- **chill**:
  - **after**: ars-h
  - **during**: *Rhus-t*↓
    - **tearing** pain: *Rhus-t*
- **cold**:
  - **air** agg.: *Kalm*
  - **applications** | **agg.**: cassia-s$_{ccrh1•}$
- **cold** agg.; becoming: phos↓
  - **tearing** pain: phos

Extremities

- **contracting**: bism$_{a1}$ mez$_{h2}$
- **convulsions**; before epileptic: cupr↓
  - **drawing** pain: cupr
- **cough** agg.; during: alum↓
  - **tearing** pain: alum
- **cramping**: calc-act$_{h1}$ mez$_{h2}$ spong$_{fd4.de}$ symph$_{fd3.de}$•
- **cutting** pain: alum$_{bg2}$ anac bar-c caust$_{k*}$ *Chel* corv-cor$_{bdg}$• lac-c manc petr-ra$_{shn4}$• *Plat* spig$_{k*}$
- **dinner** | **after**:
    - **agg.**: canth↓ thuj↓ zinc↓
      - **sore**: thuj
      - **stitching** pain: canth zinc
  - **agg.**: canth↓
    - **drawing** pain: canth$_{k*}$
- **dislocated**; as if: alum$_{b4.de*}$ bry$_{b7.de*}$ caust$_{bg2}$ euph$_{b4.de*}$ rhod$_{bg2}$ thuj$_{b4a.de*}$
- **drawing** pain: acon$_{k*}$ *Agar*$_{k*}$ aloe alum$_{k*}$ alum-p$_{k2}$ alum-sil$_{k2}$ am-m$_{k*}$ anac$_{k*}$ ang$_{k*}$ ant-c$_{k*}$ ant-t$_{k*}$ apis$_{b7a.de}$ arg-met arg-n$_{k*}$ *Ars*$_{k*}$ ars-h asaf$_{k*}$ aster aur$_{k*}$ aur-m$_{k*}$ aur-m-n$_{k*}$ *Bell*$_{k*}$ *Berb*$_{k*}$ bism$_{bg2}$ *Bry* bufo *Calc*$_{k*}$ calc-sil$_{k2}$ camph$_{k*}$ canth$_{k*}$ carb-ac$_{k*}$ *Carb-v*$_{k*}$ carbn-s card-m *Caust*$_{k*}$ chel$_{a1}$ cina$_{b7.de*}$ clem$_{k*}$ coc-c$_{k*}$ cocc$_{k*}$ coloc$_{k*}$ com$_{k*}$ con$_{k*}$ dig$_{k*}$ *Dulc* ferr-ma$_{k*}$ ferr-p gins$_{k*}$ graph grat$_{k*}$ hep$_{k*}$ ign$_{b7.de*}$ indg$_{k*}$ ip$_{k*}$ kali-bi$_{k*}$ kali-c *Kali-n*$_{k*}$ lach$_{k*}$ lact$_{k*}$ led$_{k*}$ **Lyc**$_{k*}$ mag-c mag-m mang$_{k*}$ mez$_{k*}$ mosch$_{b7a.de}$ mur-ac$_{k*}$ nat-m$_{k*}$ nat-s$_{k*}$ nit-ac *Nux-v*$_{k*}$ ol-an$_{k*}$ olnd$_{b7.de*}$ par$_{k*}$ petr$_{k*}$ *Ph-ac*$_{k*}$ *Phos* phyt$_{k*}$ *Plat* plb$_{k*}$ puls$_{b7.de*}$ *Rhod*$_{k*}$ *Rhus-t*$_{k*}$ ruta$_{b7.de*}$ sabin$_{k*}$ sacch-a$_{fd2.de}$• sanic *Sep*$_{k*}$ *Sil*$_{k*}$ sin-n spig$_{b7.de*}$ spong$_{k*}$ *Stann*$_{k*}$ staph$_{b7.de*}$ stram$_{k*}$ sul-ac *Sulph*$_{k*}$ symph$_{fd3.de}$• *Thuj*$_{k*}$ *Valer*$_{k*}$ vanil$_{fd5.de}$ verat$_{b7.de*}$ vinc zinc$_{k*}$ zinc-p$_{k2}$
  - **cramping**: grat mag-c nat-m ruta$_{h1}$ *Valer*
  - **downward**: *Agar* anac berb carb-ac carb-v kali-bi lach *Lyc* sulph
  - **paralyzed**; as if: aloe arg-met arg-n **Bell** bry$_{k*}$ *Caust* chel$_{a1}$ cina$_{k*}$ cocc con$_{k*}$ kali-c *Phos* rhus-v sabin$_{k*}$ sep
  - **paroxysmal**: ant-t$_{k*}$ mag-c
  - **pulsating** pain: ign$_{k*}$
  - **sticking** pain: spong$_{k*}$
  - **upward**: ph-ac
- **eating**; after: cina↓ clem$_{a1*}$ ind$_{sma}$
  - **tearing** pain: cina$_{a1}$
- **electric** shocks; as from: agar$_{ptk1}$ tarax valer$_{ptk1}$
- **excitement**: coloc
- **exertion** agg.: **Rhus-t**↓
  - **tearing** pain: **Rhus-t**
- **exertion**; as after: grat$_{bg2}$ guaj$_{bg2}$ phos$_{bg2}$
- **extending** the arm: anac↓
  - **agg.**: ind↓ phyt$_{k*}$ plat$_{h2*}$
    - **sore**: (↗*stretching - arm - agg. - sore)* phyt
    - **stitching** pain: ind
  - **cutting** pain: anac
- **glands**, with swollen axillary: vesp$_{ptk2}$
- **gnawing** pain: canth$_{k*}$ ferr laur$_{k*}$ mang$_{k*}$ phos ran-s$_{b7.de*}$
- **grasping** pain: mag-c$_{bg2}$
- **griping**: mag-c$_{h2}$
- **hanging** down amel.: rat↓ *Rhus-t*↓
  - **tearing** pain: rat$_{k*}$ *Rhus-t*
- **heart** disease; in: cact symph$_{fd3.de}$•
- **holding** a book agg.: coc-c↓
  - **stitching** pain: coc-c
  - **tearing** pain: coc-c
- **increasing** and decreasing suddenly: stann↓
  - **tearing** pain: stann$_{h2}$
- **intermittent**: asaf led sars
- **jerking** pain: anac$_{k*}$ ant-c$_{b7.de*}$ arn$_{bg2}$ chin cupr$_{bg2}$ hell$_{bg2}$ kali-bi$_{k*}$ lact olnd$_{b7.de*}$ puls *Ran-b* rhus-t$_{k*}$ ruta$_{k*}$ sil tarax$_{k*}$ valer$_{k*}$
- **leaning** on it: am-m↓ carbn-s↓
- **leaning** on it: ...
  - **pressing** pain: am-m$_{h2}$ carbn-s
- **lifting**:
  - **after**: berb ozone$_{sde2}$•
  - **agg.**: nat-m↓
    - **sore**: nat-m$_{h2}$
- **lying**:
  - **side**; on | **painful** side:
      - **agg.**: *Mang*
        - **boring** pain: mang
    - **painless** side:
      - **amel.**: castm↓
        - **tearing** pain: castm
  - **upper** arm agg.; on: carb-an castm↓ *Nat-m*
    - **tearing** pain: carb-an castm
- **lying** down agg.; after: ip↓
  - **drawing** pain: ip
- **massage** | **amel.**: cassia-s$_{ccrh1}$•
- **menses**; during: berb
  - **pressing** pain: berb
- **motion**:
  - **agg.**: agn↓ anag ang↓ berb *Bry* bufo calc carb-v↓ cassia-s$_{ccrh1}$• caust$_{gm1}$ *Cocc Colch* coloc↓ crot-t *Cycl*↓ dulc$_{fd4.de}$ *Euph Ferr* ferr-p fl-ac grat↓ ham↓ iris *Kalm* lac-c *Led* mag-c *Merc* nat-c↓ nux-v phyt plan↓ plat↓ sabad sabin sep↓ *Sil*↓ spong$_{fd4.de}$ staph thuj↓ vanil$_{fd5.de}$
    - **aching**: sabad *Sabin*
    - **burning** | **pricking**: coloc
    - **cutting** pain: colch$_{rsj2}$•
    - **gnawing** pain: *Ferr*
    - **pressing** pain: agn$_{hr1}$ ang berb cassia-s$_{ccrh1}$• *Colch*$_{k*}$ fl-ac$_{k*}$ led *Sabin Staph*
    - **sore**: cocc *Cycl*$_{k*}$ grat ham nat-c plan plat sep
    - **stitching** pain: **Bry** caust
    - **tearing** pain: carb-v ferr ferr-p *Sil* spong$_{fd4.de}$ thuj
  - **amel.**: am-m↓ *Arg-met* aur↓ aur-m↓ aur-m-n camph↓ chin↓ cina coc-c↓ cocc con↓ cupr *Dulc* ignis-alc↓ kali-bi *Kali-c*↓ kali-p↓ *Lyc*↓ mang↓ meph mur-ac↓ ox-ac paeon psor↓ **Rhus-t** sabad↓ sars↓ staph↓ tarax↓ thuj *Valer*↓
    - **aching**: kali-p
    - **boring** pain: cina$_{k*}$ mang
    - **cutting** pain: ignis-alc$_{es2}$•
    - **drawing** pain: *Arg-met* aur camph coc-c$_{k*}$ cocc con$_{k*}$ *Valer*
    - **pinching** pain: cina
    - **pressing** pain: aur-m$_{h2}$ aur-m-n
    - **slow** motion: *Ferr*
    - **sore**: cupr kali-c *Lyc* mur-ac
    - **stitching** pain: chin *Cocc Kali-c* **Rhus-t** sabad tarax
    - **tearing** pain: am-m *Arg-met* coc-c con$_{k*}$ *Lyc (non:*mur-ac$_{kl}$) psor *Rhus-t* sars staph$_{h1}$ thuj valer
  - **arm**; of:
    - **amel.**: mur-ac↓ sulph↓
      - **tearing** pain: mur-ac$_{h2}$ sulph
    - **backward** and forward agg.: *Nat-m*↓
      - **sore**: *Nat-m*
  - **beginning** of:
    - **agg.**: mez↓
      - **pressing** pain: mez
  - **impossible**: spong↓ tep↓
    - **tearing** pain: spong$_{fd4.de}$ tep
- **neuralgic**: corn-f$_{br1}$ hyper kalm$_{sma}$ ter$_{sma}$
- **paralyzed**; as if: agar$_{bg2}$ aloe alum$_{k*}$ ambr$_{b7.de*}$ ant-c$_{b7.de*}$ arg-met arg-n asaf$_{b7.de*}$ *Bell*$_{k*}$ bism$_{b7.de*}$ bry caps$_{h1}$ caust$_{b4.de*}$ cham *Chel*$_{k*}$ *Chin*$_{k*}$ cina$_{k*}$ cocc$_{k*}$ con$_{k*}$ cycl$_{b7.de*}$ dig$_{b4.de*}$ dulc$_{b4.de*}$ *Ferr*$_{k*}$ kali-bi kali-c$_{bg2}$ kali-n$_{b4.de*}$ led$_{b7.de*}$ mez$_{b4.de*}$ mur-ac$_{k*}$ nat-sil$_{fd3.de}$• nit-ac *Nux-v*$_{b7.de*}$ *Phos* sabin$_{b7.de*}$ sep spong$_{fd4.de}$ stann$_{b4.de*}$ *Staph*$_{k*}$ teucr$_{b7.de*}$ thuj$_{k*}$ verat$_{b7.de*}$

- **paroxysmal**: bamb-a stb2.de• gels mur-ac ozone sde2•
- **periodical**: grat↓
  - **tearing** pain: grat
- **perspiration** | **amel.**: thuj
- **pinching** pain: ang bg2 arg-met (non:calc slp) calc-act slp caust bg2 cina form a1 kali-n k* kreos bg2 laur bg2 nat-c h2* nux-m k* olnd k* osm ph-ac k* plat a1 sabad bg2 sulph bg2
- **pressing** pain: acon k* *Agn* k* alum bg2 am-m b7.de* **Anac** k* ang b7.de* arg-met b7.de* arn b7.de* asaf k* **Aur** k* aur-m-n k* **Bell** k* berb k* bism k* bry k* *Calc* k* camph k* carbn-s *Caust* chel k* cic k* clem k* colch k* coloc k* con k* crot-t k* cupr k* *Cycl* k* dulc fd4.de euph k* fl-ac k* gins k* hell k* indg k* jatr-c kali-s fd4.de kalm k* laur bg2 *Led* k* **Mez** k* mosch k* mur-ac k* nat-s k* nit-s-d a1 nux-m k* petr k* ph-ac k* phos bg2 podo fd3.de• puls b7.de* rhod bg2 sabad b7.de* *Sabin* k* sacch-a fd2.de• sars k* spig b7.de* **Stann** k* *Staph* k* sulph bg2 symph fd3.de• tarax b7.de* teucr k* tritic-vg fd5.de zinc k*
  - **burrowing**: clem k*
  - **constricting** pain: coloc k*
  - **cramping**: anac h2 asaf
  - **intermittent**: anac h2 asaf k* led k*
  - **paralyzed**; as if: **Bell** k* bism k* chel k* mez h2 ph-ac h2 staph k*
  - **tearing** pain: arg-met h1 aur k* bell h1 camph h1 led h1 stann h2 thuj k*
  - **twisting**, as if: clem k*
- **pressure**:
  - **agg.**: *Arg-met*↓ berb calc phyt sil spig↓ tritic-vg fd5.de
    - **drawing** pain: *Arg-met* spig h1
  - **amel.**: ars sne bov cassia-s↓ cina↓ indg laur mag-c↓ ruta fd4.de
    - **drawing** pain: mag-c ruta fd4.de
    - **gnawing** pain: laur k*
    - **pressing** pain: cassia-s ccrh1•
    - **sore**: bov
    - **tearing** pain: cina indg
- **pulsating** pain: ign **Kali-c** mur-ac nat-m
- **putting** on coat agg.: bry chel rhus-t sang
- **putting** the arm across the back agg.: calc
- **raising** arm agg.: abies-c oss4• agar *Bar-c* k* *Bry* bufo calc *Calc-p* carb-an↓ cassia-s↓ caust↓ cocc colch *Ferr* grat↓ kali-c↓ kali-p k2 mag-c↓ nat-c nat-m nit-ac↓ olnd phos plan↓ plb *Rhus-t* *Sang* syph teucr zinc [heroin sdj2]
  - **broken**; as if: **Cocc**
  - **drawing** pain: *Rhus-t*
  - **sore**: cassia-s ccrh1• grat kali-c nat-m nit-ac plan
  - **sprained**; as if: *Rhus-t* hr1
  - **stitching** pain: agar bry caust
  - **tearing** pain: *Agar* carb-an *Ferr* mag-c
- **raw**; as if: graph bg2
- **rest**:
  - **amel.**: cassia-s ccrh1• colch↓
    - **cutting** pain: colch rsj2•
- **rheumatic**: alumn anac↓ *Ars* aspar bell-p sp1 bry calc calc-p carbn-s card-m↓ chel *Chim* coff *Colch* crot-t dulc **Ferr** *Ferr-i* ferr-p *Fl-ac* granit-m↓ hyos iod iris *Kalm* merc nat-m phos *Phyt* ptel *Rhod* **Rhus-t** **Sang** sanic↓ urt-u verat x-ray sp1 zinc
  - **left**: rhodi br1
  - **aching**: granit-m es1•
  - **drawing** pain: anac k* card-m chel k* dulc nat-m k* sanic
  - **tearing** pain: ferr-p nat-m
  - **extending** to | **Downward**: rhodi br1
- **riding** agg.: abrot↓
  - **aching**: abrot
- **rising** | **after**:
  - **agg.**: arg-n↓
    - **drawing** pain: arg-n
  - **amel.**: bry↓ nat-c↓ sulph↓
    - **tearing** pain: bry k* nat-c k* sulph k*
- **rubbing**:
  - **amel.**: canth↓ caust↓ nat-c↓ tarax↓
    - **pinching** pain: nat-c h2*
    - **stitching** pain: caust tarax
    - **tearing** pain: canth a1 nat-c k*
- **scratching** agg.; after: mosch↓
  - **burning**: mosch
- **shooting** pain: cystein-l rly4• *Ferr* medul-os-si rly4• puls bg1 sars bg1 sulph tep
- **singing** agg.: stann
  - **aching**: stann
- **sitting**:
  - **agg.**: *Am-m*↓ anac↓ calc↓ dig↓ mur-ac↓ phos↓ *Staph*↓
    - **drawing** pain: calc k* dig k*
    - **pressing** pain: anac h2
    - **sore**: phos
    - **stitching** pain: calc
    - **tearing** pain: *Am-m* mur-ac k* *Staph*
  - **amel.**: cycl↓ jal↓
    - **pressing** pain: cycl jal
- **sleep** agg.; during: sep↓
  - **sore**: sep h2
- **sleep** agg.; on going to: *Kali-c* *Kalm*
- **sneezing** agg.: alum↓
  - **tearing** pain: alum
- **sore**: aesc agar *Agn* am-m ammc anac anthraq rly4• arg-met ars-h arum-t asaf bar-c k* bell k* bov k* *Calc* k* canth k* caust bg2 cedr cina cinnb cocc k* coff k* cot br1 croc b7.de* crot-h k* cupr k* cycl k* **Eup-per** eupi ferr b7.de* ferr-i fl-ac granit-m es1• graph grat k* *Guaj* b4a.de ham hell *Hep* k* ign indg iod iris kali-c h2* kreos laur k* led lyc lyss m-aust b7.de mag-m k* mez k* mur-ac nat-c k* *Nat-m* k* nicc *Nit-ac* k* ox-ac petr *Ph-ac* *Phos* k* phyt plan plat k* plb b7.de* puls b7.de* *Ruta* b7a.de sal-fr sle1• sarr *Sep* k* *Stann* k* stry sul-i k2 *Sulph* k* *Sumb* symph fd3.de• tep thuj k* valer b7.de* verat k* zinc k*
  - **accompanied** by | **Axilla**; swelling of glands of (See CHEST - Swelling - axilla - glands - accompanied - upper)
- **spasmodic**: agar lact mosch olnd valer
- **splinter**; as from a: agar *Nit-ac*
- **sprained**; as if: alum h2 caust h2 euph h2 *Rhus-t* ter
- **squeezed**; as if: am-m bg2 arg-met bg2 asaf bg2 calc bg2 crot-h bg2 cycl b7.de* dulc bg2 hell bg2 kali-n bg2 kreos bg2 mag-c bg2 meny bg2 merc bg2 mez bg2 mur-ac bg2 olnd bg2 petr bg2 ph-ac bg2 ruta bg2 stann bg2 valer bg2
- **standing** agg.: nat-c↓
  - **tearing** pain: nat-c h2
- **stitching** pain: abrot acon b7.de* agar agn k* all-c *Alum* k* alum-p k2 alum-sil k2 anac ant-c k* arg-met k* arn k* ars-met asaf k* aur-m-n bar-c bell k* berb *Bry* k* calc k* calc-p calc-sil k2 cann-s canth k* *Carbn-s* caust k* chel chin k* chinin-ar cina coc-c *Cocc* k* coloc con k* conch fkr1.de dig k* dulc elaps euph b4.de* euphr k* *Ferr* k* form graph grat k* *Guaj* k* hell ind indg *Kali-c* k* kali-n k* kali-s fd4.de kali-sil k2 lact laur k* *Led* k* lyc mag-c k* mag-m bg2 mang k* meny b7.de* merc-i-f mez k* nat-s k* nux-m k* nux-v bg2 olnd k* ph-ac k* *Plat* plb podo fd3.de• puls k* ran-s bg2 rhod k* *Rhus-t* k* rumx sabad k* sabin k* samb b7.de* *Sars* k* sil spong b7.de* squil b7.de* stann k* staph k* stront-c b4.de stry sulph k* symph fd3.de• tarax k* tep teucr b7.de* ther *Thuj* k* tritic-vg fd5.de valer b7.de* vanil fd5.de zinc k* [spect dfg1]
  - **boring** pain: asaf rhus-t
  - **burning**: asaf berb calc-p dig rhus-t zinc
  - **cramping**: cina
  - **drawing** pain: plb thuj
  - **jerking** pain: *Carbn-s*
  - **paroxysmal**: carbn-s tarax
  - **wandering** pain: lyc
- **stretching**:
  - **arm**:
    - **agg.**: plat↓ verat↓

- **stretching** – **arm** – **agg.**: ...
  - **sore**: (*↗extending the - agg. - sore)* plat verat
  - **amel.**: mur-ac↓
    - **tearing** pain: mur-ac k*
- **sudden**: crot-t↓ kali-c↓ meny↓
  - **tearing** pain: crot-t kali-c meny
- **tearing** pain: aesc *Agar* k* *Alum* k* alum-p k2 alum-sil k2 am-c k* *Am-m* k* anac bg2 ant-c bg2 ant-t bg2 arg-met k* arn k* **Ars** k* ars-h aur k* aur-ar k2 aur-s k2 **Bell** k* *Berb* bism k* bov k* *Bry* k* calc k* calc-sil k2 camph k* canth k* carb-an k* *Carb-v* k* carbn-s card-m castm caust k* chel k* *Chin* k* cic cimic cina k* clem coc-c cocc b7.de* colch k* coloc con k* crot-t cupr b7.de* dig k* *Dros* b7a.de* eupi ferr k* ferr-ar ferr-p *Grat* k* guaj k* hep bg2 hyos hyper ign *Indg* iod b4a.de *Kali-ar* kali-bi *Kali-c* k* kali-n k* kali-p kali-sil k2 kalm *Lach* k* lachn laur k* *Led* k* lil-t *Lyc* k* *Lyss* mag-c k* *Mag-m* k* mag-s mang k* meny k* *Merc* k* merl mez *Mur-ac* k* myric *Nat-c* k* nat-m nat-p **Nat-s** nux-v b7.de* ol-an olnd k* petr k* ph-ac phel phos k* **Plb** k* psor *Puls* k* ran-b bg2 *Rat* rheum k* *Rhus-t* k* rhus-v ruta k* sabin k* sacch-a fd2.de• sars k* sec sep k* **Sil** k* spig b7.de* spong fd4.de *Stann* k* *Staph* k* stram bg2 sul-ac k* *Sulph* k* symph fd3.de• tep *Thuj* *Valer* k* **Zinc** k* zinc-p k2
  - **alternating** with | **Hip**; tearing pain in (See hips - tearing - alternating - upper)
  - **constricting** pain: merl
  - **cramping**: meny h1
  - **drawing** pain: bry cina coc-c mur-ac h2 *Thuj*
  - **intermittent**: zinc h2
  - **jerking** pain: *Chin* mag-c h2 ph-ac sulph
  - **paralyzed**; as if: **Bell** carb-v *Chin* phos
  - **paroxysmal**: carb-v h2 led *Zinc*
  - **pressing** pain: arg-met h1 aur merl stann h2
  - **twisting** pain: cham k*
  - **twitching**: camph h1 mag-c merc merl sulph
  - **upward**: **Ars** kali-c lach led
  - **wandering** pain: merl
- **touch**:
  - **agg.**: agn arg-met *Chin* cina↓ *Cycl*↓ ferr-p k2 kreos↓ mag-c↓ mez↓ nat-c↓ ph-ac↓ propr sa3• sabin spig↓ *Staph* thuj↓
    - **aching**: arg-met sabin
    - **pressing** pain: *Agn* k* arg-met h1 ph-ac h2 sabin spig h1 *Staph* k*
    - **sore**: *Cycl* k* kreos mag-c h2 mez nat-c
    - **tearing**: cina a1 spig h1 thuj
  - **amel.**: thuj↓
    - **stitching** pain: thuj
- **turning** in bed agg.: *Sang* spong fd4.de
- **twinging**: chinin-s hipp k* melal-alt gya4 sulph
- **ulcerative** pain: bar-c bg2
- **uncovering** arm agg.: aur↓
  - **tearing** pain: aur
- **waking**; on: fl-ac↓
  - **sore**: fl-ac
- **walking**:
  - **agg.**: arg-n bry↓ camph↓ dig↓ led↓ merc-c sulph↓
    - **drawing** pain: camph k*
    - **shooting** pain: sulph
    - **stitching** pain: dig sulph
    - **tearing** pain: bry k* dig led sulph
  - **air**; in open:
    - **agg.**: anac↓ calc↓
      - **pinching** pain: calc
      - **pressing** pain: anac h2
    - **amel.**: thuj↓
      - **pressing** pain: thuj
  - **amel.**: cina↓ mur-ac↓
    - **stitching** pain: cina
    - **tearing** pain: mur-ac
- **wandering** pain: phyt
- **warm** bed agg.: caust↓
  - **tearing** pain: caust
- **warmth**:
  - **amel.**: ant-c↓ cassia-s ccrh1• ferr
    - **drawing** pain: ant-c k*
- **weather** agg.; wet: *Phyt* rhod rhus-t sanic
  - **drawing** pain: rhod sanic
- **writing** agg.: anag↓ ars-i chinin-s↓ *Cycl* *Fl-ac* galeoc-c-h↓ mur-ac↓ ozone↓ symph fd3.de• *Valer*
  - **aching**: galeoc-c-h gms1•
  - **cutting** pain: ars-i
  - **drawing** pain: anag *Valer*
  - **pressing** pain: ozone sde2•
  - **tearing** pain: mur-ac k* *Valer*
  - **twinging**: chinin-s
- **yawning**; with: mang↓
  - **burning**: mang h2

▽ - **extending** to:
  - **Axilla**: ars↓
    - **tearing** pain: ars
  - **Down** arm: alum↓ am-m↓ canth↓ castm↓ caust↓ ferr↓ guaj↓ *Lach*↓ mag-c↓ merc↓ merl↓ mur-ac↓ ol-an↓ *Rat*↓ til↓ *Zinc*↓
    - **tearing** pain: alum am-m canth castm caust ferr guaj *Lach* mag-c merc merl mur-ac ol-an *Rat* til *Zinc*
  - **Downward**: agar berb carb-v chin h1 dros ferr sne kali-bi lach *Lyc* rhus-t bg1 sulph
  - **Elbow**: caust bg1 fl-ac↓ lyc↓ mez↓ petr-ra↓ podo↓ rat↓
    - **pressing** pain: fl-ac k* mez k*
    - **stitching** pain: lyc petr-ra shn4• podo fd3.de•
    - **tearing** pain: rat
  - **Fingers**: alum↓ am-m↓ arn bg1 aur-m↓ chel hydrog srj2• rhus-t bg1
    - **aching**: hydrog srj2•
    - **stitching** pain: *Rhus-t*
    - **tearing** pain: alum am-m aur-m
  - **Forearm**: chel↓ melal-alt gya4
    - **stitching** pain: chel
  - **Hand** and thumb; into: kali-bi *Puls* spong fd4.de
  - **Head**: nicotam rly4•
  - **Neck**:
    - **menses**; during: berb
      - **pressing** pain: berb
  - **Scapula**: alum↓
    - **tearing** pain: alum
  - **Shoulder**: kali-c↓ lachn↓ laur↓ mang↓ ther↓
    - **sore**: laur
    - **stitching** pain: mang ther
    - **tearing** pain: kali-c lachn
  - **Wrist**: am-m↓ mag-c↓ ol-an↓ sars↓ symph↓ verat↓
    - **sore**: symph fd3.de• verat
    - **tearing** pain: am-m mag-c ol-an sars h2

○ - **Anterior** part: bell↓ sulph↓ zinc↓
  - **burning**: zinc
  - **pressing** pain: bell h1
  - **tearing** pain: sulph h2
- **Biceps**: brach↓ ham↓ hydr↓ iris↓ mang↓ ruta↓ tritic-vg fd5.de *Valer*↓
  - **morning**: agar
  - **bed** agg.; in: rhus-t↓
    - **burning**: rhus-t
  - **cutting** pain: hydr iris
  - **drawing** pain: mang ruta *Valer*
  - **lifting**; after: berb chinin-ar **Rhus-t** stict
  - **sore**: brach ham

- **Bones**: acon↓ agar↓ alum↓ alumn *Am-m*↓ anac ang↓ arn↓ ars-s-r arum-d aur bar-c bell↓ berb bov↓ bry calc↓ canth↓ carb-an↓ carb-v caust↓ *Chin*↓ *Cocc*↓ coloc↓ con↓ croc↓ dulc$_{fd4.de}$ euon euph↓ eupi↓ ferr *Fl-ac* gamb↓ ham **Hep**↓ hyos ign iod ip↓ kali-bi kali-n↓ led↓ *Lyc* mag-m↓ mag-s mang melal-alt↓ merc *Mez* murx nat-c↓ *Nat-s*↓ nit-ac osm ox-ac phos phyt plb↓ psor↓ rhod rhus-t ruta↓ sabin↓ sarr *Sil*↓ stann↓ staph sulph symph$_{fd3.de}$• tep↓ ter↓ thuj↓ *Valer*↓ vanil$_{fd5.de}$ verat↓ zinc↓
  - **morning**: eupi↓ ter↓
    - **drawing** pain: ter$_{k*}$
    - **tearing** pain: eupi
  - **forenoon**: agar↓ alum↓ nat-s↓
    - **drawing** pain: agar$_{k*}$
    - **tearing** pain: agar alum nat-s
  - **noon**: nicc↓
    - **tearing** pain: nicc
  - **afternoon**: fl-ac nat-s↓
    - **15** h: sarr
    - **tearing** pain: nat-s
  - **evening**: ox-ac↓ sulph↓
    - **aching**: ox-ac
    - **tearing** pain: sulph
  - **night**: dros
    - **midnight** | **before**:
      - **23** h: am-m↓
        - **tearing** pain: am-m
      - **after**: *Sulph*↓
        - **drawing** pain: *Sulph*$_{k*}$
  - **aching**: hyos iod mag-s ox-ac phyt rhod sulph
  - **boring** pain: *Carb-v* cocc kali-bi *Mang* melal-alt$_{gya4}$ tep
  - **drawing** pain: agar$_{k*}$ alum$_{k*}$ aur bar-c carb-v$_{k*}$ caust$_{k*}$ cocc$_{k*}$ euph$_{k*}$ ip$_{k*}$ kali-bi$_{k*}$ mez$_{k*}$ nit-ac$_{k*}$ plb$_{k*}$ sabin$_{k*}$ *Sulph*$_{k*}$ symph$_{fd3.de}$• ter$_{k*}$ vanil$_{fd5.de}$ verat$_{h1*}$ zinc$_{k*}$
  - **gnawing** pain: canth$_{k*}$ *Mang*$_{h2*}$
  - **lain** on: *Iod*
  - **lying** down agg.; after: ip↓
    - **drawing** pain: ip$_{k*}$
  - **motion**:
    - **agg.**: phyt↓
      - **aching**: phyt
    - **amel.**: aur↓ cocc↓ psor↓
      - **drawing** pain: aur
      - **tearing** pain: cocc$_{h1}$ psor
  - **paralyzed**, as if: nit-ac
  - **pinching** pain: gamb$_{k*}$
  - **pressing** pain: *Anac*$_{k*}$ ang$_{h1}$ bry$_{k*}$ con$_{h2}$ mez$_{h2}$ stann$_{h2}$
  - **pressure**:
    - **amel.**: canth↓
      - **tearing** pain: canth
  - **rheumatic**: *Ars-i* *Ferr* fl-ac
  - **shooting** pain: arum-d sulph
  - **sitting** agg.: *Am-m*↓ indg↓
    - **tearing** pain: *Am-m* indg
  - **sore**: ang bov *Cocc* croc ham **Hep** phos sarr *Sil* thuj zinc
  - **stitching** pain: bry calc canth coloc mez sulph symph$_{fd3.de}$•
  - **tearing** pain: acon agar alum *Am-m* ang arn bell berb bov canth carb-an caust *Chin* cocc$_{h1}$ eupi kali-n led mag-m merc nat-c *Nat-s* phos psor rhus-t$_{h1}$ ruta *Valer* zinc
    - **paralyzed**; as if: phos
  - **touch** agg.: staph
  - **ulcerative** pain: bar-c
  - **walking** agg.: psor↓ sulph↓
    - **tearing** pain: psor sulph
  - **extending** to:
    - **Elbow**: caust↓
      - **tearing** pain: caust
  - **Condyles**: ant-t↓ arg-met↓ brom↓ coc-c↓ glon↓ graph↓ indg↓ laur↓ mang↓ merc↓ phos↓ *Sabin*↓ thuj↓
- **Bones – Condyles**: ...
    - **night**: coc-c↓
      - **drawing** pain: coc-c
    - **drawing** pain: arg-met coc-c
    - **sore**: glon graph laur phos thuj
    - **stitching** pain: ant-t brom indg mang merc (non:sabad$_{kl}$) *Sabin*$_{kl}$
    - **tearing** pain: thuj
    - **twinging**: merc
    - **External**: asaf↓ chinin-s↓ sil↓ stram↓ verat-v↓
      - **evening**: chinin-s↓
        - **stitching** pain: chinin-s
      - **aching**: asaf sil verat-v
      - **stitching** pain: chinin-s stram
    - **Inner**:
      - **right**: ulm-c↓
        - **stitching** pain: ulm-c$_{jsj8}$•
  - **Elbow**; near: still↓ verat↓
    - **aching**: still verat
- **Deltoid**: agar↓ arg-met↓ *Asar* aur *Bar-c*$_{k*}$ bell↓ bufo calc card-m↓ caul caust↓ chel coc-c *Colch* **Ferr** kali-bi kali-n↓ *Kalm* lac-c merc-c nat-c↓ nat-m nux-v↓ petr↓ phos phyt rhod *Rhus-t* sal-ac↓ **Sang**$_{k*}$ sanic↓ spig↓ stann$_{mrr1}$ staph↓ stict$_{c1*}$ sulph↓ syph$_{jl2}$ viol-o zinc zinc-o$_{c2}$ zinc-val$_{c2}$
  - **right**: agar card-m caust$_{mrr1}$ *Cedr* *Kalm* lob *Lycpr*$_{c1}$ pitu-gl↓ psil$_{ft1}$ sal-ac$_{c1}$ *Urt-u*
    - **rheumatic**: urt-u$_{tl1}$
    - **tearing** pain: pitu-gl$_{skp7}$•
  - **left**: melal-alt$_{gya4}$ nux-m
    - **extending** to | **right**: ox-ac zinc-val$_{sma}$
  - **daytime**:
    - **walking** | **amel.**: syph$_{jl2}$
  - **afternoon**:
    - **17** h; until: pitu-gl↓
      - **tearing** pain: pitu-gl$_{skp7}$•
  - **night**: syph$_{jl2}$
  - **burning**: nux-v
  - **cutting** pain: caust spig
  - **drawing** pain: arg-met asar bell$_{k*}$ card-m caust kali-n$_{h2}$ sanic spig$_{h1}$ stann$_{h2}$ staph$_{h1}$
  - **hand** lies on table, while: asar
  - **motion** agg.: sal-ac$_{c1}$
  - **pinching** pain: caust$_{h2}$
  - **pressing** pain: staph$_{h1}$ sulph$_{h2}$
  - **raising** arm agg.: syph$_{jl2}$ zinc$_{ptk2}$
  - **rheumatic**: caust$_{mrr1}$ ferr-p$_{bro1}$ glyc$_{bro1}$ lycpr$_{bro1}$ med$_{bro1}$ nux-m$_{bro1}$ ox-ac$_{bro1}$ rhus-t$_{bro1}$ *Sang*$_{bro1}$ stict$_{bro1}$ *Syph*$_{bro1}$ urt-u$_{bro1*}$ viol-o$_{bro1}$ zinc-o$_{bro1}$ zing$_{bro1}$
  - **sore**: petr$_{h2}$ sal-ac$_{c1}$
  - **stitching** pain: agar caust
  - **tearing** pain: kali-n$_{h2}$ nat-c staph zinc$_{h2}$
  - **touch** agg.: sal-ac$_{c1}$
  - **warmth**:
    - **amel.** | **heat** amel.: bell-p$_{sp1}$
- **Humerus**: bov↓ *Cocc*↓ puls↓ stann↓
  - **broken**; as if: bov$_{ptk1}$ *Cocc*$_{ptk1}$ puls$_{ptk1}$
  - **crushed**; as if: stann$_{h2*}$
- **Inner** side: asaf↓ bell↓ berb↓ bov bry↓ camph↓ carb-v↓ chel con↓ crot-t laur↓ led *Lyc*↓ mang↓ merl↓ nat-s↓ nux-m↓ phel↓ rhus-t↓ rumx↓ ruta$_{fd4.de}$ samb↓ sil spig↓ stann↓ symph↓ tarax↓ tarent tritic-vg$_{fd5.de}$ zinc↓
  - **burning**: berb tarent
  - **drawing** pain: bell$_{k*}$ bry$_{k*}$ camph carb-v$_{h2}$ con$_{k*}$ led$_{k*}$ *Lyc*$_{k*}$ mang$_{k*}$ nat-s$_{k*}$ rhus-t$_{h1}$
  - **pressing** pain: spig$_{h1}$ stann$_{h2}$ symph$_{fd3.de}$•
  - **stitching** pain: asaf berb chel con led mang nux-m rumx samb$_{xxb1}$ tarax
  - **tearing** pain: berb camph laur lyc mang merl nat-s phel spig$_{h1}$ zinc

- **Inner** side: ...
  - **extending** to:
    - **Fingers**: chel
    - **Wrist**: lyc↓
      - **drawing** pain: lyc k*
- **Joints**: ign tl1
- **Lower** part: agar↓ caust↓ grat↓ led↓ mez↓ sil↓ zinc↓
  - **burning**: led mez
  - **drawing** pain: agar caust h2 grat k* sil k* zinc h2
- **Muscles**:
  - **Anterior**: bism↓
    - **cramping**: bism h1
  - **Extensor** muscles: bufo *Iod* mur-ac↓ plan plb
    - **sore**: mur-ac
  - **Flexor** muscles: asaf↓ bol-la↓ ham↓
    - **drawing** pain: asaf bol-la ham
    - **stitching** pain: asaf
- **Outer** side: ant-t↓ berb↓ mag-m↓ nat-sil fd3.de• phos↓ phyt *Sanic*↓ stann↓ thuj↓ vanil fd5.de
  - **left**: vip-l-f↓
    - **shooting** pain: vip-l-f a1
  - **drawing** pain: ant-t a1 berb a1 *Sanic* stann h2 thuj a1
  - **tearing** pain: mag-m h2 phos h2
- **Posterior** part: acon↓ agar↓ alum↓ aur↓ camph↓ con↓ ham↓ hyos jatr-c↓ lyc↓ mur-ac↓ nat-c↓ podo↓ sil↓ stann↓ *Stict* stry sul-ac↓ zinc↓
  - **aching**: ham fd3.de• jatr-c
  - **burning**: mur-ac zinc
  - **drawing** pain: acon k* con k* lyc k*
  - **pressing** pain: acon k* aur k* camph h1 stann h2
  - **shooting** pain: acon
  - **stitching** pain: acon podo fd3.de•
  - **tearing** pain: agar k* alum camph hyos nat-c sil sul-ac h2 zinc h2
- **Side** lain on: castm↓
  - **tearing** pain: castm
- **Side** not lain on: kali-bi↓
  - **tearing** pain: kali-bi
- **Skin**: arg-n↓ aur↓ nat-c↓ phos↓ sep↓ sulph↓
  - **burning**: arg-n aur nat-c phos sep sulph
- **Spots**; in: berb↓ graph↓ sulph↓
  - **burning**: berb graph sulph
- **Triceps**: *Stict*

\- **Upper** limbs (= brachialgia): abrot acon *Aesc* k* agar agath-a↓ all-c bro1 allox↓ aloe↓ *Alum* k* alum-p k2 alum-sil k2 alumn am-c b4.de* am-m b7a.de* *Ambr*↓ aml-ns ammc *Anac*↓ *Anag* bro1 androc↓ *Ang*↓ *Ant-c*↓ *Ant-t*↓ apis apoc aran↓ *Arg-met*↓ arg-n **Arn**↓ *Ars* k* ars-h ars-i ars-s-f k2 arum-t↓ arund asaf asar↓ asc-t aster↓ atra-r bnm3• aur aur-ar k2 aur-i k2 aur-m aur-m-n↓ aur-s↓ bad bapt *Bar-c* k* bar-m bar-s k2 bell k* bell-p sp1 benz-ac↓ berb beryl↓ bism↓ bit-ar↓ *Bol-la*↓ borx↓ bov brach↓ brom↓ *Brucel* sa3• **Bry** bufo but-ac↓ *Cact* caj calad↓ calam sa3• calc k* calc-i↓ *Calc-p* calc-s calc-sil k2 camph cann-i↓ cann-s b7a.de cann-xyz↓ canth↓ *Caps*↓ *Carb-ac*↓ carb-an carb-v carbn-h↓ carbn-o↓ carbn-s card-m↓ cass a1 cassia-s↓ castor-eq caul *Caust* k* *Cham* k* chel k* chin bg2 chinin-ar chinin-s↓ chlor↓ choc↓ cic bro1 cimic cina cinnb k* cist↓ cit-v k* *Clem*↓ cob-n sp1 coc-c↓ cocc k* *Coff* **Colch** k* coloc com *Con*↓ corn↓ corn-f↓ cot↓ *Croc*↓ crot-c k* crot-h *Crot-t*↓ cupr k* cupr-ar *Cur*↓ *Cycl* cystein-l↓ daph↓ *Dig*↓ dios dirc dol↓ dor↓ dros dulc k* elaps ery-a↓ **Eup-per** k* *Euph*↓ euphr↓ eupi↓ fago↓ ferr k* ferr-ar ferr-i *Ferr-m*↓ ferr-p↓ ferr-pic bro1 fl-ac form fum↓ galla-q-r nl2• gamb↓ *Gels* k* gins↓ *Glon* gran granit-m↓ *Graph* k* grat↓ gua bro1 *Guaj* k* guat sp1 gymno ham hedy a1* hell *Hep* hura hydr hydrog srj2• hyos↓ *Hyper*↓ ign ind k* indg↓ iod↓ iodof k* ip↓ jal↓ jug-c↓ jug-r↓ *Kali-ar*↓ kali-bi k* kali-c bg3 kali-i↓ kali-n kali-p kali-s fd4.de kali-sil↓ *Kalm* kola stb3• kreos bg2 *Lac-c*↓ lach lachn↓ lact↓ lat-m sp1* laur↓ *Led* lept↓ lil-t lith-c bg2 lith-m↓ lob-s↓ lyc lycpr bro1 lyss↓ m-ambo b7.de m-arct↓ m-aust↓ mag-c b4.de* mag-m b4.de* *Mag-p* mag-s k* maias-l hrn2• malar jl2 *Manc*↓ mand rsj7• mang mang-p↓ med k2 melal-alt gya4 meny↓ *Meph* merc merc-c merc-i-f merc-i-r↓ merl↓ mez k* mill morg-p fmm1• morph mosch mur-ac murx bg2 musca-d↓ myric naja *Nat-ar* **Nat-c**↓ nat-f sp1 nat-m k* *Nat-p*↓ **Nat-s**↓ nat-sil fd3.de• nicc↓ nicotam rly4• *Nit-ac*↓ nit-s-d↓ nux-m↓ *Nux-v* k* ol-an↓ ol-j *Olnd*↓ op orot-ac↓ ox-ac pall par petr ph-ac phel↓ *Phos* k* phys *Phyt* k* pic-ac↓ pin-con oss2• *Pip-m* plan plat *Plb* k* plumbg↓ plut-n↓ pneu jl2 prun↓ psil↓ *Psor*↓ ptel **Puls** puls-n↓ pyrog bg2 pyrus↓ ran-b k2 *Ran-s* raph↓ rat↓ rheum↓ rhod k* **Rhus-t** k* *Rhus-v*↓ rob↓ rumx ruta bg2 sabad↓ sabin↓ sacch↓ sacch-a↓ samb↓ *Sang* k* sarr *Sars*↓ scut↓ sec↓ senec↓ seneg↓ sep b4.de* sil sol-ni↓ sphing kk3.fr *Spig* k* spong↓ *Squil*↓ stann↓ staph k* *Stel* bro1 stict bro1 *Still*↓ stram stront-c↓ stry suis-pan↓ *Sul-ac*↓ sul-i k2 *Sulph* k* *Sumb*↓ syph k2 tab tarax↓ *Tarent* tax tell↓ tep ter↓ tetox pin2• *Teucr*↓ ther↓ thres-a sze7• thuj til↓ tritic-vg fd5.de trom tub↓ tub-m↓ tung-met↓ urt-u valer bg2 vanil fd5.de ven-m↓ *Verat* verat-v↓ verb↓ viol-o↓ viol-t↓ vip visc sp1 wye k* xan zinc k* zinc-p k2 *Zinc-s*↓ zing↓

- **alternating** sides: **Lac-c** sulph
  - **drawing** pain: sulph
  - **tearing** pain: lac-c sulph
- **right**: *Arg-n*↓ asc-t a1 bamb-a↓ bar-c↓ bell bg3 beryl tpw5 bism bg3 bit-ar↓ bry bg3 calc bg3 cassia-s ccrh1• castor-eq *Caust* chel↓ cic↓ cimic cina colch↓ coloc bg3 crot-c sk4• *Cycl* eupi *Ferr-m* bro1 ferr-pic bro1 fl-ac graph bg3 ip↓ kalm lavand-a ctl1• lil-t br1 limest-b↓ *Lyc* lycpr bro1 mand rsj7• melal-alt gya4 *Merc-i-f* nat-ar k2 nat-c↓ nit-ac↓ ozone sde2• pall phasco-ci rbp2 phos *Phyt* pip-m k* plb↓ propr sa3• ran-s bg3 rhus-v bro1 **Sang** k* sars bg3 sec bg3 sil bg3 *Spig* stroph-h **Sulph**↓ thuj sne trios rsj11• ven-m rsj12• viol-o bro1 wye bro1 xan
  - **and**:
    - **left** knee: asc-t a1
    - **left** lower limb: (↗*left - and*) *Agar* br1 asc-t k*
  - **broken**; as if: chel bg2
  - **burning**: plb
  - **drawing** pain: *Arg-n* k* bamb-a stb2.de• bar-c caust k* phos h2
  - **dull** pain: colch rsj2•
  - **heart** complaints; with: lepi br1 *Lil-t*
  - **lying** on left side agg.: *Mag-m*↓
    - **tearing** pain: *Mag-m*
  - **pinching** pain: ip h1
  - **pressing** pain: *Caust* cic a1 *Cycl* nit-ac h2
  - **sore**: bit-ar wht1• limest-b es1• *Merc-i-f* nit-ac h2
  - **stitching** pain: *Caust*
  - **tearing** pain: calc chel *Cina* nat-c ozone sde2• phos **Sulph**
  - **then** left upper limb: fl-ac
- **left**: acon bro1 *Aesc* agar k* anac bg3 arg-n arn bg3 arum-t k2 asaf bg3 asar↓ asc-t aster k* aur *Cact* bg3* cain↓ carb-ac↓ carb-v↓ carbn-s k2 cass a1 cassia-s cdd7*• cic↓ cimic bg3* cocc↓ colch bro1 croc↓ crot-h bro1* cur cycl↓ dios↓ dulc fd4.de fl-ac flav jl2 *Guaj* haliae-lc↓ ham fd3.de• hir rsj4• hydroph rsj6• iber bro1 ind iod iodof a1 ip↓ jac-c kali-c bg3 kali-m bro1 kali-n↓ kali-s fd4.de *Kalm* lac-lup hrn2• *Lach* *Lat-m* k* lyc↓ mag-s bro1 magn-gr bro1 mand rsj7• mang-p↓ meny merc-i-f↓ merc-i-r nad rly4• nat-ar↓ nat-m↓ nit-ac↓ petr-ra↓ phos↓ plat↓ pot-e↓ puls↓ rhod↓ **Rhus-t** k* sel↓ sil↓ *Spig* bro1 squil bg3 stann bg3 stram suis-pan↓ sulph bg3 sumb↓ tab k* ther tl1 trios rsj11• *Vac* jl2 ven-m rsj12• xan bro1 [*Buteo-j* sej6 helia stj7]
  - **accompanied** by | **Heart** complaints (See CHEST - Heart; complaints - accompanied - upper - left - pain)
  - **aching**: carb-ac bg1 croc bg1 dios bg1 fl-ac bg1 iber bg1 ip bg1 mand rsj7• nat-ar bg1 rhod bg1 suis-pan rly4• sumb k*
  - **and** right lower limb: (↗*right - and - left lower*) agar tl1 asc-t hr1*
  - **angina** pectoris, in: cimic dig *Lat-m*
  - **broken**; as if: cain haliae-lc srj5•
  - **burning**: cocc mang-p rly4• pot-e rly4•
  - **convulsions**; before epileptic: calc-ar
  - **cutting** pain: petr-ra shn4•
  - **drawing** pain: aur h2 carb-v h2 cycl h1 kali-c h2 lyc h2 nat-m h2 plat h2 **Rhus-t** k*
  - **pinching** pain: kali-c ptk1
  - **pressing** pain: **Kalm** k* sil h2
  - **sharp**: haliae-lc srj5•
  - **shooting** pain: sel rsj9•

- **left** – **shooting** pain: ...
  - **downward**: cimic$_{bg1}$ rhus-t$_{bg1}$
  - **sore**: arum-t$_{k2}$ cassia-s$_{ccrh1}$• merc-i-f sumb
  - **sprained**; as if: nit-ac$_{h2}$
  - **tearing** pain: asar cic kali-c kali-n phos$_{h2}$ puls$_{h1}$
  - **extending** to | **right**: cham$_{bg1}$ form
- **daytime**: borx plb sulph
  - **amel.**: adam$_{skp7}$•
  - **gnawing** pain: sulph
  - **sore**: sulph
  - **tearing** pain: *Sulph*
- **morning**: agar↓ aran↓ ars ars-i ars-s-f$_{k2}$ cham↓ chel crot-h dios dulc fago hyper↓ ign↓ jac-c lap-la$_{sde8.de}$• lyc↓ merc-i-f nux-v↓ *Ph-ac*↓ plb↓ ptel rhus-t staph stict tab↓ thuj↓ tritic-vg$_{fd5.de}$ zinc↓
  - **7.30** h: fago↓
    - **stitching** pain: fago
  - **aching**: fago
  - **bed** agg.; in: carb-v↓ eupi↓ mag-m↓
    - **tearing** pain: carb-v eupi mag-m
  - **boring** pain: aran plb
  - **burning**: agar
  - **drawing** pain: lyc
  - **motion** agg.: ars crot-h
  - **rising** agg.: merc-i-f phos staph *Vac*$_{jl2}$
  - **sore**: ign nux-v *Ph-ac* tab zinc
  - **tearing** pain: cham hyper thuj
  - **waking**; on: *Aur* cact↓ chel
    - **tearing** pain: cact
- **forenoon**: bry carbn-s castm↓ cham dulc$_{fd4.de}$ fago jac-c↓ jug-c↓ kalm petr↓ sulph tarent↓ verat-v↓
  - **11** h: sars↓
    - **tearing** pain: sars
  - **aching**: jac-c jug-c verat-v
  - **burning**: castm
  - **drawing** pain: sulph$_{k*}$
  - **pressing** pain: tarent
  - **sprained**; as if: petr
- **noon**: merc-i-r↓
  - **menses**; during: nux-v↓
    - **tearing** pain: nux-v
  - **sore**: merc-i-r
  - **walking** agg.; after: pall
- **afternoon**: calc-p chel coloc elaps↓ erig↓ fago kali-n↓ naja rumx sars↓ thuj verat-v↓ zinc zing↓
  - **14** h: propr$_{sa3}$•
  - **17** h: phys↓
    - **stitching** pain: phys
  - **aching**: erig verat-v
  - **boring** pain: coloc
  - **drawing** pain: elaps thuj$_{k*}$ zinc zing$_{k*}$
  - **pressing** pain: thuj$_{k*}$
  - **tearing** pain: kali-n sars
- **evening**: alum↓ *Ars*↓ calc cimic crot-t↓ fl-ac gamb↓ hyos hyper↓ kali-n↓ kalm lact↓ led mag-m↓ merc-c merc-i-f nat-ar phos psor *Puls* rhus-t sep↓ stann staph sulph↓ thuj↓ tritic-vg$_{fd5.de}$ zinc↓ zing↓
  - **18** h: arg-n elaps
  - **19** h: sulph↓
    - **stitching** pain: sulph
  - **19.30-20** h: ven-m$_{rsj12}$•
  - **air**; from exposure to: cham↓
    - **tearing** pain: cham
  - **amel.**: merc-i-r↓
    - **sore**: merc-i-r
  - **bed** agg.; in: carb-v kreos mag-m
  - **burning**: *Puls*
  - **drawing** pain: crot-t$_{k*}$ kali-n$_{h2}$ phos$_{h2}$ staph$_{k*}$ thuj$_{h1}$ zing$_{k*}$
- **evening**: ...
  - **pressing** pain: fl-ac$_{k*}$
  - **shooting** pain: sep sulph
  - **sore**: mag-m zinc
  - **stitching** pain: *Ars* fl-ac gamb lact sep sulph
  - **tearing** pain: alum hyper kali-n
- **night**: acon↓ adam$_{skp7}$• alum↓ am-c↓ am-m ambr anac↓ aran *Ars* asaf bry *Calc* calc-s calc-sil$_{k2}$ *Carb-v* carbn-s carc$_{gk6*}$ cass$_{a1}$ castor-eq caust cham chin↓ cit-v$_{k*}$ coloc croc crot-t dig *Dulc* *Ferr*↓ gels ham$_{fd3.de}$• hyper↓ ign *Iod* kali-n *Lyc* mag-c *Merc* merc-i-f mur-ac musca-d$_{szs1}$ nat-c↓ nux-v phos phyt plb↓ puls **Rhus-t** **Sang** sep↓ *Sil* staph stront-c↓ sulph syc$_{fmm1}$• til↓
  - **22** h: fl-ac↓
    - **stitching** pain: fl-ac
  - **midnight** | **before**:
    - **22** h: form↓
      - **tearing** pain: form
  - **after**: nux-v
    - **2** h: *Ferr*
    - **3** h: am-c↓ dios
      - **tearing** pain: am-c
    - **3-4** h: gels
    - **3-6** h: thuj
    - **4** h: verat
  - **bed** agg.; in: chin↓ stront-c↓
    - **burning**: chin
    - **tearing** pain: stront-c
  - **burning**: chin til
  - **drawing** pain: acon *Ars* *Calc* **Carb-v** caust phos$_{k*}$ puls$_{k*}$ **Rhus-t**$_{k*}$
  - **lying** on it: acon *Ars* *Carb-v* *Iod*
    - **drawing** pain: acon$_{k*}$ *Carb-v*$_{k*}$
  - **pressing** pain: *Dulc* merc
  - **sore**: anac merc-i-f plb
  - **stitching** pain: alum calc cham dulc
  - **tearing** pain: alum am-c$_{h2}$ ars *Calc* *Ferr* hyper kali-n merc nat-c$_{h2}$ plb sep$_{h2}$ stront-c
- **accompanied** by | **Hypochondria**; complaints of (See ABDOMEN - Hypochondria - accompanied - upper)
- **aching**: agath-a$_{nl2}$• allox$_{sp1}$ alum$_{k*}$ androc$_{srj1}$• arg-n$_{k*}$ *Ars* asaf bapt$_{bro1}$ benz-ac berb$_{k*}$ *Bry*$_{k*}$ but-ac$_{sp1}$ *Cact* *Calc* calc-p$_{k*}$ cann-i cann-xyz$_{bg2}$ *Carb-ac* carbn-s caust$_{k*}$ cham chinin-s choc$_{srj3}$• cocc$_{bg2}$ com croc$_{k*}$ dios dirc dol *Dulc*$_{k*}$ **Eup-per** euphr$_{k*}$ fl-ac$_{k*}$ gamb gels$_{k*}$ glon$_{k*}$ granit-m$_{es1}$• ham ip$_{k*}$ jal$_{bro1}$ jug-c kalm lac-c lach$_{k*}$ lil-t lith-c$_{bro1}$ lob-s lyc lyss melal-alt$_{gya4}$ merc merc-i-f mosch$_{k*}$ musca-d$_{szs1}$ myric naja nat-ar$_{k*}$ *Nit-ac*$_{k*}$ ol-j$_{bro1}$ orot-ac$_{rly4}$• ph-ac phyt$_{k*}$ pip-m plut-n$_{srj7}$• puls-n raph rhod$_{k*}$ sarr$_{bro1}$ staph suis-pan$_{rly4}$• *Sumb* tab$_{bg2}$ tarax thuj$_{k*}$ tung-met$_{bdx1}$• verat$_{bg2}$ verat-v zing
  - **wandering** pain: plan
- **air** agg., draft of: chin↓ verat↓
  - **drawing** pain: chin verat
- **air**; in open:
  - **amel.**: caust↓ cham merc-i-f$_{k2}$
    - **sore**: caust$_{h2}$
- **alternating** with:
  - **Eye**; pain in (See EYE - Pain - alternating with - arm)
  - **Lower** limbs: merc-i-r
  - **Stomach**; pain in (See STOMACH - Pain - alternating - limbs)
- **amputation**; after: all-c$_{k2}$ arn$_{kr1*}$ *Hyper* kalm$_{kr1*}$ ph-ac$_{kr1*}$
- **autumn** agg.: rhus-t
- **bed**:
  - **going** to bed | **when**: adam$_{skp7}$•
  - **in** bed | **agg.**: cycl *Ferr* ign iodof *Sulph* verat
  - **weight** of clothing: ferr
- **bending**:
  - **arms**:
    - **agg.**: aeth
    - **amel.**: ferr

Extremities

- **blow**; pain as from a: acon b7.de am-c b4.de* am-m b7.de* anac b4.de* *Arn* b7.de* bar-c b4.de* cic bg2 cina b7.de* con b4.de* dulc b4a.de graph b4.de* iod b4.de* kali-c b4.de* lyc bg2 m-ambo b7.de m-arct b7.de mang b4.de* mez b4.de* nit-ac bg2 nux-m bg2 nux-v bg2 olnd b7.de* petr b4.de* plat b4.de* *Puls* b7a.de sars b4.de* stann bg2 sul-ac b4.de* sulph bg2 tarax b7.de*
- **boring** pain: aran arg-n bg1 ars bg2 aur bar-c bov carb-an bg2 carb-v caust k* coloc gran mang k* mez k* nat-c *Nat-m* nux-m bg2 phos k* plb k* *Ran-s* b7a.de *Rhod* k* stann *Thuj*
- **breathing** agg.: mang hr1
- **broken**; as if: arn b7.de* borx b4a.de bov b4.de* bry bg2 cham b7.de* chel k* cocc b7.de* cupr b7a.de *Ign* b7.de* nat-m k* nux-v b7.de* phos b4.de* *Puls* k* ruta b7.de* samb b7.de* sphing kk3.fr sulph bg2 thuj b4a.de verat
- **burning**: agar alum k* alum-p k2 alum-sil k2 apis b7a.de *Ars* ars-h arum-t arund *Asaf* *Aur* aur-m aur-m-n *Bell* berb bov k* bry k* bufo calc k* *Carb-v* k* chin cocc b7.de *Com* *Con* corn crot-t *Cur* dig k* graph hep jug-c jug-r kali-bi kali-c k* kola stb3• *Led* b7a.de lith-m lyc k* lyss *M-ambo* b7.de* mag-m k* mang-p rly4• med merc k* mez k* mur-ac k* nat-c b4.de nat-m petr *Ph-ac* k* phos k* plat k* plb puls k* *Rhus-t* k* rhus-v sep b4.de sil k* spong k* stann k* stram sulph thuj tub jl2 *Urt-u* verat ptk1 zinc k* zinc-p k2
  - **accompanied** by | **nausea**: kali-bi tl1
  - **iron**; as from a hot: *Alum* b4a.de
  - **paralyzed**; as if: calc
  - **paroxysmal**: cocc *Plb*
- **burnt**; sensation as if: nux-v b7.de* prun bg2 rhus-t bg2 sil bg2
- **burrowing**: am-m b7.de* bar-c b4.de* carb-an bg2 carb-v b4.de* cina b7.de* cocc b7.de* croc b7.de* m-ambo b7.de mang b4.de* merc b4.de* mez b4.de* nat-c b4.de* *Nat-m* b4.de* *Rhod* b4.de* rhus-t b7.de* ruta b7a.de stann b4.de* thuj b4.de*
- **bursting**; sensation as if: chinin-s bg2 vip bg2
- **catarrhal** fever, during: sep ↓
  - **drawing** pain: sep h2
- **changing** position amel.: agar bg1
- **chill**:
  - **before**: *Eup-per* *Phel*
  - **during**: acon bg2 am-c bg2 apis bg2 arn bg2 *Ars* ↓ ars-h ↓ bry k* canth bg2 caps bg2 caust bg2 chel bg2 chin k* cina bg2 cocc bg2 coff bg2 dros bg2 hell bg2 ign bg2 kali-c bg2 *Kreos* bg2 lach bg2 led bg2 lyc k* meny bg2 merc bg2 mur-ac bg2 nat-m bg2 nux-v k* petr bg2 ph-ac k* phos k* puls k* rhus-t k* sabad bg2 sep bg2 spong bg2 stann bg2 stram bg2 thuj bg2 verat bg2
    - **drawing** pain: ars-h k*
    - **stitching** pain: ars-h
    - **tearing** pain: *Ars* ars-h *Rhus-t*
- **clawing**: lach k*
- **cold**:
  - **agg.**: merc-i-f k2
  - **air** agg.: *Ars* ign nit-ac *Ran-b* *Rhod*
    - **tearing** pain: ign
  - **amel.**: thuj
  - **water** | **agg.**: am-c *Ars*
- **cold** while perspiring; taking: *Dulc* ↓
  - **stitching** pain: *Dulc*
- **convulsions**; before epileptic: *Calc-ar* k* cupr ↓
  - **drawing** pain: cupr
- **corrosive**: hell b7.de* led b7.de* *Lyc* b4a.de plat b4.de* rhus-t b7.de* ruta b7.de* spong b7.de* verat b7.de*
- **coryza**; during: sep ↓
  - **drawing** pain: sep b4.de*
- **cough** agg.; during: caps ↓ dig k* *Puls* k*
  - **pressing** pain: dig
  - **shooting** pain: caps fkm1• puls
- **cough** agg.; during: ...
  - **stitching** pain: *Puls*
- **covering** agg.: rhus-v ↓
  - **burning**: rhus-v
- **cramping**: acon b7.de* alum bg2 anac b4.de* arg-met b7.de* arg-n bro1 ars b4.de* bell b4.de* bism b7.de* caust b4.de* cina b7.de* cocc b7.de* coloc bg2 cupr bro1 dig b4.de* euph b4.de* kali-bi bg2 kali-n b4.de* mosch b7.de* *Nux-v* b7.de* olnd bro1 petr bg2 *Ph-ac* bro1 plat b4.de* rhod b4.de* sabin b7.de* sec bro1 seneg b4.de* spig b7.de* stann b4.de* sul-ac bro1 verat-v bro1 viol-o b7.de* *Zinc-s* bro1
- **cutting** pain: acon b7.de* am-c am-m *Anac* k* ang b7.de* apis ars-h arund bell k* bism b7.de* caust k* con k* dig dros b7.de* hyos b7.de* *Ign* b7a.de kali-bi bg2 kali-c k* m-ambo b7.de manc mang k* mosch b7a.de mur-ac k* *Nat-c* k* ox-ac petr ph-ac k* samb b7.de* sars spig b7.de* stann k* stry sul-ac k* teucr b7.de* ven-m rsj12• verat b7.de*
- **dinner**; during: kali-n
- **dislocated**; as if: *Ant-t* bov b4.de* calc b4a.de caust b4.de* coloc bg2 ign bg2 mag-c b4.de* merc k* mez b4.de* nat-m b4.de* nit-ac b4.de* petr b4.de* phos b4.de* rhod b4.de* rhus-t sep b4.de* stann b4.de* sulph b4.de* thuj b4a.de
- **dragging**: m-ambo b7.de nat-c bg2 sep b4.de*
- **drawing** pain: acon k* aesc *Agar* aloe bg2 am-c anac *Ang* b7a.de ant-c ant-t b7.de* apis k* *Arg-met* k* *Arg-n* *Ars* ars-h k* asaf aster aur-ar k2 bapt *Bar-c* bar-s k2 bell k* bry k* cact calad *Calc* k* calc-p camph caps k* carb-ac carb-an *Carb-v* k* carbn-h carbn-s castor-eq **Caust** k* *Chel* k* chin k* chinin-ar cic cimic *Cina* k* cinnb cist cit-v k* *Clem* k* cocc k* *Coloc* k* con k* crot-h crot-t k* *Cupr* cycl k* dig k* dulc k* elaps euph euphr bg2 ferr k* ferr-ar form gins k* gran graph k* grat *Guaj* k* *Hep* b4a.de ign k* indg k* iod bg2 kali-bi k* kali-c k* *Kali-n* k* kali-p kali-sil k2 kalm kreos lach laur led *Lyc* k* *M-ambo* b7.de* m-aust b7.de *Mag-c* k* mag-m k* mand rsj7• mang k* meny b7a.de meph merc k* merc-c merl mez k* *Mur-ac* b4a.de* nat-c b4a.de nat-m k* nat-s *Nit-ac* k* nux-m k* *Nux-v* k* ol-an *Olnd* b7a.de* pall par b7a.de petr k* ph-ac k* phos k* *Phyt* *Plat* k* plb k* *Puls* k* *Rhod* k* **Rhus-t** k* *Rhus-v* sabin b7a.de sang sec k* seneg k* *Sep* k* *Sil* k* sol-ni stann k* staph k* stry k* sul-ac k* *Sulph* k* tab tell *Teucr* thres-a sze7• *Thuj* k* til *Valer* k* verat k* zinc k* zinc-p k2 zing k*
  - **cramping**: anac elaps kali-n nux-m
  - **downward**: agar k* apis aur h2 con h2 cycl k* form k* kali-c k* lyc k* *Nux-v* pall k* ph-ac k* puls k* rhus-t k* rhus-v k* seneg k* *Sep* k* sil k*
  - **drawn** forward, when reaching down; sensation as if: phos
  - **inward**: laur k*
  - **jerking** pain: nux-m k*
  - **paralyzed**; as if: am-c arg-n k* chel k* chin cina cist mag-m h2 meph *Nux-v* **Rhus-t** *Rhus-v* seneg sep h2 staph k* sul-ac h2
  - **sprained**; as if: nit-ac k*
  - **sticking** pain: am-c k*
  - **tearing** pain: *Ars* carb-v *Caust* cham k* *Cina* colch coloc k* grat k* hell ol-an k* puls k*
  - **tensive**: arg-met
  - **thread**; as from a: bry b7a.de plat b4a.de*
  - **upward**: *Ars* con h2 mag-c k* nux-v k* plat h2 sep h2
    - **up** and down on motion: con k*
  - **wandering** pain: rhus-v k*
- **dull** pain: apis b7a.de croc b7.de* hyos b7.de* melal-alt gya4
- **eating** | **after**:
  - **agg.**: ars clem ↓ cocc ↓ *Indg*
    - **aching**: cocc
    - **sore**: clem
  - **agg.**: cocc
- **electric** shock; as from an: m-ambo b7.de
- **eruptions**; after suppressed: mez ↓
  - **neuralgic**: mez
- **excitement**: alum-sil ↓
  - **burning**: alum-sil k2*
- **exertion** | **after** | **agg.**: gels ruta sacch-a fd2.de• *Sep* sil
  - **agg.**: alum androc srj1• cimic galeoc-c-h gms1• iod mand rsj7• *Merc* sulph

- **exertion**; as after: apis b7a.de arg-met b7.de* carb-an bg2 cocc b7.de* hep b4a.de kali-n bg2 merc b4.de* nux-v b7.de* par b7.de* puls b7.de* thuj b4.de* verat b7.de*
- **extending** them: *(↗extending them - amel.; stretching - agg.)* carbn-s hura sulph
  - **amel.**: *(↗extending them; stretching - agg.)* merc
- **fever**; during: *Acon* bg2 *Ant-c* bg2 apis bg2 **Arn** b7.de* *Ars* bg2 **Bell** bg2 bov bg2 bry bg2 **Calc** bg2 caps bg2 carb-v bg2 caust bg2 chin bg2 cocc bg2 *Colch* bg2 cycl bg2 euphr bg2 ferr bg2 *Ign* bg2 ip bg2 kali-c bg2 kali-n bg2 lyc bg2 meny bg2 merc bg2 **Nux-v** bg2 phel sma phos bg2 **Puls** bg2 ran-b bg2 *Rhod* bg2 *Rhus-t* bg2 ruta bg2 sabin bg2 samb bg2 *Sep* bg2 **Squil** bg2 stann bg2 staph bg2 stram bg2 sulph bg2 **Thuj** bg2 *Verat* bg2 zinc bg2
- **food** and drink:
  - **cold** agg.: *Cocc* ↓
    - **tearing** pain: *Cocc*
- **forward**, on attempting to raise arm: plb ↓
  - **drawing** pain: plb k*
- **gnawing** pain: alum *Ars* k* bry canth dros dulc graph kali-bi k* laur mag-c mang phos k* ran-s sars stront-c sulph k*
- **grasping** pain: nux-m a1*
- **grasping** something | **amel.**: lith-c sma
- **griping**: am-c b4.de* *Bell* b4.de* hyos b7a.de ign b7.de* nat-c b4.de* nat-m bg2
- **hang** down; letting arms:
  - **agg.**: alum alum-p k2 am-m ang berb *Bry* canth *Cina* ign kali-n nat-m nux-v ol-an par ph-ac phos plat ruta sabin sep stront-c sul-ac sulph thuj valer
    - **drawing** pain: *Cina* kali-n k*
  - **amel.**: *Acon* bg1 arn bg1 asar bg1 berb bg1 con bg1 lyc bg1 mag-c bg1 mag-m bg1 mang bg1 phos bg1 rat bg1 rhus-t bg1
- **jerking** pain: alum bg2 am-c b4a.de anac b4.de* ant-t b7.de* *Arn* k* **Bell** k* *Chin* b7a.de *Cic* b7.de* *Coloc* b4a.de dulc b4.de* fl-ac bg2 ip b7.de* kali-bi bg2 m-ambo b7a.de m-aust b7a.de meny b7a.de mez b4.de* nat-c b4a.de nit-ac b4.de* nux-m b7.de* nux-v b7a.de op b7a.de ph-ac b4a.de plat b4.de* *Puls* b7a.de ran-b k* rheum b7a.de rhus-v sabad b7.de* stann b4.de* sul-ac b4.de* sulph b4.de* *Valer*
- **lain** on; the one: **Carb-v** ↓ cina ↓
  - **drawing** pain: **Carb-v** cina h1
- **laughing** agg.: mang hr1
- **leaning** agg.: ruta sil thuj
- **lifting**:
  - **agg.**: ruta sep
  - **amel.**: sphing kk3.fr spig k*
  - **them** (See raising)
- **lying**:
  - **agg.**: iod ↓ sabin ↓
    - **pressing** pain: iod
    - **tearing** pain: sabin
  - **arm** under head agg.; with: staph ↓
    - **drawing** pain: staph h1
  - **back**; on:
    - **agg.**: cham ↓
      - **drawing** pain: cham
  - **side**; on:
    - **affected** side:
      - **agg.**: merc-i-f ↓
        - **sore**: merc-i-f
    - **agg.**: adam skp7• kali-n ↓
      - **tearing** pain: kali-n
    - **left**:
      - **agg.**: *Phos* ↓
        - **tearing** pain: *Phos*
    - **painful** side:
      - **agg.**: *Ars* ↓
        - **tearing** pain: *Ars*
      - **amel.**: cham ↓
        - **drawing** pain: cham
- **lying – side**; on: ...
  - **painless** side | **agg.**: crot-c sk4•
  - **still**:
    - **agg.**: rhus-t tl1
      - **tearing** pain: *Rhus-t*
  - **upper** arm agg.; on: acon anac ↓ **Ars** *Calc* *Carb-v* cocc dros *Graph* *Ign* *Iod* **Kali-c** *Spig* urt-u
    - **sore**: anac cocc
- **lying** down agg.: cassia-s ccrh1•
- **manual** labor agg.: iod ↓ *Rhus-t* ↓
  - **tearing** pain: iod *Rhus-t*
- **menses**:
  - **during**:
    - **agg.**: agar bell ↓ bry *Calc* elaps eup-pur kali-n ↓ nux-v spong stram verat
      - **drawing** pain: spong *Stram*
      - **tearing** pain: bell kali-n h2
- **motion**:
  - **agg.**: aml-ns *Ant-t* arg-met ↓ berb **Bry** bufo *Calc* ↓ calc-sil k2 cann-s *Cham* chel chin cimic cinnb **Colch** *Coloc* con ↓ croc ↓ crot-t ↓ dros ferr *Guaj* hyos iod iris kali-bi ↓ kali-c kali-n ↓ *Kalm* led limest-b ↓ mag-c mag-m mand rsj7• meph merc-i-f kr1* merc-i-r mez nat-ar ↓ nit-ac ↓ *Nux-v* olib-sac wmh1 op *Ox-ac* ph-ac phys *Phyt* *Plb* *Puls* ↓ *Ran-b* sep ↓ sil stann ↓ staph streptoc rly4• sul-i k2 sulph syph k2 urt-u ↓ zinc ↓
    - **aching**: mand rsj7• nat-ar
    - **broken**; as if: *Puls* k*
    - **burning**: crot-t
    - **drawing** pain: con h2 meph k* sulph k*
    - **pressing** pain: led h1 staph k* sulph
    - **sore**: arg-met *Calc* croc ferr kali-bi limest-b es1• plb sulph
    - **sprained**; as if: mez h2
    - **stitching** pain: urt-u zinc
    - **tearing** pain: chel dros kali-n h2 nit-ac sep h2 *Sil* stann h2
  - **amel.**: abrot k* acon agar am-m ↓ arg-met ↓ *Ars* ↓ aur ↓ aur-m-n bell ↓ camph caust ↓ cina coloc ↓ cupr cycl k* *Dulc* kali-p *Lyc* meph phos *Puls* *Rhod* **Rhus-t** sep ↓ sphing k* spig k* stel thuj *Valer* ↓
    - **drawing** pain: arg-met aur h2 bell k* camph coloc lyc *Rhod* **Rhus-t** sep h2 *Valer*
    - **pressing** pain: camph dulc
    - **slow** motion: *Ferr* ferr-p sma
    - **sore**: caust *Dulc*
    - **stitching** pain: arg-met ars dulc sep
    - **tearing** pain: *Agar* am-m arg-met *Ars* cina *Lyc* **Rhus-t** thuj
  - **arm**; of:
    - **agg.**: dig ↓
      - **pressing** pain: dig h2
  - **backward** agg.: ozone sde2•
  - **hindering** motion: nux-v
  - **passive** motion:
    - **agg.**: merc-i-f ↓
      - **sore**: merc-i-f
- **neuralgic**: *Acon* k* aesc all-c bro1 alum bro1 arn ars k* *Bry* bro1 calc c2 cham bro1 coc-c bro1 corn-f br1* crot-h *Crot-t* dirc c1 *Ferr* graph hyper c2* ign indg c2 iod kali-c bro1 *Kalm* bro1* lyc k* *Merc* bro1 merc-i-f k2 mez k2 *Nux-v* bro1 par c2* phos pip-m bro1 *Puls* bro1 ran-b *Rhus-t* k* scut bro1 sep *Staph* sulph k* ter k* teucr bro1 tub-m jl2 verat k* visc bro1
- **numbness**; with: sep ↓
  - **tearing** pain: sep h2
- **palpitation**, with (See CHEST - Palpitation - accompanied - upper)
- **paralyzed**; as if: *Acon* b7a.de alum k* am-c b4.de* am-m b7a.de* ang b7.de* ant-c vh1 arg-met b7.de* arg-n asar bg2 *Bell* b4a.de* bism b7.de* bov b4.de* brom bg2 *Calc* k* carbn-s caust bg2 *Cham* b7.de* *Chel* chin b7.de* cimic cina k* cocc k* **Colch** k* coloc k* con b4.de* croc b7.de* crot-h cur cycl b7.de* dig b4.de* dulc b4.de* ferr b7.de* guaj *Hep* b4a.de *Ign* b7a.de iod bg2 kali-c b4.de* kalm led bg2 lyc bg2 m-aust b7.de *Mag-m* b4a.de mang k* meny b7a.de meph bg2* *Merc* k* merc-i-f sma

Extremities

- **paralyzed**; as if: ...
mez b4.de* mur-ac b4.de* **Nat-m** b4.de* nit-ac bg2 **Nux-v** b7.de* op bg2 par b7.de* phos k* plat b4.de* puls b7.de* rhod b4.de* *Rhus-t* k* sabin b7a.de* sars b4.de* seneg b4.de* sep b4.de* *Sil* b4.de* stann b4.de* staph k* stront-c bg2 sul-ac b4.de* sulph bg2 thuj b4.de* **Verat** b7.de* *Zinc* b4.de*
- **paralyzed** limb: agar *Ars* bell calc caust *Cocc* crot-t *Kali-n* lat-m plb sil sulph
- **paroxysmal**: arg-met *Caust Cina Kalm* lach lyc *Mag-p* meny *Ran-b* sul-ac
- **periodical**: cinnb ↓ cist ↓
  - **year**; every: vip
  - **shooting** pain: cinnb
  - **stitching** pain: cist
- **perspiration**:
  - **amel.**: thuj
  - **during**: anac bg2 *Ant-t* bg2 *Arn* bg2 **Ars** bg2 *Bell* bg2 *Bry* bg2 **Calc** bg2 canth bg2 carb-v bg2 cham bg2 *Chin* bg2 *Coff* bg2 dig bg2 hell bg2 ign bg2 kali-n bg2 led bg2 **Lyc** bg2 **Merc** bg2 *Merc-c* bg2 **Nux-v** bg2 op bg2 phos bg2 *Puls* bg2 **Rhod** bg2 **Rhus-t** bg2 sabad bg2 *Sep* bg2 **Sulph** bg2 tarax bg2 zinc bg2
- **pinching** pain: acon bg2 arg-met b7.de* caust b4.de* cina b7.de* dig b4.de* euph b4.de* euphr b7.de* ip b7.de* meny b7.de* olnd b7.de* ph-ac b4.de* rhus-t b7.de* sabad b7.de* spong b7.de* stann b4.de* sulph b4.de*
- **playing** piano: *Gels*
- **pregnancy** agg.; during: zing ↓
  - **sore**: zing bro1
- **pressing** pain: ambr b7.de *Anac* k* ang bg2 *Ant-c* b7.de* arg-met k* arg-n a1 arn b7.de asaf a1 asar k* bell k* berb bism calc k* camph carb-v k* *Caust* k* cham k* clem k* coloc k* *Cycl* k* dig k* dros b7.de* *Dulc* k* *Fl-ac* k* ind k* iod kali-c k* *Kalm* k* lach k* led k* lil-t k* lyc k* m-arct b7.de mag-c b4.de* mag-m b4.de* manc k* mez b4.de* mur-ac nat-s k* nit-ac k* nit-s-d a1 petr k* *Ph-ac* b4a.de phos k* *Plat* b4a.de puls k* rhus-t b7.de sars k* sep b4.de* sil k* stann k* staph k* *Sul-ac* b4a.de sul-i k2 *Sulph* k* tarax b7.de* tarent thuj k*
  - **cramping**: dros h1 petr
  - **drawing** pain: thuj k*
  - **inward**: lach k*
  - **outward**: lil-t k* thuj h1*
  - **paralyzed**; as if: cham coloc k* staph
  - **tearing** pain: asar h1 led k*
- **pressing** together: nat-s bg2 spig bg2 spong bg2 stann bg2
- **pressure**:
  - **agg.**: adam skp7• berb cassia-s ↓ *Cina* ↓ merc-i-f plb ↓ *Puls* ↓ rhus-v sil *Spig*
    - **broken**; as if: *Puls* k*
    - **sore**: cassia-s ccrh1• *Cina Merc-i-f*
    - **tearing** pain: plb
  - **amel.**: cassia-s ccrh1•
- **pronation**, during: petr
- **putting** on coat: merc-i-r ↓
  - **sore**: merc-i-r
- **raising** arm agg.: *Apis* bar-c ptk caj calc cassia-s ccrh1• cocc eup-pur **Ferr** kali-p lac-c *Nit-ac* ↓ olnd phyt *Sang* sulph syph tab verat ↓ zinc
  - **drawing** pain: cocc sulph h2
  - **pressing** pain: sulph k*
  - **sore**: cassia-s ccrh1• *Nit-ac* verat h1 zinc h2
- **raw**; as if: bov bg2 cic bg2 dig bg2 nux-v bg2 phos bg2
- **rest** agg.: ang ↓ nat-c ↓ sep ↓
  - **shooting** pain: sep
  - **tearing** pain: ang h1 nat-c h2
- **rheumatic**: abrot *Aesc* agar b4.de* alumn ambr b7.de* ammc anac b4.de* ang b7.de* *Ant-c* k* *Ant-t* k* arg-n ars ars-i ars-s-f k2 asaf b7.de* asc-t a1 astac k* bacls-7 mtf11 bell k* berb borx b4a.de **Bry** k* *Cact* **Calc-p** carb-v b4.de* *Chel* k* chin *Cimic* k* coff b7.de* **Colch** k* *Coloc* com dros *Dulc* k* elaps ↓ euph b4.de* **Ferr** ferr-ar *Ferr-i* fl-ac gels bg2 gran ↓ graph b4.de* grat *Guaj* k* ham k* hydr k2 ign b7.de* iod k* iodof a1 kali-bi k* *Kalm* lach k* *Led Lyc* med meph k* **Merc** k* *Merc-i-f* mez k* *Nat-ar* nat-c nit-ac *Nux-v* k* ph-ac b4a.de phel phos k* *Phyt* k* podo *Puls* k* *Ran-b* *Rhod* k* **Rhus-t** k* rhus-v sabin b7.de* sal-ac c1 **Sang** k* squil k* stel stict stram b7.de* *Sulph* k* syc bka1* syph k2 teucr k* thuj k* ust *Valer* k* ven-m rsj12• verat k* viol-o zinc b4.de*
  - **night**: morg-g fmm1•
  - **drawing** pain: chel a1 elaps gran k* *Phyt* puls
  - **menopause**; during: sal-ac c1
  - **pressing** pain: dulc
- **rising**:
  - **amel.**: nat-c ↓
    - **tearing** pain: nat-c h2
- **rubbing**:
  - **agg.**: berb crot-t ↓ kalm merc-i-f
    - **burning**: crot-t
    - **sore**: *Merc-i-f*
  - **leaves** upper and goes to lower limbs: *Kalm*
- **scraping** pain: sulph
- **scratching**:
  - **after**: kreos ↓ led ↓ merc ↓ til ↓
    - **burning**: kreos led merc til
  - **amel.**: jug-c ↓
    - **burning**: jug-c
- **scratching**, when: berb lach
- **sewing**, when: eupi
- **shooting** pain: acon bg2 aesc agath-a nl2• brach calc-p cann-s cinnb *Con Crot-t* cupr cystein-l rly4• daph *Ferr* k* *Lith-c* mez bg2 nat-ar k2 phos k* pic-ac puls bg2 ran-b c1 *Rhus-t* k* sabin c1 sep sol-ni *Still* sulph k* valer
  - **downward**: aesc cann-s daph *Ferr Manc* phos pic-ac still
- **singing** agg.: stann ↓
  - **aching**: stann k*
- **sitting** agg.: berb ↓ bry ↓ cassia-s ccrh1• caust ↓ coloc ↓ nicc ↓ **Valer** ↓
  - **drawing** pain: **Valer**
  - **sore**: berb bry caust coloc
  - **tearing** pain: nicc **Valer**
- **sleep**:
  - **after** | **agg.**: morph
  - **siesta**: | **during**: lyc
- **smarting**: berb bg2 puls b7.de*
- **sore**: acon k* aesc agar k* all-c alum k* am-c k* am-m bg2 aml-ns ammc anac k* ang k* apis arg-met arg-n bro1 *Arn* k* ars asaf asar b7.de* aster aur b4.de* bell bg2 berb beryl sp1 bit-ar wht1• borx bov b4.de* *Bry* k* *Calc* calc-p calc-s cann-s k* *Carb-ac* carb-v k* carbn-s card-m cassia-s ccrh1• castor-eq **Caust** k* chinin-s chlor cic b7.de* cina b7.de* cist clem cocc k* coloc k* com *Con* k* cot br1 *Croc* k* crot-h crot-t cupr bro1 *Cur* dig b4.de* dros bg2 *Dulc* k* **Eup-per** *Ferr* ferr-ar graph k* grat ham fd3.de• hep k* hyper ign b7.de* indg kali-bi k* kali-c b4.de* kāli-n bg2 kali-sil k2 kreos *Lach* laur led lyc k* lyss m-arct b7.de mag-c k* malar jl2 mang bg2 meph merc merc-i-f merc-i-r mez k* nat-m k* nat-s *Nit-ac* k* nux-v ol-an olnd bro1 *Ph-ac* k* phos pip-m *Plat* k* plb k* plumbg *Puls* k* *Rhus-t* k* rhus-v rob *Ruta* k* sacch-a fd2.de• sang sarr sec bro1 *Sep* sil k* spong k* stann b4.de* stram bg2 stry sul-ac bro1 *Sulph* k* sumb tep thuj b4.de* *Verat* k* verat-v bro1 vip zinc k* *Zinc-s* bro1
  - **paralyzed**; as if: alum coloc h2 dulc
  - **upward**: cassia-s ccrh1•
- **splinter**; as from a: colch b7.de* nit-ac b4a.de plat b4a.de sil b4a.de
- **spots**; in: am-c ↓ ambr b7a.de bry ↓ merc ↓ nux-m ↓ nux-v ↓ ph-ac ↓
  - **burning**: am-c bry merc ph-ac
  - **pressing** pain: nux-m k* nux-v
- **sprained**; as if: *Ambr Arn* aur-m bell beryl sp1 borx bov *Ign* jug-c lach lact merc mez h2 nit-ac olnd petr h2 *Phos* prun ter thuj

- **squeezed**; as if: alum b4a.de ang b7a.de **Arn** b7.de* bell b4.de* bufo bg2 calad b7.de* calc b4.de* carb-v bg2 caust bg2 chel b7.de* *Cic* b7a.de cina b7.de* colch b7.de* dig b4.de* dros b7.de* graph b4.de* kali-bi bg2 kali-c b4.de* kali-n b4.de* meny b7a.de mez b4.de* mosch b7.de* nat-c b4.de* olnd b7a.de petr bg2 ph-ac b4.de* puls b7.de* ran-b b7a.de rhod b4.de* *Ruta* b7.de* sil b4.de* spig b7.de* spong b7.de stann b4.de stront-c b4.de* sulph bg2
- **steam** agg.; exposure to: kali-bi ↓
  - **burning**: kali-bi
- **stitching** pain: acon aesc all-c alum k* alum-p k2 alum-sil k2 am-c ang ant-c k* ant-t *Apis* k* arg-met k* arn ars-h asaf asar k* aur k* aur-m benz-ac berb bov brach bry k* bufo calc k* calc-p cann-s k* canth carb-v k* carbn-o *Carbn-s* castor-eq caust k* cham chel k* chlor **Cic** k* *Cina* k* cinnb cist clem k* *Cocc* k* coloc k* *Con* *Crot-t* *Cupr* cycl *Dig* b4a.de dor dros k* *Dulc* k* elaps euphr eupi fago *Ferr* k* ferr-i k2 ferr-p fl-ac form fum rly1• glon graph k* guaj k* hell hyper ind iod kali-bi *Kali-c* k* kali-i *Kali-n* b4a.de kreos b7a.de* lac-c lach k* led lept *Lith-c* *Lyc* k* m-ambo b7.de m-arct b7.de *Mag-m* k* manc *Merc* b4a.de mez k* nat-c k* nat-m k* nit-ac k* nux-v ol-an ox-ac pall petr k* ph-ac phel *Phos* k* phys *Phyt* pic-ac plat plb psor puls k* *Ran-b* k* *Ran-s* b7a.de raph rat rheum k* *Rhod* k* **Rhus-t** k* rhus-v ruta k* sabad k* sabin k* sacch *Sars* k* senec *Sep* k* sil k* sol-ni spong k* stann k* staph b7.de* *Stict* *Still* stry sul-ac bg2 *Sulph* k* tarax b7.de* *Tarent* ther bg2 *Thuj* k* urt-u valer k* viol-t k* zinc k* zinc-p k2
  - **asleep**; as if: *Sil*
  - **cramping**: *Cina*
  - **downward**: aesc cann-s cupr daph *Ferr* fl-ac *Manc* petr phos pic-ac puls **Rhus-t** still
  - **wandering** pain: arg-met ars-h castor-eq lac-c *Puls* sulph
- **stool**; before: rhus-t bg2
- **stretching**:
  - **agg.**: (↗*extending them; extending them - amel.)* alum caust sulph
  - **arm**:
    - **agg.**: sulph ↓
      - **drawing** pain: sulph h2
      - **pressing** pain: sulph k*
  - **arms**:
    - **agg.**: hipp ↓
      - **tearing** pain: hipp
  - **must** stretch: nat-m ↓
    - **drawing** pain: nat-m h2
- **supinating** forearm: cinnb
- **swollen** axillary glands, with: **Bar-c**
- **taking** hold of anything: am-c arn calc calc-sil k2 carb-v caust cham dros led plat puls **Rhus-t** sil verat
  - **amel.**: lith-c
- **taking** hold of them: *Calc* ↓
  - **sore**: *Calc*
- **talking** agg.: mang hr1
- **tearing** pain: *Acon* k* aesc agar k* *Alum* k* alum-p k2 alum-sil k2 am-c k* *Am-m* k* *Ambr* k* anac k* ang b7.de* *Ant-c* b7a.de ant-t k* apis b7a.de *Arg-met* k* *Arg-n* arn k* *Ars* k* ars-h ars-s-f k2 asaf asar k* aur aur-ar k2 aur-m aur-s k2 *Bell* k* benz-ac berb bism borx bov brom bry k* bufo *Cact* *Calc* k* calc-i k2 *Calc-p* k* camph cann-xyz bg2 canth k* *Caps* k* carb-an k* carb-v k* carbn-s **Caust** k* cham k* chel *Chin* k* chinin-ar cic k* *Cina* k* cinnb clem *Cocc* k* coff k* *Colch* k* *Coloc* *Con* crot-h crot-t *Cupr* k* dig k* dulc k* *Euph* b4a.de *Ferr* k* ferr-i ferr-m form grat *Guaj* k* hell bg2 hep k* *Hyper* ign k* indg iod *Kali-ar* *Kali-bi* *Kali-c* k* *Kali-n* k* *Kali-p* kali-s kalm kreos lach k* lachn *Led* k* *Lyc* k* lyss m-ambo b7.de *Mag-c* k* **Mag-m** k* mag-s mang k* meny meph bg2 *Merc* k* mez k* mur-ac k* nat-ar **Nat-c** k* nat-m k* *Nat-p* **Nat-s** nicc *Nit-ac* k* nux-m bg2 nux-v k* ol-an par k* *Ph-ac* k* phel *Phos* k* plat **Plb** k* *Psor* puls k* ran-b raph *Rhod* k* **Rhus-t** k* ruta sabin *Sars* k* sep k* **Sil** k* *Squil* b7a.de stann k* staph b7.de* stront-c k* stry sul-ac k* sul-i k2 **Sulph** k* tep *Teucr* *Thuj* k* **Valer** k* verb *Zinc* k* zinc-p k2
  - **cramping**: aur bell h1 bism h1 nat-c ruta
  - **downward**: acon b7a.de *Aesc* ant-t b7a.de asaf b7a.de bell b4a.de* calc k* camph canth b7a.de caps b7a.de *Carb-v* b4a.de caust h2 cham *Chin* k* cina b7a.de con b4a.de crot-t ferr b7a.de ign b7a.de kali-c k* kali-n k* lach lyc k* m-aust b7a.de mang b4a.de *Merc* b4a.de nat-c k* nit-ac b4a.de ph-ac b4a.de puls k* rhod b4a.de rhus-t b7a.de sabin sars b4a.de seneg b4a.de *Sep* b4a.de squil b7a.de *Sulph* b4a.de thuj b4a.de verat b7a.de zinc b4a.de
  - **intermittent**: kali-n h2
  - **jerking** pain: **Chin** puls sil
  - **paralyzed**; as if: *Cham* *Chin* *Cina* *Ferr-m* mag-m stann
  - **paroxysmal**: **Calc** kali-n sep
  - **twitching**: ph-ac h2 sul-ac h2
  - **upward**: *Alum* b4a.de anac b4a.de ant-c b7a.de arn *Ars* k* *Asaf* b7a.de aur b4a.de *Bell* b4a.de calc b4a.de colch b7a.de con b4a.de m-arct b7a.de mag-c b4a.de nat-c b4a.de nat-m b4a.de *Nux-v* b7a.de ph-ac b4a.de rhod b4a.de samb b7a.de sep sulph b4a.de valer b7a.de
  - **wandering** pain: *Kali-bi*
- **thinking** about it: *Ox-ac*
- **tired**; as if: beryl tpw5 *Lach* *Nux-v* verat
- **touch** agg.: agar berb carb-an **Chin** cocc crot-t ↓ euph fic-m gya1 ip ↓ lob staph ↓
  - **aching**: ip
  - **burning**: crot-t
  - **drawing** pain: staph k*
  - **pressing** pain: staph h1*
  - **tearing** pain: *Chin*
- **turning**:
  - **amel.**: sphing k*
  - **bed**; in | **agg.**: *Sang* k*
- **twinging**: pyrus *Rhus-t* k* teucr k*
- **ulcerative** pain: am-m b7.de* ang b7.de* bell b4.de* berb bov b4.de* bry b7.de* cic b7.de* graph b4.de* kali-c b4.de* mang b4.de* plat b4.de* sars b4a.de sil b4.de* thuj k*
- **uncovering**:
  - **agg.**: crot-t ↓
    - **burning**: crot-t
  - **amel.**: lac-c **Led** lyc bg1 **Puls** sulph
- **vexation**; after: nat-m ↓
  - **burning**: nat-m
- **vibrating**: berb k*
- **waking**; on: abrot chel ↓ mag-s ↓ rumx ↓ sulph ↓
  - **sore**: chel mag-s rumx sulph
- **walking**:
  - **after** | **agg.**: pall
  - **agg.**: ant-c ↓ arg-n cassia-s ↓ dios ↓
    - **sore**: cassia-s ccrh1• dios
    - **stitching** pain: ant-c
  - **amel.**: arg-met ↓ daph *Kali-s* ↓ merc-i-f k2 *Rhod* ↓ **Rhus-t** ↓ *Valer* verat
    - **drawing** pain: **Valer**
    - **sore**: verat
    - **tearing** pain: arg-met *Kali-s* *Rhod* **Rhus-t** **Valer**
  - **slowly** | **amel.**: *Ferr*
- **wandering** pain: ars ars-s-f k2 asaf cact castor-eq *Caul* chel ery-a fl-ac *Lac-c* med *Phyt* *Pip-m* psil ft1 *Puls* sol-ni sulph
- **warm** room agg.: zing ↓
  - **drawing** pain: zing k*
- **warmth**:
  - **agg.**: ant-t apis bry calc caust cham dulc *Guaj* *Lac-ac* **Led** lyc bg1 merc-i-f k2 nux-v **Puls** sabad *Stel* stront-c *Sulph* thuj zinc
  - **amel.**: **Ars** ars-s-f k2 cinnb *Graph* *Mag-p* mand rsj7• *Sil*
    - **heat** amel.: *Ferr* ↓
      - **sore**: *Ferr*
- **washing** | **after**:
  - **agg.**: bov ↓
    - **burning**: bov
  - **agg.**: am-c *Sulph*
- **waves**; in: acon b7.de*

Extremities

- **weather**:
  - **cold** agg.: agar **Calc-p** calc-sil$_{k2}$ kali-c kalm
  - **stormy**:
    - **agg.**: **Rhod Rhus-t**
      - **drawing** pain: *Rhod*
  - **wet**:
    - **agg.**: *Dulc Phyt Ran-b Rhod Rhus-t* verat
      - **drawing** pain: *Rhod Rhus-t*
- **winter** agg.: petr
- **work** amel.: caust ↓
  - **sore**: caust
- **writing**:
  - **after**: thuj ↓
    - **drawing** pain: thuj$_{k}$*
  - **agg.**: cer-s cere-b cere-s cinnb ↓ *Cycl* **Mag-p** *Merc-i-f Pip-m* sul-ac
    - **aching**: merc-i-f
    - **drawing** pain: **Mag-p** sul-ac$_{k}$*
    - **sore**: *Merc-i-f*
    - **tearing** pain: cinnb
- **yawning** agg.: nux-v

▽ • **extending** to:
  - **All** parts: chin ↓
    - **tearing** pain: chin
  - **Arms**; down: aesc ↓ nat-ar ↓
    - **shooting** pain: aesc nat-ar$_{k2}$
  - **Back**: ars caust dios
    - **tearing** pain: caust
  - **Body**; whole: apis ↓ malar ↓
    - **burning**: apis
    - **sore**: malar$_{jl2}$
  - **Chest**: caust$_{bg1}$ lach ↓ vip
    - **drawing** pain: lach
  - **Downward**: aran *Arn Aspar* carb-an *Guaj* kalm$_{k}$* lach$_{bg1}$ nat-ar **Rhod** sumb ↓
    - **aching**: sumb
  - **Elbow**: ozone$_{sde2}$•
  - **Fingers**: aesc ↓ agar ↓ alum ↓ am-m ↓ apis ↓ bry ↓ calc-p ↓ camph ↓ caps ↓ carbn-h ↓ cham ↓ chel ↓ *Chin* ↓ cist ↓ *Coloc* ↓ crot-h ↓ crot-t ↓ cycl ↓ euphr ↓ gran ↓ hydrog$_{srj2}$• kali-n ↓ *Lyc* ↓ mag-m ↓ nat-c ↓ ol-an ↓ puls ↓ *Rhus-t* ↓ rhus-v ↓ *Sep* ↓ sil ↓ staph ↓ thuj ↓
    - **aching**: calc-p euphr hydrog$_{srj2}$•
    - **boring** pain: gran
    - **burning**: mag-m
    - **drawing** pain: aesc bry carbn-h chel crot-h cycl$_{h1}$ *Lyc Rhus-t Sep* thuj$_{h1}$
      - **downward**: agar apis cist cycl lyc ol-an puls rhus-t rhus-v *Sep* sil
    - **face**; from: *Coff*
    - **heart** to fingers; from: *Aur Cocc Cycl Guaj* lat-m
    - **paralyzed**; as if: staph$_{tl1}$
    - **tearing** pain: alum am-m camph caps cham *Chin Coloc* crot-t kali-n$_{h2}$ lyc mag-m nat-c
    - **write**; difficult to: cycl ↓
      - **paralyzed**; as if: cycl$_{tl1}$
    - **First**: aesc ↓
      - **tearing** pain: aesc
    - **Fourth**: aur-m ↓ hura nat-ar sil ↓
      - **axilla** to fourth; from: nat-ar
      - **drawing** pain: sil$_{h2}$
      - **tearing** pain: aur-m
    - **Third** finger: xan$_{c1}$
    - **Tips**: cist ↓ puls ↓
      - **stitching** pain: cist puls
  - **Forearm**, into: dios ↓
    - **aching**: dios
  - **Hand**: fl-ac ↓ kali-c ↓ rhus-v ↓

• **extending** to – **Hand**: ...
  - **burning**: fl-ac
  - **drawing** pain: kali-c$_{h2}$
    - **downward**: kali-c rhus-v
- **Head**: aloe$_{bg1}$ carb-v$_{b4a.de}$
- **Lower** limbs: malar ↓
  - **sore**: malar$_{jl2}$
- **Shoulders**: cassia-s ↓ ozone ↓
  - **sore**: cassia-s$_{ccrh1}$•
  - **tearing** pain: ozone$_{sde2}$•
- **Thumb**: camph ↓ cham ↓ lyc ↓ sil ↓
  - **tearing** pain: camph cham lyc sil
- **Ulnar** nerve, along: aesc ↓ thuj ↓
  - **tearing** pain: aesc thuj
- **Up** and down: con$_{bg1}$ sil$_{bg1}$
- **Upward**: aq-mar$_{skp7}$• bufo$_{br1}$ caust$_{bg2}$ nux-v$_{bg2}$ phos$_{bg2}$
- **Wrist**: aesc ↓ am-c ↓ asc-t ↓ kali-c ↓ kali-n ↓ nat-c ↓ *Puls* ↓
  - **drawing** pain: am-c *Puls*
  - **shooting** pain: aesc
  - **stitching** pain: asc-t
  - **tearing** pain: kali-c kali-n nat-c

○ • **Bones**: acon$_{bg2}$ agar ↓ alum ↓ am-c ↓ am-m$_{b7a.de}$ anac$_{bg2}$ ang$_{bg2}$ ant-t ↓ apis$_{k}$* *Arg-met* ↓ arn ↓ ars asaf$_{b7a.de}$* aur ↓ bar-c$_{b4.de}$* bell ↓ benz-ac ↓ bism ↓ bov ↓ bry ↓ bufo ↓ cact ↓ calc ↓ calc-p ↓ canth ↓ carb-an ↓ carb-v ↓ caust ↓ cham ↓ chin$_{bg3}$ cocc$_{b7.de}$* *Coloc* ↓ con ↓ cupr ↓ *Cycl* ↓ *Dros* ↓ **Eup-per** ↓ euph ↓ fl-ac$_{bg2}$ glon$_{bg2}$ graph ↓ hell ↓ hep ↓ ign$_{b7.de}$* *Iod*$_{k}$* ip ↓ kali-bi$_{k}$* kali-c ↓ **Lach**$_{bg2}$ laur ↓ **Lyc**$_{k}$* m-arct ↓ mag-c$_{k}$* mang ↓ meph$_{bg2}$ merc$_{k}$* *Merc-c* ↓ mez$_{bg2}$ nat-c$_{bg2}$ nat-m$_{bg2}$ nit-ac$_{bg2}$ *Olnd* ↓ par ↓ petr ↓ ph-ac$_{b4a.de}$ phos ↓ plat$_{k}$* plb$_{bg2}$ puls ↓ rhod$_{bg2}$ rhus-t$_{b7.de}$* ruta$_{bg2}$ sabad sabin ↓ samb ↓ *Sars* ↓ sep ↓ sil$_{bg2}$* spig ↓ spong ↓ staph$_{b7.de}$* stront-c ↓ stroph-h$_{bg3}$ sul-ac ↓ **Sulph**$_{bg2}$ teucr thuj$_{bg2}$ *Valer* ↓ vanil$_{fd5.de}$ verat$_{b7.de}$* verb ↓ *Zinc* ↓
  - **right** arm: asc-t$_{a1}$
  - **left** arm: asc-t$_{a1}$
  - **aching**: apis *Calc-p* **Eup-per** glon
  - **boring** pain: ars kali-bi mang$_{b4a.de}$ sabad
  - **broken**; as if: nat-m$_{bg2}$
  - **burning**: par$_{b7.de}$ *Rhus-t*$_{b7a.de}$
  - **crushed**; as if: merc$_{bg2}$
  - **cutting** pain: bufo$_{bg2}$
  - **drawing** pain: acon$_{b7.de}$* alum$_{k}$* ant-t$_{b7.de}$* arn$_{b7.de}$* asaf$_{b7.de}$* bar-c$_{k}$* bry$_{b7.de}$* canth$_{b7.de}$* carb-an carb-v$_{k}$* caust$_{k}$* cham$_{b7.de}$* chin$_{b7.de}$* cocc$_{b7.de}$* coloc$_{b4.de}$* euph$_{b4.de}$* ip$_{b7.de}$* kali-bi$_{bg2}$ lyc mag-c$_{k}$* nat-m$_{k}$* nit-ac$_{k}$* plb$_{b7.de}$* puls$_{b7.de}$* *Rhod*$_{k}$* sabin$_{b7.de}$* samb$_{b7.de}$* sep$_{k}$* spig$_{b7a.de}$* staph$_{b7.de}$* teucr$_{b7a.de}$ *Thuj*$_{k}$* *Valer*$_{k}$* verat$_{b7.de}$*
  - **exertion**; as after: anac$_{bg2}$
  - **gnawing** pain: bell$_{bg2}$ kali-bi$_{bg2}$ sulph$_{bg2}$
  - **gouty**: lach$_{bg2}$
  - **grasping** pain: nat-c$_{bg2}$
  - **griping**: nat-c$_{h2}$
  - **hammering**: nit-ac$_{bg2}$
  - **jerking** pain: phos$_{b4.de}$* rhod$_{b4.de}$*
  - **motion**:
    - **amel.**: coloc ↓
      - **pressing** pain: coloc
  - **pressing** pain: *Anac*$_{k}$* ang$_{b7.de}$* *Arg-met*$_{b7a.de}$ arn$_{b7.de}$* asaf$_{b7.de}$* bism$_{b7.de}$* bry$_{b7.de}$* cham$_{b7.de}$* *Coloc*$_{k}$* con$_{k}$* cupr$_{b7a.de}$ *Cycl*$_{b7a.de}$ kali-c$_{k}$* *Mez*$_{k}$* *Olnd*$_{b7a.de}$ phos$_{k}$* plat$_{b4a.de}$ puls$_{b7a.de}$ sil$_{h2}$* spong$_{b7.de}$* staph$_{b7.de}$* thuj$_{k}$* valer$_{b7.de}$* verat$_{b7.de}$*
  - **scraping** pain: asaf$_{b7.de}$* chin$_{b7.de}$ puls$_{b7a.de}$ *Rhus-t*$_{b7a.de}$ sabad$_{b7.de}$* spig$_{b7a.de}$
  - **sore**: agar$_{b4.de}$* ang$_{b7.de}$* asaf$_{b7.de}$* bar-c$_{b4.de}$* bov$_{b4.de}$* cocc$_{b7.de}$* fl-ac$_{bg2}$ hep$_{b4.de}$* *Ign*$_{b7.de}$* nat-m$_{b4.de}$* phos$_{b4.de}$* puls$_{b7.de}$* *Ruta*$_{b7.de}$* zinc$_{b4.de}$*

- **Bones**: ...
  - **stitching** pain: acon b7.de* asaf b7.de* bufo calc k* chin b7.de* cocc b7.de* dros b7.de* graph b4a.de kali-c b4a.de lach b7a.de m-arct b7.de merc k* mez k* nat-m b4a.de par b7.de* petr k* *Sars* k* valer b7.de*
  - **tearing** pain: acon bg2 am-c bg2 am-m b7.de* ang b7.de* arg-met bg2 arn b7.de* ars b7a.de* aur k* bell b4.de* benz-ac bism b7.de* cact canth b7.de* carb-v k* caust k* cham b7.de* *Chin* k* cocc b7.de* cupr b7a.de *Cycl* b7a.de *Dros* b7a.de hell b7.de* iod k* *Kali-bi* k* lach b7a.de laur b7.de* *Lyc* bg2 meph bg2* *Merc* k* *Merc-c* b4a.de mez nat-c b4a.de nit-ac bg2 phos k* plb bg2 puls b7.de* *Rhod* k* ruta b7.de* sabin b7.de* spig b7a.de stront-c k* sul-ac b4.de* sulph k* *Teucr* b7a.de thuj bg2 verb b7.de* *Zinc* k*
- **Brachial** plexus: mez k2
- **Flexors** | **grasping** something; when: *Nat-s*
- **Inner** side: arn ↓ benz-ac ↓ carbn-o ↓ chel ↓ lept ↓ tarax ↓
  - **pressing** pain: tarax h1
  - **stitching** pain: arn benz-ac carbn-o chel lept
- **Internally**: euph ↓ sulph ↓
  - **drawing** pain: euph k* sulph k*
- **Joints**: agar ↓ alum ↓ alumn ↓ *Am-c* b4.de* anac ↓ arg-n ↓ ars ↓ aur ↓ aur-m-n bar-c ↓ *Bov* ↓ *Brom* b4a.de bry ↓ bufo ↓ cact ↓ **Calc** k* carb-an b4.de* *Carb-v* ↓ caul ↓ caust b4.de* cham ↓ *Chin* ↓ clem ↓ coloc ↓ con ↓ cupr dig b4.de* *Dros* ↓ ferr ↓ **Graph** ↓ grat ↓ hell ↓ *Hep* ↓ hyos ↓ ign b7.de* *Iod* b4a.de kali-bi ↓ kali-c b4.de* kali-n b4.de* kreos ↓ lact ↓ laur ↓ led lyc bg3 m-ambo ↓ mag-c b4.de* mag-m b4.de* mang k* merc bg3 merc-c ↓ mez ↓ *Mur-ac* ↓ nat-c b4.de* nat-m k* nit-ac ↓ par ↓ petr b4.de* **Ph-ac** ↓ phos b4.de* plb k* puls ↓ *Rheum* b7a.de rhod b4.de* rhus-t bg3 *Sars* ↓ sep b4.de* sil ↓ *Spig* ↓ *Stann* ↓ staph ↓ stram ↓ *Stront-c* ↓ sul-ac b4.de* sulph tab ↓ teucr thuj ↓ verat ↓ viol-t ↓ *Zinc* ↓
  - **morning**: stront-c ↓
    - **tearing** pain: stront-c
  - **evening**: ign
  - **bending**:
    - **agg.**: stann
    - **backward**:
      - **agg.**: ign ↓
        - **sore**: ign
  - **boring** pain: arg-n bg2 carb-v b4.de* caust b4.de* m-ambo b7.de rhod b4.de* thuj b4.de*
  - **burning**: *Carb-v* k* graph k* *Nat-c* k* stront-c k*
  - **crushed**; as if: bufo bg2
  - **cutting** pain: alum bg2
  - **drawing** pain: am-c b4.de* calc b4.de* carb-v b4.de* caul caust b4.de* cham h1 clem b4a.de graph b4.de* hyos b7.de* kali-bi k* kali-c b4a.de kreos lyc b4.de* m-ambo b7a.de *Mang* mez b4.de* nat-m b4.de* ph-ac b4.de* rhod k* sep b4.de* *Sulph* b4a.de teucr b7a.de zinc b4.de*
    - **twitching**: sulph h2
  - **fever**; during: *Calc* bg2 kali-c bg2 rhus-t bg2
  - **gnawing** pain: mag-c b4.de* mang b4.de*
  - **gouty**: caust ↓
    - **drawing** pain: caust h2
  - **jerking** pain: alum b4.de* bry b7.de* *Chin* b7a.de nat-m b4.de* sil b4.de* sul-ac b4.de* verat b7a.de
  - **motion**:
    - **agg.**: caust ↓ nat-m
      - **drawing** pain: caust h2
    - **amel.**: aur-m-n
  - **paralyzed**; as if: *Bov* b4a.de carb-v b4.de* caust b4.de* dig b4.de* kali-c b4.de* mez b4.de* nit-ac b4.de* par b7.de* sars b4.de* stann b4.de* stront-c b4.de*
  - **paroxysmal**: mang
  - **perspiration**; during: calc bg2 caust bg2 chin bg2 **Hell** bg2 kali-c bg2 kali-n bg2 led bg2 lyc bg2 *Merc* bg2 *Nux-v* bg2 ph-ac bg2 phos bg2 **Rhus-t** bg2 sars bg2 *Sep* bg2 **Sulph** bg2 *Thuj* bg2 zinc bg2
  - **pressing** pain: anac k* calc k* cham b7.de* kali-c k* mez k* nit-ac k* sep k* sulph k* zinc k*
  - **rheumatic**: anan asaf bry hep kali-bi lach *Led Lyc Merc Petr Phos* rhod *Rhus-t* sabin sars spig stann
  - **sewing**; when: arist-cl sp1

- **Upper** limbs – **Joints**: ...
  - **sitting** agg.: stront-c ↓
    - **tearing** pain: stront-c
  - **sore**: agar b4.de* alum alumn aur b4a.de aur-m-n bov b4.de* chin b7.de* *Dros* b7a.de m-ambo b7.de merc-c b4a.de *Mur-ac* b4a.de nat-m b4.de* nit-ac b4.de* ph-ac sulph b4.de*
  - **sprained**; as if: stann h2
  - **stitching** pain: ars b4.de* bar-c b4.de* bov b4.de* bry *Calc* k* carb-v b4.de* dros k* ferr graph k* hell b7.de* *Hep* b4a.de hyos b7.de* iod b4.de* *Kali-c* b4a.de kali-n k* laur led lyc *Mang* b4a.de *Merc* b4a.de nit-ac b4.de* phos k* puls sars k* *Sep* k* sil b4.de* *Spig* b7a.de *Stann* k* staph *Sul-ac* k* *Sulph* k* tab thuj k* viol-t zinc b4.de*
  - **tearing** pain: alum k* am-c k* bov k* cact calc k* carb-v k* caust k* cham b7.de* chin k* coloc con dig k* **Graph** k* grat hyos b7.de* iod k* kali-bi k* **Kali-c** k* kali-n k* lact *Led* b7a.de *Lyc* k* m-ambo b7.de nat-c k* nit-ac k* **Ph-ac** k* phos k* puls *Sars* b4a.de sep k* sil k* spig bg2 stram *Stront-c* k* *Sulph* k* *Teucr* k* *Zinc* k*
    - **wandering** pain: kali-bi
  - **writing** agg.: cinnb
  - **Bones**: *Ambr* bg2 *Lyc* bg2
  - **Joint** to joint, from: sulph ↓
    - **drawing** pain: sulph h2
  - **Side** lain on: *Ign*
- **Outer** side: mag-m ↓
  - **tearing** pain: mag-m h2
- **Outer** surface: benz-ac ↓ tarax ↓
  - **stitching** pain: benz-ac tarax
- **Part** lain on: cina ↓
  - **drawing** pain: cina h1
- **Skin**; below: berb ↓ calc-p ↓ con ↓ par ↓ sars ↓ sil ↓
  - **ulcerative** pain: berb bg2 calc-p bg2 con b4.de* par b7.de* sars b4.de* sil bg2
- **Transverse**: caust bg2

- **Veins**: puls ↓
  - **burning**: puls k2
- **Wrists**: abrot br1* *Acon* b7.de* act-sp k* agar ↓ agath-a nl2• agn ↓ aloe ↓ alum ↓ alum-sil ↓ alumn ↓ am-c k* am-m ↓ *Ambr* ↓ aml-ns ↓ ammc ↓ *Anac* ↓ anag ang ↓ *Ant-c* ant-t apis ↓ *Arg-met* ↓ *Arg-n* k* **Arn** ↓ ars k* ars-i ↓ arum-t ↓ arund k* asaf b7.de* asar ↓ asc-t k* aster ↓ **Aur** ↓ aur-ar ↓ aur-i ↓ aur-m ↓ aur-m-n ↓ aur-s ↓ bapt ↓ bar-c ↓ bar-p ↓ bar-s k2 bell berb ↓ bism bro1 bit-ar ↓ bol-la ↓ borx ↓ *Bov* ↓ brach k* *Brom* b4a.de bry k* bufo ↓ bufo-s *Calc* k* calc-ar ↓ calc-p k* calc-s k* calc-sil ↓ camph cann-i k* canth ↓ carb-ac ↓ carb-an bro1 carb-v k* carbn-s card-m ↓ cartl-s rly4• castor-eq *Caul* k* *Caust* ↓ cham k* chel k* chin ↓ chinin-ar ↓ chinin-s ↓ cic ↓ cimic k* cina cist k* clem k* cob k* coc-c ↓ cocc colch k* coloc com ↓ con ↓ conch ↓ conv ↓ cop k* cor-r k* corn ↓ croc ↓ crot-c k* cub k* cupr ↓ *Cur* ↓ *Cycl* ↓ cypra-eg ↓ dig ↓ digin ↓ dios k* dros b7.de* dulc k* erig vml3• *Eup-per* euph k* euphr ↓ ferr k* ferr-ar ferr-ma ↓ ferr-p k2 fl-ac k* form k* galla-q-r nl2• gels k* ger-i ↓ gink-b sbd1• gran ↓ *Graph* ↓ grat *Guaj* ham fd3.de• *Hell* ↓ *Hep* k* hipp k* hom-xyz c2 hura hyos k* hyper ↓ ign ↓ indg ↓ inul iod ↓ jatr-c ↓ jug-c k* kali-ar ↓ *Kali-bi* k* *Kali-c* bro1 kali-chl ↓ kali-i ↓ kali-m ↓ *Kali-n* k* kali-p ↓ kali-s fd4.de kali-sil ↓ *Kalm* k* kola stb3• kreos ↓ lac-ac k* lac-d k2 lach k* lact ↓ lap-la sde8.de• laur ↓ led k* lil-t k* limen-b-c ↓ *Lyc* lycps-v lyss ↓ m-ambo ↓ mag-c ↓ *Mag-m* ↓ mag-s manc k* mang mela ↓ melal-alt ↓ meny ↓ merc k* merc-i-f k* merc-sul ↓ merl ↓ mez k* morg-p pte1*• morph ↓ mosch ↓ mur-ac ↓ musca-d ↓ naja ↓ nat-c ↓ *Nat-m* ↓ nat-p bro1 nat-s k* nat-sil fd3.de• nept-m lsd2.fr nicc-met sk4• nit-ac ↓ nit-s-d ↓ nux-v ↓ ol-an ↓ op ↓ osm *Ox-ac* k* ozone sde2• paeon bro1 pall k* par ↓ petr ↓ *Ph-ac* ↓ phos ↓ phys k* pic-ac ↓ pip-m ↓ plan plat ↓ plb k* *Plb-act* ↓ plect c2 podo polyg-h ↓ polyp-p ↓ positr ↓ prop c2* propr sa3• prun ↓ ptel k* *Puls* pyrid ↓ ran-b ↓ ran-s ↓ *Rat* ↓ *Rhod* k* **Rhus-t** k* rhus-v k* ribo ↓ rumx ↓ *Ruta* k* sabad k* *Sabin* k* sacch-a ↓ sal-ac k* sal-fr ↓ salol c1 samb ↓ sars k* seneg ↓ sep bro1 *Sil* b4a.de* sinus rly4• sol-ni spect ↓ *Spig* ↓ spong fd4.de squil k* stann k* staph ↓ staphycoc ↓ still k* **Stront-c** ↓ stry k* sul-ac k* sulfonam ks2 **Sulph** k* symph fd3.de• tab k* tanac ↓ tarax ↓ tarent k* tax ↓ tep k* teucr ↓ thres-a sze7• thuj ↓ tritic-vg fd5.de trom *Tub* ↓ tung-met ↓ ulm-c ↓ upa ↓ urol-h ↓ urt-u k* vac jl2 vanil fd5.de vario br1* verat ↓ *Verb* ↓ *Viol-o* k* vip ↓ xan k* zinc k* zinc-p ↓ [*Buteo-j* sej6]
  - **alternating** sides: arund k* *Lac-c* lyc ↓
    - **stitching** pain: lyc

- **right**: abrom-a ks5 act-sp ang↓ arund k* bism↓ bit-ar↓ *Brucel* sa3• bufo-s **Calc**↓ calc-p k* canth↓ caust↓ chinin-s cimic k* colch k* dulc fd4.de gels↓ gink-b sbd1• ham fd3.de• lac-ac a1 lac-c led↓ limest-b↓ *Lyc* med c1 mez↓ nat-p nit-ac↓ olib-sac↓ *Ox-ac* k* ozone sde2• petr phasco-ci rbp2 plb k* plut-n↓ podo fd3.de• *Rat*↓ *Rhus-t* k* ribo↓ ruta fd4.de sal-al↓ spong fd4.de sulph symph fd3.de• tarent↓ tritic-vg fd5.de vanil fd5.de **Viol-o** k*
  - **aching**: plut-n srj7• ribo rly4•
  - **drawing** pain: gels psa
  - **dull** pain: sal-al blc1•
  - **pressing** pain: ang h1 led k* nit-ac h2 symph fd3.de•
  - **shooting** pain: tarent bg2
  - **sore**: limest-b es1•
  - **sprained**; as if: bit-ar wht1• **Calc** gels *Lyc* mez h2 *Ox-ac*
  - **stitching** pain: canth olib-sac wmh1 ruta fd4.de vanil fd5.de
  - **tearing** pain: bism calc-p caust *Rat*
- **left**: *Agar*↓ aids nl2• am-m↓ asc-t k* bism↓ brach k* brucel sa3• camph cann-i a1 cartl-s rly4• cic↓ coca-c sk4• cop k* crot-c dios k* dulc fd4.de ferr k* get↓ *Guaj* k* ham fd3.de• kali-s fd4.de kalm k* kola stb3• luf-op rsj5• lycps-v↓ mag-s melal-alt gya4 nat-sil fd3.de• nept-m lsd2.fr petr-ra↓ polyg-h↓ propr sa3• *Rhus-t*↓ rosm↓ ruta fd4.de sal-ac c1 sep↓ spong fd4.de sulph↓ symph fd3.de• tell↓ tritic-vg fd5.de vanil fd5.de [tax jsj7]
  - **aching**: lycps-v melal-alt gya4 petr-ra shn4• sulph
  - **and** right ankle: lach
  - **dislocated**; as if: get a1
  - **followed** by | **right**: kola stb3•
  - **pressing** pain: camph cic a1
  - **shooting** pain: ferr bg2 polyg-h bg2
  - **sprained**; as if: *Agar* *Rhus-t*
  - **stitching** pain: rosm lgb1 tell rsj10• [tax jsj7]
  - **tearing** pain: am-m bism h1 sep h2
  - **walking** agg.: luf-op rsj5•
- **morning**: am-c *Brucel* sa3• calc-p k* carb-v coli↓ cupr dios k* dulc k* ham fd3.de• hura iod kali-c lyc↓ lyss↓ mag-m merc-i-f k* nat-sil fd3.de• nux-v osm k* plb k* podo fd3.de• puls ruta fd4.de spong fd4.de staph stry↓ sulph symph fd3.de• tritic-vg fd5.de zinc
  - **8** h: arg-n↓
    - **boring** pain: arg-n
  - **aching**: coli rly4• stry sulph
  - **bed** agg.; in: calc hyper lyc↓ nat-c
    - **drawing** pain: calc hyper lyc h2
  - **drawing** pain: carb-v k*
  - **sprained**; as if: lyss
  - **stitching** pain: ham fd3.de• lyc k* ruta fd4.de tritic-vg fd5.de
  - **stool** agg.; after: osm↓
    - **aching**: osm
  - **tearing** pain: lyc
  - **twisting**, on: merc-i-f k*
  - **waking**; on: dulc k* merc-i-f k* propr sa3• rosm↓ sacch-a fd2.de•
    - **stitching** pain: rosm lgb1
- **forenoon**: lycps-v↓ ox-ac↓ pip-m↓ ran-b↓ sil↓ sulph↓
  - **aching**: lycps-v pip-m
  - **sprained**; as if: ox-ac
  - **tearing** pain: ran-b sil sulph
- **noon**: alumn↓
  - **sprained**; as if: alumn
- **afternoon**: am-m↓ aster↓ calc-s k* canth↓ coca-c sk4• dulc fd4.de ham fd3.de• lyc↓ lycps-v mag-s↓ nux-v propr sa3• ptel↓ ruta fd4.de sulph k* vanil fd5.de
  - **14** h: sars↓
    - **tearing** pain: sars
  - **aching**: lycps-v
  - **burning**: dulc fd4.de sulph
  - **drawing** pain: aster ptel k*
  - **stitching** pain: canth ham fd3.de• lyc k*
  - **tearing** pain: am-m lyc mag-s
- **evening**: ang↓ ars↓ bov↓ com↓ dios k* dulc fd4.de euphr↓ ham fd3.de• lach↓ *Led* k* lyc↓ nat-s nat-sil fd3.de• phos↓ phys k* pip-m k* propr sa3• rhod k* rhodi a1 rhus-v↓ ruta fd4.de sars k* staph↓ stront-c↓ tarent↓ tritic-vg fd5.de vanil fd5.de verat-v k*
  - **19** h: lyc↓
    - **tearing** pain: lyc
  - **20-23** h: fl-ac↓
    - **drawing** pain: fl-ac
  - **21** h: gels↓
    - **aching**: gels
  - **aching**: led verat-v
  - **burning**: dulc fd4.de stront-c
  - **cutting** pain: rhus-v
  - **drawing** pain: ang h1 ars h2 com k* euphr lyc k* *Rhod* ruta fd4.de staph k*
  - **exertion** agg.: lach↓
    - **sprained**; as if: lach
  - **lying** down agg.; after: nat-s↓
    - **pressing** pain: nat-s
  - **pressing** pain: ang h1 led k* nat-s k* ruta fd4.de
  - **shooting** pain: tarent
  - **sitting** agg.: **Led**↓
    - **aching**: **Led**
  - **sprained**; as if: lach
  - **stitching** pain: euphr k* rhod k* ruta fd4.de tarent vanil fd5.de
  - **tearing** pain: bov lyc phos stront-c vanil fd5.de
  - **walking** in open air agg.: hell↓
    - **stitching** pain: hell k*
- **night**: am-c↓ arg-n↓ **Ars**↓ *Aur*↓ calc↓ choc srj3• dulc fd4.de fl-ac↓ kali-n *Merc*↓ nat-m↓ podo fd3.de• rosm↓ sep↓ sil spong fd4.de tab k* tarent k* tritic-vg fd5.de vanil fd5.de
  - **23** h: nat-s↓
    - **tearing** pain: nat-s
  - **bed** agg.; in: **Ars**↓ *Merc*↓ nat-m↓
    - **tearing** pain: **Ars** *Merc* nat-m
  - **drawing** pain: *Ars* fl-ac k* nat-m k*
  - **sprained**; as if: arg-n
  - **stitching** pain: calc k* rosm lgb1
  - **tearing** pain: am-c **Ars** *Aur* kali-n h2 *Merc* sep
  - **waking**; on: mez
    - **aching**: mez
- **aching**: agath-a nl2• asaf bar-c bol-la bry calc-p carb-ac cartl-s rly4• castor-eq *Caul* cic conv br1 dios ferr-p ptk1 ger-i rly4• lac-d kr1 lach *Led* mang melal-alt gya4 mez naja nit-ac phys pip-m positr nl2• ptel rhus-t rhus-v rumx sal-fr sle1• sil stann staphycoc rly4• still tarent tung-met bdx1• urol-h rwt• [spect dfg1]
  - **cramping**: com
  - **paralyzed**; as if: nat-p
- **bed**; when going to: stront-c↓
  - **tearing** pain: stront-c
- **bending** agg.: arg-n k* brucel sa3• haliae-lc srj5• kali-s fd4.de symph fd3.de•
- **bent**; when: ferr-m↓ ferr-ma↓
  - **sprained**; as if: ferr-m ferr-ma k*
- **boring** pain: cina coloc conch fkr1.de *Hell* k* mez k* nat-s plan ran-s b7.de* rhod rhus-t b7a.de ruta fd4.de sabad b7.de* sabin b7.de*
- **bringing** thumb and first finger together: bov↓
  - **stitching** pain: bov
- **broken**; as if: borx hr1 **Eup-per** k* *Ruta* sil k* symph fd3.de•
- **burning**: agar arg-met k* arum-t arund asar berb *Bry* b7a.de bufo calc-p cartl-s rly4• cocc dulc fd4.de merc mez naja nat-c k* nat-sil fd3.de• phos plat plb pyrid rly4• ruta fd4.de sabin b7.de stront-c k* sulph symph fd3.de• thuj *Tub* vanil fd5.de zinc
- **chill**:
  - **before**: arn↓ podo↓
    - **aching**: arn podo

- **chill**: ...
  - **during**: ph-ac ↓ podo br*
    - **tearing** pain: ph-ac h2
- **clawing**: rhod k*
- **cold**:
  - **agg.**: rhus-t hr1
  - **applications** | **agg.**: abrom-a ks5
  - **washing** agg.; after: rhus-t hr1
- **cramping**: cycl tl1 xan c1
- **cutting** pain: alum bg2 bell k* bism bg2 dros bg2 dulc fd4.de mosch bg2 mur-ac bg2 ph-ac phos bg2 rhus-t bg2 rhus-v spig h1* stry teucr bg2
- **dinner**; during: kali-n ↓
  - **pulsating** pain: kali-n
- **dislocated**; as if: **Am-c** b4a.de* am-m bg2 *Ambr* b7a.de ang bg2 **Arn** k* bar-c bg2 bar-p bg bov b4.de* bry b7.de* bufo bg2 **Calc** b4.de* carb-an b4.de* carb-v b4.de* *Caust* b4.de* cina b7.de* con bg2 *Eup-per* k* ferr bg2 gels psa graph b4.de* hep b4a.de* ign b7.de* kali-n b4a.de lach bg2 lap-la sde8.de• laur bg2 led bg2 limen-b-c hrn2* lyc b4.de* m-ambo b7a.de mag-m b4.de* mez b4.de* nux-v b7.de* petr bg2 phos k* prun bg2 puls b7.de* rhod b4.de* **Rhus-t** b7.de* **Ruta** b7a.de* sabin b7.de* sars b4.de* seneg b4.de* sil b4.de* stann b4.de* *Sulph* b4.de* thuj b4.de* verb b7.de* zinc bg2
- **drawing** pain: acon k* aml-ns ammc k* anac b4a.de anag ang h1 arg-met *Ars* k* *Asaf* k* asar k* aster bapt k* bar-c k* bov k* calc k* calc-p calc-sil k2 carb-v k* carbn-s *Caul* k* *Caust* k* cham k* chel k* cina k* cist k* clem k* com k* con *Cycl* k* dig digin a1 dios k* euph euphr k* fl-ac k* guaj ham hell k* hyos k* hyper k* kali-bi k* kali-c k* kali-chl k* kali-m k2 kali-n k* kali-sil k2 led k* *Lyc* k* *Mang* mez k* morph k* mosch b7a.de nat-m k* nat-p k* nat-s k* nit-ac k* nit-s-d a1 nux-v b7.de* ph-ac k* polyp-p a1 ptel k* *Rhod* k* **Rhus-t** k* *Rhus-v* k* ruta fd4.de sabin k* samb k* sars k* sep k* sil k* spong k* squil k* stann h2 staph k* stront-c sul-ac k* *Sulph* k* symph fd3.de• tarax k* tep k* teucr b7a.de thuj k* upa k* vanil fd5.de verb vip fkr4.de zinc k*
  - **alternating** with | **Forehead**; pain in (See HEAD - Pain - forehead - alternating with - wrist)
  - **cramping**: calc-p
  - **intermittent**: ferr-ma k* stann h2
  - **outward**: caust
  - **gouty**: caust k*
  - **paralyzed**; as if: arg-met con k* *Rhus-v* k* sabin
  - **paroxysmal**: borx
  - **sprained**; as if: zinc k*
  - **sticking** pain: squil k*
  - **tearing** pain: guaj kali-bi k* mez **Rhus-t**
  - **twitching**: calc k*
- **exertion** agg.; after: alum k* berb k* kali-n k* ruta sma sacch-a fd2.de• sulph
- **exertion**; as after: lach bg2 nux-v bg2 rhod b4a.de* sabad bg2 sul-ac bg2
- **exertion** of the hand agg.: sulph ↓ vanil ↓
  - **drawing** pain: sulph k* vanil fd5.de
- **gnawing** pain: berb k* canth b7.de* dros b7.de* *Graph* phys a1 plat ran-s b7.de* verat
- **gouty**: abrot dgt1
- **grasping** something agg.: aids nl2• aur-m ↓ bov k* *Brucel* sa3• *Carb-v* ↓ iod ↓ nat-m ↓ **Rhus-t** k* tritic-vg fd5.de
  - **sprained**; as if: **Rhus-t**
  - **stitching** pain: aur-m k* bov iod k* nat-m k*
  - **tearing** pain: *Carb-v*
- **hang** down agg.; letting arms: *Sabin* ↓
  - **tearing** pain: *Sabin* k*
- **jerking** pain: anac calc bg2 rhus-t k* spig h1* squil h1 sul-ac bg2
- **knitting**, while: kali-c ↓
  - **tearing** pain: kali-c
- **lifting** agg.: alum k* iod ↓ *Rhus-t* vanil fd5.de
  - **stitching** pain: iod k* vanil fd5.de
- **lying** down agg.; after: nat-s k*
- **menses**; during: nat-p ↓
- **menses**; during: ...
  - **aching**: nat-p
  - **drawing** pain: nat-p
- **motion**:
  - **agg.**: abrom-a ks5 act-sp arn k* bov ↓ brucel sa3• *Bry* k* *Calc* ↓ calc-p ↓ calo k* carb-v k* caust ↓ dulc fd4.de euph k* *Guaj* ham fd3.de• hep hyper k* indg ↓ kali-bi ↓ kali-c k* *Kalm* lap-la sde8.de• limest-b ↓ mand rsj7• meny ↓ merc k* merl ↓ *Mez* k* ox-ac k* ozone ↓ plb podo fd3.de• propr sa3• rhod k* rhus-t ↓ rosm ↓ ruta sabad k* sal-ac c1 *Sil* ↓ stann ↓ staph stict c1* still k* sulph k* symph fd3.de• tarent tritic-vg fd5.de tub ↓ vanil fd5.de
    - **dislocated**; as if: *Arn Bry Mez* rhus-t h1 **Ruta** mp1• tub c1
    - **drawing** pain: calc-p caust k* kali-c h2 ruta fd4.de staph k*
    - **pressing** pain: ruta staph k*
    - **sore**: limest-b es1•
    - **sprained**; as if: bov *Bry* hyper mez h2
    - **stitching** pain: arn calc k* indg k* kali-c k* rosm lgb1
    - **tearing** pain: *Calc* kali-bi meny *Merc* merl ozone sde2• *Sil* stann
  - **amel.**: *Arg-met* aur-m-n k* bar-c ↓ bism carb-v ↓ con ↓ dulc ↓ hyos k* mur-ac ↓ nat-s k* prun k* *Rhod* k* **Rhus-t** k* ruta ↓ samb ↓ spong ↓ sulph k* zinc ↓
    - **drawing** pain: *Arg-met* carb-v k* con k* *Rhod* k* **Rhus-t** samb zinc
    - **pressing** pain: aur-m-n k*
    - **rapid** motion: sulph ↓
      - **sprained**; as if: sulph h2
    - **sprained**; as if: prun rhod
    - **stitching** pain: bar-c dulc ruta fd4.de samb spong k*
    - **tearing** pain: arg-met *Bism* mur-ac rhod **Rhus-t** sulph
    - **violent** motion: sulph k*
  - **wrists** agg.; of: phos ↓ sep ↓
    - **tearing** pain: phos sep
- **nap**; during: nit-ac ↓
  - **pressing** pain: nit-ac h2
- **paralyzed**; as if: acon k* agn k* arg-met asar k* bism b7.de* *Bov* b4a.de *Carb-v* k* cham chin b7.de* coc-c k* con k* *Cur* bro1 *Cycl* b7a.de dig b4a.de euph k* ham fd3.de• hipp bro1 ign b7.de* *Kali-c* b4.de* *Kalm* led b7.de* meny b7.de* merc b4a.de* mez k* nat-p k* nux-v b7.de* phos b4.de* pic-ac bro1 plb bro1 *Plb-act* bro1 rhus-v k* **Ruta** b7a.de* sil bg2 stann bro1 verb b7.de*
- **paroxysmal**: *Anac Aur* bov spig
- **pinching** pain: musca-d szs1 nat-m k* nit-ac h2* ph-ac k* stann h2*
- **pressing** pain: aloe ang k* arg-met k* arg-n k* *Asaf* b7.de* aur k* aur-m-n k* bar-c bg2 bell k* berb *Bism* k* brom k* calc-p camph cann-i k* card-m coloc k* dig digin a1 dulc fd4.de *Guaj* k* hell k* hep hyos b7.de* jatr-c kali-c bg2 kali-p fd1.de• kola stb3• *Led* k* lil-t k* meny k* *Mez* k* nat-s k* nit-ac k* nit-s-d a1 ruta b7.de* sacch-a fd2.de• *Sars* k* sil a1 *Spig* k* spong bg2 stann k* staph bg2 symph fd3.de• thuj a1 vanil fd5.de viol-o k* zinc bg2
  - **asunder**: aloe
  - **constricting** pain: ozone sde2•
  - **cramping**: bar-c h2 meny
  - **drawing** pain: coloc k* hyos h1 spong staph
  - **outward**: mang a1
  - **tearing** pain: bism h1 ruta
- **pressing** together: nat-s bg2
- **pressure** agg.: abrom-a ks5 dulc fd4.de merc
- **pulsating** pain: brach k* kali-n k* nat-sil fd3.de• polyg-h symph fd3.de•
- **raising** the arm; on: coloc ↓
  - **drawing** pain | **periosteum**; as if in: coloc
- **rest** agg.: aur-m-n ↓
  - **sore**: aur-m-n
- **resting** on hand: merl ↓
  - **tearing** pain: merl k*
- **rheumatic**: abrot bro1* *Act-sp* k* aesc ammc asc-t k* **bacls-7** pte1* bapt hr1 benz-ac bro1 calc bro1 *Caul* k* caust bro1* chel k* clem k* *Colch* k* crot-c k* ery-a k* euphr ↓ ferr-p k* form k* gran ↓ grat *Guaj* ham fd3.de•

- **rheumatic**: ...
hipp c2* hippoz mtf11 *Jug-c* k* *Kali-bi* kalm lac-ac k* *Lach* k* lyc bro1 lycpr bro1 mag-s med mtf11 morg-g pte1* morg-p pte1• nat-ar nat-p prop bro1 ptel k* *Puls* rad-br c11 *Rhod* bro1 **Rhus-t** k* rhus-v bro1 rosm lgb1 **Ruta** k* *Sabin* bro1 sacch-a fd2.de• sep bro1 stel bro1 stict streptoc jl2 syc pte1* ulm-c bro1 urt-u k* *Vac* vario bro1 *Viol-o* k* wye bro1 zinc ↓
  - **right**: morg-g fmm1• x-ray sp1
  - **night**: rosm lgb1
  - **aching**: nat-ar
  - **drawing** pain: chel k* euphr k* **Rhus-t** zinc k*
  - **tearing** pain: gran zinc
  - **writing**; after: chinin-s
- **rising** | **after**:
  - **agg.**: coloc ↓
    - **drawing** pain: coloc k*
  - **agg.**: *Brucel* sa3•
- **rubbing**:
  - **agg.**: berb ↓ dulc ↓
    - **burning**: berb dulc fd4.de
  - **amel.**: laur ↓
    - **stitching** pain: laur
- **scraping** pain: cist
- **scratching** agg.; after: calc-p ↓ plb ↓
  - **burning**: calc-p plb
- **sewing**, while: kali-c lach
- **shooting** pain: *Acon* k* agath-a nl2• bell k* brach ferr merc-sul sol-ni tarent trom
- **sitting** agg.: aur-m-n ↓ coloc ↓ led ↓ mez ↓ propr sa3•
  - **boring** pain: mez
  - **pressing** pain: aur-m-n coloc k* led
- **sore**: alumn ammc arg-met asaf k* aur-m-n bar-c bg2 bism bg2 borx bg2 bov k* brach *Calc* camph caust k* cham con bg2 croc bg2 cupr bg2 *Dros* k* **Eup-per** ham fd3.de• hep h2 led lyss mez h2 mur-ac bg2 nat-m k* nat-p nat-sil fd3.de• nit-ac k* ph-ac bg2 phos bg2 pip-m podo positr nl2• puls b7.de* rhod ptk1 rhus-t bg2 ribo rly4• **Ruta** k* sabin bg2 sacch-a fd2.de• *Salol* c1 sep sinus rly4• spong bg2 tanac thuj k* zinc k*
  - **strained**; as if: ox-ac ptk1
- **sprained**; as if: agar agath-a nl2• alumn *Am-c* ambr arg-n **Arn** bit-ar wht1• *Bov* *Bry* k* **Calc** calc-sil k2 **Carb-an** carb-v castor-eq *Caust* *Cina* cist k* dios *Eup-per* bro1 ferr graph hep hipp bro1* jug-c kali-n *Lach* laur lyc mag-c melal-alt gya4 mez nat-m nicc-met sk4* nux-v *Ox-ac* k* petr phos puls *Rhod* k* **Rhus-t** k* **Ruta** k* sabin sars seneg sil stann *Stront-c* *Sulph* tep thuj ulm-c bro1 *Verb* zinc
- **squeezed**; as if: anac bg2 asaf bg2 bar-c bg2 **Calc** bg2 cina bg2 con bg2 ferr bg2 graph bg2 kali-bi bg2 kreos bg2 laur bg2 meny bg2 merc bg2 mosch bg2 mur-ac bg2 nat-c bg2 par bg2 ph-ac bg2 plat bg2 prun bg2 ran-b bg2 rhod bg2 ruta bg2 sep bg2 spig bg2 stann bg2 staph bg2 stront-c bg2 zinc bg2
- **stitching** pain: *Acon* k* agn bg2 alum k* alum-sil k2 am-c bg2 anac k* ang bg2* apis arg-met k* arn k* ars k* ars-i aster aur k* aur-ar k2 aur-i k2 aur-m k* aur-s k2 bapt bar-c k* bell berb k* *Bov* k* brach *Bry* k* calc k* calc-ar calc-sil k2 canth carbn-s caust k* cham k* chel k* chin k* chinin-s clem k* cob k* colch k* com con k* corn cypra-eg sde6.de• dulc k* euphr k* ferr graph k* ham *Hell* k* hura hyper indg k* inul iod k* kali-bi kali-c k* kali-n k* kali-sil k2 kalm k* lach bg2 laur k* *Led* lyc k* lycps-v mang k* mela a1 meny k* *Merc* k* merc-sul k* mosch bg2 *Nat-m* k* nit-s-d a1 nux-v b7.de* op ox-ac k* phos k* plat k* plect a1 podo fd3.de• rhod k* rhus-t bg2 ruta k* sabin k* samb k* sars k* *Sep* k* *Sil* k* sol-ni spig k* spong k* squil k* staph k* *Sulph* k* tarent thuj k* tritic-vg fd5.de trom tung-met bdx1• vanil fd5.de verb b7.de* zinc k* [tax jsj7]
  - **acute**: arn bov phos
  - **needles**; as from: colch ptk1
  - **pulsating** pain: canth
  - **tearing** pain: calc rhus-t sabin
  - **twitching**: *Bry* carbn-s
- **stool** agg.; after: osm k*
- **string**; as from a: manc
- **sudden**: bar-c ↓ lyc ↓
- **sudden**: ...
  - **stitching** pain: lyc
  - **tearing** pain: bar-c
- **synchronous** with pulse: samb ↓
  - **stitching** pain: samb
- **syphilitics**; in: *Asaf* ↓
  - **drawing** pain: *Asaf*
- **tearing** pain: *Acon* k* agar alum k* am-c k* am-m k* ambr b7a.de* ammc anac k* *Arg-met* k* arn k* ars k* **Aur** k* aur-ar k2 bar-c k* bell k* berb *Bism* k* borx bov k* *Calc* k* *Calc-p* calc-sil k2 **Carb-v** k* carbn-s caust k* chel k* chin k* chinin-ar clem bg2 colch k* con bg2 cupr bg2 cycl k* dig bg2 euphr k* gran grat k* *Guaj* k* ign b7.de* inul kali-ar kali-bi *Kali-c* k* kali-chl kali-i *Kali-n* k* kali-sil k2 lach k* lact laur k* led k* lyc k* *Mag-m* k* mag-s mang bg2 meny k* *Merc* k* merl mez mur-ac nat-c nat-m **Nat-s** nit-ac k* ol-an ozone sde2• *Ph-ac* k* phos k* plb k* **Puls** bg2 ran-b k* *Rat* rhod k* **Rhus-t** k* ruta k* sabin k* *Sars* k* sep k* *Sil* k* spig b7.de* squil bg2 **Stann** k* staph k* **Stront-c** k* *Sulph* k* tarax k* teucr k* thuj k* vanil fd5.de *Zinc* k* zinc-p k2
  - **alternating** with | **Hand**; tearing in: berb
  - **convulsive**: ph-ac
  - **cramping**: aur h2
  - **drawing** pain: guaj kali-bi mez **Rhus-t**
  - **dull** pain: lyc h2
  - **jerking** pain: chin h1
  - **paralyzed**; as if: bell *Bism* meny stann
  - **pressing** pain: arg-met guaj stann
  - **sticking** pain: *Arn* calc sep staph
  - **transversely**: ph-ac
  - **twitching**: colch laur **Rhus-t**
  - **upward**: sars h2
- **touch** agg.: merc sal-ac c1
- **turning** hand: agn k* dros sma dulc fd4.de merc-i-f sma tritic-vg fd5.de
- **twisting** agg.: merc-i-f k*
- **twitching**, with: arund k* calc k* carbn-s kali-n k*
- **ulcerative** pain: bov bg2
- **walking**:
  - **agg.**: mez ↓ nat-s ↓
    - **boring** pain: mez
    - **pressing** pain: nat-s k*
  - **air** agg.; in open: clem ↓ rhod ↓
    - **stitching** pain: clem
    - **tearing** pain: rhod
- **wandering** pain: *Kalm* polyg-h *Puls*
- **warm** bed:
  - **amel.**: am-c ↓ *Ars* ↓ calc-p ↓ **Rhus-t** ↓ *Sil* ↓
    - **tearing** pain: am-c *Ars* calc-p **Rhus-t** *Sil*
- **warm**, when hands become: *Bry* ↓
  - **stitching** pain: *Bry* k*
- **warmth**:
  - **agg.**: *Guaj* ozone ↓ *Puls*
    - **tearing** pain: ozone sde2•
  - **amel.**:
    - **heat** amel.: agath-a ↓
      - **aching**: agath-a nl2•
- **washing** agg.: alum ↓
  - **stitching** pain: alum
- **weather**:
  - **change** of weather: rhus-t a1
  - **cold**:
    - **agg.**: rhus-t hr1
    - **wet**:
      - **agg.**: ruta ↓
        - **sore**: ruta
  - **rough**:
    - **agg.**: *Rhod* ↓
      - **sprained**; as if: *Rhod*

· **weather**: ...
⁝ **stormy**:
: **agg.**: rhod
. **drawing** pain: rhod
⁝ **wet** | **agg.**: erig vml3•
· **wind** agg.: carb-v
⁝ **drawing** pain: carb-v k*
· **working**; while: caust↓
⁝ **sprained**; as if: caust
⁝ **stitching** pain: caust k*
· **writing**:
⁝ **after**: hydrog↓
: **twinging**: hydrog srj2•
⁝ **agg.**: arn↓ ferr-p k* hydrog srj2• lyc **Mag-p** ox-ac↓ pip-m↓ sil↓
: **aching**: pip-m
: **sprained**; as if: lyc
: **stitching** pain: lyc ox-ac sil k*
: **tearing** pain: arn
· **writing**; as after much rapid: cor-r k*
▽ · **extending** to:
⁝ **Arm**: agath-a nl2• arg-met↓ arn bar-c↓ calc↓ com↓ jug-c plb ruta↓
: **drawing** pain: arg-met bar-c calc h2 com ruta fd4.de
⁝ **Elbow**: agath-a nl2• ham fd3.de• kali-n↓ kali-p fd1.de• lach ozone sde2• rhus-v↓ sulph↓ symph fd3.de•
: **aching**: agath-a nl2• lach
: **drawing** pain: kali-n h2 rhus-v sulph h2
: **tearing** pain: ozone sde2•
⁝ **Elbow**, along ulnar: acon↓ bell↓
: **shooting** pain: acon bell
⁝ **Fingers**: am-c↓ bar-c↓ caust↓ grat↓ lyc↓ phos↓ plb↓ plut-n srj7• *Rhus-v*↓ ruta fd4.de sep↓ squil↓ tarax↓ thuj↓ viol-o mrr1 zinc↓
: **cutting** pain: rhus-v
: **drawing** pain: caust grat *Rhus-v* ruta fd4.de squil h1 tarax thuj
: **stitching** pain: lyc sep
: **tearing** pain: am-c bar-c caust phos h2 plb tarax h1 zinc n2
: **First** finger: arund↓ asaf hell↓ xan c1
. **aching**: asaf
. **burning**: arund
. **drawing** pain: hell
. **Thumb**; and: agar↓ asar↓
burning: agar asar
drawing pain: asar
: **Fourth** finger: am-c↓ **Sulph**↓
. **burning**: **Sulph**
. **tearing** pain: am-c
: **Third** and fourth fingers:
. **hanging** down arm; on: castor-eq↓
sprained; as if: castor-eq k*
: **Third** finger: kali-c↓
. **tearing** pain: kali-c
: **Tips**: thuj↓
. **drawing** pain: thuj
: **Tips** of two smaller fingers: chel↓
. **tearing** pain: chel
⁝ **Forearm**: agath-a nl2• ferr-p ham fd3.de• nat-sil fd3.de• pall ruta fd4.de stann
: **aching**: agath-a nl2•
: **writing** agg.: agath-a nl2• ferr-p
⁝ **Hand**: fago rhod ruta fd4.de stann↓ viol-o mrr1
: **drawing** pain: ruta fd4.de stann h2
⁝ **Hand**; back of: ran-b↓
: **tearing** pain: ran-b
⁝ **Knuckles**: kali-n
: **tearing** pain: kali-n k*
⁝ **Shoulder**: sep↓ *Sil*↓
: **tearing** pain: sep *Sil*

· **extending** to: ...
⁝ **Thumb**: ozone↓ xan sma
: **tearing** pain: ozone sde2•
: **Ball**: ozone sde2•
⁝ **Ulna**: samb↓
: **drawing** pain: samb h1
⁝ **Upward**: bell↓ bry↓ canth↓ cham↓ sabin↓ staph↓
: **stitching** pain: bell bry canth cham sabin staph
: **Shoulders**: staph↓
. **stitching** pain: staph k*
○ · **Bones**: *Arg-met*↓ *Aur*↓ bapt↓ bell↓ bism↓ chin↓ cupr↓ lach↓ lact↓ nat-c↓ sabin↓ spig↓ teucr↓
⁝ **scraping** pain: chin bg2
⁝ **tearing** pain: *Arg-met Aur* bapt hr1 bell bism h1 chin cupr lach lact nat-c sabin spig teucr
· **Dorsal** side: agar k* all-c k* berb↓ caust↓ chinin-s↓ dig↓ led↓ merl↓
⁝ **evening**: all-c k*
⁝ **pinching** pain: caust k* dig h2
⁝ **stitching** pain: chinin-s led
⁝ **tearing** pain: berb caust merl
⁝ **extending** to:
: **Second** finger: caust↓
. **tearing** pain: caust
· **Palmar** side: colch↓ com k* kali-c↓ kali-n↓ plb k* tarent k*
⁝ **drawing** pain: kali-c h2 kali-n h2
⁝ **motion** agg.: plb k*
⁝ **stitching** pain: colch
⁝ **sudden**: com k*
⁝ **walking** in open air agg.; after: com k*
· **Radial** side: arg-met k* brucel sa3• hydr↓ merc-i-f a1 sabin k* samb↓ sars↓ stann k*
⁝ **drawing** pain: arg-met k* hydr k* sabin k* stann k*
⁝ **stitching** pain: arg-met k* samb xxb1 sars
· **Skin**: caps↓
⁝ **stitching** pain: caps h1
· **Ulnar** side: bell↓ berb↓ brucel sa3• calc h2* calc-s a1 chel k* cic a1 ferr-p kali-c↓ lach↓ merl↓ phys k* rumx k* sabin a1 stann↓ sulph k* zinc↓
⁝ **drawing** pain: sabin a1 stann h2
⁝ **pressing** pain: cic a1 zinc h2
⁝ **rheumatic**: ferr-p k*
⁝ **stitching** pain: bell berb
⁝ **tearing** pain: kali-c h2 lach k* merl zinc h2
⁝ **writing** agg.: ferr-p k*
⁝ **extending** to:
: **Fingers**; tips of both outer: lach↓
. **tearing** pain: lach k*

PANARIS (See Felon)

PANARITIUM (See Felon)

PARALYSIS: *(↗Dragging)* abel vh1 abrot absin br1 **Acon** k* **Agar** k* *All-c* k* aloe **Alum** k* alum-p k2 alumn k2 am-m b2.de* ambr k* *Anac* k* ang b2.de* apoc k2 arag br1 arg-met b2.de* *Arg-n* k* arn b2.de* *Ars* k* ars-s-f k2 *Art-v* asar b2.de* astra-m br1 *Aur* k* *Bapt* bar-act br1* *Bar-c* k* bar-m *Bell* k* bov b2.de* *Bry* k* **Bufo** k* *Calc* k* calc-s cann-s b2.de* carb-v k* carbn-o carbn-s **Caust** k* cham b2.de* *Chel* k* *Chin* k* *Cic* k* **Cocc** k* coff *Colch* k* coloc b2.de* *Con* k* *Crot-c* crot-h *Cupr* k* *Cur* k* cycl b2.de* dig b2.de* *Dros* k* dub bro1 *Dulc* k* elec c1 esch br1 ferr k* fl-ac bg2 *Form* k* *Gels* k* graph b2.de* grat mtf11 grin br1 guaj b2.de* *Guare* hedeo bro1 *Hell* b2.de* helo c1 helo-s c1* hep b2.de* hydr-ac k* hyos k* ign b2.de* iod b2.de* ip b2.de* ix bnm8• *Kali-ar* *Kali-c* k* *Kali-i* kali-n k* *Kali-p* k* *Kalm* k* *Lach* k* lat-h bnm5• lat-m bnm6• laur k* led b2.de* *Lol* bro1 lyc k* m-ambo b2.de* mang hr1 meph k* merc k* *Merc-c* k* mez b2.de* mill k* morph k* mur-ac b2.de* *Naja* nat-c b2.de* *Nat-m* k* *Nit-ac* k* nux-m k2 *Nux-v* k* *Olnd* k* *Op* k* ox-ac k2 petr b2.de* ph-ac k* *Phos* k* pic-ac k* *Plat* k* **Plb** k* puls k* rhod k* **Rhus-t** k* *Ruta* k* sabin b2.de* sars b2.de* *Sec* k* sel b2.de* seneg b2.de* *Sep* k* **Sil** k* spig b2.de* spong k* stann k* staph b2.de* *Stram* k* stront-c k* sul-ac b2.de* **Sulph** k* syph k2 tab k*

Extremities

Paralysis: ...
tarax b2.de* *Tarent* k* tax k* thal-xyz srj8• thuj k* vanil fd5.de *Verat* k* verin a1 vip k* xan br1 *Zinc* k*
- **right**: ars bg1 carbn-s bg1 crot-c mrr1 merc bg1
- **morning** | **bed** agg.; in: phos zinc
- **afternoon** | **17**-18 h: *Con*
- **evening**: cur sil stront-c
- **abdominal** symptoms, with: arg-n br1
- **anger**; after: nat-m k* *Nux-v* k* staph k*
- **apoplexy**; after: *Alum* anac apis *Bar-c* k* cadm-s *Caust* k* *Cocc* k* *Crot-c* *Crot-h* *Cupr* *Gels* k* ip hr1 **Lach** k* *Laur* k* *Nux-v* k* **Op** k* *Phos* *Plb* k* sec stann staph mrr1 *Stram* zinc
- **appearing** gradually: (↗*GENERALS - Paralysis - appearing)* **Caust** k*
- **ascending** (See GENERALS - Paralysis - extending - upward)
- **cholera**; after: verat k*
- **coition**; after: phos
- **cold**; after taking a: dulc k* rhod k* rhus-t k2
- **coldness** of parts, with: caust *Cocc* k* dulc graph *Nux-v* *Rhus-t*
- **descending** agg.: *Bar-c* k* merc
- **emotions** agg.: *Apis* gels k2 **Ign** nat-m nux-v stann
- **eruptions**; after suppressed: caust *Dulc* hep *Psor* *Sulph*
- **exertion** agg.; after: *Arn* hr1 ars k* *Caust* *Gels* nux-v plb k2 *Rhus-t* k*
- **fright** agg.: *Acon* vh1 stann h2
- **hemiplegia**: (↗*GENERALS - Paralysis - one)* acon *Alum* k* alum-p k2 *Anac* k* *Apis* arg-n k* *Arn* hr1 *Ars* ars-s-f k2 bapt bar-c mrr1 bar-m bell hr1 *Both* *Cadm-s* caj hr1 carbn-s c2 **Caust** k* chen-a c2 chin hr1 coc-c *Cocc* k* conin c2 cop k* dulc hr1 elaps k* *Graph* k* hell k2 hydr-ac hr1* hyos k* *Kali-c* k* *Kali-i* k* kali-m k2 kali-p *Lach* k* merc hr1 *Mur-ac* k* nat-c nux-v hr1 *Ph-ac* k* *Phos* pic-ac c2 plb k* **Rhus-t** k* *Sars* sec k2 sep hr1 *Stann* k* staph k* stram hr1 stront-c stry-xyz c2 *Sul-ac* k* syph hr1 tab thuj k* xan c1*
  - **right**: *Apis* arn k* bell k* both fne1• calc **Caust** k* colch **Crot-c** *Crot-h* elaps *Graph* irid-met c2 iris-fl c2 nat-c op k* phos *Plb* *Rhus-t* k* sang sil k* stront-c sulph
  - **left**: acon anac **Apis** arg-n arn k* ars hr1 *Bapt* bar-m bell k* brom caust k* *Elaps* hydr-ac hr1 **Lach** k* lyc nit-ac k* **Nux-v** k* ox-ac k* petr k* phys c2 podo **Rhus-t** k* santin c2 *Stann* stram k* sulph
  - **anger**; after: staph k*
  - **convulsions**; after: stann
  - **masturbation**: stann
  - **mental** excitement: stann
  - **mental** shock; after: apis
  - **numbness** of one side, the other is paralyzed: cocc
  - **pain**, caused by: nat-m
  - **twitching** of one side, the other is paralyzed: *Apis* art-v *Bell* *Stram*
- **hysterical**: *Acon* vh1 cur **Ign** nux-m k2* plb tarent
- **infantile**: plb br rhus-t k2
- **intermittent**; after suppressed: nat-m rhus-t
- **mental** symptoms, with: arg-n br1
- **nervous** disease; from: caust tl1
- **nettle** rash, after disappearance of: cop
- **old** people; in: *Bar-c* k* *Con* k* *Kali-c* k* op st
- **pain**; from: nat-m k*
- **painless**: abies-c acon aeth alum alum-p k2 ambr *Anac* *Arg-n* arn *Ars* ars-s-f k2 *Aur* aur-ar k2 aur-s k2 *Bapt* bar-c bar-s k2 bry cadm-s **Cann-i** **Cocc** colch **Con** crot-h k* *Cupr* cur **Gels** graph **Hyos** kalm *Laur* **Lyc** *Merc* nat-m *Nux-v* **Olnd** k* *Op* *Ph-ac* *Phos* **Plb** *Puls* rhod **Rhus-t** *Sec* sil stram sulph *Verat* *Zinc*
- **partial**: **Arn** hr1* *Ars* k* atro hr1 *Cocc* hr1 *Nux-v*
- **perspiration**; after suppressed: *Colch* *Rhus-t*
- **pollutions** agg.: m-aust b7.de
- **post** diphtheritic: ant-t apis arg-met arg-n hr1* arn k* *Ars* k* *Bar-c* hr1 *Camph* carb-ac *Caust* k* *Cocc* k* *Con* hr1 *Crot-h* k* cupr hr1 gels k* helon hr1 *Hyos* hr1 kali-br kali-p k* lac-c k* *Lach* k* *Nat-m* k* nux-v k* phos k* phys hr1 phyt hr1 plb hr1 rhus-t hr1 sec sulph k* thuj hr1 zinc hr1
- **progressive**: caust mrr1 con mrr1 *Lath* mrr1 *Plb* mrr1
- **rheumatic**: (↗*GENERALS - Paralysis - rheumatic)* ant-t hr1 *Arn* hr1 bar-c k* bry hr1 calc-p hr1 canth hr1 caul hr1 *Caust* chin hr1 *Cocc* k* colch hr1* ferr hr1 form hr1 gels hr1 kali-chl hr1 lath c2 lyc k* rhus-t k* sulph k*
- **rising**:
  - **agg**.: (non:phos kl)
  - **amel**.: phos kl
- **river** bath in summer: (↗*GENERALS - Paralysis - bathing - river)* *Caust*
- **sensation** of: *Abrot* acon mrr1 *Aesc* *Alum* apis ars k* bell k* *Bry* k* carbn-h *Chel* k* cinnb k* *Cocc* *Con* k* cupr *Dig* k* digin a1 dros k* ferr ferr-i a1 *Gels* **Graph** k* grat a1 hell k* hep k* *Kali-i* k* lach bg1 laur k* meph a1 merc k* *Mez* k* *Nit-ac* k* *Rhus-t* k* sabad k* sil k* thuj ptk1 tritic-vg fd5.de zinc
  - **right**: arn bg1 limen-b-c hrn2• phos bg1
  - **morning**: dulc h2 nat-c h2 sil k* zinc
    - **waking**; on: (↗*SLEEP - Waking - paralyzed)* acon vh1
  - **night**: *Led* limen-b-c mlk9.de
  - **accompanied** by | **Head**; complaints of (See HEAD - Complaints - accompanied - extremities - paralysis)
  - **bandaged**; as if: anac c1*
  - **fever**; after: sil k*
  - **headache**; during: mez h2
  - **motion** agg.: plb k*
  - **pressure** agg.: nit-ac h2
  - **walking** agg.: **Rhus-t** k*
  - **writing** agg.: aesc vh1
  - ○ **Flexors**: colch
  - **Hands**: bung-fa mtf
  - **Joints**: acon arn *Caps* cham k* croc graph h2 *Led* par k* plb rhus-t sulph tritic-vg fd5.de
    - **night**: *Led*
- **sexual** excesses: (↗*GENERALS - Paralysis - sexual)* *Calc* hr1 *Nat-m* k* *Nux-v* k* **Phos** hr1 *Rhus-t* k*
- **single** parts: anac k* *Ars* *Dulc* hr1 kara a1 nux-v k2 plb k2* xan hr1
- **spastic**: *Ben-d* vh gels vh *Hyper* vh *Lach* vh lath br1 *Nux-v* vh plect vh sec vh *Stry* vh
- **stiffness**, with: caust con lach lyc nat-m rhus-t sil
- **toxic**: *Apis* *Ars* bapt crot-h hr1 gels lac-c *Lach* mur-ac rhus-t
- **typhoid** fever; in: *Agar* *Lach* *Rhus-t*
- **vasomotor**: alumn k2
- **wet**; after getting: **Caust** k* *Dulc* hr1 *Gels* hr1 *Nux-v* hr1 *Rhus-t* k*
- **wind** agg.; cold: *Acon* vh1
- ○ **Ankles**: *Abrot* k* ang k* *Calc* b4a.de nat-m k* *Plb* mrr1 ruta k* seneg b4a.de
  - **afternoon**: cham bro1
  - **rheumatic**: ruta c1
  - **sensation** of: *Dros* k* nat-m
    - **walking** agg.: *Dros* k*
  - **sitting** agg.: nat-m k*
  - **walking** agg.: nat-m k*
  - ○ **Extensors**: *Plb* mrr1
- **Elbows**: dulc b4.de* fago mez b4.de* petr k* rhus-t ptk1 sabin
  - **sensation** of: ambr arg-met dulc h1 mez k* samb stront-c sulph k* tritic-vg fd5.de valer
    - **afternoon**: *Sulph* k*
    - **night**: stront-c
    - **motion** agg.: arg-met
    - **raising** arm agg.: mez k*
- **Feet**: ang k* apis arn k* *Ars* k* bar-m k* *Bell* k* carbn-o caust bg2* *Chin* k* *Cocc* k* colch k* *Con* crot-h k* hipp jl2 hydr-ac k* laur k* *Lyc* k* nux-v k* *Olnd* k* *Phos* k* *Plb* k* rhus-t k* stram k* sulph k* vip k* *Zinc* k*
  - **right**: kali-bi bg2
  - **night**: cham bro1
  - **fright** agg.: *Stann* k*
  - **partial**: plb k*
  - **sensation** of: asaf asar k* *Cham* k* *Chel* k* eug k* kali-bi k* led k* lipp hr1 mur-ac k* nat-m k* phos k* sil k* tab k* zinc k*
    - **morning**:
      - **bed** agg.; in: nat-m
      - **rising** agg.; after: *Phos*

• **sensation** of: ...
: **alternating** with | **tearing** pain (See Pain - feet - tearing - alternating - paralyzed)
: **stepping** agg.: asaf asar k*
• **sudden**: *Cham* k*
○ • **Flexors**: *Bar-c* k*
• **Heels**: graph
- **Fingers**: *Ars* b4a.de bry b7.de* *Calc* k* calc-p carb-v b4.de* *Caust Cocc* k* hell bg2 kali-c b4.de* *Mez* k* *Phos* k* *Plb* k* rhus-t b7a.de sabin bg2 sil bg2 stann b4a.de
• **sensation** of: acon ars k* asaf asar aur aur-ar k2 bry k* *Carb-v* k* *Chin* cycl dig euon gran k* kreos lact lil-t k* meny *Mez* phos k* plb k* staph
: **grasping**, when: carb-v k* *Mez*
: **extending** over whole side: both k*
: **Joints**: *Aur* calc-p k* par k* ptel k* verb
○ • **Extensors**: alum k2 *Ars Caust Cocc* k* *Lach* **Plb** k*
• **First**: mag-c k*
: **cramps**, with: carbn-s
: **partially**: mag-c k*
• **Flexors**: *Mez* k*
• **Fourth**: plb k*
: **sensation** of: hell k* lact k* nat-m k*
: **rest** | **amel.**: hell k*
• **Joints**: *Calc* bg2 *Calc-p* bg2 mag-c bg2 phos bg2 *Rhus-t* b7a.de *Ruta* b7a.de
• **Third**: plb k*
: **sensation** of: nat-m k*
- **Forearms**: acon b7.de* arg-n bro1 bar-c bell b4.de* calc-p caust k* colch cur bro1 dulc b4.de* ferr-act bro1 nat-m b4.de* nux-v bro1 phos plat k* *Plb* k* plb-act bro1 ruta bro1 *Sec* b7a.de **Sil** k* stront-c b4.de* sulph b4.de*
• **right**: *Plb Rhus-t*
• **left**: bar-c k* calc calc-p
• **pressure**, as from: cham k*
• **sensation** of: acon aeth a1 all-s k* ambr apis bism bov chel cocc dulc h1 fl-ac k* kali-n h2 kreos par k* plat h2 prun **Rhus-t** seneg staph stront-c sulph k* tritic-vg fd5.de
: **writing** agg.: cocc ferr-i
○ • **Muscles**:
: **Extensor** muscles: colch merc **Plb** k*
: **Flexor** muscles: ars *Gels*
: **supinated**; when: plb
- **Hands**: acon b7.de* act-sp agar *Alum* b4a.de ambr k* *Apis* arg-met b7.de* ars k* bar-c k* bar-m k* calc calc-caust calc-p k* cann-s k* carbn-o **Caust** k* *Cocc* k* colch k* cupr k* cyt-l bro1 ferr k* *Gels* k* guare hr1 hipp jl2 hydr-ac k* kali-bi bg1 kali-c k* lach laur k* merc k* nat-m k* nux-v ox-ac k2 phos k* *Plb* k* plb-act bro1 *Rhus-t* k* ruta k* *Sil* k* stann b4a.de stront-c b4.de* tab k* thyr bro1 *Zinc* k*
• **right**: **Caust** cupr bg1 elaps **Plb** k* zinc bg1
• **left**: bar-c k* calc-p *Cocc* hr1
• **sensation** of: acon k* acon-a a1 am-m k* ambr bism calc-sil k2 *Carb-an* k* **Caust** k* chel k* *Chin* elaps kali-n k* *Kalm* k* lob k* meny nat-s k* nit-ac k* nux-v phos k* pip-m k* prun sil k* staph stront-c sulph k* *Tab*
: **morning** | **rising** agg.; after: phos
: **night**:
: **midnight**:
. **after** | **3** h: plb
: **knitting**, while: am-m k*
: **motion** | **amel.**: acon k*
: **piano** playing: (↗*Playing - piano*) carb-an cur plb rhus-t zinc
: **pressure** agg.: nit-ac k*
: **rubbing** | **amel.**: chel k*
: **sleep** agg.; during: plat k*
: **writing** agg.: acon k* agar *Caust* chel k* *Cocc* k*
○ • **Palms**: plb k*
- **Hips**: *Bry* b7a.de *Coloc* b4a.de *Led* b7a.de petr b4a.de *Rhus-t* b7a.de verat b7.de*
• **sensation** of: brom con k2 nat-m phos plb *Verat*

- **Hips – sensation** of: ...
: **alternating** sides: verat
: **left**:
: **extending** to:
. **Downward** | **walking** agg.: lact br1
: **evening**: phos
: **lying** | **amel.**: phos
: **sitting** | **amel.**: phos
: **walking**:
: **agg.**: verat
: **amel.**: ph-ac
- **Knees**: ambr k* anac b4a.de* ars k* aur b4.de* bar-c b4.de* bov b4a.de carb-v b4.de* chel k* colch b7.de* lath k* mim-h a1 seneg b4a.de *Sulph* b4.de*
• **sensation** of: anac k* aur hr1 berb k* brom hr1 *Chel* k* chr-ac hr1 gels k* jug-r k* kali-c k* op k* phos k* plb hr1
: **forenoon** | **walking** agg.: bry
: **evening** | **bed** agg.; in: colch
: **ascending** stairs agg.: plb k*
: **rising** from sitting agg.: berb a1* plb
: **sitting** agg.: *Chel* k* kali-c h2
: **walking**:
: **after** | **agg.**: aur berb k* *Carb-v* k* croc k* *Hyper* lach
: **agg.**: berb k* brom k* olib-sac wmh1
: **amel.**: lach k*
• **sitting** agg.: chel k*
- **Legs**: acon b7.de aesc tl1 *Agar* bro1 alum bro1 ars b4.de* bry bro1 *Cann-i* bro1 carb-v b4.de caust b4.de chel bro1 *Cocc* bro1 con mrr1 *Crot-h* bro1 dulc bro1 gels bro1 *Gua* bro1 ix bnm8• kali-i bro1 kali-t bro1 *Lath* bro1 nat-m b4.de nux-v bro1 olnd bro1 *Plb* bro1 *Rhus-t* bro1 *Sec* b7a.de* sulfon bro1 tab bro1 *Thal* bro1 verat bro1 zinc bro1
• **beginning** in: con mrr1
• **sensation** of: *Acon* **Aesc** amyg atro bell both brom camph *Carb-v* carbn-o chel chin con k2 dros tl1 lath mag-c manc med morph *Nat-m Nit-ac* olnd plb *Rhus-v* sep tab vip
: **left**: carb-v bg1
: **chill**; during: ars ign stram
: **rheumatic**: chel ph-ac
: **walking** | **after** | **agg.**: croc
: **agg.**: stront-c
- **Lower** limbs: (↗*GENERALS - Paralysis - lower; GENERALS - Paralysis - paraplegia*) *Abrot* acon b7.de* aesc bg2* **Agar** k* *Alum* k* alum-p k2 alum-sil k2 anac k* ang k* apis k* apoc k* **Arg-n** k* arn k* **Ars** k* ars-i ars-s-f k2 bar-c bar-m k* *Bell* k* berb k* bry k* *Calc* k* calc-s calc-sil k2 *Camph* k* **Cann-i** k* cann-s b7.de* canth k* *Caps* k* *Carb-ac* k* carb-v k* carbn-s caul k* caust b4.de* cham b7.de* *Chin* b7a.de chinin-s *Cic* k* cob-n mtf *Cocc* k* colch k* coloc b4a.de *Con* k* *Crot-c* crot-t *Cupr* k* dig b4.de* diphtox jl2 *Dulc* k* elec al2 ferr b7.de* form k* *Gels* k* graph k2 *Hell* b7a.de hir mtf hydr-ac bg1 hyos k* *Ign* iod k* iris kali-ar k* *Kali-c* k* kali-sil k2 kali-t mtf kalm mtf *Lach* k* *Lath* k* *Led* b7a.de lith-c lyc k* lycps-v mag-c b4a.de mang k* merc k* *Merc-c* k* morph k* *Mygal* naja bg2* nat-m k* *Nux-m* k* **Nux-v** k* ol-an k* *Olnd* k* *Op* k* *Ox-ac* k* peti mtf ph-ac b4.de* *Phos* k* phys mtf *Pic-ac* k* pip-m mtf **Plb** k* *Psor* k* *Rhod* b4a.de rhus-r tl1 **Rhus-t** k* *Ruta* k* sars k* *Sec* k* sep k* *Sil* k* stann k* *Stram* k* *Stront-c* b4a.de sul-i k2 *Sulph* k* tab k* *Tarent* k* ter *Thal* k* *Thal-met* br1 thal-s c1 toxo-g mtf *Verat* k* verat-v k* vip-a mtf zinc k*
• **right**: abrot *Arn* hr1 lac-c k* ox-ac plb k* rhus-t hr1 thuj bg1*
: **then** left: *Ox-ac*
• **left**: alum tl1 arn hr1 *Lach* hr1 nat-c k2 ol-an bg2 sulph hr1 ter
: **then** right arm and leg: mag-c h2
• **night**: phos k*
• **accompanied** by:
: **stool**; involuntary: (↗*RECTUM - Involuntary; RECTUM - Involuntary - paralysis*) agar mtf aloe mtf *Alum* mtf apis mtf arg-n mtf ars mtf bell mtf carb-ac mtf *Caust* mtf cocc mtf coloc mtf con mtf gels mtf *Hyos* mtf ind mtf laur mtf mur-ac mtf nux-v mtf *Op* mtf ph-ac mtf phos mtf plb mtf sec mtf stram mtf stry mtf sulph mtf tarent mtf zinc mtf zinc-p mtf
: **urination**; involuntary: (↗*BLADDER - Urination - involuntary*) agar mtf *Alum* mtf arn mtf ars mtf bell mtf carb-ac mtf *Carb-an* mtf *Caust* mtf cic mtf *Con* mtf *Gels* mtf *Hyos* mtf laur mtf mur-ac mtf

Extremities

- **accompanied** by – **urination**; involuntary: ... nux-v mtf *Op* mtf phos mtf plb mtf sec mtf stram mtf stry mtf sulph mtf zinc mtf zinc-p mtf
  - ⋮ **Ankle**; clonic convulsions of: *(↗GENERALS - Paralysis - one - involuntary; GENERALS - Reflexes - increased)* anh mtf bar-c mtf cic mtf cocc mtf *Lath* mtf morph mtf *Nux-v* mtf
  - ⋮ **Uterus**; complaints of the: caul hr1*
- **anger**; after: *Nat-m*
- **apoplexy**; after: **Nux-v** *Phos*
- **cold** agg.; becoming: *Cocc* k* *Rhus-t*
- **colic**; with: *Plb* k*
- **convulsions**; after: stram
  - ⋮ **Arms**, of the: agar
- **delivery**; after: *Caust Plb* **Rhus-t**
- **eruptions**; suppressed: *Psor*
- **exertion**, following: **Nux-v** k* rhus-t
- **fulgurating** pains in abdomen, with: *Thal*
- **grief**; from: nat-m k*
- **hysterical**: ign a1*
- **injuries**; after: *(↗Injuries; GENERALS - Injuries; GENERALS - Paralysis - Injuries)* arn mtf con mtf hyper mtf nat-s mtf nit-ac mtf
  - ⋮ **Spine**; of the: *(↗BACK - Blood - spinal - injuries; BACK - Injuries - spine)* aesc mtf ben-d mtf plect mtf
- **jerking** of eyes, with: alumin arg-n
- **mercury**; abuse of: cocc k2
- **painless**: *Alum* alum-sil k2 *Arg-n Ars* bar-c bell calc camph cann-i *Carb-ac* carb-v carbn-s cic **Cocc Con** *Cupr Gels* kali-c *Lath* k* lyc *Merc* nat-m nux-m nux-v **Olnd** *Op Phos* **Plb Rhus-t** k* *Sec* k* sil stram sulph zinc zinc-p k2
- **post** diphtheritic: **Ars** *Cocc Con* gels k* *Lach* nat-m nux-v k* *Phos Plb Sec Sil*
- **sensation** of: acon **Aesc** *Alum* am-c ang vh **Aur** berb *Calc-p Chel* cupr-ar ptk1 *Dig* hyper lach phos h2 rheum *Rhus-v Sil* hr1 stront-c *Verat*
  - ⋮ **right**: phos h2
    - ⋮ **then** left: *Verat*
  - ⋮ **night**: *Calc-p* phos h2
  - ⋮ **chill**; during: ars b4a.de ign b7a.de
  - ⋮ **dinner**; during: tub ptk1
  - ⋮ **sitting** agg.: *Calc-p*
  - ⋮ **walking** agg.: aesc vh1
- **sexual** excesses: *Nat-m* k* **Nux-v** k* *Phos*
- **sitting**; after: sil k*
- **standing** agg.: sep
- **sudden**: *Nux-v Phos* hr1
  - ⋮ **unnatural** hunger, with: *Cina* hr1
- **tetanus**, followed by: nux-v
- **thrombosis** in spinal artery; from: ergot mtf sec mtf
- **vaccination**; after: *Thuj*
- **vertigo**; with: thuj bg1
- **weather** | **cold**:
  - ⋮ **wet** | **agg.**: lath c1
  - ⋮ **wet** | **agg.**: lath
- **wet**, becoming: *Nux-v* k* **Rhus-t** k*
- ▽ **extending** to | **Upper** limbs: agar alum mrr1 *Ars Con* hydr-ac *Kali-c* mang

- **Muscles**:
  - ○ **Extensor** muscles: alum k* ang hr1 ars calc *Cocc Crot-h* cur k2* **Plb** k*
  - **Flexor** muscles: caust k* *Nat-m* k*
- **Nates** | **sensation** of: sulph h2
- **Shoulders**: *Caust* k* *Cur* k* lach bg2
  - **left**: caust bg1
  - **sensation** of: aeth ambr aur-m bry elaps euph k* *Ferr-i* kreos lact k* mang mez mur-ac nat-m nux-v puls k* *Rhus-t* k* sars sep stann staph sulph tep valer verat
- **Shoulders** – **sensation** of: ...
  - ⋮ **right**: laur k* merc-c pall psor k*
  - ⋮ **left**: aur-m brom *Ign Rhus-t* k*
  - ⋮ **morning** | **rising** agg.: lach
  - ⋮ **evening**: *Ambr*
  - ⋮ **rising** agg.; after: aur-m
  - ⋮ **walking** agg.: arn
  - ○ **Joints**: *Arn* b7a.de *Ferr* b7a.de ign b7a.de puls b7.de* **Rhus-t** b7a.de verat b7a.de
- **Thighs**: acon b7.de* *Agar* bro1 alum bro1 ang b7.de* aur b4.de* bry bro1 *Cann-i* bro1 caust b4.de* *Chel* k* cocc b7.de* con mrr1 *Crot-h* bro1 dulc bro1 gels bro1 *Gue* bro1 kali-c k* kali-i bro1 kali-t a1* *Lath* bro1 manc k* nux-v bro1 *Olnd* b7.de* *Plb* bro1 *Rhus-t* bro1 sec bro1 stram k* sulfon bro1 sulph k* tab bro1 tart-ac a1 *Thal* bro1 verat bro1 zinc bro1
  - **beginning** in: con mrr1
  - **sensation** of: agar k* aur k* bar-c k* berb *Chel* cocc k* crot-t k* lach nux-v k* *Rhus-t* k* sulph h2 verat h1 zinc k*
    - ⋮ **lying** agg.: sulph h2
    - ⋮ **sitting** agg.: caust k* *Chel* k*
    - ⋮ **walking** agg.: caust k* dros k*
    - ⋮ **extending** to | **Knees**: ferr-i k* thuj k*
  - **sitting** agg.: chel k*
  - ○ **Anterior** muscles: ang h1
  - **Extensors**: *Calc* k*
  - **Inside**: *Nux-v*
  - **Posterior** muscles: led h1
- **Thumbs**: kali-c k* mag-c k*
  - **evening**: mag-c k*
  - **knitting**: kali-c k*
  - **sensation** of: lachn merc-i-f k*
    - ⋮ **right**: lachn
    - ⋮ **extending** and grasping; on: sulph
- **Toes**: ars olnd bg1
  - **turn** under while walking: *Bad* k*
  - ○ **Extensors** of: crot-h plb k*
- **Upper** arms: agar k* am-m b7.de* ambr h1 arg-met bell b4.de* calc k* calc-p chel k* *Ferr* b7a.de nux-v olnd b7.de* *Sil* b4a.de
  - **morning**: am-m k*
  - **evening**: am-m k*
  - **partial**: calc k*
  - **sensation** of: **Bell** k* *Chin* k* ferr-i k* mez h2 *Plat* k* sulph k* zinc k*
    - ⋮ **morning** | **rising** agg.; after: sulph k*
    - ⋮ **evening**: sulph k*
      - ⋮ **raising** the arm in bed; on: mez
    - ⋮ **alternating** with drawing, tearing: sulph k*
    - ⋮ **motion** | **amel.**: dulc k*.
    - ⋮ **raising** arm agg.: mez h2
    - ⋮ **sitting** agg.: cycl k*
    - ⋮ **writing** agg.: agar k* *Caust* dulc
  - ○ **Biceps**: plb k*
  - **Deltoid** muscle: *Caust* k* *Cur* k* plb a1
- **Upper** limbs: absin bg2 *Acon* k* aesc k* **Agar** ant-c bg2 ant-t k* *Apis* arg-met k* arn k* *Ars* k* ars-s-f k2 asar b7.de* *Bar-c* k* bar-m bar-s k2 *Bell* k* both k* *Brom* b4a.de bry k* *Calc* k* calc-p k* calc-s **Cann-i** k* cann-xyz bg2 carb-ac bg2 carb-v b4.de* carbn-o **Caust** k* chel k* chin k* chinin-s bg2 cimic bg2 coc-c bg2 *Cocc* k* colch k* *Con* k* *Crot-c* cupr k* dios bg2 *Dulc* k* elec al2 ferr k* ferr-i gast a1 *Gels* k* graph b4.de* *Hell* hep *Iod* bg2 ix bnm8• kali-ar *Kali-c* kali-n k* kali-sil k2 kalm *Lach* b7a.de led k* lepi a1 *Lyc* k* mag-c k* *Merc* k* *Merc-c* k* mez b4.de* morph k* nat-m bg2* *Nit-ac* k* *Nux-v* k* *Op* k* phos k* phyt k* plat k* **Plb** k* plect a1 **Rhus-t** k* *Ruta* b7.de* *Sars* b4a.de sec k* sep k* sil k* *Stann* k* *Stront-c* b4a.de sul-ac b4.de* *Sulph* k* tep k* thyr c2* verat k* verat-v vip k*
  - **right**: *Aesc* k* **Am-c** k* arn ars-s-f k2 ars-s-r bell h1 bism cann-i k* *Caust* colch k* cupr ptk1 ferr-i kali-bi bg1 **Lyc** k* nit-ac k* nux-v *Plb* sang sil **Sulph** k* tep a1 ter *Zinc* ptk1
    - ⋮ **paralysis** of tongue; with: *Caust*
    - ⋮ **Arm** and left leg: ter

- **left**: alum$_{tl1}$ brom cact *Calc*$_{k*}$ **Dig**$_{k*}$ hipp$_{jl2}$ lac-c lat-m ol-an$_{bg2}$ pall par *Rhus-t*$_{hr1}$
  - **and** numbness of right: tarent
  - **apoplexy**; after: ars
  - **hysteria**; during: sep
  - **vertigo**; during: *Arg-n*$_{k*}$
- **night**: *Nux-v*
- **accompanied** by:
  - **sciatica** (See Pain - lower limbs - sciatic - accompanied - arms)
  - **Tongue**; paralysis of: caust$_{ptk1}$
- **apoplexy**: aesc ars bar-c op **Phos**
- **coldness**:
  - **icy** during rest: *Dulc*
  - **with**: caust cocc *Dulc* nux-v plb *Rhus-t* zinc
- **diphtheria**; after: *Caust*
- **eruptions**; after suppressed: hep
- **fright** agg.: stann$_{k*}$
- **insensibility**, with: plb *Rhus-t* zinc
- **lead** poisoning; from: alumn plb
- **meningitis**, during: *Acon*
- **menses** | **before** | **agg.**: puls$_{b7.de}$
  - **during** | **agg.**: puls$_{b7.de}$
- **mercury**; after abuse of: *Hep Nit-ac*
- **neuralgia** of brachial plexus, after: crot-t ix$_{bnm8}$•
- **pain** in heart, with: (↗*CHEST - Pain - heart - region - accompanied - upp - paralysis; CHEST - Pain - heart - region - accompanied - upper - paralysis)* crot-h *Lat-m* pall
- **painless**: olnd$_{mrr1}$
- **partial**: atro$_{k*}$ cic$_{k*}$ kali-act kali-ar$_{k*}$ lac-c *Lat-m* merc *Nux-v* phos plb$_{k*}$
- **progressive**: plb$_{mrr1}$
- **rheumatic**: ant-t$_{bg2}$ chin$_{bg2}$ cocc$_{bg2}$ *Ferr*$_{bg2}$
- **sensation** of: *Abrot* acon$_{k*}$ **Aesc** agar *Alum*$_{k*}$ am-c$_{k*}$ **Am-m** ang$_{h1*}$ *Ars* ars-i bell$_{k*}$ berb$_{k*}$ brom$_{k*}$ bufo *Calc* calc-sil$_{k2}$ camph *Caust* cham chel$_{k*}$ chen-a$_{a1}$ chim$_{a1}$ *Chin* cina **Cocc Colch**$_{k*}$ coloc$_{k*}$ croc$_{k*}$ *Crot-c* crot-t *Cycl*$_{k*}$ dig dros$_{k*}$ dulc$_{k*}$ eupi$_{k*}$ *Ferr*$_{k*}$ ferr-i$_{k*}$ *Gran*$_{k*}$ graph$_{k*}$ grat$_{k*}$ hipp$_{a1*}$ hyper$_{k*}$ *Ign Iod*$_{k*}$ kali-c$_{k*}$ kiss$_{a1}$ *Lach* lepi$_{a1}$ lipp$_{a1}$ *Lith-c* lob$_{k*}$ malar$_{jl2}$ meny mez$_{k*}$ nat-m nat-s *Nux-v* ol-an$_{k*}$ par$_{k*}$ *Phos*$_{k*}$ *Plat*$_{k*}$ plb$_{k*}$ psor rhod$_{k*}$ rhus-v$_{k*}$ sars sec$_{k*}$ *Sep*$_{k*}$ *Sil* stann sul-ac sulph$_{k*}$ *Tab*$_{k*}$ tep$_{k*}$ thuj$_{k*}$ til *Verat*$_{k*}$ *Zinc* zing
  - **right**: aesc$_{k*}$ **Am-c**$_{k*}$ **Am-m**$_{k*}$ *Caust*$_{k*}$ cina$_{k*}$ ferr-i$_{k2}$ fl-ac$_{k*}$ sil$_{h2*}$
  - **left**: am-c$_{bg1}$ *Calc* nux-v pall$_{c1}$ *Plat*$_{k*}$ *Rhus-t*$_{a1}$ sep$_{h2*}$ til$_{c1}$
    - **Arm** and right foot: hyper$_{k*}$ stann
  - **morning**: chel$_{k*}$ gast$_{a1}$ *Nux-v* sil$_{h2}$
    - **bed** agg.; in: chel
    - **waking**; on: sulph$_{k*}$
  - **afternoon**:
    - **nap**; after: phos$_{k*}$
    - **walking** agg.: brom
  - **evening**: ferr-i$_{k*}$ grat$_{k*}$
  - **night**: *Nux-v* **Rhus-t**$_{k*}$ til$_{k*}$
    - **22** h: carbn-s
  - **bed** agg.; in: til$_{c1}$
  - **eating**; after: cocc$_{k*}$
  - **leaning** arm on chair agg.: plat$_{h2}$
  - **motion**:
    - **agg.**: arg-met
    - **amel.**: dulc$_{k*}$
  - **sleep** agg.; during: plat
  - **stretching** arm agg.: ang$_{h1}$
  - **writing**:
    - **agg.**: cocc ferr-i$_{k2}$ sul-ac$_{k*}$
    - **continued**; after: agar *Caust*
- **shaking**, after: nit-ac$_{h2}$

Paralysis – **Upper** limbs: ...
- **shocks**, with: **Nux-v**
- **sleep** agg.; during: mill$_{k*}$
- **sudden**: *Nux-v Rhus-t*$_{hr1}$
- **writing** agg.: agar$_{ptk1}$ cocc$_{k*}$

- **Wrists**: *Acon*$_{k*}$ *Calc*$_{b4a.de}$ calc-p$_{bg2}$ hipp$_{k*}$ *Kali-c*$_{b4.de*}$ merc$_{k*}$ mez$_{b4.de*}$ **Plb**$_{k*}$ ruta sil$_{b4a.de}$
  - **right**:
    - **Ankle**; and | **left**: nat-p
  - **morning**: hipp$_{k*}$
  - **rheumatic**: ruta$_{c1}$
  - **sensation** of: acet-ac$_{a1}$ agar bism bov carb-v$_{k*}$ hipp$_{jl2}$ kali-c lipp$_{a1}$ merc mez$_{k*}$ petr thuj$_{k*}$ tritic-vg$_{fd5.de}$
    - **right**: euphr$_{k*}$ laur lyc mez$_{a1}$ nat-p ox-ac tritic-vg$_{fd5.de}$
      - **extending** to | **Elbow**: euphr$_{k*}$
    - **left**: hipp$_{jl2}$
    - **morning**: sil$_{h2}$
      - **waking**; on: hipp$_{jl2}$
  - ○ **Extensors**: carbn-s cur **Plb**$_{k*}$ rhus-t
    - **piano** playing; from: cur *Plb* rhus-t

PARONYCHIA (See Felon - nail)

PECKING:
- ○ **Arm**: mez$_{h2}$
- **Hands**: mez$_{h2}$

PERIODICITY:
- **morning**; every alternate | **Upper** limbs: nux-v$_{bg2}$

PERSPIRATION: anh$_{sp1}$ aur aur-m *But-ac*$_{sp1}$ *Carb-v Con* convo-s$_{sp1}$ cortico$_{sp1}$ cupr dulc$_{fd4.de}$ glon kali-s$_{fd4.de}$ *Lac-ac* mag-s$_{sp1}$ mand$_{sp1}$ ol-j op plb$_{k2}$ pot-e$_{rly4}$• spong$_{fd4.de}$ stram suis-pan$_{rly4}$• tritic-vg$_{fd5.de}$ vanil$_{fd5.de}$ x-ray$_{sp1}$
- **left** arm and left leg: lac-d
- **morning**: *Carb-v* con
- **night**: aids$_{nl2}$• calc carl con kali-n
- **after**:
  - **amel.**:
    - **Lower** limbs: acon$_{bg2}$ bell$_{bg2}$ bry$_{b7a.de*}$ canth$_{b7.de*}$ cham$_{b7.de*}$ gels$_{bg2}$ *Lyc*$_{b4a.de}$ nux-v$_{b7.de*}$ puls$_{b7.de*}$ rhus-t$_{b7a.de}$ stront-c$_{b4.de*}$
    - **Upper** limbs: bov$_{b4.de*}$ canth$_{b7.de*}$ cham$_{b7.de*}$ nat-c$_{b4.de*}$ nux-v$_{b7.de*}$ puls$_{b7.de*}$
- **clammy**: ars *Cact Calc*$_{mrr1}$ camph$_{ptk1}$ carb-v$_{ptk1}$ chinin-s falco-pe$_{nl2}$• lil-t merc-c nux-m op phos pic-ac$_{ptk1}$ plb pot-e$_{rly4}$• *Tab*
  - **menses** should appear; when: *Lil-t*
- **cold**: *Ars Asaf* aur$_{kl}$ (non:aur-fu$_{kl}$) aur-i aur-m bell *Cact* calc-sil$_{k2}$ canth dros falco-pe$_{nl2}$• gard-j$_{vlr2}$• glon$_{k2}$ *Lach* lachn lat-h$_{bnm5}$• *Merc-c Morph* ox-ac$_{k2}$ phos pot-e$_{rly4}$• *Sec* spong stram *Tab Verat Verat-v*
  - **menses**, during: ars phos sec **Verat**
- **during**:
  - **agg.**:
    - **Lower** limbs: graph$_{b4.de}$ *Merc*$_{b4a.de}$ *Nux-v*$_{b7.de}$
    - **Upper** limbs: *Merc*$_{b4a.de}$
- **paralyzed** limb: ars caust cocc *Merc Rhus-t* stann
- **sticky**: mand$_{sp1}$
- **stool**, during: gamb
- ○ **Ankles**: crot-h$_{ptk1}$ naja$_{ptk1}$
- **Elbow**, flexure of: fic-m$_{gya1}$ sep$_{bg1}$ spong$_{fd4.de}$ tritic-vg$_{fd5.de}$
- **Fingers**: agn$_{k*}$ ant-c$_{k*}$ bar-c$_{k*}$ carb-v$_{k*}$ ign$_{k*}$ lyc$_{ptk1}$ m-arct$_{b7.de}$ rhod$_{k*}$ sulph$_{k*}$ tub-d$_{jl2}$ tub-m$_{jl2}$
  - **sticky** | **together**; as if fingers stuck: calc$_{bg2}$
  - ○ **Between**: sulph$_{h2}$
  - **Tips**: carb-an$_{k*}$ carb-v$_{k*}$ phos$_{bg3*}$ rhod$_{bg2}$ sep$_{h2*}$ sulph$_{bg3*}$
- **Foot**: acon$_{k*}$ aids$_{nl2}$• alum$_{bro1}$ am-c$_{k*}$ am-m$_{k*}$ anan$_{bro1}$ ang$_{k*}$ apis$_{k*}$ apoc-a$_{bro1}$ arn$_{k*}$ *Ars*$_{k*}$ *Ars-i* arund$_{bro1}$ bar-act$_{bro1}$ **Bar-c**$_{k*}$ bar-i$_{k2}$ *Bar-m* bar-ox-suc$_{rly4}$• *Bell*$_{k*}$ benz-ac brom bry$_{k*}$ **Calc**$_{k*}$ calc-i$_{k2}$ **Calc-s**$_{k*}$ camph$_{k*}$ cann-s$_{k*}$ *Canth*$_{k*}$ carb-an$_{k*}$ **Carb-v**$_{k*}$ **Carbn-s** carc$_{cd}$ cassia-s$_{ccrh1}$• *Caust* cham chel$_{k*}$ cimic$_{bg2}$ cob$_{bro1*}$ coc-c **Cocc**$_{k*}$ coff$_{k*}$ **Coloc**$_{k*}$ croc *Cupr*$_{k*}$ cycl$_{k*}$ dros$_{k*}$ **dubo-h**$_{hs1}$ dulc$_{fd4.de}$ euph$_{k*}$ fago *Fl-ac*$_{k*}$ germ-met$_{srj5}$•

- **Foot**: ...
Graph k* hell k* hep k* hura hyper ind k* **Iod** k* ip k* jab kali-ar *Kali-bi Kali-c* k* kali-m k2 kali-p kali-s kalm kreos k* *Lac-ac* k* lac-del hm2• lach k* lact led k* lil-t bg2 **Lyc** k* *Mag-m* k* mang k* med **Merc** k* mez k* morg-g pte1*• morg-p fmm1• mur-ac k* naja k* nat-ar nat-c k* *Nat-m* k* nat-p *Nit-ac* k* ol-an bro1 ox-ac *Petr* k* ph-ac k* *Phos* k* phyt k* pic-ac plb k* podo c1 *Psor* k* **Puls** k* ran-b bg2 rhus-t k* ruta fd4.de sabad k* sabin k* sal-ac bro1* sanic k* sec k* sel k* **Sep** k* **Sil** k* *Squil* k* *Staph* k* sul-i k2 **Sulph** k* symph fd3.de• tarent *Tell* bro1 thal-xyz srj8• **Thuj** k* tritic-vg fd5.de tub mrr1 vanil fd5.de *Verat* **Zinc** k* zinc-p k2 [cob-m stj2 cob-p stj2 lith-c stj2]
- • **one** foot: bar-c mtf33
- • **right**: plect vh sulph vh
- • **left**: cham nit-ac
- • **daytime**: petr-ra shn4• pic-ac
- • **morning**: am-m bry coc-c dulc fd4.de euphr vh lyc merc ruta fd4.de *Sulph* k*
  - ⋮ **bed**, in: bry dulc fd4.de lach merc phos *Puls* h1 *Sabin* k*
  - ⋮ **rising**, after: am-m
- • **forenoon**: fago
- • **afternoon**: graph lac-ac plect vh vanil fd5.de
- • **evening**: aq-mar skp7• **Calc** coc-c vh cocc graph *Mur-ac* pic-ac podo
  - ⋮ **bed**, in: calc clem k* *Mur-ac*
- • **night**: aids nl2• bar-c a1 coloc mang h2 merc bg1 *Nit-ac* staph h1 *Sulph* thuj tritic-vg fd5.de
  - ⋮ **midnight** | **before** | **23** h: hura
    - ⋮ **after** | **2** h: *Ars*
  - ⋮ **waking**, on: aids nl2• mang vh
- • **absent**: phos b4a.de *Sep* b4.de* *Sil* b4.de*
- • **accompanied** by | **Axillae**; perspiration of: tell mtf11
- • **alternating** with:
  - ⋮ **Head**; pain in (See HEAD - Pain - alternating - feet)
  - ⋮ **Joints**:
    - ⋮ **pain** (See Pain - joints - alternating with - foot)
    - ⋮ **stiffness** (See Stiffness - joints - alternating - foot)
- • **burning**, with: *Calc* k* iod tl1 *Lyc* k* mur-ac petr sep *Sulph* k* thuj
- • **carrion**, like: sil alj*
- • **children**; in: **Sil** mrr1
- • **chill**, during: cann-s
- • **clammy**: acon calc bg1* cann-i pic-ac sanic mtf33 sep stry-p br1 sulph
- • **coition** agg.: [cob-m stj2]
- • **cold**: acon *Ang* bg2 **Ant-t** bg2 apis bg2 ars ars-i k2 ars-s-f k2 aur ptk1* **Bar-c** k* bell benz-ac brass-n-o srj5• but-ac sp1 **Calc** k* calc-p bg1 *Calc-s* k* calc-sil k2 camph tl1 cann-xyz bg2 *Canth* k* **Carb-v** k* **Carbn-s** carc fd2.de• *Caust* cimic *Cocc* k* colch tl1 convo-s sp1 *Cupr* k* *Dig Dros* k* dulc fd4.de fago graph k* *Hep* k* hura ind *Ip* k* *Kali-c* kali-m k2* *Kali-p Kali-s* lach ptk1 laur *Lil-t* k* **Lyc** k* *Mag-m* k* med *Merc* k* mez k* **Mur-ac** k* nit-ac k* olib-sac wmh1 ox-ac phos k* pic-ac plb *Psor* **Puls** k* pyrog tl1 *Sanic* sec k* *Sep* k* *Sil* k* squil k* **Staph** k* stram *Sulph* k* symph fd3.de• tarent ptk1* thuj k* **Verat** k*
  - ⋮ **room**: calc k2
- • **constant**: **Sil** *Thuj*
- • **diarrhea**, during: sulph
- • **except** the feet; general perspiration: **Chin** ●* **Phos** ●*
- • **excoriating**: *Bar-c* k* *Calc Carb-v* caust bg2 coff k* **Fl-ac** k* graph k* hell k* *Iod* k* *Lyc* k* manc ptk1 nat-c bg2 nat-m bg2 *Nit-ac* k* ran-b k* *Sanic* k* *Sec Sep* k* *Sil* k* squil thuj ptk1* zinc k*
  - ⋮ **shoes**; destroying: graph ptk1* hep ptk1 naja ptk1* sanic ptk1* sec hr1* sil ptk1
  - ⋮ **socks**; destroying: sanic mtf33 sec gk **Sil** mrr1
- • **heat**, during: **Am-m** bg2 ars h2 calc bg2 ferr-p bg2 luf-op rsj5• lyc bg2 **Nat-m** bg2 nit-ac bg2 phos bg2 *Puls* bg2 *Sep* bg2 sil bg2 staph bg2 sulph bg2 thuj bg2 [cob-m stj2]
- • **injuries** of spine, in: **Nit-ac** k*
- • **leather**; like sole: cob
- • **menses**:
  - ⋮ **after**: *Calc* lil-t *Sep Sil*
- • **menses**: ...
  - ⋮ **before** and during: *Calc*
  - ⋮ **during**: ph-ac b4a.de
    - ⋮ **severity** of pain; from: verat vh
- • **offensive**: alum bro1 am-c k* am-m k* anan apis bg2 arg-n ars k* ars-i ars-s-f k2 arund aur ptk1* bamb-a stb2.de• **Bar-c** k* bar-s k2 bufo but-ac br1* *Calc* k* *Calc-s* k* carb-ac *Carbn-s* carc cd chlol c1* cob coloc cortico sp1 cycl k* dulc fd4.de *Fl-ac* **Graph** k* kali-bi gk **Kali-c** k* kali-sil k2* kalm *Lach* ptk1 **Lyc** k* med ser morg-p pte1*• nat-c bg2 nat-m **Nit-ac** k* ol-an ptk1 *Petr* k* *Phos* k* *Plb* k* *Psor* k* **Puls** k* *Rhus-t* ruta fd4.de sal-ac c1 *Sanic* k* *Sec* k* *Sep* k* **Sil** k* staph *Sulph* k* **Tell** k* **Thuj** k* vanil fd5.de *Zinc* k* zinc-p k2 [*Calc-sil* stj2 *Ferr-sil* stj2 *Mag-sil* stj2 *Mang-sil* stj2 *Nat-sil* stj2 *Sil-met* stj2]
- • **profuse**: ars arund but-ac br1 carb-an carb-v *Carbn-s* carc zzh cench k2 cham coloc cortico tpw7 fl-ac *Graph* ind *Ip Kali-c* kreos *Lac-ac* lach **Lyc** merc naja k2 **Nit-ac** petr k* phyt *Psor* puls sabad sal-ac k* *Sanic* sec *Sep* **Sil** k* staph sulph *Thuj* k* *Zinc*
- • **rotten** eggs: staph
- • **sitting**, while: bell vh symph fd3.de•
- • **sour**: *Calc* calc-sil k2 cob k* iod tl1 kali-s fkr2.de nat-m *Nit-ac* sil tritic-vg fd5.de [cob-m stj2 cob-p stj2]
  - ⋮ **evening**: *Sil*
- • **sticky**: am-c bg3* calc bg3* kali-c bg3* lyc bg3* manc bg3* sanic bg3*
- • **stool**, after: sulph
- • **suppressed**: (↗*GENERALS - Perspiration - suppression - foot)* am-c apis k* ars bad **Bar-c** k* *Bar-m* bar-s k2 *Carb-v* b4a.de cham coch colch *Cupr* k* *Form* k* graph k* haem *Kali-c* k* lyc k* merc k* nat-c k* *Nat-m* k* nit-ac k* ol-an bg2* ph-ac k* phos k* plb psor bro1 *Puls* k* *Rhus-t* k* sal-ac c2 sanic bro1 sel k* **Sep** k* **Sil** k* sulph k* *Thuj* k* x-ray sp1 **Zinc** k* zinc-p k2
- • **swelling** of feet, with: graph iod kali-c kreos *Lyc* k* petr ph-ac plb sabad
- • **urine**, like: canth coloc
- • **waking**, on: mang
- • **walking**, while: carb-v k* graph nat-c
- • **warm**: *Led* k*
- • **winter**; agg. during: arg-n *Med* al2
- ▽ • **extending** to | **Upward**: *Bell* bg2
- ○ • **Back** of: iod bg1*
- • **Heel**: ol-an bg2* phos bg1 thuj
  - ⋮ **left**: nit-ac bg2
- • **Sole**: acon k* **Am-m** k* arn k* ars bg2 *Calc* calc-sil mtf33 cassia-s ccrh1• chel k* dulc fd4.de fago fl-ac k2 glycyr-g cte1• hell kali-c k* *M-arct* b7.de* maland bg1 *Merc* k* *Nat-m* k* **Nit-ac** k* *Nux-m* petr k* pip-n bg2 *Plb* k* *Puls* sabad k* **Sil** k* *Sulph* tetox pin2•
  - ⋮ **left**: sulph bg2
  - ⋮ **morning**: aq-mar skp7•
  - ⋮ **absent**: phos b4.de*
  - ⋮ **bathing**; after: aq-mar skp7•
  - ⋮ **cold**: acon convo-s sp1 dulc fd4.de glycyr-g cte1• *Sulph*
  - ⋮ **itching**: **Sil** *Sulph*
  - ⋮ **making** sole raw: bar-c k2* *Calc* nit-ac h2 sil h2*
  - ⋮ **offensive**: aq-mar skp7• bar-c mtf33 glycyr-g cte1• *Petr Plb Sil*
  - ⋮ **profuse**: cassia-s ccrh1• glycyr-g cte1•
- **Forearm**: *Petr* k*
- **Hand**: acon k* **Agn** k* aids nl2• am-m bg2 ambr k* aml-ns anac k* *Ant-t* k* **Ars** k* ars-i bamb-a stb2.de• bar-c k* bar-i k2 bar-s k2 bell k* brom bry bg2 bufo bg2 **Calc** k* calc-i k2 *Calc-s* camph k* canth k* caps k* carb-v k* carbn-o carbn-s *Caust* cham k* chel chin bg2 cimic bg2 *Cina* k* *Cit-v* cocc k* coff k* *Coloc* k* *Con* k* cupr dig k* dirc dulc k* *Fago* k* falco-pe nl2• ferr k* *Fl-ac* k* glon graph guare hell k* *Hep* k* hura *Ign* k* iod k* *Ip* k* *Kali-bi* kali-s fd4.de kreos k* lac-ac k* laur k* *Led* k* lil-t bg2 lith-c *Lyc* k* mag-s sp1 marb-w es1• *Merc* k* *Merc-c* k* naja k2* narc-ps mp4• nat-ar nat-c k* *Nat-m* k* nat-p nat-sil fd3.de• **Nit-ac** k* *Nux-v* k* oena ol-an olib-sac wmh1 op ox-ac oxal-a rly4• *Petr* k* ph-ac k* phel **Phos** k* phys pic-ac k* pieri-b mlk9.de pneu jl2 prot jl2 puls k* pyrus rheum bg2 rhod k* *Rhus-t* k* sanic sars k* **Sep** k* **Sil** k* spig k* stict sul-i k2

- **Hand**: ...
Sulph k* syph tab thal-xyz srj8• **Thuj** k* thyr ptk1 tritic-vg fd5.de tub bg* verat k* *Zinc* k* zinc-p k2 [ind stj2 mag-lac stj2 zirc-met stj2]
  - **one** hand: bar-c mtf33
  - **daytime**: nit-ac ol-an pic-ac
  - **morning**: dulc fd4.de lyc phos puls sulph
    - **bed**, in: dulc fd4.de phos
    - **rising**, after: puls
  - **forenoon**: fago
  - **noon** until evening, daily: lac-ac
  - **afternoon**: bar-c
  - **evening**: glon ign sulph
    - **lying** down, before: sulph
  - **night**: coloc
  - **accompanied** by | **Nose**; cold: *Nux-v*
  - **air**, open: agn
  - **alternately** in one or the other: cocc
  - **anxiety**; with: bit-ar wht1•
    - **accompanied** by | **trembling** hand (See Trembling - hands - anxiety - accompanied - perspiration)
  - **chill**, during: eup-per *Ip* *Puls*
  - **clammy**: anac k* *Ars* k* both-ax tsm2 calc bg2* carb-ac coloc bg2 falco-pe nl2• ind lyss c1 merc k* nux-v k* **Phos** k* pic-ac plan pyrog k* sanic ptk1* spig k* *Stry-p* br1 sulph k* tarent ptk1 zinc
  - **cold**: acet-ac bg2 acon ambr ant-c ant-t k* *Ars* k* ars-i ars-s-f k2 *Atro* bell k* both-ax tsm2 *Brom* calc bg2* *Calc-s* calc-sil k2 **Canth** k* caps carb-ac carc fd2.de• cham k* *Cimic* k* *Cina* k* cocc dulc fd4.de falco-pe nl2• ferr bg2* gard-j vlr2• *Hep* k* iod k* *Ip* k* *Kali-bi* k* kali-cy kali-n bg2 kali-sil k2 *Lach* *Lil-t* k* *Lyc* merc-c k* morph **Nit-ac** k* nux-v k* olnd bg2 *Ox-ac* petr h2 *Ph-ac* k* *Phos* phyt pic-ac plb pot-e rly4• *Psor* rheum k* *Rhus-t* sanic pf sars *Sec* **Sep** k* *Spig* k* *Sulph* k* *Tab* tarent mtf33 *Thuj* k* **Tub** al2 *Verat* *Verat-v* zinc zinc-p k2
    - **warm** room, in: ambr
  - **coldness**, during internal: tab
  - **copious**: bamb-a stb2.de• *But-ac* sp1 *Ip* kali-sil k2 naja k2 nat-c h2 *Nit-ac* **Sil** stict ptk1 sulph ptk1
  - **coughing**, on: ant-t k* naja ptk1
  - **dysmenorrhea**: tarent
  - **excitement**; from: bamb-a stb2.de• tritic-vg fd5.de
  - **exhausting**: nat-c
  - **heat**, with: *Am-c* bg2* falco-pe nl2• ferr-p bg2* nit-ac k* thuj bg2
  - **injuries** of the spine: **Nit-ac** k*
  - **itching**, with: sulph
  - **migraine** | **during**: *Calc*
  - **offensive**: bapt hr1 calc-s coloc hep nit-ac petr mtf11 phys ptk1
  - **only**, on: agn verat h1
  - **ophthalmia**: brom cadm-s *Calc* *Con* *Dulc* **Fl-ac** k* gymno ind *Iod* *Led* *Petr* **Sulph** k*
  - **prolapsus** uteri: *Lil-t*
  - **rising**, on: am-m fago
  - **sitting**, while: calc
  - **sleep**, on going to: ars
  - **sticky**: both-ax tsm2
  - **stool**, after: *Sulph*
  - **sulphur**, odor of: sulph
  - **urine**, odor of: coloc pieri-b mlk9.de
  - **walking** in open air: agn
  - **writing**, while: coff
  - ○ **Back** of: chion bg2 lil-t lith-c k* zinc-s bg2
    - **cold**: both ptk1 chion bg1* lil-t k* zinc-s bg1*
    - **exercising**, while: thuj
  - **Between** the fingers: sulph

- **Hand**: ...
  - **Palm**: *Acon* k* agar aids nl2• *All-c* k* all-s am-m k* aml-ns k* anac k* ant-t aq-mar vml3• arg-n bg2 bapt bg2 bar-c k* bar-i k2 bar-s k2 brom bry k* cadm-s *Calc* k* calc-i k2 calc-p k* calc-sil stj2* camph k* cann-i caps k* carb-v carc fd2.de• cassia-s ccrh1• caust cench k2 *Cham* k* chel cocc bro1 coff *Con* k* crat ptk1 dig k* **Dulc** k* fago k* falco-pe nl2• ferr bg1 *Fl-ac* k* flav jl2 glon granit-m es1• gymno hell k* hep hyos **Ign** k* ind *Iod* jatr-c kali-bi bg2 *Kali-c* k* kali-p fd1.de• kali-s kali-sil k2 kola stb3• kreos k* laur k* *Led* k* lil-t lob lyc k* *M-arct* b7.de* manc k* *Merc* k* naja k* nat-m k* nat-sil fd3.de• nit-ac k* **Nux-v** k* olib-sac wmh1 oxal-a rly4• *Pert-vc* vk9 petr petr-ra shn4• *Phos* k* pic-ac bro1 pip-n bg2 *Psor* k* rheum k* rhus-t b7.de* **Sep** k* **Sil** k* spig k* *Stry-p* bro1 **Sulph** k* tab tarent trios rsj11• *Tub* tub-a jl2 vero-o rly4*• viol-o ptk1 wye bro1 [bell-p-sp dcm1]
    - **daytime**: dulc petr-ra shn4•
    - **morning**: am-m h2 aq-mar skp7• dulc fd4.de
    - **afternoon**: bar-c dulc fd4.de
    - **evening**: dulc fd4.de tab
    - **night**: *Psor*
      - **midnight** | **after**: merç
      - **waking**, on: aids nl2•
    - **bathing**; after: aq-mar skp7•
    - **clammy**: anac k* coff falco-pe nl2• spig [bell-p-sp dcm1]
    - **cold**: *Acon* calc-sil k2 carc fd2.de• *Cham* k* *Cina* b7a.de coff con bg2* convo-s sp1 dulc fd4.de falco-pe nl2• glycyr-g cte1• hydrog srj2• *Ip* b7a.de *M-arct* b7a.de nux-v k* petr-ra shn4• rheum k* spig k* sul-i k2 **Tub** al2 zinc-i bg1
    - **coldness**:
      - **back**; during coldness on: all-c
      - **back** of hand; with coldness of: hell
      - **during**: gran
    - **cough**; during: naja k2*
    - **exertion**, on: *Calc* kali-p fd1.de• *Psor*
    - **offensive**: aq-mar skp7*• glycyr-g cte1•
    - **pressed** together, when: rheum k* sanic ptk1
    - **profuse**: cassia-s ccrh1• glycyr-g cte1•
    - **room**, in: caust
    - **soup**, after: phos
    - **sticky**: sumb bg2
    - **walking** in open air: nux-v rhus-t
    - **warm**: ign ptk1*
- **Joints**: **Am-c** ars bell bry calc dros led *Lyc* mang nux-v ph-ac *Rhus-t* sars k* stann suis-pan rly4• sulph
  - **morning**: am-c lyc
  - **cold**: rhus-t
  - **painful**: am-c lyc
  - ○ **Bends** of: carc cd sep h2 suis-pan rly4•
    - **morning**: lyc h2
    - **night**: sars h2
- **Knee**: am-c k* ars k* bry k* *Calc* k* clem dros k* led k* *Lyc* k* plb sep spong k* *Sulph* k* tritic-vg fd5.de vanil fd5.de
  - **night**: ars carb-an h2
  - **circumscribed**: clem
  - **cold**: ars
  - **fever**, after: plb
  - **swelling**, with: lyc
  - ○ **Hollow** of: abrot bg2 apis bg2 arg-n bg2 ars-i bg2 bar-m bg2 bry b7.de* bufo carb-ac bg2 *Carb-an* k* con bg1* dros bg2* form bg2 ign bg1 iod bg2 kali-i bg2 puls bg2 sep bg1* *Sulph* bg2 tritic-vg fd5.de vanil fd5.de
- **Leg**: agar am-c ars k* bry k* *Calc* *Calc-p* *Caps* coc-c coloc k* dubo-h hs1 **Euph** k* hyos k* kali-bi **Mang** k* merc k* mez k* nux-v k* **Petr** k* **Podo** *Psor* puls bg1 rhod k* *Rhus-t* b7a.de rumx k* *Sep* *Stram* *Sulph* k* ter tl1 thuj til c1
  - **right**: coc-c bg1
  - **morning**: ars euph sulph k*
    - **waking**, on: coloc
  - **evening** | **bed**; in: agar ter
  - **night**: *Agar* am-c *Calc* coloc kali-bi bg1 mang *Merc* rumx bg1 *Sulph* thuj

- **night**: ...
  - **midnight**:
    - **after** | **5** h: sulph
- **clammy**: rumx
- **cold**: calc$_{tl1}$ calc-s$_{tl1}$ camph$_{tl1}$ *Caps* colch$_{tl1}$ dendr-pol$_{sk4}$• euph hep$_{tl1}$ *Merc Phos Psor* pyrog$_{tl1}$ sep$_{tl1}$ thuj$_{h1}$ verat$_{tl1}$
  - **afternoon**: calc$_{bro1}$ merc$_{bro1}$
- **except** the legs: **Lyc**$_{●}$* petr$_{hr1}$
- **fetid**: *Phos*
- **sticky**: *Calc*
- ○ **Inner** surface: agar
- **Tibia** | **Over**: dendr-pol$_{sk4}$•

\- **Lower** limbs: ars$_{k}$* asaf$_{k}$* borx$_{k}$* calc$_{k}$* coc-c coloc$_{k}$* con$_{k}$* croc$_{k}$* euph$_{b4a.de}$ euphr$_{ptk1}$ hep$_{k}$* **Hyos**$_{k}$* **Kali-n**$_{k}$* lat-h$_{bnm5}$• malar$_{jl2}$ mang$_{k}$* merc$_{k}$* nit-ac$_{b4a.de}$ nux-v petr$_{ptk1}$ *Phos*$_{k}$* podo$_{ptk1}$ *Rhod*$_{k}$* sec$_{k}$* *Sep*$_{k}$* sil$_{b4a.de}$ ter$_{k}$* thlas$_{bg2}$ *Verat Zinc*$_{k}$* zinc-p$_{k2}$

- **morning**: lyc
  - **bed**, in: rhod
    - **waking**, after: con$_{h2}$ *Sep*
- **evening**: *Tetox*$_{pin2}$•
  - **bed**; in: ter
- **night**: am-c$_{h2}$ ars calc$_{bg1}$ coloc con$_{h2}$ kali-n$_{h2}$ mang *Merc* rumx ter *Zinc*
- **clammy**: lil-t$_{ptk1}$
- **cold**: *Ang*$_{b7a.de}$ *Cann-s*$_{b7a.de}$ *Cocc*$_{b7a.de}$ *Dros*$_{b7a.de}$ ip$_{b7a.de}$ *M-arct*$_{b7a.de}$ *Puls*$_{b7a.de}$* sec$_{b7a.de}$ *Squil*$_{b7a.de}$ *Staph*$_{b7a.de}$ ter$_{ptk1}$* thuj$_{bg2}$
- **except** the lower limbs; general perspiration: **Lyc**$_{●}$*
- **fetid**: *Phos*
- **menses**, during: calc lil-t
- **menstrual** colic, during: ant-t
- **paralyzed** limbs: stram
- **suppressed**: *Apis*$_{b7a.de}$ cupr$_{b7a.de}$ *Rhus-t*$_{b7a.de}$ sel$_{b7a.de}$
- **walking**, while: ery-a

\- **Nates**: pot-e$_{rly4}$• symph$_{fd3.de}$• thuj

\- **Shoulder**: chin phasco-ci$_{rbp2}$

- **night**: phasco-ci$_{rbp2}$
- **coition**, after: agar
- ○ **Under** | **dinner** amel.: phos

\- **Thigh**: acon **Ambr**$_{k}$* arg-n$_{bg2}$ **Ars**$_{k}$* aur$_{bg2}$ *Borx* caps *Carb-an*$_{k}$* coloc$_{k}$* crot-t dros$_{k}$* eup-per eup-pur euph$_{k}$* *Hep* hyos$_{k}$* *Kali-bi* merc$_{k}$* *Nux-v*$_{k}$* ran-g$_{c2}$* rhus-t$_{k}$* *Sep*$_{k}$* sulph **Thuj**$_{k}$*

- **morning**: euph rhus-t thuj
- **afternoon**: carb-an$_{bro1}$
- **night**: *Carb-an* coloc$_{h2}$ *Merc Sep*
  - **midnight**:
    - **after**: ars nux-v
      - **3** h: borx$_{bg2}$
- **cold**: caps$_{ptk1}$ crot-t *Merc*$_{k}$* *Sep*$_{k}$* spong$_{ptk1}$
  - **afternoon**: calc$_{bro1}$ merc$_{bro1}$
- **except** the thigh; general perspiration: **Lyc**$_{●}$*
- **exertion**: carb-an$_{bro1}$
- **sensation** of: caps$_{h1}$
- **sleep**, at beginning of: ars
- **spots**, in: caps
- **walking** in open air: caps$_{h1}$
- ○ **Between**: aur *Bar-c*$_{b4a.de}$ *Carb-v*$_{b4a.de}$ *Cinnb*$_{k}$* cocc$_{b}$ hep$_{k}$* nux-v *Petr*$_{b4a.de}$ **Thuj**$_{b4a.de}$
  - **morning**: carb-an nux-v
  - **night**: aur carb-an
  - **corrosive**: cinnb
  - **offensive**: *Cinnb*
  - **walking**, while: ambr *Cinnb*
- **Inner** surface of: acon$_{bg}$ arg-n$_{b}$ kali-bi$_{b}$ sulph$_{k2}$ *Thuj*

Perspiration – Thigh: ...

- **Near** genitals: calc$_{h}$ thuj
  - **Male** genitals: crot-t
    - **offensive**: *Crot-t*

\- **Toes**: acon$_{k}$* arn$_{k}$* clem$_{k}$* *Cycl*$_{bg2}$ ferr$_{bg2}$ hell$_{bg2}$ kali-c$_{k}$* lach lyc$_{bg2}$ *Phyt Puls* ran-b$_{bg2}$ sep$_{k}$* **Sil**$_{k}$* squil$_{k}$* tarax$_{bg2}$ tell *Thuj*$_{k}$* tub-d$_{jl2}$ tub-m$_{jl2}$ zinc

- **morning** | **bed**; in: lach
- **excoriating**: bar-c$_{mtf33}$ graph$_{ptk1}$ zinc$_{ptk1}$
- **offensive**: bar-c$_{bg2}$* graph$_{bg2}$ nit-ac$_{bg2}$ puls$_{bg2}$ thuj$_{bg2}$
- **walking**, while: graph
- ○ **Between**: acon$_{k}$* anac arn$_{k}$* *Bar-c* brass-n-o$_{srj5}$• carb-v *Clem*$_{k}$* cob cupr cycl$_{k}$* ferr$_{k}$* *Fl-ac* hell$_{bg2}$ *Kali-c*$_{k}$* kali-sil$_{k2}$ *Lyc*$_{k}$* nat-sil$_{fd3.de}$• *Nit-ac Puls* ran-b$_{bg2}$ sep$_{k}$* **Sil**$_{k}$* squil$_{k}$* tarax$_{k}$* thuj$_{k}$* *Zinc*
  - **evening**: clem
  - **offensive**: *Bar-c*$_{k}$* cob cycl fl-ac$_{k2}$ *Kali-c* lyc nit-ac *Puls Sep* **Sil** *Thuj Zinc*
  - **rawness**; causing: (↗*Excoriation - toes)* **Bar-c**$_{k}$* *Carb-v* cob$_{ptk1}$ fl-ac$_{k2}$ *Graph Nit-ac Sanic*$_{k}$* *Sep Sil*$_{k}$* **Zinc**$_{k}$*
- **Under** toes: phyt$_{k}$* tarax

\- **Upper** limbs: agar asaf$_{k}$* asar$_{k}$* bar-c$_{bg2}$ bry caps carb-v$_{bg2}$ guare hyos ign$_{bg2}$ ip$_{k}$* jab kali-p$_{fd1.de}$• kali-s$_{fd4.de}$ merc **Petr**$_{k}$* ph-ac$_{k2}$ stann$_{k}$* stront-c$_{k}$* sulph$_{bg2}$ zinc

- **right**: formal$_{bro1}$
- **night**: kali-p$_{fd1.de}$• ol-j
- **amel.**: thuj$_{ptk1}$
- **coition**, after: agar
- **cold** | **clammy**: ph-ac$_{tl1}$ *Zinc*
- **no** perspiration on right arm for three months: scol$_{c1}$
- **sticky**: anac$_{b4a.de}$ camph$_{ptk1}$ carb-v$_{ptk1}$ pic-ac$_{ptk1}$
- ○ **Inner** side of: arn

\- **Wrist**: petr syph

PHLEGMASIA ALBA DOLENS (See Milk)

PICKING fingers (See MIND - Gestures - fingers - picking)

PINCHING fingertips:

\- **amel.** | **Upper** limbs: apis$_{bg2}$*

PITHY (See Numbness)

PITTING (See Indented)

PLAYING:

\- **organ**, from: lyc

\- **piano**, from: (↗*Heaviness - upper limbs - playing; Paralysis - hands - sensation - piano; Weakness - fingers - playing)* anac calc cur$_{k}$* gels kali-c mag-p *Nat-c Sep* sulph zinc

- **sensation** of heaviness: anac
- ○ **Upper** limbs: zinc$_{b4.de}$*

\- **violin**, from: calc *Kali-c* mag-p viol-o

POLLUTIONS:

\- **after**:

- **agg.**:
  - **Lower** limbs: *Sil*$_{b4a.de}$
  - **Upper** limbs: puls$_{b7.de}$* *Sil*$_{b4a.de}$ staph$_{b7.de}$*

POSITION sense lost: anh$_{sp1}$

POWERFUL (See Strength)

PREGNANCY agg.: | **Lower** limbs: vib$_{bg2}$

PRESSURE:

\- **agg.**:

- ○ **Lower** limbs: alum$_{b4.de}$* ant-c$_{b7.de}$* bell$_{bg2}$ bry$_{b7.de}$* chin$_{b7.de}$* *Cina*$_{b7.de}$* coloc$_{bg2}$ dros$_{b7.de}$* guaj$_{b4.de}$* hep$_{b4.de}$* *Iod*$_{b4a.de}$ *Kali-bi*$_{bg2}$ laur$_{b7.de}$* lyc$_{bg2}$ nux-v$_{b7.de}$* *Olnd*$_{b7.de}$* phyt$_{bg2}$ plat$_{b4.de}$* ruta$_{b7.de}$* sep$_{b4.de}$* spig$_{b7.de}$* staph$_{b7.de}$* valer$_{b7.de}$* verat$_{b7.de}$* verb$_{b7.de}$*

- **agg.**: ...
  - **Upper** limbs: am-m b7.de* ant-c b7.de* bov b4.de* bry b7.de* cann-s b7.de* caust b4.de* chel b7.de* *Cina* b7.de* dig b4.de* iod b4.de* kali-bi bg2 mang b4.de* merc b4.de* nat-m b4.de* ruta b7.de* sars b4.de* *Sil* b4a.de spig b7.de* staph b7.de* teucr b7.de* thuj b4.de* valer b7.de* verat b7.de*
- **amel.**:
  - ○ **Feet** | **Soles**: zinc-ar ptk1
  - **Lower** limbs: am-c b4.de* am-m b7.de* arg-met b7.de* ars ptk1 bell b4.de* *Bry* b7.de* calc bg2 caust bg2 chel b7.de* chin b7.de* cina b7.de* coff bg2 con bg2 dig b4.de* dros b7.de* hell b7.de* ign b7.de* kali-c b4.de* mag-p ptk1 mang b4.de* meny b7.de* *Merc* b4.de* mez b4.de* nat-c b4.de* *Puls* b7.de* rhus-t b7.de* verat b7.de*
  - **Upper** limbs: ambr b7.de* arg-met b7.de* *Bell* b4.de* bov b4.de* bry b7.de* canth b7.de* cina b7.de* ign b7.de* laur b7.de* mang b4.de* meny b7.de* puls b7.de* verat b7.de*
- **clothes**; of:
  - ○ **Lower** limbs: bufo bg2 chin bg2 nat-m bg2
  - **Upper** limbs: bufo bg2
- **shoes**; of | **Lower** limbs: bufo bg2
- **sole** of foot; against:
  - **amel.** | **Lower** limbs: rhus-t bg2
- **spine** agg; on | **Lower** limbs: phos bg2

PRICKLING; sensation of (See Tingling)

PRONATION: | **agg.** | **Upper** limbs: cinnb ptk1 petr ptk1
- ○ **Arms**; of: cupr k* plb k*

PULLING: bell k* calc-f sp1 cyt-l sp1
- ○ **Forearm** were pulled; as if hair of thuj
- **Legs** | **downward**: calc-f sp1
- **Shoulder** | **left**: luna kg1•
- **Upper** limbs: agar k* hura plb k* raph k*
  - **pregnancy** agg.; during: plb k*

PULSATION: aesc k2 ambr k2 ant-t ars bar-c bar-m k2 berb cact k2 calc-s k2 chinin-ar cystein-l rly4• cyt-l sp1 falco-pe nl2• *Ferr* ferr-i k2 glon k2 graph k2 *Ign* iod k2* *Kali-c* kali-p k2 kali-s fd4.de kali-sil k2 kreos k2 *Lach* nat-ar ol-an oxal-a rly4• *Rhus-t* sep sul-i k2 vanil fd5.de zinc
- **night**: *Ferr* sep
- **chill**; during: zinc
- **music** agg.: kreos k2
- **rest** agg.: *Ferr*
- **waking**; on: ferr-i k2
- **walking** slowly | **amel.**: ferr
- ○ **Ankles**: am-m h2 arg-met h1 bamb-a stb2.de• cench k2 dros k* kali-c k* ruta
  - **night**: dros k*
  - **lying** agg.: dros k*
- **Elbows**: agar crot-h bg2 grat k* hura indg k* kali-bi bg2 *Merc* b4a.de rhus-t k* *Still* k* ter k* thuj k*
  - **left**: gard-j vlr2• ignis-alc es2•
  - **evening**: still k*
  - **diarrhea** agg.; after: gard-j vlr2•
  - ○ **Olecranon**: agar
- **Feet**: am-m k* ang k* arg-met asaf bapt bg2 bell bg2 cact k2 cann-s carbn-s caust eup-per gels k* hydrog srj2• kali-i k* kali-s fd4.de lil-t k* mygal k* nat-m k* nux-m oxal-a rly4• plb k* plut-n srj7• ran-b b7.de* rhus-v k* vanil fd5.de
  - **right**: eup-per
  - **evening**: carbn-s
  - **dinner**; after: plb k*
  - **lying** agg.: gels k*
  - ○ **Back** of feet: cann-s k* rhus-t k*
  - **Heels**: ars-met *Nat-c* k* nat-s bg3* phos k* ran-b k*
    - **evening**: nat-c k*
    - **night**: phos k*
  - **Joints**: arg-met
  - **Outer** side of: sulph h2
  - **Soles**: arund k* cod bg1 kali-n k* kali-s fd4.de petr k* puls bg1 sacch-a fd2.de• sars k* sulph vanil fd5.de

Pulsation – Feet – Soles: ...
    - **evening**: kali-s fd4.de sulph h2
    - **rest** agg.: petr k*
    - **sitting** agg.: sars k*
    - **Hollow**: sacch-a fd2.de• sulph k* vanil fd5.de
- **Fingers**: *Am-m* k* anac bg2 anan k* apis bar-c k* borx k* carbn-o bg2 caust bg2 crot-h bg2 fago ferr-ma fl-ac k* glon hura ignis-alc es2• kali-bi kali-c k2 lith-c *M-aust* b7.de* mag-c bg2 plat positr nl2• sabad b7.de* sil bg2 *Sulph* k* teucr k* xan
  - **right** | **Second**: hydrog srj2•
  - **left**: xan c1
  - **evening**: fl-ac
  - ○ **First**: gymno hura mag-s sulph til
    - **Tips**: hura nat-m
      - **evening**: nat-m
  - **Fourth**: berb bg1 hura zinc h2
    - **Tip** of: nat-s sep
  - **Joints**: *Berb* bg2 bufo caust bg2 gels psa *Hep*
  - **Nail**:
    - **Around**: con
    - **Under**: am-m *Graph* sep sulph bg2
  - **Second**: bar-c h2 dios hura sabad
  - **Third**: crot-h sol-t-ae
  - **Tips**: aml-ns k* bell berb bg2* borx b4a.de* carb-v crot-h gels glon k* hura br1 iod k2* kreos bg2* nat-s bg1 phyt k* sep bg1 sil b4a.de stront-c b4a.de sulph b4a.de zinc b4a.de
    - **noon**: gels
- **Forearms**: bell bufo caust h2* hura hydrog srj2• kali-bi lyss olnd k* plat sabad k* stront-c bg2
  - ○ **Inner** side, near wrist: olnd
- **Hands**: am-m k* aur bg2 bry cact k2 carb-v cic coc-c dros bg2 fago fl-ac bg2 galla-q-r nl2• glon grat bg2 hydrog srj2• kali-n bg2 m-arct b7a.de mez bg2 phys plb plut-n srj7• rhus-t sabad b7.de* sumb thuj
  - **right**: hydrog srj2•
  - **left**: gels psa
  - **morning**: fago
    - **bed** agg.; in: thuj
  - **forenoon**: nicc
  - **burning**: phys k*
  - **dinner**; after: plb
  - **heat**, in: sumb
  - **motion** | **amel.**: am-m
  - **sticking**: thuj
  - **stool** agg.; straining at: cic
  - **touching** anything: glon
  - **writing** amel.: nicc
  - ○ **Back** of hands: dros nat-s
    - **motion** | **amel.**: nat-s
  - **Bones**: carb-v b4.de*
  - **Palms**: olib-sac wmh1
- **Hips**: am-c k* ars ars-h *Coloc* k* crot-h hep *Ign* mag-m k* merc rhod sil staph stront-c sk4• til k*
  - **morning**: ars-met
  - **evening**: am-c k*
- **Joints**: am-m arg-met brom led k* *Merc* k* mill rhod rhus-t *Ruta* sabad thuj
- **Knees**: *Acon* arg-met bamb-a stb2.de• brach k* brom k* calad k* *Kali-c* k* kali-n k* merc k* merc-i-f a1 olnd b7.de* spig b7.de* tarent k* thuj a1 vanil fd5.de verat-v k* zinc k*
  - **morning** | **waking**; on: verat-v k*
  - **evening**: calad k* kali-c k* merc-i-f a1
  - **night**: kali-n h2
  - **lying** agg.: calad k*
  - **motion** | **amel.**: kali-c k* vanil fd5.de
  - **painless**: merc k*
  - **sitting** agg.: bamb-a stb2.de• brom k* thuj a1 vanil fd5.de zinc k*

Extremities

- **Knees**: ...
  - **standing** agg.: arg-met
  - **walking** agg.; after: thuj a1 zinc
  - ○ **Hollow** of knees: coloc k* olnd k* vanil fd5.de
  - **Patella**: coloc k* spig k*
    - **evening**: coloc k*
- **Legs**: alum bg2 anac k* ang bg2 ant-t k* arg-met k* ars-h ars-met asaf b7.de* brom k* falco-pe nl2• kreos k* med merc-i-f nat-m bg2 nat-s k* ph-ac k* pic-ac k* plat k* rhus-t k* sil k* stann k* still k* stront-c k* vanil fd5.de [tax jsj7]
  - **evening**: still k*
  - **rest** agg.: arg-met ph-ac k*
  - **spots**, in: plat k*
  - **walking** agg.: nat-s k*
  - ○ **Calves**: allox tpw4 alum k* bov bg1 cench k2 falco-pe nl2• graph bg1 jatr-c mand rsj7• nat-m k* nux-m bg1 plat k* plb bg1 rhod bg1 vanil fd5.de
    - **morning**: alum k*
    - **evening**: mand rsj7•
    - **motion** agg.: mand rsj7•
    - **rest** | **amel.**: mand rsj7•
    - **sitting** agg.: nat-m h2 plat k*
    - **Outer** side of: graph h2
  - **Tendo** Achillis: prun k* zinc
- **Lower** limbs: alum b4.de* am-m b7.de* androc srj1• ant-t b7.de* arg-met b7a.de arn b7.de* ars-met asaf b7.de* bell b4.de* *Brom* b4a.de bry b7.de* cann-s b7.de* dig b4.de* dulc b4.de* falco-pe nl2• graph b4.de* hep b4a.de *Kali-c* k* kreos b7a.de m-aust b7.de mag-m b4.de* merc b4.de* mucs-nas rly4• mur-ac b4.de* nat-c b4.de* nat-m k* nit-ac b4.de* nux-m b7.de* nux-v k* olnd b7.de* ph-ac b4.de* phos b4.de* plat b4.de* plb b7.de* rhod b4.de* rhus-t b7.de* *Ruta* b7.de* *Sars* k* sep k* *Sulph* k* thuj b4.de* vanil fd5.de zinc b4.de*
  - **sitting**; after: sel k2
  - ○ **Joints**: arg-met b7.de* dros b7.de* ruta b7.de*
- **Nates**: cench k2 nept-m lsd2.fr phos prun ptel c1 rumx sol-t-ae zinc
  - **16** h: sol-t-ae
  - **sitting** agg.: nept-m lsd2.fr
- **Shoulders**: am-m k* arg-met bar-c k* bar-m berb brach cocc k* *Coloc* dig hura *Kali-c* k* *Led* k* m-ambo b7.de mag-m bg2 merc bg2 mez k* mur-ac k* ph-ac k* *Rhod* k* rhus-t k* *Sarr* br1 sol-t-ae stann k* sulph k* tab tarax k* thuj k*
  - **right**: am-m *Led* rhod b4a.de
  - **evening**: dig mez
  - **alternating** with tearing: bar-c
  - **cold** air | **amel.**: rhus-t
  - **motion**:
    - **agg.**: mez
    - **amel.**: am-m arg-met
  - **walking**:
    - **agg.**: dig
    - **amel.**: rhus-t
  - **warmth** agg.: rhus-t
  - ○ **Acromion**: merc
  - **Joints**: am-m b7.de *Merc* b4a.de mez b4.de ph-ac b4.de rhod b4.de thuj b4.de*
- **Thighs**: ang bg2 arg-met b7.de* ars k* asaf b7.de* berb k* bry cench k2 choc srj3• cocc b7.de* com dig h2 murx nit-ac k* plat k* ruta sec h *Sil* k* spong k* stann k* tarent k* vanil fd5.de verat-v ptk1
  - **night**: ars k*
  - ○ **Tendons** of: caust h2
- **Thumbs**: borx k* carb-v k* *Hep* hura mag-c bg2 nat-m sars staph bg2 stront-c k* zinc k*
  - **right**: hydrog srj2•
  - **night**: sars
  - **eating**; after: nat-m
  - **sitting** agg.: nat-m
  - ○ **Nails**; under: **Am-m**
  - **Tip** of: borx chinin-s ferr-ma mag-c zinc

Pulsation: ...

- **Toes**: am-m arge-pl rwt5• asaf cycl cystein-l rly4• gamb glon k2 iod k2* kali-bi kali-c k2 ph-ac plat prot jl2 zinc k*
  - ○ **Fifth**: agar plat h2
  - **First**: ars *Asaf* meph ph-ac plat rhus-t
    - **right**: hydrog srj2•
    - **Joint** of: chin-b kr1
    - **Tips**: asaf
  - **Fourth**: gamb mur-ac h2
  - **Second**: gamb mur-ac h2
  - **Third**: gamb mur-ac h2
- **Upper** arms: ars-h cocc bg2 dig k* *Kali-c* k* kali-n k* rhod k* sars k* squil sulph bg2 tarax k*
  - **left**: xan c1
  - **night**: kali-c
  - **intermittent**: kali-c h2 tarax k*
  - ○ **Deltoid**: allox tpw4 ignis-alc es2• nat-m
  - **Near** shoulder: sars
- **Upper** limbs: acon b7.de* alum anac h2 asc-t aster berb bufo bg2 carb-v k* caust k* cocc b7.de* coloc con dig k* dros b7.de* falco-pe nl2• hura ign b7.de* iod k* *Kali-c* lach k* lyss m-ambo b7.de m-arct b7.de m-aust b7.de mag-c k* mag-m k* manc merc-i-f merc-sul mur-ac k* nat-c k* nat-m nux-v olnd b7.de* petr ph-ac bg2 phys plat b4a.de sep k* sil k* squil b7.de* sulph k* tarax b7.de* teucr b7.de* thuj k* zinc k*
  - **right**: sil h2
  - **left**: nux-v xan
  - **burning**: phys
  - **eating**; after: sel k2 sil
  - **raising** arm agg.: sil h2
  - **synchronous** with pulse: graph h2
  - ○ **Bones**: sabad b7.de*
  - **Joints**: m-ambo b7.de *Merc* b4a.de
- **Wrists**: bov k* brach grat k* hura kali-bi bg2 *Lach* merc k* musca-d szs1 phos k* sal-fr sle1•
  - **evening**: bov
  - **motion** agg.: phos
  - ▽ **extending** to | **Elbow**: kali-n h2

PURRING: sep k*

- **sensation** of purring:
  - ○ **Heels**:
    - **extending** to:
      - **Toes** | **right**: oxyt bro1
- ○ **Lower** limbs: sep k*
- **Upper** limbs: sep k*

PUSHED forward in sleep; lower limbs: lyc h2

QUININE agg.; abuse of: | **Lower** limbs: puls b7a.de

QUIVERING (See Trembling)

RACHITIS (See Curving)

RAISED:

- ○ **Foot**:
  - **difficult** to raise: tab k* zinc k*
    - **forenoon**: mang k*
    - **breathing** deep agg.: carb-v h2
  - **impossible** to raise: ars k* nux-v k*
- **Leg** | **difficult** to raise: chel k* sulph k* *Vac* jl2
- **Shoulders**: (*↗Elevation - shoulders*) *Bell* b4a.de (non:ferr a1) hell bg2 mag-c bg2 merc b4.de* nat-m k* nit-ac bg2
  - **dyspnea**, with (See RESPIRATION - Difficult - accompanied - shoulders)
  - **impossible** to raise: nat-m h2*
- **Upper** arms: ferr k* nit-ac k* *Sang* k*
  - **impossible** to raise: ferr k* sang ptk1

- **Upper** limbs:
  - **difficult** to raise: alum k2 dig gran ix bnm8• mag-c phys
  - **impossible** to raise: alum cann-i ferr k* glon lyc mag-m merc nat-c k* nat-m nux-v plb sol-t-ae *Sulph*
  - **sleep** agg.; during: sep

RAISING:
- **affected** limb agg. (See Hang down - limbs - amel.)
- **lower** limbs:
  - **agg.**: bar-c b4.de* *Caust* b4a.de cocc b7.de* coff b7a.de colch b7.de* ferr b7.de* kali-bi bg2 nux-v b7a.de phos b4.de* puls b7.de* stann b4.de*
  - **amel.**: lyc b4a.de plb b7.de* ruta b7.de* stann b4.de*
- **upper** limbs:
  - **agg.**: *Acon* b7a.de ant-c b7a.de apis ptk1 arg-n ptk1 bar-c ptk1 berb ptk1 bry b7a.de* caps b7a.de chin b7a.de cocc ptk1 **Con** ptk1 dig ptk1 ferr b7a.de* graph ptk1 led b7a.de* mag-c ptk1 nit-ac ptk1 plb b7a.de ran-b b7a.de* rhus-t ptk1 *Sang* ptk1 sanic ptk1 *Spig* ptk1 sul-ac ptk1 *Sulph* ptk1 tell ptk1
    - ⁝ **Deltoid**: zinc ptk1
    - ⁝ **Shoulder**: led ptk1 phyt ptk1 rumx ptk1 sang ptk1 sanic ptk1
  - **amel.**: calc b4.de* ruta b7.de* thuj b4a.de
    - ⁝ **Shoulder**: ph-ac ptk1
  - **high** | **agg.**: alum b4a.de* ant-c b7.de* arg-met b7.de* *Bar-c* b4.de* bry b7.de* calc b4.de* caust bg2 chin b7.de* cic b7.de* *Cocc* b7.de* colch b7.de* coloc b4.de* dros b7.de* euph b4.de* *Ferr* b7.de* graph b4.de* hep b4a.de ign b7.de* kali-bi bg2 kali-c b4.de* kreos b7a.de led b7.de* *Lyc* b4.de* m-aust b7.de mag-c b4.de* mag-m b4.de* merc b4.de* mez b4.de* mur-ac bg2 nat-c b4.de* nat-m b4.de* nit-ac b4.de* nux-v b7.de* olnd b7.de* petr b4.de* phos b4.de* *Puls* b7.de* ran-b b7.de* rhus-t b7.de* sang bg2 sul-ac b4.de* sulph b4.de* teucr b7.de* verat b7.de*
  - **laterally** | **agg.**: syph ptk1

RAT running up; sensation of a: (*↗Mouse*)
- ○ - **Legs**: (*↗Alive - lower; Mouse - lower*) ail k* *Calc*
- **Upper** limbs: (*↗Alive - upper; Mouse - upper*) *Bell* ptk1 calc ptk1 sulph ptk1

RAYNAUD'S DISEASE: (*↗Coldness; Discoloration; Discoloration - fingers - white - coldness; Swelling*) ail ptk1 *Ars* ptk1* bac c2* brass-n-o srj5• cact ptk1* cortico stj* cupr stj*• ferr-p c2* germ-met srj5• hep stj* prot pte1* sec c2* sep stj* vanad dx* verat mrr1 [astra-e stj calc stj carb-v stj cyt-l stj foll stj halo stj hed stj kali-c stj kres stj lac-c stj nux-v stj perh stj sulfon stj thala stj thiop stj visc stj]
- ○ - **Fingers**: cupr sst3•
  - ○ **Second**: cupr sst3•
  - **Third**: cupr sst3•

READING agg.: | **Deltoid**: stann ptk1

REFLEXES: (*↗GENERALS - Reflexes*)
- **diminished** | **Plantar**: sulfon c1
- **increased**: thal-xyz srj8•
  - ○ **Knees** | **Patella**: anh c1* ben-d pfa2 benzol br1 cann-i bro1 cocain hs1 lath c1* mang-act bro1 zinc hs1
  - **Legs** | **Tendo** Achillis: zinc hs1
- **lost**:
  - ○ **Knees** | **Patella**: alum k4 ars a2 carbn-s hs1 cur bro1* oxyt ah1* phos vk6 plb br1* sec hs1* sulfon bro1*
  - **Legs** | **Tendo** Achillis: [arg-met stj1]
  - **Plantar**: carbn-s hs1
    - ⁝ **right**: colch br1

RELAXATION: arn ars asaf atra-r skp7• bar-c *Carb-v* *Carbn-h* *Carbn-o* *Chin* cic clem con ferr grat hell lyc nit-ac nux-m nux-v **Op** sep tab vip
- **morning**:
  - **air**; from open: *Nux-v* sep
  - **dinner**; after: nit-ac
  - **rising**; after | **amel.**: lyc
  - **waking**; on: lyc
- **sensation** of | **Deltoid**: merc-c ptk1
- ○ - **Feet**: ars *Gels* nat-c
  - **lying** agg.: ars

Relaxation: ...
- **Hands**: gels nat-c
- **Hips**:
  - ○ **Joints**: apis *Calc* *Thuj*
    - ⁝ **standing** agg.: thuj h1
- **Joints**: aids nl2• bar-c laur [calc-f stj1 mag-f stj1]
- **Knees**: lith-c phos plb sulph
  - **walking** | **amel.**: phos
- **Legs**: carb-v kali-c
- **Lower** limbs: am-m ambr k* ang camph canth cic ferr b7.de* guaj hell lach lyc nat-c nit-ac nux-m op phos plb puls stram verat
- **Upper** limbs: carb-v b4a.de colch c1* guaj hell nux-m plat k*
  - **laughing** agg.: carb-v

REST:
- **agg.**:
  - ○ **Lower** limbs: agar b4a.de am-c b4a.de ang b7.de* *Arg-met* b7.de* arn b7.de* aur b4.de* bell b4.de* bry b7.de* calc b4.de* caps b7.de* caust b4.de* cham b7.de* chin b7.de* cina b7.de* *Cocc* b7.de* coloc b4.de* con b4.de* cupr b7.de* cycl b7.de* *Dros* b7.de* *Dulc* b4a.de euphr b7a.de *Ferr* b7.de* *Graph* b4a.de hep b4a.de hyos b7.de* ign b7.de* *Kali-c* b4a.de kali-n b4.de* kreos b7a.de **Lyc** b4a.de m-ambo b7.de mag-c b4a.de *Meny* b7.de* merc b4.de* merc-c b4a.de mez b4.de* mosch b7.de* mur-ac b4.de* nat-c b4.de* nit-ac b4.de* olnd b7.de* ph-ac b4.de* phos b4.de* *Plat* b4a.de psor bg2 *Puls* b7.de* rhod b4.de* rhus-t b7.de* *Ruta* b7.de* sabin b7.de* samb b7.de* sep b4.de* sil b4a.de *Spig* b7.de* staph b7.de* stront-c b4.de* sulph b4.de* *Tarax* b7.de* *Valer* b7.de* verb b7.de* viol-t b7.de* zinc b4.de*
  - **Upper** limbs: acon b7.de* am-c b4.de* *Am-m* b7.de* ambr b7.de* anac b4.de* ang b7.de* arg-met b7.de arn b7.de* asaf b7.de* aur b4.de* bell b4.de* bism b7.de* bry b7.de* calc b4.de* carb-v b4.de* cham b7.de* chel b7.de* chin b7.de* cina b7.de* *Cocc* b7.de* coloc b4.de* con b4.de* cupr b7.de* cycl b7.de* dros b7.de* dulc b4.de* euph b4.de* *Ferr* b7.de* graph b4.de* ign b7.de* kali-n b4.de* *Lyc* b4.de* m-ambo b7.de m-arct b7.de mag-c b4.de* mang b4.de* meny b7.de* merc b4.de* mur-ac b4.de* ph-ac b4.de* phos b4.de* plat b4.de* *Puls* b7.de* ran-b b7.de* *Rhod* b4.de* **Rhus-t** b7.de* ruta b7.de* *Sabad* b7.de* sabin b7.de* samb b7.de* sars b4.de* sep b4.de* **Spig** b7.de* spong b7.de* stann b4.de* *Tarax* b7.de* *Valer* b7.de* viol-o b7.de* viol-t b7.de*
- **amel.**:
  - ○ **Lower** limbs: agn b7.de* am-m b7.de* arn b7.de* bar-c b4.de* *Bry* b7.de* chel b7.de* coloc bg2 croc b7.de* dios bg2 fl-ac bg2 *Gnaph* bg2 hep bg2 ign b7.de* kali-c b4.de* kali-n b4.de* m-aust b7.de *Merc* b4.de* mez b4.de* *Nux-v* b7.de* phos b4.de* staph b7.de* stront-c b4.de* visc bg2
  - **Upper** limbs: arn b7.de* bell b4a.de *Bry* b7.de* *Calc* b4a.de chel b7.de* cic b7.de* *Hep* b4a.de *Kali-c* b4a.de m-aust b7.de *Mag-m* b4a.de meny b7.de* nat-m b4.de* *Nux-v* b7.de* phos b4.de* sars b4.de* sep b4.de* sil b4.de* staph b7.de* sulph b4.de* verb b7.de*

RESTING the limbs (= supporting the limbs):
- **agg.**:
  - ○ **Lower** limbs: *Arn* b7a.de *Kali-c* b4.de*
  - **Upper** limbs: alum bg2 am-m b7.de* ang b7.de* asar b7.de* camph b7.de* caust b4.de* cina b7.de* con b4.de* croc b7.de* graph b4.de* *Kali-c* b4a.de mag-m b4.de* merc-c b4a.de nat-m bg2 phos b4.de* plat b4.de* rhus-t b7.de* ruta b7.de* sabin b7.de* samb b7.de* *Sil* b4.de* spong b7.de* squil b7.de* stann b4.de* sulph b4.de* thuj b4a.de valer b7.de*
- **table**; on:
  - **agg.** | **Upper** limbs: asar b7.de* nux-m b7.de*

RESTLESSNESS: (*↗MIND - Restlessness*) acon ail all-c *Alum* aml-ns **Ars** ars-s-f k2 aster aur-ar k2 bamb-a stb2.de• bell k* bit-ar wht1• bros-gau mrc1 cadm-s c1 canth carb-v *Carl* cartl-s rly4• *Caust* chel **Chin** *Chinin-ar* cic *Cimic* *Cimx* coff bro1 colch coloc cortiso sp1 *Cupr* cur bg2 *Dulc* eupi fago **Ferr** *Ferr-ar* *Glon* graph hippoc-k szs2 hyos *Iod* jal **Kali-br** k* *Kali-c* *Kali-p* k* lac-e hrn2• lac-loxod-a hrn2• limen-b-c hrn2* **Lyc** mag-c med merc merc-i-r nat-ar nat-c *Nat-m* *Nit-ac* **Nux-v** op ox-ac petr phys *Phyt* k* *Plat* **Puls** pyrog tl1 **Rhus-t** k* *Ruta* sanic sep k* **Sil** squil *Stann* stict bg2 **Stram** k* stroph-s sp1 stry suis-pan rly4• sumb tarax bg2* **Tarent** k* tub k2 vanil fd5.de **Zinc** k* zinc-p k2
- **afternoon**: ix bnm8•
- **evening**: calc **Caust** *Kali-c* mag-c meph a1 merc-i-r nat-c *Nit-ac* tarent k2

• **bed** agg.; in: **Ars** carb-v con **Kali-c** *Lyc* tarent k2
• **sitting**; after: *Mag-c*
- **night**: *Alum* bell bufo **Caust** *Colch* hep ix bnm8• *Lyc* nat-s k2 *Nit-ac* phyt **Rhus-t** *Sep* spig tung-met bdx1• **Zinc**
• **midnight** | **before**: nux-v
• **bed**; before going to: **Ars** **Kali-c** *Lyc*
- **accompanied** by | **Abdomen**; complaints of (See ABDOMEN - Complaints - accompanied - tossing)
- **convulsions**; before: bufo
- **covering** agg.: aster k*
- **lying** agg.: ars merc
- **mental** exertion | **amel.**: *Nat-c*
- **motion** | **amel.**: fago vanil fd5.de
- **music** | **amel.**: **Tarent** k1
- **sitting** agg.: merc k*
- **sleep** agg.; during: bros-gau mrc1 **Caust** coloc h2
- **tossing** from side to side: cina ptk1
- **walking** in open air | **amel.**: sumb
- **warm** bed agg.: aster k* *Lach*
○ - **Elbow**; bend of | **covered**; when: aster
- **Feet**: *(↗Motion - feet - constant)* agar k* *Alum* am k* *Ars* k* ars-s-f k2 bar-c k* calc h2 carb-v k* carbn-s caust k* *Cham* chin chinin-ar choc srj3• cimic *Cina* bro1 croc dulc fd4.de ferr-i fl-ac k* gaert pte1*• glon ign b7.de* ip k2 kali-br mrr1 kali-p k* lac-e hm2• lac-loxod-a hm2• lach bg2 lil-t mag-m k* **Med** k* *Meph* morg-p pte1*• mygal bg2 nat-c k* *Nat-m* k* nat-s ox-ac phyt bg1 plat k* plb bg2 prun *Puls* k* puls-n c2 **Rhus-t** k* sal-fr sle1• sil k* still *Stram* k* stroph-s sp1 suis-pan rly4• *Sulph* k* syc pte1*• symph fd3.de* *Tarent* k* tarent-c br1 thuj k* tub gk vanil fd5.de **Zinc** k* zinc-p k2 *Zinc-val* bro1 [helia stj7]
• **afternoon**: lac-h htj1•
• **evening**: arn mag-m nat-m
⁝ **bed** agg.; in: sulph **Zinc**
⁝ **beer**; after: nat-m
• **night**: *Cham* lyc h2 med mrr1 nat-c puls sulph h2 syc fmm1• thuj urol-h rwt• vanil fd5.de *Zinc*
⁝ **bed** agg.; in: syc bka1*•
• **beer**; after: nat-m **Sulph**
• **heat**; after: **Sulph**
• **lying** agg.: alum **Sulph**
• **menses**; during: thuj *Zinc*
• **sitting** agg.: alum bar-c chlam-tr bcx2• hydrog srj2• *Puls* sal-fr sle1• **Zinc**
• **spasmodic**: cina
• **trembling**: plat h2
• **waking**; on: ferr-i
• **walking** | **amel.**: *Nat-m*
○ • **Soles**: croc
- **Fingers**: *(↗Motion - fingers - constant)* *Agar* bg2 **Asar** vh1* camph bg2 caust mrr1 cupr bg2 hyos bg2* kali-br bg2* kali-c bg2 med mrr1 *Mosch* bg2 nat-m sne rheum bg2 rhus-t mrr1 sec bg2 spig bg2 sulph mrr1 tarent mrr1* zinc mrr1
- **Hands**: *(↗MIND - Gestures - fingers)* acet-ac *Alum* arg-n *Ars* *Asar* mrr1 aur-m-n wbt2• bell k* calc calc-ar calc-s camph cimic sne fago fl-ac gaert pte1*• glon *Hyos* k* ip k2 **Kali-br** k* kali-c kali-p fd1.de• lac-c lac-e hm2• lac-loxod-a hm2• medul-os-si rly4• mygal bg1* nat-m phos plb positr nl2• psor jl2 rhus-t sacch sst1• stram k* sulph bg2* symph fd3.de• **Tarent** k* ther ptk1 thyr ptk1* valer bg2 vanil fd5.de verat-v ptk1 zinc bro1
• **right**: lac-e hm2•
• **daytime**: rhus-t
• **night**: arg-n kali-c h2
⁝ **bed** agg.; in: lac-c
⁝ **sleep** agg.; during: rhus-t
• **delirium**; during: stram sulph sf1.de verat-v ptk1
• **sleep** agg.; during: acet-ac ars calc rhus-t
- **Hip** | **night** | **lying** agg.: bamb-a stb2.de•
• **sitting** agg.: form
- **Joints**: sil h2 sulph
- **Knees**: alumn k* *Anac* k* arg-n bg2 asar k* cartl-s rly4• ferr b7.de* lach k* *Lyc* k* mang bg2 nat-m bg2 plat bg2 puls bg2 *Rhus-t* k* spig k* staph k* tarax bg2 thuj k* zinc bg2
• **night** | **bed** agg.; in: lyc k*
- **Legs**: acon k* agar alum k* **Am-c** k* ambr gsy1 *Anac* k* *Arg-n* **Ars** k* ars-s-f k2 asaf bg2 aster *Bell* cact *Calc* k* *Calc-p* k* *Camph* *Carb-v* k* carbn-s *Caust* k* chel k* *Chin* k* *Chinin-ar* cimic k* *Cimx* colch tl1 con k* cortiso tpw7 crot-h bro1 eupi k* **Ferr** ferr-ar ferr-p *Glon* *Graph* k* hep k* hippoc-k szs2 hydrog srj2• hyos k* ind vml3• kali-br bro1 *Kali-c* k* kali-n h2 kali-s lac-c *Lach* lil-t br1* limen-b-c hm2* *Lyc* k* *Mag-c* k* **Med** k* *Meny* bro1 *Meph* k* merc k* merc-c bro1 *Mez* *Mosch* k* mygal bro1 naja nat-ar nat-c k* *Nat-m* k* nat-p *Nit-ac* k* *Nux-m* k* osm k* ox-ac *Phos* k* *Plat* k* pneu jl2 prun *Psor* rhod bg2 **Rhus-t** k* *Ruta* k* sacch sst1• scut bro1 *Sep* k* spong k* squil k* stann k* suis-pan rly4• sulfon bro1 *Sulph* k* *Tarax* k* **Tarent** k* **Tub** ust vanil fd5.de **Zinc** k* zinc-p k2 zinc-val bro1 ziz bro1 [spect dfg1 tax jsj7]
• **daytime** | **rest** agg.: hep k*
• **morning** | **bed** agg.; in: **Caust** hep k* *Psor* k*
• **evening**: alum ange-s oss1• carb-v k* *Caust* k* kali-c lyc k* *Merc* k* nat-c k* *Plat* *Sep* k* stann k* **Tarent** vanil fd5.de **Zinc**
⁝ **sleep**:
: **going** to; before: *Ars Lyc Nat-m Tarent*
: **preventing** sleep: stann h2
• **night**: *Ars* **Caust** k* *Cham* con k* eupi k* hydrog srj2• *Kola* stb3• mag-c phos *Zinc* k*
⁝ **bed**:
: **driving** out of bed: hydrog srj2•
: **in** bed | **agg.**: *Bell Carb-v Caust* k* hydrog srj2• *Lyc* med hr1 *Puls-n* **Rhus-t** k* *Ruta* **Tarent** k* zinc mrr1
: **motion** | **not** amel.: cortiso sp1
⁝ **cycling** legs vigorously in the air amel.: hydrog srj2•
⁝ **lying** agg.: ruta
⁝ **pain**; from: ph-ac h2
⁝ **put** it out of bed to cool it; must: mag-c *Sulph*
• **exertion** agg.; after: bry sys
• **heat**; during: bell borx **Calc** *Nux-v* **Rhus-t** **Sabad** sep sulph
• **insanity**, in: **Tarent** k1
• **menses**; before: pneu jl2
• **rising** agg.; after: *Psor* k*
• **sitting** agg.: alum anac *Plat* k* [tax jsj7]
• **sleep**:
⁝ **before**: **Ars** *Lyc* *Nat-m*
⁝ **during** | **agg.**: **Caust** *Nat-m*
⁝ **preventing** sleep: zinc mrr1
• **sleeplessness**; with: agar bg graph bg rhus-t a1 stann bg
• **stretching** legs | **desire**: coca-c sk4•
• **walking** agg.: anac k*
- **Lower** limbs: *(↗MIND - Insanity - restlessness - lower)* acon bg2 agar ptk1 ail alum b4.de* am-c b4.de* ambr c1 *Anac* k* ant-t bg1 aq-mar rbp6 **Ars** k* asaf b7.de* aster aur-ar k2 aur-m-n wbt2• bar-c b4.de* *Bell* k* bry b7.de* bufo bg2 calc b4.de* *Calc-p* *Cann-s* b7.de* **Carb-v** b4.de* *Caust* k* cham b7.de* chin k* *Chinin-ar* cimic bg2 con b4a.de* cop croc b7a.de dream-p sdj1• dulc fd4.de ferr b7a.de graph k* hep k* hippoc-k szs2 iod h kali-ar kali-br bg2 **Kali-c** k* kali-i bg2 kali-p k2 kreos b7a.de lap-la rsp1 lil-t bg2 *Lyc* k* mag-c b4a.de* mag-m b4a.de* marb-w es1• med k* meph bg2 *Merc* b4.de* *Mez* k* mosch k* mur-ac h2 nat-ar nat-c k* *Nat-m* k* nit-ac b4a.de* nux-m b7.de* *Nux-v* b7.de* *Olnd* b7a.de ozone sde2• petr b4.de* *Phos* k* phys bg1 *Phyt Plat* k* prun psor bg2 puls bg2 rat bg1 rhod b4a.de **Rhus-t** k* ruta b7.de* sabin b7.de* *Sep* k* sil b4a.de squil b7.de* stann k* staph b7.de* stram bg2 suis-pan rly4• sul-ac b4a.de *Sulph* k* tab **Tarent** k* *Thuj* b4a.de tub ptk1* *Valer* bg2 vanad dx vanil fd5.de **Zinc** k* *Zinc-val* bg2
• **left**:
⁝ **night**: nat-c h2
: **uncovers**: mag-c h2
• **morning** | **bed** agg.; in: **Caust**
• **evening**: alum h2 caust h2 dulc fd4.de graph kali-c lyc h2* mag-c h2 *Nit-ac* ozone sde2• phos h2 sec *Sep* stann *Sulph* tab **Tarent** tax-br oss1• vanil fd5.de

- **evening**: ...
  - ⁝ **bed** agg.; in: calc$_{h2}$ carb-v$_{h2}$ **Caust** dulc$_{fd4.de}$ hep *Lyc* mez *Nat-m* **Tarent**
  - ⁝ **pain**; from | **Calves**; in: staph$_{h1}$
- **night**: **Ars**$_{k*}$ **Caust**$_{k*}$ graph$_{h2}$ hep *Lyc* med$_{ptk1}$ nat-c nat-m ozone$_{sde2•}$ *Phyt* rhod **Tarent**$_{k*}$ zinc$_{k*}$
  - ⁝ **midnight** | **before**: nux-v$_{h1}$
  - ⁝ **bed** agg.; in: **Caust Rhus-t Tarent**
- **fever**; during: nit-ac$_{bg2}$ phos$_{bg2}$ **Rhus-t**$_{b7a.de*}$ sep$_{bg2}$ squil$_{bg2}$
- **lying**:
  - ⁝ **agg.**: alum fago hep lyc ruta$_{c1}$ sulfonam$_{ks2}$ zinc$_{bg1}$
  - ⁝ **amel.**: ars$_{h2}$
- **menses**; during: dream-p$_{sdj1•}$ lac-c$_{k*}$
- **motion** | **amel.**: ars$_{tl1}$ dulc$_{fd4.de}$ **Rhus-t Tarent**
- **pain**; from:
  - ⁝ **Calves**; in: staph$_{h1}$
  - ⁝ **Lower** limbs; in: thal$_{dx}$
- **perspiration**; during: alum$_{bg2}$ am-c$_{bg2}$ *Arn*$_{bg2}$ **Ars**$_{bg2}$ *Bell*$_{bg2}$ bov$_{bg2}$ *Bry*$_{bg2}$ **Calc**$_{bg2}$ carb-v$_{bg2}$ caust$_{bg2}$ ip$_{bg2}$ **Lyc**$_{bg2}$ *Merc*$_{bg2}$ mosch$_{bg2}$ *Nit-ac*$_{bg2}$ *Ph-ac*$_{bg2}$ *Phos*$_{bg2}$ **Rhus-t**$_{bg2}$ ruta$_{bg2}$ **Sep**$_{bg2}$ sil$_{bg2}$ squil$_{bg2}$ **Sulph**$_{bg2}$ thuj$_{bg2}$
- **room**, close: aster
- **sitting** agg.: alum anac caust$_{h2}$ dulc$_{fd4.de}$ *Lyc* mosch nat-m plat$_{k*}$ **Rhus-t**
- **sleep**:
  - ⁝ **during** | **agg.**: *Caust*$_{mtf33}$ coloc$_{h2}$ ign$_{b7.de}$ podo$_{fd3.de•}$
  - ⁝ **going** to; before: **Ars Kali-c** *Lyc Nat-m*
  - ⁝ **preventing** sleep: nux-v$_{h1}$ zinc$_{mrr1}$
- **standing** agg.: anac plat symph$_{fd3.de•}$
- **warm** bed agg.: aster **Lach** mez
- O **Joints**: staph$_{b7.de*}$

- **Shoulders**: asc-t$_{ptk1}$
- **Thighs**: *Anac*$_{k*}$ arist-m$_{a1}$ ars$_{bro1}$ *Camph* carb-v$_{k*}$ caust$_{k*}$ chin$_{bro1}$ cimic$_{bro1}$ con$_{bro1}$ crot-h$_{bro1}$ form$_{k*}$ graph$_{bro1}$ kali-br$_{bro1}$ kali-c$_{k*}$ lil-t$_{bro1}$ *Lyc*$_{bg2*}$ *Mag-m*$_{k*}$ *Med*$_{bro1}$ *Meny*$_{bro1}$ merc-c$_{bro1}$ mygal$_{bro1}$ nit-ac$_{bro1}$ ph-ac$_{k*}$ *Phos*$_{bro1}$ *Plat*$_{k*}$ puls *Rhus-t*$_{bro1}$ ruta$_{bro1}$ scut$_{bro1}$ *Sep*$_{bro1}$ squil$_{k*}$ sulfon$_{bro1}$ *Tarax*$_{bro1}$ tarent$_{bro1}$ *Zinc*$_{bro1}$ zinc-val$_{bro1}$ ziz$_{bro1}$
  - **evening** | **bed** agg.; in: mez$_{h2}$
  - **sitting** agg.: anac$_{k*}$ form$_{k*}$ ph-ac$_{k*}$ plat$_{k*}$
  - **tremulous**: plat$_{k*}$
- **Upper** arms: agar
- **Upper** limbs: acon$_{k*}$ agar$_{k*}$ ant-t$_{bg1*}$ ars$_{k*}$ aster atro bell$_{bg2}$ brom$_{k*}$ bry$_{b7.de*}$ bufo cadm-met$_{tpw6}$ calc$_{b4.de*}$ canth cartl-s$_{rly4•}$ **Caust**$_{k*}$ cham$_{k*}$ cimic$_{bg2}$ cina coloc cur$_{bg2}$ dig dirc ferr$_{k*}$ *Glon*$_{k*}$ hyos$_{bg2}$ kali-bi$_{bg2}$ *Kali-br*$_{bg2*}$ kali-c$_{bg2}$ lac-ac lac-c lyc m-ambo$_{b7.de}$ m-arct$_{b7.de}$ *Meph*$_{k*}$ merc$_{k*}$ *Mur-ac*$_{k*}$ naja$_{k*}$ nat-ar nat-c$_{k*}$ nit-ac$_{bg2}$ nux-v$_{k*}$ op phos$_{k*}$ phys$_{k*}$ psor rhus-t$_{bg2}$ rumx *Samb*$_{bg2*}$ sep$_{k*}$ sil$_{k*}$ squil$_{b7.de*}$ stict$_{bg2}$ stram$_{k*}$ *Tarent*$_{k*}$ verat-v$_{bg2}$ zinc$_{k*}$
  - **right**: merc$_{h1*}$ sil$_{h2}$
  - **left**: meph$_{a1}$
  - **morning**: alum glon
    - ⁝ **waking**; on: nit-ac$_{h2}$
  - **forenoon**: cham
    - ⁝ **air**; in open | **amel.**: cham
    - ⁝ **motion** | **amel.**: cham
  - **evening**: mur-ac nux-v
  - **night**: caust kali-bi merc nux-v$_{h1}$
    - ⁝ **sleep** agg.; during: abrot **Caust**$_{k*}$ merc
  - **tossing** from side to side | **children**; in: cina$_{mtf33}$
  - O **Joints**: calc$_{h2}$ cartl-s$_{rly4•}$
- **Wrists**: calc

RHAGADES (See Cracked)

RHEUMATIC ARTHRITIS (See Pain - joints - rheumatic)

RHEUMATIC COMPLAINTS (See Pain - rheumatic)

RIDING in a carriage: | **after**:

- **agg.** | **Lower** limbs: nat-m$_{b4.de*}$ thuj$_{b4a.de}$
- **while** | **agg.** | **Lower** limbs: valer$_{b7.de*}$
- **amel.** | **Lower** limbs: nit-ac$_{b4a.de}$

RIDING on horseback:

- **agg.** | **Lower** limbs: mag-m$_{b4.de*}$ spig$_{b7.de*}$ *Sul-ac*$_{b4a.de}$

RIGIDITY (See Stiffness)

RISING:

- **bed**; from:
  - **after**:
    - ⁝ **agg.**:
      - **Lower** limbs: *Am-m*$_{b7.de*}$ asaf$_{bg2}$ bar-c$_{b4.de*}$ caps$_{b7.de*}$ *Graph*$_{b4.de*}$ kali-c$_{b4.de*}$ kali-n$_{b4.de*}$ m-ambo$_{b7.de}$ mag-m$_{b4.de*}$ nux-m$_{b7.de}$ nux-v$_{b7.de*}$ *Olnd*$_{b7.de*}$ par$_{b7.de*}$ phos$_{b4.de*}$ plat$_{b4.de*}$ plb$_{b7.de*}$ *Rhus-t*$_{b7.de*}$ spig$_{b7.de*}$ squil$_{b7.de*}$ staph$_{b7.de*}$ thuj$_{b4.de*}$ valer$_{b7.de*}$ verat$_{b7.de*}$
      - **Upper** limbs: *Am-m*$_{b7.de*}$ cina$_{b7.de*}$ dulc$_{b4.de*}$ euph$_{b4.de*}$ kreos$_{bg2}$ mez$_{b4.de*}$ nux-m$_{b7.de*}$ nux-v$_{b7.de*}$ *Olnd*$_{b7.de*}$ puls$_{b7.de*}$ *Rhus-t*$_{b7.de*}$ *Staph*$_{b7.de*}$
    - ⁝ **amel.**:
      - **Lower** limbs: ambr$_{b7.de*}$ bry$_{b7.de*}$ caust$_{b4.de*}$ dros$_{b7.de*}$ ferr$_{b7.de*}$ ign$_{b7.de*}$ m-ambo$_{b7.de}$ m-aust$_{b7.de}$ *Nux-v*$_{b7.de*}$ plb$_{b7.de*}$ puls$_{b7.de*}$ ran-b$_{b7.de*}$ *Rhod*$_{b4a.de}$ rhus-t$_{b7.de*}$ sabad$_{b7.de*}$ sep$_{b4.de*}$ sulph$_{b4.de*}$
      - **Upper** limbs: kali-c$_{b4.de*}$ nux-v$_{b7.de*}$ puls$_{b7.de*}$ ran-b$_{b7.de*}$ sep$_{b4.de*}$
  - **agg.** | **Lower** limbs: am-m$_{b7.de*}$ ant-t$_{b7.de*}$ *Bell*$_{b4a.de}$ caps$_{b7.de*}$ carb-an$_{b4.de*}$ *Carb-v*$_{b4.de*}$ caust$_{b4.de*}$ con$_{b4.de*}$ ferr$_{b7.de*}$ ign$_{b7.de*}$ kali-n$_{bg2}$ lyc$_{b4.de*}$ *Nux-v*$_{b7.de*}$ petr$_{b4.de*}$ phos$_{b4.de*}$ puls$_{b7.de*}$ *Rhod*$_{b4a.de}$ rhus-t$_{b7.de*}$ sabin$_{b7.de*}$ sil$_{b4.de*}$ *Staph*$_{b7.de*}$ verat$_{b7.de*}$
  - **amel.**: carb-an$_{b4.de*}$ chin$_{b7.de*}$ led$_{b7.de*}$ sep$_{b4.de*}$ verat$_{b7.de*}$
    - ⁝ **Lower** limbs: chin$_{b7.de*}$ dulc$_{b4.de*}$ kali-n$_{b4.de*}$ led$_{b7.de*}$
- **sitting**; after rising from:
  - **agg.**:
    - ⁝ **Legs** | **Calves**: anac$_{ptk1}$
    - ⁝ **Lower** limbs: alum$_{b4.de*}$ anac$_{b4a.de}$ ang$_{b7.de*}$ arn$_{b7.de*}$ aur$_{b4a.de}$ bell$_{b4a.de}$ bov$_{b4.de*}$ bry$_{b7.de*}$ carb-v$_{b4.de*}$ caust$_{bg2}$ cham$_{b7.de*}$ *Chin*$_{b7.de*}$ cic$_{b7.de*}$ cocc$_{b7.de*}$ croc$_{b7.de*}$ dros$_{b7.de*}$ euph$_{b4.de*}$ ferr$_{b7.de*}$ graph$_{b4a.de}$ kali-bi$_{bg2}$ kali-c$_{b4.de*}$ lach$_{bg2}$ laur$_{b7.de*}$ led$_{b7.de*}$ lyc$_{b4.de*}$ m-ambo$_{b7.de}$ m-arct$_{b7.de}$ m-aust$_{b7.de}$ mang$_{b4.de*}$ mur-ac$_{b4.de*}$ nat-c$_{b4.de*}$ nat-m$_{b4.de*}$ *Nit-ac*$_{b4.de*}$ *Nux-v*$_{b7.de*}$ *Olnd*$_{b7.de*}$ ph-ac$_{b4.de*}$ *Puls*$_{b7.de*}$ ran-b$_{b7.de*}$ *Rhod*$_{b4a.de}$ **Rhus-t**$_{b7.de*}$ *Ruta*$_{b7.de*}$ sep$_{b4.de*}$ sil$_{b4.de*}$ spig$_{b7.de*}$ staph$_{b7.de*}$ *Sulph*$_{b4.de*}$ thuj$_{b4.de*}$ verat$_{b7.de*}$
    - ⁝ **Upper** limbs: carb-v$_{b4.de*}$
  - **amel.** | **Lower** limbs: am-m$_{b7.de*}$ aur$_{b4.de*}$ bar-c$_{b4.de*}$ caust$_{b4.de*}$ chin$_{b7.de*}$ cycl$_{b7.de*}$ kali-c$_{b4.de*}$ mag-c$_{b4.de*}$ mang$_{b4.de*}$ phos$_{b4.de*}$ rhus-t$_{b7.de*}$ spong$_{b7.de*}$ valer$_{b7.de*}$
- **stooping**; rising from:
  - **amel.**:
    - ⁝ **Lower** limbs: *Cham*$_{b7a.de}$
    - ⁝ **Upper** limbs: *Cham*$_{b7a.de}$ olnd$_{b7.de*}$ puls$_{b7.de*}$

ROLLING; sensation of:

- O **Arm**, down the: rhus-t$_{k*}$
- **Fingers**: ph-ac$_{h2}$
- **Forearms**: ph-ac$_{h2}$
- **Hand**, in: op ph-ac$_{h2}$

ROOM; in a:

- **agg.** | **Lower** limbs: alum$_{b4.de*}$ bry$_{b7.de*}$ *Croc*$_{b7.de*}$ laur$_{b7.de*}$ lyc$_{b4a.de}$ mag-c$_{b4.de*}$ meny$_{b7.de*}$ nux-v$_{b7.de*}$ *Puls*$_{b7.de*}$ ran-b$_{b7.de*}$ sulph$_{b4.de*}$ verat$_{b7.de*}$

- **amel.**:
○ • **Lower** limbs: *Bry* b7.de* cham b7.de* chel b7.de* coff b7.de* ign b7.de* laur b7.de* *Nux-v* b7.de*
• **Upper** limbs: bry b7.de* cham b7.de* nux-m b7.de* nux-v b7.de* stann b4.de*
- **entering**; when:
• **agg.** | **Lower** limbs: ran-b b7.de* verb b7.de*

ROPE around; tying (See Bandaging)

ROUGHNESS: fic-m gya1
○ - **Elbows**: til ban1•
- **Fingers**: laur bg2 par ptk1 **Petr** bg2 ph-ac psor tl1 zinc
○ • **Nails** (See Nails - roughness - fingernails)
• **Tips**: ham fd3.de• **Petr**
- **Forearms**: rhus-t k* *Sep* b4a.de sulph b4a.de
• **evening**: peti k*
- **Hands**: (↗*Chapped)* allox tpw4 alum k* bar-c k* cench k2 cortiso tpw7 dulc fd4.de *Graph* k* ham fd3.de• **Hep** k* ina-i mlk9.de kali-c k* laur k* med nat-c k* nat-m bg2 nat-sil fd3.de• nit-ac k* *Petr* k* ph-ac k* phos k* psor k2* *Rhus-t* k* rhus-v sabad k* *Sabin* b7a.de sul-ac k* *Sulph* k* *Zinc* k*
• **evening**: sulph k*
• **dead** skin: mez
• **spots**: zinc
• **weather**, cold: dulc fd4.de *Zinc*
○ • **Back** of hands: cortiso tpw7* *Nat-c*
• **Palms**: dulc fd4.de tab k*
- **Knees**: til ban1•
- **Legs**: *Sep* b4a.de sulph b4a.de
▽ • **extending** to | **Tibia**; over: alum k2
- **Upper** limbs: *Calc* b4a.de crot-h k* hep b4a.de kali-c b4a.de *Nit-ac* b4a.de ph-ac b4a.de
- **Wrists**: (non:rhus-t slp) rhus-v a1*

RUBBING:
- **agg.**:
○ • **Lower** limbs: arn b7.de* caust b4.de* coff b7.de* mur-ac b4.de* spig b7.de*
• **Upper** limbs: alum bg2 am-m b7.de* nat-c b4.de* spig b7.de*
- **amel.**:
○ • **Feet** | **Soles**: chel ptk1
• **Lower** limbs: alum bg2 am-c b4.de* am-m b7.de* anac b4.de* ang b7.de* ant-c b7.de* *Canth* b7.de* carb-an b4.de* chin b7.de* hep b4.de* kali-c b4.de* laur b7.de* nat-c b4.de* nicc bg2 ph-ac b4.de* phos b4.de* plb b7.de* stann b4.de* staph b7.de* sul-ac b4.de* sulph b4.de*
• **Upper** limbs: alum b4.de* am-m b7.de* ang b7.de* ant-c b7.de* canth b7.de* chel b7.de* chin b7.de* kali-n b4.de* laur b7.de* nit-ac b4.de* olnd b7.de* phos b4.de* plb b7.de* staph b7.de* tarax b7.de* zinc b4.de*
- **cloths** agg.; of | **Lower** limbs: *Chin* bg2

RUNAROUND (See Felon - nail - runaround)

RUNNING: | **agg.** | **Lower** limbs: arg-met b7.de* kali-c b4.de* led b7a.de sep b4.de* staph b7.de*
- **amel.** | **Lower** limbs: *Nux-v* bg2

RUPTURE of ligaments:
○ - **Legs** | **Tendo** Achillis: nat-m b4a.de

RUSH of blood (See Blood - rush)

SAND on toes; sensation of: lyc h2

SCIATICA (See Pain - lower limbs - sciatic)

SCRATCHING:
- **affected** part until sore:
• **amel.** | **Lower** limbs: led bg2
- **agg.** | **Lower** limbs: sil b4a.de
- **amel.**:
○ • **Lower** limbs: psor bg2
• **Upper** limbs: camph b7.de* cina b7.de* mag-c b4.de*
- **sensation** of | **Knees**: stann h2
○ - **Lower** limbs; scratching the squil bg2

SEASONS:
- **autumn** agg. | **Upper** limbs: *Rhus-t* b7a.de
- **summer** agg. | **Lower** limbs: kali-bi bg2 nux-v b7.de*
- **winter** agg.:
○ • **Lower** limbs: ign bg2
• **Upper** limbs: *Petr* b4.de* *Rhus-t* b7.de*

SENSITIVE: camph coff *Cupr* cycl dulc fd4.de *Ferr-p* lac-c mrr1 lath *Mang* ruta fd4.de sul-ac tarax ter thal-xyz srj8• tritic-vg fd5.de verat-v zinc
- **cold**, to: am-c ars atra-r bnm3• kali-s fd4.de
○ • **Feet**: alum am-c atra-r bnm3• zinc
• **Fingers**: agar *Cist* bro1 hep bro1 pot-e rly4• sec
⁝ **Skin** at nails: ant-c
⁝ **Tips**: berb bg1 cist lac-c bg1
• **Hands**: agar b4a.de atra-r bnm3•
• **Leg**, to a draft of air: *Zinc*
• **Upper** arms: nat-m
• **Upper** limbs: agar calc-p kali-bi bg1
- **warmth**, to: pot-e rly4• *Sulph*
- **wool**; to | **Feet**: morg-p fmm1•
○ - **Ankles**: ars-h graph sars
- **Arms** (See upper)
- **Feet**: *Acon* b7.de* agar k* aloe anac k* ant-c apis bell bg2 calc h2 calc-s flor-p rsj3• *Kali-c* k* *Lac-c* mrr1 lac-f *Lach* led **Lyc** k* mag-p br1 med *Merc-i-r* *Mez* op b7.de* *Petr* puls b7.de* rumx sars b4a.de sep bg2 *Sil* stann k* *Staph* sulph thal bg2 thal-xyz srj8•
• **touch**; to: kali-c mtf33
• **walking** agg.: alum alumn k2 ant-c tl1
○ • **Heels**: arg-n bg2 cycl bg2 euph bg2 jatr-c k* kali-bi bg2 med k* *Nux-v* bg2 ph-ac bg2 sep bg2 teucr bg2
• **Soles**: aloe *Alum* k* alumn k2 ant-c k* calc b4a.de carb-v hep b4a.de* ign b7.de* **Kali-c** k* **Lyc** **Med** k* mez nit-ac bg2 positr nl2• sabad k* sars b4a.de* *Staph* sulph b4a.de* thal dx thal-xyz srj8• ulm-c jsj8• zinc k*
- **Fingers**: agar bg2 berb ptk1 *Lac-c* k* lach *Led* k* lyc bg2 *Sec* k* thal-xyz srj8•
• **separated**; must keep fingers: lac-c k* lach k* sec mrr1
○ • **Nails**: berb *Nat-m* nux-v petr *Sil* squil sulph
⁝ **Skin** underneath the nails: ant-c b7.de*
• **Tips**: berb bg2* calc-p ptk1 cist bg2* dulc fd4.de lac-c bg2* nat-c h2* sars ptk1 *Staph* *Sulph* bg1* tarent ptk1* thal-xyz srj8•
⁝ **rubbing** | **amel.**: tarent mrr1
- **Forearms**:
• **left** | **Spots**; in: hist sp1
- **Hands**: sulph bg2
○ • **Back** of hands: con h2
• **Palms**: ars bg2 merc-c k* nat-c h2* nat-m bg2 thal-xyz srj8•
• **Skin** of hands: con bg2
- **Hips**: bapt *Coloc* galeoc-c-h gms1• mag-m h2 zinc h2
- **Joints**: arn k2
• **morning**: nit-ac h2
- **Knees**: apis bro1 ars bell bg2 berb bro1 bry k* canth b7.de* chin bg2* *Lach* lyc bg2 ph-ac bg2 rhus-t k* *Sars* *Sep* spig bg2 sulph tab bg2 verat
- **Legs**: *Acon* b7.de* arn bg2 berb *Calc* calc-s canth b7.de* chel bg2 galeoc-c-h gms1• kali-bi bg2 lach bro1 lath bro1 *Lyc* b4a.de mag-m bg2 phos bg2
• **touch**:
⁝ **sheets** agg.; of: galeoc-c-h gms1•
⁝ **slight** touch agg.: galeoc-c-h gms1•
○ • **Bones** | **Tibia**: *Puls* syph k2 thal-xyz srj8•
• **Calves**: *Nat-m* plb sil
- **Lower** limbs: *Agar* k* am-m h2 ars k* aur k* kali-bi bg2 *Mag-m* k* *Petr* k* plb sep k* sil k* staph bg2 zinc [spect dfg1]
○ • **Sciatic** nerve; down the course of the:
⁝ **left**:
⁝ **accompanied** by | **dysuria**: *Agar*
- **Nails**: calc b2.de* con b2.de* hep b2.de* m-ambo b2.de* *M-aust* b2.de merc b2.de* nat-m b2.de* *Nux-v* b2.de* petr b2.de* ph-ac b2.de* sep b2.de* *Sil* b2.de* squil b2.de* sulph b2.de* thuj b2.de*
- **Nates**: *Ars* dulc fd4.de
- **Shoulders**: *Apis* k* aspar cina con ferr lach pall pert-vc vk9

- Side not paralyzed: plb
- **Thighs**: *Agar* k* *Chin* b7.de* dulc fd4.de *Gels* lach bro1 lath bro1 *Merc* nat-c k2 rhus-t ruta sulph k*
  - **left** | **Spots**; in: hist sp1
- **Toes**: *Calc* k* *Carb-an* nit-ac bg2 positr nl2• *Sabin* b7.de* thal-xyz srj8•

○ • **Balls**: sil h2
  - **First**: ars-h eup-per k*
    - ⁝ **walking** agg.: calc colch gk
  - **Nails**: m-ambo b7.de nux-v b7.de
- **Upper** limbs: apis bg2 cina k2 kali-bi bg2 kali-s fd4.de mim-p rsj8• plb tl1 ruta fd4.de
  - **right**: mim-p rsj8•
- **Wrists**: alum b4.de* clem bg2 sulph bg2

SEPARATED sensation: hyper ptk1

○ - **Foot**; left | **walking** agg.: arg-met h1
- **Hand** feels separated from upper limbs: arb-m oss1•
- **Legs**: falco-pe nl2•
  - **body**; as if separated from his: *(↗MIND - Delusions - separated - body - extremities)* falco-pe nl2• op k* *Stram* tab bg2 tarent bg2
  - **spasmodic** drawing together; and: lyc op
  - **standing** agg.: phos k*
- **Lower** limbs: falco-pe nl2• nux-v op stram k*
  - **driving** | **agg.**: falco-pe nl2•
  - **rising** agg.: falco-pe nl2•
- **Upper** limbs: cinnb daph falco-pe nl2• *Stram*
  - **driving** | **agg.**: falco-pe nl2•
  - **riding** a horse agg.: daph
  - **writing** agg.: cinnb

SEPARATING:
- **arms** from body:
  - **amel.** | **Upper** limbs: psor bg2

SEWING agg.: | **Upper** limbs: lach b7a.de

SHAKING: kali-br k* mag-p tl1 mand rsj7• *Op*
- **noon** | **eating**; after: graph k*
- **evening**: nux-v k*
- **night**: stram k*
- **faintness**; after: am k* asaf k* colch k* kali-br kreos k* lyc k* merc-c k* sec k* stry k*
- **sleep** after dinner; during: nux-v

○ - **Feet**: kali-c h2 tab
- **Hands**: androc srj1• atro k* cann-i k* helo c1 helo-s c1* kali-c h2 lac-e hm2• lyc k* mag-p br1* nat-ox rly4• **Plb**
- **Legs**: con k* lyc k* stry k* tarent k*
- **Lower** limbs: anac b4.de* asaf b7.de* caust b4.de* mand rsj7• *Merc* k* sil b4.de* staph b7.de* tarent k*
  - **right** | **then** left: lyc h2
- **Shoulders**: agar alum bg2
  - **right**: plut-n srj7•
- **Upper** limbs: *Agar* bell k* bry k* bufo mand rsj7• merc k* op k* **Plb**

SHINING:

○ - **Elbows**: ant-c ptk1
- **Toes**: sabin bg2

SHIVERING (See Shuddering; Thrilling)

SHOCKS: *(↗Electrical)* *Agar* k* ail alum ars bg1 bell k* *Cic* k* *Cocc* k* galla-q-r nl2• **Lyc** plat h2 verat-v
- **jarring** of the carriage: *Am* k*
- **lightning**-like: plb k*
- **noise** agg.: bar-c
- **pulsating**: plat h2
- **sleep** agg.; on going to: *Agar* alum **Arg-met** **Ars** ip k* *Nit-ac* tub k13
- **waking**; on: lyc

○ - **Ankles** | **Below**: sul-ac h2
- **Elbows**: agar m-ambo b7.de nat-m phos h2 verat k*

○ • **Head**; to: agar

Shocks: ...
- **Feet**: agar all-s cadm-s *Phos* spig stann
  - **sleep** | **during** | **agg.**: all-s cadm-s
    - ⁝ **going** to; before: *Phos*

○ • **Heels**: mag-m h2
- **Fingers** touch anything; if the: *Alum*
- **Forearms**: olnd b7.de*
- **Hands**: *Agar* stann h2 sul-ac valer k* zinc
- **Hips**: agar aloe arg-met am b7.de* bell bry b7.de* cann-s b7.de* cocc b7.de* nat-m verat k*
  - **left**, then right: *Arg-met*
- **Knees**: agar arg-met *Am* b7a.de carl m-ambo b7.de puls ptk1 sul-ac valer ptk1 verat
  - **sleep**; going on to: *Agar* k* *Arg-met* k*
- **Legs**: agar plat sep
- **Lower** limbs: agar *Ars* *Cic* der m-ambo b7.de nux-v op phos plb sulph thuj *Verat* zinc
  - **right** | **falling** asleep; when: *Arg-met*
  - **painful**: ars
  - **sleep** agg.; during: *Agar* **Ars** zinc
  - **violent**, cause legs to jerk: cic
- **Nates**: cocc
- **Shoulders**: arg-met lyc bg2 m-ambo b7.de manc k*
  - **right**: *Alum* stann h2 sul-ac h2
  - **left**: agar hydrog srj2•
  - **evening** | **writing** agg.: manc k*
  - **writing** agg.: sul-ac h2
- **Thighs**: *Agar* k* dios euphr fl-ac sep

▽ • **extending** to:
    - ⁝ **Downward**: graph
    - ⁝ **Upward**: agar euphr
- **Thumb**, proximal joint: con h2
- **Toes**: am b7.de*
- **Upper** arms: *Agar* k* arg-met ruta k* tarax h1 *Valer*
- **Upper** limbs: *Agar* k* aloe apis *Arg-met* am k* asaf b7.de* aur-m k* **Cic** k* cocc b7.de* fl-ac k* hell b7.de* lyss *M-ambo* b7.de* manc k* nat-m k* *Nux-v* k* op k* phos phyt puls tarax verat b7.de*
  - **left**: agar k* arg-met *Cic* manc k*
  - **evening**: manc k*
  - **writing** agg.: manc k*

▽ • **extending** to | **Hands**: fl-ac

○ • **Joints**: m-ambo b7.de
  - **Paralyzed** part: *Nux-v*
- **Wrists**: calc h2

SHORT, sensation as if: mez ptk1 mosch ptk1

○ - **Bones**: vac jl2
- **Elbows** | **Joints**: caust bg2 lach bg2 sars bg2 sulph bg2
- **Forearms**: cham
- **Knees**: am-m bg2 graph bg2 hep bg2 lach bg2 led bg2 lyc bg2 merc bg2 nit-ac bg2 nux-v bg2 rhus-t bg2 ruta bg2 sep bg2 sulph bg2
- **Legs**:

○ • **Calves**: arg-met ptk1 carl sep bg2 *Sil* k*
    - ⁝ **descending** stairs agg.: arg-met h1*
  - **Tendo** Achillis: dios ptk1
- **Lower** limbs: acon bg2 am-m bg2 ambr k* *Berb* bg2 carb-an bg2 caust bg2 coloc b4a.de* guaj bg2 kreos bg2 lach bg2 mag-m bg2 *Mez* b4a.de* nat-m bg2 *Olnd* b7a.de* *Phos* b4a.de* sabin bg2 *Sep* b4a.de* spong bg2
  - **right**: merc
  - **left**: cinnb
- **Thighs**: guaj ptk1 kreos ptk1 sabin c1

○ • **Hamstrings**: am-m br1* bry ptk1 cimx br1 dios ptk1 guaj ptk1 nat-m ptk1
  - **Muscles** | **Flexor** muscles: visc sp1
- **Upper** limbs: aeth k* alum k* bell k* sep
- **Wrists**: carb-v

SHORTENED muscles, and tendons: *(↗Contraction; GENERALS - Shortened)* am-c k1 **Am-m** k1 ambr k1 anac k1 ars k1 aur k1 *Bar-c* k1 calc k1 carb-an k1 carb-v k1 **Caust** k1 cic k1 cimic k1 **Coloc** k1 con k1 cupr k1 dig k1 dros k1 **Graph** k1 *Guaj* k1 hell k1 hep k1 hyos k1 kali-c k1 kreos k1 lach k1 led k1 *Lyc* k1 mag-c k1 *Merc* k1 mez k1 mosch k1 *Nat-c* k1 **Nat-m** k1 nit-ac k1 *Nux-v* k1 ox-ac k1 petr k1 ph-ac k1 phos k1 plb k1 positr nl2• puls k1 ran-b k1 rheum k1 *Rhus-t* k1 ruta k1 samb k1 *Sep* k1 sil k1 stann k1 sul-ac k1 sulph k1 symph fd3.de•

○ - **Fingers**: *Caust* b4a.de

○ · **Flexors**: prot mtf11 tub-r mtf11

- **Upper limbs**: **Caust** b4a.de* *Coloc* b4a.de *Graph* b4a.de *Nat-m* b4a.de

SHORTENING (See Contraction)

SHORTER than the other; one leg: bry bg1 caust cinnb k* lycps-v mez h2 nat-m sulph til

- **right**:
  - **sensation** as if shortened: ambr hr1* crot-c k*
    - **menses**; during: tub rb2

SHRIVELLED (= shrunken): ars helo c1 helo-s c1* phyt *Rhod*

○ - **Feet**: ars merc-c k* verat verat-v bg2*

- **Fingers**: ambr k* ant-c k* crot-t k* cupr k* helo-s bnm14• merc k* ph-ac k* *Phos* sec k* *Verat*
  - **cholera**; during: *Camph* **Verat**
  - **perspiration**; during: ant-c k* canch canth **Merc** k* ph-ac k* pyrog **Verat**

○ · **Tips**: ambr k* sulph h2
    - **morning** | **waking**; on: ambr k*

- **Hands**: abies-c k* ang ant-t bg2 *Ars* bism camph hep k* *Lach Lyc* merc-c k* *Ph-ac* **Phos Verat** k* verat-v a1

○ · **Back** of hands: mur-ac h2
  - **Skin** of: aeth k* mez k*

- **Joints**: caust tl1

SHUDDERING: *(↗Thrilling)*

- **during**:
  - **agg.** | **Lower** limbs: nux-v b7.de rhus-t b7.de

○ - **Ankles**: lyc

- **Elbows**: chin b7.de
- **Feet**: mez h2
- **Hands**: chel kali-i laur k* nicc ran-b k*
- **Hips**: gran lyc ptel
- **Knees**: chin b7.de* lyc nat-m samb b7.de*
  - **walking** | **amel.**: nat-m
- **Leg**, shivering: cinnb con dig *Graph* hura kali-c k* m-aust b7.de meny k* mez plat h2 plut-n srj7•
- **Lower limbs**: acon b7.de* arn bg2 bry b7.de* camph b7.de* *Cann-s* b7.de* *Caust* b4.de* *Chin* b7.de* cina bg2 **Cocc** b7.de* coloc bg2 con bg2 graph b4.de* ign bg2 *Kali-c* bg2 lyc bg2 mag-m b4.de* meny bg2 phos b4.de* *Plat* b4.de* puls bg2 ran-b bg2 samb bg2 sars bg2 spig bg2 stront-c bg2
- **Nates**: croc
  - **sitting** agg.: croc
- **Shoulders**: mag-m h2 verat
- **Thighs**: arn b7.de cann-s b7.de chin b7.de cina b7.de ign b7.de phos h2 puls b7.de ran-b k*
  - **afternoon**: lyc
  - **shivering**: ang arn bry cann-s chin cina ign kali-bi lyc
- **Upper arms**: chin h1 ign b7.de mez h2 tritic-vg fd5.de
- **Upper limbs**: acon b7.de* arn b7.de* bar-c bg2 *Bell* b4.de* camph b7.de* *Cham* b7.de* chel b7.de* *Chin* b7.de* hell b7.de* ign bg2 laur bg2 mag-m h2 **Meny** bg2 merc bg2 mez h2* *Plat* b4.de* puls b7.de* ran-b bg2 rhus-t bg2 spig bg2 staph b7.de* sulph bg2 tritic-vg fd5.de verat b7.de*

▽ · **extending** to | **Feet**: mag-m h2

SINGING agg.:

○ - **Shoulders**: stann bro1*

- **Upper arms**: stann ptk1

SINKING DOWN, arm: acon k* kali-cy a1 *Nat-m* k*

SITTING:

- **after**:
  - **agg.**:
    - **Lower** limbs: acon b7.de* agar b4.de* alum bg2 asar b7.de* bell b4a.de bism b7.de* caps b7.de* *Carb-v* b4a.de cham b7.de* *Chin* b7.de* cocc b7.de* con b4a.de croc b7.de* dig b4a.de euph b4.de* *Hep* b4a.de *Led* b7.de* lyc b4.de* m-arct b7.de *Nit-ac* b4.de* nux-v b7.de* olnd b7.de* ph-ac b4.de* *Puls* b7.de* *Rhod* b4a.de ruta b7.de* sil b4.de* zinc b4a.de
    - **Upper** limbs: puls b7.de* ran-b b7.de*
- **chair**; in a:
  - **amel.** | **Lower** limbs: *Graph* bg2
- **hard**; on something:
  - **amel.** | **Lower** limbs: bell b4a.de
- **while**:
  - **agg.**:
    - **Knees** | **Hollow** of knees: berb ptk1
    - **Lower** limbs: acon b7.de* agar b4.de* alum b4.de* am-c b4.de* *Am-m* b7.de* anac b4.de* ang b7.de* ant-c b7.de* *Ant-t* b7.de* *Arg-met* b7.de* arn b7.de* ars b4.de* **Asaf** b7.de* aur b4.de* bar-c b4.de* *Bell* b4.de* berb bg2 bry b7.de* calc b4.de* camph b7.de* cann-s b7.de* canth b7.de* carb-an b4.de* carb-v b4.de* caust b4.de* *Cham* b7.de* chel b7.de* *Chin* b7.de* cic b7.de* cina b7.de* clem b4.de* cocc b7.de* coff b7.de* coloc b4.de* con b4.de* croc b7.de* cupr b7a.de *Cycl* b7.de* dig b4.de* dros b7.de* dulc b4.de* euph b4.de* euphr b7.de* *Ferr* b7.de* *Graph* b4a.de guaj b4.de* hell b7.de* hep b4a.de hyos b7.de* ign b7.de* *Iod* b4a.de kali-bi bg2 kali-c b4.de* kali-n b4.de* laur b7.de* led b7.de* lyc b4.de* m-ambo b7.de m-arct b7.de m-aust b7.de *Mag-c* b4a.de *Mag-m* b4a.de mang b4.de *Meny* b7.de* merc b4.de* mosch b7.de* mur-ac b4.de* nat-c b4.de* nat-m b4.de* nit-ac b4.de* nux-v b7.de* *Olnd* b7.de* par b7.de* *Ph-ac* b4a.de phos b4.de* plat b4.de* plb b7.de* **Puls** b7.de* ran-b b7.de* rheum b7.de* rhod b4a.de **Rhus-t** b7.de* *Ruta* b7.de* **Sabad** b7.de* *Sabin* b7.de* sep b4.de* *Sil* b4.de* *Spig* b7.de *Spong* b7.de* squil b7.de* stann b4.de* staph b7.de* stront-c b4.de* sul-ac b4.de* *Sulph* b4.de* **Tarax** b7.de* teucr b7.de* thuj b4.de* *Valer* b7.de* *Verat* b7.de* verb b7.de* viol-t b7.de* zinc b4.de*
    - **Nates**: staph ptk1
    - **Thighs**: lyc ptk1 mag-m ptk1 pyrog ptk1
    - **Upper** limbs: aloe bg2 am-m b7.de* anac b4.de* ant-c b7.de* ant-t b7.de* calc b4.de* cham b7.de* chel b7.de* chin b7.de* cycl b7.de* dros b7.de* ferr b7.de* meny b7.de* mur-ac b4.de* phos b4.de* puls b7.de* rhus-t b7.de* ruta b7.de* sabad b7.de* sabin b7.de* staph b7.de* sul-ac b4.de* tarax b7.de* teucr b7.de* viol-t b7.de*
  - **amel.**:
    - **Lower** limbs: alum b4.de* anac b4.de* aur b4.de* *Bry* b7.de* calc b4.de* carb-an b4.de* *Caust* b4a.de chin b7.de* cina b7.de* coff b7.de* coloc bg2 cycl b7.de* gnaph bg2 guaj b4.de* laur b7.de* mang b4.de* *Nux-v* b7.de* par b7.de* petr b4.de* plb b7.de* rhus-t b7.de* sil b4.de* spong b7.de* stann b4.de* *Tarax* b7.de* valer b7.de*
    - **Upper** limbs: agar b4.de* calc b4.de*

SITTING DOWN: | **agg.** | **Lower** limbs: am-c b4.de* bov b4.de* croc b7.de* graph b4.de* *Ip* b7a.de kali-c b4.de* *Lyc* b4a.de mang b4.de* nit-ac b4.de* ph-ac b4.de* ruta b7.de* sabin b7a.de sars b4a.de spig b7.de* thuj b4.de*

- **amel.** | **Lower** limbs: cycl b7.de*

SLEEP:

- **after**:
  - **agg.**:
    - **Lower** limbs: *Acon* b7.de* ambr b7.de* *Bry* b7.de* carb-v b4a.de chin b7.de* cocc b7.de* cycl b7.de* ign b7.de* lach b7.de* m-ambo b7.de nux-v b7.de* op b7.de* ph-ac b4a.de rheum b7.de* rhus-t b7.de* sabad b7.de* sel b7.de* sep bg2 spong b7.de staph b7.de* stram b7.de*
    - **Upper** limbs: acon b7.de* bry b7.de* chin b7.de* cocc b7.de* ign b7.de* nux-v b7.de* sel b7.de*
- **during**:
  - **agg.**:
    - **Lower** limbs: ant-t b7.de* calc b4.de* cham b7.de* ign b7.de* led b7.de* mag-c b4.de* merc b4.de* nat-c b4.de* plat bg2 puls b7.de* rhus-t b7.de* sulph b4.de* zinc b4.de*

- **during** – **agg.**: ...
  - ⁝ **Upper** limbs: acon b7.de* ant-t b7.de* caust bg2 croc b7.de* cupr b7.de* dig b4.de* hyos b7.de* ign b7.de* *Lyc* b4a.de m-aust b7.de puls b7.de* rheum b7.de* rhus-t b7.de* *Stram* b7.de* sul-ac b4.de* viol-t b7.de*
- **falling** asleep; on:
  - • **agg.**:
    - ⁝ **Lower** limbs: carb-v bg2 hyper bg2 ign b7.de* *Kali-c* bg2 merc b4.de* mur-ac b4.de* *Phos* b4.de* puls b7.de* rhus-t b7.de* sel b7.de* staph b7.de*
    - ⁝ **Upper** limbs: nit-ac b4.de*

SLIPPING Patella (See Dislocation - knees - patella)

SLOW growth of fingernails (See Nails - growth - slow - fingernails)

SMALL, seems too:
O - **Feet**: kali-c raph
- **Legs**: falco-pe nl2• kali-c

SMOKER's leg (See Berger's)

SMOKING:
- **agg.** | **Lower** limbs: clem b4.de*

SMOOTHNESS: | **sensation** as if smooth | **Fingers**: bell bg2
O - **Hands** | **Palms**: x-ray sp1

SMUTTINESS: ars k* sil

SNAKE crawling up leg; sensation of a: ail k*

SNEEZING:
- **agg.**:
O • **Lower** limbs: kali-c bg2 spig b7.de* sulph bg2
  • **Upper** limbs: alum bg2

SOFT: am-c tl1
O - **Feet**:
O • **Soles**: **Alum** ptk1 apis b7a.de ars ptk1 cann-xyz ptk1 cocc ptk1 helon ptk1 plb b7a.de *Xan* ptk1 zinc ptk1
  ⁝ **sensation** of: *(↗Swelling - feet - soles - sensation)* *Alum* k* apis b7a.de calc b4a.de helo-s rwt2• sulph b4a.de*
- **Hands**: cact br1* calc gk
- **Lower** limbs: acon bg2 alum bg2 ars bg2 cann-xyz bg2 cocc bg2 helo bg2 hyper bg2 plb bg2 sulph bg2 xanth bg2 zinc bg2
- **Nails** (See Nails - brittle)
- **Toes** | **Balls**: led b7.de*

SOFTENING of bones: | **Legs**:
O • **Bones** | **Tibia**: *Guaj*
- **Thighs** | **Femur**: sil

SORENESS (See Excoriation)

SPASM of limbs (See Convulsion)

SPINA VENTOSA: *(↗Inflammation - fingers; Nodules - fingers)* Ph-ac b4a.de

SPLIT nails (See Nails - split)

SPONGE; as if walking on a: helo ptk1 helo-s rwt2•

SPOTTED nails (See Discoloration - fingers - nails - white - spots)

SPRAINS: *(↗Dislocation; Pain - dislocated; Pain - sprained; Weakness - joints; GENERALS - Injuries - sprains)* arn tl1 bell-p sp1* **Bry** mrr1 calc mrr1 graph bro1 *Led* mrr1 petr bro1 phyt mrr1 psor mtf33 *Rhus-t* mrr1 ruta tl1* stront-c bg2* sul-ac mrr1 tritic-vg fd5.de
O - **Ankles**: anac ptk1 *Bit-ar* wht1• carb-an bro1 led bro1* nat-ar bro1 nat-c bro1* petr tl1 rhus-t tl1 ruta bro1* stront-c c2* tritic-vg fd5.de [*Stront-m* stj2]
  • **right**: bit-ar wht1• petr-ra shn4•
  • **left**: bit-ar wht1• petr-ra shn4•
  • **recurrent**: bov bro1 calc mrr1 med ptk1* nat-m mtf33 *Stront-c* bro1
- **Joints**: *(↗Weakness - joints)* carb-an bro1 hep bro1 led bro1
- **Lower** limbs: *Led* mrr1
- **Wrists**: stront-c mrr1

SPREAD APART; limbs are (See Abducted - lies)

SPUR CALCANEAL (See Exostosis - feet - heels)

SQUATTING agg.: | **Lower** limbs: calc b4a.de *Coloc* b4a.de graph b4a.de

STAGGERING (See Incoordination; VERTIGO - Accompanied - staggering)

STAMPING FEET in sleep (See MIND - Gestures - feet - stamping - sleep)

STANDING:
- **after**:
  • **agg.** | **Lower** limbs: nux-v b7.de* spig b7.de*
- **unsteadily**: ix bnm8•
  • **unobserved**; when: arg-n br1
- **while**:
  • **agg.**:
    ⁝ **Knees** | **Hollow** of knees: graph ptk1 par ptk1 rumx ptk1
    ⁝ **Lower** limbs: acon b7.de* agar b4.de* agn b7.de* alum b4.de* am-m b7.de* arn b7.de* ars b4.de* bar-c b4.de* bell b4.de* berb bg2 bry b7a.de calc b4.de* cann-s b7.de* carb-v b4.de* cham bg2 chel b7.de* chin b7.de* cina b7.de* coloc b4.de* con b4.de* croc b7.de* cupr b7.de* cycl b7.de* dig b4.de* euph b4.de* euphr b7.de* ferr b7.de* graph b4a.de* guaj b4.de* hep b4.de* ign b7.de* kali-bi bg2 kali-c b4.de* kali-n b4.de* laur b7.de* m-arct b7.de mag-c b4.de* mang b4.de* meny b7.de* merc b4.de* mez b4.de* mur-ac b4.de* nat-m b4a.de nit-ac b4.de* nux-m b7.de* nux-v b7.de* olnd b7.de* plat b4.de* plb b7.de* ran-b b7.de* rheum b7.de* *Rhus-t* b7.de* ruta b7.de* sabad b7.de* samb b7.de* sars b4.de* sil b4.de* spong b7.de* stann b4.de* staph b7.de* stront-c b4.de* sulph b4.de* tarax b7.de* thuj b4.de* **Valer** b7.de* **Verat** b7.de* verb b7.de* viol-t b7.de* zinc b4.de*
    ⁝ **Upper** limbs: agar b4.de* alum b4.de* am-m b7.de* arn b7.de* mag-c b4.de* puls b7.de* rhus-t b7.de*
  • **amel.**:
    ⁝ **Lower** limbs: agar b4.de* calc b4.de* chin b7.de* cic b7.de* cina b7.de* cocc b7.de* coloc b4.de* euph b4.de* ign b7.de* meny b7.de* mur-ac b4.de* nat-c bg2 nux-v b7.de* ran-b b7.de* ruta b7.de* spig b7.de* stann b4.de* tarax b7.de*
    ⁝ **Upper** limbs: calc b4.de* ruta b7.de* tarax b7.de*

STARTING (See Jerking)

STASIS of the venous system: | **Lower** limbs: influ jl2*

STEPPING HARD:
- **agg.**:
O • **Feet**: arg-n bg2 con bg2 visc bg2
  • **Lower** limbs: *Alum* b4.de* anac b4.de* ang b7.de* ant-c b7.de* arg-met b7.de* arg-n bg2 arn b7.de* ars b4.de* asar b7.de* bar-c b4.de* bell b4.de* berb bg2 borx b4a.de bry b7.de* calad b7.de* *Calc* b4.de* camph b7.de* canth b7.de* caust b4.de* cham b7.de* chel b7.de* chin b7.de* coff b7.de* con b4.de* dulc b4.de* euphr b7.de* ferr b7.de* *Graph* b4a.de kali-c b4.de* kali-n b4.de* lach b7.de* *Led* b7.de* lyc b4.de* m-ambo b7.de mag-c b4.de* merc b4.de* *Nat-c* b4.de* nat-m b4.de* *Nit-ac* b4.de* nux-m b7.de* nux-v b7.de* par b7.de* petr b4.de* phos b4.de* plat b4.de* plb b7.de* puls b7.de* rheum b7.de* rhod b4.de* **Rhus-t** b7.de* ruta b7.de* sabad b7.de* sabin b7.de* sep b4.de* sil b4.de* spig b7.de* spong b7.de* staph b7.de* *Sulph* b4.de* thuj b4a.de verb b7.de*
- **amel.** | **Lower** limbs: caps b7.de*

STIFFNESS: abrot absin k* acon k* adon bg2 aeth k* *Agar* aids nl2• aloe bg2 am-c am-m k* ambr bg2* androc srj1• ang b7.de* ant-c bg2 *Apis* bg2 apoc k2 *Aran* aran-ix sp1 arg-met k* arg-n bg2 *Arn* b7.de **Ars** k* ars-i ars-s-f **Asaf** atra-r bnm3• aur bg2 aur-ar k2 bamb-a stb2.de• bapt bg2 bar-s k2 *Bell* k* benz-ac bg2 berb bg2 *Bit-ar* wht1• borx bg2 bov k* brom k* **Bry** k* *Calc* k* calc-i k2 calc-p calc-s calc-sil k2 camph k* cann-i k* cann-s k* canth k* *Caps* k* *Carb-ac* *Carb-an* k* carb-v k* carbn-o *Carbn-s* carl **Caust** k* *Cham* k* **Chel** k* *Chin* k* chinin-ar chir-fl gya2 *Cic* k* *Cimic* cina b7a.de* cinnb k2 **Cocc** k* *Coff* b7.de *Colch* *Coloc* b4a.de* con b4.de* *Croc* b7.de **Cupr** k* cycl k* cyt-l sp1 dig k* dros bg2 *Dulc* k* eucal a1 eup-per k* euph b4a.de* euphr bg2 ferr bg2 ferr-ar form bg2 gink-b sbd1• graph k* *Guaj* k* guat sp1 ham bg2 hed sp1 *Hell* k* hep bg2 hip-ac sp1 hydr-ac k* *Hyos* k* ign b7.de* iod k* *Ip* b7.de jatr-c bg2 kali-ar

Extremities

Stiffness: ...
kali-bi k* *Kali-c* k* kali-cy a1 kali-i bg2 kali-n bg2 kali-p kali-s fd4.de kali-sil k2 **Kalm** *Lach* k* lath k* *Laur Lec* sne **Led** k* lil-s a1 limen-b-c hrn2* lith-c k* **Lyc** k* m-ambo b7.de m-arct b7.de m-aust b7.de mag-c b4.de mang bg2 *Med* meny *Merc* k* *Merc-c* k* merc-i-r k* merc-sul mez bg2 morg fmm1• morph a1 mosch k* musca-d szs1 naja nat-ar nat-c k* *Nat-m* k* *Nat-s* nit-ac nux-m k* *Nux-v* k* olnd k* op k* ox-ac **Petr** k* ph-ac k* *Phos* k* phys mrr1 *Phyt* k* pin-s a1 plan *Plat* k* plb k* podo bg2 prot fmm1• psor *Puls* k* pyrog jl2 ran-b bg2 rheum bg2 rhod b4a.de* **Rhus-t** k* **Ruta** bg2* sabad b7.de sabin b7.de* sal-fr sle1• *Sang* k* sarcol-ac sp1 sars k* *Sec* k* sel k* **Sep** k* **Sil** k* spig bg2 *Spong* k* stann bg2 staph b7.de* *Stram* k* stront-c b4.de stroph-s sp1 *Stry* k* sul-ac bg2 sul-i k2 **Sulph** k* suprar rly4• syph jl2 tab k* thal-xyz srj8• *Thuj* k* tritic-vg fd5.de *Tung-met* bdx1• urt-u bg2 vanil fd5.de verat k* verat-v k* visc sp1 *Zinc* k* [bell-p-sp dcm1 heroin sdj2 spect dfg1]

- **right**: am-m kali-bi
- **left**: nit-ac h2 rhus-t h1
- **morning**: am-c am-m h2 androc srj1• cact calc-p caps chlor cimic hed sp1 *Kali-bi Lach Led Petr* k* *Phos* sel k* sep spong fd4.de tritic-vg fd5.de
  - **bed** agg.; in: calc-p *Chin Lach Led* olib-sac wmh1 **Rhus-t** staph
  - **cold** bathing amel.: led
  - **rising** agg.; after: aids nl2• kali-bi k2 loxo-recl bnm10• mag-c *Petr* k* spong fd4.de
  - **waking**; on: alum k2 am-c ox-ac *Zinc*
- **forenoon**:
  - **11** h: brom
  - **standing**; after: verat
- **noon**: am-c bov
- **afternoon**: thuj k*
- **evening**: calc-s *Puls Sil* thuj k*
  - **sleep** agg.; after: cycl k*
- **night**: calc k2 hed sp1 *Nux-v* plat bg1 *Sil* spong fd4.de tus-p a1
  - **waking**; on: lach b7a.de
- **air** agg.; in open: acon k*
- **alternating** with | **convulsions** (See GENERALS - Convulsions - alternating - rigidity)
- **chill**:
  - **before**: *Chinin-s* psor *Rhus-t*
  - **during**: acon b7.de *Chinin-s* cic b7.de coff b7.de* eup-per *Nat-s* op k* *Rhus-t*
- **cold** air agg.: abies-c oss4• acon vh1 calc-sil k2 kali-c rhus-t
- **convulsions**:
  - **after**: led gt1
  - **before** | **epileptic**: bufo
  - **during**: acon alum am-c arg-met ars *Asaf Bell* k* *Camph* canth caust cham chin *Cic Cina Cocc* coloc *Dros* hell hyos *Ign* **Ip** kali-c *Laur* led *Lyc* mag-p k2* *Merc* **Mosch** nit-ac nux-m *Oena Op Petr* phos **Plat** plb sec sep sil stram sulph thuj *Verat Zinc*
- **cough**:
  - **before**: (↗*COUGH - Whooping - child - stiff*) **Cina** k*
  - **during** | **agg.**: bell caust cina *Cupr* k* ip k* led mosch
- **exertion** agg.; after: am calc calc-sil k2 mag-p k2 med k2 **Rhus-t** *Tub*
  - **disproportionate** to amount of exercise: bit-ar wht1•
- **fever**; during: canth b7.de
- **fright**; after: *Bry*
- **grasping** something agg.: am-c cham
- **headache** in occiput: *Petr*
- **menses**; during: calc-p *Rhus-t*
- **motion**:
  - **amel.**: abies-c oss4• cortiso gse rauw tpw8 symph fd3.de• tritic-vg fd5.de
  - **bed** agg.; in: calc-p k2
  - **beginning** of | **agg.**: abies-c oss4• *Agar* calc k2 *Caps* cocc mrr1 kali-p *Lyc* phos k2 podo c1 *Psor* **Rhus-t** tub nh*
- **painful**: *Ruta* mrr1 tritic-vg fd5.de
- **paralytic**: *Cocc* k* lith-c merc-c k* nat-m plb k*
- **perspiration**; after: calc-sil k2
- **resting**; after: calc-p k2 rauw tpw8 rhus-t tl1
- **rising** agg.: agar calc k2 loxo-recl bnm10• op k* plan k* psor **Rhus-t** *Ruta* mrr1
- **shivering**; during: op b7.de
- **sitting**; after: carb-an h2 carb-v h2 tritic-vg fd5.de
- **sleep** agg.; after: *Lach* morph ox-ac oxal-a rly4• **Rhus-t** *Sep*
- **standing** agg.: chin h1 tub tl1
- **swoon**, during: bov k*
- **tetanic**: absin k* ars h2 dulc a1 hyos k* *Phyt* sang k* zinc k*
- **walking**:
  - **after** | **agg.**: med k2 **Rhus-t** k* verat h1
  - **agg.**: acon k* ter
  - **amel.**: am-m h2 calc carb-v k* *Lyc Rhus-t*
- **warm** stove; when approaching a: *Laur*
- **weather** agg.; cold wet: dulc mrr1
- **wet** | **getting**: dulc mrr1

○ - **Ankles**: ars caps b7.de* carb-an **Caust** k* **Chel** k* cocc *Coloc* k* con dios dros k* graph k* hep k* *Hyper* ign b7.de* kali-c b4.de* lath k* led limen-b-c hrn2* *Lyc* k* m-arct b7.de med k* nat-m *Petr* k* plb ran-b b7.de* *Rhus-t* k* ruta sep k* **Sil** k* sul-ac k* **Sulph** k* syc pte1*• ter thal-xyz srj8• verb *Zinc* k* [heroin sdj2]
  - **right**: rhus-g tmo3•
  - **morning**: limen-b-c hrn2•
    - **rising** agg.: caps h1 carb-an limen-b-c mlk9.de
  - **evening**: sep
  - **exertion** | **amel.**: dios sulph
  - **sitting**; after: ger-i rly4• zinc h2
  - **walking** agg.: led sul-ac sumb
- **Elbows**: acon aeth alum am-c anac k* ang k* asaf bell **Bry** k* *Calc* k* *Carb-an* b4a.de *Caust* b4a.de *Chel* **Coloc** b4a.de ham *Ip* b7a.de *Kali-c* k* lac-ac lach *Led* limen-b-c hrn2* *Lyc* k* m-arct b7.de m-aust b7.de *Petr* b4a.de phos pip-m puls k* sal-fr sle1• *Sep* k* spig stann k* staphycoc rly4• sulph thuj k* tritic-vg fd5.de vanil fd5.de verat b7.de* zinc
  - **right**: crot-c sk4• limest-b es1•
  - **morning**: dios limen-b-c hrn2*
  - **evening**: com sep valer
  - **extending** the arm agg.: kali-c h2
- **Feet**: all-s k* alum k* ambr k* ang k* ant-t **Apis** k* ars k* ars-met asaf *Brom* b4a.de bry k* calc-s k* caps k* caust cham k* chel cic k* *Coloc* dios k* dros k* *Ferr* k* ferr-ar ferr-p graph k* ham fd3.de• hipp jl2 ign k* kali-ar kali-bi *Kali-c* k* kali-s kreos k* laur k* *Led* k* *Lyc* b4a.de merc mosch k* nat-m k* nux-v k* olib-sac wmh1 *Op* k* *Petr* k* phos k* plb b7a.de ran-b **Rhus-t** k* sanic *Sec* k* *Sep Stict* stry k* sul-ac *Sulph* k* tep k* thuj k* *Zinc*
  - **morning**: apis ign k* *Led* k* moni rfm1•
    - **waking**; on: alum cupr sst3•
  - **evening**: calc-s k* kali-s
    - **sitting** agg.: plat h2
    - **undressing** agg.: apis
  - **night**: **Apis** sulph h2
  - **air** open: nux-v
  - **alternating** with | **tearing** pain (See Pain - feet - tearing - alternating - stiffness)
  - **chill**; during: led b7.de
  - **cold** agg.; becoming: cham h1
  - **eating**; after: graph k*
  - **pregnancy** agg.; during: sanic tl1
  - **rising**:
    - **amel.**: alum k*
    - **sitting**; from | **agg.**: bry (non:caps kl) laur
  - **sensation**: alum bg2 plat bg2
  - **sitting** agg.: plat h2
  - **tearing** pain in, after: sulph k*
  - **waking**; on: alum k*
  - **walking**:
    - **agg.**: ign
    - **amel.**: alum k* laur k* olib-sac wmh1

○ • **Instep**: ignis-alc es2•

- **Fingers**: *Agar* k* am-c k* am-m b7.de* ambr b7.de* aml-ns k* ant-t *Apis Ars* k* ars-i aur-m bamb-a stb2.de• *Bell* k* berb bit-ar wht1• borx b4a.de bov brom b4a.de* bry k* bufo bg2 *Calc* k* *Calc-s* calc-sil k2 camph cann-i *Carb-an* k* carb-v bro1 *Carbn-s* k* *Caul* k* *Caust* cham b7.de* chin k* chinin-ar cocc b7.de* coloc con k* *Cupr* k* dig k* dios k* *Dros* k* dulc k* eup-per k* *Ferr* k* ferr-ar fl-ac k* graph k* ham k* hell helo-s bnm14• hep k* hydr-ac k* hydrog srj2• ign b7a.de iod *Kali-c* b4a.de* kali-n k* kali-s fd4.de kola stb3• kreos b7a.de lac-ac bg2 lat-m bnm6• **Led** k* lil-t k* **Lyc** k* lyss m-arct b7.de *Manc* med jl2 medul-os-si rly4• *Merc* k* merc-i-f k* mosch b7a.de nat-c bg2 nat-m k* nat-s nat-sil fd3.de• nux-v bg2 olnd k* ox-ac k* *Petr* k* pin-con oss2• plb k* *Positr* nl2• prim-o bro1 ptel puls k* **Rhus-t** k* rhus-v ruta fd4.de sacch-a fd2.de• sang sec k* *Sep* b4a.de *Sil* k* sol-ni *Spig* b7a.de spong k* stann k* stry sul-i k2 sulph k* symph fd3.de• tritic-vg fd5.de vanil fd5.de verat k* vinc [spect dfg1]
  - **left**: colch rsj2• stry bg1
  - **morning**: am-c *Ars Calc* calc-s crot-c sk4• *Ferr Lach Led* morg-p pte1*• nat-sil fd3.de• *Rhus-t* sacch-a fd2.de• symph fd3.de• thuj tritic-vg fd5.de
  - **forenoon**: fl-ac kali-s fd4.de
  - **evening**: ambr a1 petr
  - **accompanied** by | **Thumb**; flexed: lat-m bnm6•
  - **chill**; during: eup-per ferr *Rhus-t*
  - **cutting** with scissors: con k*
  - **exertion** agg.; after: mag-p k2 **Rhus-t** *Stann*
  - **extension** of them; with: carbn-s
  - **gouty**: **Agar** k* *Carb-an Lyc* petr h2 sulph
  - **grasping** something:
    - **after**: graph symph fd3.de•
    - **agg.**: am-c *Carb-an* k* *Dros* k*
  - **holding** a book agg.: lyc k*
  - **lying** agg.: hep
  - **motion** | **amel.**: colch rsj2•
  - **painful**: manc tritic-vg fd5.de
  - **spinal** affections: apis
  - **stretching** arm agg.: dulc
  - **warmth**:
    - **amel.** | **heat** amel.: colch rsj2•
  - **working**; while: lyc h2 merc h1
  - **writing** agg.: aesc cocc stann
  - ▽ **extending** to:
    - **Arm**; up | **faintness**; with: petr hr1
  - ○ **First**: acon am-m h2 arg-n *Calc Kali-c* sabad tung-met bdx1•
    - **writing** agg.: *Kali-c*
  - **Fourth**: aloe *Calc-s* con hell mur-ac *Sil*
    - **morning**: calc-s
    - **night**: mur-ac h2 sil
    - **rest** | **amel.**: hell
  - **Joints**: am-c b4a.de* am-m bg2 ambr bg2 ars b4.de* borx bg2 brom bg2 *Calc* bg2 **Carb-an** bg2 chin bg2 con bg2 dig bg2 dros b7.de* graph b4a.de* hell b7a.de* hep bg2 kali-c bg2 kali-n bg2 kreos b7a.de **Lyc** b4.de* merc b4.de mosch bg2 mur-ac bg2 nat-m b4a.de* olnd bg2 petr b4a.de* phos bg2 sabad bg2 sep bg2 *Sil* b4a.de* sulph bg2
  - **Second**: borx calc-s carb-an dros gard-j vlr2• kola stb3• *Phos* **Sil**
    - **right**: cassia-s ccrh1•
    - **Distal** joint: bell h1
  - **Third**: gard-j vlr2• mur-ac ruta fd4.de sulph til vanil fd5.de
    - **evening**: sulph
    - **night**: mur-ac
  - **Tips**: mag-p bg2
- **Forearms**: aur-m bry calc-s *Caust* k* *Cham* coloc hydr-ac morg-p pte1• plat k* prun k* *Rhus-t* k* stann k* thuj
  - **cramping**: plat stann
  - **grasping** something agg.: *Cham*
  - **painful**: **Rhus-t** thuj
  - **writing** agg.: *Caust* prun
- **Hands**: *Agar* alum k* androc srj1• *Ars* k* ars-met arum-t k* arund k* asaf k* aster aur aur-m bamb-a stb2.de• bell b4.de* bov k* *Brom* b4a.de bry k* bufo bg2 *Calc* k* *Calc-s* k* calc-sil k2 carb-ac k* *Carb-an* carbn-s cham k* chinin-ar cocc k* *Coloc* k* croc b7.de* *Cupr* cur dios k* *Ferr* k* ferr-ar ham k* hyos k* ign b7a.de* kali-ar k* kali-n bg2 kreos k* lil-t k* *Lyss* merc k* morg-p pte1*• mosch k* myris br1 nat-sil fd3.de• nit-ac k* *Nux-v* olib-sac wmh1 phos k* plat k* plb k* plut-n srj7• positr nl2• ptel k* sabad b7a.de sabin bg2 sanic sars k* sep k* sil *Stict Stry* k* thuj k* tritic-vg fd5.de vip k* wye k* zinc k*
  - **right**: olib-sac wmh1
  - **left**: *Brucel* sa3•
  - **morning** | **waking**; on: alum *Ars* bamb-a stb2.de• cupr sst3• *Ferr Lach Led* nat-sil fd3.de• positr nl2• sanic
  - **forenoon**: calc-s k*
  - **afternoon**: calc-s k*
  - **evening**: calc-s k*
  - **chilliness**: kali-chl
  - **cold** agg.; becoming: cham k* phos k*
  - **covered**, from being: sep k*
  - **cramping**: plat stann
  - **grasping** something agg.: nit-ac h2*
  - **holding** anything: mosch k* (non:nit-ac kl)
  - **motion** | **amel.**: olib-sac wmh1 tritic-vg fd5.de
  - **paralytic**: cham k*
  - **playing** piano: *Zinc*
  - **pregnancy** agg.; during: sanic tl1
  - **rheumatic**: *Agar Ars* bell chel *Ferr Kali-c Lyc Merc* nat-c ph-ac puls **Rhus-t** *Ruta* sabin sanic sep staph *Sulph* thuj viol-o
  - **waking**; on: alum k* lach led olib-sac wmh1
  - **walking** | **amel.**: alum
  - **working**; while: merc k*
  - **writing** agg.: cocc kali-m bro1*
  - ○ **Bones**: psor jl2
    - **waking**; on: psor jl2
  - **Joints**: alum bg2 *Calc* b4a.de merc b4.de* **Sil** b4a.de
  - **Palm** | **writing** agg.: kali-m ptk1
- **Hips**: acon k* agar androc srj1• ang h1 arg-met ars k* aur *Bapt* k* bar-c k* *Bell* carb-v sne cham b7.de* chin bg2 chinin-s euphr ger-i rly4• *Ham* hell led b7.de* *Lyc* k* mang-p rly4• med nat-m k* *Ph-ac* phys k* positr nl2• psor jl2 rheum k* *Rhus-t Sel* b7a.de *Sep* **Sil** *Staph Stry* succ-ac rly4• sulph k* suprar rly4• syc pte1*• *Zinc* [bell-p-sp dcm1]
  - **right**: hip-ac sp1 suprar rly4•
  - **morning**: arg-met ars chinin-s ger-i rly4• *Staph*
  - **motion** agg.; beginning of: *Ph-ac* **Rhus-t** staph
  - **rising** from sitting agg.: agar
  - **turning** over, on: *Sulph* k*
  - **walking** | **amel.**: *Ph-ac*
  - **weakness** with: lac-h htj1•
  - ○ **Joints**: acon b7a.de* ang b7.de* aur b4.de* bar-c b4a.de *Bell* b4.de* caps b7.de* coloc b4a.de* *Get* br1 gran bg2 hell b7.de* ign b7.de* kreos b7a.de m-aust b7.de nux-v bg2 rheum b7a.de* rhus-t b7a.de sep b4.de* sil bg2 staph b7.de* zinc bg2
    - **morning**: get br1
    - **motion** agg.: *Get* br1
- **Joints**: abrot k* aesc *Agar* ang c1* anh sp1 ant-s-aur apis k* apoc-a bro1 *Am* bro1* **Ars** ars-s-f k2 asc-t bro1 *Aur* aur-ar k2 bapt bar-m bro1 bar-s k2 *Bell* bry bro1* cact *Calc* k* calc-sil k2 canth *Caps* k* *Carb-an* carb-v k2 *Carbn-s* caul bro1 **Caust** k* chin bg1 *Chinin-s* cimic clem *Cocc* k* *Colch* k* *Coloc* k* dios br1* ferr-ar *Form* k* *Gins* bro1 graph *Guaj* bro1 iod bro1 kali-ar *Kali-bi Kali-c Kali-i* k* kali-s kali-sil k2 lac-ac *Lac-c* lach **Led** k* limen-b-c hm2* limest-b es1• **Lyc** k* magn-gr bro1 marb-w es1• med bro1 *Merc* bro1 mez bro1 *Nat-ar Nat-m* nat-p *Nux-v* k* ol-j c2* olib-sac wmh1 **Petr** k* *Phos Phyt* bro1 pin-s c2* psor *Puls* ran-b mrr1 rhod k2 **Rhus-t** k* sal-fr sle1• *Salol* c1 **Sep** k* **Sil** *Staph* k* *Stel* bro1 *Stict* k* stry bro1 **Sulph** k* syph k2 thal-xyz srj8• thiosin bro1 trios c2* tub-r vn* verb bro1 *Zinc*
  - **morning**: ant-s-aur caps h1 cimic get vh *Kali-bi Led* staph

Extremities

- **afternoon** | **sleeping**; after: chin
- **evening** | **21** h: phys
- **alternating** with | **Foot**; perspiration of: merc k2 sil k2
- **bath**; after a too warm: rhus-t
- **chill**; during: bry *Calc* **Caust** led *Lyc* nux-v *Op* petr rhus-t sep sulph thuj
- **chronic**: ran-b mrr1
- **cold** | **applications** | **amel.**: *Led* k*
  - **wet**: arn mrr1
- **cold** agg.; becoming: phos k2
- **edema**, with: kali-ar hr1
- **gouty**: caps tl1
- **lying** down agg.; after: caps caust
- **motion** agg.: cham h1
- **numbness**; with: colch
- **painful**: *Cocc*
- **paralytic** on rising from sleep: caps h1 chin
- **rheumatic**: *Calc* kali-ar k2 *Lyc* **Rhus-t**
- **rising** agg.: agar *Calc* *Carb-an* **Rhus-t** staph tub-r vn*
- **sitting** agg.: caust
- **sleep** agg.; after: chin
- **warmth** agg. | **heat** agg.: *Lac-c*

- **Knees**: aesc alum *Am-m* k* ambr b7.de* *Anac* k* ang ant-c k* *Apoc* *Ars* k* ars-met ars-s-f k2 **Atro** aur k* aur-ar k2 aur-m aur-s k2 bell k* *Berb* k* bov k* **Bry** k* bufo calc k* *Calc-s* calc-sil k2 *Cann-i* caps b7.de* *Carb-v* k* carbn-s card-m **Caust** k* *Chel* clem cocc k* *Coloc* k* con crot-c sk4• dig k* dios dros b7.de* elaps euph ferr-ar ferr-ma *Graph* k* guaj b4a.de hell k* hydr hyos k* *Ign* k* kali-ar *Kali-bi* kali-c k* kali-m k2 kali-sil k2 lac-ac lac-e hrn2• lac-h htj1• lach k* lath k* **Led** k* limen-b-c hrn2* lob **Lyc** k* m-aust b7.de merc k* merc-sul mez k* mim-h bro1 morg-g pte1• mur-ac *Nat-m* k* *Nat-s* *Nit-ac* k* *Nux-v* k* ol-an op *Petr* k* *Phos* k* phys phyt pin-s pip-m plan **Plat** plb k* podo *Psor* *Puls* k* rheum k* **Rhus-t** k* sal-fr sle1• sang sars k* *Sep* k* **Sil** k* spig k* *Stann* k* *Staph* **Stry** **Sulph** k* sumb symph fd3.de• tarent tep *Ter* thal-xyz srj8• vip *Zinc*
  - **alternating** sides: coloc nat-m
  - **right**: oxal-a rly4•
  - **left**: colch rsj2•
  - **morning**: ambr a1 calc-s limen-b-c hrn2* nat-m sne stry
    - **rising** agg.: *Aesc* caps h1 ign lac-e hrn2• *Lyc* nat-m sne
  - **evening**: *Plat*
  - **night**: *Lyc*
  - **alternating** with | **tearing** pain (See Pain - knees - tearing - alternating - stiffness)
  - **ascending**:
    - **stairs** | **after** | **agg.**: hydr ign
      - **agg.**: lac-e hrn2•
  - **bandaged**, as if (= enveloped): *Anac* caps fkm1•
  - **bed** in: lac-h htj1•
  - **chill**; during: *Hell* b7.de
  - **descending** stairs agg.: merc sal-fr sle1•
  - **kneeling** agg.: sep
  - **motion**:
    - **agg.**: bry tl1
    - **beginning** of:
      - **agg.**: *Carb-v* *Caust* *Euph* *Lyc* puls **Rhus-t**
      - **amel.**: colch rsj2•
  - **painful**: ant-c **Bry** *Nit-ac*
  - **paralytic**: aur
  - **rheumatic**: bacls-7 fmm1• **Bry** *Lyc* merc *Phos* **Rhus-t**
  - **rising** from sitting agg.: aesc mur-ac nat-m **Sulph**
  - **sitting**:
    - **after**: *Lach* *Lyc* **Rhus-t** stict **Sulph** symph fd3.de•
    - **agg.**: anac coloc stry
  - **sore**: stry

- **Knees**: ...
  - **squatting**, preventing: *Coloc* *Graph*
  - **standing** agg.: sil
  - **stretching** agg.: bov *Puls*
  - **sudden**: stann
  - **walking**:
    - **after** | **agg.**: ignis-alc es2• **Rhus-t**
    - **agg.**: bell *Caust* kali-bi *Led* ol-an phyt **Puls** sil sumb
    - **air** agg.; in open: hell h1 hyos
  - **warmth**:
    - **amel.** | **heat** amel.: colch rsj2•
  - ○ **Hollow** of knees: ambr h1 caust h2* dros h1 graph h2 lyc h2 mez h2 nit-ac h2 petr h2 scroph-n bg1 stann h2 sulph h2
    - **stooping**; while: sulph ptk1
  - **Patella**: caust bg2
  - **Tendons** of: hell h1
- **Legs**: alum bro1 ang bro1 arg-n bg2* arist-m br1 ars bg2 bacls-7 fmm1• bapt bro1 bar-m bro1 bell b4.de* bry b7a.de calc bro1 carb-v bg2 *Cic* bro1 colch bro1 con b4.de* dios bro1 *Eup-per* bro1 ferr b7a.de* gamb bg2 guaj bro1 *Ip* b7.de* *Lath* bro1 luf-op rsj5• mang h2* merc b4.de* morg-p fmm1• nat-m h2* nux-v bg2 petr b4.de* phys bro1 plat h2* positr nl2• ran-b b7.de* rhus-t b7a.de* sarcol-ac bro1* sars b4a.de* sep bro1 stry bro1 verat bg2 visc sp1 xero bro1 zinc b4.de*
  - **kneeling** agg.: marb-w es1•
  - **sitting**:
    - **agg.**: marb-w es1•
    - **erect** | **agg.**: marb-w es1•
  - ○ **Calves**: *Arg-n* k* cic a1 con h2 mag-m ptk1 sarcol-ac sp1 verat a1 zinc h2
    - **right**: trios rsj11•
    - **cold** applications agg.: trios rsj11•
    - **walking** agg.: caps h1
  - **Tendo** Achillis: bit-ar wht1• cic a1 cimic hr1* sulph ptk1
    - **walking**:
      - **agg.**: ant-t ptk1
      - **air** agg.; in open: cimic cp
- **Lower** limbs: *Acon* k* agar alum k* alum-p k2 alum-sil k2 am-m ambr c1 aml-ns anac k* ang k* ant-t apis b7a.de apoc *Arg-met* arg-n k* arist-m br1 ars k* ars-h atra-r bnm3• **Atro** aur aur-ar k2 *Aur-m* bacls-7 pte1• bar-c *Bell* k* **Berb** k* brom k* *Bry* k* bufo *Calc* k* calc-s calc-sil k2 caps k* carb-an *Carb-v* k* carbn-o *Carbn-s* *Caust* bg2 **Cham** b7a.de chel chin chinin-ar *Cic* k* *Cina* k* *Coc-c* *Cocc* k* con cupr k* cycl b7.de* dig k* dros k* **Eup-per** *Ferr* k* ferr-ar ferr-p galla-q-r nl2• *Guaj* b4a.de *Ham* *Hydr-ac* ign k* ignis-alc es2• jatr-c kali-c h2* kali-i *Lac-c* lact *Lath* *Led* b7.de* *Lyc* k* m-arct b7.de *Mag-p* *Mang* k* marb-w es1• *Merc* k* merc-c k* morg-p pte1• mosch b7a.de *Nat-m* k* *Nat-s* nit-ac k* **Nux-v** k* ol-an *Olnd* b7a.de op ox-ac *Petr* k* phos k* phys **Plat** plb podo positr nl2• puls ran-b rhod k* **Rhus-t** k* sal-fr sle1• sars k* sec k* **Sep** k* **Sil** *Spong* k* stram *Stry* sulph k* symph fd3.de• tab ter tetox pin2• thuj k* tritic-vg fd5.de tub k2 tung-met bdx1• *Verat* k* *Zinc* zinc-p k2 [bell-p-sp dcm1]
  - **right**: *Coc-c* galla-q-r nl2• hydrog srj2• mang h2
  - **left**: *Arg-n* phos h2 stram
  - **morning**: bar-m br1 bell *Petr* rhod **Rhus-t** spong fd4.de staph tritic-vg fd5.de *Verat*
  - **afternoon**: brom orot-ac rly4•
  - **evening**: arg-met calc-s *Lyc* *Phos* *Plat* *Puls* sil tub k2
    - **nap**, after a: *Carb-v*
    - **rising** | **amel.**: mang
  - **night**: alum *Lyc* nit-ac spong fd4.de
  - **ascending** stairs agg.: hydrog srj2•
  - **bandaged**; as if: anac c1
  - **bending** agg.: phos plan
  - **chill**:
    - **before**: petr *Phos* psor rhus-t
    - **during**: *Nat-s* *Tub*
  - **convulsions**; before epileptic: *Bufo*
  - **descending** stairs agg.: *Rhus-t* stry
  - **painful**: cic k* con br1 sec tritic-vg fd5.de

- **paralysis**; with: *Cocc* graph tl1
- **paroxysms**: stry
- **rising** agg.: agar caps h1 cycl h1 **Eup-per** *Hep* hydrog srj2• psor spong fd4.de symph fd3.de•
- **rubbing** | **amel.**: stram
- **sensation** of: alum b4a.de arg-met b7a.de arg-n bg2 asaf b7.de* caust b4.de* cham b7.de* chin b7.de* cocc b7.de* mang b4.de* merc-c b4a.de mosch b7.de* nit-ac b4.de* nux-v ptk1 plat b4.de* rhod b4.de*
- **sitting**:
  - **after**: bell *Calc* carb-an dig nux-v *Puls* **Rhus-t** *Sep* symph fd3.de• tritic-vg fd5.de zinc
  - **agg.**: mang plat
- **sleep** agg.; after: *Sep*
- **soreness**; from | **Tendo** Achillis; in: cimic
- **standing** agg.: verat k*
- **stretching** | **amel.**: hydrog srj2• spong fd4.de stram
- **walking**:
  - **after** | **agg.**: berb c1 **Rhus-t**
  - **agg.**: kali-p fd1.de• ol-an ran-b sal-fr sle1• thuj
    - **sudden** stiffness: nux-v bg2
  - **air** agg.; in open: **Berb** mang h2 puls **Rhus-t**
  - **amel.**: *Carb-v* dig
- **weather** agg.; cold wet: *Lath*
- ▽ **extending** to | **Hip** joint: sep
- ○ **Joints**: *Brom* b4a.de *Carb-an* b4a.de *Caust* b4a.de **Coloc** b4a.de dig b4.de* *Petr* b4a.de
- **Sciatic** nerve: cur *Lyc* *Nux-v*

- **Nates**:
  - **right** | **moving**; when: hydrog srj2•
- **Shoulders**: aids nl2• arge-pl rwt5• bacls-7 fmm1• bamb-a stb2.de• bapt bit-ar wht1• **Calc-s** k* carc fd2.de• caust cocc bro1 colch rsj2• com *Cupr* *Dulc* bro1 dys fmm1• elaps euph k* falco-pe nl2• *Fl-ac* gaert fmm1• *Get* br1 gran bro1 graph guaj *Ham* *Ind* k* jatr-c kali-bi kali-c kali-sil k2 lat-m bnm6• loxo-recl knl4• *Lyc* *Merc-i-f* morg-p fmm1• *Nat-c* nat-s *Petr* petr-ra shn4• phasco-ci rbp2 *Phos* *Phyt* bro1 pin-con oss2• positr nl2• prim-v bro1 **Rhus-t** k* sal-fr sle1• *Sang* bro1 senec-j bro1 sep k* sil spig k2 staph stict mrr1 stroph-s sp1 stry tub-r jl2 vanil fd5.de verat
  - **right**: bit-ar wht1• des-ac rbp6 limest-b es1• *Merc-i-f* positr nl2• staphycoc rly4•
  - **left**: aids nl2• bamb-a stb2.de• bit-ar wht1• colch rsj2• lavand-a ctl1• nat-sil fd3.de• sal-fr sle1• sep h2
  - **morning**: aids nl2• calc-s falco-pe nl2• get br1 phos staph verat a1
    - **rising** agg.; after: aids nl2•
  - **evening**: calc-s com
  - **night**: calc h2 kali-c nat-sil fd3.de•
  - **arm** over head; must put: calc h2
  - **motion** agg.: *Get* br1
  - **waking**; on: arge-pl rwt5•
  - **walking**:
    - **air** agg.; in open: lyc
    - **amel.**: calc-s
  - ○ **Joints**: *Carb-an* b4a.de caust b4.de* **Coloc** b4a.de euph b4.de* kali-bi bg2 *Petr* b4a.de *Sep* b4a.de staph b7.de* thuj b4.de* zinc b4.de*
- **Tendons**: **Ruta** mrr1
- **Thighs**: alum bro1 am-c am-m ang bro1 *Arg-n* bro1 ars k* aur k* aur-m aur-s bapt bro1 bar-m bro1 bell b4.de* bry *Calc* k* calc-s carb-v cham k* cic k* cocc colch k* *Coloc* *Con* bro1 dig dios bro1 dirc *Eup-per* bro1 gins *Graph* k* guaj bro1 hell k* hydr-ac ign k* lac-c *Lath* bro1 lil-t luf-op rsj5• merc *Nat-m* k* *Olnd* b7.de* petr k* phos phys bro1 plat bro1 puls b7.de* rhod k* rhus-t k* sarcol-ac bro1* sars sec sep bro1 *Stry* k* symph fd3.de• thuj k* valer b7.de* xero bro1
  - **left** | **walking** agg.; after: ignis-alc es2•
  - **morning**: bry *Calc*
    - **rising** agg.: carb-v bg1 ign
  - **afternoon**: *Calc-s*
  - **evening** | **rising** from a seat; when: rhod

- **Thighs**: ...
  - **contracted**, as if: sars
  - **cramp**, like a: bry
  - **motion**; continued | **amel.**: cassia-s ccrh1•
  - **paralytic**: cham cocc
  - **pressure** | **amel.**: cassia-s ccrh1•
  - **rising** from sitting agg.: cassia-s ccrh1•
  - **standing** agg.: carb-v
  - **walking**:
    - **agg.**: am-c bell *Calc* cic graph petr *Stry*
    - **beginning** to walk: *Calc*
  - ○ **Anterior** muscles: *Calc* *Stry*
  - **Posterior** part:
    - **extending** to | **Knee**: hydrog srj2•
- **Thumbs**: aeth *Calc-s* cann-i ferr *Kali-c* k* **Kreos** k* *Led* puls sabad [spect dfg1]
  - **right**: limest-b es1•
  - **left**: kreos bg2
  - **afternoon**: calc-s
  - **painful**: ferr kreos sabad
  - **sewing**, while: aeth
  - **writing** agg.: *Kali-c* k*
- **Toes**: agar k2 **Apis** k* ars brom k* *Carl* *Caul* bro1 cocc b7.de* *Coloc* dios ferr *Graph* k* *Led* k* nux-v sabin b7.de* sec b7.de* *Sil* k* stry *Sulph* k*
  - **morning**: dios hydrog srj2• rat bg1
    - **motion** | **amel.**: hydrog srj2•
  - **sitting**; after: carl
  - ○ **First**: **Atro** coloc sulph
    - **afternoon**: sulph
  - **Second**: colch
- **Upper** arms: am-m b7.de* anac bg2 gaba sa3• morg-p pte1• *Olnd* b7.de*
  - **paralytic**: acon
  - **pressure** agg.: lac-h htj1•
  - **rheumatic**: anac
  - ○ **Biceps**: agar
  - **Deltoid**: stroph-s sp1
- **Upper** limbs: agar *Am-c* k* am-m k* anac k* *Ars* b4a.de ars-h atra-r bnm3• aur-m bell k* bov bg2 calc camph canth k* caps k* *Caust* k* *Cham* k* cic b7.de* coff bg2 con k* croc b7.de* dulc k* *Ferr* k* ferr-ar *Guaj* b4a.de *Ham* hyos ip b7.de* kali-bi kali-c k* kali-i kali-n h2 lil-t lyc k* manc meny k* merc k* merc-c b4a.de merc-i-r mez bg2 morg-p fmm1• mosch b7a.de nat-c k* nat-m k* *Nux-v* k* *Op* par petr k* ph-ac k* phos k* plat puls-n *Rhus-t* k* sal-fr sle1• sars k* *Sep* k* sil k* *Spong* b7a.de stann k* tetox pin2• thuj k* tritic-vg fd5.de verat zinc k*
  - **right**: **Am-m** arn bell h1 kali-bi kali-c ven-m rsj12•
  - **left**: bry bg1* caust bg1* meny bg1* merc-i-r bg1* nat-ar bg1 par bg1* phos bg1* rhus-t bg1* sal-fr sle1• thuj bg1* vac jl2
  - **morning**: *Petr* tritic-vg fd5.de
  - **evening**: am-m petr h2
  - **night**: am-c bell h1 caust kali-c *Nux-v*
  - **accompanied** by | **heaviness**: caust bg2 petr bg2 sang bg2 sep bg2 sil bg2
  - **chill**; during: eup-per
  - **cold** agg.; becoming: am-c kali-c phos h2 *Tub*
  - **convulsions**; before: bufo ptk1
    - **epileptic**: *Bufo*
  - **extension** impossible: caps h1 morg-p fmm1•
  - **grasping** something agg.: am-c cham
  - **hang** down agg.; letting arms: sep h2
  - **manual** labor; after: **Rhus-t**
  - **motion**:
    - **after** | **agg.**: kali-c *Rhus-t*
    - **agg.**: sars h2
    - **amel.**: kali-n h2 tritic-vg fd5.de
  - **paralytic**: *Caust* cina a1 cocc tl1 graph tl1 kali-i nit-ac plat

Extremities

- **raising** | **arm** | **impossible**: nat-c h2
  - ⁝ **arm** above head agg.: caust h2
- **sensation** of: arg-met b7a.de asaf b7.de* caust b4.de* cham b7.de* cina b7.de* nit-ac b4.de* petr b4a.de plat b4.de* sabad b7.de*
- **writing** agg.: *Caust*

○ • **Joints**: alum b4a.de *Am-c* b4a.de am-m b7.de* cina b7.de kali-c b4a.de lyc b4.de* petr b4.de* plat b4a.de sep b4.de* *Sulph* b4a.de zinc b4.de*

- **Wrists**: am-c bg2 *Apis* arg-n ars asaf b7a.de *Bell* k* bov bg2 *Brom* b4a.de *Carb-an* b4a.de *Caust* b4a.de *Chel* k* **Coloc** b4a.de cub dios *Get* br1 ham helo-s bnm14• hyos b7.de* ign k* kali-c k* lact laur bg2 *Led Lyc* k* m-arct b7.de merc k* merl mez bg2 nat-ar nat-c k* nat-s petr b4a.de ph-ac k* *Phos* plb *Puls* k* rhod k* **Rhus-t** k* rhus-v ruta k* *Sabin* k* sal-fr sle1• sel *Sep* k* staph k* stroph-s sp1 *Sulph* k* thuj k* verat bg2 wye zinc
  - **right**: ran-b c1
  - **morning**: get br1 plb sel sep *Sulph*
  - **evening**: chel rhus-t hr1 sep
    - ⁝ **amel.**: arg-n
  - **holding** a glass: nat-c
  - **motion** agg.: *Get* br1 ph-ac h2
  - **paralytic**: ruta
  - **weather** agg.; cold wet: **Rhus-t** ruta

STONES: | **sensation** as if stepping on stones: aur bg2* berb ptk1 brom bg2* *Cann-xyz* ptk1 hep b4a.de* lyc bg2* nux-m ptk1 plat bg2 rhus-t bg2*

STOOL:

- **after**:
  - **amel.** | **Upper** limbs: asaf bg2
- **before**:
  - **agg.** | **Lower** limbs: kali-bi bg2
- **during**:
  - **agg.**:
    - ⁝ **Lower** limbs: apis ptk1 nux-v bg2 sec ptk1 tell bg2 verat ptk1
    - ⁝ **Thighs**: rhus-t ptk1

STOOPING:

- **agg.**:

○ • **Lower** limbs: ars bg2 bar-c b4.de* bell b4.de* bov b4.de* bry b7.de* calc b4.de* coff b7a.de croc b7.de* dros b7.de* graph b4.de* kreos b7a.de lyc b4.de* m-arct b7.de plb bg2 puls b7.de* sil b4.de*

- **Upper** limbs: samb bg2 sep b4.de* sil b4.de*

STRENGTH: *(↗Weakness)*

- **sensation** of: plut-n srj7•

○ - **Hands** feel powerful choc srj3•

- **Lower** limbs | **sensation** of: *Op* b7.de*
- **Upper** limbs | **sensation** of: *Op* b7.de*

STRETCHING OUT: *(↗Extension; GENERALS - Stretching; GENERALS - Stretching out)*

- **morning**:
  - **8** h | **11** h; until: nat-m tl1
- **convulsions**; before: calc h2
- **desire** for: stroph-s sp1
- **involuntary**: stram b7a.de
- **straightening** them out; and: phos bg2

○ - **Fingers**: [tax jsj7]

- **spasmodic**: sec
- **Foot**: phos
  - **convulsively**: cina k*
  - **inclination** to: am-c op puls
    - ⁝ **morning** | **bed**; in: *Rhus-t*
    - ⁝ **sitting**, while: *Puls*

○ • **Sole**, painful: aster

- **Hand**: bell dulc [tax jsj7]
  - **grasp** something; as if to: dulc phos
- **Leg**: cham cina ptk1 dig helo-s rwt2• hydrog srj2• lach led nat-c *Plat Rhus-t* ruta spong stann sul-ac ptk1 sulph
  - **morning**:
    - ⁝ **bed**; in: *Rhus-t*

Stretching out – **Leg** – **morning** – **bed**; in: ...
- ⁝ **waking**, on: *Plat*
- **noon**: am-c
- **evening**: nat-c
- **night**: stann
- **epilepsy**, before: *Bufo*

- **Lower** limbs: *Alum* b4a.de am-c bro1 ambr *Aml-ns* bro1 bell b4.de* cina b7.de* clem b4.de* hell bro1 helo bro1 led b7.de* m-ambo b7.de merc mez b4.de* nat-c b4.de* nat-m nux-v *Oena* ph-ac b4.de* phos puls b7.de* rhus-t b7.de* ruta bg2 sabad bg2 sec b7a.de spong stry sul-ac k*
  - **agg.**: am-m b7.de* ang b7.de* ant-c b7.de* arg-met b7.de* arn b7.de* aur b4.de* bar-c b4.de* bov b4.de* bry b7.de* bufo bg2 *Calc* b4a.de cann-s b7.de* caps b7.de* carb-v b4.de* caust b4.de* cham b7.de* chin b7.de* cina b7.de coloc bg2 con b4.de* croc b7.de* dig b4.de* dros b7.de* ferr b7.de* graph b4.de* hep b4a.de ign b7.de* *Iod* b4a.de kali-c b4.de* laur b7.de* lyc b4.de* m-aust b7.de mang b4.de* merc-c b4a.de nat-m b4.de* nux-v b7.de* petr b4.de* phos b4.de* plb b7.de* podo bg2 psor bg2 puls b7.de* *Ruta* b7.de* sabin b7.de* sep b4.de* spig b7.de* spong b7.de* *Sulph* b4.de* thuj b4.de* valer b7.de* verat b7.de*
  - **amel.**: agar b4.de* anac b4.de* asar b7.de* bell b4.de* carb-an b4.de* carb-v b4.de* cham b7.de* chel b7.de* chin b7.de* dig b4.de* dros b7.de* dulc b4.de* ferr b7.de* ign b7.de* med bg2* merc-c b4a.de nat-m b4.de* nux-m b7.de* nux-v b7.de* par b7.de* *Puls* b7.de* rhus-t b7.de* sabad b7.de* sec b7.de* sulph bg2
  - **must** stretch: nat-m h2
    - ⁝ **constantly**: med k2
- **Thigh** amel.: cham h1
- **Upper** limbs: *Alum* b4a.de am-c b4a.de bell b4.de* *Calc* b4a.de chin b7a.de led b7.de* lyc bg2 ruta b7.de* sabad b7.de* verb b7a.de
  - **accompanied** by | **Fingers**; clenched: chin ptk1
  - **agg.**: alum b4a.de am-c b4.de* am-m b7.de* anac b4.de* ang b7.de* arg-met b7.de* bry b7.de* cann-s b7.de* caust b4.de* chin b7.de* cina b7.de* clem b4.de* dig b4.de* dulc b4.de* hep b4a.de ign b7.de* kali-c b4.de* laur b7.de* lyc bg2 mang b4.de* merc b4.de* merc-c b4a.de mur-ac b4.de* nux-v b7.de* plat b4.de* puls b7.de* rhus-t b7.de* ruta b7.de* sabin b7.de* sel b7.de* *Sep* b4a.de stann b4.de* staph b7.de* sulph b4.de* thuj b4.de* verat b7.de*
  - **amel.**: am-m b7.de* mur-ac b4.de* nat-c bg2 nat-m b4.de* puls b7.de* sec b7.de* staph b7.de*
  - **palpitations**; during: cocc ptk1

STUBBING agg.: | **Toes**: colch ptk1

STUMBLING (See Awkwardness; Awkwardness - lower - stumbling)

STUNTED nails (See Nails - stunted)

SUBSULTUS (See Twitching)

SUPPURATION:

○ - **Ankles**: am k* hep k*

- **Elbows**: *(↗Abscess - elbows)* dros tep
- **Feet**: rhus-v k* *Sec* k* vip k*
  - **scurf**: *Sil*

○ • **Heels**: berb k* borx fago k*

- **Sole**, sensation of: calc k* kali-n k* lyc k* prun k* spig k*
- **Fingers**: borx k* hydrog srj2• mang k*

○ • **First** | **Nail**; around: calc k* (non:nat-s bla1)

- **Fourth** finger: *Mang* hr1
- **Nails**: *(↗Felon - root)*
  - ⁝ **vaccination**; after: **Thuj**
  - ⁝ **Around**: con nat-s bla1 ph-ac
  - ⁝ **Under**: form
- **Tips** | **sensation** of suppuration: **Sil** a1
- **Forearms**: lyc plb
- **Hips**: *(↗Hip joint) Ars* asaf asar *Aur Calc Calc-p* calc-s calc-sil **Chin** graph *Hep Merc Ph-ac Puls* rhus-t *Sep* **Sil** staph *Stram* sulph
- **Knees**: hippoz *Iod*
- **Legs**: both fne1•
- **Toes**: androc srj1•

- **Toes**: ...
  - **left** great toe; under nail of (See Nails - suppuration - toenails - left)

SWAYING: | **Leg**:
  - **to** and fro | **standing** agg.: cycl k*
- **Upper** limbs: cina ptk1
  - **to** and fro:
    - ⁝ **amel.**: sang ptk1
    - ⁝ **head**: plb a1 sec a1

SWELLING: (↗*Fullness; Raynaud's; Varices*) absin acet-ac k2 apis k* aran-ix sp1 *Arist-cl* sp1 *Arn* ars k* aur-ar k2 *Bamb-a* stb2.de• *Bar-c* both k* bros-gau mrc1 but-ac sp1 buth-a sp1 cadm-met sp1 calc-ar mrr1 calc-f sp1 carb-v k2 *Cardios-h* rly4• cary a1 chin k* chinin-s chord-umb rly4• cob-n sp1 conch a1 cortico sp1 cortiso sp1 crot-h k* *Dulc* k* fuma-ac rly4• hip-ac sp1 kali-ar k* kali-p *Kalm* lach k* lat-m sp1 med br1 merc k* **Merc-sul** morg-p fmm1• nat-ar nat-pyru rly4• op k* oxal-a rly4• *Petr* plb k* rauw sp1 rhus-t k* ribo rly4• ruta fd4.de *Sec* k* *Sil* spig k2 spong fd4.de still suis-pan rly4• tritic-vg fd5.de vanil fd5.de vip k* x-ray sp1
- **arthritic**: x-ray sp1
- **cardiac** (See heart)
- **cramp**, after: graph h2
- **doughy**: kali-s k2 vip k*
- **dropsical** (= edematous): (↗*GENERALS - Dropsy - external*) acet-ac k2 adon vh1 ant-c **Apis** apoc **Ars** *Ars-i* ars-s-f k2 *Aur* aur-ar k2 aur-i k2 aur-m k2 bell bry *Cact* carbn-s k2 chel *Chin* chinin-ar *Colch* k* **Coll** *Con Crot-h Dig Dulc* erech br1* *Eup-per Ferr* ferr-p *Fl-ac Hell Iod* kali-ar kali-c kali-n kali-p *Kalm* led *Lyc* med k2 *Merc Merc-sul* mur-ac *Naja* k* *Nat-ar* nit-ac k2 op plb prun puls pyrog k2 sabin samb seneg *Sep* squil sul-i k2 *Sulph Ter* k* xan
  - **left** side: cact bro1
  - **loss** of fluids; from: ferr br1
  - **sudden**: kali-n br1
  - ○ **Synovial** membranes: bry br1
- **flabby**, livid: both k*
- **heart** disease; from: saroth sp1
- **periodical**, every year during hot weather, dark red at first: vip
- **sensation** of: ant-c k* ars bg2 ars-met bell bg2 chin k* dulc fd4.de *Glon* k* kali-bi bg2 *Kali-br* hr1 kali-s fd4.de phos bg2 sacch-a fd2.de• tritic-vg fd5.de
  - **sudden**: tanac c1
  - ○ **Inflamed** part: *Acon* vh1
- ○ **Ankles**: agath-a nl2• agn b7.de* ambr b7.de* ant-s-aur **Apis** k* apoc *Arg-met* c1* arg-n bro1* arn k* *Ars* k* ars-s-f k2 *Asaf* k* aur-m bamb-a stb2.de• bell bg2 benz-ac bry b7a.de *Cact Calc* k* calc-sil k2 carbn-s k2 cass a1 celt a1 *Cench Cham* b7a.de *Chel* k* chir-fl bnm4• cimic bg2 *Coloc Cop Dig* k* *Eup-per Ferr* k* ferr-ar *Graph* k* ham bro1 *Hep* k* *Hydr* hyos k* kali-c b4a.de* kali-m k2 *Lac-c* lac-d lac-del hm2• *Lach* k* lat-k a1 lat-m sp1 *Led* k* lil-t k* *Lyc* k* manc k* mang k* mang-p rly4• **Med** k* merc k* merc-sul mim-h c2* nat-m b4a.de nat-pyru rly4• *Ol-j* onos *Phos* k* *Phyt* plb k* plect a1 plut-n srj7• podo prun *Psor Puls* k* rhod b4.de* *Rhus-t* k* rhus-v k* *Ruta* sal-ac samb k* sel a1 seneg b4a.de sep k* sil k* stann k* stict stront-c bro1* suis-pan rly4• sulph k* syc pte1*• urol-h rwt• vanil fd5.de verat-v xan zinc k* ziz k*
  - **left**: hir rsj4•
  - **daytime**: ser-a-c jl2
  - **evening**: cupr sst3• kali-chl ptk1 sep k* stann k* vanil fd5.de
    - ⁝ **walking** agg.: merc k*
  - **accompanied** by | **diabetes** (See GENERALS - Diabetes mellitus - accompanied - ankle)
  - **cannot** use foot: asaf ptk1
  - **chronic**, after sprain: bov c1
  - **cold** agg.: asaf k*
  - **diabetes**; in: arg-met ptk1
  - **dyspnea**, with: hep
  - **edematous**: acetan br1 apoc mrr1 bamb-a stb2.de• kali-m k2 med jl2
  - **hot**: kali-c h2
  - **menses** | **before** | **agg.**: ignis-alc es2• suis-pan rly4•
    - ⁝ **during** | **agg.**: eup-per
  - **painful**: ars h2 *Led* k* nat-sil fd3.de• plb k* vanil fd5.de

Swelling – Ankles: ...
  - **rheumatic**: cact *Chel* hep c1 *Kalm Lach*
  - **sensation** of: ham fd3.de• kali-c bg2 laur k* ox-ac k* *Phos* plat b4.de* symph fd3.de•
  - **sitting** for a long time agg.; after: *Rhus-t* hr1*
  - **stitching**: phos h2
  - **sudden**: stann k*
  - ○ **Bones**: merc staph
  - **Malleoli**, around: arist-m br1
  - **Tendons** of: phos h2
  - **Veins** of: ham fd3.de• *Lac-c Lyc* sars
- **Elbows**: acon agar agn b7.de* benz-ac *Bry* k* **Calc** b4a.de calc-f chel cic k* colch k* *Coloc* con k* dios dulc b4a.de* *Hep* bg2* hydr *Lac-ac* k* lac-c lach bg2* *Led* b7a.de mang b4a.de **Merc** k* petr k* puls k* sil spig *Sulph* b4a.de tep k* ter k* verat b7.de*
  - **evening**: sep h2
  - **hot** and red: **Merc** k*
  - **rheumatic**: agar **Bry** chel coloc com lyc
  - **sensation** of, in bend of: verat h1
  - ○ **Condyles**: **Calc-p** *Mez*
- **Feet**: acet-ac k* acon k* aesc k* alum k* am-c k* ambr k* ant-c **Apis** k* apoc apoc-a a1 arg-met arist-cl sp1 *Arn* k* **Ars** k* *Ars-i* ars-s-f k2 arund k* asaf *Aur* aur-ar k2 aur-i k2 aur-m k* aur-s a1 bar-c bar-m k* bart a1 *Bell* k* berb borx b4a.de* bov k* **Bry** k* but-ac sp1 *Cact* k* *Calc* k* *Calc-ar* calc-i k2 calc-s k* calc-sil k2 cann-s *Canth Caps* b7.de* *Carb-an* k* carb-v k* *Carbn-s* cardios-h rly4• **Caust** k* cedr k* celt a1 *Cench* cham k* *Chel* k* *Chin* k* chinin-s *Cocc* k* *Colch* k* coli rly4• coloc k* con k* cop k* corn crot-h k* *Dig* k* dor k* elae a1 *Elaps* eup-per *Ferr* k* ferr-ar *Ferr-m* ferr-p fl-ac get a1 *Glon Graph* k* *Ham* bro1 helo bro1 helo-s rwt2• helodr-cal knl2• hep k* hir rsj4• *Hyos* k* hyper iod k* kali-ar *Kali-c* k* kali-i k* kali-n k* kali-p kali-s kali-sil k2 ketogl-ac rly4• kola stb3• kreos lac-c lac-del hm2• *Lach* k* lat-k a1 **Led** k* **Lyc** k* mag-m bg2 mang k* **Med** k* *Merc* k* merc-c bro1* nad rly4• naja k2* *Nat-ar Nat-c* k* *Nat-m* k* nat-p nat-s bro1 *Nit-ac* k* nux-v k* op k* oxal-a rly4• pareir *Petr* k* ph-ac k* *Phos* k* *Phyt* k* plb k* polys sk4• positr nl2• prun k* psor al2 **Puls** k* rauw sp1 *Rhod* k* *Rhus-t* k* rhus-v k* ribo rly4• ruta k* sabad k* sacch br1* *Samb* k* sars k* *Sec* k* *Sep* k* **Sil** k* sol-ni spira a1 stann k* staph k* staphycoc rly4• *Stict* stram k* *Stront-c* k* *Stroph-h* bro1 sul-ac k* sulph k* syc fmm1• symph fd3.de• ter ther k* thuj k* tritic-vg fd5.de urol-h rwt• urt-u tl1 vanil fd5.de verat k* vesp k* vip k* wies a1 zinc k*
  - **one** foot only: kali-c ptk1 psor al1
  - **right**: ars bg1 bov bg1* crot-h bg1 elaps bg1 flor-p rsj3• kali-p bg1 lac-c ptk1 lach ptk1 lyc h2* mand rsj7• ox-ac bg1 phos bg1 polys sk4• sars bg1* sec k* spig k* spong ptk1 stront-c ptk1 sulph k*
  - **left**: *Apis* k* coloc ptk1 com k* *Elaps* kali-c ptk1 kreos bg1* lach lyc k* sang k* sil k* tell ptk1
    - ⁝ **extending** to | **right**: *Kali-c* lach bg1 rhus-r bg1
  - **daytime**: dig k*
  - **morning**: *Apis Aur* ephe-si hsj1• just bg1 *Manc* phos bg2* phyt k* sabad k* sil k* ust bg1
    - ⁝ **waking**; on: ephe-si hsj1•
  - **evening**: am-c bg1 *Apis* ars bg1 bell k* **Bry** k* carbn-s caust k* chinin-s cocc h1 crot-h k* ferr bg1 graph bg1 kali-c bg1 lach bg1 led bg1 nat-c bg1 petr bg1 *Phos* k* puls k* *Rhus-t* k* sang k* sars sep bg1 sil bg1 stann k* sulph bg1 thuj k* zinc bg1
    - ⁝ **amel.**: dig sil k*
    - ⁝ **bed** agg.; in: am-c k*
    - ⁝ **walking** agg.: mang k*
  - **night**: **Apis** aur bg2 *Carb-v* syc pte1*•
  - **alternating** with | **Eye**; inflammation of (See EYE - Inflammation - alternating - feet)
  - **apyrexia**; during: apis c1
  - **ascending** stairs agg.: *Nat-m*
  - **bed** amel.; when foot is out of: sulph
  - **blue** with red spots: elaps *Lach*
  - **burning**: canth con h2 puls h1
  - **chill**; during: ars bg2 chin bg2 *Ferr* bg2 kali-c bg2 phos bg2 puls bg2 sep bg2 sil bg2 sulph bg2

Extremities

- **chlorosis**; during: *Ferr* k*
- **cold**:
  - **agg.**: *Apis* k* *Calc* k* kreos petr hr1
  - **water** | **amel.**: led tl1
- **cramp**, after: graph h2
- **dancing**; after: *Borx* k* bov k*
- **edematous**: acet-ac acetan br1 *Anthraci* **Apis** *Apoc* apoc-a vh *Arg-met* *Arg-n* **Ars** ars-i k2 arund asaf *Aur* *Aur-m* aur-s k2 bov *Bry* *Cact* cain *Calc* *Calc-ar* calc-i k2 calc-s k* *Camph* *Canth* carb-ac carbn-s k2 card-m *Cench* **Chel** *Chin* chinin-ar *Cocc* *Colch* *Dig* k* dulc k2 *Eup-per* *Ferr* *Ferr-i* *Ferr-m* **Graph** *Hell* *Hydr* *Iod* k* *Kali-c* kali-i *Lach* led k2 **Lyc** *Lycps-v* mag-c *Mag-m* **Med** k* *Merc* **Merc-c** *Nat-ar* nat-c k2 *Nat-m* *Nat-s* *Nit-ac* *Nux-m* petr *Phos* *Plb* prun psor al2 ptel tl1* puls pyrog rhod rhus-t **Samb** k* sars senec sin-n squil vl1.nl stann *Stront-c* sul-i k2 thuj vesp *Zinc* zinc-p k2
  - **one** foot only: *Kali-c* mtf33 phos h2 puls h1
  - **left**: kali-c mtf33
- **exertion**, unusual: rhod k*
- **fever**; during: *Ars* bg2 bry bg2 caust bg2 chin bg2 **Ferr** b7a.de* **Lyc** bg2 *Puls* bg2 sec bg2 sil bg2
- **hard**: *Ars* chin h1 graph h2 vip k*
- **hot**: *Ars* k* **Bry** k* chin coli rly4• ignis-alc es2• led tl1 *Lyc* k* puls k* rhus-t
- **hydrothorax**: *Apis* merc-sul
- **inflamed**: calc carb-an k* zinc k*
- **itching**: ars k* puls k2 sol-ni
- **liver** disturbances, in: ptel vml3•
- **menses** | **before** | **agg.**: apis bro1 arist-cl sp1 bar-c bov sne *Bry* b7a.de graph bro1 *Lyc* k* oxal-a rly4• puls bro1
  - **during** | **agg.**: apis bro1* but-ac sp1 *Calc* *Graph* k* *Lyc* k* *Merc* puls k2* sulph
- **painful**: apis ars k* aur k* chin k* con h2 *Led* mand rsj7• *Merc* ph-ac phos positr nl2• rhus-t sabad sars h2 sil h2 *Sulph* thuj h1 vanil fd5.de
- **perspiration**; during: *Ars* bg2 *Calc* bg2 caust bg2 *Ferr* bg2 *Lyc* bg2 merc bg2 nat-c bg2 nat-m bg2 ph-ac bg2 phos bg2 puls bg2 *Sep* bg2 sil bg2 sul-ac bg2 *Sulph* bg2
- **phthisis**: acet-ac *Stann*
- **pregnancy**: *Merc-c* sanic tl1 *Zinc*
- **red**: ars bry *Carb-v* chin colch tl1 con graph h2 hep kali-c led tl1 merc k* mur-ac nit-ac *Puls* k* rhus-t sil stann k* thuj urt-u tl1
- **reddish** blue: ars k*
- **rheumatic**: calc-s k2 *Chel*
- **sensation** of: **Apis** k* ars bg2 ars-met *Bell* b4a.de bros-gau mrc1 bry b7.de* ham fd3.de• helo c1 helo-s c1* mang h2* merc k* nat-m k* nat-p a1 ox-ac k* oxal-a rly4• petr bg2* phos k* ribo rly4• sars k* sep k* til k* zinc b4.de*
- **shining**: alum **Ars** k* colch tl1 led tl1 *Sabin* *Sulph*
- **sitting** agg.: carb-an k* lach k*
- **stinging**: *Carb-v* lyc merc *Phos* **Puls**
- **sudden**: am-c h2 arn k* cham k* verat k*
- **tingling**: puls h1
- **walking**:
  - **after** | **agg.**: aesc k* *Lach* *Phos* k* sep k*
  - **agg.**: sil
  - **air**; in open | **after** | **agg.**: mang h2
    - **agg.**: nit-ac sulph
- **warm** | **bed** | **agg.**: sulph
  - **going** from cold to: sulph k2
- **washing** agg.; after: aesc
- **yellowish** green: ars k*

▽ • **extending** to | **Calf**: am-c puls

○ • **Back** of feet: ars k* **Bry** k* calc k* canth b7.de* carb-an h2 caust b4a.de* lat-k a1 lyc k* *Merc* k* nux-v b7.de* *Plat* b4a.de *Puls* k* rhus-t *Sep* b4a.de *Sil* b4a.de staph k* sulph bg1 *Thuj* k* vip a1
  - **edematous**: puls mtf33
  - **Blood** vessels: *Thuj* b4a.de

- **Feet**: ...
  - **Blood** vessels: ambr bg2 ant-t bg2 **Arn** bg2 *Ars* bg2 *Aur* bg2 bar-c bg2 bell bg2 calc bg2 *Carb-v* bg2 caust bg2 coloc bg2 *Cycl* bg2 *Ferr* bg2 graph bg2 kreos bg2 lach bg2 **Lyc** bg2 mag-c bg2 **Nat-m** bg2 nux-v bg2 phos bg2 **Puls** bg2 rhod bg2 rhus-t bg2 sep bg2 sil bg2 spig bg2 spong bg2 stront-c bg2 sul-ac bg2* *Sulph* bg2 **Thuj** bg2 **Zinc** bg2
  - **Bones**: staph b7.de*
  - **Heels**: ant-c k* berb con k* hyper k* kali-i k* ketogl-ac rly4• lach b7.de* merc k* petr k* plb k* raph k*
    - **red**: con h2
  - **Joints**: ars *Calc* ferr c1 hep lyc mang merc morg-p pte1*• phos *Rhod* stann sulph
  - **Soles**: agar bro1 alum bro1 ambr b7.de* ars b4.de* arund k* bamb-a stb2.de• bros-gau mrc1 *Bry* k* *Calc* k* cham k* *Chin* k* *Coloc* ferr ptk1 kali-c k* kreos b7a.de led bro1 **Lyc** k* med *Nat-c* k* *Petr* k* plat b4a.de *Puls* k* sep bg2 sulph bg2
    - **left**: bros-gau mrc1
    - **morning**: nux-v k*
    - **evening**: petr h2
    - **sensation** of: (↗*Soft - feet - soles - sensation*) *Alum* k* androc srj1• apis b7a.de bry bg2 *Calc* b4a.de *Coloc* k* zinc k*
    - **soft**: chin k*
      - **longitudinal** swelling: apis b7a.de *Plb* b7a.de
    - **stepping** agg.: kali-c k*
    - **sudden**: cham k*
- **Fingers**: act-sp aeth k* agar k* alum k* alum-sil k2 am-c k* ammc ant-c *Apis* k* arist-cl sp1 *Ars* k* ars-s-f k2 bacls-7 pte1*• benz-ac berb bg2 bit-ar wht1• borx k* *Brom* b4a.de *Bry* k* bufo calc bg2 calc-s k* canth b7.de* carb-an k* carb-v carbn-s k* cardios-h rly4• chin bg2 chord-umb rly4• cinnm bro1 *Cit-v* k* cupr k* *Dig* k* dulc fd4.de euphr fl-ac bg2 fuma-ac rly4• get a1 *Graph* k* *Hell* b7a.de helo-s bnm14• hep k* iod bg2 *Kali-bi* k* kali-c k2 kali-m bro1 *Kali-n* k* ketogl-ac rly4• lach k* led bg2 *Lith-c* bro1 *Lyc* k* *Mag-c* k* *Mang* b4a.de mang-act bro1 *Merc* k* mur-ac k* nat-c k* nat-p nat-s nat-sil fd3.de• *Nit-ac* k* nux-v k* olnd k* *Phos* k* *Phyt* pieri-b mlk9.de plb k* psor *Puls* bro1 ran-b b7.de* ran-s k* **Rhus-t** k* rhus-v k* ruta fd4.de sec *Sep* b4a.de sil k* spong k* *Sulph* k* sumb k* tab k* tep k* *Thuj* k* triat br1 tritic-vg fd5.de vanil fd5.de verat-v vip k* [spect dfg1]
  - **left** | **heart** disease; in: lycps-v c1
  - **midnight**: carb-an k*
  - **morning**: *Ars* bamb-a stb2.de• calc-s k* nat-c k* nit-ac k* ran-s sec k* sulph k* tritic-vg fd5.de vanil fd5.de
  - **forenoon**: calc-s k*
  - **afternoon**: calc-s k*
  - **evening**: stront-c sulph k*
  - **night**: carb-an h2 dig k*
  - **burning**; with: olnd
  - **constipated**, while: mag-c h2
  - **cramp**, after: graph h2
  - **dissecting** wound, from: **Ars** *Lach*
  - **eruptions**, with: anac br1 psor
  - **hang** down agg.; letting arms: am-c phos
  - **hard**: ars h2
  - **inflammatory**: nat-c bg2
  - **motion** agg.: bry tl1
  - **nodular** swellings: anac *Lyc* mag-c syc pte1•
  - **perspiration**; during: carb-an bg2
  - **red**: mag-c h2
  - **sensation** of: dulc fd4.de ham fd3.de• hydrog srj2• kali-n ptk1 kali-s fd4.de nat-sil fd3.de•
  - **walking** agg.; after: act-sp

○ • **Bones**: *Carb-an* myris br1 symph fd3.de•
  - **First**: chinin-s chord-umb rly4• *Fl-ac* fuma-ac a lac-ac k* *Lach* *Lyc* mag-c k* merc nat-sil fd3.de• phos staph sulph k* thuj k*
    - **left** | **Joints**: gink-b sbd1•
  - **Fourth**: bry k* hyos k* *Mang* rhus-t k*
    - **Middle** joint: sulph h2

- **Joints**: act-sp mtf11 agn b7.de* am-c k* ambr bg2 anag ang apis *Ars* berb *Brom* b4a.de *Bry* k* bufo *Calc* k* canth bg2 carb-v bg2 carneg-g rwt1• *Caul* caust *Cham* k* chin k* chord-umb rly4• colch euphr k* fuma-ac rly4• graph bg2 *Hep* k* hyos k* iod k* kali-bi bg2 *Lac-ac* *Led* b7a.de *Lyc* k* med *Merc* k* morg-p pte1*• *Nit-ac* k* *Phyt* psor al2 rhod *Rhus-t* k* spig mtf11 spong k* sulph b4a.de* symph fd3.de•
  - **burning** and pulsating: bufo
  - **gouty**: agn hr1 anag *Kali-i* **Lyc** stel br1 *Sulph*
  - **hot**: bry *Hep*
  - **sensation** of:
    - **grasping** something agg.: bry
    - **writing** agg.: bry a1*
  - **Middle**: lyc h2 spong fd4.de
  - **Proximal** joint: eucal a1 merc k* vinc k*
- **Nails**; close to: psil ft1
- **Periosteum**: brom b4a.de *Fl-ac* b4a.de sil b4a.de
- **Second**: apis borx calc-s k* chord-umb rly4• iris mag-c h2 morg-p fmm1• phos sulph k* syph thuj k* vanil fd5.de
  - **right**: cassia-s ccrh1•
  - **17** h: thuj
  - **afternoon**: calc-s k*
  - **Joints**: berb a1 calc-s a1 graph a1 lyc k* morg-p pte1•
    - **Distal**: carb-v h2
    - **Middle**: ars-h hr1 graph h2
- **Third**: bry k* calc olnd k* ruta fd4.de sulph k* thuj k* vanil fd5.de
  - **Middle** joint: sulph h2
- **Tips**: calc b4a.de* calc-i k2 fl-ac k* kreos k* mur-ac k* *Rhus-t* k* *Spong* b7a.de tab k* *Thuj* k* vinc bg2

\- **Forearms**: aeth c1 anac k* ant-c k* apis aran k* arn *Ars* k* aur aur-ar k2 berb k* bufo cadm-s calc k* caust k* crot-c k* crot-t k* dig k* *Ferr-p* *Graph* *Lach* k* lyc k* *Merc* k* morg-p pte1• nux-v k* op k* plb *Rhus-t* k* *Samb* b7a.de sep k* sulph k* vesp vip k*

- **right**: carneg-g rwt1• osteo-a jl2
- **dark** blue: samb
- **gangrenous**: **Lach**
- **nodular** swellings: eupi mez mur-ac nat-m zinc
- **red**: lac-d sep k* **Sil**
  - **line**: *Lach*
- **sensation** of: aran c1
- ○ **Bones** | **Radius**: *Calc*
- **Elbow**; near: lyc
- **Periosteum**: *Aur* b4.de* caust bg2
- **Posterior** part: plb
- **Veins** of: puls k2

\- **Hands**: acon k* aesc aeth c1 *Agar* k* am-c k* am-m b7.de* anac k* ang k* ap-g br1 **Apis** k* apoc-a a1 aran k* *Arg-n* c2 arn *Ars* k* ars-i ars-s-f k2 arum-d arum-t arund atro *Aur* aur-ar k2 aur-i k2 bapt bg2 bar-m k* bart a1 *Bell* k* *Brom* b4a.de brucel sa3• *Bry* k* *Bufo* *Cact* k* *Calc* k* calc-ar k2 calc-i k2 calc-sil k2 carb-ac k* carb-v k2 carbn-s caust k* cham k* chel k* chin k* chinin-ar chinin-s cit-v a1* clem k* cob-n sp1 *Cocc* k* **Colch** k* coli jl2 com k* corn crot-c a1* crot-h a1* crot-t k* cub k* cupr k* *Dig* k* dulc fd4.de elaps euphr *Ferr* k* ferr-ar ferr-p k* fl-ac k* get a1 grat k* guare k* *Hell* b7a.de helodr-cal knl2• *Hep* k* hipp a1 hyos k* iod kali-ar kali-c k* kali-n bg2 kali-p lac-c *Lach* k* lat-h bnm5• laur bg2 led k2 *Lyc* k* manc k* mang bg2 med bg2 *Merc* k* mez k* moni rfm1• morg-p pte1*• *Mosch* k* mur-ac k* naja k* nat-c k* nat-m k* *Nit-ac* k* nux-v k* olib-sac wmh1 op k* ped a1 ph-ac *Phel* *Phos* k* pieri-b mlk9.de pin-con oss2• plan plb k* *Psor* ptel bg2 rhod k* *Rhus-t* k* *Rhus-v* k* ruta k* *Samb* k* sanic *Sec* k* sep b4a.de* sil sol-ni spira a1 spong k* *Stann* k* staphycoc rly4• *Stict* stram k* sul-ac k* *Sulph* k* tep k* thuj k* tritic-vg fd5.de vanil fd5.de vesp k* vip k*

- **right**: am-c bg2 ars bg2 aur bg2 bamb-a stb2.de• *Dig* k* hep k* lyc k* nat-m k* phos sil bg2 spig bg2 viol-o bg2
- **left**: aesc bg2 am-c bg2 anac bg2 ars bg2 cact bg2 chel bg2 chin bg2 lach bg2 lycps-v bg2 merc bg2 vesp bg2
  - **accompanied** by | **Heart** symptoms (See CHEST - Heart; complaints - accompanied - hand - left - swelling)
- **daytime**: nat-m

\- **Hands**: ...

- **morning**: bamb-a stb2.de• coc-c bg1 nat-c b4a.de nat-chl br1 nat-m k* pieri-b mlk9.de tritic-vg fd5.de vanil fd5.de
  - **waking**; on: sanic
- **afternoon**: *Nat-c* k* vanil fd5.de
- **evening**: aloe lyc k* rhus-t h1 *Stann* k* sulph k*
- **night**: aran ars caust k* dig k* kali-n
  - **waking** agg.; after: samb
- **bluish**: lach bg2 samb bg2
- **chill**; during: lyc bro1
- **cough** agg.; during: acon b7.de*
- **dark**: *Bell* k* **Lach** *Vip*
- **eczema**, with: psor
- **edematous**: **Apis** apoc-a vh ars-i k2 ars-s-f k2 *Aur* *Cact* *Calc-ar* k* *Canth* chinin-ar crot-h ferr k2 iod k2 kali-c k2 kali-i k2 *Lyc* nat-c k2 *Phos* k* psor al2 sul-i k2
- **endocarditis**: *Aur-m* *Cact*
- **erysipelatous**: **Rhus-t** *Rhus-v* k*
- **feeling** as if (See sensation)
- **gangrenous**: **Ars** **Lach** **Sec**
- **hard**: graph h2
- **hot**: *Bell* *Bry* chel *Cist* *Rhus-t* k*
- **inflammatory**: aur cupr
- **intermittent**, in: *Lyc*
- **itching**: sol-ni *Urt-u* k*
- **menses**; during: *Graph* *Merc*
- **motion** | **amel.**: nat-c h2
- **nodular** swellings: ars nat-m nit-ac sul-ac
- **painful**: ars k* crot-c mre1.fr *Cur* dig k* **Lach** vesp
- **pale**: bell k* lyc k* nux-v k*
- **phlegmonous**: plb k*
- **phthisis**, in: *Stann*
- **pregnancy** agg.; during: sanic tl1
- **red**: agar tl1 lyc h2
- **reddish**: graph h2
- **room**; when entering a: aeth
- **sensation** of: aesc k* aeth k* ang bg1 aran k* bamb-a stb2.de• bapt bg1 bell bg1 chel k* chinin-s clem bg1 cocc bg1* coll bg1* dulc fd4.de gins a1 hyos bg1 kali-n br1* kali-s fd4.de laur k* lyc bg1 manc bg1 mang k* med bg1 mez k* nat-sil fd3.de• *Op* k* pen a1 ptel bg1 raph k* rhus-t bg1 sacch-a fd2.de• stront-c ptk1 ter ptk1 tritic-vg fd5.de
  - **night** | **waking**; on: aran br1
  - **grasping** something agg.: **Caust**
  - **walking** in open air agg.; after: aeth c1 mang k*
- **shining**: bell vip k*
- **walking** in open air agg.: mang h2
- **warm**; going from cold to: sulph k2
- **washing** agg.: aesc
- ▽ **extending** to:
  - **Elbow**: crot-c k* crot-h k* kali-c k2 ruta
  - **Pectoral** muscles: crot-h k*
- ○ **Back** of hands: apis b7a.de *Brucel* sa3• *Bry* b7a.de calc h2 kali-p fd1.de• **Lach** b7a.de mez h2 mur-ac h2 olnd bg2 rhus-t b7a.de
  - **left** hand: am-m h2 *Brucel* sa3• *Calc-ar* chin kali-p fd1.de•
  - **sensation** of swelling: iod ptk1
- **Behind** the thumb: am-m k*
- **Blood** vessels | **fever**; during: am-c bg2 **Arn** bg2 bar-c bg2 calc bg2 *Chin* bg2 nux-v bg2 *Phos* bg2 **Puls** bg2 rhus-t bg2 *Sulph* bg2 **Thuj** bg2
- **Bones**: *Aur*
- **Palms**: aesc bro1 agar bro1 *Apis* bro1 arg-n bro1 ars bro1 arund bro1 bry bro1 *Cact* bro1 calc bro1 cham crot-h bro1 elaps bro1 ferr-p bro1 *Lyc* nat-hchls bro1 *Rhus-d* bro1
  - **night**: ars

Extremities

- **Palms**: ...
  - **sensation** of: ars
- **Tendons**: plb k*
- **Veins**: *(↗Fullness - hands - veins)* alum k* am-c bg2* aml-ns bro1 *Ant-t* bro1 *Arn* k* ars-h bar-c k* bond a1 bry bg2 calc k* *Carb-an* bro1 castm cent a1 *Chel* k* *Chin* k* *Cic* k* crot-t k* cycl k* dig bro1 elaps bro1 *Fl-ac* gast a1 *Ham* k* *Laur* k* *Led* m-aust b7.de manc k* med hr1 meny k* merc k* mosch b7.de *Nit-ac* bro1 nit-s-d a1 *Nux-v* k* olnd k* *Op* k* ph-ac k* **Phos** k● * pilo a1 plan k* plb k* **PULS** k ●* rheum k* rhod k* *Rhus-t* k* ruta b7.de* samb bro1 sars k* spira a1 spirae a1 staph b7.de* stront-c k* **Sulph** k ●* sumb k* thuj k* thyr ptk1 *Verat* bro1 vip bg2*
  - **forenoon**: indg k*
  - **afternoon**: alum k* mez k*
    - **17** h: chel
  - **cold** washing agg.; after: am-c k*
  - **eating**; after: ruta
  - **hang** down agg.; letting arms: phos h2

- **Hips**: *Apis* bg2 arn bg2 ars b4a.de* bell bg2 borx bg2 calc bg2 echi bg2 ham bg2 iod b4.de* lach bg2 lyc bg2 merc b4a.de* ph-ac b4a.de plb k* puls bg2 pyrog bg2 rhus-t bg2 *Sep* b4.de* *Sil* b4a.de* *Staph* bg2 sulph b4a.de* vip bg2
  - **sensation** of: lil-t k*
    - **Above** hip:
      - **right**: phos h
      - **left**: chel h

- **Joints**: *Abrot* k* acon k* **Act-sp** k* agn ammc hr1 anag k* *Ant-t* k* *Apis* k* apoc k* *Arn* k* *Ars* k* ars-s-f k2 asc-c c1 asc-t k* aur k* aur-ar k2 *Aur-m* k* **Bell** k* benz-ac bro1 berb k* bov bro1 **Bry** k* bufo *Calc* k* calc-f k* canth bro1 cardios-h rly4• caust hr1* chin k* chinin-s bro1 *Cimic* k* clem k* *Cocc* **Colch** k* coli jl2 con k* dig br1* dulc k2* eup-per k2 *Ferr-p* k* *Guaj* k* *Ham* k* **Hep** k* hip-ac sp1 hippoz hr1 iod bro1 kali-ar k2* kali-bi k2* *Kali-chl* k* kali-i k* *Kali-m* bro1 *Kalm* k* *Lac-ac* k* lac-c k2* *Lach* **Led** k* *Lith-c* bro1 *Lyc* k* mang k* mang-act bro1 med k* *Merc* k* *Nat-m* k* *Nux-v* k* *Phyt* bro1 puls bro1* rham-cal bro1 *Rhod* k* *Rhus-t* k* sabin k* *Sal-ac* k* saroth sp1 sil sol-t-ae k* spong fd4.de *Stel* bro1 stict k* **Sulph** k* tarent k* *Ter* k* thuj k* verat gk *Verat-v* k*
  - **afternoon**: chin k*
  - **bluish**: **Lach** k*
  - **chronic**: diph mtf11 mang-act mtf11
  - **edematous**: *(↗GENERALS - Dropsy - internal)* ant-t k* apis k* apoc k2 arn bg2* ars-s-f k2 bov bg2 *Bry* bg2* canth bg2* *Caust* cedr bg2* chin bg2* chinin-s bg2* iod bg2* kali-i bg2* kali-m bg2* *Led* lyc bg *Nat-m* nux-v bg puls bg *Ran-b* bg2* samb bg2* *Sulph* ptk1 *Thuj*
    - **fractures**; after: bov ptk1
  - **exertion** agg.; after: act-sp k*
  - **fatigue**, from slight: act-sp ptk1*
  - **red** | **dark** red: bry bro1 kalm bro1 *Rhus-t* bro1
  - **sensation**, of: caj caps *Par* sabin
  - **shining**: *Acon* bro1 *Apis* bro1 *Bell* bro1 *Bry* bro1 dig bro1 mang-act bro1 sabin bro1
  - **white**: **Ant-c** bg2* *Apis* bro1 *Ars* bg2* aur bro1 bry bro1 *Calc* bro1 calc-p bro1 *Caust* k* cist bro1 clem bg2 *Colch* bro1 coloc ptk1 *Con* bg2* dig bro1 iod bg2* kali-s k* *Kreos* bg2* *Lach* bg2 led br1* merc bro1* *Merc-c* bro1 petr bg2 ph-ac bro1 phos bg2* puls bro1* rhod bro1 rhus-t bg2* sabin bg2 **Sil** bg2* *Staph* bg2 *Sulph* k* symph bro1 tub bro1

- **Knees**: acon *Aesc* agn b7.de* ammc anil a1 ant-c ant-t *Anthraci* *Apis* k* arge-pl rwt5• *Arn* k* *Ars* *Ars-i* ars-s-f k2 arund k* aur-m k* *Bar-c* b4a.de *Bar-m* *Bell* b4a.de* benz-ac k* **Berb** k* **Bry** k* bufo k* **Calc** k* calc-f gm1 calc-i k2 *Calc-p* calc-s calc-sil k2 *Caps* b7a.de cardios-h rly4• caust bro1 cedr bro1 *Cham* b7a.de *Chin* k* chir-fl bnm4• *Cic* k* *Clem* k* coc-c k* *Cocc* k* *Colch* k* con k* *Cop* dulc b4a.de* elat hr1 ferr k* ferr-ar *Fl-ac* **Hep** k* *Iod* k* kali-ar *Kali-c* *Kali-i* bro1 kali-s kali-sil k2 kreos k* lac-ac k* *Lac-c* k* *Lach* k* **Led** k* **Lyc** k* mag-c bro1 *Mang* b4a.de merc k* *Mez* b4a.de morg-p pte1• mur-ac k* *Nat-m* nat-pyru rly4• nat-sil fd3.de• nit-ac k* *Nux-v* k* *Petr* b4a.de *Phyt* plb a1 **Puls** k* *Rhod* k* **Rhus-t** k* ruta b7.de* *Sal-ac* k* *Sars* k* *Sep* k* **Sil** k* *Sulph* k* tarent k* ter thiam rly4• tritic-vg fd5.de *Tub* k* ven-m rsj12•
  - **right**: anthraq rly4• arge-pl rwt5• *Benz-ac* chin k* *Elat* nat-sil fd3.de• **Sulph** tarent *Ter* thiam rly4• *Tub*
  - **left**: *Aesc* *Cic* colch bg1 pot-e rly4•
  - **night**: *Calc*

- **Knees**: ...
  - **alternating** with | **Wrist**; swelling of: *(↗wrists - alternating)* kreos
  - **coldness** | **amel.**: led tl1
  - **dropsical**: *Ant-t* *Apis* k* ars-s-f k2 *Bry* *Calc* *Con* dig *Fl-ac* hyper *Iod* k* *Merc* **Rhus-t** k* *Sil* sul-i k2 **Sulph** k* [tax jsj7]
  - **fatty**: calc b4a.de dig k*
  - **gonorrhea**, after: *Clem* **Med**
  - **gouty**●: **Benz-ac** k ● **CALC** k ● **Kali-i** k ● **LED** k ● **Lyc** k ● **Plb** k ●
  - **hot**: *Bell* *Calc* *Chin* k* *Ferr-p* *Iod* **Puls** **Verat-v**
  - **inflammatory** (See Inflammation - knees)
  - **painful**: *Apis* aur-m chin h1 *Cic* dulc fd4.de *Led* *Mag-c* *Nit-ac* *Nux-v* **Puls** *Rhus-t* sal-ac sars sep tritic-vg fd5.de
  - **painless**: *Lyc* **Puls**
  - **purple**: aran k*
  - **rheumatic**: *Acon* *Apis* *Ars* berb **Bry** calc-s clem **Led** *Lyc* *Rhus-t* sal-ac verat-v
    - **cold** applications | **amel.**: *Lac-c* **Led** *Puls*
  - **scrofulous**: arn *Ars* **Calc** *Ferr* *Iod* *Lyc* **Puls** *Sil* **Sulph**
  - **sensation** of: alum k* ammc k* canth k* carb-v k* dig k* *Kali-i* k* *Lach* merc k* nat-sil fd3.de• nit-ac k* pyrus rb2 ruta fd4.de tritic-vg fd5.de
    - **afternoon**: alum k*
    - **night**: *Kali-i* k*
    - **sitting** agg.: ammc k* nat-sil fd3.de•
  - **spongy**: *Ant-c* b7a.de ars b4a.de *Calc* clem b4a.de con b4a.de iod b4a.de *Kali-i* petr b4a.de phos b4a.de **Sil** k* sulph b4a.de
  - **white** swelling (= fungus articulosum): abrot bg2 acon bro1 *Ant-c* k* apis bg2* arn k* ars-i bg2 bar-c bg2 bry b7a.de* *Calc* k* calc-f bg2 calc-i bg2 calc-p bg2* chin b7a.de* *Cist* bro1 form-ac bg2 *Hep* b4a.de *Iod* k* kali-c bg2* *Kali-i* k* *Kreos* b7a.de led bro1 *Lyc* k* nit-ac bg2 nux-v bg2 *Ol-j* ph-ac bg2* *Phos* k* psor bg2 *Puls* k* rhod b4a.de* *Rhus-t* k* *Sabin* b7.de* *Sep* b4a.de *Sil* k* slag bro1 *Stict* bro1 *Sulph* k* tub bg2* *Verat-v*
  - **women**; in: hip-ac sp1
- ○ **Bursae**: sil ptk1
- **Hollow** of knees: ars *Mag-c* k* pot-e rly4• *Rhus-t*
  - **painful**: *Mag-c* *Rhus-t*
  - **running**; sensation of gradually swelling during: nit-ac dgt
  - **sensation** of: *Nit-ac*
- **Patella**: coloc *Iod* b4a.de sep *Spong* b7a.de

- **Legs**: acet-ac k* *Acon* k* agn ambr b7.de* anil a1 *Apis* bro1 *Arist-cl* sp1 arn **Ars** k* ars-i ars-s-f k2 *Asaf* b7.de* *Aur* k* aur-ar k2 aur-i k2 *Aur-m* *Bad* borx k* bov k* *Bry* k* bufo but-ac sp1 *Cact* k* *Calc* k* calc-i k2 calc-s calc-sil k2 carb-v b4.de* carbn-s *Caust* *Cench* chel k* *Chin* k* clem k* *Colch* k* coli jl2 coloc k* cop k* cortiso sp1 *Crot-c* *Crot-h* k* *Dig* k* dulc k* elae a1 eup-per bro1 *Ferr* k* ferr-i fl-ac bro1 *Graph* k* guaj b4a.de* *Hell* helodr-cal knl2• hyos b7.de* iod k* kali-ar *Kali-bi* k* kali-c k* *Kali-chl* kali-i k* kali-m k2 kali-n k* kali-p kali-s kali-sil k2 lac-del hm2• *Lach* k* lat-m sp1* lath bro1 **Led** k* **Lyc** k* manc k* *Med* *Merc* k* morph k* nat-ar *Nat-c* k* nat-pyru rly4• nat-s k* nux-v k* phos bro1 plb k* *Puls* k* rauw sp1 *Rhod* k* rhus-t k* rhus-v k* ribo rly4• ruta **Samb** k* sec k* seneg b4a.de *Sep* k* **Sil** k* *Stann* k* *Staph* bro1 stront-br c2 stront-c b4.de* sulph k* *Syph* tanac a1 *Ter* thyr bro1 toxi a1 vip k* visc bro1 *Zinc* k*
  - **morning**: arist-m a1 *Aur* ruta fd4.de
  - **afternoon**: chel k*
    - **16** h: sang
  - **evening**: agn bufo dulc k* haem a1 mez k* nat-m sang k* stront-c
  - **accompanied** by | **diarrhea**: acet-ac mtf11
  - **bluish**: **Lach** *Led* *Puls*
  - **cold** agg.: nux-v k*
  - **edematous**: ars-i k2 aur-s k2 boerh-d zzc1• ferr mtf11 ferr-i k2 kali-m k2 nat-ar k2 ptel tl1 ruta fd4.de
  - **exertion** agg.: rhod k*
  - **hang** down; letting leg: lath br1
  - **hard**: aur h2 bov k* graph h2
  - **lymphatic** swelling: berb hr1
  - **menses** | **before** | **agg.**: ignis-alc es2• pneu jl2

- **menses**: ...
  - **during** | **agg.**: (↗*lower - menses)* sulph
- **painful**: dig k* **Led** med k2
- **purplish**: petr hr1
- **red**: aur h2 bov k*
- **riding** agg.: guaj k2
- **sensation** of: chin b7.de* staph b7.de*
- **sitting** agg.: sep k*
- **standing** agg.: merc-cy k* mez k* sep k*
- **walking** | **amel.**: *Aur Sep* k*
- ○ **Bones**: guaj b4a.de **Phos** b4.de* stront-c b4.de*
  - **Tibia**: aur b4a.de *Aur-m Calc-p* caust bg2 graph *Hep* b4a.de lach *Merc* k* **Mez** b4a.de *Nit-ac* b4a.de *Ph-ac* b4a.de *Phos* k* rhus-t *Sil* k* stann sulph thuj k* tub c1
- **Calves**: berb bry k* *Calc* carb-v k* chel bg2 chin k* *Dulc* k* graph hyos kali-n bg2 *Led* k* mez k* phos h2 puls k* *Rhus-t* b7a.de sil k* sulph k*
  - **white**: *Lyc* b4a.de mez b4a.de
  - **Veins** of: cycl h1 ham fd3.de•
- **Periosteum**: *Aur* b4.de*
- **Tendo** Achillis: berb k* kali-bi k* *Mur-ac Sep* symph b7a.de *Zinc* k*
  - **painful**: kali-bi ptk1

- **Lower** limbs: act-sp k* agav-a br1 am-c k* apis *Ars* k* arund k* aur-ar k2 aur-m *Bar-m Berb* k* brass a1 bry *Calc* k* carb-an b4.de* *Carb-v* k* carbn-s caust k* *Chel* chin b7.de* chir-fl bnm4• *Colch* b7.de* con k* crot-c mre1.fr *Dulc* k* *Graph* k* *Hell* b7.de* iod k* *Kali-ar* k* kali-bi *Kali-c* k* *Kali-m* k* *Kali-n* k* lac-c k2 lach k* *Led Lyc* k* merc k* merc-sul br1 nat-c k* nat-m k* nat-p nit-ac k* nux-v petr k* *Phos* k* plb k* polyg-h puls *Rhus-t* rhus-v k* sec b7.de* *Sep* k* **Sil** k* sol-t-ae k* streptoc jl2 sul-i k2 **Sulph** k* tritic-vg fd5.de verat vip a1
- **right**: card-m bg2
- **left**: sang bg1
- **daytime**: dig
- **morning**: nux-v b7a.de sil k*
- **evening**: am-c bry b7a.de caust b4a.de cocc k* dulc b4a.de hyper led b7a.de merc b4a.de nat-m k* phos k* puls k* rhus-t k* stann k* *Stront-c* b4a.de
- **accompanied** by:
  - **Heart**; complaints of the (See CHEST - Heart; complaints - accompanied - lower - swelling)
  - **Upper** limbs; thin: lyc bg2
- **bluish**: lach
- **china**, after abuse of: **Puls** *Sulph*
- **chronic**: streptoc jl2
- **cold** agg.: asaf led bg2
- **dropsical**: (↗*GENERALS - Dropsy - external)* acet-ac aeth gsy1 ant-t ptk1 **Apis** *Apoc* arg-met **Ars** *Ars-i* arund aur *Aur-m* bros-gau mrc1 *Cact* cain *Calc* calc-ar calc-s *Carb-ac Carbn-s Cench Chel Chim* **Chin** k* cocc *Colch* cypra-eg sde6.de• *Dig Dulc* eup-per k* *Ferr* ferr-i *Fl-ac Graph Hell Hippoz Hydr* iod *Kali-c Lach Led* **Lyc** *Mag-m Med Merc* mur-ac nat-m k2 onos phos *Phyt* plb puls rhod *Rhus-t* ruta **Samb** k* sanic sars *Senec* sul-i k2 sulph *Ter* xan *Zinc*
  - **albuminuria**, in●: *Apis Ars Calc-ar Ferr* k* *Lach Sars Ter*
  - **scarlet** fever; after: **Apis** bar-m crot-h *Hell*
- **hard**: agav-a br1 ars aur bov chin graph led mag-c mez rhus-t
  - **cellulitis**: bad c1
- **heaviness** | **sensation** of: lac-del hrn2•
- **hot**: acon am-c *Arn* ars *Bry* calc carb-an *Chin* coc-c cocc colch graph iod kali-c led lyc petr puls sars sec sep stann
- **inflammatory**: acon calc iod puls rhus-t sil
- **itching**: cocc
- **large**: sulph
- **lymphatic**: bar-c berb k*
- **menses**; during: (↗*legs - menses - during - agg.)* apis apoc ars calc graph lyc
- **painful**: acon agav-a br1 ant-c arn ars carb-an chin con daph lach mag-c merc mur-ac hr1 nux-v puls sep sil

- **Lower** limbs – **painful**: ...
  - **burning**: ant-c *Ars* mur-ac petr ph-ac puls
  - **cutting**: ph-ac
  - **drawing**: arn led puls
  - **pressing**: led
  - **pulsating**: ph-ac plat
  - **stitching**: acon am-c arn bry carb-v cocc graph iod led lyc merc petr *Puls* sars
  - **tearing**: colch led merc plat puls
  - **tense**: bry chin led sars thuj
- **phlegmasia** alba dolens (See Milk)
- **red**: acon am-c ant-c arn bry calc carb-v chin hep lach nat-c nux-v petr puls sabin sars sil stann thuj
  - **bright**: iod
  - **spots**: acon chin
    - **blisters**; or bluish black: ars
- **rheumatic**: hep
- **ropes**; like: bufo bg2
- **shining**: acon arn ars bell bry merc sabin sulph
- **soft**: chin led
- **stinging**: **Apis** graph **Led** *Puls*
- **transparent**: *Apis* sulph
- **walking**:
  - **agg.**: bros-gau mrc1 phos rhus-t
  - **air** agg.; in open: phos
- **waxy**: apis
- **white**: apis ars k* bell k* *Calc* k* chin mrr1 graph k* iod k* kreos lyc k* merc k* nux-v rhus-t sulph k*
- ○ **Blood** vessels: bry bg2 cycl b7.de* ferr b7a.de *M-aust* b7.de puls b7.de*
- **Bones**: **Asaf** b7.de* *Aur* b4.de* *Calc* b4.de* carb-an b4.de* *Coloc* b4.de* *Dulc* b4.de* guaj b4a.de *Kreos* b7a.de *Lyc* b4.de* merc b4a.de *Mez* b4.de* *Ph-ac* b4.de* *Phos* b4.de* *Rhus-t* b7.de* *Ruta* b7.de* *Sil* b4.de* spig b7.de* *Staph* b4.de* *Sulph* b4.de*
- **Periosteum**: staph b7.de*

- **Nates**: *Coloc* crot-t k* dulc k* ph-ac k* sulph
- **Shoulders**: acon k* apis bry k* calc calc-p k* carbn-o *Coloc* k* crot-h k* crot-t ferr-p k2 kali-br a1 kali-c k* kali-chl kali-i lac-ac bg2 lac-c lach k* merc merc-d a1 thuj k* vip k*
- **right**: osteo-a jl2
- **pustules**, after: kali-br a1 kali-c k*
- **vaccination**; after: apis thuj
- **Thighs**: *Acet-ac* bro1 agn *Apis* bro1 arn k* ars k* aur bro1 both k* *Cact* bro1 calad k* *Calc* b4a.de calo carbn-o carc mlr1• caust b4a.de chel bro1 chin k* colch bro1 con h2 *Dig* bro1 eup-per bro1 *Ferr* bro1 fl-ac bro1 graph bro1 *Ham* kali-c k* kali-n h2 *Lach* k* lath bro1 led lyc k* merc k* *Petr* b4a.de phos bro1 plb b7.de* puls *Rhus-t* bro1 samb bro1 sep bro1 *Staph* bro1 stront-c bro1 sulph bro1 ter thyr bro1 vip k* visc bro1
- **evening**: agn
- **sensation** of: ham fd3.de• prun k* staph b7.de*
- ○ **Bends** of thighs: dig k*
- **Femur**: *Mez* **Sil** *Stront-c*
  - **rachitic** infants; in: calc-f bro1
- **Glands**: *Calc*
- **Inner** side | **red**: stram ptk1
- **Thumbs**: ambr b7.de* berb coc-c k* cupr k* hep led bg2 morg-g pte1• naja nux-v k* phos bg2 plut-n srj7• rhus-t k* sang k* spig sulph k* trach a1 vesp k* vip k*
- **painful**: morg-g fmm1•
- **pus**, containing: sulph
- **sensation** of: berb k* plb k*
- ○ **Joints** of: ambr a1 nux-v k* phos h2 spig sulph symph fd3.de•
  - **right**: ephe-si hsj1•

Extremities

- **Toes**: am-c k* ammc *Apis* *Am* k* *Aur-m* bamb-a stb2.de• bar-c k* *Carb-an* k* *Carb-v* k* chin coc-c k* *Coloc* crot-h k* *Daph* **Graph** k* hydrog srj2• hyper k* *Led* k* *Merc* k* mur-ac k* *Nat-c* k* *Nit-ac* k* oxal-a rly4• *Paeon* k* *Ph-ac* k* *Phos* k* plat k* positr nl2• pyrus **Sabad** b7a.de *Sabin* k* spong fd4.de *Sulph* k* syph tarent k* *Thuj* k* tritic-vg fd5.de vip k* zinc k*
  - **right**: daph br1
  - **left** | **Fourth**: hydrog srj2•
  - **evening**: am-c k*
  - **night**: coc-c k*
  - **menses**; during: graph mrr1
  - **red**: am-c k* *Aur-m* carb-v thuj
  - **sensation** of: **Apis** k* pyrus rb2 sars h2 zinc ptk1
  - **wet** agg.; after getting feet: nit-ac k*
  - ○ **Balls**: *Borx* b4a.de graph h2 led b7.de* plat h2 tritic-vg fd5.de
  - **Fifth**: androc srj1• bamb-a stb2.de• dream-p sdj1• phos k* spong fd4.de tritic-vg fd5.de
    - **sensation** of: mur-ac k*
  - **First**: *Am-c* k* *Apis* aster bar-c *Benz-ac* bry k* chin coc-c k* eup-per bg2 *Led* k* *Mang* med nat-c k* plb k* positr nl2• ruta sabin k* sulph k* tep k*
    - **right**: *Benz-ac* coca-c sk4•
    - **left**: eup-per
    - **evening** | **bed** agg.; in: *Am-c*
    - **night**: chin
    - **gout**-like: aster *Benz-ac* eup-per plb k* *Rhod* sabin
    - **painful**: am-c gsy1 bar-c led tl1 rhus-t tl1 tung-met bdx1•
    - **Balls**: both br1 carb-an h2 led br1* rhus-t tl1
    - **Joints**: apis benz-ac k* get a1 ph-ac k* sang k*
  - **Joints**: *Ph-ac* b4a.de *Plat* b4a.de plb k*
  - **Second**: oxal-a rly4•
  - **Third**: crot-c k*
  - **Tips**: chin k* mur-ac k* thuj k*
- **Upper** arms: acon anac *Ant-c* b7.de* *Apis* aran arn k* berb *Bry* k* calc-p coloc k* *Graph* k* kali-c k* morg-p pte1• puls sang sep k* sulph k* tep k* vip
  - **right**: cassia-s ccrh1•
  - **cold** applications agg.: cassia-s ccrh1•
  - **hard**: *Sulph* k*
  - **hot**: *Sulph* k*
  - **motion** agg.: cassia-s ccrh1•
  - **nodular** swellings: ars nat-m zinc
  - **painful**: *Puls*
  - **rest** | **amel.**: cassia-s ccrh1•
  - **vaccination**: **Sil** *Sulph* **Thuj**
  - **warm** applications | **amel.**: cassia-s ccrh1•
  - ○ **Bone** of: guare k* tep k*
- **Upper** limbs: acon k* agar alum k* anac ant-c bg2 *Anthraci* *Apis* k* *Aran* aran-ix sp1 arist-cl sp1 *Ars* k* ars-s-f k2 bar-c k* *Bell* k* both bov b4.de* *Bry* k* *Bufo* cadm-s calc b4.de* *Calc-p* bg2 *Chin* k* chinin-s chlol cinnb k* cob-n sp1 colch cop *Crot-h* k* crot-t *Cur* dig dor dulc k* elaps ferr ferr-ar *Ferr-p* form graph *Hell* b7.de* *Hydr* iod k* kali-bi kali-c b4.de* kali-i k* *Lach* led hr1 *Lyc* k* mag-c b4.de* manc merc k* merc-c k* *Mez* k* morg-p fmm1• naja nat-s nit-ac b4.de* *Phos* k* **Rhus-t** k* rhus-v scol a1 sec b7.de* sep k* sil sol-ni stry sul-ac *Sulph* k* syph k2 vario verat k* vesp vip k*
  - **left**: lach bg1
  - **afternoon**: nat-c
  - **evening**: *Cur* rhus-t k* stann
  - **night**: *Aran* dig kali-n phos
  - **accompanied** by | **sciatica** (See Pain - lower limbs - sciatic - accompanied - arms)
  - **black**: *Carb-v* *Mur-ac*
  - **blisters**, black, putrid: *Ars*
  - **bluish**: ars bufo elaps **Lach** k* samb
  - **burning**: mur-ac olnd sulph
  - **cold** agg.: lach *Puls*
  - **cramps**, after: graph h2

Swelling – Upper limbs: ...

  - **edematous**: *Apis* ars-s-f k2 *Aur* aur-m cact calc-ar crot-h *Ferr* *Lach* *Lyc* *Merc-c* *Phos* sil
  - **erysipelatous**: scol c1
  - **hard**: ars carb-an graph h2 lach led sulph k*
  - **heart** disease; in: lycps-v
  - **hot**: ant-c *Apis* bry k* bufo *Cocc* k* *Hep* *Merc* mez *Puls* b7a.de rhus-t k* sulph k*
  - **lymphatic**: berb k*
  - **nodular** swellings: *Agar* *Ars* carb-an *Caust* dulc lyc *Mag-c* mag-m mang *Mez* mur-ac nat-m nit-ac sil stann zinc
  - **painful**: amph a1 ant-c chin hep kali-c *Lach* *Mosch* nux-v sep *Sulph* *Thuj*
  - **painless**: euphr lyc
  - **pale**: *Apis* bry nux-v
  - **paralysis**, after: sulph
  - **red**: alum h2 ant-c **Bell** *Bry* *Bufo* graph h2 *Hep* lac-d *Lyc* mag-c *Merc* sep spong *Thuj*
  - **rigidity**, with: sulph
  - **sensation** of: apis bg2 *Aran* vh1 *Ars* b4a.de *Bell* b4.de* *Caust* b4a.de cocc b7.de* glon bg2 *Kali-n* b4a.de kreos b7a.de laur b7.de* m-aust b7.de puls b7.de* sulph b4a.de verat b7.de*
  - **shining**: bry sulph
  - **stooping** agg.: sil h2
  - **uncovering** | **amel.**: chim k*
  - **white**: *Apis*
  - ○ **Bone**: aur b4a.de *Bry* b7a.de calc k* dig b4a.de dulc k* lyc k* mez k* phos b4.de* **Rhus-t** b7.de* *Sep* b4a.de *Sil* k* *Staph* b7a.de *Sulph* k*
  - **Joints**: calc
  - **Periosteum**: *Aur* *Merc* mez ph-ac bg2 **Rhus-t** bg2 **Sulph** bg2
    - **syphilitic**: calc-f sp1
  - **Veins** of: aesc bg2 agar bg2 alum b4.de *Am-c* b4.de* *Arn* b7.de* *Bar-c* b4.de* bry b7.de calc b4.de* chel b7.de chin b7.de* cic b7.de cycl b7.de fl-ac bg2 kali-bi bg2 lach bg2 laur b7a.de m-arct b7.de *Meny* b7.de* mosch b7.de *Nux-v* b7.de* *Phos* b4.de* puls b7.de* rhod b4.de ruta bg2 sars b4.de stront-c b4.de *Sulph* b4.de *Thuj* b4.de*
- **Wrists**: *Act-sp* agn b7.de* am-c am-m k* *Apis* aur k* aur-m k* bry b7.de* *Bufo* *Calc* k* carb-v k* *Crot-h* cub k* dulc k* euphr k* helo-s bnm14• *Hep* b4a.de *Iod* b4a.de kali-bi k* kreos k* *Lac-ac* k* *Lach* k* *Led* b7a.de mag-c k* mang b4a.de med c1 *Merc* k* phos k* plb k* rhod k* **Rhus-t** k* *Rhus-v* k* sabin k* sec k* sep k* sil b4a.de stict c1 stry k* sul-ac k* *Sulph* b4a.de tarent k* tep k* tritic-vg fd5.de vip k*
  - **right**: *Brucel* sa3• osteo-a jl2
  - **morning**: lac-ac k* tritic-vg fd5.de
  - **evening**: sep k*
  - **alternating** with swelling of knee: *(↗knees - alternating - wrist)* kreos
  - **bursa**-like: *Aur*
  - **motion** agg.: merc k* phos k*
  - **nodular** swellings: stann [spect dfg1]
  - **pain**; after: cub k*
  - **painful**, soft and watery: *Sec* k*
  - **red**: mag-c h2
  - **rheumatic**: act-sp med c1
  - **spots**, in: kali-bi k*
  - **sudden**: rhod
  - ○ **Palmar** surface of: carb-v k* rhus-t rhus-v a1

SWINGING (See Swaying)

TAKING OFF boots:

- **agg.** | **Lower** limbs: calc b4a.de graph b4.de*

TALKING agg.:

- ○ **Shoulders**: pyrog ptk1
- **Upper** limbs: lyc bg2

TENDERNESS (See Pain - sore; Sensitive)

TENSION: aids nl2• alum-sil k2 ang c1 aran-ix sp1 arist-cl sp1 bov *Bry* k* calc *Carl* k* *Cimx* *Cupr* gast a1 gent-l a1 hep k* iod k* kali-s fd4.de mag-m k* mang hr1 nux-v k* pieri-b mlk9.de pin-s a1 plac-s rly4• *Plat* plb k* *Puls* *Rhus-t* ruta fd4.de sec k* spong fd4.de sulph k* *Thuj* tritic-vg fd5.de valer k2 vanil fd5.de

- **morning**: *Nux-v* k*
- **afternoon**: calc
- **evening**: *Puls* hr1
  - **bed**: cupr sst3•
- **night**: hep k* *Puls* rhod sulph k*
- **chill**:
  - **before**: *Rhus-t*
  - **during**: rhus-t
- **hiccough**; after: con a1
- **increases** gradually and decreases suddenly: **Puls**
- **rising** from sitting agg.: *Rhus-t*
- **walking** agg.; after: sulph h2
- ○ **Ankles**: aesc aur h2 bell k* bry k* calc carb-an b4a.de carb-v b4.de* *Caust* k* con croc b7.de* *Lach* b7a.de lyc k* mang-m med *Merc* k* nat-c b4a.de nat-m h2 *Phos* k* plat b4a.de seneg k* sep k* sil k* spig b7.de* sulph k* tep thuj vip zinc k*
  - **morning**: con lyc
  - **drawing**, pressive: calc
  - **motion**:
    - **agg.**: **Bry**
    - **amel.**: calc zinc
  - **painful**: seneg
  - **rheumatic**: zinc
  - **sitting** agg.: nat-m h2 sil
  - **walking**:
    - **agg.**: phos sep sulph thuj
    - **air** agg.; in open: bell
  - ○ **Inner**: calc h2 ph-ac h2
  - **Sides** | **Outer**: euphr h2
- **Elbows**: acon all-s alum arg-met b7.de* berb dros k* kali-c kali-n k* kreos k* lach k* laur manc mang k* *Mez* k* *Mur-ac* k* puls k* rhus-t k* ruta fd4.de *Sep* k* stann k* sul-ac k* sulph k* tab ter teucr b7.de* zinc
  - **evening** | **yawning**; on: zinc
  - **bending** agg.; and on: berb dros h1 *Merc* ruta fd4.de
  - **raising** arm agg.: mez h2
  - **stretching** arm agg.: mang h2
  - ○ **Bends** of elbow: arg-met kali-n h2 nat-m k* *Puls* rhus-t sep h2 sulph k* thuj k*
    - **morning**: sulph k*
    - **extending** the arm agg.: **Caust** *Rhus-t*
    - **writing** agg.: thuj k*
  - **Olecranon**: arg-met stann k*
    - **bending** arms agg.: arg-met stann h2
- **Feet**: aesc k2 agar ail *Alum* k* alum-sil k2 ambr k* ant-t k* asaf b7.de* bell k* borx k* bry k* cann-s k* carb-an *Caust* k* cham k* clem eupi ger-i rly4• kali-c k* led b7.de* limen-b-c hm2* *Lyc* k* mag-m mez k* nat-m petr k* ph-ac h2 phos k* plat k* puls k* rhus-t k* sabad k* sars k* *Seneg* *Sep* stront-c k* *Sulph* k* thuj k* verat b7.de* viol-o bg2 viol-t b7.de* zinc k*
  - **morning**: sars h2 *Sulph*
  - **noon**: ambr
  - **afternoon**: nat-m
  - **evening**: *Bry* plat thuj
  - **night**: agar
  - **breakfast**; after hearty: puls
  - **burning**: alum k*
  - **dinner**; after: *Sulph*
  - **motion**:
    - **agg.**: thuj
    - **amel.**: mag-m
    - **toes**; of | **agg.**: *Sulph*
  - **sitting** agg.: **Bry** mag-m plat **Rhus-t**

Tension – Feet: ...

  - **stepping** agg.: **Bry** thuj h1
  - **walking**:
    - **agg.**: ail ant-t bell clem petr k* ph-ac h2 thuj
    - **stone** pavement agg.; on a: sep
  - ○ **Back** of feet: alum k* ant-t k* borx h2 *Bry* k* carb-an caust lyc h2 mag-m h2 nat-c h2 sec sep h2* thuj
  - **Heels**: bell a1 berb *Caust* k* led k* nicc phos thuj
    - **morning** | **bed** agg.; in: phos
    - **rising**, after long sitting: thuj
    - **standing** agg.: berb
    - **sticking**, agg. putting foot down after rising from bed: nicc
    - **walking** agg.: berb led h1 thuj
  - **Joints**: *Sep* bg2
  - **Sides** | **Outer**: *Zinc*
  - **Soles**: *Alum* k* bell k* berb *Caust* hyper lyc k* petr-ra shn4• plat h2 rhus-t b7a.de* sil h2 spig k* sulph k* *Zinc* k*
    - **forenoon**: alum k*
    - **noon**: sulph
      - **walking** agg.: sulph
    - **afternoon**: lyc
    - **evening**: zinc
    - **pressure** | **amel.**: bell
    - **sitting** agg.: lyc
    - **stepping** agg.: berb bry *Caust* spig sulph zinc
    - **stooping** agg.: plat h2
    - **Near** the heel: bell
  - **Tendons** of foot, after walking: sulph h2
- **Fingers**: aeth agn b7.de* alum k* ambr aml-ns apis arg-met k* benz-ac k* calc bg2 canth b7.de* carb-an k* caust k* coc-c croc b7a.de* *Crot-h* k* cupr bg2 ham fd3.de• hep k* hyos k* iod k* kali-bi bg2 kali-c k* lach mag-c k* mag-p bg2* mang k* nat-m k* nat-s k* nit-ac k* nux-v b7.de* olnd b7.de* ph-ac k* *Phos* k* plb b7.de* psor *Puls* k* rhod k* ruta fd4.de spong b7.de* sulph k* thuj verat b7.de*
  - **left**: phos h2
  - **evening**: ruta fd4.de sulph k*
  - **bending** agg.: caust h2 sep h2 thuj k*
  - **eruptions**; with: psor
  - **motion**:
    - **agg.**: hep k* ph-ac
    - **hindering** motion: *Coloc*
  - **pressed**, when: phos k*
  - ○ **First**: nat-m h2 sep
  - **Fourth**: canth hyper phos
  - **Joints**: carb-an k* *Caust* k* croc k* iod h* kali-c k* kali-n mag-c k* *Nat-m* nit-ac k* ph-ac bg2 phos k* puls k* rhod bg2 ruta fd4.de sep k* spong k* sulph
  - **Third**: mang h2 phos h2
- **Forearms**: agar ant-c k* arn b7.de* cadm-s calc k* camph *Caust* k* choc srj3• coloc k* com *Crot-h* crot-t graph h2* kali-c k* lach led b7.de* mag-p mang k* nat-c k* plac-s rly4• prun bg2 puls b7.de* rat sep b4a.de* stront-c k* sulph h2* teucr k* thuj zinc k*
  - **evening**: camph
  - **motion** agg.: calc
  - **stretching**:
    - **arm**:
      - **agg.**: mang h2
      - **amel.**: nat-c h2
  - ○ **Extensors** | **writing** agg.: **Mag-p** thuj
  - **Flexors**: aeth a1 nat-c h2
- **Hands**: aesc k2 alum k* am-c k* apis arg-met k* bar-c bg2* bell k* calen bg1 canth k* carb-v caust k* chin k* clem crot-h bg2* ferr bg2 ferr-ma hyper ign b7a.de ind bg1 kali-c k* lach laur k* limen-b-c hm2* lyc mang k* meny merc k* nat-c k* nat-p nat-s bg1 nat-sil fd3.de• petr-ra shn4• plb prun psor sep spong fd4.de stront-c k* sul-ac k* sulph k* thuj verb b7.de* zinc k*
  - **evening**: sulph
  - **convulsive**: lyc *Zinc*

- **hang** down agg.; letting arms: sul-ac h2
- **stretching**:
  - **agg.**: laur
  - **amel.**: nat-c
- ○ **Back** of hands: alum h2*
- **Bones**: mang h2
- **Joints**: ger-i rly4• mang h2
- **Palms**: petr-ra shn4•

- **Hips**: aeth agar am-m b7.de* ambr b7.de* asar b7.de* *Bell* k* berb bry calc h2 *Carb-v* k* *Caust* b4a.de cimic bg2 coc-c *Coloc* k* con k* crot-t euph k* ferr-ma *Lyc* k* mez h2 *Nat-m* k* nit-ac nux-v b7.de* ph-ac h2 plat k* *Puls* b7.de* *Rhus-t* k* sep stront-c k* sulph thuj k* zinc bg2
  - **right**: nit-ac
  - **left**: *Lyc* h2 *Rhus-t* sulph
  - **morning** | **waking**; on: carb-v h2
  - **afternoon**: aeth
  - **evening** | **amel.**: coc-c
  - **motion** agg.: ph-ac h2
  - **rheumatic**: lyc h2
  - **sitting** agg.: *Rhus-t*
  - **standing** agg.: lyc
  - **walking** agg.: bell h1 calc h2 carb-v lyc nit-ac sep h2 *Sulph* thuj
  - ▽ **extending** to:
    - **Downward**: berb sulph thuj
    - **Groin**: thuj
  - ○ **Joints**: *Caust* b4a.de *Coloc* b4a.de mez b4.de* nat-m b4.de* nit-ac b4.de* rhus-t b7.de* sep b4.de* sulph b4.de*
- **Joints**: am-c *Am-m* k* anac apis arg-met *Bov* *Bry* k* cact k2 *Caps* carb-an b4.de* carb-v b4.de* *Carl* k* *Caust* k* clem k* croc iod *Iris* *Kali-c* **Led** k* *Lyc* k* *Mag-c* k* *Mag-m* manc k* *Mang* *Mez* mur-ac nat-act ptk1 **Nat-m** k* *Nit-ac* orot-ac rly4• *Puls* k* rhod *Rhus-t* *Seneg* k* *Sep* k* stann sul-ac *Sulph* k* *Teucr* verat zinc
  - **evening**: *Iris*
  - **shifting**: iris
- **Knees**: acon aesc alum h2* am-m b7.de* ant-t k* arg-met b7.de* *Arn* k* ars k* *Bar-m* bell b4.de* berb *Bry* k* calc k* canth caps k* *Carb-an* b4a.de carb-v k* *Caust* k* cham k* clem coc-c colch b7.de* coloc con b4a.de* croc k* crot-t cycl b7.de* dig k* euph b4a.de euphr k* graph b4.de* hell k* ign *Iod* b4a.de kali-bi kali-c k* kali-m k2 kali-sil k2 lach laur k* *Led* k* lyc b4a.de* m-arct b7.de *Mag-c* k* merc mez k* mur-ac **Nat-m** k* *Nit-ac* k* nux-v k* ol-an pall par k* *Petr* k* *Phos* k* plat b4.de* puls k* rheum b7.de* rhod k* *Rhus-t* k* *Ruta* b7a.de samb b7.de* *Seneg* k* *Sep* k* sil spig b7.de* stann k* *Sulph* k* tab thuj verat b7.de* zinc k*
  - **right**: sulph h2 zinc h2
  - **morning** | **waking**; on: carb-v h2
  - **evening**: coloc
  - **night**: sulph h2
  - **ascending** stairs agg.: nux-v sep h2 spig h1 *Sulph*
  - **kneeling** agg.: sep
  - **motion** agg.: berb kreos nit-ac
  - **rheumatic**: mez h2
  - **rising** from sitting agg.: calc h2 petr **Rhus-t** *Sulph* thuj
  - **sitting**:
    - **after**: petr h2 [tax jsj7]
    - **agg.**: cycl
  - **sleep** agg.; after: carb-v
  - **standing** agg.: croc cycl
  - **stepping**:
    - **agg.**: petr h2 spig h1
    - **impossible**: lyc h2
  - **stretching**:
    - **agg.**: berb *Ign*
    - **impossible**: sulph h2
  - **walking** agg.: ammc borb carb-v kali-c h2 *Led* sep sil *Sulph* tab thuj zinc

- **Knees**: ...
  - ○ **Hollow** of knees: aesc *Am-m* anag ang h1 ant-c ant-t arg-met h1 ars bell *Berb* *Bry* *Calc-p* *Caps* carb-an carb-v carbn-s **Caust** cham cic *Cimx* coc-c coloc corn cycl h1 dig *Graph* hep kali-ar *Lach* lact *Lyc* lyss *Mag-c* mag-s med meny *Nat-c* **Nat-m** nit-ac *Nux-v* olnd pall petr ph-ac h2 phos *Phyt* plat *Puls* rheum **Rhus-t** *Ruta* samb sang sep stann **Sulph** *Thuj* valer verat vip zinc zinc-p k2
    - **daytime**: nat-m
    - **morning** | **rising** agg.: caust *Lyc*
    - **afternoon**: nit-ac h2
    - **cramping**: phos
    - **menses**; during: nat-p
    - **motion** agg.: ph-ac h2
    - **rising** from sitting agg.: calc-p lact nat-m **Nux-v** **Rhus-t**
    - **room**; when entering a: mag-c h2
    - **sitting** agg.: ars *Caust*
    - **standing** agg.: ars *Bar-c* graph nux-v samb verat
    - **stepping** agg.: mag-c h2
    - **stooping** agg.: *Sulph*
    - **touch** agg.: ph-ac h2
    - **walking**:
      - **agg.**: carb-an *Caust* cic coloc euphr h2 graph lact mag-c mag-s merc nat-m *Nux-v* *Phyt* **Sulph** verat
      - **air** agg.; in open: plat zinc
      - **beginning** to walk: *Caust*
      - **continued** | **amel.**: *Calc-p* carb-an *Caust* *Rhus-t*
    - **Tendons**: sep h2
- **Legs**: *Agar* *Alum* k* alum-p k2 am-c k* am-m k* *Anac* k* ant-c ant-t arg-met b7.de* arn b7.de* *Asaf* b7.de* bar-c k* bar-m borx k* bov k* *Bry* k* *Calc* k* canth b7.de* caps b7.de* carb-an k* carbn-s carc fd2.de• caust k* cham k* chel k* chin b7.de* cimx cocc b7.de* colch b7.de* coloc k* con k* cupr b7a.de dulc euph b4a.de euphr b7.de* graph k* hep k* ign k* kali-bi k* kali-c k* kreos b7a.de laur led b7.de* *Lyc* b4a.de m-ambo b7.de m-arct b7.de mag-m k* mang meny b7.de* mez k* mur-ac k* nat-c b4a.de **Nat-m** k* nat-sil fd3.de• **Nit-ac** b4a.de nux-v k* ph-ac k* phos plat b4.de* psor *Puls* k* ran-b b7.de* rheum b7.de* rhod *Rhus-t* k* ruta fd4.de sabad b7.de* sabin b7.de* *Sep* k* sil k* spig b7.de* spong stann k* staph b7.de* stram stry sulph k* tab tarax teucr b7.de* *Thuj* k* tritic-vg fd5.de valer b7.de* vanil fd5.de *Zinc* k* zinc-p k2
  - **right**: *Agar* tarax h1 ulm-c jsj8•
  - **left**: borx vanil fd5.de
  - **morning**: sulph tritic-vg fd5.de
  - **noon**: thuj
  - **afternoon**: bry sulph
  - **evening**: ant-c dulc kali-bi led h1 **Puls**
  - **night**: agar alum thuj
  - **dinner**; after: sulph
  - **kneeling**, on: (non:calc kl)
  - **lying** agg.: *Am-m*
  - **menses**; during: spong
  - **rheumatic**: mez puls
  - **rising** agg.; after: agar
  - **sitting** agg.: *Am-m* anac ant-c carl *Nat-c* hr1 rhus-t h1
  - **squatting**, on: calc h2
  - **standing** agg.: bar-c
  - **walking**:
    - **agg.**: graph kali-c h2 mang rhod *Sulph* tarax h1 thuj
    - **amel.**: *Am-m* bar-c
  - ○ **Bones**:
    - **Tibia**: zinc h2
      - **descending** agg.: bar-c h2
  - **Calves**: acon *Alum* k* alum-sil k2 am-c h2 *Anac* ang h1 *Arg-met* ars k* asaf bar-c bell k* berb bov *Bry* k* calc canth caps carb-an k* card-m castor-eq caust k* *Cham* chel cic *Cimx* cocc colch con cupr k* dulc ign k* *Kali-bi* *Kali-c* kali-i kali-m k2 kali-n kali-sil k2 kreos laur led lyc mag-m k* mur-ac nat-c **Nat-m** k* nat-p nat-sil fd3.de• nux-v k* ox-ac pall *Phos* plat

- **Calves**: ...
  Puls k* *Rhus-t* k* rhus-v ruta fd4.de *Sabad* k* sep k* *Sil* k* sol-t-ae bg1 staph k* sulph k* valer k* vanil fd5.de zinc k* zinc-p k2
  - **morning**: ferr-ma k* sulph k*
    - **walking** agg.: sulph k*
  - **forenoon**: sulph k*
  - **afternoon**: ox-ac k* ruta fd4.de
    - **17** h: **Valer**
    - **standing** agg.: valer k*
    - **walking** agg.: ox-ac k*
  - **evening**: *Alum* caust k* chel k* dulc k*
  - **ascending** stairs agg.: *Arg-met* prun sulph k*
  - **bent**, when: chel k*
  - **burning**: asaf k*
  - **cold** agg.; becoming: am-c h2
  - **cramping**: rhus-v sil
  - **descending** stairs agg.: *Arg-met*
  - **dinner**; after: canth k*
  - **drawing**: carc fd2.de• puls k*
  - **motion**:
    - **agg.**: berb cocc k* kali-n k* nat-c k*
    - **feet**; of | **agg.**: cham h1
  - **rising** from sitting agg.: alum kali-c k*
  - **sitting** agg.: lyc k* mur-ac h2 **Nat-m** plat k* **Valer**
  - **standing** agg.: alum kali-c kali-i k* stann k* vanil fd5.de
  - **stool** agg.; after: ox-ac k*
  - **stretching**:
    - **agg.**: ign k*
    - **amel.**: chel k*
  - **walking**:
    - **agg.**: *Alum* *Anac* bar-c k* berb k* caps k* *Carb-an* k* colch k* ign k* led k* nat-c k* *Nat-m* k* nit-ac h2 pall c1 phos k* psor *Rhus-t* k* sabad k* *Sil* k* spig h1 zinc
    - **air** agg.; in open: bar-c zinc
    - **amel.**: alum kali-i k* *Rhus-t* stann k*
  - **Lower** part of: nit-ac h2
- **Knee**; below | **squatting**; on: calc h2
- **Tendo** Achillis: berb *Caust* chin h1 cimic graph mag-c mur-ac phos ran-b *Sep* sulph teucr *Zinc*
  - **walking**:
    - **agg.**: mur-ac h2
    - **rapidly** | **agg.**: mag-c h2

- **Lower** limbs: adam srj5• *Alum* k* am-m b7.de* ambr b7.de* ang k* ant-c bg2 ant-t ars bg2 aur k* *Bar-c* k* berb k* bry b7a.de* calc k* camph b7.de* *Carb-an* k* carb-v k* caust k* *Cham* b7.de* clem k* *Coloc* k* con b4.de* dulc b4.de* guaj bg2 hep k* iod b4a.de kali-bi bg2 kali-c b4.de* kreos bg2 lach bg2 lyc b4.de* mag-c k* *Mag-m* k* mag-p bg2 mang k* med k2 meny bg2 meph bg2 merc k* mez k* mur-ac k* *Nat-c* k* *Nat-m* k* nit-ac k* *Nux-v* k* orot-ac rly4• petr b4.de* ph-ac k* phos k* plat k* plb bg2 *Puls* k* rhus-t k* sabin bg2 sars k* *Sep* k* sil b4a.de* stann k* staph b7.de* stram b7.de* sulph k* tritic-vg fd5.de *Zinc* k*
  - **right**: mang h2 phos h2
  - **night**: hep h2 merc nat-c *Puls*
  - **alternating** with | **Anus**; complaints of: kali-m ptk1
  - **coryza**; during: anac b4a.de
  - **cramping**: stram h1
  - **paralyzed** limb: *Nux-v*
  - **sitting** agg.: nat-c
  - **standing** agg.: *Bar-c*
  - **walking**:
    - **agg.**: mang h2 nat-c nat-m
    - **amel.**: bar-c h2 mag-m h2*
  - **warm** bed agg.: *Puls*
  - ▽ **extending** to | **Downward**: alum bg2
  - ○ **Bones**: zinc b4.de*

- **Lower** limbs: ...
  - **Joints**: ars b4.de* carb-an b4.de* carb-v b4.de* caust b4.de* graph b4.de* kali-c b4.de* lyc b4.de* mag-c b4.de* nat-m b4.de* *Rhod* b4a.de seneg b4.de* stann b4.de* sulph b4.de* zinc b4.de*
- **Nates**: aids nl2• ant-c arg-met arn bell berb *Merc* sil
  - **night**: merc
    - **sleep** agg.; during: merc
  - **lying** on back | **amel.**: merc
  - **motion** | **amel.**: aids nl2•
  - **sitting** agg.: aids nl2•
  - **stooping** agg.: bell h1
  - ○ **Gluteal** region: spig h1
- **Shoulders**: aeth anac androc srj1• *Apis* k* arge-pl rwt5• asar berb *Bov* *Bry* carb-v casc k* coc-c coloc crot-h dig k* dioxi rbp6 *Euph* k* eupi granit-m es1• ham fd3.de• hyos k* iris kali-bi *Kali-c* k* kali-i kali-n k* kali-s fd4.de lach k* lact laur k* led b7.de* *Lyc* mag-m mang marb-w es1• mez k* musca-d szs1 nat-c nat-m k* nat-p nit-ac k* olib-sac wmh1 petr k* phos podo fd3.de• ruta fd4.de *Sep* staph b7.de* sulph k* teucr bg2 tritic-vg fd5.de urol-h rwt• verat *Zinc* k*
  - **right**: cob ptm1• euph b4a.de lyc b4a.de sulph h2 zinc b4a.de
  - **morning**: calc kali-c sulph
    - **air** agg.; in open: nat-c
    - **bed** agg.; in: nat-m h2
    - **motion** of arm agg.: coloc crot-h euph phos
    - **rising** agg.; after: euph h2
    - **waking**; on: dioxi rbp6
  - **brushing** the teeth, while: phos
  - **burning**: mag-m
  - **closing** the mouth agg.: mag-c h2
  - **menses**; during: berb
  - **motion**:
    - **amel.**: sep
    - **arm**; of | **agg.**: dig
  - **paralytic**: euph
  - **raising** arm agg.: bry euph h2 hyos *Iris*
  - **rest** agg.: euph h2
  - **rheumatic**: *Lyc* puls zinc h2
  - **stooping** agg.: mag-c h2
  - **uncovering** agg.: nat-m h2
  - **waking**; on: coloc
  - **walking**:
    - **air**; in open:
      - **agg.**: lyc
      - **amel.**: euph h2
  - **writing** agg.: bov
  - ▽ **extending** to: mag-c h2
    - **Jaw**; angle of lower: mag-c h2
    - **Neck**: choc srj3•
  - ○ **Joints**: apis b7a.de asaf b7.de* bov b4.de* *Bry* b7.de* croc bg2 euph b4.de* kali-c b4.de* laur b7.de* lyc b4.de* *Mang* b4a.de nat-m b4.de* sep b4.de* teucr b7.de* zinc b4.de*
- **Tendons**: bar-c bg2 graph bg2 kali-bi bg2 ran-b bg2 ruta bg2 sep bg2 teucr bg2 zinc bg2
  - **accompanied** by | **itching**: ulm-c jsj8•
- **Thighs**: acon b7.de* *Agar* *Alum* alum-p k2 **Am-m** k* ambr k* ang b7.de* ant-c k* ant-t arg-met b7.de* arn k* asaf b7.de* aur k* aur-s k2 *Bar-c* k* bar-m bar-s k2 berb k* bry k* calc b4.de* *Camph* *Carb-v* k* **Caust** k* cham k* chel chin k* choc srj3• cic *Clem* k* *Coloc* k* crot-t eupi k* *Guaj* k* hell k* hep k* hyos b7.de* ind irid-met vml3• *Kali-bi* *Kreos* k* *Lac-d* *Lach* *Lyc* *Mag-m* k* mang meny k* *Merc* k* mez k* *Nat-m* *Nux-v* k* ol-an k* olnd k* op petr *Plat* k* plb b7.de* prun **Puls** k* rat rhod k* *Rhus-t* k* ruta *Sabin* k* *Sep* k* spig k* *Spong* k* staph k* sulph k* tab tarax *Tarent* *Thuj* k* tritic-vg fd5.de zinc-p k2
  - **morning**: carb-v tritic-vg fd5.de
    - **rising** agg.: caust h2
  - **forenoon**: sulph k*
    - **walking** agg.: sulph k*

Extremities

- **afternoon**: nat-m
- **evening**: ant-c lyc **Puls** k* rat sulph zinc-p k2
- **night**: *Alum Lyc* sulph h2
- **ascending** stairs agg.: hyos h1 nat-m
- **bearing** the weight upon the leg, with knee bent: cham k*
- **bending** knee agg.: ang h1 caust h2
- **burning**: olnd
- **drawing** tension: coloc **Puls**
  - **right** thigh: coloc h1*
- **drawing** up legs | **amel.**: zinc-p k2
- **lying** | **amel.**: bar-c
- **menses**; during: nat-m spong
- **motion**:
  - **amel.**: *Bar-c* mag-m *Puls*
  - **legs**; of | **amel.**: mag-m h2
- **rheumatic**: mez
- **sitting**:
  - **agg.**: ant-c *Camph* lyc meny k* merc k* *Plat* spig k* *Tarent* zinc-p k2
  - **amel.**: aur h2 guaj k*
- **standing** agg.: *Bar-c* cypra-eg sde6.de• nux-v rat
- **stepping** agg.: spong h1
- **walking**:
  - **agg.**: ambr aur h2 berb chin cic a1 *Guaj* ind lyc meny nat-m puls *Rhus-t* sep spig staph sulph thuj til
  - **amel.**: zinc-p k2
- **warm** bed agg.: *Puls*
- ▽ **extending** to | **Downward**: *Alum Nat-m* rhus-t sep sulph
- ○ **Anterior** part: ang h1 tritic-vg fd5.de
- **Bends** of thighs: agar arg-met h1 berb carb-an *Caust* zinc
- **Bones**: lyc
- **Hamstrings**: agar *Am-m* k* *Ambr* ant-c ant-t asar bar-c *Calc-p* carb-an **Caust** cimx dig c1 graph **Guaj** kali-ar led *Lyc* lyss med nat-c **Nat-m** nat-p *Nit-ac* phos *Phyt* puls *Rhus-t Ruta* samb sulph
  - **crossing** legs agg.: rhus-t h1
- **Posterior** part: euph h2 petr h2

- **Thumbs**: *Coloc* k* nat-c bg2 olnd bg2 phos bg2 plb bg2 prun k* ruta fd4.de staph bg2 sulph k* thuj k*
  - ○ **Balls**: cupr h2
- **Toes**: mez k* nat-s olnd b7.de* ph-ac phos k* plat k* prun sars h2 sulph k* thuj k*
  - **morning**: sars h2
  - **motion** agg.: sulph thuj
  - **stepping** agg.: thuj
  - **walking** agg.: ph-ac sulph
  - ○ **First**: plat sulph
  - **Joints**: teucr b7.de*
- **Upper** arms: agar k* alum k* *Ant-c* b7.de* asaf b7.de* asar b7.de* berb bry k* bufo carl crot-t kali-c bg2 laur b7.de* prun puls b7.de* rhus-t k* spig k* sulph zinc
  - **morning** | **bed** agg.; in: crot-t
  - **air** agg.; in open: rhus-t
  - **motion** agg.: agar k* carl
  - **walking** agg.: spig
  - ▽ **extending** to:
    - **Fingers**: crot-t
    - **Forearm**: phos
  - ○ **Biceps**: agar k*
  - **Lower** part of: kali-c h2
- **Upper** limbs: *Alum* k* alum-sil k2 anac k* ant-c bg2 arg-met k* asar bg2 aur k* bar-c k* berb k* *Caps* b7a.de carb-v k* caust k* chin k* cic k* **Cocc** bg2 coloc k* *Con* b4a.de **Dig** k* dros bg2 dulc k* graph b4.de* hyper k* kali-c k* kreos bg2 lach k* mag-p mang k* meny mez k* mur-ac k* nat-c k* nat-m k* nat-s k* nit-ac k* nux-v b7a.de ozone sde2• petr k* phos k* *Plat* b4a.de prun puls k* rhus-t k* rhus-v k* sep k* sil k* *Sulph* k* tab k* thuj vip k* zinc k*
  - **right**: ozone sde2•

Tension – **Upper** limbs: ...
  - **left**: kali-c h2
  - **cold**, as from: alum k*
  - **elevation** agg.: kali-c h2
  - **lifting** agg.: alum-sil k2
  - **numbness**; with: sep h2
  - **stretching** agg.: anac h2 cimx k*
  - **walking** agg.: cic k*
  - **writing** agg.: **Mag-p** k*
  - ▽ **extending** to | **Fingers** | **Tips**: puls
    - **Neck** | **menses**; during: berb
  - ○ **Joints**: anac b4.de* bov b4.de* caust b4.de* hep b4a.de iod b4.de* kali-c b4a.de lyc b4.de* mag-c b4.de* mang k* mez b4.de* mur-ac b4.de* nat-m b4.de* nit-ac b4.de* sep b4.de* sul-ac b4.de* zinc b4.de*
- **Varicose** veins: | **menses**; during: arist-cl sp1
- **Wrists**: am-c k* am-m k* aml-ns arg-n aur-m bar-c k* carb-an k* carb-v k* caust bg2 kali-c k* lach limen-b-c hm2* lyc mang k* *Merc* nat-p phos k* puls k* spong k* thuj verb k* zinc k*
  - **morning** | **bed** agg.; in: lyc
  - **evening** | **amel.**: arg-n
  - **bending** agg.: arg-n aur-m
  - **motion** agg.: am-c carb-an spong

THICK:
- **sensation** of being thicker | **Upper** limbs: bry bg2 manc bg2
- ○ **Fingers**: aur-m bro1
  - ○ **Tips**: *Ant-c* bro1 pop-cand bro1
- **Hands**:
  - ○ **Palms** | **Tendons**: *Plb* mrr1
- **Legs**:
  - ○ **Bones** | **Tibia**: mez hr1 thuj h1*
- **Lower** limbs: *Ars* bg2 lyc bg2 vip bg2
- **Nails** (See Nails - thick)
- **Skin**:
  - ○ **Feet**:
    - **Edge** of: lac-d k2
    - **Soles**: ant-c k2 **Ars** k* morg-p pte1*• sang k2 sulph k2
  - **Fingers** | **Tips**: am-m ptk1 pop-cand br1
  - **Hands**: psor k2 sars k2
    - **Palms**: sulph k2
- **Thighs** and buttocks (See GENERALS - Obesity - thighs)

THIN:
- ○ **Bones**: calc-p bg2
- **Nails** (See Nails - thin)

THREADS, stretched along arms, legs: lach rb2*

THRILLING sensation: *(↗Shuddering)* cann-i k2 nit-ac nux-v
- **excitement** agg.: nux-v
- ○ **Feet**: bapt
  - ○ **Soles**: ulm-c jsj8•
- **Fingers**, tips of: ail k*
- **Hands**: bapt **Cann-i**
- **Joints**: cinnb
- **Knees**: **Cann-i**
- **Legs**: **Cann-i** lyss phys stry
- **Toes**, first: benz-ac
- **Upper** limbs: **Cann-i**

THROMBOSIS: | **Lower** limbs: *Apis* bufo k2

THROWN back, shoulder: acon

THROWS hands about in sleep: nat-c h2

THRUSTS feet out of bed (See Uncover, inclination - feet - night)

TICKLING (See Itching)

TIED, sensation as if:
- ○ **Upper** limbs: abrot alum caj nux-m

- **Wrists**: glon

TIGHTNESS (See Constriction)

TILTED; Pelvis (See ABDOMEN - Displacement - pelvis - tilted)

TINGLING: (↗*Numbness)* **Acon** k* aids nl2• *Alum* alum-sil k2 *Alumn* *Ambr* anac apoc k2 arg-n *Arn* ars k* atro bell bros-gau mrc1 cadm-met sp1 calc-f sp1 calc-sil k2 camph *Carb-an* *Carb-v* carbn-o *Carbn-s* cartl-s rly4• chir-fl gya2 colch bg2 con k* croc br1 *Cupr* dulc fd4.de falco-pe nl2• fic-m gya1 *Gels* germ-met srj5• **Graph** haliae-lc srj5• hell bg2 helodr-cal knl2• hist sp1 hyos bg2 *Ign* kali-ar k2 kali-bi *Kali-c* k* kali-p ptk1 kali-s fd4.de kreos lach *Led* **Lyc** *Merc* morph nat-f sp1 *Nat-m* nat-sil fd3.de• nux-m k2 op ox-ac **Petr** *Ph-ac* **Phos** pic-ac k2 pieri-b mlk9.de plb *Positr* nl2• psor **Puls** ran-s bg2 rauw sp1 *Rhod* **Rhus-t** ruta fd4.de sanguis-s hrn2• sarcol-ac sp1 *Sec* *Sep* *Sil* spong fd4.de *Stram* stry suis-pan rly4• sulfa sp1 *Sulph* sumb suprar rly4• symph fd3.de• tanac tep teucr thal-xyz srj8• thuj tritic-vg fd5.de tung-met bdx1• vanil fd5.de *Verat* verat-v visc sp1 zinc

- **left** side: calc-f sp1
- **morning**: kali-bi spong fd4.de teucr
  - **lying** agg.: kali-c
  - **rest** agg.: anac carb-an
- **afternoon**: spong fd4.de teucr
- **night**: ham fd3.de• *Merc* spong fd4.de
  - **lying** agg.: *Sulph*
- **alternating** with | **numbness**: hist sp1
- **bed**; warm: calc-f sp1

○ - **Ankles**: ham fd3.de• nat-sil fd3.de• oxal-a rly4• ruta fd4.de staph tl1 symph fd3.de• vanil fd5.de [bell-p-sp dcm1]
  - **night**: ham fd3.de• nat-sil fd3.de• ruta fd4.de
    - ⁝ **waking**; on: bar-c
- **Elbows**: (↗*Numbness - elbows)* meny nat-sil fd3.de• petr-ra shn4• verat
- **Feet**: **Acon** k* agath-a nl2• ail all-s *Alum* alum-p k2 alum-sil k2 am-c am-m ambr k* ammc arn k* ars k* arum-d bamb-a stb2.de• *Bapt* k* bar-c berb bomb-pr mlk9.de *Calc* calc-p *Carbn-s* carc fd2.de• cartl-s rly4• caust chel k* cob-m homp• **Cocc** k* *Coch* *Colch* *Coloc* con croc des-ac rbp6 dig dulc euph graph bg2 ham hell helodr-cal knl2• hipp jl2 hydrog srj2• hyos hyper *Kali-c* kali-p ptk1 kali-s fd4.de ketogl-ac rly4• lachn lat-m bnm6• lyc mag-m manc merc-i-f mez moni rfm1• naja nat-c nat-m *Nit-ac* onos k* *Ph-ac* *Phos* positr nl2• *Puls* k* ran-s *Rhod* k* rhus-t bg2 ruta fd4.de sanguis-s hrn2• *Sec* k* *Sep* k* sil spong fd4.de stann stry strych-g br1 sul-ac sulph sumb suprar rly4• symph fd3.de• thuj trios rsj11• tritic-vg fd5.de ulm-c jsj8• vanil fd5.de visc sp1 zing [bell-p-sp dcm1 helia stj7 heroin sdj2]
  - **right**: alum carb-an fic-m gya1 ketogl-ac rly4• suprar rly4• [tax jsj7]
  - **left**: allox tpw4 crot-h des-ac rbp6 grat kali-s fd4.de
  - **morning**: calc-p dulc fd4.de fic-m gya1 tritic-vg fd5.de vanil fd5.de
    - ⁝ **bed** agg.; in: nat-c h2 vanil fd5.de
    - ⁝ **waking**; on: positr nl2•
  - **evening** | **bed** agg.; in: carb-an
  - **night**: am-m ham fd3.de• mag-m phos h2 vanil fd5.de
  - **alternating** with tingling of hands (See hands - alternating)
  - **eating**; after: kali-c
  - **lying** in bed, while: carb-an *Hyper*
  - **painful**: dulc fd4.de mag-m ruta fd4.de spong fd4.de thal-xyz srj8• vanil fd5.de
  - **rising**:
    - ⁝ **agg.**: fic-m gya1
    - ⁝ **sitting**; from | **agg.**: *Puls*
  - **sitting** agg.: dulc fd4.de euph h2 grat nat-c h2 ruta fd4.de spong fd4.de tritic-vg fd5.de
  - **standing** agg.: naja *Puls* *Sec* tritic-vg fd5.de [heroin sdj2]
  - **walking**:
    - ⁝ **agg.**: ant-c berb *Sec* tritic-vg fd5.de
    - ⁝ **amel.**: am-c *Puls*
  - **warmth** agg. | **heat** agg.: lachn

▽ • **extending** to | **Knees** | **rippling** up and down: hydrog srj2•
    - ⁝ **Upward**: **Acon** agath-a nl2•

○ • **Back** of feet: am-c chin h1 ran-s

Tingling – Feet: ...

  - **Heels**: alum am-c k* caust h2 ferr-ma *Nux-m* k* rhod
    - ⁝ **evening** | **bed** agg.; in: nit-ac h2
    - ⁝ **sitting** agg.: alum con
  - **Soles**: alum h2* am-c k* arg-n k* ars k* bell h1 *Berb* bry cain cann-i k2 **Caust** cic *Cocc* colch bg2 coloc cub k* dulc fd4.de ferr helo-s rwt2• *Hep* hydrog srj2• kali-p fd1.de• kali-s fd4.de lat-m bnm6• lyc k* nat-c k* *Nux-m* *Nux-v* *Olnd* *Rhus-t* ruta sanguis-s hrn2• *Sec* sep k* *Sil* k* staph k* stry tere-la rly4• tritic-vg fd5.de ulm-c jsj8• zing
    - ⁝ **evening**: kali-s fd4.de rhus-t tritic-vg fd5.de zing
    - ⁝ **rising** | **bed**; from | **agg.**: lyc
      - ⁝ **sitting**; from | **agg.**: *Puls*
    - ⁝ **scratching** agg.; after: sil
    - ⁝ **sitting** agg.: arg-n cic h1 **Cocc** staph zing
    - ⁝ **spot**, in one: ol-an
    - ⁝ **stool** agg.; after: petr-ra shn4•
    - ⁝ **voluptuous**: *Sil*
    - ⁝ **walking** agg.: berb bry *Olnd* *Rhus-t* *Sec* zing
- **Fingers**: abrot ptk1 **Acon** k* ail *Alum* alum-p k2 alum-sil k2 *Am-m* ambr apis arg-n bg2 *Ars* k* arum-i ptk2 *Aza* br1 bapt bg2 *Bar-c* bell cact ptk1 *Calc* calc-s *Carbn-s* cartl-s rly4• chir-fl gya2 colch bg2 con k* croc cupr-ar *Dig* dros gk dulc fd4.de falco-pe nl2• ferr bg2 fic-m gya1 form *Glon* ham fd3.de• hell bg2 hyos bg2 kali-c lac-c lach bg2 lact lil-t lob *Lyc* mag-c *Mag-m* mag-s mang bg2 merc moni rfm1• nat-c **Nat-m** k* ol-an ox-ac paeon *Par* ph-ac positr nl2• prot fmm1• ptel k* *Puls* *Ran-b* k* rat rhod k* *Rhus-t* k* sacch-a fd2.de• *Sec* sep **Sil** k* sinus rly4• spig spong fd4.de stry sul-ac sulph k* tab tere-la rly4• *Thuj* tritic-vg fd5.de *Verat*
  - **right**: hydrog srj2•
  - **morning**: dios tritic-vg fd5.de
    - ⁝ **waking**; on: ail
  - **night** | **waking**; on: bar-c
  - **grasping** something agg.: rhus-t k2
  - **sitting** agg.: alum

○ • **First**: plat
  - **Fourth**: alum carb-an ham fd3.de• sec a1 tritic-vg fd5.de ven-m rsj12•
    - ⁝ **sitting** agg.: alum
  - **Joints**: dulc fd4.de sarcol-ac sp1 verat
  - **Nail**: colch bg2*
    - ⁝ **Under**: cann-s colch *Nat-s* k* nux-m hr1
  - **Second**: apis
  - **Third**: alum ham fd3.de• sec a1 sil ven-m rsj12•
  - **Tips**: acon acon-c acon-f **Am-m** k* cact cann-s *Colch* croc cupr sst3• fl-ac *Hep* **Kali-c** k* lach nat-m *Nat-s* petr-ra shn4• positr nl2• rhod *Rhus-t* sal-fr sle1• *Sec* sep sulph *Thuj* tritic-vg fd5.de ven-m rsj12•
    - ⁝ **morning**: *Kali-c*
    - ⁝ **grasping**, when: *Rhus-t*
    - ⁝ **hang** down agg.; letting arms: sulph
- **Forearms**: (↗*Numbness - forearms)* aesc agath-a nl2• alum am-m ars both-ax tsm2 caps *Cham* *Cocc* coloc con croc fic-m gya1 galeoc-c-h gms1• *Gels* hydrog srj2• lac-c *Lyc* mag-m merc morg-p pte1• nat-m *Nit-ac* nux-v *Ph-ac* phys pip-m psor puls sec sep sulph thiam rly4•
  - **right**: agath-a nl2• am-m coloc
  - **left**: alum
  - **motion** agg.: bapt hr1

▽ • **extending** to | **Fingers**: carb-ac fic-m gya1 phys pip-m
- **Hands**: acet-ac **Acon** aesc agar ail *Alum* alum-p k2 alum-sil k2 am-c androc srj1• *Apis* arn ars arum-d aza br1 bapt bar-c bell bomb-pr mlk9.de both-ax tsm2 bros-gau mrc1 brucel sa3• *Calc* calc-p *Carb-an* *Carbn-s* cartl-s rly4• **Cocc** colch k* croc crot-h dros gk dulc fd4.de eupi falco-pe nl2• form graph ham fd3.de• hell hipp jl2 hyos k* *Kali-c* *Kali-n* ketogl-ac rly4• lac-c *Lach* lil-t *Lyc* *Mag-c* mang-p rly4• meny *Mez* mur-ac nat-c nat-m nat-s nat-sil fd3.de• *Nit-ac* *Nux-v* *Ph-ac* *Phos* ptel *Rhod* rhus-t ruta sanguis-s hrn2• *Sel* sep spong fd4.de stram stry strych-g br1 suis-pan rly4• syc pte1*• tritic-vg fd5.de ust vanil fd5.de *Verat* [heroin sdj2]
  - **right**: carb-an dulc fd4.de fic-m gya1 kali-p fd1.de• tell rsj10•
    - ⁝ **evening**: tell rsj10•
  - **left**: cact *Crot-h* ham fd3.de• hydrog srj2• *Lach*

- **morning**: calc-p form ham fd3.de• kali-c nit-ac *Phos* sacch-a fd2.de• spong fd4.de tritic-vg fd5.de
- **night**: dulc fd4.de ham fd3.de• kali-p fd1.de• mag-m sep *Sil* spong fd4.de vanil fd5.de
  - ⁝ **midnight**: rhus-t vanil fd5.de
- **accompanied** by tingling of feet: carb-an a1*
- **alternating** with tingling of feet: carb-an **Cocc** k*
- **driving** | **agg.**: falco-pe nl2•
- **grasping** something agg.: cham hydrog srj2• rhus-t
- **lain** on: am-c ambr ars *Chin* kali-c petr
- **motion**:
  - ⁝ **agg.**: bapt
  - ⁝ **amel.**: am-c carb-an sep
- **painful**: mag-m thal-xyz srj8• vanil fd5.de
- **playing** piano: sulph
- **riding** agg.: form
- **sitting** agg.: am-c *Graph* sulph
- **standing** agg.: agar
- **waking**; on: croc *Phos* sacch-a fd2.de•
- **washing** agg.; after: aesc ars
- **writing** agg.: agar

▽ • **extending** to | **Elbow**: hydrog srj2•

○ • **Back** of hands: apis dulc fd4.de ham fd3.de• jatr-c plat suis-pan rly4• tritic-vg fd5.de

- **Palms**: *Acon* bg2 am-c bg2 apis k* ars bg2 *Aza* br1 cadm-met tpw6 calad con bg2 cupr mur-ac bg2 *Rhus-t* ruta k* sanguis-s hrn2• sec bg2 seneg sep bg2 spong fd4.de staph bg2 stry suis-pan rly4• sumb tritic-vg fd5.de
  - ⁝ **left**: sel rsj9•
  - ⁝ **warm** room agg.: cadm-met tpw6

\- **Hips**: atra-r bnm3• bar-c rhus-t

- **night**: bar-c

○ • **Gluteal** muscles: calc-p

\- **Knees**: agath-a nl2• alum ant-t aur hyper ketogl-ac rly4• nat-sil fd3.de• plat rhus-t [bell-p-sp dcm1]

- **rising** from sitting agg.: chin h1
- **sitting** agg.: alum

\- **Legs**: acet-ac agar k* *Alum* bro1 am-c aran bro1 arg-met bg2 arn asaf bapt bar-c *Calc* k* calc-f sp1 *Calc-p* k* *Carb-an* *Carbn-h* carbn-s k* carc fd2.de• *Caust* bro1 cic h1 *Cocc* bro1 coloc bro1 con com *Crot-h* k* dig dulc fd4.de euph fl-ac k* gels *Gnaph* bro1 graph bro1 ham fd3.de• helodr-cal knl2• hydrog srj2• hyper ind iod *Kali-c* k* kali-i bro1 kreos lachn lact bro1 lil-t mag-m manc merc merc-i-f mez k* morg-p pte1*• naja nat-sil fd3.de• nux-m nux-v k* onos bro1* petr h2 *Phos* bro1 puls k* *Rhus-t* k* sarcol-ac bro1 *Sec* k* sep bro1 spong fd4.de *Sulph* k* tarent bro1 tela bro1 thuj *Trios* bro1 tritic-vg fd5.de vanil fd5.de verat h1 zinc bro1 [heroin sdj2]

- **left**: plb bg2
- **daytime**: *Carb-an* dulc fd4.de
- **afternoon**: *Gels*
- **evening**: *Calc* ham fd3.de• ign manc vanil fd5.de
- **bed** agg.; in: hydrog srj2• vanil fd5.de
- **excitement** agg.: calc-p
- **rising** after sitting; on: *Puls*
- **sitting**:
  - ⁝ **agg.**: am-c bar-c *Calc* camph cic h1 crot-h dulc fd4.de ham fd3.de• ign
  - ⁝ **crossed** legs; with | **agg.**: agar carb-an *Crot-h* fl-ac laur *Phos* sep
- **standing** agg.: am-c naja
- **walking** agg.: asaf

▽ • **extending** to:
  - ⁝ **Downward**: hydrog srj2•
  - ⁝ **Thigh**: hydrog srj2•

○ • **Bones**:
  - ⁝ **Tibia**: vanil fd5.de [bell-p-sp dcm1]
    - ⁝ **left** | **walking** agg.: hir rsj4•

\- **Legs**: ...

- **Calves**: ambr c1 bar-c berb caust h2 cham ham fd3.de• lach onos sacch-a fd2.de• [bell-p-sp dcm1]

\- **Lower** limbs: agar *Alum* k* alum-p k2 alum-sil k2 am-c ant-c b7.de* ant-t b7.de* arn aur bamb-a stb2.de• *Brucel* sa3• *Calc-p* cann-s b7.de* carb-ac k* carb-an *Carb-v* carbn-s caust chin bg2 coc-c bg2 com k* dig falco-pe nl2• **Graph** k* grat guaj hyper ign **Kali-c** k* lachn k* **Lyc** k* m-ambo b7.de mag-m *Merc* merc-c bg2 merc-i-f k* mez b4.de* mosch bg2 nat-m nit-ac k* nux-v op k* **Petr** k* *Ph-ac* plat b4.de* puls bg2 ran-s b7.de* rumx ruta b7.de* sanic sec bg2 *Sep* k* *Sil* k* spig k* staph b7.de* sul-ac k* *Sulph* k* tab bg2 thuj til tritic-vg fd5.de vanil fd5.de verat bg2

- **right**: carb-an kali-c h2
- **left**: lavand-a ctl1• nat-c k2
- **morning** | **bed** agg.; in: *Sulph*
- **night**: sanic
  - ⁝ **bed** agg.; in: helo sne sanic
- **kneeling**, after: op
- **lying**:
  - ⁝ **agg.**: *Kali-c* *Sulph* tritic-vg fd5.de
  - ⁝ **limb** agg.; on the: carb-an
- **menses**; during: *Graph* *Puls* sec
- **rest**; after: op
- **rising** from sitting agg.: caps h1
- **scratching** | **amel.**: sil h2
- **sitting** agg.: *Calc-p* chin *Graph* guaj h2 ign kali-c lyc mosch nux-v *Op* *Ph-ac* ros-d wla1 sep *Sil* vanil fd5.de
- **warm** room agg.: com
- **warmth** agg. | **heat** agg.: lachn c1

\- **Nates**: *Alum* calc-p dig guaj bro1 ruta fd4.de staph tl1 sulph

- **sitting** agg.: *Alum* calc dig ruta fd4.de sulph

\- **Paralyzed** parts; in: cann-i c1

\- **Shoulders**: *(↗Numbness - shoulders)* arizon-l nl2• atra-r bnm3• cham mez h2* tritic-vg fd5.de vanil fd5.de verat k* zinc

- **left**: arizon-l nl2• tritic-vg fd5.de vanil fd5.de

\- **Thighs**: *Agar* bro1 agath-a nl2• *Alum* bro1 aran bro1 arg-met calc bro1 *Calc-p* bro1 canth carbn-s bro1 caust k* cic h1 coc-c *Cocc* bro1 coloc bro1 crot-h bro1 *Gnaph* bro1 graph bro1 ham fd3.de• hep h2 kali-c bro1 kali-i bro1 kali-s fd4.de lact bro1 *Merc* k* mez bro1 nit-ac *Nux-v* bro1 onos bro1 ox-ac *Phos* bro1 *Rhus-t* bro1 sabad sarcol-ac bro1 sec k* sep bro1 sil *Sulph* bro1 tarent bro1 tela bro1 thuj *Trios* bro1 tritic-vg fd5.de vanil fd5.de verat zinc bro1 [bell-p-sp dcm1]

- **menses**; during: sec
- **painful**: caust k* thal-xyz srj8•
- **rising** from sitting agg.: chin h1
- **sitting** agg.: cic h1 sil vanil fd5.de

▽ • **extending** to | **Testes**: sabad

\- **Thumbs**: alum ambr fl-ac ham fd3.de• nat-c h2

○ • **Tip** of: am-m ambr

\- **Toes**: ail apoc-a vh1 ars arum-d aza br1 berb carc fd2.de• cic *Colch* con ham fd3.de• hell *Hep* *Lach* merc merc-i-f *Nux-m* sabad sec stry symph fd3.de• tritic-vg fd5.de vanil fd5.de verat vip [bell-p-sp dcm1]

- **right** foot | **daytime**: vip-l-f a1

○ • **First**: berb bufo-s camph carb-ac chin h1 cic nat-c h2 podo fd3.de• ran-s tung-met bdx1• vanil fd5.de
  - ⁝ **Balls**: bry bg2 kali-bi bg2 kali-c bg2 phos bg2 plb bg2 rhus-t bg2 sabad bg2 sulph bg2 zinc bg2
  - ⁝ **Tips**: mez h2

- **Fourth**; outer side of: onos
- **Nails**, under: elaps
- **Second**: crot-t
- **Tips**: acon-c **Am-m** *Nat-m*

\- **Upper** arms: *(↗Numbness - upper arms)* bros-gau mrc1 cartl-s rly4• colch rsj2• hydrog srj2• kali-s fd4.de morg-p pte1• petr-ra shn4• podo fd3.de• sep

- **right**: mand rsj7•
- **motion** | **amel.**: colch rsj2•

- **Upper** limbs: (↗*Numbness - upper limbs)* acet-ac *Acon* k* aids nl2• ail *Alum* alum-p k2 alum-sil k2 am-c am-m *Ambr* androc srj1• apis k* am ars *Aur* bapt bell cann-i cann-s caps *Carb-an Carb-v Carbn-s* caust chel chir-fl gya2 *Cocc* colch bg2 con corn *Dig* dulc fd4.de fl-ac k* **Graph** k* helodr-cal knl2• hyos k* ign kali-c kali-n m-arct b7.de *Mag-m* merc mez mill morg-p fmm1• morph nat-s ol-an paeon *Ph-ac* **Phos** k* pieri-b mlk9.de plat k* plb bg2 pot-e rly4• prot fmm1• puls rhod rhus-v ruta bg2 sabad *Sec* **Sil** k* stry sulph suprar rly4• thuj tub jl2 tung-met bdx1• ust vanil fd5.de [heroin sdj2]
  - **right**: (↗*Numbness - upper limbs - right)* am-c h2 am-m carb-an kali-bi kali-p fd1.de• sil suprar rly4•
    - **lying** on left side agg.: mag-m
    - **Arm** and left leg | **night**: kali-c
  - **left**: (↗*Numbness - upper limbs - left)* aids nl2• dig c1 dream-p sdj1• elaps suprar rly4•
    - **lying** on back agg.: kali-n
  - **morning**: ail *Mag-m*
    - **waking**; on: ail fum rly4• *Mag-m*
  - **forenoon**: dulc fd4.de mill vanil fd5.de
  - **night**: aids nl2• vanil fd5.de
    - **midnight**:
      - **before**: caust
      - **after**: aids nl2•
  - **carrying** anything, when: *Ambr*
  - **sitting** agg.: *Graph* teucr
  - **writing** agg.: spig
  - ▽ **extending** to | **Fingers**: carb-ac melal-alt gya4
  - ○ **Side** lain on: ambr arg-met ars *Bar-c* bufo *Calc* carb-an *Carb-v Chin* cop *Croc* glon *Graph* hep *Ign* kali-c *Lach Phos* **Puls** *Rheum* **Rhus-t** samb sep sil
  - **Side** not lain on: fl-ac mag-m

TIRED (See Heaviness; Weakness)

TOSSING (See Restlessness)

TOTTERING GAIT: (↗*Awkwardness - lower; Incoordination; Incoordination - lower; Unsteadiness - lower; Weakness - lower; GENERALS - Locomotor; VERTIGO - Accompanied - staggering)* acet-ac a1 acon b2.de* aesc *Agar* k* agro bro1 ail bg2* **Alum** k* am-c j5.de *Am-m* am-p br1 *Ambr* aml-ns vh1 *Anac* anan kr1 ang bro1 ant-c b2.de* *Apis* **Arg-met** k* arg-n k* arn b2.de* *Ars* k* ars-s-f kr1 *Asar* b2.de* aster bro1* astra-m br1 atro vh **Aur** k* aur-s kr1* **Bar-c** k* barbit br1 **Bell** b2.de* bov b2.de* **Bry** b2.de* bufo ptk1 *Calc* k* calc-p a1* camph k* cann-s b2.de* canth b2.de* *Caps* b2.de* *Carb-ac* carb-an k* *Carb-v* k* *Carbn-s* bro1 **Caust** k* cham b2.de* chel b2.de* *Chin* k* chinin-hcy j2 cic k* **Cocc** k* *Coff* b2.de* colch b2.de* *Coloc* bg **Con** k* croc b2.de* crot-h kr1 cupr j5.de* cupr-ar sf1.de cycl b2.de* cypra-eg sde6.de• dig sf1.de dros b2.de* dub bro1 dulc b2.de* euph b2.de* ferr b2.de* *Fl-ac* *Gels* k* *Glon* k* graph b2.de* *Hell* k* helo bro1* helo-s bnm14*• hydr-ac j5.de* hydrc sf1.de hyos k* ign k* *Iod* k* ip b2.de* kali-br bg2* kali-c b2.de* kali-n bg2 lac-ac bro1 lach j5.de* lact a1 lap-la sde8.de• *Lath* k* *Laur* b2.de* led b2.de* lil-t a1* lol bg2* lyc a1 m-ambo b2.de* m-arct b2.de* m-aust b2.de* mag-c b2.de* *Mag-m* b2.de* *Mag-p* mag-s sf1.de mang bg2* mang-act bro1 *Merc* k* *Mez* b2.de* morph a1* mosch b2.de* *Mur-ac* k* *Mygal* bro1 naja a1 *Nat-c* k* *Nat-m* k* nit-ac b2.de* *Nux-m* b2.de* **Nux-v** k* ol-an ptk1 *Olnd* b2.de* onos bro1* *Op* k* ox-ac oxyt bro1 ozone sde2• paeon bro1 par b2.de* petr b2.de* *Ph-ac* k* **Phos** k* phys a1 phyt kr1 **Pic-ac** k* plat b4a.de* **Plb** k* podo fd3.de• prun j5.de* puls b2.de* rheum b2.de* rhod k* **Rhus-t** k* ruta b2.de* sabad b2.de* samb b2.de* *Sars* k* sec k* seneg b2.de* sep b2.de* *Sil* k* spig b2.de* spong b2.de* stann bg2* stram k* stront-c b2.de* *Stry* sulfon bro1 *Sulph* k* tab bg2* tanac a1 tarax b2.de* *Tarent* tarent-c ptk1 teucr k* thal-xyz srj8• *Thuj* b2.de* trion bro1 valer b2.de* **Verat** b2.de* *Verat-v* bg2* verb k* viol-o b2.de* viol-t b2.de* vip j5.de* visc bg2 zinc b2.de* [bell-p-sp dcm1]

- **dark**; in: *Alum* bro1 *Arg-n* bro1 carbn-s bro1 dub bro1 *Gels* bro1 iodof bro1 *Stram* bro1
- **unobserved**; especially when: arg-n br1*

TOUCH:

- **agg.**: *Chel* ptk1 chin ptk1
  - ○ **Elbows** | **Tips**: graph ptk1
  - **Lower** limbs: acon b7.de* alum b4a.de* ang b7.de ant-c b7.de* arg-met b7.de* arn b7.de* ars b4.de* asar b7.de* *Bell* b4.de* borx b4a.de

Touch – agg. – **Lower** limbs: ...
bry b7.de* calc b4.de* canth b7.de* caps b7.de* caust b4.de* cham b7.de* chel b7.de* *Chin* b7.de* cina b7.de* clem b4.de* cocc b7.de* coff b7.de* colch b7.de* coloc bg2 *Cupr* b7.de* dros b7.de* dulc b4.de* ferr b7.de* guaj b4a.de hell b7.de* hep bg2 hyos b7.de* ign b7.de* *Iod* b4a.de kali-c b4.de* kali-n b4.de* lach b7.de* led b7.de* *Lyc* b4.de* m-ambo b7.de m-aust b7.de merc b4.de* mez bg2 mosch b7a.de mur-ac b4.de* nat-c b4.de* nat-m b4.de* nit-ac b4.de* nux-m b7.de* *Nux-v* b7.de* op bg2 par b7.de* ph-ac b4.de* phos b4.de* plat b4.de* plb bg2 *Puls* b7.de* ran-b b7.de* rhus-t b7.de* ruta b7.de* sabad b7.de* *Sabin* b7.de* *Sep* b4.de* sil b4.de* spig b7.de* spong b7.de* staph b7.de* *Sulph* b4.de* tab bg2 tarax b7.de* verat b7.de* visc bg2

- **Upper** limbs: acon b7.de* agar b4a.de *Agn* b7.de* ambr b7a.de anac b4.de* ang b7.de* arg-met b7.de* arn b7.de* asaf b7.de* bell b4.de* bov b4.de* *Bry* b7.de* canth b7.de* cham b7.de* *Chin* b7.de* cina b7.de* cocc b7.de* colch b7.de* *Cupr* b7.de* cycl b7.de* dros b7.de* ferr b7.de* fl-ac bg2 hep b4.de* hyos b7.de* iod b4.de* ip bg2 kali-bi bg2 kali-c b4.de* kreos b7a.de lyc b4.de* mang b4.de* merc b4.de* mez b4.de* mur-ac b4.de* nat-c b4.de* nux-v b7.de* par b7.de* petr b4.de* ph-ac b4.de* puls b7.de* rhus-t b7.de* sabad b7.de* *Sabin* b7.de* sars b4.de* sep b4a.de sil b4.de* spig b7.de* spong b7.de* **Staph** b7.de* stront-c b4.de* verat b7.de* verb b7.de* zinc b4.de*

- **amel.**:
  - ○ **Lower** limbs: agar b4.de* arn b7.de* cycl b7.de* euph b4.de* hep b4.de* meny b7.de* mur-ac b4.de* tarax b7.de*
  - **Upper** limbs: anac b4.de* bism b7.de* calc b4.de* cycl b7.de* euph b4.de* kali-c b4.de* m-arct b7.de meny b7.de* tarax b7.de* thuj b4.de*
- **feet** agg.: ars ptk1 calc ptk1 chin ptk1 kali-c ptk1 lac-f c1 sep ptk1 sulph ptk1
  - ○ **Lower** limbs: ars bg2 calc bg2 *Kali-c* bg2 sep bg2 sulph bg2 tarent bg2
- **hand** agg.: chin kr1
- ○ **Fingers** touch each other; cannot bear to have lac-c k* *Lach* k* sec k*

TOUCHING:

- **hair** agg. | **Upper** limbs: ign b7.de*

TOUGH fingernails (See Nails - tough - fingernails)

TRAUMATISM (See Injuries)

TREMBLING: abel vh1 absin a1 *Acon* k* acon-f a1 aconin a1 aeth *Agar* k* agar-ph a1 alco a1 *Alum* k* alum-p k2 alum-sil k2 alumn *Ambr Anac* k* androc srj1• ant-c k* *Apis* k* aran vh1 **Arg-n** k* arn k* **Ars** k* **Ars-i** ars-s-f k2 *Asaf* atro a1 aur-s k2 bapt k2 bar-m k* bar-s k2 bell k* borx brom k2 bry bufo buth-a sp1 *Calc* k* calc-f sp1 calc-p k2* calc-sil k2 camph k* cann-i k2 *Canth* k* caps k* carb-ac k* carb-an *Carb-v* k* carbn-o *Carbn-s* carl k* cass a1 castm **Caust** k* **Chel** k* *Chin* k* chinin-ar *Chinin-s Cic* k* *Cimic* k* *Cina* bro1 cinch a1 cob k* cob-n sp1 **Cocc** k* coff coff-t a1 coffin a1 colch k* *Con* k* cop k* *Crot-c* k* crot-h k* cupr k* cupr-ar k* cypr c1 cyt-l a1 dig digin a1 dor k* dulc k* euphr k* eupi k* ferr-i ferr-ma **Gels** k* glon k* graph helo bro1 helo-s rwt2• hep hippoc-k szs2 hydr-ac k* *Hyos* k* hyper k* iber a1 *Ign* k* **Iod** k* jab br1 kali-ar k* kali-c k* kali-i k* kali-n k* kali-p kali-s kali-sil k2 *Kalm* kola stb3• lac-ac stj5• *Lach* k* lact k* lat-h bnm5• lat-m bnm6• laur k* lob k* *Lol* bro1 lon-x bro1 lyc k* lyss *Mag-p* k* mang k* med meph **Merc** k* *Merc-c* k* *Mez* k* morph k* *Mygal* bro1 naja k2 nat-m k* nat-s k2 nicot a1 **Nit-ac** **Nux-v** k* **Op** k* ox-ac k* *Petr* ph-ac bro1 *Phos* k* phys bro1 pilo a1 *Plat* k* **Plb** k* positr nl2• *Puls* k* ran-b k* raph k* rhod **Rhus-t** k* *Rhus-v* k* sabad k* *Sec* k* sep bro1 *Sil* k* spig spira a1 *Spong* squil k* **Stram** k* stront-c *Stry* bro1 suis-pan rly4• sul-i k2 sulfon bro1 *Sulph* k* *Tab* k* *Tarent* bro1 thal bro1 thuj til k* tritic-vg fd5.de tub c1 *Valer* bro1 vanil fd5.de *Verat* k* verin a1 viol-o k* vip k* *Visc* k* wies a1 x-ray sp1 xero bro1 zinc k* zinc-m a1 zinc-p k2 zinc-s a1*

- **right**: ars bg1 dor c1
- **morning**: carb-v k* euphr k* kali-act kali-c nat-c nat-m k* **Nit-ac** *Sil* staph h1
  - **walking** agg.: euphr k*
- **afternoon**: anac k* carb-v *Gels* k* vanil fd5.de
  - **walking** agg.: ran-b k*
- **evening**: agar k* chel k* *Cocc* k* mez
  - **sleep**; when falling asleep: carb-an h2
  - **walking** agg.: dig
- **night**: calc k* hep k* rhod k*
  - **walking** agg.: nat-m k*

- **accompanied** by:
  - **mental** symptoms (See MIND - Mental symptoms - limbs)
  - **palpitations** (See CHEST - Palpitation - accompanied - limbs - trembling)
- **anger**; after: lap-la sde8.de• *Nit-ac* **Staph** mrr1
- **anxious**: ars mrr1 merc k* *Puls*
- **chagrin** (See mortification)
- **chill**; during: anac ang ars bry k* chin chinin-s cina **Cocc** con k* eup-per ferr *Gels* merc k* *Par* petr plat sabad sul-ac zinc
- **cigar**, after: op k*
- **coition**; after: *Agar*
- **colic**; after: plb k*
- **contradicted**, when: nit-ac
- **conversation**, from: *Ambr*
- **convulsive**: acon k* asaf carbn-h crot-h k* op k*
- **cough** agg.; during: bell *Cupr* *Phos*
- **crying**, while: tarent k*
- **dinner**; after: nit-ac k*
- **drawing**: lyc h2
- **drunkards**; in: **Ars** *Bar-c* *Nux-v*
- **eating**; after: alum b4a.de caust b4a.de nit-ac b4a.de
- **emissions** agg.; after: **Nat-p** k*
- **excitement**: gels k2 **Merc** phos k* **Staph** mrr1
- **exertion** agg.; after: kali-p fd1.de• *Merc* nat-m k* *Phos* k* **Rhus-t** sec k*
- **fatigue**; from: x-ray sp1
- **fever**; during: chinin-s bro1 op bro1 *Zinc* k*
- **fright**; after: **Op** k* oxal-a rly4•
- **frightened**, as if: **Op** paeon tarent
- **holding** them long in same position: staph h1
- **invisible**: *Chin*
- **menses** | **before** | **agg**.: hyos kali-c lyc *Nat-m*
  - **during** | **agg**.: *Hyos* nat-m *Nit-ac* k* plat stram
- **mental** exertion; after: plat k2
- **metabolic** causes; from: ant-t mtf crot-h mtf cupr mtf gels mtf hell mtf lach mtf nux-v mtf op mtf plb mtf stram mtf sulph mtf tab mtf zinc mtf zinc-s mtf
- **mortification**: ran-b k*
- **motion** agg.: **Merc** sulph k*
- **nervous**: thyr br1
- **one** limb: stram h1
- **periodical**: *Merc* k*
- **reflecting** agg.: borx
- **resting** against anything amel.: plb k*
- **sexual** excitement; during: graph
- **sleep**; during: ars mtf33
- **something** is to be done, when: **Kali-br**
- **standing** agg.: dirc k* *Merc-c* k* *Zinc*
- **starting** from sleep: petr h2* sil bg2
- **stool** agg.; after: ars k* carb-v *Con*
- **stretched** out, when: merc-c k*
- **suppressed** by will; can be: helo-s rwt2•
- **using** hands: ferr-i k*
- **vomiting**; after: ars k* eupi k*
- **walking**: *(↗GENERALS - Trembling - Externally - walking - agg.)*
  - **after** | **agg**.: cupr h2
  - **agg**.: acon ars cupr ferr-i **Merc** phos k2 sulph
  - **air** agg.; in open: *Nux-v* *Phos*
- **weakness**, with general: arg-n br1 lac-ac stj5•

○ - **Ankles**: asaf b7.de* mez b4.de*
- **Elbows**: bar-c b4.de* caust b4.de*
- **Feet**: am-c k* apis k* am b7.de* ars k* ars-s-f k2 asaf b7.de* aur ptk1* *Bar-c* k* bell borx k* bov k* calc camph k* canth k* caps b7.de* carbn-s chinin-s coff k* coloc k* crot-t *Cupr* cycl *Gels* bro1 *Hyos* k* ip kali-c kali-n kali-s lyc k* m-arct b7.de mag-c mag-m k* **Merc** k* mur-ac k* nat-c k* *Nat-m* k* nicc nux-m ol-an k* op ox-ac k* *Phos* bro1 *Plat* k* *Psor* k* **Puls** k* sars k* sec sep bro1 *Stram* k* *Sulph* k* sumb symph fd3.de• *Tab* *Thuj* verat k* zinc k*
  - **left**: puls h1
  - **morning**: ars nat-m
    - **rising** agg.: con crot-t merc-c
  - **forenoon**: nat-m sars
    - **11 h** | **rising** from bed agg.: nat-m

- **Feet**: ...
  - **evening**:
    - **bed** agg.; in: canth nat-m
    - **standing** agg.: nux-v k*
  - **night** | **wakes** her: nat-c h2
  - **chill**; during: canth
  - **convulsive**: hyos kali-cy
  - **descending** stairs agg.: thuj
  - **dinner**; after: mag-m
  - **falling** asleep: croc
  - **fright**; as from: coloc
  - **menses**:
    - **as** from: coloc
    - **during** | **agg**.: *Hyos* k* zinc
    - **fail** to appear; if menses: puls h1
    - **suppressed** menses; with: *Puls*
  - **motion**:
    - **agg**.: *Camph* puls h1
    - **amel**.: mag-m
  - **music** agg.: thuj k*
  - **raising** it: zinc
  - **sitting**:
    - **agg**.: mag-m plat h2 zinc
    - **amel**.: ol-an
  - **standing** agg.: *Bar-c* ol-an
  - **vomiting**: sulph h2
  - **walking**:
    - **agg**.: merc nat-c h2 par puls
    - **air**; in open | **amel**.: borx
  - **writing** agg.: bar-c mtf33

○ • **Back** of feet: kali-c h2
  - **Soles** | **Balls**: mur-ac h2
- **Fingers**: alum b4.de* am-c b4.de* ambr b7.de* anthraq rly4• ars bry k* cic cimic bg2 cupr-ar flav jl2 *Glon* hyper iod k* kali-br bro1 lac-f mtf11 lol bro1 lyss mtf11 m-ambo b7.de m-arct b7.de med mtf11 *Merc* k* morph mosch b7.de* nat-c b4.de* nat-m k* nit-ac olnd k* phos k* plat plb psor mtf11 rhus-t k* sep stront-c k* tub mtf11 vanil fd5.de x-ray mtf11 zinc bro1
  - **night**: olnd
  - **motion** agg.: plb
  - **writing** agg.: *Cimic*

○ • **First**: *Calc*
    - **convulsive**: *Calc*
  - **Second**: stann h2
- **Forearms**: agar alum b4.de* anthraq rly4• bar-c *Calc-p* carbn-s caust k* cimic colch fl-ac merc nat-c b4.de* nicotam rly4• nit-ac k* *Onos* plb *Rhus-t* b7.de* sil b4.de* spong k* stram b7a.de vanil fd5.de zing
  - **right**: *Dulc* *Nit-ac*
  - **coition**; after: nat-p ptk1
  - **grasped**; when anything is: verat
  - **writing** agg.: *Caust* k* com **Merc** k*

▽ • **extending** to:
    - **Hand**: nicotam rly4•
    - **Thumb**: agar
- **Hands**: absin vml3• *Acon* k* **Agar** k* all-c k* alum k* alum-p k2 alum-sil k2 alumn am-c k* *Aml-ns* k* *Anac* k* androc srj1• *Ant-c* k* **Ant-t** k* anthraq rly4• *Apis* k* aran mtf11 *Arg-n* k* am *Ars* k* *Ars-i* ars-s-f k2 atro aur-m bac jl2* bapt bar-c k* *Bell* k* bism k* borx b4a.de bov k* bry k* bufo bg2 cadm-met tpw6 cain **Calc** k* calc-i k2 **Calc-p** k* *Calc-s* calc-sil k2 camph cann-i k* cann-s b7.de* caps b7.de* carb-ac *Carb-an* *Carbn-h* *Carbn-s* **Caust** k* chel k* *Chin* k* chinin-ar *Cic* k* cimic k* cist coca *Cocc* k* *Coff* k* colch k* con mtf11 conv br1 *Cop* *Crot-c* *Crot-h* k* crot-t cupr cycl dig dios dulc k* elaps ephe-si hsj1• falco-pe nl2• *Ferr* k* *Gels* *Glon* k* guare ham fd3.de• helo helo-s rwt2• hep b4a.de* hippoc-k szs2 hydr-ac *Hyos* k* *Ign* ind *Iod* k* kali-ar kali-br k* *Kali-c* k* kali-i kali-n *Kali-p* kali-s kali-sil k2 *Lac-c* lac-d lac-f mtf11 lac-lup hm2• *Lach* k* lact laur k* led k* lil-t *Lol* bg2* lyc k* lycps-v bg2 lyss k* m-arct b7.de

- **Hands**: ...
mag-c k* mag-m *Mag-p* k* mag-s manc mang-p rly4• med k* **Merc** k* mez k* morph mosch bg2 nat-ar nat-c k* **Nat-m** k* nat-p nat-s nat-sil fd3.de• nicc **Nit-ac** k* *Nux-m* k* **Nux-v** k* olnd b7.de* *Onos Op* k* ox-ac k* oxal-a rly4• ozone sde2• par k* ped mtf11 ph-ac k* **Phos** k* phys *Phyt Plat* k* **Plb** k* *Psor* k* ptel c1 *Puls* k* **Querc** sne ran-b b7.de* rheum k* rhod k* rhus-t k* sabad k* sacch-a fd2.de• samb k* sars k* sel b7.de* sep k* *Sil* k* spig k* spong k* **Stann** k* staphycoc rly4• *Stram* k* stry suis-pan rly4• **Sulph** k* syph jl2 tab tarent ptk1 ter thea ther bg2 *Thuj* k* tritic-vg fd5.de tub k* valer k* vanil fd5.de x-ray mtf11 yohim c1* **Zinc** k* [lith-met stj2 tax jsj7]
  - **right**: all-c k* anac aq-mar skp7• caust hydr-ac bg1 mez k* sep h2 sulph h2*
  - **left**: both-ax tsm2 calam sa3• calc *Glon* lac-c puls sacch-a fd2.de• stann h2 vanil fd5.de
  - **morning**: ars k* aur-m calam sa3• dulc fd4.de *Kali-c* k* lyc *Nat-c* k* *Nat-m* nat-s k2 phos k* sulph k*
    - **rising** agg.: crot-t k*
  - **forenoon**: kali-s fd4.de olib-sac wmh1 sars k* sulph k* valer k*
  - **noon**: cic h1 sulph h2
  - **afternoon**: *Calc* k* dulc fd4.de lyc h2 lycps-v mez k* nat-c k* vanil fd5.de
  - **evening**: *All-c* k* caust ferr k* mez k* plan k* *Plb*
    - **bed** agg.; in: nat-m k*
  - **night**: am-c k* bufo carb-v k*
    - **wakes** her: nat-c h2
  - **accompanied** by:
    - **anxiety** and perspiration (See MIND - Anxiety - perspiration - during - hands)
    - **heat**; flushes of: plat tl1
  - **alcoholic**: phos mtf11
  - **anger**; after: hydrog srj2• sep k*
  - **anxiety**; with: am-c bov calc-f sp1 cic granit-m es1• *Plat* puls symph fd3.de• tritic-vg fd5.de
    - **accompanied** by | **perspiration** (See MIND - Anxiety - perspiration - during - hands)
  - **breakfast**; during: *Carb-an*
  - **Bright's** disease: lycps-v
  - **chill**; during: canth k* chin
  - **contradiction**, after: cop k* *Nit-ac*
  - **convulsive**: colch k* *Hyos Plb*
  - **delirium** tremens: *Coff* k* *Crot-h* sne *Kali-br Lach* **Nux-v Querc** sne *Stram*
  - **dinner** | **after** | **agg.**: ant-c h2 mag-m h2*
    - **during** | **agg.**: grat k* (non:mag-m h2) tab k*
  - **eating**; while: bism **Cocc** k* merc mrr1 olnd k* plb mrr1 stram k*
  - **emotions** agg.: nat-m plb k*
  - **exertion** agg.; after: ferr-ma hyos
  - **fever**; during: valer b7.de*
  - **fine** work, at: ham fd3.de• nat-sil fd3.de• sulph h2
  - **fright**; after: op samb
  - **grasping** something:
    - **agg.**: led ptk1 lyss mtf11 merc ptk1 plb ptk1
    - **amel.**: stann h2
  - **hanging** down, while: phos k*
  - **headache**; during: androc srj1• calc-p carb-v h2 glon k2
  - **holding** objects:
    - **hold** of anything; on taking: cann-s k* cocc k2 *Led* k* lyss k* **Merc** k* *Sil* k* stram k* verat
    - **holding** objects; on: *Agar* k* bism cann-s k* com con lap-la sde8.de• **Merc Plb** k* plut-n srj7• sabad k* *Sil* spig k* *Staph* stram k*
  - **holding** the hand:
    - **free**: cocc **Merc** plat
    - **still**: *Coff*
    - **stretched** out: caust *Cocc Coff Gels* ign **Merc** *Merc-c Phos* plat **Plb** k* *Puls* tab k*
  - **hunger**; with: olnd k*

- **Hands**: ...
  - **intermittent**: *Calc* k*
  - **manual** labor: **Merc** plb *Sil*
  - **menses**; during: agar *Hyos* k* *Zinc* k*
  - **mental** exertion; from: borx h2
  - **motion** | **agg.**:
    - **hands** agg.; of: agar k* ant-c *Camph* k* ham fd3.de• iod *Kali-br* k* *Led* k* *Plb* puls
      - **typhoid** fever; in: *Gels*
    - **amel.**: *Crot-h* zinc
  - **mouth**; when carrying something to the: kali-br **Merc** k* **Plb** k* sil ptk1
  - **nervousness**, from: kali-p c1 tritic-vg fd5.de
  - **news**, after unpleasant: (↗*MIND - Ailments - bad*) nat-m k*
  - **pain**; with: aq-mar skp7• **Caust**
  - **palpitations**; with: bov ptk1
  - **paralytic**: ant-c k* ant-t vh bell k2 *Cocc* **Merc Plb**
  - **perspiration**; during: ant-t bg2 *Bry* bg2 chin bg2 cocc bg2 *Merc* bg2 op bg2 phos bg2 *Rhus-t* bg2 *Sulph* bg2
  - **raising** them high: **Cocc** k* dubo-h hs1 gels hr1* **Merc**
  - **resting** them on table, when: stann k* *Zinc* k*
  - **rising** agg.; after: nux-m k*
  - **rubbing** | **amel.**: *Nat-m* k*
  - **sitting** agg.: *Led* sil k*
  - **sleep** agg.; after: morph k*
  - **threading** needle, while: ran-b k* *Sil*
  - **tobacco**; from: *Nux-v*
  - **typesetting**, from: plb k*
  - **typhoid** fever; in: *Arg-n Zinc*
  - **using** them, from: dulc fd4.de *Phos* k* *Sil*
  - **vertigo**:
    - **after**: *Zinc* k*
    - **from**: gran k*
  - **vomiting**; while: calc hr1 calc-p k* *Nat-s Sulph*
  - **waking**; on: ant-c k* *Nat-s* k*
  - **walking** | **after** | **agg.**: sulph k* ust k*
    - **agg.**: *Led*
  - **weakness**: *Led* k* **Merc** plb k* *Stann*
  - **weather** | **cold**:
    - **wet** | **agg.**: dulc h1
    - **wet** | **agg.**: *Dulc*
  - **worry** agg.: plb
  - **writing**:
    - **after**: thuj h1
    - **agg.**: agar *All-c* alum *Ant-c* bar-c k* bism camph caps *Carb-ac* **Caust** chel *Chin* k* *Cimic* k* *Colch* dulc fd4.de falco-pe nl2• ferr hep hydrog srj2• hyos *Ign* k* kali-br *Kali-c* lycps-v *Lyss* **Merc** k* morph *Nat-m* k* *Nat-p Nat-s* k* olnd *Ph-ac Phos* **Plb** k* *Puls* sabad samb *Sil* stann **Sulph** k* thuj h1 valer c1 yohim c1* *Zinc* k*
      - **company**; when in: ign ptk1*
      - **flatulence**; followed by offensive: ant-c br1
    - **amel.** | **fast**; writing: ferr hr1*
- **Hips**: apis bg2 asaf b7.de* m-arct b7.de valer b7.de*
  - **left**: apis bg2
- **Internal**: carb-an h2* carc fd2.de• *Chin* k* gins k* sacch-a fd2.de• staph k* sul-ac k2 [pop dhh1]
  - ○ **Legs**: bit-ar wht1•
- **Joints**: cycl mang nit-ac h2
- **Knees**: acon agar k* aids nl2• *Alum* k* alum-p k2 alum-sil k2 *Anac* k* androc srj1• ant-t arg-met k2 *Asaf* b7.de* bell k* cadm-s calad calc k* *Camph* caps k* cass a1 *Chel* chin b7.de* chinin-s coff b7.de* colch bg2 con cycl bg2 dios dros b7.de* dulc bg2 *Glon* hep k* iris kali-c k* lach laur k* *Led* k* lil-t k* lol bg2 lyss mang k* merc k* mur-ac k* nat-m k* nicc k* nux-v k* ol-an bg2 olnd k* op phos k*

Extremities

- **Knees**: ...
Plat plb psor *Puls* k* rhus-t k* *Ruta* k* sep sil stann k* staph k* stry sulph b4.de* tab bg2 tarent verb k* zinc bg2
  - **left**: aids nl2•
  - **afternoon**: nicc k*
  - **evening**:
    - **lying** down agg.; after: puls h1
    - **standing** agg.: nux-v k*
    - **walking** agg.: mang k*
  - **night**:
    - **asleep**; on falling: plut-n srj7•
    - **waking**; on: chel k*
  - **ascending** stairs agg.: canth ptk1 dros nat-m
  - **descending** stairs agg.: coff sil ptk1
  - **emissions** agg.; after: nat-p
  - **exhaustion**; from: calc-f sp1
  - **motion** | **amel**.: cassia-s ccrh1•
  - **rising** from sitting agg.: chin k* nat-p k*
  - **sitting**:
    - **agg.**: bell *Led* k*
    - **amel.**: laur k*
  - **standing** agg.: calad k* cassia-s ccrh1• nux-v ol-an a1 olnd k* tarent
  - **stepping** up a step: nat-m k*
  - **walking**:
    - **after** | **agg.**: zinc h2
    - **agg.**: dios k* dros k* *Ind* k* *Led* k* mang tarent
    - **air** agg.; in open: *Hep* laur
    - **amel.**: chin k*
  - ○ **Patella**: mur-ac h2
- **Legs**: aesc-g bro1 ail am-m arg-met k* ars bar-c k* bell k* bufo cann-i tl1 canth carbn-s carc fd2.de• *Caust* cic k* cimic tl1* *Cob* bro1 coca *Cocc* bro1 cod bro1 coff colch bro1 coloc k* *Con* bro1 cur bro1 *Cycl* dendr-pol sk4• dig dios dor k* falco-pe nl2• ferr k* ferr-m fl-ac **Gels** bro1* hippoc-k szs2 ip b7.de* kali-c k* kali-sil k2 lac-loxod-a hm2• lact lol bro1 lyc mag-m b4.de* mag-p tl1 manc med meny b7.de* merc *Mim-p* bro1 nat-c k* *Nat-m* nit-ac bro1 ol-an onos ph-ac bro1 *Phos* k* pic-ac *Plat* k* *Plb* pneu jl2 *Puls* k* *Ruta* k* *Sil* *Stry* sulph k* tab bro1 tarent viol-t b7.de* zinc k* [tax jsj7]
  - **left**: *Cic* psil ft1
  - **morning**: bufo phys k*
    - **rising** agg.; after: *Arg-met*
  - **forenoon** | **11** h: arg-n nat-m
  - **afternoon**: lac-loxod-a hm2•
  - **evening**: plat puls h1 sil h2
    - **lying** down agg.; after: plat *Puls*
  - **night**: bufo
  - **anger**; after: dendr-pol sk4•
  - **ascending** ladder: *Caust* k*
  - **coition**; after: **Calc**
  - **descending** stairs agg.: lac-c kr1
  - **exertion** agg.; slight: **Gels** mrr1
  - **menses**; before: kali-c
  - **motion** agg.: canth k*
  - **room** | **amel**.: caust
  - **sitting** agg.: *Plat*
  - **sleep**; on going to: *Cham*
  - **standing** agg.: kali-c h2
  - **stool** agg.; after: ars k*
  - **talking** of her complaints; when: falco-pe nl2•
  - **walking**:
    - **agg.**: cimic ptk *Led* puls h1
    - **air** agg.; in open: coloc
  - ○ **Calves**: meny k* nat-c h2 nat-m k* sulph k*
- **Lower** limbs: acon *Agar* am-c b4.de* am-m b7.de* *Ambr* k* anac k* apis *Arg-met* **Arg-n** k* arn k* *Ars* k* ars-i ars-s-f k2 bamb-a stb2.de• bapt bg2 bar-c b4.de* bell borx b4a.de bufo bg2 *Calc* k* calc-i k2 calc-s calc-sil k2 camph b7.de* canth k* caps carb-v k* carbn-s *Caust* k* chin chinin-ar chinin-s *Cic* k* *Cimic* k* cist cob cocc coloc k* *Con* k* corn *Crot-h* cupr dig b4.de* falco-pe nl2• fl-ac k* **Gels** bg2* *Glon* graph b4.de* helo helo-s rwt2• hep hyos iod k* ip kali-ar kali-bi k* kali-c kali-p fd1.de• kali-s **Lach** k* lact lat-m bnm6• *Lath* *Led* lyc k* manc *Med* *Merc* k* nat-ar nat-c k* *Nat-m* k* **Nit-ac** k* nux-m b7.de* **Nux-v** k* olib-sac wmh1 olnd **Op** k* par b7.de* petr phos k* phys *Phyt* pic-ac k2 pip-m plan ptk1 plat b4.de* *Plb* k* positr nl2• ptel hr1 *Puls* k* ran-b raph rhus-t k* ros-d wla1 sabad b7.de* sars k* sec seneg k* sep sil sol-ni spig b7.de* *Stann* b4a.de stram k* sulph thal-s c1 thuj bg1 *Verat* zinc
  - **left**: cic ptk1
  - **morning**: *Arg-met* *Nit-ac* olib-sac wmh1 puls k*
  - **forenoon** | **10** h: gels ptel
  - **afternoon**: olib-sac wmh1
  - **evening**: lyc olib-sac wmh1 plb k* puls
  - **night**: hep plut-n srj7•
  - **accompanied** by | **sciatica** (See Pain - lower limbs - sciatic - accompanied - trembling)
  - **air** agg.; in open: caust h2
  - **alcoholic** drinks; as from: nept-m lsd2.fr
  - **alone** amel.; being: ambr
  - **anxiety**: borx rhus-t sars
  - **ascending** stairs agg.: calc sne *Caust* corn nat-m k* nux-m
  - **carrying** a weight: graph h2
  - **chagrin**; from (See mortification)
  - **chill**, as from: caust h2
  - **coition**; after: **Calc** k* nat-p ptk1
  - **exertion**:
    - **after**:
      - **agg.**: iber c1
      - **slight** exertion: **Gels** mrr1
  - **fear**; with (See MIND - Fear - sudden - trembling)
  - **first** lower, then upper limbs: spig h1
  - **jerking**: lyc h2
  - **lying** agg.: plb
  - **menses**; during: agar caust graph hyos mag-c nat-c
  - **mortification**; from: ran-b
  - **motion** | **after** | **agg.**: phos k*
    - **amel.**: **Rhus-t**
  - **reclining**: fl-ac k*
  - **rhythmical**: *Ign*
  - **rising** after sitting; on: *Nat-m* nux-m
  - **sensation**; tremulous: rhus-t b7.de* sabad b7.de*
  - **sitting** agg.: plan plb
  - **spoken** to, when: merc
  - **standing** | **after** | **long** time; for a: *Led* olnd
    - **agg.**: caust h2
  - **stool** agg.; after: ars
  - **stooping** agg.: ars bg1
  - **vexation**; after: ran-b
  - **walking**:
    - **agg.**: caust h2 *Con* cupr bg2 cur lath br1 led merc nux-m **Nux-v** phys bg2
    - **amel.**: *Nat-m*
    - **difficult**: cimic k2*
- **Muscles** | **single** group of: plac rzf5•
- **Paralyzed** parts: **Caust** k* merc ptk1 nux-m ptk1 nux-v pd plb k*
- **Shoulders**: aesc ang b7.de* asaf k* com dros k* mang a1 puls b7.de* spig b7.de* sul-ac bg2 sulph symph fd3.de• [pop dhh1]
  - **rest**, only at: dros tl1
  - ○ **Joints**: asaf b7.de*
- **Tendons**: | **weakness**; from: *Hyos* br1*

- **Thighs**: act-sp aesc-g bro1 agar bg2 *Anac* k* apis arg-met bro1 ars-h asaf k* bar-c k* caps bg2* carbn-s cic h1 *Cob* bro1 cocc k* cod bro1 colch bro1 *Con* k* cur bro1 dor bro1 *Gels* bro1 ham fd3.de• kali-c k* kali-s fd4.de laur lil-t bg2 lol bro1 mag-m k* meny b7.de* merc bg2 *Mez* b4a.de *Mim-p* bro1 nit-ac bro1 nux-v b7.de* o p bg2 ph-ac k* phos h2* *Plat* k* rat sep k* sol-ni tab bro1 tarax b7.de* zinc bro1
  - **right**: con ham fd3.de• kali-s fd4.de lac-c rat
  - **left**: calam sa3•
  - **evening**: kali-s fd4.de rat
  - **coition**; after: **Calc**
  - **kneeling**, on: cocc k*
  - **raised**, when: act-sp k*
  - **sensation**: caust h2
  - **sitting** agg.: ham fd3.de• plat
  - **walking** agg.: *Con*
  - ○ **Muscles** of: carc jl2
- **Thumbs**: ambr h1* olnd bg2 petr-ra shn4• plat k*
  - **evening**: ambr c1
- **Toes**: *Arn* b7.de* bar-c bg2 con bg2 *Mag-c* bg2* mez b4.de* zinc bg2
- **Upper** arms: agar am-c b4.de* ant-c aran asaf k* bry b7.de* carbn-s fl-ac ign b7.de* kali-c b4.de* lyc b4.de* m-arct b7.de *Mez* b4a.de nit-ac spig b7.de* stann b4.de* tarax b7.de*
  - **motion** | **amel.**: asaf
- **Upper** limbs: acon k* *Agar* alumn ambr k* anac k* *Arg-n* *Ars* k* ars-s-f k2 bar-c k* bell k* bry k* cadm-met tpw6 calc k* calc-i k2 *Calc-p* k* calc-sil k2 cann-i tl1 caps k* *Carbn-s* carneg-g rwt1• caust k* chel *Cic* k* cimic bg2 *Cocc* k* cod bro1 coff colch com crot-h *Cupr* dor eupi ferr-m *Gels* bro1 graph helo c1 helo-s c1* *Hyos* k* hyper ind iod k* kali-ar kali-br bro1 kali-c kali-s lac-lup hm2• lact br1 lil-t lyc m-ambo b7.de m-arct b7.de manc med meph k* **Merc** k* murx nicotam rly4• **Nit-ac** k* ol-an onos **Op** k* paeon petr k* ph-ac k* *Phos* k* phys plan **Plb** k* puls b7.de* rhod k* *Rhus-t* k* sabad k* sabin k* samb b7a.de seneg k* *Sil* k* *Spig* k* spong k* *Stann* b4a.de *Stram* k* suis-pan rly4• sulph k* tab thuj k* tritic-vg fd5.de verat k* viol-o zinc k*
  - **right**: caust bg2* eupi graph bg1 nit-ac bg1 sil h2 sulph h2*
  - **left**: both-ax tsm2 com bg1 hyper lac-c bg1 puls h1 stann bg1 sulph h2 vac jl2
    - **convulsions**; before epileptic: sil ptk1
  - **morning**: *Sil* sulph
  - **forenoon**: paeon
    - **11** h: phys plb
  - **evening**: *Hyos* phys plan tritic-vg fd5.de
    - **19** h: phys
  - **night** | **waking**; on: verat
  - **brandy** amel.: plb
  - **convulsions** | **before** | **epileptic**: *Sil*
    - **during**: sulph
  - **eating** | **after** | **agg.**: bism
    - **agg.**: plb mrr1 sec stram tung-met bdx1•
  - **exertion** agg.: ix bnm8•
    - **moderate**, after: *Hyos* **Rhus-t** sil
  - **fine** work, with: sulph
  - **holding** anything: coff led lyc phos verat a1
    - **abducted** arm, with: caust h2
  - **lain** on: *Camph* k*
  - **leaning** on it, when: astac meph
  - **mental** exertion agg.: vinc
  - **motion**:
    - **after** | **agg.**: hyos
    - **agg.**: bell led plb
    - **amel.**: com **Rhus-t**
    - **slight** motion | **agg.**: bell gels iod *Mag-p*
  - **paroxysms**; during: *Op*
  - **raising** arm agg.: dubo-h hs1
  - **rising** agg.; after: alumn
  - **sensation** of: cimic bg2 con bg2 merc bg2 ol-an bg2 phos bg2 rhus-t b7.de* sabad b7.de*

Trembling – Upper limbs: ...

  - **sitting** agg.: merc
  - **sleep** agg.; during: merc
  - **standing** agg.: merc
  - **taking** hold of anything: verat k*
  - **urination** | **difficult**: dulc k*
  - **work**, fatigue: *Cupr Plb*
  - **writing**:
    - **after**: thuj
    - **agg.**: agar ant-c bar-c caust chin cimic coff colch hep kali-c **Merc** k* nat-m nat-s olnd ph-ac plb mrr1 sabad samb sep sulph thuj valer zinc k*
  - ○ **Internally**: petr h2
  - **Muscles**: carc jl2
- **Wrists**: acon k* chel glon olnd k* plb
  - **emotion**, from: plb
  - **headache**; during: glon
  - **motion** agg.: acon plb

TRICKLING:

- **drops** of water; like | **Upper** limbs: chinin-s bg2

TUBERCLES (See Eruptions - tubercles)

TUBERCULOSIS: | Hips: calc ptk1 calc-p ptk1 card-m ptk1 chin ptk1 coloc ptk1 dros gk hep ptk1 kali-c ptk1 kali-s ptk1 led ptk1 ph-ac ptk1 puls ptk1 rhus-t ptk1 sil ptk1 stram ptk1 tub ptk1*

TUMORS:

- ○ **Ankles**: cupr-ar k*
- **Elbow**:
  - **cystic**: hep b4a.de*
  - **painful**: puls h1
  - ○ **Point** of | **steatoma**: hep
- **Feet** | **benign**: hecla bc
- **Fingers** | **enchondroma**: sil hr1
- **Hands**:
  - **wen**: ph-ac plb sil
  - ○ **Between** metacarpal bones: ph-ac sang hr1 tarent
- **Knees**: ant-c
  - ○ **Hollow** of knees: calc-f phos sil
    - **fibroid**: calc-f ptk1
- **Legs**: tarent
  - **varicose**: arn
  - ○ **Calves**: kali-br *Sulph*
  - **Tibia** | **osteosarcoma** (See Cancer - bones - tibia - osteosarcoma)
- **Shoulders**: cund sne
  - **fatty**: am-m k* cund sne
- **Thighs**: merc phos sil sne
  - ○ **Between** thigh and vulva: goss
- **Toes** | **enchondroma**: sil hr1
- **Wrists**: *Cupr-ar Led*

TURNING:

- **ankles**: arn bg2 carb-an bg2 nat-c bg2 nux-v bg2 ph-ac bg2 phos bg2 ruta bg2 sil bg2 sulph bg2
- **bed**; turning over in | **agg.** | **Lower** limbs: nat-s bg2 nux-v bg2 zinc bg2
  - **amel.**:
    - **Lower** limbs: *Cham* b7a.de
    - **Upper** limbs: *Cham* b7a.de
- **convulsions**; during | **epileptic** (See GENERALS - Convulsions - epileptic - during - extremities)
- **inward**:
  - **arm**: bell h1
  - **upper** limbs: bell b4.de*
    - **Deltoid**: urt-u ptk1
- **lower** limbs | **agg.**: bry b7.de* calc bg2 cocc b7.de* coloc bg2* kali-c bg2* sabin b7a.de seneg b4.de*

Extremities

- **outwards** | **agg.** | **Lower** limbs: caps b7.de*
  - **limbs**: graph h2* nux-v bg2 ruta bg2
- **upper** limbs:
  - **agg.**: sang ptk1
    - ⁝ **Deltoid**: sang ptk1
  - **amel.**: spig ptk1
- **wrist** | **agg.**: merc-i-f ptk1

TWISTING sensation: bros-gau mrc1

○ - **Joints**: nat-c mtf11 nat-m mtf11 nat-pyru mtf11 psor mtf11
- **Knees**: dios sep zinc bg2*
- **Lower** limbs: caust bg2 graph h2 zinc bg2
- **Shoulders**: hura
- **Thighs**: carc gk6
- **Upper** arms: carc gk6
- **Upper** limbs: ars bg2 **Bell** k* cit-v dios bg2 graph h2 hyos bg2 iod nux-v bg2 sulph bg2
- **Wrists**: graph h2 plb

TWITCHING: *(↗Jerking; MIND - Gestures - tics; MIND - Tourette's)* *Agar* k* agath-a nl2• *Alum* k* alum-p k2 alum-sil k2 alumn k* ambr k* ant-c vh1 *Apis* arn k* *Ars* k* ars-i asaf atra-r bnm3• bamb-a stb2.de• **Bell** k* calad k* calc calc-f sp1 cann-i k* carb-ac k* carb-v carbn-s k2 carc mg1.de* carl k* caust *Cham* k* **Chel** k* *Chin* *Chinin-s* chlf a1 *Cic* k* cic-m a1 cimic **Cina** *Cocc* *Coff* coff-t a1 colch k* coloc croc mrr1 *Crot-c* *Cupr* k* cupr-ar a1 cypr cyt-l a1 dol c1 dros k* dulc k* ferr-p bg1 graph *Hell* helo-s rwt2• **Hyos** k* hyosin a1 **Ign** k* kali-ar kali-c k* kali-i k* kali-m k2 kali-n k* kali-p kali-s kali-sil k2 ketogl-ac rly4• kreos k* lach k* lat-m bnm6• laur k2 lipp a1 lyc h2 lyss c1 mag-p br1 meny lp *Merc* k* *Merc-c* k* morph k* mur-ac k* *Mygal* nat-ar *Nat-c* k* *Nat-m* k* nat-p nat-s nit-ac k* *Nux-m* k* *Nux-v* k* **Op** k* paeon k* pegan-ha tpi1• petr k* ph-ac k* phos k* pieri-b mlk9.de plac rzf5• plb k* puls ran-s k* **Rhus-t** k* *Rhus-v* sarcol-ac sp1 scut c1 sec k* *Sep* k* *Sil* spong fd4.de staph mrr1 **Stram** k* **Stry** k* suis-hep rly4• sul-i k2 sulph k* *Tarent* mrr1 thal-xyz srj8• tritic-vg fd5.de **Valer** k* vanil fd5.de verat mrr1 verat-v mrr1 *Visc* k* *Zinc* k* zinc-p k2 [heroin sdj2 tax jsj7]

- **side** twitching, paralysis of the other; one: *Apis* art-v *Bell* *Stram*
- **daytime**: carb-v petr k* *Sep* sil h2
- **morning**: dulc fd4.de phos h2 sulph k*
  - **rising** agg.; after: alumn
  - **sleep** agg.; during: cham
- **forenoon**: alumn k* spong fd4.de
- **afternoon** | **trying** to sleep; when: alum k*
- **evening**: carc fd2.de• caust k* dulc fd4.de graph k* spong fd4.de vanil fd5.de
  - **bed** agg.; in: *Carb-v* kali-n h2 nux-v k*
  - **sitting** agg.: am-m h2 dulc fd4.de
- **night**: ambr calc k* dulc fd4.de mag-c h2 nat-c k* phos sep k* sil h2 spong fd4.de staph stront-c
  - **bed** agg.; in: **Ars** merc-ns stry
- **backward** and inward: cupr h2
- **bed** agg.; in: merc-n k* merc-ns nux-v stry k*
- **chill**:
  - **after**: puls
  - **during**: acon dig jatr-c lyc nux-m *Nux-v* op k* ox-ac stram k* tab
- **convulsions**:
  - **after**: nux-v k*
  - **during**: *Op* k*
- **cough** agg.; during: *Cina* b7a.de cupr b7a.de*
- **cramping**: plat h2
- **electric** shocks, as from: agar *Ars* bamb-a stb2.de• colch k* nat-m k* plat k* *Ter* *Verat* h1
- **heat**; during: all-s k* dulc fd4.de op b7.de rhus-t b7a.de*
- **lightning**-like: stry k*
- **manual** labor amel.: agar
- **menses**; during: *Coff* oena
- **motion**:
  - **amel.**: *Ars* cop k* phos k* valer
  - **limbs** agg.; of: *Lyc* sep k*
- **numbness**; followed by: **Rhus-t**
- **paralytic**: cina
- **paroxysmal**: stram k*

Twitching: ...

- **sitting** agg.: **Valer**
- **sleep**:
  - **amel.**: agar k2
  - **before**: alum k*
  - **during** | **agg.**: acon k* *Alum* st ambr *Ars* k* bell cham cob k* *Colch* cupr *Hell* hep *Kali-c* k* *Lyc* k* mag-c h2 morph k* nat-c nat-m k* petr h2 puls k* *Sep* sil *Stram* k* sulph thuj *Zinc*
  - **falling** asleep | **when**: *Alum* st **Ars** *Cham* kali-c mrr1 mag-c *Nat-m* puls h1 sacch-a fd2.de• tub k13
  - **waking**; on: nit-ac h2
- **stupor**; with (See MIND - Stupor - twitching)
- **sudden**: am
- **synchronous** with respiration: hyos
- **thunderstorm**; during: phos
- **touch** agg.: puls k*
- **vexation**; after: ign petr
- **vomiting**; while: stram k*
- **waking**; on: op k*
- **wandering**: am-m h2 castm cocc coloc k* graph k* *Merc* k* nat-s k* plat
- **write**, on attempting to: nat-m h2

○ - **Ankles**: agar asaf carbn-s iod h mag-m mez *Puls* b7a.de
- **Arm** and one leg; one: apis apoc chen-a c1 hell stram tub
- **Elbows**: agn k* aloe am-c k* arg-met bar-c bg2 bell k* carbn-s caust k* cina b7.de* croc b7.de* graph k* lact k* *Mang* b4a.de *Nat-m* k* nit-ac bg2 phos h2 rheum k* rhus-t b7.de* ruta sabad k* sulph k* verat b7.de* zinc k*
  - **morning**: nat-m k*
  - **noon** | **lying** agg.: zinc k*
  - **afternoon**: nat-m
    - ⁝ **15** h: arg-met
  - **motion** | **amel.**: agn arg-met
  - **resting** on it: caust h2
  - **stretching** arm amel.: nat-m k*

▽ • **extending** to | **Wrist**: nit-ac h2

○ • **Bends** of elbow: arg-met bar-c k* plut-n srj7•
    - ⁝ **left**: plut-n srj7•
- **Feet**: agath-a nl2• *Alum* k* alum-sil k2 am-c b4.de* arg-met am k* ars b4.de* asaf k* bar-c bar-m canth k* carb-an carbn-s cedr chel *Chin* b7.de* *Cic* b7a.de cimic cina k* coff b7.de* con b4.de* crot-t cupr k* dream-p sdj1• dulc *Graph* k* **Hyos** k* ign b7.de* iod *Ip* k* laur k* led k* mag-c k* mag-m b4.de* merc k* mez b4.de* mur-ac *Nat-c* k* nat-s nux-v petr phos puls k2 ruta santin sars b4.de* *Sep* k* sil spig b7.de* **Stram** k* stry sulph k* *Thuj* k* valer b7.de* verat k* [heroin sdj2]
  - **midnight**: nat-c
    - ⁝ **after**, during sleep: nat-s
  - **daytime**: sulph
  - **morning** | **rising** agg.; after: mag-c
  - **afternoon** | **sleep**; during: ruta sep h2
  - **evening**: alum arg-met sulph h2
    - ⁝ **sleep** agg.; on going to: carb-an
  - **night**: canth lyc h2 mag-c nat-s
  - **bed** agg.; in: arg-met cimic nat-c
  - **bending** them: led
  - **crawling**: thuj
  - **lying** | **back**; on | **agg.**: nux-v
    - ⁝ **side**; on:
      - : **painless** side | **amel.**: nux-v
  - **sitting** agg.: crot-t sulph h2
  - **sleep** | **during** | **agg.**: hyos *Lyc* b4a.de nat-s sulph
    - ⁝ **going** to, on: carb-an
  - **standing** agg.: sulph h2 verat
  - **sticking**: nux-v
  - **stitches** in tibia, from: arg-met h1
  - **upward**: mag-c thuj

○ • **Back** of feet: sars h2

- **Heels**: all-c am-c eupi kalm lith-c mag-c mag-m nat-c
- **Soles**: crot-t cupr graph mur-ac a1 plat plut-n srj7• sul-ac sulph symph fd3.de• thuj h1
  - **motion** | **amel.**: sulph h2
  - **sitting** agg.: jatr-c plat h2
  - **standing** agg.: plat
    - **right** foot; on: plat a1

- **Fingers**: *Acon* k* *Agar* k* *Alum* k* am-c k* am-m b7.de* *Anac* k* apis b7a.de arn b7.de* ars k* bism k* bry k* cadm-s calc bg2 *Caust* k* cham k* chel k* *Chin* k* *Cic* k* *Cimic* k* *Cina* k* *Cocc* k* crot-t **Cupr** k* dig k* dulc k* ign k* iod k* kali-bi k* kali-br kali-c k* kali-n bg2 lach k* lith-c lyc k* m-ambo b7.de m-arct b7.de m-aust b7.de mag-c k* mag-m bg2 mang k* meny b7.de* *Merc* k* mez bg2* mosch b7.de* *Nat-c* k* nux-v k* olnd b7.de* op k* *Osm* ox-ac ph-ac k* **Phos** b4.de* plat k* plb k* puls k* ran-s b7.de* rheum b7.de* rhod k* rhus-t k* sabad k* sil b4.de* spig k* *Stann* k* staph b7.de* stront-c k* *Sul-ac* k* sulph k* tab k* valer b7.de* zinc bg2
  - **daytime**: phos k*
  - **morning**: pall
    - **rising** agg.; after: mag-c k*
  - **evening**: lyc k* puls k* sulph k*
    - **lying** down agg.; after: puls k*
  - **night**: mag-c k* nat-c k*
    - **sleep** agg.; during: nat-c
  - **accompanied** by | **Teeth**; pain in (See TEETH - Pain - accompanied - fingers - pain - twitching)
  - **cramping**: anac h2
  - **grasping** something agg.: *Nat-c* hr1
  - **motion** agg.: bry
  - **sewing**, when: kali-c
  - **shivering**; during: merc b4.de
  - **sleep** agg.; during: anac k* cupr k* lyc k* nat-c k* puls h1 rheum h* sul-ac b4a.de* sulph k*
  - **synchronous** with pulse: anac h2
  - **writing** agg.: caust k*
  - **Bones**: mez h2
  - **First**: am-m dig k* lyc k* mang k* nat-ar pall k* rhod k* sil k*
    - **evening**: am-m mang k*
    - **sitting** agg.: pall k*
  - **Fourth**: chin k* com k* kali-bi k* meny k* nat-c h2 phos k*
  - **Joints**: agar bg2 am-m bg2 chin bg2 nat-c h2 stront-c bg2 zinc bg2
  - **Second**: arn chin k* cinch a1 dulc h2 fl-ac k* kali-n k* nat-ar sil k* stann k* thuj k*
  - **Third**: chin k* cinch a1 kali-n k* mang k* nat-c k*
    - **afternoon**: mang k*
  - **Tips**: am-m b7.de* **Ars** k* merc k* phos k* staph k* sul-ac k* thuj k*
    - **chill**; during: merc b4.de

- **Forearms**: acon b7.de* agar k* aloe alum k* ars asaf k* atro bar-c calc camph b7.de* caps k* castm caust k* cina bg2 *Cupr* b7.de* fl-ac graph ign b7.de* *Led* k* merc mez nat-c k* nat-m k* nit-ac k* nux-m nux-v olnd *Op* b7.de* phos h2 plat k* plb prun bg2 puls k* ran-b b7.de* rhod k* rhus-v sabad k* sars k* sil k* *Spig* k* staph k* stram k* stry *Tarax* k* teucr bg2 thuj k* vanil fd5.de verat b7.de* zing k*
  - **morning**:
    - **waking** agg.; after: puls h1*
    - **walking** agg.; after: (non:puls h1)
  - **afternoon** | **16** h: zing
  - **chill**; during: nux-m
  - **cramping**: anac h2 asaf
  - **grasping** something agg.: *Nat-c*
  - **rest** agg.: asaf k* *Spig* staph k*
  - **sneezing** agg.: castm
  - **writing** agg.: caust k* ox-ac
  - **Extensor** side: agar h2

- **Hands**: acon b7.de* agn b7.de* aloe alumn am-m b7.de* anac b4.de* ant-t k* *Asaf* k* bar-m k* *Bell* k* brom calc bg2 canth k* caps b7.de* carbn-s k2 caust k* chin b7.de* *Cina* k* *Cocc* *Coff* colch con k* *Cupr* k* dulc k* *Graph* k* grat bg2 **Hyos** k* ign k* iod k* kreos k* *Lach* k* lact k* laur b7.de* lyc bg2 lyss k* mag-s k* manc k* mang h2 melal-alt gya4 meph k* merc k* mez k* *Nat-c* k* nat-m k* nat-s k* nit-ac k* nux-m *Nux-v* k* oena k* *Op* k* ph-ac k* phyt *Plat* k* plb k* ran-b k* rheum k* rhod k* rhus-t bg2 sabad k* santin sec k* sep k* *Stann* k* *Stram* k* stry k* *Sul-ac* k* sulph k* thuj valer k* viol-t k* visc c1 zinc k*
  - **midnight**:
    - **before**: nat-c k*
    - **after**: nat-c k*
    - **sleep** agg.; during: nat-s
  - **daytime**: sulph k*
  - **morning**: cupr k* nat-c k* rheum h
    - **rising** agg.; after: cupr k*
  - **afternoon** | **sitting** agg.: lach
  - **night**: canth k* con k* nat-c k* nat-s k*
    - **sleep** agg.; during: con k* nat-s k*
    - **waking**; on: stann k*
  - **chill**; during: nux-m nux-v
  - **chorea**-like: stram tl1
  - **convulsive**: brom k* colch colchin a1 nux-v k* phyt k*
  - **cough** agg.; during: *Cina*
  - **exertion** agg.: *Merc* k*
  - **fever**; during: *Viol-t* b7.de*
  - **fright**; after: op
  - **lying** agg.: merc k*
  - **paroxysmal**: rhod k*
  - **perspiration**; during: bry bg2 *Cham* bg2 chin bg2 cina bg2 cupr bg2 ign bg2 *Op* bg2 rheum bg2 **Rhus-t** bg2
  - **rising** agg.: cupr k* nat-m k*
  - **sitting** agg.: lach
  - **sleep** agg.; during: con k* cupr k* ign k* nat-s k* ph-ac k* viol-t k*
  - **spasm**, at beginning: sulph
  - **taking** hold of anything: nat-c k*
  - **tremulous**: sec k*
  - **Back** of hands: carc fd2.de• nat-c h2 nat-m bg2
  - **Between** fingers:
    - **First** | **Thumb**; and: mag-s k* melal-alt gya4 stann k*
  - **Hollow** of: caps k*
  - **Palms**: act-sp bro1 anac bro1 ant-c bro1 ant-t bro1 *Arg-n* bro1 arn bro1 aven bro1 calc bro1 caps h1 chel k* *Cic* bro1 *Cina* bro1 *Cocc* bro1 *Con* bro1 *Cur* bro1 *Gels* bro1 hipp bro1 lach bro1 lact-v bro1 lol bro1 *Mag-p* bro1 *Merc* bro1 *Phos* bro1 *Sarcol-ac* bro1 sars bro1 sep k* sil bro1 *Stann* bro1 *Stram* bro1 sulph bro1 tab bro1 *Zinc* bro1
  - **Ulnar** side: fago k* ox-ac k*

- **Hips**: ant-c b7.de* *Ars* k* *Calc* k* cann-s b7.de* cocc k* *Coloc* k* crot-h bg2 mag-c k* *Mag-m* k* meny bg2 mez k* nux-v b7.de* ph-ac k* pic-ac a1 sep k* sil k* stann k* sulph k* teucr b7.de* valer k*
  - **evening** | **bed** agg.; in: mag-m h2 sil k*
  - **motion** | **amel.**: sulph k*
  - **Joints**: *Coloc* b4a.de *Mez* b4a.de nux-v b7.de*

- **Joints**: alum bell bry graph nat-c h2 nat-m nit-ac h2 puls sil spig spong *Sul-ac* sulph *Verat*

- **Knees**: acon b7.de* *Agar* k* agath-a nl2• aloe am-c k* am-m b7.de* anac k* arg-met k* asaf *Bell* k* brom calc canth b7.de* carb-an caust k* chel chin k* coloc b4a.de euphr b7.de* eupi graph k* kreos b7a.de *Laur* b7.de* lyc m-aust b7.de* mag-c meny merc k* mez mur-ac a1 nat-p nit-ac k* nux-v b7.de* ox-ac phos prun puls rhod k* spig b7.de* staph sul-ac thuj k* tritic-vg fd5.de valer b7.de* verat k*
  - **right**, sitting amel.: lac-h htj1•
  - **afternoon**: caust
  - **evening**: carb-an h2 lyc
  - **chin** would be knocked together; as if knees and: nat-m bg2
  - **convulsive**: lyc

- **motion** | **amel.**: meny
- **sitting** agg.: anac h2 arg-met *Mez* staph h1 tritic-vg fd5.de
- **sleep** agg.; on going to: carb-an
- **standing** agg.: sul-ac

○ • **Hollow** of knees: agar am-m h2 bell dig laur nux-v spong
  ⁝ **bending** knee agg.: spong
  ⁝ **rhythmical**, with: dig k* puls
  ⁝ **standing** agg.: nux-v
  ⁝ **touch** | **amel.**: dig
  ⁝ **walking** in open air agg.; after: nux-v
- **Inside** of: agar *Asaf* brom canth sul-ac
  ⁝ **excitement** agg.: hydrog srj2•
- **Patella**: am-c caust mez spig thuj
  ⁝ **evening**: am-c
  ⁝ **itching**: stann h2
  ⁝ **standing** agg.: mez
  ⁝ **Below**: stann h2
- **Sides**:
  ⁝ **Outer**: arg-met *Asaf* canth
   : **intermittent**: canth k*
   : **sitting** agg.: arg-met

\- **Legs**: agar agn k* *Alum* k* alum-sil k2 am-c k* am-m b7.de* **Anac** k* ant-t k* arn b7.de* ars k* ars-i asaf k* asar b7.de* atro bell berb bry k* calc k* calc-i k2 calc-sil k2 *Camph* carb-an carb-v carbn-s k2 carl caust cedr *Chel* cina b7.de* coff b7.de* con k* crot-t *Cupr* k* cycl b7.de* dig k* goss *Graph* k* guaj k* guare *Hell* hyos ign k* iod *Ip* k* kali-n kreos *Lach* lyc k* lyss *M-aust* b7.de mag-c k* mag-m k* mang meny b7.de* merc k* *Merc-c* mez k* morph *Mosch* mygal nit-ac k* olnd b7.de* *Op* k* petr k* phos k* phyt plan plat k* plb b7.de* puls b7.de* ran-s b7.de* *Rhus-t* k* rumx sep sil squil k* stram stry suis-hep rly4• sulph k* tarax b7.de* teucr til valer *Verat* viol-t b7.de* visc c1

- **right**: helo-s rwt2•
  ⁝ **bed** agg.; in: colch rsj2•
- **afternoon** | **sitting** agg.: ars lach
- **evening**: alum am-c dig lyc mez
  ⁝ **bed** agg.; in: carb-an h2 carb-v kali-n
  ⁝ **sitting** agg.: carb-an
- **night**: bry con iris-foe mag-c stry
- **convulsive**: ars bad phyt stram
- **exertion** agg.: mang
- **motion** | **amel.**: *Valer*
- **painful**: bell petr h2 *Rhus-t*
- **rest** agg.: calc h2 meny h1
- **sitting** agg.: anac plat squil
- **sleep** | **during** | **agg.**: *Agar* cinnb crot-t lyc sep verat
  ⁝ **siesta**: | **during**: crot-t
- **stepping** out, when: *Rhus-t*
- **sticking**, with: calc
- **stitches** in sole, from: dig
- **touch** agg.: agn ars
- **upward**: kreos morph
- **walking** | **after** | **agg.**: plat h2
  ⁝ **agg.**: agn petr h2 phos

▽ • **extending** to:
  ⁝ **Downward**: plat
  ⁝ **Stomach**: lyc

○ • **Bones** | **Tibia**: mez h2
- **Calves**: agar ant-t asar bar-c chel coloc dig h2 eupi **Graph** k* jatr-c kali-bi laur mag-m merc mez h2 nat-c nat-sil fd3.de• nit-ac h2 olnd op phos h2 puls ran-s rat rhus-t tarax viol-t zinc
  ⁝ **morning**: eupi
   : **bed** agg.; in: laur puls zinc
  ⁝ **forenoon** | **sitting** agg.: nat-c
  ⁝ **convulsive**: *Op*
  ⁝ **cramping**: *Jatr-c*

\- **Legs – Calves**: ...
  ⁝ **motion** | **amel.**: coloc h2
  ⁝ **paroxysmal**: nit-ac h2
  ⁝ **sitting** agg.: nat-c h2 nat-sil fd3.de•
  ⁝ **stretching** out foot: laur
  ⁝ **synchronous** with pulse: dig h2
  ⁝ **touch**:
   : **agg.**: tarax
   : **amel.**: dig h2
- **Knee**; below: cycl h1
- **Muscles**: carc mlr1•
- **Tendo** Achillis: cedr merc tab
  ⁝ **visible**: merc

\- **Lower** limbs: agar *Alum* alum-sil k2 am-c b4a.de *Ambr* k* anac ptk1 ang bg2 arg-met k* am b7.de* ars asaf k* asar k* bamb-a stb2.de• bar-c k* bell k* berb bry b7.de* calc k* camph carb-an *Carb-v* k* carbn-s k2 caust k* *Chel* chin b7.de* cic k* *Cina* k* *Clem* b4a.de cocc k* cod br1 *Coloc* b4a.de *Cupr* dig k* dulc b4.de* glon graph k* *Hell* hep *Hyos* b7.de* ign k* **Iod** b4a.de ip k* jatr-c kali-bi bg2 kali-c k* kreos b7a.de lach k* lyc b4a.de mag-c k* manc mang k* meny bg2 merc k* merc-c b4a.de mez k* nat-c k* nat-m k* nit-ac *Nux-v* k* *Op* k* ozone sde2• *Petr* b4a.de ph-ac k* **Phos** k* phys ptk1 plac rzf5• plat k* *Puls* b7a.de rheum k* *Rhus-t* sec k* sep k* *Sil* k* spong k* *Squil* b7a.de stann b4.de* *Stram* b7.de* *Stront-c* k* *Sulph* k* tarent ptk1 *Teucr* k* thuj tritic-vg fd5.de vanil fd5.de *Verat* viol-t k* *Zinc* k* [heroin sdj2]

- **right**: dulc fd4.de sep h2 sil h2 [heroin sdj2]
- **left**: sil h2
- **forenoon** | **sitting** agg.: sep k*
- **evening**: alum am-c h2 dulc fd4.de mez k* vanil fd5.de
  ⁝ **bed** agg.; in: carb-v
  ⁝ **falling** asleep:
   : **after**: mag-c
   : **on**: sil h2
- **night**: dulc fd4.de thuj k*
  ⁝ **bed** agg.; in: *Ambr* mag-c nit-ac k* *Phos* rhus-t stront-c *Verat*
  ⁝ **sleep**; when falling asleep: stront-c
- **exertion** agg.: mang
- **lying** agg.: meny ptk1 merc k* tritic-vg fd5.de
- **menses**; during: cocc
- **motion** agg.: chel mang k*
- **nap**; during: nat-m h2
- **painful** limb: rhus-t
- **paralyzed** limb: *Nux-v*
- **rest** agg.: *Valer*
- **sitting** agg.: dulc fd4.de sep tritic-vg fd5.de
  ⁝ **hang** out of bed amel.; and letting limbs: *Verat*
- **sleep** agg.; on going to: *Agar Arg-met Ars* carb-an sep h2
- **sleeplessness**; during: thuj k*
- **stepping** out; when: *Rhus-t*
- **stool** agg.; during: verat k*
- **waking**; on: nat-m k*
- **walking** | **after** | **agg.**: cocc k* plat k*
  ⁝ **amel.**: *Valer Verat*
- **warm** bed agg.: *Rhus-t Verat*

○ • **Joints**: graph b4.de* *Mang* b4a.de mez b4.de* nit-ac b4.de*

\- **Muscles**: agar tl1 atra-r bnm3• carc mlr1• caust tl1 cimic mrr1 cina mtf33 mez tl1 tarent tl1
- **single** set of: croc br1 stram mtf33
- **undulating**: asaf tl1* rhus-t tl1

○ • **Flexor**: carc sp1 cimic cp op sarcol-ac sp1

\- **Nates**: **Agar** k* ant-c k* calc k* kali-c k* mag-c h2 mag-m k* nat-c k* nat-sil fd3.de• ph-ac phos k* prun k* sep k* spong k* stann k* symph fd3.de• tarax h1
- **evening**: ant-c k*
- **sitting** agg.: ant-c k* calc k* nat-c k*

\- **Paralyzed** parts: apis *Arg-n* merc nux-v phos *Sec* stram *Stry*

- **Shoulders**: agar k* alum k* alum-sil k2 arg-met arn k* ars-h asaf k* bell k* calc k* chel k* chin b7.de* cic k* croc b7.de* dios k* *Dros* k* fl-ac graph k* hyos k* ign ketogl-ac rly4• *Lyc* k* mag-c k* mag-m bg2 merc k* mez k* ox-ac petr k* petr-ra shn4• phos bg2 puls k* sep k* sil k* spig k* *Spong* k* stry k* sul-ac k* sulph k* tarax k* zinc k*
  - **right**: dros
  - **left**: bapt bg2
  - **rest** agg.: **Dros** k*
  - **sleep** agg.; during: hyos k*
  - **writing** agg.: sul-ac k*
  - ○ **Joints**: am-c bg2 chin bg2 merc bg2 mosch bg2 puls b7.de* *Sulph* b4a.de
  - **Posterior** margin of axilla: arg-met
- **Tendons**: *Hyos* br1*
- **Thighs**: *Anac* k* ang b7.de* ant-t k* arg-met k* arn k* ars k* ars-s-f k2 asaf k* aur k* bar-c bar-m bell b4.de* berb calc k* calc-i k2 calc-sil k2 canth b7.de* caps k* carb-an carb-v k* carbn-s k2 carc fd2.de• *Caust* k* chin k* cimic k* coloc b4.de* dig k* dulc fd4.de *Graph* k* guaj k* iod *Kali-ar* kali-bi **Kali-c** k* kali-m k2* *Kali-s* kali-sil k2 kreos b7a.de lach lact laur lyc k* *Lyss* m-aust b7.de mag-c k* *Mang* k* meny merc k* *Mez* k* mosch b7.de* mur-ac k* nat-ar nat-c k* *Nat-m* nat-sil fd3.de• nux-v k* ol-an bg2 olnd b7.de* petr k* ph-ac k* phos k* plb k* puls k* rat k* rheum k* *Rhus-t* k* sabad k* *Sep* k* sil k* spong b7.de* squil k* stann k* staph b7.de* stram k* stront-c k* sul-i k2 *Sulph* k* tarax b7.de* tep tritic-vg fd5.de valer b7.de* vanil fd5.de verat k* zinc k* zinc-p k2 zing k* [heroin sdj2]
  - **right**: arg-met vh1
  - **morning**: dulc fd4.de rat k* tritic-vg fd5.de
  - **forenoon**: merc k*
  - **afternoon**: kali-s fd4.de lyc k* nat-sil fd3.de• spong fd4.de
  - **evening**: dulc fd4.de kali-bi k* kali-s fd4.de mang h2 puls k* spong fd4.de vanil fd5.de zinc zing a1
    - **bed** agg.; in: *Berb* carb-v puls k*
  - **chilliness**; during: sep k*
  - **motion** | **amel.**: kreos k* *Rhus-t* squil
  - **pulsating**: ph-ac h2
  - **sitting** agg.: nat-sil fd3.de• spong fd4.de squil k* tritic-vg fd5.de
  - **sleep** agg.; during: **Kali-c**
  - **standing** agg.: mez h2
  - **sudden**: nat-c k*
  - **synchronous** with pulse: verat h1
  - **touch** agg.: **Kali-c**
  - **walking** agg.: sep k*
  - ○ **Femur**, as if in: sulph h2
  - **Inner** side: anac k* asaf k* chel k* mang h2 mosch k* plb spong fd4.de tritic-vg fd5.de zinc k*
    - **afternoon**: plb
    - **intermitting**: asaf k*
    - **paralytic**: mosch k*
    - **walking** agg.; after: mang h2
    - **Near** genitals: arn k*
  - **Lower** anterior part: *Berb* carc fd2.de• spong fd4.de
  - **Lower** part: mez h2
  - **Outer** side: laur k* verat h1
  - **Posterior** part: aur k* canth k* carb-v k* lyc k* ol-an k* olnd k* phos rheum symph fd3.de•
    - **morning** | **bed** agg.; in: carb-v k*
    - **crossing** legs agg.: aur k*
    - **sitting** agg.: rheum
    - **walking** in open air agg.: phos
  - **Upper** part: mosch k* thuj k*
- **Thumbs**: aeth k* agar k* alum h2 am-c k* anag apis arg-met arge-pl rwt5• ars k* asaf calc k* fl-ac k* hell k* lach k* merc bg2 mosch k* nat-c k* nux-v bg2 phos k* plat bg2 plb k* rhus-t k* sabad bg2 staph bg2 sul-ac h2* valer bg2 zinc bg2
  - **morning** | **bed** agg.; in: ars
  - **afternoon**: arg-met
    - **writing** agg.: arg-met
- **Thumbs**: ...
  - **paralytic**: mosch k*
  - **visible**: am-c k*
  - **writing** agg.: arg-met phos k*
  - ○ **Between** thumb and first finger (See hands - between - first - thumb)
  - **Proximal** joint: zinc h2
- **Toes**: acon agar k* *Am-m* b7a.de anac k* calc-p *Chin* b7.de* cic k* *Cimic* k* *Cupr* k* hell b7.de* hyper jatr-c *Merc* k* merl mez b4.de* nat-c k* par b7.de* ph-ac phos k* ran-s b7.de* sabin b7.de* stram
  - **evening**: merc
  - **night**: hyper
    - **sleep** agg.; on going to: hyper
  - **chill**; during: merc b4.de
  - **drawing**: cic
  - **shivering**; during: merc b4.de
  - **touching** first toe: ph-ac
  - **visible**: merc
  - ○ **First**: agar am-c anac ars asaf calc calc-p carl ferr-ma hell mez nat-c par phos puls ran-s symph fd3.de• tep
    - **morning**: ars mez
      - **bed** agg.; in: ars mez
    - **afternoon**: nat-c
    - **evening**: calc
      - **bed** agg.; in: calc
      - **sitting** agg.: par
    - **intermittent**: anac k*
    - **shooting**: tep
    - **sitting** agg.: par phos
    - **sticking**: hell
    - **tearing**: ars puls
    - **walking** agg.: carl
    - **Balls**: am-c h2
  - **Joints**: sabin b7.de*
  - **Second**: iris-foe
  - **Third**: sul-ac h2
  - **Tips**: *Am-m* thuj
    - **evening**: *Am-m*
- **Upper** arms: agar am-c k* ant-c b7.de* arn k* asaf k* bamb-a stb2.de• bell bg2 bry b7.de* *Calc* k* camph b7.de* carc fd2.de• caust chin b7.de* *Cina* clem cocc k* coloc bg2 crot-t cupr k* dig k* dulc k* hell k* ign b7.de* kali-bi kali-c k* kali-n kali-s fd4.de *Lyc* k* m-arct b7.de mag-m k* mang k* meny k* merc k* mez k* mur-ac k* nat-m nat-sil fd3.de• nit-ac k* olnd k* petr bg2 petr-ra shn4• ph-ac k* phos phyt plb b7.de* *Ran-b* k* *Sep* k* sil k* spig k* squil k* stann k* sulph bg2 symph fd3.de• tarax k* teucr k* thuj tritic-vg fd5.de urol-h rwt• valer b7.de* vanil fd5.de zing
  - **right**: am-c vanil fd5.de
  - **left**: dulc fd4.de kali-c h2 kali-s fd4.de lyc h2 petr-ra shn4• plut-n srj7•
  - **bending** agg.: dulc k*
  - **drawing** arm backwards: dulc k*
  - **laying** arm on something: stann h2
  - **motion** | **amel.**: ph-ac stann
  - **sleep** | **siesta**; during: bamb-a stb2.de• mez seneg k*
  - **touch** agg.: mez h2
  - **warmth** | **amel.**: ant-c h2
  - ○ **Biceps**: mag-m k* sep k* symph fd3.de• teucr k*
  - **Deltoid**: ant-c h2 bapt a1 ign nit-ac h2 *Sulph*
  - **Inner** side: caust h2 stann h2
  - **Muscles** | **Extensor** muscles: petr-ra shn4• tarax zing
  - **Outer** side: mang h2 tarax h1
- **Upper** limbs: aesc agar aloe alumn am-c am-m b7.de* ambr k* *Ant-t* k* ars k* ars-i *Asaf* k* asar b7.de* atro bamb-a stb2.de• bar-c k* bar-m bell k* berb brom bry k* calc k* calc-i k2 calc-sil k2 camph bg2 carb-ac carb-v carbn-s k2 castm *Caust* k* *Chel* chin b7.de* chlf **Cic** k* *Cina* *Clem* b4a.de cod br1 *Coff* k* *Coloc* b4a.de con *Cupr* k* dulc fl-ac *Graph* k* hell hep k* hyos k* ign k* iod k*

Extremities

- **Upper** limbs: ...
  Ip b7a.de *Kali-c* k* kali-n k* lach k* lact *Lyc* k* *M-ambo* b7.de* *M-aust* b7.de mag-c k* mag-m k* *Meny* k* *Merc* k* *Merc-c* k* mez k* morph mosch k* mygal nat-ar nat-c k* nat-m k* nit-ac k* *Nux-v* olnd k* *Op* k* ox-ac k2 petr k* *Ph-ac* b4a.de phos k* phyt plac rzf5• plan plat k* plb k* puls b7.de* ran-b k* rheum k* *Rhod* k* rhus-t k* rumx sabad k* santin sep k* sil k* spig b7a.de squil k* *Stann* k* stram stry sul-ac k* sulph bg2 tarax k* tarent teucr k* **Thuj** k* tritic-vg fd5.de *Valer* verat k* zinc k* zinc-p k2 zing
  - **right**: am-caust vh1
  - **left**: zinc h2
  - **daytime**: nat-c k*
  - **morning**: bamb-a stb2.de• caust k* rheum h
    - **bed** agg.; in: zinc h2
    - **rising** agg.; after: alumn k*
    - **sleep** agg.; during: zinc
  - **forenoon**: fl-ac k*
  - **afternoon**: bamb-a stb2.de•
  - **evening**: dulc fd4.de
    - **bed** agg.; in: carb-v k* graph k*
    - **sleep**; when falling asleep: (↗*Jerking - upper limbs - sleep - falling - when)* castm kali-c h2 sil
  - **night**: aloe bar-c bar-m k* calc k* mag-c k* tritic-vg fd5.de
    - **bed** agg.; in: hyos k*
    - **sleep**; when falling asleep: con nat-c stry
  - **backward** and inward: cupr h2
  - **bending** agg.: dulc k*
  - **grasping** on: nat-c
  - **held**, if lower limbs are: sep h2
  - **motion** | **limbs** agg.; of: chel
  - **outward**: nat-m h2
  - **painful**: meny h1
  - **sleep** agg.; during: con h2 cupr k* graph k* kali-c h2 lyc nat-c h2 puls h1 zinc k*
  - **working** hard with hands amel.: agar
  - ○ **Bones**: chin b7.de*
  - **Muscles**: carc mlr1•
- **Wrists**: agar k* am-m b7.de* anac b4a.de* *Bar-c* k* calc h2* eupi k* laur b7.de* *Mang* b4a.de nat-c k* pall k* rhod b4a.de rhus-t k* squil b7.de* stann bg2 sulph k* valer b7.de* verat k*
  - **electric** shocks, like: agar k*
  - **motion** agg.: *Rhus-t* k*
  - **sudden**: pall k*
  - ○ **Flexors** tendons: am-m h2 anac
  - **Ulnar** side: plat h2

ULCERS: bros-gau mrc1 calc-sil k2 merc-c paeon mrr1 plb k2
- **chronic**: arist-cl sp1
- **varicose**: agri mtf11 alst mtf11 arist-cl sp1 calc-i mtf11 **Card-m** vh* clem-vit mtf11 graph gk ham mtf11 lach mtf11 merc-c pyrog mtf11 sulph mtf11
- ○ **Ankles**: ars b4a.de *Calc-p* k* carb-ac cist cupr-ar bg2 fl-ac b4a.de* *Hydr* k* *Lyc* b4a.de merc-i-f merc-sul nat-m b4.de* ph-ac b4a.de puls rhus-t sars sel bg1* sep b4a.de* sil k* sulph k* *Syph* k*
  - **night**: hydr k2
  - **chronic**: *Carb-ac* hydr k2
  - **fetid**: *Calc-p Carb-ac Lyc* sulph
  - **fistulous**: *Calc-p* sil
  - **old** and deep: cist tl1 kali-bi tl1
  - **painful**: hydr k2 *Lach* rhus-t
  - **painless**: *Calc*
  - **spreading**: *Merc*
  - ○ **Malleolus**: *Calc-p*
- **Elbows**: *Calc* hydr *Iod* b4a.de lach lyc b4a.de nat-s
  - **blisters** change into ulcers: *Calc*

Ulcers: ...
- **Feet**: *Anan* **Ars** k* bar-c k* canth *Carb-ac* carbn-s caust k* cham clem *Con* crot-h *Fl-ac Graph* ip *Kali-bi* k* kali-c **Lach** b7.de* lyc merc k* nat-c nit-ac paeon br1* petr petr-ra shn4• *Phos Psor Puls Ruta* b7.de* *Sec* b7.de* sel sep k* sil k* sol-ni sul-ac *Sulph* vip *Zinc*
  - **bleeding**: *Ars*
  - **blisters**, from: **Sulph** zinc
  - **leukorrhea** agg.: ars b4a.de bell b4a.de
  - **rubbing** of the shoe; from: all-c ptk2 borx hr1* paeon ptk1*
  - **symmetrical**: petr-ra shn4•
  - ○ **Back** of feet: *Caust* b4a.de *Lyc* b4a.de* nux-v b7a.de *Psor* sars b4.de* *Sep* k* *Sil* b4.de* *Sulph* k* *Thuj* b4a.de
  - **Border**: *Merc* b4a.de sulph b4a.de
  - **Heels**: all-c br1* am-c am-m ptk1 anac aran k* *Ars* k* arund bro1 borx b4a.de *Caust* k* kali-bi k2 lach b7.de* lam br1* laur *Nat-c* k* *Sep* k* **Sil** k*
    - **left**: aran k*
    - **pus**, with bloody: ars h2*
    - **rubbing** of the shoe; from: all-c k* borx k*
    - **spreading** blister; from a: *Caust* k* *Nat-c* k* *Sep* k*
  - **Soles**: anan *Ars* k* calc caust lach phyt pip-m ruta sec **Sep** sulph
    - **blisters**, from: **Ars**
- **Fingers**: alum k* *Ars* k* arund bro1 *Borx* k* *Bov* bros-gau mrc1 *Bry Calc* carb-an carb-v k* caust k* cupr-ar *Fl-ac* b4a.de graph ptk1 **Hep** b4a.de *Kali-bi* k* kreos lyc k* mag-c mang k* mez k* nat-m k* par b7.de* petr plat k* puls ptk1 *Ran-b* k* *Sep* k* sil k* *Sulph* k* teucr b7.de* *Thuj* b4a.de
  - **painful**: lyc h2
  - ○ **Bend** of: merc bg2
  - **First**: *Calc* kali-bi lyc h2
    - **Nail** of: iod nat-s
  - **Joints**: ars k2 *Borx* k* merc b4a.de mez k* nat-c k2 nux-v b7.de* *Sep* k* staph hr1
  - **Knuckles**: kali-bi bg2 *Sep* bg2
  - **Nails**: alum k* *Am-m* b7a.de bar-c k* bell b4.de* *Borx* k* *Bov* k* bufo bg2 *Calc* b4a.de calc-p bg2 caust k* con k* *Graph* b4a.de *Hell* b7.de* *Hep* k* iod k* kali-bi bg2 kali-c k* lach k* lyc k* *M-arct* b7a.de *M-aust* b7.de* *Merc* k* *Nat-m* k* nat-s k2 **Nit-ac** b4a.de *Par* b7.de* ph-ac b4a.de phos bg2 plat k* puls k* ran-b b7.de ruta b7.de sang k* sep k* **Sil** k* sul-ac k* **Sulph** k* tet c2 teucr b7.de* *Thuj* k*
    - **Around**: alum-sil k2 **Carbn-s** chlol con hell *Nat-s* phos k* *Rhus-t Sang* **Sil** *Sulph*
    - **Under**: **Ars**
  - **Second**: aloe
  - **Tips**: alum *Am-m* b7a.de ant-t k* *Apis* b7a.de **Ars** k* **Asaf** b7a.de borx k2 *Bry* b7a.de carb-v caust bg2 fl-ac *Hell* b7a.de kali-bi bg2 *Kreos* b7a.de **Lach** b7a.de led b7a.de *M-arct* b7a.de *M-aust* b7a.de *Nat-c Petr* phos bg2* plat psor ptk1 *Puls* b7a.de sars k* *Sec Sep* teucr b7.de*
    - **burning**: **Ars** *Sep*
    - **offensive**: *Petr* k*
- **Forearms**: anac br1 kali-bi
- **Hands**: *Anan Ars* k* *Calc* b4a.de caust dros b7.de **Hep** b4a.de kali-bi k* lyc b4a.de naja *Nux-v* b7a.de ph-ac b4a.de psor *Rhus-t* b7a.de rhus-v *Sec* b7.de* sep k* sil k* stront-c k* sul-ac k* *Sulph* b4a.de
  - **cracked**: *Merc*
  - **small**: dros bg2 *Sil* bg2
  - ○ **Back** of hands: bros-gau mrc1 *Calc* b4a.de dros *Hydr* psor *Sil* b4a.de syph
    - **bleeding**: formal gm1 x-ray gm1
    - **blood** without much pain; oozing: cadm-met gm1 formal gm1 kali-tcy gm1
    - **offensive**: formal gm1 x-ray gm1
    - **painful**: formal gm1 x-ray gm1
      - **accompanied** by | **weakness**; general: x-ray gm1
  - **Palms**: *Aur* b4a.de *Lyc* pip-m psor
- **Hips**: am b7.de*
- **Joints**: *Sep* k*

- **Knees**: anac *Calc* k* carb-v b4a.de *Con* b4a.de iod b4a.de *Nux-v* bg2 ph-ac *Phos* rhus-t b7a.de *Sil* b4a.de
○ • **Cartilages**: merc-d bro1
- **Legs**: am-c anac anan ant-t k2 anth vh1 *Anthraci* apis bg2 arn bg2 **Ars** k* ars-s-f k2 *Asaf* k* *Aur* bar-c k* bar-m bar-s k2 bry b7.de* *Calc* k* calc-f bg2 calc-i bg2 calc-p k2 *Calc-s* calc-sil k2 canth **Carb-v** k* **Carbn-s** *Card-m* k* caust k* chin b7.de* *Cist* k* clem k* *Crot-h* k* echi bro1 *Ferr-m* fl-ac bg2 *Graph* k* *Grin* ham bg2 hep bg2 hydr k* iod b4a.de ip jac-c *Kali-ar* *Kali-bi* k* *Kali-c* *Kali-i* k* kali-m k2 **Kali-s** kali-sil k2 *Lac-c* **Lach** k* **Lyc** k* **Merc** k* *Merc-c* b4a.de *Mez* k* *Mur-ac* muru a1 murx *Nat-c* b4a.de* nat-m bg2 *Nit-ac* k* nux-m nux-v b7.de* paeon bg2* petr k* *Ph-ac* k* phos *Phyt* *Psor* k* *Puls* k* pyrog bg2 ran-b *Rhus-t* k* ruta k* sabin k* sacch br1* sec bg2 sel sep bg2 **Sil** k* *Sin-n* staph k* still sul-i bg2 *Sulph* k* syph k* tep trif-p bro1 vip k*
  • **burning**: **Anthraci** **Ars** *Carb-v* hydr k2 kali-ar k2 kali-bi k2 *Lyc* *Merc* *Mur-ac* hr1 *Nit-ac* puls **Sil** syph
    ⁝ **Tibia**, on: asaf hr1
  • **carious**: asaf
  • **flat**: staph h1
  • **gangrenous**: **Anthraci** **Ars** *Carb-v*
  • **herpetic**: psor jl2
  • **itching**: lyc h2 nat-c h2 psor jl2
  • **painful**: **Anthraci** **Ars** hydr k2 nat-c h2 sil staph h1
    ⁝ **night**: *Anthraci* *Carb-v* caust h2 hydr k2 *Lyc* *Nit-ac* *Sil*
  • **rubbing** agg.: staph h1
  • **rupia**: kali-br
  • **spreading**: kali-ar k2 petr hr1
  • **stitching**: ars h2 nat-c h2
  • **tearing**: lyc h2
  • **varicose**: oscilloc jl2
  • **warmth** agg.: *Carb-v* *Hydr* *Merc* mez
○ • **Bones**:
    ⁝ **Tibia**: arg-n hr1 *Asaf* k* *Cinnb* cist dulc k2 fl-ac k2* *Graph* k* lach k* *Mez* k* nit-ac *Petr* b4a.de *Ph-ac* **Psor** *Sabin* k* sang sulph *Syph* vip
      ⁝ **old** and deep: cist tl1 kali-bi tl1
  • **Calves**: dros tl1
- **Lower** limbs: agar b4.de* am-c anac anan *Anthraci* **Ars** k* *Asaf* bell *Calc* k* calc-sil k2 canth k* **Carb-v** k* *Carbn-s* card-m caust *Cist* *Com* con k2 *Crot-h* *Ferr-m* fl-ac ptk1 *Graph* k* *Grin* ham hr1 *Hydr* *Hydr-ac* ip jac-c kali-ar *Kali-bi* *Kali-c* *Kali-i* **Kali-s** *Lac-c* **Lach** k* **Lyc** k* *Merc* k* *Mez* *Mur-ac* k* murx *Nat-c* k* *Nat-m* nux-m paeon pall petr ph-ac k* phos k* *Phyt* **Psor** *Puls* ran-b *Rhus-t* rumx-p j ruta *Sabin* sang sars b4.de* **Sec** sel *Sep* k* **Sil** k* *Sin-n* still *Sul-ac* sul-i ptk1 *Sulph* k* tep thuj
  • **atonic**: pall
  • **black** base: *Anthraci* **Ars** *Asaf* **Carb-v** ip **Lach** **Lyc** **Sec** *Sil* *Sul-ac*
  • **bleeding** easily: carb-v **Merc** ph-ac
  • **bluish** areolae: aesc **Ars** **Carb-v** **Lach** *Puls* **Sil**
  • **burning**: anth vh **Anthraci** **Ars** carb-ac **Carb-v** **Carbn-s** *Caust* **Lyc** mag-c **Merc** **Puls** **Sil** sulph zinc
    ⁝ **touch** agg.: *Merc*
  • **callous** edges: kali-chl
  • **deep**: **Ars** *Aur* **Calc** **Calc-s** com **Merc** *Nit-ac* **Psor** *Puls* **Sil** **Sulph**
  • **dirty** base: lach
  • **eating** vesicles: nat-c sep
  • **elevated** margins: petr
  • **elevating** limb amel.: *Bell* *Calc* *Carb-v*
  • **fetid**: *Bry* **Carb-v** **Lach** **Merc** *Mur-ac* **Psor** **Puls** sul-ac k2
    ⁝ **dropsical** swelling; after: merc tl1
  • **fistulous**: calc ruta
  • **flat**: lach sel
  • **gangrenous**: **Arn** **Ars** *Carb-v* **Lach** **Lyc** rhus-t ptk1 **Sec**
  • **high** edges: hydr
  • **indolent**: *Carb-v* *Hydr* **Lach** *Sil* sne *Still* sulph k2
  • **irritable**: *Hydr* k* *Phyt*
  • **itching**: **Lyc** nat-c a1 *Ph-ac* *Psor* **Sil**
  • **menopause**; during: polyg-h bro1*

Ulcers – **Lower** limbs: ...
  • **mottled**: **Carb-v** **Lach** **Puls**
  • **obstinate**: petr sulph
  • **painful** | **night**: *Lyc*
  • **painless**: ars carb-v graph plat sep sil k* sulph
  • **phagedenic** blisters: *Lach* nat-c rhus-t sep
  • **puffy**: *Sabin*
  • **red** base: lac-c petr
  • **running**, oozing: petr
  • **sanious**: *Com* sulph
  • **serpiginous**: paeon
  • **smooth**: sel
  • **stinging**: ars nat-c sabin sil
  • **superficial**: lach petr
  • **tearing**: lyc
  • **varicose**: *Aesc* aq-sil hsa1 *Carb-v* k* card-m k* *Fl-ac* k2 *Graph* k* *Ham* k* hydr-ac kali-s *Nat-m* paeon gm1 psor al2 sars k2 **Sulph** k2 syph
  • **warmth** agg.: *Carb-v* *Sabin*
○ • **Bones**: *Merc* b4a.de *Sil* b4a.de sulph b4a.de
  • **Joints**: psor jl2
- **Nails**: alum k* am-m b2.de* ant-c k* **Ars** k* aur k* aur-ar k2 bar-c k* bell b2.de* borx k* bov k* calc k* *Calc-f* bg2 caust k* chin b2.de* *Cist* bg2 con k* crot-h *Fl-ac* **Graph** k* *Hell* b7.de* *Hep* k* *Lach* k* lyc k* m-arct b2.de* m-aust b2.de* *Merc* k* mur-ac b2.de* nat-m b2.de* **Nat-s** bg2 *Nit-ac* k* *Par* b7.de* petr b2.de* ph-ac b2.de* *Phos* bro1 plat b2.de* psor bro1 *Puls* k* ran-b k* rhus-t b2.de* ruta b2.de* sabad b2.de* *Sang* k* sars bro1 sec k* sep k* **Sil** k* squil k* sul-ac b2.de* *Sul-i* bg2 **Sulph** k* tet bro1 teucr b2.de* thuj k*
- **Nates**: borx k* sabin sulph vinc
  • **burning**: vinc
○ • **Upper** part of: sabin
- **Thighs**: *Ars* bro1 *Calc* k* carb-v bro1 caust b4a.de cist bro1 crot-h echi bro1 kali-c lyc bro1 merc k* *Mez* *Nat-s* nit-ac nux-v b7.de* *Petr* b4a.de ph-ac bro1 psor al2 rhus-t bro1 sabin b7.de* sacch bro1 sil k* syph thuj k* trif-p bro1 *Zinc*
  • **scratching**, from: kali-c h2
○ • **Outer** side: *Nat-s*
- **Thumbs**: caust k* kali-bi kali-i ptk1 nat-c h2*
○ • **Nails**; under: kali-bi
  • **Tip** of: borx b4a.de caust kali-i
- **Toes**: aq-mar rbp6 *Ars* k* borx k2 *Bry* carb-v k* caust k* cupr-ar *Graph* k* *Nit-ac* paeon br1 *Petr* k* plat k* *Sep* k* *Sil* k* *Sulph* k* thuj k*
  • **blisters**, originating in: ars h2 *Graph* *Petr* k*
  • **boring**: caust h2
  • **burning**: caust h2
  • **gangrenous**: *Lach*
  • **leprous**: *Graph*
○ • **Fifth**: ant-t aq-mar rbp6
  • **First**: both fne1• *Paeon* *Sil* k*
    ⁝ **Border** of: graph
  • **Joint** of: *Ars* *Borx* k* nat-c *Sep* k*
    ⁝ **phagedenic**: *Borx* k*
  • **Nails**: *Bov* b4a.de *Caust* k* graph k* *Hell* b7a.de hep k* *M-aust* merc k* ph-ac b4a.de *Sabad* b7.de sang c2 *Sep* k* **Sil** k* **Sulph** tet c2 *Teucr* b7a.de
    ⁝ **proud** flesh, with: caust h2
    ⁝ **Around**: *Phos* c2
  • **Tips**: ant-t k* *Carb-v* *Sep* b4a.de
- **Upper** arms: *Ars* b4a.de **Lach** bg2
- **Upper** limbs: *Anan* kali-bi kali-i rhus-t k* sil stront-c
  • **malignant**: lach
  • **painless**: carb-v plat *Ran-b* sep
  • **phagedenic**: rhus-v
  • **syphilitic**: phyt rhus-v
- **Wrists**: *Ars* b4a.de dor kali-bi k* lac-c mez psor **Sil** b4a.de

UNCONSCIOUS: *Agar* camph cann-s stram
- **walking** agg.: stram

UNCOORDINATED motion of limbs (See Incoordination)

UNCOVER, inclination to: *(↗Cover hands - aversion; Heat - uncovering - must)*

○ - **Feet**: *(↗Heat - feet - burning - uncovers; Heat - feet - night - uncovering; Heat - feet - uncovering; Pain - feet - uncovers - burning)* agar aloe k2 ars ptk1 calc k2 **Cham** k* *Cur* fl-ac k* glon bg1 *Lac-c* mrr1 *Mag-c* k* **Med** k* nat-m sne *Petr* *Plat* sne **Puls** k* sabin k2 *Sang* k* *Sanic* k* sec ptk1 sep **Sulph** k*
- **one** foot: lyc mtf33
- **morning**; toward: cur
- **night**: **Cham** tl1* *Fl-ac* mrr1 lac-c mtf33 lyc mrr1 *Med* tl1* puls tl1 sang tl1 sanic tl1 sulph tl1

- **Leg**:
  - **morning** | **waking**; on: *Plat*
- **Lower** limbs: crot-c *Plat* sec zinc
  - **night**: *Plat* k* zinc
- **Upper** limbs: con k* zinc
  - **sleep** agg.; during: con k*

UNCOVERING: *(↗GENERALS - Uncovering - Single)*
- **agg.**: *(↗GENERALS - Uncovering - single)* aur *Bry* con **Hep** *Nat-m* **Rhus-t** k* **Sil** squil stront-c **Thuj**

○ **Lower** limbs: aur b4.de* *Con* b4.de* hep b4a.de* *Nux-v* b7.de* rhus-t b7.de* **Sil** b4.de* stront-c b4.de* thuj ptk1
- **Upper** limbs: aur b4.de* cocc b7.de* con b4a.de nat-m b4.de* *Nux-v* b7.de* rhus-t b7.de* sil b4.de*
- **amel.**:

○ **Lower** limbs: *Puls* b7a.de
- **Upper** limbs: cann-s b7.de* mosch b7.de* puls b7.de*

UNDRESSING agg.: | **Lower** limbs: hep b4a.de nat-s bg2 sep b4.de*

UNEASINESS (See Restlessness)

UNHEALTHY SKIN: | **Fingers**: petr tl1

UNSTEADINESS, joints: ambr b7a.de bry b7a.de cann-s b7a.de hell b7a.de mang b4a.de mez nux-v b7a.de rhus-t b7a.de

○ - **Ankles**: chin b7a.de ruta b7a.de
- **Feet**: agar camph mag-m a1 merc sumb
- **Forearms**: caust bro1
- **Hands**: bell caust bro1 chlor elaps lyc
  - **writing** agg.: agar hep hydrog srj2• morph
- **Hips**: bry b7a.de chin b7a.de nat-m rhus-t b7a.de
  - **right**: lac-h htj1•
- **Knees**: *Acon* k* ars bamb-a stb2.de• *Cann-s* b7a.de carb-v chin k* cycl laur mang merc olib-sac wmh1 phys puls stry
- **Legs**: agar bry merc ptel *Sulph*
  - **afternoon**: sulph
  - **dancing**; while: hydrog srj2•
  - **walking** agg.: hydrog srj2•

○ **Calves**: nat-m h2
- **Lower** limbs: *(↗Incoordination - lower; Tottering)* acon *Agar* ptk1 ambr c1 **Arg-n** bg1* arn b7.de* bamb-a stb2.de• bapt a1 **Bar-c** b4.de* carb-v b4.de* caust k* cic ptk1 cocc ptk1 kali-br ptk1 lil-t ptk1 lycps-v nat-c b4.de* nat-m bg2 *Nux-v* phos rhod sec ptk1 stann ptk1 stram sulph b4.de* *Verb*
  - **chill**; during: *Rhus-t* a1
  - **standing** agg.: bamb-a stb2.de•
  - **walking** agg.: hydrog srj2• nat-c a1 ozone sde2• phos k2
- **Thighs**: calc ruta
- **Upper** limbs: cocc bro1 phos

UNSURE: visc sp1

URINATION agg.: | **Thighs**: berb ptk1

VARICES: *(↗Swelling; GENERALS - Varicose)* tub-r mtf11
- **bleeding**: ham mtf11
- **jar** agg.: ham k2
- **painful**: bell-p sp1 vit-b-x mtf11
- **purple** areola: aesc k2

○ - **Ankles**: ham fd3.de• sulph h2 syc bka1•

Varices – Ankles: ...
  - **left**: ferr a1 ham fd3.de•
- **Feet**: ant-t *Ferr* *Ferr-act* bro1 ham bro1 lac-c lach **Puls** sul-ac sulph *Thuj*

○ **Heels**: berb dgt1
- **Knees**: ham fd3.de• thuj bg1
- **Legs**: aesc k2 *Calc* **Carb-v** **Carbn-s** **Caust** coloc ferr *Fl-ac* graph **Ham** *Lach* mrr1 **Lyc** *Mill* *Nat-m* **Puls** sil *Sulph* **Zinc**
  - **left**: fl-ac ham fd3.de•
    - **menses**; during: ambr
  - **bleeding**: calc k2 *Ham* mill k2 *Puls* sulph k2
  - **inflamed**: arn *Ars* *Calc* *Ham* kola stb3• kreos lyc lycps-v *Puls* sil spig sulph zinc
  - **itching**: *Graph*
  - **menses**; during: *Ambr* b7.de* graph b4.de
  - **oozing**: calc k2
  - **painful**: brom *Caust* coloc h2 *Ham* kola stb3• *Lyc* *Mill* **Puls** sang mp1• *Zinc*
    - **burning**: calc k2
    - **menses**; during: ambr k2 graph
    - **pregnancy** agg.; during: mill hr1
  - **painless**: calc
  - **pregnancy** agg.; during: **Ferr** *Ham* *Lyc* *Lycps-v* *Mill* **Puls** *Zinc*
  - **pulsating**: ruta sf1.de
  - **sensitive**: *Fl-ac* graph *Ham* lach puls
  - **sore** (= bruised): arn gsy1
  - **stinging**: *Apis* graph *Ham* **Puls**
  - **stripping** the veins; after: lach cpy
  - **tearing**: sul-ac
  - **tension**: graph h2
  - **ulceration**●: *(↗GENERALS - Varicose - ulceration; SKIN - Ulcers - varicose)* ars fl-ac k2 **Lach** lyc mill k2 puls sil sulph k2
  - **walking** | **amel.**: ruta sf1.de

○ **Calves**: clem ham fd3.de• *Plb*
- **Lower** limbs: *Ambr* k* *Ant-t* b7.de* arg-n **Arn** k* *Ars* k* aur-m k2 bufo br1 **Calc** k* calc-f calc-p calc-s k2 calc-sil k2 **Carb-v** k* *Carbn-s* carc gk6 card-m k* *Caust* k* cench k2 clem coloc b4.de* con k2 *Crot-h* k* *Ferr* k* ferr-ar **Fl-ac** k* *Graph* k* **Ham** k* *Hep* *Kali-ar* kali-bi gk *Kreos* k* lac-c *Lach* k* **Lyc** k* **Lycps-v** k* *M-aust* b7.de mill k2 *Nat-m* k* paeon gm1 *Plb* psor al2 **Puls** k* sabin sars scir c1* *Sec* mrr1 sep gk sil spig k* staph gk stront-c mrr1 sul-ac k* *Sulph* k* *Thuj* k* vanil fd5.de vip **Zinc** k*
  - **cold** | **amel.**: puls mrr1 sec mrr1
  - **cramping**: graph h2
  - **distended** | **menses**; during: ambr con k2 lach puls
  - **drawing**: graph h2
  - **inflammation**; after: calc-ar ptk1
  - **menses**; during: ham mrr1
  - **painful**: calc mrr1 *Fl-ac* mrr1
    - **standing** agg.: calc mrr1
    - **walking** agg.: calc mrr1
    - **warmth** agg.: **Fl-ac** sec mrr1 **Sulph**
  - **portal** congestion; from: card-m mrr1
  - **pregnancy** agg.; during: *(↗GENERALS - Varicose - pregnancy)* acon apis *Arn* *Ars* **Carb-v** k* *Caust* *Ferr* k* **Fl-ac** *Graph* *Ham* k* kali-bi gk lach k2 *Lyc* k* *Lycps-v* mp1• *Mill* *Nux-v* psor al2 **Puls** k* *Sep* mp1• *Zinc*
- **Thighs**: aesc k2 *Calc* *Ferr* k* **Ham** lac-c *Puls* sep tritic-vg fd5.de *Zinc*
- **Upper** limbs: **Ferr-p** c1 *Nux-v* *Plb* psor al2 **Puls** stront-c k*

VARICOSITIES:
- **pregnancy**; of: bell-p sp1
- **stretching** limbs | **amel.**: allox sp1

○ - **Legs**: allox sp1 bell-p sp1 hed sp1 mand sp1
- **Thighs**: ferr bg2

VEINS showing clearly: | **Thighs**: plut-n srj7•

VEXATION:

- agg. | **Lower** limbs: bry b7.de* caust bg2 cham b7.de* *Coloc* b4a.de *Nux-v* k* ran-b bg2 *Sep* b4a.de staph b7.de*

VIBRATION; sensation of: ambr b7.de *Arn* b7.de* bism b7.de caps b7.de m-ambo b7.de m-arct b7.de mosch b7.de puls b7.de rhus-t b7.de

○ - **Elbows**: dig h2
- **Feet**: ambr h1 ars b4.de* cic b7.de* graph h2 *Olnd* b7a.de plut-n srj7•
○ • **Heels**: iod h
• **Soles**: cic h1 olnd k* ulm-c jsj8•
- **Fingers**: agn a1 nux-m bg2
○ • **Nails**; underneath: mosch b7a.de nux-m b7.de*
- **Forearms**: caps h1 plut-n srj7• sabin bg2 vanil fd5.de
- **Hands**: berb caps h1 carbn-s plut-n srj7•
- **Knees**: rhus-t b7.de*
- **Legs**: ambr ars h2 berb caust croc b7.de* m-arct b7.de olnd b7.de* plut-n srj7•
○ • **Calves**: ambr h1 phel
- **Lower** limbs: ambr b7.de* ars b4.de* bell b4.de* caust b4.de* con b4.de* kreos b7a.de moni rfm1• mosch b7.de* olnd b7.de* *Ph-ac* b4a.de puls b7.de* rhus-t b7.de* spig b7.de* sulph b4.de*
- **Muscles**: plac rzf5•
- **Thighs**: arg-met h1 bell b4.de* caust h2 graph b4.de* sabad b7.de* sep b4.de* vanil fd5.de
- **Toes**: nux-m b7.de*
- **Upper** arms: bism bg2 caps bg2 sep bg2
- **Upper** limbs: agn b7.de* am-c k* bism b7.de* caps b7.de* dig k* m-arct b7.de moni rfm1• mosch nit-ac k* olnd sep k* vib bg2
○ • **Muscles**: nit-ac h2

WAKING; on:

- **agg.**:
○ • **Lower** limbs: ambr b7.de* ars b4.de* *Brom* b4a.de bry b7.de* caust b4.de* dros b7.de* *Ign* b7.de* kali-bi bg2 kali-c b4.de* kali-n b4.de* lyc b4.de* m-ambo b7.de m-arct b7.de nat-s bg2 *Nux-v* b7.de* petr b4.de* puls b7.de* rhus-t b7.de* ruta b7.de* squil b7.de* staph b7.de* sul-ac b4.de* thuj b4.de* verat b7.de* viol-t b7.de* zinc b4.de*
• **Upper** limbs: alum bg2 aur b4.de* bry b7.de* calad bg2 caust b4.de* croc b7.de* *Ign* b7.de* iod b4.de* kali-bi bg2 kali-c b4.de* m-arct b7.de *Mag-m* b4.de* merc-c b4a.de nat-c bg2 nat-m b4.de* nit-ac b4.de* *Nux-v* b7.de* petr b4.de* phos b4.de* puls b7.de* rhus-t b7.de* ruta b7.de* thuj b4.de*
- **amel.** | **Lower** limbs: calc b4.de*

WALKING (= includes ways of walking): (*↗GENERALS - Walking)*

- **after**:
• **agg.** | **Lower** limbs: alum bg2 am-m b7a.de ars bg2 *Aur* b4a.de camph b7.de* carb-v b4.de* caust b4.de* coff b7.de* croc b7.de* cycl b7a.de *Graph* b4a.de kali-c bg2 *Kali-n* b4a.de laur b7.de* m-aust b7.de* mang b4.de* mosch b7a.de nat-c b4.de* nit-ac b4.de* olnd b7.de* plat b4.de* *Puls* b7.de* rhod b4a.de *Rhus-t* b7.de* ruta b7.de* sabin b7.de* sep bg2 spong b7.de* *Sul-ac* b4a.de *Valer* b7.de*
- **air**; in open:
• **after**:
⁝ **agg.**:
⁝ **Lower** limbs: alum b4.de* am-m b7.de* anac b4.de* borx b4a.de caust b4.de* clem b4.de* coff b7.de* ferr b7.de* graph b4.de* hep bg2 kali-c b4.de* **Lyc** b4.de* mag-c b4.de* nat-s bg2 nit-ac b4.de* nux-v b7.de* phos b4.de* rhus-t b7.de* sulph b4.de*
⁝ **Upper** limbs: am-m b7.de* ang b7.de* croc b7.de* ferr b7.de* hep b4.de* led b7.de* nux-v b7.de* phos b4.de* rhus-t b7.de* valer b7a.de
• **agg.**:
⁝ **Lower** limbs: *Ang* b7.de aur b4.de bell b4.de *Bry* b7.de calc b4.de cann-s b7.de carb-an b4.de carb-v b4.de chel b7.de *Chin* b7.de cina b7.de *Coff* b7.de *Con* b4.de dulc b4.de euph b4.de *Graph* b4.de guaj b4.de *Hell* b7.de *Hep* b4.de* hyos b7.de *Ign* b7.de laur b7.de *Lyc* b4a.de m-aust b7.de mag-m b4.de mang b4.de meny b7.de merc b4.de nit-ac b4.de *Nux-v* b7.de phos b4.de ran-b b7.de rhus-t b7.de sep b4.de sil b4.de spig b7.de spong b7.de *Staph* b7.de stront-c b4.de *Sulph* b4.de *Tarax* b7.de thuj b4.de verb b7.de

Walking – air; in open – **agg.**: ...

⁝ **Upper** limbs: am-m b7.de* anac b4.de* arn b7.de* borx b4a.de calc b4.de* chin b7.de* clem b4.de* con b4.de* croc b7a.de dulc b4.de* *Hell* b7.de* ign b7.de* m-arct b7.de mez b4.de* *Nux-v* b7.de* rhod b4.de* staph b7.de* sul-ac b4.de* *Sulph* b4.de* tarax b7.de* thuj b4.de*
• **amel.**:
⁝ **Lower** limbs: alum b4.de* ambr b7.de* arn b7.de* asaf b7.de* asar b7.de* coloc b4a.de croc b7.de* kali-c b4.de* laur b7.de* m-arct b7.de meny b7.de* nux-v b7.de* par b7.de* *Puls* b7.de* rhus-t b7.de* stront-c b4.de*
⁝ **Upper** limbs: ambr b7.de* croc b7.de* euph b4.de* hep b4.de* meny b7.de* petr b4.de* *Puls* b7.de*
- **amel.** | **Lower** limbs: am-m bg2 ferr bg2 kali-bi bg2 rhus-t bg2 verat bg2 zinc bg2
- **awkward** (See Awkwardness)
- **backwards**: ars bg2 bell bg2 canth bg2 cocc bg2 lach bg2 mang bg2* mang-act br1 oxyt bg2* ph-ac bg2 sep bg2 sil bg2 stram bg2* sulph bg2
• **agg.** | **Lower** limbs: mang bg2
• **impossible**; walking backward: cocc bg2 mang bg2
• **metacarpal**-phalangeal joint; on: mang-act bro1
- **bare** feet:
• **cannot**: mag-m dgt
• **easier** on bare feet: psor bg1*
• **likes** to walk on: sil dgt
- **beginning** of:
• **agg.** | **Lower** limbs: bry b7.de dros b7.de *Ferr* b7.de led b7.de m-ambo b7.de *Puls* b7.de ruta b7.de sabin b7.de valer b7.de
- **bent**:
• **agg.** | **Lower** limbs: bry b7.de
- **circles**, cannot walk in: oxyt ptk2
- **continued**:
• **amel.** | **Lower** limbs: dros b7.de* ferr b7.de* m-ambo b7.de *Nat-m* bg2 plb b7.de* puls b7.de* rhus-t bg2 ruta b7.de* sabin b7.de*
- **difficult**: (*↗Claudicatio; Limping)* *Ang* br1 aur cact bg2 chin iod k2 kali-i k2 olnd phys bg2 sec mrr1 sil bg2 ter [mang stj1]
• **concentrate** the mind; must: arag br1 hydrog srj2•
• **pregnancy**; during: bell-p tl1*
○ • **Leg** would go where one did not intend; as if: hydrog srj2•
- **dragging** one's feet (See Dragging - legs - walking)
- **gressus** equinus: brass-n-o srj5•
- **gressus** gallinaceous: (*↗Abducted - lower - walking)* *Aur* helo c1 helo-s c1* *Ign* **Lach** k* mag-p nux-v bg2 **Sil**
- **gressus** vaccinus: calc hr1 *Cic* hr1 *Iod* k* **Phos** hr1 *Sec*
- **hard** pavement, on: con bg3
○ • **Lower** limbs: aloe bg2 ant-c b7a.de* ars bg2 con bg2 hep b4a.de*
- **heel**:
• **ground**; doesn't touch: lath bro1
• **on**: thal dx
- **impossible**:
• **eyes** closed; with: (*↗VERTIGO - Closed)* alum bro1* arg-n br1* carbn-s bro1 dub bro1 *Gels* bro1 iodof bro1 *Stram* bro1 zinc mtf33
• **fall**; after a: arg-met ptk1
• **jump** with both legs; must (See Jumping - gait)
• **raise** one foot without lifting the other; cannot (See Jumping - gait)
- **infirm**: (*↗Incoordination - lower)* caust kali-c k* mag-c *Mag-p* nat-c ol-an phos sulph
- **involuntary** quick steps during vertigo; with: coca ptk1
- **inward**; with feet turned: cic b7.de*
• **left** foot: psor jl2
- **knees**; on: med ptk1
• **cut** off; feels legs: bar-c ptk1
- **late** learning to walk● (See GENERALS - Walk - learning)
- **lift** feet higher than usual: helo-s rwt2•
• **down** hard; and brings them: helo bro1 helo-s rwt2•

- **lifting** legs too high: agar bg2* ars b4a.de bell b4a.de* carb-v ptk1 euph bg2 merc ptk1 nat-m ptk1 onos ptk1* rhus-t ptk1 sep bg2
- **long** walk; after a:
  - **agg.** | **Lower** limbs: *Arn* b7a.de *Kreos* b7a.de *Rhus-t* b7a.de
- **miles** sensation | **Legs**: [spect dfg1]
- **must** walk (See MIND - Restlessness - driving)
- **outward**; with feet turned: bry gl1.fr• colch gl1.fr• lyc gl1.fr• mag-c b4a.de sil gl1.fr•
- **rapidly**:
  - **agg.**:
    - **Lower** limbs: ars b4.de* kali-c b4.de* led b7a.de mez b4.de* olnd b7.de* spong b7.de* staph b7.de* *Sulph* b4a.de
    - **Upper** limbs: olnd b7.de* spig b7.de* sul-ac b4.de*
  - **amel.** | **Lower** limbs: canth b7.de* nat-m b4.de*
- **rough** ground, on: hyos bg3 lil-t bg3*
- **shooting** out foot: acon bro1
- **shuffling** gait: (↗*MIND - Gestures - feet - shuffling)* arn bg2 chin bg2 colch bg2 gels fr3 lath ah1 led bg2 nux-v b7a.de* ol-an bg2* op hr1* *Psor* hr1* **Rhus-t** a1 sec hr1* sil a2 staph hr1* tab a1* vip a1* *Zinc* bg2
- **side** of foot; on:
  - O **Inner** side: chin gl1.fr• lyc gl1.fr• puls gl1.fr• staph gl1.fr•
  - **Outer** side: all-c dgt1* cic
- **side**; to one: aml-ns ptk1 verat-v ptk1
- **sideways**; unconsciously walking: absin bg2 cann-i a1
- **slow** (See MIND - Walking - slowly)
- **stooped** gait: am-m ptk1 arg-n bg2* arn bro1 *Carb-v* ptk1 cocc ptk1 coloc ptk1 con ptk1 gels ptk1 lath bro1* mang bg2* mang-act bro1 nat-m ptk1 phos bg2* sulph bg2* ter ptk1 tub bg2 verat ptk1
- **stops** in the middle of walking: *Aur* b4a.de
- **toes**; walking on: *All-c* dgt1* crot-h ptk1 lath ptk1 nit-ac bg2 sec bg2
  - **must** walk on toes: (↗*HEAD - Pain - jar agg. - walking)* calc ll1 lath br1* nit-ac h2 sec a2
- **unsteadily** (See Tottering)
- **while**:
  - **agg.**:
    - **Ankles**: lith-c ptk1 med ptk1 nit-ac ptk1
    - **Leg** | **Tendo** Achillis: am-m ptk1 ant-t ptk1 cinnb ptk1 colch ptk1
    - **Lower** limbs: *Acon* b7.de agar b4.de *Agn* b7.de alum b4.de* am-m b7.de *Ambr* b7.de* *Anac* b4.de* ang b7.de ant-c b7.de* *Ant-t* b7.de* *Arg-met* b7.de* *Arn* b7.de ars b4.de* *Asaf* b7.de *Asar* b7.de* *Aur* b4.de* bar-c b4.de *Bell* b4.de bov b4.de *Bry* b7.de* calad b7.de *Calc* b4.de* camph b7.de cann-s b7.de canth b7.de *Caps* b7a.de carb-an b4.de carb-v b4.de *Caust* b4.de* chel b7.de *Chin* b7.de cic b7.de cina b7.de clem b4.de **Cocc** b7.de coff b7.de* coloc b4.de* con b4.de cupr b7.de cycl b7.de dig b4.de *Dros* b7.de* dulc b4.de *Euphr* b7.de* ferr b7.de graph b4.de guaj b4.de *Hep* b4.de* hyos b7.de* *Ign* b7.de ip b7.de *Kali-c* b4.de* kali-n b4.de *Kreos* b7a.de *Led* b7.de *Lyc* b4.de m-ambo b7.de m-arct b7.de m-aust b7.de mag-c b4.de mag-m b4.de mang b4.de meny b7.de merc b4.de merc-c b4a.de mez b4.de *Mur-ac* b4.de* nat-c b4.de nat-m b4.de **Nit-ac** b4.de* nux-v b7.de* *Olnd* b7.de par b7.de petr b4.de *Ph-ac* b4.de* phos b4.de plb b7.de *Puls* b7.de* **Ran-b** b7.de *Rheum* b7.de* rhod b4.de rhus-t b7.de* sabad b7.de sabin b7.de samb b7.de sep b4.de sil b4.de *Spig* b7.de* spong b7.de squil b7.de stann b4.de staph b7.de* stram b7a.de stront-c b4.de sul-ac b4.de sulph b4.de tarax b7.de thuj b4.de valer b7.de verat b7.de verb b7.de viol-t b7.de *Zinc* b4.de*
    - **Upper** limbs: agar b4.de* ang b7.de* arn b7.de* bell b4.de* bry b7.de* calc b4.de* cocc b7.de* dig b4.de* ign b7.de* merc b4.de* nux-v b7.de* ran-b b7.de* sep b4.de* spig b7.de* staph b7.de* verat b7.de* viol-t b7.de*
  - **amel.**:
    - **Ankles**: caust ptk1
    - **Lower** limbs: alum b4.de* am-c b4.de anac b4.de ant-t b7.de arg-met b7.de arn b7.de ars b4.de asaf b7.de bar-c b4.de bell b4.de bry b7.de calc b4.de caps b7.de caust b4.de chin b7.de con b4.de cycl b7.de dig b4.de *Dros* b7.de dulc b4.de euph b4.de *Ferr* b7.de hyos b7.de kali-n b4.de laur b7.de led b7.de m-ambo b7.de mag-c b4.de mur-ac b4.de nat-m b4.de nit-ac b4.de ph-ac b4.de phos b4.de plat b4.de plb b7.de *Puls* b7.de rhod b4.de *Rhus-t* b7.de ruta b7.de sep b4.de sil b4.de stann b4.de stront-c b4.de sul-ac b4.de *Tarax* b7.de teucr b7.de thuj b4.de valer b7.de verb b7.de
- **wide** base; on a (See Incoordination)

WARM:
- **air**:
  - **agg.** | **Lower** limbs: nux-v b7.de*
- **applications**:
  - **agg.**:
    - **Lower** limbs: arn b7.de* bry b7.de* ign bg2 kali-bi bg2 kali-c b4.de* lac-c bg2 led b7.de* mez bg2 nux-v b7.de* plb bg2 puls b7.de* sec bg2
    - **Upper** limbs: *Calc* b4.de* caust b4.de* dulc b4.de* *Fl-ac* bg2 *Merc* b4a.de stront-c b4.de* *Thuj* b4a.de zinc b4.de*
  - **amel.**:
    - **Lower** limbs: *Ars* b4.de* *Bar-c* b4.de* bell bg2 bry b7.de* canth b7.de* *Caust* b4.de* cham b7.de* coloc bg2 graph b4.de* hep bg2 ign bg2 *Lyc* b4a.de nat-c b4.de nat-m bg2 nux-m b7.de* nux-v b7.de* ph-ac b4.de* rhus-t b7.de* sabad b7.de* staph b7.de* stront-c b4.de* sulph b4.de*
    - **Upper** limbs: am-c b4a.de ant-c b7a.de bry b7.de* cham b7.de* hell b7.de* *Kali-c* b4a.de lach b7.de* *Nit-ac* b4a.de nux-m b7.de* nux-v b7.de* rhus-t b7.de* sabad b7.de* staph b7.de*
- **becoming**:
  - **agg.** | **Upper** limbs: bry b7.de* puls b7.de* sabad b7.de*
  - **air**; in open:
    - **agg.**:
      - **Lower** limbs: bov b4.de dulc b4.de
      - **Upper** limbs: dulc b4.de*
  - **bed**; in:
    - **agg.**:
      - **Lower** limbs: am-m bg2 ant-t b7.de* carb-v b4.de* *Cham* b7.de* ferr bg2 ign bg2 kali-bi bg2 kali-c b4.de* **Led** b7.de* *Lyc* b4a.de merc b4a.de* nux-v b7.de* plb bg2 **Puls** b7.de* *Rhus-t* b7.de* sulph b4.de* visc bg2
      - **Upper** limbs: am-c b4a.de ant-t b7.de* bar-c b4.de* *Bry* b7.de* caust bg2 cham b7.de* **Led** b7.de* *Lyc* b4a.de nux-v b7.de* **Puls** b7.de* *Rhus-t* b7.de*
    - **amel.** | **Upper** limbs: bry b7.de*
- **bed**; warmth of:
  - **agg.** | **Lower** limbs: merc ptk1 syph ptk1 verat ptk1
- **room** agg.:
  - O **Lower** limbs: croc b7.de* laur b7.de* **Puls** b7.de* spig b7.de* verb b7.de*
  - **Upper** limbs: bry b7.de* caust b4.de* *Croc* b7.de* laur b7.de* nux-m b7.de* nux-v b7.de* *Puls* b7.de* sep b4.de* spig b7.de* squil b7.de* verat b7.de* verb b7.de*
- **stove**; warm:
  - **agg.** | **Lower** limbs: arn b7.de* *Puls* b7.de*

WARMTH; sensation of (See Heat)

WARTS:
- O **Ankles**: pall c1
- **Elbow**, bend of: calc a1 calc-f k* spong fd4.de tritic-vg fd5.de
- **Feet**: sulph h2 syc pte1*•
  - O **Soles**: ant-c kl* calc spa* carc gk6* con kl* dulc fd4.de lyc kl* nat-m wt* nat-s mrr1 phos ser* sep wt* sil wt* sulph wt* thuj ser* [*Ant-m* stj2 *Ant-met* stj2 *Ant-t* stj2 heroin sdj2]
    - **horny**: ant-c br1
    - **painful**: sil sne thuj mrr1
- **Fingers**: ambr k* *Bar-c* k* berb k* *Calc* carb-an k* *Caust* k* cypra-eg sde6.de• *Dulc Ferr Fl-ac* **Lac-c** lach k* lyc k* *Nat-m Nit-ac* petr k* podo fd3.de• positr nl2• psor ran-b *Rhus-t* k* sang sars *Sep* k* sil sne sinus rly4• sulph k* *Thuj* k* tritic-vg fd5.de vanil fd5.de
  - **painful**: ambr b7.de* caust bg2 fl-ac bg2 nat-c bg2 nat-m bg2 nit-ac bg2 petr bg2 thuj bg2
  - O **First**: *Caust* k* thuj
    - **horny**: (↗*SKIN - Excrescences - horny)* *Caust*
  - **Fourth**: lac-c kr1* rosm lgb1 tritic-vg fd5.de vanil fd5.de
    - **left**: rosm lgb1
  - **Joints**: sars
  - **Nails**, close to: **CAUST** k •* dulc fl-ac graph lt1.fr **Lyc** •* sep kl
  - **Second**: berb k* lach vanil fd5.de
  - **Third**: *Nat-s* k* tritic-vg fd5.de vanil fd5.de

- **Fingers**: ...
  - **Tips**: **Caust** k* dulc nat-sil fd3.de• nit-ac bg1 thuj k*
- **Forearms**: **Calc** bg2 *Sil* k*
- **Hands**: anac k* *Anil* sne *Ant-c* k* bacls-10 pte1*• **Bar-c** k* berb k* borx bg2 bov bufo k* **Calc** k* calc-sil k2 carb-an bro1 carc gk6 **Caust** k* **Dulc** k* dys fmm1• *Ferr* k* ferr-ma k* ferr-pic *Fl-ac* kali-c k* kali-chl kali-m c1* *Lach* k* *Lyc* k* mag-s c1 morg-g pte1*• morg-p fmm1• *Nat-c* k* *Nat-m* k* nat-s k2* **Nit-ac** k* *Ph-ac* phos k* *Psor Rhus-t* k* ruta bro1 *Sep* k* sil **Sulph** k* syc fmm1• **Thuj** k* verr cea1
  - **flat**: bacls-10 pte1• berb k* **Dulc** dys pte1*• lach k* morg-g pte1*• morg-p pte1*• ruta *Sep* syc pte1*•
  - **horny**: *(↗SKIN - Excrescences - horny)* *Ant-c* k* *Caust Sep Thuj*
  - **irregular** surface: syc pte1•
  - **itching**: *Sep*
  - **large**: calc-sil k2 dulc k* morg-g pte1*• syc pte1*•
  - **pointed**: bacls-10 pte1• morg-g pte1*• syc fmm1•
  - **sensitive**: nat-c
  - **small**: ferr-ma br1
  - **soft**: ant-c bro1
  - **sore**: ambr k* fl-ac ruta
  - ○ **Back** of hands: anac bg2 berb bg2 *Nat-c* b4a.de nat-m bg2 nat-s bg2 nit-ac bg2* sep bg2
  - **Knuckles**: dulc fd4.de pall
  - **Palms**: *Anac* k* ant-c bro1 berb k* borx b4a.de* calc bro1 carc gk6* *Dulc* k* ferr-ma bro1 *Ferr-pic* bro1 nat-c k* *Nat-m* k* ruta k* sulph ptk1
    - **flat**: dulc nat-m ruta
    - **painful** on pressure: nat-m
- **Lower** limbs: bar-c k2 kali-br tl1 thuj bg2
- **Nates**: con k*
- **Thighs**: med ozone sde2• tritic-vg fd5.de
- **Thumbs**: berb k* calc-sil k2* lach k* mur-ac bg1 ran-b k* thuj
- **Toes**: spig k* sulph h2* thiam rly4•
- **Upper** arms: nit-ac bg2
- **Upper** limbs: ars k* bar-c k2 borx b4a.de* bov k* **Calc** k* carb-an k* *Caust* k* dulc k* kali-c k* lyc k* merc **Nat-c** k* nat-m k* *Nat-s Nit-ac* k* petr k* phos k* rhus-t **Sep** k* *Sil* k* *Sulph* k* thuj k*
  - **soft**: ant-c bro1
- **Wrists**: ferr bg2 ferr-ma k*
  - **inflamed**: allox tpw3

WASHES:
- **always** washing her hands (See MIND - Washing - desire - hands)
- **dry** hot hands frequently: *Phos* k*

WASHING:
- **agg.** | **Hands** | **Palms**: rhus-t ptk1
  - **Upper** limbs: am-c b4.de* **Calc** b4a.de carb-v b4.de* clem b4.de* *Fl-ac* b4a.de *Laur* b7a.de lyc b4.de* phos b4.de* sep bg2 *Sulph* b4.de* tab bg2
- **amel.**:
  - ○ **Lower** limbs: asar b7.de* cann-xyz bg2
  - **Upper** limbs: asar b7.de* rhod b4.de* spig b7.de*
- **cold** washing | **amel.** | **Lower** limbs: aur ptk1 *Led* ptk1 syph ptk1
  - **feet**:
    - **amel.** | **Lower** limbs: led bg2
- **feet**:
  - **agg.** | **Lower** limbs: nux-v bg2
- **finger** tips:
  - **amel.** | **Upper** limbs: lol bg2

WASTING (See Emaciation)

WATER:
- **amel.** | **Upper** limbs: asar b7.de* spig b7.de*
- **downward**; running:
  - **cold** water | **clavicle** down to toes along a narrow line; from: caust k*
- **pouring** over:
  - **agg.** | **Upper** limbs: stront-c b4.de*

Water: ...
- **putting** hands in cold water agg.: lac-d st phos st
- **warm** water were running through marrow of bones; as if: hydrc c1
- ○ **Elbow**:
  - **cold** water were dripping from; as if: stry
  - **water** running through: graph
- **Feet**:
  - **cold** water:
    - **dipped** into cold water; as if: carb-v
    - **poured** on them; as if cold water were: verat
  - **hot** water; as if cold feet had been put in: raph
  - ○ **Sole**: merc h1
- **Hands** | **puddle** of water; sensation as if hand lying in a: lac-loxod-a hrn2•
- **Hips**:
  - **cold** water running down to toes: bell
  - **warm** water; seems bathed in: coc-c
- **Legs**:
  - **oozing** from the legs: graph **Lyc** sacch tarent-c
  - ○ **Calf**: | **runs** along; as if water: dulc h1 sulph st
- **Thighs**:
  - **cold** water trickled down front of; drops of: acon k*
  - **warm** water were running down: *Borx* k*
- **Upper** limbs:
  - **warm** water:
    - **on** hands and arms; as if warm water were: androc srj1•
    - **through** upper limbs; as if warm water were running: rhus-t h1

WEAKNESS: *(↗Strength)* abrot k* acet-ac k* acon k* acon-f a1 aeth bro1 *Agar* k* agar-ph a1 agn k2 alco a1 all-c k* allox sp1 *Alum* k* alum-p k2 alum-sil k2* alumn k2 am-c k* *Am-caust* bro1 am-m k* aml-ns ammc a1 *Anac* k* ang a1 *Ant-c* k* *Ant-t* k* anthraci vh1 *Apis* k* apoc apom a1 arag br1 **Arg-met** **Arg-n** k* **Ars** k* *Ars-h* k* *Ars-i* ars-s-f k2 asar bro1 aster astra-m br1 atp rly4• atro k* aur k* aur-m k* aur-s k2 bamb-a stb2.de• bar-c k* *Bar-m* k* bell k* bell-p bro1 berb k* beryl sp1 bism bro1 borx k* bov k* brach k* brass-n-o srj5• brom tl1 bros-gau mrc1 **Bry** k* but-ac sp1 cadm-met tpw6* cain **Calc** k* calc-f sp1 *Calc-p* k* calc-s calc-sil k2 cann-i k* cann-s k* *Canth* k* caps k* *Carb-v* k* carbn-h carbn-o carbn-s carc sp1* carl k* casc a1 **Caust** k* *Cham* k* chel k* chin k* chinin-ar *Chinin-s* chlf a1 *Cic* cimic k* cimx k* cinch a1 cinnb cit-v a1 clem k* cob k* *Coc-c* k* cocc k* coff k* colch k* **Con** k* convo-s sp1 cortico sp1 cortiso sp1 cot a1 croc k* *Crot-t Cupr* k* cupr-ar cur bro1 cycl h1 cypr bro1 cystein-l rly4• cyt-l a1* dendr-pol sk4• dig k* digin a1 digox a1 *Dulc* k* elaps eucal a1* eup-pur k* euphr k* **Ferr** k* ferr-ar *Ferr-i* k* *Ferr-m* ferr-p galeoc-c-h gms1• gast a1 **Gels** k* gent-l k* gins k* glon k* *Graph* k* grat k* guaj k2 ham k* hell k* helo-s bnm14• helon bro1 *Hep* k* hipp a1* hist sp1 hura hydr k* hydr-ac k* hyos k* hyper k* ign k* ind indg k* iod k* iris jac-c k* jatr-c *Kali-ar Kali-bi* k* *Kali-br* **Kali-c** k* kali-m k2 *Kali-n* k* *Kali-p Kali-s Kalm* k* keroso a1 kreos k* *Lach* k* lact k* lat-h bnm5• lec br1* lil-s a1 lim a1 lipp a1 lob k* **Lyc** k* mag-c k* mag-p bro1 manc k* mand rsj7• med bro1 meny k* **Merc** k* *Merc-c* k* merc-i-f k* merl k* mez k* morg-p fmm1• morph k* mur-ac k* myric bro1 *Naja* nat-ar *Nat-c* k* *Nat-m* k* nat-p nat-pyru rly4• nat-s k2 nicc-s bro1 *Nit-ac* k* *Nux-v* k* oena a1 olnd k* *Onos* bro1 op k* osm k* ox-ac k* oxyurn-sc mcp1• pall pert-vc vk9 *Petr* k* *Ph-ac* k* **Phos** k* phys k* pic-ac k* pin-s a1 plat k* **Plb** k* *Positr* nl2• prim-v bro1 pseuts-m oss1• psor ptel k* *Puls* k* *Pycnop-sa* mrz1 *Ran-b* k* raph k* rham-f a1 **Rhus-t** k* ribo rly4• rumx ruta *Sabad* k* sabin k* sapin a1 sarcol-ac bro1* sars k* scut bro1 *Sec* k* sel bro1 sep k* **Sil** k* sin-n k* sol-t-ae a1 spig k* spira a1 spong k* squil k* *Stann* k* **Staph** k* stroph-s sp1 stry k* stry-p bro1 sul-i k2 sulfon bro1 *Sulph* k* sumb k* tab k* *Tarent* k* tep k* ter k* *Thal* bro1 thal-xyz srj8• *Thuj* k* til k* tritic-vg fd5.de tung-met bdx1• upa k* valer k* vanil fd5.de **Verat** k* verat-v k* visc tl1 wies a1 xan c1 *Zinc* k* zinc-p k2 zing k* [bell-p-sp dcm1]
- **midnight**: pic-ac k*
- **daytime**: sulph
- **morning**: alum brach k* cham k* cinnb k* colch k* dulc k* *Nit-ac* ox-ac k* pall k* pert-vc vk9 peti a1 phos k* ruta fd4.de sulph k* til k*
  - **bed** agg., in: canth k* nat-m k* phos
  - **rising** agg.: bov k* coc-c k* hep k* nat-ar *Nat-m* phos k* puls k*

Extremities

- **waking**; on: arg-met bar-c crot-t k* euphr k* *Lyc* k* nat-c pic-ac k* sep k* *Zinc* k*
  - **forenoon**: ant-t cham grat lach
- **noon**: gels k* spong fd4.de zinc k*
- **afternoon**: acon k* bar-c k* brach k* mag-m k* pitu-gl skp7• ruta fd4.de spong fd4.de til k*
  - **16** h: pic-ac **Rhus-t**
  - **sitting** agg.: thuj k*
  - **walking** | **after** | **short** walk; after a: ol-an k*
    - **agg.**: gins k*
- **evening**: *Agar* k* am-c k* atra-r skp7• bar-c k* *Calc* k* dulc k* euphr k* kali-bi k* lyc k* mez k* naja *Nuph* k* paeon k* phos k* *Rhus-t* k* ruta fd4.de sabad k* spong fd4.de
  - **amel.**: pert-vc vk9
  - **lying** down agg.: naja
  - **walk**, after short: nat-m k*
- **night**: *Cham* k* *Merc* k* spong fd4.de til k*
  - **toothache**; during: clem k*
- **accompanied** by:
  - **palpitations** (See CHEST - Palpitation - accompanied - legs)
  - **vertigo** (See VERTIGO - Accompanied - extremities)
  - ○ **Teeth**; pain in (See TEETH - Pain - accompanied - limbs)
- **agg.** | **Lower** limbs: nux-v bg2
- **alternating** with:
  - **agility**: nat-m c1
  - **vision**; dim: bell h1
- **ascending** stairs agg.: bapt hr1 calc-sil vh1 sarcol-ac br1*
- **back**; after dislocation of the: ruta k2
- **bathing**; after: mand rsj7•
  - **river**; in a: ant-c
- **children**; in: irid-met br1 nat-c k2
- **chill**; during: ant-t k* cann-i k* rhus-t h1 sep k* thuj k* verat k*
- **dinner**; after: nit-ac k* tub c1
- **eating**:
  - **after**:
    - **agg.**: *Bar-c* cann-s k* *Clem* k*
    - **amel.**: paeon ruta fd4.de
- **emissions** agg.; after: nat-p mrr1 *Ph-ac*
- **exertion**; after slight: *Anac* **Ars** bry *Calc* **Carb-v** cic k* guaj k2 *Kali-c* kali-p fd1.de• nux-m br1 *Phos*
- **fever**; during: **Ars** b4a.de bell h1 *Calc* b4a.de rhod b4.de sulph b4.de
- **gout**, after: bell-p c1*
- **lying**:
  - **amel.**: atra-r skp7•
  - **bed**; in | **agg.**: carl sulph
  - **side**; on:
    - **left** | **agg.**: merc-i-f
- **menses**; during: calc-p k* mag-m k*
- **mental** exertion; from: ph-ac phos k2
- **motion**:
  - **agg.**: rumx
  - **amel.**: caps k* cham k* *Lyc* phos k* pimp a1 **Rhus-t** k*
- **overheated**; from being: phos k2
- **paralytic**: agar k2 alum k* am-m h2 ambr k2 *Anac* ars k* bar-c k2 bell k* cann-i k2 carb-v **Caust** k* *Cham* k* cimic k2 cocc k2 *Con* mrr1 ferr k2 ferr-ar gels k2 graph k2 *Kali-bi* *Kali-br* *Kali-c* merc-c k* nux-m k2 nux-v k* phos k* psor al2 rhus-t k2 ruta k2 sabad k* sarcol-ac sp1 thal-xyz srj8• **Verat**
  - **spasmodic** jerks, after: cic hr1
  - **strain**; after: ulm-c jsj8•
- **periodical**: ars *Calc* kreos k*
- **perspiration**; during: anac b4a.de ars b4a.de dig b4a.de sulph b4.de
- **pregnancy** agg.; during: calc-p k*
- **pressure** agg.: nit-ac k*
- **rheumatic**: *Ars* bro1 bov calc-p bro1 *Chin* bro1 chinin-s bro1 *Colch* bro1 ferr-c bro1 sulph bro1
- **rising**:
  - **after** | **agg.**: chel k*
- **rising**: ...
  - **amel.**: arg-met lyc k* nat-m k*
  - **bed**; from | **agg.**: phos *Puls*
  - **sitting**; from | **agg.**: caust dig *Ruta* mrr1
- **sensation** of:
  - ○ **Feet**: camph bg2 cham bg2 coff bg2 rhus-t bg2
    - **Joints**: nux-v bg2
  - **Hips**: cina bg2
  - **Knees**: am-c bg2 ant-c bg2 asar bg2 caust bg2 cocc bg2 *Con* bg2 croc bg2 dig bg2 euphr bg2 ferr bg2 ip bg2 kali-n bg2 mag-c bg2 *Nux-m* bg2 plat bg2 plb bg2 *Puls* bg2 rheum bg2 ruta bg2 sabad bg2 staph bg2 valer bg2
  - **Legs**: bell bg2 canth bg2 coff bg2 croc bg2 dig bg2 kali-c bg2 merc bg2 puls bg2 stront-c bg2 sulph bg2 thuj bg2 valer bg2 verat bg2 verb bg2
    - **Calves**: aloe bg2
  - **Lower** limbs: acon bg2 agar bg2 aloe bg2 alum bg2 am-c bg2 anac bg2 ant-c bg2 ars bg2 asar bg2 bell bg2 bov bg2 calc bg2 carb-an bg2 caust bg2 colch bg2 con bg2 croc bg2 dulc bg2 *Graph* bg2 hell bg2 hep bg2 ign bg2 ip bg2 kali-bi bg2 kali-n bg2 led bg2 *Lyc* bg2 mag-c bg2 mez bg2 nat-m bg2 nux-v bg2 par bg2 *Phos* bg2 plat bg2 *Puls* bg2 rhus-t bg2 ruta bg2 sabin bg2 samb bg2 sars bg2 seneg bg2 spong bg2 stann bg2 stram bg2 *Sulph* bg2 verb bg2
  - **Thighs**: hell bg2 merc bg2 nux-v bg2 rheum bg2 rhod bg2 squil bg2 staph bg2 thuj bg2
- **sexual** excesses; after: phos k2
- **sitting**:
  - **agg.**: arg-met chel k* merc k* nux-v k* ruta thuj
  - **long** time agg.; for a | **after**: sars k*
- **sleep**:
  - **after** | **agg.**: merc-c
  - **during**:
    - **agg.** | **hang** vertically from the joints; as if bones: dendr-pol sk4•
  - **insufficient** sleep | **after**: am-c
- **standing** agg.: anac berb k* cortiso sp1 dirc k* hell k* stann k* zinc k*
- **stiffness**, with: caust con lach lyc nat-m rhus-t sil
- **stool** agg.; after: *Ars* k* colch k*
- **sudden**: alum bg2 arg-n bg2 bell bg2 **Cham** k* lyc k* naja nat-p thuj bg2
  - **evening**: atra-r skp7*•
  - **hunger**; with: *Zinc*
  - **walking** agg.: nat-p k2
- **sunstroke**; from: phos k2
- **surprise**; from: gels k2
- **urination**; after | **amel.**: spira
- **using** hands; from: ferr-i k2
- **waking**; on: chin k* kali-n k* sol-t-ae k* tep k*
- **walking**:
  - **agg.**: *Anac* **Arg-met** berb k* *Bry* cob k* colch k* ferr-i k2 ham k* kali-s fd4.de lyc naja nat-p petr k* ruta fd4.de
  - **air**; in open:
    - **agg.**: am-c h2 colch *Dig* euph ferr mag-m merl nux-v pic-ac raph ruta fd4.de sang *Zinc*
    - **amel.**: am-c cham clem
  - **amel.**: gins k* hipp a1 phos k* sulph k*
- **warmth** agg. | **heat** agg.: coloc k*
- **weeping**; after: con
- ▽ **extending** to:
  - ○ **Back**; through | **chill**; during: thuj k*
- ○ **Ankles**: abrot k* *Acon* b7.de* agn aloe k* *Alum* b4a.de arg-n am ars k* ars-s-f k2 arund a1 bry b7.de* calc k* *Calc-p* c2* calc-s calc-sil mtf33 **Carb-an** k* carbn-s carc fb *Caust* k* *Cham* bro1 chlf k* cic k* com k* cori-r a1 dios k* dulc fd4.de falco-pe nl2• *Ferr* ferr-ar glon k* graph bg2 *Ham* c2* hipp a1 kali-c k* kali-sil k2 *Lac-d* laur bg2 led br1* lyc b4a.de mag-m bro1 mang b4a.de* mang-act br1* mang-m c2 med k* merc k* mez k* **Nat-ar** k* **Nat-c** k* *Nat-m* k* **Nat-p** k* **Nat-s** k* **Nit-ac** k* nux-v k* ph-ac k2* phos bro1* phys k* pieri-b mlk9.de pin-s c2* plb k* plut-n srj7• polyp-p a1 positr nl2• psor bg2* puls *Rhus-t* k* *Rhus-v* k* ruta bro1* *Sec* ptk1 *Sep* **Sil** k* sphing kk3.fr stront-c b4.de* *Sul-ac* *Sulph* k* tung-met bdx1• valer k* vanil fd5.de

- **morning**: agn coca
  - **walking** agg.: agn com a1 valer k*
- **afternoon**: cham ptk1
- **night**: sulph k*
- **children**; in: sil mtf33
  - **learning** to walk: **Carb-an** k* mang ptk1 nat-c k2 nat-p nat-s ptk1
- **motion** agg.: laur k* nux-v k*
- **running** agg.: mez k*
- **sensation** of: ulm-c jsj8•
- **sitting**:
  - **agg.**: paeon k*
  - **walking**; after: caust
- **standing** agg.: calc k*
- **stepping** agg.: phos h2
- **sudden**: com k*
- **walking**:
  - **agg.**: agn aloe bit-ar wht1• *Calc-p* st1 carb-an k* com k* med *Nat-c* **Nit-ac** nux-v k* plb k* ruta fd4.de sulph h2 vanil fd5.de
  - **air** agg.; in open: mez h2
  - **amel.**: caust k*
  - **beginning** to walk: mez h2
- **warm** bathing; after: calc
- ○ **Sides** | **Outer**: petr h2

- **Elbows**: adeps-s k1 ang k* aur bg2 bros-gau mrc1 caj a1 chinin-s coloc k* dios k* fago k* glon k* hyper k* kali-m bg1 led k* nat-s k* op k* phos h2* plb k* positr nl2• raph k* sars k* staph k* *Sulph* k* thuj k* valer k*
  - **17 h**: valer
  - **dinner**; after: nit-ac h2
  - ○ **Bend**, of: cann-i k*
- **Feet**: acon bro1 *Aesc* bro1 agar k* am-c k* ambr k* ant-c b7.de* ant-t a1 arg-met bg2* **Ars** k* ars-s-f k2 aspar a1 bar-c b4.de* bell k* borx *Bov* k* bry a1 *Calc* k* calc-sil k2 camph b7.de* cann-s bro1 canth k* caps b7.de* carb-ac k* carbn-o carbn-s caust bg2 *Cham* k* *Chin* k* chinin-s chlf k* cinch a1 clem k* coca coff k* colch k* croc k* crot-t k* cycl k* eup-per eup-pur k* ferr k* ferr-ar k2 franz a1 gamb k* gard-j vlr2• gels k* gins k* glon k* graph k* grat k* *Hell* k* hipp bro1* hyos k* ign k* indg k* ip k* *Lach* k* lath k* laur k* lipp a1 *Lyc* k* mag-c k* mag-s k* merc k* *Mez* narz a1 nat-ar nat-c k* *Nat-m* k* nat-sil fd3.de• nicc nit-ac k* nux-v k* *Ol-an* k* *Olnd* k* ox-ac ptk1 petr k* phel k* *Phos* k* phys k* *Plat* k* plb k* plect a1 polyp-p a1 *Puls* k* querc-r svu1• rad-br bg1 ran-r c2* ran-s k* *Rhus-t* k* ruta k* sabad k* sars k* sec k* seneg k* *Sil* k* stann k* stram k* stront-c *Sulph* k* sumb k* *Tab* k* tep k* thuj k* verat k* verb b7a.de xan k* zinc k*
  - **right**: agar bg1
  - **morning**: caust k* lyc k* mag-m k* sapin a1
    - **bed** agg.; in: zinc k*
    - **rising** agg.: nat-m k*
    - **walking** agg.: lyc k* mag-c k* mag-m k*
  - **forenoon**: seneg k*
  - **noon**: kali-bi k*
  - **afternoon**: alum k* bov k* hydr-ac k* lith-c lyc k* nux-v k*
    - **16 h**: **Lyc**
    - **17 h**: cham
    - **walking** agg.: lyc k*
  - **evening**: agar k* ign k* merc-c k* pic-ac k* puls k*
    - **19 h**: ant-c k*
    - **walking** | **after** | **agg.**: coc-c
      - **agg.**: mag-m h2
  - **night**: *Carb-an* k* cham h1 mag-s k* mang a1 nit-ac k*
    - **midnight**:
      - **after** | **4 h**: plb
    - **menses**; before: mang k*
  - **accompanied** by | **Head**; complaints of (See HEAD - Complaints - accompanied - feet - weak)
  - **ascending** stairs agg.: acon k* borx bry k* lyc k* mag-c k* nux-v k*
  - **bending** agg.: led k*

- **Feet**: ...
  - **chilliness**; during: hell k*
  - **coition**; after: calc-p k*
  - **dinner**; after: mag-m k*
  - **eating**; after: cain ferr k* nat-c h2
  - **fever**; after: nat-s k*
  - **headache**; during: ol-an k*
  - **lying** | **amel.**: mag-c k* *Nat-m* k*
  - **menses**; during: ant-t k* castm *Graph* mang ol-an k* zinc k*
  - **paralytic**: cham k* nat-m k* nat-sil fd3.de• olnd k* tab k* thal-xyz srj8•
  - **raise**, trying to: merc k*
  - **riding** amel.; while: *Nat-m*
  - **sitting**:
    - **agg.**: anac k* card-b a1 card-m ptk1 coc-c k* *Led* k* plat k* *Rhus-t* k* thuj k*
    - **amel.**: *Nat-m* k*
  - **standing** agg.: kali-n k* *Nat-m* k* sars k*
  - **trembling**: caps k*
  - **waking**; on: nat-m k*
  - **walking**:
    - **agg.**: camph k* chin clem k* croc k* *Graph* grat a1 ham k* kali-n k* par k* **Rhus-t** a1 thuj a1
    - **air**; in open | **after** | **agg.**: borx h2
      - **agg.**: agar arn olnd thuj
    - **amel.**: laur k* nat-m k* zinc k*
    - **beginning** to walk: mag-m h2
  - ○ **Heel**:
    - **motion** | **amel.**: gard-j vlr2•
  - **Muscles** | **Extensor** muscles: *Kali-br* hr1
  - **Soles**: bism bg2 cain calc-f sha carbn-s k* croc k* hipp a1* kreos k* led k* nux-v k* olnd k* plb k* sumb k* tep k* thuj k*
    - **dinner**; after: carbn-s
    - **sitting** agg.: plb k* thuj k*
    - **walking** agg.: nux-v k* olnd k* thuj k*
- **Fingers**: acon bg2 ambr k* **Ars** k* *Bov* k* *Calc* bg2* carb-an *Carb-v* k* cic k* crot-h k* cur k* fago k* *Gels* bro1 hell b7.de* hipp k* hura kali-bi k2 kali-c b4a.de* kali-m ptk1 *Kali-n* k* lact led k* lyc k* medul-os-si rly4• *Nat-m* par k* phos k* **Rhus-t** k* sep ptk1 sil k* zinc
  - **daytime**: nit-s-d a1 phos k*
  - **night**: ambr
  - **drops** things: *Ars* bov ptk1 carb-an *Nat-m* *Sil* *Stann* k*
  - **grasping**, when: **Ars** carb-an carb-v k* kali-br *Sil*
  - **paralytic**: **Ars** carb-v
  - **playing** piano: *(↗Playing - piano)* agar ptk1 bov ptk1 *Calc* ptk1 **Caust** ptk1 *Cham* ptk1 cimic ptk1 cocc ptk1 *Cur* k* *Cycl* ptk1 *Dros* ptk1 gels ptk1 **Kali-c** ptk1 mag-p ptk1 **Nat-m** ptk1 phos ptk1 pic-ac ptk1 plat ptk1 sep ptk1 *Sil* ptk1 *Stann* k* *Valer* ptk1 *Zinc* k*
  - **writing** agg.: fago k* kali-c
  - ○ **First**: alco a1 kali-c k* nat-m k*
    - **writing** agg.: kali-c k*
  - **Second**: nat-m k*
  - **Third**: plb k*
  - **Tips**: *Mez*
- **Forearms**: acon bg2 aeth k* agar k* ang k* anthraq rly4• arg-met arg-n mtf11 **Ars** k* aur k* aur-m-n k* **Bell** k* beryl tpw5 bufo camph k* cham k* chel b7.de* chinin-ar k2 coloc k* con k* cycl b7.de* *Dig* k* dros bg2 dulc k* galla-q-r nl2• indg k* kali-n k* merc k* mez k* nat-m k* nicotam rly4• nit-ac k* nux-v k* op k* osm k* phos k* plb k* rhod k* **Rhus-t** k* sabin k* streptoc rly4• stront-c sumb k* thuj k* tung-met bdx1• verat k*
  - **right**: arg-met *Sil*
  - **morning** | **waking**; on: arg-met
  - **evening**: *Dig*
  - **night**: kali-n k*
  - **heart** disease; in: dig c1

- **knitting**, while: aeth k*
- **paralytic**: kali-n h2
  - ⁝ **accompanied** by | **Fingers**; contraction of: arg-met ptk1
- **writing** agg.: agar k* arg-met coloc k*

\- **Hands**: acon acon-a a1 act-sp bg2 alum k2 alumn k* ang k* arg-met k2 arn k* ars k* aven br1 bell k* bism k* *Bov* k* bry b7.de* bufo k* calc bg2* canth k* caps carb-v k* caust k* cham k* chin k* chinin-s cimic k* *Cina* k* colch k* com k* croc k* cupr k* cur dios k* euph b4a.de *Fl-ac* k* galla-q-r nl2• gard-j vlr2• gels k* get a1 glon k* ham fd3.de• hell k* hep bg2 hipp k* jug-r k* *Kali-bi* k* kali-c k* *Kali-n* k* kreos k* lach k* luf-op rsj5• lyc k* mag-p bg2 med ptk1 melal-alt gya4 menth-pu a1 *Merc* k* *Merc-c* b4a.de merc-i-f k* merc-n a1 **Mez** k* nat-ar nat-c k* nat-m k* nat-p *Nat-s* k* nat-sil fd3.de• *Nit-ac* k* nit-s-d a1 nux-m k* nux-v k* ol-an bg2 ox-ac ptk1 phos k* phys k* plb k* plut-n srj7• positr nl2• rhod k* rhus-t k* *Ruta* k* sabin k* sec k* sep k* sil k* spong fd4.de *Stann* k* streptoc rly4• sulph k* sumb k* tab k* verat h1* zinc k*

- **right** | **writing** agg.: lac-e hrn2•
- **left**: cact k2 spong fd4.de [spect dfg1]
- **morning**: calc h2 caust h2 dios k* lyc k* nat-m k* sapin a1
  - ⁝ **bed** agg.; in: nat-m k*
  - ⁝ **rising** agg.: nat-m k* plb k* sulph k*
  - ⁝ **waking**; on: caust k* mag-c a1 mag-m a1
- **afternoon**: bov k*
  - ⁝ **17** h: cham
  - ⁝ **sleep** agg.; after: nux-v
- **evening**: dios k* ham fd3.de•
- **night**: kali-n k*
  - ⁝ **fever**; after: nat-s
  - ⁝ **waking**; on: mez h2
- **chill**; during: laur k* sabin b7.de
- **cramping**: caust h2
- **dinner**; after: mag-m k*
- **eating**; after: bar-c nat-c h2
- **grasping** objects, on: get a1 hydrog srj2• kali-p fd1.de• melal-alt gya4 nat-m k* *Nat-s*
- **headache**; during: ol-an k*
- **laughing** agg.: carb-v h2
- **lying**:
  - ⁝ **agg.** | **hard**; on something: nat-m
  - ⁝ **amel.**: mag-c
  - ⁝ **hand** on table agg.; lying: stann
- **menses**: alumn k* ol-an k* zinc k*
- **motion** agg.: plb k* thuj k*
- **numb** as from electric shocks: fl-ac k*
- **paralytic**: act-sp **Alumn** k* ang k* **Ars** bism *Bov* crot-h k* gels k2 nat-m k* nat-sil fd3.de• *Sil* *Stann*
- **playing** piano: **Cur** mrr1
- **pressure** agg.: mez k* nit-ac k*
- **rising** agg.; after: nux-m k* plb k*
- **sprained**, as if: indg k*
- **supper** agg.; after: nat-m k*
- **trembling**: bism a1 lycps-v *Stann*
- **waking**; on: mez k*
- **walking** agg.: grat k* plb k*
- **warm** room agg.: *Caust* k*
- **writing**:
  - ⁝ **after**: plb k*
  - ⁝ **agg.**: *Aesc* aml-ns ant-c br1 bamb-a stb2.de• bism brach k* caps carb-v h2 chel k* *Lol* a1 **Mez** k* plect a1 sabin k* sil ptk1 *Stann* k* *Zinc* k*

\- **Hips**: adeps-s k1 agar k* *All-c* k* apis k* arg-met brach k* calc-p bg1* carb-v k* chin k* cina b7.de* cinnb k* der a1 ham k* ign k* *Kali-c* k* kreos b7a.de mang k* murx *Ox-ac* k* *Pic-ac* podo k* prun a1 ruta ptk1 sars k* sep k* syph tarent k* thuj k* tril-p ptk1 *Verat* zing k* [viol-t xyz62]

- **right**: *Arg-met*
  - ⁝ **then** left: *Verat*

\- **Hips**: ...

- **left**: podo c1
- **morning**: chin k* mang k*
  - ⁝ **waking**; on: arg-met
- **evening**: ammc a1 tarent k*
  - ⁝ **bed**; before going to: chinin-s
- **ascending** stairs agg.: podo k*
- **coition**, preventing finishing: all-c k*
- **motion** | **amel.**: chin h1
- **paralytic**: arg-met *Kali-c* mang h2
- **rising** from seat agg.: sep k*
- **standing** agg.: zing k*
- **vertigo**; with: acon bg1 arg-met h1 con bg1 olnd bg1
- **walking**:
  - ⁝ **agg.**: chinin-s cob ptk1 coca *Verat*
  - ⁝ **continued** | **amel.**: sep

○ • **Joints**: *Acon* b7a.de agar bg2 agn b7.de* apis b7a.de arg-met bg2 *Calc* b4a.de *Calc-p* bg2 chin b7.de* dros bg2 ferr-p bg2 ign bg2 irid-met bg2 mang bg2 sars bg2 sep bg2 *Staph* b7a.de thuj b4.de*

\- **Joints**: (↗*Sprains; Sprains - joints)* *Acon* k* aesc k* agn c1 *Aloe* *Arg-met* **Arn** k* ars k* ars-s-f k2 atp rly4• aur aur-ar k2 aur-s k2 bar-c h2 bar-m bro1 bell-p bro1 borx k* bov k* *Bry* **Calc** k* calc-sil k2 caps k2 *Carb-an* k* carb-v k* carbn-s *Caust* k* cent a1 cham k* chel k* *Chin* k* chinin-ar cimic k* clem k* coloc k* **Con** k* cypr bro1 dig c1 dios hr1 euph k* *Ferr* k* ferr-ar ferr-p graph hipp bro1 **Kali-c** k* *Kali-s* kali-sil k2 *Lach* *Led* k* **Lyc** k* mang k* **Merc** k* merc-c k* mez k* morph k* murx k* *Nat-m* *Nit-ac* k* *Nux-v* *Petr* k* *Phos* k* plb k* podo k* **Psor** k* *Puls* k* raph k* rhod **Rhus-t** k* **Sep** k* *Sil* k* *Staph* k* stront-c sk4• **Sulph** k* tab bg2 *Verat* zing k*

- **morning**:
  - ⁝ **bed** agg.; in: carb-v
  - ⁝ **motion** agg.: cimic
- **forenoon**: ars k*
- **chill**; during: raph k*
- **diarrhea** agg.; after: borx
- **motion**:
  - ⁝ **agg.**: chlf k* chlor con k*
  - ⁝ **beginning** of | **agg.**: *Euph* k*
- **pregnancy** agg.; during: murx ptk1
- **rising** | **amel.**: carb-v k*
- **sitting** agg.: ars k* graph k* phos k*
- **sprain**; after: phos k2 rhus-t k2
- **stooping** agg.: graph
- **walking** | **after** | **agg.**: borx h2 zing k*
  - ⁝ **amel.**: borx

\- **Knees**: abrot k* acon k* act-sp k* *Agar* k* agn b7.de* aids nl2• alco a1 all-s *Alum* k* alum-p k2 am-c b4.de *Ambr* *Anac* k* androc srj1• ang k* ant-t k* *Arg-met* *Arg-n* k* arn k* *Ars* k* ars-h ars-i ars-s-f k2 arund k* asar k* aur k* aur-ar k2 aur-i k2 aur-s k2 bamb-a stb2.de• bapt k* *Bar-c* bar-i k2 bart a1 bell k* *Bol-la* borx k* *Bov* k* bros-gau mrc1 *Bry* k* cain caj k* calad k* *Calc* k* calc-ar calc-i k2 calc-s calc-sil k2 *Camph* k* *Cann-i* k* cann-s b7.de* *Canth* k* carb-v k* carbn-s carl k* *Caust* k* cham k* chel k* *Chin* k* *Chinin-ar* *Chinin-s* cimic k* cinnb clem k* cob k* **Cocc** k* colch k* *Coloc* k* **Con** k* conin a1 cor-r cot a1 croc k* *Cupr* k* cycl k* des-ac rbp6 *Dig* k* *Dios* k* *Dulc* k* euphr k* fago k* *Ferr* k* ferr-ar *Ferr-p* gard-j vlr2• *Gels* k* gins k* *Glon* k* graph k* *Hell* hep b4a.de hipp bro1* hura *Hydr* hyos k* *Ign* k* indg k* iod k* iodof a1 *Ip* k* *Iris* ix bnm8• jac-c k* jatr-c kali-bi kali-br k* *Kali-c* k* *Kali-n* k* kali-s kali-sil k2 kreos k* lac-ac k* *Lach* k* lact lap-la sde8.de• *Lec* *Led* k* lil-t bg2 lim a1 lith-c lol bg2 *Lyc* k* mag-c b4.de mag-m k* mand rsj7• mang med *Merc* k* merc-i-r k* merc-sul a1 mez k* mosch k* mur-ac ptk1 murx bg2 **Nat-m** k* nat-p bg2 nat-pyru rly4• **Nat-s** k* *Nit-ac* k* *Nux-m* k* *Nux-v* k* ol-an k* olib-sac wmh1 olnd k* op k* osm k* ox-ac ozone sde2• petr k* *Ph-ac* k* *Phos* k* pic-ac k* plac rzf5• *Plat* k* **Plb** k* podo k* positr nl2• *Psor* puls k* ran-b k* rheum b7.de* *Rhus-v* k* *Ruta* k* sabad k* sarr *Sars* k* sep k* *Sil* k* sphing kk3.fr spirae a1 spong b7.de* *Stann* k* *Staph* k* stront-c b4.de* stry k* sul-ac k* sul-i k* sulph k* syph tab k* tax k* tell k* thea *Thuj* k* valer b7.de* vanil fd5.de verat k* zinc k*

- **alternating** sides: cic

- **right**: ars$_{bg1}$ kali-s$_{fd4.de}$ [spect$_{dfg1}$]
- **left**: chel gard-j$_{vlr2•}$ ruta$_{fd4.de}$ [tax$_{jsj7}$]
- **morning**: chin$_{k*}$ *Dios*$_{k*}$ *Nat-m*$_{k*}$ plac$_{rzf5•}$
  - **bed** agg.; in: sulph
  - **rising** agg.; after: petr$_{k*}$ phos$_{k*}$ staph$_{k*}$
- **forenoon**: dulc$_{fd4.de}$ sulph$_{k*}$ valer$_{k*}$
- **noon**: aids$_{nl2•}$
- **afternoon**: caust$_{k*}$ chinin-s ham$_{k*}$ ped$_{a1}$ ruta$_{fd4.de}$
  - **13 h**: ozone$_{sde2•}$
  - **walking** agg.: caust$_{k*}$
- **evening**: anac$_{k*}$ bry$_{k*}$ dios$_{k*}$ nat-m$_{k*}$ nat-pyru$_{rly4•}$ ruta$_{fd4.de}$ sang$_{k*}$ sarr
- **night**: calc$_{k*}$
- **ascending** stairs agg.: *Bry*$_{k*}$ *Canth* cass$_{a1}$ caust$_{k*}$ **Con**$_{k*}$ dig$_{k*}$ dios hura hyos$_{k*}$ iod$_{k*}$ iodof$_{a1}$ *Kali-c*$_{k*}$ kali-s$_{fd4.de}$ merc ox-ac$_{k*}$ *Plat*$_{k*}$ plb$_{k*}$ *Ruta*$_{k*}$ *Stann Sulph Thuj*
- **coition**; after: agar **Calc**$_{k*}$ con dios$_{bg1}$ kali-c lyc petr *Sep*$_{k*}$ sil
- **descending** stairs agg.: bell dios$_{a1}$ gels$_{ptk1}$ hura *Kali-c*$_{k*}$ lac-ac$_{k*}$ merc$_{a1}$ ruta$_{bg1*}$ stroph-s$_{sp1}$
- **dinner**; after: nit-ac$_{h2}$ phel$_{k*}$ til$_{k*}$
- **eating**; after: anac$_{k*}$ *Lach*$_{k*}$
- **exertion** agg.: cob$_{k*}$ equis-h
- **extending** and flexing amel.: ferr$_{k*}$
- **fright**; after: cinnb merc
- **kneeling** agg.: *Tarent*$_{k*}$
- **knock** together, as if they would: *Agar*$_{k*}$ aids$_{nl2•}$ arg-met$_{k2}$ berb cinnb *Cocc*$_{k*}$ *Colch*$_{k*}$ **Nux-v**$_{k*}$
- **menses**; during: *Ph-ac*$_{b4a.de}$
- **mental** exertion; from: borx$_{h2}$
- **motion**:
  - **agg.**: cycl$_{k*}$ phos$_{k*}$
  - **amel.**: chin$_{k*}$ phos$_{k*}$
- **paralytic**: mosch$_{k*}$ stann$_{k*}$
- **pollutions** in sleep, from: dios$_{ptk1}$
- **raising** leg: colch$_{k*}$
- **rest** | **amel.**: **Bry**$_{k*}$
- **rising** agg.; after: ferr-ma
  - **seat**; from a: bamb-a$_{stb2.de•}$ berb laur puls
- **shifting** from side to side (See alternating)
- **sitting**:
  - **agg.**: camph$_{k*}$ cic$_{k*}$ coloc$_{k*}$ mag-c$_{k*}$ mosch phos$_{k*}$
  - **amel.**: staph$_{k*}$
- **standing** agg.: acon *Anac*$_{k*}$ calad$_{k*}$ carb-v$_{k*}$ chin$_{h1}$ *Cic*$_{k*}$ *Cupr* dios$_{a1}$ hipp$_{a1}$ iod$_{k*}$ iodof$_{a1}$ merc$_{k*}$ *Mosch* olnd$_{ptk1}$ plat$_{k*}$ prun$_{k*}$ sul-ac$_{k*}$
- **stool** agg.; after: trom$_{k*}$
- **sudden**: cham$_{k*}$
- **sun** agg.; walking in the: stann$_{bg1}$
- **touch** agg.: chin$_{k*}$
- **vexation**; after: caust
- **walk**, as after a long: cocc$_{k*}$ cor-r$_{k*}$ dulc$_{k*}$ euph euphr$_{k*}$
- **walking**:
  - **after** | **agg.**: aur calc-s caust clem$_{h2}$ ind phyt *Rhus-t* ruta
  - **agg.**: acon agar anac$_{h2}$ bell$_{h1}$ *Bry* calc carb-v caul chel *Chin* **Cocc**$_{k*}$ **Coloc**$_{k*}$ con *Cupr* cycl dig dios dulc$_{fd4.de}$ hyos kali-c kali-n$_{h2}$ kali-s$_{fd4.de}$ *Lec Led* lil-t mag-c nat-n *Nat-s* petr plat puls ruta$_{fd4.de}$ spong stann$_{bg1}$ staph zinc
  - **air** agg.; in open: calad hyos *Zinc*
  - **amel.**: cham dios petr phos ruta$_{h1}$
- **warm** bathing; after: calc
- ▽ **extending** to | **Downward**: chlf$_{br1}$

- Knees: ...
  - ○ **Hollow** of knees: adeps-s$_{k1}$ aur blatta-o$_{bg1}$ bov$_{k*}$ ferr$_{k*}$ ham$_{bg1}$ laur$_{bg1}$ led$_{bg1}$ onos$_{vml3•}$ plat$_{k*}$ rad-br$_{bg1}$ rheum staph$_{k*}$ valer$_{k*}$ zinc$_{k*}$
    - **morning**: valer$_{k*}$
    - **rising** from sitting agg.: ferr$_{k*}$ staph$_{k*}$
    - **sitting** agg.: plat$_{k*}$
    - **standing** agg.: rheum
    - **walking**:
      - **agg.**: zinc
        - **standing**; after: ferr
      - **impossible**: adeps-s$_{k1}$
- **Legs**: acet-ac$_{k*}$ acon$_{k*}$ act-sp$_{k*}$ *Aesc*$_{k*}$ *Agar*$_{k*}$ all-c allox$_{sp1}$ aloe *Alum*$_{k*}$ alum-sil$_{k2}$ alumn$_{k*}$ *Am-c*$_{k*}$ am-m$_{k*}$ ambr$_{k*}$ amyg$_{a1}$ anan androc$_{srj1•}$ ang$_{b7a.de}$ ant-t$_{bg1}$ apis$_{b7a.de}$ *Arg-met*$_{k*}$ *Arg-n*$_{k*}$ arn$_{b7.de*}$ *Ars*$_{k*}$ arund$_{k*}$ asaf asar$_{b7a.de}$ aspar$_{k*}$ atra-r$_{bnm3•}$ atro$_{k*}$ *Bar-c*$_{k*}$ bar-m$_{bro1}$ bell$_{k*}$ benz-ac berb$_{bro1}$ beryl$_{tpw5}$ borx *Bov*$_{k*}$ brom$_{k*}$ bry$_{k*}$ bufo *Cact*$_{k*}$ *Calc*$_{k*}$ *Calc-p*$_{k*}$ *Calc-s* calc-sil$_{k2}$ camph$_{k*}$ *Cann-i*$_{k*}$ *Canth*$_{k*}$ carb-v carbn-o carbn-s *Caust*$_{k*}$ cent$_{a1}$ cerv$_{a1}$ cham$_{k*}$ chin$_{b7.de*}$ chinin-ar$_{k2}$ chinin-s chlor$_{k*}$ choc$_{srj3•}$ *Cic*$_{k*}$ cimic$_{k*}$ clem$_{k*}$ cob$_{bro1}$ **Cocc**$_{k*}$ coff$_{b7.de}$ colch$_{bro1}$ coloc$_{k*}$ **Con**$_{k*}$ conin$_{a1}$ cop corn$_{k*}$ croc$_{b7.de*}$ *Cupr*$_{k*}$ cur$_{bro1}$ cycl$_{k*}$ des-ac$_{rbp6}$ dig$_{k*}$ digin$_{a1}$ dios$_{k*}$ dub$_{a1}$ dulc$_{k*}$ elaps eup-per$_{k*}$ euph$_{k*}$ *Ferr*$_{k*}$ ferr-ar$_{k2}$ *Ferr-m* ferr-p fl-ac$_{k*}$ form$_{k*}$ gels$_{k*}$ gins$_{k*}$ *Glon* grat$_{k*}$ guaj haem$_{a1}$ *Ham*$_{k*}$ hell$_{k*}$ hep$_{b4a.de}$ hura *Hydr Hydrog*$_{srj2•}$ hydroph$_{rsj6•}$ hyos$_{k*}$ ind indg$_{k*}$ iris jab$_{k*}$ jatr-c *Kali-bi*$_{k*}$ *Kali-c*$_{k*}$ *Kali-cy*$_{k*}$ *Kali-n*$_{k*}$ kalm$_{k*}$ kreos$_{k*}$ lac-loxod-a$_{hrn2•}$ *Lach*$_{k*}$ lat-m *Lec*$_{sne}$ led$_{k*}$ lepi$_{a1}$ lil-t$_{k*}$ *Lyc*$_{k*}$ m-arct$_{b7.de}$ *Mag-c* mag-s$_{k*}$ mand$_{rsj7•}$ mang med$_{k*}$ medul-os-si$_{rly4•}$ *Merc*$_{k*}$ merc-c$_{b4a.de}$ mez$_{k*}$ mim-p$_{rsj8•}$ murx$_{k*}$ *Nat-ar Nat-c*$_{k*}$ nat-m$_{k*}$ nat-p **Nat-s**$_{k*}$ nit-ac$_{k*}$ nuph$_{k*}$ **Nux-m Nux-v**$_{k*}$ ol-an$_{bg2}$ *Olnd*$_{k*}$ onos$_{k*}$ *Op*$_{k*}$ ox-ac$_{k*}$ ozone$_{sde2•}$ paeon$_{bro1}$ paull$_{a1}$ peti$_{a1}$ *Petr* **Ph-ac**$_{k*}$ phel$_{bro1}$ *Phos*$_{k*}$ phys$_{k*}$ phyt *Pic-ac*$_{k*}$ *Plat*$_{k*}$ **Plb**$_{k*}$ positr$_{nl2•}$ psor$_{k*}$ puls$_{k*}$ *Rhod*$_{b4a.de}$ **Rhus-t**$_{k*}$ ribo$_{rly4•}$ rumx ruta$_{k*}$ sabad$_{k*}$ sabin$_{a1}$ *Sarcol-ac*$_{bro1}$ sarr$_{bro1}$ sars$_{k*}$ seneg *Sep*$_{k*}$ *Sil*$_{k*}$ spong$_{fd4.de}$ *Stann*$_{bro1}$ staph$_{k*}$ stront-c$_{k*}$ stry$_{k*}$ sulfonam$_{ks2}$ *Sulph*$_{k*}$ sumb$_{a1}$ tanac$_{a1}$ tarax$_{b7.de*}$ tarent$_{k*}$ tell$_{rsj10•}$ *Thuj*$_{k*}$ tub$_{c1}$ vac$_{jl2}$ valer$_{k*}$ verat$_{k*}$ verb$_{b7.de}$ vib$_{bro1}$ vip$_{k*}$ xan$_{k*}$ *Zinc*$_{k*}$ zinc-p$_{k2}$ [heroin$_{sdj2}$ spect$_{dfg1}$ tax$_{jsj7}$]
  - **right**: bov$_{bg1}$ con$_{bg1}$ tarax$_{h1*}$
  - **left**: anthraq$_{rly4•}$ cortico$_{tpw7*}$
  - **morning**: acon$_{k*}$ ambr$_{k*}$ *Arg-met* ars$_{k*}$ bar-c$_{k*}$ brach$_{k*}$ chlor$_{k*}$ dios$_{k*}$ nux-v stach$_{a1}$ sulph$_{k*}$
    - **bed** agg.; in: ran-a$_{a1}$ sulph$_{k*}$
    - **rising** agg.: *Arg-met* hura ran-a$_{a1}$ rat$_{k*}$ rhod$_{k*}$
    - **waking**; on: *Arg-met* caust$_{k*}$ sumb$_{k*}$
  - **forenoon**: coloc$_{k*}$ ptel$_{k*}$ ran-b rhus-t$_{k*}$ sars$_{k*}$ tell$_{rsj10•}$
  - **noon**: *Rhus-t*$_{k*}$
  - **afternoon**: am-m$_{k*}$ erio$_{a1}$ hura lac-loxod-a$_{hrn2•}$ nat-c$_{k*}$ peti$_{a1}$ rat$_{k*}$ [heroin$_{sdj2}$]
    - **walking** agg.: *Rhus-t*$_{k*}$
  - **evening**: abrot$_{k*}$ atra-r$_{bnm3•}$ brach$_{k*}$ coc-c$_{k*}$ kali-n$_{k*}$ merc$_{k*}$ onos phys$_{k*}$ propr$_{sa3•}$ stach$_{a1}$
    - **ascending** stairs agg.: rhus-t rumx
    - **walking** agg.: onos
  - **night**: am-m$_{k*}$ sulph$_{k*}$
  - **accompanied** by:
    - **faintness**: beryl$_{tpw5}$
    - **palpitations** (See CHEST - Palpitation - accompanied - legs)
    - **Spinal** meningitis (See BACK - Inflammation - membranes - accompanied - lower)
  - **ascending**:
    - **agg.**: lyss$_{c1}$ *Ruta*
    - **stairs** | **agg.**: acon$_{k*}$ alum-sil$_{k2}$ *Bry*$_{k*}$ corn *Hura* hyos ruta tarax$_{a1}$
  - **crossing** legs agg.: verb$_{h}$
  - **delivery**; after: *Caust Rhus-t*
  - **diarrhea** agg.; after: borx$_{kl}$ (non:bov$_{kl}$)
  - **dinner**; after: agar
  - **eating** agg.: hyos$_{k*}$

Extremities

- **exertion**; after slight: cic vac jl2 ziz
- **journey**, after: pic-ac k*
- **menses**; during: bov k* sars k* sulph zinc
- **motion**:
  - **agg.**: clem k* nat-s k* pic-ac k*
  - **amel.**: aur-m-n k* cham k* dios k* nat-s k* stront-c
- **overworked**; as if: ozone sde2•
- **painful**: calc k* cann-i k* crot-h k* plat h2
- **paralytic**: bell k* cod k* *Con* mrr1 kali-n k* pic-ac tl1
- **rising**:
  - **after** | **amel.**: caust k*
  - **agg.**: bry k*
  - **sitting**; from | **agg.**: atro puls
- **room** | **amel.**: grat
- **seminal** emissions, after: *Kali-br* hr1
- **sexual** excesses; after: aur bro1 calc bro1 calc-p bro1 *Chin* bro1 *Cob* bro1 con bro1 cupr bro1 dam bro1 dig bro1 *Dios* bro1 ery-a bro1 form bro1 gels bro1 *Kali-c* bro1 lyc bro1 med bro1 nat-p bro1 *Nux-v* bro1 *Ph-ac* bro1 *Pic-ac* bro1 sars bro1 sel bro1 staph k* *Sulph* bro1 zinc bro1
- **sitting**:
  - **agg.**: acon k* alum tl1 alumn k* aur-m-n k* bry tl1 camph k* cic k* indg plat k* **Rhus-t** k* sulph k* *Thuj*
  - **amel.**: valer k*
- **sleep** | **amel.**: tell k*
- **standing** agg.: aster k* chin cinch a1 nat-p k* ol-an k* samb k* stroph-s sp1 valer k*
- **stepping** agg.: plat h2
- **stool** agg.; after: con k*
- **studying**; from: pic-ac tl1 [tax jsj7]
- **temperature**; change of: act-sp
- **waking**; on: arg-met
- **walking**:
  - **after** | **agg.**: kali-n h2 rhus-t tl1
  - **agg.**: agar k* am-c k* *Caust* k* chel k* chin k* *Con* k* ery-m a1 *Gran* k* ind indg a1 lyc k* mez k* nat-p a1 nat-s a1 nit-ac k* **Nux-m** onos ph-ac h2* plat k* plb k* positr nl2• *Rhus-t* k* stram *Sulph* k* tarax k* tarent k* zinc k*
  - **air** agg.; in open: grat
  - **beginning** to walk: *Bry* k*

○ • **Calves**: aesc aloe *Arg-n* k* borx ptk1 but-ac sp1 calc k* calc-i k* *Calc-p* calc-s k* calc-sil k2 carb-v k* castm cham k* chinin-s coc-c k* croc k* dulc k* ferr k* ferr-i k* hipp a1 hydrog srj2• kali-c k* kali-n k* *Kalm* kola stb3• kreos k* *Nat-m* nicc k* osm plb k* ribo rly4• sil k* stront-c sulfonam ks2 sulph k* thuj k* valer k* zinc k*
  - **afternoon**: castm valer k*
  - **evening**: dulc k* eupi k*
  - **night**: *Sulph* k*
  - **accompanied** by | **palpitations**: calc-p ptk1
  - **ascending** agg.: bell h1
  - **chill**; during: thuj k*
  - **kneeling** agg.: ars-i k*
  - **motion** agg.: castm
  - **rising** from sitting agg.: zinc k*
  - **sitting**:
    - **agg.**: stront-c
    - **amel.**: nicc k*
  - **walking**:
    - **after** | **amel.**: calc-s
    - **agg.**: aloe croc k* gran k* nicc k* osm
    - **amel.**: plb k*
- **Muscles** | **Extensor** muscles: *Kali-br* hr1
- **Tendo** Achillis: lyc k* valer k*
  - **morning**: lyc k*
  - **sitting** agg.: valer k*

\- **Lower** limbs: *(↗Tottering)* acet-ac acon k* **Aesc** aeth k* *Agar* k* ail k* all-s k* aloe **Alum** k* alum-p k2 *Alum-sil* k4 alumn am-c k* *Am-m* k* ambr k* *Anac* b4.de* androc srj1• *Ang* k* ant-c b7.de ant-t b7.de* *Apis* **Arg-met** **Arg-n** k* am b7.de* **Ars** k* ars-s-f k2 asar k* **Aur** aur-ar k2 aur-i k2 aur-s k2 bamb-a stb2.de• *Bapt* k* bar-c bar-s k2 bell k* benz-ac k* berb k* beryl sp1 borx k* bov b4.de brach k* bros-gau mrc1 *Bry* k* *Bufo* k* but-ac sp1 cadm-met sp1 calad **Calc** k* calc-ar k2 calc-f sp1 calc-i k* calc-s camph b7.de* cann-i k* cann-s k* canth b7.de* **Carb-ac** carb-an b4.de *Carb-v* k* *Carbn-s* carc sp1 cartl-s rly4• cassia-s ccrh1• castm **Caust** k* cham k* chel k* *Chin* k* *Chinin-ar* *Cic* *Cina* cist k* clem b4.de* coc-c k* **Cocc** k* colch k* **Con** k* *Corn* cortico sp1 croc b7.de* *Crot-c* *Crot-t* k* *Cupr* k* cycl a1 des-ac rbp6 dig k* diosm br1 dros b7.de* dulc b4.de* ery-a k* eup-per bg2 *Euph* b4a.de euphr k* ferr b7.de* *Ferr-i* k* fuma-ac rly4• **Gels** k* **Glon** k* granit-m es1• *Graph* k* grat guaj k* ham k* *Hell* k* hep b4.de* hipp k* *Hydr* k* *Hyos* k* ign b7.de* ind k* iod b4.de* ip k* *Kali-ar* kali-bi k* *Kali-br* *Kali-c* k* *Kali-n* k* kali-ox a1 *Kali-p* *Kreos* b7a.de lac-h sk4• lapa a1 lat-m bnm6• *Lath* mrr1 laur b7.de* led b7.de* lil-t k* lob-c a1 luna kg1• *Lyc* k* m-arct b7.de m-aust b7.de mag-c b4.de* *Mag-m* k* mand rsj7• mang b4.de* *Med* merc k* *Merc-c* b4a.de *Mez* k* mosch b7.de* **Mur-ac** k* murx *Nat-ar* **Nat-c** k* *Nat-m* k* nat-n bg2 nat-p nat-s k2* nat-sil fd3.de• nicc k* *Nit-ac* k* *Nux-m* k* **Nux-v** k* olib-sac wmh1 olnd k* onos ptk1* *Op* k* ox-ac k* ozone sde2• par b7.de *Petr* petr-ra shn4• *Ph-ac* k* **Phos** k* **Pic-ac** k* *Plat* k* **Plb** k* podo c1 psil ft1 ptel hr1 puls k* *Ran-b* k* *Rat* bg2 rhod k* **Rhus-t** k* ros-d wla1 *Ruta* k* sabin b7.de* samb b7.de sang k* sarcol-ac sp1 *Sars* k* *Sec* k* sel c1* seneg k* *Sep* k* **Sil** k* spig b7.de* spong k* *Stann* k* stram b7.de* *Stront-c* k* stroph-s sp1 stry *Sul-ac* sulfonam ks2 *Sulph* k* tab k* tarent k* thal a1 thal-xyz srj8• *Thuj* k* til tritic-vg fd5.de vanil fd5.de verat verb k* vip k* wies a1 xan k* **Zinc** k* zinc-p k2 [heroin sdj2]

- **one side** | **epileptic** convulsion; after: cadm-s ptk1 phos ptk1
- **right**: nat-m h2 stann h2 sulph h2
- **left**: petr k2
- **daytime**: cassia-s ccrh1•
- **morning**: ambr h1 ant-t *Arg-met* bar-c bar-m br1 carb-an k* iod h mur-ac k* *Nat-m* k* **Nux-v** k* *Phos* k* plect a1 *Rhus-t* ruta fd4.de sep h2 *Sil* k* solin a1 sulph k*
  - **bed** agg.; in: nat-m k* plb k* sulph k* *Zinc* k*
  - **waking**; on: *Arg-met* nat-m k* petr-ra shn4• sep h2
- **forenoon**: arg-n dulc fd4.de nat-m ptel k* *Ran-b* k*
  - **11 h**: arg-n nat-m zinc
- **noon**: *Calc* a1 kali-c h2
- **afternoon**: *Arg-n* k* bamb-a stb2.de• carb-v h2 mag-m h2 nat-c nux-v k* pip-m k* plb k* rumx ruta fd4.de spong fd4.de vanil fd5.de zinc
  - **13 h**: ham
- **evening**: atra-r skp7• bamb-a stb2.de• hydr-ac k* indg k* nit-ac h2 plect a1 rhus-g a1 ruta fd4.de spong fd4.de sulph k* zinc k*
  - **menses**; during: kali-n h2 mag-m k*
  - **walking** agg.: sang k* thuj verat
- **night**: spong fd4.de
  - **22 h**: plan
  - **amel.**: cassia-s ccrh1•
- **accompanied** by:
  - **Knees**; pain in: xan c1
  - **Meninges** of spine; inflammation of (See BACK - Inflammation - membranes - accompanied - lower)
  - **Teeth**; pain in (See TEETH - Pain - accompanied - limbs)
- **ascending** stairs agg.: agar *Ars* asar bell h1 **Calc** lyc nicc nux-v phos pic-ac rhus-t k2 *Ruta* k* sars thuj
- **catarrhal** fever; during: sep
- **child** late learning to walk: **Calc**
- **chill**; during: ars b4a.de chin b7.de *Hell* b7.de ign b7a.de *Seneg* b4a.de verat b7.de
- **coition**; after: *Calc*
- **delivery**; after: caust ptk1 *Rhus-t* k*
- **descending** stairs agg.: arg-met ptk1 nux-m petr-ra shn4• *Ruta* k* sep bg1 sil k* stann sulph
- **diarrhea**; during: borx h2
- **dinner**; after: am-c h2
- **eating**; after: mur-ac

- **exertion** agg.; after: *Anac* **Calc** **Gels** k* **Rhus-t**
- **false** step, from: ph-ac
- **fear**; with (See MIND - Fear - sudden - trembling)
- **fever**; during: ars b4a.de chin b7.de sulph b4.de
- **hunger**; during: *Zinc*
- **leukorrhea** agg.: kreos b7a.de
- **menses**; during: arg-n *Cocc* kali-n mag-m *Nit-ac* nux-m k* petr-ra shn4• sulph *Zinc*
- **motion** | **amel.**: cassia-s ccrh1•
- **painful**: aloe nux-m k* plan k* stann h2 *Staph* hr1
- **paralytic**: agar k2 ambr k2 anac arg-n k* **Cocc** k* dig h2 rhus-t k2 ruta ptk1 sars k2 thuj ptk1
- **pregnancy** agg.; during: agar k2* bell-p bro1 plb k*
- **progressive**: *Con* mrr1 *Lath* mrr1
- **rising**:
  - **kneeling**; from: **Con** mrr1
  - **sitting**; from | **agg.**: *Glon* k* mag-c k* nat-m k* nat-sil fd3.de• ruta k* zinc k*
- **sitting** agg.: ars cassia-s ccrh1• led mag-c k* plat h2 stann ptk1
- **sitting** down agg.: diosm br1
- **smoking** agg.: *Clem* k*
- **standing** agg.: agar *Anac* bar-act a1 berb *Bry* dirc hell nat-m h2 **Nux-m** petr-ra shn4• plat k* stann tarent mtf33 zinc
- **stool** agg.; after: plect k*
- **sun** agg.; walking in the: bros-gau mrc1
- **temperature**; change of: act-sp
- **tremulous**: bamb-a stb2.de• caps h1 dig h2 iber vml3•
- **vertigo**; with: con bg1
- **vexation**; after: caust lyc nat-m *Nux-v*
- **walking**:
  - **after** | **agg.**: **Aesc** **Arg-met** bapt k* berb *Bry* **Calc** *Calc-s* carl k* **Con** **Gels** glon k* hell k* kali-n led **Mag-m** mosch *Mur-ac* nux-v k* petr-ra shn4• phos k2 *Plb* *Ran-b* k* **Rhus-t** *Ruta* *Sil* stann k* sulph k* zinc k*
  - **agg.**: botul br1 calc tl1 kali-c mtf33 mang-act br1 *Nux-m* ptk1 sang a1 vanil fd5.de
  - **air** agg.; in open: grat mag-m h2* ruta fd4.de sang seneg verat
  - **amel.**: borx h2 cann-s k* cassia-s ccrh1• cic a1 dros h1 nat-m zinc k*
  - **continued**:
    - **air**; in open | **amel.**: zinc
  - **learning** to walk; when (See GENERALS - Walking - learning - accompanied - lower)
- **wet** agg.; after getting feet: phos *Rhus-t*
- ○ **Bones**, sitting: sulph h2
- **Joints**: cinnb k* nit-ac k* plumbg a1 rhus-t k* *Seneg* b4a.de stront-c

- **Nates**: cortico tpw7
  - **left**: cortico sp1
- **Shoulders**: acon aloe alumn arg-met bapt k* borx bov k* brom k* carb-an k* carb-v k* cedr k* chinin-ar cic k* clem k* *Com* k* cupr-ar k* ger-i rly4• gins k* kali-n k* kola stb3• laur k* mag-c k* nat-m k* nit-s-d a1 nux-v k* phos h2 pic-ac k* plat k* plect a1 ran-s k* sep k* sil k* stry k* symph fd3.de• thlas bg1 thuj k* zing
  - **right**: carb-v k*
  - **left**: alumn
  - **morning** | **waking**; on: arg-met
  - **bending** forward agg.: alumn
  - **painful**: cedr k* chinin-ar *Lach*
  - **paralytic**: arg-met carb-v k* ferr c1
  - **walking** agg.; after: bapt k*
  - ○ **Joints**: aloe bg2 arg-met bg2 bapt bg2 bov bg2 carb-an bg2 carb-v bg2 cic bg2 com bg2 dros b7.de* kali-n bg2 laur bg2 mag-c bg2 pic-ac bg2 plat bg2 sabin bg2 sep bg2 sil bg2 thuj bg2
- **Thighs**: acon k* aesc bro1 agar k* all-c aloe *Alum* k* alum-p k2 alum-sil k2 *Alumn* bro1 am-c k* am-m b7.de* ammc k* anac k* androc srj1• ang b7.de* arg-met k* arg-n bro1 *Arn* b7.de* *Ars* k* arund k* asar h1 aur b4a.de bar-m bro1

- **Thighs**: ...
berb bro1 borx h2 bov b4.de* brach k* bry k* *Calc* k* *Calc-p* bro1 calc-sil k2 *Cann-i* bro1 caps k* carb-an carbn-s *Carc* jl2* caust k* cham k* chel k* *Chin* k* chinin-ar chinin-s cimic bro1 cina tl1 clem k* cob bro1 coc-c k* **Cocc** k* colch bro1 coloc k* **Con** k* croc k* crot-h k* cupr bro1 cur bro1 cycl b7.de* dig b4.de* dulc k* eup-per ptk1 euph k* ferr c1* *Form* bro1 *Gels* bro1* gins k* *Glon* k* graph k* *Guaj* k* ham k* hell k* hep b4a.de hipp a1 hura ip k* kali-bi k* *Kali-c* k* kali-i k* kali-m k2 kali-n b4.de* kali-sil k2 kalm bro1 lac-ac k* lach bro1 lappa ptk1 lil-t k* lyc k* mag-s k* mand rsj7• mang k* med bro1 *Merc* k* *Merc-c* k* mez k* mosch b7.de* **Mur-ac** k* nat-ar nat-c k* nat-m k* nat-p **Nat-s** k* nit-ac *Nux-v* k* *Olnd* k* onos bro1 op bg2 ozone sde2• paeon bro1 ph-ac k* phel bro1 *Phos* k* *Pic-ac* bro1 pip-m k* *Plat* k* *Plb* k* puls k* raph rat k* *Rheum* k* rhod b4.de rhus-t bro1 *Ruta* k* *Sarcol-ac* bro1 sarr bro1 sars k* *Seneg* k* sep k* sil k* sol-ni spig k* squil k* *Stann* k* staph k* stront-c k* sulph k* tarent k* thuj k* urt-u ptk1 vanil fd5.de verat k* verb k* vib bro1
  - **right**: *Con* *Kali-c*
  - **left**: brach bg1 chel cic bg1 glon ham bg1 hura bg1 nit-ac bg1 sulph bg1 tarent bg1
  - **midnight** | **after**: merc
  - **morning**: brach k* *Calc* nat-c ruta fd4.de
    - **chill**; during: verat k*
    - **rising** agg.; after: phos k* rhod k* squil k*
    - **walking**; beginning to: *Calc*
  - **afternoon**: fago k* kali-c h2
  - **evening**: *Agn* hr1 chin cinch a1 fago k* mag-c k* stront-c tarent k* vanil fd5.de
  - **night**: ham k*
    - **sleep** agg.; during: sep
  - **ascending** steps, during: ars *Bry* k* coloc k* mez sep k*
  - **coition**; after: agar gsy1 *Calc*
  - **emissions** agg.; after: *Agar* calc
  - **exertion**; violent | **amel.**: carc mg1.de*
  - **menses** | **before** | **agg.**: carb-an b4.de
    - **during** | **agg.**: am-c k* am-m k* bov k* carb-an k* castm nicc k* sars k*
  - **overworked**; as if: ozone sde2•
  - **painful**: stann h2
  - **paralytic**: arg-met *Con* mrr1 ferr c1 puls k*
  - **pregnancy**: *Ip*
  - **rising**:
    - **agg.**: cic a1 thuj
    - **sitting**; from | **agg.**: ruta
  - **sitting**; after: acon k* anac arg-met croc k* mag-c k* mag-s k* mang-m k* ph-ac k* plat k*
  - **sleep**; short | **amel.**: carc mg1.de*
  - **standing** agg.: mag-m k* plat k* stann h2
  - **stool** | **after** | **agg.**: lyc k* *Ph-ac* b4a.de *Phos* b4a.de
    - **during** | **agg.**: germ-met srj5• *Ph-ac* b4a.de *Phos* b4a.de
  - **sudden**: cic k* hep h2
  - **waking** | **amel.**: sep
  - **walking**:
    - **after** | **agg.**: ind k* nit-ac k* sol-t-ae k*
    - **agg.**: anac arg-met aur k* bufo *Calc* k* caust h2 chel chin con k* euph-a a1 hep k* *Kali-i* lycps-v mag-c mag-s k* merc mez k* *Olnd* k* puls k* *Ruta* stach a1
    - **air** agg.; in open: ang arg-met spig h1
    - **amel.**: mag-m k* rat
  - ○ **Anterior**: arn bg1 lappa ptk1
  - **Bones**: stann h2
- **Thumbs**: alco a1 kali-c k* nat-m k* plb a1 sil k* sulph k*
  - **writing** agg.: kali-c k*
- **Toes**: ars k* crot-h k* glon k*
- **Upper** arms: acon k* *Arg-met* k* arg-n bell k* brach k* bry k* calc bg2 carl k* cham bg2 cic k* clem k* colch k* crot-t k* cycl b7.de* dulc fd4.de gins k* grat bg2 guaj b4a.de* jatr-c k* kali-n k* lact k* mang k* merc-c b4a.de mim-p rsj8• nat-m k* *Phos* k* phyt sep k* sil stann k* *Sulph* k* symph fd3.de• *Thuj* k*

- **left**: olib-sac wmh1
- **morning** | **waking**; on: arg-met
- **night** | **sleep**; during: sep h2
- **exertion** agg.; after: *Arg-met*
- **flexion** agg.: phyt
- **motion**:
  - **agg.**: grat k* phyt
  - **amel.**: arg-met
- **paralytic**: *Arg-met* bell h1 ferr c1 kali-n k*
- **raised**, when: grat k*
- **rising** agg.: thuj k*
- **sudden**: mang h2
- **waking** agg.; after: arg-met
- **writing** agg.: carl k* cic k* con k*

▽ • **extending** to | **Hand**: crot-t k*

○ • **Deltoid**: stann mrr1

- **Upper** limbs: abrot *Acon* k* **Aesc** k* agar k* *All-c* k* aloe bg2 *Alum* k* alum-p k2 alum-sil k2 alumn k* *Am-c* k* aml-ns bg2 ammc *Anac* k* *Ang* b7a.de ant-c *Apis* arg-met arn k* *Ars* k* ars-i ars-s-f k2 arund asar k* aur k* aur-ar k2 aur-i k2 aur-s k2 bapt k* **Bell** k* berb k* beryl sp1 *Bism* k* borx bov k* brach k* brom k* bry k* bufo k* cact k* *Calc* k* calc-i k2 calc-p k* *Calc-s* camph k* carb-v k* *Carbn-s* cartl-s rly4• *Caust* k* cere-b a1 cham k* *Chel* k* *Chin* k* chinin-ar chinin-s **Cic** k* cod a1 coff b7.de* coloc k* com k* **Con** k* corn *Crot-c* k* *Crot-t* k* *Cupr* k* *Cur* k* cystein-l rly4• **Dig** k* dios k* dros k* dulc b4.de* elaps ptk1 euph k* eupi k* ferr c1 ferr-m k* *Gels* k* gins k* *Glon* k* *Gran* k* granit-m es1• graph grat k* *Guaj* k* ham k* hell b7.de* hep k* hipp a1 hura hydroph rsj6• hyper k* ign k* *Iod* k* ix bnm8• kali-ar k* kali-bi k* **Kali-c** k* kali-i k* kali-n k* kali-s *Kalm* *Lach* k* lact k* laur bg2 led k* lil-t k* *Lyc* k* lyss m-aust b7.de* macro a1 mag-c bg2 mag-p bg2* malar jl2 mand rsj7• mang k* med bro1 merc b4.de* *Merc-c* b4a.de merc-i-f k* merc-sul k* mez k* nat-ar nat-c k* *Nat-m* k* nat-p k* nat-s nicotam rly4• nit-ac k* nit-s-d a1 *Nux-v* k* ol-an bg2* op b7a.de par k* peti a1 *Petr* k* *Ph-ac* k* *Phos* k* phyt plat k* plb k* psil ft1 psor *Rhod* k* *Rhus-t* k* ruta k* sabad sabin b7a.de* sarcol-ac bro1* sars sec k* seneg b4.de* *Sep* k* *Sil* k* spig bg2 spong k* **Stann** k* *Staph* k* stict stram k* stront-c k* sul-ac b4.de* *Sulph* k* sumb k* symph fd3.de• tab k* tarent k* ter k* tere-la rly4• *Thuj* k* til k* tub al valer k* vanil fd5.de verat bg2 zinc k*
  - **one side** | **accompanied** by:
    - **Lower** limbs; weakness:
      - **one side** | **epileptic** convulsions; after: cadm-s ptk1 phos ptk1
    - **apoplexy**; after: cadm-s ptk1 phos ptk1
  - **right**: am-c h2* anac bg1 *Bism* k* carb-v *Caust* k* chel bg1 colch bg1 eup-per bg1 ferr-i bg1 gels bg2 gins bg1 ham bg1 lyc bg1 merc-i-f bg1 ozone sde2• plat h2 rhod zinc bg1
  - **left**: agar k* alumn arn brom *Calc* k* *Dig* k* nat-s *Nux-v* sars spong fd4.de *Sumb* *Tab*
    - **accompanied** by | **Heart** disease (See CHEST - Heart; complaints - accompanied - upper - left - weakness)
  - **morning**: carbn-s dulc *Kali-c* lyc k* *Nux-v* k* peti a1 sil k* sulph valer k*
    - **bed** agg.; in: kali-c sil k*
    - **rising** agg.: caj k* card-m
    - **waking**; on: arg-met nit-ac k* sep
  - **forenoon**: indg k* ph-ac k* plect a1
  - **noon**: colch k* con k*
  - **afternoon**: chinin-s nux-v k*
    - **14** h: sarr
  - **evening**: brach k* ferr-i k* nat-m k* plect a1 spong fd4.de vanil fd5.de
    - **bed** agg.; in: phos k*
    - **vomiting**; after: sulph k*
  - **night**: ambr lyc k*
  - **accompanied** by:
    - **Elbow**; pain in: bapt hr1
    - **Teeth**; pain in (See TEETH - Pain - accompanied; TEETH - Pain - accompanied - limbs)
  - **anger**, after a fit of: nat-m
  - **ascending** stairs agg.: nux-v

Weakness – Upper limbs: ...

  - **chilliness**; during: gins k* *Ph-ac*
  - **clenching** hands, on: chin k*
  - **cold**, from exposure to: *Rhod*
  - **convulsions**; after: **Cic**
  - **dinner**; after: grat k* plect a1
  - **eating**; after: bar-c
  - **ejaculations**; after: staph
  - **exertion**; after slight: *Cic* *Lach* *Stann*
  - **hanging** down amel.: asar k*
  - **laughing** agg.: carb-v h2
  - **motion**:
    - **agg.**: carb-v k* *Stann*
      - **pain** in chest; from extreme: stict c1
    - **amel.**: acon *Lyc* plat *Rhod* k* stront-c
  - **paralytic**: anan vh1 ph-ac h2 stann h2
    - **motion** agg.: *Stann* h1*
  - **playing** piano: gels
  - **sudden**: calc
  - **taking** hold of something: arn **Ars** k* bov carb-v choc srj3• cina colch nat-m sil spong fd4.de
  - **walking** agg.; after: bapt a1
  - **weather** agg.; stormy: *Rhod*
  - **writing** agg.: acon agar brach carb-v k* *Caust* cocc kali-c k* lyss c1 merc-i-f k* **mez** k* sabin

▽ • **extending** to:
    - **Body**; whole: malar jl2
    - **Lower** limbs: malar jl2

- **Wrists**: aloe k* arn k* ars k* bov bg2 brach k* *Carb-v* *Caust* choc srj3• cot a1 *Cur* dig k* dor *Glon* ham fd3.de• hura kali-bi bg1 kali-c k* kalm k* lil-t k* lyc k* *Merc* k* mez k* nat-m k* nat-p k* phos k* phys k* *Plb* k* podo k* *Positr* nl2• rhod k* sep k* *Sil* k* spong k* sul-ac k* sulph k* symph fd3.de• tung-met bdx1• valer bg1* vanil fd5.de [tax jsj7]
  - **right**: *Sil*
    - **Ankle**; and | **left**: nat-p k*
  - **morning**: lil-t k*
  - **evening**: ham fd3.de• phos k* vanil fd5.de
  - **menses**; after: nat-p k*
  - **motion**:
    - **agg.**: dig k*
    - **amel.**: rhod k*
  - **paralytic**: *Carb-v* phos k*
  - **sprained**, as if: kali-c k*
  - **using** hand: sep k* vanil fd5.de
  - **writing** agg.: calad *Kali-br* lavand-a ctl1• sarcol-ac sp1

WEATHER:

- **change** of:
  - **agg.**:
    - **Lower** limbs: *Bry* b7a.de nat-s bg2 phyt ptk1 *Rhus-t* b7a.de sil b4.de*
    - **Thighs**: phyt ptk1
- **cold** | **dry**:
  - **agg.** | **Lower** limbs: acon bg2 caust bg2 hep bg2 nux-v bg2 sep bg2
  - **wet**:
    - **agg.**:
      - **Lower** limbs: *Rhod* b4.de* *Sep* b4.de*
      - **Upper** limbs: dulc b4.de* *Merc* b4a.de nux-m b7a.de *Rhod* b4.de* ruta b7a.de *Stann* b4a.de
- **rough**:
  - **agg.** | **Upper** limbs: rhod b4.de*
- **thunderstorm** agg. | **Lower** limbs: caust b4.de* nat-c b4.de* petr b4.de* *Phos* b4.de* *Sil* b4.de*

- wet:
  - **agg.** | **Lower** limbs: *Borx* b4a.de lyc b4a.de *Merc* b4a.de nux-m b7.de* *Rhod* b4.de* *Sep* b4.de* still bg2 verat b7.de*

WEIGHT; sensation of a (See Heaviness)

WENS on hands: ph-ac k* plb k* sil k*

WET:
- **agg.**:
  - ○ **Lower** limbs: calc-p bg2 dulc bg2 nux-v bg2 puls bg2 rhus-t bg2 sep bg2 sil bg2
  - **Upper** limbs: nat-s bg2
- **room** agg. | **Lower** limbs: ars bg2

WETTING a part:
- ○ **Feet** agg.: all-c ptk1 cham k* cupr ptk1 *Dulc* ptk1 merc k* *Nat-c* k* *Nat-m* k* *Phos* k* *Puls* k* rhus-t k* *Sep* k* **Sil** k* xan
- **Upper** limbs | **amel.**: spig b7.de*

WHIRLING: glon k*

WHITLOW (See Felon)

WHIZZING, thigh: bell h1

WIND: | **agg.** | **Lower** limbs: ham bg2 nux-v b7.de* staph bg2
- **east**:
  - **agg.** | **Upper** limbs: carb-v b4.de* *Stann* b4a.de

WIND; sensation of:
- ○ **Hands**: plat h2
- **Legs**: samb h1
  - ○ **Calves** | **cool** wind streaming up calves; sensation of: helon br1*
- **Lower** limbs | **sensation** as from cool wind: bar-c h2 calc h2 chin-b c1 helon c1 lil-t k* m-aust b7.de mosch b7.de* rhus-t b7.de* samb bg2
- **Shoulder**, sensation of:
  - **passing** over and extending to fingers: fl-ac k*
  - **wind** blowing on: lyc k*
- **Toes**: cupr h2
- **Upper** Arm, extensor muscles | **coldness**; as if: phos
- **Upper** limbs | **cold** wind was blowing on it; as if: aster k*

WINDOW; at the:
- **agg.** | **Upper** limbs: chin b7.de*

WINE agg.: | **Lower** limbs: *Carb-v* b4.de* nit-ac b4a.de **Zinc** b4.de*

WITHERED: *(↗Emaciation)* phyt a1
- ○ **Feet** | **Soles**: ant-c ptk1
- **Fingers** | **Tips**: ant-t b7.de* puls b7a.de
- **Skin** of hands: bar-c b4a.de bell b4a.de graph b4a.de* **Lyc** k* nat-c k* nat-m k* petr bg2 ph-ac k* sabad b7.de* sulph b4a.de
  - ○ **Palms**: diph ptk1 sang ptk1

WOODEN sensation: *(↗MIND - Delusions - tongue - wood; MIND - Delusions - wood - he)* kali-n mrr1 thuj ptk2
- ○ **Feet**: carl k* plb b7a.de* rhus-t b7a.de*
  - ○ **Soles**: ars k* plb a1
- **Hands**: **Kali-n** k*
- **Legs**: thuj tl1
- **Lower** limbs: *Arg-n* k* *Ars* k* chinin-s nux-v hr1 phos hr1 plb bg2 rhus-t bg2* sec hr1 thuj b4a.de*
  - **walking** agg.: **Kali-n** k* plb k* rhus-t k* sec gk thuj k*
- **Thighs**:
  - ○ **Muscles** | **Extensor** muscles: stry a1
- **Upper** limbs: kali-n b4.de*

WOOL; as if stepping on: helo-s rwt2•

WOUNDS (See Injuries)

WRAPPING UP:
- **agg.**:
  - ○ **Lower** limbs: cham b7.de* *Puls* b7a.de
  - **Upper** limbs: *Puls* b7a.de

Wrapping up: ...
- **amel.** | **Lower** limbs: nux-v b7.de*
- **hands**; wrapping up:
  - **amel.** | **Upper** limbs: hell b7.de*

WRINKLED: ars *Sec* k*
- ○ **Feet**: ars
- **Fingers**: ambr k* cupr k* fl-ac bg2 *Ph-ac* k* psil ft1 sol-ni sulph bg2
  - **perspiration**; during: ambr bg2 **Ant-c** bg2 cupr bg2 **Merc** b4.de* *Ph-ac* b4a.de* verat bg2
  - **shivering**; during: ant-c b7.de
  - ○ **Tips**: ambr b7.de* ant-c b7.de* *Cupr* b7a.de sulph bg2 verat b7a.de
    - **perspiration**; during: ant-c b7.de
- **Hands**: both-ax tsm2
  - ○ **Back** of hands: mur-ac *Ph-ac* k*
  - **Hands** | **Palms**: sang k2
- **Legs**: rhod
- **Lower** limbs: *Rhod* b4a.de
- **Upper** limbs: ambr b7.de* ant-c b7.de* cupr b7a.de merc b4.de* mur-ac b4.de* ph-ac b4.de* sabad b7.de* sulph b4.de*

WRIST-DROP (See Paralysis - wrists)

WRITER'S cramp (See Cramps - fingers - writing; Cramps - hands - writing; Pain - fingers - writing; Pain - hands - writing - agg.)

WRITING:
- **agg.**:
  - ○ **Forearms**: merc-i-r ptk1 ran-b ptk1
  - **Upper** limbs: acon b7.de* agar b4.de* aloe bg2 alum bg2 am-m b7.de* ant-c b7.de* arn b7.de* bar-c b4a.de* bry b7.de* cann-s b7.de* **Carb-v** b4.de* caust b4.de* chin b7.de* cic b7.de* cocc b7.de* coff bg2 colch bg2 euph b4.de* grat bg2 hep b4a.de* **Kali-c** b4.de* meny b7.de* merc bg2 merc-i-f ptk1 mez b4.de mur-ac b4.de* nat-c bg2 nat-m bg2 nux-v b7.de* olnd b7.de* ph-ac b4.de* phos bg2 prun bg2 puls bg2 rhus-t bg2 ruta bg2 sabad b7.de* sabin b7.de* samb b7.de* sil b4.de* spig b7.de* stann b4.de* staph bg2 sul-ac b4.de* sulph bg2 tarax bg2 teucr bg2 thuj b4.de* *Valer* b7.de* viol-t bg2 zinc b4.de*
  - **Wrists**: lyc ptk1 *Mag-p* ptk1
- **amel.** | **Upper** limbs: zinc-ar ptk1
- **difficult** and slow | **breakfast**; after: carb-v h2

YAWNING:
- **agg.**:
  - ○ **Lower** limbs: nux-v b7.de* sabad b7.de* sars b4.de* stann b4.de* zinc b4.de*
  - **Upper** limbs: am-c b4.de* mag-c b4.de* *Nux-v* b7.de* sabad b7.de*

ANKLES; complaints of: acon b2.de* agar b2.de agn b2.de* alum b2.de am-c b2.de am-m b2.de* ambr b2.de* anac b2.de ang b2.de* ant-c b2.de* arg-met b2.de* arn b2.de* ars b2.de* asaf b2.de* asar b2.de aur b2.de bar-c b2.de bell b2.de bism b2.de* borx b2.de bov b2.de bry b2.de* calc b2.de* camph b2.de* caps b2.de* carb-an b2.de carb-v b2.de **Caust** b2.de* chel b2.de* chin b2.de* cic b2.de* cocc b2.de* colch b2.de* coloc b2.de con b2.de croc b2.de* cycl b2.de* dig b2.de dros b2.de* dulc b2.de euph b2.de euphr b2.de* ferr b2.de* graph b2.de* guaj b2.de hell b2.de* hep b2.de* hyos b2.de* ign b2.de* iod b2.de kali-c b2.de* kali-n b2.de kreos b2.de* lach b2.de* led b2.de* **Lyc** b2.de* m-ambo b2.de* m-arct b2.de* m-aust b2.de* mag-m b2.de mang b2.de* merc b2.de* mez b2.de* mosch b2.de mur-ac b2.de nat-c b2.de* **Nat-m** b2.de* nit-ac b2.de* nux-v b2.de* olnd b2.de* par b2.de* petr b2.de* ph-ac b2.de* phos b2.de* plat b2.de plb b2.de* puls b2.de* ran-b b2.de* ran-s b2.de* rheum b2.de* rhod b2.de **Rhus-t** b2.de* rumx ptk1 ruta b2.de* samb b2.de* sars b2.de sec b2.de* sel b2.de* seneg b2.de **Sep** b2.de* sil b2.de* spig b2.de* spong b2.de* stann b2.de* staph b2.de* stront-c b2.de* sul-ac b2.de **Sulph** b2.de* tarax b2.de* teucr b2.de* thuj b2.de* valer b2.de* verat b2.de* viol-t b2.de* zinc b2.de*
- **left**: toxi mtf2•
- **extending** to:
  - ○ **Calves**: meny ptk1
  - **Toes**: nat-c ptk1
  - **Upward**: guaj ptk1
- **nervous**: mag-m ptk1

Extremities

ARMS; complaints of (See Upper limbs)

BLOOD CIRCULATION; complaints of: tub-a jl2

ELBOW; complaints of: acon b2.de* agar b2.de* agn b2.de* alum b2.de* am-c b2.de* am-m b2.de* *Ambr* b2.de* anac b2.de* ang b2.de* *Ant-c* b2.de* ant-t b2.de* *Arg-met* b2.de* arn b2.de* ars b2.de* asaf b2.de* aur b2.de* bar-c b2.de* bell b2.de* bov b2.de* bry b2.de* calad b2.de* calc b2.de* camph b2.de* canth b2.de* caps b2.de* carb-an b2.de* carb-v b2.de* **Caust** b2.de* cham b2.de* chel b2.de* chin b2.de* cic b2.de* cina b2.de* clem b2.de* cocc b2.de* colch b2.de* coloc b2.de* con b2.de* croc b2.de* cupr b2.de* dig b2.de* dros b2.de* dulc b2.de* euphr b2.de* graph b2.de* hell b2.de* *Hep* b2.de* hyos b2.de* ign b2.de* iod b2.de* **Kali-c** b2.de* *Kali-n* b2.de* kreos b2.de* laur b2.de* led b2.de* *Lyc* b2.de* m-ambo b2.de* m-arct b2.de* m-aust b2.de* mag-c b2.de* mag-m b2.de* mang b2.de* meny b2.de* *Merc* b2.de* mez b2.de* mosch b7.de mur-ac b2.de* nat-c b2.de* nat-m b2.de* nux-m b2.de* nux-v b2.de* olnd b2.de* par b2.de* petr b2.de* ph-ac b2.de* phos b2.de* plat b2.de* puls b2.de* ran-b b2.de* ran-s b2.de* rheum b2.de* rhod b2.de* **Rhus-t** b2.de* ruta b2.de* sabad b2.de* sabin b2.de* samb b2.de* sars b2.de* sec b2.de* seneg b2.de* **Sep** b2.de* spig b2.de* spong b2.de* stann b2.de* staph b2.de* stront-c b2.de* sul-ac b2.de* **Sulph** b2.de* tarax b2.de* teucr b2.de* thuj b2.de* valer b2.de* verat b2.de* verb b2.de* viol-o b2.de* viol-t b2.de* zinc b2.de*

▽ - **extending** to:

○ · **Axilla**: ars ptk1

· **Hand**: cinnb ptk1

· **Shoulder**: ther ptk1

○ - **Bend** of: agn b2.de* alum b2.de* am-m b2.de* *Anac* b2.de* ant-c b2.de* *Arn* b2.de* bar-c b2.de* bell b2.de* calc b2.de* canth b2.de* carb-an b2.de* *Caust* b2.de* cic b2.de* cina b2.de* clem b2.de* colch b2.de* coloc b2.de con b2.de* cupr b2.de* dros b2.de* dulc b2.de* graph b2.de* hell b2.de* hep b2.de* hyos b2.de* iod b2.de* **Kali-c** b2.de* kali-n b2.de* *Laur* b2.de* lyc b2.de* meny b2.de* mur-ac b2.de* petr b2.de* ph-ac b2.de* *Phos* b2.de* *Puls* b2.de* *Sep* b2.de* spig b2.de* staph b2.de* *Sulph* b2.de* teucr b2.de* thuj b2.de* valer b2.de* verat b2.de* zinc b2.de*

- **Tip**: agar b2.de* alum b2.de* arg-met b2.de* asaf b2.de* bar-c b2.de* bry b2.de* carb-an b2.de* carb-v b2.de* caust b2.de* dulc b2.de* graph b2.de* **Hep** b2.de* hyos b2.de* kreos b2.de* lyc b2.de* merc b2.de* mur-ac b2.de* nat-m b2.de* olnd b2.de* ph-ac b2.de* puls b2.de* rhus-t b2.de* sabin b2.de* sars b2.de* sep b2.de* spig b2.de* spong b2.de* *Stann* b2.de* sul-ac b2.de* valer b2.de*

EXTENSOR MUSCLES; complaints of: | **Sides** of: anac bg2 card-m bg2 kreos bg2 merc bg2 sabin bg2

FEET; complaints of: acon b2.de* agar b2.de agn b2.de* alum b2.de* am-c b2.de* am-m b2.de* ambr b2.de* anac b2.de* ang b2.de* ant-c b2.de* ant-t b2.de* arg-met b2.de* **Arn** b2.de* **Ars** b2.de* asaf b2.de* asar b2.de* aur b2.de* bar-c b2.de* **Bell** b2.de* bism b2.de* borx b2.de bov b2.de bry b2.de* calad b2.de* calc b2.de* camph b2.de* cann-s b2.de* canth b2.de* caps b2.de* carb-an b2.de* carb-v b2.de* caust b2.de* cham b2.de* chel b2.de* chin b2.de* cic b2.de* cina b2.de* clem b2.de cocc b2.de* coff b2.de* colch b2.de* coloc b2.de con b2.de* croc b2.de* cupr b2.de* cycl b2.de* dig b2.de dros b2.de* dulc b2.de euph b2.de ferr b2.de* graph b2.de* guaj b2.de hell b2.de* hep b2.de* hyos b2.de* ign b2.de* iod b2.de ip b2.de* kali-c b2.de* kali-n b2.de kreos b2.de* lach b2.de* laur b2.de* led b2.de* **Lyc** b2.de* m-arct b2.de* m-aust b2.de* mag-c b2.de mag-m b2.de* mang b2.de meny b2.de* merc b2.de* mez b2.de mur-ac b2.de* nat-c b2.de* nat-m b2.de* nit-ac b2.de* nux-m b2.de* nux-v b2.de* olnd b2.de* op b2.de* par b2.de* petr b2.de* ph-ac b2.de* phos b2.de* plat b2.de* plb b2.de* **Puls** b2.de* ran-b b2.de* ran-s b2.de* rheum b2.de* rhod b2.de* rhus-t b2.de* ruta b2.de* sabad b2.de* sabin b2.de* samb b2.de* sars b2.de* sec b2.de* sel b2.de* **Sep** b2.de* **Sil** b2.de* spig b2.de* spong b2.de* squil b2.de* stann b2.de* staph b2.de* stram b2.de* stront-c b2.de* sul-ac b2.de* sulph b2.de* tarax b2.de* thuj b2.de* valer b2.de* verat b2.de* verb b2.de* viol-t b2.de* zinc b2.de* zinc-chl ptk1

○ - **Back** of: agar b2.de* anac b2.de* ang b2.de* ant-t b2.de arg-met b2.de* ars b2.de asaf b2.de* aur b2.de bell b2.de bism b2.de* bry b2.de* calc b2.de* **Camph** b2.de* cann-s b2.de canth b2.de* carb-an b2.de* **Caust** b2.de* chel b2.de chin b2.de* cocc b2.de colch b2.de* coloc b2.de* con b2.de cupr b2.de* cycl b2.de* dig b2.de graph b2.de guaj b2.de **Hep** b2.de* ign b2.de* kali-c b2.de* lach b2.de* led b2.de* lyc b2.de* mag-m b2.de* mang b2.de merc b2.de* mez b2.de mosch b2.de mur-ac b2.de* nat-c b2.de* nat-m b2.de nit-ac b2.de nux-v b2.de* olnd b2.de* par b2.de* petr b2.de phos b2.de plat b2.de* plb b2.de* puls b2.de* ran-b b2.de* ran-s b2.de* rheum b2.de* rhus-t b2.de* ruta b2.de sabin b2.de* sars b2.de*

Feet; complaints of – **Back** of: ...
sep b2.de* sil b2.de* **Spig** b2.de* spong b2.de stann b2.de staph b2.de* stram b2.de* sulph b2.de* **Tarax** b2.de* thuj b2.de* viol-t b2.de zinc b2.de*

- **Feet | Heels**: *Agar* b2.de* agn b2.de* alum b2.de am-c b2.de* am-m b2.de* ambr b2.de* anac b2.de* ang b2.de* ant-c b2.de* ant-t b2.de *Aran* bg2 arg-met b2.de* arn b2.de* ars b2.de aur b2.de bar-c b2.de bell b2.de berb bg2 bism b2.de* borx b2.de bry b2.de* calc b2.de* cann-s b2.de* canth b2.de caps b2.de* carb-an b2.de **Caust** b2.de* cham b2.de* chin b2.de* cic b2.de* cina b2.de* clem b2.de cocc b2.de* colch b2.de* coloc bg2 con bg2* cycl b2.de* dros b2.de* euph b2.de* ferr ptk1 gard-j vlr2• **Graph** b2.de* hell b2.de* hep b2.de **Ign** b2.de* iod b2.de kali-c b2.de* kali-n b2.de kreos b2.de lach b2.de* laur b2.de* **Led** b2.de* lyc b2.de* *M-ambo* b2.de* *M-arct* b2.de* mag-c b2.de* mag-m b2.de mang bg2* meny b2.de* merc b2.de* mez b2.de mur-ac b2.de* **Nat-c** b2.de* *Nat-s* bg2 nit-ac b2.de nux-v b2.de* olnd b2.de* par b2.de* petr b2.de* ph-ac b2.de* phos b2.de* phyt bg2 plat b2.de plb b2.de* **Puls** b2.de* ran-b b2.de* ran-s b2.de* rheum b2.de* rhod b2.de* rhus-t b2.de* ruta b2.de* **Sabin** b2.de* sars b2.de sel b2.de* **Sep** b2.de* sil b2.de* spong b2.de* stann b2.de* staph b2.de* stront-c b2.de* sul-ac b2.de sulph b2.de* thuj b2.de valer b2.de* verat b2.de* viol-t b2.de* *Zinc* b2.de*

- **Side**: ang bg2 arn bg2 calc bg2 chin bg2 coloc bg2 graph bg2* kali-bi ptk1 led bg2* lith-c ptk1 ol-an bg2 sabin bg2 sep bg2 sulph bg2 tarax bg2 thuj bg2 zinc ptk1

○ · **Outer**: nat-s bg2

- **Sole** of: acon b2.de* agar b2.de agn b2.de* alum b2.de* am-c b2.de* am-m b2.de* ambr b2.de* anac b2.de* ang b2.de* *Ant-c* b2.de* ant-t b2.de* arg-met b2.de* arn b2.de* ars b2.de* asaf b2.de asar b2.de* aur b2.de bar-c b2.de* bell b2.de* *Berb* bg2 bism b2.de* borx b2.de bov b2.de bry b2.de* calad b2.de* **Calc** b2.de* canth b2.de* carb-an b2.de carb-v b2.de* caust b2.de* cham b2.de* chel b2.de* chin b2.de* cic b2.de* cina b2.de clem b2.de coff b2.de* colch b2.de* coloc b2.de con b2.de croc b2.de* **Cupr** b2.de* dig b2.de dros b2.de* dulc b2.de euph b2.de ferr b2.de* gels bg2 graph b2.de* hell b2.de* hep b2.de* hyos b2.de* ign b2.de* kali-c b2.de* kali-n b2.de kali-p bg2 kreos b2.de* lach b2.de* laur b2.de* **Led** b2.de* *Lyc* b2.de* m-ambo b2.de* m-arct b2.de* m-aust b2.de* mag-m b2.de mang b2.de *Med* bg2 meny b2.de* merc b2.de* mez b2.de* mur-ac b2.de* **Nat-c** b2.de* nat-m b2.de nit-ac b2.de nux-m b2.de* nux-v b2.de* olnd b2.de* par b2.de* petr b2.de* **Ph-ac** b2.de* phos b2.de* plat b2.de* plb b2.de* **Puls** b2.de* ran-s b2.de* rheum b2.de* rhod b2.de rhus-t b2.de* ruta b2.de* sabad b2.de* sabin b2.de* samb b2.de* sars b2.de* sec b2.de sel b2.de* sep b2.de* **Sil** b2.de* spig b2.de* squil b2.de stann b2.de* staph b2.de* stront-c b2.de* sul-ac b2.de **Sulph** b2.de* **Tarax** b2.de* thuj b2.de valer b2.de* verat b2.de* verb b2.de* viol-t b2.de* zinc b2.de*

▽ · **extending** to | **Knees**: lith-c ptk1

FINGERS; complaints of: *Acon* b2.de* agar b2.de* agn b2.de* alum b2.de* *Am-c* b2.de* **Am-m** b2.de* *Ambr* b2.de* anac b2.de* ang b2.de* ant-c b2.de* ant-t b2.de* arg-met b2.de* arn b2.de* ars b2.de* asaf b2.de* asar b2.de* aur b2.de* bar-c b2.de* bell b2.de* bism b2.de* borx b2.de* bov b2.de* bry b2.de* *Calc* b2.de* camph b2.de* cann-s b2.de* canth b2.de* caps b7.de carb-an b2.de* carb-v b2.de* *Caul* bg2 *Caust* b2.de* cham b2.de* *Chel* b2.de* chin b2.de* cic b2.de* cina b2.de* clem b2.de* cocc b2.de* coff b2.de* colch b2.de* coloc b2.de* con b2.de* croc b2.de* cupr b2.de* *Cycl* b2.de* dig b2.de* dros b2.de* dulc b2.de* euph b2.de* euphr b2.de* ferr b2.de* *Graph* b2.de* guaj b2.de* hell b2.de* hep b2.de* hyos b2.de* ign b2.de* iod b2.de* *Kali-c* b2.de* kali-n b2.de* *Kreos* b2.de* lach b2.de* laur b2.de* led b2.de* **Lyc** b2.de* m-ambo b2.de* m-arct b2.de* m-aust b2.de* *Mag-c* b2.de* mag-m b2.de* mang b2.de* meny b2.de* *Merc* b2.de* mez b2.de* mosch b2.de* mur-ac b2.de* nat-c b2.de* *Nat-m* b2.de* nat-s br1 *Nit-ac* b2.de* nux-m b7.de nux-v b2.de* *Olnd* b2.de* op b2.de* par b2.de* petr b2.de* *Ph-ac* b2.de* *Phos* b2.de* plat b2.de* plb b2.de* *Puls* b2.de* *Ran-b* b2.de* *Ran-s* b2.de* rheum b2.de* *Rhod* b2.de* **Rhus-t** b2.de* ruta b2.de* *Sabad* b2.de* sabin b2.de* sars b2.de* *Sec* b2.de* sel b2.de* *Sep* b2.de* **Sil** b2.de* *Spig* b2.de* spong b2.de* squil b7.de *Stann* b2.de* *Staph* b2.de* stront-c b2.de* *Sul-ac* b2.de* **Sulph** b2.de* tarax b2.de* *Teucr* b2.de* **Thuj** b2.de* valer b2.de* verat b2.de* verb b2.de* viol-t b2.de* zinc b2.de*

- **alternating** between different fingers: lappa bg2

○ - **Between**: am-m b2.de* ambr b2.de* ars b2.de* aur b2.de* camph b2.de* caust b2.de* cycl b2.de* ferr b2.de* **Graph** b2.de* *Hell* b2.de* kreos b2.de lach b2.de* *Laur* b2.de* nit-ac b2.de* plb b2.de* *Puls* b2.de* ran-s b2.de* rhod b2.de* rhus-t b2.de* **Sel** b2.de* sep b2.de* sul-ac b2.de* zinc b2.de*

- **Joints**: acon b2.de* agn b2.de* alum b2.de* am-c b2.de* am-m b2.de* ambr b2.de* anac b2.de* ang b2.de* ant-c b2.de* ant-t b2.de* arg-met b2.de* arn b2.de* ars b2.de* asar b2.de* aur b2.de* bar-c b2.de* bell b2.de* bism b2.de*

- **Joints**: ...
borx b2.de* bov b2.de* bry b2.de* **Calc** b2.de* calc-f ptk1 camph b2.de* cann-s b2.de* caps b2.de* carb-an b2.de* carb-v b2.de* *Caul* bg2* *Caust* b2.de* *Cham* b2.de* chel b2.de* chin b2.de* cina b2.de* clem bg2 cocc b2.de* coff b2.de* colch b2.de* coloc b2.de* con b2.de* croc b2.de* cupr b2.de* cycl b2.de* dig b2.de* dros b2.de* dulc b2.de* euph b2.de euphr bg2 ferr b2.de* *Graph* b2.de* *Hell* b2.de* hep b2.de* ign b2.de* iod b2.de* *Kali-c* b2.de* *Kali-n* b2.de* kreos b2.de* lach bg2 *Led* b2.de* *Lith-c* bg2 *Lyc* b2.de* m-ambo b2.de* m-arct b2.de* m-aust b2.de mag-c b2.de* mang b2.de* meny b2.de* merc b2.de* mosch b2.de* nat-c b2.de* *Nat-m* b2.de* nit-ac b2.de* nux-m b2.de* nux-v b2.de* olnd b2.de* par b2.de* petr b2.de* ph-ac b2.de* phos b2.de* plat b2.de* plb b2.de* *Puls* b2.de* ran-s b2.de* rheum b2.de* rhod b2.de* *Rhus-t* b2.de* ruta b2.de* sabad b2.de* sabin b2.de* samb b2.de* sars b2.de* sec b2.de* seneg b2.de* **Sep** b2.de* *Sil* b2.de* **Spig** b2.de* spong b2.de* stann b2.de* staph b2.de* stront-c b2.de* sul-ac b2.de* **Sulph** b2.de* teucr b2.de* verat b2.de* verb b2.de* zinc b2.de*
- **Nails**: *Alum* b2.de am-m b2.de ant-c b2.de ars b2.de bar-c b2.de bell b2.de borx b2.de bov b2.de calc b2.de caust b2.de chel b2.de chin b2.de cocc b2.de con b2.de dig b2.de dros b2.de *Graph* b2.de hell b2.de hep b2.de iod b2.de kali-c b2.de lach b2.de lyc b2.de m-aust b2.de *Merc* b2.de mur-ac b2.de nat-m b2.de nit-ac b2.de par b2.de ph-ac b2.de plat b2.de puls b2.de ran-b b2.de ruta b2.de sabad b2.de *Sep* b2.de **Sil** b2.de squil b2.de sul-ac b2.de *Sulph* b2.de teucr b2.de thuj b2.de
- **Tips**: acon b2.de* agar b2.de* **Am-m** b2.de* ambr b2.de* ang b2.de* ant-c b2.de* *Ant-t* b2.de* ars b2.de* asaf b2.de* bar-c b2.de* bell b2.de* bism b2.de* borx b2.de* calc b2.de* *Calc-p* ptk1 cann-s b2.de* canth b2.de* caust bg2 cham b2.de* *Chel* b2.de* chin b2.de* coff b2.de* colch b2.de* con b2.de* *Croc* b2.de* cupr b2.de* dros b2.de* ferr b2.de* hell b2.de* hep b2.de* kali-c ptk1 *Kreos* b2.de* lach b2.de* laur b2.de* m-ambo b2.de* m-arct b2.de* *M-aust* b2.de* merc b2.de* mez b2.de* mur-ac b2.de* nux-m b7.de olnd b2.de* ph-ac b2.de* *Phos* b2.de* puls b2.de* ran-b b2.de* ran-s b2.de* rhus-t b2.de* sabad b2.de* sabin b2.de* sars b2.de* *Sec* b2.de* sel b2.de* sep b2.de* *Sil* b2.de* *Spig* b2.de* spong b2.de* stann b2.de* *Staph* b2.de* stront-c b2.de* sul-ac b2.de* *Sulph* b2.de* tarax b2.de* **Teucr** b2.de* **Thuj** b2.de* valer b2.de* verat b2.de* verb b2.de* viol-o b7.de zinc b2.de*

FLEXOR MUSCLES; complaints of: cupr bg2 graph bg2 kali-c bg2 kreos bg2 led bg2 nat-m bg2 nux-v bg2 phos bg2 psor bg2 sep bg2 zinc bg2

FOREARM; complaints of: acon b2.de* agar b2.de* agn b2.de* alum b2.de* am-c b2.de* am-m b2.de* ambr b2.de* *Anac* b2.de* ang b2.de* ant-c b2.de* ant-t b2.de* *Arg-met* b2.de* arn b2.de* asaf b2.de* aur b2.de* bar-c b2.de* bell b2.de* *Bism* b2.de* bov b2.de* bry b2.de* calad b2.de* **Calc** b2.de* camph b2.de* canth b2.de* caps b2.de* carb-an b2.de* *Carb-v* b2.de* **Caust** b2.de* cham b2.de* chel b2.de* *Chin* b2.de* cic b2.de* cina b2.de* clem b2.de* cocc b2.de* colch b2.de* coloc b2.de* con b2.de* croc b2.de* cupr b2.de* cycl b2.de* dig b2.de* dros b2.de* *Dulc* b2.de* euph b2.de* euphr b2.de* ferr bg2 graph b2.de* guaj b2.de* hell b2.de* hep b2.de* hyos b2.de* ign b2.de* *Kali-c* b2.de* kali-n bg2 kreos b2.de* laur b2.de* led b2.de* *Lyc* b2.de* m-ambo b2.de* m-arct b2.de* m-aust b2.de* mag-c b2.de* mag-m b2.de* mang b2.de* meny b2.de* **Merc** b2.de* *Mez* b2.de* mosch b2.de* mur-ac b2.de* nat-c b2.de* nat-m b2.de* *Nit-ac* b2.de* nux-m b7.de nux-v b2.de* olnd b2.de* op b2.de* par b2.de* petr b2.de* ph-ac b2.de* phos b2.de* phyt ptk1 plat b2.de* plb b2.de* prun bg2 puls b2.de* ran-b b2.de* ran-s b2.de* rheum b2.de* rhod b2.de* **Rhus-t** b2.de* ruta b2.de* sabad b2.de* sabin b2.de* samb b2.de* *Sars* b2.de* sec b2.de* *Sel* b2.de* seneg b2.de* **Sep** b2.de* *Sil* b2.de* spig b2.de* spong b2.de* stann b2.de* **Staph** b2.de* stram b2.de* stront-c b2.de* sul-ac b2.de* **Sulph** b2.de* tarax b2.de* teucr b2.de* thuj b2.de* valer b2.de* verat b2.de* verb b2.de* viol-t b2.de* zinc b2.de*
- **accompanied** by:
○ • **Hip**; complaints of | **left**: merc-i-f ptk1
○ - **Bones**: arg-n bg2 kali-bi bg2 nat-m bg2 spig bg2 spong bg2

HANDS; complaints of: *Acon* b2.de* agar b2.de* agn b2.de* alum b2.de* am-c b2.de* am-m b2.de* ambr b2.de* *Anac* b2.de* ang b2.de* ant-c b2.de* ant-t b2.de* arg-met b2.de* arn b2.de* ars b2.de* asaf b2.de* asar b2.de* aur b2.de* bar-c b2.de* *Bell* b2.de* bism b2.de* borx b2.de* bov b2.de* *Bry* b2.de* **Calc** b2.de* camph b2.de* cann-s b2.de* canth b2.de* caps b2.de* carb-an b2.de* carb-v b2.de* *Caul* bg2* caust b2.de* cham b2.de* chel b2.de* chin b2.de* cic b2.de* cina b2.de* clem b2.de* cocc b2.de* coff b2.de* colch b2.de* coloc b2.de* con b2.de* croc b2.de* cupr b2.de* cycl b2.de* dig b2.de* dros b2.de* dulc b2.de* euph b2.de* euphr b2.de* ferr b2.de* graph b2.de* guaj b2.de* hell b2.de* hep b2.de* hyos b2.de* ign b2.de* iod b2.de* ip b2.de* kali-c b2.de* kali-n b2.de* *Kreos* b2.de* lach b2.de* laur b2.de* led b2.de* **Lyc** b2.de* m-ambo b2.de* m-arct b2.de* m-aust b2.de* mag-c b2.de* mag-m b2.de*

Hands; complaints of: ...
mang b2.de* meny b2.de* merc b2.de* mez b2.de* mosch b2.de* mur-ac b2.de* nat-c b2.de* nat-m b2.de* nit-ac b2.de* nux-m b2.de* **Nux-v** b2.de* olnd b2.de* op b2.de* par b2.de* petr b2.de* *Ph-ac* b2.de* phos b2.de* plat b2.de* plb b2.de* puls b2.de* ran-b b2.de* ran-s b2.de* rheum b2.de* rhod b2.de* *Rhus-t* b2.de* ruta b2.de* sabad b2.de* sabin b2.de* samb b2.de* sars b2.de* sec b2.de* *Sel* b2.de* seneg b2.de* **Sep** b2.de* sil b2.de* spig b2.de* spong b2.de* squil b2.de* *Stann* b2.de* staph b2.de* stram b2.de* stront-c b2.de* sul-ac b2.de* **Sulph** b2.de* tarax b2.de* teucr b2.de* thuj b2.de* valer b2.de* verat b2.de* verb b2.de* viol-o b2.de* viol-t b2.de* *Zinc* b2.de*
- **alternating** sides: phyt bg2

○ - **Back** of hand: alum b2.de* ang b2.de* ars b2.de* borx b2.de* bov b2.de* bry b2.de* *Calc* b2.de* camph b2.de* caust b2.de* cina b2.de* cycl b2.de* dig b2.de* euph b2.de* *Kreos* b2.de* lyc b2.de* merc b2.de* mur-ac b2.de* **Nat-c** b2.de* nux-v b2.de* petr b2.de* ph-ac b2.de* puls b2.de* rheum b2.de* **Rhus-t** b2.de* *Samb* b2.de* **Sep** b2.de* sil b2.de* spig b2.de* stann b2.de* *Sulph* b2.de*
- **Palm**: *Acon* b2.de* agar b2.de* alum b2.de* am-m b2.de* ambr b2.de* **Anac** b2.de* asar b2.de* bar-c b2.de* bism b2.de* *Borx* b2.de* *Bry* b2.de* camph b2.de* canth b2.de* caps b2.de* carb-v b2.de* caust b2.de* cham b2.de* chel b2.de* chin b2.de* coff b2.de* con b2.de* dig b2.de* *Dulc* b2.de* graph ptk1 hell b2.de* hep b2.de* ign b2.de* ip b2.de* kali-c b2.de* *Kreos* b2.de* lach b2.de* laur b2.de* led b2.de* *Lyc* b2.de* m-ambo b2.de* m-arct b2.de* mag-c b2.de* mang b2.de* *Merc* b2.de* mez b2.de* mur-ac b2.de* nat-c b2.de* nat-m b2.de* *Nux-v* b2.de* petr b2.de* phos b2.de* puls b2.de* **Ran-b** b2.de* *Ran-s* b2.de* rheum b2.de* rhus-t b2.de* ruta b2.de* *Samb* b2.de* **Sel** b2.de* sep b2.de* **Spig** b2.de* spong b2.de* *Stann* b2.de* staph b2.de* *Sulph* b2.de*

HIP; complaints of: acon b2.de* **Agar** b2.de* agn b2.de alum b2.de* am-c b2.de* am-m b2.de* ambr b2.de* anac b2.de ang b2.de* ant-c b2.de* ant-t b2.de* arg-met b2.de* arn b2.de* ars b2.de* asaf b2.de* asar b2.de* *Aur* b2.de* bar-c b2.de bell b2.de* bov b2.de *Bry* b2.de* calc b2.de* camph b2.de* cann-s b2.de* canth b2.de* carb-an b2.de carb-v b2.de* *Caust* b2.de* cham b2.de* chel b2.de* chin b2.de* cic b2.de* **Cina** b2.de* clem b2.de* cocc b2.de* coff b2.de* colch b2.de* coloc b2.de* con b2.de* crot-h bg2 cycl b2.de* dig b2.de* dros b2.de* *Dulc* b2.de* **Euph** b2.de* ferr b2.de* graph b2.de* hell b2.de* hep b2.de* hyos b2.de* ign b2.de iod b2.de* kali-bi bg2 kali-c b2.de* kali-n b2.de* *Kreos* b2.de* lach b2.de* laur b2.de* led b2.de* *Lyc* b2.de* m-arct b2.de* m-aust b2.de* mag-c b2.de* mag-m b2.de mang b2.de meny b2.de* merc b2.de mez b2.de* mosch b2.de* mur-ac b2.de nat-c b2.de* nat-m b2.de* nit-ac b2.de* **Nux-v** b2.de* olnd b2.de* par b2.de* petr b2.de ph-ac b2.de* phos b2.de phyt ptk1 plat b2.de plb b2.de* **Puls** b2.de* ran-b b2.de* ran-s b2.de rheum b2.de* rhod b2.de* rhus-t b2.de* *Ruta* b2.de* sabad b2.de* sabin b2.de* samb b2.de* sars b2.de sec b2.de sel b2.de seneg b2.de **Sep** b2.de* sil b2.de* spig b2.de* spong b2.de *Stann* b2.de* staph b2.de* stram b2.de* stront-c b2.de* *Sulph* b2.de* tarax b2.de teucr b2.de* thuj b2.de* valer b2.de* verat b2.de* verb b2.de viol-o b2.de viol-t b2.de zinc b2.de*
- **alternating** sides: cimic bg2 cocc bg2 euon bg2* lil-t bg2
- **right**: chel mtf11
- **left**:
  - • **accompanied** by | **Forearms**; complaints of (See Forearm - accompanied - hip - left)
- **accompanied** by | **pneumonia**: chel mtf11

○ - **Joints**: acon b2.de* agn b2.de* alum b2.de am-c b2.de am-m b2.de* ang b2.de* ant-c b2.de* ant-t b2.de* arg-met b2.de* arn b2.de* asaf b2.de* asar b2.de* aur b2.de bar-c b2.de bell b2.de* **Bry** b2.de* **Calc** b2.de* camph b2.de* canth b7.de caps b2.de* carb-an b2.de **Caust** b2.de* cham b2.de* chel b2.de* chin b2.de* cina b7.de cocc b2.de* colch b2.de* coloc b2.de* con b2.de croc b2.de* dros b2.de* dulc b2.de* euph b2.de* euphr b2.de ferr b2.de* graph b2.de hell b2.de* hep b2.de hyos b2.de ign b2.de* iod b2.de kali-c b2.de* kali-n b2.de kreos b2.de* **Led** b2.de* lyc b2.de* m-ambo b7.de m-arct b2.de* m-aust b2.de* mag-c b2.de* mag-m b2.de meny b2.de* merc b2.de* mez b2.de nat-m b2.de* nit-ac b2.de* nux-v b2.de* par b2.de* petr b2.de* ph-ac b2.de* phos b2.de* plat b2.de plb b2.de* puls b2.de* **Rhus-t** b2.de* ruta b7.de sabin b7.de samb b2.de* seneg b2.de sep b2.de* sil b2.de* stann b2.de* staph b2.de* still bg2 stram ptk1 stront-c b2.de* sulph b2.de* thuj b2.de* verat b2.de* zinc b2.de

HOOF: | **clubfoot** (See Clubfoot)

KNEES; complaints of: acon b2.de* agar b2.de agn b2.de* alum b2.de* am-c b2.de* am-m b2.de* ambr b2.de* anac b2.de* ang b2.de* ant-c b2.de* ant-t b2.de* **Apis** bg2* arg-met b2.de* arn b2.de* ars b2.de* asaf b2.de* asar b2.de* aur b2.de* bar-c b2.de bell b2.de* benz-ac ptk1 borx b2.de bry b2.de* calad b2.de* calc b2.de* camph b2.de* cann-s b2.de* canth b2.de* caps b2.de*

Knees; complaints of: ...
carb-an b2.de carb-v b2.de* **Caust** b2.de* cham b2.de* chel b2.de* **Chin** b2.de* cic b7.de cina b2.de* clem b2.de cocc b2.de* coff b2.de* colch b2.de* coloc b2.de con b2.de* croc b2.de* cupr b2.de* cycl b2.de* dig b2.de* dros b2.de* dulc b2.de euph b2.de euphr b2.de* ferr b2.de* *Gels* ptk1 graph b2.de* guaj b2.de hell b2.de* hep b2.de* hyos b2.de* ign b2.de* iod b2.de* ip b2.de* kali-c b2.de* kali-n b2.de kreos b2.de lach b2.de* laur b2.de* **Led** b2.de* lyc b2.de* m-ambo b2.de* m-arct b2.de* m-aust b2.de* mag-c b2.de* mag-m b2.de mang b2.de meny b2.de* merc b2.de* mez b2.de mosch b2.de mur-ac b2.de* nat-c b2.de* **Nat-m** b2.de* nit-ac b2.de* nux-m b2.de* **Nux-v** b2.de* olnd b2.de* par b2.de* **Petr** b2.de* ph-ac b2.de* phos b2.de* plat b2.de* plb b2.de* **Puls** b2.de* ran-b b2.de* ran-s b2.de* rheum b2.de* rhod b2.de* **Rhus-t** b2.de* ruta b2.de* sabad b2.de* sabin b2.de* samb b2.de* sars b2.de* sel b2.de* seneg b2.de **Sep** b2.de* sil b2.de* spig b2.de* spong b2.de* squil b7.de stann b2.de* staph b2.de* stront-c b2.de* sul-ac b2.de* **Sulph** b2.de* tarax b2.de* teucr b2.de thuj b2.de* valer b2.de* verat b2.de* verb b2.de* viol-t b2.de* zinc b2.de* [*Mang-i* stj2 *Mang-s* stj2]

- **left**: toxi mtf2•

○ - **Bend** of: alum b2.de am-c b2.de am-m b2.de ambr b2.de* ang b2.de* ant-t b2.de ars b2.de* asaf b2.de asar b2.de **Bell** b2.de* borx b2.de bry b2.de* calc b2.de cann-s b2.de carb-an b2.de caust b2.de* chel b2.de* chin b2.de* cocc b2.de coloc b2.de con b2.de* dig b2.de dros b2.de euph b2.de euphr b2.de ferr b2.de graph b2.de* guaj b2.de hell b2.de hep b2.de kali-c b2.de kreos b2.de* lach b2.de laur b2.de led b2.de* lyc b2.de* m-aust b2.de mag-c b2.de* mang b2.de* meny b2.de merc b2.de* mez b2.de* mur-ac b2.de nat-c b2.de* **Nat-m** b2.de* nit-ac b2.de* nux-v b2.de* olnd b2.de onos ptk1 par b2.de petr b2.de* ph-ac b2.de phos b2.de* plat b2.de puls b2.de* ran-b b2.de ran-s b2.de rheum b2.de* rhus-t b2.de* ruta b2.de samb b2.de sars b2.de* sep b2.de spong b2.de* squil b2.de stann b2.de* staph b2.de* sul-ac b2.de sulph b2.de* tarax b2.de* thuj b2.de* valer b2.de* verat b2.de zinc b2.de

▽ • **extending** to | **Heel**: alum ptk1

- **Knees** | **Patella**: alum b2.de* am-c b2.de anac b2.de ang b2.de arg-met b2.de* arn b2.de asaf b2.de* **Bell** b2.de* bry b2.de* calc b2.de* **Camph** b2.de* cann-s b2.de* carb-v b2.de caust b2.de* chel b2.de* chin b2.de* cocc b2.de con b2.de* graph b2.de guaj b2.de hell b2.de kreos b2.de* led b2.de* lyc b2.de *M-aust* b2.de meny b2.de mez b2.de mur-ac b2.de nit-ac b2.de* nux-v b2.de* par b2.de ph-ac b2.de phos b2.de ran-b b2.de rhus-t b2.de* samb b2.de sars b2.de sep b2.de spig b2.de* stann b2.de* staph b2.de* stront-c b2.de sulph b2.de tarax b2.de teucr b2.de thuj b2.de verb b2.de viol-t b2.de* zinc b2.de*
- **Sides** | **Inner**: phos bg2

KNEES; position of:

- **inward** (= genu valgum): bar-c st ix bnm8• lach st maland c2 nux-v st sep bg2 staph bg2
- **outward** (= genu varum): calc st nux-v st *Ph-ac* b4a.de *Staph* b7a.de sulph b4a.de*

LEGS; complaints of: acon b2.de* agar b2.de* agn b2.de* alum b2.de* am-c b2.de* am-m b2.de* ambr b2.de* anac b2.de* ang b2.de* ant-c b2.de* ant-t b2.de* arg-met b2.de* arn b2.de* ars b2.de* asaf b2.de* asar b2.de* aur b2.de bar-c b2.de* bell b2.de* bism b2.de* borx b2.de* bov b2.de* bry b2.de* calad b2.de* **Calc** b2.de* camph b2.de* cann-s b2.de* canth b2.de* caps b2.de* carb-an b2.de carb-v b2.de caust b2.de* cham b2.de* chel b2.de* chin b2.de* cic b2.de* cina b2.de* clem b2.de cocc b2.de* coff b2.de* colch b2.de* coloc b2.de* con b2.de* croc b2.de* cupr b2.de* cycl b2.de* dig b2.de* dros b2.de* dulc b2.de euph b2.de* euphr b2.de* ferr b2.de* fic-m gya1 graph b2.de* guaj b2.de* hell b2.de* hep b2.de hyos b2.de* ign b2.de* iod b2.de* ip b2.de* kali-c b2.de* kali-n b2.de* kreos b2.de* lach b2.de* laur b2.de* led b2.de* **Lyc** b2.de* m-ambo b2.de* m-arct b2.de* m-aust b2.de* mag-c b2.de* mag-m b2.de mang b2.de meny b2.de* merc b2.de* mez b2.de* mosch b2.de* mur-ac b2.de nat-c b2.de* nat-m b2.de* nit-ac b2.de* nux-m b2.de* nux-v b2.de* olnd b2.de* op b2.de* par b2.de* petr b2.de* ph-ac b2.de* phos b2.de* phyt ptk1 plat b2.de* plb b2.de* **Puls** b2.de* ran-b b2.de* ran-s b2.de* rheum b2.de* rhod b2.de* rhus-t b2.de* ruta b2.de* sabad b2.de* sabin b2.de* samb b2.de* sars b2.de sec b2.de* sel b2.de* seneg b2.de **Sep** b2.de* **Sil** b2.de* spig b2.de* spong b2.de* squil b2.de* stann b2.de* **Staph** b2.de* stram b2.de* stront-c b2.de sul-ac b2.de sul-i ptk1 sulph b2.de* tarax b2.de* teucr b2.de* thuj b2.de* valer b2.de* verat b2.de* verb b2.de* viol-t b2.de* zinc b2.de*

○ - **Legs**:

○ • **Bones**:

⁝ **Tibia**: **Agar** b2.de* agn b2.de* alum b2.de am-c b2.de ambr b2.de anac b2.de* ang b2.de* ant-c b2.de arn b2.de* ars b2.de* **Asaf** b2.de* asar b2.de aur b2.de bar-c b2.de bell b2.de* bism b2.de* bry b2.de

Legs; complaints of – **Legs – Bones – Tibia**: ...
Calc b2.de* cann-s b2.de carb-an b2.de **Carb-v** bg2* caust b2.de* cham b2.de chel b2.de chin b2.de* cina b2.de cinnb ptk1 clem b2.de cocc b2.de coff b2.de* colch b2.de coloc b2.de* con b2.de* cycl b2.de* dig b2.de* dros b2.de* dulc b2.de* euph b2.de* euphr b2.de guaj b2.de hyos b2.de ign b2.de* kali-c b2.de* kreos b2.de* lach b2.de* laur b2.de* lyc b2.de* m-ambo b2.de m-arct b2.de m-aust b2.de mag-c b2.de* mag-m b2.de mang b2.de* meny b2.de* **Merc** b2.de* **Mez** b2.de* mosch b2.de* mur-ac b2.de* nat-c b2.de* nit-ac b2.de nux-v b2.de par b2.de petr b2.de* ph-ac b2.de* **Phos** b2.de* phyt ptk1 plat b2.de* plb b2.de **Puls** b2.de* rhod b2.de* rhus-t b2.de* sabad b2.de* sabin b2.de* samb b2.de sars b2.de* sep b2.de* sil b2.de* spig b2.de* spong b2.de* stann b2.de staph b2.de still ptk1 sul-ac b2.de sulph b2.de tarax b2.de* thuj b2.de* valer b2.de verat b2.de viol-t b2.de zinc b2.de*

⁝ **syphilitic**: merc ptk1 phyt ptk1 still ptk1 sul-i ptk1

⁝ **Periosteum**: mang ptk1

• **Calves**: agar b2.de* agn b2.de **Alum** b2.de* am-c b2.de am-m b2.de ambr b2.de* anac b2.de* ang b2.de ant-c b2.de* ant-t b2.de* arg-met b2.de* *Arg-n* bg2* arn b2.de* **Ars** b2.de* asaf b2.de* asar b2.de bar-c b2.de bell b2.de bism b2.de borx b2.de bov b2.de* bry b2.de* **Calc** b2.de* camph b2.de* cann-s b2.de* canth b2.de* caps b2.de* carb-an b2.de carb-v b2.de* caust b2.de* cham b2.de* chel b2.de* chin b2.de* cina b2.de cocc b2.de* coff b2.de colch b2.de coloc b2.de* con b2.de* croc b2.de* cupr b2.de* cycl b2.de dig b2.de dulc b2.de* euph b2.de euphr b2.de* ferr b2.de* **Graph** b2.de* guaj b2.de* hep b2.de hyos b2.de* ign b2.de* ip b2.de* kali-c b2.de kali-n b2.de kreos b2.de lach b2.de laur b2.de led b2.de* lyc b2.de* m-ambo b2.de m-arct b2.de *M-aust* b2.de mag-c b2.de* mag-m b2.de mang b2.de* meny b2.de merc b2.de* mur-ac b2.de* nat-c b2.de* nat-m b2.de* **Nit-ac** b2.de* nux-v b2.de* olnd b2.de* par b2.de petr b2.de* ph-ac b2.de phos b2.de plat b2.de* plb b2.de **Puls** b2.de* rheum b2.de **Rhus-t** b2.de* ruta b2.de sabad b2.de* sabin b2.de* samb b2.de sars b2.de sec b2.de sel b2.de **Sep** b2.de* sil b2.de* spig b2.de* **Stann** b2.de* **Staph** b2.de* stram b2.de stront-c b2.de* **Sulph** b2.de* tarax b2.de* teucr b2.de thuj b2.de* **Valer** b2.de* verat b2.de* viol-t b2.de* zinc b2.de*

⁝ **extending** to | **Sacrum**: merc-i-r ptk1

• **Tendo** Achillis: acon b2.de* alum b2.de* **Anac** b2.de* ant-c b2.de* arg-met b2.de* arn b2.de* aur bg2 bell b2.de* benz-ac ptk1 bism b2.de* bry b2.de camph b2.de cann-xyz bg2 carb-an b2.de* *Caust* b2.de* chel b2.de* chin bg2 dulc b2.de* euphr b2.de* graph bg2 *Hep* b2.de* kali-bi ptk1 kali-c b2.de kreos b2.de laur bg2 mag-c bg2 meny bg2 *Merc* bg2 mez b2.de* **Mur-ac** b2.de* nat-c b2.de* nat-m b2.de* plat b2.de *Prun* bg2 puls b2.de* ran-b b2.de* rheum b2.de rhod b2.de* rhus-t b2.de* **Sabin** b2.de* sel bg2 *Sep* b2.de* stann b2.de* staph b2.de* sul-ac b2.de* sulph b2.de* teucr b2.de* thuj b2.de* valer b2.de* **Zinc** b2.de*

LOWER LIMBS; complaints of: alum ptk1 *Ars* ptk1 bell ptk1 *Calc* ptk1 **Caust** ptk1 graph ptk1 *Kali-c* ptk1 lach ptk1 led ptk1 **Lyc** ptk1 *Mang* ptk1 merc ptk1 nit-ac ptk1 nux-v ptk1 **Puls** ptk1 **Rhus-t** ptk1 sep ptk1 **Sil** ptk1 **Sulph** ptk1 valer ptk1 zinc ptk1

- **alternating** sides: acon ptk1 aloe ptk1 ars ptk1 **Bry** ptk1 calc-p ptk1 cham ptk1 cic ptk1 cina bg2 coloc ptk1 cupr ptk1 dios ptk1 graph ptk1 *Kali-bi* ptk1 kali-c ptk1 kali-n ptk1 lach ptk1 lil-t ptk1 mag-p ptk1 *Nat-m* ptk1 nat-s ptk1 *Puls* ptk1 *Rhus-t* ptk1 sep ptk1 sil ptk1 *Sulph* ptk1
- **right**: *Acon* b7a.de* agar b4a.de* agn b7a.de* *Alum* b4a.de* am-c b4a.de* am-m b7a.de* ambr b7a.de* anac b4a.de* *Ang* b7a.de* ant-c b7a.de* ant-t b7a.de* apis b7a.de* aran bg2 *Arg-met* b7a.de* *Arn* b7a.de* **Ars** b4a.de* asaf b7a.de* asar b7a.de* *Aur* b4a.de* bar-c b4a.de* **Bell** b4a.de* bism b7a.de* borx b4a.de* bov b4a.de* brom b4a.de* **Bry** b7a.de* calad b7a.de* *Calc* b4a.de* *Camph* b7a.de* cann-s b7a.de* *Canth* b7a.de* caps b7a.de* *Carb-an* b4a.de* *Carb-v* b4a.de* *Caust* b4a.de* cham b7a.de* chel b7a.de* *Chin* b7a.de* cic b7a.de* cina b7a.de* clem b4a.de* *Cocc* b7a.de* *Coff* b7a.de* colch b7a.de* **Coloc** b4a.de* *Con* b4a.de* croc b7a.de* *Cupr* b7a.de* cycl b7a.de* dig b4a.de* *Dros* b7a.de* dulc b4a.de* euph b4a.de* euphr b7a.de* ferr b7a.de* fl-ac b4a.de* **Graph** b4a.de* *Guaj* b4a.de* hell b7a.de* *Hep* b4a.de* hyos b7a.de* *Ign* b7a.de* iod b4a.de* ip b7a.de* kali-c b4a.de* *Kali-n* b4a.de* kreos b7a.de* **Lach** b7a.de* *Laur* b7a.de* *Led* b7a.de* *Lyc* b4a.de* m-ambo b7a.de* m-arct b7a.de* m-aust b7a.de* *Mag-c* b4a.de* mag-m b4a.de* mang b4a.de* *Meny* b7a.de* *Merc* b4a.de* *Mez* b4a.de* mill b7a.de mosch b7a.de* mur-ac b4a.de* *Nat-c* b4a.de* *Nat-m* b4a.de* *Nit-ac* b4a.de* *Nux-m* b7a.de* **Nux-v** b7a.de* *Olnd* b7a.de* op b7a.de* *Par* b7a.de* *Petr* b4a.de* *Ph-ac* b4a.de* **Phos** b4a.de* plat b4a.de* plb b7a.de* **Psor** b4a.de* **Puls** b7a.de* ran-b b7a.de* *Ran-s* b7a.de* rheum b7a.de* **Rhod** b4a.de* *Rhus-t* b7a.de*

- **right**: ... ruta b7a.de* *Sabad* b7a.de* *Sabin* b7a.de* *Samb* b7a.de* **Sars** b4a.de* **Sec** b7a.de* sel b7a.de* seneg b4a.de* **Sep** b4a.de* *Sil* b4a.de* spig b7a.de* *Spong* b7a.de* squil b7a.de* stann b4a.de* *Staph* b7a.de* *Stram* b7a.de* stront-c b4a.de* sul-ac b4a.de* *Sulph* b4a.de* *Tarax* b7a.de* teucr b7a.de* *Thuj* b4a.de* valer b7a.de* *Verat* b7a.de* *Verb* b7a.de* viol-o b7a.de* *Viol-t* b7a.de* *Zinc* b4a.de*
- **left**: *Acon* b7a.de* *Agar* b4a.de* *Agn* b7a.de* alum b4a.de* am-c b4a.de* *Am-m* b7a.de* **Ambr** b7a.de* *Anac* b4a.de* ang b7a.de* ant-c b7a.de* *Ant-t* b7a.de* apis b7a.de* *Arg-met* b7a.de* arn b7a.de* *Ars* b4a.de* **Asaf** b7a.de* *Asar* b7a.de* aur b4a.de* *Bar-c* b4a.de* *Bell* b4a.de* bism b7a.de* *Borx* b4a.de* *Bov* b4a.de* brom b4a.de *Bry* b7a.de* *Calad* b7a.de* **Calc** b4a.de* camph b7a.de* cann-s b7a.de* canth b7a.de* caps b7a.de* carb-an b4a.de* *Carb-v* b4a.de* *Caust* b4a.de* cham b7a.de* *Chel* b7a.de* chin b7a.de* *Cic* b7a.de* **Cina** b7a.de* *Clem* b4a.de* *Cocc* b7a.de* coff b7a.de* colch b7a.de* *Coloc* b4a.de* *Con* b4a.de* *Croc* b7a.de* cupr b7a.de* cycl b7a.de* *Dig* b4a.de* dros b7a.de* *Dulc* b4a.de* *Euph* b4a.de* *Euphr* b7a.de* **Ferr** b7a.de* fic-m gya1 fl-ac b4a.de* *Graph* b4a.de* *Guaj* b4a.de* *Hell* b7a.de* **Hep** b4a.de* *Hyos* b7a.de* *Ign* b7a.de* *Iod* b4a.de* ip b7a.de* iris bg2 *Kali-bi* bg2 kali-c b4a.de* kali-n b4a.de* *Kreos* b7a.de* *Lach* b7a.de* laur b7a.de* *Led* b7a.de* **Lyc** b4a.de* *M-ambo* b7a.de* m-arct b7a.de* *M-aust* b7a.de* *Mag-c* b4a.de* mag-m b4a.de* mang b4a.de* meny b7a.de* *Merc* b4a.de* *Mez* b4a.de* mill b7a.de *Mosch* b7a.de* mur-ac b4a.de* nat-c b4a.de* nat-m b4a.de* *Nat-s* bg2 **Nit-ac** b4a.de* nux-m b7a.de* *Nux-v* b7a.de* olnd b7a.de* op b7a.de* par b7a.de* *Petr* b4a.de* ph-ac b4a.de* *Phos* b4a.de* *Plat* b4a.de* plb b7a.de* psor b4a.de* *Puls* b7a.de* *Ran-b* b7a.de* ran-s b7a.de* *Rheum* b7a.de* rhod b4a.de* **Rhus-t** b7a.de* *Ruta* b7a.de* sabad b7a.de* *Sabin* b7a.de* samb b7a.de* sars b4a.de* sec b7a.de* *Sel* b7a.de* *Seneg* b4a.de* *Sep* b4a.de* **Sil** b4a.de* *Spig* b7a.de* spong b7a.de* squil b7a.de* *Stann* b4a.de* staph b7a.de* stram b7a.de* *Stront-c* b4a.de* *Sul-ac* b4a.de* **Sulph** b4a.de* tarax b7a.de* *Teucr* b7a.de* thuj b4a.de* toxi mtf2• *Valer* b7a.de* verat b7a.de* verb b7a.de* viol-o b7a.de* viol-t b7a.de* *Zinc* b4a.de*

▽ · **extending** to | **right**: coloc bg2 mag-c ptk1

- **accompanied** by:
  - **constipation** (See RECTUM - Constipation - accompanied - lower)
  - **diarrhea** (See RECTUM - Diarrhea - accompanied - lower)
  - **hemorrhoids** (See RECTUM - Hemorrhoids - accompanied - lower)
  - **nausea**: *Ip* b7a.de
  - **respiration**; difficult (See RESPIRATION - Difficult - accompanied - lower)
  - **restlessness**; with (See MIND - Restlessness - lower)
  - **screaming**; with (See MIND - Shrieking - lower)
  - ○ **Head**; pain in (See HEAD - Pain - accompanied - lower)
  - **Lumbar** region; pain in (See BACK - Pain - lumbar - accompanied - lower)
- **alternating** with | **Upper** limbs; complaints of (See Upper limbs - alternating with - lower)
- **paroxysmal**: bell bg2 dios bg2 ign bg2 zinc-val bg2
- **periodical**: arg-n bg2 ars bg2 bell bg2 ign bg2 nat-m bg2 nat-s bg2

▽ - **extending** to:
  - ○ **Chest**: caust bg2 phos bg2 rhus-t bg2
  - **Downward**: ant-t bg2 bell bg2 caust bg2 coloc bg2 kali-c bg2 mez bg2 phyt bg2 tell bg2
  - **Inguinal** region: caust bg2
  - **Other** parts: cimic bg2 iris bg2 lach bg2 puls bg2

○ - **Bones**: agar b2.de* alum b2.de am-c b2.de am-m b2.de* anac b2.de ang b2.de* *Aran* bg2 arg-met b7.de ars b2.de asaf b2.de* aur b2.de* bar-c b2.de* bell b2.de bism b2.de* borx b2.de bry b2.de* calc b2.de* cann-s b2.de* canth b2.de* caps b2.de carb-an b2.de carb-v b2.de caust b2.de chin b2.de* cocc b2.de* coloc b2.de con b2.de* cupr b2.de cycl b2.de* dros b2.de* dulc b2.de* euph b2.de* graph b2.de* guaj b2.de* hep b2.de* iod b2.de ip b2.de* kali-c b2.de* kali-n b2.de* kreos b2.de* lach b2.de* laur b2.de* led b2.de* lyc b2.de* mag-c b2.de mag-m b2.de mang b2.de **Merc** b2.de* mez b2.de mosch b2.de mur-ac b2.de nat-c b2.de nit-ac b2.de* nux-v b2.de olnd b2.de* petr b2.de ph-ac b2.de* **Phos** b2.de* **Puls** b2.de* rhod b2.de* rhus-t b2.de* **Ruta** b2.de* sabad b2.de* sabin b2.de* samb b2.de* sars b2.de sep b2.de* **Sil** b2.de* spig b2.de* **Staph** b2.de*

- **Lower** limbs – **Bones**: ... stront-c b2.de* sulph b2.de* teucr b2.de thuj b2.de valer b2.de* verat b2.de* viol-t b2.de* zinc b2.de*
- **Joints**: acon b2.de* agar b2.de agn b2.de alum b2.de am-c b2.de* am-m b2.de* ambr b2.de anac b2.de ang b2.de* ant-c b2.de ant-t b2.de arg-met b2.de* arn b2.de* ars b2.de asaf b2.de asar b2.de aur b2.de* bar-c b2.de bell b2.de* bism b2.de borx b2.de bov b2.de bry b2.de* calad b2.de **Calc** b2.de* camph b2.de cann-s b2.de canth b2.de caps b2.de* carb-an b2.de* carb-v b2.de **Caust** b2.de* cham b2.de chel b2.de chin b2.de* cic b2.de cina b2.de clem b2.de cocc b2.de* coff b2.de colch b2.de coloc b2.de* con b2.de* croc b2.de cupr b2.de cycl b2.de* dig b2.de* dros b2.de* dulc b2.de euph b2.de euphr b2.de ferr b2.de* graph b2.de* guaj b2.de hell b2.de* hep b2.de hyos b2.de* ign b2.de* iod b2.de ip b2.de **Kali-c** b2.de* kali-n b2.de kreos b2.de lach b2.de laur b2.de **Led** b2.de* **Lyc** b2.de* m-ambo b2.de m-arct b2.de m-aust b2.de mag-c b2.de* mag-m b2.de mang b2.de meny b2.de merc b2.de* mez b2.de* mosch b2.de mur-ac b2.de nat-c b2.de **Nat-m** b2.de* nit-ac b2.de* nux-m b2.de nux-v b2.de* olnd b2.de par b2.de petr b2.de* ph-ac b2.de* phos b2.de* plat b2.de plb b2.de puls b2.de* ran-b b2.de ran-s b2.de rheum b2.de rhod b2.de **Rhus-t** b2.de* ruta b2.de* sabad b2.de sabin b2.de* samb b2.de sars b2.de sec b2.de sel b2.de seneg b2.de **Sep** b2.de* **Sil** b2.de* spig b2.de* spong b2.de squil b2.de stann b2.de* staph b2.de* **Stront-c** b2.de* sul-ac b2.de **Sulph** b2.de* tarax b2.de* teucr b2.de* thuj b2.de valer b2.de verat b2.de* verb b2.de viol-t b2.de zinc b2.de*

NAILS; complaints of: *Alum* b2.de* am-m b2.de* ambr bg2 ant-c b2.de* arg-n bg2 ars b2.de* aur b2.de* bar-c b2.de* bell b2.de* bism bg2 borx b2.de* bov b2.de* calc b2.de* carb-v bg2 castor-eq br1* *Caust* b2.de* chel b2.de* chin b2.de* cocc b2.de* colch b2.de* **Con** b2.de* **Crot-h** bg2 dig b2.de* dros b2.de* ferr bg2 **Graph** b2.de* hell b2.de* **Hep** b2.de* hyper bro1 iod b2.de* **Kali-c** b2.de* kali-n bg2 **Lach** b2.de* lyc b2.de* m-ambo b2.de* m-arct b2.de *M-aust* b2.de *Merc* b2.de* mez bg2 mosch b2.de* mur-ac b2.de* *Nat-m* b2.de* *Nit-ac* b2.de* nux-v b2.de* par b2.de* petr b2.de* ph-ac b2.de* phos bg2 plat b2.de* puls b2.de* ran-b b2.de* rhod bg2 rhus-t b2.de* ruta b2.de* *Sabad* b2.de* sec b2.de* **Sep** b2.de* **Sil** b2.de* *Squil* b2.de* staph bg2 sul-ac b2.de* **Sulph** b2.de* teucr b2.de* thuj b2.de* upa bro1 ust ptk1 x-ray bro1

- **abscess**: | **Fingernails**; around (See Abscess - fingers - nail)
- **adhesion** of the fold of skin to growing nail (See growth - fold)
- **almond** shaped nails: tub hr1
- **atrophy** of nails: sil bro1
- **biting** nails (See MIND - Biting - nails)
- **blood**:
  - **oozing** from fingernails (See Blood - oozing)
  - **rush** of blood to fingernails (See Blood - rush - fingers - nails)
- **breaking** easily (See brittle)
- **brittle** nails: *(↗exfoliation)* alum b2.de* anan bro1 *Ant-c* bro1 ars bg2* **Calc** b2.de* *Calc-f* bg2 calc-sil mtf33 caust bro1 chlam-tr bcx2• clem ptk1 dios bro1 fl-ac b4a.de* gink-b sbd1• **Graph** b2.de* hydrog srj2• lept bg2* med jl2 merc b2.de* morg-p pte1*• nat-m bg2* nat-sil fd3.de• plb bro1* psor ptk1* sabad b2.de* sec bro1 senec bro1* sep b2.de* *Sil* b2.de* spig bg2 squil ptk1 *Sulph* b2.de* syc pte1*• syph jl2 thuj b4a.de* tritic-vg fd5.de x-ray bro1 [heroin sdj2]
  - ○ **Fingernails**: *Alum* k* alum-sil k2 *Ambr* ant-c ars but-ac sp1 calc calc-f gm1 calc-p sne calc-sil k2 castor-eq chin sma *Cupr* vh *Dios* k* *Fl-ac* **Graph** k* hep k2 hydrog srj2• *Lyc* vh med vh merc k* *Nit-ac* k* ozone sde2• *Phos* vh plac rzf5• podo fd3.de• **Psor** k* rhus-g tmo3• sabad st1 *Senec* c1* sep *Sil* k* squil staph zf *Sulph* k* symph fd3.de• *Thuj* k* tritic-vg fd5.de tub xxb [heroin sdj2]
    - ⁝ **crumbling**: but-ac br1*
  - **Toenails**: *Alum* b4a.de castor-eq *Graph* b4a.de ozone sde2• senec c2 *Sil* syc pte1*• *Thuj* k* tritic-vg fd5.de
    - ⁝ **crumbling**: ars sep *Sil* *Thuj* tritic-vg fd5.de
- **burning**; as if (See Pain - fingers - nails - under - burning)
- **burrowing** (See Pain - fingers - nails - burrowing)
- **coldness** under fingernails (See Coldness - fingers - nails)
- **constriction**:
  - ○ **Fingers** | **cramping** under fingernails (See Constriction - fingers - nails)
- **corrugated** nails: ars calc k2 fl-ac sabad **Sil** *Thuj* k*
  - ○ **Fingernails**: calc-f gm1 *Sabad* b7.de* thuj ser
  - **Toenails**: *Sabad* b7.de*
  - **Transversely**: ars med ez*

- **cracked** nails (See split)
- **crippled** nails (See stunted)
- **curved** fingernails: *Nit-ac* k*
  - **consumption**; in: med k* tub k*
- **cut** short; as if: sulph bg2*
- **deformed** (See distorted)
- **discoloration**: graph ptk1 nit-ac ptk1 thuj ptk1
  - **blue**: *Aur* b2.de* *Chel* b2.de* chin b2.de* cocc b2.de* *Dig* b2.de* dros b2.de* *Ip* bg2 lyc bg2 manc bg2 *Nat-m* b2.de* nit-ac ptk1 *Nux-v* b2.de* ox-ac bro1* petr b2.de* plb bg2 *Sil* b2.de* *Verat* ptk1 verat-v bg2
    - **fever**; before: chin b7a.de *Cocc* b7a.de
    - **perspiration**; during: nit-ac b4a.de
  - **gray**: merc-c ptk1
  - **spots**: nit-ac ptk1 sil ptk1
  - **yellow**: con bro1
  - ○ **Fingernails** (See Discoloration - fingers - nails)
  - **Toenails** (See Discoloration - toes - nails)
- **distorted** nails: aloe dgt1 alum k* anan ant-c ptk1 ars-br vh bamb-a stb2.de• calc k* calc-f ptk1 carc mlr1• *Fl-ac* k* **Graph** k* hydrc mtf11 med jl2 merc nat-m mrr1 nit-ac k2 sabad k* *Sep* k* **Sil** k* sulph k* syph ptk1* *Thuj* k*
  - **accompanied** by:
    - **breaking** easily: thuj mtf11
    - **Skin**; hard (See SKIN - Hard - accompanied - nails)
  - ○ **Toenails**: anan ant-c bro1 **Graph** k* merc sep sil bro1 sulph mrr1 thuj
- **dryness**: senec sne
  - ○ **Fingernails**; about (See Dryness - fingers - nails)
  - **Toenails** (See Dryness - toes - nails)
- **excrescences**: | **horny** excrescences under nails (See Excrescences - horny - nails)
- **exfoliation** of nails: *(↗brittle)* alum ant-c apis ars borx kr1 **Calc** mrr1 castor-eq chlor crot-h ferr bg2 form **Graph** k* *Hell* hep k2 *Merc* k* pyrog bg3* rhus-t sabin *Sec* sep *Sil* k* squil sulph thuj k* *Ust*
  - ○ **Fingernails**: merc b4.de* *Sil* b4a.de thuj b4a.de
- **falling** out of nails: *Ant-c* b2.de* *Ars* b2.de* borx bg2* brass bro1 but-ac bro1 canth bg2 chlol bg2 croc bg2 form bg2 *Graph* bg2* *Hell* b2.de* hell-f c2* merc b2.de* oena sne pyrog ptk2 ruta fd4.de sec b2.de* *Sil* bg2* **Squil** b2.de* sulph bg2 thuj b2.de* *Ust* bg2*
  - **accompanied** by:
    - **eczema**:
      - **Fingers** (See Eruptions - fingers - eczema - accompanied - falling)
      - **Toes** (See Eruptions - toes - eczema - accompanied - falling)
    - **granulating** surface; leaving an unhealthy and: sec a1*
  - **sensation** as if: apis b7a.de* med bg2 pyrog bg2* ust ptk1
  - ○ **Fingernails**: apis b7a.de *Ars* b4a.de bell b4a.de hell b7a.de merc b4.de *Thuj* b4.de* x-ray sp1
  - **Toenails**: *Ars* b4a.de bell b4a.de *Thuj* b4a.de
- **felon**:
  - **beginning** in nail (See Felon - nail)
  - **hangnails**; from (See Felon - hangnails)
  - **onychia** (See Felon - root)
  - **panaritium** (See Felon)
  - **paronychia** (See Felon - nail)
  - **prick** with a needle under the nail; from (See Felon - prick)
  - **whitlow** (See Felon)
  - ○ **Root** of nail; at (See Felon - root)
  - **Under** nail (See Felon - under)
- **fold** of skin remains attached to the growing nail (See growth - fold)
- **fragile** (See brittle)
- **fungus**: sil mrr1
- **furrowed** (See roughness - ribbed)
- **growth** of nails:
  - **arrested**: *Ant-c* k* rad-br ptk1 staph ptk1
- **growth** of nails: ...
  - **fold** of skin remains attached to the growing nail: carc jl2 osm br1*
  - **interrupted**: kali-s ptk1
  - **rapid**: falco-pe nl2• fl-ac k* graph bro1 ruta fd4.de wies c1
    - **Fingernails**: falco-pe nl2• ozone sde2• ruta fd4.de
  - **slow**: ant-c b7.de* sil bg2
    - **Fingernails**: *Ant-c* k*
- **hangnails**: *Calc* k* carc gk6 kali-chl c2 lyc k* *Merc* k* **Nat-m** k* nat-s bg3* positr nl2• pycnop-sa mrz1 *Rhus-t* k* sabad k* sanic c1 sep *Sil* k* *Stann* k* **Sulph** k* *Thuj* k* upa a1*
  - **inflamed**: kali-chl k* lyc h2* nat-m mtf11 upa a1
  - **painful**: lyc h2* nat-m gk sel k* stann k* upa a1
  - **painless**: plut-n srj7•
  - ○ **Fingers**: calc b4a.de lyc b4a.de *Merc* b4a.de *Nat-m* b4.de *Rhus-t* b7.de sabad b7.de* *Stann* b4.de* *Sulph* b4.de*
    - **Third** | **right**: wye c1
  - **Thumbs** | **Root** of nail: bros-gau mrc1
- **hardness**: graph mtf33
  - ○ **Fingernails**: ars calc-sil k2 falco-pe nl2• *Graph* mrr1 hep k2 ruta fd4.de sec gk
- **heat** | **Fingernails** (See Heat - fingers - nails)
- **horny**: *(↗Callosities - horny)* sabad br1
  - ○ **Fingernails**: ant-c hr1*
  - **Toenails**: graph hr1 sulph a1
- **inflammation**:
  - ○ **Fingernails** (See Inflammation - fingers - nails)
  - **Pulp** of nail (See Felon - root)
  - **Toenails**; under (See Inflammation - toes - nails)
- **ingrowing** toenails: alum alum-p k2 *Ant-c* sne bufo gk calc mrr1 *Caust* k* colch k* fl-ac ptk1 **Graph** k* hep bro1* kali-c k* kali-chl kali-m c2 *Lach* sne lyc zf **M-aust** k* mag-p bro1 *Nat-m* *Nit-ac* k* *Ph-ac* phos sne plb sang hr1* **Sil** k* staph c2* *Sul-i* bg2* *Sulph* k* tet c2* **Teucr** k* *Thuj* k* tub
  - **paralysis**: alum st
  - **sensation** of: x-ray sp1
  - **ulceration**, with: *Nit-ac* sang hr1 **Sil** *Teucr* k*
  - **unhealthy** granulation, with: **Lach** k ● sang
- **injuries**: | **Fingernails**; of (See Injuries - fingers - nails)
- **itching**:
  - ○ **Fingernails** (See Itching - fingers - nails)
  - **Thumb**; under nail of the (See Itching - thumbs - nails)
  - **Toes**; under nail of the (See Itching - toes - nails - under)
- **looseness** of nails (See falling)
- **loss** of nails (See falling)
- **lunula** of nails absent: sulph a1
- **mycoses**: graph mtf11
- **numbness** (See Tingling - fingers - nail; Tingling - toes - nails)
- **nutritional** changes; from: rad-br c11*
- **prickling** (See Tingling - fingers - nail)
- **pulsation**:
  - ○ **Fingernails** (See Pulsation - fingers - nail)
  - **Thumb**; under nail of the (See Pulsation - thumbs - nails)
- **recedes**; skin (See skin)
- **roughness**:
  - **ribbed**: ars bg2 *Fl-ac* ptk1* psor jl2 sabad b2.de* sil sne sulph sne thuj ptk1*
    - **Transversely**: ars ptk1
  - ○ **Fingernails**: *Graph* k* kali-p fd1.de• **Sil** k* tritic-vg fd5.de
    - **ribbed**: psor jl2 thuj
    - **ridges**, longitudinal: fl-ac kali-p fd1.de• tritic-vg fd5.de
- **sensitive** | **Fingernails** (See Sensitive - fingers - nails)
- **skin** recedes from the nails with formation of pus: eug br1 sec bro1
- **soft** nails (See brittle)
- **split** nails: **Ant-c** k* ars bg2 *Fl-ac* bg2* gink-b sbd1• graph mtf33 ina-i mlk9.de lept bg1* nat-m bg2 ruta bg2* sabad bg2 **Sil** k* *Squil* k* stann c2 sulph k* thuj ptk1
  - ○ **Centre**; down the: aur-m mrr1
  - **Fingernails**: but-ac sp1 *Squil* b7a.de

- **Toenails**: *Squil* b7a.de
- **spotted** nails (See discoloration - spots; Discoloration - fingers - nails - white - spots)
- **stunted** nails: alum b2.de* *Ant-c* bg2 ars bg2 calc b2.de* calc-f bg2 carc mlr1• *Caust* bg2 ferr bg2 **Graph** b2.de* merc b2.de* nit-ac mtf33 *Sabad* b2.de* sep b2.de* sil b2.de* sulph b2.de* thuj bg2*

○ · **Fingernails**: alum k* but-ac br1 calc b4a.de *Caust* k* fl-ac k2 **Graph** k* *Nit-ac Sabad Sep* k* **Sil** k* sulph *Thuj* k*

· **Toenails**: ars *Caust* k* fl-ac k2 **Graph** k* merc b4.de *Nat-ar Nit-ac* sabad sep k* **Sil** k* *Thuj* k*

- **suppuration**: ars bg2

○ · **Fingernails** (See Felon - nail)

· **Toenails**: ant-c b7a.de *Hell* b7a.de squil b7a.de

⁝ **left** great toe; under nail of: caust

- **thick** nails: alum k* *Ant-c* k* ars bg2 calc k* calc-f bg2* *Caust* bg2 falco-pe nl2• ferr bg2 fl-ac k2 **Graph** k* laur ptk1 merc k* sabad k* sep k* **Sil** k* sulph k* thuj bg2 *Ust*

○ · **Fingernails**: alum falco-pe nl2• **Graph** k* sabad k* *Sil* b4a.de *Thuj* b4a.de ust hr1*

· **Toenails**: ant-c bro1 *Graph* k* *Sabad* b7.de* sec sil bro1 sulph mrr1

- **thin** nails: ars calc-f gm1 fl-ac k2 lept ptk1 op
- **tingling**: colch ptk1

○ · **Fingernails**; under (See Tingling - fingers - nail)

· **Toenails**; under (See Tingling - toes - nails)

- **tough** | **Fingernails**: chin-b kr1 chinin-s
- **trophic** (See nutritional)
- **ulcers** (See Ulcers - nails)
- **warts**: | **Fingernails**; close to (See Warts - fingers - nails)

○ - **Around** nails: *Calc-p* bg2 psor ptk1

- **Base**: calc-p ptk1 caps ptk1
- **Corner**: lach ptk1
- **Edges**: calc-p ptk1 rad-br ptk1
- **Under**: alum ptk1 berb ptk1 bism ptk1 sars ptk1 sep ptk1

NATES; complaints of: alum b2.de am-c b2.de* ambr b2.de ang b2.de ant-c b2.de* asaf b2.de bar-c b2.de* bell b2.de borx b2.de* calc b2.de* camph b2.de cann-s b2.de canth b2.de* carb-v b2.de* caust b2.de* chin b2.de cina b2.de cocc b2.de coff b2.de con b2.de* croc b2.de cycl b2.de* dig b2.de dros b2.de dulc b2.de **Graph** b2.de* guaj b2.de hep b2.de hyos b2.de* ign b2.de iod b2.de kali-c b2.de* laur b2.de* lyc b2.de* mag-c b2.de mang b2.de* meny b2.de* merc b2.de* mez b2.de* mur-ac b2.de nat-c b2.de nat-m b2.de nit-ac b2.de nux-v b2.de olnd b2.de* **Ph-ac** b2.de* phos b2.de* plat b2.de* puls b2.de rhus-t b2.de* samb b2.de sars b2.de* sel b2.de* sep b2.de* sil b2.de* spig b2.de stann b2.de **Staph** b2.de* stront-c b2.de sulph b2.de* tarax b2.de thuj b2.de verat b2.de viol-t b2.de zinc b2.de*

- **extending** to | **Upward** to lumbar region: staph ptk1

SHOULDERS; complaints of: *(↗Shoulders - joints)* **Acon** b2.de* aesc bg2 agar b2.de* agn b2.de* *Alum* b2.de* am-c b2.de* *Am-m* b2.de* *Ambr* b2.de* anac b2.de* ang b2.de* ant-c b2.de* ant-t b2.de* arg-met b2.de* arn b2.de* ars b2.de* asaf b2.de* asar b2.de* bar-c b2.de* **Bell** b2.de* borx b2.de* bov b2.de* **Bry** b2.de* calc b2.de* calc-p bg2 camph b2.de* cann-s b2.de* canth b2.de* carb-an b2.de* carb-v b2.de* caust b2.de* *Chin* b2.de* cic b2.de* cina b2.de* cocc b2.de* colch b2.de* croc b2.de* cupr b2.de* dig b2.de* dros b2.de* euph b2.de* *Ferr* b2.de* ferr-p ptk1 graph b2.de* guaj b2.de* ham bg2 hep b2.de* hyos b2.de* ign b2.de* *Kali-bi* bg2 **Kali-c** b2.de* kali-n b2.de* kalm ptk1 kreos b2.de* lach bg2 laur b2.de* *Led* b2.de* *Lyc* b2.de* m-ambo b2.de* **Mag-c** b2.de* *Mag-m* b2.de* mang b2.de* meny b2.de* merc b2.de* mez b2.de* mosch b2.de* mur-ac b2.de* *Nat-c* b2.de* nat-m b2.de* *Nit-ac* bg2 nux-m b7.de nux-v b2.de* olnd b2.de* op b2.de* par b2.de* petr b2.de* ph-ac b2.de* *Phos* b2.de phyt ptk1 plat b2.de* plb b2.de* **Puls** b2.de* ran-b b2.de* ran-s b2.de* rhod b2.de* **Rhus-t** b2.de* sabad b2.de* sabin b2.de* sang ptk1 sars b2.de* sep b2.de* sil b2.de* spig b2.de* spong b2.de* squil b2.de* stann b2.de* staph b2.de* stram b2.de* stront-c b2.de* sul-ac b2.de* **Sulph** b2.de* tarax b2.de* teucr b2.de* thuj b2.de* valer b2.de* verat b2.de verat-v bg2 verb b2.de* zinc b2.de* [*Ferr-sil* stj2]

- **alternating** sides: lyc ptk1
- **right**: chel bg2 ferr ptk1 kali-m bg2* kalm ptk1 phyt ptk1 sang bg2* stict bg2* stront-c ptk1
- **left**: *Ferr* ptk1 ferr-p ptk1 kalm bg2 led ptk1 mag-c ptk1 nux-m ptk1 *Phos* bg2 rumx ptk1 sulph ptk1 verat bg2

Shoulders; complaints of – **left**: ...

▽ · **extending** to:

⁝ **right**: lyc ptk1

⁝ **Neck**: spig ptk1

- **accompanied** by | **Teeth**; complaints of (See TEETH - Complaints - accompanied - shoulders)

▽ - **extending** to:

○ · **Chest**: ferr-p ptk1

· **Wrist**: ferr-p ptk1

○ - **Joints**: *(↗Shoulders)* acon b2.de* agn b2.de* am-c b2.de* am-m b2.de* *Ambr* b2.de* ant-t b2.de* arg-met b2.de* arn b2.de* *Asaf* b2.de* asar b2.de* bism b2.de* *Bov* b2.de* **Bry** b2.de* **Calc** b2.de* canth b2.de* caps b2.de* carb-an b2.de* *Carb-v* b2.de* caust b2.de* cham b2.de* chel b2.de* chin b2.de* cic b2.de* cocc b2.de* coloc b2.de* *Croc* b2.de* dig b2.de* dros b2.de* euph b2.de* **Ferr** b2.de* ferr-p bg2* graph b2.de* hell b2.de* hep b2.de* hyos b2.de* **Ign** b2.de* iod b2.de* kali-bi bg2 **Kali-c** b2.de* kali-i bg2 kreos b2.de* lach bg2 laur b2.de* led b2.de* lyc b2.de* m-ambo b2.de* m-arct b2.de* mag-c b2.de* mag-m b2.de* mang b2.de* **Merc** b2.de* mez b2.de* mosch bg2 mur-ac b2.de* nat-c b2.de* **Nat-m** b2.de* nit-ac b2.de* nux-m b2.de* nux-v b2.de* olnd b2.de* op b2.de* *Petr* b2.de* ph-ac b2.de* phos b2.de* **Puls** b2.de* ran-b b2.de* rhod b2.de* **Rhus-t** b2.de* ruta b2.de* sabad b2.de* sabin b2.de* *Sang* ptk1 sars b2.de* **Sep** b2.de* sil b2.de* spig b2.de* stann b2.de* **Staph** b2.de* *Stront-c* b2.de* sul-ac b2.de* **Sulph** b2.de* teucr b2.de* thuj b2.de* valer b2.de* verat b2.de* viol-t b2.de* zinc b2.de*

THIGHS; complaints of: acon b2.de* agar b2.de* agn b2.de* alum b2.de am-c b2.de am-m b2.de* ambr b2.de* anac b2.de* ang b2.de* ant-c b2.de* ant-t b2.de* arg-met b2.de* arn b2.de* ars b2.de* asaf b2.de* asar b2.de* aur b2.de* bar-c b2.de bell b2.de* bism b2.de* borx b2.de bov b2.de bry b2.de* calad b2.de* calc b2.de* camph b2.de* cann-s b2.de* canth b2.de* caps b2.de* carb-an b2.de* carb-v b2.de* caust b2.de* cham b2.de* chel b2.de* **Chin** b2.de* cic b2.de* cina b2.de* clem b2.de* cocc b2.de* coff b2.de* colch b2.de* coloc b2.de* con b2.de croc b2.de* cupr b2.de cycl b2.de* dig b2.de* dros b2.de* dulc b2.de euph b2.de* euphr b2.de* ferr b2.de* graph b2.de* **Guaj** b2.de* hell b2.de* hep b2.de* hyos b2.de* ign b2.de* iod b2.de ip b2.de* kali-c b2.de* kali-n b2.de kreos b2.de lach b2.de* laur b2.de* led b2.de* lyc b2.de m-ambo b2.de* m-arct b2.de* m-aust b2.de* mag-c b2.de mag-m b2.de mang b2.de* meny b2.de* **Merc** b2.de* mez b2.de* mosch b2.de* mur-ac b2.de* nat-c b2.de* nat-m b2.de* nat-n bg2 nit-ac b2.de* nux-m b2.de* nux-v b2.de* olnd b2.de* par b2.de* petr b2.de* ph-ac b2.de* phos b2.de **Phyt** bg2* plat b2.de* plb b2.de* puls b2.de* pyrog ptk1 ran-b b2.de* ran-s b2.de* rheum b2.de* rhod b2.de* rhus-t b2.de* ruta b2.de* sabad b2.de* sabin b2.de* samb b2.de* sars b2.de* sel b2.de* seneg b2.de sep b2.de* sil b2.de* spig b2.de* spong b2.de* squil b2.de* stann b2.de* staph b2.de* stram b2.de* stront-c b2.de sul-ac b2.de sulph b2.de* tarax b2.de* teucr b2.de* thuj b2.de* valer b2.de* verat b2.de* verb b2.de* viol-t b2.de* zinc b2.de

- **alternating** sides: acon bg2

▽ - **extending** to | **Knee**; middle of: ind ptk1

○ - **Anterior** part: agar b2.de* ambr b2.de **Anac** b2.de* ang b2.de* ant-c b2.de aran bg2 arg-met b2.de* arn bg2 asaf b2.de* aur b2.de bar-c b2.de* bell b2.de bell-p ptk1 bov b2.de bry b2.de* calc b2.de cann-s b2.de* chel b2.de* chin b2.de* cimic bg2* cina b2.de coff bg2 coloc b2.de* con b2.de dig b2.de* dros b2.de dulc b2.de* euph b2.de* euphr b2.de* graph bg2 hep b2.de ign bg2 kali-bi bg2 kali-c b2.de laur b2.de **Lil-t** bg2 lyc b2.de mag-c b2.de* mang b2.de meny b2.de* merc b2.de mosch b2.de mur-ac b2.de* nat-c b2.de nat-m b2.de* nit-ac b2.de nux-v b2.de olnd b2.de* ph-ac b2.de* phyt bg2 plat b2.de podo bg2 puls b2.de rhus-t b2.de ruta bg2 sabad b2.de sabin b2.de* samb b2.de sars b2.de sil b2.de* spig b2.de **Spong** b2.de* stann b2.de* staph b2.de sulph bg2 tarax b2.de thuj b2.de valer b2.de* viol-t b2.de* xan ptk1 xanth bg2 zinc b2.de

- **Femur**: *Stront-c* br1
- **Inner** Side: agn b2.de alum b2.de anac b2.de ant-c b2.de arg-met b2.de arn b2.de* ars b2.de asaf b2.de* bar-c b2.de* bell b2.de calc b2.de* camph b2.de* caps b2.de carb-an b2.de* carb-v b2.de* caust b2.de* chin b2.de cocc b2.de coff b2.de dig b2.de graph b2.de* hep b2.de* ign b2.de iod b2.de kali-c b2.de* kreos b2.de* laur b2.de **Lil-t** bg2 lyc b2.de* m-arct b2.de m-aust b2.de mag-m b2.de mang b2.de* meny b2.de merc b2.de* mez b2.de mosch b2.de mur-ac b2.de nat-c b2.de nat-m b2.de nit-ac b2.de* nux-v b2.de olnd b2.de par b2.de **Petr** b2.de* plat b2.de plb b2.de* podo bg2 ran-b b2.de **Rhod** b2.de* rhus-t b2.de ruta b2.de sabad b2.de sabin b2.de* samb b2.de* sars b2.de sel b2.de* sep b2.de spong b2.de* **Stann** b2.de* staph b2.de* sul-ac b2.de **Sulph** b2.de* tarax b2.de* thuj b2.de verb b2.de viol-t b2.de* zinc b2.de

Extremities

- **Outer** Side: agar b2.de agn b2.de alum b2.de* anac b2.de* ang b2.de ant-c b2.de arn b2.de asaf b2.de aur b2.de* bar-c b2.de bell b2.de* bism b2.de canth b2.de* carb-an b2.de carb-v b2.de caust b2.de* chin b2.de coc-c bg2 cocc b2.de* colch b2.de euph b2.de* gels bg2 helon ptk1 laur b2.de mag-c b2.de mang b2.de meny b2.de merc b2.de mez b2.de mosch b2.de mur-ac b2.de nat-c b2.de nit-ac b2.de nux-v b2.de olnd b2.de **Ph-ac** b2.de* phyt bg2* rhus-t b2.de ruta b2.de sars b2.de spig b2.de* stann b2.de* staph b2.de sulph b2.de* tarax b2.de valer b2.de* zinc b2.de*
- **Posterior** part: agar b2.de alum b2.de* am-c b2.de* ambr b2.de anac b2.de ang b2.de ant-c b2.de* arg-n bg2 asaf b2.de aur b2.de bar-c b2.de* bell b2.de borx b2.de* calc b2.de* camph b2.de cann-s b2.de canth b2.de* caps b2.de* carb-v b2.de* caust b2.de* chin b2.de cina b2.de cocc b2.de coff b2.de* coloc ptk1 con b2.de* croc b2.de cycl b2.de* dig b2.de dros b2.de dulc b2.de euph b2.de euphr b2.de gnaph ptk1 graph b2.de* guaj b2.de hep b2.de hyos b2.de* ign b2.de* iod b2.de kali-bi bg2 kali-c b2.de* laur b2.de led b2.de* lyc b2.de* mag-c b2.de mag-m b2.de mang b2.de* meny b2.de* merc b2.de* mez b2.de* mosch b2.de* mur-ac b2.de nat-c b2.de nat-m b2.de nit-ac b2.de nux-v b2.de olnd b2.de par b2.de* ph-ac b2.de* phos b2.de* plat b2.de* puls b2.de ran-b b2.de rheum b2.de rhus-t b2.de* samb b2.de* sars b2.de sel b2.de* seneg b2.de sep b2.de* sil b2.de* spig b2.de stann b2.de* staph b2.de* stront-c b2.de sul-ac b2.de **Sulph** b2.de* tarax b2.de thuj b2.de valer b2.de verat b2.de* viol-t b2.de **Zinc** b2.de*

THUMBS; complaints of: am-m bg2 ambr bg2 anac bg2 arn bg2 asaf bg2 bar-c bg2 _Calc-p_ bg2 carb-v bg2 caust bg2 clem bg2 _Graph_ bg2 _Hep_ bg2 ign bg2 kali-n bg2 _Lach_ bg2 laur bg2 _Led_ bg2 lyc bg2 merc bg2 mez bg2 _Nat-c_ bg2 nat-m bg2 nit-ac bg2 _Nux-v_ bg2 petr bg2 ph-ac bg2 phos bg2 rheum bg2 sep bg2 sil bg2 spig bg2 staph bg2 stront-c bg2 _Sul-ac_ bg2 sulph bg2 verat bg2

▽ - **extending** to | **Upward**, arms and shoulder: cedr ptk1 naja ptk1

TOES; complaints of: acon b2.de* agar b2.de* agn b2.de* alum b2.de* am-c b2.de* am-m b2.de* ambr b2.de* anac b2.de ant-c b2.de* ant-t b2.de arg-met b2.de* **Arn** b2.de* ars b2.de* asaf b2.de* asar b2.de* aur b2.de* bar-c b2.de* bell b2.de bism b2.de* borx b2.de* bov b2.de bry b2.de calad b2.de* calc b2.de* camph b2.de* cann-s b2.de canth b7.de caps b2.de* carb-an b2.de* carb-v b2.de* **Caust** b2.de* cham b2.de* chel b2.de* chin b2.de* cic b2.de* cina b2.de* clem b2.de cocc b2.de* colch b2.de* con b2.de cupr b2.de* cycl b2.de* dig b2.de dros b2.de* dulc b2.de euphr b2.de* ferr b2.de **Graph** b2.de* guaj b2.de hell b2.de* hep b2.de* hyos b2.de* ign b2.de* kali-c b2.de* kali-n b2.de kreos b2.de lach b2.de* laur b2.de* led b2.de* lyc b2.de* m-ambo b2.de* m-arct b2.de* m-aust b2.de* mag-c b2.de* mag-m b2.de merc b2.de* mez b2.de* mosch b2.de* mur-ac b2.de nat-c b2.de* nat-m b2.de* nat-s br1 nit-ac b2.de* nux-m b2.de* nux-v b2.de* olnd b2.de* par b2.de* petr b2.de* ph-ac b2.de* phos b2.de* **Plat** b2.de* plb b2.de* **Puls** b2.de* ran-b b2.de* **Ran-s** b2.de* rheum b2.de* rhod b2.de* rhus-t b2.de* ruta b2.de* sabad b2.de* **Sabin** b2.de* sars b2.de sec b2.de* sep b2.de* sil b2.de* spig b2.de* spong b2.de* squil b2.de* staph b2.de* stront-c b2.de* sul-ac b2.de **Sulph** b2.de* tarax b2.de* teucr b2.de* **Thuj** b2.de* valer b2.de* verat b2.de* verb b2.de viol-t b2.de* zinc b2.de*

- **alternating** sides: nat-s bg2

▽ - **extending** to:

○ · **Hip**: pall ptk1

· **Instep**: anac ptk1

· **Thighs**: nux-v ptk1 thal ptk1

○ - **Back** of: cann-s bro1

- **Balls**: agar b2.de am-c b2.de am-m b2.de* ambr b2.de* ant-c b2.de* ant-t b2.de ars b2.de* asaf b2.de* bar-c b2.de* berb ptk1 bry b2.de* cann-s b2.de* carb-an b2.de caust b2.de cina b2.de* coff b2.de colch b2.de* con b2.de cupr b2.de* dros b2.de* graph b2.de* hell b2.de* kali-c b2.de* laur b2.de* **Led** b2.de* lyc b2.de mez b2.de mur-ac b2.de nit-ac b2.de* **Petr** b2.de* ph-ac b2.de* plat b2.de plb b2.de **Puls** b2.de* ran-s b2.de* rhus-t b2.de* sabad b2.de sabin b2.de* **Spig** b2.de* squil b2.de* tarax b2.de* viol-t b2.de*
- **First** toe: agar b2.de alum b2.de* am-c b2.de* am-m b2.de* ambr b2.de* anac b2.de* ant-c b2.de* **Arn** b2.de* ars b2.de **Asaf** b2.de* aur b2.de* bar-c b2.de bism b2.de calc b2.de* cann-s b2.de* caps b2.de carb-an b2.de **Caust** b2.de* chin b2.de clem b2.de cocc b2.de* colch b2.de* con b2.de* cupr b2.de cycl b2.de* dulc b2.de* graph b2.de* hell b2.de* hep b2.de* iod b2.de **Kali-c** b2.de* laur b2.de led b2.de* _M-arct_ b2.de mag-c b2.de* merc b2.de* mez b2.de* mur-ac b2.de nat-c b2.de* nat-m b2.de nat-s ptk1 nit-ac b2.de* nux-v b2.de olnd b2.de* petr b2.de ph-ac b2.de phos b2.de* **Plat** b2.de* plb b2.de puls b2.de* rad-br ptk1 ran-b b2.de ran-s b2.de rhus-t b2.de* ruta b2.de sabin b2.de* sars b2.de* sep b2.de* **Sil** b2.de* staph b2.de* sul-ac b2.de sulph b2.de* tarax b2.de* teucr b2.de* thuj b2.de* verat b2.de viol-t b2.de **Zinc** b2.de*

○ · **Ball**: bry bg2 kali-bi bg2 kali-c bg2 phos bg2 puls bg2 rhus-t bg2 sabad bg2 sulph bg2 zinc bg2

Toes; complaints of: ...

- **Joints**: agn b2.de* am-c b2.de* ambr b2.de* ant-c b2.de* ant-t b2.de* arg-met b2.de* arn b2.de* **Aur** b2.de* bell b2.de bism b2.de* bry b2.de calc b2.de* caps b2.de* carb-an b2.de* carb-v b2.de **Caust** b2.de* cham b2.de* chel b2.de* chin b2.de* cina b2.de cocc b2.de con b2.de cupr b2.de cycl b2.de* dros b2.de ferr b2.de* graph b2.de* hell b2.de hep b2.de hyos b2.de* **Kali-c** b2.de* **Led** b2.de* lyc b2.de* mag-c b2.de merc b2.de* mez b2.de nat-c b2.de nat-m b2.de* nit-ac b2.de nux-v b2.de* petr b2.de* ph-ac b2.de phos b2.de* plat b2.de plb b2.de* puls b2.de* ran-b b2.de* ran-s b2.de rhus-t b2.de* ruta b2.de **Sabin** b2.de* sec b2.de* **Sep** b2.de* sil b2.de* spig b2.de* staph b2.de stront-c b2.de* **Sulph** b2.de* tarax b2.de* **Teucr** b2.de* verat b2.de **Zinc** b2.de*
- **Nails**: alum b2.de* ant-c b2.de ars b2.de* borx b2.de bov b2.de* calc b2.de caust b2.de* colch b2.de con b2.de* dig b2.de* **Graph** b2.de* hell b2.de* hep b2.de* m-ambo b2.de m-aust b2.de merc b2.de* mosch b2.de mur-ac b2.de nat-c b2.de* nat-m b2.de nit-ac b2.de nux-v b2.de par b2.de ph-ac b2.de puls b2.de ran-b b2.de **Sabad** b2.de* sep b2.de* sil b2.de* squil b2.de* sulph b2.de teucr b2.de* thuj b2.de

○ · **Under**: ant-c ptk1 fl-ac ptk1 graph ptk1 teucr ptk1

- **Tip** of: alum b2.de am-c b2.de* am-m b2.de* ambr b2.de arn b2.de* ars b2.de asaf b2.de bism b2.de* calc b2.de camph b2.de* canth b2.de caps b2.de* chin b2.de* cocc bg2 hep b2.de **Kali-c** b2.de* lach b2.de m-ambo b2.de m-aust b2.de mosch b2.de* mur-ac b2.de* olnd b2.de* phos b2.de puls b2.de* ran-b b2.de* **Sep** b2.de* sil b2.de* spig b2.de thuj b2.de* zinc b2.de*

UPPER ARMS; complaints of: acon b2.de* agar b2.de* agn b2.de* alum b2.de* am-c b2.de* am-m b2.de* ambr b2.de* anac b2.de* ang b2.de* _Ant-c_ b2.de* ant-t b2.de* _Arg-met_ b2.de* arn b2.de* ars b2.de* asaf b2.de* asar b2.de* aur b2.de* _Bar-c_ b2.de* bell b2.de* bism b2.de* borx b2.de* bov b2.de* **Bry** b2.de* calc b2.de* camph b2.de* cann-s b7.de _Canth_ b2.de* carb-an b2.de* carb-v b2.de* caust b2.de* chel b2.de* chin b2.de* cina b2.de* clem b2.de* **Cocc** b2.de* coff b2.de* colch b2.de* coloc b2.de* con b2.de* croc b2.de* crot-h bg2 cupr b2.de* cycl b2.de* dig b2.de* dros b2.de* dulc b2.de* euph b2.de* euphr b2.de* **Ferr** b2.de* graph b2.de* guaj b2.de* hell b2.de* hep b2.de* ign b2.de* iod b2.de* ip b2.de* _Kali-c_ b2.de* kali-n b2.de* kreos b2.de* _Lach_ b2.de* laur b2.de* led b2.de* lyc b2.de* m-arct b2.de* m-aust b2.de* mag-c b2.de* mag-m b2.de* mang b2.de* meny b2.de* merc b2.de* mez b2.de* mosch b2.de* _Mur-ac_ b2.de* nat-c b2.de* nat-m b2.de* nit-ac b2.de* nux-m b2.de* nux-v b2.de* _Olnd_ b2.de* par b2.de* petr b2.de* ph-ac b2.de* phos b2.de* plat b2.de* _Plb_ b2.de* puls b2.de* ran-b b2.de* ran-s b2.de* rheum b2.de* rhod b2.de* rhus-t b2.de* ruta b2.de* sabad b2.de* sabin b2.de* samb b2.de* sars b2.de* **Sep** b2.de* sil b2.de* spig b2.de* spong b2.de* squil b2.de* stann b2.de* staph b2.de* stront-c b2.de* sul-ac b2.de* _Sulph_ b2.de* tarax b2.de* teucr b2.de* thuj b2.de* valer b2.de* verat b2.de* zinc b2.de*

○ - **Bones**: bar-c bg2 bell bg2

- **Deltoid**: bar-c ptk1 ferr ptk1 ferr-p ptk1 syph ptk1 urt-u ptk1 viol-o ptk1

· **right**: coloc ptk1 kalm ptk1 lycpr ptk1 mag-c bg2* mag-m bg2 phyt ptk1 _Sang_ bg2* staph ptk1

· **left**: ferr ptk1 nux-m bg2

UPPER LIMBS; complaints of: _Acon_ bg2 agar bg2 agn bg2 _Alum_ bg2 am-c bg2 am-m bg2* ambr bg2 **Anac** bg2 ang bg2 ant-c bg2 ant-t bg2 _Apis_ bg2 arg-met bg2 **Arn** bg2 _Ars_ bg2* **Asaf** bg2 asar bg2 aur bg2 _Bar-c_ bg2 bell bg2* bism bg2 borx bg2 bov bg2 brom bg2 bry bg2 **Cact** bg2 calad bg2 calc bg2* calc-p bg2 camph bg2 cann-xyz bg2 canth bg2 _Caps_ bg2 carb-an bg2 carb-v bg2 caust bg2* _Cham_ bg2 chel bg2 chin bg2 cic bg2 cina bg2 clem bg2 cocc bg2* coff bg2 colch bg2 coloc bg2 con bg2 croc bg2 cupr bg2 cycl bg2 dig bg2 dros bg2 dulc bg2 euph bg2 euphr bg2 ferr bg2* _Fl-ac_ bg2 graph bg2 guaj bg2 hell bg2 _Hep_ bg2 hyos bg2 _Ign_ bg2 iod bg2 ip bg2 **Kali-c** bg2* kali-n bg2 kalm bg2 _Kreos_ bg2 **Lach** bg2 laur bg2 led bg2 **Lyc** bg2* mag-c bg2 _Mag-m_ bg2 mang bg2 meny bg2 merc bg2* mez bg2 mosch bg2 mur-ac bg2 nat-c bg2 nat-m bg2 **Nit-ac** bg2 nux-m bg2 nux-v bg2* _Olnd_ bg2 op bg2 par bg2 _Petr_ bg2 _Ph-ac_ bg2 _Phos_ bg2* plat bg2 plb bg2 psor bg2 _Puls_ bg2* ran-b bg2 ran-s bg2 rheum bg2 rhod bg2 **Rhus-t** bg2* ruta bg2 sabad bg2 **Sabin** bg2 samb bg2 sars bg2 sec bg2 sel bg2 _Seneg_ bg2 sep bg2* sil bg2* _Spig_ bg2 spong bg2 **Squil** bg2 **Stann** bg2 staph bg2 **Stram** bg2 stront-c bg2 sul-ac bg2 **Sulph** bg2* _Tarax_ bg2 _Teucr_ bg2 thuj bg2 _Valer_ bg2 verat bg2 _Verb_ bg2 viol-o bg2 _Viol-t_ bg2 zinc bg2

- **alternating** sides: acon ptk1 alum ptk1 _Calc_ ptk1 caust bg2* cham ptk1 chin ptk1 _Cocc_ bg2* colch ptk1 echi bg2 _Lac-c_ ptk1 lyc bg2* mag-m ptk1 mang ptk1 plat bg2* sep ptk1 _Zinc_ ptk1
- **right**: _Acon_ b7a.de* agar b4a.de* _Agn_ b7a.de* alum b4a.de* am-c b4a.de* _Am-m_ b7a.de* _Ambr_ b7a.de* anac b4a.de* _Ang_ b7a.de* ant-c b7a.de* ant-t b7a.de* apis b7a.de* arg-met b7a.de* arn b7a.de* _Ars_ b4a.de* asaf b7a.de* asar b7a.de*

- **right**: ...
Aur b4a.de* bar-c b4a.de* **Bell** b4a.de* **Bism** b7a.de* *Borx* b4a.de* *Bov* b4a.de* brom b4a.de* **Bry** b7a.de* calad b7a.de* **Calc** b4a.de* camph b7a.de* **Cann-s** b7a.de* *Canth* b7a.de* caps b7a.de* carb-an b4a.de* *Carb-v* b4a.de* **Caust** b4a.de* *Cham* b7a.de* *Chel* b7a.de* chin b7a.de* cic b7a.de* cina b7a.de* clem b4a.de* *Cocc* b7a.de* coff b7a.de* *Colch* b7a.de* **Coloc** b4a.de* *Con* b4a.de* croc b7a.de* *Cupr* b7a.de* cycl b7a.de* *Dig* b4a.de* *Dros* b7a.de* *Dulc* b4a.de* euph b4a.de* euphr b7a.de* *Ferr* b7a.de* fl-ac b4a.de* **Graph** b4a.de* guaj bg2* hell b7a.de* hep b4a.de* hyos b7a.de* *Ign* b7a.de* iod b4a.de* *Ip* b7a.de* kali-c b4a.de* kali-n b4a.de* *Kreos* b7a.de* *Lach* b7a.de* laur b7a.de* led b7a.de* *Lyc* b4a.de* *M-ambo* b7a.de* m-arct b7a.de* m-aust b7a.de* *Mag-c* b4a.de* mag-m b4a.de* *Mang* b4a.de* meny b7a.de* merc b4a.de* mez b4a.de* mill b7a.de mosch b7a.de* mur-ac b4a.de* **Nat-c** b4a.de* *Nat-m* b4a.de* nit-ac b4a.de* nux-m b7a.de* *Nux-v* b7a.de* olnd b7a.de* *Op* b7a.de* par b7a.de* *Petr* b4a.de* ph-ac b4a.de* *Phos* b4a.de* plat b4a.de* *Plb* b7a.de* psor b4a.de* *Puls* b7a.de* ran-a ptk1 *Ran-b* b7a.de* **Ran-s** b7a.de* rheum b7a.de* rhod b4a.de* *Rhus-t* b7a.de* ruta b7a.de* *Sabad* b7a.de* sabin b7a.de* samb b7a.de* sang bg2 **Sars** b4a.de* **Sec** b7a.de* sel b7a.de* seneg b4a.de* sep b4a.de* *Sil* b4a.de* spig b7a.de* spong b7a.de* squil b7a.de* stann b4a.de* *Staph* b7a.de* stict bg2 stram b7a.de* **Stront-c** b4a.de* *Sul-ac* b4a.de* sulph b4a.de* tarax b7a.de* teucr b7a.de* thuj b4a.de* valer b7a.de* *Verat* b7a.de* verb b7a.de* viol-o b7a.de* viol-t b7a.de* zinc b4a.de*

▽ • **extending** to | **left**: fl-ac bg2

- **left**: *Acon* b7a.de* agar b4a.de* agn b7a.de* *Alum* b4a.de* am-c b4a.de* am-m b7a.de* ambr b7a.de* **Anac** b4a.de* ang b7a.de* ant-c b7a.de* *Ant-t* b7a.de* *Apis* b7a.de arg-met b7a.de* **Arn** b7a.de* *Ars* b4a.de* **Asaf** b7a.de* asar b7a.de* *Aur* b4a.de* *Bar-c* b4a.de* *Bell* b4a.de* bism b7a.de* borx b7a.de* bov b4a.de* brom b4a.de *Bry* b7a.de* cact ptk1 *Calad* b7a.de* *Calc* b4a.de* *Camph* fse1.de cann-s b7a.de* canth b7a.de* *Caps* b7a.de* carb-an b4a.de* *Carb-v* b4a.de* caust b4a.de* *Cham* b7a.de* chel b7a.de* *Chin* b7a.de* *Cic* b7a.de* cimic ptk1 *Cina* b7a.de* *Clem* b4a.de* *Cocc* b7a.de* *Coff* b7a.de* colch b7a.de* coloc b4a.de* *Con* b4a.de* *Croc* b7a.de* cupr b7a.de* *Cycl* b7a.de* *Dig* b4a.de* dros b7a.de* dulc b4a.de* euph b4a.de* euphr b7a.de* *Ferr* b7a.de* *Fl-ac* b4a.de graph b4a.de* guaj b4a.de* hell b7a.de* *Hep* b4a.de* *Hyos* b7a.de* *Ign* b7a.de* *Iod* b4a.de* ip b7a.de* **Kali-c** b4a.de* *Kali-n* b4a.de* kali-sula ptk1 *Kreos* b7a.de* *Lach* b7a.de* laur b7a.de* *Led* b7a.de* *Lyc* b4a.de* m-ambo b7a.de* *M-arct* b7a.de* **M-aust** b7a.de* *Mag-c* b4a.de* *Mag-m* b4a.de* mang b4a.de* *Meny* b7a.de* *Merc* b4a.de* mez b4a.de* mill b7a.de *Mosch* b7a.de* *Mur-ac* b4a.de* nat-c b4a.de* *Nat-m* b4a.de* **Nit-ac** b4a.de* *Nux-m* b7a.de* *Nux-v* b7a.de* *Olnd* b7a.de* *Op* b7a.de* par b7a.de* *Petr* b4a.de* *Ph-ac* b4a.de* *Phos* b4a.de* plat b4a.de* plb b7a.de* psor b4a.de *Puls* b7a.de* ran-b b7a.de* ran-s b7a.de* rheum b7a.de* rhod b4a.de* **Rhus-t** b7a.de* ruta b7a.de* sabad b7a.de* **Sabin** b7a.de* samb b7a.de* sars b4a.de* sec b7a.de* *Sel* b7a.de* *Seneg* b4a.de* *Sep* b4a.de* *Sil* b4a.de* *Spig* b7a.de* spong b7a.de* **Squil** b7a.de* **Stann** b4a.de* *Staph* b7a.de* **Stram** b7a.de* *Stront-c* b4a.de* sul-ac b4a.de* **Sulph** b4a.de* *Tarax* b7a.de* *Teucr* b7a.de* *Thuj* b4a.de* *Valer* b7a.de* *Verat* b7a.de* *Verb* b7a.de* viol-o b7a.de* *Viol-t* b7a.de* *Zinc* b4a.de*

- **accompanied** by:

▽ • **nausea**: *Ip* b7a.de

• **pain** in general (See GENERALS - Pain - accompanied - upper)

○ • **Heart**; complaints of (See CHEST - Heart; complaints - accompanied - upper - right - complaints)

• **Teeth**; complaints of (See TEETH - Complaints - accompanied - upper)

- **alternating** with | **Lower** limbs; complaints of: cocc ptk1 fago ptk1 kali-bi ptk1 kali-m ptk1 kalm ptk1 nat-c ptk1 *Sil* ptk1 *Valer* ptk1 visc ptk1

▽ - **extending** to:

○ • **Back**: caust bg2

• **Chest**: sulph bg2 vip bg2

⁝ **Sides** | **left**: caust bg2

• **Outward**: caust bg2

○ - **Bones**: acon b2.de* agar b2.de* alum b2.de* am-c b2.de* am-m b2.de* anac b2.de* ang b2.de* ant-t b2.de* arg-met b2.de* arn b2.de* **Asaf** b2.de* *Aur* b2.de* bar-c b2.de bell b2.de bism b2.de* bov b2.de* *Bry* b2.de* calc b2.de* canth b2.de* caps b7.de carb-an b2.de* *Carb-v* b2.de* caust b2.de* *Cham* b2.de* *Chel* bg2 *Chin* b2.de* **Cocc** b2.de* coloc b2.de* con b2.de* cupr b2.de* cycl b2.de* dig b2.de* *Dros* b2.de* dulc b2.de* euph b2.de* euphr bg2 hell b2.de* hep b2.de* ign b2.de* iod b2.de* ip b2.de* kali-c b2.de* kali-n bg2 *Lach* b2.de* laur b2.de*

Upper limbs – **Bones**: ...
led bg2 *Lyc* b2.de* m-arct b2.de* mag-c b2.de* mag-m bg2 *Mang* b2.de* *Merc* b2.de* mez b2.de* *Nat-c* b2.de* nat-m b2.de nit-ac b2.de* olnd b2.de* par b2.de* petr b2.de* *Ph-ac* b2.de* phos b2.de* plat b2.de* plb b2.de* *Puls* b2.de* ran-s bg2 rhod b2.de* **Rhus-t** b2.de* *Ruta* b2.de* sabad b2.de* *Sabin* b2.de* samb b2.de* sars b2.de* sep b2.de* *Sil* b2.de* spig b2.de spong b2.de* *Stann* bg2 *Staph* b2.de* stront-c b2.de* sul-ac b2.de* sulph b2.de* teucr b2.de* *Thuj* b2.de* valer b2.de* verat b2.de* verb b2.de* zinc b2.de*

- **Joints**: acon b2.de* agar b2.de* *Agn* b2.de* alum b2.de* *Am-c* b2.de* am-m b2.de* *Ambr* b2.de* anac b2.de* ang b2.de* ant-c b2.de* ant-t b2.de* arg-met b2.de* arn b2.de* ars b2.de* asaf b2.de* asar b2.de* aur b2.de* bar-c b2.de* bell b2.de* bism b2.de* borx b2.de* *Bov* b2.de* *Bry* b2.de* calad b2.de* **Calc** b2.de* camph b2.de* cann-s b2.de* canth b2.de* caps b2.de* carb-an b2.de* *Carb-v* b2.de* **Caust** b2.de* cham b2.de* chel b2.de* chin b2.de* cic b2.de* cina b2.de* clem b2.de* cocc b2.de* coff b2.de* colch b2.de* coloc b2.de* con b2.de* croc b2.de* cupr b2.de* cycl b2.de* dig b2.de* *Dros* b2.de* dulc b2.de* euph b2.de* euphr b2.de* ferr b2.de* *Graph* b2.de* guaj b2.de* *Hell* b2.de* hep b2.de* hyos b2.de* *Ign* b2.de* iod b2.de* **Kali-c** b2.de* *Kali-n* b2.de* kreos b2.de* lach b2.de* laur b2.de* **Led** b2.de* **Lyc** b2.de* *M-ambo* b2.de m-arct b2.de m-aust b2.de mag-c b2.de* mag-m b2.de* *Mang* b2.de* meny b2.de* **Merc** b2.de* mez b2.de* mosch b2.de* mur-ac b2.de* nat-c b2.de* *Nat-m* b2.de* nit-ac b2.de* nux-m b2.de* nux-v b2.de* olnd b2.de* op b2.de* par b2.de* *Petr* b2.de* ph-ac b2.de* *Phos* b2.de* plat b2.de* plb b2.de* *Puls* b2.de* ran-b b2.de* ran-s b2.de* rheum b2.de* *Rhod* b2.de* **Rhus-t** b2.de* *Ruta* b2.de* sabad b2.de* *Sabin* b2.de* samb b2.de* sars b2.de* sec b2.de* sel b2.de* seneg b2.de* **Sep** b2.de* *Sil* b2.de* *Spig* b2.de* spong b2.de* squil b2.de* *Stann* b2.de* *Staph* b2.de* *Stront-c* b2.de* *Sul-ac* b2.de* **Sulph** b2.de* tarax b2.de* teucr b2.de* *Thuj* b2.de* valer b2.de* verat b2.de* verb b2.de* viol-o b2.de* viol-t b2.de* *Zinc* b2.de*

- **Single** parts | **alternating** between single parts: fl-ac bg2

- **Veins**: nux-v ptk1 plb ptk1 *Puls* ptk1 thyr ptk1

WRIST; complaints of: *Acon* b2.de* agn b2.de* alum b2.de* **Am-c** b2.de* am-m b2.de* ambr b2.de* *Anac* b2.de* ant-c b2.de* ant-t b2.de* arg-met b2.de* arn b2.de* ars b2.de* *Asaf* b2.de* asar b2.de* aur b2.de* bar-c b2.de* bell b2.de* bism b2.de* **Bov** b2.de* *Bry* b2.de* **Calc** b2.de* *Calc-p* bg2 canth b2.de* caps b2.de* carb-an b2.de* carb-v b2.de* **Caust** b2.de* cham b2.de* chel b2.de* chin b2.de* cic b2.de* cina b2.de* clem b2.de* colch b2.de* coloc b2.de* con b2.de* croc b2.de* cycl b2.de* dig b2.de* dros b2.de* dulc b2.de* euph b2.de* euphr b2.de* *Graph* b2.de* guaj b2.de* hell b2.de* hep b2.de* hyos b2.de* ign b2.de* iod b2.de* **Kali-c** b2.de* *Kali-n* b2.de* kreos b2.de* *Lach* b2.de* laur b2.de* led b2.de* lyc b2.de* m-ambo b2.de m-arct b2.de* mag-c b2.de* mag-m b2.de* mang b2.de* meny b2.de* merc b2.de* mez b2.de* nat-c b2.de* nat-m b2.de* nit-ac b2.de* nux-v b2.de* petr b2.de* ph-ac b2.de* phos b2.de* plb b2.de* puls b2.de* ran-b b2.de* ran-s b2.de* rheum b2.de* *Rhod* b2.de* **Rhus-t** b2.de* **Ruta** b2.de* sabad b2.de* **Sabin** b2.de* samb b2.de* *Sars* b2.de* sec b2.de* sel b2.de* seneg b2.de* **Sep** b2.de* sil b2.de* spig b2.de* spong b2.de* squil b2.de* stann b2.de* staph b2.de* stront-c b2.de* sul-ac b2.de* **Sulph** b2.de* tarax b2.de* teucr b2.de* thuj b2.de* valer b2.de* verb b2.de* viol-o b7.de* viol-t b2.de zinc b2.de*

- **right**: ox-ac ptk1 viol-o ptk1

Extremities

AFFECTED (See Disturbed)

ALTERNATING with: | **rage** (See MIND - Rage - alternating - sleep)

ANXIOUS: (↗*DREAMS - Anxious; DREAMS - Nightmares)* *Acon* b2.de* aids nl2• **Ars** b2.de* aster kr1 *Bell* b2.de* bry j5.de cham b2.de* *Cocc* b2.de* dor a1 dulc b2.de* ferr b2.de* *Hep* b2.de* ip b2.de* *Kali-c* b2.de* *Kali-i* kr1 kali-n j5.de lat-m jl3 mag-c j5.de mand rsj7• merc b2.de* *Merc-c* kr1 *Nat-c* j5.de nit-ac bg2 op b2.de* petr b2.de* positr nl2• rhus-t b2.de* samb b2.de* sil a1 verat b2.de* zinc kr1 [heroin sdj2]
- **morning**; towards: inul a1
- **wake** up on time; to (See MIND - Anxiety - time - wake)

ASLEEP, falling (See Falling)

AWAKE during sleep; sensation as if he was (See Conscious)

AWARE of one's surroundings during sleep (See Conscious)

BAD: (↗*Confused; Disturbed; Interrupted; Restless; Unrefreshing)* acet-ac sf1.de *Agar* k* agath-a nl2• aloe ange-s jl3 arist-cl mg1.de asar j5.de* *Bamb-a* stb2.de• bell j5.de bell-p mg1.de caj a1 canth k* chin a1 choc srj3• cob ptm1• des-ac jl3 dirc k* ferr-i k* gran a1 gymno ham k* hippoc-k szs2 inul k* iod k* *Kola* stb3• lac-e hrn2• lach k* lyc a1 lycps-v a1 mag-c k* mec a1 melal-alt gya4 meli a1 merc k* merc-c a1 mill mit a1 *Moni* rfm1• morph a1 naja nat-ar nit-ac k* nux-v a1 olib-sac wmh1 rib-ac jl3 spong fd4.de tab k* trif-p a1 tub jl2 vanil fd5.de [bell-p-sp dcm1 beryl stj2]
- **midnight**:
  - **before**: naja a1
  - **after**: arum-d a1 merc a1 **Rhus-t** a1
- **morning** | **amel.**: lyc a1
- **menses**; before: arist-cl mg1.de
- **sleepiness** in evening, after: aloe a1

CATNAPS (See Short - catnaps)

CHILL; sleeps during (See Falling - chill)

CLAIRVOYANT STATE, like a: com a1 stann j5.de

COMA VIGIL: (↗*Comatose; MIND - Coma)* **Acon** b2.de* *Agar* b2.de* alum b2.de* *Anac* b2.de* ang b2.de* ant-c b2.de* ars j5.de bell b2.de* *Bry* b2.de* camph b7.de* *Cham* b7.de* chin b7.de *Cocc* b7.de* croc b2.de* cur a1* cycl b2.de* hell a1* hydr-ac j5.de* hyos b7.de* ign b2.de* lach b2.de* laur b7.de* lon-x c1* lyc b2.de* m-ambo b2.de* *M-arct* b2.de merc-c bg2 mosch b7a.de mur-ac ptk1* nat-m b2.de* nux-m bg2 nux-v a1 olnd b7.de **Op** b2.de* petr b2.de* *Phos* b2.de* plat b2.de* ran-s b7.de rheum b2.de* rob a1 ruta b7.de sep b2.de* sil b2.de* spig b2.de* *Spong* b2.de* stann b2.de* staph b7.de stram b2.de* *Sulph* b2.de* teucr b2.de* verat b7.de* zinc-s mtf

COMATOSE: (↗*Coma vigil; Deep; Heavy; Oppressive; Prolonged; Waking - difficult; MIND - Coma)* acon k* aeth k* *Agar* k* *Agn* k* **Ail** bg2 alco a1 anac b2.de* ang b2.de* *Ant-c* k* **Ant-t** k* *Anthraci* kr1 *Apis* k* **Arg-n** k* *Arn* k* *Ars* k* ars-s-f k2* *Art-v* hr1* *Asaf* k* atra-r bnm3• atro hr1* aur aur-ar k2 aur-m k* aur-s k2 **Bapt** k* *Bar-c* k* **Bell** k* benzol br1 *Borx* *Bry* k* *Bufo* *Calad* k* *Calc* b2.de* *Camph* k* canth j5.de *Caps* j5.de* carb-ac k* carb-v b2.de* casc j5.de *Caust* k* *Cench* st1 cerv a1 cham k* *Chin* k* chlf *Chlol* k* *Chlor* *Cic* k* *Cimic* clem b2.de* cocc k* *Colch* coloc k* *Con* k* **Croc** k* *Crot-c* *Crot-h* k* cub k* *Cupr* k* cupr-act kr1 cupr-c j5.de cycl b2.de* cyt-l mg1.de *Dig* k* diph-pert-t mp4• *Dor* k* dulc a1 euph b2.de* euphr b2.de* ferr b2.de* ferr-p bg2 *Gels* k* *Graph* b2.de* *Grat* j5.de* *Hell* k* *Hep* b2.de* hydr-ac j5.de hyos k* *Ign* b2.de* *Iris* kr1 kali-br hr1 kali-c b2.de* kali-chl j5.de *Kali-i* hr1* kali-n k* *Kali-perm* kr1 kreos ptk1 *Lach* k* *Lact* j5.de* *Laur* k* *Led* k* lup j5.de *Lyc* k* m-ambo b2.de* m-arct b2.de* merc k* merc-c b4a.de* *Merc-cy* hr1* mosch k* *Mur-ac* hr1* naja gm1 *Nat-m* k* nit-ac b2.de* **Nux-m** k* nux-v k* *Oena* sne olnd b2.de* **Op** k* petr b2.de* petr-ra shn4• *Ph-ac* k* *Phos* k* *Phys* hr1* plat j5.de* *Plb* k* *Puls* k* pycnop-sa mrz1 ran-b b2.de* *Rhus-t* k* ruta b2.de* sabad j5.de *Sec* k* *Seneg* b2.de* sep k* spig b2.de* spong hr1* stann b2.de* *Stram* k* *Sulph* k* tab bg2 *Tarent* hr1* ter k* thal-xyz srj8• ther hr1 urt-u hr1* valer b2.de* **Verat** k* vip j5.de *Zinc* k* zinc-p k2 zing k*
- **day** and night: anac j5.de bar-c lup j5.de
- **daytime**: aeth j5.de dig j5.de hep j5.de lup j5.de plb hr1* sabad j5.de
- **morning**: **Calc-p** sne euphr h2 *Nux-v* hr1* phos
  - **sunrise**, after: euphr b7.de* m-ambo b7.de* merc bg2 nux-v b7.de* puls b7.de*
- **forenoon**: ant-c b7a.de* ant-t verat j5.de

Comatose – forenoon: ...
  - **all** forenoon: sel a1
- **noon**: ther hr1*
- **afternoon**: euph j5.de kali-c j5.de zing k*
- **evening**: ant-t ars k* asaf j5.de verat j5.de
  - **to** evening; from evening: lup j5.de
- **night**: **Puls** hr1*
- **accompanied** by:
  - **bronchitis** (See CHEST - Inflammation - bronchial - accompanied - sleep; comatose)
  - **cough** (See COUGH - Accompanied - sleep; comatose)
- **alternating** with:
  - **delirium** (See MIND - Delirium - alternating - sleep - comatose)
  - **sleeplessness**: *Camph*
- **apoplexy**, in: *Crot-h* hr1* *Op* j5.de
- **children**; in: sep j5.de
- **continued**: (↗*Prolonged)* anac j5.de lach j5.de op j5.de
  - **three** days: *Hyos* kr1 *Verat* j5.de
  - **two** days: hyos j5.de
  - **week**, a whole: *Hell* hr1*
- **convulsions**: (↗*Falling - convulsions)*
  - **after**: *Atro* hr1* *Bufo* kr1 *Caust* hr1* *Cic* sne cupr sne *Ign* hr1* *Kali-br* hr1* *Oena* sne plb hr1*
  - **before**: *Sulph* hr1*
  - **between**: agar aur *Bufo* *Ign* **Oena** **Op** k* plb
  - **during**: op b7a.de* *Plat* hr1* *Sulph* hr1* vip-a j5.de
- **delirium**; with: acon j5.de ant-c j5.de **Ant-t** hr1* arn j5.de **Bapt** hr1* *Bry* j5.de* camph j5.de coloc j5.de puls j5.de sec j5.de *Verat* hr1*
- **delivery**; during: lach
- **dinner**; after: dig j5.de ign j5.de
- **eating**; after: rhus-t b7a.de
- **eruptions**; after suppressed: *Zinc*
- **eyes**:
  - **one** eye open: verat j5.de
  - **open**, with: caps j5.de coloc j5.de samb j5.de
  - **opening** difficult: aeth j5.de cham j5.de cocc j5.de m-arct j5.de
- **fever**; before: puls b7a.de
- **heat**; with: *Acon* bg2 *Agar* hr1* anac j5.de **Ant-t** b7.de* **Apis** bg2 bell j5.de* bry j5.de calc bg2 *Camph* bg2 cham j5.de cic bg2 coloc j5.de con bg2 croc bg2 gels k2 hep bg2 hyos bg2 ign bg2 led bg2 *Nux-m* bg2 *Op* b7.de* *Ph-ac* bg2 *Phos* bg2 *Puls* j5.de* rhus-t bg2 sec bg2 spong bg2* stram bg2 *Tarent* hr1* valer bg2 *Verat* bg2
- **hunger**; with: bell j5.de
- **pain**; after: lach j5.de
- **periodical** | **day**; every third: sep
- **perspiration** during the night; with: chin b7.de op b7.de **Puls** b7.de* rhus-t b7.de
- **respiration**, with ailments of: acon j5.de cham j5.de op j5.de stram j5.de vip j5.de
- **sitting** agg.: aur j5.de*
- **snoring**, with: bell j5.de carb-v j5.de laur j5.de *Op* j5.de* rhus-t j5.de *Stram* j5.de
- **sudden**: m-arct j5.de
- **sunstroke**, from: *Op* hr1*
- **thirst**; with: anac j5.de bell j5.de cham j5.de op j5.de verat j5.de
- **uremia**, in: agar kr1 anac kr1 ars kr1 aur kr1 lach st lact kr1 op kr1 plb tl1 ter kr1
- **vomiting**:
  - **after**: aeth ptk1 *Cupr* hr1*
  - **with**: dig j5.de vip-a j5.de
- **yawning**; with: (↗*Yawning - coma)* cimic ptk1 laur j5.de

CONFUSED: (↗*Bad)* dios a1 kali-bi a1 lyc a1 op a1
- **alternating** with:
  - **delusions** | **morning**, before 6 h (See MIND - Delusions - night - towards - alternating - sleep)

CONSCIOUS sleep: (↗*MIND - Awareness)* lavand-a ctl1• m-aust cea1 morph a1

CONVULSIONS; sleeps during (See Falling - convulsions)

DEEP: *(↗Comatose; Heavy; Oppressive; Waking - difficult)* acon b2.de* aesc k* aeth k* aether a1 agar k* agar-cit a1 agn b2.de* *Aids* nl2• ail k* alco a1 all-c k* *Alum* k* alum-p k2* am-c bro1 ambr j5.de* ampe-qu a1 amyg a1 anac k* androc srj1• ant-c k* ant-s-aur a1* **Ant-t** k* *Apis* k* apoc aran k* **Arg-n** k* arge-pl rwt5• *Arn* k* *Ars* k* ars-s-f k2* atha j5.de* atro k* aur aur-ar k2 **Bapt** k* *Bar-c* k* bar-s k2* **Bell** k* ben-n a1 benz-ac k* berb bit-ar wht1• borx b2.de* bov j5.de brom k* brucel sa3• brucin a1 *Bry* k* cact *Calad* calam sa3• *Calc* k* *Camph* k* cann-i k* canth j5.de carb-ac k* **Carb-v** carbn-dox knl3• **Carbn-h Carbn-o Carbn-s** carc zzh *Cardios-h* rly4• *Carl* k* *Caust* k* cedr k* *Cench* k2* cere-b a1 cham k* *Chel* k* *Chin* k* chin-b hr1 chinin-ar chinin-s k* chlf k* chlol k* *Chlor* hr1* choc srj3• chord-umb rly4• *Cic* k* *Cina Cinch* a1 cinnm k* cob-n sp1* coca coca-c sk4• cocc k* coch hr1* coff j5.de *Colch* k* **Con** k* conch fkr1• corn k* **Croc** k* crot-c a1 *Crot-h* crot-t k* cund a1 *Cupr* k* cupr-act a1 *Cycl* k* cyclosp sa3• dat-m a1 des-ac rbp6 dig k* digin a1 dios hr1* dulc fd4.de elaps erig mg1.de eug k* euph k* falco-pe nl2* ferr-ma a1 *Fl-ac* k* galeoc-c-h gms1• *Gels* k* ger-i rly4• gins j5.de* glon k* granit-m es1• **Graph** k* grat k* guan a1 haliae-lc srj5• ham fd3.de• *Hell* k* helodr-cal knl2• *Hep* hippoc-k szs2 hydr-ac hr1* *Hydrog* srj2• *Hyos* k* *Ign* k* ina-i mlk9.de jab k* jac-c a1 jal a1 kali-bi bg2 kali-br k* kali-i k* *Kali-n* kali-p kali-s fd4.de ketogl-ac rly4• **Kreos** k* lac-h htj1• *Lac-loxod-a* hrn2• *Lach* k* *Lact* k* lact-v bro1 *Laur* k* **Led** k* lepi a1 linu-c a1 lob k* lol a1 lon-x a1* luna kg1• lup bro1 *Lyc* k* *M-ambo* b2.de* *M-arct* b2.de* mag-c mg1.de **Merc** k* *Merc-c* k* mez j5.de morph k* *Mosch* b2.de* musca-d szs1 nad rly4• *Naja* k* nat-ar nat-c k* *Nat-m* nat-p nat-sil fd3.de• nep srb2.fr **Nux-m** k* **Nux-v** olib-sac wmh1 **Op** k* ox-ac k* peti a1 petr b2.de* petr-ra shn4• *Ph-ac* k* phor-t mie3• *Phos* k* *Phys* k* pip-m k* pisc a1* plac-s rly4• plat j5.de *Plb* k* plut-n srj7• *Podo* k* positr nl2• pot-e rly4• psor ptel hr1* **Puls** k* rad-br sze8• *Rhod* k* *Rhus-t* k* ruta b2.de* sabad b2.de* sacch-a fd2.de• sal-fr sle1• *Sec* k* sel b2.de* *Seneg* k* *Sep* b2.de* sinus rly4• sol-mm j5.de* sol-ni spig k* spong stann k* *Stram* k* suis-pan rly4• sul-ac *Sulph* k* symph fd3.de• tab k* tarent hr1 tax k* ther k* thioc-ac rly4• thuj hr1* tritic-vg fd5.de *Valer* k* vanil fd5.de vario hr1 **Verat** k* verat-v a1 xan hr1* *Zinc* k* [alumin-s stj2 aur-s stj2 calc-n stj1 chr-s stj2 cinnb stj2 gal-s stj2 lith-s stj2 mang-p stj2 mang-s stj2 mang-sil stj2 nicc-s stj2 tung-met stj2]

- **daytime**: ant-t j5.de borx j5.de dig j5.de erig mg1.de eug j5.de* ign j5.de ketogl-ac rly4• *Lact* j5.de led manc k* *Merc* j5.de *Ph-ac* h2* phos k* pycnop-sa mrz1 sel j5.de tab j5.de
- **morning**●: alum k* bell brom bry calc calc-ar k* **Calc-p** carbn-s con k* cortiso gse gels hr1* gins k* *Graph* k* hep kali-s fd4.de led lyc h2* m-arct j5.de nat-c j5.de **Nux-v** k ●* op ph-ac j5.de phos **Sulph** k ●* thuj k*
  - **6** h: atro kr1 calad euphr
- **forenoon** | **10** h: peti a1
- **noon**: eug k* eup-per hr1* ketogl-ac rly4•
  - **and** afternoon: borx j5.de eug j5.de ign j5.de sel j5.de tab j5.de
- **afternoon**: borx j5.de euph k* (non:euphr kl) ign j5.de merc-i-r k* nad rly4• osteo-a jl2 petr-ra shn4• sel sil k*
  - **catalepsy**; after: grat k*
  - **heat**; after: cina
- **evening**: arg-n k* *Ars* astac a1 *Lyc* a1* sacch-a fd2.de•
  - **first** sleep, in the: ambr h1 aur h2 bell h1 cycl h1 mang h2 puls h1 thuj h1
- **night**: asc-c hr1* chord-umb rly4• osteo-a jl2 tab hr1*
  - **midnight**:
    - **before**: rhod
    - **after**: nat-m stram j5.de
      - **3** h; until: bapt a1
      - **morning** toward | **amel.**: op a1
      - **5** h | **after**: phys
  - **sleeplessness**; after: *Nep* mg1.de*
- **accompanied** by:
  - **diphtheria** (See THROAT - Diphtheria - accompanied - sleep)
  - ○ **Brain**; inflammation of (See HEAD - Inflammation - brain - accompanied - sleep)
  - **Lungs**; inflammation of (See CHEST - Inflammation - lungs - accompanied - sleep)
- **alternating** with:
  - **delirium** (See MIND - Delirium - alternating - sleep - deep)

Deep – alternating with: ...

  - **excitement** (See MIND - Excitement - alternating - sleep; deep)
  - **headache** and dyspnea: plb a1
  - **respiration**; difficult (See RESPIRATION - Difficult - alternating - sleep)
  - **sleeplessness**, periods of: benz-ac k2
- **amenorrhea**, in: *Cina* kr1
- **beer**; after: sulph a1
- **children**; in: (non:cupr k*) cupr-act a1*
- **chill**:
  - **after**: *Ars*
  - **during**: bell *Hep* laur *Nat-m Nux-m* hr1* **Op** k*
- **coma** vigil, after: hell a1
- **convulsions**:
  - **after**: aeth sf *Bufo* canth *Caust* cupr sne cupr-act bro1 dat-s a1 *Hell Hyos* k* *Ign Lach* **Nux-v** *Oena* **Op** k* plb sec *Sulph* tarent zinc bro1
    - **epileptic**: aeth bro1 hyos bro1 kali-br bro1 lach bro1 *Op* bro1
  - **between**: agar *Bufo Ign* **Oena Op** plb
- **delirium**:
  - **after**: *(↗reflexes - delirium)* agar br1 bry phos stram a1
  - **during**: cocc plb stram vip
- **dinner**; after: agar k* chel k* til k*
- **disturbed**, yet: dulc fd4.de kali-br hr1*
- **drunken**, as if: kali-n a1 *Led* b7a.de *Nux-m* b7a.de
- **excitement** or exertion, from: *Podo* hr1*
- **exhausting** | **dreams**; with: zinc kr1
- **fear** of death, after: vario hr1*
- **heat**:
  - **after**: *Cina* hr1
  - **during**: *All-c* **Apis** aran *Arn* ars cact *Calad* chinin-ar con gels k2 ign *Lach* hr1* laur *Mez Nux-m* hr1* *Nux-v* **Op** k* *Phos* **Rob** sec sep spong syph al
- **interrupted** by dreams, with chilliness: *Lyc* hr1*
- **menses**; during: **Nux-m** k* *Phos* k* sulph
- **old** people; in: op ptk1
- **palpitations**; with: *Podo* hr1*
- **rage**, after: sec hr1*
- **reflexes**; with diminished | **delirium**; after: *(↗delirium - after)* agar br1
- **sitting** agg.: ox-ac
- **spells** of deep sleep with snoring and stertorous breathing: laur br1
- **sudden**: chin-b hr1*
- **unrefreshing**: *Granit-m* es1• mand rsj7• melal-alt gya4 musca-d szs1 pic-ac ptk1 ruta fd4.de *Zinc* hr1*
- **uremia**, in: agar anac ars aur-m kr1 bell lach st1 lact op ter kr1
- **vomiting**:
  - **after**: crot-t
  - **between**: cic-m a1
- **writing** agg.: ph-ac

DELIRIOUS: ail k2* morph a1 sal-fr sle1• vanil fd5.de

DISTURBED: *(↗Bad; Interrupted; Light; Restless; Restless - dreams; Waking - frequent)* acon k* acon-c a1 agath-a nl2• ail k* alco a1 alum k2* alum-sil k2 amn-l sp1 amph a1 ange-s jl3 anis a1 *Apis* arist-m a1 arn k* *Ars* k* asaf k* *Asar* mrr1 aster k* aur-m-n wbt2• bar-act a1* (non:bar-c k*) bell k* bell-p sp1 bit-ar wht1• borx mrr1 brass-n-o srj5• cact k* calad k* calc k2 *Calc-p* carc mg1.de* cassia-s cdd7*• chlorpr pin1• cit-v br1 *Clem* br1 cob k* coca corn-a br1 cortiso jl3 cupr-ar k* cystein-l rly4• del a1 dig k* dirc k* dulc k* equis-h a1 fago k* form k* gels k2 **Graph** k* haliae-lc srj5• ham k* hippoc-k szs2 hyos k* iber a1 ind a1 jab a1 jac-c a1 jal a1 (non:kali-bi k*) kali-br a1* kali-i k* kali-s fd4.de *Lac-h* sk4• *Laur* lavand-a ctl1• loxo-recl bnm10• lycps-v m-arct c1* macro a1 mag-m mrr1 mand rsj7• merc k* moni rfm1• morph k* myris a1 naja nat-ar nat-m k* op k* perh jl3 petr-ra shn4• phasco-ci rbp2 phys k* pip-m a1 pitu-gl skp7• plan k* plb k* plect a1 polyp-p a1 positr nl2• (non:puls k*) puls-n a1* ran-b k* rhus-g a1 ruta fd4.de santin a1 sarcol-ac sp1 sel rsj9• sep k* sol-t-ae a1 spong fd4.de staph hr1 stram mrr1 suis-em rly4• **Sulph** k* tab k* tetox pin2• thea a1 tritic-vg fd5.de vanil fd5.de vesp k* [heroin sdj2 sol-ecl cky1]

Disturbed: ...
- **morning**: rhod a1 sabin k*
  - **7-8 h**: coca-c sk4•
- **night**: hir skp7•
  - **midnight**: dendr-pol sk4• [sol-ecl cky1]
    - **before**: calc-p phyt
    - **after**: med jl2 sapin a1 stront-c a1
      - **2 h**: bung-fa mtf
      - **2-3 h**: luf-op rsj5•
      - **3 h**: lac-h sk4•
        - **3-5 h**: cimic
      - **4 h**: borx mrr1 med jl2
      - **5 h**: ham lavand-a ctl1•
- **anxiety**, from: *(↗Sleeplessness - anxiety)* *Acon* j5.de alum j5.de am-c j5.de ambr j5.de ant-c j5.de aq-mar rbp6 arg-met j5.de *Ars* h2* bar-c j5.de *Bell* j5.de bov j5.de *Bry* j5.de calc j5.de calc-f sp1 cann-s j5.de carb-an j5.de *Carb-v* j5.de carc mlr1• *Castm* j5.de *Caust* j5.de cham j5.de *Chin* j5.de *Cocc* j5.de coff j5.de con j5.de cycl a1 dig j5.de dulc j5.de *Ferr* j5.de *Graph* j5.de *Hep* j5.de *Hyos* j5.de *Ign* j5.de *Kali-c* j5.de kreos j5.de lach j5.de lact j5.de lyc j5.de *Mag-c* j5.de mag-m j5.de mang j5.de *Merc* j5.de merc-c j5.de nat-c j5.de *Nat-m* j5.de nat-sil fd3.de• nicc j5.de *Nit-ac* j5.de nux-v j5.de petr j5.de ph-ac j5.de phel j5.de *Phos* j5.de plat j5.de positr nl2• puls j5.de ran-s j5.de rat j5.de sabin j5.de *Sep* j5.de *Sil* j5.de spong j5.de squil j5.de stront-c j5.de *Sulph* j5.de tab j5.de verat h1* zinc j5.de [heroin sdj2]
  - **moon**; full: sulph j5.de
- **childbed**, in (See delivery)
- **children**; in: | **newborns**: *Cham* hr1*
- **chill**; during: alum j5.de *Am-c* j5.de calc j5.de caust j5.de daph j5.de graph j5.de grat j5.de hep j5.de mag-c j5.de nat-c j5.de *Phos* j5.de rhus-t j5.de sep j5.de sil j5.de *Sulph* j5.de verat j5.de
- **ciphers** before the eyes; by: ph-ac sulph j5.de
- **coldness**; during: ars j5.de borx j5.de cor-r j5.de euphr j5.de ferr-ma j5.de kali-c j5.de kreos j5.de mang j5.de nit-ac j5.de sabad j5.de sars j5.de sulph j5.de tab j5.de tart-ac j5.de
- **congestion**, by: alumn am-c j5.de asar j5.de borx j5.de bruc j5.de *Bry* j5.de calc j5.de carb-an j5.de dulc j5.de graph j5.de hep j5.de ign j5.de mag-c j5.de medul-os-si rly4• *Merc* j5.de mur-ac j5.de *Nat-m* j5.de phos j5.de rhus-t j5.de sabin j5.de samb j5.de senn j5.de *Sil* j5.de sulph j5.de
- **convulsions**, by: cocc j5.de hyos j5.de kali-c j5.de mag-c j5.de *Puls* j5.de *Rhus-t* j5.de *Sil* j5.de
- **cough**, by: *(↗COUGH - Sleep - disturbing)* *Acon* a1 agar j5.de alum j5.de am-m j5.de apis b7a.de arn b7.de* ars j5.de calc bg2 caust j5.de cham b7.de* *Cina* hr1 con j5.de hep j5.de *Hyos* b7a.de kali-c j5.de kali-n a1 *Lach* b7.de* lact j5.de lyc j5.de m-ambo b7.de m-aust b7.de mag-s a1 mur-ac j5.de nat-c j5.de* nat-m j5.de nat-sil fd3.de• *Nit-ac* j5.de rhod a1 *Sep* j5.de *Sil* j5.de sul-ac j5.de *Sulph* j5.de tritic-vg fd5.de [heroin sdj2]
- **delirium**; during: *Acon* j5.de arn j5.de *Bry* j5.de coloc j5.de kali-c j5.de *Nux-v* j5.de op j5.de *Puls* j5.de sec j5.de sulph j5.de
- **delivery**; after: lyc j5.de
- **delusions**; by: bell j5.de canth j5.de carb-v j5.de cham j5.de colch j5.de dulc j5.de merc j5.de par j5.de *Plb* hr1* sulph j5.de
- **dreams**, by: abrom-a ks5 absin vh1 acon k* agar agath-a nl2• alco a1 allox sp1* *Alum* kr1 *Alumn* hr1 am-c gsy1 am-m j5.de ambr k* ammc j5.de* ang j5.de* ant-s-aur kr1 **Ant-t** j5.de* *Apis* b7a.de* aran-ix mg1.de* arg-met jl *Arg-n* hr1* arn k* *Ars* k* ars-s-r hr1* atro k* bell k* benz-ac k* berb hr1* bol-la a1* bond a1 bov hr1* brach hr1* bruc j5.de bry k* cact k* cain kr1 *Calc* j5.de* calc-ar k2 calc-f hr1* calc-p k* calc-s hr1* calen hr1* camph b7a.de cann-i hr1* *Caps* hr1* carb-an j5.de *Carb-v* h2* carbn-s *Card-m* a1* carl k* castor-eq kr1 caust j5.de cham k* *Chel* hr1* *Chin* j5.de chinin-s j5.de chir-fl gya2 cimic k* cit-v hr1* *Clem* j5.de* cob a1 coc-c k* cocc j5.de* coff j5.de coloc k* com hr1* *Con* h2* cor-r j5.de *Corn* a1* croc j5.de crot-t k* (non:cupr k*) cupr-act a1* *Cycl* k* cyt-l sp1 daph j5.de dig k* digin a1 digox a1 dios hr1* dulc k* euphr k* *Ferr* k* ferr-i k* flor-p rsj3• gamb k* gast a1 glon k* *Gran* j5.de *Graph* k* guare hr1* ham a1* hell k* *Hep* j5.de hir jl3 hydrog srj2• iber a1* ign k* ind a1 iod hr1* iodof hr1* jab a1 kali-ar k2* kali-c jl3 kali-chl j5.de* kali-s fd4.de kreos j5.de kres mg1.de *Lach* hr1* *Laur* *Lob* j5.de lyc k* lycps-v kr1 lyss m-arct j5.de mag-c k* mag-m j5.de mag-s k* mand sp1* *Menis* a1 merc k* merc-sul hr1* mez j5.de mosch j5.de mur-ac k* *Murx* hr1* myric a1 nat-c j5.de nat-m k* *Nat-s* j5.de nat-sil fd3.de• nicc j5.de nit-ac k* nux-m j5.de nux-v k* op k* paeon k* par k* peti a1 petr j5.de petr-ra shn4• ph-ac j5.de *Phos* j5.de* pip-m a1 plan hr1* plat j5.de plb k* prun j5.de psil ft1 psor k* ptel k* *Puls* j5.de* *Pycnop-sa* mrz1 *Raph* hr1* rauw tpw8* rhod k* rhus-g a1

- **dreams**, by: ... *Rhus-t* j5.de* rhus-v hr1* sabad j5.de sabin j5.de* sec j5.de sel j5.de* seneg j5.de *Sep* j5.de* *Sil* j5.de* sin-n k* sol-ni solin a1 spig k* *Spong* k* staph h1 stront-c j5.de sulph k* tab k* tarax hr1* *Tarent* hr1* tell rsj10• *Ter* j5.de* teucr j5.de *Thuj* j5.de* tril-p c1 trios rsj11• v-a-b jl3 valer k* vanil fd5.de vario hr1* ven-m rsj12• verat j5.de verb j5.de visc c1 wies a1 *Zinc* j5.de* zinc-o j5.de zinc-ox j5.de
  - **morning**: aur hr1* cham a1 *Cycl* hr1* *Fl-ac* hr1* jab a1 *Kali-chl* a1* *Kali-m* kr1
  - **noon**: ther hr1*
    - **sleep** | **siesta**; during: **Nat-m** hr1*
  - **night**:
    - **midnight**:
      - **before**: *Chel* hr1*
      - **after**: ph-ac hr1* stront-c a1
        - **5 h**: ham a1
  - **amorous**: lith-c a1* *Sil* hr1
  - **exciting**: carc sp1
  - **frightful**: alumn hr1* aran-ix mg1.de calc-f sp1 kres mg1.de lach k2 mand rsj7• mim-p rsj8• petros hr1* sec a1
  - **menses**; during: *Kali-c* hr1*
- **driven** out of bed; sensation of being: rhus-t j5.de
- **easily**: agath-a nl2• coff j5.de* cortico mg1.de cortiso mg1.de* *Lach* j5.de *Lyc* j5.de merc j5.de nicc j5.de *Op* sf1.de puls j5.de saroth mg1.de sel sf1.de *Sulph* sf1.de
- **erections**; during: *(↗Restless - sexual)* alum j5.de* ambr j5.de ant-c j5.de aur j5.de carb-v j5.de *Caust* b4a.de chin b7.de* coloc j5.de dig b4a.de hep j5.de kali-c j5.de lach j5.de led j5.de lith-c kr1 merc b4.de* merc-act j5.de *Nat-c* j5.de nat-m j5.de* *Nit-ac* b4a.de ol-an j5.de op j5.de par j5.de ph-ac b4.de* pic-ac hr1* plat j5.de plb j5.de ran-b j5.de sep j5.de *Sil* j5.de *Stann* j5.de thuj b4.de*
  - **painful**: cact hr1*
- **fainting**, by: ars j5.de bar-c j5.de calc j5.de carb-v j5.de *Sep* j5.de sil j5.de *Ther* j5.de
- **fear**; by: am-c j5.de bell j5.de *Con* j5.de ip j5.de lyc j5.de merc j5.de nat-c j5.de nat-m j5.de ph-ac j5.de phos j5.de rat j5.de *Sil* j5.de stann j5.de *Sulph* j5.de zinc j5.de
  - **apoplexy**, of: arn j5.de carb-v j5.de nat-c j5.de
  - **future**, of the: dulc j5.de
  - **ghosts**; of: cocc j5.de sulph j5.de
  - **mice**, of: colch j5.de
  - **robbers**, of: merc j5.de nat-m j5.de sil j5.de
- **fever**; after: *Chin* b7a.de
- **flatulence**; from: *(↗Sleeplessness - flatulence; ABDOMEN - Flatulence - sleep - preventing)* nux-m a1
- **heat**; by: alum j5.de am-c j5.de anac b4a.de* arn j5.de *Ars* j5.de *Bar-c* j5.de *Bell* j5.de borx j5.de *Bry* b7.de* *Calc* j5.de cann-s j5.de carb-an j5.de carb-v j5.de caust j5.de *Chin* j5.de cina j5.de clem j5.de coff j5.de *Con* j5.de cor-r j5.de cycl k* dulc b4.de* ferr-ma j5.de* *Graph* j5.de* grat j5.de hep k* ign j5.de kali-c k* kreos j5.de lach b7.de* lact j5.de laur j5.de led b7a.de* m-arct b7.de* *Mag-c* j5.de *Mag-m* j5.de* mang j5.de merc b4.de* merc-c b4a.de* mosch j5.de mur-ac j5.de nat-c j5.de *Nat-m* j5.de *Nicc* j5.de *Nit-ac* j5.de paeon k* petr b4a.de* ph-ac b4.de* phos j5.de *Puls* b7.de* ran-b b7.de* ran-s j5.de rheum b7.de* *Rhus-t* b7.de* ruta fd4.de sabad j5.de sabin j5.de sec j5.de sep j5.de *Sil* j5.de sol-t-ae k* staph j5.de sul-ac j5.de *Sulph* j5.de teucr j5.de *Thuj* j5.de *Verat* j5.de viol-t b7a.de* wies a1
  - **sunrise**; toward: ars j5.de
- **hunger**; by: abies-n chin ign lyc k* ph-ac b4.de phos j5.de teucr
- **menses**:
  - **after** | **agg.**: agar bg2 kali-br bg2 nat-m bg2 thuj bg2
  - **before** | **agg.**: agar bg2 *Alum* calc-p bg2 cycl bg2 kali-c bg2 sars bg2 sep bg2 sul-ac bg2
  - **during** | **agg.**: agar bg2 alet bg2 alum bg2 am-c bg2 bell bg2 cact bg2 calc bg2 cann-xyz bg2 carb-an bg2 castm bg2 caust bg2 con bg2 ham bg2 helo bg2 ign b7a.de* **Kali-c** bg2 kreos b7a.de laur bg2 lyc bg2 *Mag-c* bg2 mag-m bg2 merc bg2 *Nat-m* bg2 **Nux-m** bg2 *Phos* bg2 plat bg2 puls bg2 rhus-t bg2 senec bg2 sep bg2 spong bg2 sulph bg2 uran-n bg2
- **moon**; full: ham fd3.de• lap-la sde8.de• nat-c j5.de sulph j5.de
- **nausea**; by: am-c j5.de ambr j5.de bar-c j5.de bry j5.de carb-v j5.de cham j5.de con j5.de cycl bg* *Graph* j5.de hell bg* hep j5.de kali-c j5.de *Lach* j5.de lyc j5.de mang j5.de mez j5.de *Mur-ac* j5.de nicc j5.de nit-ac j5.de phel j5.de phos j5.de rat j5.de rhus-t j5.de* ruta j5.de sacch-a fd2.de• seneg j5.de *Sep* j5.de sil j5.de squil j5.de *Sulph* j5.de symph fd3.de• ther j5.de thuj j5.de vip j5.de

Sleep

- **nightmare**; by a: acon j5.de alum j5.de brucel sa3• calc mrr1 carc mlr1• castm j5.de cinnb j5.de con j5.de cycl j5.de daph j5.de guaj j5.de kali-n j5.de lavand-a ctl1• *Lyc* j5.de meph j5.de merc a1 mez j5.de *Nat-c* j5.de *Nat-m* j5.de *Nit-ac* j5.de op j5.de puls j5.de sec a1 sel rsj9• *Sil* j5.de sulph j5.de ter j5.de trios rsj11• tritic-vg fd5.de
  - **moon**; full: nat-c j5.de
- **noise**; by the slightest: *(↗Waking - noise - slight)* acon j5.de alum j5.de alumn j5.de* am-c j5.de ang j5.de* apis j5.de* ars j5.de *Asar* j5.de* *Bell* j5.de *Calad* j5.de calc-br j5.de carb-v j5.de cham j5.de chin j5.de* cocc j5.de *Coff* j5.de* dulc fd4.de grat j5.de ham fd3.de• *Ign* j5.de* kali-n j5.de kali-p fd1.de• lach j5.de *Merc* j5.de narcot j5.de* nat-p j5.de nat-sil fd3.de• nux-v j5.de ol-an j5.de* op j5.de phos j5.de pycnop-sa mrz1 ruta j5.de saroth j5.de* sel j5.de sep j5.de* spong fd4.de sul-ac j5.de *Sulph* h2* tarent j5.de valer j5.de vanil fd5.de zinc-val j5.de
- **oppression** of chest; by: alum j5.de am-c j5.de carb-v j5.de kali-c j5.de lach j5.de lact j5.de mag-m j5.de nat-c j5.de nat-m j5.de nit-ac j5.de phos j5.de seneg j5.de stront-c j5.de sulph j5.de
- **pain**; by: alum j5.de aur j5.de bell j5.de coc-c a1 kali-n j5.de lach j5.de *Lyc* j5.de *Merc* j5.de merc-i-f a1 mosch j5.de mur-ac j5.de *Nit-ac* j5.de ruta fd4.de vanil fd5.de vip j5.de
  - **abdomen**: am-m j5.de bry j5.de calc j5.de caust j5.de cina j5.de cycl a1 dor a1 kali-c j5.de lach j5.de mag-m j5.de mag-s a1 merc j5.de mur-ac j5.de nat-c j5.de phos a1 *Rhus-t* j5.de ruta fd4.de sep j5.de zinc j5.de
  - **headache**: alum j5.de chinin-s j5.de con j5.de eug j5.de grat j5.de lact j5.de *Lyc* j5.de mag-m j5.de mur-ac j5.de nat-m j5.de nat-s j5.de nat-sil fd3.de• nicc j5.de *Nit-ac* j5.de phos j5.de rhus-t j5.de ruta fd4.de stram j5.de *Sulph* j5.de* symph fd3.de• vanil fd5.de
  - **legs**: cyn-d jl3 ruta fd4.de
  - **muscles**: mand rsj7•
  - **stomach**: *Nit-ac* j5.de *Sil* j5.de valer a1
- **palpitations**; by: *(↗Sleeplessness - palpitations)* am-c j5.de **Aur-m** mrr1 calc j5.de calc-ar k2 ham fd3.de• ign j5.de lact j5.de *Lyc* j5.de lycps-v mrr1 merc b4.de* nat-c j5.de *Nat-m* j5.de nat-sil fd3.de• *Nit-ac* j5.de *Ph-ac* b4a.de phos j5.de rhus-t j5.de sep j5.de *Sil* j5.de *Sulph* j5.de zinc j5.de
  - **lying** on side, when: ign j5.de lyc j5.de nat-c j5.de
    - **left**: lyc j5.de nat-c j5.de
- **perspiration**, by: alum j5.de am-c j5.de bar-c j5.de cann-s j5.de carb-v j5.de *Caust* j5.de chel j5.de *Chin* j5.de *Chinin-s* j5.de *Cic* j5.de con j5.de croc j5.de daph j5.de *Dros* j5.de *Dulc* j5.de ferr-ma j5.de* graph j5.de *Hyos* j5.de ign j5.de kali-c j5.de kali-n j5.de kreos j5.de lach j5.de led j5.de mang j5.de merc j5.de *Mur-ac* j5.de *Nat-m* j5.de nat-s j5.de nicc j5.de *Nit-ac* j5.de ph-ac j5.de puls j5.de pycnop-sa mrz1 ran-b j5.de *Raph* j5.de rat j5.de rhus-t j5.de sabad j5.de sabin j5.de sars j5.de sep j5.de *Sil* j5.de *Sulph* j5.de symph fd3.de• thuj j5.de verat j5.de vip j5.de zinc-o j5.de zinc-ox j5.de
  - **anxiety**, from: graph j5.de *Nat-m* j5.de nicc j5.de sil j5.de
  - **cold**: am-c j5.de graph j mang j5.de *Nat-m* j nicc j sabad j5.de sil j ther j5.de
- **pollutions**, by: am j5.de camph j5.de cann-s b7.de* carb-an j5.de chel j5.de coloc j5.de con j5.de crot-t j5.de cycl j5.de dig j5.de ferr b7.de* kali-chl j5.de lach j5.de lact j5.de m-ambo b7.de* nat-c j5.de nat-m j5.de *Nux-v* j5.de par b7.de* petr j5.de *Ph-ac* j5.de phos j5.de plat j5.de plb j5.de *Puls* j5.de ran-b b7.de* samb j5.de sars j5.de *Sep* j5.de *Sil* j5.de spig j5.de stann j5.de staph j5.de stram j5.de *Sulph* j5.de *Thuj* j5.de
- **pulsations**, by: nat-m j5.de nit-ac j5.de rhus-t j5.de sabad j5.de sep j5.de sil j5.de sulph j5.de
- **scraping** throat; from: ozone sde2•
- **shuddering**; by: ant-c j5.de berb j5.de bry j5.de carb-v j5.de carc mtf33 caust j5.de kali-c j5.de raph j5.de sabin j5.de sulph j5.de
- **sliding** in bed, by: mur-ac j5.de
- **suffocation**, by: agar bg2 *Am-caust* vh1 *Hep* b4a.de lach k2 nat-sil fd3.de• op b7.de* phos b4a.de samb b7.de* spong b7a.de
- **thoughts**; by: agar j5.de agath-a nl2• borx j5.de *Bry* j5.de *Calc* j5.de caust j5.de *Chin* j5.de cocc j5.de *Coff* a1 coloc j5.de con j5.de *Graph* j5.de hep j5.de *Hyos* j5.de kali-c j5.de kali-n j5.de kali-s fd4.de lyc j5.de *M-arct* j5.de *Nux-v* j5.de olib-sac wmh1 ph-ac j5.de plat j5.de *Puls* j5.de rhus-t j5.de sabad j5.de *Sep* j5.de sil j5.de spong j5.de staph j5.de sulph j5.de tritic-vg fd5.de vanil fd5.de viol-t j5.de zinc j5.de
  - **business**; of: bell j5.de ham a1 hyos j5.de sulph j5.de
  - **scientific**: spong j5.de
- **twitching**, by: alum j5.de ant-t j5.de *Ars* j5.de *Bell* j5.de calc j5.de carb-v j5.de castm j5.de crot-h j5.de *Cupr* j5.de dulc j5.de *Graph* j5.de hyos j5.de *Kali-c* j5.de *Lyc* j5.de mag-c j5.de nat-c j5.de *Nat-m* j5.de *Nit-ac* j5.de *Op* j5.de *Puls* j5.de rhus-t j5.de sel j5.de *Sep* j5.de *Sil* j5.de sul-ac j5.de *Sulph* j5.de viol-t j5.de zinc j5.de

Disturbed: ...

- **uneasiness**, by: agar j5.de cina j5.de clem j5.de cocc j5.de gast a1 lach j5.de merc j5.de nat-c j5.de nicc j5.de* petr j5.de puls j5.de sabad j5.de
  - **4 h.** | **agg.**: plan a1
- **vertigo**; with: am-c j5.de calc j5.de caust j5.de chin j5.de cor-r j5.de lach j5.de lyc j5.de merc j5.de nat-c j5.de nicc j5.de op j5.de *Phos* j5.de sacch-a fd2.de• sep j5.de *Sil* j5.de stront-c j5.de *Sulph* j5.de *Ther* j5.de
- **visions**; by: acon alum alum-sil k2* apis *Arg-n Am* bell *Calc* camph j5.de *Carb-an* carb-v *Cham* j5.de chin coff dulc j5.de *Graph* j5.de hell j5.de ign lach led lyc k* m-arct b7.de merc nat-c j5.de* nat-m j5.de nit-ac j5.de nux-m j5.de *Op* j5.de ph-ac phos plat j5.de puls j5.de rhus-t *Sep* j5.de sil spong stram b7.de* sulph thuj
  - **anxious**: calc j5.de phos j5.de sep j5.de
  - **closing** eyes; on: apis bell j5.de *Calc* camph j5.de *Graph* j5.de lach led lyc spong *Sulph* j5.de *Thuj* k*
  - **erotic**: ambr j5.de calc sil j5.de
  - **frightful**: bell calc *Carb-an* carb-v chin j5.de lyc j5.de merc *Nux-v Op* j5.de sil spong j5.de sulph
- **vivacity**; by: *Ang* j5.de ant-c j5.de am j5.de aur j5.de borx j5.de *Calc* j5.de caps j5.de carc mlr1• *Coff* j5.de *Lach* j5.de lam j5.de lyc j5.de m-aust j5.de *Merc* j5.de *Nat-m* j5.de *Nit-ac* j5.de *Nux-v* j5.de phos j5.de *Prun* j5.de *Puls* j5.de ran-b j5.de ran-s j5.de rhus-t j5.de sel j5.de sep j5.de sil j5.de *Spig* j5.de staph j5.de sul-ac j5.de *Sulph* j5.de zinc j5.de
- **vomiting**; by: chrys-ac a1 hep j5.de kali-c j5.de *Lach* j5.de mur-ac j5.de nit-ac j5.de rat j5.de *Sil* j5.de *Ther* j5.de thuj j5.de verat j5.de vip j5.de
- **walking** in bed; child is: rheum j5.de

DOZING: *(↗Light; Semi-conscious)* acon k* alum j5.de ambr b7.de* anac b4.de* ant-c j5.de ant-t b7.de arn k* *Ars* k* aur b4.de* bell k* borx h2 bry calc j5.de *Camph* b7.de canth k* *Cham* k* chel b7.de* chin b7.de cic clem b4.de cob st1 coc-c a1 *Cocc* coff b7.de coloc j5.de dig k* dulc k* euph k* falco-pe nl2• ferr b7.de* gala br1 graph k* *Hell* b7.de* *Hep* k* hyos k* ign k* juni-v a1 (non:kali-bi k*) kali-br a1* kali-c k* *Kali-n* b4.de* *Lach* mang-p rly4• merc k* naja narcot a1 nat-c h2 nat-m h2 nit-ac k* *Nux-v* b7.de op k* *Par Petr* k* phos k* plat b4.de* *Puls* b7.de* pyrid rly4• ran-b b7.de ran-s k* raph j5.de rhus-t k* sabad k* samb k* sel k* sil k* sol-mm a1 spong b7.de stann b4.de staph b7.de* stram b7.de sul-ac k* sulph h2* teucr b7.de vanil fd5.de *Verat* b7.de

- **daytime**: anac j5.de coloc j5.de euph j5.de *Hep* j5.de ign j5.de melal-alt gya4 *Nux-v* j5.de raph j5.de
- **morning**: aloe ambr b7.de **Apis** b7a.de coff k* **Nux-v** b7.de pic-ac k* puls b7.de ran-b b7.de
  - **menses**; during: kali-c b4.de
- **noon**: aloe a1
- **afternoon**: chinin-s a1 euph j5.de falco-pe nl2•
  - **13 h**: falco-pe nl2•
  - **alternating** with waking: cann-i a1
- **night**:
  - **midnight**:
    - **after**: coff j5.de ran-s j5.de
      - **3 h** | **after**: *Coff*
      - **morning**; towards: aloe a1 ambr j5.de coff j5.de nux-v j5.de ran-s j5.de
- **chill**; during: *Camph* b7.de *Verat* b7.de
- **closed**; as soon as eyes are: adon st
- **constantly**: merc a1
- **convulsions**; with: aeth k2
- **fever**; during: acon b7a.de camph b7.de *Op* b7.de phos b4a.de spong b7.de verat b7.de
- **menses**; during: *Goss* st
- **sitting** agg.: narcot a1 vanil fd5.de
  - **reading** or studying: coca a1
- **stool** agg.; after: aeth k2
- **vomiting**; after: *Aeth* k*
- **waking** agg.; after: aloe a1 clem a1 vanil fd5.de

DREAMING: *(↗DREAMS - Many)* acon tl1 borx tl1 caps tl1 crot-h tl1 ign tl1

- **daytime**, during sleep: aur j5.de bism j5.de carb-v j5.de eug j5.de ign j5.de lach j5.de lyc j5.de nux-m j5.de *Nux-v* j5.de par j5.de petr j5.de plat j5.de sel j5.de stann j5.de tarax j5.de ther j5.de
  - **periodically**: cann-i kr1

- **morning**: ambr a1 ang a1 atro a1 aur hr1* calc j5.de chel a1 chr-ac a1 chr-o a1 con j5.de *Cycl* h1* *Fl-ac* a1* glon a1 goss a1 hell j5.de *Kali-chl* a1* *Kali-m* kr1 lact j5.de led j5.de lyc j5.de m-arct j5.de m-aust j5.de methys jl3 mez j5.de nat-m j5.de* nit-ac j5.de *Nux-v* j5.de ph-ac j5.de phos j5.de puls j5.de ran-b j5.de rhod j5.de rhus-t j5.de sabin j5.de* spig j5.de zinc j5.de
- **forenoon**: bism j5.de lact a1
  - **sleep**; when falling asleep: nat-m a1
- **noon**: ther a1
  - **afternoon**, and: nux-v j5.de sel j5.de ther j5.de
  - **sleep | siesta**; during: aur j5.de eug j5.de ign j5.de lach j5.de lyc j5.de **Nat-m** kr1 *Nux-v* j5.de par j5.de petr j5.de pip-m a1 plat j5.de sel j5.de* *Ther* j5.de*
- **evening**:
  - **bed | going** to bed | **before**: ign j5.de nat-m j5.de nux-v j5.de plat j5.de sulph j5.de
    - **in** bed | **agg.**: arn j5.de aur a1 calc j5.de chin j5.de ferr-ma j5.de hell j5.de kali-i j5.de merc j5.de nat-c j5.de nux-v j5.de puls j5.de *Sep* j5.de
- **night**:
  - **midnight**: m-arct j5.de sep j5.de
    - **before**: am-m a1 ambr j5.de ant-c j5.de arn j5.de aur j5.de bell j5.de calc j5.de *Chel* kr1 chin j5.de ferr-ma j5.de fl-ac a1 hell j5.de hep j5.de hyos j5.de ign j5.de kali-c j5.de kali-i j5.de kali-n a1 kreos j5.de lyc a1 m-arct j5.de mag-m j5.de merc j5.de nat-c j5.de nux-v j5.de puls j5.de sep j5.de *Sil* j5.de spong j5.de staph j5.de stront-c a1 *Sulph* j5.de* tarax j5.de teucr j5.de thuj j5.de
    - **after**: am-m a1 ang j5.de cinnb j5.de con j5.de fl-ac a1 hell j5.de kali-n a1 lyc a1 mang j5.de merc j5.de merc-act j5.de ph-ac j5.de plat j5.de plb j5.de puls j5.de rhus-t j5.de sil j5.de* spig j5.de stront-c a1 *Sulph* j5.de teucr j5.de
      - **3** h: eupi a1 *Rhus-t* a1
      - **5** h: ham a1 lycps-v a1
      - **sleep**; on going to: bell a1 hep a1 sil a1 staph a1 stram a1 thuj a1
- **awake**, while: *(↗MIND - Absorbed)* *Acon* k* all-s a1 am-c b2.de* anac b2.de* ang b2.de* ant-t j5.de* arn k* ars b2.de* *Bell* b2.de* berb j5.de bry k* calc b2.de* camph b2.de* carbn-chl a1 cedr a1 cham k* chin cinnb a1 graph k* ham a1 hell b2.de* hep k* hyos b2.de* *Ign* lach b2.de* led j5.de lil-t a1 m-ambo b2.de* m-arct j5.de merc k* narcot a1 nux-m b2.de* *Nux-v* k* olnd b2.de* *Op* k* petr *Ph-ac* b2.de* *Phos* k* puls b2.de* ran-r j5.de ran-s b2.de* rheum k* rhus-g tmo3• samb b2.de* sang hr1 sel b2.de* sep *Sil* k* spig j5.de spong j5.de stram k* *Sulph* thuj b2.de* ust a1 verat b2.de*
- **bed**; driving out of: sep h2
- **chill**; with: acon bg **Ars** bg bry bg chin bg *Nux-v* bg ph-ac bg **Phos** bg *Puls* bg rhus-t bg sabad bg **Sep** bg sil j5.de *Spig* bg spong j5.de staph bg sulph j5.de thuj bg
- **closing** the eyes agg.: graph j5.de led j5.de lyc j5.de plat j5.de *Sep* j5.de *Spong* j5.de stann j5.de sulph a1
- **coition**; after: rhod a1
- **followed** by:
  - **vomiting**: verat j5.de
  - ○ **Head**; pain in: *(↗DREAMS - Headache - before; DREAMS - Unpleasant - followed)* celt a1 murx k*
- **headache**; before (See followed - head)
- **heat**; during: *Acon* bg2 bry bg2 chin bg2 ferr-ma j5.de ign j5.de lact j5.de *Nat-m* j5.de **Nux-v** bg2 *Ph-ac* bg2 phos bg2 **Puls** j5.de* *Rhus-t* j5.de* sabad j5.de* sep j5.de* sil bg2 **Spig** b7.de* staph bg2 sulph j5.de* thuj bg2
- **lying | back**; on | **agg.**: *Arn* kr1* kali-chl j5.de m-arct j5.de mag-c j5.de mang h2
  - **side**; on:
    - **agg.**: ign j5.de mag-c j5.de thuj j5.de
    - **left | agg.**: lyc bg2 phos bg2 puls bg2 sep bg2* sulph dgt thuj bg2*
- **menses | before**:
  - **agg.**: alum k* calc k* canth k* caust k* con k* kali-c k* *Merc* bg2 spong bg2 sul-ac
    - **falling** asleep, after: ferr-ma a1 glon a1
  - **during | agg.**: agar bg2 alet bg2 alum k* am-c bg2 bell bg2 cact bg2 calc k* cann-s bg cann-xyz bg2 carb-an bg2 castm k* caust k* con k* ham bg2 helo bg2 ign bg2 kali-c k* laur bg2 lyc bg2 mag-c k* mag-m bg2 merc bg2 nat-c *Nat-m* k* **Nux-m** bg2* *Phos* bg2 plat bg2 puls bg2 rhus-t bg2 senec bg2 sep bg2 spong bg2 sulph bg2 thuj uran-n bg2
- **nausea**, followed by: sulph j5.de

Dreaming: ...
- **nightmare** (See DREAMS - Nightmares)
- **palpitations**; with: ign j5.de merc j5.de rhus-t j5.de *Sil* j5.de zinc j5.de
- **perspiration**:
  - **cold | with**: nat-m j5.de nicc j5.de
  - **during**: acon bg2 **Ars** bg2 bry bg2 chin bg2 *Nux-v* bg2 ph-ac bg2 **Phos** bg2 *Puls* bg2 rhus-t bg2 sabad bg2 **Sep** bg2 *Sil* bg2 *Spig* bg2 staph bg2 *Sulph* bg2 thuj bg2
  - **with**: bar-c j5.de chord-umb rly4• dulc j5.de ferr-ma j5.de ham fd3.de• ign j5.de kali-n j5.de kreos j5.de *Led* j5.de mag-s j5.de mur-ac j5.de *Nat-m* j5.de nat-s j5.de nicc j5.de nit-ac j5.de petr j5.de *Puls* j5.de rat j5.de sabad j5.de **Sep** j5.de *Sil* j5.de *Sulph* j5.de zinc-o j5.de zinc-ox j5.de
    - **cold** perspiration; when waking: sabad j5.de sil j5.de
- **prolonged**: ign br1
- **sensation** of dreaming: buth-a jl3
- **sexual** gratification: arg-n br1
- **sleep**:
  - **falling** asleep: petr-ra shn4•
  - **going** to sleep; on | **agg.**: ambr j5.de ant-c j5.de aur j5.de bell j5.de calc j5.de chin j5.de cocc j5.de cor-r j5.de ferr-ma j5.de hep j5.de hyos j5.de *Kali-c* j5.de kreos j5.de m-arct j5.de mag-m j5.de mang j5.de mur-ac j5.de *Nat-m* j5.de olib-sac wmh1 petr-ra shn4• phos j5.de rhus-t j5.de *Sil* j5.de *Spong* j5.de *Staph* j5.de tarax j5.de *Thuj* j5.de verat j5.de zinc j5.de
  - **throughout**: petr-ra shn4•
- **thirst**, followed by: mag-c j5.de rat j5.de sulph j5.de

DREAMLESS (See DREAMS - Unremembered)

DREAMS (See DREAMS)

DROWSINESS (See Sleepiness)

DULL: *(↗Heavy; Oppressive)* aesc sf1.de anac j5.de ant-t j5.de bell a1* bry sf1.de calad b7.de* calc j5.de chin sf1.de *Con* sf1.de cupr-act a1 dig a1 eug j5.de* *Graph* j5.de* grat j5.de *Hep* j5.de kali-n j5.de lach b7.de* led sf1.de lyc sf1.de merc j5.de nux-v sf1.de op j5.de petr sf1.de *Phos* j5.de *Puls* j5.de* vanil fd5.de zinc sf1.de
- **daytime**: *Hep* j5.de
- **morning**: alum j5.de euphr j5.de graph j5.de phos j5.de
  - **eating**; after: carb-v a1

ENOUGH (See Waking - slept)

EXCESSIVE (See Prolonged)

EXHAUSTING: *(↗Unrefreshing)* aeth k2 cann-s j5.de colch a1 dream-p sdj1• hydrog srj2• phos j5.de* positr nl2• sec j5.de zinc j5.de*
- **deep**, with dreams: zinc kr1
- **pollution**, after: cann-s b7.de*

FAINTING (See Falling - faintness)

FALLING ASLEEP:
- **daytime**: *(↗Sleepiness - overpowering)* erig mg1.de granit-m es1• lac-h sk4• meph a1 merc a1 pant-ac rly4• thuj a1
- **morning**: *Atro* hr1* coca hep k* kali-c h2 lyc k* sacch-a fd2.de• spig h1
  - **reading**, in chair; after: coca a1
- **forenoon**: ant-t a1 *Calc* k* vanil fd5.de
  - **9** h: coca a1
  - **reading** agg.: agar h2 nat-s
- **noon**: aloe op a1 pitu-gl skp7•
  - **eating** agg.: puls
- **afternoon**: aur h2 bar-c cina dios k* fago k* fic-m gya1 ham fd3.de• hyos k* mag-c k* nat-m k* phys k* pip-m a1 sabad k* scroph-n a1 sep k* sin-a a1 spong fd4.de vanil fd5.de
  - **13.30-14.30** h: pip-m a1
  - **16** h: cass a1 plut-n srj7•
  - **16.30** h: ferr-p a1
  - **17** h | **sitting** agg.: nat-m
  - **17** h; after: nat-m a1
  - **sitting** agg.: aur h2 nat-m vanil fd5.de
  - **studying**: gels a1
  - **working**; while: zinc h2

Sleep

- **evening**: am-c carc fd2.de• graph h2 mez k* plat h2 plb a1 sol-mm a1 vanil fd5.de
  - **eating**; after: am-c gels
  - **reading** agg.: mez
  - **sitting** agg.: apis hep **NUX-V** k ●* plat h2 tell vanil fd5.de
  - **twilight**; in the: borx h1*
- **alternating** with | **rage** (See MIND - Rage - alternating - sleep)
- **answering**, when (See MIND - Answering - stupor)
- **beer**; after: thea
- **breakfast** agg.; after: sumb
- **chill**:
  - **after**: *Ars* kr1 *Camph* kr1 gels kr1 *Mez* kr1 spong kr1 *Verat* kr1
  - **during**: *(↗heat - during)* ambr k* ant-c ant-t k* **Apis** k* borx b4a.de calad b7.de camph b7.de caps b7a.de cimx *Cina* b7a.de fic-m gya1 gels *Kali-i* ketogl-ac rly4• lyc merc *Mez* *Nat-m* **Nux-m** k* nux-v b7.de* **Op** k* *Phos* b4a.de* podo psor rhus-t b7.de sabad b7a.de sil *Verat* kr1
- **coition** | **during**: bar-c k* *Lyc* k*
- **company** agg.: caust h2 meph k*
- **conversation**, during a: caust nat-sil fd3.de• tarax vanil fd5.de
- **convulsions**: *(↗Comatose - convulsions)*
  - **after**: *Art-v* kr1 cupr kr1 *Hyos* kr1 *Lach* kr1 **Nux-v** kr1 *Oena* kr1 **Op** kr1 *Tarent* kr1
  - **during**: rheum
- **difficult**: *(↗Sleeplessness)* amp rly4• aq-mar rbp6 *Arg-met* kr1* arge-pl rwt5• bit-ar wht1• carbn-s a1 carc fb* *Carl* a1 cham a1 chord-umb rly4• clem a1 coca-c sk4• coli rly4• cortiso tpw7 cupr a1* cystein-l rly4• des-ac jl3 dig a1 digin a1 dulc fd4.de ephe-si hsj1• ferr h1 ger-i rly4• granit-m es1• helo-s rwt2• hep a1 kali-s fd4.de ketogl-ac rly4• lac-loxod-a hrn2• lach a1 lavand-a ctl1• lyc a1 mag-c a1 mag-m a1 mag-s a1 mang-p rly4• medul-os-si rly4• merc a1 mez a1 mur-ac a1* nat-ar a1 *Nat-c* a1 nat-m a1 nat-ox rly4• nit-ac hr1* *Olib-sac* wmh1 onop jl3 orot-ac rly4• *Phos* a1 plac-s rly4• plan a1 positr nl2• pot-e rly4• propr sa3• ptel a1 ruta a1 sacch-a fd2.de• saroth sp1 sel a1* sil a1 sinus rly4• spong fd4.de streptoc rly4• suis-em rly4• suis-hep rly4• suis-pan rly4• *Sulph* a1* suprar rly4• symph fd3.de• thiam rly4• thyr jl3 tritic-vg fd5.de upa a1 ust a1 vanil fd5.de [ant-m stj2 arg-n stj2 arg-p stj2 aur-m stj2 beryl-m stj2 cadm-m stj2 chlor stj2 chr-m stj2 cob-m stj2 cupr-m stj2 lith-m stj2 mang-m stj2 merc-d stj2 nicc stj1 nicc-met stj2 plb-m stj2 stront-m stj2 zinc-n stj2]
  - **children**; in: agre jl3 tritic-vg fd5.de
  - **coition**; after: bov j5.de
  - **heart** complaints; from: olib-sac wmh1
  - **hours**; needs several: *(↗late)* carc sst2•
  - **perspiration**; with: *Sulph* hr1*
  - **sleepiness**; with: kali-s fd4.de nat-c a1 tritic-vg fd5.de vanil fd5.de
  - **thoughts**; from a rush of (See Sleeplessness - thoughts - activity)
  - **waking** agg.; after: *(↗Sleeplessness; Sleeplessness - waking)* dulc fd4.de ketogl-ac rly4• mag-s jl3 nat-c a1 *Nat-m* hr1* ph-ac a1 *Phos* a1* plac-s rly4• pot-e rly4• ruta fd4.de thal jl3
    - **3** h: *(↗Sleeplessness - thoughts - activity)* pic-ac a1 [bell-p-sp dcm1]
- **dinner**; after: ant-t k* aur h2 calc h2 caust k* coca cur **Kali-c** hr1* *Mag-c* k* ph-ac h2 tab k*
- **early**: *(↗Need - great; Prolonged)* alum k* am-m k* ant-c borx graph k* grat k* ignis-alc es2• ketogl-ac rly4• lach a1 lact k* mang-p rly4• mez a1 musca-d szs1 nat-m k* petr-ra shn4• ph-ac k* pycnop-sa mrz1 sep spong stann k* staphycoc rly4• sulfonam ks2 sulph k* suprar rly4• tritic-vg fd5.de
  - **supper** agg.; after: gels a1
  - **weakness**, as from: ph-ac a1 spong fd4.de
- **easy**: chord-umb rly4• keroso a1 lyc a1 mag-c a1 mit a1 plat a1 sacch-a fd2.de• suprar rly4•
  - **11**-15 h: nat-c
  - **daytime**: sapin a1
  - **evening**: chord-umb rly4• form a1
  - **disturbed**, after being: form a1
  - **knitting** and talking: plb a1
  - **light** is on; when: stram tl1
- **eating**; after: arum-t bov k* calc-p k* der a1 gamb k* graph h2 *Hed* mg1.de ignis-alc es2• lyc k* mur-ac k* nat-m k* ruta h1
- **exertion**; from the least mental: *(↗reading)* **Ars** chlor ferr k* fic-m gya1 **Hyos** k* ign kali-br *Kali-c* nat-s *Nux-v* tarax
- **faintness** | **palpitation**; sleeps after fainting with: *Nux-m* kr1
- **falling**, with sensation of: *(↗MIND - Delusions - bed - falling; MIND - Delusions - bed - falling - through)* calen kr1
- **flushes** of heat; with: *Carb-v* kr1
- **heat**:
  - **after**: *Apis* kr1 *Ars* kr1 *Sep* kr1
  - **and** chill; between: **Nux-v** kr1
  - **during**: *(↗chill - during)* *Acon* bg1 **Ant-t** *Apis* **Calad** k* caps k* cedr chel k* *Chin* chinin-ar k2 **Eup-per** k* flor-p rsj3• gels k* *Ign* **Lach** k* lachn laur luf-op rsj5• lyc k* med kr1 **Mez** k* **Nat-m** *Nux-m* **Op** k* **Podo** k* rhus-t k* **Rob** **Samb** stram k*
    - **children**; in: *Op* kr1
    - **old** people; in: *Op* kr1
- **late**: *(↗difficult - hours; Sleeplessness; Sleeplessness - evening)* acon b2.de* agar b2.de* agn b2.de* agre jl3 alum b2.de* alum-p k2 *Am-c* b2.de* *Am-m* b2.de* *Ambr* b2.de* ammc j5.de* anac b2.de* anag a1* *Ang* b2.de* *Anh* mg1.de ant-c b2.de* ant-t b2.de* apis bg2 aran-ix jl3 arn b2.de* **Ars** b2.de* ars-s-f k2 asar b2.de* asc-t a1 aur b2.de* bacls-7 fmm1• bapt bg2 bar-c b2.de* bar-s k2 bart a1 *Bell* b2.de* berb j5.de bism b2.de* *Borx* b2.de* **Bry** b2.de* *Calad* b2.de* **Calc** b2.de* camph b2.de* cann-s b2.de* canth b2.de* caps b2.de* *Carb-an* b2.de* **Carb-v** b2.de* carbn-s k2 carc jl2* *Carl* a1 cass a1 castm j5.de caust b2.de* cench k2 cham b2.de* chel b2.de* *Chin* b2.de* chinin-ar k2 chr-ac a1* cimic jl3 clem b2.de* cob a1 cob-n mg1.de coca-c sk4• *Cocc* b2.de* *Coff* b2.de* coloc b2.de* *Con* b2.de* cor-r j5.de *Crot-t* j5.de cupr j5.de *Cur* j5.de* cycl b2.de* des-ac mtf11 dig b2.de* dirc a1 dulc b2.de* euph b2.de* euphr b2.de* *Ferr* b2.de* *Ferr-act* sf1.de *Ferr-p* bg2* fl-ac bg2 gaert pte1*• gels bg2 *Gent-l* j5.de *Graph* b2.de* grat j5.de guaj b2.de* *Hep* b2.de* hipp a1* hyos b2.de* hyper a1 *Ign* b2.de* ignis-alc es2• indg j5.de* ip b2.de* *Kali-ar* k2 *Kali-c* b2.de* kali-n b2.de* kali-s fd4.de kreos b2.de* *Lac-c* kr1 lac-h sk4• *Lach* b2.de* *Lam* j5.de *Laur* b2.de* *Led* b2.de* *Lyc* b2.de* lycpr j5.de m-ambo b2.de m-arct b2.de* *M-aust* b2.de* *Mag-c* b2.de* *Mag-m* b2.de* *Mag-s* j5.de mang b2.de* meph jl3 **Merc** b2.de* *Mez* b2.de* mill kr1 *Moni* rfm1• mosch b2.de* *Mur-ac* b2.de* nat-ar k2 *Nat-c* b2.de* *Nat-m* b2.de* nat-n bg2* *Nat-s* j5.de nat-sil k2 *Nit-ac* b2.de* nux-m b2.de* **Nux-v** b2.de* *Ol-an* j5.de* *Op* j5.de opl a1 par b2.de* perh jl3 pert-vc vk9 *Petr* b2.de* *Petros* j5.de* *Ph-ac* b2.de* phel j5.de **Phos** b2.de* pieri-b mlk9.de *Plat* b2.de* *Plb* b2.de* *Prun* j5.de psor jl2 **Puls** b2.de* *Ran-b* b2.de* ran-s b2.de* rat j5.de rheum b2.de* rhod b2.de* **Rhus-t** b2.de* ruta fd4.de sabad b2.de* sabin b2.de* samb b2.de* sarcol-ac jl3 saroth mg1.de *Sars* b2.de* *Sel* b2.de* seneg b2.de* **Sep** b2.de* *Sil* b2.de* *Spig* b2.de* spira a1 spong b2.de* *Stann* b2.de* *Staph* b2.de* stront-c b2.de* *Sul-ac* b2.de* *Sulph* b2.de* syc fmm1• tab j5.de* tarax b2.de* ter j5.de *Teucr* b2.de* thea a1 ther a1 *Thuj* b2.de* tritic-vg fd5.de tub-m jl2 *Valer* b2.de* vanil fd5.de verat b2.de* verb b2.de* viol-t b2.de* visc sp1 *Zinc* b2.de* zinc-p k2 [chr-s stj2 cinnb stj2]
  - **bed** were in motion; from sensation as if: clem bg2
  - **coition**; after: bov b4.de*
  - **contractions**; from: bell bg2
  - **distension**; from sensation of | **abdomen**; in: alum bg2
  - **excitement**; after: chlor a1
  - **fear** of falling; from: cimic bg2
  - **four** hours, after: phos j5.de ran-b j5.de
  - **going** to bed late, after: am-c j5.de sep j5.de*
  - **heaviness**; from:
    - **Abdomen**; in: ambr bg2 mag-m bg2
    - **Upper** limbs; in: alum bg2
  - **lascivious** thoughts; from: *(↗sexual)* calc bg2* dros bg2
  - **menses**; during: mag-m b4.de
  - **nervousness**; from: arg-n bg2 valer bg2
  - **one** hour, after: sulph j5.de
  - **one** hour and a half, after: sil j5.de
  - **pain**; from: bufo bg2 **Cham** bg2 coloc bg2
    - **Back**; in: bell bg2 nat-m bg2
    - **Extremities**; in: kreos bg2
  - **rising** late, and: aster hr1* tritic-vg fd5.de
  - **sadness**; from: ign bg2

- **saliva** running down throat; from: kali-c bg2
- **sexual** excitement agg.: *(↗lascivious)* ph-ac bg2
- **sleepiness**; with:
  - **daytime**; in the: ammc a1 carb-v a1
    - **evening**; and in the: ang j5.de borx j5.de clem a1 nat-n sf1.de *Nux-v* j5.de sel j5.de
- **thirst**; from: mag-m bg2
- **three** hours, after: ferr j5.de
- **two** hours, after: bacls-7 fmm1• ferr j5.de graph j5.de *Merc* j5.de phos j5.de ran-b j5.de ter j5.de thuj j5.de tritic-vg fd5.de
- **vertigo**; from: arg-met bg2
- **waking**:
  - **dreams**, from: bell bg* lach bg* sil bg* sulph bg*
  - **early**, with: borx h2* cycl kr1* dios kr1 guaj j5.de *Lyc* kr1 ol-an j5.de pert-vc vk9 prun j5.de puls j5.de ran-b j5.de sel j5.de sep j5.de staph j5.de sul-ac kr1 sulph j5.de vanil fd5.de visc jl3 zinc j5.de
- **warmth** agg. | **heat** agg.: caust a1
- **warmth** of bed; from: *Puls* bg2 **Sulph** bg2

- **laughing**; after: phos k*
- **listening** to conversation, when: cinnb tarax
- **lying** on back, with right arm clamped between legs; when: *(↗Position - back - arms - right)* plb a1
- **menses**; during: phos h2
- **pain**:
  - **after**: phyt
  - **during** | **noon**, at: kali-i a1
- **palpitations**; with: calc sf1.de nat-m sf1.de sil sf1.de **Sulph** hr1*
- **perspiration**:
  - **after** | **agg.**: **Ars** kr1 ars-h kr1
  - **during**: arn *Ars* bell carb-an chel chin cic cina cupr sf1.de cycl euphr ferr hyos ign kali-c lob mez mur-ac nit-ac nux-v **Op** ph-ac phos plat **Podo** psor *Puls* **Rhus-t** sabad *Spong* kr1
  - **with**: **Ars** kr1* tarax kr1* *Thuj* sf1.de verat sf1.de
- **reading** agg.: *(↗exertion)* ang k* aur h2 cimic *Colch* ham fd3.de• ign iris kali-p fd1.de• kola stb3• lyc malar jl2 mez *Nat-m* nat-s phos h2 plat prun ruta sep sil h2
- **sewing**: ferr
- **shocks**; with: [niob-met stj2]
  - **electric**-like (See GENERALS - Shock - electric-like - sleep - going)
- **sitting** agg.: acon ang ant-t apis ars arum-t aur calc-p chin cimx *Cina* fago ferr ferr-ma form ham fd3.de• hep ign *Kali-br* k* kali-c kali-p fd1.de• kali-s fd4.de kola stb3• lyc merc mur-ac nat-c *Nat-hchls* *Nat-m* nat-p nat-sil fd3.de• **Nux-v** petr h2 phos h2 podo fd3.de• puls sacch-a fd2.de• *Sep* staph h1 sulph h2 tarent tell thuj vanil fd5.de verat h1 [cadm-met stj2 cadm-s stj2]
  - **floor**, on: tarent a1
  - **heat**; during: chel a1
  - **soup** agg.: form a1
  - **working**; while: nat-c a1
- **sleepiness**; without: cob-n mg1.de
- **standing** agg.: acon cor-r mag-c morph nit-ac sf1.de
  - **dinner**; after: *Mag-c*
- **stool** agg.; after: *Aeth* k* elaps sabad a1 *Sulph* k*
- **studying**; while (See exertion)
- **suffocation**, with: *Am-c* hr1* bad hr1* bell sf1.de carb-an sf1.de cina tl1 *Dig* sf1.de **Grin** hr1* **Lach** hr1* *Op* hr1* *Spong* hr1* valer hr1*
- **talk** of others agg.: arn gt bapt gt* hyos gt
- **talking** | **after** | **excitedly**: thea a1
  - **agg.**: caust *Chel* mag-c morph ph-ac plat h2
    - **dinner**; after: *Mag-c* ph-ac h2
- **thinking**, after: nat-s a1 suis-em rly4•
  - **intense**: thea a1
- **vertigo**; with: sacch-a fd2.de• tell hr1*
- **vomiting**: *(↗Sleepiness - vomiting)*
  - **after**: aeth c1* bell ip c1* sanic gt1* stram kr1
  - **while**: *Aeth*

Falling asleep – **late**: ...

- **walking** agg.: acon sf1.de nit-ac sf1.de
- **weakness**; from: crot-t a1 petr k* phos k* pilo a1 psil ft1* spong fd4.de
- **wine** agg.: thea
- **working**; while: bism j5.de* lact j5.de* mur-ac j5.de* ol-an a1 phel j5.de* ran-b j5.de* sulph j5.de* zinc j5.de*
- **writing** agg.: ph-ac thuj

FEIGNED: *Sep* hr1*

HALF ASLEEP (See Dozing)

HEAT:

- **sleepiness** during heat (See Sleepiness - heat - during)
- **sleeps** during heat (See Falling - heat - during)

HEAVY: *(↗Comatose; Deep; Dull; Oppressive; Waking - difficult)* acon k* aesc k* agar k* agath-a nl2• aids nl2• ail k* all-c k* (non:ant-c k*) ant-t a1* aq-mar rbp6 arizon-l nl2• asc-c k* bell k* berb k* brucel sa3• bufo calam sa3• carb-ac k* carbn-s carc mlr1• coloc k* crot-t j5.de cyn-d jl3 des-ac rbp6 ferr h1* fum rly1*• gast a1 ger-i rly4• gink-b jl3 glon k* hippoc-k szs2 hoit jl3 hydr-ac j5.de hydrc k* iodof a1 jab k* kali-c jl3 kali-n j5.de lach j5.de lact k* lavand-a ctl1• lepi a1 lob k* lol a1 lyc k* manc k* morph k* nat-c k* nit-ac k* nux-v j5.de op k* ozone sde2• penic jl3* phys k* pic-ac a1 pip-m a1 plan k* *Podo* k* propr sa3• ptel k* rhus-t st1 spig k* stann jl3 sulph k* tab k* tere-la rly4• thuj k* til k* vanil fd5.de verat k* vult-gr sze5• xan k* [heroin sdj2 tung-met stj2]

- **morning**: ferr k* glon k* hydr-ac j5.de iber a1 kali-i k* *Lach* k* meny k* nat-hchls a1 thuj k*
- **afternoon** | **14** h: pip-m a1
- **evening** | **lying** down agg.; after: seneg kr1
- **children**; in: lach j5.de sulph mtf33
- **delirium**; after: sec k*

INSUFFICIENT (See Short)

INTERRUPTED: *(↗Bad; Disturbed; Restless; Waking - frequent)* acet-ac k* acon k* agar k* agath-a nl2• *Alum* k* alum-sil k2* am-c k* *Am-m* j5.de ambr k* *Anac* j5.de ang j5.de ant-s-aur a1 ant-t k* aran j5.de ars k* asaf j5.de aur-m-n wbt2• *Bamb-a* stb2.de• *Bar-c* j5.de berb j5.de bov j5.de cact k* *Calc* j5.de calen j5.de *Camph* hr1* cann-i k* *Cann-s* j5.de canth k* caps h1* carb-ac hr1* carb-an j5.de *Carb-v* j5.de carc gk6* caust j5.de *Chin* j5.de* chinin-ar chlol k* cob-n mg1.de coc-c k* coca cocc k* *Coff* j5.de colch j5.de coli rly4• con k* croc j5.de cund a1 cycl k* dig k* digin a1 *Dros* j5.de dulc k* equis-h *Euph* j5.de euphr k* ferr k* form k* *Graph* j5.de grat j5.de hell-v a1 hippoc-k szs2 hura hydr-ac j5.de *Hyos* j5.de ign j5.de ina-i mlk9.de indg j5.de ip k* kali-c k* kali-chl j5.de* kali-cy a1 kali-i j5.de kali-n j5.de kali-s fd4.de kreos j5.de kres jl3* lac-del hrn2• lach k* lact j5.de led j5.de lyc k* m-arct b7.de mag-c j5.de* mag-m j5.de mag-s j5.de mang j5.de medul-os-si rly4• merc k* merc-c k* mez j5.de morph k* mosch j5.de *Mur-ac* b4.de* myric k* nabal a1 naja nat-c j5.de nat-m k* nat-s j5.de nicc j5.de nit-ac k* *Nux-v* j5.de *Ol-an* j5.de op k* par k* petr k* ph-ac k* phel j5.de phos k* psil ft1 ptel k* *Puls* j5.de *Ran-b* k* ran-g a1 ran-s k* raph j5.de *Rat* j5.de *Rhod* j5.de rhus-g tmo3• rhus-t b7.de* rumx ruta j5.de sabin j5.de sacch-a fd2.de• samb j5.de *Sanguis-s* hrn2• sars b4.de* *Sec* hr1* sel hr1* *Seneg* j5.de *Sep* h2* sil k* sol-ni a1 sol-t a1 *Spig* j5.de spong j5.de squil j5.de stann j5.de *Staph* b7.de* *Stram* k* *Stront-c* j5.de sul-ac j5.de sulph k* sumb a1 tab k* tarax j5.de *Ter* j5.de tere-la rly4• teucr j5.de thuj k* tritic-vg fd5.de vanil fd5.de verat b7.de* viol-t j5.de zinc k*

- **morning**: ambr j5.de arist-cl sp1 ars j5.de coff j5.de dulc fd4.de euph j5.de kali-s fd4.de merc-c a1 mez j5.de stront-c j5.de teucr j5.de
- **night**:
  - **midnight**:
    - **before**: *Rhod* b4a.de tab j5.de
    - **after**: ars j5.de dulc fd4.de euph j5.de graph b4a.de lyc mez j5.de nat-m pip-m a1 ran-s sulph b4a.de teucr j5.de
      - **2-4** h: arist-cl sp1
- **breakfast** agg.; after: peti a1
- **burning** in veins, from: verat
- **children**; in: borx j5.de dulc fd4.de tritic-vg fd5.de vanil fd5.de
- **cramps**, by:
  - **jaw**: carbn-h a1
  - **toes**: carbn-h
- **heat**, by sensation of: *Bar-c*
  - **hands** and head: verat-v a1
- **jerking**; by | **Limbs**; in: merc a1 sumb

Sleep

- **menses** | **after** | **agg.**: agar hr1*
  - **during** | **agg.**: am-c k*
- **oppression** of chest; by: seneg
- **pain**; from: ruta fd4.de stann a1 vanil fd5.de
- **pollutions**, from: petr
- **restlessness** agg.: agar a1 dulc fd4.de lac-del hrn2• lat-m bnm6•
- **starting**; from: caps h1* carbn-s a1 merc h1* op a1
- **thirst**; by: nat-m k* sacch-a fd2.de• tritic-vg fd5.de
- **toothache**; by: castm
- **urinate**; with desire to: bros-gau mrc1 dulc fd4.de nat-m a1 petr h2* sacch-a fd2.de• tritic-vg fd5.de vanil fd5.de
- **weather**; during hot: sel a1

INTOXICATED; as if: petr-ra shn4•

INVERTED sleep pattern (See Sleeplessness - night - sleeps)

LIGHT: *(↗Disturbed; Dozing; Semi-conscious; Waking - easy)* *Acon* b7.de* agar j5.de* agath-a nl2• *Alum* b4a.de* alumn a1* am-c b4.de* anac b4.de* ant-t b7.de* *Ars* b4.de* *Aur-m-n* wbt2• aur-s wbt2• bacls-7 fmm1• bell a1 bond a1 brass-n-o srj5• brom a1 bruc j5.de **Bry** b7.de* buni-o jl3 calad b7.de* *Calc* hr1* *Cann-s* b7.de* canth b7.de* carb-an b4.de* carl a1 caust j5.de cerv a1 *Cham* hr1* *Chin* b7.de* choc srj3• *Coff* j5.de* com a1 cortiso jl3 crot-t a1 cystein-l rly4• des-ac jl3 dig b4.de* dioxi rbp6 dulc fd4.de *Ferr* b7.de* ferr-act sf1.de *Gels* hr1* *Graph* hr1* grat j5.de* **Hell** hr1* hydrog srj2• hydroph rsj6• hyos bg2 *Ign* b7.de* itu a1 kali-n j5.de* kali-s fd4.de *Kola* stb3• lac-del hrn2• lac-lup hrn2• **Lach** j5.de* lap-la sde8.de• lavand-a ctl1• *Lyc* b4.de* *Merc* b4.de* merc-c b4a.de* morg-p fmm1• mur-ac a1 nabal a1 narcot a1 nat-m h2* nep mg1.de* nicc j5.de nux-m b7.de* *Nux-v* b7.de* ol-an j5.de onop jl3 *Op* bg2* ozone sde2• penic jl3* phos j5.de* positr nl2• puls j5.de* pycnop-sa mrz1 *Ran-s* hr1* raph a1 *Rhus-t* hr1* ros-d wla1 ruta b7.de* sacch-a fd2.de• sarcol-ac jl3 saroth mg1.de* sec hr1* *Sel* b7.de* senec a1* sep j5.de* *Sil* b4.de* sol-t-ae a1 *Stram* hr1* sul-ac b4.de* *Sulph* b4a.de* sumb a1 tab a1 tarent a1 thal jl3 tritic-vg fd5.de vip-a jl3 *Zinc* hr1* [calc-sil stj2 cupr stj2 ferr-sil stj2 heroin sdj2 kali-sil stj2 mag-sil stj2 nat-caust stj2 nat-lac stj2 nat-sil stj2 sil-met stj2]

- **morning**: clem a1 kali-n hr1* lycps-v a1 mag-s a1
- **noon**: ang a1
- **night**:
  - **midnight**:
    - **before**: canth a1
    - **after**: ant-s-aur a1 carl a1 coc-c a1 grat a1 ran-s kr1
      - **4.30-8 h**: lavand-a ctl1•
      - **5 h** | **until**: pip-m a1
      - **morning**; towards: *Ars* kr1
- **breakfast** agg.; after: peti a1
- **hears** every sound: acon ptk1 alum ptk1 alumn bg* am-c k* ang a1 apis kr1 ars j5.de* *Asar Calad* carb-v j5.de chin cocc *Coff* kr1* dulc fd4.de grat *Ign* bg2* kali-n j5.de kali-s stj1* lach j5.de* *Merc* j5.de* narcot a1 nat-p nat-sil fd3.de• nux-v ol-an op k* phos k* ruta j5.de saroth mg1.de* sel k* sep st1 sul-ac j5.de *Sulph* h2*
- **refreshing**; though: ozone sde2•
- **rising** to urinate, after: sapin a1
- **tossing** around; much: *(↗Position - changed; MIND - Restlessness - bed - tossing)* am-c bg2 hipp jl2 petr bg2 [ferr-sil stj2 mag-sil stj2 nat-sil stj2 sil stj2 sil-met stj2]

LIGHT ON; wants the: gaert jl2* psor jl2

LONG sleep (See Prolonged)

MUCH (See Need - great)

NARCOLEPSY (See Sleepiness - overpowering)

NEED OF SLEEP:

- **great**: *(↗Falling - early; Prolonged; Waking - late)* bit-ar wht1• brucel sa3• carbn-dox knl3• carc mlr1• *Caust* st1* chin st1* diaz sa3• gink-b sbd1• hippoc-k szs2 nux-v st1* pitu-gl skp7• sacch-a fd2.de• saroth mg1.de* spong fd4.de *Staph* st1* *Sulph* st1* tritic-vg fd5.de vanil fd5.de [*Alum* stj2 *Nat-caust* stj2 *Oxyg* stj2 *Sil* stj2 titan stj2 titan-s stj2]
- **little**: *(↗GENERALS - Sleep - short - amel.)* cob-n mg1.de galeoc-c-h gms1• gink-b sbd1• ina-i mlk9.de lavand-a ctl1• pulm-a srb2.fr tritic-vg fd5.de
  - **children**; in: rheum mtf33
- **no**: ap-g vml3• cinnb a1 iod a1 sin-n a1

NEURALGIA (See Sleepiness - pain - after - neuralgia)

NOT REFRESHED by sleep (See Unrefreshing)

OPPRESSIVE: *(↗Comatose; Deep; Dull; Heavy)* am-c k* cham k* mur-ac k*

- **night**:
  - **midnight** | **after**: des-ac jl3
- **working**; while: mur-ac

OVERPOWERING (See Sleepiness - overpowering)

PAIN:

- **sleepiness** during pain (See Sleepiness - pain - during)
- **sleeps** during pain (See Falling - pain - during)

PATTERN: | **reversed** (See Sleeplessness - night - sleeps)

PERIODICITY:

- **night** | **alternate**: form bg2

PERSPIRATION:

- **during** sleep; perspiration (See PERSPIRATION - Sleep - during)
- **sleeps** during perspiration (See Falling - perspiration - during)

POSITION:

- **abdomen**, on: abrot st1 acet-ac k* *Aloe* sne am-c bro1* amp rly4• aq-mar rbp6 arge-pl rwt5• ars k* *Bell* k* *Bell-p* sf1.de bry cadm-s bg2 calc k* *Calc-p* k* carc cd* caust vh cina k* cocc k* *Coloc* k* crot-t k* cupr a1 dulc fd4.de falco-pe nl2• halo jl3 ham fd3.de• ign k* kali-s fd4.de *Kola* stb3• *Lac-c* k* lach a1 *Lyc* vh* **Med** bg2* *Nat-m* vh petr-ra shn4• *Phos* vh* phyt bg2* *Plb* bg2* podo k* psil ft1 *Puls* b2.de* **Sep** a1* stann k* *Stram* k* *Sulph* vh symph fd3.de• *Tub* vh* [calc-lac stj2 calc-m stj1 calc-met stj2 calc-sil stj2]
  - **arm** over the head; with one: ars ptk1 cimic ptk1 dig lac-c ptk1 nux-v ptk1 *Puls* ptk1
  - **arm** under the head; with one: androc srj1• ars ptk1 bell ptk1 cocc plat ptk1
  - **hands** above head: aq-mar rbp6 carc cd
  - **pelvis**; spasmodically throwing up the: *Cupr* st
  - **pregnancy**; during: podo st*
  - **sleep**; when falling asleep: kali-s fd4.de lac-c st1
- **arms**:
  - **abdomen**; on: bell bg2 calc bg2 cocc k* coloc bg2 ign bg2 m-ambo b2.de* **Puls** k* stram bg2
  - **apart**: *Cham* ptk1 plat ptk1 psor ptk1
  - **head**:
    - **above**; stretched: castor-eq gt verat gt
      - **fingers** while asleep; cracks: castor-eq gt*
    - **over**: aloe sne *Arg-met* st ars st* aur sne bry gt calc k* carc mlr1• castor-eq kr1* chin k* cimic bg2 coloc k* euph ferr-ma *Lac-c* k* med nit-ac **Nux-v** k ●* *Plat* b2.de* plb sne **PULS** k ●* rheum k* ruta k* **Sulph** k●* thuj k* verat k* viol-o
      - **one** or both arms: nux-v gt
    - **under** the: acon k* aloe sne ambr k* ant-t k* ars k* bell k* caj a1 cedr bg2 chin st cocc k* coloc k* ign k* m-ambo b2.de* m-aust b2.de meny k* *Nux-v* k* plat k* *Puls* k* rhus-t k* sabad k* sanic vh spig k* viol-o k*
      - **one** or both arms: nux-v gt
  - **heart** area; clenched over: coca-c sk4•
- **back**; on: acet-ac a1 acon k* *Aids* nl2• aloe am-c bro1* ambr k* androc srj1• ant-c k* ant-t k* *Apis* arn k* ars k* aur k* bism k* **Bry** k* *Calc* k* carbn-h a1 carc cd cham a1 chin k* chlor a1 choc srj3• *Cic* k* cina bro1* *Coca Colch* k* coloc k* conch fkr1• crot-t j5.de* cupr a1 cupr-act a1 cupr-ar a1 cypra-eg sde6.de• dig k* digin a1 dros k* dulc fd4.de *Ferr* k* gink-b sbd1• guaj j5.de *Hell* k* hep k* hyos hr1 hyper a1 *Ign* k* iris-foe a1 kali-chl j5.de* kali-p kreos k* *Lac-c* k* *Lyc* k* m-ambo b2.de* m-arct b2.de* m-aust b2.de* mang k* med k* **Merc-c** k* mez k* morph a1 mur-ac h2* nat-ar a1 nat-m nit-ac j5.de **Nux-v** k ●* olib-sac wmh1 op k* ox-ac k* par k* *Phos* k* *Plat* k* positr nl2• **PULS** k ●* rhod k* **RHUS-T** k ●* ribo rly4• ruta k* sabad k* sars k* sol-ni spig k* stann k* *Stram* k* **Sulph** k ●* vanil fd5.de verat k* viol-o k* zinc k*
  - **evening** | **impossible**: mag-m j5.de

- **night**:
  - **midnight** | **after**: mez j5.de
- **alternating** with sudden sitting up, then lying again: hyos gt*
- **arms**:
  - **head**; lying over: carc mtf33 neon srj5• vanil fd5.de [calc stj1]
    - **left** arm lying over head: aids nl2• dig a1 ign h*
  - **right** arm clamped between legs, on falling asleep: (↗*Falling - lying)* plb a1
- **feet** drawn up: *Puls* a1
- **foot** rests on opposite knee with one leg drawn upward: *Lac-c* mrr1
- **hands**:
  - **crossed** over abdomen: **Puls** j5.de*
  - **flat** under occiput: aloe sne ambr h1 ars k* coloc h2 ign *Nux-v* k1* phos h2
    - **left** hand only: acon a1
      - **other** arm over the head: coloc a1
  - **head**:
    - **above**: carc fb* *Lac-c* med kr1* plat h2 **Puls** a1* viol-o st
    - **behind**: aids nl2•
    - **on** the: carc jl2
    - **over** the: aloe sne carc gk6 *Lac-c* k* med kr1* ozone sde2• plat h2 **Puls** a1* viol-o st
      - **thighs** drawn up upon abdomen, lower limbs uncovered: *Plat* kr1*
    - **under** the head: carc mlr1• [nat-ar stj2]
      - **folded** under head; hands: [ars stj2 ars-met stj2]
- **head**:
  - **low**: cench st1 *Dig* nux-v
  - **upright**: m-aust st1
- **impossible**: acet-ac k* acon b7.de* lact j5.de mag-m j5.de petr-ra shn4• phos b4a.de positr nl2• *Sulph* k*
- **knees** bent: aloe sne bry ptk1 hell ptk1 lach ptk1 **Merc-c** a1* stram ptk1
  - **spread** apart; and: plat ptk1
- **only** on back: dig j5.de *Ferr* j5.de* rhus-t j5.de sulph j5.de

- **changed** frequently: (↗*Light - tossing; Restless)* acon bg2 arn bg2 **Ars** bg2* aur j5.de *Bad* hr1* bell bg2 *Cact* hr1* calen j5.de* caste jl3 coli rly4• *Eup-per* sf1.de *Ferr* sne form hr1* gels bg2 helodr-cal knl2• *Hep* hr1* hipp jl2 *Ign* j5.de* kali-c j5.de *Kola* stb3• lac-del hm2• lac-h sze9• lach j5.de* lyc j5.de* lycpr j5.de m-aust j5.de malar jl2 merc bg2 mosch hr1* mur-ac bg2 *Nat-s* sf1.de nux-v bg2 phos j5.de plac-s rly4• plat j5.de positr nl2• puls bg2 *Pyrog* bg2* rhus-t sf1.de *Ruta* sne sabin j5.de sel rsj9• sulph bg2 tritic-vg fd5.de vanil fd5.de zinc bg2* [calc-sil stj2 rubd-met stj2]
  - **morning**: aur j5.de malar jl2
  - **evening**: kali-c j5.de lach j5.de
  - **night**:
    - **midnight**:
      - **after** midnight; and: dulc bg2 plat j5.de
        - **3** h: tub jl2
  - **palpitations**, because of: cact st1
  - **turning** three hundred and sixty degrees all night: lac-del hrn2•
- **curled** up: med tl1 musca-d szs1
  - **dog**; like a: aids nl2• ars k* bapt k* bry k* psor dgt [heroin sdj2 mag-br stj1]
- **diagonally**: con bg2*
- **face**; on the: cina tl1 *Lac-c* kr1* med tl1 stram b7.de*
- **fingers** spread apart: lac-c st *Lach* st *Sec* st
- **genupectoral** (See knees - chest)
- **hands**:
  - **abdomen**; on: *Puls* b7.de
  - **and** knees; on hands: aids nl2• cina bro1* med tl1
  - **head**:
    - **on**: cham a1
    - **over**: ars bro1 nit-ac a1 nux-v bro1 plat a1* puls br1* sulph bro1 verat bro1 viol-o a1
      - **left** hand: dig j5.de* viol-o kr1
- **hands – head – over**: ...
      - **both** hands: castor-eq a1 nit-ac a1 plat a1 rheum a1 viol-o a1
      - **one** hand: rheum kr1
        - **one** hand under the head: coloc j5.de* ign j5.de
    - **under**: acon b7.de* ambr b7.de ant-t b7.de* arist-cl rbp3• ars b4.de* bell bro1 cadm-s a1 chin bro1 coloc b4.de* ign b7.de* iris-foe a1 m-ambo b7.de m-aust b7.de nux-v b7.de phos a1 plat b4.de* puls b7.de viol-o b7.de*
      - **morning**: cocc j5.de ph-ac j5.de
  - **heart** region; clenched over: coca-c sk4•
  - **nape** of neck; on: *Nux-v* a1*
  - **pit** of stomach; one hand on: plat j5.de*
    - **right** hand: acon j5.de plat j5.de
    - **left** hand: ant-t j5.de m-aust j5.de phos j5.de viol-o j5.de
  - **stomach**; on: m-ambo b7.de
- **hard**; every position seems: laur j5.de mag-c j5.de phos j5.de
- **head**:
  - **backwards**; bent: alum kr1* *Bell* k* chin k* cic k* *Cina* k* cupr k* dig dros gk *Hep* b2.de* hyos k* hyper bg2 ign k* m-ambo b2.de* *Nux-v* k* rheum h* sep k* *Spong* k* stann k* viol-t k*
  - **bored** into pillow: *Apis* sf1.de arn st1 bell a1* carc mlr1• *Hell* sf1.de *Hep* st1 hyper st1 lach sf1.de *Spong* st1 stram a1 verat sf1.de *Zinc* sf1.de
    - **occiput**: *Zinc* hr1*
  - **covered** with sheet: aloe sne calc sne *Cor-r* st1 rumx sne *Sil* sne
  - **forwards**; bent: acon k* cic k* crot-h j5.de cupr k* phos j5.de puls j5.de *Stann* kr1 staph k* viol-o k*
  - **low**; with: absin a1 arn k* cadm-s cedr bg2 *Dig* hep k* *Nux-v* k* sil **Spong** b2.de* sulph zinc
    - **dislikes**: m-aust j5.de
    - **impossible** | **midnight**; after: m-aust j5.de
  - **occiput** impossible; lying on: dulc j5.de
  - **side**, to one: cina k* dulc fd4.de spong k* tarax k*
    - **right**: cina j5.de
  - **table**, on the: *Ars* kr1*
  - **upright**: ant-t j5.de* led a1
- **impossible**; lying: *Cham* glon a1 lap-la rsp1 lyc sulph tarent a1
- **kneeling**: *Med* st1 stram k*
- **knees**:
  - **bent**: aloe sne ambr k* m-ambo b2.de* **Merc-c** b petr-ra shn4• *Plat* hr1* viol-o k*
  - **chest** position; knee: *Calc-p* fb* *Carc* fb* cina mtf33 con sf1.de euph sf1.de lac-c mtf33 lob ptk1 *Lyc* sf1.de* **Med** hr1* musca-d szs1 olib-sac wmh1 *Phos* fb* sep fb* stram mtf33 *Tub* st1*
    - **children**; in: carc gk6
  - **elbows** bent; knees and: ambr bg2 carc sp1* lyc bg2 m-ambo bg2 med bro1 stram bg2 viol-o bg2
    - **infants**; in: carc jl2*
  - **face** forced into pillow; and: *Calc-p* st* *Carc* vh* cina h1 eup-per c1 *Lyc* st* **Med** k1* *Phos* st* *Sep* st* *Tub* st* zinc h2
  - **spread** apart: *Cham* b2.de* m-ambo b2.de* *Plat* b2.de* puls b2.de* viol-o b2.de*
- **limbs**, lower:
  - **crossed**: kali-p fd1.de• rhod k* thuj bg2
    - **ankles**; at: rhod mrr1
  - **drawn** up: abies-c a1 anac k* *Carb-v* k* *Cham* k* chin k* *Hell* *Lac-c* k* mang k* meny k* **Merc-c** nat-m op ox-ac *Plat* k* plb **Puls** b2.de* rhod k* *Stram* k* symph fd3.de• tritic-vg fd5.de ulm-c jsj8• vanil fd5.de viol-o [tax jsj7]
    - **left**: stann j5.de
  - **spread** apart: bell st *Cham* k* mag-c nux-v plat k* *Puls* k1* rhod bg2 rhus-t st viol-o
  - **stretched** out: agar k* bell k* cham k* chin k* dulc k* plat k* *Puls* k* rhus-t k* *Stann* j5.de
    - **one** stretched out:
      - **right** one: aids nl2• stann j5.de
      - **other** drawn up; the: aids nl2• lac-c k* stann k*

Sleep

- **uncovered**; inclined to have lower limbs: con st plat
- **motionless**: lyc a1
- **naked**: ara-maca sej7• fl-ac a1 med gk merc st1 puls st1 sabin gk **Sulph** st1 thuj gk
- **restless** (See changed)
- **reverse**: coff j5.de
- **side**; on: acon k* alum k* *Am* kr1 **Bar-c** k* borx k* *Calc-s* vh caust k* *Colch* k* coli rly4• ferr k* fuma-ac rly4• glycyr-g cte1• kali-n k* ketogl-ac rly4• m-arct b2.de merc k* mosch k* myos-a rly4• nat-c k* *Nat-s* vh nux-v k* oxal-a rly4• *Phos* k* pot-e rly4• ran-b k* sabad k* sabin k* spig k* sulph k* vanil fd5.de [mag-br stj1]
  - **curled** up: bapt ptk1
  - **impossible**: acon aur ferr k* *Lach* st *Merc* moni rfm1• mosch k* nat-c j5.de **Phos** b4a.de* puls j5.de ran-b k* rhus-t k* sabad k* sulph
  - **left** side; on: acon a1 am-c a1 atro a1 bar-c k* borx k* bry vh* bufo a1 calc vh* carc pd* cench k2 chel vh3* chin vh coca-c sk4• elaps gk fuma-ac rly4• gels a1 iris vh kali-p fd1.de• *Mag-m* k1* myos-a rly4• nat-c h2* nat-m mrr1 *Nat-s* vh* pert-vc vk9 *Phos* vh pot-e rly4• psor a1 sabin k* sep vh *Sulph* kr1* *Thuj* mrr1 tritic-vg fd5.de [merc stj2 nat-f stj2]
    - **feet** drawn up: phos a1 tritic-vg fd5.de
    - **hand** on chest as if protecting the heart: kali-ar mrr1
    - **head** on left arm: cob a1
    - **impossible**●: (↗*Sleeplessness - lying - side - left - inability)* arb-m oss1• *Ars* vh cean gk2 cimic gk *Cocc* colch coloc vh elaps gk kali-c k2 *Kali-s* vh *Lach* k* lyc k* naja a1* nat-c j5.de op a1 phasco-ci rbp2 **Phos** k* puls k2 sep k2 tab a1 thea a1
    - **only** sleep on; can: carc gk6
  - **painful** side; on: bry sf1.de coloc sf1.de *Cupr-act* kr1*
  - **right** side; on: ail arge-pl rwt5• *Ars* vh carc mrr1* cham a1 chin vh coli rly4• ign vh iris-foe a1 kali-c jl *Kali-s* vh ketogl-ac rly4• lach k* limest-b es1• *Lyc* st* merc vh musca-d szs1 *Nat-s* vh pert-vc vk9 *Phel* vh **Phos** k* positr nl2• *Sulph* vh sumb a1 symph fd3.de• vanil fd5.de vero-o rly4*• [alumin-p stj2 arg-met stj1* arg-n stj2 arg-p stj2 calc-m stj1 cupr-p stj2 lith-p stj2 mang-p stj2 plb-p stj2 titan stj2 titan-s stj2 zinc-p stj2]
    - **abdomen** on waking; but on: pert-vc vk9
    - **back** on waking; but on: *Lyc* kr1*
    - **impossible**: *Acet-ac* st arg-n k2* aur j5.de *Borx* k* bry chin vh merc j5.de* prun a1 psor k* puls j5.de ran-b a1 sulph a1
- **sitting**●: acon bg2 *Ars* k* bar-c bell k* borx b2.de* cann-s k* caps k* carb-v k* chin k* cic k* *Cina* k* dig k* hep k* *Kali-c* kali-n k* **Lyc** k ●* nat-m h2* **Phos** k ●* **Puls** k ●* **Rhus-t** k ●* sabin k* spig k* *Stram* hr1* **Sulph** k ●*
  - **erect**: cina b7.de*
  - **head**:
    - **backward**; sitting erect and head held a little: *Cina* a1* *Phos* st
    - **bent**:
      - **forward**: acon a1
        - **or** to the side: puls a1
      - **side** | **right**; to: *Cina* a1
    - **table**; on the: *Ars* st
  - **only** when sitting; sleep possible: acon j5.de puls j5.de sulph j5.de
  - **up** suddenly, then lying on back again: hyos gt*
- **sitting** up in bed (unconscious): puls b7.de stann b4.de
- **stiff**: *Cham* st1 mag-s st1 plat st1
- **stomach**; on: [ant-c stj2 calc-m stj1 calc-n stj1]
- **straight**: abrot a1 glycyr-g cte1•
- **strange**: berb a1 calc-p dgt plb k2* [tax jsj7]
- **turning** 180 degrees (See reverse)

PROFOUND (See Deep)

PROLONGED: (↗*Comatose; Comatose - continued; Falling - early; Need - great; Waking - late)* acon-l a1 aeth k2* agar k* aids nl2• alum b4.de* anac k* anan a1 androc srj1• *Ant-c* b7.de* *Apis* k* arge-pl rwt5• arn b7.de* atha j5.de bamb-a stb2.de• *Bar-c* b4a.de bell b4.de* berb k* bit-ar wht1• *Borx* k* brom b4a.de* calc b4.de* camph k* cann-i k* carb-an k* carb-v b4.de* carbn-h carbn-o carbn-s carl k* *Caust* b4.de* chin gl1.fr• chinin-s chlol k* choc srj3• *Cob* a1* cocc b7.de* con h2 daph a1 dig b4.de* dulc fd4.de falco-pe nl2• ferr j5.de fl-ac a1 galla-q-r nl2• gels k* gins j5.de* goss a1 granit-m es1• haliae-lc srj5• ham k* *Hep* k* hura hydr-ac k* *Hyos* k* hypoth jl3 ign b7.de* indg a1 *Kali-c* b4.de* kali-p fd1.de• kali-s fd4.de kreos j5.de* *Lach* j5.de lact j5.de* lact-v c2 laur b7.de* led b7.de* limest-b es1• linu-c a1 luna kg1•

Prolonged: ...
M-arct j5.de m-aust j5.de mag-m j5.de mag-s k* **Merc** b4.de* merl k* mez k* mill a1 morph k* nat-c k* nat-hchls a1 nat-m b4.de* *Nux-m* hr1* nux-v k* ol-an k* olib-sac wmh1 op k* ox-ac k* peti a1 petr j5.de petr-ra shn4• ph-ac b4.de* phel k* phos k* plac-s rly4• plat k* propr sa3• *Puls* b7.de* sacch-a fd2.de• sal-fr sle1• *Sec* j5.de* sel bg2 senec bg2 sep k* sil b4.de* sol-o c2 spong fd4.de *Stann* j5.de* *Staph* gl1.fr• stram k* suis-pan rly4• *Sulph* k* sumb k* symph fd3.de• tarent k* ther k* tritic-vg fd5.de vanil fd5.de verat k* vichy-g a1 vip-a jl3 zinc j5.de [bell-p-sp dcm1 bor-pur stj2 heroin sdj2]

- **day** and night: mag-c mg1.de
- **daytime**: calc j5.de eug j5.de* *Hep* j5.de *Hyos* j5.de *Lact* j5.de meph j5.de merc j5.de sacch-a fd2.de• saroth mg1.de scroph-n j5.de ther j5.de verat j5.de
- **morning**: apis kr1 *Cycl* hr1* dulc fd4.de ol-an a1 phos a1 plat h2 sacch-a fd2.de• spong fd4.de sumb a1 tritic-vg fd5.de zinc h2
- **noon**: calc k* petr-ra shn4• spig k*
  - **afternoon**; and: calc j5.de eug j5.de *Hyos* j5.de scroph-n j5.de ther j5.de
  - **sleep** | **siesta**; during: eug a1
- **amenorrhea**, with: *Cycl* kr1
- **children**; in: *Borx* j5.de* dulc fd4.de spong fd4.de tritic-vg fd5.de
- **continuous**: anac j5.de kali-p fd1.de• lach j5.de merc j5.de petr j5.de
- **days**; for several: *Verat* j5.de*
- **dinner**; after: agar a1 til a1
- **sensation** as after a: bapt a1
- **unrefreshing** (See Unrefreshing - prolonged)

REFRESHING: ozone sde2• phor-t mie3• sal-al blc1• vero-o rly3•
- **short** sleep is (See GENERALS - Sleep - short)

RESTLESS: (↗*Bad; Disturbed; Interrupted; Position - changed; Sleeplessness - restlessness; Waking - frequent)* abrot a1 acet-ac hr1* **Acon** k* acon-c a1 adlu jl3 adon bg2* aeth k* agar k* agath-a nl2• agn k* agre jl3 *Aids* nl2• *Ail* hr1* alco a1 *All-c* k* all-s k* aloe *Alum* k* alum-p k2* alum-sil k2* alumn k* *Am-c* k* am-caust j5.de am-m k* *Ambr* k* aml-ns ammc j5.de* amn-l sp1 anac k* anag k* androc srj1• ang k* ant-c k* ant-s-aur kr1 *Ant-t* k* *Anthraci* kr1 *Apis* k* apoc k* ara-maca sej7• aran k* aran-sc a1 *Arg-met* *Arg-n* k* arge-pl rwt5• arist-cl mg1.de arist-m a1 arizon-l nl2• *Arn* k* **Ars** k* ars-h hr1* *Ars-i* k* ars-s-f k2* arum-t k* *Asaf* k* asar k* asc-t hr1* aspar hr1* astac a1* aster k* atro k* *Aur* k* aur-ar k2 aur-i k2* aur-s k2* *Bac* jl2 bacls-7 fmm1• bad hr1 *Bamb-a* stb2.de• *Bapt* hr1* bar-act a1 **Bar-c** k* *Bar-m* bar-s k2 bart a1 **Bell** k* berb k* *Bism* k* borx k* bov k* brach k* brom k* *Brucel* sa3• *Bry* k* buni-o jl3 but-ac sp1* *Cact* k* cadm-met tpw6* cain calad k* *Calc* k* **Calc-ar** k* calc-i k2* calc-p k* calc-s calc-sil k2* calen j5.de* camph k* *Cann-i* bro1 cann-s k* canth b2.de* caps b2.de* carb-ac k* carb-an k* *Carb-v* k* *Carbn-s* carc mg1.de* *Card-m* k* cardios-h rly4• *Carl* k* casc j5.de* caste jl3 castm k* castor-eq caul tl1 *Caust* k* cedr k* cench k2* cerv a1 *Cham* k* *Chel* k* **Chin** k* *Chinin-ar* chinin-s k* chlol hr1 choc srj3• chord-umb rly4• chr-ac hr1* cic k* *Cimic* k* cimx k* **Cina** k* cinch a1 *Cinnb* k* cit-v hr1* clem k* *Cob* a1* cob-n sp1 coc-c k* coca k* coca-c sk4• cocain bro1 **Cocc** k* cod hr1* coff k* coff-t a1 colch k* coli rly4• *Coloc* k* colocin a1 con k* convo-s sp1 *Cop* k* cor-r j5.de cortiso tpw7* croc k* crot-t k* culx k2* cund a1 **Cupr** k* cupr-act a1* cupr-ar hr1* *Cur* hr1* *Cycl* k* cypr sf1.de cystein-l rly4• daph j5.de del a1 delphin a1 dendr-pol sk4• des-ac jl3 dicha mg1.de *Dig* k* digin a1 dios k* dirc k* dor k* dream-p sdj1• dros b2.de* *Dulc* k* dys pte1*• elaps ephe-si hsj1• *Erig* mg1.de erio a1 esp-g jl3 eup-per bro1 *Eup-pur* k* euph b2.de* euphr k* falco-pe nl2• *Ferr* k* ferr-ar ferr-i k* ferr-m ferr-p k* fil hr1* flor-p rsj3* form hr1 fuma-ac rly4• gaert pte1*• galeoc-c-h gms1• gamb k* gard-j vlr2• gast a1 *Gels* k* gent-c a1 gent-l j5.de* *Glon* hr1* gran k* **Graph** k* *Guaj* b2.de* ham k* hell k* hell-f a1 *Hep* k* hipp a1* hippoc-k szs2 hir mg1.de* hura *Hydr* k* hydrog srj2• hydroph rsj6* *Hyos* k* hyper k* iber jl3 *Ign* k* ina-i mlk9.de *Indg* j5.de inul k* *Iod* k* iodof a1* ip k* iris iris-foe a1 jac-c k* *Jal* bro1 jug-c k* jug-r k* **Kali-ar** k* *Kali-bi* bg2* kali-br hr1* *Kali-c* k* kali-chl k* kali-i k* kali-m k2 *Kali-n* k* kali-p *Kali-s* kali-sil k2* *Kalm* hr1* ketogl-ac rly4• kola stb3• *Kreos* k* kres mg1.de lac-ac hr1* *Lac-c* hr1* lac-d hr1* lac-del hrn2• lac-e hrn2• lac-h sk4• lac-leo hrn2• lac-loxod-a hrn2• lac-lup hrn2• *Lach* k* lachn k* lact k* lam j5.de lat-m sp1* *Laur* b2.de* *Lavand-a* ctl1• led k* lil-t k* limest-b es1• *Lith-c* kr1 *Lob* j5.de lob-s a1 **Lyc** k* lycpr j5.de lyss hr1* m-ambo b2.de m-arct b2.de* m-aust b2.de* *Mag-c* k* *Mag-m* k* *Mag-p* hr1* mag-s k* malar jl2 manc k* mand mg1.de* mang k* marb-w es1• med melal-alt gya4 mentho bro1 meny k* meph jl3 merc k* merc-c k* *Merc-cy* hr1* merc-sul hr1* merl k* mez k* mim-p rsj8• moni rfm1• morg-p pte1*• morph k* mosch k* mucs-nas rly4• *Mur-ac* k* muru a1 *Murx* hr1* musca-d szs1 *Mygal* hr1* myris a1* nad rly4• naja bg2* *Nat-ar* k* *Nat-c* k* *Nat-m* k* nat-ox rly4• nat-p k* *Nat-s* k* nat-sil k2*

Restless: ...
nep jl3* nicc k* *Nit-ac* k* *Nuph* hr1* nux-m k* *Nux-v* k* ol-an k* olib-sac wmh1 olnd b2.de* onop jl3 **Op** k* osm a1* ox-ac k* oxal-a rly4• oxyt ptk2 paeon k* pant-ac rly4• par k* passi br1* paull a1 ped a1 penic srb2.fr *Petr* k* petr-ra shn4• ph-ac k* phos k* phys k* phyt k* *Pic-ac* k* pieri-b mlk9.de pimp a1 plac-s rly4• plan k* plat k* *Plb* k* plect a1 plut-n srj7• *Podo* k* polyg-h a1 polyp-p a1 positr nl2• propr sa3• prun k* psil ft1 psor k* ptel k* **Puls** k* *Pycnop-sa* mrz1 pyrog bg2* rad-br c11* ran-b k* *Ran-s* k* *Raph* k* rat k* *Rheum* k* rhod k* rhus-g a1 **Rhus-t** k* rhus-v k* ribo rly4• rob k* ros-d wla1 *Rumx* ruta k* *Sabad* k* *Sabin* k* sacch-a fd2.de• sal-al blc1• *Sal-fr* sle1• samb k* sang k* *Sanguis-s* hrn2• sanic c1 santin a1* sarcol-ac bro1 sars k* *Scut* bro1 sec k* sel b2.de* senec k* seneg k* *Senn* j5.de* *Sep* k* **Sil** k* sol-t-ae a1 solin a1 *Spig* k* spong k* *Squil* k* *Stann* k* staph k* staphycoc rly4• *Stram* k* streptoc jl2 *Stront-c* k* suis-em rly4• sul-ac b2.de* sul-i k2* sulfon bro1 **Sulph** k* syc pte1*• symph fd3.de• *Syph* hr1* tab k* *Tarax* b2.de* tarent k* tax k* tell rsj10• ter k* teucr k* thea bro1 *Ther* thiam rly4• thioc-ac rly4• thiop jl3 *Thuj* k* til k* tril-p c1 *Trios* rsj11• tritic-vg fd5.de trom k* tub hr1* tus-p a1 upa k* uran-n sf1.de urol-h rwt• ust hr1* v-a-b jl3* vac a1* valer k* vanil fd5.de ven-m rsj12* verat b2.de* verat-v a1* verb k* vesp hr1* vib hr1* vinc j5.de viol-t k* wildb a1 zinc k* zinc-m a1 zinc-o j5.de zinc-ox j5.de [ars-met stj2 bell-p-sp dcm1 heroin sdj2 lac-mat sst4 *Spect* dfg1]

- **morning**: aur j5.de calc k* dulc j5.de galeoc-c-h gms1• ham k* hell k* inul a1 kali-bi k* kreos j5.de mag-s k* mygal sf1.de nit-ac h2 ran-b j5.de ran-s j5.de rhod j5.de sulph j5.de teucr j5.de zinc j5.de
- **afternoon**: colch k* glon k* mez k* tarent k*
- **evening**: caust sf1.de mur-ac j5.de pin-s a1 thuj j5.de
  - **23** h; until: pic-ac a1
- **night**:
  - **midnight**:
    - **before**: aeth alum *Arg-n* kr1 ars-h kr1 asc-t a1* *Bell* *Calc-p* kr1 cassia-s ccrh1• *Chel* coloc cor-r j5.de euph j5.de mur-ac h2* nux-v op pic-ac teucr j5.de thuj j5.de
      - **2** h; until: puls
    - **at**: malar jl2 zinc a1
    - **after**: alum am-m aster bry **Caps** bg1 coc-c **Coff** bg1 coli rly4• coloc dor a1 dulc hr1 gast a1 *Gels* kr1 hippoc-k szs2 iodof kr1 *Kali-c* bg1* kreos j5.de *Lach* kr1 lyc mag-c j5.de mag-s *Nit-ac* kr1 **Nux-v** bg1 pic-ac pip-m a1 ran-b j5.de ran-s **Rhus-t** sabin c1 sep **Sil** bg1 sulph teucr j5.de verat zinc j5.de*
      - **1-4** h: mag-c h2
      - **2** h: galeoc-c-h gms1•
        - **after**: bapt dios kr1 pitu-gl skp7•
        - **until**: galeoc-c-h gms1• puls a1
      - **3** h:
        - **3-5** h: cimic
        - **after**: **Ars** *Bapt* hr1 *Dulc* kr1 sulph
        - **until**: verat
      - **4** h | **after**: aur coli rly4• dulc plan a1
      - **morning**; towards: dulc fd4.de *Gels* kr1 syph jl2
  - **paroxysms**; before: *Chin*
- **anxiety**; with: cham sf1.de
- **apoplexy**, in: *Arn* hr1*
- **bed** | **driving** out of bed | **heat**; from: clem a1
  - **early**; when going to bed: am-c a1
- **bodily** restlessness, from: alum b4.de* am-c b4.de* anac b4.de* ars b4.de* asaf b7.de* *Bar-c* b4.de* bell b4.de* bov b4.de* bros-gau mrc1 bry b7.de* calc b4.de* *Cann-s* b7.de* caust b4.de* chin b7.de* cina b7.de* croc b7.de* graph b4.de* hell b7.de* ign b7.de* kali-n b4.de* lac-del hrn2• laur b7.de* mag-c b4.de* merc b4.de* mur-ac b4.de* nat-c b4.de* nat-m b4.de* petr b4.de* ph-ac b4.de* phos b4.de* rhus-t b7.de* ruta b7.de* seneg b4.de* *Sep* b4.de* sulph b4.de* thuj b4.de*
- **children**; in: agre jl3 bac jl2 bell j5.de bry j5.de carc mtf33 *Cina* kr1* coff j5.de dulc fd4.de hyos j5.de ign hr1* ip mtf33 *Jal* j5.de kali-c j5.de lach j5.de* rheum j5.de senn j5.de sil j5.de staph j5.de tritic-vg fd5.de valer j5.de
- **chill**:
  - **after**: *Eup-pur* hr1* spong k*
  - **before**: anthraci arn *Chin*
  - **during**: *Anthraci* kr1
- **chorea**, in: *Chlol* hr1* *Mygal* hr1*
- **coldness** of body, from: ambr k* mur-ac h2
- **convulsions**; during epileptic: *Cic* hr1*
- **cool** place, tries to find a: *Sulph* hr1*
- **digestive** complaints, from: but-ac jl
- **dreams**; from: (↗*Disturbed*) acon b7.de* agar b4.de* agath-a nl2• *Alum* b4a.de ambr b7.de* ang b7.de* ant-c j5.de am b7.de* ars b4.de* *Asaf* b7.de* aster jl3 *Aur* b4.de* bac jl2 berb a1 *Bry* b7.de* calad b7.de* caps b7.de* carb-v b4.de* chel b7.de* **Chin** b7.de* clem b4.de* *Coloc* b4.de* dig b4.de* dulc b4.de* euph b4.de* ferr b7.de* *Ferr-p* hr1* *Fl-ac* b4a.de gran j5.de guaj b4.de* ign b7.de* ip b7.de* *Kali-c* b4.de* *Kreos* b7a.de *Lach* b7.de* lat-m bnm6• led b7.de* lyc b4.de* *M-ambo* b7.de* m-arct b7.de* mag-c b4a.de mang b4a.de meph jl3 merc-sul hr1* mez b4.de mosch b7.de* nat-c b4.de* nat-m j5.de* nit-ac b4.de* *Nux-v* b7.de* *Olnd* b7.de* op b7.de* par b7.de* petr b4.de* phos b4.de* plb b7.de* *Puls* b7.de* pyrog bg2 ran-s j5.de rhod b4.de* rhus-t b7.de* ruta b7.de* *Sabad* b7.de* sabin b7.de* sacch-a fd2.de• samb b4.de* sars b4.de* sec b7.de* sel b7.de* seneg b4.de* *Sep* b4.de* sil b4a.de* *Spig* b7.de* spong b7.de* *Stann* b4.de* staph b7.de* stram b7.de* streptoc jl2 stront-c b4.de* sulph b4.de* tell rsj10• teucr b7.de* thiop jl3 thuj b4.de* *Trios* rsj11• valer b7.de* vanil fd5.de verb b7.de* zinc b4.de*
  - **frightful**: castm br1
  - **voluptuous**: bism ptk1
- **eating** | **after** | **agg.**: carb-v k*
  - **satiety** agg.; after eating to: phos h2
- **erections**; with: ol-an a1*
- **feet** | **out** of bed, towards morning; puts feet: *Cur* kr1
- **heat**:
  - **before**: *Chin* hr1*
  - **during**: **Ars** hr1* *Calc* hr1* *Carb-v* hr1* *Cimx* hr1* *Dig* hr1* dulc fd4.de galeoc-c-h gms1• mag-c h2 ph-ac h2 rhod a1 sabin hr1* sep h2* spong hr1* tritic-vg fd5.de
  - **from** | **body**; of: bar-c ptk1 galeoc-c-h gms1• mag-m ptk1
- **heaviness**; from | **Abdomen**; in: mag-m h2
- **imagines** to have to go through deep water: carb-v kr1
- **liver** complaints; in: *Podo* hr1* *Sep* hr1*
- **loss** of sleep; from: *Lac-d* kr1
- **lying** on left side agg.: lyc
- **menses**:
  - **after** | **agg.**: nat-p k*
  - **before** | **agg.**: alum k* arist-cl mg1.de calc j5.de caust sf1.de con sf1.de *Kali-c* h2* sep hr1*
  - **during** | **agg.**: am-c k* calc k* goss st1 kali-c k* mag-c b4.de nat-p k*
- **mental** derangement, in: *Con* hr1*
- **metrorrhagia**:
  - **after**: *Sep* hr1*
  - **in**: *Sabin* hr1*
- **mortification**; from: *Ign* hr1*
- **over**-fatigue, from: am br1
- **overstudy**; from: *Cupr-act* kr1
- **pain**; with: aur a1 bell b4.de* dulc fd4.de galeoc-c-h gms1• glon a1 kali-c b4.de* kali-n b4.de* mur-ac b4.de* nit-ac b4.de* petr b4.de* phos b4.de* sulph b4.de* [spect dfg1]
  - ○ **Head**; of: petr-ra shn4•
  - **Limbs**, of: sil
- **periodically**:
  - **night** | **every** other: asar a1
- **perspiration**; during: suis-em rly4• *Sulph* kr1
  - **head**, on: *Calc* kr1
- **pollution**, after: aloe
  - **amel.**: phos a1
- **position** is right; no: caust ptk1 trios rsj11•
- **sexual** causes, from: (↗*Disturbed - erections; MALE GENITALIA/SEX - Sexual desire - increased - sleep - disturbing*) astac vh aur ptk1 canth ptk1 kali-br ptk1 raph ptk1
- **shocks**; from: mag-m ptk1
- **summer** complaints, in: *Ferr-p* hr1*
- **toothache**; from: alum bg2*
- **turning** body | **left** to right all night: lac-del hrn2•
- **twitching**; with | **Limbs**; of: ambr

Sleep

- **uncovering**, with: alum hr1* calad hr1* dulc fd4.de galeoc-c-h gms1• hep bro1 mosch hr1* nat-sil fd3.de• op bro1 *Rhus-t* hr1* sanic bro1 *Sulph* bro1
  - **covers** agg.: galeoc-c-h gms1•
- **vaccination**; after: *Thuj* hr1*
- **vexation**; after: petr h2
- **visions**, with: *Stram* hr1*
- **worms**; from: *Nat-p* hr1* santin br1

REVERSED sleep pattern (See Sleeplessness - night - sleeps)

RISE:

- **aversion** to: *(↗Unrefreshing)* aesc kr1 ambr j5.de androc srj1• arizon-l nl2• ars j5.de bry j5.de canth j5.de *Carb-v* kr1 *Card-m* kr1 cob-n mg1.de crot-h j5.de cycl j5.de* dros j5.de dulc fd4.de falco-pe nl2• ferr-ma j5.de graph j5.de ham fd3.de• kali-p fd1.de• lach j5.de lyc mtf33 *Nat-m* j5.de nat-sil fd3.de• *Nux-v* j5.de sacch-a fd2.de• sal-fr sle1• saroth mg1.de *Sep* j5.de* spong fd4.de *Sulph* j5.de* *Thuj* j5.de vanil fd5.de verat j5.de
  - **waking**; after: bry j5.de falco-pe nl2• kali-p fd1.de• nux-v j5.de puls j5.de sacch-a fd2.de• ulm-c jsj8•
- **must** rise: acon j5.de *Ars* j5.de bry j5.de carb-an j5.de *Carb-v* j5.de cham j5.de choc srj3• con j5.de *Graph* j5.de hydrog srj2• *Lyc* j5.de *Mag-c* j5.de mag-m j5.de nat-c j5.de nat-m j5.de nicc j5.de nit-ac j5.de puls j5.de *Rhus-t* j5.de* sep j5.de sil j5.de ther j5.de
  - **evening** | **before** falling asleep: *Carb-v* j5.de puls j5.de
  - **night**:
    - ⁝ **midnight** | **after**: mag-m j5.de
  - **sleeplessness**; during: con j5.de *Nux-v* j5.de phos j5.de *Rhus-t* j5.de
  - **thunderstorm**; during: nat-m j5.de
  - **waking**; on: anac j5.de *Lac-c* kr1
- **remain** in bed; desire to (See MIND - Bed - remain)

RUNNING in his sleep (See MIND - Runs - sleep)

SEMI-CONSCIOUS: *(↗Dozing; Light)* *Acon* b7.de* agar sf1.de agath-a nl2• alum j5.de* ambr j5.de* anac j5.de* ant-c j5.de ars j5.de* aur st1 bapt hr1* **Bell** berb k* bry k* calc canth j5.de* carb-v a1 casc k* **Cham** j5.de* chel st1 chin a1 chinin-s choc srj3• cocc hr1 *Coff* sf1.de* coloc j5.de* con a1 dig k* ferr j5.de* *Gels* *Graph* j5.de* grat sf1.de hipp a1 hydr-ac j5.de hyos j5.de ign k* kali-br a1 *Kali-c* k* *Kali-n* j5.de* kola stb3• lach j5.de* led j5.de *M-arct* b7.de* manc a1 merc j5.de* merc-i-r k* morph a1 nat-c j5.de nat-m h2 *Nit-ac* h2* olib-sac wmh1 olnd *Op* b7.de* *Par* j5.de paro-i jl3 *Petr* j5.de* petr-ra shn4• phos sf1.de plat a1 prun j5.de *Puls* h1* ran-s raph j5.de* rhus-t j5.de* ruta sabad j5.de sacch-a fd2.de• sec hr1* *Sel* sf1.de* sil j5.de* spig b7.de* spong sf1.de staph j5.de* stront-c j5.de *Sulph* sf1.de* sumb a1 *Verat* j5.de

- **daytime**: verat j5.de
- **evening**: bamb-a stb2.de• rhus-t j5.de sabad j5.de verat j5.de
  - **first** sleep; and in the: bell h1
- **night**:
  - **midnight**: mang a1
    - ⁝ **before**: bamb-a stb2.de• rhus-t j5.de sabad j5.de verat j5.de
    - ⁝ **after**: coff j5.de pip-m a1 ran-s j5.de
  - **sleepy** by day: bry sf1.de
- **hears** everything: *(↗HEARING - Acute - sleep agg.)* alumn kr1 am-c ang a1 apis kr1 ars j5.de *Asar* *Calad* carb-v j5.de chin cocc *Coff* kr1* grat *Ign* kr1* kali-n j5.de lac-del hm2• lach j5.de *Merc* j5.de narcot a1 nat-p nux-v ol-an op phos ruta j5.de saroth mg1.de* sel sep st sul-ac j5.de *Sulph* h2*
  - **conversation** around; semi-conscious of: dios a1
- **sitting**; but sleepy while: ign a1

SHORT: *(↗Sleeplessness; Waking - slept - short)* acon k* agar k* anag k* ange-s jl3 ant-c k* ant-t k* *Anthraci* kr1 apis kr1 aran-sc vh1 *Arg-n* k* arn k* ars bg1 ars-i k* *Bar-c* hr1* *Borx* j5.de bov k* *Bry* j5.de *Calc* j5.de* *Camph* hr1* carb-ac hr1* *Caust* j5.de cerv a1 chin j5.de* *Croc* j5.de cund a1 cupr k* *Fl-ac* a1* galeoc-c-h gms1• ignis-alc es2• kali-c k* *Lach* hr1* lap-la sde8.de• *Laur* hr1* lyc k* lyss hr1* mag-c k* mag-m j5.de marb-w es1• med mtf33 meph jl3 merc k* morph k* myric k* nat-ar nat-c k* nat-sil fd3.de• nit-ac k* nux-v k* *Ol-an* j5.de ox-ac k* par k* ped a1 *Petr* hr1* petr-ra shn4• *Ph-ac* j5.de* phos k* plat k* plb j5.de *Prun* j5.de *Rhus-t* hr1* *Rumx* a1* ruta *Sal-ac* hr1* *Sec* hr1* sep j5.de sin-n k* spong k* staph j5.de sul-ac bg2 ther j5.de thuj k* tritic-vg fd5.de tus-fr a1 vanil fd5.de verat-v k* verb j5.de* *Zinc* j5.de* [tax jsj7]

- **afternoon**: petr-ra shn4• teucr a1

Short: ...

- **evening**: castm a1 spong fd4.de
- **night**:
  - **midnight**:
    - ⁝ **before**:
      - ⁚ **22-4** h: sep j5.de
      - ⁚ **23-4** h: staph j5.de
    - ⁝ **at** | **morning**; until: merc j5.de
    - ⁝ **after**:
      - ⁚ **4.30-6.30** h: ham a1 lac-leo hrn2•
      - ⁚ **5** h | **after**: phys a1
- **amel.** (See GENERALS - Sleep - short)
- **catnaps**, in: androc srj1• *Camph* hr1* carb-ac hr1* carc fd2.de• olib-sac wmh1 phos mtf33 *Rhus-t* hr1* rumx a1 *Sec* hr1* *Sel* bg2* sulph bg2*
- **dinner**; after: aloe a1
- **fatigue**, does not: ap-g vh
- **pain**; from: plb a1
- **refreshing**; short sleep is (See GENERALS - Sleep - short)
- **repeated**, while sitting: narcot a1 olib-sac wmh1
- **sensation** of short sleep: dig a1 dros a1 glon a1 mosch a1 myric a1 nat-sil fd3.de• ost a1
  - **morning**: *Ars* a1 carb-an a1 con a1 grat a1 kali-bi a1 kali-c a1 phos a1 til a1
  - **forenoon**: viol-t a1
  - **evening**: grat a1
  - **sitting** and reading, while: euphr a1
  - **waking**; on: myric a1 nat-sil fd3.de• trif-p a1

SLEEPINESS: *(↗MIND - Prostration)* abel jl3 abies-c k* abies-n k* abrot k* *Acon* k* acon-a a1 acon-ac rly4• acon-c a1 acon-f a1 acon-l a1 aconin a1 adam srj5• adlu jl3 adox a1* aesc k* *Aeth* k* *Agar* k* agar-cpn a1 agar-cps a1 agar-pa a1 agar-ph a1 agar-pr a1 *Agath-a* nl2• agn k* aids nl2• ail k* alet hr1* alf br1 all-c k* allox tpw4 *Aloe* k* **Alum** k* alum-p k2* am-br k* *Am-c* k* am-caust a1 am-m k* ambr k* aml-ns *Ammc* j5.de* amyg a1* *Anac* k* *Anag* hr1* anan vh1 ancis-p tsm2 *Androc* srj1• ang b2.de* anh mg1.de* anil a1 *Ant-ar* sf1.de **Ant-c** k* ant-m a1* **Ant-t** k* antip br1 ap-g br1 **Apis** k* *Apoc* k* apoc-a a1 apom a1 arg-met k* arg-n k* *Arn* k* **Ars** k* *Ars-h* ars-i k* ars-met a1* ars-s-r hr1* arum-m a1* arum-t k* arund k* *Asaf* k* asar k* asc-c k* asc-t k* aspar j5.de* aster k* atro k* aur k* aur-ar k2 aur-i k2* aur-m k* bamb-a stb2.de• **Bapt** k* bar-act a1 *Bar-c* k* *Bar-m* k* bart a1 **Bell** k* ben-n a1 benz-ac k* *Berb* k* beryl sp1* bism k* *Bit-ar* wht1• bomb-pr a1* bond a1 borx k* both k* both-ax tsm2 *Bov* k* brach k* *Brom* k* bruc j5.de *Bry* k* bufo bufo-s a1 bung-fa tsm2 buth-a sp1 cact k* cadm-met tpw6* cain calad b2.de* *Calc* k* calc-ar k* calc-f sp1 *Calc-p* k* calc-s k* calen hr1* *Camph* k* **Cann-i** k* cann-s k* *Canth* k* caps k* carb-ac k* carb-an b2.de* **Carb-v** k* carbn-chl a1 carbn-dox knl3• carbn-o k* **Carbn-s** k* *Carl* k* casc k* cass a1 cassia-s ccrh1• castm catal a1 **Caust** k* cedr k* cench a1 cent a1 cere-b a1 cerv a1 *Cham* k* **Chel** k* chim k* **Chin** k* *Chinin-ar* chinin-s k* chlf k* chlol k* chlor k* chlorpr pin1• choc srj3• chord-umb rly4• chr-ac a1 cic k* cic-m a1 cich a1 cimic a1 *Cimx* k* cina k* cinch a1 cinnb k* cinnm a1 cist k* *Clem* k* *Cloth* tsm2 cob-n sp1 coc-c k* coca k* coca-c sk4• *Cocc* k* cod k* coff k* *Colch* k* colchin a1 coli jl2 coll k* *Coloc* k* *Con* k* convo-d a1 convo-s sp1 *Cop* k* *Cor-r* k* corn k* corn-f bro1 cot a1 **Croc** k* *Crot-c* k* *Crot-h* j5.de* crot-t k* cryp a1 cupr k* cupr-act a1 cupr-ar a1 *Cycl* k* cyt-l a1* dat-f a1 dat-m a1 dendr-pol tsm2* *Dig* k* digin a1 diosm br1 dirc k* dros b2.de* dub a1* dubo-h a1 dubo-m a1* *Dulc* k* echi bg2* elae a1 elaps emetin a1 ephe-si hsj1• equis-h ery-a k* esch br1 eucal a1* eug k* *Eup-pur* k* *Euph* k* euph-hy a1 euphr k* eupi k* eys sp1 *Ferr* k* ferr-ar ferr-i k* ferr-ma j5.de* *Ferr-p* k* ferul a1 fil br1 *Fl-ac* k* form k* galla-q-r nl2• *Gamb* k* gard-j vlr2• gast a1 *Gels* k* gent-l j5.de ger-i rly4• germ-met srj5• gins j5.de* *Glon* k* *Glycyr-g* cte1• gran k* **Graph** k* *Grat* k* guaj k* guare k* guat sp1 *Haem* a1* haliae-lc srj5• halo jl3 ham k* hecla jl hell k* helo-s bnm14• *Helon* k* *Hep* k* hip-ac sp1 hipp a1* hippoc-k szs2 *Hir* rsj4*• hura hydr k* hydr-ac k* hydrc k* *Hydrog* srj2• hydroph jl3 *Hyos* k* hyosin a1 hyper k* iber a1 ign k* *Ind* k* indg k* *Indol* br1* iod k* iodof a1* ip k* iris iris-fl a1 jab k* jac-c k* jatr-c jug-c k* jug-r k* **Kali-ar** *Kali-bi* k* *Kali-br* k* *Kali-c* k* kali-chl k* kali-cy k* kali-i k* *Kali-m* kr1 *Kali-n* k* kali-p kali-s kali-tel a1 kalm k* ketogl-ac rly4• kiss a1 *Kola* stb3• *Kreos* k* lac-c lac-d k* lac-del hrn2• *Lac-h* sk4• **Lach** k* lachn k* lact k* lath br1* *Laur* k* *Led* k* lepi a1 levo jl3 lil-s a1 lil-t k* lim a1 lina a1* linu-c a1 lip jl3 lipp a1 lob k* lob-c a1 lob-p bro1 lob-s a1 lobin a1 lol a1 lon-x a1 loxo-recl bnm10• luf-op rsj5• lup j5.de* *Lyc* k* lyss k* *M-ambo* b2.de *M-arct* b2.de* m-aust b2.de* *Mag-c* k* *Mag-m* k* mag-p bg2 mag-s k* *Manc* k* mand a1*

Sleepiness: ...
Mang k* mangi br1 mec a1 med hr1* mela a1 melal-alt gya4 meph k* *Merc* k* **Merc-c** k* merc-cy k* merc-d a1 merc-i-f k* merc-pr-a a1 merc-sul k* *Merl* k* methys jl3 mez k* mill k* mit a1 morg-g fmm1• morph k* *Mosch* k* mucs-nas rly4• *Mur-ac* k* muru a1 murx j5.de* musca-d szs1 myric k* naja k* narc-ps a1* narcin a1 narcot a1 narz a1 nat-ar nat-br a1 *Nat-c* k* *Nat-hchls* nat-lac a1 *Nat-m* k* *Nat-n* bg2* nat-ox rly4• nat-p k* nat-pyru rly4• nat-s k* nat-sal br1 nat-sil fd3.de• neon srj5• nicc k* nicc-met sk4• nicot a1 nicotam rly4• nid jl3 *Nit-ac* k* nit-s-d a1* nitro-o a1 **Nux-m** k* **Nux-v** k* oci-sa sp1* oena k* *Ol-an* k* olib-sac wmh1 olnd k* **Op** k* orot-ac rly4• osm k* osteo-a jl2 ox-ac k* ozone sde2• pall bg2* pana a1 *Par* k* paro-i jl3 paull a1 ped a1 pegan-ha tpi1• pert jl2 pert-vc vk9 peti a1 petr k* petr-ra shn4• **Ph-ac** k* phal a1 *Phel* k* **Phos** k* phys k* phyt k* **Pic-ac** k* picro a1 pin-s a1 pip-m a1* pip-n bg2* pitu-gl skp7• plac-s rly4• plan k* plat k* *Plb* k* plect a1 plumbg a1 **Podo** k* propr sa3• psil jl3* psor k* ptel k* **Puls** k* puls-n a1 pyrid rly4• *Pyrog* bro1 rad-br c11 ran-b k* ran-s k* raph k* rat k* rauw tpw8* reser jl3 rham-f a1 rheum k* *Rhod* k* *Rhus-t* k* rib-ac jl3 ribo rly4• ric a1 rob k* rosm a1* rumx *Ruta* k* sabad k* sabin b2.de* *Samb* k* sang k* santin a1 sapin a1 sarcol-ac bro1 saroth mg1.de sarr k* sars k* scor a1* *Scroph-n* j5.de* scroph-xyz c2 *Sec* k* sel k* *Senec* k* seneg k* *Sep* k* serp a1 sieg mg1.de *Sil* k* sol-mm j5.de sol-ni a1 sol-ps a1* solin a1 sphing a1 spig k* spig-m a1 spira a1* spirae a1 spong k* squil b2.de* *Stann* k* *Staph* k* still k* *Stram* k* stront-c k* stry k* suis-hep rly4• suis-pan rly4• *Sul-ac* k* sul-i k* sulfon bro1 **Sulph** k* sumb k* suprar rly4• symph fd3.de• tab k* tanac a1 taosc iwa1• tarax k* tarent k* tax k* tax-br oss1• tep k* ter k* teucr b2.de* thea k* ther k* thev a1* thiam rly4• thiop jl3 **Thuj** k* thymol sp1 til k* tong a1 toxo-g jl2 trinit br1 trios a1 tritic-vg fd5.de trom k* tub k* tub-r jl2* uran-n bg2* valer k* vanil fd5.de *Verat* k* verat-v k* verb k* vero-o rly4• vesp hr1* vichy-g a1 viol-o k* viol-t b2.de* vip k* vip-a j5.de* visc a1* voes a1 wies a1 x-ray jl* xan k* zinc k* zinc-act a1 zinc-s a1 zing k* ziz a1* [ant-met stj2 arg-p stj2 bar-i stj2 cadm-m stj2 cadm-s stj2 heroin sdj2 lith-i stj2 mang-i stj2 moly-met stj2 niob-met stj2 rhodi stj2 rubd-met stj2 ruth-met stj2 stront-m stj2 stront-met stj2 techn stj2 tell stj2 yttr-met stj2 zinc-i stj2 zirc-met stj2]

- **day** and night: *Bar-c* b4a.de
- **daytime**: aeth ptk1 *Agar* bro1 alum bro1 am-c bro1* anac bro1 ant-c bro1* ant-t tl1* apis ptk1 ars ptk1 *Asar* sne *Bapt* ptk1 bell ptk1 cadm-met sp1 calc bro1* calc-p bro1 cann-s bro1 carb-v bro1* cartl-s rly4• caust ptk1 *Chel* ptk1 chin bro1* cinnb bro1 clem ptk1 coca-c sk4• *Colch* bro1 *Croc* ptk1 crot-c sk4• cyclosp sa3• dulc fd4.de euphr bro1 *Ferr-p* ptk1 flor-p rsj3• *Gels* ptk1 graph bro1* hippoc-k szs2 hydrog srj2• indol bro1 kali-c bro1 ketogl-ac rly4• lac-h sk4• lac-leo sk4• lach ptk1 lavand-a ctl1• lept ptk1 lup bro1 *Lyc* bro1 mag-m bro1 mag-s sp1 malar jl2 merc bro1 merc-c bro1* moni rfm1• mosch ptk1 muru a1 *Nat-c* bro1 nat-m bro1* nicc-met sk4• **Nux-m** bro1* nux-v ptk1* *Op* bro1* petr a1 petr-ra shn4• *Ph-ac* ptk1 phos bro1* pic-ac ptk1 pin-con oss2• podo ptk1 psor jl2 puls ptk1* rhus-t h1* *Sep* bro1 sil bro1 spong bro1 staph bro1 *Sulph* bro1* *Ter* ptk1 tere-la rly4• tetox pin2• thuj ptk1 *Tub* bro1* [bell-p-sp dcm1 *Spect* dfg1]
  - **evening** awake, night sleepless: *Abies-n* bro1 cinnb bro1 colch bro1 graph bro1 lach bro1 *Lyc* bro1 merc bro1 ph-ac bro1 puls he1* sil bro1 staph bro1 thea bro1
  - **anxious** at night: haliae-lc srj5•
  - **asleep** late; and falling: ammc a1 carb-v a1
  - **debility**, with vertigo; from: **Nit-ac** st
  - **lying** down | **impossible**: cham mtf33
  - **moon**; at new: sep sf1.de
  - **restless** sleep | **night**: *Bac* jl2 hyos a1 mag-m a1*
  - **sleeplessness**; with: cham mtf33
    - **night** (See Sleeplessness - sleepiness - with - daytime)
- **morning**: (↗*Unrefreshing*) aesc k* *Agar* k* ail k* *All-c* k* aloe kr1 alum k* alum-p k2* alum-sil k2* am-c j5.de* ambr b2.de* ammc j5.de* anac k* ang b2.de* ant-c k* *Ant-t* b2.de* *Apis* aq-pet a1 am b2.de* ars j5.de* arum-i a1 asaf b2.de* asar hr1 *Asc-t* k* aspar a1 aur h2 bamb-a stb2.de• bart k* bell b2.de* berb k* bism k* borx b2.de* bry b2.de* cact k* cain k* calad k* **Calc** k* calc-act a1 calc-ar k* **Calc-p** k* calc-sil k2* camph k* canth k* carb-v b2.de* **Carbn-s** k2 cardios-h rly4• *Carl* k* cartl-s rly4• castm a1 castor-eq a1 *Caust* k* chin bg2* chlorpr jl3 cinnb k* cinnm a1 *Clem* k* cob-n sp1 coc-c a1 coca cocc k* *Con* k* corn a1 cortico sp1 croc b2.de* crot-c k* cur k* cycl k* cyclosp sa3• des-ac rbp6 dig b2.de* dros h1 dulc b2.de* *Echi* bg2* equis-h a1 *Euphr* k* ferr-i k* fl-ac k* form k* gamb k* granit-m es1• **Graph** k* grat j5.de* guare k* hell j5.de hep k* hydrog srj2• hyos k* ign b2.de* ind k* indg j5.de kali-c b2.de* kali-n b2.de* kali-s fd4.de ketogl-ac rly4• *Kola* stb3• kreos b2.de* lac-h sk4• lach k* laur k*

- **morning**: ...
led k* lith-c k* lyc k* lyss hr1* *M-ambo* b2.de* *M-arct* j5.de m-aust b2.de* mag-c k* *Mag-m* k* menis a1 *Meph* k* *Merc* k* merc-d a1 mur-ac k* myric k* *Nat-c* k* nat-m k* *Nat-n* bg2* *Nat-s* k* nicc-met sk4• nit-ac b2.de* nux-m k* **Nux-v** k* op k* ox-ac k* ozone sde2• petr k* petr-ra shn4• *Ph-ac* k* *Phos* k* phys k* plat k* *Podo* k* *Puls* k* ran-b b2.de* rat k* rhod b2.de* rhus-t k* ribo rly4• sabad k* scroph-n j5.de sel c1 **Sep** k* *Sil* k* sin-n a1 *Spig* k* staph k* stram b2.de* suis-hep rly4• sul-ac k* sul-i k2* **Sulph** k* sumb k* tarent k* *Teucr* bg2* ther k* thuj k* **Tub** al* upa k* vanil fd5.de verat b2.de* verb b2.de* wies a1 xan k* zinc k* zing k* [spect dfg1]
  - **6** h: hyos a1
    - **waking**; on: sep a1
  - **7** h: calad a1 wies a1
  - **8** h: op sulph
  - **air**; in open | **amel.**: asc-t kr1
  - **bed** agg.; in: con h2 hell h1 hep h2 petr h2 vanil fd5.de
  - **diarrhea** agg.; after: *Nux-v* a1
  - **eating**; after: lach
  - **heat**; after: nit-ac sep k*
  - **nausea**; with: calad a1*
  - **reading** or writing, when: nat-s kr1
  - **restless** night: zinc sf1.de
  - **riding** agg.: phys
  - **rising**:
    - **after**:
      - **agg.**: agar k* all-c k* ant-c k* ars ars-met a1* bell k* *Bism* k* calad k* cocc b7.de* con b4.de* kali-n k* mag-c b4.de* mur-ac k* nat-m b4.de* nit-ac k* plat b4.de* sil b4.de* spig k* sulph k* verb k* zinc b4.de*
      - **amel.**: kali-c h2 nat-m a1
    - **agg.**: aesc ammc k* cact k* cob-n sp1 con k* kali-s fd4.de merc-sul k* nit-ac j5.de nux-v j5.de ph-ac j5.de rhod k*
  - **sitting** agg.: cimx phos
  - **sleepless** night: *Teucr* sf1.de
  - **sunrise**; after: m-ambo b7.de m-aust b7.de nux-v b7.de *Sulph* b4a.de
  - **turning** in bed | **amel.**: meph a1
  - **waking** | **after** | **agg.**: neon srj5• sul-ac h2
    - **on**: (↗*Unrefreshing*) aids nl2• bamb-a stb2.de• bry carb-v clem con ephe-si hsj1• grat hura ignis-alc es2• *Kola* stb3• lac-loxod-a hrn2• lac-lup hrn2• limest-b es1• moni rfm1• nat-m sne oci-sa sk4• petr-ra shn4• sep vanil fd5.de
- **forenoon**: agar k* *Agath-a* nl2• ail k* alum k* alum-p k2* alum-sil k2* am-c k* anac bro1 ang k* **Ant-c** k* ant-t k* am k* ars h2 bar-c b2.de* bart k* bell j5.de *Bism* k* bruc j5.de cadm-s *Calc* k* *Calc-p* k* calc-sil k2* *Cann-s* k* *Carb-an* k* *Carb-v* k* chel chinin-s con b2.de* crot-h cycl k* dros b2.de* dulc b2.de* fl-ac k* gels k* graph k* hell k* hydr kali-c b2.de* kali-n h2* lach k* lipp a1 lyc k* mag-c k* mag-m k* merc-sul k* *Mosch* k* myric k* narcot a1 *Nat-c* k* nat-m k* *Nat-p* k* *Nat-s* k* nicc j5.de *Nux-v* k* petr bro1 petr-ra shn4• *Phos* phys k* pin-s a1 plat k* *Podo* k* puls b2.de* rhus-t k* ruta **Sabad** k* sars k* scor a1 scroph-n j5.de sel b2.de* sep k* sil k* sol-ni spig b2.de* spong j5.de staph b2.de* sul-ac b2.de* tab k* thuj k* til k* vanil fd5.de zinc b2.de*
  - **9** h: cench k2 phys pip-m a1 sep
    - **sitting** agg.: indg
  - **10** h: ant-t chel hydr merc merc-d a1 nat-p thiam rly4•
    - **10**-12 h: calc-s
  - **10**.30 h: equis-h petr-ra shn4•
  - **11** h: ars-met kr1 arum-t cench k2 des-ac rbp6 hydr nux-v rhus-t thuj
    - **11**-12 h: kali-n
    - **listening** to a lecture, while: cinnb
    - **until**: phos
  - **11**.30 h: crot-h petr-ra shn4• phys stry
  - **motion** agg.: *Carb-v* a1
  - **reading** agg.: agar carb-v nat-s ruta fd4.de
  - **rumbling** in bowels, with: *Podo* k*
  - **sitting** agg.: carb-v indg nicc vanil fd5.de
  - **smoking** agg.; after: bufo

- **standing** agg.: chinin-s
- **walking** agg.: rhus-t
- **writing** agg.: nat-s

- **noon**: acon k* agar aloe asc-t k* aur bamb-a stb2.de• borx bry k* (non:bufo slp) bufo-s a1* calc calc-ar camph k* *Chin* clem k* coloc k* crot-h k* crot-t k* dros eupi k* falco-pe nl2• ferr-i k* galla-q-r nl2• graph k* gymno hura hydr-ac a1 kali-bi a1 kali-c h2* kali-n a1 ketogl-ac rly4• lach a1 lyc a1 ol-an op k* pana a1 petr k* phos h2 phys k* sep k* spong fd4.de suis-hep rly4• sulph k* tab tritic-vg fd5.de verat a1
  - **12**-15 h: hyos
  - **chilliness**; during: ferr-i k*
  - **eating**; after: cycl k* euph k* *Graph* k* *Puls* k*
  - **until**: bamb-a stb2.de•
  - **walking** agg.; after: puls k*

- **afternoon**: *Acon* k* acon-ac rly4• adlu jl3 aeth k* *Agar* k* *Agath-a* nl2• aids nl2• alum b2.de* am-c k* amp rly4• amyg a1 *Anac* k* androc srj1• ant-c k* ant-t b2.de* apoc k* *Arg-n* k* *Ars* k* ars-s-f k2* *Arum-t* a1* asaf b2.de* asar h1 asc-t aur k* aur-ar k2 aur-s k2* bar-act a1* (non:bar-c k*) bar-m bar-s k2* bart a1 bell b2.de* borx h2 bov k* brom k* *Bruc* j5.de bry k* buth-a sp1 cadm-met tpw6 cain calc b2.de* calc-s k* cann-i k* canth k* caps b2.de* carb-ac k* carb-an k* carb-v k* carbn-s k* cartl-s rly4• caust k* chel k* **Chin** k* chinin-ar chinin-s chloram jl3 chord-umb rly4• cic k* cimic k* cina k* cit-ac rly4• clem k* coc-c k* coff b2.de* colch k* con k* *Croc* k* crot-t j5.de cur a1 cycl k* dios k* dulc b2.de* ery-a a1 euph b2.de* euphr k* eys sp1* fago k* falco-pe nl2• *Ferr* k* ferr-ar fl-ac k* form k* galla-q-r nl2• gard-j vlr2• gels k* ger-i rly4• granit-m es1• graph k* *Grat* k* guaj k* ham k* hera a1 hydrog srj2• hyos k* ign b2.de* ind k* indg k* kali-ar kali-bi a1 kali-c k* kali-chl k13 kali-i k* kali-m k2 kali-n h2* kali-s kali-sil k2* ketogl-ac rly4• kola stb3• lac-h htj1• lac-leo hrn2• *Lach* k* laur k* lec limen-b-c hrn2* limest-b es1• lyc k* lyss hr1* mag-c mang-p rly4• melal-alt gya4 meli a1 merc b2.de* merc-c k* merc-sul k* mez b2.de* mosch k* mucs-nas rly4• mur-ac k* *Nabal* a1 nat-ar nat-c k* nat-m k* nat-p k* nat-pyru rly4• nat-s k* nat-sil fd3.de• nauf-helv-li elm2• nicc j5.de nit-ac k* nux-m b2.de* **Nux-v** k* ol-an j5.de* orot-ac rly4• osteo-a jl2 oxal-a rly4• ozone sde2• paeon k* pall pant-ac rly4• par k* petr b2.de* petr-ra shn4• ph-ac k* *Phos* k* phys k* pip-m a1 plac-s rly4• plat b2.de* plumbg a1 positr nl2• psil ft1 ptel a1 *Puls* k* puls-n a1 ran-b k* raph k* rheum b2.de* rhod k* rhus-g tmo3• **Rhus-t** k* ribo rly4• *Rosm* lgb1 *Ruta* k* sabad k* sacch-a fd2.de• sal-fr sle1• sapin a1 sep k* sil k* sin-a a1 spig b2.de* *Spong* k* squil b2.de* *Staph* k* stront-c k* suis-pan rly4• sul-ac b2.de* **Sulph** k* sumb k* suprar rly4• teucr j5.de thuj k* tritic-vg fd5.de tung-met bdx1• vanil fd5.de verat k* verb k* viol-o j5.de viol-t k* zinc k* zinc-p k2* zing k* [bell-p-sp dcm1 heroin sdj2 tax jsj7]
  - **13** h: corn a1 hura a1 lac-leo hrn2• mag-c a1 oxal-a rly4• phys a1 ribo rly4• [heroin sdj2]
    - **13**-14 h: ail falco-pe nl2•
  - **14** h: aids nl2• *Chel* elaps k* equis-h falco-pe nl2• glon hura ign kali-cy a1 lyc zinc
    - **14**-15 h: sulph
    - **14**-16 h: falco-pe nl2• ign k* melal-alt gya4 staph
    - **14**-17 h: clem petr-ra shn4• sil
    - **after**: gels a1 kali-i a1
    - **air**; in open | **amel**.: castm a1
    - **house**; in: lyc a1
    - **streetcar**, in: chinin-s a1
    - **until**: clem a1
  - **14**.30 h: carb-v grat petr-ra shn4•
  - **15** h: aids nl2• arum-t a1 bry a1 carbn-s k2 choc srj3• kalm murx nit-m-ac a1 pall petr-ra shn4• phys pip-m a1 pneu j1.de* ptel a1* suprar rly4• (non:tell slp)
    - **15**-16 h: lac-loxod-a hrn2• pall st
    - **15**-19 h: carbn-s nat-m
    - **evening** | **until**: nat-p a1
    - **after**: carbn-s a1 lac-leo hrn2•
  - **15**.30 h: galla-q-r nl2• pitu-gl skp7•
  - **16** h: aids nl2• coca a1 limen-b-c hrn2* ol-an a1 plac-s rly4• plut-n srj7• suis-pan rly4•
    - **16**-17 h: oci-sa sk4•
    - **16**-18 h: ind
  - **16**.30 h: arum-t a1 ery-a a1 ferr-p galla-q-r nl2• sep

- **afternoon**: ...
  - **17** h: aids nl2• arg-n bov chloram jl clem dios equis-h hyper jab lach nat-m petr-ra shn4• thuj
    - **17**-23 h: bell a1
    - **18** h; or: coca a1
    - **after**: nat-m a1
  - **17**.30 h: coca a1 lac-h htj1• [bell-p-sp dcm1]
  - **23** h; until: nit-m-ac a1
  - **evening**; until: asc-c a1
  - **air**; in open | **amel**.: myric a1 zing a1
  - **carriage**, in a: chinin-s a1 lyc a1
  - **church**, in: chinin-s
  - **eating**; after: chin-b kr1 fum rly4• hyper a1 positr nl2• rumx sep k*
  - **lecture**, during: *Agath-a* nl2• myric a1
  - **reading** agg.: anac a1
  - **sitting** agg.: anac a1 ant-c a1 dulc fd4.de nat-sil fd3.de• nicc a1 sacch-a fd2.de• staph a1 tritic-vg fd5.de vanil fd5.de
  - **sleepless**; but | **night** and evening; at: gard-j vlr2• **Sulph** st
  - **studying**: gels a1 ulm-c jsj8•
  - **sunset**; and after | **wakeful** at night; and: **Sulph** hr1*
  - **walking** agg.: ars-met a1
  - **working**; while: nat-ar a1

- **evening**: *Agar* k* agath-a nl2• aloe *Alum* k* alum-p k2* alum-sil k2* am-c b2.de* **Am-m** k* **Ambr** k* anac k* ang b2.de* **Ant-c** k* **Ant-t** b2.de* *Apis* arg-n a1 *Arn* k* *Ars* k* ars-i ars-met a1 arum-t k* asaf k* bapt k* bar-c k* bar-m bar-s k2* bell k* benz-ac k* berb k* bit-ar wht1• borx k* *Bov* k* brom k* bruc j5.de bry j5.de cain st1 calad k* **Calc** k* calc-act a1 *Calc-ar* calc-caust a1 calc-i k2* *Calc-p* k* **Calc-s** k* *Calc-sil* k2* camph k* cann-i k* canth j5.de carb-an k* *Carb-v* k* *Carbn-s* castor-eq kr1 caust k* cench k2* chel k* chin k* chinin-ar chinin-s chlol k* chord-umb rly4• chr-ac a1* *Cic* cimic k* cimx k* cina k* *Clem* k* cob k* coca cocc b2.de* coff k* colch k* *Con* k* convo-d a1 *Croc* k* crot-c sk4• crot-h k* cub a1 cycl k* dig k* dros k* dulc b2.de* euphr k* eys sp1* fago k* falco-pe nl2• ferr k* ferr-ar ferr-i k* ferr-p *Fl-ac* k* form k* glon k* gran k* *Graph* k* grat j5.de* hecla jl hell k* *Hep* k* hipp a1 hura hydrog srj2• ictod j5.de* ign b2.de* ind k* indg k* iod k* kali-ar kali-bi k* **Kali-c** k* kali-chl k13 kali-m k2 kali-p *Kali-s* *Kali-sil* k2* ketogl-ac rly4• kola stb3• lac-c lach sk4• *Lach* k* lact j5.de *Laur* k* lil-t k* limen-b-c hrn2* lith-c lyc k* m-arct b2.de* m-aust b2.de* mag-c mag-m k* mag-s k* mang k* medul-os-si rly4• merc j5.de merc-c k* merc-i-r k* merl k* mez k* mim-h a1 mosch b2.de* mur-ac k* murx k* *Nabal* a1 naja *Nat-c* j5.de* nat-m k* nat-n bg2 nat-ox rly4• nat-s j5.de nauf-helv-li elm2• nept-m lsd2.fr nit-ac k* nux-m k* **Nux-v** k* pall k* par k* *Petr* k* petr-ra shn4• *Ph-ac* k* *Phos* k* phys pic-ac k* pip-m a1 plat k* plb k* podo k* polyp-p a1 psor k* **Puls** k* ran-b k* ran-s k* rhod b2.de* rhus-t k* ruta k* sal-fr sle1• sapin a1 sars k* sel k* seneg k* *Sep* k* *Sil* k* sol-mm a1 spig k* squil k* *Stann* j5.de* staph k* still a1 stram k* sul-i k2* *Sulph* k* tab k* tarent k* ter k* thuj k* tritic-vg fd5.de tung-met bdx1• valer k* vanil fd5.de vichy-g a1 wildb a1 xan k* yuc a1 zinc j5.de* zing k* [bell-p-sp dcm1 heroin sdj2]
  - **18** h: ant-c bamb-a stb2.de• hyper laur myric *Nat-m* nauf-helv-li elm2• nept-m lsd2.fr olib-sac wmh1 sumb
  - **18**.30 h: pip-m a1
  - **19** h: *Ant-c* falco-pe nl2• sil
    - **19**-21 h: chel a1 narcot a1
  - **19**.30 h: sol-t-ae a1
  - **20** h: agar agath-a nl2• kali-cy lyc mang h2 mang-p rly4• sep sol-t-ae a1 tarax trom
  - **20**.30 h: limen-b-c hrn2•
  - **21** h: cench k2 coca lyss kr1 nat-m nat-s pic-ac plumbg a1 [bell-p-sp dcm1]
    - **until**: ang a1 sil a1
  - **23** h; until: nit-m-ac a1
  - **air**; in open | **amel**.: myric a1 pic-ac a1
  - **anger**; after: puls
  - **asleep** late and difficult; falling: ang j5.de borx j5.de clem a1 nat-n sf1.de *Nux-v* j5.de sel j5.de
  - **conversation**, amel.: fago a1

- **early**: adlu jl3 am-m a1* ant-t a1 *Apis* kr1 *Arn* a1* ars-i a1* berb hr1* bov a1* calad a1* calc a1* *Carb-v* h2* castor-eq kr1 caust a1 chel a1 cimx a1 cinnb hr1 crot-h a1 dig a1 euphr a1 fago a1 fl-ac a1 glon hr1* hipp a1 ictod kr1 *Kali-c* a1* kali-cy a1 lil-t a1* lyc a1 mag-m a1 mang hr1* mang-act bro1 mang-p rly4• mez a1 nat-m a1 *Nux-v* bro1 par a1 ph-ac a1 phos a1* plb a1 podo a1 puls a1* sel a1 *Sep* a1* sil a1 squil a1 still a1 *Sulph* bro1 tell a1
- **eating**; after: am-c sne **Calc** sne chin-b hr1 gels sne hep sne nat-m tl1 nid sne *Nit-ac* sne rumx a1 tell sne
- **heat**; after: nit-ac a1
- **light** amel.; by: am-m j5.de*
- **reading** agg.: ang sf1.de brom a1
- **riding** in a carriage agg.: nept-m lsd2.fr pall a1
- **sitting** agg.: ang a1 arg-n a1 bamb-a stb2.de• *Nux-v* kr1 petr a1 vanil fd5.de
  - **reading**; and: nux-v bro1
- **sleepless** in bed: des-ac jl3
- **sunset**:
  - **after** sunset: dros bg2
  - **at** sunset: anis a1 arum-t kr1 dros k* **Sulph** kr1
- **thirst**; with: benz-ac a1* ferr a1
- **twilight**; at: **Am-m** k* borx h2
- **walking** agg.; after: nat-m a1 sumb a1
- **warm** room agg.: ant-t hr1* ind kr1 merl a1
- **wine** agg.: carbn-s a1 fl-ac a1
- **writing** agg.: brom a1

- **night**: muru a1
- **accompanied** by:
  - **abdominal** complaints: ant-c kr1 cupr-s kr1 *Nux-m* kr1 podo kr1
  - **bronchitis** (See CHEST - Inflammation - bronchial - accompanied - sleepiness)
  - **complaints**; other: acon b2.de* agar b2.de* ambr b2.de* ant-t b2.de* arg-met b2.de* *Ars* b2.de* asaf b2.de asar bg2 bell b2.de* *Borx* b2.de* calad b2.de* caps b2.de* *Cham* b2.de* chel b2.de* chin b2.de* cic b2.de* cina b2.de* cocc b2.de* *Con* b2.de* croc b2.de* crot-h br1 cycl b2.de* dig b2.de* euphr b2.de* ferr b2.de* hell b2.de* hep b2.de* *Ign* b2.de* *Kali-c* b2.de* kreos b2.de* lach b2.de* *Laur* b2.de* led b2.de* m-ambo b2.de* m-arct b2.de m-aust b2.de mag-c b2.de* merc b2.de* *Mez* b2.de* *Nat-m* b2.de* *Nit-ac* b2.de* nux-m b2.de* nux-v b2.de* op b2.de* petr b2.de* *Ph-ac* b2.de* phos b2.de* *Plat* b2.de* plb b2.de* **Puls** b2.de* *Ran-b* b2.de* *Rhod* b2.de* rhus-t b2.de* *Sabad* b2.de* sabin b2.de* sep b2.de* stann b2.de* *Staph* b2.de* stram b2.de* stront-c b2.de* sul-ac b2.de* tarax b2.de* thuj b2.de* verat b2.de* verb b2.de* viol-o b2.de* viol-t b2.de*
  - **cough** (See COUGH - Accompanied - sleepiness)
  - **headache** (See HEAD - Pain - accompanied - sleepiness)
  - **intestinal** complaints (See ABDOMEN - Complaints - intestines - accompanied - sleepiness)
  - **neurological** complaints (See GENERALS - Neurological - accompanied - sleepiness)
  - **sleeplessness** (See Sleeplessness - accompanied - sleepiness - daytime)
  - **vision**; complaints of (See VISION - Complaints - accompanied - sleepiness)
  - ○ **Face**:
    - **heat** of: glon bg2
    - **pale** discoloration of: glon bg2
    - **red** discoloration of: am-m bg2
      - **children**; in: op b7a.de
  - **Jaw**; clenched (See FACE - Clenched - accompanied - sleepiness)
  - **Liver**; complaints of: **Chel** kr1 *Lept* kr1 *Myric* kr1 *Nat-m* kr1 *Sil* kr1
  - **Stomach**; complaints of (See STOMACH - Complaints - accompanied - sleepiness)
  - **Teeth**; pain in (See TEETH - Pain - accompanied - sleepiness)
  - **Uterus**; prolapse of: *Agar* kr1

- **air**; in open:
  - **agg.**: acon ant-t bufo chel guare kali-bi k* mosch j5.de nux-v j5.de plat h2
    - **walking** | **amel.**: asar jl
  - **amel.**: aeth j5.de* agar a1 alum b4.de* castm j5.de chel a1 clem a1 ignis-alc es2• limen-b-c mlk9.de *Ol-an* j5.de* plb j5.de* tab j5.de* zinc j5.de
  - **being**; after: bufo bg2
- **albuminuria**, in: *Helo-s* rwt2• *Helon* hr1*
- **alcohol**; after drinking: *Glon* kr1
- **alcoholism**; with (See drunkenness)
- **alone** agg.: *Bry* k* *Hell* k*
- **alternating** with:
  - **excitement** (See MIND - Excitement - alternating - sleepiness)
  - **restlessness** (See MIND - Restlessness - alternating - sleepiness)
  - **sleeplessness**: asim hr1* benz-ac k2* caust k* *Hyos* k* lach sep
  - **vertigo**: ant-t k*
  - ○ **Head**:
    - **complaints** (See HEAD - Complaints - alternating - sleepiness)
    - **pain** (See HEAD - Pain - alternating - sleepiness; HEAD - Pain - alternating - stomach)
- **anemia**, in: hyper sf1.de *Sabin* kr1
- **anxiety**; with: ars j5.de asaf a1 bell a1 borx b4a.de* bov hr1 led j5.de merc a1 nux-v j5.de rhus-t j5.de*
- **apoplexy**:
  - **as** before an apoplexy: coff j5.de
  - **in**: apis bg2 *Bar-c* hr1* hell bg2 *Hyos* hr1* kali-i bg2 *Nux-v* hr1* *Op* hr1*
- **bathing** | **sea**; in the: *Lim* br1
- **bed**:
  - **going** to bed | **amel.**: euphr a1
  - **in** bed:
    - **agg.**: dulc fd4.de eupi a1
    - **hard**; too: psor sf1.de
  - **shuns** the: cann-s kr1
- **beer**; after: sulph k* thea
- **breakfast** | **after** | **agg.**: bapt a1 calad k* clem k* lach k* manc k* nat-s k* peti a1 still k* sumb ther k* verat k*
  - **before** | **agg.**: *Calc* hr1*
- **brooding**, with: carb-an j5.de
- **caused** by other complaints (See accompanied - complaints)
- **cheerfulness**; after: bell calc
- **children**; in: all-s hr1* borx j5.de chir-fl bnm4• dulc fd4.de op wbt• podo hr1*
- **chill**:
  - **after**: gels hr1* hipp a1 nux-v b7a.de* rhus-t bg2
  - **before**: ars k* nicc k* puls sabad k* ther k*
  - **between**: *Nux-m* k*
  - **during**: acon bg2 aeth am-c j5.de ambr k* ant-c k* *Ant-t* k* apis b7a.de* ars b4a.de* aster a1* bell bg2 borx b4a.de* *Calad* j5.de* calc j5.de camph bg2* caps b7.de* cham bg2 chel ptk1 cimic bg2* cimx k* cina b7a.de* croc j5.de* cycl b7.de* *Gels* bg2* hell k* hyos bg2 hyper sf1.de ign bg2 iris kali-bi k* *Kali-i* k* kali-n sf1.de led bg2 lept bg2 lyc j5.de merc b4.de* mez k* *Nat-m* k* nit-ac j5.de *Nux-m* k* nux-v k* **Op** k* ph-ac bg2 phos k* plat b4.de* puls bg2 *Rhus-t* b7a.de* *Sabad* bg2 *Sabin* bg2 sars h2 sep bg2 staph b7.de* tarax ter bg2 *Verat* bg2*
- **chilliness**: am-m a1 ang j5.de ars k* aspar k* calad j5.de calc a1* chlf a1 croc j5.de crot-h hr1 cycl a1* hell k* kali-c a1* led sf lyc a1* nat-m k* sumb k* thuj k*
  - **after**: nux-v k* sabin hr1
  - **during**: ang j5.de ars aspar calad j5.de croc j5.de cycl kr1 hell led sf1.de mez h2 nat-m phos h2 plat h2 sabin kr1 sumb thuj uran-n sf1.de
- **cholera** infantum:
  - **after**: *Chin* hr1*
  - **in**: *Arn* hr1*
- **coffee**: | **after**: bart a1

Sleep

- **coition**:
  - **after**: agar k* bar-c bg2 lyc bg2 sep k*
  - **during**: bar-c k* *Lyc* k*
- **coldness**; with: crot-h j5.de [tax jsj7]
- **company** agg.: caust h2 meph k*
- **complaints** causing sleepiness: acon b2.de* agar b2.de* am-c b2.de* anac b2.de* ang b2.de* ant-c b2.de* **Ant-t** b2.de* arn b2.de* ars b2.de* asaf b2.de* asar b2.de* aur b2.de* bar-c b2.de* bism b2.de* bov b2.de* bry b2.de* calc b2.de* caps b2.de* carb-v b2.de* caust b2.de* cham b2.de* chel b2.de* *Chin* b2.de* cic b2.de* cina b2.de* clem b2.de* cocc b2.de* coff b2.de* con b2.de* croc b2.de* cycl b2.de* dros b2.de* euphr b2.de* ferr b2.de* graph b2.de* hyos b2.de* *Ign* b2.de* *Kali-c* b2.de* *Lach* b2.de* laur b2.de* lyc b2.de* m-ambo b2.de* m-aust b2.de mag-c b2.de* merc b2.de* mosch b2.de* mur-ac b2.de* nat-c b2.de* *Nat-m* b2.de* nit-ac b2.de* **Nux-m** b2.de* *Nux-v* b2.de* op b2.de* par b2.de* petr b2.de* ph-ac b2.de* *Phos* b2.de* plat b2.de* plb b2.de* puls b2.de* ran-b b2.de* rheum b2.de* **Rhus-t** b2.de* ruta b2.de* *Sabad* b2.de* sabin b2.de* sel b2.de* sep b2.de* *Sil* b2.de* spig b2.de* stann b2.de* staph b2.de* *Sulph* b2.de* *Tarax* b2.de* thuj b2.de* verb b2.de* *Zinc* b2.de*
- **complaints**; during (See accompanied - complaints)
- **confusion**, with (See MIND - Confusion - sleepiness)
- **consciousness**; as if loosing: phys ptk1
- **constant**: *Bell* j5.de *Bruc* j5.de caust j5.de chin j5.de* clem j5.de* croc a1 ferr j5.de* fl-ac a1 hipp a1 hydr-ac hr1 hyper a1* kali-br a1 kali-c j5.de* kreos j5.de m-arct j5.de nux-m hr1 puls a1 rhus-t a1 spig j5.de taosc iwa1• thuj j5.de* zinc j5.de*
- **conversation**; during: caust k* cench k2* chinin-s lach a1 mang-p rly4• tarax k* vanil fd5.de
- **convulsions**:
  - **after**: aeth c1 calc b4a.de cic mrr1* cur hr1* *Dros* b7a.de *Hyos* b7a.de *Op* b7a.de *Stram* hr1*
  - **before**: *Nux-v* hr1*
    - **and** after: glon hr1 *Nux-m* hr1*
  - **during**: bell bro1 *Hydr-ac* hr1* *Op* hr1* **Tarent** hr1* vip j5.de
- **coryza**; during: *Ant-t* b7a.de *Cham* b7.de* **Gels** bg2 nux-v b7.de* petr b4.de*
- **cough**:
  - **after**: *Anac* bg2* *Ant-t* kr1 *Ign* k*
  - **between** attacks: euph-l bro1
  - **with**: ant-c **Ant-t** k* *Ip* k* *Kreos* k* nux-m b7.de* op
- **dark**, at: cench k2*
- **delirium**; during: acon ant-c j5.de arn *Bell* hr1* *Bry* camph k* coloc *Crot-h* hr1* lach b7.de* **Op** hr1* *Puls* sec j5.de
- **delivery**; after: phel ptk1*
- **diarrhea**:
  - **after** | **agg.**: aeth sne ars-met kr1 *Nux-v*
  - **during**: *Ant-t* kr1 asim kr1 *Calc* kr1 *Corn* kr1 *Nux-m* kr1 vanil fd5.de
    - **children**; in: *Ant-t* kr1 chin mtf33 sulph mtf33 vanil fd5.de
  - **tenesmus**, after: *Colch* kr1* **Sulph** kr1*
- **diet**; errors in: nux-m mrr1
- **dinner**:
  - **after**:
    - **agg.**: acon k* adlu jl3 **Agar** k* alum k* alum-p k2* alum-sil k2* *Am-c* j5.de *Anac* k* androc srj1• ant-c ant-t k* *Apis* arn j5.de ars h2* arum-m j5.de* *Aur* k* aur-s k2* bapt k* bar-c k* bar-m bar-s k2* bell j5.de berb k* borx j5.de *Bov* k* bruc j5.de bry j5.de cadm-met mg1.de calc k* *Calc-p* k* calc-sil k2* cann-s k* canth k* caps carb-an k* *Carb-v* k* carbn-s caust k* cham j5.de chel k* *Chin* k* *Cic* cimic k* cinnb k* clem k* coca croc k* crot-h j5.de crot-t j5.de cur cycl k* dios k* eug j5.de* euph h2* euph-a a1 euphr k* ferr k* graph k* grat k* ham k* hura hydr-ac j5.de ign k* kali-bi k* kali-c k* kali-chl k13 kali-m k2 kali-n k* kali-sil k2* *Lach* k* laur k* levo jl3 linu-c a1 lipp a1 **Lyc** k* mag-c k* mag-m k* mez k* *Mur-ac* k* nat-c h2* *Nat-m* k* nat-p k* nat-s k* nep srb2.fr nit-ac j5.de *Nux-m* k* **Nux-v** ol-an k* ox-ac k* par k* peti a1 ph-ac k* *Phos* k* phys k* plat k* plb k* prun j5.de* *Puls* j5.de ran-b k* *Rat* j5.de* reser jl3 *Rhus-t* *Ruta* j5.de scroph-n j5.de seneg j5.de sep j5.de sil sphing a1* squil k* staph j5.de stict c1 sulph k* symph fd3.de• tab k* tarax k* thuj k* til k* tong a1 tritic-vg fd5.de **Tub** st1* verb k* vib k* zinc k*
      - **16 h** | **until**: coca a1
      - **air**; in open | **amel.**: kali-c a1 ol-an a1 rat a1
      - **reading**, when: prun a1
- **dinner – after – agg.**: ...
      - **showers** amel.; cold: cadm-met mg1.de
      - **writing** agg.: coca a1
  - **before**: calad k* calc-p k* lach k* nux-v a1 phos h2 scroph-n a1 sil a1 thuj k*
  - **during** | **agg.**: ang k* borx bov k* *Calc-p* k* cham k* hyper k* *Kali-c* kali-n a1 puls k* rat k* sarr k*
- **drinking**:
  - **after**:
    - **agg.**: nux-m hr1* ph-ac k*
    - **milk**: agar zr
- **driving**:
  - **agg.**: limen-b-c hrn2• [heroin sdj2]
  - **air**; in open | **amel.**: limen-b-c hrn2•
- **dropsy**, in: apoc bg2 *Hell* hr1*
- **drunkenness**; during: bell gl1.fr• *Op* kr1*
- **dullness**, with: arn j5.de bell a1 cact hr1* calad j5.de calc-p j5.de* carb-an j5.de caust j5.de coff j5.de *Cupr* hr1* dig j5.de* ferr j5.de *Gels* hr1* *Hyos* hr1* kreos j5.de lac-ac hr1* *Merc* hr1* nat-m j5.de nux-m j5.de *Phos* hr1* plb a1 *Rhod* b4a.de sep j5.de staph j5.de zinc j5.de
- **dyspnea** agg.: ran-b k2
- **eating**:
  - **after**:
    - **agg.**: acon k* **Agar** k* all-s k* aloe am-c k* *Anac* k* ant-c k* ant-t bg2* *Apis* arn bg2* ars b4a.de* arum-m k* *Arum-t* k* asaf b7.de* aur b4.de* bar-act sf1.de bar-c b4.de* berb a1* beryl tpw5* bism bro1 *Bov* k* bry k* bufo k* **Calc** k* calc-p k* *Calc-sil* k2* canth k* caps k* *Carb-v* k* *Carbn-s* *Carl* k* caust b4.de* chel k* *Chin* k* chinin-s kr1 choc srj3• cic k* cinnb k* clem k* coc-c k* coff b7.de* con b4.de* cortiso gse croc k* cub a1 cycl k* dig k* *Echi* sf1.de epiph br1 *Fel* a1* ferr b7.de* fruc-m-s yl1 gamb k* granit-m es1• graph k* grat k* hyos k* ign hr1* ignis-alc es2• *Kali-c* k* *Kali-chl* k13 *Kali-m* k2 kali-p k* kali-s lach k* laur b7a.de* *Lyc* k* lyss k* meph k* morg-g pte1*• *Mur-ac* k* *Nat-c* b4.de* *Nat-hchls* a1 *Nat-m* k* nauf-helv-li elm2• nit-ac k* *Nux-m* b7.de* **Nux-v** k* *Op* k* par b7.de* paull bro1 petr k* ph-ac k* *Phos* k* pip-n bg plat b4.de* psil ft1 psor al2 puls b7a.de* ran-b b7.de* rheum b7.de* *Rhus-t* k* *Rosm* lgb1 rumx *Ruta* k* scroph-n bro1 sep b4.de* *Sil* k* sin-a a1 *Squil* bg2* *Staph* k* still hr1* *Sulph* k* symph fd3.de• tarax k* *Tell* k* *Thuj* k* tritic-vg fd5.de *Verb* k* vib k* wildb a1 zinc k* zinc-p k2*
      - **and** drinking: ph-ac j5.de
      - **motion** | **amel.**: *Caps* sf1.de
  - **before** | **agg.**: calad lach a1 nat-m k*
  - **while** | **agg.**: agar k* bov hr1* calc ptk1 *Calc-p* hr1* caps ptk1 cham b7.de* chin bg3* **Kali-c** k* *Nux-v* bg3* *Phos* k* ptel c1 puls b7.de* rhus-t bg3* sarr a1* *Sulph* bg3*
- **excitement**; after: *Nux-m* k* *Podo* hr1* stram k* ziz a1
- **exertion**:
  - **after**; as: anac j5.de petr-ra shn4•
  - **agg.**: ars ptk1 bar-c ptk1 nux-m kr1* sel ptk1
    - **slightest** exertion: nux-m c1
  - **amel.**: melal-alt gya4 phys a1
- **eyes**:
  - **burning**; with: laur b7.de*
  - **closed**: *Acon* kr1
  - **half**-closed: *Bry* kr1 *Kreos* kr1
  - **heat**, with sensation of: kreos j5.de plat b4.de*
  - **opening** difficult: am-m j5.de ant-c j5.de ant-t j5.de ars-h kr1 bar-c j5.de canth j5.de castm j5.de chin j5.de cic j5.de cocc j5.de coff j5.de *Con* j5.de grat j5.de hell j5.de ign j5.de *Lach* kr1 m-arct j5.de merc j5.de mosch j5.de mur-ac j5.de nux-m j5.de oci-sa sk4• ph-ac j5.de *Phel* j5.de prun j5.de *Sabad* j5.de spig j5.de stann j5.de *Staph* j5.de tarax j5.de thuj j5.de verb j5.de
  - **pressing**; with: euphr b7.de*
- **face**:
  - **hot**; with: *Glon* kr1
  - **pallor**: *Glon* kr1
- **faintness**:
  - **after**: kali-n hr1 merc b4.de*

• **air** agg.; in open: *Crot-t* kr1
• **with**: stram j5.de
- **fever**:
• **after**: *Arn* b7a.de *Ars* b4a.de cham b7a.de op b7a.de plb b7a.de rhus-t b7a.de
⁝ **paroxysms**: podo ptk1
• **before**: rhus-t b7a.de
• **during** | **agg.**: (↗ *heat - during*) acon b7a.de ant-t bro1 apis bro1 bapt tl1 cham b7a.de corn-f bro1 gels bro1 nux-m mrr1 nux-v b7a.de* op bro1 puls b7a.de
• **septic**: stram ptk1
- **fright**:
• **after**: op ptk
• **with**: merc j5.de
- **fullness**, with sensation of: scroph-n j5.de
- **grief**; from: ign mrr1 *Op* hr1* **Ph-ac** kr1
- **groaning**, with: *Cham* hr1*
- **hallucinations**, with: lachn hr1*
- **head** to one side; child hangs: *Cina* kr1
- **headache**:
• **before**: sulph ptk1
• **during**: acon aesc agar ail k* aml-ns ammc kr1 ant-t bro1 ars arund kr1 asar *Bell* kr1 bism kr1 bran bro1 *Brom* b4a.de *Bruc* k1* calc j5.de calc-p kr1 camph cham k* chel j5.de* chinin-s *Coll* kr1 con *Corn* *Crot-h* kr1 cub kr1 d u b bro1 equis-h *Gamb* kr1 gels k* gins glon k* grat hipp hydr hydrog srj2• ign k* ind k* iodof kr1 ip jug-r kali-n kreos k* *Lach* k* laur k* lept bro1 lob merc-i-r mur-ac myric k* *Nat-m* kr1 nat-s *Nux-m* *Nux-v* kr1 **Op** bg2* pall kr1 petr-ra shn4• *Ph-ac* kr1 phos plb psil ft1 puls ran-b rhus-t bg2 sanguis-s hrn2• sep j5.de *Stann* stel bro1 still kr1 stront-c sul-ac tanac ter bg2 vip vip-a j5.de xan c1 zinc
- **heat**:
• **after**: caps a1*
• **before**: ant-t b7a.de *Puls* b7a.de* rhus-t b7a.de* sabad b7a.de
• **during**: (↗ *fever - during - agg.*) *Acon* b7a.de* ail bg2* *Ambr* kr1 *Ant-c* k* **Ant-t** b7a.de* *Apis* k* aran kr1 **Arn** bg2* *Ars* b4a.de* asaf k* aspar a1 bell bg2 borx b4a.de* bry c1 **Calad** k* calc camph caps bg2 cedr *Cham* b7a.de* chel chin cocc kr1 croc bg2 crot-h cycl bg2 **Eup-per** k* *Gels* k* *Hell* hep k* hyos kr1 ign k* kali-c bg2 *Kali-i* kr1 **Lach** k* lachn laur *Lyc* k* **Mez** k* mosch bg2 nat-c k* **Nat-m** k* nit-ac *Nux-m* k* nux-v bg2 **Op** k* petr bg2 *Ph-ac* k* *Phos* k* **Plb** b7.de* **Podo** k* *Puls* k* ran-b k2 rhus-t k* **Rob** ruta sabad k* **Samb** k* *Sep* b4.de* stram k* sulph bg2 syph al *Ter* kr1 thuj verat k* verat-v viol-t bg2
- **heaviness**, with: aesc hr1* apoc-a a1 atro a1 carb-ac a1* caust j5.de coli jl2 *Kreos* hr1* morph a1 *Puls* hr1* sil a1 staph j5.de tarent a1 tere-la rly4•
• **head**, of: *Bar-c* kr1 corn kr1 hydr a1
- **house**, in the: plat tab
- **hypochondriasis**, in: *Arg-n* hr1*
- **hysteria**; during: **Nux-m** hr1*
- **impatience**, with: nit-ac j5.de*
- **indifference**, with: corn hr1*
- **indolence**, with: acon j5.de* alum a1 am-m j5.de ammc j5.de *Ant-t* j5.de ars j5.de carb-an j5.de* carb-v j5.de* chel j5.de* cinnb j5.de colch a1 croc j5.de* dig j5.de* dulc j5.de* grat j5.de ip j5.de laur j5.de* lyc j5.de* mag-c j5.de* mag-m j5.de* nat-c j5.de* nat-m a1 nat-s a1 rat j5.de* sars j5.de tong j5.de* verb j5.de* *Zinc* j5.de*
- **influenza**; during: bapt tl1 *Gels* hr1* *Sabad* hr1*
- **injuries**; after: | **head**; of the: op mrr1
- **intermittent**: ars a1 cann-i a1 carbn-s a1 guare a1
• **afternoon**: fl-ac a1
- **intoxicated**; as if: agar hr1* agath-a nl2• *Led* k* **Nux-m** k* petr-ra shn4•
- **irresistible**: crot-h bg2 kali-n bg2 nux-m bg2
- **irresolution**; with: hyos j5.de
- **irritability**; with: ind j5.de*
- **labor** pain; during: gels mrr1 *Op* b7a.de *Puls* k*
• **contraction**; after each: gels st
- **laughing**; after: phos ptk1
- **laughter**, with inclination to: *Nux-m* j5.de*
- **lectophobia**; with (See bed - shuns)
- **lids**, with contraction of: acon b7.de* agar b4.de* *Ant-t* k* chel b7.de* chin b7.de* cic b7.de* cocc b7.de* *Con* k* croc k* euphr b7.de* ferr b7.de* ham bg2 kali-c k* m-arct b7.de m-aust b7a.de merc b4.de* plat b4.de* sabad b7.de* staph b7.de* tarax b7.de* thuj k* verb b7.de* viol-o b7.de* viol-t b7.de*
- **liver** complaints; in (See accompanied - liver)
- **looking** long at one place, on: cic k*
- **lying**:
• **agg.**: dulc fd4.de ferr-ma a1 lyc b4.de* plat b4.de* sel bg2*
• **inclination** to lying down: *Alum* hr1* am-c j5.de berb j5.de bism j5.de calad j5.de **Caust** j5.de* cina j5.de clem j5.de *Cocc* hr1* coff j5.de coloc j5.de con h2* crot-t j5.de cycl j5.de *Graph* j5.de* *Hell* j5.de hep j5.de *Ign* j5.de* kali-c j5.de lact j5.de led j5.de *Mur-ac* hr1* nat-c j5.de nat-m j5.de ol-an j5.de* olnd j5.de petr j5.de rhus-t j5.de ruta fd4.de staph j5.de tritic-vg fd5.de vanil fd5.de [tax jsj7]
• **quietly** | **amel.**: phos a1
• **side**; on:
⁝ **left** | **agg.**: thuj ptk1
- **meal**; after (See eating - after - agg.)
- **measles**; during: *Apis* kr1 xan kr1
- **meeting**, in interesting: pip-m a1
- **menses**:
• **before** | **agg.**: calc-p k* melal-alt gya4 ozone sde2• puls b7.de* sulph b4a.de
• **during** | **agg.**: choc srj3• eupi k* *Kali-c* k* mag-c b4.de* **Nux-m** k* ph-ac b4a.de *Phos* k* *Sulph* k* uran-n
• **suppressed** menses; from: *Cycl* kr1 nux-m br1 senec ptk1
- **mental** exertion:
• **agg.**: **Ars** k* ferr k* *Gels* k* *Hyos* k* kali-c ptk1 kali-s fd4.de nat-s nux-m hr1* nux-v k* *Op* mrr1 ph-ac ptk1 *Podo* hr1* sabad hr1* sel ptk1 tarax k*
• **amel.**: croc b7.de*
- **metrorrhagia**; during: *Sec* hr1*
- **moon**; at new: sep sf1.de
- **moroseness**, with: calc j5.de calen j5.de carb-an j5.de carb-v j5.de cycl ptk1 hyos j5.de kali-c j5.de ol-an j5.de ph-ac j5.de sabad j5.de sep j5.de
- **motion**:
• **agg.**: *Carb-v* kr1 sil b4.de*
• **amel.**: caps bg2 carb-v b4.de* *Cycl* b7a.de *Mur-ac* b4a.de* nicc j5.de phos a1 tarax b7.de*
- **music** agg.: stann k*
- **narcolepsy**; from (See overpowering)
- **nausea**:
• **after**: aeth lp ant-t lp chinin-ar k2 ip lp*
• **with**: am-c b4a.de ant-t bg2 apoc bro1* calad hr1* ind a1* ip bg2 *Nux-m* j5.de* plan hr1* ran-b b7.de* rhus-t b7a.de seneg j5.de vanil fd5.de
- **news**, after sad (See sad news)
- **occupation** amel.: melal-alt gya4
- **old** people: ant-c br1
- **overestimation** of time and distance; with: nux-m j5.de
- **overpowering**: (↗ *Falling - daytime*) aeth c1 agar j5.de* agar-pa a1 agn b7.de* alco a1 all-c a1* alum a1* *Am-c* bg2 androc srj1* ang b7.de* *Ant-c* j5.de **Ant-t** b7.de* *Ars* j5.de* arum-i a1* arum-m j5.de *Atox* bro1* *Aur* k* bar-act a1 bar-c bell bg2 brom a1 *Bry* b7.de* buth-a mg1.de calc k* camph k* cann-s k* canth j5.de carb-v k* carbn-s cartl-s rly4• *Caust* b4.de* *Chin* h1* *Cimx* k* cina j5.de clem b4.de* cocc k* coff k* colch a1 coloc k* colocin a1 *Con* b4a.de* conin a1 *Cor-r* k* **Croc** b7.de* *Crot-h* j5.de* crot-t j5.de* cycl j5.de cyn-d st1 echi bg2 euph j5.de* euphr a1 ferr k* ferr-p bg2 fl-ac bg2 gels k* grat j5.de* guar vml3• *Haem* j5.de* hep a1 *Hydr-ac* j5.de* hydrog srj2• hyos k* hypoth jl3 kali-bi a1 *Kali-br* hr1 kali-c b4.de* *Kali-n* a1* *Kola* stb3• *Lach* k* lact k* laur k* lina br1* lyc k* *M-ambo* b7.de* m-arct b7.de mag-s j5.de* mang-p rly4• melal-alt gya4 *Merc* j5.de merl a1 *Mez* k* *Moni* rfm1• musca-d szs1 naja nat-ar bro1 nat-c k* nat-m k* nat-n a1 nicotam rly4• nit-ac k* **Nux-m** k* *Nux-v* k* **Op** k* osm a1 pall a1 petr h2 petr-ra shn4• ph-ac b4.de* phos k* *Phys* a1* pimp a1 pip-m a1 pisc st1 plb j5.de podo bg2 psil ft1 psor st1 *Puls* b7.de* rauw sp1 rhod j5.de* *Rhus-t* j5.de* *Sabad* j5.de* scroph-n j5.de sel jl3 *Sep* j5.de *Sil* j5.de* sol-t-ae a1 spig k* stann k* sulph k* suprar rly4• tab j5.de taosc iwa1• *Tarax* j5.de* tarent k* tax-br oss1• thal-xyz srj8• tritic-vg fd5.de tub br1 vanil fd5.de verb j5.de viol-t a1 voes a1 *Zinc* b4.de* [**Spect** dfg1]

Sleep

- morning: arum-i ptk2 cartl-s rly4• clem a1 ger-i rly4• mag-s k* nux-v k* sacch-a fd2.de•
- forenoon: cann-s k* lyc sil a1 spig k*
- noon: kali-n a1 lyc k* verat a1
- afternoon: colch a1 kali-c h2* nat-c k* nicotam rly4• **Puls** k*
  - 13 h: lyc a1
  - 15 h: pall a1
  - 17 h: hyos a1 nicotam rly4• petr-ra shn4• [tax jsj7]
    - 17-18 h: petr-ra shn4•
- evening: carb-v k* cina a1 hep a1 kali-bi a1 kali-c h2* lyc k* mag-s k* spig k*
- accompanied by:
  - bronchitis (See CHEST - Inflammation - bronchial - accompanied - sleepiness)
  - cough (See COUGH - Accompanied - sleepiness)
  - tetanus (See GENERALS - Tetanus - accompanied - narcolepsy)
- air agg.; in open: merl a1
- concentrating; when: *Op* mrr1
- dinner; after: aur k* carb-v h2* kali-bi a1 laur k* lyc a1 mez a1 phos a1
- eating; after: calc k* carb-v k* guar vml3• lyc a1 nit-ac k* *Nux-v* a1
- periodical:
  - hour | returns at the same: tarent a1
- reading by lamplight; on: mang a1
- waking; on: ferr a1
- working: bism j5.de lact j5.de mur-ac j5.de phel j5.de ran-b j5.de sulph j5.de tarent a1 zinc j5.de

- pain:
  - after: lach bg2 phyt k* ruta fd4.de
    - neuralgia; after an attack of: *Cocc-s* hr1*
  - during: ant-t b7a.de *Ars* bg aur bg bell bg carb-an bg1 cham bg graph bg lyc bg *Merc* bg *Nit-ac* bg nux-m k* *Op* bg2 phos bg2 psil ft1* sul-ac bg sulph bg til bg tritic-vg fd5.de
    - Abdomen: ant-t *Nux-m* b7a.de
      - children; in: cham b7a.de
    - Eyes: kali-c bg2 lyc bg2 mang bg2
      - tearing: plb bg2
    - Hypochondrium: sep st
    - Stomach: galeoc-c-h gms1•
    - Teeth (See TEETH - Pain - accompanied - sleepiness)
- palpitations; with: aur h2 chin k* crot-t merc j5.de nux-v j5.de *Podo* kr1 tab j5.de
- periodical: fl-ac bg2* *Sep* b4a.de
  - day:
    - every other day: bry b7.de* lach b7.de*
    - every third day: sep a1
  - morning | every two hours: fl-ac a1
  - afternoon: fl-ac a1
    - day; every other: **Lach** hr1*
  - evening | day; every other: lach
- perspiration; with: *Acon* bg2 ant-c bg2 **Ant-t** bg2* *Apis* bg2 am bg2 ars bg2 *Asaf* bg2* **Bell** bg2 borx bg2 **Calad** bg2 caps bg2 **Cham** bg2 *Cina* bg2 *Com* kr1 croc bg2 cycl bg2 *Hep* bg2 *Ign* bg2 kali-c bg2 lach bg2 lyc bg2 **Mez** bg2 mosch bg2 nat-c bg2 nat-m bg2 *Nit-ac* bg2 *Nux-m* bg2* nux-v bg2 **Op** bg2 petr bg2 *Ph-ac* bg2* *Phos* bg2 *Plb* bg2 podo bg2 **Puls** bg2 rhus-t bg2* **Sabad** bg2 sep bg2 stram bg2 sulph bg2 verat bg2 viol-t bg2
  - face; of: calc-p kr1
  - work; after | amel.: phys a1
- pneumonia; in: *Ant-t* tl1* chel ptk1* *Op* tl1* phos ptk1*
- pollutions, after: aq-mar jl3* glycyr-g cte1• *Sep* kr1
- pregnancy agg.; during: gels k* *Helon* k* mag-c mrr1 *Nux-m* k*
- prostration, with: acon a1 ant-t a1 calc-p hr1 cann-s j5.de canth j5.de chel a1 con h2* croc j5.de* crot-t a1 kali-bi a1 lach a1 mur-ac a1 [bell-p-sp dcm1]
- pulse, with slow: tela vh
- purpura, after: *Hell* hr1*
- reading:
  - agg.: alum k2 anac k* ang k* aster aur b4.de* bism h1 brom k* *Carb-v* *Carbn-s* cimic k* *Colch* k* coloc *Con* k* *Ferr* hr1 *Gels* ign k* iris lac-h sk4• lyc mang mez mosch b7.de* nat-c b4.de* *Nat-m* nat-s k* pimp a1 plat prun *Puls* b7a.de ruta k* *Sabad* b7.de* sang sel b7.de* sep sil h2 *Sulph* tab tarax k* urt-u verat
  - amel.: croc ptk1
- rest agg.: caust ckh1 kali-n j5.de*
- restlessness; with: ars j5.de bufo kr1 coloc j5.de *Con* hr1* crot-h j5.de *Hep* hr1* lact hr1* *Merc* hr1* *Petr* hr1* rhus-t j5.de* *Sep* hr1* *Stram* hr1* tab a1
- rheumatism; during: *Lyc* hr1* *Puls* hr1*
- riding:
  - agg.: bapt brom carb-ac carc dgt card-m chinin-s ham fd3.de• limen-b-c mlk9.de lyc op pall phys sulph tet a1 tritic-vg fd5.de vanil fd5.de
  - air; in open | agg.: ant-t
  - horse; a: | agg.: lyc
  - streetcar; on a | agg.: chinin-s
- rising:
  - agg.: merc a1
  - amel.: nat-m a1 nicc j5.de
- room, in the: asar b7.de* plb b7.de*
  - warm: ant-t chinin-s cinnb colch sne conv sne hip-ac sne ind merl sil sne thlas sne
- sad news; after: *(↗MIND - Ailments - bad)* ign k*
- sadness; with (See MIND - Sadness - sleepiness)
- scarlatina:
  - after: *Ter* hr1*
  - in: *Nat-m* a1*
- sedentary habits, in persons of: *Gels* kr1
- sewing: ferr k*
- shivering:
  - after: sabin b7.de*
  - during: cina b7.de led b7.de nat-m b4.de rhus-t b7.de sabad b7.de *Sabin* b7a.de staph b7.de
- shock, after mental: *Pic-ac* hr1*
- sitting agg.: acon aesc agar am-c j5.de anac k* ang ant-c ant-t k* apis aran-sc a1 arg-met j5.de arg-n ars ars-met kr1 arum-t aur k* bapt bruc j5.de cadm-s calc h2 calc-p carb-v b4.de* caust b4.de* *Cham* k* chin k* chinin-s cimx cina k* clem k* coca coff b7.de* cycl k* dulc fd4.de fago ferr k* ferr-ma form gels *Hep* ign k* indg j5.de kali-br kali-c k* kali-s fd4.de lac-leo sk4• lyc k* merc k* mez mur-ac k* narcot a1 nat-c k* *Nat-hchls* *Nat-m* k* nat-p k* nicc *Nux-m* b7.de* **Nux-v** k* par petr k* phel j5.de plat j5.de plb b7.de* psor puls k* ran-b j5.de rat rhus-t b7.de* *Sabad* b7.de* sacch-a fd2.de• *Sep* k* spig j5.de staph k* *Sulph* b4.de* tarax k* tarent tell thuj k* tritic-vg fd5.de vanil fd5.de verat j5.de *Zinc* kr1
  - conversation; during: chinin-s a1*
  - room; in a warm: bung-fa mtf ind a1
  - sleepless while lying, and: cham k*
  - waking agg.; after: rhus-t
  - working; while: *Sulph* *Zinc* kr1
- sleeplessness, during (See Sleeplessness - accompanied - sleepiness)
- smallpox, in: *Nat-m* hr1*
- smoking agg.: bufo
- sopor: anh mg1.de cyt-l mg1.de
- soporific; as after a: *Mand* mg1.de
- soreness, with: eug j5.de m-arct j5.de
- speaking difficult: am j5.de
- standing agg.: acon k* alum k* cor-r k* mag-c k* merc b4.de* merl a1 morph k* nit-ac j5.de* phel k* tritic-vg fd5.de
  - working; while: phel k* tritic-vg fd5.de
- starting, with: am-m a1 ang j5.de ant-t j5.de bell a1 *Cham* hr1* chel j5.de kali-i j5.de mag-c j5.de* merc j5.de* plat j5.de* *Puls* hr1* sars j5.de* seneg j5.de *Tarent* hr1* verat j5.de*
- stool:
  - after | agg.: aeth k* bry k* colch k* coloc k* elaps ferr-p bg2 lact c1 *Nux-m* k* nux-v bg2 *Sulph* k*

- **stool**: ...
  - **amel.**: grat a1
  - **during** | **agg.**: ant-t bg2 bry k* elaps lact mtf *Manc* a1* nux-m k* puls bg2
- **stretching**; with: am-c j5.de ant-t j5.de bar-c j5.de bell j5.de* chel a1 chin j5.de* hell j5.de lach j5.de* laur a1 mag-c j5.de* meph j5.de* nit-ac j5.de* ol-an a1 ph-ac j5.de phos j5.de* sabad j5.de
- **students**, in: ferr ptk1 *Gels* k* mag-p ptk1
- **stupefaction**; with (See MIND - Stupefaction - sleepiness)
- **stupor**, with: cyt-l mg1.de gels a1 nat-m hr1
- **sudden**: chir-fl gya2 *Fl-ac* bg2* grat j5.de hydrog srj2• m-arct j5.de merc j5.de n a d rly4• nept-m lsd2.fr rumx ptk1 tritic-vg fd5.de ulm-c jsj8•
  - **evening**: fl-ac a1
    - **18** h: rhus-t a1
  - **wine** agg.: fl-ac a1
- **summer** colds, in: *Gels* kr1
- **summer** heat with general debility, in: *Corn* kr1
- **supper** agg.; after: am-c arum-t **Calc** carb-v chim-m chin clem colch hep kr1 lach mag-c mez nit-ac
- **syphilis**; during: *Syph* hr1*
- **talking** agg.: ars j5.de caust k* *Chel* k* *Mag-c* k* morph ph-ac k* plat j5.de plb j5.de*
- **thoughts**, with activity of: agre jl3 teucr j5.de
- **thunderstorm**; during: (↗*weather - stormy - agg.)* sil k*
- **uneasiness**, with: am-c j5.de nat-m a1 nicc j5.de* phos a1
- **unoccupied**; when: am-c b4.de* nat-m b4.de*
- **uterus**; with prolapse of (See accompanied - uterus)
- **vertigo**, with (See VERTIGO - Sleepiness)
- **vomiting**: (↗*Falling - vomiting)*
  - **after**: *Aeth* k* ant-c k* ant-t b7.de* apom bg2 ars bg2 bell k* cupr k* dig k* **Ip** k* kali-bi bg2 sanic ptk1
  - **during**: *Aeth* bro1 *Ant-t* bro1 *Apoc* kr1 dig b4a.de* ip bro1 mag-c bro1 vip-a j5.de
  - **weakness** and slow pulse, with: apoc k*
- **waking** | **after** | **agg.**: (↗*Unrefreshing)* bell h1 neon srj5• sul-ac h2
  - **on**: bell a1 bry j5.de* calad kr1 calc j5.de calc-f sp1 caust j5.de chel a1 choc srj3• falco-pe nl2• laur j5.de lyc a1 *Nux-m* a1* stram a1 tere-la rly4•
- **walking**:
  - **about** | **amel.**: mosch gt
  - **after**; as: rhus-t j5.de
    - **air**; in open: arn carb-an con lach lyc nat-m phos phys stann *Sulph* sumb
    - **long** walk; a: anac j5.de
  - **agg.**: acon k* arg-met j5.de caust k* chinin-s kali-n k* lyc h2* nat-c h2 nit-ac b4.de* rhus-t k* verat k*
  - **air**; in open:
    - **after** | **agg.**: arn b7.de* lach b7.de* phos b4.de* puls b7.de* rhus-t b7.de* sep b4.de* stann b4.de*
    - **agg.**: acon b7a.de ant-t b7.de* (non:ars slp) ars-met kr1* *Chel* con eug *Euphr* b7a.de kali-c b4a.de* m-aust b7.de* mosch k* nux-v k* rhus-t h1 sil stann b4.de*
    - **amel.**: asar jl
  - **amel.**: ignis-alc es2• merc a1 nat-m a1 ph-ac b4.de*
  - **cold** air; in | **agg.**: nux-m k2
- **watching** TV (See mental)
- **weakness**:
  - **as** from: anac j5.de
  - **literary** occupation in evening amel.: *Croc* kr1
  - **nursing** or night watching, after: *Sulph* kr1
  - **vertigo**; with: **Nit-ac** kr1*
  - **with**: aeth j5.de am-c bg2* anac j5.de ang j5.de ant-t a1 arg-met j5.de aur j5.de bar-c a1 bism bg2 brom a1 bruc j5.de canth j5.de chin j5.de cic a1 clem j5.de *Croc* j5.de* cupr j5.de* *Cycl* hr1* echi bg2 eucal bg2* grat j5.de* hell j5.de kali-bi a1 kali-n j5.de* lach j5.de lact j5.de laur j5.de* lyc a1 mag-c a1 merc-sul hr1* merl a1 *Mez* a1* mur-ac a1 nat-c j5.de nat-m a1 *Nit-ac* j5.de* pall bg2 petr j5.de ph-ac j5.de* phel j5.de plat j5.de puls a1 ran-b a1 scroph-n j5.de sil j5.de squil j5.de *Sulph* j5.de* thuj a1 tritic-vg fd5.de uran-n bg2 valer j5.de verat j5.de* vip-a j5.de [tax jsj7]

Sleepiness: ...

- **weariness**; with: am-c j5.de anac j5.de* ant-c j5.de* ars j5.de bar-c j5.de berb j5.de borx j5.de calad j5.de calc j5.de* camph j5.de caust j5.de* chel a1 chen-v hr1* *Cic* hr1* clem j5.de* **Coca** hr1* colch a1 con h2* croc j5.de cycl a1 dig j5.de ferr j5.de **Gels** hr1* graph j5.de* grat hr1* hell j5.de* hep j5.de ign j5.de ip j5.de kali-c a1 *Kreos* hr1* lact j5.de laur j5.de* led sf1.de lyc a1 m-aust j5.de mang j5.de* merl a1 murx sf1.de nat-c j5.de nat-m j5.de nat-s a1 nit-ac a1 *Nux-v* hr1* pall sf1.de petr j5.de ph-ac j5.de* phel a1 podo fd3.de• ruta fd4.de sang hr1* sel sf1.de sep j5.de sil hr1* sin-n hr1* sol-mm j5.de spig j5.de spong a1* staph j5.de still hr1* *Sulph* j5.de* ther j5.de uran-n sf1.de vanil fd5.de ziz hr1*
  - **eating**; while: kali-c ptk1
- **weather**:
  - **cloudy** weather: | **agg.**: physal-al bg1
  - **hot**: **Ant-c** kr1 *Corn* kr1 *Gels* hr1 *Nux-v* kr1 sel b7.de* tritic-vg fd5.de
    - **first** hot weather; at: vip a1
  - **stormy**:
    - **agg.**: (↗*thunderstorm)* sil h2*
    - **before**: form gels bg2* sil h2*
- **weep**, with inclination to: cham hr1* tritic-vg fd5.de
- **whooping** cough; after: *Ant-t* kr1 *Caust* kr1
- **wine** agg.: ail k* carbn-s conch fkr1• fl-ac a1 phos b4.de*
- **work**:
  - **aversion** to work, with: am-m j5.de clem j5.de colch j5.de coloc j5.de mag-m j5.de ther bg2*
  - **during**: am-c j5.de aur-m k* bism k* caust k* euphr a1 ign b7.de* lact j5.de* lyc k* mez a1 mur-ac b4.de* nat-c k* oci-sa sk4• phel j5.de* ran-b j5.de* sulph k* tarent a1 til a1 tritic-vg fd5.de zinc b4.de*
    - **amel.**: am-c b4.de* bar-c j5.de nat-c h2
  - **not** at work; when: am-c h2* mosch
  - **scientific** work, during: tarax j5.de
    - **amel.**: croc j5.de
- **worms**; with: *Nux-m* kr1
- **writing**:
  - **agg.**: bapt brom k* nat-s j5.de* ph-ac k* thuj
  - **amel.**: croc ptk1
- **yawning**:
  - **with** (See Yawning - sleepiness - during)
  - **without**: chel tl1

SLEEPLESSNESS: (↗*Falling - difficult; Falling - difficult - waking; Falling - late; Short)* abrom-a bnj1 abrot k* absin k* acetan vh1 achy-a bnj1 *Acon* k* acon-c a1 acon-f a1 adon bg2* aeth k* aether a1 *Agar* k* agav-t jl3 *Agn* k* aids nl2* alco a1 alet sf1.de alf br1* all-s br1 allox sp1 *Aloe* alum k* alum-p k2* alumn k* am-br k* am-c k* am-caust a1 am-m k* am-pic br1 ambr k* *Ammc* hr1* anac k* *Androc* srj1• ang k* anh br1* anil a1 ant-c k* ant-o a1 **Ant-t** k* anthraci anthraco kr1 aphis a1* *Apis* k* apoc k* apoc-a a1 apom bro1 aqui br1* ara-maca sej7* aran k* aran-ix mg1.de* arg-cy a1 arg-met **Arg-n** k* arge-pl rwt5• arist-cl sp1 *Arn* k* **Ars** k* ars-h a1* *Ars-i* k* **Ars-s-f** k2* *Arum-t* k* arund k* asaf b2.de* asar b2.de* asc-t k* asim hr1* *Aster* hr1* *Atro* k* *Aur* k* aur-m k* *Aur-m-n* wbt2• aur-s a1* *Aven* bg1* aza jl3 *Bamb-a* stb2.de• *Bapt* k* bar-c k* bar-m bar-s k2* **Bell** k* bell-p c1* ben a1* *Benz-ac* k* benzo c1 bism b2.de* blum-o bnj1 boerh-d zzc1• bond a1 *Borx* k* bov mrr1 brach a1 brass-n-o srj5• bros-gau mrc1 brucel sa3• brucin a1 **Bry** k* bufo-s but-ac br1* buth-a sp1 **Cact** k* cadm-met cadm-s cain calad k* calam sa3• **Calc** k* calc-ar hr1* calc-br c1* calc-caust a1* calc-hp sf1.de calc-i k2* *Calc-p* k* calc-s k* calc-sil k2* calo a1 *Camph* k* *Camph-mbr* bro1 canch a1 cann-i k* cann-s k* *Canth* k* caps k* carb-an k* *Carb-v* k* carbn-dox knl3• *Carbn-s* *Carc* mg1.de* cardios-h rly4• *Carl* k* cassia-s ccrh1• castm bg2* caul k2* *Caust* k* cean sf1.de cedr k* cench k2* cere-b a1 cerv a1 **Cham** k* chel b2.de* **Chin** k* *Chinin-ar* *Chinin-s* k* chlf hr1* chlol k* chol br1 chrysan bro1 *Cic* k* cimic k* *Cina* k* cinnb k* **Cit-v** k* clem k* cob k* cob-n sp1 coc-c k* coca k* coca-c sk4• cocain br1* *Cocc* k* *Cocc-s* hr1* coch hr1* cod a1 **Coff** k* coff-t a1 coffin a1* colch k* colchin c1* *Coloc* k* *Con* k* conch a1 convo-s sp1 cop k* corn hr1* corn-f hr1 cortico mg1.de* cortiso mg1.de* cot a1 croc bg2* crot-c a1* *Crot-h* k* crot-t k* *Cupr* k* cupr-act a1 cupr-ar hr1* **Cycl** k* **Cypr** hr1* cyt-l a1* daph k* dendr-pol sk4• *Dig* k* digin a1 dios k* diosm br1 dip bro1 dirc k* *Dros* k* *Dulc* k* dys pte1*• eaux a1 elaps ergot jl3 ery-a k* eucal hr1* eug k* eup-per bg2* eup-pur k* euph euph-pe a1 euphr b2.de* fago k* *Ferr* k* *Ferr-ar* ferr-i k* ferr-p k* ferul a1 fil hr1* *Fl-ac* k* form k* gad a1 gamb k* gast a1 *Gels* k*

Sleeplessness: ...
get a1 *Glon* k* *Glycyr-g* cte1• gran k* *Graph* k* grin sf1.de *Guaj* k* guar a1* guat sp1 haem a1 halo jl3 hedy a1 *Hell* k* helo bg2 helo-s rwt2• helon br1* **Hep** k* hipp a1 hippoz hr1* hir skp7• hist sp1 hura hydr k* hydr-ac a1 *Hydrog* srj2*• hydroph rsj6• **Hyos** k* *Hyosin* a1* hyosin-hbr br1* iber a1 *Ign* k* ina-i mlk9.de inul a1 *Iod* k* iodof a1 *Ip* k* iris iris-t c1* jab k* jac-c k* *Jal* jatr-c jug-c k* jug-r k* **Kali-ar** k* *Kali-bi* k* *Kali-br* k* **Kali-c** k* kali-chl k13 kali-cy k* *Kali-i* k* kali-m k2* kali-n k* kali-p k* kali-perm a1 *Kali-s* kalm k* ketogl-ac rly4• kiss a1 *Kola* stb3• *Kreos* k* lac-ac k* *Lac-c* k* *Lac-d* k2* lac-f wza1• *Lac-h* sk4*• lac-leo hrn2• **Lach** k* *Lachn* k* lact k* lam a1 lat-h bnm5• lat-m sp1* laur k* lec br1* *Led* k* lepi a1 lept k* lil-t k* linu-c a1 lipp a1 *Lith-c* kr1* lob-s a1 *Lup* bro1* *Lyc* k* *Lycps-v* kr1 lyss hr1* m-arct b2.de m-aust b2.de *Mag-c* k* *Mag-m* k* mag-p bro1 *Mag-s* k* *Maias-l* hrn2• malar jl2 manc k* mand sp1 mang b2.de* mate a1 *Med* k* meningoc jl2 menis a1 meph hr1* **Merc** k* **Merc-c** k* merc-cy k* merc-i-f k* merc-i-r k* merc-n a1 merc-ns a1 merc-sul a1 merl k* mez k* morg-g pte1*• morg-p pte1*• morph k* mosch k* mur-ac k* myric br1 myris k* naja nat-ar k* *Nat-c* k* nat-hchls a1 *Nat-m* k* nat-ox rly4• *Nat-p* *Nat-s* k* nep srb2.fr nicc k* nicot a1 *Nit-ac* k* nitro-o a1 *Nux-m* k* **Nux-v** k* oci-sa sk4• ol-an a1 ol-j c2 olib-sac wmh1 olnd k* **Op** k* orot-ac rly4• osm a1 ost a1 ox-ac bg* oxal-a rly4• parathyr jl2 *Passi* bg1* paull a1 pegan-ha tpi1• peti a1 petr k* petr-ra shn4• *Ph-ac* k* phel c1 **Phos** k* phys k* phyt k* pic-ac k* pin-s a1 pip-m a1 plac-s rly4• plan k* *Plat* k* **Plb** k* plb-chr a1 plect a1 *Podo* hr1* *Positr* nl2• *Propr* sa3• prun k* pseuts-m oss1• psor k* ptel k* **Puls** k* puls-n a1 querc-r svu1• ran-b k* ran-g a1 ran-s k* raph k* rauw sp1 rheum b2.de* rhod k* **Rhus-t** k* rhus-v k* rosm a1 *Rumx* rumx-act a1 ruta b2.de* sabad k* sabin k* sacch a1 samb b2.de* sang k* sapin a1* sarcol-ac sp1 saroth sp1 sarr k* sars k* scopin-hbr br1 scopla br1 *Scut* c1* *Sec* k* *Sel* k* *Senec* k* senn c1* **Sep** k* **Sil** k* sin-n k* sol-t-ae k* spig k* spira a1 spong k* squil k* **Stann** k* **Staph** k* stict c1* stram k* strept-ent jl2 stront-c b2.de* stry k* stry-n mtf11 suis-pan rly4• sul-ac k* sulfon bro1 **Sulph** k* sumb k* syc pte1*• **Syph** k* *Tab* k* tarax b2.de* *Tarent* k* tax k* tela c1* tell hr1* term-a bnj1 teucr b2.de* thal sf1.de thal-xyz srj8• thea k* *Ther* mrr1 thiop jl3 **Thuj** k* thyreotr jl3 til k* trach a1 tril-c a1 (non:tril-p a1*) trinit br1 trion bwa3 tritic-vg fd5.de *Tub* bg2* tub-m jl2 uran-n c2 *Ust* hr1* *Valer* k* vanil fd5.de verat k* verb b2.de* verbe-o br1 vero-o rly4*• vesp k* vinc k* viol-o b2.de* *Viol-t* b2.de* vip k* wies a1 x-ray sp1 xan hr1* yohim c1* zinc k* zinc-m a1* zinc-o c1* zinc-ox c zinc-p c1* zinc-val bg2* zing k* ziz a1 [alumin-s stj2 ant-met stj2 ars-met stj2 *Astat* stj2 *Bar-br* stj2 *Bar-i* stj2 *Bar-met* stj2 bell-p-sp dcm1 *Bism-sn* stj2 brom stj2 caes-met stj2 ferr-f stj2 ferr-lac stj2 ferr-n stj2 ferr-sil stj2 *Hafn-met* stj2 heroin sdj2 *Irid-met* stj2 kali-met stj2 *Lanth-met* stj2 lith-f stj2 lith-i stj2 lith-met stj2 lith-p stj2 lith-s stj2 *Merc-d* stj2 *Osm-met* stj2 *Plb-m* stj2 *Plb-p* stj2 *Polon-met* stj2 *Rhen-met* stj2 rubd-met stj2 *Spect* dfg1 stront-m stj2 stront-met stj2 *Tant-met* stj2 *Thal-met* stj2 *Tung-met* stj2 zinc-i stj2 zinc-n stj2]

- **daytime**: bros-gau mrc1
  - **children**; in: *(↗total)* chel a1
    - **and** night: psor st
- **morning**: bros-gau mrc1 cinnb k* coli jl2 cycl k* dulc k* kali-i k* merc-i-r k* *Nat-m* ol-an k* sol-t-ae k*
  - **5** h; after: coca-c sk4•
  - **images**; from: acon
  - **until**: aur mtf33
- **afternoon**: *Ars-s-f* k2* bros-gau mrc1 pip-m a1 sil a1
  - **13** h | **13**-14 h: pip-m a1
  - **14**.30 h: pall a1
  - **16** h | **until**: nat-p a1
- **evening**: *(↗Falling - late)* aloe *Arn* k* *Ars-s-f* k2* borx brom k* bry k* cact k* calc k* calc-p k* calc-s k* canth k* carb-an k* clem h2* cob k* coca *Coff* k* dios hr1* dor a1* *Ferr* hr1* fl-ac k* ger-i rly4• grat k* guaj k* *Kola* stb3• **Lach** k* lyc k* lycps-v a1 *Mag-c* merc k* mez k* mucs-nas rly4• nat-c k* ol-an k* olib-sac wmh1 petr k* *Phos* k* psor k* **Puls** k* *Rhus-t* k* sang spirae a1 staph k* stront-c **Sulph** k* tab k* tub-m ih *Valer* k* zing k*
  - **21** h: kali-cy a1
  - **bed**; after going to: **Ambr** k* bamb-a stb2.de• bell sf1.de* borx carb-v carc mg1.de* cham k2 cob-n mg1.de* cortiso sp1 *Kola* stb3• mag-c *Mag-m* ozone sde2• *Ph-ac* *Phos*
    - **closing** eyes; and: *Mag-m*
    - **restlessness**; from physical: bamb-a stb2.de•
    - **sleepiness** before; but: petr-ra shn4•
  - **congestion**, from: rhus-t a1

- **evening**: ...
  - **cough** agg.: phos a1
  - **joyful** news, from: aloe a1
  - **menses**; during: mag-m k*
  - **pulsation** in vessels, from: rhus-t a1
  - **restlessness**; with: phos a1
  - **sleepiness**; with | **morning**: *Teucr* sf1.de
  - **starting**, from: *Puls* k*
  - **thoughts**, from activity of: bar-c a1 fl-ac st1 rhus-t a1 sabad a1 sil a1
  - **toothache**; from: rat a1
  - **walking** agg.; after: fl-ac k*
  - **warmth** agg. | **heat** agg.: calc **Puls** rhus-t
  - **wine** agg.: fl-ac k*
- **night**: am-c j5.de ambr j5.de ant-t j5.de aphis j5.de *Ars* j5.de aur j5.de *Aur-m-n* wbt2• borx j5.de bry j5.de camph j5.de caps j5.de carb-v h2* carbn-dox knl3• *Caust* j5.de cham j5.de* *Chin* j5.de *Cina* j5.de cinnb h1* clem j5.de cocc j5.de *Coff* j5.de coloc j5.de *Con* j5.de cyclosp sa3• dros j5.de dulc j5.de *Ferr* j5.de granit-m es1• *Graph* j5.de hep j5.de hydr-ac j5.de *Hyos* j5.de ign j5.de jal j5.de *Kali-c* j5.de kali-chl k13 kali-i j5.de kali-m k2 kreos j5.de *Lac-lup* hrn2• lach j5.de lact j5.de laur j5.de m-aust j5.de *Mag-c* j5.de merc j5.de *Mosch* j5.de *Nat-m* j5.de *Nit-ac* j5.de *Nux-v* j5.de olib-sac wmh1 *Olnd* j5.de *Op* j5.de orot-ac rly4• petr j5.de petr-ra shn4• *Phos* j5.de *Plb* j5.de positr nl2• prun j5.de rat j5.de *Rhus-t* j5.de ruta j5.de sabin j5.de sec j5.de sel j5.de sep j5.de *Sil* j5.de *Spig* j5.de spong fd4.de *Squil* j5.de stram j5.de stront-c j5.de sul-ac j5.de *Sulph* j5.de thea j5.de *Thuj* j5.de valer j5.de vinc j5.de vip-a j5.de zinc j5.de
  - **midnight**: lac-h htj1•
    - **before**: abies-c oss4• acon k* *Agar* k* *Aloe* *Alum* k* *Alum-p* k2 alum-sil k2 am-c k* am-m k* **Ambr** k* anac k* *Ang* b2.de* ant-c k* ant-t k* *Arg-n* arn k* **Ars** k* ars-s-f k2 asar k* aur k* aur-ar k2 aur-s k2 bamb-a stb2.de• bar-c k* bar-m bar-s k2 *Bell* k* bism k* *Borx* k* both-ax tsm2 **Bry** k* bufo bg2 cact *Calad* k* **Calc** k* **Calc-p** k* calc-s *Calc-sil* k2 camph k* cann-s k* canth k* caps k* *Carb-an* k* **Carb-v** k* *Carbn-s* carc fd2.de• cassia-s ccrh1• caust k* cench k2 *Cham* k* chel k* *Chin* k* chinin-ar cinnb clem k* coc-c a1 coca a1 cocc k* **Coff** k* coloc k* **Con** k* cor-r cortico sp1 cupr cycl k* dig k* dor dulc k* euph k* euphr k* *Ferr* k* ferr-ar ferr-p form frax a1 galeoc-c-h gms1• *Gels* gent-l *Graph* k* *Guaj* k* guar ham *Hep* k* *Hydr* kr1 hyos k* *Ign* k* ip k* kali-ar **Kali-c** k* kali-n k* kali-s kali-sil k2* kreos k* *Lac-c* lac-leo hrn2• lach k* laur k* *Led* k* lil-t k* **Lyc** k* lycps-v m-ambo b2.de* m-arct b2.de *M-aust* b2.de* mag-c k* **Mag-m** k* mag-s mang b2.de* *Med* **Merc** k* merc-i-f *Mez* k* mosch k* *Mur-ac* k* **Nat-ar** **Nat-c** k* *Nat-m* k* *Nat-p* nat-sil k2 nit-ac k* nux-m b2.de* *Nux-v* k* par k* petr k* petr-ra shn4• *Ph-ac* k* **Phos** k* phys **Pic-ac** k* pin-con oss2• pip-m a1 plat k* plb k* *Podo* kr1 **Puls** k* *Ran-b* k* ran-s k* rheum b2.de* rhod b2.de* **Rhus-t** k* sabad k* sabin b2.de* sacch-a fd2.de• samb b2.de* sars k* *Sel* k* seneg k* **Sep** k* **Sil** k* sin-n a1 *Spig* k* spong k* *Stann* k* *Staph* k* *Stront-c* k* *Sul-ac* k* **Sulph** k* tab tarax k* tarent k2* ter *Teucr* k* ther *Thuj* k* tritic-vg fd5.de usn a2 *Valer* k* verat k* verb k* viol-t k* zinc k* zinc-p k2
    - **0** h:
      - **until**: aloe a1 alum j5.de* *Am-m* j5.de ambr a1 *Ang* j5.de ant-c j5.de ant-t j5.de* ars a1 *Bry* a1 caust j5.de chin a1 coc-c a1 coca a1 coff j5.de con j5.de* cor-r j5.de* dor a1* euph j5.de* euphr a1 graph j5.de guare a1 kali-c j5.de kali-n j5.de* kreos j5.de lach j5.de led j5.de *Lyc* j5.de* *M-aust* j5.de mag-c j5.de* mag-s a1 merc j5.de* mur-ac j5.de* *Nux-v* j5.de phos j5.de* phys a1 plat a1 puls j5.de *Rhus-t* j5.de* sacch-a fd2.de• sars j5.de sep j5.de sil a1 sin-n a1 spig j5.de* spong j5.de* *Staph* j5.de* **Sulph** j5.de* teucr j5.de thuj j5.de verat j5.de
        - **activity** of thoughts; from: calc a1
        - **fixed** thoughts; from: puls a1
        - **heat** and anxiety; from: graph a1
        - **sleepiness**; with: bar-s k2
    - **1** h:
      - **until**: am-c atra-r jl atro bamb-a stb2.de• bry calad *Carb-v* caust cench k2 con cortico jl* gels kali-c j5.de kreos lac-h htj1• laur mag-c merc merc-i-f nat-p nit-ac petr-ra shn4• phos plan thuj
        - **restlessness**; from: phos a1
        - **sensation** of heat; from: still a1
    - **1** or 2 h | **until**: bry kreos petr-ra shn4• *Sulph*

- **midnight – before**: ...
  - 2 h:
    - **until**: aids nl2• all-c allox jl* anac arn j5.de berb borx j5.de bry calc j5.de calc-p j5.de carb-an j5.de* *Cham* choc srj3• coca com (non:cupr slp) cupr-ar a1* dulc euphr graph hist mg1.de* kali-c j5.de kreos j5.de lyss macro a1 *Merc* j5.de morph nat-m pall petr-ra shn4• phel phos j5.de *Puls* raph j5.de sanguis-s hrn2• sil
      - **thoughts**; from activity of: aids nl2• *Sil* a1
  - 2 or 3 h | **until**: *Arn* calc calc-p hist mg1.de*
  - 3 h | 3-5 h | **except**: chin j5.de
    - **until**: am-m arn j5.de ars *Bell-p* st bry calc j5.de calc-p j5.de cench k2 chin chinin-ar choc srj3• cob-n sp1 com euphr eupi hist mg1.de mag-c mand sp1 *Merc* mez mill nat-p petr-ra shn4• positr nl2• psil ft1 ran-s rhus-t syc fmm1•
      - **rising** agg.; after: aloe a1
      - **thoughts**; from activity of: nat-p a1
  - 3 or 4 h | **until**: cupr-s a1 nit-ac a1
  - 4 h | **until**: acon-c aloe *Am-c Borx* bry j5.de calc k2 *Chel* kr1 cupr-s ignis-alc es2• kreos j5.de nit-ac petr-ra shn4• psil ft1 syph jl2 tarent thuj wildb a1
  - 4 or 5 h | **until**: aloe a1
  - 5 h:
    - **until**: aids nl2• arn j5.de carb-an tarent
      - **except** two hours in evening: arn a1
  - 22 h:
    - 22-1 h; except for: nux-v a1
    - 22-2 h: thea a1
    - 22-4 h; except for: sep a1
    - **after**: pip-m a1
  - 23 h:
    - 23-1 h: am-c carb-v j5.de kali-c j5.de kreos j5.de laur j5.de merc j5.de nit-ac j5.de
      - **except**: nux-v a1
    - 23-2 h: coca
      - **or** 23-3 h: arn kr1
    - **after**: chel
    - **until**: chel *Kali-c* j5.de laur j5.de mag-m j5.de *Nux-v* j5.de staph j5.de*
  - **morning**; until: **Ant-t** kr1* *Arn Atro* kr1 **Aur** k* bar-c mtf33 buni-o jl *Cact* kr1* cain chin chinin-s cimic *Coff* crot-h cycl *Fl-ac* hyos kali-i j5.de *Kreos Lyss* m-aust j5.de meph merc *Nat-c* nat-m nit-ac h2 *Prun* j5.de *Psor* kr1* *Puls* h1* sil spirae a1 *Staph* sul-ac j5.de sulph h2 thuj a1 *Valer* zinc zing a1*
  - **midnight**; until after: lyc j5.de olib-sac wmh1 plat j5.de
  - **heat** and anxiety; from: graph a1
  - **sunrise**; until: hyos j5.de *Nux-v* j5.de
  - **talkativeness**; with: *Lach* kr1
  - **thirst**; with: bry kr1
  - **thoughts**; from activity of: cact a1 calc a1 lac-leo hrn2• nat-sil fd3.de•
  - **weakness**:
    - **with**: *Lach* j5.de* mosch j5.de
    - **without** | **morning**: cinnb j5.de
- **after**: abies-c gt *Acon* k* adlu jl alum b2.de* am-c b2.de* am-m k* ambr b2.de* anan vh androc srj1• ang b2.de* ant-c k* ant-t b2.de* apis arn b2.de* **Ars** k* ars-i k2 ars-s-f k2 *Asaf* k* *Asar Aur* k* aur-ar k2 aur-s k2 *Bamb-a* stb2.de• bapt a1 bar-c b2.de* bell *Benz-ac* borx b2.de* both-ax tsm2 bry k* calad b2.de* calc b2.de* camph j5.de *Cann-s* k* canth b2.de* **Caps** k* carb-v b2.de* caust k* cham b2.de* chin k* chlorpr pin1• cocc b2.de* **Coff** k* colch con b2.de* croc b2.de* cycl b2.de* cypr gbk dros b2.de* *Dulc* k* esp-g jl euph b2.de euphr k* ferr b2.de* fl-ac b4a.de graph b2.de* guaj b2.de* hell b2.de* **Hep** k* *Hipp* jl2 ign b2.de* *Iod* k* **Kali-ar Kali-c** k* kali-n b2.de* kali-p kali-sil k2* kreos b2.de* *Lac-e* hrn2• lach b2.de* laur lyc k* m-arct b2.de m-aust b2.de *Mag-c* k* mang b2.de* merc b2.de* merc-c b4a.de merc-sul mez b2.de* mosch j5.de mur-ac k* *Nat-ar Nat-c* k* nat-m k* nat-ox rly4• nat-p *Nat-sil* k2 nit-ac b2.de* **Nux-v** k* olnd k* **Ph-ac** k* phos b2.de* plat b2.de* plb b2.de* *Psor* puls k* *Ran-b* k* *Ran-s* k* rat *Rhod* k* *Rhus-t* k* sabad b2.de* sabin k* samb b2.de* sars b2.de* sel b2.de* *Sep* k* **Sil** k* spong b2.de*

- **midnight – after**: ...
  squil b2.de* staph b2.de* *Sul-ac* k* sul-i k2 sulph b2.de* *Syph* thuj b2.de* tub jl2 v-a-b jl2* verat b2.de* verb b2.de* viol-t b2.de*
  - 1 h: bell-p ptk1 mag-c ptk1 nux-v ptk1 sep ptk1 spig [bell-p-sp dcm1]
    - 1-2 h: *Sulph*
      - **except** for: calc a1
    - 1-3 h: am-m h2* chlorpr jl
      - **except** for: calc a1
    - 1-4 h: borx phos [kali-ar stj2]
    - 1-5 h: mag-c
    - **after**: ambr j5.de* cocc j5.de* kali-n j5.de* mag-c j5.de* nat-c j5.de nit-ac h2* nux-v h1* sep j5.de*
    - **until**: ambr atra-r bnm3• *Carb-v* kr1 carc fd2.de• cench k2 *Cocc* cortico tpw7* ham fd3.de• kali-n lac-h htj1• merc-i-f nat-c oci-sa sk4• petr-ra shn4• sep ulm-c jsj8•
  - 1.30-2.30 h: agar perh jl
  - 1 or 2 h:
    - **after**: **Kali-c**
    - **until**: lac-h sk4• sulph kr1*
  - 2 h: *Cham* kr1 propr sa3• *Puls* kr1
    - 2-3 h: ap-g bro1 bapt bro1* bell-p bro1 bry bro1 *Calc* bro1 chin bro1 *Coff* bro1 gels bro1 gink-b jl kali-c bro1* kalm bro1 mag-m a1 merc bg1 nat-c bro1 nat-m bro1 nit-ac bro1 *Nux-v* bro1 *Sel* bro1 sep bro1
    - 2-4 h: am-m h2 arist-cl mg1.de mag-m merc j5.de ph-ac
    - 2-5 h: arist-cl mg1.de *Bell* k1* borx chloram jl sulph sf1.de
    - **after**: all-c bapt benz-ac caust coff dios graph kali-bi **Kali-c** kali-sil k2 *Lec* k* *Mag-c* mag-m mez nat-m **Nit-ac** pall *Ptel* puls st sars h2 *Sil* thuj *Verat* h1*
    - **until**: allox tpw3* borx calc k2 cham st cupr hist sp1 lyss st mag-c oci-sa sk4• pall kr1* *Puls* kr1* sacch-a fd2.de• [bell-p-sp dcm1]
  - 2 or 3 h:
    - **after**: ars-s-f k2 bamb-a stb2.de• mag-c
    - **until**: *Calc* kr1* petr-ra shn4•
  - 2.30 h:
    - **after**: carb-an h2
    - **until**: lyc a1 pip-m a1
  - 3 h: bry bg1 galeoc-c-h gms1• hir skp7• *Lac-e* hrn2• tetox pin2• tub c* [kali-met stj2 kali-sil stj2]
    - 3-4 h: arist-cl mg1.de chel mag-c mrr1 nux-v sf1.de rib-ac jl [tax jsj7]
    - 3-5 h: arist-cl mg1.de bell-p mg1.de* calc-f mg1.de* cob-n mg1.de kali-c k2 lac-e hrn2• mand jl sulph tl1
      - **except** for: chin a1
      - **warmth** agg. | **heat** agg.: **Borx**
    - **after**: am-m j5.de* ammc **Ars** k1 ars-s-f k2 bamb-a stb2.de• *Bapt* kr1* *Bell-p* st *Borx* bry bg1* *Calc* k* calc-ar *Calc-s Chin* clem coff euphr graph jug-c kreos **Mag-c** k* mag-m mag-s mg1.de mez nat-m sf1.de nicc **Nux-v** k ●* ol-an op petr-ra shn4• pitu-gl skp7• plat *Psor* ran-s raph j5.de **Rhus-t** k ● *Sel* **SEP** k ● staph **SULPH** k ● **Thuj** k1* **Tub** st* zinc-p k2 [bell-p-sp dcm1 kali-m stj1]
    - **until**: ap-g vh ars st cench k2 cob-n sp1 hist mg1.de mand sp1 merc st nat-p sulph syc pte1*•
  - 3.30 h:
    - **after**: arg-met st maias-l hrn2•
    - **until**: bit-ar wht1•
  - 4 h: carc fb hir skp7• puls-n a1 [tax jsj7]
    - 4-6.30 h: cycl a1
    - **after**: aur mtf33 bar-c mtf33 borx bufo carc fb* caust cycl hyper st ignis-alc es2• lyc k* *Mur-ac* **Nux-v** mrr1 *Petr* j5.de ph-ac phos plan plut-n srj7• ruta sacch-a fd2.de• sapin a1 **Sep** k ● staph **SULPH** k ● tab sf1.de thuj j5.de trom verb zinc j5.de
    - **pollution**, after: pip-m a1
    - **until**: am-c ap-g vh arb-m oss1• calc k2 chel kr1 hep *Nicc* kr1* op thuj
  - 4.30 h | **after**: crot-c sk4• sep a1
  - 5 h:
    - **after**: androc srj1• aur-s zr chin h1 fago **Nat-m** k ● *Ph-ac* **SULPH** k● [tax jsj7]
    - **until**: aloe maias-l hrn2• ran-b
  - 5.30 h:
    - **after**: sapin a1

Sleep

- **midnight** – **after** – 5.30 h: ...
  - **until**: crot-c sk4•
  - **morning**:
    - **towards**: calc-ar k2 lina a1 pip-m a1 spong fd4.de zing kr1
    - **until**: **Ant-t** kr1* *Atro* kr1* bar-c mtf33 both-ax tsm2 *Cact* kr1* chinin-s a1* cycl a1* *Fl-ac* a1* hydrog srj2• *Hyos* kr1* kola stb3• merc a1* nat-c a1* *Psor* kr1* puls kr1* *Sil* j5.de* spirae a1* syph jl2 valer kr1* zing st
      - **6** h: syph jl2
- **part** of the night:
  - **first** (See midnight - before)
  - **large** part: carc tpw*
  - **latter** (See midnight - after - morning - towards)
  - **middle**: sel a1
    - **except** for the middle part: *Crot-h* kr1
    - **reading** | **amel.**: sel a1
- **all** night; not sleeping (See total)
- **bed**; after going to: form a1 gent-l a1 ham a1 lycps-v a1 ran-b a1 spong fd4.de wies a1
- **every** other night (See periodical - night - alternate)
- **first** part of the (See midnight - before)
- **heat**; during: nat-sil k2
- **later** part of night (See midnight - after)
- **middle** of the night (See part - middle)
- **several** nights running: anac ptk1 hedy a1*
- **sleepiness**; with (See sleepiness - with - daytime)
- **sleeps** by day: anh sp1 guat sp1 lach bg2 luf-op rsj5• sil bg2 staph bg2

- **abdominal** complaints; from: *Alum* kr1 ant-t bro1 bar-c a1* caust j5.de coff j5.de coll kr1 *Coloc* kr1 cupr bro1 cycl a1 *Dulc* j5.de* gent-l j5.de *Lach* j5.de* *Lyc* kr1 *Mag-c* j5.de* mag-s j5.de* nat-m j5.de nept-m lsd2.fr ox-ac k2 plan kr1 *Plb* j5.de* sulph a1* verat j5.de
- **accident**, after an: *Stict* st1
- **accompanied** by:
  - **appetite**; loss of: parathyr jl2
  - **complaints**; other (= complaints causing sleeplessness): acon b2.de* agar b2.de* agn b2.de* alum b2.de* am-c b2.de* am-m b2.de* ambr b2.de* anac b2.de* ant-c b2.de* arn b2.de* **Ars** b2.de* asar b2.de* aur b2.de* bar-c b2.de* *Bell* b2.de* bism b2.de* borx b2.de* **Bry** b2.de* *Calad* b2.de* **Calc** b2.de* camph b2.de* canth b2.de* caps b2.de* *Carb-an* b2.de* **Carb-v** b2.de* caust b2.de* cham b2.de* chel b2.de* *Chin* b2.de* clem b2.de* cocc b2.de* coff b2.de* coloc b2.de* con b2.de* cycl b2.de* dig b2.de* dulc b2.de* euph b2.de* euphr b2.de* *Graph* b2.de* guaj b2.de* *Hep* b2.de* *Ign* b2.de* ip b2.de* *Kali-c* b2.de* kali-n b2.de* *Kreos* b2.de* lach b2.de* laur b2.de* led b2.de* *Lyc* b2.de* m-ambo b2.de* m-arct b2.de m-aust b2.de mag-c b2.de* mag-m b2.de* mang b2.de* **Merc** b2.de* mez b2.de* mosch b2.de* mur-ac b2.de* nat-c b2.de* nat-m b2.de* nit-ac b2.de* nux-m b2.de* nux-v b2.de* par b2.de* petr b2.de* ph-ac b2.de* **Phos** b2.de* plat b2.de* plb b2.de* **Puls** b2.de* ran-b b2.de* rheum b2.de* rhod b2.de* **Rhus-t** b2.de* sabad b2.de* sabin b2.de* samb b2.de* *Sars* b2.de* sel b2.de* seneg b2.de* **Sep** b2.de* sil b2.de* spig b2.de* spong b2.de* stann b2.de* staph b2.de* stront-c b2.de* sul-ac b2.de* *Sulph* b2.de* tarax b2.de* teucr b2.de* thuj b2.de* verat b2.de* verb b2.de* viol-t b2.de* zinc b2.de*
  - **nausea**: chinin-s bg2 parathyr jl2 petr-ra shn4•
  - **sleepiness**: ambr bro1 *Apis* bro1 *Bell* bro1 canni-i bro1 caust bro1 *Cham* bro1 coca bro1 coff bro1 cupr bro1 ferr bro1 *Gels* bro1 lach bro1 lavand-a ctl1• morph bro1 *Op* bro1 sil bro1 stram bro1
    - **daytime**: *(↗weariness)* *Acon* *Agar* k* am-c k* am-m ambr sf1.de anh mg1.de* ant-c st *Ant-t* kr1 apis apoc *Arg-n* bg1* arn k* ars ars-met a1* aur-s a1 bar-act sf1.de bar-c bar-s k2 **Bell** k* borx k* *Bry* k* bufo kr1 calad *Calc* calc-sil k2 camph cann-i canth carb-an h2 carb-v k* carbn-s k* caul tl1 *Caust* **Cham** k* **Chel** chin k* chr-ac a1* cic cina cinnb bg1 clem k* cob-n mg1.de cocc k* cod a1 *Coff* *Con* corn *Crot-h* crot-t j5.de *Cupr* daph dirc elaps kr1 epil a1 euphr eupi *Ferr* k* ferr-ar ferr-p fl-ac bg1 *Gels* bg* gent-l j5.de *Graph* k* guat sp1 *Hep* hura a1 hyos k* kali-ar *Kali-c* k* kali-p kali-sil k2 *Kreos* tl1 lac-d st *Lach* k* lact j5.de laur lil-s a1 lyc m-aust j5.de mag-c k2* mag-m med *Merc* k* mosch k* mur-ac bg1 nat-ar *Nat-c* nat-hchls a1 *Nat-m* k* nat-p nat-sil k2

- **accompanied** by – **sleepiness** – **daytime**: ... nit-ac *Nux-m* kr1* *Nux-v* k* **Op** k* *Petr* kr1 *Ph-ac* k* **Phos** k* *Phys* kr1 pic-ac k2 plan bg1 plb polyg-h kr1 psor st **Puls** k* ran-b k* rhod *Rhus-t* k* sabad sabin *Samb* sapin a1 sel *Senec* sf1.de **Sep** k* *Sil* k* sol-mm j5.de* solin a1 spig k* spong fd4.de **Staph** k* *Stram* k* sul-ac sul-i k2 **Sulph** k* syph *Tarent* bg* ter sf1.de teucr j5.de thuj verat viol-o vip-a j5.de zinc
  - **vertigo** (See VERTIGO - Accompanied - sleeplessness)
  - ○ **Head**:
    - **heaviness** (See HEAD - Heaviness - accompanied - sleeplessness)
    - **pain** | **bursting** (See HEAD - Pain - bursting - accompanied - sleeplessness)
  - **Heart**; complaints of: *Aur-m* kr1 **Borx** a1 *Colch* kr1 crat br1* *Dig* kr1* merc a1 merc-c a1 naja bg2 *Op* kr1 spig bg2 *Tab* kr1* verat a1
  - **Nerves**; inflammation of (See GENERALS - Inflammation - nerves - accompanied - sleeplessness)
  - **Occiput**; pain in (See HEAD - Pain - occiput - accompanied - sleeplessness)
  - **Skin**; complaints of: **Chlol** mrr1
- **agony**, in: *Acet-ac* kr1
- **alcohol** | **agg.**: agav-t jl
- **alone** agg.: gaert pte1*• kali-br mrr1 kali-c k2* syc fmm1• tritic-vg fd5.de
- **alternate** night, on (See periodical - night - alternate)
- **alternating** with:
  - **coma**: *Camph* hr1*
  - **delirium** (See MIND - Delirium - alternating - sleeplessness)
  - **dreams**: coff-t a1
  - **sleep**: crot-h k2
  - **sleepiness**: asim hr1* *Hyos* hr1*
- **amenorrhea**, in: *Senec* kr1 *Xan* kr1
- **anger**; after: *Acon* sf1.de *Cham* sf1.de coff sf1.de **Coloc** j5.de* falco-pe nl2• galla-q-r nl2• *Nux-v* sf1.de op sf1.de
- **anticipation**; from: carc mlr1• cupr sst3• gels mrr1
  - **failure**: carc mlr1•
- **anxiety**, from: *(↗Disturbed - anxiety; MIND - Anxiety)* abrot sf1.de *Acon* j5.de* agar h2* alum bg2* ant-c b7a.de apis k2 arg-n k2* arn **Ars** k* atro sf1.de bar-c b4a.de* bell k* bry *Calad* b7a.de calc b4a.de* calc-br sf1.de carb-an k* carb-v b4.de* carc mlr1• *Caust* k* cench k2* *Cham* j5.de* **Cocc** k* coff j5.de coloc hr1* con h2* *Crot-h* hr1* cupr cupr-ar sf1.de *Dig* sf1.de *Ferr* j5.de glycyr-g cte1• graph h2* haliae-lc srj5• hep b4a.de *Hyos* h1* ign hr1* *Kali-br* hr1* kali-c b4.de* kali-i kali-s fd4.de *Lach* b7a.de* laur k* lyss m-arct j5.de mag-c mag-m k* mang h2 merc k* merc-c b4a.de* nat-c nat-m nux-v oci-sa sk4• phos b4.de* positr nl2• puls b7.de* ran-b j5.de* ran-s j5.de rhus-t k* sabin j5.de sal-fr sle1• samb b7a.de* *Sep* b4.de* *Sil* h2* stram sulph tax-br oss1• thuj tritic-vg fd5.de verat j5.de* vip sf1.de wies a1 [heroin sdj2]
  - **menses**; after: agar hr1*
- **aortic** disease, in: crat bro1
- **apoplexy**, before: *Aster* hr1*
- **apyrexia**; during: ars bro1
- **bed**:
  - **hard**; feels too: arn bro1 bry bro1 cit-ac rly4• hep b4a.de mag-c b4.de* *Pyrog* bro1 ruta fd4.de
  - **hot**; feels too: op bro1 ruta fd4.de
  - **late**, when going to bed: am-c h2 [ant-c stj2 cadm-s stj2 gal-s stj2 mang-p stj2 mang-s stj2 mang-sil stj2 nicc-s stj2]
  - **sit** up in bed; must: ars bg1
- **beer**: | **amel.**: thea a1
- **biting**; from | **Skin**; in: cocc b7.de*
- **blood**; after loss of: phos sf1.de
- **blood** rushed through the body; from sensation as if: alumn k2 puls tl1
- **Bright's** disease; from: kali-br tl1
- **burning**; from:
  - **eruptions**; of: kreos b7a.de rhus-t b7.de*
  - **ulcers**, sores; in: staph b7.de*
  - ○ **Chest**; in: apis b7a.de
    - **Ribs**; under the: apis b7a.de

- **Soles**, of: *Lach* kr1
- **Stomach**; in: am-c h2
- **Veins**; in the: *Ars*

- **calamity**, after domestic: *Lach* hr1*
- **cares**; from: (↗*MIND - Ailments - cares; MIND - Anxiety; MIND - Cares full)* ambr bg2* calc bg2 carc mlr1• cerv a1 *Cocc* mrr1 graph b4a.de haliae-lc srj5• ign br1* kali-br a11* kali-p hr1* nat-sil fd3.de• nux-v a1 puls h1* urol-h rwt• [lac-mat sst4]
  - **business**, of: (↗*thoughts - business) Ambr* hr1* *Calc* sf1.de **Hyos** hr1* ign hr1 nux-v k2*
  - **daily**: *Ambr* hr1* bamb-a stb2.de• *Calc* sf1.de graph j5.de ign hr1* kali-p hr1* sacch-a fd2.de•
  - **imaginary**: **Hyos** hr1*
- **caressed**, unless: *Kreos* hr1*
- **carried**, unless: cham
- **causeless**: ambr hr1* aur b4.de* *Calc* b4a.de carc mlr1• glycyr-g cte1• kali-c b4.de* mag-c b4.de* merc b4.de* mur-ac b4.de* spig b7.de* *Squil* b7.de* sulph b4.de*
  - **children**; in: carc mlr1•
- **childbed**, in (See delivery)
- **children**; in: *Absin* br1* acon bg2* *Ars* bro1* arund a1 bac jl2 *Bell* b4a.de* borx bg2 calc-br bro1 **Carc** c1* *Cham* b7a.de* *Cina* bro1 **Coff** b7a.de* *Cypr* hr1* hyos bro1 kali-br bro1 lac-f wza1• lat-m bnm6• *Mag-m* st1 *Op* b7a.de* *Passi* bro1* phos bro1 podo hr1 puls bro1 rheum bg2 *Stict* hr1* sulph bro1 syph dgt tub-m jl2 zinc-val br1
  - **evening**: lyc a1
  - **caressed**; child must be: *Kreos* kr1
  - **carried**, child must be: cham
  - **fretful** from bedtime to morning; next day lively: *Psor* kr1*
  - **held**; child must be: stram mtf33
  - **infants**: carc fb* psor tl1*
  - **laughing**; with: cypr br1*
  - **newborns**: *Bell* j5.de* cham j5.de coff kr1 cypr kr1 op kr1 psor kr1 sulph kr1
  - **play** and laugh; child wants to: cypr br1*
  - **rocked**, child must be: (↗*MIND - Rocking - amel.) Carc* st1* cina *Stict* st1
  - **weaning**; after: bell bro1
  - **weeping**; with: carc cd
- **chill**; with: acon bg2 am-c bg2 ambr b7.de* anac bg2 ant-c j5.de* **Aran** kr1 ars bg2 bell bg2 borx bg2 bry calc bg2 *Cham* b7.de* chin bg2 coff bg2 euphr b7.de* graph h2 *Hep* b4a.de* ip b7.de* kreos b7a.de* *Lach* kr1 lyc k* mang bg2 merc bg2 *Mur-ac* nat-m bg2 nit-ac bg2 nux-v b7.de* phos bg2 plat bg2 *Puls* b7.de* rhod bg2 rhus-t bg2 sabin j5.de sep bg2 sil bg2 sulph bg2 thuj b4a.de* vanil fd5.de
- **chilliness**; with: graph h2* *Lac-c* hr1* *Lyc* hr1* olib-sac wmh1
- **cholera** infantum, in: *Cadm-s* kr1
- **chronic**: apis kr1 *Ars-h* hr1* aur mrr1 coli jl2 *Crot-h* hr1* cupr-ar sf1.de hydr-ac hr1* *Hyos* hr1* **Lach** hr1* lat-m bnm6• *Plat* hr1* sulfag mtf11 syph mtf33 thuj ptk1* *Verat* hr1*
- **clouds** were passing through brain; as if: *Hep* b4a.de
- **coffee**:
  - **abuse** of coffee agg.: cham bro1 **Coff** kr1 dulc fd4.de nux-v k*
  - **unless** he drinks: merc h1
- **coition**; after: calc cop k* kali-c k2* nit-ac sep sil
- **cold**; after taking a: *Jatr-c* kr1
- **coldness**, from: *Acon* bro1 aloe alum am-c ambr k* arg-n ars k* borx b4a.de bov calc camph bro1 carb-v k* cist bro1 daph euph bg2 euphr b7.de ferr gink-b sbd1• graph k* kreos lac-c mag-s merc mur-ac nat-m k* nat-s nux-v ozone sde2• phos k* plect a1 puls b7.de* staph sulph k* thuj k* tritic-vg fd5.de *Verat* bro1 [heroin sdj2]
  - ○ **Feet**, of: aloe am-m k* aran bg2* *Carb-v* chel lec oss• mag-m dgt2 nit-ac petr *Phos* k* raph rhod sil tritic-vg fd5.de verat a1 zinc k*
  - **Hands**, of: aloe kr1 verat-v a1
  - **Knees**, of: apis bro1 *Carb-v* bro1 verat a1
- **complaints**:
  - **before** other complaints develop; sleeplessness: chin ptk1

- **complaints**: ...
  - **causing** sleeplessness: acon b2.de* agar b2.de* alum b2.de* am-c b2.de* am-m b2.de* ambr b2.de* anac b2.de* ang b2.de* ant-c b2.de* ant-t b2.de* arn b2.de* **Ars** b2.de* asaf b2.de* aur b2.de* bar-c b2.de* *Bell* b2.de* bism b2.de* borx b2.de* **Bry** b2.de* *Calad* b2.de* **Calc** b2.de* camph b2.de* cann-s b2.de* canth b2.de* caps b2.de* carb-an b2.de* *Carb-v* b2.de* caust b2.de* **Cham** b2.de* chel b2.de* **Chin** b2.de* cic b2.de* cina b2.de* clem b2.de* cocc b2.de* **Coff** b2.de* colch b2.de* *Con* b2.de* cupr b2.de* cycl b2.de* dig b2.de* dros b2.de* dulc b2.de* euphr b2.de* ferr b2.de* *Graph* b2.de* guaj b2.de* hell b2.de* *Hep* b2.de* *Hyos* b2.de* *Ign* b2.de* iod b2.de* ip b2.de* *Kali-c* b2.de* kali-n b2.de* *Kreos* b2.de* lach b2.de* laur b2.de* led b2.de* *Lyc* b2.de* m-arct b2.de m-aust b2.de *Mag-c* b2.de* *Mag-m* b2.de* mang b2.de* **Merc** b2.de* mez b2.de* mosch b2.de* mur-ac b2.de* nat-c b2.de* *Nat-m* b2.de* nit-ac b2.de* nux-m b2.de* nux-v b2.de* olnd b2.de* op b2.de* petr b2.de* ph-ac b2.de* **Phos** b2.de* plat b2.de* plb b2.de* **Puls** b2.de* ran-b b2.de* *Ran-s* b2.de* rheum b2.de* *Rhod* b2.de* **Rhus-t** b2.de* ruta b2.de* sabad b2.de* *Sabin* b2.de* samb b2.de* *Sars* b2.de* *Sel* b2.de* **Sep** b2.de* *Sil* b2.de* spig b2.de* spong b2.de* squil b2.de* stann b2.de* staph b2.de* stram b2.de* stront-c b2.de* sul-ac b2.de* *Sulph* b2.de* tarax b2.de* teucr b2.de* thuj b2.de* valer b2.de* verat b2.de* viol-t b2.de* zinc b2.de*
- **complete** (See total)
- **congestion**, from: alumn am-c sf1.de ambr sf1.de asar bry *Calc* calc-br sf1.de *Carb-v* a1* eucal sf1.de graph a1 hep h2* ign mag-c *Merc* mosch j5.de mur-ac h2 nit-ac a1 *Phos Puls* ran-b rhus-t sabin j5.de senn sf1.de *Sep* **Sil** spong kr1 *Sulph* wies a1
  - **head**, to: am-m b7a.de *Borx* kr1 *Carb-v* kr1* cycl b7.de* *Puls* b7.de*
- **convalescence**, during: alf kr1* aven kr1* castm kr1* coff hr1* cypr kr1* *Hyos* hr1* kali-br hr1* scut kr1* stann kr1* *Tub* kr1* tub-a kr1*
- **conversation**:
  - **after** a: **Ambr** k* hep j5.de* kola stb3•
  - **amel.**: thea a1
- **convulsions**; with: alum kr1 art-v hr1* bell kr1 bry b7a.de* calc kr1 carb-an kr1 carb-v kr1 *Cic* hr1* cupr kr1 cypr hr1* hep kr1 hyos b7.de* ign b7a.de* ip b7a.de* **Kali-br** hr1* kali-c kr1 merc kr1 mosch b7a.de* nux-v kr1 ph-ac kr1 phos kr1 puls b7a.de* rheum b7a.de* rhus-t b7a.de* sel kr1 sep kr1 sil kr1 stront-c kr1 thuj kr1
- **coryza**, from: *Ars* b4.de* mag-m a1 *Puls* b7a.de
- **cough**, from: am-m b7.de* *Apis* b7a.de* bism b7.de* calad b7.de* *Caps* hr1* *Caust* b4.de* *Chin* b7a.de *Chlol* hr1* *Daph* hr1* dig b4a.de eup-per bg2* *Gels* hr1 *Hep* b4a.de *Hyos* b7.de* irid-met srj5• *Kali-bi* hr1* *Kali-cy* hr1* *Kali-n* b4a.de lyc b4.de* m-arct b7.de* **Nit-ac** b4.de* *Nux-v* b7.de* *Ol-j* hr1* *Phel* hr1* *Phos* b4.de* puls b7.de* *Rhus-t* b7.de* ruta fd4.de sabad b7.de* sep b4.de* spong fd4.de *Stict* bg2* *Stront-c* b4a.de *Sulph* b4.de* *Syph* hr1* teucr b7.de* tritic-vg fd5.de *Tub* jl2
  - **midnight**, after: *Kali-c* hr1*
  - **children**, in: *Stict* st1
  - **irritation** to cough; from: ars b4.de*
  - **lying** down, on: *Ol-j* hr1*
  - **whooping** cough, in: *Caust* hr1* kali-br tl1
- **country**; in the: prot jl2
- **cramps**, from: arg-met bro1 coloc bro1 cupr bro1
  - ○ **Calves**, in: (↗*Waking - cramps - calves)* cham kr1* coff kr1* *Cupr-act* kr1* ferr kr1* *Meny* kr1 *Mez* kr1 nux-v kr1* *Verat* kr1*
  - **hands** and feet, in: valer k2
- **crawling**; from | **Calves** and feet; in: sulph h2
- **dark** room agg.; in a: (↗*MIND - Fear - death - alone - evening - bed)* calc grin vh **Puls** st* staph st* **Stram** k* *Sulph* st*
  - **children**; in: stram tl1
- **delirium**:
  - **delusions**; with: arg-n kr1 *Bell* kr1 op kr1
  - **with** (See MIND - Delirium - sleeplessness - with)
- **delirium** tremens; in: aven br1 *Cimic* kr1* **Gels** k1 hyos sf1.de* kali-p sf1.de *Nux-v Sumb* br1
- **delivery**:
  - **after**: *Acon* bg2 bell bg2 cham b7.de* *Coff* b7.de* hyos bg2 ign bg2 mosch bg2 *Nat-s* hr1* nux-v bg2 op b7.de* puls bg2
  - **before**: *Con* a1*
- **dentition**; during: acon bg2* bell bro1 borx bg2* calc-br sf1.de* *Cham* bg2* coff bg2* *Cypr* bro1 ferr-p bg2* *Gels* hr1* kali-br tl1 kali-c ggd1 kreos bro1 mag-c bg2* passi bro1 phos bg2* scut bro1 ter hr1*

Sleep

- **despair**; from: carc mlr1• lyss kr1 psor sf1.de
- **diabetics**, in: *Uran-n* kr1
- **diarrhea**; during: borx b4a.de **Bufo** kr1 *Coloc* kr1 cuph ah1 *Dulc* kr1 gast a1 *Merc-c* kr1 *Nat-s* kr1 **Phos** kr1
  - **autumn** agg.: *Merc* kr1
- **diphtheria**; in: *Chinin-ar* kr1 *Kali-chl* hr1 *Kali-m* kr1 *Kalm* kr1
- **disappointment**; from: carc mlr1•
- **discharges**; from suppressed: *Lach* sf1.de
- **disorder**, when room is in: ars k2
- **dispute**, after: staph k2*
- **drawing**; from | **Legs**; in: carb-v k* *Sep* b4a.de
- **dreams**; from: *(↗nightmares)* adon ptk1 ambr h1 ars b4a.de* bell b4.de* carb-an h2 chin b7.de* laur b7.de* nat-m bg2 rhus-t hr1 sep b4.de* *Tell* rsj10•
- **drugs**; after: *(↗narcotics)* ars bro1 aven bro1 cann-i bro1 chlol kr1 *Cimic* bro1 *Gels* bro1 *Hyos* bro1 mosch kr1 *Nux-v* bro1 op bro1* sec bro1* stram bro1 *Sumb* bro1
  - **mercury**: *Kali-br* hr1*
  - **opium**: *Bell* hr1* *Nux-v* hr1*
- **drunkards**; in: *(↗drunkenness)* *Apom* br1 ars bro1 aven br1* cann-i bro1 *Cimic* bro1 *Gels* bro1 *Hyos* bro1 lach ptk1 nux-v bro1* op bro1* passi sf1.de sec bro1 stram bro1 *Sumb* c1*
- **drunkenness**; during: *(↗drunkards)* coff gl1.fr• hyos sf1.de* kali-p sf1.de* nux-v gl1.fr•
- **dryness**; from | **nose**; of: *Sil* b4a.de
- **dysmenorrhea**; in: *Cocc* kr1
- **eating**:
  - **after**:
    - **agg.**: *(↗supper)* acon bg2 agar bg2 am-c bg2 anac bg2 arn bg2 ars bg2 aur bg2 bar-c bg2 bell bg2 borx bg2 bov bg2 bry bg2 *Calc* bg2 canth bg2 carb-an bg2 *Carb-v* bg2 caust bg2 cham bg2 chel bg2 **Chin** bg2 cic bg2 clem bg2 croc bg2 crot-h bg2 cycl bg2 dig bg2 euph bg2 (non:fel a1*) ferr bg2 graph bg2 grat bg2 kali-c bg2 **Lach** bg2 laur bg2 lyc bg2 mag-c bg2 mag-m bg2 nat-c bg2 *Nat-m* bg2 *Nit-ac* bg2 nux-m bg2 **Nux-v** bg2 ph-ac bg2 **Phos** bg2 plb bg2 prun bg2 *Puls* bg2 ran-b bg2 *Rhus-t* bg2 ruta bg2 seneg bg2 sep bg2 **Sil** bg2 squil bg2 staph bg2 verb bg2 zinc bg2
      - **late** and much; too: *Puls* kr1
    - **amel.**: hed mg1.de *Phos* bg2* tub mtf33
- **erections** agg.: ant-c j5.de *Calc* b4a.de dig b4a.de *Plat* kr1 sep k* *Thuj* b4a.de*
  - **painful**: **Thuj** kr1
- **eructations** agg.: bar-c h2 carb-v b4.de*
- **erysipelas**, during: *Apis* kr1 *Verat-v* hr1*
- **excesses**; after: nux-v bg2
- **excitement** agg.: abrot bg2* absin bro1 *Acon* bro1 agar bg2* *Alf* bro1 am-val bro1 *Ambr* k* anac sf1.de *Apis* bg2 *Arg-n* aur bro1 *Aur-m* hr1* aur-m-n wbt2• bry bro1 *Calc* bg2* camph k* *Cann-i* bro1 canth k* caps carb-an h2* *Carc* mlr1• cham bro1 chin k* chinin-ar bro1 chlol bro1 cimic bg2* coca kr1* **Coff** k* *Colch* k* coloc bro1 croc bg2* cupr-ar sf1.de cypr sf1.de ferr sf1.de gels k2* haliae-lc srj5• *Hep* k1 hydrog srj2• **Hyos** k* hyosin-hbr bro1 *Ign* bro1 *Kali-br* bro1 kali-p k* *Lach* laur k* *Lyc* lyss hr1* mag-c bg2* meph bg2* *Merc* mez j5.de mosch k* nat-m bro1 nit-ac **Nux-v** k* oci-sa sk4• *Op* b7.de* passi bro1 *Ph-ac* b4a.de* *Phos* hr1* plat bg2* positr nl2• *Puls* k* ran-b senec bg2* *Sep* k* spong bg2* staph bg2 *Stram* bro1 sul-ac sulph k* tarent mtf33 teucr k* thea bro1 tritic-vg fd5.de valer bro1 zinc-val bro1
  - **theater**, at: *Phos* kr1
- **exertion** agg.; after: arn kr1* **Ars** bg2* aven bro1 *Calc* sf1.de cann-i bro1 chin bro1* chinin-s bro1 *Chlol* hr1* cimic bro1* coca bro1 *Cocc* bro1 coff tl1 *Colch* bro1 *Dig* sf1.de dip bro1 *Gels* bro1 helon sf1.de hyos bro1 kali-br bro1 *Nux-v* bro1* passi bro1 *Phos* bro1 pisc bro1 *Sil* sf1.de
- **exhaustion**: aven ptk1 cact mtf11 chlol ptk1 coca ptk1 cocc ptk1 *Coff* ptk1 cypr hr1 gels hr1* ozone sde2•
- **eyes**:
  - **close**; from sensation as if eyes will not: phos b4.de*
  - **closed** eyes; with: dulc h1 staph h1
  - **open**; with inability to: carb-v
- **faces**; from seeing hideous: *Bell* b4a.de calc b4a.de carb-an b4a.de *Carb-v* b4a.de
- **fagged**, yet: aur kr1
- **faintness**; with: ars j5.de calc j5.de graph j5.de
- **falling**, sensation of: *Bell* bg2
- **fancies**, from (= fantasies, phantasies, illusions,): *Acon* b7a.de alum k* ambr k2 anh mg1.de ant-t b7.de* arg-n k* *Bell* k* *Calc* b4a.de *Carb-an* b4a.de *Carb-v* b4a.de *Cham* b7.de* chin b7.de* coff b7.de* ign b7.de* led b7.de* merc k* nat-c k* *Op* j5.de* petr j5.de ph-ac k* phos k* rhus-t b7.de* *Sil* b4a.de* spong b7a.de* thuj k* [arg-met stj1]
  - **heroic**: **Chin** mrr1
- **fear**; from: **Acon** b7a.de* alum b4a.de* am-c b4.de* androc srj1• arn b7.de* ars b4.de* bamb-a stb2.de• bell b4.de* *Bry* b7.de* calc b4.de* *Cann-s* b7a.de carb-an b4a.de carb-v b4.de* caust b4.de* cham b7.de* *Chin* b7a.de *Cocc* b7.de* coff b7.de* *Con* b4a.de dig b4.de* graph b4.de* hyos b7.de* *Ign* hr1* kali-c b4.de* *Lach* b7a.de* *Laur* b7a.de lyc b4.de* mag-c b4.de* mag-m b4.de* merc b4.de* merc-c b4a.de* nat-m b4.de* nit-ac b4.de* nux-v b7.de* phos b4.de* *Plat* b4a.de plb b7a.de *Puls* b7.de* ran-s b7.de* *Rhus-t* b7.de* *Sabin* b7a.de *Samb* b7a.de sep b4.de* sil b4.de* sulph b4.de* syph bro1 thuj b4.de* *Verat* b7.de* vip bg2 zinc b4.de*
  - **die**; that she must: cench k2
  - **ghosts**; of (See MIND - Fear - ghosts - sleeplessness)
- **fetus**; from painful motion of: arn k2
- **fever**:
  - **asthenic** fever; during: *Cact* hr1* *Stram*
  - **during** | **agg.**: acon bg2 ant-t bro1
- **flatulence**; from: *(↗Disturbed - flatulence; ABDOMEN - Flatulence - sleep - preventing)* ambr bg2 borx b4a.de m-aust b7.de *Nux-m* b7.de* nux-v bg2 *Op* b7a.de *Valer* b7a.de
- **flushes** of heat; from: puls k2 ran-b k2
- **formication**, from: bamb-a stb2.de• bar-c b4a.de bufo bg2 carb-v b4.de* guare a1 lyc b4.de* osm bg2*
  - ○ **Feet**; of: sulph bro1
  - **Fingers**; of: mez b4a.de
  - **Legs**, of: *Sulph* b4a.de* zinc
- **fracture**, after reposition of: *Stict* st1
- **fright**; after: **Acon** b7a.de* bamb-a stb2.de• *Ign* hr1* op b7a.de*
  - **pregnancy**; in: *Ign* kr1
- **frightened** easily: [stront-m stj2 stront-met stj2]
- **girls**; in: puls st1
- **going** to bed, after (See evening - bed)
- **gonorrhea**; during: *Tarent* kr1
- **gout**, in: *Mang* hr1*
- **grief**; from●: *(↗MIND - Ailments - grief)* *Gels* hr1* graph h2* *Ign* k* *Kali-br* k* lach k2* **Nat-m** k* *Sulph* j5.de*
- **hair**; bristling of (= standing on end): carb-v b4.de*
- **head**, from wild feeling in: lil-t br1*
- **headache**; from: acon a1 acon-ac rly4• alum b4a.de ammc a1* *Arg-n* hr1* ars-i hr1* **Aur** hr1* bac jl2 brach hr1* bufo a1 calc-caust sf1.de canth b7a.de carbn-o a1 carc zzh *Chel* hr1* **Chin** b7a.de* *Chlol* hr1* chloram jl3 *Coff* bro1 *Croc* hr1* elaps kr1 epil a1* glycyr-g cte1• ind bro1 kreos b7a.de *Lach* hr1* lyc a1 m-arct b7a.de mag-s j5.de* manc h * *Merc* a1 *Merl* hr1* mosch j5.de mur-ac h2 nicc j5.de nit-ac j5.de osm a1 pal hr1* petr-ra shn4• *Phos* b4a.de *Phys* hr1* pitu-gl skp7• *Puls* hr1* ruta fd4.de sars bg2* *Sil* b4.de* *Spig* hr1* spong j5.de **Sulph** hr1* *Syph* hr1* verat b7.de* zinc-val bro1
- **heart**; with disease of (See accompanied - heart)
- **heat**:
  - **after**: *Hell* hr1*
  - **during**: acon bro1* ail k2* aloe kr1 alum k* alumn a1* am-c b4.de* am-m b7.de* **Anac** b4.de* ang h1 ant-t **Apis** b7a.de* *Aran* hr1* arg-met bg2 arn b7.de* *Ars* k* *Ars-h* hr1* *Bapt* hr1* *Bar-c* k* bell b4.de* **Borx** k* *Bry* k* *Cact* hr1* *Calc* k* cann-s k* *Carb-v* k* carbn-s *Caust* k* *Cham* b7.de* chin b7.de* chinin-s *Cina* kr1 cit-v hr1* clem k* coc-c k* cocc k* *Coff* b7.de* colch k* *Coloc* hr1* con k* eucal a1 *Ferr* galeoc-c-h gms1• graph k* hep k* *Hyos* hr1* ign b7.de* iod sf1.de kali-br bro1 kali-n b4a.de* kreos j5.de* *Lachn* hr1* laur b7.de* led bg2 m-arct b7.de* *Mag-c* b4.de* mag-m k* mang bg2 meph bro1 merc b4a.de* merc-c bg2 mosch b7.de* nat-m k* nat-p k* nat-sil k2 *Nit-ac* k* nux-m b7.de* nux-v k* ol-an a1 *Ol-j* hr1* *Op* bro1* *Petr* b4.de* *Ph-ac* k* *Phos* k* plect a1 puls k* ran-b b7.de* ran-s k* **Rhod** b4a.de* *Rhus-t* k* sabad b7.de* *Sabin* b7.de* *Sanic* bro1 sars k* sec j5.de sep k* *Sil* b4.de* spong hr1 *Staph* b7.de* *Stram* hr1* stront-c b4a.de* **Sulph** b4.de* thuj k* verat b7.de* wies a1
    - **anxious**: bry a1 ign hr1* *Puls* hr1*
    - **dry**: *Caust* b4.de* clem b4.de* graph b4.de* nit-ac a1 sulph hr1 *Thuj* b4a.de wies a1

• **during**: ...
⁝ **Feet**; in: *Led* b7a.de staph b7a.de
⁝ **Hands**; of: *Led* b7a.de staph b7a.de
⁝ **Head**; in: am-m **Borx** k* *Sil* b4a.de verat
• **sensation** of; from: bry b7.de* iod bg2 kreos b7a.de op bg2 puls b7.de* ran-b st1
- **heavy** blow, after a: *Ambr* sf1.de *Con* sf1.de
- **heavy** feeling; from:
○ • **Arms**; in: alum k*
• **Limbs**; in: *Caust* j5.de gran a1 mag-c b4.de* maias-l hrn2•
⁝ **Lower**: caust h2
• **Stomach**; in: all-s vh1
- **hemorrhages**; from: *Chin* phos hr1*
- **hemorrhoids**; from: abrot vh1 *Ars* kr1 *Kali-c* kr1
- **hiccough**; with: *Nux-v* hr1*
- **homesickness**, from (See MIND - Homesickness - sleeplessness)
- **hunger**; from: abies-n k* ap-g bro1* *Chin* k* *Cina* bro1 *Ign* k* **Lyc** k ●* nat-c k2 **Phos** k ●* psor bg2* sanic sulph bro1* teucr k* tritic-vg fd5.de tub kl*
- **hydrophobia**, in: *Lyss* hr1*
- **hypochondriasis**, in: *Arg-n* hr1* *Bar-c* hr1* graph j5.de valer hr1*
- **hypogastrium**; from complaints of: ambr b7.de* graph b4.de* mag-c b4.de* mag-m b4.de* nux-m b7.de* *Plb* b7a.de *Rhus-t* b7a.de
- **hysterical**: *Croc* sf1.de mosch k* *Senec* hr1* *Stict* hr1*
- **indigestion**; from: mag-p br1
- **influenza**; after: *Aven* bg2*
- **injuries**; after: *Arn* hr1* *Rhus-t* hr1* *Stict* hr1*
- **insane** people, in: bell st1* carc mlr1• **Cimic** sne *Hyos* st1* *Kali-br* sne *Lach* hr1* *Manc* hr1* *Meli* sne op j5.de *Tarent* hr1*
- **intermittent**: (↗*periodical)* carbn-s a1
- **irresolution**; from: psor bg2
- **irritability**; from: *Acon* hr1* *Arg-n* hr1* *Bapt* hr1* *Chinin-s* kr1 *Chlol* hr1* *Coff* sf1.de *Gels* hr1* hydrog srj2• **Hyos** hr1* *Kali-p* hr1* *Lach* hr1* lyss hr1* mosch hr1* *Nat-m* hr1* plat hr1* *Stict* hr1*
- **itching**; from: acon bro1 *Agar* bro1 alum bro1 am-c h2* anac k* ant-c *Apis* b7a.de* *Arn* b7.de* bar-c k* bell bg2 *Bov* hr1* calad k2* carb-v k* caust hr1* chlol k* *Cit-v* a1 cocc j5.de con b4.de* cop hr1* dol c1* dulc h1* elae a1 euphr b7.de* *Gels* k* gink-b sbd1• jug-r vml3• kali-c h2* kreos b7a.de* lach k* lyss k* *Merc* k* *Mez* k* **Psor** k* *Puls* k* ran-b b7.de* raph k* ros-d wla1 sars b4.de* spong fd4.de staph hr1* *Sulph* b4.de* teucr bro1 valer bro1 zinc k*
• **pregnancy** agg.; during: *Dol* hr1*
• **senilis**, pruritus: med jl2 *Mez* hr1*
• **tetters**: staph b7.de*
• **thigh**: ulm-c jsj8•
○ • **Anus**; of: *Aloe* k2* alum bro1 coff bro1 ferr gt ign bro1 *Indg* bro1
• **Arms**; of: ign br1 spong fd4.de
• **Ears**; in: nux-v b7.de*
• **Head**: gels c1
• **Rectum**; in: ferr b7.de*
• **Scrotum**: urt-u kr1*
- **jars**, concussions; from sensation of: sil b4.de*
○ • **Limbs**; in: ip b7.de* kreos b7a.de
- **jerks**; from: arg-met bg2 *Ars* bg2 **Bell** bg2 *Bry* b7a.de calc bg2 carb-v bg2 cham bg2 cimic k2 colch b7.de* dulc j5.de hyos j5.de ign b7a.de* *Ip* b7a.de m-arct b7a.de puls b7a.de* *Rhus-t* b7a.de sel bg2 *Sep* bg2 sulph bg2 zinc mrr1
○ • **Head**; in: cycl bg2 m-arct b7a.de sil b4.de*
• **Limbs**; in: ip b7a.de
- **joy**, from excessive: *(↗MIND - Ailments - joy - excessive; MIND - Ailments - surprises - pleasant)* **Coff** k* ozone sde2• tritic-vg fd5.de
- **legs** crossed, unless: *Rhod* hr1*
- **leukorrhea**; before: *Senec* kr1
- **light**; from | **room** agg.; in an illuminated: *Coff* kr1 lach st* nux-v st* **Staph** st*
- **liver** complaints; in: acet-ac hr1* *Dol* hr1*
- **locomotor** ataxia; in: camph-br hl9*
- **long**, for hours: aur b4.de calc b4.de caust b4.de con b4.de dulc b4.de lyc b4.de mag-c b4.de mang b4.de merc b4.de *Nat-m* b4.de ph-ac b4.de phos b4.de sars b4.de sep b4.de sil b4.de sul-ac b4.de sulph b4.de zinc b4.de
- **longing**; from | **friend**; for a distant: plb b7a.de
- **loss** of sleep:
• **after**: cocc bg2*
• **sensation** as from loss of sleep: euph a1 guaj a1 op a1 ost a1 puls a1
⁝ **morning**: graph a1 naja a1 sol-ni a1
⁝ **rising** agg.; after: merc a1
- **lying**:
• **agg.**: *Bell* b4a.de *Cham* chin lyss puls b7.de*
• **back**; on | **agg.**: sulph oss•
• **side**; on:
⁝ **agg.**: card-m a1 ferr b7.de*
⁝ **left**:
⁝ **agg.**: card-m bg ter bg2 thuj mlk1* x-ray sp1
⁝ **inability** to lie on the left side; because of: *(↗Position - side - left - impossible)* card-m ptk1 *Colch* thuj ptk1
⁝ **right** | **agg.**: colch rsj2• merc b4.de* trios rsj11•
• **uncomfortable** agg.; lying: lavand-a ctl1•
- **mania**, in: *Apis* kr1 **Cimic** sne *Cocc* *Meli* sne *Nux-v* kr1 *Stram* kr1 *Verat-v* kr1
- **masturbation**; with: staph mrr1
- **measles**; during: calc bro1 coff bro1 *Ferr-p* hr1*
- **menopause**; during: *(↗GENERALS - Heat - flushes - night; GENERALS - Orgasm - night)* *Acon* kr1* *Arn* st *Bell* st *Cimic* sf1.de cocc sf1.de *Coff* kr1* dig bg1 *Gels* st *Kali-br* hr1* *Senec* kr1* *Sulph* kr1* valer st *Zinc* kr1
- **menses**:
• **after** | **agg.**: cimic bro1 kali-br hr1* thuj hr1*
• **before** | **agg.**: agar a1* carc sst• cycl k* dendr-pol sk4• goss st1 kreos b7a.de* petr-ra shn4• senec bro1 tub gt1*
• **beginning**, at: agar kr1*
• **during**:
⁝ **agg.**: agar k* am-c k* cimic eupi k* gent-c k* ign mag-m k* nat-m k* senec k* sep k*
⁝ **dysmenorrhea**, with: *Cocc* kr1
⁝ **menorrhagia**, in: cann-i hr1*
- **mental** exertion; after: agar ambr arn kr1* **Ars** *Aur-m* aven sf1.de cact mtf11 calc sf1.de carc mlr1• *Chlol* hr1* cocc sf1.de *Coff* ferr **Hyos** k* ign kali-br *Kali-c* *Kali-p* *Lach* *Lyc* **Nux-v** k* *Ph-ac* *Pic-ac* *Sil* sf1.de vanil fd5.de
• **children**; in: carc mlr1•
- **miscarriage**:
• **after**: *Cypr* hr1*
• **during**: *Helon* hr1*
- **money**; from loss of: stann gl1.fr•
- **moon**:
• **full**: bamb-a stb2.de• *Lac-e* hrn2• nux-v vh *Sil* vh
• **new**; at: *Sep* bg2*
- **mortification**; from: *(↗MIND - Ailments - mortification)* *Calc* hr1* *Coloc* *Ign* hr1* staph k2
- **motion**:
• **desire** for motion; from (See restlessness)
• **fetus**, of (See fetus)
- **mountain** climbing; from: coca br1
- **muttering**, with: **Hyos** hr1*
- **narcotics**: *(↗drugs)*
• **after**: *Bell* kr1 *Nux-v* kr1 stram a1
• **in** spite of: lyss hr1*
• **without**: *Kali-i* kr1
- **nausea**; from: am-c j5.de ambr bg2 cham j5.de cocc hr1* cycl bg2 *Graph* h2* hell bg2 rhus-t b7.de* ruta fd4.de sacch-a fd2.de• [tax jsj7]
- **nervous**: acon ptk1 calc ptk1 chin ptk1 coff bg2* diosm br1 elec mtf11 gels ptk1 hyos ptk1 lach ptk1 lyc ptk1 mosch ptk1 *Nux-v* ptk1 *Plat* ptk1 scut ptk1 stict ptk1 teucr ptk1 thea br1
- **news**, after surprising: *Coff* kr1
- **night** watching; from: cocc k2* colch tl1
- **nightmares**; after: *(↗dreams)* ambr bg2
- **noise**, from slight: alumn kr1 am-c ang a1 apis kr1 ars j5.de *Asar* *Calad* k* carb-v b4.de* chin k* cocc *Coff* kr1* grat ign kr1* kali-n j5.de lach j5.de* *Merc* j5.de narcot a1 nat-p *Nux-v* ol-an **Op** kr1* phos k* ruta j5.de saroth mg1.de* *Sel* sep st1 spong fd4.de sul-ac j5.de *Sulph* h2* *Ther* mrr1 tritic-vg fd5.de vanil fd5.de

Sleep

- **numbness**; from: cimic k* cina
- **nursing** the child, after: *Cimic* hr1*
- **nursing** the sick, from: cimic hr1 **Cocc** k* *Coff* k* zinc-act st
- **old** people; in: *Acon* kr1* ars bro1 *Bar-c* k* carc jl2 op bro1 passi bro1 phos bro1 sulph st1 **Syph** st1
- **operation**; after: *Stict* c1*
- **oppression**; from:

○ • **Abdomen**; of: *Mag-c* b4.de* mag-m b4.de*

• **Chest**; of: acon b7a.de *Calc* b4a.de *Hep* b4a.de *Ip* b7a.de kali-c j5.de nux-m b7.de nux-v bg2 physal-al bro1 polys sk4• ran-b b7.de* ran-s b7.de* *Samb* b7a.de

• **Hypogastrium**; of: mag-c h2

- **orgasm** of blood; from: acon b7a.de* am-c b4.de* *Ars* b4a.de asar b7.de* borx b4a.de bry b7.de* calc b4.de* carb-an b4a.de carb-v b4.de* *Con* b4a.de dulc b4.de* hep b4a.de ign b7.de* kali-c b4.de* *Laur* b7a.de mag-c b4.de* merc b4.de* nat-m b4.de* nit-ac b4.de* *Phos* b4a.de *Plat* b4a.de *Puls* b7.de* ran-b b7a.de *Rhus-t* b7.de* sabin b7.de* *Samb* b7a.de sars b4.de* sep b4.de* **Sil** b4.de* sulph b4.de*

○ • **Chest**; to: *Puls* b7a.de

• **Head**; to: cycl b7a.de puls b7a.de

- **over**-fatigue; from mental and physical (See exertion; mental)
- **overheated**; after being: borx mrr1
- **overloaded** stomach; from: *Puls* b7a.de
- **overwork**; from (See tension - mental)
- **pain**; from: acon j5.de ars bro1 arum-t bg2* cann-i bro1 *Cham* bro1 cimic bg2 coloc bro1 *Dol* a1 dulc fd4.de eup-per bg2* eupi a1 *Ferr-p* hr1* helo-s bnm14• *Iris* kr1 kreos j5.de *Lach* hr1* loxo-lae bnm12• mag-c j5.de mag-m bro1 mag-s c1 *Merc* j5.de* passi bro1 phyt a1 plb a1 positr nl2• ptel a1 puls bro1 *Rhus-t* hr1* ruta fd4.de sin-n bro1 *Staph* ptk1 stram a1 *Sulph* hr1* syph al* tritic-vg fd5.de vip-a j5.de

• **not** from pain: coff tl1

• **parts** lain on: *Thuj* hr1*

• **rheumatic** pains: *Ant-t* kr1 *Ars* kr1 atro kr1 bell bro1 cact kr1 calc bro1 *Caul* kr1 coff bro1 *Coloc* kr1 *Dulc* kr1 ign bro1 *Puls* kr1 *Stict* kr1

• **sleep**; when falling asleep: galeoc-c-h gms1• lil-t **Merc** kr1

○ • **Abdomen**: alum b4.de* ars b4.de* bar-c b4.de* calc b4.de* canth b7.de* cham b7.de* cina b7.de* coff b7.de* ferr b7.de* kali-c b4.de* kreos b7a.de *Mag-c* b4a.de mag-m b4.de* mag-s c1 mang b4.de* nat-m b4.de* nit-ac b4.de* nux-m b7.de* phos b4.de* plb b7.de* *Rhus-t* b7a.de sars b4.de* sep b4.de* sulph b4.de* verat b7.de*

• **Arms**: calc h2 caust bg2 mag-s a1 mosch b7.de* thea a1 tritic-vg fd5.de

• **Back**: *Calc* b4a.de con hr1* *Dulc* hr1* lac-ac hr1* *Lac-c* hr1* mag-s hr1* *Nat-m* b4a.de ptel a1* sin-n hr1* *Syph* hr1* thuj b4a.de

• **Body** sore, whole: caust h2

⁝ **sleepiness** all day; with: am-c vh ant-c dm arg-n dm lac-d dm mag-c k2 mosch dm pic-ac k2 **Staph** sulph dm

• **Bones**: anac j5.de daph j5.de* *Kalm* hr1* *Merc* hr1* plb hr1*

• **Calf**: staph b7.de*

• **Chest**: all-s vh1 alum b4a.de am-m b7.de anac b4a.de ars b4a.de calc b4a.de cupr b7.de* *Graph* b4a.de lyc b4.de* mag-m b4.de* merc-c b4a.de nux-m b7.de nux-v b7.de* sabad b7a.de

• **Epigastrium**: calad b7.de*

• **Eyes**: carb-v b4.de* kreos b7a.de rheum b7.de* verat b7.de*

• **Face**: caps b7.de* plan a1 verb b7.de*

• **Feet**: lach b7.de* phos a1

• **Gums**: *Dol* c1* stann h2

• **Head**: acon a1 am-c k* ammc a1* *Arg-n* kr1 ars-i kr1 **Aur** kr1 brach kr1 bufo bg2* calc-caust sf1.de carbn-o a1 caust bg2 *Chel* kr1 **Chin** j5.de *Chlol* kr1 chloram jl3 *Croc* kr1 elaps kr1 *Lach* kr1 lyc bg2* mag-s j5.de* manc kr1 merc bg2 *Merl* kr1 mosch j5.de mur-ac bg2 nat-m bg2 nicc j5.de nit-ac j5.de osm bg2* pall kr1 *Phys* kr1 *Puls* kr1 ruta fd4.de sars sf1.de sol-ni bg2 *Spig* kr1 spong j5.de staph bg2 stram bg2 **Sulph** kr1 *Syph* kr1 tarax b7.de* verat h1

• **Heart**: mand sp1

• **Hips**: sin-n a1

• **Hypochondria**: apis b7a.de calad b7.de*

• **Jaw**; upper: cassia-s ccrh1•

- **pain**; from: ...

• **Joints**: sol-t-ae a1

• **Knee**: gard-j vlr2• spig b7.de*

⁝ **sitting** up in bed | **amel.**: acon vh1

• **Legs**: agar j5.de *Kali-bi* hr1* med hr1* *Mez* hr1* *Rhus-t* hr1* staph j5.de *Syph* hr1* visc c1

⁝ **right**: visc c1

○ • **Limbs**: aeth a1* *Ars* b4a.de bar-c b4.de* bell b4.de* calc b4a.de caust b4.de* cham b7.de* chin b7.de* con b4.de* guaj b4a.de hep b4.de* kali-c b4.de* kreos j5.de mag-c j5.de merc b4.de* merc-c b4a.de mosch b7a.de nat-c bg2 nat-m b4.de nit-ac b4.de* phos b4.de* plb b7.de* *Puls* b7.de* ran-s b7.de* *Rhod* b4.de* rhus-t b7.de* spig b7.de* sulph b4.de* syph k2 zinc b4.de*

⁝ **sore**: cham h1

⁝ **Lower**: agar h2

• **Lumbar** region: am-m b7.de* kreos b7a.de mag-m h2 *Rhus-t* b7a.de

• **Mouth**: merc-pr-r a1

• **Muscles**: arge br1 helon bro1 lavand-a ctl1•

• **Rectum**: am-c gsy1*

• **Skin**: petr a1

• **Spleen**: apis b7a.de

• **Stomach**: ars b4a.de calc b4a.de carbn-o a1 cocc b7.de* galeoc-c-h gms1• graph b4a.de *Ign* b7.de* ox-ac k2* phos a1 rhus-t b7.de* seneg b4a.de valer b7.de*

⁝ **pressing** pain: *Alum* b4a.de *Calc* b4a.de

• **Teeth** (See TEETH - Pain - accompanied - sleeplessness)

• **Toes**: positr nl2•

- **palpitations**; from: *(↗Disturbed - palpitations)* acon b7a.de* adon bg2* agar b4a.de alum bro1 am-c bro1 ars b4a.de *Aur-m* k* bar-c b4a.de bell bg2 *Benz-ac* *Cact* bro1* *Calc* k* cimic bro1* coca bro1 *Coff* hr1* crot-t k* dig digin a1 dulc b4a.de* *Ign* bro1* *Iod* bro1 jatr-c bg2 kali-bi *Kali-p* hr1* *Kola* stb3• lact j5.de lil-t bro1 lyc b4.de* lycps-v bro1* merc b4a.de mur-ac b4a.de nat-c b4a.de *Nat-m* k* oci-sa sk4• psor k* puls b7a.de* *Rhus-t* bro1* saroth mg1.de sars k* sep bro1 sil k* spig bro1* vanil fd5.de
- **pecuniary** loss; from (See money)
- **periodical**: *(↗intermittent)*

• **night** | **alternate** nights, on: anac k* chin bro1 lach k*

• **alternating** with | **deep** sleep (See Deep - alternating - sleeplessness)

• **hours**:

⁝ **four** hours; for: sulfonam ks2

⁝ **half** hours; for: anac a1

⁝ **three** hours:

⁝ **every**: puls a1

⁝ **for**: sulfonam ks2

- **perspiration**:

• **from**: anac b4a.de *Ars* bry b7.de* cham b7.de* chel b7.de* *Chin* b7a.de chinin-s j5.de cic b7a.de *Clem* b4a.de *Coff* b7.de* **Con** *Dros* b7a.de dulc j5.de ferr graph j5.de *Merc* b4a.de mosch j5.de *Nux-v* hr1* petr j5.de ph-ac b4.de* ran-b b7.de* *Rhus-t* b7.de* sabad b7.de* sabin b7.de* *Sel* b7.de* sulph tarax k* verat k*

⁝ **Forehead**: sars b4.de*

⁝ **Lower** limbs: borx b4a.de

• **with**: alum bg2 am-c bg2 am-m bg2 **Anac** bg2 *Apis* bg2 arn bg2 *Ars* bg2 bar-c bg2 bell bg2 borx bg2 *Bry* b7.de* *Calc* bg2 cann-xyz bg2 carb-v bg2 caust bg2 *Cham* b7.de* *Chel* b7.de* **Chin** bg2 cic h1* *Clem* bg2 cocc bg2 **Coff** b7.de* con bg2 dros bg2 graph bg2 hep bg2 ign bg2 kali-n bg2 kreos bg2 laur bg2 led bg2 luf-op rsj5• mag-c bg2 mag-m bg2 mang bg2 *Merc* bg2 merc-c bg2 mosch bg2 nat-m bg2 *Nit-ac* bg2 nux-m bg2 nux-v bg2 petr bg2 **Ph-ac** bg2 *Phos* bg2 *Puls* bg2 *Ran-b* b7.de* ran-s bg2 *Rhod* bg2 **Rhus-t** b7.de* *Sabad* b7.de* *Sabin* b7.de* sars bg2 *Sel* b7.de* sep bg2 sil bg2 staph bg2 stront-c bg2 *Sulph* bg2 syph al *Tarax* bg2 *Thuj* bg2 *Verat* bg2

- **planning** for the next day (See anticipation)
- **playing** and laughing, child is: coff sf1.de* cypr sf1.de* med kr1
- **pleasant**: cortico mg1.de cortiso mg1.de
- **pneumonia**:

• **after**: *Kali-c* hr1*

- • **in**: *Ant-t* hr1* *Bell* hr1* *Chel* hr1* *Elaps* kr1 *Merc* hr1*
- **position** is right, no: kali-c j5.de lach b7.de* laur j5.de lycpr j5.de nat-c j5.de plat j5.de ran-b j5.de staph j5.de
- **pregnancy** agg.; during: *Acon* hr1* ambr hr1* *Bell* hr1* cact hr1* cham hr1* chin hr1* *Cimic* hr1* *Coff* hr1* cypr k* gels hr1* hyos hr1* ign hr1* kali-bi hr1 *Kali-br* hr1* lyc hr1* mag-p hr1* mosch hr1* nux-v hr1* *Op* hr1* *Puls* hr1* rhus-t hr1* staph hr1* stram hr1* sulph bro1 tarent hr1*
  - • **cramps** in calves, from: cham kr1* coff kr1* *Cupr-act* kr1* ferr kr1* nux-v kr1 *Verat* kr1
  - • **sleepiness**; with: *Nux-m* st1
- **protracted**: cadm-s br1 spong fd4.de
- **pulsation**, from: acon bro1 ammc a1 *Bell* bro1 *Cact* bg2* *Glon* bro1 pall a1 rhus-t j5.de* sec bro1 *Sel* bro1* sulph bro1 thea bro1
  - ○ • **Blood** vessels; in: rhus-t b7.de* sabad b7.de* *Sel* b7.de*
  - • **Body**: kali-c k2
    - ⁝ **abdomen**; particularly in the: *Sel* k1
  - • **Different** parts of body; in: cact br1
  - • **Ear**, in the: sil k*
  - • **Head**, in: ars h2 cycl b7.de* kreos b7a.de sil b4.de*
  - • **Lower** limbs, in: agar h2
- **reading**; after: sel j5.de*
- **remaining** up later than usual, on: grat a1
- **renal** affections, in: *Hyos* hr1* *Plb* hr1*
- **respiration**:
  - • **arrested**; from: ars bg2 bry b7.de* grin bg2 *Lach* bg2
  - • **difficult**: *Arg-n* hr1* ars sf1.de *Borx* kr1 *Calc* b4a.de carb-an j5.de *Cham* hr1* *Chlol* hr1* *Kali-br* hr1* *Kali-c* bg2* *Kali-i* hr1* lact j5.de *Morph* hr1* *Ran-b* hr1* *Stann* hr1* *Syph* hr1*
    - ⁝ **children**; in: *Kali-br* hr1*
- **restlessness**, from: (↗*Restless)* abies-n hr1* abrot hr1* **Acon** j5.de* agar b4a.de *Alum* b4.de* am-c h2* anac h2* anthraco j5.de **Apis** bg2* aran-ix mg1.de arn hr1* **Ars** b4a.de* arum-t sf1.de asar b7.de* aur j5.de bamb-a stb2.de• bell b4a.de* borx b4a.de* *Bry* b7.de* *Calc* b4a.de carb-an b4a.de* *Carb-v* b4a.de* caust b4a.de* cham ptk1 *Chin* j5.de *Cina* j5.de* clem b4a.de cocc j5.de *Coff* hr1* coloc b4.de* *Con* b4a.de* cor-r j5.de *Cupr* j5.de* *Cypr* hr1* dicha mg1.de dig b4a.de dulc j5.de euph j5.de* euphr kr1 eupi a1 ferr bg2 gels bg gent-l j5.de graph b4.de* guaj b4.de* hep b4a.de *Ign* hr1* ind a1 iod j5.de* jal j5.de kali-c sf1.de kali-n h2* *Kreos* b7a.de* lac-leo hm2• *Lach* b7.de* lam j5.de laur b7.de* *Led* j5.de* *Lyc* j5.de* lycpr j5.de m-aust b7.de* mag-c b4.de* mag-m b4.de* mag-s a1 mang b4.de* *Meph* hr1* *Merc* b4.de* **Merc-c** hr1* mosch a1 mur-ac j5.de* nat-c b4a.de* *Nat-m* h2* nat-s j5.de* *Nit-ac* j5.de olnd j5.de *Op* j5.de* par b7.de* *Petr* b4.de* ph-ac b4a.de *Phos* b4.de* plat b4a.de plut-n srj7• positr nl2• *Psor* hr1* *Puls* b7.de* ran-b b7.de* *Rhod* b4a.de *Rhus-t* b7.de* ruta j5.de sabin b7.de* sars h2* sec j5.de senn sf1.de *Sep* b4.de* *Sil* b4a.de* *Spig* j5.de spong b7.de* stann b4a.de* sulph h2* tarent a1 ter hr1* *Teucr* b7a.de thal jl3 *Thuj* b4.de* tritic-vg fd5.de ulm-c jsj8• vinc j5.de zinc mrr1 zinc-val sf1.de
  - • **anxious**: merc bg2
  - • **internal** restlessness: lach bg2
  - • **old** people; in: bar-c bg2
  - ○ • **Arms**; of: kali-bi bg2
  - • **Body**; of: **Acon** b7.de* alum b4a.de* *Am-c* b4a.de *Anac* b4a.de *Ant-c* b7a.de **Ars** b4.de* arum-t bg2 asaf b7.de* aur b4.de* borx b4a.de *Bry* b7.de* calc b4.de* canth b7.de* carb-an b4a.de *Carb-v* b4.de* *Caust* b4a.de **Cham** b7.de* *Chin* b7.de* *Cic* b7.de* *Cina* b7a.de cocc b7.de* *Coff* b7.de* *Con* b4.de* dulc b4.de* *Euphr* b7a.de *Guaj* b4a.de hell b7a.de hyos b7.de* *Ign* bg2 iod b4.de* *Ip* b7.de* kali-n b4.de* kreos b7a.de *Laur* b7a.de led b7.de* lyc b4.de* m-aust b7.de mag-c b4a.de mag-m b4.de* mang b4.de* merc b4.de* merc-c b4a.de mur-ac b4.de* nat-m b4.de* nux-m b7.de* nux-v b7.de* olnd b7.de* op b7a.de petr b4.de* *Phos* b4.de* *Plat* b4.de* *Puls* b7.de* ran-s b7a.de rheum b7a.de *Rhod* b4.de* *Rhus-t* b7.de* ruta b7.de* *Sabin* b7a.de sil b4.de* spig b7.de* *Stram* b7.de* sulph b4.de* tarax b7.de* *Teucr* b7a.de thuj b4.de* *Valer* b7a.de
  - • **Legs**, in: agar b4.de* graph b4.de* lyc k2 *Mag-c* b4a.de perh jl3 *Rhod* b4a.de rhus-t a1 saroth mg1.de stann b4.de*
    - ⁝ **twitching** in abdomen; and: caust h2
- **retching**; from: merc-c b4a.de
- **retiring**, after (See evening - bed)
- **riding**:
  - • **carriage**; in a:
    - ⁝ **agg.**: *Alum* st1* *Calc* st1* sel st1*
    - ⁝ **amel.**: tarent a1
- **rising** up in throat; from something: *Calc* b4a.de
- **rocked**, child must be: *Carc* st1* cina *Stict* st1
- **sad** events; from: ign tl1 *Nat-m* kr1* vanil fd5.de
- **sadness**:
  - • **from**: acet-ac kr1 *Aur* kr1 *Carc* mlr1• cimic mtf11 *Ign* kr1 *Kali-br* kr1 kali-c j5.de positr nl2• rhus-t j5.de sulph j5.de *Thuj* kr1*
  - • **with** (See MIND - Sadness - sleeplessness - with)
- **saliva**:
  - • **flow** of; with constant: *Ign* kr1
  - • **running** down throat, from saliva: epil c1 kali-c bg1
- **scarlatina**; during: *Ail* hr1* am-c br1 *Merc-i-r* hr1* *Phyt* hr1* *Verat-v* hr1*
- **screaming**; with: cina j5.de hyos j5.de jal j5.de senn j5.de
  - • **children**; in: passi sf1.de
- **scruples**, from: ferr j5.de
- **secretion**; from suppressed (See discharges)
- **senses**; from acuteness of: asar bro1 *Bell* bro1 calad bro1 calc-br bro1 cham bro1 cocc bro1 *Coff* bro1 ign bro1 nux-v bro1 *Op* bro1 tarent bro1 valer bro1 zinc-val bro1
- **sexual** | **excitement** agg.: anan vh ant-c j5.de* aur b4a.de* cann-i bro1 canth bro1* galeoc-c-h gms1• kali-br br1* raph br1*
- **sexual** desire; from: anan vh calc k2*
- **sexual** thoughts agg.: calad k2* calc k2 staph mrr1
- **shaking** chills; from: am-c b4.de* carb-v b4.de*
- **shivering**; from: bry k* kali-c b4.de*
- **shocks**, from: agar k* alum **Arg-met** k* **Ars** *Bell* k* hyper a1 ip nat-ar *Nat-m* *Nit-ac* k* *Phos*
- **skin** disorders; from (See accompanied - skin)
- **sleepiness**: (↗*weariness - in)*
  - • **with**: *Acon* k* adam skp7• *Agar* k* am-c k* am-m k* ambr sf *Ant-t* hr1 *Apis* bg2* apoc k* arg-n a1 arn k* ars k* bar-c k* **Bell** k* borx b2.de* *Bry* k* calad k* *Calc* k* *Calc-sil* k13 camph k* cann-i canth k* carb-v k* *Caust* k* **Cham** k* **Chel** k* chin k* chr-ac a1* cic k* cina b2.de* clem k* cob-n mg cocc k* cod a1 *Coff* k* *Con* k* corn k* corn-f hr1 *Crot-h* k* crot-t j5.de *Cupr* daph k* dirc k* epil a1* euphr k* eupi *Ferr* k* ferr-ar ferr-p gels bg1 gent-l j5.de graph k* *Hep* k* hyos k* kali-ar *Kali-c* k* kali-p kali-sil k13 *Lach* k* lact j5.de laur k* *Lec* sne lil-s a1 lyc k* m-arct b2.de m-aust b2.de* mag-m k* med *Merc* k* mosch k* *Nat-c* k* *Nat-m* k* nat-p nat-sil k13 nit-ac k* *Nux-m* hr1* *Nux-v* k* **Op** k* *Petr* hr1 petr-ra shn4• *Ph-ac* k* **Phos** k* *Phys* hr1 plb k* **Puls** k* ran-b k* rhod k* *Rhus-t* k* sabad k* sabin k* *Samb* k* sapin a1 sel k* *Senec* sf **Sep** k* *Sil* k* solin a1 spig k* staph k* *Stram* sul-ac k* sul-i k13 *Sulph* k* syph *Tarent* hr1* ter sf teucr j5.de thuj k* verat k* viol-o k* vip-a j5.de zinc k*
    - ⁝ **daytime**: aln vva1• am-c bg2* anh sp1 apeir-s mlk9.de arg-n bg2* arn bg2 bar-act bg2 bell bg2 bry bg2 carc mlr1• cyclosp sa3• guat sp1 kali-c bg2 mag-c mtf33 mosch bg2 nat-m bg2 nit-ac tl1 ph-ac bg2 sil bg2* staph mtf33 stront-c sk4• sulph bg2*
      - ⁚ **body** aches all over (See pain - body - sleepiness)
      - ⁚ **mental** exertion; after: pic-ac k2
    - ⁝ **morning**: cycl a1 hydrog srj2•
      - ⁚ **and** after sunset: **Sulph** hr1*
    - ⁝ **afternoon**: abrot a1
      - ⁚ **and** evening: **Sulph** st
    - ⁝ **night**:
      - ⁚ **midnight**:
        - . **after** | **5** h: myric a1
    - ⁝ **going** to sleep; before: galeoc-c-h gms1•
    - ⁝ **heat**; during: **Puls** a1
    - ⁝ **measles**; after: *Caust* hr1*
    - ⁝ **moon**; at new: sep sf1.de
    - ⁝ **pregnancy** agg.; during: *Nux-m* hr1*
    - ⁝ **restlessness**; with: *Graph* hr1* *Petr* hr1*
    - ⁝ **thoughts**; from: agar a1
  - • **without**: ars-s-r hr1* aur hr1* chin-b hr1* *Fl-ac* hr1*

Sleep

- **smallpox**, in: *Sarr* hr1*
- **soreness**, with: carb-v j5.de mag-s j5.de

○ • **Mouth** and throat, in: arum-t bro1 merc bro1
- **sounds** in the heart, from: x-ray sp1
- **starting**; from: alum b4a.de am-m b7.de* ambr b7a.de* am b7.de* *Ars* b4.de* bell b4.de* bism b7.de* borx b4a.de bry b7.de* calc b4.de* canth b7.de* caust b4a.de chel b7a.de *Chin* b7.de* coff b7a.de *Dig* bg2 dulc b4.de* euph b4a.de guaj b4.de* hep b4.de* hyos j5.de ign b7.de* kali-bi bg2 kali-c b4.de* *Kali-n* b4a.de led b7.de* lyc b4.de* mag-c b4.de* merc b4.de* *Merc-c* b4a.de nat-c b4.de* nat-m b4.de* nit-ac b4.de* nux-v b7.de* phos b4.de* plb b7.de* psor j5.de* *Rhus-t* b7.de* sars b4.de* sel b7.de* sep b4.de* stront-c b4.de* sulph b4.de* verat b7.de*
- **stitching**; from:

○ • **Body**; in: euph b4a.de

• **Skin**; in: apis b7a.de arg-met bg2 cann-s b7a.de cocc b7.de*
- **stubborn** (See chronic)
- **students**: tub-m jl2 v-a-b jl2*
- **stupefaction**, with: calc j5.de *Nux-v* j5.de
- **sudden**: carc mlr1• scut a1
- **supper**; after late: *(↗eating - after - agg.)* *Puls* hr1*
- **talk**; with desire to: *Cypr* hr1* [tax jsj7]
- **tea**; after abuse of: camph-mbr bro1 chin bro1 dulc fd4.de *Nux-v* bro1 puls bro1 thea br1
- **teething**; during (See dentition)
- **tension**; from:

• **mental** tension; from: *Bamb-a* stb2.de•

• **muscles**; from tension in the (See pain - muscles)

○ • **Face**; in: apis b7a.de
- **thinking** amel.: thea a1
- **thirst**; from: all-s hr1* borx b4a.de *Bry* b7a.de calad b7.de* *Calc* b4a.de *Cham* b7a.de gamb a1 ign hr1* nit-ac b4.de* *Ran-s* b7a.de

• **menses**; during: *Sep* a1
- **thoughts**:

• **morning**, towards: ars h2

• **activity** of thoughts; from: *(↗Falling - difficult - waking - 3; MIND - Thoughts - rush - sleeplessness)* acon bro1 adon ptk1 *Aesc* agar aln vva1• aloe k* alum *Ambr* anh mg1.de* ant-t ap-g bro1 apis bg2* aran-ix mg1.de* *Arg-n* **Ars** k* aur kr1 *Aur-m-n* wbt2• *Bamb-a* stb2.de• bar-c bell k* borx k* bros-gau mrc1 *Bry* k* cact calad b7.de* **Calc** k* calc-f jl *Calc-s* calc-sil k2 canth bg2 *Carbn-s* *Carc* mg1.de* caust *Chin* k* chlam-tr bcx2• cinnb coca-c sk4• *Cocc* k* **Coff** k* coloc con cortico mg1.de* cortiso mg1.de* cupr sst3• cupr-act a1 *Cypr* k* dig a1 dios dulc fd4.de fago falco-pe nl2• *Ferr* *Fl-ac* *Gels* k* *Glycyr-g* cte1• *Graph* k* grat ham k* hell **Hep** k* hist mg1.de* hydrog srj2• *Hyos* k* hyper hypoth jl ign k* irid-met srj5• jatr-c bg2 kali-ar *Kali-c* k* kali-n j5.de kali-sil k2 *Kola* stb3• lac-h sk4• lac-leo hrn2• lac-loxod-a hrn2• lac-lup hrn2• *Lach* k* lavand-a ctl1• lil-t oss• *Lyc* k* marb-w es1• meph bro1 *Nat-m* nat-p nat-sil fd3.de• nux-m bg2 **Nux-v** k* olib-sac wmh1 *Op* b7.de* ozone sde2• petr-ra shn4• *Pic-ac* k* pieri-b mlk9.de pin-con oss2• plat j5.de* plb plut-n srj7• podo c1 polys sk4• positr nl2• *Psor* **Puls** k* *Pyrog* k* *Rhus-t* b7.de* ruta fd4.de sabad k* sabin b7a.de sacch-a fd2.de• sal-fr sle1• saroth mg1.de* *Sep* k* *Sil* k* spig k* spong fd4.de *Staph* k* *Sulph* k* teucr k* thea a1 thuj tritic-vg fd5.de *Tub* tung-met bdx1• vanil fd5.de verat b7.de* viol-o viol-t b7.de* yohim bro1 *Zinc* k* [bell-p-sp dcm1]

• **business**, of: *(↗cares; from - business)* bell a1 *Cocc* a1* **Nux-v** mrr1 phos k2

• **disagreeable** things; of: **Nat-m** mrr1

• **dreams** from previous night, of: cench k2

• **erotic** (See sexual thoughts)

• **foggy** thoughts: carc az1.de•

• **lascivious** (See sexual thoughts)

• **melody**; thinking of the same: puls h1*

• **same** thought, always the: bar-c *Calc* k* *Coff* *Graph* k* petr plat k* **Puls** k* thuj bg2

• **songs**; of: plut-n srj7•
- **throat**; from pain in: atra-r bnm3•
- **thrusts**; from | **upward**: *Bell* b4a.de
- **thunderstorm**; before: agar sil
- **tiredness** (See weariness)
- **tobacco**; after abuse of: gels br1* nux-v plan br1*
- **toothache**; from: alum b4a.de *Aur* hr1* *Bar-c* b4.de* *Cham* hr1* *Cocc-s* hr1* hell a1 mag-m b4.de* merc-c b4a.de* rat a1 **Sep** a1* *Sil* hr1* *Spig* b7.de* staph hr1* trom hr1*
- **tossing** about | **not** from tossing about: ars tl1 coff tl1 hyos tl1
- **total**: *(↗daytime - children)* am-c j5.de ambr j5.de ars j5.de aur j5.de *Calc* j5.de *Canth* j5.de carc sst*• chin j5.de cic j5.de clem j5.de coloc j5.de *Daph* j5.de* dulc j5.de *Graph* j5.de hep j5.de iod j5.de ip j5.de *Kreos* j5.de mag-c j5.de merc j5.de mosch j5.de nat-c j5.de *Nit-ac* j5.de *Nux-v* j5.de phel c2 prun j5.de rhus-t j5.de sars j5.de sep j5.de sil j5.de spong j5.de staph j5.de *Sul-ac* j5.de *Sulph* j5.de syph al tax j5.de vip j5.de
- **trembling**; from: calc j5.de euph b4a.de* lyc h2* nat-m b4a.de

○ • **Nerves**; in: *Nat-m* b4a.de
- **tuberculosis**, in: all-s bro1 *Coff* bro1 dig bro1 *Iod* hr1* *Sang* hr1* sil kr1*
- **twitching**; from:

○ • **Lids**; of: *Apis* b7a.de

• **Limbs**; of: agar vh1 *Alum* k* ambr k* arg-n bg2 **Ars** k* bell k* calc k* canth carb-v bg2 carc gk6* *Cypr* kr1 hep b4a.de ign k* *Kali-c* k* lyc bg2 m-ambo b7a.de *Merc* b4a.de merc-c nat-m bg2 op bg2 *Phos* b4a.de **Puls** k* rhus-t k* sel k* sep k* stront-c k* sulph ptk1 tab bg1
- **unaccountable** (See causeless)
- **uncomfortable** sensation; from: *Puls* b7.de*
- **uncovering** the ear; from: lec oss•
- **uneasiness**; from: agar h2* alum a1 am-c a1 *Bry* hr1* *Carb-v* hr1* *Cina* j5.de *Merc* j5.de* nat-c h2 orni tl1 petr j5.de phos h2*

• **anxiety** with heat, must uncover which causes chilliness; and: *Mag-c*

• **not** from discomfort: coff tl1
- **urination** | **urging** to urinate; with: bamb-a stb2.de• dig kr1 graph j5.de luf-op rsj5• nat-c j5.de ran-b b7.de* ruta j5.de vanil fd5.de
- **urination**; from frequent: *Nat-m* b4a.de
- **uterine** colic; caused by: cann-i c1*
- **vaccination**; after: carc mlr1• *Mez* hr1* *Thuj* hr1*
- **vertigo**; from: am-c arg-n calad calc lac-ac hr1* malar jl2 *Merc-c* k* nat-c nat-m phos k* rhus-t b7.de* sacch-a fd2.de• spong sulph tell ther k*
- **vexation**; after: acon ars calc hr1* cham *Coloc* b4a.de* kali-p nux-v k* petr *Staph*
- **visions**; from: ambr k2* androc srj1• *Arg-n* bry calc carb-an *Cham* hr1* dulc fd4.de *Ign* hr1* lyc merc *Op* hr1* sulph

• **anxious**: androc srj1• *Carb-an* hr1*

• **ciphers** in front of his eyes; sees: ph-ac b4a.de

• **closing** eyes; on: *Led* kr1 *Thuj* kr1
- **vivacity**; from: *(↗MIND - Vivacious)* ambr b7a.de *Ang* b7a.de* ant-c b7.de* am j5.de aur k* bamb-a stb2.de• borx j5.de *Calc* k* canth b7a.de caps b7a.de* carc mlr1• caust b4.de* chin b7.de* *Coff* b7.de* cypr sf1.de graph k* hyos b7.de* kali-c k* kola stb3• lach b7.de* lam j5.de lyc j5.de m-aust b7.de* merc k* mez k* *Nat-m* h2* *Nit-ac* k* nux-v j5.de phos j5.de *Prun* j5.de *Puls* b7.de* *Ran-b* b7.de* *Ran-s* b7.de* rhus-t b7.de* ruta b7.de* sel j5.de sep k* sil k* spig j5.de staph j5.de sul-ac b4a.de* *Sulph* k* verat h1
- **waking** agg.; after: *(↗Falling - difficult - waking)* aeth a1* agar h2 am-c k* am-m j5.de anan vh1 androc srj1• **Ars** k* ars-s-f k2* *Aur* k* aur-ar k2 *Bamb-a* stb2.de• bar-c k* *Bell* k* bell-p tl1* berb j5.de borx k* brach k* calc k* calc-f jl3 calc-sil k2* caps k* carb-v k* carbn-s carc gk6* caust k* chr-ac a1* clem k* cocc k* con b2.de* cycl b2.de* *Dulc* k* *Ferr* k* ferr-m ferr-ma a1 ferr-p graph k* ina-i mlk9.de jug-c sf1.de kali-ar kali-c k* kali-n j5.de kali-sil k2* kola stb3• **Lach** k* laur k* led b2.de* loxo-recl knl4• lyc k* **Mag-c** k* mag-m k* mang k* *Merc* k* mez k* mur-ac k* *Nat-c* h2* **Nat-m** k* *Nit-ac* h2* nux-m bg2 *Nux-v* k* ol-an k* orot-ac rly4• ox-ac oxal-a rly4• ozone sde2• petr j5.de ph-ac k* *Phos* k* phyt k* pip-n bg2 plac-s rly4• plut-n srj7• prun j5.de* psor sf1.de puls k* *Ran-b* k* ran-s k* rat rhod j5.de rhus-t k* ruta k* sabin k* sal-fr sle1• *Sars* k* sel k* *Sep* k* **Sil** k* spong k* stront-c j5.de suis-pan rly4• sul-ac k* *Sulph* k* vanil fd5.de zinc k* zinc-p k2* [bell-p-sp dcm1]

• **midnight**, before: *Mur-ac* j5.de

• **noise**, by a: ox-ac a1
- **walking** in open air agg.; after: kali-c j5.de
- **warm** coverings, though limbs are cold; with: **Camph** **Led** *Med* **Sec**
- **warmth**, from: carb-an h2 kali-n h2 mag-c h2 mur-ac h2 petr-ra shn4•
- **weakness**; from: *(↗weakness; weariness - from)* ammc a1 cypr hr1* *Gels* hr1* gran a1 helon br1* *Kali-br* hr1* *Kreos* b7a.de* *Mag-p* hr1* meph sf1.de merc j5.de *Ph-ac* sf1.de phos sf1.de *Pic-ac* hr1* ran-s b7.de stann sf1.de *Tub* hr1*

- **weaning** child, on: bell ptk1
- **weariness**: (↗*accompanied - sleepiness - daytime)*
  - **from**: (↗*weakness)* **Ars** cact hr1* carc mlr1• *Chlol* hr1* helon sf1.de **Ign** sne kali-br tl1
  - **in** spite of weariness: (↗*sleepiness)* ambr bg2* apis bg2* apoc bg2* *Bell* bg2* bit-ar wht1• calc j5.de *Cham* bg2* dulc j5.de helo bg2 hep bg2* kali-c bg2* kreos j5.de lach j5.de meph bg2 moni rfm1• mur-ac bg2 nat-m bg2* nux-v bg2* olib-sac wmh1 op bg2* ph-ac bg2 phos bg2* pic-ac bg2 puls bg2* ran-s j5.de* ruta fd4.de *Senec* bg2* *Sep* bg2* sil bg2* spong fd4.de stann bg2 sulph bg2* *Tarent* bg2* ter bg2* **Ther** mrr1 tritic-vg fd5.de vanil fd5.de
    - **women**; in: castm bg2
  - **without**: bamb-a stb2.de• kola stb3•
  - ○ **Legs**: *Sep* b4a.de
  - **Lower** limbs; from tiredness of: agar h2
- **windy** weather; during: adam srj5•
- **wine**, after abuse of: (↗*MIND - Libertinism)* coff fl-ac k* **Nux-v**
- **women**; especially in: ergot jl
  - **excited**: senec sf1.de
  - **exhausted**: castm sf1.de
- **worms**; from: *Ferr* hr1* teucr hr1* *Valer* hr1*
- **worry**; from (See cares; from)
- **yawning**, with spasmodic: cimic ptk1 croc bg2* kali-bi bg plat bg2* vanil fd5.de

SLEEPS (See Falling)

SLUMBER (See Dozing)

SOMNOLENCE (See Sleepiness)

SOPOR (See Deep)

STUPEFYING:
- **morning**: anac b2.de* ang b2.de* ant-t b2.de* *Bell* b2.de* *Brom* b4a.de bry b2.de* *Calc* b2.de* carb-v b2.de* caust b2.de* clem b2.de* cocc b2.de* **Con** b2.de* croc b2.de* dig b2.de* euphr b2.de* **Graph** b2.de* hep b2.de* hyos b2.de* ign b2.de* kali-c b2.de* kali-n b2.de* *Led* b2.de* lyc b2.de* m-ambo b2.de* nat-c b4.de nat-m b2.de* **Nux-v** b2.de* ph-ac b2.de* *Phos* b2.de* puls b2.de* ran-b b2.de* sep b4.de spig b2.de* stram b2.de* verat b2.de* zinc b2.de*
- **perspiration**; during: acon bg2 **Ant-t** bg2 *Apis* bg2 bell bg2 calc bg2 camph bg2 *Chin* bg2 cic bg2 con bg2 croc bg2 hep bg2 hyos bg2 ip bg2 led bg2 nux-m bg2 **Op** bg2 ph-ac bg2 phos bg2 **Puls** bg2 **Rhus-t** bg2 sec bg2 spong bg2 stram bg2 valer bg2 verat bg2

STUPOR, drowsy: arg-n br1 cyt-l sp1 hir skp7• **Op** br1*
- **children**; in:
  - **nurslings** | **vomiting**; after: aeth tl1 ip tl1 sanic tl1

SUDDEN: pisc a1*
- **daytime**: *Chin* j5.de
- **evening**: fl-ac a1
  - **19**-21 h: calc a1
- **sitting** agg.: chin j5.de

SUPERFICIAL (See Light)

TIREDNESS; without: chir-fl gya2

TOSSING; much (See Position - changed)

UNREFRESHING: (↗*Bad; Exhausting; Rise - aversion; Sleepiness - morning; Sleepiness - morning - waking - on; Sleepiness - waking - after - agg.)* abrom-a ks5 abrot k* acon k* aesc sf1.de agar k* agath-a nl2• *Aids* nl2• ail k* alco a1 *Alum* k* alum-p k2* alum-sil k2* *Am-c* k* am-m b2.de* ambr k* ammc j5.de* anac b2.de* anag hr1* *Anan* vh1 androc srj1• ange-s oss1• ant-c k* ant-o a1 ant-s-aur a1 ant-t k* anthraci kr1 ap-g bro1 apis apoc-a a1 *Arg-met* kr1* *Arg-n* k* arge-pl rwt5• arn k* *Ars* k* ars-h hr1* ars-s-f k2* asaf b2.de* asim a1* aster hr1* aur k* aur-ar k2 aur-m hr1* *Aur-m-n* wbt2• bar-act a1 *Bar-c* k* *Bell* k* berb k* bism k* borx k* bov b2.de* brom k* bros-gau mrc1 *Brucel* sa3• bry k* calad hr1* calam sa3• **Calc** k* calc-f k* calc-s hr1 calc-sil k2* camph k* cann-s k* *Caps* b2.de* carb-ac k* *Carb-an* b2.de* carb-v k* carbn-s k* carc tpw2* cardios-h rly4• *Carl* k* carneg-g rwt1• **Caust** k* cham k* *Chel* k* *Chin* k* chinin-ar chinin-s k* chlol k* chlorpr jl3 cic k* cina b2.de* cinch a1 cinnb k* *Clem* k* *Cob* k* cob-n mg1.de* *Cocc* k* cod a1* coff b2.de* colch k* coli rly4• coloc con k* corn k* cortiso sp1* croc b2.de* culx k2* cupr k*

Unrefreshing: ...
cupr-act a1* cupr-ar k* *Cycl* k* daph k* des-ac jl3* *Dig* k* dream-p sdj1• dros b2.de* dulc j5.de *Echi* bg2* equis-h *Erig* mg1.de euph b2.de* euphr k* falco-pe nl2• ferr b2.de* ferr-ma k* *Fl-ac* hr1* form k* fum rly1*• gard-j vlr2• gast a1 glon gnaph k* graph k* *Guaj* k* halo jl3 ham **Hell** hr1* hell-v a1 *Helon* hr1* hep k* hipp a1 hippoc-k szs2 hir skp7• hydrog srj2• hyos k* hyper hr1* ign k* ignis-alc es2• ina-i mlk9.de ind a1 ip b2.de* jac-c k* jug-c k* kali-bi k* kali-c b2.de* kali-i k* kali-n b2.de* kali-p fd1.de• kali-s fd4.de kiss a1 *Kola* stb3• kreos k* lac-cp sk4• lac-del hrn2• *Lac-e* hrn2• lac-h sk4• lac-leo hrn2• **Lach** k* lact k* laur b2.de* *Lavand-a* ctl1• *Lec* k* led b2.de* lil-t bro1 *Luna* kg1• **Lyc** k* m-ambo b2.de* m-arct b2.de *M-aust* j5.de **Mag-c** k* **Mag-m** k* malar jl2 mand sp1* med al melal-alt gya4 meny b2.de* *Meph* j5.de* merc b2.de* merc-c bro1 merl k* mez k* mit a1 *Moni* rfm1• mosch b2.de* mur-ac b2.de* myric k* nabal a1 nat-ar nat-c k* *Nat-m* k* nat-n k* nat-p k* nat-sil k2* nicc j5.de **Nit-ac** k* nux-m b2.de* *Nux-v* k* oci-sa sk4• olib-sac wmh1 olnd b2.de* *Op* k* orot-ac rly4• ozone sde2• paeon k* pert-vc vk9 *Petr* k* petr-ra shn4• *Ph-ac* b2.de* **Phos** k* **Phys** sne pic-ac k* pin-con oss2• plac rzf5• plan k* plat h2* *Podo* k* polyg-h a1 *Positr* nl2• prun j5.de psil ft1 psor k* ptel k* *Puls* k* puls-n a1 querc-r svu1• rad-br sze8• ran-b k* rheum b2.de* rhod b2.de* rhus-g tmo3• rhus-t b2.de* rib-ac jl3 ros-d wla1 rumx ruta b2.de* sabad k* sacch sst• *Sal-ac* hr1* sal-fr sle1• samb b2.de* sang a1 santin sarcol-ac bro1* saroth mg1.de* sarr k* sars k* sec b2.de* sel k* *Sep* k* *Sil* k* skat br1 *Spig* k* spong b2.de* squil b2.de* stann k* staph k* *Stram* b2.de* stront-c b2.de* sul-ac j5.de sul-i k* *Sulph* k* syph bro1* tarax b2.de* tax-br oss1• teucr k* thuj k* thymol bro1 tritic-vg fd5.de **Tub** br1* tung-met bdx1• upa k* vac jl2 valer b2.de* vanil fd5.de verat b2.de* vib hr1* viol-t b2.de* visc sp1 wies a1 x-ray sp1 xan br1 *Zinc* k* zinc-p k2* zing k* [bell-p-sp dcm1 chr-m stj2 chr-met stj1* chr-s stj2 heroin sdj2 lac-mat sst4 mag-f stj1 mag-lac stj2 mag-met stj2 mag-n stj2 *Mag-s* stj1 mag-sil stj2 mang stj1 mang-act stj2 mang-i stj2 mang-m stj2 mang-met stj2 mang-n stj2 mang-p stj2 mang-s stj2 mang-sil stj2 sol-ecl cky1 **Spect** dfg1 tax jsj7]
- **daytime**: caust j5.de ign j5.de
- **morning**: aml-ns kr1 ang h1 aq-mar skp7• brom a1 bry chir-fl gya2 *Clem* hr1* *Cocc* hr1* *Cod* hr1* con cortiso tpw7 *Gnaph* k* *Graph* hep kali-p fd1.de• kali-s fd4.de *Lyc* mrr1 *Mag-c* mrr1 **Mag-m** mrr1 marb-w es1• mill hr1* moni rfm1• musca-d szs1 *Nat-m* hr1* *Nux-v* olib-sac wmh1 op pert-vc vk9 petr-ra shn4• *Podo* hr1* *Sep* hr1* spong fd4.de **Sulph** k* ulm-c jsj8• zinc-p k2*
  - **tired** in morning than in evening; more: **Mag-c** kr1* malar jl2
  - **waking**; on (See morning)
- **noon**: digin a1 ign a1
  - **and** afternoon: ign j5.de
- **afternoon**: bar-c k* colch a1 dream-p sdj1• glon a1 ign h1 nat-m h2 petr-ra shn4• sal-fr sle1•
  - **3-4** h: ruta a1
  - **3-5** h: cimic a1
- **deep** sleep (See Deep - unrefreshing)
- **dreams**; from: agath-a nl2• calc-f a1* celt a1 *Chel* hr1* *Cod* hr1* dioxi rbp6 sacch-a fd2.de•
- **fever**; during: *Ars* hr1* *Dig* hr1* *Ip* hr1* *Phos* hr1*
- **menses**; during: *Nux-m* hr1*
- **overstudy**; from: *Cupr-act* kr1
- **prolonged** sleep: **Nux-v** bg2
- **rising**, indisposed to: aesc kr1 ambr j5.de ars j5.de bry j5.de canth j5.de *Carb-v* kr1 *Card-m* kr1 cob-n mg1.de crot-h j5.de cycl j5.de* des-ac rbp6 dros j5.de ferr-ma j5.de graph j5.de ham fd3.de• kali-p fd1.de• kali-s fd4.de lach j5.de malar jl2 *Nat-m* j5.de nat-sil fd3.de• *Nux-v* j5.de olib-sac wmh1 petr-ra shn4• ros-d wla1 saroth mg1.de *Sep* j5.de* spong fd4.de *Sulph* j5.de* *Thuj* j5.de verat j5.de
- **sleep** | **siesta** agg., after: (↗*GENERALS - Sleep - after - afternoon - agg.)* calc-s hr1* cob-n mg1.de pert-vc vk9 **Staph** mrr1
- **tired** on rising than on retiring; more (See morning - tired)

VOMITING; sleeps after (See Falling - vomiting - after)

WAKING:
- **morning**:
  - **6** h: aq-mar rbp6 *Arg-n* kr1 arist-cl rbp3• carc fd2.de• olib-sac wmh1 syc bka1•
    - **dream**, from: rhus-t a1
  - **6.30** h: hippoc-k szs2
  - **7** h: cadm-met tpw6 [tax jsj7]
  - **dreams**, from: lyc a1

Sleep

- **heat** of face, coldness of hands and soles; with: con a1
- **sleep**; immediately on going to: nat-m a1
- **sunrise**, at: **Lyc** k ● lycps-v

- **afternoon**: [tax jsj7]
  - **15** h: propr sa3•
  - **16**-17 h: *Kali-i* kr1 lac-lup hrn2•
  - **alternating** with | **dozing** (See Dozing - afternoon - alternating)
- **evening** | **falling** asleep, soon after: ambr j5.de bry j5.de ferr j5.de hydr-ac j5.de kali-c j5.de phos j5.de *Prun* j5.de puls j5.de sul-ac j5.de
- **night**: alum a1 astac a1 cann-i a1 *Kali-c* hr1* merc-c a1 mim-h a1 *Mur-ac* a1 olib-sac wmh1 *Puls* a1 spong fd4.de tell rsj10• tritic-vg fd5.de [heroin sdj2]
  - **midnight**:
    - **before**: borx chel b7.de* chin b7.de* merc j5.de mez j5.de mur-ac nat-m nicc j5.de phel phos j5.de plb j5.de puls k* sil tab
      - **23** h: *Bell* kr1 chel cimic **Coc-c** kr1 nat-m sil h2* ther kr1
        - **stool**; with urging to: mag-c a1
        - **vertigo**, with: ther a1
      - **23**.30 h: lyss kr1
    - **at**: agar am-m j5.de amph a1 anan vh1 ant-t j5.de *Arg-n* kr1 bar-c j5.de bry j5.de *Calc* j5.de* camph chel cimic con j5.de crot-t j5.de cystein-l rly4• gent-l graph j5.de ketogl-ac rly4• lat-m bnm6• laur j5.de *Lyc* kr1 m-arct j5.de *Mag-c* j5.de malar jl2 mang j5.de merc-c nat-c nat-m nat-p nat-sil fd3.de• nicc kr1 nit-ac kr1 olib-sac wmh1 phos j5.de plat plect a1 rat j5.de rhus-t j5.de ruta kr1 sep j5.de sil spong sul-ac b4.de* sulph thuj j5.de vac kr1
      - **dream**; after: fl-ac zinc
    - **after**: alum h2* *Am-c* j5.de am-m kr1 brucel sa3• calc h2 canth caps carb-an j5.de cardios-h rly4• chin b7.de* cystein-l rly4• dulc fd4.de *Euphr* b7.de* germ-met srj5• *Graph* kr1 grat j5.de *Ign* kr1 kreos b7a.de* lac-leo hrn2• *Lach* kr1 lap-la sde8.de• laur b7.de* *Lyc* j5.de m-ambo b7.de* m-arct j5.de mag-c j5.de *Merc* kr1 *Mez* j5.de* nat-m j5.de nux-v k* phel phos h2 plac-s rly4• pot-e rly4• ran-b j5.de *Ran-s* b7.de* ruta fd4.de sabin b7.de* sars j5.de sel j5.de *Sep* bg2 *Sil* h2* sinus rly4• spig k* **Spong** b7.de* squil b7.de* staph b7.de* suis-em rly4• suis-hep rly4• sul-ac sulph gt syph kr1 tritic-vg fd5.de tung-met bdx1•
      - **0**-1 h: adlu jl *Ars* mrr1
      - **1** h: ant-t j5.de borx caul kr1 *Cocc* kr1 cystein-l rly4• **Kali-c** kali-n j5.de *Mag-c* j5.de mang j5.de *Merc* kr1 merc-sul kr1 nat-c nat-m nit-ac j5.de nux-v ph-ac phos j5.de pieri-b mlk9.de rat *Sep* j5.de spig j5.de squil j5.de stann j5.de stront-c ter kr1
        - **1**-1.30 h: flav jl2
        - **1**-2 h: ephe-si hsj1• *Rumx* kr1
        - **1**-3 h: *Ph-ac* kr1*
        - **1**-5 h: rauw sp1
      - **1.30**-2.30 h: mang-p rly4• sel jl
      - **1** or 2 h: lach a1
      - **2** h: agar kr1 *All-c* kr1 *Am-m* j5.de* ant-c h2* arist-cl mg1.de bamb-a stb2.de• *Bapt Benz-ac* calc mtf33 carb-an j5.de *Caust Dios* kr1 ferr flor-p jl* graph hydrog srj2• *Kali-bi* kr1 **Kali-c** kreos j5.de lac-leo hrn2• lach lachn kr1 luf-op rsj5• lyc *M-arct* j5.de mag-m j5.de mang-p rly4• merc j5.de mez nat-c j5.de nat-s **Nit-ac** k* ozone sde2• phys pot-e rly4• **Ptel** *Rat* rumx sars sil h2* staph stront-c suis-em rly4• sulph sf1.de syc bka1• symph fd3.de• *Urol-h* rwt• ven-m jl* [bell-p-sp dcm1 heroin sdj2]
        - **2**-3 h: arist-cl sp1 bamb-a stb2.de• bapt sf1.de choc srj3• kali-bi sf1.de mag-c nat-c h2 petr-ra shn4• sep sf1.de syc bka1• tung-met bdx1• [spect dfg1]
        - **2**-4 h: berb **Kali-c** k* merc petr-ra shn4• suis-em rly4• syph mrr1
        - **2**-6 h: arist-cl sp1 visc sp1
        - **before**: ferr a1
        - **causeless**: staph a1
        - **chill**, from: *Nat-m* kr1 [heroin sdj2]
        - **cough**, from: sulph a1
        - **dream**, from: mez a1
        - **heat**, from: benz-ac a1
        - **moon**; at full: ozone sde2•

- **night** – **midnight** – **after** – **2** h: ...
  - **pain**; from:
    - **Finger**; in: lac-leo hrn2•
    - **Teeth**; in: nat-s a1
  - **2** or 3 h: bacls-7 pte1*• dys fmm1• *Samb* kr1 syc fmm1•
  - **2.30** h: cob ptm1• cupr oss• olib-sac wmh1 [heroin sdj2]
    - **2.30**-4.30 h: hydroph jl*
  - **3** h: am-c j5.de am-m j5.de* aq-mar rbp6 arge-pl rwt5• arist-cl mg1.de ars bell-p st* benz-ac sf1.de *Borx* k1 bry sf1.de calc j5.de* calc-f sp1 carb-v h2* cardios-h rly4• carl cassia-s ccrh1• *Chin* k1 cob ptm1• *Coff* cupr sst3• cyclosp sa3• euphr j5.de* ferr-ma j5.de glon graph ham kr1 *Hed* mg1.de* jug-c sf1.de kali-bi sf1.de *Kali-c* kola stb3• lac-leo hrn2• lil-t *Lyc* h2* *Mag-c* j5.de* mag-m mag-s st* methys jl mez mim-p rsj8• nat-c j5.de nat-m nat-sil fd3.de• nept-m lsd2.fr nicc nit-ac j5.de **Nux-v** k* olib-sac wmh1 petr-ra shn4• *Phyt* kr1 *Pic-ac* pin-con oss2• plat ran-s j5.de *Raph* j5.de *Rat* j5.de rauw sp1 rhus-t j5.de sacch-a fd2.de• saroth sp1 sarr sel j5.de seneg j5.de sep sil h2* succ-ac rly4• suis-pan rly4• **Sulph** symph fd3.de• thuj mrr1 *Urol-h* rwt• zinc-p k2 zing [bell-p-sp dcm1 ferr-p stj1 heroin sdj2 kali-m stj1 kali-n stj1 tax jsj7]
    - **3**-4 h: bad bamb-a stb2.de• bufo fago galla-q-r nl2• ind nat-m *Nux-v* petr-ra shn4• rauw sp1 *Sulph*
      - **constriction** of heart, with: saroth mg1.de
    - **3**-5 h: carneg-g rwt1• mand mg1.de saroth mg1.de **Sulph** kr1
      - **thoughts**, from activity of: calc-f sp1
    - **cough**, from: cain a1 op a1
    - **sore** throat; with: lac-leo hrn2•
    - **stool**; with urging to: cob ptm1• mag-c a1 olib-sac wmh1
  - **3**.30 h: ind a1 nat-m a1 symph fd3.de• [heroin sdj2]
  - **3** or 4 h: bufo a1 fago a1 ind a1
  - **4** h: aq-mar rbp6 ars kr1 aur sf1.de aur-m-n wbt2• bamb-a stb2.de• borx carb-v h2 carc fb* caust j5.de* chel st chir-fl gya2 coloc kr1 con h2 cortico mg1.de cortiso mg1.de cupr sst3• cycl sf1.de dream-p sdj1• galla-q-r nl2• ham fd3.de• hippoc-k szs2 hydrog srj2• ignis-alc es2• kali-c h2* kali-p fd1.de• kali-s fkr2.de kola stb3• lac-h htj1• *Lyc* *Mag-c* j5.de* mang h2* merc j5.de *Moni* rfm1• mur-ac nat-m neon srj5• nept-m lsd2.fr nit-ac *Nux-v* k* ozone sde2• penic jl* perh jl pert-vc vk9 peti a1 petr j5.de phos pin-con oss2• plb plut-n srj7• ptel ruta j5.de sacch-a fd2.de• sars sf1.de sep sil j5.de stann jl staph suis-em rly4• *Sulph* syc bka1• symph fd3.de• tab sf1.de thuj j5.de* trom ulm-c jsj8• urol-h rwt• *Verb* j5.de* zinc j5.de [heroin sdj2 tax jsj7]
    - **4**-5 h: aur-m-n wbt2• aur-s wbt2• cortico tpw7 sulph sf1.de verat kr1
    - **aggravation**, with: cycl sf1.de
    - **fresh**; feeling: pert-vc vk9
    - **headache**, from: stram a1
    - **stool**; with urging to: rumx a1
    - **toothache**, with: nat-c a1
  - **4.30** h: cortico tpw7* ozone sde2• plut-n srj7•
    - **4.30**-5 h: trios rsj11•
  - **4.50** h: cob ptm1•
  - **5** h: aloe aml-ns kr1 androc srj1• aq-mar rbp6 aspar kr1 aur-s zr bamb-a stb2.de• carc fd2.de• chr-ac kr1 con dream-p sdj1• fago galeoc-c-h gms1• ham fd3.de• helon hydrog srj2• kali-i kr1 kali-p fd1.de• lac-h sze9• lavand-a ctl1• lyc lycps-v mez nat-m nat-p nat-sil fd3.de• neon srj5• oxal-a rly4• ozone sde2• propr sa3• *Sulph* symph fd3.de• taosc iwa1• thiam rly4• tub al* tung-met bdx1• [cob stj2 cob-m stj2 cob-p stj2 sel stj2 tax jsj7]
    - **5**-6 h: *Kali-c* kr1 sacch-a fd2.de• trios rsj11•
    - **accompanied** by | **Heart**; pain in (See CHEST - Pain - heart - night - midnight - after - 5)
    - **stool**; with urging to: *Aloe* olib-sac wmh1 op **Sulph**
  - **morning**, toward: *Am-m* kr1 arg-n kr1 arum-d kr1 bell-p st* chel kr1 chr-ac kr1 dream-p sdj1• *Form* kr1 lap-la sde8.de• mur-ac kr1 phel phos squil kr1 staph stront-c a1
  - **menses**, after: kali-c j5.de
  - **toothache**, with: nat-m a1
- **abdominal** complaints; from: kali-c jl rhus-t h1 ruta fd4.de
- **alarmed**: *Agn* hr1* cact hr1*

- **alert** (See MIND - Alert - waking)
- **anger**, with (See MIND - Anger - morning - waking)
- **anxiety**, as from: (*↗MIND - Anxiety - waking*) acon b7.de agar h2 alum b4a.de am-c b4.de* ant-c b7a.de am b7.de* *Ars* b4.de* bar-c b4a.de bell b4.de* borx b4a.de calc b4.de* carb-v b4.de* caust b4.de* chin b7.de* cocc b7.de* con b4a.de* dig b4.de* ferr b7a.de graph b4.de* hep b4.de* ign b7.de ip b7.de* kali-c b4.de* lac-h sk4• lyc b4.de* mag-c b4.de* nat-m b4.de* nat-sil fd3.de• nit-ac b4.de* nux-v b7.de* petr b4a.de ph-ac b4.de* phos b4.de* plat b4.de* *Puls* b7.de* *Samb* b7a.de sep b4.de* sil b4.de* squil b7.de* stram b7a.de sulph b4.de* taosc iwa1• zinc h2
  - **burning** in the blood vessels; with: *Ars* b4a.de
- **bed** were in motion, as if: *Lac-c* kr1*
- **breath**, to get: (*↗RESPIRATION - Difficult - sleep - during - agg.; RESPIRATION - Difficult - waking*) acon vh1* aeth mrr1 ant-t k* grin mrr1 **Lach** mrr1 naja mrr1
- **breathing**; from arrest of: kali-c b4.de*
- **call**, as from a: dulc j5.de kreos j5.de rhod b4a.de* *Sep* hr1*
- **causeless**: ang b7.de* caust b4.de* *Cina* b7.de* ign b7.de* mag-c b4.de* merc b4.de* nat-c b4.de* ruta fd4.de *Sep* b4a.de sul-ac b4.de* sulph b4.de* thyr jl3 viol-t b7.de*
- **children**; in:
  - **pushes** everything away and wants everybody to go away; child: staph mtf33
  - **put** down in bed; when being: stram mtf33
- **chill**, with: alum b4.de am-c b4.de ambr b7.de ars b4.de aur b4.de carb-an b4a.de carb-v b4.de caust b4.de hep b4a.de lyc b4.de mag-m b4.de *Mur-ac* b4.de* nat-m b4.de nit-ac b4.de phos b4.de plat b4a.de sabad b7.de sars b4.de sep b4.de sil b4.de* spong fd4.de staph b7.de sulph b4.de verat b7.de zinc b4.de
- **clothes** feel damp or tight: *Guaj* kr1
- **coldness**, from: all-s hr1* ambr am j5.de clem j5.de con k* ferr-ma j5.de* malar jl2 mang k* ozone sde2• sabad b7.de* sars k* sulph j5.de thuj b4a.de
  - ○ **Feet**, of: puls b7.de*
  - **Leg**; left: agar h2
  - **Limbs**, of: **Carb-v**
  - **Stomach**; in: germ-met srj5•
- **complaint**; as from some: calc-act a1
- **confusion**, with (See MIND - Confusion - waking)
- **congestion**, with: *Nat-m* hr1*
- **cough**, from: **Acon** hr1* alum k* alum-sil hr1* am-m b7a.de *Anac* hr1* *Arg-n* hr1* ars k* *Bell* hr1* bism k* brom hr1* calc k* card-m hr1* caust k* *Chel* hr1* chin b7.de* coc-c k* cocc b7.de* con hr1* *Dios* hr1* dulc fd4.de falco-pe nl2• graph k* *Hep* k* **Hyos** k* *Kali-c* bg2* *Lach* b7a.de* mag-m k* (non:mang slp) mang-o a1* nat-sil fd3.de• nit-ac k* *Nux-v* k* *Op* k* *Phos* hr1* psor k* **Puls** k* rhus-t k* *Rumx* kr1 *Ruta* kr1 samb ptk1 *Sang* hr1* *Sel* hr1* sep k* sil k* spong sf1.de stront-c k* suis-pan rly4• **Sulph** k* syc bka1• syph jl2 tab k* tell jl3 thuj k* tritic-vg fd5.de vanil fd5.de
  - **menses**, during: zinc k*
  - **whooping** cough:
    - **morning** | **6**-7 h: coc-c bro1
- **cramps**; from | **Calves**; in: (*↗Sleeplessness - cramps - calves; EXTREMITIES - Cramps - legs - calves - waking*) lach b7a.de staph b7.de*
- **difficult**: (*↗Comatose; Deep; Heavy*) agar k* aids nl2• aloe *Alum* j5.de amyg a1 *Ant-t* j5.de arge a1 arge-pl rwt5• bell j5.de berb k* bry k* *Calc* k* calc-f jl3 *Calc-p* k* *Camph* k* *Carb-v* k* carbn-s *Cardios-h* rly4• *Cench* st1 cham k* *Cic* k* clem k* coli rly4• *Con* j5.de cupr-act a1 cystein-l rly4• dulc fd4.de ferr j5.de fum rly1*• fuma-ac rly4• gels k* gins j5.de* *Glon* k* granit-m es1• graph k* ham fd3.de• hydr a1* hyos k* iodof hr1* *Kali-br* k* kali-s fd4.de ketogl-ac rly4• kreos lac-h htj1*• lact j5.de led j5.de lob k* *Luna* kg1• lyc k* mag-m k* melal-alt gya4 mur-ac k* nat-c k* nat-m k* nat-sil fd3.de• nit-ac k* *Nux-v* k* *Op* j5.de oxal-a rly4• petr-ra shn4• ph-ac phos phys a1 podo k* positr nl2• pot-e rly4• ruta *Sep* k* sinus rly4• spong fd4.de (non:stram k*) suis-em rly4• suis-pan rly4• sulph k* sumb k* *Tab* j5.de tere-la rly4• teucr k* thiop jl3 viol-t j5.de visc sp1 [alumin-s stj2 calc-n stj1]
  - **morning**: *Alum* k* *Calc* k* **Calc-p** k* caust cham a1 clem a1 cortiso gse cystein-l rly4• dulc fd4.de ferr h1 granit-m es1• ham fd3.de• kali-s fd4.de lyc h2 nat-sil fd3.de• nit-ac h2 **Nux-v** k ● oxal-a rly4• ozone sde2• *Ph-ac* k* podo fd3.de• psil ft1 spong fd4.de stram suis-em rly4• suis-pan rly4• thuj k* tung-met bdx1• ulm-c jsj8•
- **difficult**: ...
  - **afternoon**: ferr a1 petr-ra shn4•
    - **siesta**, after: eug a1*
  - **dreams**; from: pert-vc vk9 pot-e rly4•
- **dreams**, by: (*↗DREAMS - Frightful - waking; DREAMS - Rousing*) *Acon* j5.de* agar agath-a nl2• am-c j5.de *Am-m* h2* amp rly4• ang kr1 ant-c h2 *Ant-t* j5.de* arg-met j5.de arg-n kr1* *Arn* k* *Ars* h2* asc-t kr1 atro aur k* bad bar-c *Bell* k* *Bov* j5.de brucel sa3• bry k* cain kr1 *Calc* b4.de* calc-f kr1* calc-p k2 *Camph* kr1 cann-s b7.de* carb-v h2* carc sp1* casc a1* cench k2 *Cham* k* chel b7.de* *Chin* b7.de* chlam-tr bcx2• chr-ac kr1 *Cic* b7.de* *Cina* b7.de* cinnb j5.de clem h2 coca coff b7.de* colch coloc k* con h2 com a1 cupr j5.de cycl j5.de cyclosp sa3• dicha mg1.de *Dig* h2* dros j5.de dulc j5.de *Erig* mg1.de euph h2* *Ferr-ma* j5.de gink-b sbd1• gran graph grat j5.de ham fd3.de• *Hep* *Hydroph* rsj6• hyper *Ign* b7.de* ina-i mlk9.de indg j5.de ip j5.de kali-bi bg2 *Kali-c* j5.de *Kali-chl* j5.de *Kali-i* j5.de kali-n b4.de* ketogl-ac rly4• *Kola* stb3• kreos j5.de lac-h sze9• lac-leo hrn2• lac-lup hrn2• *Lach* b7.de* lam j5.de laur j5.de led b7.de* lob kr1 lyc lycpr j5.de lyss *M-arct* j5.de m-aust b7.de* mag-c k* *Mag-s* j5.de *Mang* j5.de *Meph* a1* *Merc* *Mez* b4.de* mur-ac j5.de murx j5.de *Nat-c* j5.de nat-m k* *Nat-s* j5.de* *Nicc* j5.de nit-ac j5.de *Nux-v* k* olnd j5.de *Op* j5.de ozone sde2• par j5.de *Petr* j5.de petr-ra shn4• *Ph-ac* phos k* plac-s rly4• plan plat h2 plut-n srj7• propl ub1• puls k* pycnop-sa mrz1 rat j5.de rheum b7.de* rhus-t j5.de ribo rly4• ruta h1 sabad j5.de *Sabin* b7.de* sal-fr sle1• sars k* *Sep* h2* sil k* *Spig* j5.de spong j5.de* stann staph k* *Stront-c* b4.de* **Sulph** k* tab j5.de* *Teucr* j5.de *Thuj* b4.de* trios rsj11• tritic-vg fd5.de tung-met bdx1• verat h1* verb j5.de *Zinc* b4.de*
  - **anxious** (See MIND - Anxiety - dreams)
  - **falling**; of: thuj mrr1
  - **sad**: calc-f sp1 gink-b sbd1•
- **dryness** of mouth; from: (*↗MOUTH - Dryness - morning - waking; MOUTH - Dryness - night - waking*) bung-fa mtf
- **early**; too: acon b2.de* agar aids nl2• aloe a1 alum k* alum-sil k2 am-c b2.de* am-m k* ambr k* anag androc srj1• ang b2.de* ant-c k* ant-t k* arist-cl sp1 arizon-l nl2• am k* *Ars* k* ars-i ars-s-f k2 asaf k* astac a1 *Aur* k* aur-ar k2 aur-i k2 aur-m-n wbt2• bar-c b2.de* bart a1 bell bell-p sp1 berb j5.de *Borx* k* brach kr1 brom bry k* bufo bg2 cadm-met tpw6* calad b2.de* *Calc* k* calc-f sp1 calc-i k2 calc-p calc-sil k2 cann-s b2.de* canth b2.de* caps k* carb-an j5.de carb-v k* carbn-s carc fd2.de* *Caust* k* cham k* chel chin k* chinin-ar chinin-s chord-umb rly4• chr-ac a1* cob coca *Cocc* k* *Coff* k* con k* cop corn cortico mg1.de* cortiso mg1.de croc k* cycl k* dios dros k* *Dulc* k* ery-a euphr k* falco-pe nl2• ferr k* ferr-ar ferr-i k2 fl-ac *Form* gast a1 gels germ-met srj5• glon *Graph* k* grat j5.de guaj k* haliae-lc srj5• ham fd3.de• hell k* hep k* hippoc-k szs2 hura hydr hydrog srj2• hydroph rsj6• hyos hyper ign k* ina-i mlk9.de ind iod k* junc-e a1 *Kali-ar* kali-bi **Kali-c** k* kali-m k2 kali-n k* kali-p kali-s kali-sil k2 ketogl-ac rly4• *Kola* stb3• kreos k* lac-h htj1• *Lach* k* lavand-a ctl1• *Lyc* k* lycps-v m-arct b2.de* m-aust b2.de *Mag-c* k* mag-s sp1 mang k* menth-pu a1 *Meph* *Merc* k* merc-c b4a.de merc-i-f mez k* morph mucs-nas rly4• *Mur-ac* k* **Nat-ar** **Nat-c** k* *Nat-m* k* nat-ox rly4• *Nat-p* nat-sil k2 nep mg1.de* **Nit-ac** k* **Nux-v** k* ol-an olib-sac wmh1 olnd b2.de* orot-ac rly4• ozone sde2• ped a1 penic jl *Ph-ac* k* phasco-ci rbp2 phel phos k* **Pic-ac** k* plat k* plb b2.de* *Positr* nl2• prun pseuts-m oss1• ptel kr1 puls k* pycnop-sa mrz1 **Ran-b** k* ran-s k* rauw sp1 rhod k* rhus-t k* ruta fd4.de sabad b2.de* sabin b2.de* sacch sst1• sal-fr sle1• samb b2.de* sang saroth mg1.de* sars k* *Sel* k* seneg bg2 *Sep* k* *Sil* k* sphing a1* spong k* squil b2.de* staph k* staphycoc rly4• suis-em rly4• *Sul-ac* k* sul-i k2 **Sulph** k* syph kr1 thiam rly4• thiop jl *Thuj* k* *Trios* rsj11• tritic-vg fd5.de trom kr1 tub br1* *Tung-met* bdx1• urol-h rwt• vanil fd5.de verat k* verb k* viol-t k* *Zinc* zinc-p k2 zing [heroin sdj2 *Spect* dfg1 tax jsj7]
  - **3** or 4 hours after falling asleep: *Kali-c* mrr1 **Sulph** mrr1
  - **asleep** late; and falling: borx j5.de cycl kr1* dios kr1 guaj j5.de ignis-alc es2• *Lyc* kr1 ol-an j5.de prun j5.de puls j5.de ran-b j5.de sel j5.de sep j5.de staph j5.de sul-ac kr1 sulph j5.de vanil fd5.de visc jl zinc j5.de
  - **down** early in evening; if she does not lie: sep a1
  - **feels** worse if he sleeps again: *Nux-v* kr1
- **easy**: (*↗noise; Light*) ars-s-f k2 aur-s k2 brom a1 euph a1 fl-ac a1 galeoc-c-h gms1• medul-os-si rly4• merc a1 merc-cy a1 *Petr* a1 sul-ac a1
  - **night**:
    - **midnight** | **before**: puls a1
  - **senses**; acute: galeoc-c-h gms1•
- **enough**; as if he slept (See slept)

Sleep

- **erections**, by: ambr b7.de* am hr1* borx j5.de calc b4a.de carb-v j5.de *Card-m* hr1* gnaph hr1* *Hep* b4a.de* kali-c j5.de lach j5.de nat-c j5.de nat-m j5.de ox-ac a1 petr j5.de *Ph-ac* hr1* podo fd3.de• puls b7.de* sel b7a.de sil j5.de* stann j5.de thuj j5.de
- **falling**; with sensation of: *(↗DREAMS - Falling)* bell bg2* bism kr1 dig bg2* *Guaj* kr1* *Ph-ac* kr1 sang kr1
- **fear** of ghosts; from: *(↗MIND - Fear - ghosts - waking)* cocc b7.de*
- **flatulence**; from painful: nat-s ptk
- **fluttering** in body; from: hyos bg2
- **formication**; from | **Extremities**; in: bamb-a stb2.de•
- **frequent**: *(↗Disturbed; Interrupted; Restless)* *Acon* k* aeth k* agar k* agath-a nl2• agn k* all-s k* allox sp1 **Alum** k* *Alum-p* k2* *Alum-sil* k2* am-c k* am-m k* *Ambr* k* aml-ns ammc a1 anac k* androc srj1• ang k* *Ant-c* k* ant-t k* anth a1 apis k* aran k* *Arg-n* arn k* *Ars* k* ars-s-f k2* asaf b7.de* atp rly4• atro k* aur k* aur-ar k2 aur-m-n wbt2• aza jl3 bac jl2 *Bamb-a* stb2.de• bapt hr1* bar-act a1 **Bar-c** k* *Bar-m* bart a1 *Bell* k* benz-ac berb k* bism k* bomb-pr a1* *Borx* k* *Bov* k* *Bry* k* bufo k* buni-o jl3 cain kr1 calad k* **Calc** k* *Calc-ar* calc-p j5.de calc-sil k2* calen j5.de* cann-s k* canth k* caps k* *Carb-ac* k* *Carb-an* k* *Carb-v* k* *Carbn-s* carc mg1.de* *Card-m* k* cardios-h rly4• *Carl* k* caste jl3 castm *Caust* k* cedr k* cerv a1 cham k* chel k* *Chin* k* chinin-ar chinin-s a1 choc srj3• chord-umb rly4• *Cic* k* cimic k* *Cimx* k* cina k* cinch a1 cinnb k* clem k* cob ptm1• cob-n mg1.de coca cocc k* cod a1 *Coff* k* colch k* coloc k* con k* cop k* croc k* culx k2* cupr k* cycl k* cystein-l rly4• daph j5.de des-ac jl3 *Dig* k* digin a1 *Dros* k* dulc k* esp-g jl3 *Euph* k* *Euphr* k* ferr b2.de* ferr-i k* fl-ac k* franz a1 fuma-ac rly4• galeoc-c-h gms1• gins j5.de* granit-m es1• *Graph* k* grat j5.de guaj k* guare k* haliae-lc srj5• ham st1 hed sp1 **Hep** k* hippoc-k szs2 hura hydr-ac j5.de *Hydrog* srj2• hyos k* ign k* ina-i mlk9.de indg k* ip k* irid-met srj5• kali-ar *Kali-c* k* kali-chl j5.de *Kali-i* j5.de* kali-n k* kali-s kali-sil k2* ketogl-ac rly4• *Kola* stb3• kreos b2.de* lac-e hm2• lac-h sk4• lac-leo hm2• lac-loxod-a hm2• *Lach* k* lact j5.de lam j5.de laur b2.de* led k* limen-b-c hm2* lipp a1 *Lyc* k* lycpr j5.de lyss hr1* m-ambo b2.de* m-arct b2.de* m-aust b2.de* *Mag-c* k* mag-m k* mag-s k* mang k* meny k* **Merc** b2.de* merc-c k* merl k* methys jl3 mez k* mosch k* mucs-nas rly4• **Mur-ac** k* myric k* naja nat-ar nat-c k* *Nat-m* k* nat-p nat-s k* nat-sil k2* nicc k* *Nit-ac* k* nux-m k* *Nux-v* k* *Ol-an* j5.de* *Olib-sac* wmh1 olnd k* op b2.de* orig a1 orot-ac rly4• ox-ac k* ozone sde2• par k* ped a1 petr k* ph-ac k* phasco-ci rbp2 phel k* **Phos** k* phys k* pin-con oss2• plan k* *Plat* k* plect a1 plut-n srj7• positr nl2• pot-e rly4• propr sa3• **Puls** k* pycnop-sa mrz1 *Ran-b* k* ran-s b2.de* raph j5.de rat k* rheum b2.de* rhod k* *Rhus-t* k* ribo rly4• ruta k* sabad k* sabin k* sacch-a fd2.de• sal-fr sle1• sal-p a1 samb k* sang k* sanguis-s hm2• sarcol-ac bro1 sars k* sel k* senec k* seneg k* **Sep** k* *Sil* k* *Spig* k* spong k* squil k* *Stann* k* *Staph* k* stram k* *Stront-c* k* suis-pan rly4• sul-ac k* **Sulph** k* symph fd3.de• syph mrr1 *Tab* j5.de* taosc iwa1• tarax k* ter k* teucr k* thal jl3 thea thuj k* til k* tritic-vg fd5.de tung-met bdx1• upa k* valer b2.de* vanil fd5.de verat k* viol-o k* viol-t k* wies a1 wildb a1 *Zinc* k* zinc-p k2* [alumin-s stj2 aur-s stj2 bell-p-sp dcm1 cadm-s stj2 chr-s stj2 gal-s stj2 heroin sdj2 lac-mat sst4 lith-s stj2 mang-p stj2 mang-s stj2 mang-sil stj2 nicc-s stj2 spect dfg1]
  - **morning** | **twilight**; at: lac-loxod-a hm2•
  - **afternoon**: cann-i a1
  - **night**: brucel sa3• lac-e hm2•
    - **midnight**:
      - **before**: alum h2 chel
      - **about**: bell a1
      - **after**: am-m *Bamb-a* stb2.de• caps h1 gink-b sbd1• grat hippoc-k szs2 lac-e hm2• lyc h2 mag-s melal-alt gya4 mez sep sil spig h1 spong fd4.de staph h1 **Sulph**
        - **2** h: gink-b sbd1• lac-e hm2•
        - **3** h: euphr h2 gink-b sbd1• lac-loxod-a hm2•
          - **3-4** h: *Lac-e* hm2•
          - **after**: ulm-c jsj8•
        - **4** h | **after**: aur h2 gink-b sbd1• ulm-c jsj8•
        - **morning** | **towards**: chinin-s a1 coff j5.de* myric a1 rhod a1 spong fd4.de
        - **periodical** | **hours**; every two: bamb-a stb2.de•
  - **anxiety**, with: *Dig* a1* lyc k* [heroin sdj2]
  - **causeless**: caust a1 granit-m es1•
  - **children**; in: borx mtf33 phos mtf33 sep mtf33 staph mtf33 tritic-vg fd5.de vanil fd5.de
    - **newborns**; in: *Borx* kr1

- **frequent**: ...
  - **dreams**, from: agath-a nl2• *Alum* hr1* bry a1 cedr a1 cina a1 euphr a1 galeoc-c-h gms1• granit-m es1• lyc a1 nat-m a1 nat-s hr1 ribo rly4• stront-c sf1.de tab sf1.de vanil fd5.de
  - **falling**, as if: guaj a1
  - **fancies**, illusions; from: *Sulph* b4a.de
  - **fever**; during: anac b4.de mang b4.de nat-m b4.de nit-ac b4.de
  - **fright**, as from: *Agn* hr1 *Bism* a1* cocc h1* coff a1 graph h2* guaj a1 lac-e hm2• merc a1 nat-c a1
  - **heat**:
    - **bed**; of: culx k2
    - **from**: cocc a1*
  - **hour**; same (See periodical - hour - same)
  - **menses**, during: mag-c a1
  - **oppression** of chest, with: stann jl3
  - **pain**, from: spong fd4.de
    - **midnight**, before: *Ars* a1
  - **restlessness**, with: *Lach* hr1*
  - **sufficient** sleep; as from: *(↗slept)* calc-act a1 **Merc** a1* tarax a1
  - **thinking** of business, with: ham a1
  - **two** hours; every: thiam rly4•
- **fright**, as from: abrot mtf33 achy jl3 acon b7.de* adam skp7• aesc st1 agn k* alum k2* *Am-c* k* *Am-m* j5.de *Ambr* k* anac j5.de *Ant-c* k* ant-t j5.de *Apis* kr1 am b7.de* *Ars* j5.de aur k* bar-c j5.de* *Bell* k* *Bism* k* **Borx** k* bov j5.de* *Bry* b7a.de* bufo bg2 cact k2* calad b7a.de **Calc** j5.de* calc-s hr1* cann-s b7.de* canth b7.de* *Caps* k* carb-ac bg2 *Carb-an* j5.de *Carb-v* j5.de* carc mlr1• cassia-s ccrh1• castm j5.de *Caust* b4.de* *Cham* b7a.de* chel k* *Chin* chinin-ar k2 chlol k* cimic k* cina k* *Cocc* k* coff k* colch b7.de* *Con* b4.de* croc b7a.de crot-h k13 daph j5.de *Dig* k* *Dros* b7a.de* *Dulc* b4.de* *Euphr* k* ferr-ma j5.de gins j5.de graph k* guaj k* ham fd3.de* *Hep* b4a.de hydrog srj2• **Hyos** b7.de* *Ign* b7.de* *Indg* j5.de *Ip* b7a.de* kali-bi sf1.de kali-br sf1.de *Kali-c* k* kali-i j5.de kali-n j5.de kali-p k* *Lach* b7.de* lap-la sde8.de• laur k* led b7.de* limest-b es1• **Lyc** k* *M-arct* b7.de* *M-aust* j5.de *Mag-c* j5.de *Mag-m* j5.de* *Mag-s* j5.de *Med* hr1* meny h1 merc k* mez j5.de *Murx* j5.de nat-ar nat-c k* *Nat-m* k* nat-p bg2 nat-s j5.de* nicc j5.de *Nit-ac* b4a.de* *Nux-v* k* op bg2* ozone sde2• paeon ptk1 *Petr* j5.de *Ph-ac* j5.de *Phos* j5.de* *Phys* sne plat j5.de *Puls* k* rat rheum b7a.de ruta b7.de* *Sabad* b7.de* sabin b7.de* sal-fr sle1• *Samb* b7a.de* sang sars b4.de* sec j5.de *Sep* k* *Sil* j5.de* sinus rly4• *Spong* k* stann j5.de* staph b7a.de* *Stram* k* *Stront-c* j5.de suis-pan rly4• sul-ac **Sulph** k* tell jl3 ter bg2 teucr b7a.de* *Thuj* j5.de* **Tub** al* ulm-c jsj8• vanil fd5.de *Verat* b7.de* visc c1 xan c1 **Zinc** j5.de*
  - **night**:
    - **midnight** | **before** | **23** h: cimic
      - **after** | **2-3** h: calc mtf33
  - **dreams**; frightened from: bell a1* bung-fa mtf casc kr1 corn a1 dicha mg1.de *Erig* mg1.de **Lyc** kr1 *Meph* a1* mez h2* op gk psor al2* *Stram* rti2 *Sulph* a1* ulm-c jsj8•
    - **menses**; before: sul-ac ptk1
  - **falling** asleep; when just: bell tl1
  - **lump** which lodges in her throat; imagines she has swallowed a: *Sep* kr1*
  - **noise**, from slightest: apis kr1 kali-p fd1.de• *Nux-v* hr1* sars a1
  - **perspiration**; during: *Acon* bg2 apis bg2 am bg2 **Bell** bg2 bry bg2 *Cham* bg2 chin bg2 ip bg2 *Lyc* bg2 nux-v bg2 phos bg2 **Puls** bg2 samb bg2 *Sep* bg2 sil bg2 sulph bg2
  - **trembling**, with: abrot k*
  - **trifling**, about something: *Lach* hr1*
- **glottis**; from spasm of: chlor gt
- **grinding** of teeth; with: ant-c b7.de* hyos b7.de* phos bg2
- **hawking** up mucus; from: bov b4.de* spig b7.de*
- **heart** symptoms, with: both-ax tsm2 chr-ac hr1* *Kali-i* hr1* *Lach* hr1* *Merc* hr1* *Phyt* hr1* *Stict* hr1*
  - **night**:
    - **midnight** | **after**: **Spong** kr1
- **heat**:
  - **morning**: alum kr1 *Arn* kr1 sel rsj9•

- **night**:
  - **midnight**:
    - **after**:
      - **2** h: *Benz-ac*
      - **3** h: *Ars* kr1 bapt kr1
- **from** and with: alum k* amp rly4• anac k* ange-s oss1• arn b7.de ars k* bamb-a stb2.de• **Bar-c** k* *Bell* j5.de* *Benz-ac* borx j5.de calc k* carb-an b4a.de carb-v b4a.de* caust k* chinin-s j5.de choc srj3• cina j5.de cocc b7.de con k* dulc b4a.de ferr j5.de graph k* *Hep* b4a.de *Kali-bi* kr1 kali-c j5.de kali-n b4a.de* kali-p fd1.de• kola stb3• kreos b7a.de *M-arct* b7.de* *Mag-c* k* mag-m b4a.de* merc b4a.de mosch b7a.de* nat-m k* nicc j5.de **Nit-ac** k* petr k* ph-ac k* **Phos** k* puls b7.de* ran-s b7.de* rhod b4a.de ruta fd4.de sabad j5.de sel rsj9• sep k* sil k* stront-c b4a.de sul-ac k* sulph k* tarax b7.de teucr j5.de thuj k* vanil fd5.de [spect dfg1]
  - **head**, from heat in: arn h1
  - **passes** off; which: calad hr1*
- **hepatic** symptoms, with: bry hr1* *Carb-v* hr1* ptel hr1*
  - **night**:
    - **midnight**:
      - **after** | **4** h: ptel kr1
- **hunger**, from: *Aeth* sf1.de alum sf1.de am-c sf1.de *Ant-c* kr1 *Aran* sf1.de bamb-a stb2.de• chin *Ign* kr1 kola stb3• **Lyc** k* *Lyss* kr1 nat-m sne *Petr* h2* *Ph-ac* k* psil ft1* *Psor* k*
  - **ravenous** appetite; from: petr bg2 ph-ac b4.de*
- **ideas**; from disagreeable: calc gt
- **impossible**: acon k* bell k* chlf k* chlol a1 coff k* con k* *Crot-h* k* op k* tab k*
  - **morning**: adam skp7• bell a1 *Ph-ac* a1 tab a1
- **impression** of having slept for hours, although it was only thirty minutes (See slept - short)
- **incomplete**, not fully: m-arct b7.de*
- **itching**; from: agar hr1* ant-c b7.de* dulc h2 gamb a1 ina-i mlk9.de *Jug-c* hr1* *Led* hr1* *Merc* hr1* nat-sil fd3.de• sabad b7.de* *Stram* hr1* [spect dfg1]
  - ○ **Scalp**, of: jug-c vml3• merc-c b4a.de
- **jars**, concussion; from sensation of: ign b7.de
- **jerks**, by: **Bell** bg2* canni-i c1 hep b4a.de m-arct b7.de* merc b4a.de mez b4a.de *Nat-c* b4a.de oci-sa sk4• *Sulph* b4a.de zinc b4a.de*
  - ○ **Feet**; in: phos b4a.de
- **just** awakened, sensation as if: cycl a1
  - **dream**, from a: atro a1
- **late**; too: (*↗Need - great; Prolonged; MIND - Bed - remain - morning*) agar k* aids nl2• alum k* ambr k* *Anac* k* androc srj1• ang b2.de* ant-c k* ant-t k* *Apis* arn k* asaf k* aster atha a1 bell k* berb bism b2.de* borx k* brom bry k* bufo **Calc** k* **Calc-p** k* canth b2.de* carb-v k* carbn-dox knl3• carbn-s *Caust* k* cham clem k* *Coca* cocc k* coloc *Con* k* corn croc b2.de* cur *Cycl* cypra-eg sde6.de• dig k* dulc k* *Euphr* k* falco-pe nl2• ferr j5.de fl-ac galeoc-c-h gms1• glon **Graph** k* hep k* hyos k* hyper ign k* indg kali-c k* kali-n k* kali-s fd4.de kreos b2.de* *Lach* laur k* led k* lyc k* *M-ambo* b2.de* m-arct b2.de mag-c k* *Mag-m* k* mag-s j5.de manc menis a1 *Merc* k* mez morph musca-d szs1 nabal a1 *Nat-c* k* nat-m k* *Nat-p* nit-ac k* **Nux-v** k* ol-an peti a1 petr k* petr-ra shn4• *Ph-ac* k* phasco-ci rbp2 phel *Phos* k* plac-s rly4• plat k* positr nl2• puls b2.de* ran-b k* rhod k* rhus-t k* sal-fr sle1• sang scut a1 **Sep** k* *Sil* b2.de* spig k* stann stram k* sul-ac k* **Sulph** k* sumb tere-la rly4• verat k* verb k* zinc k* [tax jsj7]
- **lying** on painful side, while: *Borx* kr1
- **menses**:
  - **before**: sars b4.de* sul-ac
  - **during**: mag-c
    - **gushing** flow; from: coca kr1*
    - **pain**, from: sel rsj9*
- **mesmerized**; as if: m-arct b7.de*
- **move**, unable to: erig hr1* lyc hr1* sil j5.de
- **movements** of child in pregnancy, from: *Thuj* hr1*
- **nausea**, from: alum b4a.de* am-c b4.de* *Ambr* b7.de* ars j5.de arund hr1* aspar hr1* bry b7.de* calad hr1* calc b4.de* caust b4.de* *Con* hr1* cupr-ar hr1* *Dig* b4.de* euphr j5.de ferr-p hr1* *Goss* hr1* graph b4.de* *Ham* hr1* *Hyper* hr1* lach j5.de lyc b4.de* mag-c j5.de mang-p rly4• merc k* mez j5.de nat-sil fd3.de• nicc j5.de olnd j5.de op b7.de* phel j5.de phos b4.de* *Rat* j5.de rhus-t b7.de* ruta j5.de seneg b4.de* sep j5.de sil j5.de squil b7.de* *Sulph* j5.de *Ther* j5.de thuj j5.de tritic-vg fd5.de vanil fd5.de
- **noise**: (*↗easy*)
  - **from** a; as: bell kr1 dulc fd4.de merc j5.de nat-c h2 nat-m j5.de positr nl2• sars h2*
  - **rattling** of paper, by: calad
  - **slight** noise, from: (*↗Disturbed - noise*) alumn kr1* am-c ang a1 apis kr1 ars j5.de* *Asar* k* *Aur-m-n* wbt2• *Aur-s* wbt2• bamb-a stb2.de• *Calad* k* carb-v j5.de *Caust* mtf33 chin cocc *Coff* bg1* dulc fd4.de grat ham fd3.de• *Ign* kr1* kali-n j5.de kali-p fd1.de• lach j5.de marb-w es1• *Merc* j5.de narcot a1 nat-p nat-sil fd3.de• nux-v k* ol-an *Op* bg1* petr-ra shn4• phos pitu-a vml2• ruta j5.de saroth mg1.de* sel k* sep st spong fd4.de sul-ac j5.de sulph st vanil fd5.de [nat-caust stj2 nat-lac stj2]
- **numbness**, with: ambr j5.de bry j5.de *Erig* k* lyc j5.de mez j5.de phel j5.de puls j5.de
- **orgasm** of blood; from: am-c b4.de* bar-c b4a.de calc b4.de* kali-c b4.de* mag-c b4.de* nat-c b4a.de nat-m b4.de* nux-v b7.de* phos b4a.de sabin b7a.de sep b4.de* sil b4.de* sulph b4.de*
- **pain**, with: am-m bg2 *Aml-ns* kr1 ant-c bg2 **Ars** bg2* ars-h hr1* bapt hr1* both-ax tsm2 cham b7.de* *Chin* hr1* chir-fl bnm4• chr-ac hr1* dulc fd4.de *Eup-per* hr1* galeoc-c-h gms1• hydrog srj2• *Kali-c* hr1* kali-n j5.de kali-s fd4.de **Lach** hr1* merc-c a1 mur-ac j5.de myric hr1* *Nat-m* hr1* petr-ra shn4• ph-ac hr1* plac-s rly4• ran-a a1 raph hr1* ruta fd4.de sacch-a fd2.de• sel jl3 spong fd4.de staph bg2 tell jl3 tritic-vg fd5.de vanil fd5.de [spect dfg1]
  - **midnight**, especially: **Ars** kr1
  - **ulcers**; in: rhus-t b7.de*
  - ○ **Back**; in: *Am-m* b7a.de
  - **Ear**; in: acon mtf11 ferr-p mtf11
  - **Epigastrium**; in: ambr b7.de* bry b7.de* rhus-t b7.de*
  - **Foot**; in: lac-leo hrn2•
  - **Heart**; in | **burning** pain: benz-ac ptk1
  - **Limbs**; in: am-c b4.de am-m bg2 calc b4a.de carb-an b4.de* caust b4.de* croc b7.de* euph b4.de* hep b4a.de lach b7a.de lyc b4.de* mur-ac b4.de* nit-ac b4.de* rhod b4.de* sep b4.de* sil b4.de* sulph b4.de* viol-o b7a.de
- **palpitations**, with●: (*↗CHEST - Palpitation - waking*) agar sf1.de alum kr1* am-c *Ars* kr1 *Asar* mrr1 **Aur-m** mrr1 benz-ac k* bufo bg2 *Calc* k* *Camph* b7a.de* *Canni-i* kr1 *Carb-an* kr1* chin bg2 coc-c a1 ham fd3.de• hyos a1 ina-i mlk9.de iris bg2 kali-bi k* *Kola* stb3• limen-b-c mlk9.de *Lyc* h2* macro a1 mag-s mg1.de* *Merc* k* *Merc-c* k* mur-ac h2 *Nat-c* k* nat-m j5.de* nat-sil fd3.de• nit-ac j5.de ox-ac bg2* petr j5.de phasco-ci rbp2 *Phos* sf1.de pot-e rly4• rad-br ptk1 rhus-t b7.de* sars h2 *Sep* k* *Sil* j5.de *Spong* kr1 stram a1 sulph thuj sf1.de zinc
- **paralyzed** feeling, with: (*↗EXTREMITIES - Paralysis - sensation - morning - waking*) acon vh1 ferr-i kr1 kreos j5.de nat-c j5.de phos j5.de
- **periodical** | **day** | **every** other day: olib-sac wmh1
  - **hour**:
    - **same**; at the: rhod j5.de *Sel* k*
    - **every**: allox tpw4* *Arg-n* kr1 arn a1 ars-h kr1 carb-v j5.de ferr j5.de* *Galeoc-c-h* gms1• lavand-a ctl1• marb-w es1• nat-m j5.de sacch-a fd2.de• staph j5.de *Sulph* a1
    - **half** hour; every: agar a1 am-c j5.de mosch j5.de* *Nat-m* j5.de* *Sulph* j5.de*
    - **quarter** of an hour; every: cic j5.de lact j5.de merc j5.de* mur-ac h2*
    - **one** and a half hour; every: plut-n srj7•
    - **two** hours; every: nat-m j5.de
    - **three** hours; every: nat-m j5.de puls j5.de
- **perspiration**, from: alum b4a.de am-m j5.de anac b4.de androc srj1• ant-c hr1* ant-t hr1* ars ptk1 astac hr1* bamb-a stb2.de• bar-c j5.de *Bell* sf1.de berb a1* calc j5.de calc-p hr1* *Caust* j5.de* *Chel* b7a.de* chin j5.de* *Chinin-ar* kr1 chir-fl gya2 choc srj3• *Cic* b7a.de* clem b4a.de* **Con** k* croc j5.de daph j5.de **Dros** b7.de* dulc fd4.de euphr j5.de* *Ferr* hr1* ferr-ma j5.de* form hr1* gamb hr1* haliae-lc srj5• *Hep* sf1.de kali-p fd1.de• kola stb3• kreos j5.de *Lac-c* hr1* *Lac-d* hr1* *Lach* hr1* laur j5.de *Led* j5.de* *Lyc* hr1* mang b4.de merc j5.de *Nat-m* b4.de* nat-s j5.de nicc j5.de nit-ac b4.de *Ptel* hr1* *Puls* b7.de* ran-b b7.de* *Rat* j5.de rumx kr1 ruta fd4.de sabad j5.de *Samb* hr1* sel rsj9• sep j5.de *Sil* j5.de suis-em rly4• sulph sf1.de tarax b7.de* ther j5.de tub c1 vanil fd5.de
- **pollutions**; from: aloe a1 arn j5.de cain a1 crot-t j5.de cycl j5.de dig j5.de petr j5.de phos j5.de *Sel* kr1 sil j5.de *Thuj* j5.de*
  - **sensation** as before a pollution; with a: mur-ac a1
- **prickling**; from: bell bg2
- **pulled** at the nose; as if: nat-c h2
- **restlessness**; from | **leg**; of: hydrog srj2•

Sleep ○

- **salivation**; from: (↗*MOUTH - Salivation - sleep; MOUTH - Salivation - Sleep - during - agg.)* merc bg2
- **same** hour; at the (See periodical - hour - same)
- **scratching**; from | **Larynx**; in: bov b4.de* hep b4a.de
- **sensation** as if waking:
  - **deep** sleep; after a: phys a1
  - **long** sleep; after a: plut-n srj7•
- **sexual** excitement, from: carb-ac hr1* galeoc-c-h gms1• lyc bg2 ruta fd4.de
- **shocks**, from: *Arg-met* k* ars-h kr1 carc mlr1• dig ptk1 *Mag-m* k* manc k* merc a1
  - **electric**-like shocks in head: aster vh
  - ○ **Brain**; in: coca ptk1
- **shuddering**; with: nit-ac bg2
- **singing** in sleep, by: m-arct b7.de sulph bg2*
- **slept** one's fill; as having: (↗*frequent - sufficient)* agar a1 calc-act a1 caps j5.de choc srj3• cycl j5.de dig j5.de dros j5.de dulc fd4.de *Ferr* j5.de *Form* a1* i p j5.de kreos j5.de *Lyc* j5.de melal-alt gya4 **Merc** j5.de* olib-sac wmh1 prun j5.de *Puls* j5.de *Ran-b* j5.de ran-r j5.de ran-s j5.de *Ruta* j5.de* samb j5.de *Sel* j5.de spig j5.de spong fd4.de stann j5.de sul-ac j5.de taosc iwa1• tarax j5.de* *Tung-met* bdx1• [tax jsj7]
  - **night**:
    - **midnight**:
      - **after**:
        - **3** h: form a1
        - **4** h: borx h2
  - **obliged** to rise and to occupy himself: *Lac-c* kr1
  - **short** sleep; even after a: (↗*Short)* ham fd3.de• med kr1 spong fd4.de
- **sneezing**, from: am-m b7a.de dig a1 hep a1 olib-sac wmh1 tritic-vg fd5.de
- **soreness**, with: aesc a1* *Arn* hr1* olib-sac wmh1 *Rhus-t* a1*
- **stool**; from urging to: (↗*RECTUM - Urging - night - waking)* aloe a1 *Aur* b4a.de ferr-i a1
- **sudden**: ars k* bry k* carb-ac k* cinnb h1* crot-t k* ferr-ma k* kali-c jl3 *Kali-i* hr1* kreos k* m-arct j5.de medul-os-si rly4• nat-c h2* phys k* positr nl2• sal-fr sle1• sec k* sel rsj9• spira a1 spirae a1 staphycoc rly4• suis-em rly4• suis-pan rly4• sulph j5.de* til k*
  - **night**: hir skp7•
    - **midnight**:
      - **after**: ant-s-aur a1
        - **1**.30-2.30 h: sel rsj9•
        - **2** h; or: benz-ac kreos
        - **3** h; or: bry
  - **called**, as if: kreos a1 positr nl2• rhod ptk1 sep ptk1
  - **dream**, as from a: cinnb h1* positr nl2•
  - **dropping** from posterior nares; by: hydr st
  - **nightmare**, from: streptoc rly4• thea a1
  - **pollution**, after a: crot-t a1
  - **stool**; from | **night**:
    - **midnight**:
      - **after**:
        - **1** h: caul kr1
        - **5** h: **Sulph** kr1
        - **6** h: arg-n kr1
    - **desire** for: *Bry* kr1 *Dios* kr1 *Kali-bi* kr1
- **suffocation**, from: ant-t k* bry b7.de* *Calc* b4a.de carb-an b4a.de dig mrr1 graph a1 *Grin* mrr1 *Hep* b4a.de hyos b7a.de *Ip* b7a.de kali-i ptk1 lach mrr1 *Op* mrr1 phos b4a.de puls b7.de* ruta fd4.de samb b7a.de* spong b7a.de* sulph mrr1 valer ptk1 xanth bg2
  - **sleep**; on going to: **Lach** mrr1 naja k2
- **talking**, with: arn a1 bry bg2* *Sulph* hr1*
- **taste** in mouth; from bad: rhus-t b7.de*
- **thirst**, by: aloe kr1* ant-t b7.de* berb hr1* borx j5.de bung-fa mtf *Calad* hr1* c a l c b4a.de carb-v j5.de chinin-s j5.de chord-umb rly4• **Coff** b7.de* dros b7.de* e u g j5.de* gamb a1 kali-n j5.de kali-s fd4.de *Lil-t* hr1* mag-c j5.de mag-m b4a.de *Nat-s* hr1* nit-ac b4a.de* ph-ac b4a.de plat j5.de pot-e rly4• ran-s j5.de *Rat* j5.de rhus-t b7.de* ruta fd4.de *Sel* b7.de* sep j5.de spong fd4.de *Stram* hr1* sul-ac b4.de* sulph b4a.de* thiam rly4• thuj j5.de tritic-vg fd5.de [bell-p-sp dcm1 spect dfg1]
- **thoughts** with: nat-sil fd3.de• ruta fd4.de tritic-vg fd5.de vanil fd5.de

Waking – thoughts with: ...

  - **business**; of: hyos a1 [tax jsj7]
  - **careful**: *Ambr* sf1.de *Calc* sf1.de kali-s fd4.de vanil fd5.de
  - **rush** of; from: m-arct b7.de **Nux-v** b7.de
- **tight**; everything seems too: *Guaj* kr1
- **toothache**, by: am-m j5.de ars j5.de bell hr1* *Calc* hr1* *Carb-an* hr1* castm j5.de cham j5.de dulc fd4.de *Glon* hr1* lach j5.de mez a1 nat-c j5.de nat-m j5.de phos j5.de sabin b7.de* sep j5.de* spig b7.de*
- **tossing** about, when: ant-s-aur kr1
- **touch**, from slightest: galeoc-c-h gms1• ruta b7a.de*
- **twitching**; from: carc mg1.de*
- **uncovering**; with aversion to: clem b4a.de
- **urinate**; with desire to: allox tpw3 ant-c b7a.de aran kr1 bros-gau mrc1 card-m kr1 cystein-l rly4• dulc fd4.de fuma-ac rly4• ger-i rly4• ham fd3.de• *Hep* kr1 *Kali-bi* kr1 *Kali-c* kr1 kali-s fd4.de kreos kr1 melal-alt gya4 nat-m kr1 plac-s rly4• podo fd3.de• pot-e rly4• ruta fd4.de sacch-a fd2.de• sarr kr1 sil kr1 spong fd4.de suis-em rly4• suis-pan rly4• tritic-vg fd5.de vanil fd5.de ven-m rsj12• [spect dfg1]
- **vertigo**, from: ant-t hr1* chin hr1* *Dulc* hr1* euphr j5.de *Hyper* hr1* *Kali-c* hr1* kali-i hr1* lach j5.de lap-la sde8.de• lyc j5.de malar jl2 *Med* hr1* merc j5.de nicc j5.de **Nux-v** hr1* op j5.de *Phos* j5.de sil j5.de stram j5.de *Sulph* j5.de ther j5.de*
- **vivacity**; as if from: cycl b7.de* dros b7.de* ip b7.de* merc b4.de* ph-ac b4a.de *Ran-b* b7.de* ruta b7.de* samb b7.de* *Sep* b4a.de tarax b7.de* viol-t b7.de*
- **vomiting**; from: dig bg2 petr b4.de* sil b4.de*
- **warmth**, from: cocc j5.de kreos j5.de sep j5.de suis-em rly4•
  - **bed**; of: culx k2
- **weeping**; on: aids nl2• cic c1 positr nl2•
- **worms**, from: calc-f a1*
- **wrong**; sensation that something is wrong within her (See MIND - Delusions - wrong - something - waking)
- **yawning**; by (See Yawning - waking)

WALKING in bed; child is (See MIND - Walking - bed)

WINDOW open; with: ara-maca sej7•

YAWNING: abies-c k* abrot a1 *Acon* k* acon-c a1 *Aesc* k* agar k* all-c k* alum k* alum-sil k2* *Am-c* k* am-m k* ambr k* *Aml-ns* br1* ammc k* amyg a1* anac k* androc srj1• ang k* ant-c k* *Ant-t* k* *Apis* k* apom a1 *Aran* hr1* arg-met k* *Arg-n* k* *Arn* k* **Ars** k* ars-h hr1* ars-i k* arum-t k* arund a1* asaf k* asar k* aspar k* astac a1 atro k* aur k* aur-m k* bamb-a stb2.de• bar-c k* bart a1 bell k* bit-ar wht1• *Bol-la* a1 bomb-pr mlk9.de bond a1 borx k* bov k* b r a c h hr1* *Brom* k* *Bry* k* bufo cadm-met tpw6 cain caj a1 calad k* *Calc* k* *Calc-ar* calc-caust a1 *Calc-p* k* calc-sil k2* camph k* cann-s k* canth k* caps k* carb-ac k* carb-an k* carb-v k* carbn-dox knl3• carbn-s card-b a1 card-m hr1* *Carl* k* castm a1* **Caust** k* cedr a1* cere-b a1 cerv a1 *Cham* k* **Chel** k* chen-v hr1* chin k* chinin-ar chinin-s k* chlf k* cic b2.de* cimic a1* cimx k* **Cina** k* cinch a1 *Cit-v* k* *Clem* k* cob k* cob-n sp1 coc-c k* coca *Cocc* k* coff k* colch k* coloc k* con k* cor-r k* **Croc** k* crot-c a1 crot-h k* crot-t k* cryp a1 *Cupr* k* cupr-act a1 cycl k* cystein-l rly4• daph k* dig k* digin a1 dream-p sdj1• dros k* dulc k* elat k* eup-pur k* euph k* euphr k* eupi k* eys sp1 fago k* falco-pe nl2• ferr k* ferr-ma k* form k* galeoc-c-h gms1• gamb k* gast a1 gels k* gent-l k* germ-met stj2*• gins a1 glon k* gran k* **Graph** k* grat k* guaj k* *Haem* a1* haliae-lc srj5• hecla jl hell k* hep k* hipp a1* hura hydr k* hydr-ac k* hydrc k* hydrog srj2• hyos k* hyosin a1 hyper k* **Ign** k* ind *Indg* j5.de* iod k* ip k* jab k* jatr-c jug-c k* jug-r k* **Kali-ar** kali-bi k* *Kali-c* k* kali-cy a1 kali-i k* kali-n k* kali-p k* kiss a1 kola stb3• **Kreos** k* lach k* lachn k* lact k* lact-v c1* **Lath** br1* *Laur* k* led k* lepi a1 levo jl3 lil-s a1 *Lil-t* k* lim a1 lina a1 lipp a1 lob k* l o l sf1.de *Lyc* k* lycps-v lyss k* m-ambo b2.de* *M-arct* b2.de* m-aust b2.de* *Mag-c* k* mag-m k* mag-p ptk1 malar jl2 *Mang* k* med k* melal-alt gya4 *Menis* a1 meny k* meph k* merc k* *Merc-c* bg2* merc-sul hr1* merl k* mez k* mill k* m i m - h a1 morph k* mosch k* *Mur-ac* k* naja nat-ar nat-c k* nat-lac a1 *Nat-m* k* nat-s k* neon stj2*• nep srb2.fr nicc k* nit-ac k* nux-m k* **Nux-v** k* oci-sa sk4• *Ol-an* k* *Olib-sac* wmh1 *Olnd* k* **Op** k* ost a1 ox-ac k* *Par* k* peti a1 petr k* petr-ra shn4• ph-ac k* phel k* *Phos* k* phys k* phyt k* pieri-b mlk9.de p i m p a1 pin-con oss2• plat k* plb k* podo hr1* polyp-p a1 positr nl2• psor k* ptel a1* *Puls* k* puls-n a1 quas a1 ran-b k* raph k* rat k* rheum k* rhod k* **Rhus-t** k* rosm a1 rumx ruta k* *Sabad* k* sabin b2.de* *Sal-ac* hr1* sang k* sarr *Sars* k* sec k* sedi a1 sel k* senec k* seneg k* *Sep* k* sieg mg1.de *Sil* k* sphing a1 spig k* spira br1 spong k* *Squil* k* *Stann* k* *Staph* k* stram k* stront-c k* sul-ac k* sulph k* tab k* tarax k* tarent k* tart-ac a1 tax k* tell k* ter k* teucr k* thea thres-a sze7• thuj k* til k* tong a1 trom hr1* valer k* vanil fd5.de

Yawning: ...
Verat k* verb k* vinc k* *Viol-o* k* *Viol-t* hr1* vip a1 xan k* zinc k* zinc-val bg3* [*Spect* dfg1 zirc-met stj2]

- **daytime**: agar aspar j5.de* bit-ar wht1• brach k* **Castm** sne cob-n sp1 coca-c sk4• croc k* flor-p rsj3• kreos j5.de lyc k* mag-m j5.de *Nat-c* k* **Nux-v** k* oci-sa sk4• olib-sac wmh1 petr-ra shn4• ph-ac k* phys k* phyt k* *Sulph* k* zinc j5.de
- **morning**: agar k* alum h2 am-m k* ang k* ant-t k* apis a1 aspar k* bar-c k* brom k* bry k* carl k* cedr *Cocc* j5.de* croc k* crot-t st1 cycl k* ferr k* hyper k* ign k* kreos j5.de lach k* m-arct j5.de mag-c k* mag-m j5.de mang k* mur-ac k* nat-c k* nat-m k* nicc k* *Nux-v* k* petr-ra shn4• rat j5.de rhus-t k* sep h2 tab k* tarent k* verat k* viol-o k* zinc h2* zing k*
  - **7** h: cedr a1
  - **8** h: nicc a1
  - **9** h; until: mag-c a1
  - **noon**, till: hep a1
  - **air**, in open: croc a1
  - **bed**, in: m-arct j5.de mag-m j5.de sep k*
  - **incessantly**: *Cocc* hr1*
  - **rising**:
    - **after**: apis mag-c h2 *Nux-v* k*
    - **on**: acon k* alum k* ign j5.de m-arct j5.de mag-m j5.de plat k* rhus-t k* senec k*
  - **room** in: croc a1
  - **waking**, on: agar k* alum j5.de bar-c j5.de bit-ar wht1• cocc j5.de mag-m h2* nux-v j5.de verat j5.de
  - **walking** in open air: agar k*
- **forenoon**: agar k* aloe ant-t k* bart a1 *Calc-p* k* *Carb-an* k* caust k* cham k* coca crot-t k* graph k* hell k* hep k* hyos k* indg j5.de* kali-c h2 kali-n h2* lyc h2 mag-c k* mag-m k* mez k* nat-c h2* rhus-t k* sars h2* senec k* spig h1* vanil fd5.de zinc k*
  - **9** h: carl a1 lyc h2
  - **10** h: arg-n
  - **11** h: arum-t caust mit a1 rhus-t
- **noon**: bry k* falco-pe nl2• ign k* menis a1 merc j5.de psor k* sep j5.de vanil fd5.de verat k*
  - **and** afternoon: ars j5.de asar j5.de bell j5.de bov j5.de bry j5.de canth j5.de caust h2* *Ign* j5.de lact j5.de laur j5.de mag-c j5.de mag-m j5.de merc j5.de nat-c j5.de nicc j5.de nit-ac j5.de par j5.de phel j5.de phos j5.de plat j5.de plb j5.de rat j5.de sep j5.de sul-ac j5.de tab j5.de tong j5.de
  - **riding**, while: mill a1
  - **siesta**, after: bar-c j5.de ign a1 verat a1
  - **walking**, after: sep k*
- **afternoon**: *Arg-n* k* arum-t k* *Asar* k* bamb-a stb2.de• bell j5.de bov k* canth k* caust k* dulc fd4.de erig a1 falco-pe nl2• ign k* *Ip* hr1 jug-r k* kali-c h2 kali-chl k* kali-p fd1.de* laur j5.de mag-c h2* nat-ar nat-c h2* nicc j5.de nux-v k* par k* petr-ra shn4• plat k* positr nl2• ran-s k* sang a1 sep j5.de spirae a1 *Spong* k* stry k* symph fd3.de• tong j5.de trom c1 vanil fd5.de
  - **13** h: form
    - **13-14** h: petr-ra shn4•
  - **14** h: chel falco-pe nl2• grat melal-alt gya4
  - **15** h: com
    - **15-20** h: ped a1
  - **16** h: olib-sac wmh1 plan a1
    - **16-18** h: ph-ac
    - **walking** in open air | **amel**.: plan a1
  - **17** h: arg-n euphr
    - **17-18** h: fago a1
  - **amel**.: phel a1
  - **sitting**, while: nicc k*
  - **walking**, after: sep k*
- **evening**: abrom-a ks5 aloe am-c k* am-m k* *Arn* j5.de* bell k* bov k* *Calc* hr1* cann-s k* carl k* castm caust h2* *Cedr* a1* chel k* chinin-s coc-c k* cocc k* cupr k* cycl k* dulc fd4.de erig a1 euphr k* graph h2* hecla jl *Hep* hr1* hura ign j5.de ip j5.de* lach k* lyc k* mag-c h2* merc j5.de mez k* nat-c h2* nit-ac h2* nux-v k* ox-ac k* petr-ra shn4• ph-ac j5.de* phos k* psor k* *Puls* b7a.de rat k*

- **evening**: ...
rhus-t k* sal-fr sle1• sulph k* sumb k* symph fd3.de• thuj k* vanil fd5.de verat k* zinc h2
  - **19** h: mag-c
    - **after** | **amel**.: nat-m a1
  - **20** h: aloe
  - **21** h: *Cedr* kr1
    - **21**.30 h: lyc a1
    - **21-22** h: ph-ac
  - **agg**.: mill a1 ph-ac a1
  - **bed**, in: cocc j5.de nat-m k*
  - **reading**, after: lyc k*
  - **twilight**, in the: bell h1*
- **night**: bell h1 *Caust* k* nit-ac h2
  - **midnight** | **after**: *Thuj* kr1
  - **eating**; after: ruta a1
- **abdominal** symptoms, with: bov bg1* *Castm* kr1* haem bg1* hep j5.de m-arct j5.de
- **abortion**, in threatening: *Cham* hr1*
- **accompanied** by:
  - **complaints**; other: acon b2.de agar b2.de am-c b2.de am-m b2.de anac b2.de ang b2.de ant-t b2.de arg-met b2.de *Arn* b2.de ars b2.de aur b2.de bar-c b2.de bell b2.de borx b2.de bry b2.de calad b2.de calc b2.de canth b2.de caps b2.de carb-an b2.de *Caust* b2.de *Chel* b2.de chin b2.de **Cina** b2.de cocc b2.de croc b2.de cycl b2.de dig b2.de ferr b2.de *Graph* b2.de hep b2.de **Ign** b2.de ip b2.de kali-c b2.de **Kreos** b2.de laur b2.de lyc b2.de *M-arct* b2.de m-aust b2.de mag-c b2.de mag-m b2.de mang b2.de *Meny* b2.de mez b2.de *Mur-ac* b2.de nat-c b2.de nat-m b2.de **Nux-v** b2.de *Olnd* b2.de op b2.de par b2.de petr b2.de ph-ac b2.de *Phos* b2.de plat b2.de puls b2.de **Rhus-t** b2.de ruta b2.de *Sabad* b2.de **Sars** b2.de sep b2.de sil b2.de stann b2.de *Staph* b2.de sul-ac b2.de sulph b2.de teucr b2.de thuj b2.de verat b2.de viol-o b2.de zinc b2.de
  - **coryza** (See NOSE - Coryza - yawning)
  - **neurological** complaints (See GENERALS - Neurological - accompanied - yawning)
  - ○ **Chest**; sensation of a band about (See CHEST - Constriction - band - accompanied - yawning)
- **air**, in open: cystein-l rly4• eug j5.de* *Euph* b4a.de euphr h2* sacch-a fd2.de• stann h2*
  - **amel**.: clem a1 ol-an j5.de*
  - **walking**; after (See walking - after - air)
- **alternating** with:
  - **cough**: *Ant-t* hr1*
  - **eructations**: berb hr1*
- **anemia**, in: *Graph* kr1
- **anxiety**, during: *Plb* hr1*
- **appetite**, with wanting: kreos j5.de*
- **breakfast** | **agg**.: carl a1
- **bulimia**, with: *Lyc* hr1*
- **children**, in: *Cham* hr1* ign j5.de
- **chill**:
  - **before**: aesc ant-t *Aran* hr1* arn k* ars chin elat *Eup-per* k* ign k* ip k* nat-m nicc k* nux-v rhus-t
    - **mouth** remains open for a long time: ant-t
  - **during**: acon b7.de* agar h2* am-c b4a.de* ant-t b7.de* apis b7a.de* arn bg2 ars k* ars-h k* bol-la k* **Brom** b4a.de* bry k* calad k* calc b4a.de caps k* carb-an ptk1 caust k* chin b7.de* cimx cina k* cob k* croc k* cycl bg2 dig b4.de* **Elat** **Eup-per** k* eupi c1 gamb k* graph h2* ign bg2 ip bg2 kali-c bg2 *Kreos* j5.de* laur k* lyc k* m-arct b7.de m-aust b7.de* mag-m k* *Meny* k* merc mez k* *Mur-ac* k* murx **Nat-m** k* nat-s k* **Nux-v** b7.de* *Olnd* k* par k* phos k* plat b4.de* puls bg2 *Rhus-t* b7.de* ruta k* sabad bg2 *Sars* bg2 *Sep* k* sil k* staph bg2 teucr b7.de* thuj k* zinc h2
- **chilliness**, with: acon b7.de* am-c b4.de* ant-t b7.de* ars b4.de* bar-act a1 bol-la kr1 *Bry* b7.de* *Calc* b4.de* caps b7.de* *Caust* b4a.de chin b7.de* chinin-s j5.de *Cina* kr1 cob kr1 croc b7.de* daph kr1 dig b4a.de* *Gels* kr1 *Ip* kr1 *Kreos* b7a.de* lyc b4.de* m-arct b7.de m-aust b7.de mag-m h2 merc-sul kr1 *Mur-ac* b4a.de

Sleep

- **chiliness**: ...
Nat-m b4a.de* Nat-s kr1 olnd par k* phos sf1.de puls kr1 rhus-t b7.de* ruta b7.de* sep k* sil b4.de* teucr b7.de*
  • **menses**, before: **Puls** hr1*
- **church**, in: pic-ac a1
- **coldness**, with: caust h2 nat-c k*
- **coma**; during: (↗*Comatose - yawning)* aml-ns ptk1 kali-c ptk1
- **complaints**, during other: agar c1 castm c1 cina c1* kreos c1 sars c1
- **conference**, during a: caust st1
- **constant**: aesc a1 am-m j5.de asar j5.de *Bry* j5.de calc j5.de calc-p c1 caps h1* carb-ac a1 card-b a1 carl a1 castm ptk1 chin j5.de chinin-s a1 *Cocc* h1* crot-c a1 eug j5.de hep j5.de lath br1* mag-c j5.de malar jl2 nat-c j5.de nux-v j5.de op j5.de par j5.de phos j5.de* plat j5.de sars j5.de spig j5.de staph j5.de sulph j5.de trom a1 zinc j5.de
  • **lying** down, after: *Cocc* h1*
- **constriction** of throat, from: nat-m a1
- **conversation**, listening to a: *Caust* st1 *Lyss* hr1*
- **convulsions**:
  • **before**: agar h2* *Tarent* hr1*
  • **in**: agar h2 *Aml-ns* kr1 cic sne *Graph* hr1* hep c1 *Ign* hr1* kali-bi kl *Op* hr1*
- **coughing**:
  • **after**: all-c bg2* *Anac* b4a.de* ant-c k* **Ant-t** k* arn hr1* *Ip* k* **Kreos** k* *Nux-v* kl op k* sang hr1*
  • **causes** cough (See COUGH - Yawning)
  • **children**; especially in: **Ant-t** kr1
  • **when** (See COUGH - Accompanied - yawning; COUGH - Yawning)
- **cramps** in stomach, with: calc h2
- **delirium**, before: agar br1*
- **diarrhea**:
  • **after**: nux-v
  • **during**: *Caps* kr1 *Cupr* kr1
- **dinner**:
  • **after**: ant-t sf1.de ars k* bry j5.de canth k* cob k* colch k* dig k* *Ign* j5.de* kali-bi k* laur j5.de *Lyc* k* mag-c k* mag-m k* nat-c k* nat-m k* nit-ac j5.de phel k* phos j5.de* plat j5.de* plb k* rat j5.de* *Squil* sf1.de sul-ac k* tab k* zinc k*
  • **before**: alum k* *Bry* k* *Calc-p* hr1* lyc k* merc k*
  • **during**: *Calc-p* hr1* ign j5.de lact j5.de zinc k*
- **drinking**:
  • **agg.**: carl a1
  • **cold** water, when drinking: thuj
- **dyspnea**:
  • **after**: sulph a1
  • **with**: bapt kr1 *Brom* kr1* sulph
- **eating**, after: ambr c1 *Aran* kr1 ars k* aur-m caps b7a.de* chin bg2 chinin-s sf1.de con ign k* ip k* *Kali-c* h2* *Nat-c* bg2* nat-s ptk1 nit-ac plat squil bg2* *Sulph* bg2*
  • **amel.**: chen-v kr1 hydrog srj2•
- **emptiness** of stomach, from: ammc a1
- **eructations**:
  • **amel.**: thuj bg1
  • **with** yawning: berb bg2* lol sf1.de nat-m bg2 phos bg2 tell ptk1
- **exertion**:
  • **as** from: petr-ra shn4•
  • **during**: petr-ra shn4•
- **frequent**: *Acon* k* agar h2* alum h2* am-c h2 am-m h2 aml-ns ptk1 ang h1* ant-c h2* ant-t k* *Arn* j5.de *Ars* h2* asar h1 bar-act a1 bar-c k* *Bell* h1* bit-ar wht1• blatta-a a1 bov j5.de *Brom* k* bry k* calc h2* camph h1* cann-s k* canth j5.de *Caps* k* *Carb-v* h2* caust k* *Cham* h1* **Chel** k* chin st1 chinin-ar k2 chinin-s j5.de cic h1* cimx k* cina j5.de *Cit-v* k* clem a1 cob a1 *Cocc* k* coff k* colch j5.de* con j5.de cor-r k* croc k* crot-h j5.de *Crot-t* j5.de *Cupr* k* cycl a1 dig j5.de dros j5.de dulc h1* elat k* euph k* euphr j5.de *Gran* j5.de **Graph** k* grat k* *Guaj* j5.de haem j5.de *Hep* h2* hera a1 *Hydr-ac* j5.de* *Ign* k* ip k* kali-c h2* kali-i k* kali-sil k2* kreos k* lach j5.de *Lact* j5.de laur k* *Lyc* k* lyss *M-arct* j5.de m-aust j5.de mag-c k* mag-m k* *Mang* h2* marb-w es1• melal-alt gya4 meny h1 meph k* merc k* *Merc-c* k* merc-sul a1 mosch k* myric k* nat-ar nat-c k* nat-m k* nat-s k*

- **frequent**: ...
nit-ac h2 nux-v j5.de ol-an k* *Olib-sac* wmh1 *Olnd* k* onis j5.de* ozone sde2• par j5.de ph-ac k* phel k* *Phos* j5.de phyt c1 plat j5.de *Plb* j5.de plut-n srj7• *Puls* j5.de rheum j5.de rhod j5.de rhus-t k* ruta j5.de sabad j5.de sars k* *Sep* j5.de *Sil* h2* solin a1 spig k* spong fd4.de squil k* stann k* staph k* stront-c j5.de sul-ac j5.de **Sulph** k* tab tarax j5.de tart-ac j5.de tax j5.de* vanil fd5.de *Verat* j5.de verb j5.de vinc j5.de vip fkr4.de xan c1 zinc k* zinc-act a1
  • **morning**: *Cocc* k* lycps-v ozone sde2• rhus-t a1 verat h1
  • **forenoon**: caust a1 indg k* lyc k* nat-c k* nat-m k* ph-ac k* sars k*
  • **afternoon**: caust a1 erig c1 hera a1 mag-c k* olib-sac wmh1 spong fd4.de
    ⁝ **menses**, during: nat-m k*
  • **evening**: bell h1 erig c1 hep k* lyc k* mag-c k* nat-c k* ph-ac k*
    ⁝ **18** h, after: mag-c a1
    ⁝ **reading**, after: lyc k*
    ⁝ **restlessness**, with: aran kr1
    ⁝ **riding** in a carriage: nat-m k*
    ⁝ **sleepiness** and restlessness, with: *Con* kr1 *Kali-i* kr1
  • **dinner**, after: *Lyc* a1
  • **menses**, during: mag-m a1
  • **sleep**, after: ign a1
  • **sleeping** off the intoxication, after: alco a1
  • **supper**, after: *Lyc* a1
  • **wine** | **amel.**: nat-m a1
- **headache**:
  • **before**: agar h2* nux-v sne
  • **with**: *All-c* hr1* am-c h2* bar-c bg chinin-ar kr1 cycl b7.de* form bg1* *Glon* a1* ign h1 jug-r vml3• kreos b7a.de mag-c bg mur-ac bg nux-m bg nux-v b7.de* *Phos* hr1* rhus-t a1 staph ptk1 zinc bg
- **heat**:
  • **before**: ars b4a.de* bry b7a.de caps b7a.de *Elat* hr1* ign b7a.de *Ip* hr1* lyc b4a.de *Nux-v* hr1* puls b7a.de *Rhus-t* b7a.de* sil b4a.de sulph b4a.de
  • **during**: aesc *Apis* kr1 arn bg2 *Ars* bg2* bry bg2 calc calc-p k* carl a1 *Caust* b4.de* chinin-s k* cina k* croc bg2 *Elat* hr1* eup-per hr1* *Ign* bg2 kali-c k* kreos bg2 *Nat-m* b4a.de **Nit-ac** bg2 nux-v b7.de* *Op* bg2 *Phos* b4.de* plat bg2 *Rhus-t* k* ruta sabad k* sep bg2 thuj k*
- **hiccough**, with: aml-ns ptk1 carl a1 caust b4.de* cocc ptk1 crot-t a1 mag-c b4.de* nat-m bg2
- **honor**, from wounded: *Nux-v* hr1*
- **hysteria**, in: *Kali-p* hr1* tarent hr1*
- **indoors**: ruta a1*
- **ineffectual**: acon k* ambr h1 aml-ns vh1 ant-t k* cham k* cocc a1 croc k* ign k* lach j5.de* **Lyc** k ●* manc k* phos k* ruta k* spira a1 stann k*
  • **efforts** to yawn: lach st **Lyc** k ●
    ⁝ **children**; in: *Lyc* kr1
  • **oppression** of chest, from: *Phos* a1
- **injuries**, from: *Lach* hr1*
- **interrupted**: acon b7.de* ars h2 cham j5.de cocc h1* ign b7.de* lyc k* ruta b7.de*
- **intoxication**, as from: bell a1
- **irresistible**: cit-v br1
- **lachrymation**, with: ammc kr1 ant-t k* bell b4.de calc-p k* ferr b7.de* hell bg2 ign k* *Kali-c* kr1 kreos b7a.de mag-p ptk1 meph k* *Nux-v* k* ph-ac b4.de* rhus-t k* *Sabad* k* sars k* staph k* viol-o k*
  • **overflowing** with tears; eyes are: bar-c b4.de* ign b7.de* kreos b7a.de
- **laughter**, followed by involuntary: agar k*
- **leaning** towards left | **amel.**: phel a1
- **listening** to conversation, when: *Caust* k* *Lyss* kr1*
- **loud**: ferr-ma j5.de
  • **siesta**, after: aloe a1
- **lying** down, after: *Cocc* k* plan k*
- **menorrhagia**, in: *Apis* kr1
- **menses**:
  • **after**: carb-an bg2*
  • **before**: am-c bro1 carl k* phel k* **Puls** k*
  • **during**: *Am-c* k* bell k* *Bry* b7a.de *Carb-an* k* *Dig* hr1* kali-i j5.de mag-m k* nat-m *Phos* b4.de puls bro1

- **metrorrhagia**, in: *Apis* kr1
- **nausea**, with: euphr a1 gran a1 *Kali-bi* bg2* *Kali-c* hr1* lach a1 lol sf1.de nat-m bg2
- **neuralgia**, before the attack of: *Chel* hr1*
- **oppression** of chest, with: *Brom* b4a.de croc b7.de* ign b7.de* stann k*
- **pain**:
  - **during** the: nux-v bg2 phos bg2* puls bg2 *Sulph* b4a.de
    - **Abdomen**; in: caust bg2 puls b7.de*
    - **Elbow**; in: mang a1
  - **paroxysms** of pain:
    - **before**: agar h2*
    - **with**: agar h2 aran ptk1 ph-ac h2 phos ptk1
  - ○ **Chest**; in: bov bg2 canth b7.de* hep b4a.de
  - **Stomach**; in: chel b7.de* kali-bi bg2
- **paralysis**; sensation of | **Palate**: meny b7.de*
- **paroxysmal**: agar h2* ang j5.de ferr j5.de til a1
- **parturition**, after: *Plat* hr1*
- **periodical**: arum-t a1
- **perspiration**, during: am bg2 *Ars* bg2 bry bg2 calad a1* caust bg2 cina bg2 croc bg2 ign bg2 *Kali-c* bg2 kreos bg2 *Nit-ac* bg2 **Nux-v** bg2 op bg2 phos bg2 plat bg2 *Rhus-t* bg2 *Sabad* bg2 **Sep** bg2
- **pressing**; with | **Stomach**; in: caust b4a.de sul-ac b4.de*
- **reading**, while: euphr k* nat-c k* thuj
  - **aloud**: hyos k* thuj k*
- **respiration**:
  - **after**: sulph a1
  - **difficult**; with: bapt kr1 *Brom* bg2* sulph
- **restlessness**, with: *Lach* hr1* plb hr1*
- **retching**; after: tell ptk1
- **rheumatism**, in: *Bry* hr1*
- **sadness**, in: merc-sul hr1*
- **salivation**; with: am-c b4.de* ant-t b7.de* *Kali-c* b4a.de
- **shuddering**, during: am b7.de* calad k* *Cina* k* cycl b7.de* hydr-ac j5.de* ip b7.de* kali-c h2 laur k* mag-m j5.de meny b7.de* mez h2 nux-v b7.de* *Olnd* k* par b7a.de phos b4.de* plat b4.de sars b4.de* sep a1
- **sighing**; with: ign bg2 [tax jsj7 zirc-met stj2]
- **sitting**, while: atro hr1* borx j5.de carl k* clem k* coca nat-c k* nicc j5.de tarax k*
- **sleep**, during: *All-c* hr1* all-s ptk1 castm k*
- **sleepiness**:
  - **during**: *All-c* hr1* alum b4.de* am-c j5.de ars j5.de* aspar j5.de bar-c b4.de* bell j5.de bov j5.de calc b4.de* carb-an j5.de carb-v b4.de* cham b7.de* chel b7.de* *Chin* b7.de* cic jl3 cina a1 clem b4.de* coff j5.de con b4.de* croc b7.de* *Cupr* b7.de* dulc b4.de* euphr b7.de* *Graph* j5.de* grat j5.de haem bg2* hell b7.de* indg j5.de kali-bi bg2 *Kali-c* j5.de *Kali-n* j5.de* *Kreos* b7a.de* lact j5.de *Laur* b7.de* lyc j5.de *M-arct* j5.de *M-aust* j5.de *Mag-c* j5.de *Mag-m* hr1* mag-s a1 mang a1 melal-alt gya4 merc b4.de* mez b4.de* mill a1 mosch b7.de* mur-ac j5.de *Nat-c* b4.de* nat-m b4.de* nicc j5.de *Nux-v* j5.de* *Ol-an* j5.de* *Par* b7.de* ph-ac b4.de* phel j5.de phos b4.de* plb b7.de* plut-n srj7• rat j5.de *Rhus-t* bg2* ruta j5.de senec sf1.de spig b7.de* *Spong* b7.de* *Squil* sf1.de stann b4.de* *Sulph* j5.de* verb b7.de* zinc b4.de* [cadm-met stj2 cadm-s stj2 tax jsj7]
  - **without**: acon k* alum k* am-m k* ang b2.de* ant-t k* arn k* bry k* canth k* caust k* cham k* chin k* *Croc* bg2* cupr k* cycl k* grat j5.de* hep k* *Ign* k* indg j5.de kali-i k* lach k* lact j5.de laur k* lyss m-arct b2.de* *M-aust* b2.de mag-c k* mang h2* mosch k* nat-m k* ol-an j5.de* phel j5.de* phos k* **Plat** k* rat a1 rhod j5.de **Rhus-t** k* *Sep* k* spig k* squil k* staph k* sulph k* tax j5.de* viol-o k* zinc j5.de
- **soreness**, with: bar-c j5.de
- **spasmodic**: acon k* agar k* am-c k* ang k* ant-t k* arn k* ars hr1* bov hr1* bry k* calc carl a1 chinin-ar st *Cina* k* cocc k* coloc k* *Cor-r* croc k* cupr k* euphr k* gran j5.de* *Hep* k* hipp a1 *Ign* k* *Kali-c* b4a.de lach b7.de* laur k* *M-arct* b2.de* m-aust b2.de* *Mag-p* k* med k* mosch k* *Nat-m* k* nux-v pana a1 **Plat** k* **Rhus-t** k* sep k* squil k* *Staph* k* sulph k* tarent k* til a1
  - **morning**: ign k*
  - **evening**: am-c k* ign k* sulph k*
  - **amenorrhea**, in: *Cina* kr1
  - **heat**, during: ars sf1.de nux-v sf1.de rhus-t sf1.de
  - **sleep**, after deep: nat-m a1

Yawning – spasmodic: ...

  - **sleeplessness**, during: croc sf1.de plat sf1.de
  - **wine** | **amel.**: nat-m a1
- **spasms**, before: agar ptk1 merc bg1* tarent ptk1
- **stool**:
  - **after**: anac k* nux-v bg2 op k*
  - **before**: form k* lyc bg2 *Sulph* bg2 *Verat* bg2
- **stretching**, with: acon b2.de* aesc hr1* *Agar* b2.de* all-c bro1 *Alum* b2.de* *Am-c* b2.de* ambr b2.de* aml-ns bro1* ang b2.de* ant-t b2.de* am b2.de* **Ars** b2.de* asar bro1 bar-c b2.de* *Bell* b2.de* borx b2.de* bov b2.de* *Bry* b2.de* *Calc* b2.de* calc-p ptk1 camph h1 cann-s b2.de* canth b2.de* caps b2.de* *Carb-v* b2.de* carl a1* castm bro1 *Caust* b2.de* **Cham** b2.de* *Chel* bro1 *Chin* b2.de* chinin-s j5.de *Cina* bro1 coca bro1 cocc b2.de* crot-h bro1 cupr-act bro1 cur hr1* daph hr1 dig h2* dros b2.de* elat bro1* euphr bro1 ferr b2.de* *Form* bg2* *Gels* bro1 gran j5.de *Graph* b2.de* *Guaj* b2.de* hell b2.de* hep b2.de* hydr-ac bro1 *Ign* b2.de* *Ip* b2.de* kali-c bro1 kreos b2.de* *Lach* j5.de* lact j5.de laur b2.de* led b2.de* lyc bro1 mag-c b2.de* malar jl2 mang j5.de* meph j5.de merc b2.de* merc-c bg2 mez b2.de* morph bro1 mur-ac b2.de* nat-m h2* nit-ac b2.de* **Nux-v** b2.de* *Olnd* b2.de* onis j5.de petr b2.de* ph-ac b2.de* phos b2.de* plat b2.de* plb b2.de* plut-n srj7• *Puls* b2.de* ran-b b2.de* rhod j5.de **Rhus-t** b2.de* ruta b2.de* *Sabad* b2.de* sec b2.de* sel b7a.de senec sf1.de seneg b2.de* *Sep* b2.de* sil b2.de* *Spong* b2.de* *Squil* b2.de* stann b2.de* *Staph* b2.de* *Sulph* b2.de* tab j5.de tart-ac j5.de tong j5.de valer b2.de* verat b2.de* verb b2.de* viol-o hr1* zinc b2.de*
  - **forenoon**: ant-t j5.de
  - **wretched** feeling; with: form ptk1
- **stupefaction**, with: jatr-c kr1 meph j5.de
- **suffocating**, as from: *Cit-v* a1
- **summer** complaints, in: *Ars* hr1*
- **supper**:
  - **after**: coca croc a1 *Lyc* k* ruta
  - **before**: merc k*
- **taste**; with putrid: kreos b7a.de
- **thirst**, with: bry b7.de*
- **trembling**, with: *Cina* b7.de* olnd b7.de*
  - **internal**: nux-v j5.de
- **uneasiness**, with: am-c j5.de ang j5.de nicc j5.de
- **vertigo**, with: agar k* petr k*
- **violent**, vehement: agar am-c j5.de aml-ns ptk1 ant-t j5.de* ars h2 caust cham j5.de cina *Cocc* j5.de coff *Cor-r* croc j5.de dulc a1 euphr j5.de ferr-ma j5.de gran j5.de hep k* hyos *Ign* k* indg j5.de kola stb3• lach j5.de *M-arct* j5.de mag-c mag-p ptk1 mez j5.de mosch nat-m nit-ac j5.de nux-v j5.de *Plat* k* rat j5.de *Rhus-t* k* sil ptk1 staph bg3* sulph j5.de til verat j5.de
  - **siesta**, after: aloe a1
  - **wine** | **amel.**: nat-m a1
- **vomiting**, between acts of: apom a1
- **wakefulness**; with: cham j5.de kali-bi bg2
- **waking**, on: alum j5.de bar-c j5.de cocc j5.de dig a1 mag-m j5.de* nux-v j5.de verat j5.de
- **walking** | **after** | **air**; in open: alum h2* euph ptk1 nat-m k* sep j5.de
  - **while**: bart a1 camph k* chlf k*
    - **air**; in open: eug k* euphr k* kali-c h2* lycps-v sacch-a fd2.de• stann k*
      - **amel.**: berb kr1 ox-ac plan
- **warm**:
  - **bed**, in: chinin-s
  - **room**, in: mez
- **weakness**, with: alum h2 camph h1
- **weariness**, with: *Am-c* hr1* ars j5.de bar-c j5.de bit-ar wht1• *Calc* j5.de* choc srj3• crot-t j5.de dulc j5.de eug j5.de* graph j5.de grat j5.de kali-n j5.de kreos b7a.de* laur j5.de mag-c j5.de mag-m j5.de melal-alt gya4 nit-ac j5.de nux-v j5.de* olib-sac wmh1 *Olnd* sf1.de *Plan* hr1* rat j5.de *Rhus-t* hr1* ruta fd4.de sulph j5.de vanil fd5.de zinc j5.de
- **wine** | **amel.**: nat-m
- **work**:
  - **aversion** to work; with: ang j5.de mag-m j5.de tong j5.de
  - **not** at work, when: mosch a1

Sleep

DREAMS in general: am-m ptk1 arn ptk1 ars ptk1 bry ptk1 calc ptk1 *Chin* ptk1 *Graph* ptk1 lach ptk1 lyc ptk1 *Mag-c* ptk1 *Nat-m* ptk1 **Nux-v** ptk1 **Phos** ptk1 **Puls** ptk1 *Rhus-t* ptk1 *Sil* ptk1 *Sulph* ptk1 thuj ptk1

ABATTOIRS: sal-fr sle1•

ABDOMEN: (↗*Body; parts)*
- **constricted**; as if the abdomen was: nat-m a1
- **cut** in; a big: ozone sde2•
  - **blood** and pus in; with: ozone sde2•
  - **tumor**; under which grows a: ozone sde2•
- **pain** in: (↗*Disease)* apis a1 choc srj3•
- **someone** is lying across his abdomen and chest | **respiration**; impeding: (↗*Chest - figure - respiration; RESPIRATION - Impeded - dreams)* kali-bi a1
- **ulcers**; covered with: (↗*Disease)* choc srj3• junc-e a1
- **warts**; covered with (See Warts - abdomen)

ABORIGINAL people: | **Maori**: plut-n srj7•

ABORTION: ign a musca-d szs1 petr-ra shn4•

ABSURD: (↗*Strange; MIND - Foolish)* apis chin k* cina k* colch jl coloc ferr-ma *Glon* mag-m h2 mygal pip-m plan a1 psil ft rumx *Sulph* thuj tritic-vg fd5.de
- **midnight**, after: *Chin* a1

ABUSED; being: (↗*Children - abused; Insults; Quarrels)* falco-pe nl2• maias-l hrn2•
- **defend** himself | **weak** to; too: ambr a1

ABUSED SEXUALLY; being: (↗*Children - abused; Insults; Quarrels)* bung-fa mtf plut-n srj7• [heroin sdj2]

ABUSING:
- **betrayed** him; those who: rhus-g tmo3•
- **pinched** her breast; the lady who: bung-fa mtf

ABYSS: (↗*Falling - abyss; Falling - height)* *All-c* kr1 dulc fd4.de kali-p fd1.de• *Lac-ac* kr1 ruta fd4.de
- **descending** perpendicularly into: chin h1
- **steep**: anac h2* nat-sil fd3.de• podo fd3.de• ruta fd4.de symph fd3.de•

ACCIDENTS: (↗*Disaster; Explosion; Misfortune)* allox tpw3* am-m androc srj1• ant-c k* arg-met a arn k* **Ars** k* bamb-a stb2.de• bell k* bros-gau mrc1 calc bro1 cham chin chlam-tr bcx2• cinnb coca-c sk4• con dendr-pol sk4• *Dig* bro1 dulc fd4.de falco-pe nl2• germ-met stj2*• **Graph** k* helodr-cal knl2• ina-i mlk9.de ind iod k* iodof jab kali-c kali-s k2 kola stb3• kreos lac-del hrn2• lac-h sze9• lac-lup hrn2• lyc k* mag-m h2 *Maias-l* hrn2• mand mg1.de mez h2 nat-s nit-ac bro1 *Nux-v* oci-sa sk4• petr-ra shn4• phasco-ci rbp2 plac-s rly4• polys sk4• puls rumx sars sil bro1 spong fd4.de sul-ac sulph thuj tritic-vg fd5.de verat bro1 viol-o mfm [ant-met stj2 aur stj2 aur-m stj2 aur-s stj2 bar-i stj2 heroin sdj2 mang-i stj2 mang-m stj2 mang-met stj2 mang-p stj2 mang-s stj2 merc-i-f stj2 nicc-met stj2 nicc-s stj2 sel stj2 stann stj2 tax jsj7 zinc stj2 zinc-i stj2 zinc-m stj2 zinc-n stj2 zinc-p stj2]
- **airplane**; crash of an (See Airplanes - crash)
- **annoying**: ind a1*
- **bloody**: brucel sa3•
- **boat** foundering (See Boat - foundering)
- **car**; with a: helodr-cal knl2• lac-e hrn2• lac-lup hrn2• *Maias-l* hrn2• tritic-vg fd5.de viol-o mfm [heroin sdj2]
  - **fear** of: helodr-cal knl2• plut-n srj7•
  - **hit-and-run**: lac-e hrn2•
  - **run** over by car; nearly: bung-fa mtf plut-n srj7•
- **drowning** (See Drowning)
- **explosion** (See Explosion)
- **fatal** accident: (↗*MIND - Fatalistic)* cham hr1 **Graph** gt* kali-m bg *Nux-v* hr1 puls gt sars gt* spong fd4.de sul-ac gt
- **machine**; while operating: coca-c sk4•
- **mutilated** body in mangled car: maias-l hrn2•
- **struck** by lightning, being (See Lightning - struck)
- **trains** | **collision** of three trains: oci-sa sk4•
- **unaffected** by; being: dendr-pol sk4•

ACCOMPANIED BY: | **Head**; pain in: menis br1

ACCUSATIONS: (↗*Defamation; Theft - accused)* clem j5.de lac-del hrn2• lac-leo hrn2• lach j5.de nat-m j5.de petr-ra shn4• thuj j5.de

Accusations: ...
- **chemicals**; having: lac-del hrn2•
- **crime**, wrongful of: (↗*Defamation; Murder; Wrong)* choc srj3• chr-ac a1 clem dendr-pol sk4• falco-pe nl2• hydrog srj2• lac-h sk4• lac-leo hrn2• petr-ra shn4• plut-n srj7• polys sk4• sil h2*
- **denying**: lac-del hrn2•

ACHIEVEMENT, of: adam srj5•

ACQUAINTANCES: choc srj3• dulc fd4.de ham fd3.de• ruta fd4.de spong fd4.de tritic-vg fd5.de vanil fd5.de [sel stj2]
- **distant**: fl-ac plat a1 plb sel
- **walking** on water: ped a1

ACROBATS swinging from trapezes: hydrog srj2*• plut-n srj7• tritic-vg fd5.de

ACTIVE: bell gt falco-pe nl2•

ACTIVITY: arizon-l nl2•
- **completed**, never: arizon-l nl2•

ACTORS; about: bung-fa mtf
- **green**, yellow and black; turning: sol-t-ae a1

ADOLESCENTS: lac-leo hrn2• *Limen-b-c* hrn2• nept-m lsd2.fr
- **disturbed** by adults at critical time: limen-b-c hrn2•
- **teaching** French and piano to: lac-leo hrn2•
- **time** of: lac-e hrn2•
- **wish** to be an: limen-b-c hrn2•

ADOPTION: lac-d sk4•
- **dogs**; injured: lac-d sk4•

ADVENTUROUS: agath-a nl2• bar-c j5.de coli rly4• lac-e hrn2• lac-h sk4• ozone sde2• petr-ra shn4• senec a1 sulph j5.de
- **day**; adventures of the: bry gt cic gt rhus-t gt

ADVICE: | **not** heeding: lac-cp sk4•

AFFECTING the mind: (↗*Exciting)* bry chin dulc fd4.de *Ign Lach* nat-m *Nux-v* olnd ph-ac phos ruta fd4.de sabad sabin spong fd4.de sulph thuj tritic-vg fd5.de viol-t

AFFECTIONATE: androc srj1• coc-c a1 polys sk4•

AGGRESSIVE: (↗*Fights)* bit-ar wht1• rad-br sze8• thiam rly4•

AGREEABLE (See Pleasant)

AIDS: (↗*Disease)* aids nl2• bamb-a stb2.de• lac-h htj1•
- **child** having AIDS; her: irid-met srj5•

AIR: (↗*Battles; Fights; War)*
- **sleeping** in (See Sleeping - air)

AIR ATTACKS: (↗*Battles; Fights; War)* dulc fd4.de germ-met srj5• visc jl*

AIRPLANES: lac-del hrn2• lac-leo hrn2• lac-lup hrn2• nept-m lsd2.fr pot-e rly4• vanil fd5.de
- **crash** of an airplane: (↗*Death - dying - teammates)* graph dgt mand mg1.de sulph dgt
- **choosing** comfortable seats: lac-del hrn2•
- **on** an airplane; being: (↗*Journeys - airplane)* nat-ox rly4• nept-m lsd2.fr pot-e rly4• vanil fd5.de
- **parachuting** from: lac-leo hrn2•

AIRPORTS: arizon-l nl2• falco-pe nl2• nept-m lsd2.fr

AL CAPONE: ara-maca sej7•

ALARMS: hipp a1 mim-p rsj8• [heroin sdj2]

ALIEN from outer space:
- **killing** him; trying to: lac-e hrn2•
- **psychic**: lac-e hrn2•

ALONE; being (See Forsaken)

ALTERNATING: | **Head**, pain in (See HEAD - Pain - alternating - dreams)

Dreams

AMOROUS: *(↗Coition; Lascivious; Sexual; MIND - Amorous)* acon k* adam srj5• aesc aether a1 agath-a nl2• agn b2.de* aids nl2• aln vva1• *Alum* k* alum-sil k2 am-c **Am-m** k* ambr anag kr1 *Androc* srj1• ang **Ant-c** k* aphis j5.de* aq-mar rbp6 *Arg-n* k* arist-m a1 arn k* ars k* ars-i ars-s-f kr1* astac aster jl *Aur* k* aur-ar k2 aur-i k2 aur-s k2 bamb-a stb2.de• bar-c bar-i k2 *Bar-m* bell bg2 *Bism* k* bit-ar wht1• bomb-chr mlk9.de borx k* bov b2.de* bros-gau mrc1 cact k* cain caj a1 *Calc* k* calc-ar calc-i k2 calc-p calc-sil k2 *Camph* k* *Cann-i* cann-s cann-xyz bg2 **Canth** k* *Carb-ac* carb-an k* carb-v carbn-s carl carneg-g rwt1• castm caust k* *Cench* k2* cent a1 chel k* *Chin* b2.de* chinin-s a1 chir-fl gya2 chlam-tr bcx2• *Cic* cinnb clem k* *Cob* cob-n mg1.de* coc-c coca coca-c sk4• cocc b2.de* coloc k* **Con** k* cop *Crot-c* sk4• *Cycl* des-ac jl *Dig Dios* k* dioxi rbp6 dream-p sdj1• dros bg2 dulc fd4.de ery-a euph k* falco-pe nl2• form k* fum rly1• gal-ac a1 gast a1 *Gels* ger-i rly4• germ-met srj5• gins a1 goss st **Graph** k* haliae-lc srj5• ham k* helodr-cal knl2• hipp a1 hura hydr hydrog srj2• **Hyos** k* hyper **Ign** k* ind inul iod irid-met srj5• *Iris* kali-ar *Kali-br Kali-c* k* kali-chl kali-fcy a1 kali-m kr1* kali-n kali-p kali-s fd4.de *Kalm* ketogl-ac rly4• kola stb3• kreos k* lac-ac *Lac-cp* sk4• lac-del hrn2• lac-e hrn2• lac-h sze9• lac-leo hrn2*• lac-loxod-a hrn2• **Lach** k* lact a1 *Led* k* *Lil-t* linu-c a1 lith-c luna kg1• *Lyc* k* lyss kr1 m-ambo b2.de* m-arct b2.de* mag-c b2.de* mag-m k* mag-s maias-l hrn2• medul-os-si rly4• melal-alt gya4 meny k* *Merc* k* merc-c k* merc-i-f merc-i-r kr1 merc-sul a1* mez k* mur-ac k* myric nad rly4• nat-ar **Nat-c** k* *Nat-m* k* nat-p k* nat-sil fd3.de* nept-m lsd2.fr nicc j5.de* nicc-met sk4• nit-ac k* nitro-o a1 nux-m k* **Nux-v** k* olib-sac wmh1 **Olnd** k* **Op** k* *Orig* a1* (non:orig-v kr1) orot-ac rly4• ox-ac oxal-a rly4• ozone sde2• paeon par k* ped a1 pen a1 pert-vc vk9 *Petr* k* petr-ra shn4• **Ph-ac** k* phasco-ci rbp2 **Phos** k* phys pic-ac pip-m plac-s rly4• plan **Plat** k* plb k* plut-n srj7• *Positr* nl2• psil ft1 *Psor* **Puls** k* ran-b k* raph rauw jl *Rhod* k* rhus-v ribo rly4• ros-d wla1 ruta fd4.de **Sabad** k* sacch-a fd2.de• sal-al blc1• *Samb* k* sanic bg1 sapin a1 *Sars* k* sel k* senec k* **Sep** k* serp a1 **Sil** k* sin-n sol-t-ae *Spig* k* spira a1 spirae a1 spong fd4.de squil *Stann* k* **Staph** k* *Stram* k* streptoc rly4• sul-ac sul-i k2 *Sulph* k* sumb symph fd3.de• *Tarax* k* thiam rly4• **Thuj** k* thymol sp1 tritic-vg fd5.de trom *Urol-h* rwt• ust v-a-b jl2* valer k* vanil fd5.de verat b2.de* vinc viol-o j5.de **Viol-t** k* visc c1 x-ray sp1 yuc a1 zinc b2.de* *Zinc-pic* bg2* [heroin sdj2]

- **morning**: aln vva1• aloe colch grat lil-t plb sabad sil sumb
- **afternoon**: par a1
- **evening**: coloc a1 puls h1 sil a1
- **night**:
  - **midnight**:
    - **before**: coloc a1
    - **after**: cann-s kr1 des-ac jl olib-sac wmh1 paeon a1
      - **3** h: pip-m a1
      - **5** h: merc-i-r a1
- **bonds**: dioxi rbp6
- **boyfriends**, old: aids nl2•
- **boys**, young: aids nl2• tritic-vg fd5.de
- **coition**:
  - **after**: kali-c j5.de
  - **two** women; with: nept-m lsd2.fr nicc-met sk4•
- **dead**; with the: positr nl2•
- **debility**; with (See weakness)
- **embraced** threateningly from behind (See Threats - embraced)
- **erections**:
  - **priapism**, with: *Camph* kr1 *Pic-ac* kr1
  - **with**: aur j5.de cact kr1* camph st cann-i a1* clem a1 coloc j5.de ketogl-ac rly4• kreos j5.de lac-ac kr1* led j5.de merc j5.de mur-ac h2* *Nat-c* j5.de nat-m j5.de par j5.de ph-ac h2* pic-ac st plat h2 plb j5.de* ran-b j5.de rhod kr1* *Sars* kr1* sep a1 sil h2* sin-n a1* *Spig* a1 stann h2* thuj j5.de
  - **without**: sars gt
- **fallen** in love; has: bamb-a stb2.de• carbn-dox knl3• kola stb3• plut-n srj7• ruta fd4.de [ind stj2 tax jsj7]
- **gentle**: [heroin sdj2]
- **homosexuality**: crot-c sk4•
- **leukorrhea**, with: *Petr* j5.de*
- **looking** in her eyes: ozone sde2•
- **lying**:
  - **back**; on: coloc a1
  - **side**; on right: sars a1

Amorous: ...

- **menses**:
  - **before**: *Calc* k* *Kali-c* k*
  - **during**: bamb-a stb2.de• calc sf1.de goss st
- **orgasm**; with: bamb-a stb2.de• nux-v btw1*
- **penis**, with relaxed: sabad kr1
- **perverse**: ind c1
- **pollutions**, with: *(↗MALE GENITALIA/SEX - Pollutions - dreams - with)* *Alum* j5.de ambr bro1 ang j5.de *Ant-c* j5.de* aphis j5.de* arist-m a1 arn j5.de* ars j5.de* ars-s-f kr1* aur j5.de bar-c j5.de* bism j5.de* borx j5.de bov j5.de bros-gau mrc1 cain kr1* *Calad* bro1 *Calc* j5.de* calc-act a1 calc-p a1 *Camph* kr1* cann-i a1* cann-s sf1.de canth sf1.de carb-ac a1* carb-an j5.de* caust j5.de* chin j5.de *Cic* kr1 *Cob* a1* coloc j5.de* con bro1 cycl k2 *Dig* j5.de* dios kr1* euph j5.de ferr j5.de form a1* *Gels* kr1 *Graph* kr1* grat j5.de* ham a1* hura a1 hydr a1 ind a1 iod k2 *Iris* a1* *Kali-br* kr1* *Kali-c* j5.de* kali-chl j5.de *Kali-m* kr1* kali-s k2 lac-cp sk4• lac-del hrn2• lach j5.de* lact j5.de *Lil-t* a1* lipp a1 lyc a1* lyss a1* merc-i-f kr1* merc-sul a1 myric a1 *Nat-c* j5.de* nat-m j5.de nat-p a1* **Nux-v** j5.de* *Olnd* j5.de* op kr1* paeon a1 par j5.de *Ph-ac* j5.de* *Phos* j5.de* *Pic-ac* kr1* plat st plb j5.de *Puls* a1* rhod j5.de* *Rosm* lgb1 ruta fd4.de sabad j5.de samb j5.de *Sars* j5.de* sel kr1* senec a1* *Sep* j5.de* *Sil* j5.de* sin-n a1* *Spig* j5.de* spira a1 stann j5.de* staph j5.de* stram j5.de sulph a1 thuj j5.de* thymol bro1* ust kr1* *Viol-t* a1*
  - **erections**, with long continued: rhod kr1
  - **every** second or third night: **Nux-v** kr1
  - **one** or three a week: sars kr1
  - **painful**: *Sars* kr1
  - **profuse**: cann-i kr1 *Kali-c* kr1 merc-i-f kr1 *Olnd* kr1
  - **sleep**, as soon as he falls: *Pic-ac* kr1
  - **sticky** emission with aversion to coition: *Plat* kr1
- **raw**: [heroin sdj2]
- **sadness**, during: *Aur* kr1
- **sleep**:
  - **interrupting** sleep (See SLEEP - Disturbed - dreams - amorous)
  - **restless**, with: cain kr1
- **vivid**: bism kr1
- **weakness**, with: plat gt*

AMPUTATION: nat-sil fd3.de•

- **arm**; of: *(↗Arm - cutting; Children - arms - shortened)* irid-met srj5• lob kr1
- **leg**; of: atro a1 suis-em rly4•
  - **woman** has legs amputated because of him: ozone sde2•

AMUSEMENT PARKS: hippoc-k szs2

AMUSING: lac-del hrn2•

ANGEL: [heroin sdj2 spect dfg1 tax jsj7]

- **crying** about one: [heroin sdj2]
- **fallen**: plut-n srj7•

ANGER: *(↗Quarrels; Vexatious; MIND - Anger)* agar j all-c alum k* am-c ambr h1 androc srj1• ant-c k* apis *Arn* ars j asar aster aur bell-p jl* bit-ar wht1• borx j bov j brom k* *Bry* bung-fa mtf (non:calc slp) calc-act a1* calc-sil k2 canth carl cartl-s rly4• castm caust cham *Chin* j con j convo-d a1 crot-c a1 crot-h dream-p sdj1• dros h1 dulc fd4.de hep j ina-i mlk9.de kali-chl j kali-n ketogl-ac rly4• kola stb3• *Lac-d* sk4• lac-del hrn2• lac-e hrn2• lac-leo hrn2• lac-lup hrn2• lach lipp a1 m-arct j m-aust j *Mag-c* k* mag-m j5.de mag-s mang h2 melal-alt gya4 merc-i-r mosch j5.de mur-ac j myris nat-ar nat-c j nat-m nicc *Nit-ac* j **Nux-v** op j paeon peti a1 petr j ph-ac phel j *Phos* positr nl2• puls rat rheum h rob a1 rumx ruta j sabin sal-fr sle1• sanguis-s hrn2• sars h2 sel sep sil sol-a a1 spong h1 stann *Staph* sul-ac h2 tarax toxi mtf2• verat zinc [am-br stj2 bar-br stj2 bell-p-sp dcm1 heroin sdj2]

- **authority**; against: *Lac-d* sk4•
- **himself**; at: lac-lup hrn2•
- **indignant**:
  - **event** she is unable to stop; over: lac-leo hrn2•
  - **lack** of morality in others; at the: agath-a nl2•
- **injustice** (See Injustice)
- **man** who becomes nearly beside himself; about a: apis a1*

- **pupils**; because he has square: ozone sde2•

ANIMALS: *(↗Bats; Bear; Bees; Beetles; Birds; Bugs; Cats; Cattle; Chickens; Deer; Dogs; Elephants; Elk; Fish; Goats; Horses; Insects; Lions; Lizards; Maggots; Marmots; Moths; Opossums; Otter; Pigeons; Pigs; Rabbits; Raccoons; Rats; Scorpions; Seal; Shellfish; Skunks; Snakes; Spiders; Tigers; Trout; Turtles; Weasels; Wolves)* adam srj5• agath-a nl2• aids nl2• aloe alum h2 am-c k* *Am-m* k* apeir-s mlk9.de aq-mar rbp6 arg-n bro1* arge-pl rwt5• **Arn** k* bamb-a stb2.de• bell k* bov k* bros-gau mrc1 carneg-g rwt1• cench k2 cham chlorpr jl choc srj3• cimic al crot-c sk4• daph k* *Dendr-pol* sk4• des-ac rbp6 dulc fd4.de galla-q-r nl2• gran ham fd3.de• helodr-cal knl2• hura hydr hydrog srj2*• hyos k* hyosin c1 ina-i mlk9.de kali-p fd1.de• kali-s fd4.de *Kola* stb3• lac-c bro1 lac-cp sk4• *Lac-d* sk4• lac-del hrn2• lac-e hrn2• lac-h sk4• *Lac-leo* hrn2• lac-loxod-a hrn2• *Lac-lup* hrn2• limen-b-c hrn2* lyc m-aust b2.de mag-m j *Maias-l* hrn2• medul-os-si rly4• *Merc* k* merl c1 nat-p fkr6.de nicc j nicc-met sk4• *Nux-v* k* op bro1* oxal-a rly4• petr-ra shn4• phasco-ci rbp2 *Phos* k* phys plut-n srj7• polys sk4• positr nl2• *Puls* k* rad-br sze8• ran-s k* *Ros-d* wla1 ruta fd4.de sal-fr sle1• sanguis-s hrn2• sedi a1 sil k* spong fd4.de staph h1 suis-pan rly4• sul-ac k* sulph symph fd3.de• tarent tritic-vg fd5.de *Urol-h* rwt• vanil fd5.de verat j zinc j* [spect dfg1 zinc-i stj2 zinc-m stj2 zinc-n stj2 zinc-p stj2]

- **attacked** by a wild beast; of being: haliae-lc srj5•
- **baby**: lac-h htj1•
- **beaten**: lac-d sk4•
- **biting** (See Bitten - animals)
- **black**: am j5.de petr-ra shn4• *Puls*
- **cardboard** boxes; in: phasco-ci rbp2
- **changed** into; women are (See Women - changed)
- **changing** form: adam srj5• symph fd3.de•
- **copulating**: cench k2
- **dangerous**: galla-q-r nl2•
- **dead**: aids nl2• ptel a1*
- **devouring** meat in market: hura a1
- **dirty**: galla-q-r nl2•
- **domestic** animals: | **pets**: lac-lup hrn2•
- **eaten** by animals (See Eaten - animals)
- **eating** living animals: falco-pe nl2• hydrog srj2•
  - **giving** someone living animals to eat: falco-pe nl2•
- **farm**; of the: brucel sa3•
- **fetuses**: *(↗Fetuses)* lac-loxod-a hrn2•
- **fighting** | **with** animals: crot-h vml3• staph a1
- **flying**: kola stb3•
- **growing** rapidly: ozone sde2•
  - **destroy** them; has to | **toilet**; sticks them into the: ozone sde2•
- **half** human half animal: helodr-cal knl2•
- **injured**: aids nl2• myos-a rly4•
- **killing**: dendr-pol sk4•
- **large**: coca-c sk4•
  - **huge**: lac-h sk4•
- **monstrous** animals: sedi a1
- **poisonous**: *(↗Poison; of; Poison; of - taken; Poisoned)* positr nl2• tarent a
- **protecting**; he is: *Plut-n* srj7•
- **restrained** by collars: lac-e hrn2•
- **road**; crossing | **dangerous** road: plut-n srj7•
- **room**; trying to break into a: coca-c sk4•
- **sick**: myos-a rly4•
- **slaughtered**: phasco-ci rbp2
- **spots**; with: lac-h htj1•
- **suffering**: aids nl2• hydrog srj2•
- **suspended** animation; in: limen-b-c hrn2•
- **tails**: helo-s rwt2•
- **talking**: plut-n srj7•
- **tied**: lac-d sk4•
- **wild**: aids nl2• dulc fd4.de guan a1 helodr-cal knl2• hura a1 hyos j5.de kali-s fd4.de lac-d sk4• lac-h sk4• *Lac-leo* sk4• lyc a1 melal-alt gya4 nat-sil fd3.de• nux-v k* rad-br sze8• sil sulph tarent a1 tax-br oss1•
  - **playing** with: dulc fd4.de guan a1
  - **pursuing** him (See Pursued - animals - wild)

ANNOYING: absin gt

ANOTHER PERSON lying in bed with him (See People - bed)

ANTISOCIAL elements: lac-cp sk4•

ANTS; millions of: gink-b sbd1•

ANXIOUS: *(↗Frightful; Nightmares; Unpleasant; MIND - Anxiety; SLEEP - Anxious)* abies-n bro1 abrot **Acon** k* adam srj5• adlu jl aesc aeth agar k* agath-a nl2• agn k* all-c all-s **Alum** k* alum-p k2 alum-sil k2 **Am-c** k* **Am-m** k* *Ambr* k* aml-ns ammc *Anac* k* anag anan androc srj1• ang k* ant-c k* ant-o a1 ant-s-aur a1 ant-t k* apis k* aq-mar rbp6 *Arg-met* k* *Arg-n* k* **Arn** k* **Ars** k* *Ars-i* ars-s-f k2 asar k* asc-t k* astac kr1 *Aur* k* aur-ar k2 aur-i k2 aur-m aur-s k2 *Bapt* k* **Bar-c** k* bar-i k2 *Bar-m* bar-s k2 bart *Bell* k* benz-ac gt berb bism k* *Borx* k* bov k* bruc j5.de *Bry* k* bufo bg2 cact ptk1 calad **Calc** k* calc-caust a1 calc-i k2 calc-p calc-s *Calc-sil* k2 *Camph* cann-i k* cann-s k* *Canth* k* caps k* carb-ac carb-an k* *Carb-v* k* **Carbn-s** carc sst*• carl carneg-g rwt1• caste gt *Caust* k* *Cham* k* chel k* *Chin* k* chinin-ar chinin-s a1 chir-fl gya2 chord-umb rly4• chr-ac a1* cic *Cimic* cina k* cinnb *Cist* clem k* coc-c a1 coca coca-c sk4• **Cocc** k* coff k* colch coloc k* com *Con* k* cor-r cortico jl *Croc* k* crot-c sk4• crot-h k* crot-t cupr cupr-act a1 cycl cyt-l mg1.de* dig k* digox a1 dios *Dros* k* dulc b4.de* elaps erio a1 ery-a euph k* euph-l bro1 euphr k* eupi falco-pe nl2• *Ferr* k* *Ferr-ar* ferr-i *Ferr-p* k* *Gamb* gink-b sbd1• glon **Graph** k* guaj k* guare *Hell* k* *Hep* k* hipp a1 hydr hydr-ac j5.de *Hyos* k* *Hyper* *Ign* k* ina-i mlk9.de indg j5.de *Iod* k* ip k* iris jal a1 jug-c *Kali-ar* **Kali-c** k* kali-chl kali-i *Kali-m* kr1* kali-n k* kali-p kali-s *Kali-sil* k2 *Kola* stb3• *Kreos* k* kres mg1.de lac-cp sk4• lac-del hrn2• lac-h sk4• lac-leo hrn2• *Lach* k* lachn lact lam j5.de* *Laur* k* *Led* k* levo jl lil-t limen-b-c hrn2* linu-c a1 lipp a1 lob luf-op vml3• **Lyc** k* lycps-v m-ambo b2.de* m-arct b2.de* m-aust b2.de* **Mag-c** k* *Mag-m* k* *Mag-s* mand mg1.de *Mang* k* mang-p rly4• melal-alt gya4 menth-pu c1 *Merc* k* merc-c k* merc-i-r mez k* mosch gt *Mur-ac* k* murx nad rly4• *Nat-ar* **Nat-c** k* **Nat-m** k* nat-p k* *Nat-s* **Nat-sil** k2 nicc nicotam rly4• **Nit-ac** k* **Nux-v** k* oci-sa sk4• *Ol-an* j5.de olib-sac wmh1 *Op* k* orig a1 oxal-a rly4• oxyt bro1 ozone sde2• paeon k* palo jl par k* *Petr* k* petros j5.de* *Ph-ac* k* **Phos** k* plac-s rly4• plan *Plat* k* plb k* polys sk4• positr nl2• propl ub1• *Psor* k* **Puls** k* pycnop-sa mrz1 *Pyrog* bg2* *Ran-b* k* *Ran-s* k* raph rat j5.de rauw sp1 *Rheum* k* rhod k* rhus-g tmo3• **Rhus-t** k* rumx ruta fd4.de sabad k* sabin k* sal-fr sle1• sang sanguis-s hrn2• *Sars* k* sec k* sel k* *Sep* k* **Sil** k* sin-a kr1 spig k* **Spong** k* squil k* stann k* staph k* *Stram* k* stront-c k* suis-pan rly4• *Sul-ac* k* sul-i k2 **Sulph** k* tab tarax k* ter teucr k* **Thuj** k* thyreotr jl til tritic-vg fd5.de tub c* ust valer k* vanil fd5.de *Verat* k* verat-v bg2 verb k* wildb a1 *Zinc* k* zinc-p k2 zing [heroin sdj2 tax jsj7]

- **morning**: alum a1 calc h2* lyc a1 nit-ac h2 phos h2 puls h1* zinc h2*
  - **waking**; on:
    - **amel.**; anxiety is: am-c j5.de arg-met j5.de bov j5.de calc j5.de cann-s j5.de caust j5.de *Chin* j5.de *Graph* j5.de lach j5.de led j5.de nat-m j5.de nit-ac j5.de *Phos* j5.de *Sil* j5.de *Sulph* j5.de
    - **continued**; anxiety is: zinc kr1
- **afternoon**: adlu jl
  - **siesta**; during: nat-m h2
- **night**:
  - **midnight**: all-s a1
    - **before**: mez a1 sulph h2*
    - **after**: merc a1 *Sulph* h2*
      - **3.30 h**: *Nat-m* a1
      - **morning**; toward: *Kali-m* kr1 zinc kr1
- **accompanied** by impeded respiration (See RESPIRATION - Impeded - dreams)
- **business**; about: bry a1
- **children**, in: *Ambr* kr1 bung-fa mtf
- **conscious** anxiety had gone into her subconscious; as if all her: [heroin sdj2]
- **cried** out, so that he: nat-m a1
- **dinner**, after: sin-n kr1
- **eating**; after: nat-m b4a.de
- **falling** asleep, on: ars h2 cori-r a1 dig fl-ac mez *Nat-c* nat-m nit-ac phos h2 staph h1 thuj h1
- **fever**, in remittent: *Hyos* kr1
- **fire**; of (See Fire - danger)
- **hemiopia**, in: *Aur* kr1
- **inflammation** of brain, in: *Merc* kr1

Dreams

- **influenza**, in: *Sabad* kr1
- **lying** on left side, when: lyc phos *Puls* sep *Thuj* k*
- **menses**:
  - **before**: canth *Caust* k* con k*
    - **after** menses; and: sul-ac ptk1
  - **during**: alum calc caust con kali-c mag-c nat-c nat-m thuj
- **mortification**, after: *Puls*
- **moving**, of: *Lyc* kr1
- **palpitation**, with: arg-met kr1
- **performance**; about her: galeoc-c-h gms1•
- **perspiration**; with: lat-m bnm6• nat-m j nicc j
- **pleasant**, partly: dros kr1
- **prepared**; was not: galeoc-c-h gms1•
- **quarrels** | **friends**; between: stront-c sk4•
- **racking** his brain: kalm kr1
- **repeating**: ign ptk1
- **restlessness**, with: ars ll1 led h1*
- **respiration**; with impeded: graph b4.de*
- **suffocated**, as if: agar kr1
- **tormenting**: aur-m kr1
- **typhus**, in: *Am* kr1
- **waking** from anxious dreams (See MIND - Anxiety - dreams)
- **weeping** during sleep; with: *Nat-m* kr1

APE (See Monkey)

APOCALYPTIC, trying to save the world: plut-n srj7• rad-br sze8•

APOLOGIZING: lac-e hrn2•

APPEARANCE: | **concern** about: lac-e hrn2•

APPLAUDED; being: ars-h hr1

AQUARIUMS: hippoc-k szs2

ARCHITECTURE: ulm-c jsj8•

ARGUMENTS: nicc-met sk4•
- **friends**; with: lac-cp sk4•

ARM: *(↗Body; parts)*
- **amputation** (See Amputation - arm)
- **blisters**; arms covered with (See Blisters - arms)
- **cauterizing** of: bomb-pr a1*
- **cutting** his arm; he is: *(↗Amputation - arm; Children - arms - shortened)* gink-b sbd1•
- **hurt**, mother's arm: chin a1
- **pain** in: *(↗Disease)* nicc a1
- **paralyzed**: nicc a1

ARMAGEDDON: positr nl2•

ARMIES: aids nl2• ptel c1
- **rising** from their graves: *(↗Graves)* ptel a1

ARMOR: | **men** in armor: sarr a1

ARMY: | **more** time in the army; he has to serve: rhus-g tmo3•

ARRESTED; being: *(↗MIND - Delusions - arrested)* clem k* mag-c petr-ra shn4• taosc iwa1•
- **deceitful** cabdriver: nicc-met sk4•
- **imprisonment** (See Imprisonment; Prisoner - being)
- **innocently**: clem h2
- **murder**; for: sil a1

ARROWS: | **piercing** muscles: bomb-pr a1*

ARTIFICIAL things: | **copies** of nature: plut-n srj7•

ASCENDING: adam srj5• brass-n-o srj5• brom dulc fd4.de hydrog srj2• hyper kali-p fd1.de• mur-ac rhus-t vanil fd5.de
- **descending**; and: nept-m lsd2.fr
- **hill** (See Hill - ascending)
- **stairs** (See Stairs - ascending)

ASPIRING: zing a1

ASSEMBLIES, large: cere-b a

ASSERTING herself: falco-pe nl2•

ASTERIX and Obelix: ozone sde2•

ASTRAY, going: *(↗Lost - mountains)* adam srj5• am-m b7.de crot-c sk4• irid-met srj5• lac-h sk4• mag-c j5.de mag-m j5.de nat-c h2* olib-sac wmh1 sep j5.de spong fd4.de tritic-vg fd5.de vanil fd5.de

ASYLUM; INSANE: lyss kr1

ATTACKED, of being: adam srj5• germ-met srj5• lac-d sk4• *Nicc-met* sk4• positr nl2• toxi mtf2• tritic-vg fd5.de [buteo-j sej6 merc stj2]
- **above**; from: maias-l hrn2•
- **high** school bullies; by | **child**; being a: lac-lup hrn2•
- **Indians**; by | **child**; being a: lac-lup hrn2•
- **knife**; with a: crot-c sk4•
  - **abdomen**; in: coli gmj1
- **men**; by big: oci-sa sk4•
- **son**: lac-del hrn2•
- **submitting** it, lest he lose his friends; and: positr nl2•
- **wild** beast; by a (See Animals - attacked)

AUTHORITY: sal-al blc1•

AUTOPSIES: *(↗Dissecting - dead)* fic-m gya1 rumx
- **dissecting** dead bodies (See Dissecting - dead)

AWAY: | **go** away; she wants to: bell h1

BACK: *(↗Body; parts)*
- **burnt**: mag-c a1
- **pain** in back: ephe-si hsj1•
- **pinched**, back and breast are: phos h2*
- **warts**; covered with (See Warts - back)

BACKWARDS IN TIME; going: plut-n srj7• sil cd1

BAFFLED, being: verat-v a1

BALLOONS: *Agath-a* nl2• galla-q-r nl2• rad-br sze8• [tax jsj7]
- **abdomen**; has a balloon in front of: ozone sde2•

BALLS: *(↗Dancing; Entertainment)* mag-c a1 mag-s a1 pieri-b mlk9.de vanil fd5.de [tax jsj7]

BANK; of robbing a (See Robbing - bank)

BANQUET: *(↗Carousing; Eating; Feasting)* bomb-chr mlk9.de dulc fd4.de irid-met srj5• kola stb3• mag-c j mag-s nit-ac j5.de ph-ac pieri-b mlk9.de positr nl2• ruta fd4.de spong fd4.de *Tung-met* bdx1•

BASEBALL; playing: atro a1*

BASKETBALL:
- **playing**: carbn-dox knl3• helodr-cal knl2•
  - **water**, under: galeoc-c-h gms1•

BATS: *(↗Animals)* gard-j vlr2• limen-b-c hrn2• neon srj5•
- **double**-bodied | **wings**; with three: plut-n srj7•
- **flying** in the room; there was a bat: ham a1* [plut-n stj2]
- **invading** out of the sky: ignis-alc es2•

BATHING: *(↗Water)* lac-h sk4• vanil fd5.de [niob-met stj2]
- **boiling** water; child is bathing in: mag-c
- **cold** showers: arizon-l nl2•
- **people** are bathing (See People - bathing)
- **sea** water; in: lac-h sk4•

BATHROOMS:
- **cannot** find the bathroom: lac-e hrn2• limen-b-c hrn2•
- **in**: galeoc-c-h gms1•

BATHTUB:
- **black** spots in a white bathtub: ozone sde2•
- **dirty** with black border: ozone sde2•

BATTLES: *(↗Air; Air attacks; Blood - bloodshed; Cannonading; Enemies; Fights; War; MIND - Talking - battles)* *All-c* bamb-a stb2.de• bell bry crot-c a1 dendr-pol sk4• ferr k* guaj hyos j5.de *Kola* stb3• *Meny* vh nat-m a1 nat-s cda phos zf plat k* ran-s rat a1* sil sol-t-ae a stann thuj tung-met bdx1• verb [ferr-f stj2 ferr-lac stj2 ferr-n stj2 ferr-sil stj2 plut-n stj2]

BEACH: falco-pe nl2• hippoc-k szs2 limen-b-c hrn1 musca-d szs1 nept-m lsd2.fr

- **dirty**: falco-pe nl2•
- **walking** on the sand: limen-b-c hrn2•

BEAR: *(↗Animals)* lac-e hrn2• *Lac-lup* hrn2• limen-b-c hrn2•

BEARD, having a: arizon-l nl2•
- **women**; in (See Women - bearded)

BEATEN, being: *(↗Mouth - blow)* agath-a nl2• dendr-pol sk4• galeoc-c-h gms1• kali-c a1 kali-n lac-d sk4• lac-e hrn2• nat-m h2* puls a1*
- **children** (See Children - beaten)
- **father** was about to beat him: kali-c h2*
- **teacher**; by: oci-sa sk4•

BEAUTIFUL dreams: *(↗Buildings - beautiful; Country - beautiful; Girl - beautiful; Landscape - beautiful; Regions)* bamb-a stb2.de• cyclosp sa3• dulc fd4.de ham fd3.de• hippoc-k szs2 irid-met srj5• *Kola* stb3• podo fd3.de• polys sk4• spong fd4.de [tax jsj7]

BEAUTY: | **awe** with: lac-e hrn2•

BED:
- **another** person lying in bed with him (See People - bed)
- **crowded**: coca-c sk4•
- **narrow**; too: lac-cp sk4•
- **place** to sleep; she had to hunt all night for a: lac-cp sk4•
- **small**; too: *(↗Lying)* ferr-i a1
- **someone** is sleeping in her bed: falco-pe nl2•

BEES: *(↗Animals; Insects)* cystein-l rly4• puls j5.de* spong fd4.de

BEETLES: *(↗Animals; Bugs; Cockroaches; Insects)* coca a1 kres mg1.de* limen-b-c hrn2* ran-s c1* [heroin sdj2]
- **black**: [heroin sdj2]
  - **eating**: [heroin sdj2]

BEGGARS: mag-c j5.de

BELONGING: | **she** knows where she belongs: galla-q-r nl2•

BETRAYED, having been: adam srj5• lac-e hrn2• musca-d szs1 petr-ra shn4• podo fd3.de• sal-fr sle1• sil h2
- **friends**; by: adam skp7• crot-c sk4•

BICYCLE; riding a: galeoc-c-h gms1• kola stb3• nicc-met sk4• vanil fd5.de
- **difficult**; is: aids nl2• lac-leo hm2• visc sp1
- **exhausting**: ephe-si hsj1•
- **maximal** force; with: ephe-si hsj1•
- **sand**; on: ephe-si hsj1•

BIRDS: *(↗Animals)* apeir-s mlk9.de com a1 dulc fd4.de falco-pe nl2• hippoc-k szs2 ina-i mlk9.de kola stb3• limen-b-c hrn2* positr nl2• ros-d wla1 spong fd4.de vanil fd5.de [buteo-j sej6 yttr-met stj2]
- **cage**; in a: helodr-cal knl2•
- **cranes**; white: irid-met srj5•
- **eagles**: plac-s rly4• [buteo-j sej6]
- **escaping** | **cage**; out of their: carbn-dox knl3•
- **exotic**: [buteo-j sej6]
- **falcon**: positr nl2•
- **geese**: zinc h2* [buteo-j sej6 zinc-i stj2]
  - **biting** him: zinc a1
- **kites**: falco-pe nl2•
- **large** black: choc srj3• corv-cor bdg•
- **owl**: [buteo-j sej6 spect dfg1]
- **swans**: positr nl2•
- **water** birds: [buteo-j sej6]

BIRTHDAYS: sal-fr sle1• vanil fd5.de

BITING: androc srj1• [tax jsj7]

BITTEN; being: [nicc-met stj2 nicc-s stj2 tax jsj7]
- **animals**; by: aln vva1• am-m bov j5.de calc j5.de cench k2 daph gink-b sbd1• lyss m-aust j5.de *Maias-l* hm2• merc nicc j5.de *Phos* k* puls k* sulph j5.de* verat j5.de zinc j5.de
  - **rear**; from | **heads** bitten off: maias-l hrn2•
- **arms**, into the: aln vva1• am-m a1 m-aust j5.de nicc j5.de

Bitten; being: ...
- **dogs**, by (See Dogs - bitten)
- **goose**; by (See Birds - geese - biting)
- **horse**, by a (See Horses - bitten)
- **snakes**, by (See Snakes - biting)
- **wasps**; by: marb-w es1•

BLASPHEMY: plut-n srj7•

BLESSED VIRGIN: ulm-c jsj8•

BLIND; being: *(↗Disease)* phys k*

BLINDNESS: haliae-lc srj5• kola stb3•

BLISTERS: *(↗Disease)*
- **burning**: castm j5.de*
- **arms** covered with: castm j5.de* lac-h sk4•

BLOOD: *(↗Disease)* irid-met srj5• kali-m ccrh1• lac-h sk4• *Moni* rfm1• musca-d szs1 *Phos* bg1 polys sk4• rad-br bg rhus-t bg1 sol-t-ae bg1
- **bleeding**, during metrorrhagia: petr-ra shn4• *Sec* kr1
- **bloodshed**: *(↗Battles; War)* *Moni* rfm1• petr-ra shn4• plat b4.de* thuj gt tung-met bdx1• verb gt
- **dripping** from one's heart: ignis-alc es2•
- **mouth**; in: [plut-n stj2]
- **pools** of: sol-t-ae a1*
- **strains**: bros-gau mrc1
- **spitting** blood (See Hemoptysis)
- **transfusion**: limen-b-c hm2•

BOARS, WILD: ina-i mlk9.de (non:merc a1) merl a1

BOASTING: asc-t a1 m-ambo b7.de*

BOAT: helodr-cal knl2• lac-loxod-a hrn2• loxo-recl knl4• musca-d szs1 sal-al blc1• sal-fr sle1• vanil fd5.de [heroin sdj2]
- **building** a: sal-fr sle1•
- **foundering**: agath-a nl2• alum asim a2 bamb-a stb2.de• bit-ar wht1• lyc sil
- **motorboat** (See Motorboats)
- **river**; on a: plut-n srj7•
- **rowboat** (See Rowboat)
- **rubber** boat going up a mountain stream: ozone sde2•

BODY:
- **deformed**: positr nl2• rad-br sze8• sep h2
- **disfigured**: falco-pe nl2• petr-ra shn4•
- **emaciated**; becoming: *(↗Emaciated)* kali-n a1* kreos k*
- **embalmed**: carb-ac
- **lightness** of: [buteo-j sej6]
- **mutilated**: *(↗Mutilation)* am ptk1 bros-gau mrc1 maias-l hm2•
- **paralyzed**: [am-br stj2]
  - **right** side: irid-met srj5•
- **pieces**; of being in: bros-gau mrc1 dict bg1
- **structure**: positr nl2•
- **swollen**: *(↗Disease)* carbn-s a1 squil k* suis-em rly4•
- **turns** into | **stuffed** doll: lac-e hrn2•
- **wrapped** in newspapers: phasco-ci rbp2

BODY; PARTS OF: *(↗Abdomen; Arm; Back; Cheek; Chest; Ears; Eyes; Face; Fingernails; Fingers; Foot; Hair; Hands; Head; Jaws; Larynx; Leg; Limbs; Liver; Mammae; Mouth; Muscles; Penis; Teeth; Throat; Thyroid; Toe; Tongue; Vocal)* (non:mag-c a1*) maias-l hrn2•
- **dead**: maias-l hm2•
- **diseased** parts of body: kali-c h2*
- **three** dimensional lifelike images; have become: arizon-l nl2•

BOILS: *(↗Disease)* plut-n srj7• prun k*

BOMBS: lac-e hrn2• musca-d szs1 rad-br sze8•
- **bomb** threat: *(↗Danger - impending)* limen-b-c hm2•
- **explosion** of (See Explosion - bombs)
- **falling**: polys sk4•
- **time** bomb: rhus-g tmo3•

BOOKS: irid-met srj5• positr nl2• ruta fd4.de

BOOTS: | **warm** and fluffy: positr nl2•

BORED: | **people** are: lac-e hrn2•

BOREDOM: plut-n srj7•

BORN; being: [bell-p-sp dcm1]

BOULDERS; of (See Rocks)

BOUND; being:
- **mouth**; across (See Mouth - chain)
- **ropes**; with: coca a1

BOUNDARY crossed: dioxi rbp6

BOWLING: | **dark** alley in: maias-l hrn2•

BOX; flying: ozone sde2•

BOY: | **girl**; looking like a: dendr-pol sk4•

BOYFRIEND: dulc fd4.de galeoc-c-h gms1• hydrog srj2• sal-fr sle1•
- **affair**, having an: sal-fr sle1•
- **leaving** her (See Forsaken - girl)
- **old** boyfriend: aids nl2• arizon-l nl2• hydrog srj2• plut-n srj7• sal-fr sle1• *Urol-h* rwt• [heroin sdj2]
  - **amazed** at how hairy he'd become: lac-leo hrn2•
- **returning**: galeoc-c-h gms1•

BRAKES:
- **find** while driving; cannot: lac-cp sk4•
- **function** any more; do not: bamb-a stb2.de• crot-c sk4• maias-l hrn2•

BREAST FED: | **guru**; by one's: phasco-ci rbp2

BREATHING under water: hippoc-k szs2 ozone sde2•

BRIDGE: [tax jsj7]
- **building** bridges; of: lac-leo hrn2•
- **collapse**; that might: allox tpw3
- **river**; crossing over flooded: bros-gau mrc1 lac-h sk4•

BROTHER: plut-n srj7• vanil fd5.de

BRUISING himself: nicc a1

BRUTALITY: *(↗Violence)* ara-maca sej7• *Moni* rfm1•

BUBBLES; colorful: | **sky**; in the: polys sk4•

BUFFALOES: | **spotted**: polys sk4•

BUGS: *(↗Animals; Beetles; Cockroaches; Insects)* kres mg1.de* limen-b-c hrn2* myric a1 oxyt a2 staphycoc rly4•
- **attacking** his head; enormous bugs: myric a1

BUILDING SITES: positr nl2•

BUILDINGS: *(↗House)* aids nl2• aln vva1• *Androc* srj1• choc srj3• dulc fd4.de falco-pe nl2• ham fd3.de• helodr-cal knl2• hippoc-k szs2 hura a1 ina-i mlk9.de kola stb3• lac-e hrn2• lac-h htj1• limen-b-c hrn2* myris a1 orot-ac rly4• pall a1* positr nl2• ruta fd4.de spong fd4.de symph fd3.de• tung-met bdx1• vanil fd5.de [am-c stj1]
- **admirable**: fic-m gya1 graph gl1.fr• helodr-cal knl2•
- **beautiful**: *(↗Beautiful)* aids nl2•
- **big**; seeing: aids nl2• falco-pe nl2• ina-i mlk9.de nat-m dgt vanil fd5.de
  - **beautiful**; and: limen-b-c hrn2•
- **bigger** inside than they appear: aids nl2•
- **collapsing**: lac-h htj1•
- **dark** and old: limen-b-c hrn2•
- **demolition** of public building: hura a1
- **drab** and decrepit: limen-b-c hrn2•
- **falling** apart | **earthquake**; as if split by: lac-e hrn2•
- **glass** buildings: musca-d szs1
- **looking** for a particular: coca-c sk4•
- **neglected**: aids nl2•
  - **outside** but beautiful inside: aids nl2•
- **ornate**: aids nl2•
- **palatial**: aids nl2•
  - **wandering** in: lac-h sk4•
- **ruined** (See Ruins)
- **squalid** (See Dirty - buildings)
- **structure** of: *Positr* nl2•

Buildings: ...
- **temple**: [bell-p-sp dcm1]
  - **collapsing**: nept-m lsd2.fr
  - **sacred** temple made of gauze: limen-b-c hrn2•
- **white** | **get** in; trying to: galeoc-c-h gms1•

BULL:
- **crashing** through the window: [buteo-j sej6]
- **pursuing** him (See Pursued - bulls)

BULLYING: *(↗Ill-treatment)* peti a1 positr nl2•

BURIED; being: *(↗Funerals)*
- **alive**; being buried: adam srj5• aids nl2• *Am* chel ign
  - **explosives**, with: aids nl2•

BURIED; things are: tung-met bdx1•

BURNED; being: xan a2

BURNING tinder or sulphur; dreams of smelling (= spunk - amadou): anac k*

BURNS: mag-c b4.de mag-m b4.de
- **smoke** screen; something as a: phasco-ci rbp2

BUS: *(↗Climbing - bus; Journeys - bus)*
- **wrong** place; bus takes him/her to the: maias-l hrn2•

BUSINESS: *(↗Striving; Work)* aether a1 anac apis arist-m a1 asaf bell *Bry* k* bufo calc calc-act a1 calc-sil k2 camph canth carb-v carc gk6* carl celt a1 *Chel* cic cina j cinnb a1 croc *Cur* dulc fd4.de elaps gels ger-i rly4• hep hura hyper a1 ina-i mlk9.de kali-c lac-e hrn2• *Lach* *Lyc* merc myris c1 **Nux-v** oxal-a rly4• phos psor k* *Puls* pyrog **Rhus-t** ruta fd4.de sang sars sel c1* *Sil* staph tarent k* [arg-met stj2 plat stj2 stann stj2]
- **absorbing**: nux-v a
- **day**, of the: *(↗Events - previous - day)* abrom-a ks5 acon k* alum bg2 anac j5.de* anan a1 apis bg2 arg-met k* asaf bg2 asc-t bg2 bapt bg2 *Bell* b2.de* **Bry** k* calc bg2 calc-f camph bg2 canth b2.de* carb-v bg2 chel k* *Cic* k* *Cina* b2.de* croc j5.de cur euph b2.de* fl-ac gels bg2 graph hep b2.de* kali-c k* kali-chl **Lach** k* *Lyc* k* **Mag-c** k* mag-m bg2 *Merc* k* naja a1* nit-ac h2 **Nux-v** k* ph-ac b2.de* *Phos* b2.de* plat b2.de* psor bg2 **Puls** k* pyrog bg2 **Rhus-t** k* sabin b2.de* sars k* sel b2.de* sep **Sil** k* sol-t-ae a1 stann k* staph b2.de* sulph b2.de* visc c1 [tax jsj7]
  - **morning**: nit-ac h2
- **difficulties**; in (See Difficulties - work)
- **falling** asleep, on: rhus-t staph a1
- **fever**, in typhoid: **Rhus-t** kr1
- **foreign** to his daily life: myris a1
- **forgot** during the day; about business he: sel c1*
- **neglected**: hyper myris sil stann
- **operations** on a large scale: hura a1
- **pressure** of business: hyper a1*
- **projects**, of: camph a
- **succeed**; does not: *(↗Unsuccessful)* mag-m *Phos* sabad
- **unable** to finish: *Phos* h2*

BUSY, being: *(↗Busy; Hurry; MIND - Busy)* ambr anac androc srj1• apis bapt dx1 bell **Bry** camph canth carb-ac carc fd2.de* *Carl* coca dulc fd4.de fic-m gya1 hydr *Hydrog* srj2• hyos hyper ign kalm lac-lup hrn2• lach led lil-t a1 loxo-recl knl4• lyc mosch osm phos pip-m a1 polyg-h a1 rad-br gk1 sabad sabin sang sep spig h1 [buteo-j sej6 spect dfg1]

BUTTERFLY: *(↗Moths)* rhus-g tmo3•

CAGE: | **wire** cage filled with whipped cream: maias-l hrn2•

CESAREAN with a long scar: phasco-ci rbp2

CALCULATING: sel b7a.de* sep kl

CALLING OUT: *(↗Voice)* kali-c thuj
- **help**; for: *(↗Shrieking - help)* kali-c lil-s a1 plat dx1
- **mother**; for his: chin a1
- **someone** is calling●: ant-c merc sep

CALM: lac-e hrn2•

CAMELS: hydrog srj2*• ozone sde2•

CAMPING: lac-h htj1•

CANCER: *(↗Disease)* aster sze10• halo jl kola stb3• lac-h htj1• rad-br sze8• tritic-vg fd5.de
- **mammae**: aster sze10•

CANDLES: galla-q-r nl2•

CANNONADING: *(↗Battles; Fights; War)* menis a1

CANNONS: choc srj3•

CANYON: | **side** of; being on: [buteo-j sej6]

CAR: apeir-s mlk9.de bomb-chr mlk9.de choc srj3• des-ac rbp6 ina-i mlk9.de lac-del hrn2• lac-h sk4• lac-loxod-a hrn2• *Lac-lup* hrn2• limen-b-c hrn2* ozone sde2• petr-ra shn4• sal-fr sle1• tere-la rly4• vanil fd5.de
- **control**; taking: des-ac rbp6
- **driving** a car (See Driving - car)
- **find** the car; cannot: sanguis-s hrn2•
- **function** anymore, while driving; does not: ozone sde2•
- **limousine** | **white** limousine with black roof: maias-l hrn2•
- **luxury** car is washed with mud; white: ozone sde2•
- **racing**: dendr-pol sk4•
- **red** sports car: dioxi rbp6
  - **sell** it, but he does not succeed; wants to: ozone sde2•
- **secondhand** cars: lac-lup hrn2•
- **shrinking**: stront-c sk4•
- **small** car; cannot hold a: ozone sde2•
- **spinning**, going out of control: coca-c sk4•
- **split** in half; passing houses: hydrog srj2•
- **threatening**: falco-pe nl2•
- **water**; filled with: nicc-met sk4•
- **wheels** detaching from body: choc srj3•

CARE-TAKING: lac-leo hrn2•
- **family** member; taking care of: | **paralyzed** legs; with: [buteo-j sej6]

CAREFREE: falco-pe nl2• sal-fr sle1•

CARES, FULL OF: *(↗Grief; Harassing; Sad)* alum a1 apis gt* *Ars* j5.de* carl a1 castm j5.de corv-cor bdg• crot-t j5.de hydr a1 ina-i mlk9.de lac-leo hrn2• mur-ac j5.de nux-v j5.de sabad a1 stront-c a1 thuj a2 [tax jsj7]
- **children**; about one's: *(↗Children - responsibility)* lac-leo hrn2• sanguis-s hrn2•
- **patients**; for his: lac-leo hrn2•

CARING: | **another** person; about: [buteo-j sej6 tax jsj7]

CAROUSING: *(↗Banquet; Drinking; Eating; Feasting)* ars j calc j carb-an j carb-v j cham j chin j con j dulc fd4.de graph kali-c kali-n j led j lyc mur-ac j nat-c nat-m nit-ac nux-v petr pieri-b mlk9.de sep j sil spong j sulph zinc

CASUALTIES, of (See Accidents)

CATARRH from nose, of: hydrog srj

CATCH:
- **trying** to | **flew** above his head; something that: crot-c sk4•

CATS: *(↗Animals)* adam srj5• aids nl2• arn b7.de* ars calc-p *Daph* falco-pe nl2• graph hippoc-k szs2 hydrog srj2*• hyos k* ignis-alc es2• irid-met srj5• kali-s fd4.de kola stb3• lac-c *Lac-e* hrn2• lac-f mtr lac-h sze9• *Lac-leo* hrn2• melal-alt gya4 mez musca-d szs1 nux-v ozone sde2• positr nl2• puls ros-d wla1 ruta fd4.de samb bat1• taosc iwa1• thuj bg1 [heroin sdj2]
- **angry**: hyos a1 lac-e hrn2•
- **army** of: calc-p a
- **big**: positr nl2•
- **black**: am a1 daph k* lac-lup hrn2• [heroin sdj2]
  - **eaten** by a black cat (See Eaten - animals - cat)
  - **grabbing** his hand; evil black cat: daph a1
  - **sex**; having: [heroin sdj2]
- **dead**: positr nl2•
- **frightened** by: puls a
- **gone** crazy; from being alone all night: lac-leo hrn2•
- **kitten**: lac-leo hrn2•
- **lost**, missing: lac-leo hrn2•
- **many** cats surrounding her: ephe-si hsj1•
- **outside**: ozone sde2•

Cats: ...
- **pursued** by cats; being (See Pursued - cats)
- **pursuing** a mouse: coca-c sk4• oci-sa sk4•
- **running**: pert-vc vk9
- **white** cat; big: lac-h sk4•
- **wild**: ozone sde2•
- **wounded** abdomen; with: ozone sde2•

CATTLE: *(↗Animals)* lac-loxod-a hrn2•

CAUGHT; of being: coca-c sk4• crot-c sk4• lac-cp sk4•

CAUTERIZING of arm (See Arm - cauterizing)

CEILING: | **collapsing**: nept-m lsd2.fr

CELEBRATIONS: falco-pe nl2• vanil fd5.de

CELLAR; being in a: *(↗Crushed)* taosc iwa1•
- **walls** are falling; and: *(↗Crushed)* bov

CEMETERY (See Churchyard)

CENSORIOUS: positr nl2•

CEREMONIES: positr nl2•

CHANDELIERS: aids nl2•

CHANGING:
- **curse** into a blessing: positr nl2•
- **everything** is changed: ozone sde2•
- **places** often: *(↗Places - public - changing)* all-s a* led lyc
- **subjects**; rapid changing of: *(↗Things - changing)* mang h1 [bell-p-sp dcm1]

CHAOS: polys sk4•

CHAOTIC: falco-pe nl2•

CHARMING, she is: irid-met srj5•

CHASED; of being (See Pursued)

CHASING (See Pursued)

CHEATED; being: dendr-pol sk4• lac-d sk4• oci-sa sk4•
- **friends**; by: oci-sa sk4•

CHEATING: bit-ar wht1•

CHEEK: *(↗Body; parts)*
- **burnt**: mag-c a1
- **swollen**: *(↗Disease)* kali-n h2*

CHEERFUL (See Happy)

CHEST: *(↗Body; parts)*
- **figure** sitting on chest: paeon hr1
  - **respiration**; impeding: *(↗Abdomen - someone - respiration)* paeon a1
- **ghost** sitting on chest (See Ghosts - chest)
- **open** the chest and to look into it; wished to: paull a1
- **pain** in chest: sacch-l c1
- **pressed**; being: am-m a1
- **someone** is lying across his chest | **respiration**; impeding (See Abdomen - someone - respiration)

CHICKENS: *(↗Animals)* limen-b-c hrn2•

CHILD; being a: | **he** is a: plut-n srj7•

CHILDBIRTH: falco-pe nl2• lac-h sk4• lac-leo hrn2• ozone sde2• [bell-p-sp dcm1]
- **baby** is moribund: falco-pe nl2•
- **delivering** baby herself: lac-leo hrn2•
- **delivery** alone; she had to conduct a: dendr-pol sk4•
- **distressing**: lac-h sk4•
- **premature**: lac-h sk4• rad-br sze8•
- **terror**; with: falco-pe nl2•
- **water**; in: nept-m lsd2.fr
- **worthlessness**, with feeling of: falco-pe nl2•

Dreams

CHILDREN; about: aids nl2• am-m bamb-a stb2.de• brass-n-o srj cass a1 chir-fl gya2 choc srj3• chord-umb rly4• dulc fd4.de fic-m gya1 galeoc-c-h gms1• hippoc-k szs2 hura *Hydrog* srj2*• kali-br tl1 kali-n kola stb3• lac-del hrn2• lac-e hrn2• lac-h htj1• lac-leo hrn2• lac-lup hrn2• limen-b-c hrn2* lipp a1 mag-c maias-l hrn2• (non:merc a1) merl k* nept-m lsd2.fr oci a1 oxal-a rly4• ozone sde2• pant-ac rly4• petr-ra shn4• plut-n srj7• ruta fd4.de sal-fr sle1• *Sanguis-s* hrn2• sil tl1 suprar rly4• taosc iwa1• tritic-vg fd5.de ulm-c jsj8• vanil fd5.de [ant-m stj2 aur-m stj2 beryl-m stj2 cadm-m stj2 chlor stj2 cob-m stj2 lith-m stj2 mag-met stj2 mang-m stj2 merc-d stj2 mur-ac stj2 plb-m stj2 spect dfg1 stront-m stj2 zinc-m stj2]
- **abused**; being: *(↗Abused; Abused; being)* lac-loxod-a hrn2• ozone sde2• plut-n srj7•
- **adopting** them: limen-b-c hrn2•
- **AIDS**; her child has (See Aids - child)
- **alcoholic**; her son was an: coca-c sk4•
- **animal** costumes; in: galeoc-c-h gms1•
- **arms** | **shortened** arms and no hands; with: *(↗Amputation - arm; Arm - cutting)* positr nl2•
- **baby**-sitting: lac-del hrn2• lac-lup hrn2• [heroin sdj2]
- **beaten**, being: kali-c a1 kali-n nat-m a1
- **birthday** party: lac-lup hrn2•
- **black**: *(↗People - black)* sanguis-s hrn2•
  - **blond** hair and three eyes; with: maias-l hrn2•
    - **but** could not see, needed help: maias-l hrn2•
- **captive**; held: lac-h sk4•
- **caring** for debilitated child: dendr-pol sk4•
- **coma**; in: ozone sde2•
- **control** her son; she was trying to: coca-c sk4•
- **danger**; in: lac-lup hrn2• nept-m lsd2.fr ozone sde2• plut-n srj7•
  - **unprotected** | **adults**; children feel unprotected by: *Limen-b-c* hrn2•
  - **water**: lac-del hrn2•
- **daughter** (See Daughter)
- **dead** (See Dead; of - children)
- **deformed**: rad-br sze8•
- **dirty**: lac-d sk4•
- **Advent** spiral; doing an: lac-lup hrn2•
- **educating**: galeoc-c-h gms1•
- **fondness** for: lac-del hrn2•
  - **own** child; her: [tax jsj7]
- **garden**; in a | **pear** tree; under a: plut-n srj7•
- **gassed**; being: lac-lup hrn2•
- **got** a three year old child; she: mag-c a1
- **hair** pulled by violent man; having: lac-lup hrn2•
- **happened** to; something has: hydrog srj2• kali-n a1 kreos a1* lac-del hrn2• lac-leo hrn2• maias-l hrn2•
- **help**; requested to | **unescorted**: nicc-met sk4•
- **hordes**, disturbing her idyllic fancy: ozone sde2•
- **injured**: positr nl2•
- **kidnapped**; being: *(↗Kidnappers; Kidnapping)* lac-leo hrn2• nept-m lsd2.fr
- **looking** after: aids nl2• sal-fr sle1• [bell-p-sp dcm1]
- **looking** for: lac-del hrn2•
- **loosing** in water: lac-del hrn2•
- **lost**: galla-q-r nl2• nept-m lsd2.fr
  - **crowd**; in: bamb-a stb2.de•
- **love** for her child; great: | **cared** for by another women; yet: limen-b-c hrn2•
- **murdered**, being: lac-lup hrn2• thea a1 tritic-vg fd5.de
- **mutilated**: *(↗Mutilation)* lac-e hrn2•
- **neglecting** her child: bamb-a stb2.de• dendr-pol sk4• lac-h sze9• limen-b-c hrn2• sanguis-s hrn2•
- **newborns**: *(↗Nursing) Adam* srj5• aids nl2• bit-ar wht1• bomb-pr mlk9.de choc srj3• ephe-si hsj1• granit-m es1• helodr-cal knl2• hippoc-k szs2 ina-i mlk9.de lac-h htj1*• limen-b-c hrn2• maias-l hrn2• pant-ac rly4• petr-ra shn4• *Plut-n* srj7• positr nl2• [bell-p-sp dcm1 spect dfg1]
  - **drowned**, a baby is being: dream-p sdj1•
  - **extraordinary**: des-ac rbp6
  - **falling** from old fashioned railways; babies: lac-h htj1•
  - **feeding** from dismembered breast: *(↗Nursing)* positr nl2•

Children; about – **newborns**: ...
  - **found** a living premature baby on city street: maias-l hrn2•
  - **Frankenstein** baby: positr nl2•
  - **handicapped**: adam srj5•
  - **healthy** | **premature**; though: lac-h sk4•
  - **leukemia**; with: ozone sde2•
  - **naked** babies from the cold; trying to save (See Saving - children - newborns - naked)
  - **back** of mother; on: lac-leo hrn2•
  - **protecting** from harm: adam srj5• aids nl2•
  - **sick**: musca-d szs1
  - **smaller** and smaller, getting: aids nl2•
  - **snow** with baby; walking in: kreos hs1
  - **talking** to her, a baby is: sal-fr sle1•
  - **twins**: ignis-alc es2•
  - **yearning** for a baby | **friend** yearning for a baby; of a: lac-h htj1•
- **playing**: *Agath-a* nl2• lac-lup hrn2• nept-m lsd2.fr sal-fr sle1•
  - **dangerous** liquid; with: lac-lup hrn2•
- **precocious** and arrogant: lac-e hrn2•
- **protecting** them from falling: ozone sde2•
- **rescuing**; of: *(↗Saving - children)* aids nl2• cass a1 *Hydrog* srj2• maias-l hrn2• melal-alt gya4 plut-n srj7• positr nl2• sal-fr sle1• suprar rly4• tritic-vg fd5.de
  - **abandoned**: nicc-met sk4•
- **responsibility** for: *(↗Cares - children; Responsibility)* lac-del hrn2• lac-h sze9• *Limen-b-c* hrn2•
  - **adults** overwhelmed by: *Limen-b-c* hrn2•
  - **does** not want: lac-del hrn2•
- **sick**: sal-fr sle1•
- **something** has happened to (See happened)
- **starving**: lac-loxod-a hrn2•
- **taking** care of endangered parents: limen-b-c hrn2•
- **tear**-filled eyes; with: nicc-met sk4•
- **teenager** | **jumping** of building, screaming, dies: lac-lup hrn2•
- **tortured**; being: lac-lup hrn2•
- **violated**; being: lac-lup hrn2•
- **weeping**: lac-lup hrn2•
- **wildness** of: limen-b-c hrn2•
- **younger**; were ten years: ozone sde2•

CHIMNEY: | **climbing** inside a: agath-a nl2•

CHOICES: arizon-l nl2•

CHOIRS singing: *Lac-lup* hrn2•

CHOKED; being: *(↗Suffocation; Throat - grasped)* lac-h sk4• phos k* sil zinc k* zinc-m hr1* [zinc-i stj2 zinc-n stj2 zinc-p stj2]

CHOLERA: *(↗Disease)* linu-c a1
- **dying** from: musca-d szs1

CHRISTMAS: falco-pe nl2•

CHURCHES: *(↗Fire - cathedral; Praying; Preaching; Religious)* aids nl2• asc-t bros-gau mrc1 coc-c galeoc-c-h gms1• lap-la sde8.de• lyss melal-alt gya4 nept-m lsd2.fr ozone sde2• symph fd3.de• tung-met bdx1• vanil fd5.de zing [nicc-met stj2 nicc-s stj2]
- **ornate**: aids nl2•
- **rubble**, on a pile of: galla-q-r nl2•

CHURCHYARD: *(↗Funerals; Graves)* bros-gau mrc1 crot-h k2 gink-b sbd1• hura a1 kali-p fd1.de• ruta fd4.de
- **dead** child in a churchyard; finding a (See Dead bodies - churchyard)

CIGARETTES: vero-o rly3•

CINEMA; going to: pant-ac rly4•

CIRCLE: arge-pl rwt5• lac-lup hrn2•
- **center** of | **he** is in: lac-del hrn2•
- **going** clockwise toward a: lac-del hrn2•

- **standing** outside a circle: lac-del hrn2•
  - **looking** in: lac-del hrn2•
- **walking** in a: lac-del hrn2•

CIRCUS: galla-q-r nl2• hydrog srj2*• tritic-vg fd5.de

CITIES: bamb-a stb2.de• dulc fd4.de falco-pe nl2• nat-m a1 ruta fd4.de vanil fd5.de
- **beautiful** cities: bamb-a stb2.de•
- **destroyed**:
  - **bombs**; by: plut-n srj7•
  - **fire**; by (See Fire - city)
- **jungle** encroaching on each other; and: dream-p sdj1•
- **strange**: kola stb3• ozone sde2•

CIVIL WAR: *(↗War)* op gl1.fr•

CLAIRVOYANT: *(↗Events - future; Prophetic; Visionary; MIND - Clairvoyance; MIND - Fear - happen; MIND - Prophesying)* Acon k1* adam srj5• asaf bov *Cann-i* carc zzh carneg-g rwt1• com hr1* cortico sp1 fuma-ac rly4• lac-del hrn2• m-arct j5.de mang k* nat-p mrr1 olib-sac wmh1 ph-ac phos ptel gk rad-br bg (non:rad-met) spong fd4.de *Sulph* k* ther dw tritic-vg fd5.de [arg-n stj2 calc-sil stj2 ferr-sil stj2 heroin sdj2 kali-sil stj2 mag-sil stj2 mang-sil stj2 nat-sil stj2 sil stj2 sil-met stj2 spect dfg1]
- **drunkenness**; during: lach gl1.fr•
- **solving** important questions of the day: acon gl•

CLARITY; about: sanguis-s hrn2•

CLASSROOM: | **turned** out of: lac-h sk4•

CLEANING: aids nl2• anthraq rly4• dulc fd4.de hydrog srj2• lac-f wza1• nauf-helv-li elm2• olib-sac wmh1 positr nl2• [heroin sdj2 tax jsj7]
- **everything**: carc az1.de•
- **spilled** milk: lac-leo hrn2•

CLEANLINESS: positr nl2•

CLIFF:
- **edge** of a; he is at the: lac-h sk4•
- **standing** on a: *Agath-a* nl2• arizon-l nl2•

CLIMBING: *(↗Declivities)* *Agath-a* nl2• arizon-l nl2• brom k* dulc fd4.de falco-pe nl2• hyper kola stb3• loxo-recl knl4• mur-ac myos-a rly4• *Positr* nl2• rhus-t spong fd4.de tung-met bdx1• vanil fd5.de verat a2
- **bus** steps: *(↗Bus)* androc srj1•
- **double**-helix staircase; a: plut-n srj7•
- **exerting**: rhus-t c1
- **falling**; and: loxo-recl knl4•
- **high** fence with ease: coca-c sk4•
- **ladders**: androc srj1• nept-m lsd2.fr
  - **broken** ladder; a: crot-c sk4•
  - **tall** ladders: maias-l hrn2•
- **manure**; over piles of: maias-l hrn2•
- **mountains**; in the: kola stb3• vanil fd5.de
- **obstructed** | **snow**; by: plut-n srj7•
- **tree** to escape flood; into a: am-m a1

CLOSET: *(↗Excrements)*
- **being** on: *(↗Excrements)* musca-d szs1 ozone sde2• phasco-ci rbp2 polys sk4• positr nl2• psor a1 tung-met bdx1• [spect dfg1]
- **dirty**: *(↗Dirty)* ozone sde2•
- **sitting** on: ozone sde2•
  - **opens** constantly; door: ozone sde2•

CLOTHES: adam srj5• melal-alt gya4 [alumin-s stj2 lith-s stj2 sulph stj2]
- **blue**; dark: bros-gau mrc1
- **brightly** colored: hippoc-k szs2
- **changing** clothes in public: hippoc-k szs2
- **coat** | **bright** pink fuzzy: galeoc-c-h gms1•
- **hidden** her clothes; someone has: bamb-a stb2.de• lac-leo hrn2•
- **inappropriate**: [buteo-j sej6]
- **large** enough to grow into: positr nl2•
- **make** up; did not wish to: mag-c a1
- **red** dress: musca-d szs1
- **underwear**: galla-q-r nl2•
  - **unclean**: marb-w es1•

Clothes: ...
- **wearing** many layers of: hydrog srj2•

COBWEBS: galla-q-r nl2•

COCCINELLA (See Ladybugs)

COCKROACHES: *(↗Beetles; Bugs; Insects)*
- **swarming** out of a little hole in the ground: dioxi rbp6
- **trousers**; in her: lac-cp sk4•

COCOON: rhus-g tmo3•
- **propelled** from: rhus-g tmo3•

CODES: aids nl2•
- **identification** codes | **back**; worn on: plut-n srj7•

COFFINS: *(↗Funerals; Graves)* bomb-pr mlk9.de brom k* crot-c wn form a1 ignis-alc es2• lipp a1 merc-i-f k* symph fd3.de• [tax jsj7]
- **unknown** corpse; with an: *(↗Dead bodies)* gink-b sbd1• lac-v-f c1

COITION: *(↗Amorous; Sexual)* am-c gt am-m j5.de bamb-a stb2.de• bit-ar wht1• borx j5.de* bros-gau mrc1 chir-fl gya2 corn-a c1 falco-pe nl2• ind a1 iod a1 kali-s fd4.de lac-ac kr1* lyc j5.de maias-l hrn2• nat-m fr nat-p a plat hr1* plut-n srj7• polym bg ruta fd4.de sacch-a fd2.de• sanguis-s hrn2• sil j5.de* sul-ac h2* sumb a* thuj j5.de tritic-vg fd5.de tung-met bdx1• vanil fd5.de *Zinc-pic* sf1.de
- **aversion** to: positr nl2•
- **desire** for, of: sel a
- **erections** without emission: lac-ac kr1 pert-vc vk9
- **forced**: arizon-l nl2• falco-pe nl2•
  - **dangerous**; with a man known to be: arizon-l nl2•
- **girlfriend** who turns into a man; with: bit-ar wht1•
- **observed**: lac-e hrn2•
- **pollution**; without: pert-vc vk9
- **presence** of others; in the: *Plut-n* srj7•
- **stranger** preventing the act; entrance of: nat-p a1
- **unsuccessful**: ind a1* iod a1* [bar-i stj2 merc-i-f stj2]
- **urinating** during coition: kreos ry1 puls ry1
- **waking** up; without: pert-vc vk9

COLLEGE:
- **campus**: helodr-cal knl2•
- **colorful**: polys sk4•

COLORED: *(↗Fantastic)* adam srj5• bamb-a stb2.de• bros-gau mrc1 coca-c sk4• coli rly4• cystein-l rly4• cyt-l sp falco-pe nl2• gink-b sbd1• hydrog srj2• *Kola* stb3• lac-del hrn2• nat-m jsa nat-ox rly4• neon srj5• ozone sde2• pot-e rly4• psil dx1 ruta fd4.de sacch-a fd2.de• saroth mg1.de* suis-pan rly4• sulph jsa thiam rly4• tung-met bdx1• [buteo-j sej6 tax jsj7]
- **beige**: ozone sde2•
- **black**: helo-s rwt2• ozone sde2•
  - **white**; and: hippoc-k szs2
- **blue**: ara-maca sej7• arist-cl rbp3• ozone sde2• til ban1• [buteo-j sej6]
- **bright**: ara-maca sej7•
- **exaggerated** colors and proportions: hippoc-k szs2 lac-del hrn2•
- **green**: apeir-s mlk9.de irid-met srj5• *Lac-d* sk4• neon srj5• ozone sde2• til ban1•
- **orange**: androc srj1• arizon-l nl2• chir-fl gya2 coca-c sk4•
- **purple**: galla-q-r nl2• lac-leo hrn2•
- **red**: androc srj1• ara-maca sej7• helo-s rwt2• phasco-ci rbp2 [nicc-met stj2 nicc-s stj2]
- **vivid** (See bright)
- **white**: helo-s rwt2• hippoc-k szs2 ozone sde2• positr nl2• rad-br sze8• sanguis-s hrn2•
- **yellow**: androc srj1• chir-fl gya2 galla-q-r nl2• helo-s rwt2• phasco-ci rbp2 til ban1• [cadm-met stj2]

COMEDY: choc srj3• sol-t-ae a1

COMET: | **earth**; hurtling toward: plut-n srj7• tritic-vg fd5.de

COMICAL: *(↗Grotesque; Joyous; Laughing; Ludicrous)* choc srj3• *Glon* lach j5.de plut-n srj7• *Sulph* tritic-vg fd5.de
- **heads** with comical expression; seeing multitudes of: glon gt
- **laughter**; with loud: sulph gt

COMMUNE: nept-m lsd2.fr

Dreams

- **country**; in the: phasco-ci rbp2
- **living** in: galeoc-c-h gms1•

COMPANIES, of (See People - companies)

COMPETITION: chir-fl gya2 lac-e hrn2• lac-lup hrn2•

COMPLAINING; of: marb-w es•

COMPLICATED and containing its explanation; dream is: *(↗Lucid - revealing)* asc-t a1

COMPLIMENTS: falco-pe nl2•

COMPUTERS: choc srj3•
- **broken**: lac-loxod-a hrn2•

CONCILIATION: bamb-a stb2.de•

CONCRETE; things made of: corv-cor bdg•
- **blocks**, slabs, walls: corv-cor bdg•

CONFERENCE: bros-gau mrc1

CONFIDENCE; breach of: lac-e hrn2•

CONFIDENCE:
- **increased** | **done**; to get things: lac-e hrn2•

CONFIDENT and assertive, she is: adam srj5• dream-p sdj1• falco-pe nl2• nept-m lsd2.fr

CONFLAGRATION (See Fire - conflagration)

CONFUSED: *(↗Disconnected)* *Acon* k* (non:agar slp) agar-ph a1* agath-a nl2• aloe *Alum* k* alum-sil k2 am-c ammc anag androc srj1• ang b2.de* ant-t apis arg-n asc-t kr1 bamb-a stb2.de• bar-act a1 bar-c k* bart a1 bism brach bruc j5.de *Bry* k* cadm-s kr1 calad *Calc* calc-act a1 calc-f calc-sil k2 camph *Cann-s* k* canth k* carb-an carl caust k* cedr cench k2 *Chel* *Chin* k* chinin-s chir-fl gya2 choc srj3• *Cic* k* cina b2.de* clem (non:coff slp) coff-t a1* coloc con *Croc* k* *Cupr-act* kr1 cycl cypra-eg sde6.de• cystein-l rly4• cyt-l mg1.de dig digin a1 digox a1 *Dulc* k* equis-h erig ery-a eug j5.de* euph k* euphr eupi falco-pe nl2• *Ferr* ferr-i ferr-ma j5.de ferr-p gast a1 *Glon* k* granit-m es1• grat j5.de *Hell* k* hydr hydr-ac bro1 hydrog srj2• hyper *Ign* k* ina-i mlk9.de iod iodof kr1 *Kali-br* kali-cy a1 kiss a1 kola stb3• lac-h htj1• laur k* led k* lina a1 *Lyc* k* *Lyss* kr1 m-arct b2.de* m-aust b2.de* mag-c k* mag-s mang k* *Menis* a1 mez k* nat-ar *Nat-c* k* *Nat-m* nat-p nat-sil fd3.de• nicc nit-ac *Nux-v* pert-vc vk9 petr k* petr-ra shn4• phos k* pip-m br1 plat k* plb b2.de* podo c1* **Puls** k* puls-n a1 rumx ruta k* *Sabad* k* sabin k* sanguis-s hrn2• sel senec *Sep* *Sil* k* sin-a a1 sol-t-ae a1 spig k* spirae a1 *Stann* k* stram sul-i *Sulph* k* thuj k* til tritic-vg fd5.de valer k* vanil fd5.de verat k* wildb a1 [heroin sdj2]
- **morning**: chinin-s a1 mag-c a
- **afternoon**:
  - **14** h: sulph a1
  - **siesta**; during: eug kr1 plat h2
- **night**:
  - **midnight** | **after**: chin
- **awake**; half: nicc a
- **being** confused; of: [heroin sdj2]
- **broken**: cadm-s kr1
- **falling** asleep, on: nat-c h2
- **prostatitis**; in: *Sel* kr1
- **sexual** identity; about (See Sexual identity)
- **sleep**; during restless: *Sep* kr1
- **vivid**: *Ruta* kr1
- **walking**:
  - **unknown** streets; in: kola stb3• ozone sde2•
  - **snow**; obstructed by piles of: *(↗Snow - wading)* ozone sde2•

CONNECTED: acon a1 am-c h2* ammc a1 ars a1 calc a1 carl a1 coloc a1 *Ign* a1 lyc a1 nat-m a1 petr a1 plan a1 staph b7.de*

CONNECTED WITH OTHERS; being: [buteo-j sej6]

CONSCIOUS (See SLEEP - Dreaming - awake)

CONSOLING:
- **relatives**: | **dead** person; of: dendr-pol sk4•

CONSPIRACIES: bros-gau mrc1 mosch a1 ped a1 podo fd3.de•

CONSTRICTED, as if the abdomen was (See Abdomen - constricted)

CONSTRUCTING; about: helo-s rwt2•

CONTAMINATION: melal-alt gya4 [heroin sdj2]

CONTEMPT: tarent a1

CONTINUATION: *(↗Persistent)*
- **dreams**, of:
  - **sleep**; former dream is continued on going to: anthraq rly4• ars bac bn calad carl kl chir-fl gya2 chord-umb rly4• gink-b sbd1• hydrog srj2• lam j5.de nat-c nat-m j5.de nit-ac h2* petr j5.de
  - **waking**, after: acon b2.de* all-s am-c st anac b2.de* ant-c dx1 arg-met arn b2.de* bry b2.de* calad gt calc k* carl a1 caust st *Chin* k* euph b2.de* graph b2.de* ign k* lach st led st *Lyc* merc b2.de* nat-c k* *Nat-m* k* nit-ac st phos st pot-e rly4• *Psor* puls b2.de* sep b2.de* sil b2.de* sulph st zinc k*
- **ideas**; of former: ant-t k* asaf k* ign k* m-aust b2.de* puls k* rhus-t

CONTINUOUS: *(↗Persistent)* anac j5.de bapt a1 bar-c j5.de bros-gau mrc1 echi bg indol ah mosch j5.de nat-s j5.de *Phos* j5.de plat j5.de rhus-g tmo3• sabin j5.de xan bg

CONTRABAND (See Smuggled)

CONTRADICTORY to his intentions; actions are: *(↗MIND - Contradictory - actions)* bamb-a stb2.de•

CONVERSATIONS: *(↗Entertainment; Talking)* [tax jsj7]
- **carries** on; he: cham h1
  - **sister**, though she lives far away; with: germ-met srj5•
- **dead** people; with (See Dead; of - talking)
- **ending**; never: ozone sde2•
  - **forgetting** people that are waiting for her: ozone sde2•
- **happy** conversation; quarrel changing into (See Quarrels - happy)
- **previous** day; of: jatr-c a1 nat-c j5.de
- **women**; with: cedr j5.de spong fd4.de

CONVULSIONS: *(↗Disease)* calc-s kr1*

COOKING: *(↗Eating; Food)* arizon-l nl2• bros-gau mrc1 canth j5.de dream-p sdj1• dulc fd4.de falco-pe nl2• *Galeoc-c-h* gms1• kola stb3• lac-loxod-a hrn2• melal-alt gya4 pant-ac rly4• ruta fd4.de [heroin sdj2]
- **learning**: stront-c sk4•
- **meat**: falco-pe nl2• [heroin sdj2]
- **not** getting the cooking ready: am-m a1
- **soup**, not enough and without cups: ozone sde2•

COOPERATING: | **complaining** neighbor; with: dendr-pol sk4•

COPYING: | **others**: plut-n srj7•

CORONATION: upa a1

CORPSES (See Dead bodies)

CORRIDORS: galla-q-r nl2•
- **narrow**: galla-q-r nl2•

CORRUPTION: musca-d szs1

COTTAGE; small, dirty, bare: coca-c sk4•

COUGH: *(↗Disease)* eupi

COUNTERCLOCKWISE motion: plut-n srj7•

COUNTRY: asc-t a1 thiam rly4•
- **beautiful**: *(↗Beautiful; Earth - beautiful; Regions)* agath-a nl2• dream-p sdj1• melal-alt gya4 ol-an a1 podo fd3.de• rumx a taosc iwa1•
- **far** off: sil h2
- **foreign**: *(↗Journeys)* aids nl2• bros-gau mrc1 corian-s knl6• helo-s rwt2• ind kr1 kola stb3• loxo-recl knl4• melal-alt gya4 ozone sde2• pieri-b mlk9.de plat j5.de* plut-n srj7• positr nl2• ruta fd4.de sil j5.de sin-a a1* spong fd4.de tritic-vg fd5.de tung-met bdx1• vanil fd5.de
  - **massage**; doing foot: galeoc-c-h gms1•
- **native** country: ant-c h2* gink-b sbd1• lach j5.de* mur-ac h2* nicc-met sk4• rhus-g tmo3• thiam rly4•

- **open** country (See Walking - country)

COUPLE; old loving: coca-c sk4•

COURT; judicial: lac-cp sk4•
- **before** a court; of standing: bamb-a stb2.de•

COUSIN: *(↗Family)* *Lac-h* sk4• lac-lup hrn2•
- **disease**: lac-h sk4•
- **emaciated**: lac-h sk4•
- **handicapped** | **helping**; she was: lac-h sk4•
- **murdered**; being: lac-h sk4•
- **reassuring** frightened cousin: lac-h sk4•
- **scolding**; she is: lac-h sk4•
- **teaching** | **younger** cousins: lac-h sk4•

COWS: dulc fd4.de [hydrog stj2]
- **dying**: hydrog srj2•
- **keep** cow away; trying to | **grandmother**; from his old: nicc-met sk4•

CRASH (See Accidents)

CRAZY; being (See Insane)

CREDIT:
- **deserved**; she | **someone** else; being given to: stront-c sk4•

CRIME: *(↗Defamation; Guilt; Wrong)* agath-a nl2• apeir-s mlk9.de carbn-s a1 cocc j5.de helodr-cal knl2• hura hydrog srj2*• lac-loxod-a hrn2• nat-m nat-s nit-ac petr j5.de rumx ruta fd4.de [gal-met stj2]
- **accused** wrongfully of crime, being (See Accusations - crime; Murder)
- **acquits** him of a crime; conscience: thuj a1*
- **answer**; for which he is held to: nat-m a
- **committing** a crime: *(↗Wrong - he)* hydrog srj2•
  - **he** had committed a crime: apeir-s mlk9.de bros-gau mrc1 cocc k* germ-met srj5• nat-s nat-sil fd3.de• nit-ac a1 petr petr-ra shn4•
    - **serial** killer looking for an alibi: plut-n srj7•
- **concealment** of: lac-loxod-a hrn2•

CRIMINALS, of: haliae-lc srj5• loxo-recl knl4• melal-alt gya4 musca-d szs1 podo fd3.de• thioc-ac rly4•

CRIPPLED man: *(↗Disabled; People - deformed)*
- **carried** on his back: lac-d sk4•

CRITICAL: lac-lup hrn2•

CRITICIZED; being: galeoc-c-h gms1• toxi mtf2•

CROCODILES: dendr-pol sk4• led mp1• sedi a1
- **sneezing**; he drives the crocodiles away by: sedi a1

CRONES: musca-d szs1

CROSSROADS: adam srj5• ulm-c jsj8• [spect dfg1]

CROWDS (See People - crowds)

CRUELTY: *(↗Ill-treatment; Mutilation; Violence)* cub a1 falco-pe nl2• *Ign* j5.de kola stb3• lac-h sze9• lil-t a1 nat-m nux-v oxal-a rly4• plut-n srj7• rob a1 sel k* sil stann k* tung-met bdx1•
- **anger**; without: lil-t a
- **animals**, to: falco-pe nl2•

CRUSHED, being: *(↗Cellar; Cellar - walls)* *Sulph* tung-met bdx1•
- **people** being crushed: choc srj3•

CRYPT: musca-d szs1

CRYSTALS: aids nl2• positr nl2•
- **trapped** inside a crystal; being: *(↗Trap - being)* aids nl2•

CURIOUS; of being: lac-leo hrn2•

CURIOUS dream: *(↗Strange)* lach hr1 paeon hs1 pip-m a1*

CURSING: caj a

CURTAINS: galla-q-r nl2•
- **blowing** upwards: galla-q-r nl2•
- **dark**: galla-q-r nl2•
- **separation**; making a: galla-q-r nl2•

CUT, being: *(↗Knives)* falco-pe nl2• frax a1 guaj nat-s a1 positr nl2•
- **pieces**; to: lil-s a1
- **sliced** through to get at the stuff inside her: positr nl2•
- **stigmata**: positr nl2•

CUTTING: *(↗Head - cut)* androc srj1• calc-f chin falco-pe nl2• fuma-ac rly4• hura mag-m nat-c nicc op ribo rly4• tung-met bdx1•
- **others**; cutting or mutilating: ant-c gt
- **parts** of body (See Body; parts)
- **person** cut up: merc-sul tung-met bdx1•
- **trying** to cut off finger: nicc a
- **woman** for salting, cutting up: calc-f

CYLINDERS: adam srj5•

DAISIES: polys sk4•

DANCING: *(↗Balls; Entertainment; MIND - Dancing)* agath-a nl2• dendr-pol sk4• dulc fd4.de falco-pe nl2• gamb kola stb3• mag-c k* mag-m k* mag-s myos-a rly4• pert-vc vk9 polys sk4• ruta fd4.de sanguis-s hrn2• spong fd4.de thioc-ac rly4• zing [heroin sdj2]
- **circle**; in a: [heroin sdj2]
- **eccentric** dance steps; following: coca-c sk4•
- **spiral**; in a: falco-pe nl2•
- **tango**; a: rosm lgb1
  - **gypsies**; with two: *(↗Gypsies)* rosm lgb1
    - **fear** of being robbed by them; with: rosm lgb1

DANGER: *(↗Hiding - danger; Threatened; MIND - Fear - danger)* adam srj5• agath-a nl2• aids nl2• aloe am-c anac k* arizon-l nl2• *Ars* ars-met a1* bell bomb-chr mlk9.de calc-f calc-p *Cann-i* k* carbn-dox knl3• carbn-s carc fd2.de• chin coca-c sk4• con *Crot-c* sk4• dulc fd4.de galeoc-c-h gms1• galla-q-r nl2• graph ham fd3.de• *Hep* hydrog srj2*• indg j5.de iod k* kali-bi kali-c kali-i kali-n k* kali-s fd4.de *Kola* stb3• *Lac-d* sk4• lac-del hrn2• *Lac-leo* sk4• lac-lup hrn2• *Lach* limen-b-c mlk9.de linu-c a1 lyc macro a1 mag-c mag-s maias-l hrn2• mang nat-c k* nat-s j5.de nicc-met sk4• nux-v oci-sa sk4• ozone sde2• petr-ra shn4• phos plut-n srj7• podo fd3.de• polys sk4• *Positr* nl2• psor k* puls *Pycnop-sa* mrz1 ran-b k* rumx ruta fd4.de sacch-a fd2.de• sal-fr sle1• sanguis-s hrn2• sin-a a1 spong fd4.de *Staph* b7a.de sul-ac h2* sulph symph fd3.de• taosc iwa1• tarent thuj k* toxi mtf2• tritic-vg fd5.de *Tung-met* bdx1• vanil fd5.de [bar-i stj2 *Bell-p-sp* dcm1 buteo-j sej6 heroin sdj2 lith-i stj2 mang-i stj2 mang-m stj2 mang-met stj2 mang-s stj2 merc-i-f stj2 zinc-i stj2]
- **amusement** park rides; dangerous: maias-l hrn2•
- **animals**; from (See Animals - dangerous)
- **boat** capsizing: crot-c sk4•
- **children**; to (See Children - danger)
- **cry** out; can not: aloe kr1
- **death**, of: agath-a nl2• bell b4.de* carc fd2.de• dulc fd4.de lac-h sk4• lac-leo sk4• lac-lup hrn2• mag-m j5.de mang a1 merc-c b4a.de oci-sa sk4• plut-n srj7• ran-b j5.de sul-ac b4.de* sulph b4.de* thuj b4.de*
- **drowning**, of (See Drowning - danger)
- **electric** cable in water; of: maias-l hrn2•
- **escaping** from a danger: dulc fd4.de hep hippoc-k szs2 kali-s fd4.de petr-ra shn4• ruta fd4.de spong fd4.de taosc iwa1• tritic-vg fd5.de tung-met bdx1•
  - **fruitless** efforts to escape: dulc fd4.de ind a1*
- **falling**, of (See Falling - danger)
- **family**; of his: lac-h sk4•
- **fear** without: agath-a nl2• positr nl2•
- **fire**, from (See Fire - danger)
- **friends** in danger: nicc-met sk4•
- **impending** danger: *(↗Bombs - bomb)* calc-f a1* ind vml3• lac-lup hrn2• nat-c a1 vanil fd5.de
- **lying** on left side: thuj k*
- **murder**; of: oci-sa sk4•
- **personal** danger: til a1
- **protecting** others from: nicc-met sk4•
- **relatives** in danger: nicc-met sk4•
- **sense** of danger lacking: galla-q-r nl2• nept-m lsd2.fr
- **threatened** by gang of teenage drug abusers (See Threatened)
- **travelling**; while: plut-n srj7•
- **unnoticed** by authority figures: limen-b-c hrn2•
- **want**; and: am-c kr1

Dreams

- **water**: *(↗Flood; Water)*
  - **in** water; from danger (See Water - danger - in)
  - **on** the water: ran-b c1
- **wind**; from: fic-m gya1

DARKNESS: *(↗MIND - Darkness - agg.; MIND - Light - desire)* ars k* aur k* choc srj3• dulc fd4.de lac-h sze9• maias-l hrn2• neon srj5• nept-m lsd2.fr rhus-g tmo3• ruta fd4.de spong fd4.de taosc iwa1• tritic-vg fd5.de [aur-m stj2 aur-s stj2 tax jsj7]

DAUGHTER: *(↗Family)* lac-lup hrn2• nept-m lsd2.fr [tax jsj7]
- **criminal**; is: galeoc-c-h gms1•
- **apoplectic** fit; daughter has an: *(↗Disease)* nat-s
- **struck** with paralysis: nat-s a1
- **thief** and he is agonized over turning her in; that his daughter is a: plut-n srj7•
- **wheelchair**; in a | **proving** remedy; has taken a: plut-n srj7•
- **young**; when: galeoc-c-h gms1•

DEAD BODIES: *(↗Coffins - unknown; Skeletons)* agath-a nl2• alum j alumn am-c **Anac** k* arn j aur bar-c h2* bit-ar wht1• bomb-pr mlk9.de brom b4a.de* bros-gau mrc1 bry j5.de *Calc Calc-sil* cann-i kr1* cann-s carb-ac caust j *Chel* k* cocc j con j corv-cor bdg• *Crot-c* k* crot-h k2 dirc dulc fd4.de elaps fl-ac j fum rly1*• gard-j vlr2• gink-b jl* granit-m es1• graph j grat j5.de hura hydr-ac j5.de iod j5.de iris jac-c kali-c j5.de kali-m ccrh1• *Kola* stb3• lac-h sze9• lac-v a1 laur j5.de loxo-recl knl4• mag-c j mag-m mag-s merc moni rfm1• nat-c nat-p neon srj5• nit-ac oci-sa sk4• ozone sde2• ped a peti a1 petr-ra shn4• ph-ac j5.de phos h2 plat j plut-n srj7• ran-s k* rumx sars j sil j sinus rly4• sol-t-ae sul-ac j sulph b4a.de* syc bka1*• tarent *Thuj* tritic-vg fd5.de vanil fd5.de verb zinc [heroin sdj2 spect dfg1]
- **alive** after funeral; coming: allox sp1
- **arms** cut off; with: hura a
- **bed** with her; put in: ozone sde2•
- **children**; of:
  - **burned**: positr nl2•
  - **infants**: limen-b-c hrn2•
- **churchyard**; finding dead child in a: mag-s a1
- **dissecting** dead bodies (See Dissecting - dead)
- **embracing**: elaps al*
- **jumped** from dissecting table: chel a
- **knife** into wounds of; digging: elaps a
- **mutilated** bodies: hura a1
- **returning** to life: bomb-chr mlk9.de petr-ra shn4• rumx a1 tritic-vg fd5.de
- **searching** for: maias-l hrn2•
- **shroud**; putting dead body in: elaps a1*
- **skin** taken from: mag-m a1
- **sleeping** on left side; when: thuj kr1
- **smell** of dead bodies: calc crot-h k2 tritic-vg fd5.de

DEAD; of the: alum b2.de* am-c b2.de* *Anac* k* ange-s jl ant-c bg2 *Arg-n* arge-pl rwt5• arizon-l nl2• *Arn* k* **Ars** k* ars-i ars-s-f k2 aur k* aur-ar k2 aur-s k2 bar-act a1 bar-c k* *Brom* b4a.de bry k* calad *Calc* k* calc-act a1 calc-ar calc-f calc-i k2 *Calc-sil* cann-i cann-xyz bg2* carbn-s caust cench k* *Chel* k1 chin-b k1 coca a1 cocc b2.de* cod a1 con k* convo-d a1 croc b7.de *Crot-h* k* culx k2* elaps k* ferr ferr-i k2 goss st *Graph* k* hydrog srj2• iod k* iris kali-ar *Kali-c* k* kali-n j5.de kali-s fd4.de kali-sil k2 lac-lup hrn2• laur k* lepi a1 lil-t c1 lipp a1 *Lyc* k* m-arct b2.de **Mag-c** k* mag-m k* mag-s *Med* k* merc-c b4a.de mur-ac b2.de* nat-c j5.de* nat-p a1* nat-s j5.de nicc j5.de nit-ac b2.de* nux-v j5.de ol-an ozone sde2• paull a1 ph-ac k* *Phos* k* plat k* plumbg a1 podo fd3.de• ran-b b2.de* ran-s b2.de* rat j5.de rauw sp1 rheum b2.de* ruta fd4.de saroth mg1.de* sars b2.de* sil k* sin-a a1* sin-n spong b2.de* sul-ac k* sul-i k2 *Sulph* k* syc pte1• symph fd3.de• thres-a sze7• **Thuj** k* tung-met bdx1• vanil fd5.de verb b2.de* vip-a jl zinc b2.de* [heroin sdj2]
- **children**: arge-pl rwt5• granit-m es1• lac-h htj1*• limen-b-c hrn2• suis-pan rly4• vanil fd5.de
  - **embolism**; being responsible for the death of one's child by causing an: limen-b-c hrn2•
  - **infants**: cench k2 limen-b-c hrn2* oci-sa sk4•
  - **newborns**: adam srj5•
- **friends**: arg-n k* cedr a1 coca a1 con h2 ferr k* gard-j vlr2• musca-d szs1 nat-c vanil fd5.de [ant-m stj2 ferr-f stj2 ferr-lac stj2 ferr-n stj2 ferr-sil stj2]
  - **hanging** by his legs; a dead friend: coca a1

Dead; of the – **friends**: ...
  - **long** deceased: *Arg-n* k* cedr a1 coca a1 con h2 ferr *Lac-lup* hrn2• nat-c vanil fd5.de
  - **talking** with deceased friends: *(↗talking)* corv-cor bdg1• *Lac-lup* hrn2• lepi a1* sep ggj thuj a1
- **menses**, during: goss st
- **relatives**: bros-gau mrc1 caust h2 coca-c sk4• echi c1 ferr fl-ac hippoc-k szs2 hydrog srj2• kali-c h2 kali-s fd4.de lac-h sk4• lac-loxod-a hrn2• limen-b-c hrn2* mag-c mag-s musca-d szs1 nicc-met sk4• olib-sac wmh1 plac-s rly4• rheum ruta fd4.de sars spong fd4.de tax-br oss1• tung-met bdx1• vanil fd5.de [mag-lac stj2 mag-met stj2 mag-sil stj2 spect dfg1 temp elm1]
  - **beloved**: limen-b-c hrn2•
  - **talking** with dead relatives: *(↗talking)* calc-sil sk2•
- **sleeping** on back, while: am
  - **left** side, on the: *Thuj* k*
- **talking** with dead people: *(↗friends - talking; relatives - talking)* lepi a1*
- **wife**: aran-ix mg1.de
- **woman** coming back to life; dead: hydrog srj2•

DEATH: allox tpw3* alum alum-p k2 alum-sil k2 alumn am-c anac c1 arn k* ars k* ars-s-f k2 aur k* aur-ar k2 aur-br vh1 aur-s k2* *Bit-ar* wht1• brom k* *Calc* k* calc-f calc-sil k2 camph cann-i bro1 carbn-s k2 carc gk6 castm chel chin k* chin-b kr1* (non:chinin-ar slp) cocc (non:coff slp) coff-t slp con cortico sp1 corv-cor bdg• crot-c bro1 crot-h k2* dendr-pol sk4• dulc fd4.de elaps bro1 ferr-i fl-ac galla-q-r nl2• ger-i rly4• grat haliae-lc srj5• hura hydr-ac c1 *Hydrog* srj2• kali-ar kali-c kali-chl kali-m k2 kali-n kali-s k* kali-sil k2 kola stb3• **Lach** k* luna c1 lyc mag-m mag-s maias-l hrn2• merc-c nat-m nat-s j5.de neon srj5• nicc j5.de nit-ac k* oxal-a rly4• ozone sde2• paeon plan plat j5.de* plut-n srj7• ran-s bro1 raph rat rauw sp1 rheum j5.de rhus-v ruta fd4.de saroth sp1 sil sin-a svr6 sol-mm a1 spong a1 suis-pan rly4• *Sulph* tarent thuj j5.de* tritic-vg fd5.de vanil fd5.de ven-m jl* [am-br stj2 ant-c stj2 ant-met stj2 aur-m stj2 bar-br stj2 bar-i stj2 bell-p-sp dcm1 ferr stj2 ferr-f stj2 mang-i stj2 merc-i-f stj2 nicc-met stj2 nicc-s stj2 tax jsj7 zinc-i stj2]
- **morning**: calc a1
- **acquaintance**; of: nicc a
- **afterlife**; and the: plut-n srj7•
- **approaching**: coli gmj1 kali-c kali-chl ruta fd4.de sil *Sulph* tab
- **brother**, of (See relatives - brother)
- **dying**: am-c bg2 cortico tpw7 lac-del hrn2• ozone sde2• plut-n srj7•
  - **he** has to die: arn kr1 lach k2 nit-ac sil
  - **he** is: *(↗Funerals)* am-c arn bov j5.de brom camph carc sde• chel cocc j5.de cortico tpw7* dream-p sdj1• dulc fl-ac gard-j vlr2• gels c1 ignis-alc es2• kali-chl j5.de prot ptj• rauw sp1 rhus-g tmo3• sulph *Thuj* tritic-vg fd5.de vanil fd5.de [buteo-j sej6]
    - **removal** of the corpse from the house; and orders the rapid: fl-ac rauw sp
    - **shots** in abdomen; with two: coli gmj1
  - **man** suckling at her breast; dying: sal-fr sle1•
  - **teammates** in a airplane crash: *(↗Airplanes - crash)* lac-leo hrn2•
- **family**, in (See relatives)
- **father**; of (See relatives - father)
- **fear** of death; losing the: irid-met srj5•
- **friend**, of a: allox tpw3* aster sze10• bamb-a stb2.de• (non:coff slp) coff-t a1* coli gmj1 con cortico jl* fl-ac gard-j vlr2• kali-n kola stb3• lac-h sk4• lach a1 nicc oxal-a rly4• petr-ra shn4• ruta fd4.de vanil fd5.de [chlor stj2]
- **husband**, of her (See relatives - husband)
- **lying** on the left side, while: thuj j5.de*
- **mother**; of (See relatives - mother)
- **parents** (See relatives - parents)
- **pets**; of dead: positr nl2•
- **preachers**; of religious: bung-fa mtf
- **pope**; of: *Rhus-g* tmo3•
- **relatives**; of: alumn aran-ix jl *Calc-f* castm chin chlam-tr bcx2• choc srj3• elaps gk fl-ac gard-j vlr2• ger-i rly4• gink-b sbd1• grat hydrog srj2• lac-h htj1• levo jl loxo-recl knl4• mag-s mur-ac nicc paeon *Pegan-ha* tpi1• pitu-a vml2• plan plat plut-n srj7• sacch-a fd2.de• stront-c sk4• tritic-vg fd5.de vanil fd5.de [*Calc-sil* stj2 chlor stj2 tax jsj7]
  - **brother**; of his: lac-d sk4• plan a1*

- **relatives**; of: ...
  - **daughter**; of his little: calc-f a1
  - **father**; of his: alumn a1* hydrog srj2• kola stb3• mag-s a1 plut-n srj7• stront-c sk4• vanil fd5.de
    - **distant**; being: mag-s a1
  - **grandmother**; of: *Galeoc-c-h* gms1•
  - **husband**; of her: bung-fa mtf dream-p sdj1•
  - **long** deceased: galeoc-c-h gms1•
  - **mother**; of his: arizon-l nl2• chin a1 mag-c a1 mur-ac h2* oxal-a rly4• petr-ra shn4• plac-s rly4• suis-em rly4• tritic-vg fd5.de
  - **parents**; of: castm a1* coli gmj1
  - **sister**; of distant: gard-j vlr2• plat h2*
- **shadow** of death; about the: haliae-lc srj5•
- **teacher**; of her: bung-fa mtf
- **waking**; lasting after: alum a

DECADENT: | **being**: galeoc-c-h gms1•

DECAY: dream-p sdj1•

DECEIT: falco-pe nl2• lac-cp sk4• tritic-vg fd5.de vanil fd5.de
- **deceitful**; being: dendr-pol sk4•

DECEIVED; BEING: lac-cp sk4• stront-c sk4• ulm-c jsj8•

DECLIVITIES: *(↗Climbing)* anac j5.de dulc fd4.de ruta fd4.de tritic-vg fd5.de vanil fd5.de

DECOMPOSITION: musca-d szs1

DEER: *(↗Animals)* lac-lup hrn2•

DEFAMATION: *(↗Accusations; Accusations - crime; Crime)* mosch

DEFENDING: | **relatives**: dendr-pol sk4•

DEFIANT; being: agath-a nl2•

DELIBERATIONS: *Ign* kr1

DELIVERING a baby: choc srj3• granit-m es1• *Kola* stb3• neon srj5• symph fd3.de•

DEMONSTRATING: | **machine**; the operation of a: coca-c sk4•

DEPARTURE (See Away - go)

DERAILING (See Journeys - train - derailing)

DESCENDING escalators; unable to find way back up: brass-n-o srj5•

DESERT: kola stb3• sil j5.de
- **seashells** and cacti like seaweed: maias-l hrn2•

DESERTED; of being (See Forsaken)

DESIRED; being: | **man**; by a: lac-del hrn2•

DESPAIR: lac-lup hrn2• rad-br sze8•

DESSERTS: | **detail**; in great: loxo-recl knl4•

DESTINATION:
- **reaching** | **unable**: *(↗Unsuccessful)* cadm-met jl1 *Galeoc-c-h* gms1• hippoc-k szs2 petr-ra shn4• [tax jsj7]

DETECTIVE; she is a: haliae-lc srj5•

DEVILS: agath-a nl2• apis arg-met k* carc sde• cypra-eg sde6.de• kali-c lac-c *Moni* rfm1• nat-c nicc op gl1.fr• ozone sde2• petr-ra shn4• positr nl2• sin-a a1 sin-n [nicc-met stj2 nicc-s stj2 tax jsj7]
- **communication** with: pegan-ha tpi1•
- **cooking** babies on a volcano and eating them: ozone sde2•

DIAMONDS: aids nl2•

DIARRHEA: *(↗Disease)* allox tpw3* apis a1 helodr-cal knl2• psil ft1

DIED; someone (See Death)

DIET: oci-sa sk4•

DIFFICULTIES: *(↗Embarrassment; Failures; Unsuccessful)* **Am-m** anac ant-t k* **Ars** cann-s caps croc dream-p sdj1• fic-m gya1 gink-b sbd1• *Graph* *Mag-c* mag-m mur-ac nat-ar a1 *Phos* plat positr nl2• raph a1 rhus-t *Tung-met* bdx1• [tax jsj7]
- **bicycle**; while riding a (See Bicycle - difficult)
- **communication**; on: [bell-p-sp dcm1]
- **journeys**, on: *(↗Missing - train)* aids nl2• am-m a1 bros-gau mrc1 calc-p a1 falco-pe nl2• hippoc-k szs2 lac-e hrn2• mag-s a1 merc a1* mez a1 nat-c a1 petr-ra shn4• plut-n srj7• positr nl2• sal-fr sle1• [*Bell-p-sp* dcm1 heroin sdj2 spect dfg1]
- **work**; in his daily: am-m ptk1 ars ptk1 *Bry* ptk1 nux-v ptk1 puls ptk1 *Rhus-t* bla1*

DIGGING: positr nl2•

DINOSAURS: kola stb3•

DIRT: *(↗Disgusted - dirt; Water - dirty)* aids nl2• bros-gau mrc1 dulc fd4.de falco-pe nl2• galla-q-r nl2• kreos j5.de lac-d sk4• musca-d szs1 nat-sil fd3.de• olib-sac wmh1 polys sk4• positr nl2• prun j5.de ruta fd4.de sanguis-s hrn2• tritic-vg fd5.de tung-met bdx1• [sel stj2]
- **toothpaste** on the walls: ozone sde2•
- **wading** in dirt: iod j5.de

DIRTY: *(↗Closet - dirty)*
- **buildings**: aids nl2•
- **factories**: falco-pe nl2•
- **linen**: *(↗Disgusted - dirty)* dulc fd4.de kali-n a1 *Kreos* a1* ozone sde2•
  - **love** in dirty linen; couple making: ozone sde2•
- **place**: *(↗Places)* galla-q-r nl2•
  - **beautiful** view of the sea; with a: nicc-met sk4•
- **roads**: apis a1 olib-sac wmh1
- **table**: *(↗Writing - dirty)* prun k*
- **underwear** (See Clothes - underwear - unclean)

DISABLED people: *(↗Crippled; People - deformed)* helodr-cal knl2• positr nl2• [buteo-j sej6]

DISAGREEABLE (See Unpleasant)

DISAPPOINTMENTS: *(↗Exasperation; MIND - Ailments - love)* adam skp7• cann-s echi bg ign k* positr nl2• rumx taosc iwa1• ust

DISASTER: *(↗Accidents; Misfortune)* arge-pl rwt5• bros-gau mrc1 corv-cor bdg• dulc fd4.de lac-h htj1• pyrid rly4• sars symph fd3.de•
- **averted**; being: lac-h sk4•

DISCONNECTED: *(↗Confused)* agar *Apis* kr1 *Arn* cadm-s a1* chel chin cina cinnb coca crot-t equis-h grat guare a1 hir jl* ina-i mlk9.de lyc *Lyss* kr1 myris phos plan plat *Puls* ruta fd4.de sil sol-t-ae sulph [bell-p-sp dcm1]
- **4 h**, after: plan a
- **evening**, while napping: plat a
- **closing** eyes; on: lyc a
- **drowsiness**; during: guare a
- **sleep**; with disturbed: *Lyss* kr1

DISEASE: *(↗Abdomen - pain; Abdomen - ulcers; Aids; Arm - pain; Blind; being; Blisters; Blood; Body - swollen; Boils; Cancer; Cheek - swollen; Cholera; Convulsions; Cough; Daughter - apoplectic; Diarrhea; Doctors; Ears - lump; Emaciated; Epidemic; Epilepsy; Eruptions; Events - painful; Excrescences; Expectoration; Eyes - lids; Eyes - stitches; Face - abscesses; Face - pustules; Face - swollen; Fainting; Fever; Fingers - stiff; Foot - stitching; Hair - falling; Hands - burning; Headache; Hemorrhage; Hyperthyroidism; Injuries; Insane - becoming; Jaws - broken; Knee; Leper; Lethargy; Limbs - broken; Maxillary - pain; Miscarriage; Mother - ill; Nausea; Pain; Poisoned; Rabies; Rash; Sick people; Smallpox; Suffering; Suffocation; Teeth - breaking; Teeth - falling; Throat; Unconsciousness; Urinating - strangury; Vertigo; Warts; Wind colic; Worms - vomited; Wounded; Wounds)* aids nl2• am-c j5.de am-m k* anac k* anan apis asar k* bar-c borx k* both-ax tsm2 bros-gau mrc1 bry vh cadm-met gm1 *Calc* k* calc-act a1 calc-sil k2* castor-eq a1* caust cocc b2.de* con k* dros k* eupi fago graph hep k* kali-c k* kali-n kali-s k* kola stb3• *Kreos* k* lac-c lac-loxod-a hrn2• *Lyc* m-arct b2.de mag-c melal-alt gya4 meph nat-m bg2 nat-s **Nux-v** k* ozone sde2• peti a1 petr-ra shn4• phos k* podo fd3.de• positr nl2• prun rad-br sze8• rat ruta fd4.de sarr a sil k* squil b2.de* stront-c sk4• sulph sumb syph thiam rly4• tritic-vg fd5.de upa vanil fd5.de

Dreams

Disease: ...
ven-m jl* zinc b2.de* [ant-c stj2 ant-met stj2 chlor stj2 mang-m stj2 stront-m stj2 zinc-i stj2 zinc-m stj2 zinc-n stj2 zinc-p stj2]
- **contagious**: anan a1* sarr a1
- **family**; in the: peti a1
- **loathsome** disease: anac k* lac-h sk4• stront-c sk4•
- **own** disease, his: sumb a *Syph* kr1

DISGUISE: falco-pe nl2• [heroin sdj2]

DISGUSTED; being: *(↗Unpleasant; MIND - Disgust; MIND - Thoughts - disgusting)* aids nl2• aloe alumn am-c anac arg-met arist-m a1 borx a1 castn-v chel (non:chin slp) chin-b kr1* chr-ac kr1* coca-c sk4• con eupi a1* falco-pe nl2• hydrog srj2*• inul kali-n h2* kola stb3• *Kreos* lac-d sk4• lac-e hrn2• lac-h sk4• lac-loxod-a hrn2• lach a1 mag-m mag-s j5.de maias-l hrn2• mur-ac musca-d szs1 nat-m (non:nux-m k1) *Nux-v* k1 ozone sde2• phasco-ci rbp2 phos plan a1 *Polys* sk4• *Positr* nl2• *Puls* rheum a1 sil h2* sulph tung-met bdx1• zinc
- **morning**: inul a1
- **dirt**: *(↗Dirt)* kreos j5.de prun j5.de
- **dirty** linen: *(↗Dirty - linen)* kali-n a1 *Kreos* k1*
- **herself**; with: lac-h sk4•
- **smeared** with excrements (See Excrements - smeared)
- **soiling** himself with excrements: aloe castn-v iod zinc
- **wading** in dirt: iod j5.de

DISGUSTING: *(↗Unpleasant; MIND - Disgust; MIND - Thoughts - disgusting)* alet bg2 am-c b2.de* anac b2.de* chel b2.de* dulc fd4.de kreos b2.de* lach bg2* mag-m b2.de* merc bg2 mur-ac b2.de* nat-m b2.de* *Nux-v* b2.de* phos b2.de* puls b2.de* sulph b2.de* zinc b2.de*

DISORIENTED: lac-del hrn2•

DISPUTE: | **legal** | **poisoning** by toxins in paint; about: lac-del hrn2•
- **money**; about (See Money - disputing)

DISSECTED; being: gink-b sbd1•

DISSECTING:
- **dead** bodies: *(↗Autopsies)* cench k2 chel a1 fic-m gya1 iris lac-e hrn2• ped a1 petr-ra shn4• sang tung-met bdx1•
- **people**: cench k2

DISTANT THINGS: plb a1*
- **people**: sel a1*
- **things**; strange and distant: fl-ac a1 plat a1

DISTORTED:
- **everything** is: carl a1
- **images**: *Graph* h2*

DISTORTING everything: lac-del hrn2•

DISTURBING (See Unpleasant)

DIVIDED: | **two** parts; into: conch fkr1•

DIVING: fic-m gya1 sal-al blc1•
- **sea**; in the: nauf-helv-li elm2• [tax jsj7]

DIVORCED; of getting: | **abusive** husband; because of: [buteo-j sej6]

DOCTORS (= physicians): *(↗Disease; Sick people)* canna a1 dulc fd4.de falco-pe nl2• lac-h sze9• mang a1 tritic-vg fd5.de
- **consulting** | **succession**; many doctors in: dendr-pol sk4•
- **conversation** with his doctor: mang a1
- **neglectful**: polys sk4•
- **uterus** and ovaries on a board; drawing an: ozone sde2•

DOGS: *(↗Animals)* abrot agath-a nl2• aids nl2• am-c b4.de* apeir-s mlk9.de *Arn* k* bomb-chr mlk9.de calc carbn-dox knl3• cere-b a1 cina k2 crot-c sk4• dendr-pol sk4• dulc fd4.de falco-pe nl2• graph guar vml3• haliae-lc srj5• helodr-cal knl2• hippoc-k szs2 hyos b7.de* ina-i mlk9.de kali-s fd4.de lac-c mrr1 lac-del hrn2• lac-h sze9• lac-loxod-a hrn2• lac-lup hrn2• limen-b-c hrn2* lyc lyss maias-l hrn2• merc k* nux-v paull pieri-b mlk9.de pitu-a ft* positr nl2• puls querc-r svu1• rad-br sze8• ros-d wla1 rumx *Sil* spong fd4.de *Sulph* tritic-vg fd5.de vanil fd5.de verat zinc [spect dfg1]
- **bitten** by dogs; being: aids nl2• bomb-chr mlk9.de calc lyss med hu merc ozone sde2• *Sulph* verat k*

Dogs: ...
- **black**: aids nl2• arizon-l nl2• *Arn* bomb-chr mlk9.de musca-d szs1 puls h1* ros-d wla1 tub dx1
- **buttons** instead of eyes: hippoc-k szs2
- **clung** to him; as if many young: lyc h2
- **fins** and fish tails; with: plut-n srj7•
- **frightened** by a black dog: puls
- **harassed** by: dendr-pol sk4•
- **mad** dog: abrot rumx
  - **killing** a mad dog (See Killing - dog)
- **missing**: galeoc-c-h gms1•
- **multiple** heads; with: plut-n srj7•
- **problems**, a dog is telling her his: aids nl2•
- **puppies** | **chasing** cat: maias-l hrn2•
- **pursued** by dogs, being (See Pursued - dogs)
- **revive** suffocating dog: dendr-pol sk4•
- **turns** into a dog; she: irid-met srj5•
- **typhus**, in: *Arn* kr1

DOLPHINS: dendr-pol sk4• phasco-ci rbp2
- **riding** on: phasco-ci rbp2

DOMINOES: adam srj5•

DONKEY: ulm-c jsj8•

DOORS:
- **closing**: sal-fr sle1•
- **ill-fitting**: arizon-l nl2•
- **knocking** on doors; one is: arizon-l nl2• neon stj2*•

DOWN'S SYNDROME: rad-br sze8•
- **baby**; of a: neon srj5•

DOWSERS: galeoc-c-h gms1•

DRAGONS: kali-s fd4.de *Kola* stb3• olib-sac wmh1 op [titan stj2]

DREAMING, of: adam srj5• *Plut-n* srj7• sal-fr sle1• spong fd4.de
- **forgotten** and then remembered; dreams: sal-fr sle1•

DRESSING: falco-pe nl2•

DRESSING UP: lac-d sk4•
- **wedding**; for a: oci-sa sk4•

DRINKING: *(↗Carousing)* ars bro1 dros k* med k* nat-m bro1 phos bro1
- **impossible**: arist-m a1

DRIVING:
- **car**; a: aq-mar mgm• chlam-tr bcx2• choc srj3• des-ac rbp6 falco-pe nl2• helo-s rwt2• hydrog srj2• ina-i mlk9.de *Kola* stb3• loxo-recl knl4• ozone sde2• petr-ra shn4• vanil fd5.de
  - **busy** street; down a: coca-c sk4•
  - **detour**; led on a: des-ac rbp6
  - **fast**: falco-pe nl2• galla-q-r nl2•
  - **hill** with son; driving up a: *Hydrog* srj2•
  - **itself**; car is driving: choc srj3•
  - **learning**: stront-c sk4•
  - **recklessly**: petr-ra shn4• plut-n srj7•
  - **steep**, rough track in a large car; driving a: fic-m gya1 marb-w es1•
- **mule**; a (See Mule)

DROWNED, BEING: *(↗MIND - Fear - drowned)* ign j5.de rumx a1 [tax jsj7]

DROWNING: *(↗Water)* aether a1 agath-a nl2• alum ara-maca sej7• bov ign k* kali-c kola stb3• lac-cp sk4• lac-leo hrn2• lyc mag-s j5.de merc k* merc-act h1* merc-i-f k* musca-d szs1 nat-s c1* nicc ran-b k* rauw tpw8* rumx samb k* sil k* tarent a1* verat verat-v hr1* zinc k* [ant-m stj2 aur-m stj2 beryl-m stj2 cadm-m stj2 chlor stj2 cob-m stj2 cupr-m stj2 heroin sdj2 lith-m stj2 mang-m stj2 merc-d stj2 mur-ac stj2 nicc-met stj2 nicc-s stj2 plb-m stj2 sel stj2 stront-m stj2 tax jsj7 zinc-m stj2]
- **baby**; they are trying to drown my: dream-p sdj1•
- **boat** owner indifferent to man drowning: lac-lup hrn2•

- **boat**, on a foundering (See Boat - foundering)
- **children** are drowning: [chr-m stj2]
- **danger** of: bov a1 lac-lup hrn2• limen-b-c hrn2* oci-sa sk4• plut-n srj7• tritic-vg fd5.de
- **man** is drowning: dendr-pol sk4• *Lyc* kr1 sil h2 sol-t-ae
  - **save** him: dendr-pol sk4•
- **mother** is drowning: nicc k* rauw sp1
- **people** are drowning: agath-a nl2• lyc hr1* mag-s j5.de verat a1
- **someone** trying to open her mouth, and: aether a1
- **son** is drowning; fear: lac-del hrn2•
- **two** people in pool: ozone sde2•

DRUG dealers: positr nl2• [heroin sdj2]

DRUGS: dioxi rbp6
- **psychotropic** drugs: kola stb3•
- **son** is selling; his: bamb-a stb2.de•

DRUGS; hallucinations as if induced by: dioxi rbp6

DRUNKEN people (See People - drunken)

DUCKS: hippoc-k szs2
- **mothers** and babies: hippoc-k szs2

DUELS: *(↗Enemies; Fights)* asc-t

DUVETS: haliae-lc srj5•

DWARVES: plut-n srj7•

DYING (See Death - dying)

EARS: *(↗Body; parts)*
- **cut** off; having ears: nat-c
- **lump** in right ear; having a: *(↗Disease)* cinnb a1
  - **throat**; and in: cinnb a1

EARTH: | **beautiful**; earth is: *(↗Country - beautiful; Landscape - beautiful; Regions)* lac-e hrn2•

EARTHQUAKE: cartl-s rly4• helodr-cal knl2• lac-f c1* loxo-recl knl4• oxal-a rly4• ozone sde2• rat sil sil-mar hs1
- **houses**, buildings falling: lac-e hrn2• ozone sde2•
- **people** fall down a crack in the ground; seeing one's: [aur stj2]

EATEN:
- **animals**; by: gink-b sbd1•
  - **cat**; by a black: gink-b sbd1•

EATING: *(↗Banquet; Carousing; Cooking; Food; Picnics)* agath-a nl2• bros-gau mrc1 *Corv-cor* bdg• dulc fd4.de *Iod* k* kola stb3• lac-h sk4• maias-l hrn2• ruta fd4.de spong fd4.de thres-a sze7• vanil fd5.de [bar-i stj2 hydrog stj2 lith-i stj2 mang-i stj2 merc-i-f stj2 tax jsj7 zinc-i stj2]
- **night**; at: lac-leo hrn2•
- **animals**; living (See Animals - eating)
- **canine** flesh: alum j5.de
- **human** flesh: falco-pe nl2• sol-t-ae
- **live** animals: hydrog srj
- **lots** of food: pseuts-m oss1•
- **meat**: rhus-g tmo3•
  - **raw**: falco-pe nl2•
- **snow**: crot-c sk4•

ECCENTRIC: jac-c a

ECSTASY; of: cann-i a maias-l hrn2•

EDUCATION: lac-leo hrn2•

EFFICIENCY: lac-f wza1•

EJACULATION (See Amorous - pollutions; Pollution)

ELDERS, respect for: dream-p sdj1•

ELECTRIC shock: fic-m gya1

ELECTROCUTION: hydrog srj2•

ELEPHANTS: *(↗Animals)* des-ac rbp6 kali-m ccrh1• ozone sde2•
- **riding** on an elephant's back: lac-loxod-a hrn2•
- **small**, the size of a dog; very: ozone sde2•

ELEVATOR (See Lift)

ELK: *(↗Animals)* lac-loxod-a hrn2•

ELVES: plut-n srj7•

EMACIATED; becoming: *(↗Body - emaciated; Disease; MIND - Delusions - emaciation)* kreos

EMBARRASSMENT: *(↗Difficulties; Unsuccessful; MIND - Ailments - embarrassment)* allox sp1 alum k* *Am-m* k* anac b2.de* ant-t b2.de* *Ars* k* bell bg2 cann-s b2.de* caps b2.de* chir-fl gya2 croc b2.de* crot-c sk4• des-ac rbp6 galeoc-c-h gms1• graph k* lac-d sk4• lac-leo sk4• limen-b-c hrn2* lyc fry mag-c k* mag-m b2.de* merc-c b4a.de mur-ac b2.de* nicc-met sk4• oci-sa sk4• oxal-a rly4• petr-ra shn4• phos k* plat b2.de* plut-n srj7• *Polys* sk4• positr nl2• rhus-t b2.de* sep bg2 thiam rly4• [tax jsj7]
- **dark** spot on her dress from menses: bung-fa mtf
- **mother** was pregnant; his: oci-sa sk4•
- **slipping** on the floor; after: bung-fa mtf
- **remember** names; can't: galeoc-c-h gms1•

EMISSION which did not take place: thuj a1

EMOTIONS: ozone sde2•
- **stress**: ozone sde2•
- **suppressing**: hydrog srj2• sal-fr sle1•
- **without**: lac-loxod-a hrn2• *Polys* sk4• [bell-p-sp dcm1]

ENCAGED in ropy wires: [lappa stj]

ENCIRCLED tightly, being: lac-del hrn2• ruta

ENDLESS: sep h2

ENEMIES: *(↗Battles; Duels; Fights; Pursued - enemies; War)* arg-met k* con hydrog srj2• ina-i mlk9.de *Kola* stb3• lac-del hrn2• petr-ra shn4• ptel
- **avoids**: lac-del hrn2•

ENLARGED: *(↗Exaggerated; Large - everything)*
- **objects** are: lac-del hrn2•

ENRAGED, impassioned: limen-b-c hrn2•

ENTERTAINMENT: *(↗Balls; Conversations; Dancing)* nat-c a1

EPIDEMIC; of an: *(↗Disease)* anan a1 sarr a1
- **ear** epidemic: adam srj5•

EPILEPSY: *(↗Disease)* iris-foe mag-c k1 sil

EQUILIBRIUM; unstable: nept-m lsd2.fr

ERECTIONS: kreos b7a.de plut-n srj7•

ERRORS (See Mistakes)

ERUPTIONS: *(↗Disease)* am-c j5.de am-m b7.de* anac j5.de bamb-a stb2.de• bros-gau mrc1 castm j5.de plut-n srj7• stront-c sk4•

ESCAPING: *(↗Fleeing; Running)* agath-a nl2• dendr-pol sk4• dulc fd4.de hydrog srj2• ina-i mlk9.de *Lac-e* hrn2• nat-sil fd3.de• ozone sde2• petr-ra shn4• plut-n srj7• ruta fd4.de symph fd3.de• tritic-vg fd5.de ulm-c jsj8• [bar-i stj2 merc-i-f stj2 tax jsj7 zinc-i stj2]
- **danger**; from: lac-e hrn2•
- **Mafia**; from the: crot-c sk4•
- **monastery**; from a Buddhist: marb-w es1•
- **unable** to: bit-ar wht1•

ETIQUETTE: positr nl2•

EULOGY for man died of AIDS: maias-l hrn2•

EUNUCHS: dendr-pol sk4•

EUPHORIC (See Pleasant)

EVENTS: aster a1 crot-t a1 dulc fd4.de plan a1
- **book**, from: calc-f kr1
- **contorted**: graph h2
- **daily**: pert-vc vk9
- **during** weeks and months; as if events transpired in dreams were: sang gt

Dreams

- **forgotten**; long: acon a1 am-c a1 anac a1 bov a1 calad cere-b a1 chin a1 ferr-i a1 gink-b sbd1• nat-c a1 plut-n srj7• sel senec a1 **Sil** a1 spig a1 sulph a1 sumb a1
- **future**, of: *(↗Clairvoyant; MIND - Clairvoyance; MIND - Fear - happen)* **Acon** k1* asaf bov j5.de *Cann-i* cortico tpw7* fic-m gya1 hydrog srj2• m-arct j5.de mang ph-ac phos (non:rad-met) spong fd4.de *Sulph* thiam rly4• tritic-vg fd5.de ulm-c jsj8•
- **important**: osm a1
- **long** duration; as if from: *Sang* kr1
- **not** yet taken place (See future)
- **painful**: *(↗Disease; Pain)* osm kr1
- **past**; long: *(↗Historic)* acon a1 am-c anac j5.de* androc srj1• bov j5.de* brucel sa3• calad calc j5.de cere-b a1 chin a1 chlam-tr bcx2• corian-s knl6• ferr ferr-i fic-m gya1 gink-b sbd1• hydrog srj2• kali-s fd4.de nat-c j5.de* *Pert-vc* vk9 plut-n srj7• sel k* senec **Sil** k* spig spong fd4.de sulph a1 sumb a1 tritic-vg fd5.de vanil fd5.de [spect dfg1 tax jsj7]
  - **continues** the same dream; after awaking falls to sleep again and: calad nat-c
  - **present** events; mixed with: ozone sde2•
  - **understanding** and learning from events long past: plut-n srj7•
- **previous**: *Acon* aeth agav-t jl am-c anac *Ant-t* arg-met asaf aster bov *Bry* calad calc h2* *Calc-p* caps h1 carbn-s chel chin *Cic* coca cocc *Croc* crot-t elaps euph ferr-i fl-ac graph ind jatr-c kali-c kali-chl kali-m k2 kali-sil k2 *Lach* nat-c nat-p nat-sil k2 nit-ac nux-v osm ozone sde2• ph-ac phos plan *Rhus-t* sang sars sel senec sep **Sil** sol-t-ae spig spong fd4.de sulph sumb thuj tritic-vg fd5.de ulm-c jsj8• vanil fd5.de
  - **day**, of the previous: *(↗Business - day)* *Acon* aeth a1 agav-t jl arg-met k* bals-p a1 **Bry** k* calc-f calc-p a1 chel *Cic Croc* a1 cur elaps a1 euph j5.de* ferr fl-ac graph hep bg1 ind a1 kali-c kali-chl kali-sil k2 lach lyc mag-c merc methys jl naja a nat-c j5.de nit-ac a1 *Nux-v* ph-ac j5.de phos a1 *Puls* pyrog bg rhus-t sars sel j5.de* senec a1 sep sil sol-t-ae a1 spong fd4.de stann vanil fd5.de visc c1
  - **evening**, of the previous: nat-c h2 ph-ac thuj a1
  - **morning**; of the previous: *Camph* kr1
  - **vivid**: *Sil* kr1
  - **years**: calad kr1
- **read**: *Bry* kr1 calc-f kr1 *Calc-p* a1*
  - **previously** heard, read, talked or thought about: *Ant-t* a1 asaf a1 bov a1 bry a1 calc-f hr1 calc-p a1 carbn-s a1 coca a1 fic-m gya1 fl-ac a1 graph h2* jatr-c a1 nat-c a1 nux-v a1 *Rhus-t* a1 sars a1 sil hr1 thuj a1
- **room**; in the next: sumb a1
- **unfortunate**: *(↗Misfortune)* cocc a1 dulc fd4.de sulph a1
- **whirlwind**-like; many: coca-c sk4•

EVIL; of: *(↗Good)* corian-s knl6• plut-n srj7•
- **impending**: cimic br1* *Kola* stb3• lac-loxod-a hrn2• oci-sa sk4•
  - **child** to a: ozone sde2•
- **power** of evil; the: ara-maca sej7•
- **rise** of evil; the: ara-maca sej7•

EXAGGERATED: *(↗Enlarged)* [tax jsj7]
- **colors** and proportions: lac-del hrn2•

EXAMINATIONS: aids nl2• galeoc-c-h gms1• lac-h sk4• maias-l hrn2• positr nl2• thres-a sze7• vanil fd5.de
- **failing** an exam: *(↗Failures)* [*Zinc* stj1 zinc-i stj2]
- **ink** on exam paper; spilling: ign mtf
- **missing** an exam: maias-l hrn2•
  - **oversleeping**; from: pert-vc vk9
- **unprepared** for an exam; being: nat-m hu2 [zinc stj2 zinc-i stj2]

EXASPERATION: *(↗Disappointments)* staph j5.de taosc iwa1•

EXCELLING:
- **capable**; being: [buteo-j sej6]
- **mental** work; in: *(↗Mental)* acon anac am *Bry* camph carb-an graph *Ign* lach *Nux-v* puls rhus-t sabad *Sabin Thuj*

EXCITING: *(↗Affecting)* bell-p mg1.de* cact k2 carc mg1.de* choc srj3• cob-n sp1 cod a1 coloc dicha mg1.de elaps mg falco-pe nl2• helodr-cal knl2• hydrog srj2• kali-cy kali-s fd4.de *Kola* stb3• lac-e hrn2• lyss kr1* mag-s sp1 nat-m nux-v orig a1 *Phos* kr1 pip-m a1 ruta fd4.de saroth mg1.de*
- **starting**; with: saroth mg1.de

EXCREMENTS: *(↗Closet; Closet - being)* aloe bros-gau mrc1 castn-v dulc fd4.de hippoc-k szs2 iod maias-l hrn2• musca-d szs1 plut-n srj7• polys sk4• positr nl2• psor sars taosc iwa1• zinc [bell-p-sp dcm1 heroin sdj2]
- **morning**: aloe a
- **closets**: aids nl2• bros-gau mrc1 psor a1
- **large** amounts: hydrog srj
- **smeared** with excrements, being: dulc fd4.de zinc k* [bar-i stj2 iod stj2 lith-i stj2 mang-i stj2 merc-i-f stj2 zinc-i stj2]
- **soiling** himself with excrements: aloe k* castn-v iod sars k13 zinc
- **stool** (See Stool)
- **wading** in excrements: coca-c sk4• (non:iod j5.de) polys sk4•

EXCRESCENCES: *(↗Disease)* hydrog srj2• mez j5.de

EXERTION; of physical: *(↗Striving; Work)* apis bro1 *Ars* k* atro a1 bapt bro1 brom kr1 *Bry* bro1 dicha mg1.de dulc fd4.de kola stb3• lac-h sk4•• med kr1 nat-m bro1 nux-v bro1 phos bro1 puls bro1 rhus-t k* sel bro1 spong fd4.de staph bro1 tritic-vg fd5.de tung-met bdx1• [arn xyz62 bar-i stj2 echi xyz62 iod stj2 lith-i stj2 mang-i stj2 merc-i-f stj2 sabin xyz62 stann stj2 zinc-i stj2]

EXHAUSTING: *(↗Harassing)* aeth alum ant-c ant-o a1 ant-t apis b7a.de arn k* ars j5.de asc-t atro aur bac bn bell bov a1 bry carbn-s carc sst* cina b7.de* croc j5.de dream-p sdj1• dulc fd4.de echi bg equis-h a1 ferr j5.de graph hyper k* iod k* lach lyc k* lyss kr1 mag-c mang j5.de med hr1* nat-m a1 nux-v b7a.de op j5.de petr j5.de ph-ac phos polyg-h a1 *Puls* rhod j5.de rhus-t b7.de* ruta k* sabin b7.de* sep a1 spig spong k* valer j5.de verat k* vichy-g a1 *Zinc* j5.de* [bar-i stj2 lith-i stj2 mag-lac stj2 mag-met stj2 mag-n stj2 mag-sil stj2 mang-i stj2 merc-i-f stj2 zinc-i stj2]
- **fatigued**; much: lyss kr1
- **perspiration** on waking; with: *Lyc* kr1

EXPECTORATION; purulent: *(↗Disease)* hep b4a.de*

EXPLOITED; of being: dendr-pol sk4•

EXPLOSION: *(↗Accidents)* arist-cl rbp3• ham fd3.de• kola stb3• *Moni* rfm1• nat-sil fd3.de• positr nl2• rad-br sze8• stann k* tritic-vg fd5.de tung-met bdx1• [tax jsj7]
- **bombs**; of: dulc fd4.de fic-m gya1 gink-b sbd1• irid-met srj5• *Moni* rfm1• nat-ox rly4•
  - **atomic** bomb: lac-h sze9• ozone sde2• plut-n srj7• tritic-vg fd5.de
- **nuclear**: ozone sde2•
- **thumb**; of: polys sk4•

EXPOSING:
- **breast**; her: bung-fa mtf
  - **left**: bung-fa mtf
- **friend** is exposing her breast: bung-fa mtf
- **husband** is exposing his genitals: bung-fa mtf

EYES: *(↗Body; parts)* maias-l hrn2•
- **lids** itching: *(↗Disease)* upa a1
- **pupils** are square: ozone sde2•
- **size** | **pupil**; disparity in: lac-e hrn2•
- **stitches** in eyes: *(↗Disease)* *Calc* kr1
- **three**; having: maias-l hrn2•

FACE: *(↗Body; parts)* maias-l hrn2•
- **abscesses**; covered with: *(↗Disease)*
  - **large**, bloody: dendr-pol sk4•
- **cut** away, having one side of face: mag-m a1
- **disfigured**: sep h2*
- **emotionless** face: lac-d sk4•
- **half** blue: maias-l hrn2•
- **horrible** face: lac-h sk4• polys sk4•
- **mirror**; in the | **own** face; is not his: plut-n srj7•
- **pustules**; covered with: *(↗Disease)* anac
  - **white**, ugly: anac j5.de
- **smallpox** marks; covered with: *(↗Smallpox)* anac h2
- **swollen**: *(↗Disease)* kali-n j5.de
  - **right**: dendr-pol sk4•
- **transformed** into a devil's head with horns; face: coca-c sk4•
- **two** faces:
  - **having** two faces: *(↗Trinity - women - three)* maias-l hrn2•
  - **only** sees one; there are two faces but he: loxo-recl knl4•

- **white** | **lips**; with red: kola stb3•
- **worm** climbing out of the forehead: galla-q-r nl2•

FACTORY: musca-d szs1

FAILURES: *(↗Difficulties; Examinations - failing; Mistakes; Unsuccessful)* am-m a1 dulc fd4.de fago a1 ign j5.de mosch j5.de nat-sil fd3.de• op j5.de plac-s rly4• positr nl2• psor jl2 spong fd4.de [bar-i stj2 cob stj2 cob-m stj2 iod stj2 lith-i stj2 mang-met stj2 merc-i-f stj2 osm-met stj2 scand-met stj2 sel stj2 tant-met stj2 zinc-i stj2]
- **examination**: allox tpw3

FAINTING: *(↗Disease)* bamb-a stb2.de• graph stront-c sk4•

FAIRY TALE; as in a: ozone sde2•

FALLING: *(↗SLEEP - Waking - falling)* acon agath-a nl2• allox tpw3* alum k* alum-p k2 *Am-m* k* ange-s jl aur k* **Bell** k* bism bomb-pr mlk9.de *Cact* k* cain calc canth caps k* cartl-s rly4• chel chin k* choc srj3• cimic bg2 cob-n jl *Crot-c* sk4• *Dig* k* dulc elaps eupi falco-pe nl2• ferr k* ferr-p glycyr-g cte1• *Guaj* k* hell bg1 *Hep* b2.de* ign k* kali-c kali-i kali-n b2.de* kali-p *Kreos* k* lac-h sze9• m-arct b2.de* mag-m k* *Merc* k* mez k* musca-d szs1 nat-s nicc nux-m nux-v op oxal-a rly4• ph-ac phos bg2 plac-s rly4• plb k* polys sk4• *Puls* rad-br sze8• rumx sabad sabin k* sang *Sars* k* sep sol-t-ae *Sulph* k* sumb k* symph fd3.de• tab bg2 **Thuj** k* ulm-c jsj8• zinc k* zinc-o j5.de zinc-p k2* [ant-c stj2 ant-m stj2 ant-met stj2 ant-t stj2 arg-met stj2 arg-n stj2 arg-p stj2 astat stj2 aur-m stj2 aur-s stj2 bar-br stj2 bar-i stj2 bar-met stj2 bism-sn stj2 cadm-m stj2 cadm-met stj2 cadm-s stj2 caes-met stj2 cinnb stj2 cupr stj2 cupr-f stj2 cupr-m stj2 cupr-p stj2 ferr-f stj2 ferr-lac stj2 ferr-n stj2 ferr-sil stj2 hafn-met stj2 heroin sdj2 ind stj2 iod stj2 irid-met stj2 lanth-met stj2 lith-i stj2 mag-lac stj2 mag-met stj2 mag-n stj2 mag-sil stj2 mang-i stj2 mang-met stj2 merc-d stj2 merc-i-f stj2 moly-met stj2 nicc-met stj2 nicc-s stj2 niob-met stj2 osm-met stj2 plat stj2 plb-m stj2 plb-p stj2 polon-met stj2 rhen-met stj2 rhodi stj2 rubd-met stj2 ruth-met stj2 scand-met stj2 sel stj2 stann stj2 stront-m stj2 stront-met stj2 tant-met stj2 tax jsj7 techn stj2 tell stj2 thal-met stj2 tung-met stj2 yttr-met stj2 zinc-i stj2 zinc-m stj2 zinc-n stj2 zirc-met stj2]
- **abyss**, into an: *(↗height; Abyss)* atro hs1 cartl-s rly4• *Cham* elaps eupi hep a1 lap-la rsp1 ozone sde2• stram zr2 [spect dfg1]
- **confidence**, with: falco-pe nl2• nept-m lsd2.fr
- **danger** of: agath-a nl2• alum a1 am-m a1 dulc fd4.de kali-s fd4.de lac-h sk4• macro a1 positr nl2• spong fd4.de tung-met bdx1• [heroin sdj2]
  - **flood**; into (See flood)
  - **height**, from a: alum a1 carc fd2.de•
- **elevator**; in an: gink-b sbd1• ozone sde2• staph dtp
- **fear** of falling (See Fear - falling)
- **flood**, into a: *(↗Flood)* am-m spong fd4.de
- **grave**, into a (See Graves - falling)
- **hammock**; from: phos a
- **height**, from a: *(↗abyss; Abyss)* acon agath-a nl2• alum am-m anan aur bomb-pr mlk9.de caps ptk1 chin cimic bg1 *Crot-c* sk4• dendr-pol sk4• *Dig* guaj hep ina-i mlk9.de kali-c kali-n a1 *Kreos* merc merc-c a1 *Mez* nat-s nicc nux-m k* op petr-ra shn4• ph-ac h2 phos plut-n srj7• positr nl2• rad-br sze8• sep sin-a a1 sol-t-ae *Sulph* sumb **Thuj** k* zinc [hydrog stj2]
  - **bridge**; faulty: lac-h htj1•
  - **men** are killed by falling from a height: arizon-l nl2• sabin j5.de*
  - **pushed** off from behind: *Crot-c* sk4•
- **high** places; from (See height)
- **horse**, from: tarent a1
- **ladder**; from a: *Crot-c* sk4•
- **loft**, from: nicc a1
- **motorcycle**: nicc-met sk4•
- **pit**, into a: elaps a1
- **precipice**; into a (See abyss)
- **starting** out from sleep: glycyr-g cte1•
- **water**, into: *(↗Water)* *Am-m* *Dig* eupi *Ferr* ign ina-i mlk9.de iod mag-m mag-s melal-alt gya4 merc mez j musca-d szs1 nicc ph-ac h2 plb j plut-n srj7• puls j sars j sep j sulph j zinc j [lith-s stj2 nicc-met stj2 nicc-s stj2 spect dfg1]
  - **child** is falling; her: eupi
  - **daughter** is falling: iod k* [merc-i-f stj2]
  - **husband** is falling: nept-m lsd2.fr
  - **mother** is falling: nicc
- **window** | **friends** falling from a window: choc srj3•

FAMILIES; of: limen-b-c hrn2•

FAMILY, own: *(↗Cousin; Daughter; Father; Grandparents; Mother; Parents; People - family; Relatives; Sister; Son)* *Androc* srj1• ant-c j5.de *Aq-mar* rbp6 ara-maca sej7• bit-ar wht1• bros-gau mrc1 choc srj3• dulc fd4.de galeoc-c-h gms1• germ-met stj2*• granit-m es1• haliae-lc srj5• lac-e hrn2• lac-h htj1• lac-lup hrn2• limen-b-c mlk9.de maias-l hrn2• melal-alt gya4 oxal-a rly4• *Plut-n* srj7• pyrid rly4• rad-br sze8• ruta fd4.de spong fd4.de vanil fd5.de [buteo-j sej6 calc-sil stj2 ferr-sil stj2 kali-sil stj2 mag-sil stj2 mang-sil stj2 nat-sil stj2 sil stj2 sil-met stj2 spect dfg1 tax jsj7]
- **large** family; a: lac-h sk4•
- **loses** his (See Losing - family)
- **poisonous** and dying; whole family eating something: [calc-sil stj2]
- **two** families | **same** house; living in the: lac-h sk4•

FAMINE, but escaping by crawling out; being left in a dungeon to die of: *(↗Hunger)* ped a1

FANTASTIC: *(↗Colored; Visionary)* acon am-c ambr k* ant-t k* arg-n ars k* ars-h kr1 bamb-a stb2.de• bar-c k* bros-gau mrc1 bufo bg2* **Calc** k* calc-i ptk1 calc-sil k2 **Carb-an** k* *Carb-v* k* *Carbn-s* cench k2 *Cham* k* *Chin* j5.de coff j5.de *Con* k* ferr-i *Graph* k* hell k* hippoc-k szs2 hydrog srj2*• *Ign* j5.de ina-i mlk9.de ip b7a.de kali-ar *Kali-c* k* kali-n k* kali-sil k2 kalm lac-e hrn2• **Lach** k* lact j5.de led j5.de lyc k* maias-l hrn2• merc k* morph mur-ac j5.de *Nat-c* k* **Nat-m** k* *Nat-s* nicc j5.de nit-ac k* nux-v k* olib-sac wmh1 **Op** k* oxal-a rly4• ozone sde2• pen a1 petr b4a.de* plan prun j5.de ptel puls j5.de *Sep* b2.de* sil k* spong k* *Sulph* k* zinc k* zinc-o j5.de [aur stj2 aur-m stj2 aur-s stj2 tax jsj7]

FARMING: galeoc-c-h gms1• mag-s merc-i-r

FAT; being (See Obese)

FATHER: *(↗Family)* alumn a1 am-m a1 bit-ar wht1• castm a1 crot-h a1 fic-m gya1 granit-m es1• kali-c a1 lac-lup hrn2• loxo-recl knl4• mag-s a1 nept-m lsd2.fr pert-vc vk9 plut-n srj7• pot-e rly4• spong fd4.de vanil fd5.de [bell-p-sp dcm1 buteo-j sej6 mur-ac stj2 tax jsj7]
- **advising**:
  - **son** | **correct** path; to take: dendr-pol sk4•
- **hurt** by: plut-n srj7•
- **seduce** her; trying to: plut-n srj7•
- **wanting** love from his: plut-n srj7•

FATIGUING (See Exhausting)

FEAR: lac-h sze9•
- **car** accidents (See Accidents - car - fear)
- **children**; in: kali-br tl1
- **doing** something I should not have been doing: [buteo-j sej6]
- **falling**; of: lac-lup hrn2• rad-br sze8• rhus-g tmo3•
  - **cliff**; from a: lac-lup hrn2•
  - **ravine**; into a: lac-lup hrn2•
- **followed** by: aids nl2• alum j5.de *Am-m* j5.de *Chin* j5.de *Cocc* j5.de *Con* j5.de falco-pe nl2• hep j5.de lyc j5.de mag-s j5.de melal-alt gya4 mur-ac j5.de nat-c j5.de ph-ac j5.de sal-fr sle1• sil j5.de sulph j5.de zinc j5.de
- **injuries**: phasco-ci rbp2
- **sister**; his:
  - **discover**; will: | **secret** room; his: oci-sa sk4•
- **sudden**: arge-pl rwt5•
- **trouble**; of getting into: lac-lup hrn2•
- **water**; of: graph h2

FEARLESS: lac-del hrn2•

FEASTING: *(↗Banquet; Carousing)* anan ant-c k* arist-cl rbp3• asaf hura *Kola* stb3• m-ambo b2.de* mag-s nit-ac k* petr-ra shn4• ph-ac k* spong fd4.de tril-p tung-met bdx1• zinc [tax jsj7]

FEATHER: lac-leo hrn2•
- **room** filled with feathers: galla-q-r nl2•
- **vagina**; putting a feather in her: aids nl2•

FEEDING: | **people**: lac-loxod-a hrn2•

FEELINGS; far removed from: dioxi rbp6

FEET; cold: dioxi rbp6

FENCES:
- **black**: galla-q-r nl2•

- **walls** and: galla-q-r nl2•

FETUSES: *(↗Animals - fetuses)* ephe-si hsj1•

FEVER: *(↗Disease)* kali-chl j5.de sulph k*

FEVERISH: euphr a1 lachn a1

FIELDS: positr nl2•
- **large**, open: *Corv-cor* bdg•
- **ploughed**: falco-pe nl2•

FIGHTING; one is: bros-gau mrc1 lac-loxod-a hrn2• nat-s ptk1 positr nl2• ran-b ptk1
- **animals** (See Animals - fighting - with)

FIGHTS: *(↗Aggressive; Air; Air attacks; Battles; Cannonading; Duels; Enemies; Quarrels; Stabbed; War; Wounded)* aesc *All-c* allox sp1 aza jl bapt bell bomb-chr mlk9.de brass-n-o srj5• brom k* bros-gau mrc1 bry calad ceph a1 coca con crot-c k* culx k2 elaps *Ferr* k* ferr-i k* fum rly1*• gink-b sbd1• guaj guare hyper ina-i mlk9.de indg iris jab jac-c kali-bi kali-c j5.de kali-n j5.de *Kola* stb3• lac-e hrn2• lac-h sk4• lac-lup hrn2• loxo-recl knl4• lyc lyss kr1 m-aust j5.de mag-c mag-s j5.de maias-l hrn2• mosch nat-ar nat-c j5.de *Nat-m* nat-s nicc j5.de nicc-met sk4• nux-v tl1 petr-ra shn4• phel j5.de phos pip-m plat k* polys sk4• positr nl2• ptel puls j5.de pycnop-sa mrz1 *Ran-s* rat rhus-g tmo3• sacch-a fd2.de• sars j5.de senec sil sol-t-ae stann k* *Staph* staphycoc rly4• *Stram* kr1 taosc iwa1• term-a bnj1 tung-met bdx1• vanil fd5.de verb [am-br stj2 bar-br stj2 ferr-f stj2 ferr-lac stj2 ferr-n stj2 ferr-sil stj2 merc stj2 plut-n stj2 tax jsj7]
- **conquers** always: bapt
- **existence**; for | **man** who caused deep offense; with: limen-b-c hrn2•
- **ghosts**, with: sars sep sil j5.de
- **herself**; for: oci-sa sk4•
- **karate** with his teacher: ozone sde2•
- **man**; fighting a | **attacked** his group; who: lac-h sk4•
- **men**; with | **no** one hurt: maias-l hrn2•
- **mother**; with: pseuts-m oss1•
- **police**; with: taosc iwa1•
- **reading**; suggested by: coca a1
- **rights**; for her: crot-c sk4• lac-h sk4• oci-sa sk4•
- **robbers**, with: *(↗Robbers - fighting)* allox tpw3 ferr-i jac-c a1 mag-c nat-c sil

FINGERNAILS: *(↗Body; parts)*
- **long**: falco-pe nl2•

FINGERS: *(↗Body; parts)*
- **seized** by the fingers (See Seized)
- **stiff** fingers: *(↗Disease)* calc-s j5.de*

FIRE: agath-a nl2• aids nl2• alum k* am-c b2.de* **Anac** k* ant-t k* arist-cl rbp3• *Ars* k* aur ptk1* bar-c k* *Bell* k* calc k* *Calc-p* calc-sil k2* cann-i sf1.de cann-xyz bg2* *Carb-ac* carb-v k* cass a1 cench k2 chin choc srj3• clem k* corv-cor bdg• *Croc* k* *Cur* cystein-l rly4• daph dulc fd4.de euphr k* fl-ac graph k* ham fd3.de• helo-s rwt2• **Hep** k* hyos ptk1 irid-met srj5• iris kali-ar kali-c kali-n kali-sil k2 kiss a1 *Kola* stb3• *Kreos* k* lac-h sk4• *Lac-lup* hrn2• lach bro1 **Laur** k* lyc ptk1 *M-aust* b2.de* **Mag-c** k* **Mag-m** k* *Mag-s* manc ptk1 meny ptk1 *Meph* *(non:*merc slp*)* merc-act slp merc-c k* merc-sul moni rfm1• musca-d szs1 naja nat-c *Nat-m* k* nat-p nat-s nit-s-d a1 osm *Phos* k* pip-m a1 plat k* plut-n srj7• positr nl2• rad-br c11* rhod k* *Rhus-t* k* ruta ptk1* sel jl* sil k* sol-t-ae a1 spig k* spong stann k* stront-c k* sul-ac k* *Sulph* k* til ban1• tritic-vg fd5.de tub ptk1 tung-met stj2*• vanil fd5.de zinc k* zinc-o j5.de zing [ant-c stj2 ant-met stj2 aur-m stj2 aur-s stj2 bar-i stj2 germ-met stj2 heroin sdj2 iod stj2 lith-i stj2 mang-i stj2 merc-i-f stj2 osm-met stj2 spect dfg1 stront-met stj2 tax jsj7 zinc-i stj2]
- **burned** and scorched; everything was: oci-sa sk4•
- **building** on fire: lac-lup hrn2•
- **cathedral** was on fire: *(↗Churches)* kali-c a1
- **city**; destroying a: sol-t-ae a1
- **conflagration**: anac h2 nat-m h2*
- **danger**, of: ant-t a1 bell a1 clem a1 dulc fd4.de merc-act a1 nit-s-d a1 tung-met bdx1•
  - **burn** down the house; someone wants to: lac-lup hrn2•
  - **chasing** a group of people; fire: lac-lup hrn2•
- **drills**: falco-pe nl2•
- **evil** little creature in oven; trying to burn: lac-lup hrn2•

Fire: ...
- **fireball**: lac-lup hrn2•
- **firetruck**: lac-lup hrn2•
  - **riding** on the back of a: lac-lup hrn2•
- **heaven**; coming down from: *Sulph*
- **hot**; that is not: til ban1•
- **house** on fire; setting a: gink-b sbd1•
- **kept** fires going: lac-lup hrn2•
- **lightning**, from: euphr a1
- **people** on fire: aids nl2•
- **trees** on fire: agath-a nl2•
- **world** on fire: ignis-alc es2• positr nl2• *Rhus-t*

FIREWORKS: positr nl2• tritic-vg fd5.de

FISH: *(↗Animals; Fishing; Trout; Water)* adam srj5• aids nl2• arg-n k* arizon-l nl2• carc fd2.de• chin-b kr1* fic-m gya1 haliae-lc srj5• hippoc-k szs2 kali-c b4.de* kali-m ccrh1• lac-del hrn2• lac-h sk4• lac-loxod-a hrn2• lac-lup hrn2• limen-b-c hrn2* mag-c b4.de* melal-alt gya4 musca-d szs1 positr nl2• ros-d wla1 thres-a sze7• vanil fd5.de
- **big** as a room: ozone sde2•
- **dead**: falco-pe nl2•
- **gold** metal: choc srj3•
- **goldfish**: ignis-alc es2• vanil fd5.de
- **people** who are fish: hippoc-k szs2
- **rescuing**: fic-m gya1
- **silver**: ignis-alc es2•

FISHING: *(↗Fish)* arg-met chin zzl (non:chin-b hr1) chinin-s k* cinch kl mag-c k* melal-alt gya4 positr nl2• verat-v k*
- **deep** sea: [buteo-j sej6]

FIT; he had a: iris mag-c sil

FIXED ideas (See Persistent - fixed)

FLAGPOLES: | **holding**: galeoc-c-h gms1•

FLASHES, like still pictures in a movie format: chir-fl gya2

FLAYED; people being (= skinned): ara-maca sej7• arn h1* mag-m a1 ulm-c jsj8•

FLEEING: *(↗Escaping; Pursued)* agath-a nl2• asc-t a1 crot-c sk4• *Kola* stb3• lac-h sk4• polys sk4• zinc k* [iod stj2 lith-i stj2 mang-i stj2 zinc-i stj2 zinc-m stj2 zinc-n stj2 zinc-p stj2]
- **strict** government; from a: rhus-g tmo3•

FLIES: *(↗Insects)* aids nl2• ina-i mlk9.de
- **housefly**; aunt had a pet: oci-sa sk4•
- **wall**; fly on the: ara-maca sej7•

FLIPPING over: lac-lup hrn2•

FLIRTATION (See Amorous)

FLOATING: *(↗Flying)* coca-c sk4• hell lap-la rsp1 musca-d szs1 olib-sac wmh1 ribo rly4• sanguis-s hrn2• urol-h rwt• [buteo-j sej6]
- **water**; on: plut-n srj7•

FLOOD: *(↗Danger - water; Falling - flood; Water)* am-m a1* bamb-a stb2.de• bomb-chr mlk9.de falco-pe nl2• fic-m gya1 galla-q-r nl2• helodr-cal knl2• lac-del hrn2• lac-h sk4• mag-c merc moni rfm1• musca-d szs1 nat-c ozone sde2• pyrid rly4• rumx sanguis-s hrn2• *Sil* til ban1• ulm-c jsj8• [heroin sdj2 mag-m stj1]
- **calm** in a: lac-del hrn2•
- **floor** of house; on: galeoc-c-h gms1•
- **house** is in a: lac-del hrn2•
- **streets** flooded: lac-h sk4•
- **swept** away and dismembered by a: [heroin sdj2]

FLOWERS: agath-a nl2• dulc fd4.de falco-pe nl2• galla-q-r nl2• gard-j vlr2• ina-i mlk9.de irid-met srj5• kola stb3• lac-cp sk4• lac-e hrn2• mag-c maias-l hrn2• nat-s oxal-a rly4• positr nl2• ruta fd4.de spong fd4.de tritic-vg fd5.de vanil fd5.de
- **roses**; beautiful, white: maias-l hrn2•

FLY EGGS: phasco-ci rbp2

FLYING: *(↗Floating; Lifted)* adam srj5• aids nl2• all-s mgm• apeir-s mlk9.de *Apis* k* asc-t a1 atro bell bg2* bomb-chr mlk9.de bomb-pr mlk9.de camph mgm• cann-i mgm• carc dgt2 chir-fl gya2 choc srj3• convo-d a1 dulc fd4.de falco-pe nl2• fuma-ac rly4• ina-i mlk9.de indg kali-s fd4.de *Kola* stb3• lac-h sk4• lat-m ptk1 loxo-recl knl4• lyc maias-l hrn2• musca-d szs1 nat-s k* *Olib-sac* wmh1 plut-n srj7• positr nl2• *Rhus-g* bg1* sal-fr sle1• samb bat1• spong fd4.de stict br1* suis-pan rly4• tritic-vg fd5.de vesp mgm• xan xanth bg2 [buteo-j sej6 heroin sdj2 hydrog stj2]
- **airplane**: adam srj5• agath-a nl2• aids nl2• allox tpw4* falco-pe nl2• hydrog srj2• ina-i mlk9.de orot-ac rly4• spong fd4.de
  - **desk** becomes an airplane; his: aids nl2•
- **America**; across: haliae-lc srj5•
- **away**: lat-m dp•
- **flapping** | **anxious** about landing: maias-l hrn2•
- **holding** a young girl: plut-n srj7•
- **people**: chir-fl gya2 hydrog srj2•
- **room**; from room to: musca-d szs1

FOAM on forehead; white: ozone sde2•

FOG: suprar rly4•

FOLLOWED BY: | **Head**; pain in (See SLEEP - Dreaming - followed - head)

FOOD: *(↗Cooking; Eating)* adam srj5• choc srj3• corian-s knl6• corv-cor bdg• dendr-pol sk4• dulc fd4.de falco-pe nl2• galeoc-c-h gms1• irid-met srj5• lac-del hrn2• lac-loxod-a hrn2• ptel a1 stront-c sk4• [bell-p-sp dcm1 spect dfg1 tax jsj7]
- **dirty** food | **ate** it anyway: lac-lup hrn2•
- **disgusting**: agath-a nl2• falco-pe nl2•
- **green**: neon srj5•
- **horrible**: falco-pe nl2•
- **insufficient**: falco-pe nl2•
- **pizza**: stront-c sk4•
- **preparing** food: loxo-recl knl4•
  - **desserts**: loxo-recl knl4•
- **revolting** (See disgusting)
- **synthetic**: coca-c sk4•
- **war** camp; distributing in a: coca-c sk4•

FOOLISH: colch rsj2• merc-i-r a1 suis-em rly4•

FOOT: *(↗Body; parts)*
- **soles** are tickled: phos j5.de*
- **stitching** in the foot: *(↗Disease)* asar a1

FOREIGN COUNTRY (See Country - foreign)

FOREIGN LANGUAGE; she had to converse in a: coca-c sk4•

FOREIGNERS: *(↗Strangers)* lac-e hrn2•
- **among** foreigners; being: plut-n srj7•
- **danger**; in: | **violent** persons; from: nicc-met sk4•
- **destroying** the earth: polys sk4•

FOREST: *(↗Walking - woods)* canth com a1 dulc fd4.de fuma-ac rly4• limen-b-c hrn2* mag-m pieri-b mlk9.de ruta fd4.de sep spong fd4.de tritic-vg fd5.de vanil fd5.de [tax jsj7]
- **astray** in a; going: mag-m j5.de sep j5.de
- **roaming**: lac-h sk4•

FORGETFULNESS: | **streets**; of well-known: lac-leo hrn2•

FORGOTTEN something; one has: loxo-recl knl4• sel bro1 tritic-vg fd5.de
- **medicine**: cimic ggj

FORMS: *(↗Things)* bry bg2* calc bg2* cina bg2*
- **black**: am ars op br1* puls
  - **darkening** the sun; a black form: ped a1
- **grotesque** forms dancing before her: narcot a1
- **horrid**, presenting a bottle: merc-c a1
- **sitting** on chest: paeon a1*

FORSAKEN; being: falco-pe nl2• kola stb3• *Lac-h* sk4*• lac-leo hrn2• oci-sa sk4• rad-br sze8• stront-c sk4• vanil fd5.de [tax jsj7]
- **everyone**; by: dream-p sdj1• falco-pe nl2• positr nl2•

Forsaken; being: ...
- **father** on a journey; he could not accompany his: mag-s a1
- **friends**; by: *Lac-h* sk4• oci-sa sk4•
- **girl** forsaken by her boyfriend: adam srj5• lac-h sk4•
- **helpless**; and: *Lac-d* sk4•
- **mother**; by her: gink-b sbd1•
- **mountain**; on a huge: crot-c sk4•

FOUNDERING boat (See Boat)

FRAGMENTED: *Agath-a* nl2• haliae-lc srj5• rhus-g tmo3• sal-fr sle1• tritic-vg fd5.de

FREEDOM: lac-h sze9• [buteo-j sej6 tax jsj7]
- **desire** for: [buteo-j sej6]
- **yearning** for: olib-sac wmh1

FREEZING: grat kola stb3•

FRIENDLY, being: ped a1
- **frightened**; though being: lac-leo hrn2•

FRIENDS: aids nl2• aln vva1• ant-c h2 aq-mar rbp6 ara-maca sej7• bros-gau mrc1 bung-fa mtf chlam-tr bcx2• dulc fd4.de ferr galeoc-c-h gms1• ham fd3.de• kali-s fd4.de lac-e hrn2• lac-h htj1• lac-lup hrn2• oci a1 oci-sa sk4• ozone sde2• petr-ra shn4• plac-s rly4• positr nl2• rumx sal-al blc1• samb bat1• spong fd4.de streptoc rly4• tritic-vg fd5.de vanil fd5.de [bell-p-sp dcm1 calc-sil stj2 ferr-sil stj2 kali-sil stj2 mag-sil stj2 mang-sil stj2 mur-ac stj2 nat-sil stj2 sil stj2 sil-met stj2 tax jsj7]
- **apartment**; in wrong: ozone sde2•
- **beating** up his friend | **happy** to be: polys sk4•
- **birthday** | **formality**; treating as a: polys sk4•
- **chauffeur**; being used as a: polys sk4•
- **childhood** friends: lac-lup hrn2•
- **company**; being in: lac-h sk4•
- **dead** (See Dead; of - friends)
- **death** of (See Death - friend)
- **falling** from a window (See Falling - window - friends)
- **loosing** in the city: ozone sde2•
- **meeting** friends: calc-p a1 chlam-tr bcx2• *Galeoc-c-h* gms1• *Ina-i* mlk9.de lac-d sk4• lac-lup hrn2• nept-m lsd2.fr
  - **old** friends; meeting: *(↗Seeing)* bros-gau mrc1 samb bat1•
- **mourning** the departure of: lac-leo hrn2•
- **old**: *(↗Seeing)* aids nl2• ant-c h2* bamb-a stb2.de• bros-gau mrc1 carbn-dox knl3• carneg-g rwt1• dulc fd4.de ferr granit-m es1• helodr-cal knl2• ina-i mlk9.de *Lac-cp* sk4• lac-d sk4• lac-del hrn2• *Lac-leo* hrn2*• lac-lup hrn2• loxo-recl knl4• ozone sde2• petr-ra shn4• plut-n srj7• polys sk4• pyrid rly4• rumx streptoc rly4• tritic-vg fd5.de *Tung-met* bdx1• vanil fd5.de [buteo-j sej6 heroin sdj2]
  - **meeting** old friends (See meeting - old)
  - **relieved** to have harmony with: lac-leo hrn2•
- **punished** by: lac-h sk4•
- **save** her friends; attempting to: lac-d sk4•
- **seeing** friends: *(↗Seeing)* chir-fl gya2 lac-del hrn2• lac-lup hrn2• plac-s rly4• rumx a1
  - **cheerful** mood; in a: nicc-met sk4•
- **separated** from her friend: lac-d sk4•
- **sick** friends; assisting: lac-h sk4•

FRIGHTFUL: *(↗Anxious; Grimaces)* abrot acon adon st aeth aether a1 agar agath-a nl2• agn alco a1 alet sf1.de all-c all-s alum b4.de* alumn am-c **Am-m** k* ammc k1 *Anac* sf1.de* androc srj1• ang *Ant-c* apis *Aran* aran-ix mg1.de* *Arg-met* *Arg-n* k* *Arn* k* **Ars** k* ars-i k2 ars-s-f k2 asc-t kr1 atro **Aur** aur-ar k2 aur-i k2 aur-m aur-m-n wbt2• aur-s a1* bad *Bapt* bar-c k* bar-m bar-s k2 *Bell* k* *Bism* bol-la a1 **Borx** bov bruc j5.de *Bry* bufo cact br1 **Calc** calc-act a1 **Calc-ar** *Calc-f* *Calc-p* *Calc-s* *Calc-sil* k2 *Camph* cann-i *Cann-s* carb-an k* **Carb-v** carbn-s *Carc* mlr1• *Carl* k1 casc castm caust *Cench* k2* *Cham* k* *Chel* *Chin* k* chinin-ar chinin-s *Chlol* chord-umb rly4• cimic **Cina** clem **Cocc** k* cod coff *Colch* coloc **Con** cop corn *Croc* k* **Crot-c** k* crot-h k2* *Cycl* dendr-pol sk4• dig digin a1 digox a1 dios dor dros dulc elaps *Erig* mg1.de *Eup-pur* euphr fl-ac gink-b sbd1• **Graph** k* grat guaj k* ham a1 hep hipp a1 hydr hydrog srj2• *Hyos* hyper iber ign k* indg ip iris jac-c jug-c jug-r **Kali-ar** kali-bi **Kali-br** **Kali-c** k* kali-cy a1 *Kali-i* kali-m k2 kali-n kali-p *Kali-s* k* *Kali-sil* k2 kalm ketogl-ac rly4• kiss a1 *Kola* stb3• kreos *Lac-d* sk4• lac-e hrn2• lac-h sk4• lach lat-m bnm6• *Laur* k* led b7.de* lil-s a1 lil-t **Lyc** k* lyss *Mag-c* *Mag-m* mag-s j5.de

Dreams

Frightful: ...
manc mand jl mang k* *Med Merc* k* merc-c merc-i-f merc-i-r merc-sul mez mit a1 morph a1 mosch mur-ac k* myric naja *Nat-ar Nat-c* **Nat-m** nat-p *Nat-s* nat-sil k2 **Nicc** *Nit-ac* nux-m *Nux-v* k* oci-sa sk4• op k* ox-ac oxal-a rly4• paeon *Par* kr1 petr k* ph-ac k* phel *Phos* k* phys pitu-a vml2• plac-s rly4• plan plat plb j5.de podo fd3.de• psil ft1 *Psor* k1 ptel **Puls** k* *Pyrog* k2* *Ran-b* sf1.de *Ran-s* rat rhus-t k* ribo rly4• ruta fd4.de sabad sang sarr sars k* scroph-n a1 scut a1 sec sel kr1 sep serp a1 **Sil** sin-n sol-ni a1 spig *Spong* b7a.de* stann k* staph stram stront-c k* suis-em rly4• sul-ac b4.de* *Sulph* k* symph fd3.de• tab *Tarax* kr1 tax-br oss1• thea thuj til ust verat k* verat-v verb k* wildb a1 *Zinc* k* zinc-p k2 zing
- **morning**: *Con* a1 ign a1
- **afternoon**: ign a1
- **night**:
  - **midnight**: all-s a1
    - **after**: dor a1 ph-ac h2* plan a1 stront-c a1
- **alone**, when: kali-c k2
- **alternating** with | **Head**; pain in (See HEAD - Pain - alternating - frightful)
- **closing** eyes, on: chin a1
- **dysmenorrhea**, in: *Cycl* kr1
- **falling** asleep, on: chin
- **falling** downstairs, after: *Rhus-t* kr1
- **followed** by | **fear**: oci-sa sk4•
- **true** | **waking**; seeming true after: cina k2 nat-m a1
- **waking** him: *(↗SLEEP - Waking - dreams)* bell a1 carneg-g rwt1• casc kr1 com a1 dicha mg1.de dulc fd4.de *Erig* mg1.de **Lyc** kr1 *Meph* a1* ribo rly4• sal-fr sle1• samb bat1• *Sulph* a1*

FROG: allox tpw4
- **bed**; in: allox jl*

FRUITS: castor-eq choc srj3• fic-m gya1 jac-c a1 lac-cp sk4• mag-c b4.de* nept-m lsd2.fr polys sk4• spong fd4.de

FRUSTRATION: *Lac-e* hrn2• melal-alt gya4

FUN: | **hurting** others; by: lac-h sk4•

FUNERALS: *(↗Buried; Churchyard; Coffins; Death - dying - he is; Graves)* adam srj5• allox sp1 alum ange-s jl bart brom k* *Chel* k* form galla-q-r nl2• hura ignis-alc es2• kali-s fd4.de kola stb3• lac-h sk4• lach hr1 mag-c nat-c h2* nicc rat ros-d wla1 [am-br stj2 bar-br stj2 heroin sdj2 nicc-met stj2 nicc-s stj2]
- **corpse** coming alive:
  - **after** a funeral: allox sp1
  - **before** funeral: allox tpw4
- **own** funeral; his: lach hr1
  - **alive**; being buried (See Buried - alive)
  - **knell**; his own funeral: aether a1

FUR coats: galla-q-r nl2•

FURNITURE; high: | **collapsing**: nept-m lsd2.fr

FUTURE:
- **planning** one's life; about: ulm-c jsj8•
- **told**; being: stront-c sk4•

GALILEO' S wheels and models of the universe: plut-n srj7•

GAMBLING: bit-ar wht1• dioxi rbp6 [tax jsj7]

GAMES: musca-d szs1
- **cat** and mouse; like: coca-c sk4•
- **enjoying**: dioxi rbp6
- **new** games; playing: stront-c sk4•
- **sex**; of: coca-c sk4•
  - **aunt**; with: lac-cp sk4•

GARDENS: agath-a nl2• apeir-s mlk9.de com a1 falco-pe nl2• gard-j vlr2• hippoc-k szs2 ina-i mlk9.de lac-h sk4• maias-l hrn2• nat-s j5.de* nept-m lsd2.fr phel j5.de* plut-n srj7• positr nl2•
- **overgrown**: chir-fl gya2
- **water** gardens: irid-met srj5•

GARMENT, made the previous day: aeth a1

GAS MASKS; people wearing: ozone sde2•

GATES: | **opening** and shutting in succession: oci-sa sk4•

GENEALOGY, of: haliae-lc srj5•

GENITALIA; female: | **enlarged** like male genitals: coca-c sk4•

GEOMETRICAL FIGURES:
- **cube**: ulm-c jsj8•
- **squares**: ulm-c jsj8•

GERMAN language; in: plut-n srj7•

GHOSTS: aesc alum k* am-c *Arg-n* k* asc-t atro bell bov k* *Camph* *Carb-v* k* carbn-s cham chlol kr1 cina k2 convo-d a1 *Crot-c* dendr-pol sk4• eupi *Graph* haliae-lc srj5• ign k* *Kali-c* k* kali-s k* kali-sil k2 lach j5.de mag-s manc *Med* musca-d szs1 nat-c nat-m nat-sil k2 *Ol-j* kr1 op orot-ac rly4• paeon petr-ra shn4• puls rhus-g tmo3• sars k* sep *Sil* k* sinus rly4• spig k* *Sulph* [ant-t stj2 zinc stj2 zinc-i stj2 zinc-m stj2 zinc-n stj2 zinc-p stj2]
- **approaching** her; shadow: ozone sde2•
- **black**: ars cerv a1
- **chest**; sitting on: paeon gt*
- **fighting** with ghosts: sars sep sil j5.de
- **flying**: positr nl2•
- **interchangeably** good and bad: positr nl2•
- **miserable** phantoms: bell a1
- **pursued** by ghosts; being (See Pursued - ghosts)
- **white**: ozone sde2• sars
  - **scarves**; in: ozone sde2•
    - **narcosis**; under: ozone sde2•

GIANTS: agath-a nl2• bamb-a stb2.de• bell lyc plut-n srj7•
- **pursued** by giants, being: agath-a nl2• bell

GIRL: tritic-vg fd5.de vanil fd5.de
- **attention** of a; trying to attract the: lac-cp sk4•
- **beautiful** girls; of: *(↗Beautiful)* caust a1 lac-cp sk4• positr nl2•
- **being** a: apis
- **running** after: lac-cp sk4•

GIRLFRIEND: | **old** girlfriend is beating current girlfriend: plut-n srj7•

GIVING things away: adam srj5• sal-fr sle1•

GLADIATOR; being a: phasco-ci rbp2

GLASS: lac-lup hrn2•
- **broken**: lac-del hrn2•
- **covered** up: lac-del hrn2•
- **feet**; in my: carbn-dox knl3•
- **sheet**, very hot and dangerous | **mother** burned hand on: limen-b-c hrn2•

GLOB: | **black**, oily: musca-d szs1

GLOOMY: plan ptk1 ruta fd4.de

GLORIFICATION OF ONESELF: saroth mg1.de

GOATS: *(↗Animals)* choc srj3• lac-cp sk4• nicc-met sk4•

GOBLINS: | **frighten** people, set to: positr nl2•

GOD; of: *(↗Religious)* toxi mtf2•
- **repudiating** him: hyper a1
- **word** of God; talking about one's love for: maias-l hrn2•

GODDESS; of: *Sanguis-s* hrn2• [bell-p-sp dcm1]

GOOD AND EVIL: *(↗Evil)* ara-maca sej7•

GOOSE (See Birds - geese)

GRACEFUL: | **she** had to be silent and graceful: marb-w es1•

GRANDPARENTS; of: *(↗Family)* granit-m es1•
- **grandmother**:
  - **old** | **isolated**: polys sk4•

GRASS: hippoc-k szs2 musca-d szs1

GRAVES: *(↗Armies - rising; Churchyard; Coffins; Funerals)* anac *Arn* dulc fd4.de hura iris kola stb3• mag-c k* ptel [nicc-met stj2 nicc-s stj2]
- **falling** into a grave: iris
- **living** in tombs: nicc
- **putting** tapers on tombs: hura
- **rising** from their graves; armies (See Armies - rising)
- **thrown** into a grave, being: mag-c a1

GREAT LEAPS (See Jumping - leaps)

GREATNESS: bufo bg2*

GREENHOUSE: sal-fr sle1•
- **roses**; full of blue and gold: sal-fr sle1•

GRIEF: *(↗Cares)* arn fyz7 *Ars* h2* carl a1 lyc c1 mag-s a1 stront-c a1*

GRIMACES, horrible: *(↗Frightful)* op j5.de

GROOMING of body hair (See Hair - body - grooming)

GROTESQUE: *(↗Comical)* carneg-g rwt1• lil-t

GROUPS: lac-e hrn2• lac-leo hrn2• lac-loxod-a hrn2•
- **fit** in a group; unable to: [buteo-j sej6]
- **mourning** departure of friends (See Friends - mourning)
- **screwed** over by attorney: lac-e hrn2•
- **spiritual**: nept-m lsd2.fr
- **working** well together: *(↗Teamwork)* *Lac-e* hrn2•

GROWING things: choc srj3• kreos j5.de

GUESTS: *Lac-cp* sk4•
- **bed** by guests; deprived of their: lac-cp sk4•
- **unable** to ask a guest to stop what he is doing: *Lac-cp* sk4•

GUIDANCE or advice; looking for: stront-c sk4•
- **parents** for; asking: *Limen-b-c* hrn2•
  - **receiving** unsatisfactory: limen-b-c hrn2•

GUIDED; being: stront-c sk4• [tax jsj7]
- **lost**; when: nicc-met sk4•
- **policeman**; by a: nicc-met sk4•

GUIDING: olib-sac wmh1

GUILT: *(↗Crime; Mortification)* androc srj1• arist-cl rbp3• asar jl bros-gau mrc1 gard-j vlr2• *Kola* stb3• lac-del hrn2• lac-e hrn2• lac-h sze9• positr nl2• [heroin sdj2]
- **not** feeling guilt: *(↗Remorse - want)* lac-h sk4•

GUITAR; buying a: coca-c sk4•

GUNNING (See Hunting)

GUNS: *(↗Shooting; Shot)* bit-ar wht1• choc srj3• hippoc-k szs2 loxo-recl knl4• oci-sa sk4• pot-e rly4• ruta fd4.de

GYMNASTIC exercises; he is performing: bell a1 galla-q-r nl2• hydrog srj2•

GYPSIES: *(↗Dancing - tango - gypsies)* choc srj3• pieri-b mlk9.de

HAIR: *(↗Body; parts)*
- **axillae**; of:
  - **long** and admirable: positr nl2•
  - **shaving**: [heroin sdj2]
- **body** hair:
  - **grooming**: lac-leo hrn2•
  - **licking**: lac-leo hrn2•
- **cut**; having hair: coca-c sk4• dream-p sdj1• lac-loxod-a hrn2• vanil fd5.de [heroin sdj2]
  - **occiput**: cob a1
  - **short**: gink-b sbd1•
  - **son's** head was shaved: brass-n-o srj5•
- **dress** the hair of the company; obliged to: mag-c k*
- **drying** her: aids nl2•
- **falling** out: *(↗Disease)* aids nl2• mag-c sal-fr sle1•
- **gray**: gink-b sbd1• lac-h sk4•
- **graying**: polys sk4•
- **red**: musca-d szs1

Hair: ...
- **white**, turning: aids nl2•

HAMMERING: | **finger**; on:
  - **woman**; of a: galeoc-c-h gms1•
    - **oriental**: galeoc-c-h gms1•
- **hands**; on | **woman**; of a: galeoc-c-h gms1•

HANDCUFFED: positr nl2•

HANDICAPPED people (See Disabled)

HANDS: *(↗Body; parts)*
- **burning** hands by washing: *(↗Disease)* mag-m a1
- **cut**, being: positr nl2•
- **cut** to pieces, being: sol-t-ae a1
- **losing** control over her hands: bung-fa mtf

HANGING: | **cliff**; on to a | **arm**; by right: agath-a nl2• lac-lup hrn2•
- **down**; upside: plut-n srj7•

HAPPEN to him, everything is going to: arg-n k2

HAPPY: falco-pe nl2• mang h2 sphing kk3.fr sulph bro1
- **alive**; to be: lac-e hrn2•
- **ending**: nept-m lsd2.fr
- **notice** it; she is happy but does not: ozone sde2•

HARASSING: *(↗Cares; Exhausting)* thuj a1*

HARBORS: lac-h sze9• [temp elm1]

HARE; white: | **butcher** it; cannot: ozone sde2•

HEAD: *(↗Body; parts)*
- **ape**-like people; seeing heads from: plut-n srj7•
- **bitten** off by animals: maias-l hrn2•
- **comical** heads; seeing: glon hr1*
- **cut** off: *(↗Cutting)* androc srj1• hura a1 nicc a1
- **picking** up small heads: jac-c a1
- **pustular** eruptions on: stront-c sk4•
- **skull**; milky white: lac-leo hrn2•
- **upper** part of his head is torn away: lil-s a1

HEADACHE; about: *(↗Disease)* hydrog srj2• pip-m a1 polyg-h a1 polyg-pe vml2•
- **before** the headache appears: *(↗SLEEP - Dreaming - followed - head)* celt a1 hydrog srj2*•
- O - **Temples**; in: lyc a1

HEARING talking: stram a1

HEART FAILURE; she is having a: ignis-alc es2•

HEAVINESS: plut-n srj7•

HEAVY: acon bg2 arn b7.de* ars bg2 bell bg2 calc bg2 chin b7.de* dig bg2 dulc b4.de* elaps al lach b7.de* laur b7.de* m-ambo b7.de* mag-c bg2 mang a1 nat-m b4.de* *Nux-v* b7.de* *Ph-ac* b4.de* *Phos* b4a.de pic-ac bg2 plb b7.de* polyg-h bg2 sars b4.de* sec b7.de* sil bg2 sul-ac bg2 tab bg2 *Thuj* b4.de*

HELD:
- **finger**; held by (See Seized)
- **hand**; tightly held by: am-m a1

HELL; of: *(↗Purgatory)* *Moni* rfm1• sanguis-s hrn2•

HELPED; being: helodr-cal knl2• sal-al blc1• [tax jsj7]
- **strangers**; by: lac-h sk4•

HELPING: *(↗Saving)*
- **friends**; his: bung-fa mtf *Lac-h* sk4•
- **people**: carc fd2.de• coca-c sk4• corv-cor bdg• ina-i mlk9.de lac-e hrn2• lac-h sk4• maias-l hrn2• sabad j5.de sal-al blc1• [tax jsj7]
  - **aversion** to: maias-l hrn2•
  - **distress**; in: polys sk4•
  - **unable** to help others: crot-c sk4•
  - **weaker** than himself: *Nicc-met* sk4•
- **rejected** by those he tries to help: lac-e hrn2•
- **shrieking** for help (See Shrieking - help)
- **trying** to help: lac-lup hrn2•

Dreams

HELPLESS feeling: allox tpw3 bit-ar wht1• gink-b sbd1• hippoc-k szs2 lac-loxod-a hrn2• lac-lup hrn2• *Pycnop-sa* mrz1 spong fd4.de [buteo-j sej6 sel stj2]
- **end** of the world; as if it is the: fic-m gya1 hydrog srj2• [temp elm1]

HEMOPTYSIS: hep meph phos j5.de

HEMORRHAGE: *(↗Disease)* phos k* sol-t-ae st thiam rly4•

HERO; of being the: aur-s wbt•

HICCOUGH; constant: pert-vc vk9
- **relieve** it; not able to: pert-vc vk9

HIDING: lac-lup hrn2• phasco-ci rbp2 tritic-vg fd5.de [heroin sdj2 tax jsj7]
- **danger**; from: *(↗Danger)* hippoc-k szs2 lac-d sk4• lac-del hrn2• lac-e hrn2• lac-h sk4• lac-leo hrn2• lac-lup hrn2• tritic-vg fd5.de

HIGH places: all-c anac arizon-l nl2• brom k* bros-gau mrc1 chin cortico tpw7* dulc fd4.de falco-pe nl2• hydrog srj2• kola stb3• lac-h sk4• laur lyss macro a1 maias-l hrn2• *Plut-n* srj7• positr nl2• ros-d wla1 tung-met stj2*• ulm-c jsj8• [am-br stj2 ant-c stj2 ant-m stj2 ant-met stj2 ant-t stj2 arg-met stj2 arg-n stj2 arg-p stj2 astat stj2 aur stj2 aur-m stj2 aur-s stj2 bar-br stj2 bar-i stj2 bar-met stj2 bism-sn stj2 cadm-m stj2 cadm-met stj2 cadm-s stj2 caes-met stj2 cinnb stj2 hafn-met stj2 ind stj2 iod stj2 irid-met stj2 lanth-met stj2 lith-i stj2 mang-i stj2 merc stj2 merc-d stj2 merc-i-f stj2 moly-met stj2 niob-met stj2 osm-met stj2 pall stj2 plat stj2 plb stj2 plb-m stj2 plb-p stj2 polon-met stj2 rhen-met stj2 rhodi stj2 rubd-met stj2 ruth-met stj2 stann stj2 stront-m stj2 stront-met stj2 tant-met stj2 tax jsj7 techn stj2 tell stj2 thal-met stj2 yttr-met stj2 zinc stj2 zinc-i stj2 zinc-m stj2 zinc-n stj2 zinc-p stj2 zirc-met stj2]
- **falling** from (See Falling - height)
- **ledge** | **hanging** from a: lac-h sk4•

HILL:
- **ascending** | **see** everywhere from top; could: brass-n-o srj5•
- **road** curved and narrow; with: nicc-met sk4•
- **sliding** down a steep hill (See Sliding - hill)
- **standing** on a hill: ephe-si hsj1•

HISTORIC: *(↗Events - past)* acon bg2 am-c ant-t k* brom bg2 caust k* *Cham* k* cic bg2 croc k* cypra-eg sde6.de• graph bg2 hell k* hyos j5.de *M-ambo* b2.de* m-arct b2.de* *Mag-c* k* merc k* olib-sac wmh1 *Phos* k* plut-n srj7• sel k* *Sil* k* stram k*

HOLES: lac-lup hrn2•
- **leggings**; in: lac-lup hrn2•
- **legs**; in: lac-lup hrn2*
- **stockings**: lac-lup hrn2•

HOLIDAYS: falco-pe nl2• tritic-vg fd5.de vanil fd5.de
- **being** on holiday: galeoc-c-h gms1• vanil fd5.de [bell-p-sp dcm1]

HOME: *(↗House; Household)* galeoc-c-h gms1• lac-lup hrn2• lach a1 mur-ac a1*
- **away** far from; being taken: crot-c sk4•
- **childhood** home; of (See House - youth)
- **running**: *(↗Running - home)* galeoc-c-h gms1•
- **turned** out of: lac-h sk4•

HOMELESS:
- **being** homeless: bros-gau mrc1 galla-q-r nl2• phasco-ci rbp2 positr nl2•
- **looking** for accommodation: galla-q-r nl2• positr nl2•
- **men**: coca-c sk4•
- **people** are: lac-loxod-a hrn2•

HOMEOPATHIC REMEDIES: lac-e hrn2• lac-loxod-a hrn2• tritic-vg fd5.de

HOMESICKNESS: galeoc-c-h gms1• *Glon* a1* kola stb3• lac-d sk4•

HOMOSEXUALITY: musca-d szs1
- **children**; amongst: dendr-pol sk4•
- **concealed**: *Plut-n* srj7•
- **contacts**; he has homosexual: pegan-ha tpi1•
- **he** is homosexual: pegan-ha tpi1•
- **open**, unabashed: *Plut-n* srj7•
- **tell** her she is homosexual; people: galeoc-c-h gms1•

HOPELESS: aq-mar rbp6 lac-loxod-a hrn2•

HORRIBLE: adon bro1* aids nl2• ant-c gt *Arg-n* bro1 *Aur* bro1 bapt bro1 *Bell* bro1 bit-ar wht1• *Cact* bro1 calc bro1 cann-i bro1 castm bro1 *Cham* bro1 *Chin* bro1 chlol ptk1 *Colch* bro1 eupi bro1 graph gt* *Hyos* bro1 kali-br hr1* kali-c bro1 lac-h sze9• *Lil-t* bro1 lyc bro1 mand rsj7• *Merc-c* bro1 nux-v bro1 op bro1 phos bro1 psor bro1 puls bro1 ran-s bro1 *Rhus-t* bro1 sec bro1 sep bro1 sil tl1 stram bro1 *Sulph* bro1 thea bro1 *Zinc-m* bro1 [heroin sdj2]

HORSES: *(↗Animals)* *Agath-a* nl2• alum am-c b4.de* am-m k* apeir-s mlk9.de asc-t atro bamb-a stb2.de• bomb-chr mlk9.de choc srj3• crot-c gink-b sbd1• helodr-cal knl2• hyper a1 ina-i mlk9.de indg lac-del hrn2• *Lac-e* hrn2• lac-loxod-a hrn2• m-aust b7.de* mag-m j5.de mag-s merc merl a1 musca-d szs1 phos ruta fd4.de senec a1 spong fd4.de sul-ac b4.de* tarent ther vero-o rly4*• zinc
- **bitten** by a horse; being:
  - **arm**; in the: am-m k*
  - **ferocious** black horse; by: phos a1
- **black** with a big white spot on chest: ozone sde2•
- **changing** into dogs: zinc
- **cleaning** two carthorses with a small dishcloth: lac-h htj1•
- **drowning**: crot-c a1 (non:crot-h a1)
- **eating** corn in a garage: ozone sde2•
- **falling** from horse: tarent a1
- **kicking**: *Mag-s*
- **pursuing** him: allox jl* alum
- **racing**: lac-del hrn2•
- **riding**: bamb-a stb2.de• chr-ac kr1 helodr-cal knl2• nat-c spong fd4.de ther
- **running**: atro indg lipp a1
- **small**; very: ozone sde2•
- **theft** of a horse: aether a1 rumx
- **ugly**: (non:merc a1) merl k* phos
- **wild**: marb-w es1•
- **wounded** by: mag-s a1

HOSE, garden: | **taking** a plastic plug from a woman's faucet and putting it on his own: lac-lup hrn2•

HOSPITALS: galla-q-r nl2• hippoc-k szs2 positr nl2• tritic-vg fd5.de vanil fd5.de [tax jsj7 temp elm1]

HOSTAGES:
- **taken** as | **sexual** torture; for: maias-l hrn2•

HOTELS: aln vva1•
- **no** room at the hotel: galla-q-r nl2•

HOUSE: *(↗Buildings; Home)* *Aids* nl2• aln vva1• chir-fl gya2 *Galeoc-c-h* gms1• ina-i mlk9.de kola stb3• *Lac-leo* hrn2• limen-b-c hrn2* maias-l hrn2• musca-d szs1 orot-ac rly4• ozone sde2• pall kr1 plut-n srj7• positr nl2• suis-em rly4• tritic-vg fd5.de vanil fd5.de [heroin sdj2]
- **big**: aids nl2• arizon-l nl2• gink-b sbd1• ham fd3.de• polys sk4• symph fd3.de• vanil fd5.de [pall stj2]
  - **curtains**; with flowing: limen-b-c hrn2•
  - **mansion**: aids nl2•
- **building** a house: helodr-cal knl2•
- **bright**; very: ozone sde2•
- **built**; houses being: hura a1 myris c1
  - **upper** stories first: myris c1
- **clearing** from excess: chlam-tr bcx2•
- **cold**, lifeless, nearly threatening: ozone sde2•
- **collapsing**: nept-m lsd2.fr
- **community** centre: lac-del hrn2•
  - **rundown**: lac-del hrn2•
  - **wooden**: lac-del hrn2•
- **country**; in the: chlam-tr bcx2• *Lac-leo* hrn2• nicc-met sk4•
- **crystal** and marble; built of: ozone sde2•
- **decorating**: aids nl2•
- **dirty**: ozone sde2•
- **door**; without: polys sk4•
- **entrance**; with hidden: ozone sde2•
- **exploring**: fic-m gya1
- **facade**; only a: phasco-ci rbp2
- **family**; for a big: ozone sde2•
- **find** house where he wants to go; cannot: ozone sde2•
- **glass**; with walls of: ozone sde2•

- **grandmother's** house; like her: galeoc-c-h gms1•
- **looking** around in: ozone sde2•
- **majestic**: polys sk4•
- **mother's** house; her: ozone sde2•
- **moving**: aids nl2• [heroin sdj2 spect dfg1]
- **old**: bung-fa mtf limen-b-c hrn2• tritic-vg fd5.de
  - **dirty**; and: falco-pe nl2•
- **old**-fashioned: plut-n srj7•
  - **places** that are not modernized: plut-n srj7•
- **ornate** house: aids nl2•
- **other** people's; being in: galeoc-c-h gms1•
- **people** in her house: [buteo-j sej6]
- **privacy**; without: polys sk4•
- **rooms**; with many: helodr-cal knl2•
- **rural** (See country)
- **sexual** liaisons; for: maias-l hm2•
- **showing** her around their; people: galeoc-c-h gms1•
- **white** with refugees; painted: ozone sde2•
- **youth**; like the house of her: aids nl2• carbn-dox knl3• helodr-cal knl2• kola stb3• lac-lup hrn2• ozone sde2• plut-n srj7•

HOUSEHOLD: *(↗Home; Shopping)* bell *Bry* k*

HOUSEWORK: plut-n srj7•

HUGGING: chlam-tr bcx2• moni rfm1•

HUMILIATION: *(↗Mortification; Shameful)* alum k* am-c k* arn k* *Asar* k* bros-gau mrc1 chir-fl gya2 coca-c sk4• con k* dulc fd4.de falco-pe nl2• ign kola stb3• lac-del hrn2• led k* mag-m k* mosch k* mur-ac k* ozone sde2• podo fd3.de• *Sil* staph k* [heroin sdj2 mang-i stj2 mang-m stj2 mang-met stj2 mang-p stj2 mang-s stj2]
- **sexual**: falco-pe nl2• [heroin sdj2]

HUNG; being:
- **falling** down an interminable lift shaft; hanged man: choc srj3•
- **himself**: am-m bros-gau mrc1
- **genitals**; by: bros-gau mrc1
- **persons**: bros-gau mrc1 merc-sul

HUNGER: *(↗Famine)* adam srj5• *Arg-n* k* bry calc *Corv-cor* bdg• ign
- **people**; of hungry: lac-loxod-a hrn2•

HUNTING: *(↗Safari)* dulc fd4.de hura hyper junc-e a1 maias-l hrn2• merc-i-r spong fd4.de verat [tax jsj7]

HURRICANE (See Storms - hurricane)

HURRY: *(↗Busy)* arist-cl rbp3• choc srj3• coca hydrog srj2• ina-i mlk9.de merc-c nat-sil fd3.de• nux-v b7a.de ruta fd4.de tritic-vg fd5.de vanil fd5.de
- **perform** some labor; to: rhus-t gt

HYDROPHOBIA (See Fear - water; Rabies)

HYPERTHYROIDISM; having: *(↗Disease)* crot-c sk4•

ICE: hippoc-k szs2 positr nl2• [tax jsj7]

IDENTITY:
- **lost**: lac-lup hm2•
- **search** for her: galeoc-c-h gms1•

IGNORED, she is: positr nl2•

IGUANAS: aids nl2•

ILL-TREATMENT: *(↗Bullying; Cruelty; Mutilation; Violence)* ambr j5.de dros j5.de* oxal-a rly4• podo fd3.de• tung-met bdx1•

ILLEGAL; is somewhere: ozone sde2•

ILLUMINATIONS: crot-c rad-br sze8• [tax jsj7]

IMPATIENCE; of: sanguis-s hrn2•

IMPORTANT PERSON, she is an: irid-met srj5•

IMPOVERISHED (See Poverty - being)

IMPRESSIVE: acon bg2 arn bg2 camph bg2 carb-an bg2 graph bg2 ign bg2 lach bg2 nux-v bg2 puls bg2 ruta fd4.de sabin bg2 suprar rly4• thuj bg2

IMPRISONMENT: *(↗Prisoner - being)* bov j5.de cerv a1 dulc fd4.de hydrog srj2• positr nl2• taosc iwa1• [irid-met stj2 temp elm1]

INADEQUATE; of feeling: lac-del hrn2•

INCEST: marb-w es1• polys sk4• positr nl2• sal-fr sle1• [nat-f stj2]
- **father** is normal; with: sal-fr sle1•

INDECENT BEHAVIOR of men and women: cench k2 lac-del hrn2• petr-ra shn4•

INDECENT PROPOSAL: crot-c sk4•

INDIANS, being among: jug-c lac-lup hrn2•

INDIFFERENCE:
- **friend** being murdered; to: dendr-pol sk4•
- **people**; of: ozone sde2•
- **suffering**; to: helodr-cal knl2•

INDIFFERENT: lac-lup hrn2•

INDIGNANT (See Anger - indignant)

INDIGNATION: arist-cl rbp3• *Lac-e* hrn2• [tax jsj7]
- **salesman**; as a: lac-del hm2•

INDUSTRIOUS: apis gt arn ptk1 bry ptk1 echi ptk1 lac-h sk4• puls ptk1 rhus-t gt*

INDUSTRY: limen-b-c hrn2•

INFECTION; of an: aids nl2• positr nl2•

INFORMATION, seeking: positr nl2•

INJECTIONS: | **receiving** many: [buteo-j sej6]

INJURIES: *(↗Disease; Wounded)* allox tpw3* am-m ant-c cench k2 chel a1 chin choc srj3• cortico sp1 fuma-ac rly4• galeoc-c-h gms1• ham fd3.de• helodr-cal knl2• kali-s fd4.de kola stb3• lob kr1 *Mag-s* j5.de nat-s nat-sil fd3.de• nicc j5.de petr-ra shn4• phasco-ci rbp2 phos rhus-g tmo3• suis-pan rly4• sumb symph fd3.de• thiam rly4• [cadm-met stj2]
- **fear** of (See Fear - injuries)
- **fingernails** digging in; by: falco-pe nl2•
- **machinery**, by: cortico tpw7*
- **mothers** hand burned by hot glass sheet (See Glass - sheet - mother)
- **self**-inflicted: nicc

INJUSTICE: *Nicc-met* sk4•
- **mother**; done to his: nicc-met sk4•

INSANE: *(↗MIND - Insanity)*
- **becoming** insane: *(↗Disease)* aloe a1* chlam-tr bcx2• ferr-p bg2 lac-h sk4•
  - **man** becomes insane: (non:apis vh1)
- **being** insane: aloe k* apis
  - **man**; a: (non:apis vh1)
- **eyes**; a wild man with crazy: coca-c sk4•

INSECTS: *(↗Animals; Bees; Beetles; Bugs; Cockroaches; Flies; Lice; Maggots; Moths; Vermin; Wasps)* arg-n arizon-l nl2• cystein-l rly4• falco-pe nl2• fic-m gya1 hist mg1.de* lac-leo sk4• *Lac-lup* hrn2• oxal-a rly4• phos a1 ribo rly4• ros-d wla1 sarr a1 (non:sphing a1) spig a1* [heroin sdj2]
- **crawling**: bros-gau mrc1
- **cut** out of his heel; had to be: arg-n a1
- **eating**: [heroin sdj2]
- **heel**; burrowing in his: arg-n a1
- **is** an insect; she: coca-c sk4•
- **trousers**; in her: lac-cp sk4•
- **stinging** (See Stung)

INSECURE; he is: pin-con oss2•

INSTRUCTIVE: falco-pe nl2•

INSULTS: *(↗Abused; Abused; being; Quarrels)* asar chir-fl gya2 falco-pe nl2• lac-leo hrn2• mosch b7a.de nat-s phasco-ci rbp2 tarent [calc-sil stj2]

INSURRECTIONS: *(↗Revolution; Riot)* ped a1

INTELLECTUAL: *(↗Scientific)* all-s a1 anac a1 ars a1 bufo-s a1 carb-ac a1 carb-an a1 cham a1 cinnb a1 coloc a1 ferr a1 fl-ac a1 guaj a1 ign b2.de* ind a1 kali-n j5.de lyc a1 m-arct b2.de* nat-p a1 phos a1 sabin a1 *Senec* a1* sil a1 thuj a1 ust a1

- **morning**: ign a1
- **night** | **midnight**, after: mag-c a1

INTERROGATION: positr nl2•

INTERRUPTED; of being: limen-b-c hrn2•

INTIMIDATING; of: con gt

INTOXICATED persons; of: *(↗People - drunken)* coca-c sk4•
- **sister**; her: rhus-g tmo3•

INTRIGUES: bros-gau mrc1 lach k* podo fd3.de•

INTRUDERS (See Robbers)

INVADERS; of (See Robbers)

INVENTION, full of: apis kali-n j5.de lach sabin

INVISIBLE; she is: adam srj5•

IRIDOLOGY, of: neon srj5•

ISLAND: musca-d szs1
- **searching** for a place to stay on an island: coca-c sk4•

ISOLATED; of being: phasco-ci rbp2 polys sk4• rad-br sze8•
- **contact**; can't make any: phasco-ci rbp2
- **feeling** isolated while amongst others: plut-n srj7•

ITALY: musca-d szs1

JAMES BOND; sees: fic-m gya1

JAWS: *(↗Body; parts)*
- **broken**: *(↗Disease)* rauw sp1
- **piece** of the jaw becoming loose and easily coming out; a: coca a1
- **stuck** together: crot-c sk4•

JEALOUSY: androc srj1• bamb-a stb2.de• dream-p sdj1• falco-pe nl2• ina-i mlk9.de *Kola* stb3• lac-leo hrn2• lyc gl1.fr• ruta fd4.de sacch-a fd2.de• sal-fr sle1• sanguis-s hrn2• spong fd4.de [heroin sdj2]

JET AIRPLANE (See Airplanes)

JEWELRY: *(↗MIND - Jewelry - desire)* aids nl2• hippoc-k szs2 irid-met srj5• [cadm-met stj2 osm-met stj2]

JOB (See Work)

JOKE, relating a: coca a1 lac-e hrn2•
- **money**; about: lac-e hrn2•

JOURNEYS: *(↗Country - foreign)* all-s kr1 am-c k* am-m k* anan *Apis* k* arizon-l nl2• bamb-a stb2.de• bart a1 bomb-chr mlk9.de brom k* bros-gau mrc1 bufo k* calc-f *Calc-p* *Carb-ac* carc sp1* chel (non:chin slp) chin-b kr1* choc srj3• cortico tpw7* corv-cor bdg• *Crot-h* dendr-pol sk4• dream-p sdj1• dulc fd4.de elaps galla-q-r nl2• haliae-lc srj5• hippoc-k szs2 hura hydr hydrog srj2• hyper ina-i mlk9.de ind indg **Kali-n** k* kali-s fd4.de *Kola* stb3• lac-c k* lac-d *Lac-h* sk4*• lac-leo hrn2*• *Lac-lup* hrn2• *Lach* k* linu-c a1 *Mag-c* k* mag-m k* mag-s melal-alt gya4 merc merc-c b4a.de* merc-i-r mez *Nat-c* k* nat-m nat-pyru rly4• neon srj5• nicc-met sk4• *Op* k* oxal-a rly4• ozone sde2• petr-ra shn4• pieri-b mlk9.de pip-m a1 *Plut-n* srj7• positr nl2• propl ub1• psor k* rauw tpw8* *Rhus-t* ruta fd4.de sang k* sel *Sil* k* sin-a a1 spong fd4.de suis-em rly4• ther *Tub* st urol-h rwt• vanil fd5.de [spect dfg1 tax jsj7]
- **airplane**; by: *(↗Airplanes - on)* helo-s rwt2• helodr-cal knl2• ozone sde2• petr-ra shn4• plut-n srj7• vanil fd5.de
- **bus**; by: *(↗Bus)* helo-s rwt2• ozone sde2• plut-n srj7•
- **car**; by (See Driving)
- **China**; to: bamb-a stb2.de•
- **cruise** around the world: bamb-a stb2.de•
- **desert**; in the: ozone sde2•
- **difficulties**; with (See Difficulties - journeys)
- **foreign** countries; in: plut-n srj7• vanil fd5.de
- **friends**; with: lach-h sk4•
- **horseback**, on: nat-c ther
- **island**; on an: ozone sde2•
- **long**: nat-m a1
- **night**, in the: adam srj5•
- **Peking**; to: ozone sde2•

Journeys: ...
- **preparing**: cortico tpw7
- **railroad**, by (See train)
- **returning** home from a trip: galeoc-c-h gms1•
- **road**:
  - **deserted**; through: lac-h sk4•
  - **ups** and downs; with: lac-h sk4•
- **Russia**; to: ozone sde2•
- **train**: *(↗Train)* adam srj5• apis cortico tpw7* haliae-lc srj5• ignis-alc es2• *Lac-h* sk4• ozone sde2• petr-ra shn4• ruta fd4.de
  - **derailing**: lac-h sk4•
- **travelling** forward while looking backward: plut-n srj7•
- **water**, by: *(↗Sailing; Water)* alum j5.de chin-b kr1* dulc fd4.de nat-s j5.de sal-fr sle1• sang j5.de valer j5.de

JOYOUS: *(↗Comical; Ludicrous; Pleasant)* ant-t a1 ars j5.de asaf b2.de* caust b2.de* coff b2.de* croc b2.de* dig b2.de* dros j5.de* dulc fd4.de grat j5.de* lac-e hrn2• lach b2.de* laur b2.de* m-ambo b2.de* mag-c b2.de* mag-m j5.de mez b2.de* mur-ac a1 olib-sac wmh1 **Op** b2.de* ozone sde2• palo jl ph-ac h2 phos b2.de* ruta fd4.de spong fd4.de squil b2.de* sulph b2.de*

JUGGLERS: positr nl2•

JUMPING: limen-b-c hrn2* ruta fd4.de verat
- **height**; from a: bit-ar wht1• haliae-lc srj5•
  - **airplane**; out of an: helodr-cal knl2•
  - **landing** easily; and: bit-ar wht1• marb-w es1•
  - **tall** building | **water**; into the: nicc-met sk4•
- **leaps**; great: apis a1 galla-q-r nl2• hydrog srj2• ruta fd4.de
  - **air**; like a bird through the: apis a1 ruta fd4.de
- **water**: *(↗Water)*
  - **he** is jumping into: bomb-chr mlk9.de tarent a1
  - **men** jumping into: bomb-chr mlk9.de mag-s

JUNGLE: carbn-dox knl3•
- **tropical** rainforest: limen-b-c hrn2•
  - **woman's** lover hiding in deep ravine: limen-b-c hrn2•

JUSTIFYING himself: plut-n srj7•

KANGAROO: coca-c sk4• ger-i rly4• melal-alt gya4

KEY; has taken the wrong: ozone sde2•

KEYHOLE; peeping through: neon srj5•

KICKED: | **abdomen**; in: nicc-met sk4•

KIDNAPPERS: *(↗Children - kidnapped; Pursued - man - kidnapper)* bamb-a stb2.de• *Kola* stb3• lac-leo hrn2•

KIDNAPPING: *(↗Children - kidnapped)*
- **friend** is kidnapped by a shepherd dog: ozone sde2•

KILLED; being (See Murdered - being)

KILLING: *(↗Murder; Murdering)* adam srj5• castm a1 crot-c sk4• hippoc-k szs2 *Lac-e* hrn2• medul-os-si rly4• moni rfm1• pseuts-m oss1• pyrid rly4• spong fd4.de suis-pan rly4• [aur stj2 aur-m stj2 aur-s stj2]
- **dog**; a mad: rumx
- **brother** is; her | **sister**; her: nicc-met sk4•
- **father**, her: *(↗MIND - Ailments - quarrelling - father)* castm a1
- **friend**, a: allox tpw3*
  - **knife**; with a: allox tpw3*
- **idea** of; but did not like the: *Lac-e* hrn2•

KINDNESS: positr nl2•

KINGS: kola stb3•
- **royalty**: hippoc-k szs2

KISSED: bit-ar wht1• tritic-vg fd5.de
- **he** was kissed:
  - **black** figure; by a | **pink** lips; with: lac-cp sk4•

KITES (See Birds - kites)

KNEE: *(↗Disease)*
- **eczema**; wet: coca-c sk4•

- **pain** in: zinc a1
- **swollen**: *Cocc*

KNELL (See Funerals - own - knell)

KNIVES: *(↗Cut being; Stabbed)* aids nl2• am-m b7.de* arizon-l nl2• falco-pe nl2• guaj *Kola* stb3• lach k* nat-c k* ozone sde2• plut-n srj7• positr nl2• ribo rly4• ruta fd4.de tung-met bdx1• [buteo-j sej6]
- **threatened** with; is: ozone sde2•

LABOR, of being in (See Delivering)

LABORIOUS (See Industrious)

LABYRINTH: [tax jsj7]
- **circular** spiral or cobweb: galla-q-r nl2•

LADYBIRDS (See Ladybugs)

LADYBUGS: ulm-c jsj8•

LANDLORD: musca-d szs1

LANDSCAPE:
- **beautiful**: *(↗Beautiful; Earth - beautiful)* dulc fd4.de gink-b sbd1• ina-i mlk9.de *Kola* stb3• nat-sil fd3.de• nept-m lsd2.fr ozone sde2• ruta fd4.de spong fd4.de tritic-vg fd5.de vanil fd5.de
- **desolate**: maias-l hm2• [heroin sdj2]

LANGUAGE:
- **German** (See German)
- **talking** in a foreign language; people: maias-l hm2•

LARGE: | **everything** was: *(↗Enlarged)* lac-del hm2•

LARYNX: *(↗Body; parts)*
- **constricted**; being gradually: kali-c a1

LASCIVIOUS: *(↗Amorous)* arg-n bro1 ars bro1 *Cann-i* bro1 canth bro1 *Cob* bro1 *Dios* bro1 grat a1 ham bro1 *Hyos* bro1 ign bro1 lac-cp sk4• lac-d sk4• musca-d szs1 nat-m bro1 nit-ac bro1 op bro1 orig a1* petr-ra shn4• ph-ac bro1 *Phos* bro1 sal-n br1 sil bro1 *Staph* bro1 stront-c sk4• thuj bro1 ust bro1 verat-v bro1
- **orgasm**; with: musca-d szs1
- **smutty**: maias-l hm2•

LATIN; SPEAKING: lyss a1*

LAUGHED AT; being: bung-fa mtf toxi mtf2•

LAUGHING: *(↗Comical; Ludicrous)* alum bro1 caust k* coca croc hyos bro1 kola stb3• kreos lac-h sk4*• lyc bro1 melal-alt gya4 ruta fd4.de

LAWSUITS: sal-fr sle1• sep h2

LEASH:
- **connected** by | **gloved** hand to: [buteo-j sej6]

LEAVE; desire to: phasco-ci rbp2

LECTURE: bros-gau mrc1

LEG: *(↗Body; parts)*
- **amputation** (See Amputation - leg)
- **eruptions**; covered with: lac-h sk4•
- **she** has no legs: haliae-lc srj5•
- **ulcers** | **right** leg: stront-c sk4•

LEPER; being a: *(↗Disease)* guar vml3• paull a1

LETHARGY: *(↗Disease)* graph h2* op j5.de

LEWD: musca-d szs1 petr-ra shn4• plut-n srj7•
- **orgasm**; with: musca-d szs1

LICE: *(↗Insects; Vermin)* am-c chel k* falco-pe nl2• gamb mur-ac k* *Nux-v* k* ped a1 phos k*
- **combing** hair full of: falco-pe nl2•

LICKING: | **body** hair (See Hair - body - licking)

LIFE; about the meaning of: ignis-alc es2•

LIFT: bit-ar wht1• musca-d szs1

LIFTED out of her body; she was: *(↗Flying; MIND - Delusions - body - out)* coca-c sk4• rhus-g tmo3•
- **death**; at: rhus-g tmo3•

LIGHT; of: *Galeoc-c-h* gms1• kola stb3• nept-m lsd2.fr sanguis-s hrn2•
- **candle** light: loxo-recl knl4•
- **neon**: hippoc-k szs2
- **sunlight** (See Sun - being)
- **switching** the light (See Switch)

LIGHTNING: *(↗Thunderstorm)* *Arn* euphr k* phel spig
- **struck** by lightning, being: *Arn*
  - **shoulder** is; his: spig j5.de

LIMBS: *(↗Body; parts)*
- **broken**: *(↗Disease)* cimic

LIONS: *(↗Animals)* dendr-pol sk4• kali-m ccrh1• lac-h sk4• lac-loxod-a hrn2• lac-lup hrn2• [spect dfg1 titan stj2]
- **being** a lion: phys
- **bite**; which do not: crot-c a1

LISTENERS: | **explode** like balloons: ozone sde2•

LISTENING: | **pretending** to be: ara-maca sej7•

LIVER comes out: *(↗Body; parts)* ozone sde2•
- **blood** of menses; with: ozone sde2•

LIZARDS: *(↗Animals)* crot-c sk4• limen-b-c hrn2• [heroin sdj2]

LLAMAS; a zoo full of: bamb-a stb2.de•

LOCKED UP: | **half**-open gate; with: lac-cp sk4•

LOCKING and unlocking: hippoc-k szs2

LONG: *Acon* androc srj1• bry calc chin chir-fl gya2 chord-umb rly4• *Coff* euph h2* hydrog srj2• *Ign* naja a1 nat-c puls spig j5.de suis-pan rly4• tarent a1 thuj h1* tritic-vg fd5.de vanil fd5.de
- **object**, the same: *(↗Persistent)* petr h2 spig h1
- **weeks** and months duration; events in her dreams were not for hours, but for: sang rb2

LOOKING:
- **down** from above: musca-d szs1
- **far** away, more than usual: ulm-c jsj8•
- **someone**; for (See Searching - someone)

LOOTING (See Plundering)

LOSING: dulc fd4.de spong fd4.de vanil fd5.de
- **family**; his: choc srj3•
- **patients** (See Patients - losing)
- **things**: nat-ox rly4• plut-n srj7• vanil fd5.de
- **wallet** (See Wallet - lost)

LOSS: *(↗Misfortune)*
- **disheartening**: *(↗Misfortune)* *Meph* a1
- **sensation** of loss; with: ozone sde2•

LOST; being: adam srj5• chir-fl gya2 nicc sk4• phasco-ci rbp2 plut-n srj7• positr nl2• sal-fr sle1• sep a1 sol-br vml3• tritic-vg fd5.de ulm-c jsj8•
- **city**; in a: aln vva1• ozone sde2• phasco-ci rbp2
- **forest**; in a: am-m ind k* mag-c mag-m mag-s sep
- **home**, at: choc srj3• mag-c h2* [am-c stj1 am-m stj1]
- **hospital**; in a: carbn-dox knl3•
- **hotel**; in a: aln vva1•
- **house**; in a: aln vva1•
- **mountains**, in the: *(↗Astray)* ind a1* tritic-vg fd5.de
- **strange** place; in a: nicc-met sk4• tritic-vg fd5.de
- **street**; cannot find the right: ozone sde2•
- **town**; in an empty (See city)

LOTTERY: bit-ar wht1• mag-c a1 nat-s j5.de* ruta fd4.de
- **winning**: streptoc rly4•

LOVE; fallen in (See Amorous - fallen)

LUCID: acon mtf fl-ac a1 lac-lup hrn2• olib-sac wmh1 ruta fd4.de sal-fr sle1•
- **revealing** a perplexed situation when waking: *(↗Complicated)* acon h1* olib-sac wmh1

Dreams

LUDICROUS: *(↗Comical; Joyous; Laughing)* bell cod a1 falco-pe nl2• glon k* grat a1 iber a1* jug-c lac-lup hrn2• lach merc-c k* merc-i-r a1 mez k* mygal phos k* pin-con oss2• sedi a1 sol-t-ae a1 *Sulph* k*
- **lying** while:
  - **back**; on: *Arn* st
  - **left** side, on: sep st

LUGGAGE; of: sal-fr sle1•

LURID (See Vivid - lurid)

LYING: *(↗Bed - small)*
- **bed** with another person; in (See People - bed)
- **under** him; someone is lying: nit-ac h2

MACHINES: spong fd4.de
- **flying** machine, making a: falco-pe nl2•
- **perpetual** motion or seismic activity monitor: haliae-lc srj5•

MAGGOTS: *(↗Animals; Insects; Worms)* lac-lup hrn2•

MAGIC: aids nl2• arist-cl rbp3• coca-c sk4• hippoc-k szs2 oxal-a rly4• petr-ra shn4• plac-s rly4• sol-t-ae a1 [tax jsj7]
- **black** magic, voodoo: lac-lup hrn2•
- **gifts**, magical: *(↗MIND - Delusions - magician)* aids nl2•

MAKE UP: nept-m lsd2.fr

MAMMAE: *(↗Body; parts; Women - breasts)* *Lac-e* hrn2• lac-leo hrn2•
- **huge**: aster sze10•
  - **nipple** pulled itself inward; with: aster sze10•
- **naked**: *(↗Nakedness)* galla-q-r nl2•

MAN (See Men)

MANURE: maias-l hrn2•

MANY: *(↗SLEEP - Dreaming)* abrot a1 acon k* aconin a1 agar k* agath-a nl2• agn b2.de* alco a1 all-c a1 **Alum** b2.de* *Am-c* b2.de* *Am-m* b2.de* ambr b2.de* aml-ns a1 ammc a1 amp rly4• anac b2.de* ang k* ant-c b2.de* ant-s-aur a1 ant-t b2.de* *Apis* k* arg-met b2.de* arg-n a1 arist-m a1 *Arn* b2.de* *Ars* b2.de* asaf k* asar b2.de* asc-t a1 astac a1 atro a1 aur b2.de* bals-p a1 bapt a1 bar-c k* bart a1 **Bell** b2.de* benz-ac a1 berb a1 bism b2.de* bol-la a1 bond a1 borx b2.de* both-a rb3 bov k* brach a1 brom bro1 brucel sa3• **Bry** b2.de* bufo-s a1 cact a1 caj a1 calad b2.de* calam sa3• **Calc** b2.de* calc-caust a1 calc-f a1 calc-p j5.de* camph b2.de* cann-i a1 cann-s b2.de* canth b2.de* caps k* carb-ac a1 carb-an b2.de* *Carb-v* k* carbn-s a1 card-m a1 carl a1 casc a1 castor-eq a1 *Caust* b2.de* celt a1 *Cham* b2.de* chel b2.de* **Chin** b2.de* chinin-s a1 chord-umb rly4• chr-ac a1 cic k* cimic a1* cina b2.de* cinnb a1 clem k* cob a1 coc-c a1 coca a1 cocc b2.de* cod a1 coff b2.de* coff-t a1 colch a1 *Coloc* b2.de* com a1 **Con** b2.de* cor-r j5.de cori-r a1 cortico mg1.de cortiso mg1.de croc b2.de* crot-t j5.de* culx k2 cund a1 cupr h2* cupr-act a1 *Cycl* b2.de* dig b2.de* digin a1 digox a1 dios a1 dirc a1 dros b2.de* dulc b2.de* equis-h a1 euph b2.de* euphr b2.de* eupi a1 fago a1 *Ferr* b2.de* ferr-i a1 ferr-p k2 fl-ac a1 form a1 franz a1 gal-ac a1 galeoc-c-h gms1• gamb a1 gast a1 gels a1 gins a1 glon a1 *Gran* j5.de* *Graph* b2.de* grat j5.de guaj b2.de* hall a1 ham a1 *Hell* b2.de* helodr-cal knl2• *Hep* b2.de* hipp a1 hydr a1 hyos b2.de* hyosin a1 hypo a1 *Ign* b2.de* ina-i mlk9.de ind a1 iod h* ip b2.de* jab a1 jal a1 jug-r a1 kali-bi a1 kali-br a1 **Kali-c** b2.de* kali-cy a1 kali-n b2.de* kali-s k2 kiss a1 **Kreos** b2.de* lac-ac a1 lac-del hrn2• *Lach* k* lact j5.de* laur b2.de* led b2.de* lil-t a1 lob j5.de lob-c a1 **Lyc** b2.de* lycps-v a1 *M-ambo* b2.de* *M-arct* b2.de* m-aust b2.de *Mag-c* k* mag-m k* mag-s *Mang* k* mang-p rly4• menis a1 meny b2.de* meph jl *Merc* b2.de* merc-i-r a1 merc-sul a1 merl a1 *Mez* b2.de* mosch b2.de* mur-ac b2.de* myric a1 naja a1 nat-ar a1 nat-c k* *Nat-m* b2.de* nat-ox rly4• nat-p a1 *Nat-s* j5.de nicc j5.de **Nit-ac** b2.de* nux-m b2.de* **Nux-v** b2.de* olnd b2.de* op b2.de* ox-ac a1 paeon a1 *Par* k* peti a1 petr k* **Ph-ac** b2.de* **Phos** b2.de* phys a1 pic-ac a1 pieri-b mlk9.de pimp a1 pip-m a1 plac-s rly4• plan a1 plat b2.de* plb k* plut-n srj7• polyg-h a1 pot-e rly4• prun j5.de* psor a1 ptel a1 **Puls** b2.de* puls-n a1 ran-b b2.de* ran-s b2.de* rheum b2.de* *Rhod* b2.de* rhus-g a1 *Rhus-t* k* rhus-v a1 ros-d wla1 ruta b2.de* sabad k* sabin b2.de* sacch-a fd2.de• sars b2.de* sec b2.de* sel b2.de* senec a1* seneg b2.de* *Sep* b2.de* **Sil** b2.de* sin-n a1 sol-ni a1 solin a1 spig b2.de* *Spong* b2.de* squil b2.de* *Stann* k* *Staph* b2.de* stram k* stront-c k* succ-ac rly4• suis-em rly4• sul-ac b2.de* **Sulph** b2.de* sumb a1 tab a1 tarax k* tarent a1 *Ter* teucr b2.de* ther thuj k* tril-c a1 (non:tril-p a1) **Tub** st* *Tung-met* bdx1• tus-p a1 valer b2.de* vanil fd5.de verat b2.de* verat-v a1

Many: ...
verb b2.de* viol-t b2.de* visc c1 wies a1 wildb a1 *Zinc* b2.de* zing a1 [bell-p-sp dcm1 spect dfg1 tax jsj7]
- **alternating** with | **Head**; pain in (See HEAD - Pain - alternating - dreams)
- **children**, in: valer j5.de
- **crowding** one upon another: kali-c j5.de sep j5.de *Sil* j5.de* thuj j5.de

MAPS: dream-p sdj1• [temp elm1]
- **old**: haliae-lc srj5•

MARKETS: choc srj3•
- **Indian** markets: choc srj3•

MARMOTS: *(↗Animals)* lac-e hrn2•

MARRIAGES (See Wedding)

MASCULINE and feminine energies; of: plut-n srj7•

MASKS: kali-c h2* mag-c a1 ran-r j5.de tritic-vg fd5.de

MAXILLARY joint: | **pain** in: *(↗Disease)* agar kr1

MATURE; of being: stront-c sk4•

MEADOW: murx a1 ruta fd4.de spong fd4.de tritic-vg fd5.de vanil fd5.de
- **green** meadows: lac-cp sk4•

MEANINGFUL: lac-del hrn2•

MEASURING STICKS: galeoc-c-h gms1•

MEAT: falco-pe nl2• sal-fr sle1• tritic-vg fd5.de
- **buying** and selling: falco-pe nl2•
- **cut** off bone; needed to be: [buteo-j sej6]
- **legs** and feet, with: falco-pe nl2•
- **mouth**; thrust into: alum j5.de* falco-pe nl2•
- **pork**: falco-pe nl2•
- **raw**: falco-pe nl2• nept-m lsd2.fr tritic-vg fd5.de
- **roasted** | **vegetarians**; fed to: ozone sde2•

REFLECTING during dreams: *(↗Mental)* acon b2.de* anac b2.de* arn b2.de* bry b2.de* camph b2.de* carb-an b2.de* graph b2.de* *Ign* b2.de* lach b2.de* m-arct b2.de* m-aust b2.de* *Nux-v* b2.de* puls b2.de* rhus-t b2.de* sabad b2.de* sabin b2.de* thuj b2.de*

MEMORY:
- **weakness** of memory | **person** with whom she is talking on the phone; does not recollect knowing the: bung-fa mtf

MEN: dulc fd4.de frax a1 maias-l hrn2• melal-alt gya4 nicc phasco-ci rbp2 *Puls* k1* ruta fd4.de sanguis-s hrn2• spong fd4.de urol-h rwt• vanil fd5.de
- **breast**; men's: phasco-ci rbp2
- **caressing** her back: ozone sde2•
- **crotch**; man putting hand on her: lac-del hrn2•
- **excited** about | **arrival**: maias-l hrn2•
- **feminine**: coca-c sk4• plut-n srj7•
- **following** to violate her: *Cench* st kali-n a1 kreos
- **green**: sol-t-ae a1
- **huge** and strong man; a: bung-fa mtf
  - **controlling** her; was: bung-fa mtf
- **massaging**; a man is | **legs**; woman's: dendr-pol sk4•
- **naked**: cench k2 eupi *Puls*
- **obnoxious**:
  - **held** back by an: lac-h sk4•
  - **macho**; big: coca-c sk4•
    - **suitcase**; in a small: lac-h sk4•
- **older** man in alley: limen-b-c hrn2•
- **rough** | **unshaven**: maias-l hrn2•
- **running** after men; he is (See Running - men)
- **staring**; a man is | **women** in shower though eyeglass; at: maias-l hrn2•
- **threatening**: arizon-l nl2• vanil fd5.de
  - **alternating** with friendliness: arizon-l nl2•
- **tiny** | **bottle**; trapped in a: *(↗Trap - being)* lac-h sk4•

MENSES: tritic-vg fd5.de
- **flooding**, wherever she goes: aids nl2•

- **having** her menses: bung-fa mtf
- **reappearing**: lam a1 laur a1

MENTAL EXERTION: (↗*Excelling - mental; Reflecting; Work)* *Acon* k* alum ambr k* *Anac* k* *Arn* k* ars b2.de* aur h2* bell h1* berb j5.de *Bry* k* calc-p j5.de camph k* carb-an b2.de* cham j5.de *Chin* k* cic k* clem k* coff j5.de coloc dulc b2.de* *Graph* k* **Ign** k* iod b2.de* kali-n b2.de* *Lach* k* laur k* led k* m-ambo b2.de* m-arct b2.de* m-aust b2.de* mosch k* mur-ac b2.de* *Nat-m* k* **Nux-v** k* *Olnd* k* op b2.de* par b2.de* *Ph-ac* k* *Phos* k* plb b2.de* **Puls** k •* *Rhus-t* k* *Sabad* k* sabin k* sars k* sec k* spong k* staph k* *Sulph* k* teucr b2.de* *Thuj* k* *Viol-t* k* zinc k* zinc-p k2 [buteo-j sej6]

MERRY: asaf gt dulc fd4.de op gt

METAL; about: bamb-a stb2.de•

METAMORPHOSIS; about: limen-b-c hrn2• tritic-vg fd5.de ulm-c jsj8•
- **bug** or beetle to moth: limen-b-c hrn2•
- **man** to bat: limen-b-c hrn2•

MICE: colch k* mag-s marb-w es• pot-e rly4• ruta fd4.de sep vanil fd5.de
- **head** and mass of entrails; with | **kill** it; has to step on it and: marb-w es1•
- **neck**; crawling up her: coca-c sk4•
- **trap** a fleeing mice; to: coca-c sk4•
- **yellow**: mag-s

MILITARY: rad-br sze8• til ban1• [bell-p-sp dcm1]

MILK:
- **cleaning** spilled (See Cleaning - spilled)
- **pressing** out milk of her right breast: positr nl2•
- **lake** of white milk: lac-h htj1•

MIRROR; of broken: ulm-c jsj8•

MISCARRIAGE: (↗*Disease)* m-arct j5.de petr-ra shn4•

MISERY: ozone sde2•

MISFORTUNE: (↗*Accidents; Disaster; Events - unfortunate; Loss; Loss - disheartening)* alum k* *Am-m* k* anac k* ant-c k* *Arn* k* *Ars* k* ars-s-f k2 aur-m a1 bamb-a stb2.de• bar-c k* bar-m bar-s k2 *Bell* k* cann-s k* carb-an k* carc fd2.de• *Cham* k* *Chin* k* chinin-ar clem cocc k* croc k* **Graph** k* guaj k* ham fd3.de• ign k* iod j5.de *Kali-ar* kali-bi gt *Kali-c* k* kali-m k2 kali-n k* kali-p kali-s kreos j5.de laur k* led k* **Lyc** k* mag-c mag-m j5.de mang k* *Merc* k* mur-ac k* nat-s j5.de nicc j5.de **Nux-v** k* op k* ozone sde2• petr b2.de* ph-ac k* *Phos* k* **Puls** k* ran-b k* rhus-t k* rhus-v j5.de* sars k* sel k* spong k* stann k* staph k* *Sul-ac* k* *Sulph* k* tarent **Thuj** k* tub jl2 verat k* verb k* zinc k* zinc-p k2

MISSING: | **train**; the: (↗*Difficulties - journeys; Unsuccessful)* lac-c hr1 lac-d al2 vanil fd5.de

MISTAKES; of making: (↗*Failures)* am-m bg2 chlam-tr bcx2• coca-c sk4• *Galeoc-c-h* gms1• haliae-lc srj5• lac-e hrn2• ozone sde2• polys sk4• positr nl2• suis-em rly4• tritic-vg fd5.de [niob-met stj2]
- **diagnosis**; in: lac-e hrn2•
- **remember** names; can't: galeoc-c-h gms1•
- **time**; in: rhus-g tmo3•

MISUNDERSTOOD: | **mother**; by: lac-e hrn2•

MODEL; famous: dendr-pol sk4•

MONEY: alum k* apeir-s mlk9.de aq-mar rbp6 bamb-a stb2.de• bros-gau mrc1 *Cycl* k* cypra-eg sde6.de• dioxi rbp6 dulc fd4.de hydrog srj2• kola stb3• lac-e hrn2• lac-h sk4*• mag-c mag-m k* maias-l hrn2• melal-alt gya4 musca-d szs1 nept-m lsd2.fr orot-ac rly4• oxal-a rly4• phos positr nl2• puls k* spong fd4.de suis-pan rly4• tritic-vg fd5.de vanil fd5.de zinc bg2 zinc-o j5.de [heroin sdj2 tant-met stj2 tax jsj7]
- **counterfeit**: aids nl2• zinc-o
- **disputing** about money: (non:chin slp) chin-b slp lac-h sze9• maias-l hrn2• petr-ra shn4• positr nl2•
- **finding**: positr nl2•
- **fund**-raising for clinic: maias-l hrn2•
- **gold**, of: *Cycl* cypra-eg sde6.de• polys sk4• puls
- **lending**: lac-leo hrn2•
- **nuts**; distributing: bung-fa mtf
- **overcharged** by cashier: lac-leo hrn2•

Money: ...
- **problems** with: lac-e hrn2• lac-h sze9•
- **receiving**: dulc fd4.de mag-c a1 tritic-vg fd5.de vanil fd5.de
- **stolen**: (↗*Stealing - money)* lac-h sze9• maias-l hrn2• ozone sde2•
- **without**; left behind: ozone sde2•

MONK:
- **erection**; with: dendr-pol sk4•
- **lecturing** | **religious** place; in a: nicc-met sk4•
- **singing** and dancing: ozone sde2•

MONKEY: bung-fa mtf
- **black**: polys sk4•
- **cross** a lake; wants to: bros-gau mrc1
- **food** and plaything; utilized as: polys sk4•

MONSTERS: agath-a nl2• aloe hydr lac-leo hrn2• maias-l hrn2• musca-d szs1 olib-sac wmh1 ruta fd4.de [arg-n stj2 zinc stj2 zinc-i stj2 zinc-m stj2 zinc-n stj2 zinc-p stj2]

MONSTROUS: arg-n st

MONUMENTS: | **large**; very: bamb-a stb2.de•

MOON: kola stb3•
- **multiple**: hippoc-k szs2
- **orange**: hippoc-k szs2

MOPED: | **driving** one hundred kilometers an hour: ozone sde2•

MORAL FEELING:
- **lack** of | **others**; in: lac-e hrn2•

MORTIFICATION: (↗*Guilt; Humiliation)* asar h1* bac mhn1 ign b2.de* kola stb3• mosch b2.de* podo fd3.de• rheum b2.de* sil h2 staph b2.de* taosc iwa1• tub al2

MOTHER: (↗*Family)* adam srj5• arizon-l nl2• dulc fd4.de granit-m es1• helodr-cal knl2• hydrog srj2• lac-d sk4• lac-del hrn2• lac-lup hrn2• maias-l hrn2• melal-alt gya4 *Plut-n* srj7• ruta fd4.de sanguis-s hrn2• spong fd4.de suis-em rly4• toxi mtf2• tritic-vg fd5.de vanil fd5.de [ant-m stj2 aur-m stj2 beryl-m stj2 cadm-m stj2 chlor stj2 chr-m stj2 cob-m stj2 cupr-m stj2 lith-m stj2 mang-m stj2 merc-d stj2 mur-ac stj2 plb-m stj2 stront-m stj2 zinc-m stj2]
- **dead** mother appearing: hippoc-k szs2 mag-s a1 [heroin sdj2]
- **beautiful** look on her face: maias-l hm2•
- **bed**; with her in: rhus-g tmo3•
- **contraceptives**; advising on: lac-h htj1•
- **find** biological mother; trying to: galeoc-c-h gms1•
- **flying** around the world: hydrog srj2•
- **hitting** her daughter: bit-ar wht1•
- **ill**; being: (↗*Disease)* castor-eq a1 dream-p sdj1•
- **milk**; asking for: lac-h sk4•
- **old**; being: lac-loxod-a hrn2•
- **penis**; has a: rhus-g tmo3•
- **possessed**; is: fic-m gya1
- **pregnant**; is: helodr-cal knl2•
- **protecting** | **child**; her: plut-n srj7•
- **road**; taking the wrong: ozone sde2•
- **searching** for: plut-n srj7•
- **strangled** by her daughter: bit-ar wht1•
- **swinging** on a pendulum; with mother: hydrog srj2•

MOTHS: (↗*Animals; Butterfly; Insects)* chir-fl gya2 limen-b-c hrn2•

MOTION; of: lyc gt* [buteo-j sej6]
- **fast**: galla-q-r nl2• helo-s rwt2• [buteo-j sej6]

MOTORBOATS: lac-lup hrn2•

MOTORCYCLES: lac-loxod-a hrn2• lac-lup hrn2• vanil fd5.de

MOUNTAINS: ozone sde2• tritic-vg fd5.de vanil fd5.de [tax jsj7]
- **descending** | **injured** leg; in spite of her: coca-c sk4•
- **expedition**; mountaineering: coca-c sk4•
- **snow**; covered with: lac-h sk4•
- **walking** in the: falco-pe nl2• kola stb3• neon srj5• [tax jsj7]

MOUTH: (↗*Body; parts)*
- **blood** in mouth (See Blood - mouth)
- **blow** on the mouth; receiving a: (↗*Beaten)* menth-pu a1
- **chain** across mouth; being bound with a: bapt a1

Dreams

- **opening** of mouth impossible: agar kr1

MOVIE ACTRESS: *Polys* sk4•
- **advantage** being taken of: polys sk4•
- **money** to; to lend: polys sk4•
- **recognize**; failing to: polys sk4•

MOWING people (See People - mowing)

MUD: | **stuck** in: dream-p sdj1•

MUDDY water (See Water - muddy)

MULE, driving a: (non:chin-b k*) (non:cinch hr1*)

MUMMY; wrapped up like a: phasco-ci rbp2

MURDER: *(↗Accusations - crime; Killing)* agath-a nl2• am-m androc srj1• aq-mar rbp6 *Arn* aur-m-n wbt2• aur-s c1* bamb-a stb2.de• bell bit-ar wht1• *Brom* b4a.de calad calc calc-sil k2* carb-an carc mg1.de* cartl-s rly4• castm chel choc srj3• crot-h k2 dendr-pol sk4• falco-pe nl2• galla-q-r nl2• guaj hura hydrog srj2• ign kali-i kali-s k2* kalm kiss a1 *Kola* stb3• *Kreos* lac-del hrn2• lac-h sk4*• lac-leo sk4• lac-loxod-a hrn2• lach lact led k* lyc *M-arct* b7.de* *Mag-m* maias-l hrn2• *Mand* mg1.de *Merc* k* *Merc-c* k* *Moni* rfm1• musca-d szs1 *Naja* *Nat-ar* *Nat-c* *Nat-m* nat-ox rly4• nat-sil k2 nicc nicc-met stj2*• ol-an orot-ac rly4• pegan-ha tpi1• *Petr* petr-ra shn4• plut-n srj7• podo fd3.de• puls rhus-t rhus-v j5.de rumx ruta fd4.de sal-fr sle1• sanic saroth jl* sedi a1 sel jl* sep gt* *Sil* sol-a a1 spong k* *Staph* k* sulph symph fd3.de• thuj tung-met bdx1• urol-h rwt• vanil fd5.de ven-m jl verb b7a.de zinc k* [gal-met stj2 nicc-s stj2 tax jsj7 zinc-i stj2 zinc-m stj2 zinc-n stj2 zinc-p stj2]
- **arrested** for murder (See Arrested - murder)
- **disposing** of corpse: polys sk4•
- **violent**: lac-loxod-a hrn2•

MURDERED:
- **about** to be: positr nl2•
- **being**: *(↗Poisoned)* acon-ac rly4• agath-a nl2• am-m bomb-chr mlk9.de chel chr-ac kr1 dendr-pol sk4• guaj ign kali-i *Kreos* kr1 lac-e hrn2• *Lach* lact lyc mag-m a1 merc merc-act j5.de merc-c a1 petr-ra shn4• phos j5.de pot-e rly4• rauw tpw8 ruta fd4.de sil xan a2 zinc k*
  - **amiable** to keep from being murdered; being: lac-e hrn2•
  - **mother**; by: fic-m gya1
- **everyone** | **decree**; by: lac-h sk4•
- **men**, murdered: dulc fd4.de rumx

MURDERER: ara-maca sej7•
- **being** a murderer: plut-n srj7•

MURDERING: *(↗Killing)*
- **Arab** with four stabs in chest: ozone sde2•
- **boys** and girls: thea a1
- **father**, her: *(↗MIND - Ailments - quarrelling - father)* castm a1 positr nl2•

MUSCLES: *(↗Body; parts)*
- **pierced** with arrows (See Arrows - piercing)

MUSHROOMS: dulc fd4.de
- **colorful**: psil ft1

MUSIC: aids nl2• dream-p sdj1• dulc fd4.de helodr-cal knl2• hippoc-k szs2 kola stb3• lac-del hrn2• lac-e hrn2• lac-lup hrn2• limen-b-c hrn2* loxo-recl knl4• luf-op vml3• mag-s j5.de orot-ac rly4• positr nl2• ruta fd4.de sarr spong fd4.de tritic-vg fd5.de vanil fd5.de
- **drumming**: aids nl2• galla-q-r nl2•
- **Jamaican** reggae: limen-b-c hrn2•
  - **lively** even though people are poor: limen-b-c hrn2•
- **loud**: dioxi rbp6
- **religious** Middle Eastern music: sanguis-s hm2•

MUSICAL INSTRUMENTS:
- **playing** | **tuba**: galeoc-c-h gms1•

MUTILATION: *(↗Body - mutilated; Children - mutilated; Cruelty; Ill-treatment)* adam srj5• androc srj1• ant-c k* arn j5.de* con hura m-arct j5.de mag-c mag-m h2* merc *Nux-v* k* tung-met bdx1•
- **dead** bodies; mutilated (See Dead bodies - mutilated)
- **others**; of (See Cutting - others)

MYSTIC: hippoc-k szs2

MYTHICAL CREATURES: agath-a nl2•

NAKED people: *(↗Women - naked)* cench k2 dulc fd4.de galla-q-r nl2• haliae-lc srj5• positr nl2• ros-d wla1 tritic-vg fd5.de [nat-f stj2 tax jsj7]
- **bathing** in swimming pool of hotel: *(↗People - bathing)* ozone sde2•
- **husband**; her: bung-fa mtf
  - **caressed** at the genitals by a lady doctor; being: bung-fa mtf
- **man** with dried up penis: galla-q-r nl2•
- **snow**; small boy, naked in: phasco-ci rbp2

NAKEDNESS: *(↗Mammae - naked; Shoes - socks)* aids nl2• androc srj1• cench k2 dendr-pol sk4• erech a1 falco-pe nl2• fic-m gya1 galla-q-r nl2• ham fd3.de• kali-p k2 lac-e hrn2• *Lac-leo* hrn2• limen-b-c hrn2* maias-l hrn2• medul-os-si rly4• petr-ra shn4• ros-d wla1 rumx thiam rly4• vanil fd5.de
- **alone**; being naked when: lac-h sk4•
- **cover** herself; she must: lac-h sk4• plut-n srj7•
- **unashamed**: maias-l hrn2•
- **wraps** self in rug: lac-leo hm2•

NARROW place: *(↗Places)* galla-q-r nl2• oci-sa sk4• rad-br sze8•

NATIVE COUNTRY (See Country - native)

NATIVE PEOPLE (See People - native)

NAUSEA: *(↗Disease)* *Arg-met* k*

NECROPHILIA (See Amorous - dead)

NEEDLES: *(↗Pins)* androc srj1• positr nl2•
- **swallowed** a needle; he accidentally: lac-h sk4•

NEGLECTED being: bung-fa mtf lac-d sk4•
- **friends**; by: crot-c sk4•

NEGLECTING others: | **children** (See Children - neglecting)

NEIGHBOR: bamb-a stb2.de• irid-met srj5•

NEST: | **moving** birds nest to a safe place: limen-b-c hm2•

NEW SCENES, places etc.: *(↗Places)* calc-f kr1

NIGHTMARES: *(↗Anxious; Unsuccessful - shriek; MIND - Fear - terror - night; MIND - Weeping - nightmare; SLEEP - Anxious)* achy jl *Acon* k* acon-ac rly4• aether a1 aloe *Alum* k* *Alum-sil* k2 alumn *Am-c* k* am-m k* ambr k* ammc j5.de ange-s jl ant-t k* arg-n a1* arn j5.de* ars k* ars-i ars-s-f k2 arum-t asar jl aur b4a.de* *Aur-br* bro1* aur-m a1* aur-m-n wbt2• aur-s c1* bamb-a stb2.de• *Bapt* k* bar-c mrr1 bar-ox-suc rly4• bell k* berb j5.de* *Bit-ar* wht1• *Borx* brucel sa3• *Bry* k* bufo k* cadm-s *Calc* k* calc-i k2 calc-sil k2 *Camph* *Cann-i* k* canth k* carb-an b4a.de carb-v k2 carc fb* card-m kr1 *Carl* a1 cartl-s rly4• castm j5.de* cench c1* *Cham* chel *Chin* j5.de* chinin-s a1 chlol bro1 chlorpr mtf11 chord-umb rly4• cina k* *Cinnb* clem a1 colch a1 *Con* k* cot a1 *Crot-t* j5.de *Cycl* k* cypr bro1* daph k* (non:dig slp) digin slp dulc j5.de* elaps *Ferr* k* ferr-i ferr-p gard-j vlr2• gels k* gink-b jl *Guaj* k* ham fd3.de• heli-n mtf11 hep hir jl hydr-ac j5.de hydroph jl* hyos a1* ign ind *Iod* k* iris kali-ar kali-bi k* *Kali-br* bg2* kali-c k* kali-chl j5.de* *Kali-i* kali-n k* kali-p k2* kali-s k2 kali-sil k2 ketogl-ac rly4• *Kola* stb3• kres mg1.de* lach mrr1 lact a1 laur j5.de* lavand-a ctl1• *Led* k* lob j5.de lyc k* m-ambo b7.de* mag-c sf1.de mag-m k* mag-s jl maias-l hrn2• mand rsj7• mang j5.de* med kr1 meph merc k* *Merc-c* j5.de merc-i-f a1* mez k* mucs-nas rly4• murx j5.de naja jl nat-ar *Nat-c* k* nat-m k* nat-ox rly4• nat-p nat-s j5.de* nat-sil k2 nicotam rly4• *Nit-ac* k* nitro-o a1 *Nux-v* k* op k* osm a1 **Paeon** k* pariet a1* pegan-ha tpi1• ph-ac b4a.de phos k* pic-ac sf1.de plac-s rly4• plb k* pot-e rly4• ptel k* puls k* *Pycnop-sa* mrz1 rhod b4.de* rhus-t k* ribo rly4• ruta k* sars j5.de* scut bro1 sec j5.de* sep b4a.de *Sil* k* sinus rly4• sol-ni bro1 spong fd4.de staph gl1.fr• stram bg2* streptoc rly4* suis-pan rly4• sul-ac bg2* sul-i k2 **Sulph** k* syc pte1*• tab tax-br oss1• tell ter thea a1 thiop jl thuj tritic-vg fd5.de tub jl2* valer k* vanil fd5.de *Zinc* k* [bell-p-sp dcm1]
- **morning**: nicotam rly4• phos a1
- **afternoon**: mez a1
- **night**:
  - **midnight**: merc-act a1 mez a1 pot-e rly4•
    - **before**: cycl j5.de kali-c j5.de
    - **after**: cinnb j5.de *Mez* j5.de*
      - **4 h**: alum kr1 kali-bi a1 pot-e rly4•
- **amorous** dreams, during: nit-ac a1

- **children**, in: achy jl borx k2* calc mtf33 *Carc* mlr1• kali-p k2 spong fd4.de *Stram* mrr1
  - **behavior** problems; with (See MIND - Behavior - children - nightmares)
- **falling** asleep, on: am-c h2* *Cann-i* a1* cycl j5.de* digin a1 gels a1 nit-ac h2* ter j5.de*
- **first** sleep; during: am-c bg2 cann-xyz bg2 cycl bg2 gels bg2 nit-ac bg2
- **fever**; during: hydrog srj2•
- **lying** on the back: card-m guaj ind a1* ptel gk **Sulph** k* [alumin-s stj2 cadm-s stj2 chr-s stj2 gal-s stj2 lith-s stj2 mang-s stj2 nicc-s stj2 titan-s stj2]
- **menses**:
  - **after**: sul-ac k2 thuj
  - **before**: sul-ac k*
  - **end** of; at: sul-ac k2
- **moon**; at full: nat-c j5.de*
- **periodical**:
  - **night** | **sleep**; on going to: cann-i c1
- **room** must be searched | **appeased**; before: *Cham* kr1
- **waking**, on: ozone sde2• ptel a1

NO DREAMS (See Unremembered)

NOAH'S ARK: bamb-a stb2.de•

NOBLE; she was: irid-met srj5•

NOISE: atro a1 cere-b a1 luf-op vml3• lyc a1 stann a1*

NONE (See Unremembered)

NOSE:
- **discharge** from nose:
  - **bluish**: lac-h sk4•
  - **profuse**: hydrog srj2*•
  - **watery**: ped a1
  - **yellow**: hydrog srj2*•
- **pulling** him by his nose; somebody: nat-c h2*
- **small** nose: sal-fr sle1•

NOSTALGIC: bros-gau mrc1

NUCLEAR POWER STATION: ozone sde2•
- **protecting** a: plut-n srj7•

NUMBERS; of: galeoc-c-h gms1• [tax jsj7]
- **seven**: arist-cl rbp3• sanguis-s hm2•
- **three**; about cipher: positr nl2•

NUNS: musca-d szs1 positr nl2•
- **ordered** to become a: falco-pe nl2•

NURSING newborns: *(↗Children - newborns; Children - newborns - feeding)* lac-del hrn2•

OBESE; being: galeoc-c-h gms1• ulm-c jsj8•

OBJECTS (See Things)

OBSCENE: bros-gau mrc1 cob-n sp1* x-ray al2*

OBSERVER: ara-maca sej7• [bell-p-sp dcm1]

OBSERVING:
- **alternating** with | **acting**: *Plut-n* srj7•
- **as** if, although in the dream: bit-ar wht1•
- **participating** in her dreams; rather than: haliae-lc srj5• *Positr* nl2• [heroin sdj2]

OBSTACLES:
- **easily** dealt with: maias-l hm2•
- **path**; in his: lac-h sk4•

OCCIPITAL tension gone with head off: maias-l hrn2•

OCCURRENCES in the next room (See Events - room)

OCEAN: hippoc-k szs2
- **being** in an ocean: [buteo-j sej6]
- **overlooking** the: fic-m gya1
- **street**; crashing down on: coca-c sk4•

OCTOPUS: ozone sde2• plut-n srj7•

ODORS (See Smelling)

OFFERING:
- **seat**; his | **woman**; to a: nicc-met sk4•

OIL RIGS: | **destruction**: corv-cor bdg•

ONENESS; feeling of: [buteo-j sej6]

ONIONS: kola stb3•

OPOSSUMS: *(↗Animals)* limen-b-c hrn2•

OPPORTUNITY: | **lost**: lac-e hm2•

OPPRESSED; being: oci-sa sk4•

OPPRESSIVE regime: plut-n srj7•

ORGANIZING: adam srj5• lac-e hrn2• lac-f wza1•

ORGASM; with (See Amorous - orgasm)

ORIENT; about the: olib-sac wmh1

ORGIES: limen-b-c hrn2•

OTTER: *(↗Animals)* lac-lup hrn2•

OUTSIDER:
- **being** an outsider: *Lac-lup* hm2• phasco-ci rbp2 plut-n srj7•
  - **bystander**; he was a: lac-lup hrn2•
  - **spirit** watching; felt more like a: lac-lup hrn2•

OVARIES: | **pain** in ovaries: choc srj3•

OXEN:
- **pursuing** him; are (See Pursued - ox)
- **putrid**: hura a1

PAIN: *(↗Disease; Events - painful; Suffering)* asar b7.de* bry a1 cain kr1 carbn-h a1 cocc b7.de* kola stb3• lyc h2 *Med* kr1* ozone sde2• tritic-vg fd5.de
- **abdomen** (See Abdomen - pain)
- **arm** (See Arm - pain)
- **back** (See Back - pain)
- **hand** from hot and dangerous glass sheet; burning pain in (See Glass - sheet)
- **knees** (See Knee - pain)
- **maxillary** joint (See Maxillary - pain)
- **ovaries** (See Ovaries - pain)
- **temples** (See Headache - temples)
- **uterus** (See Uterus - pain)

PAIRS; matching: *Plut-n* srj7• [tax jsj7]

PALACES: irid-met srj5•

PALPITATION of the heart: merc h1 [arg-met stj2]

PANTHER: lac-h sk4•

PARADISE; view of: hippoc-k szs2

PARALLEL lines: haliae-lc srj5•

PARALYZED: hippoc-k szs2
- **fear**; she was paralyzed with: coca-c sk4•

PARANORMAL phenomenon: hippoc-k szs2
- **children**: hippoc-k szs2

PARASITES: melal-alt gya4

PARENTS; about his: *(↗Family)* ara-maca sej7• *Plut-n* srj7• vanil fd5.de
- **split** up; parents: germ-met srj5•

PARROT:
- **kill** it with a knife; trying to: corv-cor bdg•
- **large** black: corv-cor bdg•
- **talking**: corv-cor bdg•

Dreams

PARTIES: *(↗Picnics; MIND - Amusement - desire)* bros-gau mrc1 corian-s knl6• crot-c a1 dendr-pol sk4• dulc fd4.de falco-pe nl2• hura a1 ina-i mlk9.de lac-del hrn2• lac-h sk4• loxo-recl knl4• maias-l hrn2• nat-c a1 pert-vc vk9 petr-ra shn4• phel a1 pieri-b mlk9.de pip-m a1 *Plut-n* srj7• sal-fr sle1• taosc iwa1• vanil fd5.de [ant-c stj2 ant-met stj2 cadm-met stj2 mag-lac stj2 mag-met stj2 mag-n stj2 mag-sil stj2 stann stj2 zinc stj2 zinc-i stj2 zinc-m stj2 zinc-n stj2 zinc-p stj2]
- **forgot** to offer drink to his best friend; where he: pert-vc vk9
- **pleasure**; of: bros-gau mrc1 lac-e hrn2•

PASSION, outburst of: mag-c j5.de

PASSIVE: | **change** the situation; unable to: ara-maca sej7•

PAST (See Events - past)

PASTURES, green and blue sky: lac-e hrn2•

PATHS: | **two**: arizon-l nl2•

PATIENTS: *(↗Sick people)*
- **losing**: lac-e hrn2•
- **suicidal**: *(↗Sick people; Suicide)* lac-loxod-a hrn2•

PEACEFUL: *(↗Pleasant; Quiet)* crot-c sk4• hippoc-k szs2 nux-m a1 pyrid rly4• rhus-g tmo3• spig a1 taosc iwa1•
- **wants** to be | **violence**; yet forced to: lac-e hrn2•

PEDOPHILIA: musca-d szs1

PEEVISH: mang a1 nat-m a1

PENINSULA: | **ocean** and mountain; of: coca-c sk4•

PENIS: *(↗Body; parts)* galla-q-r nl2•
- **breaking** off: kali-n a1
- **cut** off: positr nl2•
- **detachable**: lac-loxod-a hrn2•
- **enormous**: plut-n srj7•
- **glans** penis breaking off: kreos j5.de
- **prepuce** sloughed off: linu-c
- **shriveled**: galla-q-r nl2•

PEOPLE: apis a1* ars-h kr1* art-v kr1 aster a1 bell bros-gau mrc1 calc-ar choc srj3• coc-c a1 *Dios* kr1 dulc fd4.de **Equis-h** a1* galeoc-c-h gms1• gels a1 ina-i mlk9.de kola stb3• lac-lup hrn2• lyss kr1 merc nat-m a1 oxal-a rly4• *Puls* j5.de* pycnop-sa mrz1 ruta fd4.de *Sanguis-s* hrn2• spong fd4.de tritic-vg fd5.de vanil fd5.de [spect dfg1]
- **another** person lying in bed with him (See bed)
- **assembled** (See crowd)
- **bathing**, are: *(↗Naked people - bathing; Swimming)* chin-b k* dulc fd4.de tung-met bdx1•
- **bed** with him; another person is lying in: chlam-tr bcx2• dulc fd4.de petr
- **black**: *(↗Children - black)* *Sanguis-s* hm2• [tax jsj7]
- **changing**; people are | **sullen** to genial; from: positr nl2•
- **companies**: canth j5.de phel j5.de
- **creeping** in each other: ozone sde2•
- **crowds** of: aids nl2• apis kr1* ars-h kr1* canth j5.de cere-b a1 choc srj3• dulc fd4.de **Equis-h** kr1* galeoc-c-h gms1• hydrog srj2• ina-i mlk9.de lac-lup hrn2• loxo-recl knl4• nept-m lsd2.fr phel j5.de pieri-b mlk9.de polys sk4• ruta fd4.de tritic-vg fd5.de vanil fd5.de
  - **racing**: coca-c sk4•
- **dear** to him, vivid dreams, two nights in succession: nat-m a1
- **deformed** people: *(↗Crippled; Disabled)* m-arct b7.de*
- **disappearing**; a person was | **box**; into a small: oci-sa sk4•
- **drunken**: *(↗Intoxicated)* cench k2 rad-br sze8• sal-fr sle1•
- **emaciated**: gink-b sbd1•
- **escape**; attempting to: bit-ar wht1•
- **family**: *(↗Family)* lac-h sze9• lac-lup hrn2•
- **gatherings**:
  - **groups**, school boards, church commune: galeoc-c-h gms1•
  - **sacred** drums; with: galeoc-c-h gms1•
- **human**, half animal; half: *Plut-n* srj7•
- **hungry** (See Hunger - people)
- **influential** persons: lyss kr1 tung-met bdx1•
- **jumping**: hydrog srj2•
- **loved** by him: bros-gau mrc1

People: ...
- **many** people; she is occupied with: bell h1
- **mowing**: glon a1
- **nasty** and unhelpful: lac-e hrn2•
- **native** | **Americans**: *Lac-e* hrn2•
- **old**: lac-lup hrn2• [tax jsj7]
  - **young**; being: hippoc-k szs2
- **parties** (See Parties)
- **picnics** (See Picnics)
- **powerful**, important: dendr-pol sk4•
- **same** people; with the: bros-gau mrc1
- **scantily** dressed: dendr-pol sk4•
- **seen** for years; people not: calad kr1 calc-ar kr1* gard-j vlr2• hydrog srj2• lac-lup hrn2• oxal-a rly4• samb bat1• tritic-vg fd5.de tung-met bdx1• *Urol-h* rwt•
- **strange** things; doing: hydrog srj2• lac-del hrn2• limen-b-c hrn2• spong fd4.de
- **transformed**: hippoc-k szs2
- **unknown**: hydrog srj2• ruta fd4.de
- **white** coats; in: *Plut-n* srj7•
- **window**; people are before the (See Window - people)
- **wounded**: brucel sa3•

PERFORMANCE: nicc-met sk4•
- **teacher**; of:
  - **observed** by adolescent | **inadequate**; is: limen-b-c hrn2•

PERFORMING: *(↗Theater - performing)* aids nl2• galeoc-c-h gms1• positr nl2•
- **unprepared** to perform on stage: galeoc-c-h gms1•

PERSISTENT: *(↗Continuation; Continuous; Long - object)* *Acon* b2.de* agav-t jl anac b2.de* ant-t b2.de* arn b2.de* asaf b2.de* bar-c j5.de *Bry* b2.de* *Calc* b2.de* *Chin* b2.de* coff b2.de* euph b2.de* graph b2.de* **Ign** b2.de* lach b2.de* m-aust b2.de* merc b2.de* mosch j5.de *Nat-c* b2.de* nat-m b2.de* nat-s j5.de *Phos* j5.de plat j5.de *Puls* b2.de* sabin j5.de sep b2.de* sil b2.de* spig b2.de* staph b2.de* zinc b2.de*
- **fixed** ideas in dreams: acon j ign b7.de* puls b7.de* stann j

PERSONS (See People)

PETS: | **dead** and beloved: hippoc-k szs2

PHONE (See Telephones)

PHOTOGRAPHS, taking: galla-q-r nl2• [heroin sdj2]

PHYSICIAN (See Doctors)

PIANO:
- **playing** piano: galeoc-c-h gms1•
  - **public**; in: marb-w es1•
- **two** pianos:
  - **friend** had two pianos; her | **none**; while she had: lac-h sk4•

PICKING sores till bleeding: musca-d szs1

PICNICS: *(↗Eating; Parties)* falco-pe nl2• lac-h sk4• nat-s a1 nept-m lsd2.fr nicc-met sk4• oci-sa sk4• petr-ra shn4•
- **disgusting** food; with: falco-pe nl2•

PICTURE FRAME: | **empty**, hung on the wall: positr nl2•

PIGEONS: *(↗Animals)* lac-leo hrn2• *Lac-lup* hrn2•

PICTURES:
- **showing**; sister was | **semi**-nude: oci-sa sk4•

PIGS: *(↗Animals)* coca-c sk4• falco-pe nl2• positr nl2•

PINCHED at back and breast, being (See Back - pinched)

PINS, swallowing: *(↗Needles)* merc j5.de*

PLACES: *(↗Dirty - place; Narrow; New; Wet)*
- **high** places (See High)
- **public**: dulc fd4.de equis-h a1 lyc a1 merc-i-r a1
  - **changing** often: *(↗Changing - places)* all-s led lyc olib-sac wmh1
  - **new** (See New)
- **strange**: stront-c sk4•

PLANTS: arge-pl rwt5• hippoc-k szs2 nept-m lsd2.fr
- **growing**:
  - **fast**: loxo-recl knl4•
  - **water**; in: hippoc-k szs2

PLAYFUL: lac-leo hrn2•

PLAYING: lac-leo hrn2•
- **baseball** (See Baseball)
- **children** (See Children - playing)
- **death** of a friend; though informed about the: nicc-met sk4•

PLAYMATE: | **childhood**; since: lac-del hrn2•

PLEASANT: *(↗Joyous; Peaceful; Quiet; Wonderful)* acon k* aether a1 agar h2* agath-a nl2• agn k* all-c a1 alum k* alum-sil k2 am-c k* am-m k* ambr k* *Ant-c* k* ant-t k* *Arn* k* ars k* ars-h kr1 asaf k* atro a1 *Aur* b2.de* aur-s k2 bamb-a stb2.de• bar-c k* bar-m bell k* bism k* borx k* bov k* bry **Calc** k* cann-i a1 cann-s k* canth k* *Carb-an* k* carb-v k* caust k* cench k2 cham k* chel k* chin k* cic k* cinnb a1 clem k* cocc k* cod a1 *Coff* k* coloc k* com *Con* k* *Croc* k* cycl k* dig k* dros k* erig a1 eug j5.de euph k* fago a1 gins a1 *Graph* k* grat ham fd3.de• hell k* hura a1 hyos k* ign k* ina-i mlk9.de *Kali-c* k* kali-cy a1 kali-i kali-m k2 kali-n k* kali-p kola stb3• kreos k* lach-h sk4• *Lach* k* laur k* led k* luna kg1• lyc k* *M-ambo* b2.de m-arct b2.de *Mag-c* k* mag-m k* mag-s maias-l hrn2• manc mang k* menis a1 meny k* merc k* mez k* morph a1 mur-ac k* nat-ar **Nat-c** k* *Nat-m* k* *Nat-p* nat-s j5.de nat-sil k2 nept-m lsd2.fr nicc nicc-met sk4• nit-ac k* nitro-o a1 nux-m k* *Nux-v* k* oci-sa sk4• ol-an j5.de olib-sac wmh1 olnd k* **Op** k* orot-ac rly4• ox-ac a1 oxal-a rly4• par k* ped a1 petr k* petr-ra shn4• *Ph-ac* k* phel a1 *Phos* k* phys a1 *Plat* k* plb k* podo fd3.de• **Puls** k* ran-b k* rhod k* ros-d wla1 *Sabad* b2.de* samb b2.de* saroth mg1.de* sars b2.de* senec k1 **Sep** b2.de* *Sil* b2.de* spig b2.de* spong k* squil k* stann k* **Staph** k* stram k* stront-c k* *Sulph* k* sumb a1 tarax k* tarent tep *Teucr* b2.de* thiam rly4• thuj k* valer k* verat k* vero-o rly4*• **Viol-t** k* zinc k* zing
- **afternoon**: mez a1
- **evening**: zing a1
- **night**:
  - **midnight** | **after** | **2** h; after: tarent a1
    - **before** midnight pleasant, after midnight frightful: ph-ac h2*
- **laughter**; provoking: bell gt

PLEASE: | **superiors**; desire to please: lac-lup hrn2•

PLUNDERING: *(↗Stealing)* tung-met bdx1•

POETIC: ars-h kr1 bufo-s lach k* nat-m j5.de til

POISON; of: *(↗Animals - poisonous; Water - poisoned)* kreos b7a.de lac-lup hrn2•
- **taken** poison; having: *(↗Animals - poisonous)* chlam-tr bcx2• *Kreos* k* plut-n srj7•
- **water**; in: phasco-ci rbp2

POISONED, being: *(↗Animals - poisonous; Disease; Murdered - being)* chr-ac a1 falco-pe nl2• helo-s rwt2• kali-bi hs1 kali-n a1* *Kreos* k* lac-h sk4• melal-alt gya4 nat-m k* oci k* [ant-c stj2 ant-met stj2 chr-met stj2 tant-met stj2]
- **family** eating something poisonous; her whole (See Family - poisonous)
- **herself**; by: kali-n a1
- **woman** and her children being gassed and poisoned; a: lac-lup hrn2•

POLICE: adam srj5• aids nl2• bamb-a stb2.de• coca-c sk4• dulc fd4.de frax a1 helodr-cal knl2• hippoc-k szs2 kola stb3• lac-e hrn2• lac-leo hrn2• musca-d szs1 *Nicc-met* sk4• ozone sde2• petr-ra shn4• taosc iwa1• vanil fd5.de [tax jsj7]
- **marijuana** cigarette in the presence of; unconcernedly rolling a: coca-c sk4•
- **pursued** by (See Pursued - police)
- **tell**; she must | **killed** her sister; that her brother: nicc-met sk4•

POLITICAL: asc-t a1

POLLUTION; environmental: falco-pe nl2• positr nl2•

POOL of water (See Water - pools)

POOR; being (See Poverty)

POSTMASTERS and POSTMISTRESSES: hydrog srj2•

POVERTY: gink-b sbd1• lac-loxod-a hrn2• limen-b-c hrn2*
- **being** poor; of: oci-sa sk4•

POWERFUL: adam srj5• hippoc-k szs2
- **male** feeling; and | **woman**; in a: coca-c sk4•

PRAYING: *(↗Churches; Religious)* ars-h bung-fa mtf lac-h sk4• petr-ra shn4• pip-m a1

PREACHING: *(↗Churches; Religious)* allox jl* anac ant-t

PRECARIOUS POSITION: | **feeling** safe is a: lac-lup hrn2•

PRECIPICE (See Abyss)

PRECISION: lac-e hrn2•

PREGNANT:
- **being**: choc srj3• corian-s knl6• falco-pe nl2• galla-q-r nl2• granit-m es1• hydrog srj2• *Kola* stb3• lyc zf musca-d szs1 neon srj5• pic-ac plut-n srj7• rhus-g tmo3• suis-em rly4• tritic-vg fd5.de [bell-p-sp dcm1 heroin sdj2 *Spect* dfg1]
  - **terrified** about delivery: falco-pe nl2•
- **husband** is; her: plut-n srj7•

PREPARED: | **was** not: galeoc-c-h gms1•

PRINCESS, partner had relationship with a: irid-met srj5•

PRISONER: [tax jsj7]
- **being** taken a: *(↗Imprisonment)* allox tpw3* haliae-lc srj5• maias-l hrn2• nat-m positr nl2• thiam rly4• tung-met bdx1• [titan stj2]
- **release** of prisoners: hura a1
- **riots**: *(↗Riots - prison)* rhus-g tmo3•

PROCESSION: irid-met srj5• kali-p fd1.de• [cadm-met stj2]
- **giant**: lac-h sk4•
- **political**: nicc-met sk4•

PROFOUND: saroth sp1

PROJECTS: anac j5.de bufo bg2 camph j5.de* dulc fd4.de rhus-t j5.de
- **coming** true in the dreams: rhus-t j5.de
- **mixed** up with the projects he had made: anac h2*

PROMISCUITY: plut-n srj7• [tax jsj7]

PROPHETIC: *(↗Clairvoyant; MIND - Clairvoyance; MIND - Fear - happen)* **Acon** k1* ara-maca sej7• asaf bov *Cann-i* cortico sp1 lac-del hrn2• lac-h htj1• lap-la sde8.de• m-arct j5.de mang olib-sac wmh1 ph-ac phos plac-s rly4• ptel gk pycnop-sa mrz1 rad-br bg sinus rly4• *Sulph* [spect dfg1 tax jsj7]
- **death**; prophesying: kali-c j5.de kali-chl j5.de

PROSPERITY: [heroin sdj2]

PROSTITUTES: musca-d szs1

PROTECTED; being: | **not** being protected from harm: bung-fa mtf

PROTECTING: *Nicc-met* sk4• rhus-g tmo3•
- **animals**; wild: corv-cor bdg•
- **boy** who fell overboard; wanting to protect a young: nicc-met sk4•
- **woman**; feeling protective towards a foreign: nicc-met sk4•

PROVING a remedy: bit-ar wht1• merc-i-f a1* pip-m a1 spong fd4.de

PROVOKED, being: *(↗Quarrels)* chir-fl gya2 verat-v a1

PRUDE, being: **Tub** st

PUB in former sanatorium: ozone sde2•

PUNCHES:
- **men** | **blows** not felt: maias-l hrn2•

PUNISHMENT: | **dismissed** from work: bros-gau mrc1

PURCHASE, making (See Shopping)

PURGATORY: *(↗Hell)* ignis-alc es2•

PURSE: | **organizing**: lac-lup hrn2•

PURSUED, being: (↗*Fleeing; Running)* adam srj5• *Agath-a* nl2• aids nl2• allox tpw3* anac mrr1 androc srj1• arg-met k* arge-pl rwt5• arizon-l nl2• atro aur-m-n wbt2• bell bit-ar wht1• bomb-chr mlk9.de carc fd2.de• corv-cor bdg1• *Crot-c* sk4• dream-p sdj1• dulc fd4.de falco-pe nl2• germ-met stj2*• helodr-cal knl2• hir jl* hydr a1 ina-i mlk9.de kali-s fd4.de ketogl-ac rly4• *Kola* stb3• kreos lac-cp sk4• lac-d sk4• lac-del hrn2• *Lac-e* hrn2• lac-h htj1*• lac-leo hrn2• mag-m dgt mag-s j5.de *Maias-l* hrn2• musca-d szs1 nat-ox rly4• nat-sil fd3.de• nept-m lsd2.fr nux-m k* nux-v oci-sa sk4• ped a1 petr-ra shn4• ph-ac plac-s rly4• plut-n srj7• polys sk4• positr nl2• pot-e rly4• pseuts-m oss1• pycnop-sa mrz1 ros-d wla1 ruta fd4.de sep *Sil* k* sinus rly4• spong fd4.de stront-c sk4• succ-ac rly4• *Sulph* symph fd3.de• tritic-vg fd5.de tung-met bdx1• vanil fd5.de verat *Zinc* k* [mang-s stj2 niob-met stj2 pall stj2 tax jsj7 zinc-i stj2 zinc-m stj2 zinc-n stj2 zinc-p stj2]

- **alligators**; by: nicc-met sk4•
- **animals**; by: allox jl* alum carc fd2.de• cench k2 dulc fd4.de eupi hipp a1 ind kali-s fd4.de lac-leo hrn2• *Maias-l* hrn2• nux-v petr-ra shn4• positr nl2• sil k* suis-pan rly4• *Sulph* k* tarent tet a1 toxi mtf2• verat
  - **wild**: allox jl* alum cench k2 dioxi rbp6 dulc fd4.de eupi hipp a1 hydr a1 ind kali-s fd4.de lac-leo sk4• led a1 nux-v pyrid rly4• sil succ-ac rly4• *Sulph* tarent tet a1 verat
- **bulls**, by: arist-cl rbp3• ind petr-ra shn4• tarent k*
  - **mad**: ind k*
- **cats**; by: lac-leo hrn2• *Nux-v* sil verat
- **crocodiles**, by: sedi a1
- **dogs**; by: *Nux-v* ozone sde2• sil verat
- **elephant**; by an: lac-h sk4•
- **enemies**, by: (↗*Enemies)* con lac-del hrn2•
- **ghosts**, by: sil tritic-vg fd5.de
- **giants**, by: agath-a nl2• bell
- **horses**, by: allox tpw3* alum
- **looking** down at a pursuer from a mountain: lac-e hrn2•
- **Mafia**; by the: crot-c sk4•
- **man**; by a: lac-e hrn2• spong fd4.de
  - **bird** of prey, with a: aids nl2•
  - **kidnapper**: (↗*Kidnappers)* lac-leo hrn2• petr-ra shn4•
  - **teased**; and: lac-h sk4•
  - **violate** her; to: agath-a nl2• *Cench* st kali-n a1 kreos
- **murderers**; by: dendr-pol sk4• nept-m lsd2.fr oci-sa sk4•
- **ox**; by an: eupi hipp a1 (non:manc a1) tet a1
- **police**; by: arizon-l nl2• bros-gau mrc1 galla-q-r nl2• lac-e hrn2• lac-h htj1• lac-leo hrn2• lac-loxod-a hrn2• mag-m dgt marb-w es1•
- **robbers**, by: helodr-cal knl2• mag-m
- **run** backwards, must: sep
- **snakes**; by: dendr-pol sk4• petr-ra shn4•
- **soldiers**, by: dulc fd4.de mag-s
- **witch**; by: (↗*Witches - creeping)* ozone sde2•

PURSUING; of: dendr-pol sk4•

- **chase** mice; she helped cats: coca-c sk4•

PUZZLES: lac-e hrn2•

PYTHON (See Snakes - python)

QUARRELS: (↗*Abused; Abused; being; Anger; Fights; Insults; Provoked; Reconciliation; Vaccinations - arguing; Vexatious)* alum k* alum-sil k2 am-c k* am-m bg2 anan ant-c k* apis k* aran-ix jl *Arn* k* ars bg2* aur k* aza jl *Bapt* bar-c *Bell* k* brom k* brucel sa3• *Bry* k* calc k* calc-act a1 canth k* carl castm *Caust* k* cham k* chin bg2 chir-fl gya2 con k* *Crot-h* culx k2 dulc fd4.de echi ptk1 ferr-p bg2 guaj k* guare hep k* hydr bg2 ina-i mlk9.de indg j5.de kali-c j5.de *Kali-n* kali-p fd1.de• *Kola* stb3• lac-cp sk4• lac-del hrn2• lac-h sk4• lyc bg2 m-aust b2.de• *Mag-c* k* mag-s *Merc* j5.de mosch nat-c k* nat-m k* nat-s nat-sil fd3.de• nicc nicc-met stj2*• nit-ac bg2 **Nux-v** k* oci-sa sk4• op k* oxyg st oxyt ptk2 ozone sde2• paeon ph-ac k* phasco-ci rbp2 *Phos* k* plat k* plut-n srj7• positr nl2• *Puls* k* raph bg1 rat j5.de rheum bg2 sabin k* *Sel* b2.de• sep sil spig k* spong fd4.de *Stann* k* staph k* *Stram* bg2 tarax k* tung-met bdx1• verat k* zinc k* [aur-m stj2 aur-s stj2 nicc-s stj2 zinc-i stj2 zinc-m stj2 zinc-n stj2 zinc-p stj2]

- **dead** persons; with: cedr a1 kali-c h2*
- **father**; with his: (↗*MIND - Ailments - quarrelling - father)* crot-h a1

Quarrels: ...

- **friends**; with: lac-h sk4• [arg-met stj2]
- **happy** conversation with another person; quarrel changing into: ferr-p c1
- **money**, about (See Money - disputing)
- **mother**; with: dendr-pol sk4•
- **vaccinations**: lavand-a ctl1•

QUESTIONS: | **spread** out over the universe: sal-fr sle1•

QUIET: (↗*Peaceful; Pleasant)* agath-a nl2• atro kr1

RACCOONS: (↗*Animals)* lac-lup hrn2• limen-b-c hrn2•

RADIOACTIVITY: ozone sde2•

QUILT: | **beautiful** brown: maias-l hrn2•

RABBITS: (↗*Animals)* lac-cp sk4• lac-e hrn2•

RABIES: (↗*Disease)* anan k*

RACETRACK: | **racing** horses on: lac-e hrn2•

RAILWAY lines and roads: positr nl2•

RAIN: [tax jsj7]

- **soaked** in; being: oci-sa sk4•

RAINBOWS: coff-t a1 irid-met stj2*• neon srj5• [spect dfg1]

RAPE: aids nl2• arist-cl rbp3• *Cench* k2* fum rly4• germ-met srj5• haliae-lc srj5• kola stb3• kreos j5.de *Moni* rfm1• musca-d szs1 nat-p fkr6.de petr plac-s rly4• positr nl2• sep j5.de streptoc rly4• suis-pan rly4•

- **being** raped: granit-m es1• positr nl2• [bell-p-sp dcm1 germ-met stj2]
- **children** of: positr nl2•
- **committed**; that he has: lac-h sk4•
- **pursued** for rape; being (See Pursued - man - violate)
- **threats** of rape: cench k2 dendr-pol sk4• sep
  - **indifferent** to: polys sk4•

RASH; body covered with: (↗*Disease)* am-m rad-br sze8•

RATS: (↗*Animals)* allox jl* des-ac rbp6 ignis-alc es2• lac-h sk4• lac-loxod-a hrn2• lac-lup hrn2• limen-b-c hrn2* pieri-b mlk9.de polys sk4• positr nl2• sep

- **bed**; in: allox tpw4*
- **creeping** under the clothes: menis a1*

READ previous day; of what he had: bry gt

READING:

- **about**: pert-vc vk9
- **walking** up and down in his room and reading (See Walking - reading)

READY; he is not (See Failures)

REBELLING: (↗*Revolution)* dream-p sdj1*•

- **Christianity**; against: *Plut-n* srj7•

RECALLING things (See Events - forgotten)

RECONCILIATION: (↗*Quarrels)* mang h2* [bell-p-sp dcm1 mang-met stj2]

REFRIGERATOR: | **replacing** the: galeoc-c-h gms1•

REGIONS, beautiful: (↗*Beautiful; Country - beautiful; Earth - beautiful)* agath-a nl2• dulc fd4.de nat-sil fd3.de• ol-an a1 podo fd3.de• rumx a1 spong fd4.de symph fd3.de•

REJECTED; being: (↗*MIND - Ailments - rejected)* *Lac-e* hrn2•

- **helped**; by those he had: lac-e hrn2•

RELATIONSHIPS: *Aq-mar* rbp6 sal-al blc1•

- **difficulty** in; having: [buteo-j sej6]

RELATIVES: (↗*Family)* bros-gau mrc1 dulc fd4.de falco-pe nl2• ger-i rly4• *Lac-h* htj1• maias-l hrn2• merc-i-r a1 oci a1 oci-sa sk4• ruta fd4.de sal-al blc1• spong fd4.de suis-em rly4• tung-met bdx1• vanil fd5.de [buteo-j sej6]

- **dead** relatives (See Dead; of - relatives)
- **death** of relatives (See Death - relatives)
- **sick** (See Sick people - relatives)

RELIGIOUS: *(↗Churches; God; Praying; Preaching; Remorse)* hydrog srj2*• nept-m lsd2.fr nicc-met sk4• plac-s rly4• positr nl2• sol-t-ae a1 suis-pan rly4•

RELOCATION; of: galla-q-r nl2• ina-i mlk9.de

REMEMBERED: adam srj5• ammc a1 amp rly4• atp rly4• bell j5.de* brom a1 bry b7.de* cann-s b7.de* carb-v j5.de carl a1 casc a1 caust a1 cham a1 clem j5.de* cob-n mg1.de* coli rly4• con j5.de fl-ac a1 franz a1 ger-i rly4• gins a1 glon a1 graph j5.de* ina-i mlk9.de indg a1 lavand-a ctl1• lyc a1 mag-c a1 mag-s a1 mang j5.de medul-os-si rly4• mez j5.de* *Nat-m* j5.de* nicotam rly4• *Nuph* a1 nux-v b7.de* oxal-a rly4• pall a1 phos j5.de* plat a1 pot-e rly4• pyrid rly4• sin-a a1 streptoc rly4• suis-em rly4• suis-hep rly4• suis-pan rly4• *Sulph* a1 suprar rly4• tarent a1 thiam rly4• [bell-p-sp dcm1]
- **morning**, which was very unusual to him; in the: chir-fl gya2 nat-m a1
- **cannot** be remembered (See Unremembered)
- **in** the dream: sal-fr sle1•

REMORSE: *(↗Religious; Reproaches)* aether a1 apeir-s mlk9.de aq-mar rbp6 arn j5.de* ars h2* bros-gau mrc1 elaps a1 fl-ac a1 helodr-cal knl2• hyper a1 lach j5.de led j5.de limen-b-c hrn2* nat-c j5.de nat-m a1 sanic
- **death** of child; over: | **carelessness**; due to maternal: limen-b-c hrn2•
- **want** of remorse: *(↗Guilt - not)* androc srj1• plut-n srj7•

REMOVING; anxious dreams about: merc-i-r a1

REPEATING: *Arn* bamb-a stb2.de• cere-b a1 eupi a1 galeoc-c-h gms1• ign *Kola* stb3• nat-m ozone sde2• petr h2 phasco-ci rbp2 ulm-c jsj8• [sel stj2]
- **each** dream: plut-n srj7•
  - **perspective**; from a different: plut-n srj7•
- **themes** | **different** scenes: galeoc-c-h gms1•

REPENTANCE (See Remorse)

REPRIMANDED: plut-n srj7•
- **friend**; by: lac-h sk4•
- **mother**; by | **rude** behavior; for: lac-h sk4•
- **teacher**; by: lac-h sk4•

REPROACHES himself: *(↗Remorse)* dulc fd4.de lac-del hrn2• nat-m h2*
- **studied** for exams; for not having: nicc-met sk4•

RESCUED; being: | **brother**; by: lac-h sk4•

RESCUING; he is: tung-met bdx1•
- **children**; he is rescuing (See Children - rescuing)

RESOLVING: | **relationships**; old: helo-s rwt2•

RESPIRATORY complaints; with: cinnb j5.de ign j5.de kali-chl j5.de thuj j5.de tritic-vg fd5.de

RESPONSIBILITY: *(↗Children - responsibility)* dioxi rbp6 gard-j vlr2• lac-leo hrn2• *Limen-b-c* hrn2•
- **adults**; towards disabled young: lac-leo hrn2•
- **children**; for (See Children - responsibility)

RESTAURANT: maias-l hrn2• tritic-vg fd5.de
- **pay** for meal; cannot: maias-l hrn2•
  - **expensive**: maias-l hrn2•
- **venison**; eating: maias-l hrn2•

RESTLESS: agav-t jl1 ambr b7.de* anac jl ange-s jl arg-n a1 *Ars* b4.de* brom a1 bry a1 calad a1 calc j5.de calc-caust a1 carb-v j5.de carbn-s a1 carl a1 caste jl cham a1 cic b7.de* *Clem* b4.de* colch a1 coli jl2 esp-g jl euph a1 graph b4.de* indg a1 *Iod* b4.de* jug-r a1 *Kali-c* j5.de* kali-n b4a.de* lac-leo hrn2• *Led* b7.de* lith-c a1 lyc a1 mez a1 mosch b7.de* mur-ac b4.de* nat-c j5.de* nat-m j5.de* nid jl nux-v b7.de* *Olnd* b7.de* op b7.de* par b7.de* ph-ac j5.de phos b4.de* propl ub1• psor a1 ptel a1 sabad b7.de* sal-fr sle1• *Sil* a1 stann a1 staph b7.de* *Sulph* b4.de* tab a1 teucr b7.de* thuj a1 *Viol-t* b7.de* visc sp1 zinc b4a.de [bar-i stj2 lith-i stj2 mang-i stj2 merc-i-f stj2 zinc-i stj2]

RESURRECTION: allox jl

REUNION: ara-maca sej7•

REVEALING a perplexed situation when waking: acon j5.de*

REVELATION:
- **dead**; from the: lac-del hrn2•
- **die**; we never really: lac-lup hrn2•
- **intruder** in his own world; he was an: lac-lup hrn2•

REVENGE: lach j5.de* positr nl2•

REVERED PERSON is sexually abusive: lac-h sk4•

REVIVE:
- **unable** to; he was | **dying** friend; his: coca-c sk4•

REVOLUTION: *(↗Insurrections; Rebelling; Riots)* hura a1 merc a1

RHINOCEROS: ozone sde2•

RIDICULOUS (See Humiliation; Ludicrous)

RIDING: carc fd2.de• chr-ac kr1 dulc fd4.de ina-i mlk9.de maias-l hrn2• nat-c ther [tax jsj7]
- **backwards**: falco-pe nl2•
- **bicycle**; his old: lac-h sk4•
- **carriage**; in a: bell a1 dulc fd4.de falco-pe nl2• indg j5.de nat-s j5.de sacch-a fd2.de•
  - **fast**: falco-pe nl2•
  - **wild** riding: coca-c sk4•
- **train**; on a: phasco-ci rbp2

RINGS: aids nl2• hippoc-k szs2 nept-m lsd2.fr

RIOTS: *(↗Insurrections; Revolution)* bry con crot-c sk4• guaj indg kali-c lyc merc j5.de nat-c nat-m phos puls stann k* tung-met bdx1• [tax jsj7]
- **prison**: *(↗Prisoner - riots)* rhus-g tmo3•

RISEN AND DRESSED, having: sumb a1

RIVER: corv-cor bdg• dream-p sdj1*• galla-q-r nl2• ina-i mlk9.de limen-b-c hrn2• nept-m lsd2.fr tetox pin2• tritic-vg fd5.de vanil fd5.de [temp elm1]
- **banks** crumbling; river: chir-fl gya2
- **flowing** | **away** from the sea: plut-n srj7•
- **ocean**; becoming: neon srj5•
- **riding** up narrow flooded river: nicc-met sk4•
- **underworld**; in the: plut-n srj7•

ROAD:
- **absent**, they cannot go on: ozone sde2•
- **curved**: lac-h sk4• [tax jsj7]

ROAMING over fields: *(↗Walking; Wandering)* dulc fd4.de **Rhus-t**

ROBBERS: *(↗Thugs)* aids nl2• allox jl* **Alum** k* alum-p k2 *Arn* *Aur* k* aur-s c1* bamb-a stb2.de• bell k* bros-gau mrc1 calc-p carb-v castm cench k2 dendr-pol sk4• dream-p sdj1• ferr-i k* galla-q-r nl2• germ-met srj5• hippoc-k szs2 jac-c *Kali-c* k* kali-s k2* *Kola* stb3• lac-d sk4• lac-h sze9• lac-lup hrn2• lil-s a1 loxo-recl knl4• **Mag-c** k* mag-m k* mag-s melal-alt gya4 *Merc* k* merc-act j5.de* nat-c k* **Nat-m** k* neon srj5• ozone sde2• petr k* petr-ra shn4• phel phos plb b2.de* plut-n srj7• positr nl2• psil ft1 psor k* ptel rumx a1 sanguis-s hrn2• *Sanic* k* sel jl* *Sil* k* sin-n sinus rly4• verat k* *Zinc* k* [nat-ar stj2 oxyg stj tax jsj7]
- **chased** out of the house: germ-met srj5•
- **detecting** robbers: merc-i-r
- **father's** house; in his: mag-s a1
- **fighting** with robbers: *(↗Fights - robbers)* allox tpw3* ferr-i jac-c a1 *Kola* stb3• mag-c nat-c psil ft1 sil
- **menses**, during: *Nat-m*
- **own** world felt like a revelation; that he was an intruder in his (See Revelation - intruder)
- **pursuing** her (See Pursued - robbers)
- **sleep**, until the house is searched; and cannot: **Nat-m** sanic

ROBBERY (See Robbing)

ROBBING: carbn-dox knl3• dendr-pol sk4• hydrog srj2•
- **bank**; a: hydrog srj2• plut-n srj7•
- **guards** are assisting a robbery: dendr-pol sk4•
- **house**; robbers want to go into: ozone sde2•
- **library**, a: galla-q-r nl2•

Dreams

ROBOTS: dream-p sdj1•

ROCKET:
- **unmanned** | **computerized**: polys sk4•

ROCKS:
- **dragged** by men with ropes: maias-l hrn2•
- **large**, white rocks; of: lac-del hrn2•

ROLES:
- **two** roles; playing | **one** dream; in: plut-n srj7•

ROLLER COASTERS and helter-skelters: positr nl2•

ROMANTIC: am-c aq-mar rbp6 bung-fa mtf coca-c sk4• luna kg1•

ROME; ancient: plut-n srj7•

ROOMS: tritic-vg fd5.de vanil fd5.de
- **many**: pall c1
- **not** enough: galla-q-r nl2•
- **water** closets; full of: ozone sde2•
- **white**: sanguis-s hrn2•

ROUNDABOUTS: falco-pe nl2•

ROUSING the patient: *(↗SLEEP - Waking - dreams)* *Acon* j5.de* agar agath-a nl2• am-c j5.de *Am-m* h2* aml-ns gt ang kr1 ant-c h2 *Ant-t* j5.de* arg-met j5.de arg-n kr1 *Arn Ars* h2* asc-t kr1 atro aur bad bar-c *Bell Bov* j5.de bry cain kr1 calad gt *Calc* h2* calc-f kr1* *Camph* kr1 cann-s j5.de* carb-v h2* carc sp1* casc a1* *Cham Chin* j5.de* chr-ac kr1 *Cina* j5.de cinnb j5.de clem h2 cob gt coca colch coloc con h2 corn a1 cupr j5.de cycl j5.de dicha mg1.de *Dig* j5.de* dros j5.de dulc j5.de *Erig* mg1.de euph j5.de *Ferr-ma* j5.de gran graph grat j5.de *Hep* hyos gt hyper *Ign* j5.de indg j5.de ip j5.de *Kali-c* j5.de *Kali-chl* j5.de *Kali-i* j5.de kali-n h2* kreos j5.de *Lach* j5.de lam j5.de laur j5.de led h1* lob kr1 lyc lycpr j5.de lyss *M-arct* j5.de m-aust j5.de mag-c k1 *Mag-s* j5.de *Mang* j5.de melal-alt gya4 *Meph* a1* *Merc Mez* j5.de* mosch gt mur-ac j5.de murx j5.de *Nat-c* j5.de nat-m *Nat-s* j5.de* *Nicc* j5.de nit-ac j5.de *Nux-v* olnd j5.de *Op* j5.de par j5.de *Petr* j5.de *Ph-ac* phos plan plat h2 positr nl2• puls rat j5.de rhus-t j5.de ruta h1* sabad j5.de *Sabin* j5.de sars *Sep* h2* sil *Spig* j5.de spong j5.de stann staph *Stront-c* j5.de* **Sulph** tab j5.de* *Teucr* j5.de *Thuj* h1* tritic-vg fd5.de verat h1* verb j5.de *Zinc* h2*
- **daytime**, while sitting: acon a1
- **morning**: lyc a1
  - **6** h: rhus-t a1
- **forenoon** | **sitting**; while: ant-t a1
- **evening**: sulph a1
- **night**:
  - **midnight**: fl-ac a1 zinc a1
    - **after**: mez a1
  - **lying** down; after: acon a1
- **ejaculation**; dream of coition, after awaking sensation as after an: am-c gt
- **frequently**: alum kr1 cina a1 euphr a1 lyc a1 nat-m a1 stront-c sf1.de tab sf1.de
- **sensation** of waking from a dream, during a dream: glon a1

ROWBOAT: lac-del hrn2•
- **transport**; is mode of: lac-del hrn2•

ROWDY, feeling disposed to act like a: caj a1

ROWING: *(↗Water)* rhus-t

RUBBISH: positr nl2•
- **falling** on her; is: mag-m

RUINS: positr nl2•
- **places**; of historical: lac-h sk4•
- **walking** among ruins (See Walking - ruins)

RUNNING: *(↗Escaping; Pursued)* bell a1 dream-p sdj1• dulc fd4.de *Galeoc-c-h* gms1• *Kola* stb3• lac-e hrn2• lac-h sk4• oci-sa sk4• petr-ra shn4• ruta fd4.de sep a1 spong fd4.de stront-c sk4• taosc iwa1•
- **fatigue**; without: dendr-pol sk4•
- **home**: *(↗Home - running)* bros-gau mrc1 galeoc-c-h gms1•
- **men**; after: *(↗someone)*
  - **he** is running after men: *Nicc* a1 petr-ra shn4•
- **snow**; in (See Snow - running)
- **someone**; after: *(↗men)* cadm-met sp1* [cadm-s stj2]

Running: ...
- **up** and down: ambr st pall a1*
- **vainly**: *(↗Unsuccessful - run)* cit-ac rly4• croc j5.de ind a1

RUSSIA; being in: marb-w es1•

SACKS: | **putting** things all of one kind in sacks: galla-q-r nl2•

SACRED:
- **objects**: galeoc-c-h gms1•
- **places**: ozone sde2•

SAD: *(↗Cares; Weeping)* am-m b7.de* *Ars* asc-t (non:aur slp) aur-m kr1* bamb-a stb2.de• cann-i caps k* carb-an carbn-s castm j5.de caust k* crot-t j5.de galla-q-r nl2• graph guar vml3• guare ign k* junc-e a1 *Kola* stb3• lac-h htj1• laur k* lepi lyc k* mag-c manc mur-ac k* nat-c b4.de* *Nat-m* k* nat-sil fd3.de• nit-ac *Nux-v* op k* ozone sde2• paeon paull a1 peti a1 phos k* plan *Puls* rat j5.de *Rheum* k* spong k* stront-c symph fd3.de• taosc iwa1• tarent ust zinc

SAFARI: *(↗Hunting)* maias-l hrn2•

SAILING: *(↗Journeys - water; Water)* adam srj5• alum j5.de chin crot-c sk4• dulc fd4.de hura nat-s sang k* senec spong fd4.de valer j5.de vanil fd5.de verat-v
- **promised** land, to the: sal-fr sle1•

SAINTS: stront-c sk4•
- **different** religions; from | **together**; coming: lac-h sk4•

SALT: melal-alt gya4

SAND CASTLES: | **building**: lac-h sk4•

SAVING: *(↗Helping)*
- **children**: *(↗Children - rescuing)*
  - **newborns**: | **naked** babies from the cold; trying to save: lac-h htj1•
- **someone**; he had to save: coca-c sk4•

SAVIOR; of being the: aur-s wbt•

SCENES, new: calc-f kr1 olib-sac wmh1
- **vulgar**: chin-b kr1*

SCHOOL: galeoc-c-h gms1• lac-leo hrn2• limen-b-c hrn2• tritic-vg fd5.de vanil fd5.de [tax jsj7]
- **high** school: limen-b-c hrn2•
- **old**; goes back to: chir-fl gya2

SCHOOLMATE: | **meeting** of old: lac-leo hrn2•

SCIENTIFIC: *(↗Intellectual)* carb-an h2* guaj h2* *Ign* b7.de* m-arct b7.de* spong j5.de

SCORPIONS: *(↗Animals)* helo-s rwt2• lac-lup hrn2• sanguis-s hrn2•

SCOLDING someone: | **not** being a good citizen: [buteo-j sej6]

SCROTUM:
- **swollen** | **ulcerated**; and: nicc-met sk4•

SEA: *(↗Storms - sea; Water)* adam srj5• *Agath-a* nl2• all-c androc srj1• bit-ar wht1• bros-gau mrc1 (non:chin slp) chin-b kr1* chir-fl gya2 choc srj3• falco-pe nl2• fic-m gya1 hydrog srj2• kali-s fd4.de lac-loxod-a hrn2• lac-lup hrn2• melal-alt gya4 murx j5.de sal-fr sle1• spong fd4.de [ant-m stj2 aur-m stj2 beryl-m stj2 cadm-m stj2 chlor stj2 chr-m stj2 cob-m stj2 cupr-m stj2 lith-m stj2 mang-m stj2 merc-d stj2 mur-ac stj2 plb-m stj2 spect dfg1 stront-m stj2 yttr-met stj2 zinc-m stj2]
- **silver**: ignis-alc es2•
- **torches** in the sea: ozone sde2•

SEAL: *(↗Animals)* lac-lup hrn2•

SEARCHING: ulm-c jsj8• [tax jsj7]
- **someone**; for: arizon-l nl2• carc mg1.de* tritic-vg fd5.de [tax jsj7]
  - **failing** to find him; and: carc mlr1• plut-n srj7•
- **treasure**; for ancient secret: *(↗Treasure - digging)* dendr-pol sk4•

SECRET: kola stb3• lac-del hrn2• tung-met bdx1•
- **discovery** of: limen-b-c hrn2•
  - **performing** difficult trick; for: limen-b-c hrn2•
- **keep** a; must: plut-n srj7•

SEDUCING: | **exposing** thighs and breasts; by: bung-fa mtf

SEDUCTION: *Lac-e* hrn2• plut-n srj7• [tax jsj7]
- **unwanted**: lac-e hm2•

SEEING AGAIN an old schoolmate: *(↗Friends - meeting - old; Friends - old; Friends - seeing)* ant-c j5.de* ferr a1 thres-a sze7• [kali-sil stj2 sil stj2 sil-met stj2]

SEIZED by the finger; being: sil h2*

SEMINAR: | **leading** a: lac-del hrn2•

SENSIBLE: aur a1 olib-sac wmh1

SEPARATED; being:
- **people**: ozone sde2•
- **relatives**; from: oci-sa sk4•

SERIOUS NATURE OF: but-ac br1

SEVENTH son of a seventh son: irid-met srj5•

SEWERS; about: musca-d szs1

SEXUAL: *(↗Amorous; Coition)* chir-fl gya2 corian-s knl6• helo-s rwt2• lac-h sze9• loxo-recl knl4• maias-l hrn2• mand rsj7• musca-d szs1 sanguis-s hrn2• tritic-vg fd5.de [tax jsj7]
- **anal** intercourse: crot-c sk4•
- **captivity**; of: maias-l hm2•
- **disgust** | **sex** and death with: maias-l hrn2•
- **perversity**: helodr-cal knl2• lac-h sze9•
  - **followed** by | **remorse** (See MIND - Remorse - dream)
- **rain**; having sex in the: lac-cp sk4•
- **seduced** wife's sister: maias-l hm2•
- **several** people, having sex with: aids nl2• tritic-vg fd5.de [heroin sdj2]
  - **indifferent** at the same time; and being: carc az1.de•
- **sexual** activity | **broadcast** on television; being: lac-cp sk4•
- **sleeping** bag; in a | **quick** and rough: maias-l hrn2•
- **vicar**; having sex with a: positr nl2•
- **violence**: musca-d szs1

SEXUAL IDENTITY; ambiguous about one's: *(↗MIND - Confusion - identity - sexual)* irid-met srj5• plut-n srj7• positr nl2• [heroin sdj2]

SHAMEFUL: *(↗Humiliation)* acon a1 alum arn j5.de bros-gau mrc1 con k* dulc fd4.de erech a1 falco-pe nl2• hydrog srj2• *Lac-e* hrn2• led h1* mag-m h2* mur-ac h2 olib-sac wmh1 ozone sde2• plut-n srj7• polys sk4• spong fd4.de tub al* [heroin sdj2 oxyg stj2]
- **house** is dirty and sloppy; because her: ozone sde2•

SHAMELESS: crot-c sk4• *Lac-cp* sk4• lac-h sk4•
- **behavior** of guest: lac-cp sk4•

SHARING: nept-m lsd2.fr

SHARKS: musca-d szs1
- **dangerous** because they have no fins: positr nl2•

SHED, being under a: merc-i-r a1

SHEEP: positr nl2•
- **young** lambs: positr nl2•

SHEETS: | **circling** in a drying machine: galla-q-r nl2•

SHELLFISH: *(↗Animals)* limen-b-c hrn2•

SHELLS: falco-pe nl2•

SHELTER: | **warmth**; for: phasco-ci rbp2

SHIP: arizon-l nl2• bamb-a stb2.de• bit-ar wht1• fic-m gya1 gink-b sbd1• tritic-vg fd5.de vanil fd5.de [tax jsj7]
- **submarine**: dioxi rbp6 [heroin sdj2]
  - **stone**; made of: hippoc-k szs2
- **wartime**; in: hydrog srj2•

SHIT: dioxi rbp6

SHOCKING: lac-del hrn2• ph-ac a1
- **events** | **emotions**; without: polys sk4•

SHOES: dream-p sdj1•
- **dancing** shoes; cannot get on: chir-fl gya2

Shoes: ...
- **heavy** shoes; wearing: ulm-c jsj8•
- **high**-heeled: sanguis-s hm2•
- **socks**; having neither shoes nor: *(↗Nakedness)* falco-pe nl2•

SHOOTING; about: *(↗Guns; Shot)* allox tpw4 *Am-m* k* bit-ar wht1• coca-c sk4• hep k* lac-h sk4• lact-v a1 mag-s j5.de *Merc* k* merc-i-r a1* plut-n srj7• positr nl2• spong j5.de streptoc rly4• taosc iwa1• thiam rly4• til ban1•
- **unsuccessful** efforts: taosc iwa1•

SHOOTING; is: aids nl2• plut-n srj7•
- **person** that owes him money: ozone sde2•

SHOPPING: *(↗Household)* aids nl2• arizon-l nl2• bit-ar wht1• dulc fd4.de hura a1 ina-i mlk9.de lac-h htj1• oxal-a rly4• petr-ra shn4• ruta fd4.de [heroin sdj2 tax jsj7]

SHOT; being: *(↗Guns; Shooting)* asim a2 haliae-lc srj5• mag-s a1 plut-n srj7• streptoc rly4•
- **going** to be shot: chel hs1
- **soldier** is shot, a: am-m k*
- **woman** is accidentally: lac-e hm2•
- **wounded** by a shot; being: acon-ac rly4• bell coli gmj1 irid-met srj5• lact j5.de lob k* mag-s mang h1* streptoc rly4• [mang-i stj2 mang-m stj2 mang-met stj2 mang-p stj2 mang-s stj2 titan stj2]

SHOTS; hearing: cerv a1 germ-met srj5• hep k* hura a1 lac-lup hrn2• ozone sde2• spong hr1

SHOWERS: falco-pe nl2• nept-m lsd2.fr
- **shower** head falls out of her hand: ozone sde2•

SHRIEKING: [tax jsj7]
- **help**; for: *(↗Calling - help)* kali-c h2*
- **unable** to shriek (See Unsuccessful - shriek)

SHUDDERING: calc-act a1

SICK PEOPLE: *(↗Disease; Doctors; Patients; Patients - suicidal)* both-ax tsm2 (non:calc slp) calc-act slp calc-sil k2 castor-eq a1 dulc fd4.de ign lac-h sk4• mosch nat-s a1 nat-sil fd3.de• peti a1 rat rheum ruta fd4.de staph thiam rly4•
- **blond** woman: coca-c sk4•
- **grandmother** | **doctor**; has to rush to the: oci-sa sk4•
- **help** them; cannot: ozone sde2•
- **mother**; his: lac-h sk4•
- **relatives**: lac-loxod-a hm2• toxi mtf2•

SICKNESS; of (See Disease)

SILKWORM: *(↗Worms)* rhus-g tmo3•

SILVER: ignis-alc es2•

SINGING: asc-t bg2 galeoc-c-h gms1• kola stb3• *Lac-e* hrn2• loxo-recl knl4• sanguis-s hrn2•
- **political** songs: asc-t a1

SISTER: *(↗Family)* helodr-cal knl2• lac-h sze9• plut-n srj7• [buteo-j sej6]

SKATING: musca-d szs1
- **water**; in the: ped a1

SKELETONS: *(↗Dead bodies)* bomb-pr mlk9.de op pieri-b mlk9.de

SKULL:
- **breaking**; his skull is: gink-b sbd1*•
- **lined** up on a table; skulls: positr nl2•

SKUNKS: *(↗Animals)* lac-loxod-a hrn2• lac-lup hrn2•

SKY:
- **purplish**: coca-c sk4•
- **stormy**: [temp elm1]

SLAP on the face: phasco-ci rbp2

SLEEP:
- **falling** asleep | **mother's** lap; in: nicc-met sk4•

SLEEPING: kola stb3•
- **air**; in: acon a1
- **thousand** years; for a | **woman** would sleep: plut-n srj7•

Dreams

SLEIGH-RIDES: sars a1 spong fd4.de tril-c a1 (non:tril-p a1*)

SLIDING: positr nl2•
- **hill**; sliding down a steep: plut-n srj7•

SLIPPING: | **staircase**; down a: bros-gau mrc1

SLOWER; companion is: plut-n srj7•

SMALL, she is: galla-q-r nl2•

SMALLPOX: *(↗Disease; Face - smallpox)* anac h2

SMEARED with excrements, being (See Excrements - smeared)

SMELLING something:
- **sulphur**; burning: anac k*
- **tinder**; burning: anac k*

SMOKING: ina-i mlk9.de spong fd4.de tell tritic-vg fd5.de vanil fd5.de vero-o rly4*•

SMUGGLED GOODS: mag-c a1

SMUGGLING: plut-n srj7•

SNAKES: *(↗Animals; Water - wading - snakes)* aids nl2• alum k* arg-met gt *Arg-n* k* bell tl1 bit-ar wht1• bov k* carc fb* cench k2 chord-umb rly4• colch a crot-c sk4• daph bro1 dendr-pol sk4• dulc fd4.de falco-pe nl2• galla-q-r nl2• grat hyos tl1 indol ah iris kali-c k* kali-s fd4.de kalm kr1* kola stb3• *Lac-c* k* *Lac-h* sk4*• lac-leo hrn2• lach st* med hu2 merl a1 op bro1 ozone sde2• pitu-a ft* ptel pycnop-sa mrz1 *Ran-b* kr1* *Ran-s* k* rat rhus-g tmo3• ruta fd4.de sep sil k* sol-ni sphing k* spig bg2 stront-c sk4• tab teucr bg teucr-s bg1 thiam rly4• tub al2 vero-o rly4*• [nat-f stj2 tax jsj7]
- **bed**, in: *Lac-c* kr1
- **biting** him: adam skp7• aids nl2• bov k* cench k2 crot-c sk4• dendr-pol sk4• dulc fd4.de irid-met srj5• kola stb3• med hu ozone sde2• pert-vc vk9 [tax jsj7]
- **black** and white: dendr-pol sk4•
- **blue** and white: polys sk4•
- **converted** into liquid: lac-h sk4•
- **escape** him: lac-h sk4•
- **fear**, without: galla-q-r nl2•
- **golden**: lac-h sk4•
- **horrifying**: *Arg-n* a
- **killing**: lac-h sk4•
- **leaping** out at her: loxo-recl knl4•
- **python**: rosm lgb1
  - **abdomen**; encircling the | **pregnant** friend; of her: lac-h sk4•
  - **throwing** her into a pool full of caimans: rosm lgb1
- **splitting** in parts that keep moving: ozone sde2•
- **surrounded** by: lac-h sk4•
- **tiny**: lac-h sk4•
- **tongue** turns into a horrible snake; a boy's: aids nl2•

SNEAKING: lac-lup hrn2•
- **house**; about the: rhus-g tmo3•

SNORKELING: | **dry** land; on: maias-l hm2•

SNOW: art-v bapt brass-n-o srj5• crot-c sk4• dulc fd4.de falco-pe nl2• hippoc-k szs2 hydrog srj2*• kali-n a1 kali-p fd1.de• *Kreos* lac-h htj1*• limen-b-c mlk9.de ozone sde2• ruta fd4.de spong fd4.de tritic-vg fd5.de vanil fd5.de [tax jsj7]
- **children** playing in: galeoc-c-h gms1•
  - **anxious** they will be cold: galeoc-c-h gms1•
- **hills**; on:
  - **ice**; with: *Plut-n* srj7•
  - **descending** on a snowboard: ozone sde2•
- **open** air while it snows; being in: kreos a1*
- **polluted** by poisonous industry: ozone sde2•
- **running** through deep: dulc fd4.de rhus-t gt
- **smothered** in the snow; being: bapt a1
- **snow** storms: *Kreos*
- **strange** dark cities filled with: limen-b-c hm2•
- **wading** through deep: *(↗Confused - walking - unknown - snow)* rhus-t gt
- **working** in snow: bapt k* ruta fd4.de

SOAKED with rain, being: mag-c

SOCIAL INFERIORITY; of: lac-lup hrn2•

SOCIETY and community: arge-pl rwt5• dream-p sdj1•

SOFT and sweet: positr nl2•

SOILING himself (See Excrements - soiling)

SOLDIER: bry j5.de carbn-dox knl3• chel dulc fd4.de haliae-lc srj5• hippoc-k szs2 lac-h sze9• musca-d szs1 nat-c j5.de ozone sde2• phasco-ci rbp2 positr nl2• tritic-vg fd5.de tung-met bdx1• [mang-i stj2 mang-m stj2 mang-met stj2 mang-p stj2 mang-s stj2]
- **being** a: chel a1 [tax jsj7]
  - **Russian** soldier: musca-d szs1
- **porcelain**: galla-q-r nl2•
- **pursuing** him: dulc fd4.de mag-s
- **shot**, is: am-m
- **singing**: kola stb3•
- **toy**: positr nl2•

SOLEMNITIES: ant-c h2* carc fd2.de• ina-i mlk9.de pieri-b mlk9.de ruta fd4.de

SOLES are tickled (See Foot - soles)

SOMERSAULTS: zing a1*

SOMNAMBULISTIC: sil a1

SOMNOLENCE: dulc fd4.de graph j5.de op j5.de

SON: *(↗Family)* lac-lup hrn2•

SORCERY: rhus-g tmo3•

SORTING (See Organizing)

SPACESHIP: sal-al blc1•

SPEECH; making a: hydrog srj2• lac-leo hrn2• thres-a sze7•
- **inspirational**: lac-leo hm2•
- **Latin**; in (See Latin)
- **long** speech; a: am j5.de bros-gau mrc1 cham j5.de

SPEEDING: lac-h sk4• petr-ra shn4•
- **dry** dusty roads: helo-s rwt2•

SPENDING money: falco-pe nl2•

SPIDERS: *(↗Animals)* agath-a nl2• bomb-chr mlk9.de carc zzh carneg-g rwt1• cinnb convo-d mgm• crot-c k* lac-c samkn lat-m bnm6• oxal-a rly4• oxyt a2* plut-n srj7• sanguis-s hrn2• sars h2* symph fd3.de• ven-m jl* [spect dfg1]
- **black**: ozone sde2•
  - **mouth**; creeping in corner of: ozone sde2•
- **enormous**, hairy spiders: *Crot-c* a1
- **face** and can feel its throbbing legs; spider is on: agath-a nl2•
- **ox**; as large as a: cinnb k*
- **ruby** red abdomen: agath-a nl2•

SPIED upon; being: polys sk4•

SPIES; about: dream-p sdj1• positr nl2• sal-fr sle1•
- **she** is a spy: plut-n srj7•

SPINNING: lac-lup hrn2• (non:lach a4) lachn a1 (non:sars a4)

SPIRALS: falco-pe nl2• galla-q-r nl2•
- **bringing** order to chaos: falco-pe nl2•
- **moving**: galla-q-r nl2•

SPIRITS (See Ghosts)

SPIRITUAL: hippoc-k szs2

SPLENDOR: stann j5.de

SPORTS: lac-e hrn2• tritic-vg fd5.de
- **bicycling**: lac-e hm2•
- **bowling** | **metal** platter; with: lac-e hrn2•
- **football**: lac-e hm2•

SPRIT; he is solely a: rhus-g tmo3•

STAB:
- **antagonist**, his: nat-c a1 ozone sde2•
- **friend**, his: allox jl*
- **others**, will: lach j5.de ozone sde2• positr nl2•

STABBED, being: (↗*Fights; Knives*) chin guaj lil-s a1 nat-c op petr-ra shn4• positr nl2• ruta fd4.de [tax jsj7]
- **behind**; from: dendr-pol sk4•
- **fear** of being stabbed: lach
- **groin**; in the | **ripped** up through the head; and: coca-c sk4•

STABLES: galla-q-r nl2•

STAGS: canth j5.de

STAIRS: aids nl2• galla-q-r nl2• ina-i mlk9.de pall hr1* tritic-vg fd5.de ulm-c jsj8•
- **ascending**: dulc fd4.de neon srj5•
  - **countless** stairs: ozone sde2•
- **banisters**: aids nl2•
- **grand**: aids nl2•
- **secret**: aids nl2•
- **wide**: aids nl2• pall hr1*

STANDING: lac-leo hrn2•

STARS: dulc fd4.de irid-met srj5• neon srj5•
- **falling** stars: alum
- **quasars**: neon srj5•

STATUE: | **life**; coming to: lac-d sk4•

STEALING: (↗*Plundering; Theft - committed*) helodr-cal knl2• *Lac-lup* hrn2• rad-br sze8•
- **fruit**: plb
- **garden** hose, but he would return it when nearby again: lac-lup hrn2•
- **horse**; a: rumx
  - **someone** is stealing his: aether a1
- **impulse** to: lac-leo hrn2•
- **money**: (↗*Money - stolen*) marb-w es1•
- **paintings**, his: sal-fr sle1•
- **screen** out of a backpack; a computer: rosm lgb1
- **young** man; from a: rosm lgb1

STONES: *Maias-l* hrn2•
- **floor**: hippoc-k szs2
- **lying** on him; stone: kali-c
- **message**; stone with a: falco-pe nl2•

STOOL: aloe k* androc srj1• bros-gau mrc1 castn-v dulc fd4.de falco-pe nl2• polys sk4• positr nl2• psor sars ulm-c jsj8• zinc k* [heroin sdj2 zinc-i stj2 zinc-m stj2 zinc-p stj2]
- **incontinence**: dulc fd4.de haliae-lc srj5•
- **smelly**: falco-pe nl2•
- **urging** to pass: nicc-met sk4•

STORMS: aids nl2• all-s *Ars* jac-c kali-s fd4.de lac-lup hrn2• mag-c phasco-ci rbp2 *Sil* [oxyg stj2]
- **destroying**: lac-lup hrn2•
- **hurricane**:
  - **approaching** | **sunny** and calm; yet: limen-b-c hrn2•
- **sea**, at: (↗*Sea; Water*) all-c sil
- **snow** storms (See Snow - snow)
- **thunderstorm** (See Lightning; Thunderstorm)

STOVE, hot: apis a1

STRANGE: (↗*Absurd; Curious*) acon a1 ant-t a1 bar-act a1 chinin-s j5.de dream-p sdj1• dulc fd4.de fuma-ac rly4• ketogl-ac rly4• *Lach* j5.de* lact j5.de lat-m bnm6• limen-b-c hrn2* nat-ox rly4• nit-ac j5.de oxal-a rly4• ph-ac j5.de propr sa3• rhus-g tmo3• ribo rly4• sanguis-s hrn2• sarr a1 spong fd4.de staphycoc rly4• stram a1 streptoc rly4• *Stront-c* sk4• suis-pan rly4• thiam rly4•

STRANGE THINGS: fl-ac a1 plat a1

STRANGERS: (↗*Foreigners*) lac-del hrn2• *Plut-n* srj7•
- **entering** house; stranger: nat-ox rly4•

Strangers: ...
- **head** divided into two; stranger with: stront-c sk4•

STRANGLED; being (See Choked; Suffocation)

STREAM: (↗*Water*) com dulc fd4.de nept-m lsd2.fr
- **crossing** a stream on horseback: chr-ac a1*
- **everything** moving in a stream from right to left: galla-q-r nl2•

STRIKING:
- **betrayed** him; those who: rhus-g tmo3•
- **father**; his: oci-sa sk4•
- **men**; two | **obscene** comment; who passed an: nicc-met sk4•

STRIVING: (↗*Business; Exertion; Vexatious; Work*) cina b2.de* croc j5.de dulc fd4.de graph h2* nux-v b2.de* **Rhus-t** ●* sabin b2.de* tung-met bdx1•

STRUCK by lightning, being (See Lightning - struck)

STRUGGLING; of: coca-c sk4•

STUDENTS do not obey: ozone sde2•

STUNG by an insect, being: (↗*Wasps*) marb-w es1• oxal-a rly4• phos k* [arg-n stj2]

SUBORDINATION like a servant: lyss a1*

SUCTION: lac-lup hrn2•

SUFFERING: (↗*Disease; Pain*) cimic a1 [hydrog stj2]
- **others**; of: lac-loxod-a hrn2•

SUFFOCATION: (↗*Choked; Disease; Throat - closing; Throat - swollen*) arn bapt a1 dream-p sdj1• hippoc-k szs2 iris kali-bi kali-c h2 led vml4 petr-ra shn4• spong fd4.de xan c1* [bell-p-sp dcm1 tax jsj7]

SUGAR: kola stb3•

SUGGESTIONS; giving: | **passenger**; to the other: bung-fa mtf

SUICIDE: (↗*Patients - suicidal*) cisplat dgt2 hydrog srj2• lact dgt2 naja petr-ra shn4• term-a bnj1 [merc stj2]

SUN:
- **being** in the: *Agath-a* nl2• haliae-lc srj5• lac-e hrn2• [heroin sdj2]
- **sunrise**: kola stb3•

SUPERNATURAL things: asc-t a1

SURGERY: lac-leo hrn2• musca-d szs1
- **grateful** to have sperm and egg combined and put in uterus: lac-del hrn2•
- **returns** to work before anesthetic wore off: lac-leo hrn2•
- **undergoing** unnecessary; as example for medical students: lac-leo hrn2•

SURPRISED; of being: ulm-c jsj8•

SURREAL: lac-del hrn2•

SURVIVAL: ozone sde2• tung-met bdx1•

SWALLOWING pins: merc j5.de*

SWEAR, disposed to: caj a1

SWIMMING: (↗*People - bathing; Water*) adam srj5• *Agath-a* nl2• apeir-s mlk9.de *Bell* chin-b kr1* falco-pe nl2• fum rly1*• galla-q-r nl2• hura ina-i mlk9.de iod lac-lup hrn2• limen-b-c mlk9.de loxo-recl knl4• lyc melal-alt gya4 merc-i-r musca-d szs1 nat-p fkr6.de nauf-helv-li elm2• ran-b rhus-t sal-al blc1• sol-t-ae spong fd4.de taosc iwa1• vanil fd5.de [heroin sdj2]
- **people**: musca-d szs1
- **sea**; in the: nauf-helv-li elm2•
- **sensation**, languid feeling: lac-del hrn2•
- **underwater**: falco-pe nl2• vanil fd5.de

SWINGING: hydrog srj2• ina-i mlk9.de sang j5.de

SWIRLING: | **pleasurable**: [buteo-j sej6]

SWITCH; light: positr nl2•

SYMPATHETIC: lac-leo hrn2•
- **mourning** a friend's departure; with those who are: lac-leo hrn2•

TABLE is being set for him: ozone sde2•

- **tablecloth** is too beautiful: ozone sde2•

TAKING: | **more** than wanted to give: [buteo-j sej6]

TALKING with someone: *(↗Conversations; MIND - Talking - sleep)* plb a1 ruta fd4.de spong fd4.de
- **school** friends; two: pert-vc vk9
- **dead** people; with (See Dead; of - talking)
- **doctor**; with his (See Doctors - conversation)

TALL, being very: ferr-i

TANKS: | **battle** tanks: bamb-a stb2.de•

TAPEWORMS: | **she** has: plut-n srj7•

TEACHER:
- **incompetent** (See Performance - teacher - observed - inadequate)
- **sarcastic**; being: nicc-met sk4•
- **spiritual**; of a: helo-s rwt2• neon srj5•
- **yelling** at me; old teacher: chir-fl gya2

TEACHING: corv-cor bdg• *Lac-e* hrn2• lac-leo hrn2• lac-lup hrn2•
- **adolescents**: lac-leo hrn2•
- **homeopathy**: carbn-dox knl3•

TEAMWORK: *(↗Groups - working)* *Lac-e* hrn2•

TEETH: *(↗Body; parts)* [sil-met stj2]
- **breaking** off: *(↗Disease)* crot-c sk4• irid-met srj5• kali-n kali-p fd1.de• rauw sp1 sul-ac j5.de ther thuj [tax jsj7]
  - **molar**: ephe-si hsj1•
- **cleaning**: bit-ar wht1•
- **falling** out: *(↗Disease)* aids nl2• bamb-a stb2.de• coca a1 cocc convo-d a1 cypra-eg sde6.de• nicc nux-v k* positr nl2• sul-ac j5.de tab [nicc-met stj2 nicc-s stj2]
- **filling** is falling out: nux-v a1
- **fillings** put in son's teeth: brass-n-o srj5•
- **becoming** loose: coca a1
  - **one** tooth and a piece of the jaw easily coming out; and: coca a1
- **pulled** out; being: cench k2 nat-m plut-n srj7•

TELEPHONES: irid-met srj5•
- **answering** the phone: galeoc-c-h gms1•
- **under** water; phone: galeoc-c-h gms1•

TEMPLES: | **pain** in (See Headache - temples)

TENT: | **erecting** a large tent; men: hydrog srj2•

TERRAPIN: cench k2

TERROR: maias-l hrn2•

TERRORISTS: ozone sde2• petr-ra shn4•
- **fire** in cinema hall; who open: nicc-met sk4•

TEST; taking a (See Examinations)

THEATER:
- **going** to the: tritic-vg fd5.de
  - **dressed**; but could not get (See Unsuccessful - dress - theater)
- **in**: galeoc-c-h gms1•
- **people**, full of: aids nl2•
- **performing** in: *(↗Performing)* galeoc-c-h gms1•

THEFT: ina-i mlk9.de taosc iwa1•
- **accused** of; being: *(↗Accusations; MIND - Admonition - agg.)* choc srj3• lach
  - **wife** accused of theft: lac-leo hrn2•
- **committed** a theft, having: *(↗Stealing)* alum lac-leo hrn2• oxal-a rly4• plb ros-d wla1 taosc iwa1•
  - **object** of no value except to owner: lac-leo hrn2•

THINGS: *(↗Forms)*
- **bigger** and overpowering; things are: bamb-a stb2.de•
- **black**: nat-ar a1
- **changing** quickly: *(↗Changing - subjects)* *Mang* h2*

Things: ...
- **desired**: sil h2
- **fixed** upon the same things, dreams: acon ign petr h2 puls spig h1* stann
- **growing**: kali-n a1 kreos j5.de
- **important** things; of very: lach a1
  - **forgotten** waking: lach a1
- **shining**: melal-alt gya4
  - **entering** body: melal-alt gya4
- **small**, seem: ferr-i a1
- **varied**: am-c j5.de cann-i a1 carl a1 coloc a1 equis-h a1 *Gran* a1 iber a1 iris-foe a1 lachn a1 mang a1 mez a1 *Nat-c* j5.de *Nat-m* j5.de op a1 pip-m a1 plan a1 stram a1 zing a1 [bell-p-sp dcm1]

THINKING:
- **difficulty** in | **afternoon**: lac-h sk4•

THIRSTY, being: aids nl2• dros k* mag-c **Nat-m**

THREATENED; of being: *(↗Danger)* galla-q-r nl2• musca-d szs1 positr nl2•

THREATENING: | **professor**; he is threatening his: crot-c sk4• lac-h sk4•

THREATS: aids nl2• anac jl arist-cl rbp3• ars dream-p sdj1• hippoc-k szs2 sep tung-met bdx1• ulm-c jsj8•
- **embraced** threateningly from behind; of being: positr nl2•
- **rape**, of (See Rape - threats)

THROAT: *(↗Body; parts; Disease)*
- **closing**; that the throat is: *(↗Suffocation)* xan a2*
- **grasped** by the throat; being: *(↗Choked)* phos a1 sul-ac a1
- **lump** in the throat; having a: cinnb a1
  - **right** ear; and in: cinnb a1
- **sore** throat: bar-c a1 borx h2* pip-m a1
- **stoppage** of the throat: kreos a1
- **swollen**; is: *(↗Suffocation)* led vml4

THROWING:
- **bottles**: coca-c sk4•
- **everything** away: (non:rhus-t h1)
- **someone** out of the window: bry a1*
- **things** | **anger**; from: bung-fa mtf

THROWN; being:
- **carriage**; from a: nat-s a1
- **downwards**: calc vh1
- **grave**, into a (See Graves - thrown)
- **high** place; from a: crot-c sk2•
- **trash**; into a (See Trash - thrown)

THUGS: *(↗Robbers)* plut-n srj7•

THUNDERSTORM: *(↗Lightning)* *Arn* k* *Ars* k* euphr k* nat-c k* phel j5.de spig j5.de* tritic-vg fd5.de

THYROID GLAND: *(↗Body; parts)*
- **enlarged**: plut-n srj7•

TICKLED on the soles, being (See Foot - soles)

TIDE; coming in: fic-m gya1

TIED up; of being: positr nl2•

TIGERS: *(↗Animals)* lac-leo hrn2• lac-lup hrn2• positr nl2•
- **surrounded** by: lac-d sk4•

TIME:
- **exaggeration** of time (= passes too slowly): sang hr1
- **lost** conception of: bamb-a stb2.de•
- **short** of time; he is running: *Rhus-g* tmo3•
- **travelling** through: rhus-g tmo3•

TIREDNESS; of: arizon-l nl2• vanil fd5.de

TIRING (See Exhausting)

TOAD: allox tpw4 tritic-vg fd5.de
- **bed**; in: allox jj*
- **bitten** by a: aids nl2•

TOE: *(↗Body; parts)*
- **cut** off; toe: lac-e hrn2• nat-s j5.de
  - **child**; of | **found** in truck: lac-e hrn2•
- **falling** off: hippoc-k szs2

TOILETS (See Closet)

TONGUE: *(↗Body; parts)*
- **large**; too: chir-fl gya2 tab j5.de

TORNADOES on the sea: fic-m gya1

TORPEDO: ozone sde2•

TORTURED; of being: dendr-pol sk4•

TOSSING someone out of the window (See Window - tossing)

TOWER: | **blown** up: positr nl2•

TOXIC orange cloud: phasco-ci rbp2

TRAFFIC: lac-e hrn2•

TRAIN: *(↗Journeys - train)* aids nl2• haliae-lc srj5• lac-h htj1*• maias-l hrn2• vanil fd5.de [bell-p-sp dcm1 cadm-met stj2]
- **catch**; trying to: hydrog srj2• vanil fd5.de [tax jsj7]
- **changing** track: dioxi rbp6
- **missing** (See Missing - train)
- **riding** (See Riding - train)
- **sitting** in train with sister: pert-vc vk9
- **stop** where he thinks it will; does not: ozone sde2•
- **troop** train carrying money: maias-l hrn2•

TRAM: des-ac rbp6
- **derailed**: des-ac rbp6

TRANSFORMATION: rhus-g tmo3•

TRAP: dendr-pol sk4•
- **being** trapped: *(↗Crystals - trapped; Men - tiny - bottle; MIND - Delusions - trapped)* coca-c sk4• falco-pe nl2• oci-sa sk4• sal-fr sle1•
  - **water**; under: *Lac-lup* hrn2•

TRASH: | **thrown** into a trash; being: lac-e hrn2•

TRAVELLING (See Journeys)

TREASURE: aids nl2• hippoc-k szs2 ulm-c jsj8• [spect dfg1]
- **digging** for: *(↗Searching - treasure)* aids nl2•
- **finding**: [spect dfg1]

TREATMENT, medical: canna a1

TREES: fic-m gya1 kola stb3• lac-e hrn2• lac-loxod-a hrn2• *Lyc* kr1 spong fd4.de symph fd3.de• tritic-vg fd5.de vanil fd5.de [heroin sdj2]
- **bordering** | **premises**: nicc-met sk4•
- **chopping** down (See cut; being)
- **cut** off: [erech stj]
- **cut**; being: coca-c sk4• lac-e hrn2•
- **removing** and replanting: chir-fl gya2

TRINITY:
- **women**; of: | **three** faces; or one woman with: *(↗Face - two - having)* plut-n srj7•

TRIUMPH: bapt a1 bit-ar wht1•

TROLLS: musca-d szs1

TROPICAL PLACES: ara-maca sej7•

TROUBLE: linu-c a1 rumx a1*
- **being** in: allox sp1 cimic a1* rumx a1
- **causing** some trouble: x-ray sp1

TROUT: *(↗Animals; Fish)* lac-lup hrn2•

TRUCK: chlam-tr bcx2•
- **big** red: polys sk4•
- **crushing** | **smaller**, lighter vehicles: polys sk4•
- **loaded**; heavily | **towards** them; tilting: oci-sa sk4•

TRUE ON WAKING; dreams seem: am-m anac j5.de* *Arg-met* k* arn j5.de cina k2 hydrog srj2• hyos k2 ina-i mlk9.de nat-c k* nat-m podo fd3.de• rad-br ptk1 ruta fd4.de symph fd3.de• vanil fd5.de verat [spect dfg1]

TRUE; dreams are coming (See Clairvoyant)

TUMOR: musca-d szs1

TUNNEL: aids nl2• hippoc-k szs2 musca-d szs1 vanil fd5.de [heroin sdj2 tax jsj7]
- **moving** up and down a tunnel | **end**; but never finding its: coca-c sk4•

TURBULENT: coca-c sk4•

TURN:
- **around**; turning: lac-lup hrn2• lact j5.de* ozone sde2•
- **central** point, about which everything must turn; he is the: thuj a1

TURTLES: *(↗Animals)* lac-loxod-a hrn2•

TWENTY spokes radiating outwards: neon srj5•

TWINS: crot-c sk4• haliae-lc srj5• nept-m lsd2.fr *Plut-n* srj7• ruta fd4.de

TWISTERS: [temp elm1]

TYRANNY; world of: positr nl2•

TYRANT: | **power** of a; being under the: lac-h sk4•

UFO's: lac-h sze9• rhus-g tmo3•

UGLY: ara-maca sej7•

UGLY; being: stront-c sk4•

UNCLE; maternal: pert-vc vk9

UNCONSCIOUSNESS; about: *(↗Disease)* graph h2*

UNCOVERING; with: kreos j5.de nat-m j5.de

UNDERGROUND: plut-n srj7•

UNDERWEAR (See Clothes - underwear)

UNDERWORLD; in the: plut-n srj7• ulm-c jsj8•

UNICORN: ignis-alc es2•

UNIFICATION, of: adam srj5•

UNIFORMS: hippoc-k szs2

UNIMPORTANT: alum b2.de* anac b2.de* arg-met b2.de* ars b2.de* bell b2.de* *Bry* b2.de* canth b2.de* cham b2.de* chel b2.de* *Chin* b2.de* cic b2.de* cina b2.de* clem b2.de* cocc b2.de* coff b2.de* con b2.de* euph b2.de* ferr-i a1 hep b2.de* ign b2.de* kali-c b2.de* kali-n a1 lach b2.de* lyc b2.de* lycps-v a1 *Mag-c* b2.de* merc b2.de* nat-m b2.de* *Nux-v* b2.de* peti a1 *Ph-ac* b2.de* phos b2.de* plat b2.de* *Puls* b2.de* rhod b2.de* *Rhus-t* b2.de* sabin b2.de* sars b2.de* sel b2.de* *Sep* b2.de* sil b2.de* stann b2.de* staph b2.de* stront-c b2.de* *Sulph* b2.de* viol-t b2.de*
- **being**: crot-c sk4•

UNPLEASANT: *(↗Anxious; Disgusted; Disgusting; Vexatious)* abies-n a1* agar agath-a nl2• aids nl2• allox tpw4* alum k* ang k* ant-c b7.de* ant-t apis aran-ix sp1 arg-met arg-n k2 ars a1 asar b7.de* *Bell* kr1 brucel sa3• bry k* calc calc-caust a1 calc-f kr1* cann-i a1 *Cann-s* k* carbn-s caust b4a.de* cham chin b7.de* chir-fl gya2 chr-ac a1 cic *Cimic* cina b7.de* cit-v a1 cob-n jl coca (non:coff slp) coff-t a1* con a1 *Corn* a1* cycl a1 cyt-l sp1 dig dream-p sdj1• fago ferr ferr-i fl-ac *Gels* k* glon hall a1 ham hippoc-k szs2 hydrog srj2• iber jl ign b7.de* ina-i mlk9.de iod iris a1 kali-bi k* kalm *Lac-c* kr1 lach k* lat-m bnm6• laur levo jl lil-t luna kg1• lyc j5.de* lyss kr1 m-arct b7.de mag-s sp1 maias-l hrn2• mand jl* mang-p rly4• melal-alt gya4 merc merc-c k* merc-d a1 mosch b7.de* mucs-nas rly4• myric a1 nat-m *Nat-s* kr1 nux-m nux-v b7.de* op b7.de* ox-ac peti a1 *Petr* kr1 plan polyg-h a1 psil jl* ptel pycnop-sa mrz1 rauw sp1 rheum b7.de* rhus-t b7.de* rumx ruta b7.de* sacch-a fd2.de• sang k* senec kr1 sep sil a1 staph k* stry **Sulph** k* tarent tell jl* tep a1 til a1 tung-met bdx1• ust wildb a1 ziz a1 [spect dfg1 tax jsj7]
- **falling** asleep, on: lyss kr1
- **followed** by headache: *(↗SLEEP - Dreaming - followed - head)* aids nl2• murx k*
- **fear**; from: calc-f sp1

Dreams

- **physically** and mentally: des-ac rbp6

UNREAL; everything seems: ulm-c jsj8•

UNREMEMBERED: acon-ac rly4• adam skp7• agar *Agath-a* nl2• agn k* aloe arg-met arge-pl rwt5• *Arn* k* ars j5.de *Aur* k* *Aur-m-n* wbt2• bamb-a stb2.de• bapt *Bell* k* bit-ar wht1• bov k* *Bry* k* bufo-s cact calc k* calc-act slp (non:calc-ar slp) calc-caust a1 canth k* *Carb-ac* carb-an k* carb-v k* *Carl Chel* chir-fl gya2 choc srj3• chord-umb rly4• chr-ac a1* *Cic* k* cinnb cob k* coca cocc k* con k* croc b2.de* cystein-l rly4• dream-p sdj1• ephe-si hsj1• eupi falco-pe nl2• fl-ac franz a1 galeoc-c-h gms1• galla-q-r nl2• goss st gran haliae-lc srj5• *Hell* k* helodr-cal knl2• hipp a1 hydr *Hydrog* srj2• hyper ign b2.de* iod k* ip k* kali-i ketogl-ac rly4• kola stb3• lac-e hrn2• *Lac-loxod-a* hrn2• lach k* lact j5.de laur k* lavand-a ctl1• lipp a1 *Lyc* k* *M-arct* b2.de* mag-c k* mag-m k* mang meny k* merc k* mez k* mur-ac k* myric naja nat-c *Nat-m* k* nat-s nicc nux-m j5.de ol-an ox-ac oxal-a rly4• ozone sde2• paeon pert-vc vk9 peti a1 petr h2* ph-ac k* phel phos k* pip-m a1 plac-s rly4• plan plat k* plect a1 plut-n srj7• positr nl2• rad-br sze8• rhus-g tmo3• rhus-t b2.de* ruta fd4.de *Sabad* k* sal-al blc1• samb k* sars b2.de* *Sel* k* seneg k* sin-a a1 *Spig* k* spirae a1 spong fd4.de stann k* staph k* stram b2.de* suis-em rly4• suis-pan rly4• sul-ac k* *Sulph* k* suprar rly4• *Tarax* k* tarent thiam rly4• til tritic-vg fd5.de ulm-c jsj8• vanil fd5.de *Verat* k* [bell-p-sp dcm1 cob-m stj2 cob-p stj2 heroin sdj2 tax jsj7]

- **morning** | **sleep**; in: lac-del hrn2•
- **door** shut; as if a: dream-p sdj1•

UNSUCCESSFUL EFFORTS: *(↗Business - succeed; Destination - reaching - unable; Difficulties; Embarrassment; Failures; Missing - train)* am-m androc srj1• cadm-m mg1.de* calc calc-f cann-s j5.de carl cham j5.de choc srj3• coca-c sk4• croc dig dulc fd4.de galla-q-r nl2• ign lac-e hrn2• mag-c mag-s mosch mur-ac h2 nat-c j5.de op ph-ac phos mtf plat ros-d wla1 ruta fd4.de stann j5.de staph dtp tab taosc iwa1• tritic-vg fd5.de tung-met bdx1• [ars stj2 ars-met stj2 bar-br stj2 brom stj2 calc-lac stj2 calc-met stj2 calc-sil stj2 cupr-m stj2 ferr-sil stj2 gal-met stj2 gal-s stj2 germ-met stj2 kali-ar stj2 kali-met stj2 kali-sil stj2 mang-m stj2 nat-ar stj2 sel stj2 zinc stj2 zinc-i stj2 zinc-m stj2 zinc-n stj2 zinc-p stj2]

- **brakes** of the car do not function any more (See Brakes - function)
- **business**, in: mag-m *Phos* sabin
- **climbing** | **sand** dune: loxo-recl knl4•
- **coition**, in: ind a1* iod a1
- **do** various things; to: arist-cl rbp3• lac-e hrn2• nicc-met sk4• ozone sde2• ulm-c jsj8•
- **dress**; to:
  - **ball**; for a: mag-c mag-s
  - **theater**, for going to: mag-s a1*
- **escape** from danger; to (See Danger - escaping - fruitless)
- **finding**; in:
  - **house** where he wants to go: kola stb3•
  - **toilet**; the: ign mtf lac-c mtf mag-c mtf mag-m mtf mag-p mtf mag-s mtf phos mtf
  - **way** in his own house: mag-c
- **go** away; to: bell h1
- **harm** other; to: crot-c sk4•
- **jumping** long distance contest: ozone sde2•
- **open** the mouth, to (See Mouth - opening)
- **reach** a distant place, to: croc melal-alt gya4 petr-ra shn4• plat ros-d wla1
- **run**; to: *(↗Running - vainly)* croc j5.de ind a1
- **shriek**; to: *(↗Nightmares)* am-m a1 ars j5.de castm j5.de mag-m j5.de sil j5.de tab j5.de*
- **swim**; to: lac-h sk4•
- **talk**; to: mag-c

URGENCY; of: lac-lup hrn2•

URINATING: am-br bamb-a stb2.de• bell k2 bomb-chr mlk9.de chr-ac kr1 ger-i rly4• kola stb3• *Kreos* k* lac-c k* lac-leo hrn2• loxo-recl knl4• lyc merc-i-f plut-n srj7• pycnop-sa mrz1 rad-br sze8• sapin a1 *Seneg* k* *Sep* k* sulph

- **chamber** pot; into the: sep a1* sulph a1*
- **desire** for: agath-a nl2• kali-n a1 kreos j5.de merc-i-f a1
- **hide** he is; tries: phasco-ci rbp2
- **public**; in: arge-pl rwt5• loxo-recl knl4•
- **strangury**; he had an attack of: *(↗Disease)* chr-ac a1*

URINE: arge-pl rwt5•

- **soiled** with; being: zinc j5.de

UTERUS: | **pain** in uterus: choc srj3•

VACCINATIONS: | **arguing** about vaccinations: *(↗Quarrels)* lavand-a ctl1•

VALUABLE, delicate objects: [tax jsj7]

- **preserving**: polys sk4•

VAMPIRES: chord-umb rly4• ignis-alc es2• pegan-ha tpi1• psil ft1*

VEGETABLES: androc srj1• lac-cp sk4• loxo-recl knl4• nept-m lsd2.fr

VEGETATION, greenery: nept-m lsd2.fr

VEHICLES: lac-leo hrn2• *Lac-lup* hrn2• rad-br sze8•

- **airplane** (See Airplanes)
- **beverage** truck: lac-lup hrn2•
- **cars** (See Car)
- **commercial** airliner: lac-lup hrn2•
- **firetruck** (See Fire - firetruck)
- **go**-cart: lac-lup hrn2•
- **motorcycles** (See Motorcycles)
- **parachute**: lac-lup hrn2•
- **raft**; river raft: lac-lup hrn2•
- **snowmobiles**: lac-lup hrn2•
- **toy** vehicle: lac-lup hrn2•

VENGEANCE (See Revenge)

VERMIN: *(↗Insects; Lice)* alum bg2 am-c bell bg2 bov j chel k* colch falco-pe nl2• gamb kali-c j lac-c k* mag-s mur-ac k* *Nux-v* k* ped c1 phasco-ci rbp2 phos k* ran-s j sep sil bg2 sphing kk3.fr

VERSES, he composes: *(↗MIND - Verses - making)* falco-pe nl2• nat-m a1

VERTIGO: *(↗Disease)* agath-a nl2• brucel sa3• plut-n srj7• *Sil* k*

VEXATIOUS: *(↗Anger; Quarrels; Striving; Unpleasant; MIND - Ailments - reproaches)* acon b2.de* *Aeth* a1 agar k* *Alum* k* alum-p k2 alum-sil k2 am-c k* am-m k* *Ambr* k* anac k* ang b2.de* ant-c k* ant-t a1 apis arn b2.de* *Ars* k* ars-s-f k2 **Asar** k* asc-t a1 aur a1 aur-m a1 aur-s a1 bapt a1 bell-p mg1.de* borx k* bov k* *Bry* k* calc k* calc-sil k2 *Cann-i* cann-s b2.de* carbn-s k2 *Caust* k* cham k* chel b2.de* chin k* chinin-ar choc srj3• *Cimic* bg2* cina k* cinnb a1 coca a1 cocc b2.de* coloc a1 *Con* k* dig k* dros k* elaps a1 erio a1 *Gamb Gels* **Graph** k* grat j5.de hep k* hydr a1 hydrog srj2• *Ign* k* iris a1 jug-c a1 junc-e kali-chl kali-m k2 kali-n kiss a1 kreos b2.de* lac-e hrn2• lach b2.de* led b2.de* lil-t a1 linu-c a1 lyc k* lycps-v a1 m-ambo b2.de* *M-arct* b2.de* m-aust b2.de* macro a1 mag-c mag-m k* mag-s mang menth-pu a1 merc-i-r a1 mit a1 *Mosch* k* mur-ac k* murx a1 nat-ar nat-c k* *Nat-m* k* nat-p nat-s *Nit-ac* k* *Nux-v* k* op k* petr b2.de* ph-ac k* phel j5.de phos k* plan plat k* plb a1 ptel puls b2.de* rat rheum b2.de* rhus-g a1 *Rhus-t* k* rumx a1 ruta b2.de* sabad a1 sabin b2.de* sang a1 sars k* scut a1 sep k* sil k* sol-t-ae spong k* *Staph* k* stront-c b2.de* sul-ac j5.de **Sulph** k* tarent a1 thuj a1 ust a1 zinc k*

- **children**, in: *Ambr* kr1

VICTIM: | **at** the mercy of an amusement park ride operator: lac-lup hrn2•

VIOLENCE: *(↗Brutality; Cruelty; Ill-treatment)* adam srj5• agath-a nl2• aids nl2• androc srj1• apoc-a a1 ara-maca sej7• aran-ix mg1.de arg-n k2* arizon-l nl2• aur a1* bell k2 cact k2 carbn-dox knl3• corian-s knl6• germ-met stj2*• granit-m es1• ham fd3.de• helo-s rwt2• helodr-cal knl2• *Kola* stb3• lac-del hrn2• lac-e hrn2• led musca-d szs1 oxal-a rly4• plut-n srj7• podo fd3.de• pycnop-sa mrz1 *Rhus-g* tmo3• sanguis-s hrn2• spong fd4.de streptoc jl2 toxi mtf2• tung-met bdx1• ven-m jl [aur-m stj2 aur-s stj2 merc stj2]

- **betrayed** him; toward those who: *Rhus-g* tmo3•
- **striking** with a stick: lac-e hrn2•

VISIONARY: *(↗Clairvoyant; Fantastic; MIND - Clairvoyance; MIND - Fear - happen; MIND - Prophesying)* aloe am-c *Anh* mg1.de* arn ars j5.de bell *Calc* calc-sil k2 camph carb-an *Carb-v* j5.de cham chin coloc *Con* j5.de dulc fd4.de graph hippoc-k szs2 *Kali-c Kali-n* kali-sil k2 *Lach* lachn led j5.de *Lyc* mur-ac nat-c k* *Nat-m* k* nicc nit-ac j5.de *Nux-v* olib-sac wmh1 *Op Petr* plan prun j5.de ptel gk sep *Sil Spong* sulph zinc j5.de zinc-o j5.de [ant-t stj2]

- **frightful**: bell a1

VISITS:
- **brother**; from: nicc j5.de*
- **homeopaths**; by: galeoc-c-h gms1•
- **making** visits: chir-fl gya2 dulc fd4.de ina-i mlk9.de mag-s j5.de* maias-l hm2•
  - **friend** who is not at home: ozone sde2•
  - **relatives**; to: lac-h sk4•
- **social**: lac-h sk4•

VIVID: *(↗Wild)* *Acon* k* adam srj5• agar k* agath-a nl2• alco a1 all-s kr1 am-c ambr k* amp rly4• **Anac** k* *Androc* srj1• ang k* *Ant-t* b2.de* aran-ix mg1.de* arg-met k* *Arg-n* bro1 *Arn* k* ars k* ars-i ars-s-f k2 ars-s-r kr1 asaf aster atp rly4• **Aur** k* aur-ar k2 aur-i k2 aur-s k2 bamb-a stb2.de• bapt kr1 bar-act a1 bar-c k* bar-i k2 bar-m bar-s k2 *Bell* k* bism k* brom k* bruc j5.de *Bry* k* calad k* *Calc* k* calc-act a1 calc-f calc-i k2 *Calc-p* calc-sil k2 cann-i k* cann-s k* canth k* caps b2.de* *Carb-an* k* **Carb-v** k* carbn-dox knl3• *Carbn-s* cardios-h rly4• carl *Cench* k2* *Cham* k* *Chel* chin k* chinin-ar choc srj3• chord-umb rly4• chr-ac kr1 chr-o a1 *Cic* k* cinnb clem k* cob cob-n mg1.de coc-c coca coca-c sk4• *Cocc* k* *Coff* k* colch coli rly4• coloc k* *Con* k* croc k* *Cycl* cyclosp sa3• cystein-l rly4• daph bro1 dig dios bro1 dream-p sdj1• dros k* dulc fd4.de euph k* *Ferr* k* *Ferr-i* ferr-p k* fl-ac k* form franz a1 fum rly1*• fuma-ac rly4• gast a1 ger-i rly4• gins a1 **Graph** k* guaj k* haliae-lc srj5• ham a1 helodr-cal knl2• hippoc-k szs2 hydr-ac j5.de* hydrog srj2• *Hyos* bg3* hyper ign k* ina-i mlk9.de ind indol bro1 *Iod* k* ip k* irid-met srj5• jug-c kali-ar kali-bi kali-c k* kali-cy kali-m k2 kali-n kali-p kali-s kali-sil k2 ketogl-ac rly4• *Kola* stb3• lac-c mrr *Lac-h* htj1• *Lac-loxod-a* hrn2• lac-lup hrn2• lach k* lact *Lam* j5.de* laur k* led k* lipp a1 lob kr1 **Luna** kg1• **Lyc** k* *M-ambo* b2.de* *M-arct* b2.de* m-aust b2.de* *Mag-c* k* mag-m k* mag-s jl *Mang* k* mang-act bro1 mang-p rly4• medul-os-si rly4• meny k* meph *Merc* k* merc-c merc-sul mez k* moni rfm1• mosch k* mur-ac k* musca-d szs1 myos-a rly4• naja nat-ar *Nat-c* k* **Nat-m** k* nat-ox rly4• *Nat-p* nat-pyru rly4• **Nat-sil** k2 nicotam rly4• nit-ac k* nux-m k* *Nux-v* k* ol-j op k* orig a1 ox-ac oxal-a rly4• ozone sde2• paeon pant-ac rly4• *Petr* k* *Ph-ac* k* **Phos** k* phys pin-s a1 plac-s rly4• plan plat k* plut-n srj7• polys sk4• pot-e rly4• psil ft1 psor ptel *Puls* k* pycnop-sa mrz1 pyrog bro1 rad-br c11* ran-b k* ran-s raph *Rheum* k* rhod j5.de **Rhus-t** k* rhus-v rumx *Ruta* k* *Sabad* k* samb k* sel rsj9• senec *Sep* k* **Sil** k* sin-n a1* sinus rly4• spig k* spirae a1 squil j5.de *Stann* k* *Staph* b2.de* stram k* streptoc rly4• *Stront-c* bg2* succ-ac rly4• suis-em rly4• suis-pan rly4• sul-i k2 **Sulph** k* sumb suprar rly4• tab tarax k* *Teucr* k* thioc-ac rly4• thuj k* til tub br1* valer k* vanil fd5.de ven-m rsj12• verat b2.de* verat-v k* vero-o rly4*• viol-o j5.de viol-t k* visc sp1 zinc k* zinc-p k2 zing [bell-p-sp dcm1 heroin sdj2]
- **morning**: chinin-s a1 kali-bi a1 mag-c a1 sulph a1 sumb a1
  - **towards**: mez h2 staph h1
- **afternoon**: ang a1 sin-a a1
- **night**:
  - **midnight**: zinc a1
    - **before**: mez a1
    - **after**: coloc a1 mez a1 nat-m a1 *Puls* h1* zinc h2*
- **erections**, with: sulph a1
- **lurid**: luna kg1•
- **lying** with head down: plat a1
- **not** one's own; but seemed as if: sal-fr sle1•
- **remember**; could not: cic tl1 lac-e hrn2• plut-n srj7•

VOCAL CORDS; mucus on: *(↗Body; parts)* ozone sde2•

VOICE: *(↗Calling)* rhus-t a1
- **absent** persons; of: cham gt
- **calling** his name: kola stb3•

VOMITING: helodr-cal knl2• ruta fd4.de
- **blood**: bamb-a stb2.de•
- **defecating** simultaneously; and: adam srj5•
- **dry**: falco-pe nl2•
- **flesh**; a piece of: aids nl2•
- **pus**: bamb-a stb2.de•
- **worms** (See Worms - vomited)

VULGAR SCENES: chin-b kr1*

WADING:
- **snow**; in (See Snow - wading)
- **water**; in (See Water - wading)

WAGONS: nux-v gl1.fr• senec a1

WAITING: plut-n srj7• [tax jsj7]

WALKING: *(↗Roaming; Wandering)* agar kr1 bell a1 bros-gau mrc1 canth j5.de* cench k2 dulc fd4.de elaps a1 kola stb3• med nat-c a1 nat-s j5.de pall a1 positr nl2• rhus-t k* ruta fd4.de spong fd4.de tritic-vg fd5.de vanil fd5.de
- **apartments**, through: pall a1 spong fd4.de
- **country**; through open: kola stb3•
- **dark**; in: loxo-recl knl4•
- **floor**, on hot: apis a1*
- **isolated** street; in an: coca-c sk4•
- **mud**, in: *Galeoc-c-h* gms1• iod k* [bar-i stj2 merc-i-f stj2]
- **nature**; in: lac-loxod-a hrn2•
- **reading**; walking up and down in his room and: agar hr1
- **roads**, over dirty: apis a1
- **ruins**, among: hura a1 iod a1* tung-met bdx1• [bar-i stj2 merc-i-f stj2 zinc-i stj2]
- **staircase**; in: bros-gau mrc1 pall a1
- **stilts**; with: nept-m lsd2.fr
- **water**: *(↗Water)*
  - **in** the water (See Water - wading)
  - **on** the water (See Water - walking)
- **woods**, in: *(↗Forest)* canth a1 tritic-vg fd5.de vanil fd5.de

WALLET: | **lost**: lac-e hrn2• lac-lup hrn2•

WANDERING: *(↗Roaming; Walking)* cench k2 chir-fl gya2 dulc fd4.de stram a1 symph fd3.de• tritic-vg fd5.de ulm-c jsj8• vanil fd5.de zing a1

WANT: am-c a1

WAR: *(↗Air; Air attacks; Battles; Blood - bloodshed; Cannonading; Civil; Enemies; Fights)* aids nl2• arist-cl rbp3• carbn-dox knl3• corian-s knl6• corv-cor bdg• crot-c sk4• dendr-pol sk4• elaps fkr8.de falco-pe nl2• ferr b2.de* germ-met stj2*• gink-b sbd1• lac-h htj1*• *Meny* vh musca-d szs1 ozone sde2• pitu-a vml2• plat b2.de* polys sk4• positr nl2• ruta fd4.de stann jl *Thuj* b2.de* tung-met bdx1• vanil fd5.de verb b2.de* visc jl [ferr-f stj2 ferr-lac stj2 ferr-n stj2 ferr-sil stj2 irid-met stj2 merc stj2 plut-n stj2]
- **camp**; being in a war: coca-c sk4•
- **civil** war: op gl1.fr•
- **dismantling** of an idyll by: plut-n srj7•
- **space** war: lac-leo hrn2•

WARTS: *(↗Disease)* mez tritic-vg fd5.de
- **abdomen** covered with warts: junc-e a1
- **back** covered with warts: mez a1

WASHING: ulm-c jsj8•
- **cars** and lorries: falco-pe nl2•
- **clothes**: falco-pe nl2•
- **oneself** in river: dream-p sdj1*• falco-pe nl2•

WASPS: *(↗Insects; Stung)* agath-a nl2• falco-pe nl2• rauw sp1 symph fd3.de• [spect dfg1]

WASTELAND: tung-met bdx1•

WATCHED; being: [tax jsj7]

WATCHING:
- **helicopter**: loxo-recl knl4•
- **herself** from above: haliae-lc srj5• [buteo-j sej6]
- **me**; two men: lac-lup hrn2•

WATER: *(↗Bathing; Danger - water; Drowning; Falling - water; Fish; Flood; Journeys - water; Jumping - water; Rowing; Sailing; Sea; Storms - sea; Stream; Swimming; Walking - water)* adam srj5• agath-a nl2• *All-c* *All-s* alum k* **Am-m** k* androc srj1• apeir-s mlk9.de ara-maca sej7• arg-n k* arge-pl rwt5• arist-cl rbp3• arn k2 *Ars* *Bamb-a* stb2.de• *Bell* bit-ar wht1• bol-la a1 bomb-chr mlk9.de bomb-pr mlk9.de bov k* carb-v carc fd2.de• chin mhn1 chin-b slp chr-ac a1* com corv-cor bdg• *Dig* k* dulc fd4.de eupi falco-pe nl2• *Ferr* k* fic-m gya1 galeoc-c-h gms1• gink-b sbd1• *Graph* k* ham fd3.de• helodr-cal knl2• hippoc-k szs2 hura ign k* ina-i mlk9.de iod k* *Kali-c* k* kali-n k* kali-p fd1.de• kali-s fd4.de kali-sil k2 kalm kola stb3• lac-del hrn2• lac-h sk4*• lac-leo hrn2• lac-loxod-a hrn2• *Lac-lup* hrn2• lap-la sde8.de• limen-b-c mlk9.de loxo-recl knl4• *Lyc* mag-c k* mag-m k* mag-s maias-l hrn2• melal-alt gya4 *Meph* *Merc* k* merc-i-r murx musca-d szs1 nat-c k* nat-m nat-p fkr6.de nat-s k* nat-sil fd3.de• neon srj5• nept-m lsd2.fr nicc orot-ac rly4• ox-ac oxal-a rly4• ozone sde2• phasco-ci rbp2

Dreams

Water: ...
ran-b k* rhus-t ruta fd4.de sang sanguis-s hrn2• *Sil* k* sol-t-ae spong fd4.de suis-hep rly4• suis-pan rly4• sulph suprar rly4• tarent tetox pin2• *Thuj* mlk1 tritic-vg fd5.de urol-h rwt• valer k* vanil fd5.de verat *Verat-v* k* zinc k* [ant-m stj2 ant-t stj2 aur-m stj2 bar-i stj2 beryl-m stj2 cadm-m stj2 chlor stj2 chr-m stj2 cob-m stj2 cupr-m stj2 ferr-f stj2 ferr-lac stj2 ferr-n stj2 ferr-sil stj2 germ-met stj2 heroin sdj2 lith-i stj2 lith-m stj2 mag-met stj2 mang-i stj2 mang-m stj2 merc-d stj2 merc-i-f stj2 mur-ac stj2 nicc-met stj2 nicc-s stj2 niob-met stj2 plb-m stj2 sel stj2 spect dfg1 stront-m stj2 tax jsj7 yttr-met stj2 zinc-i stj2 zinc-m stj2 zinc-n stj2 zinc-p stj2]

- **noon**: nat-m a1
- **black**: *Ars* k* ozone sde2• til ban1•
  - **tar**; like: ozone sde2•
- **boat** owner indifferent to man drowning (See Drowning - boat owner)
- **boat**; foundering (See Boat; Boat - foundering)
- **bottom** of: *Lac-lup* hrn2•
- **clear** water: ara-maca sej7•
- **danger**: | **in** water; from danger: ars ars-met kr1* fic-m gya1 *Graph* kali-n lac-lup hrn2• *Mag-c* mag-m h2* (non:merc slp) merc-act j5.de* nat-c k* **Nat-s** stront-c sk4• sulph [heroin sdj2]
- **daughter** is in water and crying for help: nat-s [bar-i stj2]
- **dirty**: *(↗Dirt)* lac-h sk4• musca-d szs1 ozone sde2•
  - **bathing** impossible: ozone sde2•
- **falling**: falco-pe nl2•
  - **ice**; through: ozone sde2•
  - **icy** cold: ozone sde2•
- **flood**; of a (See Flood)
- **flooding** (See Flood)
- **high** waves: ozone sde2• phasco-ci rbp2
  - **feet**; on his: ozone sde2•
- **high** water; waves of (See high waves)
- **house** was on: oci-sa sk4•
- **lake**:
  - **bathing**; people: ozone sde2•
  - **crossing** a: bros-gau mrc1
- **leaking**: chlam-tr bcx2• galeoc-c-h gms1•
  - **bed**; in: chlam-tr bcx2•
- **muddy**; of: ars gt [heroin sdj2]
- **ocean**; being in an (See Ocean - being)
- **poisoned**: *(↗Poison; of)* ozone sde2•
- **pools** of water; of: ignis-alc es2• kola stb3• nauf-helv-li elm2•
  - **being** in a pool of water: [buteo-j sej6]
  - **dark** and murky: sanguis-s hrn2•
- **poured** upon him, is: ox-ac
- **putrid**: *Arg-n* k*
- **rising** | **storm**; during a: coca-c sk4•
- **running**: aln vva1• *Galeoc-c-h* gms1• nat-s br
  - **refrigerator**; through: galeoc-c-h gms1•
- **sailing** (See Sailing)
- **sea** (See Sea)
- **smells**: agath-a nl2•
- **swimming** in: acon-ac rly4• hippoc-k szs2 lac-h sk4• lac-lup hrn2• limen-b-c hrn2• musca-d szs1 nept-m lsd2.fr suprar rly4•
  - **dove** to get friend who went under rough water: lac-lup hrn2•
- **under** water: helo-s rwt2•
- **wading**; in: ant-t j5.de dulc fd4.de melal-alt gya4 merc-i-r nept-m lsd2.fr ruta fd4.de spong fd4.de [buteo-j sej6]
  - **snakes**; with: *(↗Snakes)* alum dulc fd4.de
- **walking** on the water: *Agath-a* nl2• ozone sde2•
  - **acquaintances** walking on the water; sees: ped a1
- **wall** of: falco-pe nl2•
- **waterfall**: adam srj5• corv-cor bdg• kali-p fd1.de•
- **waves** (See Waves)
- **yellow**: hura

WATER-SKIING: adam srj5•

WATER PIPES: fic-m gya1
- **boiling** water spurting out of bursting water pipes: dioxi rbp6

WAVES: bit-ar wht1• chir-fl gya2 corv-cor bdg• dendr-pol sk4• [ant-m stj2 aur-m stj2 beryl-m stj2 cadm-m stj2 chlor stj2 chr-m stj2 cob-m stj2 cupr-m stj2 lith-m stj2 mang-m stj2 merc-d stj2 mur-ac stj2 plb-m stj2 stront-m stj2 zinc-m stj2]
- **coming** over him: ign mrr3* lac-del hm2•
- **drain**; coming out of: bamb-a stb2.de•
- **head**; in | **vertigo**; causing: bamb-a stb2.de•
- **huge** wave approaching: dendr-pol sk4•
- **tidal** wave: bit-ar wht1• dulc fd4.de germ-met srj5• haliae-lc srj5• limen-b-c hrn2• rad-br sze8• ruta fd4.de [spect dfg1 temp elm1]

WAX from candle dripping on her black trousers: ozone sde2•

WEAKNESS: ambr j5.de [tax jsj7]

WEASELS: *(↗Animals)* lac-loxod-a hrn2•

WEATHER: | **cloudy**: nicc-met sk4•

WEAVING: lac-loxod-a hrn2•

WEDDING: alum k* aq-mar rbp6 arizon-l nl2• bamb-a stb2.de• bros-gau mrc1 chel haliae-lc srj5• ina-i mlk9.de irid-met srj5• lac-d sk4• lac-leo hrn2• mag-c k* mag-m b4.de* mag-s k* musca-d szs1 nat-c k* nat-s neon srj5• nept-m lsd2.fr oci-sa sk4• petr-ra shn4• polys sk4• sil h1* thres-a sze7• toxi mtf2• urol-h rwt• [cadm-s stj2 gal-s stj2 mag-lac stj2 mag-met stj2 mag-n stj2 mag-sil stj2 titan-s stj2]
- **cousin** is getting married: bung-fa mtf lac-h sk4•
  - **person** she is divorcing from; to the: bung-fa mtf
- **everyone** going | **except** her: hydrog srj2•
- **forced** to marry:
  - **ugly** man; an | **skin** disease; with a: oci-sa sk4•
- **preparing**: ozone sde2•
- **repeated**, since only one half of the body has been married; wedding has to be: bamb-a stb2.de•
- **spiritual**: irid-met srj5•
- **two** women; with: nat-c j5.de
- **widow** | **marry** a; tricked into: polys sk4•

WEEPING; about: *(↗Sad; MIND - Weeping - dreaming)* ang k* calc-f ptk1 dendr-pol sk4• elaps fl-ac bg2 *Glon* k* kali-c kola stb3• *Kreos* k* lac-e hrn2• lac-lup hrn2• limen-b-c hrn2* mag-c nat-m a1 nux-v bg2 oxal-a rly4• plan ptk1 positr nl2• ruta fd4.de *Sil* k* sol-mm a1 spong stram bg2* suis-em rly4• [tax jsj7]
- **love** of the word of God: maias-l hrn2•
- **mother** would die; the idea that her: oci-sa sk4•
- **music**: lac-lup hrn2•
- **reprimands**; from: lac-h sk4•
- **song**; from: kola stb3•

WELLS: *All-c* merc-c

WET places: *(↗Places)* galla-q-r nl2•

WHALES: irid-met srj5• kola stb3• lac-lup hrn2•
- **black** whale | **oil**-coated or burnt: plut-n srj7•
- **turning** over and over like a skewer: lac-lup hrn2•

WHIPPED, getting: falco-pe nl2• positr nl2• ptel a1

WILD: *(↗Vivid)* aloe apis bell bro1 cann-i dor dulc fd4.de glon hyos bro1 kalm lac-lup hrn2• limen-b-c hrn2* nat-ox rly4• op ozone sde2• pip-m a1 ruta fd4.de *Sanguis-s* hrn2• tab

WIND COLIC: *(↗Disease)* fago a1

WINDOW: aids nl2• neon srj5•
- **broken**: hep neon srj5•
- **jumping** from window: bit-ar wht1• mag-m
- **making** a: dream-p sdj1•
- **people** are before the: melal-alt gya4 merc h1
- **shutting** windows: arizon-l nl2• tritic-vg fd5.de
  - **never** completed: arizon-l nl2•
- **smashing** the window: am-c j5.de
- **tossing** someone out of the: bry a1

WIRES:
- **electric**, many: coca-c sk4•
- **sparking** | **randomly** arranged: polys sk4•

WITCHES: *Kola* stb3• lap-la sde8.de• pyrid rly4• ruta fd4.de sol-t-ae a1 tritic-vg fd5.de [ant-c stj2 ant-met stj2]
- **creeping** from under the door like a haze: *(↗Pursued - witch)* ozone sde2•

WITNESS; she was a: haliae-lc srj5•

WOLVES: *(↗Animals)* aids nl2• lac-loxod-a hrn2• limen-b-c hrn2•

WOMEN: *Dios* kr1* dulc fd4.de lac-e hrn2• ruta fd4.de sanguis-s hrn2• spong fd4.de tritic-vg fd5.de vanil fd5.de
- **arrogant**, with exaggerated confidence: ozone sde2•
- **bearded**: positr nl2•
- **boy**; short-haired, thin, blond, no curves, like a: galeoc-c-h gms1•
- **breasts**; with big: *(↗Mammae)* phasco-ci rbp2
- **changed** into animals: sol-t-ae a1
- **clothing**; without much: maias-l hrn2•
- **coming** to my house | **inspecting** me and my house: galeoc-c-h gms1•
- **curled** up; sitting: galeoc-c-h gms1•
- **depressed**, came to party: lac-del hrn2•
- **discrimination**; against: galeoc-c-h gms1•
- **friends**: sal-fr sle1•
- **guiding** her: lac-h sk4•
- **he** is a woman: pegan-ha tpi1•
- **huge**, black with wild and fierce face: sanguis-s hrn2•
- **looking** under their skirts: ozone sde2•
  - **naked** indecently, with spread legs: ozone sde2•
- **naked**: *(↗Naked people)* ozone sde2•
- **old** women: ina-i mlk9.de positr nl2•
  - **irritating** and harassing others: oci-sa sk4•
- **pregnant** | **screaming** and hitting her: limen-b-c hrn2•
- **underwear**; dressed in winter: galeoc-c-h gms1•
- **widows**; we were: galeoc-c-h gms1•

WONDERFUL: *(↗Pleasant)* agath-a nl2• bamb-a stb2.de• chinin-s a1 lac-loxod-a hrn2• op a1 paeon a1 ph-ac a1

WOODWORK; doing: galeoc-c-h gms1•

WORK: *(↗Business; Exertion; Mental; Striving)* agath-a nl2• ambr j5.de amp rly4• carc mg1.de* chord-umb rly4• dulc fd4.de falco-pe nl2• gels a1 ger-i rly4• lac-e hrn2• lac-leo hrn2• melal-alt gya4 ozone sde2• rhus-t sf1.de* ruta fd4.de sal-fr sle1• sel jl* spong fd4.de vanil fd5.de [pyre-p stj tax jsj7]
- **night**, treats patients; whole: carc az1.de•
- **complex**, having to do: [pyre-p stj]
- **lose** her job; she would: coca-c sk4•
- **shop**, working in a: falco-pe nl2•
- **snow**; working in: bapt

WORLD:
- **dark** and cold, another world that is: arist-cl rbp3• galla-q-r nl2•
- **fire**; on (See Fire - world)

WORLD PEACE; of: haliae-lc srj5•

WORMS: *(↗Maggots; Silkworm)* arge-pl rwt5• choc srj3• coca-c sk4• musca-d szs1 positr nl2• [alum stj2 bell-p-sp dcm1 oxyg stj2 sil stj2]
- **covered** with: gink-b sbd1•
- **creeping**: alum j am-c bov j esp-g jl ina-i mlk9.de kali-c j mur-ac nux-v phos ran-s j ruta fd4.de sil j [oxyg stj]
- **tapeworm** (See Tapeworms - she)
- **vomited**; are: *(↗Disease)* *Chin* mhn1 *Chin-b* k*

WORRIES; full of: apis b7a.de ars b4.de* bros-gau mrc1 graph b4a.de mur-ac b4.de* phos b4a.de rhus-t b7.de*

WOUNDED, being: *(↗Disease; Fights; Injuries)* ant-c k* chel a1 dream-p sdj1• lob kr1 *Mag-s* j5.de plut-n srj7•
- **shot**; by a (See Shot - wounded)

WOUNDS: *(↗Disease)* ant-c chel a1 *Mag-s* j5.de plut-n srj7•
- **pus**; with lots of: dioxi rbp6

WRITING: falco-pe nl2• senec
- **dirty** table; on: *(↗Dirty - table)* prun
- **offensive** and provocative things: plut-n srj7•
- **pens**; with: irid-met srj5•

Writing: ...
- **written** page; on a much: coca-c sk4•

WRONG; DOING: *(↗Accusations - crime; Crime)*
- **he** has done wrong: *(↗Crime - committing)* cocc a2 germ-met srj5• ozone sde2• positr nl2•
- **order**; doing things in wrong: ulm-c jsj8•
- **others**; the wrong doing of: dros gt*

YOUTH, TIME OF: gink-b sbd1• hippoc-k szs2 limen-b-c hrn2* olib-sac wmh1 ozone sde2• sil j5.de*

ZOOMING through stars: [buteo-j sej6]

CHILL in general (= coldness): acon k* acon-f c2 adam srj5• *Aesc* aeth *Agar* k* agn k* ail allox tpw4 alst *Alum* k* alum-p k2 am-c k* am-m k* *Ambr* k* *Anac* k* androc bnm2• ang b2.de* anh sp1 *Ant-c* k* **Ant-t** k* *Anthraci* **Apis** k* **Aran** k* arg-met k* *Arist-cl* sp1 **Arn** k* **Ars** k* ars-i arum-t asaf k* asar k* atra-r bnm3• aur k* aur-m bapt bar-c k* bar-m k2 *Bell* k* bell-p sp1 berb bism b2.de* bol-la borx k* both fne1• bov k* brom k* *Bry* k* bufo buth-a sp1 cact cadm-met sp1 cadm-s calad k* *Calc* k* *Calc-ar* calc-i k2 *Calc-p* k* *Camph* k* cann-i **Cann-s** b2.de* **Canth** k* *Caps* k* *Carb-an* k* **Carb-v** k* **Carbn-s** castm caust k* **Cedr** *Cham* k* **Chel** k* **Chin** k* **Chinin-s** k* chir-fl gya2 chlam-tr bcx2• *Cic* k* cimic k* *Cimx* cina k* clem b2.de* cloth tsm2 cob-n sp1 coca cocc k* coff k* *Colch* k* coli jl2 coloc k* con k* cop corian-s knl6• corn croc k* crot-h crot-t cupr k* cupr-ar *Cycl* k* cyt-l sp1 daph *Dig* k* dios *Diphtox* jl2 dros k* dulc k* *Elaps* elat euon **Eup-per** k* *Eup-pur* **Euph** b2.de* euphr b2.de* eupi *Ferr* k* ferr-ar k2 fic-m gya1 fl-ac bg2 fram jl2 gamb **Gels** k* *Graph* k* grat guaj k* hell k* **Helo** *Hep* k* *Hyos* k* **Ign** k* influ jl2* *Iod* k* **Ip** k* kali-bi *Kali-c* k* *Kali-i* *Kali-n* b2.de* kreos k* lac-c lac-d ptk1 lac-lup hrn2• *Lach* k* *Lachn* lap-la sde8.de* lat-m sp1* laur k* **Led** k* lil-t lith-c lob loxo-recl bnm10• **Lyc** k* lyss m-ambo b2.de* m-arct b2.de* m-aust b2.de* mag-c k* mag-m k* mag-s k* malar jl2 mang k* melal-alt gya4 **Meny** k* merc k* merc-c k* **Mez** k* *Mosch* k* *Mur-ac* k* naja *Nat-ar* nat-c k* **Nat-m** k* nat-p nicc **Nit-ac** k* **Nux-m** k* **Nux-v** k* *Olib-sac* wmh1 *Olnd* b2.de* *Op* k* oscilloc jl2 par k* *Petr* k* *Ph-ac* k* phel *Phos* k* physala-p bnm7• phyt pime c2 plan plat k* plb k* *Podo* *Propl* ub1• *Psor* k* **Puls** k* pyrog jl2 pyrus c2 ran-b k* ran-s b2.de* rauw sp1 rheum b2.de* *Rhod* b2.de* **Rhus-t** k* *Rob* *Ruta* k* **Sabad** k* sabin k* sal-fr sle1• *Samb* k* sang sarr sars k* **Sec** k* sel k* senec seneg k* **Sep** k* *Sil* k* spig k* spong k* squil b2.de* stann k* **Staph** k* *Stram* k* stront-c b2.de* *Sul-ac* k* sulph k* *Sumb* syc bka1• symph ptk1 *Tarax* k* *Tarent* teucr k* ther **Thuj** k* thyr ptk1 tub-a jl2 vac jl2 valer k* vanil fd5.de vario c2 **Verat** k* **Verat-v** verb h* viol-o bg2 viol-t b2.de* vip *Zinc* b2.de* [bell-p-sp dcm1 heroin sdj2 spect dfg1]

ONE SIDE: acon bg2 alum k* alum-p k2 alum-sil k2 ambr k* anac k* ant-t k* *Arn* k* ars bg2 *Bar-c* k* bar-s k2 bell k* **Bry** k* **Carb-v** k* **Caust** k* *Cham* k* *Chel* k* chin k* cocc k* con ptk1 croc k* dig k* dros k* elat ferr ign k* ip bg2 kali-c k* kali-p kali-s fkr2.de kali-sil k2 *Lach* k* **Lyc** k* **Mosch** bg2* nat-c k* nat-m nat-p **Nux-v** k* *Par* k* petr bg2 ph-ac k* *Phos* k* plat k* **Puls** k* ran-b k* rheum bg2 **Rhus-t** k* ruta k* sabad k* sabin k* sars k* *Sep* **Sil** k* spig k* stann k* stram k* sul-ac k* *Sulph* k* *Thuj* k* verat *Verb* k*

- **coldness** of right side and heat of left: *Rhus-t*
  - **numbness**: *Puls*

RIGHT: apis bg1 arn **Bry** k* caust k* **Chel** k* eupi *Lyc* k* *Nat-m* nux-v k* *Par* k* petr bg2 ph-ac bg2 *Phos* k* plat bg2 puls k* ran-b k* **Rhus-t** k* sabin k* thuj sne

LEFT: ant-c h2 arn bg2 ars bg2 *Bar-c* k* bar-s k2 **Carb-v** k* **Caust** k* chin bg2 **Dros** b7a.de* elaps ferr *Lach* k* **Lyc** k* nat-c nat-m bg2 par bg2 phos bg2 *Rhus-t* k* ruta k* *Sil* k* spig k* *Stann* k* sulph k* **Thuj** k*

- **convulsions**; before epileptic: *Sil*

DAY:

- **cold** day; on a (See Cold - agg. - day)
- **lasting** all day: cupr bg2
- **periodically** returning every seventh day (See Periodical - week)

DAY AND NIGHT: *Graph* b4a.de sars b4a.de

DAYTIME: alum k* ant-c k* ant-t bg2 ars k* arund asar k* bapt k* camph carb-an k* **Chin** dros k* ephe-si hsj1• gels k* graph k* **Hell** b7a.de* hep b4a.de* kali-ar kali-c k* kali-p lyc k* mag-s k* merc mosch k* nat-c k* *Nat-m* k* nat-s k* nit-ac k* plan k* *Rhod* b4a.de* sabin k* sars *Sil* k* spig b7.de* *Sul-ac* b4a.de* tarent k* verat b7.de* viol-o bg2 [bell-p-sp dcm1]

- **fever**; with | **night**: alum bapt a1
- **perspiration**; with | **night**: ars

MORNING (= 6-9 h): abrom-a ks5 acon k* agar k* alum k2 am-c k* am-m k* ambr b7.de* anac b4.de* **Ang** k* ant-c bg2 ant-t b7.de* *Apis* k* *Arn* k* *Ars* k* *Bamb-a* stb2.de• bar-c k* bar-m bar-s k2 bell k* berb k* **Bov** k* **Bry** k* calad bg2 *Calc* k* calc-sil k2 calen canth k* carb-an h2* carb-v k* carbn-s k1 (non:caust k*) cedr chin k* chinin-ar chinin-s bro1 cimx k* cina b7.de* cocc k* coff b7.de* coloc bg2 **Con** k* *Cycl* k* dios k* dros k* dulc fd4.de **Eup-per** k* euph hr1 euphr b7.de* *Ferr* k* *Ferr-ar* *Gels* k* *Graph* k* *Hell* k* helo-s rwt2• *Hep* k* hir skp7• hydr hr1 kali-ar kali-c k* kali-m k2 kali-n kali-p kali-sil k2 kreos b7a.de* *Led* k* *Lyc* k* m-arct b7.de mag-c k* mag-m k* mag-s k* mang b4.de* meny *Merc* k* mez k* *Mur-ac* k* nat-ar nat-c k* **Nat-m** k* nat-s k* **Nit-ac** k* nux-m k* **Nux-v** k* petr k* ph-ac bg2 *Phos* k* phyt k* plb b7.de*

Morning: ...
Podo k* puls b7.de* rheum b7.de* *Rhod* b4a.de* rhus-t bg2 *Rhus-v* k* ruta sars b4.de* **Sep** k* sil k* *Spig* k* spong fd4.de *Staph* k* sul-ac b4.de* *Sulph* k* *Sumb* k* tere-la rly4• ther thuj k* tritic-vg fd5.de **Verat** k*

- **6** h: *Arn* *Bov* dros eup-per *Ferr* graph *Hep* hura *Lyc* nat-m *Nux-v* ph-ac rhus-t hr1 sil stram **Verat**
  - **6**-7 h: podo bro1
  - **6**-9 h: bov chinin-s eup-per nux-v
- **6**.30 h: hura
- **7** h: am-m bov dios dros **Eup-per** ferr graph *Hep* hura nat-m nux-v **Podo** k* sil stram
  - **7**-9 h: dros **Eup-per** k* nat-m *Podo*
    - **violent** chill one day, and a light chill the next day at noon: **Eup-per** k*
- **7**.30 h: ferr
- **8** h: ail k2* bov chinin-s cocc dios dros **Eup-per** lyc mez nat-m phos podo puls sil sulph
  - **8**-9 h: ars asaf dros eup-per hura
- **8**.30 h: chinin-ar sanic c1
- **bed** agg.; in: *Ang* k* apis *Arn* *Bov* carb-an h2 carbn-s caust chin chinin-ar *Chinin-s* con dulc fd4.de *Graph* k* hep h2 kali-c k* kali-n *Led* k* lyc mag-s **Merc** k* *Mur-ac* k* **Nat-m** *Nit-ac* k* **Nux-v** rhod k* sars k* staph k* sulph k* **Verat**
- **continuing**:
  - **forenoon**; through the: *Arn* ars eup-per *Nat-m* petr plb
  - **evening**; until: bapt hell mag-c nat-c plb
- **menses**; after faintness during: **Nux-v**
- **perspiration**, after: mag-s k* op k*
- **pollutions**, after: merc
- **rising** | **after** | **agg.**: acon k* aloe *Am-m* bg2 borx k* bry bg2 **Calc** k* calc-p canth k* carb-v bg2 *Cham* bg2 coloc b4.de* dulc fd4.de euphr b7.de* graph bg2 *Hell* b7a.de* hep *Lach* bg2 laur b7.de* mag-m mang k* meny k* merc k* mez bg2 nat-c k* nat-m bg2 nat-s nux-v k* *Phos* b4a.de* puls b7.de* ran-b bg2 *Rhus-t* bg2 *Spig* k* spong fd4.de staph b7.de* sulph b4a.de* **Verat** k*
  - **agg.**: puls h1
- **room** agg.: sul-ac h2
- **sleep** agg.; during: caust k* nat-m k*
- **uncovered**, if: clem k* **Nux-v**
- **violent** chill morning of one day, light in afternoon of next: *Eup-per* k*
- **waking**; on: ant-t arn ars ars-s-f k2 *Bamb-a* stb2.de• bell h1 bry canth *Chel* k* cimic k* con *Lyc* k* mag-s k* *Merc* k* nat-c nat-s k* nit-ac rhus-t k* sep k* spong fd4.de sulph k* tarent thuj k* trom k* zinc
- **warm** stove, by a: *Ferr-i* k* lyc k* mag-c k*

FORENOON (= 9-12 h): aeth k* agar k* alst alum k* alum-p k2 alum-sil k2 am-c k* *Ambr* k* **Ang** k* *Ant-c* k* ant-t k* arg-n k* *Arn* k* **Ars** k* ars-s-f k2 *Asar* k* asc-t bamb-a stb2.de• bapt k* bar-c k* bar-s k2 bell bg2 berb k* bov k* bry bg2 **Cact** **Calc** k* calc-sil k2 calen cann-xyz bg2 carb-an b4.de* *Carb-v* b4a.de* cham bg2 *Chin* k* *Chinin-ar* chinin-s cimic k* cocc con k* cop **Cycl** k* **Dros** k* *Eup-per* k* eup-pur euphr k* formal bro1 gamb k* graph k* grat k* guaj k* kali-ar kali-c k* kali-n h2* kali-p kali-sil k2 laur k* *Led* k* lyc k* mag-c b4.de* mag-m k* merc b4.de* merc-i-r k* merl k* mez k* mur-ac b4.de* *Nat-ar* *Nat-c* k* **Nat-m** k* nit-ac bg2 **Nux-v** k* op bg2 par b7.de* petr k* *Ph-ac* k* phos k* plat b4.de* plb b7.de* podo puls b7a.de* ran-b bg2 rhod bg2 rhus-t b7.de* *Sabad* bg2 sars k* senec *Sep* bg2 sil k* spong fd4.de stann k* staph k* stram bg2 *Stront-c* k* *Sul-ac* bg2 **Sulph** k* thuj k* vanil fd5.de *Viol-t* k* zinc k*

- **9** h: alst ang ant-t asaf carb-ac cham tl1 dros **Eup-per** hydr ip kali-c *Lyc* mag-c merc-sul mez *Nat-m* ph-ac rhus-t sep staph sulph
  - **9**-10 h: bov eup-per ferr-i nat-m tl1 rhus-t
  - **9**-11 h: *Alst* bapt bro1 bol-la bro1 cench k2 mag-s bro1 **Nat-m** k* *Stann* wye bro1
- **10** h: alst *Ars* ars-s-f k2 bapt berb bol-la cact carb-v chin chinin-s cimic colch eup-per fago ferr-i gels led mag-s merc **Nat-m** petr k* ph-ac phos puls rhus-t sep sil **Stann** sulph thuj
  - **10**-11 h: agar *Ars* carb-v lob **Nat-m** k* *Nux-v* sulph
  - **10**-14 h: merc-sul
  - **10**-15 h: sil sulph
  - **10**-17 h: *Sulph*

Chill

- **10**.30 h: cact *Caps* hura lob nat-m
- **11** h: *Bapt*$_{k*}$ berb$_{k*}$ bol-la **Cact** calc canth carb-v castm cench$_{k2}$ cham *Chinin-s* *Cocc* epil$_{a1*}$ hyos *Ip* lob nat-c **Nat-m** **Nux-v** op podo puls *Sep*$_{k*}$ sil sulph
  - **11**-12 h: cob ip kali-c sulph
  - **11**-13 h: nat-m$_{tl1}$
  - **11**-16 h: *Cact* gels
  - **23** h; and: **Cact**$_{k*}$
  - **alternating** with 16 h the next day: *Calc*$_{k*}$
  - **disgust** at even the smell of food; with: *Cocc*
- **17** h; until: sulph
- **sleep** agg.; during: phos$_{k*}$
- **stool** agg.; after: dios
- **sudden** chill, with goose flesh and hair standing on end: bar-c
- **waking**; on: canth
- **warm** | **room** | **agg.**: sil
  - **stove**; by a: bapt ferr-i lyc

NOON (= 12-13 h): agar alum$_{k*}$ alum-p$_{k2}$ alum-sil$_{k2}$ anac ant-c$_{k*}$ apis arg-met$_{k*}$ *Arg-n* *Arn* *Ars* ars-s-f$_{k2}$ asar$_{bg2}$ bapt bar-c bar-s$_{k2}$ *Borx*$_{k*}$ *bry*$_{k*}$ calc$_{bg2}$ chel chinin-ar chinin-s cic cina cocc colch$_{k*}$ croc dig *Elaps* *Elat*$_{k*}$ *Eup-per*$_{k*}$ ferr$_{k*}$ ferr-ar ferr-i$_{k*}$ gels$_{k*}$ graph$_{k*}$ ham$_{fd3.de•}$ kali-bi kali-c$_{k*}$ kali-p kali-sil$_{k2}$ lac-ac$_{k*}$ lach$_{k*}$ **Lob**$_{k*}$ **Lyc** mag-c$_{bg2}$ malar$_{jl2}$ merc$_{k*}$ merl **Nat-m**$_{k*}$ nit-ac nux-v$_{bg2}$ op petr$_{k*}$ ph-ac phos$_{k*}$ **Puls**$_{k*}$ ran-b$_{k*}$ rob sabad samb sarr sars$_{h2}$ senec$_{k*}$ sil$_{k*}$ spira$_{k*}$ spong$_{fd4.de}$ staph stram$_{bg2}$ *Sulph*$_{k*}$ thuj$_{k*}$ tub vanil$_{fd5.de}$ zinc zing$_{a1}$

- **12** h: agar *Ant-c* apis *Chin* colch *Elaps* elat eup-per ferr ferr-i gels graph *Kali-c* *Lach* lob merc nat-m nux-v petr phos senec *Sil* *Sulph* thuj zing
  - **12**-14 h: **Ars** ars-s-f$_{k2}$ bol-la *Lach* sulph
- **bathing**; after: sulph
- **dinner**; after: alum$_{h2}$ grat mag-s puls$_{h1}$
- **heat**, followed by: colch$_{k*}$
- **menses**; during: phos$_{h2}$
- **sleep** agg.; after: bry

AFTERNOON (= 13-18 h): acon$_{k*}$ alum$_{k*}$ alum-p$_{k2}$ alum-sil$_{k2}$ am-c$_{k*}$ am-m$_{bg2}$ anac$_{k*}$ *Ang*$_{k*}$ ant-c$_{k*}$ ant-t$_{k*}$ **Apis**$_{k*}$ *Arg-met*$_{k*}$ arg-n$_{k*}$ *Arn*$_{k*}$ **Ars**$_{k*}$ ars-s-f$_{k2}$ arum-t$_{k*}$ *Asaf*$_{k*}$ asar$_{bg2}$ bapt$_{k*}$ bar-c$_{k*}$ bar-s$_{k2}$ bell$_{bg2}$ berb$_{k*}$ *Borx*$_{k*}$ *Bry*$_{k*}$ calc$_{bg2}$ camph$_{bg2}$ canth$_{k*}$ caps$_{k*}$ **Carb-an**$_{k*}$ carb-v$_{bg2}$ carbn-s castm *Caust*$_{k*}$ cedr$_{k*}$ cham$_{b7.de*}$ *Chel*$_{k*}$ **Chin**$_{k*}$ **Chinin-ar** **Chinin-s** cic$_{k*}$ cimic$_{k*}$ *Cina*$_{k*}$ *Cocc*$_{k*}$ coff$_{b7.de*}$ colch$_{k*}$ *Con*$_{k*}$ cop croc$_{k*}$ cur dig$_{k*}$ digin$_{a1}$ *Dros*$_{k*}$ dulc$_{fd4.de}$ elaps eup-per$_{k*}$ euphr$_{k*}$ **Ferr**$_{k*}$ ferr-p **Gels**$_{k*}$ *Graph*$_{k*}$ **Guaj**$_{b4a.de*}$ hyos$_{bg2}$ ign$_{b7.de*}$ ip$_{k*}$ *Kali-ar* kali-bi$_{k*}$ kali-c$_{k*}$ kali-i$_{k*}$ kali-m$_{k2}$ kali-n$_{k*}$ kali-p kali-sil$_{k2}$ kreos$_{k*}$ *Lach*$_{k*}$ *laur*$_{k*}$ **Lyc**$_{k*}$ m-aust$_{b7.de}$ mag-c$_{b4.de*}$ mag-m$_{k*}$ mand$_{sp1}$ merc$_{b4.de*}$ merl$_{k*}$ mez$_{bg2}$ nat-c$_{bg2}$ nat-m$_{k*}$ *Nit-ac*$_{k*}$ **Nux-v**$_{k*}$ op$_{k*}$ ox-ac$_{k*}$ petr$_{k*}$ *Ph-ac*$_{k*}$ phos$_{k*}$ plan$_{k*}$ plb podo$_{k*}$ *Psor* **Puls**$_{k*}$ *Ran-b*$_{k*}$ *Rhus-t*$_{k*}$ *Sabad*$_{k*}$ samb$_{hr1}$ sarr$_{k*}$ sars$_{a1}$ sep$_{b4a.de*}$ *Sil*$_{k*}$ *Spig*$_{k*}$ *Spong*$_{b7.de*}$ stann$_{bg2}$ *Staph*$_{k*}$ *Stram*$_{k*}$ sul-ac$_{b4.de*}$ *Sulph*$_{k*}$ teucr$_{b7.de*}$ *Thuj*$_{k*}$ tub$_{jl2}$ verat$_{k*}$ zinc$_{k*}$ zinc-p$_{k2}$

- **13** h: **Ars** ars-s-f$_{k2}$ *Cact* canth chel cina coff colch elat eup-per ferr-p$_{k*}$ gels ham$_{fd3.de•}$ kali-ar$_{k2}$ *Lach* merc nat-ar nux-m phos **Puls** sabad sars sil sulph
  - **13**-14 h: arg-met **Ars** eup-per ferr merc nat-m *Puls*
- **14** h: **Ars** ars-s-f$_{k2}$ *Calc*$_{k*}$ canth caust chel cic cur *Eup-per* *Ferr* gels hell *Lach*$_{k*}$ laur lob nat-ar *Nit-ac* plan$_{k*}$ *Puls* sang sarr sil sulph
  - **14**-15 h: cur *Lach*
  - **14**-16 h: gels
  - **14**-18 h: borx$_{k*}$
- **14**.30 h: led
- **15** h: **Ang** **Ant-t** **Apis**$_{k*}$ **Ars** ars-h asaf *Bell* bol-la calc canth **Cedr** cench$_{k2}$ *Chel* **Chinin-s**$_{k*}$ cic coff con cur ferr kali-ar kali-c kali-n$_{h2}$ lyc nux-v petr puls sabad *Samb* sil **Staph**$_{k*}$ **Thuj**
  - **15**-3 h: **Canth**$_{k*}$
  - **15**-16 h: *Apis* asaf canth *Lach* lyc$_{bro1}$ med puls thuj$_{bro1}$
  - **15**-17 h: **Apis** *Con* ferr ven-m$_{rsj12•}$
  - **15**-18 h: *Ars* eup-per ferr
  - **15**-21 h: cedr
  - **bed** time; until: puls

Afternoon: ...

- **16** h: aesc$_{k*}$ anac **Apis** ars asaf bol-la bov canth caust$_{k*}$ **Cedr** cham chel chinin-s con eupi gamb gels graph hell *Hep* ip kali-ar kali-c kali-i lec **Lyc** mag-m nat-m *Nat-s* *Nux-v* petr ph-ac phel **Puls** samb sep sil sulph [heroin$_{sdj2}$]
  - **16**-17 h: **Apis** cob gels$_{c1}$ graph mag-m$_{h2}$
  - **16**-18 h: nat-m sulph$_{k*}$
  - **16**-19 h: kali-c kali-i nat-m
  - **16**-20 h: *Bov* graph hell hep kali-i **Lyc**$_{k*}$ mag-m$_{k*}$ *Nat-s* sabad zinc
    - **coldness** and goose flesh; with icy: nat-s
    - **numb** hands and feet icy cold; with | **19** h: *Lyc*
  - **16**-22 h: phel
  - **alternating** with 11 h the next day: *Calc*$_{k*}$
- **17** h: alum am-m apis ars ars-s-f$_{k2}$ bov canth caps carb-an castm *Cedr* chel chin$_{k*}$ cimic coloc con dig eup-per ferr gamb gels graph hell *Hep* hura ip **Kali-c** kali-i kali-s **Lyc** mag-c *Nat-m* nux-m nux-v phos *Rhus-t* sabad samb sanic$_{c1}$ sarr sep sil sulph *Tarent* **Thuj** *Tub*$_{k*}$
  - **17**-18 h: am-m caps *Cedr* chel hell *Kali-c*$_{k*}$ phos puls sulph *Thuj*
  - **17**-19 h: canth *Hep*
  - **17**-20 h: alum *Carb-an* gamb *Hep* *Nat-m* nat-s sulph
- **17**.30 h: *Nat-m*
- **morning**; until: canth kali-i sars
- **air** agg.; in open: caust$_{h2}$
- **constantly** increasing chilliness without subsequent heat or perspiration: lyc
- **diarrhea** agg.; after: ox-ac
- **dinner**; after: **Anac** borx *Carb-an* caust coc-c colch$_{k*}$ cycl mag-m merc merl$_{k*}$ nit-ac nux-v puls spig *Sulph* thuj
- **heat**:
  - **following**: nux-v$_{k*}$ **Puls** stram
  - **perspiration**; with heat and | **17** h: nux-v
- **lasting** four hours: nux-v
- **long** lasting (See Predominating - afternoon)
- **menses** | **during** | **agg.**: nat-c$_{k*}$ nat-m$_{k*}$ *Nat-s*$_{k*}$ phos$_{h2}$
  - **first** day of: nat-m$_{k*}$
- **perspiration**:
  - **cold**: gels sarr
  - **with**: dig nat-m
- **sleep** | **after** | **agg.**: acon anac$_{h2}$ *Bry* con cycl merc sabad
  - **until** going to sleep in the evening: graph
- **violent** chill with thirst and red face: **Ferr**
- **walking** agg.; after: graph$_{k*}$
- **warm** room, even in a: acon$_{a1}$ mag-m nat-m$_{a1}$ rat$_{a1}$ rhus-t

EVENING (= 18-22 h): acon$_{k*}$ aesc$_{k*}$ agar$_{k*}$ *Agn*$_{bg2}$ **Alum**$_{k*}$ alum-sil$_{k2}$ **Am-c**$_{k*}$ *Am-m*$_{k*}$ ambr$_{b7.de*}$ androc$_{srj1•}$ ant-c$_{bg2}$ ant-t$_{k*}$ **Apis**$_{k*}$ aran$_{k*}$ arg-met$_{k*}$ arg-n$_{k*}$ **Arn**$_{k*}$ ars$_{k*}$ asar$_{b7.de*}$ aur$_{k*}$ bapt$_{k*}$ bar-c$_{k*}$ bar-m bar-s$_{k2}$ **Bell**$_{k*}$ berb$_{k*}$ bol-la$_{bro1}$ *Borx*$_{k*}$ *Bov*$_{k*}$ **Bry**$_{k*}$ bufo$_{bg2}$ *Calad*$_{k*}$ *Calc*$_{k*}$ calc-s calc-sil$_{k2}$ camph$_{h1*}$ *Canth*$_{k*}$ *Caps*$_{k*}$ carb-ac$_{hr1}$ *Carb-an*$_{k*}$ *Carb-v*$_{k*}$ *Carbn-s* castm caust$_{k*}$ *Cedr*$_{k*}$ cham$_{k*}$ *Chel*$_{k*}$ **Chin**$_{k*}$ chinin-ar *Chinin-s* cimx **Cina**$_{k*}$ cob-n$_{sp1}$ *Cocc*$_{k*}$ colch$_{k*}$ coloc$_{bg2}$ con$_{bg2}$ croc$_{k*}$ **Cycl**$_{k*}$ dios$_{k*}$ dulc$_{k*}$ elaps *Ferr*$_{k*}$ ferr-ar ferr-i$_{k2}$ *Gamb*$_{k*}$ *Gels* *Graph*$_{k*}$ grat$_{k*}$ guaj$_{b4.de*}$ ham$_{fd3.de•}$ hell$_{b7.de*}$ **Hep**$_{k*}$ hydr$_{k*}$ hyos$_{k*}$ *Ign*$_{k*}$ *Ip*$_{bg2*}$ kali-ar kali-bi$_{k*}$ *Kali-c*$_{k*}$ kali-m$_{k2}$ kali-n$_{k*}$ *Kali-p* **Kali-s** kali-sil$_{k2}$ lac-leo$_{hrn2•}$ *Lach*$_{k*}$ lachn lap-la$_{sde8.de•}$ laur$_{k*}$ led$_{k*}$ **Lyc**$_{k*}$ mag-c$_{k*}$ *Mag-m*$_{k*}$ mag-s$_{k*}$ mang$_{k*}$ meph$_{a1}$ **Merc**$_{k*}$ *Merc-c*$_{b4a.de*}$ merl$_{k*}$ mez$_{k*}$ *Mur-ac*$_{k*}$ naja nat-ar nat-c$_{k*}$ nat-m$_{k*}$ nat-p nat-s$_{k*}$ nicc$_{k*}$ *Nit-ac*$_{k*}$ nux-m$_{k*}$ nux-v$_{k*}$ olib-sac$_{wmh1}$ op$_{b7.de*}$ ox-ac$_{k*}$ *Par*$_{b7.de*}$ *Petr*$_{k*}$ *Ph-ac*$_{k*}$ phel$_{k*}$ **Phos**$_{k*}$ plac$_{rzf5•}$ plat$_{k*}$ plb$_{k*}$ podo psor$_{k*}$ **Puls**$_{k*}$ **Pyrog** *Ran-b*$_{b7.de*}$ ran-s$_{bg2}$ rat$_{k*}$ *Rhod*$_{b4a.de*}$ **Rhus-t**$_{k*}$ ruta$_{fd4.de}$ sabad$_{k*}$ sabin$_{b7.de*}$ samb$_{k*}$ sarr$_{k*}$ sars$_{b4.de*}$ sel$_{k*}$ **Sep**$_{k*}$ sil$_{k*}$ spig$_{k*}$ *Spong*$_{b7.de*}$ *Squil*$_{b7.de*}$ stann$_{k*}$ *Staph*$_{k*}$ stram$_{bg2}$ stront-c$_{b4.de*}$ sul-ac$_{bg2}$ **Sulph**$_{k*}$ *Tarent*$_{k*}$ teucr$_{b7.de*}$ thuj$_{k*}$ tritic-vg$_{fd5.de}$ tub$_{k13}$ vanil$_{fd5.de}$ verat$_{b7.de*}$ vip$_{fkr4.de}$ *Zinc*$_{k*}$ zinc-p$_{k2}$ zing$_{a1}$

- **18** h: adam$_{srj5•}$ am-m ant-t arg-n ars ars-s-f$_{k2}$ bell bov canth caps carb-an *Cedr* cham chel gamb graph hell **Hep** **Kali-c** kali-i kali-n kali-p kali-s lyc mag-m *Nat-m* nat-s nux-m *Nux-v* *Petr* ph-ac phel phos puls rhus-t samb sep *Sil* sulph tarent thuj
  - **18**-4 h: gamb
  - **18**-5 h: gamb **Hep** nicc

- **18** h: ...
  - **18**-19 h: hep mur-ac nicc stram *Tub*
  - **18**-19.30 h: thuj h1
  - **18**-20 h: ars *Hep* kali-i mag-m naja sulph
  - **18**-21 h: nat-s k2
  - **18**-22 h: kali-i phel
  - **18**-0 h: lachn
- **19** h: alum am-m ars ars-s-f k2 *Bov* calc canth carb-an carbn-s castm caust *Cedr* chel *Chinin-s* colch elaps *Ferr* *Gamb* graph hell **Hep** kali-i kali-n *Lyc* mag-c mag-m mang nat-m **Nat-s** nux-v petr ph-ac phel phos *Puls* **Pyrog** k* **Rhus-t** sil *Sulph* *Tarent* thuj *Tub* k*
  - **19**-19.30 h: calc-caust c1
  - **19**-21 h: chel mag-c
  - **19**-22 h: bov phos
  - **dashed** with ice-cold water; as if:
    - **cold** blood were running through the blood vessels; or as if:
      - **moving**; cold when | **eating** and drinking agg.: **Rhus-t**
- **19**.30 h: calc castm caust *Ferr* mag-s thuj
- **20** h: alum ars ars-s-f k2 bar-c *Bov* canth carb-an carbn-s castm chel *Coff* *Elaps* form gamb graph hell *Hep* kali-ar k2 kali-i lyc mag-c mag-m mag-s mur-ac h2 naja nux-v ph-ac phel phys pip-m rat *Rhus-t* sil sulph tarax
- **21** h: *Ars* bol-la *Bov* *Bry* canth carb-an cedr croc cycl gamb gels ham fd3.de• hydr kali-n laur mag-c mag-m mag-s merc merl nept-m lsd2.fr nux-m nux-v ph-ac phel rat sabad sulph
  - **21**-10 h: *Mag-s*
  - **21**-22 h: elaps mag-c mag-m sarr
  - **21**-0 h: am-c
- **21**.30 h: hir skp7•
  - **21**.30-0.30 h: sulfonam ks2
- **abdomen**, with burning in the: nat-c *Phos*
- **bed**:
  - **in** bed:
    - **agg.**: *Acon* hr1 agar **Alum** k* alum-p k2 alum-sil k2 am-c k* ars k* ars-s-f k2 aur k* bamb-a stb2.de• bell h1 bov hr1 bry k* *Calc* k* calc-ar carb-an k* castm *Chel* *Chin* chinin-s coc-c k* colch k* *Dros* k* ferr k* guare hep hr1 kali-c h2 kali-n lyc k* mag-c k* mag-s *Merc* k* mur-ac nat-ar nat-c nat-m k* nat-p *Nat-s* hr1 nicc hr1 *Nit-ac* k* nux-v k* op k* petr k* *Phos* k* raph k* rhus-t k* sang k* *Sil* k* spig h1 *Sulph* k* tarent thuj k* tritic-vg fd5.de *Tub* vanil fd5.de
    - **amel.**: chinin-s mag-c mag-m *Nat-s* *Rat*
- **cold**, from external: nux-m k*
- **colic**; with: led
- **continuing**:
  - **all** night: bov cina gamb k* hyos ip lyc nux-v puls rhus-t sarr
  - **midnight**; until: calad *Merc* phos *Tub*
- **drinking** agg.; after: nat-m
- **eating** | **after** | **agg.**: *Calc* con h2 *Kali-c* nux-v
  - **while** | **agg.**: bov (non:con kl)
- **falling** asleep:
  - **before**: carb-v lyc nux-v *Phos* samb h1 staph h1
  - **on**: calc graph lyc h2 sil
- **flushes** of heat; with: petr thuj
- **followed** by:
  - **convulsions** and heat lasting all night: cina
  - **fever** all night: *Cina* hr1
  - **perspiration**: carb-an cedr sabad
- **heat** | **without** subsequent: calc lyc sabad sulph
- **lying** down | **after** | **agg.**: acon am-m *Aur* bov bry camph caps *Cham* grat hell lac-c lyc merc nat-c nat-m nicc nit-ac *Nux-v* par ph-ac phos *Podo* **Puls** sabad sars spig h1
  - **amel.**: sulph h2
- **menses**; during: nat-c h2
- **mingled** with heat, then heat no perspiration: *Kali-s*
- **motion** agg.: apis brom k* bry calad k* colch nux-v
- **pains**, with the: cycl ign **Puls**
- **rising** agg.: borx canth

Evening: ...
- **sleep**, with stupefying: lyc
- **stool** agg.; during: alum k* sulph k*
- **sunset**, at: *Ars* k* carb-ac *Ign* k* *Puls* k* thuj
- **tea** agg.: ox-ac
- **undressing**: acon bell h1 calc cocc fago mag-c k* *Merc* nat-ar nit-ac op plat k* *Rhus-t* spig tarent *Tub*
- **waking**; on: nat-c nux-m k* ph-ac h2
- **walking** agg.: petr k*
- **warm** room, in a: arg-n chlor k* laur nat-m puls k*
- **warmth**; external:
  - **during**: *Mur-ac*
  - **not** amel. by: calc canth chin cina laur **Nux-v** rhus-t
- **writing** agg.: sulph k*

NIGHT (= 22-6 h): acon k* agar b4.de* *Alum* k* am-c b4.de* *Am-m* k* ambr k* ang bg2 ant-t b7.de* apis arg-met b7a.de* arist-cl sp1 *Ars* k* *Ars-i* ars-s-f k2 arum-t k* **Aur** b4.de* bamb-a stb2.de• bar-c k* bar-s k2 *Bell* k* berb k* borx k* bov k* bry k* cact k* calad k* calc b4.de* canth k* caps k* **Carb-an** k* carb-v k* carbn-s *Caust* k* cench k2 cham k* chel chin k* chinin-ar coff bg2 coli jl2 con k* dios a1 dros k* **Eup-per** k* euphr bg2 **Ferr** k* **Ferr-ar** **Ferr-i** ferr-p gamb k* graph h2 **Hep** k* **Hyos** k* iod k* ip k* kali-ar kali-c k* kali-i k* kali-n h2 kali-s kali-sil k2 kreos b7a.de* lac-lup hrn2• *Lach* k* lap-la rsp1 laur b7.de* lyc k* mag-c k* mag-m b4.de* mag-s k* mang bg2 meny **Merc** k* *Merc-c* b4a.de* merl mur-ac k* nat-m b4.de* *Nit-ac* k* **Nux-v** k* op k* **Par** k* petr bg2 ph-ac bg2 **Phos** k* *Phyt* hr1 puls k* pyrog ptk1 ran-s bg2 rhus-t k* ruta fd4.de sabad k* sarr sars b4.de* sep k* sil k* spig bg2 *Spong* bg2* squil b7.de* staph b7.de* stram k* **Sulph** k* thuj k* *Tub* verat k* zinc b4.de*
- **midnight**: ars k* ars-s-f k2 cact k* canth k* **Caust** k* *Chin* chinin-ar grat k* lyc h2 mez k* mur-ac nat-m k* nux-v bro1 raph k* sep k* *Sulph* k*
  - **before**: alum am-c k* *Arg-met* k* arund aur bg2 cact calad b7.de* carb-an k* caust chin bg2 kali-p fd1.de• *Mur-ac* k* nit-ac k* *Phos* k* **Puls** k* rhod b4a.de* sabad k* sulph k* verat k*
    - **22** h: *Ars* ars-h *Bov* cact canth carb-an cench k2 *Chinin-s* elaps euph hydr *Kali-i* lach mag-c *Petr* ph-ac phel sabad
    - **22.30** h: chel olib-sac wmh1
    - **23** h: *Ars* **Cact** canth *Carb-an* euph lec naja olib-sac wmh1 sulph tub k2
  - **at**: *Ars* k* cact canth **Caust** k* *Chin* chinin-ar grat hep bg2 mez mur-ac nat-m nit-ac raph sep sil bg2 stram bg2 *Sulph*
  - **after**: am-m h2* **Ars** k* *Borx* b4a.de* **Calad** k* canth bg2 caust bg2 cham bg2 cocc bg2 coff k* dros k* ferr bg2 *Hep* kali-c bg2 kali-n bg2 laur bg2 mag-s k* mang h2 merc merc-c a1 mez h2 *Nux-v* bg2 *Op* k* petr k* phos bg2 ran-s bg2 rhus-t bg2 sil squil bg2 sulph h2* *Thuj* k*
    - **1** h: **Ars** ars-s-f k2 canth kali-ar nat-m puls sil
      - **1**-2 h: aloe ars bro1 dios
    - **2** h: ars canth caust hep lach nat-ar nat-m kr1 puls rhus-t sarr sil tax
      - **2**-4 h: borx k*
    - **3** h: aloe am-m canth *Cedr* cimic cina eup-per **Ferr** led lyss nat-m rhus-t sil *Thuj* k*
      - **waking**; on: cimic k1 **Ferr** k1
    - **4** h: *Alum* am-m **Arn** **Cedr** con ferr k* lac-h sk4• nat-m ph-ac sil
      - **4**-5 h: bry *Nux-v* *Sulph*
      - **16** h; and: ars-s-f k2 cedr
      - **followed** by perspiration: **Cedr** k1
    - **5** h: ant-t *Apis* bol-la *Bov* *Chin* k* chinin-m kr1 coff con dios dros nat-m rhus-t hr1 sep sil
      - **fever**; after thirty-six hours of: apis
    - **frequent** chills | **1**-7 h: *Sil*
  - **menses**; before: lyc h2
- **bed**:
  - **in** bed:
    - **agg.**: adam srj5• ars-i k2 canch canth **Carb-an** dros euphr k* *Ferr-i* ferr-p mag-c mag-m h2 mag-s k* meny nat-ar k2 olib-sac wmh1 sars k* sul-i k2 *Sulph* k*
    - **amel.**: phos h2
- **hot** head, with: colch k*
- **menses**; during: arist-cl sp1
- **nausea**; after: phyt k*
- **never** at night: chin
- **perspiration**; during: eup-per

Chill

- **putting** hand out of bed, on: *Canth Hep Sil* k*
- **rising**:
  - **agg**.: ant-t k*
  - **amel**.: sul-i k2
- **waking**; on: aloe am-m gsy1 carb-an k* chel k* graph k* phos h2 sars k* sil k*
- **warm** room agg.: rat

ABSENT (See FEVER - Chill absent)

ACCOMPANIED BY:
- **abortion** (See FEMALE - Abortion - accompanied - chills)
- **beer**; desire for (See GENERALS - Food and - beer - desire - chill)
- **cold** drinks; desire for (See GENERALS - Food and - cold drink - desire - chill)
- **complaints**; other: *Acon* b2.de* agar b2.de* agn b2.de* alum b2.de* am-c b2.de* am-m b2.de* ambr b2.de* anac b2.de* ant-c b2.de* ant-t b2.de* am b2.de* **Ars** b2.de* asar b2.de* aur b2.de* bar-c b2.de* bell b2.de* *Borx* b2.de* bov b2.de* **Bry** b2.de* calad b2.de* *Calc* b2.de* camph b2.de* cann-s b2.de* canth b2.de* *Caps* b2.de* carb-an b2.de* carb-v b2.de* caust b2.de* *Cham* b2.de* chel b2.de* *Chin* b2.de* cic b2.de* cina b2.de* cocc b2.de* coff b2.de* coloc b2.de* con b2.de* croc b2.de* cupr b2.de* cycl b2.de* dig b2.de* dros b2.de* dulc b2.de* euph b2.de* ferr b2.de* graph b2.de* *Hell* b2.de* *Hep* b2.de* hyos b2.de* *Ign* b2.de* iod b2.de* ip b2.de* kali-c b2.de* kali-n b2.de* *Kreos* b2.de* lach b2.de* laur b2.de* led b2.de* *Lyc* b2.de* m-arct b2.de m-aust b2.de mag-m b2.de* mang b2.de* meny b2.de* merc b2.de* mez b2.de* mur-ac b2.de* nat-c b2.de* *Nat-m* b2.de* nit-ac b2.de* nux-m b2.de* **Nux-v** b2.de* olnd b2.de* op b2.de* par b2.de* petr b2.de* ph-ac b2.de* phos b2.de* plat b2.de* plb b2.de* **Puls** b2.de* ran-b b2.de* rhod b2.de* **Rhus-t** b2.de* ruta b2.de* *Sabad* b2.de* sabin b2.de* samb b2.de* sars b2.de* sec b2.de* sel b2.de* seneg b2.de* sep b2.de* sil b2.de* spig b2.de* spong b2.de* squil b2.de* stann b2.de* staph b2.de* stram b2.de* stront-c b2.de* sul-ac b2.de* sulph b2.de* tarax b2.de* teucr b2.de* thuj b2.de* valer b2.de* *Verat* b2.de* viol-t b2.de* zinc b2.de*
- **hot** breath (See RESPIRATION - Hot - chill)
- **influenza** (See GENERALS - Influenza - accompanied - chill)
- **other** complaints: ars b4a.de *Ign* b7a.de *M-arct* b7a.de *Puls* b7a.de *Rhus-t* b7a.de sabad ptk1
- **warm** drinks; desire for (See GENERALS - Food and - warm drinks - desire - chill)

○ - **Teeth**; pain in (See TEETH - Pain - accompanied - chill)

ACIDS agg.: lach bro1

AFFECTED parts: *Ang* b7a.de ars bry bg3 caust cocc k* colch bg3 dulc graph lach k* *Led* k* m-arct b7.de merc mez bg3 nux-v petr plat plb k* pyrog jl2 rhod *Rhus-t* k* sec bg3 *Sil* k* thuj

AIR:
- **walking** (See Walking - air - agg.)
- **warm** (See Warm - room)

AIR; DRAFT OF: | **slightest**: *Acon* bro1 agar bro1 agra bro1 am-p bro1 arg-n bro1 *Ars* bro1 ars-i bro1 astac bro1 *Bar-c* bar-s k2 bell k* bry **Calc** k* *Calc-p* bro1 calen bro1 canch bro1 canth k* **Caps** k* carb-an *Cham* **Chin** k* dulc hep k* kali-c k* kali-sil k2 mag-c *Merc* k* merc-c bro1 mez bro1 **Nux-v** k* positr nl2• *Psor* bro1 pyrus rhod rhus-t gk1 sel k* sep bro1 sil k* sulph k* tub bro1 *Zinc*

AIR; IN OPEN:
- **agg**.: **Agar** k* *Alum* k* alum-sil k2 *Am-c* k* **Anac** k* *Ant-t* **Ars** k* ars-s-f k2 **Asar** k* bamb-a stb2.de• **Bapt** *Bar-c* bar-s k2 bell k* bol-la borx k* bov brom *Bry* k* bufo k* calad k* **Calc** calc-p calc-sil k2 calen *Camph* cann-s k* canth *Caps* carb-ac carb-an k* carb-v k* caust b4.de* *Cham* k* *Chel* k* **Chin** k* *Chinin-ar* cocc k* **Coff** k* colch *Con* k* **Cycl** dulc k* *Euph* k* guaj k* ham fd3.de• **Hep** k* **Ign** k* *Kali-ar* kali-c k* *Kali-chl* kali-m k2 kali-n k* kali-p kali-sil k2 kreos k* *Laur* k* m-aust b7.de mag-m k* mag-s mang k* **Merc** k* *Merc-c* k* *Mosch* k* nat-m *Nit-ac* k* **Nux-m** k* **Nux-v** k* **Petr** k* ph-ac k* phos **Plat** k* **Plb** k* *Puls* *Ran-b* k* rhod k* *Rhus-t* k* sars k* sel bg2 *Seneg* k* **Sep** k* *Sil* k* spig k* stram k* stront-c k* sul-ac k* sulph k* tab *Tarax* k* thuj k* viol-t k* *Zinc* k* zing
- **amel**.: acon k* alum k* *Ang* k* ant-c k* **Apis** arg-met k* **Asar** k* bar-c bg2 **Bry** k* **Caps** cic bg2 cocc croc bg2 *Graph* k* hell bg2 **Ip** k* lil-t bg2 lyc bg2 *Mag-c* k* *Mag-m* k* meny bg2 *Mez* k* nat-m k* petr-ra shn4• phos k* pip-n bg2 **Puls** k* ran-s bg2 *Sabin* k* spong bg2 stann bg2 *Staph* k* **Sul-ac** k* sulph bg2

ALCOHOL; from abuse of: (↗*MIND - Libertinism)* led *Nux-v*

ALTERNATING WITH:
- **flushes** of heat (See GENERALS - Heat - flushes - alternating - chills)
- **heat** (See FEVER - Alternating - chills)
- **mental** symptoms: croc bg2 *Plat* b4a.de*
- **pain**: chin bg2 *Hell* b7a.de* kali-c bg2 nat-m bg2
- **perspiration**: ant-c ars k* ars-s-f k2 calc chin st* euph glon bg1 led lyc mez st* nux-v k* *Phos* sabad sang ptk1 spig st spong fd4.de sulph thuj verat
  - **heat**; with: plut-n srj7•

○ - **Face**; flushes of heat in (See FACE - Heat - flushes - alternating - chills)
- **Head**; heat in (See HEAD - Heat - alternating - chilliness)

ANGER; after: *(↗MIND - Anger)* acon k* ars k* aur bro1 **Bry** k* *Cham* k* **Nux-v** k* teucr k*
- **alternating** with | **heat** (See FEVER - Anger - alternating - chill)

ANNUAL chill: *Ars* **Carb-v** **Lach** *Nat-m* *Psor* *Rhus-r* **Rhus-v** *Sulph* *Thuj* tub *Urt-u*
- **semi**-annual: lach *Sep*

ANTERIOR part of body: stram h1

ANTICIPATING: ant-t apis ptk1 **Ars** k* bell **Bry** k* cham k* chin k* chinin-ar **Chinin-s** k* eup-per k* gamb k* ign **Nat-m** k* **Nux-v** k* sep
- **about** 2 hours each attack: *Chinin-s*
- **every**:
  - **day** 2 hours: cham k*
  - **other** day: nat-m nux-v
    - **one** hour: ars chin ign nat-m nux-v
    - **tertian**, several hours: ant-t
    - **two** hours: nux-m
- **postponing**; or: *Bry* k* chin gamb *Ign* k*

ANXIETY, caused by: *(↗MIND - Anxiety)* acon k* ars gels *Tub*

ARSENIC; from abuse of: ip

ASCENDING agg.: *(↗BACK - Coldness - extending - up the)* *Acon* k* am-m k* ammc ang ars ars-s-f k2 bar-c k* ben-n bufo bg2 calc *Calc-p* k* canth carb-an k* caust chel bg2 cimx *Cina* k* coff croc k* *Dig* k* dulc k* eup-per eup-pur br1 *Gels* k* *Hyos* k* kali-bi k* kali-i kali-p k2 *Lach* k* mag-c k* mag-s meny bg2 merl nat-s nux-m bg2 *Nux-v* bg2* ox-ac *Phos* k* *Puls* k* rhus-t bg2 ruta bg2 **Sabad** k* *Sars* k* *Sep* k* spig h1* staph k* **Sulph** k* thuj bg2 verat k* vesp br1

ASCENDING to head: glon ptk1

AUTUMN and spring: apis ars **Lach** *Psor* sep

○ - **Part** of body: cham bg3 *Cocc* bg3 **Ign** bg3 *Rhus-t* bg3 stront-c bg3

AUTUMNAL: **Aesc** ars bapt **Bry** chin **Colch** **Nat-m** *Nux-v* rhus-t **Sep** verat

BATHING: *(↗Water)* bell calc calc-s caps tl1 eupi sulph *Tub*

BED:
- **coldness** out of bed; heat in bed and: mez
- **in** bed:
  - **agg**.: acon k* **Agn** bg2 **Alum** k* am-c k* am-m k* ambr k* *Ang* k* ant-t k* arg-met k* arn k* *Ars* k* ars-i **Aur** k* aur-i k2 aur-s k2 bamb-a stb2.de• bar-c k* bar-m bar-s k2 *Bell* k* berb bg1 borx k* bov k* *Bry* k* calad k* calc k* calc-sil k2 canth k* caps k* **Carb-an** k* carb-v k* caust k* cench k2 **Chel** k* **Chin** k* chinin-ar clem k* colch coloc k* dios **Dros** k* **Ferr** k* ferr-ar graph k* guaj k* hell k* **Hep** k* **Hyos** k* iod k* ip k* *Kali-c* k* kali-m k2 kali-n k* *Kali-p* kreos k* laur k* *Lec* *Led* k* **Lyc** k* mag-c k* mag-m k* mang k* meny k* **Merc** k* *Merc-c* k* *Mur-ac* k* nat-ar nat-c k* nat-m k* *Nat-s* k* **Nit-ac** k* *Nux-v* k* op b7.de *Par* k* petr k* *Ph-ac* k* *Phos* k* plat k* **Puls** k* *Rhod* k* rhus-t k* sabad k* sabin k* samb k* sang sars k* sel k* sep k* **Sil** k* spig k* spong k* squil k* stann k* staph k* stront-c k* sul-ac bg2 **Sulph** k* thuj k* vanil fd5.de verat k* *Zinc* k* zinc-p k2
  - **amel**.: am-c borx b4a.de bry k* canth k* **Caust** k* **Cham** b7.de cimx cocc k* con k* hell k* **Kali-c** k* *Kali-i* kali-n k* *Lachn* mag-c k* **Mag-m** k* mag-s mez k* mosch nat-c k* nit-ac k* *Nux-v* k* *Podo* puls k* **Pyrog** *Rhus-t* k* sars k* *Squil* k* stram k* sulph k*

- **putting** hand out of bed: **Bar-c** k* *Canth* **Hep** k* **Nux-v** ptk1 phos **Rhus-t** k* *Sil* tarent ptk1 **Tub** ptk1
- **rising** from:
  - **agg.**: acon b7.de* *Am-m* bg2 bar-c bism borx k* bry bg2 **Calc** k* *Canth* k* carb-v bg2 cham k* coloc b4.de* euphr b7.de* ferr-i graph bg2 *Hell* b7a.de* *Lach* bg2 laur b7.de* mag-c mang b4.de* meny bg2 **Merc** k* mez k* nat-c b4.de* nat-m bg2 **Nux-v** k* *Phos* k* puls b7.de* ran-b bg2 *Rhus-t* k* *Sil* *Spig* b7.de* staph b7.de* sulph b4a.de* verat b7.de*
  - **amel.**: am-c ambr ant-t arg-met ars aur bell dros euph ferr ferr-i k2 ign **Iod** led *Lyc* mag-c merc merc-c *Nat-c* plat *Puls* rhod rhus-t sel *Sep* stront-c sulph *Verat*
- **turning** over in: acon k* agar h2 alum-sil k2 *Bry* k* caps k* ham fd3.de• hep k* lyc k* nat-m k* **Nux-v** k* **Puls** k* sec a1 sil k* staph k* *Stram* sulph k*

BEGINNING in (= extending from):

○ - **Abdomen**: ambr ptk1 **Apis** k* *Ars* ptk1 *Bell* calad k* calc *Camph* cann-s coloc k* cur **Ign** k* merc par k* phos ptk1 sep ptk1 teucr k* verat k*

▽ • **extending** to | **Fingers** and toes: calad

- **Ankles**: chin lach puls
- **Anus** running down legs: syph c1
- **Arms**: **Bell** k* dig **Hell** *Ign* lyc bg2 mez k* plat sulph h2
  - **right**, and right side: *Merl*
  - **left**, and lower limbs: *Nux-m*
  - **and**:
    - **Hand**: *Carb-v*
    - **Thighs**: psor

○ • **Both** at once: *Bell* hell mez

- **Back**: ant-t *Arg-met* k* ars-s-f k2 bapt bell k* *Bol-la* bov **Bry** sne cact canth **Caps** k* caust ptk1 cedr cocc c1* conv br1 croc k* **Dulc** k* *Eup-per* k* *Eup-pur* *Gamb* k* gels k* hipp c1* *Hyos* k* kali-i **Lach** k* led lept *Lyc* k* merc sne nat-m k* nit-ac bg2 *Nux-v* puls k* *Pyrog* *Rhus-t* k* sarr sec ptk1 sep k* spig spong staph k* stront-c ptk1 sulph h2* verat

○ • **Between** the scapulae (See dorsal - between)

- • **Cervical** region: psil ft1
- • **Dorsal** region: *Eup-per* gels **Lach** nat-m
  - **Between** the scapulae: bol-la **Caps** led *Pyrog* k* rhus-t sarr *Sep*
    - **followed** by:
      - **Bones**; coldness of: pyrog tl1
      - **Extremities**; coldness of: pyrog tl1
    - **extending** down the back: *Caps* hr1
- • **Lumbar** region: bell bg2 eup-per bg2 *Eup-pur* gels ptk1 hydrc *Hyos* bg2* lach k* **Nat-m** k* rhod bg2 stront-c k* sulph bg2* tarent
- **Bladder**: sars ptk1

○ • **Neck** of bladder after urinating: sars

- **Body**:
  - **right** side of: bry nat-m rhus-t
  - **left** side of: *Carb-v* caust
- **Buttocks**: puls
- **Calves**: *Lach* lyc ox-ac
- **Chest**: **Apis** k* ars *Carb-an* k* *Cic* k* cina kreos lith-c merl nux-v rhus-t *Sep* k* spig k* sulph h2
  - **right** side: *Merl*
  - **left** side: visc c1
- **Face**: acon arn bar-c k* berb k* borx calc carb-ac *Caust* k* *Cham* ign kreos laur merc petr phos puls *Rhod* ruta staph stram
- **Feet**: acon bg2 alum h2 apis arn bar-c k* borx calc calc-s *Chel* cimx dig k* ferr lp **Gels** k* helo-s rwt2* *Hyos* k* kali-bi lyc mag-c **Nat-m** nux-m *Nux-v* puls *Rhus-t* k* sabad sarr *Sep* spig h1* *Sulph* k*
  - **right** foot: chel lyc sabin

○ • **Soles** and palms (See hands - palms)

- • **Toes** (See toes)
- **Fingers**: *Bry* coff dig **Nat-m** nux-v *Sep* *Sulph*

○ • **Tips** of: **Bry** nat-m puls

- **Toes**; and: **Bry** cycl dig meny nat-m **Sep** stann *Sulph*
- **Hands**: bry *Chel* dig k* eup-per **Gels** k* ip merc bg2 nat-m bg2 *Nux-v* puls rhus-t sabad *Sep* *Sulph*
  - **right** hand: merl
  - **left** hand: *Carb-v* nux-m

Beginning in – **Hands**: ...

- • **feet**; and: apis bry carb-v chel dig *Ferr* *Gels* **Nat-m** nux-m op puls k2 rhus-t sne sabin samb sulph

○ • **Palms** and soles: dig k*

- **Head**: bar-c mosch k* nat-m stann valer

○ • **Occiput**: agar bg2 *Valer* bg2

- • **Vertex**: arum-t k* kalm bg2
- **Knees**: apis benz-ac puls thuj
- **Legs**: cedr *Chin* cocc c1 kali-bi *Nux-m* ox-ac puls rhus-t sep thuj
- **Lips**: **Bry** k*
- **Lumbar** region: *Hyos* bg2 lach bg2
- **Neck**: arg-n bg2 lyc bg2 puls staph thuj bg2 valer k*
- **Nose**: nat-c sabad sulph tarax tub zinc
- **Palms** and soles (See hands - palms)
- **Sacrum**: bell h1 puls
- **Scalp**: mosch
- **Scapula**: *Rhus-t* bg2
- **Scrobiculus** cordis (See stomach)
- **Spine**:

▽ • **extending** to | **Arms**: lept ptk1

- **Stomach**: iris bg2 sec bg2

○ • **Pit** of: *Arn* k* bar-c k* *Bell* k* cadm-s **Calc** k* caust cur *Helon* merl mez h2 spig k*

- **Thighs**: cedr *Cham* *Rhus-t* ther **Thuj** k*
- **Throat**: sep
- **Toes**: *Bry* coff ferr lp **Nat-m** *Sep* sulph
- **Umbilicus**: puls
- **Wrist** | **left**: *Nux-m*

BREAKFAST: | **after** | **agg.**: calc-s k* carb-an eupi gels graph h2 puls bro1 verat

- **during**: carb-an k* eupi k* gels k* graph k* kiss a1 verat k*

CHANGING type: (↗*MIND - Capriciousness; MIND - Mood - changeable*) *Elat* *Eup-per* **Ign** k* meny **Puls** k* sep

CHILLINESS: (↗*GENERALS - Cold - feeling; GENERALS - Heat - lack*) abies-c bro1 abrot acon k* *Aesc* aeth k* *Agar* k* **Agn** b2.de* *Alum* k* am-c k* am-m k* ambr b2.de* **Anac** k* ang k* ant-c k* ant-t k* *Apis* k* *Aq-mar* skp7• *Aran* k* *Arg-n* k* arizon-l nl2• **Arn** k* *Ars* k* *Ars-i* bro1 *Asaf* asar k* asc-t astac bro1 aur aur-m aur-s k2 *Bamb-a* stb2.de• *Bapt* k* **Bar-c** k* *Bar-m* **Bell** k* berb bro1 bism k* bol-la borx b2.de* bov k* brom k* **Bry** k* *Cact* *Cadm-s* br1 calad k* **Calc** k* *Calc-ar* br1* calc-p bro1 *Calc-sil* br1* calen bro1 **Camph** k* cann-s b2.de* canth b2.de* caps k* *Carb-an* k* **Carb-v** k* **Carbn-s** castm bro1 **Caust** k* cedr k* cench k2 *Cham* k* **Chel** k* *Chin* k* *Chinin-s* chir-fl bnm4• *Cic* k* cimx k* cina b2.de* cist *Clem* cocain bro1 cocc k* coff k* **Colch** k* con k* corn corn-f bro1 crat bro1 croc k* crot-t cupr k* des-ac rbp6 dig k* *Dros* k* dulc k* *Echi* bro1 eup-per k2 eup-pur bro1 euph b2.de* **Euphr** k* **Ferr** k* ferr-p gamb k* *Gels* k* **Graph** k* guaj b2.de* hell b2.de* helo bg2* *Helo-s* rwt2• **Hep** k* hom-xyz br1 hydr hydrog srj2• *Hyos* b2.de* *Ign* k* *Ip* k* jatr-c bro1 kali-ar k2* kali-bi k* kali-br a1 kali-c k* kali-n b4.de* kali-p k* *Kali-s* kalm mrr1 kola stb3• kreos k* lac-ac lac-cp vml2• lac-d bro1 lach k* lachn lact *Laur* k* *Led* k* lept lob-p bro1 **Lyc** k* *M-arct* b2.de m-aust b2.de* mag-m mrr1* *Mag-p* bro1 meny k* *Merc* k* *Merc-c* k* **Mez** k* mill morph bro1 mosch k* mur-ac k* nat-ar k* nat-c k* *Nat-m* k* nat-p *Nat-s* nept-m lsd2.fr **Nit-ac** k* **Nux-m** k* **Nux-v** k* *Olnd* k* op k* ox-ac ozone sde2• par k* pert-vc vk9 *Petr* k* ph-ac k* *Phos* k* pieri-b mlk9.de pimp c2* *Plat* k* **Plb** k* podo **Psor** bro1* **Puls** k* pulx br1 pyrus bro1 rad-br bro1 ran-b k* ran-s b2.de* rhod b2.de *Rhus-t* k* ruta b2.de* *Sabad* k* **Sabin** k* sal-fr sle1• samb b2.de* sanic mrr1* sars b2.de* *Sec* bro1 seneg b2.de* **Sep** k* *Sil* k* sphing kk3.fr spig k* spong b2.de* squil k* *Stann* b2.de* staph b2.de* stram k* stront-c k* sul-ac h2* **Sulph** k* sumb syph k2 *Tab* bro1 **Tarax** k* *Tarent* k* *Tela* bro1 ter **Teucr** k* ther bg2 thuj b2.de* tritic-vg fd5.de tub br1 *V-a-b* jl2 vac br1 valer k* vanil fd5.de verat b2.de* viol-t k* visc c1 zinc k* [bell-p-sp dcm1 lac-mat sst4 spect dfg1]

- **left** | **then** right: olib-sac wmh1
- **morning**: am-c anac ang arg-met *Arn* asaf bov calc bro1 carb-an cench k2 chin h1 chinin-ar con dulc fd4.de eup-per euph ferr k* gels c1 hep kali-ar k2 mag-s mang mur-ac nat-m nit-ac rhod spong fd4.de symph fd3.de• tritic-vg fd5.de
  - **lasting**:
    - **day**; all: ferr kali-p k2 mag-c mang mez nat-m sabin **Sil**
    - **forenoon**; all: *Arn*

• **rising** agg.; after: acon arg-n dulc fd4.de mag-m h2 mang mur-ac nat-c nux-v sep h2 spong fd4.de
• **waking**; on: ang *Arn* chel dulc fd4.de mag-s rhod rhus-t a1 spong fd4.de symph fd3.de• zinc
- **forenoon**: aeth agar ambr arg-n asar bar-c chinin-s cycl a1 dulc fd4.de gamb k* guaj kali-c laur led mag-c mag-m mur-ac nat-c hr1 **Nat-m** plat h2 symph fd3.de• vanil fd5.de
• **dinner**, eating amel.; before: ambr
• **hair** standing on end: mag-m
- **noon**: apis lac-ac lob spong fd4.de vanil fd5.de
• **sleep** agg.; after: bry
- **afternoon**: *Acon* am-c arg-met *Bar-c* carb-an caust chinin-s cina con *Croc* cycl dulc ferr a1 graph kali-chl kali-n *Lyc* mag-m meny nat-c h2 nit-ac petr phos k* ran-b sil h2 spong fd4.de stram sulph h2 symph fd3.de• [bell-p-sp dcm1]
• **16** h: mag-c mag-m a1 mag-p a1 sep h2
• **dinner**; after: anac ars bell h1 carb-an mag-p bro1
• **menses**; during: nat-m
• **not** relieved by heat of stove, but relieved by covering up warmly in bed: *Podo*
• **sleep** | **siesta** agg.; after: anac *Bry* cycl a1 merc
• **subsequent** heat, without: nit-ac ph-ac
- **evening**: *Acon* k* agar agn hr1 all-c alum h2* am-c k* *Am-m* ambr apis arg-met arg-n a1 arn ars bro1 aur aur-ar k2 bell bov brom bry calad *Calc* canth caps carb-an carb-v carbn-s cedr bro1 cham choc srj3• cimx cocc colch crot-c sk4• cycl h1 dulc k* *Ferr* ferr-i k2 graph guaj hep ign kali-c kali-i kali-m k2 kali-n kali-s kali-sil k2 kreos lyc mag-c bro1 mag-m mag-p bro1 mag-s mang mentho bro1 meny merc k* *Merc-c* *Mur-ac* nat-c nat-m *Nat-p* *Nat-s* nat-sil fd3.de• nit-ac ol-j bro1 petr phos k* plac rzf5• podo propr sa3• *Psor* **Puls** k* ran-b *Rhus-t* k* ruta fd4.de sep k* **Sil** a1 spong fd4.de squil h1 sulph *Tarent* thuj tritic-vg fd5.de tub k2 vanil fd5.de verat a1 zinc
• **eating**; after: croc *Kali-c*
• **flushes** of heat in the face; with: nit-ac petr
• **hair** standing on end, sensation of: am-c *Bar-c* calc *Dulc* nit-ac
• **headache**; during: *Acon* bry
• **lasting** all night, with cold legs: aur
• **lying**:
⁝ **bed**; in:
⁝ **agg.**: am-m aur bov bry caps a1 cench k2 colch kali-sil k2 lyc *Merc* merc-c *Mur-ac* podo tritic-vg fd5.de vanil fd5.de *Zinc*
⁝ **amel.**: kali-i kali-n mag-m mag-s tub k2
• **nausea** and cold limbs, with: apis
• **sleep**; when falling asleep: lyc phos k*
• **sleepiness**; with: lycps-v nat-m op
• **wakes**, as often as she: **Am-m**
• **walking** agg.: puls
• **warm** stove agg.: merc
- **night**: acon k* agar aloe alum bro1 am-c k* ambr h1 ars bro1 aur-ar k2 bamb-a stb2.de• bov caps carb-v h2 *Card-m* caust cedr bro1 croc des-ac rbp6 dulc bro1* ferr h1* graph hep c1 iris c1 kali-i kali-s fd4.de mag-c bro1 mag-p bro1 mentho bro1 *Merc* bro1 mur-ac a1 nat-sil fd3.de• ol-j bro1 ozone sde2• *Phos* bro1 *Puls* bro1 ruta fd4.de sep bro1 spong fd4.de staph h1 symph fd3.de• verat k2
• **21**.30 h has to go to bed, followed by shaking chill: *Sabad*
• **lying** down, and as often as she wakes without thirst; after: **Am-m**
• **menses** | **before** | **agg.**: aloe
⁝ **during** | **agg.**: *Lach*
• **sleep** agg.; during: am-c grat nat-c h2 *Sil* h2* symph fd3.de•
• **undressing**: acon *Merc-c* op
- **accompanied** by:
• **hot** breath (See RESPIRATION - Hot - chill)
• **illness**; recurrent acute (See GENERALS - Complaints - acute - recurrent - accompanied - heat)
• **voice**; complaints of: **Merc** bg2 nat-c bg2 nux-v bg2
- **air**:
• **chest** is chilly in the air; the well-covered: ran-b
- **air**: ...
• **cold** air were blowing on uncovered parts; as if: mosch
- **air** agg.; draft of: arizon-l nl2• caust h2 nux-v tl1 olib-sac wmh1 ozone sde2•
- **air** agg.; in open: anac c1 cycl a1
• **evening**: bapt a1
• **and** heat in the room: *Chin*
⁝ **whole** body, but not in cold air; over the: caust
- **apyrexia**, during the: anac *Ars* bry caps cocc daph dig *Hep* led nat-m puls ran-s sabad sil verat
- **bad** news; after: sulph
- **bed**, but heat in bed; outside of: mez
- **children**; in: | **newborns**: coli jl2
- **coffee** agg.; abuse of: *Cham* *Nux-v* [tax jsj7]
- **coition**; after: nat-m k*
- **drinking** | **after** | **agg.**: caps hr1* tarax h1*
• **agg.**: ars kali-ar k2 verat k2
- **eating** | **after** | **agg.**: alum-p k2 *Ars* asar calc carb-an caust cycl a1 kali-c kali-sil k2 nux-v rhus-t sil sulph tarax teucr zinc
• **while** | **agg.**: carb-an euph ran-s staph h1
- **exciting** news: gels sulph
- **fever**, during (See FEVER - Chilliness)
- **frequent** attacks of: camph tl1 diphtox jl2
• **intermediate** sleep; with: **Nux-m**
• **short** attacks of: ferr
- **frightful** dream; after: crot-c sk4•
- **hair** standing on end, sensation of: am-c bar-c calc caust dulc grat mag-m mur-ac nit-ac
- **headache**:
• **after**: alum kr1 *Rhus-t* kr1
⁝ **pulsating** in occiput; after: dros kr1
• **during**: agar kr1 am-c kr1 anthraci c1 arg-n a1 cadm-s c1 **Calc** kr1 **Caust** kr1 cist kr1 coca kr1* **Coff** kr1 **Coloc** kr1 con h2 **Cupr** kr1 cycl hr1 dulc fd4.de elat kr1 eupi c1 *Ferr* kr1 ham fd3.de• ign hr1 **Kali-c** kr1 kali-s fd4.de *Kola* stb3• lac-ac c1 **Lac-d** kr1 lac-loxod-a hrn2• lach k13 limen-b-c hrn2* **Merc** kr1 mez kr1 **Mosch** kr1 nit-ac kr1 *Nux-v* kr1 ozone sde2• **Puls** kr1 rhus-t a1 ruta fd4.de *Sang* a1* *Sil* kr1 spong fd4.de *Sulph* kr1 *Thuj* kr1 tritic-vg fd5.de verat k2 zing kr1
⁝ **one** side: **Ign** kr1
⁝ **menorrhagia**, during: chinin-s kr1
⁝ **Temple** | **right**: ziz kr1
- **heat**; before flushes of: sang kr1
- **influenza**; after: chin tl1
- **itching**; with: petr alj puls alj
○ • **Abdomen**: mag-c h2
- **labor** pains:
• **after**: *Kali-c* *Kali-i*
• **first**; from: gels c1
• **with**: gels hr1
- **lasting** all night (See night)
- **laughter** | **after**: hura bg1
- **lifting** the bed clothes: agar h2
- **menses**: *(↗menses - before - agg.; Menses)*
• **before** | **agg.**: *(↗menses; Menses)* acon bg2 aloe am-c k* ant-c bg2 ant-t bg2* apis bro1 *Calc* k* *Caul* cham bro1 cimic bg2* coloc bg2 gels bg2 glyc bro1 graph bro1 ign bg2 ip bg2 *Kali-c* k* kali-i bg2 *Kreos* k* **Lyc** k* *Mag-c* k* mang bg2 nat-c bg2 nat-m nux-v k* phos bg2 plat bro1 **Puls** k* ruta bg2 sec bro1 *Sep* k* **Sil** k* *Sulph* bg2* thuj bg2 verat k* zinc bg2
• **during** | **agg.**: am-c k* apis bro1 bell berb k* *Bry* bufo calc k* *Carb-an* carbn-s castm *Caul* cham bro1 cimic hr1 *Cocc* cycl eupi c1 glyc bro1 *Graph* k* ip kali-i kreos led k2 mag-c nat-c a1 nat-m nat-p *Nux-v* k* *Phos* plat bro1 **Puls** k* *Sec* k* **Sep** k* **Sil** k* **Sulph** k* *Tab* vanil fd5.de verat k2* zinc zing
- **motion**; from slightest: ars bro1 nux-v bro1* spig br1*
- **movement** of the bedclothes; slightest●: acon **Arn** k* *Calc* **NUX-V** k●* rhus-t stram sulph
- **nausea**; during: cadm-s br1 ruta fd4.de
- **nervous**: dulc fd4.de gels hr1* [tax jsj7]

- **pain**; with: alum-sil k2 *Ars* bar-c kr1 bry kr1 calc kr1 caps a1* *Caust* dulc kr1 euphr kr1 graph kr1 kali-c kr1 kali-n kr1 led kr1 lyc kr1 mez kr1* nat-m kr1 *Puls* rhus-t kr1 ruta fd4.de sep j5.de squil kr1 syph gk tub gk
  - **abdomen**; in: merc h1
    - **burning**: caps h1 mag-c h2
  - **burning** pains, with: caps kr1
  - **throbbing** pains; with burning: hep kr1
- **part** touched: spig
- **perspiration**; with: acon ail am-c aml-ns ant-c arg-n ars bry *Calc* calc-i k2 *Caps* chin cocc br1 dig **Eup-per** eup-pur euph led mur-ac a1 *Nat-m* **Nux-v** petr phos psor puls *Pyrog* ruta fd4.de sabad sang sulph thuj **Tub**
  - **warm** in bed; as soon as he gets: arg-n
- **sneezing**:
  - **after**: petr-ra shn4•
  - **with**: ox-ac c1
- **stool**:
  - **after** | **agg.**: ambr a1 bufo grat mag-m *Plat*
  - **before**: *Ars* k* bapt bar-c benz-ac calad camph bro1 dig elat bro1 ip mang *Merc* k* *Mez* nat-c phos k* puls verat k*
  - **during** | **agg.**: aesc alum bg2 *Ars* k* bell k* calc-s castm bg2 *Colch* bro1 con bg2 dig bg2 hyos b7.de* ip bro1 *Jatr-c* bro1 kali-c bg2 *Mag-m* *Mag-p* hr1 merc bg2* mez k* podo c1 ptel bg2 *Puls* b7a.de* rheum k* ric bro1 *Sec* bro1 *Sil* spig b7.de* stann sulph bg2 trom bro1 **Verat** k*
  - **urging** to | **during**: mag-m h2
- **subsequent** heat, without: agn dulc fd4.de lyc nat-c hr1
- **sun** amel.: anac c1
- **uncovering** agg.: nux-v bro1
- **urination**:
  - **after**:
    - **agg.**: arn **Plat** puls sep sulph thuj
    - **amel.**: med
  - **before**: *Med* nit-ac
  - **during** | **agg.**: gels br1 *Lyc* *Nit-ac* **Plat** sep *Stram* thuj
  - **urging** to urinate:
    - **after**: caust h2
    - **followed** by: senec
    - **on**: hyper *Med*
- **vertigo**; after: nat-c a1
- **vomiting**:
  - **after**: aeth c1
  - **while**: ars bro1 dulc k* puls bro1 tab bro1
- **waking**; on: card-m staph
- **walking** | **after** | **agg.**: gins kali-ar k2
  - **air** agg.; in open: acon cham chin dig euph led merc-c plb
- **warm**:
  - **bathing** | **amel.**: ozone sde2•
  - **breath**; with hot (See RESPIRATION - Hot - chill)
  - **room**:
    - **agg.**: ant-c c1* arg-n a1 carb-ac cinnb dulc fd4.de grat iod kali-br hr1* lact ozone sde2• *Puls* **Sil** a1 spong fd4.de symph fd3.de•
      - **more** in a warm room than in the open air: bry grat *Puls*
    - **entering** a warm room; when | **air**; from open: am-c ars bar-c bry [tax jsj7]
  - **touch**; yet warm to: corn-f br1 dulc fd4.de
- **washing** agg.: bry zinc
- **waves**; in: bufo bg2

CHOLERA; during (See RECTUM - Cholera - accompanied - coldness)

COLD:
- **agg.** | **day** in the summer; on a: acon aran cham dulc rhus-t
- **air**:
  - **entering** cold air:
    - **agg.**: aesc **Agar** k* *Ars* k* ars-s-f k2 berb bg2 bry k* *Calc* calc-sil k2 *Camph* k* **Caps** k* caust k* cham k* **Coff** k* **Cycl** k* dig k* ferr-i k2 ham fd3.de• hell k* hep k* kali-ar kali-c k* kali-sil k2 **Mez** k* mosch k* nat-ar nat-c nat-p nux-m k* **Nux-v** k* petr k* phos k* *Rhod* k* *Rhus-t* k* sabad k* sep k* sil k* spig k* verat k* *Zinc* zinc-p k2
    - **amel.**: meph a1
  - **entering** cold air from a warm room agg.: *Puls*
- **bathing** | **agg.**: aran cedr
- **drinks** | **agg.**: rhus-t ptk1

COLD; AFTER TAKING A: acon bg2 ars bg2 bell bg2 *Bry* bg2 calc bg2 *Camph* b7.de* cham bg2 chin bg2 graph bg2 *Lyc* b4a.de* *Merc* bg2 *Nux-v* bg2 phos bg2 *Puls* bg2 rhus-t bg2 *Sep* b4a.de* sil bg2 spig bg2 sulph bg2 verat bg2

COLDNESS (= objective): acon b2.de* agar b2.de agn b2.de alum b2.de alum-p k2 am-c b2.de* *Am-m* b2.de* ambr b2.de* anac b2.de* ang b2.de ant-c b2.de *Ant-t* b2.de* apis bg2 aran bg2 *Arn* b2.de* **Ars** b2.de* asaf b2.de* asar b2.de* *Aur* b2.de* bar-c b2.de* bar-m k2 bell b2.de* *Bism* b2.de* borx b2.de* bov b2.de* brom bg2 *Bry* b2.de* *Calad* b2.de* calc b2.de* calc-i k2 **Camph** b2.de* *Cann-s* b2.de* *Canth* b2.de* caps b2.de* carb-an b2.de* *Carb-v* b2.de* *Caust* b2.de* *Cham* b2.de* *Chel* b2.de* chin b2.de* cic b2.de* cina b2.de cocc b2.de* coff b2.de* colch b2.de* *Coloc* b2.de* *Con* b2.de* *Croc* b2.de* crot-h bg2 **Cupr** b2.de* cycl b2.de* dig b2.de* dros b2.de* *Dulc* b2.de* *Euph* b2.de* euphr b2.de* *Ferr* b2.de* ferr-ar k2 graph b2.de* *Hell* b2.de* *Helo-s* rwt2• hep b2.de* *Hyos* b2.de* ign b2.de* iod b2.de* ip b2.de* kali-c b2.de *Kali-n* b2.de* kreos b2.de* *Lach* b2.de* *Laur* b2.de* *Led* b2.de* *Lyc* b2.de* m-ambo b2.de* m-arct b2.de m-aust b2.de *Mag-c* b2.de* mag-m b2.de mang b2.de* meny b2.de* merc b2.de* merc-c b4a.de* **Mez** b2.de* *Mosch* b2.de* mur-ac b2.de* *Nat-c* b2.de* *Nat-m* b2.de* nit-ac b2.de* nux-m b2.de* *Nux-v* b2.de* olnd b2.de* **Op** b2.de* par b2.de* petr b2.de* ph-ac b2.de* phos b2.de* plat b2.de* *Plb* b2.de* **Puls** b2.de* *Ran-b* b2.de* rhod b2.de *Rhus-t* b2.de* ruta b2.de* sabad b2.de* sabin b2.de* samb b2.de* *Sars* b2.de* sec b2.de* sel b2.de* seneg b2.de *Sep* b2.de* sil b2.de* spig b2.de* spong b2.de* squil b2.de* stann b2.de **Staph** b2.de* *Stram* b2.de* stront-c b2.de* sul-ac b2.de sulph b2.de* tab bg2 tarax b2.de teucr b2.de thuj b2.de* valer b2.de* **Verat** b2.de* verb b2.de* zinc b2.de* [tax jsj7]
- **one** side: alum b2.de ambr b2.de anac b2.de ant-t b2.de arn b2.de bar-c b2.de bell b2.de bry b2.de *Caust* b2.de cham b2.de chin b2.de cocc b2.de croc b2.de dig b2.de ign b2.de kali-c b2.de lyc b2.de nat-c b2.de *Nux-v* b2.de par b2.de ph-ac b2.de phos b2.de plat b2.de **Puls** b2.de **Rhus-t** b2.de ruta b2.de sabad b2.de sars b2.de spig b2.de stann b2.de stram b2.de sul-ac b2.de sulph b2.de thuj b2.de verb b2.de
- **morning**: acon b7.de *Ars* b4a.de carb-an b4.de con b4.de dros b7a.de hell b7.de mez b4.de nat-c b4.de verat b7.de
- **forenoon**: cycl b7.de rhod b4.de sars b4.de
- **afternoon**: bar-c b4.de camph b7.de canth b7.de caust b4.de hyos b7.de *Kali-n* b4.de* nux-v b7.de phos b4.de *Ran-b* b7.de*
- **evening**: *Am-m* b7.de* ars b4.de bry b7.de* calc b4.de camph b7.de carb-v b4.de *Chin* b7.de* dulc b4a.de *Ferr* b7.de* kali-n b4.de laur b7.de m-aust b7.de mag-c b4.de mang b4.de *Merc* b4a.de par b7.de petr b4a.de ran-b b7.de rhod b4.de rhus-t b7.de* sabad b7a.de *Staph* b7.de
- **night**: *Ambr* b7.de* ars b4a.de bar-c b4a.de caps b7.de *Con* b4a.de euphr b7a.de *Hyos* b7.de* merc b4a.de *Nit-ac* b4.de* *Puls* b7.de* sabad b7.de thuj b4a.de
- **chilliness**; without external: led tl1
- **general**; in (See Chill in)
- ○ **Blood** vessels, in (See Internal - coldness - blood)
- **Body**; of (See Chill in; Icy; SKIN - Coldness)
- **Bones**, in (See Internal - coldness - bones)
- **External** parts | **sensation** of: acon b2.de* agar b2.de* am-m b2.de* ambr b2.de* ant-t b2.de* *Arn* b2.de* ars b2.de* asar b2.de* bar-c b2.de* bell b2.de* borx b2.de* bov b2.de* bry b2.de* *Calc* b2.de* camph b2.de* cann-s b2.de* canth b2.de* caps b2.de* carb-v b2.de* *Caust* b2.de* *Chel* b2.de* chin b2.de* cic b2.de* cocc b2.de* coff b2.de* coloc b2.de* con b2.de* croc b2.de* *Dig* b2.de* dulc b2.de* euph b2.de* graph b2.de* hell b2.de* hyos b2.de* ign b2.de* ip b2.de* kreos b2.de* lach b2.de* laur b2.de* led b2.de* lyc b2.de* m-ambo b2.de* m-arct b2.de *M-aust* b2.de mag-c b2.de* mang b2.de* meny b2.de* **Merc** b2.de* mez b2.de* **Mosch** b2.de* mur-ac b2.de* nat-c b2.de* nux-m b2.de* olnd b2.de* par b2.de* petr b2.de* ph-ac b2.de* phos b2.de* **Plat** b2.de* plb b2.de* *Puls* b2.de* ran-b b2.de* ran-s b2.de* rhod b2.de* **Rhus-t** b2.de* ruta b2.de* sabad b2.de* sabin b2.de* samb b2.de* **Sec** b2.de* sep b2.de* spig b2.de* spong b2.de* staph b2.de* stront-c b2.de* sulph b2.de* thuj b2.de* valer b2.de* **Verat** b2.de* verb b2.de* viol-t b2.de*
- **Hands**; with cold: buth-a sp1

- **Internal** parts | **sensation** of: acon b2.de alum b2.de ambr b2.de ant-c b2.de ant-t b2.de arn b2.de *Ars* b2.de asaf b2.de bar-c b2.de bell b2.de bov b2.de bry b2.de **Calc** b2.de camph b2.de caps b2.de carb-an b2.de carb-v b2.de caust b2.de chel b2.de chin b2.de colch b2.de con b2.de croc b2.de dros b2.de graph b2.de hell b2.de ign b2.de ip b2.de kali-c b2.de kali-n b2.de kreos b2.de lach b2.de **Laur** b2.de *Lyc* b2.de m-aust b2.de mag-c b2.de mang b2.de *Meny* b2.de merc b2.de mez b2.de mosch b2.de nat-c b2.de nat-m b2.de nit-ac b2.de *Nux-v* b2.de olnd b2.de *Par* b2.de ph-ac b2.de phos b2.de plat b2.de plb b2.de puls b2.de rhus-t b2.de ruta b2.de sabad b2.de sars b2.de sec b2.de *Sep* b2.de spong b2.de sul-ac b2.de *Sulph* b2.de valer b2.de verat b2.de zinc b2.de
- **Single** parts: *Acon* b2.de* agar b2.de* *Agn* b2.de* alum b2.de* am-c b2.de* am-m b2.de* *Ambr* b2.de* anac b2.de* ang b2.de* ant-c b2.de* *Ant-t* b2.de* *Arn* b2.de* *Ars* b2.de* asaf b2.de* asar b2.de* *Aur* b2.de* bar-c b2.de* *Bell* b2.de* bism b2.de* borx b2.de* bov b2.de* bry b2.de* **Calad** b2.de* *Calc* b2.de* *Camph* b2.de* cann-s b2.de* canth b2.de* caps b2.de* carb-an b2.de* carb-v b2.de* **Caust** b2.de* cham b2.de* *Chel* b2.de* *Chin* b2.de* cic b2.de* cina b2.de* cocc b2.de* coff b2.de* colch b2.de* coloc b2.de* *Con* b2.de* croc b2.de* cupr b2.de* cycl b2.de* *Dig* b2.de* dros b2.de* dulc b2.de* euphr b2.de* ferr b2.de* glon bg2 *Graph* b2.de* hell b2.de* hep b2.de* hyos b2.de* ign b2.de* **Ip** b2.de* *Kali-c* b2.de* *Kali-n* b2.de* kreos b2.de* lach b2.de* laur b2.de* led b2.de* lyc b2.de* m-ambo b2.de m-arct b2.de* m-aust b2.de mag-c b2.de* mag-m b2.de* mang b2.de* meny b2.de* *Merc* b2.de* *Mez* b2.de* mosch b2.de* mur-ac b2.de* nat-c b2.de* nat-m b2.de* *Nit-ac* b2.de* nux-m b2.de* *Nux-v* b2.de* olnd b2.de* op b2.de* par b2.de* petr b2.de* ph-ac b2.de* *Phos* b2.de* plat b2.de* plb b2.de* *Puls* b2.de* ran-b b2.de* rhod b2.de* **Rhus-t** b2.de* ruta b2.de* sabad b2.de* sabin b2.de* samb b2.de* sars b2.de* sec b2.de* sel b2.de* seneg b2.de* **Sep** b2.de* sil b2.de* spig b2.de* spong b2.de* squil b2.de* stann b2.de* staph b2.de* stram b2.de* stront-c b2.de* sul-ac b2.de* **Sulph** b2.de* tarax b2.de* teucr b2.de* *Thuj* b2.de* **Verat** b2.de* verb b2.de* zinc b2.de*

COMA; with (See MIND - Coma - chills)

COMPLAINTS starting with chill: *Acon* b7a.de

CONGESTIVE (See Pernicious)

CONVULSIONS; after epileptic: ars bg2 calc k* camph bg2 carb-v bg2 caust tl1 cocc bg2 **Cupr** k* sil bg2 sulph k* verat bg2

CORYZA:
- **agg.**: anac bg2 *Ant-t* bg2 bry bg2 calad bg2 caps bg2 caust bg2 *Cham* bg2 **Graph** bg2 hep bg2 nat-c bg2 *Nux-v* bg2 **Puls** bg2 spig bg2 spong bg2 sulph bg2
- **with** (See NOSE - Coryza - chilliness)

COUGH agg.: apis ptk1 *Ars* k* bry k* calc k* carb-v k* *Con* k* cupr k* eup-per ptk1 hyos k* lyc pd *Mez* k* nat-c nux-v k* phos k* **Puls** k* *Rhus-t* k* *Sabad* k* sep k* sulph k* thuj ptk1 tub bg verat k*

COVERED (See External; Uncovering)

CREEPING: *(↗SKIN - Goose)* acon all-c aloe am-m aml-ns anac k* *Ang* k* ant-t k* apis ars ars-h asaf k* berb k* bol-la *Bry* k* calad calc k* calc-p k* camph k* cham k* chlor k* cimx clem k* crot-h k* crot-t k* dig k* dros k* equis-h c1 ferr a1 frax a1* gast a1 grat k* hir skp7• kali-i lac-c bg3* lyc k* meny merc k* merc-sul mez *Nat-m* k* ph-ac k* *Psor* k* rhus-t ruta samb k* sec k* *Spig* k* stram k* sul-ac *Sulph Thuj* k* til k* *Tub* valer k* verat k* zinc a1 zing k*
- **morning**: cina lyc k* spig k* viol-t k*
  - **rising** from bed, creeping coldness of abdomen; on: meny
- **forenoon**: chlor
  - **warm** room; when entering a: aloe
- **afternoon**: alum k* arg-n calc k* calen carb-an caust psor k*
  - **16**-18 h: alum arg-n
  - **dinner**; after: thuj k*
  - **sleep** | **siesta** agg.; after: bry
- **evening**: am-m arg-n *Ars* ars-h ars-s-f k2 bell calc k* chlor gins k* kali-i lyc k* nat-m psor *Puls* rhus-t k* sul-ac k* thuj k* *Tub* zing k*
- **night**: hep merc-c k* puls tub
- **alternating** with heat: anthraci
- **cold** air agg.: anac bufo
- **cold**; before taking a: merc tl1
- **menses**; before: ant-t alj1*
- **motion** agg.: acon sin-a k*
- **rising** from sitting, when: coff k*
- **standing** agg.: coloc k* ham k*

Creeping: ...
- **stool**:
  - **after** | **agg.**: ambr grat
  - **before**: *Mez*
  - **during** | **agg.**: nat-m k*
- **urination** agg.; after: eug plat sars sep
- **warm** room, in a: aloe *Puls* ran-b k*

DELIVERY: | **during**: sulph bg2

DESCENDING: *(↗BACK - Coldness - extending - down)*
- **agg.**: *(↗BACK - Coldness - extending - down)* acon **Agar** k* am-m aml-ns apis ars k* ars-h arum-t bar-c k* *Bell* k* borx k* brom calad canth k* carb-ac caust k* cedr chel *Cic* k* cocc k* *Coff* k* colch k* croc k* *Eup-per* eup-pur *Gels* bg2 kalm bg2 kreos k* lach k* lil-t lob lyc bg2 mag-c k* merc bg2 *Mez* k* **Mosch** k* nat-m bg2 *Phos* k* plat bg2 *Psor* ruta bg2 *Sabad* k* *Staph* k* **Stram** k* stront-c bg2 *Sul-ac* k* sulph k* thuj k* *Valer* k* **Verat** k* zinc k*
- **head** to toes: verat

DIARRHEA:
- **after** | **agg.**: ambr b7.de puls b7.de
- **before**: ant-t b7.de *Verat* b7.de
- **during**: aloe ambr k* apis cop br1 kali-n k* sulph k*
  - **mucous** colitis: cop br1

DISORDERED stomach: ant-c **Ip** *Puls*

DRINKING:
- **agg.**: adam srj5• alum ant-t k* arn k* **Ars** k* ars-s-f k2 asaf bg2 **Asar** k* bry k* cadm-s **Calc** k* cann-s cann-xyz bg2 **Caps** k* *Chel* k* **Chin** k* *Chinin-ar* cimx cocc k* *Con* croc k* *Elaps* k* **Eup-per** k* hep k* kali-ar lach bg2* *Lob* lyc merc sne mez k* nat-m k* nit-ac k* **Nux-v** k* puls k* *Rhus-t* k* sep k* sil k* sulph k* *Tarax* k* *Tarent* k* thuj k* **Verat** k*
- **amel.**: bry k* carb-an k* **Caust** k* **Cupr** k* *Graph* k* *Ip* k* manc ptk1 mosch k* nux-v k* oci-sa sp1 olnd k* *Phos* k* rhus-t k* sil k* spig k* tarax k*
- **cold** water is felt as if pouring over outside of thorax: *Verat*
- **cough**, causes: cimx *Psor*
- **hastens** and increases the chill and causes nausea: *Eup-per*
- **ice** water were rising and falling; as if | **lung**; through a cylindrical opening in left: elaps
- **increases** the chill and causes vomiting: **Ars** cadm-s nux-v
- **unbearable**; makes headache and all the other symptoms: **Cimx**

EATING:
- **after**:
  - **agg.**: acon bg2 agar k* alum k* alum-sil k2 am-c k* am-m k* anac k* ant-t bg2 *Arg-n* **Ars** k* ars-s-f k2 **Asar** k* aster vh **Bell** k* borx k* *Bry* k* *Calc* k* calc-sil k2 camph cann-i c1 **Carb-an** k* *Carb-v* k* carbn-s *Caust* k* cham k* chin k* cist bg2 coc-c k* coli jl2 coloc k* con k* cor-r bg2 croc k* cycl k* dig *Graph* k* ign k* *Ip* k* iris bg2 kali-ar kali-bi bg2* **Kali-c** k* kali-p lach k* *Lyc* k* nat-c k* nat-m k* nat-p nit-ac k* *Nux-v* k* par bg2 *Petr* k* ph-ac k* phos k* puls k* **Ran-b** k* *Rhus-t* k* sel k* sep k* sil k* staph k* *Sulph* k* **Tarax** k* teucr k* ther verat k* zinc k* zinc-p k2
  - **amel.**: acon **Ambr** k* *Ars* k* bov k* cann-s cann-xyz bg2 chel k* cop cupr bg2 *Cur Ferr* k* hir skp7• ign k* **Iod** k* kali-c k* kola stb3• laur k* mez k* *Nat-c* k* petr k* *Phos* k* rhus-t k* sabad k* squil k* stront-c k* thlas bg2
  - **immediately** after: coli jl2
- **before** | **agg.**: ambr b7.de* bov bg2 calc bg2 *Carb-an* b4.de* carb-v bg2 chin bg2 euph b4.de* graph b4.de* iod bg2 laur bg2 lyc bg2 *Nat-c* bg2 phos bg2 puls bg2 rhus-t bg2 sep bg2 sulph bg2
- **overeating** agg.; after: ant-c cycl **Ip** *Nux-m* **Puls**
- **while** | **agg.**: apis bov carb-an k* carb-v k* cocc k* con k* *Euph* k* kali-c k* lyc k* nit-ac k* *Ran-s* k* raph k* *Rhus-t* sep k* sil k* staph k* sulph sne

EMISSIONS; after: graph bg2 merc b4.de* nat-m bg2

EXCITEMENT; after (= cold shivers; emotional): asar bg2* calc cic crat br1 **Gels** k* goss br1 ign rhus-v bg2 teucr valer pd zinc-val ptk1

EXERTION: | **after** | **agg.**: arn *Ars* bar-c bry bg2 crat br1 eup-per kali-s merc nux-v rhus-t sil sulph zinc-val ptk1
- **amel.** | **air**; in open: alum **Caps** mag-c mag-m **Puls** spong staph sul-ac

EXPOSURE, after: *Acon* ang ant-c *Aran* arn *Ars* bar-c bol-la *Bry* cact **Calc** canth carb-v **Cedr** *Chin* *Chinin-s* cimx$_{bro1}$ dros *Dulc* eucal eup-per *Hep* kali-c lach led nat-m *Nat-s* plac$_{rzf5}$• **Rhus-t** sep spig *Tarent* zinc
- **cold** bathing, too frequent: ant-c *Calc* *Rhus-t* *Tarent*
- **draft**; to a: *Acon* bar-c *Calc* canth *Ferr* *Hep* *Merc* *Tarent* tub$_{k2}$
  - **heated**; when: acon carb-v ran-b$_{k2}$ rhus-t$_{gk}$ sil tub$_{gk}$
- **malarial** influences: **Arn** carb-ac **Cedr** *Chin* chinin-ar *Chinin-s* corn$_{br1}$ corn-f$_{br1}$ *Eucal* eup-per *Ferr* ip *Nat-m* *Nat-s* *Nux-v* **Psor** *Sulph*
  - **chronic**: corn$_{br1}$ corn-f$_{br1}$
- **rains**; during: *Aran* bell *Calc* cedr cur *Dulc* *Ferr* **Nat-s** **Rhus-t** zinc
- **seaside**, residing at: *Nat-m* *Nat-s*
- **soil** freshly turned up: *Nat-m*
- **sun**; to the heat of: bell *Cact* glon lach nat-c
- **swamps**: *Ang* *Cedr* chin *Chinin-s* corn$_{br1}$ corn-f$_{br1}$ eucal *Nat-m* **Nat-s** nux-v
  - **chronic**: corn$_{br1}$ corn-f$_{br1}$
- **tropical** countries: *Ang* *Bry* **Cedr** chin corn$_{br1}$ corn-f$_{br1}$ *Nat-m* **Nat-s** podo ter
  - **chronic**: corn$_{br1}$ corn-f$_{br1}$
- **water**:
  - **standing** in water: arn *Calc* led *Rhus-t*
  - **water** courses; from living at: *Calc* *Nat-m* *Nat-s* *Nux-v*
- **weather** | **warm** (See Summer; Weather - hot)
- **wet**: *(↗Weather - cold; GENERALS - Wet - getting)*
  - **becoming**; from: acon *Aran*$_{k*}$ bar-c bell *Bry* *Calc* *Cedr* *Dulc* *Nat-s* **Rhus-t** sep *Tarent*
    - ⁝ **overheated**; when: acon *Calc* *Clem* colch **Rhus-t** sep sil
  - **rooms**; sleeping in wet: aran$_{k*}$ *Ars* *Calc* carb-v chinin-ar lach *Nat-s* *Rhus-t*
- **wind**, to violent: nit-ac$_{h2}$
- **working**:
  - **clay**; in: **Calc**
  - **water**; in: **Calc** *Rhus-t*

EXTENDING:
- **downward** (See Descending - agg.)
- **from** (See Beginning)
- **upward** (See Ascending agg.)

EXTERNAL: **Acon**$_{k*}$ *Aeth*$_{k*}$ agar$_{k*}$ *Alum*$_{k*}$ alum-sil$_{k2}$ am-c am-caust$_{a1}$ **Am-m**$_{k*}$ *Ant-t*$_{k*}$ *Apis* aran arn$_{k*}$ **Ars**$_{k*}$ *Ars-i* ars-s-f$_{k2}$ bar-c *Bar-m*$_{k*}$ bar-s$_{k2}$ bell$_{k*}$ bry calc$_{k*}$ calc-i$_{k2}$ calc-sil$_{k2}$ **Camph**$_{k*}$ *Cann-s*$_{b7a.de}$ canth$_{k*}$ caps *Caust*$_{k*}$ cham$_{k*}$ chel$_{k*}$ chin$_{k*}$ cimic$_{k*}$ cimx$_{k*}$ cina colch$_{k*}$ con$_{k*}$ crat$_{br1}$ cupr$_{b7.de*}$ cupr-ar$_{k*}$ *Dig*$_{k*}$ dulc euph$_{bg2}$ *Euphr*$_{k*}$ ferr-m$_{k*}$ gamb$_{k*}$ gels$_{k*}$ hyos$_{k*}$ **Ign**$_{k*}$ iod$_{k*}$ *Ip*$_{k*}$ kali-ar$_{k*}$ kali-bi$_{k*}$ kali-c$_{k*}$ kali-chl$_{k*}$ kali-m$_{k2}$ kali-n$_{pd}$ kali-p kali-sil$_{k2}$ lach$_{k*}$ laur led$_{b7.de}$ mag-c$_{k*}$ meny *Merc*$_{k*}$ *Merc-c*$_{k*}$ *Mez*$_{k*}$ mosch$_{k*}$ mur-ac$_{k*}$ naja nat-m$_{k*}$ nat-s$_{k*}$ **Nit-ac**$_{k*}$ *Nux-m*$_{b7a.de}$ nux-v **Olnd**$_{k*}$ *Op*$_{b7a.de}$ petr$_{k*}$ *Phos*$_{k*}$ plb$_{k*}$ ran-b$_{bg2}$ rhus-t$_{k*}$ *Sabad*$_{k*}$ *Sec*$_{k*}$ sil$_{k*}$ squil$_{b7.de}$ sul-ac$_{k*}$ *Sulph*$_{k*}$ til **Verat**$_{k*}$ *Verat-v*$_{k*}$ *Verb*$_{k*}$ **Zinc**$_{k*}$ zinc-p$_{k2}$
- **morning**: acon$_{k*}$ aeth$_{k*}$
- **afternoon**: chel ol-an$_{a1}$ puls
  - **sweat**; during: gels
- **evening**: am-c calc$_{k*}$ dulc$_{k*}$ *Gamb*$_{k*}$ nux-m$_{k*}$ ran-b$_{k*}$ rhus-t$_{k*}$
  - **bed** agg.; in: nat-m$_{k*}$
  - **lasting** until 4 h: gamb
- **night**: nit-ac$_{k*}$ phos$_{k*}$
  - **sleep** agg.; during: crot-h
  - **waking** agg.; after: bov bry
- **cholera**, as in: **Camph** colch$_{k*}$ *Sec* **Verat**
- **excitement** agg.: crat$_{br1}$
- **exertion** agg.: crat$_{br1}$
- **hair** were standing on end; with sensation as if the: am-c *Bar-c* calc cina dulc meny nit-ac puls *Sil*
- **only** external: *Ars*$_{b4a.de}$ nit-ac$_{b4a.de}$
- **spots**, in: *Ambr* ars bell bry **Caust** *Cham* hep **Ign** *Led* lyc merc **Mez** mosch nux-v *Par*$_{k*}$ petr plat$_{sne}$ **Puls** rhus-t **Sep** *Sil* *Spig* thuj
- **stool** | **urging** to; during: ant-c$_{k*}$
- **stupor**; during: hep$_{k*}$

External: ...
- **thirty** six hours; during:
  - **with** thirst | **without** desire for warmth nor dread of open air, nor without subsequent heat: *Mez*
- **uncovering** agg.: arg-met cor-r$_{br1}$

FEVER; without: cadm-met$_{sp1}$

FLOWERS; from smell of: lac-c$_{ptk1}$

FOLLOWED BY: | **Head**; pain in (See HEAD - Pain - forehead - chill - before)

FREEZING; bad effects of: arist-cl$_{sp1}$

FREQUENT (= several a day): *Bac*$_{jl2}$ bell$_{h1}$ both$_{fne1}$•

FRIGHT agg.: *(↗MIND - Ailments - fright)* acon$_{k*}$ bell$_{bg2}$ **Gels**$_{k*}$ ign$_{k*}$ lyc *Merc*$_{k*}$ nux-v$_{k*}$ op$_{k*}$ plat$_{k*}$ *Puls*$_{k*}$ sep$_{dgt}$ sil$_{k*}$ *Verat*$_{k*}$

GOOSE FLESH (See SKIN - Goose)

GRIEF; from: *(↗MIND - Ailments - grief)* *Gels*$_{k*}$ *Ign*$_{k*}$

HEADACHE in forehead, with: mang$_{h2}$

HEAT:
- **external**: ars$_{h2}$ mur-ac$_{h2}$
- **overheated**; when: acon$_{k*}$ *Ant-c*$_{k*}$ ant-t bell$_{k*}$ *Bry*$_{k*}$ camph$_{k*}$ **Carb-v**$_{k*}$ chir-fl$_{gya2}$ dig$_{k*}$ glon$_{bg2}$ *Kali-c*$_{k*}$ nat-m$_{k*}$ *Nat-s* *Nux-v*$_{k*}$ op$_{k*}$ phos$_{k*}$ **Puls**$_{k*}$ rhus-t$_{k*}$ samb$_{ptk1}$ sep$_{k*}$ **Sil**$_{k*}$ *Thuj*$_{k*}$ verat$_{ptk1}$ zinc$_{k*}$
- **with** (See FEVER - Chill; with)
- **without** subsequent: *(↗FEVER - Succession - chill - followed - perspiration - intervening)* acon agar$_{h2}$ *Aran* bov calc camph chin ferr$_{ip}$ *Hep* led lyc mez *Mur-ac* nit-ac ph-ac ran-b sabad sep staph sulph

HELD down, desire to be: *Gels*$_{k*}$ *Lach*$_{k*}$

HEPATIC: | **night**: mag-s$_{sp1}$

HOLDING cold things in hand: bell$_{bg2}$ nat-m$_{bg2}$ sil$_{bg2}$ *Zinc*$_{bg2*}$

ICY COLDNESS of the body: *(↗Internal - icy)* acon-f ant-t aran$_{bg2}$ **Ars**$_{k*}$ bism *Bry* cadm-s *Calc* **Camph** **Carb-v** carbn-s carc$_{fd2.de}$• cic con cory$_{br1}$ **Cupr** cupr-ar$_{bg2}$ cypra-eg$_{sde6.de}$• hell helo$_{bg2}$ *Helo-s*$_{rwt2}$• hydr-ac$_{bg2}$ lachn laur$_{bg2}$ marb-w$_{es1}$• *Merc-c* nat-m$_{k*}$ nat-s nux-v olib-sac$_{wmh1}$ rad-br$_{sze8}$• ruta$_{fd4.de}$ **Sec** *Sep* **Sil** stram tab$_{bg2}$ *Tarent* verat$_{k*}$ zinc [heroin$_{sdj2}$]
- **accompanied** by:
  - ○ **Head** and redness of face; heat of (See HEAD - Heat - accompanied - face - redness - coldness)
  - **Head**; pain in (See HEAD - Pain - accompanied - coldness)
- **covered**, with clammy sweat and blueness; cannot bear to be: **Sec**
- **headache**; with (See HEAD - Pain - accompanied - coldness)
- **lying** on ice; as if: lyc$_{k*}$
- **menses**; during: *Sil*
- **single**; in:
  - **places**: ars calad camph *Meny*
  - **spots**: arg-met par petr verat
- **skin**; of:
  - **blue**, yet wants to be uncovered; skin dry and: camph
  - **perspiration** and also livid hands and feet; covered with a cold: *Stram* verat
  - **whole** body; the: cory$_{br1}$
    - ⁝ **cold** breath; with: camph$_{k13}$ **Carb-v** verat
- **uncover**, with desire to: *Camph*$_{k*}$ carb-v$_{mrr1}$ **Sec**
- **waking**; on: malar$_{jl2}$

INSPIRATION agg.: chin$_{bg2}$

INTERNAL: *Acon*$_{k*}$ adam$_{srj5}$• aeth$_{k*}$ agar$_{h2}$ *Agn*$_{k*}$ all-c$_{k*}$ *Alum*$_{k*}$ alum-p$_{k2}$ alum-sil$_{k2}$ am-c$_{ptk1}$ ambr$_{b2.de*}$ **Anac**$_{k*}$ ang$_{k*}$ ant-c$_{k*}$ ant-t$_{b2.de*}$ anth$_{vh}$ **ANTIP**$_{vh}$ **Apis** aran$_{ptk1}$ *Arn*$_{k*}$ **Ars**$_{k*}$ ars-i ars-s-f$_{k2}$ asaf$_{b2.de*}$ asar$_{bg2}$ astac$_{kr1}$ bamb-a$_{stb2.de}$• bar-c$_{k*}$ *Bell*$_{k*}$ *Berb* bov$_{k*}$ *Bry*$_{k*}$ **Calc**$_{k*}$ calc-i$_{k2}$ calc-sil$_{k2}$ camph$_{b2.de*}$ *Canth*$_{k*}$ *Caps*$_{k*}$ carb-an$_{b2.de*}$ carb-v$_{k*}$ **Caust**$_{k*}$ *Cham*$_{k*}$ *Chel*$_{k*}$ **Chin**$_{k*}$ *Chinin-s* cic$_{b7.de*}$ cimic$_{k*}$ cinnb$_{ptk1}$ **Cocc**$_{k*}$ *Coff*$_{k*}$ colch$_{k*}$ coloc *Con*$_{k*}$ cor-r croc$_{k*}$ cypra-eg$_{sde6.de}$• **Dig**$_{k*}$

Internal: ...
Dros k* elaps k* *Euphr* k* eupi k* graph b2.de* guaj k* hell k* **Hep** k* ign k* iod *Ip* k* kali-ar kali-bi ptk1 kali-c k* kali-p kali-s fd4.de kali-sil k2 kreos b2.de* lac-c lach k* lap-la sde8.de• laur k* lyc k* m-aust b2.de* mag-c b2.de* mang b2.de* meny b2.de* **Merc** k* merc-c mez k* mosch b2.de* mur-ac b4a.de nat-ar nat-c k* *Nat-m* k* nat-p *Nat-s* k* nit-ac b2.de* **Nux-v** k* olnd b2.de* paeon k* par k* petr k* ph-ac k* **Phos** k* plat b2.de* plb k* *Psor* **Puls** k* ran-b k* rheum b2.de* *Rhus-t* k* ruta k* sabad b2.de* samb bat1• sars b2.de* sec b2.de* *Sep* k* *Sil* k* spig k* spong b2.de* squil k* stront-c b2.de* sul-ac b2.de* sul-i k2 **Sulph** k* *Tarent* ther thuj k* valer b2.de* verat k* *Verb* bg2 zinc b2.de*

- **morning**: arg-n k* *Con* ham fd3.de• *Lyc* k* merc k* sulph
  - **bed** agg.; in: lyc merc k*
- **forenoon**: euph a1 euphr h2 lyc h2 *Merc* sulph k*
- **noon**: kali-c k* psor k*
- **afternoon**: *Ars* k* cocc guaj phos k* psor
  - **15** h: staph h1
  - **following** heat: guaj
  - **without** subsequent heat: ang
- **evening**: atro k* caust cocc k* eupi k* *Gamb* k* guaj k* kali-s fd4.de lyc mang h2 nit-ac k* par k* petr phos plac rzf5• plb psor
  - **lying** down agg.: **Hell** squil h1
  - **sleep**; when falling asleep: phos
- **night**: ambr k* *Dros* nux-v k* petr k* *Sil* k* squil h1*
  - **midnight**: caust k*
  - **air** agg.; in open: anac
  - **cold** air were streaming through the bones; as if: verat
  - **sleep**; during first: dig
  - **waking**; on: arn k*
  - **warm** room, in a: *Anac* cist k* kreos k* puls k*
- **accompanied** by | **external** chill: calc bg2
- **breakfast**; during: ther k*
- **coldness**: *(↗GENERALS - Cold - feeling; GENERALS - Cold - feeling - inner)*
  - **ice**; as if touched with: agar bg2 cocc bg2 ol-an bg2
  - **through** her; as if the cold was going: plac rzf5•
  - **warm** to touch, yet: corn-f br1
  - ○ **Blood** vessels; in: *(↗GENERALS - Cold - feeling - blood)* abies-c bg **Acon** k* ant-c ant-t k* **Ars** k* bry a1 caust a1 lyc k* op b7.de par a1 **Rhus-t** k* sapin a1 **Verat**
  - **Bones**; as if in the: *(↗GENERALS - Cold - feeling - bones)* adam srj5• aran mtf11 berb k* elaps k* galla-q-r nl2• merc k* ozone sde2• pyrog bro1* *Sulph* sne verat k* zinc bro1
  - **Joints**; as if in the: positr nl2•
  - **Skin**; as if under: acon bg2 am-m bg2 arg-n bg2 ip bg2
- **external** heat agg.: *Ip*
- **icy** coldness: *(↗Icy)* antip vh
- **warm** hot water bottle | **amel.**: bamb-a stb2.de•
- ▽ **extending** to | **Outward**: ant-t bg2

IRREGULAR (See Periodicity - irregular)

LONG LASTING (See Shaking - long)

LYING:
- **after** | **amel.**: kali-i merl nit-ac rhus-t sulph
- **agg.**: acon bg1 am-m berb bg1 cham *Cimx* k* fic-m gya1 graph bg1 nat-c bg1 nux-v phel podo puls ptk1 sabin bg1 sars bg1 ther bg1 thuj bg1
- **amel.**: arn k* asar k* bar-c bg2 bell bg2 *Bry* k* calc bg2 canth k* cocc bg2 colch k* kali-n k* nat-m k* *Nux-v* k* phos h2 sil squil bg2 zinc
- **back**; on | **agg.**: tell bg2*
- **desire** to lie down; with | **chilliness**; from: dros h1
- ○ **Part** lain on: arn bg2 calc bg2

LYING DOWN:
- **agg.**: am-c b4.de ars b4.de aur b4.de *Bry* b7.de* calc b4a.de caps b7.de *Chin* b7.de* graph h2 hell b7.de lyc b4a.de *Mag-c* b4a.de *Merc* b4.de* *Nit-ac* b4.de* nux-v b7.de par b7.de puls b7.de sabin b7.de samb b7.de sars b4.de *Sel* b7a.de spig b7.de spong b7.de squil b7.de thuj b4a.de
- **amel.**: mag-m b4a.de

MENSES: *(↗Chilliness - menses; Chilliness - menses - before - agg.)*
- **after** | **agg.**: borx bg2 chinin-s bg2 *Graph* b4.de* jug-r kali-c k* kreos bg2 lyc bg2 nat-m k* *Nux-v* k* phos k* *Puls* k*
- **before** | **agg.**: acon bg2 aloe bg2 am-c k* ant-t bg2* bar-c bg2 berb k* *Calc* k* carb-v bg2 cham bg2 coloc b4a.de* con bg2 *Kali-c* k* *Kreos* k* **Lyc** k* mag-c ptk1 mang bg2 merc bg2 nux-v k* phos bg2 **Puls** k* ruta b7.de* sep k* **Sil** k* sulph k* thuj k* verat k*
- **during**:
  - **agg.**: acon bg2 agar bg2 aloe k* *Am-c* k* am-m bg2 *Bell* k* berb k* bry k* bufo k* cact bg2 *Calc* k* carb-an k* castm k* caul k* caust *Cham* k* cimic bg2 cocc bg2 coff k* cupr bg2 *Cycl* k* eupi gels bg2 *Graph* k* ign bg2 ip k* kali-c bg2 kali-i k* kali-n h2 *Kreos* k* lach k* *Led* lyc k* mag-c k* nat-c b4.de* nat-m k* nat-p k* *Nat-s* k* *Nux-v* k* ozone sde2• *Phos* k* **Puls** k* rhus-t bg2 *Sec* k* **Sep** k* **Sil** k* **Sulph** k* tab bg2 thuj k* vanil fd5.de verat k* *Vib* zinc k*
    - **intermission**, on: eupi
    - **uncovered**, when: mag-c
    - **walking** agg.: mag-c
  - **beginning** of menses | **agg.**: berb bg2 jab ptk1 kola stb3• sil bg2 vanil fd5.de verat bg2
  - **constant**: castm cycl *Kreos* rhus-t

MENTAL EXERTION; after: aur colch nat-m bg2 *Nux-v* k* tub k2 zinc-val ptk1

MONTHLY (See Periodical - month - every)

MOTION:
- **after**:
  - **agg.**: agar k* **Ars** k* cadm-s cann-xyz bg2 kali-c k* nux-v k* phos k* **Puls** k* rat **Rhus-t** k* sep k* *Spig* ptk1 stann k* valer k* zinc k*
    - **foot**; of: merc bg2
    - **hand**; of: caust h2
- **agg.**: *Acon* k* *Agar* aloe alum k* ant-c *Ant-t* k* **Apis** k* arn k* ars ars-i ars-s-f k2 asaf k* asar k* bar-c bg2 *Bell* k* brom **Bry** k* *Camph* cann-s k* *Canth* **Caps** casc caust k* cedr cench k2 cham chel bg2 chin k* cocc bg2 **Coff** k* colch k* coloc sne con k* crot-t *Cur* cycl eup-per gels ham fd3.de• hell k* *Hep* k* iod kali-ar *Kali-c* k* kali-n k* kali-sil k2 led bg2 merc k* **Merc-c** k* mez k* *Nat-m* k* *Nit-ac* **Nux-v** k* ozone sde2• petr plan *Plb* k* podo psor ran-b bg2 **Rhus-t** k* rumx sang sel bg2 **Sep** k* **Sil** k* *Spig* k* **Squil** k* staph k* sul-ac sulph *Thuj* k*
  - **shivering**; during: nux-v b7.de
- **amel.**: *Acon* apis arn asar bell *Caps* cycl *Dros* k* *Kreos* k* mag-m merc mez nit-ac nux-v podo **Puls** k* rhus-t sabin bg2 sep sil spig spong fd4.de staph k* sul-ac k* *Tarent*
- **arms**; of | **agg.**: rhus-t ptk1

NAUSEA; with: arg-n br1

NERVOUS (See Excitement)

NOISE agg.: ther ptk1

OVERHEATED (See Heat - overheated)

PAIN:
- **after**: kali-c b4a.de*
- **with**: *Agar* ptk1 alum-sil pd ang k* *Aran* k* *Ars* k* asaf k* aur bamb-a stb2.de* bar-c k* borx bg2 **Bov** k* bry k* calc-p bg2* *Camph* ptk1 caps k* caust bg2 cocc k* **Coloc** k* cupr bg2 cycl **Dulc** k* *Euph* k* *Graph* k* hep k* *Ign* k* *Kali-bi* k* kali-c k* **Kali-n** k* kali-sil k2 lach k* *Led* k* lyc k* *M-arct* b7a.de **Mez** k* mosch pd nat-c nat-m k* nat-s bg2 petr phyt bg2 plat bg2 plb k* **Puls** k* ran-b k* *Rhus-t* k* sars b4a.de* **Sep** k* sil k* *Squil* k* sulph k* syph gk tell c1 tritic-vg fd5.de
  - ○ **Abdomen**; in (See ABDOMEN - Pain - accompanied - chill)
  - **Back**; in (See BACK - Pain - chill - during)
  - **Neck**; in (See BACK - Pain - cervical - chill)
  - **Teeth**; in (See TEETH - Pain - accompanied - coldness)

PARTIAL (See Single)

PERIODICAL: lyc bg2 rhus-t mrr1
- **day**:
  - **second** day; every: **Brom** b4a.de *Carb-an* b4a.de lach b7a.de lyc b4a.de malar jl2
  - **ten** to fourteen days: kali-bi bg2

- **afternoon** | **every** other: bapt hr1
- **hour**:
  - **2** h: ars bg2 benz-ac bg2 **Kali-c** bg2 rhus-t bg2
  - **3** h: thuj bg2
  - **10**-11 h: borx bg2 **Nat-m** bg2
  - **11** h: gels bg2
  - **15** h: ang bg2 **Bell** bg2 thuj bg2
    - **toward** 15 h: *Apis* bg2 *Con* bg2 staph bg2 thuj bg2
  - **16** h: dios bg2 *Puls* bg2 valer bg2
    - **16**-20 h: bell bg2 *Bov* bg2 graph bg2 hell bg2 *Hep* bg2 **Lyc** bg2 *Mag-m* bg2 zinc bg2
  - **19** h: rhus-t bg2
  - **same** hour: *Ant-c* bg2 apis bg2 aran bg2 ars bg2 **Bov** bg2 bufo bg2 cact bg2 **Cedr** bg2 *Chinin-s* bg2 cina bg2 con bg2 graph bg2 *Hell* bg2 hep bg2 ign bg2 kali-bi bg2 *Kali-c* bg2 *Lyc* bg2 mag-m bg2 phos bg2 **Sabad** b7a.de* **Spig** b7a.de* stann bg2 staph bg2 *Thuj* bg2
- **week**:
  - **three**; every: chinin-s mag-c psor sulph *Tub*
  - **two**; every: am-m **Ars** k* *Calc* k* *Chin* k* *Chinin-s* **Lach** plan psor *Puls* k*
    - **night**; never at: chin bro1
  - **every**: am-m canth *Chin* k* lyc plan
    - **night**; never at: chin bro1
- **month** | **every**: nux-m **Nux-v** puls **Sep** tub
- **year** | **every**: ars bg2 carb-v bg2 crot-h bg2 lach bg2 rhus-t bg2 sulph bg2 tarent bg2 thuj bg2 vip bg2

PERIODICITY:
- **irregular**: **Ars** k* *Eup-per* ign *Ip* k* kali-ar *Meny* mill **Nux-v** k* **Psor** k* **Puls** k* samb **Sep** k* ter hr1
- **marked**, not: acon am-m ambr bell camph canth carb-an carb-v caust chel cic coloc mag-c **Psor** **Sep**
- **regular** and distinct: aesc ang apis **Aran** k* *Ars* bro1 ars-i k2 bol-la bro1 *Bov* **Cact** k* *Caps* **Cedr** k* chin bro1 **Chinin-s** k* cina k* *Eucal* bro1 *Ferr* *Gels* *Hell* ip bro1 lyc *Nat-s* podo *Pyrog* *Sabad* *Spig* stann staph *Tarent* thuj
  - **clock**-like: *Aran* cact *Cedr* chinin-s gm1 gels c1

PERNICIOUS: acon pd* apis **Arn** k* *Ars* k* ars-s-f k2 *Bell* *Cact* *Camph* k* *Caps* chinin-s cur elat **Gels** k* *Hyos* k* ip k2 *Lyc* *Nat-s* **Nux-v** k* *Op* **Psor** k* *Puls* *Stram* sul-ac sulph tarent **Verat** k* verat-v [*Cob* stj2]
- **congestion**, violent: | **head**, cold body with thirst; of | **stomach**, body feels bruised; chill most severely in pit of: **Arn**
  - **warm** room, and chill beginning in chest; with suffocation in: *Apis*
- **red** face when sitting up, delirium and bursting headache; with | **pale** face when lying down: *Bell*

PERSPIRATION:
- **after** chill; perspiration: ant-c ars ars-s-f k2 bamb-a stb2.de• bell h1 bry calad **Caps** *Carb-v* carbn-s k2 **Caust** cham dig eup-per kali-c lach **Lyc** mag-s mez nat-m op petr ph-ac phos puls rhus-t sabad sarr *Sep* sulph *Thuj* verat
- **followed** by perspiration | **heat**; without intervening (See FEVER - Succession - chill - followed - perspiration)
- **more** he sweats the colder he becomes; the: *Cinnb* cist
- **with** perspiration; chill: alum am-c h2 *Ars* k* ars-s-f k2 calc calc-i k2 cedr **Cham** k* chir-fl gya2 cinnb cocc bro1 cupr dig *Eup-per* k* euph ferr gels granit-m es1• jab br1 kali-ar lach ptk1 lap-la rsp1 led lyc nat-m nux-v k* **Puls** k* pyrog k* *Rhus-t* sabad k* sang sars sulph tab ptk1 thuj tub ptk1 verat [bell-p-sp dcm1]

POSTERIOR part of body: *Cham* bg2 **Cocc** bg2 *Croc* b7.de* **Ign** b7.de* *Rhus-t* bg2 stront-c bg2

POSTPONING: alst bry canth bg2 chin k* cina **Gamb** k* ign k* *Ip* k* kali-bi bg2 phos bg2
- **two** hours: sanic c1

PREDOMINATING: alum k* am-m k* **Ant-c** k* *Ant-t* k* *Apis* **Aran** k* **Arn** k* ars aur k* bol-la borx *Bov* k* **Bry** **Camph** k* **Canth** k* **Caps** k* carb-v k* *Caust* k* **Cedr** **Chin** k* **Chinin-s** cimic cimx hr1 cina *Cocc* k* cycl k* dig hr1 dros k* elat eup-per k* euphr hr1 *Gamb* graph hep k* kali-c *Kali-i* hr1 kali-n laur led k* *Lyc* k* **Meny** k* meph k* merc merl k* **Mez** k* mur-ac k* nat-c

Predominating: ...
Nat-m k* nicc k* **Nux-v** k* *Petr* k* ph-ac phos plat k* plb k* podo *Puls* rhus-t k* *Rob* **Sabad** k* sarr sars k* **Sec** sep k* **Staph** k* sulph thuj k* **Verat** k*
- **morning**: bry **Eup-per** hep **Nat-m** **Nux-v** *Podo* sep **Verat**
- **noon**: *Ant-c* elat **Sulph**
- **afternoon**: apis arn **Ars** **Lyc** plb **Puls** *Rhus-t* thuj
- **evening**: alum arn *Cina* cycl *Hep* *Kali-s* mur-ac ph-ac *Phos* **Puls** **Rhus-t** *Sulph*
- **night**: apis gamb *Merc* phos
- **long** lasting chill:
  - **heat**, no thirst; little: *Lyc* puls
  - **without** heat, sweat or thirst: **Aran** bov
- **only** of chill; the paroxysm consists: aran bov camph canth hep led *Lyc* mez mur-ac ran-b sabad
- **without** heat or thirst: mur-ac sep staph sulph

PRESSURE:
- **amel.**: *Bry* ptk1 phos ptk1
- **hand**; of | **agg.**: meny bg2

QUARTAN (= Every 72 hours): acon anac ant-c apis *Arn* **Ars** **Ars-i** ars-s-f k2 baj bro1 bapt bell brom bry bufo carb-v chin k* chinin-ar chinin-s k* **Cimx** cina clem coff cor-r *Elat* hell bro1 **Hyos** *Ign* **Iod** ip kali-ar lach **Lyc** *Meny* mill *Nat-m* nux-m *Nux-v* oci-sa sp1 plan podo **Puls** rhus-t **Sabad** sep sul-i k2 sulph thuj **Verat**
- **double**: *Ars* chin **Dulc** eup-per *Eup-pur* gamb lyc nux-m puls rhus-t
  - **diarrhea**; on the days free from fever with constant: **Iod**

○ - **Tongue**; with discoloration of | **white**: *Ip* kr1*

QUOTIDIAN (= Every day): *(↗FEVER - Periodical - day - every)* acon aesc agar alum alum-p k2 anac *Ang* ant-c ant-t apis **Aran** *Arn* **Ars** k* ars-s-f k2 arund asaf bapt bar-c bell bol-la k* bry **Cact** *Calc* camph *Caps* carb-v *Cedr* cham chel chin chinin-ar *Chinin-s* k* cic *Cina* con *Cur* cycl *Dros* elaps elat *Eup-per* eup-pur *Ferr* ferr-ar gamb k* *Gels* graph hep ign k* **Ip** *Kali-ar* kali-bi *Kali-br* hr1 kali-c kali-n bro1 kali-s lach led lob k* *Lyc* mag-c meny **Nat-m** *Nat-s* nit-ac **Nux-v** k* op petr *Phos* plan plb bro1 *Podo* **Puls** *Pyrog* *Rhus-t* sabad *Samb* sarr sep *Spig* stann staph stram sulph *Tarent* k* thuj verat
- **double**: ant-c apis ars bapt *Bell* *Chin* dulc **Elat** **Graph** led nux-m *Puls* rhus-t *Stram* *Sulph*
- **violent** chill; morning of one day, light chill but in the afternoon of next day: eup-per

RIDING on horseback: kali-c h2

RIGOR (See Shaking)

RISING:
- **agg.**: acon arn ars *Bell* *Bry* cham merc **Merc-c** k* mur-ac nux-v phos puls *Rhus-t* squil sulph verat
- **amel.**: *Rhus-t*
- **bed**; from:
  - **after**:
    - **agg.**: euphr h2
    - **amel.**: am-c bg2 *Ambr* bg2 ant-t bg2 arg-met bg2 ars bg2 **Aur** bg2 bell bg2 dros bg2 euph bg2 ferr bg2 ign bg2 *Iod* bg2 led bg2 lyc bg2 mag-c bg2 merc bg2 merc-c bg2 *Nat-c* bg2 plat bg2 *Puls* bg2 rhod bg2 rhus-t bg2 sel bg2 *Sep* bg2 stront-c bg2 sulph bg2 verat bg2
- **stooping**; from | **agg.**: acon bg2 arn bg2 ars bg2 *Bell* bg2 *Bry* bg2 cham bg2 merc bg2 **Merc-c** bg2 mur-ac bg2 *Nux-v* bg2 phos bg2 puls bg2 rhus-t bg2 squil bg2 sulph bg2 verat bg2

ROOM; in a: | **amel.** (See Warm - room - amel.)

SAD NEWS, from: *(↗MIND - Ailments - bad; MIND - Sadness)* calc cic ign teucr

SCRATCHING agg.; after: agar bg2* mez ptk1 petr ptk1 staph bg2

SEWER gas: bapt c1 phyt c1 *Pyrog* *Tub* st

SHAKING (= shivering, rigors): abrom-a ks5 acon k* adam srj5• *Aesc* agar k* aloe k* alum k* alum-p k2 alum-sil k2 *Am-c* k* am-m b2.de* anac k* androc srj1• ang k* ant-c k* *Ant-t* k* *Apis* k* *Aran* arg-met k* arg-n k* arn k* **Ars** k* *Ars-i* asaf k* asar k* *Astac* c2 aster atra-r bnm3• aur k* aur-ar k2 aur-i k2 aur-s k2 bamb-a stb2.de• bapt k* bar-c k* bar-m bar-s k2 *Bell* k* berb beryl tpw5

Chill

Shaking: ...
bol-la borx k* bov k* *Brom* k* *Bry* k* bufo bg2 *Cact* calad k* *Calc* k* *Calc-i* k2 calc-p calc-s calc-sil k2 **Camph** k* *Cann-s* k* *Canth* k* *Caps* k* *Carb-an* k* *Carb-v* k* **Caust** k* cedr cench k2 cham k* **Chel** k* **Chin** k* *Chinin-ar* **Chinin-s** k* cic b2.de* *Cina* k* *Clem* k* *Cocc* k* *Coff* k* **Colch** k* *Coloc* k* con k* croc k* cupr k* cycl k* cypra-eg sde6.de• dig k* *Dros* k* dulc k* *Elaps* *Eup-per* k* *Eup-pur* *Euph* k* *Euphr* bg2 eupi **Ferr** k* **Ferr-i** ferr-p form-ac bg2 *Gamb* *Gels* k* graph k* guaj k* hell k* helo-s rwt2• **Hep** k* hydrog srj2• hyos k* **Ign** k* *Iod* k* *Ip* k* kali-ar kali-bi bg2 *Kali-br* a1* *Kali-c* k* kali-chl *Kali-i* kali-m k2 kali-n k* kali-p kali-s kalm kola stb3• kreos k* *Lach* k* lat-h bnm5• *Laur* k* **Led** k* *Lob* loxo-lae bnm12• **Lyc** k* lyss m-ambo b2.de* m-arct b2.de* *M-aust* b2.de* *Mag-c* k* mag-m k* mag-s mang k* marb-w es1• *Meny* k* *Merc* k* merc-c k* *Mez* k* moni rfm1• *Mosch* k* *Mur-ac* k* *Nat-ar* *Nat-c* k* **Nat-m** k* nat-p *Nat-s* nat-sil fd3.de• nit-ac k* nux-m k* **Nux-v** k* olib-sac wmh1 olnd k* *Op* k* ox-ac bg2* par k* *Petr* k* *Ph-ac* k* **Phos** k* plac rzf5• plan *Plat* k* plb k* *Podo* **Psor** ptel c1 **Puls** k* pycnop-sa mrz1 **Pyrog** k* ran-b b2.de* rheum b2.de* rhod b2.de **Rhus-t** k* **Ruta** k* *Sabad* k* sabin k* *Samb* k* sang k* sarr sars b2.de* *Sec* k* seneg b2.de* **Sep** k* *Sil* k* spig k* spong k* squil b2.de* stann k* *Staph* k* stram k* stront-c b2.de sul-ac b2.de* sul-i k2 **Sulph** k* symph fd3.de• *Tab* k* *Tarax* k* *Tarent* ter k* ther c1* **Thuj** k* til ban1• tub jl2 v a i e r b2.de* vanil fd5.de verat k* verat-v bg2 *Verb* k* viol-o b2.de* visc c1 yohim vml4 zinc k* zinc-p k2

- **one** side: alum b2.de* ambr b2.de* anac b2.de* ant-t b2.de* am b2.de* bar-c b2.de* *Bell* b2.de* bry b2.de* *Caust* b2.de* cham b2.de* chin b2.de* *Cocc* b2.de* croc b2.de* dig b2.de* ign b2.de* kali-c b2.de* lyc b2.de* nat-c b2.de* **Nux-v** b2.de* par b2.de* ph-ac b2.de* phos b2.de* plat b2.de* *Puls* b2.de* *Rhus-t* b2.de* ruta b2.de* sabad b2.de* sars b2.de* spig b2.de* stann b2.de* stram b2.de* sul-ac b2.de* sulph b2.de* thuj b2.de* verb b2.de*
- **daytime**: kali-c b4a.de *Sil* b4a.de viol-o b7a.de
- **morning**: ant-c k* ars calc b4.de caps carb-v chin k* cocc k* coff coloc b4.de con b4.de* cor-r k* cycl b7.de *Hell* k* kali-c b4.de kali-n h2 mag-m b4.de* *Mang* k* *Merc* nat-ar nat-c k* *Nat-m* nux-m k* nux-v b7.de *Podo* rat k* rhus-t b7.de sarr s e p b4.de* spong k* staph b7.de *Verat* k*
  - **8** h: sulph h2
  - **bed** agg.; in: chin coff mag-s k* nat-c k* nat-s
  - **heat**, without subsequent: cocc
  - **rising** agg.: acon kreos mag-m a1 mag-s k* nux-v rhus-t h1
  - **waking** agg.; after: sep h2
  - **walking** agg.: sep k*
- **forenoon**: ang k* arg-n *Ars* b4.de carb-an chin b7.de chinin-s eup-per k2 hep b4a.de kali-c b4.de kali-n h2 mag-m b4.de* nat-c b4.de* **Nat-m** nit-ac b4.de* *Nux-v* op ph-ac k* **Phos** k* podo puls sars b4.de* spong fd4.de *Stann* b4.de* s t a p h k* stront-c b4.de
  - **11**-16 h: sep
  - **flying** heat, with: bov
  - **heat**, without subsequent: kali-n nat-c
- **noon**: ant-c sars h2 *Sep* k*
  - **dinner** | **after** | **agg.**: mag-m
    - **during** | **agg.**: grat
- **afternoon**: aeth a1 alum b4.de alum-sil k2 *Ang* k* apis b7a.de **Ars** k* ars-s-f k2 *Asaf* b7a.de bell b4.de *Canth* k* castm cham k* chel *Chin* chinin-s cocc k* coff con croc dig b4.de* **Ferr** ign b7.de ip kali-n h2 lyc b4.de m-arct b7.de m-aust b7.de mag-m b4.de nat-c b4.de* nux-v b7.de* petr ph-ac k* **Phos** psor puls b7.de *Rhus-t* k* sabad spong b7.de* *Staph* k* sulph k*
  - **16**-20 h: zinc h2
  - **17** h: nat-c h2
  - **air**; slightest contact with open: nux-v
  - **coldness** and blue nails for four hours; with | **followed** by heat without subsequent sweat: *Nux-v*
  - **dashed** with cold water; as if: sabad
  - **lasting** until next morning: kali-i
- **evening**: abrom-a ks5 acon k* agar k* alum b4.de **Am-c** k* **Ars** k* ars-s-f k2 asar *Aur* b4.de* bell b4.de* bov b4.de* **Calc** b4a.de canth b7.de *Caps* k* *Carb-v* k* caust b4.de cench k2 cham k* **Chel** k* *Chin* k* *Cocc* k* croc cycl b7.de* dulc b4.de *Elaps* *Ferr* k* gamb k* graph k* grat k* *Hep* hyos **Ign** k* kali-i kali-n h2 **Kali-s** kali-sil k2 *Lach* **Lyc** mag-c k* mag-m k* mag-s k* mang k* *Merc* k* nat-c b4.de nat-m k* nat-s nat-sil fd3.de* nit-ac nux-m k* nux-v b7.de ox-ac k* ozone sde2• *Petr* k* ph-ac k* *Phos* k* *Puls-n* **Pyrog** rat k* rhus-t b7.de *Sabad* b7.de sabin b7.de

- **evening**: ...
  sars b4.de* *Sep* *Sil* k* spig b7.de staph b7.de* stront-c sulph k* tab k* *Tarent* thuj verat b7.de *Zinc* k*
  - **19** h: petr hr1
  - **19**-4 h: gamb
  - **20** h | **commencing** in the feet with hair standing on end: bar-c
  - **21**-10 h: mag-s
  - **air** agg.; in open: abrom-a ks5 mang k*
  - **bed**:
    - **in** bed:
      - **agg.**: agar h2 am-c bamb-a stb2.de• cench k2 *Chel* k* chin inul hr1 mag-c mag-m a1 *Merc* k* *Mez* nat-m rhus-t k* sabad **Sil** k* sulph h2 t a b k* thuj k*
      - **amel.**: mag-m mag-s sars h2
  - **heat**, without subsequent: *Led*
  - **house**, in the: mang k*
  - **sleep** agg.; on going to: am-c phos staph
  - **undressing**:
    - **after**: spong k*
    - **while**: agar mag-c
  - **walking** in open air agg.: **Ars** k* *Chin*
- **night**: acon arg-met b7a.de bar-c b4a.de beryl tpw5 borx b4a.de bry b7.de *Calc* k* caust b4.de cench k2 dros gamb k* hep b4a.de kali-c k* kali-i k* m-arct b7.de merc k* nat-m nat-s olib-sac wmh1 petr k* *Phos* k* rhus-t k* sars k* staph b7.de* sulph k*
  - **air** agg.; in open: **Ars** calc calc-p caust *Cham* chel chin coff lach mag-m nux-v plat rhus-t tab
  - **bed**: beryl tpw5
    - **going** to bed | **before**: cocc laur nat-m *Samb*
  - **lying** down agg.: *Acon*
  - **waking**; on: caust h2 phos h2 sulph h2
- **accompanied** by:
  - **other** complaints (See GENERALS - Complaints - accompanied - shivering)
  - **vertigo** (See VERTIGO - Accompanied - shivering)
  - **Head**; pain in (See HEAD - Pain - accompanied - chill)
  - **Stomach**; pain in (See STOMACH - Pain - accompanied - shivering)
  - **Teeth**; complaints of (See TEETH - Complaints - accompanied - shivering)
- **air** agg.; draft of: acon bar-c bry *Caps* **Chin** mosch phys verat
- **air** agg.; in open: abrom-a ks5 coff hs1 coff-t a1*
  - **covering**; not amel. by: rhus-t
- **alternating** with heat (See FEVER - Alternating - shivering)
- **apyrexia**; during: ign a1
- **bed**, on putting hand out of: **Hep** phos **Rhus-t**
- **beginning** in:
  - ○ **Arms**: *Hell* bg2
  - **Back**: bov bg2 **Croc** bg2
  - **Feet**: vesp ptk2
  - **Head**: *Mosch* bg2 phys bg2 valer bg2
- **chill**; before: ip h1
- **cold**, taking hold of anything: *Zinc* k*
- **coldness**; without: chel b7.de dros b7.de *Meny* b7a.de rheum b7.de
- **convulsions**; rigors during: *Hell*
- **delivery**; during: caul bro1
- **drinking** | **after** | **agg.**: verat a1
  - **agg.**: alum am ars calc k* calc-s cann-s **Caps** k* chel *Chin* elaps e u p - p e r k2 lyc **Nux-v**
- **dyspnea**; during: oxyt ptk2
- **eating** | **after** | **agg.**: rhus-t a1
  - **while** | **agg.**: caps graph k* lyc mag-m
- **entering** the house from the open air; on: aeth arg-n caust chin

- **face**, livid: *Rhus-t*
- **fright** agg.: merc k*
- **hair** standing on end; with: *Am-c* bar-c calc caust cina dulc meny nit-ac puls sil
- **heat**:
  - **with**: **Arn** k* *Ars* k* *Bell* bry cann-i k* cham k* *Chel* k* *Chin* cocc *Hell* k* hep hyos k* ign k* *Lach* k* merc k* mosch k* puls k* *Rhus-t* k* sep k* tab k*
    - **face**; of: staph h1 *Thuj*
    - **head**; of: **Arn Bell** bry *Cact* mang ptel c1
      - **forehead**: ant-c h2
  - **without** subsequent heat: **Aran** bov camph canth cocc graph hep kali-c kali-n led lyc mez mur-ac **Staph** sulph verat
    - **menses**; during: nat-c h2
    - **perspiration**; or: **Aran** bov canth castm
    - **thirst**; or: **Sep** *Staph Sulph*
- **held**, so he would not shake so hard; wants to be: (*↗Violent*) *Gels Lach*
- **inspiration** agg.: **Brom** k*
- **long** lasting: (*↗FEVER - Succession*) ant-t **Aran** k* *Ars* bapt bol-la bro1 bov cact bro1 calad camph canch bro1 canth caps k* *Chinin-s* bro1 cina eup-pur bro1 *Gamb* hell hyos ip bro1 kali-i kalm kreos *Led Lyc* meny bro1 *Mez* nat-c nat-m bro1 *Nux-v* k* plb bro1 podo k* puls k* *Pyrog* bro1 *Rhus-t Sabad* bro1 sec *Sep Verat* k* verat-v bro1
  - **heat**, no thirst; little: puls
  - **relieved** by anything; not: **Aran** *Nux-v*
  - **thirty**-six hours, with subsequent heat: mez
  - **twelve** hours: canth
  - **twenty**-four hours, with heat, perspiration or thirst: *Aran*
  - **whole** day | **drawing** pains in throat and back; with: verat
  - **without**:
    - **heat** or perspiration: **Aran** bov canth *Lyc*
    - **subsequent** heat: **Aran** bov camph hep led lyc mez verat
- **maniacal** delirium, with: cimx tarent
- **menses** | **before** | **agg.**: *Sep* bg2
  - **during** | **agg.**: nat-c h2 phos h2
- **motion** agg.: alum ant-t beryl tpw5 *Caps* cedr eup-per sang sil sul-i k2 sulph thuj
- **pain**; during: *Ars* sulph h2
- **partial**: *Ars Bry* caps caust *Chin* cocc graph hell hep ign ptel c1 *Puls* rhus-t sabin samb spig spong staph thuj *Verat*
- **perspiration**; with: alum cedr cupr *Eup-per* **Nux-v** *Rhus-r Rhus-t* til ban1• verat
  - **cold**: til ban1•
- **pulsating** pain in occiput, with: borx
- **skin** cold and blue, with: *Camph* k* carb-v chin nux-m nux-v *Rhus-t Sec* k*
- **sleep** | **siesta**; during: sep h2
- **sleep** and snoring; with deep: *Op*
- **stool**:
  - **after**:
    - **agg.**: ang b7.de* canth b7.de* carb-an k* *Kali-c* b4a.de mag-m h2* *Merc* b4.de* mez b4.de* *Plat* k* *Rheum* bg2
      - **frequent**: verat a1
  - **before**: carb-an k* caust k* chinin-s mag-m k* mang bg2 merc k* mez k*
  - **during** | **agg.**: *Bell* k* *Coloc* b4a.de mag-m k* nit-ac k* ptel c1 rheum b7.de* stann k* *Sulph* b4a.de verat b7.de* vip bg2
- **swallowing**; during and after: merc-c
- **urination** | **after** | **agg.**: *Kali-c* b4a.de plat bg2 rhod bg2
  - **during** | **agg.**: stram ptk1 thuj ptk1
- **vomiting**; after: gard-j vlr2• thuj k* zinc
- **walking** in open air agg.: chel mang h2 tarax h1
- **wandering**: nux-v b7a.de
- **warm** | **applications** | **agg.**: beryl tpw5
  - **room**; on going into a: colch plat h2 rhus-t
- **wind** agg.: psor jl2 zinc h2
- **without** shaking: *Puls* b7a.de
- **yawning** agg.: arn cina plat h2 thuj pd*

Shaking: ...
▽ - **extending** to:
○ • **Body**; over: acon bg2 agar bg2 alum bg2 **Anac** bg2 *Ang* bg2 ant-t bg2 **Asaf** bg2 **Asar** bg2 aur bg2 *Bar-c* bg2 bell bg2 bry bg2 cann-xyz bg2 cham bg2 chin bg2 **Colch** bg2 *Con* bg2 croc bg2 form bg2 **Kali-c** bg2 led bg2 *Meny* bg2 mez bg2 nat-m bg2 nux-v bg2 par bg2 ph-ac bg2 **Puls** bg2 rhus-t bg2 *Ruta* bg2 sabad bg2 **Samb** bg2 sars bg2 sec bg2 sil bg2 **Spig** bg2 sul-ac bg2 thuj bg2 valer bg2 vario bg2 verat bg2 verb bg2
  - **Brain**; into: caust bg2
  - **Downward**: agar bg2 *Bell* bg2 calc-p k2 caust bg2 *Chel* bg2 coff bg2 colch bg2 *Croc* bg2 mosch bg2 phys bg2 *Sabad* bg2 staph bg2 sul-ac bg2 *Valer* bg2 vario bg2 *Zinc* bg2
  - **Upward**: *Acon* bg2 agar bg2 carb-an bg2 *Cina* bg2 colch bg2 hyos bg2 *Lach* bg2 puls bg2 sabad bg2 *Sars* bg2 spig bg2 stront-c bg2 sulph bg2

○ - **Affected** parts: *Ang* b7a.de ars b4.de*
  - **Internally**: *Chel* bg2 **Coff** b7.de* dros bg2 hell bg2 **Ign** bg2 **Phos** bg2 rheum bg2
  - **Single** parts: acon b2.de* am-c b2.de* ang b2.de* arg-met b2.de* arn b2.de* *Ars* b2.de* asaf b2.de* aur b2.de* bar-c b2.de* **Bell** b2.de* borx b2.de* bov b2.de* bry b2.de* camph b2.de* cann-s b2.de* canth b2.de* caps b2.de* carb-v b2.de* *Caust* b2.de* *Cham* b2.de* chel b2.de* *Chin* b2.de* cina b2.de* *Cocc* b2.de* coff b2.de* coloc b2.de* croc b2.de* dig b2.de* *Graph* b2.de* guaj b2.de* hell b2.de* hep b2.de* ign b2.de* ip b7.de kali-c b2.de* kali-n b2.de* lach b2.de* laur b2.de* led b2.de* m-arct b2.de m-aust b2.de mag-m b2.de* mang b2.de* meny b2.de* merc b2.de* mez b2.de* mosch b2.de* nat-c b2.de* nat-m b2.de* nux-v b2.de* par b2.de* ph-ac b2.de* phos b2.de* plat b2.de* **Puls** b2.de* ran-b b2.de* rhod b2.de* rhus-t b2.de* ruta b2.de* sabad b2.de* sabin b2.de* samb b2.de* seneg b2.de* sep b2.de* sil b2.de* spig b2.de* spong b2.de* **Staph** b2.de* stram b2.de* stront-c b2.de* sulph b2.de* thuj b2.de* valer b2.de* **Verat** b2.de* zinc b2.de*
  - **Upper** half of body: *Meny* b7a.de

SHIVERING (See Shaking)

SITTING:
- **agg.**: ambr bg2 caps bg2 con bg2 **Dros** bg2 hell b7.de* ip b7a.de* **Kreos** bg2 lyc bg2 ph-ac bg2 *Phos* b4.de* plat bg2 *Puls* bg2 rhus-t bg2 sep bg2
- **amel.**: *Bry* bg2 colch bg2 cupr bg2 dros bg2 ign k* merc bg2 nux-v k* **Squil** bg2

SITTING UP in bed agg.: nit-ac h2

SLEEP:
- **after**:
  - **agg.**: acon *Agar* **Alum Am-m** *Ambr* arn k* ars bry k* cadm-s calc caust con crot-t cycl *Lyc* k* merc nit-ac nux-v phos puls rhus-t sabad samb sars sep sil staph sulph tarent thuj verat zinc zinc-p k2
    - **afternoon** sleep: merc bg2
  - **amel.**: arn k* ars k* bry calad k* calc caps k* chin k* colch k* cupr k* ferr fl-ac bg2 kreos k* *Nux-v* k* **Phos** k* psil ft1 rhus-t samb k* sep k*
- **alternating** with attacks of coldness: *Nux-m*
- **beginning** to: tub c1*
- **during** | **agg.**: acon bg2 aeth alum bg2 *Am-c* k* ambr bg2 arge-pl rwt5• *Ars* k* aur bg2 bell k* **Borx** k* bov bry k* cadm-s calad a1 calc carb-an k* carb-v k* carbn-s caust k* cham k* chin k* grat hep k* hyos *Ign* indg lyc k* merc bg2 mur-ac k* *Nat-m* k* *Op* k* *Ph-ac* k* phos k* *Puls* k* sabad k* samb sars bg2 sep k* sil bg2 staph bg2 sulph k* verat bg2 x-ray sp1 zinc k*

SLIGHT chill: *Ars* bro1 aza bro1 carb-v bro1 chin bro1 cina bro1 eup-per bro1 eup-pur bro1 *Ip* bro1

SOUR FOOD agg.: verat bg2

SPRING agg.: *Ant-t Ars* canth *Carb-v* k* cham *Gels* **Lach** k* nux-m **Psor** sep sulph k*

STAGES; succession of (See FEVER - Succession)

STANDING agg.: hell b7.de

STARTING from slightest noise with chill through and through: ang h1

STOOL:
- **after** | **agg.**: aloe bro1 ambr k* ang bg2 ars bg2* bov b4a.de* bufo k* calc bg2 camph bro1 *Canth* k* caps bg2* carb-an bg2 carb-v bg2* caust bg2 coloc bg2 dios form bro1 graph bg2 grat k* ip bro1 *Kali-c* bg2 lach bg2 lyc mag-m bg2 mag-p med bg2* *Merc* bg2* merc-c k* mez k* nit-ac bg2 nux-v bg2 ox-ac

Chill

- **after** – **agg.**: ... paeon petr phel sne phos bg2 *Plat* k* **Puls** b7.de* rheum bg2* *Sec* bro1 sel bg2 staph bg2 stram bg2 stront-c sulph h2* tab bro1 verat bg2*
- **before**: aloe ang bg2 ant-c ant-t b7.de* *Ars* k* bapt *Bar-c* k* benz-ac bry bg2 calad k* caps bg2 carb-an bg2 carb-v bg2 caust bg2 cham bg2 chinin-s colch bg2 dig k* graph bg2 ip m-arct b7.de *M-aust* b7.de* mag-m k* mang b4.de* *Merc* k* *Mez* k* nat-c k* nat-m bg2 nux-m bg2 nux-v bg2 *Phos* puls k* rheum bg2 spig b7.de* *Verat* k*
- **during** | **agg.**: aloe k* alum k* alum-sil k2 ang bg2 ars k* bell k* bry cact calad k* calc k* calc-sil k2 calen a1 caps castm cham bg2 chin bg2 coloc k* con k* dig b4a.de* *Ferr-m* germ-met srj5• grat hyos bg2 ind ip jatr-c lac-c ptk1 lyc mag-m k* *Merc* k* merc-c b4a.de* nat-c k* nat-m bg2 nit-ac bg2 phos k* plat *Podo* k* ptel bg2* *Puls* k* rheum k* *Rhus-t* k* sec k* sep bg2 sil k* sol-t-ae vml3• spig k* stann k* staph bg2 *Sulph* k* trom *Verat* k* vib
- **urging** to: dulc ptk1

SUDDEN: acon tl1 camph tl1 croc bg2 graph h2 rhus-t mrr1
- **causeless**: hir rsj4•

SUMMER agg.: caps casc cedr lach nat-m **Psor** k*
- **weather**; in hot (See Weather - hot)

SUNSHINE:
- **agg.**: nat-m ptk1
- **amel.**: anac k* con k* plat bg2 stront-c bg2

SWALLOWING agg.: *Merc-c* k* sulph bg2

TALKING agg.: ars h2* ph-ac bg2 *Teucr* b7.de*
- **unpleasant** subjects; of: calc bg2 *Teucr* bg2

TERTIAN: aesc alum anac ant-c ant-t *Apis* **Aran** arn **Ars** ars-i ars-s-f k2 bar-c *Bar-m* bell bol-la borx h2 *Brom* **Bry** *Calc* k* calc-i k2 *Canth* **Caps** carb-an carb-v *Cedr* *Cham* *Chin* k* *Chinin-ar* *Chinin-s* k* cic *Cimx* cina cor-r dros dulc elat **Eup-per** **Eup-pur** *Ferr* ferr-ar gamb k* gels hyos ign iod **Ip** k* kali-ar *Lach* *Lyc* k* *Mez* mill *Nat-m* nux-m **Nux-v** petr plan *Podo* **Puls** *Rhus-t* sabad sarr sep staph sul-i k2 sulph *Thuj* verat
- **double**: aesc apis **Ars** chin dulc elat eup-pur gamb k* lyc nux-m puls **Rhus-t** thuj verat

THINKING of the chill agg.: chinin-ar

TOUCH:
- **agg.**: (↗*MIND - Touched - aversion*) **Acon** k* ang k* apis k* bell k* cham k* **Chin** k* colch k* hep k* hyos k* *Kali-c* bro1 kali-i bg2 *Lyc* k* **Nux-v** k* phos k* plb bg2 puls k* ran-b bg2 sabin bg2 sep k* *Sil* bro1 spig k* staph k* sulph k*
- **bedclothes** agg.; of: aran c1
- **clothes** agg.; of: cupr-ar bg2

TOUCHING anything: zinc hr1
- **cold** agg.: *Zinc* b4a.de

TREMBLING and shivering: acon k* *Agar* *Agn* k* **Anac** k* anag vh1 anan vh1 **Ant-t** k* apis k* arn k* ars k* ars-s-f k2 asaf k* bell k* berb k* borx k* bov k* brom k* bry k* bufo bg2 calc k* calc-sil k2 camph bg2 cann-s k* canth k* caps k* carb-an k* cham chin k* chinin-s choc srj3• cic k* cimic cina k* cob-n sp1 cocc k* con k* *Croc* k* dig bg2 *Eup-per* k* ferr k* ferr-ar gels mrr1 graph bg2 hyos bg2 kali-bi bg2 kali-n k* *Led* k* mag-s sp1 merc k* merc-i-f mygal nat-c k* nat-m k* nux-v k* olib-sac wmh1 olnd k* op k* par k* petr k* ph-ac k* phos k* pip-n bg2 **Plat** k* psor *Puls* k* pycnop-sa mrz1 rhus-t k* sabad k* **Sil** k* spong fd4.de stram k* sulph k* *Tarent* k* teucr k* ther tritic-vg fd5.de tub bg2 vac jl2 *Valer* k* vanil fd5.de verat bg2 zinc k*
- **morning**: anac
- **noon**: gels k*
- **afternoon**: asaf carb-an spong fd4.de
- **evening**: cench k2 nat-m ph-ac h2 plat k* spong fd4.de teucr k* tritic-vg fd5.de
- **night**: borx olib-sac wmh1
- **internal**: par
  - **forenoon**: lyc par
  - **evening**: par

TURNING over in bed (See Bed - turning)

UNCOVERED; desire to be:
- **abdomen**: tab bro1
- **cold**, dry skin; with | **covered** during heat and perspiration; but desire to be: *Camph* k*

UNCOVERING, undressing: *Acon* k* **Agar** k* am-c *Am-m* k* *Apis* ptk1 *Arg-met* k* *Arg-n* **Arn** k* *Ars* k* ars-h asar k* astac kr1 aur k* aur-ar k2 *Bell* k* *Borx* k* bry bg2 *Calc* k* calc-s ptk1 calc-sil k2 camph ptk1 canth k* *Caps* k* carb-an card-m **Cham** k* **Chin** k* chinin-ar *Clem* k* cocc k* colch k* con k* cor-r br1 **Cycl** k* dig k* dros k* *Eup-per* *Ferr* **Hep** k* *Ip* ptk1 kali-n lach k* led ptk1 *Mag-c* k* *Merc* merl mez k* *Mosch* k* nat-m nit-ac *Nux-m* k* **Nux-v** k* *Phos* k* plat k* *Puls* k* rhod k* **Rhus-t** k* samb k* *Sec* ptk1 *Sep* k* **Sil** k* spong k* *Squil* k* **Stram** k* stront-c k* *Tarent* *Thuj* k* tub k2* vero-o rly4•
- **amel.**: *Apis* calc-s pd **Camph** k* carb-v mrr1 hep bro1 ign k2 *Ip* led bg2* med k* puls sanic bro1 **Sec** k* *Sep* sulph bro1
- **aversion** to: **Camph** mrr1 *Cycl* b7a.de *Nux-v* b7a.de stram b7a.de
- **hot** when covered; yet too: cor-r br1
- **smothered** if wrapped up; yet feels: arg-n br1*

○ - **Hands**: mag-c ptk1

UPPER part of body: agar bg2 arg-met h1 bar-c bg2 **Cina** bg2 euph h2* *Ip* mag-m h2 meny h1* nat-p fkr6.de nept-m lsd2.fr plat h2 rhus-t bg2

URINATION:
- **after**:
  - **agg.**: ang c1 *Arn* k* calc k* caust bg2 eug hep k* iod bg2* *Med* k* nat-m k* petr bg2 **Plat** k* puls k* rhod k* sars k* sep k* stram bg2 sulph k* thuj k*
    - **begins** in neck of bladder and spreads upwards: sars
- **before**: arn k* borx k* bry k* coloc k* hyper med **Nit-ac** k* nux-v k* puls k* rhus-t k* sulph k* thuj k*
- **during**:
  - **agg.**: *Acon* bro1 all-c sne bell k* eug *Gels* k* *Lyc* k* merc k* *Nit-ac* k* nux-v k* petr hr1 phos k* **Plat** k* puls k* *Sars* bg2* senec sep k* squil bg2 *Stram* sulph k* *Thuj* k* verat k*
    - **shivering**, during painful: petros pd
- **urging** to urinate: dulc ptk1 hyper k13 *Med* k13

VERTIGO:
- **after**: corn-f br1
- **with** (See VERTIGO - Chill - during)

VEXATION; after: acon ars bry gels merc *Nux-v* *Rhus-t* *Tarent*

VIOLENT chill: (↗*Shaking - held*) acon tl1
- **bluish**, cold face and hands, mottled skin; with: **Nux-v** *Rhus-t*
- **delirium**; with: *Arn* *Ars* *Bell* bry cham **Chin** ip k2 **Nat-m** nux-v puls *Sep* stram sulph *Verat*
- **heat**; without subsequent: **Aran** bov camph hep *Led* *Mez*
- **red** face and thirst; with: **Ferr** *Ign*
- **unconsciousness**; with: *Ars* *Bell* camph *Hep* lach **Nat-m** nux-v op puls stram valer

VOMITING:
- **after** (See STOMACH - Vomiting - chill - before)
- **before** (See STOMACH - Vomiting - chill - after)

WAKING; on: **Alum** k* *Ambr* k* **Arn** k* ars k* *Bry* k* calc k* card-m caust k* ham fd3.de• hep k* *Lyc* k* mag-c h2 merc k* nit-ac k* *Nux-v* k* phos k* puls k* rhus-t sabad k* samb k* sars k* *Sep* k* sil k* staph k* sulph k* tarent thuj k* verat k* zinc
- **as** often as he awakes: **Am-m** k* arn

WALKING:
- **after** | **agg.**: calc h2 mag-c h2
- **agg.**: arn asaf cham *Chin* k* cocc b7.de hell b7.de meny h1 *Squil* b7a.de
- **air**; in open:
  - **after** | **agg.**: agar bg2 am-c k* anac k* *Ars* k* *Bry* k* cann-s cann-xyz bg2 carb-v k* kali-c k* laur k* nit-ac k* nux-v k* *Puls* k* *Rhus-t* k* *Sep* k* spong k* staph k* zinc k*
  - **agg.**: acon anac k* *Ant-t* k* **Ars** k* ars-s-f k2 bamb-a stb2.de• bell k* borx k* bry k* carb-an k* carb-v k* cham **Chel** k* **Chin** k* chinin-ar cocc k* colch k* con k* dig k* **Euph** k* hep k* mag-m mang k* *Merc* k* *Merc-c* k* nux-m k* **Nux-v** k* petr h2 ph-ac k* sel k* *Sil* k* *Spig* k* sul-ac k* *Sulph* k* tarax k*
  - **amel.**: *Alum* bg2 aur bg2 *Caps* bg2* dulc bg2 lyc bg2 mag-c bg2 mag-m bg2 **Puls** bg2 rhus-t bg2 sabin bg2 sep bg2 spong bg2 **Staph** bg2 **Sul-ac** bg2
- **backward** agg.: merc bg2
- **rapidly** | **amel.**: mang h2

WARM:

- **applications** | **agg.**: apis bro1 canch bro1 chin bro1 chinin-s bro1 nux-v bro1
- **bed** | **not** amel.: lachn sul-i k2
- **desire** for warmth which does not relieve: acon alum alum-p k2 apeir-s mlk9.de **Aran** k* asar ptk1 bamb-a stb2.de• bell bov *Cadm-s* bro1 calc calc-i k2 calc-sil k2 camph caust bro1 cench k2 *Chin* chinin-s bro1 cic *Cina* cocc colch con dros k* ferr *Hep* kali-i **Lach** laur bro1 lyc k* mag-p bro1 meny *Merc* k* *Nat-m* **Nux-v** ozone sde2• *Phos* podo puls bro1 pulx bro1 *Pyrog* sil k* spong fd4.de *Tarent* verat
- **drinks**:
  - **agg.**: *Alum* k* bell ptk1 cham *Puls* ptk1
  - **amel.**: alum-sil k2 bry eupi kola stb3•
  - **tolerated**; are: *Ars* casc *Cedr Eup-per Lyc Nux-v Rhus-t* sulph
- **fire**; from heat of: ip bg2 pulx ptk1
- **food** | **agg.**: *Alum* k* aster vh *Bell* k* bry k* **Puls** k*
- **hot** water bottle amel.: bamb-a stb2.de•
- **irons**:
  - **amel.**:
    - **hot** irons: *Caps* **Lachn**
    - **covering**; but not by external: lachn
- **room**:
  - **agg.**: *Acon Alum* b4.de* **Anac** b4.de* **Ant-c** b7a.de* **Apis** k* *Arg-n Arn* bg2 ars b4.de* asar b7.de* bar-c b4.de* bar-s k2 *Bov* bg2 bry k* canth bg2 caust bg2 chin b7.de* *Cina* b7a.de* cinnb *Clem* bg2 **Cocc** b7.de* colch bg2 croc b7.de* *Dulc* bg2 graph bg2 grat k2 *Guaj* bg2 hell bg2 **Iod** b4.de* **Ip** k* kali-c bg2 lach bg2 *Laur* b7.de* lyc bg2 m-aust b7.de *Mag-m* bg2 meny bg2 merc k* **Mez** b4.de* mur-ac b4.de* nat-m k* nux-v bg2 ol-an bg2 ph-ac b4.de* *Phos* b4.de* plat bg2 puls k* ran-b b7.de* rhus-t b7.de* *Ruta* b7a.de* sabin bg2 *Sars* b4.de* **Sec** *Sep* k* sil b4.de* *Spong* bg2 staph k* **Sul-ac** b4a.de* sulph bg2 teucr b7.de* thuj bg2*
    - **smothering** in: **Apis**
  - **amel.**: *Aesc* agar k* am-c k* **Ars** k* *Bar-c* k* bell brom calad bg2 camph k* canth k* carb-an k* carb-v k* *Caust* k* cham bg2 **Chel** k* *Chin* k* chinin-ar *Cic* k* coff bg2 con k* gels guaj bg2 hell k* *Hep* k* **Ign** k* **Kali-ar** *Kali-bi* **Kali-c** k* kali-sil k2 kreos k* *Lach* k* laur k* mag-c k* mang k* **Meny** k* merc k* merc-c k* mez nat-ar **Nux-m** k* *Nux-v* k* petr k* *Plat* k* ran-b k* rat rhod k* *Rhus-t* k* **Sabad** k* sel k* *Sep* k* sil k* spig k* *Sul-ac* k* sulph k* *Tarent Ther* valer k* zinc k*
  - **entering** a warm room; when | **air**; from open: am-c h2 *Arg-n* ars h2 bar-c h2 chin h1 plat h2 rhus-t h1
  - **feels** cold: spong fd4.de thuj
  - **not** amel. in warm room nor by a warm stove: *Acon Alum* alum-p k2 **Anac** *Ant-c* **Apis** aran arg-n ars ars-i ars-s-f k2 asar bamb-a stb2.de• *Bapt* bell **Bov Bry** cact calc canth carb-ac *Chin* choc srj3• cic *Cina* cinnb clem **Cocc** colch dios dros *Dulc* euphr *Ferr-i* graph h2 guaj hell hep iod **Ip** kali-i *Kreos* lach *Laur* lyc *Mag-m* meny h1 *Merc* **Mez** *Nat-m* nit-ac h2 nux-m **Nux-v** ph-ac *Phos Podo* **Puls** *Ruta* sabin sars *Sep Sil Spong Staph* stry *Sul-ac* sulph teucr thuj til **Verat** visc c1
- **stove**:
  - **desire** to be near: *Gels* mosch *Rhus-t*
    - **cold**, and gets sick near; he feels: *Laur* k* pulx br1
    - **increases** the chill; but it: chin
  - **not** amel.: kali-i kreos podo *Tarent*
  - **sitting** near a warm stove; when: *Alum* b4a.de* *Anac* b4a.de* ant-c bg2 **Apis** bg2 *Ars* bg2 asar bg2 bar-c bg2 *Bov* b4a.de* bry bg2 canth b7a.de* caust bg2 chin bg2 *Cina* b7a.de* **Cocc** b7.de* colch bg2 croc bg2 *Dios* a1 *Dulc* b4a.de* graph bg2 *Guaj* b4a.de* hell bg2 iod b4a.de* **Ip** b7.de* kali-c b4a.de* lach bg2 *Laur* b7.de* lyc bg2 *Mag-m* b4a.de* meny b7.de* *Merc* b4.de* **Mez** bg2 mur-ac bg2 nat-m bg2 *Nux-v* b7.de* ph-ac bg2 *Phos* b4a.de* plat bg2 **Puls** b7a.de* ran-b bg2 rhus-t b7.de* *Ruta* b7a.de* sabin bg2 *Sars* b4a.de* sep bg2 sil bg2 *Spong* b7.de* *Staph* b7.de* sul-ac bg2 sulph bg2 teucr bg2 thuj b4.de*
- **sun**; desire for: anac con

WARMTH:

- **agg.** | **unbearable**: **Apis** *Camph* **Ip** *Mez* b4a.de **Puls Sec Sep** staph

Warmth: ...

- **external**:
  - **amel.**: *Aesc* arg-met arn **Ars** k* aur bg2 *Bar-c* k* **Bell** camph bg2 canth k* **Caps** k* carb-an *Caust* k* chel *Chin Chinin-ar* cic k* cimx clem bg2 cocc colch con k* cor-r *Eup-per* ferr *Gels Hell* k* *Hep* k* hyos **Ign** k* **Kali-c** k* kali-i kali-sil k2 kola stb3• *Lach* k* *Lachn* laur k* **Meny** k* merl *Mez* mosch k* nat-c **Nux-m** k* **Nux-v** k* *Plat* k* *Podo* pyrog k2 rhod bg2 **Rhus-t** k* **Sabad** k* samb k* sep sil k* *Squil* k* *Stram* stront-c k* sulph k* *Tarent Ther* tub k2
  - **not** amel.: aran bro1
- **wrapping** up, followed by severe fever and sweat; amel. by: cench k2 kola stb3• sil

WATER: (↗*Bathing*)

- **dashed** over him; as if cold water were: *Agar* k* ail alum bg2 *Anac* bg2 ant-t k* apis **Arn** k* ars *Bar-c* k* bry *Chel Chin* k* croc bg2 *Led* bg2 lil-t lyc mag-c bg2 merc k* mez k* nat-m nux-v k* phel *Phos* k* *Puls* k* **Rhus-t** k* *Sabad* k* spig thuj k* valer bg2 vario bg2 *Verat* k* verb k*
- **getting** wet; from: acon *Aran* bar-c *Bell Bry Calc* cedr *Dulc Nat-s* **Rhus-t** *Sep* sil
  - **overheated**; when: acon *Calc Clem* colch *Rhus-t* sep sil
- **poured** over him; as if: *Anac Ant-t Arn* b7a.de ars *Bar-c* canth ptk1 *Chin* cimx *Led* k* *Mag-c* **Merc** k* mez k* *Puls* b7a.de* *Rhus-t* k* stram *Thuj* b4a.de *Verat* b7a.de *Verb* b7a.de
- **running** down the back; as if: agar alumn ars
  - **clavicles** across the chest down to the toes, along the narrow space; from the: caust
- **spurted** upon the back; as if: caust lyc
- **standing** in cold water; as if: gels bg2
- **trickled** down the back; as if: ars caps caust
- **working** in, from: **Calc** *Rhus-t*

WAVES; in: carb-an ptk1

WEATHER:

- **cold** damp: (↗*Exposure - wet*) am-c k* *Aran* k* *Calc* k* *Dulc* lyc k* mang k* merc k* **Nux-m** k* *Rhus-t* k* sulph k* verat k*
- **hot**, in summer: ang bapt bell bry chin
- **stormy**:
  - **agg.**: *Bry* k* cham k* chin k* nux-m k* nux-v k* phos k* puls k* rhod k* *Rhus-t* k* **Zinc** k*
  - **before**: bry bg2 gels bg2 zinc bg2
- **warm** | **agg.**: ant-c *Ars* bapt *Bell Bry* calc **Caps** carb-v *Cedr* chin cina *Ip* **Lach** nat-m psor jl2 puls **Sulph** *Thuj*

WET: | **agg.**: aran bro1 lappa ptk1 led ptk1 *Rhus-t* ptk1 thuj ptk1

WET agg.; getting: bell bg2 *Bry* bg2 calc bg2 colch bg2 hep bg2 lyc bg2 nux-m bg2 puls bg2 *Rhus-t* bg2 sars bg2 **Sep** b4a.de*

WIND:

- **agg.**: lyc bg2 sanic ptk1 zinc bg2
- **cold** | **agg.**: agra br1
- **sensation** of:
  - **blowing** cold upon the body; it were: acon bg2 agar bg2 asaf bg2 asar k* bar-c bg2 calc bg2 camph k* canth bg2 caps bg2 caust k* chel bg2 *Chin* k* cimic bg2 cimx coloc bg2 *Cor-r* bg2 croc k* cupr k* hep lac-d bg2* *Laur* k* m-arct b2.de *M-aust* b2.de* mez bg2 mosch k* nat-m bg2 nux-v bg2 ol-an bg2 olnd bg2 petr bg2 ph-ac h2* phos bg2 plat bg2 puls bg2 ran-b bg2 rhus-t k* samb k* sulph bg2 valer bg2 verat bg2
  - **blowing** upon soles while body was sweating; as if wind were: acon
  - **cold** air were extending from the spine over the body; as if | **epileptic** aura; like an: agar
  - **shoulder** blades; between the: *Caust*
  - **walking** agg.: chin

WINE agg.: cina bg2

WRITING agg.: agar k* zinc h2

YAWNING: | **with** (See SLEEP - Yawning - chill - during)

BODY:

○ - **Forepart** of body: *Cham* bg2 puls bg2 sulph bg2

Chill

- **Lower** part of body: acon bg2 **Arn** bg2 nux-v bg2 puls bg2 sars bg2
- **Posterior** part: *Rhus-t* bg2

SIDE lain on: arn k* calc bg2 mur-ac

SIDE not lain on: ant-c h2 ferr-ma

SINGLE parts: abies-c sne *Acon* b2.de* agar b2.de* agn b2.de* alum b2.de* am-c bg2 am-m bg2 **Ambr** k* anac b2.de* ant-t bg2 anth vh apis bg2 arg-met b2.de* arn b2.de* ars k* *Asar* k* aur b2.de* bamb-a stb2.de• bar-c k* bell k* borx b2.de* bov b2.de* brom bg2 bry k* calad k* *Calc* k* camph b2.de* cann-xyz bg2 canth bg2 caps bg2 carb-an bg2 carb-v b2.de* *Caust* k* cham k* chel bg2* chin b2.de* cic bg2 cocc bg2 coff b2.de* colch b2.de* coloc bg2 con bg2 croc b2.de* cupr bg2 dig b2.de* dros b2.de* dulc b2.de* euph bg2 euphr b2.de* graph bg2 guaj b2.de* hell b2.de* hep k* hyos b2.de* **Ign** k* iod bg2 ip b2.de* kali-bi bro1 kali-c b2.de* kali-n bg2 *Kreos* b2.de* lach bg2 laur bg2 *Led* k* lyc k* m-arct b2.de m-aust b2.de mag-c b2.de* mang bg2 meny b2.de* *Merc* b2.de* merc-c bg2 **Mez** k* *Mosch* k* mur-ac b2.de* nat-c b2.de* nat-m b2.de* nit-ac bg2 nux-m bg2 nux-v k* olnd bg2 op b2.de* *Par* b2.de* petr b2.de* *Ph-ac* b2.de* phos b2.de* **Plat** b2.de* plb b2.de* **Puls** k* *Ran-b* b2.de* rhod bg2 rhus-t k* ruta bg2 sabad bg2 sabin bg2 samb b2.de* sars bg2 sec bg2* seneg bg2 **Sep** k* sil k* spig b2.de* spong b2.de* squil b2.de* stann b2.de* staph b2.de* stram bg2 stront-c b2.de* sulph b2.de* thuj k* valer bg2 verat k* verb b2.de* viol-t bg2 zinc b2.de*

- **night**: aloe bg2 alum bg2 ant-c bg2 bov bg2 bry bg2 calad bg2 *Calc* bg2 com bg2 cop bg2 ferr bg2 iod bg2 naja bg2 nit-ac bg2 petr bg2 phos bg2 psor bg2 rhod bg2 sars bg2 sep bg2 *Sil* bg2 sulph bg2 thuj bg2 verat bg2 zinc bg2
- **accompanied** by | **heat** of other parts: chin bg2 *Ign* bg2 nux-v bg2 *Rhus-t* bg2 sabad bg2
- **bed** agg.; in: am-m bg2 ars bg2 bov bg2 calc bg2 carb-v bg2 graph bg2 kali-c bg2 merc bg2 nit-ac bg2 phos bg2 rhod bg2 rhus-t bg2 sep bg2 sil bg2 sulph bg2 zinc bg2

FEVER, heat in general: abrom-a ks5 acet-ac c2 **Acon** k* aesc aeth agar agn agrosti-vg br1 alet c2 all-s c2* alst k* alum am-act c2 am-c am-m *Ambr* anac *Ang* ant-c k* **Ant-t** k* anthraci **Apis** k* aran arg-met *Arist-cl* sp1 **Arn** k* **Ars** k* ars-h arum-i c2 *Arum-t* asaf asim c2* astac c2 aur c2 aur-m aur-s k2 *Bapt* *Bar-c* bar-ox-suc rly4• basil jsx1.fr **Bell** k* bell-p sp1 ben c2 benz-ac benzo c2 berb c2 bid-p jsx1.fr bit-ar wht1• bol-la k* both fne1• brom **Bry** k* **Cact** cadm-s cain calad mrr1 *Calc* calen c2 calo c2 camph *Canch* br1 *Canth* k* *Caps* k* carb-an carb-v k* *Carbn-s* card-b c2 card-m c2 casc caul caust k* cedr k* cent c2 *Cham* k* *Chel* chim c2 *Chin* k* **Chinin-s** k* chir-fl bnm4• cic h1 cimic cimx *Cina* k* cinch c2 cloth tsm2 coca c2 *Cocc* *Coff* *Colch* colchin c2 coloc h2 colum-p sze2• **Con** k* convo-s sp1 conyz-sm jsx1.fr cop corn-a br1 corn-f croc crot-h cupr *Cur* *Cycl* cymbop-ci jsx1.fr daph c2 *Dig* k* diph jl2 diph-pert-t mp4• diph-t-tpt jl2 dor c2 dros *Dulc* eberth jl2 echi mtf11 *Elaps* elat epil c1* ery-m c2 eucal eup-a br1 *Eup-per* eup-pur euph euphr k2 eys sp1 *Ferr* ferr-ar k2 **Ferr-p** k* fic-m gya1 *Fl-ac* galv c2 gard-t jsx1.fr **Gels** k* gent-l c2 *Graph* guaj c2 guiz-sc jsx1.fr gymno c2 hedy a1* *Hell* *Hep* *Hyos* k* hyosin c2 *Ign* k* *Iod* **Ip** k* iris-t c2 ix bnm8• kali-bi kali-c kali-chl **Kali-i** kali-s ptk1 *Kreos* *Lac-c* lacer a1 *Lach* k* lachn lat-m bnm6• *Laur* *Led* leptos-ih jl2 lim c2 lob loxo-lae bnm12• loxo-recl bnm10• **Lyc** k* lyss c2 *Mag-c* mag-m mag-s k* malar c2* mang markh-l jsx1.fr med ptk1 meny *Merc* k* *Merc-c* k* *Merc-cy* *Merl* **Mez** k* micr br1 mik-c jsx1.fr mill mom-ch jsx1.fr mosch *Mur-ac* muru a1 nat-c **Nat-m** k* nat-p k2 nat-s nat-sal c2 *Nit-ac* *Nux-m* **Nux-v** k* oci-g jsx1.fr oci-sa sp1 ol-j c2 olib-sac wmh1 *Op* k* oper br1 oxyt c2 *Parathyr* jl2 parth c2* pert jl2 pert-vc vk9 petr petr-ra shn4• *Ph-ac* phenac c2 **Phos** k* physala-p bnm7• pic-ac ptk1 pimp c2 pisc c2 plb plect c2 plumbg c2 *Podo* k* positr nl2• prim-v c2 prin c1* *Psor* ptel c1 **Puls** k* pyre-p c2 pyrog jl2 queb c1* ran-a c2 raph c2 rhod c2 **Rhus-t** k* *Rhus-v* ruta h1* sabad *Sabin* sal-n c2 sal-p c2 salol c1* *Samb* *Sang* k* sapin c2 saroth sp1 sarr sars h2 scarl jl2 **Sec** senec-ma jsx1.fr seneg *Sep* ser-a-c jl2 **Sil** spig **Spong** **Squil** *Stann* *Staph* **Stram** *Sul-ac* *Sulph* k* *Sumb* **Tarax** k* *Tarent* ter teucr thuj toxo-g jl2 triclis-g jsx1.fr trios c2 tritic-vg fd5.de tub-a jl2 tub-m jl2 urt-u mrr1 *Valer* vario c2 **Verat** k* *Verat-v* vern-am jsx1.fr *Viol-t* wye c2 yohim lp2 zinc [alam dbx1.fr androp-sn dbx1.fr aphlo-t dbx1.fr arund-p dbx1.fr calli-al dbx1.fr cyath dbx1.fr haru-pa dbx1.fr sal-ma dbx1.fr scirp-p dbx1.fr spect dfg1 trem-g dbx1.fr]

SIDE:

- **one** side: (↗*Body*) acon bg2 agar bg2 *Agn* bg2 **Alum** k* am-m bg2 ambr b2.de anac b2.de* ang bg2 ant-c bg2 ant-t b2.de* arn k* ars bg2 asaf k* asar bg2 bar-c b2.de* *Bell* k* borx bg2 bov bg2 brom bg2 **Bry** k* calc bg2 cann-xyz bg2 caps bg2 carb-an bg2 carb-v k* *Caust* k* **Cham** k* chel k* chin b2.de cina bg2 *Clem* k* cocc b2.de* coff bg2 colch bg2 coloc bg2 croc b2.de cycl bg2 **Dig** k* dros bg2 dulc bg2 euph bg2 *Graph* k* hell bg2 hyos bg2 ign b2.de* *Kali-c* k* laur bg2 **Lyc** k* mag-c bg2 mag-m bg2 mang k* meny bg2 merc bg2 mez bg2 **Mosch** k* mur-ac k* nat-c k* nat-m bg2 nit-ac bg2 **Nux-v** k* olnd bg2 **Par** k* *Ph-ac* k* *Phos* k* plat k* plb bg2 **Puls** k* ran-b bg2 rheum bg2 *Rhus-t* k* ruta b2.de* sabad b2.de* sars b2.de* seneg bg2 sep bg2 spig k* squil bg2 stann b2.de* staph k* stram b2.de *Stront-c* bg2 sul-ac k* *Sulph* k* *Tarax* k* teucr bg2 thuj k* verat k* verb k* viol-o k* zinc k*
  - **right**: **Alum** k* am-m bg2 ambr b7a.de ant-c bg2 ant-t bg2 ars bg2 asaf bg2 asar bg2 bar-c bg2 *Bell* k* borx bg2 bov bg2 brom bg2 *Bry* k* cann-xyz bg2 carb-v k* caust b4a.de *Cham* k* chin b7a.de clem bg2 cocc b7a.de colch bg2 coloc bg2 dros b7a.de* dulc bg2 fl-ac k* ign bg2 kali-c k* laur bg2 lyc bg2 *Mag-c* k* mag-m k* mosch k* mur-ac bg2 nat-c k* *Nux-v* k* olnd bg2 **Phos** k* plb bg2 *Puls* k* *Ran-b* k* rhus-t bg2 sabad sabin b7a.de sep bg2 spig k* squil bg2 staph bg2 stront-c bg2 thuj bg2 tub verb k*
  - **left**: acon bg2 agar b4a.de* agn b7a.de ambr b7a.de anac k* ant-c k* arn b7a.de bar-c b4a.de bell k* calc bg2 caps bg2 carb-v b4a.de caust b4a.de cham b7a.de chel bg2 *Chin* b7a.de cina bg2 cocc bg2 coff bg2 cycl bg2 dig b4a.de euph bg2 graph bg2 hell bg2 hyos bg2 ign bg2 **Lyc** k* meny bg2 merc k* *Mez* k* nat-m k* nit-ac bg2 nux-v k* *Par* k* ph-ac k* *Plat* k* puls b7a.de *Ran-b* k* rheum bg2 **Rhus-t** k* ruta b7a.de* sars bg2 seneg bg2 sep bg2 spig b7a.de* **Stann** k* sul-ac bg2 *Sulph* k* tarax bg2 teucr bg2 thuj k* verb b7a.de viol-o bg2 zinc bg2
    - **coldness** of right; with: par **Rhus-t**
- **cheek** red and hot, the other pale and cold; one: **Acon**
- **hand** and foot are red and cold; one side of body | **other** side, hand and foot are hot in the evening and at night; and the: *Puls*

DAY:

- **febrile** heat only during the: ail ant-t k* bell berb carb-v *Eup-per* ox-ac sep k* sulph thuj
- **periodically** during the: sil

MORNING (= 6-9 h): aeth ail am-c h2 am-m b7a.de* anac b4.de *Ang* **Apis** k* aq-mar skp7• *Arn* k* ars k* ars-s-f k2 bamb-a stb2.de• bell k* **Bism** b7.de* borx k* bry k* *Calc* k* carb-an *Caust* k* *Cham* k* chel chin k* cimic cina b7.de coff k* con b4.de cycl k* dros dulc b4a.de* eup-per euph b4a.de* ferr b7.de fl-ac glon graph b4.de hell b7.de *Hep* k* ign k* ip b7.de* kali-bi kali-c k* *Kali-i* k* lach laur b7.de* lyc bg2 m-ambo b7.de* mag-c k* malar jl2 meph a1 mez b4.de* *Nat-m* k* nicc nit-ac b4.de nux-m nux-v k* op b7.de ox-ac petr k* petr-ra shn4• ph-ac b4.de phos b4.de* phyt k* podo puls b7.de* *Rhus-t* k* sabad k* sang k* sarr *Sep* b4.de* sil b4.de spong h1 staph b7.de* stram b7.de *Sulph* k* teucr k* thuj k* vanil fd5.de verat b7.de vip [spect dfg1]

- **8**-14 h: dor kr1*
- **bed** agg.; in: ars dulc fd4.de ign kali-c h2* nicc nux-v petr k* petr-ra shn4• **Puls** *Sep* sne sulph vanil fd5.de
  - **5** h (See Night - midnight - after - 5h - bed)
- **chill**, without (See Chill absent - morning)
- **chilliness**; with: **Apis** am **Ars** caust cham coff kali-bi kali-c kali-i sulph thuj
- **coffee** agg.: cham h1
- **ejaculation**; after: petr h2
- **rising** agg.; after: am-m h2 *Antip* vh1 calc carb-an coloc h2 lach mag-c rhus-t sabad
  - **and** walking about: aeth camph chel petr sep sulph
- **sensation** of: bamb-a stb2.de•
- **sleep** agg.; during: sulph h2
- **waking**; on: acon-c aeth alum bg2 anac bg2 antip vh am b7.de* ars bg2 bamb-a stb2.de* bapt bg2 bell b4.de* **Borx** b4a.de* calad b7.de* calc bg2 camph caust bg2 chel cina b7.de* cocc b7.de* con bg2 eup-per *Ferr* b7.de* hep bg2 hydrog srj2• ip b7.de* kali-i a1 kreos bg2 lac-c lyc bg2 m-arct b7.de mag-c bg2 mag-m bg2 merc bg2 *Mosch* bg2 nit-ac bg2 petr k* ph-ac bg2 *Phos* b4.de* ptel bg2 puls b7.de* ran-s b7.de* *Samb* bg2 sel bg2 sep k* sil bg2 stront-c bg2 sulph k* **Tarax** b7.de* thuj b4.de*
  - **amel.**: sulph h2
  - **rising** amel., shortly after: antip vh
- **walking** in open air agg.; after: nux-v

FORENOON (= 9-12 h): alum *Am-c* k* am-m k* ant-c b7a.de* arg-met k* arg-n hr1 ars k* *Bapt* bell b4.de berb bry k* cact calc k* calc-sil k2 cann-xyz bg2 caps cedr **Cham** k* **Chin** b7.de* dros b7.de *Eup-per* euphr k2 gels ham k* ign b7.de* kali-c k* lyc *Mag-c* k* nat-c bg2 **Nat-m** k* nux-m k* *Nux-v* op b7.de petr b4.de petr-ra shn4• *Phos* k* *Rhus-t* k* sabad b7.de* sars k* sep k* sil k* sol-ni spig stann bg2 staph b7.de* stram b7.de* sulph k* thuj valer b7.de* verat k* zinc k*

- **9** h: am-c **Cham** k* corh br1 lac-d k2
  - **midnight**, until: corh br1 petr-ra shn4•
- **9** and 17 h: *Kali-c*
- **10** h: aq-mar skp7• *Rhus-t* hr1*
  - **10**-20 h: sil h2
  - **midnight**, until: corh br1
  - **hot** water, or hot water running through the blood vessels; as if dashed with: **Rhus-t**
- **11** h: caps hr1 ozone sde2•
  - **11**-12 h: calc h2
  - **11**-13 h: arg-met k*
  - **11**-17 h: ph-ac h2
  - **thirst** and chilliness; with: sil
- **alternating** with chill: calc cham thuj
- **chilliness**; with: ars *Bapt* **Cham** kali-c sil sulph thuj
- **heat** of the whole body except the head: arg-met
- **menses**; before: am-c

NOON (= 12-13 h): ars k* ars-h bell h1 dulc fd4.de ferr-i k* mag-c h2 merc spig *Stram* k* sulph k* tritic-vg fd5.de

- **14** h; until: ars mrr1
- **15** h; until: ars mrr1

AFTERNOON (= 13-18 h): acon k* agar k* alum k* alum-p k2 alum-sil k2 am-m k* ambr k* *Anac* k* *Ang* k* ant-c b7.de ant-t k* **Apis** arg-n k* *Arn* *Ars* k* ars-i k2* ars-s-f k2 *Asaf* k* asar k* aster aza br1* bapt hr1 **Bell** k* berb bov k* *Bry* k* cain calad k* calc k* calc-ar calc-i k2 calc-s calc-sil k2 calen *Canth* k* caps caust k* cench k2 *Chel* *Chin* k* cina k* coff k* *Colch* k* con k* croc cur dig k* dros k* dulc fd4.de epil a1 eup-per euphr k2 eupi ferr k* *Ferr-ar* ferr-i k* **Gels** k* graph b4.de hep k* hyos k* **Ign** k* iod k* ip k* iris *Kali-ar* *Kali-c* k*

Fever

Afternoon: ...
Kali-n kali-p kali-sil k2 lac-ac *Lach* k* laur b7.de* lil-t br1 *Lyc* lyss m-arct b7.de m-aust b7.de mag-c k* mag-m k* mag-s mez b4.de *Nat-m* k* nicc *Nit-ac* k* nux-v k* par b7.de* ph-ac k* **Phos** k* phyt plb b7.de* podo psor **Puls** k* ran-b k* rhod rhus-t k* *Ruta* k* sabad b7.de sabin b7.de* samb b7.de* *Sang* k* sarr sars h2 senec k* *Sep* k* *Sil* k* spig b7.de spong k* *Squil* k* **Stann** b4.de* *Staph* k* stram k* sul-ac k* sul-i k2 sulph k* thuj b4.de tritic-vg fd5.de trom k* verat b7.de zinc k*
- **13** h: ars cact hura lyc still
  - **13**-16 h | **headache**; with severe: lac-ac
- **14** h: chlor mag-c mag-s **Puls** rhus-t sang sol-ni
  - **14**-15 h: phos h2
  - **followed** by chill at 16 h: **Puls**
- **15** h: acon apis hr1* cench k2 coff ferr lyc nicc *Sang*
  - **15**-16 h: clem crot-c sk4• lyc
  - **midnight**; until: cench k2
- **16** h: anac chel *Hep* ip *Lyc*
  - **after**: *Anac* bg2 lyc bg2 *Stann* bg2
  - **16**-17 h: stann
  - **16**-20 h: *Hell Lyc*
  - **midnight**; until: phos k2 *Stram*
  - **periodical** every day, eating amel.: *Anac*
- **17** h: con kali-c kali-n nat-c nit-ac phos rhus-t sulph thuj
- **alternating** with chill: **Calc** kali-n sul-i k2 sulph h2
- **chilliness**:
  - **followed** by: kali-n
    - **air** agg.; in open: kali-c
  - **with**: anac **Apis** *Ars* caust coff *Colch* cur hyos kali-c *Podo* *Rhus-t* sil sulph
- **coldness**; with external: sulph
- **dinner** | **after** | **agg.**: alum bar-c dig *Lach* nit-ac phos plan ptel raph sabin sul-ac til
  - **during** | **agg.**: *Mag-m* sul-ac thuj valer
- **lying** down agg.; after: bry carb-an chel coff mag-m nicc **Puls** sul-ac sulph zinc
- **sleep** agg.; after: borx *Calad* ferr nat-m
- **tuberculosis**; in beginning: ars-i br1
- **walking**:
  - **agg.**: bry thuj
  - **air**; in open:
    - **after** | **agg.**: meny

EVENING (= 18-22 h): **Acon** k* aesc *Agar* k* **Agn** b7.de* alum k* alum-p k2 alum-sil k2 am-c k* am-m b7.de* ambr b7.de* anac k* ang k* ant-c b7a.de* ant-t k* anthraci apis k* aran arg-met arn k* *Ars* k* ars-br vh ars-h ars-s-f k2 **Asar** bg2 astac kr1 aster k* bapt bar-c bar-m bar-s k2 **Bell** k* *Berb* borx k* bov k* bry k* bufo bg2 calad k* *Calc* k* *Calc-s* k* calc-sil k2 calen caps k* carb-an b4a.de* *Carb-v* k* carbn-s cassia-s ccrh1• caust k* cench k2 *Cham* k* *Chel* k* **Chin** k* chinin-s *Cina* k* clem coc-c k* cocc k* coff k* coloc k* con k* croc cycl k* diphtox jl2 dros k* elaps epil a1 euphr k* ferr k* ferr-ar ferr-i graph b4.de* **Guaj** b4.de* hell k* *Hep* k* hipp jl2 *Hyos* k* ign k* iod b4a.de* ip k* kali-ar *Kali-c* k* kali-i k* kali-n k* kali-p kali-s kali-sil k2 **Lach** k* **Laur** b7.de* lec led k* **Lyc** k* m-arct b7.de mag-c bg2* mag-m k* meny b7.de* *Merc* k* *Mez* k* mosch k* mur-ac k* nat-c b4.de* nat-m k* nicc nit-ac k* nux-m nux-v k* op b7.de par b7.de* pert-vc vk9 petr k* petr-ra shn4• *Ph-ac* k* **Phos** k* pitu-gl skp7• plat k* plb k* *Psor* **Puls** k* ran-b k* **Ran-s** b7.de* rhod k* **Rhus-t** k* ruta b7.de* sabad k* sabin k* samb b7.de* *Sars* k* sel bg2 *Sep* k* **Sil** k* spig k* spong b7.de* squil k* stann k* staph k* stram k* stront-c bg2 sul-ac k* *Sulph* k* tetox pin2• **Teucr** b7.de* *Thuj* k* tritic-vg fd5.de tub gk **Valer** b7.de* verat k* vip k* zinc k* zinc-p k2
- **18** h: adam srj5• ant-t arg-n berb borx carb-v h2 caust chin cocc hep kali-c lac-ac limen-b-c hm2* malar jl2 nux-v rhod *Rhus-t*
  - **18**-19 h: calc h2 phos h2
  - **18**-20 h: calc caust h2* **Lyc** *Sulph* vh
  - **18**-0 h: lachn a1
- **19** h: ambr bov elaps *Lyc* mag-s petr pitu-gl skp7• puls rhus-t
- **20** h: alum-sil k2 ant-t coff ferr hep lachn mur-ac naja nicc *Phos* sol-ni sulph
  - **20**-21 h: ars sulph

Evening: ...
- **21** h: **Bry** lac-d kr1* lyc mag-s nit-ac
  - **21**-0 h: bry k2
- **morning**; and: *Hep*
- **bed** agg.; in: *Acon* agn anac h2 arg-met borx calc h2 calen coc-c coff hep kali-c kali-i a1 kali-n h2 mosch ruta fd4.de sars sulph h2 thuj
  - **lying** down agg.; after: *Acon* asar bar-c **Bry** carb-ac chel coff hell mag-m ruta fd4.de samb h1 sul-ac h2 sulph h2 zinc h2
  - **perspiration**; with: borx bov calc verat h1
- **chill**; after: acon apis ars berb graph guaj petr k* sulph
- **chilliness**; with: *Acon* anac apis am ars ars-s-f k2 bapt borx carb-v caust *Cham* choc srj3• coff *Elaps* ferr-i hep kali-c kali-i mur-ac k2 nat-m pert-vc vk9 sabin *Sil* sulph thuj tritic-vg fd5.de
- **cough** agg.; during: *Con* b4a.de
- **delirium**; with: *Psor*
- **eating**; after: anac ang raph ruta fd4.de
- **lasting**:
  - **from** 19-0 h, following 16 h chill: *Aesc* k*
  - **all** night: acon bol-la cocc graph hep lach lyc puls *Rhus-t* sarr sil tarent k2
    - **followed** by shuddering: cocc
- **room**, on entering the: ang nicc **Puls** sul-ac sulph zinc

NIGHT: (↗*Bed - in*) *Acon* k* aesc bro1 *Agar* k* *Alum* k* alum-sil k2 am-c k* am-m k* anac k* androc srj1• ang k* ant-c k* ant-t k* *Apis* k* arn b7.de* *Ars* k* ars-h *Ars-i* arum-t arund aur-ar k2 bamb-a stb2.de• **Bapt** k* *Bar-c* k* *Bar-m* bar-s k2 **Bell** k* berb bol-la borx **Bry** k* bufo bg2 cact k* cadm-s calad k* *Calc* k* calc-s calc-sil k2 camph b7.de* *Cann-s* b7a.de* *Canth* k* caps carb-an k* *Carb-v* k* **Carbn-s** caust k* cedr *Cham* k* chin b7.de* chinin-ar k2 chir-fl gya2 cic *Cimic* **Cina** k* *Cinnb* **Clem** b4.de* coca cocc k* coff k* **Colch** k* con k* cur cycl dig *Dros* k* dulc k* elaps epil a1 ferr *Ferr-ar* ferr-p bg2 fic-m gya1 fl-ac bg2* *Gels* k* glon **Graph** k* *Hep* k* hura hydr hydrog srj2• hyos b7.de ign k* *Iod* bg2* *Kali-bi* kali-c h2* kali-i bg2* kali-n b4.de* kali-p kali-s k* kali-sil k2 lac-d al2* **Lach** k* laur b7a.de* led b7.de* lil-t *Lyc* k* *M-ambo* b7.de* m-arct b7.de mag-c k* mag-m k* mag-s malar jl2 **Merc** k* *Merc-cy* *Morph* *Mur-ac* *Nat-ar* nat-c h2 nat-m k* *Nat-s* nicc *Nit-ac* k* nux-m b7.de* *Nux-v* k* ol-j br1 *Op* k* paeon *Petr* k* petr-ra shn4• *Ph-ac* k* **Phos** k* pitu-gl skp7• plb k* psor **Puls** k* ran-b b7.de* **Ran-s** b7a.de* raph rheum b7.de* rhod b4.de* **Rhus-t** k* *Sabad* k* sabin b7.de* sarr sec bg2 *Sep* k* **Sil** k* **Spig** b7.de* spong b7.de* *Squil* b7.de* stann bro1 staph k* *Stram* k* **Stront-c** b4.de* sul-ac k2 **Sulph** k* **Tarax** b7.de* *Tarent* tetox pin2• thuj k* tritic-vg fd5.de *Tub* urt-u bro1* ust verat k* **Viol-t** b7.de* vip bg2 zinc k* zinc-p k2
- **midnight**: **Ars** coc-c elaps lyc mag-m mag-s nux-v petr *Rhus-t* sep *Stram* k* sulph tritic-vg fd5.de verat k*
  - **before**: acon agar alum k* am-m bg2 ant-c k* ars bapt k2 **Bry** k* cadm-s **Calad** k* *Carb-v* cham k* *Chin* b7.de *Chinin-s* elaps eug ferr b7.de* *Graph* hydr lach k2 *Laur* k* lyc k* *Mag-m* k* mag-s nit-ac nux-v k2 petr ph-ac h2 phos puls k* rhus-t h1* sabad k* sep k* sulph h2 verat k*
    - **22** h: alum-sil k2 ars elaps hydr lach petr
    - **23** h: cench k2 mag-m
      - **23**-0 h: pitu-gl skp7•
  - **after**: ang k* ant-c h2 **Ars** k* ars-s-f k2 borx bry bg2 calc b4.de* caust chin k* cic cimic coff b7.de* dros elaps ferr *Ferr-ar* gamb al4 ign k* *Kali-c* k* kreos b7a.de* *Lyc* m-ambo b7.de mag-c mag-m merc k* nat-m nit-ac h2 **Petr** bg2 ph-ac bg2 phos k* puls b7.de* ran-b *Ran-s* k* *Rhod* b4a.de* rhus-t bg2 sabad k* *Samb* b7a.de* sars spong b7.de* **Staph** b7.de* sul-ac h2 sulph k* thuj k*
    - **0**-2 h: *Ars* mrr1
    - **2** h: *Ars* borx tax
      - **2**-3 h: benz-ac bg2
    - **3** h: ang thuj
      - **3**-5 h: kali-c k2
      - **until**: *Ars* mrr1
    - **4**-5 h: sep a1
    - **5** h:
      - **bed** agg.; in: cench k2
      - **followed** by shaking chill: *Apis* k*
  - **8** h; until: sil h2
  - **and** noon: ars *Elaps* spig stram sulph

- **midnight**: ...
  - **menses**; before: lyc
  - **perspiration**, when lying on the back; with: *Cham*
  - **sleep**, passing away on waking; during: *Calad*
- **anxiety** and perspiration; with: alum calc
- **chilliness**; with: acon *Agar* apis *Ars* ars-s-f k2 bapt carb-v carbn-s caust cham choc srj3• coca coff *Colch* cur *Elaps Graph Kali-bi Rhus-t Sil* **Sulph** thuj tub
- **chilly** during day, heat at night: dros k*
- **dry** burning heat: **Acon** alum-p k2 anac arn **Ars** *Bar-c* **Bell Bry** calc carb-v caust cedr chel chinin-s *Cina* coc-c coff *Colch* coloc *Con* dulc *Graph* hep kali-n *Lach* lyc *Nit-ac* nux-m *Nux-v* **Phos** *Puls* ran-s rhod **Rhus-t** rhus-v spig thuj *Tub*
  - **anxiety**; with: acon *Apis* **Ars** bar-c bry rhus-t
  - **sleeplessness**; with: bar-c *Cham* graph hyos *Phos*
  - **thirst**; without: *Apis* **Ars**
- **high** temperature; very: bry k2 hyos k2 rhus-t k2 stram k2
- **hunger**; with: kali-p k2
- **perspiration**; with: agar alum am-m *Ant-c* **Bell** borx bry calc caps carb-an cedr cina *Colch Con* ferr glon hydrog srj2• ign mag-c mag-m **Merc** nat-m nit-ac nux-v op **Phos** *Psor* **Puls Rhus-t** sabad *Sep* spig h1 staph stram **Sulph** thuj verat
  - **clammy** perspiration and quick pulse: cimic
- **waking**:
  - **on**: **Bar-c** benz-ac carb-v coloc gamb al4 mag-m h2 sil h2 **Sulph** tarax h1 zinc
  - **amel.**: *Calad*
- **water** were poured over one; as if hot water: ars

ABORTION; after: bell tl1 puls tl1

ACCOMPANIED BY:
- **asthmatic** respiration (See RESPIRATION - Asthmatic - accompanied - fever)
- **beer**; desire for (See GENERALS - Food and - beer - desire - fever - during)
- **bilious** complaints: ant-c b7.de* ars b4a.de bry b7a.de *Cham* b7.de* *Chin* b7.de* *Cocc* b7.de* dig b4a.de ign b7.de* *Nux-v* b7.de* puls b7.de*
- **blood** poisoning: ail tl1
- **cold** drinks; desire for (See GENERALS - Food and - cold drink - desire - fever)
- **coryza**: acon bg2 anac bg2 ars bg2 bell bg2 bry bg2 calc bg2 camph bg2 cham bg2 cina bg2 hep bg2 *Lach* bg2 *Lyc* bg2 merc bg2 merc-c bg2 mosch bg2 *Nux-v* bg2 puls bg2 rhus-t bg2 sabad bg2 seneg bg2 *Spig* bg2
- **diphtheria** (See THROAT - Diphtheria - accompanied - fever)
- **drinks**; aversion to (See GENERALS - Food and - drinks - aversion - heat)
- **flushes** of heat: bac jl2 glon tl1
- **migraine**: tub-d jl2
- **pneumonia** (See CHEST - Inflammation - lungs - accompanied - fever)
- **suppuration**: acon bro1 bell bro1 merc bro1 *Rhus-t* bro1
- **thirst** (See STOMACH - Thirst - fever - during)
- **thirstlessness** (See STOMACH - Thirstless - fever)
- **warm** drinks; desire for (See GENERALS - Food and - warm drinks - desire - fever)

○ - **Brain**; complaints of ars b4a.de *Bell* b4a.de hyos b7.de lyc b4a.de op b7.de stram b7.de verat b7.de
- **Stomach**; complaints of: *Ant-c* b7.de* cham b7.de* cocc b7.de* *Ign* b7a.de *Ip* b7.de* *Nux-v* b7.de* puls b7.de* rhus-t b7a.de sabad b7.de*

ACIDS: | agg.: lach bg2

ADYNAMIC FEVER (See GENERALS - Weakness - fever - during - agg.)

AFFECTED parts: acon k* arn bell bry k* guaj h2* sulph

AIDS: carc mlr1•

AIR: | **intolerance** of both cold and warm: cocc

AIR; IN OPEN:
- **agg.**: ang h1 chin cur **Nux-v** staph h1

Air; in open: ...
- **amel.**: canth cassia-s ccrh1• mosch *Nat-m* petr-ra shn4• phos b4.de*

ALTERNATING with:
- **chilliness**, dry, burning heat: *Bell* sang
- **chills**: abies-n br1* acon k* agar *Agn* k* all-c all-s alum alum-p k2 am-c k* **Am-m** k* androc srj1• ange-s oss1• *Ant-t* k* *Apis* bro1 arn **Ars** k* *Ars-i* ars-s-f k2 asar h1 aster atp rly4• aur h2 bamb-a stb2.de• *Bapt* k* *Bar-c* bar-s k2 **Bell** k* bol-la k* borx bov brom **Bry** k* bufo **Calc** k* calc-i k2 calc-sil k2 carb-ac caust cench k2 *Cham* k* chel **Chin** k* chinin-ar choc srj3• cimic sne **Cocc** k* colch cupr cycl k* cypra-eg sde6.de• *Dig* k* dros *Dulc* hr1 *Elaps* eup-per k* **Gels** ptk1 granit-m es1• graph k* *Hell* k* helon k* **Hep** k* hydr ptk1 hydrog srj2• *Hyos* k* *Ign Iod* k* *Ip* k* kali-bi k* kali-c kali-i k* kali-n k* kali-p *Kalm* k* *Kreos* lach k* lachn c1 lat-m bnm6• laur k* lob *Lyc* k* *Mag-m* mag-s k* marb-w es1• med meny **Merc** k* merc-c k* mosch nat-c h2 nat-m nat-ox rly4• nat-s nux-m ptk1 **Nux-v** k* ol-an ptk1 olib-sac wmh1 ozone sde2• petr-ra shn4• *Ph-ac* k* *Phos* k* phyt bro1 plat h2 *Psor* puls k* pycnop-sa mrz1 rheum rhod k* **Rhus-t** k* sabad k* sacch sst1• sal-al blc1• samb k* *Sang* k* *Sec Sel* k* *Sep* k* *Sil* sol-ni k* solid bro1 spig k* spong fd4.de stram sul-ac sulph k* *Tarent* k* tere-la rly4• thuj tung-met bdx1• *Verat* k* *Zinc* zinc-m a1 zinc-p k2 [bell-p-sp dcm1 lac-mat sst4 *Spect* dfg1]
  - **forenoon**: *Calc* k* chin k* (non:colch kl) elaps thuj
  - **noon**: kali-n h2
  - **afternoon**: bamb-a stb2.de• calc k* *Chin* k* chinin-s kali-n k* lob myric nad rly4• rhus-t k* sep sulph
    - **18** h: buth-a sp1
    - **air** agg.; in open: *Chin*
    - **eating**; after: sep
  - **evening**: all-c all-s alum k* am-c k* ant-s-aur *Bar-c* k* cench k2 cocc kali-c k* kali-n lyc k* merc nat-m h2 ph-ac k* puls h1 sep h2 sulph h2
    - **20** h: elaps
    - **bed** agg.; in: am-c k*
  - **night**: **Acon** k* ang k* atp rly4• *Bar-c* hir skp7• hura ip mag-s k* *Merc* phos sabad sacch sst1• sep k* sol-t-ae a1 sulph k* [spect dfg1]
    - **with** perspiration: atp rly4• *Ip*
  - **anger**; from (See Anger - alternating - chill)
  - **coryza**; during: graph b4.de* *Nux-v* b7a.de
  - **cough** agg.; during: *Nux-v* b7a.de rhus-t b7a.de
  - **fright**: lyc
  - **menses**; during: am-c k* thuj k* wies zr
  - **motion** agg.: ant-t
  - **twitches**, with hot: *Nat-m*
- **insanity** (See MIND - Insanity - alternating - fever)
- **perspiration**: apis k* ars ars-s-f k2 bell calad calc *Euph* kali-bi kali-c h2 kali-i kali-sil k2 *Led* lyc nux-v phos puls sabad sacch sulph thuj *Verat*
- **shivering**: acon agar ars k* bell bov *Bry* calc caust chin k* *Cocc* cycl *Dros Elaps* hep *Ip* kali-bi lach lob merc mez ptk1 mosch nicc *Nux-v* k* ph-ac *Plat* podo sabad sang spig ptk1 wies a1
- **shuddering**: ars mag-s mosch

ANGER; after: *(↗MIND - Anger; MIND - Anger - heat - with)* acon k* bry bg2 **Cham** k* *Cocc* k* coloc ign nat-m nux-v k* *Petr* k* **Sep** k* **Staph** k*
- **alternating** with | **chill**: **Nux-v** kr1
- **perspiration**; with: *Petr* kr1

ANTICIPATING: acon b7a.de ars b4a.de chin b7a.de chinin-s hr1 ign b7a.de nat-m b4a.de **Nux-v** k* sep b4a.de

ANXIOUS heat (See MIND - Anxiety - fever - during)

APPEARING:
- **gradually**: chin bg2 *Plat* bg2 stann bg2 stront-c bg2
  - **disappearing** | **suddenly**: bell bg2 sul-ac bg2
- **suddenly**:
  - **disappearing** | **suddenly**: thuj bg2

APYREXIA: apis c1 cimx br1 ign a1 puls br1

ASCENDING agg.: *Acon* k* agar k* alum alum-p k2 am-m k* ang ant-t arg-met bg2 arund bell calad k* canth k* carb-an k* *Cina* k* colch k* crot-t dig k* eberth jl2 glon k* *Hyos* k* kali-c k* *Lach* k* led k* lyc k* mag-c bg2 mang k* *Nat-m* **Phos** k* plb k* puls bg2 sabad k* sars k* **Sep** k* spig bg2 stann bg2 staph bg2 stront-c bg2 **Sulph** k* sumb ulm-c jsj8• *Verat*

AUTUMNAL: aesc *Ars* bapt **Bry** *Calc Carb-ac* carb-v chin **Colch** *Eup-per* lach **Nat-m** *Nux-v* puls *Rhus-t* **Sep** *Verat*

BED:

- **in** bed: *(↗Night; Warmth; Warmth - agg.)* *Acon* k* agar agn k* alum bg2 am-c am-m k* ant-c k* ant-t *Apis* k* arg-met *Arn* k* asar k* bapt borx k* *Bry* k* *Calc* k* calen canth b7.de carb-an k* *Carb-v* k* caust bg2 cench k2 cham k* chel k* chinin-s clem coc-c **Coff** k* con dulc fd4.de eug graph bg2 hell k* hep k* ign b7.de *Kali-c* k* kali-chl kali-m k2 kali-p *Led* k* lyc bg2 m-ambo b7.de* mag-c **Mag-m** k* mag-s **Merc** k* *Mez* k* mosch k* nicc nit-ac nux-v k* **Petr** bg2 ph-ac k* phos k* **Puls** k* *Rhus-t* k* ruta fd4.de samb k* sars sil spong k* squil k* staph b7.de **Sul-ac** k* *Sulph* k* teucr b7.de thuj k* verat b7.de *Viol-t* b7.de*
  - **amel.**: agar k* bell k* brom bg2 canth k* *Caust* cic k* cocc k* con k* hyos k* lach k* *Laur* k* *Nux-v* k* sil k* squil k* staph k* stram k*
  - **driving** him out of bed at night: graph *Merc*
  - **feeling** of heat in bed, yet aversion to uncovering: *Coff* merc
- **putting** hand out of; from (See Chilliness - putting)

BEER; drinking: *Bell* k* *Ferr* k* rhus-t k* sulph k*

- **amel.**: verat bg2

BILIOUS: **Acon** b7a.de* alum bg2 ant-c b7a.de* ant-t b7a.de* arn b7a.de* *Ars* bg2 asaf b7a.de* asar b7a.de* aur bg2 bapt bro1* **Bell** bg2 **Bry** b7a.de* calc bg2 card-m bg2 **Cham** b7a.de* chin b7a.de* cocc b7a.de* *Coff* bg2 **Coloc** bg2* croc bg2 *Crot-h* bro1 cupr bg2 *Dig* bg2 euon bro1 *Eup-per* bro1 gels bro1 *Graph* bg2 hyos bg2 **Ign** b7a.de* ip b7a.de* *Lach* bg2 lept bro1 *Lyc* bg2 mag-c bg2 mag-m bg2 *Merc* bg2* *Merc-c* bro1 merc-d bro1 mez bg2 *Mur-ac* bg2 nat-c bg2 nat-m bg2 *Nat-s* bg2 nux-m bg2 **Nux-v** b7a.de* nyct bro1 oci-sa sp1 *Op* bg2 petr bg2 ph-ac bg2 *Phos* bg2 **Plat** bg2 podo bro1 polyp-p br1 *Puls* b7a.de* ran-b bg2 rhus-t b7a.de* samb bg2 sec b7a.de* sel bg2 seneg bg2 sep bg2 sil bg2 spong bg2 stann bg2 **Staph** b7a.de* stram bg2 stront-c bg2 sulph bg2 tarax b7a.de* verat b7a.de* verb bg2 zinc bg2

BLACKWATER fever (= febris hemoglobinurica): *Ars* ptk1 crot-h ptk1 lyc ptk1

BLOOD is hot at night; sensation as if: nit-ac h2*

BODY: *(↗Side - one)*

○ - **Anterior** part: am-m bg2 canth k* caps k* *Cham* k* cic bg2 cina k* croc k* **Ign** k* iod k* led k* mez k* mosch bg2 ran-b bg2 **Rhus-t** k* sec k* sel k*

- **Lower** part: caust k* hep k* kali-c bg2 lyc k* nat-c k* nat-m k* *Op* k* ph-ac bg2 puls bg2 stann k*
- **Posterior** part: am-c bg2 calc bg2 carb-an k* carb-v k* caust bg2 **Cham** k* lyc k* meny bg2 mur-ac k* nat-c k* nat-m k* rhus-t b7a.de* sep k* sil bg2 stann bg2 sulph k* thuj k*
- **Upper** part: acon bg2 **Agar** k* *Aml-ns* bg2 *Anac* k* *Arn* k* bism bg2 bry k* carb-an h2 cina k* croc bg2 dros k* euph h2* iris bg2 meny h1* nux-v k* *Par* k* plat h2 *Puls* pycnop-sa mrz1 rhus-t k* sabad bg2 sel k* ulm-c jsj8•
  - **head**; but less of the: *Arg-met*
  - **ice-cold** feet; with: lact

BREAKFAST agg.; after: agar bg2 bar-c k* borx bg2 calc k* cham bg2 croc k* ign k* iod k* laur b7.de* mag-m b4.de* phos b4.de* plb b7.de* sabad k* sars b4.de* staph k* sulph

BUBONIC-plague (See GENERALS - Pest - bubonic)

BURNING heat: **Acon** k* agar bg2* *Agn* bg2 ant-t **Apis** k* arg-n bg2 arn k* **Ars** k* *Asar* bg2 aur-ar k2 bapt k* bar-c bar-m bar-s k2 **Bell** k* bism k* brom b4a.de* *Bry* k* bufo k* cact k* *Cann-s* b7a.de* canth k* caps k* carb-an bg2 *Carb-v* k* carbn-s *Cham* k* chel chin k* chinin-ar *Chlor Cina* cocc bg2 coloc bg2 *Con* k* crot-h cur dig *Dulc* k* *Elaps* eup-per k2* euph bg2 formal bro1 **Gels** k* glon bg2 guaj k2 hell k* *Hep* k* **Hyos** bg2 ign k* ip k* *Kali-ar* kreos bg2 lach k* laur b7a.de* *Led* bg2 *Lyc* k* mag-c k* manc *Med* k* merc k* *Merc-c* k* mosch k* mur-ac k* nat-m nit-ac *Nux-v* k* **Op** k* petr k* **Phos** k* phyt bg2 plat bg2 plb podo bg2 **Puls** k* rhod bg2 *Rhus-t* k* sabad bg2 sabin k* *Samb* k* sarr *Sec* k* sel bg2 sep h2 sil h2* spig bg2 *Spong* k* *Squil* b7a.de* stann k* staph k* stram k* sulph *Tarent* thuj k* **Tub** verat k*

- **morning**: ars *Bry Cham* ign nat-m nux-v rhus-t sep h2 sulph thuj
- **forenoon**: bry lyc **Nat-m** *Nux-v Phos* rhus-t sulph thuj verat
  - **9**-12 h: **Cham**
- **afternoon**: **Apis** *Ars* ars-s-f k2 **Bell** berb *Bry Hep* hyos ign lyc nat-m nit-ac nux-v **Phos** *Puls* rhus-t stram sulph
  - **16** h:
    - **lasting** all night: *Hep*

Burning heat – **afternoon** – **16** h: ...

- - - **lasting** several hours: **Lyc**
  - **transient** chill; with: cur
- **evening**: *Acon* agar apis *Ars* ars-s-f k2 **Bell** berb *Bry Carb-v Cham* cina hell hep *Hyos* ign ip **Lyc** *Merc-c* mosch nat-m nit-ac nux-v **Phos Puls Rhus-t** staph sulph thuj verat
- **night**: **Acon** agar apis **Ars** ars-s-f k2 arund *Bapt* **Bell** *Berb Bry* **Cact** cann-s canth *Carb-v* carbn-s *Cham* cina con *Hep* ign lyc merc nat-m nit-ac nux-v *Op* petr **Phos Puls** *Rhus-t* staph *Stram* sulph thuj verat
  - **midnight**: **Ars** lyc *Rhus-t* stram sulph verat
    - **before**: agar ars **Bry** *Cham* laur puls sep verat
      - **21**-0 h: *Bry*
    - **after**: **Ars** ign lyc merc nat-m *Phos* sulph thuj
      - **3** h: *Thuj*
  - **bed**, intolerable burning heat; in: **Puls**
- **agg.**: rat ptk1 zinc-val ptk1
- **alternating** with:
  - **chill**: *Laur*
  - **chilliness**: **Bell**
- **amel.**: alum ptk1 *Ars* ptk1 caps ptk1 carb-v ptk1 lyc ptk1 sec ptk1
- **distended** blood vessels, with: aloe *Bell* **Chin** chinin-s cycl dig ferr *Hyos Led* **Merl** *Puls* sars
- **dry**, burning heat:
  - **agg.** all symptoms: bry bg3*
  - **extending** from head and face:
    - **accompanied** by | **thirst** for cold drinks: *Acon*
- **except** head and face, which are covered with sweat: stram
- **feel**, which he does not: canth
- **furious** delirium, with: **Bell** canth **Stram** verat
- **heat** outside, cold inside: **Ars**
- **internal**:
  - **blood** seems to burn mostly in the veins: **Ars** *Bry Med* **Rhus-t**
  - **parts**: euph ptk1 merc-c ptk1 mez k*
- **interrupted** by shaking chills, then internal burning heat with great thirst: sec
- **lasting** all day: chin thuj
- **painful**: phos bg2
- **parts** lain on: lyss manc
- **perspiration**:
  - **red** face; heat, even when bathed in perspiration, with a: op
  - **with** (See PERSPIRATION - Hot)
- **pricking** over the whole body, with: **Chin** gels
- **sleep** agg.; during: gins **Samb** thuj
- **sparks**: *(↗BACK - Pain - burning - sparks)* alum k* am-c bg2 ant-c k* bar-c bg2 calad bg2 cina bg2 *Clem* bg2 graph bg2 kali-c bg2 led k* lyc k* mag-m bg2 mez k* nat-m bg2 nit-ac bg2 ol-an bg2 rheum bg2 sec k* *Sel* bg2 *Sulph* k* viol-o bg2
- **spot**, which is cold to the touch; in one: *Arn*
- **spots**, in single: agar bro1 apis bro1 sel zinc h2
- **spreading** from the hands over the whole body: **Chel**
- **stinging** sensations, with: *Apis* merc-c
- **thirst**:
  - **covered**; and desire to be: manc
  - **drinks**; for cold: *Acon* **Phos**
  - **unquenchable**, with: *(↗STOMACH - Thirst - unquenchable - fever)* **Ars** bell colch hep **Phos**
- **walking** in open air agg.: chin
- **within** and without, body turning hot: **Bell**

○ - **Abdomen** | **croup**; in: cub c1

- **Skin** and flesh; between: brom bg2

CATARRHAL fever: **Acon** k* arn bg2 *Ars* k* asc-c c2 bapt tl1 bar-m *Bell* bg2 **Bry** k* camph bg2 carb-v caust bg2 **Cham** b7a.de* chin bg2 cocc bg2 coff bg2 con k* *Dulc* bg2 eug c2 euphr k2 *Ferr-p* **Hep** k* ign b7a.de* ip bg2 kali-chl *Kali-i* lach mang bg2 **Merc** k* merc-k-i c2 myrt-c c2 **Nux-v** b7a.de* ph-ac k* phos bg2 pimp a1 plect a1 pop-cand c2 *Puls* b7a.de* *Rhus-t* k* *Sabad* k* sep k* sil h2* spig b7a.de* squil bg2 stann bg2 *Sulph* bg2 verat bg2

- **menses**; during: *Graph* k*

CATHETER fever: acon$_{c1}$* camph-ac$_{bro1}$ petros$_{c2}$*
- **prophylaxis**: camph-ac$_{bro1}$*

CEREBROSPINAL fever: *(↗BACK - Inflammation - membranes; GENERALS - Convulsions - meningitis; HEAD - Inflammation - meninges; MIND - Delirium - meningitis)* acon$_{k}$* aeth agar am-c ant-t **Apis** *Arg-n* arn$_{k}$* ars$_{k}$* bapt$_{k}$* **Bell** bry$_{k}$* cact *Calc*$_{sne}$ camph canth *Carb-v*$_{sne}$ *Cic* *Cimic*$_{k}$* cocc crot-h$_{k}$* cupr$_{k}$* cupr-act$_{hr1}$* dig **Gels**$_{k}$* glon hell$_{k}$* hydr-ac hyos$_{k}$* *Ign* lyc$_{k}$* *Nat-m* **Nat-s**$_{k}$* *Nux-v* **Op** *Phos* phys$_{br1}$ plb$_{k}$* psor$_{sne}$ pyrog$_{c1}$* **Rhus-r**$_{sne}$ *Rhus-t* sal-ac$_{tl1}$ *Sil*$_{sne}$ sol-ni stram$_{a2}$ *Sulph*$_{sne}$ tarent verat **Verat-v**$_{k}$* *Zinc*

CHANGING, paroxysms: *(↗MIND - Capriciousness; MIND - Mood - changeable)* *Elat* eupi **Ign** lat-m$_{bnm6}$• meny *Psor* **Puls** sep staphycoc$_{jl2}$
- **abuse** of; after:
  - **homeopathic** potencies: **Sep**
  - **quinine**: arn ars calc$_{tl1}$ *Elat* *Eup-per* ferr ign *Ip* nux-v **Puls**
- **frequently**: *Elat* ign *Psor* *Puls* verat-v$_{tl1}$
- **no** two paroxysms alike: **Puls**

CHILDREN; in: | **infants**: **Acon**$_{bg2}$ bell$_{bg2}$ borx$_{bg2}$ *Cham*$_{bg2}$ *Coff*$_{bg2}$ ign$_{bg2}$ merc$_{bg2}$ nux-v$_{bg2}$ sil$_{bg2}$

CHILL absent (= fever without chill): acet-ac acon aesc alum ambr *Anac* *Ang* ant-c **Apis**$_{k}$* *Arn* **Ars**$_{k}$* *Bapt* **Bell**$_{k}$* benz-ac bov **Bry**$_{k}$* cact *Calc* carb-v carbn-s caust **Cham**$_{k}$* *Chin* chinin-ar *Cina* clem coff con corh$_{br1}$ cur elaps eup-per *Ferr* *Ferr-ar* *Ferr-p* **Gels**$_{k}$* graph hep *Ip* kali-ar kali-bi kali-c kali-s$_{k2}$ lach *Lyc* lyss mang merl nat-m nicc nux-m *Nux-v* petr podo puls **Rhus-t**$_{k}$* spig stann *Stram* sulph *Thuj*
- **morning**: arn ars bry calc caust eup-per hep kali-bi kali-c nat-m petr podo rhus-t sulph thuj
  - **6**-10 h: rhus-t
  - **7** h: podo
- **forenoon**: ars bapt cact calc *Cham* eup-pur$_{hr1}$ **Gels** lyc nat-m nux-m nux-v rhus-t spig sulph thuj
  - **9** h: kali-c
  - **9**-12 h: **Cham**
  - **10** h: **Gels** **Nat-m** *Rhus-t* thuj
    - **10**-11 h: gels **Nat-m** thuj
  - **11** h: *Bapt* cact *Calc* med **Nat-m** thuj
- **noon**: ars spig stram sulph
  - **12**-13 h: sil
- **afternoon**: aesc anac ang apis **Ars** **Bell** *Bry* calc caust chin chinin-ar clem coff con cur eup-per ferr ferr-ar *Gels* graph ip kali-ar kali-bi kali-c lyc nat-m nux-v puls rhus-t *Sang* *Sil* sulph
  - **13** h | **13**-14 h: **Ars**
  - **14** h: **Puls**
    - **14**-15 h: cur kali-c
  - **15** h: ars coff cur ferr lyc nicc
    - **15**-16 h: **Apis** clem lyc *Sang*
  - **16** h: **Anac** *Apis* ars graph hep *Ip* kali-bi **Lyc**
    - **16**-20 h: *Lyc*
    - **lasting** all night: ars *Hep* puls stann
  - **17** h: con kali-bi kali-c petr sabin stann
    - **17**-18 h: petr
      - **ill** humored; very: con
  - **17**.30 h | **pricking** in tongue; with: cedr
- **evening**: acon aesc alum ambr anac ang ant-t apis arn ars *Bapt* **Bell** borx **Bry** calc carb-v caust *Cham* chin chinin-ar *Cina* coff coloc eup-per ferr ferr-ar ferr-p hep ip kali-ar kali-bi kali-c kali-s$_{k2}$ lach lyc nat-m nicc nux-m nux-v *Petr* plat podo **Puls** **Rhus-t** stann sulph thuj
  - **18** h: calc carb-v caust kali-c **Nux-v** petr
    - **18**-19 h: *Calc* nux-v
    - **18**-20 h: ant-t caust
    - **18**-0 h: lachn
    - **lasting** all night: cham lyc *Nux-v* *Rhus-t*
  - **19** h: aesc bov *Calc* lyc *Nux-v* petr rhus-t
    - **19**-20 h: ambr
    - **19**-0 h: aesc

Chill absent – **evening**: ...
  - **20** h: coff ferr hep sulph
  - **periodical**, at same hour, daily fever, with short breath: cina
- **night**: acon ang ant-t apis **Ars** ars-s-f$_{k2}$ **Bapt** **Bell** **Bry** *Calc* *Carb-v* caust cham *Cina* coff ferr *Ferr-ar* gels hep ip *Kali-bi* lachn lyc nat-m nicc nux-v petr *Phos* podo *Puls* **Rhus-t** stram sulph thuj
  - **midnight**:
    - **before**: acon ant-c ars **Bry** *Carb-v* cham elaps lyc mag-m mag-s nat-m petr puls sabad
      - **22** h: ars elaps *Hydr* lach petr sabad
      - **23** h: cact *Calc* mag-m
    - **at**: **Ars** nux-v stram sulph
      - **0**-2 h: **Ars**
      - **0**-3 h: **Ars** kali-c med
    - **after**: **Ars** borx ferr kali-c lyc nat-m sulph tax thuj
      - **1** h | **1**-2 h: **Ars**
      - **2** h: **Ars** benz-ac
        - **2**-4 h: kali-c
      - **3** h: ang thuj
      - **4** h: arn
- **menses**; before: calc$_{b4.de}$

CHILL; with: **Acon**$_{k}$* ambr anac *Anders*$_{zzc1}$• ant-c ant-t$_{bro1}$ apis$_{bro1}$ apoc$_{k2}$ arg-n$_{hr1}$ **Ars**$_{k}$* ars-i ars-s-f$_{k2}$ asar bamb-a$_{stb2.de}$• bapt$_{mtf}$ bar-m$_{k2}$ **Bell**$_{k}$* benz-ac bros-gau$_{mrc1}$ *Bry*$_{k}$* bufo caesal-b$_{zzc1}$• **Calc** caps carb-v$_{k}$* cassia-s$_{cdd7}$*• **Cham**$_{k}$* *Chel* chin$_{k}$* *Chinin-s*$_{k}$* choc$_{srj3}$• cina$_{h1}$ *Cocc* coff coloc cycl$_{h1}$ *Dig* *Dros* *Ferr* ferr-ar *Gels*$_{ptk1}$ granit-m$_{es1}$• *Graph* **Hell**$_{k}$* helo-s$_{bnm14}$• **Ign**$_{k}$* iod ip kali-ar kreos lac-del$_{hrn2}$• lac-lup$_{hrn2}$• lat-h$_{bnm5}$• lat-m$_{sp1}$ *Led* loxo-lae$_{bnm12}$• lyc *Merc* *Mez* nat-c nat-m *Nat-s* nicc **Nit-ac**$_{k}$* **Nux-v**$_{k}$* *Olnd* petr phos pitu-gl$_{skp7}$• *Plb* *Podo* positr$_{nl2}$• *Puls* *Pyrog* ran-b **Rhus-t**$_{k}$* sabad sabin *Samb* *Sang* *Sep* ser-a-c$_{jl2}$ sil spig staph staphycoc$_{jl2}$ *Stram* sulfonam$_{ks2}$ **Sulph**$_{k}$* *Tarent*$_{k}$* *Thuj* tub$_{c}$* *Verat*$_{k}$* *Zinc* [bell-p-sp$_{dcm1}$ trem-g$_{dbx1.fr}$]
- **morning** | **8**-10 h: caesal-b$_{zzc1}$•
- **afternoon** | **14**-16 h: caesal-b$_{zzc1}$•
- **night**: *Anders*$_{zzc1}$•
- **heat** and perspiration: cassia-s$_{cdd7}$• *Jab* *Mez* *Nux-v*
- **intermittent**: tub$_{jl2}$
- **long** time, for a: podo$_{ptk1}$ pyrog$_{ptk1}$
- **perspiration**; without subsequent: *Graph*
- **shaking**: *Sec*
- **uncovering** agg.: tub$_{jl2}$
- **warmly** covered in bed: hipp$_{jl2}$

CHILLINESS; with: acon agar *Anac* androc$_{srj1}$• **Apis** *Arn* *Ars* bapt bar-m *Bell* borx **Calc** camph$_{h1}$ carb-v carbn-s$_{k2}$ *Caust* *Cham* *Coch* **Coff** *Colch* cur dros dulc$_{fd4.de}$ *Elaps* ephe-si$_{hsj1}$• hep kali-ar **Kali-bi** *Kali-c* kali-i *Kali-s* lach lachn led lyss$_{c1}$ *Merc* nat-m ozone$_{sde2}$• phos *Podo* **Puls**$_{k}$* pycnop-sa$_{mrz1}$ *Pyrog* sabin sec *Sep* sil *Spig* *Squil* *Sulph* *Tarent* **Thuj** tritic-vg$_{fd5.de}$ *Tub* **Verat** *Zinc*
- **21**.30 h has to go to bed, followed by shaking chill: *Sabad*
- **alternating** with heat not perceptible to the touch: merc
- **fire**; with desire to be near a: cic$_{c1}$
- **long** into the heat; continues: *Podo* *Pyrog*
- **motion**; on the least (See Motion - chilliness)
- **putting** the hands out of bed, from: *(↗GENERALS - Cold; becoming - agg. - part - hand; GENERALS - Cold; becoming - agg. - part - hand - bed)* arn *Bar-c* borx *Hep* **Nux-v** pyrog stram *Tarent* **Tub**
- **sleep**; during: borx$_{c1}$

▽ - **extending** to | **Extremities**: cic$_{c1}$

CHOLERA (See RECTUM - Cholera)

CHRONIC: cact$_{ptk1}$ chinin-ar$_{mtf11}$ chinin-s$_{ptk1}$ fl-ac$_{br1}$ kali-p$_{ptk1}$ mastoid$_{mtf11}$ nat-sal$_{ptk1}$

CLOTHING:
- **loosening** of clothing: | **amel.**: bov$_{bg2}$ calc$_{bg2}$ lyc$_{bg2}$ nux-v$_{bg2}$

COFFEE; drinking: canth$_{k}$* cham$_{k}$* rhus-t$_{k}$*
- **amel.**: ars$_{k}$*

COITION; after: calc$_{bg2}$ graph$_{k}$* kali-c$_{bg2}$ kreos$_{bg2}$ lach$_{bg2}$ mag-m$_{bg2}$ nux-v$_{k}$* sep$_{bg2}$

Fever

COLD:
- **air** agg.: hydroph rsj6•
- **amel**.: am-m bg2 aur bg2 *Sulph* bg2
- **washing** agg.: mez bg2

COLD; AFTER TAKING A: acon b7a.de cham b7a.de chin b7a.de coff b7a.de hyos b7a.de ip b7a.de nux-m b7a.de nux-v b7a.de puls b7a.de sel b7a.de

COLDNESS:
- **external**, with: arn *Ars* k* bell bry calc canth bro1 carb-v h2 chin euph hell iod merc mez mosch ph-ac phos plat k2 puls rhus-t sabad spong stann sulph h2 verat [bell-p-sp dcm1]
- **icy**: cadm-s br1
- **internal**; with: helo mtf11
- **predominates**: bry b7a.de cact br1 canth b7a.de caps b7a.de ip b7a.de puls b7a.de ran-b b7a.de sabad b7a.de staph b7a.de verat b7a.de

○ - **Arms**; in the | **eyes**; with staring of: cic c1
- **Thighs**; in the | **eyes**; with staring of: cic c1

COLORS: | **black** | **agg.**: med vk4
- **yellow** | **agg.**: aur vk4 sep vk4 syph vk4

COMA; with (See MIND - Coma - fever - during)

CONSTANTLY HIGH TEMPERATURE (See Intense - constant)

CONTINUED fever: *(↗Intense - constant; Irritative - slow; Septic; Typhoid; Typhus)* ail am-c ant-c k2 anthraci apis apoc vh1 arg-n **Arn** k2 **Ars** ars-s-f k2 **Arum-t** **Bapt** **Bry** cadm-s k2 calad calc camph *Canth Caps* carb-ac *Carb-an* **Carb-v** carc cd cham chel **Chin** *Chinin-ar Chinin-s* chlol gm1 **Chlor** cic *Cocc* **Colch** **Crot-h** **Echi** **Gels** *Hell* hydr-ac **Hyos** k* iod ip *Kali-p Kalm* br1 lac-lup hrn2• **Lach** lachn c1 *Lyc* lycps-v mang merc *Mill* br1 *Mosch Mur-ac Nit-ac* nux-m *Op* pest al2 petr *Ph-ac* **Phos** plb gk *Psor* puls *Pyrog* k* **Rhus-t** *Rhus-v* sal-al blc1• sang sars h2 *Sec Sil* **Stram** k* sulph *Ter* tub c1 verat verat-v zinc
- **afternoon**: agar apis *Ars Bry Canth* chin colch dig *Gels Hyos* ip **Lach** lyc *Nit-ac* nux-v ph-ac **Phos** puls rhus-t stram sul-ac sulph
  - **16** h until midnight: *Stram*
  - **16**-20 h: *Lyc*
  - **17** h: kali-n rhus-t sulph
- **evening**: arn *Ars* **Bry** *Carb-v Cham* chin hell ign ip *Lach* **Lyc** *Mur-ac* nit-ac nux-v **Ph-ac** **Phos** **Puls** **Rhus-t** sul-ac *Sulph*
  - **19** h: *Lyc Rhus-t*
  - **20** h: hep mur-ac phos sulph
  - **21**-0 h: *Bry*
- **night**: am-c apis **Ars** ars-s-f k2 arum-t **Bapt** **Bry** calad **Carb-v** cham **Chin** **Chinin-ar** cocc *Colch Kali-bi* **Lach** lyc **Merc** *Mur-ac Nux-v Op Ph-ac Phos Puls* **Rhus-t** *Stram* sul-ac **Sulph**
  - **midnight**: *Ars* lyc *Rhus-t Stram Sulph Verat*
    - **before**: ars *Bapt* **Bry** calad **Carb-v** lach lyc nux-v *Stram*
      - **22** h: lach
    - **after**: **Ars** bry chin chinin-ar lyc nux-v **Phos** **Rhus-t** *Sulph*
  - **temperature** running very high: **Bell** *Bry Hyos* rhus-t *Stram*
- **abdominal** (See Typhoid)
- **accompanied** by | **tympanites**: kalm br1
- **cerebral**: *Apis* arn *Bapt Bry* canth cic *Gels* **Hyos** *Lach Lyc* nux-m *Op Ph-ac Phos Rhus-t* **Stram** verat verat-v
- **congestive**: arn *Bry Gels* glon *Lach* sang verat
  - **cerebral** paralysis; with threatened: hell *Lach Lyc* **Op** *Ph-ac Phos* tarent zinc
  - **collapse**, with: carb-v
  - **paralysis** of lungs; with: *Ant-t* ars carb-v *Lyc* mosch *Phos* sulph
- **eruptive**: *Acon* bro1 *Ail* **Apis** arn k* ars k* arum-t *Bapt* bro1 **Bell** k* bry k* calc camph bro1 carb-v chlor *Euphr Ferr-p* bro1 gels bro1 ip bro1 kalm bro1 lach merc k* mur-ac nux-m nux-v bro1 ph-ac phos puls bro1 **Rhus-t** k* sec stann sulph
  - **cold**, viscous perspiration; with: chlor
- **hemorrhagic** (See Typhoid - hemorrhagic)
- **pectoral**: am-c *Ant-t* **Bry** *Carb-v* chel chin *Hyos* kali-bi *Lyc* nit-ac **Phos** *Rhus-t Sulph* tub c1*

Continued fever: ...
- **petechial** (See Typhus - petechial)
- **stupid** form: apis *Arn Ars* arum-t **Bapt** *Bry* **Carb-v** *Chin* chinin-s cic cocc *Crot-h Gels* **Hell** **Hyos** *Lach* lyc **Mur-ac** nux-v **Op** **Ph-ac** *Phos Rhus-t* sec *Stram* verat **Zinc**
- **stupor**, complete: **Hell** **Hyos** lyc **Op** *Ph-ac* plb gk stram
- **typhus** fever with swelled parotid gland and sensitive bones (See Typhus - accompanied - bones; Typhus - accompanied - parotid)

CONVERSATION, from: sep k*

CONVULSIONS; after: *(↗Intense - convulsions)* arn b7a.de* ars bg2 calc h2* chin b7a.de* hyos b7a.de* ign b7a.de* rhus-t b7a.de*

COUGHING increases the heat: am-c k* ambr k* ant-t k* *Arn* k* *Ars* k* bell k* carb-v k* chin ptk1 *Coc-c* bg2* hep k* hyos k* ign ptk1 iod k* ip k* kali-n bg2 kreos k* lach k* led k* lyc k* m-arct b7.de mag-m k* mur-ac ptk1 nat-c k* nat-m ptk1 nux-v k* phos k* puls k* sabad k* sep h2 squil k* sulph k* thuj ptk1

COVERING: | **slightest**; can bear only: corh br1

DENGUE fever: acon c1* ars bro1 bell bro1 bry bro1 canth bro1 chin bro1 *Eup-per* c2* *Gels* c2* ip bro1 nux-v bro1 *Rhus-t* bro1 rhus-v bro1

DENTITION; during: *Acon* bg2* agar bg2 *Ars* b4a.de* *Bell* b4a.de* borx bg2 bry bg2 **Calc** b4a.de* *Cham* b7a.de* cic bg2 coff bg2 cupr bg2 ferr-p bg2* *Gels* bg2* hep bg2 hyos bg2 ign b7a.de* ip bg2 lach bg2 merc b4a.de* merc-c bg2 nit-ac bg2 *Nux-v* b7a.de* phyt hr1 puls bg2 *Rheum* b7a.de* rhus-t bg2 sec bg2 *Sil* b4a.de* stann b4a.de stram bg2 *Sulph* b4a.de* thuj bg2 *Verat-v* kr1

DESCENDING agg.: acon k* agar k* *Alum* k* bar-c k* *Bell* k* calc-p k* canth k* *Caust* k* chel k* cic k* coff k* colch k* croc k* euphr k* laur k* mag-c k* mez k* mosch k* nat-c k* op k* par k* ruta k* sabad bg2 sabin staph k* stront-c k* sul-ac k* thuj k* valer k* verat k* zinc k*

DIARRHEA: | **after** | **agg.**: ars h2
- **during**: coli jl2

DINNER: | **after** | **agg.**: bar-c bell h1 *Dig* nit-ac phos plan ptel sabin sep sul-ac til
- **during** | **agg.**: mag-m sul-ac thuj valer

DISCORDANT with temperature (See GENERALS - Pulse - discordant)

DRINKING:
- **agg.**: bar-c calc cham cocc malar jl2
- **amel.**: bamb-a stb2.de•
- **cold** water | **agg.** | **shivering** from it: *Bell* calen **Caps** eup-per *Nux-v*
  - **amel.**: bism k* **Caust** k* cupr k* fl-ac k* lob op k* *Phos* k* sep k*

DRY heat: acet-ac **Acon** k* aesc aeth hr1 ail alum b2.de* am-c am-m b2.de* ambr b2.de* aml-ns anac k* ant-c b2.de* ant-t k* *Apis* k* arg-met b2.de* *Arn* k* **Ars** k* ars-i ars-s-f k2 arum-t bapt bar-c k* bar-m **Bell** k* bism k* bol-la **Bry** k* cact *Calc* k* calc-p camph k* cann-s b2.de* canth b2.de* caps b2.de* carb-an carb-v k* carbn-s caust k* *Cedr Cham* k* chel k* *Chin* k* chinin-ar chlor cimx cina clem k* cocc k* coff k* *Colch* k* coloc k* con k* cor-r corh br1 croc b2.de* crot-h cupr b2.de* cycl b2.de* **Dulc** k* elaps ephe-si hsj1• *Ferr* k* *Ferr-ar* ferr-i *Ferr-p* gels ptk1 *Graph* b2.de* hell k* hep k* hyos k* hyper ign k* *Iod* k* ip k* *Kali-ar Kali-c* k* kali-cy kali-n k* kali-p kali-s kali-sil k2 kreos b2.de* lach k* lact laur b2.de* led k* lil-t bg2 *Lyc* k* m-ambo b2.de* m-arct b2.de m-aust b2.de* mag-s mang b2.de* meny *Merc* k* *Merc-c* b4a.de mosch b2.de* *Mur-ac* k* nat-ar nat-c b2.de* nat-m b2.de* nat-s nit-ac k* nux-m b2.de* **Nux-v** k* *Op* k* par b2.de* *Petr Ph-ac* k* **Phos** k* phys plb k* ptel *Puls* k* pycnop-sa mrz1 pyrog k2 ran-b b2.de* ran-s k* rheum b2.de* rhod b2.de* *Rhus-t* k* ruta b2.de* sabad b2.de* sabin b2.de* *Samb* k* *Sec* k* sel b2.de* sep k* sil k* spig k* *Spong* k* squil k* stann k* staph k* *Stram* k* stront-c k* sul-ac b2.de* *Sulph* k* *Sumb* k* tarax b2.de* *Tarent* thuj k* tub ptk1 tub-m vn* valer b2.de* verat b2.de* *Viol-t* b2.de* zinc b2.de*
- **daytime**: bar-m
- **morning**: ail *Arn Bry* calc cocc nit-ac petr h2 sulph
  - **waking**; on: *Arn*
- **afternoon**: alum *Ars* elaps ferr gels nat-s
  - **14** h:
    - **alternating** with | **chill**, as if dashed with cold water: chel
  - **chilliness**; with: arg-n

- **afternoon**: ...
  - **sleep** agg.; during: alum
- **evening**: aesc apis ars bapt bell *Calc-p* carb-v **Chin** coff coloc dulc fd4.de elaps graph *Kali-c* *Plb* **Puls** sul-ac h2
  - **19**-21 h:
    - ⁝ **followed** by chill | **22** h; until: elaps
  - **bed**, with chilliness in back; in: coff
  - **distended** veins and burning hands that seek out cool places: **Puls**
  - **sleep** agg.; on going to: ph-ac h2
- **night**: **Acon** anac ant-t arn **Ars** bapt *Bar-c* *Bar-m* **Bell** *Bry* calc calc-sil k2 carb-an carb-v *Carbn-s* *Caust* *Cedr* chel chinin-ar chinin-s cina *Clem* *Cocc* coff *Colch* coloc con dulc *Ferr* graph hep kali-n *Lach* lyc mur-ac *Nit-ac* nux-m *Nux-v* ph-ac h2 **Phos** *Puls* ran-s raph **Rhus-t** *Rhus-v* samb ptk1 spig h1 *Sumb* *Tarent* thea thuj
  - **bed**; driving out of: ant-t
  - **delirium**; with: **Ars** **Bell** *Bry* *Chinin-s* *Coff* *Lach* *Lyc* *Phos* **Rhus-t**
  - **gagging**, with spasmodic: **Cimx**
  - **hot** vapors rise up to the brain, as if: ant-t sarr sulph
  - **menses**; before: con
  - **motion** agg.: *Bry*
  - **noise** agg.: bry
  - **pricking** as from needles, with: bol-la chin gels nit-ac
  - **rising** heat and glowing redness of cheeks, without thirst, after sleep: cina
  - **sleep** | **during** | **agg.**: bov bry gins ph-ac **Samb** k* thuj viol-t
    - ⁝ **going** to sleep; on | **agg.**: **Samb**
  - **sweaty** hands when put out of bed, with: *Hep* k*
  - **swollen** veins of arms and hands without thirst: **Chin** sumb
- **alternating** with | **perspiration**: apis ptk1*
- **coition**; after: *Nux-v* k*
- **menses**; before: carb-an b4a.de con b4.de* kali-c b4.de* merc b4.de*
- **walking** in open air agg.: arg-met nat-m *Sumb*

○ - **Covered** parts, of: (↗*covered; Covered*) *Thuj*
- **Skin**; with dry: convo-s sp1

DYSENTERIC (See RECTUM - Dysentery - accompanied - fever)

EATING:
- **after**:
  - **agg.**: acon b7.de* alum k* *Ang* k* arg-met bg2 arg-n asaf k* bar-c h2 bell borx *Bry* k* calc k* *Caust* k* cham k* chlor hr1 con b4.de* cycl k* dig k* fl-ac graph k* ign ind *Lach* k* lachn lact k1 *Lyc* k* mag-c k* mag-m k* nat-m k* *Nit-ac* k* *Nux-v* k* par b7.de* petr k* **Phos** k* psor pyrog ran-b c1 raph ruta fd4.de *Sep* k* sil k* staph bg2 sul-ac k* sulph k* tub ptk1 valer bg2 viol-t k* zinc b4.de*
  - **amel.**: **Anac** k* ars k* cann-xyz bg2 **Chin** k* cupr bg2* cur ferr k* ign k* iod k* lach bg2 mez bg2 nat-c k* phos k* rhus-t k* stront-c k* zinc bg2
- **before** | **agg.**: ferr bg2 fl-ac bg2 phos bg2 sabin bg2
- **overeating** agg.; after: ant-c bg2 *Bry* bg2 caps bg2
- **while**:
  - **agg.**: am-c k* *Bar-c* cham k* chlor hr1 mag-m k* nux-v k* psor sil k* spig k* staph bg2* sul-ac k* tab bg2* thuj valer k* viol-t
  - **amel.**: **Anac** ign lach mez zinc

ELEVATED TEMPERATURE (See Intense)

ERUPTIVE fevers:
- **measles**: **Acon** k* ail bro1 *Am-c* *Ant-c* k* ant-t bro1 **Apis** k* ars k* *Ars-i* bro1 *Bell* bg2* **Bry** k* camph k* *Carb-v* k* cham k* *Chel* chin k* *Chlor* *Coff* k* con bro1 cop *Crot-h* *Dros* k* dulc bro1 eup-per bro1 **Euphr** k* ferr-p bro1 *Gels* k* hep hyos k* ign k* ip k* *Kali-bi* k* kali-c bg2 kali-m bro1 kali-n bg2 lach bro1 mag-c bg2 merc bg2* merc-c bro1 merc-pr-r bro1 nux-v bg2 op bro1 *Phos* k* **Puls** k* *Rhus-t* k* spong bro1 *Squil* k* stict bro1 *Stram* k* **Sulph** k* ter bg2 tub bg2 verat k* viol-o bro1 zinc
- **scarlatina**: *Acon* bro1 **Ail** k* **Am-c** k* **Apis** k* *Arg-n* arn *Ars* k* *Arum-t* k* *Asim* bro1 bapt k2 **Bell** k* *Bry* k* *Calc* canth k* *Carb-ac* k* *Carb-v* *Cham* chim k* chinin-ar bro1 com bro1 *Crot-c* *Crot-h* k* *Cupr* k* cupr-act bro1 dub bro1 **Echi** k*

Eruptive fevers – **scarlatina**: ...
eucal bro1 *Gels* k* hep k* hyos k* ip k* kali-chl bro1 kali-p k2 kali-s bro1 lac-c bro1 **Lach** k* **Lyc** k* **Merc** k* merc-i-r bro1 mur-ac k* **Nit-ac** nux-m op bro1 *Ph-ac* *Phos* phyt bro1 **Rhus-t** k* sang bro1 sec sil bro1 sol-ni bro1 spig bro1 *Stram* k* *Sulph* **Ter** k* *Zinc* k*
- **smallpox**; after: *Acon* bro1 ant-t bro1 *Bapt* bro1 *Bell* bro1 gels bro1 vario bro1 *Verat-v* bro1

EXANTHEMATOUS fever (See Eruptive)

EXCITEMENT agg.: aloe bg2 **Aml-ns** bg2 calc c2 caps bg2* carc fb cob-n sp1 cocc pd coff bg2 phos bg2 psor bg2 puls bg2 zinc bg2

EXERTION:
- **after**:
  - **agg.**: am-m brom fl-ac pyrog rhus-t sep
  - **amel.**: ign k* *Sep* k* stann k*
- **agg.**: acon alum k* *Ant-c* ant-t arg-met ars calc k2 *Camph* *Chin* ferr merc k* nat-m bg2 nit-ac nux-v k* olnd k* ox-ac *Rhus-t* ruta fd4.de samb *Sep* sil bg2 spig spong stann stram *Sumb* valer

EXTERNAL heat: **Acon** k* aeth agar b2.de **Agn** bg2 ail alum k* alum-sil k2 am-c k* am-m b2.de ambr b2.de *Anac* k* ang b2.de ant-c b2.de* *Ant-t* k* apis arg-met b2.de *Arn* k* **Ars** k* *Ars-i* asaf k* asar b2.de* bapt bar-c b2.de* **Bell** k* bism k* borx b2.de bov b2.de **Bry** k* calad b2.de *Calc* k* camph b2.de* cann-s b2.de **Canth** k* *Caps* k* carb-an b2.de *Carb-v* k* carbn-s caust b2.de cedr **Cham** k* chel k* *Chin* k* *Chinin-s* chlor cic k* cimic cina b2.de coc-c *Cocc* k* coff k* colch k* coloc k* con k* cor-r croc b2.de crot-h cupr k* cycl b2.de dig k* dros b2.de dulc k* *Euph* b2.de ferr b2.de graph b2.de guaj b2.de* hell k* hep k* hydrog srj2• *Hyos* k* **Ign** k* iod k* ip k* jatr-c kali-ar kali-bi kali-c k* kali-chl kali-i kali-n k* kali-sil k2 kreos b2.de *Lach* k* laur b2.de* led b2.de *Lyc* k* m-ambo b2.de m-arct b2.de m-aust b2.de* mag-c k* mag-m b2.de mang b2.de meny b2.de* *Merc* k* *Merc-c* k* mez b2.de mosch b2.de mur-ac b2.de* nat-c b2.de nat-m b2.de nit-ac b2.de* nux-m b2.de *Nux-v* k* olnd b2.de *Op* k* par b2.de petr b2.de ph-ac b2.de* *Phos* k* phyt plat b2.de plb k* **Puls** k* ran-b b2.de ran-s b2.de *Rheum* b2.de* rhod b2.de **Rhus-t** k* ruta k* sabad b2.de sabin b2.de samb b2.de sars b2.de sec k* sel k* seneg b2.de sep k* **Sil** k* spig k* spong b2.de* **Squil** b2.de* stann b2.de staph b2.de* **Stram** k* stront-c b2.de sul-ac k* sul-i k2 *Sulph* k* tarax b2.de *Tarent* teucr b2.de *Thuj* b2.de* valer b2.de* verat k* viol-t b2.de zinc k*
- **morning**: bell
- **forenoon** | **10**-15 h: canth
- **afternoon**:
  - **16** h: coff ptel
  - **chilliness**; with: ars
    - ⁝ **and** redness without internal heat: **Ign**
- **evening**: anac iod plb rhus-t sulph
  - **20** h: coff nat-ar
  - **21** h: elaps
  - **22** h: ars
  - **lying** down agg.; after: coff squil h1
- **night**: *Bry* *Colch* kali-bi phos rhus-t
  - **23** h: nat-m
  - **midnight**; after:
    - ⁝ **2** h | **waking**; on: hep
- **chilliness**; with: *Acon* agn alum alum-sil k2 *Anac* *Arn* **Ars** ars-s-f k2 asar atro *Bell* berb *Bry* **Calc** *Calc-ar* calc-sil k2 cann-i *Cocc* *Coff* coloc dig dros gamb *Hell* hep **Ign** *Kali-n* lac-c *Lach* *Laur* *Lyc* *Meny* merc mur-ac nat-m **Nux-v** par *Phos* plb **Pyrog** ran-b raph rat rheum **Sep** *Sil* *Squil* sul-i k2 *Sulph* tab **Thuj** *Verat*
- **coldness** of the whole body; with sensation of: bar-c
- **dinner**; after: ptel
- **fanned** in place of thirst during the heat; desire to be: **Carb-v**
- **sensation** of external heat | **without** heat: **Cham** ign ruta fd4.de
- **yellow** skin, with: merc-c

○ - **Single** parts: *Acon* b2.de* agar b2.de* agn b2.de* alum b2.de* am-c b2.de* am-m b2.de* ambr b2.de* anac b2.de* ang b2.de* ant-c b2.de* ant-t b2.de* arg-met b2.de* *Arn* b2.de* **Ars** b2.de* asaf b2.de* asar b2.de* aur b2.de* *Bar-c* b2.de* **Bell** b2.de* bism b2.de* borx b2.de* bov b2.de* *Bry* b2.de* calad b2.de* *Calc* b2.de* camph b2.de* cann-s b2.de* canth b2.de* caps b2.de* carb-an b2.de* *Carb-v* b2.de* *Caust* b2.de* cham b2.de* chel b2.de* chin b2.de* cic b2.de* cina b2.de* clem b2.de* cocc b2.de* coff b2.de* colch b2.de* coloc b2.de* con b2.de*

Fever

- **Single** parts: ...
croc b2.de* cupr b2.de* cycl b2.de* dig b2.de* dros b2.de* dulc b2.de* euph b2.de* euphr b2.de* ferr b2.de* *Graph* b2.de* guaj b2.de* hell b2.de* hep b2.de* hyos b2.de* ign b2.de* ip b2.de* *Kali-c* b2.de* kali-n b2.de* kreos b2.de* lach b2.de* laur b2.de* led b2.de* *Lyc* b2.de* m-ambo b2.de* m-arct b2.de m-aust b2.de mag-c b2.de* mag-m b2.de* mang b2.de* meny b2.de* **Merc** b2.de* mez b2.de* mosch b2.de* mur-ac b2.de* nat-c b2.de* nat-m b2.de* nit-ac b2.de* nux-m b2.de* *Nux-v* b2.de* olnd b2.de* op b2.de* par b2.de* petr b2.de* **Ph-ac** b2.de* **Phos** b2.de* plat b2.de* plb b2.de* puls b2.de* ran-b b2.de* ran-s b2.de* rheum b2.de* rhod b2.de* rhus-t b2.de* ruta b2.de* sabad b2.de* sabin b2.de* samb b2.de* sars b2.de* sec b2.de* sel b2.de* seneg b2.de* *Sep* b2.de* sil b2.de* *Spig* b2.de* spong b2.de* squil b2.de* *Stann* b2.de* *Staph* b2.de* stram b2.de* stront-c b2.de* sul-ac b2.de* **Sulph** b2.de* tarax b2.de* teucr b2.de* thuj b2.de* valer b2.de* verat b2.de* verb b2.de* viol-o b2.de* viol-t b2.de* zinc b2.de*

FLUSHES (See Heat - flushes)

FRIGHT; after: chen-a hr1*

GANGRENE; during: ran-b tl1

GASTRIC FEVER: *Acon* k* **Ant-c** k* **Ant-t** k* **Ars** k* asaf b7a.de* *Asar* b7a.de* aur bg2 bapt k* *Bell* k* **Bry** k* calc bro1 canth carb-v k* card-m k2 *Cham* k* *Chel* chin k* *Cocc* b7a.de* coff b7a.de* colch k* coloc k* cupr k* cycl b7a.de* *Dig* bg2 eup-per ferr-p ptk1 *Gels* hydr bro1 ign k* **Ip** k* iris kali-sula a1* lyc bro1 mag-m k* mag-s *Merc* k* mez bg2 mur-ac k* nat-c bg2 nat-s *Nux-v* k* ph-ac bro1 *Phos* plb b7a.de* *Podo* **Puls** k* rheum k* *Rhus-t* k* santin bro1 *Sec* k* squil b7a.de* staph b7a.de* *Sulph* k* tarax k* trios c2 *Verat* k*

GLANDULAR (See GENERALS - Mononucleosis)

HAT, putting on: agar h2

HEAD, except: ang h1 sulph h2

HEAT: abies-n bro1 acet-ac bro1 **Acon** k* aesc k* aeth k* agar k* agn k* *Agro* bro1 all-s bro1 alst alum k* am-c k* am-m k* *Ambr* k* anac k* androc srj1• *Ang* k* ant-c k* **Ant-t** k* apis b7a.de* aran arg-met b2.de* **Arn** k* **Ars** k* ars-h *Arum-t* asaf k* asar b2.de* atra-r bnm3• aur bg2 aur-m aur-s k2 *Bapt* k* *Bar-c* k* **Bell** k* benz-ac bism b2.de* borx b2.de* bov b2.de* brom k* **Bry** k* **Cact** calad b2.de* *Calc* k* calo bro1 camph k* cann-s b2.de* *Canth* k* *Caps* k* carb-an k* carb-v k* casc cassia-s cdd7• caul caust k* cedr *Cham* k* *Chel* k* *Chin* k* chinin-ar bro1 cic b2.de* cimic k* cimx cina b2.de* clem b2.de* *Cocc* k* *Coff* k* *Colch* k* coloc b2.de* **Con** k* cop corn-f croc k* crot-h cupr k* *Cur* *Cycl* k* *Dig* k* dros k* *Dulc* k* elat eucal k* *Eup-per* eup-pur euph k* euphr bg2* *Ferr* k* ferr-ar k2 **Ferr-p** k* fic-m gya1 *Fl-ac* k* **Gels** k* glon bro1 *Granit-m* es1• *Graph* k* guaj b2.de* *Hell* k* *Hep* k* *Hydrog* srj2• *Hyos* k* *Ign* k* *Iod* k* **Ip** k* kali-bi kali-c k* kali-chl **Kali-i** kali-n b2.de* *Kreos* k* *Lac-c* *Lach* k* lachn *Laur* k* *Led* k* lob **Lyc** k* m-ambo b2.de m-arct b2.de* m-aust b2.de* *Mag-c* k* mag-m k* mag-s mang k* meny k* *Merc* k* *Merc-c* k* *Merc-cy* *Merl* **Mez** k* mill k* morph bro1 mosch k* *Mur-ac* k* nat-c k* **Nat-m** k* nat-p k2 nat-s *Nit-ac* k* *Nux-m* k* **Nux-v** k* olnd b2.de* *Op* k* par b2.de* petr k* *Ph-ac* k* **Phos** k* phyt bro1 plat b2.de* plb k* *Podo* *Psor* **Puls** k* pulx bro1 ran-b b2.de* **Ran-s** b2.de* **Rheum** b2.de* rhod b2.de* **Rhus-t** k* *Rhus-v* ruta b2.de* sabad k* *Sabin* k* *Samb* k* *Sang* sarr sars b2.de* **Sec** k* sel b2.de* seneg k* *Sep* k* **Sil** k* spig k* spira bro1 *Spirae* bro1 **Spong** k* **Squil** k* *Stann* k* *Staph* k* **Stram** k* stront-c b2.de* *Sul-ac* k* *Sulph* k* *Sumb* **Tarax** k* *Tarent* ter k* teucr k* thuj k* vac jl2 *Valer* k* **Verat** k* *Verat-v* k* verb bg2 viol-o bg2 *Viol-t* k* zinc k*

- **absent**: agar am-m **Aran** ben *Bov* camph canth *Caps* *Caust* *Cimx* cocc gamb graph *Hep* kali-c kali-n led *Lyc* mag-c *Mez* mur-ac nat-c ph-ac ran-b rhus-t *Sabad* **Staph** sul-ac **Sulph** *Thuj* *Verat*
- **accompanied** by:
  - • **complaints**; other: **Acon** b2.de* agar b2.de* agn b2.de* alum b2.de* am-c b2.de* am-m b2.de* anac b2.de* ang b2.de* ant-c bg2 ant-t b2.de* arg-met b2.de* arn b2.de* **Ars** b2.de* asaf b2.de* asar b2.de* **Bell** b2.de* borx b2.de* bov b2.de* *Bry* b2.de* calad b2.de* calc b2.de* camph b2.de* canth b2.de* caps b2.de* *Carb-v* b2.de* *Cham* b2.de* chel b2.de* chin b2.de* cic b2.de* cina b2.de* cocc b2.de* coff b2.de* colch b2.de* coloc b2.de* con b2.de* croc b2.de* cupr b2.de* cycl b2.de* dig b2.de* dros b2.de* *Dulc* b2.de* euph b2.de* ferr b2.de* graph b2.de* hell b2.de* hep b2.de* *Hyos* b2.de* *Ign* b2.de* iod b2.de* *Ip* b2.de* kali-c b2.de* kreos b2.de* lach b2.de* laur b2.de* led b2.de* *Lyc* b2.de* m-ambo b2.de* m-arct b2.de m-aust b2.de mag-c b2.de* mag-m b2.de* mang b2.de* meny b2.de* merc b2.de* mosch b2.de* mur-ac b2.de* nat-c b2.de* **Nat-m** b2.de* nit-ac b2.de* **Nux-v** b2.de* olnd b2.de* **Op** b2.de* par b2.de* petr b2.de* *Ph-ac* b2.de* phos b2.de* plat b2.de* plb b2.de* **Puls** b2.de* ran-b b2.de*

Heat – accompanied by – **complaints**; other: ...
ran-s b2.de* rheum b2.de* rhod b2.de* *Rhus-t* b2.de* ruta b2.de* sabad b2.de* *Sabin* b2.de* samb b2.de* sars b2.de* *Sep* b2.de* sil b2.de* spig b2.de* spong b2.de* squil b2.de* staph b2.de* stram b2.de* sulph b2.de* tarax b2.de* teucr b2.de* *Thuj* b2.de* valer b2.de* *Verat* b2.de* viol-t b2.de* zinc b2.de*

- • **perspiration** (See Perspiration - heat)
- **beginning** in:
  - ○ • **Abdomen**: *Rhus-t* bg2
  - • **Back**: spong bg2
  - • **Ears**: acon bg2 calc bg2 kali-c bg2 olnd bg2 *Sep* bg2
  - • **Face**: *Acon* bg2 alum bg2
  - • **Feet**: *Lach* bg2 led bg2
  - • **Hands**: hep bg2 lach bg2 led bg2 mez bg2 phos bg2
  - • **Head**: *Acon* bg2 alum bg2 *Op* bg2
  - • **Lumbar** region: bapt bg2
  - • **Stomach**: nat-m bg2 *Op* bg2
- **continued**: ars bro1 bol-la bro1 granit-m es1• ign bro1
- **decreasing**:
  - • **night**:
    - ⁝ **midnight** | **after**: gels bro1
- **descending** agg.: alum hr1
- **flushes**; in: acet-ac bro1 *Aml-ns* bro1 antip bro1 *Ars* bro1 ars-i bro1 bell-p sp1 bol-la bro1 calc bro1 *Carl* bro1 chim bro1 *Dig* bro1 erech bro1 ferr-r bro1 frax bro1 hep bro1 ign bro1 indg bro1 iod bro1 jab bro1 *Kali-c* bro1 lach bro1 lyc bro1 med bro1 merc bro1 *Nicc* bro1 petr bro1 *Phos* bro1 puls bro1 *Sang* bro1 *Sep* bro1 *Sul-ac* bro1 *Sulph* bro1 urt-u bro1 valer bro1 visc bro1 yohim bro1
- **head**; heavy: pitu-gl skp7•
- **internally**; only (See Internal)
- **mild**:
  - • **accompanied** by | **insanity**: hyos tl1
- **periodical**:
  - • **day** | **every** few days: granit-m es1•
- **predominates**: ars bg2 *Bell* bg2 benz-ac bg2 *Bry* bg2 ip bg2 *Lach* bg2 verat bg2
- **radiating**: vario jl2
- **spots**; in: **Apis** bg2 carb-v bg2 sel bg2 zinc bg2

○ - **Affected** parts: *Acon* b7.de alum bg2 *Bry* b7.de* *Guaj* b4a.de lach bg2 m-ambo b7.de phos bg2 *Puls* b7.de* *Sulph* b4a.de

- **Single** parts: *Acon* b2.de* agar b2.de* agn b2.de* alum b2.de* am-c b2.de* am-m b2.de* ambr b2.de* **Aml-ns** bg2 anac b2.de* ang b2.de* ant-c b2.de* ant-t b2.de* *Apis* ptk1 arg-met b2.de* *Arn* b2.de* **Ars** b2.de* asaf b2.de* asar b2.de* aur b2.de* bapt bg2 bar-c b2.de* **Bell** b2.de* bism b2.de* borx b2.de* bov b2.de* **Bry** b2.de* calad b2.de* *Calc* b2.de* camph b2.de* cann-s b2.de* *Canth* b2.de* caps b2.de* carb-an b2.de* *Carb-v* b2.de* caust b2.de* *Cham* b2.de* chel b2.de* chin b2.de* cic b2.de* cina b2.de* clem b2.de* cocc b2.de* coff b2.de* colch b2.de* coloc b2.de* con b2.de* croc b2.de* cupr b2.de* cycl b2.de* dig b2.de* dros b2.de* dulc b2.de* euph b2.de* euphr b2.de* ferr b2.de* *Graph* b2.de* guaj b2.de* hell b2.de* hep b2.de* hyos b2.de* ign b2.de* iod b2.de* ip b2.de* kali-c b2.de* kali-n b2.de* kreos b2.de* lach b2.de* *Laur* b2.de* led b2.de* *Lyc* b2.de* m-ambo b2.de* m-arct b2.de m-aust b2.de mag-c b2.de* mag-m b2.de* mang b2.de* meny b2.de* **Merc** b2.de* *Mez* b2.de* mosch b2.de* mur-ac b2.de* nat-c b2.de* nat-m b2.de* nit-ac b2.de* nux-m b2.de* *Nux-v* b2.de* olnd b2.de* op b2.de* par b2.de* petr b2.de* **Ph-ac** b2.de* **Phos** b2.de* plat b2.de* plb b2.de* *Puls* b2.de* ran-b b2.de* ran-s b2.de* rheum b2.de* rhod b2.de* rhus-t b2.de* ruta b2.de* *Sabad* b2.de* sabin b2.de* samb b2.de* sars b2.de* sec b2.de* sel b2.de* seneg b2.de* *Sep* b2.de* sil b2.de* spig b2.de* spong b2.de* squil b2.de* *Stann* b2.de* staph b2.de* stram b2.de* stront-c b2.de* sul-ac b2.de* **Sulph** b2.de* tarax b2.de* teucr b2.de* thuj b2.de* valer b2.de* verat b2.de* verat-v ptk1 verb b2.de* viol-o b2.de* viol-t b2.de* zinc b2.de*
  - • **iron**; as from hot: alum bg2 mag-c bg2
- **Stomach**; pit of: cub c1

HECTIC FEVER: abrot k* *Acet-ac* k* acon bro1 am-c ambro c2 ant-t gcj1* arg-met k* arn **Ars** k* **Ars-i** k* ars-s-f k2 asar hr1* aur-m aur-m-n c2 bals-p c2* bapt c2* bar-c b4a.de* bell bg2 bol-la bry k* *Calc* k* calc-hp bg2* calc-i k2* *Calc-p* *Calc-s* k* calc-sil k2 calen hr1* **Caps** k* carb-an *Carb-v* k* card-m hl1* chim hr1* *Chin* k* *Chinin-ar* k* chinin-s hr1* *Chlor* cocc k* con b4a.de* corh br1 crot-h *Cupr* k* dig bg2* dros bg2 dulc b4a.de* echit a1 erio ll1

Hectic fever: ...
eucal hr1* eup-per hr1* eup-pur hl9* ferr bg2* ferr-act ll1 ferr-p k* fl-ac hr1* gels hr1* get ll1 graph b4a.de* guaj b4a.de* hell bg2 hep k* hippoz hr1 hydr hr1 hyos hr1 hyper bg2 ign bg2 **Iod** k* ip k* **Kali-ar** *Kali-c* k* kali-i bg2 *Kali-p* *Kali-s* kreos hr1 lac-d k2 *Lach* k* led bg2 lob-e c2 **Lyc** k* med k* *Merc* k* merc-c b4a.de* mez mill nat-ar hr1* nat-c bg2 nat-m b4a.de* nit-ac k* nux-v k* ol-j a1* olib-sac wmh1 petr hr1* *Ph-ac* k* phel bro1 **Phos** k* plb a1* ptel hr1* *Puls* k* *Pyrog* k* rhus-g hl1 rob hr1* **Sang** k* *Senec* **Sep** k* **Sil** k* *Stann* k* staph bg2 stront-c ll1 sul-ac k* sul-i k2 *Sulph* k* *Tarent* thuj k* tril-p hr1 **Tub** k* verat bg2 zinc bg2

- **forenoon**:
  - **9-10 h** | **midnight**; until: corh br1
- **hemoptysis**, with: mill
- **nostalgia**, from: **Caps** hr1
- **periodical**:
  - **day**; every | **forenoon** | **11**-12 or 13 h: arg-met
    - **afternoon** | **17** h: med hr1*

HEMORRHAGE: | **amel.**: bell k2

HIGH FEVER (See Intense)

ICE-WATER; after abuse of: carb-v tl1

IDIOPATHIC: pyrog tl1

INFECTION; from: ail bg2 ars bg2 arum-t bg2 **Bapt** bg2 caust bg2 chinin-ar bg2 **Eup-per** bg2 ferr-p bg2 *Gels* bg2 merc bg2 *Rhus-t* bg2 sulph bg2

INFLAMMATORY fever: acet-ac *Acon* k* apis k* arn k* ars k* bapt bro1 bar-c bg2 **Bell** k* **Bry** k* *Cact* calad bg2 calc bg2 camph b7a.de* cann-s b7a.de* canth k* caust bg2 *Cham* k* chin k* cocc bg2 coff bg2 *Colch* k* coloc bg2 con k* dig k* dros b7a.de* dulc k* *Gels* gink-b sbd1• hep k* hyos k* ign b7a.de* ip k* kali-c k* *Kali-n* bg2 kola stb3• *Lach* k* laur b7a.de* lyc k* **Merc** k* mez bg2 nat-c bg2 nat-m bg2 nit-ac k* nux-v k* op b7a.de* ph-ac bg2 *Phos* k* **Puls** k* **Rhus-t** k* sabad bg2 sabin b7a.de sec bg2 seneg bg2 sep k* sil k* spig b7a.de* spong b7a.de* squil b7a.de* staph bg2 stram b7a.de* sul-ac k* *Sulph* k* tub c1 verat k*

- **alternating** with insanity (See MIND - Insanity - alternating - fever)
- **face**; with red: acon tl1
  - **pale** face; or alternating red and: acon tl1
- **skin**; with dry: acon tl1
- **thirst**; with violent: acon tl1

INSIDIOUS fever: acet-ac *Ars* k* bell b4a.de carc jl2 *Chin* k* cocc k* colch con k* iod b4a.de merc-c b4a.de *Sec* k* sep b4a.de stann b4a.de *Sulph* k* *Tub* k*

INSPIRATION agg.: bry bg2 rhod bg2

INTENSE heat: abrot **Acon** k* ant-t anthraci jl2 *Apis* **Arn** **Ars** k* *Arum-t* *Aur* aur-ar k2 bapt ptk1 **Bell** *Bry* k* buth-a sp1 cact canth caps carbn-s k2 carc jl2 chel chin chinin-ar ptk1 *Chinin-s* k* cina coff *Colch* **Con** convo-s sp1 croc crot-h k* cuph br1 cupr cyt-l sp1 dig k* dulc eberth jl2 epil a1* *Eup-per* mrr1 ferr-ar *Ferr-p* mrr1 **Gels** hep hyos influ jl2 iod ptk1* ip b7a.de *Kali-ar* kali-i *Lach* loxo-lae bnm12• loxo-recl bnm10• *Lyc* mag-c meny merc-c **Mez** morb jl2 mur-ac br1* musca-d szs1 naja bg2 **Nat-m** nat-s nit-ac nux-m *Nux-v* k* *Op* oscilloc jl2 ourl jl2 ph-ac *Phos* k* psor k2* **Puls** **Pyrog** k* **Rhus-t** k* sabad b7a.de sal-ac tl samb sang **Sec** *Sil* staph *Stram* sulph ptk1 thuj toxo-g jl2 *Tub* k* tub-a jl2 vac jl2 valer b7a.de vario al2* verat b7a.de verat-v tl1* yers jl2 yohim br1*

- **morning**: malar jl2
- **night**: malar jl2
- **accompanied** by:
  - **diphtheria** (See THROAT - Diphtheria - accompanied - fever - intense)
  - O **Lungs**; hepatization of | **rapid** (See CHEST - Hepatization - rapid - accompanied - fever)
- **children**; in: buth-a sp1 iod mtf33
- **coma**; with (See MIND - Coma - fever - during)
- **constant**: (↗*Continued; Typhoid*)
  - **accompanied** by:
    - **diarrhea** | **children**; in tuberculous: lob-e c1
- **convulsions**; with: (↗*Convulsions; GENERALS - Convulsions - heat*) **Bell** k* *Cic* diph-pert-t mp4• *Hyos* op prot fmm1• **Stram**

Intense heat: ...

- **delirium**; with: ant-t anthraci jl2 *Apis* **Ars** **Bell** *Bry* carb-v chin *Chinin-s* *Chlor* *Clem* hr1 coff hep hyos iod lachn c1 **Nat-m** nux-v **Op** **Puls** sarr sec **Stram** k*
  - **night**:
    - **midnight**:
      - **after** | **1**-2 h: lachn c1
- **dyspnea**; with: (↗*RESPIRATION - Difficult - fever*) diph mtf11
- **followed** by | **prostration**: (↗*MIND - Prostration - fever - after*) camph mtf11
- **head** and face, body cold; of: **Arn** *Bell* *Op* *Stram*
- **meningitis**; during: apis mrr1
- **sleep** | **after** | **agg.**: cina op
  - **during** | **agg.**: *Ant-t* apis caps chin gels *Lach* lyc **Mez** *Nat-m* *Nux-m* **Op** rhus-t stram
- **stupefaction** and unconsciousness, with: *Bell* *Cact* **Nat-m** **Op** k* *Phos*

INTERMITTENT: (↗*Remittent*) abies-n br1 acon bg2* aesc c2 agar k* *Alst* bro1 alum k* am-c bg2 am-m bg2* *Am-pic* bro1 *Aml-ns* bro1 anac bg2 ang c1* ant-c bg2* ant-t bg2* apis k* aran bg2* arg-met bg2 arist-cl sp1 arn bg2* **Ars** k* ars-br br1* *Ars-i* k* ars-s-f k2 arum-t bg2 asaf bg2 asar bg2 astac c2 atra-r bnm3• aur bg2 aza c2* baj bro1 bapt bro1 bar-c bg2 bell bg2* benz-ac bg2 bol-la bwa3* bov bg2 bry bg2* bufo bg2* buth-a sp1 cact bg2* calad bg2* **Calc** k* calc-ar c2* *Calc-p* calc-s camph bg2 *Camph-mbr* bro1 canch c2* cann-xyz bg2 canth bg2 *Caps* bg2* *Carb-ac* k* carb-an bg2 *Carb-v* k* card-m c2 casc c2 caust bg2* *Cean* c2* *Cedr* bg2* cent c2* cham bg2 chel bg2* chelo bro1 chim c2 *Chin* bg2* *Chinin-ar* k* chinin-m c2* *Chinin-s* bg2* chion bro1 cic bg2 cimx c2* cina bg2* cist bg2* clem bg2 cocc bg2* coff bg2* colch bg2* coloc bg2 corn c2 corn-a c2 corn-f c2* croc bg2 crot-h bg2* cupr bg2 cycl bg2 dros bg2 *Echi* bro1 elat c2* eucal bg2* eup-per bg2* *Eup-pur* c2* euphr bg2 **Ferr** k* ferr-ar *Ferr-i* ferr-p c2* fl-ac bg2 gels bg2* gent-q c2 graph k* guare c2 *Helia* bro1 hell bg2 *Hep* k* hydr bg2* hyos bg2 ign bg2* ilx-a c2* *Iod* k* *Ip* bg2* iris bg2 iris-t c2 kali-ar kali-bi bg2* kali-c k* kali-i bg2 kali-n bg2* **Kali-s** k* lach k* laur bro1 lept bg2 lil-t bg2 **Lyc** k* mag-c bg2 mag-m bg2 mag-p bg2 maland bro1 malar bro1 meny bg2* merc bg2 methyl bro1 mez bg2 mosch bg2 mur-ac bg2* naja bg2 narc-ps mp4• nat-c bg2 **Nat-m** k* nat-p bg2* **Nat-s** k* nicc bg2 **Nit-ac** k* nux-m bg2* nux-v k* ol-j c2 op bg2* ost c2* pambt br1* par bg2 parth bro1 *Petr* bg2 petros c2* ph-ac bg2* phel c2* *Phlor* c1 *Phos* k* plb bg2 plb-xyz c2 plect c2 podo bg2* *Polym* bro1 polyp-p c2* **Psor** k* ptel c2 *Puls* bg2* **Pyrog** k* quas c2 querc-r c1* ran-b bg2 ran-s bg2 rheum bg2 rhod bg2 rhus-t bg2* rob c2 sabad bg2* sabin bg2 sal-al bwa3 samb bg2 sang bg2 sanic c2 sars c2 sec bg2 sel bg2 senec bg2 *Sep* k* *Sil* k* sin-n c2 *Spig* bg2* spong bg2 stann bg2 *Staph* bg2 stram bg2* sul-ac bg2* **Sulph** k* tarax bg2* **Tarent** k* tarent-c c2 *Tela* bro1 tell bg2 teucr bg2 ther bg2 *Thuj* bg2* **Tub** k* urt-u bg2* valer bg2 *Verat* bg2* verat-v bro1 verb bro1 verbe-o br1 vichy-g c2 vip bg2 zinc bg2

- **accompanied** by:
  - **anemia** (See GENERALS - Anemia - accompanied - fever - intermittent)
  - **weariness**: cimx br1
- **bronchopneumonia**, following: chinin-m kr1 chinin-s kr1
- **chronic**: eup-per br1 helia br1
- **congestive**: camph bro1 *Op* bro1 *Verat* bro1
- **gout**; with: ferr led
- **incomplete**: aran bro1 *Ars* k* cact bro1 *Carb-v* bro1 eup-per bro1 eup-pur bro1 *Ip* bro1 nat-m bro1 nux-v bro1 puls k2
- **liver**; with enlarged (= liver-cake): caps bwa3 chinin-ar k2* eup-per hr1* ferr ll1 ferr-ar ferr-i *Lyc* nat-m **Nit-ac** k* nux-m he1* nyct bwa3
- **long** lasting heat; with: **Ant-t** cact canth colch *Ferr* hep ip sec sil *Tarent*
- **masked** (= dumb ague): *Ars* k* bol-la hl1 cedr bro1 chelo c1* chinin-pur hl1 chinin-s bwa3* gels br1* ip k* maland bro1 malar al2 nux-v k* *Sep* k* spig k* stry hl1 *Tarent* k* *Tub*
- **old** people, with coma: alum nux-m *Op*
- **periosteum**; with pain in: mur-ac hr1
- **pernicious**: ars bro1 camph bro1 chinin-brh bro1 *Chinin-s* bro1 crot-h bro1 *Tarent* bro1
- **prophylaxis**: ars bro1* chinin-s bro1*
- **pulmonary** hemorrhage, with: *Arg-n*
- **recent** cases: acon bro1 aran bro1 ars bro1 chin bro1 chinin-s bro1 ip bro1 tarent bro1
- **rheumatism**; with: chinin-s bro1 cortiso sp1 hed sp1 led morg-p fmm1•

Fever

- **spleen**; with enlarged: *(↗GENERALS - Malaria - accompanied - spleen)* aran hr1* ars btw2 berb he1 bol-la bwa3 caps bwa3 *Carb-ac* cean bn2* chin btw1 ferr-ar (non:ferr-i c1*) hell br1 ign hr1 ilx-a hl9 lyc a2 morph ll1 nit-ac bwa5 nux-m he1* nyct bwa3 parth ah1 polym bwa3 querc-r c1 rhus-t hr1 sul-ac hr1* urt-u tl2
- **spoiled**: abies-n bro1 am-m bro1 aran bro1 ars k* ars-br bro1 *Calc* calc-ar bro1 canch bro1 carb-v bro1 corn bro1 corn-f bro1 *Ferr Helia* bro1 ign bro1 *Ip* nat-m k* nux-v *Puls* bro1 pyrog bro1 querc bro1 **Sep** sulph *Tarent* tela bro1
- **tuberculosis**, in: acon bro1 all-s bro1 ars bro1 ars-i bro1 bapt bg1* calc-i bro1 chin bro1 *Chinin-ar* bro1 *Ferr-p* bro1 iod bro1 lyc bro1 nit-ac bro1 phos bro1 sang bro1 sil bro1 stann bro1
- **typhoid** fever; that tends toward: *Ars* gels
- **vertigo**; with: corn-f br1
- **weather** agg.; warm: canch br1

INTERNAL heat: **Acon** k* aloe alum b2.de* am-c b2.de* am-m b2.de* ambr b2.de* anac k* ang b2.de* ant-c b2.de* ant-t b2.de* apis b7a.de* arg-met b2.de* **Arn** k* **Ars** k* ars-i asaf b2.de* asar b2.de* bar-c b2.de* **Bell** k* berb bism b2.de* borx b2.de* bov b2.de* *Brom* b4a.de* **Bry** k* calad k* *Calc* k* camph b2.de* cann-s b2.de* *Canth* k* caps k* carb-an b2.de* *Carb-v* k* *Caust* k* *Cham* k* chel k* chin k* *Cic* k* cina b2.de* clem b4.de* cocc b2.de* **Coff** b2.de* colch b2.de* coloc b2.de* *Con* k* croc k* *Cupr* b2.de* **Cycl** bg2 dig b2.de* dros b2.de* dulc b2.de* *Euph* b2.de* *Ferr* ferr-ar ferr-i *Ferr-p Fl-ac* graph b2.de* guaj b2.de* *Hell* k* hep b2.de* hydrog srj2• hyos k* ign k* *Iod* k* ip k* *Kali-ar Kali-c* k* kali-n b2.de* kali-p kreos b2.de* lach k* **Laur** k* *Led* b2.de* *Lyc* k* m-ambo b2.de* m-arct b2.de* m-aust b2.de* **Mag-c** k* mag-m k* mang b2.de* *Med Meny* b2.de* **Merc** k* merc-c bg2* *Mez* k* *Mosch* b2.de* *Mur-ac* b2.de* nat-c b2.de* nat-m b2.de* *Nit-ac* k* nux-m b2.de* **Nux-v** k* olnd b2.de* op b2.de* par b2.de* petr b2.de* **Ph-ac** k* **Phos** k* plat b2.de* *Plb* b2.de* *Puls* k* ran-b b2.de* ran-s b2.de* rheum b7.de *Rhod* b2.de* **Rhus-t** k* ruta b2.de* *Sabad* k* sabin b2.de* samb b2.de* sars b2.de* *Sec* k* seneg b2.de* *Sep* k* *Sil* k* *Spig* k* spong b2.de* squil b2.de* *Stann* k* *Staph* b2.de* stram b2.de* stront-c b2.de* sul-ac b2.de* **Sulph** k* tarax b2.de* teucr b2.de* thuj b2.de* valer b2.de* *Verat* k* viol-t b2.de* *Zinc* k*

- **morning**: alum k* carb-v h2 petr h2
  - • **8** h: caust
- **afternoon**: graph h2
- **evening**: anac k* calc h2 limen-b-c hm2* *Puls* spig h1 zinc h2
- **night**: calc h2 clem h2 mag-m h2 petr h2 spig h1
  - • **uncover**, which causes chilliness; must: **Mag-c**
- **burning**: *Ars* bell h1 brom caps hyos mez *Mosch* petr-ra shn4• **Sec**
  - • **forenoon** | **9**h: brom
- ○ • **Blood** vessels; in: agar **Ars** k* *Aur Bry* k* *Calc* k* *Hyos Med* k* nat-m nit-ac op **Rhus-t** k* *Syph* k* verat
- **chilliness**; with: graph h2
- **cold** to the touch; while body feels: acon vh1 *Carb-v Ferr* sars sec gk
- **coldness** of single parts; with: chin ign *Nux-v Rhus-t*
- **external** chill; with: **Acon** k* ant-t bg2 apis bg2 *Arn* k* **Ars** k* ars-i *Bell* k* bry *Calc* k* **Camph** k* caps k* carb-v bg2 *Cham* k* *Chel* cic bg2 cina bg2 dig bg2 dros bg2 *Ferr* ferr-ar *Ferr-i* hyos bg2 *Ign* k* *Iod* k* *Ip* k* *Kali-ar Kali-c* k* kali-n ptk1 *Mez* k* **Mosch** k* nat-c h2 nit-ac k* nux-v bg2 *Ph-ac* k* *Phos* plat bg2 *Puls Rhus-t* k* sabad sang *Sec* k* *Sil* squil sul-ac sul-i ptk1 sulph k* til ban1• **Verat** k* *Zinc*
- **menses**; during: nat-m h2
- **perspiration**; with cold: anac
- ○ - **Blood** vessels; in: chin bg1 com bg1 phos bg1 plb bg1 xan bg1
- **Single** parts: **Acon** b2.de* alum b2.de* am-c b2.de* am-m b2.de* ambr b2.de* ang b2.de* ant-c b2.de* ant-t b2.de* arg-met b2.de* *Arn* b2.de* *Ars* b2.de* asaf b2.de* asar b2.de* aur b2.de* bar-c b2.de* **Bell** b2.de* bism b2.de* borx b2.de* bov b2.de* **Bry** b2.de* calad b2.de* *Calc* b2.de* *Camph* b2.de* cann-s b2.de* **Canth** b2.de* caps b2.de* carb-an b2.de* *Carb-v* b2.de* caust b2.de* *Cham* b2.de* chel b2.de* chin b2.de* cic b2.de* cina b2.de* cocc b2.de* coff b2.de* colch b2.de* coloc b2.de* con b2.de* croc b2.de* cupr b2.de* dig b2.de* dros b2.de* dulc b2.de* *Euph* b2.de* euphr b2.de* ferr b2.de* glon bg2 graph b2.de* guaj b2.de* hell b2.de* hep b2.de* hyos b2.de* ign b2.de* iod b2.de* ip b2.de* kali-c b2.de* kali-n b2.de* kreos b2.de* lach b2.de* **Laur** b2.de* led b2.de* *Lyc* b2.de* m-ambo b2.de* m-arct b2.de m-aust b2.de mag-c b2.de* mag-m b2.de* mang b2.de* meny b2.de* **Merc** b2.de* *Mez* b2.de* mosch b2.de* mur-ac b2.de* nat-c b2.de* nat-m b2.de* nit-ac b2.de* nux-m b2.de* *Nux-v* b2.de* olnd b2.de* op b2.de* par b2.de* petr b2.de* *Ph-ac* b2.de* **Phos** b2.de* plat b2.de* plb b2.de* *Puls* b2.de* ran-b b2.de* ran-s b2.de* rhod b2.de* rhus-t b2.de* ruta b2.de* *Sabad* b2.de* sabin b2.de* sars b2.de* *Sec* b2.de* seneg b2.de* *Sep* b2.de* sil b2.de* spig b2.de*

Internal heat – **Single** parts: ...
spong b2.de* squil b2.de* stann b2.de* staph b2.de* stram b2.de* stront-c b2.de* sul-ac b2.de* **Sulph** b2.de* tarax b2.de* thuj b2.de* verat b2.de* viol-o b2.de* viol-t b2.de* zinc b2.de*

INTOXICATION: | **after**: acon bg2 bell bg2 stram bg2

IRREGULAR stages: **Ars Bry** *Ip* **Nux-v** op pyrog jl2 *Sep*

IRRITATIVE fever: *(↗MIND - Irritability)* acon arn **Ars** k* bapt bell *Bry Camph* canth *Carb-v* cham k* *Chin Cina* bro1 *Cocc* crot-t cupr dig *Gels* k* *Graph* hr1 hell hyos ign bro1 ip bro1 **Lach** *Lyc* merc k* *Mur-ac Nat-m Nux-v* k* op *Ph-ac* podo k* *Puls Rhus-t* rhus-v hr1 sang bro1 *Sec* sulph k* verat k* *Verat-v* hr1
- **slow**: *(↗Continued) Acet-ac* **Ars** *Bry* calc-s *Camph* canth *Chin* cocc hell lach *Lyc Mur-ac Ph-ac Phos* plb rhus-t tl1 *Sec* sil sulph thuj

LACTATION; during: acon b7a.de arn b7a.de bry b7a.de cham b7a.de coff b7a.de ign b7a.de op b7a.de rhus-t b7a.de

LONG lasting heat: acon *Ant-t* apis *Arn Ars* aster bar-m *Bell* bol-la *Cact* calc-f *Caps* carc mlr1• **Cham** chin colch elaps eup-per *Ferr* **Gels** graph *Hep* hyos lach laur loxo-lae bnm12• lyc nat-m *Nux-v Parathyr* jl2 *Sec* sil *Sulph Tarent*
- **followed** by chill: apis
- **sleep**, with: *Chin*

LOW FEVER (See GENERALS - Weakness - fever - during - agg.)

LYING: | **quietly** | **agg.**: arn b7.de
- **affected** part agg.; on the: sulph bg2

LYING DOWN agg.; after: *Agn* b7a.de *Chel* b7a.de *Coff* b7a.de *Hell* b7.de* puls b7.de rhus-t b7.de *Samb* b7.de* spong b7.de squil b7.de

MALARIA (See GENERALS - Malaria)

MARSH fever: helo-s rwt2•

MEAT agg.: agar bg2 mag-c b4a.de* merc bg2

MENOPAUSE; during: calc bg2 sul-ac bg2

MENSES:
- **after** | **agg.**: nat-m bg2
- **before** | **agg.**: alum bg2 am-c k* apis bg2 bufo bg2 calc k* carb-an k* cham bg2 con k* cupr k* graph bg2 iod k* kali-c k* lac-c bg2 lyc k* *Merc* bg2 nat-m bg2 nit-ac k* puls k* sep k* sulph bg2 thuj k* tub-sp vn*
- **during** | **agg.**: *Acon* k* aesc k* am-c bg2 *Bell* k* bry *Calc* k* carb-an carb-v bg2 cham bg2 *Coc-c* bg2* ferr bg2 gels k* *Graph* k* helo bg2 helon k* *Hyos* bg2 ign bg2 kali-bi k* kali-c bg2 kali-i bg2 kreos lach bg2 lob bg2 lyc bg2 mag-c k* mag-m k* mag-s bg2 merc k* nat-m k* nit-ac h2* nux-v k* petr bg2 *Phos* k* puls bg2 *Pyrog* bg3* rhod k* **Sep** k* *Sulph* k* thuj bro1 verat-v bg2
- **suppressed** menses; from: *Acon* bg2 con bg2 hell bg2 lyc bg2 *Puls* bg2 sil bg2 sulph bg2

MENTAL EXERTION:
- **after**: ambr bell caps tl1 cocc tl1 nux-v olnd k* phos sep k* sil spong ptk1
- **amel.**: ferr nat-c bg2 nat-m

MILD fever: glycyr-g cte1• loxo-lae bnm12•
- **time**; no definite: glycyr-g cte1•
- **type**; no definite: glycyr-g cte1•

MILK agg.: acon bg2

MOTION:
- **after** | **agg.**: am-c b4.de* **Am-m** bg2 ars bg2 canth b7.de* caust b4.de* nit-ac b4.de* petr bg2 phos b4.de* rhus-t bg2 *Sep* b4.de* spig b7.de* *Spong* b7.de* *Stann* b4.de* **Sul-ac** b4.de*
- **agg.**: agar alum am-m k* ant-c k* ant-t k* ars k* bell k* bry k* *Camph* k* canth **Chin** k* chinin-s con cur *Fl-ac* bg2 led b7.de* merc bg2 *Nux-v* k* olnd b7.de* phos bg2 samb b7.de* *Sep* k* spig b7.de* spong h1 squil b7.de* stann k* staph bg2 stram k* sul-ac valer b7.de*
- **amel.**: agar ambr bg2 apis k* asaf bg2 aur bg2 bism bg2 **Caps** k* con bg2 cycl k* dulc bg2 euph bg2 ferr k* kali-n bg2 *Lyc* k* merc-c k* phos bg2* puls k* rhus-t k* sabad k* samb k* sel k* tarax k* valer k* [spect dfg1]
- **chilliness**, brings on: ant-t *Apis Arn Chinin-s Merc* **Nux-v** k* *Podo* **Rhus-t** *Stram*
- **quiet** in any stage; wants to be: **Bry** gels

MUCUS; with complaints from: ars b4a.de *Asar* b7a.de bell b4a.de bry b7a.de *Caps* b7a.de cham b7a.de chin b7a.de cina b7a.de dig b4a.de dulc b4a.de *Ign* b7a.de ip b7a.de merc b4a.de *Merc-c* b4a.de mez b4a.de *Nux-v* b7a.de *Puls* b7a.de rheum b7a.de rhus-t b7a.de spig b7a.de stann b4a.de sul-ac b4a.de sulph b4a.de

NERVOUS (See Excitement)

NERVOUS complaints; characterized by: camph b7a.de chin b7a.de cocc b7a.de cupr b7a.de ferr b7a.de hell b7a.de ign b7a.de nux-v b7a.de staph b7a.de verat b7a.de

NOISE agg.: bry k* caust bg2 coff bg2 sep bg2

NURSING; from: acon mp1• arn mp1• *Bell* mp1• **Bry** mp1• coff mp1• rhus-t mp1•
- **anger**; after: *Cham* mp1•
- **rheumatic** pain in breast: **Bry** mp1•

OPERATION; after: | **mastoid**: caps tl1

PAIN:
- **after** pain; fever: phyt bg2
- **during** pain; fever: carb-v b4a.de mag-m bg2 phos bg2 sang bg2
- **from** pain; fever: *Acon* bg2 arn bg2 ars h2* bell bg2 bry bg2 carb-v k* cham k* hell bg2 ign bg2 puls bg2 *Rhus-t* bg2 *Sil* bg2 staph bg2 sulph bg2

○ • **Abdomen**; in: sec ptk1

• **Stomach**, in: *(↗STOMACH - Pain - fever)* sec

PAROXYSMAL fever: acon tl1 am-m arund *Bry* *Calc* camph cham cocc cupr-act tl1 cystein-l rly4• hep kali-sula a1* lyc *Merc* nit-ac op tub-d jl2 zinc
- **morning**: eup-per kali-bi
- **forenoon** | **11** h: cact br1 calc
- **afternoon**: agar h2 aza bro1 calc sil
  - • **15** h: lyc
- **evening**: calc lyc
  - • **19** h: lyc
- **night**: kali-bi **Merc**
- **convulsions**; during: ign bro1
- **short** attacks: agn bg2 am-c bg2 *Am-m* bg2 **Ambr** bg2 ant-t bg2 **Arn** bg2 asar bg2 aur bg2 *Bar-c* bg2 bell bg2 borx bg2 **Calc** bg2 carb-v bg2* cham bg2 chin bg2 **Cocc** bg2 *Cupr* bg2 dig bg2 *Euphr* bg2 **Hell** bg2 **Hep** bg2 hyos bg2 *Ign* bg2 iod bg2 ip bg2 kali-c bg2 kreos bg2 lach bg2 laur bg2 led bg2 **Lyc** bg2 **Nux-v** bg2 olnd bg2 petr bg2 ph-ac bg2 **Phos** bg2 *Rhus-t* bg2 ruta bg2 **Sep** bg2 *Sil* bg2 *Stann* bg2 sul-ac bg2 **Sulph** bg2 *Teucr* bg2 **Thuj** bg2 *Verat* bg2 zinc bg2

PAROXYSMS increasing in severity: ars *Bry* eup-per *Nat-m* nux-v *Psor* **Puls**
- **irregular**: **Ars** k* carb-v *Eup-per* ign *Ip* *Meny* **Nux-v** k* **Psor** k* **Puls** k* samb **Sep** k*
  - • **long** chill, little heat, no thirst: **Puls**
  - • **short** chill, long heat, no thirst: **Ip**
  - • **stage** wanting; one: *Apis* aran **Ars** bov camph dros led lyc meny mez verat
- **regular**: *Chin* **Chinin-s** cina

PERIODICAL: acon bg2 agar bg2 *Alum* bg2 am-c bg2 am-m bg2 anac bg2 ant-c bg2 ant-t bg2 *Apis* bg2 aran bg2 arg-met bg2 arn bg2 **Ars** bg2 arum-t bg2 asaf bg2 asar bg2 aur bg2 bar-c bg2 *Bell* bg2 benz-ac bg2 bov bg2 *Bry* bg2 bufo bg2 cact bg2 calad bg2 *Calc* bg2 camph bg2 cann-xyz bg2 canth bg2 **Caps** bg2 carb-an bg2 carb-v bg2 carc fb caust bg2 *Cedr* bg2 cham bg2 chel bg2 **Chin** bg2* chinin-s bg2* cic bg2 *Cina* bg2 cist bg2 clem bg2 cocc bg2 coff bg2 colch bg2 coloc bg2 croc bg2 crot-h bg2 cupr bg2 cycl bg2 dros bg2 eucal bg2 eup-per bg2* euphr bg2 *Ferr* bg2 fl-ac bg2* gels bg2 graph bg2 hell bg2 hep bg2 hydr bg2 hyos bg2 *Ign* bg2 iod bg2 **Ip** bg2 iris bg2 kali-bi bg2 kali-c bg2 kali-i bg2 kali-n bg2 *Lach* bg2 lept bg2 lil-t bg2 lyc bg2 mag-c bg2 mag-m bg2 mag-p bg2 meny bg2 merc bg2 mez bg2 mosch bg2 mur-ac bg2 naja bg2 nat-c bg2 nat-m bg2* nat-p bg2 **Nat-s** bg2 nicc bg2 nig-s mp4• nit-ac bg2 nux-m bg2 **Nux-v** bg2 op bg2 par bg2 *Petr* bg2 ph-ac bg2 phos bg2 plb bg2 podo bg2 **Puls** bg2 ran-b bg2 ran-s bg2 rheum bg2 rhod bg2 rhus-t bg2* *Sabad* bg2 sabin bg2 samb bg2 sang bg2 sec bg2 sel bg2 senec bg2 *Sep* bg2 sil bg2 *Spig* bg2 spong bg2 stann bg2 *Staph* bg2 stram bg2 sul-ac bg2 **Sulph** bg2 tarax bg2 tarent bg2 tell bg2 teucr bg2 ther bg2 *Thuj* bg2 urt-u bg2 valer bg2 *Verat* bg2 vip bg2 zinc bg2

Periodical: ...
- **day**:
  - • **alternate**: *Alum* b4a.de* anac b4a.de* *Ant-c* bg2 *Apis* bg2 arn bg2 **Ars** b4a.de* bar-c bg2 *Bell* b4a.de* *Bry* b7a.de* *Calc* b4a.de* **Canth** bg2 *Caps* b7a.de* carb-v b4a.de* *Cham* b7a.de* **Chin** b7a.de* cic bg2 cina b7a.de* crot-h bg2 dros b7a.de* dulc bg2 ferr b7a.de* hell bg2 hyos bg2 ign b7a.de* **Ip** b7a.de* *Lach* bg2 lyc b4a.de* meny bg2 merc bg2 mez bg2 *Nat-m* b4a.de* nux-m bg2 **Nux-v** b7a.de* petr bg2 **Puls** b7a.de* ran-b bg2 *Rhus-t* b7a.de* *Sabad* b7a.de* sep bg2 sil bg2 staph b7a.de* *Sulph* b4a.de* *Thuj* bg2 *Verat* b7a.de* zinc bg2
    - ⁝ **double**: apis bg2 **Ars** b4a.de* bell bg2 chin bg2 dulc bg2 graph bg2 nux-m bg2 *Puls* bg2 **Rhus-t** b7a.de* stram bg2 thuj bg2 verat bg2
  - • **eighth**; every: sulph bg2
  - • **fourth**; every: ars bg2 eup-per bg2
  - • **second** to third; every: anac bg2 verat bg2
  - • **tenth** to fourteenth; every: lach bg2
  - • **tenth**; every: kali-p bg2 lach bg2
  - • **third** or fourth; every: asar bg2 aur bg2 caps bg2
  - • **every** (= quotidian): *(↗CHILL - Quotidian)* *Acon* bg2 alum bg2 apis bg2 **Aran** bg2 *Arn* bg2 **Ars** b4a.de* bell b4a.de* bol-la br1 *Bry* bg2 calc b4a.de* camph bg2 **Caps** b7a.de* carb-v b4a.de* cham bg2 *Chin* b7a.de* cic bg2 cina b7a.de* con bg2 *Cycl* bg2 dros b7a.de* ferr bg2 graph b4a.de* hyos bg2 *Ign* b7a.de* **Ip** b7a.de* kali-c b4a.de* kali-n b4a.de* *Lach* b7a.de* lyc bg2 meny bg2 *Nat-m* b4a.de* nit-ac b4a.de* **Nux-v** b7a.de* op b7a.de* petr bg2 **Puls** b7a.de* rhus-t b7a.de* sabad b7a.de* *Samb* bg2 sep bg2 spig b7a.de* stann b4a.de* staph b7a.de* *Stram* bg2 *Sulph* b4a.de* thuj bg2 verat b7a.de*
    - ⁝ **13**-18 h: cedr mtf11
    - ⁝ **16**-20 h: hell bg2 *Lyc* bg2
    - ⁝ **double**: *Ars* bg2 *Bell* b4a.de* chin b7a.de* dulc bg2 *Graph* b4a.de* nux-m bg2 *Puls* bg2 rhus-t bg2 *Stram* b7a.de* sulph bg2
    - ⁝ **one** to four days: sabad bg2
    - ⁝ **one** to three days: nux-v bg2
  - • **third**; every: anac bg2 eup-per bg2 hydr bg2
  - • **twice** a day: verb bg2
- **afternoon** | **every** other: bapt hr1
- **hour** | **same** hour; at the: ant-c bg2 cact br1 cedr bg2 *Cina* bg2* coc-c bg2 ign bg2 ip bg2 **Sabad** b7a.de* sel bg2 *Sil* bg2 spig b7a.de *Stann* bg2
- **week**:
  - • **second**; every: ars bg2 calc bg2 chel bg2 chinin-s bg2 ign bg2 lach bg2 nicc bg2 phyt bg2 puls bg2 sulph bg2
  - • **every**: am-m bg2 ars bg2 calc bg2 canth bg2 cedr bg2 croc bg2 eup-per bg2 iris bg2 kali-c bg2 lac-d bg2 nux-m bg2 phos bg2 sabad bg2 sang bg2 sil bg2 sulph bg2
  - • **third**; every: aur bg2
  - • **two** weeks, then two weeks less fever; during: mag-m bg2
- **month** | **second** or third; every: lept bg2 valer bg2
- **year**; every: *Ars* b4a.de *Carb-v* b4a.de crot-h bg2 urt-u bg2

PERSPIRATION:
- **absent**: acon k* alum k* am-c anac h2 *Apis* k* *Aran* k* arg-n arn k* **Ars** k* ars-i ars-s-f k2 **Bell** k* bism k* *Bov* **Bry** k* **Cact** k* calc k* caps carb-v bro1 carbn-s *Cham* k* chin k* coff k* colch k* cor-r corh br1 corn crot-h cystein-l rly4• dulc k* *Eup-per* k* **Gels** k* *Graph* k* *Hyos* k* ign k* iod k* *Ip* k* kali-ar kali-bi *Kali-c* kali-p *Kali-s* kali-sil k2 lach k* led k* *Lyc* k* mag-c k* merl nat-ar nat-c k* nat-m k* nit-ac k* **Nux-m** k* nux-v k* olib-sac wmh1 olnd k* op k* *Ph-ac* k* phel *Phos* k* *Plat* k* *Plb* k* *Psor* k* puls k* pycnop-sa mrz1 ran-b k* *Rhus-t* k* sabad k* sang sec k* sil k* spong k* squil k* staph k* sul-i k2 *Sulph* k* tub verb k* [am-br stj2 bar-br stj2]
- **amel.**: ars ptk1 lyc ptk1 rhus-t ptk1
- **cold** agg.: convo-s sp1 plb bro1
- **heat**; with: acon b7a.de* agar k* **Alum** am-m k* anac h2 androc srj1• *Ant-c* k* ant-t apis aran bro1 arist-cl rbp3• ars b4a.de* ars-i br1 ars-s-f k2 asc-t aza bro1 bac jl2 *Bell* k* berb k* *Bol-la* bro1 borx *Brucel* sa3• bry k* *Calc* k* calc-sil k2 camph canth **Caps** k* carb-an carb-v cassia-s cdd7• cedr k* *Cham* k* chel chin k* *Chinin-s* bro1 choc srj3• cimx bro1 cina k* cob k* colch k* **Con** k* conv bro1 convo-s sp1 cor-r *Dig* eup-per k* euph h2 *Ferr* k* fic-m gya1 gamb k* glon *Granit-m* es1• guare **Hell** k* hep k* hydr-ac ign k* *Ip* k* kali-bi *Kali-i* k* kali-n h2 lac-c k* laur k* lyc bro1 mag-c mag-m *Merc* k* **Mez** **Nat-c** k* nat-m k*

- **heat**; with: ...
nat-p *Nat-s* nit-ac k* *Nux-v* k* **Op** k* ox-ac k* *Par* ph-ac h2* **Phos** k* *Podo* **Psor** k* **Puls** pycnop-sa mrz1 **Pyrog** raph *Rhus-t* k* ruta fd4.de *Sabad* k* samb k* *Sep* k* sol-t-ae spig h1 spong fd4.de **Stann** k* *Staph* k* **Stram** k* stront-c **Sul-ac** k* **Sulph** k* *Sumb* thuj tritic-vg fd5.de **Tub** k* ulm-c jsj8• valer k* *Verat* k* wye bro1 [bell-p-sp dcm1]
  - **pain** | **amel.**: nat-m bro1
- **suppressed** perspiration; from: rhus-t k2

POSTPONING: chin b7a.de cina b7a.de

PRESSURE agg.: pip-n bg2

PUERPERAL FEVER: *(↗Septic; Zymotic; ABDOMEN - Inflammation - peritoneum - delivery)* *Acon* b7.de* ail hr1* ant-c bg2 *Apis* *Arg-n* arn k* ars k* *Bapt* k* bell k* borx bg2 *Bry* k* *Calc* bg2* camph k2 canth hr1* carb-ac bg2* carb-an bg2 carb-v bg2* **Carbn-s** cham k* chin bg2 chinin-ar bg2* *Chinin-s* bro1 chlol btw2 cimic k* cocc bg2* coff k* *Colch* hr1 coloc k* con bg2 croc bg2 **Crot-h** hr1* dulc bg2 **Echi** k* *Ferr* k* gels *Hydr-ac* bro1 *Hyos* k* ign k* ip k* kali-br ll1 kali-c k* kali-chl hr1 kali-m a2* kali-p c2* kreos bg2* **Lach** k* **Lyc** k* med c1 merc bg2* *Merc-c* c2* mill k* *Mur-ac* k* nux-v k* op k* petr a2* *Ph-ac* bg2 phos k* *Phyt* hr1 plat k* **Puls** k* **Pyrog** k* raja-s jl1 **Rhus-r** **Rhus-t** k* sabal c2 sabin bg2 sal-ac c2 sec k* **Sep** bg2* sil k* squil bg2 staph bg2 stram b7a.de* streptoc vml3• **Sulph** k* ter hr1* thyr c2 verat k* verat-v k* zinc bg2*
- **lochia**; from suppressed: *Lyc* k* mill puls **Sulph** k*
- **malignant**: ail tl1
- **prophylaxis**: arn btw2 calen mhn1 verat-v btw1
- **subacute**: coli jl2

PULSE: | **temperature**; discordant with (See GENERALS - Pulse - discordant)

PUTRID (See Zymotic)

QUARTAN FEVER: acon bg2 alum bg2 *Anac* b7a.de* apis bg2 *Arn* bg2 **Ars** b4a.de* bell bg2 bry bg2 *Carb-v* b4a.de* chin bg2 cina bg2 *Clem* b4a.de* *Hyos* b7a.de* *Ign* bg2 iod bg2 ip bg2 *Lach* bg2 **Lyc** b4a.de* nat-c bg2 *Nat-m* b4a.de* nit-ac bg2 nux-m bg2 *Nux-v* bg2 petr bg2 **Puls** b7a.de* rhus-t bg2 **Sabad** b7a.de* sep bg2 sulph bg2 thuj bg2 *Verat* bg2
○ - **Tongue** | **white** discoloration of the tongue; with: *Ip* kr1*

QUININE; after abuse of: am-c bg2 ant-t bg2 *Apis* bg2 **Arn** bg2 **Ars** bg2 asaf bg2 *Bell* bg2 bry bg2 *Calc* bg2 caps bg2 **Carb-v** bg2 cham bg2 *Cina* bg2 cupr bg2 cycl bg2 dig bg2 **Ferr** bg2 hell bg2 **Ip** bg2 *Lach* bg2 mang bg2 merc bg2 **Nat-m** bg2 nux-m bg2 nux-v bg2 *Ph-ac* bg2 phos bg2 plb bg2 **Puls** bg2 samb bg2 *Sep* bg2 stann bg2 sul-ac bg2 *Sulph* bg2 *Verat* bg2

REACTION; lack of: *(↗GENERALS - Reaction - lack)*
- **no** fever when fever is expected: carc cpd*•
  - **children**; in: carc cpd*•

READING agg.: ambr b7a.de* bell bg2 **Nux-v** bg2 **Olnd** b7a.de* phos bg2 *Sep* bg2 sil bg2

RECURRENT (See Relapsing)

RELAPSING: *Acon* bro1 arn mrr1 ars k* ars-i br1 *Bapt* c2* *Bry* c2* **Calc** k* carc fb* cedr mrr1 chinin-s mrr1 cimic bro1 *Eucal* br1* *Eup-per* c2* **Ferr** k* (non:granit-m es1) ip mrr1 lac-lup hrn2• nat-m mrr1 **Psor** k* *Rhus-t* c2* stann mrr1 **Sulph** k* *Tub* k*
- **children**; in: carc fb
- **diet**; from errors in: ip bro1

REMITTENT: *(↗Intermittent)* **Acon** k* ant-c c2* *Ant-t* arn **Ars** k* ars-s-f k2 bapt **Bell** k* bol-la **Bry** k* cassia-s ccrh1• **Cham** k* chin k* *Chinin-s* c2* cina c2* *Cocc* coff coloc *Crot-h* c2* eup-per k* ferr ferr-p k2 **Gels** k* granit-m es1• hyos bro1 ign *Ip* k* *Lach* lept *Lyc* mag-c mag-s **Merc** k* mur-ac *Nat-s* nit-ac bro1 *Nux-v* k* *Nyct* c1* ph-ac phos *Podo* polyp-p br1 puls k* rhus-t k* sep stram k* *Sulph* k* tarax tub gk verat
- **morning**: *Arn* bry mag-c podo *Rhus-t* sulph
- **afternoon**: **Ars** ars-s-f k2 **Bell** *Bry* chin **Gels** ign **Lach** *Lyc* nux-v tub mrr1
- **evening**: *Acon* arn ars-s-f k2 **Bell** *Bry* chin lach **Lyc** mag-c merc mur-ac nux-v ph-ac *Phos* puls **Rhus-t** *Sulph* verat hr1
  - **syphilis**; in: kali-i br1
- **night**: acon ant-t **Ars** ars-s-f k2 bapt cham coff lyc mag-c mag-s **Merc** nux-v ph-ac *Phos* *Puls* **Rhus-t** *Sulph* tub mrr1

Remittent: ...
- **accompanied** by:
○ • **Liver**; enlarged: merc hr1 nyct bwa3
  - **Spleen**; enlarged: nyct bwa3
  - **Tongue**:
    ⋮ **brown** discoloration | **yellowish** brown: crot-h kr1*
- **amel.**: chinin-s mrr1
- **autumn**; every: carb-ac
- **bilious**: merc-d br1* nyct br1
- **chronic**: nyct br1
- **infantile**: **Acon** ant-c bro1 ars **Bell** *Bry* **Cham** cina bro1 **Gels** k* *Ip* k* lept c2* nux-v puls bro1 santin c2* sulph
- **redness** of one cheek, paleness of the other; with: *Acon* **Cham**
- **typhoid** fever; prone to become: ant-t **Ars** *Bapt* **Bry** carb-ac colch *Gels* *Mur-ac* ph-ac phos **Psor** **Rhus-t** sec ter tub
  - **abuse** of quinine; from: arn **Ars** *Ip* puls **Rhus-t**

REST agg.: [spect dfg1]

RHEUMATIC: **Acon** b7a.de* ant-c b7a.de* ant-t b7a.de* apis bg2 *Arn* b7a.de* *Ars* b4a.de* bell b4a.de* benz-ac bg2 **Bry** b7a.de* calc b4a.de* camph b7a.de* cann-s b7a.de* carb-v b4a.de* caul bg2 caust b4a.de* **Cham** b7a.de* *Chin* b7a.de* coff bg2 *Colch* b7a.de* cupr b7a.de* dulc b4a.de* euphr b7a.de* *Ferr-p* bg2 ign b7a.de* ip bg2 lac-c mrr1 lach bg2 *Merc* b4a.de* mez b4a.de* *Nux-v* b7a.de* phos b4a.de* *Puls* b7a.de* ran-b b7a.de* rhod b4a.de* rhus-t b7a.de* sabad bg2 sil b4a.de* squil b7a.de* stann b4a.de* staph bg2 *Sulph* bg2 thuj b4a.de* valer b7a.de* verat b7a.de*
- **periodical**: senec bg2 teucr bg2

RIDING:
- **amel.**: kali-n k* *Nit-ac* k*
- **carriage**; in a | **agg.**: graph k* *Psor* sel bg2 sep bg2
- **wind**; in the | **after**: nit-ac

RISING:
- **bed**; from:
  - **after**:
    ⋮ **agg.**: acon agn am-c ambr ant-t ars asar bell *Bism* bg2 calc carb-an carb-v chel chin coloc dros *Hell* ign iod kali-c kali-n bg2 mang *Merc* mez petr plat sel sep spig stront-c sul-ac sulph valer *Verat*
    ⋮ **amel.**: acon bg2 agn bg2 am-c bg2 ambr bg2 ant-t bg2 ars bg2 asar bg2 bell bg2 calc bg2 carb-an bg2 carb-v bg2 chel bg2 chin bg2 coloc bg2 dros bg2 euph bg2 *Hell* bg2 ign bg2 iod bg2 kali-c bg2 mang bg2 merc bg2 mez bg2 petr bg2 plat bg2 rhod bg2 sel bg2 sep bg2 spig bg2 stront-c bg2 sul-ac bg2 sulph bg2 valer bg2 verat bg2
  - **agg.**: *Thuj*
    ⋮ **walking** about; and: nicc

ROOM: | **in** a room | **amel.**: anac bg2 bell bg2 carb-v bg2 cocc bg2 coff bg2 con bg2 guaj bg2 hep bg2 lach bg2 merc-c bg2 nux-m bg2 nux-v bg2 sil bg2 spig bg2
- **warm** room; in a (See Warm - room - agg.)

RUBBING:
- **agg.**: sulph bg2
- **amel.**: nat-m bg2

SADNESS; with (See MIND - Sadness - fever)

SCARLET FEVER: *(↗SKIN - Eruptions - scarlatina)* ail k2* **Am-c** b4a.de* apis mrr1 arum-t mrr1 bapt k2 bell b4a.de* carb-ac br1 croc ptk1 crot-h tl1 cupr br1 dubo-m br1 euph bg2 hep b4a.de hyos bg2 *Iod* b4a.de lach k2* merc b4a.de* phos k2 rhus-t mrr1 sulph k2 thuj bg2
- **accompanied** by:
  - **blood** poisoning: mur-ac tl1
  - **cellulitis**: ail bro1 am-c bro1 *Apis* bro1 lach bro1 *Rhus-t* bro1
  - **convulsions** (See GENERALS - Convulsions - accompanied - scarlatina)
  - **diarrhea**: ail bro1 ars bro1 asim bro1 phos bro1 rhus-t bro1
  - **pain** | **alternating** sides: lac-c tl1
  - **restlessness** (See MIND - Restlessness - feverish - scarlet)
  - **salivation**: **Arum-t** st1 caps st1 **Lach** st1 *Merc* st1 *Sulph* st1

- **accompanied** by: ...
  - • **vomiting** (See STOMACH - Vomiting - accompanied - scarlatina)
  - ○ • **Larynx**; inflammation of: brom bro1 spong bro1
  - • **Skin**:
    - ⁝ **dry**: ferr-p tl1
    - ⁝ **hot**: ferr-p tl1
  - • **Tongue**:
    - ⁝ **black** discoloration: *Kali-c* kr1*
    - ⁝ **red** discoloration of the tongue | **bright** red: *Apis* kr1* **Bell** kr1* sulph kr1*
- **chronic**: calc bro1 hep bro1 rhus-t bro1
- **coarse** dark rash: ail gm1 phyt gm1 rhus-t gm1 sulph gm1
- **followed** by cough (See COUGH - Scarlatina)
- **irregular**: *Acon* bg2 **Am-c** bg2 am-m bg2 *Apis* bg2 arn bg2 *Ars* bg2 bar-c bg2 **Bell** bg2 *Bry* bg2 carb-v bg2 caust bg2 cham bg2 coff bg2 *Croc* bg2 dulc bg2 euph bg2 hep bg2 *Hyos* bg2 iod bg2 ip bg2 *Lach* bg2 *Merc* bg2 ph-ac bg2 phos bg2 rhus-t bg2 stram bg2 *Sulph* bg2 thuj bg2 *Zinc* bg2
- **malignant**: *Ail* bro1 am-c bro1* *Apis* bro1 ars bro1 arum-t bro1 bapt bro1 *Carb-ac* bro1 carb-v bro1 *Crot-h* bro1 cupr-act bro1 echi bro1 hydr-ac bro1 *Lach* bro1 merc-cy bro1 *Mur-ac* bro1 phos bro1 *Rhus-t* bro1 tab bro1 zinc bro1
  - • **accompanied** by | **salivation**: **Am-c** st1
- **miliary**: *Acon* bro1 ail bro1 am-c bro1 apis bro1 ars bro1 bry bro1 *Coff* bro1 kali-ar bro1 lach bro1 rhus-t bro1
- **prophylaxis**: ail gm1 bell br1* eucal bro1* phyt gm1 rhus-t gm1 sulph gm1
- **smooth** rash: bell gm1
- **stupor**; with (See MIND - Stupor - scarlatina)

SCRATCHING agg.: sulph bg2

SEASONS:
- **spring**; in: caps b7a.de cina b7a.de ip b7a.de *Lach* b7a.de *Verat* b7a.de
- **summer**; in (See Summer)
- **winter**; in (See Winter)

SEPTIC FEVER: (↗*Continued; Puerperal; Zymotic*) acet-ac ail bg2* am-c bg2* **Anthraci** k* *Apis* *Arg-n* bg2* **Arn** k* **Ars** k* **Bapt** k* *Bell* k* berb **Bry** k* bufo bg2 *Cadm-s* calc ptk1 carb-ac bg2 *Carb-v* k* carbn-s k2 *Chin* ptk1 chinin-ar bg2 colch ptk1 **Crot-c** k* **Crot-h** k* *Cur* **Echi** k* elaps bg2* ferr bg2* ferr-p bg2 gels ptk1 hyos ptk1 kali-bi k2 kali-c ptk1 **Kali-p** k* kreos bg2* **Lach** k* **Lyc** k* *Merc* k* merc-cy bg2* **Mur-ac** k* naja bg2* *Nat-m* ptk1 nit-ac bg2* nux-v ptk1 op k* *Ph-ac* k* **Phos** k* *Puls* k* **Pyrog** k* *Rhus-t* k* *Rhus-v* sec ptk1 stram ptk1 sul-ac bg2* **Sulph** k* tarent bg2 **Tarent-c** k* ter bg2 vario ptk1 verat bg2* verat-v bg2* vip bg2 zinc ptk1

SHIVERING; with: acon k* anac androc bnm2• ant-t *Apis* **Arn** k* ars ptk1 asar b7.de *Bell* borx c1 bov bry k* *Calc* carb-v carbn-s **Caust** k* *Cham* k* chin chinin-s cina cocc coff coloc h2 *Cur* cycl *Dros* *Elaps* *Eup-per* ferr c1 **Gels** k* graph **Hell** k* *Hep* ign kali-i ptk1 kali-n c1 *Lach* lap-la rsp1 m-aust b7.de mag-m *Mag-p* meny merc mur-ac a1 **Nux-v** k* petr ph-ac *Podo* positr nl2• psor puls k* pycnop-sa mrz1 *Rhus-t* k* sabad sec ptk1 sep spig b7.de **Sulph** k* *Tarent* verat *Zinc* [bell-p-sp dcm1 spect dfg1]
- **accompanied** by:
  - • **complaints**; other: *Ars* b4a.de
  - • **heat**; internal: arn b7.de
- **air**; in open:
  - • **agg.**: am-c b4.de *Ars* b4.de* bell b4.de caust b4.de cham b7.de *Chin* b7.de hep b4.de* laur b7.de mag-m b4.de *Nit-ac* b4a.de nux-v b7.de ph-ac b4.de plat b4.de* *Tarax* b7.de* zinc b4.de
  - • **amel.**: ang b7.de staph b7.de
- **alcoholic** drinks; after: *Cina* b7a.de
- **alternating** with heat (See Alternating - shivering)
- **and** perspiration with heat: **Nux-v** podo *Rhus-t* *Sulph*
- **bed** agg.; in: acon b7.de *Aur* b4.de* bell b4.de *Bry* b7a.de *Dros* b7a.de kali-c b4.de m-arct b7.de merc b4.de nat-c b4.de rhus-t b7.de *Sel* b7a.de staph b7.de
- **cold** air agg.: cham b7.de* mosch b7a.de
- **combing** hair; from: sel b7a.de
- **drinking** agg.: *Ars* b4a.de bell cann-s b7.de **Caps** k* *Chin* b7.de* *Eup-per* m-aust b7.de **Nux-v** k* verat b7.de*

Shivering; with: ...
- **eating** | **after** | **agg.**: agar b4.de alum b4.de am-m b7a.de *Ars* b4a.de ign b7.de *Ip* b7a.de lyc b4.de rhus-t b7.de* staph b7.de sulph b4.de *Verat* b7.de
  - • **while** | **agg.**: lyc b4a.de staph b7.de
- **hair** standing on end; with: meny b7.de puls b7.de
- **internally**: *Hell* b7a.de ign b7.de
- **lying** | **amel.**: nux-v b7.de
- **lying** down agg.: sabin b7.de
- **menses**; before: am-c b4.de sep b4.de
- **motion** agg.: alum b4.de apis arn caps b7.de chin b7.de con b4a.de merc b4.de **Nux-v** k* podo sil b4a.de stram
  - • **slightest** motion: beryl sp1
- **pain**; during: *Ars* b4a.de bar-c b4a.de *Coloc* b4a.de euph b4a.de *Mez* b4a.de ran-b b7a.de *Sep* b4a.de
- **rest** agg.: *Dros* b7.de*
- **rising** from bed agg.: rhus-t b7.de staph b7.de
- **room**:
  - • **agg.**: alum b4.de *Ars* b4a.de caust b4.de mag-m b4.de meny b7.de mez b4a.de plat b4.de
  - • **amel.**: chin b7.de
- **sleep**; during: cina b7.de sabad b7.de
- **stool** | **after** | **agg.**: ang b7.de canth b7.de
  - • **during** | **agg.**: rheum b7.de *Verat* b7.de
- **touch** agg.: chin b7.de *Spig* b7a.de
- **turning** around in bed; when: puls b7.de
- **uncovering** agg.: apis arg-met b7.de **Arn** bar-c borx c1 *Calc* *Cham* b7.de* chin *Chinin-s* clem b4.de lach **Nux-v** *Psor* *Puls* b7a.de *Rhus-t* stram *Tarent* thuj b4.de **Tub**
- **vomiting**; before: *Verat* b7.de
- **warm** | **applications** | **agg.**: apis b7a.de
  - • **stove**:
    - ⁝ **agg.**: cina b7a.de guaj b4a.de merc b4a.de ruta b7a.de
    - ⁝ **amel.**: ars b4.de bar-c b4.de ign b7.de kali-c b4.de nux-v b7a.de rhus-t b7.de
- **yawing**; while: arn b7.de cina b7.de cycl b7.de ip b7.de meny b7.de mur-ac b4.de nux-v b7.de olnd b7.de phos b4.de sars b4.de

SHUDDERING: borx c1
- **alternating** with heat: bov
- **with** the heat: acon aeth c1 *Bell* caps **Cham** *Hell* ign *Kali-i* nat-m *Nux-v* rheum *Rhus-t* zinc
  - • **constant**, with one cheek hot and red: coff
- ○ **Toes** and fingers; especially stict c1

SITTING:
- **agg.**: alum b4.de* anac bg2 calc b4a.de* graph b4.de* lyc bg2 mang b4.de* phos k* rhus-t b7.de* sep k* valer b7.de*
- **amel.**: acon bg2 ant-t bg2 bry bg2 colch bg2 cupr bg2 iod bg2 merc bg2 nat-m bg2 nux-v k* squil bg2

SLEEP, heat comes on:
- **after**: agar anac arn ars *Bell* *Borx* k* calad k* calc caust cic cina k* cocc coloc con k* *Ferr* k* ferr-ar ferr-p hep ip kreos lyc mag-m merc mez ptk1 *Mosch* nat-m nit-ac *Op* k* petr ph-ac *Phos* ptel puls *Samb* k* *Sep* *Sil* **Sulph** **Tarax** thuj zinc
  - • **amel.**: **Calad** k* chin colch hell k* nux-v *Phos* k* *Sep* k*
  - • **noon** after eating; at: anac bg2 phos bg2 puls bg2 *Sel* bg2 staph bg2 sulph bg2
- **during**: *Acon* k* *Alum* k* anac k* ant-t k* apis k* *Arn* b7a.de* *Ars* k* astac *Bar-c* bell k* *Borx* bov *Bry* k* **Calad** k* *Calc* caps k* cham k* chin chinin-ar cic *Cina* con k* cycl *Dulc* k* gels gins *Hep* b4.de* ign k* *Lach* k* led k* lil-t *Lyc* m-arct b7a.de merc k* merc-c bg2 **Mez** *Nat-c* k* *Nat-m* k* nat-p *Nit-ac* *Nux-m* **Op** k* *Petr* k* ph-ac k* *Phos* k* *Puls* k* ran-b k* *Rheum* k* *Rhus-t* k* sabad b7a.de* **Samb** k* sep k* *Sil* k* stram k* **Sulph** bg2* tarax thuj k* *Ust* *Valer* bg2 vario *Verat* b7.de* viol-t k*
  - • **cold** feet and sweat on waking: **Samb**
  - • **dry** heat: samb thuj

SMALLPOX; during (See SKIN - Eruptions - smallpox - accompanied - fever)

SMOKING:
- **agg.**: cic b7.de* ign bg2 *Sep* b4.de*

- **amel.**: hep bg2 sep bg2

SOUR FOOD agg.: *Lach* bg2

STAGES:
- **first** stages: *Ferr-p* br1
- **irregular** stages (See Irregular)
- **succession** of stages (See Succession)

STANDING:
- **agg.**: arg-met k* con k* *Mang* k* puls k* rhus-t k*
- **amel.**: bell k* cann-s cann-xyz bg2 iod k* ip k* phos k* sel k*

STOOL:
- **after**:
  - **agg.**: ars k* bry caust k* **Iris** bg2 nux-v k* rhus-t k* sel k*
  - **amel.**: bry bg2 colch bg2 rhus-t bg2 spig bg2
- **before**: calc k* caust bg2 crot-t k* cupr k* *Mag-c* k* *Merc* k* *Phos* k* samb verat k*
- **during** | **agg.**: **Aloe** bg2 ars k* bell bg2 **Caps** bg2 cham k* **Iris** bg2 merc b4.de* merc-c b4a.de nat-c b4.de puls k* rhus-t k* sulph k*

STOOPING:
- **agg.**: bry k* *Gamb* bg2 *Kali-c* k* **Merc-c** k* sep k*
  - **coldness** when rising from: *Merc-c*
- **amel.**: colch bg2 hyos bg2

STORM:
- **before**: sil h2*
- **during**: sil h2

SUCCESSION of stages: (↗*CHILL - Shaking - long)*
- **chill**:
  - **accompanied** by:
    - **heat**: **Acon** b2.de* agn bg2 alum b2.de* am-c bg2 anac b2.de* ant-t b2.de* *Arn* bg2 **Ars** b2.de* bar-c b2.de* *Bell* b2.de* bov b2.de* bry b2.de* **Calc** b2.de* camph b2.de* canth b2.de* carb-v b2.de* **Cham** b2.de* chin b2.de* cina b2.de* *Cocc* b2.de* **Coff** b2.de* colch bg2 coloc b2.de* *Dig* bg2 euph b2.de* graph b2.de* *Hell* b2.de* **Ign** b2.de* iod b2.de* kali-c b2.de* lach b2.de* led bg2 lyc b2.de* *Merc* b2.de* *Mez* b2.de* mosch b2.de* nat-c b2.de* **Nit-ac** b2.de* nux-v b2.de* olnd b2.de* *Par* bg2 *Petr* b2.de* ph-ac bg2 phos b2.de* plat b2.de* **Plb** b2.de* *Puls* b2.de* ran-b bg2 **Rhus-t** b2.de* sabad b2.de* samb b2.de* sel bg2 *Sep* b2.de* sil bg2 *Spig* b2.de* spong b2.de* *Squil* b2.de* *Sulph* b2.de* **Thuj** b2.de* **Verat** b2.de* *Zinc* b2.de*
      - **flushes** of heat: ars b4.de* merc b4.de* plat b4.de* *Puls* bg2
      - **internal**: **Acon** b7.de* arn bg2 **Ars** b4.de* bell bg2 *Bry* b7a.de* calc b4a.de* *Cham* b7a.de* chel bg2 chin bg2 *Euph* b4a.de* hell bg2 *Ign* b7a.de* iod bg2 *Kali-c* bg2 merc bg2 *Mez* b4a.de* *Mosch* b7a.de* nat-m bg2 nit-ac b4.de* nux-v bg2 olnd b7a.de* ph-ac bg2 *Puls* bg2 *Rhus-t* bg2 sabad bg2 sec bg2 spong bg2 *Squil* bg2 stann bg2 *Sulph* bg2 **Verat** b7a.de* *Zinc* b4a.de*
        - **thirst**; with: calc b4.de* kali-c b4.de*
      - **perspiration**; without: sulph b4.de*
      - **External** heat: acon bg2 agn bg2 *Anac* b4a.de* *Arn* bg2 *Ars* bg2 *Bell* b4a.de* bry bg2 **Calc** b4a.de* chin b7a.de* *Cocc* bg2 *Coff* bg2 colch bg2 *Dig* bg2 *Hell* bg2 **Ign** b7a.de* kali-bi bg2 kali-n bg2 lach b7a.de* laur bg2 lyc bg2 *Meny* bg2 merc b4a.de* mez bg2 **Nux-v** b7a.de* phos bg2 plb bg2 *Ran-b* bg2 rheum bg2 sel bg2 **Sep** bg2 *Sil* bg2 *Squil* bg2 sulph bg2 *Thuj* b4a.de*
      - **Internal** heat: olnd bg2
    - **heat** and perspiration: nux-v b2.de* *Verat* bg2
    - **perspiration**: ars b2.de* calc b2.de* *Euph* b2.de* led b2.de* lil-t bg2 lyc b2.de* nux-v b2.de* puls b2.de* sabad b2.de* sulph b2.de* thuj b2.de* *Verat* bg2
    - **thirst**:
      - **then** heat: cina b7.de*
        - **then** perspiration:
          - **thirst**:
            - **with**: spong b7.de*
            - **without**: ign b7.de* kali-c b4.de m-arct b7.de
        - **thirst**:
          - **with**: ant-c b7a.de*
          - **without**: *Hep* b4a.de *Kali-n* b4a.de

Succession of stages – **chill**: ...
  - **alternating** with:
    - **heat**: *Agn* b2.de* am-c b2.de* **Am-m** b2.de* *Ambr* bg2 *Ant-t* b2.de* arn bg2 **Ars** b2.de* *Asar* b2.de* aur b2.de* bapt bg2 *Bar-c* b2.de* **Bell** b2.de* borx b2.de* *Bry* b2.de* bufo bg2 **Calc** b2.de* canth b2.de* caust b2.de* *Cham* b2.de* chel b2.de* **Chin** b2.de* *Cocc* b2.de* coff b2.de* *Coloc* b2.de* *Dig* bg2 dros b2.de* graph b2.de* **Hep** b2.de* *Hyos* bg2 iod b2.de* kali-c b2.de* kali-n b2.de* *Kreos* b2.de* **Lach** b2.de* laur b2.de* led bg2 *Lyc* b2.de* **Merc** b2.de* mosch b2.de* nat-m b2.de* nit-ac b2.de* nux-v b2.de* *Ph-ac* b2.de* *Phos* b2.de* polyg-h bg2 rheum b2.de* rhod b2.de* **Rhus-t** b2.de* sabad b2.de* **Samb** b7a.de* *Sel* b2.de* *Sep* b2.de* sil b2.de* *Spig* b2.de* stram b2.de* sulph b2.de* ter bg2 valer bg2 *Verat* b2.de* *Zinc* b4a.de*
      - **face**; of: caust b4.de
      - **followed** by | **heat**: verat bg2
      - **menses**; during: am-c b4.de rhod b4.de
      - **perspiration**; then: bry bg2 *Kali-c* b4.de* spig bg2
    - **thirst**, then perspiration: sabad
  - **followed** by:
    - **heat**: **Acon** k* *Alum* k* am-c k* am-m k* ambr k* ang ant-c k* *Ant-t* k* apis k* aran *Arn* k* ars k* asar k* bapt bar-c k* *Bell* k* berb borx k* bry k* cact calc k* camph canth k* **Caps** k* carb-an k* *Carb-v* k* cassia-s cdd7*• caust k* cham k* *Chin* k* chinin-ar k2 *Cina* k* clem a1 coff k* *Colch* con h2 conv br1 *Corn* croc k* **Cycl** k* dig k* *Dros* k* dulc k* elaps *Eup-per* ferr-ar k2 granit-m es1• *Graph* k* guaj k* hell k* *Hep* k* hir skp7• hydrog srj2• **Hyos** k* **Ign** k* **Iod** k* **Ip** k* kali-bi kali-c k* kali-n k* kreos k* lach k* laur k* **Lyc** k* m-aust b2.de* *Mag-c* k* mag-m k* malar mtf11 mang h2 meny b2.de* merc k* *Merc-c* k* mez mur-ac h2 *Nat-c* k* **Nat-m** k* *Nat-s* nit-ac k* nux-m k* **Nux-v** k* *Op* k* *Petr* k* ph-ac k* *Phos* k* plat h2 psor **Puls** k* **Rhus-t** k* sabad k* **Sang** *Sec* k* seneg sep k* sil *Spig* k* *Spong* k* squil k* staph k* *Stram* k* sul-i k2 **Sulph** k* thuj k* *Valer* k* vario al2 *Verat* k* visc c1
      - **alternating** with chill | **then** perspiration: aur bg2 sabad b7.de*
      - **face**; especially of: acon b7.de* *Ambr* b7a.de* chin b7.de* cycl b7a.de* kali-c b4.de* kreos b7a.de* *Nux-v* b7.de* op b7.de* *Petr* b4.de* stram b7.de*
        - **accompanied** by restlessness | **menses**; before: lyc b4.de
      - **head**; of: ip bg2
      - **sensation** of: meny b7.de* sulph b4.de*
      - **spots**; in single: cycl bg2
      - **then** chill: sulph b2.de* thuj ptk1
        - **thirst**; with: sulph b4.de
      - **then** perspiration: am-c k* am-m k* apis k* **Ars** k* bell k* borx h2* bov k* *Bry* k* cact caps k* carb-an k* carb-v k* cassia-s cdd7*• caust k* cedr cham k* **Chin** k* chinin-ar k2 cina k* cocc k* conv br1 corn dig k* dros k* *Eup-per* *Eup-pur* gels *Graph* k* hep k* *Ign* k* **Ip** k* kali-c k* kali-n h2 *Lach* k* lyc k* lyss c1 m-arct b2.de mag-m k* nat-c k* *Nat-m* k* *Nat-s* nit-ac k* **Nux-v** k* op k* ox-ac k2 plb b2.de* podo c1 **Puls** k* *Rhus-t* k* *Sabad* k* sabin k* samb k* sep k* *Spong* k* staph k* *Sulph* k* thuj k* *Verat* k*
        - **hiccough**; then: ars bg2
        - **internal** chill; with: phos
        - **little**: conv br1
        - **sour**: lyc k*
        - **with** thirst: ant-c h2 rhus-t k*
        - **without** thirst: am-m k* nit-ac k*
      - **thirst**:
        - **with**: *Acon* b7.de* *Bell* b4.de* borx b4a.de* cina b7.de* dros b7.de* *Hep* b4.de* merc b4.de* *Puls* b7a.de* *Rhus-t* b7.de* sec b7.de* spig b7.de* sulph b4.de*
          - **followed** by:
            - **heat** without thirst: *Hep* bg2 kali-n bg2
            - **perspiration** without thirst:
              - **followed** by | heat with thirst: ant-c bg2
          - **internal** chill; and:
            - **followed** by | **heat** and perspiration: phos b4.de*
        - **without**: am-m b7.de* borx b4a.de* canth b7.de* cina b7.de* coff b7.de* nux-m b7.de* ph-ac b4.de* rhus-t b7.de* *Spig* b7.de* sulph b4.de*

- **followed** by – **heat** – **thrist** – **without**: ...
  - **followed** by:
    - **heat** with thirst: petr bg2
    - **perspiration**: kali-c bg2
  - **menses**; during: phos b4.de*
  - **perspiration**; without: sep b4.de*
- : **with** perspiration: _Acon_ k* agn hr1 alum anac ant-t k* **Bell** k* bry k* _Caps_ k* carb-v k* cassia-s ccrh1• **Cham** k* _Chin_ k* choc srj3• cina k* con b2.de dig b2.de* eup-per _Ferr_ ferr-i k2 graph k* hell k* _Hep_ k* ign k* ip b2.de kali-c k* kali-sula c1* m-aust b2.de* merc b2.de mez k* nat-m nit-ac k* _Nux-v_ k* **Op** k* phos k* _Puls_ k* **Rhus-t** k* _Sabad_ k* sars h2 spig k* stann b2.de staph b2.de stram b2.de sulph k* tub k2 valer b2.de verat b2.de
  - . **face**; of the: alum k*
- : **without** perspiration: _Caps_ hr1 graph k* nat-m k* tarent k2
- : **Single** parts with perspiration of another part; of: aml-ns bg2
- ⁝ **perspiration**:
  - : **followed** by:
    - . **heat**: **Bell** k*
    - . **thirst**: lyc b4.de*
  - : **intervening** heat; without: (↗_CHILL - Heat - without_) alum h2 am-m k* arg-met h1 ars h2 _Bry_ k* cact **Caps** k* _Carb-an_ k* carb-v k* carbn-s **Caust** k* cedr cham k* chel k* cimx _Clem_ k* _Dig_ k* graph h2 hell k* hep b2.de hyos k* kali-c kali-n k* **Lyc** k* _M-aust_ b2.de* mag-c h2 mag-m h2 merc k* merc-c k* **Mez** k* mur-ac h2 nat-m k* nat-s nux-v k* op k* **Petr** k* ph-ac k* phos k* _Rhus-t_ k* sabad k* sep k* spig k* sulph h2 **Thuj** k* _Verat_ k*
    - . **and** without thirst: am-m k* bry k* caust k* _Staph_
  - : **perspiration**; cold | **intervening** heat; without: ars k* verat k*
  - : **without** heat or thirst (See intervening - and)
- ⁝ **shaking**:
  - : **then** heat | **menses**; during: phos b4.de
- ⁝ **thirst**:
  - : **then** heat without thirst: _Hep_ kali-n nat-m
  - : **then** perspiration: kali-c thuj b4.de*
- • **thirst**; without:
  - ⁝ **then** heat:
    - : **thirst**; with: petr b4.de sulph bg2
      - . **then** perspiration without thirst | **then** heat with thirst: ant-c b7a.de
    - : **thirst**; without: ars b4.de* cycl b7.de* dros b7.de* hell b7.de* ph-ac b4.de*

○ • **External** | **followed** by | **heat**: ars b4a.de merc b4a.de sulph b4a.de
- ⁝ **heat**; with internal: _Acon_ b2.de* agar b2.de* am-m b2.de* anac b2.de* _Arn_ b2.de* _Ars_ b2.de* asar b2.de* bar-c b2.de* bell b2.de* bry b2.de* calad b2.de* calc b2.de* camph b2.de* cann-s b2.de* canth b2.de* carb-v b2.de* caust b2.de* cham b2.de* _Chel_ b2.de* chin b2.de* cic b2.de* cocc b2.de* con b2.de* croc b2.de* cupr b2.de* dig b2.de* dulc b2.de* euph b2.de* graph b2.de* hell b2.de* ign b2.de* ip b2.de* kali-c b2.de* laur b2.de* lyc b2.de* m-aust b2.de* mag-c b2.de* mag-m b2.de* mang b2.de* merc b2.de* mez b2.de* **Mosch** b2.de* mur-ac b2.de* nat-c b2.de* nit-ac b2.de* nux-v b2.de* _Ph-ac_ b2.de* phos b2.de* plat b2.de* _Puls_ b2.de* ran-b b2.de* ran-s b2.de* rhod b2.de* **Rhus-t** b2.de* ruta b2.de* sabad b2.de* samb b2.de* sars b2.de* _Sec_ b2.de* sep b2.de* sil b2.de* spig b2.de* spong b2.de* squil b2.de* stann b2.de* staph b2.de* _Sulph_ b2.de* valer b2.de* _Verat_ b2.de* zinc b2.de*

• **Internal**:
- ⁝ **heat**; with external: _Acon_ b2.de* agar b2.de* agn b2.de* alum b2.de* ambr b2.de* _Anac_ b2.de* arg-met b2.de* arn b2.de* _Ars_ b2.de* asaf b2.de* bar-c b2.de* _Bell_ b2.de* bism b2.de* bry b2.de* calad b2.de* **Calc** b2.de* camph b2.de* cann-s b2.de* caps b2.de* carb-an b2.de* carb-v b2.de* caust b2.de* cham b2.de* chel b2.de* chin b2.de* cic b2.de* cocc b2.de* _Coff_ b2.de* colch b2.de* coloc b2.de* cupr b2.de* cycl b2.de* dig b2.de* dros b2.de* dulc b2.de* euph b2.de* hell b2.de* hep b2.de* hyos b2.de* _Ign_ b2.de* iod b2.de* ip b2.de* kali-c b2.de* _Kali-n_ b2.de* kreos b2.de* _Lach_ b2.de* **Laur** b2.de* _Lyc_ b2.de* m-aust b2.de* mang b2.de* _Meny_ b2.de* merc b2.de* mez b2.de* mur-ac b2.de* nat-c b2.de* nat-m b2.de* **Nux-v** b2.de* olnd b2.de* op b2.de* _Par_ b2.de* ph-ac b2.de*

- **chill** – **Internal** – **heat**; with external: ...
  Phos b2.de* plb b2.de* puls b2.de* ran-b b2.de* rhus-t b2.de* sabad b2.de* samb b2.de* sec b2.de* sel b2.de* **Sep** b2.de* _Sil_ b2.de* spig b2.de* spong b2.de* _Squil_ b2.de* stann b2.de* staph b2.de* stram b2.de* _Sulph_ b2.de* tarax b2.de* thuj b2.de* verat b2.de* zinc b2.de*
  - ⁝ **heat**; with internal: petr b4.de*
- **general**; in (= compound fevers): _Acon_ b2.de* agn b2.de* alum b2.de* am-c b2.de* am-m b2.de* ambr b2.de* anac b2.de* ang b2.de* ant-c b2.de* ant-t b2.de* arn b2.de* **Ars** b2.de* asar b2.de* aur b2.de* bar-c b2.de* **Bell** b2.de* borx b2.de* bov b2.de* **Bry** b2.de* calad b2.de* _Calc_ b2.de* camph b2.de* canth b2.de* _Caps_ b2.de* carb-an b2.de* carb-v b2.de* caust b2.de* _Cham_ b2.de* chel b2.de* _Chin_ b2.de* cina b2.de* clem b2.de* cocc b2.de* coff b2.de* coloc b2.de* con b2.de* croc b2.de* cycl b2.de* dig b2.de* dros b2.de* dulc b2.de* euph b2.de* _Graph_ b2.de* guaj b2.de* _Hell_ b2.de* _Hep_ b2.de* hyos b2.de* _Ign_ b2.de* iod b2.de* ip b2.de* kali-c b2.de* kali-n b2.de* kreos b2.de* lach b2.de* laur b2.de* led b2.de* lyc b2.de* m-ambo b2.de* m-arct b2.de* _M-aust_ b2.de* meny b2.de* _Merc_ b2.de* mez b2.de* mosch b2.de* nat-c b2.de* nat-m b2.de* nit-ac b2.de* nux-m b2.de* **Nux-v** b2.de* olnd b2.de* op b2.de* petr b2.de* ph-ac b2.de* _Phos_ b2.de* plat b2.de* plb b2.de* _Puls_ b2.de* ran-s b2.de* rheum b2.de* rhod b2.de* **Rhus-t** b2.de* _Sabad_ b2.de* sabin b2.de* samb b2.de* sec b2.de* sel b2.de* _Sep_ b2.de* sil b2.de* spig b2.de* spong b2.de* squil b2.de* stann b2.de* staph b2.de* stram b2.de* stront-c b2.de* _Sulph_ b2.de* tarax b2.de* thuj b2.de* valer b2.de* _Verat_ b2.de* zinc b2.de*
- **heat**:
  - • **accompanied** by:
    - ⁝ **chill**:
      - : **internal** chill: acon bg2 _Anac_ b4a.de* ars bg2 _Bell_ b4a.de* bry b7.de* calc b4.de* coff bg2 _Ign_ b7a.de* kali-n bg2 _Lach_ b7a.de* laur bg2 lyc bg2 meny bg2 merc b4.de* _Nux-v_ b7a.de* phos bg2 sep bg2 sil bg2 thuj b4.de*
        - . **then** perspiration: caps b7.de*
    - ⁝ **coldness** | **Single** parts; of: chin b7.de* ign b7a.de* _Nux-v_ b7a.de* rhus-t b7a.de*
    - ⁝ **perspiration**: acon b2.de* alum b2.de* am-m b2.de* ant-t b2.de _Bell_ b2.de* bry b2.de* _Calc_ bg2 canth bg2 **Caps** b2.de* _Cham_ b2.de* chin b2.de* cina b2.de* _Con_ b2.de* dig b2.de euph bg2 glon bg2 graph b2.de **Hell** b2.de* _Hep_ b2.de* ign b2.de* _Ip_ b2.de* kali-c b2.de laur bg2 m-aust b2.de _Med_ bg2 merc b2.de* **Nat-c** bg2 nit-ac b2.de* _Nux-v_ b2.de* **Op** b2.de* par bg2 phos b2.de* plb b2.de* puls b2.de* **Rhus-t** b2.de* _Sabad_ b2.de* _Sars_ bg2 sep bg2 spig b2.de* spong b2.de* **Stann** b2.de* _Staph_ b2.de* **Stram** b2.de* stry bg2 **Sul-ac** bg2 sulph b2.de* tarax b2.de* thuj bg2 _Valer_ b2.de* _Verat_ b2.de* viol-t b7a.de*
      - : **clammy**: **Op** bg2
      - : **coldness**; with external | **then** chill: stann b4.de
      - : **then** chilliness: stann b2.de
      - : **thirst**:
        - . **with**: con b4.de* hep b4.de* merc b4a.de* rhus-t b7.de*
          - **then** chilliness: stann b4.de*
        - . **without**: am-m b7.de* bell b4.de* bry b7.de* caps b7.de* hep b4.de* nux-v b7.de* phos b4.de* spig b7.de* stram b7.de* verat b7.de*
    - ⁝ **shivering**: _Acon_ b2.de* anac b2.de arn b2.de* _Ars_ b2.de* asar b2.de* _Bell_ b2.de* bry b2.de* bufo bg2 calc b2.de caps b2.de _Cham_ b2.de* _Chin_ bg2 coff b2.de* dros b2.de _Hell_ b2.de* ign b2.de* _Ip_ bg2 kali-c b2.de m-aust b2.de* merc b2.de* mosch b2.de* _Nux-v_ b2.de* puls b2.de* _Rhus-t_ b2.de* _Samb_ bg2 sep b2.de* spig b2.de* sulph b2.de* _Verat_ bg2 _Zinc_ b2.de*
      - : **thirst**:
        - . **with**: caps b7.de*
        - . **without**: _Hell_ b7a.de* spig b7.de*
    - ⁝ **thirst** | **alternating** with | **chill**: calc b4.de*
      - : **then** perspiration: coff b7.de*
  - • **alternating** with:
    - ⁝ **chill**: yohim br1*
      - : **followed** by perspiration: kali-c meny verat
      - : **then** heat: verat
        - . **finally** perspiration: bry kali-c spig
    - ⁝ **perspiration**: _Am-m_ bg2 bell b2.de* _Chin_ b7a.de* colch b7a.de* lach bg2 **Led** b2.de* nat-c bg2 nux-v bg2 _Samb_ bg2 sep bg2 sulph bg2

Fever

- **alternating** with: ...
  - **shivering**: acon b2.de* am-c b2.de* **Ars** b2.de* asar b2.de* *Bell* b2.de* borx b2.de* **Bry** b2.de* calc b2.de* caust b2.de* *Cham* b2.de* chel b2.de* chin b2.de* *Cocc* b2.de* coff b2.de* coloc b2.de* graph b2.de* hep b2.de* *Ip* b7a.de* kali-c b2.de* lach b2.de* **Merc** b2.de* mosch b2.de* *Nux-v* b2.de* ph-ac b2.de* phos b2.de* *Plat* bg2 rheum b2.de* rhus-t b2.de* sabad b2.de* *Sep* b2.de* sil b2.de* spig b2.de* *Sulph* b2.de* verat b2.de*
- **face**; of:
  - **shivering**; with: sulph b4.de*
  - **then** chill: *Calc* b4.de* lyc b4.de* meny b7.de* staph b7.de* sulph b4.de*
- **followed** by:
  - **chill**: ail alum h2 am-m ang k* apis k* ars h2 asar *Bell* k* *Bry* k* calad k* **Calc** k* caps k* *Caust* k* chin k* coloc dros h1 dulc k* elaps eup-pur *Hell* k* ign k* kali-c lyc k* meny k* merc k* nat-m nicc nit-ac k* **Nux-v** k* petr k* *Phos* k* **Puls** k* *Pyrog* ruta fd4.de **Sep** k* **Stann** k* *Staph* k* sul-ac bg2 *Sulph* k* thuj k* *Tub* verat b7a.de [tax jsj7]
    - **then** heat: am-m stram k*
      - **then** perspiration: *Rhus-t* k*
  - **coldness**: bufo bg2 calc b4.de* caust b4.de* *Nux-v* b7.de* sang bg2 sep b4.de* sulph b4.de*
    - **icy** coldness: bufo bg2
  - **perspiration**: agar h2 alum h2 *Am-m* k* ant-c k* ant-t k* **Ars** k* bar-c b4a.de bell k* borx k* bry k* calc k* carb-an k* *Carb-v* k* cassia-s ccrh1 • **Cham** k* *Chin* k* cina k* **Coff** k* corn dros k2 graph k* hell k* hep k* *Ign* k* *Ip* k* kali-c h2 kali-n h2 kreos k* lach k* lob lyc k* *Mang* nit-ac k* *Nux-v* k* op k* ox-ac k2 petr k* puls k* *Ran-s* k* rhod k* **Rhus-t** k* sep h2 *Sil* k* spong k* staph k* stront-c k* sulph k* **Verat** k*
    - **perspiration**; cold: aml-ns bg2 caps k* gard-j vlr2 • *Verat* k*
    - **then** chill: calad b2.de* kali-bi bg2* tab bg2
    - **then** heat: **Ant-c** b7a.de
    - **thirst**; then: calad bg2
      - **heat**; then: ant-c bg2
  - **shivering**: alum bg2 *Ang* bg2 caps b2.de* cocc b2.de* hell b2.de* nat-m b2.de* puls b2.de* rhus-t b2.de* *Sulph* b2.de*
- **head**; in:
  - **alternating** with:
    - **chilliness**: sep b4.de* stram b7.de*
    - **then** coldness, then heat: stram b7.de*
- **internal**:
  - **accompanied** by | **external** coldness: *Bell* b4a.de *Calc* b4a.de euph b4a.de iod b4a.de mez b4a.de phos b4.de* *Verat* b7a.de
- **with**:
  - **external** coldness: arn bg2 *Ars* bg2 *Bell* bg2 bry bg2 *Calc* bg2 chin bg2 euph bg2 hell bg2 iod bg2 merc bg2 *Mez* bg2 mosch bg2 ph-ac bg2 phos bg2 puls bg2 rhus-t bg2 *Sabad* bg2 spong bg2 stann bg2 tab bg2 *Verat* bg2
    - **then** chill, then heat with external coldness: *Phos*
    - **then** heat: aloe am-c ant-c ant-t calad calc carb-v hell ign ran-s sil
    - **thirst**; and violent: acon bg2 ars bg2 bell bg2 bry bg2 calc bg2 cham bg2 puls bg2 rhus-t bg2 sep bg2 sil bg2 sulph bg2 verat bg2

- **perspiration**:
  - **alternating** with:
    - **chilliness**: ant-c calc nux-v sacch
    - **dry** skin: *Apis* b7a.de*
  - **followed** by:
    - **chill**: caps b7.de *Carb-v* k* euphr h2 *Hep* k* *Nux-v* k*
      - **then** perspiration: ars bg2 chin bg2 mez bg2 *Nux-m* b2.de nux-v k* spig bg2
        - **with** heat: nux-v
    - **heat**: caps bg2 *Nux-v* b2.de*
      - **followed** by | **chill**: eucal bg2
  - **following** chill:
    - **alternating** with heat: carb-ac corn kali-c meny verat
      - **then** heat: bry
    - **with** heat: calc caps sulph
  - **long** after the heat has subsided, with renewal of the earlier symptoms; appears: ars

Succession of stages – **perspiration**: ...
  - **with**:
    - **heat**:
      - **and** coldness, irregular intermingle: cedr
      - **followed** by dry heat: ant-c
      - **following** chill: acon k* agn bg2 alum am-m bg2 anac ant-c ant-t bg2 bell k* bry bg2 calc bg2 canth bg2 caps k* carb-an bg2 *Caust* bg2 *Cham* k* chin k* cina k* clem bg2 cocc bg2 dros bg2 graph k* hell k* hep k* ign k* ip bg2 kali-c k* kreos bg2 lach bg2 *Lyc* bg2 merc bg2 mosch bg2 nat-m k* nicc nit-ac k* nux-v k* op k* phos k* puls k* rheum bg2 rhus-t k* sabad k* samb bg2 sel bg2 sep bg2 spig k* stram bg2 sulph k* verat bg2

- **regular**: chin bro1 *Chinin-s* bro1
- **shivering**:
  - **accompanied** by:
    - **heat**: acon bg2 anac bg2 arn bg2 ars bg2 asar bg2 **Bell** b4a.de* bry bg2 calc bg2 caps bg2 *Cham* bg2 coff bg2 dros bg2 **Hell** bg2 ign bg2 kali-c bg2 merc bg2 mosch bg2 *Nux-v* bg2 puls bg2 rheum bg2 *Rhus-t* bg2 sep bg2 spig bg2 sulph bg2 *Zinc* b4a.de*
      - **face**; of | **thirst**; without: anac b4.de* ars b4.de* calc b4.de* dros b7.de* kali-c b4.de*
      - **hands**; of: nat-c b4.de
    - **perspiration**: acon b2.de* alum bg2 m-ambo b2.de* m-aust b2.de* *Rhus-t* b2.de*
  - **followed** by:
    - **chill**: ars b2.de* *Bry* b2.de* ip b2.de* lach b2.de*
      - **then** heat without perspiration: ars b4.de*
      - **thirst**; without: ip b7.de*
    - **heat**: ang b2.de* apis b7a.de* asar bg2 *Bell* b2.de* bry b2.de* canth b2.de* carb-v b2.de* cocc b2.de* con b2.de* cycl b2.de* graph b2.de* ign b2.de* lach b2.de* laur b2.de* led b2.de* m-arct b2.de* m-aust b2.de* mosch b2.de* nux-v b2.de* puls b7a.de sabad b7a.de *Sep* b2.de* sil b2.de* staph b2.de* *Sulph* b2.de*
      - **chill**; with: bry b7.de* lach b7a.de*
      - **face**; of: cocc b7.de m-aust b7a.de sep b4.de
      - **thirst**; with: con b4.de* sulph b4.de*
    - **perspiration**: bry b2.de* caps b2.de* caust b2.de* *Clem* b2.de* dig b2.de* graph b2.de* m-ambo b2.de *M-aust* b2.de *Nat-m* b2.de* *Rhus-t* b2.de*

SUDDEN (See Paroxysmal)

SUMMER, hot season: ant-c *Arn* b7a.de *Ars Bell Bry* k* *Calc Caps* k* carb-v cedr chin cina k* dulc fd4.de eup-per *Gels Ip* k* *Lach* k* nat-m puls *Sulph* thuj verat

SUN:
- **heat** of; in the: *Ant-c* k* *Bell Cact* dulc fd4.de *Glon* lyss nat-c k* puls k* sep k*
- **walking** in: ant-c

SUPPER; after: | **amel.**: anac bg2

SUPPRESSION: | **discharges**: cham ptk1 merc k2*

SYMPTOMS; without other: chinin-s mrr1 **Ferr-p** mrr1 mur-ac mrr1 nat-m mrr1

TALKING agg.: *Ars* b4a.de* nux-v bg2 olnd bg2 sel b7a.de* *Sep* b4a.de* squil b7.de* teucr bg2

TEETH, with pains in: ant-c h2 nat-c h2

TERTIAN (See Periodical - day - alternate)

THINKING agg.: phos bg2 spong bg2

THIRSTLESS (See STOMACH - Thirstless - fever)

TOBACCO smoking: cic ign sep

TRAUMATIC fever: acon bg2* apis bg2 *Arn* bg2* *Ars* c2* bry bg2 cact c2 *Calen* hr1* carb-v bg2 *Chin* c2* *Coff* hr1* croc bg2 euphr bg2 hep bg2 *Iod* hr1* *Lach* bg2* *Lyss* hr1* merc bg2* nat-c bg2 *Nit-ac* bg2 ph-ac bg2 phos bg2 *Puls* bg2 *Rhus-t* bg2 *Staph* bg2 *Sul-ac* bg2 *Sulph* bg2*

TROPICAL: **Cedr** corn br1 corn-f br1 *Gels* nat-s **Psor** *Ter*
- **chronic**: corn br1 corn-f br1

TYPHOID FEVER: *(↗Continued; Intense - constant; Typhus; GENERALS - Food poisoning)* absin c2 acon bg2 *Agar* c2* agarin bro1 ail c2* am-m br1 ant-t apis k* arg-met bg2 arg-n bro1 arn k* *Ars* k* arum-t c2* *Bapt* k* bapt-c c2 bell bg2* ben c2 berb-a c2 **Bry** k* but-ac sp1 calad c2 calc bg2* calc-ar c2 camph bg2 canth caps carb-ac carb-v bg2* cham bg2 chin b7a.de* cina bro1 cocc bg2 **Colch** k* coli jl2 crot-h bro1 cupr bg2 cupr-ar bro1 dor c2 dulc c2 eberth jl2 echi c2* eucal c2* ferr-m c2 *Gels* bro1 glon bro1 hell bg2* hydr bro1 hyos b7a.de* hyosin-hbr bro1 ign b7a.de iod bro1 ip k* kali-c bg2* kali-n bg2 kali-p bro1 *Lach* bg2* laur bro1 lob-p c2 *Lyc* k* manc c2 *Merc* bg2* merc-c bg2 merc-cy bro1 *Methyl* br1* mez bg2 morb tl1 mosch c2* *Mur-ac* k* naphtin c2 nat-m bg2 *Nit-ac* k* nit-s-d c2 nuph c2 nux-m b7a.de* *Nux-v* b7a.de* *Op* b7a.de* parathyr jl2 *Ph-ac* k* phenac c2 **Phos** k* puls b7a.de* pyrog br1* **Rhus-t** k* *Sec* k* sel bro1 septi c2 sol-ni c2 *Stram* bg2* stry bro1 sul-ac bg2* sul-h c2 *Sulph* k* sumb c2* tarax bg2* *Ter* k* trios c2 vacc-m bro1 valer bro1 vario jl2 verat k* verat-v c2 xero bro1 zinc c2* zinc-m c2

- **accompanied** by:
  - **abscesses**: ars bro1 hep bro1 sil bro1
  - **chilliness**; great: psor jl2
  - **constipation**: *Bry* bro1 hydr bro1 nux-v bro1 op bro1
  - **decubitus**: arn bro1 *Ars* bro1 bapt bro1 carb-v bro1 *Lach* bro1 mur-ac bro1 pyrog bro1 *Sec* bro1
  - **fever**: ars bro1 *Bapt* bro1 bell bro1 gels bro1 methyl bro1 rhus-t bro1 stram bro1
  - **gastrointestinal** complaints: cupr-ar br1
  - **mucus**; discharge of: alum bg2 ars bg2 *Asar* bg2 bell bg2 borx bg2 bry bg2 **Calc** bg2 cham bg2 *Chin* bg2 cina bg2 dig bg2 *Dulc* bg2 graph bg2 hyos bg2 *Ign* bg2 ip bg2 lyc bg2 *Merc* bg2 merc-c bg2 mez bg2 *Nux-v* bg2 par bg2 **Phos** bg2 **Puls** bg2 rheum bg2 *Rhus-t* bg2 sel bg2 seneg bg2 sep bg2 spig bg2 stann bg2 sul-ac bg2 **Sulph** bg2 **Thuj** bg2 zinc bg2
  - **perspiration**; cold: psor tl1
  - **saliva** | **frothy**: *Bry* kr1*
  - **sleeplessness**: bell bro1 *Coff* bro1 gels bro1 *Hyos* bro1 *Hyosin-hbr* bro1 op bro1 rhus-t bro1
  - **urination** | **profuse**: gels bro1 mur-ac bro1 *Ph-ac* bro1
  - **yawning** agg.: ign hr
  - O **Abdomen** | **distention**; tympanitic: *Ars* bro1 *Asaf* bro1 bapt bro1 *Carb-v* bro1 chin bro1 cocc bro1 coch bro1 lyc bro1 methyl br1* mill bro1 mur-ac bro1 *Nux-m* bro1 *Ph-ac* bro1 rhus-t bro1 *Ter* bro1
  - **Larynx**; complaints of: apis bro1 merc-c bro1
  - **Liver**; enlarged: absin cp1 lyc ry1 merc-i-f btw1 phos hr1
  - **Spleen**; enlarged: absin cp1 merc-i-f btw1 phos hr1 querc-r c1
  - **Tongue**:
    - **biting** | **sleep**; during: **Ph-ac** kr1*
    - **black** discoloration: nux-v kr1*
    - **brown** discoloration: *Bapt* kr1* *Iris* kr1* *Phos* kr1* *Zinc* kr1*
      - **centre**: *Apis* kr1*
      - **reddish** brown discoloration: zinc kr1*
      - **yellowish** brown: *Lachn* kr1*
    - **clean** tongue: *Cocc* kr1* *Dulc* kr1* *Gels* kr1*
    - **cracked**: phos kr1* **Rhus-t** kr1* *Zinc* kr1*
      - **edges**: nux-v kr1*
    - **dirty** discoloration: merc kr1*
    - **dryness** of tongue: *Lachn* kr1*
    - **mucus**:
      - **brown**: **Rhus-t** kr1*
      - **white**: *Apis* kr1* phos kr1*
    - **paralysis** of tongue: *Cocc* kr1* *Hyos* kr1* *Mur-ac* kr1*
    - **red** discoloration of the tongue | **Sides** of the tongue: *Iris* kr1* nux-v kr1* phos kr1*
    - **smooth**: phos kr1*
    - **white** discoloration: *Glon* kr1* phos kr1*
      - **Sides** of tongue; at: **Mur-ac** kr1*
    - **yellow** discoloration of the tongue: *Gels* kr1*
- **collapse**; in stage of: xan c1
- **delirium**; with (See MIND - Delirium - typhoid)

Typhoid fever: ...

- **developing** | **slowly**: *Ars* bg2 bell bg2 camph bg2 chin bg2 cocc bg2 con bg2 cupr bg2 dig bg2 ferr bg2 hell bg2 hyos bg2 ign bg2 iod bg2 merc bg2 merc-c bg2 nux-v bg2 **Ph-ac** bg2 **Phos** bg2 sep bg2 stann bg2 staph bg2 verat bg2
- **early** stage: xero br1
- **followed** by | **hair**; falling out of (See HEAD - Hair - falling - typhoid)
- **hemorrhagic**: alum bro1 *Alumn* bro1 ars bro1 *Bapt* bro1 carb-v k* chin bro1 **Crot-h** k* elaps bro1 *Ham* bro1 hydrin-s bro1 ip bro1 kreos bro1 *Lach* k* *Mill* k* *Mur-ac* bro1 *Nit-ac* bro1 nux-m bro1 ph-ac br1* **Phos** sec bro1 *Sul-ac* *Ter* bro1
  - **oozing** of dark thin blood from capillaries: *Arn* bro1 *Ars* bro1 carb-v bro1 crot-h mur-ac bro1 *Sul-ac*
- **icteric** skin, with: cham chin *Crot-h* lyc merc *Nat-s* sulph
- **rainy** season; during: oci-sa sp1
- **resistant**: streptom mtf11
- **scarlet** fever; after: ail bro1 arum-t bro1 *Hyos* bro1 lach bro1 *Rhus-t* bro1 stram bro1
- **septic** conditions; with: bapt mtf11
- **spasmodic**: prot jl2
- **symptoms** closely related to: arn br1 oci-sa sp1

O - **Abdominal** (See Typhoid)

TYPHUS FEVER: *(↗Continued; Typhoid)* acet-ac bro1 *Agar* c2* ail c2* alum c2 apis c2* arn bg2* *Ars* bg2* arum-t bro1 asar c2 bapt c2* bell bg2* bry bg2* calad c2 calc bro1 *Camph* bro1 caps hr1 carb-v bg2* castm c2 chin bro1 *Chinin-s* c2* chlf c2 chlor c2 crot-h bro1 dig bg2 hell bro1 hydr c2 hyos bg2* hyosin c2 ign bg2 kreos bro1 *Lach* bg2* *Merc* bg2* merc-c bg2 merc-i-r c2* mur-ac bg2* nit-ac bro1 nux-m bg2 nux-v bg2 op bg2* pest c2 ph-ac bg2* *Phos* bg2* puls bg2 pyrog br1* *Rhus-t* bg2* stram bg2* sul-ac bg2 *Sulph* bg2 ter tl1 verat bg2*

- **accompanied** by:
  - **cellulitis**: bell bro1 chinin-s bro1 *Merc-i-r* bro1
  - **salivation**: agar kr1*
  - **septicemia**: *Ars* bro1 *Mur-ac* bro1 pyrog bro1 rhus-t bro1
  - O **Bones**; sensitive: *Mang*
  - **Glands**; inflammation of salivary: bell bro1 chinin-s bro1 *Merc-i-r* bro1
  - **Parotid** gland; swollen: *Mang*
  - **Tongue**:
    - **aphthae** on tongue: moni jl2 *Mur-ac* kr1* *Sulph* kr1*
    - **black** discoloration: arg-n kr1* arn kr1* *Ars* kr1* *Hyos* kr1*
    - **brown** discoloration: ars kr1* *Chlor* kr1* nux-v kr1*
      - **yellowish** brown: bapt kr1*
    - **cracked**: *Apis* kr1* *Ars* kr1* *Atro* kr1* *Bapt* kr1*
    - **dirty** discoloration: *Camph* kr1* *Carb-v* kr1*
    - **induration** of tongue: *Arg-n* kr1* *Atro-s* kr1*
    - **trembling**: *Agar* kr1* *Apis* kr1* *Ars* kr1* aur kr1* *Gels* kr1* *Lach* kr1*
    - **ulcers**: *Apis* kr1* **Bapt** kr1*
    - **white** discoloration: *Bapt* kr1* **Bry** kr1* *Carb-v* kr1* *Gels* kr1* *Rhus-t* kr1*
      - **heavily** coated: *Bapt* kr1*
      - **yellowish** white: *Bapt* kr1*
- **petechial**: anthraci *Arn* *Ars* *Bapt* camph caps *Carb-v* *Chin* **Chlor** *Lach* **Mur-ac** nit-ac *Phos* *Rhus-t* *Sec* sulph
  - **fetid** stool, intestinal hemorrhage, sopor | **weak** that he settles down in bed into a heap; so: **Mur-ac**
  - **foul** breath, says there is nothing the matter with him: **Arn**
  - **putrid**, foul, cadaverous smell of stool | **tongue** and extreme prostration; brown, leathery-looking: **Ars**

UNCOVERING:

- **agg.**: *Merc* bro1 *Nux-v* bro1 samb bro1 stront-c bro1
  - **pain** from uncovering: *Aur* b4a.de carb-an b4a.de con b4a.de *Merc* b4a.de *Sil* b4a.de stram h1 stront-c b4a.de
  - **yet** too cold when uncovered: camph tl1 cor-r br1
- **amel.**: acon k* *Ars* *Bov* calc bg2 *Cham* k* chin k* chinin-ar coloc dulc fd4.de ferr k* ign k* *Led* lyc k* mur-ac k* nux-v k* plat k* *Puls* k* *Staph* k* verat k*

Fever

- **aversion** to: acon k* agar b2.de* am-c b4.de* androc srj1• ant-c b2.de arg-met b2.de *Arg-n* arn b2.de ars k* asar b2.de aur k* aur-ar k2 **Bell** k* borx b2.de bry b2.de *Calc Camph* k* canth b2.de caps b2.de* carb-an k* carb-v bg2 cham b2.de chin b2.de* *Chinin-s* cic b2.de* clem k* cocc b2.de* coff k* *Colch* k* con k* *Gels* granit-m es1• *Graph* k* *Hell* k* *Hep* k* ign b2.de* kali-c bg2 kreos b2.de* lach b2.de* led b2.de m-aust b2.de* **Mag-c** k* *Mag-m* k* manc meny b2.de *Merc* k* mur-ac b2.de nat-c k* nat-m b2.de nat-s ptk nux-m k* **Nux-v** k* *Petr* bg2 ph-ac k* phos k* **Psor Puls** k* **Pyrog** rheum b2.de rhod b2.de* **Rhus-t** k* sabad b2.de* **Samb** k* sep b2.de* *Sil* k* spig bg2 **Squil** k* stann bro1 staph b2.de **Stram** k* *Stront-c* k* sul-ac h2 *Tarent* thuj b2.de **Tub**
  - **shivering**; during: chin b7.de
- **chilliness** from: acon agar *Apis* **Arn** bar-c *Bell Calc* carb-an cham **Chin** *Chinin-s* **Nux-v** k* *Psor* pyrog **Rhus-t** sarr *Sep* squil *Tarent* **Tub**
  - **and** pain: squil
  - **any** stage of paroxysm; in: arn ars aur carb-an *Chin Gels* graph hell *Hep* **Nux-v** *Pyrog* **Rhus-t Samb** squil stram *Tarent*
- **desire** for: **Acon** k* **Apis** k* *Arn Ars* k* *Ars-i* ars-s-f k2 asar k* aur b2.de *Bar-c Borx* k* *Bov* k* bry k* calad calc k* carb-v b2.de cham k* **Chin** k* *Chinin-ar Coff* k* cor-r br1 **Euph** k* **Ferr** k* ferr-i fl-ac k* *Hep* hyos tl1 **Ign** k* iod k* ip bro1 kali-i k2 *Lach* k* led k* lyc k* *M-ambo* b2.de* **M-arct** b2.de* *Mag-c* med merc b2.de **Mosch** k* **Mur-ac** k* **Nat-m** *Nit-ac* k* nux-v b2.de* **Op** k* **Petr** ph-ac bg2 *Phos* k* *Plat* k* **Puls** k* rhus-t k* **Sec** k* seneg b2.de* sep b2.de spig k* **Staph** k* sul-i k2 *Sulph* k* thuj k* *Verat* k* [tax jsj7]

UNDULANT (See GENERALS - Brucellosis)

URINATION:
- **after** | **agg.**: phos bg2 rhus-t bg2
- **agg.**: clem bg2
- **amel.**: clem bg2

VACCINATION: | **after**: carc fb*

VERTIGO; with: (↗*VERTIGO - Fever - during; VERTIGO - Fever - During - agg.)* cassia-s ccrh1• corn-f br1 urt-u ptk1

VEXATION; heat from: acon *Cham* k* nux-v *Petr* k* ph-ac phos **Sep** k* staph

VIOLENT (See Intense)

VOMITING:
- **amel.**: acon k* dig k* puls k* sec k*
- **during**: ant-c k* ant-t ptk1 *Arn* k* ars k* bapt ptk1 cassia-s ccrh1• cham k* eup-per ptk1 lach k* nat-m ptk1 nux-v k* op bro1 phos bg2 stram k* verat k*

WAKING: | **after** | **amel.**: **Calad** bg2 chin bg2 colch bg2 hell bg2 nux-v bg2 phos bg2 sep bg2
- **on**: laur bro1

WALKING:
- **agg.**: rhus-t bg2 samb b7.de
- **air**; in open:
  - **after** | **agg.**: ars k* calc h2 caust k* meny b7.de* ol-an bg2 *Petr* k* **Ran-s** k* *Rhus-t* k* sabin k* *Sep* k* tub-m jl2
  - **agg.**: am-c k* am-m k* arg-met k* bell k* borx k* bry **Camph** k* caust chin k* con h2 cur guaj bg2 hep k* hyos led h1 m-aust b7.de meny mur-ac bg2 *Nux-v* k* ph-ac k* rhus-t k* sabad *Sep* k* spig k* staph k* tarax k* thuj
  - **amel.**: alum k* asar k* caps k* cic lyc k* mag-c k* mosch k* *Phos* k* *Puls* k* sabin k* tarax k*

WARM:
- **covering** agg.: acon k* **Apis** k* borx bg2 calc k* *Cham* k* chin bg2* coff ferr k* **Ign** k* *Led* k* lyc k* mur-ac k* nat-m ptk1 nux-v k* op k* *Petr* plat bg2 **Puls** k* rhus-t k* staph k* sulph verat k*
- **drinks** | **agg.**: sumb k*
- **intolerance** of both cold and warm air: cocc
- **room**:
  - **agg.**: *Am-m* k* ang k* **Apis** k* aster bg2 *Bry* caust bg2 croc bg2 fl-ac bg2 *Ip* k* kali-c h2 kali-n b4.de* *Lyc* k* mag-m k* nat-m nicc nit-ac bg2 phos bg2 plan **Puls** k* **Ran-s** bg2 rhod b4a.de* rhus-t b7.de* sul-ac *Sulph* valer bg2 zinc
  - **intolerable**; heat of the room is: **Apis**

WARMTH: *(↗Bed - in)*
- **agg.**: *(↗Bed - in)* **Apis** bry ign op **Puls** staph

Warmth: ...
- **amel.**: alum bg2 **Ars** bg2 caps bg2 carb-v bg2 lyc bg2
- **intolerance** of: *Ign* b7a.de

WASHING:
- **agg.**: am-c k* anac bg2 calc bg2 rhus-t k* sep k* sil bg2 sulph k*
- **amel.**: am-m bg2 **Apis** k* asar bg2 bapt caust bg2 **Fl-ac** k* **Puls** k* spig bg2

WATER:
- **dashed** with hot water; as if (See GENERALS - Heat - flushes - warm water - dashed)
- **drinking** agg.: calc canth k* ign k* m-arct b7.de *Rhus-t* k* sep k*

WEATHER:
- **cold** agg.: hydroph rsj6•
- **warm** | **agg.**: nit-ac h2

WET ROOMS: | **living** in: chinin-ar k2

WHOOPING COUGH; with: dros ptk1

WINE:
- **agg.**: ars k* *Carb-v* k* fl-ac k* gins iod nat-m k* nux-v k* sil k*
- **amel.**: acon bg2 con bg2 op bg2

WINTER: calc carb-v chin nux-m puls *Rhus-t* sulph verat

WORMS; from: **Acon** bg2 ambr bg2 anac bg2 ars bg2 asar bg2 bell bg2* *Calc* b4a.de* *Chin* bg2 cic b7a.de* **Cina** b7a.de* dig b4a.de* *Ferr* bg2 *Graph* bg2 hyos b7a.de* ign bg2 kali-c bg2 lach bg2 *Merc* b4a.de* nat-m bg2 nux-v b7a.de* passi br1 petr bg2 phos bg2 *Plat* bg2 puls bg2 ruta bg2 **Sabad** b7a.de* sabin bg2 santin bro1 **Sil** b4a.de* *Spig* b7a.de* spong bg2 stann b4a.de* stram b7a.de* **Sulph** b4a.de* teucr bg2 thuj bg2 valer b7a.de*

YAWNING agg.: agar bg2

YELLOW fever: acon k* all-c c2 am-c bg2 ant-t bg2* *Apis* bg2* arg-met b7a.de* arg-n k* *Arn* b7a.de* **Ars** k* *Ars-h* k* bell k* *Bry* k* *Cadm-s* k* calc k* camph k* **Canth** k* caps c2 carb-ac bro1 **Carb-v** k* cham bg2 *Chin* k* chinin-s bro1 coff k* coloc bg2 crot-c bro1 **Crot-h** k* cupr c2* daph dig b7a.de* gels bro1 gua bro1 hell b7a.de* hep k* *Hyos* bro1 ip k* lach k* lept c2 lob k* **Merc** b7a.de* mur-ac k2 *Nat-s* k* nit-ac b7a.de* **Nux-v** k* op bro1 *Phos* k* plb b7a.de* *Psor* puls b7a.de* rhus-t k* sabad b7a.de* sabin bro1 *Sep* bg2 *Sul-ac* bg2* sulph bg2 *Ter* k* verat k*
- **accompanied** by:
  - ○ **Tongue**:
    - **black** discoloration: *Ars* kr1* *Cadm-s* kr1* **Carb-v** kr1*
    - **brown** discoloration: *Sulph* kr1* *Verat* kr1*
    - **cracked**: *Verat* kr1*
- **perspiration** is checked from exposure to a draft of air; when: *Cadm-s*
- **prophylaxis**, of: ars ptk1* crot-h gm1
- **third** stage:
  - **hemorrhages**:
    - **paleness** of face and violent headache; with great | **heaviness** of limbs and trembling of the body; with great: **Carb-v**

ZYMOTIC FEVERS: *(↗Puerperal; Septic)* acet-ac ail k2* anthraci apis **Arn** k* **Ars** k* ars-s-f k2 arum-t k2 **Bapt** *Bell* k* berb **Bry** k* *Cadm-s* canth bg2 carb-v k* **Carbn-s** *Chin* bg2 **Crot-h** *Cur* dig bg2 **Echi** echi-p c2 hippoz c2 hyos k* ip k* kali-bi k2 **Kali-p Lach Lyc** merc k* merc-c bg2 **Mur-ac** k* nux-m k* nux-v k* op k* ph-ac k* *Phos* k* *Puls* k* *Pyrog* k* **Rhus-t** k* rhus-v **Sulph** k* tarent

COVERED PARTS: *(↗Dry - covered)* arg-met k1 (non:arg-n k*) borx b4a.de cham h1 *Thuj* k*

SIDE LAIN ON: arn gsy1 mag-m k*

SINGLE PARTS: cham h1 cycl h1 *Ign* b7a.de *Rhus-t* b7a.de stann tub zinc

PERSPIRATION in general: absin a1 *Acet-ac* k* *Acon* k* aesc k* aeth k* *Agar* k* agar-ph a1 agath-a nl2• agn b2.de* ail k1 alco a1 all-c k* alst k* alum k* am-act c2 am-c k* am-caust a1 am-m k* ambr k* aml-ns ammc hr1 ampe-qu a1 anac k* ang k* *Ant-c* k* **Ant-t** k* anthraci anthraco apis k* apoc k* arg-met k* arg-n k* arn k* *Ars* k* ars-h hr1 ars-i k* *Ars-s-f* hr1 arund k* asaf k* asar b2.de* asc-c k* asc-t hr1 astac a1 atro hr1 aur k* bapt k* *Bar-c* k* *Bell* k* ben c2 benz-ac k* berb k* bism bg2 bol-la bond a1 borx b2.de* bov k* brom k* *Bry* k* bufo cact k* cain calad k* **Calc** k* calc-hp c2 calc-i k2 calc-p bg2* calo br1 camph k* canch k1 cann-i k* cann-s b2.de* (non:canth b2.de*) *Caps* k* carb-ac k* *Carb-an* k* *Carb-v* k* caust k* *Cedr* cham k* chel k* **Chin** k* *Chinin-s* chir-fl bnm4• cic k* cimx k* cina k* cinnb k* cist k2 cit-ac rly4• clem k* *Cocc* k* coch hr1 coff k* colch k* coli jl2 coloc k* colum-p sze2• con k* corn k* croc b2.de* crot-c k* crot-h k* crot-t k* cupr k* cur k* cycl k* daph k* *Dig* k* dios k* dros k* dubo-h hs1 *Dulc* k* *Elaps* *Elat* eup-per k* eup-pur euph b2.de* euphr b2.de* eupi falco-pe nl2• **Ferr** k* ferr-ar k2 ferr-i mrr1 fl-ac k* flor-p rsj3• form hr1 gamb *Gels* k* germ-met srj5• glon k* *Graph* k* grat k* *Guaj* k* haliae-lc srj5• hell k* helo-s bnm14• **Hep** k* hydr hr1 hydr-ac k* *Hyos* k* ign k* *Iod* k* **Ip** k* iris jab k* jatr-c kali-ar k2 kali-bi kali-c k* kali-i k* kali-n k* kali-s k* kali-sula a1* kalm k* kreos k* lac-ac k* lach k* lachn k* lat-h bnm5• lat-m bnm6• laur k* led k* lil-t k* lith-c bg2 lob k* luf-op rsj5• **Lyc** k* m-ambo b2.de* m-arct b2.de* m-aust b2.de *Mag-c* k* mag-m b2.de* mag-s k* malar jl2 mang k* med hr1* meny k* *Merc* k* merc-c k* merc-cy k* merl k* *Mez* k* morph k* mosch k* mur-ac k* myric k* naja *Nat-ar* nat-c k* **Nat-m** k* nat-ox rly4• nicc k* nicotam rly4• nit-ac k* nux-m k* **Nux-v** k* *Olib-sac* wmh1 **Op** k* *Ox-ac* k* oxal-a rly4• par k* parathyr jl2 pert jl2 *Petr* k* petr-ra shn4• *Ph-ac* k* **Phos** k* phys k* pin-con oss2• plan k* plat k* plb k* plect bro1 *Podo* **Psor** k* puls k* pyrid rly4• ran-b b2.de* *Ran-s* k* rheum k* rhod k* *Rhus-t* k* rob ruta b2.de* sabad k* sabin k* sal-ac k* **Samb** k* sang k* sarr k* sars b2.de* *Sec* k* sel k* senec seneg b2.de* **Sep** k* **Sil** k* spig k* spong k* squil b2.de* stann k* staph k* stram k* stront-c b2.de* stry k* sul-ac k* *Sulph* k* sumb k* tab k* tarax k* tarent k* tax k* teucr thal-xyz srj8• ther k* thuj k* thyr br1 trios *Valer* k* **Verat** k* *Verat-v* k* viol-o b2.de* viol-t b2.de* vip k* visc sp1 wye k2 zinc k* *Zing* k* ziz k* [aur-m stj2 aur-s stj2 cadm-m stj2 cadm-s stj2 calc-s stj1 chr-s stj2 gal-s stj2 lith-s stj2 mang-p stj2 mang-s stj2 merc-d stj2 nicc-s stj2 titan-s stj2]

- **amel.** (See GENERALS - Perspiration - during - amel.)

ONE SIDE: acon alum b2.de* *Ambr* k* anac b2.de* ant-t b2.de* arn b2.de* aur-m-n *Bar-c* k* bell k* *Bry* k* carb-v bg2 *Caust* b2.de* cham k* *Chin* k* *Cocc* b2.de* croc b2.de dig b2.de* fl-ac k* ign b2.de* jab br1* kali-c b2.de lyc k* merc merl nat-c b2.de nux-m **Nux-v** k* par b2.de **Petr** k* ph-ac b2.de *Phos* k* plat b2.de psor al **PULS** k ●* ran-b k* rheum bg2 rhus-t k* ruta b2.de *Sabad* b2.de* sabin k* sars b2.de *Spig* b2.de* stann b2.de* stram sul-ac b2.de *Sulph* k* **Thuj** k* verb b2.de

ALTERNATING SIDES: agar ptk1

RIGHT side: aur-m-n bell k* bry k* fic-m gya1 fl-ac bg2 jab kr1 merl nux-v k* *Phos* k* psor al *Puls* k* ran-b k* sabin k*

LEFT side: ambr bg2* anac bg2* **Bar-c** k* *Chin* k* fl-ac k* jab kr1 kali-c bg2 phos k* **Puls** k* rhus-t k* spig bg2* stann bg2* sulph k*

SIDE:

○ - **Affected** side: *Ambr* b7.de*

DAY AND NIGHT: | **relief**; without: **Hep** samb sep h2

DAYTIME: agar k* am-c k* am-m k* ambr k* anac *Ant-t* bell k* bry k* **Calc** k* *Carb-an* k* carb-v bg2* carbn-s caust b4.de* *Chin* k* *Con* k* *Dulc* k* **Ferr** k* ferr-ar *Ferr-p* granit-m es1• *Graph* k* guaj *Hep* k* kali-bi **Kali-c** k* kali-sil k2 lach laur led **Lyc** k* mag-c h2* *Merc* k* **Nat-c** k* **Nat-m** k* *Nat-p* *Nit-ac* nux-v bg2* **Ph-ac** k* *Phos* b4.de* puls k* *Rheum* rhus-t bg2 *Sel* k* **Sep** k* sil k* *Staph* k* *Stram* sul-ac k* **Sulph** k* verat k* zinc k*

- **awake**, while: **Samb** k* sep tl1
- **closing** the eyes agg.: chin h1 **Con** k*
- **nausea** and languor, with: **Merc**
- **sleep** agg.; during: bell caust con k* lyc k* sel a1

MORNING (= 6-9 h): acon k* *Alum* k* alum-p k2 alum-sil k2 **Am-c** k* am-m k* ambr k* ang k* *Ant-c* k* ant-t hr1 apis bg2 arg-met bg2 *Arg-n* k* arn b7.de* *Ars* k* ars-i ars-s-f k2 aur k* aur-i k2 aur-s k2• bamb-a stb2.de• bell k* borx k* bov k* *Bry* k* bufo k* **Calc** k* calc-i k2 calc-sil k2 canth k* caps k* carb-an k* **Carb-v** k* *Carbn-s* *Caust* k* cham k* *Chel* k* *Chin* k* *Chinin-ar* chinin-s cic k* cimic bg2 cimx k* clem k* cocc k* *Coff* k* coloc k* con k* dig b4.de* dros k* dulc k* elaps eug k* *Euph* k* euphr b7.de* eupi k* falco-pe nl2• **Ferr** k* *Ferr-ar* ferr-i ferr-p gamb k* graph k* grat k* guaj k* *Hell* k*

Morning: ...
Hep k* hyper k* ign b7.de* ina-i mlk9.de iod k* kali-ar kali-c k* kali-m k2 kali-n k* kali-p kali-s kali-sil k2 kalm hr1 kreos k* lac-h htj1• lach bg2* lachn k* laur b7a.de* led b7.de* *Lyc* k* m-ambo b7.de m-arct b7.de m-aust b7.de *Mag-c* k* mag-m k* mag-s k* **Merc** k* *Merc-c* b4a.de* merl k* mez k* *Mosch* k* mur-ac k* nat-ar nat-c k* nat-m k* nat-p nat-s hr1* nicc k* **Nit-ac** k* nux-v k* op k* ox-ac k* par k* petr b4a.de* *Ph-ac* k* **Phos** k* *Puls* k* ran-b k* *Ran-s* b7.de* rhod b4.de* *Rhus-t* k* *Ruta* b7a.de* *Sabad* k* **Samb** k* sang k* *Sel* b7.de* senec k* *Sep* k* **Sil** k* spig k* spong k* *Stann* k* *Stront-c* b4.de* sul-ac k* sul-i k2 *Sulph* k* tarax b7.de* thuj k* til a1 tritic-vg fd5.de vanil fd5.de **Verat** k* vip fkr4.de zinc k*

- **6** h: alum sil
  - **6**-7 h: sulph
- **7**-12 h: phos
- **noon**; until: *Ferr*
- **early** morning: stann bro1
- **bed** agg.; in: alum h2 am-m k* ant-c h2 *Bamb-a* stb2.de• benz-ac k* bov hr1 bufo **Calc** caps chin con euph hr1 **Ferr** k* graph h2 kali-c k* kali-i k* kali-n k* lyc k* nat-c k* nicc k* ol-an a1 phos k* ruta fd4.de *Sep* h2* spong fd4.de
- **coffee** agg.: cham k*
- **heat**; after: ars k* graph k* nit-ac k* **Puls** k*
- **menses**; before: nat-s
- **periodical** (See Periodical - morning)
- **restless** night, after a: arg-n lyc k*
- **side**; perspiration every morning, agg. on the affected: ambr k1
- **sleep** agg.; during: **Ant-c** bell borx h2* *Bov* bufo *Chel* *Chin* *Chinin-s* con **Ferr** ign lachn nat-m h2 ph-ac h2 **Puls** k* spong fd4.de *Sulph* h2* vanil fd5.de zinc k*
- **waking**:
  - **after** | **agg.**: acon-c alum-sil k2 androc srj1• *Ant-c* ant-t ars h2 bry carb-an carb-v chel chin con dig ferr gamb hyper mag-s *Nux-v* ph-ac phos phys ran-b c1 **Samb** **Sep** spong fd4.de **Sulph**
  - **amel.**: chel tl1
  - **on**: am-m h2 ant-c h2 carb-v h2 con h2 dig h2 dros ptk1 ephe-si hsj1• euphr h2 falco-pe nl2• iod h par ptk1 ptel c1 ros-d wla1 *Samb* ptk1 sel rsj9• sep h2* spong h1 sulph ptk1 tere-la rly4• tritic-vg fd5.de vanil fd5.de

FORENOON (= 9-12 h): acon b7.de* **Agar** k* ars k* bamb-a stb2.de• carb-v bg2 cic b7.de* **Ferr** k* **Hep** b4a.de* ign k* merc b4.de* *Nat-c* bg2 nat-m bg2 phos b4.de* ruta fd4.de sabad bg2 *Sel* b7.de* sep k* sil bg2 staph bg2 stront-c b4.de* sul-ac k* sulph k* tritic-vg fd5.de *Valer* b7.de*

- **9** h | **stool** agg.; after: sumb
- **exertion** agg.: gels k* sulph k* valer k*
- **menses**; during: agar ars sep sulph
- **sleep** agg.; during: nux-m

NOON (= 12-13 h): acon k* *Arn* hr1 cham k* cinnb k* clem k* spong fd4.de tritic-vg fd5.de valer k*

AFTERNOON (= 13-18 h): agar b4.de* all-s k* alum bg2 am-m k* ars k* *Bell* b4.de* *Berb* k* calad b7.de* calc-s k* canth k* caps b7.de* cartl-s rly4• chel hr1 cina dendr-pol sk4• ferr-i k* fl-ac k* *Hep* k* kali-i hr1 kali-n k* laur b7.de* lyc bg2 mag-m k* mag-s nat-ar *Nat-m* nat-p k* nicc k* nit-ac *Nux-v* k* op k* *Ph-ac* hr1 phos bg2 ptel k* puls bg2 rhus-t bg2 ruta fd4.de *Sel* b7.de* sil k* stann b4.de* staph k* sulph k* thuj bg2 tritic-vg fd5.de zinc bg2

- **13** h:
  - **13**-15 h: kali-c
  - **13**-16 h: phos
- **15** h: atp rly4• ferr mag-s
  - **15**-17 h: bamb-a stb2.de• sil
- **16** h, until midnight: bell h1
- **17** h: cartl-s rly4• psil ft1 puls sarr
- **coldness**; during: gels k*
- **heat**; during: ferr k* gamb k* nit-ac k* ruta fd4.de
- **sleep** agg.; during: ant-t calad carb-an nat-m k* nit-ac

EVENING (= 18-22 h): acon bg2 *Agar* k* am-m bg2 anac k* ant-t bg2 anthraco apis bg2 *Arg-n* hr1 ars b4.de* asar b7.de* bamb-a stb2.de• bar-c b4.de* bell k* berb borx bg2 bov k* bry bg2 cain calad k* *Calc* b4.de* calc-s k* canth caps bg2 carb-v k* carbn-s caust bg2 **Cham** b7.de* chel **Chin** b7.de* chinin-s cocc k* coloc k* con k* *Fl-ac* b4a.de* graph bg2 *Hell* b7a.de* *Hep* b4.de* hyos bg2 ip bg2 kali-c bg2 kali-n bg2 lach k* lyc bg2 mag-c k* mag-m h2 *Meny* k* merc k* merc-c k* *Mur-ac* k* nat-m k* nat-p k* nat-pyru rly4• op bg2 ph-ac bg2* *Phos* k* psor k* puls bg2 rat k* rhus-t k* samb b7.de* *Sarr* *Sars* b4.de* *Sel* b7.de*

Perspiration

Evening: ...
senec hr1 sep k* sil bg2 spig k* _Spong_ bg2 stram bg2 sul-ac bg2 _Sulph_ k* sumb k* _Tarax_ b7.de* thuj k* verat k* zinc bg2

- **18** h: dig plb _Psor_
- **19** h: elaps mag-s
  - • **19**-1 h: **Samb**
- **20** h: ferr mag-s sumb
  - • **nausea** and heat; with: ferr
- **bed** agg.; in: _Agar_ ars asar k* calc k* eug ferr kali-n h2 _Meny_ k* **Merc** k* nat-sil fd3.de• rat k* **Sulph** k* ter hr1 verat k*
- **heat**, with the: carb-v ferr a1
- **lasting** all night: bol-la chel cocc k* **Hep** _Kali-c_ led _Meny_ k* **Puls**
- **rest**, even when at: cain _Sarr_

NIGHT (= 22-6 h): abies-c br1 _Acet-ac_ k* acon k* _Agar_ k* agn aloe _Alum_ k* alum-p k2 alum-sil k2 am-c k* _Am-m_ k* _Ambr_ k* _Anac_ k* androc srj1• ang ant-c b7.de* ant-t k* anthraci anthraco apis bg2 arg-met k* _Arg-n_ k* arist-cl sp1 _Arn_ k* **Ars** k* ars-h k* _Ars-i_ k* ars-met ars-s-f k2 arum-i a1 asar k* asc-t k* astac a1 aur k* aur-i k2 aur-s k2 bac vh bamb-a stb2.de• bar-c k* bar-m bell k* benz-ac bg2* berb k* beryl tpw5 bol-la borx k* bov b4.de* brucel sa3• bry k* _Calc_ k* calc-i k2 _Calc-p_ k* calc-s calc-sil k2* camph-ac bwa3 _Canth_ k* caps b7.de* carb-ac k* **Carb-an** k* **Carb-v** k* _Carbn-s_ carl a1 casc **Caust** k* cham k* _Chel_ b7.de* _Chin_ k* _Chinin-ar_ chlor hr1 _Cic_ k* cimx cina cist k* _Clem_ k* cob-n sp1 coca _Cocc_ k* coff b7.de* colch k* coloc k* **Con** k* corian-s knl6• croc b7.de* cupr k* cur cycl k* des-ac rbp6 dig k* dios k* diosm br1 dros k* _Dulc_ k* dys fmm1• _Eup-per_ k* euph b4a.de* euphr k* eupi k* fago _Ferr_ k* _Ferr-ar_ _Ferr-i_ _Ferr-p_ foll oss• form bg2 gaert pte1*• gal-ac c1 gamb k* gard-j vlr2• _Graph_ k* guaj k* haliae-lc srj5• ham fd3.de• hell k* **Hep** k* hura hydrog srj2• hyos b7.de* ign k* ina-i mlk9.de _Iod_ k* _Ip_ k* jab br1 **Kali-ar** kali-bi k* kali-br a1 **Kali-c** k* kali-i bg2* kali-m k2 kali-n k* _Kali-p_ **Kali-s** k* kali-sil k2* _Kalm_ hr1 kreos bg2* **Lach** k* lap-la sde8.de• laur k* lec _Led_ k* lob _Lyc_ k* m-ambo b7.de m-arct b7.de m-aust b7.de mag-c b4.de* mag-m b4.de* mag-s k* manc k* mang k* med k* meny b7.de* **Merc** k* merc-c k* _Mez_ hr1 _Mur-ac_ k* musca-d szs1 myos-a hr1* _Nat-ar_ _Nat-c_ k* _Nat-m_ k* nat-p nat-s k* _Nit-ac_ k* nux-v k* ol-j a1* olib-sac wmh1 op k* ox-ac k* ozone sde2• pant-ac rly4• petr k* ph-ac k* phel hr1* phos k* phyt k* plat b4.de* plb k* _Pop_ br1 _Prun_ ptk1 psor k* ptel k* **Puls** k* pyrog bg2* ran-g a1 raph k* rat k* rheum rhod b4.de* _Rhus-t_ k* ribo rly4• ros-d wla1 ruta fd4.de sabad b7.de* sabin k* **Samb** k* sang bg2* sars hr1 _Sel_ b7a.de* senec hr1 **Sep** k* **Sil** k* sinus rly4• spig k* spong k* stach a1 stann k* _Staph_ k* stram k* _Stront-c_ k* sul-ac bg2* sul-i k2 **Sulph** k* sumb k* syc fmm1• syph bg1* tab k* **Tarax** k* tarent k* tax br1 thal-met br1* ther k* **Thuj** k* til k* tritic-vg fd5.de tub bg2* urol-h rwt• _Ust_ hr1 _Valer_ k* vanil fd5.de _Verat_ k* vero-o rly4*• viol-o b7.de* viol-t k* vip fkr4.de zinc k* zinc-p k2 [ferr-sil stj2 mag-sil stj2 mang-sil stj2 nat-sil stj2 sil-met stj2 zinc-n stj2]

- **midnight**: acon k* alum am-m k* arg-met arn k* _Ars_ bar-c k* bar-m bell hr1 berb k* canth k* clem con k* dig k* dros k* _Ferr_ k* _Fl-ac_ vh hep k* ip k* kali-ar kali-c kali-m k2 lach lat-m bnm6• lyc k* mag-m k* mag-s k* merl _Mur-ac_ k* nat-m k* nux-v k* op k* par ph-ac k* _Phos_ k* plat h2 rhus-t k* sabad k* _Samb_ k* sil staph k*
  - • **before**: am-m bg2 ant-t bg2 _Ars_ b4.de* asar bg2 bell bg2 bry bg2 _Calc_ k* canth b7.de* _Carb-an_ bg2 carb-v k* cham b7.de* chin bg2 **Con** b4.de* eug a1 hep b4.de* kali-n bg2 _Lach_ bg2 laur b7a.de* led bg2 _Lyc_ bg2 mag-c bg2 _Meny_ bg2 _Merc_ bg2 _Mur-ac_ k* nat-c bg2 nat-m b4.de* op b7.de* ph-ac h2* phos h2 ran-b bg2 rhus-t b7.de* sabad bg2 samb b7.de* sars bg2 _Sep_ b4.de* staph h1* _Sulph_ b4.de* **Tarax** b7.de* thuj b4.de* valer bg2 _Verat_ b7a.de*
    - ⁝ **22** h: borx
      - : **22**-10 h: _Bry_
      - : **until** morning: laur
      - : **chilliness**; during: _Bry_
    - ⁝ **23** h: lac-leo hrn2• sil
      - : **23**-2 h: carb-an h2
  - • **after**: acon k* _Agar_ alum k* am-m k* _Ambr_ k* arg-met k* ars k* ars-h hr1 _Aur_ bg2 bamb-a stb2.de• _Bar-c_ k* bar-s k2 bell b4.de* bol-la borx k2 _Bry_ b7.de* _Calc_ bg2 calc-sil k2 caps bg2 carb-an k* _Chel_ k* _Chin_ b7.de* clem k* coloc k* con b4.de* _Dros_ k* **Ferr** k* graph k* hell k* hep b4.de* hyos b7.de* kali-c k* kali-p fd1.de• kali-s _Lach_ hr1 lachn k* laur b7a.de* lyc k* m-ambo b7.de m-arct b7.de mag-c k* _Mag-m_ k* merc k* merl nat-m b4.de* nat-s k2 nicc k* nux-v k* ph-ac b4.de* phos k* plb bg2 puls k* ran-s b7.de* _Rhus-t_ b7a.de* sabad k* samb b7.de* _Sil_ k* spong fd4.de **Stann** bg2 staph b7.de* sulph k* _Tarax_ bg2 thuj bg2 **Tub** k*
    - ⁝ **1** h: ars k2 mag-c

Night – midnight – after – 1 h: ...

- : **1**-2 h: ars k2
- ⁝ **2** h:
  - : **2**-3 h: merc
  - : **2**-5 h: puls
- ⁝ **3** h: am-c k2 bry k* _Calc_ calc-ar carb-an clem ferr-m merl nat-c nux-v par **Psor** stann sulph
  - : **3**-16 h: eupi rhus-t
  - : **sleep** agg.; during: _Merl_ nat-c
- ⁝ **4** h: bamb-a stb2.de• _Caust_ _Chel_ _Ferr_ gamb sep _Stann_ tell
  - : **4**-6 h: arg-n bg2
  - : **sleep** agg.; during: _Carb-an_ **Chel**
  - : **until**: syc bka1•
- ⁝ **5**-6 h: bamb-a stb2.de• bov ham fd3.de•
- ⁝ **early**: bov bg2 mag-c bg2 mag-m bg2 med bg2 phos bg2 rhus-t bg2 stann bg2 sulph bg2 tab bg2 thuj bg2
- ⁝ **morning**; towards: med mtf33
- ⁝ **waking**; on: bell h1

- • **morning**; until: mag-c mag-m _Phos_
- • **lying** on back agg.: cham k*
- • **waking**; on: bell k* bol-la colch k* con k* phos k* sulph k*

- **accompanied** by | **phthisis** pulmonalis (See CHEST - Phthisis - accompanied - perspiration - night)
- **alternating** with dryness of skin: _Apis_ **Nat-c** k*
- **apyrexia**, during: cimx
- **bed** agg.; in: dulc fd4.de granit-m es1• ruta fd4.de spong fd4.de [beryl stj2]
- **coition**; after: _Agar_ b4.de* **Calc** bg2 _Chin_ bg2 graph bg2 kali-c bg2 lach bg2 nat-c b4a.de* petr bg2 _Sel_ bg2 **Sep** bg2 sulph bg2
- **covering**, when: nit-ac h2 ruta fd4.de tritic-vg fd5.de
  - • **little**; ever so: _Chin_
- **effort**; on slight: calc-f sp1
- **followed** by:
  - • **chills** | **uncovering**; when: vero-o rly3•
- **heat**; during: _Acet-ac_ bro1 carb-v hep bro1 hydrog srj2• ruta fd4.de stront-c sulph
- **lasting** all night:
  - • **loquacity**, with: **Puls**
  - • **without** relief: **Hep** kali-c k* meny hr1 **Merc**
- **long** lasting musty night perspiration: _Cimx_
- **lying** down agg.; after: ang k* ham hr1 _Hep_ k* meny k* rhus-t k* sabad k* sil k*
- **menopause**; during: stront-c ptk1
- **menses** | **before** | **agg**.: bell graph sulph **Verat** k*
  - • **during** | **agg**.: arist-cl sp1 asar bell k* borx h2 kali-c kreos b7a.de sulph
- **miliary** itching eruption, with: _Rhus-t_ k*
- **sleep** agg.; during: agar k* anac ant-t _Bell_ calc h2 carb-an chel _Chin_ chinin-s chlor a1 con k* cycl des-ac rbp6 dig h2 eup-per euphr k* hyos kali-n h2 kali-s fd4.de merc sne mur-ac h2 nat-c nit-ac k* phos **Puls** spong fd4.de stach a1 thuj
- **stupid** slumber, during: **Puls**
- **stupor**, with: puls
- **syphilis**; in: kali-i br1
- **wakefulness**, with: calc h2 cham hep h2
- **waking**; on: alum anac h2 bamb-a stb2.de• bell h1 canth card-m vml3• _Chin_ choc srj3• _Cycl_ dros dulc fd4.de gard-j vlr2• (non:hep kl) kola stb3• led _Mang_ merc-c nat-m nit-ac h2 nux-v par pd plut-n srj7• **Samb** bg2* sep sil h2 staph sulph h2 thuj

ABSENT: _Bell_ ptk1 bry ptk1 calc ptk1 **Cham** ptk1 **Chin** ptk1 colch ptk1 coloc ptk1 _Dulc_ ptk1 helo-s bnm14• _Lach_ ptk1 nux-m tl1 psor ptk1 **Rhus-t** ptk1 _Sil_ ptk1 squil ptk1 _Stram_ ptk1 _Sulph_ ptk1 [tax jsj7]

- **fever**; during (See FEVER - Perspiration - absent)
- **inability** to perspire (See SKIN - Dry - perspire)

○ - **Affected** parts; on: scol vwe2

ACCOMPANIED BY:
- **anxiety** and trembling of hands (See MIND - Anxiety - perspiration - during - hands)
- **apoplexy** (See GENERALS - Apoplexy - accompanied - perspiration)
- **complaints**; other: *Acon* b2.de* ambr b2.de* anac b2.de* ant-c b2.de* *Ant-t* b2.de* am b2.de* **Ars** b2.de* bar-c b2.de* bell b2.de* **Bry** b2.de* calc b2.de* camph b2.de* cann-s b2.de* carb-v b2.de* **Caust** b2.de* **Cham** b2.de* chel b2.de* chin b2.de* cina bg2 cocc b2.de* coff b2.de* coloc b2.de* con b2.de* croc b2.de* dig b2.de* dros b2.de* dulc b2.de* ferr b2.de* graph b2.de* hyos b2.de* *Ign* b2.de* *Ip* b2.de* kali-n b2.de* kreos b2.de* led b2.de* lyc b2.de* m-arct b2.de* m-aust b2.de* *Mang* b2.de* **Merc** b2.de* mez b2.de* mosch b2.de* mur-ac b2.de* *Nat-c* b2.de* nat-m b2.de* *Nit-ac* b2.de* **Nux-v** b2.de* **Op** b2.de* par b2.de* ph-ac b2.de* *Phos* b2.de* plb b2.de* *Puls* b2.de* ran-b b2.de* rhod b2.de* **Rhus-t** b2.de* *Sabad* b2.de* sabin b2.de* samb b2.de* sel b2.de* **Sep** b2.de* spong b2.de* stann b2.de* staph b2.de* **Stram** b2.de* stront-c b2.de* **Sulph** b2.de* tarax b2.de* thuj b2.de* valer b2.de* **Verat** b2.de*
- **emaciation** (See GENERALS - Emaciation - accompanied - perspiration)
- **falling** hair (See SKIN - Hair - falling - perspiration)
- **pneumonia** (See CHEST - Inflammation - lungs - right - lower - accompanied - perspiration)
- **pulse**; violent (See GENERALS - Pulse - violent - accompanied - perspiration)
- **respiration**:
  - **complaints** of (See RESPIRATION - Complaints - accompanied - perspiration)
  - **difficult** (See RESPIRATION - Difficult - accompanied - perspiration)
- **vertigo** (See VERTIGO - Accompanied - perspiration)
- **weakness** (See GENERALS - Weakness - perspiration - from)
- ○ - **Head**; pain in (See HEAD - Pain - perspiration - with)
- **Skin**; red (See SKIN - Discoloration - red - accompanied - perspiration)
- **Stomach**; pain in (See STOMACH - Pain - accompanied - perspiration)

ACRID: all-s k* *Caps* k* **Cham** k* *Con* k* fl-ac k* graph iod ip k* *Lac-ac* k* lac-leo hrn2• lyc k* merc *Nit-ac* bg1* par k* rhus-t spong fd4.de tarax k* tarent ptk1 tritic-vg fd5.de

ACUTE DISEASES; after: psor bro1

AFFECTED parts, on: acon c* **Ambr** k* **Ant-t** k* anthraco j5.de ars k* *Asaf* b7a.de asar sf1.de both-ax tsm2 bry k* calc bg2* *Caust* k* chin sf1.de *Cocc* k* *Coff* fl-ac k* guaj sf1.de hell sf1.de kali-c bg2* lyc bg2 **Merc** k* nat-c k* nit-ac k* nux-v k* petr sf1.de puls sf1.de **Rhus-t** k* *Sep* k* sil k* *Stann* k* stram k* stront-c k* tarent-c ptk1 thuj sf1.de
- **morning**: *Ambr*

AGGRAVATES the symptoms (See GENERALS - Perspiration - during - agg.)

AIR; IN OPEN:
- **agg.**: agar b4.de* anac b4.de* bell b4.de* *Bry* k* **Calc** k* caps k* *Carb-an* k* carb-v k* *Caust* k* cham bg2 *Chin* k* ferr bg2 guaj k* hep k* ip k* kali-c k* lach k* lyc bg2 nux-v bg2 petr bg2 ph-ac b4.de* **Psor** k* rhod k* ruta sel bg2 sep b4a.de* *Sil* k* stram bg2 sul-ac bg2 thuj k* valer k*
- **amel.**: alum *Ars* b4a.de graph

ALTERNATING with heat (See FEVER - Alternating - perspiration)

AMELIORATES the symptoms (See GENERALS - Perspiration - during - amel.)

ANGER; after: *(↗Vexation; MIND - Anger)* acon k* bry k* *Cham* k* cupr ferr-p k2 lyc k* nux-v mtf33 *Petr* k* **Sep** k* staph k*
- **heat**; with (See FEVER - Anger - perspiration)

ANXIETY, during: *(↗MIND - Anxiety)* acon b2.de* alum k* alum-p k2 am-c *Ambr* anac b2.de ant-c k* arn k* **Ars** k* ars-s-f k2 aur-m-n wbt2• bar-c k* bell b2.de* benz-ac k* berb bov bg2 bry k* **Calc** k* calc-p calc-sil k2 cann-s canth bg2 *Carb-v* k* carbn-s *Caust* k* **Cham** k* **Chin** k* chinin-ar cic k* cimx clem h2 cocc k* *Coff* bg2 croc b2.de* *Dys* fmm1• **Ferr** k* *Ferr-ar* **Fl-ac** k*

Anxiety, during: ...
graph k* ham fd3.de• hep bg2 ign b2.de* ignis-alc es2• kali-bi k* kali-n k* kola stb3• kreos k* lyc b2.de* *Mag-c* k* **Mang** k* *Merc* k* *Merc-c* k* mez k* mur-ac k* *Nat-ar* *Nat-c* k* nat-m k* *Nat-p* nat-sil fd3.de• nit-ac k* *Nux-v* k* oxal-a rly4• **Ph-ac** k* *Phos* k* plb k* *Puls* k* rheum bg2 *Rhus-t* k* ribo rly4• sabad b2.de* samb k* sel k* **Sep** k* sil k* spong k* stann k* staph k* stram k* sul-ac h2 *Sulph* k* tab k* tarent *Thuj* k* vanil fd5.de verat k*
- **evening**: ambr sulph k*
- **night**: **Ars** carb-an k* *Carb-v* nat-m k*
- **dinner**; after: calc k*

ASCENDING agg.: arn *Bell*

AWAKE, only while: ars bg2 bell bg2 bry bg2 carb-an bg2 chin bg2 con bro1 *Hell* b7a.de hep b4a.de* *Merc* bg2* *Nux-v* bg2 ph-ac b4a.de* *Phos* bg2* **Puls** b7a.de* **Samb** k* sep k* thuj bg2

BED:
- **getting** out of amel.: ars bell *Calc* *Camph* *Hell* hep lach lyc *Merc* *Puls* **Rhus-t** *Sep* sulph **Verat**
- **in** bed:
  - **agg.**: *Alum* k* am-m k* ambr bg2 ang k* ant-c b7.de* ant-t bg2 aphis br1 ars k* ars-i ars-s-f k2 asar k* bell b4.de* beryl tpw5 bry k* bufo k* **Calc** k* calc-i k2 *Camph* caps carb-an bg2 carb-v bg2 caust b4a.de* *Cham* k* chin b7.de* cop a1 dirc k* dulc k* eug **Euph** b4a.de* **Ferr** k* ferr-ar ferr-i *Hell* k* hep bg2* iod kali-ar kali-c k* kali-n k* lyc k* mag-c bg2 **Meny** bg2* *Merc* k* *Mur-ac* k* nat-ar nat-c *Nit-ac* k* nux-v k* op bg2 ph-ac bg2 phos k* plb podo fd3.de• *Puls* b7a.de* ran-b bg2 *Rhus-t* k* **Ruta** b7a.de* sabad b7.de* *Samb* k* sars bg2 *Sel* k* sep k* sil bg2* sol-ni staph b7.de* sul-i k2 *Sulph* k* tarax b7.de* thuj bg2 tritic-vg fd5.de valer b7.de* verat k*
    - **warm** bathing; after: lat-m bnm6•

BEGINNING in: | **Face**: *Samb* bg2

BLOODY: *Anag* kr1 arn k* ars bg2* calc k* cann-i sf1.de cann-xyz bg2 cantha *Carb-v* b4a.de* cham k* chin k* clem k* cocc hr1* **Crot-h** k* *Cur* k* dulc b4a.de* graph mtf33 hell bg2* **Lach** k* *Lyc* k* *Nux-m* k* *Nux-v* k* petr phos bg2* sulph mtf33
- **night**: *Cur*

BREAKFAST agg.; after: *Carb-v* k* grat k*

BURNING: merc k* *Mez* k* **Nat-c** k* verat k*

CLAMMY: abies-c br1 absin a1 acet-ac k* acon k* act-sp hr1* aeth br1* agar bg2* aloe bg2* am-c b2.de* aml-ns anac k* ant-c k* *Ant-t* k* apis apoc hr1 arge-pl rwt5• arn k* **Ars** k* ars-s-f k2 atra-r bnm3• ben-n a1 both fne1• brom k* *Bry* b2.de* *Calc* k* **Camph** k* canth k* carb-ac bg2* carb-an k* carb-v k* carbn-h a1 caust hr1 *Cench* a1* **Cham** k* chin k* chin-b hr1 chlor hr1 cimic k* cocc k* coff coff-t a1* colch k* coloc b4a.de* *Corn* k* corn-f br1 corv-cor bdg• *Crot-c* k* crot-h crot-t a1* cub a1* cupr k* *Cupr-ar* a1* daph k* dig k* elat fago k* falco-pe nl2• **Ferr** k* **Ferr-ar** *Ferr-i* ferr-m a1 **Ferr-p** k* *Fl-ac* k* gast a1 glon k* guat sp1 *Hell* k* *Hep* k* hydr a1 hydr-ac a1* hydrog srj2• hyos k* iod k* jatr-c k* kali-bi bg2 kali-br hr1 kali-cy a1 kali-n a1 kali-ox a1 lach k* lachn lat-m bnm6• lil-t bg2* limen-b-c hrn2* lob a1 lup br1 **Lyc** k* lyss hr1* med jl2 **Merc** k* *Merc-c* k* merc-pr-r a1 merc-sul a1 mez k* morph k* *Mosch* k* mur-ac a1 *Naja* bg2* napht a1 nat-m bg2 nat-sil k2 *Nux-v* k* op k* ox-ac k* oxyurn-sc mcp1• **Ph-ac** k* phal c1 **Phos** k* phys a1 pic-ac hr1 *Plb* k* *Psor* k* pyrog tl1 rauw jl sabin hr1 *Sec* k* sil hr1 sol-t a1 *Spig* k* *Spong* k* stann k* stram a1 stry a1 *Sul-ac* k* sul-i k2 sulph a1 sumb k* **Tab** bg2* tanac a1 ter k* trach a1 *Tub* k* **Verat** k* *Verat-v* ptk1 vip k* wies a1 zinc zinc-m a1 zinc-s a1
- **right** side of body: haliae-lc srj5•
- **morning**: mosch k*
- **evening**: clem k* limen-b-c hrn2* sumb k*
- **night**: cupr fago k* hep k* *Lyc* kr1 *Merc* kr1 ox-ac hr1
  - **sleep**; during: hydrog srj2•
- **bed** agg.; in: plb kr1
- **menopause**; during: *Crot-h* st *Lach* st *Lyc* st *Sul-ac* st *Ter* st
- **sleep**; on going to: daph kr1
- **starting** from sleep, with: daph k*

CLOSING THE EYES; on: bell bg2 *Bry* k* calc k* carb-an k* caust bg2 chin bg2 **Con** k* graph bg2 *Lach* k* mag-m bg2 puls bg2 sanic tl1 sep bg2 sulph bg2 thuj k*

CLOTHS; as from wet: tub bg2 verat-v bg2

COFFEE agg.: cham b7.de

Perspiration

COITION; after: *Agar* k* *Calc* chin *Eug* k* **Graph** k* nat-c k* sel **Sep** k*

COLD: abies-c bro1 acet-ac k* *Acon* k* act-sp k* aeth k* *Agar* k* agar-ph a1 ail k* alco a1 aloe bg2* alumn a1* **Am-c** k* am-caust a1 ambr b2.de* *Aml-ns* bro1 *Anac* k* ang b2.de anh sp1 ant-ar bro1 *Ant-c* k* **Ant-t** k* *Anthraci* apis apoc hr1 aran jl arg-n hr1 *Arn* k* **Ars** k* ars-i ars-s-f k2 asaf b2.de* aur bg2 *Aur-m* k* bar-c k* bar-m k* bar-s k2 bell k* benz-ac k* bol-lu a1 both bros-gau mrc1 *Bry* k* *Bufo* k* buth-a sp1 cact k2* cadm-s k2 caj a1 calad k* *Calc* k* calc-i k2 calc-p bg2* calc-s calc-sil k2 **Camph** k* *Cann-i* a1* cann-s k* canth k* caps k* *Carb-ac* k* **Carb-v** k* *Carbn-s* castm ptk1 *Cench* st cent a1 cham k* **Chin** k* **Chinin-ar** chlol hr1* *Chlor* k* cimic k* *Cina* k* *Cist* k* cit-ac rly4• **Cocc** k* coff k* coff-t a1 colch k2* coloc k* con bg2 convo-s jl* corn k* corn-f bro1 croc k* *Crot-c* crot-h k* cupr k* *Cupr-act* a1* *Cupr-ar* kr1* cupr-s hr1 *Cur* k* cyt-l jl* dendr-pol sk4• dig k* digin a1 *Dios* hr1 *Dros* k* dulc k* *Elaps* k* ephe-si hsj1• esp-g kk1.de *Euph* b2.de* euph-l bro1 euphr **Ferr** k* *Ferr-ar* *Ferr-i* ferr-p bg2 formal bro1 frag a1 gels k* gink-b sbd1• *Glon* hr1 *Graph* b2.de* *Ham* hr1 *Hell* k* **Hep** k* hura *Hydr* kr1 *Hydr-ac* bg2* hydrog srj2• *Hyos* k* *Ign* k* iod k* **Ip** k* jatr-c k* kali-ar kali-bi bg2* *Kali-c* k2* kali-cy a1 kali-n kali-p bg2* kalm k* kola stb3• (non:lac-ac hr1) lac-c k* *Lach* k* lachn k* lat-m bnm6• laur k* lil-t bg2* *Lob* k* lol a1 lon-x br1 lup bro1 **Lyc** k* lyss hr1 m-ambo b2.de* *M-arct* b2.de* mag-m b2.de manc k* mang b2.de* med hr1* *Merc* k* **Merc-c** k* *Merc-cy* hr1* merc-pr-r a1 *Mez* k* morph mur-ac k* *Naja* bg2 narc-ps c1* narcot a1 *Nat-ar* *Nat-c* k* nat-f sp1 nat-m nat-p nit-ac k* *Nux-v* k* op k* ox-ac k* paeon hr1* pareir hr1 penic srb2.fr *Petr* k* *Ph-ac* b2.de* phase-vg a1 *Phos* k* pic-ac hr1 plan plb k* podo k* *Psor* *Puls* k* pyrog k* ran-s bg2 *Rheum* b2.de* rhus-t k* *Rob* hr1 *Ruta* k* sabad b2.de* sang k* sanic bro1* **Sec** k* seneg k* **Sep** k* sil k* *Spig* k* *Spong* k* squil b2.de stann k* *Staph* k* *Stram* k* suis-em rly4• sul-ac k* sul-i k2 sulo-ac jl *Sulph* k* sumb *Tab* k* tela bro1 ter k* tere-ch jl thea a1 *Ther* k* *Thuj* k* *Tub* k* vanil fd5.de **Verat** k* **Verat-v** k* vip k* vip-a jl wye a1 zinc k* zinc-p k2

- **morning**: *Ant-c* canth chin esp-g kk1.de euph k* ruta vanil fd5.de
  - • **rising** from bed: bry a1
- **afternoon**: des-ac rbp6 **Gels** phos verat-v
- **evening**: anac hura phos a1 seneg hr1 spong fd4.de
  - • **18** h: psor
- **night**: am-c bros-gau mrc1 buth-a jl chin cit-ac rly4• coloc croc k* cupr k* cur k* *Dig* k* fago iod lob mang h2 op plut-n srj7• rhus-t **Sep** spong fd4.de suis-em rly4• thuj
- **accompanied** by:
  - • **palpitation** (See CHEST - Palpitation - accompanied - perspiration)
  - • **vomiting** (See STOMACH - Vomiting - accompanied - perspiration - cold)
- **air**; perspiration in cold: ars k* **Bry** k* **Calc** k* carb-an k* caust bg2 chin bg2 guaj bg2 hep bg2 kali-c bg2 *Lyc* k* nux-v bg2 rhus-t bg2 sep k* verat k*
- **amel.**: nux-v k*
- **anguish**; with great: cact br1
- **anxiety**; from: hydrog srj2• vanil fd5.de
  - • **waking**; on: hydrog srj2•
- **cigar**; after: op a1
- **clammy** sweats with: lat-h bnm5• verat-v tl1
  - • **accompanied** by | **Lumbar** region; pain in (See BACK - Pain - lumbar - accompanied - perspiration)
  - • **chill**: corn cupr hr1* lyss kr1 **Verat** kr1
  - • **hemorrhage**: **Chin** k*
- **coffee**; after: digin a1
- **convulsions**, during: camph k2* *Cupr* hr1* *Ferr* k* stram k* *Verat* hr1*
- **cough**:
  - • **after**: dros ptk1
  - • **during** (See COUGH - Accompanied - perspiration)
- **delirium** | **after** loquacious delirium: cupr ptk1
- **diarrhea**; in: aeth kr1 aloe sne ant-t kr1 *Ars* kr1 calc kr1 *Camph* kr1 cupr kr1 graph ptk hell kr1 jatr-c kr1 pic-ac kr1 *Sec* kr1 *Sil* kr1 sulph kr1 *Tab* kr1 ter kr1 *Verat* kr1
- **dysmenorrhea**; in: *Sars* kr1 *Verat* kr1
- **eating**: **Merc** k*
  - • **after**: digin a1 sang hr1 sul-ac k*
- **exertion** of body or mind; after the slightest: act-sp *Calc* **Hep** k* kali-c mtf33 nat-sil mtf33 **Sep** k*

Cold: ...

- **fear**; with (See MIND - Fear - perspiration - cold)
- **fever**; during: ip b7.de verat b7.de*
- **headache**:
  - • **after**: gels a1
  - • **with**: **Gels** hr1* graph k* ruta fd4.de *Verat* kr1
- **heat**; with sensation of internal: anac jl bros-gau mrc1 til ban1•
- **icy**: tab bg2
- **lying**: thea a1
- **mania**; during (See MIND - Mania - perspiration)
- **menses**:
  - • **before**: mang b4.de *Thuj* b4a.de
  - • **during**: ars coff phos *Sars* k* *Sec* **Verat** k*
- **motion**, on: ant-c k* des-ac rbp6 sep
- **nausea**; with: ant-t ptk1 *Calc* kr1 *Ip* kr1 *Lach* kr1 lob ptk1 **Petr** kr1* ruta fd4.de *Tab* kr1 *Verat* kr1* verat-v kr1
  - • **and** vertigo: ail vanil fd5.de
- **nightmare** | **waking** from; on: hydrog srj2• suis-em rly4•
- **over** the body, warm perspiration on the palms: *Dig*
- **perspiration** increases the coldness of the body (See CHILL - Perspiration - more)
- **sensation** as if: glon bg2
- **sleep**; during: brass-n-o srj5•
- **stool**, during: *Ars* b4a.de *Dulc* b4a.de merc k* plb ptk1 sulph k* thuj verat
- **sudden** attacks of perspiration: *Crot-h* k* tab ptk1
- **terminal** patients; in: ant-t mrr1
- **urination**, after: bell k*
- **vertigo**; with: ail kr1 ign b7.de* *Merc-c* kr1 ther kr1 thuj b4a.de vanil fd5.de verat b7.de*
- **vomiting**; with (See STOMACH - Vomiting - accompanied - perspiration - cold)
- **waking**; on: carb-v k2 vanil fd5.de
- **walking**: rhus-t a1
  - • **air**; in cold open: rhus-t h1

COLDNESS:

- **after**: aml-ns carbn-s corn k* kali-cy k* mela a1 mur-ac k* ol-j a1 petr senec k* sil sulph k* thuj k*
- **during**: *Arg-n* k* cit-ac rly4• gels hydrog srj2• lachn k* psor k* *Puls* raph k* **Verat** verat-v a1 [nat-sil stj2]

O - **Hands**; with coldness of nit-ac h2

- **Legs**; with coldness of: calc h2

COLIC, during: mez k* nux-v plan k* plb k* sulph

COLLIQUATIVE: acet-ac agar ptk1 **Ant-t** k* *Ars* *Ars-h* kr1 asc-t ptk1 camph *Carb-v* **Chin** k* crat br1 **Eupi** ferr c1 *Iod* kr1 *Jab* kr1* *Lach* *Lyc* mill k* *Nit-ac* k* op a1 *Psor* k* *Sec* k* verat-v a1

COMA; with (See MIND - Coma - perspiration)

COMPANY agg.: thuj ptk1

CONVERSATION, from: *Ambr* k*

CONVULSIONS:

- **after**: acon ars k* art-v c1 *Bry* kr1 calc hr1 cedr cupr k* *Ferr* b7a.de* ign b7a.de* mag-c bg2 *Olnd* b7a.de plb bg2* sec k* *Sil* bg2* stram b7a.de* stry k*
  - • **epileptic**: *Cupr* b7a.de plb b7a.de
- **before**: *Merc* b4a.de
- **during**: ars k* art-v hr1* atro a1 *Bell* k* **Bufo** k* camph k* carb-an bg2 *Merc* b4a.de nux-v k* op k* plb a1 sep k* stram k2 verat b7a.de

COPIOUS (See Profuse)

CORYZA; during: ars bg2 *Calc* bg2 cham bg2 kali-c bg2 lyc bg2 **Merc** b4a.de* nat-m bg2 *Sil* bg2

COUGH:

- **after**: brom bg2 sep bg2
- **agg.**: acon k* agar k2* ant-c k* ant-t k* apis arg-n **Ars** k* ars-h sne ars-s-f k2 bell k* brom k* bry k* *Calc* k* calc-s ptk1 calc-sil k2 caps k* carb-an *Carb-v* k* carbn-s *Caust* *Cham* chin k* chinin-ar cimx dig k* *Dros* k* eug eupi k* *Ferr* ferr-ar guare k* **Hep** k* *Ip* k* irid-met srj5• kali-bi tl1 kali-c k* *Kali-n* k* lach lyc k* *Merc* k* nat-ar nat-c k* nat-m k* nat-p nit-ac k2 *Nux-v* k* ph-ac k* **Phos** k* psor

- **agg.**: ...
puls *Rhus-t* k* *Sabad* k* **Samb** k* sel k* seneg **Sep** k* sil *Spong* k* squil sulph k* tab *Thuj* tub dp* *Verat* k*
  - **night**: chin dig eug kali-bi lyc *Merc* nat-c nit-ac k* psor sulph
- **during**:
  - **agg.** | **paroxysms** of cough end with perspiration: ars brom *Ign*

COVERED: | **wants** to be; yet: aeth c1* chin bro1 hep bro1

CRITICAL: *Acon* sf1.de bapt bell sf1.de bry *Canth* sf1.de chlor pneu sf1.de *Pyrog* k* rhus-t sf1.de

DEBILITATING: *(↗Profuse - debilitating; GENERALS - Weakness; GENERALS - Weakness - perspiration - from)* bry ptk1 calc-p ptk1 camph ptk1 carb-an ptk1 chin ptk1 chinin-s ptk1 ferr ptk1 **Iod** ptk1* merc ptk1 nit-ac ptk1 phos ptk1 psor ptk1 **Samb** ptk1* sep ptk1 tub ptk1
- **delivery**; after: samb ptk1
- **fever**; after: castm ptk1
- **foul**: croc ptk1
- **injuries** of spine; from: nit-ac ptk1

DELIVERY: | **after**: **Acon** bg2 **Bry** bg2 calc k2 cham bro1 *Chin* bg2 kali-c bro1 samb bro1 stram bro1 sulph bg2 verat bg2

DESCENDING agg.: sep k*

DIARRHEA:
- **after** (See RECTUM - Diarrhea - followed - perspiration)
- **during**: *Acon* k* aloe sne asc-t ptk1* bac jl2 bry k2 con k* sulph k* tub tl1* **Verat** k*

DINNER; after: *Carb-an* dig k* mag-m k* phos k* ptel k* sep k* thuj k*

DREAMING; while: led b7.de*

DRINKING:
- **after** | **agg.**: aloe k* ars k* carb-v bro1 castm cham k* chin k* *Cocc* con k* ferr bg2 hep bg2 kali-c bro1 kali-p malar jl2 *Merc* k* phos bg2 *Puls* k* rhod bg2 rhus-t k* *Sel* k* sil bg2 stram b7.de* sulph k* sumb k* tarax bg2 *Verat* bg2
- **agg.**: con b4.de
- **amel.**: *Caust Chinin-s* cupr nux-v *Phos* sil thuj
- **cold** drinks | **agg.** (See GENERALS - Food and - cold drink - agg. - perspiring)
- **warm** drinks | **agg.**: bry k* kali-c k* mag-c k2 *Merc* k* phos k* *Rhus-t* a1 sil k2 spong fd4.de sul-ac k* sumb a1 tritic-vg fd5.de
- **water** | **amel.**: apis bg2 bry bg2 **Caust** bg2 *Cupr* bg2 ip bg2 *Nux-v* bg2 *Op* bg2 *Phos* bg2 puls bg2 sep bg2 *Sil* bg2 spig bg2 tarax bg2 thuj bg2

DYSPNEA, with: *(↗RESPIRATION - Difficult - perspiration)* anac *Ant-t* antip vh apis **Ars** k* arund k* brom tl1 **Carb-v** k* kali-s gg6 *Lach* lyc mang samb gg6 sil spong fd4.de sulph k* thuj verat

EASILY; perspires (See Exertion - agg. - slight)

EATING:
- **after**:
  - **agg.**: alum bg2 am-c hr1 arg-met ars k* bar-c hr1 benz-ac bg2* borx b4a.de* **Bry** k* **Calc** k* calc-sil k2 **Carb-an** k* **Carb-v** k* **Carbn-s** castm bg2 *Caust* k* *Cham* k* chin bg2 con k* *Crot-c* k* crot-h ferr ferr-ar graph k* guare a1* *Kali-c* k* kali-sil k2 *Laur* k* *Lyc* k* nat-c bg2 nat-m k* **Nit-ac** k* *Nux-v* k* par b7.de* petr k* ph-ac k* **Phos** k* psor rhus-t bg2 sel k* **Sep** k* *Sil* k* sul-ac bg2* **Sulph** k* thuj k* verat bg2 *Viol-t* k*
  - **amel.**: alum k* *Anac Chin* k* cupr bg2 cur *Ferr* k* fl-ac bg2* ign bg2 kali-c bg2 **Lach** *Nat-c* k* nit-ac tl1 petr bg2 *Phos* k* *Rhus-t* k* sep k* verat k*
- **amel.**: ignis-alc es2• lach ptk1
- **while**:
  - **agg.**: am-c bg2 ant-t k* arg-met ars k* ars-s-f k2 bamb-a stb2.de• *Bar-c* k* bar-s k2 *Benz-ac* k* borx bry k* *Calc* k* calc-sil k2 **Carb-an** k* **Carb-v** k* **Carbn-s** caust bg2 cham bg2 cocc *Con* k* eupi c1 graph k* guare k* hep bg2 ign k* kali-ar kali-bi gk **Kali-c** k* *Kali-p* k* kali-sil k2 laur bg2 lyc bg2 mag-m b4.de* **Merc** k* nat-c k* *Nat-m* k* **Nit-ac** k* nux-v k* ol-an k* phos k* psor al2 *Puls* k* ruta fd4.de sars k* **Sep** k* sil k* spig bg2 sul-ac k* teucr bg2 tritic-vg fd5.de valer k* viol-t k* vip fkr4.de
    - ⁝ **anxiety** and cold perspiration: **Merc**
  - **amel.**: anac k* *Ign* k* lach k* mez k* **Phos** k* zinc k*

EMISSIONS agg.; after: *Calc* nat-m bg2 phys ptk1 puls rhus-t ptk1 *Sep* k* sulph

EXCITEMENT; after: ars-s-f k2 bamb-a stb2.de• bar-c k* graph lach k2 *Tarent* a1 tritic-vg fd5.de

EXCORIATING: coff bg2 **Fl-ac** bg2 graph bg2 *Hell* bg2 iod bg2 lyc bg2 nat-m bg2 *Nit-ac* bg2 ran-b bg2 rhus-t bg2 sil bg2 zinc bg2

EXERTION:
- **after**:
  - **agg.**: *Brom* b4a.de calc mrr1 calc-f sp1 nat-sil fd3.de• *Sep* bg2 sul-ac bg2 tub jl2
    - ⁝ **Front** part of body; often only in: agar k1
  - **amel.**: agar bry *Ign* bg2 polyg-h polyg-pe vml2• sep k* stann bg2
- **agg.**:
  - **air**; in open: *Bry* calc carb-an caust *Chin*
  - **slight** exertion: *(↗Profuse - exertion - slight; Walking - agg.)* acon k* aeth k* **Agar** k* alum-p k2 am-c bg2 am-m bg2 ambr k* aml-ns k* anac b2.de* ant-c k2* *Ant-t* b2.de* *Ars* k* **Ars-i** ars-s-f k2 asar k* bamb-a stb2.de• bapt bell k* benz-ac berb borx bg2 *Brom* k* *Bry* k* bufo bg2 but-ac br1* **Calc** k* *Calc-i* k2 calc-p bg2 **Calc-s** k* calc-sil k2 camph canth k* caps carb-an k* carb-v k* *Carbn-s* caust k* cham bg2 *Chel* **Chin** k* *Chinin-ar* chinin-s cinnb k* *Cist Cocc* k* coloc b2.de* con b2.de* corn *Cupr* dulc b2.de* eup-pur bro1 *Eupi* k* **Ferr** k* ferr-ar **Ferr-i** *Ferr-m* ferr-p fl-ac bg2 *Gels* k* gink-b sbd1• **Graph** k* guaj b2.de* ham fd3.de• *Hep* k* *Hyos* bg2 ign b2.de* **Iod** k* *Ip* b2.de* *Jab* ptk1 kali-ar **Kali-c** k* kali-n k* **Kali-p** *Kali-s* k* kali-sil k2 kreos k* lach k* lap-la sde8.de• led k* **Lyc** k* mag-c k* mag-m b2.de* malar jl2 med ptk1* meph bg2 *Merc* k* merc-c bro1 merc-cy ptk1 *Nat-ar* **Nat-c** k* *Nat-m* k* nat-n bg2 *Nat-p* **Nat-s** nat-sil fd3.de• **Nit-ac** k* nux-v b2.de* op k* ox-ac ptk1 ozone sde2• petr b2.de* **Ph-ac** b2.de* **Phos** k* phyt plut-n srj7• podo fd3.de• **Psor** k* **Puls** b2.de* rheum k* *Rhod* b2.de* **Rhus-t** k* ruta fd4.de sabad k* samb ptk1 sars b2.de* sel k* seneg b2.de* **Sep** k* *Sil* k* spig k* spong b2.de* stann k* **Staph** b2.de* *Stram* b2.de* sul-ac k* sul-i k2 **Sulph** k* tab thuj k* tritic-vg fd5.de **Tub** al2* valer k* verat k* yohim vml4 **Zinc** b2.de* [alumin-s stj2 aur-m stj2 aur-s stj2 cadm-m stj2 cadm-s stj2 chr-s stj2 gal-s stj2 lith-s stj2 mang-p stj2 mang-s stj2 merc-d stj2 nicc-s stj2 spect dfg1 tell stj2 titan-s stj2]
    - ⁝ **daytime**: agar b4a.de anac b4a.de bell b4a.de *Calc* b4a.de *Carb-an* b4a.de *Dulc* b4a.de *Graph* b4a.de guaj b4a.de **Hep** b4a.de **Kali-c** b4a.de *Lyc* b4a.de merc b4a.de *Nat-c* b4a.de *Nat-m* b4a.de nit-ac b4a.de ph-ac b4a.de *Sep* b4a.de sil b4a.de sul-ac b4a.de *Sulph* b4a.de *Zinc* b4a.de

EXHAUSTING: *(↗GENERALS - Weakness - perspiration - from)*
- **not** exhausting: *Ars* bg2 *Bov* bg2 bry bg2 *Calad* b7.de* calc bg2 carb-an b4.de* cic b7.de* *Coloc* bg2 **Cupr** bg2 hell bg2 **Lyc** bg2 m-ambo b7.de nat-c bg2 *Phos* bg2 **Puls** bg2 **Rhus-t** b7.de* sep b4.de* *Spig* bg2 tarax b7.de* **Thuj** bg2

FACE, of the whole body except the (See FACE - Perspiration - except)

FEET, except (See EXTREMITIES - Perspiration - foot - except)

FEVER:
- **after**: ant-t k* **Ars** k* *Bell* k* bov k* bry k* *Calad* k* calc k* *Caps* hr1 carb-v k* cassia-s cdd7• *Chin* k* *Chinin-ar Chinin-s* coloc k* *Cupr* k* *Ferr* ferr-p k2 *Gels* k* glon k* graph hell k* *Hep* k* kali-n *Lach* k* *Lyc* k* merc ptk1 nat-ar nat-c k* nat-m k* *Nat-s Nux-v* k* ol-j a1 op ptk1 ph-ac ptk1 *Phos* k* *Puls* k* pyrog ptk1 *Rhus-t* k* *Sil* hr1 spig k* spong h1 stram ptk1 sulph ptk1 tab k* thuj k* tub ptk1* verat-v ptk1 *Zinc* k*
  - **hectic** fever: stront-c bg2
- **before**: caps b7a.de chin b7a.de nux-v b7a.de samb b7a.de
- **during** (See FEVER - Perspiration - heat)

FLATUS, when passing: *(↗FACE - Perspiration - flatus)* kali-bi k*

FLIES, attracting the: bry bg2* *Calad* k* puls k* sep bg2 sumb thuj k*

FOLLOWED BY: | **vomiting**: sulph h2

Perspiration

FOOD: | **warm** agg. (See Warm - food - after)

FOREHEAD; general perspiration except (See HEAD - Perspiration of - forehead - except)

FRIGHT agg.: *(↗MIND - Ailments - fright)* acon bg2 *Anac* k* bamb-a stb2.de• *Bell* k* gels lyc k* **Op** k* psor al2 sil sulph bg2

HEAD; general perspiration except (See HEAD - Perspiration of - except)

HEADACHE:
- **after**: asc-c c1
- **during** (See HEAD - Pain - perspiration - with)

HOT: *(↗Warm - hot - exertion)* **Acon** k* *Aesc* k* am-m b2.de aml-ns bg2* anac bg2 ange-s oss1• ant-c b2.de* aphis br1* asar bg2 asc-t k* aur bg2* *Bell* k* bism bg2* bry k* calc k* calc-sil k2 camph b2.de* canth b2.de* *Caps* b2.de* *Carb-v* k* **Cham** k* chel chin k* cina b2.de cocc *Coff* bg2* colch rsj2• **Con** k* corn k* dig k* dros b2.de* *Hell* b2.de* hep b2.de hydrog srj2• **Ign** k* ignis-alc es2• **Ip** k* kreos bg2 lach bg2* led b2.de* lyc bg2* *Merc* b2.de* merc-i-r k* nat-c k* **Nux-v** k* **Op** k* par b2.de* penic srb2.fr *Ph-ac* b2.de* phos k* pip-n bg2 plb b2.de plut-n srj7• **Psor** k* puls k* pycnop-sa mrz1 *Pyrog* rauw sp1 *Rhus-t* b2.de* sabad k* sang ptk1 **Sep** k* sil k* spig b2.de spong b2.de *Stann* k* staph k* *Stram* k* *Sulph* k* tarax b2.de thuj k* til bro1* valer b2.de verat k* verat-v bro1 viol-t k* [spect dfg1]
- **accompanied** by | **Mammae**; tumors of the (See CHEST - Tumors - mammae - accompanied - perspiration)
- **exertion**; from (See Warm - hot - exertion)
- **fever**; during: glon ptk1 tub jl2
- **lower** limbs, except: op pd*

INCREASING AND DECREASING SUDDENLY (See Intermittent)

INSANITY; attacks of: | **after**: *Cupr* b7.de*

INTERMITTENT: ant-c bell chin k2 coloc cupr-ar ferr kali-n nux-v *Sep* sil

LONG-LASTING: am-c am-m anthraco *Ars* **Caust** k* cimx con cupr k* dulc h2 **Ferr** k* *Ferr-ar Gels* **Hep** k* lach bg2 *Led* merc bg2* **Samb** k* *Verat*
- **apyrexia**; continuing through: *Verat*

LOWER LIMBS, except (See EXTREMITIES - Perspiration - lower - except)

LUMINOUS: phos b4.de*

LYING:
- **agg.**: ars k* bry b7.de* *Caps* k* cham bg2 chel k* **Ferr** k* ferr-ar ham k* hep k* hyos bg2 lyc k* *Mag-s* **Meny** k* merc nat-c bg2 op k* ph-ac bg2 podo puls rhod bg2 **Rhus-t** k* **Samb** k* *Sep* k* sil bg2 tarax k* tarent k* valer bg2
- **bed**; in | **amel.**: ars bg2 **Bell** bg2 **Bry** bg2 calc bg2 caust bg2 con bg2 hep bg2 kali-c bg2 lach bg2 lyc bg2 **Nux-v** bg2 rhus-t bg2 sil bg2 squil bg2 staph bg2 *Stram* bg2 sulph bg2
- **side**; on:
  - **right** | **agg.**: *Lach* bg2*

LYING DOWN agg.: ars bg2 asar b7.de* con bg2 lyc bg2 **Meny** b7.de* *Merc* bg2 *Puls* b7a.de* rhus-t bg2 samb bg2 sel bg2 *Tarax* b7.de* verat b7a.de*

MENOPAUSE; during: bell bg2 *Calc* bg2 hep bro1 jab bg2* lach bg2 nux-v bg2 sep bg2 **Sul-ac** bg2 til bro1 valer bg2

MENSES:
- **after** | **agg.**: med jl2 ph-ac h2 *Sep* bg2
- **before** | **agg.**: bar-c bg2 bell k* borx bg2 bov bg2 calc k* dulc fd4.de *Graph* k* *Hyos* k* kola stb3• lyc bg2 mang bg2 nat-s phos sep bg2 *Sulph* k* *Thuj* k* **Verat** k*
- **during**:
  - **agg.**: agar k* ars asar k* bell k* *Borx* k* bry bg2 calc bg2 *Caust* k* cham bg2 chin bg2 coc-c bg2 coff k* *Graph* k* *Hyos* k* kali-c k* kola stb3• kreos k* lyc bg2 mag-c k* *Mag-m* k* murx k* nat-s bg2 nux-v ptk1 phos bg2 sec k* *Sep* k* sil bg2 sulph k* tritic-vg fd5.de **Verat** k* wies a1
  - **beginning** of menses | **agg.**: acon bg2 caust bg2 cham bg2 *Hyos* b7.de* *Phos* bg2 sep bg2 verat bg2

MENTAL EXERTION:
- **agg.**: act-sp aur h2 bell k* borx k* **Calc** k* calc-sil k2 graph k* **Hep** k* hyos k* *Kali-c* k* kali-p fd1.de* **Lach** k* lyc k* nat-m k* nux-v k* phos pip-n bg2 *Psor* **Sep** k* sil k* **Staph** k* *Sulph* k* tub k*
- **amel.**: ferr k* nat-c k*

MENTAL SHOCK; after: anac bro1 sep bro1

MOTION:
- **after** | **agg.**: agar bg2 *Ars* bg2 carb-v bg2 caust bg2 hyos bg2 kali-c bg2 **Rhus-t** bg2 **Sep** b4a.de* stann bg2 stram bg2 *Sul-ac* b4a.de* *Valer* bg2
- **agg.**: acon bg2 agar k* alum k* alum-sil k2 am-m k* *Ambr* k* anac k* ant-c ant-t k* *Ars* k* ars-i ars-s-f k2 arund k* asar bg2 bar-c bg2 bell k* beryl tpw5 **Brom** b4a.de* **Bry** k* **Calc** k* calc-i k2 calc-sil k2 camph canth k* *Carb-an* k* carb-v k* **Carbn-s** *Caust* k* cham k* **Chin** k* chinin-ar *Chinin-s* clem a1 *Cocc* k* cur dulc bg2 **Ferr** k* ferr-ar ferr-i *Fl-ac* b4a.de* gels k* gran a1 **Graph** k* guaj bg2 **Hep** k* iod k* ip k* kali-ar *Kali-bi* **Kali-c** k* *Kali-n* b4a.de* kali-sil k2 lach b7.de* *Led* b7.de* lil-s a1 **Lyc** b4.de* mag-c k* mag-m k* **Merc** k* merc-c ptk1 nat-ar *Nat-c* k* *Nat-m* k* *Nit-ac* k* **Nux-v** k* op b7.de* petr bg2 ph-ac bg2 phos k* **Psor** k* puls k* *Rheum* b7.de* rhod bg2 rhus-t bg2 sabad bg2 samb bg2 *Sel* k* **Sep** k* sil k* spig b7.de* **Stann** k* staph bg2 *Stram* k* sul-ac k* sul-i k2 **Sulph** k* thuj k* *Valer* b7.de* **Verat** k* *Zinc* k*
- **amel.**: anac bg2 *Ars* k* asar bg2 bell bg2 calc bg2 **Caps** k* con k* cycl bg2 dulc bg2 ferr k* lyc bg2 **Merc** k* ph-ac bg2 *Puls* k* **Rhus-t** k* sabad k* **Samb** k* sel bg2 sep k* sil bg2 spong bg2 *Sul-ac* k* sulph k* tarax bg2 thuj k* *Valer* k* verat k*
  - **disappears** and heat comes on; on making any motion, perspiration: *Lyc* k*
- **brings** on chilliness: eup-per k* eup-pur k* hep **Nux-v** psor *Tub*

MUSIC agg.: sabin kr1 tarent c1*

NAUSEA; with (See STOMACH - Nausea - accompanied - perspiration)

NERVOUS: jab ptk1 rhus-t ptk1 sep ptk1 [zirc-met stj2]

NEVER perspiring (See Absent)

NEWS, from unpleasant: *(↗MIND - Ailments - bad)* calc-p k*

NO PERSPIRATION (See Absent)

OCCUPATION, during: berb

ODOR:
- **acrid**: *(↗pungent)* lac-leo hm2•
- **aromatic**: all-c bg2 benz-ac k* guare k* petr bg2 rhod k* sep bg2 urt-u bg2
- **bathing**; after: nat-ox rly4•
- **bitter**: dig bg2 *Verat* b2.de*
  - **morning**: verat
- **blood**: *Lyc* k*
- **bread**; white: ign b7a.de*
- **burnt**: **Bell** b2.de* *Bry* b7a.de* m-ambo b2.de* mag-c bg2 sulph k* thuj b4a.de*
- **cadaverous** like carrion: *Ars* art-v lach alj* *Psor* kr1* pyrog k2* thuj k*
- **camphor**: camph b2.de*
- **cheesy**: con bg2 *Hep* k* phos ptk1 plb k* sanic ptk1 sep ptk1 sulph k*
- **coffee**; like fresh: bamb-a stb2.de•
- **drugs**, like corresponding: asaf k* ben camph k* carbn-h chen-a a1 chinin-ar a1 iod k* ol-an a1 phos sulph k* tab k* ter a1 valer k*
- **eggs**; spoiled: plb fse1.de staph k* sulph k*
- **elder**-blossoms: *Sep* k*
- **fecal** before stool: sacch-l bg2*
- **fetid**: aesc k* all-s kr1 aloe kr1 am-c k* am-m bg2 ambr kr1 anac aq-mar jl arn k* *Ars* b2.de* art-v bro1 aur-m kr1 *Bapt* bg2* **Bar-c** b2.de* bell bg2 bov bg2* *But-ac* bro1 calc bro1 *Canth* b2.de* *Carb-ac* carb-an k* *Carb-v* b4a.de* cass a1 cimic kr1 cimx bro1 coloc bg2 con k* crot-h bg2* *Cycl* b2.de* *Daph* br1* dios bg2 *Dulc* k* *Euphr* b2.de* ferr k* fl-ac b4a.de* **Graph** b2.de* *Guaj* b2.de* **Hep** k* *Kali-c* b2.de* kali-i bro1 *Kali-p* bg2* lac-c bg2* lach bg2 led k* lyc k* m-arct b2.de* *Mag-c* b2.de* mag-m bg2* med c1* *Merc* k* merc-c b4a.de* **Nit-ac** b2.de* **Nux-v** b2.de* ol-an bro1 osm bro1 *Petr* bg2* **Phos** b2.de* plb bg2 *Psor* k* **Puls** b2.de* pyrog k* *Rhod* b2.de* *Rhus-t* b2.de* rob samb xxb1 **Sel** bg2 *Sep* b2.de* **Sil** b2.de* sol-t bro1 spig b2.de* spong fd4.de stann bro1 **Staph** b2.de* stram bg2* sulph b2.de* *Tax* bro1 tell thuj k* tritic-vg fd5.de *Tub* vanil fd5.de vario kr1* *Verat* b2.de* zinc k*
  - **coughing**, after: *Hep*

- **fetid**: ...
  - **eruptions**, with: *Dulc* med c1
- **fishy**: calc ptk1 graph ptk1 med ptk1* ol-an ptk1 sanic ptk1 sep ptk1 tell ptk1 thuj ptk1
- **garlic**: *Art-v* bg2* asaf vh bov ptk1 kalag br1 kali-p ptk1 lach kr1* lyc ptk1 phos mtf33 sulph st thuj k2* [*Tell* stj2]
- **herring**; pickled: vario st
- **honey**: thuj k*
- **leek**: thuj st
- **lilac**: sep
- **mice**: canth mgm• sil ptk1 tub st
- **musk**: *Apis* k* bism bg2 ger-i rly4• mosch k* puls k* *Sulph* k* sumb
- **musty**: arn *Cimx* k* m-arct b2.de* merc b4a.de* merc-c bg2 nux-v k* ol-an ptk1 pot-e rly4• *Psor* k* *Puls* k* *Rhus-t* k* *Stann* k* sulph sne syph alj* thuj bg1* thyr ptk1 [tax jsj7]
- **offensive**: acon b2.de* all-s k* aloe am-c k* ambr b2.de* ange-s oss1• apis aq-mar vml3• **Arn** k* *Ars* k* ars-s-f k2 art-v k* asar b2.de* aur-m k* bamb-a stb2.de• *Bapt* k* bar-c b2.de* **Bar-m** bar-ox-suc rly4• bar-s j5.de* bell k* bov b2.de* bry b2.de* calc-sil k2 camph b2.de* *Canth* b2.de* caps mrr1 carb-ac br1 **Carb-an** k* *Carb-v* k* **Carbn-s** carc gk6 caust b2.de* cham b2.de* chin bro1 cimic cimx cit-ac rly4• cocc coloc b2.de* con k* croc ptk1 cycl k* daph k* *Dulc* k* euphr k* *Ferr* k* ferr-ar *Fl-ac* gink-b sbd1• **Graph** k* guaj k* haliae-lc srj5• **Hep** k* hyos b2.de* ign b2.de* iod b2.de* ip b2.de* kali-act a1 kali-ar kali-c k* kali-p kali-sil k2 *Lach* led k* **Lyc** k* m-ambo b2.de* m-arct b2.de* *Mag-c* k* mand sp1 med k* **Merc** k* merc-c ptk1 *Merl* mosch b2.de* murx k2 nat-m b2.de* nat-pyru rly4• nat-sil fd3.de• **Nit-ac** k* **Nux-v** k* oci-sa sp1 oena a1 osm br1* ozone sde2• pant-ac rly4• **Petr** k* *Phos* k* plac-s rly4• plb b2.de* plut-n srj7• podo k2* *Psor* k* **Puls** k* pulx bro1 *Pyrog* k* rheum b2.de* rhod k* *Rhus-t* k* rob ros-d wla1 sacch-l c1 sal-al blc1• sanic mrr1 sec ptk1 *Sel* **Sep** k* **Sil** k* sinus rly4• sol-t-ae c1 spig k* spong fd4.de stann k* *Staph* k* stram b2.de* **Sulph** k* syph k2 tann-ac br1 tarax tax a1 *Tell* k* tere-la rly4• **Thuj** k* tung-met bdx1• vario br1* *Verat* k* wies c1 zinc b2.de* [alumin-s stj2 ant-c stj2 aur-s stj2 cadm-m stj2 cadm-s stj2 calc-s stj1 chr-s stj2 cinnb stj2 gal-s stj2 kali-s stj1 lith-s stj2 mang-p stj2 merc-d stj2 nicc-s stj2 sol-ecl cky1 titan-s stj2]
  - **one side**: **Bar-c**
  - **morning**: carb-v con hr1 dulc k* merc-c k* nux-v
  - **afternoon**: *Fl-ac* k*
  - **night**: ars **Carb-an** k* carb-v k* con k* cycl dulc euphr k* *Ferr* kr1* graph k* *Guaj* kr1 *Lyc* kr1 mag-c k* **Merc** nit-ac k* nux-v k* puls h1 rhus-t k* *Sep* kr1 spig *Staph* k* *Tell* thuj k*
    - **midnight**: mag-c merl k*
      - **after**: ambr h1
    - **sleep**; during: cycl
  - **cough**, after: hep k* merl
  - **exertion**, on: nat-sil fd3.de• nit-ac k*
  - **menses**, during: stram
  - **motion**, on: eupi k* mag-c
  - **parts** | **lain** on: sanic mrr1
- **onions**: art-v bg2* bov b2.de* *Calc* h2* ignis-alc es2• kali-i ptk1 kali-p bg2* lach bg2* *Lyc* b2.de* medul-os-si rly4• osm bg2 ozone sde2• petr ptk1 phos bg2 sin-n bg2 tell bg2* thuj ptk1 tung-met bdx1•
  - **convulsions**; after: art-v ptk1
- **peaches**: psor jl2 suprar rly4•
- **penetrating**: bapt k2
- **potato** soup; like: ozone sde2•
- **pungent**: *(↗acrid)* *Cop* kr1 fl-ac ptk1 gast a1 *Ip* kr1 rhus-t b2.de* *Sep* a1* spong fd4.de sulph k2 thuj k2*
- **putrid**: *Ars* b4a.de *Bapt* k* both-ax tsm2 **Carb-v** k* con kali-p k2 led *Mag-c* k* med c1 nux-v bg2 **Psor** pulx br1* pyrog k2* rhus-t k* sil bg2 *Spig* **Staph** k* stram k* verat [merc stj2]
- **rancid** | **night**: thuj k*
- **rank**: art-v *Bov* cop dulc fd4.de ferr goss kali-s fd4.de *Lac-c* kr1 *Lach* *Lyc* *Sep* spong fd4.de *Tell*
  - **menses**; during: *Stram* *Tell*
- **rhubarb**: rheum h*
- **sickly**: *Chin* chinin-s a1 thuj
- **smoky**: bell
- **sour**: *Acon* k* alco a1 all-s a1 *Arn* k* **Ars** k* ars-s-f k2 *Asar* k* bapt k2 *Bell* b2.de* **Bry** k* bufo bg2 calc k* calc-s calc-sil k2 *Carb-v* k* *Carbn-s* *Caust* k* *Cham* k*

Odor – sour: ...
chel k* chin b7a.de* *Cimx* cina k2 clem st **Colch** k* *Cupr* kr1 des-ac rbp6 ferr k* ferr-ar ferr-m ferr-ma k* *Fl-ac* k* gast a1 *Graph* k* ham fd3.de• **Hep** k* hyos k* ign k* **Iod** k* *Ip* k* *Iris* k* kali-c k* kalm hr1* kreos bro1 lac-ac k* lac-d bro1 *Lach* hr1* lat-h bnm5• led k* **Lyc** k* **Mag-c** k* **Merc** k* nat-m k* *Nat-p* k* nat-sil fd3.de• **Nit-ac** k* *Nux-v* k* pilo a1 **Psor** k* puls k* pyrog bro1 *Rheum* k* *Rhus-t* k* rob br1* *Ruta* kr1 *Samb* hr1* sanic bro1 **Sep** k* **Sil** k* spig bg2 spong fd4.de staph bg2 sul-ac k* sul-i k2 **Sulph** k* sumb k* tarent tep a1 *Thuj* k* tritic-vg fd5.de **Verat** k* zinc k* [cob stj2 cob-m stj2 cob-p stj2 spect dfg1]
  - **morning**: *Bry* k* *Carb-v* *Iod* k* lyc k* nat-m k* rhus-t k* sep h2 spong fd4.de sul-ac k* **Sulph** k*
  - **forenoon**: sulph k*
  - **afternoon**: *Fl-ac* k* ham fd3.de•
  - **night**: *Arn* k* ars asar kr1 bry k* carbn-s *Caust* k* cop a1 *Graph* k* **Hep** k* iod *Kali-c* h2* lyc mag-c k* **Merc** kr1 nat-m nit-ac k* *Phyt* kr1 plect a1 *Sep* k* sil h2 *Sulph* k* *Thuj* k* *Zinc* h2
    - **sleep**, during: bros-gau mrc1 bry
- **spicy**: rhod k*
- **straw** | **rotten**: brucel sa3•
- **sulfuretted** hydrogen: plb bg2 *Staph* bg2 sulph b2.de*
- **sulphur**: phos k* *Sulph* a1
- **sulphuric** acid: plb bg2 *Staph* bg2 sulph bg2
- **sweetish**: agath-a nl2• apis *Ars* hr1* bamb-a stb2.de• *Calad* k* merc k* puls sal-al blc1• *Sep* kr1 spong fd4.de thuj k* *Uran-n* kr1 vanil fd5.de
- **sweetish**-sour: bry b2.de* **Puls** b7a.de*
- **urine**: benz-ac k2 berb k* bov st **Canth** k* card-m bg1 caust coloc k* ery-a k* graph bg2* lyc bg2* nat-m bg1 **Nit-ac** k* pieri-b mlk9.de plb bg1 podo fd3.de• rhus-t bg1 sec bg1 thyr bg1 urt-u bg1
  - **evening**: ery-a br1
  - **cats**; of: ulm-c jsj8•
  - **horses**: **Nit-ac** k* *Nux-v* kr1
- **vinegar**: iris c1*
- **vinous**: sec bg2

ODORLESS: ant-c b7.de* rhus-t b7.de* sep b4.de* sul-ac bg2

OILY: agar k* arg-met arn bg1 *Ars* hr1* aur b2.de* **Bry** k* bufo k* calc k* carb-v bro1 **Chin** k* *Fl-ac* b4a.de* lup br1* lyc st **Mag-c** k* med bg1 **Merc** k* *Nat-m* b2.de* nat-sil fd3.de• nux-v ol-j a1 petr bg1 phos mtf33 plb b2.de* *Psor* hr1* pycnop-sa mrz1 rhus-t bg2 *Rob* ruta fd4.de sal-al blc1• *Sel* k* **Stram** k* sumb k* **Thuj** k* thyr ptk1
- **daytime**: bry k*
- **morning**: bry chin k*
- **night**: *Agar* kr1 bry croc mag-c h2 **Merc** k* ruta fd4.de

OILY FOOD agg.: pin-con oss2•

PAINFUL parts: both-ax tsm2 kali-c k*

PAINS:
- **after** disappearance of: chel
- **from**: acon k* *Ant-t* k* *Ars* bg2 bell k* *Bry* k* calc k* caust k* *Cham* k* *Chel* k* chin k* cocc h1 *Coloc* k* dios bg1 dulc k* form gels bg2* *Hep* k* hyos k* iris bg1 kali-bi gk **Lach** k* lyc k* **Merc** k* **Nat-c** k* nit-ac k2 phos h2 *Podo* k* psor al2 puls ptk1 *Rhus-t* k* ruta fd4.de sel k* **Sep** k* spig k* still k* stram k* sul-ac h2 *Sulph* k* sumb k* *Tab* thuj k* til k* tritic-vg fd5.de verat k*

PALPITATION; with: agar k* ars k* calc ptk1 caust h2 con tl1 *Lach* k*

PAROXYSMAL: *Valer* b7a.de
- **short** attacks: acon bg2 cham bg2 cupr bg2 *Ip* bg2 *Nat-c* bg2 spig bg2 *Stann* bg2 *Sul-ac* bg2 *Valer* b7a.de*

PARTIAL (See Single)

PERIODICAL: alum bg2 **Ant-c** b7a.de* *Ars* k* **Bar-c** b4a.de* *Bov* bg2 calc bg2 caps bg2 carb-v bg2 **Chin** bg2 *Ferr* b7a.de* *Ip* bg2 kali-c bg2 kali-n b4a.de lach bg2 lyc bg2 mur-ac b4a.de* **Nat-m** bg2 *Nit-ac* b4a.de* rhus-t bg2 *Sep* b4a.de* sil k* staph bg2 stry bg2 sulph bg2 verat bg2
- **day** | **alternate**: ant-c bg2 bar-c bg2 **Ferr** bg2 kali-n bg2 *Nit-ac* bg2
- **morning** | **alternate** morning; every: *Ant-c* k* *Ferr* k*
- **evening**:
  - **alternate** evening: *Bar-c*
  - **every** evening, lasting all night: anthraco meny

Perspiration

- **night**; alternate: bar-c kali-c bg2 kali-n **Nit-ac** sep bg2
- **hour**; at the same: ant-c h2* *Bov* bg2 cina bg2 ign bg2 **Sabad** bg2 spig bg2

PERSPIRATION agg. (See Symptoms - agg. - during)

PROFUSE: abrot absin a1 acet-ac br1* *Acon* k* aesc k* aeth k* agar k* *Agarin* bro1 agath-a nl2• agn hr1 alco a1 *All-c* hr1 alum am-act bro1 am-c k* am-caust a1 am-m ambr k* aml-ns k* androc srj1*• ange-s oss1• anh sp1 ant-c **Ant-t** k* anthraco *Antip* br1* apis k* apoc gk arg-n k* arge-pl rwt5• arist-cl sp1 **Ars** k* ars-i k* arund hr1 asar asc-c k* *Asc-t* vh astac hr1 atra-r bnm3• atro hr1 aur k* aur-i k2 *Aur-m* k* **Aur-m-n** k* aur-s k2 bacls-7 pte1*• *Bamb-a* stb2.de• bapt k* *Bar-c* **Bell** k* ben benz-ac a1* bol-la k* bond a1 both fne1• both-ax tsm2 *Brom* br1 bros-gau mrc1 **Bry** k* bufo buth-a sp1 cact caj a1* **Calc** k* calc-ar k2 calc-hp ptk1 calc-i k2 calc-p hr1 calc-s calc-sil k2* *Camph* k* cann-i tl1 canth k* *Caps* k* carb-ac **Carb-an** k* **Carb-v** k* **Carbn-s** carc fb* casc cass a1 castm *Caust* k* **Cedr** k* cham k* chel k* **Chin** k* **Chinin-ar Chinin-s** chlor k* *Cist* clem coc-c coca ptk1 coca-c sk4• cocc k* *Colch* k* *Coloc* con k* cop k* corn crat br1 croc bro1 *Crot-c Cupr* k* cupr-s hr1 cypra-eg sde6.de• *Dig* dulc k* elaps elat esin c2* eup-per k* eup-pur fago a1 **Ferr** k* **Ferr-ar** *Ferr-i* k* *Ferr-p* k* *Fl-ac* k* flor-p rsj3• *Gels* k* glon hr1 granit-m es1• graph k* guaj k2* *Ham* hr1 hed sp1 helo-s bnm14• **Hep** k* *Hydrc* br1 hydroph rsj6• hyos k* hyper bro1 iod k* *Ip* k* **Jab** br1* **Kali-ar Kali-bi** k* **Kali-c** k* kali-i hr1 kali-n k* **Kali-p** k* kali-s *Lac-ac* k* lac-c lac-e hrn2• *Lach* k* lact k* lat-m sp1* lith-c lob k* lob-e c1 loxo-recl bnm10• lup br1 **Lyc** k* *Mag-c* k* *Maias-l* hrn2• malar jl2 mang k* **Merc** k* merc-c k* merc-cy br1* *Mez* morph bro1 *Nat-ar Nat-c* k* nat-f sp1 **Nat-m** *Nat-p* nat-sil stj2*• *Nit-ac* k* *Nux-v* k* oci-sa sp1 olib-sac wmh1 *Op* k* oxal-a rly4• oxyurn-sc mcp1• ozone sde2• par petr k* petr-ra shn4• **Ph-ac** k* phase-vg a1 phel hr1 *Phos* k* phys a1 physala-p bnm7• *Pilo* bro1 pisc c2 pitu-p sp1 plb a1 plut-n srj7• podo polyp-p bro1 pot-e rly4• propr sa3• **Psor** k* *Puls* k* pyre-p a1 pyrog k* rham-cal br1 *Rhod* hr1 *Rhus-t* k* rob ros-d wla1 ruta fd4.de *Sabad* k* sal-ac k* sal-al blc1• **Samb** k* sang k* sanic bro1 sarr hr1 sars *Sec* k* *Sel* k* **Sep** k* **Sil** k* *Spong* k* stann k* staph k* stram k* sul-ac hr1* *Sulph* k* syc fmm1• tab k2* *Tarax* k* tarent ptk1 ter a1* thal-xyz srj8• thiam rly4• *Thuj* k* thyr ptk1 til bro1* tritic-vg fd5.de **Tub** k* tung-met bdx1• urol-h rwt• ust hr1 valer k* vanil fd5.de vario hr1* **Verat** k* verat-v zinc k* zinc-p k2 zing hr1 [ferr-sil stj2 kali-sil stj2 lith-f stj2 lith-m stj2 lith-met stj2 lith-p stj2 mag-lac stj2 mag-s stj1 mag-sil stj2 mang-sil stj2 nat-caust stj2 *Sil-met* stj2 sol-ecl cky1 tell stj2 zinc-n stj2]

- **day** and night: **Hep** *Merc* k* phos tl1 *Samb*
- **daytime**, during sleep: *Caust*
- **morning**: acon am-c am-m ars k* bry **Calc** h2* carb-v caust chin **Chinin-s** dulc **Ferr** *Ferr-ar* **Mag-c** *Merc* nat-c nat-m nat-p *Nit-ac* **Op** petr hr1 *Ph-ac* k* **Phos** *Puls* k* *Rhus-t* k* sep k* **Sil** spong fd4.de tritic-vg fd5.de vanil fd5.de
  - **bed** agg.; in: am-m **Ferr** kali-i a1 spong fd4.de
  - **hot**: *Cham* chin **Op** k* phos
  - **lasting** all day: ferr
  - **sleep** agg.; during: *Chinin-s Puls* spong fd4.de *Sulph* hr1 vanil fd5.de
  - **waking** agg.; after: ephe-si hsj1• *Ferr Sep* k* spong fd4.de **Sulph** k* tritic-vg fd5.de vanil fd5.de
- **afternoon**: chel hr1 *Fl-ac* pot-e rly4• spong fd4.de
  - **heat**; with: staph
- **evening**: bar-c chel con fl-ac nat-sil fd3.de• ruta fd4.de samb sarr sulph
  - **19-1 h** | **dry** heat returns on going to sleep: **Samb**
  - **fever**, with high: con
  - **lasting** all night: bol-la sep h2*
  - **periodical** | **alternate** evening; every: bar-c
- **night**: acet-ac am-m ambr hr1 ant-c *Ant-t* k* anthraco arg-n k* *Ars* ars-i ars-s-f k2 asar bac vh bamb-a stb2.de• bar-c ben benz-ac a1 berb k* bol-la brucel sa3• *Bry* k* buth-a sp1 cact *Calc-p* k* canth caps carb-ac *Carb-an Carb-v Carbn-s* casc caust cham k* chel k* *Chin* k* chinin-s *Cic Clem* k* coloc corian-s knl6• cupr k* dig c1 dulc fd4.de elaps gk fago *Ferr-p* gal-ac c1 graph **Hep** k* iod k* jab hr1 **Kali-ar Kali-c** *Kali-p* kali-sil k2 kola stb3• *Lob* k* *Lyc* k* mag-c h2* med hr1* **Merc** k* merc-i-r merc-sul k* moni rfm1• nat-ar *Nat-c* *Nat-m* k* nat-p nat-sil fd3.de• **Nit-ac** k* op gk ozone sde2• petr h2 *Ph-ac* k* phel vml3• **Phos** k* plb hr1 *Psor* k* pycnop-sa mrz1 pyre-p a1 pyrog k2 ruta fd4.de sabad *Samb* k* sarr sars h2 *Sep* h2* **Sil** k* *Spong* k* staph a1 stram k* sul-ac hr1 sul-i k2 **Sulph** k* *Tarax* k* tell a1 **Thuj** k* til a1 trios rsj11• tritic-vg fd5.de **Tub** vh valer k* vanil fd5.de *Verat* xan c1 [spect dfg1]
  - **midnight**:
    - **before**: *Carb-v*

Profuse – night – midnight: ...

- - - **after**: acon alum am-m ambr ars bol-la clem coloc dulc fd4.de graph **Kali-c** mag-c mag-m nat-sil fd3.de• phos sil spong fd4.de sulph
      - **3 h**: bry clem nat-c par
      - **4 h**: *Stann*
    - **morning**; until: graph mag-c *Phos*
  - **children**; in: sacch sst1•
  - **dreams**; from: kola stb3•
  - **sleep** agg.; during: *Acon* hr1 carb-an *Chin* chinin-s dulc fd4.de kola stb3• nat-c *Phos* ruta fd4.de spong fd4.de *Thuj* vanil fd5.de
  - **sleeplessness**; with: bar-c *Cham* k* cic k* corn iod **Sulph**
  - **waking** and returns again on falling asleep; ceases on: cham
- **accompanied** by:
  - **anemia** (See GENERALS - Anemia - accompanied - perspiration)
  - **asthma** (See RESPIRATION - Asthmatic - accompanied - perspiration)
  - **cholera** (See RECTUM - Cholera - accompanied - perspiration)
  - **circulation** of blood; weak (See GENERALS - Circulation - weak - accompanied - perspiration)
  - ○ **Bones**; caries of (See GENERALS - Caries - bone - accompanied - perspiration)
- **awake**, only while: *Samb* k* sep
- **chill**; after congestive: hed sp1 nux-v
- **coition**; after: *Agar*
- **debilitating**: (↗*Debilitating; GENERALS - Weakness - perspiration - from)* *Acet-ac* bro1 bry camph bro1 carb-an bro1 *Carb-v* bro1 castm bro1 *Chin* k* chinin-s chrysan bro1 eup-per bro1 ferr br1* gels k* kali-n bro1 *Merc* k* nit-ac bro1 *Op* bro1 *Ph-ac* k* phel bro1 *Phos* k* pyrog bro1 rhod k* rhus-g bro1 *Salv* bro1 samb hr1* stann bro1 sul-ac bro1
  - **fetid**, and: carb-an merc
  - **not**: casc rhus-t **Samb** k*
- **delirium**; during: carb-ac stram
- **delivery**; after: samb ptk1
- **diarrhea**; with: sulph mtf33
  - **and** copious urination: *Acon*
  - **and** frequent, copious urination: acon k1
  - **chronic**: tub ptk1
- **dyspnea**, with: mang
- **exertion** agg.: trios rsj11•
  - **slight**; from: (↗*Exertion - agg. - slight)* *Eupi* br1 kali-c mtf33 malar jl2 phos mtf33 psor tl1* rheum mrr1
- **fever**; after: hed sp1
- **followed** by | **chills**: sal-al blc1•
- **heart** complaints; with relief of: dig
- **influenza**; after: aml-ns ptk1
- **menopause**; during: aml-ns bro1 bell bro1 crot-h bro1 hep bro1 *Jab* bro1 lach bro1 nux-v bro1 *Sep* bro1 til bro1 valer bro1
- **menses** | **before** | **agg.**: hyos thuj
  - **during**:
    - **agg.**: *Graph Hyos Murx Verat*
    - **beginning** of menses | **agg.**: bamb-a stb2.de•
- **music** agg.: *Tarent*
- **nylon** and synthetic materials: [*Nat-caust* stj2]
- **periodical** | **night**; alternate: bar-c kali-n *Nit-ac*
- **relief**; without: cham bg2 form bg2 **Hep** *Merc* k* phos tl1 rhus-t bg2 *Samb*
- **sitting** quietly, while: **Kali-bi**
- **sleep** | **during** | **agg.**: aral br1* camph carb-an carc fd2.de• casc a1 *Chin* chinin-s coca-c sk4• con k2* dulc h1 merc k2 mur-ac h2* nat-c *Op* ozone sde2• *Phos* podo samb tl1* sanic tl1 spong fd4.de *Thuj*
  - **siesta**: | **during**: *Caust* sel
- **uncovered** parts, except the head; on: *Thuj* k*
- **urination** and diarrhea; copious: *Acon*
- **waking**; on: am-m canth chin dros k2 dulc fd4.de *Ferr* ham fd3.de• lac-d k2 **Samb** k* *Sep* spong fd4.de **Sulph**
  - **deep** sleep; from: rumx ptk1

- **walking**:
  - **agg.**: bry canth chinin-s kali-c *Merc* **Psor** sel *Sep* *Sulph*
  - **air** agg.; in open: **Caust** *Chin* lyc h2 ph-ac h2 rhod sel *Zinc*
- **weather** agg.; warm: lyc gm1 spong fd4.de
- **winter**; during: carc fb

O - **Affected** parts, on: ambr tl1 **Ant-t** k* con tl1 merc tl1 rhus-t tl1
- **Covered** parts, on: bell **Cham** **Chin** *Ferr* *Nit-ac* nux-v sec *Thuj*

PURULENT: sulph mtf33

RAGE; during: acon ant-t ars *Bell* hyos lyc merc nat-c nat-m nit-ac nux-v *Op* ph-ac phos puls *Stram* verat

REST:
- **agg.**: anac bg2 apis bg2 *Ars* bg2 *Asar* bg2 *Calc* bg2 caps bg2 *Con* bg2 **Ferr** bg2 lyc bg2 ph-ac bg2 rhus-t bg2 *Samb* bg2 **Sep** bg2 sil bg2 spong bg2 staph bg2 sul-ac bg2 *Sulph* bg2 tarax bg2 valer bg2
- **amel.**: ant-t bg2 *Bell* bg2 *Bry* bg2 calad bg2 camph bg2 carb-an bg2 hep bg2 ip bg2 *Led* bg2 merc bg2 nat-c bg2 nat-m bg2 **Nux-v** bg2 phos bg2 plat bg2 *Sel* bg2 staph bg2

RISING:
- **bed**; from | **after** | **amel.**: alum bg2 ambr bg2 ant-c bg2 ant-t bg2 *Ars* bg2 *Bell* bg2 bry bg2 **Calc** bg2 caps bg2 carb-an bg2 caust bg2 *Chin* bg2 con bg2 cycl bg2 dulc bg2 ferr bg2 hell bg2 ign bg2 iod bg2 kali-c bg2 *Lyc* bg2 meny bg2 merc bg2 mur-ac bg2 nux-v bg2 *Puls* bg2 **Rhus-t** bg2 ruta bg2 sabad bg2 *Sel* bg2 **Sep** bg2 *Spig* bg2 staph bg2 *Sulph* bg2 tarax bg2 thuj bg2 *Valer* bg2 verat bg2 *Viol-t* bg2
  - **agg.**: apis bg2 *Bry* b7.de* **Calc** bg2 carb-v bg2 cham bg2 hep bg2 *Lach* bg2 lyc bg2 nat-m bg2 nux-v bg2 ph-ac bg2 phos bg2 rhod bg2 **Rhus-t** bg2 *Samb* bg2 *Sel* bg2 sep bg2 sil bg2 staph bg2 sul-ac bg2 sulph bg2 thuj bg2

ROOM, in the: acon k* agn bg2 *Apis* k* *Bell* bg2 bry k* calc bg2 caps bg2 carb-an bg2 carb-v bg2 caust k* *Cham* bg2 chin bg2 cist k* *Con* bg2 ferr bg2 *Fl-ac* k* **Ip** k* lach bg2 *Merc* bg2 *Nux-v* k* petr bg2 *Phos* k* **Puls** k* rhod k* rhus-t k* **Sel** bg2 sep k* **Sil** bg2 spig bg2 stram bg2 sulph k* thuj bg2 valer k*

SADNESS; from: calc-p k* jab bro1

SALTY deposits after perspiration: nat-m bg2* sal-al blc1• sel st*

SCANTY SWEAT: alum ptk1* ant-c apis k* apoc ptk2* bol-la br1 calad k* casc chinin-s cimx *Cina* conv bro1 croc cycl dulc elaps *Eup-per* k* eup-pur gamb graph ptk1 ign *Ip* kali-c kali-i lac-h htj1• lach k* led nux-m k* nux-v k* phel ran-b c1 sang ptk1 sep sil thal-xyz srj8• verat k2 [alumin stj2 alumin-p stj2 alumin-s stj2 beryl-m stj2]
- **chill**; after a severe: eup-per

SCRATCH, must (See SKIN - Itching - perspiration - agg.)

SENSATION as if about to perspire, but no moisture appears: alum k* *Am-c* ars-i bg2 asar b7a.de* bapt berb bg2 borx k* bov calc k* camph caps bg2 cimx coff bg2 croc k* *Ferr* glon k* **Ign** k* iod k* kola stb3• lyc bg2 nicc phos k* podo bg2 pop-cand c1 puls k* ran-b bg2 *Raph* sars k* senec **Stann** k* sul-ac k* sulph k* thuj verat bg2 verat-v bg2 x-ray rb2

SEXUAL excitement: | **with**: lil-t k2

SHIVERING: | **with**: aml-ns ant-t arg-n cedr coff eup-per hell led lyc *Merc* **Nux-v** k* puls pyrog raph *Rhus-t* sep sulph tab verat

SHUDDERING, after: dig c1 rhus-v k* stry k* thuj k*

SICKNESS:
- **after**: ars bg2 bell bg2 bry bg2 calc bg2 caust bg2 cham bg2 chin bg2 **Cupr** bg2 ferr bg2 hep bg2 ign bg2 mag-c bg2 merc bg2 nux-v bg2 *Olnd* bg2 plb bg2 samb bg2 sec bg2 sel bg2 *Sep* bg2 sil bg2 stram bg2 *Sulph* bg2 verat bg2
- **before** the: *Merc* bg2
- **during**: calc bg2 camph bg2 cham bg2 **Merc** bg2 *Nux-v* bg2 rhus-t bg2 sel bg2 **Sep** bg2 sulph bg2 *Verat* bg2

SITTING agg.: am-c *Anac* k* **Ars** k* *Asar* k* *Calc* k* caps k* caust k* chin k* *Con* k* *Ferr* k* *Kali-bi* lyc k* mang k* nat-c k* nit-s-d a1 ph-ac k* phos k* rhod k* *Rhus-t* k* sep k* spong k* *Staph* k* sul-ac k* sulph k* tarax k* tell a1 valer k*

SLEEP:
- **before**: bry bg2 chin bg2 dros bg2 hep bg2 jatr-c bg2 *Merc* b4.de* nux-v bg2 ph-ac bg2 *Phos* b4a.de* **Samb** bg2 sep b4a.de*

Sleep: ...
- **beginning** to, on: aeth am-c ant-c k* **Ars** k* *Bell* b4a.de bry bg2 *Calc* k* carb-an k* carb-v bg2 chin bg2 *Con* k* graph bg2 hep bg2* lyc k* *Mag-c* k* **Merc** k* mez k* **Mur-ac** k* op k* *Phos* k* puls rhus-t k* *Sanic* sars k* *Sep* k* sil **Sulph** k* tab **Tarax** k* **Thuj** k* verat k*
- **during**:
  - **agg.**: *Acet-ac* bro1 acon bg2 aeth bro1 agar k* *Agarin* bro1 am-c h2 anac k* ange-s oss1• *Ant-c* k* *Ant-t* k* *Apis* bg2 aral bg2* arn bg2 *Ars* k* *Ars-i* bro1 ars-s-f k2 *Bamb-a* stb2.de• bar-c k* bar-s k2 **Bell** k* bol-la bro1 borx k* *Bov* b4a.de bros-gau mrc1 bry k* bufo k* *Calad* bg2 calc k* calc-sil k2 camph k* **Caps** bg2 *Carb-an* k* carb-v k* carbn-s carc gk6 *Caust* **Cham** k* **Chel** k* **Chin** k* *Chinin-ar* *Chinin-s* chrysan bro1 cic k* cina k* clem **Con** k* corn-f bro1 croc bg2 cycl k* dig k* dros dulc k* eup-per euphr k* *Ferr* k* *Ferr-ar* *Ferr-p* k* hep k* hydrog srj2• **Hyos** k* ign k* ina-i mlk9.de *Iod* bro1 ip bro1 *Jab* bro1 kali-ar kali-c k* kali-i bro1 *Kali-p* kali-s fd4.de kali-sil k2 ketogl-ac rly4• *Lac-c* lach bg2* lachn led bg2 lyc k* m-ambo b7.de m-arct b7.de m-aust b7.de *Merc* k* merc-c bg2 **Mez** k* mur-ac myos-s bro1 nat-c k* *Nat-m* k* nat-tel bro1 nit-ac k* nux-m bg2 nux-v k* *Op* k* petr bg2* *Ph-ac* k* *Phos* k* phyt bro1 picro bro1 *Pilo* bro1 plac-s rly4• **Plat** k* plb bg2 **Podo** k* *Pop* bro1 prun bg2 psor k* **Puls** k* rhod bg2 **Rhus-t** k* *Sabad* k* *Salv* bro1 sang bro1 sanic bro1 sec bg2 **Sel** k* *Sep* k* **Sil** k* spong bg2* stann bro1 staph bro1 stram k* stront-c bro1 suis-em rly4• *Sulph* k* suprar rly4• syc pte1• symph fd3.de• tarax k* thal bro1 **Thuj** k* til c1* tritic-vg fd5.de tub valer bg2 vanil fd5.de verat k* zinc k* zinc-p k2 [thal-met stj2]
    - **closing** the eyes; even when: carb-an k* **Con** k*
    - **deep** sleep: puls ptk1
    - **dry** heat, perspiration on waking: **Samb** k*
    - **first** sleep, but soon ceases: ars bg2
  - **amel.**: ars k* bell k* bry k* carb-an k* chin k* *Hell* b7a.de hep k* *Merc* k* *Nux-v* k* ph-ac k* *Phos* k* puls k* **Samb** k* sep bg2 thuj bg2
- **falling** asleep | **amel.**: bry bg2 *Merc* bg2 nux-v bg2 ph-ac bg2 phos bg2 **Samb** bg2
- **nightmares**; from: carc zzh gard-j vlr2•
- **sleep**; on going to | **amel.**: bry *Merc* nux-m ph-ac phos **Samb** *Sep*
- **waking** agg.; after: alum k* am-m bg2 ambr bg2 anac *Ant-c* k* ant-o arn k* *Ars* k* ars-s-f k2 bamb-a stb2.de• bar-c k* bell k* borx bg2 bov bry k* *Calad* *Calc* k* calc-sil k2 canth caps bg2 carb-ac bg2 carb-an k* carb-v k* carbn-s caust k* cedr cham bg2 *Chel* k* *Chin* k* *Chinin-ar* cic k* *Clem* k* colch coloc bg2 con k* corn croc bg2 crot-c sk4• cycl k* des-ac rbp6 dig *Dros* k* dulc bg2 euphr k* eupi *Ferr* k* ferr-ar gard-j vlr2• glon graph hep k* hyper ign ip bg2 jug-c kali-c bg2 kreos bg2 lac-c laur bg2 led k* lyc k* mag-c k* mag-s mang *Merc* k* merc-c mez bg2 nat-c bg2 nat-m k* nicc nit-ac bg2 *Nux-v* k* **Par** b7.de* ph-ac k* *Phos* k* pip-m ptel puls b7.de* ran-b k* rat rumx sabad bg2 **Samb** k* **Sep** k* sil k* spong b7.de* stann staph k* **Sulph** k* *Tarax* k* thuj bg2 til
  - **amel.**: ant-c k* apis bg2 *Ars* k* bell k* *Cham* k* **Chel** k* chin k* cycl k* *Euphr* k* ferr bg2 *Hell* k* hyos bg2 m-arct b7.de **Nux-v** k* op k* **Phos** k* *Plat* k* **Puls** k* rhus-t bg2 sel k* *Sep* k* sil k* stram k* *Sulph* k* **Thuj** k*

SMELL (See Odor)

SMOKING agg.: ars bg2 ign bg2 ip bg2 lach bg2 nat-m b4.de* sel bg2 spig bg2 staph bg2 tarax bg2 thuj b4.de*

SPOTS, in: merc k* petr ptk1 tell c1*

STAGES; succession of (See FEVER - Succession)

STAINING the linen: agar dgt1 *Arn* b2.de* ars k* bar-c bar-m **Bell** k* benz-ac st *Calc* b2.de* carb-an k* carl st cham b2.de* chin k* clem b2.de* dulc b2.de* *Graph* k* *Lac-c* st **Lach** k* *Lyc* b2.de* mag-c k* med al2* *Merc* k* nux-m b2.de* *Nux-v* b2.de* rheum k* ruta fd4.de *Sel* k* thuj hr1* vanil fd5.de [mag-lac stj2 mag-met stj2 mag-n stj2 mag-sil stj2]
- **bloody**: anag st *Arn* st ars st calc cann-i st *Cham* st chin st *Clem* k* cocc st crot-h *Cur* dulc st hell st **Lach** *Lyc* k* merc st **Nux-m** k* *Nux-v* st phos st *Sel* st
  - **night**: cur st
- **blue**: *Indg* st iod st kali-i st
- **brown**: iod a1* nit-ac a1* sep a1* vanil fd5.de wies a1*
- **brownish** yellow: ars k* *Bell* k* carb-an k* graph bg2 lac-c st *Lach* bg2* mag-c bg2 sel bg2* thuj bg2*
- **dark**: bell st
- **difficult** to wash out: *Lac-d* kr1* *Mag-c* k* *Merc* k* sep alj* spong fd4.de
- **green**: agar bg2 cupr k* sulph mtf33

- **red**: *Arn* k* *Calc* b2.de* *Carb-v* cham b2.de* chin b2.de* clem b2.de* *Crot-h* bg2* *Dulc* k* ferr st gast a1* **Lach** k* *Lyc* b2.de* **Nux-m** k* *Nux-v* k* thuj k*
- **spots**; in: merc b2.de *Sel* b2.de
- **white**: agar dgt1 *Sel* b7.de*
- **yellow**: ars k* *Bell* k* ben-n a1 bry cadm-s **Carb-an** k* carl a1* *Chin* chinin-ar cit-ac rly4• *Crot-c* elat hr1 *Ferr* ferr-ar **Graph** k* guat sp1 hep bg1 *Ip* k* lac-c st lac-d **Lach** k* lyc bro1 *Mag-c* k* **Merc** k* podo fd3.de• *Rheum* b2.de* ruta fd4.de samb xxb1 **Sel** k* *Thuj* k* tub k* *Verat* b7a.de*
  - **difficult** to wash out: merc bg2

STEAMING: psor ptk1

STICKY: abies-c br1* agar ant-t anthraci k* anthraco aq-mar skp7• ars bamb-a stb2.de• both brom cann-i k* canth caust chlor crot-h ferr fl-ac k* gels mrr1 guat sp1 ham fd3.de• hep k* iod kali-bi k* kali-br lachn lyc bro1* *Merc* bro1 nat-sil fd3.de• op phal c2* phos k* plb psor jl2 pycnop-sa mrz1 spong fd4.de tab tax vanil fd5.de
- **evening**: anthraco fl-ac k*

STIFFENING:
- **hair**: sel ptk1
- **linen**: **Merc** k* nat-m ptk1 sel k*

STOOL:
- **after**:
  - **agg.**: acet-ac bro1 **Acon** k* aloe k* ant-t bro1 ars k* bros-gau mrc1 calc k* camph k* carb-v k* **Caust** k* chin k* com hr1 con bg2 crot-t k* kali-c k* lach k* *Merc* k* merc-c pd nat-c ptk1 ph-ac bro1 phos k* plb ptk1 rhus-t k* *Samb* *Sel* k* sep k* sulph k* sumb k* tab bro1 tub bro1 **Verat** k*
  - **amel.**: borx bg2 **Bry** bg2 puls bg2 **Rhus-t** bg2 *Spig* bg2 sulph bg2 thuj h1* verat bg2
- **before**: *Acon* k* ant-t k* *Bell* k* bry k* calc k* caps k* caust k* dulc k* kali-c k* kola stb3• **Merc** k* op k* phos k* rhus-t k* **Trom** k* *Verat* k*
- **during**:
  - **agg.**: acon k* agar k* alum k2 ars k* atro a1 bac jl2 bell k* calc k* carb-v k* cham k* chin k* *Cocc* hr1 crot-t k* *Dulc* k* ferr k* ferr-ar gamb hr1 hep k* ip k* kali-bi bg2* kola stb3• lipp a1 **Merc** k* nat-c bg2 nat-m k* ptel hr1 rat hr1 rhus-t k* seneg a1 sep k* *Stram* k* *Sulph* k* tab mrr1 trom k* **Verat** k* [mur-ac stj2]
    - **cold** perspiration (See Cold - stool)

STORM; before: rhus-t bg2

STRANGERS; in the presence of: *(↗MIND - Stranger - presence - agg.)* ambr k* **Bar-c** k* lyc k* *Sep* k* stram k* thuj pd*

SUDDEN: aml-ns apis bg1 ars k* bell k* carb-v ptk1 *Carbn-s* clem k* *Crot-h* k* fic-m gya1 helo-s bnm14• hyos bg1 *Ip* k* merc-cy bg1 phos bg2* ros-d wla1 spong fd4.de *Tab* ptk1 tritic-vg fd5.de valer bg1*
- **afternoon**: clem
- **chill**; with: tab ptk1
- **disappearing** suddenly; and: **Bell** k* colch ptk1
- **walking** in the open air, with chilliness; while: led

SUPPRESSED (See GENERALS - Perspiration - suppression)

SUPPRESSION of discharges: | **agg.**: *Bar-c* b4a.de **Bell** b4.de* *Bry* bg2 calc bg2 caust bg2 *Cham* bg2 **Chin** bg2 hep bg2 *Ip* bg2 kali-c bg2 lach bg2 lyc bg2 nat-c bg2 *Nux-v* bg2 op bg2 ph-ac bg2 **Rhus-t** bg2 sel bg2 *Sep* bg2 *Sulph* bg2 thuj bg2 verat bg2

SYMPTOMS:
- **agg.**:
  - **after** perspiration: *Acon* ant-t calc cham **Chin** *Con* ip *Merc* **Ph-ac** phos *Puls* **Sep** sil *Staph* *Sulph*
  - **during** perspiration: *Acon* ant-t arn **Ars** calc calc-i k2 **Caust** **Cham** *Chin* chinin-ar cimx cinnb k2 cist k2 croc eup-per euphr k2 *Ferr* ferr-ar **Form** ign *Ip* kali-ar k2 lyc med k2 **Merc** mur-ac k2 nat-ar nat-c *Nux-v* **Op** phos *Psor* puls rhod c1 **Rhus-t** samb ptk1 **Sep** spong **Stram** **Sulph** **Verat** wye k2
- **amel.** during perspiration: *(↗GENERALS - Perspiration - during - amel.)* *Acon* aesc aeth apis *Ars* *Bapt* k* bell *Bov* **Bry** *Calad* camph canth *Cham* *Chinin-s* cimx **Cupr** elat eup-per fl-ac hr1 **Gels** *Graph* *Hep* *Lach* lyc **Nat-m** psor **Rhus-t** samb sec *Stront-c* *Thuj* *Verat*
  - **headache**, except the: *Nat-m*

Symptoms – amel. during perspiration – **headache**: ...
- ⁝ ~~which~~ is agg.: ars chinin-s **Eup-per** k*

TALKING:
- **agg.**: alum bg2 ambr anac bg2 bry bg2 *Calc* bg2 carb-an bg2 carb-v bg2 cham bg2 chin bg2 *Fl-ac* bg2 gink-b sbd1• graph k* hep bg2 *Iod* k* *Merc* bg2 nat-c bg2 nat-m bg2 nux-v bg2 *Ph-ac* bg2 **Rhus-t** bg2 **Sel** bg2 sep bg2 sil h2 sul-ac bg2 *Sulph* k* verat bg2
- **amel.**: ferr bg2 *Hep* bg2 nat-c bg2

TALKING IN PUBLIC; when: bamb-a stb2.de•

TASTE: | **salty**: *Sel* st*

THIGHS, except (See EXTREMITIES - Perspiration - thigh - except)

THINKING agg.: phos bg2

UNCOVERING:
- **agg.**: staph h1
  - **pain** from uncovering: hep b4a.de nat-c b4a.de stront-c b4a.de
- **amel.**: acon k* *Bell* k* calc k* *Camph* **Cham** k* *Chin* k* ferr bg2 *Ign* bg2 led k* **Lyc** k* *Nit-ac* k* nux-v bg2 *Puls* k* ruta fd4.de sec ptk1 spig k* *Staph* k* sulph k* *Thuj* k* verat k*
- **aversion** to: acon k* aeth k* agar b2.de am-c bg2 ant-c b2.de arg-met b2.de arn k* ars k* asar b2.de aur k* bar-c bell b2.de borx b2.de bry b2.de *Calc* camph b2.de canth b2.de caps b2.de carb-an k* carb-v bg2 cham b2.de chin k* cic b2.de* *Clem* k* cocc b2.de* coff b2.de* colch k* con k* *Eup-per* gels **Graph** b2.de* *Hell* k* hep k* ign b2.de jab bg2 kali-c bg2 kreos b2.de* lach b2.de* led b2.de m-aust b2.de *Mag-c* b2.de* mag-m k* meny b2.de merc b2.de* mur-ac b2.de nat-ar *Nat-c* k* nat-m b2.de* nux-m k* **Nux-v** k* *Petr* bg2 ph-ac b2.de phos b2.de puls b2.de rheum b2.de rhod b2.de* **Rhus-t** k* sabad b2.de* **Samb** k* sec bg2 *Sep* b2.de* sil k* squil k* staph b2.de *Stram* k* *Stront-c* k* thuj b2.de tub viol-t bg2
- **desire** for: *Acon* k* apis bg2 ars b2.de asar b2.de* aur b2.de borx b2.de *Bov* bg2 bros-gau mrc1 bry b2.de calc k* *Camph* carb-v b2.de cham b2.de* chin b2.de coff b2.de* *Euph* bg2 ferr k* *Fl-ac* bg2 ign b2.de* iod k* lach b2.de **Led** k* *Lyc* b2.de* *M-ambo* b2.de **M-arct** b2.de med jl2 merc b2.de *Mosch* b2.de* *Mur-ac* k* *Nat-m* *Nit-ac* b2.de* nux-v b2.de olib-sac wmh1 *Op* k* ph-ac bg2 phasco-ci rbp2 phos b2.de* plat b2.de* *Puls* b2.de* rhus-t b2.de **Sec** k* seneg b2.de* sep b2.de spig k* staph k* *Sulph* b2.de* thuj b2.de* tub jl2 verat k* *Zinc*
  - **night**: phasco-ci rbp2

URINATION:
- **after** | **agg.**: bell b4.de* coloc bg2 *Hep* bg2 merc bg2* merc-c bro1 nat-m bg2 sel bg2 staph bg2 sulph bg2 *Thuj* bg2
- **before**: ant-t bg2 bry bg2 coloc b4a.de* ph-ac bg2 *Rhus-t* bg2
- **during** | **agg.**: acon b7.de bell b4.de* *Hep* bg2 ip bg2 lyc bg2 **Merc** b4a.de* merc-c bro1 ph-ac bg2 sep bg2 sulph bg2 *Thuj* bg2

VEXATION; after: *(↗Anger)* acon bry *Cham* lyc *Petr* k* **Sep** k* staph verat

VISCOUS: *Plb* b7.de* pyrog jl2

VOMITING:
- **after** vomiting; perspiration: acon b7a.de bell b4a.de carb-an b4a.de phos b4a.de sep b4a.de
- **amel.**: *Phos* b4a.de *Thuj* b4a.de
- **before** vomiting; perspiration: apom br1
- **during** the stage of perspiration; vomiting (See STOMACH - Vomiting - perspiration - during)
- **when** vomiting; perspiration (See STOMACH - Vomiting - accompanied - perspiration)

WALKING:
- **agg.**: *(↗Exertion - agg. - slight)* *Agar* k* am-m bg2 ambr k* anac bg2 ant-t bg2 asar bg2 bar-c bg2 bar-s k2 *Bell* b4.de* benz-ac brom bg2 *Bry* k* calad bg2 **Calc** k* calc-sil k2 canth k* carb-an k* carb-v bg2 caust k* chin bg2 chinin-s *Coc-c* **Cocc** bg2 coloc dulc bg2 eug ferr k* ferr-m fl-ac bg2 *Graph* bg2 *Guaj* b4.de* *Hep* b4a.de* hydr-ac **Iod** b4a.de* ip k* *Kali-c* k* kali-n bg2 kali-sil k2 lach bg2 led k* lyc b4a.de* mag-c bg2 *Merc* k* nat-c b4a.de* nat-m k* nit-ac bg2 **Nux-v** k* op k* petr bg2 ph-ac b4.de* phos bg2 **Psor** k* *Puls* bg2 *Rheum* bg2 *Rhod* b4.de* rhus-t bg2 sel k* seneg b4.de* **Sep** k* sil k* spig bg2 *Stann* bg2 staph bg2 stram bg2 sul-ac bg2 **Sulph** k* sumb ther thuj bg2 til valer k* verat bg2 zinc bg2

- **air**; in open:
  - **after** | **agg.**: alum bg2 ant-c b7.de* bry b7.de* canth bg2 ferr bg2 led b7.de* meny bg2 *Petr* b4a.de* phos b4.de* *Rhod* b4a.de* rhus-t h1* *Ruta* b7.de* **Sep** b4a.de*
  - **agg.**: **Agn** b7a.de* am-m bg2 ant-c bell k* **Bry** k* *Calc* *Carb-an* k* carb-v k* **Caust** k* cham bg2 **Chin** k* coloc k* ferr bg2 *Guaj* b4a.de* hep h2* kali-c bg2 led k* lyc h2* *Merc* bg2 nit-ac k* *Nux-v* b7.de* ph-ac h2* *Phos* k* rhod k* rhus-t bg2 ruta *Sel* b7.de* sep bg2 spig bg2 stram bg2 *Sulph* k* sumb thuj bg2 zinc k*
  - **amel.**: alum k* **Ars** k* bry *Caps* bg2 con bg2 dulc bg2 graph lyc bg2 nux-v bg2 phos bg2 puls k* rhod bg2 rhus-t bg2 sep bg2 sulph h2 tarax bg2 thuj k* viol-t bg2 zinc h2
- **amel.**: cham chel *Puls* k* *Thuj* k*

WARM: acon ant-c k* ant-t sne anth a1 ars-h hr1 asar ben both-ax tsm2 camph k* canth b7.de carb-v cham cocc dig j5.de dros k* ign k* ip b7a.de kali-c k* kreos j5.de lach led k* nat-m nux-v op phos puls j5.de sep sil j5.de staph stram thuj h1* verat j5.de

- **evening**: anac j5.de puls j5.de
- **night**: staph j5.de thuj j5.de
- **amel.**: acon ptk1
- **applications** | **agg.**: beryl tpw5
- **convulsions** | **after** | **epileptic**: sil gt1*
  - **with**: sil j5.de
- **food** | **after**: bell bg2 *Bry* k* carb-an k* *Carb-v* k* cham k* euph bg2 *Ferr* k* kali-bi gk *Kali-c* k* lach k* mag-c k2 ph-ac k* **Phos** k* puls k* sep k* **Sul-ac** k* *Thuj* k*
- **hot** | **exertion**; from: (↗*Hot*) limest-b es1•
- **moist**; and: visc c1
- **periodical**: carb-v j5.de
  - **morning**; alternate: ant-c j5.de
- **room**:
  - **agg.**: carb-v h2 cist k2
    - : **cannot** bear heat of the room: plan
- **sitting** agg.: asar j5.de
- **somnolence**; with: op j5.de
- **stool**; becomes cold and sticky after: **Merc**
- **uneasiness**; causing: **Calc** cham glycyr-g cte1• nux-v *Puls* **Sep** *Sulph*
- **waking** | **amel.**: thuj j5.de

WARM IN BED agg.; becoming: | **chilliness** and perspiration as soon as he gets warm: arg-n

WASH OFF; difficult to (See Staining - difficult)

WASHING:

- **agg.**: graph bg2
- **amel.**: apis bg2 *Asar* bg2 *Calc* bg2 caust bg2 *Euphr* b7.de* **Fl-ac** bg2 **Nux-v** b7.de* *Puls* bg2 rhod bg2 sabad bg2 spig bg2 thuj k*

WIND agg., cold: ars bg2 **Bell** bg2 cham bg2 chin bg2 cur lyc bg2 phos bg2

WINE amel.; drinking: acon k* apis k* con k* lach k* *Op* k* sul-ac k* thuj k*

WRITING agg.: borx *Hep* k* *Kali-c* k* kali-p fd1.de• *Psor* k* **Sep** k* *Sulph* k* tell a1 *Tub* k*

COVERED parts: **Acon** k* **Bell** k* both-ax tsm2 *Cham* k* **Chin** k* *Ferr* led k* lyc bg2 *Nit-ac* k* nux-v k* *Puls* k* sanic tl1 sec sil k13 spig k* *Thuj* k* tritic-vg fd5.de

SINGLE parts: *Acon* k* agar b2.de* agn b2.de* am-c b2.de* am-m b2.de* *Ambr* k* anac b2.de* ang b2.de* ant-t b2.de* apis ptk1 arg-met b2.de* arn b2.de* ars k* ars-s-f k2 asaf b2.de* asar b2.de* aur b2.de* bar-c k* bar-s k2 bell k* borx b2.de* bov b2.de* *Bry* k* calad b2.de* **Calc** k* *Calc-p* k* calc-sil k2 camph b2.de* cann-s k* canth b2.de* caps k* carb-an b2.de* carb-v b2.de* **Caust** k* *Cham* k* chel b2.de* chin k* cic b2.de* cina b2.de* clem b2.de* cocc b2.de* coff b2.de* coloc b2.de* con b2.de* croc b2.de* cupr b2.de* cycl b2.de* dig b2.de* dros b2.de* dulc b2.de* euph b2.de* euphr b2.de* ferr b2.de* *Graph* b2.de* guaj b2.de* hell k* hep k* hyos b2.de* **Ign** k* iod b2.de* ip k* kali-c b2.de* kali-n b2.de* kreos b2.de* lat-m bnm6• laur b2.de* *Led* k* *Lyc* k* m-ambo b2.de* m-arct b2.de m-aust b2.de mag-m b2.de* mang b2.de* merc k* merc-c ptk1 **Mez** k* mosch b2.de* nat-c b2.de* nat-m b2.de* nit-ac b2.de* nux-v k* op b2.de* osm br1 par k* *Petr* k* ph-ac b2.de* *Phos* b2.de* plat b2.de* plb b2.de* plect c2 *Psor* **Puls** k* *Pyrog* ran-s b2.de* *Rheum* b2.de* rhod b2.de* rhus-t k*

Single parts: ...
ruta b2.de* sabad b2.de* sabin b2.de* samb b2.de* sars b2.de* sec b2.de* *Sel* k* **Sep** k* *Sil* k* *Spig* k* spong k* squil b2.de* *Stann* k* staph b2.de* stram b2.de* stront-c b2.de* sul-ac b2.de* *Sulph* k* tarax b2.de* thal-xyz srj8• *Thuj* k* *Tub* valer b2.de* verat k* viol-t b2.de* zinc k*

- ○ **Back** part of body: acon b2.de ars bg2 calc bg2 caust bg2 *Chin* b2.de* coff b2.de *Dulc* bg2 ferr bg2 guaj bg2 ip b2.de lach bg2 led b2.de* m-ambo b2.de mang bg2 mosch bg2 *Mur-ac* bg2 nat-c bg2 *Nux-v* b2.de par b2.de* petr b2.de* *Ph-ac* bg2 puls b2.de* sabin b2.de* **Sep** b2.de* sil b2.de *Stann* b2.de* stram b2.de* sulph b2.de*
- **Front** of body: agar k* ambr bg2 anac b2.de* **Arg-met** k* arn k* *Asar* b2.de* bell b2.de* *Bov* b2.de* *Calc* k* canth k* cina bg2 **Cocc** k* dros bg2 *Euphr* b2.de* *Graph* k* ip bg2 kali-n k* laur bg2 m-arct b2.de m-aust b2.de merc k* merc-c bg2 nat-m bg2 nux-v **Phos** k* plb b2.de* rheum bg2 *Rhus-t* b2.de* ruta bg2 sabad b2.de* sec b2.de* **Sel** k* *Sep* b2.de* staph bg2
- **Joints**; on: *Am-c* b4a.de* ars bg2 bell bg2 bry bg2 *Calc* bg2 dros bg2 led bg2 *Lyc* b4a.de* mang bg2 nux-v bg2 ph-ac bg2 *Rhus-t* bg2 stann bg2 *Sulph* bg2
  - ○ **Bend** of joints: sep bg2 zinc bg2
- **Lower** part of body: am-c k* am-m k* apis k* ars k* asaf bg2 aur bg2 bry bg2 calc bg2 chel b2.de cinnb *Cocc* hr1* coloc k* con bg2 **Croc** k* cycl k* dros bg2 euph k* ferr b2.de* *Hyos* k* *Iod* b2.de* kali-n bg2 mang k* merc k* nit-ac k* nux-v bg2 *Phos* h2* ran-a bro1 sabin b2.de sanic bro1 sep k* sil bg2 tarax b2.de thuj k* *Zinc* b2.de*
- **Side**:
  - **one** side of the body: bar-c mtf33
  - **right**: phos mtf33
- **Side** lain on: *Acon* k* *Ars* b4a.de *Bell* k* benzol pls1 bry **Chin** k* fl-ac b4a.de nat-c b4.de* **Nit-ac** k* nux-v k* podo fd3.de• puls k* *Sanic* k* sep b4a.de vesp br1*
- **Side** not lain on: acon ptk1 *Ben* k* benz-ac dgt1 benzol br1 nux-v ptk1 thuj k*
- **Touching** each other; parts: nicc-s bro1*
- **Upper** part of body: acon bg2 agar b2.de* agn b2.de *Anac* b2.de* *Ant-t* b2.de* arg-met k* arn bg2 **Asar** k* aza bro1 bar-c bg2 bell h1* berb k* *Bov* b2.de* calc bro1* camph k* canth bg2 *Caps* b2.de* *Carb-v* k* caust bg2 *Cham* k* chin k* cic b2.de cina k* coc-c bg2 dig k* dulc k* eup-per euphr bg2 fl-ac k* graph bg2 *Guaj* b2.de* *Ign* b2.de* ip k* **Kali-c** k* laur k* m-ambo b2.de m-aust b2.de mag-c bg2 mag-m bg2 mag-s j5.de merc-c bg2 mosch b2.de* mur-ac bg2 nat-c bg2 *Nit-ac* k* nux-v k* **Op** k* **Par** k* petr bg2 ph-ac bg2 phos bg2 plat b2.de plb bg2 psor al2 puls bg2 *Ran-s* b2.de* *Rheum* k* rhus-t bg2 *Ruta* b2.de* sabad bg2 *Samb* b2.de* *Sars* b2.de* *Sec* k* sel b2.de* sep k* sil k* spig k* spong b2.de *Stann* b2.de* stram b2.de stront-c b2.de sul-ac k* thuj k* tub ptk1 valer k* verat k* viol-t b2.de [tax jsj7]
  - **sleep**; before: berb

UNCOVERED parts; on: bell st* *Puls* k1* *Thuj* b4a.de*

Perspiration

AFTERNOON: | **13**-22 h: adam skp7•

EVENING: am-m br1 bufo bg2

NIGHT: bufo bg2 mez tl1

ABSCESSES (See GENERALS - Abscesses)

ACANTHOSIS nigricans: ars mtf con mtf nux-v mtf thuj mtf

ACRID: | **Under** cuticle; as if something acrid had been secreted: cupr-ar rb2

ACTINOMYCOSIS: bry sne hecla bro1* hippoz bro1 kali-i c2* nit-ac c2*

ADHERENT: *Arn* k* *Ars* par k*

○ - **Bone**; to (= hidebound) arn k* *Asaf* k* aur k* chin k* *Crot-t* k* hell k* merc k* *Ph-ac* k* puls k* ruta k* sabin k* *Sil* k* staph k*

• **sensation** as if skin were: kali-i rb2 phos rb2

AIR: | **draft** of air; sensitive to (See Sensitiveness - air agg.; draft)

AIR AGG.; IN OPEN: *Calc* b4.de* kali-c b4.de* *Lyc* b4a.de *Nat-c* b4.de nux-m bg2 petr b4.de* plb bg2

ALIVE:

○ - **In** skin; as if insects or something were alive brom rb2

- **Under** skin; as if something alive were creeping: sec rb2

○ • **Abdomen**, of: spong rb2

ALLERGY to milk: (↗*GENERALS - Allergic*) **Tub** vh

ANESTHESIA: acon k* *All-s* *Alum* alum-p k2 alum-sil k2 ambr k* *Anac* k* ang bg2 ant-t b7.de* *Arg-n* arn *Ars* ars-i bell k* bry cadm-s k2 calc *Camph* cann-i k* *Caps* *Carb-ac* k* *Carbn-s* k* carl caul caust cham k* **Chin** chinin-ar chinin-s chlol k* *Cic* cocain br1 *Cocc* con k* cupr-ar cycl k* hell hyos hyper bg2 iod *Kali-br* k* *Kali-i* kreos bg2 lach b7.de* lat-m bnm6• laur loxo-lae bnm12• lyc k* m-ambo bg2 meph *Merc* k* mosch naja gm1 nat-m **Nux-v** k* oena **Olnd** k* *Op* k* *Petr* ph-ac k* *Phos* k* plat k* *Plb* k* pop-cand br1 psil ft1 **Puls** k* **Rhus-t** *Sec* k* sep k* stram k* sul-i k2 sulph k* tarent ter verat-v vinc *Zinc* zinc-p k2

- **morning** | **waking**; on: *Ambr*
- **eruptions**; after suppressed: *Zinc*
- **patches**: bufo k2
- **spots**; in small: bufo br1

○ - **Mucous** membranes carbn-s k2

ANHIDROSIS (See Dry - perspire; Inactivity)

ANTS:

- **biting**; as if an ant were (See Biting - ants)
- **bitten** by an ant; as if (See Bitten - ant)
- **covered** with ants; as if: m-arct rb2 zinc rb2
- **crawling**; as if an ant were:

○ • **In** the skin: ham fd3.de• sabad rb2

• **Over** the skin: anan rb2 ign rb2 ph-ac rb2* pic-ac rb2

• **Waist**; around the: tab rb2

ASLEEP: | **touched**; as if skin were asleep in places when: nux-v rb2

ATROPHY: ars bro1 cocc bro1 graph bro1 sabad bro1 sulph bro1 thal bro1

BATH; as if he were in a vapor: acon rb2

BEDSORES (See Decubitus)

BEES stinging; as if (See Pain - stinging)

BITES of insects (See Stings; GENERALS - Wounds - bites)

BITING: *Agar* k* agn k* aloe bg2 alum k* alum-p k2 alum-sil k2 am-c k* *Am-m* k* ant-c k* arn k* bar-m k* bell k* berb borx k* bov k* *Bry* k* bufo bg2 *Calad* *Calc* k* camph k* canth k* caps k* carb-an k* *Carb-v* k* *Caust* k* cham k* chel k* chin k* coc-c k* cocc k* *Colch* k* coloc k* *Con* k* dros k* **Euph** k* *Euphr* ptk1 *Gamb* hell k* *Ip* k* kreos k* *Lach* k* **Led** k* *Lyc* k* lyss m-arct b2.de m-aust b2.de* mag-c k* mang k* merc k* merc-c b4a.de *Mez* k* mur-ac k* nat-c k* nat-m k* nat-p nicc *Nux-v* k* *Olnd* k* op k* pall petr k* ph-ac k* phel phos k* plat k* **Puls** k* ran-b k* ran-s k* rhod k* rhus-t k* ruta k* sel k* sep k* sil k* spig k* *Spong* k* stront-c k* *Sulph* k* syph ptk1 tarent k2 thuj k* verat k* viol-t k* zinc k*

Biting: ...

- **night**:

• **bed** agg.; in: coc-c mag-c h2 sulph h2

⁝ **sleep**; before: coc-c

- **ants** were biting; as if: gamb rb2 lach rb2
- **chill**; during: gamb
- **fever**; during: *Cham* b7.de* puls bg2
- **fleas** were biting; as if: arg-met rb2 bell bg2 cact rb2 dulc bg2* graph bg2 merc rb2 mez bg2* nat-c rb2 nuph rb2 nux-v rb2 phos bg2 pulx rb2 sec bg2 sil bg2* staph bg2* symph fd3.de• syph ptk1 tab bg2* tell rb2 teucr bg2* visc bg2*

○ • **Abdomen**, arms and legs; on: thuj rb2

• **Knee**; the: pall rb2

⁝ **Above** the knee: pall rb2

- **insects** were biting; as if: cop rb2

• **touched**; on the spot: antho rb2

- **leeches** were biting; as if: carbn-s rb2
- **nettles** were biting; as if: paeon rb2
- **perspiration**; from: cham h1* spong fd4.de tarax k* thuj alj
- **scratching** agg.; after: am-c k* *Am-m* k* bry k* calc k* canth k* carb-an k* carb-v k* carbn-s *Caust* k* chin k* con k* dros k* *Euph* k* hell k* ip k* kreos k* **Lach** k* *Led* k* *Lyc* k* m-arct b2.de mang k* merc k* *Mez* k* nat-c k* nat-m k* nux-v k* **Olnd** k* petr k* ph-ac k* *Puls* k* ran-b k* ruta k* sel k* sep k* sil k* *Spong* k* *Sulph* k* zinc k* zinc-p k2

• **changing** place on scratching: sulph h2

- **spots**, in: nat-m k*
- **vermin** were biting; as if: atro rb2

BITTEN; as if:

- **ant**; by an: tarent rb2
- **bug**; by a: kali-bi ptk1 syph rb2* tell ptk1
- **insect**; by an: cop rb2 lycps-v rb2 [heroin sdj2]

○ - **Abdomen**; on the: carb-ac rb2

BLADDER rose under skin and burst; as if a: sil rb2

BLOOD would start through skin; as if: aml-ns rb2

BLOTCHES (See Eruptions - blotches)

BODY were under the skin; as if a foreign: bomb-pr rb2*

- **small** foreign bodies (See Foreign)

BRAN-LIKE, furfuraceous covering of skin (See Eruptions - scaly - bran-like)

BRUISED Pain (See Pain - bruised)

BUBBLING sensation: berb rb2 calc k*

BUGS; sensation of: *Cocain* br1

BURNING (= smarting): acet-ac bro1 **Acon** k* agar k* all-c k* alum k* alum-p k2 alum-sil k2 am-c k* am-m k* *Ambr* k* anac k* anan ant-c k* *Anthraci* k* **Apis** k* *Arg-met* k* *Arn* k* **Ars** k* ars-i asaf k* asar k* aur k* aur-ar k2 aur-i k2 aur-s k2 bapt bro1 bar-c k* bar-m bar-s k2 **Bell** k* bell-p sp1 berb beryl sp1 bism k* both fne1• bov k* *Brom* b4a.de **Bry** k* *Bufo* k* buth-a sp1 calad k* *Calc* k* calc-i k2 *Calc-s* camph k* cann-s k* canth k* *Caps* k* *Carb-an* k* *Carb-v* k* *Caust* k* cham k* chel k* chin k* chinin-ar chir-fl bnm4• *Cic* k* clem k* *Cocc* k* coff k* colch k* coloc k* con k* cop k* *Crot-t* k* cupr k* cycl k* dig k* dros k* *Dulc* k* elat hr1 eup-per k2 *Euph* k* euph-l a1 *Ferr* k* ferr-ar ferr-i ferr-p fl-ac bg2 *Form* bro1 graph k* grin bro1 guaj k* hell k* *Hep* k* hip-ac sp1 hist sp1 *Hyos* k* *Ign* k* ina-i mlk9.de iod k* kali-ar **Kali-bi** k* *Kali-c* k* kali-i k2 kali-m k2* *Kali-n* k* kali-p *Kali-s* k* kali-sula a1* kreos k* **Lach** k* lat-h bnm5• lat-m bnm6• laur k* led k* loxo-lae bnm12• **Lyc** k* m-ambo b2.de* m-arct b2.de m-aust b2.de mag-c k* mag-m k* mang k* medus bro1 meny k* *Merc* k* merc-c b4a.de* *Mez* k* mosch k* mur-ac k* nat-ar nat-c k* *Nat-m* k* nat-p nat-sil fd3.de• nit-ac k* *Nux-v* k* ol-an olnd k* *Op* k* par k* petr k* petr-ra shn4• ph-ac k* **Phos** k* physala-p bnm7• plat k* plb k* positr nl2• *Puls* k* rad-br bro1 *Ran-b* k* rhod k* **Rhus-t** k* ruta k* sabad k* sabin k* samb k* sang bro1 sars k* sec k* sel k* seneg k* *Sep* k* **Sil** k* *Spig* k* spong k* *Squil* k* stann k* *Staph* k* stram k* stront-c k* sul-ac k* sul-i k2 sulfa sp1 **Sulph** k* tarent k* *Tarent-c* tl1* teucr k* thuj k* tril-p c1 tub jl2 *Urt-u* k* vac jl2 valer k* verat k* verat-v ptk1 vesp bro1 viol-o k* viol-t k* x-ray sp1 zinc k*

- **morning** | **bed** agg.; in: carb-v h2
- **evening** | **rising** agg.: mang h2
- **night**: *Ars* *Carb-v* cinnb clem *Con* *Dol* *Merc* nux-v *Olnd* rhus-t

- **night**: ...
  - **midnight**:
    - **after** | **4** h: colch rsj2•
- **chill**; during: petr bg2 sars bg2 verat bg2
- **coal** | **rash**; as if a glowing coal lay on: mez rb2
- **coition**; after: agar
- **cold** water; after working in: olib-sac wmh1 thuj
- **fever**; during: petr b4a.de*
- **fire** were falling on body; as if sparks of: sec rb2
- **flames**; as from: viol-o k*
- **fleabites**; burning as if from: merc rb2
- **hand** has lain on; where: hyos h1*
- **heated**; when getting: bry h1
- **itching** (See Itching - burning)
- **lying** | **amel.**: mang h2*
- **mental** excitement; from: *Bry* k*
- **mustard** plaster; as from: kali-c ptk1
- **nettles**; as from: calc-p cocc dulc a1 **Urt-u**
- **parts** lain on: lyss manc *Sulph* k*
- **perspiration**:
  - **from**: acon bg2 **Ars** bg2 bell bg2 bry bg2 caps bg2 lach bg2 lyc bg2 merc k* **Mez** k* **Nat-c** k* petr bg2 phos bg2 puls bg2 *Rhus-t* bg2 **Sep** bg2 sil bg2 stann bg2 verat k*
  - **without**: colch rsj2•
- **scratching**; after: adam skp7• agar k* alum bro1 *Am-c* k* am-m k* ambr k* anac k* ant-c arn k* *Ars* k* ars-s-f k2 bar-c *Bell* k* bov k* *Bry* k* calad k* calc k* calc-sil k2 cann-s k* canth k* caps k* carb-an k* carb-v k* carbn-s **Caust** k* chel k* cic k* cocc k* coff con k* crot-t k* cycl k* dros k* *Dulc* k* euph k* graph k* *Hep* k* kali-ar kali-c k* kali-p *Kali-s* kali-sil k2 kola stb3• *Kreos* k* *Lac-c* lac-d k2 **Lach** k* laur k* *Led* k* *Lyc* k* m-ambo b2.de* m-arct b2.de* mag-c k* mag-m k* mang k* **Merc** k* mez k* mosch k* murx bro1 nat-c nat-m nat-s nit-ac nux-v k* **Olnd** k* par k* *Petr* ph-ac k* *Phos* k* pix bro1 plb b7.de positr nl2• psor bg2* puls k* ran-b k* rhod k* **Rhus-t** k* sabad k* sabin k* samb k* sars k* sel k* seneg k* **Sep** k* **Sil** k* spig k* spong k* *Squil* k* *Staph* k* stront-c k* **Sulph** k* thuj k* *Til* k* tril-p c1 verat k* viol-t k* zinc k* zinc-p k2
  - **amel.**: *Kali-n*
- **sleep** agg.; after: *Urt-u*
- **sparks**; as from: agar arg-met calc *Calc-p* k* nat-m **Sec** k* sel k*
- **spots**: agar am-c k* *Am-m* k* apis k* *Ars* k* ars-s-f k2 bell k* canth k* *Carb-v* caust chel k* croc k* cupr cycl b7a.de eos br1 ferr k* *Fl-ac* iod k* kali-ar *Kali-c* k* lach lyc k* mag-c k* mag-m *Merc* k* *Mez* k* nat-s nat-sil fd3.de• **Ph-ac** k* plat *Rhus-t* k* sang bg1 sel k* *Sul-ac* k* **Sulph** k* tab thuj viol-o zinc
  - **wandering**: puls sne
- **sun**; as if burned from heat of: lach rb2
- **touch**; on: *Canth* k* caps fkm1• caust h2 *Ferr* k* sabin thal-xyz srj8•
  - **cold** to touch; burning sensation, but really: sec k2
- **vapor** were emitted from the pores of the body; as if burning: fl-ac rb2
- **walking** agg.: petr h2
- **warm** water; from: olib-sac wmh1

BURNS (See GENERALS - Burns)

BURNT EASILY (See GENERALS - Sun - sunburn)

BURST; as if skin would: tarent rb2 [heroin sdj2]

CALLOUS skin (See Hard - callosities)

CANCER: **Ars-br** rmk1• **Ars-i** rmk1• cund sne kali-ar mrr1 kali-s mrr1 rad-br br1 x-ray br1*
- **cicatrices**: graph gm1
  - **operation**; from: graph gm1
- **epithelioma**: acet-ac br1 ars bg2 carc mlr1• cund mtf11 des-ac rbp6 hydr bg2 kali-s tl1 kreos tl1 lap-a bg2 merc tl1 ran-b mtf11 sep tl1 sil bg2 thuj bg2
- **melanoma**: (↗*GENERALS - Cancerous - melanoma)* carc mlr1•
- **sunlight** agg.; from: carc mlr1•

CHAPPING: (↗*Cracks)* *Aesc* alum k* alum-sil k2 ant-c k* arn k* aur k* bry k* **Calc** k* calc-sil k2 carbn-s k2 cham k* *Cycl* k* **Graph** k* **Hep** k* *Kali-c* k* kreos k* *Lach* k* lyc k* mag-c k* mang k* merc k* nat-c k* nat-m k* nit-ac k* petr k* **Puls** k* **Rhus-t** k* ruta k* **Sars** k* **Sep** k* sil k* **Sulph** k* viol-t k* zinc k*

CHILBLAINS (See EXTREMITIES - Chilblains)

CICATRICES: (↗*Cicatrices - blisters; Keloid; Ulcers - cicatrices; BACK - Abscess - cervical - cicatrices; CHEST - Abscess - mammae - threatening; CHEST - Cancer - mammae - cicatrices; CHEST - Cicatrices; CHEST - Induration - mammae - cicatrices; CHEST - Swelling - mammae - cicatrices; EXTREMITIES - Cicatrices; FACE - Cicatrices; GENERALS - Cancerous - cicatrices; GENERALS - Cicatrices; GENERALS - Wounds - granulations)* bell-p bg2 calc-f bg2* carb-v bg2 caust bg2* chir-fl bnm4• crot-h bg2 dros tl1 *Fl-ac* bg2* gast c2 glon bg2 graph bg2* hyper c2* iod bg2* kali-bi bg2 kali-c bg2 lach bg2 *Merc* ptk1 mez bg2 naja ptk1 nat-m bg2 nit-ac bg2* ozone sde2• petr ptk1 phos bg2 *Phyt* bg2* pyrog jl2 sabin bg2 *Sil* bg2* sul-ac bro1 syph ptk1 ↓thiosin c1* vip bg2
- **adherent**: dros bg1
- **black**: asaf k* graph k2
  - ○ • **Centre**; near: loxo-recl bnm1•
- **bleeding**: both fne1• *Lach* k* phos k* sep h2*
- **blisters** form on cicatrices: (↗*Cicatrices)* mag-c
- **blue**: ant-c k* asaf k2 *Bad* cench ferr bg2 lach k* lyss c1 rhus-t bg2 sep pd sul-ac k* thuj bg2
- **break** open: asaf k* *Borx* both fne1• calc-p *Carb-an* k* carb-v h2* *Caust* k* con croc k* *Crot-h* k* dream-p sdj1• fl-ac bg3* glon a* *Graph* bro1* *Iod* k* *Lach* k* m-ambo bro1 nat-c *Nat-m* k* nit-ac a **Phos** k* ruta fd4.de **Sil** k* sulph vip sf1.de
  - **accompanied** by | **suppuration**: croc ptk1
  - **black**; become: asaf ptk1
  - **painful** | **burning**: sars ptk1
  - **sensation** as if: junc-e rb2
- **brown**: crot-h bg2* lach bg2*
- **cracked**: kali-c bg2*
- **depressed**: carb-an *Kali-bi* k* kali-i k* sil syph ptk1
- **dusky** mottled: loxo-recl bnm1•
- **elevated**: *Bad* k* fl-ac c1
- **eruptions**; after: kali-br ptk1
- **green**: led bro1*
- **hard**: calc-f bg3* dros tl1 fl-ac bg3 *Graph* k* kali-bi bg2* sil tl1
- **itching**: alum k* aq-mar rbp6 *Fl-ac* k* gast a1 *Iod* k* led ptk1 naja bg3* ozone sde2• *Phos* b7a.de sil sne symph fd3.de• tritic-vg fd5.de
- **keloid** (See Keloid)
- **nodules**: fl-ac bg2* sil
- **operation**; after: arist-cl sp1
- **painful**: all-c bg2* asaf k2* aster a bamb-a stb2.de• both-ax tsm2 calen oss• *Carb-an* carb-v bg2* con h2 crot-h eug hr1 gink-b sbd1• graph *Hyper* k* kali-c kali-sil k2 *Lach* k* limen-b-c hm2* lyss *Mag-m* h2 *Nat-m* k* *Nit-ac* nux-v h1 phos plut-n srj7• **Sil** k* staph k2* sul-ac tritic-vg fd5.de
  - **air** agg.; in open: graph h2
  - **become** (See painful)
  - **burning**: ars k* *Carb-an* k* carb-v bg2* caust tl1 *Graph* k* hyper k2 lach k* tell ptk1
  - **drawing**: graph h2 phyt bg2* sep h2
  - **pressing**: carb-v h2 kali-c h2 petr h2 sulph h2
  - **shooting** upwards: hyper k2
  - **sore**; become: caust *Fl-ac* graph a nux-v **Sil**
  - **stinging**: *Carb-an* hyper k2 *Sil* *Sul-ac*
  - **stitching**: chin h1 mez h2* petr h2 *Sil* sul-ac bg2* thuj bg2*
  - **tearing**: carb-v h2* graph h2 petr h2 sep h2
  - **touch** agg.: hep h2 puls h1
  - **weather**; change of: carb-an *Nit-ac* k*
  - ○ • **Bones**: mag-m h2
- **pimply**: fl-ac bg2* iod k*
- **purple**: asaf tl1* loxo-recl bnm10•
  - **accompanied** by | **ulceration**: asaf ptk1
  - **followed** by | **black**: loxo-recl bnm10•
- **red**; become: ant-c bad cench k2 *Fl-ac* k* **Lach** k* limen-b-c hm2* *Merc* k* nat-m k* sil stram k* *Sul-ac* k*
  - ○ • **Edges** around: *Fl-ac*
- **round**: rhus-t bg2
- **scaly**: fl-ac bg2*
- **sensitive**: staph mrr1

- **shining**: sil k*
- **tension**; in: kali-c h2* lach bg2
- **unsightly**: carb-an ptk1
- **veins**; studded with: asaf a* cench
- **vesicles**; surrounded by: *Fl-ac* k*
- **white**: kali-bi bg2 rad-br ptk1 syph bg2*
  - **brown** scars turned white; old: berb vl

CLAMMY (See PERSPIRATION - Clammy)

CLOTHING: | **agg.**: coc-c k2

COAL (See Burning - coal - rash)

COBWEB; sensation of a: arg-n br1

COLD:
- **agg.**: agar ptk1 *Hep* ptk1 lac-d ptk1 petr ptk1 *Psor* ptk1 *Rhus-t* ptk1
- **air** agg.: psor k2
- **bathing** agg.: *Ant-c* ptk1 thuj ptk1

COLDNESS: abies-c br1* acet-ac hr1* acon k* aeth br1 agar k* agn k* ail k* alum k* alum-p k2 alum-sil k2 am-c k* am-caust a1 am-m k* ambr k* amyg a1* anac k* *Anan* k* ant-c k* ant-m bro1 *Ant-t* k* apis apoc hr1 arn k* **Ars** k* *Ars-i* ars-s-f k2 asaf k* asar k* asc-c hr1 aur k* aur-ar k2 aur-i k2 aur-s k2 bar-c k* bar-m k* bar-s k2 *Bell* k* benz-ac a1* bism k* borx b2.de both bro1 bov k* brach hr1 bry k* *Cact* k* calad k* **Calc** k* calc-i k2 **Calc-p** k* calc-sil k2 **Camph** k* cann-i hr1 cann-s k* canth k* *Caps* k* carb-ac k* carb-an k* *Carb-v* k* **Carbn-s** *Caust* k* *Cham* k* *Chel* k* *Chin* k* *Chinin-ar* k* *Cic* k* cimic a1* cina k* cinnb a1* cit-l a1* cocc k* *Coff* k* coff-t a1 *Colch* k* coloc k* con k* cory br1 crat br1* croc k* *Crot-h* k* *Cupr* k* cupr-ar a1* cupr-n a1 cupr-s a1* cycl k* cyt-l a1* **Dig** k* *Dios* dros k* dulc k* eup-pur k* euph k* euphr k* *Ferr* k* ferr-ar *Ferr-i* ferr-p gal-ac br1 galla-q-r nl2• *Gamb* a1* gels a1* *Graph* k* guare a1* ham fd3.de• *Hell* k* **Helo** *Helo-s* rwt2• hep k* hip-ac sp1 **Hydr-ac** k* hyos k* *Ign* k* ina-i mlk9.de inul hr1 *Iod* k* **Ip** k* *Jatr-c* bro1 *Kali-ar* k* *Kali-br* k* *Kali-c* k* kali-chl k* kali-m kali-n b2.de* kali-p k* *Kali-s* k* kali-sil k2 kali-sula a1* **Kalm** a1* kreos k* lac-d k2* *Lach* k* lachn k* lat-m br1* **Laur** k* *Led* k* *Lyc* k* lyss hr1 m-ambo b2.de m-arct b2.de **M-aust** b2.de mag-c k* mag-m k* mang k* med bro1* meny k* *Merc* k* *Merc-c* k* *Merc-cy* k* merc-sul hr1 *Mez* k* mosch k* mur-ac k* nat-ar nat-c k* nat-f sp1 nat-m k* nat-p nat-s a1 *Nit-ac* k* **Nux-m** k* *Nux-v* k* oena a1* ol-an a1 olnd k* *Op* k* **Ox-ac** k* par k* petr k* ph-ac k* *Phos* k* phys a1 *Phyt* k* pitu-p sp1 *Plat* k* *Plb* k* *Podo* k* puls k* pyrog k2* ran-b k* ran-s b2.de rhod k* **Rhus-t** k* ruta k* sabad k* sabin k* *Samb* k* sang k* sars k* **Sec** k* sel k* seneg k* **Sep** k* *Sil* k* spig k* spong k* squil k* stann k* staph k* stram k* stront-c k* sul-ac k* sul-i k2 **Sulph** k* *Sumb* k* *Tab* k* tarax k* teucr k* *Ther* thuj k* thymol sp1 valer k* ven-m rsj12• **Verat** k* verat-v k* verb k* viol-t b2.de zinc k* zinc-p k2 zinc-s a1 zing a1
- **one** side | **convulsions**, during: *Sil*
- **left**: caust dros k* *Lach* k* *Sil* k*
  - **epilepsy**, before: *Sil*
- **evening**: dulc a1
- **night**: all-s hr1 *Ars* k* *Camph* *Carb-v* k* eup-per hr1 ham fd3.de• *Hyos* k* *Mosch* nit-ac a1 phos a1*
- **accompanied** by:
  - **dryness** of skin (See Dry - accompanied - coldness)
  - **hemorrhages**; passive (See GENERALS - Hemorrhage - passive - accompanied - skin)
  - ○ **Heart**; complaints of the (See CHEST - Heart; complaints - accompanied - skin - coldness)
- **alternating** with | **heat**: petr-ra shn4• stram
- **coma**; with (See MIND - Coma - skin - coldness)
- **convulsions**; during: anan *Camph* caust cic *Hell* hyos mosch **Oena** op stram *Verat*
  - **side** of body; one (See one - convulsions)
- **diarrhea**; during: aeth *Camph* *Jatr-c* *Laur* tab *Verat*
- **eating**; after: camph ran-b
- **exercise**; during: plb *Sil* valer pd
- **fever**; during: *Camph* *Iod* kali-sula a1
- **heat**; with internal (See GENERALS - Heat - sensation - internally)
- **icy**: *(↗GENERALS - Cold - feeling - icy)* agar ptk1 ant-t k* *Apis* ptk1 *Ars* k* cact ptk1 cadm-s *Calc* k* **Camph** k* **Carb-v** k* chinin-ar br1 chlol br1 cupr k* elaps ptk1 hell k* *Helo* ptk1 hydr-ac ptk1 lachn k* *Lyc* ptk1 med ptk1 meny ptk1 *Nat-m* k* nit-ac ptk1 ol-an ptk1 phos ptk1 *Sec* k* *Sil* ptk1 tarent k* valer k2 *Verat* k*

Coldness – icy: ...
  - **chill**; during: verat bro1
  - **spots**; in: *Agar* arg-met *Par* petr positr nl2• **Verat**
- **injured** parts: **Led**
- **labor**; during: coff
- **marble**; as: lat-m br1
- **menses**:
  - **after**: graph
  - **before**: *Sil*
  - **during**: arg-n k2 coff k* dig k* *Led* *Tab* k* thuj k* *Verat* k*
- **nausea**; with (See STOMACH - Nausea - accompanied - skin; STOMACH - Nausea - accompanied - skin - cold)
- **pain**; during: ars
- **pregnancy**; during: *Nux-m*
- **rings** around body; as if: helo-s rwt2•
- **scratching**; after: agar k* mez k* petr k*
- **sensation** of: arn k* *Calc* caust chel galla-q-r nl2• kali-br tl1 lac-d k2 malar jl2 *Merc* *Mosch* nat-m tl1 *Plat* positr nl2• puls *Rhus-t* sec *Verat-v*
  - ○ **Under** skin: ip rb2
- **sleep** | **during**: ambr br1
- **spots**: *Agar* arg-met berb caust mez k2 mosch *Par* k* petr plat sne tarent bg1 **Verat**
  - **scratching**; after: mez
- **stool**:
  - **after**: crot-t
  - **during**: sul-ac b4a.de
- **suffering** parts: caps caust *Led* merc mez *Sil* k*
- **trembling**; with: mosch op
- **uncover**; must: *Camph* med lp* *Sec* k*
- **vomiting** | **after**: asc-c c1
- **waves** over: helo-s rwt2•
- ○ **Nerves**; along painful *Led* merc sil
- **Upper** part of body: ip k*

COMEDONES (See FACE - Eruptions - comedones)

COMPLAINTS of skin: aethi-a ll1* aln br1 ambr ptk1 anac c2 anag br1 *Anan* br1 ant-c bg2 anthraco br1 *Apis* bg2* **Ars** bg2* asaf bg2 astac br1 *Bell* bg2* berb-a br1 bov bg2 bry ptk1 bufo br1 *Calc* bg2* caust ptk1 chlol br1 chrysar bwa3* cic br1 clem br1 *Com* br1 *Cop* br1 *Crot-t* bg2* daph br1 *Dol* br1 *Dulc* br1 *Euph* br1 fuli br1 *Graph* bg2* hep bg2* hera br1 hydrc br1 ichth br1 lach bg2* *Lappa* br1 lev c2 lyc bg2* mag-s br1 *Manc* br1 menth br1 **Merc** bg2* *Mez* bg2* morg fmm1• morg-g fmm1• morg-p fmm1• nat-m br1 nit-ac ptk1 oena br1 *Olnd* br1 ov br1 pall br1 petr bg2* phos ptk1 pip-m br1 *Pix* br1 *Prim-o* br1 *Psor* bg2* puls bg2* rad-br br1 *Ran-b* br1* ran-s ptk1 *Rhus-t* bg2* rhus-v br1 sabad ptk1 sars ptk1 scroph-n br1 sep bg2* sil bg2* staph br1 stram br1 sul-i br1 *Sulph* bg2* tell br1 thuj bg2* thyr ptk1 titan br1 tub br1 ust ptk1 verbe-o br1 vesp br1 vinc br1 viol-o ptk1 viol-t ptk1 [bell-p-sp dcm1]
- **accompanied** by:
  - **arthritis** (See GENERALS - Inflammation - joints - accompanied - skin)
  - **coryza** (See NOSE - Coryza - accompanied - skin)
  - **respiration**; asthmatic (See RESPIRATION - Asthmatic - accompanied - skin)
  - **sleeplessness** (See SLEEP - Sleeplessness - accompanied - skin)
  - **waking**; frequent: ant-c b7.de* carb-v b4.de* zinc b4.de*
  - ○ **Bladder**; complaints of the (See BLADDER - Complaints of bladder - accompanied - skin)
  - **Kidneys**; complaints of (See KIDNEYS - Complaints - accompanied - skin)
  - **Testes**; inflammation of (See testes; MALE GENITALIA/SEX - Inflammation - testes - accompanied - skin)
- **alternating** with:
  - **gastrointestinal** complaints: graph ptk1

- **alternating** with: ...
  - • **internal** affections (See GENERALS - Complaints - internal - alternating - eruptions)
  - • **other** symptoms: ant-c ptk1 ars ptk1 calad ptk1 graph ptk1 hep ptk1 staph ptk1 sulph ptk1
  - • **respiration**; complaints of (See RESPIRATION - Complaints - alternating - skin)
  - O • **Joints**; pain in (See EXTREMITIES - Pain - joints - alternating with - skin)
- **chronic**: eryth vwe2 gali br1 kali-ar br1
- **dirty** filthy people: sulph tl1
- **eruptions**; after suppressed: psor mtf33
- **rheumatism**; after: dulc bro1
- **syphilitic**: phos br1
- O - **Folds** of skin: ars ptk1 calc ptk1 carb-v ptk1 graph bg2* hep ptk1 lyc ptk1* merc ptk1 morg-p mtf *Nat-m* ptk1 ol-an ptk1 petr ptk1* psor bg2* puls ptk1 sel ptk1 sep ptk1 sil ptk1 sulph bg2*
- **Mucocutaneous** borders: graph ptk1 hep ptk1 nat-p ptk1 nit-ac br1* petr ptk1 psor ptk1 *Sulph* ptk1
- **Sebaceous** glands: lyc bro1 psor bro1 raph bro1 sil bro1 sulph bro1
- **Under** the skin: acon bg2* aesc ptk1 agar bg2* alum ptk1 arg-met bg2 bell bg2* brom bg2* cic bg2* coca ptk1 cocain bg2 euph ptk1 ip bg2 lach bg2* mag-m bg2 phos bg2* sec bg2* thuj ptk1 zinc bg2*

CONDYLOMATA (See Excrescences - condylomata)

CONGESTION: *Morg* fmm1•
- **spots**; in: antip br1

CONTRACTION: alum k* am-m k* anac k* asar k* bell k* bism k* bry k* carb-v k* *Chin* k* cocc k* cupr k* ferr k* *Graph* k* kali-c k* kreos k* lyc k* merc k* nat-m k* nit-ac k* *Nux-v* k* olnd k* op a1 par k* petr k* phos k* *Plat* k* plb k* puls k* ran-s k* rhod k* **Rhus-t** k* ruta k* sabad k* sec k* *Sel* k* sep k* sil k* spig k* stann k* stront-c k* sul-ac k* sulph k* zinc k* [heroin sdj2]
- **chill**; during: *Caps* bg2 chin bg2 graph bg2 lyc bg2 nat-m bg2 nit-ac bg2 nux-v bg2 *Par* b7.de* rhus-t bg2 sep bg2

CORD lay under the skin; as if a thin: euph rb2*

CRACKLING: | **Under** skin: carb-v ptk1

CRACKS: *(↗Chapping)* *Aesc* aloe alum k* alum-sil k2 am-c *Ant-c* k* ant-t ptk1 anthraci bro1 anthraco c2* *Arn* k* ars bg2* ars-s-f bro1 *Aur* k* *Bad* k* bals-p c2 bar-c k* bar-s k2 benz-ac c2 bov bg2* bry k* bufo bg2* cadm-s br1 **Calc** k* calc-f bro1* calc-s k* *Carb-an* k* carb-v k* **Carbn-s** *Caust* bg2* *Cham* k* cist bg2* com corn-a br1 *Cund* c2* *Cycl* k* eug bro1 falco-pe nl2• *Ferr* ptk1 fl-ac bg2* **Graph** k* *Hep* k* hydr k* *Ign* ptk1 iris kali-ar bro1 kali-bi gk kali-c k* *Kali-s* kali-sil k2 *Kreos* k* *Lach* k* led bro1 *Lyc* k* mag-c k* mag-p c2 maland bro1* *Mang* k* mang-act bro1 *Merc* k* merc-c ptk1 merc-i-r bg2* merc-pr-r bro1 mez ptk1* mur-ac ptk1 *Nat-c* k* *Nat-m* k* *Nit-ac* k* olnd k* osm *Paeon* **Petr** k* petr-ra shn4• phos k* pix bro1 *Psor* k* ptel gk **Puls** k* ran-b bro1 rat bro1* *Rhus-t* k* rhus-v a* ruta k* sanic bg2* **Sars** k* *Sed-ac* br1 **Sep** k* *Sil* k* sinus rly4• **Sulph** k* suprar rly4• teucr k* viol-t k* x-ray bro1 xero bro1 *Zinc* k* zinc-p k2
- **burning**: petr sars zinc
- **deep**, bloody: alum bg2* graph bg2* *Merc* k* moni jl2 **Nit-ac** k* parth vml3• **Petr** k* psor k2* puls k* rhus-v a *Sars* k* sil a *Sulph* k*
- **fetid**: *Merc*
- **humid**: aloe
- **itching**: merc *Petr* k*
- **linear**: moni jl2
- **mercurial**: *Hep* *Nit-ac* *Sulph*
- **new** skin cracks and burns: *Sars* k*
- **painful**: *Graph* k* mang moni jl2 nit-ac vh petr vh rhus-v vh sars vh x-ray bg zinc
- **patterned**; geometrically: mez mrr1
- **skin** and mucous membranes meet; where (See mucocutaneous)
- **small**: merc-i-r ptk1
- **summer** agg.: coc-c bg1
- **ulcerated**: bry merc
- **washing**; after: alum *Ant-c* k* bry k* **Calc** k* *Calc-s* cham k* hep a kali-c k* lyc k* merc a nit-ac k* psor a *Puls* k* rhus-t k* sars k* **Sep** k* **Sulph** k* zinc k*
- **winter** agg.: alum **Calc** k* *Calc-s* **Carbn-s** k* cist a *Graph* k* merc a **Petr** k* *Psor* sanic a* **Sep** k* **Sulph** k*

Cracks: ...
- **yellow**: merc k*
- O - **Folds** of skin: mang ptk1
- **Mucocutaneous** borders: graph mrr1 nit-ac mtf11 paeon mtf11
- **Orifices** cracked: ant-c vh cund mp4*• graph mtf11 **Nit-ac** bg3* sulph bg2

CRAWLING (See Formication)

CREEPING (See Formication)

CUTTING (See Pain - cutting)

CYSTS (See GENERALS - Tumors - cystic)

DECUBITUS (= becomes sore): *Agar* k* all-c c1* am-c k* am-m k* ambr k* ang b2.de* ant-c k* apis bg2 *Arg-n* k* **Arn** k* ars k* bapt k* bar-c k* bell k* bov k* bry bg2 bufo bg2 *Calc* k* calc-p **Calen** vml3• camph c2 canth k* carb-ac bro1 carb-an k* *Carb-v* k* caust k* cham k* **Chin** k* chinin-s bg2 chlol c2 coff k* colch k* crot-h dros k* echi bg2* euph euphr b2.de* fl-ac k* **Graph** k* *Hep* k* hippoz c2* hydr k* *Ign* k* kali-ar kali-c k* kreos k* **Lach** k* lap-a br1 lat-m bnm6• *Lyc* k* m-arct b2.de mag-m k* mang k* *Merc* k* merc-c bg2 mez k* mur-ac bg2* *Nat-c* k* nat-m k* nit-ac k* nux-m bro1 nux-v k* olnd k* op k* paeon c2* **Petr** k* ph-ac k* phos k* plb k* podo bg2 *Puls* k* pulx br1 pyrog bg2* rhus-t k* ruta k* sars bg2 sel k* **Sep** k* **Sil** k* spig k* squil k* *Sul-ac* k* *Sulph* k* ter k* *Tub* st1 valer c2* vinc bg2 vip bro1 zinc k*
- **children**; in: ant-c k* bar-c k* bell k* *Calc* k* carb-v bg2 **Cham** k* *Chin* k* ign k* kreos k* *Lyc* k* **Med** vh merc k* puls k* **Rhus-t** b7a.de ruta k* *Sep* k* sil k* squil k* **Sulph** k* [lac-ac stj]
- **gangrenous**: caust mtf33
- **sensitive**: **Chin** bg2
- O - **Bend** of joints: sep bg2
- **Folds**; in: graph a3 lyc mta1 sulph al1

DENTITION agg.; during: borx ptk1 cham ptk1 merc ptk1 sulph ptk1

DEPIGMENTATION (See Discoloration - white - spots)

DERMATITIS (See Inflammation)

DERMATOGRAPHISM (See Discoloration - red - scratching - streaks)

DESQUAMATION (See Eruptions - desquamating)

DIRTY: allox tpw4* *Apis* *Ars* k* bry *Caps* ferr k* ferr-pic bg3 guat sp1 iod k* merc k* nat-m tl1 petr bg3 phos **Psor** k* *Sanic* sec **Sulph** k* thuj k*
- **oily** oozing: *Psor* jl2
  - • **odor**: *Psor* jl2
    - ⁝ **flesh**; of rotten: psor jl2
    - ⁝ **nauseating**: psor jl2
    - ⁝ **unhealthy**: *Psor* jl2

DISCOLORATION:
- **blackish**: acon k* ant-c k* ant-t ptk1 *Apis* *Arg-n* arn br1* **Ars** k* asaf k* aur bapt ptk1 both fne1• carb-ac ptk1 *Carb-v* k* chel *Chin* ptk1 *Crot-h* k* cycl ptk1 elaps ptk1 ferr ptk1 gels ptk1 hell ptk1 kreos ptk1 lac-e hrn2• *Lach* k* mag-m ptk1 *Merc* ptk1 merc-c ptk1 nit-ac k* nux-v ptk1 op ptk1 ph-ac phos ptk1 phyt **Plb** k* **Sec** k* sol-t-ae c2 spig k* staph ptk1 stram ptk1 sul-ac ptk1 verat ptk1
  - • **pores**: sabin c1*
  - • **spots**: aeth anac bg2 arn br1 *Ars* k* both br1 cic a1 *Crot-h* k* ferr *Lach* k* phos k2 rhus-t k* sars k2 sec k* *Vip* k*
    - ⁝ **gray**: loxo-recl bnm1•
- **bluish**: acon k* *Aeth* ail am-c k* ang b2.de* *Ant-t* k* *Apis* k* *Arg-n* k* arn k* *Ars* k* aur k* aur-ar k2 *Bapt* k* *Bell* k* bism k* both fne1• *Brom* k* bry k* bufo cadm-s calc k* calc-sil k2 *Camph* k* *Carb-an* k* **Carb-v** k* *Carbn-s* chin chinin-ar coca cocc k* con k* cop **Crot-c** *Crot-h* k* *Cupr* k* cur **Dig** k* elaps ptk1 *Ferr-p* ptk1 gels glon bg2 *Hydr-ac* k* kali-bi *Kali-br* k* kreos ptk1 lac-e hrn2• lac-h sze9• **Lach** k* lat-m sp1 *Laur* k* led mang ptk1 merc k* *Merc-c* b4a.de merc-cy ptk1 mur-ac k* naja nat-m k* *Nux-m* **Nux-v** k* **Op** k* *Ox-ac* k* oxyurn-sc mcp1• petr a1 ph-ac k* phos k* *Phyt* k* plb k* puls k* rhus-t k* ruta fd4.de samb k* *Sec* k* sil k* spong k* *Stram* sulph k2* syph *Tarent* tarent-c ptk1 thuj k* thymol sp1 **Verat** k* **Verat-v** k* vip
  - • **accompanied** by:
    - ⁝ **pain** | **burning**: anthraci ptk1 ars ptk1 lach ptk1
  - • **chill**; during: *Apis* b7a.de* cocc bg2 *Lach* bg2 merc bg2 *Nux-v* b7.de* verat bg2
  - • **deep** blue: anthraci mrr1

• **gray**: *Acetan* vh1

• **indurated**: *Sars*

• **periodical** | **year**; every: *Crot-h*

• **spots**: aeth *Agar* bg2 anan ant-c k* anthraci apis arg-n **Arn** k* *Ars* k* ars-s-f k2 bad *Bapt* bg2 bar-c k* bar-m berb borx *Bry* k* calc *Carb-an* *Carb-v* chlol *Con* k* crot-c mre1.fr **Crot-h** k* dulc euphr *Ferr* k* hell ptk1 *Hep* kreos bg2 *Lac-c* k* **Lach** k* laur *Led* k* *Lyc* *Mag-m* b4a.de merc moni rfm1• mosch k* nit-ac k* *Nux-m* k* *Nux-v* k* *Op* k* **Ph-ac** k* **Phos** k* *Plat* plb *Puls* k* rhus-t k* ruta k* *Sars* **Sec** k* *Sep* bg2 sil k* **Sul-ac** k* *Sulph* k* tarent tarent-c mrr1 ter verat b7a.de *Vip* bg2 [echi stj]

⋮ **eruptions**; after: abrot ptk1 ant-t ptk1

○ • **Affected** part: ars bg2 asaf bg2 aur bg2 carb-an ptk1 con bg2 hep bg2 lach bg2* merc bg2 sec ptk1 sil bg2 verat bg2

- **bronzed**: tub ptk1
- **brown**: ant-c bg2 arg-n bg2* *Ars* bg2* aur bg2 bapt ptk1 berb ptk1 borx bg2 *Bry* ptk1 calc-p bg2 cann-xyz bg2 carb-v ptk1 carc cd* chel ptk1 crot-h tl1 dulc fd4.de hyos bg2* iod bg2* kreos ptk1 *Lach* bg2 lyc ptk1 lycps-v ptk1 manc ptk1 nat-m bg2 nit-ac bg2* op bg2* petr ptk1 phos bg2* plb bg2 *Rhus-t* ptk1 sec bg2* **Sep** bg2* staph ptk1 *Sulph* ptk1 thuj ptk1* verat ptk1

• **coffee** with milk: carc jl2*

• **dark** brown: ars-h br1

• **elevated**: caust h2

• **inflamed**: ferr h1

• **itching**: caust h2 lyc h2 sulph h2

• **liver** spots: am-c k* *Ant-c* k* ant-t k* *Arg-n* arn k* *Ars* k* ars-i ars-s-f k2 *Aur* k* aur-ar k2 bad borx bry k* cadm-s calc k* calc-p calc-s calc-sil k2 canth k* *Carb-v* k* *Carbn-s* carc bg* caul bg2 caust k* chel bg2 *Con* k* cop cor-r crot-h **Cur** k* dros k* *Dulc* k* ferr k* ferr-ar k2 ferr-i graph k* *Hyos* k* *Iod* k* kali-ar kali-bi k* kali-c k* kali-p kali-s k2 kali-sil k2 **Lach** k* *Laur* k* led bg2 **Lyc** k* **Merc** k* *Merc-c* b4a.de merc-i-r *Mez* k* moni rfm1• nat-ar *Nat-c* k* nat-hsulo mtf11 nat-m bg2 nat-p **Nit-ac** k* *Nux-v* k* ozone sde2• petr k* *Phos* k* *Plb* k* psor al2 puls k* ruta k* sabad k* **Sep** k* sil k* stann k* sul-ac sul-i k2 **Sulph** k* tarent *Thuj* k* trios rsj11• *Tub* [am-m stj1]

• **pigmentation** following ezcematous inflammation: berb bro1* lach bro1 *Lyc* bro1 med bro1 merc bro1 merc-d bro1 *Nit-ac* bro1 sil bro1 sulph bro1 ust bro1

• **spots**: bac bro1 carc mlr1• card-m bro1 con bro1 crot-h ptk1 iod bro1* lach ptk1 lyc ptk1 merc ptk1 petr ptk1 phos bro1* sanic ptk1 sep bro1* sulph ptk1 thuj bro1*

⋮ **coffee** with milk: carc fb*

⋮ **eruptions**; after: berb ptk1*

• **suppurating**: ferr h1

- **chloasma**: (↗*FACE - Chloasma*) *Arg-n* bro1 aur bro1 cadm-s bro1 card-m bro1* **Caul** ●* cob bro1 cur bro1 guar bro1* laur bro1 **Lyc** ●* *Nat-hp* bro1 nux-v bg3* paull bro1 petr bro1 plb bro1 raph mgm• rob bg3 **Sep** ●* sulph c2* thuj bro1
- **contusion**; after: *Arn* bg2 bell bg2 con bg2 lach bg2 puls bg2 sul-ac bg2
- **coppery**: carb-an ptk1 cor-r ptk1 merc ptk1 mez ptk1 nit-ac ptk1 *Rhus-t* ptk1 syph ptk1

• **spots**: benz-ac ptk1 lach ptk1 med ptk1 nit-ac ptk1

⋮ **eruptions**; after: med ptk1

- **dark**: calc-p bg2
- **darkening**: pitu-p sp1
- **dirty**: ars k* borx bry k* bufo k* caust br1 *Ferr* k* *Ferr-i* ferr-pic ptk1 *Iod* k* kali-ar a1 merc k* *Nat-m* k* *Nit-ac* petr ptk1 phos k* *Plb* k* **Psor** k* sec k* stram **Sulph** k* tarent *Thuj* k* tub

• **gray**: (↗*white - dirty*) *Iod*

• **spots**: berb sabin *Sec*

- **dusky**: ail ptk1 *Ant-t* ptk1 arg-n bg2* ars ptk1 ars-i ptk1 *Bapt* ptk1 *Calc-p* bg2* camph ptk1 carb-v k2 crot-h ptk1 gels bg2* *Hell* ptk1 kali-p k2 lach ptk1 merc ptk1 *Nit-ac* ptk1 *Nux-v* ptk1 *Op* ptk1 sec ptk1 verat k2

• **silver** salts over a long period; from taking (= argyria): arg-n tl1

- **gray**: *Acetan* vh1 arg-met bg2 dig bg2 kreos bg2 lach bg2 laur bg2 merc bg2 phos bg2 plb bg2 scarl jl2 sec bg2 tab bg2 tub-m jl2 tub-r jl2 zinc bg2

• **spots**: iod nit-ac

- **green**: bufo bg2 con bg2 cupr bg2 nat-s mrr1
- **green**: ...

• **spots**: *Arn* k* ars k* *Bufo* k* carb-v **Con** k* crot-h kali-n b2.de* *Lach* k* med nit-ac sep k* sul-ac k* verat vip

- **injuries**; remains long after: led br1
- **lead** colored: *Plb* b7.de* *Sec* b7.de
- **liver** spots (See brown - liver)
- **livid**: agar bro1 *Ail* br1* *Ant-t* bro1 arn bro1 *Ars* bro1 cadm-s bro1 camph bro1 *Carb-an* bro1 *Carb-v* bro1 chin bro1 crat bro1 crot-h bro1 *Cupr* bro1 *Dig* bro1 hell bro1 ip bro1 kali-i bro1 lach bro1* *Laur* bro1 *Morph* bro1 mur-ac bro1 *Pyrog* jl2 *Sec* bro1 sul-ac k2* *Tarent-c* bro1 *Verat* bro1 vip bro1

• **spots**: agav-a bro1 *Ail* bro1 bapt a1* both bro1 *Morph* bro1 ox-ac bro1 sec bro1 *Sul-ac* bro1

- **mottled**: ail k2* am-c k2* arn k2 ars k* bapt ptk1 bell k2* bond a1 *Carb-v* k* chlol cic k2 con ptk1 cop k* *Crot-h* k* glon ptk1 kali-bi ptk1 kali-m ptk1 **Lach** k* led k2* lil-t ptk1 loxo-recl bnm1• manc ptk1 nat-m ptk1* nux-m k* *Nux-v* k* ox-ac k* phos ptk1 puls k2* rhus-t ptk1 sars ptk1 sulph ptk1 syph ptk1 thuj ptk1* *Verat-v* k*

• **chill**; during: arn crot-h kali-br hr1 *Nux-v* rhus-t

• **washing**; after: kali-c

- **orange**: elat br1
- **pale**: *Acet-ac* am-c k2 *Anan* androc srj1• *Apis* *Ars* k* ars-s-f k2 atra-r bnm3• bar-c k* bar-s k2 **Bell** k* benz-ac k* borx k2 **Calc** k* calc-p k2 *Calc-s* calc-sil k2 *Carb-ac* carb-an k* *Carb-v* k* carc jl2* caust k* *Chin* k* *Chinin-ar* **Cocc** k* *Con* k* crat br1 *Cupr* *Dig* k* diph jl2 diphtox jl2 **Ferr** k* *Ferr-ar* *Ferr-p* *Fl-ac* k* graph k* *Hell* k* *Helon* ign k* kali-ar kali-br a1 *Kali-c* k* *Kreos* loxo-recl bnm10• **Lyc** k* mang *Merc* *Merc-c* k* *Nat-c* hr1 *Nat-m* k* *Nat-s* k* **Nit-ac** k* *Nux-v* k* olnd k* op k* ph-ac k* *Phos* k* **Plat** k* *Plb* k* *Podo* **Puls** k* pyrog k2 sabin k* sang **Sec** *Sep* k* *Sil* k* *Spig* k* staph k* *Sul-ac* k* **Sulph** k* sumb syph mrr1 tab k* thuj k2 tub k2 valer k* **Verat** k* zinc k* zinc-s a1 [am-br stj2]

• **children**; in: calc br1 chir-fl bnm4•

• **chill**; during: *Camph* b7.de

• **fever**; during: cocc bg2 ferr bg2 *Lyc* bg2 **Mosch** bg2 nit-ac bg2 *Puls* bg2 sulph bg2

• **spots**: lach k*

⋮ **cold** agg.; becoming: *Sabad* b7a.de

- **pink** spots: colch ptk1
- **purple**: acon ptk1 *Ail* br1 *Arn* ptk1 *Ars* ptk1 bapt ptk1 camph ptk1 carb-an ptk1 *Carb-v* ptk1 *Crot-h* ptk1 **Cupr** ptk1 **Dig** ptk1 elaps ptk1 *Ferr-p* ptk1 ham k2 kreos ptk1 **Lach** ptk1* laur ptk1 led mrr1 mang ptk1 merc-cy ptk1 mur-ac hr1* *Nux-v* ptk1 *Op* ptk1 ox-ac ptk1 rhus-t ptk1 sec k2* sep ptk1 sil ptk1 sulph ptk1 tarent tl1* tarent-c ptk1* thuj ptk1 toxo-g jl2 *Verat* ptk1 **Verat-v** ptk1

• **spots**: sec k2

⋮ **eruptions**; after: abrot ptk1*

• **suppression** of eruption; after: abrot br1*

- **red**: *Acon* k* **Agar** k* agn k* ail k2 *Am-c* k* anh sp1 ant-c k* **Apis** k* *Arn* k* **Bell** k* bell-p sp1 bov k* *Bry* k* bufo bg2 buth-a sp1 calc k* calc-p bg2 calc-sil k2 camph k* canth k* caps k2 carb-v k* celt a1 chin k* chinin-s bg2 cinnb k2 cob-n sp1 coc-c cocc k* coll *Com* con k* cop *Crot-c* k* *Crot-h* *Crot-t* k* cub c1 cur cycl k* cypr br1 dig br1 *Dulc* k* euph k* euph-l br1 euphr b7.de ferr-p **Graph** k* hist sp1* hyos k* ign k* kreos k* lach k* led k* *Lyc* k* m-ambo b2.de* *Manc* k* **Merc** k* mez bg2* nat-f sp1 *Nat-m* k* nit-ac k* *Nux-v* k* olnd k* *Op* k* paeon petr k* *Ph-ac* k* *Phos* k* phyt k* pitu-gl skp7• pitu-p sp1 plb k* psor k2 *Puls* k* rad-br sze8• rauw sp1 **Rhus-t** k* *Ruta* k* *Sabad* k* sec k* sep k* sil k* spong k* squil k* stann k* **Stram** k* sul-ac k* sulfa sp1 *Sulph* k* *Tarax* k* tell ter bg2 teucr k* til k* toxo-g jl2 tub al vesp ptk2 x-ray sp1 zinc k* zing a1

• **accompanied** by:

⋮ **dropsy** (See GENERALS - Dropsy - general - accompanied - skin)

⋮ **perspiration**: lat-m bnm6• rauw sp1

• **bee** stings; from: dulc fd4.de **Sep** ●*

• **bluish** red | **stool** agg.; during: ars b4a.de *Carb-v* b4a.de

• **dark** red: tarent tl1

⋮ **mottled**: nat-m b4.de thuj b4.de

• **fever**; during: *Apis* b7a.de* **Ars** b4a.de* bell bg2 canth b7.de* **Ign** b7a.de* merc bg2 *Nux-v* bg2 *Op* bg2 ph-ac bg2 *Puls* bg2 rhus-t bg2

• **fiery** red: stram b7a.de

• **flush** over whole body; with: cub c1

• **heat** | **with**: ars h2 bell h1 pitu-gl skp7•

• **mottled**: carb-v bg2 *Caust* bg2 lyc bg2 plat bg2 thuj bg2

- **network**; like a: *Brom* b4a.de
- **parts** on which he had been lying: petr a1
- **points**: ant-c b7.de calad b7a.de canth b7.de caps b7.de lach b7.de *Sabad* b7a.de
- **scarlet**: am-c tl1 am-m b7a.de bell bg2* chinin-s bg2 chlol bg1 *Croc* b7.de* *Stram* b7a.de
- **scratching**; after: adam skp7• agar k* am-c k* ant-c k* arn k* *Bell* k* b o v k* canth k* chin k* dulc k* *Graph* k* kreos k* lyc k* *Merc* k* *Nat-m* k* nux-v k* *Olnd* k* op k* ozone sde2• petr k* ph-ac k* psor jl2 puls k* **Rhus-t** k* ros-d wla1 ruta k* spong k* tarax k* teucr k*
  - **streaks**: calc carb-v k* dulc fd4.de euph k* mez mrr1 par k* ph-ac k* **Phos** k ●* *Sabad* k* thal dx
- **spots**: *(↗FACE - Discoloration - red - spots)* acon k* aeth agar bro1 agn k* ail bg2* *Alum* k* alum-p k2 **Am-c** k* am-caust a1 am-m k* *Ambr* k* *Ant-c* k* ant-t k* *Apis* k* *Arn* k* **Ars** k* ars-i ars-s-f k2 aur k* bar-c k* bar-s k2 barbit bro1 **Bell** k* benz-ac *Berb* brom *Bry* k* buth-a sp1 calad k* **Calc** k* calc-i k2 calc-sil k2 canth k* caps k* *Carb-an* k* *Carb-v* k* carbn-s k2 caust k* cham k* chel chin k* *Chlol* cinnb cist clem k* *Coc-c* k* **Cocc** k* coff k* *Con* k* cor-r croc k* crot-c mre1.fr *Crot-h* *Crot-t* cupr k* *Cycl* k* *Dros* k* *Dulc* k* elaps ferr ferr-ar ferr-i *Graph* k* hep k* hyos k* iod k* *Ip* k* *Jug-c* kali-ar kali-c k* kali-i k* kali-n k* kali-s kali-sil k2 **Lach** k* led k* *Lyc* k* m-ambo b2.de* m-arct b2.de* *Mag-c* k* mag-m k* mang **Merc** k* mez k* nat-ar nat-c k* nat-m k* nat-p **Nit-ac** k* nux-v k* oena ol-j o p k* par k* *Petr* k* *Ph-ac* k* **Phos** k* phyt *Pic-ac* bg2 *Plb* k* propl ub1• p t e l c1 puls k* rhod k* *Rhus-t* k* ros-d wla1 **Sabad** k* *Samb* sars k* scol a1* sec k* **Sep** k* *Sil* k* spong k* squil k* *Stann* k* *Stram* k* **Sul-ac** k* sul-i k2 **Sulph** k* sumb *Tab* *Teucr* k* thuj k* verat k* vip k* zinc k* zinc-p k2 [calc-n stj1 *Spect* dfg1]
  - **air**; cold: sabad
  - **bathing**; after: *Am-c*
    - **soap**; with: **Sulph** ●*
  - **bluish** red: *Anthraci* apis k* *Ars* *Bell* k* calc bg2 *Cor-r* bg2 crot-h elaps *Lach* **Phos** k* phyt ptk1 plb ptk1 *Sul-ac* b4a.de
    - **nodules**: *(↗Eruptions - erythema nodosum)* lyss hr1
  - **brownish** red: calc cann-s k* *Carb-v* **Nit-ac** k* *Phos* k* **Sep** thuj k*
  - **burning**: lyc h2* sulph h2*
  - **coppery**: alum k* *Ars* k* bad bg2 calc k* cann-s k* **Carb-an** k* carb-v k* *Cor-r* k* crot-t *Kreos* k* **Lach** k* led k* lyc bg2 merc pd *Mez* k* *Nit-ac* phos k* phyt *Rhus-t* k* ruta k* syph k* ust k* *Verat* k*
    - **desquamation**; after: *Carb-an* chol
    - **syphilitic**: *Carb-an* bro1 carb-v bro1 *Cor-r* bro1 kali-i bro1 lyc bro1 m e r c bro1 nit-ac bro1 sulph bro1
  - **coral**-colored: cor-r br1
  - **dark** red: bell b4.de cor-r br1
  - **desquamation**; after: *Carb-an* *Fl-ac*
  - **eruptions**; after: arum-t bg3*
  - **fiery** red: acon k* bell k* ferr-ma stram k*
  - **flesh** is thin over bones; where: ph-ac k2
  - **inflammation**; after: bry bg2
  - **itching**: cocc mrr1 con h2* dulc h2* graph h2* ina-i mlk9.de lyc h2*
  - **moist**: crot-t
  - **pale** in cold; turning: *Sabad* b2.de*
  - **pale** red: *Apis* bg2 *Arn* b7a.de nat-c k* phos k* *Sil* k* teucr k*
  - **red** wine; like: *Cocc* k* **Sep** k*
  - **rose**-colored: apis bg2 bell bg2 cann-s carb-an carb-v cocc cop *Nat-c* b4a.de* rhod sars sep *Sil* b4a.de tep teucr vip bg2
  - **scarlet**: acon k* **Am-c** k* am-m k* antip vh1 arn k* *Ars* k* bar-c k* **Bell** k* *Bry* k* *Carb-an* carb-v k* caust k* cham k* coff k* *Croc* k* dulc k* euph k* hep k* *Hyos* k* iod k* ip k* lach k* **Merc** k* ph-ac k* phos k* r h u s - t k* *Stram* k* *Sulph* k*
  - **smooth**, indurated: *Carb-an*
  - **swollen**: plb b7a.de
  - **violet**: con bg2 ferr nit-ac phos k* verat k*
  - **warmth** agg.: fl-ac
- **streaks**: *Sabad* b7a.de
- **swelling**; with: androc bnm2• celt a1 tarent tl1

○ • **Orifices**: aloe ptk1 nit-ac ptk1* pyrog ptk1 *Sulph* br1*

- **rosy**: apis br1
  - **children**; in: cina br1*
    - **nurslings**: acon tl1
- **spots**: agar *Carc* mlr1• crot-h ptk1 dulc fd4.de lat-m bnm6• morb jl2 thuj mtf33
  - **burnt**; as if: ant-c k* *Ars* k* carb-v k* caust k* chir-fl bnm4• *Cycl* k* e u p h k* hyos k* kreos k* rhus-t k* sec k* stram k* tritic-vg fd5.de
  - **circumscribed**: croc b7.de m-arct b7.de
  - **confluent**: *Bell* b2.de* *Cic* b2.de* hyos b2.de* ph-ac b2.de* valer b2.de*
  - **dark** spots:
    - **eruptions**; after: sulph mtf
    - **old** people; in●: ars k* aur bar-c k* *Carb-an* *Con* k* *Lach* k* *Lyc* op k* *Sec*
  - **elevated**: kali-c bg2 kali-i bg2 merc b4.de nat-s bg2 sil bg2
  - **eruptions**; after: ferr bg2 lach bg2 rhus-t bg2 thuj bg2
  - **fleabites**; like: *Acon* k* ant-t bg2 bell bg2 dulc bg2 graph bg2 *Jug-c* bg2 lac-c kr1 mez bg2 pall sec bg2 stram b7.de*
  - **glistening**: *Calc* k* phos
  - **granular**: par b7.de
  - **lenticular**: calc rhus-t vip
  - **moist**: ant-c ars carb-v *Crot-t* *Hell* kali-c lach sel **Sil** *Sulph* tarax
  - **periodical** | **year**; every: *Crot-h*
  - **scratching**; after: *Am-c* k* ant-c k* bell k* calc k* cocc k* cycl k* graph k* mag-c k* mang k* merc k* nit-ac k* ph-ac k* *Phos* k* *Rhus-t* k* sabad k* sep k* sil k* sul-ac k* *Sulph* k* tell bg2 verat k*
  - **small**: ant-t bry lach led lyc merc op rat squil *Sul-ac* vip
  - **smarting**: bry k* *Ferr* k* fl-ac bg2 hep k* *Led* k* nat-m k* ph-ac k* *Puls* sil k* verat k*
  - **smooth**: carb-an carb-v cor-r lach mag-c petr sumb
  - **star** shaped: stram
  - **stinging**: canth k* chel k* lach lyc merc *Nit-ac* k* *Puls* k* **Sil**
    - **tetters**; like: merc b4a.de nat-m b4a.de sep b4a.de
- **streaks**: all-c ptk1 apis bg2 *Bell* ptk1 bufo bg2* carb-v b4a.de* euph b4a.de* *Hep* ptk1 merc ptk1 mygal ptk1 ph-ac h2* *Phos* ptk1 sabin ptk1 sil ptk1 sulph bg2
- **vermilion**: hyos b7.de*
- **violet**: bell h1* loxo-lae bnm12• *Verat* b7.de
  - **gray**: *Acetan* vh1
- **white**: **Apis** **Ars** ars-s-f br1* calc carb-v cob-n mtf11 *Fl-ac* **Kali-c** lac-c mica mtf11 *Nat-c* hr1 nat-f sp1 nat-m bro1 nit-ac bro1 pitu-p mtf11 sil mrr1 sumb k* zinc-p bro1
  - **brownish** white | **spots**: thuj bg2
  - **dirty**: *(↗dirty - gray)* *Caust* br1
  - **milky**: nat-c br1
  - **spots**: *(↗Eruptions - herpetic - circinate; Eruptions - pityriasis versicolor; Vitiligo; EXTREMITIES - Discoloration - white - spots)* *Alum* k* am-c k* ant-t vh **Ars** k* ars-s-f k2* *Aur* k* *Berb* *Calc* k* c a l c - f ptk1 calc-sil k2 carb-an k* coca graph bro1* ign dgt *Merc* k* **Mica** vs *Nat-c* k* nat-m ptk1 nit-ac k* ozone sde2• *Phos* k* sel ptk1 **Sep** b2.de* **Sil** k* *Sulph* k* zinc bg2
    - **bluish**; becoming: *Calc*
    - **borders**; with dark: *Calc*
    - **children**; in: merc mtf33 sep vh*
    - **dreams** of white things; after: ozone sde2•
- **wine** colored: sep ptk1
- **yellow** (= jaundice, etc.): acal br1 acetan vh1 **Acon** k* aesc c2* agar k* agar-ph mtf11 agn *Aloe* k* alum alum-p k2 alumn k2 *Am-m* k* *Ambr* k* anders mtf11 *Ant-c* k* ant-i c1 *Ant-t* arg-n bro1 *Arn* k* *Ars* k* ars-i asaf k* astac k* *Aur* k* aur-m-n k* aur-s c1* barbit bro1 *Bell* k* *Berb* k* blatta-a c2 both fne1• bov c2 brass-n-o srj5• brom b4a.de* *Bry* k* bufo k* cadm-s br1 *Calc* k* calc-ar mtf11 *Calc-p* k* calc-s calc-sil k2 calen c2* cann-s k* *Canth* k* *Carb-v* k* carbn-s **Card-m** k* cas-s br1* *Caust* k* cean c2* cedr *Cham* k* **Chel** k* chelo c2* chen-a hr1* chim c2 **Chin** k* *Chinin-ar* **Chion** k* chol c2* cina k* coca cocc k* **Con** k* convo-s sp1 *Corn* k* corn-f croc k* **Crot-h** k* cupr k* *Dig* k* diph-t-tpt jl2 *Dol* c2* dulc k* elaps gk elat k* eup-per k* euph k* fab br1 fel br1* *Ferr* k* ferr-ar *Ferr-i* ferr-pic c2 fl-ac mtf11 gels k* granit-m es1• graph k* *Guat* sp1 hed sp1 hell k* *Hep* k* hier-p lsr4.de• hip-ac sp1 *Hydr* k* *Ign* k* ilx-a c2 ins mtf11 **Iod** k* iris *Jug-c* br1* kali-ar kali-bi k* kali-c k* kali-i mtf11 kali-m c2* kali-p *Kali-pic* c1*

- **yellow**: ...
kali-s k2 kali-sil k2 lac-h sze9• **Lach** k* lact mtf11 lat-m bnm6• laur k* *Lept* k* leptos-ih jl2 lina br1* lipp c2 loxo-lae bnm12• loxo-recl bnm10• **Lyc** k* mag-m k* mag-s sp1 malar jl2 mang k* mang-act br1 med **Merc** k* *Merc-c* k* merc-d bro1* morg-p pte1*• mur-ac sne myric k* nat-ar nat-c k* nat-ch mtf11 nat-f sp1 *Nat-m* k* nat-p k* **Nat-s** k* **Nit-ac** k* **Nux-v** k* olnd *Op* k* oscilloc jl2 ost bro1 petr k* ph-ac k* **Phos** k* pic-ac c2* **Plb** k* plb-xyz c2 *Podo* k* psor bg2* *Ptel* k* *Puls* k* quas mtf11 ran-b k* rheum k* rhus-t k* ric c2 rumx bro1 ruta br1* sabad k* *Sang* saroth sp1 *Sec* k* **Sep** k* *Sil* k* *Spig* k* still bro1 sul-ac k* sul-i k2 sulfa sp1 *Sulph* k* tab tarax b2.de* tarent ter c2 thuj tinas gsb1 toxo-g jl2 trinit br1* verat k* vip k* yers jl2 *Yuc* bro1 [spect dfg1 stann stj2]
  - **accompanied** by:
    - **apyrexia**: ars bro1 bol-la bro1 card-m bro1 nux-v bro1 podo bro1
    - **catarrh**: mag-s sp1
    - **catarrh**; gastroduodenal: acon mp1• kali-m mp1• kali-s mp1• nat-m mp1•
    - **constipation**: chion bro1
    - **dropsy**; external (See GENERALS - Dropsy - external - accompanied - skin - discoloration)
    - **dryness**: sang ptk1
    - **flatulence**: carb-v bg2 cham bg2 chin bg2 ign bg2 lyc bg2 nit-ac a1 nux-v bg2 plb bg2 sep dh1*
    - **hemorrhages** (See GENERALS - Hemorrhage - accompanied - skin)
    - **itching**: *Dol* mrr1* *Hep* k13
    - **stones**; obstruction with: chel mtf11
    - **stool**; alternately black and white: aur-m-n fr2*
    - **vomiting** (See STOMACH - Vomiting - accompanied - skin)
    - **Abdomen**; itching of: cham ptk1* merc mp1•
    - **Brain**; complaints of the (See HEAD - Brain; complaints of - accompanied - skin)
    - **Heart**; complaints of the (See CHEST - Heart; complaints - accompanied - skin - discoloration)
    - **Hypochondria**; complaints of: aloe bg2 am-m bg2 bry bg2 chion bg2 eup-per bg2 guaj bg2 lyc bg2 nux-v bg2 podo bg2 tarax bg2
    - **Liver**:
      - **congestion** of (See ABDOMEN - Congestion - liver - accompanied - skin)
      - **enlargement** of (See ABDOMEN - Enlarged - liver - accompanied - skin - discoloration)
      - **inactivity** of (See ABDOMEN - Inactivity - liver - accompanied - skin)
      - **induration** of (See ABDOMEN - Hard - liver - accompanied - skin - discoloration)
      - **pain** (See ABDOMEN - Pain - liver - region - accompanied - skin)
    - **Lungs**; inflammation of (See CHEST - Inflammation - lungs - accompanied - skin)
    - **Portal** congestion (See ABDOMEN - Portal - accompanied - skin)
    - **Tongue**:
      - **mucus**; white: *Dig* kr1*
      - **white** discoloration of the tongue: *Iod* kr1* **Merc** kr1* *Myric* kr1* *Nux-v* vk1
  - **albuminuria**; with: *Dig* mp1•
  - **anemia**, with: phos mp1•
  - **anger**; after: acon tl1* *Aur* kr1 *Aur-m-n* kr1 *Bry* cham k* chin mp1• ign mp1• nat-m mp1• *Nat-s* k* **Nux-v** k* sulph mp1•
  - **atrophy**, from acute: *Phos* mp1•
  - **bile**; from deficiency of: iris tl1
  - **brain** disease, with: phos ptk1*
  - **catarrhal**: am-m bro1 *Chel* bro1 *Chin* bro1 chion br1* dig bro1 *Hydr* bro1 *Lob* br1* *Merc* bro1 nux-v bro1 podo bro1
  - **children**, new born●: *Acon* k* astac mp1• *Bov* k* cham bro1 chel mrr1 *Chin* k* elat c1* *Lup* br1* *Merc* bg2* merc-d bro1 myric bro1* *Nat-s* k* ph-ac mp1• *Podo* k13 sep k* toxo-g jl2

Discoloration – yellow – children, new born: ...
    - **anger**, with: nat-s zr
  - **chill**; during: ambr bg2 ant-c bg2 *Apis* bg2 ars bg2 bell bg2 bry bg2 calc bg2 *Cham* bg2 *Chin* bg2 con bg2 dig bg2 ferr bg2 hell bg2 ign bg2 nat-m bg2 *Nux-v* bg2 op bg2 *Puls* bg2 *Rhus-t* bg2 sep bg2
  - **chronic**: aur bro1* chel ptk1* chion mp1• chol ptk1 con bro1* corn br1 iod bro1* phos bro1* sulph mp1• ter mp1•
  - **cider**, from: cham mp1• chion ptk1
  - **cold**; after taking a: acon mp1• cham mp1• dulc mp1• merc mp1• nux-v mp1•
  - **confusion**:
    - **after**: agar mp1• **Nux-v** mp1•
    - **with**: phos mp1•
  - **convulsions**:
    - **after**: agar mp1• **Nux-v** mp1•
    - **with**: agar
  - **dark** yellow: iod mtf33
    - **spots**: ant-t bg2 crot-h bg2
  - **diarrhea** | **after** | **agg.**: chin ptk1*
    - **during**: dig ptk1 *Lycps-v* mp1• *Merc* mp1• *Nux-v* mp1• *Podo* mp1• *Puls* mp1•
  - **emotions**; from: acon bg2 bry bro1* *Cham* bg2* lach bro1* nux-v bg2* vip bro1*
  - **fever**; during: ambr b7.de* *Ant-c* bg2 **Apis** b7a.de* ars bg2 bry b7.de* **Cham** b7.de* *Chin* b7.de* cocc bg2 con bg2 dig bg2 **Ferr** b7.de* ign bg2 lach bg2 **Merc-c** bg2 **Nux-v** b7.de* op b7.de* *Puls* b7.de* rhus-t b7a.de* sep bg2 sulph bg2
  - **fright**; after: acon tl1*
  - **fruit**; from unripe: rheum ptk1
  - **heat**; during: card-m ptk1* chel sne *Ferr* lach *Nux-v* vip ptk1*
  - **hemolytic**: crot-h mp1• hir mtf11
  - **intermittent** fever; after: am-c *Ars Chinin-s Con* ferr nat-c *Nat-m Nux-v Sang* **Sep** *Tub*
  - **loss** of vital fluids; from: chin ptk1
  - **malignant**: acon bro1 *Ars* bro1 crot-h bro1* lach bro1 merc bro1 *Phos* bro1
  - **masturbation**; after: chin ptk1
  - **menses**, from suppressed: chion br1* *Phos* b4a.de
  - **mortification**; after: bry *Lyc*
  - **nervous** excitement; from: phos ptk1
  - **pregnancy** agg.; during: acon vh1 aur k* phos c2*
  - **rheumatism** of arms, with: chel mp1•
  - **rich** food agg.: carb-v ptk1*
  - **rings**: *Nat-c* nat-m k*
  - **sallow** (= grayish greenish): cadm-s br1 syc bka1*•
  - **sexual** excess; after: chin ptk1
  - **spots**: alum-sil k2 ambr k* ant-t k* **Arn** k* ars k* aur-ar k2 calc-i k2 canth k* **Con** k* crot-c cur st dol br1 elaps **Ferr** k* hydrc iod k* kali-ar kali-c k* *Lach* k* *Lyc* k* *Nat-c* k* nat-p k* nux-v st **Petr** k* **Phos** k* plb bro1 *Psor* ptel hr1 *Rhus-t* b7a.de *Ruta* k* sabad k* **Sep** k* stann k* sul-i k2 **Sulph** k* *Thuj* vip
    - **brownish**: sep mtf11
    - **green**; turning: con bro1
    - **old** people; in: lyc br1
  - **sudden** attacks: crot-h tl1
  - **summer**; every: chinin-ar k* *Chion* k*
  - **toxic**: crot-h mtf11
  - **vexation** agg.: *Cham* k* kali-c k* *Nat-c Nat-s* ptk1

DRAWING:
- **cobweb**, or dried albuminous substance, withered and dried up; as from a: arg-n br1
- **inward**; as if skin were drawn: rat rb2

DRIED ALBUMINOUS SUBSTANCE: | **sensation**; of (See Drawing - cobweb)

DRY: *(↗FACE - Dryness)* *Acon* k* acon-f k* aeth hr1 agar h2* *Alum* k* alum-p k2 alum-sil k2 *Am-c* k* ambr k* ant-c k* *Ant-t* k* *Anthraci* anthraq rly4• *Apis* k* arg-met k* arg-n arizon-l nl2• *Arn* k* **Ars** k* *Ars-i* k* asaf k* bapt bg2 bar-c k* bar-m bar-ox-suc rly4• **Bell** k* *Bism* k* borx k* bov sne **Bry** k* bufo cain c1* *Calad* ptk1 **Calc** k* calc-i k2 calc-s calc-sil k2 *Camph* k* *Cann-s* k* canth k* carb-an k* *Carb-v* k* *Carbn-s* caust k* **Cham** k* *Chel* k* **Chin** k* *Chinin-ar* choc srj3• cina a1 clem k* cocc k* *Coff* k* **Colch** k* coli rly4• coloc k* con k* convo-s sp1 cortico tpw7* cortiso tpw7 *Crot-h* k* cypra-eg sde6.de• diph ptk1 **Dulc** k* **Eup-per** k* falco-pe nl2• *Ferr* k* ferr-ar ferr-i k2 ferr-p fic-m gya1 fl-ac ptk1 gels c1 gink-b sbd1• *Graph* k* guat sp1 hell k* hep k* *Hydr-ac* k* hydrc bro1 *Hyos* k* ign k* *Iod* k* *Ip* k* ix bnm8• jab br1 **Kali-ar** k* kali-bi k* **Kali-c** k* kali-i bg2 kali-m k2 kali-n k* kali-p kali-s kali-sil k2 ketogl-ac rly4• kreos k* *Lach* k* lap-la sde8.de• laur k* lavand-a ctl1• **Led** k* limest-b es1• *Lith-c* loxo-recl bnm1• **Lyc** k* m-ambo b2.de* m-aust b2.de *Mag-c* k* mag-m ptk1 maland jl2 malar jl2 mang k* mang-p rly4• meli ptk1 menis br1 *Merc* k* merc-c b4a.de* mez k* mim-p rsj8• mosch mur-ac k* *Nat-ar* *Nat-c* k* *Nat-m* k* nat-p nat-s ptk1 nat-sil fd3.de• *Nit-ac* k* nit-s-d br1 **Nux-m** k* nux-v k* olib-sac wmh1 **Olnd** k* **Op** k* pant-ac rly4• par k* parth vml3• **Petr** k* petr-ra shn4• *Ph-ac* k* **Phos** k* *Phyt* k* pilo bro1 pitu-p sp1 *Plat* k* **Plb** k* plut-n srj7• polyg-h bg2 positr nl2• *Psor* k* ptel c1* *Puls* k* rad-br sze8• ran-b k* ran-s k* rauw sp1 rhod k* *Rhus-t* k* ribo rly4• rumx ruta k* *Sabad* k* sacch sst1• sal-al blc1• sal-fr sle1• samb k* sang hr1* sanguis-s hrn2• sanic ptk1 sars bro1* **Sec** k* sel rsj9• **Seneg** k* *Sep* k* **Sil** k* *Skook* br1 spig k* *Spong* k* *Squil* k* *Staph* k* **Stram** k* stront-c k* sul-ac k* sul-i k2 **Sulph** k* *Sumb* k* tab bg2 tell rsj10• **Teucr** k* thal-xyz srj8• thuj k* thyr ptk1 tril-p c1 tritic-vg fd5.de tub ptk1* tub-m vn* tub-r jl2 uran-n br1 ust k* v-a-b jl2 vac jl2 valer k* vanil fd5.de vario br1* *Verat* k* **Verb** k* vero-o rly4*• *Viol-o* k* viol-t k* visc ptk1 vit-b-x mtf11 zinc k* [*Alumin-s* stj2]

- **morning** | **bed** agg.; in: mag-c h2
- **night**: nat-c h2*
- **accompanied** by:
  - **coldness** of skin: camph ptk1 nux-m ptk1
  - **dropsy** (See ABDOMEN - Dropsy - ascites - accompanied - skin; GENERALS - Dropsy - external - accompanied - skin - dry)
  - **fever**; dry (See FEVER - Dry - skin)
  - **inflammatory** fever (See FEVER - Inflammatory - skin)
  - ○ **Mucous** membranes | **discharges**; increased (See GENERALS - Mucous secretions - increased - accompanied - skin)
- **alternating** with | **perspiration**: *Nat-c* b4a.de
- **bathing** agg.: lavand-a ctl1•
- **burning**: acet-ac br1 **Acon** k* alum k* am-m k* ambr k* anac k* ant-c k* ant-t k* *Apis* arg-met k* *Arn* k* **Ars** k* ars-s-f k2 bar-c k* bar-m bar-s k2 **Bell** k* bism k* **Bry** k* *Calc* k* camph k* cann-s k* canth k* caps k* carb-v k* carbn-s caust k* cham k* *Chel* k* chin k* clem k* *Cocc* k* *Coff* k* colch k* coloc k* con k* croc k* cupr k* cycl k* *Dulc* k* ferr k* glon k2 graph k* *Hell* k* hep k* hyos k* ign k* ip k* *Kali-ar* *Kali-c* k* kali-n k* kali-s kreos k* **Lach** k* laur k* *Led* k* **Lyc** k* m-ambo b2.de* m-arct b2.de m-aust b2.de mag-c k2 mang k* *Merc* k* mosch k* mur-ac k* nat-c k* nat-m k* nat-p *Nit-ac* k* nux-m k* **Nux-v** k* **Op** k* par k* *Ph-ac* k* **Phos** k* phyt bg2 **Puls** k* ran-b k* rheum k* rhod k* *Rhus-t* k* ruta k* sabad k* sabin k* *Samb* k* *Sec* k* sel k* *Sep* k* *Sil* k* spig k* spong k* *Squil* k* *Stann* k* *Staph* k* **Stram** k* stront-c k* sul-ac k* *Sulph* k* tarax k* thuj k* **Valer** k* verat k* viol-t k* visc c1 zinc k* zinc-p k2
- **cracking**; as if: murx ptk1
- **fever**; during: acon b7a.de* bell bro1 *Ip* b7a.de *Op* b7a.de pyrog bro1
  - **alternating** with | **perspiration** (See FEVER - Dry - alternating - perspiration)
- **hot**: cic a1 iod mtf33 tell c1 tril-p c1 ust ptk1
- **parchment**; like: *Ars* b4a.de sabad ptk1
- **perspiration**; although: petr-ra shn4•
- **perspire**; inability to: *(↗Inactivity)* acet-ac bro1 acon k* *Aeth* bro1 *Alum* k* am-c ambr *Anac* apis apoc k* arg-met arg-n bro1 arizon-l nl2• arn **Ars** k* *Ars-i* **Bell** k* *Berb-a* bro1 bism brass-n-o srj5• bry k* calc k* calc-sil k2 cann-s *Cham* *Chin* k* coff **Colch** k* *Con* crot-t bro1 cupr *Dulc* k* *Eup-pur* **Graph** k* hyos iod k* ip kali-ar k* **Kali-c** k* kali-i bro1 kali-s kali-sil k2 lach c2* laur *Led* *Lyc* k* mag-c k* *Maland* bro1 merc merc-c nat-c bro1 nat-m nit-ac **Nux-m** k* nux-v olnd k* op k* *Petr* bro1 *Ph-ac* phos k* plat **Plb** k* plb-m bro1 *Psor* k* puls

Dry – perspire; inability to: ...
Rhus-t sabad *Samb* sanic bro1 sars bro1 sec k* seneg sep **Sil** k* spong **Squil** *Staph* sulph k* teucr thuj thyr bro1 verb viol-o [alumin stj2 alumin-p stj2]

  - **exertion** agg.: arg-met *Calc* *Nat-m* **Plb** k*
- **pollution**; after: bar-c h2
- **rough**: fic-m gya1 hep tl1 iod *Lith-c* merc nat-c sil tl1 sulph tl1
- **scratching** agg.: lavand-a ctl1• tell rsj10•
- **sensation** as if skin had dried: tub rb2
- **sensation** of dryness: *Alumn* br1 camph b7.de*
- **sleep**; during: thea bro1
- ○ **Single** parts: acon ptk1 alum ptk1 *Bell* ptk1 bry ptk1 graph ptk1 kali-bi ptk1 *Lyc* ptk1 *Nat-m* ptk1 **Nux-m** ptk1 petr ptk1 *Phos* ptk1 **Puls** ptk1 rhus-t ptk1 stram ptk1 **Sulph** ptk1 verat ptk1

EATING agg.: calc-p bg2 caust bg2 dulc bg2 nux-v bg2 puls bg2

ECCHYMOSES: *(↗Purpura; GENERALS - Hematoma)* aeth hr1* allox mgm• ancis-p tsm2 anth arg-n arge-pl rwt5• **Arn** k* ars bro1* bad bar-c k* bar-m bell bg2* bell-p bro1* bit-ar wht1• both bro1 both-ax tsm2 *Bry* k* calc k* canth tl1 *Carb-v* k* carc mrr1 cench tsm2 cham k* chin k* chlol k* chlor bro1 cic bg2 cloth tsm2 coca *Con* k* crot-c tsm2 *Crot-h* k* dulc k* erig ptk2 euphr k* *Ferr* k* flav jl2 ham k2* helo-s bnm14• *Hep* k* *Hyper* bg2 iod bg2* kreos bro1* *Lach* k* laur k* **Led** k* loxo-lae bnm12• loxo-recl bnm1• *Mag-m* b4a.de mill k2 mur-ac ptk1 nat-m sne *Nux-v* k* par k* petr bg2* petr-ra shn4• **Ph-ac** k* **Phos** k* physala-p bnm7• plb k* *Puls* k* pyrog ptk1 rad-br sze8• rhus-t k* ruta k* **Sec** k* solid ptk1 stront-c mrr1 **Sul-ac** k* *Sulph* k* suprar bro1 *Tarent* k* *Ter* k* thal-xyz srj8• *Thlas* bg2 vanil fd5.de verbe-o br1 vip tsm2 [bell-p-sp dcm1]

- **blow**; from the slightest: agar ptk1 arn ptk1 flav jl2
- **periodical** | **year**; every: crot-h
- **sensation** of: *Arn* b7.de* calc bg2 chin b7.de* ferr b7.de* nux-v bg2 par b7.de* ruta b7.de* sec b7.de* sul-ac bg2
- **spots**: morb jl2 tarent mtf33

ELASTICITY; want of (See Inelasticity)

ELECTRIC: | **sparks**; sensation as from electric: *(↗Sticking - electric)* agar *Arg-met* calc *Calc-p* melal-alt gya4 nat-m **Sec** *Sel* thal-xyz srj8• ulm-c jsj8•

ERUPTIONS: *(↗FACE - Eruptions)* acet-ac *Acon* k* acon-c c2 aeth mrr1 agar k* agn k* agri mtf11 alum k* alum-sil k2 alumn *Am-c* k* am-m k* ambr k* anac k* ang b2.de* *Ant-c* k* ant-t k* anthraci mrr1 *Apis* aq-mar jl aran a1 arg-met k* arn k* **Ars** k* **Ars-i** k* ars-s-f k2 arund asaf k* asar k* aster aur k* aur-s k2 **Bar-c** k* bar-m k* bell k* bism k* borx k* bov k* brom bg2 *Bry* k* calad k* **Calc** k* calc-i k2 **Calc-s** k* camph k* cann-s k* canth k* caps k* *Carb-an* k* *Carb-v* k* *Carbn-s* k* **Caust** k* cham k* chel k* chin k* chinin-ar chinin-s chlor k* chord-umb rly4• *Cic* k* cimic cina k* *Cist* clem k* cob cocc k* coch c2 coff k* colch k* coli rly4• coloc k* *Con* k* cop k* cor-r c2 crat br1 croc k* *Crot-t* cub a1 cupr k* cupr-act c2 cupr-ar a1 *Cycl* k* cystein-l rly4• dig k* dros k* *Dulc* k* elaps ery-m c2 euph k* euph-a c2 euphr k* fago a1 falco-pe nl2• ferr b2.de* fl-ac fum rly1*• germ-met srj5• gink-b sbd1• *Graph* k* guaj k* guare a1 *Hell* k* hep k* hyos k* ign k* iod k* *Ip* k* **Jug-c** k* **Jug-r** k* *Kali-ar* kali-bi k* *Kali-br* **Kali-c** k* kali-i a1 kali-m k2 kali-n k* kali-p **Kali-s** k* ketogl-ac rly4• *Kreos* k* lac-ac a1 lacer c1* lach k* lact a1 lappa c2 laur k* led k* **Luna** kg1• **Lyc** k* m-ambo b2.de* m-arct b2.de m-aust b2.de mag-c k* mag-m b2.de* mang b2.de* meny b2.de* **Merc** k* **Mez** k* morb jl2 morg fmm1• morg-p pte1*• morph a1 mosch k* mur-ac k* musca-d szs1 *Nat-ar* nat-c k* **Nat-m** k* nat-ox rly4• nat-p nat-pyru rly4• nat-s k2 nicotam rly4• *Nit-ac* k* nux-m b2.de* nux-v b2.de* *Olnd* k* op k* ox-ac a1 par k* **Petr** k* ph-ac k* phos k* phys a1 pix c2 plat k* plb k* prot fmm1• **Psor** k* *Puls* k* ran-b k* ran-s k* rheum k* rhod k* **Rhus-t** k* *Rhus-v* k* ric c2 *Rumx* ruta k* sabad k* sabin b2.de* samb k* sarr a1 sars k* sec k* sel k* seneg k* **Sep** k* **Sil** k* solid c2 spig k* spong k* squil k* stann k* *Staph* k* stram k* stront-c k* suis-hep rly4• suis-pan rly4• sul-ac k* *Sul-i* **Sulph** k* suprar rly4• syph k2 tarax k* tax c2 tell mrr1 tep c2 teucr k* thiam rly4• *Thuj* k* thymol sp1 tritic-vg fd5.de tub valer k* vanil fd5.de verat k* verb k* vero-o rly4*• *Viol-t* k* wies a1 zinc k* zinc-p k2

- **left** side; worse on the: myos-a rly4*• nat-f sp1
- **afternoon** | **16** h; starting up: lyc tl1
- **accompanied** by:
  - **cough**: *Carb-v* b4a.de

- diarrhea in summer (See RECTUM - Diarrhea - summer - accompanied - eruptions)
- **leukorrhea** (See FEMALE - Leukorrhea - accompanied - eruptions)

○ • **Glands**; swelling of: *Calc* bg2 **Sil** bg2

- **acne**: (↗*FACE - Eruptions - acne)* aster ptk1 bar-c ptk1 bell ptk1 carb-v ptk1 cycl ptk1 graph ptk1 **Hep** bg2* **Kali-br** bg2* *Merc* ptk1 nux-v ptk1 sel ptk1 sep ptk1 sul-i ptk1 sulph ptk1 thal-xyz srj8•
  - **accompanied** by | **emaciation** (See GENERALS - Emaciation - accompanied - acne)
  - **black**: ars ptk1 aster ptk1
  - **chronic**: lappa ptk1
  - **hard**: ars-i ptk1
  - **painful** | **sore**: arn ptk1
  - **pustular**: calc-hp ptk1
    - ⁝ **menses**; during: kali-br ptk1
  - **seasons** | **summer**: bov ptk1
  - **women**; in young: cycl ptk1
- **acute** | **agg.** after acute eruptions: **Apis** b7a.de
- **air** agg.; in open: *Nit-ac* b4a.de
- **air** amel.; if covered from the: carc dtp
- **alternating** with:
  - **asthma** (See RESPIRATION - Asthmatic - alternating - eruptions)
  - **complaints**; other: ant-c ptk1 ars ptk1 *Calad* b7a.de* graph ptk1 hep ptk1 *Rhus-t* b7a.de staph ptk1 sulph ptk1
  - **cough** (See COUGH - Alternating - eruptions)
  - **diarrhea** (See RECTUM - Diarrhea - alternating - eruptions)
  - **digestive** complaints: graph hr1
  - **dysentery** (See RECTUM - Dysentery - alternating - eruptions)
  - **internal** affections (See GENERALS - Complaints - internal - alternating - eruptions)
  - **respiratory** symptoms (See RESPIRATION - Complaints - alternating - eruptions)

○ • **Chest**; tightness of (See CHEST - Oppression - alternating - eruptions)

  - **Limbs**; pain in (See EXTREMITIES - Pain - alternating with - eruptions)
- **amel.**: merc-c b4a.de
- **anger** agg.: positr nl2•
- **angioedema**: *(↗urticaria; FACE - Eruptions - angioedema; FACE - Swelling - lips - angioedema; LARYNX - Swelling - larynx - angioedema; MOUTH - Swelling - tongue - angioedema)* agar bro1* *Anac* bro1 antip bro1* apis ptk1* bacls-7 mtf11 bol-lu c2* calc-m mp4• hell br1* hep br1* kali-i ptk1 pitu-p sp1 prot ptj1* santin c2 vesp mrr5
- **angioma**: *(↗Spider)* lyc bg1 sulph bg1
- **anthrax** (See carbuncle)
- **antibiotics**; from: *(↗GENERALS - History - antibiotics)* rhus-v gm1
- **appear** (See break - sensation)
- **areola**; with: anac bg2 ant-t bg2 borx bg2 cic bg2 cocc bg2 kali-bi bg2 sil bg2 thuj bg2
- **baker's** itch: calc bg2 dulc bg2 graph bg2 *Lyc* bg2 rhus-t bg2 sulph bg2
- **bathing** | **agg.**: ant-c mrr1
- **biting**: *Agar* bg2 agn k* alum k* alum-p k2 am-c k* *Am-m* k* ant-c k* arn k* ars k* bell k* borx k* bov k* *Bry* k* *Calc* k* calc-sil k2 camph k* canth k* caps k* carb-an k* carb-v k* carbn-s *Caust* k* cham k* chel k* chin k* cocc k* *Colch* k* coloc k* con k* dros k* **Euph** k* hell k* *Ip* k* *Lach* k* **Led** k* *Lyc* k* m-arct b2.de m-aust b2.de mag-c k* mang k* merc k* *Mez* k* mur-ac k* nat-c k* nat-m k* nux-v k* *Olnd* k* op k* petr k* ph-ac k* phos k* plat k* **Puls** k* ran-b k* ran-s k* rhod k* *Rhus-t* sel k* sil k* spig k* *Spong* k* still stront-c k* *Sulph* k* thuj k* til a1 verat k* viol-t k*
  - **night**: ars h2*
- **blackish**: ant-c k* **Ars** k* asaf k* *Bell* k* *Bry* k* chin con crot-h hyos k* *Lach* k* mur-ac k* nit-ac k* ran-b *Rhus-t* k* *Sec* k* sep k* *Sil* k* spig k* *Still* vip
- **bleeding**: aeth hr1* alum am-m ptk1 ant-t apis ars bry bg2 calc dulc k* euph falco-pe nl2• hep kali-ar kali-c kali-n *Lach* lyc k* mang k2 med **Merc** k* merc-c *Nit-ac* olnd *Par* *Petr* k* *Psor* k* *Sep* **Sulph** k* tritic-vg fd5.de
  - **scratching**; after: alum *Ars* ars-s-f k2 arum-t ptk1 *Bov* *Calc* k* chin k* cocc cupr-ar *Dulc* *Lach* k* *Lyc* k* mez h2 nux-v k* petr plut-n srj7• *Psor* k* **Sulph** *Til* tritic-vg fd5.de
  - **touch** agg.: nit-ac mtf33 [bell-p-sp dcm1]
- **blisters**: ail k2 all-c tl1 alum alum-sil k2 am-c *Anac* **Ant-c** k* apis bro1 *Ars* k* ars-s-f k2 aur aur-ar k2 aur-s k2 borx bry *Bufo* canth k* carb-an carbn-s **Caust** k* *Cham* chir-fl bnm4• *Clem* k* crot-h k* *Dulc* dys fmm1• *Graph* hep k* *Kali-ar* kali-bi k2 *Kali-c* k* kali-s kali-sil k2 lach k* loxo-lae bnm12• *Mag-c* med gk *Merc* k* nat-ar *Nat-c* nat-m k* nat-p nat-s k2 nit-ac *Petr* phos physala-p bnm7• positr nl2• prim-o br1 *Ran-b* *Ran-s* **Rhus-t** k* rhus-v sec bro1 *Sep* k* *Sil* k* *Sulph* syc fmm1• urt-u tl1 verat vip zinc [heroin sdj2]
  - **blood** filled: lach k2 podo fd3.de• sec ptk1
  - **burn**; as from a: ambr aur bell *Canth* k* carb-an clem lyc nat-c phos plut-n srj7• positr nl2• sep sulph urt-u tl1
  - **burning**: ran-b tl1 rhus-t tl1
  - **cyanotic**: loxo-recl bnm1•
  - **itching**: crot-t bg2 kali-i bro1 kreos bro1 mag-c bro1 moni rfm1• *Nat-m* bro1 ran-b tl1 rhus-t bg2* rhus-v bro1 [heroin sdj2]
  - **syphilitic**: kali-i bro1 syph bro1
- **blotches**: aloe bg2 anac *Ant-c* arn *Ars* k* ars-s-f k2 *Asaf* bar-c *Bell* k* berb k* *Bry* k* calc caps chel chlol k* chord-umb rly4• cocc k* coff con croc *Crot-h* crot-t dulc fl-ac k* hell *Hep* *Hyos* ign kali-ar k2 kali-bi c2 kali-c kali-sil k2 kreos *Lach* *Led* lyc *Mag-c* *Mang* *Merc* nat-c k* nat-m *Nit-ac* *Nux-v* op *Petr* ph-ac *Phos* k* *Puls* *Rhus-t* *Rhus-v* ruta sabin samb-c c2 *Sars* *Sec* sel sep k* *Sil* spig *Squil* staph stram suis-hep rly4• sul-ac sulph *Urin* c1 valer verat vip
  - **indurated**: am-m phos k* sars
  - **inflamed**: hep mang *Merc* *Phos* *Sil*
  - **irregular**: arg-n br1
  - **itching**, oozing: **Graph** k* ina-i mlk9.de sul-ac k2
  - **red**: arg-n carb-v chord-umb rly4• crot-t cypra-eg sde6.de• fl-ac k* merc mur-ac op k* phos sul-ac k2 *Tell* rsj10• urt-u k* vip fkr4.de
    - ⁝ **desquamating**: fl-ac
    - ⁝ **elevated**: fl-ac k* *Rhus-t*
  - **scratching**; after: kali-c lach lyc mang hr1 merc nat-c nit-ac op rhus-t spig suis-hep rly4• verat zinc
  - **stinging**: *Petr* sars stram zinc
  - **syphilitic**: calo br1
  - **watery**: graph mag-c
  - **yellow**: ant-c sulph
- **bluish**: ail bg2 ant-t ptk1 carb-an bg2 carb-v bg2 cupr bg2 dig bg2 hydr-ac ptk1 nux-v bg2 op bg2 ox-ac bg2 verat bg2 vip bg2
  - **black**: **Arg-n** hr1 ars bg2 bell bg2 con bg2 kali-chl bg2 *Lach* bg2 *Ran-b* bg2 rhus-t bg2
  - **dark**: *Ail* arg-n *Crot-h* *Lach* *Ran-b* sars *Sulph*
- **boils**: *(↗carbuncle)* abrot k* achy-a mtf11 aeth bro1 agar aln vva1• aloe bg2 alum k* alum-p k2 alum-sil k2 alumn am-c k* am-m k* ambro c2 *Anac* k* anan c2* *Ant-c* k* ant-t k* anth *Antho* bg2 anthraci c2* *Apis* k* **Arn** k* *Ars* k* *Ars-i* ars-s-f k2 ars-s-r c2 aur k* aur-ar k2 aur-s k2 *Bar-c* **Bell** k* bell-p c2* brom k* bry k* bufo k* cadm-s c2 *Calc* k* calc-chln c2 calc-hp bro1 calc-i k2 *Calc-m* c2 calc-p *Calc-pic* bro1 *Calc-s* k* calc-sil k2 carb-an k* carb-v k* carbn-s carc mrr1 caust mrr1 chin k* chinin-ar cist coc-c cocc k* coccal awy1• colch bg2 coli rly4• *Con* *Crot-h* k* cystein-l rly4• dulc echi br1* elaps elat c2 *Euph* k* *Ferr-i* bro1 gaert fmm1• gels bro1 glon br1 *Graph* k* **Hep** k* hippoz c2* *Hyos* k* *Ichth* bro1 ign k* ins br1 *Iod* k* iris bg2 jug-r kali-bi k2 *Kali-i* kali-n k* kreos k* **Lach** k* lappa mtf11 laur k* *Led* k* **Lyc** k* m-ambo b2.de* mag-c k* mag-m k* maland c2* mand sp1 mang-coll br1 med br* **Merc** k* mez k* mur-ac k* nat-ar nat-c k* *Nat-m* k* nat-p nat-sal c2 *Nit-ac* k* nux-m k* *Nux-v* k* ol-myr bro1 op bg2 oper bro1 osteo-a jl2 ozone sde2* **Petr** k* *Ph-ac* k* *Phos* k* *Phyt* k* pic-ac k* positr nl2• prot fmm1• **Psor** k* puls k* pyrog jl2 rhus-r bro1 **Rhus-t** k* rhus-v c2 sabin c2 sapin c2 sars k* *Sec* k* *Sep* k* *Sil* k* sol-a c2 spong k* stann *Staph* k* staphycoc jl2* stram k* strept-ent jl2 strych-g c2* *Sul-ac* k* sul-i bg2* **Sulph** k* suprar rly4• tarent k* *Tarent-c* bro1* *Thuj* k* tritic-vg fd5.de tub bro1 *Urin* c1* vesp ptk2 viol-t ptk1 zinc k* zinc-o bro1 zinc-p k2 [bell-p-sp dcm1 mag-s stj1]
  - **right** side: osteo-a jl2

Skin

- **accompanied** by:
  - **diabetes** (See GENERALS - Diabetes mellitus - accompanied - boils)
  - **impotence**: pic-ac ptk1
- **another**, as soon as the first boil is healed; succeeded by: nat-p tl1 sil tl1 sulph c1
- **beginning** stage: bell mtf11
- **blind**: [*Spect* dfg1]
- **blood** boils: alum alum-p k2 anthraci bro1* arn k* ars b2.de* *Bell* bry k* *Calc* crot-h bro1* euph hyos *Iod* iris kali-bi lach bg2* *Led* *Lyc* mag-c *Mag-m* k* *Mur-ac* *Nat-m* nit-ac ph-ac k* **Phos** k* pyrog bro1* sec k* sep *Sil* sul-ac sul-i k2 sulph thuj k* visc c1 zinc h2*
- **blue**: *Anthraci* bufo crot-h lach tarent tl1
- **burning**: *Antho* bg2 **Anthraci** br1* ars bg2* carb-v bg2 lach tl1 sil tl1 tarent bg2* tarent-c tl1*
- **children**; in: mag-c ptk1
- **chronic**: stram mtf33
- **crops**: *(↗small - crops)* anthraci br1 echi ptk1 ferr-i br1 lappa br1 *Sil* hr1* sulph ptk1 syph ptk1
- **edema** around: crot-h tl1
  - **blood**; with black, non coagulable: crot-h tl1
- **fever**:
  - **after**: *Euph* b4a.de
  - **during** | **agg.**: *Euph* b4a.de
- **foul** smelling: lach mtf11
- **injured** places: *Dulc* k*
- **itching**: cassia-s ccrh1• cephd-i zzc1• *Kali-br* hr1
  - **scratching**; after: cassia-s ccrh1•
- **large**: ant-t k* *Apis* bufo *Hep* k* hyos k* *Lach* *Lyc* k* merc nat-c k* *Nit-ac* k* nux-v phos k* sil viol-t
- **menses**; during: merc ptk1
- **painful**: arn bg2* cassia-s ccrh1• **Hep** bg2 suprar rly4•
- **periodical**: anthraci br1 **Ars** k* hyos *Iod* **Lyc** k ●* *Merc* nit-ac phos phyt sil staph **Sulph** k ●
- **purple**: lach mrr1
- **pus**:
  - **greenish**: *Sec* k*
  - **yellowish**: cassia-s ccrh1• [bell-p-sp dcm1]
- **receding**: lyc ptk1
- **recurrent** (See GENERALS - History - boils)
- **red**:
  - **dark** bluish red: lach bg2 sec bg2
  - **scarlet** red: apis bg2 bell bg2
- **slowly**:
  - **healing**: [bell-p-sp dcm1]
  - **maturing**: hep sanic tl1* sil sulph [bell-p-sp dcm1]
- **small**: abrot tl1 **Arn** k* bar-c bell-p tl1 cassia-s cdd7*• cystein-l rly4• dulc *Fl-ac* **Kali-i** lappa ptk1 *Lyc* m-ambo b2.de* mag-c k* mag-m nat-m nux-v pic-ac ptk1 sec ptk1 sulph k* tarent tub ptk1 viol-t zinc k*
  - **crops**: *(↗crops)* anthraci tl1 arn br1* bell-p tl1 *Kali-br* hr1 plut-n srj7• sulph tl1 tarent-c tl1
- **smallpox**; after: *Hep* bro1 phos bro1 sulph bro1
- **spring**; in: bell k* *Crot-h* *Lach*
- **stinging**:
  - **burning**: apis bg2
  - **touch** agg.: mur-ac ozone sde2• sars h2* sil
- **vaccinations**; from: sil tl1 thuj tl1
- **warm** bed agg.: merc-sul tl1

- **break** out:
  - **fails** to break out; when an eruption: *(↗rash - slow; slow; suppressed)* *Ail* k* am-c k* ant-t k* apis ptk1 ars ptk1 asaf ptk1 *Bry* bg2* cupr bg2* dulc bg2* ip ptk1 petr ptk1 ph-ac ptk1 psor bg2* *Stram* k* *Sulph* k* *Zinc* k*

- **break** out: ...
  - **sensation** as if an eruption would break out: lachn rb2 pop rb2 samb rb2
- **brownish**: anag dulc nit-ac ph-ac phos puls k2 syph jl2 tritic-vg fd5.de
  - **yellowish** brown: [lac-mat sst4]
- **burn**; as from a: *Ran-b* b7a.de
- **burning**: acon bg2 agar k* alum k* alum-p k2 alum-sil k2 *Am-c* k* am-m k* *Ambr* k* anac k* ant-c k* ant-t k* anthraci br1 **Apis** arg-met k* arn a1 **Ars** k* ars-s-f k2 aur k* aur-s k2 bar-c k* bar-s k2 *Bell* k* berb bov k* *Bry* k* bufo k* calad k* *Calc* k* calc-p k2 *Calc-s* calc-sil k2 cann-s k* canth k* caps k* **Carb-ac** *Carb-an* k* *Carb-v* k* *Carbn-s* **Caust** k* chin k* chinin-ar **Cic** k* *Clem* k* cocc k* coff k* colch k* com *Con* k* com a1 crot-t k* cub dig k* dulc k* euph k* gast a1 **Graph** guaj k* hell k* *Hep* k* ign k* jug-c a1 kali-ar k* *Kali-bi* k* *Kali-c* k* kali-i k* kali-n k* kali-s kali-sil k2 kreos k* *Lach* k* laur k* led k* *Lyc* k* m-ambo b2.de* m-arct b2.de m-aust b2.de* mang k* medus br1 **Merc** k* *Mez* k* mosch a1 nat-ar nat-c k* nat-m k* nat-p nit-ac *Nux-v* k* olnd k* par k* petr k* ph-ac k* *Phos* k* plat k* plb k* *Psor* *Puls* k* rad-br mrr1 *Ran-b* k* **Rhus-t** k* sabad k* sars k* seneg k* sep k* *Sil* k* spig k* spiros-af oss• spong k* squil k* stann k* *Staph* k* stram k* stront-c k* *Sulph* k* tarent-c mrr1 teucr k* thuj k* tritic-vg fd5.de urt-u k* verat k* viol-o k* *Viol-t* k* zinc k* zinc-p k2
  - **night**: ars caust *Merc* **Rhus-t** k* staph til k*
  - **air** agg.; in open: led k*
  - **cold** washing agg.; after: clem thuj k*
  - **rubbing**; after: sars h2
  - **scratching**; after (See Burning - scratching)
  - **touch** agg.: cann-s canth *Merc*
  - **washing**; when: *Merc* olib-sac wmh1
- **carbuncle**: *(↗boils)* acon bro1 agar ant-t k* **Antho** bg2 *Anthraci* k* *Apis* k* *Arn* k* **Ars** k* ars-s-f k2 asim c2 **Bell** k* both bro1 bov bg2 bry bro1 *Bufo* k* *Calc-chln* c2* calc-s c2 calen c2 caps k* carb-ac c1* carb-an *Carb-v* c2* *Chin* bro1 coloc *Crot-c* *Crot-h* k* cupr-ar bro1 *Echi* k* euph bro1 *Hep* k* hippoz c2* *Hyos* k* ins br1 iod bg2 jug-r vh kali-p c2 kreos c2* *Lach* k* *Lappa* bro1 led br1* **Lyc** bg2 merc mtf11 mur-ac k* myris br1 nit-ac k* op bg2 ph-ac k2 phyt k* pic-ac pyrog bro1* *Rhus-t* k* sang hr1 *Scol* bro1 *Sec* k* ser-febr-s mtf11 **Sil** k* staphycoc jl2* stram k2* strych-g c2 sul-ac bro1* *Sulph* k* tarent bg2* *Tarent-c* k*
  - **accompanied** by:
    - **diabetes** (See GENERALS - Diabetes mellitus - accompanied - carbuncles)
    - **pain**; bursting: vip ptk1*
  - **burning**: *Anthraci* *Apis* *Ars* coloc *Crot-c* crot-h hep **Tarent-c** k*
  - **chronic**: stram mtf33
  - **first** stage: echi br1 rhus-t br1
  - **foul** smelling: anthraci jl2 lach mtf11
  - **openings**; with many: hep bg2 lyc bg2 nit-ac bg2
  - **purple** | **vesicles** around; with small: *Crot-c* **Lach**
  - **red**:
    - **bluish** red: lach ptk1
    - **scarlet** red: apis ptk1 bell ptk1
  - **stinging**: **Apis** k* carb-an *Nit-ac* k*
- **chancres**: *(↗GENERALS - Chancre)* merc-i-r k2
- **chemicals**; from | **tar** and petroleum chemicals: *Petr* mrr1
- **chickenpox**: acon k* **Ant-c** k* *Ant-t* k* apis bro1* ars k* asaf k* *Bell* k* bry bro1 canth *Carb-v* k* caust k* coff con cycl k* *Dulc* bro1 hyos ip k* kali-m bro1 *Led* k* *Merc* k* merc-c k2 nat-c k* nat-m k* **Puls** k* rhus-d c2* *Rhus-t* k* sec b2.de* *Sep* k* sil k* **Sulph** k* syc fmm1* *Thuj* k* tub jl2 urt-u bro1* vac jl2 vario bro1* [*Ant-m* stj2 *Ant-met* stj2]
  - **painful** on pressure: ant-c c1
- **children**; in: | **newborns**; in: dulc ptk1 tub mrr1
- **chronic**: mang ptk1 sul-i ptk1 syph br1 vac br1
- **clustered**: *Agar* k* alum bg2 *Calc* k* crot-t ptk1 nat-m bg3* ph-ac k* ran-b k* rhus-t k* staph tell bg2 verat k*
- **coalescent** (See confluent)
- **cold**:
  - **air**:
    - **agg.**: *Apis* caust dulc k* kali-c mang *Nit-ac* **Rhus-t** rhus-v bg1 *Rumx* *Sars* b4a.de sep
    - **amel.**: calc k* hep b4a.de

- **applications** | **amel.**: led mrr1
- **bathing**:
  - ⁝ **agg.**: thuj ptk1
  - ⁝ **amel.**: ant-c br1
- **washing** agg.: **Clem** *Dulc* olib-sac wmh1 sulph

- **cold** agg.; becoming: **Ars** dulc k* sars
- **confluent**: agar k* *Ant-t* k* antip vh1 bell bg3* *Caps* k* *Chlol* k* *Cic* k* cop a1 hyos k* kali-bi bg2 kola stb3• morb jl2 *Ph-ac* k* phos rhus-t bg3* rhus-v sarr hl1* valer k*
- **coppery**: alum k* alum-p k2 *Ars* k* *Ars-i* aur *Calc* k* calc-i bro1 cann-s k* **Carb-an** k* carb-v k* coc-c bg2 cor-r k* hydrc ptk1 *Kali-i* *Kreos* k* led k* *Lyc* *Merc* k* merc-d ptk1 *Mez* k* *Nit-ac* k* phos *Psor* *Rhus-t* k* ruta k* sars k2* syph k* *Verat* k*
  - **dense**: agar calc
  - **fumes** agg.: ip ptk1 merc ptk1 puls ptk1
  - **spots**: cor-r br1 med hr1 *Merc* *Merc-d* hr1 *Mez* *Nit-ac* syph hr1* ust k*
- **cosmetics**; from: bov ptk1
- **crusty**: aethi-m br1 *Agar* *Alum* k* alum-p k2 alumn k2 am-c k* am-m k* ambr k* *Anac* k* anag *Anan* **Ant-c** k* ant-t *Anthraci* apis **Ars** k* **Ars-i** *Aur* aur-ar k2 *Aur-m* aur-s k2 *Bar-c* k* bar-m bar-s k2 *Bell* k* bov k* *Bry* k* **Calc** k* calc-i k2 **Calc-s** calc-sil k2 caps k* *Carb-an* k* carb-v k* **Carbn-s** *Caust* cham k* *Chel* chrysar br1 *Cic* k* *Cist* *Clem* k* com **Con** k* **Dulc** k* elaps *Fl-ac* **Graph** k* hell k* *Hep* k* *Jug-c* *Kali-ar* *Kali-bi* *Kali-c* k* kali-chl *Kali-i* kali-m k2 kali-p *Kali-s* kreos k* *Lach* *Lappa* *Led* k* *Lith-c* **Lyc** k* mag-c k* mag-m ptk1 manc br1* med br1 **Merc** k* *Merc-i-r* **Mez** k* mur-ac k* **Nat-m** k* nat-p **Nit-ac** k* nux-v k* **Olnd** k* paeon par k* **Petr** k* ph-ac *Phos* k* *Phyt* plb k* *Psor* k* *Puls* k* rad-br ptk1 **Ran-b** k* **Rhus-t** k* *Rhus-v* k* *Sabad* k* sabin k* sang *Sars* k* *Sep* k* **Sil** k* *Spong* k* squil k* *Staph* k* sul-ac **Sulph** k* tarent bg2 tell thuj k* vac vanil fd5.de verat k* vinc k* *Viol-t* k* zinc k* zinc-p k2
  - **black**: *Ars* bell chin vip k*
  - **bleeding**: merc k* *Mez* *Sulph* ptk1
  - **body**; over whole: ars **Dulc** k* *Psor* k*
  - **brown**: am-c ant-c k* berb dulc k2 manc ptk1 olnd ptk1
    - ⁝ **yellow**: dulc ptk1
  - **burning**: am-c *Ant-c* k* calc cic puls sars
  - **conical**: sil ptk1 syph ptk1
  - **cracked**: viol-t ptk1
  - **dirty**: psor ptk1
  - **dry**: *Ars* *Ars-i* **Aur** **Aur-m** *Bar-c* *Calc* chinin-s graph lach led merc *Ran-b* sulph thuj *Viol-t*
  - **elevated**: mez k2
  - **falling**: nit-ac ptk1
  - **fetid**: graph lyc med c1 *Merc* plb *Psor* staph **Sulph**
  - **gray**: ars merc k* *Sulph*
  - **greenish**: ant-c calc petr sulph
  - **gummy**: viol-t ptk1
  - **hard**: **Ran-b** k*
  - **hay**; allergic to: *(↗GENERALS - Allergic)* **Graph** vh
  - **honey** colored: ant-c bg2 carb-v cic bg2 kreos bg2
  - **horny**: *(↗Excrescences - horny)* ant-c k* graph **Ran-b** k*
  - **inflamed**: **Calc** *Lyc*
  - **irritating**: aethi-m br1
  - **lead** colored: ars b4a.de
  - **mercury**; after abuse of: **Kali-i**
  - **moist**: alum anac *Anthraci* **Ars** *Bar-c* **Calc** **Carbn-s** *Cic* clem dulc k2 **Graph** *Hell* *Hep* *Kali-s* **Lyc** **Merc** k* **Mez** nit-ac ptk1 *Olnd* petr k2 phos plb ran-b **Rhus-t** ruta sep *Sil* **Staph** k* **Sulph** vinc ptk1 viol-t ptk1
  - **offensive**: med gk mez k2
  - **oozing**:
    - ⁝ **greenish**, bloody: ant-c k*
    - ⁝ **water**: staph bg2
  - **painful**: *(↗smarting)* aethi-m br1
  - **patches**: dys fmm1• hydr hydrc kali-c *Merc* **Nit-ac** sabin sil thuj zinc
  - **pus** underneath; with: bov ptk1 lyc ptk1 mez bg2* nit-ac bg2 thuj ptk1
  - **red**: merc b4a.de

- **crusty**: ...
  - **renewed** daily: crot-t
  - **scratching**; after: alum k* am-c k* am-m k* ant-c k* ars k* ars-s-f k2 *Bar-c* k* bell k* bov k* bry k* *Calc* k* caps k* carb-an k* carb-v k* carbn-s cic k* *Con* k* *Dulc* k* *Graph* k* *Hep* k* kali-ar kali-c k* kali-s kali-sil k2 kreos k* led k* **Lyc** k* *Merc* k* mez k* nat-m k* petr k* phos k* psor jl2 puls k* ran-b k* **Rhus-t** k* sabad k* sabin k* sars k* sep k* sil k* *Staph* k* **Sulph** k* thuj k* verat k* viol-t k* zinc k* zinc-p k2
  - **serpiginous**: *Clem* *Psor* sulph
  - **shiny**: olnd ptk1
  - **smarting**: *(↗painful)* puls
  - **sticky**: arg-n ptk1 lyc ptk1*
  - **suppurating**: *Ars* plb sil *Sulph*
  - **thick**: bov ptk1 *Calc* ptk1 clem ptk1 dulc ptk1 kali-bi ptk1 mez k2* petr ptk1 staph ptk1*
    - ⁝ **offensive**: vinc ptk1
  - **weather**; warm: bov
  - **white**: *Alum* ars ptk1 *Calc* *Mez* k* **Nat-m** tell thuj zinc b4a.de
  - **yellow**: *Ant-c* k* aur aur-m *Bar-m* *Calc* *Calc-s* carb-v *Cic* cupr dulc graph ptk1 hyper iod *Kali-bi* *Kali-s* kreos med br1 *Merc* k* *Mez* nat-p nit-ac b4a.de *Petr* ph-ac *Spong* *Staph* sulph *Viol-t*
    - ⁝ **yellow**-white: *Mez*
- **dark**: ail bg2 apis bg2 sec bg2
- **desquamating**: acet-ac *Acon* b2.de* agar k* **Am-c** k* *Am-m* k* anac vh1 ant-t k* apis k* *Ars* k* *Ars-i* k* ars-s-f k2 *Arum-t* *Aur* k* bar-c k* **Bell** k* borx *Bov* k* bufo k2 calc k* calc-s calc-sil k2 canth k* caps k* carb-an k* caust k* cham k* *Clem* k* *Coloc* k* com bg2 con k* crot-h crot-t cupr k* dig k* *Dulc* k* elaps k* euph k* ferr k* ferr-p fl-ac bg2 ger-i rly4• *Graph* k* *Hell* k* hell-f c2 hep bro1* ign bro1 iod k* *Kali-ar* k* *Kali-c* k* kali-m ptk1 **Kali-s** k* kali-sil k2 kreos lach k* *Laur* k* *Led* k* *Mag-c* k* manc medus c1 *Merc* k* merc-c b4a.de* **Mez** k* morb jl2 mosch k* *Nat-ar* nat-c k* nat-m k* nat-p nit-ac ptk1 **Olnd** k* op k* par k* petr k2 *Ph-ac* k* *Phos* k* pip-n bg2 pix c2 plat k* plb k* **Psor** ptel c1 *Puls* k* ran-b k* ran-s k* retin-ac mtf11 *Rhus-t* k* *Rhus-v* sabad k* samb xxb1 sars ptk1 *Sec* k* sel k* **Sep** k* *Sil* k* spig k* *Staph* k* sul-ac k* sul-i k2 *Sulph* k* tarax k* teucr k* thuj k* thyr ptk1 urt-u verat k* vip ptk1
  - **scales**; white: ars bg2 calc bg2 com bg2 crot-t bg2 dulc bg2 lyc bg2 merc bg2 sep bg2 sil bg2 thuj bg2
  - **scarlet** fever; after: arum-t bro1
  - **sensation** of desquamation: *Agar* b2.de* alum b2.de* am-c b2.de* *Bar-c* b2.de* bufo bg2 calc b2.de* *Lach* b2.de* merc b2.de* *Ph-ac* b2.de* *Phos* b2.de* phyt ptk1 rhus-t ptk1 sep b2.de* sulph b2.de*

○ • **Affected** parts; on: rhus-t bg2

- **dirty**: merc *Psor* k* *Sulph* k* syph k*
- **discharging** (= moist): aethi-a c1 *Aethi-m* bro1 alum k* alum-p k2 alum-sil k2 *Anac* anag *Ant-c* k* ant-t bro1 *Ars* k* *Ars-i* ars-s-f k2 *Bar-c* k* bell k* *Bov* k* bry k* bufo cact cadm-s *Calc* k* *Calc-s* canth caps carb-an k* **Carb-v** k* **Carbn-s** *Caust* k* cham chrysar bro1 *Cic* k* cist *Clem* k* *Con* k* crot-h *Crot-t* k* cupr **Dulc** k* **Graph** k* *Hell* k* *Hep* k* hydr iod *Jug-c* *Kali-ar* *Kali-br* *Kali-c* k* kali-m bg2 kali-p *Kali-s* kali-sil k2 *Kreos* k* lacer a1* *Lach* k* led k* **Lyc** k* *Manc* k* med gk *Merc* k* **Mez** k* mur-ac narc-ps br1* nat-ar nat-c k* **Nat-m** k* nat-p *Nat-s* nit-ac k* olnd k* *Petr* k* *Ph-ac* k* *Phos* k* phyt *Psor* k* ran-b **Rhus-t** k* rhus-v ruta k* sabin k* *Sars* sec k2 *Sel* k* **Sep** k* **Sil** k* **Sol-ni** squil k* *Staph* k* still stront-c bro1 sul-ac k* *Sul-i* *Sulph* k* tarax k* *Tell* *Thuj* k* tub-d jl2 vario bro1 vinc viol-t k* zinc k* zinc-p k2
  - **amel.**: psor jl2 sulfa sp1
  - **bloody**: ant-c calc carc cd crot-h lach merc k* nux-v sulph mtf33
    - ⁝ **scratching**; after: alum bg2 calc bg2 chin b7.de* kali-c bg2 *Lach* bg2 *Lyc* bg2 nux-v bg2 psor bg2
    - ⁝ **watery** | **scratching**; after: alum bg2 ars bg2 cocc b7.de
  - **corrosive**: *Ars* k* ars-s-f k2 *Calc* k* caps carbn-s *Clem* k* con h2* *Graph* k* kali-bi tl1 merc merc-i-f merc-i-r k* *Nat-m* k* ran-s *Rhus-t* k* *Squil* b7a.de staph hr1* **Sulph** k* *Thuj* k*
  - **destroying** hair: ars lyc merc mez k2 *Nat-m* k* *Rhus-t* staph sne
  - **gluey** (See sticky)
  - **glutinous**: bufo gk *Calc* *Carbn-s* **Graph** k* lappa ptk1 manc br1 mez k2 *Nat-m* sulph
    - ⁝ **scratching**; after: graph bg2 lyc bg2
  - **golden** crystals; dries into: **Graph** mrr1

Skin

- **greenish**: *Acon* ptk1 ant-c apis ptk1 **Ars** ptk1 *Carb-v* ptk1 cham ptk1 con ptk1 ip ptk1 kali-bi ptk1 *Kali-chl* kali-i ptk1 lyc ptk1 mag-c ptk1 med ptk1 **Merc** ptk1 *Nat-s* ptk1 par ptk1 phos ptk1 **Puls** ptk1 rhus-t k* sec k2* *Sep* ptk1 stann ptk1 sul-ac ptk1 *Sulph* ptk1 *Verat* ptk1
- **honey**; like: ant-c mrr1 graph nh1* nat-p k2
- **ichorous**: ant-t anthraci jl2 clem nat-s ptk ran-s k* *Rhus-t* k* staph mtf33
- **offensive**: anthraci jl2 carc cd chrysar bwa3* graph mtf33 kali-p k2 med gk psor tl1* *Staph* b7a.de
  - **cadaverous** like carrion: psor mtf33
- **pus**: clem dulc h2* emetin mp4• graph k* *Hep* lyc med gk mez k2 nat-c h2* nat-m *Nit-ac* psor k2 sec k2 *Sulph*
- **scratching**; after: alum k* alum-p k2 alum-sil k2 ars k* bar-c k* bell k* bov k* bry k* calc k* carb-an k* *Carb-v* k* cassia-s cdd7• caust k* cic k* con k* dulc k* **Graph** k* hell k* hep k* *Kali-c* k* *Kreos* k* **Lach** k* led k* **Lyc** k* m-ambo bg2 merc k* mez k* nat-c k* nat-m k* nit-ac k* *Olnd* k* *Petr* k* rad-br ptk1 **Rhus-t** k* ruta k* sabin k* sars sel k* *Sep* k* sil k* squil k* *Staph* k* sul-ac k* sulph k* tarax k* thuj k* viol-t k*
- **sticky** (See glutinous)
- **thick**: **Graph** mrr1 nat-c k2 psor k2
- **thin**: cupr *Dulc* hell **Nat-m** petr tl1 psor k2 *Rhus-t* rhus-v sol-ni
- **viscid**: graph tl1
- **weeping**: beryl sp1
- **white**: borx **Calc** calc-sil k2 *Carb-v* caust *Dulc* graph lyc merc mez k2 *Nat-m* *Phos* psor k2 **Puls** sep **Sil**
- **yellow**: *Alum* alum-p k2 *Anac* **Ant-c** ars ars-s-f k2 bar-c bar-s k2 *Calc* canth carb-an **Carb-v** **Carbn-s** caust *Clem* cupr *Dulc* *Graph* k* *Hep* iod *Kali-c* *Kali-s* k* lach *Lyc* med gk merc mez k2 nat-c k2 *Nat-m* nat-p **Nat-s** k* **Nit-ac** **Phos** psor k2* **Puls** *Rhus-t* **Sep** **Sil** sol-ni staph hr1 **Sulph** k* *Thuj* *Viol-t*

- **dry**: acon-ac rly4• *Alum* k* alum-p k2 *Alum-sil* k4 alumn bro1 anac anag k* ant-c bro1 **Ars** k* **Ars-i** k* ars-s-f k2 **Aur** k* **Aur-m** **Bar-c** k* bar-s k2 *Berb-a* bro1 (non:borx hr1) *Bov* k* *Bry* k* bufo cact cadm-s bro1 calad k* **Calc** k* **Calc-s** k* canth hr1* *Carb-v* k* *Carbn-s* caust k* chrysar br1 clem k* cocc k* corn k* cory bro1 *Cupr* k* *Dulc* k* euph-l bro1 *Fl-ac* k* fum rly1*• *Graph* k* guare a1* *Hep* k* hydr-ac *Hydrc* bro1 hyos k* *Iod* bro1 *Kali-ar* k* *Kali-c* k* *Kali-chl* kali-i kali-m bro1 kali-n bg2 kali-s k* kali-sil k2 *Kreos* k* **Led** k* lith-c bro1 *Lyc* k* *Mag-c* k* *Maland* bro1 *Merc* k* **Mez** k* mim-p rsj8• nat-c k* nat-m k* nat-p nit-ac bro1 par k* *Petr* k* *Ph-ac* k* **Phos** k* phyt bro1 pip-m bro1 pix bro1 *Psor* k* rad-br mrr1 rhus-t k* sacch-a fd2.de• *Sars* k* sel k* **Sep** k* **Sil** k* sinus rly4• stann k* *Staph* k* *Sulph* k* teucr k* thuj tub bro1 valer k* **Verat** k* *Viol-t* k* xero bro1 *Zinc* k*
  - **bleeding** | **scratching**; after: alum *Ars* *Calc* *Lyc* *Petr* *Sulph*
  - **itching**: sulph tl1
- **eating** (See phagedenic)
- **ecthyma**: ant-c k* ant-t k* anthraco c2 arg-n k* ars k* bell hr1* borx cham cic k* cist bro1 *Crot-c* *Crot-t* k* euph-pe c2 hydr bro1 *Jug-c* k* jug-r c2* kali-ar a1 *Kali-bi* k* kali-br kali-i k* kreos bro1 *Lach* bro1 lyc merc k* nit-ac k* petr k* pop-cand c2 rhus-t k* sec k* *Sil* k* staph staphycoc jl2 sulph k* thuj k*
- **eczema**: acon hr1 aeth hr1* aethi-a c1 *Aethi-m* bro1 aln bro1 alum k* alum-p k2 alum-sil k2 *Alumn* c2 am-c k* am-m k* anac k* ant-c k* ant-t hr1 **Anthraci** mrr1 anthraco bro1* aq-mar rbp6 arb c1* arg-n arn mrr1 **Ars** k* **Ars-i** k* ars-s-f k2 ars-s-r c2 arum-t mrr1 astac aur k* aur-ar k2 *Aur-m* k* *Aur-m-n* wbt2• aur-s k2* **Bar-c** k* **Bar-m** bell k* *Berb* bro1 berb-a c2* borx k* **Bov** c2* brom k* bry k* bufo gk* *Calad* k* **Calc** k* *Calc-p* hr1 **Calc-s** k* calc-sil k2 canth k* caps bro1 carb-ac k* *Carb-v* k* carbn-s carc fb* cardios-h rly4• castor-eq bro1 *Caust* k* cere-b c2 *Chel* hr1 chin c1 chrysar bro1 **Cic** k* *Cist* hr1 clem k* cod c2 colch tl1 com c2* *Con* hr1* cop k* corn hr1* corn-a c2* **Crot-t** k* cund hr1 cur hr1* cycl **Dulc** k* dys fmm1• euph bro1 fago c2* falco-pe nl2• ferr-i hr1 ferr-s c2 fl-ac k* frax bro1 fuli br1* fum vs1.fr ger-i rly4• **GRAPH** k ●* **Hep** k* hippoz bro1 hom-xyz mgm• hydr k* *Hydrc* hr1* ins br1 iodof c2 *Iris* k* **Jug-c** k* **Jug-r** *Kali-ar* k* kali-bi k* kali-br hr1 kali-c *Kali-chl* k* kali-i a1* kali-m c2* *Kali-s* k* kali-sil k2 *Kreos* bro1* lac-f wza1• lach **Lappa** k* led k* *Lith-c* **Lyc** k ●* mang mrr1* *Mang-act* bro1 **Med** vh* *Merc* k* *Merc-c* c2* merc-d bro1 merc-i-r c2 merc-pr-r bro1 **Mez** k* moni rfm1• morg fmm1• morg-p fmm1* *Mur-ac* hr1* naphtin c2 nat-ar bro1 *Nat-c* hr1* nat-hp mtf **Nat-m** k ●* nat-p k* *Nat-s* k* nit-ac k* nux-v bro1 **Olnd** k* op wbt• osm c2* ox-ac hr1 penic mtf11 **Petr** k* ph-ac k2 **Phos** k ●* *Phyt* k* pilo bro1 pip-m c2 pix c2 *Plb* bro1 podo bro1 polyg-xyz c2 positr nl2• pot-e rly4• prim-o c2 prim-v c2* **Psor** k* puls mrr1 pyrog c2 rad-br c11* *Ran-b* k* rhus-d c2* **RHUS-T** k ●* rhus-v k* sanic c2*

- **eczema**: ...
Sars k* scroph-n mtf11 **Sep** k ●* *Sil* k* skook c2* solid ptk1 spira c2 *Staph* k* streptoc jl2 strych-g br1 sul-ac hr1* **Sul-i** k* **SULPH** k ●* sumb hr1 *Syph* hr1* tarent k2* tarent-c mrr1 tell c1* ter hr1* *Thuj* k* thyr c2* thyroiod mtf titan br1 **Tub** al* tub-d jl2 urt-u mrr1 ust hr1* vac c2 *Vinc* c2* *Viol-t* k* visc hs2 x-ray bro1 xero br1* zinc hr1* [lac-mat sst4]
  - **night**: psor tl1
  - **accompanied** by:
    - **acid** symptoms: nat-p tl1
    - **gout** (See EXTREMITIES - Pain - joints - gouty - accompanied - eczema)
    - **herpes**: petr mrr1
    - **motion** sickness: petr mrr1
    - **redness**; intense: crot-t mtf11
    - **respiration**; asthmatic (See RESPIRATION - Asthmatic - accompanied - eczema)
    - **rheumatism** (See EXTREMITIES - Pain - rheumatic - accompanied - eczema)
    - **swelling** of skin: apis mrr1
    - **urine** | **complaints** of: lyc ptk1
    - **Liver**; complaints of: lyc bro1*
    - **Stomach**; complaints of (See STOMACH - Complaints - accompanied - eczema)
    - **Urinary** organs; complaints of (See URINARY - Complaints - accompanied - eczema)
  - **acute**: acon bro1 anac bro1 bell bro1 canth bro1 *Chinin-s* bro1 *Crot-t* bro1 mez bro1 *Rhus-t* bro1 sep bro1 vac jl2*
  - **air**; in open:
    - **agg.**: tub jl2
    - **amel.**: pert-vc vk9 psor tl1
  - **allergic**: nat-pyru mtf11
  - **alternating** with:
    - **asthmatic** respiration (See RESPIRATION - Asthmatic - alternating - eczema)
    - **internal** affections (See GENERALS - Complaints - internal - alternating - eczema)
  - **atopic** (See eczema)
  - **bathing** in the sea: *Mang* mrr1
  - **burning**; with: **Anthraci** mrr1 *Ars* mrr1* pert-vc vk9 rhus-t tl1
  - **childhood**; since: carc gk6* med mrr1 tub mrr1
  - **children**; in: calc fr3 calc-m mtf calc-s c1 carc dgt1 dulc mtf psor mtf33 sep mtf33 staph mtf33 viol-t br1
    - **infants**: frax br1 med gk5* strept-ent jl2
  - **chronic**: am-c bg2 bar-c bg2 calc-f bg2 com mtf11 cupr bg2 cur bg2 guaj bg2 ichth mtf11 lev mtf11 mang-c mtf11 merc mtf11 *Nat-c* bg2 psor bg2* sec bg2 sep bg2* sul-ac mtf11 sul-i bg2 *Sulph* bg2 tub mtf33 viol-t bg2
    - **accompanied** by | **anxiety**: asthm-r mtf11
  - **cold** applications | **amel.**: apis mrr1
  - **desquamating**: ars mtf11 bac jl2 streptoc jl2
  - **discharging**: *(↗FACE - Eruptions - eczema - moist)* alumn mtf11 cic bro1 con bro1 dulc bro1 graph bro1 hep bro1 kali-m bro1 kreos ptk1 lappa ptk1 maland jl2 merc-c bro1 merc-pr-r bro1 mez bro1 sep bro1 staph bro1* sul-i br1* tub bro1 vinc ptk1 viol-t bro1
    - **accompanied** by | **scrofulous** skin conditions: lap-a mtf11 lyc mtf11
    - **copious**: mez tl1 rhus-t fr3*
    - **offensive**: lappa ptk1
    - **salt** rheum: **Ambr** k* **Ars** k* calc b2.de* calc-s k2 chin b2.de* *Graph* k* hep bg2 lach bg2 lyc k* merc k* nat-c b2.de* petr k* phos k* puls k* rhus-t bg2 sep k* *Sil* k* *Staph* k* sulph k* zinc b2.de*
    - **vaccination**; after: *(↗vaccination)* maland jl2
    - **yellow** moisture under crusts: staph tl1
  - **dry**: sep mtf33 streptoc jl2 tarent mtf33
    - **children**; in: calc-s tl1* dulc ptk1 frax ptk1 sep mtf33 tarent ptk1* viol-t ptk1
  - **excoriating**: bac jl2 rhus-t tl1

- **fissures**; with: *Tub* jl2
  - **dry**: tub jl2
  - **oozing**: tub jl2
  - **painful**: tub jl2
  - **red** look; deep: tub jl2
- **gastric** complaints; with (See STOMACH - Complaints - accompanied - eczema)
- **herpetiform**: tub jl2
- **itching**: ars mtf11 cygn-ol sze3• ins br1 led tl1 mez tl1 rhus-t tl1 staph mtf33 *Tub* jl2
  - **night**: psor mtf11
  - **not** itching: cic br1*
- **menses** agg.: mang br1* mang-act bro1
- **moist** (See discharging)
- **neurasthenic** persons; in: *Anac* bro1 ars bro1 phos bro1 *Stry-ar* bro1 stry-p bro1 viol-t bro1 zinc-p bro1
- **neurotic** persons; in: anac bwa3* zinc ptk1
- **offensive**: lappa ptk1 vinc ptk1
- **psoriasiform**: tub jl2
- **scales**; with hard horny: ant-c tl1 ran-b tl1 *Tub* jl2
- **scrofulous** persons; in: *Aethi-m* bro1 *Ars-i* bro1 calc bro1 *Calc-i* bro1 calc-p bro1 caust bro1 cist bro1 crot-t bro1 *Hep* bro1 merc bro1 merc-c bro1 rumx bro1 sep bro1 sil bro1 tub bro1
- **seaside**; at the: *Nat-m* bro1*
- **summer** | **amel.**: *Petr* tl1
- **sun**, from: *Mur-ac* hr1*
- **syphilitic**: *Ars* bro1 *Graph* bro1 kreos bro1 merc bro1 petr bro1 phyt bro1 *Sars* bro1
- **urine** agg.; suppression of: solid ptk1
- **vaccination**; from: (↗*discharging - vaccination*) mez bro1 skook c1 *Thuj* tl1 vac jl2
- **warm** applications agg.: psor tl1
- **water** | **agg.**: ars-i ptk1 tub jl2
- **weeping** (See discharging)
- **winter** agg.: petr tl1

○ • **Folds** of the Skin: moni jl2 tub jl2

- **edematous**: | **itching** (See itching - edematous)
- **elevated**: anac ars asaf *Bry* k* calc carb-v caust cic b7.de cop k* crot-h cupr-ar dulc graph kola stb3• lach medul-os-si rly4• merc k* mez op phos k* podo fd3.de• sulph k* tab tarax valer vanil fd5.de
- **erysipelas** (See Erysipelas)
- **erythema**: (↗*erythema; BACK - Eruptions - erythema; CHEST - Discoloration - redness - erythematous; EXTREMITIES - Eruptions - erythematous; EXTREMITIES - Eruptions - upper limbs - erythematous; FACE - Discoloration - red - erythema; MALE GENITALIA/SEX - Eruptions - penis - erythematous*) acon bro1 androc bnm2• antip c2* apis bro1 *Am* bro1 ars ptk1 ars-i bro1 atra-r bnm3• *Bell* c2* bor-ac c2 bufo bro1 *Canth* bro1 cardios-h rly4• chir-fl bnm4• *Chlol* br1* diph-t-tpt jl2 eberth jl2 echi bro1 euph-l bro1 gaul bro1 grin c2* ins br1 kali-c bro1 lac-ac bro1 lat-h bnm5• lat-m bnm6• *Leptos-ih* jl2 loxo-lae bnm12• loxo-recl bnm1• merc bro1* *Mez* c2* morg-p pte1*• narc-ps br1* nux-v bro1 physala-p bnm7• pic-ac c2 plan c2 plb-chr c2* prot fmm1• psor jl2 ran-b tl1 *Rhus-t* bro1 rob bro1 scarl jl2 sulph ptk1 syc fmm1• ter c2* toxo-g jl2 tub c2 urt-u c2* ust bro1 verat-v bro1 xero bro1
  - **acute**: zinc-s mtf11
  - **cracks**: syc fmm1•
  - **followed** by | **gangrene**: ran-b tl1
  - **itching**: fago br1
  - **lenticular**: syph jl2
  - **multiforme**: antip bro1 bor-ac bro1 cop bro1 vesp bro1
    - **acute**: antip br1
  - **purpuric**: toxo-g jl2
  - **toxic** treatment; after: zinc-s mtf11
  - **weather** agg.; wet: narc-ps br1*
- **erythema** nodosum: (↗*Discoloration - red - spots - bluish - nodules*) *Acon* c2* ant-c bro1 apis c2* *Am* bro1 ars bro1 chin bro1 chinin-ar bro1 *Chinin-s* bro1* diph-t-tpt jl2 ferr bro1 jug-c c2 kali-br c2* kali-i c2 led c2* narc-ps mp1• nat-c bro1 phyt c2 ptel bro1 rhus-t bro1* rhus-v c2* streptoc jl2 sul-ac c2 toxo-g jl2 tub jl2* v-a-b jl2 yers jl2
  - **accompanied** by | **Joints**; inflammation of (See EXTREMITIES - Inflammation - joints - accompanied - erythema; EXTREMITIES - Inflammation - joints - evening)
  - **indurated**: tub jl2
  - **patches**; with bronze: tub jl2
  - **punctiforms**: tub jl2
  - **subcutaneous**: tub jl2
- **excoriated** (See Excoriation)
- **exertion** agg.: *Con* b4a.de merc vh nat-m b4a.de
- **fails** to break out (See break - fails)
- **favus**-like: aethi-a c1 ars ptk1 sulph ptk1
- **fetid**: *Ars* k* ars-s-f k2 *Graph* k* *Hep* k* kali-p *Lach* *Lyc* k* *Merc* k* mez k* *Nit-ac* k* **Psor** k* rhus-t k* *Sep* k* *Sil* k* staph k* **Sulph** k* tell br1 vinc k* zinc k*
- **fever**; during: ars bg2 bry bg2 calc bg2 *Con* b4.de* ip bg2 lyc bg2 nat-m bg2 puls bg2 **Rhus-t** bg2 sep bg2 sulph bg2
- **fine**: carb-v ptk1 nat-m ptk1 rhus-t ptk1 thiam rly4•
- **fish**; after: ars bg3* sep bg3*
- **flat**: *Am-c* k* ang b2.de* ant-c k* ant-t k* *Ars* k* *Asaf* k* **Bell** k* carb-an k* euph k* **Lach** k* *Lyc* k* merc k* *Nat-c* k* nit-ac k* petr k* *Ph-ac* k* phos k* puls k* *Ran-b* k* *Sel* k* *Sep* k* *Sil* k* staph k* sulph k* thuj k*
- **fleabites**; like: graph h2 jug-r vml3• loxo-recl bnm10• olib-sac wmh1 [heroin sdj2]
- **fright**; from: aethi-a c1
- **furuncles** (See boils)
- **gastric** symptoms; with: ant-c br1
- **German** measles (See rubella)
- **granular**: (↗*rash*) *Acon* bg2 *Agar* k* alum b2.de* am-c k* ars k* *Bell* b2.de* *Bry* b2.de* bufo bg2 *Carb-v* k* clem b2.de* cocc k* con b2.de* dulc b2.de* graph k* hep k* iod b2.de* *Ip* b2.de* kreos k* led k* manc bg2 merc b2.de* merc-c b4a.de mez b2.de* nat-m k* nux-v k* op bg2 par k* ph-ac b2.de* phos k* psor bg2 puls b2.de* *Rhus-t* b2.de* sars b2.de* stram bg2 sulph b2.de* valer k* (non:vinc kl) zinc k*
  - **honey** colored: ant-c ptk1
- **granuloma**; eosinophilic: loxo-lae bnm12•
- **grape** shaped: agar k* **Calc** k* rhus-t k* staph k* verat k*
- **gritty**: am-c k* falco-pe nl2• graph k* *Hep* k* nat-m k* phos k* zinc k*
- **hard**: agar *Ant-c* k* aur bov bg2 carb-an bg2 caust fl-ac k2 graph bg2 kali-bi bg2 mez nit-ac bg2 *Ran-b* k* rhus-t k* spig k* valer k*

○ • **Under** the skin: chlam-tr bcx2•

- **heat** rash (See miliaria rubra)
- **herpes** zoster (= zona): acon bro1 aethi-m bro1 agar k* aln bro1 anac bro1 anan bro1 anthraco bro1 apis bro1* arg-n k* arn k* *Ars* k* aster bro1 bar-c bro1 borx c2* bry k* bufo k* calc bro1 canth k* *Carb-ac* bro1 carbn-o c2* carbn-s caust k* cedr k* cham k* chrysar bro1 cist k* *Clem* k* com k* crot-h crot-t k* diph-t-tpt jl2 dol k* dulc bg2* eucal bro1 euph k* *Graph* k* grin br1* *Hep* k* hyper bro1 iod **Iris** k* kali-ar c2* *Kali-bi* k* *Kali-chl* k* kali-i kali-m c2* kalm c2* *Lach* k* lith-c bro1 luf-op mtf11 maland mtf11 **Merc** k* **Mez** k* morph bro1 nat-c k* *Nat-m* k* *Nit-ac* bro1 *Petr* k* ph-ac bro1 phyt hr1 pip-m bro1 prot mtf11 *Prun* c2* psor bro1 puls k* **Ran-b** k* ran-s c2* **Rhus-t** k* sal-ac bro1 *Sars* bro1 sel k* semp br1* *Sep* k* *Sil* k* staph k* staphycoc jl2 stry-ar bro1 *Sulph* k* syc mtf11 tell bro1 thal gk *Thuj* k* vac jl2* *Vario* k* xero bro1 zinc k* zinc-p c2* zinc-val bro1
  - **accompanied** by:
    - **neuralgic** pain: ars bro1 dol bro1 *Kalm* bro1 *Mez* bro1 ran-b bro1 still bro1 zinc bro1
    - **Stomach**; complaints of: iris ptk1
  - **chronic**: ars bro1 semp bro1
  - **cold** applications | **amel.**: apis mrr1
  - **followed** by:
    - **eruptions**: kali-m ptk1
    - **pain**: dol bg2 vario bg2 zinc bg2*
    - **ulcers**: euph bg2 petr bg2 sil bg2 thuj bg2 tub bg2
  - **warm** applications | **amel.**: ars tl1

- **herpetic**: acet-ac k* acon bg3* aeth c2 aethi-a c1 agar k* agath-a nl2• all-s hr1 aln c2 *Alum* k* alum-p k2 alum-sil k2 am-c k* ambr anac k* *Anan* k* anthraco c2* *Apis* **Ars** k* ars-br br1* *Ars-i* ars-s-f k2 aster k* aur aur-ar k2 aur-i k2 aur-s k2 bac ptk1 *Bar-c* k* *Bar-m* k* bar-s k2 bell k* berb k* berb-a c2 borx k* **Bov** k* *Bry* k* bufo cadm-s calad **Calc** k* calc-f c2* calc-i k2 **Calc-s** k* calc-sil k2 caps k* *Carb-an* k* *Carb-v* k* **Carbn-s** *Caust* k* chel chrys-ac c1 chrysar bwa3 *Cic* k* *Cist* k* **Clem** k* cocc coloc hr1* com k* **Con** k* cortico sp1 crot-h k* *Crot-t* k* cupr k* cycl dol k* **Dulc** k* dys fmm1• equis-a br1 ery-m c2 eucal hr1 eup-per hr1 gaert fmm1• gink-b sbd1• **Graph** k* grat k* hell *Hep* k* hydrog srj2• hyos ictod c2 iod k* iris jug-c c2 jug-r c2 *Kali-ar* kali-bi hr1* *Kali-c* k* *Kali-chl* *Kali-i* k* kali-m k2 kali-n kali-p *Kali-s* kalm k* *Kreos* k* *Lac-c* k* lac-d k2 lac-e hm2• *Lach* k* *Led* k* **Lyc** k* mag-c k* *Mag-m* k* manc k* mang k* med jl2* **Merc** k* mez k* morg-g fmm1• mosch mur-ac musca-d szs1 *Nat-ar* *Nat-c* k* **Nat-m** k* nat-p *Nat-s* k* nit-ac k* nux-v oci-sa sp1 ol-j hr1 *Olnd* k* par k* *Petr* k* ph-ac *Phos* k* phyt ptk1 plat mrr1 plb prot jl2* *Psor* k* puls *Ran-b* k* ran-s k* rhod **Rhus-t** k* rhus-v c2 rob k* rumx ruta sabad sarr c2 *Sars* k* semp ptk2 **Sep** k* **Sil** k* sol-o c2 spig k* spong k* squil stann *Staph* k* sul-ac sul-i k2 **Sulph** k* syph jl2 tarax **Tell** k* teucr thal-xyz srj8• thuj k* ulm-c c2 vac jl2 valer vario bg3* verat viol-t zinc k* zinc-p k2
  - **right** side: iris hr1
  - **accompanied** by:
    - **eczema** (See eczema - accompanied - herpes)
    - **pemphigus**: ran-b mtf11
    - **Glands**; swelling of: dulc bro1
    - **Head** pain (See HEAD - Pain - accompanied - herpes)
  - **alternating** with | **Chest** complaints and dysenteric stools: rhus-t k*
  - **bleeding**: anac dulc k* lyc
  - **burning**: agar alum alum-p k2 am-c ambr k* anac k* **Ars** k* aur aur-i k2 bar-c bell bov bry calad *Calc* k* caps carb-an carb-v **Caust** cic clem cocc *Con* k* dulc hell hep *Kali-c* k* kali-n kali-sil k2 kreos lach led *Lyc* *Mang* **Merc** k* mez mosch hr1 nat-c nat-m nux-v olnd par petr ph-ac phos plb *Psor* puls ran-b **Rhus-t** sabad sars sep k* *Sil* spig spong squil staph k* stram *Sulph* teucr thuj verat viol-t zinc
  - **chapping**: alum aur bry cadm-s *Calc* k* cycl graph hep kali-c kreos lach lyc mag-c mang merc nat-c nat-m nit-ac petr *Puls* *Rhus-t* ruta sars **Sep** sil **Sulph** viol-t zinc
  - **chronic**: aln bro1* anthraco br1
  - **circinate**: *(↗pityriasis versicolor; ringworm; Discoloration - white - spots)* anac anag k* ars-s-f bro1* bacls-10 fmm1• *Bar-c* k* bar-s k2 *Brom* b4a.de *Calc* k* calc-act bro1 calc-ar mp1• carc gk chrysar bwa3* clem k* dulc k* dys mp1• equis-a bro1 equis-h mp1• *Eup-per* *Graph* k* hell hep k* iod k* *Lith-c* mag-c k* med mp1• morg fmm1• morg-p fmm1• *Nat-c* k* **NAT-M** k •* parth vml3• phos **Phyt** psor al2 rad-br vh4* sanic mp1• semp ptk2 **SEP** k •* spong sulph k* syc mp1• **TELL** k •* ter bg2 **Thuj** k* tor mp1• **TUB** k •*
    - **rings**, in intersecting: tell bro1*
    - **spots**, in isolated: sep bro1*
    - **spring**; every: **Sep**
  - **clusters**; in: dulc
  - **cold** water agg.: clem *Dulc* *Sulph*
  - **corrosive**: alum alum-p k2 am-c bar-c *Calc* carb-v caust chel *Clem* *Con* k* **Graph** hell hep kali-c kali-sil k2 lach lyc mag-c mang merc mur-ac nat-c nit-ac nux-v olnd par *Petr* ph-ac phos plb *Rhus-t* *Sep* **Sil** squil staph *Sulph* tarax viol-t
  - **crusty**: alum alum-p k2 am-c ambr anac *Ars* *Aur* *Aur-m* bar-c bell bov bry **Calc** calc-sil k2 caps carb-an carb-v cic *Clem* k* **Con** k* cupr *Dulc* k* **Graph** hell hep kali-c kali-sil k2 kreos lach *Led* **Lyc** k* mag-c **Merc** *Mez* k* mur-ac nat-m nit-ac nux-v olnd par petr ph-ac phos plb puls ran-b **Rhus-t** k* sars *Sep* k* *Sil* squil staph **Sulph** k* thuj k* verat *Viol-t* zinc
  - **dry**: alum alum-sil k2 ars *Bar-c* *Bov* k* bry cact k* *Calc* calc-sil k2 carb-v caust clem k* cocc cupr dol k* *Dulc* k* fl-ac bro1 graph *Hep* k* hyos hyper hr1 kali-i kreos k* **Led** k* lyc mag-c mang-act bro1 med k* *Merc* k* nat-c nat-m nit-ac k* par petr ph-ac k* **Phos** k* psor k* rhus-t k* sars **Sep** k* **Sil** k* stann *Staph* k* sulph k* teucr k* thuj k* valer verat viol-t *Zinc* k*
  - **fevers**; in: carb-v **Nat-m** rhus-t
  - **gastric** complaints; with: iris br1
  - **glands**; covered with: dulc graph

- **herpetic**: ...
  - **gray**: ars
  - **indolent**: lyc mag-c psor
  - **itching**: aeth a1 agar agath-a nl2• alum k* alum-p k2 alum-sil k2 am-c ambr anac *Ant-t* **Ars** k* aur-i k2 bar-c bell *Bov* bry calad calc calc-sil k2 caps k* carb-an carb-v k* *Caust* chel k* cic **Clem** k* cocc con cupr k* dulc *Graph* guaj hr1 hep jug-r kali-ar k2 *Kali-c* k* *Kali-i* hr1 kali-sil k2 kreos *Lac-d* hr1 lach *Led* lyc mag-c mag-m mang k* med jl2 *Merc* k* mez nat-c nat-m k* *Nit-ac* k* nux-v olnd par petr ph-ac phos plb *Psor* hr1 puls ran-b ran-s **Rhus-t** k* sabad sars **Sep** k* *Sil* spig spong squil stann *Staph* k* *Sulph* k* tarax thuj k* valer verat viol-t zinc
    - **menses**; before: carb-v h2
  - **jerking** pain; with: calc caust cupr lyc puls **Rhus-t** sep sil *Staph*
  - **mealy**: am-c **Ars** aur bov bry **Calc** cic *Dulc* graph kreos led *Lyc* merc mur-ac **Phos** *Sep* **Sil** sulph thuj k* verat
  - **menses** | **before** | **agg.**: *Dulc* bg2
    - **during** | **agg.**: gink-b sbd1• petr kr1
  - **mercurial**: aur mosch k* *Nit-ac*
  - **moist**: alum am-c anac anan ars bar-c k* bell *Bov* k* bry cact cadm-s **Calc** k* caps hr1 carb-an *Carb-v* k* **Caust** k* cic k* cist *Clem* k* con k* **Dulc** k* **Graph** k* grat hell hep k* kali-c k* **Kreos** k* lach led k* **Lyc** k* **Merc** k* mez k* nat-c k* nat-m k* nit-ac *Olnd* k* petr **Ph-ac** k* phos *Psor* k* ran-b **Rhus-t** k* ruta **Sep** k* *Sil* k* squil staph sul-ac **Sulph** k* tarax *Tell* thuj viol-t
  - **neuralgia**; post herpetic: *(↗GENERALS - Pain - eruptions - herpetic - neuralgic)* kalm k2* mez bro1 ran-b bro1 still bro1 vario bro1
  - **noise**; with sensitivity to (See MIND - Sensitive - noise - herpes)
  - **patches**: *Ant-c* caust con crot-h *Graph* hyos **Lyc** **Merc** mur-ac *Nat-c* nat-m nit-ac petr phos sabad sars **Sep** sil **Sulph** zinc
    - **brown**: **Sep**
  - **pimples** or pustules; surrounded by | **confluent**: hep bro1
  - **pregnancy** agg.; during: sep bro1
  - **recurrent**: hed mtf11 rib-ac mtf11
  - **red**: am-c k* ars *Bry* cic *Clem* *Dulc* k* kreos *Lach* k* led *Lyc* *Mag-c* mag-s *Merc* olnd petr ph-ac staph tax tell
  - **scaly**: agar anac anan k* ars k* aur bell bov k* cact cadm-s **Calc** k* carbn-s k2 cic k* *Clem* k* *Con* k* cupr *Dulc* k* *Graph* k* hep hyos kali-ar k2 kali-c kreos hr1 lach hr1 led k* *Lyc* k* mag-c k* **Merc** k* nat-m k* olnd ph-ac k* *Phos* k* plb *Psor* ran-b rhus-t *Sep* k* sil staph k* *Sulph* k* teucr thuj k*
    - **white**: anac ars graph lyc thuj zinc
      - **dry**, mealy: ars calc dulc lyc sep sil thuj
  - **simplex**: vac mtf11
  - **spreading**: alum caps carbn-s clem k2 dulc **Merc** nat-c h2
  - **spring**, every: *Sep*
  - **stinging**: alum alum-p k2 alum-sil k2 anac hr1 *Ars* bar-c bell bov bry calc calc-sil k2 caps carb-v caust **Clem** cocc con cycl graph hell hep kali-c kali-sil k2 kreos led lyc mag-c melal-alt gya4 *Merc* mez mur-ac nat-c nat-m *Nit-ac* nux-v petr phos *Puls* ran-b ran-s *Rhus-t* sabad **Sep** *Sil* spong squil staph *Sulph* thuj viol-t zinc
  - **suppressed**: alum ambr ars hr1 *Calc* *Lach* *Lyc* nat-c sep *Sulph*
  - **suppurating**: ars k* bell cadm-s cic clem cocc con cycl *Dulc* k* hep jug-c led *Lyc* mag-c **Merc** *Nat-c* k* nat-m *Petr* plb puls **Rhus-t** sars **Sep** sil spig staph sulph tarax thuj verat viol-t zinc k*
  - **tearing**: ars bell bry *Calc* carb-v carbn-s k2 caust clem cocc dulc graph kali-c **Lyc** merc *Mez* nat-c nit-ac nux-v phos puls rhus-t *Sep* *Sil* staph *Sulph* *Zinc*
  - **washing**; pain from: lac-c kr1
  - **whitish**: anac thuj k* zinc
  - **yellowish**: agar ars carbn-s cic cocc cupr *Dulc* hell kreos led *Lyc* *Merc* nat-c k* nit-ac par sep *Sulph*
    - **brown**: carbn-s cupr dulc lyc *Nat-c*
  - ○ **Body**; all over: dulc *Psor* *Ran-b*
- **hives** (See urticaria)
- **hormonal** change; during any: sulph zr

- **horny**: *(↗Excrescences - horny)* *Ant-c* k* ars bg2* borx ptk1 graph ptk1 *Ran-b* k* sil ptk1 sulph ptk1 tritic-vg fd5.de
- **humid** (See discharging)
- **impetigo**: aln c2* alum am-c ang hr1 **ANT-C** k* ant-s-aur bro1 *Ant-t* c2* anthraco c2 apis mrr1 arg-n hr1* *Ars* k* ars-i **Arum-t** bg2* bac jl2* bar-c bor-ac c2 calc k* *Calc-m* c2* *Calc-p* hr1 calc-s mrr1 carb-ac k* carb-v k* carbn-s c2 caust k* cic k* *Cinnb* hr1 clem k* con k* crot-t k* *Dulc* k* euph bro1 ferr-i br graph k* *Hep* k* hydrc hr1 *Iris* k* *Jug-c* k* jug-r vml3• *Kali-bi* k* *Kali-i* a1* kali-n bro1 kreos lact lyc k* maland c2* med jl2 merc k* *Mez* c2* nat-c nat-m k* *Nit-ac* k* olnd k* petr-ra shn4• *Ph-ac* phos k* psor jl2* *Rhus-t* k* rhus-v hr1* sars k* sep k* sil k* staph k* staphycoc jl2* sulph k* syc bka1• tarent bg3* thuj hr1* tub mtf11 tub-m jl2 vario mtf11 viol-t k*
- **indented**: bov ptk1 thuj ptk1 vario ptk1
- **inflamed**: am-c h2* ars calc dulc fd4.de led mrr1 *Lyc* ruta fd4.de tritic-vg fd5.de
  - **bad** smelling: psor jl2
  - **herpetiform**: sulfa sp1
  - **itching**: psor jl2
  - **oozing**: psor jl2
  - **scratching**; from: psor jl2
- **injured** parts: arn mrr1 calc-p alj
- **itching**: *(↗tetters)* acon k* aeth a1* *Agar* k* agn k* allox sp1 *Alum* k* alum-p k2 alum-sil k2 *Am-c* k* am-m k* ambr k* *Anac* k* anag k* *Ant-c* k* *Ant-t* k* anthraci vh1 *Apis* bg2 arg-met k* *Arn* k* **Ars** k* *Ars-i* ars-s-f k2 asaf k* aur-m-n hr1* bamb-a stb2.de• bar-c k* bar-s k2 bell k* borx br1 bov k* *Bry* k* bufo *Calad* k* *Calc* k* *Calc-p* k* *Calc-s* calc-sil k2 *Canth* k* caps k* carb-an k* carb-v k* carbn-s carl a1 **Caust** k* *Cham* k* chel k* chinin-s cic k* cimic k* cina k* **Clem** k* cocc k* cod hr1 colch hr1 *Com* bg2 con k* *Cop* a1 cortiso sp1* *Crot-t* k* cupr k* dig k* dros gk dulc k* fago a1 ferr a1 fl-ac k2 fuli br1 gast a1 gink-b sbd1• goss a1 **Graph** k* guaj hr1 guare k* *Hep* k* hippoc-k szs2 *Ign* k* iod a1 ip k* iris *Jug-c* k* *Jug-r* k* *Kali-ar* k* kali-bi k* kali-br k* *Kali-c* k* *Kali-i* k* kali-n k* kali-p *Kali-s* kali-sil k2 kalm a1 *Kreos* k* lac-d hr1 lac-e hm2• *Lach* k* lat-m sp1 laur k* *Led* k* *Lyc* k* m-ambo b2.de* m-arct b2.de* m-aust b2.de* mag-c k* mag-m k* mang k* *Merc* k* **Mez** k* morg fmm1• morg-p pte1• myos-a rly4• nat-ar nat-c k* nat-f sp1 **Nat-m** k* **Nit-ac** k* **Nux-v** k* *Olnd* k* ox-ac a1 *Par* k* *Petr* k* ph-ac k* *Phos* k* *Phyt* k* pic-ac bg2 pitu-gl skp7• pix br1 plac-s rly4• plb k* positr nl2• pot-e rly4• *Psor* k* *Puls* k* *Ran-b* k* ran-s k* **Rhus-t** k* ruta k2 sabad k* sabin k* sacch-a gmj3 *Sars* k* *Sel* k* **Sep** k* *Sil* k* spig k* spong k* *Squil* k* stann k* **Staph** k* stram k* stront-c k* sul-ac k* **Sulph** k* tarax k* tarent k2 teucr k* thuj k* til a1 tritic-vg fd5.de tub-m jl2 *Vac* jl2 valer k* verat k* vero-o rly4*• vinc hr1 *Viol-t* k* zinc k* zinc-p k2 [*Spect* dfg1]
  - **evening**: aeth a1 *Alum* borx graph kreos k* mag-m mez h2* staph
  - **night**: ant-c ant-t *Ars* k* ars-i asc-t a1 *Clem* crot-t graph *Iris* kali-bi k* kreos **Merc** *Merc-i-f* hr1 *Mez* olnd *Psor* mrr1 puls mrr1 *Rhus-t* k* staph k* thyr ptk1 ust k* verat viol-t k*
  - **air** agg.; in open: led *Nit-ac*
  - **cold**:
    - **air**:
      - **agg.**: *Kali-ar* k* *Psor Rumx*
      - **amel.**: kali-bi *Kali-i* vh
    - **washing** agg.: *Clem*
  - **dentition**; during: calc alj
  - **edematous**: pitu-gl skp7•
  - **heat**:
    - **stove**; of:
      - **agg.**: **Kali-i** vh
      - **amel.**: *Rumx Tub*
  - **heat** of bed | **agg.** (See Itching - warm; becoming - bed - agg.)
  - **menses**:
    - **after** | **agg.**: coloc bg2 con bg2 kali-c bg2 kreos bg2 nat-m bg2 tarent bg2
    - **before** | **agg.**: carb-v h2*
    - **during** | **agg.**: agar bg2 am-c bg2 apis bg2 bell bg2 calc bg2 carb-v k* cham bg2 chin bg2 con bg2 crot-h bg2 dulc bg2 **Graph** bg2 hep bg2 *Kali-c* k* kali-n bg2 lac-c bg2 lyc bg2 mag-c bg2 med bg2 merc bg2 nat-s bg2 nux-m bg2 nux-v bg2 petr bg2 *Phos* bg2 puls bg2 sang bg2 sep bg2 sil bg2 sulph bg2 zinc bg2
  - **overheated**; when: *Kali-i* vh
- **itching**: ...
  - **patches**:
    - **bleeding** after scratching: **Sulph**
    - **circumscribed**:
      - **lenticular**: cop br1
      - **mottled**: cop br1
    - **dry** and red (See patches - dry - itching)
  - **rubbing** | **amel.**: cortiso gse
  - **scratching** agg.: sacch-a gmj3
  - **storm**; before: graph k*
  - **touch** agg.: mez
  - **undressing**; when: *Ars-i* *Kali-ar* k* nat-s **Rumx**
  - **waking**; on: trios rsj11•
  - **wandering**: gink-b sbd1•
  - **warm** | **bed** | **agg.**: aeth *Alum* anac ant-c caust *Clem* cocc *Kali-act* kreos mag-m merc mur-ac **Psor** k* *Puls Rhus-t* sars staph **Sulph** *Til* verat
    - **room** | **agg.**: alum-p k2 *Sep* sulfonam ks2
  - **warmth**:
    - **agg.**: *Alum* alum-sil k2 *Aur-s* wbt2• bov *Caust Clem Kali-i* vh *Led Lyc* **Med Merc** *Mez* morg fmm1• nat-ar *Psor* k* *Puls* k* *Sulph* verat h1*
    - **amel.**: morg fmm1•
    - **fire**, of: *Mez*
  - **washing** | **agg.**: gink-b sbd1• mez sulph
  - **without**: chord-umb rly4• cic ptk1 cupr-act ptk1
- **jerking** pain; with: asaf b2.de* asar calc k* *Caust* k* cham k* chin k* cupr k* lyc k* *Puls* k* **Rhus-t** k* sep k* sil k* *Staph* k*
- **knotty**, tuberculous (See tubercles)
- **lactation**; during: *Sep*
- **leprosy**: all-s bnj1 alum k* am-c hr1 ambr hr1 anac k* ant-t k* *Ars* k* *Aza* bnj1 *Bad* bro1 bar-c k* bix pls1 boerh-d bnj1 *Calc* k* calo a2* canch bwa3 *Carb-ac* k* *Carb-an* k* *Carb-v* k* *Carbn-s* *Caust* k* chaul bro1* coloc hr1 com k* con k* crot-h k* cupr b7.de* cupr-act a1* cur bwa3* daph hr1* dip mp1• drym-cor jsx1.fr elae c2* form k* *Graph* k* guan bro1 *Gymno* bro1 haem mp1• hell k* hemidsm bnj1 hura c2* hydrc k* iod k* *Iris* jatr-g bro1 kali-ar hr1 kali-c k* *Kali-i* k* *Lach* k* maeso-f jsx1.fr mag-c k* mang k* *Meph* merc bro1* merc-sul hr1 mitra-st jsx1.fr *Nat-c* k* nat-m k* nit-ac k* *Nuph* k* oena bwa3* pentac-m jsx1.fr petr k* *Phos* k* pip-m c2* *Psor* psoral gsb1 ricino-h jsx1.fr **Sec** k* *Sep* k* *Sil* k* still hr1 strych-g c2* **Sulph** k* syph c1 *Thyr* c2* tinas vma2 *Tub* k* *Vac* c2 zinc k*
  - **borderline**: alum mtf anac mtf tub mtf
  - **chronic**: cupr-act br1
  - **lepromatous**: hura mtf hydrc bnj1
  - **tuberculoid**: elae mtf lepr vml3• strych-g mtf
- **lichen**: *(↗papular)* acon ptk1 agar c2* alum bro1 am-m bro1 *Anan* bro1 *Ant-c* bro1 anthraco c2 *Apis* c2* *Ars* c2* *Ars-i* c2 *Bell* bro1 bov bro1 bry bro1* *Calad* bro1 castn-v bro1 *Cic* ptk1 cocc ptk1 dulc c2* jug-c c2* kali-ar bro1 *Kreos* bro1 *Led* bro1 *Lyc* bro1* mang c2 merc bro1 mur-ac ptk1 nabal bro1 nat-c bro1 nat-m ptk1 phyt c2* *Plan* bro1 *Rumx* c2* sep bro1 sul-i bro1 *Sulph* c2* til c2*
- **lichen** planus: agar bro1 anac bro1 *Ant-c* bro1 apis bro1 *Ars* bro1 *Ars-i* bro1 chinin-ar bro1 iod bro1 *Jug-c* bro1 *Kali-bi* bro1 kali-i bro1 led bro1 merc bro1 sars bro1 staph bro1 sul-i c2* sulph mtf11 syph jl2*
- **liver** spots: bell-p sp1
- **malignant**: syc fmm1•
- **mealy**: am-c **Ars** aur bov bry bufo **Calc** cic *Dulc* graph kali-ar k2 kreos led *Lyc* merc mur-ac nit-ac petr k2 **Phos** *Sep* **Sil** sulph thuj verat
  - **white**: *Ars Calc* dulc **Kali-chl** k* lyc sep sil thuj
- **measles**: *(↗GENERALS - Measles - ailments)* **Acon** k* ail a1* *All-c* hr1 *Am-c* k* am-m k2 *Anan* hr1 *Ant-c* k* ant-t hr1 antip vh **Apis** k* *Arn* k* *Ars* k* *Ars-i* c2 *Bell* k* borx bg2 **Bry** k* caj a1 camph k* caps c2 *Carb-v* k* *Carbn-s* cham k* *Chel* k* chin k* *Chlor* k* *Coff* k* con hr1 *Cop* k* cor-r hr1* *Crot-h* k* cub bg2 cupr c2 *Cupr-act* c2 *Dros* k* dulc hr1* elat c1* eup-per hr1* **Euphr** k* *Ferr-p* k* *Gels* k* hell hr1 hep hr1 *Hydr* hr1 hyos k* ign k* influ jl2* *Ip* k* kali-ar c2 *Kali-bi* k* *Kali-chl* hr1 kali-m ptk1 kali-s k* lach c2 lip-as bta1• mag-c k* maland c2 *Merc* hr1* *Merc-c* c2 morb bg2* mur-ac c2 *Murx* hr1 nux-v k* *Op* bg2* *Phos* k* phyt k* pix bg2 psor hr1 **Puls** k* puls-n c2 *Rhus-t* k* rhus-v c2 *Sabad* hr1 sep hr1 *Spong* hr1 *Squil* k* *Stict* hr1* *Stram* k* streptoc mtf11 sulfon bg2 **Sulph** k* ter bg2 toxo-g jl2 tub bg2* tub-a c2* verat k* verat-v c2 viol-o hr1 xan c1 zinc k*

- **accompanied** by:
  - **catarrh** (See GENERALS - Catarrh - accompanied - measles)
  - **convulsions** (See GENERALS - Convulsions - measles)
  - **cornea**; pustules on: kali-bi tl1
  - **coryza** and profuse lachrymation: kali-bi tl1 puls tl1
  - **cough**; croupy: acon bro1 coff bro1 dros bro1 euphr bro1 gels bro1 *Hep* bro1 kali-bi bro1 *Spong* bro1 stict bro1
  - **fever**; low: *Ail* bro1 *Ars* bro1 bapt bro1 carb-v bro1 crot-h bro1 *Lach* bro1 *Mur-ac* bro1 *Rhus-t* bro1 sulph bro1
  - **meningeal** complications (See HEAD - Complaints - meninges - accompanied - measles)
  - **rheumatism** (See GENERALS - Pain - rheumatic - measles)
  - **salivation**: nat-m kr1*
  - **secretions**; watery yellowish green: kali-bi tl1 puls tl1
  - **voice**; complaints of: cinnb bg2
  - **Ear**; pain in: puls bro1
  - **Eyes**:
    - **complaints**: ars bro1 *Euphr* bro1 kali-bi bro1 puls bro1
    - **swelling**, almost closed: gels tl1
  - **Larynx**; inflammation of: dros bro1 gels bro1 *Kali-bi* bro1 viol-o bro1
  - **Tongue**; root of | **brown** discoloration; dark: *Lach* kr1*
- **followed** by | **voice**; complaints of: bell bg2 bry bg2 **Carb-v** bg2 cham bg2 *Dros* bg2 dulc bg2 sulph bg2
- **German** measles (See rubella)
- **hemorrhagic**: *Crot-h* ptk1 ferr-p tl1*
- **livid**: ail tl1
- **malignant**: ail bro1 *Ars* bro1 crot-h bro1 lach bro1
- **prophylaxis**: *Acon* bro1* ars bro1* puls bro1*
- **receding**; suddenly: ail tl1 *Bry* ptk1 phos ptk1 puls ptk1 rhus-t ptk1
- **suppressed**: ail tl1 ant-t bro1 apis bro1 *Bry* bro1 camph bro1 *Cupr-act* bro1 *Ip* bro1 *Lach* bro1 *Stram* bro1
- **tardy** development: ant-t bro1 apis bro1 bry bro1* cupr bro1 dulc bro1 gels bro1 ip bro1 *Stram* bro1 sulph bro1 tub bro1 verat-v bro1 *Zinc* bro1

- **measles**-like: *Acon* b7a.de *Bell* b7a.de benzol br1* *Coff* b7a.de
- **menses**:
  - **after** | **agg.**: kreos bro1
  - **before** | **agg.**: all-s bro1 apis bg2* *Bell* bro1 bell-p bro1 bufo bg2 calc bg2* carb-v bg2* chlam-tr bcx2• *Cimic* bro1 clem bg2 con bg2* dulc b4a.de* eug bro1 graph bg2* *Kali-ar* bro1 kali-c bro1 *Mag-m* bg2* mang-act bro1 *Med* bro1 *Nat-m* bg2 phos bg2 psor bg2* sang bg2* sars bg2* sil bro1 *Sulph* bg2* thuj bg2* verat bg2*
  - **during** | **agg.**: all-s bro1 apis bg2* *Bell* bro1 bell-p bro1 calc bro1 *Cimic* bro1 con b4a.de* *Dulc* k* eug bro1 *Graph* k* hyos gt1 *Kali-ar* bro1 kali-c gt1* kali-n hr1* kreos bg2 mag-m bro1 mang-act bro1 *Med* bro1 nux-m petr gt1 positr nl2• psor bro1 sang bro1 *Sars* bro1 sil bro1 thuj bro1 verat bro1
- **mercury**; after abuse of: *Calc* b4a.de *Staph* b7a.de *Sulph* b4a.de
- **miliaria** alba (See vesicular - sudamina)
- **miliaria** crystallina (See vesicular - sudamina)
- **miliaria** rubra: acon b2.de* am-m bro1 ars bro1 bell b2.de* bov ptk1 *Bry* bro1 cact bro1 carb-v ptk1 cent bro1 *Coff* b2.de* con ptk1 hura bro1 *Jab* bro1 led bro1 morb jl2 nat-m bg2* psor ptk1 puls ptk1 raph bro1 *Rhus-t* b7a.de sulph j2 syzyg bro1 tub-m jl2 urt-u bro1
  - **children**; in: | **infants**: **Acon** bg2 *Cham* bg2 sulph bg2
- **miliary**: acon ptk1 ars ptk1 bry ptk1 coff ptk1 *Dulc* ptk1 *Ip* ptk1 merc ptk1 phyt ptk1 *Sulph* ptk1
  - **agg.** after miliary eruptions: **Apis** b7a.de
  - **scratching**; after: spong b7a.de
- **milium**: *Calc-i* bro1 staph bro1 tab bro1
- **milk** agg.: calc h2 sep h2
- **moist** (See discharging)
- **molluscum**: *Brom* bro1 bry bro1 calc bro1 *Calc-ar* bro1 kali-i bro1 lyc bro1 merc bro1 nat-m bro1 sil bro1 sulph bro1 teucr bro1 vac mtf11
- **molluscum**: ...
  - **contagiosum**; molluscum: calc c1* carc sst2* kali-i ll lyc ll sil c1* sulfa sp1 thuj ll
  - **fibrosum**; molluscum: sil c1*
- **moon**; with full:
  - **decrease**; eruptions: antho c1
  - **increase**; eruptions: clem c1
- **morbiliform**: lat-m bnm6• loxo-lae bnm12• sulfa sp1 vario jl2
- **nettle** rash (See urticaria)
- **newborns** (See children - newborns)
- **offensive**: *Graph* bg2 *Petr* bg2 **Staph** bg2 *Vinc* bg2
- **oozing** (See discharging)
- **overheated**; from being: *Bov Carb-v Con* **Nat-m** *Psor Puls*
- **painful**: agar k* alum alum-sil k2 ambr k* ant-c k* *Ant-t* a1 apis arg-met k* **Arn** k* *Ars* k* ars-s-f k2 *Asaf* k* aur k* aur-ar k2 bar-c k* bar-s k2 **Bell** k* berb bov calc calc-sil k2 cann-s k* canth k* caps k* cassia-s cdd7• chel *Chin* k* cic *Clem* k* coli rly4• *Con* k* *Cupr* k* cycl b7.de dros b7.de *Dulc* k* galeoc-c-h gms1• guaj k* hell b7.de *Hep* k* kali-ar *Kali-c* k* kali-s kali-sil k2 *Lach* k* led k* *Lyc* k* m-arct b2.de m-aust b2.de* *Mag-c* k* *Mag-m* k* merc k* nat-ar nat-c k* nat-p **Nux-v** k* par k* petr k* **Ph-ac** k* phos k* *Puls* k* ran-b k* ran-s k* rhus-t k* ruta k* samb b7.de sel k* seneg k* *Sep* k* **Sil** k* *Spig* k* *Spong* k* squil k* staph b7.de succ-ac rly4• **Sulph** k* thuj k* valer k* vanil fd5.de *Verat* k* verb k* vip fkr4.de
  - **brushing** hair: galeoc-c-h gms1•
    - **sore**: sulfa sp1
  - **drawing**: m-ambo b7.de
  - **sore**: *Arg-met* b7a.de *Hep* b4a.de nat-m b4a.de *Ph-ac* b4a.de *Rhus-t* b7a.de ruta b7a.de sil b4a.de *Spig* b7a.de verat b7a.de
  - **splinters**; as from | **touch** agg.: *Hep Nit-ac*
  - **spots**: luna kg1•
  - **touch** agg.: galeoc-c-h gms1• [bell-p-sp dcm1]
  - **ulcerative** | **Below** the skin: puls b7.de staph b7.de tarax b7.de
- **painless**: *Ambr* k* anac k* ant-c k* ant-t k* bell k* cham k* *Cocc* k* *Con* k* cycl k* dros k* *Hell* k* *Hyos* k* lach k* laur k* **Lyc** k* *Olnd* k* ph-ac k* phos k* puls k* rhus-t k* samb k* *Sec* k* spig k* staph k* *Stram* k* *Sulph* k*
- **papular**: *(↗lichen)* *Acon* ptk1 allox sp1 anthraco br1 aur bac jl2 beryl sp1 *Bry* ptk1 *Calc* caps a1 *Caust* cham cycl *Dulc* ptk1 galeoc-c-h gms1• gels *Grin* hippoz *Hydrc Iod Kali-bi Kali-c* **Kali-i** k* kali-s kerose a1 lat-m bnm6• loxo-lae bnm12• loxo-recl bnm10• lyc *Merc* k* morb jl2 narc-ps br1* nat-f sp1 *Petr* petr-ra shn4• phos pic-ac psor k2* *Sep* sil suis-hep rly4• sulfa sp1 *Sulph* k* *Syph* k* tere-la rly4• thiop mtf11 toxo-g jl2 x-ray sp1 zinc
  - **healing** quickly: allox tpw3 galeoc-c-h gms1•
  - **heat**: beryl sp1
  - **itching**: acon bro1 allox tpw3* aln bro1 *Ambr* bro1 anthraco bro1 *Ars* bro1 *Ars-i* bro1 ars-s-f bro1 bac jl2 beryl tpw5* carb-ac bro1 *Chlol* bro1 dios bro1 *Dol* bro1 gink-b sbd1• kali-bi bro1 *Lyc* bro1 *Merc* bro1 *Mez* bro1 *Nit-ac* bro1 *Olnd* bro1 ov br1* ped bro1 psor jl2 *Rhus-t* bro1 *Rhus-v* bro1 *Rumx* bro1 sil bro1 *Sulph* bro1 ter bro1
    - **bathing**: allox sp1
    - **scratching** agg.: beryl tpw5*
    - **warm** applications agg.: beryl tpw5
    - **without** fever or itching: cub c1
  - **syphilitic**: *Calo* bro1 kali-i bro1 lach bro1 merc bro1 merc-c bro1 *Merc-i-r* bro1
  - **white**: suis-hep rly4•
- **patches**: acon-ac rly4• agar ail k* apis ptk1 ars k* berb k* *Calc* k* *Carb-v* coli rly4• *Graph* ina-i mlk9.de *Iris* jug-c *Kali-bi Kali-c Lith-c* mang petr k2 phos k* pot-e rly4• *Puls Sars* sec ptk1 *Sep* sinus rly4• thuj tritic-vg fd5.de *Viol-t*
  - **circumscribed**, lenticular | **mottled** appearance; with itching and (See itching - patches - circumscribed - lenticular - mottled)
  - **dry** red patches | **itching** violent: granit-m es1• sulfonam ks2
- **peas**-size: vac jl2
- **pemphigus**: *(↗EXTREMITIES - Eruptions - fingers - pemphigus; EXTREMITIES - Eruptions - hand - back - pemphigus; EXTREMITIES - Eruptions - thumb - pemphigus; EXTREMITIES - Eruptions - upper limbs - pemphigus; EXTREMITIES - Eruptions - wrist - pemphigus; MOUTH - Eruptions - pemphigus)* acon k* ail tl1 *Anac* k* antip br* *Ars* k* *Arum-t* bg3* bell k* bry hr1 bufo k* calc k* calth a1* canth k* carbn-o a1* caust k*

- **pemphigus**: ...
chin k* chlol hr1 cop a1* cortiso sp1 *Crot-h* k* cur a1 *Dulc* k* gamb hr1 hep k* hydrc k* jug-c k* **Lach** k* lipp a1 *Lyc* k* manc br* *Merc* k* *Merc-c* c2* merc-pr-r bro1 *Nat-m* k* *Nat-s* k* nat-sal br* *Nit-ac* k* ph-ac k* phos k* *Psor* k* *Ran-a* bro1 ran-b k* ran-s k* raph c2* *Rhus-t* k* *Sars* k* scroph-xyz c2 *Sep* k* *Sil* k* sul-ac k* sulfa sp1 *Sulph* k* syph c2* thuj k*
- **periodical**: apis bg2 calc bg2 dulc bg2 kreos bg2 *Rhus-t* b7a.de tub bg2
- **perspiration**; during: *Apis* bg2 ars bg2 bry bg2 calc bg2 *Con* b4.de* ip bg2 lyc bg2 nat-m bg2 **Op** b7.de* puls bg2 **Rhus-t** b7a.de* **Sep** b4a.de* sulph bg2 *Thuj* b4a.de*
- **petechiae**: ail ptk1 apoc *Arn* k* **Ars** k* ars-s-f k2 aur-m *Bapt* bell k* berb borx bg2 **Bry** k* calc bro1 *Camph* canth *Chel* b7a.de chin bg2 chlf bg2 chlol bg2 *Con* cop bg2 *Crot-h* k* cub bg2 cupr k* cur bro1 dulc eup-per ferr mtf11 hep bg2 hir mtf11 *Hyos* k* iod bg2 iodof bg2 kali-chl bg2 *Kreos* bg2 *Lach* k* led k* leptos-ih jl2 loxo-recl bnm10• merc bg2 mur-ac bro1* nat-m nux-v k* *Ph-ac* k* phel **Phos** k* plb bg2 *Pyrog* bg2 **Rhus-t** k* ruta k* *Sec* k* sil k* squil stram k* sul-ac k* tab bg2 ter vario al2*
  - **moist** after scratching: ars h2*
  - **old** people; in: *Con*
  - **painful** | **evening**; in: ars h2
  - **purple**: arn tl1 crot-h tl1 led tl1 phos tl1
  - **tendency** to: sec mtf11
- **phagedenic**: alum k* alum-sil k2 am-c k* **Ars** bg2 *Arum-t* bg2 *Bar-c* k* bar-s k2 *Borx* k* *Calc* k* calc-sil k2 carb-an bg2 carb-v k* carbn-s caust k* **Cham** k* chel k* *Clem* k* *Con* k* croc k* **Graph** k* hell k* *Hep* k* hydr bg2 kali-ar kali-c k* kali-sil k2 lach k* lyc k* mag-c k* mang k* merc k* mur-ac k* *Nat-c* k* nat-m nat-p *Nit-ac* k* nux-v k* olnd k* par k* **Petr** k* ph-ac k* phos k* plb k* psor k2 *Rhus-t* k* sars *Sep* k* **Sil** k* *Squil* k* *Staph* k* sulph k* tarax k* *Viol-t* k*
- **pimples**: acetan bg2 *Acon* k* *Agar* k* aloe alum k* alum-p k2 am-c k* am-m k* ambr k* anac k* **Ant-c** k* *Ant-t* k* aran k* arg-met k* arg-n bg2 arn k* **Ars** k* ars-h hr1 ars-i arum-d hr1 arum-t hr1 aster k* *Aur* k* aur-ar k2 aur-m hr1 bar-c k* *Bar-m* bar-s k2 *Bell* k* benz-ac bg2 berb k* borx bg2 bov k* brom k* *Bry* k* bufo k* *Calad* k* calc k* *Calc-p* k* *Calc-s* k* calc-sil k2 *Canth* k* caps k* carb-ac bg2 *Carb-an* k* carb-v k* *Carbn-s* **Caust** k* *Cham* k* chel k* chin k* chinin-ar chlf bg2 chlol bg2 chord-umb rly4• cimic cina k* *Cist* clem k* coc-c k* *Cocc* k* coli rly4• *Con* k* cop bg2 crot-h k* crot-t cub k* cund hr1 cupr k* cycl k* dig bg2* dros k* *Dulc* k* eug c2 euph-l br1 euphr k* falco-pe nl2• *Fl-ac* k* *Gamb* gels k* gink-b sbd1• granit-m es1• *Graph* k* guaj bg2 hell k* helodr-cal knl2• *Hep* k* hippoc-k szs2 hydr hr1 hydr-ac bg2 hyos bg2* hyper a1* ina-i mlk9.de indg a1* iod k* iodof bg2 jab bg2 *Kali-ar* kali-bi bg2 kali-br k* *Kali-c* k* kali-chl k* kali-m k2 kali-n k* kali-p kali-s *Kreos* k* lac-e hrn2• *Lach* k* lachn c1 *Led* k* **Luna** kg1• *Lyc* k* m-ambo b2.de* mag-c k* mag-m k* mang k* meny hr1 meph k* **Merc** k* *Merc-c* k* *Mez* k* mosch k* *Mur-ac* k* myric hr1 nat-ar *Nat-c* k* **Nat-m** k* *Nat-p* k* *Nat-s* **Nit-ac** k* *Nux-v* k* op bg2 pall k* par k* petr k* **Ph-ac** k* **Phos** k* pieri-b mlk9.de pip-n bg2 pix bg2 plb k* psor bg2* **Puls** k* querc-r svu1• rat c2 rhus-g tmo3• **Rhus-t** k* ruta sabad k* sabin hr1 *Sars* k* sel k* *Seneg* k* **Sep** k* *Sil* k* spig k* *Spong* k* *Squil* k* stann k* *Staph* k* stram bg2 stront-c k* suis-hep rly4• sul-ac k* sul-i k2 sulfon bg2 **Sulph** k* tab k* tarax k* tarent k* tell *Thuj* k* *Til* k* toxi mtf2• tritic-vg fd5.de trom hr1 *Urin* c1 vac hr1 valer k* vanil fd5.de verat k* viol-t k* **Zinc** k*
  - **night**; only at: anthraco c1
  - **appear** on body; as if pimples were about to: cinnb rb2
  - **black**: carb-v spig
    - **Center**: carb-v bg2 kali-bi bg2 psor bg2
    - **Tips**: carb-v ptk1
  - **bleeding**: *Cist* falco-pe nl2• par rhus-t stront-c thuj [bell-p-sp dcm1]
  - **burning**: agar k* **Ars** k* berb hr1 bov k* canth caust cocc c1 cub hr1 graph kali-c mag-m merc k* nat-s ph-ac *Rhus-t* squil staph stront-c sulph til
    - **scratching**; after: caust h2 graph h2 mag-m h2 sulph h2
  - **close** together: cham staph thuj verat
  - **confluent**: cic mur-ac ph-ac tarent k* valer
  - **copper**-colored: kali-i
  - **crusts**; with: calc merc squil
    - **green**: *Calc*
  - **drunkards**; in: kreos lach led nux-v ptk1
  - **gnawing**, itching: ant-c ant-t *Caust* mang nit-ac
  - **groups**; in: berb hr1

- **pimples**: ...
  - **hard**: agar k* arum-t hr1 *Bov* calc-s hr1 nit-ac rhus-t k* sabin ther hr1 valer verat
  - **inflamed**: agar berb bry *Chel* k* dulc fd4.de falco-pe nl2• nit-ac petr ruta fd4.de stann sulph k* tritic-vg fd5.de vanil fd5.de
  - **itching**: acal br1 acon k* ambr ammc anan vh1 *Ant-c* anthraco br1 *Apis* *Ars* k* asc-t hr1 bar-c bov k* *Bry* calc carb-an carbn-s *Caust* k* cham cina h1* coc-c hr1 cocc k* *Con* k* dulc k* falco-pe nl2• **Graph** k* *Hep* k* kali-c kali-sil k2 laur led h1* lyc mag-c h2* mag-m merc k* mur-ac nat-c nat-m nat-s *Nit-ac* ph-ac propr sa3• *Psor* puls *Sep* k* *Sil* k* squil h1* staph k* stront-c *Sulph* k* *Syzyg* br1 **Tell** til zinc k* ziz hr1
    - **warm**; when: caust **Kali-i** vh sars *Tell* til
  - **lenticular**: cic c1
  - **menses** | **after** | **agg.**: gink-b sbd1•
    - **during** | **agg.**: ger-i rly4• lac-c kr1
  - **moist**: *Calc* graph kali-c nat-s ol-an puls sil sulph thuj k* zinc
  - **painful**: ant-c apis arg-met arn ars-s-f k2 *Cist* cocc con dulc eug hr1 falco-pe nl2• graph *Hep* hr1 ind hr1 kali-c k* kali-chl kali-i lach mur-ac nat-c nit-ac nux-v phos plb puls ruta fd4.de seneg spong squil staph sulph k* tritic-vg fd5.de vanil fd5.de verat
  - **perspiring** parts; on: con
  - **pus**; containing: *Ant-c* b7a.de *Ant-t* b7a.de sars b4a.de
  - **red**: syzyg br1
    - **menses**; during: con al1*
  - **scratching** agg.; after: agar h2* am-c k* am-m k* *Ant-c* k* bar-c bry k* *Caust* k* chin k* cocc k* con k* cycl k* dros k* dulc k* graph k* hep k* kali-c k* laur k* merc k* nat-c k* nat-m k* *Nit-ac* k* petr k* ph-ac k* phos k* *Puls* k* *Rhus-t* k* sabad k* sabin k* sars k* sel k* **Sep** k* sil k* spong k* squil k* staph k* stront-c k* *Sulph* k* verat k* *Zinc* k*
    - **white** after scratching; pimples become: agar *Ars* bov bry ip sulph
  - **small**: arn br1 mag-s ptk1 muru a1 ruta fd4.de syzyg br1 tritic-vg fd5.de
  - **smarting**: agar bell calc cham coloc dig *Hep* hr1 kali-c kali-n lyc merc teucr verat
  - **sore**, as if excoriated: alum arg-met bell bov calc clem cob hr1 **Eug** hr1 guaj *Hep* k* hyos ind hr1 lac-c hr1 mez ph-ac *Rhus-t* sabin sel spig stann teucr verat zinc k*
  - **splinter**, pain like a: arn k* hep *Nit-ac*
  - **stinging**: alum *Anan* hr1 ant-c k* apoc vh1 arn *Bell* calc-p *Canth* caps caust cocc hell kali-c kali-n kreos mez h2* nat-c petr squil staph
  - **tearing**: dulc
  - **tensive**: arn bov con mang nat-s
  - **tingling**: canth
  - **titillating**: bell caust mag-m verat
  - **touch**, sensitive to: berb calad dulc fd4.de **Hep** [bell-p-sp dcm1]
  - **ulcerated**: kali-c hr1 *Merc* k* nit-ac ph-ac sabin sep
  - **watery**: lachn c1
  - **whitish**: borx c1
    - **red** areola; with: borx ptk1
  - ○ **Folds**; on: cupr ptk1
- **pityriasis** (See scaly)
- **pityriasis** versicolor: *(↗herpetic - circinate; Discoloration - white - spots)* bac c2* carb-ac c1* caul c1 chrys-ac c2 *Chrysar* bro1 dulc mrr1 lyc mtf11 mez c2* *Nat-ar* bro1 psor jl2 *Sep* c2* *Sulo-ac* c2 sulph bro1 *Tell* c2*
- **pocks**: *Ant-c* *Ant-t* k* *Arn* *Ars* bell bry caust clem cocc euon hyos *Kali-bi* *Kreos* *Merc* mill psor puls *Rhus-t* sil sulph thuj
  - **black**: *(↗smallpox - black)* *Ars* bell hyos lach mur-ac *Rhus-t* sec
  - **burning**: **Ars** lach merc
  - **large**: ant-t b7a.de
  - **suppurating**: bell *Merc* sulph
  - **whitish**: iod lyc
- **pointed**: ant-c ptk1 ant-t ptk1 *Ars* ptk1 hydr ptk1 puls ptk1 *Sil* ptk1
- **psoriasis**: *(↗EXTREMITIES - Inflammation - joints - psoriatic)* agar b2.de* alum k* am-c k* ambr k* *Ant-t* c2* arizon-l nl2• arn mrr1 *Ars* k* **Ars-i** k* ars-s-f k2 ars-s-r c2 aster bro1 aur k* aur-ar k2 aur-m-n bro1* bell b2.de* bell-p c2 berb-a bg3* borx k* bry k* bufo *Calc* k* *Calc-s* *Canth* k* carb-ac k*

- **psoriasis**: ...
carb-v k13 carc mlr1• *Chin* k* *Chrys-ac* c1* chrysar bwa3* cic b2.de* *Clem* k* cor-r k* cortiso sp1 cupr k* cupr-act bro1 dros gk dulc k* dys pte1*• emetin mp4• falco-pe nl2• *Fl-ac* hr1* gali c2 *Graph* kr1* hep b2.de* hydrc c1* hyos b2.de* ichth mtf11 iod k* *Iris* k* *Kali-ar* k* kali-br k* *Kali-c* k* kali-m ptk1 kali-p *Kali-s* k* led k* *Lob* k* **Lyc** k* mag-c k* manc mrr1 *Mang* k* *Mang-act* bro1 *Merc* k* merc-aur bro1 merc-c merc-i-r k* merc-k-i gm1 merc-sul hr1 *Mez* k* morg-g pte1*• mur-ac bro1 naphtin c2* nat-ar br1* nat-m bro1* *Nit-ac* k* nit-m-ac br1* nuph k* olnd b2.de* pall sne *Petr* k* ph-ac *Phos* k* **Phyt** k* pix c2 plat bro1 plb b2.de* positr nl2• *Psor* k* *Puls* k* rad-br c11* ran-b k* *Rhus-t* k* *Sarr* k* *Sars* **Sep** k* *Sil* k* staph b2.de* stel c2* still c2 stry-ar bro1 stry-p bro1 sul-i k2 *Sulph* k* syph jl2* tell k* ter bro1 teucr k* thuj k* thyr bg3* tritic-vg fd5.de tub br1* ust br1* verat gk x-ray br1* [*Gal-met* stj lac-mat sst4]
  - **accompanied** by:
    - **diabetes** (See GENERALS - Diabetes mellitus - accompanied - psoriasis)
    - **Bones**; pain in (See GENERALS - Pain - bones - accompanied - psoriasis)
    - **Head**; pain in (See HEAD - Pain - accompanied - psoriasis)
  - **children**; in: calc mtf33 cupr mtf33 sep mtf33 **Staph** mrr1 tub mtf33
  - **chronic**: cupr mtf33 cupr-act br1
  - **desquamating**: ars mtf11
  - **diffusa**: ars ars-i k* calc k* cic k* clem k* dulc k* *Graph* k* lyc k* merc-i-r k* *Mez* mur-ac k* rhus-t k* sulph k* thuj k*
  - **fright**; after: manc mrr1
  - **grief** or suppressed emotions; after: **Staph** mrr1
  - **inveterata**: calc k* carb-ac k* clem k* *Kali-ar* k* *Mang* k* merc k* petr k* puls rhus-t k* *Sep* k* *Sil* k* sulph k*
  - **itching**; without: cupr-act ptk1
  - **purplish**: phyt mrr1
  - **swollen** persons: scarl jl2
  - **syphilitic**: ars **Ars-i** asaf bro1 aur aur-m-n br1 *Cor-r* *Graph* bro1 *Kali-bi* bro1 *Kali-br* k* **Merc** k* *Nit-ac* k* phos bro1 **Phyt** *Sars* thuj
- **purulent**: ant-c b7a.de* ant-t bg2 *Ars* b4a.de* bell b4a.de* cic b7.de* clem b4a.de* cocc b7.de* con b4a.de* cycl b7a.de* *Dulc* bg2 euphr b7a.de* *Graph* bg2 hep b4a.de* *Kali-bi* bg2 led b7.de* *Lyc* b4a.de* m-ambo b7.de* mag-c b4a.de* **Merc** b4a.de* **Nat-c** b4a.de* nat-m bg2 petr b4a.de* plb b7a.de* *Psor* bg2 puls b7a.de* **Rhus-t** b7.de* samb b7.de* sars b4a.de* sec b7a.de* **Sep** b4a.de* sil b4a.de* spig b7.de* *Staph* b7a.de* sulph b4a.de* tarax b7.de* thuj b4a.de* verat b7.de* viol-o bg2 viol-t b7.de* *Zinc* bg2
- **pustules**: agar aln bro1 am-c am-m k* anac k* *Ant-c* k* *Ant-s-aur* **Ant-t** k* arn k* **Ars** k* ars-br vh ars-i ars-s-f hr1* *Aur* aur-m hr1 aur-s k2 *Bell* k* *Berb* bro1 brom hr1 bry k* bufo k* calad *Calc* k* calc-p *Calc-s* calc-sil k2 *Carb-ac* k* *Carb-v* *Carbn-s* *Caust* k* cham k* *Chel* k* *Cic* k* cina cinnb k2 *Clem* k* cocc k* *Con* cop k* *Crot-h* k* *Crot-t* k* cund hr1 cupr-ar cycl k* *Dulc* k* echi br1* euph k* fl-ac k* gnaph graph k* *Hep* k* hippoz k* *Hydrc* *Hyos* k* iod *Iris* k* jug-c k* jug-r k* kali-ar k* *Kali-bi* k* *Kali-br* kali-c *Kali-chl* hr1 *Kali-i* k* kali-s kali-sil k2 *Kreos* k* lach k* lat-m bnm6• lyc bg3* *Mag-m* hr1 *Merc* k* merc-c bro1 merc-i-f bg2 merc-i-r bg2 *Mez* narc-ps br1* nat-c hr1* *Nat-m* k* *Nit-ac* k* nux-v op b2.de* *Petr* k* ph-ac phos phyt bro1 pieri-b mlk9.de podo c1* positr nl2• *Psor* k* *Puls* k* rad-br sze8• ran-b br1* **Rhus-t** k* rhus-v k* *Sars* sec k* *Sep* k* *Sil* k* sol-o c2 squil **Staph** k* staphycoc jl2 still hr1 streptoc jl2 strych-g br1 succ-ac rly4• sul-i k2* sulfa sp1 **Sulph** k* syph jl2 tab k* tarent tl1 tarent-c mrr1 tax br1* tell k* thal-xyz srj8• thap-g hsa1 thuj k* thyr ptk1 vario bg3* viol-t zinc [bell-p-sp dcm1]
  - **bathing** agg.: *Dulc*
  - **black**: ant-c b7a.de ant-t **Anthraci**· bry hyos b7a.de kali-bi bg1 **Lach** k* *Mur-ac* nat-c k* rhus-t k* sec b7a.de thuj bg1
    - **Tips**: anthraci ptk1 kali-bi ptk1 lach ptk1
  - **bleeding**: ant-t
  - **bloody** | **Tips**: carb-ac ptk1
  - **blue** spots, leaving: rheum h
  - **bluish**: rheum h
  - **brown**: ant-t syph jl2
    - **Tips**: verat ptk1
  - **burning**: am-c k* bar-c hr1 berb hr1 ind hr1 jug-r *Lach* hr1 petr k*
    - **touch** agg.: canth
    - **uncovering**; when: mez h2

- **pustules**: ...
  - **confluent**: ant-t **Cic** k* *Crot-t* hr1 *Lach* hr1 *Merc*
  - **cracked**: rhus-t
  - **crust**; covered with a: anac bg2 ant-t bg2 *Bov* bg2 crot-t bg2 kali-bi bg2 tarent bg2
  - **dry**: *Merc*
  - **fetid**: anthraci k* ars bufo thuj mtf33 viol-t
  - **greasy**: kreos k*
  - **green**: jug-r *Sec* viol-t
  - **hair** in center; with a: kali-bi bg2 petr bg2*
  - **hard**: anac ant-c crot-h nit-ac
  - **humid**: bell
  - **indolent**: *Kali-br* *Kreos* hr1 *Psor*
  - **inflamed**: anac crot-t *Kali-bi* k* rhus-t k* sep stram k*
  - **itching**: ant-t anthraci vh1 anthraco arg-n hr1 asim hr1 bar-c hr1 berb k* *Crot-t* k* *Dulc* k* graph hydr-ac *Kali-bi* *Lach* hr1 maland jl2 merc merc-i-r hr1 nux-v olib-sac wmh1 petr k* *Rhus-t* k* sars *Sil* hr1 spig hr1 *Sulph* k* zinc hr1 zinc-s bg2
    - **evening**: maland jl2
    - **night**: *Kali-bi*
  - **itch**-like: clem grat k*
  - **lumpy**: anthraci vh1 anthraco cham
  - **malignant**: **Anthraci** k* apis **Ars** k* *Bell* k* *Bufo* k* canth *Carb-v* k* cench *Crot-h* k* **Lach** k* maland jl2 *Ran-b* *Rhus-t* k* scol c1* *Sec* k* *Sil* k* *Tarent-c*
  - **offensive**: vario ptk1*
  - **painful**: ant-t ars berb *Kali-br* stram k* viol-t k*
  - **purpura**: staphycoc jl2
  - **red**: anac ant-t ars k* berb k* caust **Cic** cimic cinnb hr1 crot-h crot-t graph hydr-ac hydrc kali-c mez *Nit-ac* olib-sac wmh1 syph jl2 vac jl2 [bell-p-sp dcm1]
    - **fever**; during: vac jl2
    - **Areola**: anac ant-t borx calad lach nit-ac par thuj
  - **rose**-colored: ars aur hr1 dulc *Kali-br* hr1
  - **scaly**: merc
  - **scratching**; after: am-m k* ant-c k* ars k* bell k* bry k* cycl k* hyos k* merc k* puls k* **Rhus-t** k* sil k* staph k* *Sulph* k*
  - **scurfy**: anac k* ant-c ant-t k* bov k* crot-t dulc *Kali-chl* merc
  - **small**: ant-t ars hr1 *Hep* hr1 hydrc k* *Kali-bi* hr1 kali-i k* kali-n k* loxo-lae bnm12• merc-i-r hr1 puls sep hr1 zinc hr1
  - **sore**: calad merc k*
  - **spots** covered with: jug-r lyc
  - **spring**; in: sul-ac hr1
  - **stinging**: am-c berb k* dros ind hr1 *Lach* hr1 rhus-t *Sep*
  - **sunken** | **Tips**: thuj ptk1
  - **syphilitic**: *Ant-t* bro1 asaf bro1 *Calo* bro1 fl-ac bro1 *Hep* bro1 ign bro1 *Kali-bi* k* kali-i bro1 lach bro1 *Merc-n* bro1 mez bro1 *Nit-ac* bro1
  - **tensive**: ant-t crot-h kali-n mag-s
  - **tetters**; on the: kreos k*
  - **thin** pustules:
    - **breaking** and discharging ichorous pus | **corroding** the skin and spreading about: ant-t
  - **titillating**: mez
  - **ulcerated**: ant-t *Ars* crot-t cupr-ar *Dulc* mag-m *Merc* nat-c k* ol-myr hsa1 *Sars* sil
  - **vesicles**; mixed with: ant-t
  - **water**; containing: kali-i rhus-t stram
  - **white**: calad cimic k* cop cycl
    - **tips**: *Ant-c* k* ant-t k* puls k*
  - **yellow**: anac calc-s tl1 carb-v clem k2 hyos *Merc* staph viol-t k*
    - **yellow**-green pus: vac jl2
- **pyoderma**: hep mtf11

- **rash**: (↗*granular)* **Acon** k* aeth mrr1 *Agar* k* *Ail* k* alum k* alum-p k2 **Am-c** k* am-m k* anac *Anan Ant-c* k* *Ant-t* k* antip vh1 *Apis* k* aq-mar jl *Arn* k* **Ars** k* ars-i ars-s-f k2 arund asaf k* bar-c bar-m bar-s k2 **Bell** k* bov k* brass-n-o srj5• **Bry** k* bufo k* *Calad* k* *Calc* k* calc-i k2 *Calc-s* calc-sil k2 camph *Canth* k* *Carb-v* k* carbn-s cardios-h rly4• cassia-s cdd7• **Caust** k* **Cham** k* chel chin b2.de* chinin-s *Chlol Clem* k* cocc k* *Coff* k* *Com* con cop corian-s knl6• corn crot-t cupr k* dig k* dros *Dulc* k* elaps euph k* euphr k* germ-met srj5• *Graph* k* hell k* *Hep* k* hippoc-k szs2 *Hyos* k* iod *Ip* k* *Jug-c Kali-ar Kali-bi Kali-br Kali-s* kreos k* lac-f wza1• *Lach* k* lat-h bnm5• *Led* k* loxo-recl bnm1• lyc manc bg2 **Merc** k* merc-c b4a.de **Mez** k* *Nat-m* k* nicotam rly4• nit-ac nux-v k* op k* par k* petr **Ph-ac** k* phos k* phyt k* plac-s rly4• *Psor* k* **Puls** k* rad-br sze8• rheum k* **Rhus-t** k* ruta b2.de* sars k* *Sec* k* *Sel* k* *Sep* k* *Sil* k* spong k* *Staph* k* **Stram** k* sul-i k2 **Sulph** k* syph tab teucr k* tub c urt-u valer k* verat k* viol-t k* zinc k* zinc-p k2
  - **night**: chlol k*
  - **accompanied** by | **diarrhea** (See RECTUM - Diarrhea - accompanied - rash)
  - **allergic**: galph mtf11
  - **alternating** with:
    - ⁝ **asthma** (See RESPIRATION - Asthmatic - alternating - rash)
    - ⁝ **Chest**; oppression of: *Calad*
  - **bee** stings; from: sep h2
  - **belladonna**, after abuse of: hyos
  - **black**: *Lach*
  - **blotches**: *Agar* lyc
  - **bluish**: **Acon** *Ail* am-c bell *Coff* hydr-ac ptk1 **Lach** *Phos* phyt gm1 sep stram *Sulph*
  - **brownish**: mez k*
  - **burning**: *Ars* hr1 bov hr1 ph-ac h2*
    - ⁝ **itching**, and: agar clem teucr
  - **children**; in: acon *Bry* k* *Cham* k* ip sulph
    - ⁝ **infants**: cham mtf33
  - **chronic**: am-c clem mez olib-sac wmh1 *Staph*
  - **close**, white, with burning: agar bry nux-v
    - ⁝ **itching**; and: agar bry calad sulph
  - **cold** air agg.: apis dulc sars k* sep
  - **delivery**; during: *Bry* cupr *Ip*
  - **dentition**; during: apis bro1 *Borx* bro1 calc bro1 *Cham* bro1 cic bro1 led bro1 rhus-t bro1 *Spira* bro1 sumb bro1
  - **excoriated** skin, with: *Sulph*
  - **itching**: ant-c hr1 bov hr1 *Calc* hr1 corian-s knl6• grin hr1 *Hep* hr1 *Mez* hr1 nicotam rly4• sep h2* zinc hr1
  - **menses** | **before** | **agg.**: *Dulc* k*
    - ⁝ **during** | **agg.**: *Con*
  - **moist**: carb-v
  - **overheated**; when: apis lyc
  - **patches**: *Ail*
  - **periodical** | **year**; every: ail vh1
  - **purple**: thal-xyz srj8•
  - **receding** in eruptive fevers: (↗*slow)* **Bry** k*
  - **red**: eryth vwe2
    - ⁝ **dark**: mez k2
    - ⁝ **fiery**: **Acon Bell** stram sulph
  - **room** agg.: *Calc* b2.de
  - **scarlet**: **Acon** k* **Am-c** k* ars k* arum-t k2 **Bell** k* **Bry** k* calc k* carb-v k* caust k* *Chlol Coff* k* com con dulc k* hyos k* iod *Ip* k* *Kali-bi* lach k* lat-m bnm6• *Merc* k* ph-ac k* phos k* phyt k2 rhus-t k* sulph k* zinc
  - **scratching** agg.; after: am-c k* am-m k* ant-c k* bov k* bry k* calc k* carbn-s caust k* dulc k* graph k* ip k* *Lach* k* led k* *Merc* k* mez k* ph-ac k* phos k* puls k* *Rhus-t* k* sars k* sel k* sil k* spong k* staph k* *Sulph* k* verat k* viol-t k* zinc k*
  - **shiny** and smooth: bell k2
  - **slow** evolution of rash in eruptive fevers: (↗*receding; break - fails)* apis bro1 ars bro1 **Bry** k* lach bro1 rhus-t bro1 stram ptk1 zinc bro1

- **rash**: ...
  - **stinging**, biting: nat-m k* viol-t k*
  - **sunlight** agg.; from: (↗*sun)* **Camph** mrr1
  - **suppressed**: hell ptk1 ip rhus-t k2
  - **tightness** of chest (See alternating - chest)
  - **warm** room; when entering a | **air**; from open: apis ars
  - **weather**; change of: *Apis* k*
  - **white**: agar k* *Apis* **Ars** k* bov k* *Bry* k* calad k* ip k* nux-v *Phos* k* rhus-v k* *Sulph* k* **Valer** k*
    - ⁝ **air** agg.; in open: sars k*
    - ⁝ **room** agg.: calc
- **receding**: ant-t ptk1 ars ptk1 bry ptk1 camph ptk1 caust ptk1 cupr ptk1 lyc ptk1 op ptk1 sulph ptk1 *Zinc* ptk1
- **recurrent**: ambr bg2 *Calc* bg2 graph bg2 lyc bg2 *Sulph* bg2 tub bg2
- **red**: acon k* *Agar* **Am-c** anac k* *Anan* ant-c k* ant-t a1 apis *Arn* k* *Ars* k* asim a1* aur k* aur-ar k2 bell a1 berb bry b7.de* calad b7a.de *Calc* k* caust bg2 cham k* chel k* chinin-s chir-fl bnm4• *Chlol* k* cic k* cina b7.de *Clem* k* cocc k* *Com* con cop k* crot-t cycl k* *Dulc* fl-ac goss a1 *Graph* ina-i mlk9.de *Kali-bi* k* **Kali-c** kali-s ketogl-ac rly4• lach k* *Led* b7.de* lipp a1 lyc m-ambo b7.de *Mag-c* **Merc** k* *Mez* k* *Nit-ac* k* op b7.de ox-ac k* petr ph-ac **Phos** k* plb b7.de psor jl2 ran-b tl1 *Rhus-t* k* sabad k* sars sep k* sil spig k* squil b7.de staph k* *Stram* k* **Sul-ac Sulph** tab hr1 thuj k* til tritic-vg fd5.de tub k2 valer k* vanil fd5.de verat b7.de verb b7a.de vero-o rly4*• vip [calc-n stj1]
  - **insect** stings; like: bell h1 podo fd3.de• tritic-vg fd5.de
  - **scarlet**: anac a1* *Anan* k* cop dulc a1 phyt k2
  - **spotted**: ail tl1 dulc a1 ketogl-ac rly4• merc olib-sac wmh1 tritic-vg fd5.de tub-m jl2 vanil fd5.de verat
  - **striped**: rhus-t a1
  - ○ **Areola**: anac ant-c b7a.de ant-t k* borx cocc k* dulc h1 tab
- **retarded**: arist-cl sp1
- **rhus** poisoning (= poison oak poisoning): agar k* am-c k* **Anac** k* anac-oc c2 anag mrr1 (non:anan a1) ang vh apis bro1 arn k* ars-i sne astac bro1 *Bry* k* cimic bro1 clem k2 **Crot-t** k* cupr cypr br1* echi c2* *Erech* br1* euph-l br1* *Graph* k* *Grin* k* hedeo br1* hydro-v c2* kali-s k* led k* lob k* mez bro1 *Nuph* k* plan k* prim-o bro1 ran-b k2 **Rhus-d** bro1* rhus-t c2* *Sang* k* *Sep* k* sulph k* tanac br1* urt-u bro1 vanil bro1 verb bro1 verbe-o br1 verbe-u c2 xero br1*
- **ringworm**: (↗*herpetic - circinate)* anac-oc c2 anag c2* ant-c bro1 ant-t c2* *Apis* b7a.de *Ars* c2* *Bac* c2* bapt c2 bar-m c2 *Calc* c2* calc-i bro1 chim c2 chrys-ac c2 chrysar bwa3* cupr c2 dulc mrr1 eup-per c2 *Graph* bro1* hep bro1 jug-c c2* jug-r c2* kali-i br1 kali-s bro1 lappa c2 lyc bro1* mez c2* nat-m mrr1 oci-sa sp1 ol-j c2* phyt c2 psor c2* rad-br mrr1 ran-b ptk1 rhus-t bro1 semp br1* *Sep* c2* sil mrr1 *Sulph* c2* *Tela* c2 tell bro1* thuj mrr1 tub bro1* viol-t c2* [spect dfg1]
  - **intersecting** rings: tell bro1
  - **spots**; in | **Upper** parts of body: sep bro1
- **roseola**: **Acon** k* ail k2 bad br1 *Bell* k* **Bry** k* carb-v *Coff* cop hr1* *Corn* hr1 cub c1* *Hyos* k* ip kali-i bg3* *Merc* k* nux-v k* phos k* **Puls** k* rhus-t sars k* sulph
  - **syphilitic**: iod bg2 **Kali-i** k* merc bg2* merc-c bro1 merc-i-r bro1 nit-ac bg2 *Phos* k* phyt bro1 sars bg2
- **rough**: ail gm1 alum tl1 phyt gm1 rhus-t gm1 sulph gm1
- **rubella**: **Acon** b2.de* antip c2 *Apis* b7a.de ars b4.de *Bell* b2.de* **Bry** b2.de* carb-v b2.de* *Coff* b2.de* *Euphr* b7a.de ip b2.de* mag-c b4a.de merc b2.de* phos b2.de* **Puls** b2.de* rhus-t b2.de* sulph b2.de*
  - **slow** development of: bry b7a.de *Nux-v* b7a.de
  - **suppressed**: **Bry** b7a.de **Puls** b7a.de *Rhus-t* b7a.de
- **rubeola** (See measles)
- **rupia**: aethi-m bro1 alum k* ant-t bro1 **Ars** k* *Berb-a* bro1 borx calc k* caust k* cham k* clem k* *Fl-ac Graph* k* *Hep* k* hydr bro1 kali-c *Kali-i* k* lach bro1 lyc *Maland* merc k* merc-i-r bro1 *Mez (non:*nat-act hr1*)* nat-c *Nat-m* k* *Nat-s* k* nit-ac k* petr k* *Phyt* k* rhus-t k* sec bro1 sep k* sil k* staph k* sulph k* *Syph* k* thuj k* thyr c2*
- **scabby** (See crusty)
- **scabies**: aloe bro1 ambr k* *Ant-c* k* ant-t k* anthraco c2* **Ars** k* *Aster Bar-m* bry k* *Calc* k* canth k* carb-ac carb-an k* **Carb-v** k* **Carbn-s Caust** k* chrysar bro1 *Cic* bro1 *Clem* k* coloc k* con k* cop crot-t k* *Cupr* k* *Dulc* k* *Graph* k* guaj k* *Hep* k* **Kali-s** *Kreos* k* *Lach* k* led k* *Lyc* k* m-ambo b2.de* *Mang* k* *Merc* k* merc-i-f mez k* mur-ac bro1 *Nat-c* k* nat-m bro1 nat-s k2 neor-m jsx1.fr nux-v bro1 ol-lav fr4 olnd petr k* *Ph-ac* k* **Psor** k* puls k* rhus-v c2* sabad k* **Sel** k* **Sep** k* *Sil* k* squil k* staph k* *Sul-ac* k* **Sulph** k*

Skin

- **scabies**: ...
tarax k* ter c2 valer k* *Verat* k* vinc bro1 viol-t bro1 *Zinc* k* [crasp-v dbx1.fr eppa-an dbx1.fr gynu-ce dbx1.fr maesa-t dbx1.fr raphis-g dbx1.fr senec-fa dbx1.fr tod-a dbx1.fr]
  - **bleeding**: calc k* dulc k* *Merc* k* sulph k*
  - **dry**: *Ars* k* calc k* carb-v k* caust k* clem k* cupr k* dulc k* graph k* *Hep* k* kreos k* *Led* k* lyc k* *Merc* k* merc-i-f nat-c k* petr k* ph-ac k* *Psor* **Sep** k* **Sil** k* staph k* *Sulph* k* valer k* *Verat* k* zinc k*
  - **fatty**: ant-c k* *Caust* k* clem k* cupr k* *Kreos* k* **Merc** k* *Merc-c* b4a.de sel k* *Sep* k* squil k* **Staph** b7a.de sulph k*
  - **moist**: calc k* *Carb-v* k* carbn-s k2 caust k* clem k* con k* dulc k* *Graph* k* kreos k* *Lyc* k* merc k* petr k* sep k* sil k* squil k* staph k* sulph k*
  - **prairie**: *Apis* led bro1 rhus-t bro1 rumx k* sulph bro1
  - **recurrent**: psor mrr1
  - **suppressed**: alum k* ambr k* ant-c k* ant-t k* *Ars* k* *Carb-v* k* *Caust* k* *Dulc* k* graph k* kreos k* lach k* nat-c k* nat-m k* ph-ac k* psor mrr1 *Sel* k* *Sep* k* sil k* **Sulph** k* verat k* zinc k*
    - **mercury** and sulphur; by: agn k* ars k* bell k* calc k* carb-v k* **Caust** k* *Chin* k* dulc k* hep k* iod k* nit-ac k* **Psor** *Puls* k* rhus-t k* sars k* *Sel* k* **Sep** k* sil k* *Staph* k* thuj k* valer k*

- **scaly**: agar k* alumn k2 *Am-m* k* anac ant-c k* **Ars** k* *Ars-i* k* *Aur* k* aur-ar k2 bac c2* *Bar-m* *Bell* k* berb-a c2* borx k* bry hr1 bufo cact cadm-s k* *Calad* *Calc* k* calc-s calc-sil k2 canth k* carb-ac bro1 caul c2 chaul mtf11 chrysar br1 cic k* cist k2 **Clem** k* *Colch* bro1 com cupr k* cycl dulc k* dys fmm1• *Fl-ac* k* fum rly1*• gali br1 granit-m es1• *Graph* bg2* guat sp1 hep k* *Hydrc* hyos k* iod kali-ar k* *Kali-bi* *Kali-br* hr1 kali-c k* kali-i hr1 kali-m k2* kali-p k2 *Kali-s* kali-sil k2 kola stb3• **Kreos** hr1* lach hr1 *Led* k* lyc bg2* *Mag-c* k* maland jl2 manc ptk1 mang hr1* mang-act bro1 med ptk1 *Merc* k* merc-pr-r bro1 mez k* mim-p rsj8• morg-p fmm1• *Nat-ar* k* nat-c ptk1 *Nat-m* k* nat-pyru rly4• *Nit-ac* k* nuph hr1 *Olnd* k* petr k* **Phos** k* **Phyt** k* pip-m bro1 pix br1 *Plb* k* *Psor* k* ptel hr1 quill br1 *Rhus-t* k* ruta fd4.de samb c2 sang *Sars* **Sep** k* *Sil* k* staph k* suis-pan rly4• *Sul-ac* bro1 sul-i k2* *Sulph* k* tell bro1 ter c2* teucr k* thiam rly4• thuj k* thyr bro1* tritic-vg fd5.de
  - **bran**-like: agar alum am-c anac arg-met **Ars** k* ars-i ars-s-f k2 aur k* aur-ar k2 borx bry k* bufo bg2 **Calc** k* calc-p ptk1 canth carb-ac carb-an carb-v chlor *Cic* clem *Dulc* k* graph k* iod k* *Kali-ar* k* **Kali-chl** k* kali-i kali-m k2 **Kreos** k* lach led *Lyc* k* mag-c k* mang merc mez *Nat-ar* nat-m *Nit-ac* olnd petr phos k* **Phyt** rad-br ptk1 ran-b rhus-t sanic ptk1 *Sep* k* **Sil** k* staph sulph k* *Thuj* k* thyr ptk1 tub ptk1
  - **brown**: am-m ptk1
  - **fine**: morb jl2
  - **ichthyosis**: anag *Ars* k* *Ars-i* k* aur k* calc chin k* clem k* coloc graph k* hep *Hydrc* c2* iod bro1 kali-i bro1 lac-c k* lac-d mtf11 lyc merc bro1 mez *Nat-c* c2* oena br1* ol-j petr **Phos** k* pip-m c2 platan bro1 platan-oc br1 platan-or c2 plb k* *Plb-xyz* c2 sep sil sulph k* syph br1* thuj k* thyr c2* v-a-b jl2*
    - **offensive** odor; with: psor tl1
  - **red**: nat-pyru rly4•
  - **rosy**: toxo-g jl2 tub jl2 tub-m jl2
  - **shining**: *Euphr* bg2 iris ptk1 rhus-t bg2
  - **silvery**: *Nuph* a1
  - **spots**: hydrc kali-c *Merc* **Nit-ac** *Puls* sabin sacch-a fd2.de• sil thuj zinc
  - **syphilitic**: (↗*syphilitic)* *Ars* bro1 ars-i bro1 ars-s-f br1* borx bro1 *Cinnb* bro1 fl-ac bro1 kali-i bro1 merc bro1 merc-c bro1 merc-i-f bro1 merc-n bro1 *Merc-pr-r* bro1 merc-tn bro1 *Nit-ac* bro1 *Phos* bro1 phyt bro1 *Sars* bro1 sulph bro1
  - **white**: anac *Ars* graph **Kali-chl** k* kali-m k2 lyc nat-ar k2 thuj tritic-vg fd5.de tub al* zinc
  - **yellow**: bar-m k2 *Cic* hr1 **Kali-c** k* **Kali-s** nat-p hr1*

- **scarlatina**: (↗*FEVER - Scarlet)* acon k* **Ail** k* **Am-c** k* am-m b2.de* antip c2* **Apis** k* arg-n c2 am k* *Ars* k* *Arum-t* k* asim c2* bar-c k* **Bell** k* *Bry* k* *Calc* k* calc-s c2 *Canth* c2 *Carb-ac* k* *Carb-v* k* caust b2.de* *Cham* k* chin bg2 chinin-ar c2 chinin-s c2 cina c2 coc-c a1 coff b2.de* *Croc* b2.de* *Crot-h* k* *Cupr* k* *Cupr-act* c2 dulc b2.de* *Echi* c2 euph b2.de* *Gels* k* hell c2 hell-f c2 hep k* *Hyos* k* iod b2.de* ip b2.de* jug-c c2 **Lach** k* **Lyc** k* **Merc** k* morb jl2 *Mur-ac* hr1* **Nit-ac** k* *Ph-ac* k* *Phos* k* phyt k* **Rhus-t** k* sol-ni c2 *Spig* c2 *Stram* k* *Sulph* k* *Ter* c2 tub jl2 verat c2 *Zinc* k*

- **scarlatina**: ...
  - **accompanied** by:
    - **convulsions** (See GENERALS - Convulsions - accompanied - scarlatina)
    - **epistaxis**: *Acon* b7a.de
    - **rheumatic** pain: bry bro1 *Rhus-t* bro1 spig bro1
    - **saliva** | **viscid**: hippoz kr1* **Lach** kr1*
    - **salivation**: **Arum-t** kr1* *Caps* kr1* **Lach** kr1* *Merc* kr1* *Sulph* kr1*
    - **Kidneys**; inflammation of (See KIDNEYS - Inflammation - accompanied - scarlatina)
    - **Throat**:
      - **dark** red discoloration (See THROAT - Discoloration - redness - dark; THROAT - Discoloration - redness - dark - accompanied - scarlatina)
      - **pain** | **sore** (See THROAT - Pain - sore - accompanied - scarlatina)
    - **Tongue**:
      - **black** discoloration: *Carb-ac* kr1*
      - **brown** discoloration: phyt kr1*
        - **Tip**: *Merc* kr1*
      - **cracked**: *Apis* kr1* *Nit-ac* kr1*
      - **dryness** of tongue: *Merc* kr1* *Nit-ac* kr1*
      - **pale**: *Ail* kr1*
      - **paralysis** of tongue: *Stram* kr1*
      - **swelling**: am-m kr1*
      - **white** discoloration of the tongue | **dirty** tongue: *Dig* kr1*
  - **bleeding**: arum-t bro1 crot-h bro1 *Lach* bro1 mur-ac bro1 phos bro1
  - **gangrenous**: *Ail* k* **Am-c** k* *Ars* k* **Carb-ac** k* *Lach* k* *Phos*
  - **itching**: arum-t bro1
  - **like**: com a1 vario jl2
  - **livid**: *Ail* bro1 *Lach* bro1 mur-ac bro1 sol-ni bro1
  - **malignant**: ail br1 am-c br1 carb-ac br1 crot-h br1
  - **patches**; in: *Ail* k*
  - **raw**: arum-t bro1
  - **receding**: *Am-c* k* *Apis* bro1 *Ars* hr1* *Bry* hr1* calc bro1 *Camph* bro1 crot-h hr1 cupr bro1 *Cupr-act* bro1 *Gels* hr1 *Op* hr1 ph-ac hr1 *Phos* k* *Stram* bro1 *Sulph* k* verat bro1 **Zinc** k*
  - **smooth**: *Am-c* k* **Bell** k* euph b2.de* euphr hyos k* merc k*
  - **suppressed**: **Apis** b7a.de *Bry* b7a.de *Lach* b7a.de
- **scars**; with unsightly: carb-an ptk1 cop ptk1 kali-br ptk1
- **scorbutic**, spots: anan merc merc-c
- **scratching** agg.; after: agar k* alum k* **Am-c** k* am-m k* ant-c k* am k* *Ars* k* *Bar-c* k* bar-s k2 bell k* bov k* bry k* *Calc* k* canth k* carb-an k* carb-v k* carbn-s **Caust** k* chin k* cic k* con k* *Cycl* k* *Dulc* k* euph k* graph k* hell k* *Hep* k* ip k* *Kali-c* k* kali-s *Kreos* k* lach k* laur k* **Lyc** k* mag-c k* *Merc* k* mez k* nat-c k* nat-m k* nit-ac k* nux-v k* *Olnd* k* *Petr* k* ph-ac k* phos k* plb k* *Puls* k* rhod k* **Rhus-t** k* sabin k* *Sars* k* *Sep* k* *Sil* k* spong k* squil k* *Staph* k* stront-c k* sul-ac k* **Sulph** k* thuj k* verat k* viol-t k* zinc k*
- **scrofulous**: (↗*Scrofuloderma)* aethi-a c1 psor jl2
- **scurfy** (See scaly)
- **sensitive**: ant-c arg-met bell fum rly4• **Hep** k* lach led nit-ac par sabad spig stann *Urt-u* mrr1 valer
- **serpiginous**: ars bg3* ars-i bg2 *Calc* bg2 *Clem* k* *Hep* k* *Psor* *Sars* k* *Sulph* k*
  - **symmetrical**: thyr ptk1
- **shingles** (See herpes)
- **shining** through: merc k*
- **slow** evolution in eruptive diseases: (↗*break - fails)* ail k2
- **small**: vac jl2
  - **fever**; during: vac jl2
- **smallpox**: *Acon* bro1 agar am-c bro1 am-m k* anac bg2* anac-oc c2 *Ant-c* k* **Ant-t** k* anthraci c2 *Apis* k* arg-n c2 am b2.de* *Ars* k* bapt c2* *Bell* k* *Bry* k* bufo bg2 canth k* *Carb-ac* k* carb-v caust h2* cham k* *Chinin-s* c2* cimic bro1 clem k* cocc k* *Crot-h* c2* cund c2 cupr tl1 cupr-act c2* gels bro1 *Ham* c2 *Hep* bro1 *Hydr* br1* hyos k* *Iod* b4a.de kali-bi bg2* kali-i c2 kali-m c2 kreos bg2 lach c2* maland c2* **Merc** k* mill bro1 *Nat-m* nit-ac k* op bro1 phos c2* *Puls* k*

- **smallpox**: ...
Rhus-t k* *Salol* c1* sarr c1* sep sil k* sin-n c2* sol-ni c2 stram k* *Sulph* k* *Thuj* k* vac c2* vario k* verat-v bro1 *Zinc* [clem-sax dbx1.fr]
  - **accompanied** by:
    - **fever**: am-m bg2 ant-c bg2 *Ant-t* bg2 apis bg2 arn bg2 ars bg2 bell bg2 clem bg2 cocc bg2 hyos bg2 *Merc* bg2 mur-ac bg2 nit-ac bg2 puls bg2 *Rhus-t* bg2 sil bg2 sulph bg2 **Thuj** bg2 *Vario* bg2
    - **Epigastrium**; pain in: mill br1
  - **black**: *(↗pocks - black)* ant-c k* **Ars** k* *Bell* k* bry k* hyos k* *Lach* k* *Mur-ac* k* **Rhus-t** k* *Sec* k* sep k* sil k* spig k*
  - **bleeding**: ars bro1 *Crot-h* bro1 *Ham* bro1 *Lach* bro1 nat-n bro1 *Phos* bro1 *Sec* bro1 sulph bro1
  - **confluent**: ars bro1 hippoz bro1 *Merc* bro1 phos bro1 sulph bro1 vario bro1
  - **discrete**: *Ant-t* bro1 bapt bro1 bell bro1 gels bro1 sulph bro1
  - **hemorrhagic**: nat-n br1
  - **malignant**: am-c bro1 ant-t bro1 *Ars* bro1 bapt bro1 *Carb-ac* bro1 *Crot-h* bro1 *Lach* bro1 *Mur-ac* bro1 ph-ac bro1 phos bro1 *Rhus-t* bro1 sec bro1 sulph bro1 vario bro1
  - **prophylaxis** to: ant-t bro1 hydr bro1 kali-cy bro1 *Maland* br1* thuj bro1 vac bro1* vario br1*
  - **receding**: ars bro1 *Camph* bro1 cupr bro1 sulph bro1 zinc bro1
  - **similar** to smallpox: *Acon* b7a.de ant-t tl1 *Bell* b7a.de *Puls* b7a.de rhus-t b7a.de vario jl2
- **smarting**: acon k* agar k* *Alum* k* alum-p k2 ambr k* ant-c k* apis **Arg-met** k* ars k* *Aur* k* aur-ar k2 bar-c k* bar-s k2 *Bry* k* bufo bg2 *Calc* k* cann-s k* canth k* caps k* carb-an k* carbn-s chel k* chin k* *Cic* k* coff k* *Colch* k* dol *Dros* k* ferr k* **Graph** k* hell k* **Hep** k* ign k* kali-c k* *Kali-s* kali-sil k2 lach led lyc k* m-ambo b2.de* m-aust b2.de mag-c k* *Mang* k* merc k* mez k* nat-c k* nat-hchls c2 *Nat-m* k* *Nit-ac* k* nux-v k* olnd k* *Par* k* *Petr* k* *Ph-ac* k* phos k* phyt bg2 plat *Puls* k* ran-b k* *Rhus-t* k* ruta k* sabin k* sars k* sel k* **Sep** k* sil k* *Spig* k* spong k* *Squil* k* staph k* *Sulph* k* teucr k* valer k* *Verat* k* *Zinc* k* zinc-p k2
- **soap**; application of | **agg.**: nat-c ptk1 [heroin sdj2]
- **spring**; in: ars-br ah1 graph alj *Nat-s* k* **Psor** alj* rhus-t sang bro1* *Sars* k* *Sep* k*
- **stinging**: acon k* alum k* alum-p k2 alum-sil k2 am-m k* *Anac* k* ant-c k* **Apis** am k* *Ars* k* ars-s-f k2 asaf k* *Bar-c* k* bar-m bar-s k2 *Bell* k* borx br1 bov k* *Bry* k* calc k* calc-sil k2 camph k* canth k* caps k* carb-v k* caust k* cham k* chin k* **Clem** k* cocc k* *Con* k* *Cycl* k* des-ac rbp6 dig k* *Dros* k* graph k* guaj k* hell k* *Hep* k* ign k* kali-ar k* kali-c k* kali-s k2 kali-sil k2 kreos k* *Led* k* lyc k* m-ambo b2.de* m-arct b2.de* mag-c k* *Merc* k* mez k* mur-ac k* nat-ar nat-c k* *Nat-m* k* **Nit-ac** k* nux-v k* petr k* phos k* *Plat* k* **Puls** k* *Ran-b* k* ran-s k* *Rhus-t* k* sabad k* *Sabin* k* sars h2* sel k* **Sep** k* **Sil** k* spong k* squil k* *Staph* k* stram h1* stront-c k* **Sulph** k* tell br1 thuj k* *Urt-u* k* verb k* *Viol-t* k* zinc k*
- **stings** of insects; like red (See red - insect)
- **strawberries**: bry j5.de
- **sudamina** (See vesicular - sudamina)
- **summer**: *(↗GENERALS - Allergic)* calc bg2 *Kali-bi* k* led mur-ac h2 sars br1
  - **amel.**: *Petr* mrr1
- **sun**; from: *(↗rash - sunlight)* apis a aur-m-n wbt2• bell a* camph cortiso sp1 fago a graph a kali-i a mur-ac a nat-c a nat-m gsy1 psor a ros-d wla1 sacch-a fd2.de• sol a staph a sulfa sp1 urt-u a [heroin sdj2 nat-n stj1]
- **suppressed**: *(↗break - fails; GENERALS - History - eruptions - suppressed; GENERALS - Reaction - lack - suppression - eruptions)* abrot mrr1 acon k* agar hr1 ail bg2* alum k* am-c k* ambr k* anac c1 ant-c hr1* ant-t bg2* apis bg2* *Ars* k* *Ars-i* ars-s-f k2* asaf c1* bad hr1* bar-c k2* *Bell* k* **Bry** k* calad k* calc k* *Camph* bg2* caps bg2 carb-an k* *Carb-v* k* carc dtp *Caust* k* *Cham* k* chin bg2 *Cic* hr1* clem sf1.de con k* *Cupr* k* cupr-act c1 cupr-ar c1 **Dulc** k* fl-ac bg *Gels* *Graph* k* *Hell* c1* *Hep* k* hyos hr1* iod b2.de* **Ip** k* **Kali-bi** bg2 kali-c k* *Kali-s* k* kalm k2 *Kreos* bg2 lach k* laur sf1.de *Lyc* k* mag-c bg2 mag-s bro1 merc k* *Mez* k* mill hr1 *Nat-c* k* nit-ac k* *Nux-m* k* **Nux-v** bg2 op k* **Petr** k* **Ph-ac** k* phos k* plb c1* **Psor** k* ptel c1 *Puls* k* ran-b tl1 *Rhus-t* k* sars k* sel k* senec bg2 *Sep* k* sil k* *Staph* k* **Stram** k* sul-ac k* sul-i k2 **Sulph** k* thuj k* *Tub* k* *Tub-k* c1 *Urt-u* hr1* verat k* verat-v sf1.de *Viol-t* k* x-ray bro1* **Zinc** k*
- **suppurating**: alum am-c **Ant-c** k* ant-t k* apis *Ars* k* ars-s-f k2 *Bar-c* bar-s k2 bell k* *Borx* k* bufo gk cadm-s *Calc* k* calc-s k* calc-sil k2 carb-v *Carbn-s* caust k* **Cham** chel chinin-s bg2 *Cic* k* *Clem* k* cocc k* *Con* k* croc cycl k* *Dulc* k* euphr k* **Graph** hell *Hep* k* jug-c kali-c *Kali-s* lach led k* **Lyc** k* m-ambo b2.de mag-c k* mang **Merc** k* mur-ac *Nat-ar* *Nat-c* k* nat-m k* nat-p **Nit-ac** nux-v olnd par **Petr** k* ph-ac phos phys tl1 plb k* polys sk4• *Psor* k* puls k* **Rhus-t** k* ruta fd4.de *Samb* k* *Sars* k* sec k* **Sep** k* **Sil** k* spig k* *Squil* *Staph* k* *Sulph* k* tarax k* thuj k* vanil fd5.de verat k* viol-o k* *Viol-t* k* *Zinc* k* zinc-p k2
- **swelling**; with: acon k* am-c k* arn k* ars k* *Bell* k* bry k* calc k* canth k* carb-v k* caust k* chin k* cic k* con k* euph k* hep k* *Kali-c* k* lyc k* mag-c k* **Merc** k* nat-c k* nat-m k* nit-ac k* petr k* ph-ac k* phos k* *Puls* k* **Rhus-t** k* ruta k* *Samb* k* sars k* *Sep* k* sil k* *Sulph* k* *Thuj* k*
- **symmetrical**: arn ptk* crot-t a1 lac-d hr1 nat-m gsd1 nept-m lsd2.fr sep hr1 sil a1 thyr ptk
- **syphilitic**: *(↗scaly - syphilitic)* *Arg-n* k* ars k* ars-br vh **Ars-i** k* *Aur* k* aur-ar k2 bad *Calc-i* hr1 chopn br1 *Cist* hr1 cund hr1 dulc k* *Fl-ac* *Guaj* k* *Hep* k* *Kali-bi* k* kali-chl **Kali-i** k* kreos *Lach* k* *Lyc* k* **Merc** k* **Merc-c** k* *Merc-d* hr1 **Merc-i-f** k* **Merc-i-r** k* morb jl2 **Nit-ac** k* petr k* *Phyt* k* plat k* rhus-t k* rumx sang k* sars k* sep k* *Sil* k* staph k* still k* sulph hr1 **Syph** k* *Thuj* k*
  - **rosy**: morb jl2
- **tearing** pain; with: acon k* arn k* ars k* bell b2.de* *Bry* k* *Calc* k* canth k* carb-v k* caust k* clem k* cocc k* dulc k* graph k* kali-c k* **Lyc** k* merc k* *Mez* k* nat-c k* nit-ac k* nux-v b2.de* phos k* puls k* *Rhus-t* k* *Sep* k* *Sil* k* *Staph* k* *Sulph* k* zinc k*
- **tense**: alum k* ant-t k* *Arn* k* bar-c k* bell k* bry k* canth k* carb-an k* **Caust** k* cocc k* con k* hep k* kali-c k* mez k* olnd k* *Phos* k* puls k* **Rhus-t** k* sabin k* sep k* spong k* staph k* *Stront-c* k* sulph k* thuj k*
  - **bacon**; after: *Puls* b7a.de
- **tetters**: *(↗itching)* agar b2.de* alum b2.de* am-c b2.de* ambr b2.de* anac b2.de* **Ars** b2.de* aur b2.de* bar-c b2.de* bell b2.de* borx bg2 **Bov** b2.de* *Bry* b2.de* bufo bg2 calad b2.de* **Calc** b2.de* caps b2.de* carb-ac bg2 carb-an b2.de* carb-v b2.de* *Caust* b2.de* cham ptk1 chel b2.de* cic b2.de* **Clem** b2.de* cocc b2.de* **Con** b2.de* cupr b2.de* cycl b2.de* **Dulc** b2.de* *Fl-ac* bg2 **Graph** b2.de* hell b2.de* hep b2.de* hyos b2.de* kali-c b2.de* kali-n b2.de* *Kreos* b2.de* lach b2.de* *Led* b2.de* **Lyc** b2.de* m-arct b2.de mag-c b2.de* mag-m b2.de* mang b2.de* **Merc** b2.de* mez b2.de* mosch b2.de* mur-ac b2.de* *Nat-c* b2.de* nat-m b2.de* nit-ac b2.de* nux-v b2.de* olnd b2.de* op bg2 par b2.de* *Petr* b2.de* ph-ac b2.de* *Phos* b2.de* plb b2.de* puls b2.de* ran-b b2.de* ran-s b2.de* **Rhus-t** b2.de* ruta b2.de* sabad b2.de* sars b2.de* **Sep** b2.de* **Sil** b2.de* spig b2.de* spong b2.de* squil b2.de* stann b2.de* *Staph* b2.de* sul-ac b2.de* sulph b2.de* tarax b2.de* *Tell* bg2 teucr b2.de* thuj b2.de* valer b2.de* verat b2.de* vib ptk1 viol-t b2.de* zinc b2.de*
  - **burning**: agar b2.de* alum b2.de* am-c b2.de* ambr b2.de* anac b2.de* **Ars** b2.de* aur b2.de* bar-c b2.de* bell b2.de* bov b2.de* bry b2.de* bufo bg2 calad b2.de* calc b2.de* caps b2.de* carb-an b2.de* carb-v b2.de* **Caust** b2.de* cic b2.de* clem b2.de* cocc b2.de* *Con* b2.de* dulc b2.de* hell b2.de* hep b2.de* kali-c b2.de* kali-n b2.de* kreos b2.de* lach b2.de* led b2.de* *Lyc* b2.de* m-arct b2.de* mang b2.de* **Merc** b2.de* mez b2.de* *Mosch* b7.de* nat-c b2.de* nat-m b2.de* nux-v b2.de* olnd b2.de* par b2.de* petr b2.de* ph-ac b2.de* phos b2.de* plb b2.de* puls b2.de* ran-b b2.de* **Rhus-t** b2.de* sabad b2.de* sars b2.de* sep b2.de* *Sil* b2.de* spig b2.de* spong b2.de* squil b2.de* stann b2.de* staph b2.de* *Sulph* b2.de* teucr b2.de* thuj b2.de* verat b2.de* viol-t b2.de* zinc b2.de*
  - **chapped**, cracked: alum b2.de* aur b2.de* bry b2.de* *Calc* b2.de* cycl b2.de* graph b2.de* hep b2.de* kali-c b2.de* kreos b2.de* lach b2.de* lyc b2.de* mag-c b2.de* mang b2.de* merc b2.de* nat-c b2.de* nat-m b2.de* nit-ac b2.de* petr b2.de* *Puls* b2.de* *Rhus-t* b2.de* ruta b2.de* *Sars* b2.de* **Sep** b2.de* sil b2.de* **Sulph** b2.de* viol-t b2.de* zinc b2.de*
  - **crusty** (= scurfy): alum b2.de* am-c b2.de* ambr b2.de* ars b2.de* bar-c b2.de* bell b2.de* bov b2.de* bry b2.de* bufo bg2 **Calc** b2.de* caps b2.de* carb-an b2.de* carb-v b2.de* cic b2.de* clem b2.de* **Con** b2.de* *Dulc* b2.de* **Graph** b2.de* hell b2.de* hep b2.de* kali-c b2.de* kreos b2.de* led b2.de* **Lyc** b2.de* mag-c b2.de* *Merc* b2.de* mez b2.de* mur-ac b2.de* nat-m b2.de* nit-ac b2.de* nux-v b2.de* olnd b2.de* par b2.de* petr b2.de* phos b2.de* plb b2.de* puls b2.de* ran-b b2.de* **Rhus-t** b2.de* sars b2.de* *Sep* b2.de* *Sil* b2.de* squil b2.de* staph b2.de* **Sulph** b2.de* thuj b2.de* verat b2.de* viol-t b2.de* zinc b2.de*
    - **white**: ars b2.de* *Graph* b2.de* *Lyc* b2.de* zinc b2.de*

Skin

- **dry**: alum b2.de* ars b2.de* *Bar-c* b2.de* *Bov* b2.de* bry b2.de* *Calc* b2.de* carb-v b2.de* caust b2.de* clem b2.de* cocc b2.de* cupr b2.de* *Dulc* b2.de* **Fl-ac** b4a.de graph b2.de* hyos b2.de* kreos b2.de* *Led* b2.de* lyc b2.de* mag-c b2.de* *Merc* b2.de* nat-c b2.de* nat-m b2.de* par b2.de* petr b2.de* ph-ac b2.de* phos b2.de* rhus-t b2.de* sars b2.de* **Sep** b2.de* **Sil** b2.de* stann b2.de* staph b2.de* sulph b2.de* teucr b2.de* **Thuj** b4a.de valer b2.de* *Verat* b2.de* viol-t b2.de* zinc b2.de*
- **gray**: ars b2.de*
- **inflamed**: hep bg2
- **insensible**: nux-v b7.de
- **itching**: agar b2.de* alum b2.de* am-c b2.de* ambr b2.de* anac b2.de* ars b2.de* bar-c b2.de* bell b2.de* *Bov* b2.de* bry b2.de* bufo bg2 calad b2.de* calc b2.de* caps b2.de* carb-an b2.de* carb-v b2.de* *Caust* b2.de* chel b2.de* cic b2.de* **Clem** b2.de* cocc b2.de* con b2.de* cupr b2.de* dulc b2.de* *Graph* b2.de* hep b2.de* ip b7.de kali-c b2.de* kreos b2.de* lach b2.de* led b2.de* lyc b2.de* m-arct b2.de mag-c b2.de* mag-m b2.de* mang b2.de* *Merc* b2.de* mez b2.de* mur-ac b4a.de nat-c b2.de* nat-m b2.de* *Nit-ac* b2.de* nux-v b2.de* olnd b2.de* par b2.de* petr b2.de* ph-ac b2.de* phos b2.de* plb b2.de* puls b2.de* ran-b b2.de* ran-s b2.de* **Rhus-t** b2.de* sabad b2.de* sars b2.de* **Sep** b2.de* *Sil* b2.de* spig b2.de* spong b2.de* squil b2.de* stann b2.de* *Staph* b2.de* *Sulph* b2.de* tarax b2.de* teucr b2.de thuj b2.de* valer b2.de* verat b2.de* viol-t b2.de* zinc b2.de*
  - **evening**: **Staph** b7a.de
  - **night**: *Staph* b7a.de
  - **menses** | **before** | **agg.**: carb-v b4.de* mez b4a.de
    - **during** | **agg.**: carb-v b4.de
- **menses** | **during** | **agg.**: graph b4a.de
  - **suppression** of: bell b4a.de
- **oozing** (= discharging moisture): alum b2.de* ars b2.de* bar-c b2.de* bell b2.de* *Bov* b2.de* bry b2.de* bufo bg2 calc b2.de* carb-an b2.de* *Carb-v* b2.de* caust b2.de* cic b2.de* clem b2.de* con b2.de* dulc b2.de* **Graph** b2.de* hell b2.de* hep b2.de* kali-c b2.de* kreos b2.de* lach b2.de* led b2.de* **Lyc** b2.de* merc b2.de* *Merc-c* b4a.de mez b2.de* nat-c b2.de* nat-m b2.de* nit-ac b2.de* olnd b2.de* petr b2.de* ph-ac b2.de* phos b2.de* **Rhus-t** b2.de* ruta b2.de* *Sep* b2.de* sil b2.de* squil b2.de* staph b2.de* sul-ac b2.de* sulph b2.de* tarax b2.de* thuj b2.de* viol-t b2.de*
- **painful**: *Clem* b4a.de *Dulc* b4a.de
- **painless**: lyc b4a.de *Mag-c* b4a.de
- **phagedenic**: alum b2.de* am-c b2.de* bar-c b2.de* *Calc* b2.de* caps b7.de carb-v b2.de* caust b2.de* chel b2.de* *Clem* b2.de* *Con* b2.de* **Graph** b2.de* hell b2.de* hep b2.de* kali-c b2.de* lach b2.de* lyc b2.de* mag-c b2.de* mang b2.de* merc b2.de* mur-ac b2.de* nat-c b2.de* nit-ac b2.de* nux-v b2.de* olnd b2.de* par b2.de* *Petr* b2.de* ph-ac b2.de* phos b2.de* plb b2.de* *Rhus-t* b2.de* *Sep* b2.de* **Sil** b2.de* squil b2.de* staph b2.de* sulph b2.de* tarax b2.de* viol-t b2.de*
- **red**: am-c b2.de* bry b2.de* cic b2.de* *Clem* b2.de* *Dulc* b2.de* led b2.de* *Lyc* b2.de* *Mag-c* b2.de* *Merc* b2.de* petr b2.de* ph-ac b2.de* staph b2.de*
- **stitching**: alum b2.de* anac b4a.de *Ars* b2.de* bar-c b2.de* bell b2.de* bov b2.de* bry b2.de* calc b2.de* caps b2.de* carb-v b2.de* caust b2.de* **Clem** b2.de* cocc b2.de* con b2.de* cycl b2.de* graph b2.de* hell b2.de* hep b2.de* kali-c b2.de* kreos b2.de* led b2.de* lyc b2.de* m-arct b2.de mag-c b2.de* *Merc* b2.de* mez b2.de* mur-ac b2.de* nat-c b2.de* nat-m b2.de* *Nit-ac* b2.de* nux-v b2.de* petr b2.de* phos b2.de* *Puls* b2.de* ran-b b2.de* ran-s b2.de* *Rhus-t* b2.de* sabad b2.de* **Sep** b2.de* *Sil* b2.de* spong b2.de* squil b2.de* staph b2.de* *Sulph* b2.de* thuj b2.de* viol-t b2.de* zinc b2.de*
- **suppressed**: ambr b7a.de *Rhus-t* b7a.de
- **suppurating**: ars b2.de* bell b2.de* cic b2.de* clem b2.de* cocc b2.de* con b2.de* cycl b2.de* *Dulc* b2.de* hep b2.de* led b2.de* *Lyc* b2.de* mag-c b2.de* **Merc** b2.de* *Nat-c* b2.de* nat-m b2.de* petr b2.de* plb b2.de* puls b2.de* **Rhus-t** b2.de* sars b2.de* **Sep** b2.de* sil b2.de* spig b2.de* staph b2.de* sulph b2.de* tarax b2.de* teucr b2.de thuj b2.de* verat b2.de* viol-t b2.de* zinc b2.de*
- **tearing**: ars b2.de* bell b2.de* bry b2.de* *Calc* b2.de* carb-v b2.de* caust b2.de* clem b2.de* cocc b2.de* dulc b2.de* graph b2.de* kali-c b2.de* **Lyc** b2.de* m-arct b2.de* merc b2.de* mez b2.de* nat-c b2.de* nit-ac b2.de* nux-v b2.de* phos b2.de* puls b2.de* rhus-t b2.de* *Sep* b2.de* *Sil* b2.de* staph b2.de* *Sulph* b2.de* zinc b2.de*

- **tetters**: ...
  - **twitching**: calc b2.de* caust b2.de* cupr b2.de* lyc b2.de* puls b2.de* **Rhus-t** b2.de* sep b2.de* sil b2.de* *Staph* b2.de*
  - **yellow** brown: lyc b2.de* *Nat-c* b2.de*
  - **yellowish**: agar b2.de* ars b2.de* bufo bg2 cic b2.de* cocc b2.de* cupr b2.de* hell b2.de* kreos b2.de* led b2.de* lyc b2.de* *Merc* b2.de* nat-c b2.de* nit-ac b2.de* par b2.de* sep b2.de*

○ • **Cicatrices**; on: calc-p bg2

- **touch** agg.: apis ptk1 chin ptk1 coc-c ptk1 coff ptk1 hep ptk1 lach ptk1 mang ptk1 plb ptk1 thuj ptk1
- **transient**: diph-t-tpt jl2
- **transparent**: cina k* *Merc* k* **Ran-b** k*
- **tubercles**: agar alum am-c *Am-m* anac ang *Ant-c* apis aran k* *Ars* aur *Bar-c* k* bar-m bar-s k2 *Bell* hr1 *Bry* **Calc** k* calc-p k* calc-s *Carb-an* *Carb-v* carbn-s **Caust** *Cic* cocc *Con* crot-h k* *Dulc* *Fl-ac* k* *Graph* hell *Hep* hydrc k* kali-ar *Kali-bi* k* *Kali-br* kali-c *Kali-i* k* kali-n kali-s **Lach** **Led** *Lyc* mag-c mag-m mag-s mang *Merc* k* merc-c *Mez* *Mur-ac* nat-ar *Nat-c* *Nat-m* *Nit-ac* k* nux-v *Olnd* *Petr* ph-ac *Phos* *Rhus-t* sec sel sep *Sil* stann *Staph* sul-ac *Sulph* syph k2 tarax *Thuj* k* tub k2 valer verat *Zinc*
  - **burning**: am-c am-m calc *Carb-an* cocc dulc kali-i mag-m mag-s mang *Merc* mur-ac nicc *Nit-ac* phos *Staph*
  - **desquamating**: sang bg1
  - **drawing**, painful: cham
  - **erysipelatous**: *Nat-c* *Phos* sil
  - **gnawing**: rhus-t
  - **hard**: am-c am-m ant-c bar-c bov *Bry* con *Lach* *Mag-c* *Mag-s* nat-m phos rhus-t valer
  - **humid**: kali-n sel thuj hr1
  - **inflamed**: am-m rhus-t
  - **itching**: am-m h2* aur canth carb-an cham cocc dulc graph kali-c kali-n lach lyc mag-c mag-s mur-ac nat-m nit-ac k* op rhus-t staph stram stront-c tub zinc
  - **leprous**: *Nat-c* k* phos *Sil*
  - **malignant**: ars
  - **miliary**: nat-m
  - **mucous**: *Fl-ac* *Nit-ac* *Thuj*
  - **painful**: am-c ars bell bov lach lyc ph-ac zinc
  - **painless**: arn bell graph ign led olnd squil verat
  - **purple**: tub
  - **raised**: olnd rhus-v valer
  - **red**: *Am-c* berb bov carb-an carb-v dig *Hep* kali-chl kali-i *Lach* *Led* mag-c mag-m *Merc* mur-ac nat-m nit-ac op ph-ac puls sep spig sulph *Thuj* verat
    - **Areola**: cocc dulc ph-ac
  - **scratching** agg.; after: mang h2* zinc h2*
  - **scurfy**: sulph
  - **smooth**: ph-ac
  - **soft**: bell crot-h lach
  - **sore**: *Nit-ac* hr1 sep
    - **painful**; as if: ant-c caust ph-ac
  - **stab** wound; after: sep
  - **stinging**: calc caust dulc kali-i led mag-c phos rhus-t squil stram
  - **summer**: *Kali-bi*
  - **suppurating**: am-c bov *Caust* *Fl-ac* k* *Kali-bi* k* nat-ar k2 nat-c nit-ac *Sil*
  - **syphilitic**: ars k* *Ars-i* aur bro1 *Carb-an* bro1 dulc fl-ac k* hep hydrc bro1 kali-bi *Kali-i* k* *Merc* merc-i-r bro1 *Nit-ac* phyt sil still bro1 thuj k*
  - **tearing**: cham con
  - **tensive**: caust mur-ac
  - **tuberous**: *Kali-bi* *Nat-c* phos sil *Tub*
  - **ulcerating**: am-c bov *Caust* *Fl-ac* *Kali-i* hr1 *Nat-c* k* sec
  - **umbilicated**: *Kali-bi* *Kali-br*
  - **wart**-shaped: lyc *Thuj*
  - **watery**: graph mag-c k*

- **white**: ant-c dulc sep sulph valer
- **winter**: *Kali-br* k*
- **yellow**: *Ant-c* rhus-t

- **ulcerating**: clem bg2 rhus-t bg2
- **ulcerative** pain; with: am-c k* *Am-m* k* ant-c k* ars k* bar-c k* caps k* caust k* con k* graph k* kali-c k* laur k* *Mang* k* merc k* *Phos* k* *Puls* k* *Rhus-t* k* *Sep* k* **Sil** k* *Staph* k* sulph k* tarax k* zinc k*
- **umbilicated**: ant-t bg2 kali-bi bg2
- **urticaria**: *(↗angioedema; GENERALS - Allergic)* *Acon* k* agar k* all-c k* alum-p k2 alum-sil k2 am-c k* am-m k* amyg c2 anac bg2* anan hr1 *Ant-c* k* ant-t k* anthraco c2* antip bg1* ap-g c2* **Apis** k* arn k* **Ars** k* *Ars-i* ars-s-f k2 arum-d hr1* arum-dru c1* asim hr1 **Astac** k* aur aur-ar k2 aur-s k2 bapt hr1 bar-c k* bar-m bar-s k2 bell k* bell-p sp1 benz-ac k* berb bg2* bomb-pr c2* bond a1 *Bov* k* *Bry* k* bufo k* *Calad* k* **Calc** k* *Calc-ln* c1 **Calc-s** k* camph bg2* carb-ac mrr1 carb-an k* *Carb-v* k* **Carbn-s** card-b a1 cardios-h rly4• **Caust** k* cham k* chin k* chinin-ar *Chinin-s* k* **Chlol** k* chlor k* cic k* cimic k* cina bro1 clem hr1 cob-n sp1 coca cocc k* *Con* k* **Cop** k* *Corn* k* cortico mtf11 crot-c mrr1 *Crot-h* k* crot-t k* cub k* cund bro1 *Cupr* cypra-eg sde6.de• diph jl2 diph-t-tpt jl2 *Dol* hr1 **Dulc** k* dys fmm1* *Elat* k* fago bro1 ferr-i k* ferr-s c2 form bg2 frag c2* gaert pte1* gal-ac c1* *Graph* k* guar hr1* gymno br1 helia c2 **Hep** k* hist sp1* hom-xyz bro1* hydr k* hygroph-s zzc1• *Ichth* bro1 ign k* ina-i mlk9.de iod k* ip k* *Kali-ar* *Kali-br* k* *Kali-c* k* kali-chl bro1 kali-i k* kali-m bg2 kali-p k* kali-s k* kola stb3• *Kreos* k* lach k* lat-h bnm5• lat-k c2 lat-m bnm6• **Led** k* lepr mtf11 linu-u c2* lipp c2 *Lyc* k* lycps-v mag-c k* med c2* medus c2* merc k* *Mez* k* mim-p vml3• morg-g fmm1• myric c2 nat-ar nat-c k* nat-f sp1 **Nat-m** k* *Nat-p* k* nat-s bg2 nit-ac k* *Nux-v* k* op bg2 pall k* *Petr* k* ph-ac k* *Phos* k* physala-p c2 pic-ac bg2 pin-s a1* pip-n bg2 pitu-p sp1 podo c1* polyg-h ptk1 positr nl2• prot fmm1• *Psor* k* *Puls* k* **Rhus-t** k* rhus-v c2* rob bg2* rumx k* ruta k* sabin bg2 *Sal-ac* k* sanic bro1 sarr a1 sars k* sec k* sel k* *Sep* k* sil k* skook c2* sol-a c2 sol-o c2 stann bro1 staph k* stram k* *Stroph-h* br1* stry-p bro1 *Sul-ac* k* *Sul-i* sulfa sp1 sulfonam ks2 **Sulph** k* tell rsj10• ter k* tet c2* tetox pin2• thiosin c1 thuj k* thyr mtf11 *Til* k* trios c2* tub jl2 *Urin* c1 **Urt-u** k* ust k* uva br1 valer k* vario jl2 *Verat* k* vesp k* voes c2 zinc k* zinc-p k2 [heroin sdj2 mang stj1 senec-abv dbx1.fr]
  - **morning**: *Bell* k*
    - **waking**; on: bov ptk1
  - **forenoon**: bov bro1
  - **afternoon**: chlol k*
    - **16 h**: sulfonam ks2
  - **evening**: *Bell* hr1 hyper hr1 *Kreos* k* *Nux-v* k*
  - **night**: ant-c bro1 **Apis** ars bro1 *Bov* *Chlol* k* *Cop* k* hydr *Nux-v* *Puls* k*
  - **accompanied** by:
    - **edema**: *Apis* bro1 vesp bro1
    - **erysipelas** (See Erysipelas - accompanied - urticaria)
    - **indigestion** (See STOMACH - Indigestion - accompanied - urticaria)
    - **pinworm**: urt-u ptk1
    - **rheumatic** complaints (See GENERALS - Pain - rheumatic - accompanied - urticaria)
    - **shuddering**: ap-g ptk1
    - **Bronchial** tubes; complaints of the (See CHEST - Complaints - bronchial tubes - accompanied - urticaria)
  - **acute**: adren br1
  - **air** | **change** of air agg.: *Apis*
  - **air**; in open:
    - **agg.**: chlol bro1 *Dulc* bro1 nit-ac h2* rhus-t bro1 sep bro1
    - **amel.**: calc bro1
  - **alternating** with:
    - **asthma** (See RESPIRATION - Asthmatic - alternating - urticaria)
    - **respiration**; difficult (See RESPIRATION - Difficult - alternating - urticaria)
    - **rheumatism**: *Urt-u* k*
    - **Chest**; oppression of (See CHEST - Oppression - alternating - urticaria)
    - **Stomach**, pain in: ap-g vh
  - **apyrexia**; during: apis c1

- **urticaria**: ...
  - **ascarides**; with: urt-u bg3*
  - **asthmatic** troubles; in: *Apis*
  - **bathing**; after: bov bro1* phos *Urt-u*
  - **bluish**-white margins; with: cob-n sp1
  - **buckwheat**; from: puls bro1
  - **burning**: apis tl1 *Chlol* mrr1 **Crot-c** mrr1 hygroph-s zzc1• rhus-t tl1 urt-u tl1
  - **children**; in: cop bro1
  - **chill**:
    - **after**: **Apis** a1 chlol hr1 *Elat* k* *Hep* k*
    - **before**: *Hep* k*
    - **during**: apis k* *Ars* k* ign k* **Nat-m** k* **Rhus-t** k*
  - **chronic**: *Anac* bro1 *Ant-c* bro1 antip bro1 *Ars* bro1 *Astac* bro1 *Bov* bro1 calc bro1 *Chlol* bro1 *Cop* bro1 cund bro1 *Dulc* bro1 hep bro1 *Ichth* br1* *Lyc* bro1* nat-m bro1 *Rhus-t* bro1 sep bro1 stroph-h bro1* *Sulph* bro1 urt-u bro1
    - **children**; in: cop ptk1
  - **clothes**; from pressure of: med al2 thal-xyz srj8•
  - **cold**:
    - **air**:
      - **agg.**●: ars bro1 caust dulc hr1* kali-br nat-s *Nit-ac* k* **RHUS-T** k ●* rumx k* **Sep** k ●* sulph gk
      - **amel.**: *Calc* k* *Dulc* k* hygroph-s zzc1•
    - **applications** | **amel.**: apis mtf calc-s mtf hygroph-s zzc1• sulph mtf
    - **bathing**:
      - **after**: *Calc-p* k*
        - **amel.**: apis bro1 dulc bro1
  - **cold**; after taking a: *Dulc* ptk1
  - **cold** agg., becoming: **Dulc** k* sulph gk
  - **constipation**; with: cop br1*
  - **crops**; in: **Crot-c** mrr1
  - **diarrhea**, with: apis bro1 bov bro1* puls bro1*
  - **drinking** cold water agg.: bell k*
  - **excitement**; after: anac bro1 bov br1* ign bro1 kali-br bro1
  - **exertion**; after violent●: apis bro1 calc bro1 *Con* k* hep bro1 *Nat-m* k* *Psor* k* sanic bro1 *Urt-u* k*
  - **fever**:
    - **during**:
      - **agg.**: **Apis** k* **Carb-v** lmj chlor *Cop* k* cub hygroph-s zzc1• **Ign** k* **Rhus-t** k* *Rhus-v* *Sulph*
        - **bathing** agg.: *Hygroph-s* zzc1•
        - **children**; in: **Apis** lmj **Carb-v** lmj chlor lmj cop lmj cub lmj ign lmj **Rhus-t** lmj *Rhus-v* lmj *Sulph* lmj
        - **woolen** clothes agg.: *Hygroph-s* zzc1•
    - **prodrome** of; during: *Hep* al4
    - **suppressed**: elat c1
  - **fish** agg.: ars ptk1
  - **flat**: form ptk1 lob ptk1
  - **fruit**; from: puls bro1
  - **gigantea** (See angioedema)
  - **hot** drinks | **amel.**: chlol bro1
  - **increasing** and decreasing suddenly: antip bro1
  - **indigestion**; after: ant-c mtf ars mtf carb-v mtf cop mtf dulc mtf nux-v mtf puls mtf rob mtf trios mtf
  - **itching** | **without** itching: uva br1*
  - **liver** symptoms, with: astac bg3* myric bg3* ptel ptk1*
  - **livid**: *Apis*
  - **location**, rapid change of: ap-g vml3•
  - **lying** | **amel.**: urt-u
  - **malaria**; from suppressed: elat br1*
  - **meat** agg.: **Ant-c** k*
  - **menopause**; during: morph bro1 ust bro1

- **menses**:
  - **after** | **agg.**: kreos ptk1
  - **before** | **agg.**: *Dulc Kali-c* k*
  - **delayed**, with: puls ptk1
  - **during**:
    - **agg.**: bell k* *Cimic* bro1 dulc bro1* *Kali-c* k* mag-c bro1 puls k* sec ust bro1
      - **profuse** menses: bov ptk1
- **nausea**:
  - **after**: sang hr1*
  - **before**: sang k*
- **nervous**: hist-m mtf11
- **nodular**: *Agar* k* ail bg2 *Alum* k* alum-p k2 alum-sil k2 am-c k* am-m k* anac k* *Ant-c* k* ant-t k* antho bg2 **Apis** k* arn ars k* ars-s-f k2 aur k* bar-c k* bar-m bar-s k2 bell k* berb bg2 beryl sp1 borx bg2 bov bg2* brom bg2 *Bry* k* **Calc** k* calc-sil k2 cann-s k* canth k* caps k* *Carb-an* k* *Carb-v* k* carbn-s *Caul* bg2 **Caust** k* *Chel* k* chin k* *Chlol* k* chlor cic k* clem bg2 cocc k* con k* *Cop* crot-h bg2 crot-t bg2 dig k* dros k* **Dulc** k* euph bg2 graph k* hell k* *Hep* k* hydr bg2 ign k* *Iod* k* ip k* iris bg2 *Jug-c* kali-ar *Kali-bi* bg2 *Kali-br* k* kali-c k* kali-i k* kali-n k* kali-s k* kali-sil k2 kreos k* **Lach** k* *Led* k* *Lyc* k* m-ambo b2.de* m-arct b2.de* *Mag-c* k* mag-m k* *Mang* k* merc k* merc-i-f bg2 merc-i-r bg2 **Mez** k* mur-ac k* nat-ar nat-c k* *Nat-m* k* nat-p nat-s bg2* nit-ac k* nux-v k* olnd k* op k* pall *Petr* k* ph-ac k* phos k* phyt bg2 *Puls* k* **Rhod** bg2 **Rhus-t** k* rhus-v *Ruta* k* sabin k* *Sars* bg2 *Sec* k* sel k* *Sep* k* *Sil* k* spig k* spong k* squil k* stann k* *Staph* k* stram k* sul-ac k* *Sulph* k* tarax k* thuj k* *Urt-u* k* valer k* *Verat* k* verb k* viol-t k* zinc k* zinc-s bg2
  - **rosy** (= erythema): antip vh *Bell Bry Chlol Chlor* coca cop crot-t gels jug-c kali-br kali-i merc *Nat-c* k* nat-m bg2 petr phos k* phyt **Rhus-t** sil k* **Stram** ter
- **oxyuris**; with: urt-u dm
- **periodical** | **year**; every: urt-u bro1*
- **perspiration**; during: **Apis** k* **Rhus-t**
- **pigmentary**: tub jl2
  - **syphilitic**: calc-s bro1 nit-ac bro1
- **pork**; from: puls bro1
- **purple**: chinin-s ptk1
- **recurrent** (See GENERALS - History - urticaria)
- **rheumatism**; during: *Bov* bro1 dulc bro1 **Rhus-t** k* **Urt-u** k*
- **rubbing** | **amel.**: elat hr1*
- **scratching**; after: agar k* alum k* am-c k* am-m k* ant-c k* ars k* ars-s-f k2 bar-c k* bry k* *Calc* k* calc-sil k2 carb-an k* carb-v k* carbn-s *Caust* k* chin chinin-ar cic k* cocc k* con k* **Dulc** k* *Graph* k* hell k* *Hep* k* ip k* **Lach** k* led k* *Lyc* k* mag-c k* mag-m k* mang k* merc k* **Mez** k* nat-c k* nat-m k* nit-ac k* nux-v k* olnd k* op b7.de *Petr* k* puls k* **Rhus-t** k* ruta k* sel k* sep k* sil k* spig k* *Staph* k* sulph k* thuj k* verat k* zinc k* zinc-p k2
- **seaside**; at: ars mag-m
- **shellfish**: (*↗GENERALS - Food and - shellfish - agg.)* apis c1 camph bro1 ter bg3* urt-u bg3*
- **spirituous** liquors; after: chlol br1* tritic-vg fd5.de
- **spring**; every: rhus-t
- **stomach**, preceded by pressure in: ap-g vml3•
- **strawberries**; from: bry j5.de frag br1
- **sudden** violent attack: camph bro1
- **sun**; exposure to: ign gk
- **suppressed**: urt-u ptk1
- **tuberosa**; urticaria (See angioedema)
- **undressing** agg.: puls ptk1
- **vaccination**; from: skook srj
- **walking**:
  - **agg.**: bov bro1
  - **cold** air; in | **agg.**: *Sep*
- **warm** drinks:
  - **amel.** | **hot** drinks: chlol bro1

- **urticaria**: ...
  - **warmth** agg. | **heat** agg.: hygroph-s zzc1•
  - **warmth** and exercise: anac brm *Apis* k* *Bov* calc-p brm cic brm *Con* k* *Dulc* k* kali-c bro1 *Kali-i Led Lyc* k* **Nat-m** k* nit-ac *Psor* k* *Puls Sulph* k* **Urt-u** k*
    - **amel.**: ars bro1 chlol bro1 *Hep* k* lyc ptk1 *Sep* k*
  - **weather**; change of: *Apis* k*
  - **wet**; from becoming: **RHUS-T** k ●
  - **white**: nat-m ptk1
    - **Apex**: *Ant-c* ptk1 puls ptk1
  - **wine**; from: *Chlol* k*
- **vaccination**; after: mez br1 sars hr1* thuj tl1
- **varicella** (See chickenpox)
- **variola** (See smallpox)
- **vesication** (See blisters)
- **vesicular**: agar alum k* alum-p k2 alum-sil k2 am-c k* *Am-m* k* *Anac* k* ancis-p tsm2 *Ant-c* k* *Ant-t* k* anthraci anthraco br1 aq-mar jl arb br1 arg-met k* arist-cl sp1 arn k* **Ars** k* ars-s-f k2 arum-m hr1 arum-t ptk1* aster mgm• aur k* aur-ar k2 aur-s k2 *Bar-c* k* bar-s k2 *Bell* k* bell-p sp1 *Benz-ac* hr1 both tsm2 both-ax tsm2 *Bov* k* *Brucel* sa3• *Bry* k* *Bufo* k* calad k* *Calc* k* calc-p *Calc-s* calc-sil k2 calen hr1 *Cann-s* k* **Canth** k* caps **Carb-ac** k* *Carb-an* k* carb-v k* carbn-s k2 cassia-s cdd7• **Caust** k* cench tsm2 cham k* chel hr1 *Chin* k* chinin-ar chinin-s bg2 chrysar br1 *Cic* k* cist **Clem** k* cloth tsm2 cocc k* coch hr1 com k* con k* cop *Corn* k* crot-h k* **Crot-t** k* cupr-ar cycl k* dig **Dulc** k* **Euph** k* euph-cy c2 euphr ptk1 *Fl-ac Graph* k* grin k* *Hell* k* *Hep* k* hyos k* ign k* *Iris Jug-r* kali-ar *Kali-bi* k* *Kali-c* k* *Kali-chl* k* *Kali-i* k* kali-m k2 *Kali-n* k* kali-p k2 *Kali-s* k* kali-sil k2 kola stb3• *Kreos* k* lac-c k* **Lach** k* *Lact* lat-m bnm6• laur k* loxo-lae bnm12• *Lyc* k* m-ambo b2.de* m-arct b2.de* *Mag-c* k* **Manc** k* mand sp1 mang k* med ptk1* *Merc* k* *Merc-c* k* *Mez* k* morg-p pte1*• narc-ps br1* nat-ar **Nat-c** k* **Nat-m** k* *Nat-p* nat-s k* **Nit-ac** k* olnd k* op k* osm *Petr* k* ph-ac k* **Phos** k* plat k* plb k* positr nl2• *Psor* k* ptel c1 *Puls* k* **Ran-b** k* *Ran-s* k* rheum k* rhod b4.de* **Rhus-t** k* *Rhus-v* k* *Rumx* ruta k* sabad k* *Sabin* k* sal-ac sars k* *Sec* k* *Sel* k* seneg k* *Sep* k* *Sil* k* spig k* spong k* *Squil* k* staph k* staphycoc jl2 still hr1 stram k* streptoc jl2 succ-ac mtf11 sul-ac k* **Sulph** k* syc bka1*• syph ptk1 tarax k* *Tell* k* ter k* tetox pin2• thuj k* toxo-g jl2 tub-d jl2 urt-u ptk1 valer b7.de* vario mtf11 verat k* verat-v hr1 vip x-ray sp1 zinc k* zinc-p k2
  - **abscess**; over: rhus-t ptk1
  - **accompanied** by:
    - **aphthae** (See MOUTH - Aphthae - accompanied - eruptions)
    - **infectious** disorders: fl-ac mtf11
    - **Liver**; complaints of (See ABDOMEN - Liver - accompanied - vesicular)
  - **acrid** fluid; filled with: acon bg2 bufo bg2 caust bg2 crot-h bg2 *Graph* bg2 ran-b bg2 rhus-t bg2
  - **air**; in: asaf ptk1
  - **black**: *Anthraci* k* arg-n **Ars** k* **Lach** k* nat-c petr *Sec* hr1 vip
  - **blood**; filled with: *Ail* k* **Ars** k* aur k* bry k* camph canth k* carb-ac k* fl-ac graph kali-p **Lach** nat-c *Nat-m* k* *Phos* bg2 *Sec* k* sep bg2 sulph k*
  - **bluish**: *Anthraci* k* **Ars** k* bell k* con k* crot-h bg2 **Lach** k* **Ran-b** k* rhus-t k* vip
    - **Center**: calc bg2 kali-bi bg2
  - **brown**: anag ant-c carb-v lyc mez k* nit-ac phos sep thuj
  - **burning**: agar am-c k* am-m k* *Anac* anag ars aur *Bar-c* bov k* calc canth hr1* carb-ac br1 carb-v a1 caust k* clem mrr1 com bg2 *Crot-t* k* dulc bg2 graph guare k* hep kali-n h2* lach k* mag-c mag-m mang merc *Mez* k* *Mur-ac* nat-c nat-m k* nit-ac phos plat *Ran-b* k* rhus-t h1* seneg k* sep sil *Spig* spong k* staph sulph k* vip bg2
  - **bursting**: mez bg2
  - **cicatrices**; on: fl-ac bg2
  - **close** to each other: ran-b rhus-t verat
  - **cold** air agg.: *Dulc*
  - **confluent**: alum *Bell* hr1 *Cic* crot-t hr1 *Mez* hr1 phel rhus-t k* *Sulph*
  - **cracked**, breaking: anag mrr1 *Bry Crot-h Lach* mang k2 phos *Vip*
  - **crusty**: bov mrr1 chrysar br1 mez mrr1 ran-b mrr1
  - **cutting**: graph

- **dark**: ail ptk1 anthraci ptk1
- **denuded** surface, forming on: anag rhus-t staph
- **desquamating**: anag mrr1 *Bry* puls rhus-t
- **discharges**, from: tell ptk1
- **drawing**, painful: clem
- **dry**: rhus-t
- **erysipelatous** (See Erysipelas)
- **frostbite**; after: mag-c b4.de nit-ac b4.de rhus-t b7.de
- **gangrenous**: acon b2.de* *Ars* k* bell k* *Bufo Camph* k* **Canth** b7a.de carb-v k* **Lach** k* mur-ac k* phos bg2 *Ran-b* k* *Sabin* k* *Sec* k* sil
- **grape** shaped: bufo rhus-t
- **grouped**: anag br1 rhus-v sulph
- **hard**: *Kali-s* hr1 lach ph-ac phos h2* sil
- **heat** of sun; as from: clem
- **humid**: con hr1 hell hep lach mang *Merc* k* phos ran-b ran-s **Rhus-t** k* sulph vip
- **inflamed**: am-m anac bar-c bell *Crot-t* dulc kali-n med gk rhus-t rhus-v
- **itching**: aeth k* am-c gsy1 am-m *Anac* ant-c ant-t apis ars-h k* bry **Calc** k* *Canth* k* *Carb-ac* k* caust clem k2 con bg2 crot-t k* daph k* dulc bg2* *Fl-ac* k* *Graph* k* *Jug-r* kola stb3• *Lach* k* mag-c med gk *Mez* k* *Nat-c* k* phos bg2 plb bg2 positr nl2• psil ft1 psor bg2 *Rhus-t* k* rumx ruta fd4.de sel k* *Sep* k* sil k* sulph tab bg2 tell
  - **evening**: kali-c k*
  - **night**: *Graph* k*
  - **cold** air agg.: *Rumx*
  - **scars**; around old: *Fl-ac*
  - **uncovered**; where: *Rumx*
  - **warm**:
    - **bed** agg.; in: aeth
    - **room** | **agg.**: apis
- **large**: bufo ptk1 manc ptk1
- **miliary**: acon bg3 carb-ac hr1
- **mucous** membrane: am-c bg2 apis bg2 bar-c bg2 berb bg2 borx bg2 canth bg2 caps bg2 carb-v bg2 caust bg2 mez mtf11 nat-m bg2 nit-ac bg2 staph bg2 thuj bg2
- **painful**: bell canth hr1 clem kali-c phos k* psil ft1 **Rhus-t** hr1 *Tarent* hr1
  - **shooting** pains: **Nat-c** k*
  - **touch** agg.: nat-c hr1
  - **ulcerated**; as if: mez mur-ac
- **painless**: stront-c sulph
- **peeling** off (See desquamating)
- **periodical**: anag mrr1
- **phagedenic**: (↗*ulcerated*) am-c ars borx *Calc* caust cham clem graph hep kali-c *Mag-c* mang k2 merc k* nat-c *Nit-ac Petr* sep *Sil Sulph*
- **purpura**: staphycoc jl2 toxo-g jl2
- **red**: *Ant-c* k* calc-p cic crot-h cycl fl-ac lach mang merc k* nat-c k* *Nat-m* k* ol-an physala-p bnm7• rhus-v hr1 sil valer
  - **Areola** (See areola - red)
- **scratching**; after: *Am-c* k* *Am-m* k* ant-c k* ars k* ars-s-f k2 bar-c k* bar-s k2 bell k* bry k* calc caust k* chin k* *Cycl* k* dulc k* graph k* grat *Hep* k* kali-ar kali-c k* kreos k* **Lach** k* laur k* m-ambo b2.de* mag-c h2 mang k* merc k* nat-c k* nat-m k* nicc ol-an *Phos* k* psor bg2 *Ran-b* k* **Rhus-t** k* sabin k* sars k* sel k* sep k* spong k* *Sulph* k*
- **scurfy**: am-m hr1 anac bell hr1 hell kali-bi merc k2 nat-c nat-m k* nit-ac ran-b k* sil sulph
- **small**: ail k2 am-m anac hr1 cann-s crot-t bg2 fl-ac graph hell indg hr1 *Kali-chl* hr1 lach mang k* merc k* *Merc-c* hr1 nat-m nicc hr1 nit-ac psor hr1 rhus-t k* sel hr1 *Sil* hr1 stram hr1 *Sulph* hr1 thuj
- **smarting**: con graph hell mag-c mang nat-c ph-ac phel plat rhod rhus-t rhus-v sil staph thuj
- **spots**:
  - **covered** with: dulc iod lach merc rhus-t spong
  - **leaving**: caust
- **spreading** when opened by the fluid contained: arn bg2
- **stab** wound; after a: sep pd

- **vesicular**: ...
  - **stinging**: am-c calc cham clem k2 crot-t k* nat-m **Nit-ac** psil ft1 *Rhus-t* sne sil spong *Staph Tell*
  - **sudamina**: agar b4a.de* am-c k* am-m bro1 apis ars k* bell k* *Bry* k* canth k* chinin-s crot-t k* graph k* *Hep* k* lac-c k* lach k* **Nat-m** k* ph-ac k* phos b4a.de **Rhus-t** k* spong sul-ac k* sulph b4a.de urt-u bro1 valer k*
  - **sun**; from exposure to: acon c1 camph *Kali-i* vh sacch-a fd2.de• *Staph* vh
  - **suppurating**: *Am-m* arum-t vh aur bov calc carb-v graph mag-c med gk *Nat-c* nit-ac petr phos puls ran-b ran-s rhus-t sars sulph vip zinc
  - **syphilitic**: *Cinnb* bro1 merc-c bro1 *Merc-i-r* bro1 thuj bro1
  - **tensive**: am-m k* hura c1* kali-n mag-c mag-m mur-ac nat-c
  - **transparent**: con h2* kali-c lach *Mag-c* mag-m mang merc nat-s bg2 *Ran-b* k* rhus-t hr1 urt-u hr1
  - **ulcerated**: (↗*phagedenic*) *Calc* caust *Clem* cupr-ar graph *Merc* nat-c petr k2 **Sulph** *Zinc*
  - **ulcers**; around (See Ulcers - vesicles)
  - **varioloid**: acon b2.de* *Bell* b2.de* *Puls* b2.de* rhus-t b2.de*
  - **violet**: anthraci jl2
  - **watery**: ars h2* *Bell* bov canth clem k* cupr graph kali-c kali-n m-ambo b7a.de merc nat-c nat-s k2 ol-an plat plb *Rhus-t* rhus-v sec *Sulph* tab vip zinc
  - **white**: am-c berb cann-s caust clem con h2* galeoc-c-h gms1• graph hell hep k* *Kali-chl Lach Merc* mez *Nat-c* phos rhus-t h1* sabad sulph *Thuj* valer k*
    - **healed** quickly: galeoc-c-h gms1•
    - **partly** white: bor-ac bg2
  - **wound**; around a: *Lach* rhus-t
  - **yellow**: *Agar* am-m anac k* anag ant-c anthraci ars ars-s-f k2 bufo calc-p carbn-s k* chel cic clem com k* crot-h crot-t **Dulc** k* euph ptk1 *Euphr Hydr* k* *Kali-n* k* *Kreos* lach k* *Manc Merc* k* mur-ac nat-c nat-s k* ph-ac psor ran-b ran-s k* raph k* **Rhus-t** *Rhus-v* sep sulph tab k* vip k*
    - **spots**: cur st lyc st nux-v st sep st sulph st
  - ○ **Areola** | **red**: anac *Calc* cann-s crot-h crot-t kali-c kali-chl lach hr1 *Nat-c* psil ft1 sil sulph tab k* vip
- **wandering**: gink-b sbd1•
- **warm** bed agg.: alum tl1 sulph k2
- **warmth** agg.: cortiso sp1
  - **radiant** heat: **Ant-c** mrr1
- **washing** agg.●: canth **Clem** k* *Dulc* hydr mez morg-p pte1• phos podo fd3.de• *Psor* sars **Sulph** urt-u
- **weaning**; after: dulc ptk1
- **weather** agg.; wet: narc-ps cda1*
- **wet** agg.; getting: arist-cl sp1
- **whitish**: agar k* anan ant-c ant-t bg2 apis bg2 **Ars** k* *Ars-i* borx k* bov k* bry k* com con h2* hep h2* ip k* merc *Mez* k* olib-sac wmh1 op bg2 phos k* plac-s rly4• plb bg2 *Puls* sec bg2 sulph k* thuj k* *Valer* k* zinc k*
  - **chalk**; like: calc bg2*
  - **milky**: zinc bg2
  - ○ **Areola**; with red: borx c1
- **winter**:
  - **agg.**: *Aloe* bro1 alum bro1* ars bro1* *Calc Dulc Hep* kali-br hr1 kali-c *Mang Merc Mez Petr* bro1* *Psor* bro1* **Rhus-t** sabad bro1* *Sep Stront-c* sulph tub ptk1
  - **amel.**: kali-bi bro1* sars bro1*
- **withered**: kali-c bg2 mang bg2 ph-ac bg2
- **yellow**: *Agar* k* anac *Ant-c* ars k* aur *Bar-c* bar-m bufo cadm-s calc-s chel *Cic* k* cocc k* cupr k* *Dulc Euph* k* hell k* iod mtf33 kali-c *Kali-chl* kreos k* lach led k* lyc k* **Merc** k* *Nat-c* k* nat-s *Nit-ac* k* par k* ph-ac ran-s raph *Rhus-t* sep k* *Spong* tab valer k*

○ - **Bend** of joints: cupr bg2 graph bg2* kreos bg2 nat-m bg2 psor bg2 sep bg2
- **Covered** parts; on: *Led* k* *Thuj* k*
- **Folds** of skin; in: *Ars* mtf calc mtf carb-v mtf graph mtf hep mtf lyc mtf merc mtf *Nat-m* fr2* *Petr* mtf **Psor** mtf puls mtf sel mtf sep mtf sil mtf sulph mtf
- **Hairy** parts; on: agar calc kali-c b2.de* kali-i lach *Lith-c* lyc k* *Merc* k* *Nat-m* k* nit-ac k* ph-ac k* **Rhus-t** k* sil
- **Uncovered** parts: thuj tl1

Skin

- **Under** skin; sensation as if eruptions are: hyper ptk1*

ERYSIPELAS: **Acon** k* *Am-c* k* am-m k* *Anac* k* anac-oc c2* anan k* ant-c k* *Anthraci* k* **Apis** k* arg-n c2 arist-cl sp1 *Arn* k* *Ars* k* *Ars-i* ars-s-f k2 arund k* atro hr1* *Aur* k* aur-ar k2 aur-s k2 bar-c k* bar-m **Bell** k* bell-p tl1* *Borx* k* *Bry* k* bufo k* cadm-s *Calc* k* *Calc-f* hr1 calc-i k2 calc-sil k2 calen hr1* *Camph* k* *Canth* k* carb-ac k* *Carb-an* k* carb-v k* *Carbn-s* caust k* *Cham* k* chel k* *Chin* k* chlol c2 cinnm hr1 cist c2* *Clem* k* colch k* com k* con c2 cop br1* *Crot-c* *Crot-h* k* crot-t k* cund hr1 cupr k* *Cupr-act* c2 diph-t-tpt jl2 dor c2 dulc k* *Echi* k* elat hr1* **Euph** k* euph-cy c2 euph-l br1 euph-pe c2 ferr-m ptk2 *Ferr-p* c2 frag c2 gast a1 *Gels* k* **Graph** k* gymno c2 *Hep* k* hippoz c2* *Hydr* bg2* hyos k* inul c2 *Iod* k* *Ip* k* jab c2 *Jug-c* k* jug-r bro1 kali-ar kali-bi gk *Kali-c* k* *Kali-chl* k* kali-i kali-m k2 *Kali-p* kali-s k* kali-sil k2 kalm hr1 lac-c k2 **Lach** k* led k* *Lyc* k* mag-c k* mag-s sp1* manc mtf11 mang k* meph a1 **Merc** k* mur-ac k* nat-ar nat-c k* nat-m k* nat-p k* nat-s k* *Nit-ac* k* nux-v hr1 passi c2* petr k* *Ph-ac* k* *Phos* k* plan c2 plat hr1 plb k* podo hr1* prim-o bro1 psor bro1* ptel hr1* *Puls* k* pyrog bg2* ran-a c2 ran-b k* ran-s bg2 rhod k* rhus-d c2 **Rhus-t** k* *Rhus-v* k* *Ruta* k* sabad k* samb k* sars k* sec ptk1 semp ptk2 sep k* *Sil* k* spong b2.de* stann b2.de* staph b2.de* stram b2.de* strept-ent jl2 streptoc jl2 sul-i k2 *Sulph* k* *Tarent-c* tax bro1 tep c2 *Ter* k* *Thuj* k* tub bg2* vac mtf11 verat k* *Verat-v* c2* vesp vip bg2* *Xero* bro1 zinc k* zinc-act c2

- **alternating** sides: lac-c k2*
- **right**:
  - ▽ • **extending** to | **left**: *Apis* arund *Graph* k* *Kali-c* hr1 *Lyc* *Rhus-t* hr1 sulph
- **left**:
  - ▽ • **extending** to | **right**: lach k* *Rhus-t* k*
- **accompanied** by:
  - • **urticaria**: astac ptk1 frag bro1
  - ○ • **Tongue**:
    - ⁝ **trembling**: lach kr1*
    - ⁝ **white** discoloration of the tongue: **Apis** kr1*
- **acute**: gali mtf11
- **bleeding**: ars b4a.de bar-c b4a.de bell b4a.de euph b4a.de graph b4a.de hep b4a.de petr b4a.de sep b4a.de sulph b4a.de
- **brain** complaints; with: am-c gsy1 verat-v ptk1
- **children**; in: *Lach* hr1 psor mtf33
  - • **newborns**: bell bro1* camph bro1* carb-an pd
- **chronic**: *Graph* k* lappa mtf11 *Ter* k*
- **dark** red spots: rhus-t mrr1
- **discharge**; with slimy: *Rhus-t* a1
- **erratic**: apis bro1 arn k* *Ars* bro1 bell k* chin bro1 *Graph* bro1 hep bro1 hydr bro1 mang k* *Mur-ac* k* *Puls* k* rhus-t sabin k* sulph k*
- **fever**; without: *Graph* bro1 hep bro1 lyc bro1
- **gangrenous**: acon k* *Anthraci* *Apis* **Ars** k* *Bell* k* *Camph* k* **Carb-v** k* chin k* com **Crot-c** *Hippoz* k* hyos k* **Lach** k* mur-ac k* *Rhus-t* k* *Sabin* k* **Sec** k* *Sil* k* ter
- **inflamed**: bell-p sp1
- **injuries**; after: calen bro1 led k2 psor bro1
- **malignant**: both mtf11
  - • **accompanied** by | **Lymphatic** glands; swollen: both mtf11
- **menses**; during: *Graph* k*
- **newborns** (See children - newborns)
- **old** people; in: am-c k* carb-an bro1* *Lach* hr1
- **phlegmonosum**: ferr-m ptk2
- **place**; changing: **Puls** b7.de*
- **prophylaxis**: graph bro1*
- **putrid** odor: kali-p k2
- **receding**: lyc ptk1
- **recurrent** (See GENERALS - History - erysipelas)
- **scarlet** red: **Am-c** b4a.de *Am* b7a.de *Ars* b4a.de *Bar-c* b4a.de *Bell* b4.de *Bry* b7a.de carb-v b4a.de cham b7a.de euphr b7.de hep b4a.de *Hyos* b7a.de *Iod* b4a.de ip b7a.de merc b4a.de *Phos* b4a.de *Sulph* b4a.de
- **scratching**; after | **agg.**: *Am-c* k* ant-c k* arn k* ars k* *Bell* k* borx k* bry k* calc k* calc-sil k2 canth k* carb-an k* carb-v k* *Graph* k* *Hep* k* hyos k* *Lach* k* *Lyc* k* mag-c k* **Merc** k* nat-ar nat-c k* nit-ac k* petr k* phos k* puls k* ran-b k* **Rhus-t** k* samb k* sil k* spong k* *Sulph* k* thuj k*
- **smooth**: *Acon* hr1 *Apis* **Bell** colch hr1 kali-p k2 nat-s hr1 *Puls* hr1
- **streaks**; running in: *Graph*

Erysipelas: ...

- **suppressed**: acon bg2 am-c bg2 ars bg2 bell bg2 bry bg2 calc bg2 dulc bg2 graph bg2 hep bg2 ip bg2 lyc bg2 merc bg2 ph-ac bg2 phos bg2 puls bg2 rhus-t bg2 sulph bg2 thuj bg2
- **swelling**; with: *Acon* k* am-c k* **Apis** k* *Arn* k* *Ars* k* aur bro1 *Bar-c* b4.de **Bell** k* borx c1 bry k* *Calc* k* calc-sil k2 canth k* *Carb-an* b4.de* carb-v k* carbn-s caust k* chin k* *Clem* b4a.de **Crot-c** euph k* *Graph* k* *Hep* k* kali-c k* *Lach* led k2 lyc k* mag-c k* mang b4.de **Merc** k* mur-ac b4a.de nat-ar nat-c k* nat-m k* nit-ac k* petr k* ph-ac k* phos k* puls k* rhod b4.de **Rhus-t** k* rhus-v ruta k* samb k* sars k* sep k* sil k* stann b4.de *Sulph* k* *Thuj* k* *Verat-v* zinc k*
- **traumatic**: apis pd calen ptk1 psor ptk1
- **vesicular**: am-c k* *Anac* anac-oc bro1 am bro1 *Ars* k* astac bar-c k* *Bell* k* bry k* *Canth* k* *Carb-ac* bro1 carb-an k* *Carbn-s* caust bro1 chin b2.de* cist hr1 com crot-t k* euph b2.de* *Graph* k* *Hep* k* *Kali-c* hr1 *Kali-chl* k* kali-s *Lach* k* mez k* petr k* phos k* puls k* ran-b k* **Rhus-t** k* *Rhus-v* k* sabad k* *Sep* k* staph k* stram k* *Sulph* k* ter hr1* urt-u k* vac jl2 verat-v hr1* verb bro1 verbe-o br1
  - • **dark**; becoming: canth ptk1 ran-b ptk1
- **wandering**: *Graph* ptk1 hydr ptk1 rhus-t ptk1 sulph ptk1 syph ptk1
- **wounds**; of: apis hr1*

○ - **Joints**; of: **Bry** b7a.de

EXCORIATION: *(↗Intertrigo)* Aeth c2 alum *Arg-met* arn c2* *Ars* *Ars-i* ars-s-f k2 **Arum-t** ptk1 aur k* bamb-a stb2.de• **Bar-c** k* bar-s k2 bell bry **Calc** k* **Calc-s** k* canth *Carb-v* k* **Carbn-s** *Caust* *Cham* k* *Chin* ptk1 chrysar br1 clem colch dros **Graph** k* *Hep* k* hydr **Ign** ptk1 iod kali-ar kali-c *Kali-chl* kali-m k2 kali-s kreos mrr1 laur **Lyc** k* **Merc** k* *Merc-c* k* **Nat-m** nat-p **Nit-ac** k* *Olnd* k* par **Petr** k* ph-ac phos psor k2* puls k* **Rhus-t** k* ruta k* sabin c1 sanic c2 sars **Sep** k* sul-i k2 **Sulph** k* viol-t

- **acrid** discharges; from: sulph tl1
- **mechanical**: arist-cl sp1
- **menses**; before: kali-c bg2 sep bg2
- **scratching**; after: agar b2.de* am-c b2.de* anac bg2 ang b2.de* ant-c b2.de* am b2.de* bar-c b2.de* calc b2.de* caust b2.de* chin b2.de* dros b2.de* **Graph** b2.de* hep b2.de* kali-c b2.de* kreos b2.de* *Lach* b2.de* *Lyc* b2.de* mang b2.de* merc b2.de* *Olnd* b2.de* **Petr** b2.de* phos b2.de* plb b2.de* **Psor** bg2 puls b2.de* rhus-t b2.de* ruta b2.de* sabin b2.de* sel bg2 *Sep* b2.de* sil b2.de* squil b2.de* sul-ac b2.de* sulph b2.de*
  - • **must** scratch it raw: *(↗Itching - scratching - agg. - raw)* agar *Alum* am-c ant-c arg-met k2 arn *Bar-c* bov calc calc-sil k2 *Carbn-s* caust chin dros **Graph** hep kali-c kali-sil k2 kreos *Lach* *Lyc* mang merc *Olnd* **Petr** phos plb psor k2* puls rhus-t ruta sabin *Sep* sil squil sul-ac *Sulph* tarax h1 *Til*
- **sensation** as if excoriated: canth rb2
  - • **touch** agg.: ferr rb2
- **urine**; from (See URINE - Acrid)

○ - **Folds** of skin: carb-v hr1 merc hs2 sulph mtf33

EXCRESCENCES: *(↗Warts)* *Ant-c* k* ant-t *Arg-n* hr1 ars aur aur-s k2 bell k* **Calc** k* calc-sil k2 *Carb-an* *Carb-v* *Carbn-s* carc gk6* **Caust** k* clem cocc *Fl-ac* **Graph** k* *Hep* iod lach **Lyc** med br1* merc-n c2 nat-m k* **Nit-ac** k* nux-v petr b4a.de ph-ac k* phos plb puls ran-b k* rhus-t sabin *Sil* k* sinus rly4• **Staph** k* sul-ac b4a.de sul-i k2 *Sulph* k* **Thuj** k*

- **benign**: med jl2
- **condylomata**: *(↗Warts)* acet-ac alumn anac ant-c ptk1 ant-t k* *Apis* k* arg-n ars ptk1 *Aur* k* *Aur-m* k* aur-m-n bar-c ptk1 bell bg2 benz-ac bry bg2 *Calc* k* *Carb-an* ptk1 caust k* cham k* *Cinnb* k* clem ptk1 **Dulc** b4a.de* euph *Euphr* k* graph bg2 *Hep* k* iod bg2 *Kali-chl* *Kali-i* k* lac-c **Lach** bg2* *Lyc* k* m-aust b2.de* **Med** k* *Merc* k* **Merc-c** k* merc-d c2 merc-n c1* mez bg2 nat-c ptk1 **Nat-s** k* **Nit-ac** k* nux-v bg2 petr ptk1 **Ph-ac** k* *Phos* k* phyt k* pic-ac c2 plat-m c2 psor k* ran-b ptk1 rhus-t bg2* *Sabin* k* sang ptk1 sanic c2 *Sars* k* sec bg2 sel bg2 *Sep* k* sil bg2* *Staph* k* *Sulph* k* *Teucr* **Thuj** k*
  - • **bleeding**: *Cinnb* k* *Med* **Nit-ac** k* phos ptk1 sulph **Thuj**
  - • **broad**: nit-ac *Thuj*
  - • **burning**: apis *Cinnb* *Nit-ac* ph-ac sabin k* *Thuj*
    - ⁝ **itching**: *Sabin* b7a.de
  - • **dry**: lyc merc merc-c nit-ac sars *Staph* k* sulph thuj
  - • **fan**-shaped: *Cinnb* k* sulph *Thuj*
  - • **flat**: acet-ac
  - • **horny**: *(↗horny)* thuj
  - • **inflamed**: plut-n srj7•

- **condylomata**: ...
  - **itching**: lyc med gk psor *Sabin* k* sep sne staph thuj
  - **moist**: *Apis* caust euphr med merc merc-c **Nit-ac** psor sabin staph sulph **Thuj**
  - **offensive**: calc hep med *Nit-ac* thuj
  - **pediculated**: caust lyc med jl2 nit-ac ph-ac *Staph* hr1 thuj
  - **rapid** growing: *Thuj*
  - **sensitive**: staph k2
  - **sticking** pain: **Nit-ac**
  - **stubborn**: merc mtf11
  - **suppressed**: med gk merc k2* nit-ac k2* staph k2* *Thuj* k2*
  - **suppurating**: *Thuj*
  - **syphilitic**: aur aur-m aur-m-n *Cinnb* cory br1 kali-i *Merc* **Nit-ac** staph *Thuj*
- **conical**: *(↗Warts - conical)* ant-c ptk1 ant-t ptk1 *Ars* ptk1 hydr ptk1 puls ptk1 *Sil* ptk1 syph ptk1
- **epithelioma**: abr br1 ferr-pic br1 mag-s sp1 scroph-n br1
- **fibromatous**: calc-ar bro1 calc-s tl1 *Con* bro1 *Iod* bro1 kali-br bro1 lyc bro1 sec bro1 thuj bro1
  - **bleeding**: vario jl2
- **fleshy**: ars calc ptk1 merc ptk1 nat-s mtf33 nit-ac ptk1 *Staph* k* *Thuj* k*
- **fungus** (= cauliflower): alum bg2 **Ant-c** k* ant-t bg2 *Ars* k* aur bg2 bell bg2 calc bg2 **Carb-an** b4a.de* carb-v bg2 caust b4a.de* cham bg2 clem k* *Con* k* dulc b4a.de graph bg2 hep bg2 iod k* *Kreos* k* lac-c **Lach** k* lyc bg2 manc bro1 merc bg2 mez bg2 *Nit-ac* k* nux-v bg2 petr k* ph-ac bg2 phos k* rhus-t k* sabin k* sang *Sep* bg2 **Sil** k* *Staph* k* sulph k* **Thuj** k*
  - **medullary**: bell k* *Carb-an* k* *Phos* k* sil k* sulph k* *Thuj* k*
  - **syphilitic**: *Ars* **Ars-i** aur aur-m aur-m-n cory br1 *Iod* **Lach** *Manc* **Merc** **Merc-c** **Nit-ac** **Sil** staph thuj
- **fungus** haematodes: *(↗CHEST - Cancer - clavicles - fungus; EXTREMITIES - Fungus; GENERALS - Tumors - angioma)* abrot mtf33 ant-c ptk1 ant-t k* **Ars** k* aur ptk1 bar-c ptk1 bell k* calc k* **Carb-an** k* *Carb-v* k* *Caust* ptk1 clem k* *Dulc* ptk1 hydr sne *Kreos* k* *Lach* k* **Lyc** k ●* manc bro1 med ptk1 *Merc* k* merc-c ptk1 nat-c ptk1 *Nat-m* *Nat-s* ptk1 *Nit-ac* k* nux-v k* petr ptk1 *Ph-ac* ptk1 **Phos** k* phyt ptk1 plan sne ran-b ptk1 *Rhus-t* k* *Sabin* ptk1 sang ptk1 sep k* **Sil** k* staph k* **Sul-ac** b4a.de *Sulph* k* **Thuj** k*
- **hard**: ant-c b7a.de ran-b b7a.de*
- **horny**: *(↗condylomata - horny; Eruptions - crusty - horny; Eruptions - horny; Indurations - horny; Warts - horny; EXTREMITIES - Callosities - horny; EXTREMITIES - Corns - feet - soles - horny; EXTREMITIES - Corns - horny; EXTREMITIES - Excrescences - horny; EXTREMITIES - Warts - fingers - first - horny; EXTREMITIES - Warts - hand - horny)* **Ant-c** k* mez *Ran-b* k* ruta fd4.de sep sil ptk1 sulph k* thuj
- **humid**: merc-c *Nit-ac* psor *Sabin* staph sulph **Thuj**
- **malignant**: nat-cac ptk2
- **painful**: staph mrr1
- **pedunculated**: lyc bg2* *Nit-ac* ptk1 *Sabin* ptk1 staph ptk1 thuj ptk1
- **red**: **Nat-s** k* thuj
- **sensitive**: staph ptk1*
- **smooth**: nat-s mtf33 sars bg2 sulph bg2 *Thuj*
- **swelling**, inflamed, puffy bunches: ars k* carb-an k* graph bg2 hep k* *Nat-c* k* *Phos* k* *Sil* k* sulph k*
- **syphilitic**: ars-br br1

EXPULSION: | **splinters**; of: *(↗GENERALS - Abscesses - foreign)* anac bro1* anag br1* hep bro1 sil bro1*

FATTY DEGENERATION of the muscles: lac-d k2

FECES passed through skin; itching as if: graph hr1*

FESTERING; as if something was: bufo ptk2

FILTHY skin (See Dirty)

FISSURES (See Cracks)

FLABBINESS: abrot br1* agar k* ang b2.de* ant-t k* *Apis* ars bro1 aster bro1 bar-c bro1 borx k* **Calc** k* *Camph* *Caps* k* cham k* chel bro1 *Chin* k* *Cist* mrr1 *Clem* k* *Cocc* k* con k* cory br1 croc k* *Cupr* k* dig k* euph k* *Ferr* k* graph k* hell k* *Hep* bro1 *Hyos* k* iod k* ip k* *Lach* k* *Lyc* k* mag-c k* merc k* morph bro1 nat-c k* nat-m bro1 op bro1 puls k* rheum k* sabad k* salv bro1

Flabbiness: ... sanic bro1 sars k2* sec k* seneg k* sil k* *Spong* k* sul-ac k* sulph k* thyr bro1 *Verat* k*

FOREIGN BODIES or grains of sand were under the skin; sensation as if small: coca mrr1 **Cocain** k*

FORMICATION: *(↗FACE - Formication)* *Acon* k* acon-f k* aesc *Agar* k* agn k* all-s k* *Alum* k* alum-p k2 alum-sil k2 am-c k* ambr bro1 anac anh sp1 ap-g bro1 apis *Aran* arg-met k* *Ars* k* *Ars-i* ars-s-f k2 arund k* asaf b7.de aur k* aur-ar k2 aur-s k2 *Bar-c* k* bar-m bar-s k2 bell k* borx k* both fne1• bov k* bry bg2 bufo k* buth-a sp1 cadm-s k2 calad calc k* calc-p k* calc-s calc-sil k2 calen bro1 cann-i k* cann-s k* canth caps k* carb-v k* *Carbn-s* caust k* cham chel k* chin k* *Chinin-ar* cina b7.de cist **Coca** mrr1 *Cocain* bro1 *Cocc* cod bro1 colch b7.de con k* croc k* *Crot-c* dulc k* *Ferr* ferr-p fl-ac bg2 germ-met srj5• hip-ac sp1 hist sp1 *Hyper* k* ign b7.de* *Iod* kali-c k* kali-m k2 kali-p fd1.de• kali-s *Kalm* bg2 lach k* lat-h thj1 lat-m sp1 *Laur* k* led k* **Lyc** k* m-ambo b7.de m-arct b7.de m-aust b2.de* mag-c k* *Mag-m* k* mang k* *Med* medus bro1 mentho br1 merc k* merc-c k* *Mez* k* *Morph* bro1 mur-ac k* nat-ar *Nat-c* k* *Nat-m* nat-p nat-sil fd3.de• nit-ac k* *Nux-v* k* *Olnd* k* onos op bg2 osm bg1 pall sne *Par* b7.de* **Ph-ac** k* *Phos* k* *Pic-ac* k* *Plat* k* plb k* podo fd3.de• psor k2 *Puls* pycnop-sa mrz1 *Ran-b* k* ran-s k* **Rhod** k* **Rhus-t** k* rumx bro1 *Sabad* k* **Sec** k* sel b7.de* *Sil* k* spig k* spong k* *Staph* k* stram b7.de* *Sul-ac* bro1 sul-i k2 **Sulph** k* tab k* tarax b2.de* **Tarent** k* thuj k* tritic-vg fd5.de tub k2 *Urt-u* k* valer bro1 *Viol-t* k* *Visc* bg2 *Zinc* k* zinc-p k2

- **morning**: ferr k* mag-c k* staph h1*
- **forenoon**: mag-c k* sars k*
- **evening**: gent-c k* mag-c k* nat-sil fd3.de• **Sulph** k*
  - **lying** agg.: *Cist* ph-ac h2
  - **undressing**; when: sil h2
- **night**: arge-pl rwt5• bar-c k* *Cist* dulc a1 mag-m k* nat-sil fd3.de• sulph
  - **chill**; during: gamb
  - **lying** down agg.; after: *Cist* ph-ac
  - **waking**; on: bar-c h2 carb-v
- **bad** news; after: calc-p ptk1*
- **chill**; during: gamb samb b7.de*
- **emission**; after: ph-ac
- **erection**; during: tarent
- **fever**; during: **Croc** b7.de* plat bg2 *Puls* bg2 rhus-t bg2 sep bg2 spig bg2 sulph bg2 thuj bg2
- **fleas**; as if from: gent-c rb2 nat-c rb2 nicc rb2 pall rb2* podo fd3.de• ptel rb2 pulx rb2 spong rb2
  - **bag** full of fleas; he were in a: ars rb2
- **flies**; as if from: calad rb2 cench rb2 cod rb2 galla-q-r nl2• gymno rb2* laur rb2
- **frostbite**; after: colch b7.de
- **grains**; as from (See Foreign)
- **house**; on entering: phos
- **insects**; as if from: arund rb2 calad ptk1 carb-an ptk1 dulc rb2* helo rb2 lac-c rb2* led tl1 mez rb2* myric ptk1 nat-c rb2* oena ptk1 osm ptk1 ph-ac rb2* pic-ac ptk1 sec rb2 stram ptk1 tab rb2* tarent rb2*
  - **rapidly**; crawling: dulc rb2
  - ○ **Shoulders**, neck and hands; on: lac-c rb2
- **itching**; with: buth-a sp1 cina a1 **Colch** bg1 pall sne podo fd3.de•
- **lice**; as if from: lat-h thj1 led rb2
- **mouse** were crawling under the skin; as if a: ign rb2 sec rb2
- **mucous** membranes: anh sp1
- **nervous**: astac ptk1*
- **numbness**; with: euphr
- **perspiration**; during: apis bg2 am bg2 **Ars** bg2 *Cocc* bg2 colch bg2 *Croc* bg2 *Nux-v* bg2 plat bg2 *Puls* bg2 rhod k* **Rhus-t** bg2 sel bg2 *Sep* bg2 spig bg2 sulph bg2 *Tarax* bg2 thuj bg2
- **rubbing** | **amel.**: sec ptk1 zinc
- **sand**; as from (See Foreign)
- **scratching**:
  - **after**: acon bg2 bar-c bg2 caust bg2 colch bg2 kali-c bg2 plat bg2 puls bg2 rhus-t bg2 sabad bg2 sulph bg2
  - **agg.**: dulc k*
  - **amel.**: cina a1 croc k* zinc
- **sexual** excitement; during: mez tarent
- **shivering**; during: nux-v b7.de

- **spider**; as if from a: dulc rb2 visc c1*
- **warmth** | **amel.**: acon
- **worms** boring and crawling on body; as if (See Worms - boring)

▽ - **extending** upwards; beginning at feet and nat-m

○ - **Hair**: ph-ac k2

- **Paralyzed** parts; in: cadm-s ptk1 *Phos* k* plb
- **Under** the skin: cadm-s ptk1 calc ptk1 cocain ptk1 phos ptk1 **Sec** ptk1 tub jl2 zinc ptk1

FRECKLES: adren c2 *Am-c* k* *Ant-c* k* ant-t k* bad bro1 bry k* *Calc* k* carb-v k* carc mlr1• con k* dros k* *Dulc* k* *Ferr* *Graph* k* hyos k* iod k* iris-g c2 kali-c k* lach k* laur k* **LYC** k ●* merc k* mez k* *Mur-ac* k* *Nat-c* k* nat-p *Nit-ac* k* nux-m k* petr k* **PHOS** k ●* plb k* psor al2 *Puls* k* sec **Sep** k ●* sil k* sol c2 stann k* sul-i k2 **Sulph** k ●* tab c2* thuj k*

- **burning**: am-c mtf11
- **dark**: nit-ac h2*
- **itching**: am-c mtf11
- **sun** agg.; in: mur-ac ptk1

FUNGUS HAEMATODES (See Excrescences - fungus haematodes)

GANGLIA: *(↗EXTREMITIES - Ganglion; GENERALS - Tumors - ganglion)* am-c k* apis ptk1 arn k* aur-m benz-ac ptk1 *Carb-v* k* carc mlr1• *Nat-m* ptk1 ph-ac *Phos* k* plb rhus-t *Ruta* k* sil k* *Stict* ptk1 sulph k* zinc

GANGRENE: *(↗GENERALS - Circulation; GENERALS - Inflammation - gangrenous)* acet-ac hr1 aesc hl9 *Agar* ail bro1 alco a1 alum am-c gsy1 ant-c k* *Anthraci* k* apis k* **Ars** k* *Asaf* bell bg3* bism hr1 both bro1 both-a rb3 brass bro1 brom bro1 calc calen bro1 *Canth* k* carb-ac bro1 carb-an bro1 *Carb-v* k* **Caust** chin bg3* chlor br1* chr-o bro1 cist ptk1 crot-h ptk1 crot-t bro1 cupr-ar bro1 cycl echi br1* euph k* euph-l br1 euph-re mtf ferr-p bro1 kali-chl bro1 kali-p br1* *Kreos* k* lach k* loxo-recl bnm1• mag-c merc k2 mur-ac ptk1 ph-ac plb bg3* *Polyg-pe* bro1 ran-a bro1 *Rhus-t* ruta sal-ac bro1 sars k2 **Sec** k* sil bg3* solid ptk1 *Stram* sul-ac k2* tarent-c bro1* vip ptk1

- **accompanied** by | **diabetes** (See GENERALS - Diabetes mellitus - accompanied - gangrene)
- **cold**: ant-t k* apis bg2 **Ars** k* *Asaf* k* bell k* brom bg2 *Canth* caps *Carb-v* k* con k* crot-h k* *Euph* k* iod bg2 kreos bg2 *Lach* k* merc k* *Merc-c* bg2 **Plb** k* ran-b k* **Sec** k* *Sil* k* *Squil* k* sul-ac k* sulph k* tarent-c
- **dry**: ant-c ptk1 sec ptk1
- **hot**: acon k* ant-t ars k* bell k* mur-ac k* op bg2 *Sabin* k* *Sec* k*
- **injuries**; after: arn bro1* ars k2 lach bro1* sec ptk1 sul-ac br1*
- **moist**: *Bell* b7a.de brom bg2 *Carb-v* k* **Chin** k* *Hell* k* ph-ac phos bg3* *Squil* tarent *Vip* bg2
- **old** people; in: all-c bro1* am-c bro1 ars bro1 *Carb-v* k* euph ptk1 euph-re mtf ph-ac ptk1 sars k2 **Sec** k* sul-ac bro1*
- **red** streaks following course of lymphatics: pyrog tl1
- **spots**: crot-h cycl k* *Hyos* k* loxo-lae bnm12• sec k*

GNAWING (See Pain - gnawing)

GOOSE FLESH: *(↗CHILL - Creeping; EXTREMITIES - Goose)* *Acon* k* aesc aeth agar *Ang* k* ant-t k* anth c1 arg-n *Ars* k* asar k* aur k* bar-c k* bar-m *Bell* k* berb borx k* bov *Bry* k* bufo ptk1* *Calc* calc-sil k2 calen vml3• *Camph* k* *Cann-s* k* canth k* carb-an cardios-h rly4• *Caust* k* chel k* *Chin* k* chinin-ar k* chlor chord-umb rly4• *Croc* k* crot-t cypra-eg sde6.de• fum rly1*• gels hr1 ham fd3.de• **Hell** k* ign k* kali-i k* kali-p fd1.de• *Lach* bg1* lachn c1 lat-m bnm6• laur k* *Led* k* *Lyc* mag-m mang k* merc merl mez k* mur-ac k* nat-c bg2 *Nat-m* k* *Nat-s* nit-ac **Nux-v** k* ozone sde2• *Par* k* *Phos* k* plac rzf5• plat ran-b b2.de* rhod b2.de* ruta k* *Sabad* k* sabin k* sars k* *Sil* sphing k* spig k* stann k* staph k* streptoc rly4• sul-ac k* symph fd3.de• tab tarent *Thuj* k* vanil fd5.de **Verat** k* [bell-p-sp dcm1]

- **morning**: chinin-s mang sep h2*
- **evening**: mang h2* vanil fd5.de
- **accompanied** by:
  - **epistaxis** (See NOSE - Epistaxis - accompanied - goose)
  - **weakness** | **Cervical** region (See BACK - Weakness - cervical - accompanied - goose)
- **air** agg.; in open: *Acon* bg2 aeth a1 agar caust k* chin sars k* staph bg2 sulph bg2
- **chill**; during: asar bg2 canth bg2 hell bg2 nux-v bg2 ozone sde2• sabad bg2 sec bg2
- **drinking** agg.; after: cadm-s k* *Chin* verat h1*

Goose flesh: ...

- **eating**; while: mag-m
- **fever**; during | **sensation** of goose flesh: crot-t rb2
- **house**; in: calc
- **news**; when seeing or hearing the: ozone sde2•
- **room** agg.: *Calc* b4.de*
- **shivering**; with: ang b7.de* aur bg2 bar-c bg2 *Camph* bg2 *Cann-s* b7.de* *Caust* bg2 chin b7.de* ign b7.de* laur b7.de* led bg2 mez bg2 *Sabad* b7.de* sabin b7.de* sars bg2 stann bg2 staph b7.de* sul-ac bg2 thuj bg2 verat b7.de*
- **stool** agg.; after: grat
- **sudden** chill with hair standing on end: bar-c dulc
- **swallowing** agg.: opun-s a1
- **walking** agg.: lyc
- **warm** room; in: adam srj5• mez

GRASPED TOGETHER; as if: acon bg1 ther bg1

GREASY: agar b2.de* aur b2.de* bar-c bg2 *Bry* b2.de* bufo bg2 calc b2.de* *Chin* b2.de* mag-c b2.de* *Merc* b2.de* musca-d szs1 *Nat-m* b2.de* plb b2.de* psor bg2 sel b2.de* stram b2.de* sulph bg2 thuj bg2

HAIR: *(↗GENERALS - Hair)*

- **end**; stands on: irid-met srj5• lat-m bnm6•
- **falling** out: *(↗BACK - Hair - falling; BACK - Hair - falling - cervical; CHEST - Hair - falling; FEMALE - Hair; HEAD - Hair - falling; MALE GENITALIA/SEX - Hair; SKIN)* *Alum* k* ars k* bac jl2 *Calc* k* carb-an *Carb-v* k* *Graph* k* hell k* hist mtf11 kali-c k* lach lat-m sp1 *Nat-m* k* op k* ph-ac mrr1 phos k* pitu-p sp1 prot jl2 sabin k* *Sec* k* *Sel* k* streptoc jl2 sulph k* syph jl2 thal st thuj mtf33 tub al
  - **perspiration**; during: lat-m sp1
  - **spots**; in: *Carb-v* b4a.de *Graph* b4a.de
- **gray**; becomes: phos kl sep kl
  - **early**: syph jl2
- **growth** of hair; excessive: carb-v lmj carc lmj cortiso sp1 med bg3* nat-m lmj puls lmj rauw sp1 **Sep** lmj sulph lmj thuj bg3* thyr ptk1
  - **children**; in: carb-v lmj carc lmj nat-m lmj puls lmj **Sep** lmj sulph lmj *Thuj* lmj*
  - **fine** hairs: tub mtf33
- **tearing** out her/his hair (See MIND - Pulling - hair)

○ - **Unusual** parts; on: carc mlr1• lyc bg2 med bg3 thuj k* thyr bg2*

HARD: am-c b2.de* anag br1 *Ant-c* b2.de* *Ant-t* ptk1 arg-n bg2* ars b2.de* bov b2.de* calc-f ptk1 chin b2.de* choc srj3• cic b2.de* cist ptk1 clem b2.de* cortiso tpw7 dulc b2.de* graph b2.de* kali-c b2.de* lach b2.de* led b2.de* lyc b2.de* par b2.de* petr ptk1 phos b2.de* *Ran-b* b2.de* *Rhus-t* b2.de* sars ptk1 *Sep* b2.de* sil b2.de* squil b2.de* *Sulph* b2.de* syph jl2 thuj b2.de* tub mtf33 verat b2.de*

- **accompanied** by | **nails**; distorted: med jl2
- **callosities**, like: am-c k* *Ant-c* k* bar-c bg2 borx k* *Dulc* dys fmm1• elae bro1 *Ferr-pic* bro1 fl-ac k2 **Graph** k* hydr bro1 lach k* led lyc k* morg fmm1• *Nit-ac* bro1 petr bro1 rad-br c11 *Ran-b* k* *Rhus-t* k* sal-ac bro1 sars bro1 sec gk **Sep** k* *Sil* k* sulph k* thuj k*
  - **cracks**; with deep: cist ptk1 graph ptk1
  - **hang** down agg.; letting limbs: ran-s ptk1*
  - **pressure**; from slight: ant-c ptk1*
  - **soft**: *Sil* ptk1
- **desquamating**: am-c k* ant-c k* borx k* dulc *Graph* k* *Lach* ran-b k* *Rhus-t* *Sep* k* *Sil* k* sulph k*
- **leather**, like: parth vml3•
- **parchment**; like: acon aeth anac ptk1 **Ars** k* **Bar-c** ptk1 calc-f ptk1 camph *Chin* k* cop crot-h dig dulc k* kali-c k* led k* *Lith-c* *Lyc* k* mag-c br1 op kl petr ptk1 phos k* rhus-t *Sars* *Sep* mrr1 *Sil* k* squil k* sulph ptk1
  - **fever**; during: *Ars* bg2 chin bg2 **Ip** b7a.de* lyc bg2 sil bg2
- **thickening**; with (See Thick)

HEAT:

- **accompanied** by | **coldness** (See GENERALS - Heat - lack - accompanied - skin)
- **coma**; with (See MIND - Coma - skin - heat)
- **fever**; with: acon bro1 cub c1
- **fever**; without: acon bg2* aeth a1 all-c br1 aloe k* apis ptk1 apoc k2 arn ars k* bell k* borx bry k* caust bg2 chin cocc k* coloc dig c1 dulc ephe-si hsj1• fl-ac bg2* gels c1 glon k2 *Graph* k* haliae-lc srj5• hep hyos iod k* kali-bi k* *Lach* k*

- **fever**; without: ...
lat-h bnm5• lavand-a ctl1• lyc h2* mag-c malar jl2 medus br1 mez k2 mur-ac nit-ac h2* nux-v petr k2 phos k* plut-n srj7• pop br1 prot fmm1• ptel tl1 puls *Rad-br* ptk1 rhus-t k* sang sec k2 sep sil k* stram bg2* sulph k* *Ter* ptk1 tril-p c1 tub jl2 *Ust* ptk1 vac jl2 vario jl2
  - **night**: fl-ac **Graph** nat-m sel rsj9•
  - **coition**; after: *Graph*
  - **dinner**; during nausea, after: ptel hr1
  - **exertion** agg.: calc nat-m
  - **moist**; and: visc c1
  - **scratching**; after: spong sulph
  - **spots**: bry b7.de rhus-t b7.de
  - **waking**; on: fl-ac nat-m puls *Sil*
- **scratching**; after: spong b7a.de
- **sensation** of: agath-a nl2• hyos b7.de suprar rly4•
- **tingling** over whole body; feverish: cub c1
- **water** seems hot; warm: olib-sac wmh1

○ - **Small** areas; in: cadm-met sp1
- **Under** skin: ter ptk1

HIDEBOUND; sensation as if (See Adherent - bone)

HOT (See Heat - fever; without)

HYPERESTHESIA (See Decubitus; Sensitiveness)

ICE:
- **ice**-cold needles; or sensation of: *Agar* k* *Ars*
- **water** on skin: acon bg3

ICHTHYOSIS (See Eruptions - scaly; Eruptions - scaly - ichthyosis)

IMPRESSIONS: | **deep**; instruments leave: (↗*Indented*) apis bg2 ars bg2 *Bov* b2.de* phos bg2 verat b2.de

INACTIVITY: (↗*Dry - perspire)* alum k* ambr k* **Anac** k* ang b2.de* ant-c k* ant-t k* *Ars* k* ars-i ars-s-f k2 bell k* *Bry* k* *Calc* k* camph k* carb-an k* carb-v k* caust k* cham k* chin k* cocc k* **Con** k* cycl k* dig k* *Dulc* k* graph k* hell k* hep k* iod k* *Ip* k* **Kali-c** k* **Kali-p** k* kali-s lach k* *Laur* k* led k* **Lyc** k* merc k* mur-ac k* *Nat-c* k* nat-m k* *Nat-p* *Nit-ac* k* nux-v k* *Olnd* k* op k* petr k* **Ph-ac** k* phos k* plat k* plb k* *Psor* puls k* rhod k* rhus-t k* ruta k* sabin k* sars k* *Sec* k* sep k* *Sil* k* spong k* squil k* staph k* stram k* sul-i k2 *Sulph* k* thuj k* verat k* zinc k*

INDENTED easily from pressure: (↗*Impressions - deep)* apis ptk1 ars k* **Bov** k* **Bry** caps ptk1 phos ptk1 verat k*

INDURATIONS, nodules, etc.: aeth hr1 *Agar* k* ail bg2 alum bg2* alumn k2 am-c k* am-m bg2 anac b4.de* **Ant-c** k* *Ant-t* bg2 antho bg2 *Apis* b7a.de arg-met ptk1 arg-n ars k* *Ars-i* ars-s-f k2 aur k* *Bar-c* k* bell bg2 berb bg2 borx k* bov b2.de* brom bg2 *Bry* b7.de* bufo **Calc** k* calc-sil k2 cann-s bg2 canth bg2 caps bg2 *Carb-an* k* carb-v b4a.de* carbn-s k2 *Caul* bg2* caust k* *Chel* k* chin k* chlol bg2 cic k* cinnb ptk1 *Clem* k* cocc bg2 **Con** k* crot-h bg2 crot-t bg2 dig bg2 dros bg2 *Dulc* k* euph bg2 *Graph* k* guaj ptk1 hell b7.de* *Hep* b4a.de* hydr bg2 ign b7.de* *Iod* k* ip bg2 iris bg2 *Kali-bi* bg2 kali-br bg2 *Kali-c* k* kali-i bg2* kali-n bg2 kali-s bg2* kali-sil k2 kreos b7a.de* lach k* *Led* k* loxo-recl bnm10• **Lyc** k* mag-c bg2* mag-m bg2 maland jl2 *Mang* k* *Merc* k* merc-i-f bg2 merc-i-r bg2 mez bg2* *Mur-ac* k* nat-c bg2 *Nat-m* bg2 nat-s bg2 nit-ac bg2 nux-v bg2 olnd bg2 op bg2 par k* petr b4.de* ph-ac b4.de* **Phos** k* phyt bg2 psor k2 **Puls** b7.de* *Ran-b* k* **Rhod** bg2* **Rhus-t** k* *Ruta* b7.de* sabin b7.de* sars k* *Sec* b7.de* sel b7.de* **Sep** k* **Sil** k* spig bg2 spong bg2 squil k* stann bg2 *Staph* k* stram b7.de* sul-ac b4.de* **Sulph** k* tarax bg2 ther ptk1 *Thuj* k* tritic-vg fd5.de tub c1 urt-u bg2 valer bg2 verat k* verb b7.de* viol-t bg2 zinc bg2 zinc-s bg2
- **bathing**; after: cortiso sp1
- **bluish**: *Mang* mur-ac
  - **spots**: *Phos* *Sars* k*
- **burning**: *Hep* k*
  - **scratching** agg.; after: staph h1
- **chagrin**; after (See mortification)
- **children**; in: | **newborn**: camph tl1
- **hard**: kali-i ptk1 mag-c ptk1 nat-s ptk1 sil ptk1
- **horny**: (↗*Excrescences - horny)* *Ant-c* graph tritic-vg fd5.de x-ray sp1
- **itching**: staph h1

Indurations, nodules: ...
- **moist** after scratching: staph h1
- **mortification**; after: *Coloc* vh
- **painful**: phyt ptk1
- **purple**: lach k2 sep k2
- **red**: med ptk1 sabad toxo-g jl2
  - **hard** and tender: petr k*
- **rheumatic**: bacls-7 fmm1•
- **scratching**; after: cortiso sp1 kali-c h2
- **sensitive**: staph k2
- **stitching**: caust h2
- **warm** applications agg.: cortiso sp1
- **white** nodules: agar bg2
  - **scratching**; after: agar b2.de* *Ars* b2.de* bov b2.de* bry b2.de* crot-h bg2 ip b2.de* sulph b2.de*

○ - **Under** skin: alum ptk1 kali-ar ptk1 mag-c ptk1

INELASTICITY: am-caust a1 ant-c k* apis bg2 ars k* *Bov* k* bufo bg2 caps ptk1 *Cupr* k* dulc k* kalm dp• lach k* morph a1 phos bg2* ran-b k* *Rhus-t* k* sep k* verat k*

INFLAMMATION (= dermatitis): *Acon* k* agn k* alum k* *Anac* ant-c k* *Apis* k* arist-cl sp1 *Arn* k* *Ars* k* ars-s-f k2 ars-s-r bro1 *Asaf* k* *Aur* bad bar-c k* *Bar-m* bell k* bell-p tl1* beryl sp1 borx k* bov bro1 bry k* bufo gk *Calc* k* camph k* cann-s k* canth k* caust k* **Cham** k* chin bro1 chir-fl bnm4• chlol cina k* cocc k* colch k* com con k* cortico sp1 croc k* crot-h crot-t br1* *Dulc* euph k* falco-pe nl2• *Gels* k* graph k* **Hep** k* hyos k* *Kali-s* kreos k* lach k* loxo-lae bnm12• lyc k* m-arct b2.de* manc br1 mand sp1 mang k* **Merc** k* mez k* moni jl2 myris br1 nat-c k* nat-m k* *Nit-ac* k* ped bro1 petr k* ph-ac k2 phos k* physala-p bnm7• *Plb* k* plb-i bro1 positr nl2• prot fmm1• psor bro1* **Puls** k* ran-b k* **Rhus-t** k* ruta k* *Sec* bro1 sedi bro1 sep k* **Sil** k* spiros-af oss• *Staph* k* *Sulph* k* tarent-c k* verat k* x-ray sp1 zinc k*
- **antibiotics**; after: moni jl2
- **chronic**: sil mrr1
- **desquamation**; with: cortico sp1
  - **newborn**; in: viol-t mtf11
- **detergent** | **agg.**: syc fmm1•
- **excitement** agg.: syc fmm1•
- **exfoliative** (See desquamation)
- **fibrinous**: streptoc jl2
- **flour** | **agg.**: syc fmm1•
- **inclination** to: alum k* ars k* *Asaf* k* *Bar-c* k* bell k* *Borx* k* *Brom* b4a.de calc k* camph k* canth k* **Cham** k* chel k* con k* croc k* euph k* graph k* *Hep* k* hyos k* lach k* mang k* *Merc* k* merc-c b4a.de nat-c k* nat-m k* *Nit-ac* k* *Petr* k* plb k* positr nl2• *Puls* k* ran-b k* **Sil** k* staph k* *Sulph* k*
- **itching**: syc fmm1•
  - **night**: syc fmm1•
  - **warmth** agg. | **heat** agg.: syc fmm1•
- **malignant**: com c2*
- **painful**: *Phos* b4a.de
- **superficial**: lyc b4a.de mang b4a.de *Merc* b4a.de sulph b4a.de

○ - **Epidermis**: morb jl2

INJURIES agg.; slight: alum ptk1

INTERTRIGO: (↗*Excoriation)* acon k* *Aeth* bro1 agn bro1 *Am-c* *Ambr* ant-t hr1 arist-cl sp1 arn ars k* *Bar-c* bell hr1* *Borx* k* calc k* *Calc-s* calc-sil k2 *Carb-v* k* **Caust** k* *Cham* k* *Chin* k* fago c2* **Graph** k* *Hep* *Hydr* *Ign* k* jug-r bro1 kali-ar kali-br bro1 *Kali-c* kali-chl kali-m k2 kali-s k2 kali-sil k2 **Kreos** *Lyc* k* *Mang* *Merc* k* mez bro1 *Nat-m* nat-p c2 nat-s k2 *Nit-ac* nux-v ol-an olib-sac wmh1 olnd k* ox-ac bro1 *Petr* k* ph-ac phos *Phyt* plb psor bro1 puls k* rhus-t ruta sabin *Sep* k* *Sil* squil *Sul-ac* k* **Sulph** k* syph tub bro1 zinc-o mtf11
- **dentition**; during: caust alj* lyc bro1
- **infants**; in: acon bg2 *Borx* bg2 *Carb-v* bg2 caust bg2 cham bg2* graph bg2 ign bg2 lyc bg2 *Merc* bg2 puls bg2 sep bg2 sil bg2 sulph bg2

IRRITATION: rad-br ptk1

ITCHING: (↗*FACE - Itching)* abrot tl1 acon k* adam skp7*• aesc k2 **Agar** k* agath-a nl2• *Agn* k* aids nl2• ail aloe k* *Alum* k* alumn c2 *Am-c* k* am-m k* *Ambr* k* anac k* anac-oc bro1 anag k* *Anan* ang b2.de* *Ant-c* k* ant-t k* *Anthraci* anthraco br1 anthraq rly4• *Antip* bro1 ap-g vml3• **Apis** k* apoc vh1 *Arg-met* k* arge-pl rwt5• arist-cl sp1 arizon-l nl2• arn k* **Ars** k* *Ars-i* k* ars-s-f k2 arum-d c2 asaf k* asar k* *Astac* aur k* aur-m aur-m-n aur-s k2

Itching: ...
bamb-a stb2.de• *Bar-c* k* bar-m bar-ox-suc rly4• bell k* bell-p sp1 benzol pls1 beryl sp1 bism k* borx k* both fne1• **Bov** k* brass-n-o srj5• *Bry* k* bufo bg2 buth-a sp1 cadm-met tpw6* cadm-s br1 *Calad* k* *Calc* k* calc-f sp1 *Calc-p* k* calc-s calc-sil k2 camph k* cann-i k2 cann-s k* canth k* caps k* *Carb-ac* k* *Carb-an* k* **Carb-v** k* **Carbn-s** carl br1 carneg-g rwt1• cassia-s cdd7*• **Caust** k* cench k2 cham k* **Chel** k* chin k* *Chinin-ar* chion br1 chir-fl bnm4• **Chlol** k* choc srj3• chrysar bro1 *Cic* k* cina k* cinnb k* *Cist* k* *Clem* k* cob-n sp1 coc-c k* coca-c sk4• *Cocc* k* cod c2* coff k* coff-t a1 colch k* coli rly4• coll coloc k* com bg2 *Con* k* cop bg2* corian-s knl6• cortico sp1 cortiso sp1 croc k* *Crot-h* *Crot-t* k* *Cupr* k* cupr-ar *Cycl* k* cypra-eg sde6.de• cyt-l sp1 *Dig* k* dios k* *Dol* k* dream-p sdj1• dros k* *Dulc* k* elae bro1 elat hr1 euph k* euph-l br1 euphr k* eupi c2 *Fago* br1* falco-pe nl2• fic-m gya1 *Fl-ac* k* flor-p rsj3• form bg2* gal-ac a1* galla-q-r nl2• *Gamb* *Gels* k* ger-i rly4• germ-met srj5• glon br1* glycyr-g cte1• gran bro1 **Graph** k* grin bro1 guaj k* guan bro1 guat sp1 haliae-lc srj5• hell k* hep k* hist sp1 hom-xyz c2* *Hydrc* k* hyos k* hyper bro1 ichth bro1 ign k* ina-i mlk9.de indg k* iod k* *Ip* k* jug-c k* *Jug-r* *Kali-ar* k* *Kali-bi* k* kali-br k* *Kali-c* k* kali-n k* kali-p *Kali-s* kali-sil k2 *Kreos* k* lac-d k2 *Lach* k* lap-a c2* lap-la sde8.de• lat-h bnm5• lat-m bnm6• laur k* lavand-a ctl1• *Led* k* limest-b es1• loxo-lae bnm12• loxo-recl bnm10• **Lyc** k* m-ambo b2.de* m-arct b2.de* m-aust b2.de* **Mag-c** k* mag-m k* mag-s sp1 maland bro1* mang k* mang-act bro1 *Med* k* medul-os-si rly4• menis br1 menth c2 mentho br1* meny k* **Merc** k* merc-c b4a.de* merc-i-f k* **Mez** k* mim-p rsj8• *Moni* rfm1• morph br1* mosch k* mur-ac k* naphtin mtf11 *Nat-ar* *Nat-c* k* **Nat-m** k* nat-p k* *Nat-s* neon srj5• nicc bro1 nicotam rly4• *Nit-ac* k* *Nux-v* k* **Ol-an** k* *Olib-sac* wmh1 *Olnd* k* *Op* k* pall ptk1 par k* *Petr* k* petr-ra shn4• *Ph-ac* k* *Phos* k* physala-p bnm7• pic-ac bg2 pieri-b mlk9.de pin-con oss2• pitu-gl skp7• *Pix* bro1 plac-s rly4• *Plat* k* plb k* plut-n srj7• podo bg2 polys sk4• *Positr* nl2• prim-o bro1 prot fmm1• pseuts-m oss1• **Psor** k* ptel k* **Puls** k* pulx bro1 **Pycnop-sa** mrz1 rad-br c11* ran-b k* ran-s k* rheum k* rhod k* **Rhus-t** k* *Rhus-v* bro1 rumx k* *Ruta* k* *Sabad* k* sabin k* sal-ac sal-fr sle1• samb k* *Sanguis-s* hrn2• *Sars* k* sec k* sel k* seneg k* **Sep** k* **Sil** k* sphing kk3.fr spig k* **Spong** k* *Squil* k* stann k* **Staph** k* stram k* streptoc rly4• stront-c k* strych-g br1 suis-em rly4• suis-hep rly4• sul-ac k* sul-i k2* **Sulph** k* symph fd3.de• syzyg bro1 *Tab* k* tarax k* **Tarent** k* *Tarent-c* br1* tell k* teucr k* ther k2 thioc-ac rly4• *Thuj* k* *Til* k* tril-p c1 *Trios* rsj11• tritic-vg fd5.de **Tub** al2* **Urt-u** k* valer k* vanil fd5.de ven-m rsj12• verat k* *Vesp* k* viol-o k* *Viol-t* k* visc sp1 x-ray sp1 xero bro1 zinc k* zinc-p k2 [*Alumin-p* stj2 *Alumin-s* stj2 heroin sdj2 lac-mat sst4 sol-ecl cky1 spect dfg1 temp elm1]

- **right**: con h2*
- **daytime**: *Graph* b4a.de
- **morning**: am-c k* am-m b7a.de ant-c b7.de bov b4.de bry b7.de coloc b4.de cycl b7.de guat sp1 hell b7.de *Hep* b4.de* kali-c b4.de* kali-n b4a.de lach b7.de* m-arct b7.de mang b4.de nux-v b7.de petr b4.de puls b7.de *Rhus-t* k* ruta b7.de sars k* sep b4.de spong b7.de* staph k* stram sulph k*
  - **bed** agg.; in: *Calc* coloc petr *Rhus-t* spong sulph
  - **rising** | **after** | **agg.**: cimic a1 coloc b4.de *Hep* b4a.de mag-m h2* ruta b7.de sars b4.de
    - **agg.**: coloc h2* hep h2* *Rumx* ruta h1 *Sars*
  - **waking**; on: coloc b4.de* led h1 m-arct b7.de spong b7.de* stram sulph b4.de
- **forenoon**: cycl b7.de lach b7.de
  - **9** h: ven-m rsj12•
- **afternoon**: ant-c b7.de chel b7.de coloc b4.de laur b7.de rhus-t b7.de valer b7.de
- **evening**: *Agn* b7.de* alum k* am-m k* anac k* ang b7.de ant-c b7.de* apis arge-pl rwt5• ars b4.de* bar-c b4.de bov b4.de bry b7.de* cadm-met tpw6 calad calc b4a.de camph b7.de *Carb-an* k* carb-v k* *Caust* b4a.de chin b7.de cocc k* coloc k* *Con* k* cycl k* fl-ac k* hell b7.de *Ign* b7.de ip b7.de kali-c b4.de* kali-n b4.de* **Kreos** k* laur b7.de led b7.de lyc k* m-arct b7.de *M-aust* b7.de mag-m h2* *Merc* k* mez k* mur-ac k* *Nux-v* k* olnd k* op b7.de ph-ac b4.de plat b4.de plb b7.de *Puls* k* *Ran-b* b7.de *Ran-s* b7.de *Rhod* b4.de* **Rhus-t** b7.de* sabad b7.de sars k* sel k* seneg b4.de sep b4.de sil k* spong fd4.de stann b4a.de **Staph** b7.de symph fd3.de• tarax b7.de teucr b7.de thuj k* tritic-vg fd5.de zinc k*
  - **22** h: tell rsj10•
  - **amel.**: cact
  - **bed**:
    - **in** bed:
      - **agg.**: *Alum* anan vh ang h1 bar-c bell h1 calad calc h2 calc-s k2 camph h1 *Carb-an* carb-v chin c1 coloc con cycl kali-m k2 kali-n h2 lyc merc mez h2 mur-ac nat-c nux-v ph-ac h2 plat h2 *Puls* sars spong fd4.de sulph k2 tell thuj til tub c zinc

- **evening** – **bed** – **in** bed: ...
      - **amel.**: kali-c h2 sars h2
  - **tired**; when: tell rsj10•
- **night**: aids nl2• ail alum-p k2 am-c k* am-m k* ant-c b7.de* ap-g vh1* arg-n k* ars b4.de bar-c k* bar-s k2 berb k* bov bry b7.de cadm-s calad b7.de cann-s b7.de carb-v b4.de* **Carbn-s** card-m carneg-g rwt1• cassia-s ccrh1• *Caust* k* *Cham* b7.de* chin b7.de **Chlol** cina b7.de *Cist* *Clem* cocc k* con b4.de croc k* cycl hr1 dig b4.de *Dol* k* dulc b4.de* euphr k* fic-m gya1 gamb gels *Graph* ign b7.de iris kali-ar *Kali-bi* k* kali-c h2* kali-m k2 kreos *Lach* k* lachn *Led* lyss mag-c h2* mag-m b4.de manc med br1 merc k* merc-i-f k* *Mez* k* *Moni* rfm1• nux-v k* olnd k* op wbt* parth vml3• petr h2* petr-ra shn4• phos b4.de* plan k* plat h2* positr nl2• *Psor* mrr1 puls k* *Rhus-t* b7a.de *Sabad* b7a.de sabin b7.de sars k* *Sil* k* spong b7.de* *Staph* b7a.de stram **Sulph** k* tell lp thioc-ac rly4• thuj k* tub al* **Urt-u** ven-m rsj12• verat b7.de* *Viol-t* b7.de zinc k*
  - **midnight**: cob-n sp1
    - **before**: bry b7.de *Puls* b7.de
    - **after**: dulc b4.de sabad b7.de sabin b7.de spong b7.de
      - **0**-3 h: dulc h2
      - **4** h, until: ap-g vml3•
  - **hot**: syph pd
- **accompanied** by:
  - **constipation** (See RECTUM - Constipation - accompanied - skin - itching)
  - **diabetes** (See GENERALS - Diabetes mellitus - accompanied - skin)
  - **heat** of skin; sensation of: *(↗GENERALS - Pain - internally - burning - accompanied - itching)* cod br1
  - **hemorrhoids** (See RECTUM - Hemorrhoids - accompanied - skin)
  - **nausea**: *Ip* b7a.de
  - **numbness** of skin: brass-n-o srj5• cod br1
- **air**; in open:
  - **agg.**: led b7a.de *Nit-ac* b4a.de sulph b4.de
  - **amel.**: conch fkr1•
- **bacon**; after: *Puls* b7a.de
- **bathing**:
  - **after**: bov bg2 clem b4a.de* *Dulc* b4a.de
  - **agg.**: bov ptk1 calc ptk1 clem ptk1 *Mag-c* bg1* *Sulph* mrr1 tritic-vg fd5.de
  - **amel.**: clem k* sanguis-s hrn2• spong fd4.de
- **bed** agg.; in: alum b4.de anac b4a.de ang b7.de ant-c b7a.de *Bov* b4a.de calc b4a.de camph b7.de *Carb-an* b4.de* **Carb-v** b4.de* *Caust* b4a.de *Cham* b7a.de chin b7.de cic b7a.de clem b4.de *Cocc* b7.de* *Coloc* b4.de* con b4.de* *Cycl* b7.de* kali-ar ptk1 kreos b7a.de led ptk1 lyc b4a.de m-arct b7.de *M-aust* b7.de *Merc* b4a.de mez b4a.de mur-ac b4a.de **Nux-v** b7.de* ph-ac b4.de pic-ac ptk1 plat b4.de *Psor* ptk1 *Puls* b7.de* *Rhus-t* b7a.de sars b4a.de seneg b4.de sil ptk1 staph b7.de* *Sulph* b4.de* thuj b4a.de verat b7a.de *Zinc* b4.de*
- **biting**: **Agar** k* *Agn* k* alum k* alum-p k2 am-c k* *Am-m* k* ant-c k* ant-t a1 arn k* bar-m bell k* berb borx k* *Bov* k* *Bry* k* *Calc* k* calc-p k* calc-sil k2 camph k* canth k* caps k* carb-an k* *Carb-v* k* *Caust* k* cham k* chel k* chin k* cimic coc-c cocc k* colch k* coloc k* *Con* k* dros k* *Dulc* *Euph* k* hell k* ip k* kali-n *Lach* k* **Led** k* *Lyc* k* m-arct b2.de* m-aust b2.de mag-c k* mang k* *Merc* k* *Mez* k* mur-ac k* *Nat-c* k* nat-m k* nat-p nicc *Nux-v* k* **Ol-an** k* **Olnd** k* op k* *Paeon* *Petr* k* *Ph-ac* k* phos k* plat k* *Psor* ptel **Puls** k* pycnop-sa mrz1 ran-b k* ran-s k* rhod k* rhus-t k* *Rumx* ruta sel k* sep k* *Sil* k* spig k* *Spong* k* *Staph* ptk1 stront-c k* *Sulph* k* *Tarent* *Tell* *Thuj* k* **Urt-u** k* verat k* viol-t k* wies a1 zinc k* zinc-p k2
  - **perspiration**; after: cocc mang h2 spong fd4.de
- **bleeding** | **scratching**; after: alum b2.de* arg-met bg2 calc b2.de* chin b2.de* cocc b2.de* coff bg2 cycl b2.de* *Dulc* b2.de* euph b2.de* hep b2.de* hyos b2.de* kali-c b2.de* kali-n b2.de* *Lach* b2.de* lyc b2.de* m-ambo b2.de* **Merc** b2.de* moni rfm1• nit-ac b2.de* *Par* b2.de* petr b2.de* psor bg2 sphing kk3.fr spig kk3.fr sulph b2.de*
- **burning**: *Acon* k* adam srj aegop-p aem1• *Agar* k* agath-a nl *Agn* aids nl alum k* alum-p k2 am-c k* ambr k* anac k* ant-c k* *Apis* k* arg-met k* arizon-l nl2• arn k* **Ars** k* ars-i ars-s-f k2 asaf k* asar b2.de* aur k* aur-s k2 *Bar-c* k* bar-s k2 *Bell* k* berb bism k* *Bov* k* **Bry** k* *Calad* k* *Calc* k* *Calc-p* k* calc-s calc-sil k2 camph k* cand bnd1• cann-s k* canth k* caps k* carb-an k* carb-v k* cardios-h rpd1 cartl-s rly• cassia-s cdd *Caust* k* cham k* chin k*

- **burning**: ...
chinin-ar **Chlol** *Cic* k* cinnb clem k* coca-c sk• cocc k* coff k* colch k* coloc k* *Com* k* *Con* k* crass-o rcb2• crot-t gk1 cupr k* cyclosp sa2• cypra-eg sde6.de• dig k* dros k* dulc k* euph k* ger-i rly• germ-met srj granit-m es1• **Graph** k* guaj k* hell k* *Hep* k* hyos k* ign k* iod k* *Jug-c* *Kali-ar* *Kali-bi* k* *Kali-c* k* kali-m k2 kali-n k* *Kali-s* kali-sil k2 ketogl-ac rly• kreos k* lac-cp sk• lac-del sk• lac-leo sk• **Lach** k* lachn k* laur k* led k* **Lyc** k* m-ambo b2.de* m-arct b2.de* m-aust b2.de mag-c k* mang k* meny k* *Merc* k* *Merc-c* b4a.de *Mez* k* mucs-nas rly• mur-ac k* nat-ar nat-c k* nat-m k* nat-ox rly• nat-p neon srj nit-ac k* nux-v k* olnd k* op k* orot-ac rly• oxal-a rly• pall pant-ac rly• pern-c mie1• petr k* ph-ac k* phel phor-t mie• *Phos* k* plat k* plb k* positr nl2• propl ub1• psil ft1 **Puls** k* rad-br gk1 ran-b k* rhod k* **Rhus-t** k* rubu-c vv• ruta k* sabad k* samb k* sars k* sec k* sel k* seneg k* *Sep* k* seq-s bhk1• **Sil** k* simul vv• sinus rly• *Spig* k* spong k* *Squil* k* stann k* staph k* stram k* streptom-s vk2 stront-c k* succ-ac kgp1• sul-ac k* sul-i k2 sulfonam ks **Sulph** k* teucr k* thioc-ac rly• thuj k* tyl-i ks *Urt-u* k* valer k* verat k* vero-o rly• vibh jzk viol-o k* viol-t k* zinc k* zinc-p k2 [cladon fdr1]
  - **night**: *Bov* lachn k* *Mez* olib-sac wmh1 *Til*
  - **nettles**; as from: bry h1 calc-p **Chlol** cocc positr nl2• **Urt-u**
  - **spots**; in: limest-b es1•
    - **night**: limest-b es1•
  - **washing**; after: olib-sac wmh1
- **changing** place: am-c ptk1
  - **rapidly**: sulfonam ks2
- **chill**:
  - **after**: graph h2*
  - **during**: alum bg2 *Am-c* bg2 ars bg2 bry bg2 graph bg2 *Hep* *Led* bg2 lyc bg2 m-aust b7.de *Mang* bg2 merc bg2 mez bg2* nat-m bg2 nux-v bg2 *Petr* k* rhus-t bg2 sars bg2 sulph bg2
- **chronic**: hip-ac mtf11
- **coition**; after: *Agar*
- **cold**:
  - **air**:
    - **agg.**: apis cadm-met tpw6 cadm-s calad pd dulc bro1 *Hep* bro1 kali-ar lac-ac led gk nat-s bro1 nit-ac *Olnd* bro1 petr bro1 rhus-t bro1 *Rumx* k* sep spong *Staph* sulph gk tell *Tub*
    - **amel.**: *Kali-bi* kali-i mrr1 mez mrr1 pycnop-sa mrz1
  - **amel.**: berb bro1 fago bro1 graph bro1 mez bro1
  - **applications** | **amel.**: [sol-ecl cky1]
  - **bathing**:
    - **agg.**: clem pd *Fago* vh*
    - **amel.**: berb mtf dol mrr1 fago bg1 graph mtf kali-i mrr1 mez mtf
  - **water**:
    - **agg.**: clem bro1 olib-sac wmh1 tub bro1
    - **amel.**: berb mtf calad mtf canth mtf **Fago** vh graph mtf led gk mez k* spong fd4.de
- **cold** agg.; becoming: *Ars* b4a.de *Caust* b4a.de clem ptk1 sars b4a.de *Sil* b4a.de *Spong* b7.de* thuj ptk1 tub ptk1
- **contact** | **agg.**: ran-b br1*
- **corrosive**: agar b2.de* **Agn** b2.de* alum b2.de* ambr b2.de* anac b2.de* ant-c b2.de* arg-met b2.de* ars b2.de* *Bar-c* b2.de* bell b2.de* bism b2.de* bry b2.de* canth b2.de* caps b2.de* cham b2.de* clem b2.de* cocc b2.de* con b2.de* cycl b2.de* dig b2.de* dros b2.de* euph b2.de* graph b2.de* guaj b2.de* hell b2.de* hyos b2.de* kali-c b2.de* *Led* b2.de* **Lyc** b2.de* m-ambo b2.de* m-aust b2.de* meny b2.de* merc b2.de* mez b2.de* nat-c b2.de* nux-v b2.de* **Olnd** b2.de* par b2.de* ph-ac b2.de* phos b2.de* **Plat** b2.de* puls b2.de* ran-s b2.de* rhod b2.de* rhus-t b2.de* ruta b2.de* sep b2.de* spig b2.de* *Spong* b2.de* squil b2.de* stann b2.de* **Staph** b2.de* sulph b2.de* tarax b2.de* thuj b2.de* verat b2.de* vinc ptk1
- **crawling**: *Acon* k* **Agar** k* agn aloe bg2 *Alum* k* alum-p k2 am-c k* ambr k* ant-c k* *Arg-met* k* *Arn* k* ars k* ars-s-f k2 asaf k* aur aur-s k2 *Bar-c* k* bar-s k2 bell k* borx bov bry k* calad calc k* calc-s calc-sil k2 camph k* cann-s canth k* caps k* carb-v k* *Carbn-s* *Caust* k* chel k* chin k* cina k* cist k2 cocc **Colch** k* *Con* k* croc k* *Dig* dulc fd4.de euphr k* graph k* guaj k* hep k* ign k* ina-i mlk9.de kali-ar *Kali-c* k* kali-m k2 kali-p kali-s kali-sil k2 lach k* laur led k* **Lyc** k* m-ambo b2.de* m-arct b2.de* m-aust b2.de mag-c mag-m mang *Merc* k* mur-ac k* nat-ar *Nat-c* k* nat-m k* nat-p nit-ac *Nux-v* k* ol-an bg2 *Olnd* pall par k* *Ph-ac* k* phos **Plat** k* **Plb** k* **Puls** k* *Ran-b* k* ran-s k* *Rhod* k* **Rhus-t** k* *Sabad* k* sabin k* *Sec* k* sel k* **Sep** k* *Sil* k* **Spig** k* spong k* squil k* **Staph** k* sul-ac k* **Sulph** k* tab bg2 **Tarent** k* tell ptk1 teucr k* thuj k* verat k* viol-t k* zinc k* zinc-p k2
- **despair** from itching: *Dol* mrr1 ham fd3.de• olib-sac wmh1 **Psor**
- **diabetics**; in: *Cephd-i* zzc1•
- **dinner**; after: parth vml3•
- **drawing**: staph b7.de
- **dressing**; while: nux-v b7.de
- **drunkards**: carb-v lach nux-v sulph
- **dryness**; from: cortico tpw7 hep tl1 sil tl1 sulph tl1
- **eating**:
  - **after** | **agg.**: calc-p dulc a1
  - **amel.**: chel ptk1
  - **small** quantities | **amel.**: guat sp1
- **eruptions**:
  - **suppressed** eruptions; after: *Ars*
  - **where** eruptions have been: calc-act h1
  - **without**: agar k2 **Alum** k* alum-sil k2 **Ars** k* bar-act br1 bar-c vml calc-sil k2 carc mlr1• cist k* clem a1 cupr ptk1 *Dol* k* fago c1 gal-ac br1 galeoc-c-h gms1• *Gels* gink-b sbd1• graph k2 hist sp1 kali-s fkr2.de kola stb3• lach med *Merc* **Mez** k* nat-m st ozone sde2• *Petr* plac-s rly4• *Psor* pycnop-sa mrz1 *Ros-d* wla1 rosm lgb1 sil mg spong k2 *Sulph* thyr ptk1 ulm-c jsj8• [heroin sdj2 sol-ecl cky1]
- **excitement**; on: bry h1
- **exertion**; after:
  - **agg.**: *Nat-m* vanil fd5.de
  - **amel.**: agar k2
- **feather** bed; in: *Cocc* b7.de*
- **fever**; during: **Am-c** b4.de* *Ant-c* bg2 ars bg2 bry bg2 *Cham* bg2 ign br1 kali-br lyc bg2 **Mang** b4.de* merc bg2 nux-v bg2 *Puls* bg2 rhus-t bg2 sil bg2 **Spong** b7.de* staph bg2 sulph bg2
- **fleabites**; like: inul rb2 myric rb2 nicc rb2 olnd rb2 pall sne ptel hr1 puls rb2 pycnop-sa mrz1 *Staph* sne tab pd visc sp1
- **followed** by:
  - **other** complaints: ign bg2 kali-bi bg2 puls bg2
  - **perspiration**: *Coloc* b4a.de
- **gnawing**: dros b7.de* tarax b7.de*
- **hairy** parts: dol bro1* fago bro1 rhus-t b7a.de*
- **heat**:
  - **flushes** of heat; after: sep h2
  - **stove**; of | **amel.**: calc-sil k2 clem ptk1 *Rumx* k* sal-fr sle1• **Tub** k*
- **heated**; when: arg-n bg2 ign bg2 mang b4a.de* puls bg2
  - **daytime**: bov b4a.de *Ign* b7.de* *Lyc* b4.de mang b4.de petr b4a.de puls b7.de sabad b7.de
- **insect**; after bite of: calad b7.de* dulc fd4.de nat-sil fd3.de•
- **intense** (See violent)
- **intolerable**: ina-i mlk9.de kali-ar ptk1 podo c1
- **jaundice**; during: *Dol* ptk1* *Hep* k* myric ptk1 pic-ac ptk1 ran-b ptk1 thyr ptk1
- **jerking**: calc k* *Carbn-s* caust k* *Lyc* k* nat-m k* puls k* rhus-t k*
- **keloid**: carc gk6
- **lying**:
  - **agg.**: guat sp1
  - **amel.**: urt-u
- **lying** down agg.; after: bry b7.de camph b7.de *Ign* b7.de ip b7.de kreos b7a.de m-ambo b7.de m-arct b7.de m-aust b7.de nux-v b7.de* tarax b7.de
- **March**; month of: fl-ac k*
- **meat** agg.: rumx ptk1 ruta k*
- **menopause**; during: calad bro1
- **menses**:
  - **amel.**: cycl ptk1
  - **before** | **agg.**: calc bro1 *Graph* bro1 hep bro1 inul bro1 kali-c bro1 *Sil* bro1 sulph bro1
  - **during** | **agg.**: calc bro1 *Graph* k* hep bro1 inul bro1 *Kali-c* k* mag-c b4.de phos k* *Sil* bro1 sulph bro1
- **mental** exertion agg.: *Agar*
- **motion** agg.: apis b7a.de cortiso sp1 guat sp1
- **nausea**:
  - **before**: lob ptk1 sang k*
  - **scratch** until he vomits; must: *(↗STOMACH - Nausea - itching)* lp k*

- **nervous**: arg-met ptk1
- **old** people; in: alum ptk1 arg-n bg2 ars bg2* bar-act br1* bar-c bg2 con bg2 dol bg1* dulc ptk1 fago bg1* fl-ac mg kreos bg2 mag-p bg2 merc bg3* *Mez* k* nat-sil br1 olnd bg3* op bg2 sul-ac bg2 sulph bg3* urt-u ptk1
- **overheated**; when: ign jug-c vml3• *Lyc*
- **pain** ceases; when: ign lyc stront-c
  - **scratching**; after: ars h2 bar-c h2 sulph h2
- **painful** parts: alum ptk1 bar-c bg3 carbn-s ign thuj
- **paroxysmal**: corn bg1
- **parts**:
  - **lain** on: (↗*Side lain)* carb-v bg2
  - **not** lain on: chin h1*
  - **suffering**: dig h2
  - **various** (See single)
- **perspiration**:
  - **after** | **agg.**: bry b7.de *Lyc* b4a.de *Mang* b4a.de op b7.de
  - **agg.**: *Apis* bg2 cham bg2 coloc bg2 lyc bg2 (non:mang h2*) **Mang-m** kl *Merc* k* mur-ac h2 nat-m h2 petr-ra shn4• rhod k* rhus-t bg2
  - **during**: *Am-c* bg2 ant-c bg2 bar-c bg2 benz-ac bg2 bry bg2 **Calc** b4a.de* cann-s b7.de caust bg2 cham b7a.de* *Coloc* b4a.de* *Fl-ac* b4a.de* ip b7.de* *Led* b7.de* **Lyc** b4a.de* **Mang** b4.de* merc bg2 op b7.de* par b7.de* puls bg2 **Rhod** b4a.de* **Rhus-t** b7a.de* *Sabad* b7.de* sil bg2 **Spong** b7a.de* staph bg2 *Sulph* b4a.de* thuj bg2 viol-t bg2
  - **waking**; on: led tl1
- **perspiring** parts●: (↗*spots - perspire)* all-s am-c k* benz-ac bry bg2 calc k* cann-s cann-xyz bg2 cedr *Cham* k* coloc k* fl-ac k* ip k* led k* *Lyc* k* **Mang** k* mur-ac h2 nat-m h2 op k* par k* parth vml3• rhod k* rhus-t k* sabad k* spong k* sulph k* vesp br1
- **pregnancy** agg.; during: *Calad* sne chlol hr1 cocc alj coll br1 dol alj* ichth br sabin ptk1 sep hr1 tab hr1*
  - **insupportable** over whole body: *Tab* br*
- **respiration**; with:
  - **complaints**: sabad ptk1
  - **short**: lob bg1
- **rubbing** | **amel.**: cortiso gse crot-t bro1* dios ptk1 med ptk1 parth vml3•
- **scratching**:
  - **agg.**: *Agar Alum* alum-p k2 alum-sil k2 am-m k* **Anac** k* anag **Apis** bg2 *Arg-met* arg-n hr1 *Arn* k* **Ars** k* ars-s-f k2 bar-c berb bro1 *Bism* k* *Bov* k* brucel sa3• *Calad* k* calc k* calc-sil k2 cann-s k* canth k* **Caps** k* carb-an k* carb-v *Caust* k* cham k* chel k* cinnb coff coli rly4• *Con* k* crot-t bg2* cupr k* *Dol* dros k* guaj k* ina-i mlk9.de ip kali-ar k2 kali-sil k2 kreos k* lach bg2 lachn *Led* k* lyss c1 m-ambo b2.de* mag-c k* mang k* merc k* *Mez* k* *Moni* rfm1• mur-ac k* nat-ar nat-c k* onos sne par k* petr-ra shn4• ph-ac k* phos k* phyt positr nl2• **Puls** k* **Rhus-t** k* rhus-v sal-fr sle1• sars h2* seneg k* sep k* *Sil* k* spig k* spong k* squil k* stann k* *Staph* k* stram k* *Stront-c* k* **Sulph** k* tell rsj10• *Til* tril-p c1 tub k2
    - **bleeds**; must scratch until it: *Agar Alum* k* *Arg-met* k* **Ars** k* *Bar-c* k* bell mtf33 *Bism* a1 *Bov* carb-v *Chlol* choc srj3• coff ptk1 *Crot-t* bro1 dol k2 gink-b sbd1• *Graph* mrr1 kali-n h2 led *Med* mez h2* murx bro1 nit-ac h2 phos h2 pix bro1 *Psor* k* *Puls* sep bro1 *Sulph* bro1 til bro1 [tax jsj7]
    - **changing** place on scratching: *Agar* k* alum anac k* ap-g vml3• apoc vh arn bg2* asaf bg2* calc k* *Canth* carb-an k* chel k* con h2 cycl k* dulc fd4.de *Ign* k* kali-s fkr2.de m-arct b2.de* mag-c k* mag-m k* *Mez* k* neon srj5• nit-ac bg2 pall podo fd3.de• ruta k2 sars h2* *Spong* k* *Staph* k* *Sul-ac* k* tub c1* zinc k* [tax jsj7]
    - **raw**; must scratch until it is: (↗*Excoriation - scratching - must) Agar Alum* am-c ant-c arg-met k2 arn ars k2 bar-c bov calc *Carbn-s* caust chin cist k2 dros dulc k2 **Graph** k* hep kali-c kali-sil k2 kreos *Lach Lyc* mang merc mez k2 *Olnd* **Petr** k* phos plb *Psor* k* puls rhus-t ruta sabin *Sep* sil squil sul-ac *Sulph Til*
    - **slight** scratching agg.; hard scratching amel.: crot-t bg2
  - **amel.**: agar k* *Agn* k* alum k* alum-sil k2 am-c k* am-m k* ambr k* anac k* ang b2.de* ant-c k* ant-t k* apis arn k* ars **Asaf** k* bar-c b2.de* bell k* borx k* bov k* *Brom* k* bros-gau mrc1 *Bry* k* cadm-s k* **Calc** k* calc-s camph k* *Cann-s* k* *Canth* k* caps k* carb-an k* cassia-s ccrh1• caust k* chel k* chin k* cic k* *Cina* k* clem k* coloc k* com con k* conch fkr1* *Crot-t* **Cycl** k* cypra-eg sde6.de• dig k* *Dros* k* *Fl-ac* bg2 form *Guaj* k* hep k* hydr *Ign* k* *Jug-c* kali-ar *Kali-c* k* kali-m k2 kali-n k* kali-s *Kreos* k* lac-leo hrn2• laur k* led k* m-arct b2.de* m-aust b2.de* *Mag-c* k* mag-m k* *Mang* k* mang-act bro1 medul-os-si rly4• meny k* merc k* mez k* mosch k* **Mur-ac** k* **Nat-c** k* nat-p nit-ac k* nux-v k* olnd k* petr-ra shn4• ph-ac k* **Phos** k* plat k* *Plb* k* positr nl2• prun pycnop-sa mrz1 ran-b k* rhus-t k* *Ruta* k* sabad k* sabin k* sal-ac samb k* *Sars* k* sec k* sel k* seneg k* *Sep* k* spig k* spong k* squil k* stann k* staph k* streptoc rly4• sul-ac k* *Sulph* k* tarax k* *Thuj* k* valer k* viol-t k* *Zinc* k*
    - **transient**: *Agn* b7.de anac b4a.de bar-c b4.de caps b7.de chel b7.de chin b7.de clem b4.de coloc b4.de cycl b7.de dig b4.de *Led* b7.de mag-m b4.de merc b4.de mez b4a.de nux-v b7.de olnd b7.de ph-ac b4.de plat b4.de plb b7.de ruta b7.de sabin b7.de spig b7.de *Squil* b7.de staph b7.de viol-t b7.de
    - **while**; only after a: dulc b4.de
  - **must** scratch: agar bg2* alum mrr1 arg-met bg2* coff bg2* cycl bg2 granit-m es1• positr nl2• psor bg2* staph bg2* suis-hep rly4• tritic-vg fd5.de vanil fd5.de
  - **unchanged** by scratching: acon k* agar k* agn k* *Alum* k* am-c k* am-m k* ambr k* *Ang* b2.de* ant-c k* ant-t k* *Arg-met* k* arn k* asaf k* aur k* bar-c k* bar-s k2 bell k* bism k* borx k* *Bov* k* *Calad* k* camph k* carb-an k* carb-v k* caust k* cham k* chel k* cina k* clem k* cocc k* coff k* colch k* coli rly4• coloc k* croc k* cupr k* dig k* dulc k2 euph k* euphr k* *Hell* k* hyos k* iod k* *Ip* k* laur k* *M-ambo* b2.de* m-arct b2.de* m-aust b2.de *Mag-m* k* *Med* merc-i-f kr1 mur-ac k* nat-c k* nux-v k* op k* petr-ra shn4• plac-s rly4• *Plat* k* prun **Puls** k* *Ran-s* k* rheum k* rhus-t k* ruta k* samb k* sars h2* sec k* seneg k* sil k* *Spig* k* **Spong** k* stann k* stram k* sul-ac k* tarax k* teucr k* valer k* visc bg2
- **shivering**; during: led b7.de
- **single** parts: adam skp7• hydroph rsj6•
- **sitting** agg.: chel b7.de cycl b7.de
- **sleep**:
  - **amel.**: positr nl2•
  - **during** | **agg.**: agn b7a.de am-c k* ars k* bamb-a stb2.de• *Bar-c* k* carb-v k* caust k* con k* dulc k* mag-m k* *Phos* k* sars k* sulph k* zinc k*
  - **going** to sleep; on | **agg.**: *Osm*
- **smarting**: alum k* am-m ambr k* apis bg2 *Arg-met* k* arg-n aur k* berb bry k* bufo bg2 calc k* cann-s k* cic b2.de* colch k* dros k* *Graph* k* hep k* kali-c k* kali-sil k2 led k* lyc k* m-ambo b2.de* m-arct b2.de* mag-c k* mang k* merc k* mez k* mur-ac nat-c k* nat-m b2.de* nit-ac b2.de* nux-v k* olnd k* par k* petr k* **Plat** k* puls k* *Rhus-t* k* ruta k* sabin k* sars k* *Sep* k* sil k* squil k* staph k* *Sulph* k* valer k* verat k* *Zinc* k*
- **spots**: agn k* alum h2* am-m k* arn k* aster *Berb* caps h1* *Con* k* dros k* euph k* *Fl-ac* galla-q-r nl2• *Graph* k* *Iod* k* jug-c k* *Kali-c* k* lac-h sk4• *Lach* *Led* k* luna kg1• *Lyc* k* m-ambo b2.de* merc k* merc-i-f kr1 mez k* *Nat-m* k* neon srj5• *Nit-ac* olib-sac wmh1 op k* ozone sde2• par k* petr k2 sel c1* sep k* *Sil* k* spong k* *Sul-ac* k* **Sulph** k* *Zinc* k* [bell-p-sp dcm1]
  - **liver** spots: *Caust*
  - **perspire**; which: (↗*perspiring) Tell*
- **spreading** | **scratching**; after: anac b4.de* cann-s b7.de chel b7.de spong b7.de
- **spring**; in: fl-ac lach
- **stinging**: acon k* *Agar* agn k* alum k* alum-p k2 am-c k* am-m b2.de* anac k* ang b2.de* ant-c k* **Apis** k* arg-met k* *Arn* k* ars k* ars-i ars-s-f k2 asaf k* asar k* aur k* aur-s k2 *Bar-c* k* bar-s k2 bell k* bov k* **Bry** k* calad k* calc k* calc-sil k2 camph k* cann-s k* canth k* caps k* carb-an k* carb-v k* carbn-s *Caust* k* cham k* chel k* chin k* **Chlol** clem k* coc-c *Cocc* k* coff colch k* *Con* k* *Cop* crot-h *Cycl* k* dig k* *Dros* k* dulc k* euph k* euphr k* **Graph** k* guaj k* hell k* hep k* hyos k* ign k* iod k* kali-ar *Kali-c* k* kali-m k2 kali-n k* kali-p kali-s kali-sil k2 kreos k* lach k* laur k* led k* lyc k* m-ambo b2.de* m-arct b2.de* m-aust b2.de* mag-c k* mag-m k* mang k* meny k* *Merc* k* mez k* mosch k* *Mur-ac* k* nat-c k* *Nat-m* k* nat-p nit-ac k* nux-v k* olnd k* op k* par k* petr k* ph-ac k* phos k* plat k* plb k* **Puls** k* pulx br1 ran-b k* ran-s k* rheum k* rhod k* **Rhus-t** k* ruta k* *Sabad* k* sabin k* samb k* sars k* sel k* *Sep* k* *Sil* k* *Spig* k* **Spong** k* squil k* *Stann* k* *Staph* k* stram k* stront-c k* sul-ac k* *Sulph* k* tarax k* tell teucr k* *Thuj* k* *Til* **Urt-u** verat k* **Viol-t** k* zinc k* zinc-p k2
  - **morning** | **rising** agg.: sars h2*
  - **evening**: petr h2* sars h2* spong fd4.de
    - **bed** agg.; in: nat-m h2* spong fd4.de

- **scratching**; after: sulph h2
- **sun** exposure; from: brass-n-o srj5• glycyr-g cte1•
  - **winter**; even in: glycyr-g cte1•
- **symmetrical**: rhus-g tmo3•
- **tearing**: *Bell* k* bry k* *Lyc* k* sil k* *Staph* k* sulph k* zinc k*
  - **scratching**; after: bell h1
- **thinking of it** agg.: med ptk1*
- **tickling**: acon k* agar k* alum k* am-m k* *Ambr* k* apis ptk1 *Arg-met* k* bry k* bufo calc k* canth k* caps k* caust ptk1 *Cham* ptk1 chel k* chin k* cist ptk1 coc-c ptk1 cocc k* *Colch* *Con* ptk1 dig k* dros k* euph k* euphr k* ferr ptk1 hyos ptk1 ign k* **Iod** ptk1 ip ptk1 kali-bi ptk1 kali-c ptk1 *Lach* ptk1 lob ptk1 mang k* melal-alt gya4 *Merc* k* mur-ac k* nat-m ptk1 **Nux-v** ptk1 phos k* *Plat* k* prun *Puls* k* ran-b *Rhus-t* k* *Rumx* ptk1 ruta k* *Sabad* k* sang ptk1 sec sel *Sep* k* **Sil** k* *Spig* k* spong k* squil k* stann ptk1 staph k* *Sulph* k* sumb ptk1 tarax k* teucr k*
  - **scratching**; after: agar k* ambr k* caps k* chin k* cocc k* merc k* **Sabad** k* *Sil* k* spig k* teucr k*
- **touch** agg.: cadm-s a1 caps b7.de* cocc alj mez hr1* nat-m h2 rhus-t hr1 tub al
- **ulcers**; leading to: kali-bi tl1
- **undressing** agg.●: (↗*GENERALS - Uncovering - agg.; GENERALS - Undressing) Alum* bro1 am-m k* anac ant-c bro1 *Ap-g* vh1 apoc vh1 ars k* asim k* bell-p bro1 bov bro1 cact carb-v bro1 carc gk6* card-m bro1 cist bro1 *Cocc* k* dios bg2 *Dros* k* dulc bro1 gamb k* hep alj hyper k* *Jug-c* bro1 kali-ar k* kali-bi bg2 kali-br kreos bro1 led bro1 lyc bro1 mag-c *Menis* bro1 *Merc* bro1 merc-i-f bro1 mez k* mur-ac nat-m alj *Nat-s* k* nit-ac ptk1 nux-v k* *Olnd* k* pall k* parth vml3• ph-ac *Psor* alj* puls b7.de* rhod k* rhus-g tmo3• rhus-t b7.de* **Rumx** k* sang bro1 sep bro1 sil k* stann k* *Staph* k* sulph bro1* tell ptk1* *Tub* k*
- **violent**: agar arge-pl rwt5• cem ah1 cub c1 cypra-eg sde6.de• dros dulc granit-m es1• graph h2* ip kreos tl1 lach lyc k2 merc k2 mez k* op pall sne petr-ra shn4• prot pte1* psor al2 pycnop-sa mrz1 rad-br c11 ther k2
- **voluptuous**: ambr k* anac k* ang k* arg-met k* carc fd2.de• m-arct b2.de* mang-p rly4• meny k* *Merc* k* mur-ac k* parth vml3• plat k* positr nl2• puls k* sabad k* sep k* *Sil* k* spig k* spong k* suis-em rly4• **Sulph** k*
- **vomiting** | **amel.**: *Ip* k*
- **walking**:
  - **agg.**: kali-ar pd
  - **air** agg.; in open: cinnb *Sulph*
- **wandering**: (↗*FACE - Itching - wandering) Agar* arge-pl rwt5• *Bar-c* berb calc-i c1 camph h1* *Canth* caust cench k2 cham *Con* dulc h2* gink-b sbd1• graph jug-c kali-c kali-p fd1.de• mag-m k* mang *Merc* mez *Olib-sac* wmh1 olnd podo fd3.de• *Puls* pycnop-sa mrz1 rat rhus-v ruta fd4.de sil bg1 spong staph streptoc rly4• suis-em rly4• *Sulph* bg1 tub c1 zinc
  - **night**: cina a1
- **warm** | **applications** | **amel.**: *Anac* mtf ars mtf clem mtf kali-bi mtf *Kali-s* mtf *Rhus-v* mtf rumx mtf thuj mtf
  - **bathing**:
    - **agg.**: spong fd4.de trios rsj11• tritic-vg fd5.de
      - **hot** bath: calc bg2* mez k2
    - **amel.**: anac mtf ars mtf petr mtf rhus-v mtf rumx mtf
      - **hot** bath: anac mrr1 kali-s mtf rhus-t k2* rhus-v bro1* sil bg2 syph ptk1
- **warm**; becoming:
  - **agg.**: *Aeth* k* *Alum* k* arg-n bov k* clem cob cocc k* com *Dol* gels ign *Kali-ar* kali-i mrr1 *Led* *Lyc* k* mang h2 **Merc** k* mez k* mur-ac *Nat-ar* op wbt• parth vml3• phos mrr1 **Psor** k* *Puls* k* sars b4a.de* *Sil* b4a.de *Staph* b7.de* **Sulph** k* **Urt-u** k* verat b7.de*
  - **amel.**: tub mrr1
  - **bed**; in | **agg.**: *Aeth* *Alum* k* alum-p k2 alum-sil k2 *Anac* *Ant-c* k* *Apis* arg-n bar-c bar-s k2 *Bov* k* cadm-s calad k* *Calc* k* calc-s cann-s b7.de carb-an *Carb-v* k* *Carbn-s* card-m caust k* chin b7.de cinnb *Clem* k* cob k* coc-c bg2 *Cocc* k* coloc cortiso sp1 cupr-ar *Cycl* dol vml3• dulc a1 *Gels* *Graph* k* *Kali-ar* k* *Kali-bi* kali-br kali-c kali-chl *Kali-s* *Led* k* *Lyc* k* lyss m-ambo b7.de mag-c *Merc* k* *Mez* k* mur-ac k* *Nat-m* *Nat-p* nux-v k* petr mrr1 ph-ac *Phos* pic-ac bg2 **Psor** k* *Puls* k* *Rhus-t* k* sabad b7a.de sars k* *Sep* k* sil b4a.de* spong k* **Sulph** k* *Tell* lp thuj *Til* *Urt-u* verat b7a.de zinc k* zinc-p k2
- **warmth**:
  - **agg.**: chin b7.de cocc b7.de* *Euphr* b7a.de nux-v b7.de puls b7.de *Staph* b7a.de teucr b7.de verat b7a.de
  - **amel.**: ars bro1 petr bro1 rumx bro1

Itching: ...
- **washing** with cold water (See cold - water - agg.)
- **wiping** with hand | **amel.**: dros ptk1
- **wool** agg.●: (↗*GENERALS - Clothing - intolerance - woolen)* Hep nat-m gk phos k* podo fd3.de• psor puls sulph k*

○ - **Affected** parts: *Acon* b7a.de agar ptk1 dig h
- **Bend** of joints: psor bg2
- **Folds**; of: sel br1
- **Orifices**: ambr bg2* caust bg2* fl-ac bro1 petr bg2* sulph bg2
- **Paralyzed** parts; in: phos
- **Side** lain on: (↗*parts - lain)* carb-v b4.de* chin k* con b4.de* vesp ptk2
- **Side** not lain on: chin b7.de ruta b7a.de
- **Under** skin: agar bg2
- **Upper** part of body: *Ars* b4a.de

JAUNDICE (See Discoloration - yellow)

KELOID: (↗*Cicatrices; GENERALS - Wounds - granulations)* alum ptk1 ars st1 bell-p bg2* calc st1 calc-f bg2* calen vml3• carb-v st1 carc pc* caust bg2* crot-h st1 cupre-l c1* diphtox ggd1 dros ggd1 *Fl-ac* bro1* gast st **Graph** bg2* hyper st1 *Iod* bg2* junc-e st1 kali-bi bg2 lach st1 loxo-lae bnm12• lyss mrr1 maland c1* merc st1 **Nit-ac** c1* nux-v st1 phos st1 phyt st1 psor st1* rhus-t st1 sabin bro1* **Sil** k* sul-ac st1 *Sulph* c1* thiosin st1 thuj ggd1 tub st1* vac c1* *Vip* st* x-ray ggd1

KERATOSES (See Indurations - horny)

LEECHES were drawing at spots on skin; as if (See Sticking - leeches)

LOOSE; as if the skin were hanging: ant-c k* bell k* bufo bg2* carb-an ptk1 kreos k* lach bg2 **Phos** k* plb bg2 sabad k*

LOUSINESS: (↗*HEAD - Lice; MALE GENITALIA/SEX - Crab; SKIN)* am-c ars k* bac bro1 bros-gau mrc1 canth b7a.de cocc bro1 lach k* *Lyc* k* m-ambo b2.de* *Merc* k* *Nat-m* bro1 nit-ac olnd k* *Psor* k* *Sabad* k* staph k* *Sulph* k* vinc
- **itching**: led ptk1

LUPUS: (↗*FACE - Cancer - lupus; GENERALS - Cancerous - lupus)* abr c2* agar alum alum-sil k2 alumn ant-c apis bro1 arg-n **Ars** k* ars-i k* aur-ar c2* aur-i bro1* aur-m k* *Bar-c* bell calc k* calc-i bro1 calc-s br1* calc-sil k2 calo c2 *Carb-ac* *Carb-v* *Caust* chr-o c2 cic *Cist* k* cund br1* ferr-pic c2* form br1* form-ac bro1 germ-met srj5• graph k* guar bro1 guare k* hep k* *Hydr* c2* *Hydrc* k* irid-met br1* kali-ar *Kali-bi* k* kali-c *Kali-chl* *Kali-i* bro1 *Kali-s* kali-sil k2 *Kreos* k* lach **Lyc** k* m-arct merc bg3 merc-i-r nat-m bg3 **Nit-ac** k* nux-v mrr1 ol-j *Phyt* k* *Psor* puls mrr1 ran-b k2 rhus-t sabin sep *Sil* sol c1* spong staph k* sulph k* thiosin c1* **Thuj** k* titan br1 tub c2* urea bro1 x-ray bro1
- **discoid**: tub mrr1
- **erythematosus**: apis bro1 cist bro1 cortiso sp1 guar bro1 *Hydrc* bro1 *Iod* bro1 *Kali-bi* bro1 morb jl2 *Phos* bro1 sep bro1 sulfa sp1 *Thyr* bro1 tub-m jl2
- **hypertrophicus**: ars ll1* ars-i ll1 aur ll1 calo ll1 carb-an ll1 carb-v ll1 cic ll1 con ll1 graph ll1* kali-bi ll1 kali-i ll1 lyc ll1 nit-ac ll1 phos ll1 sep ll1 sil ll1 sulph ll1 *Thuj* ll1
- **red** | **ochre**: guare br1

LUSTERLESS: psor jl2

MARBLED (See Discoloration - mottled)

MELANOSIS: chlorpr mtf11

MENSES:
- **absent** | **agg.**: kali-m bg2 sulph bg2
- **before** | **agg.**: borx bg3* calc-p ptk1 carb-v bg2* clem bg2 *Dulc* bg2* *Graph* bg3* kali-c bg3* kali-m ptk1 mag-m bg3* *Nat-m* bg3* psor bg2 sang bg3* sars bg2* sep bg2* stram bg3* sulph bg2 thuj bg2 verat bg3*
- **during** | **agg.**: nux-m bg2
- **scanty** agg.: con ptk1

MOISTURE: alum k* ant-t bg2 ars k* ars-i bg2 bar-c k* bell k* *Bov* k* bry k* bufo bg2 calc k* canth bg2 caps k2 carb-an k* **Carb-v** k* caust k* chion br1 cic k* *Clem* k* con k* cub c1 cupr-n a1 dulc k* **Graph** k* hell k* hep k* kali-ar *Kali-c* k* *Kreos* k* *Lach* k* *Led* k* **Lyc** k* m-ambo b2.de* merc k* mez k* nat-c k* nat-m k* nit-ac k* olnd k* *Petr* k* ph-ac k* phos k* psor b4a.de* **Rhus-t** k* ruta k* sabin k* *Sel* k* *Sep* k* sil k* squil k* *Staph* k* sul-ac k* sulph k* tarax k* thuj k* viol-t k*

Skin

- **accompanied** by | **nausea** (See STOMACH - Nausea - accompanied - skin - moist)
- **chill**; during: bufo bg2
- **scratching** agg.; after: *Alum* k* ars k* ars-s-f k2 bar-c k* bar-s k2 bell k* bov k* bry k* calc k* calc-sil k2 carb-an k* *Carb-v* k* caust k* cic k* cocc h1* con k* dulc k* **Graph** k* hell k* hep k* kali-act kali-ar *Kali-c* k* kali-s kali-sil k2 *Kreos* k* **Lach** k* led k* **Lyc** k* m-ambo b2.de merc k* *Mez* k* nat-c k* nat-m k* nit-ac k* *Olnd* k* *Petr* k* **Rhus-t** k* ruta k* sabin k* sars sel k* *Sep* k* sil k* squil k* *Staph* k* sul-ac k* sulph k* tarax k* thuj k* viol-t k*
- **spots**; in: ant-c carb-v *Hell* kali-c lach led petr k* sabin sel **Sil** *Sulph* tarax vinc
- **warm**; and: visc c1

MOLES: *(↗BACK - Moles)* *Calc* k* carb-v carc fb* graph k* nit-ac petr k* ph-ac k* pitu-p sp1 positr nl2• **Puls** rad-br c11* sil k* sul-ac k* *Sulph* k* tarent *Thuj* k*
- **dark**: **Carc** mrr1
- **itching** and stinging: thuj
- **red**: con bg2 *Iod* bg2 lach bg2 led bg2 *Lyc* bg2 merc bg2 ox-ac bg2 *Sep* bg2 sulph bg2

MOON AGG.; FULL AND NEW: *Alum* ptk1

MOTTLED (See Discoloration - mottled)

NAKED; as if one were: sulph rb2

NETWORK of blood vessels: ant-t bg2 *Ars* bg2 bell bg2 berb *Calc* k* carb-an bg2 *Carb-v* k* *Caust* k* clem k* *Crot-h* k* ferr-p bg2 graph bg2 hydr bg2 kreos bg2 lach bg2 lyc k* merc bg2 nat-m k* nit-ac bg2 nux-v bg2 ox-ac petr bg2 *Phos* bg2 plat k* puls bg2 rhus-t bg2 sabad sec bg2 *Sep* bg2 sil bg2 staph bg2 sul-ac bg2 sulph bg2 thuj k*

NEURODERMATITIS (See Eruptions - eczema)

NEVI: *(↗FACE - Veins - spider)* abrot bg2* **Acet-ac** k* arn ptk1 ars ptk1 bell-p br1* *Calc* k* calc-f bg2* carb-an ptk1 *Carb-v* k* carc st* cund hr1* *Ferr-p* bg2* **Fl-ac** k* *Graph* b2.de* *Ham* bg2* lach ptk1* *Lyc* k* med st nit-ac b2.de* *Nux-v* k* *Petr* b2.de* *Ph-ac* b2.de* **Phos** k* plat ptk1 rad-br bg2* *Rumx* bg2* *Sep* ptk1 *Sil* b2.de* sul-ac b2.de* *Sulph* b2.de* *Thuj* k* ust ptk1 vac k* vanil fd5.de
- **flat**: mur-ac ptk1
- **mottled**: con ptk1 phos ptk1 sep ptk1 thuj ptk1
- **red**: med bg2

NODOSITIES (See Indurations)

NUMBNESS: acon *Ambr* k* **Anac** k* ang b2.de anh sp1 ant-t k* arg-n ptk1 calc-f sp1 cann-i cham k* choc srj3• cic c1 con k* *Crot-c* cycl k* cyt-l sp1 euphr *Hyos* *Hyper* lach k* lat-m bnm6• *Lyc* k* m-ambo b2.de* medus br1 mentho br1 *Nux-v* k* *Olnd* k* *Ph-ac* k* phos k* plat k* plb k* *Puls* **Sec** k* sep k* stram k* sulph k* thal-xyz srj8•
- **morning** | **waking**; on: *Ambr*
- **night** | **waking**; on: ambr a1
- **accompanied** by | **itching** (See Itching - accompanied - numbness)
- **cold**; exposure to: acon k2
- **itching**; after: cycl h1*
- **scratching** agg.; after: alum bg2 ambr k* *Anac* k* ang b2.de* cham con k* cycl k* *Lach* k* lyc k* **Olnd** k* ph-ac k* phos k* plb k* sep k* *Sulph* k*
- **spots**: bufo ptk1 calc-f sp1 gels k2

ODOR, offensive (See PERSPIRATION - Odor - offensive)

OILY (See FACE - Greasy; FACE - Shiny - oily)

OVEREATING: | **agg.**: bry bg2 **Ip** bg2 puls bg2

PAIN: *Acon* ↓ *Agar* ↓ **Agn** ↓ *Alum* ↓ am-c ↓ **Am-m** ↓ ambr ↓ anac ↓ ang ↓ *Ant-c* ↓ **Apis** ↓ arg-met ↓ arg-n ↓ arge-pl ↓ *Arn* ↓ *Ars* ↓ ars-i ↓ ars-s-f ↓ **Asaf** ↓ atra-r ↓ aur ↓ aur-ar ↓ aur-s ↓ *Bad* ↓ *Bar-c* ↓ bar-s ↓ **Bell** ↓ bell-p ↓ berb ↓ bism ↓ borx ↓ bov ↓ brass-n-o ↓ *Bry* ↓ calad ↓ *Calc* ↓ calc-sil ↓ calen ↓ *Camph* ↓ cann-s ↓ canth ↓ caps ↓ carb-an ↓ carb-v ↓ carbn-s ↓ caust ↓ cham ↓ chel ↓ *Chin* ↓ chinin-ar ↓ chinin-s ↓ chir-fl ↓ chlor ↓ *Cic* ↓ **Cimic** ↓ cina ↓ clem ↓ *Cocc* ↓ coff ↓ colch ↓ coloc ↓ con ↓ cot ↓ crot-h ↓ crot-t ↓ *Cycl* ↓ *Dig* ↓ *Dol* ↓ *Dros* ↓ dulc ↓ **Eup-per** ↓ euph ↓ euphr ↓ fago ↓ ferr ↓ ferr-ar ↓ ferr-p ↓ galeoc-c-h ↓ *Glon* ↓ **Graph** ↓ guaj ↓ **Ham** ↓ hell ↓ **Hep** ↓ heroin ↓ hyos ↓ *Ign* ↓ iod ↓ kali-ar ↓ *Kali-bi* ↓ *Kali-c* ↓ *Kali-i* ↓ kali-n ↓ kali-s ↓ kali-sil ↓ *Kreos* ↓ lach ↓ lat-m ↓ laur ↓ led ↓ loxo-recl ↓ **Lyc** ↓

Pain: ...
m-ambo ↓ m-arct ↓ m-aust ↓ mag-c ↓ mag-m ↓ *Mang* ↓ *Meny* ↓ *Merc* ↓ *Merc-c* ↓ *Mez* ↓ morg ↓ mosch ↓ mur-ac ↓ *Nat-c* ↓ *Nat-m* ↓ *Nat-p* ↓ **Nit-ac** ↓ nux-m ↓ *Nux-v* ↓ olib-sac ↓ **Olnd** ↓ osm ↓ paeon ↓ par ↓ *Petr* ↓ ph-ac ↓ *Phos* ↓ plan ↓ **Plat** ↓ plb ↓ prot ↓ *Psor* ↓ **Puls** ↓ ran-b ↓ *Ran-s* ↓ rhod ↓ rhus-d ↓ **Rhus-t** ↓ rumx ↓ *Ruta* ↓ sabad ↓ sabin ↓ samb ↓ saroth ↓ sars ↓ sel ↓ semp ↓ **Sep** ↓ *Sil* ↓ spig ↓ *Spong* ↓ squil ↓ stann ↓ **Staph** ↓ *Still* ↓ stront-c ↓ *Sul-ac* ↓ *Sulph* ↓ symph ↓ *Tarax* ↓ tarent ↓ tarent-c ↓ teucr ↓ *Ther* ↓ **Thuj** ↓ tub ↓ **Urt-u** ↓ vac ↓ valer ↓ *Verat* ↓ *Vinc* ↓ *Viol-t* ↓ xero ↓ **Zinc** ↓
- **evening**:
  - **warm** in bed agg.; becoming: sep ↓ sulph ↓
    - **stinging**: sep h2 sulph h2
- **biting** pain: bell-p sp1
- **bruised**; as if: arg-met k* *Arn* k* bell-p mtf11 calen mtf11 cic k* dros k* dulc k* morg fmm1• olnd k* plat k* rhus-t k* saroth sp1 sul-ac k* symph mtf11
- **brushing** hair: v-a-b jl2
- **burning** (See Burning)
- **cold**:
  - **agg.**: agar ptk1 aur ptk1 plb ptk1 rhus-t ptk1
  - **air** agg.: rhus-t h1
- **cutting** pain: **Bell** k* calc k* dros k* graph k* ign k* lyc k* mur-ac k* *Nat-c* k* ph-ac k* rhus-t k* sep k* sil k* sul-ac k* *Viol-t* k*
  - **knife**; as if cut or sliced with a: bell rb2
- **dull** pain: lat-m bnm6•
- **excitement** agg.: *Bry* ↓
  - **stinging**: *Bry* h1
- **fever**; during: *Chin* mrr1
- **gnawing** pain (= eating): *Agar* k* **Agn** k* alum k* ambr k* anac k* ant-c k* arg-met k* ars k* *Bar-c* k* bell k* bism k* bry k* canth k* caps k* cham k* clem k* cocc k* con k* *Cycl* k* *Dig* k* *Dros* k* euph k* graph k* guaj k* hell k* hyos k* kali-c k* led k* **Lyc** k* m-ambo b2.de* m-aust b2.de* *Meny* k* merc k* mez k* nat-c k* nat-p nux-v k* **Olnd** k* par k* ph-ac k* phos k* **Plat** k* puls k* *Ran-s* k* rhod k* rhus-t k* *Ruta* k* sep k* spig k* *Spong* k* squil k* stann k* **Staph** k* sulph k* tarax k* thuj k* *Verat* k*
- **heat**; during: apis ↓ bry ↓ chin ↓ **Merc-c** ↓ nit-ac ↓ *Olnd* ↓ puls ↓ *Rhus-t* ↓ *Sabad* ↓ *Spong* ↓ viol-t ↓
  - **stinging**: apis bg2 bry bg2 chin b7.de* **Merc-c** bg2 nit-ac bg2 *Olnd* b7.de* puls bg2 *Rhus-t* bg2 *Sabad* b7.de* *Spong* bg2 viol-t bg2
- **herpes** zoster; before: staph ptk1
- **jumping** out; sensation as if: thuj ↓
  - **stinging**: thuj ptk1
- **patches**; in: limest-b ↓
  - **sore** | **burning**: limest-b es1•
- **perspiration**; during: **Cham** ↓ *Con* ↓ *Ip* ↓ *Par* ↓ puls ↓ tarax ↓
  - **biting** pain: **Cham** bg2 *Con* bg2 *Ip* bg2 *Par* bg2 puls bg2 tarax bg2
- **pressure** | **amel.**: ign ptk1
- **prickling** pain: tub jl2
- **rubbing** of trousers: cot ↓
  - **stinging**: cot br1
- **scratching**; after: agar k* agn ↓ *Alum* k* alum-p k2 am-c ↓ **Am-m** ↓ ambr ↓ ant-c ↓ arg-met ↓ arn ↓ *Ars* k* ars-s-f k2 asaf ↓ **Bar-c** k* bar-s k2 bell k* bry ↓ calc k* cann-s ↓ canth ↓ caps k* carb-an bg2 carb-v ↓ caust ↓ chin k* cic ↓ cocc k* con k* cycl ↓ dros ↓ euphr k* *Graph* ↓ *Hep* ↓ ign bg2 kali-c ↓ kola stb3• kreos k* led k* *Lyc* ↓ m-ambo b2.de* m-aust ↓ mag-c ↓ mag-m ↓ mang ↓ merc ↓ *Mez* ↓ nat-c ↓ nat-m k* nit-ac ↓ nux-v k* **Olnd** ↓ par k* *Petr* k* ph-ac k* *Phos* ↓ phyt bg2 plat ↓ plb k* psor ↓ puls k* ran-b ↓ rhus-t k* ruta ↓ sabin ↓ sars ↓ sel k* sep k* **Sil** k* spig ↓ spong ↓ squil k* staph k* sul-ac ↓ **Sulph** k* tarax ↓ thuj k* verat k* zinc b4.de
  - **drawing**: cycl b7.de
  - **gnawing** pain: agar k* agn bg2 alum k* ant-c k* bar-c k* canth k* caps k* cycl k* dros k* kali-c k* led k* *Lyc* k* **Olnd** k* par k* ph-ac k* phos k* plat bg2 puls k* rhus-t k* ruta k* spong k* staph k* tarax k* verat k*
  - **sore**: agar b2.de* alum b2.de* ambr b2.de* ant-c b2.de* arg-met b2.de* bar-c b2.de* bry b2.de* calc b2.de* cann-s b2.de* canth b2.de* caps b2.de* cic b2.de* dros b2.de* graph b2.de* *Hep* b2.de* kali-c b2.de* led b2.de*

- **scratching**; after – **sore**: ...
  lyc b2.de* m-ambo b2.de* m-aust b2.de* mag-c b2.de* mang b2.de* merc b2.de* *Mez* b2.de* nat-c b2.de* nat-m b2.de* nit-ac b2.de* nux-v b2.de* **Olnd** b2.de* par b2.de* *Petr* b2.de* ph-ac b2.de* phos b2.de* psor bg2 puls b2.de* **Rhus-t** b2.de* sabin b2.de* sars b2.de* sel b2.de* **Sep** b2.de* sil b2.de* squil b2.de* *Staph* b2.de* **Sulph** b2.de* verat b2.de* zinc b2.de*
  - **tearing** pain: ars k* bell k* bry k* calc k* cycl k* *Lyc* k* m-ambo b2.de* puls k* rhus-t k* sep k* sil k* staph k* **Sulph** k*
  - **ulcerative** pain: am-c k* **Am-m** k* arn k* asaf k* bar-c k* bell k* bry k* calc k* carb-v k* caust k* chin k* cic k* con k* cycl k* *Graph* k* hep k* kali-c k* led k* mag-m k* mang k* merc k* nat-m k* petr k* *Phos* k* *Puls* k* ran-b k* **Rhus-t** k* sep k* **Sil** k* spig k* staph k* sul-ac k* *Sulph* k* thuj k* verat k* zinc k*
- **sore**: acon k* agar b2.de* *Alum* k* ambr k* *Ant-c* k* apis bro1 arg-met k* *Arn* k* *Ars* k* aur k* aur-ar k2 aur-s k2 *Bad* bro1 bar-c k* bell bro1 bell-p bro1 borx k* bov bro1 brass-n-o srj5• *Bry* k* *Calc* k* calc-sil k2 cann-s k* canth k* caps k* carb-an k* carb-v k* caust k* chel k* chin k* chinin-ar chinin-s bro1 *Cic* k* **Cimic** k* coff k* colch k* con bro1 crot-h crot-t bro1 *Dol* bro1 *Dros* k* **Eup-per** k* euph bro1 fago bro1 ferr k* ferr-ar ferr-p galeoc-c-h gms1• *Glon* *Graph* k* ham hell k* **Hep** k* *Ign* k* kali-c k* kali-s kali-sil k2 lach bro1 led k* lyc k* m-ambo b2.de* m-arct b2.de m-aust b2.de* mag-c k* mang k* *Merc* k* mez k* mosch k* nat-c k* *Nat-m* k* *Nat-p* *Nit-ac* k* nux-m bro1 *Nux-v* k* olib-sac wmh1 olnd k* osm bro1 paeon bro1 par k* *Petr* k* ph-ac k* phos k* *Plat* k* *Psor* bro1 *Puls* k* ran-b k* ran-s bro1 rhus-d bro1 *Rhus-t* k* rumx bro1 ruta k* sabin k* sars k* sel k* semp bro1 **Sep** k* sil k* spig k* spong k* squil k* staph k* *Still* sul-ac k* *Sulph* k* tarent-c bro1 teucr k* *Ther* bro1 **Thuj** b4a.de valer k* verat k* *Vinc* bro1 xero bro1 **Zinc** k*
  - **covered**; as if: arg-met bg2 sulph bg2
- **splinter**; as from a: calad **Hep** **Nit-ac**
- **sticking** (See Sticking)
- **stinging**: *Acon* agar b2.de agn b2.de alum k* am-m b2.de anac k* ant-c b2.de **Apis** arg-met arge-pl rwt5• arn k* ars k* ars-i ars-s-f k2 **Asaf** k* atra-r bnm3• bar-c k* bar-s k2 bell k* *Bry* k* calc k* calc-sil k2 cann-s k* canth k* caps k* carb-v k* caust k* chel b2.de *Chin* b2.de chir-fl bnm4• cina clem b2.de *Cocc* k* colch k* con k* cot br1 *Cycl* b2.de dig k* dros k* dulc k* euphr b2.de **Graph** b2.de guaj b2.de **Ham** k* hell k* hep k* hyos k* ign k* iod k* *Kali-bi* kali-c k* kali-n b2.de kreos b2.de lach k* loxo-recl bnm10• *Lyc* k* m-ambo b2.de m-arct b2.de mag-c k* meny k* *Merc* k* *Mez* k* mur-ac b2.de nat-c b2.de nat-m b2.de *Nit-ac* b2.de *Nux-v* k* olnd k* par b2.de ph-ac k* phos k* plat k* plb b2.de prot pte1• *Puls* k* ran-b k* ran-s k* rhod b2.de *Rhus-t* k* ruta b2.de sabad k* sabin b2.de samb sars b2.de sel k* sep k* *Sil* k* spig k* spong k* squil k* stann k* **Staph** k* stront-c b2.de *Sul-ac* k* *Sulph* k* *Tarax* b2.de teucr b2.de ther ptk1 **Thuj** k* **Urt-u** k* vac jl2 verat b2.de viol-t k* zinc b2.de
  - **burning**: *Acon* b2.de* alum b2.de* anac b2.de* arg-met b2.de* arn b2.de* ars b2.de* **Asaf** b2.de* bar-c b2.de* bell b2.de* *Bry* b2.de* calc b2.de* cann-s b2.de* caps b2.de* carb-v b2.de* caust b2.de* cina b2.de* *Cocc* b2.de* colch b2.de* dig b2.de* dros b2.de* dulc b2.de* hell b2.de* hep b2.de* hyos b2.de* ign b2.de* iod b2.de* kali-c b2.de* lach b2.de* *Lyc* b2.de* m-ambo b2.de* m-arct b2.de* m-aust b2.de* mag-c b2.de* meny b2.de* *Merc* b2.de* *Merc-c* b4a.de *Mez* b2.de* *Nux-v* b2.de* olnd b2.de* ph-ac b2.de* phos b2.de* plat b2.de* *Puls* b2.de* ran-b b2.de* ran-s b2.de* *Rhus-t* b2.de* sabad b2.de* samb b2.de* sel b2.de* sep b2.de* *Sil* b2.de* spig b2.de* spong b2.de* squil b2.de* stann b2.de* **Staph** b2.de* *Sul-ac* b2.de* *Sulph* b2.de* **Thuj** b2.de* viol-t b2.de*
  - **needles** and pins; as from: tarent mrr1 [heroin sdj2]
- **tearing** pain: ambr anac arg-n bar-c bell berb *Camph* cann-s chlor coloc *Graph* *Kreos* *Nit-ac* *Phos* plan
- **touch** agg.: *Canth* ↓
  - **ulcerative** pain: *Canth*
- **ulcerative** pain: alum k* am-c k* **Am-m** k* ambr k* anac k* ang b2.de* ars k* bell k* bov k* *Bry* k* canth k* caps k* carbn-s caust k* cham k* *Chin* k* *Cic* k* cocc k* dros k* ferr k* **Graph** k* hep k* ign k* kali-ar *Kali-c* k* *Kali-i* kali-n k* kali-s kali-sil k2 kreos k* lach k* laur k* mag-c k* mag-m k* *Mang* k* merc k* mur-ac k* nat-c k* *Nat-m* k* nat-p nit-ac k* nux-v k* petr k* ph-ac k* *Phos* k* **Puls** k* **Rhus-t** k* ruta k* sars k* *Sep* k* sil k* spig k* spong k* stann k* staph k* *Sul-ac* k* sulph k* tarax k* *Thuj* k* verat k* zinc k*

○ - **Below** skin:
  - **scratching**; after: arn ↓ asaf ↓ bar-c ↓ bry ↓ calc ↓ carb-v ↓ con ↓ cycl ↓ *Graph* ↓ hep ↓ kali-c ↓ led ↓ nat-m ↓ petr ↓ *Phos* ↓ *Puls* ↓ ran-b ↓ *Rhus-t* ↓ **Sil** ↓ staph ↓ *Sulph* ↓ zinc ↓

Pain – Below skin – **scratching**: ...
  - **ulcerative** pain: arn bg2 asaf bg2 bar-c bg2 bry bg2 calc bg2 carb-v bg2 con bg2 cycl bg2 *Graph* bg2 hep bg2 kali-c bg2 led bg2 nat-m bg2 petr bg2 *Phos* bg2 *Puls* bg2 ran-b bg2 *Rhus-t* bg2 **Sil** bg2 staph b7.de* *Sulph* bg2 zinc bg2
- **Flesh**; between skin and: *Zinc* b4a.de
- **Folds**; on: caust ↓
  - **sore**: caust ptk1
- **Mucocutaneous** borders: *Nit-ac* ↓
  - **splinter**; as from a: *Nit-ac* br1
- **Spots**; in: aloe arn ↓ **Sulph**
  - **sore**: arn mtf11

PARCHMENT (See Hard - parchment)

PERIODICITY: tub bg2 vip bg2

PERSPIRATION; no (See Dry - perspire; Inactivity)

PETECHIAE (See Eruptions - petechiae)

PITYRIASIS (See Eruptions - scaly)

PRESSURE agg.; slight: sulph ptk1

PRICKLING: *Acon* aesc k2 aeth a1 agar k* agath-a nl2• *Anag* br1 ant-t k* **Apis** k* arg-met k2 ars bg2 bar-c bell k* berb calc-p bg2 cann-i cann-s b2.de* carb-ac c1 carbn-s k2 cartl-s rly4• celt a1 cham bg2 chir-fl bnm4• cimic cist k2 clem a1 cod br1 *Colch* croc k* dig c1 dros k* dulc fd4.de **Ham** k* kali-ar kali-c ptk1 kali-s fd4.de kalm bg2 lat-m bnm6• **Lob** k* loxo-recl bnm10• **Lyc** k* mag-m mand rsj7• med melal-alt gya4 merc-c bg2 mez k* mosch k* nat-m nat-sil fd3.de• neon srj5• nit-ac nux-v ph-ac k2 **Plat** k* plut-n srj7• positr nl2• prot pte1*• psor k2 pycnop-sa mrz1 ran-b k2 *Ran-s* k* rhod bg2 **Rhus-t** sabad k* sang hr1 sel c1 sep k* **Staph** sne suis-em rly4• suis-hep rly4• sul-ac **Sulph** k* sumb taosc iwa1• tell rsj10• thal-xyz srj8• *Urt-u* vanil fd5.de zinc k*
- **feverish** tingling: cub c1
- **fleas**; as if from: merc rb2 podo fd3.de• symph fd3.de•
- **needles**; as from: celt a1
- **nettles**; as from | **fever**; during: apis bg2 bry bg2 rhus-t bg2
- **perspiration**; during: apis bg2 arn bg2 **Ars** bg2 *Cocc* b7.de* colch bg2 *Croc* bg2 *Nux-v* b7.de* plat bg2 *Puls* bg2 **Rhod** bg2 **Rhus-t** bg2 sel bg2 *Sep* bg2 spig bg2 sulph bg2 *Tarax* b7.de* thuj bg2
- **spots**, in (= circumscribed parts): kali-s fd4.de nat-sil fd3.de• nicc-met sk4• positr nl2• sel c1 vanil fd5.de
- **walking** in open air agg.: *Sulph*
- **warm**; when: ant-c ptk1 gels psa kali-ar morg-p pte1• sumb urt-u ptk1
  - **bed** agg.; in: **Sulph**

PRURITUS (See Itching)

PSORIASIS (See Eruptions - psoriasis)

PURPURA: *(↗Ecchymoses; GENERALS - Thrombocytopenia)* *Acon* c2* *Arn* c2* *Ars* c2* bapt bro1 bell bro1 bry bro1 carb-v c2* cary c2 chinin-s bro1 chlol c2* cor-r c2 *Crot-h* c2* *Ham* c2* jug-r c2* kali-chl c2 kali-i br1* *Lach* c2* led mrr1 *Merc* c2* *Ph-ac* c2* *Phos* c2* rhus-t bro1 *Rhus-v* c2* sal-ac bro1* sec c2* staphytox jl2 sul-ac c2* sulfon bro1 tax c2 ter bro1* verat-v bro1
- **colic**; with: bov bro1 coloc bro1 cupr bro1 merc-c bro1 thuj bro1
- **formication**; with: phos alj
- **hemorrhagica**: aln bro1* *Arn* k* ars k* ars-i ars-s-f k2 bell berb both bro1* bov bry k* *Carb-v* chinin-s chlol *Cimic* sne cor-r *Crot-h* k* *Cupr* ferr-pic bro1* *Ham* k* hir mtf11 hyos iod k* ip bro1* *Kali-i* **Lach** k* **Led** k* merc bro1* merc-c bro1* mill bro1* naja bro1* nat-n br1* nux-v *Ph-ac* k* **Phos** k* *Rhus-t* rhus-v bro1* ruta **Sec** k* sil stram **Sul-ac** k* sulph **Ter** k* thlas bro1*
- **idiopathica**: *(↗GENERALS - Thrombocytopenia)* acon mp1• *Arn* mp1• ars mp1• bapt mp1• bell mp1• bry mp1• carb-v mp1• chinin-s mp1• chlor mp1• *Crot-h* mp1• ham mp1• jug-r mp1• kali-i mp1• *Lach* mp1• merc mp1• *Nat-m* sne ph-ac mp1• *Phos* mp1• rhus-t mp1• sal-ac mp1• *Sec* mp1• sul-ac mp1• sulfon mp1• ter mp1• verat-v mp1• [rhen-met stj]
- **itching**: phos alj
- **miliaris**: acon k* am-c am-m arn bell bry c2 *Cact* c2 coff dulc euph-cy c2 *Jab* c2 sul-ac sulph
- **rheumatica**: acon bro1* ars bro1* *Bry* bro1* merc bro1* *Rhus-t* bro1* rhus-v bro1*

Skin

- **senilis**: ars bar-c bry con *Lach* op rhus-t sars ptk1 **Sec** sul-ac
- **weakness**; with: am bro1 *Ars* bro1 carb-v bro1 lach bro1 merc bro1 *Sul-ac* bro1

RADIANT; unnaturally: [heroin sdj2]

RAWNESS (See Excoriation)

RELAXED:
- **accompanied** by | **nausea** (See STOMACH - Nausea - accompanied - skin - relaxed)

RHAGADES (See Cracks)

RINGWORM (See Eruptions - herpetic - circinate)

ROOM agg.: sulph bg2

ROUGH: alum h2* *Alumn* k* *Am-c* b4a.de anag *Apis* b7a.de apoc k2 ars k* *Ars-i* bar-c bell b2.de* bry k* **Calc** k* calen ptk1 crot-t k* dig a1 fl-ac bg2* *Graph* k* hep k* *Hyos* b7a.de hyper a1 *Iod* k* kali-c b2.de* kali-i k* laur b2.de* *Lith-c* k* mang k2 merc k* merc-c b4a.de mez k* *Nat-c* k* *Nat-m* nit-ac bg2* olnd k* op a1 parth vml3• **Petr** k* ph-ac k* phos k* phyt bg3* *Plb* psor bg2* *Rhus-t* k* ruta b2.de* sabad bg1* sars k* *Sec* k* seneg b4a.de **Sep** k* sil tl1 spong fd4.de stram k* **Sulph** k* thal-xyz srj8• tub ptk1* zinc bg1
- **knots**; as from small: hyper ptk1
- **winter** agg.: alumn kl
- ○ - **Folds**; on: mang ptk1

RUBBING:
- **clothes**; of: | **agg.**: bad ptk1 olnd ptk1
- **constant** | **agg.**: sep ptk1
- **slight** | **agg.**: sulph ptk1 vinc ptk1

RUPIA (See Eruptions - rupia)

SCALY: | **eruptions**; with (See Eruptions - scaly)

SCARS (See Cicatrices)

SCLEROSIS: x-ray sp1

SCROFULODERMA: (↗*Eruptions - scrofulous*) calc-i bro1 *Calc-s* bro1 petr bro1 scroph-n bro1 ther bro1

SEASONS:
- **summer**:
  - **agg.**: kali-c bg2 lach bg2 mur-ac bg2 nat-m bg2
  - **amel.**: aesc bg2 petr bg2 psor bg2
- **winter** agg.: alum bg2* graph bg2 petr bg2 psor bg2

SEBORRHEA (See FACE - Greasy)

SENSITIVENESS: *Acon* k* *Agar* k* alum k* alum-sil k2 am-c b2.de* am-m ambr k2 ant-c k* ant-t k* **Apis** k* *Arg-n* arist-cl sp1 arn k* ars k* ars-s-f k2 asaf ptk1 aur k* aur-ar k2 aur-s k2 bamb-a stb2.de• bar-c k* bar-s k2 **Bell** k* bov k* brass-n-o srj5• *Bry* k* bufo cadm-s k2 calad k2 *Calc* k* calc-f sp1 calc-p a1 *Calc-s* calc-sil k2 camph k* cann-s k* canth k* caps k* carb-an k* carb-v k* caust k13 cham k* **Chin** k* *Chinin-ar* chir-fl bnm4• *Chlor* k* choc srj3• cimic cina k2 *Coc-c* bg2* coca-c sk4• *Coff* k* colch k* *Con* k* cot br1 *Crot-c* cupr k* cupr-ar bg2 cycl cyt-l sp1 dulc fd4.de *Ferr* k* ferr-ar *Ferr-p* fl-ac bg2 foll jl3 galeoc-c-h gms1• gels helo-s bnm14• **Hep** k* *Hyos* k* ign k* *Ip* k* kali-ar kali-c k* *Kali-p* *Kali-s* *Kreos* k* lac-c k2 lac-d k2 **Lach** k* lat-m sp1* *Led* k* lyc k* **Lyss** k* m-arct b2.de m-aust b2.de* *Mag-c* k* mag-p k2 mand sp1 mang bg2* meny sf **Merc** k* mez *Mosch* k* nat-c k* *Nat-m* k* nat-p *Nit-ac* ptk1 *Nux-m* k* *Nux-v* k* olib-sac wmh1 olnd k* op bg2* ox-ac par k* **Petr** k* **Ph-ac** k* phos k* plan bg2* **Plb** k* puls k* *Pycnop-sa* mrz1 pyrid rly4• ran-b k* ran-s k* rhus-d c2 *Rhus-t* k* ruta ptk1 sabad b7.de* sacch-a fd2.de• *Sang* sars b2.de* *Sec* k* *Sel* k* *Sep* k* **Sil** k* *Spig* k* spong k* squil k* stann k* staph k* sul-ac k* **Sulph** k* symph fd3.de• tarent bg2* tell jl3 thal-xyz srj8• *Thuj* k* trios rsj11• tritic-vg fd5.de tub ptk1* *Urt-u* mrr1 v-a-b jl2 vanil fd5.de verat k* vult-gr sze5• *Zinc* k* zinc-p k2 [heroin sdj2 spect dfg1 tax jsj7]
- **right** side: *Crot-h*
- **left** side: ign gk *Lach* pycnop-sa mrz1
- **accompanied** by | **paralysis** (See GENERALS - Paralysis - accompanied - skin - sensitiveness)
- **air** agg.; draft of: *Acon* b7.de ambr b7.de *Anac* b4a.de bell b4.de* *Calc* b4.de* *Caps* b7.de* *Caust* b4.de cham b7.de *Chin* b7.de graph b4a.de hep b4a.de ign b7.de* kali-c b4a.de lach b7a.de *Nat-c* b4.de *Nux-v* b7.de phos b4.de* puls b7.de *Sel* b7.de sep b4.de* sil b4.de* spig b7.de sulph b4.de* valer b7.de verb b7.de
- **air** agg.; dry: *Carb-an* b4a.de *Sep* b4a.de

Sensitiveness: ...
- **air** agg.; in open: am-c b4a.de anac b4a.de bell b4.de calc b4.de* *Carb-an* b4a.de *Caust* b4.de *Cham* b7.de *Cocc* b7.de *Coff* b7.de* graph b4a.de *Hep* b4a.de *Ign* b7.de *Kali-c* b4.de lyc b4.de* m-aust b7a.de merc b4a.de mosch b7a.de *Nat-c* b4.de* nit-ac b4.de *Nux-v* b7.de* op b7.de *Petr* b4.de ph-ac b4.de *Phos* b4.de* *Plb* b7.de* puls b7a.de *Rhus-t* b7.de *Sep* b4a.de sil b4.de *Sulph* b4.de verb b7.de viol-t b7a.de
- **air** agg.; wet: agar b4.de *Am-c* b4.de* aur b4a.de *Calc* b4.de carb-an b4.de* carb-v b4.de* dulc b4.de* *Lyc* b4a.de mag-c b4a.de *Mang* b4a.de *Mur-ac* b4a.de nat-c b4.de *Nux-m* b7.de *Rhod* b4.de *Sep* b4.de verat b7.de zinc b4a.de
- **air**; to: calc bg2 ign bg2 plb bg2
- **chill**; during: camph bg2 ign bro1 nux-v b7.de*
- **cold** air | **wet**: *Nux-m* b7a.de
- **cold**; to: bacls-7 fmm1• mag-c br1
  - **air** agg.: *Agar* b4.de* *Am-c* b4.de *Anac* b4a.de *Ant-c* b7a.de **Aur** b4.de* bell b4.de *Calc* b4.de camph b7.de *Caps* b7.de* *Carb-an* b4a.de carb-v b4.de **Caust** b4.de* *Cham* b7.de *Cocc* b7a.de *Coff* b7a.de ip b7.de lyc b4a.de *Mez* b4.de mosch b7.de* nat-m b4a.de *Nux-m* b7.de petr b4.de ph-ac b4a.de *Phos* b4a.de rhod b4.de* *Rhus-t* b7.de* sabad b7.de* *Sep* b4.de* **Spig** b7.de* stram b7.de viol-t b7.de
  - **objects**; to cold: **Lac-d** vh
- **diminished**: acet-ac br1* *Acon* bro1 ars bro1 aur bro1 bufo bro1 *Cann-i* bro1 *Carbn-o* bro1 carbn-s bro1 elae bro1 hyos bro1 *Ign* bro1 kali-br bro1 merc bro1 *Nux-v* bro1 *Plb* bro1 pop-cand bro1 sec bro1 *Zinc* bro1
- **feel** my skin; as if I can: galeoc-c-h gms1•
- **fever**; during: *Chin* mrr1
- **light**; to: prot fmm1•
  - **ultraviolet**: prot fmm1•
- **pressure**; to: helo-s bnm14• mand sp1
- **rubbing**; to: arist-cl sp1
- **sore**, prickly: galeoc-c-h gms1•
- **spots**; in: ferr ptk1 hep ptk1
- **striking**; to slight: colch bg2 sep bg2
- **sun**, to: morg-p pte1*• psor jl2 *Ros-d* wla1 sel jl
- **touch**; to: *Acon* b7a.de *Ang* b7.de ant-c b7.de *Ant-t* b7a.de arg-met vh1 bry b7a.de calc-f sp1 calc-s tl1 camph b7.de chin tl1* cina b7.de* coff tl1 *Colch* b7.de fum rly1• hep tl1 lac-c tl1 lach tl1 laur b7.de led tl1 mand sp1 nat-pyru rly4• nux-m b7a.de nux-v b7.de *Olnd* b7.de* puls b7.de *Ran-b* tl1 sabad b7.de sanic tl1 **Spig** b7.de* ther tl1 [heroin sdj2 tax jsj7]
  - **hard** pressure | **amel.**: chin vml
- **warm**:
  - **air** agg.: anac b4.de aur b4.de* calc b4.de* carb-v b4a.de *Cocc* b7a.de ign b7a.de *Iod* b4a.de ip b7.de phos b4.de* *Puls* b7.de rhus-t b7a.de seneg b4a.de sep b4.de* *Sulph* b4a.de
  - **water**:
    - **agg.**: olib-sac wmh1
    - **hot** water; to: bamb-a stb2.de•
- **weather**; change of: dulc bro1 hep bro1 kali-c bro1 psor bro1 *Sulph* bro1
- **wet** agg.; getting: *Am-c* b4a.de *Calc* b4a.de carb-v b4a.de dulc b4a.de mur-ac b4a.de rhod b4a.de sep b4a.de
- **wind**; to: *Cham* b7.de* chin b7a.de *Nux-v* b7.de puls b7.de
- **wool**: morg-p fmm1•

SHINING: acon bg3* **Apis** k* *Aur* ptk1 **Bell** k* *Bry* ptk1 calc-f ptk1 carb-ac ptk1 caust ptk1 *Chel* cist ptk1 *Colch* euphr ptk1 glon ptk1 *Kali-bi* ptk1 *Kreos* **Lac-c** ptk1 lach ptk1 mang ptk1 med k* nat-m k2* *Phos* ptk1 plb k2 rhus-t ptk1 rhus-v a1 sabin ptk1 sel k2 sil ptk1 syph ptk1 *Ter* ptk1 thuj k2

SHRIVELLED (See Wrinkled)

SMALL; he were crowded in a skin several times too: meny rb2

SMARTING (See Biting; Burning)

SOFT:
- **feels**: ars ptk1 caps ptk1 haliae-lc srj5• kali-c ptk1 lach ptk1 sil ptk1 thuj ptk1
  - **children**; in: borx mtf33

SORE:
- **becomes** sore (See Decubitus)
- **feeling** (See Pain - sore)

SOUR FOOD agg.: *Bell* bg2 *Rhus-t* bg2

SPIDER angioma: _(↗Eruptions - angioma; GENERALS - Tumors - angioma)_ card-m mrr1 plb mtf33
- **portal** congestion; from: card-m mrr1
- **red**: med ptk1

SPLINTER; pain as from (See Pain - splinter)

SPOTS (See Discoloration - spots)

STICKING: _Acon_ k* _Agar_ k* agn k* alum k* am-c am-m k* anac k* ant-c k* **Apis** k* _Arn_ k* ars k* ars-i _Asaf_ k* **Bar-c** k* bell k* **Bry** k* bufo _Calc_ k* _Cann-s_ k* _Canth_ k* caps k* carb-v k* _Carbn-s_ _Caust_ k* chel k* _Chin_ k* chinin-ar clem k* coc-c _Cocc_ k* coff _Colch_ k* con k* _Crot-h_ _Crot-t_ _Cycl_ k* dig k* dios dros k* dulc k* euphr k* **Graph** k* guaj k* ham fd3.de• hell k* hep k* hyos k* ign k* iod k* kali-ar kali-c k* kali-n k* kali-p kali-s kreos k* lach k* **Lyc** k* m-ambo b2.de* m-arct b2.de mag-c k* meny k* _Merc_ k* merc-c b4a.de* mez k* mur-ac k* nat-c k* nat-m k* nat-p _Nit-ac_ k* nux-v k* olnd k* par k* ph-ac k* _Phos_ k* plan plat k* plb k* **Puls** k* ran-b k* ran-s k* rhod k* **Rhus-t** k* ruta k* _Sabad_ k* sabin k* sars k* sel k* _Sep_ k* _Sil_ k* spig k* **Spong** k* squil k* _Stann_ k* _Staph_ k* stront-c k* sul-ac k* _Sulph_ k* symph fd3.de• _Tarax_ k* tell teucr k* _Thuj_ k* verat k* **Viol-t** k* visc bg2 zinc k* zinc-p k2
- **evening** | **bed** agg.; in: alum cycl symph fd3.de• thuj zinc
- **night**: am-c h2* anac cann-s merc thuj
- **chill**; during: bry bg2 nat-m bg2 rhus-t bg2 _Samb_ bg2
- **electric**: _(↗Electric - sparks)_ agar
- **leeches** were drawing at spots on skin; as if: coc-c a1*
- **perspiration**; with: cann-s k2 spong fd4.de
- **scratching**; after: agar bg2 alum k* am-m k* anac bg2 arn k* ars k* asaf k* **Bar-c** k* bell k* _Bry_ k* calad bg2 calc k* calc-sil k2 cann-s k* canth k* carbn-s _Caust_ k* chel k* chin k* cocc k* con k* _Cycl_ k* dros k* dulc k* _Graph_ k* hell k* kali-ar kali-c k* kali-s _Lach_ k* lyc k* m-arct b2.de _Merc_ k* mez k* nit-ac k* nux-v par k* ph-ac k* _Puls_ k* ran-b k* **Rhus-t** k* ruta k* _Sabad_ k* sars k* sel k* sep k* sil k* _Spong_ k* _Squil_ k* staph k* stront-c k* **Sulph** k* tarax k* teucr k* thuj k* _Viol-t_ k* visc bg2 zinc k*
  - **amel.**: cina a1
- **shivering**; during: samb b7.de
- **splinter**; as from a (See Pain - splinter)

STIFFNESS: kalm ptk1 _Rhus-t_ ptk1 verat ptk1

STINGING (See Pain - stinging)

STINGS of insects: _(↗GENERALS - Wounds - bites)_ acet-ac c2* acon k* aids nl2• am-c mp1• am-caust mp1• am-m b7a.de* androc srj1• ant-c k* _Anthraci_ _Apis_ k* _Arn_ k* ars k* bamb-a stb2.de• _Bell_ k* bry bufo _Calad_ k* camph mp1• caps b7a.de _Carb-ac_ caust k* _Cedr_ k* cham b7a.de coloc k* crot-h c2* _Cycl_ b7a.de dulc fd4.de echi br1* **Gent-l** sne grin c1* gua mp1• gymne mp1• _Hydr-ac_ c2 hyper k* ip st _Kali-n_ b4a.de kali-perm mp1• kreos _Lach_ k* lat-m ptk1* **Led** k* merc k* _Mosch_ c2 _Nat-m_ nat-sil fd3.de• nux-v b7a.de podo fd3.de• prot fmm1• pulx ptk1* pyrog mp1• sacch-a fd2.de• samb b7a.de scor c1 semp ptk2 seneg k* sep k* sil k* sisy mp1• spirae mp1• **Staph** sne sul-ac sulph k* tab c1* tarent **Urt-u** k*
- **bees**; from: apis mrr1* arn tl1 carb-ac mtf11 led ptk1 tab ptk1 urt-u tl1* viol-o br1
- **itching** and burning: _Calad_ b7a.de
- **mosquitoes**; from: calad ptk1 led tl1 tab ptk1
- **sensation** as if: graph h2
- **wasps**; of: arn tl1 mez sys

STRIAE: cortiso sp1

SWELLING: acal bro1 _Acet-ac_ bro1 acon k* _Agar_ bro1 agn k* aloe am-c k* _Anac_ bro1 anil br1 _Ant-c_ k* **Apis** k* _Arn_ k* **Ars** k* _Ars-i_ ars-s-f k2 _Asaf_ k* aur k* _Bar-c_ k* bar-m _Bell_ k* bell-p bro1 beryl sp1 borx k* both bro1 brass-n-o srj5• **Bry** k* bufo bg2 calc k* canth k* caps tl1* carb-an k* carb-v k* carc fd2.de• caust k* celt a1 chel k* _Chin_ k* chinin-ar chir-fl bnm4• **Cic** cina k* clem k* cocc k* colch k* coloc k* _Con_ k* _Cop_ crot-h k* cupr ptk1 cycl b2.de* dig k* _Dulc_ k* elat bro1 **Euph** k* ferr k* ferr-ar ferr-i k* fl-ac graph k* hell k* hep k* hippoz bro1 _Hydrc_ hyos k* iod k* _Kali-ar_ kali-bi kali-br kali-c k* kali-n k* kali-s kreos k* _Lach_ k* lat-m bnm6• _Led_ k* loxo-lae bnm12• loxo-recl bnm10• _Lyc_ k* mag-c k* mang k* **Merc** k* mez k* mur-ac k* nat-ar nat-c k* _Nat-m_ k* nat-p nat-sal bro1 nit-ac k* **Nux-v** k* olnd k* op k* petr k* ph-ac k* _Phos_ k* plb k* prim-o bro1 _Prun_ bro1 **Puls** k* rhod k* **Rhus-t** k* ruta k* _Sabin_ k* _Samb_ k* sars k* sec k* seneg k* sep k* sil k* spig k* spong k* squil k* stram k* stront-c k* sul-ac k* **Sulph** k* syph ptk1 thuj k* _Thyr_ bro1 verat k*

Swelling: ...
- **accompanied** by | **eczema** (See Eruptions - eczema - accompanied - swelling)
- **baglike**: apis bg2 cann-xyz bg2 chin bg2 kali-c bg2
- **bluish** black: acon k* am-c k* _Arn_ k* **Ars** k* aur k* _Bell_ k* carb-v k* con k* _Dig_ k* hep k* **Lach** k* mang k* _Merc_ k* nux-v k* _Op_ k* ph-ac k* phos k* plb k* **Puls** k* samb k* sec k* seneg k* sil k* sul-ac k* _Verat_ k*
- **burning**: _Acon_ k* am-c b4a.de ant-c k* _Apis_ b7a.de _Arn_ k* **Ars** k* _Asaf_ b7.de* _Bell_ k* **Bry** k* calc k* canth b7.de* carb-an k* carb-v k* caust k* chin k* _Clem_ b4a.de cocc k* colch k* coloc k* crot-h dulc k* euph k* hell k* hep k* hyos k* iod k* kali-ar kali-c k* _Lach_ k* led k* **Lyc** k* mang k* _Merc_ k* mez k* _Mur-ac_ b4a.de nat-ar nat-c k* nux-v k* olnd b7a.de op k* petr b4a.de ph-ac k* **Phos** k* _Puls_ k* _Rhus-t_ k* samb k* sars b4a.de sec k* sep k* _Sil_ k* _Spig_ k* spong k* squil k* stann k* sul-i k2 **Sulph** k*
- **cold**: _Ars_ k* asaf k* bell k* cocc k* _Con_ k* cycl k* _Dig_ b4a.de* dulc k* lach k* rhod k* sec k* spig k*
- **crackling**: bell b4a.de
- **crawling**: acon k* _Arn_ k* caust k* chel k* colch k* con k* lach k* _Merc_ k* nat-c k* nux-v k* ph-ac k* _Puls_ k* **Rhus-t** k* sec k* _Sep_ k* spig k* _Sulph_ k*
- **drawing** pain; with: arn b7a.de led b7a.de
- **dropsical**: _(↗GENERALS - Dropsy - external)_ acet-ac br1 acon k* **Ant-c** k* apis b7a.de* apoc k2 **Ars** k* _Ars-i_ aur k* aur-ar k2 _Bell_ k* **Bry** k* cain br1 calad c2 canth k* chel k* **Chin** k* chinin-ar _Colch_ k* coloc k* con k* _Dig_ k* _Dulc_ k* elat br1 eup-per euph k* _Ferr_ k* _Ferr-ar_ guaj k* **Hell** k* hyos k* iod k* kali-ar kali-c k* kali-n k* kali-s kali-sil k2 kola stb3• lach k* _Led_ k* _Lyc_ k* _Merc_ k* mez k* mur-ac k* nat-c k* _Nat-m_ nat-p _Nat-s_ nit-ac k* _Nux-m_ olnd k* op k* phos k* plb k* psor al2 **Puls** k* rhod k* _Rhus-t_ k* ruta k* _Sabin_ k* _Samb_ k* sars k* sec k* seneg k* sep k* sil k* **Squil** k* stram k* sul-i k2 **Sulph** k* **Tell** verat k*
  - **intermittent** fever; after: _Ars_ b4a.de dulc b4a.de kali-c b4a.de sep b4a.de
  - **menses**; with suppressed: cham b7a.de*
  - **miliary** eruption; after: _Ars_ b4a.de bry b7a.de carb-an b4a.de _Hell_ b7a.de kali-c b4a.de _Rhus-t_ b7a.de
  - **scarlatina**; after: **Lach** b7a.de
  - **wound**; around: lat-h bnm5•
- **flat**: _Apis_ b7a.de
- **gouty**: acon b7a.de ant-c b7a.de arn b7a.de asaf b7a.de _Bry_ b7a.de chin b7a.de cocc b7a.de _Colch_ b7a.de _Led_ b7a.de _Puls_ b7a.de _Rhus-t_ b7a.de _Sabin_ b7a.de
- **greasy**, oily: ant-c b7.de sabin b7.de*
- **hard**: acon k* agn k* all-s a1 ant-c k* _Arn_ k* ars k* asaf k* bell k* **Bry** k* bufo bg2 calc k* _Caust_ k* chin k* cina k* con k* dig k2 dulc k* graph k* hell k* hep k* lach k* _Led_ k* loxo-lae bnm12• lyc k* merc k* mez k* nux-v k* ph-ac k* **Phos** k* plb k* **Puls** k* **Rhus-t** k* sabin k* _Samb_ k* sep k* sil k* spong k* squil k* _Stront-c_ k* _Sulph_ k* _Ther_
- **inflamed**: _Acon_ k* agn k* am-c k* ant-c k* arn k* _Ars_ k* asaf k* bell k* borx k* **Bry** k* calc k* canth k* carb-v k* caust k* cocc k* colch k* con k* crot-h _Hep_ k* hyos k* _Iod_ bg2 lach k* lyc k* mang k* **Merc** k* mez k* mur-ac k* nat-c k* nit-ac k* petr k* phos k* **Puls** k* _Rhus-t_ k* sars k* sep k* _Sil_ k* _Sulph_ k* thuj k* verat k*
  - **tetter**; of: graph h2
- **itching**: **Apis** bg2
- **metastatic**: dulc b4a.de
- **painful**: acon b7a.de ant-c b7a.de _Arn_ b7a.de canth b7a.de chin b7a.de nux-v b7a.de _Puls_ b7a.de _Rhus-t_ b7a.de _Spig_ b7a.de _Staph_ b7a.de
- **painless**: _Euphr_ b7a.de _Rhus-t_ b7a.de
- **pale**: _Ant-c_ k* **Apis** k* _Arn_ k* _Ars_ k* bell k* **Bry** k* calc k* chin k* cocc k* con k* dig k* euph k* ferr k* graph k* hell k* hep k* _Iod_ k* kali-c k* kreos k* lach k* **Lyc** k* merc k* nit-ac k* nux-v k* phos k* plb k* _Puls_ k* rhod k* _Rhus-t_ k* _Sabin_ k* sep k* sil k* spig k* sul-i k2 _Sulph_ k* _Thuj_ b4a.de
- **red**: am-c b4a.de _Carb-v_ b4a.de merc-c b4a.de nat-c b4a.de petr b4a.de sars b4a.de _Thuj_ b4a.de
  - **bright** red: _Apis_ b7a.de
  - **dark** red: _Ant-c_ b7a.de _Arn_ b7a.de _Asaf_ b7a.de _Bry_ b7a.de _Chin_ b7a.de nux-v b7a.de olnd b7a.de _Puls_ b7a.de _Rhus-t_ b7a.de _Sabin_ b7a.de
  - **streaks**: apis b7a.de
- **scratching**; after: ant-c k* arn k* ars k* bell k* bry k* calc k* canth k* caust k* chin k* con k* dulc k* hep k* kali-c k* kali-sil k2 kreos k* **Lach** k* led k* _Lyc_ k* mang k* _Merc_ k* mez k* nat-ar k2 nat-m k* nit-ac k* phos k* _Puls_ k* ran-b b7.de _Rhus-t_ k* sabin k* samb k* sep k* sil k* sul-ac k* _Sulph_ k*
- **shining**: _Arn_ k* _Ars_ k* **Bry** k* merc k* _Puls_ bg2 _Rhus-t_ k* sabin k* _Sulph_ k*
- **sore** pain; with: rhus-t b7a.de

- **spongy**: *Ant-c* k* **Ars** k* ars-i bar-c b4a.de bell k* calc k* *Carb-an* k* carb-v k* caust k* clem k* con k* graph k* iod k* kreos k* **Lach** k* lyc k* merc k* mez b4a.de nit-ac k* nux-v k* petr k* ph-ac k* *Phos* k* rhus-t k* sabin k* *Seneg* b4a.de sep k* **Sil** k* sul-i k2 *Sulph* k* thuj k*
- **spots**; in: antip br1
- **stinging**: acon k* agn k* ant-c k* **Apis** k* arn k* ars k* **Bry** k* canth k* **Caust** k* chel k* chin k* *Cocc* k* con k* cycl k* dig k* ferr k* graph k* kali-n k* lach k* led k* mag-c k* mang k* mez k* *Nit-ac* k* nux-v k* phos bg2 **Puls** k* *Rhus-t* k* ruta k* sabad k* sep k* sil spong k* *Sulph* k* *Thuj* k*
- **suppurating**: sil b4a.de *Staph* b7a.de sulph b4a.de
- **tearing**: colch b7a.de *Led* b7a.de
- **tense**: ant-c b7.de* bry b7.de* chin b7a.de led b7.de* *Puls* b7.de *Rhus-t* b7.de* *Sabin* b7a.de *Samb* b7a.de

○ - **Affected** parts; on: acon k* agn k* ant-c k* arn k* ars k* asaf k* aur k* **Bell** k* *Bry* k* *Calc* k* *Canth* k* carb-an k* carb-v k* *Caust* k* chin k* chir-fl bnm4• clem k* cocc k* con k* cypr br1 dig k* dulc k* euph k* ferr k* graph k* hell k* *Hep* k* iod k* **Kali-c** k* lach k* led k* *Lyc* k* mag-c k* mang k* **Merc** k* mur-ac k* nat-c k* nat-p *Nit-ac* k* nux-v k* petr k* ph-ac k* *Phos* k* plb k* **Puls** k* rhod k* **Rhus-t** k* ruta k* sabin k* *Samb* k* sars k* sec k* **Sep** k* *Sil* k* spig k* *Spong* k* stram k* **Sulph** k* thuj k*
- **Orifices**: nit-ac ptk1*
- **Paralyzed** parts; of: plb b7a.de
- **Single** parts: acon b7.de ant-c b7.de* arn b7.de* *Bry* b7.de canth b7.de chin b7.de* cocc b7.de* colch b7.de* lach b7.de* **Puls** b7.de* rhus-t b7.de* spig b7.de
- **Ulcers**; about: lyc bg2 *Rhus-t* bg2
- **Uncovered** parts; of: rhus-t b7a.de

SWOLLEN sensation: alum k* *Am-m* k* ant-c k* arn k* *Ars* k* aur k* **Bell** k* *Bry* k* canth k* caps k* carb-v k* *Chin* k* cic b7.de cocc k* con k* dig k* dulc k* guaj k* hep k* hyos k* ign k* *Kali-n* k* kreos k* lach k* *Laur* k* merc k* nit-ac k* nux-m k* nux-v k* *Par* k* plat k* **Puls** k* **Rhus-t** k* sabin k* sars k* seneg k* sep k* sil k* *Spig* k* spong k* stann k* *Staph* k* sul-ac k* sulph k* verat k* zinc k*

TEARING (See Pain - tearing)

TENSION: acon k* agn k* alum k* alum-p k2 alum-sil k2 am-c k* am-m k* anac k* *Ang* b2.de* ant-c k* apis bg2 arg-met k* *Arg-n* k* *Arn* k* ars k* ars-i asaf k* asar k* aur k* aur-ar k2 *Bapt* *Bar-c* k* bar-m bar-s k2 bell k* berb borx k* bry k* bufo bg2 cact ptk1 calc k* cann-i k2 canth k* carb-an k* carb-v k* **Caust** k* cham k* chin k* chinin-s bg2 colch k* *Coloc* k* *Con* k* crot-h k* crot-t br1 dig k* dulc k* euph k* guaj k* hell k* hep k* hura br1 iod k* kali-c k* kali-s kali-sil k2 kreos k* lach k* laur k* led k* lyc k* m-arct b2.de mag-m k* mang k* meny k* merc k* mez k* mosch k* mur-ac k* nat-c k* nat-m k* nat-s k* **Nit-ac** k* *Nux-v* k* olnd k* par k* petr k* ph-ac k* phel bg2 **Phos** k* pic-ac bg2 *Plat* k* plb k* *Puls* k* rhod k* *Rhus-t* k* ruta k* sabad k* sabin k* sars k* *Sep* k* sil k* *Spig* k* spong k* stann k* staph k* **Stront-c** k* sul-i k2 *Sulph* k* tarax k* thuj k* verat k* verb k* *Viol-o* k* viol-t k* zinc k*
- **egg** white were dried on the skin; as if: alum ptk1 ol-an ptk1 sul-ac ptk1
- **scratching**; after: ang b2.de* caust k* *Lach* k* m-arct b2.de ph-ac k* ruta k* spig k* *Stront-c* b2.de* *Stront-met*
- **sensation** of: pic-ac bg2

THICK: alum k2 am-c k* anac k* **Ant-c** k* *Ars* k* bell bg2 borx k* bros-gau mrc1 *Calc* castor-eq br1* choc srj3• cic k* cist ptk1 clem k* cupr bg2 *Dulc* k* *Graph* k* hydr-ac hydrc ptk1 kali-c *Lach* k* *Lyc* par k* parth vml3• petr ptk1 phos psor k2 rad-br ptk1 *Ran-b* k* **Rhus-t** k* sars mrr1 **Sep** k* sil k* sulph k* thiosin br1 thuj k* verat k* viol-t bg2
- **scratching**; skin becomes thick after: ant-c k* ars k* cic k* *Dulc* k* graph k* *Iod* *Kali-bi* *Lach* k* *Ran-b* k* **Rhus-t** k* sep k* thuj k* verat k*
- **sensation** as if skin were thick: sanguis-s hm2•
  - **drawn** into wrinkles; and could not be: par rb2

THIN (= transparent): nat-m mrr1 phos br1* syph mrr1
- **sensation** of a: (↗*FACE - Thin - skin - sensation)* bamb-a stb2.de• thuj bg1

THRILLING sensation: celt a1

TINEA VERSICOLOR (See Eruptions - pityriasis versicolor)

TINGLING (See Prickling)

TOUCH:
- **agg.**: asaf bg2 mez tl1 plb bg2

Touch: ...
- **clothes** agg.; of: | **Under** skin: oena ptk1

TREMBLING: mang ptk1 phos ptk1 sec ptk1 tab ptk1
- **fever**; during: rhus-t b7.de

TUMORS (See Excrescences)

ULCERATIVE pain (See Pain - ulcerative)

ULCERS: abr c2* acon k* aesc k2 agar agn b2.de* all-c k* alst-s mtf11 *Alum* k* alum-p k2 alum-sil k2 alumn k* *Am-c* k* am-m c2 ambr k* anac k* anac-oc bro1 anag hr1 anan c2* ang b2.de* ant-c k* ant-t k* *Anthraci* k* anthraco br1 arg-met k* *Arg-n* k* arn k* **Ars** k* **Ars-i** k* **Asaf** k* *Aster* c2* *Aur* k* aur-ar k2 aur-i k2 aur-s k2 bals-p c2* bar-c k* *Bar-m* *Bell* k* benz-ac k* berb k* beryl sp1 borx k* bov k* brass-n-o c2 *Brom* k* *Bry* k* bufo k2 *Calc* k* calc-p k* *Calc-s* k* calc-sil c2* *Calen* hr1* camph k* canth k* carb-ac k* carb-an k* **Carb-v** k* carbn-s k2* card-m hr1 *Caust* k* cetr c2 *Cham* k* chel k* chin k* chinin-ar chlor k* chr-o c2 cic k* cina k* *Cinnb* cist k* clem k* cocc k* coch c2 coff k* colch k* com c2* *Con* k* croc k* *Crot-h* c2* cund hr1* *Cupr* k* cupr-ar bro1 cycl k* dig k* dros k* dulc k* echi c2* euph k* ferr k* ferr-ar ferr-p *Fl-ac* k* gali c2* *Gaul* bro1 ger bro1* get c2 *Graph* k* grin c2 guaj k* *Ham* c2* hed sp1 hell c2 hell-v c2 **Hep** k* hippoz c2* hydr k* hydrin-m c2 hyos k* hyper hr1 ign k* *Iod* k* ip k* jug-r bro1 *Kali-ar* k* **Kali-bi** k* *Kali-c* k* **Kali-chl** k* kali-i c2* kali-p k* **Kali-s** k* kali-sil k2 *Kreos* k* lac-c c2* **Lach** k* lap-a hr1 lappa c2 led k* liat c2* **Lyc** k* lyss c2 m-ambo b2.de* m-arct b2.de m-aust b2.de mang k* **Merc** k* merc-act c2 merc-c bro1 *Mez* k* mill hr1 mur-ac k* *Nat-ar* *Nat-c* k* *Nat-m* k* nat-p nat-s bro1 **Nit-ac** k* nux-m k* nux-v k* *Paeon* k* par k* *Petr* k* *Ph-ac* k* *Phos* k* **Phyt** k* *Pip-m* a1 plb k* plb-i c2 polyg-xyz c2 *Psor* k* **Puls** k* *Pyrog* k* rad-br c11* ran-a c2* ran-b k* ran-fl c1 ran-s k* rhus-g br1 *Rhus-t* k* ruta k* sabin k* samb k* sang k* *Sars* k* scroph-n bro1 *Sec* k* sel k* seneg k* *Sep* k* **Sil** k* sol-ni c2 spiros-af oss• spong k* squil k* *Staph* k* stram k* stront-c k* strych-g c2 sul-ac k* sul-i k2* **Sulph** k* symph br1* syph c2* syzyg c2 tarax k* tarent mrr1 tarent-c bro1* tep c2 teucr b2.de *Thuj* k* trach-xyz c2 uncar-tom mp4• verat k* vesp a1 viol-t hr1 vip ptk1 xan c1* *Zinc* k* zinc-o mtf11 zinc-p k2
- **absorption** of pus: *Iod* bg2 *Phos* bg2 sil bg2
- **accompanied** by:
  - **diabetes** (See GENERALS - Diabetes mellitus - accompanied - ulcers)
  - **dropsy** (See GENERALS - Dropsy - general - accompanied - ulcers)
  - **weakness** (See GENERALS - Weakness - accompanied - ulcers)
- **black**: ant-t k* **Anthraci** k* **Ars** k* *Asaf* k* bell k* bism ptk1 **Carb-v** k* *Carbn-s* *Con* k* euph k* grin ham k2 ip k* kali-ar ptk1 kali-bi bg2 **Lach** k* **Lyc** k* *Mur-ac* k* *Plb* k* rhus-t k* sars **Sec** k* *Sil* k* squil k* *Sul-ac* k* *Sulph* k*
  - **bluish** black: carb-v bg2 crot-h bg2 lach bg2 tarent bg2 vip bg2
  - **spots** | **Centre**; on: *Kali-bi*

○ • **Base**: **Ars** k* calc-f bro1 carb-an bro1 ip k* lach k* mur-ac bro1 plb k* sil k* sulph k* tarent-c bro1 thuj
  - **Margins**: *Ars* k* con **Lach** k* sil k* sulph k*
- **bleeding**: acet-ac k2 ant-t k* arg-met k* *Arg-n* arn k* **Ars** k* *Ars-i* ars-s-f k2 *Asaf* k* bar-m k2 bell k* cadm-met gm1 *Calc* k* calc-s calen hr1 carb-an k* *Carb-v* k* carbn-s caust k* *Con* k* croc k* *Crot-h* k* dros k* dulc k2 formal gm1 *Graph* k* ham k* **Hep** k* hydr hyos k* *Iod* k* kali-ar *Kali-c* k* kali-s kali-sil k2 kalm k* kreos k* **Lach** k* **Lyc** k* m-ambo b2.de* **Merc** k* *Mez* k* mill k2 nat-m k* **Nit-ac** k* **Ph-ac** k* **Phos** k* *Puls* k* pyrog k2 *Ran-b* k* rhus-t k* ruta k* sabin k* **Sang** rmk1• *Sec* k* sep k* *Sil* k* *Sul-ac* k* sul-i k2 *Sulph* k* thlas ptk1 thuj k* x-ray gm1 zinc k* zinc-p k2
  - **night**: *Kali-c* k*
  - **black** blood: ham k2 lach k2
    - **clotted**: ars h2 puls k2
  - **menses** | **before** | **agg.**: phos b4.de*
    - **during** | **agg.**: **Phos** k*
  - **offensive**: caust bg2
  - **touch** agg.: ars bro1 *Carb-v* k* dulc bro1 ham alj **Hep** k* *Hydr* kreos bro1 *Lach* k* merc bro1 merc-c alj *Mez* k* *Nit-ac* k* *Petr* bro1 *Phos* bro1

○ • **Edges**: **Ars** k* asaf k* caust k* hep k* lach k* *Lyc* k* *Merc* k* ph-ac k* phos k* puls k* sep k* *Sil* k* sulph k* thuj k*

- **bluish**: aesc k2 arn k* **Ars** k* *Asaf* k* *Aur* k* aur-ar k2 bell k* bism hr1 bry k* calc k* calc-sil k2 carb-an *Carb-v* k* *Con* k* crot-h ptk1 *Hep* k* hippoz hr1 *Kali-i* k* **Lach** k* *Lyc* k* *Mang* k* *Merc* k* mur-ac ptk1 ph-ac k* sec k* seneg k* **Sil** k* staph k* tarent-c ptk1 thuj ptk1 verat k* vip ptk1 [echi stj]

○ • **Edges**: *Asaf* kali-s *Mang* k* nit-ac

- **boils**: | **from**: *Calc-p*
- **burning**: alumn bro1 ambr k* anth vh **Anthraci** k* apis b7a.de* **Ars** k* ars-s-f k2 asaf k* aur k* aur-ar k2 aur-s k2 bar-c k* bar-m bell k* bov k* *Brom* b4a.de bry k* *Bufo* calc k* calc-s calc-sil k2 canth k* *Carb-ac* carb-an k* **Carb-v** k* **Carbn-s** **Caust** k* *Cham* k* chin k* chinin-ar cinnb *Clem* k* coloc hr1 *Con* k* *Dros* k* ferr-ar graph k* ham hr1 *Hep* k* *Hydr* ign k* kali-ar k* kali-bi bg2 *Kali-c* k* kali-m k2 kali-p kali-s kali-sil k2 *Kreos* k* lach k* **Lyc** k* mang k* **Merc** k* *Mez* k* mur-ac k* *Nat-ar* *Nat-c* k* nat-m k* nat-p *Nit-ac* k* nux-v k* petr k* ph-ac k* *Phos* b2.de* *Plb* k* **Puls** k* *Ran-b* k* **Rhus-t** k* ruta b7.de sars k* sec k* sel k* sep k* **Sil** k* squil k* *Staph* k* stront-c k* sul-ac b4.de* **Sulph** k* syph tarent tl1 tarent-c mrr1 *Thuj* k* zinc k* zinc-p k2
  - **night**: *Anthraci* bell h1* *Carb-v* k* cham h1* *Hep* k* *Lach* k* *Merc* rhus-t sep h2* *Staph*
  - **chill**; during: ars b4a.de* merc bg2
  - **menses**; during: *Carb-v*
  - **touch** agg.: ars bell canth carb-v *Lach* *Lyc* merc mez puls rhus-t sil sulph

○ • **Around** about: *Ars* k* *Asaf* k* bell k* *Caust* k* cham k* hep k* *Lach* k* *Lyc* k* *Merc* k* mez k* mur-ac k* nat-c k* nux-v k* petr k* phos k* **Puls** k* *Rhus-t* k* sep k* *Sil* k* staph k*

  - **Margins**; in: **Ars** k* asaf k* carb-an k* *Caust* k* clem k* *Hep* k* *Lach* k* **Lyc** k* **Merc** k* mur-ac k* petr k* ph-ac k* phos k* puls k* ran-b k* sep k* **Sil** k* staph k* sulph k* thuj k*

- **burrowing** (See undermined)
- **cancerous**: *Ambr* k* ant-c k* *Anthraci* k* apis **Aran** b7a.de **Ars** k* *Ars-i* **Ars-s-f** k2 *Aster* bro1 aur k* aur-ar k2 aur-i k2 **Aur-s** k2* bell k* **Brom** b4a.de **Bufo** calc k* *Calc-s* calc-sil k2 *Carb-ac* k* *Carb-an* k* *Carb-v* k* *Carbn-s* caust k* chel k* chim c1* chinin-s j5.de* clem k* coenz-q mtf11 *Con* k* *Crot-c* cund k* dor a1 dulc k* *Ferr* bg2* fl-ac sf1.de fuli bro1 *Gali* br1* *Graph* **Hep** k* *Hippoz* hydr k* *Jug-c* sne kali-ar k* kali-bi k2* kali-c *Kali-i* k* *Kreos* k* *Lach* k* **Lyc** k* *Lyss* k* mang *Merc* k* *Mill* hr1* mur-ac *Nit-ac* k* *Petr* *Ph-ac* *Phos* k* *Phyt* k* *Rhus-t* k* rumx sabin b7.de *Sang* rmk1• sars k* *Sep* k* **Sil** k* spong k* squil k* *Staph* k* stram b7a.de sul-i k2 **Sulph** k* tarent-c bro1 *Thuj* k* *Zinc* b4a.de
- **chancres**: (*↗GENERALS - Chancre*) cinnb k2 protg br1
- **chronic**: cadm-met gm1 carc mlr1• formal gm1 fuli br1 grat br1 kali-tcy gm1 maland jl2 petr hr1 pyrog mtf11 strych-g br1 syzyg br1 x-ray gm1
- **cicatrices**; in: (*↗Cicatrices*) asaf k2* calc-p ptk1 paeon gm1
- **coalescing**: merc bro1
- **coition** agg.: kreos ptk1
- **cold**:
  - **air** | **amel.**: *Dros* **Led** k* **Puls** sec a1
  - **application** amel. the pain; cold: *Cham* *Fl-ac* **Led** *Lyc* **Puls**
  - **feeling** in them; with a cold: ang b2.de* *Ars* k* **Bry** k* *Dig* bg2 merc k* petr k* plb k* *Rhus-t* k* *Sil* k* thuj k*
- **confluent**: ant-t b7.de
- **copper** colored | **Edges**: kali-bi bro1
- **corroded** edges: **Borx** bg2
- **crawling**; with: acon k* ant-t k* **Arn** k* bell k* caust k* *Cham* k* *Clem* k* colch k* *Con* k* croc k* graph k* hep k* kali-c k* *Lach* k* merc k* nat-c k* nat-m k* nat-p nux-v k* ph-ac k* phos b4.de plb k* puls k* ran-b k* **Rhus-t** k* sabin k* sec k* **Sep** k* spong k* staph k* sul-ac k* sulph k* thuj k*
- **crusty**: anac bg2 ant-c b7.de* ars k* ars-s-f k2 bar-c k* *Bell* k* bov k* bry k* **Calc** k* *Calc-s* calc-sil k2 carb-an k* chr-met dx cic k* clem k* **Con** k* *Graph* k* hell b7.de *Hep* k* *Kali-bi* k* kali-i bg2 *Kali-s* led k* **Lyc** k* **Merc** k* **Mez** k* mur-ac k* nux-v b7.de olnd k* par b7.de petr bg2 *Ph-ac* plb b7.de puls k* ran-b k* **Rhus-t** k* sabin b7.de sars k* *Sep* k* **Sil** k* spong b7.de* staph k* **Sulph** k* viol-t k*
  - **black** scab: bell h1* **Kali-bi**
- **deep**: *Agar* k* *Ant-c* k* *Anthraci* **Ars** k* ars-s-f k2 *Asaf* k* *Aur* k* aur-ar k2 *Aur-m-n* hr1 aur-s k2 *Bell* k* *Bov* **Calc** k* **Calc-s** k* calc-sil k2 *Carb-v* k* carbn-s caust k* chel k* clem k* *Com* k* *Con* k* *Hep* k* *Hippoz* k* *Hydr* **Kali-bi** k* kali-c ptk1 *Kali-i* k* kreos k* **Lach** k* led k* *Lyc* k* m-ambo b2.de* **Merc** k* *Merc-c* k* mez ptk1 *Mur-ac* k* nat-ar nat-c k* nat-m k* nat-p **Nit-ac** k* *Petr* k* ph-ac k* phos k* *Psor* k* **Puls** k* rad-br ptk1 ran-b ptk1 rat ptk1 rhus-t k* ruta k* sabin k* *Sars* sel k* *Sep* k* **Sil** k* staph k* stram k* **Sulph** k* *Syph* tarent ptk1 tarent-c bro1 thuj k*
- **diabetic** (See GENERALS - Diabetes mellitus - accompanied - ulcers)
- **dirty**: *Arn* *Ars* k* calc k* **Lach** k* *Lyc* k* **Merc** k* mosch **Nit-ac** k* sabin k* *Sulph* k* *Thuj* k*
- **discharges**: hep tl1 kali-ar ptk1 kali-s ptk1 nat-s ptk1 *Rhus-t* ptk1 zinc-s ptk1
  - **albuminous**: *Calc* k* loxo-lae bnm12• *Puls* k*
  - **blackish**: *Anthraci* bry chin ham k2 lyc sec k2 *Sulph*
  - **bloody**: ant-t k* *Anthraci* *Apis* b7a.de arg-met k* arn k* **Ars** k* *Ars-i* **Asaf** k* bell k* calc-s canth k* carb-an *Carb-v* k* carbn-s *Caust* k* com *Con* k* croc k* *Dros* k* graph k* ham k2 **Hep** k* hyos k* iod k* kali-ar *Kali-c* k* kali-s kali-sil k2 kreos k* lach k* *Lyc* k* m-ambo b2.de* **Merc** k* mez k* nat-m k* *Nit-ac* k* *Petr* k* ph-ac k* phos k* *Puls* k* pyrog rhus-t k* ruta k* sabin k* *Sars* sec k* sep k* *Sil* k* sul-ac k* sul-i k2 sulph k* thuj k* zinc k* zinc-p k2
    - **black**: carb-v k2 elaps br
  - **brownish**: anac k* *Anthraci* ars k* *Bry* k* calc k* carb-v k* con k* nit-ac k2 puls k* rhus-t k* *Sil* k*
    - **dark** brown: ars b4.de *Sil* b4a.de
  - **cheesy**: merc k* *Sil* bg2
  - **copious**: acon k* ap-g br* arg-met b2.de* arg-n *Ars* k* *Asaf* k* *Bell* bg2 bry k* *Calc* k* calen hr1 canth k* carbn-s *Chin* k* cic k* cist k2 *Fl-ac* k* graph k* hep bg2 **Iod** k* *Kali-c* k* kali-sil k2 kreos k* lach bg2 lyc k* mang k* *Merc* k* mez k* nat-c k* ph-ac k* *Phos* k* plb bg2 **Puls** k* *Rhus-t* k* ruta k* sabin k* **Sep** k* *Sil* k* squil k* *Staph* k* *Sul-ac* b4a.de sul-i k2 sulph k* thuj k*
  - **corrosive**: agar k* am-c k* anac k* **Ars** k* **Ars-i** ars-s-f k2 bell k* calc k* carb-an *Carb-v* k* **Caust** k* cham k* chel k* cist k2 clem k* con k* crot-c cupr k* *Fl-ac* *Graph* k* *Hep* k* hippoz k* ign k* *Iod* k* **Kali-bi** k* *Kali-i* kreos k* lach k* *Lyc* k* **Merc** k* mez k* nat-c k* nat-m k* *Nit-ac* k* nux-v k* *Petr* k* *Phos* k* plb k* puls k* *Ran-b* k* *Ran-s* k* **Rhus-t** k* ruta k* sep k* **Sil** k* spig k* *Squil* k* *Staph* k* sul-ac k* sul-i k2 sulph k* zinc k*
  - **gelatinous**: arg-met k* arn k* bar-c k* cham k* ferr k* merc k* sep k* *Sil* k*
  - **gray**: ambr k* ars k* carb-ac carb-an b2.de* **Caust** k* chin k* *Kali-chl* lyc k* merc k* sep k* *Sil* k* thuj k*
  - **green**: *Ars* k* ars-i sne *Asaf* k* aur k* aur-ar k2 calc-sil k2 *Carb-v* k* *Caust* k* clem k* com k* kali-chl *Kali-i* kreos k* *Lyc* merc k* naja nat-c k* *Nat-s* k* *Nux-v* k* par *Phos* k* *Puls* k* rhus-t k* sec k* sep k* *Sil* k* staph k* *Sulph* k*
    - **yellow**: aur b4a.de *Brom* b4a.de *Caust* b4a.de clem b4a.de merc b4a.de sep b4a.de sil b4.de*
  - **hot**: puls mtf33
  - **ichorous**: am-c k* ant-t k* *Anthraci* k* **Ars** k* *Asaf* k* aster bro1 aur k* aur-ar k2 bov k* calc k* *Carb-ac* bro1 *Carb-an* **Carb-v** k* *Carbn-s* *Caust* k* *Chin* k* cic k* clem k* *Con* k* cor-r bro1 cund hr1 *Dros* k* graph k* ham hr1 *Hep* k* *Kali-ar* *Kali-c* k* kali-i *Kali-p* k* kali-sil k2 kreos k* *Lach* k* **Lyc** k* mang k* **Merc** k* *Mez* k* mur-ac k* **Nit-ac** k* nux-v k* ph-ac k* *Phos* k* plb k* *Psor* k* *Ran-b* k* *Ran-s* k* **Rhus-t** k* *Sang* sec k* sep k* **Sil** k* squil k* *Staph* k* *Sul-ac* b4a.de sulph k* viol-t hr1
  - **maggots**; with: ars k* calc k* merc k* *Sabad* k* *Sil* k* sulph k*
  - **odorless**: calc b4a.de caust b4a.de
  - **offensive**: alum alum-p k2 *Am-c* k* *Anan* bro1 *Anthraci* k* *Apis* **Ars** k* ars-i sne ars-s-f k2 *Asaf* k* aur k* aur-ar k2 aur-s k2 **Bapt** k* bell k* bov k* *Bry* k* *Calc* k* calc-f bro1 calc-p *Calc-s* calc-sil k2 *Calen* bro1 *Carb-ac* k* **Carb-an** k* **Carb-v** k* **Carbn-s** caust k* *Chel* k* *Chin* k* chr-met dx chrysar br1 cic k* clem k* com k* *Con* k* crot-h k* crot-t bro1 cycl k* *Echi* bro1 eucal bro1 *Ferr* bg2 fl-ac k2* gels bro1 *Ger* bro1 *Graph* k* grin *Guaj* **Hep** k* hydr *Hyper* k* *Kali-p* k* kreos k* **Lach** k* **Lyc** k* mang k* *Merc* k* merc-c bro1 *Mez* k* *Mur-ac* k* nat-c k* *Nat-p* **Nit-ac** k* nux-m k* nux-v k* **Paeon** k* *Petr* k* **Ph-ac** k* *Phos* k* plb k* *Psor* k* *Puls* k* pyrog k* rhus-t k* ruta k* sabin k* *Sars* *Sec* k* *Sep* k* **Sil** k* **Staph** k* sul-ac k* **Sulph** k* thuj k* vinc
    - **cadaverous**: *Brom* b4a.de carb-v b4a.de
    - **cheese**; like old: calc bg2 *Con* bg2 *Hep* k* sulph k*
    - **eggs**; like rotten: *Brom* b4a.de calc b4a.de* [calc-s stj1 kali-s stj1]
    - **herring** brine; like: *Graph* k* *Lach* b7a.de *Tell*

Skin

- **offensive**: ...
  - ⋮ **putrid**: *Am-c* k* *Anthraci* k* **Ars** k* **Asaf** bapt bell borx *Brom* b4a.de *Calc* k* *Calc-s* **Chel** chin k* cycl graph **Hep** k* kali-p k2 lach lyc *Merc* **Mur-ac** k* *Nit-ac Ph-ac Phos* **Psor** k* **Puls** pyrog k2 rhus-t k* *Sars Sep* **Sil** sulph
- **oily**: ham bg2 mez bg2
- **purulent**: sulph mtf33
- **retarded**: **Hep** b4a.de **Merc** b4a.de *Merc-c* b4a.de sil b4a.de
- **salty**: *Ambr* b7.de sil b4a.de staph b7.de
- **scanty**: acon k* *Ars* k* bar-c k* *Bell* k* bov k* bry k* **Calc** k* carb-v k* caust k* chin k* cina k* clem k* *Coff* k* *Cupr* k* dros k* *Dulc* k* *Graph* k* *Hep* k* *Hydr* hr1 hyos k* ign k* ip k* kali-bi bg2 kreos k* **Lach** k* led k* lyc k* *Mag-c* k* **Merc** k* nux-v k* *Petr* k* *Phos* k* *Plat* k* plb k* puls k* rhus-t k* sars k* *Sep* k* **Sil** k* spong k* *Staph* k* sulph k* *Verat* k*
- **sour** smelling: calc k* graph k* **Hep** k* lyc mtf33 *Merc* k* nat-c k* sep k* *Sulph* k*
- **staining** | **black**: bry b2.de* chin b2.de* lyc b2.de* *Sulph* b2.de*
- **sticky**: sep bg2
- **tallow**; like: *Merc* k* *Merc-c*
- **tenacious**: ars k* asaf k* *Bov* k* cham k* *Con* k* *Graph* k* *Hydr* **Kali-bi** bg2* merc k* mez k* ph-ac k* phos k* sep k* sil k* staph k* viol-t k*
- **thick**: ars-i sne calc-s k2 caps b7.de merc b4a.de sep b4a.de **Sil** b4.de*
- **thin**: ant-t k* *Ars* k* ars-s-f k2 **Asaf** k* calc-sil k2 *Carb-v* k* **Caust** k* dros k* fl-ac k2 *Iod* k* *Kali-c* k* *Kali-i* k* kali-sil k2 *Lyc* k* **Merc** k* nit-ac k* *Phos* k* plb k* puls k* *Pyrog* ran-b k* ran-s k* rhus-t k* ruta k* sec bg2 *Sil* k* staph k* sul-ac k2 sul-i k2 *Sulph* k* thuj k*
- **watery**: ant-t k* *Ars* k* ars-i ars-s-f k2 *Asaf* k* calc k* carb-v k* **Caust** k* clem k* con k* *Dros* k* fl-ac k2 *Graph* k* hell bg2 *Iod* k* *Kali-c* k* lyc k* **Merc** k* nit-ac k* nux-v k* *Petr* k* ph-ac k2 plb k* psor bg2 puls k* *Ran-b* k* *Ran-s* k* *Rhus-t* k* ruta k* *Sil* k* squil k* staph k* sul-i k2 sulph k* thuj k*
  - ⋮ **bloody**: carb-ac ptk1 kali-ar ptk1 rhus-t ptk1
- **whitish**: *Am-c* k* *Apis* b7a.de ars k* *Calc* k* carb-v k* hell k* lach bg2 *Lyc* k* **Mez** *Puls* k* sep k* sil k* sulph k* thuj bg2
- **yellow**: acon k* alum alum-p k2 am-c k* ambr k* anac k* ang b2.de* arg-met k* ars k* ars-i k2 ars-s-f k2 aur k* aur-ar k2 aur-i k2 aur-s k2 bov k* bry k* *Calc* k* calc-s calc-sil k2 *Calen* bg2 canth hr1 caps k* *Carb-v* k* carbn-s *Caust* k* cic k* *Clem* k* con k* croc k* dulc k* graph k* hep k* *Hydr* iod k* **Kali-bi** kali-n k* *Kali-p* k* kali-s k* *Kreos* k* lyc k* mang k* *Merc* k* **Mez** nat-ar nat-c k* nat-m k* nat-p *Nit-ac* k* nux-v k* *Phos* k* **Puls** k* ran-b k* rhus-t k* ruta k* sec k* sel k* *Sep* k* *Sil* k* spig k* *Staph* k* sul-ac k* sul-i k2 sulph k* thuj k* viol-t k*
  - ⋮ **brownish**: aur b4a.de *Sil* b4.de
  - ⋮ **grayish** yellow: *Caust* b4a.de merc b4.de
- **drunkards**: sul-ac k2
- **dry**: **Kali-bi** k* mag-c k2 mang ptk1 sec k2
- ○ • **Edges**: *Sang*
- **eczematous** | **Edges**: kali-bi bro1
- **egg**-shaped: eberth jl2
- **elevated**: merc b4a.de ph-ac b4a.de *Thuj* b4a.de
- **elevated** and indurated margins; with: *Apis* **Ars** k* asaf k* bry k* carb-an k* caust k* cic k* cina k* cinnb clem k* *Hep* k* hydr *Kali-ar Kali-bi* lach k* **Lyc** k* *Merc* k* mur-ac k* *Nit-ac Petr* k* ph-ac k* *Phos* k* *Puls* k* ran-b k* sep k* **Sil** k* staph k* *Sulph* k* thuj k*
- **elevated** margins; with: ars bro1 calen bro1 nit-ac bro1 ph-ac bro1 *Sil* bro1
- **fistulous**: *Agar* k* ant-c k* ars k* *Asaf* k* aur k* aur-ar k2 aur-s k2 bar-c k* *Bell* k* *Berb* bg2 **Bry** k* **Calc** k* *Calc-f* bg2* *Calc-p* k* calc-s calc-sil k2 calen bro1 carb-ac *Carb-v* k* carbn-s **Caust** k* chel k* *Cinnb* k* clem k* *Con* k* eucal hr1 *Fl-ac* k* *Hep* k* *Hippoz* k* kali-i bro1 kreos k* *Lach* b2.de* led k* **Lyc** k* *Merc* k* *Mill* hr1* nat-c k* *Nat-m* k* nat-p *Nit-ac* k* *Petr* k* ph-ac b2.de* **Phos** k* phyt bro1 **Puls** k* pyrog mtf11 rhus-t k* ruta k* sabin k* sel k* sep k* **Sil** k* stann j5.de *Staph* k* stram k* *Sulph* k* syph mtf11 *Ter* bg2 *Thuj* k* tub-k mtf11
- **flat**: (↗*superficial*) *Am-c* k* ang b2.de* ant-c b2.de* ant-t b2.de* *Ars* k* *Asaf* k* bell k* carb-an b2.de* carb-v b2.de* *Chin* k* cor-r k* **Lach** k* **Lyc** k* **Merc** k* nat-c b2.de* **Nit-ac** k* petr b2.de* *Ph-ac* k* phos b2.de* *Puls* k* *Ran-b* k* sel k* *Sep* k* *Sil* k* staph b2.de* sulph b2.de* *Thuj* k*
- **flesh**; like raw | **Base**: ars bro1 merc bro1 nit-ac bro1
- **foul**: ail bg2 *Am-c* k* *Anthraci Ars* k* *Asaf* k* aur k* aur-ar k2 bapt bg2 bell k* borx bov b2.de* bry k* *Calc* k* *Calc-s* calc-sil k2 carb-ac mtf11 *Carb-v* k* caust k* chel k* *Chin* k* cic k* con k* crot-h bg2 cycl k* echi br1 ger br1 *Graph* k* **Hep** k* kali-ar ptk1 kreos k* *Lach* bg2 lyc k* mang k* merc k* mez k* **Mur-ac** k* nat-c k* nit-ac k* nux-m k* nux-v k* *Ph-ac* k* phos k* plb k* puls k* *Rhus-t* k* ruta k* sabin k* sec k* sep k* **Sil** k* staph k* sul-ac k* *Sulph* k* thuj k*
  - • **asa** foetida; like: carb-v ptk1
- **fungous**: alum alumn ant-c *Arg-n* **Ars** bell *Calc Carb-an Carb-v Carbn-s* caust *Cham* cinnb clem *Crot-c* graph *Hydr* kreos *Lach Merc* mur-ac bro1 *Nit-ac Petr* phos sabin **Sep** **Sil** staph *Sulph Thuj*
- **gangrenous**: am-c k* am-m bg2 ant-t bg2 antho bg2 *Anthraci* **Ars** k* *Asaf* k* aur bg2 **Bapt** k* bell b4a.de* bism both fne1• caps gm1 *Carb-v* k* *Chin* k* *Cinnb* cist tl1 com bg2 *Con* k* *Crot-c Crot-h* k* euph k* kali-bi k* kali-p *Kreos* k* **Lach** k* loxo-lae bnm12• **Lyc** merc bg2 mill *Mur-ac* nat-pyru mtf11 petr b4a.de ph-ac b4a.de plb bg2 ran-b bg2 rhus-t sabin *Sars* **Sec** k* **Sep** *Sil* k* squil k* sul-ac k* sulph b4a.de* vip bg2
  - • **hot** (= inflammatory): acon bg2 **Ars** bg2 **Bell** bg2 mur-ac bg2 *Sabin* bg2 *Sec* bg2
- ○ • **Edges**: anthraci bro1 *Ars* bro1 *Carb-v* bro1 kreos bro1 lach bro1 nit-ac bro1 sec bro1 *Sul-ac* bro1 tarent-c bro1
- **glistening** (See shining)
- **gray** | **Base**: nit-ac bg2 thuj bg2
- **healing** slowly (See indolent)
- **herpetic**: agath-a nl2• *Sars*
- **honeycomb**; like: cinnb ptk1
- **hot**: *Acon* b7.de bry b7.de lyc b4a.de ruta b7.de sep b4.de
- **indolent**: (↗*GENERALS - Diabetes mellitus - accompanied - ulcers*) *Agar* k* agn k* alum alum-p k2 *Alumn* anac k* *Anag* bro1 **Ars** k* *Ars-i* ars-s-f k2 *Asaf* vh aster bro1 bals-p mtf11 bar-c bro1 *Calc* k* calc-f bro1 *Calc-i* bro1 *Calc-p* k* calc-s calc-sil k2 *Calen* br1 camph k* carb-an k* *Carb-v* k* carbn-s chel bro1 com **Con** k* crot-h cupr bro1 *Dulc* k* eucal bro1 *Euph* k* fl-ac k* fuli bro1 *Ger* br1* *Graph* k* *Hippoz* k* *Hydr* k* *Iod* k* ip k* kali-ar **Kali-bi** bg2* kali-c k* *Kali-i* bro1 kali-s kali-sil k2 **Lach** k* *Laur* k* loxo-lae bnm12• **Lyc** k* m-ambo b2.de mang k2 merc bg2* mill hr1 *Mur-ac* k* *Nit-ac* k* olnd k* *Op* k* paeon bro1 petr **Ph-ac** k* phos k* phyt bro1 plb k* *Psor* k* *Puls* k* pyrog k2* rad-br br1 rhus-t k* sal-ac hr1 *Sang Sars Sec* k* *Sep* k* **Sil** k* *Still* stram k* sul-ac k2 sul-i k2 **Sulph** k* syph bro1 syzyg bro1 xan hr1 zinc k* zinc-p k2 [bell-p-sp dcm1]
- **indurated**: agn k* alum k2 *Alumn Arg-met* arn k* *Ars* k* ars-i ars-s-f k2 *Asaf* k* *Aur* k* aur-ar k2 bar-c k* **Bell** k* brom *Bry* k* **Calc** k* calc-s calc-sil k2 *Carb-an* k* *Carb-v* k* *Carbn-s* caust k* cham k* chel k* *Chin* k* cic k* cina k* *Clem* k* *Con* k* cupr k* cycl k* *Dulc* k* *Fl-ac* graph k* *Hep* k* *Hydr* hyos k* iod k* *Kali-bi* k* *Lach* k* led k* **Lyc** k* *Mang Merc* k* *Merc-i-f Merc-i-r* mez k* nat-c k* nux-v k* petr k* phos k* plb k* **Puls** k* ran-b k* ran-s k* sel k* sep k* **Sil** k* staph k* sul-i k2 sulph k* syph jl2 thuj k* verat k*
  - • **shining**: fl-ac phos *Puls* k* sil
- ○ • **Areola** (See areola - indurated)
  - • **Base**: alumn br1* calc k2 *Calc-f* bro1 com bro1 con bro1
  - • **Margins**: alum alumn **Ars** k* *Asaf* k* bry k* **Calc** calc-f bro1 *Carb-an* k* *Carb-v Caust* k* cic k* cina k* clem k* *Com* k* *Fl-ac* graph k2 *Hep* k* *Lach* k* **Lyc** k* **Merc** k* mur-ac b2.de *Nit-ac* k* paeon bro1 petr k* ph-ac k* *Phos* k* *Puls* k* ran-b k* *Sang* sep k* **Sil** k* staph k* **Sulph** k* thuj k*
- **inflamed**: **Acon** k* agn k* ant-c k* arn k* **Ars** k* ars-s-f k2 asaf k* bar-c k* *Bell* k* borx k* bov k* *Bry* k* *Calc* k* calen hr1* carb-an bro1 caust k* *Cham* k* cina k* cinnb k* cocc k* colch k* con k* croc k* cupr k* dig k* *Ferr-p* hr1 graph bg2 hed sp1 **Hep** k* hyos k* ign k* kreos k* *Lac-c* k* *Lach* k* led k* *Lyc* k* m-arct b2.de mang k* **Merc** k* mez k* *Nat-c* k* *Nat-m* k* nat-p *Nit-ac* k* nux-v k* petr k* **Phos** k* phyt bro1 plb k* *Puls* k* ran-b k* *Rhus-t* k* ruta k* sal-ac hr1 sars k* sep k* **Sil** k* *Staph* k* sul-ac bg2 *Sulph* k* thuj k* verat k* zinc k*
- ○ • **Edges**: merc bg2
- **injury**; after slight: arn bro1 con bro1 mang ptk1
- **insensibility** in: *Iod*
- **irregular** margins; with: ars ptk1 kali-bi ptk1 merc bro1* nit-ac bro1 phyt ptk1 sars ptk1 sil ptk1
- **itching**: agath-a nl2• alum k* alum-p k2 alum-sil k2 am-c k* ambr k* anac k* ant-c k* ant-t k* arn k* *Ars* k* bar-c k* bell k* bov k* bry k* calc k* canth k* carb-v k* *Caust* k* cham k* chel k* *Chin* k* clem k* con k* dros k* *Graph* k* **Hep** k* ip k* kali-ar ptk1 kali-n k* kreos k* lach k* led k* **Lyc** k* *Merc* k* **Mez** k* nat-c k* nat-m k* *Nit-ac* k* nux-v k* petr k* *Ph-ac* k* phos k* *Psor Puls* k* *Ran-b* k* *Rhus-t* k* ruta k* sabad k* sars k* sel k* *Sep* k* **Sil** k* squil k* *Staph* k* *Sulph* k* *Thuj* k* verat k* viol-t k* zinc k* zinc-p k2
  - • **night**: *Lyc Staph*

○ · **Around** about: agn k* ang ant-t b2.de* ars k* bell k* caust k* clem k* **Hep** k* *Lach* k* *Lyc* k* merc k* mez k* nat-c k* nux-v k* petr k* ph-ac k* phos k* **Puls** k* *Ran-b* rhus-t k* sabin k* sep k* **Sil** k staph k* sulph k*
- **jagged** margins; with: *Ars* *Carb-v* hep k* lach k* **Merc** k* *Nit-ac* *Petr* **Ph-ac** k* *Sil* k* staph k* sulph k* *Thuj* k*
  · **zigzag**: *Merc* ptk1 *Nit-ac* k* *Ph-ac* ptk1
- **lardaceous**: ant-c k* *Ars* k* cupr k* *Hep* k* kali-bi kreos k* **Merc** k* *Nit-ac* k* *Phyt* sabin k* sil bg2 sulph k* thuj k*

○ · **Bases**: ars k* hep k* *Merc* k* nit-ac k* phyt bro1
- **malignant**: *Anthraci* br1 arg-n ptk1 ars b4a.de* *Brom* b4a.de calc b4a.de* carb-an bg2* carb-v bg2* caust ptk1 chel ptk1 cist tl1 con b4a.de* hippoz gm1 hydr bg2* kreos tl1 lach mtf33 lyc ptk1 mang ptk1 merc ptk1 *Merc-c* ptk1 **Nit-ac** ptk1 petr ptk1 ran-b ptk1 ran-s ptk1 sil b4a.de* thuj bg2*
- **menses**; during: graph b4.de*
- **mercurial**: *Asaf* *Aur* k* bell b4a.de *Carb-v* *Cist* **Hep** k* *Kali-bi* **Kali-i** *Lach* *Lyc* *Mez* b4a.de mur-ac c2 **Nit-ac** k* **Ph-ac** **Phyt** **Sars** k* sep **Sil** k* *Staph* b7a.de* *Sulph* k* *Thuj* b4a.de
- **mottled** areola (See areola - mottled)
- **multiple**: *Bar-m*
- **mustard** poultice; from: calc-p ptk1
- **necrosis**: | **radiation** therapy; from: cadm-i gm1
- **old**: croc b7a.de *Cupr* b7a.de *Lach* b7a.de ran-b b7a.de rhus-t b7a.de staph b7a.de
- **old** people; in: tarent-c ptk1
- **oozing** blood (See bleeding)
- **painful**: agath-a nl2• alum-sil k2 ang b7.de* arn k* **Ars** k* ars-i k2 ars-s-f k2 *Asaf* k* aur **Bell** k* calc-s calen hr1 *Carb-an* k* *Carb-v* k* carbn-s *Caust* k* cham b7.de* chin k* cic b7a.de *Cocc* b7a.de coff b7.de con k* cor-r croc b7.de cupr dig b4.de dulc k* *Fl-ac* k* *Graph* k* *Hep* k* hyos k* iod b4.de *Kali-bi* *Kreos* k* **Lach** b7a.de *Led* *Lyc* k* *Merc* k* mez b4.de* *Mur-ac* k* nat-c b4.de nat-m k* *Nit-ac* k* *Nux-v* k* *Ph-ac* k* phos k* *Phyt* *Puls* k* ran-b rhus-t b7.de sabin b7.de* *Sep* b4a.de *Sil* k* *Staph* hr1 sulph zinc
  · **morning**: ars h2*
  · **night**: *Asaf* k* cham k* *Cinnb* *Con* k* *Merc* *Mez* hr1
  · **aching**: bell camph carb-v chin *Graph* par sil
  · **biting**: ars k* bell k* bry k* calc k* carb-an k* caust k* cham k* chin k* colch k* coloc b4.de dig k* *Euph* k* graph k* kali-bi bg2 *Lach* k* *Led* k* *Lyc* k* mang k* merc k* mez k* nat-c k* nat-p petr k* ph-ac k* **Puls** k* ran-b k* rhus-t k* ruta k* sel k* sil k* staph k* sul-ac b2.de* *Sulph* k* thuj k* zinc
    ⁝ **night**: cham h1 rhus-t
    ⁝ **walking** in open air agg.: rhus-t h1
  · **boring**; with: arg-met k* aur k* bell k* calc k* caust k* chin k* hep k* *Kali-c* k* nat-c k* nat-m k* puls k* ran-s k* sep k* *Sil* k* *Sulph* k* thuj k*
  · **bruised** pain; with: ang b2.de* *Arn* k* cham k* chin k* cocc k* *Con* k* **Hep** k* hyos k* nat-m k* nux-v k* rhus-t k* ruta k* *Sulph* k*
    ⁝ **motion**; from: hyos h1
  · **burnt**; as if: alum k* ant-c k* **Ars** k* bar-c k* bell k* bry k* calc k* *Carb-v* k* caust k* *Cycl* k* hyos k* ign k* kreos k* lach k* *Nux-v* k* puls k* sabad k* *Sec* k* sep k* stram k*
  · **burrowing** pain; with: *Asaf* bg2 bell bg2 bry bg2 bufo bg2 calc bg2 chin b7.de* nat-c bg2 phos bg2 ruta bg2 sep bg2 stront-c bg2 sulph bg2
  · **cold** applications | **amel.**: *Led* lyc k2
  · **cough** agg.; during: con b4.de*
  · **cutting**; with: *Arn* **Bell** k* *Calc* k* cic *Clem* dros k* graph k* ign k* kali-ar ptk1 *Lyc* k* mag-m **Merc** bg2* mur-ac k* *Nat-c* k* ph-ac k* plat rhus-t k* *Ruta* sep k* *Sil* k* sul-ac k*
  · **drawing** pain; with: *Calc* b4a.de clem b4.de graph b4.de mez b4.de* nit-ac b4.de staph b7.de
  · **eating**; before: puls h1
  · **gnawing** pain; with: agar *Agn* k* *Apis* b7a.de **Ars** b4.de* bar-c k* bell k* bufo bg2 calc k* carb-v b4.de *Cham* k* *Chel* b7.de* *Con* b4.de cupr b7a.de cycl k* **Dros** k* *Hep* k* hyos k* *Kali-c* k* *Kreos* b7a.de lach led k* lyc k* manc mang b2.de* *Merc* k* mez k* nat-c k* nit-ac b4a.de ph-ac k* *Phos* k* *Plat* k* *Puls* k* ran-b b7.de* *Ran-s* k* rhus-t k* *Ruta* k* sep k* *Sil* b4.de **Staph** k* sul-ac k* *Sulph* k* thuj k* zinc b4a.de
  · **jerking** pain; with: arn k* *Asaf* k* aur k* bell k* bry k* *Calc* k* **Caust** k* cham k* chin k* clem k* cupr k* graph k* lyc k* merc k* nat-c k* *Nat-m* k* nit-ac k* *Nux-v* k* petr k* phyt **Puls** k* *Rhus-t* k* ruta sep k* **Sil** k* *Staph* k* sulph k*
    ⁝ **Around** about: staph h1

- **painful**: ...
  · **menses**; during: *Cham*
  · **pressing**: camph k* carb-v k* chin k* *Graph* k* mez **Paeon** par k* *Phyt* **Sil** k*
  · **shooting**: **Ars** *Asaf* clem *Hep* **Lyc** *Phyt* *Puls* *Staph*
  · **smarting**: alum k* alum-p k2 ambr k* ant-c k* arn k* ars k* bell k* bry k* calc k* canth caust k* *Cham* cic k* *Graph* k* **Hep** k* hyos k* ign k* kali-c k* kali-sil k2 *Lyc* k* m-ambo b2.de* m-aust b2.de* *Merc* k* mez k* *Nat-m* k* nux-v k* *Ph-ac* k* *Phos* k* **Puls** k* *Rhus-t* k* *Sep* k* sil k* *Staph* k* sul-ac k* *Sulph* k* *Thuj* k* zinc k* zinc-p k2
    ⁝ **night**: *Hep* lyc *Merc* rhus-t
  · **stinging**, stitching: acon k* alum k* alum-p k2 alum-sil k2 ant-c k* *Apis* k* arn k* **Ars** k* ars-s-f k2 *Asaf* k* bar-c k* *Bell* k* bov k* *Bry* k* bufo bg2 calc k* calc-sil k2 camph k* canth k* *Carb-an* carb-v k* carbn-s *Caust* cham k* chin k* chinin-ar *Cinnb* clem k* cocc k* con k* cycl k* *Graph* k* *Hep* k* *Hydr* kali-n k* led k* *Lyc* k* m-arct b2.de* mag-c k* mang k* **Merc** k* mez k* mur-ac k* nat-ar *Nat-c* k* nat-m k* nat-p **Nit-ac** k* nux-v k* *Petr* k* ph-ac h2 phos k* **Puls** k* ran-b k* *Rhus-t* k* sabad k* sabin k* sars k* sel k* *Sep* k* **Sil** k* spong k* squil k* *Staph* k* sul-ac k2 **Sulph** k* *Thuj* k*
    ⁝ **evening**: mez h2
    ⁝ **night**: mang h2 rhus-t sep h2
    ⁝ **laughing** agg.: hep h2
    ⁝ **splinters**; as from: ham bro1 hep k* **Nit-ac** k*
    ⁝ **Areola**; in: acon k* *Ars* k* **Asaf** k* bell k* cham k* cocc k* hep k* lyc k* *Merc* k* mez k* mur-ac k* nat-c k* nit-ac h2 nux-v k* petr k* phos k* **Puls** k* rhus-t k* sabin k* sep k* *Sil* k* staph k* *Sulph* k*
    ⁝ **Margins**: **Ars** k* ars-s-f k2 *Asaf* k* bry k* clem k* *Hep* k* *Lyc* k* **Merc** k* mez h2 mur-ac k* petr k* phos k* *Puls* k* ran-b k* sep k* *Sil* k* staph k* *Sulph* k* thuj k*
      ⁝ **touch** agg.: clem
  · **suppurative** pain; with: am-c k* anac k* arn k* ars k* *Asaf* k* aur k* bar-c k* *Bry* k* *Calc* k* *Carb-v* k* chin k* colch k* *Con* k* cycl k* dros k* euph k* *Graph* k* hep k* hyos k* iod k* kali-c k* kreos k* led k* nat-m k* nit-ac k* nux-v k* par k* petr k* **Phos** k* **Puls** k* *Ran-b* k* *Rhus-t* k* ruta k* sars k* sec k* **Sil** k* staph k* *Sulph* k* valer k* verat k* zinc k*
  · **tearing**; with: *Ars* k* bell k* bry k* *Calc* k* canth k* carb-v k* caust k* clem k* cocc k* *Cycl* k* *Graph* k* kali-c k* kali-sil k2 **Lyc** k* m-ambo b2.de* *Merc* k* mez k* nat-c k* nit-ac k* *Nux-v* k* phos k* puls k* rhus-t k* *Sep* k* sil k* *Staph* k* **Sulph** k* zinc k*
    ⁝ **motion** agg.: bell h1
    ⁝ **Around** about: calc h2 staph h1
  · **touch** agg.: nat-c hr1
  · **ulcerative** | **Below** surface of ulcer: am-c bg2 anac bg2 arn bg2 ars b4.de* *Asaf* bg2 aur bg2 bar-c b4.de* *Bry* bg2 *Calc* bg2 *Carb-v* bg2 chin bg2 colch bg2 *Con* b4.de* cycl bg2 dros bg2 euph bg2 *Graph* b4.de* hep bg2 hyos bg2 iod bg2 kali-c b4.de* kreos bg2 led bg2 nat-m bg2 nit-ac bg2 nux-v bg2 par bg2 petr bg2 **Phos** b4.de* **Puls** b7.de* *Ran-b* bg2 *Rhus-t* bg2 ruta bg2 sars bg2 sec bg2 **Sil** b4.de* staph b7.de* *Sulph* b4.de* tarax b7.de valer bg2 verat bg2 zinc b4.de*
  · **warmth** of bed; from: cinnb dros fl-ac bro1 *Merc* *Puls*
  · **weather** agg.; cold: *Kali-bi*

○ · **Around** about: *Ars* asaf k* hep *Lach* **Puls**
    ⁝ **touch** agg.: mez h2*
  · **Margins**: *Ars* k* asaf k* caust bg2 clem bg2 hep k* lach k* lyc k* *Merc* k* mur-ac bg2 petr bg2 ph-ac bg2 phos bg2 puls bg2 ran-b b7.de* sep bg2 *Sil* k* sulph bg2 thuj bg2
- **painless**: ambr k* anac k* ant-t k* arn k* *Ars* k* aur k* *Bapt* k* bar-c k* *Bell* k* bov k* *Bry* k* cadm-met gm1 *Calc* k* camph k* carb-an k* *Carb-v* k* cham k* chel k* chin k* cic k* *Cocc* k* *Con* k* croc k* *Dulc* k* eberth jl2 fl-ac k* formal gm1 graph k* *Hell* k* hep ptk1 hydr ptk1 *Hyos* k* ign k* ip k* *Lach* k* laur k* led k* **Lyc** k* m-ambo b2.de* merc k* nit-ac k* nux-m k* nux-v k* *Olnd* k* **Op** k* **Ph-ac** k* *Phos* k* phyt bg2 plat k* *Puls* k* rhus-t k* *Sec* k* *Sep* k* *Sil* ptk1 staph k* *Stram* k* sulph k* verat k* x-ray gm1 zinc k* zinc-p k2
- **perforating**: *Kali-bi* bg2 merc-c bg2 **Sil** bg2
- **phagedenic**: agar *Anthraci* **Ars** k* ars-s-f k2 aur-m-n *Bapt* hr1 borx brom k2 *Calc* calc-sil k2 **Carb-v** k* carbn-s k2 **Caust** k* cham **Chel** k* cic cinnb cist k2* clem con *Crot-c* *Crot-h* k* dulc *Graph* *Hep* k* hydr k2 hydrc *Hyper* *Kali-ar* k* *Kali-c* *Kali-p* kali-sil k2 *Lach* led **Lyc** k* **Merc** k* merc-c bro1* merc-cy ptk1

Skin

- **phagedenic**: ...
merc-d bro1 *Merc-i-r* *Mez* k* nat-ar *Nat-c* *Nat-m* **Nit-ac** k* **Petr** k* phos k2 *Puls* **Ran-b** **Ran-s** *Rhus-t* sars *Sep* **Sil** k* squil staph *Sul-ac* *Sulph* k* zinc
- **pimples**; surrounded by: acon k* *Ars* k* bell k* **Carb-v** k* *Caust* k* cham k* fl-ac grin bro1 *Hep* k* **Lach** k* lyc k* m-ambo b2.de* merc k* *Mez* k* mur-ac k* nat-c k* *Petr* k* phos k* *Puls* k* ran-s *Rhus-t* k* *Sep* k* sil k* staph k* *Sulph* k*
- **plug** inside; with a hard: sabin b7.de
- **proud** flesh: alum b2.de* ant-c b2.de* ap-g bro1 ars b2.de* aur ptk1 bar-c ptk1 bell b2.de* *Calc* ptk1 carb-an b2.de* carb-v b2.de* caust b2.de* *Cham* b2.de* clem b2.de* *Dulc* ptk1 fl-ac bro1 graph b2.de* kreos b2.de* *Lach* b2.de* *Lyc* ptk1 med ptk1 merc b2.de* merc-c ptk1 nat-c ptk1 *Nat-s* ptk1 **Nit-ac** bro1* *Petr* b2.de* *Ph-ac* bro1* phos b2.de* phyt ptk1 ran-b ptk1 rhus-t ptk1 sabin b2.de* sang ptk1 **Sep** b2.de* **Sil** b2.de* staph b2.de* *Sulph* b2.de* thuj b2.de*
- **pulsating**: acon k* *Apis* b7a.de am k* ars k* ars-s-f k2 *Asaf* k* bar-c k* bell k* bov k* *Bry* k* *Calc* k* calc-s caust k* cham k* chin k* clem k* con k* *Hep* k* hyos k* ign k* *Kali-c* k* kali-s kali-sil k2 kalm **Lach** bg2 *Lyc* k* m-ambo b2.de* **Merc** k* mez k* mur-ac k* *Nat-c* k* nat-m k* nit-ac k* petr k* ph-ac k* phos k* puls k* rhus-t k* ruta k* sabad k* sars k* sep k* *Sil* k* staph k* **Sulph** k* thuj k*
  - **night**: *Asaf* a2 *Hep* **Merc**
  - **walking** agg.: mur-ac ptk1
- **punched** out: anan vh1 kali-bi bg2* merc ptk1 phos bro1 phyt bg2*
- **pustules** around: calc caust clem *Hep* *Mez* *Mur-ac* ph-ac rhus-t *Sil* sulph
- **recurrent**: lach bg2 sil bg2 sulph bg2 vip bg2
- **red**: cor-r br1 lac-c tl1
  - ○ **Areola** (See areola - red)
- **regular** margins; with: kali-bi k*
- **reopening** of old: *Ars* *Carb-v* bg2* caust bg2 con bg2 croc bg2 crot-h k* glon bg2 *Kreos* k* *Lach* k* nat-c bg2 *Nat-m* bg2 **Phos** bg2 *Sep* sil k* sulph bg2 vip bg2*
  - **healed**; when partly: **Kreos**
  - **spring** agg.: cench *Lach*
- **round** ulcers: **Kali-bi** bg2
- **rubbing**; from: ang h1
- **salt** rheum; like (See Eruptions - eczema - discharging - salt)
- **sarcomatous**: ant-c *Apis* *Ars* **Hep** kreos *Merc* **Nit-ac** *Phos* sabin sulph thuj
- **scooped** out: vario ptk1
- **scratching**; after: ang b2.de* ant-c k* *Ars* k* *Asaf* k* *Asar* b7a.de bar-c k* bell k* bry k* calc k* carb-an k* carb-v k* *Caust* k* chin k* con k* graph k* *Hep* k* *Iod* kreos k* **Lach** k* *Lyc* k* mang k* *Merc* k* mez k* nat-c k* *Nit-ac* k* *Petr* k* ph-ac k* phos k* puls k* ran-b k* *Rhus-t* k* sabin k* sep k* *Sil* k* staph k* **Sulph** k* thuj k*
- **scrofulous**: aethi-m bro1 ars-i bro1 bar-i bro1 *Cal-ren* bro1 *Calc* bro1 *Calc-act* bro1 *Calc-ar* bro1 *Calc-br* bro1 *Calc-caust* bro1 *Calc-cn* bro1 *Calc-f* bro1 *Calc-hp* bro1 *Calc-i* bro1 *Calc-lac* bro1 *Calc-lp* bro1 *Calc-m* bro1 *Calc-ox* bro1 *Calc-p* bro1 *Calc-pic* bro1 *Calc-s* bro1 *Calc-sil* bro1 *Calc-st-s* bro1 chin bro1 hep bro1 *Kali-br* hr1 *Lap-a* bro1 merc bro1 merc-act bro1 merc-aur bro1 merc-br bro1 merc-c bro1 merc-cy bro1 merc-d bro1 merc-i-f bro1 merc-i-r bro1 merc-ns bro1 merc-p bro1 merc-pr-r bro1 merc-tn bro1 nit-ac bro1 *Sil* bro1 sulph bro1
- **sensitive**: alum k* alum-p k2 am-c k* anac k* ang b2.de* arg-n k2 **Arn** k* *Ars* k* ars-i **Asaf** k* aur k* aur-ar k2 aur-i k2 aur-s k2 *Bell* k* *Calen* bro1 carb-an k* carb-v carbn-s *Caust* k* cham k* *Chin* k* chinin-ar cic k* *Clem* k* *Cocc* k* coff k* con k* *Cor-r* croc k* cupr k* dig k* *Dulc* k* *Ferr* bg2 *Graph* k* **Guaj** b4a.de **Hep** k* *Hydr* hyos k* *Iod* k* *Kali-bi* bg2 kreos k* **Lach** k* led k* **Lyc** k* *Merc* k* *Mez* k* mur-ac k* nat-c k* nat-m k* nat-p nit-ac k* *Nux-v* k* *Paeon* k* *Petr* k* *Ph-ac* k* phos k* **Puls** k* ran-b k* ran-s k* rhus-t k* sabin k* *Sec* sel k* *Sep* k* *Sil* k* squil k* *Staph* k* sul-ac k2 sul-i k2 sulph k* tarent-c bro1 thuj k* verat k*
  - **weather** agg.; cold: kali-bi bg2
  - ○ **Around** about: *Ars* k* **Asaf** k* bell k* caust k* cocc k* *Hep* k* **Lach** k* loxo-lae bnm12• lyc k* merc k* mez k* mur-ac k* nat-c k* nux-v k* petr k* phos k* **Puls** k* rhus-t k* sep k* sil k*
  - **Margins**: **Ars** k* **Asaf** k* caust k* clem k* **Hep** k* *Lach* k* *Lyc* k* **Merc** k* mur-ac k* petr k* ph-ac k* phos k* puls k* ran-b k* sep k* **Sil** k* sulph k* *Thuj* k*
- **serpiginous**: *Ars* borx calc chel bro1 kali-bi sne *Merc* k* merc-c bro1 merc-i-f bg2 ph-ac bro1 *Phyt* sabad *Sars* *Sil* staph
- **shaggy** (See jagged)
- **shining**: *Lac-c* k* mag-c k2 *Phos* puls sec k2 staph syph
  - ○ **Base**: hydr bg2
- **shining**: ...
  - **Margins**: fl-ac phos puls sil
- **small**: arg-n ptk1 ars ptk1 kali-bi ptk1 med ptk1
- **small** ulcers; surrounded by: phos bro1 sil bro1
- **spongy**: alum k* *Ant-c* k* ant-t k* **Ars** k* bell k* calc k* **Carb-an** k* *Carb-v* k* *Carbn-s* caust k* cham k* *Clem* k* con k* *Ferr* bg2 graph k* *Hep* *Iod* k* *Kreos* k* **Lach** k* *Lyc* k* **Merc** k* nit-ac k* nux-v k* *Petr* k* *Ph-ac* k* *Phos* k* rhus-t k* sabin k* *Sep* k* **Sil** k* *Staph* k* sul-ac b4a.de sul-i k2 *Sulph* k* *Thuj* k*
  - ○ **Margins**; at: **Ars** k* *Carb-an* k* caust k* clem k* *Lach* k* lyc k* merc k* petr k* ph-ac k* phos k* sep k* **Sil** k* staph k* sulph k* thuj k*
- **spotted**: arn b2.de* ars b2.de* **Con** b2.de* ip b2.de* *Lach* b2.de* sul-ac b2.de*
- **spreading**: borx bg2 hydrc bg2 merc bg2 phos bg2 ran-s bg2
- **spring**; in: *Calc* *Cench* *Lach*
- **stupor**; with (See MIND - Stupor - ulcers)
- **superficial**: (↗*flat*) am-c ant-c ant-t *Ars* k* *Asaf* bell carb-an carb-v *Chin* eberth jl2 hydr ptk1 **Lach** k* **Lyc** k* *Merc* k* *Mez* nat-c *Nat-m* *Nit-ac* k* petr *Ph-ac* phos puls ran-b *Sel* *Sep* *Sil* staph sulph thuj k*
  - **menopause**; during: polyg-h ptk1
- **suppressed**: ars bg2 bry bg2 clem bg2* cupr bg2 dulc bg2 *Lach* bg2* **Sulph** bg2*
- **suppurating**: acon k* am-c k* ambr k* anac k* ang b2.de* ant-c k* ant-t k* arg-met k* arn k* **Ars** k* ars-i ars-s-f k2 **Asaf** k* aur k* aur-ar k2 aur-s k2 bar-c k* *Bell* k* borx k* bov k* bry k* calc k* *Canth* k* caps k* carb-an k* *Carb-v* k* carbn-s **Caust** k* cham k* chel k* chin k* cic k* clem k* cocc k* coloc b4a.de con k* croc k* dros k* dulc k* graph k* hell k* **Hep** k* hyos k* ign k* **Iod** k* ip k* kali-ar kali-c k* kali-m k2 kali-n k* *Kali-s* kali-sil k2 kreos k* lach k* led k* *Lyc* k* m-ambo b2.de* mang k* **Merc** k* mez k* mur-ac k* *Nat-c* k* nat-m k* nat-p *Nit-ac* k* nux-v k* petr k* *Ph-ac* k* *Phos* k* phyt bg2 plb k* **Puls** k* ran-b k* ran-s k* **Rhus-t** k* ruta k* sabad k* sabin k* sars k* sec k* sel k* *Sep* k* **Sil** k* spig k* spong k* squil k* *Staph* k* sul-ac k* sul-i k2 **Sulph** k* thuj k* viol-t k* zinc k*
- **swelling**; surrounded by (See Swelling - ulcers)
- **swollen**: acon k* agath-a nl2• agn k* arn k* *Ars* k* aur k* bar-c k* *Bell* k* *Bry* k* *Calc* k* carb-an k* carb-v k* caust k* cham k* cic k* cocc k* *Con* k* dulc k* graph k* hell bg2 *Hep* k* iod k* *Kali-c* k* led k* **Lyc** k* mang k* **Merc** k* *Nat-c* k* *Nat-m* k* nat-p *Nit-ac* k* nux-v k* *Petr* k* ph-ac k* *Phos* k* plb k* **Puls** k* **Rhus-t** k* sabin k* samb k* **Sep** k* **Sil** k* squil bg2 staph k* **Sulph** k* *Vip*
  - ○ **Areola**: acon k* ars k* *Bell* k* caust k* cham k* graph h2* *Hep* k* lyc k* *Merc* k* nat-c k* nux-v k* petr k* phos k* **Puls** k* *Rhus-t* k* *Sep* k* sil k* staph k*
  - **Margins**: *Ars* k* bry k* *Calc* carb-an k* caust k* cic k* *Hep* k* lyc k* **Merc** k* petr k* ph-ac k* phos k* *Puls* k* *Rhus-t* bg2 *Sep* k* **Sil** k* *Sulph* k*
- **syphilitic**: anan **Ars** k* ars-i k2 asaf br1* *Aur* k* aur-ar k2 *Aur-m* k* *Aur-m-n* aur-s k2 *Bapt* hr1 calo br1 *Carb-v* k* *Cinnb* br1* *Cist* k* *Cor-r* bro1 *Crot-c* *Cund* bro1 *Fl-ac* bro1 graph bro1 *Hep* k* **Iod** k* *Kali-bi* k* *Kali-chl* **Kali-i** k* lac-c *Lach* k* lyc bro1 **Merc** k* **Merc-c** k* merc-cy br1* merc-d bro1 *Merc-i-r* k* *Merc-pr-r* bro1 mez k* **Nit-ac** k* *Petr* k* **Phyt** k* rumx sang *Sars* k* sil bro1 *Staph* k* *Still* k* stram sulph bro1 *Syph* k* **Thuj** k*
- **tense**: arn k* *Asaf* k* aur k* *Bar-c* k* bell k* bry k* calc k* carb-an k* carb-v k* *Caust* k* cham k* chin k* clem k* cocc k* **Con** k* graph hep k* *Iod* k* kali-c k* kreos k* *Lach* k* lyc k* *Merc* k* mez k* mur-ac k* nat-c k* nit-ac k* nux-v k* petr k* ph-ac k* *Phos* k* *Phyt* **Puls** k* *Rhus-t* k* sabin k* sep k* sil k* *Spong* k* staph k* **Stront-c** k* **Sulph** k* thuj k* zinc k*
  - ○ **Areola**: *Asaf* k* bell k* caust k* cham k* cocc k* hep k* *Lach* k* lyc k* merc k* mez k* mur-ac k* nat-c k* nux-v k* petr k* ph-ac k* phos k* **Puls** k* rhus-t k* sabin k* sep k* sil k* staph k* *Stront-c* k* *Sulph* k*
- **thrusts** inside; with: ang b2.de* *Arn* b2.de* cic b2.de* *Clem* b2.de* mez b2.de* mur-ac b2.de* plat b2.de* *Ruta* b2.de* sul-ac b2.de*
- **tingling**: acon arn bell caust cham clem con hep lach phos rhus-t sec sep sulph
  - **night**: rhus-t
- **tumor**; after removal: hydr ptk1
- **undermined**: *Asaf* k* bell k* bry k* calc k* carb-v chin k* lyc nat-c k* phos k* ruta k* sep k* stront-c k* sulph k*
  - ○ **Margins**: kali-bi bg2
- **unhealthy**: alum k* alum-p k2 am-c k* *Apis* b7a.de bar-c k* borx *Calc* k* calc-sil k2 caps gm1 carb-v k* caust k* *Cham* k* **Chel** k* clem k* *Con* k* croc k* *Graph* k* hell k* **Hep** k* *Hippoz* kali-c k* *Lach* k* lyc k* mag-c k* mang k* *Merc* k* mur-ac k* nat-c k* nat-p **Nit-ac** k* nux-v k* op bg2 *Petr* k* ph-ac k* phos k* plb k* *Rhus-t* k* *Sep* k* **Sil** k* squil k* *Staph* k* *Sulph* k* viol-t

- **varicose**: (↗*EXTREMITIES - Varices - leg - ulceration; GENERALS - Varicose - ulceration)* aesc bg2 alco a1 anac ant-t k* *Arn* hr1 *Ars* k* *Calc* k* calc-f bro1 calen hr1* *Carb-v* k* *Card-m* k* **Caust** k* cinnb clem-vit bro1 coll hr1 crot-h k* crot-t bg2 cund br1* cur a1 eucal hr1* *Fl-ac* k* gast c2 graph k* grin ham k* hydr k* kreos *Lach* k* **Lyc** k* merc k* mez k* morg-p fmm1• phyt bro1 psor bro1 **Puls** k* pyrog k* *Rhus-t* k* sars sec k* *Sil* k* sul-ac *Sulph* k* thuj *Zinc* k* [am-s stj1]
- **vascular**: aur bg2 lyc bg2 merc bg2
- **vesicles**; surrounded by: *Ars* k* bell k* caust k* *Fl-ac* k* *Hep* k* **Lach** k* m-ambo b2.de* merc k* **Mez** k* nat-c k* *Nat-m* petr k* phos k* puls bg2 *Rhus-t* k* sep k* *Thuj*
- **warmth**:
  - **agg.**: *Cham* k* dros k* euph k* *Fl-ac* k* hydr led k* *Lyc* k* *Merc* k* puls bg2* *Sabin* k* *Sec* k*
  - **amel.**: *Ars* k* clem bg2* con bg2* hep bg2* **Lach** k* rhus-t bg2* **Sil** k* *Syph* k*
- **wart** shaped: ars calc *Nat-c* phos thuj b4a.de
- **washing** agg.: *Hydr*
- **white** spots; with: *Ars* k* calc con k* **Lach** k* **Merc** k* phos k* sep k* **Sil** k* sulph k* thuj
- **winter** agg.: petr hr1
- **yellow**: calc cor-r kali-bi tl1 nit-ac plb k* staph sulph zinc

○ - **Areola**:
  - **boils**: hep ptk1
  - **dark**: aesc ptk1 *Lach* ptk1
  - **elevated**: ars ptk1 asaf ptk1 *Merc* ptk1 *Sil* ptk1
    - **indurated**; and: ars ptk1 lyc ptk1 sil ptk1
  - **eruptions**: carb-v ptk1 *Hep* ptk1 lach ptk1
  - **fungoid**: lach ptk1
  - **hanging** over: kali-bi ptk1
  - **indurated**: arn k* *Ars* k* **Asaf** k* *Bell* k* caust k* cham k* cina k* fl-ac ptk1 graph ptk1 hep k* **Lach** k* *Lyc* k* merc k* mez k* nat-c k* nux-v k* petr k* phos k* **Puls** k* sep k* sil k* staph k* sulph k*
    - **red**: puls ptk1
  - **mottled**: arn *Ars* **Carb-v** k* **Con** *Crot-h* ip **Lach** *Led* **Puls** *Sul-ac*
  - **red**: *Acon* k* ant-c k* arn k* **Ars** k* ars-s-f k2 *Asaf* k* bar-c k* bell k* borx k* bry k* *Calc* k* caust h2 *Cham* k* cocc k* cupr k* fl-ac graph h2 **Hep** k* hyos k* ign k* *Kali-bi* k* kreos k* *Lach* k* led k* *Lyc* k* *Merc* k* **Mez** k* nat-c k* nat-p nit-ac k* nux-v k* *Petr* k* ph-ac k* phos k* plb k* **Puls** k* ran-b k* *Rhus-t* k* sars k* sep k* **Sil** k* **Staph** k* **Sulph** k* thuj k* verat k* zinc k*
    - **dark** red: aesc bg2 lach bg2 mez bg2 puls bg2 sil bg2 staph bg2
  - **sensitive**: asaf ptk1
  - **shiny**: puls ptk1
  - **small**: calc ptk1 hep ptk1 mez ptk1 phos ptk1 rhus-t ptk1
  - **with**: ars ptk1 asaf ptk1 hep ptk1 lach ptk1 lyc ptk1 merc ptk1 *Puls* ptk1 *Sil* ptk1
- **Folds**; in: carb-v hr1
- **Mucocutaneous** borders: nit-ac mtf11 paeon mtf11
- **Mucosal** margins: lach k2
- **Under** the skin: cic bg2 sec bg2

UNCOVERING agg.: kali-ar bg2 olnd bg2 sec bg2

UNHEALTHY: alum k* **ALUM-P** k2 alum-sil k2 am-c k* anag c2 ant-c ptk1 *Apis Arn* ptk1 ars h2* *Bar-c* k* *Bar-m* **Borx** k* *Bufo* k* **Calc** k* calc-s k* calen bro1 caps *Carb-v* k* **Carbn-s** k* carc mlr1• **Caust** k* **Cham** k* chel k* clem k* con k* croc k* crot-h *Fl-ac* **Graph** k* ham hell k* **Hep** k* hydr bro1 kali-bi ptk1 kali-c k* kreos bg2 **Lach** k* liat br1 *Lyc* k* mag-c k* maland c2 *Mang* k* merc k* mez ptk1 moni rfm1• mur-ac k* nat-c k* nat-m tl1 nat-p nit-ac k* nux-v k* olnd b2.de* op bg2 par b2.de* **Petr** k* ph-ac k* *Phos* k* pip-m bro1 plb k* **Psor** k* puls k* *Pyrog* bro1 **Rhus-t** k* *Sars* k* sec k2 sel c1* *Sep* k* **Sil** k* spong fd4.de squil k* *Staph* k* still sul-ac bg2 *Sulph* k* tab bg2 tarax k* *Tarent* k* thuj k2* tub-r jl2 vanil fd5.de *Viol-t* b2.de*

○ - **Joints**; around: mang ptk1

VACCINATION; after: thuj br1

VITILIGO: (↗*Discoloration - white - spots)* alum stj2* ant-t hr1* ars mrr5 ars-s-f mrr5 calc mrr5 cob-n jl3* ign dgt1 kres jl3 merc mrr5* nat-c dgt1* nat-caust stj2* nat-m mrr5 ozone sde2• phos mrr5 pitu-a mtf* pitu-gl mp4* pitu-p jl3 sep sej1* sil stj2* thuj mtf* [cob stj2 moly-met stj2 oxyg stj2 stann stj2]

WARM: | **applications** | **agg.**: mez tl1
- **bed** | **agg.**: mez tl1 psor bg2 *Sulph* bg2

WARMTH: | **sensation** of (See Heat - sensation)

WARTS: (↗*Excrescences; Excrescences - condylomata)* acet-ac k* alum am-c k* ambr k* anac k* anac-oc c2* anag br1* anan *Ant-c* k* ant-t bro1 arg-n k* *Ars* k* ars-br bro1 ars-i bg2 *Aur* k* aur-ar k2 aur-m k* aur-m-n k* **Bar-c** k* **Bell** k* bell-p sp1 *Benz-ac* berb bg2 borx b2.de* *Bov* k* bufo k* **Calc** k* calc-cn ah1 calc-o-t c2 **Calc-s** carb-an k* carb-v k* carc mlr1* castm c2* castor-eq c2* **Caust** k* chel k* chr-o c2* cina mrr1 cinnb c2* clem ptk1 colch bg2 cupr k* cupre-l c2 **Dulc** k* euph k* euphr k* ferr ferr-ma c2 ferr-p ferr-pic bg2* fic-c br1* *Fl-ac* k* graph k* *Hep* k* kali-ar kali-bi c2 kali-br bg2 kali-c k* *Kali-chl* kali-m c2* kali-perm c2* kiss c2 *Lac-c* k* *Lach* k* limx hsa1 lyc k* m-aust b2.de *Mag-c* b4a.de mag-s c2* *Med* k* *Merc* ptk1 **Merc-c** k* merc-i-f k* mill *Nat-c* k* nat-m k* nat-p **Nat-s** k* **Nit-ac** k* nit-s-d c2 *Ox-ac* pall c2 penic mtf11 petr k* *Ph-ac* k* phase-xyz c2 phos k* phyt k* pic-ac bg2 plac-s rly4• *Psor* k* puls pd* ran-b k* *Rhus-t* k* ruta k* sabin k* sang hr1* sars k* semp kr1* *Sep* k* sil k* sinus rly4• spig k* spong fd4.de staph k* sul-ac k* **Sulph** k* syc pte1*• syph k2 thiam rly4• **Thuj** k* tritic-vg fd5.de x-ray bro1* [gomph-f dbx1.fr heroin sdj2]
- **bathing** agg.: psor tl1
- **black**: calc bg2 hecla bg2
- **bleeding**: ambr bg2 **Caust** k* cinnb k* cupre-l sne hep k* lyc k* nat-c k* *Nit-ac* k* ph-ac *Rhus-t* k* staph **Thuj** k* [bell-p-sp dcm1]
  - **touch** agg.: nit-ac mtf33
  - **washing**; from: *Nit-ac* k*
- **broad**: caust bg2 dulc bg2
- **brown**: dulc fd4.de *Sep* k* *Thuj* k*
  - **children**; in: | **young** girls: thuj mtf33
- **burning**: am-c k* ars k* hep lyc k* *Petr* k* phos k* *Rhus-t* k* sabin br1 sep k* sulph k* thuj k2
- **cold** washing agg.: dulc
- **conical**: (↗*Excrescences - conical)* ant-t bg2 nat-m bg2
- **cracked**: lyc bro1
- **cylindrical**: carc az1.de•
- **discharging**: nit-ac bro1
- **drawing**: con h2*
- **dry**: dulc b4a.de* fl-ac k2 sars hr1* *Staph* k* *Sulph* b4a.de
- **filiform**: med alj staph c1 thuj c1
- **fissured**: thuj bg2
- **flat**: acet-ac bacls-10 fmm1• berb k* calc bg2 *Caust* k* con hr1 **Dulc** k* dys fmm1• fl-ac k* lach k* med jl2* merc-i-f ptk1 morg-g fmm1• morg-p fmm1• nat-m bg2 ruta k* *Sep* k* syc bka1*• *Thuj* k*
- **fleshy**: *Calc* carc az1.de• *Caust* k* cupre-l sne *Dulc* k* nat-m sne sil k*
- **girls**; young: sep hr1 thuj hr1
- **granular**: arg-n ptk1
- **growing**: kali-c h2*
- **hard**: *Ant-c* k* borx sne *Calc* k* calc-sil k2 *Caust* k* dulc k* fl-ac k* lach k* ran-b k* *Sep* k* *Sil* k* *Sulph* k* thuj bg2*
- **hollow**; become: *Calc*
- **horny**: (↗*Excrescences - horny)* **Ant-c** k* *Calc* k* *Caust* dulc k* graph k* nat-c h2* *Nit-ac* k* ran-b k* rhus-t bro1 *Sep* k* sil bg2* *Sulph* k* thuj k*
- **indented**: calc k* euphr k* lyc k* nit-ac k* *Ph-ac* k* rhus-t k* sabin k* sep staph k* *Thuj* k*
- **inflamed**: am-c k* bell bov k* *Calc* k* calc-sil k2 *Caust* k* *Hep* k* lyc k* nat-c k* *Nit-ac* k* rhus-t k* sars sep k* *Sil* k* staph k* sulph k* thuj
- **isolated**: *Lyc* k* *Thuj*
- **itching**: carb-an h2* con sne euphr k* graph h2* *Kali-c* k* kali-n h2* *Nit-ac* k* phos k* psor k* sabin br1 *Sep* k* spong fd4.de sulph h2* thuj k* tritic-vg fd5.de
- **jagged**: bacls-10 fmm1• calc b2.de* **Caust** k* euphr b2.de *Lyc* k* morg-g fmm1• **Nit-ac** k* ph-ac k* rhus-t k* sabin b2.de* *Sep* staph k* **Thuj** k*
- **large**: *Caust* k* **Dulc** k* ferr-pic sne kali-c k* lyc hr1 mag-s ptk1 morg-g fmm1• nat-c k* **Nit-ac** k* ph-ac *Rhus-t* k* *Sep* k* *Sil* k* staph sne syc bka1*• **Thuj** k*
- **lupoid**: ferr-pic c2*
- **mercury**; after abuse of: *Aur Nit-ac Staph*
- **moist**: *Caust* k* lyc k* **Nit-ac** k* ph-ac psor k* *Rhus-t* k* staph **Thuj** k*

- **old**: *Calc* k* *Caust* k* *Kali-c* k* *Nit-ac* k* rhod bg2 rhus-t k* sars hr1 sulph k* *Thuj* k*
- **painful**: am-c ambr h1* *Bov* k* *Calc* k* calc-sil k2 *Caust* k* ferr-pic sne hep k* kali-c k* kali-s kali-sil k2 lach lyc k* nat-c k* nat-m k* *Nit-ac* k* petr k* phos k* plac-s rly4• rhus-t k* ruta sabin sep k* sil k* sulph k* thiam rly4• *Thuj* [bell-p-sp dcm1]
- **pedunculated**: **Caust** k* *Dulc* k* *Lyc* k* *Med* k* nat-s bg2 **Nit-ac** k* ph-ac k* *Rhus-t* k* sabin bg2* sil *Staph* k* *Thuj* k* tritic-vg fd5.de [tax jsj7]
- **pointed**: med jl2 *Thuj* b4a.de
- **pulsating**: *Calc* k* kali-c k* lyc k* *Petr* k* sep k* *Sil* k* sulph k*
- **red**: *Calc* k* nat-s k* *Thuj* k*
- **rough**: caust bg2 syc fmm1•
- **round**: *Calc* k*
- **sensitive** to touch: *Caust Cupr* hep *Nat-c* k* nat-m **Nit-ac** hr1 **Staph** *Thuj* k*
- **shining**: sil bro1
- **small**: bar-c k* bar-s k2 berb k* *Calc* k* carc az1.de• *Caust* k* con hr1 dulc k* ferr k* ferr-p hep k* lach k* med hr1 *Nit-ac* k* psor bg2 rhus-t k* *Sars* k* *Sep* k* *Sulph* k* *Thuj* k* tritic-vg fd5.de
- **smelling** like old cheese: *Calc Graph Hep* k* **Thuj** k*
- **smooth**: **Ant-c** k* calc bro1 **Dulc** k* lach bg2 nat-m bg2 nat-s bg2 nit-ac bg2 psor bg2 ruta k* thuj bg2
- **soft**: *Ant-c* k* *Calc* k* calen hr1 carc az1.de• dulc ptk1 mag-s ptk1 med jl2 nat-s bg2 **Nit-ac** k* sil thiam rly4• *Thuj* k*
- **stinging**: am-c k* ant-c k* bar-c k* bar-s k2 *Calc* k* calc-sil k2 caust k* graph h2* *Hep* k* kali-sil k2 lyc k* **Nit-ac** k* rhus-t k* sep k* sil k* staph k* sulph k* **Thuj** k*
- **stitching** in warts: ant-c b2.de* bar-c b2.de* *Bov* k* *Calc* b2.de* caust b2.de* **Hep** k* lyc b2.de* **Nit-ac** k* rhus-t b2.de* sep b2.de* sil b2.de* staph b2.de* sulph b2.de*
- **suppressed**: mang k2* meny ptk1 merc k2 nit-ac k2* staph k2* *Thuj* k2*
- **suppurating**: ars k* *Bov* k* *Calc* k* calc-sil k2 *Caust* k* *Hep* k* kali-sil k2 *Nat-c Sil* k* *Thuj* k*
- **syphilitic**: *Aur* k* aur-ar k2 aur-m aur-m-n aur-s k2 *Hep Merc* **Nit-ac** k* staph *Thuj* k*
- **tearing**: am-c k*
- **thick**: dulc bg2
- **thin** epidermis; with: *Nit-ac*
- **ulcers**:
  - **become** ulcers; warts: *Ars* b4a.de calc h2 caust ptk1 hell ptk1
  - **surrounded** by a circle of ulcers; warts: ant-c *Ars* k* *Calc* caust bg2 *Nat-c* k* phos k*
- **venereal**: med mtf11 nit-ac mtf11 thuj mtf11
- **warm** bed agg.: psor tl1

WASHING agg.: ars ptk1 *Sulph* ptk1

WAXY: **Acet-ac** k* **Apis** k* **Ars** k* atra-r bnm3• calc bg2 calc-p k2 chin colch bg2 *Cupr* **Ferr** *Ip* lyc **Lycps-v** nat-m k2* *Phos* k* *Sil* k* tub k2

WEATHER: | **cold** | **agg.**: dulc tl1
- **wet** | **agg.**: dulc tl1

WEIGHT were drawing downward under skin; as if a: spong rb2

WENS: *Agar* am-c k* anac ant-c ars sne **Bar-c** k* benz-ac c2* brom bro1 **Calc** k* calc-f sne calc-sil k2* caust mha clem sne coloc *Con* bg2* daph bro1 **Graph** k* hell sne *Hep* k* kali-bi sne kali-br hr1* kali-c k* kali-i c2* lach bg2 lob c2 lyc sne* merc sne mez bro1 *Nit-ac* k* nux-v sne petr sne ph-ac k* *Phos* bg2 *Phyt* c2* plb bg2* psor al2 puls sne rhus-t k* ruta sne *Sabin* sep sne *Sil* k* spong staph c1 sulph thuj k* zinc bg2

WIND:
- **agg.**: psor ptk1
- **cold** wind were blowing out from skin; as if a: carc fd2.de• cupr rb2

WITHERED: *Ars* k* calc k* calc-sil k2 camph caps cham **Chin** k* clem cocc k* croc cupr ptk1 *Ferr* k* *Ferr-ar Ferr-p* hyos *Iod* k* kali-c kali-sil k2 lyc k* merc nat-m bg2 *Ph-ac* k* phos plb bg2* rheum rhod *Sars* **Sec** k* seneg sil k* spong sulph k* *Verat* k*

WOOL:
- **agg.**: (↗*GENERALS - Clothing - intolerance - woolen)* com bg1
- **drawn** over skin; as if woolen cloth were: staph h1*

WORMS; sensation of: ars ptk1 coca ptk1 merc ptk1 nat-c ptk1 nit-ac ptk1 sel ptk1 sil ptk1 sulph ptk1
- **boring** and crawling on body; as if worms were: tarent rb2

O - **Under** the skin: coca ptk1 **Cocain** k*

WORN-OUT (See Wrinkled)

WOUNDS (See GENERALS - Wounds)

WRINKLED, shrivelled: abrot bg2* am-c k* ambr k* *Ant-c* k* apis arg-n bg2 *Ars* k* bar-c bg2 berb k2 *Borx* k* bry k* bufo bg2 calc k* camph k* caps b2.de* cham k* **Chin** b2.de* chlor k* clem b2.de* cocc b2.de* *Con* k* croc b2.de* *Cupr* k* *Dulc* b4a.de falco-pe nl2• *Ferr* b2.de* graph k* hell k* hep hyos b2.de* iod b2.de* *Kali-ar* kali-br bg2* kali-c b2.de* *Kreos* k* laur bg2 *Lyc* k* manc k* merc k* merc-c bg2* *Mez* k* morph a1 mur-ac k* nat-m k2 nux-v k* op bg2* ph-ac k* phos k* phyt k* plb k* psor k2* rheum k* rhod k* rhus-t k* rumx ptk1 sabad k* *Sars* k* **Sec** k* seneg b2.de* *Sep* k* *Sil* b2.de* spig k* spong b2.de* stram k* *Sulph* k* tritic-vg fd5.de urt-u k* *Verat* k* verat-v viol-o k* zinc k2
- **emaciation**; from: abrot bro1 *Arg-n* bro1 fl-ac bro1 kreos bro1 op bro1 sanic bro1 sars bro1 sil bro1 *Sulph* bro1
- **folds**; hanging in: sulph mtf33
  - **emaciation**; after: sars mrr1
- **old** people; in: sec br1

BONES; complaints of skin covering: agar bg2

SIDE:

- **one** side; symptoms on: *Aesc* *Agar* k* agn k* **Alum** k* **Alumn** kr1 am-c k* am-m k* *Ambr* k* **Anac** k* ang b2.de* ant-c k* ant-t k* aphis *Apis* kr1 *Arg-met* k* *Arg-n* arn k* ars k* **Asaf** k* asar k* aur k* *Bar-c* k* bar-m bell k* bism k* borx k* *Bov* b2.de* brom sf1.de **Bry** k* *Calc* k* calc-act sf1.de camph k* cann-s k* *Canth* k* caps k* carb-ac a1 carb-an k* carb-v k* carc mlr1• caust k* cham k* chel k* chin k* *Chinin-s* sf1.de cic k* *Cina* k* clem k* *Coc-c* kr1 cocc k* coff k* colch k* coloc k* con k* croc k* cupr k* *Cycl* k* dig k* dros k* *Dulc* k* euph k* euphr k* ferr k* ferr-s a1 graph k* *Guaj* k* hell k* hep k* hura a1 *Hydrog* srj2• hyos k* ign k* iod k* iris **Kali-c** k* kali-m k2 kali-n k* **Kali-p** **Kreos** k* **Lach** k* laur k* led k* **Lyc** k* **Lyss** m-arct b2.de m-aust b2.de mag-c k* mag-m k* mang k* meny k* merc k* merc-c b4a.de *Mez* k* mosch k* *Mur-ac* k* nat-c k* nat-m k* nit-ac b2.de* nux-m k* nux-v k* oena a1 *Olnd* k* orig a1 *Par* k* petr k* **Ph-ac** k* *Phos* k* **Plat** k* *Plb* k* puls k* ran-b k* ran-s k* rheum k* rhod k* rhus-t k* ruta k* *Sabad* k* *Sabin* k* samb k* **Sars** k* sel k* seneg k* sep k* sil k* *Spig* k* spong k* squil k* stann k* *Staph* k* *Stront-c* k* **Sul-ac** k* sul-i k2 sulph k* tarax k* *Tarent* kr1 tell a1 teucr k* thala jl thuj k* valer k* verat k* **Verb** k* viol-o k* viol-t k* vip sf1.de xan a1 *Zinc* k* zinc-p k2
- **alternating** sides: (↗*MIND - Capriciousness; MIND - Mood - changeable)* agar androc srj1• ant-c k* apis tl1 arg-n tl1 asaf tl1 bry tl1 calc tl1 carc fb* chel tl1 cimic k* cina bg2 **Cocc** bg2 coloc tl1 iris k* kali-bi tl1 kali-s fd4.de **Lac-c** k* mang sf1.de merc k* neon srj5• onos phos k* plat k* podo fd3.de• puls k* ran-s tl1 sep k* sulph tl1 symph fd3.de• xan mgm•
- **right**: abies-c abrom-a ks5 *Acon* k* adam srj5• adlu jl3 *Aesc* k* *Agar* b2.de* agath-a nl2• *Agn* k* *Alum* k* *Alumn* kr1 *Am-c* k* *Am-m* b2.de* ambr b7a.de* anac b2.de* *Androc* srj1• *Ang* b2.de* ant-c b7a.de ant-t b2.de* **Apis** k* **Arg-met** k* arist-m a1 *Arn* k* **Ars** k* ars-i ars-s-f k2* art-v hr1* arum-t hr1* asaf b2.de* asar b7a.de aster hr1* atro vh **Aur** k* aur-ar k2 *Aur-i* k2* *Aur-m-n* wbt2* aur-s k2* aza jl3 **Bapt** k* bar-c b2.de* *Bar-s* k2* **Bell** k* benzol br1 *Bism* k* **Borx** k* *Both* bg2* *Bov* b2.de* brach a1 brom k* **Bry** k* calad b7a.de **Calc** k* calc-i k2* calc-p k* camph b2.de* cann-i k* cann-s k* **Canth** k* caps k* carb-ac bg2* *Carb-an* b2.de* carb-v b2.de* carc fd2.de• card-m bg2* *Caust* k* cedr k* cer-s a1 cere-s a1 cham k* **Chel** k* chen-a vml3• chin k* chir-fl gya2 chloram jl3 choc srj3• cic b2.de* cimic jl3 cina b2.de* cinnb bro1 clem b2.de* *Cocc* k* *Coff* b2.de* *Colch* k* coli jl2 **Coloc** k* **Con** k* conch fkr1• corn hr1* croc b2.de* **Crot-c** **Crot-h** k* culx k2* cupr b2.de* cur bro1* cycl b2.de* cyn-d jl3 dicha jl3 *Dig* b2.de* dol br1* *Dros* k* dulc k* *Elaps* bg2* *Elat* hr1* equis-h bro1 euph b2.de* euphr k* ferr b7a.de* ferr-p bro1* fl-ac b4a.de* form k* galeoc-c-h gms1* *Gels* ptk1 gink-b jl3* gins j5.de glon a1 graph b2.de* guaj k* guat jl3 haliae-lc srj5• harp jl3 hell b2.de* *Hep* k* hip-ac br1* *Hydrog* srj2*• hyos b2.de* hypoth jl3 *Ign* k* *Indg* bg2 iod b2.de* *Ip* k* *Iris* k* *Kali-bi* bg2* kali-br mrr1 *Kali-c* b2.de* kali-m k2 *Kali-n* b2.de* kalm k* kreos k* lac-ac stj5• **Lach** b7a.de laur b2.de* led b2.de* lil-t *Lith-c* k* **Lyc** k* lycpr bro1 **Lyss** k* m-ambo b7a.de m-arct b2.de* m-aust b2.de* mag-c b2.de* *Mag-m* k* *Mag-p* bg2* mand mg1.de* *Mang* k* meny k* *Merc* k* *Merc-i-f* k* methys jl3 *Mez* k* mill b7a.de mim-p jl3 moly-met jl3 *Mosch* k* mur-ac k* murx bg2* naja ptk1 nat-ar k* *Nat-c* k* nat-m b2.de* nat-s ptk1* neon stj2*• nit-ac k* *Nux-m* k* **Nux-v** k* oci-sa jl* oena a1 olnd b2.de* op k* osteo-a jl2 *Pall* par k* penic srb2.fr *Petr* k* *Ph-ac* b2.de* phasco-ci rbp2 phel st1 phor-t mie3• phos b2.de* phyt k* pic-ac a1 plat b2.de* *Plb* k* *Podo* k* prim-o br1 *Prun* psil jl3 psor b4a.de* ptel a1 **Puls** k* *Ran-b* k* **Ran-s** k* **Rat** k* rheum b2.de* *Rhod* k* *Rhus-t* b2.de* rumx bg1* *Ruta* b2.de* *Sabad* k* *Sabin* k* samb b7a.de *Sang* k* **Sars** k* **Sec** k* sel b2.de* *Seneg* b2.de* sep b2.de* ser-a-c jl2 *Sil* k* sinus rly4• spig k* spong b2.de* *Squil* b2.de* stann b2.de* *Staph* k* stram b7a.de *Stront-c* k* **Sul-ac** k* *Sul-i* k2* sulfonam ks2 *Sulph* k* syph jl2 tarax k* *Tarent* a1* tell *Teucr* k* thiop jl3 thuj k* thyr jl3 tub jl2* *Valer* b2.de* vanad dx* vario jl2 ven-m jl3 verat b7a.de verb b2.de* vero-o rly4*• viol-o k* viol-t k* wye a1 yuc a1 *Zinc* k* [alumin-p stj2 am-f stj2 am-p stj1 arg-p stj2 ars-met stj2 astat stj2 bar-f stj1 bar-i stj2 bar-met stj2 bar-p stj1 bell-p-sp dcm1 bism-sn stj2 caes-met stj2 calc-f stj1 *Chr-met* stj1* cob stj2 cupr-f stj2 cupr-p stj2 ferr-f stj2 ferr-i stj1 ferr-lac stj2 ferr-sil stj2 *Fl-pur* stj2 gal-met stj2 hafn-met stj2 irid-met stj2 kali-ar stj2 kali-f stj1 kali-i stj1 kali-p stj1 kali-sil stj2 lanth-met stj2 lith-f stj2 lith-i stj2 lith-p stj2 mag-f stj1 mag-i stj1 mag-lac stj2 mag-met stj2 mag-sil stj2 mang-i stj2 mang-p stj2 nat-f stj1* nat-i stj1 nat-p stj1 nat-sil stj2 nicc stj1 nicc-met stj2 osm-met stj2 plb-p stj2 polon-met stj2 rhen-met stj2 tant-met stj2 thal-met stj2 titan stj2 tung-met stj2 zinc-i stj2 zinc-p stj2]
  - **coldness** of (See Coldness - right)
  - **heat** of (See Heat - affected - right)
  - **then** left side: acet-ac acon k* am-c st* ambr st* anac st androc srj1• *Apis* bg2* ars a1 ars-met aspar bar-c st bell k* benz-ac bg2* bros-gau mrc1 bry bg2 calc-p ptk1 canth bg2* *Caust* st* chel tl1* choc srj3• cupr ptk1 dendr-pol sk4• form sne galla-q-r nl2• hydrog srj2• lac-c tl1 lil-t st* **Lyc** k* merc-i-f st* mez ox-ac bg2* *Phos* st* podo fd3.de• ptel a1 rad-br mrr1 rheum st rumx st* **Sabad** j5.de* sang k* saroth a1 *Sil* ptk1 spong sul-ac st* sulph symph fd3.de• syph ptk1 thiop jl *Verat* st* [pop dhh1]
- **left**: achy jl3 acon k* adam srj5• adon sf1.de agar b2.de* agath-a nl2• agn b2.de* *Aids* nl2• *All-c* k* aloe alum b2.de* alum-sil k2 alumn hr1* *Am-br* k* am-c b2.de* am-m b2.de* *Ambr* b2.de* *Anac* k* *Androc* srj1• ang b2.de* ange-s jl3 *Ant-c* k* *Ant-t* k* *Apis* k* *Arg-met* k* **Arg-n** k* *Arn* k* *Ars* b2.de* ars-i bg2* *Art-v* hr1* arum-t **Asaf** k* **Asar** k* *Asc-t* *Aster* k* atra-r jl3* *Aur* b2.de* aur-m-n bapt hr1* bar-act sf1.de bar-c b2.de* bar-m k* bell b2.de* *Bell-p* hr1* benz-ac a1 *Berb* bism k* borx b2.de* bov b2.de* *Brom* k* bros-gau mrc1 *Bry* k* buni-o jl3 cact mrr1 calad b7a.de *Calc* k* calc-ar k2* calc-f mg1.de* *Camph* b2.de* cann-s k* canth k* **Caps** k* carb-an b4a.de carb-v b2.de* car.de* kalm a1 **Kreos** k* lac-ac hr1* **Lach** k* lat-m jl3 laur b2.de* led b2.de* lepi a1* *Lil-t* bg2* *Lith-c* *Luf-op* rsj5• *Lyc* b2.de* lycps-v a1 m-ambo b7a.de m-arct b2.de* m-aust b2.de* mag-c b2.de* mag-m k* mang k* meny k* meph jl3 *Merc* k* *Merc-c* merc-i-f a1 *Merc-i-r* k* **Mez** k* mill b7a.de mim-p rsj8*• mosch k* *Mur-ac* k* naja k* nat-ar a1 nat-c b2.de* nat-f mg1.de* nat-m b2.de* nat-s k* nat-sil fd3.de• neon srj5• nept-m lsd2.fr nid jl3 *Nit-ac* k* nux-m k* *Nux-v* b2.de* oena a1 ol-j a1 **Olnd** k* onop jl3 *Onos* op b7a.de* *Osm* ox-ac k* *Par* k* paro-i jl3 perh jl3 *Petr* b2.de* ph-ac b2.de* phasco-ci rbp2 **Phos** k* phys pic-ac a1 plan a1 plat b2.de* plb k* *Podo* hr1* positr nl2• psil ft1 psor b4a.de puls b2.de* puls-n a1 pulx br1* ran-b k* *Ran-s* k* *Rheum* b7a.de* *Rhod* k* *Rhus-t* b2.de* rumx bro1 *Ruta* b7a.de sabad b2.de* *Sabin* k* sal-ac sal-fr sle1• samb b2.de* sapo bro1 sars b2.de* sec b2.de* **Sel** k* seneg b2.de* **Sep** k* sieg mg1.de *Sil* k* *Spig* k* spong b2.de* **Squil** k* **Stann** k* staph k* *Stram* b7a.de stront-c k* stroph-s jl3 sul-ac k* sulfa jl3 sulfonam jl3 **Sulph** k* tab *Tarax* k* tell jl3* teucr k* thala jl3 ther k* thuj k* toxi mtf2• ulm-c jsj8• ust k* v-a-b jl3* vac jl2 valer b2.de* *Verat* b2.de* *Verb* b2.de* vesp *Viol-o* k* *Viol-t* k* vip-a jl3 xan *Zinc* b2.de* [alumin-s stj2 am-s stj1 *Ant-m* stj2 ant-met stj2 aur-m stj2 *Aur-s* stj2 bar-br stj2 bar-n stj1 bar-s stj1 bell-p-sp dcm1 beryl stj2 beryl-m stj2 cadm-m stj2 cadm-met stj2 *Cadm-s* stj2 calc-br stj1 calc-lac stj2 calc-m stj1 calc-met stj2 calc-n stj1 calc-s stj1 *Chlor* stj2 chr-m stj2 *Chr-s* stj2 cob-m stj2 cupr-ac[illegible] cupr-m stj2 ferr-m stj1 ferr-n stj2 *Gal-s* stj2 helia stj kali-br stj1 kali-s stj1 lith[illegible] stj2 *Lith-s* stj2 mag-br stj1 mag-n stj2 mang-m stj2 mang-n stj2 *Many-s* stj2 merc-d stj2 moly-met stj2 nat-br stj2 nat-n stj1 *Nicc-s* stj2 niob-met st[illegible] *litro* stj2 pall stj2 plb-m stj2 rhodi stj2 rubd-met stj2 ruth-met stj2 stront-m stj2 stront-met stj2 tax jsj7 techn stj2 titan-s stj2 yttr-met stj2 zinc-m stj2 zinc-n stj2 zirc-met stj2]
  - **coldness** of (See Coldness - left)
  - **heat** of (See Heat - affected - left)
  - **then** right side: acon adam srj5• all-c k2* aloe androc srj1• arg-n bg2 ars ptk1 benz-ac st brom ptk1* bros-gau mrc1 calc st* calc-p *Colch* cupr br1 dulc elaps ferr st* *Form* bg2* form-ac sf1.de hed mg1.de* hydrog srj2• ign gk *Iod* st ip k2* kali-c kreos lac-c bro1* **Lach** k* merc-i-r ptk1 naja nat-m gk neon srj5• nit-m-ac nux-m ptk1 phyt podo fd3.de• psil ft1 puls ptk1 rad-br mrr1 rhus-t k* sabad bg2* stann ptk1 tarax ptk1
- **crosswise**: agar b2.de* *Alum* ptk1 ambr bg2* ant-c tl1 apis ptk1 *Bell* ptk1 berb ptk1 borx ptk1 both br1* calc b2.de* carc pd* *Chel* ptk1 *Chin* ptk1 ferr ptk1 fl-ac bg2 glon bg2 hell ptk1 kali-bi ptk1 kali-i ptk1 kali-m ptk1 *Kalm* ptk1 lac-c bg2* lach bg2* lyc bg2* *Mang* b2.de* murx ptk1 nat-c ptk1 nit-ac b2.de* nux-v ptk1 *Phos* ptk1 **Rhus-t** ptk1 [illegible] sil b2.de* stict ptk1 sul-ac bg2* *Sulph* ptk1 tarax ptk1 valer b2.de* vera[illegible] bg2* zinc ptk1
  - **right** upper and left lower: acon k* *Agar* b4a.de* agn k* am-c k* am-m k* **Ambr** k* ang b7a.de* *Ant-c* k* ant-t k* arg-met k* ars b4a.de ars-i asar k* asc-t a1* bism k* *Borx* k* *Both* st *Bov* k* *Brom* b4a.de* bry k* calad k* *Calc* k* cann-s k* carb-v k* *Caust* k* chel k* cic k* cina k* colch k* coloc k* croc k* cupr k* dig k* dulc k* euph k* euphr b7a.de* *Ferr* k* graph k* hell k* hyos k* ign k* iod k* ip k* kali-n h2 *Lyc* k* m-ambo b7a.de* mag-c k* mang k* med bro1 *Merc-i-f* mez k* mur-ac k* *Nat-c* k* nux-v k* perh jl petr b4a.de ph-ac b4a.de **Phos** k* plat k* *Plb* k* ran-b k* rheum k* rhod b4a.de rhus-t k* ruta k* sel k* *Sil* k* spig k* **Sul-ac** k* viol-o k*

• **left** upper and right lower: **Agar** k* *Alum* k* *Anac* k* ant-t bro1* *Arn* k* ars k* asc-t a1* bar-c k* bell k* *Both* st brom k* camph k* caps k* *Carb-an* k* cham k* chel chin k* coff k* con k* cupr b7a.de cycl k* euphr k* *Fl-ac* k* hep k* hydrog srj2• hyper *Kali-c* k* kali-n k* lach k* laur k* **Led** k* m-arct b7a.de* m-aust b7a.de* mag-m k* meny k* merc k* mill k* mur-ac k* nat-m k* nit-ac k* nux-m k* nux-v k* olnd k* op k* par k* ph-ac k* *Puls* k* ran-s k* rhod k* **Rhus-t** k* sabad k* sabin k* samb k* sars k* sec k* seneg k* sep b4a.de spong k* *Squil* k* *Stann* k* staph k* stram k* sulph k* **Tarax** k* teucr k* *Thuj* k* valer k* *Verat* k* *Verb* k* *Viol-t* k* zinc b4a.de

O - **Lain** on; pain goes to side ars bg* *Bry* bg* calc bg* hep ptk1 *Kali-c* bg* merc bg* mosch ptk1 nux-m ptk1 *Ph-ac* bg* **Puls** bg* ruta tl1 sep bg* sil bg* symph tl1 teucr ptk1

- **Not** lain on; pain goes to side: bry bg* cupr bg* fl-ac bg* graph bg* *Ign* bg* kali-bi bg* kali-c ptk1 puls bg* *Rhus-t* bg* teucr ptk1

DAYTIME: *Agar* bg1* *Alum* am-c bg2* am-m k* arg-met bg2* arg-n bg2* calc bg2* calc-sil k2 caust bg2* cimic k* euph ptk1 *Euphr* bg2* *Ferr* k* guaj k* *Hydrog* srj2• lac-d k2* lach bg2* *Med* k* *Nat-ar* k* nat-c k* *Nat-m* k* *Nit-ac* k* nux-v bg2* phos bg2* *Puls* k* *Rhus-t* k* *Sang* k* **Sep** k* **Stann** k* **Sulph** k*

- **advances**; when day:
  • **agg.**: acon bg2 bry bg2 echi bg2 glon bg2 sang bg2 spig bg2 stram bg2
  • **amel.**: agar bg2 cycl bg2 helo bg2
- **amel.**: acon sf1.de *Agar* bg2* alum ptk1 am bg2* bry bg2* cham bg2* cob-n sp1 *Cycl* bg2* helo bg2 helon sf1.de hydrog srj2• *Jal* bg2* kali-c b4a.de* *Mag-p* bg2* merc k2* nat-p k2* nat-s k2* *Petr* bg2* sep bg2* syph bro1*

MORNING (= 6-9 h): *Abies-n* abrot absin *Acal* kr1* *Acon* k* aesc **Agar** k* agn k* *Aids* nl2• all-c bg2* *Aloe* k* *Alum* k* **Alum-p** kr1* alumn kr1* am-c k* **Am-m** k* *Ambr* k* *Anac* k* ang b2.de* *Ant-c* k* ant-s-aur kr1* *Ant-t* b2.de* *Apis* k* aran bg2* aran-ix mg1.de **Arg-met** k* *Arg-n* k* arist-cl mg1.de *Arn* k* *Ars* k* **Ars-i** k* ars-s-f kr1* asaf k* asar k* asc-t c1 **Aur** k* aur-ar k2 aur-i k2* *Aur-m-n* wbt2• **Aur-s** k2* bac c1* *Bapt* *Bar-c* k* bar-i k2* *Bar-m* *Bar-s* k2* bell k* benz-ac *Berb* bism k* *Borx* k* *Bov* k* *Brucel* sa3• **Bry** k* bufo k* cadm-met kr1* calad k* **Calc** k* calc-i kr1* **Calc-p** k* *Calc-sil* k2* cann-i kr1* cann-s k* cann-xyz ptk1 *Canth* k* *Caps* k* **Carb-an** k* **Carb-v** k* **Carbn-s** cassia-s cdd7*• castm bg2* *Caust* k* **Cham** k* **Chel** k* chin k* *Chr-ac* cic k* cimic **Cina** k* *Cinnb* *Cist* k* clem k* cob bg2* cob-n kr1* coc-c k* *Coca* *Cocc* k* cod *Coff* k* colch k* coloc k* *Con* k* convo-s kr1* corn cortico kr1* cortiso kr1* **Croc** k* crot-h k* crot-t k* cupr k* cycl k* cystein-l rly4• daph j5.de* *Dig* k* *Dios* k* *Dros* k* *Dulc* k* echi kr1* elaps bg2* erig mg1.de *Eup-per* k* euph k* *Euphr* k* *Ferr* k* *Ferr-ar* k* ferr-i *Ferr-p* k* *Fl-ac* bg2* form *Gamb* *Gels* gink-b sbd1• glon kr1* glycyr-g cte1• gran *Graph* k* grat *Guaj* k* harp jl hed kr1* hell k* helo-s rwt2• *Hep* k* *Hydr* *Hydrog* srj2• hydroph kr1* hyos k* *Ign* k* iod k* ip k* iris bg2* *Kali-ar* k* **Kali-bi** k* *Kali-c* k* kali-chl k13 *Kali-i* kali-m k2 **Kali-n** k* *Kali-p* k* kali-sil k2* *Kalm* *Kreos* k* lac-ac stj2*• lac-c kr1* *Lac-leo* sk4• **Lach** k* laur k* led k* lept bg2* lil-t bg2* lith-c kr1* lob bg2* *Luna* kg1• lyc k* m-ambo b2.de* *M-arct* b2.de* *M-aust* b2.de* *Mag-c* k* mag-f kr1* *Mag-m* k* mag-s kr1* magn-gr kr1* mang k* med kr1* meny k* meph j5.de *Merc* k* merc-c k* *Merc-i-f* mez k* mosch k* mur-ac k* mygal kr1* naja bg2* **Nat-ar** *Nat-c* k* **Nat-m** k* nat-n bg2* *Nat-p* **Nat-s** k* nat-sil kr1* nicc k* nicc-s br1 **Nit-ac** k* nuph kr1* *Nux-m* k* **Nux-v** k* oci-sa kr1* olnd b2.de* **Onos** k* *Op* k* ox-ac par k* pareir perh jl **Petr** k* **Ph-ac** k* **Phos** k* *Phyt* pic-ac *Plan* *Plat* k* plb k* **Podo** k* positr nl2• prot jl2 *Psor* ptel **Puls** k* *Ran-b* k* ran-s k* *Rheum* k* **Rhod** k* **Rhus-t** k* **Rumx** k* ruta k* sabad k* sabal c1 *Sabin* k* sacch sst1• *Sal-ac* sal-fr sle1• samb k* *Sang* k* *Sars* k* sec k* *Sel* k* *Senec* *Seneg* k* **Sep** k* *Sil* k* sol-t-ae vml3• **Spig** k* spong k* **Squil** k* *Stann* k* *Staph* k* stel kr1* *Stram* k* stront-c k* stry kr1* stry-p kr1* **Sul-ac** b2.de* sul-i kr1* **Sulph** k* symph fd3.de• tab *Tarax* k* *Tarent* hr1* teli kr1* teucr k* *Thuj* k* **Tub** kr1* *Tung-met* bdx1• vac jl2 **Valer** k* vanil fd5.de ven-m kr1* *Verat* k* *Verat-v* verb k* viol-o k* viol-t k* visc kr1* xero kr1 *Zinc* k* *Zinc-p* kr1* [gal-met stj2 heroin sdj2 sol-ecl cky1 *Spect* dfg1]

- **6** h: aloe k* *Alum* ptk1 am ptk1 bov ptk1 calc-p coloc mrr1 ferr ptk1 *Hep* ptk1 lyc ptk1 mim-p vml3• *Nux-v* ptk1 ox-ac sep sil k* sulph k* verat k*
  • **6**-10 h: mim-p rsj8*•
- **7** h: carc fd2.de• eup-per k* hep ptk1 nat-c ptk1 *Nux-v* ptk1 podo k* sep ptk1 [mag-br stj1 mag-f stj1 mag-i stj1 mag-lac stj2 *Mag-m* stj1 *Mag-met* stj2 mag-n stj2 mag-p stj1 mag-s stj1 *Mag-sil* stj2 *Titan* stj2 titan-s stj2 *Vanad* stj1*]
  • **7**-9 h: carc fd2.de• eup-per ptk
- **8** h: *Eup-per* k* nux-v k* [bor-pur stj2]
  • **8**-12 h: cact ptk1 *Chinin-s* ptk1 *Eup-per* ptk1 *Gels* ptk1 nat-c ptk1 **Nat-m** ptk1 nux-v ptk1 phos ptk1 sabad ptk1 sep ptk1 stann ptk1 sulph ptk1
- **noon**; until: rhus-g tmo3•
- **afternoon**; and: sars bg2

Morning – afternoon; and: ...
  • **evening**; and: nit-ac bg2
- **evening**; and: alum bg2* bov bg2* *Calc* ptk1 caust ptk1 coc-c ptk1 graph bg2* guaj bg2 kali-c bg2* lach ptk1 **Lyc** ptk1 phos bg2* psor ptk1 *Rhus-t* ptk1 sal-fr sle1• sang ptk1 **Sep** ptk1 *Stram* ptk1 *Stront-c* ptk1 *Thuj* ptk1 verat ptk1 zinc bg2
- **night**; and: iod bg2 nat-c bg2
- **amel.**: acon bg2* am-m bg2* ambr j5.de apis bro1 carc zzh cench k2* chel ptk1 jug-c bro1 merc j5.de* phos bg2* psor jl2 puls vh sang bg2* still bro1 xero bro1 zinc j5.de*
- **bed** agg.; in: aloe ptk1 *Am-m* ptk1 *Ambr* ptk1 bry ptk1 con ptk1 *Kali-c* ptk1 *Lyc* ptk1 *Nux-v* ptk1 phos ptk1 sep ptk1 *Sulph* ptk1 symph fd3.de•
- **daytime** begins (See sunrise)
- **one** day and the afternoon of the next; morning of: eup-per ptk1 lac-c bg2*
- **rising** agg.: *Rhus-t* mrr1
- **sunrise**:
  • **after**: cham k* m-ambo b2.de* m-aust b2.de* *Nux-v* k* puls k* syph st1
    : **amel.**: colch ptk1 syph ptk1
    : **sunset**; until: arg-n bg2 bry bg2 echi bg2 gels bg2 glon bg2* *Med* bro1* nat-m bg2 stann bg2* stront-c bg2
  • **before**: lyc bg2
- **waking**; on: (↗Sleep - after - morning) *Aids* nl2• *Alum* mrr1 apoc vh1 bell-p mg1.de cadm-met mg1.de* cob-n mg1.de* dulc fd4.de ferr-ar k2* flav jl3* *Graph* mrr1 hom-xyz mgm• *Hydroph* rsj6• *Lac-h* htj1• lac-loxod-a hrn2• **Luna** kg1• *Lyc* mrr1 mag-c mg1.de *Mag-m* mrr1 plut-n srj7• positr nl2• prot jl3 psil vml3• raph mgm• sal-fr sle1• symph fd3.de• vanil fd5.de [tax jsj7]

FORENOON (= 9-12 h): aloe alum k* alum-p kr1* alum-sil k2 *Alumn* kr1 am-c k* am-m k* ambr k* anac bg2 ang b2.de* ant-c k* ant-t k* aran *Arg-met* k* arg-n bg2* ars k* ars-s-f kr1* asaf k* aur k* aur-ar k2 aur-s k2* bar-c k* bar-i k2 bar-m *Bar-s* k2* bell k* borx k* bov k* *Bry* k* cact calc k* calc-sil k2* **Cann-i** kr1 **Cann-s** k* **Cann-xyz** ptk1 canth k* carb-an k* *Carb-v* k* carbn-s caust k* cedr cham k* chel k* chin k* cocc k* coloc k* con b2.de* cupr k* cycl k* dros k* dulc k* euph k* euphr k* ferr k* *Fl-ac* bg2* germ-met srj5• gink-b sbd1• graph b2.de* *Guaj* k* haliae-lc srj5• halo jl hell k* *Hep* b2.de* hydrog srj2• hydroph rsj6• ign k* ip k* kali-ar kali-c k* kali-chl k13 kali-m k2 kali-n k* kali-p kali-sil k2* kreos k* lach k* *Laur* k* lyc b2.de* m-arct b2.de* m-aust b2.de* mag-c k* mag-m k* *Mang* k* merc k* mez k* mosch k* mur-ac k* *Nat-ar* **Nat-c** k* **Nat-m** k* nat-p *Nat-sil* kr1* neon srj5• nit-ac k* *Nux-m* k* nux-v k* par k* *Pareir* kr1 petr k* ph-ac k* phos k* plat b2.de* plb k* **Podo** k* puls k* *Ran-b* k* rhod k* *Rhus-t* k* rumx **Sabad** k* *Sars* k* *Sec* k* sel k* seneg k* **Sep** k* *Sil* k* *Spig* k* spong b2.de* **Stann** k* *Staph* b2.de* *Stram* bg2* stront-c k* **Sul-ac** k* **Sulph** k* *Tarax* k* *Teucr* k* valer k* verat b2.de* verb k* *Viol-t* k* zinc k* zinc-p kr1*

- **9** h: bry ptk1 carneg-g rwt1• *Cedr* mrr1 *Cham* k* *Eup-per* ptk1 kali-bi ptk1 kali-c k* lac-c ptk1 nat-m tl1* nat-s ptk1 nux-v ptk1 podo sep ptk1 sul-ac ptk1 sumb urol-h rwt• *Verb* ptk1 [alum stj2 *Alumin* stj2 alumin-p stj2 alumin-s stj2 arg-n stj2 arg-p stj2 bar-n stj1 calc-n stj1 ferr-n stj2 mag-n stj2 mang-n stj2 nat-n stj1 *Nitro* stj2 *Zinc-n* stj2]
  • **9**-11 h: stann sf1.de [pop dhh1]
  • **9**-14 h: nat-m sf1.de
  • **9**-16 h: verb ptk1
- **10** h: *Ars* ptk1 borx ptk1* carc fb cench k2 chin ptk1 chinin-s ptk1 cimic *Eup-per* ptk1 gels k* *Iod* ptk1 med ptk1 **NAT-M** k ●* nux-v petr ptk1 *Phos* ptk1 *Rhus-t* ptk1 sep ptk1 sil ptk1 *Stann* ptk1 *Sulph* ptk1 thuj ptk1
  • **10**-11 h: gels bro1 *Nat-m* bro1* *Sep* bro1 sulph bro1
  • **10**-13 h: both-a rb3
  • **10**-15 h: chinin-s ptk1 nat-m ptk1 tub bg*
- **11** h: arg-met arg-n sf1.de* ars k* arum-t asaf ptk1 asar bapt ptk1 bell mrr1 berb cact k* *Chinin-s* ptk1 cimic cob cocc ptk1 falco-pe nl2• *Gels* ptk1 hydr k* hyos k* ind sf1.de ip k* lach sf1.de* mag-p ptk1 nat-c ptk1 **Nat-m** k* nat-p ptk1* *Nux-v* ptk1 *Phos* ptk1 phyt *Puls* ptk1 *Rhus-t* ptk1 *Sep* ptk1 *Stann* ptk1 **SULPH** k ●* viol-t a *Zinc* ptk1 [calc-sil stj2 ferr-sil stj2 kali-sil stj2 *Mag-sil* stj2 mang-sil stj2 nat-ar stj2 nat-br stj2 nat-caust stj2 nat-f stj2 nat-lac stj2 *Nat-met* stj2 nat-sil stj2 ruth-met stj2 sil stj2 sil-met stj2]
  • **11**-12 h: haliae-lc srj5•
- **amel.**: *Alum* k* fl-ac a1 lil-t bro1* **Lyc** k* nat-sil k2*

NOON (= 12-13 h): alum ant-c ptk1 apis k* **Arg-met** k* arg-n bg2 arge br1 ars bruc j5.de cact br1 carb-v k* carc fd2.de• cham bg2 chel bg2* chin ptk1 cic coloc bg2 conch fkr1• elaps ptk1 *Eup-per* ptk1 falco-pe nl2• gels ptk1 kali-bi k* kali-c ptk1 lach ptk1 mag-c bg2 nat-m bg2* *Nux-m* k* nux-v bg2* paeon phos k* sang bg2 *Sel* bg2 sep k* *Sil* ptk1 spig ptk1 *Stram* k* *Sulph* k* *Valer* k* verb ptk1 *Zinc* k*

- **12**-16 h: alum ptk1 ars ptk1 bell ptk1 lach ptk1 lyc ptk1 puls ptk1 sil ptk1 thuj ptk1 zinc ptk1
- **12**-0 h: lach sf1.de*
- **eating**:
  - **after**:
    - **agg.**: grat bg2 halo jl *Mag-m* sf1.de *Nat-c* sf1.de nat-sil fd3.de• nux-m sf1.de valer sf1.de
    - **amel.**: **Chel** k* nat-s sf1.de
- **increasing** till noon, then decreasing; symptoms: *Arg-n* sf1.de echi sf1.de gels sf1.de glon sf1.de kalm k2* *Sang* st sanic st spig st stann sf1.de stront-c sf1.de

AFTERNOON (= 13-18 h): acon aesc bro1 aeth *Agar* k* aids nl2• all-c *Aloe* k* *Alum* k* **Alum-p** k2* alum-sil k2* **Alumn** hr1 *Am-c* k* *Am-m* k* *Ambr* k* anac k* ang b2.de* *Ant-c* k* ant-t k* *Apis* k* *Arg-met* k* *Arg-n* arn k* *Ars* k* ars-i ars-s-f k2 *Asaf* k* *Asar* k* aur k* aur-ar k2 aur-i k2* aur-s k2* aza jl3 *Bamb-a* stb2.de• bar-c k* bar-i k2* *Bar-m* bar-s k2* **Bell** k* *Bism* k* borx k* *Bov* k* *Bry* k* buth-a sp1* cact calad k* calc k* calc-i k2* *Calc-p* calc-sil k2* camph k* cann-s k* *Canth* k* caps k* carb-an k* carb-v k* carbn-s carc tpw2* caust k* cedr *Cench* bro1* cham k* *Chel* k* chin k* *Cic* k* *Cimic* k* cina k* coc-c k* cocc k* coff k* colch k* *Coloc* k* con k* conch fkr1• croc k* cycl k* cyn-d jl3 cyt-l mg1.de* *Dig* k* dios dros k* *Dulc* k* euphr k* eys sp1 fago bro1 ferr k* ferr-ar ferr-i ferr-m hr1* ferr-p *Fl-ac* bg2 gels gink-b sbd1• graph b2.de* grat j5.de guaj bg2 hell k* hep b2.de* hip-ac sp1* hydrog srj2• hyos k* *Ign* k* iod k* ip k* kali-ar *Kali-bi* k* kali-c k* kali-chl k13 kali-cy bro1 kali-m k2 **Kali-n** k* kali-p kali-s fkr2.de kali-sil k2* kreos k* lach k* *Laur* k* *Led* lil-t bro1 lob bro1 luna kg1• **Lyc** k* m-arct b2.de* m-aust b2.de* mag-c k* mag-m k* *Mang* k* meli meny k* *Merc* k* merc-sul c1 mez k* *Mosch* k* *Mur-ac* k* naja jl nat-ar nat-c b2.de* *Nat-m* k* nicc *Nit-ac* k* nux-m k* *Nux-v* k* *Ol-an* op k* par k* petr k* *Ph-ac* k* *Phos* k* phyt plan plat b2.de* plb k* psil ft1 *Ptel* **Puls** k* *Ran-b* k* ran-s k* rheum k* rhod k* **Rhus-t** k* *Rumx* ruta k* sabad k* sabin k* sal-ac *Sang* *Sars* k* *Sel* k* *Seneg* k* **Sep** k* **Sil** k* **Sin-n** spig k* spong b2.de* squil k* stann k* *Staph* b2.de* *Still* k* stront-c b2.de* sul-ac k* sul-i k2* *Sulph* k* tarax k* *Teucr* k* thea c1 thiop jl **Thuj** k* urol-h rwt• *Valer* k* *Ven-m* jl3 verat b2.de* verb k* *Viol-t* k* wye k2* x-ray bro1 xero bro1 **Zinc** k* **Zinc-p** k2 [heroin sdj2]

- **13** h: arg-met k* *Ars* k2* cact ptk1 calc vh chel ptk1 cina ptk1 grat ptk1 kali-c ptk1 *Lach* ptk1 mag-c phos ptk1 *Puls* ptk1 thuj vh [arg-n stj2 *Ind* stj2 nicc stj1 nicc-met stj2 nicc-s stj2 *Pall* stj2 *Stann* stj2]
  - **13**-14.30 h: lac-h htj1•
  - **13**-14 h: ars k2
  - **13**-18 h: bamb-a stb2.de• both-ax tsm2 carc gk6* galeoc-c-h gms1•
  - **13**-21 h: chel sf1.de
- **14** h: ars k2* bros-gau mrc1 calc chel ptk1* cur st *Eup-per* ptk1 falco-pe nl2• ferr ptk1 gels ptk1 irid-met srj5• lach k* lob mag-p ptk1 nit-ac k* ol-an puls k* sang [tax jsj7]
  - **14**, 15 or 16 h until morning: syph sf1.de
  - **14**-15 h: *Aur-m-n* wbt2•
  - **14**-16 h: **Sep** mrr1
- **14**.30 h: hell
- **15** h: *Ang* bg3 ant-t bg3* *Apis* k* ars k* asaf bg3* asar **Bell** k* bry k2* calc vh cedr bg3* cench chel bg3* *Chinin-s* bg3* clem con bg3* nat-m bg3 plut-n srj7• samb bg3* sang bg3* sil staph k* sulph *Thuj* k* [beryl stj2 calc-lac stj2 calc-m stj1 *Calc-met* stj2 calc-p stj1 calc-sil stj2 heroin sdj2]
  - **15**-3 h: bell k2
  - **15**-17 h: sep k*
  - **15**-18 h: apis sf1.de rhus-g tmo3•
  - **15**-19 h: **Lyc** mrr1
  - **15**-20 h: neon srj5•
- **16** h: *Aesc* ptk1 alum anac k* *Apis* ptk1 ars ptk1 arum-t *Aur-m-n* wbt2• berb bc bry vh cact ptk1 calc-p carb-v *Caust* k* *Cedr* ptk1 cench k2 chel k* chinin-s ptk1 cob *Coloc* k* fum rly1• gels k* germ-met srj5• *Hell* k* ign hr1 ip ptk1 kali-c kali-p fd1.de• lachn **Lyc** k* mag-m mang ptk1 meli br1 merc-sul vh mur-ac nat-s k* nit-ac ptk1 nux-m ptk1 *Nux-v* ptk1 puls k* rhus-t ptk1 stront-c sulph ptk1 verb ptk1 [heroin sdj2]

Afternoon – 16 h: ...

- **16**-4 h: thuj sf1.de
- **16**-17 h: allox jl coloc mrr1 merc-sul c1*
- **16**-18 h: alum h2 both-ax tsm2 eys jl* gels sf1.de **Sep** ●* stann mrr1 [heroin sdj2]
- **16**-19 h: coloc sf1.de *Lyc* sf1.de vero-o rly3•
- **16**-20 h: alum k* *Apis* ptk1 bov buth-a mg1.de* *Caust* ptk1 chinin-s vh coloc ptk1 *Hell* k* hyos ptk1 **LYC** k ●* mag-m morg-g fmm1• nit-ac ptk1 nux-m k* phos ptk1 plat ptk1 *Puls* ptk1 *Rhus-t* ptk1 sabad bro1 sulph k* **Thuj** ptk1 tub ptk1 valer ptk1
- **16**-22 h: alum chel plat

- **17** h: alum ptk1 *Aur-m-n* wbt2• *Bamb-a* stb2.de• bov ptk1 caust ptk1 cedr ptk1 *Chin* ptk1 cimic *Coloc* k* con k* falco-pe nl2• galeoc-c-h gms1• *Gels* ptk1 haliae-lc srj5• *Hep* k* hyper ptk1 kali-c k* lac-ac stj2*• *Lyc* ptk1 nat-m ptk1 *Nux-v* ptk1 psil ft1 **Puls** k1* *Rhus-t* ptk1 sulph ptk1 *Thuj* ptk1 tub ptk1 valer ptk1 [*Cadm-met* stj2 cadm-s stj2 calc-lac stj2 *Cupr* stj2 cupr-act stj2 cupr-f stj2 cupr-m stj2 cupr-p stj2 ferr-lac stj2 heroin sdj2 mag-lac stj2 mang-act stj2 mang-i stj2 mang-m stj2 mang-n stj2 mang-p stj2 mang-s stj2 mang-sil stj2 nat-lac stj2 neon stj2 nicc stj1 nicc-met stj2 nicc-s stj2 rhodi stj2 *Stann* stj2 *Zinc* stj2 zinc-i stj2 zinc-m stj2 zinc-p stj2]
  - **17**.30 h: loxo-recl knl4•
  - **17**-5 h: plb dx thal dx
  - **17**-18 h: ange-s carc gk6* methys scir c1*
  - **17**-19 h: **Luna** kg1•
  - **17**-20 h: *Lil-t*
- **evening**; and: kali-n bg2
- **daylight**; until: syph ptk1
- **amel.**: anac b4a.de cinnb k* cob-n jl3 cortico tpw7* erig vml3• gels ptk1 gink-b sbd1• hecla jl hed jl3 hydrog srj2• kali-c jl med jl2 *Nat-s* bg2* neon srj5• phyt bg2* podo fd3.de• *Positr* nl2• rhus-t bg2* sacch-a fd2.de• sal-fr sle1• *Sep* bg2*
  - **16** h: germ-met srj5•
    - **bed**; until going to: alum
- **late**: *Apis* bro1 aran bro1 carb-v bro1 colch bro1 *Coloc* bro1 *Hell* bro1 *Lyc* bro1 mag-p bro1 med bro1 meli bro1 ol-an bro1 *Puls* bro1 sabad bro1 zinc bro1

EVENING (= 18-22 h): abrot *Acon* k* aeth hr1* agar k* agn k* alf bro1 *All-c* k* aloe k* **Alum** k* alum-sil k2* alumn kr1 am-br bro1 **Am-c** k* *Am-m* k* **Ambr** k* *Anac* k* *Androc* srj1• *Ang* b2.de* **Ant-c** k* **Ant-t** k* apis k* *Arg-met* k* *Arg-n* k* **Arn** k* *Ars* k* *Ars-i* ars-s-f k2 *Asaf* k* *Asar* k* aur k* aur-ar k2 aur-i k2* aur-m-n wbt2• *Aur-s* k2* *Bapt* *Bar-c* k* bar-i k2* bar-m bar-s k2* **Bell** k* berb berb-a jl3 bism k* *Borx* k* *Bov* k* *Brom* **Bry** k* bufo bg2 buth-a sp1 caj bro1 *Calad* k* **Calc** k* calc-ar k2* *Calc-i* k2* calc-p *Calc-s* **Calc-sil** k2* camph k* cann-s k* canth k* **Caps** k* **Carb-an** k* **Carb-v** k* **Carbn-s** carc sp1* cassia-s cdd7*• **Caust** k* cedr *Cench* k2* **Cham** k* chel k* chin k* chlorpr pin1* cic k* *Cimic* cina k* clem k* *Cocc* k* coff k* **Colch** k* *Coloc* k* com *Con* k* *Croc* k* crot-h k* crot-t sf1.de cupr k* *Cupr-s* hr1* **Cycl** k* cyn-d jl3 cyt-l mg1.de* daph sf* dig k* dios bro1 diphtox jl2 dirc dros k* *Dulc* k* euon bro1 **Euphr** k* eys sp1* *Ferr* k* *Ferr-ar* *Ferr-i* *Ferr-p* k* *Ferr-t* *Fl-ac* k* flor-p jl3 form sf1.de *Gamb* gink-b sbd1• glycyr-g cte1• *Graph* k* *Guaj* k* hecla jl **Hell** k* *Hep* k* hipp jl2 *Hydrog* srj2• **Hyos** k* *Ign* k* *Iod* k* *Ip* k* iris br1 jatr-c *Kali-ar* *Kali-bi* k* *Kali-c* k* kali-chl k13 *Kali-i* kali-m k2 **Kali-n** k* *Kali-p* *Kali-s* k* kali-sil k2* *Kalm* kreos k* **Lach** k* *Laur* k* *Led* k* *Lil-t* **Lyc** k* m-ambo b2.de* *M-arct* b2.de* *M-aust* b2.de* **Mag-c** k* *Mag-m* k* *Mang* k* **Meny** k* meph j5.de **Merc** k* merc-c bro1 *Merc-i-r* **Mez** k* mosch k* mur-ac k* *Nat-ar* *Nat-c* k* *Nat-m* k* **Nat-p** k* nat-s k2 *Nat-sil* k2* neon srj5• nep mg1.de* nicc **Nit-ac** k* *Nux-m* k* *Nux-v* k* olnd b2.de* op k* osm *Ox-ac* palo jl3 *Par* b2.de* penic srb2.fr *Petr* k* **Ph-ac** k* **Phos** k* phyt pic-ac pitu jl3 plan **Plat** k* **Plb** k* polys sk4• *Psor* *Ptel* **Puls** k* *Ran-b* k* **Ran-s** k* rheum k* *Rhod* k* *Rhus-t* k* **Rumx** k* **Ruta** k* sabad k* *Sabin* k* sal-ac sal-fr sle1• *Samb* k* *Sang* k* *Sars* k* sel k* *Seneg* k* **Sep** k* **Sil** k* **Sin-n** spig k* *Spong* k* squil k* **Stann** k* staph k* stict **Stront-c** k* **Sul-ac** k* *Sul-i* k2* sulfonam jl3* **Sulph** k* *Sumb* symph fd3.de• *Syph* k2* *Tab* k* tarax k* tarent hr1* teucr k* thiop jl *Thuj* k* trios jl tub mrr1 v-a-b jl3* **Valer** k* vanil fd5.de verat k* verb k* vib k* viol-o k* viol-t k* x-ray bro1* **Zinc** k* zinc-p k2 [stront-met stj2]

- **2** h; until: asaf vh
- **18** h: ampe-qu br1 ant-t ptk1 bapt calc st calc-p caust *Cedr* ptk1 choc srj3• dig hep k* hyper *Kali-c* ptk1 kali-i lachn mim-p vml3• nat-m ptk1 neon srj5• **Nux-v** ptk1 penic srb2.fr petr ptk1 *Puls* ptk1 *Rhus-t* ptk1 *Sep* ptk1 *Sil* ptk1 *Sumb* k*
  - **18**-4 h: guaj st*

- **18** h: ...
  - **18**-6 h: kreos k* lil-t sf1.de *Syph*
  - **18**-19 h: carc mg1.de* culx k2 *Hep*
  - **18**-20 h: carc fd2.de• rauw jl
  - **18**-21 h: androc srj1• bamb-a stb2.de• carc gk6* choc srj3• galeoc-c-h gms1• pall sne [osm-met stj2]
    - **amel.**: ozone sde2•
  - **18**-22 h: kali-c mim-p rsj8*•
- **19** h: alum ptk1 ant-c bov k* bry vh *Cedr* ptk1 chinin-s ptk1 culx k2 elaps al ferr ptk1 gamb ptk1 gels ptk1 glycyr-g cte1• *Hep* ptk1 *Ip* ptk1 *Lyc* k* nat-m ptk1 *Nat-s* ptk1 *Nux-v* ptk1 petr k* puls ptk1 pyrog ptk1 rhus-t k* sep ptk1 sulph ptk1 tarent ptk1 [beryl-m stj2 *Graph* stj2 lith-c stj2 thal-met stj2]
- **20** h: alum ptk1 *Bov* ptk1 caust ptk1 coff ptk1 elaps ptk1 hep ptk1 mag-c ptk1 merc ptk1 merc-i-r nat-sil fd3.de• phos ptk1 plut-n srj7• *Rhus-t* ptk1 **Sulph** ptk1 tarax vanil fd5.de
  - **20**-0 h: arg-n ptk1 *Bov* ptk1 **Bry** ptk1 carb-v ptk1 gels ptk1 lyc ptk1 mur-ac ptk1 phos ptk1 puls ptk1 rumx ptk1 stann ptk1 sulph ptk1
  - **20**-3 h: syph sf1.de
  - **20**-21 h: neon srj5•
- **21** h: ars ptk1 *Bov* ptk1 **Bry** k* calc st cham vh galeoc-c-h gms1• *Gels* ptk1 hydrog srj2*• luna kg1• merc ptk1* mur-ac k* sanic vh sulph [alumin-p stj2 am-f stj2 arg-p stj2 bar-f stj1 calc-f stj1 calc-p stj1 cinnb stj2 cob-p stj2 cupr-f stj2 cupr-p stj2 ferr-f stj2 fl-ac stj2 fl-pur stj2 kali-f stj1 kali-p stj1 lith-f stj2 lith-p stj2 mag-p stj1 mang-p stj2 merc-i-f stj2 nat-f stj1* nat-p stj1 ph-ac stj1 phos stj2 plb-p stj2 sul-ac stj1 tell stj2 zinc-p stj2]
  - **21**-5 h: ammc vh
  - **21**-22 h: cham mrr1
  - **21**-0 h: sanic mrr1
  - **amel.**: ara-maca sej7• *Med* vh
- **night**; and: cench k2 lil-t sf1.de mag-c bg2
- **midnight**; until: anac ptk1
- **air** agg.; in open: *Am-c* k* carb-an carb-v k* *Merc* b2.de* *Merc-c* nit-ac k* sulph k*
- **amel.**: *Agar* sf1.de* *Alum* k* am-m sf1.de ang sf1.de aran-ix mg1.de arg-met k* am asaf **Aur** k* *Aur-m-n* wbt2• borx bro1* bruc j5.de calc-caust zf carc fb* castm sf1.de chel chin vh cob-n sp1 conch fkr1• cortiso jl3 cypra-eg sde6.de• erig vml3• halo jl hed mg1.de* hydrog srj2• *Ign* zf ina-i mlk9.de kali-n b4a.de* *Lac-e* hrn2• lac-leo sk4• lob bro1 *Lyc* k* mag-c mg1.de mag-m dgt *Med* k* nat-m sf1.de nat-s vh nicc bro1 nux-v bro1 podo sf1.de *Puls* j5.de* rat vh sacch sst1• *Sep* k* stel bro1 tarent zf thyr jl3 visc sp1* zinc mrr1 [aur-m stj2 aur-s stj2 beryl stj2]
- **eating**:
  - **after**:
    - **agg.**: indg petr h2 vanil fd5.de
    - **amel.**: *Sep*
- **every** other evening: *Puls*
- **lying** down:
  - **after**:
    - **agg.**: ars graph sf1.de hep sf1.de *Ign* *Led* *Merc* sf1.de *Phos* puls sf1.de sel sf1.de stront-c *Sulph* thuj
    - **amel.**: kali-n
- **sleep**; before going to: *Plat* k*
- **sunset**:
  - **after**: ang bg2 aur ptk1* bry k* ign k* kreos ptk1 lycps-v bg2 *Merc* ptk1 phyt ptk1 *Puls* k* rhus-g tmo3• rhus-t k* *Syph* ptk1
    - **amel.**: alum vh coca bg2* lil-t bg1* med bg1* sel bg2*
  - **sunrise**; until: *Aur* k* cimic colch k* merc bg2* phyt bro1 plut-n srj7• **Syph** bg2*
- **twilight**; in the:
  - **agg.**: (↗*Twilight - agg.*) *Acon* vh1 *Am-m* k* ang b2.de* arg-n bg2 **Ars** k* ars-s-f k2* borx b4a.de **Calc** k* *Caust* k* cham bg2 dig k* graph bg2 (non:mang) nat-m k* **Phos** k* plat sf plb k* **Puls** k* **Rhus-t** k* staph k* sul-ac k* valer k*
  - **amel.**: (↗*Twilight - amel.*) alum bry k* lac-e hrn2• meny bg2 *Phos* k* tab bg2

NIGHT (= 22-6 h): abel jl3 abrot acet-ac **Acon** k* agar k* agn k* agre jl3 aloe alum k* **Alum-p** k2* alum-sil k2* alumn kr1 *Am-br* am-c k* *Am-m* k* ambr k* *Ammc* k* anac k* androc srj1• ang b2.de* *Ant-c* k* *Ant-t* k* apis bg2* apoc *Aral*

Night: ...
aran bg2* arg-met k* **Arg-n** k* arist-cl sp1 **Arn** k* **Ars** k* **Ars-i** k* **Ars-s-f** k2* *Asaf* k* asar k* aster bro1 *Aur* k* aur-ar k2 aur-i k2* aur-m k2* *Aur-m-n* wbt2• **Aur-s** k2* bac bro1* *Bar-c* k* bar-i k2* *Bar-m* *Bar-s* k2 *Bell* k* benz-ac k* benzol br1 berb-a jl3 bism k* borx k* *Bov* k* *Brom* *Bry* k* bufo bg2 buni-o jl3 but-ac bro1 cact caj bro1 calad k* **Calc** k* calc-ar k2* **Calc-i** **Calc-p** k* **Calc-s** k* **Calc-sil** k2* *Camph* k* *Cann-i* *Cann-s* k* *Canth* k* *Caps* k* carb-ac **Carb-an** k* *Carb-v* k* **Carbn-s** carc gk6* cassia-s cdd7*• *Caust* k* cedr *Cench* k2* **Cham** k* *Chel* k* **Chin** k* chinin-ar chion bro1 cic k* cimic bg2* *Cina* b2.de* **Cinnb** k* clem k* coc-c k* *Cocc* k* *Cod* **Coff** k* **Colch** k* *Coloc* k* com bro1 **Con** k* convo-s jl3 cor-r sf cory br1 *Croc* k* crot-c bro1 *Crot-h* crot-t j5.de *Cupr* k* **Cycl** k* cyt-l sp1 daph ptk2 der vml3• *Dig* k* dios k* dol k* *Dros* k* **Dulc** k* elaps *Equis-h* erig mg1.de eucal *Euphr* k* **Ferr** k* **Ferr-ar** **Ferr-i** *Ferr-p* k* *Fl-ac* k* flav jl3 *Gamb* k* gink-b sbd1• **Graph** k* grat j5.de guaj k* haliae-lc srj5• hed sp1 *Hell* k* **Hep** k* hip-ac jl3 *Hydrog* srj2• **Hyos** k* *Ign* k* **Iod** k* **Ip** k* iris br1* jal bg2* just sf **Kali-ar** **Kali-bi** k* *Kali-br* k* **Kali-c** k* *Kali-chl* **Kali-i** k* *Kali-m* kali-n k* *Kali-p* k* *Kali-sil* k2* kalm k2* kreos k* **Lach** k* laur k* *Led* k* **Lil-t** k* lob bg2* luna kg1• *Lyc* k* m-ambo b2.de* m-arct b2.de* m-aust b2.de* **Mag-c** k* **Mag-m** k* mag-p bg2* mand sp1 **Mang** k* meny k* meph bg2* **Merc** k* *Merc-c* k* *Merc-i-f* **Merc-k-i** gm1 *Mez* k* moly-met jl3 mosch k* *Mur-ac* k* naja mrr1 *Nat-ar* *Nat-c* k* *Nat-m* k* *Nat-p* *Nat-s* k* *Nat-sil* k2* nep mg1.de* **Nit-ac** k* *Nux-m* k* *Nux-v* k* *Olnd* k* *Op* k* orni tl1 osteo-a jl2 *Ox-ac* k* par k* pareir hr1* parth vml3• *Petr* k* *Ph-ac* k* phenob srb2.fr **Phos** k* *Phyt* k* *Pic-ac* plat k* **Plb** k* pneu jl3 prot jl3* **Psor** k* **Puls** k* pyrog bg2* rad-br mrr1 ran-b k* ran-s k* rat bg2* *Rheum* k* rhod k* **Rhus-t** k* **Rumx** k* ruta b7.de* *Sabad* k* sabin k* sal-ac *Samb* k* sang k* sarcol-ac jl3 *Sars* k* scir hbh *Sec* k* *Sel* k* senec seneg k* **Sep** k* sieg mg1.de **Sil** k* sin-n *Spig* k* *Spong* k* squil k* *Stann* k* *Staph* k* stict k* still bg2* stram k* **Stront-c** k* *Sul-ac* k* **Sul-i** k2* **Sulph** k* symph fd3.de• **Syph** bg2* tarax k* tarent **Tell** k* ter bg2* teucr k* thal jl3 thal-xyz srj8• thea bro1 ther c1 *Thuj* k* trios jl3 valer k* verat k* verb c1 vib bro1 *Viol-t* k* vip bg2* visc jl3 x-ray bro1 yohim lp2 **Zinc** k* **Zinc-p** k2 [bar-br stj2 bar-met stj2 bell-p-sp dcm1 bism-sn stj2 caes-met stj2 hafn-met stj2 lanth-met stj2 lith-c stj2 lith-f stj2 lith-met stj2 lith-s stj2 osm-met stj2 plb-p stj2 rhen-met stj2 tant-met stj2 tung-met stj2]

- **midnight**: **Acon** ptk1* aran bro1 arg-n bg2* *Ars* bg2* ars-i sf1.de brom sf1.de calad ptk1 calc ptk1 canth ptk1 *Caust* ptk1 chin k2* cocc tl1 dig ptk1 dros bg2* ferr bg2* hed jl3 kali-ar k2 kali-c ptk1 lach j5.de* lyc ptk1 mag-m ptk1 mez bro1 mur-ac ptk1 nat-ar bl nat-m ptk1 nux-m ptk1 nux-v bg2* op bg2* phos ptk1 puls bg2* *Rhus-t* ptk1 samb bg2* spong bg2 stram ptk1 sulph ptk1* verat ptk1 zinc gl1.fr•
  - **before**: acon vh1 alum k* alum-p k2* am-m k* ambr k* anac k* ang b2.de* *Ant-t* k* apis **Arg-n** k* arn k* **Ars** k* ars-s-f k2 asar k* *Bell* k* brom k* *Bry* k* calad b2.de* cann-s k* caps bg2 **Carb-v** k* *Carbn-s* *Caust* k* **Cham** k* chel k* chin k* **Coff** k* colch *Cupr* k* cycl k* dulc k* ferr k* ferr-ar *Fl-ac* bg2 *Graph* k* *Hep* k* ign k* **Kali-ar** kali-c k* kali-chl k13 kali-m k2 lac-h htj1• *Lach* k* **Led** k* **Lyc** k* m-arct b2.de* m-aust b2.de* mag-c bg2 *Mang* k* *Merc* k* *Mez* k* mosch k* *Mur-ac* k* nat-m k* nat-p k2* nat-s k2* *Nit-ac* k* nux-v k* osm petr k* **Phos** k* phyt plat k* *Psor* **Puls** k* *Ran-b* k* **Ran-s** k* rhod k* *Rhus-t* k* **Rumx** k* *Ruta* **Sabad** k* samb k* *Sep* k* *Spig* k* *Spong* k* **Stann** k* *Staph* k* *Stront-c* k* sulph k* teucr k* thuj k* ulm-c jsj8• *Valer* k* verat bg2 viol-t k*
    - **22** h: *Ars* ptk1 *Bov* ptk1 cham **Chinin-s** ptk1 *Graph* ptk1 ign ptk1 lach ptk1 petr ptk1 podo puls
      - **22**-4 h: acon vh1
    - **23** h: aral ptk1 ars ptk1 bell k* *Cact* k* calc ptk1 carb-an ptk1 lach rumx k* sil sulph ptk1 [*Ant-c* stj2 ant-m stj2 *Ant-met* stj2 ant-t stj2 aur-m stj2 beryl-m stj2 *Bism-sn* stj2 cadm-m stj2 *Chlor* stj2 chr-m stj2 cob-m stj2 cupr-m stj2 lith-m stj2 mang-m stj2 merc-d stj2 mur-ac stj2 plb-m stj2 stront-m stj2 tax jsj7 zinc-m stj2]
      - **23**-5 h: aral vh1
      - **amel.**: borx ptk1
  - **at** | **amel.**: *Lyc* mrr1
  - **after**: acon k* alum k* alum-p k2* alum-sil k2* alumn am-c b4.de* am-m k* ambr k* ang b2.de* ant-c k* ant-t k* apis bro1 arist-cl sp1 **Ars** k* *Ars-i* ars-s-f k2 asaf k* aur k* aur-ar k2 bamb-a stb2.de• bar-c k* bar-i k2* bar-m bar-s k2* bell k* borx k* *Bry* k* calad b2.de* *Calc* k* *Calc-i* k2* *Calc-sil* k2* *Cann-s* k* canth k* caps k* carb-an b2.de* carb-v k* caust k* cham k* *Chel* chin k* coc-c cocc k* coff k* con k* croc k* *Cupr* **Dros** k* dulc k* euph kr1 euphr k* *Ferr* k* *Ferr-ar* ferr-i ferr-p *Gels* k* graph k* hed sp1 hell k* hep k* *Ign* k* iod k* **Kali-c** k* kali-chl k13 kali-m k2 **Kali-n** k* kali-p *Kali-sil* k2* lyc b2.de* m-ambo b2.de* m-arct b2.de* m-aust b2.de* *Mag-c* k* mand mg1.de* *Mang* k* *Merc* k* **Merc-c** b4a.de *Mez* k* mur-ac

- **midnight – after**: ...
Nat-ar nat-c k* nat-m k* nat-p nat-s nat-sil k2* nit-ac k* **Nux-v** k* par *Ph-ac* k* **Phos** k* phyt plat k* **Podo** k* *Puls* k* ran-b k* *Ran-s* k* rhod k* **Rhus-t** k* rumx sabad k* sabin k* *Samb* k* sars k* seneg k* sep k* **Sil** k* spig k* *Spong* k* squil k* staph k* stram k* sul-ac k* sul-i k2* *Sulph* k* tarax k* **Thuj** k* tung-met bdx1• viol-o k*
⋮ **until** noon: *Ars* k* cist
⋮ **0**-1 h: **Ars** mrr1
⋮ **0**-2 h: **Ars** mrr1
⋮ **0**-4 h: am-c ptk1 *Ars* ptk1 caust ptk1 cedr ptk1 dros ptk1 kali-bi ptk1 lach ptk1 *Nat-m* ptk1 nux-v ptk1 **Podo** ptk1 rumx ptk1 *Sulph* ptk1 thuj sf1.de verat ptk1
⋮ **1** h: **Ars** k* carb-v ptk1 caul cocc kali-bi mrr1 lachn mag-m k* mur-ac psor *Puls* ptk1 [*Ars-met* stj2 *Kali-ar* stj2 lith-p stj2 nat-ar stj2 thal-met stj2]
⋮ **1**-2 h: *Ars* k2*
⋮ **1**-3 h: *Kali-ar* k2
⋮ **2** h: all-c (non:ars k1*) aur-m benz-ac k* canth ptk1 *Caust* ptk1 com ptk1 cur st dros k* ferr k* galeoc-c-h gms1• graph ptk1 *Hep* k* iris ptk1 (non:kali-ar k1*) *Kali-bi* k* *Kali-br* **Kali-c** k* kali-p ptk1 lach ptk1 lachn k* lyc ptk1 mag-c k* med vh mez ptk1 nat-m ptk1 nat-s ptk1 *Nit-ac* ptk1 ptel ptk1 *Puls* ptk1 rumx k* sars ptk1 *Sil* ptk1 spig ptk1 sulph ptk1
⋮ **2**-3 h: galeoc-c-h gms1• gink-b jl kali-bi sf1.de nat-s tl1
⋮ **2**-4 h: arist-cl mg1.de* kali-bi tl1 **Kali-c** k* syph mrr1
⋮ **2**-5 h: bell-p mg1.de hed mg1.de kali-i mrr1 nat-m gk tub br1
⋮ **2**-11 h: aesc bro1 aeth bro1 *Aloe* bro1 am-c bro1 bac bro1 bell bro1 chel bro1 cina bro1 coc-c bro1 cur bro1 *Kali-bi* bro1 *Kali-c* bro1 kali-cy bro1 kali-p bro1 nat-s bro1 *Nux-v* bro1 ox-ac bro1 *Podo* bro1 ptel bro1 rhod bro1 *Rumx* bro1 *Sulph* bro1 thuj bro1 tub bro1
⋮ **3** h: adlu jl aeth tl1 am-br vh* *Am-c* k* *Am-m* ptk1* ant-c ant-t k* *Ars* k1* bapt borx *Bry* tl1* calc k* canth ptk1 *Cedr* ptk1 chin k* con dulc euphr ferr ptk1* hed mg1.de* iris k* *Kali-ar* k1* kali-bi k2 **Kali-c** k* kali-n k* kali-p st* kali-s mrr* mag-c mg1.de* mag-f mg1.de* mag-m k* nat-m ptk1 nux-v k* plut-n srj7• podo k* *Psor* ptk1 *Rhus-t* ptk1 sec *Sel* ptk1 sep k* sil ptk1 staph *Sulph* ptk1 *Thuj* k* urol-h rwt• zinc [am-caust stj2 am-f stj2 am-p stj1 am-s stj1 aur stj2 aur-m stj2 aur-s stj2 bell-p-sp dcm1 *Cupr* stj2 cupr-act stj2 cupr-f stj2 cupr-m stj2 cupr-p stj2 ferr-f stj2 ferr-i stj1 ferr-lac stj2 ferr-m stj1 ferr-n stj2 ferr-p stj1 ferr-s stj1 ferr-sil stj2 kali-f stj1 kali-i stj1 *Kali-m* stj1 *Kali-met* stj2 kali-sil stj2 merc-d stj2 plb-m stj2 stront-m stj2 stront-met stj2 thal-met stj2]
⋮ **after**: tub jl2
⋮ **3**-4 h: aeth c1* am-m sf1.de arist-cl mg1.de caust sf1.de kali-bi sf1.de kali-c sf1.de mag-c mrr1 med c1* nux-v sf1.de
⋮ **3**-5 h: borx sf1.de calc-f mg1.de kali-bi tl1 mag-c mg1.de mand mg1.de syph sf1.de
⋮ **3**-6 h: dys fmm1•
⋮ **4** h: *Alum* ptk1 alumn am-m ptk1 anac ptk1 apis ptk1 *Arn* ptk1 *Borx* ptk1 *Caust* ptk1 **Cedr** ptk1 chel k* coloc ptk1 *Con* ptk1 cycl sf1.de ferr ptk1 haliae-lc srj5• *Ign* hr1* kali-c ptk1 *Lyc* ptk1 mag-c mg1.de *Mur-ac* ptk1 nat-act ptk1 *Nat-c* ptk1 nit-ac ptk1 **Nux-v** ptk1 penic jl* podo k* *Puls* ptk1 rad-br ptk1 sep ptk1 sil ptk1 stann ptk1 *Sulph* ptk1 tanac c verat ptk1 xan vh
⋮ **4**-6 h: both-a rb3 ferr-p ptk
⋮ **4**-8 h: alum ptk1 arn ptk1 aur ptk1 bry ptk1 chel ptk1 eup-per ptk1 hep ptk1 kali-bi ptk1 lach ptk1 *Nat-m* ptk1 nux-v ptk1 **Podo** ptk1 rumx ptk1 sulph ptk1 verat ptk1
⋮ **4**-11 h: phor-t mie3•
⋮ **4**-16 h: kali-c ptk1 kali-cy st **Med** st nux-v
⋮ **5** h: aloe ptk1 apis sf1.de* bov **Chin** ptk1 cob k* dros ptk1 galeoc-c-h gms1• haliae-lc srj5• ham fd3.de• helon kali-c k2* kali-i k* nat-c k2 *Nat-m* ptk1 nat-p ptk1 ph-ac ptk1 *Podo* k* rumx ptk1 sep ptk1 sil ptk1 *Sulph* ptk1* [alumin-s stj2 am-s stj1 ang stj4 *Ant-c* stj2 aur-s stj2 bar-i stj2 bar-s stj1 cadm-met stj2 cadm-s stj2 calc-s stj1 chr-m stj2 *Chr-met* stj1* *Chr-s* stj2 cinnb stj2 cob-m stj2 cob-p stj2 ferr-i stj1 ferr-s stj1 gal-s stj2 germ-met stj2 *Iod* stj2 kali-s stj1 lith-i stj2 lith-s stj2 mag-i stj1 mag-s stj1 mang-i stj2 *Mang-met* stj2 mang-s stj2 merc-i-f stj2 nat-i stj1 neon stj2 nicc-s stj2 rubd-met stj2 *Sel* stj2 sul-ac stj1 tell stj2 titan-s stj2 zinc-i stj2]
⋮ **5**-6 h: [tung-met stj2]
⋮ **5**-9 h: both-ax tsm2 galeoc-c-h gms1• lac-lup hrn2• ozone sde2• ulm-c jsj8• [hydrog stj2]
⋮ **amel.**: anac ptk1 form ptk1 **Lyc** k* mand sp1 nat-p k2* nat-s k2* ran-s ptk1

Night – midnight – after – amel.: ...
⋮ **until** noon: puls bro1*
⋮ **sunrise**; until | **agg.**: both-a rb3
- **air** agg.; night: acon ptk1 am-c bg2* **Carb-v** bg2* lach bg2 lyc bg2 **Merc** bg2* *Nat-s* bg2* *Nit-ac* bg2* nux-m bg2 *Sulph* bg2*
- **amel.**: alum j5.de* ang bg2* arg-met bg2 caust bg2* cupr-act bro1 granit-m es1• laur j5.de* loxo-lae bnm12• mand a1* med st* *Petr* bg2* phasco-ci rbp2
- **bed**:
  - **in** bed:
    ⋮ **agg.**: pneu jl2
    ⋮ **amel.**: mand sp1
- **lasting** all night: **Colch** bg2
- **periodical** | **alternate** nights; on: *Puls*

ABSCESSES: (↗*Fistulae; Reaction - lack - suppuration; Wounds - suppurating)* acon a1 all-c kr1 aln vva1• am-c kka *Anan* k* ant-c k* ant-t k* **Anthraci** k* *Apis* kr1* **Arn** kr1* ars k* *Ars-i* k* ars-s-f k2 *Asaf* k* *Bar-c* bar-m a1 *Bell* b4a.de* *Bell-p* st borx lsa1.de both a1 *Bry* k* bufo bg2* calc k* calc-f k2* *Calc-hp* bg2* **Calc-i** k* **Calc-s** k* calc-sil k2* **Calen** kr1* *Canth* kr1 caps k* carb-an sf1.de *Carb-v* carc mrr1 *Caust* kr1 cench k2 *Cham* j5.de* *Chin* c1* chinin-ar mg1.de chinin-s a1 cic k* *Cist* kr1* clem lsa1.de cocc k* con k* conch a1 *Croc* k* crot-h k* cupr sf1.de digox c1* *Dulc* k* *Echi* bg2* elaps gk elat c1* eucal lsa1.de *Fl-ac* kr1* graph mrr1 *Guaj* k* *Gunp* st1 **Hep** k* *Hippoz* kr1* hydrog srj2• kali-bi gk kali-c k* kali-chl kali-i mrr1 kali-s ptk1 *Kreos* b7a.de* **Lach** k* *Lap-a* kr1 led kr1* *Lyc* b4a.de* mag-c k* *Mang* kr1* mang-act br1 matth c1* med gk **Merc** k* merc-d bg methyl c1* mez k* *Myris* c1* nat-c k* nat-m k* nat-sal c1* nat-sil k2 *Nit-ac* nux-v *Ol-j* k2* (non:olnd k1) paeon petr k* ph-ac k2* **Phos** j5.de* *Phyt* kr1* pic-ac mrr1 plb a1 psil ft1 psor sf1.de* ptel a1 puls k* *Pyrog* k* raja-s jl3 *Rhus-t* j5.de* *Sec* k* sep k* sieg mg1.de* **Sil** k* sil-mar br1 staph k* *Stram* k* *Sul-ac* kr1* sul-i bg2* *Sulph* k* symph c1* syph bg* tarent kr1* *Tarent-c* k* thuj mrr1 thyr c1* tub sf1.de vesp a1* *Vip* j5.de wies a1 [amar-t dbx1.fr cassia-l dbx1.fr kali-f stj1 mag-f stj1 sol-er dbx1.fr]
- **abort**; remedies to: apis bro1 arn st bell bro1 bry bro1 calc k2 *Calc-s* kr1 *Hep* bro1 *Merc* bro1
- **accompanied** by:
  - **bleeding**:
    ⋮ **dark**: crot-h tl1 lach tl1
    ⋮ **uncoagulable**: crot-h tl1 lach tl1
  - **diabetes** (See Diabetes mellitus - accompanied - abscesses)
  - **fever** (See FEVER - Accompanied - suppuration)
  - **swelling**: hyper tl1
○ • **Tongue** | **red** discoloration of the tongue: *Apis* kr1*
- **acute**: acon bro1 *Anan* bro1 anthraci bro1 apis bro1 *Arn* bro1 ars bro1 *Bell* bro1 calc-hp bro1 *Calc-s* bro1 calen bro1 *Carb-ac* bro1 chin bro1 chinin-s bro1 crot-h bro1 fl-ac bro1 *Hep* bro1 hippoz bro1 *Lach* bro1 lap-a bro1 lyc bro1 *Merc* bro1 *Myris* bro1 *Nit-ac* bro1 ph-ac bro1 phos bro1 *Rhus-t* bro1 *Sil* bro1 sil-mar bro1 *Sulph* bro1 syph bro1 *Tarent-c* bro1 vesp bro1
- **blind**: *(↗hasten)* lyc ptk1
- **bluish**: tarent-c ptk1
  - **mottled**: tarent tl1 tarent-c tl1*
- **burning**: **Anthraci** k* **Ars** k* lach tl1 merc k2 *Pyrog* k* sil tl1 tarent tl1 **Tarent-c** k*
- **chronic**: *Anthraci* vh arg-met jl arn bro1 *Asaf* hr1* aur hr1* calc hr1* calc-f bro1* calc-i bro1 calc-p bro1 calc-s sf1.de *Carb-v* k* cham bro1 chin bro1 con hr1* fl-ac bro1* graph bro1 *Hep* hr1* *Iod* hr1* iodof bro1 kali-bi ptk1 kali-i bro1 laur hr1* lyc hr1* mag-f jl3 mang hr1* *Merc* hr1* merc-c hr1* merc-i-r bro1 *Nit-ac* hr1* ol-j c1* phos hr1* sars hr1* sep hr1* **Sil** hr1* stram tl1* *Sulph* hr1* syph mtf11
- **cold** applications | **amel.**: led tl1 lyc tl1
- **coldness**; sensation of: merc ptk1 ol-j ptk1
- **deep**: calc ptk1 caps ptk1 tarent ptk1*
- **discharge**; causing abscesses to (See hasten)
- **effects** from: abrot sf1.de *Chin* sf1.de chinin-ar sf1.de ferr sf1.de kali-c sf1.de nat-m sf1.de ph-ac sf1.de *Phos* sf1.de
- **exertion**; from physical: *Carb-ac* c1*
- **fever**:
  - **after** | **recurrent** fever: ph-ac ptk1
  - **continued**: ph-ac st1
  - **during** | **agg.**: ars ptk1 hep ptk1 sil ptk1

- **fistulous** opening; with a (See Fistulae - abscess)
- **foreign** bodies; elimination of: *(↗SKIN - Expulsion - splinters)* arn st cortiso mtf *Hep* kr1* *Lob* c1* **Sil** kr1*
- **gangrenous**: anthraci vh *Ars* hr1* *Asaf* hr1* *Carb-v* hr1* *Chin* hr1* chinin-s kr1 *Hep* hr1* *Kreos* hr1* **Lach** hr1* *Merc* hr1* *Nit-ac* hr1* phos hr1* *Sil* hr1* *Sul-ac* hr1*
- **hasten** suppuration; remedies to: *(↗blind)* arn br1 ars bg2 bell bg2 calc bg2 echi br1 guaj br1* *Hep* b4a.de* kreos bg2 lach bg2* lyc bg2 manc ptk1 *Merc* b4a.de* myris k2* nat-sil k2 oper bro1 phos bro1 phyt bro1* puls bg2 *Sil* b4a.de* sulph k2 tarent mtf33
- **incipient**: apis sf1.de *Arn* hr1* ars sf1.de *Bar-c* hr1* *Bell* bg* *Carb-an* bg* euph sf1.de guaj sf1.de *Hep* bg* *Lach* bg* *Merc* bg* rhus-t sf1.de sil-mar br1
- **insect** stings; from: tarent tl1
- **malignant**: *Tarent-c* br1
- **maturing**; not (See hasten)
- **menses**, at: merc k2*
- **painful**: anthraci tl1 ars tl1 hep mrr1 *Pyrog* br1 tarent tl1 tarent-c br1*
- **purple**: tarent-c br1
- **pus**:
  - **absorption**: iod b4a.de* **Lach** bg2 *Phos* b4a.de* *Sil* b4a.de*
    - **Glands**; of: *Iod* b4a.de *Phos* b4a.de *Sil* b4a.de
  - **acrid**: ail ptk1 **Ars** j5.de* *Asaf* sf1.de *Bell-p* ptk1 brom ptk1 *Carb-v* j5.de* **Caust** j5.de* *Cham* j5.de* *Clem* j5.de* echi ptk1 euphr ptk1 fl-ac k2* gels ptk1 *Hep* j5.de *Ign* mtf33 iod mtf33 *Kali-i* ptk1 lach j5.de *Lyc* j5.de* *Merc* j5.de* mez j5.de *Nat-c* j5.de* nat-m j5.de **Nit-ac** j5.de* nux-v j5.de *Petr* hr1* phos j5.de plb j5.de puls j5.de* *Ran-b* j5.de* ran-s j5.de *Rhus-t* j5.de* ruta j5.de sabad ptk1 sanic ptk1 sars ptk1 *Sep* j5.de* *Sil* j5.de* spig j5.de squil j5.de *Staph* j5.de* *Sul-ac* j5.de* *Sulph* j5.de* zinc j5.de*
  - **air** bubbles; full of: sulph bg3*
  - **black**: bry j5.de chin j5.de* lyc j5.de *Sulph* j5.de*
  - **bland**: bell hr1* *Calc* hr1* *Hep* hr1* *Lach* hr1* mang hr1* *Merc* hr1* phos hr1* **Puls** hr1* rhus-t hr1* *Sil* hr1* staph hr1* *Sulph* hr1*
  - **bloody**: arg-n j5.de* arn j5.de *Ars* j5.de* **Asaf** j5.de* bell j5.de* calc-s k2* *Carb-v* j5.de* *Caust* j5.de* con j5.de croc j5.de crot-h ptk1 dros j5.de graph mtf33 **Hep** j5.de* iod j5.de kali-bi gk kali-c j5.de kreos j5.de lach j5.de *Lyc* j5.de* **Merc** j5.de* mez j5.de nat-m j5.de *Nit-ac* j5.de* ph-ac j5.de phos j5.de* *Phyt* hr1* *Puls* j5.de* *Rhus-t* j5.de* ruta j5.de sabin j5.de sec j5.de *Sep* j5.de *Sil* j5.de* sul-ac j5.de sulph j5.de* zinc j5.de*
    - **streaked**: merc br1
  - **brown**: anac j5.de *Ars* j5.de* bry j5.de* calc j5.de *Carb-v* j5.de* con j5.de puls j5.de *Rhus-t* j5.de* *Sil* j5.de*
  - **destroying** hair: bell-p ptk1 lyc ptk1 merc ptk1 rhus-t ptk1
  - **excoriating**: am-c j5.de anac j5.de *Asaf* j5.de* bell j5.de calc j5.de chel j5.de con j5.de cupr j5.de graph j5.de ign j5.de* iod j5.de* kreos j5.de lyc mtf33 puls mtf33 sep mtf33 sulph mtf33 zinc mtf33
  - **fetid**: am-c j5.de ant-t j5.de *Anthraci* kr1 arn st1 *Ars* j5.de* **Asaf** j5.de* aur j5.de bapt ptk1 bar-m j5.de *Bell* j5.de bov j5.de bry j5.de *Calc* j5.de* calc-f ptk1 *Carb-an* hr1* **Carb-v** j5.de* *Caust* j5.de* chel j5.de *Chin* j5.de* chinin-s j5.de* cic j5.de clem j5.de con j5.de* cycl j5.de dros j5.de fl-ac sf1.de *Graph* j5.de* **Hep** j5.de* kali-c j5.de *Kali-p* hr1* **Kreos** j5.de* *Lach* j5.de* led ptk1 *Lyc* j5.de* mag-m ptk1 mang j5.de *Merc* j5.de* mez j5.de mur-ac j5.de nat-c j5.de *Nit-ac* j5.de* nux-m j5.de *Nux-v* j5.de* paeon sf1.de petr sf1.de *Ph-ac* j5.de* phos j5.de* *Phyt* hr1* plb j5.de *Psor* bg2* *Puls* j5.de* *Pyrog* ptk1 ran-b j5.de *Ran-s* j5.de *Rhus-t* j5.de* ruta j5.de sabin j5.de sec j5.de *Sep* j5.de* **Sil** j5.de* squil j5.de stann j5.de *Staph* j5.de sul-ac j5.de* **Sulph** j5.de* syph ptk1* thuj j5.de vip j5.de* vip-a j5.de
    - **asa** foetida; as from: carb-v ptk1
  - **gelatinous**: arg-met j5.de arn j5.de bar-c j5.de cham j5.de* ferr j5.de merc j5.de* sep j5.de *Sil* j5.de*
  - **gray**: *Ambr* j5.de *Ars* j5.de* carb-an j5.de *Caust* j5.de* chin j5.de lyc j5.de merc j5.de* sep j5.de *Sil* j5.de* thuj j5.de
  - **greenish**: ars j5.de *Asaf* j5.de* *Aur* j5.de* carb-v j5.de *Caust* j5.de* kreos j5.de **Merc** j5.de* nat-c j5.de nux-v j5.de phos j5.de *Puls* j5.de* rhus-t j5.de* sec k2* sep j5.de* sil j5.de* staph j5.de sulph mtf33 syph ptk1 tub ptk1
  - **hot**: puls mtf33
  - **lumpy**: calc-s mtf33
  - **oozing**: carb-v mtf33
  - **scanty**: calc-s bg2 hep bg2 sil bg2 sulph bg2
- **pus**: ...
  - **sour**, smelling: calc j5.de* graph j5.de *Hep* j5.de* kalm j5.de* lyc mtf33 *Merc* j5.de* nat-c j5.de sep j5.de sulph j5.de*
  - **suppressed**: ars bg bell bg *Bry* ptk1 *Calc* bg* cham kr1 dulc ptk1 **Hep** bg* kreos bg *Lach* kr1* lyc bg *Merc* bg* puls ptk1 *Sil* kr1* stram ptk1 *Sulph* ptk1
  - **tenacious**: ars j5.de asaf j5.de* borx ptk1 bov j5.de* cham j5.de coc-c ptk1 *Con* j5.de* hydr bg* kali-bi bg* merc j5.de* mez j5.de ph-ac j5.de phos kr1 sep j5.de* sil j5.de sulph j5.de
  - **thick**: arg-n bg2* calc-s tl1* *Calc-sil* k2* euphr ptk1 hep bg2* *Kali-bi* ptk1 kali-s bg2 puls bg2* sanic ptk1
  - **thin**: agar-cps a1 ars bg2* *Asaf* j5.de* carb-v j5.de* *Caust* j5.de* dros j5.de fl-ac bg2* iod j5.de* kali-c j5.de *Lyc* j5.de* mag-m ptk1 *Merc* j5.de* nit-ac k* phos ptk1 plb j5.de puls j5.de ran-b j5.de* ran-s j5.de rhus-t j5.de* ruta j5.de *Sil* j5.de* staph j5.de* *Sulph* j5.de* thuj j5.de
  - **watery**: agar-cps a1 *Ars* j5.de* **Asaf** j5.de* calc j5.de* *Carb-v* j5.de* *Caust* j5.de* cench k2* cham hr1* clem j5.de con j5.de dros j5.de *Graph* j5.de *Iod* j5.de* kali-c j5.de lach j5.de *Lyc* j5.de* *Merc* j5.de* *Nit-ac* j5.de* nux-v j5.de *Phyt* hr1* plb j5.de puls j5.de ran-b j5.de* *Ran-s* j5.de rhus-t sf1.de *Sil* sf1.de* sulph mtf33
  - **whitish**: am-c j5.de ars j5.de *Calc* j5.de* carb-v j5.de hell j5.de *Lyc* j5.de* nat-m j5.de puls j5.de sep j5.de sil j5.de sulph j5.de
  - **yellow**: acon j5.de am-c j5.de ambr j5.de anac j5.de ang j5.de arg-met j5.de arg-n ptk2 ars j5.de* aur j5.de bov j5.de *Bry* j5.de *Calc* j5.de* calc-s k2* caps j5.de *Carb-v* j5.de* *Caust* j5.de* cench k2* *Cic* j5.de *Clem* j5.de con j5.de croc j5.de dulc j5.de euphr ptk1 graph j5.de **Hep** j5.de* iod j5.de kali-n j5.de kreos j5.de lyc j5.de mag-c j5.de mag-m ptk1 mang j5.de *Merc* j5.de* *Mez* bg2* *Nat-c* j5.de* nat-m j5.de *Nit-ac* j5.de* *Nux-v* j5.de *Phos* j5.de* **Puls** j5.de* *Rhus-t* j5.de* ruta j5.de sanic ptk1 sec j5.de sel j5.de *Sep* j5.de* *Sil* j5.de* spig j5.de *Staph* j5.de* sul-ac j5.de *Sulph* hr1* thuj j5.de viol-t j5.de
  - **yellow**-green: ars-i bg2* *Calc-sil* k2* kali-bi bg2* kali-s bg2* merc k2* *Puls* bg2*
- **recurrent** (See History - abscesses)
- **spring**; in: crot-h k2
- **stabbing** pain; with: tarent-c mrr1
- **stinging**: tarent-c br1
- **suppressed**: ars ptk1 bell ptk1 calc ptk1 *Hep* ptk1 kreos ptk1 lach ptk1 lyc ptk1 merc ptk1 sil ptk1
- **threatening**: bell bg2 *Calc-f* br1 carb-an bg2 *Hep* bg2 lach bg2 merc bg2
- **warm** applications | **amel.**: ars tl1

○ - **Blood** vessels; of: ant-t bg2 *Ars* bg2 kreos bg2 *Lach* bg2 **Lyc** bg2 *Puls* bg2 *Sil* bg2 sulph bg2
- **Bones**, of: ang b7a.de* aran bg2 arg-met bg2* arg-n sf1.de arn bg2 *Ars* bg2 arund-d mtf11 asaf b7.de* aur bg2* bell k* bry k* *Calc* k* calc-f bg2* *Calc-hp* bro1* calc-i bg2 calc-p bg2* caps bg2 carb-an bg2 chin bg2 cist bg2 clem bg2 *Con* b4a.de* cupr b7a.de* dulc bg2 euph bg2 fl-ac bg2* *Graph* bg2 guaj bg2* hecla bg2 *Hep* bg2 iod bg2 kali-bi bg2 *Kali-c* bg2 kali-i bg2 kreos b7a.de* lach bg2 **Lyc** bg2 mang bro1 **Merc** b4a.de* merc-aur sf1.de *Mez* bg2 nat-m bg2 *Nit-ac* bg2 op bg2 petr bg2 *Ph-ac* bg2 phos bg2* *Plat* bg2 psor bg2 puls bg2* rhus-t bg2 ruta bg2 sabin bg2 sec bg2* *Sep* bg2 sil b4a.de* spong bg2 staph b7.de* stront-c bg2 *Sulph* bg2 symph bro1* ther bg2 thuj bg2 tub bg2 tub-m jl2 vitr-cor mtf11
  - **chronic**: calc-ar mtf11 calc-i mtf11
  - **fractures**: sil bg2
- **Cartilages**: stram k2
- **Connective** tissue: calc-s mtf11 mez ptk1 phos mtf11
- **Glands**: *(↗Glands)* anthraci jl2 ars tl1 *Aur* j5.de *Aur-m-n* kr1 bad bg2* *Bar-c* bg2* bar-m *Bell* k* brom **Calc** k* calc-f mg1.de *Calc-hp* bg2* calc-i bro1 calc-p mg1.de **Calc-s** k* canth k* carb-an bg2* carb-v k* cinnb k2 cist k* clem bg2* coloc k* crot-h *Dulc* k* echi sf1.de fl-ac bg2* *Form* bg2* *Guaj* guare kr1 **Hep** k* hyos k* ign k* jug-r c1 **Kali-i** k* kreos k* *Lach* k* lap-a br1* *Lyc* k* **Merc** k* moni rfm1• myris mg1.de *Nit-ac* k* petr k* *Phos* k* *Phyt* bg2 *Pyrog* k* *Rhus-t* k* *Sars* k* sec c1 *Sep* k* **Sil** k* sil-mar c1 spig bg2 squil k* *Stram* sul-ac bg2 **Sulph** k* *Syph* k* teucr-s sf1.de* toxo-g jl2 *Tub* k* v-a-b jl2 zinc bg2
  - **children**; in: med jl2
  - **slow** and slow to heal: sil tl1
  - **sudden** and rapid: hep tl1
- **Internal** organs, of: anthraci mtf11 *Canth* hr1* **Lach** hr1* paro-i mtf11 pyrog mtf11
- **Joints**: *(↗EXTREMITIES - Abscess - joints)* *Ang* kr1 ars-i sf1.de bac sf1.de calc sf1.de calc-f sf1.de *Calc-hp* bro1* *Calc-p* bg2* calc-s sf1.de conch a1 fl-ac sf1.de guaj k2 kali-c sf1.de kali-i sf1.de *Merc* bg2* myris c1 nit-ac sf1.de ol-j c1* ph-ac sf1.de

- **Joints**: ...
Phos bg2* Psor bg2* puls sf1.de Sil kr1* stram mtf33 ter sf1.de Teucr sf1.de thuj sf1.de tub sf1.de
  • **chronic**: stram mtf33
○ • **About** the joints: calc-hp ptk1 mang hr1* merc ptk1 phos ptk1 psor ptk1 sil ptk1
- **Mucous** membranes: borx b4a.de Sil b4.de
- **Muscles**, of: *(↗Complaints - muscles)* calc k2
○ • **Deep** muscles: Calc br1*
- **Periosteum**: ant-c bg2 **Asaf** bg2 aur bg2 bell bg2 Chin bg2 cycl bg2 hell bg2 Kali-bi bg2 Merc bg2 mez bg2 Ph-ac bg2 puls bg2 rhod bg2 rhus-t bg2 ruta bg2 sabin bg2 Sil bg2 staph bg2
- **Thorax**: hep tl1
- **Vesicles**; on: rhus-t ptk1

ABSENCES (See MIND - Unconsciousness - frequent)

ABSORPTION of exudates; to facilitate the: Arn b7.de* ars mtf11 kali-i ptk1 merc-d ptk1 sul-i ptk1 Sulph res1*

ACCUMULATION:
- **fluid** | **Serous** membranes (See Dropsy - internal - serous)

ACETONEMIA: carb-ac c2 carc dgt1 Senn br1*
- **children**; in: phenob jl3* senn br1*

ACIDOSIS: *(↗Sourness)* carc mg1.de* gaert fmm1• loxo-lae bnm12• nat-m tl1 nat-p br1* phos bg* syc pte1*•
- **children**; in: carc mlr1•
- **lactic**: germ-met srj5• nat-p br1
- **respiratory** | **coma**; with (See MIND - Coma - acidosis)

ACONITE; after abuse of: sulph bro1

ACRIDITY, excoriations, etc.: *(↗Mucous secretions - acrid)* all-c bg **Ars** bg ars-i bg arum-d br1 arum-i br1 arum-m br1 arum-t bg* Brom bg Caust bg cham bg Graph bg hep bg Iod bg Kreos bg lyc bg **Merc** bg merc-c bg Nit-ac bg phos bg Rhus-t bg Sep bg Sil bg **Sulph** bg

ACROMEGALY: carc mlr1• Pitu xyz61 pitu-gl bro1* thyr c2*
- **children**; in: carc mlr1•

ACTIVITY: bacls-10 fmm1• calc-p bg chlol a1 coff bg form a1* lac-ac stj5• lach bg mang bg morg-p fmm1• nux-v bg* op bg rhus-t bg stram bg tarent bg valer bg
- **amel.**: *(↗MIND - Exertion - physical - amel.; MIND - Mental exertion - amel.; MIND - Occupation - amel.)* cortico sp1 cycl bg2 dulc fd4.de helo bg2 ignis-alc es2• iod bg2* kali-bi bg2 lil-t bg2 mur-ac bg2 olib-sac wmh1 pieri-b mlk9.de positr nl2• sep bg2 spong fd4.de tritic-vg fd5.de tung-met bdx1• vanil fd5.de [spect dfg1]
- **desire** for: Acon hr1* ars hr1* aur hr1* eucal hr1* hyper a1 ignis-alc es2• led a1 nat-s a1 nicc-met sk4• tung-met bdx1•
- **increased**: *(↗Energy - excess)* Acon hr1* Agar hr1* ant-c hr1* ant-t hr1* boerh-d ckh1 camph hr1* carc mlr1• cic jl3 Coff br1 conch fkr1• dioxi rbp6 eucal hr1* flor-p rsj3• Hyos hr1* ignis-alc es2• lac-h sk4• lyss hr1* nep jl3* nept-m lsd2.fr Olib-sac wmh1 Op hr1* Ox-ac hr1* plat hr1* sacch-a fd2.de• Stram hr1*
  • **afternoon**; until: nicc-met sk4•
  • **evening**: conch fkr1•
  • **nervous**: coff br1 viol-o ptk1
  • **vascular**: coff br1
○ • **Organs**; of: coff br1
- **outer** activity ceases: anh sp1
- **physical**: *(↗Energy - excess; Exertion)* ars a1 coca a1* fl-ac st1 lycps-v a1 nat-s a1 nep jl3* nept-m lsd2.fr olib-sac wmh1 Op a1 phos a1 positr nl2•
  • **afternoon**: rhus-t a1
  • **evening**: lac-h sk4• lycps-v a1
  • **midnight**, until: **Coff** a1 olib-sac wmh1
    ⁝ **followed** by utter prostration: olib-sac wmh1

Activity – physical: ...
  • **aversion** (See Exertion - aversion)

ADENITIS (See Inflammation - glands)

ADENOIDS (See NOSE - Adenoids)

ADENOPATHY (See Abscesses - glands; Cancerous - glands; Indurations - glands; Inflammation - glands; Swelling - glands)

ADHESIONS: calc-f a* calc-s a fl-ac a graph a sil a suis-chord-umb mtf11 thiosin a*
- **sensation** of adhesion | **Inner** parts; of: arn b2.de* berb ptk1 Bov ptk1 bry b2.de* calc ptk1 coloc b2.de* Dig st1 euph b2.de* hep b2.de* ign ptk1 kali-bi ptk1 kali-c bg2 kali-i ptk1 kali-n b2.de* m-ambo b2.de merc st1 merc-c ptk1 Mez b2.de* nux-v b2.de* ol-an ptk1 osm ptk1 par b2.de* petr b2.de* phos b2.de* Plb b2.de* puls b2.de* Ran-b bg2 **Rhus-t** b2.de* rumx ptk1 seneg b2.de* Sep b2.de* Sulph b2.de* thuj b2.de* ust ptk1 verb b2.de*

ADIPOSOGENITAL DYSTROPHY: cortiso mtf11 suis-chord-umb mtf11

AGGLUTINATION for blood: bapt tl1

AGILITY: *(↗MIND - Agility)* agar hr1* androc srj5• apis ptk1 asar a1 bell a1 bond a1 calc-p bg2 chlol a1 choc srj3• clem hs1 coca a1 coff bg2* form a1* gamb hs1 lach bg2* luna c1 m-aust h1 mang bg2 nux-v ptk1 op bg2 rhus-t bg2 stram bg2* tarent ptk1 valer ptk1
- **alternating** with | **weakness** (See EXTREMITIES - Weakness - alternating - agility)

AGRANULOCYTOSIS: chloram mtf11 cortico sp1* lach mg1.de sulfa sp1*

AGUE (See Malaria)

AIDS: *(↗Autoimmune; Collagen)* acet-ac mtf am-caust mtf anan vh2 arg-met vh2 carb-v mtf crot-h gk4 germ-met srj5• med mtf phos mtf plut-n srj7• tub mtf tub-r mtf uncar-tom mtf urin mtf
- **accompanied** by | **diarrhea**: sulph gk4

AILMENTS from:
- **disease**; never recovered | **children**; in: Ars lmj calc-p lmj **Carb-v** lmj Carc lmj Caust lmj Chin lmj Ph-ac lmj **Psor** lmj Tub lmj
- **fright**: acon tl1
- **mobile** phone: [bell-p-sp dcm1]
- **physical** symptoms; suppression of: carc sst2•
- **weaning** milk: *(↗Lactation)* arg-n mtf **Bell** bg2* bry bg2* Calc bg2 carb-an hr1 chin mtf con k* cycl br1* frag hr1* lac-c bg2* lac-d hr1 puls k* urt-u hr1

AIR:
- **agg.** | **thick** and heavy; as if: agn ptk1
- **cold** | **agg.** (See Cold - air - agg.)
- **drawing** in air | **agg.**: alum b2.de* **Ant-c** b2.de* Bell b2.de* bry b2.de* calc b2.de* caust b2.de* chin b2.de* cic b2.de* cina b2.de* hyos b2.de* ign b2.de* ip b2.de* kali-n b2.de* m-ambo b2.de* M-arct b2.de* Merc b2.de* mez b2.de* nat-m b2.de* nux-m b2.de* Nux-v b2.de* par b2.de* petr b2.de* ph-ac b2.de* phos b2.de* Puls b2.de* sabad b2.de* Sabin b2.de* sars b2.de* sel b2.de* Sep b2.de* Sil b2.de* Spig b2.de* Staph b2.de* sulph b2.de* thuj b2.de* verb b2.de*
- **indoor** air (= in the room or house):
  • **agg.**: Acon kr1 all-c ptk1 alum ptk1 **Alumn** kr1 am-c kr1 am-m kr1 Ambr kr1 Anac kr1 Ang kr1 Ant-c kr1 Apis ptk1 Arg-met kr1* arg-n ptk1* Arn kr1 ars kr1* ars-i ptk1 Asaf kr1 Asar kr1 Aur kr1* Bar-c kr1 bell kr1 Borx kr1 Bov kr1 bry kr1* calc kr1 camph kr1 cann-s kr1 cann-xyz ptk1 canth kr1 caps kr1 carb-an kr1 carb-v kr1* Caust kr1 chel kr1 chir-fl gya2 Cic kr1 cina kr1 coff kr1 Colch kr1 con kr1 **Croc** kr1* dig kr1 dulc kr1 ferr ptk1 glon ptk1 graph kr1* Hell kr1 hep kr1 hyos kr1 ign kr1 Iod kr1* ip kr1 kali-c kr1 Kali-i ptk1 kali-n kr1 **Lach** ptk1 Laur kr1 lil-t ptk1 Lyc kr1* **Mag-c** kr1* Mag-m kr1* mang kr1 med ptk1 Meny kr1 merc kr1 Mez kr1 mosch kr1 mur-ac kr1 nat-c kr1 Nat-m kr1 nat-s ptk1 nit-ac kr1 nux-v kr1 Op kr1* Ph-ac kr1 Phos kr1 Plat kr1 Plb kr1 prun ptk1 **Puls** kr1* rad-br ptk1 Ran-b kr1 Ran-s kr1 Rhod kr1 rhus-t kr1* ruta kr1 Sabad ptk1 **Sabin** kr1* Sars kr1 sel kr1 Seneg kr1* sep kr1 spig kr1 Spong kr1 Stann kr1 staph kr1 Stront-c kr1 sul-ac kr1 Sulph kr1* tab ptk1 Tarax kr1 tarent ptk1 thuj kr1 til ptk1 tritic-vg fd5.de tub ptk1 Verat kr1 Verb kr1 viol-t kr1 Zinc kr1 [arg-p stj2 ferr-lac stj2 ferr-n stj2 ind stj2 mang-act stj2 mang-m stj2 mang-n stj2 nitro stj2 zinc-n stj2]

- **indoor** air: ...
  - **amel.**: *Agar* kr1* alumn kr1 *Am-c* kr1 *Am-m* kr1 ambr kr1 anac kr1 ang kr1 *Ant-c* kr1 arn kr1 ars kr1 bar-c kr1 *Bell* kr1 borx kr1 bov kr1 bry kr1 *Calad* kr1 *Calc* kr1 *Camph* kr1 *Cann-s* kr1 *Canth* kr1 *Caps* kr1 *Carb-an* kr1 *Carb-v* kr1 caust kr1 **Cham** kr1 *Chel* kr1 *Chin* kr1 chir-fl gya2 cic kr1 *Cina* kr1 cit-v kr1 **Cocc** kr1 *Coff* kr1 *Coloc* kr1 *Con* kr1 cycl ptk1 dig kr1 *Dros* kr1 dulc kr1 *Euph* kr1 *Ferr* kr1 graph kr1 **Guaj** kr1 hell kr1 hep kr1 hyos kr1 *Ign* kr1* iod kr1 *Ip* kr1 kali-c kr1 *Kali-n* kr1 *Kreos* kr1 lach kr1 laur kr1 *Led* kr1 lyc kr1 mag-c kr1 mag-m kr1 mang kr1* meny kr1 *Merc* kr1 mez kr1 *Mosch* kr1 *Mur-ac* kr1 *Nat-c* kr1 nat-m kr1 *Nit-ac* kr1 **Nux-m** kr1 **Nux-v** kr1 oci-sa kr1* *Olnd* kr1 op kr1 *Petr* kr1 ph-ac kr1 phos kr1 plat kr1 plb kr1 puls kr1 ran-b kr1 *Rheum* kr1 rhod kr1 *Rhus-t* kr1 *Ruta* kr1 *Sabad* kr1 sabin kr1 sars kr1 *Sel* kr1 seneg kr1 sep kr1 **Sil** kr1 *Spig* kr1 stann kr1 *Staph* kr1 *Stram* kr1 stront-c kr1 *Sul-ac* kr1 sulph kr1 tarent kr1 *Teucr* kr1 *Thuj* kr1 *Valer* kr1 verat kr1 verb kr1 *Viol-t* kr1 zinc kr1 [mang-met stj2]
  - **open** air; and | **agg.**: ars ptk1 aur ptk1 iod ptk1 mez ptk1
- **night** air (See Night - air)
- **passing**; sensation of air:
  - **him**; through: calc bg2 coloc bg2
  - ○ **Glands**; through: spong k*
- **unclean** | **sensation** of: trif-p ptk1
- **warm** agg. (See Warm - air - agg.)
- **wet** air agg.: *Carb-v* b4a.de *Dulc* b4a.de *Fl-ac* b4a.de lach b7a.de nux-m b7.de* *Rhus-t* b7a.de ruta b7a.de *Stann* b4a.de verat b7.de
  - **coition**; after: sep bg2

AIR; DRAFT OF:

- **agg.**: acon k* alum k2* am-p br1 ambr b7.de anac k* aral br1* *Ars* k* ars-s-f k2* astac kr1 aur aur-m-n wbt2* *Bapt* hr1* **Bell** k* benz-ac k* bov k* brom k2* *Bry* k* cadm-s k* **Calc** k* calc-f k2* **Calc-p** k* *Calc-s* calc-sil k2* camph *Canth* b7a.de* *Caps* k* carb-an *Carbn-s* k1* *Caust* k* cench k2* *Cham* k* *Chin* k* chr-met dx cic br1* cimic zr* *Cist* k* cocc coff k2 colch bg2* coloc k* crot-c sk4• crot-h bg2 dulc k2* echi bng elaps lsa1.de *Ferr* gels gink-b sbd1• *Graph* k* *Hep* k* *Hyos* b7a.de* *Ign* k* kali-ar k* *Kali-bi* bg2* **Kali-c** k* kali-chl k13 kali-fcy zr kali-m k2* kali-n kali-p kali-s k* kali-sil k2* kola stb3• lac-c lac-d k2* *Lach* k* led k* lob vh* **Lyc** k* *Lyss* k* m-aust b2.de* *Mag-c* k* *Mag-p* k* *Med* k* *Merc* k* mim-p jl3 mur-ac k* naja al *Nat-c* k* *Nat-m* k* nat-p nat-sil k2* *Nit-ac* k* *Nux-m* k* *Nux-v* k* *Ol-j* onop jl *Petr* *Ph-ac* k* phasco-ci rbp2 *Phos* k* polys sk4• positr nl2• psil jl* *Psor* k* **Puls** k* rad-br sze8• *Ran-b* k* rhod lsa1.de **Rhus-t** k* *Rumx* sabad lsa1.de sacch-a fd2.de• sang bg2* *Sanic* sars k* **Sel** k* senec k2* *Sep* k* **Sil** k* *Spig* k* spong fd4.de squil k2* *Stann* k2* *Stram* k* stront-c k* **Sulph** k* *Sumb* tep a1 tritic-vg fd5.de tub bg1* valer k* vanil fd5.de verat a1 verb k* vichy-g a1 x-ray sp1 *Zinc* k* zinc-p k2* [am-br stj2 bar-br stj2 cadm-met stj2 erech stj *Ferr-sil* stj2 kali-br stj1 kali-f stj1 kali-i stj1 *Kali-met* stj2 *Mag-sil* stj2 mang-i stj2 *Mang-sil* stj2 nat-br stj2 niob-met stj2 oxyg stj2 stront-m stj2 stront-met stj2]
- **amel.**: aesc bc ferr ptk1 iod ptk1 lycps-v bg2* sec ptk1 tub ptk1
- **cold** draft of air:
  - **agg.**: acon b7a.de *Camph* b7a.de nux-v b7.de rhus-t b7.de
    - **perspiration**; during: brom mtf33 dulc k2 merc-i-f c1 rhus-t gk
  - **amel.**: **Puls** b7.de
- **sensation** of a draft: *(↗Fanned; Wind - sensation)* aur al camph canth caust sf1.de *Chel* coloc sf1.de cor-r croc fl-ac graph helo-s rwt2• hydrog srj2• *Lac-d* *Laur* *Mez* sf1.de *Mosch* *Nux-v* olnd puls rhus-t sabin samb spig squil stram *Thuj* sf1.de *Zinc*
  - **fanned**; as if: aur ptk1 *Camph* ptk1 *Chel* ptk1 *Chin* ptk1 *Cor-r* ptk1 croc ptk1 *Culx* ptk1 **Fl-ac** ptk1 helo ptk1 helo-s rwt2• **Hep** ptk1 lac-d ptk1 laur ptk1 lil-t ptk1 med ptk1 mosch ptk1 naja ptk1 nat-m ptk1 nux-v ptk1 petr ptk1 sel ptk1 sep ptk1 sulph ptk1 syph ptk1 ther ptk1 thuj ptk1 thyr ptk1 zinc ptk1
- **slight** draft of air agg.: caps ptk1
  - **motion** of person; caused by: streptoc jl2
- **warm** draft of air:
  - **agg.**: caps a1 sel ptk1
  - **amel.**: thuj ptk1

AIR HUNGER (See Fanned - desire)

AIR; IN OPEN:

- **agg.**: *Acon* k* *Agar* k* agn k* agre jl alco a1 all-c bg2* all-s vh alum k* alumn kr1 *Am-c* k* am-m k* ambr k* anac k* ang b2.de* ant-c k* *Ant-t* apoc k2 aran ptk1 arg-met bg2 arn k* *Ars* k* *Ars-s-f* k2 asar bg2 aur k* aur-ar k2 aur-s k2 aza jl *Bar-c* k* bar-m *Bell* k* benz-ac k2* berb j5.de borx k* bov k* bruc j5.de brucel sa3• *Bry* k* bufo k* cact br1 cadm-s bro1* calad k* *Calc* k* calc-i k2 *Calc-p* k* *Camph* b2.de* cann-s b2.de* canth k* *Caps* k* *Carb-an* k* *Carb-v* k* carbn-o a1 carbn-s bro1 *Caust* k* cedr *Cham* k* *Chel* k* **Chin** k* chinin-ar cic k* cimic bg2 cina k* cist bg2* *Clem* k* **Cocc** k* *Coff* k* coff-t st colch bg2* *Coloc* k* *Con* k* cor-r bg2* crot-h bro1 crot-t cycl bro1* dig k* dros b2.de* *Dulc* k* epiph bro1 euph k* euphr bro1 *Ferr* k* ferr-ar ferr-p fl-ac bg2 form *Graph* k* **Guaj** k* *Ham* hell k* *Helon* **Hep** k* hyos k* ign k* iod k* ip k* *Kali-ar* *Kali-bi* k* **Kali-c** k* kali-m k2 *Kali-n* k* *Kali-p* kali-sil k2* kalm k* *Kreos* k* *Lach* k* laur k* led b2.de* lina bro1 *Lyc* k* lycpr bro1 *Lyss* m-ambo b2.de* m-arct b2.de* m-aust b2.de* mag-c k* mag-m b2.de* mag-p bg2* *Mang* k* meny k* **Merc** k* *Merc-c* k* mez b2.de* mosch b2.de* *Mur-ac* k* nat-ar *Nat-c* k* nat-m k* nat-p nat-sil k2* **Nit-ac** k* **Nux-m** k* **Nux-v** k* olnd k* op k* par *Petr* k* *Ph-ac* k* *Phos* k* phyt k* plat b2.de* plb k* psil ft1 *Psor* k* puls k* ran-b k* rheum k* rhod k* *Rhus-t* k* **Rumx** k* ruta k* sabad b2.de* sabin b2.de* sang bg2 sars b2.de* *Sel* k* senec *Seneg* b2.de* *Sep* k* **Sil** k* *Spig* k* spong b2.de* *Stann* k* staph b2.de* *Stram* k* *Stront-c* k* *Sul-ac* k* **Sulph** k* tarax b2.de* *Teucr* k* thea bro1 thuj k* urt-u ptk1 *Valer* k* verat k* verb k* viol-o ptk1 viol-t k* voes a1 x-ray bro1 *Zinc* k* [am-caust stj2 am-p stj1 calc-sil stj2 ferr-sil stj2 mag-sil stj2 mang-act stj2 mang-m stj2 mang-met stj2 mang-sil stj2 sil-met stj2]
  - **stool** | **after** | **agg.**: mez b4.de*
    - **before**: mez b4.de*
- **amel.**: abrom-a ks5 abrot *Acon* k* adam srj5• aesc bg2* aeth c1* agar *Agn* k* *All-c* k* aloe k* **Alum** k* alum-p k2 alum-sil k2 **Alumn** kr1 am-c b2.de* *Am-m* k* ambr k* *Aml-ns* k* *Anac* b2.de* *Androc* srj1• ang b2.de* ange-s jl *Ant-c* k* ant-t bro1* ap-g vh *Apis* k* aran bg2 aran-ix mg1.de aran-sc vh1 *Arg-met* k* **Arg-n** k* arist-cl mg1.de arn k* **Ars** k* ars-i ars-s-f k2 *Asaf* k* *Asar* k* *Atro* *Aur* k* aur-i k2 aur-m k2* bamb-a stb2.de• bapt bg2* bar-c b2.de* bar-i k2* bar-s k2 bell b2.de* bism kr1 borx b2.de* *Bov* k* brom b4a.de* *Bry* k* bufo bro1 buni-o jl *Cact* k* caj *Calad* calc b2.de* calc-i k2 *Calc-s* calc-sil k2 *Camph* k* **Cann-i** k* cann-s k* canth k* *Caps* b2.de* carb-ac carb-an k* *Carb-v* k* *Carbn-s* carc mg1.de* card-m vml3• caust b2.de* *Chel* k* *Chin* bro1 chir-fl gya2 *Chlor* choc srj3• cic k* *Cimic* k* cina b2.de* *Cinnb* k* clem bro1 cob ptm1*• coc-c k* coca k* *Coff* k* colch b2.de* coloc k* com k* *Con* k* conch fkr1* conv br1* crat bro1 **Croc** k* *Crot-c* culx k2 cypra-eg sde6.de• dicha jl dig k* *Dios* k* dor c1 dream-p sdj1• dros bro1* *Dulc* b2.de* erig mg1.de euon bro1 euphr k* falco-pe nl2• ferr-i *Fl-ac* k* flor-p jl *Gamb* gels k* germ-met srj5• gink-b sbd1• glon bg2* *Graph* k* grat k2 hed mg1.de *Hell* k* helodr-cal knl2• hep b2.de* hip-ac jl* hippoc-k szs2 *Hydr-ac* hydrog srj2*• hyos k* *Iber* bg1* ign b2.de* ignis-alc es2• ind k* **Iod** k* *Ip* k* irid-met stj2*• *Kali-bi* k* kali-c b2.de* kali-cy gm1 **Kali-i** k* *Kali-n* k* *Kali-s* k* kola stb3• *Lac-ac* stj2*• *Lac-c* st *Lach* k* lact laur k* *Lil-t* k* limen-b-c hm2* limest-b es1• lob vh *Lyc* k* m-arct b2.de* m-aust b2.de* **Mag-c** k* **Mag-m** k* mag-p bg2 mag-s k* malar jl2 mang k* *Med* st* *Meli* meny k* merc b2.de* merc-i-f k2* merc-i-r k* *Mez* k* *Mosch* k* mur-ac k* myrt-c naja al* naphtin nat-c k* *Nat-m* k* **Nat-s** k* nep mg1.de nicc nit-ac b2.de* nux-v b2.de* ol-an c1* olnd b7.de op k* *Osm* pall sne* pant-ac rly4• petr-ra shn4• ph-ac k* phasco-ci rbp2 phel vml3• *Phos* k* *Phyt* pic-ac k* *Pieri-b* mlk9.de pip-n bg2 pitu jl *Plat* k* plb k* pneu jl2 psil ft1 psor bg2* *Ptel* **Puls** k* pycnop-sa mrz1 rad-br c11* ran-b k* *Ran-s* k* rat rauw jl* *Rhod* b2.de* **Rhus-t** k* ruta b2.de* **Sabad** k* **Sabin** k* sacch-a fd2.de• sal-ac sang *Sanic* saroth sp1 sars b2.de* *Sec* k* sel b2.de* *Seneg* k* *Sep* k* spig k* *Spong* k* squil b7a.de stann b2.de* staph b2.de* stel bro1 stront-c b2.de* stry bro1 stry-p br1 sul-ac b2.de* sul-i k2 *Sulph* k* symph fd3.de• *Tab* k* tarax k* *Tarent* k2* *Tell* k* teucr ptk2 thiop jl *Thlas* bg1* thuj k* tril-p tritic-vg fd5.de **TUB** ●* tub-r jl2 *Tung-met* stj2*• valer bg2 vanil fd5.de verat b2.de* verb b2.de* *Vib* k* viol-t k* visc sp1 *Zinc* k* zinc-p k2 [alumin-s stj2 am-br stj2 am-f stj2 ant-m stj2 ant-met stj2 arg-p stj2 astat stj2 aur-s stj2 bar-br stj2 bar-f stj1 bar-met stj2 beryl stj2 beryl-m stj2 bism-sn stj2 cadm-m stj2 *Cadm-met* stj2 cadm-s stj2 caes-met stj2 calc-br stj1 calc-f stj1 calc-lac stj2 calc-n stj1 chr-s stj2 cob-m stj2 cob-p stj2 ferr-f stj2 ferr-lac stj2 ferr-n stj2 ferr-s stj1 gal-s stj2 hafn-met stj2 heroin sdj2 kali-br stj1 lanth-met stj2 lith-f stj2 lith-s stj2 mag-br stj1 mag-f stj1 mag-i stj1 mag-lac stj2 mag-n stj2 mang-i stj2 mang-n stj2 mang-s stj2 mang-sil stj2 merc-d stj2 moly-met stj2 nat-br stj2 nat-caust stj2 nat-f stj1* nat-i stj1 nat-lac stj2 nicc-s stj2 niob-met stj2 nitro stj2 osm-met stj2 oxyg stj2 plb-m stj2 plb-p stj2 polon-met stj2 rhen-met stj2 rhodi stj2 rubd-met stj2 ruth-met stj2 sol-ecl cky1 stront-m stj2 stront-met stj2 tant-met stj2 techn stj2 thal-met stj2 *Titan* stj2 *Titan-s* stj2 yttr-met stj2 zinc-i stj2 zinc-n stj2 zirc-met stj2]
  - **pine**-forest amel.: tub vh

- **exertion** in open air amel.: rauw sp1 sacch-a fd2.de•
- **going** into; when: *Nux-v* b7.de ran-b b7.de* *Verb* b7a.de

AIR; OPEN:

- **aversion** to open air: agar k* alum k* **Am-c** k* *Am-m* k* ambr k* anac k* androc srj1• ang b2.de* apis b7a.de aran bg2 arn b2.de* *Ars* b2.de* ars-s-f k2 aur b2.de* **Bapt** *Bell* k* *Bry* k* **Calc** k* calc-ar k2 **Calc-p** calc-sil k2 camph k* cann-s b2.de* canth k* *Caps* k* carb-an k* carb-v k* *Caust* k* **Cham** k* chel k* *Chin* k* cic b2.de* cina k* *Cist* **Cocc** k* **Coff** k* coloc k* *Con* k* *Cycl* dig k* dros b2.de* *Ferr* k* *Ferr-ar* graph k* *Guaj* k* *Helon* *Hep* k* **Ign** k* ip k* kali-ar **Kali-c** k* kali-m k2 kali-n k* kali-p kali-sil k2 kreos k* *Lach* k* laur k* led b2.de* *Lyc* k* *Lyss* m-ambo b2.de *M-aust* b2.de* mag-m b2.de* mang k* meny k* *Merc* k* merc-c *Mosch* k* mur-ac b2.de* **Nat-c** k* *Nat-m* k* *Nat-p* **Nat-sil** k2* nit-ac k* *Nux-m* k* **Nux-v** k* op k* **Petr** k* ph-ac k* phos k* plat b2.de* *Plb* k* *Psor* puls b2.de* rhod k* *Rhus-t* k* **Rumx** ruta b2.de* sabin b2.de* sars b2.de* sel k* seneg k* *Sep* k* **Sil** k* *Spig* k* staph b2.de* stram b2.de* stront-c k* *Sul-ac* k* **Sulph** k* teucr k* thuj k* tub bg2 valer k* verat b2.de* verb k* *Viol-t* k* zinc b2.de*
  - **alternating** with desire for: ars-s-f k2
- **desire** for open air: *(↗Cold - air - desire)* acon k* adam srj5• *Agn* k* aloe bg2 *Alum* k* alum-p k2 alum-sil k2 am-c b2.de* am-m k* ambr k* aml-ns a1 anac k* *Androc* srj1• ang b2.de* ange-s jl *Ant-c* k* ant-t *Apis* k* aran-ix mg1.de arg-met k* **Arg-n** bg2* *Arn* k* *Ars* k* *Ars-i* k* *Asaf* k* *Asar* k* aster **Aur** k* aur-ar k2 aur-i k2 **Aur-m** **Aur-s** k2 *Bamb-a* stb2.de* *Bapt* sf1.de *Bar-c* k* bar-i k2 bar-m bar-s k2 bell b2.de* *Borx* k* bov k* brass-n-o srj5• *Brom* brucel sa3• *Bry* k* bufo calc b2.de* **Calc-i** *Calc-s* cann-s b2.de* caps b2.de* carb-an k* **Carb-v** k* carbn-h *Carbn-s* carc fd2.de• caust k* chel a1 chlam-tr bcx2• choc srj3• cic b2.de* cimic jl cina b2.de* cit-v a1 coca a1 conch fkr1* crat br1 **Croc** k* dig k* dream-p sdj1• *Elaps* *Fl-ac* gels *Graph* k* ham fd3.de• *Hell* k* hep b2.de* hippoc-k szs2 hydrog srj2• hyos a1 ignis-alc es2• **Iod** k* *Ip* sf1.de irid-met srj5• kali-bi bg2 kali-c k* **Kali-i** k* kali-n k* kali-p fd1.de• **Kali-s** kola stb3• lac-leo sk4• *Lach* k* lact a1 laur k* *Lec* sne *Lil-t* k* limen-b-c hm2* **Lyc** k* *M-arct* b2.de* *Mag-c* k* *Mag-m* k* mang k* med k2* meli sne meny k* *Mez* k* mim-p skp7• mosch b2.de* mur-ac k* nat-c k* *Nat-m* k* *Nat-s* nat-sil fd3.de• nicc-met sk4• olib-sac wmh1 op k* orot-ac rly4• ozone sde2• petr-ra shn4• ph-ac k* phasco-ci rbp2 phos k* pin-con oss2• *Plat* k* plb b2.de* podo fd3.de• *Ptel* **Puls** k* rad-br c11 rhod b2.de* rhus-t k* ruta b2.de* sabin k* sacch-a fd2.de• sanguis-s hm2• *Sanic* sars k* *Sec* k* sel b2.de* seneg k* sep k* *Spig* spong k* stann k* staph b2.de* *Stram* k* stront-c b2.de* suis-em rly4• sul-ac b2.de* sul-i k2 **Sulph** k* symph fd3.de• *Tab* taosc iwa1• *Tarax* k* *Tarent* k* *Tell* *Teucr* k* thuj k* tritic-vg fd5.de *Tub* nh* tub-r jl2* vanil fd5.de verat b2.de* viol-t k* zinc k* zinc-p k2 [spect dfg1 tax jsj7]
  - **night**: adam srj5• haliae-lc srj5•
  - **abortion**; during: puls bro1
  - **accompanied** by:
    - **coldness** of body: ars mrr1
    - **flatulence**: kali-i ptk1 zinc ptk1
  - **alternating** with aversion (See aversion - alternating)
  - **but** draft agg.: acon st anac st *Ars* st borx st *Bry* st *Calc-s* st carb-an st *Carbn-s* st *Caust* st *Graph* st kali-bi gk **Kali-c** st **Kali-s** a *Lach* st **Lyc** st *Mag-c* st med a mur-ac st *Nat-c* st *Nat-m* st nat-sil fd3.de• *Ph-ac* st *Phos* st **Puls** st **Rhus-t** st sanic a sars st *Sep* st *Spig* st *Stram* st **Sulph** st tub a *Zinc* st
  - **diarrhea**; during: arg-n zr
  - **menses** | **before** | **agg.**: lach bg2
    - **during** | **agg.**: mag-c vh
  - **mountain** air: haliae-lc srj5•

AIRPLANE sickness (See STOMACH - Nausea - airplane)

AKINESIA (See Motion - aversion; Paralysis; Weakness - paralytic)

ALBUMINURIA (See URINE - Albuminous)

ALCOHOLIC stimulants (See Food and - alcoholic)

ALCOHOLISM (See MIND - Alcoholism)

ALIVE sensation, internally: anac b2.de* arund vh asar b2.de* bell b2.de* berb bg2* calc bg2 calc-p ptk1 cann-s b2.de* *Cann-xyz* ptk1 *Caust* ptk1 chel bg2 cocc b2.de* **Croc** b2.de* cycl tl1* galeoc-c-h gms1• hyos b2.de* *Ign* b2.de* kali-i bg2 lach b2.de* led b2.de* m-ambo b2.de mag-m b2.de* meny b2.de* merc b2.de* nat-m b2.de* op ptk1 pall tl1 petr b2.de* phos bg2 plb b2.de* puls ptk1 rhod b2.de* sabad b2.de* *Sabin* ptk1 sang bg2* sec b2.de* sil b2.de* spong b2.de* sulph b2.de* tarax b2.de* tarent tl1 ther tl1* **Thuj** b2.de* viol-t b2.de*

○ - **Glands**: ign bg2 merc bg2 rhod bg2 *Spong* b7.de* sulph bg2

ALLERGIC constitution: *(↗Dust - agg.; Food and; Shock; anaphylactic; Smoke - inspiration - agg.; NOSE - Hay; RESPIRATION - Asthmatic - allergic; SKIN - Allergy; SKIN - Eruptions - crusty - hay; SKIN - Eruptions - summer; SKIN - Eruptions - urticaria)* all-c mrr1 am-c mrr1 **Apis** mrr1 ars mrr1 ars-i mrr1 arum-t mrr1 arund mrr1 blatta-o mrr1 borx mrr1 bov mrr1 calc-s mrr1 carc jl2* caust mrr1 chlam-tr bcx2• clem mrr1 cortico sp1 cycl mrr1 diph-t-tpt jl2 *Dulc* mrr1 enteroc jl2 euphr mrr1 fl-ac mrr1 flav jl2 fuma-ac mtf11 galph mtf11 hep mrr1 *Iod* mrr1 kali-ar mrr1 kali-bi mrr1 kali-c mrr1 kali-i mrr1 kali-n mrr1 kali-s mrr1 lac-c mrr1 lyc mrr1 med mrr1 naja mrr1 nat-ar mrr1 *Nat-c* mrr1 nat-m mrr1 nat-p mrr1 nat-pyru mtf11 nat-s mrr1 nux-m mrr1 nux-v mrr1 petr mrr1 phos mrr1 prot jl2 psor jl2* puls mrr1 ran-b mrr1 sabad mrr1 samb mrr1 sang mrr1 sanguis-s mtf11 sanic mrr1 sin-n mrr1 stict mrr1 suis-cu mtf11 sul-ac mrr1 sulph mrr1 ther mrr1 thuj mrr1 tub jl2*

- **accompanied** by | **sour** food; desire for (See Food and - sour food - desire - accompanied - allergy)
- **antibiotics**; to: coli mtf11 med mtf11 oxyte-ch! mtf11 penic mtf11 succ-ac mtf11 sulph mtf11
- **aspirin**; to: *(↗Aspirin)* **Calc** mrr1
- **cats**; to: ars mrr5 dulc mrr1 kali-c mrr1 lac-f wza1• puls mrr1 sulph mrr1 **Tub** mrr1
- **chemical** hypersensitivity: *(↗Aluminium; Coal gas; Iron; Lead; Smoke - inspiration - agg.)* nat-m mrr1 nux-v mrr1 phos mrr1 sul-ac mrr1 verat mrr1
- **detergents**; to: syc mtf11
- **dust**; to (See Dust - agg.)
- **flour**; to (See Food and - farinaceous - agg.)
- **food** allergy (See Convulsions - errors; Food and - diet - agg. - errors; RECTUM - Diarrhea - indiscretion)
- **lactose** (See Food and - milk - agg.)
- **lemons**: med mtf11
- **milk**; to (See Food and - milk - agg.)
- **molds**; to: blatta-o mrr1
- **multiple**: carc mlr1*
- **oranges** (See Food and - oranges - agg.)
- **petrochemical** fumes; to: *(↗Coal gas; Smoke - inspiration - agg.)* dioxi rbp6 nux-v mrr1 petr mrr1 phos mrr1 sep mrr1 sul-ac mrr1
- **pollen**; airborne (See NOSE - Hay)
- **shellfish**; to (See Food and - shellfish - agg.; SKIN - Eruptions - urticaria - shellfish)
- **sugar** (See Food and - sugar - agg.)

ALONE; being: | **amel.**: ambr b2.de* *Bar-c* b2.de* carb-an b2.de* con b2.de* hell b2.de* *Lyc* b2.de* mag-c b2.de* nat-c b2.de* nat-m b2.de* *Pall* bg2 petr b2.de* phos b2.de* *Plb* b2.de* **Sep** b2.de* stann b2.de* stram b2.de* sulph b2.de*

ALOPECIA (See HEAD - Hair - falling; SKIN - Hair - falling)

ALTERNATING states: *(↗Change - symptoms - constant; Contradictory; Metastasis; Pain - wandering; MIND - Mental symptoms - alternating - physical)* **Abrot** bg2* acon bg2 agar bg **Aloe** sne *Ars* k2 asaf bg2 bell bg bry bg2 cact bg2 calc bg2 carc sst* caust bg2 cimic bg2 cocc bg2 con bg2 croc bg crot-h bg2 crot-t bg2 dig bg2 diph-t-tpt jl2 dulc bg2 glon bg graph bg2* grat bg2 ham bg2* ign bg2 ip bg2 **Kali-bi** bg2* kali-c bg2 kali-s fd4.de kalm bg2 **Lac-c** bg lach bg2 lil-t bg2 lith-c bg2 *Lyc* bg2 mez bg2 nat-m bg2 nux-v bg2 onop bg* phos bg2 plat bg2 podo bg2 prot jl3 *Puls* bg2* rhus-t bg2 sabad bg2 sec bg2 senec bg2 sep bg2 sil bg2 sulph bg2 tril-p bg2 ust bg2 zinc bg2

- **accompanied** by | **reaction**; lack of: *Valer* ptk1
- **food** and drinks; alternating desires and aversions of: carc mtf33
- **rapid** alternation: croc ptk1

ALTITUDE agg. (See Ascending high - agg.)

ALTITUDE sickness: cordyc mp4•

ALUMINIUM poisoning: *(↗Allergic - chemical; ABDOMEN - Cancer - aluminium; STOMACH - Cancer - aluminium)* alum tl1* bar-c gm1 *Bry* hr1* cadm-met gm1 *Cadm-o* st* calc-ox gm1 camph hr1* cham hr1* ip hr1* plb gm1 puls hr1*

- **dialysis**; from: alum mtf bar-c mtf gels mtf kali-p mtf ph-ac mtf pic-ac mtf plb mtf zinc-p mtf

ALZHEIMER'S DISEASE: alum mrr1 cordyc mp4• hell mrr1 nux-m mrr1 zinc mtf

AMEBIASIS: emetin mp4•
- **accompanied** by | **Tongue**; ulcers on: tub vk1

AMYOTROPHIC LATERAL SCLEROSIS: *(↗Neurological)* ang sne arg-n bro1* calc sne cupr bro1* *Cur* mrr1 diph jl2 dub sne hyper bro1 lath bro1* medul-spi mtf11 ms mtf11 nux-v sne pic-ac sne plb bro1* polio mtf11 rhus-t sne sulph mrr1 zinc sne

ANALGESIA: *(↗Anesthesia [=insensibility]; Irritability - lack; Painlessness)* anh mg1.de ant-c sf1.de atra-r bnm3• bapt sf1.de bell cann-i k2 chel *Cic* **Cocc** con galla-q-r nl2• hell *Hyos* ign kali-br laur **Lyc** mand mg1.de merc mosch **Olnd** **Op** **Ph-ac** phos phys br1* pic-ac **Plb** k* positr nl2• puls rhus-t k* sec **Stram** *Sulph* tub jl2 tung-met bdx1• [heroin sdj2]
- **alternating** with painfulness: asaf vh
- O - **Affected** parts: anac asaf bapt st *Cocc* con *Lyc* *Olnd* op mrr1 **Plat** k* puls rhus-t
- **Inner** parts: ars bell bov hyos **Op** **Plat** spig

ANALGESICS; from: *(↗Medicine - allopathic - abuse; KIDNEYS - Analgesics)* am-c gm1 bell tl1 carb-v gm1 lach gm1 op gm1

ANAPHYLAXIS (See Shock; anaphylactic)

ANASARCA (See Dropsy - external)

ANEMIA: *(↗Faintness - anemia; Weakness - anemia)* abel jl3 abies-c oss4• *Acet-ac* k* acetan br1* acon k* agar k* agn k2* *Alet* c1* aloe sf1.de alst-s br1 alum k* alum-p k2* alum-sil k2* am-c sf1.de ambr k* anil a1* ant-c k* *Ant-t* b7a.de* *Apis* kr1 apoc k2* aq-mar sf1.de *Arg-met* *Arg-n* k* *Arg-o* bro1 *Arn* k* **Ars** k* ars-h br1* *Ars-i* **Ars-s-f** k2* aur-ar c1* *Bell* k* ben-d c1* berb k2* beryl sp1* bism hr1* bit-ar wht1• bol-la kr1 **Borx** k* both tsm2 both-ax tsm2 bov k* *Bry* k* cadm-met sp1* **Calc** k* calc-ar bro1 calc-i k2* calc-lac bro1* **Calc-p** k* calc-sil k2* calen sf1.de calo bro1 carb-an k2* *Carb-v* k* *Carbn-s* kr1* carc cd* casc hr1* *Caust* k* cedr cham k* **Chin** k* chinin-ar k* chinin-fcit bro1 *Chinin-s* bro1 chlol hr1* chloram jl3 chlorpr jl3 cic bro1 cina k* cob-n sp1* cocc k* coff k* colch a1 coloc k* *Con* k* cordyc mp4• cortico sp1 cortiso sp1 crat br1* *Crot-h* k* cund hr1 cupr k* cupr-ar bro1 cupr-s a1 *Cycl* k* dig k* dys fmm1• eucal sf1.de **Ferr** k* ferr-act bro1 **Ferr-ar** k* ferr-c bro1 *Ferr-i* k* *Ferr-m* c1* ferr-ox bro1 *Ferr-p* k* ferr-pic sf1.de ferr-prox br1 *Ferr-r* bro1 ferr-val bwa3 **Germ-met** stj2*• goss br1* **Graph** k* *Ham* hr1* **Hell** k* *Helon* k* hep bg2* *Hydr* hr1* *Ign* k* iod k* ip c1* *Irid-met* c1* **Kali-ar** k* *Kali-bi* k* *Kali-br* hr1* **Kali-c** k* kali-chl br1 **Kali-fcy** zr kali-n sf1.de **Kali-p** k* kalm hr1* kres mg1.de* lac-ac c1 lac-d bg2* *Lach* k* lec br1* loxo-lae bnm12• loxo-recl bnm10• lyc k* lyss hr1 m-ambo b2.de m-aust b2.de mag-c k* mag-m k* malar jl2 **Mang** k* *Mang-act* br1* **Med** k* **Merc** k* *Merc-c* merc-k-i gm1 mez k* **Mosch** b7a.de* *Mucor* jl2 nat-ar k* *Nat-c* k* **Nat-m** k* nat-n c1* *Nat-p* k* *Nat-s* k* **Nit-ac** k* nux-m k* *Nux-v* k* ol-j k* *Olnd* osteo-mye-scl mtf11 oxyg c1* petr k* *Ph-ac* k* **Phos** k* phyt bro1 *Pic-ac* k* **Plat** b4a.de* **Plb** k* *Plb-act* bro1 plb-xyz c2 psor **Puls** k* rhod k* *Rhus-t* k* ric a1 rub-t c1* ruta k* sabin k* sacch br1* sal-ac hr1 sang hr1 *Sec* k* *Senec* k* *Sep* k* sil k* spig k* **Squil** k* *Stann* k* **Staph** k* *Strept-ent* jl2 stroph-h c1* *Stry-af-cit* bro1 succ-ac mtf11 **Sul-ac** k* sulfa sp1* sulfag mtf11 sulfonam jl3 **Sulph** k* syc bka1*• tab a1* ter hr1 tetrac mtf11 ther k* *Thyr* c1* trinit br1 tub hr1* tub-sp vn* urt-u c1* *Ust* hr1 valer k* vanad br1* verat k* *Verat-v* hr1 *X-ray* br1* *Yohim* bwa3* *Zinc* k* zinc-ar bro1 zinc-m bro1 zinc-s a1 [*Am-br* stj2 *Ars-met* stj2 *Brom* stj2 *Calc-met* stj2 *Chr-m* stj2 *Chr-met* stj2 *Cob* stj2 *Cob-m* stj2 *Cob-p* stj2 *Cupr-f* stj2 *Cupr-m* stj2 *Cupr-p* stj2 *Ferr-f* stj2 *Ferr-lac* stj2 *Ferr-n* stj2 *Ferr-sil* stj2 *Gal-met* stj2 *Kali-met* stj2 *Mang-m* stj2 mang-met stj2 *Mang-n* stj2 *Mang-p* stj2 *Mang-s* stj2 *Mang-sil* stj2 *Nat-br* stj2 *Nicc-met* stj2 *Nicc-s* stj2 *Scand-met* stj2 *Sel* stj2 *Titan* stj2 *Titan-s* stj2 *Zinc-i* stj2 *Zinc-n* stj2 *Zinc-p* stj2]
- **accompanied** by:
  - **abortion**: alet sf1.de carb-v bg2 ferr bg2* ferr-act sf1.de kali-c sf1.de kali-n sf1.de kali-perm sf1.de sec sf1.de *Sep* bg2 sulph bg2
  - **anemic** look: calc-p tl1
  - **bone** marrow failure: chloram mtf cortiso mtf x-ray mtf
  - **constipation**: alum bg2* alum-sil gm1 alumn gm1 chin bg2 cycl bg2 ferr bg2 graph bg2 hydr bg2 kali-c bg2 mang bg2 nat-m bg2 nux-v bg2 plb gm1 puls bg2 sulph bg2
  - **coryza**: bry bg2 chin bg2 ferr bg2 hydr bg2 kali-c bg2 puls bg2

Anemia – **accompanied** by: ...
  - **dropsy** (See Dropsy - external - accompanied - anemia)
  - **emaciation**: plb hr1*
  - **faintness** (See Faintness - anemia)
  - **fever** | **intermittent**: nit-ac br1
  - **fever** and dizziness; asthenic: ferr mtf11
  - **gastrointestinal** complaints: cycl br1
  - **genital** complaints: cycl br1
  - **malaria** (See Malaria - accompanied - anemia)
  - **nervousness**: ferr mtf11
  - **palpitations** (See CHEST - Palpitation - accompanied - anemia)
  - **perspiration**; profuse: acet-ac br1
  - **pulsation** all over the body: kali-c tl1
  - **respiration**; difficult: acet-ac br1 calc tl1 stroph-h br1
  - **urinary** complaints: cycl br1
  - **urine**; copious: acet-ac br1
  - **vertigo**: alet bg2 carb-v bg2 chin bg2 crot-h bg2 cycl bg2 eucal bg2 ferr bg2 kali-c bg2 led bg2 phos bg2 senec bg2
  - **vomiting**: acet-ac br1
  - **weakness** (See Weakness - anemia)
  - O **Face**; red discoloration of: ferr tl1* graph br1
  - **Head**; pain in: ars bro1 calc-p bro1 *Chin* bro1 cycl bro1 ferr bro1 *Ferr-p* bro1 *Ferr-r* bro1 kalm bro1 nat-m bro1 *Ph-ac* bro1 zinc bro1
  - **Heart**; weak: acet-ac br1
  - **Liver**; complaints of the (See ABDOMEN - Liver - accompanied - anemia)
  - **Mucous** membrane; pale: ferr tl1 graph tl1
  - **Spleen**; complaints of the (See ABDOMEN - Spleen - accompanied - anemia)
  - **Stomach**; pain in: *Ferr* bro1 glon bro1 graph bro1
- **aplastic**: cortico sp1 x-ray sp1
- **children**; in: *Calc-p* br1* loxo-lae bnm12• med jl2
  - **nurslings**: borx mtf33 lap-a br1
- **corpuscles**; from reduced red: plb tl1
- **dialysis**; from: ferr-act mtf ferr-cit mtf rub-t mtf
- **disease**; from exhausting: acet-ac bro1 alst bro1 *Calc-p* br1* *Chin* bro1 chinin-s bro1 *Ferr* bro1* helon bro1 kali-c bro1 *Nat-m* bro1 *Ph-ac* bro1 *Phos* kr1* sec kr1
- **erythrocytic**: pic-ac bro1 x-ray sp1
- **followed** by:
  - **blood**; loss of: *Chin* tl1
  - **dropsy**: *Chin* tl1
- **girls**; in young: alum tl1 tub jl2
- **grief**; from: nat-m bro1* ph-ac bro1*
- **heart** disease; from: ars bro1* crat bro1* stroph-h bro1*
- **hemorrhage**; after: *Arg-o* bro1 *Ars* bro1 bit-ar wht1• *Calc* k* *Carb-v* **Chin** k* crot-h bro1 **Ferr** k* *Helon* hr1* hydr hr1* ign bro1 *Lach* nat-br bro1 *Nat-m* *Nux-v* *Ph-ac* *Phos* k* sabin k2* staph hr1* *Sulph*
- **hypochromic**: beryl sp1
- **lead** in water; from: alum tl1
- **macrocytic**: beryl sp1
- **malaria**; from: alst bro1 *Ars* bro1 *Nat-m* bro1 *Ost* br1* rob bro1
- **menorrhagia**, from: *(↗FEMALE - Metrorrhagia - anemia)* arg-o bro1 ars bro1 *Calc* bro1 calc-p bro1 *Cann-i* hr1* crat bro1 *Cycl* bro1 *Ferr* bro1 *Graph* bro1 helon c *Hydr* hr1* *Kali-c* bro1 kali-fcy zr lyss mtf11 mang-act bro1 *Nat-m* bro1 *Phos* a1 *Puls* bro1 sec a1 sep bro1
- **menses** | **after** | **agg.**: ant-c bg2 calc bg2 chin bg2 ferr bg2 nat-m bg2
  - **suppressed**; from: sabal bro1
- **nursing** mothers: acet-ac br1
- **nutritional** imbalance; from: alet bro1 alum bro1 *Calc-p* bro1 ferr bro1 ferr-p mp1• helon bro1 nux-v bro1
- **pernicious**: *Ars* bro1* calc k2* carc fb* *Crot-h* hr1* ferr-pic a mang k2* med mtf11 nat-m k2 *Phos* c1* pic-ac hr1* rad-br sze8• *Thyr* c1* [cob stj]
  - **family**; in: carc mlr1•
- **progressive**: pic-ac br1

- **radium** treatments; after: phos gm1
- **sickle**-cell: cob-n sp1
- **syphilitic**: *Ars* bro1 *Aur* bro1 *Calo* br1* carb-an bro1 carb-v bro1 ferr-i bro1 ferr-lac bro1 *Iod* bro1 merc bro1 sars bro1
- **young** people; in: ferr br1

ANESTHESIA [=insensibility]: (↗*Analgesia; Irritability - lack; Neurological)* abrot k1* absin a1* *Acon* a1* aethyl-n a1 alco a1* ambr j5.de* *Anac* kr1* ant-t b7.de* arg-n k1* *Ars* j5.de* ars-i k2* atro a1* bar-m j5.de* bell j5.de* benzol br1 berb k1* cadm-s k2* *Camph* b7.de* cann-i a1* canth b7.de *Caps* kr1* carb-ac a1* carbn-chl a1* carbn-h a1* carbn-o a1* carbn-s a1* caul kr1* *Caust* k1* cham k1* chel b7.de chlf a1* chlol a1* *Cic* b7.de* cocain br1 cocc b7a.de* *Croc* b7a.de crot-chlol c1* cupr b7.de cupr-act j5.de* cycl a1* cyt-l br1 *Eucal* kr1* haliae-lc srj5• *Hell* b7a.de* **Hydr-ac** j5.de* hyos b7a.de* *Hyper* k1* ign b7.de* kali-br c1* *Kali-i* kr1* keroso a1* laur b7.de* lyc j5.de* m-ambo b7.de m-arct j5.de* mand k1* merc a1* meth-ae-ae a1* methyl a1* mosch b7.de nit-s-d br1 nitro-o a1* *Nux-m* b7.de* nux-v b7.de* *Olnd* b7a.de* *Op* b7.de* ox-ac k1* ph-ac k1* *Plat* br1 **Plb** b7.de* psil ft1 puls b7a.de* ran-a j5.de* rhod j5.de* *Sec* j5.de* spig k1* stram b7.de* stront-c k1* tab a1* ter kr1* verat j5.de* *Verat-v* kr1* vip j5.de* zinc j5.de* [heroin sdj2]

- **right** side, of: plb a1
- **chill** | **during**: cocc bg2 hyos bg2 lyc bg2 mosch bg2 *Op* bg2 ph-ac bg2 phos bg2 *Puls* bg2 rhus-t bg2 spong bg2 *Stann* bg2 stram bg2
- **hysterical**: ign mrr1
- **perspiration** | **during**: ars bg2 *Bell* bg2 calc bg2 cann-xyz bg2 caust bg2 *Hyos* bg2 ign bg2 *Lyc* bg2 **Mur-ac** bg2 *Op* b7.de* *Ph-ac* bg2 *Phos* bg2 puls bg2 rhus-t bg2 *Stram* bg2 thuj bg2
- **sensation** of: coca-c sk4•
- **shivering** | **during**: op b7.de
- **wandering**: cocc bg2 phos bg2
- **warm** applications; to: kara a1

○ - **Affected** parts, of: plb a1*
- **Lower** half of body: spong bg2
- **Mucous** membranes: carbn-s br1 kali-br br1

ANESTHESIA [=narcosis]: | **ailments**; from: (↗*Chloroform; Medicine - allopathic - abuse - morphine)* acet-ac bro1* adren br1 am-caust bro1 aml-ns bro1* crot-chlol c2 hep bro1* keroso c2 op cpd• phos bro1* plb c2

ANEURYSM: (↗*CHEST - Aneurysm)* *Ars-i* c2 aur bg* *Bar-c* c2* bar-m c2* cact c2* calc-f bg* carb-an c2 carb-v bg* eucal c2 guaj c2 ign sne *Kali-i* c2* lach bg* lith-c c2 *Lyc* b4a.de* lycps-v c2 magn-gr c2 plb-xyz c2 puls bg* ran-b tl1 ran-s c2* sec gk spong c2 sulph bg* syph mrr1 thuj bg*

- **anastomosis**; from (= connection of blood vessels): thuj ptk1
- **small** aneurysms all over the body: plb ptk1
- **tendency** to: aur bg bar-c bg carb-v bg conv br1 lach bg *Lyc* bg puls bg sulph bg thuj bg

○ - **Capillary**: *Calc-f* bro1 fl-ac bro1 tub bro1

ANTHRAX poison; complaints from: **Ars** b2.de*

ANTIBIOTICS; from (See History - antibiotics)

ANTIPYRETICS; from: am-c gm1 carb-v gm1 lach gm1 op gm1

ANXIETY, general physical: (↗*MIND - Anxiety)* acon k* agar alum j5.de am-m k* ambr j5.de *Aml-ns* androc srj1• *Ant-t* **Arg-n** arn j5.de **Ars** k* ars-i **Ars-s-f** k2 bar-c k* bar-m bar-s k2 bell j5.de borx j5.de* *Brom* k* *Bry* k* *Calc* k* calc-ar k2 calc-i k2 **Camph** cann-s k* *Canth* k* carb-v k* caust j5.de cench k2 **Cham** k* *Chel* *Chin* k* chlor a1 cic k* cocc k* *Coff* k* *Colch* k* con k* *Cupr* k* **Dig** euph k* *Ferr* k* *Ferr-ar* *Ferr-i* ferr-p k* guaj k* hydrog srj2• ign k* *Iod* **Ip** kreos j5.de laur k* lob *Lyc* k* m-ambo b2.de* mag-c j5.de meph j5.de merc k* mez k* mosch k* mur-ac k* nat-c j5.de nat-m k* nat-s k1 nux-m j5.de **Nux-v** k* op j5.de petr j5.de **Ph-ac** k* **Phos** plat k* plb k* prun j5.de **Puls** k* ran-b j5.de rhod j5.de rhus-t k* ruta j5.de sabad k* sabin k* sars j5.de *Sec* k* seneg k* *Sep* k* sil j5.de spig j5.de squil j5.de *Stann* k* *Staph* k* stram k* sul-ac k* sul-i k2 **Sulph** k* tarent k2 *Teucr* k* ther k2 thiam rly4• thuj k* *Verat* k* *Zinc* zinc-p k2

APHTHAE: (↗*CHEST - Aphthae; CHEST - Aphthae - mammae - nipples; FACE - Aphthae; FEMALE - Aphthae; GENERALS; MALE GENITALIA/SEX - Aphthae; MOUTH - Aphthae; RECTUM - Aphthous; THROAT - Aphthae)* *Ant-t* c2 *Ars* c2 asim c2 *Borx* c2* bov mrr1 bry c2 chin c2 chin-b c2 chlor c2 corn c2 cub c2 eup-a c2 ferr-s c2 ferul c2 hell c2

Aphthae: ...
Kali-chl c2 kali-m c2 merc c2 *Merc-c* c2 moni jl2 *Mur-ac* c2 *Nat-m* c2 ric c2 sul-ac c2 sulph tl1

- **fetid**, sour smelling: mur-ac tl1
- **inflamed**: aeth tl1 merc tl1

APOPLEXY: (↗*Circulation; Convulsions - apoplectic; Paralysis - one - apoplexy; Weakness - apoplexy; HEAD - Apoplexy)* **Acon** k* agar mg1.de *Alco* a1 aloe hr **Anac** b2.de* ant-c b2.de* ant-t b2.de* apis c1* *Arn* k* *Ars* bg2* ars-s-f hr1* asar b2.de* *Aster* hr1* *Aur* k* bapt c1* bar-c k* **Bell** k* both mrr1 brom c1* **Bry** b2.de* bufo gk cact hr1* cadm-br c1* cadm-s bg2* calc b2.de* *Camph* k* carb-v k* carbn-h c1* carbn-s c1 caust hr1* chen-a c1* *Chin* k* chlol c1* **Cocc** k* *Coff* k* con k* croc b2.de* *Crot-h* k* *Cupr* k* cupr-act c1* dig b2.de* erig mg1.de *Ferr* k* fl-ac c1* *Form* hr1* gast c1* **Gels** k* germ-met srj5• **Glon** bg2* guare c1* hell hr1* hep b2.de* *Hydr-ac* a1* *Hyos* k* ign b2.de* iod hr1* **Ip** k* juni-v a1* kali-br c1* kali-cy c1* kali-i bro1 kali-n mg1.de kreos b2.de* **Lach** k* lat-m bnm6• laur k* lim c1* lith-br c1* lol a1 *Lyc* k* merc k* *Mill* a1* morph a1 nat-m k* nat-n mg1.de nat-ns c1* nit-ac k* *Nux-m* k* *Nux-v* k* *Oena* hr1* olnd b2.de* **Op** k* ox-ac a1 pap-r mtf11 *Phos* k* plb k* *Puls* k* ran-g c1* rhus-t k* sabad b2.de* samb b2.de* sang hr1 sars b2.de* sec k* sep k* *Sil* k* sin-n hr1* sol-a c1* staph mrr1 *Stram* k* stront-c c1* sulph b2.de* tab a1* verat b2.de* *Verat-v* a1* viol-o b2.de* vip bg2*

- **accompanied** by:
  - **fever**: *Acon* bg2 *Bell* bg2 calc bg2 cocc bg2 hyos bg2 *Lach* bg2 lyc bg2 **Nux-v** bg2 **Op** bg2 *Sep* bg2 sil bg2 stram bg2 thuj bg2
  - **hypertension**: glon tl1 op tl1
  - **perspiration**: acon bg2 *Bell* bg2 calc bg2 cocc bg2 hyos bg2 lach bg2 lyc bg2 *Nux-v* bg2 **Op** bg2 sep bg2 sil bg2 stram bg2 thuj bg2
  - **pulse**:
    - **irritable**: acon ptk1
    - **slow** and full: op ptk1
    - **small**: lach ptk1
    - **weak**: lach ptk1
  - **salivation**: *Anac* kr1* **Nux-v** kr1*
  - **speech** disorder: laur mtf11
  - **uremia**: kali-br br1

○ · **Face**:
    - **bluish**, pale discoloration of: lach ptk1
    - **congestion** of: arn mrr1 lach mrr1 op mrr1 sulph mrr1
    - **red** discoloration of: arn br1 op ptk1
  - **Head**:
    - **burning** pain in (See HEAD - Pain - burning - accompanied - apoplexy)
    - **congestion** in waves (See HEAD - Congestion - waves - accompanied - apoplexy)
    - **pulsating** (See HEAD - Pulsating - accompanied - apoplexy)
  - **Pupils** | **contracted**: op ptk1
- **coma**; with (See MIND - Coma - apoplectic)
- **fever**; during: nux-v b7.de
- **hemorrhagic**, sanguine: *Acon* b2.de* ant-c bg2 ant-t bg2 ars bg2 *Aur* b2.de* bell b2.de* bry b2.de* calc b2.de* camph b2.de* chin b2.de* cocc b2.de* coff b2.de* ferr b2.de* ign b2.de* ip b2.de* kreos b2.de* lach b2.de* *Lyc* b2.de* merc b2.de* nux-v b2.de* olnd b2.de* ph-ac bg2 puls bg2 rhus-t b2.de* sabad b2.de* samb b2.de* sep b2.de* stram bg2 sulph b2.de* thuj bg2 verat bg2 viol-o b2.de*
- **holding** head with hands (See HEAD - Hands - holds - apoplexy)
- **later** stages: methyl br1
- **nervous**: arn b2.de* asar b2.de* bar-c b2.de* bell b2.de* bry b2.de* *Chin* b2.de* *Coff* b2.de* cupr b2.de* dig b2.de* hyos b2.de* ign b2.de* ip bg2 laur b2.de* merc b2.de* nux-v b2.de* phos b2.de* puls b2.de* rhus-t b2.de* sil b2.de* stram b2.de* viol-o b2.de*
- **sensation** of impending: ran-g a
- **serous**: dig b4a.de merc b4a.de
- **threatened**: *Aster* hr1* *Bell* hr1* bry k2 cact k2 calc-f br1 **Coff** hr1* *Fl-ac* hr1* *Glon* hr1* ign hr1* kali-n mg1.de lach mrr1 *Laur* hr1* prim-v c1* *Stront-c* kr1*
  - **beer** drinkers; in: gua br1

APPEARANCE (See Complexion)

APPEARING SUDDENLY: | **disappearing** suddenly; and (See Complaints - appearing - suddenly - disappearing - suddenly)

ARMS AWAY FROM THE BODY amel.; holding the (See CHEST - Oppression - arms; RESPIRATION - Asthmatic - arms; RESPIRATION - Difficult - arms)

ARSENICAL poisoning: (↗*Paralysis - toxic - arsenic)* camph k* *Carb-v* hr1* chin k* chinin-s kr1* dig hr1* euph c1 *Ferr* k* graph k* **Hep** hr1* iod k* *Ip* k* lach hr1* *Merc* k* nux-m c1 nux-v k* *Phos* hr1* plb hr1* samb k* sulph c1 tab hr1* thuj st1 *Verat* k*

- **fumes**; from arsenical: camph b7a.de* ip b7a.de* *Merc* bg2 nux-v b7a.de*

ARTERIOSCLEROSIS: (↗*Blood vessels - complaints - arteries; Blood vessels - degeneration; Circulation; Diabetes mellitus - accompanied - arteriosclerosis; Ossification - arteries; CHEST - Arteriosclerosis)* adren br1* *Am-i* bro1* am-van bro1 aml-ns sf1.de ant-ar bro1 arg-n mg1.de *Arn* bg2* ars bro1* *Ars-i* br1* asar vh aster jl3 *Aur* bg2* aur-br sf1.de *Aur-i* bro1* aur-m ptk1 aur-m-n br1* *Bar-c* br1* bar-i sf1.de* bar-m br1* bell-p mg1.de* benz-ac sf1.de cact br1* cal-ren sf1.de *Calc* bg2* calc-ar bg2 calc-f br1* chinin-s bro1 chlam-tr bcx2• chlol st1 con br1* crat br1* *Cupr* bg2* ergot bro1 fl-ac bg2* form bg2 form-ac sf1.de fuc mg1.de *Glon* bro1* hed mg1.de* hyper mg1.de iod bg2* kali-bi vh *Kali-i* bro1* kali-sal bro1 kres mg1.de* lach bro1* lith-c bro1 mag-f mg1.de mand jl3 naja mg1.de *Nat-i* bro1 nit-ac sf1.de phos bro1 *Plb* bg2* *Plb-i* c1* *Polyg-a* bro1 rad-br mg1.de rauw mg1.de *Sec* bg2* sil mg1.de solid sf1.de spartin-s br1 *Stront-c* bg2* *Stront-i* bro1* stroph-h br1* sulph gk sumb br1* syph jl2 *Tab* bg2* thlas sf1.de thyroiod bro1 *Vanad* br1* *Visc* bg2* zinc-p sf1.de [bar-p stj1 bar-s stj1 kali-f stj1 kali-n stj1 nat-n stj1]

- **accompanied** by | **diabetes** (See Diabetes mellitus - accompanied - arteriosclerosis)
- **memory**; with weakness of (See MIND - Memory - weakness - arteriosclerotic)
- **old** people; in: bar-c br1 stroph-h br1

ARTHRALGIA (See Pain - joints)

ARTHRITIS (See Inflammation - joints)

ASCENDING:

- **agg.**: acet-ac k* acon k* agar bg2* aloe alum k* alum-sil k2* *Alumn* kr1 *Am-c* k* anac k* *Ang* b2.de* ant-c k* arg-met k* arg-n arn k* **Ars** k* ars-s-f k2* asar k* aur k* aur-ar k2 aur-i k2* aur-s k2 *Bar-c* k* bar-m *Bar-s* k2* bell k* blatta-o mrr1 *Borx* k* **Bry** k* but-ac br1* *Cact* hr1* cadm-s **Calc** k* calc-ar k2* *Calc-p* k* calc-sil k2* cann-i cann-s k* canth k* *Carb-v* k* *Carbn-s* caust k* chin k* **Coca** k* coff k* *Con* bg2* conv *Cupr* k* dig k* dios dros k* euph k* *Ferr* bg2* gels gins a1 *Glon* k* glycyr-g cte1• graph k* hell k* hep k* hyos k* ign k* iod bg2* kali-ar kali-c k* *Kali-i* k* *Kali-n* k* kali-p *Kalm* k* kreos k* lach k* led k* lyc k* m-ambo b2.de m-arct b2.de m-aust b2.de mag-c k* mag-m k* meny k* *Merc* k* mosch k* mur-ac k* nat-ar nat-c k* *Nat-m* k* nat-n bg2* nat-p nat-sil fd3.de• nit-ac k* nux-m k* *Nux-v* k* olnd bg2* *Ox-ac* k* par k* petr k* ph-ac k* *Phos* k* plat k* plb k* prot jl3* *Puls* bg2* ran-b k* rhod hr1* rhus-t k* *Ruta* k* sabad k* *Sabin* hr1* *Seneg* k* *Sep* k* sil k* *Spig* k* **Spong** k* squil k* *Stann* k* staph k* sul-ac k* *Sulph* k* *Tab* k* *Tarax* k* thuj k* (non:tub lmj) *Valer* hr1* verb k* vip-a jl3 *Zinc* k* zinc-p k2* [fl-ac stj2 hydrog stj2 lith-c stj2 lith-f stj2]
- **amel.**: allox jl3 am-m b2.de* arg-met b2.de* bar-c b2.de* bell b2.de* bry b2.de* canth b2.de* coff b2.de* *Con* b2.de* *Ferr* b2.de* lyc b2.de* meny b2.de* nit-ac b2.de* plb b2.de* ran-b b7.de *Rhod* b2.de* rhus-t b2.de* ruta b2.de* sabin b2.de* stann b2.de* sulph b2.de* tub vh4 *Valer* b2.de* verb b2.de*
- **stairs** | **agg.**: *Acon* b7a.de *Alum* b4.de *Am-c* b4a.de anac b4a.de *Ang* b7a.de ant-c b7.de arn b7.de *Ars* b4.de* asar b7.de *Bar-c* b4.de* bell b4.de *Borx* b4a.de *Bry* b7.de* *Calc* b4.de *Cann-s* b7.de* carb-v b4.de caust b4.de chin b7.de coff b7.de cupr b7.de dig b4.de dros b7.de hell b7.de* hyos b7.de* ign b7.de kali-c b4.de *Kali-n* b4a.de led b7.de lyc b4.de m-arct b7.de m-aust b7.de mag-c b4.de *Meny* b7.de* *Merc* b4.de* mur-ac b4.de *Nat-c* b4a.de nat-m b4.de nit-ac b4a.de nux-m b7.de *Nux-v* b7.de* par b7a.de petr b4.de ph-ac b4a.de phos b4.de plat b4.de *Plb* b7.de* *Rhus-t* b7.de *Ruta* b7.de* sabad b7.de *Seneg* b4a.de *Sep* b4.de* spig b7.de *Spong* b7.de *Stann* b4.de* *Staph* b7.de *Sulph* b4.de* tarax b7.de *Thuj* b4.de verb b7.de*

ASCENDING high:

- **agg.**: (↗*Mountain - sickness; MIND - High places - agg.)* acon k* *Ars* lmj bry k* **Calc** b2.de* calc-p lmj carb-v lmj **Coca** k1* *Conv* **Med** lmj *Olnd* k* *Spig* k* sulph k* **Tub** lmj verat lmj

Ascending high – **agg.**: ...

- **children**; in: *Acon* lmj *Ars* lmj bry lmj calc lmj calc-p lmj carb-v lmj **Coca** lmj **Med** lmj sulph lmj **Tub** lmj verat lmj
- **amel.**: prot a syph tf tub a

ASPHYXIA (See RESPIRATION - Asphyxia)

ASPIRIN; from: (↗*Allergic - aspirin)* arn ptk1 carb-v ptk1 lach ptk1 mag-p ptk1*

ASSIMILATION of nutrition defective (See Caries - bone; Children; Development; Emaciation; Growth; Softening bones; STOMACH - Indigestion)

ATHEROMA (See Tumors - atheroma)

ATHLETIC persons: | **running**; long distance: cordyc mp4•

ATMOSPHERIC pressure; great changes in: nitro rly4• [arg-n stj2 mag-n stj2 mang-n stj2]

ATROPHY: (↗*Paralysis - Atrophy; Shrinkage; Shrinkage - Lymphatic)* alf br1 ars bg2* bar-c bg2* calc-sil c2 cetr c2 chin bg2 cupr bg2 hep bg2 *Iod* c2* kali-c bg2 kali-p c2 mez tl1 *Nat-m* c2 nux-v bg2 phos bg2 plb bg2 plb-i c2 plb-xyz c2 sabal c2 sec bg2 stann bg2

- **accompanied** by:
  - **coldness**: cina bg2 sil bg2
  - **flatulence**: lach bg2
  - **formication**: bell bg2 calc bg2 nit-ac bg2 nux-v bg2
  - **palpitations**; nervous: calc-ar bg2
  - **restlessness** (See MIND - Restlessness - atrophy)
  - **trembling**: absin bg2
  - **vertigo**: caust bg2 hyos bg2 indg bg2 lach bg2 sil bg2 visc bg2
- **wounds**; from: form ptk1
- ○ - **Circulation**; of the blood calc-act bg2 lach bg2 nat-m bg2 op bg2 sulph bg2
- **Glands**: (↗*Emaciation - glands)* anan ars k* *Aur* bar-c carb-an *Cham* k* chim kr1 chin k* **Con** k* **Iod** k* kali-ar kali-c k* **Kali-i** k* kali-p kreos lac-d *Nit-ac* k* nux-m k* ph-ac k* plb sars *Sec* k* sil k* *Staph* sul-i k2 verat k*
- **Muscles**; of: (↗*Dystrophy - muscles; Muscles; Myatrophy; EXTREMITIES - Emaciation)* arg-n sne ars bg2* ars-i bg2 brass-n-o srj5• calc ptk1 carbn-s c2* *Caust* bg2* cupr bg2* germ-met srj5• kali-i bg2 lach sne lat-h bnm5• led bg2 nux-v sne phos bg2* phys c2* pic-ac sne plb bg2* plb-i mtf11 plb-xyz c2 sec bg2 sep sne stry sne sulph sne syph jl2 thal ptk1 thal-met br1 thuj bg2* zinc bg2
  - **progressive**: crot-h ptk1 kali-p ptk1 mang ptk1 phos ptk1 phys ptk1 *Plb* br1* verat-v ptk1
  - **spinal** sclerosis; from: plb mtf33
- **Single** parts: sel bro1

ATTENTION: | **not** directing full attention to his complaint; when: *Camph* b2.de cic b2.de *Hell* b2.de

AUTOIMMUNE diseases: (↗*Aids; Collagen)* acet-ac mtf carc mtf cortiso mtf crot-h mtf cyclop mtf cyclosp mtf med mtf mur-ac mtf phos mtf stann mtf sulph mtf syph mtf tub mtf uncar-tom mtf urin mtf

AVIATOR'S DISEASE: (↗*Jet; MIND - Fear - flying - airplane; STOMACH - Nausea - airplane)* *Acon* mtf *Arg-n* mtf arn mtf ars mtf bell st1* borx st* cham mtf *Coca* st* cocc kl* gels mtf kali-m mtf petr ptk2* phos mtf psor st1

BALL internally; sensation of: (↗*Foreign; Knotted; Plug; Shot)* acon k* *Arg-n* k* arn bg2* asaf k* atri sf1.de bamb-a stb2.de• *Bell* brom bry k* calc k* *Cann-i* caust k* cham ptk1 chin ptk1 cob ptk1 coc-c coloc con k* crot-t cupr gels ptk1 graph k* **Hep** st1 **Ign** k* kali-ar bg2* kali-c k* kali-m ptk1 lac-c ptk1 *Lach* k* *Lil-t* bg2* lyc bg* mag-m k* merc-d ptk1 merc-i-r ptk1 mosch bg2* nat-m k* nat-s ptk1 nit-ac ptk1 nux-m k* *Nux-v* bg3* par k* phos ptk1 phyt k* plan ptk1 plat k* *Plb* k* *Puls* ptk1 raph rhus-t k* ruta k* sabad bg2 senec k* **Sep** k* sil k* spig staph k* stram k* sulph k* tab teucr ptk1 ust ptk1 valer k* zinc bg3*

- **hard**: nux-m ptk1
- **hot**: carb-ac ptk1 lyc ptk1 phyt ptk1 raph ptk1

BAND; sensation of (See Constriction - internally - band)

BANDAGING: | **amel.**: *Arg-n* ptk1 bry ptk1 lac-d ptk1 *Mag-m* ptk1 pic-ac ptk1 tril-p ptk1

BASEDOW'S disease (See EXTERNAL - Goitre - exophthalmic)

BATHING:

- **agg.**: *Aesc* k* aeth k* **Am-c** k* am-m k* **Ant-c** k* ant-t *Apis* sf1.de *Aran* k* ars bg2* *Ars-i* k* ars-s-f k2* *Bar-c* k* bar-s k2* *Bell* k* bell-p bro1* borx k* bov k* bry k* **Calc** k* **Calc-s** k* calc-sil k2* *Canth* k* caps k2* *Carb-v* k* *Carbn-s* *Caust* k* *Cham* k* cist k2 **Clem** k* coloc b4a.de* con k* *Crot-c* bro1 *Dulc* k* ferr bro1 *Form* bg2* *Graph* ham fd3.de• *Hep* hr1* hydrog srj2• *Ign* bg2* *Kali-c* k* kali-chl k13 kali-m k2 *Kali-n* k* kali-s kali-sil k2* kreos bro1 *Lac-d* laur k* lil-t bro1 *Lyc* k* lyss a mag-c k* *Mag-p* k* *Mang* k* *Merc* k* merc-c *Mez* k* mur-ac k* nat-c k* nat-m k* nat-p bc *Nat-s* bro1 *Nit-ac* k* nux-m k* nux-v k* ol-an bg2 *Op* bg2* *Petr* *Phos* k* phys bg2* phyt c1 psor k2* puls k* rad-br c11* **Rhus-t** k* *Rumx* *Sars* k* **Sep** k* sil k* *Spig* k* stann k* staph k* stram mtf33 *Stront-c* k* sul-ac k* **Sulph** k* thuj b4a.de* urt-u bro1 zinc k* zinc-p k2* [alumin-s stj2 am-br stj2 am-caust stj2 am-f stj2 am-s stj1 aur-s stj2 cadm-s stj2 chr-s stj2 cinnb stj2 lith-s stj2 mang-s stj2 mang-sil stj2 nicc-s stj2 stront-met stj2 titan-s stj2]
- **amel.**: *(↗MIND - Washing - desire - hands)* acon k* agar all-c ptk1 *Alum* k* *Alumn* hr1* *Am-m* k* ant-t k* *Apis* k* arg-n bg2* ars k* **Asar** k* aur k* *Bism* b7a.de *Borx* k* bros-gau mrc1 bry k* bufo k2* calc hr1* calc-s ptk1 cann-i *Caust* k* cham k* *Chel* k* *Euphr* k* *Fl-ac* k* form hell hr1* hyper bg2* kali-chl *Lac-c* lac-h htj1• laur k* **Led** k* mag-c k* mez k* mur-ac k* nat-m bg2* nauf-helv-li elm2• nept-m lsd2.fr nux-v k* phos bg2* phyt *Pic-ac* k* *Psor* k* **Puls** k* rhod k* sabad k* sep k* *Spig* k* staph k* *Stram* thlas bg2* thuj bg2 zinc k* [spect dfg1]
- **aversion** to bathing (= dread of bathing): *(↗MIND - Dirty; MIND - Hydrophobia)* aloe sne **Am-c** k* am-m k* **Ant-c** k* aq-mar jl3* bar-c k* bar-m *Bell* k* bell-p st *Borx* k* bov k* *Bry* k* *Calc* k* calc-s ptk1 calc-sil k2* *Canth* k* *Carb-v* k* carc mlr1• *Cham* k* **Clem** k* *Con* k* dulc k* glon vh *Hep* hr1* kali-c k* kali-chl k13 kali-m k2 *Kali-n* k* kali-s fd4.de kali-sil k2* *Laur* k* lyc k* lyss a mag-c k* marb-w es1• merc k* *Mez* k* mur-ac k* nat-c k* nat-p nit-ac k* nux-m k* nux-v k* phos k* phys a1* podo fd3.de• psil ft1 **Psor** k* *Puls* k* rad-br ptk1 **Rhus-t** k* sanguis-s hm2• *Sars* k* **Sep** k* sil k* **Spig** k* stann k* *Staph* k* *Stront-c* k* sul-ac k* **Sulph** k* syph jl2 tritic-vg fd5.de *Zinc* k* [gal-s stj2]
- **desire** for: nept-m lsd2.fr sacch-a fd2.de• tarent a1 zea-i br
- **dread** of (See aversion)
- **ice**-cold bathing | **desire** for: meph br1
- **lukewarm** bathing | **agg.**: acon bg2 *Ang* b2.de* phos bg2
- **sea**; bathing in the:
  - **agg.**: *(↗Weakness - sea-bath)* aq-mar vh1 *Ars* k* brom ptk1 carc vh* kali-i mrr1 lim c1* *Mag-m* k* med st *Mur-ac* mrr1 nat-m bg2 *Rhus-t* k* sep k* *Zinc* bg2*
  - **amel.**: ambr tsm1 aq-mar vh1 chir-fl gya2 *Med* st*
- **vinegar** | **amel.**: vesp bro1

○ - **Affected** part; bathing the plut-n srj7•
  - **amel.**: alum *Am-m* ant-t ars **Asar** borx bry *Caust* cham *Chel* clem a cycl a *Euphr* helo-s bnm14• laur mag-c mez mur-ac nux-v **Puls** rhod sabad sep *Spig* staph zinc
  - **ice** cold water; in | **amel.**: helo-s bnm14•
- **Face**; bathing:
  - **agg.**: fl-ac k2 plan bg2
  - **amel.**: *Asar* k* *Calc-s* k* fl-ac k2 *Lac-d* bg1* mez k* nat-m kr1 *Phos* bg1* sabad k*
- **Feet**; bathing:
  - **cold** water; in | **amel.**: led bro1* puls tl1 sec bro1
  - **hot** water; in | **amel.**: bufo br1
  - **warm** water; in | **amel.**: bufo k2 pneu jl2
- **Head**; bathing:
  - **warm** | **amel.**: Phos vh

BEARING DOWN (See ABDOMEN - Pain - dragging; FEMALE - Pain - bearing)

BELLADONNA; after abuse of: hyos bro1 op bro1

BENDING, turning:

- **affected** part:
  - **agg.**: *(↗Bent - agg.; Drawing backward; Drawing up)* acon b2.de* am-c b2.de* *Am-m* b2.de* anac b2.de* ang b2.de* *Ant-c* b2.de* ant-t b2.de* arg-met b2.de* *Arn* b2.de* asaf b2.de* aur b2.de* bar-c b2.de* *Bell* b2.de* borx b2.de* bov b2.de* *Bry* b2.de* **Calc** b2.de* camph b2.de* caps b2.de*

Bending, turning – **affected** part – **agg.**: ...
carb-an b2.de* carb-v b2.de* caust b2.de* cham b2.de* *Chel* b2.de* *Chin* b2.de* *Cic* b2.de* cina b2.de* cocc b2.de* *Coff* b2.de* con b2.de* croc b2.de* cupr b2.de* cycl b2.de* dig b2.de* dros b2.de* dulc b2.de* graph b2.de* hep b2.de* hyos b2.de* **Ign** b2.de* iod b2.de* ip b2.de* *Kali-c* b2.de* lach b2.de* laur b2.de* led b2.de* *Lyc* b2.de* m-ambo b2.de* m-arct b2.de m-aust b2.de *Mag-c* b2.de* merc b2.de* mez b2.de* mur-ac b2.de* *Nat-m* b2.de* nit-ac b2.de* *Nux-v* b2.de* olnd b2.de* par b2.de* petr b2.de* ph-ac b2.de* plat b2.de* plb b2.de* *Puls* b2.de* ran-b b2.de* rhod b2.de* *Rhus-t* b2.de* ruta b2.de* sabad b2.de* sabin b2.de* samb b2.de* *Sel* b2.de* seneg b4.de *Sep* b2.de* *Spig* b2.de* *Spong* b2.de* stann b2.de* staph b2.de* sulph b2.de* tarax b2.de* teucr b2.de* thuj b2.de* valer b2.de* verat b2.de* zinc b2.de*

  - **amel.**: *(↗Bent - amel.; Lying)* acon b2.de* am-m b2.de* anac bg2 ant-c b7a.de arg-met b2.de* arg-n bg2 **Bell** b2.de* bov bg2 bry b7a.de calc b2.de* cann-s b2.de* caust bg2 *Cham* b2.de* *Chin* b2.de* cocc tl1 colch bg2 *Coloc* bg2 guaj b2.de* hep b2.de* kali-c b2.de* lach b2.de* m-aust b2.de mag-c bg2 mag-p bg2 mang b2.de* meny b2.de* *Merc* bg2 *Merc-c* bg2 mur-ac b2.de* nux-v b2.de* petr b2.de* *Plb* bg2 *Puls* b2.de* rheum b2.de* rhus-t b2.de* *Ruta* b7a.de sabad b2.de* sabin b2.de* *Squil* b2.de* teucr b2.de* *Thuj* b2.de* verat b2.de*
- **agg.**: *Am-m* b2.de* anac jl ang b2.de* ant-t b2.de* arn b2.de* *Bell* b2.de* bov b2.de* *Bry* b2.de* calc b2.de* camph b2.de* caps b2.de* carb-an b2.de* carb-v b2.de* cham b2.de* *Chin* b2.de* *Cic* b2.de* cocc b2.de* coloc bg2 con b2.de* cycl b2.de* dros b2.de* dulc b2.de* euph b2.de* guaj b2.de* *Hep* b2.de* *Ign* b2.de* iod b2.de* ip b2.de* lach b2.de* laur b2.de* m-arct b2.de* mag-c b2.de* merc b2.de* mez b2.de* mur-ac b2.de* *Nat-m* b2.de* nit-ac b2.de* nux-v b2.de* petr b2.de* ph-ac b2.de* plat b2.de* plb b2.de* puls b2.de* ran-b b2.de* rhod b2.de* *Rhus-t* b2.de* sabad b2.de* sabin b2.de* samb b2.de* *Sel* b2.de* spig b2.de* *Spong* b2.de* *Stann* b2.de* staph b2.de* thuj b2.de* verat b2.de* visc jl zinc b2.de*
- **amel.**: cann-s b7.de meny b7.de petr b4.de
- **backward**:
  - **agg.**: *(↗Stretching - agg.)* am-c b2.de* *Anac* b2.de* ant-c b2.de* aran-ix jl asaf b2.de* atra-r jl* aur b2.de* *Bar-c* b2.de* bov b4.de *Calc* b2.de* caps b2.de* carb-v b2.de* caust b2.de* *Chel* b2.de* cina b2.de* coff b2.de* *Con* b2.de* cupr b2.de* dig b2.de* dros b2.de* dulc b2.de* *Ign* b2.de* *Kali-c* b2.de* kali-i j5.de kreos j5.de lac-c bg2 lach j5.de lith-c bg2* m-arct b2.de* m-aust b2.de* mag-c j5.de mang j5.de nat-m b2.de* nat-s j5.de *Nit-ac* b2.de* nux-v b2.de* ph-ac j5.de *Plat* b2.de* plb b2.de* *Puls* b2.de* rhod b2.de* rhus-t b2.de* ruta j5.de samb j5.de **Sep** b2.de* stann b2.de* *Sulph* b2.de* teucr b2.de* thuj b2.de* tong j5.de valer b2.de* zinc j5.de
    - **and** forward agg.: asaf b2.de* *Chel* b2.de* coff b2.de* nux-v b2.de* thuj b2.de*
  - **amel.**: *(↗Stretching - amel.)* acon b2.de* ant-c j5.de *Bell* b2.de* bism bg2* bry j5.de calen j5.de cann-s b2.de* *Cham* b2.de* chin b2.de* cimic bg2* dios sf1.de* **Dros** bg2 fl-ac bg2* hep bg2* iod jl kali-c b2.de* kreos bg2* lac-c bg2 *Lach* b2.de* m-aust b2.de* mag-m jl mand mg1.de* merc j5.de nux-v b2.de* puls b2.de* rhus-t b2.de* sabad b2.de* sabin b2.de* sep j5.de spong j5.de squil j5.de *Thuj* b2.de* verat b2.de* zinc bg2* zinc-o j5.de
    - **and** forward amel.: tril-p ptk1
  - **stretching** limbs; and:
    - **agg.**: acon ptk1 *Calc* ptk1 **Cham** ptk1 chel ptk1 cinnb ptk1 **Colch** ptk1 iod ptk1 kalm ptk1 merc-c ptk1 **Plat** ptk1 *Puls* ptk1 rad-br ptk1 *Ran-b* ptk1 **Rheum** ptk1 **Rhus-t** ptk1 *Sep* ptk1 **Staph** ptk1 *Sulph* ptk1 *Thuj* ptk1
    - **amel.**: *Alum* ptk1 **Ant-t** ptk1 arn ptk1 bell ptk1 *Calc* ptk1 cham ptk1 chel ptk1 cocc ptk1 *Dios* ptk1 fl-ac ptk1 *Guaj* ptk1 hep ptk1 hyper ptk1 *Ign* ptk1 lach ptk1 lyss ptk1 *Nux-v* ptk1 plb ptk1 *Puls* ptk1 rhus-t ptk1 sabin ptk1 sec ptk1 seneg ptk1
- **bed** agg.; turning in: *Acon* kr1 agar kr1 am-m kr1 anac kr1 *Ars* kr1 asar kr1 *Borx* kr1 **Bry** kr1 calc kr1 *Cann-s* kr1 *Caps* kr1 *Carb-v* kr1 *Caust* kr1 chin kr1 cina kr1 cocc kr1 *Con* kr1 cupr kr1 dros kr1 *Euph* kr1 *Ferr* kr1 graph kr1 *Hep* kr1 kali-c kr1 lach kr1 led kr1 *Lyc* kr1 mag-c kr1 merc kr1 *Nat-m* kr1 nit-ac kr1 *Nux-v* kr1 petr kr1 *Phos* kr1 plat kr1 plb kr1 **Puls** kr1 ran-b kr1 *Rhod* kr1 *Rhus-t* kr1 ruta kr1 *Sabad* kr1 sabin kr1 *Samb* kr1 sars kr1 *Sil* kr1 *Staph* kr1 *Sulph* kr1 thuj kr1 valer kr1
- **double**:
  - **agg.**: dios bro1

- **double**: ...
  - **amel.**: *(↗Bent - amel.; Doubling)* aloe bro1 androc srj1• arg-n sf1.de* bov sf1.de caust sf1.de chin bro1* choc srj3• colch b7.de* *Coloc* bro1* dulc fd4.de mag-c sf1.de* *Mag-p* bro1* mand jl plb sf1.de [mag-br stj1 mag-f stj1 mag-lac stj2 *Mag-met* stj2 mag-n stj2 mag-sil stj2 stann stj2]
- **forward**:
  - **agg.**: aesc st asaf b2.de* *Bell* bro1 chel b2.de* *Coff* b2.de* kalm bro1 lyss jl2 mag-m jl mang j5.de nux-v b2.de* pieri-b mlk9.de thiop jl thuj b2.de*
  - **amel.**: acon ptk1 all-s vh apis k2 *Aur* k* *Calc* ptk1 caps ptk1 caust ptk1 cham ptk1 chin ptk1 choc srj3• cimic ptk1 coloc st* gels br1* graph ptk1 *Kali-c* bro1* lil-t ptk1 lyc ptk1 mag-m ptk1 *Mag-p* ptk1 merc-c ptk1 pareir ptk1 plat ptk1 puls ptk1 *Rheum* ptk1 *Rhus-t* ptk1 sec ptk1 *Sep* ptk1 *Sulph* ptk1 *Teucr* k* thres-a sze7• thuj ptk1 tril-p c1*
- **head**:
  - **backward**:
    - **agg.**: bell b2.de* bry b2.de* caust b2.de* chin b2.de* *Cic* b2.de* cimic bg2 cupr b2.de* cycl b2.de* dig b2.de* dros b2.de* kali-c b2.de* merc bg2 *Puls* b2.de* *Sep* b2.de* spong b2.de* valer b2.de* viol-o b2.de* viol-t bg2
    - **amel.**: bell b2.de* *Cham* b2.de* *Hep* b2.de* hyper bro1 m-aust b2.de* rhus-t b2.de* seneg bro1 thuj b2.de* verat b2.de*
  - **forwards**:
    - **agg.**: viol-o b2.de*
    - **lying** | **amel.**: coloc bro1
  - **sideways**:
    - **agg.**: chin b2.de* *Spong* b2.de*
    - **amel.**: meny b2.de* puls b2.de* sep b2.de*
- **inward**:
  - **agg.**: am-m b2.de* *Ign* b2.de* staph b2.de* verat b2.de*
  - **amel.**: am-m b2.de* *Bell* b2.de*
- **outward** | **agg.**: caps b2.de* caust bg2
- **right**; to:
  - **agg.**: spig b2.de*
  - **walking** agg.: helo ptk1
- **shoulders**:
  - **backward** | **amel.**: *Calc* b2.de* cycl b2.de*
- **sideways**:
  - **agg.**: *Bell* b2.de* borx b2.de* *Calc* b2.de* canth b2.de* chel b2.de* chin b2.de* cocc b2.de* *Kali-c* b2.de* lyc b2.de* *Nat-m* b2.de* plb b2.de* stann b2.de* staph b2.de*
  - **amel.**: meny b2.de* *Puls* b2.de*

BENT; holding the part:
- **agg.**: *(↗Bending - affected - agg.)* hyos b2.de* lyc bg2 *Spong* b2.de* teucr b2.de* valer b2.de*
- **amel.**: *(↗Bending - affected - amel.; Bending - double - amel.)* bov bg2 bry bg2 *Coloc* bg2 nat-m bg2 puls b2.de* rhus-t b2.de* *Squil* b2.de* sulph bg2 verat bg2

BERIBERI: ars ptk1 *Elat* br1* lath br1* rhus-t bro1*

BESNIER-BOECK-SCHAUMANN, morbus: *(↗CHEST - Fibrosis; CHEST - Sarcoidosis)* aq-mar jl aran-ix jl asar jl beryl jl hip-ac jl hist jl kres jl lyc mrr1 mand jl parathyr jl puls mrr1 thiop jl tub-m jl2 v-a-b jl

BINDING UP, bandaging amel.: *(↗EXTREMITIES - Bandaging - amel.)* apis bg2* *Arg-n* bg2* bry b7.de* chin bg2* gels bg2* hep b4a.de kali-c b4.de *Mag-m* bg2* meny bg2 mim-p jl3 pic-ac ptk2 puls b7.de* rhod bg2* sep b4.de sil b4.de* tril-p bg2

BINDING UP HAIR: *(↗EXTREMITIES - Bandaging - amel.)*
- **amel.**: kali-n b2.de*

BITES (See Wounds - bites)

BITING:
- **teeth** together; biting (= clenching teeth):
  - **agg.**: alum b2.de* **Am-c** b2.de* anac b2.de* bell b2.de* bry b2.de* carb-an b2.de* caust b2.de* chin b2.de* coff b2.de* colch b2.de* dig b2.de* graph b2.de* *Guaj* b2.de* hell b2.de* *Hep* b2.de* *Hyos* b2.de* *Ip* b2.de* lach b2.de* mang b2.de* merc b2.de* petr b2.de* puls b2.de* *Rhus-t* b2.de* sars b2.de* *Sep* b2.de* sil b2.de* spong b2.de* staph b2.de* *Sul-ac* b2.de* sulph b2.de* *Verb* b2.de*

Biting – **teeth** together; biting: ...
  - **amel.**: ars b2.de* caust bg3 chin b2.de* cocc b2.de* coff b2.de* euph b2.de* mag-m b2.de* mur-ac bg3 ol-an bg3 *Phyt* mrr1 *Podo* bg3 *Staph* b2.de*

BLACKNESS of external parts: *(↗Inflammation - internally - gangrenous)* *Acon* k* agar k* all-c hr1* alum k* am-c k* ang b2.de* *Ant-c* k* ant-t j5.de* *Anthraci* apis *Arg-n* k* arn k* **Ars** k* ars-i asaf k* asar k* aur k* bar-c k* bell k* bism k* bit-ar wht1• both a1* brass a1* bry k* calc k* *Calc-ar* hr1* camph k* canth k* *Caps* j5.de* carb-ac bg* *Carb-an* k* *Carb-v* k* carbn-o a1 caust k* cham k* chin k* chinin-ar chr-ac hr1* chr-o c1 cic k* cina k* cocc k* com sf1.de *Con* k* *Crot-h* k* **Cupr** k* cycl k* *Dig* k* dros k* *Echi* ergot c1 euph j5.de* euph-c sf1.de *Ham* hell j5.de hyos k* ign b2.de* iod k* ip k* jasm a1 *Kali-p* hr1* *Kreos* k* kres srb2.fr *Lach* k* *Lyc* k* mag-c **Merc** k* *Merc-cy* sf1.de mur-ac j5.de nat-m k* nit-ac k* *Nux-v* k* **Op** k* *Ph-ac* k* *Phos* k* phyt k* *Plb* k* puls k* ran-a c1 ran-b j5.de* ran-s a1 rhus-t j5.de ric c1 ruta sabad k* *Sabin* j5.de *Samb* k* sars k* **Sec** k* sep k* sil k* spig k* spong k* squil k* stann staph b2.de* stram k* sul-ac j5.de* sulph j5.de* *Tarent* a1* ter hr1* thuj k* **Verat** k* *Vip* j5.de* *Vip-a* j5.de
- **cold**: ant-t **Ars** *Asaf* bell *Canth* caps *Carb-v* chin kr1 con crot-h *Euph* *Lach* merc **Plb** ran-b **Sec** sil squil sul-ac sulph tarent-c *Ter* kr1
- **diabetic**: *Ars* sf1.de* *Kreos* sf1.de* kres mg1.de* *Sec* kr1*
- **hot**: acon ars bell mur-ac *Sabin* *Sec*
- **moist**: *Carb-v* **Chin** *Hell* lach sf1.de ph-ac tarent *Vip* sf1.de
- **old** people; in: adren sf1.de all-c kr1* am-c kr1 *Ars* kr1* *Carb-v* chin kr1 con kr1 crot-h sf1.de cupr st1 echi sf1.de ergot sf1.de euph kr1 *Kreos* sf1.de **Lach** kr1* *Ph-ac* kr1 *Plb* kr1* **Sec** vip sf1.de
- **traumatic**: am-m kr1 *Arn* kr1 *Calen* kr1 *Hyper* kr1 **Lach** kr1 *Sul-ac* kr1

BLEEDING (See Hemorrhage)

BLINKING of the eyes: | **amel.**: asaf b2.de* croc b2.de* stann b2.de*

BLOND complexion (See Complexion - fair)

BLOOD CIRCULATION (See Circulation)

BLOOD PRESSURE (See Hypertension; Hypotension)

BLOOD VESSELS:
- **complaints** of: *(↗Circulation)* acon ptk1 aml-ns ptk1 apis ptk1 arn ptk1* *Bell* ptk1 bell-p br1 **Carb-v** ptk1 card-m br1 chlam-tr bcx2• ferr ptk1 *Fl-ac* ptk1 gels ptk1 glon ptk1 *Ham* ptk1 *Hyos* ptk1 influ mtf11 ins mtf11 *Lach* ptk1 lyc ptk1 nat-m ptk1 *Phos* ptk1 **Puls** ptk1 sacch br1 sang ptk1 sec ptk1* sep ptk1 sul-ac ptk1 sulph ptk1 *Thuj* ptk1 tril-p ptk1 vip ptk1 zinc ptk1 [bell-p-sp dcm1]
  - ○ **Arteries**; of: *(↗Arteriosclerosis; Inflammation - blood - arteries; Ossification - arteries; Tension - arteries)* *Cact* br1
- **constriction**: iod br1
- **degeneration** of: *(↗Arteriosclerosis)* bar-c br1 bar-m br1 vanad br1
  - **fatty** degeneration (See Fatty - blood)
- **menses**:
  - **before** | **Veins**: ferr bg2
- **spasms** of: act-sp br1 aran-ix sp1
- **swelling** (See Swelling - blood)

BLOWING THE NOSE:
- **agg.**: acon b2.de* agn b2.de* alum b2.de* am-c b2.de* ambr b2.de* ang b2.de* ant-t b2.de* arg-met b2.de* *Arn* b2.de* **Aur** b2.de* bar-c b2.de* *Bell* b2.de* bry b2.de* *Calc* b2.de* cann-s b2.de* *Canth* b2.de* caps b2.de* carb-an b2.de* carb-v b2.de* *Caust* b2.de* cham b2.de* chel b2.de* chin b2.de* cina b2.de* coff b2.de* *Colch* b2.de* con b2.de* dig b2.de* euph b2.de* euphr b2.de* graph ptk1 **Hep** b2.de* hyos b2.de* iod b2.de* kali-bi ptk1 *Kali-c* b2.de* kali-n b2.de* kreos b2.de* lach ptk1 led b2.de* lyc b2.de* mag-c b2.de* mag-m b2.de* mang b2.de* meny b2.de* **Merc** b2.de* mez b2.de* nat-m b2.de* nit-ac b2.de* *Nux-v* b2.de* par b2.de* *Ph-ac* b2.de* phos b2.de* **Puls** b2.de* *Ran-b* b2.de* sabin b2.de* sars b2.de* sel b2.de* *Sep* b2.de* sil b2.de* **Spig** b2.de* spong b2.de* stann b2.de* *Staph* b2.de* stram b2.de* stront-c b2.de* *Sulph* b2.de* tarax b2.de* teucr b2.de* thuj b2.de* verat b2.de* zinc ptk1
- **amel.**: *Mang* b2.de* merc b2.de* *Sil* b2.de* stann b2.de*

BLOWS (See Injuries)

BOILING sensation: am-m br1* led ptk1 ust ptk1

○ - **Side** lain on: mag-m ptk1*

BORING with fingers in ear and nose: *(↗EAR - Boring; NOSE - Boring)*
- **agg.**: chel b7.de chin b7.de ruta b7.de

- **amel.**: *(↗EAR - Boring; NOSE - Boring)* arum-t ptk1 bell b2.de* *Chel* b2.de* lach b2.de* **Nat-c** b2.de* par b2.de* *Phos* b2.de* rheum b2.de* rhus-t b2.de* *Spig* b2.de* sulph b2.de* *Thuj* b2.de* zinc b2.de*

BORRELIOSIS (See Lyme)

BREAKFAST:

- **after**:
  - **agg.**: *Agar Am-m* k* ambr k* anac k* ars k* bell k* borx k* *Bry* k* *Calc* k* calc-sil k2* carb-an k* carb-v k* carbn-s *Caust* k* **Cham** k* chin k* chir-fl gya2 *Con* k* cycl k* *Dig* k* euph k* ferr form *Graph* k* grat bg2 *Guaj* bg2 hell k* ign k* iris bg2 *Kali-c* k* *Kali-n* k* laur k* lyc k* mag-c k* mang k* *Nat-c* k* *Nat-m* k* *Nat-s* ptk1 nit-ac k* nux-m k* **Nux-v** k* par k* petr k* ph-ac k* **Phos** k* plb k* puls k* rhod k* rhus-t k* sars k* *Sep* k* sil k* stront-c k* *Sulph* k* *Thuj* k* tritic-vg fd5.de valer k* verat k* **Zinc** k* zinc-p k2*
  - **amel.**: acon b2.de* alum b2.de* am-c b2.de* *Am-m* b2.de* *Ambr* b2.de* anac b2.de* ars b2.de* *Bar-c* b2.de* *Bov* b2.de* bry b2.de* *Calc* k* *Cann-s* b2.de* canth b2.de* *Carb-an* b2.de* carb-v b2.de* caust b2.de* *Chel* b2.de* chin b2.de* cina b2.de* *Croc* k* ferr k* graph b2.de* hell b2.de* *Hep* b2.de* *Ign* b2.de* *Iod* k* kali-c b2.de* *Lach* b2.de* *Laur* b2.de* *Lyc* b2.de* mag-c b2.de* mag-m b2.de* merc b2.de* *Mez* b2.de* myric ptk1 nat-c b2.de* nat-m nat-p k2* nat-s bg2* nit-ac b2.de* *Nux-v* b2.de* *Petr* b2.de* phos b2.de* *Plat* b2.de* *Plb* b2.de* *Ptel* vml3• puls b2.de* *Ran-b* b2.de* ran-s b2.de* rhod b2.de* *Rhus-t* b2.de* *Sabad* b2.de* sacch sst1• sacch-a fd2.de• *Sep* b2.de* *Spig* b2.de* *Squil* hr1* *Staph* k* *Stront-c* b2.de* *Sulph* b2.de* *Tarax* b2.de* teucr b2.de* valer k* verat b2.de* *Verb* b2.de* zinc-p k2
- **before** | **agg.**: alumn kr1 croc br1*

BREATHING:

- **agg.**: *Acon* b2.de* agar b2.de* alum b2.de* am-c b2.de* *Am-m* b2.de* *Anac* b2.de* ant-c b2.de* arg-met b2.de* arn b2.de* ars b2.de* asaf b2.de* asar b2.de* aur b2.de* *Bell* b2.de* bism b2.de* borx b2.de* bov b2.de* **Bry** b2.de* *Calc* b2.de* *Cann-s* b2.de* *Caps* b2.de* cham b2.de* chin b2.de* *Cina* b2.de* clem b2.de* cocc b2.de* **Colch** b2.de* coloc b2.de* con b2.de* croc b2.de* cupr b2.de* dig b2.de* dros b2.de* dulc b2.de* euphr b2.de* graph b2.de* *Hep* b2.de* hyos b2.de* *Kali-c* b2.de* kali-n b2.de* led b2.de* lyc b2.de* m-ambo b2.de* *Mag-c* b2.de* merc b2.de* mez b2.de* *Mur-ac* b2.de* nat-c b2.de* *Nat-m* b2.de* *Nit-ac* b2.de* nux-v b2.de* ph-ac b2.de* plat b2.de* *Puls* b2.de* ran-b b2.de* rhod b2.de* *Rhus-t* b2.de* *Sabad* b2.de* sars b2.de* *Sel* b2.de* seneg b2.de* **Sep** b2.de* sil b2.de* **Spig** b2.de* squil b2.de* stann b2.de* sul-ac b2.de* *Sulph* b2.de* thuj b2.de* verat b2.de*
- **amel.**: asaf b7.de cina b7.de tarax b7.de
- **Cheyne**-Stokes respiration (See Cheyne-stokes)
- **deep**:
  - **agg.**: **Acon** b2.de* *Agn* b2.de* am-m b2.de* arg-met b2.de* *Arn* b2.de* asaf b2.de* asc-t ptk1 *Bell* bg2 *Borx* b2.de* both-a rb3 brom bg2 **Bry** b2.de* calad b2.de* calc b2.de* *Canth* b2.de* caps b2.de* carb-an b2.de* caust b2.de* cina b2.de* dros b2.de* dulc b2.de* fl-ac bg2 *Graph* b2.de* *Hell* b2.de* hep b2.de* hist jl hyos b7a.de* ign b2.de* ip b2.de* *Kali-c* b2.de* *Kali-n* b2.de* kreos b2.de* lach b7a.de* *Lyc* b2.de* mag-m b2.de* mang b2.de* *Merc* b2.de* merc-c bg2 mosch b2.de* nat-c b2.de* nat-m b2.de* nux-m b2.de* nux-v b2.de* *Olnd* b2.de* *Phos* bg2* plb b2.de* puls b2.de* ran-b ptk1 *Ran-s* b2.de* rheum b2.de* **Rhus-t** b2.de* rumx ptk1 *Sabad* b2.de* **Sabin** b2.de* sang ptk1 seneg b2.de* sep b2.de* *Sil* b2.de* spig b2.de* spong b2.de* *Squil* b2.de* stram b7a.de* *Sulph* b4a.de* thuj b2.de* valer b2.de* verb b2.de*
  - **amel.**: *(↗MIND - Delusions - complaints)* acon k* agar bg2 agath-a nl2• asaf k* bar-c k* *Cann-i* cann-xyz ptk1 chin k* chir-fl gya2 *Colch* k* *Cupr* k* dig k* dros k* ign k* iod k* *Lach* k* meny k* mygal bg2 nat-m bg2* olnd k* osm k* ox-ac ptk1 puls k* *Seneg* k* sep k* *Spig* k* **Stann** k* staph k* sulph bg2 ter thuj b4.de verb bg2* viol-t k* [ind stj2]
  - **desire** to breath deeply: acet-ac achy jl acon alum alumn am-br aml-ns sf1.de ant-c sf1.de *Aur* bapt *Borx* brom **Bry Cact Calc** *Calc-p* camph sf1.de cann-i sf1.de *Caps* k* *Carb-ac Carb-v Card-m Caust* cedr *Chin* chir-fl gya2 cimx coca croc **Crot-t** k1* *Cupr* sf1.de *Dig* euon eup-per *Glon* hydr ictod **Ign** *Ind Ip* sf1.de *Kali-c Kali-n* sf1.de *Kreos* **Lach** *Lact* lil-t *Lob* sf1.de *Lyc* med kr1 *Merc* mez mosch **Nat-s** nux-m *Op* sf1.de ozone sde2• *Par Phos* podo prun ran-b samb *Sang* **Sel** *Seneg* sep sil sf1.de stann stram **Sulph** ther tub k2 verb xan
- **holding** the breath: *(↗not)* dros b2.de *Kali-n* b2.de led b2.de meny b2.de merc b2.de *Spig* b2.de

- **Breathing – holding** the breath: ...
  - **agg.**: *(↗Not)* cact ptk1 dros b7.de* *Kali-n* b4a.de* led b7.de* meny b7.de* merc b4a.de* *Spig* b7.de*
  - **amel.**: *Bell* b2.de*
- **irregular** breathing agg.: cact ptk1 rumx ptk1
- **not** breathing; when: *(↗holding; holding - agg.)* asaf b2.de* cina b2.de* *Ign* b2.de* *Merc* b2.de* spig b2.de* tarax b2.de*

BRIGHT colors: | **amel.**: *Stram* bro1 tarent bro1

BRIGHT'S DISEASE (See KIDNEYS - Inflammation)

BRITTLE BONES: *(↗Bones; Caries - bone; Injuries - bones; Osteoporosis; Softening; Softening bones)* *Asaf* bg2* bufo bg2* *Calc* k* calc-f ptk1 calc-p ptk1 carc a* chel ptk1 cupr ptk1 fl-ac ptk1 *Lac-ac* hr1 **Lyc** bg2* **Merc** bg2* par ptk1 *Ph-ac* bg2* phos br1 rad-br ptk1 ruta ptk1 **Sil** bg2* **Sulph** bg2* *Symph* k* syph jl2 thuj bg2* thyr br

BROMIDES, abuse of: *(↗Convulsions - bromides)* am-c kr1 camph kr1* cham bg2* helon bro1* kali-br br1* lach bg2* mag-c kr1 nux-v bro1* op kr1 phos bg2* zinc bro1* zinc-p bg2*

BROWN-SÉGUARD syndrome: *(↗Paralysis - accompanied - skin - sensitiveness; Paralysis - injuries; Paralysis - one; BACK - Injuries - spine)* am-br mtf atro-s mtf *Bell* btw1* cocc mtf ergot hl1* kali-br mtf nux-v mtf *Sec* mtf stry mtf

BRUCELLOSIS: bapt bro1 brucel jl2* bry bro1 *Colch* bro1 malar jl2 merc bro1 merc-k-i gm1 rhus-t bro1 tub jl2

- **chronic**: botul jl2

BRUISED (See Pain - sore)

BRUISES (See Injuries)

BRUNET (See Complexion - dark)

BRUNETTE (See Complexion - dark)

BRUSHING TEETH (= cleaning teeth):

- **agg.**: carb-v b2.de* coc-c bg2* lyc b2.de* ruta b2.de* *Staph* b2.de*

BUBBLING: *(↗Welling)* *Acon* bg2 agar b2.de* **Aloe** bg2 alum b2.de* am-c b2.de* ambr k* anac b2.de* ang b2.de* ant-c k* ant-t b2.de* arn b2.de* ars b2.de* asaf k* asar b2.de* bar-c b2.de* bell k* berb k* bov b2.de* bry b2.de* calc b2.de* caps a1 carb-an b2.de* carb-v b2.de* cham b2.de* chel b2.de* chin b2.de* cina b2.de* cocc b2.de* colch k* croc b2.de* *Crot-t* bg2 dig b2.de* *Gamb* bg2 graph b2.de* hell b2.de* ip *Jatr-c* bg2 junc-e br1* kali-c b2.de* kreos b2.de* lyc k* m-arct b2.de m-aust b2.de* mag-c b2.de* mag-m b2.de* mang b2.de* meny b2.de* merc b2.de* nat-m b2.de *Nat-s* bg2 nux-v k* olnd b2.de* par b2.de* petr b2.de* ph-ac b2.de* phos b2.de* pip-n bg2 plat b2.de* plb b2.de* plut-n srj7• *Puls* k* *Rheum* k* rhus-t b2.de* ruta b2.de* sabin b2.de* sars b2.de* sep b2.de* sil b2.de* spig k* spong b2.de* squil k* stann b2.de* staph b2.de* stront-c b2.de* sul-ac b2.de* sulph b2.de* tarax k* teucr b2.de* urol-h rwt• valer b2.de* verb b2.de* viol-t b2.de* zinc b2.de*

○ - **Blood** vessels: aur bg2

BUBONIC plague (See Pest - bubonic)

BULBAR paralysis (See HEAD - Paralysis - medulla)

BURNING (See Heat; Pain - burning)

BURNS: *(↗MOUTH - Burns)* acet-ac hr1* *Acon* j5.de* agar k* aloe mg1.de alum k* alumn hr1* ant-c k* arist-cl mg1.de* arn hr1* **Ars** k* *Bar-c* j5.de *Bell* j5.de *Bry* j5.de calc k* calc-p hr1* calc-s hr1* *Calen* hr1* camph bro1* **Canth** k* caps tl1 carb-ac k* *Carb-v* k* *Carbn-s* kr1* *Caust* k* chin j5.de cic hr1* clem b4a.de cortiso sp1 crot-h hr1* cycl k* des-ac jl3 dulc fd4.de echi sf1.de euph k* ferr j5.de gaul bro1* germ-met srj5• grin br1* *Ham* hr1* hed sp1 *Hep* hr1* hoit jl3 hyos j5.de* *Hyper* hr1* *Ign* j5.de ignis-alc es2• iris tl1 jab c1* *Kali-bi* c1* kali-c j5.de kali-chl hr1* kali-m kr1* *Kreos* k* lac-lup hrn2• lach k* mag-c k* *Mag-m* j5.de *Merc* j5.de* mez tl1 mom-b mtf11 *Nat-c* j5.de* *Nux-v* j5.de op j5.de par j5.de passi c1* petr hr1* phos j5.de* pic-ac c1* *Plan* hr1* plat j5.de plb k* positr nl2• *Puls* j5.de* rad-br c1* ran-b st1 *Rhus-t* k* ruta k* sabad j5.de *Sec* k* sep j5.de *Sil* hr1* spira c1* spong fd4.de *Stram* k* *Sul-ac* j5.de *Ter* hr1* thuj j5.de tritic-vg fd5.de *Urt-u* j5.de* vanil fd5.de verat j5.de zinc-o mtf11 [euph-sp dbx1.fr vauc-s dbx1.fr]

- **ailments** from burns (See Convalescence - burns)
- **cicatrices**: caust tl1
- **gangrenous**: anthraci ptk1 ars ptk1 caust ptk1* sec ptk1
- **granulations**; unhealthy: petr ptk1 plan ptk1

- **healing** slowly: carb-ac bro1* *Caust* bro1* x-ray br1
- **painless**: lac-h sze9• pic-ac tl1
- **radium**, from: phos ptk1 rad-br c11
- **superficial** burns: urt-u tl1
- **suppurating**: calc-s ptk1*
- **vapor**; from hot: kali-bi ptk1
- **warm** applications | **amel.**: ars tl1 led tl1
- **x-ray**; from: *Cadm-i* sne calc-f st* fl-ac sne phos st* rad-br a* sil sne x-ray st*

BURROWING, DIGGING (See Pain - digging)

BURSAE (See Inflammation - bursae)

BUSINESS, work, occupation; complaints from: arn bg2 caust bg2 gels bg2 mag-p bg2 nux-v bg2 pic-ac bg2 sil bg2 zinc bg2

BUZZING: bit-ar wht1•

CACHEXIA: (↗*Cancerous - cachectic; Emaciation*) acet-ac kr1* arg-met kr1* arg-n a1* arn kr1* **Ars** k* ars-i kr1* bad hr1* bond a1* calc kr1* caps hr1* carb-ac a1* chim k* chin j5.de* clem k* *Coc-c* hr1* cund hr1* fl-ac kr1* *Form* hr1* hippoz br1 hydr kr1* *Iod* k* irid-met br1 *Kali-bi* k* lath br1 mang kr1* merc a1* merc-n a1 merc-ns a1* morph a1* mur-ac a1* nat-m k* **Nit-ac** k* phos kr1* phyt kr1* pic-ac kr1* plb a1* sacch br1 sec kr1* seneg hr1* suis-chord-umb mtf11 thal kr1* thuj kr1* uran-met sf1.de vanad br1 vip a1* x-ray kr1*

- **accompanied** by cough: nux-v bg2 *Phos* bg2 puls bg2 stann bg2
- **cancer**; from: alum bg2 ars bg2 bar-c bg2 calc bg2 carb-v bg2 carc br1 caust bg2 con bg2 cory br1 cund bg2 graph bg2 hydr bg2 iod bg2 kali-chl bg2 kali-i bg2 *Kreos* bg2 lyc bg2 nit-ac bg2 phyt bg2 rad-br bg2 sil bg2 sulph bg2 thuj bg2*
- **dentition**; during: *Kreos* bro1 nux-v bro1 op bro1
- **fever** | **intermittent**: am-m bro1 aran bro1 arn bro1 *Ars* bro1 ars-i bro1 *Calc-ar* bro1 carb-v bro1 cean bro1 chelo bro1 *Chinin-ar* bro1 eucal bro1 eup-per br1* ferr bro1 *Hydr* bro1 *Ip* bro1 *Lach* bro1 maland bro1 malar bro1 *Nat-m* bro1 nit-ac br1 *Polym* bro1 puls bro1 sulph bro1 verat bro1
- **malaria**; from: ars br1
- **radium** treatments; after: phos gm1
- **syphilis**; from: *Ars* bro1 *Aur* bro1 calo bro1 carb-an bro1 carb-v bro1 ferr-i bro1 ferr-lac bro1 *Iod* bro1 merc bro1 nit-ac br1 sars bro1
- **tuberculosis**; from: all-s bro1 ars bro1 *Ars-i* bro1 calc-p bro1 erio br1* ferr-p br1 hippoz br1 *Iod* bro1 kreos mtf11 lec br1 myos-s bro1 nit-ac br1 phos bro1 sil bro1 silpho bro1 *Tub* bro1

CAGED in wires, twisted tighter and tighter (See Constriction - external - caged)

CAMPHOR; from: canth bro1 carb-v gm1 coff bro1 *Kali-n* b4a.de op bro1

- **odor** of camphor agg.: kali-n bg2*

CANCEROUS affections: (↗*Hodgkin's; Leukemia; Malignant; Tumors*) **Abrot** sne acet-ac k* alum alumn k* *Ambr* anan c1* anil c1 *Ant-m* bro1 *Apis* k* apoc st1 arg-met k2 arg-n mg1.de **Ars** k* ars-br br1* *Ars-i* k* *Aster* k* *Aur* k* aur-ar c1* aur-i k2* *Aur-m* k* aur-m-n c2* aur-s k2* *Bapt* c1* bar-c k2* bar-i c1* bell hr1* bell-p ptk1 bism k* **Brom** k* *Bry* c1* *Bufo* k* cadm-ar sne *Cadm-s* *Calc* k* *Calc-i* c1* calc-ox c1* *Calc-p* sne *Calc-s* *Calen* hr1* calth c1 *Carb-ac* k* **Carb-an** k* *Carb-v* k* *Carbn-s* k* carc br1* caust k* *Cham* sne chel c1* chlam-tr bcx2• cholin bro1 *Cic* c1* cinnm c1* *Cist* k* *Cit-ac* hr1* cit-l c1 clem k* **Con** k* cory br1* crot-h c1 *Cund* hr1* cupr k* cupr-act bro1 cur c1 dulc elaps c1 eos br1* epiph c1 eucal st1 euph c1* euph-he c1 ferr-i c1 ferr-p hr1* ferr-pic st1 form br1* form-ac bro1 formal br1 fuli br1* *Gaert* sne *Gali* c1* gent-l st1 germ-met stj2*• *Graph* k* gua br1* guaj st *Ham* c1* hell mrr1 hep k* *Hippoz* hr1* *Hydr* k* hydrin-m c1 *Iod* c1* *Jug-c* sne *Kali-ar* k* *Kali-bi* *Kali-cy* hr1* *Kali-i* c1* *Kali-p* br1* *Kali-s* k* *Kreos* k* kres mg1.de *Lach* k* *Lap-a* k* lob-e c1 **Lyc** k* maland br1* matth c1 med bro1* *Merc* k* merc-c gm1 *Merc-i-f* merc-k-i gm1 methyl c1 *Mill* hr1* *Morph* hr1* morph-act yl1 myric sne nat-cac ptk2 nat-m k* nat-s mrr1 nectrin c1* **Nit-ac** k* nux-m sne *Ol-an* c1 *Op* c1 orni c1 oxyg c1 parathyr jl2 petr ptk1 ph-ac k* **Phos** k* **Phyt** k* pic-ac c1 plat mrr1 pneu jl2 psor c1* rad-br bro1* ran-b k2 rumx-act bro1 *Sang* c1* sarcol-ac mg1.de *Scir* c1* *Sec* ptk1 sed-r bro1 *Semp* br1* sep k* sieg mg1.de **Sil** k* silphu c1 sol c1 squil j5.de *Strych-g* br1 sul-ac *Sulph* k* symph bg* syph k2* tarax jl3* tax bro1 *Ter* hr1* thiosin gm1 *Thuj* k* toxo-g jl2 trif-p c1* tub mrr1 uncar-tom mp4• viol-o c1 visc mg1.de* *X-ray* jl* zinc [bar-met stj2 cupr-f stj2 ferr-f stj2 hafn-met stj2 lanth-met stj2 nicc-met stj2 polon-met stj2 scand-met stj2 yttr-met stj2]

- **accompanied** by:

○ • **Liver**; complaints of: scir rmk1•

Cancerous affections – **accompanied** by: ...

• **Mouth**; offensive odor of (See MOUTH - Odor - offensive - accompanied - cancer)

- **advanced** stage: alum-sil gm1 anan gm1 ant-ar gm1 ant-i gm1 arg-met gm1 bell-p gm1 benzq gm1 cadm-act gm1 cadm-ar gm1 cadm-br gm1 cadm-chl gm1 cadm-chr gm1 cadm-f gm1 cadm-gl gm1 cadm-i gm1 cadm-m gm1 cadm-met gm1 cadm-n gm1 cadm-o gm1 cadm-s gm1 cadm-sel gm1 calc-f gm1 con gm1 hydr gm1 kali-tcy gm1 lap-a gm1 oxyg gm1 phos gm1 phyt gm1 scir gm1 scroph-n gm1 symph gm1
- **angioma** (See Tumors - angioma)
- **beginning** stage: parathyr jl2 toxo-g jl2
- **cachectic** emaciation; with: (↗*Cachexia; Emaciation - cancerous*) acon st carb-an sne carc gk6 *Card-m* sne *Hydr* kr1* pic-ac c1* thuj k2
  - • **pronounced**: cory br1
- **cicatrices**, in old: (↗*SKIN - Cicatrices*) graph k2* sil bg2
- **colloid** cancer: (↗*Tumors - colloid*) (non:carb-ac hr1) carb-an gcj1* hydr hr1 *Lach* hr1* lob-e ktp6• *Phos* hr1*
- **contusions**, after: arn sne bell-p sne *Con* hr1* ruta sne
- **encephaloma** (See Tumors - encephaloma)
- **endotheliosarcoma** (See sarcoma - kaposi)
- **epithelioma**: (↗*Tumors - papillomata*) abr c1* acet-ac k* alum k2* alumn hr1* ant-m gm1 arg-met arg-n k* *Ars* k* **Ars-i** k* ars-s-f k2* ars-s-r gm1 aur k* aur-ar k2 *Bell* k* brom k* bufo gm1 cadm-met gm1 calc calc-p k* calc-sil k2* carb-ac sf1.de carb-an hr1* carc mlr1• cic c1* clem k* **Con** k* *Cund* hr1* epiph gm1 euph bro1 ferr-pic bro1 formal gm1 fuli br1* hippoz gm1 *Hydr* k* *Hydrc* sf1.de kali-ar c1* kali-bi gm1 kali-chl hr1* kali-m sf1.de *Kali-s* k* kali-tcy gm1 *Kreos* k* lach k2 *Lap-a* hr1* lob bro1 **Lyc** k* mag-m jl3 mag-s c1* merc k* merc-c hr1* methyl c1* nat-cac bro1 nat-m hr1* nectrin c1* nit-ac hr1* phos k* *Phyt* k* puls hr1* rad-br c11 rad-met bro1 raja-s jl3 *Ran-b* ran-s ptk1 scroph-n bro1 sep k* *Sil* k* sol gm1 *Strych-g* bro1 sulph k* thuj k* uran-n kr1 x-ray gm1
  - • **accompanied** by:
    - ⁝ **Tongue**:
      - ⁝ **indented** tongue: *Kali-m* kr1*
      - ⁝ **purple** discoloration of the tongue: *Kali-m* kr1*
  - • **flat**: cund ptk1
- **fungus** haematodes (See SKIN - Excrescences - fungus haematodes)
- **hemangioma** (See Tumors - angioma)
- **Hodgkin's** disease (See Hodgkin's)
- **irritability**: alum tl1
- **lupus**; carcinomatous: (↗*FACE - Cancer - lupus; SKIN - Lupus*) agar alum alumn k* ant-c arg-n **Ars** k* *Ars-i* ars-s-f k2 aur-ar gm1 aur-m *Bar-c* calc k* calc-sil k2 *Carb-ac* *Carb-v* *Carbn-s* caust *Cist* con k2 graph k* hep hippoz gm1 *Hydrc* kali-ar *Kali-bi* k* kali-c *Kali-chl* kali-s *Kreos* lach **Lyc** k* merc ptk1 nat-m ptk1 *Nit-ac* *Phyt* *Psor* rhus-t ptk1 sep k* *Sil* k* sol gm1 spong staph k* sulph k* thiosin gm1 **Thuj** titan br
  - • **rings**; in: *Sep*
- **lymphoma**: (↗*Hodgkin's*) ars ptk1* ars-i ptk1* aur-m mtf *Bar-c* mtf bar-i mtf calc sne *Calc-f* mtf carb-an mrr1* carc mtf cist mtf con mrr1* *Iod* mtf kali-m mtf mur-ac mtf nat-m mtf ph-ac mtf phos mtf phyt mtf rad-br ptk1 saroth mtf scroph-n sne* sec ptk1 sil sne syph mtf *Thuj* mtf tub mrr1
- **melanoma**: (↗*SKIN - Cancer - melanoma*) *Arg-n* ars-br rmk1• brom sne bry sne *Calc* sne carc mlr1• card-m hydr sne hyos sne *Lach* k* merc-c sne ph-ac plb sne sil sne
  - • **sunlight** agg.; from: carc mlr1•
- **myeloma**: *Hecla* rmk1•
  - • **multiple**: aur mtf calc-f mtf lach mtf nit-ac mtf phos mtf syph mtf
- **offensive** smell (See Odor of - offensive - cancerous)
- **osteosarcoma** (See EXTREMITIES - Cancer - bones - osteosarcoma)
- **pains** of; to relief (See Pain - cancerous)
- **sadness**; with (See MIND - Sadness - cancer)
- **sarcoma**: (↗*Tumors - fibrosarcoma; Tumors - rhabdomyosarcoma*) agar mtf ars ptk1 *Aur* mtf bar-c k* cadm-met mtf calc mtf calc-f carb-ac k* carb-an ptk1* carb-v mtf *Crot-h* hr1* cupr-s st1 *Euph* mtf graph hr1* *Hecla* kr1* hydr mtf *Kali-chl* hr1 *Kali-m* kr1 *Lach* ptk1* *Lap-a* hr1* nat-act sne nat-cac sne nat-m sne *Nit-ac* mtf ph-ac mtf *Phos* ptk1* rad-br mtf sil ptk1* *Symph* ptk1* **Thuj** ptk1* visc mtf x-ray mtf
  - • **accompanied** by | **pain**; burning: bar-c ptk1

- **sarcoma**: ...
  - • **inoperable**: cupr-s$_{mtf11}$
  - • **Kaposi** sarcoma (= Ewing's sarcoma; Ewing's tumor): aur$_{mtf}$ calc-f$_{mtf}$ fl-ac$_{mtf}$ med$_{mtf}$ nit-ac$_{mtf}$ syph$_{mtf}$ thuj$_{mtf}$
  - • **spindle**-cell: carc$_{mtf}$ syph$_{mtf}$
  - ○ • **Bones** (See EXTREMITIES - Cancer - bones - osteosarcoma)
  - • **Tibia** (See EXTREMITIES - Cancer - bones - tibia - osteosarcoma)
- **scirrhus**: alumn$_{k*}$ *Anac*$_{hr1*}$ apis$_{tl1}$ arg-met arn$_{hr1*}$ *Ars* ars-s-f$_{k2*}$ *Aster*$_{k*}$ *Bell*$_{k*}$ bell-p$_{bg*}$ borx$_{hr1}$ *Calc-s* calen$_{hr1*}$ **Carb-an**$_{k*}$ *Carb-v*$_{k*}$ *Carbn-s* clem$_{k1*}$ **Con**$_{k*}$ cund$_{hr1*}$ ferr-i$_{hr1}$ *Graph* *Hydr*$_{k*}$ *Lap-a*$_{k*}$ nux-v$_{hr1*}$ petr$_{ptk1}$ *Phos* *Phyt*$_{k*}$ sep$_{k*}$ **Sil**$_{k*}$ squil$_{h1}$ staph$_{k*}$ *Sulph*$_{k*}$
  - • **painful**: apis$_{tl1}$ con$_{tl1}$
- **smell**; offensive (See Odor of - offensive - cancerous)
- **smoking**; from: con$_{ptk1}$
- **stage**; advanced (See advanced)
- **surgery**; after: carc$_{mlr1}$•
- **syphilitic**: kali-i$_{gm1}$
- **tubercular** base; on: kali-i$_{gm1}$
- **ulceration**; before: hydr$_{br1}$ lap-a$_{br1}$
- **ulcers**: aur$_{ptk1}$ trif-p$_{hl1*}$
  - • **painful**: raja-s$_{mtf11}$
  - ○ • **Glands**: arn$_{k*}$ **Ars**$_{k*}$ ars-i$_{k2*}$ aur$_{k*}$ *Bell*$_{k*}$ **Bufo** calc$_{k*}$ carb-an$_{k*}$ carb-v$_{k*}$ caust$_{k*}$ clem$_{k*}$ **Con**$_{k*}$ cupr$_{k*}$ dulc$_{k*}$ *Hep*$_{k*}$ kali-ar$_{k2}$ kali-c$_{k*}$ *Kreos*$_{k*}$ lyc$_{k*}$ merc$_{k*}$ merc-i-f nit-ac$_{k*}$ ph-ac$_{k*}$ phos$_{k*}$ rhus-t$_{k*}$ *Sep*$_{k*}$ *Sil*$_{k*}$ squil$_{b2.de*}$ sul-ac$_{k*}$ **Sulph**$_{k*}$ zinc$_{k*}$
  - • **Skin**, of (See SKIN - Ulcers - cancerous)

▽ - **extending** to:
  - ○ • **Bones**; metastasis in: *Con*$_{rmk1}$• *Hecla*$_{rmk1}$• *Symph*$_{rmk1}$•
  - • **Lungs**; metastasis in: *Lyc*$_{rmk1}$•

○ - **Blood** vessels: bell-p$_{gm1}$
- **Bones**, of: asaf$_{gm1}$ aur$_{sne}$ aur-ar$_{gm1}$ aur-i$_{bro1}$ aur-m-n$_{gm1}$ *Bry*$_{sne}$ cadm-calc-f$_{gm1}$ cadm-met$_{gm1}$ calc-f$_{sne*}$ calc-p$_{sne}$ calc-sil$_{sne}$ carc$_{sne}$ con$_{hr1*}$ euph$_{gm1}$ euph-re$_{mtf}$ **Hecla**$_{c1*}$ hippoz$_{gm1}$ lap-a$_{gm1}$ merc-k-i$_{gm1}$ methyl$_{gm1}$ *Phos*$_{c1*}$ *Rhus-t*$_{sne}$ ruta$_{sne}$ sil$_{sne}$ stront-c$_{gm1}$ **Symph**$_{c1*}$ syph$_{al}$ toxi$_{gm1}$
  - ○ • **Periosteum**: *Symph*$_{rmk1}$•
- **Glands**: arg-met$_{gm1}$ ars-br$_{br1}$ aur-ar$_{gm1}$ *Aur-m*$_{k*}$ aur-m-n$_{gm1}$ **Bar-c**$_{rmk1}$• **Bar-i**$_{rmk1}$• brom$_{gm1}$ buni-o$_{jl3}$ **Carb-an**$_{k*}$ *Carc*$_{mlr1}$• cist$_{gm1}$ **Con**$_{k*}$ ferr-i$_{gm1}$ hippoz$_{gm1}$ iod$_{gm1}$ lap-a$_{hr1*}$ merc-k-i$_{gm1}$ myris$_{gm1}$ nat-sil-f$_{nta1}$ sars$_{gm1}$ scroph-n$_{mtf11}$ semp$_{mtf11}$ sieg$_{mg1.de}$ sil$_{gm1}$ strych-g$_{br1*}$ sul-i$_{k2}$ syph$_{st1}$ thiosin$_{gm1}$ toxo-g$_{jl2}$ v-a-b$_{jl2}$ [bar-m$_{stj1}$ bar-p$_{stj1}$ bar-s$_{stj1}$]
  - • **children**; in: med$_{jl2}$

CANTHARIS: | **agg.**: apis$_{bg2*}$ *Camph*$_{bg2*}$

CAP (See Compression)

CAPILLARIES (See CHEST - Capillary)

CAR EXHAUST (See Smoke)

CARIES:

○ - **Bone**, of: (↗*Bones; Brittle; Necrosis - bone; Softening; Softening bones; Spongy - bones)* **Ang**$_{k*}$ *Anthraco*$_{kr1}$ *Arg-met*$_{kr1*}$ *Arn*$_{hr1*}$ *Ars*$_{k*}$ **Asaf**$_{k*}$ *Aur*$_{k*}$ aur-ar$_{k2}$ aur-i$_{k2*}$ *Aur-m*$_{k*}$ *Aur-m-n*$_{k*}$ bell$_{k*}$ both$_{a1}$ bry$_{k*}$ *Calc*$_{k*}$ *Calc-f*$_{k*}$ *Calc-p*$_{k*}$ calc-s calc-sil$_{k2*}$ caps$_{k*}$ carb-ac$_{k*}$ caust$_{hr1*}$ chin$_{k*}$ cinnm$_{hr1*}$ *Cist* clem$_{k*}$ colch$_{gk}$ con$_{k*}$ *Cupr*$_{k*}$ dulc$_{k*}$ euph$_{k*}$ ferr$_{k*}$ **Fl-ac**$_{k*}$ graph$_{k*}$ *Guaj*$_{k*}$ *Guare*$_{k*}$ hecla$_{br1*}$ *Hep*$_{k*}$ *Iod*$_{k*}$ kali-bi *Kali-c*$_{bg2}$ **Kali-i**$_{k*}$ kreos$_{k*}$ lach$_{k*}$ **Lyc**$_{k*}$ mang$_{k2*}$ **Merc**$_{k*}$ *Mez*$_{k*}$ nat-c$_{mrr1}$ nat-m$_{k*}$ nat-sil$_{br1}$ *Nit-ac*$_{k*}$ *Ol-j*$_{hr1*}$ op$_{k*}$ petr$_{k*}$ *Ph-ac*$_{k*}$ *Phos*$_{k*}$ *Psor*$_{hr1*}$ *Puls*$_{k*}$ rad-br$_{ptk1}$ rhod$_{k*}$ rhus-t$_{k*}$ ruta$_{k*}$ sabin$_{k*}$ sal-ac$_{hr1*}$ sec$_{k*}$ *Sep*$_{k*}$ **Sil**$_{k*}$ spong$_{k*}$ *Staph*$_{k*}$ stront-c$_{mg1.de}$ *Sulph*$_{k*}$ syph$_{k2*}$ tarent$_{hr1*}$ tell$_{ptk1}$ ter$_{hr1*}$ **Ther**$_{k*}$ thuj$_{k*}$ tub$_{c2*}$ tub-k$_{c1}$ [kali-p$_{stj1}$ nat-p$_{stj1}$]
  - • **accompanied** by | **perspiration**; profuse: chin$_{ptk1*}$
  - • **heat** in affected parts; with: calc-f$_{br1}$
  - • **insidious**: *Arg-met*$_{br1}$
  - • **painful** (See Pain - bones - caries; Pain - bones - caries - boring)
  - ○ • **Long** bones: ang$_{br1}$

Caries: ...
- **Periosteum**, of: ant-c$_{k*}$ **Asaf**$_{k*}$ aur$_{k*}$ bell$_{k*}$ calc$_{br1}$ calc-f$_{dp}$• *Chin*$_{k*}$ cycl$_{k*}$ hell$_{k*}$ kali-i$_{k2}$ *Merc*$_{k*}$ mez$_{k*}$ **Ph-ac**$_{k*}$ puls$_{k*}$ rhod$_{k*}$ rhus-t$_{k*}$ ruta$_{k*}$ sabin$_{k*}$ *Sil*$_{k*}$ staph$_{k*}$

CARRIED; being: | **amel.**: (↗*MIND - Carried - desire)* ant-c$_{bg2}$ ant-t$_{b2.de*}$ ars$_{bg2}$ bell$_{b2.de}$ *Cham*$_{b2.de*}$ coloc$_{bg2}$ ip$_{bg2}$ kali-c$_{bg2}$ merc$_{b2.de}$

CARRYING:
- **agg.**: ambr$_{b7a.de}$ both-a$_{rb3}$ carb-ac$_{st}$ caust$_{st}$ ruta$_{c1}$
  - • **burdens**; carrying: cadm-s$_{br1*}$ ruta$_{ptk1}$
- **back** agg.; on the: alum$_{k*}$
- **head** agg.; on the: calc$_{k*}$ ruta$_{ptk1}$ tarent$_{ptk1}$

CARSICKNESS (See Riding - streetcar; on - agg.; STOMACH - Nausea - riding; STOMACH - Vomiting - riding)

CARTILAGES, affection of: (↗*Inflammation - cartilages; Swelling - cartilages; Tumors - enchondroma)* **Arg-met**$_{kr1*}$ calc-p$_{ptk1}$ cimic$_{sf1.de}$ guaj$_{sf1.de}$ led$_{sf1.de}$ merc$_{sf1.de}$ nat-m$_{kr1*}$ olnd$_{sf1.de}$ plb$_{sf1.de}$ ruta$_{br1*}$ *Sil*$_{k2*}$ sulph$_{ptk1}$ symph$_{ptk1}$ [bell-p-sp$_{dcm1}$]
- **syphilitic**: arg-met$_{bro1}$ *Asaf*$_{bro1}$ *Aur*$_{bro1}$ aur-m$_{bro1}$ calc-f$_{bro1}$ carb-v$_{bro1}$ *Fl-ac*$_{bro1}$ hep$_{bro1}$ *Kali-bi*$_{bro1}$ *Kali-i*$_{bro1}$ lach$_{bro1}$ *Merc*$_{bro1}$ *Mez*$_{bro1}$ *Nit-ac*$_{bro1}$ ph-ac$_{bro1}$ *Phos*$_{bro1}$ phyt$_{bro1}$ sars$_{bro1}$ *Sil*$_{bro1}$ staph$_{bro1}$ still$_{bro1}$ sulph$_{bro1}$
- **ulcers** of: merc-c$_{k*}$ merc-d$_{ptk1}$

CATALEPSY: (↗*MIND - Gestures; MIND - Gestures - hands - brushing; MIND - Sitting; MIND - Unconsciousness - conduct)* abies-c$_{c1}$ *Acon*$_{k*}$ acon-c$_{a1*}$ aether$_{a1*}$ *Agar*$_{k*}$ aran$_{k*}$ art-v$_{k*}$ asaf$_{sf1.de}$ bell$_{k*}$ camph-mbr$_{bro1}$ *Cann-i*$_{k*}$ **Cann-s**$_{b7a.de}$ canth$_{a1}$ caust$_{sf1.de}$ cham$_{k*}$ chlol$_{k*}$ cic$_{k*}$ *Cocc* *Coff*$_{k*}$ *Con* *Crot-c*$_{bro1}$ crot-h$_{sf1.de}$ *Cupr*$_{sf1.de}$ cur$_{k*}$ *Ferr*$_{k*}$ gels$_{k*}$ graph$_{k*}$ hipp$_{jl2}$ hydr-ac$_{j5.de*}$ hyos$_{k*}$ ign$_{k*}$ indg$_{c1}$ iod$_{a1}$ *Ip*$_{k*}$ lach$_{k*}$ laur$_{j5.de}$ mag-c$_{ptk}$ *Mag-m*$_{sf1.de}$ merc$_{j5.de*}$ *Morph*$_{bro1}$ *Mosch*$_{j5.de*}$ *Nat-m*$_{k*}$ nux-m$_{k*}$ ol-an$_{sf1.de}$ *Op*$_{k*}$ *Petr*$_{k*}$ *Ph-ac*$_{k*}$ pip-m$_{c1*}$ *Plat*$_{k*}$ plb$_{a1}$ *Puls*$_{b7a.de}$ raph$_{c1*}$ reser$_{jl3}$ sabad$_{k2*}$ sep$_{hr1}$ spong$_{c1*}$ staph$_{k*}$ stram$_{k*}$ stry$_{a1}$ sulph$_{k*}$ tab$_{c1*}$ tanac$_{a1}$ thuj$_{k*}$ *Valer*$_{sf1.de}$ verat$_{k*}$ *Zinc*$_{sf1.de}$
- **afternoon**: grat$_{a1}$
- **evening** | **bed** agg.; in: cur
- **anger**; after: bry$_{kr1*}$ *Cham*$_{kr1}$
- **extremities** can be moved by others: stram$_{ptk1}$
- **fright**; after: (↗*MIND - Ailments - fright)* *Acon*$_{k*}$ bell$_{k*}$ *Gels*$_{k*}$ ign$_{k*}$ **Op**$_{k*}$
- **grief**; from: (↗*MIND - Ailments - grief)* *Ign*$_{k*}$ *Ph-ac*$_{k*}$ puls$_{a}$ staph$_{k*}$
- **jealousy**; from: (↗*MIND - Ailments - jealousy)* *Hyos*$_{k*}$ **Lach**$_{k*}$
- **joy** agg.: (↗*MIND - Ailments - joy - excessive)* **Coff**$_{k*}$
- **love**; from disappointed: hyos *Ign* lach *Ph-ac*
- **menses** | **before** | **agg.**: mosch$_{bro1}$
  - • **during** | **agg.**: mosch$_{bro1}$ *Plat*$_{k*}$
- **religious** excitement, from: (↗*MIND - Religious - too)* stram$_{k*}$ sulph$_{k*}$ verat$_{k*}$
- **sexual** | **excitement** agg.: *Con*$_{k*}$ *Plat*$_{k*}$ stram
- **sexual** excesses; after: chin$_{kr1}$ nux-v$_{kr1}$
- **worm** complaints; in: sabad$_{hr1*}$

CATARRH: arund$_{br1}$ calen$_{br1}$ grat$_{br1}$ *Hydr*$_{br1}$ *Kali-bi*$_{br1}$ *Kali-m*$_{br1}$ lem-m$_{br1}$ lyc$_{br1}$ nicc-met$_{br1}$ petr$_{br1}$ seneg$_{br1}$ *Skook*$_{br1}$ thuj$_{mtf33}$ *Verb*$_{br1}$
- **accompanied** by:
  - • **measles**: all-c$_{bro1}$ ars$_{bro1}$ dulc$_{bro1}$ *Euphr*$_{bro1}$ gels$_{bro1}$ kali-bi$_{bro1}$ merc$_{bro1}$ *Puls*$_{bro1}$ sabad$_{bro1}$ *Stict*$_{bro1}$
  - ○ • **Face**; pain in: verb$_{bro1}$
- **acute**: iod$_{br1}$ sangin-n$_{br1}$
- **chronic**: berb-a$_{br1}$ beta$_{br1}$ kali-bi$_{br1}$ sangin-n$_{br1}$
  - • **children**; in: med$_{br1}$
  - ○ • **Mucous** membranes: alum$_{bg2}$ arg-met$_{bg2}$ bar-c$_{bg2}$ benz-ac$_{bg2}$ carb-an$_{bg2}$ caust$_{bg2}$ clem$_{bg2}$ con$_{bg2}$ dulc$_{bg2}$ kali-i$_{bg2}$ mang$_{bg2}$ nit-ac$_{bg2}$ plb$_{bg2}$ sil$_{bg2}$ sul-ac$_{bg2}$ sulph$_{bg2}$ thuj$_{bg2}$
- **suppressed** (See NOSE - Discharge - suppressed)
- **weather** | **cold**, wet: asc-t$_{br1}$

CATHETERISM, ailments from: (↗*BLADDER - Inflammation - catheterization; BLADDER - Urination - involuntary - catheterization)* acon$_{ptk1}$ arn$_{bg2*}$ kali-c$_{bg2}$ mag-p$_{bg2*}$ nux-v$_{bg2*}$ petros$_{ptk1}$

CAUTERY with argentum nitricum; antidote to: nat-m$_{c1}$

CELIBACY (See Sexual desire - suppression - agg.)

CELLARS (See Wet - getting - rooms)

CELLULITIS (See Inflammation - cellulitis)

CEREBRAL accident (See Apoplexy)

CHANCRE: *(↗Chancre; Syphilis; FEMALE - Ulcers - chancres; GENERALS; MALE GENITALIA/SEX - Ulcers - penis - chancres; MALE GENITALIA/SEX - Ulcers - scrotum - chancres; SKIN - Eruptions - chancres; SKIN - Ulcers - chancres; URETHRA - Ulceration - chancres)* acet-ac br1 ail c2 anan bro1 *Apis* c2* arg-n c2* ars bro1 asaf bro1 asc-t c2 aur-m c2 carb-an ptk1 cinnb c2* cor-r c2* crot-h c2 *Hep* b4a.de* iodof c2 jac-c c2* jug-r c2 kali-bi bro1 kali-i bro1* lac-c c2 lach c2 lyc bro1 merc b4.de* merc-act c2 *Merc-c* c2* merc-i-f c2* merc-i-r br1* *Nit-ac* b4a.de* ph-ac c2* phos bro1 plat bro1 plat-m c2* sil bro1 sulph c2*

- **agg.**: *Ars* bro1 hecla bro1 *Hep* bro1 lach bro1 *Sil* bro1 sulph bro1 thuj bro1
- **induration** remaining long: merc-i-f br1
- **soft**: cor-r ptk1 merc ptk1 nit-ac ptk1 thuj ptk1
- **soften** and cause formation of pus; to: acet-ac br1

CHANGE: ruta sne

- **impressions**; change of | **agg.**: *Ign* vh
- **organ** to another organ; from one (See Metastasis)
- **position**:
  - **agg.**: acon k* *Bry* k* **Caps** k* *Carb-v* k* caust k* *Chel* k* *Con* k* **Euph** k* **Ferr** k* *Lach* k* *Lyc* k* petr k* ph-ac k* *Phos* k* plat k* plb k* **Puls** k* ran-b k* rhod k* rhus-t k* sabad k* *Samb* k* sil k* thuj k*
  - **amel.**: agar k* apis bro1 arn bg2* ars k* buni-o jl calc-f sne caust al1* cench k2 *Cham* k* *Dulc* bg2* **Ferr** sne **Ign** k* *Meli* k* *Nat-s* k* *Ph-ac* k* *Plb* bg1* puls k* pyrog ptk1* **Rhus-t** k* sep bg1* staph bg1 syph ptk1 tab bg2 teucr k* valer k* zinc k*
  - **desire** for change of: *Acon* bg2* alum j5.de* *Arn* j5.de* **Ars** bg2* bapt bg2* bell j5.de* **Bry** j5.de* caust bg2* cham bg2* *Eup-per* bg2* *Ferr* sne ign bg2* lyc j5.de* nat-s bg2* **Rhus-t** bg2* sil j5.de* tarax j5.de* zinc bg2* *Zinc-val* bg2*
  - **not** amel.: acon bg2 caust bg2 nat-s bg2
- **symptoms**; change of: ambr bg2 bry b7a.de cimic bg2 *Croc* b7a.de *Ign* b7a.de* *Nat-m* bg2 **Plat** bg2 plb bg2 **Puls** b7a.de* rhus-t b7a.de
  - **constant**: *(↗Alternating; Contradictory; Metastasis)* apis bro1 bell bro1 benz-ac bro1 berb bro1* carc c1* cimic k2* *Croc* br1* crot-t k2 *Dios* bro1 *Ign* bg2* *Kali-bi* k2* kali-c k2 *Kali-s* bro1 *Lac-c* bro1* lil-s k2 lil-t bro1 mag-p bro1 magn-gr bro1 *Mang-act* bro1 merl sne paraf bro1 phyt bro1 podo k2 *Puls* br1* sabin k2 sang ptk1 sanic bro1* syph bro1 *Tub* k1* valer k2
  - **rapid**: ambr bg2* ant-c k2 arn bg2* asaf ptk1 bac jl2 benz-ac bg2* *Berb* bg2* caul bg2* caust bg2* cimic bg2* croc br1* dios ptk1 ign br1 kalm bg2* led bg2* meph a1 plat bg2 plb bg2 puls bg2* rhod ptk1 sal-ac sf1.de sep ptk1 sul-ac sf1.de tab ptk1 tarent ptk1 tub bg2* valer bg2*
- **temperature**; of (See Temperature - change)
- **weather**; of (See Weather - change)

CHEMICAL hypersensitivity (See Allergic - chemical)

CHEMOTHERAPY agg.: *(↗Weakness - chemotherapy; STOMACH - Nausea - Medicine - allopathic - chemotherapy)* kali-p mrr1 sep mrr1 uncar-tom mp4• [lith-f stj2 lith-m stj2 lith-met stj2 lith-p stj2 lith-s stj2]

CHEWING:

- **after** chewing agg.: sabin b2.de* staph b2.de*
- **agg.**: acon b2.de* aloe ptk1 *Alum* b2.de* **Am-c** b2.de* **Am-m** b2.de* anac b2.de* arg-met b2.de* arg-n bg2 arn b2.de* ars b2.de* aur b2.de* bell b2.de* borx b2.de* bov b2.de* *Bry* b2.de* calc b2.de* cann-s b2.de* carb-an b2.de* carb-v b2.de* caust b2.de* *Chin* b2.de* cocc b2.de* coff b2.de* colch b2.de* dig b2.de* euph b2.de* *Euphr* b2.de* graph b2.de* *Guaj* b2.de* **Hep** b2.de* *Hyos* b2.de* *Ign* b2.de* ip b2.de* kali-c b2.de* lach b2.de* m-ambo b2.de* mag-c b2.de* mang b2.de* **Meny** b2.de* merc b2.de* *Mez* ptk1 nat-c b2.de* *Nat-m* b2.de* nit-ac b2.de* nux-v b2.de* *Olnd* b2.de* petr b2.de* *Ph-ac* b2.de* *Phos* b2.de* podo ptk1 *Puls* b2.de* ran-b b2.de* **Rhus-t** b2.de* *Sabin* b2.de* sars b2.de* seneg b2.de* *Sep* b2.de* sil b2.de* spig b2.de* spong b2.de* squil b2.de* *Staph* b2.de* sul-ac b2.de* sulph b2.de* tarax b2.de* teucr b2.de* *Thuj* b2.de* verat b2.de* *Verb* b2.de* *Zinc* b2.de*
- **amel.**: bry b2.de* cocc ptk1 cupr-act bro1* olnd bg2 seneg b2.de* *Staph* ptk1

CHEYNE-STOKES respiration: *(↗RESPIRATION - Intermittent; RESPIRATION - Irregular)* acon k* *Acon-f* c1* am-c sf1.de ang sf1.de antip c1* atro c1* *Bell* k* *Camph* sf1.de cann-i sf1.de carb-v bg1* carbn-o bg1 chlol st coca st* cocain bro1* crot-h sf1.de *Cupr* sf1.de cupr-act mtf11 cupr-ar sf1.de *Dig* sf1.de *Grin* c1* *Hydr-ac* sf1.de* *Ign* iod sf1.de ip sf1.de kali-cy c1* lach sf1.de *Laur* br1* led sf1.de lob sf1.de *Morph* bro1* nat-taur br1 nux-v olnd sf1.de *Op* bg2* parth c1* *Saroth* bro1* spartin-s br1 spong sul-ac bg2* *Sulph* bg2* vanad st verat sf1.de

- **accompanied** by | **coma** (See MIND - Unconsciousness - cheyne-stokes)

CHILDBED; ailments from (See FEMALE - Delivery - after)

CHILDREN; complaints in: *(↗Complaints - acute - children; Development; Development - arrested; Emaciation - children; Growth; Growth - length; TEETH - Dentition)* abrot sf1.de* acet-ac c1 acon b2.de* *Aeth* k* agar k* *All-c* alum bg2* *Ambr* k* *Ang* b2.de* ant-c b2.de* **Ant-t** b2.de* apis sf1.de arg-n mtf33 arn k* ars k* asaf k* *Aur* k* *Bar-c* k* **Bell** k* beta br1 **Borx** k* brom mtf33 *Bry* k* bufo mtf33 **Calc** k* calc-f jl *Calc-p* bg2* calc-s mtf33 calc-sil mtf33 camph k* canth k* **Caps** k* carb-v mtf33 carc mg1.de* caust bg2* **Cham** b2.de* chel kr1 chin k* chlol kr1 chlorpr jl *Cic* k* cic-m c1 *Cina* b2.de* clem k* coc-c sf1.de *Cocc* k* *Cocc-s* kr1 *Coff* bg2* con k* *Croc* k* cupr k* dig k* dros k* euph k* ferr k* ferr-p bg2* *Gels* graph k* hell k* hep bg2 **Hyos** k* *Ign* k* *Iod* k* **Ip** b2.de* *Kali-br* kr1* kali-c k* *Kali-m* kr1 *Kali-p* kr1* kali-sil mtf33 *Kreos* k* lac-c mtf33 *Lach* k* laur k* **Lyc** k* mag-c k* mag-m mtf33 mag-p kr1 med mtf33 meph jl **Merc** b2.de* **Merc-c** b4a.de *Mill* kr1 *Mosch* kr1 mur-ac k* naja mtf33 nat-c k* *Nat-m* b4a.de* nat-s mtf33 nat-sil mtf33 nit-ac mtf33 *Nux-m* k* *Nux-v* k* **Op** k* ped c1 phos sf1.de* phyt ptk1 plat mtf33 plb k* *Podo* bg* *Psor* k* **Puls** b2.de* *Rheum* b2.de* rhus-t k* rib-ac jl ruta k* sabad k* sabin k* *Samb* bg2* sanic mrr1* sec k* seneg k* senn j5.de sep b2.de* **Sil** b2.de* spig k* *Spong* k* *Squil* k* stann k* staph k* stram c1* sul-ac k* **Sulph** b2.de* syph mtf33 tarent mtf33 ter kr1 *Teucr* k* thuj k* thyr jl tub mrr1* verat k* viol-o k* viol-t k* zinc k*

- **biting** nails (See MIND - Biting - nails)
- **born** too late: borx mtf33
- **delicate**, puny, sickly: *(↗Emaciation - children - boys)* alum br1* aur c2 brom bg2* calc-p bg2* *Caust* kr1* irid-met c1* *Lyc* bg2* mag-c c1* mag-m mtf33 phos bg2* psor kr1* sanic mrr1 *Sil* mrr1 tub mrr1*
  - **artificial** baby foods; from: alum br1
  - ○ **Liver**; with complaints of (See ABDOMEN - Liver - children - puny)
- **fingers** in the mouth; put (See MIND - Gestures - fingers - mouth)
- **growing** too fast (See Growth)
- **newborns**: *(↗Nurslings)* acon vh1
- **nurslings**: arn b7a.de borx ptk1 *Bry* b7a.de calc ptk1 calc-p ptk1 *Cham* b7a.de *Cina* b7a.de ign b7a.de *Ip* b7a.de kali-bi ptk1 mag-c ptk1 *Nux-v* b7a.de ph-ac ptk1 puls ptk1 *Rheum* b7a.de rhus-t b7a.de sulph ptk1
  - **dying** soon after birth: arg-n ptk1
- **scrofulous**: bar-c br1
- **teenagers**: tub-m vs

CHILL, feels better before: psor

CHILLY persons (See Heat - lack)

CHINA; abuse of (See Quinine)

CHLORAL agg.: cann-i bro1

CHLORATE OF POTASH agg.: hydr bro1

CHLOROFORM; ailments from: *(↗Anesthesia [=narcosis] - ailments)* acet-ac k2 am-caust br1 phos bg*

CHLOROSIS: *Abrot* hr1* *Absin* hr1* *Acet-ac* adren br1 *Alet* k* *Alum* k* alum-p k2* alumn *Am-c* k* *Ambr* hr1* *Ant-c* k* *Ant-t* hr1* aq-mar sf1.de *Arg-met* k* arg-n k* **Ars** k* ars-i ars-s-f k2* aur-ar c1* bar-c k* **Bell** k* bry c1* cadm-met jl3 **Calc** k* calc-ar k2* calc-i k2 **Calc-p** k* carb-an k* *Carb-v* k* **Carbn-s** k* caust k* cham c1 *Chin* k* *Chinin-ar* chlor c1* cimic k2 cina kr1 cob-n jl3 **Cocc** k* coch hr1* *Con* k* *Cupr* k* cupr-ar br1 *Cycl* k* dig k* **Ferr** k* **Ferr-ar** k* *Ferr-i* k* **Ferr-m** ferr-p k* *Ferr-s* hr1* franz c1* **Graph** k* *Guar* hr1* *Hell* k* *Helon* k* *Hep* k* ign k* *Ip* hr1* *Kali-ar* kali-bi sf1.de *Kali-c* k* *Kali-fcy* k* *Kali-p* k* kali-perm sf1.de kali-s lac-c sf1.de lach c1 **Lyc** k* *Lyss* k* **Mang** k* mang-act br1 *Med* st merc k* *Mill* hr1* *Nat-c* k* nat-hchls c1* **Nat-m** k* nat-p **Nit-ac** k* *Nux-v* k* olnd k* *Petr* k* ph-ac k* **Phos** k* phyt hr1* pic-ac **Plat** k*

Chlorosis: ...
Plb k* Puls k* sabin k* sacch a1* sarr br1 Senec k* Sep k* Sin-n hr1* Spig k* staph k* sul-ac k* Sulph k* thuj k* ust k* valer k* vanad st1 verat hr1 Xan hr1* zinc k* zinc-p k2

- **accompanied** by:
  - **apyrexia**: chin bro1 puls bro1
  - **asthma** (See RESPIRATION - Asthmatic - accompanied - chlorosis)
  - **charcoal**; desire for (See Food and - charcoal - desire - accompanied - chlorosis)
  - **leukorrhea**: calc tl1
  - ○ **Tongue** | **pale**: Ferr kr1*
- **alternate** days; symptoms agg. on: alum
- **hysteria**; with (See MIND - Hysteria - chlorosis)
- **winter** agg.: Ferr k*

CHOLERINE (See RECTUM - Cholera - beginning)

CHOLESTEROL; increased (See Hyperlipidemia)

CHORDEE (See URETHRA - Chordee)

CHOREA: (↗Neurological; EXTREMITIES - Athetosis; MIND - Tourette's) Abrot hr1* absin br1* acon k* Agar k* agar-ph c1* agarin bro1 agre jl3 Ambr hr1* Aml-ns kr1* ant-c c1* Ant-t k* apis Arg-n k* arn c1* Ars k* ars-i ars-s-f k2* Art-v k* Asaf k* aster k* Atro hr1* aven bro1 Bell k* Bufo k* Cact k* Calc k* calc-i k2* Calc-p c1* Castm kr1* caul k* Caust k* cedr k* Cham k* Chel k* chin k* chlol k* Cic k* Cimic k* Cina k* cocain bro1 Cocc k* coch hr1* Cod hr1* coff k* con k* Croc k* crot-c crot-h k* Cupr k* Cupr-act c1* Cupr-ar k* cypr k* Dios k* diph-t-tpt jl2 dulc k* dys fmm1* elec c1* eup-a br1* Ferr k* ferr-ar ferr-cit sf1.de ferr-cy bro1 Ferr-i Ferr-r bro1 Ferr-s hr1* form k* Gels hr1* Guar hr1* Hipp k* hippoz mtf11 Hyos k* Ign k* Iod k* ip k* kali-ar Kali-br k* kali-c kali-i kali-p Kali-s hr1* Lach k* lat-k c1* lat-m bro1 laur k* levo jl3 Lil-t k* lyc b4a.de lyss mg1.de Mag-p k* Mand jl3 Mang st1 merc k* methyl br1 mez Mill hr1* Morph hr1* mur-ac c1* Mygal k* narc-ps ah1* Nat-m k* Nit-ac Nux-m k* Nux-v k* ol-an sf1.de Op k* passi sf1.de petr b4a.de ph-ac k* Phos k* phys hr1* phyt hr1* picro bro1 plat plb k* psor k* Puls k* rhod k* Rhus-t k* russ c1* sabin k* Samb Santin bro1 Scut c1* Sec k* Sep k* Sil k* Sin-n hr1* sol-ni c1* Spig bro1 stann k* staph vh* stict hr1* Stram k* streptoc mtf11 Stry bro1 stry-p br1* sul-ter c1* sulfon br1* Sulph k* Sumb k* syc bka1• tanac c1* Tarent k* tarent-c c1* Ter hr1* thal a1* thal-xyz srj8• thiop jl3 thuj k* toxo-g jl2 Tub st1 valer sf1.de verat hr1 verat-v k* vib tl1 visc k* Zinc k* zinc-ar bro1 Zinc-br c1* zinc-cy c1* zinc-p k2* zinc-val bro1* ziz hr1* [brom stj1 calc-br stj1 mag-br stj1]

- **one-sided**: Calc k* Cocc k* Cupr k* nat-s k* phys k* tarent st
- **right**: Ars Caust k* Nat-s phys Tarent zinc kl
- **left**: Cimic Cupr rhod
- **daytime**: art-v tarent
- **morning**: arg-n gsy1* mygal k*
- **noon**: arg-n gsy1*
- **afternoon**: Nat-s
- **evening**: Zinc k*
- **night**: Arg-n Caust k* cupr k2* zinc mrr1
  - **amel.**: Art-v hr1* Tarent hr1*
- **accompanied** by:
  - **chronic** diseases: sulph tl1
  - **drops** things: agar tl1
  - **gasping**: laur ptk1
  - **palpitations** (See CHEST - Palpitation - tumultuous - accompanied - chorea)
  - **paroxysms**; convulsive: ter tl1
  - **spasms**: hyos tl1 mag-p tl1
  - **trembling**: calc tl1 visc tl1
  - **weakness**; paralytic: cocc tl1
  - ○ **Muscles**; twitching of: agar tl1 hyos tl1 ign tl1 mygal tl1 stram tl1
  - **Tongue**:
    - **brown** discoloration: cupr kr1*
    - **complaints**: caust bro1
    - **motion** of the tongue; constant: verat-v kr1*
    - **protruding** tongue: sumb kr1*
      - **difficulty**; with: ars-i vk1

Chorea – accompanied by – Tongue: ...
    - **roughness**: cupr kr1*
    - **swelling**: asaf kr1* Morph kr1* sulph kr1*
    - **trembling**: cupr kr1*
    - **white** discoloration of the tongue: Asaf kr1* cupr kr1* Nat-m kr1*
- **alternating** with rheumatism: cimic k2
- **anemia**; from: ars bro1 chin bro1 Ferr-r bro1 hyos bro1
- **anxiety**, from: stram sf1.de
- **beginning** in:
  - **face** | **body**; and spreads over: Sec
- **children** who have grown too fast: (↗puberty) phos k*
- **chronic**: chlol ptk1
- **coition** in a woman; after: Agar k* Cedr k*
- **cold**:
  - **agg.**: ign bro1
  - **bathing** | **after**: Rhus-t k*
- **colors**; sight of bright | **amel.**: tarent bro1*
- **cordis**: cimic ptk1 tarent ptk1
- **corybantism**; from: bell bro1 hyos bro1 stram bro1
- **dancing**: | **excessive**; after: bell ptk1 hyos ptk1 stram ptk1
- **dentition**; during second: bell bro1 Calc hr1*
- **dinner**; after: zinc k* ziz hr1*
- **ear**; from piercing the: lach ptk1
- **eating**; after: ign k*
- **emissions**; with seminal: dios ptk1
- **eruptions**; after suppressed: Caust k* cupr sf1.de Sulph zinc k*
- **excitement** agg.: agar arg-n sf1.de Asaf bro1 bell bro1 cimic k2* Cocc bro1 croc bro1 gels bro1 hyos bro1 Ign k* kali-br bro1 Laur k* mag-p ptk1 nat-m sf1.de Op k* Phos stict bro1 stram bro1 Tarent kr1
- **exertion** | **amel.**: Zinc k*
- **falling**; with: Calc hr1*
- **fear**; from: calc st1
- **fright** agg.: acon k* agar arg-n sf1.de Calc k* Caust k* cimic bro1 cupr k* Cupr-act kr1 cupr-ar sf1.de* Gels k* Ign k* Kali-br k* Laur k* Nat-m k* Op k* phos Stram k* tarent bro1 visc c1* Zinc k*
- **grief**; from: caust vh Cupr-act kr1 ign k* nat-m vh staph vh
- **hands** in pockets amel., putting: aster ptk1*
- **hemorrhages** | **after**: stict ptk1
- **holding** | **amel.**: asaf ptk1
- **hyperesthesia**, excessive: Tarent kr1
- **hysterical**: croc ptk1 tarent mtf33
- **imitation**, from: Caust k* Cupr k* mygal Tarent k*
- **jerks** constant cannot keep still: hyos tl1 laur ptk1
- **light**; from: ign bro1 ziz hr1*
- **loss** of animal fluids, from: Chin
- **lying** on back | **amel.**: (non:cupr ptk1*) cupr-act kr1* Ign k*
- **masturbation**; from: agar bro1 Calc k* chin k* cina kr1
- **menopause**; during: cimic sf1.de
- **menses**:
  - **absent** or difficult, with: cimic tl1 puls ptk1
  - **after** | **amel.**: sep hr1*
  - **before** | **agg.**: caul sf1.de cimic bro1
  - **delayed**: caul k2
  - **during** | **agg.**: caul sf1.de caust k2* cimic bro1* Zinc k*
  - **suppressed** menses; from: hell b7a.de
- **misses** getting hold of anything: asaf ptk1
- **moon**:
  - **full** moon: nat-m kl
  - **new** moon: (↗Moon - new - agg.) cupr sf1.de
- **motion**:
  - **agg.**: anh sp1 Cupr-act kr1 ziz kr1
  - **backward**, with: Bell kr1
  - **gyratory**, with: stram tl1*
  - **rhythmical**, with: agar bro1 caust bro1 cham bro1 cimic bro1 lyc bro1 Tarent bro1
- **music** | **amel.**: tarent k2*
- **noise** agg.: ign bro1 ziz hr1*
- **numbness** of affected part, with: nux-v kl

- **nymphomania**; with: *Tarent* hr1*
- **old** people; in: aeth ptk1 aven br1
- **periodical**: *Cupr* *Cupr-act* kr1 nat-s
  - **hour**; at the same: ign ptk1
  - **week**; every: croc kr1*
- **perspiration**; from suppressed | **foot**, at: form ptk1
- **pocket**; keeping hand in | **amel.** (See hands)
- **pollutions**, with: *Dios* kr1
- **pregnancy** agg.; during: bell bro1* *Caust* k* *Chlol* hr1* *Cupr* k* gels ptk1 *Hyos* zr
- **pressure** agg.: cimic mrr1
- **puberty**, in: (↗*children)* agar sf1.de asaf bro1* caul hr1* *Cimic* k2* ign bro1* puls bro1* zinc bl
- **punishment**, from: agar kr1 caust vh *Ign* hr1* nat-m vh staph vh
- **rest** agg.: *Zinc* k*
- **rheumatic**: **Caust** k* *Cimic* k* kali-i k* *Rhus-t* k* spig bro1* stict k*
- **run** or jump, cannot walk must: bufo k* kali-br k* **Nat-m** k ●* *Stram* kr1
  - **better** than walking: tarent ptk1
- **scrofulous**: calc bro1 *Calc-p* bro1 caust bro1 *Iod* bro1 phos bro1 psor bro1
- **sleep**:
  - **during**:
    - **agg.**: **Caust** bl *Cupr-ar* sf1.de tarent bro1* verat-v tl1* zinc ptk1 *Ziz* kr1*
    - **amel.**: **Agar** k* cupr bro1* hell k* mag-p ptk1* mygal ptk1* ziz
- **stool** agg.; during: mag-p ptk1
- **strabismus**, with: *Stram* hr1*
- **swallow**; cannot: art-v ptk1
- **Sydenham's** chorea: agar mtf11 agarin mtf11 art-v mtf11 cupr mtf11 streptoc jl2 zinc mtf11 zinc-cy mtf11 ziz mtf11
- **sympathetic**: caust ptk1
- **thinking** of it, when: *Caust*
- **thunderstorm**:
  - **agg.**: *Phos*
  - **before**: *Agar* k* *Rhod* k* sep k*
- **touch** agg.: ziz hr1*
- **waking**; on: *Chlol* hr1*
- **weather** agg.; dry: *Caust*
- **wet**; after getting: *Rhus-t* k*
- **wine** agg.: *Zinc* k*
- **worms**; from: asaf bro1 *Calc* k* *Cina* k* santin bro1 *Spig* bro1 tanac br*

▽ - **extending** to | **Tongue**: cina k2

O - **Crosswise**:
  - **left** arm and right leg: agar bro1* *Cimic* bro1* *Stram* kr1
  - **right** arm and left leg: tarent bro1*
- **Face**:
  - **agg.**: *Cupr* kr1
  - **begins** in face (See beginning - face)
- **Feet** | **cold** clammy feet up to knee; with: laur ptk
- **Muscles**; of local: hyos ptk
- **Side** lain on: cimic k*
- **Single** muscles: hyos ptk1
- **Single** parts | **wandering**: stram bro1
- **Spinal**: asaf k* cic k* cocc k* cupr k* mygal k* nux-v k*
- **Tongue**; with protrusion of: sumb ptk
- **Uterine**: *Caul* hr1* **Cimic** hr1* croc hr1* *Ign* hr1* *Lil-t* hr1* *Nat-m* hr1* *Puls* hr1* sec hr1* *Sep* hr1*

CHRONIC DISEASES, to begin treatment: calc bro1 calc-p bro1 morb tl1 *Nux-v* bro1 psor puls a1* *Sulph* bro1 tub tl1
- **parasitic** micro organisms; caused by: thuj tl1
- **scarlet** fever; after: psor tl1

CHRONIC FATIGUE SYNDROME: (↗*Mononucleosis - chronic; Weakness; Weakness - exertion - agg. - slight; Weariness)* acet-ac mp4• am-c mrr1 ant-c mrr1 aq-pur mp4• arg-met mrr4• arg-n mrr4* atro vh1 aur mrr1 bapt vh1 berb vh1 beryl mp4• brass-c mp4• brom vh1 calc mrr1 calc-p mrr1 camph mrr4* cann-i mrr1 carb-v mrr4* carc sej3* chin mrr1 cocc mrr1 coff mrr1 cordyc mp4• dam mp4• ferr mrr1 gels mrr1* germ-met srj5• granit-m mp4• ign mrr1 ind mp4• kali-p mrr4* lyc k2* mag-c mrr1 mag-m mrr4* *Mur-ac* mrr1 nat-m mrr1 nux-v mrr4• onos mrr1 op mrr1 ozone vml3• penic mp4• ph-ac mrr1* phos mrr1 *Pic-ac* mrr1 sarcol-ac mp4• scut mrr1* sel mrr1 sep mrr4* sil mrr1 *Stann* mrr1 sulph mrr1 thuj mrr1 uncar-tom mp4•

CHRONICITY (See Complaints - chronic)

CHURCH BELLS; ringing of: | **agg.**: ant-c b2.de*

CICATRICES: (↗*SKIN - Cicatrices)*

O - **Glands**; of: dros tl1

CLAMPS; sensation of iron: *Coloc* b2.de*

CLEAR (See Weather - clear)

CLENCHING: | **teeth** together (See Biting - teeth)

CLOSING:

O - **Eyes**:
  - **agg.**: agar b2.de* alum bg2 arn b2.de* ars b2.de* *Bell* b2.de* **Bry** b2.de* c a l a d b2.de* *Calc* b2.de* camph bg2 carb-an b2.de* caust b2.de* chel b2.de* *Chin* b2.de* *Clem* b2.de* con b2.de* croc b2.de* dig b2.de* ferr b2.de* *Graph* bg2 *Hell* b2.de* hep b2.de* ign b2.de* kali-c b2.de* *Lach* b2.de* led b2.de* m-aust b2.de* *Mag-m* b2.de* mang b2.de* nux-v b2.de* op b2.de* ph-ac b2.de* phos b2.de* *Puls* b2.de* sars b2.de* sec bg2 sep b2.de* spong b2.de* staph b2.de* stram bg2 *Stront-c* bg2 sulph b2.de* *Ther* bg2* thuj b2.de*
  - **amel.**: acon b2.de arn b2.de* aur b2.de* bell b2.de borx b2.de* *Bry* b2.de *Calc* b2.de* canth b2.de* chin b2.de cic b2.de* *Clem* b2.de* coff b2.de con b2.de* *Croc* b2.de* euph b2.de hell b7.de *Ign* b2.de ip b7.de kali-c b4.de* *Lyc* b2.de* m-ambo b2.de mag-m b2.de *Nux-v* b2.de ph-ac b4.de phos b2.de plat b2.de* seneg b4.de *Spig* b2.de* zinc b2.de*
- **Mouth** | **agg.**: *Mez* b2.de* nux-v b2.de*

CLOTHES:
- **cold**; as if: ars-i ptk1
- **fire**; as if on: ars-i ptk1
- **fit** him; would not: verat-v ptk1
- **heavy**; too: con h2* euph h2* *Lac-c* hr1* merc h1*
- **large**; too: psor bg2* thuj bg2*
- **tight**; too: apis hr1* arg-met kr1* ars-met kr1 benz-ac kr1 caust ptk1 chel ptk1 chin h1 glon a* nux-v ptk1 rumx ptk1 thuj cd1
- **wet**; as if: calc bg2* guaj bg2* lac-d ptk1 lyc bg2* phos bg2* ran-b ptk1 sanic bg2* sep bg2* tub bg2* verat-v bg2*

CLOTHING:
- **intolerance** of: (↗*Covers - agg.; Warm - desire)* *Am-c* k* ant-t a1* *Apis* **Arg-n** arn k* asaf k* asar k* *Bov* *Bry* k* **Calc** k* *Caps* k* *Carb-v* k* *Carbn-s* *C a u s t* k* cench k2* chel bg* chin k* clem bg2* *Coc-c* k2* coff k* con **Crot-c** *Crot-h* dios sf1.de euph a1 *Glon* sf1.de *Graph* *Hep* k* ign k* kali-bi kali-c k* k a l i - c h l hr1 kali-i sf1.de kali-m kr1 kali-n k* kola stb3• kreos k* *Lac-c* st1 *Lac-e* hm2• **Lach** k* *Lept* vh lil-t bg* lith-c sf1.de **Lyc** k* manc vh merc j5.de* *Nat-m* bg *Nat-s* **Nux-v** k* olnd k* **Onos** op k* *Phos* bg1* plb sf1.de polyg-h kr1* *Puls* k* *Ran-b* k* *Sanic* *Sars* k* *Sep* k* *Spig* **Spong** k* *Stann* k* sulph k* *Tarent* verat-v bg2* vip sf1.de [hydrog stj2]
  - **fever**; during: acon bg2 **Bov** bg2 calc bg2 **Euph** bg2 ferr bg2 *Lyc* bg2 s p i g bg2 verat bg2
  - **woolen**: (↗*SKIN - Itching - wool; SKIN - Wool - agg.)* com bg2 hep bg2 merc bg2* morg-p pte1*• phos k* psor k* puls k* rhus-t bg* sal-fr sle1• *Sulph* k* [lith-p stj2]
    - **working** with undressed wool, ailments from: **Anthraci** vh
- **loosening** of clothing amel.: am-c k* am k* ars kr1 asar k* *Bry* k* **Calc** k* *Cann-i* *Caps* k* *Carb-v* k* *Caust* k* cench br1 chel chin k* coff k* glycyr-g cte1• *Hep* k* ignis-alc es2• **Lach** **Lyc** k* mag-m h2 nat-s tl1 **Nit-ac** **Nux-v** k* olnd k* o p k* orni tl1 *Puls* k* ran-b k* sabin gk *Sanic* *Sars* k* *Sep* k* *Spig* *Spong* k* *Stann* k* *Sulph* k*
- **pressure** of clothing: am-c b2.de* aml-ns bg2* apis bg2* *Arg-n* bg2* arn b2.de* *Asar* b2.de* bov bg2* *Bry* b2.de* **Calc** b2.de* *Caps* b2.de* *Carb-v* b2.de* *Caust* b2.de* cench kr1* chin b2.de* coc-c bg2* *Coff* b2.de* con bg2* glon kr1* *Hep* b2.de* ignis-alc es2• kali-bi bg2* kali-i bg2* **Lach** bg2* lil-t kr1* **Lyc** b2.de* merc bg2* *Nat-m* bg2* nat-s bg2* nit-ac kr1* nux-m bg2* **Nux-v** b2.de* olnd b2.de* onos kr1* op b2.de* ovi-p br1 phos bg2* psor kr1* puls b2.de* *Ran-b* b2.de* sabin gk *Sars* b2.de* sec kr1* *Sep* b2.de* **Spong** b2.de* *Stann* b2.de* *Sulph* b2.de* tub kr1* vip bg2* [ferr-n stj2 mag-n stj2 mang-n stj2 nitro stj2 zinc-n stj2]
  - **amel.**: fl-ac bg2 glycyr-g cte1• nat-m bg2 psor ptk1 sabad ptk1 [mag-n stj2]
- **woolen** | **amel.**: spig bg2

CLUCKING: | **Muscles**: mang h2

CLUTCHING (See Pain - cramping; Pain - grasping)

COAGULATED, CURDLED; sensation as if: | **Bone** marrow: ang b2.de*

COAL GAS, from: (*↗Allergic - chemical; Allergic - petrochemical; Death - carbon; Sewer-gas; RESPIRATION - Asphyxia - coal)* acet-ac bro1* am-c bro1* arn k* bell hr1* borx st bov k* carb-v *Carbn-s* k* coff bro1* ip hr1* lach st1 *Op* kr1* phos c1 sec bg2*

COAL TAR drugs: am-c gm1 bov bro1* carb-v gm1 lach gm1 mag-p gm1 op gm1

COBWEB, sensation of a: (*↗Formication)* alum b2.de* alumn kr1 *Bar-c* b2.de* *Borx* b2.de* brom bg2* calad hr1 *Calc* b2.de* carl k13 chin bg2 con kr1* *Graph* b2.de* laur a1 mag-c b2.de* mez a1 morph a1 ph-ac b2.de* phos bg2 plb b2.de* *Ran-s* b2.de* rat a1 sul-ac b2.de* sulph k13 sumb bg2* wies a1

COD-LIVER OIL agg.: (*↗Medicine - allopathic - abuse - cod-liver)* hep bro1

COITION: (*↗GENERALS; MALE - Coition; MALE GENITALIA/SEX - Coition)*

- **after**: agar k* agn k* alum j5.de am-c ambr sf1.de anac k* anan arg-n asaf k* bar-c k* berb j5.de borx b2.de* *Bov* k* *Calad* k* **Calc** k* calc-i k13 canth k* carb-an j5.de carb-v bg2 *Cedr* k* *Chin* k* *Con* k* daph j5.de dig j5.de eug j5.de *Graph* k* kali-bi bg2 **Kali-c** k* **Kali-p** *Kreos* j5.de* led j5.de lyc k* mag-m k* merc j5.de* mez j5.de mosch k* *Nat-c* k* nat-m k* nat-p k* nat-sil k13 nit-ac k* *Nux-v* k* *Petr* k* *Ph-ac* k* *Phos* k* plb k* puls bg2 rhod k* *Sel* k* **Sep** k* **Sil** k* *Staph* k* sul-ac j5.de sulph bg tab j5.de tarent ther ziz hr1
  - **agg.**: **Agar** k* agn alum j5.de* am-c ambr sf1.de anac anan *Apis* arg-n k* asaf bar-c berb j5.de borx both-a rb3 both-ax tsm2 *Bov* *Calad* k* **Calc** calc-i k2 calc-s bro1 calc-sil k2* canth carb-an j5.de *Cedr* k* *Chin* k* *Con* daph j5.de dig j5.de* eug j5.de *Graph* **Kali-c** k* kali-i c1 **Kali-p** k* *Kali-sil* vh* kreos j5.de lac-c mrr1 led j5.de lil-t mrr1 lyc mag-m merc j5.de mez j5.de mosch *Nat-c* nat-m *Nat-p* nat-sil k2* *Nit-ac* *Nux-v* k* *Petr* *Ph-ac* k* *Phos* k* plb rhod *Sel* k* **Sep** k* **Sil** k* *Staph* sul-ac j5.de tab j5.de tarent ther [alumin stj2 alumin-p stj2 alumin-s stj2 arg-met stj2 arg-p stj2 ferr-sil stj2 ind stj2 kali-ar stj2 kali-met stj2 mag-sil stj2 mang-sil stj2 sil-met stj2 stann stj2]
  - **amel.**: bamb-a stb2.de• *Canth* mgm• **Con** bg2* lac-h htj1• merc bg2 *Staph* bg2* [heroin sdj2]
- **during**: alum bg2 anac b2.de* asaf b2.de* bar-c b2.de* *Bufo* bg2 calad b2.de* **Graph** b2.de* *Kali-c* b2.de* kreos bg2 lyc b2.de* plat b2.de* *Sel* b2.de*
  - **agg.**: **Agar** ptk1 alum j5.de anac asaf bar-c berb j5.de borx j5.de bufo ptk1 calad k* calc j5.de* *Canth* k* *Carb-v* j5.de caust j5.de chin ptk1 clem j5.de ferr *Graph* k* *Kali-c* k* kali-p ptk1 kreos k* lyc k* *Nat-c* ptk1 *Nat-m* ptk1 nat-p ptk1 nit-ac j5.de *Nux-v* j5.de petr j5.de ph-ac ptk1 plat plb j5.de *Sel* k* sep k* *Sil* ptk1 spig ptk1 stann ptk1 staph ptk1 sulph ptk1 tax j5.de thuj
  - **amel.**: **Con** ptk1 merc ptk1 *Staph* ptk1
- **fright** (See MIND - Fear - coition - during)
- **interrupted** coition agg.: bell bg2* bell-p sf1.de

COLCHICUM agg.: led bro1

COLD:

- **agg.**: abrot gt1* acet-ac k2* *Acetan* br1* achy jl3 *Acon* k* *Act-sp* bg2 adon sf1.de aesc *Agar* k* *Agn* k1* all-s bro1 allox tpw3 *Alum* k* alum-p k2 *Alum-sil* k2* alumn k* *Am-c* k* am-m k2* ambr br1* ammc br1 anac b2.de* *Ant-c* k* ant-t ptk1* anth br1* *Apoc* aran k* aran-ix mg1.de* *Arg-met* k* arg-n arist-cl mg1.de* arn k* **Ars** k* ars-i bg2* ars-s-f k2 *Asar* k* *Aur* k* aur-ar gt1 aur-s k2 bac bro1 *Bad* k* *Bamb-a* stb2.de• **Bar-c** k* *Bar-m* k1* bar-s k2 *Bell* k* bell-p mg1.de* benz-ac gt1* berb k2 *Borx* k* *Bov* k* *Brom* bg2* bros-gau mrc1 *Bry* k* cadm-s k* **Calc** k* **Calc-ar** **Calc-f** k* **Calc-p** k* calc-s **Calc-sil** k* calen bro1 **Camph** b2.de* *Canth* b2.de* **Caps** k* *Carb-an* k* *Carb-v* k* *Carbn-s* k* carc hbh* card-m k2 *Carl* a1 castm bg2 *Caul* k2* **Caust** k* cench k2 *Cham* k* chel k* **Chin** k* *Chinin-ar* choc srj3• *Cic* k* *Cimic* k* cinnb *Cist* k* clem k* coc-c k2 coca-c sk4• *Cocc* k* coch c1 *Coff* b2.de* *Colch* k* coli jl2 coll bro1 *Coloc* k* *Con* k* cop a1 crot-c bro1* cupr bro1 *Cycl* k* cyt-l mg1.de* *Dig* k* diphtox jl2 **Dulc** k* elaps *Eup-per* bg* *Euphr* st1 falco-pe nl2• **Ferr** b2.de* *Ferr-ar* ferr-p a1 flav jl3* *Form* a1* franz a1 gels br1 germ-met stj2*• gins a1 **Graph** k* *Guaj* gymno ham k2* hed mg1.de *Hell* k* *Helon* **Hep** k* hydr hydrog srj2• *Hyos* k* **Hyper** k* hypoth jl3 *Ign* k* ina-i mlk9.de iod a1 *Ip* k* *Iris* vh **Kali-ar** k* *Kali-bi* k* **Kali-c** k* kali-i a1* kali-m k2* **Kali-p** k* kali-s fd4.de *Kali-sil* st1* *Kalm* k* *Kreos* k* lac-ac a1 *Lac-d* k* lach k*

Cold – agg.: ...

lact br1 laur k* *Led* k* lob bro1* luna kg1• **Lyc** k* lycps-v m-ambo b2.de* m-aust b2.de* **Mag-c** b2.de* *Mag-m* b2.de* **Mag-p** k* mand jl3 *Mang* k* med k2 meny k* *Merc* k* *Mez* k* mit a1 moly-met jl3* **Mosch** k* *Mur-ac* b2.de* *Naja* br1* **Nat-ar** *Nat-c* b2.de* *Nat-m* k* *Nat-p* nat-s k2 nat-sil k2* nicc-met sk4• **Nit-ac** k* nit-s-d bro1 *Nux-m* k* **Nux-v** k* oci-sa jl* olib-sac wmh1 onop jl3 oscilloc jl2 *Ox-ac* parth vml3• *Petr* k* *Ph-ac* k* **Phos** k* phys a1* *Phyt* k* pimp a1 plac rzf5• plat k2 *Plb* k1* *Podo* st1 polyg-h a1 polyg-pe c1 polys sk4• prot jl2 pseuts-m oss1• psil jl3* **Psor** k* ptel a1 *Puls* k* *Pycnop-sa* mrz1 pyre-p a1 **Pyrog** k* raja-s jl3 **Ran-b** k* rheum k* *Rhod* k* **Rhus-t** k* rib-ac jl3 **Rumx** k* *Ruta* k* **Sabad** k* sacch-a gmj3 samb k* sanic mrr1 saroth mg1.de *Sars* b2.de* sec a1 sel bro1 senec seneg k* **Sep** k* sieg mg1.de **Sil** k* sol-ni a1 sol-t-ae bg2 **Spig** k* spong k* squil k* *Stann* k* staph k* stram k* **Stront-c** k* stry a1* *Sul-ac* k* *Sulph* k* *Sumb* symph fd3.de• tab bro1 *Tarent* k* tax-br oss1• teucr thala a1 *Ther* *Thuj* k* thyr br1 tritic-vg fd5.de *Tub* k* tub-sp zs valer gt1* verat b2.de* verb k* vichy-g a1 *Viol-t* b2.de* x-ray jl xero bro1 *Zinc* k* [am-caust stj2 am-p stj1 *Ant-m* stj2 *Ant-met* stj2 bar-p stj1 beryl stj2 bor-pur stj2 *Cadm-met* stj2 calc-lac stj2 calc-met stj2 cob stj2 cob-m stj2 cob-p stj2 ferr-sil stj2 ind stj2 *Kali-met* stj2 lith-c stj2 mag-lac stj2 mag-met stj2 *Mag-sil* stj2 mang-p stj2 mang-sil stj2 *Niob-met* stj2 *Pall* stj2 pop dhh1 *Rhodi* stj2 *Rubd-met* stj2 *Ruth-met* stj2 *Sil-met* stj2 *Stront-m* stj2 *Stront-met* stj2 tax jsj7 *Techn* stj2 tung-met stj2 *Yttr-met* stj2 zinc-m stj2 zinc-p stj2 *Zirc-met* stj2]

- **air**:
  - **agg.**: *Abrot* k* *Acon* k* adam srj5• *Aesc* k* **Agar** k* agn k2 **All-c** *Alum* k* alum-p k2* alum-sil k2* *Alumn* k* am-br hr1* *Am-c* k* ammc anac b2.de* ant-c k* ant-t k2* anth br1* apis bg2 apoc k2* aral vh1 *Aran* k* arn k* **Ars** k* ars-s-f k2* asar k* astac hr1* atra-r bnm3• **Aur** k* aur-ar k2 aur-m bro1* aur-s k2* bac bro1* bacls-7 fmm1• **Bad** k* bamb-a stb2.de• *Bapt* hr1* **Bar-c** k* *Bar-m* k* bar-s k2* *Bell* k* borx k* bov k* brass-n-o srj5• brom a1* brucel sa3• *Bry* k* bufo bg2* cadm-s k* **Calc** k* **Calc-p** k* calc-sil k2* calen hr1* **Camph** k* canth k* caps k* *Carb-ac* *Carb-an* k* *Carb-v* k* *Carbn-s* *Carl* a1 caul tl1 **Caust** k* cham k* chin k* chinin-ar cic k* **Cimic** k* cina k* **Cist** k* clem sf1.de *Coc-c* hr1* *Coca* *Cocc* k* coff k* *Colch* k* *Coloc* k* *Con* k* cor-r sf1.de cupr bro1* cur bro1 *Cycl* hr1* *Dig* k* **Dulc** k* dys fmm1• elaps eup-per k2 euph-l bro1 *Ferr* k* ferr-ar ferr-p k* fl-ac *Graph* k* ham k2* **Hell** k* **Hep** k* hydrog srj2*• *Hyos* k* **Hyper** k* *Ign* k* ind hr1* *Ip* k* **Kali-ar** k* *Kali-bi* k* **Kali-c** k* kali-chl k13 kali-m k2* kali-p k* kali-s mrr1* *Kreos* k* lac-ac a1* lac-c a1 *Lac-d* lach k* laur k* lob mrr1 **Lyc** k* lycps-v lyss hr1* m-ambo b2.de* m-arct b2.de m-aust b2.de *Mag-c* k* mag-m k* **Mag-p** k* *Mang* k* med hr1* meny k* *Merc* k* *Merc-i-r* hr1* mez k* **Mosch** k* mur-ac k* *Nat-ar* k* nat-c k* nat-m k* *Nat-p* k* *Nat-s* bg2* nat-sil k2* nit-ac k* nit-s-d hr1* **Nux-m** k* **Nux-v** k* *Osm* ox-ac k2* par k* *Petr* k* *Ph-ac* k* phor-t mie3• *Phos* k* *Phyt* tl1 *Plan* plb sf* psil jl **Psor** k* ptel a1 *Puls* k* pyrog tl1* **Ran-b** k* **Rhod** k* **Rhus-t** k* **Rumx** k* ruta k* **Sabad** k* samb k* sang sf1.de sars k* sel bro1* senec a1 seneg k* **Sep** k* **Sil** k* sol-ni spig k* spong k* squil k* staph k* stram k* **Stront-c** k* *Sul-ac* k* *Sulph* k* *Sumb* syc fmm1• *Tarent* *Thuj* k* tub br1* urt-u bro1 *Verat* k* *Verat-v* hr1* verb k* viol-o bro1 viol-t k* visc bro1 *Zinc* k* zinc-p k2* *Zing* hr1* [alumin-p stj2 alumin-s stj2 am-caust stj2 am-m stj1 am-p stj1 ant-met stj2 arg-met stj2 *Ars-met* stj2 astat stj2 bar-br stj2 *Bar-met* stj2 bar-p stj1 bism-sn stj2 cadm-met stj2 caes-met stj2 calc-lac stj2 calc-m stj1 *Calc-met* stj2 chr-met stj1* cupr-act stj2 cupr-m stj2 cupr-p stj2 ferr-s stj1 *Ferr-sil* stj2 germ-met stj2 hafn-met stj2 irid-met stj2 kali-met stj2 kali-n stj1 *Kali-sil* stj2 lanth-met stj2 lith-p stj2 mag-br stj1 *Mag-met* stj2 mag-n stj2 *Mag-sil* stj2 mang-act stj2 mang-m stj2 mang-met stj2 mang-n stj2 mang-p stj2 *Mang-sil* stj2 merc-d stj2 moly-met stj2 neon stj2 nicc-met stj2 niob-met stj2 osm-met stj2 pall stj2 plat stj2 plb-p stj2 polon-met stj2 rhen-met stj2 rhodi stj2 rubd-met stj2 ruth-met stj2 scand-met stj2 *Sil-met* stj2 stann stj2 stront-m stj2 *Stront-met* stj2 tant-met stj2 techn stj2 thal-met stj2 titan stj2 titan-s stj2 tung-met stj2 vanad stj1* yttr-met stj2 zirc-met stj2]
    - **overheated**; when: carbn-s k2 ran-b k2
  - **amel.**: *Acon* st aesc sf1.de* agn b2.de *All-c* k2* aloe sf1.de *Alum* sf1.de am-m sf1.de ambr b2.de* anac b2.de* anan hr1* androc srj1• ang sf1.de *Ant-c* b2.de* ant-t b2.de* *Apis* sf1.de aran sf1.de aran-ix jl3 *Arg-n* sf1.de* arist-cl jl3 asaf sf1.de *Asar* b2.de* aur b2.de* aur-i k2 bapt k2* bar-i k2* bell-p jl3 beryl jl3 *Bry* b2.de* *Bufo* k2 calad b2.de* calc b2.de* calc-f jl3 camph tl1 cann-i hr1* cann-s b2.de *Carb-v* b2.de* carc gk6 cham b2.de* *Chin* hr1 cimic sf1.de cina b2.de* cit-v hr1* *Coc-c* hr1* cocc b2.de *Colch* b2.de* croc b2.de* *Dros* b2.de* dulc sf1.de euph b2.de* foll jl3 *Glon* k2* glycyr-g cte1• hed jl3 iber jl3 ign b2.de* **Iod** b2.de* ip b2.de* kali-bi kr1*

- **amel.**: ...
Kali-i hr1* Kali-s k2* Lac-c mrr1 Lach b2.de* Led b2.de* Lil-t sf1.de luf-op jl3 **Lyc** b2.de* m-arct b2.de mag-m k2* mag-p sf1.de med k2* meph jl merc b2.de* mosch sf1.de Nat-m b2.de* nep jl3* Nit-ac b2.de* nux-m tl1 nux-v b2.de* Op b2.de* ozone sde2• phos b2.de* Pic-ac k2* pitu jl3 plat b2.de* psil jl **Puls** b2.de* rauw jl3 rhus-t b2.de* ruta fd4.de sabin b2.de* Sec b2.de* Sel b2.de* seneg b2.de* Sep b2.de* stront-c sf1.de Sulph b2.de* syph k2* Tab sf1.de tere-ch jl3 teucr b2.de* thala jl3 thuj b2.de* tritic-vg fd5.de tub st tub-r jl3 vanil fd5.de visc jl3
  - **windows** open; must have: (↗RESPIRATION - Difficult - open; RESPIRATION - Difficult - open - doors; RESPIRATION - Difficult - open - window) Aml-ns bro1 apis sf1.de Arg-n bro1* bapt bro1* bry k2 (non:calc bro1*) camph k2 carb-v br1* Carbn-s k2 carc fd2.de• con gk dulc fd4.de glon k2 graph k2 ham fd3.de• iod sf1.de Ip sf1.de kali-p fd1.de• kali-s fd4.de Lach k2* lyc sf1.de med bro1* podo fd3.de• Puls k2* sabin k2 sacch-a fd2.de• sec k2 Sulph k2* tritic-vg fd5.de tub k2 vanil fd5.de
- **aversion** to: am-c sf1.de Aran sf1.de Ars sf1.de bart a1 bell sf1.de bry sf1.de Calc sf1.de caps a1* caust sf1.de Cham sf1.de chin sf1.de dulc fd4.de graph sf1.de grat sf1.de Hep sf1.de hydrog srj2• Kali-c sf1.de nat-c sf1.de nat-m sf1.de nux-m sf1.de Nux-v sf1.de Petr sf1.de sanguis-s hrn2• sel sf1.de Sil sf1.de spong fd4.de sulph sf1.de tub sf1.de
- **desire** for: (↗Air; open - desire) achy jl aloe Apis arg-n k2* asaf k* asar k* Aur k* camph k2* carb-v k* cic a1 Croc k* gran a1 Iod k* kali-s k2* lil-t k* mim-p skp7• Puls k2* ruta fd4.de sabin gk Sec k* sul-i k2* sulph k* tritic-vg fd5.de tub br1 vanil fd5.de
- **drawing** in cold air:
  - **agg.**: alum b2.de* ant-c b2.de* Ars b2.de* Aur b2.de* Bell b2.de* Bry b2.de* Calc b2.de* camph b2.de* **Caust** b2.de* cham b2.de* cina b2.de* cist bg2 dulc b2.de* Hep b2.de* **Hyos** b2.de* kali-bi bg2 Kali-c b2.de* m-ambo b2.de* m-arct b2.de* **Merc** b2.de* mosch b2.de* nat-m b2.de* Nux-m b2.de* **Nux-v** b2.de* par b2.de* petr b2.de* phos b2.de* puls b2.de* Rhod b2.de* Rhus-t b2.de* **Rumx** bg2 **Sabad** b2.de* sars b2.de* seneg b2.de* Sep b2.de* sil b2.de* spig b2.de* staph b2.de* Stront-c b2.de* sulph b2.de* thuj b2.de* verat b2.de*
  - **amel.**: nux-v b7.de puls b7.de
- **inspiration**:
  - **agg.**: aesc ptk1 Am-c ptk1 ars ptk1 **Caust** ptk1 Cimic ptk1 cist ptk1 hep ptk1 hydr ptk1 Hyos ptk1 Ign ptk1 Merc ptk1 Nux-v ptk1 Psor ptk1 Rumx ptk1 Sabad ptk1 sel jl3 seneg ptk1 sep ptk1 syph ptk1
  - **amel.**: hom-xyz mgm• sel ptk1*
- **sensation** of cold air: benz-ac ptk1 chin ptk1 lac-d ptk1 laur ptk1 Lyss ptk1 M-aust b7a.de menth br1 mez ptk1 mosch ptk1 thyr ptk1

- **amel.**: acon b2.de* aesc k2* agn b2.de all-c bro1* aloe k2* alum b2.de alumn kr1 am-m sf1.de Ambr b2.de* Anac b2.de* Ant-c b2.de* Ant-t b2.de* Apis k2* arg-n br1* arge-pl rwt5• arn b2.de* Asar b2.de* aur b2.de* aur-i k2 bapt kr1* bar-c b2.de* bell b2.de* bell-p bro1 beryl jl borx b2.de* Bry b2.de* Calad b2.de* calc b2.de* calc-f kr1* calc-i k2 camph ptk1 Cann-i kr1 cann-s b2.de canth mrr1 carb-v b2.de* carc hbh* cassia-s cdd7*• caust b2.de* Cham b2.de* chin b2.de* cimic kr1* Cina b2.de* coc-c k2 cocc b2.de* Colch b2.de* coloc b2.de* Croc b2.de* Dros b2.de* dulc b2.de* Euph b2.de* fago bro1 ferr b2.de* **Fl-ac** kr1* germ-met srj5• glycyr-g cte1• graph b2.de* guaj st* hell b2.de* hep b2.de* hist sp1 **Hyos** kr1 iber jl ign b2.de* ind vml3• **Iod** b2.de* Ip b2.de* kali-c b2.de* kali-i ptk1 Kali-s ptk1* Lac-c k2 lach b2.de* laur b2.de* Led b2.de* lil-t sf1.de Lyc b2.de* lyss jl2 m-ambo b2.de m-arct b2.de mag-m sf1.de mag-s sp1 med st merc b2.de* mez b2.de* moly-met jl mur-ac b2.de* nat-c b2.de* Nat-m b2.de* nit-ac b2.de* nux-m b2.de* nux-v b2.de* onos bro1 Op b2.de* ph-ac b2.de* Phos b2.de* Plat b2.de* psor ptk1 **Puls** b2.de* rhus-t b2.de* sabad b2.de* Sabin b2.de* Sec b2.de* Sel b2.de* Seneg b2.de* sep b2.de* sil b2.de* spig b2.de* spong b2.de* staph b2.de* Sulph b2.de* syph ptk1 tab ptk1 Teucr b2.de* Thuj b2.de* trios jl tritic-vg fd5.de verat b2.de*
- **applications**:
  - **agg.**: ars bg2 chir-fl bnm4• graph bg2 hep bg2 lach bg2 nit-ac bg2 petr bg2 ph-ac bg2 ruta bg2 sil bg2
    - **chill**; during: Cycl b7.de*
  - **amel.**: acon bg2 aloe mrr1 alum bro1 **Apis** bg2* Arg-n bg2* ars b4a.de asar bro1 bell bro1 bry bg2* canth mrr1 ferr-p bro1 iod bg2 kali-m bro1 led bg2 loxo-lae bnm12• lyc bg2 merc bro1 nux-v bg2 phos bro1 puls bg2* sabin bro1 sec bg2 sep bg2 sil b4a.de zinc b4a.de
- **bathing**:
  - **agg.**: acon k2 **Am-c** kr1* am-m kr1 **Ant-c** k* **Ant-t** k2* apoc st ars-i sf1.de atra-r bnm3• Bar-c Bell k* bell-p st* Borx kr1 bov kr1 Bry kr1 bufo kr1 **Calc** kr1 calc-sil k2 Canth kr1 Caps Carb-v kr1 carbn-s Caust Cham kr1 chim st cimic st **Clem** bg2* Colch Con kr1 Dulc bg2* elaps Form k* glon bg2 **Ign** bg2* Kali-c kr1 kali-m bg2 Kali-n kr1* Kreos Lac-d lach st Laur kr1 lob mrr1 Lyc kr1* mag-c kr1 **Mag-p** k* Merc kr1* Mez bg1* mosch bg2 mur-ac nat-c kr1 Nit-ac k* Nux-m kr1* nux-v kr1* phos k* Phys c1* psil ft1 psor k2 puls kr1 **Rhus-t** k* ruta st sars k* Sep k* Sil sf1.de* Spig kr1 spong fd4.de stann kr1 Staph kr1 Stront-c kr1 sul-ac kr1 **Sulph** kr1* symph fd3.de• thyr jl **Tub** k* urt-u ptk1 Zinc kr1*
  - **amel.**: alum sf1.de ant-t sf1.de Apis bg2* Arg-n k* Arn Asar bg2* aster jl aur bg2* Aur-m aur-m-n wbt2• bell mtf33 bell-p ptk1 berb-a jl bism Bry sf1.de* bufo bro1* calc-f jl Calc-s camph mrr1 cann-xyz bg2 caust bg2 coc-c ptk1 cycl hr1 Fl-ac k* galla-q-r nl2• glycyr-g cte1• hed mg1.de* hyper sf1.de* ind k* iod k* kali-cy gm1 kali-i vh lac-c mtf33 Led bg2* mag-s jl* meph k* Nat-m k* phyt ptk1 pic-ac k2* podo fd3.de• Psor sf1.de Puls bg2* pyrog jl2 rat ptk1 sec bg2 sep bro1* spig sf1.de sulph ptk1 syph st* tung-met bdx1•
    - **at** first amel. then agg.: vesp a
    - **face** and hand; of: vesp k2
  - **desire** for cold bathing: (↗FACE - Wash) aloe sf1.de Apis sf1.de arg-n sf1.de asar sf1.de aster bell mtf33 caust sf1.de chel sf1.de dulc fd4.de euphr sf1.de fl-ac a1* Hyper sf1.de iod sf1.de lac-cp sk4• Led sf1.de meph nat-m k* petr-ra shn4• phyt puls sf1.de sep sf1.de vanil fd5.de
    - **warm** bathing; with intolerance for: lac-cp sk4•
- **bed**; lying in: falco-pe nl2• Ign vh phos ptk1 positr nl2• sil ptk1 spong fd4.de
  - **night**: CARB-AN mrr1
- **dry** weather (See Weather - cold - dry)
- **faintness** (See Faintness - cold)
- **feeling**: (↗Heat - lack; CHILL - Chilliness; CHILL - Internal - coldness)
  - **one** side cold, the other warm: apis ptk1 chin b7a.de Ign b7a.de par ptk1* pime bro1 Rhus-t b7a.de
  - **right** side: bar-c ptk1 bry ptk1 chel ptk1 rhus-t ptk1 sabad ptk1
    - **heat** of left side; with: par br1*
  - **left** side: carb-v ptk1 caust ptk1 dros ptk1 lyc ptk1 sulph ptk1 thuj ptk1
  - **air** | **draft** of | **from**: am-p br1
    - **inspired** air feels cold: lith-c ptk1*
  - **eating**; after: nux-v b7a.de ran-b b7a.de sulph b4a.de
  - **frozen**; as if: mez mrr1
  - **icy** cold: (↗SKIN - Coldness - icy) acon bg2 agar bg2 bar-m ptk1 calc bg2 jatr-c ptk1
    - **accompanied** by | **nausea** and vomiting (See STOMACH - Nausea - accompanied - coldness; STOMACH - Vomiting - accompanied - coldness)
    - **menses**; during: sil ptk1
    - **pain**; during: dulc ptk1
  - **spots**; in: agar bg2* am-m bg2 arn bg2 ars bg2 calc-p ptk1 canth bg2 mang bg2 par bg2 petr bg2* rhus-t bg2 sep ptk1 stront-c ptk1 tarent bg2* Verat ptk1
  - ○ **Affected** parts; in: (↗Coldness) Ang bg2 ars b4a.de* bry bg2 caust bg2 cocc bg2 crot-h bg2 dulc b4a.de* graph bg2 lach bg2 Led bg2 merc bg2* mez bg2 petr b4a.de* plat b4a.de* plb bg2 rhod b4a.de* Rhus-t bg2 sil b4a.de* Spig br1 thuj b4a.de*
  - **Blood** vessels; in: (↗CHILL - Internal - coldness - blood) abies-c bg2* **Acon** k* ant-c ant-t k* **Ars** k* bell sf1.de kali-chl ptk lyc k* op b7.de* plb bg2 pyrog ptk1 **Rhus-t** k* sul-ac ptk1 sulph sf1.de Verat k*
  - **Bones**: (↗CHILL - Internal - coldness - bones) Aran k* Ars k* Berb bg2* Calc k* coca-c sk4• dulc bg2* elaps k* Eup-per ptk1 galla-q-r nl2• graph bg2 hep k2 kali-i ptk1 lavand-a ctl1• lyc k* merc k* mez mrr1 pyrog ptk1 sep k* sulph k* Verat k* zinc k*
  - **External**: am-m ptk1 ars ptk1 camph ptk1 Ign ptk1 kali-n ptk1 nit-ac ptk1 Nux-v ptk1 olnd ptk1 verat ptk1* Zinc ptk1
    - **accompanied** by:
      - **pain**; burning | **Internal**: sec ptk1

- **Inner** parts: (↗internal; CHILL - Internal - coldness) acon b2.de* alum b2.de* ambr b2.de* anac ptk1 anh mg1.de ant-c b2.de* ant-t b2.de* Antip vh1 Apis ptk1 aran vh1 arn b2.de* ars k* asaf b2.de* bar-c b2.de* bell b2.de* bov b2.de* bry b2.de* Calc k* camph b2.de* caps b2.de* carb-an b2.de* carb-v b2.de* caust b2.de* chel b2.de* chin b2.de* cocc ptk1 colch b2.de* con b2.de* cory br1 croc b2.de* dig ptk1 dros b2.de* elaps ptk1 graph b2.de* hell b2.de* Helo-s rwt2• hep ptk1 Hura st ign b2.de* ip b2.de* kali-c b2.de* kali-n b2.de* kreos b2.de* lach b2.de* Laur k* lyc k* m-aust b2.de* mag-c b2.de* mang b2.de* mang-p rly4• meny k* merc b2.de* mez b2.de* mosch b2.de* nat-c b2.de* nat-m b2.de* nit-ac b2.de* nux-v k* olnd b2.de* par k* petr mrr1 ph-ac b2.de* phos b2.de* plat b2.de* plb b2.de* positr nl2• puls b2.de* rhus-t b2.de* ruta b2.de* sabad b2.de* sars b2.de* sec b2.de* sep k* spong b2.de* sul-ac b2.de* sulph k* ther ptk1 valer b2.de* Verat b2.de* zinc b2.de*
- **Lower** part of body:
  - **accompanied** by:
    - **heat**; sensation of | **Upper** part of body (See Heat - sensation - upper - accompanied - coldness)
- **Nerves**: acon k2 agar br1 ferr-t c1 ferul a1 kali-c k2 ter c1
- **Parts** lain on: arn ptk1 mur-ac ptk1
- **Single** parts: agar mg1.de aran mg1.de aran-ix mg1.de Ars ptk1 asar br1 berb ptk1 buth-a mg1.de calad br1 calc ptk1 Carb-v ptk1* chel ptk1 chin ptk1 Cist br1* Dulc ptk1 elaps mg1.de helo mg1.de Ign ptk1 kali-c ptk1 kali-chl ptk1 lyc ptk1 meny ptk1 mosch mrr1 nat-m ptk1 ph-ac ptk1 Plat br1* **Puls** ptk1 Rhus-t ptk1 sec ptk1 Sep ptk1 sil ptk1 Spig ptk1 sulph ptk1 **Verat** ptk1
- **Tips** of fingers, toes and nose: meny bg2
- **Upper** part of body: Ip hr1*

- **heat** and cold: allox tpw3 Alum alum-p k2* ang bg2* ange-s oss1• Ant-c k* ant-t st1 arn bg* Ars-i asar bg2 aur-s k2* bar-c k2 bar-s k2* bell vh brom k2 cadm-i gm1 Calc bg2* calc-s k2* caps bg2 carb-v ptk Carbn-s carc pd* Caust k* celt a1 cimic hr1* cina bg2 cinnb Cocc Cor-r bg1* falco-pe nl2• ferr sf1.de* **Fl-ac** k* flav jl3 Glon bg1* Graph k* hell bg* Ip k* kali-c k* Lach k* **Lyc** k ●* mag-m Merc k* merc-k-i gm1 nat-c k* **Nat-m** k ●* nux-v h1* Ph-ac k* Phys bg1* pin-con oss2• plan c1 Psor k* puls k* Ran-b rob st1 sanic bg2 Sep k* Sil k* sul-ac bg1* Sulph k* Syph bg2* tab bg2* thala jl3 thuj ptk1 Tub gt1*
- **hot** days with cold nights: acon ptk1 dulc ptk1 merc-c ptk1 rumx ptk1
- **internal** coldness with external heat: (↗feeling - inner) lap-la rsp1 laur st
- **painful** coldness: arn ptk1 camph mrr1 cist ptk1 med ptk1 mez ptk1 mosch ptk1 syph ptk1
- **paralysis** (See Paralysis - cold - agg.)
- **room**:
  - **amel.**: puls bg2
  - **entering** a cold room; after: **Ars** k* bell ptk1 calc-p Camph b2.de* carb-v k* caust k* con k* cor-r br1 Dulc k* Ferr Ferr-ar Graph Hep ip bg2* **Kali-ar** k* kali-c k* kali-p kali-sil k2 mosch k* nux-m k* Nux-v k* Petr phos k* Psor Puls k* **Ran-b** k* Rhus-t Sabad k* **Sep** k* Sil k* spong k* stront-c k* Tub Verb k*
    - **from** a warm room: cor-r br1
- **spots**: agar mrr1 calc-p ptk1 camph mrr1 caps k2 Helo br1 Helo-s br1* mez mrr1 petr tl1* sep ptk1 tarent ptk1 Verat ptk1
  - **painful**: ran-b mrr1
- **water**:
  - **sensation** of:
    - **being** in cold water: led ptk1
    - **running**:
      - **Blood** vessels; through: abies-c bg2 borx bg2 op b7.de*
      - **Bones**; through: graph bg2
    - **Body**; on: ran-b tl1
- **weather** (See Weather - cold)
- **wet** agg.: ant-c tl1 ant-t bro1 Aran bro1 arn br1* ars bro1 ars-i bro1 bry tl1 calc bro1 calc-sil bro1 colch tl1 coli jl2 dulc bro1* Nat-s bro1 nux-m bro1 Phyt tl1* Rhus-t bro1 ter bro1 [arg-met stj1 bar-m stj1 bar-p stj1 mang-met stj1]

COLD; BECOMING:

- **after** | **agg.**: (↗Uncovering - agg.; Uncovering - single) acetan br1 Acon k* agar k* Alum k* alum-p k2 alum-sil k2 Alumn Am-c k* anac bg2* Ant-c bg2* Ant-t Arg-n arn k* **Ars** k* ars-s-f k2 aur k* aur-s k2 **Bar-c** k* bar-s a1* **Bell** k* borx k* **Bry** k* **Calc** k* **Calc-p** calc-s calc-sil k2 camph k* Carb-v k* Carbn-s Caust bg2* **Cham** k* **Chin** k* cimic bg2 cocc k* Coff k*

Cold; becoming – after – **agg.**: ...
colch k2 Coloc k* con k* croc k* cupr k* cupr-s kr1 Cycl k* dig k* dros k* **Dulc** k* eup-per k2 ferr ferr-ar k2 **Fl-ac** bg2 **Graph** k* guaj bg2 **Hep** k* hydr bg2 **Hyos** k* hyper ign k* Ip k* kali-ar k2 Kali-bi k* Kali-c k* kali-m k2 kali-p Kali-sil k2 kalm led k* Lyc k* m-ambo b7.de* mag-c k* Mang k* Med **Merc** k* moni rfm1• Mosch b7a.de nat-c k* Nat-m k* nat-p nat-sil k2 Nit-ac k* Nux-m k* **Nux-v** k* op k* Petr k* Ph-ac k* **Phos** k* phyt k2 plat k* polyg-h bg2 Psor k* **Puls** k* **Pyrog Ran-b** k* **Rhus-t** k* ruta k* sabin k* Samb k* sang k2 sars k* sel k* **Sep** k* **Sil** k* **Spig** k* spong b7.de Stann k* staph k* stront-c k* **Sul-ac** k* sul-i k2 Sulph k* Tarent Thuj tub k2 valer k* Verat k* Xan kr1 zinc-p k2

- **agg.**: Acetan vh1 acon k* aesc Agar k* agath-a nl2• allox tpw3 alum-p k2 Alumn Am-c k* ant-c k* Anth vh1 arg-n Arn k* **Ars** k* ars-i ars-s-f k2 asar k* **Aur** k* Aur-m-n wbt2• aur-s k2 Bad Bamb-a stb2.de• **Bar-c** k* bar-m bar-s k2 bell k* borx k* both-ax tsm2 bov k* Bry k* Calc k* Calc-p calc-sil k2 Camph k* canth k* Caps k* Carb-an k* Carb-v k* Carbn-s Caust k* Cham k* chin k* chinin-ar cic k* Cimic clem k* Cocc k* Con k* Dig k* diphtox jl2 Dulc k* elaps Ferr k* ferr-ar ferr-p gard-j vlr2• Graph k* hell k* **Hep** k* Hydrog srj2• Hyos k* Hyper ign k* **Kali-ar Kali-bi Kali-c** k* kali-m k2 kali-p kali-s kali-sil k2 kalm c1 Kreos k* lach k* **Lyc** k* m-ambo b2.de* m-aust b2.de Mag-c k* mag-m k* Mag-p mang k* Med meny k* merc k* merc-i-r mez k* **Mosch** k* mur-ac k* Nat-ar nat-c k* nat-m k* Nat-p nicc nit-ac k* nux-m k* **Nux-v** k* Petr k* **Ph-ac** k* Phos k* phyt c1 Psor pycnop-sa mrz1 **Pyrog Ran-b** k* rhod k* **Rhus-t** k* Rumx ruta k* **Sabad** k* samb k* sars k* **Sep** k* **Sil** k* spig k* spong k* squil k* staph k* stram k* Stront-c k* **Sul-ac** k* sul-i k2 Sulph k* Sumb Tarent Thuj k* tub k2 Verat b2.de* verb k* viol-t k* Zinc k* zinc-p k2
  - **overheating**; after: acon bg1* Bell-p st bry bg1* caps bg2 (non:carb-v h2*) cycl dulc vh kali-ar k2 kali-c k2 kali-s c1* puls bl ran-b k2 rhus-t a* sil k2
  - **pain**; from: calc-p tl1
  - **perspiration**; during: **Acon** bg2* Ars-s-f k2 calc mrr1 calc-sil k2 dulc st med gk merc-i-f st nit-ac st rhus-t hr* sang ms* sars dgt2 sil vh sul-i k2
    - **hot** perspiration: nux-v bg2
  - **sitting** on cold steps: ars ptk1 calc ptk1 caust ptk1 dulc a* Nux-v ptk1 rhod ptk1 sil ptk1
  - ○ **Part** of body agg.: (↗Uncovering - single) agar ptk1 am-c ptk1 Bar-c Bell k* Calc ptk1 cham k* Hell k* **Hep** k* ip kr1 led b2.de* Nux-v ptk1 ph-ac Phos ptk1 psor ptk1 puls k* **Rhus-t** k* Sep k* **Sil** k* tarent ptk1 thuj ptk1 zinc ptk1
    - **Back**: pilo st
    - **Extremities**: aur Bry con **Hep** Nat-m **Rhus-t Sil** squil stront-c **Thuj**
    - **Feet**: alum bg2 am-c bg2 ars bg2 Bar-c k* bufo bg2 cham k* clem bg2 **Con** k ●* cupr k* dulc ptk2* kali-ar bg2 kali-c bg2 Lach bg2 **Lyc** ●* mag-p bg2 nit-ac bg2 nux-m bg2 **NUX-V** ●* phos bg2 phys bg2 **Puls** ●* sep bg2 **Sil** k* stann h2 sulph ptk tub a vip fkr4.de zinc bg2
    - **Hand**: (↗FEVER - Chilliness - putting) acon bg2 merc bg2 phos bg2
      - **bed**; out of: (↗FEVER - Chilliness - putting) **Bar-c** borx a1 canth Con **Hep** phos **Rhus-t** Sil
    - **Head**: am-c h2 arg-n bg2 **BELL** k ●* Hep bg2 hyos bg2 led k* nux-v bg2 **Puls** k ●* rhus-t bg2 **SEP** k ●* **Sil** k*
- **amel.**: acon k* aesc bg2 agn k* all-c bg2 aloe bg2 alum k* alumn kr1 am-c bg2 am-m bg2 ambr k* anac b2.de* ang bg2 ant-c k* ant-t k* Apis bg2 Arg-n k* arn k* asaf bg2 asar b2.de* aur k* bapt bg2 bar-c k* bell k* bov k* brom bg2 Bry k* calad k* calc b2.de* calc-i k2 cann-i kr1 cann-s k* carb-v k* carc mlr1• caust b2.de* Cham k* chin b2.de* cina b2.de* clem k* coc-c bg2 cocc k* coff k* colch k* coloc k* croc k* Dros k* dulc k* euph k* Fl-ac bg2 Glon Graph b2.de* guaj bg2 hell k* ign b2.de* **Iod** k* ip k* kali-bi kr1 kali-c b2.de* kali-i bg2 kali-s bg2 kalm bg2 Lac-c Lach k* Led k* lil-t bg2 **Lyc** k* m-ambo b2.de m-arct b2.de mang k* Merc k* mez k* mur-ac k* nat-c k* Nat-m k* nit-ac k* Nux-m b2.de* nux-v b2.de* olnd k* op k* Petr k* ph-ac k* phos k* plat k* psil ft1 **Puls** k* rhus-t b2.de* sabad k* Sabin k* sars k* Sec k* sel k* seneg k* sep b2.de* sil b2.de* spig k* spong k* staph k* Sulph k* teucr k* thuj k* verat k*

COLD; TAKING A:

- **after**: Acon b2.de agar b2.de alum b2.de am-c b2.de anac b2.de Ant-c b2.de arn b2.de ars b2.de aur b2.de bar-c b2.de **Bell** b2.de borx b2.de **Bry** b2.de Calc b2.de camph b2.de Carb-v b2.de caust b2.de **Cham** b2.de Chin b2.de cocc b2.de Coff b2.de Coloc b2.de Con b2.de croc b2.de cupr b2.de Cycl b2.de dig b2.de dros b2.de **Dulc** b2.de Graph b2.de Hep b2.de **Hyos** b2.de ign b2.de Ip b2.de kali-c b2.de led b2.de Lyc b2.de m-ambo b2.de m-arct b2.de m-aust b2.de mag-c b2.de Mang b2.de **Merc** b2.de nat-c b2.de Nat-m b2.de

- **after**: ...
Nit-ac b2.de nux-m b2.de **Nux-v** b2.de op b2.de petr b2.de ph-ac b2.de **Phos** b2.de plat b2.de **Puls** b2.de ran-b b2.de **Rhus-t** b2.de ruta b2.de sabin b2.de *Samb* b2.de sars b2.de sel b2.de *Sep* b2.de **Sil** b2.de **Spig** b2.de stann b2.de staph b2.de stront-c b2.de sul-ac b2.de *Sulph* b2.de valer b2.de *Verat* b2.de
  - **agg.**: *Acon* b7.de* agar b4.de alum b4a.de am-c b4.de anac b4.de *Ant-c* b7.de *Arn* b7a.de ars b4a.de aur b4.de bar-c b4.de* *Bell* b4.de* borx b4a.de *Bry* b7.de* *Calc* b4.de camph b7.de* *Carb-v* b4.de caust b4.de *Cham* b7.de* *Chin* b7.de cocc b7.de* *Coff* b7.de* coloc b4.de* con b4.de* croc b7.de* cupr b7.de *Cycl* b7.de dig b4.de dros b7.de *Dulc* b4.de* graph b4.de* *Hep* b4.de *Hyos* b7.de* *Ign* b7.de* *Ip* b7.de kali-c b4.de led b7a.de *Lyc* b4.de m-ambo b7.de m-arct b7.de m-aust b7.de mag-c b4.de *Mang* b4a.de **Merc** b4a.de *Nat-c* b4.de nat-m b4.de* *Nit-ac* b4.de* *Nux-m* b7.de* **Nux-v** b7.de *Op* b7.de petr b4.de ph-ac b4.de *Phos* b4.de* *Plat* b4.de *Puls* b7.de *Ran-b* b7a.de *Rhus-t* b7.de* ruta b7.de sabin b7.de *Samb* b7.de *Sars* b4.de* *Sel* b7.de* *Sep* b4.de* *Sil* b4.de* **Spig** b7.de stann b4.de *Staph* b7.de stront-c b4.de sul-ac b4a.de *Sulph* b4a.de valer b7a.de verat b7.de*
  - ○ **Feet**; of: cham b2.de *Puls* b2.de **Sil** b2.de
  - **Head**; of: **Bell** b2.de led b2.de puls b2.de **Sep** b2.de
  - **Stomach**; of: puls b7a.de
- **tendency**: *(↗Complaints - acute - recurrent; History - coryza; NOSE - Coryza - periodical)* abies-c oss4• **Acon** k* aesc sf1.de agar sf1.de agra br1* all-c sf1.de **Alum** k* alum-p k2 alum-sil k2 alumn k2 am-c k* am-m anac k* *Ant-c* k* ant-t aral sf1.de aran sf1.de *Arg-n* arn k* ars k* ars-i k* ars-s-f k2 *Bac* br1* **BAR-C** k* bar-i k2 bar-m sf1.de bar-s k2 *Bell* k* benz-ac bg2 borx k* bov bg2 **Bry** k* calad sf1.de *Calc* k* calc-i k2* **Calc-p** k* *Calc-s* calc-sil k2 *Calen* br1* camph k* caps mg1.de carb-an sf1.de* *Carb-v* k* *Carbn-s* carc fb* carl br1 caust k* **Cham** k* chin k* chinin-ar choc srj3• cimic k2* cinnb sf1.de **Cist** sf1.de* clem sf1.de coc-c cocc k* coff k* colch k2 coloc k* *Con* k* croc k* crot-h j5.de cupr k* cycl sf1.de dig k* dios dros b2.de* **Dulc** k* dys fmm1• elaps sf1.de eup-per k2 euphr sf1.de *Ferr* k* ferr-ar ferr-i ferr-p k* flav jl2 *Form* k* gast a1* *Gels* k* goss *Graph* k* ham hed mg1.de* **Hep** k* hydr bro1 *Hydrog* srj2• *Hyos* k* hyper sf1.de ign k* iod k* ip k* **Kali-ar** *Kali-bi* **Kali-c** k* **Kali-i** k2 kali-n ptk1 kali-p k1* kali-s kali-sil k2 *Lac-d* lach j5.de* led k* **Lyc** k* m-ambo b2.de* m-arct b2.de* m-aust b2.de* mag-c mg1.de* mag-m k* **Med** k2* **Merc** k* mez k* moni rfm1• naja bg2 **Nat-ar** *Nat-c* k* **Nat-m** k* nat-p nat-sil k2 **Nit-ac** k* *Nux-m* k* **Nux-v** k* ol-j sf1.de* op k* osm c1 *Petr* k* *Ph-ac* k* *Phos* k* plat k* pseuts-m oss1• **Psor** k* *Puls* k* pycnop-sa mrz1 rhod c1* *Rhus-t* k* **Rumx** ruta k* sabad sabin k* samb k* sang sars k* sel k* senec k2* **Sep** k* **Sil** k* solid bro1 spig k* stach a1 stann k* staph k* succ-ac rly4• *Sul-ac* k* sul-i k2 *Sulph* k* *Thuj* kr1* **TUB** k* tub-m jl2 v-a-b jl2* valer k* verat k* verb sf1.de zinc sf1.de [bell-p-sp dcm1]
  - **accompanied** by:
    - **sneezing**; violent and frequent: all-c tl1 cist tl1
    - **vomiting**: cocc tl1
  - **ailments** from: coloc c1 dulc vh kali-c c1 puls vh rhod c1
    - **spring** agg.: all-c c1
  - **air** agg.; in open: all-c tl1
  - **air** on chest agg.; draft of: ph-ac ptk1
  - **beginning** stage: all-c tl1 ferr-p tl1
  - **children**; in: bar-c br1 calc-i br1 carc tpw* sep mtf33
  - **cold** agg.; after becoming: acon tl1
  - **cold** air agg.: *Kali-c* tl1
  - **eyes**; acrid discharge from: all-c tl1
  - **indoors**: all-c tl1
  - **lean**, dry people; in: alum br1
  - **menses** | **before** | **agg.**: calc bg2 lac-c bg2
    - **during**:
      - **agg.**: *Acon* b7a.de
        - **first** menses: calc-p ptk1
  - **overheated**; after being: kali-c ptk1
  - **perspiration**, after: *Ip* b7a.de nit-ac ptk1* *Rhus-t* b7a.de
  - **weather**:
    - **stormy** | **agg.**: nit-s-d br1
    - **warm**:
      - **wet** | **agg.**: *Ip* br1
    - **wet** | **agg.**: **Calen** br1*

Cold; taking a – **tendency**: ...
  - **winds**; after damp cold: all-c tl1
  - **women**; in: | **obese**: am-c br1

COLDBLOODED persons (See Heat - lack)

COLDNESS of affected parts: *(↗Cold - feeling - affected; Heat - lack)* acon bg2 agar bg2 aids nl2• aln vva1• alum-sil k2 *Arn* bg2 ars ptk1 asar bg2 bar-c bg2 bell bg2 bov bg2 bry bg2* bufo bg2 *Calc* bg2* camph bg2 cann-xyz bg2 canth bg2 caps k2* *Caust* bg2* chel bg2 *Chin* bg2 *Cocc* bg2* coff bg2 colch ptk1 croc bg2 cypra-eg sde6.de• dig bg2 dros bg2 dulc bg2 euph bg2 graph bg2 hell bg2 ign bg2 kali-i k2 kreos bg2 lach bg2* **Laur** bg2 led ptk1 *Lyc* bg2 mag-c bg2 mand rsj7• melal-alt gya4 meny bg2* *Merc* bg2 mez bg2* **Mosch** bg2 **Mur-ac** bg2 ozone sde2• par bg2 ph-ac bg2 phos bg2 *Plat* bg2 plb bg2 **Puls** bg2 pyrog jl2 rhod bg2 **Rhus-t** bg2* ruta bg2 *Sec* bg2* **Sep** bg2 sil ptk1 *Spig* bg2* spong bg2 stann bg2 staph bg2 **Sulph** bg2 thal dx *Verat* bg2 **Verb** bg2 zinc bg2
- **one** side of the body in septic fever: meny h1 *Puls* h1 rhus-t h1
- **right** side: ars a1 par a1 rhus-t a1
- **left** side: bry a1 caust a1 lyc a1 sapin a1
- **drinking** agg.; after: asaf b7a.de
- **pain**; during: agar br1 ars b4a.de euph b4a.de
- **wounds** become cold (See Wounds - cold)
- ○ **Blood** vessels; in (See Cold - feeling - blood; CHILL - Internal - coldness - blood)
- **Body**; of the whole (See Heat - lack; SKIN - Coldness)
- **Bones**; of the (See Cold - feeling - bones; CHILL - Internal - coldness - bones)
- **Paralyzed** parts: *Cocc* b7a.de dulc ptk2 *Plb* b7a.de *Rhus-t* b7a.de
- **Side** lain on:
  - **morning** | **bed** agg.; in: arn h1
- **Trunk** | **menses**; before: mang b4.de thuj b4a.de

COLLAGEN DISEASES: *(↗Aids; Autoimmune)* ars mtf ars-i mtf calen mtf carc mtf cortiso mtf des-ac mtf11 graph mtf kali-ar mtf lach mtf med mtf merc mtf nit-ac mtf penic mtf11 psor mtf rhus-t mtf saroth mtf11 suis-chord-umb mtf11 syph mtf thuj mtf tub-r mtf

COLLAPSE: *(↗Faintness; Weakness; MIND - Prostration)* acet-ac k* acetan br1* acon a1* aconin a1 adren st1 aeth ptk1 agar-ph mtf11 **Am-c** k* ampe-qu a1 amyg k* *Ant-ar* sf1.de *Ant-t* bg* anthraci jl2 apis aran-ix mg1.de arn bg* **Ars** k* *Ars-h* k* atra-r bnm3• *Bapt* sf1.de bar-c k* beryl sp1 borx br1 calc mrr1 **Camph** k* cann-i k* canth *Carb-ac* k* carb-an hr1* **Carb-v** k* **Carbn-s** k* carc gk6* caust sf1.de cench a1 **Chin** hr1* chir-fl bnm4* cina cit-l a1* *Colch* bro1* colchin a1 coli jl2 con ptk1 crat br1* *Crot-h* k* crot-t k* *Cupr* k* cupr-act br1* *Cupr-ar* k* cupr-s k* cystein-l rly4• cyt-l a1* *Dig* c1* diph bro1* dor k* euon k* *Gels* sf1.de hell k* home a1* *Hydr-ac* br1* hydrog srj2• *Hyos* hr1* iod k* ip ptk1 jab k* kali-br sf1.de kali-c tl1 kali-chl a1 kali-chr a1 kali-cy a1 kali-n k* kola stb3• kou br1 *Lach* a1* lat-m sp1 *Laur* k* lith-c sf1.de lob bro1 lob-p bro1 lol a1 lyc sf1.de *Med* k* merc k* merc-c k* merc-cy bg* merc-n a1 merc-ns a1 merc-pr-a a1 morph k* *Mosch* hr1* mur-ac bro1* naja k* nicot c1* nit-s-d a1 *Nux-v* mrr1 olnd k* op k* ox-ac k* oxyurn-sc mcp1• ozone sde2* *Ph-ac* mrr1 *Phos* k* phys k* pitu sp1 pitu-p sp1 plb k* rhus-t sf1.de sabad sf* santin a1 scam a1 *Sec* k* sel mrr1 *Seneg* hr1* sep ptk1* *Sil* mrr1 stram k* *Stront-c* mrr1 succ c sul-ac k* sulph ptk1 tab k* tarent mg1.de tarent-c sf1.de tax k* *Verat* k* *Verat-v* sf1.de* vip k* *Zinc* bro1*
- **accompanied** by:
  - **cholera**: *(↗diarrhea)* *Ars* bg2 **Camph** bg2 carb-v bg2* op bg2 *Sulph* bg2 **Verat** bg2
  - **palpitations** (See CHEST - Palpitation - accompanied - collapse)
  - **vertigo**: colch bg2
    - **nausea**; and: cocc mtf11
  - ○ **Abdomen**; cramping pain in: aeth bro1 camph bro1 cupr bro1 *Verat* bro1
  - **Heart**; complaints of (See CHEST - Heart; complaints - accompanied - collapse)
  - **Lungs**; complaints of the: hydr-ac br1
- **coldness**; with: camph mrr1 carb-v mtf33 *Verat* br1*
- **convulsions**; after: nicot bro1
- **delivery**; during: ip bro1

- **diarrhea** agg.; after: (*↗accompanied - cholera; Faintness - diarrhea - after - agg.; Weakness - diarrhea - from)* ant-c kr1 anthraci vh1 **Ars** k* **Camph** k* **Carb-v** k* *Ph-ac* mrr1 ric a1 sec ptk1 **Verat** k*
- **injuries**; from: acet-ac ptk1 sul-ac ptk1
- **menses**; at start of: merc ptk1
- **motion**; from: dig c1
- **needle**; from prick of a: calc h2
- **nervous**: am-c ptk1 laur ptk1
- **overwork**; from: *Nux-v* mrr1
- **pain**; from: bamb-a stb2.de•
- **paralysis**, at beginning of general: con k*
- **perspiration**:
  - **with**: colch ptk1
  - **without**: am-c ptk1 camph bg3* phys ptk1
- **smallpox**; after: *Ars* bro1 carb-v bro1 lach bro1 *Mur-ac* bro1 ph-ac bro1
- **stool** agg.; after: ant-t bg2 ars bg2 cocc bg2 con bg2 crot-t bg2 hydr bg2 kali-p bg2 mez bg2 petr bg2 podo bg2 stann bg2 verat bg2
- **sudden**: (*↗Weakness - rapid; Weakness - sudden)* **Ars** k* **Camph** sne chir-fl gya2 *Colch* hr1* crot-h ptk1 graph ptk1 hydr-ac ptk1 phos k* sep ptk1
- **tendency** to: colch br1 coli jl2 pyrog jl2 ser-a-c jl2
- **typhoid** fever; of: *Ars* bro1 *Camph* bro1 carb-v br1* chin bro1 crat br1 hyosin-hbr bro1 *Laur* bro1 mur-ac bro1 sec bro1 verat bro1
- **vision**; after illusions of: sep bg3*
- **vomiting**:
  - **after**: **Ars** k* lob k* phys k* ric a1 *Verat* k*
  - **during**: aeth bro1 *Ant-t* bro1 *Ars* k* cadm-s bro1 crot-h bro1 euph-c bro1 *Lob* bro1 ric a1 *Tab* bro1 *Verat* hr1* verat-v hr1*

COMBING hair:
- **agg.**: *Asar* hr1* bell k2* *Bry* b2.de* carb-ac ptk1 chin b2.de* form ptk1 glon ptk1 ign b2.de* kreos b2.de* mez ptk1 nat-s bg2 *Puls* b7a.de *Sel* b2.de* sep brm sil ptk1 tub ser
- **amel.**: carb-ac bg2 form bg2* glon bg2 tarent ptk1

COMFORTABLE feeling: acon a1 agar a1 ars a1 aur a1 chir-fl gya2 chlor a1 coca a1 dat-a a1 gast a1 kali-br a1 lach a1 mec a1 nat-p a1 op a1 phos a1 pic-ac a1 ruta fd4.de spong fd4.de

COMMON COLD (See NOSE - Coryza)

COMPANY: | **agg.** | **pleasant** company: hell bg2
- **amel.**: *Ars* b2.de bov b2.de con b2.de *Dros* b2.de kali-c b2.de **Lyc** b2.de mez b2.de *Phos* b2.de sil b2.de **Stram** b2.de zinc b2.de

COMPLAINTS:
- **morning** | **sun**; increasing and decreasing with the: kalm ptk1 *Nat-m* ptk1 *Sang* ptk1 sel ptk1 spig ptk1
- **accompanied** by:
  - **mental** symptoms (= mental symptoms are concomitants): **Acon** bg2 agar bg2 *Alum* bg2 *Am-c* bg2 am-m bg2 ambr bg2 anac bg2 *Ant-c* bg2 *Ant-t* bg2 arg-met bg2 arg-n bg2 arn bg2 ars bg2 asaf bg2 aur bg2 *Bar-c* bg2 *Bell* bg2 bov bg2 *Bry* bg2 calad bg2 **Calc** bg2 camph bg2 *Canth* bg2 *Carb-an* bg2 carb-v bg2 caust bg2 cham bg2 chel bg2 *Chin* bg2 cic bg2 cina bg2 *Cocc* bg2 coff bg2 coloc bg2 con bg2 *Croc* bg2 *Cupr* bg2 dig bg2 dulc bg2 *Ferr* bg2 graph bg2 hell bg2 *Hep* bg2 *Hyos* bg2 *Ign* bg2 iod bg2 *Ip* bg2 kali-c bg2 kali-n bg2 lach bg2 laur bg2 led bg2 *Lyc* bg2 *Mag-c* bg2 *Mag-m* bg2 merc bg2 mez bg2 mosch bg2 *Nat-m* bg2 *Nit-ac* bg2 *Nux-m* bg2 **Nux-v** bg2 olnd bg2 op bg2 par bg2 *Petr* bg2 ph-ac bg2 **Phos** bg2 plat bg2 plb bg2 **Puls** bg2 ran-s bg2 rhod bg2 *Rhus-t* bg2 ruta bg2 *Sabad* bg2 *Sabin* bg2 sars bg2 sec bg2 sel bg2 seneg bg2 *Sep* bg2 sil bg2 *Spig* bg2 spong bg2 squil bg2 stann bg2 staph bg2 **Stram** bg2 *Stront-c* bg2 *Sulph* bg2 verat bg2 verb bg2 zinc bg2
  - **shivering**: sabad ptk1
  - **sleepiness** (See SLEEP - Sleepiness - accompanied - complaints)
  - ○ **Teeth**; pain in: calc-p bg2
- **acute**: (*↗Sudden)* *Acon* br1
  - **children**; in: (*↗Children)* cham mrr1
  - **recurrent**: (*↗Cold; taking - tendency; Convalescence)* bar-c mrr1 calc mrr1 carc mrr1* merc mrr1 *Psor* mrr1 *Sil* mrr1 sulph mrr1 tub mrr1
    - **accompanied** by | **heat**; lack of vital: psor mrr1

Complaints: ...
- **alternating** with | **diarrhea** (See RECTUM - Diarrhea - alternating - other)
- **appearing**:
  - **atypical**: mosch bro1
  - **distant** parts; from complaints in: ars bg2 sabad bg2
  - **gradually**: (*↗Pain - appear gradually)* bry br1
    - **disappearing**; and:
      - **gradually**: arg-n ptk1 ars ptk1 gels ptk1 *Glon* ptk1 kali-bi ptk1 kalm ptk1 lach ptk1 *Nat-m* ptk1 phos ptk1 **Plat** ptk1 puls ptk1 *Sang* ptk1 *Spig* ptk1 **Stann** ptk1 **Stront-c** ptk1 sulph ptk1 syph ptk1
      - **suddenly**: *Arg-met* ptk1 caust ptk1 *Ign* ptk1 *Puls* ptk1 *Sul-ac* ptk1
  - **suddenly**: (*↗Pain - appear suddenly; Sudden)*
    - **disappearing**; and:
      - **gradually**: puls ptk1 sabin ptk1
      - **suddenly** (= rapidly): arg-n ptk1 *Bell* ptk1 *Chr-ac* br1 *Kali-bi* ptk1 *Nit-ac* ptk1 spig ptk1 sulph ptk1 tub jl2 [ang stj4]
- **body** weight; regulation of: thyr mtf11
- **chronic**: *Alum* ptk1 arg-met bg2 arg-n ptk1 *Ars* ptk1 calc bg2* carb-v br1 carc mlr1• *Caust* ptk1 *Con* ptk1 iod br1 kali-bi ptk1 kali-i ptk1 lyc br1* mang ptk1 med jl2 nat-s bg2 nit-ac br1 phos ptk1 plb ptk1 psor ptk1 *Sep* ptk1 sil bg2 sulph bg2* syph ptk1 thuj bg2 tub ptk1 vac br1
  - **accompanied** by | **relaxation**; physical (See Relaxation - physical - chronic)
  - **indefinite**: kali-i br1 thuj tl1
  - **sadness**; with (See MIND - Sadness - chronic)
- **followed** by | **Head**; pain in: carb-ac bg2 coff bg2
- **groups**; appear in: caust bg2 cham bg2 cocc bg2 coloc bg2 cupr bg2 hyos bg2 rhod bg2 sil bg2
- **internal** complaints:
  - **alternating** with:
    - **eczema**: *Graph*
    - **eruptions**: ars ptk1* crot-t pd* graph rhus-t ptk1 sulph mtf33
- **radiating**: agar ptk1 arg-n ptk1 ars ptk1 bapt ptk1 *Berb* ptk1 caust ptk1 cham ptk1 cimic ptk1 *Coloc* ptk1 *Cupr* ptk1 *Dios* ptk1 kali-bi ptk1 kali-c ptk1 kalm ptk1 mag-p ptk1 *Merc* ptk1 mez ptk1 nux-v ptk1 phyt ptk1 plat ptk1 plb ptk1 sec ptk1 sil ptk1 spig ptk1 xanth ptk1
- **recurrent** (See History - complaints)
- **spitting**; with (See MIND - Spitting - complaints)
- **spots**; in (See Spots - symptom)
- **subacute**: kali-bi br1
- **superficial**: *Ign* br1
- **symmetrical**: arn ptk1 bac bn kali-i ptk1 lac-d ptk1 nat-m gk syph ptk1 thyr ptk1
- **viral** infections: syph jl2 uncar-tom mp4•
- **wandering**: acon ptk1 agar ptk1 *Am-c* ptk1 bar-c ptk1 calc ptk1 chel ptk1 chin ptk1 cimic ptk1 cina ptk1 **Cocc** ptk1 graph ptk1 **Ign** ptk1 lyc ptk1 mag-c ptk1 mag-p ptk1 op ptk1 ph-ac ptk1 phos ptk1 rat ptk1 rhus-t ptk1 sec ptk1 stann ptk1 staph ptk1 *Sulph* ptk1 *Thuj* ptk1 *Valer* ptk1 verat-v ptk1 *Zinc* ptk1
- ▽ **extending** to:
  - ○ **Anus**: carb-an bg2
  - **Backward**: bar-c ptk1 *Bell* ptk1 *Bry* ptk1 *Chel* ptk1 con ptk1 crot-t ptk1 cupr ptk1 gels ptk1 *Kali-bi* ptk1 kali-c ptk1 kali-i ptk1 lil-t ptk1 merc ptk1 nat-m ptk1 par ptk1 phos ptk1 phyt ptk1 prun ptk1 puls ptk1 *Sep* ptk1 spig ptk1 **Sulph** ptk1
  - **Distant** parts: berb ptk1 cupr ptk1 dios ptk1 mag-p ptk1 plb ptk1 tell ptk1 valer ptk1 xan ptk1
  - **Downward**: (*↗Pain - extending - downward)* aloe ptk1 arn ptk1 aur ptk1 bar-c ptk1 *Berb* ptk1 *Borx* bro1 bry ptk1 cact bro1 caps ptk1 cic ptk1 coff ptk1 hyper ptk1 **Kalm** bro1* lach ptk1 lyc bro1* puls ptk1 rhod ptk1 rhus-t ptk1 *Sanic* bro1 sel ptk1 zinc ptk1
  - **Forward**: berb ptk1 bry ptk1 carb-v ptk1 *Gels* ptk1 lac-c ptk1 *Sabin* ptk1 *Sang* ptk1 sep ptk1 sil ptk1 **Spig** ptk1
  - **Head**: dig bg2
  - **Heart**: aur ptk1 kalm ptk1 lach ptk1 lyc ptk1 lycps-v bg2
  - **Outward**: *Asaf* ptk1 bell ptk1 berb ptk1 bry ptk1 chin ptk1 kali-bi ptk1 kali-c bro1 kali-m ptk1 kalm ptk1 lith-c ptk1 prun ptk1 sep ptk1 sil ptk1 *Sulph* bro1 *Valer* ptk1 zinc ptk1
  - **Stomach**: bism ptk1 colch ptk1 dulc ptk1 kali-bi ptk1 lappa ptk1

- **extending** to: ...
  - **Teeth**: staph bg2
  - **Upward**: *(↗Pain - extending - upward)* acon ptk1 **Asaf** ptk1 *Bell* ptk1 ben bro1 calc ptk1 cimic ptk1 con ptk1 croc ptk1 cupr ptk1 dulc ptk1 eup-per bro1 gels ptk1 glon ptk1 **Ign** ptk1 kali-bi ptk1 kalm ptk1 kreos ptk1 **Lach** ptk1 *Led* bro1* *Naja* ptk1 op ptk1 **Phos** ptk1 *Puls* ptk1 sabad ptk1 **Sang** ptk1 sep br1* **Sil** ptk1 stroph-h ptk1 *Sulph* ptk1 thuj ptk1 zinc ptk1

○ - **Axis**; Cranio-spinal cocc tl1
- **Blood** circulation; of (See Circulation)
- **Blood** vessels (See Blood vessels)
- **Bones** (See Bones)
- **Cartilage** (See Cartilages)
- **Connective** tissue (See Connective)
- **Fibrous** tissues: *Guaj* br1 kali-i br1 *Phyt* br1 rhod tl1 *Rhus-t* br1* sabin br1
- **Glands** (See Glands)
- **Joints** (See Joints)
- **Ligaments**: *Arg-met* br1
- **Lower** half of body: bac-t bro1
- **Lymphatic** system: am-c tl1 bar-i br1 calc mtf11 merc mtf
- **Mucous** membranes (See Mucous membranes)
- **Muscles**; of: *(↗Abscesses - muscles; Indurations - muscles; Inflammation - muscles; Injuries - muscles; Jerking - muscles; Pain - muscles; Paralysis - muscles; Relaxation - muscles; Shortened; Stiffness - muscles; Tension - muscles; Weakness - muscular)* bell-p br1 camph br1 *Cimic* br1 *Colch* br1 daph br1 *Ran-b* br1 stroph-h br1
  - **chronic**: colch br1

○ • **Attachment** of: *Rhus-t* br1
  - **Flexor** muscles: cimx br1
- **Nervous** system (See Neurological)
- **Organs**; of: merc br1
- **Orifices**: *Aesc* ptk1 aloe ptk1 *Bell* ptk1 *Caust* ptk1 graph ptk1 ign ptk1 kali-c ptk1 lach ptk1 lyc ptk1 *Merc* ptk1 mur-ac ptk1 nat-m ptk1 **Nit-ac** ptk1 **Nux-v** ptk1 phos ptk1 podo ptk1 rat ptk1 *Sep* ptk1 *Sil* ptk1 **Sulph** ptk1
- **Parts** lain on: cimic ptk1 graph ptk1 mosch ptk1 nat-m ptk1 phys ptk1 tell ptk1
- **Peripheral**: plb br1
- **Pituitary** gland (= hypophysis): calc br1
  - **accompanied** by | **Adrenal** cortex: cortico mtf11
- **Serous** tissues (See Mucous membranes - serous)
- **Single** parts: agar ptk1 alum ptk1 bar-c ptk1 caust ptk1 con ptk1 dulc ptk1 kali-c ptk1 ol-an ptk1 plb ptk1 rhod ptk1 sec ptk1 sul-i ptk1 valer ptk1
- **Tendons**: *Rhus-t* br1

COMPLEXION (= color of eyes, face, hair):

- **brown** hair: **Carc** mrr1 iod mrr1 nux-v mtf33 prot jl2 [ars stj2 ars-met stj2 kali-i stj1 mag-i stj1]
  - **women**; in: euon-a br1 sep br1
- **café** au lait (See brown)
- **dark**: *(↗HEAD - Hair - dark)* acon k1* alum k* anac k* arn k* ars k* aur kr1* bacls-10 pte1• bacls-7 pte1• brom c1 *Bry* k* *Calc* k* calc-i sf1.de calc-p mtf33 caps sf1.de carc mrr1* **Caust** k* cham c1 *Chin* kr1* cina bg2* coff kr1* con c1 dys fmm1• ferr gk ferr-pic br1 graph c1 hep gk **Ign** k* iod c1* **Kali-c** k* kreos k* lac-c kr1 lach bg2 lyc c1 lycpr c1 mag-p sf1.de morg-g fmm1• mur-ac c1 nat-m k* **Nit-ac** k* *Nux-v* k* *Petr* br1 ph-ac ptk1 phos k1* pic-ac c1 **Plat** k* prot fmm1• puls k1* **Rhus-t** st sang c1 sec sf1.de sep k* staph k13* sulph k* syc fmm1• thuj c1* viol-o c1* [aur-m stj2 aur-s stj2 bar-i stj2 bar-met stj2 bism-sn stj2 cinnb stj2 hafn-met stj2 irid-met stj2 kali-ar stj2 lanth-met stj2 lith-i stj2 mang-i stj2 merc stj2 merc-d stj2 merc-i-f stj2 nat-i stj1 osm-met stj2 plb stj2 plb-m stj2 plb-p stj2 rhen-met stj2 tant-met stj2 thal-met stj2 tung-met stj2 zinc-i stj2]
  - **blue** eyes and dark hair: lach a lyc kl nat-m kl sep kl
  - **rigid** fibre, with: *Acon* kr1 *Anac* kr1 arn kr1 *Ars* kr1 *Bry* kr1* *Caust* kr1* kalm kr1 nat-m kr1 *Nit-ac* kr1 **Nux-v** kr1* *Plat* kr1 puls kr1 *Sep* kr1 staph kr1 sulph kr1

○ • **Eyes**: aur c1 calc-p mtf33 graph c1 iod c1* lach c1 lycpr c1 mur-ac c1 nit-ac c1* sep gk
- **fair**, blond, light: *(↗HEAD - Hair - fair)* agar k* *Apis* aur c1 bacls-10 pte1• bell j5.de* borx *Brom* k* bry k* **Calc** k* *Camph* br1 *Caps* k* cham c1* chel c1 clem c1 cocc c1* coloc c1 con c1 cupr c1 cycl c1 dig c1 dys fmm1• gaert fmm1• *Graph* k* *Hep* k* hyos k* ip j5.de* *Kali-bi* k* kreos c1 lac-ac stj5• lachn br1 lob k* lycps-v c1 merc k* mez c1 nat-c c1* oena sne op c1 **Petr** k* **Phos** k* **Puls** k* *Rhus-t* k* sabad k* sel c1* seneg ptk1 sep j5.de* *Sil* k* spig c1 **Spong** k* stann-i bg2* sul-ac c1 *Sulph* k* thuj c1* tritic-vg fd5.de *Tub* br1

Complexion – fair, blond, light: ...
vanad dx* vario c1 viol-o c1 [am-br stj2 bar-br stj2 calc-br stj1 fl-ac stj2 hydrog stj2 kali-br stj1 lith-f stj2 mag-br stj1 mur-ac stj2 nat-br stj2]
  - **lax** fibre, with: *(↗Relaxation - connective)* agar c1* *Bell* c1 **Brom** c1 **Calc** c1* *Caps* c1 *Cham* c1* clem c1 cocc c1 con c1 dig c1 **Graph** c1 hep br1 hyos c1 *Kali-bi* c1 lach c1 *Lyc* c1 *Merc* c1* op mtf33 *Rhus-t* c1 sil c1 spong br1 **Sulph** c1 thuj mtf33 tub br1
  - **women**: *Cocc* br1

○ • **Eyes**: bell c1* brom c1* caps c1 lob c1 puls c1 spong c1
- **florid**: *(↗FACE - Discoloration - rosy)* bacls-10 fmm1• ferr-p tl1 morg-g fmm1• morg-p fmm1• op tl1 prot fmm1• tub tl1 tub-d jl2
- **gray** (See FACE - Discoloration - grayish)
- **red** hair: calc-p kl cina b7a.de ferr-p a kali-p a lach kr1* nit-ac b4a.de* nux-v b7a.de phos kr1* **Puls** b7a.de* **Rhus-t** b7a.de* sabad b7a.de sep kr1* sil mtf33 spig b7a.de sulph c1* [alumin-p stj2 arg-p stj2 cupr-p stj2 ferr stj2 ferr-f stj2 ferr-lac stj2 ferr-n stj2 ferr-sil stj2 lith-p stj2 mang-p stj2 plb-p stj2 zinc-p stj2]
- **rosy** (See florid)
- **yellow**: blatta-a br1

COMPRESSION amel.: acon b7.de apis bg2 carb-an bg2 lil-t bg2 sep bg2

CONDITION after a given complaint; impaired (See Convalescence)

CONDYLOMATA (See SKIN - Excrescences - condylomata)

CONGESTION:

- **blood**; of: *(↗Circulation; Heat - flushes; Orgasm; Plethora)* **Acon** k* act-sp kr1 adren c2 **Aesc** k* agar bg2 agn bg2 *Aloe* k* *Alum* k* alum-p k2 alum-sil k2 am-c k* am-m k* ambr k* aml-ns bro1* ang bg2 anis kr1 ant-c k* ant-t bg2 *Anthraci* kr1 *Apis* k* aq-mar jl3 arist-cl sp1 *Arn* k* ars bg2* asaf k* aster jl3 *Aur* k* aur-ar k2 aur-i k2 aur-s k2 bar-c k* bar-i k2 **Bell** k* *Borx* k* bov k* brom bg2 *Bry* k* **Cact** k* calad bg2 *Calc* k* calc-hp c1* calc-sil k2 camph k* cann-s k* canth k* carb-an k* *Carb-v* k* *Carbn-s* caust k* cent bro1 cham k* chel k* chen-a vml3• **Chin** k* chinin-s j5.de cinnb st1 clem k* cocc k* *Coff* k* colch coll br1 coloc k* con k* conv croc k* cupr k* cycl k* dig k* dulc k* erig sf1.de eucal sf1.de euphr bg2 **Ferr** k* *Ferr-i* ferr-p k* *Ferr-s* kr1* fl-ac bg2* gad bro1 gels bg* **Glon** k* *Graph* k* guaj k* *Ham* k* *Hell* k* hep k* hir jl3 hydr sf1.de hydr-ac a1 *Hyos* k* hypoth jl3 ign k* iod k* ip bg2 jab c1 kali-c k* kali-i bro1* kali-n k* kreos sf1.de *Lach* k* laur k* led k* lil-t bro1* lon-c bro1 *Lyc* k* m-arct b2.de m-aust b2.de mag-c k* mag-m k* mand mg1.de mang k* **Meli** k* meli-xyz c2 merc k* merc-c bg2 mez k* *Mill* j5.de* *Morg* fmm1• mosch k* nat-c k* *Nat-m* k* nat-s ptk1 *Nit-ac* k* nux-m k* **Nux-v** k* op k* petr k* ph-ac k* **Phos** k* plat k* plb k* podo sf1.de *Psor* ptel tl1 **Puls** k* raja-s jl3 *Ran-b* k* rhod k* *Rhus-t* k* sabin k* samb k* *Sang* bg* sars bg2 sec k* sel bg2 *Seneg* k* *Sep* k* *Sil* k* spig k* spira br1 *Spong* k* squil k* staph k* stel br1* *Stram* k* *Stront-c* sf1.de *Stront-i* sf1.de sul-ac k* **Sulph** k* tarax k* ter ptk1 thuj k* ust br1 valer k* verat k* verat-v k* **Viol-o** k* vip ptk1 zinc bg2
  - **accompanied** by:
    - **hemorrhage** (See Hemorrhage - accompanied - congestion)
    - **nausea**: verat-v br1
    - **sciatica**: acon bro1 bell bro1 gels bro1
    - **vomiting**: verat-v br1
    - **Lungs**; hemorrhage of (See CHEST - Hemorrhage - accompanied - congestion)
    - **Ovaries**; complaints of: vib br1
    - **Uterus**; complaints of: vib br1
  - **coldness** of legs, with: *Bell* kl *Nat-m* kl *Stram* kl
  - **hemorrhage**; after: mill k2
  - **menopause**; during: *(↗Heat - flushes - menopause)* ust br1
  - **night**: senn br1
  - **passive**: verbe-o br1
  - **sudden**: acon ptk1 bell ptk1 cact k2 glon br1* verat-v ptk1
  - **superficial**: aml-ns br1 iod br1
  - **violent**: glon br1

▽ • **extending** to:
    - **Downward**: aur ptk1 meph ptk1 thyr ptk1

- **blood**; of – **extending** to: ...
  - ⁝ **Upward**: acon ptk1 arn ptk1 bell ptk1 bry ptk1 ferr ptk1 glon ptk1 kali-i ptk1 meli ptk1 naja br1 phos ptk1 sang ptk1 stront-c ptk1

○ • **Internally**: *Aloe* *Apis* ars k* aur-i k2 bar-i k2 **Cact** calc-sil k2 *Camph* k* canth k* *Colch* conv cupr k* *Glon* *Hell* **Meli** *Phos* sars k2 sep *Verat* k* verat-v

• **Single** parts; to: **Acon** bg2 alum bg2 am-c bg2 am-m bg2 ambr bg2 ant-c bg2 *Arn* bg2 asaf bg2 *Aur* bg2 bar-c bg2 **Bell** bg2 borx bg2 bov bg2 *Bry* bg2 *Calc* bg2 camph bg2 cann-xyz bg2 canth bg2 carb-an bg2 **Carb-v** bg2 caust bg2 cham bg2 chel bg2 **Chin** bg2 clem bg2 cocc bg2 coff bg2 coloc bg2 con bg2 croc bg2 cupr bg2 cycl bg2 dig bg2 dulc bg2 **Ferr** bg2 *Graph* bg2 guaj bg2 *Ham* bg2 hell bg2 hep bg2 *Hyos* bg2 ign bg2 iod bg2 kali-c bg2 kali-n bg2 lach bg2 laur bg2 led bg2 *Lyc* bg2 mag-c bg2 mag-m bg2 mang bg2 merc bg2 mez bg2 mosch bg2 nat-c bg2 *Nat-m* bg2 *Nit-ac* bg2 nux-m bg2 *Nux-v* bg2 op bg2 petr bg2 ph-ac bg2 *Phos* bg2 plat bg2 plb bg2 **Puls** bg2 *Ran-b* bg2 rhod bg2 *Rhus-t* bg2 sabin bg2 samb bg2 sec bg2 *Seneg* bg2 **Sep** bg2 *Sil* bg2 spig bg2 *Spong* bg2 squil bg2 staph bg2 *Stram* bg2 sul-ac bg2 **Sulph** bg2 tarax bg2 thuj bg2 valer bg2 verat bg2 **Viol-o** bg2

○ - **Glands**; of: aur-i k2 con br1 dig c1 ferr-i k2
- **Joints**; of: morg fmm1•
- **Nerve** centres; of:
  - • **accompanied** by | **paralysis** (See Paralysis - accompanied - congestion - nerve)
- **Portal** (See ABDOMEN - Portal)
- **Single** parts: con br1 ferr-p br1 ust br1

CONNECTIVE TISSUE; affections of: (↗*Dermatomyositis; Sjögren's*) *Acon* br1 apis mrr1 arg-met mrr1 arg-n mrr1 aur mrr1 bry ptk1* calc ptk1* calc-f ptk1 camph br1 *Caust* mrr1 colch ptk1 dulc mrr1 **Fl-ac** ptk1 graph ptk1* **Guaj** ptk1 *Iod* br1 kali-bi br1 kali-c mrr1 kali-i br1 *Kali-m* ptk1 kalm mrr1 lac-c mrr1 lach mrr1 lap-a br1 lyc ptk1* merc mrr1 nat-m mrr1 nat-s mrr1 nux-v mrr1 phos mrr1 *Phyt* br1* psor mrr1 puls mrr1 rad-br mrr1 *Ran-b* mrr1 rhod ptk1 *Rhus-t* br1* ruta ptk1* sabin ptk1 *Sec* ptk1 sep mrr1 sil ptk1* staph ptk1* sulph mrr1 thuj mrr1 tub mrr1
- **induration**: alum bg2 calc-f bg2 *Carb-an* bg2 clem bg2 *Con* bg2 fl-ac bg2 hydrc br1 kali-i br1 *Lap-a* bg2 sil bg2

○ - **Glands**; about: *Lap-a* br1

CONSCIOUS of inner organs: bamb-a stb2.de•

CONSTIPATION:
- **agg.**: alet bg2 aloe ptk1 arg-n bg2* chin bg2 fl-ac k2 kali-bi bg2 nat-m bg2 nux-v bg2 phos bg2 sul-i bg2
- **amel.**: *Calc* k* carb-v bg2 merc k* nit-ac a *Psor* k* ust ptk1

CONSTITUTION:
- **carbo**-nitrogenous: arg-n bg2 cupr bg2 sulph bg2
- **dyscratic**: ars bg2 carb-an bg2 hydr bg2 iod bg2 kali-bi bg2 kali-i bg2 lyc bg2 nat-m bg2 nit-ac bg2 sil bg2 sul-ac bg2 sulph bg2
- **hydrogenoid**: aran bg2 dulc bg2* kali-n bg2 nat-m bg2* nat-p bg2 nat-s bg2* nit-ac bg2 thuj bg2*
- **lithemic**: ant-c bg2 aran bg2 arn bg2 berb bg2 bry bg2 calc bg2 caust bg2 chin bg2 coc-c bg2 dulc bg2 form bg2 guaj bg2 kali-c bg2 kalm bg2 led bg2 lith-c bg2 lyc bg2 med bg2 mez bg2 nat-s bg2 rhod bg2 rhus-t bg2 sars bg2 sep bg2 sulph bg2 ter bg2
- **neuropathic**: agar bg2 ambr bg2 arg-n bg2 asaf bg2 asar bg2 aur bg2 bell bg2 castm bg2 caust bg2 cham bg2 cimic bg2 cina bg2 cocc bg2 coff bg2 croc bg2 *Ign* bg2 iod bg2 kali-bi bg2 kali-p bg2 led bg2 lil-t bg2 mag-m bg2 mag-p bg2 mosch bg2 *Nux-v* bg2 ph-ac bg2 phos bg2 pic-ac bg2 puls bg2 sel bg2 sil bg2 valer bg2 zinc bg2
- **oxygenoid**: ars-i bg2 ferr bg2 ferr-i bg2 iod bg2 kali-i bg2
- **psoric**: ant-c bg2 bar-c bg2 brom bg2 calc bg2 calc-p bg2 carb-an bg2 carb-v bg2 cupr bg2 graph bg2 hep bg2 iod bg2 kali-i bg2 lyc bg2 nat-c bg2 nat-m bg2 nit-ac bg2 petr bg2 psor bg2 sil bg2 *Sulph* bg2 tub bg2
- **sycotic**: apis bg2 ars bg2 calc bg2 caust bg2 cupr-act bg2 graph bg2 lach bg2 med bg2 nat-s bg2 nit-ac bg2 sabin bg2 sel bg2 *Thuj* bg2
- **syphilitic**: ars bg2 asaf bg2 aur bg2 carb-an bg2 cor-r bg2 iod bg2 jatr-c bg2 kali-bi bg2 kali-i bg2 kalm bg2 led bg2 *Merc* bg2 mez bg2 nit-ac bg2 phyt bg2 sars bg2 sil bg2 sulph bg2 syph bg2 thuj bg2

CONSTRICTION: acon bg2 alum-sil bro1 *Anac* bro1 arg-n bg2 arn bg2 asar bro1 *Cact* bro1 caps bro1 *Carb-ac* bro1 chin bg2 coloc bro1 iod bro1 lach bro1 mag-p bro1 naja bro1 nat-m bro1 *Nit-ac* bro1 plb bro1 puls bg2 sec bro1 *Sulph* bro1 ther bg2 zinc bg2
- **accompanied** by | **paralysis** (See Paralysis - accompanied - constriction)
- **pain**; during: coloc ptk1 ign ptk1 lyc ptk1
- **string**; as if constricted by a: plb bg2

○ - **Arteries**; of: *Cact* br1
- **Blood** vessels; of (See Blood vessels - constriction)
- **Bones**; of: am-m k* anac k* aur k* chin k* cocc k* *Coloc* *Con* k* gels bg2 *Graph* k* kreos k* lyc k* merc k* nat-m k* **Nit-ac** k* nux-v k* petr k* phos k* **Puls** k* rhod k* *Rhus-t* k* *Ruta* k* sabad k* sep k* sil k* stront-c k* **Sulph** k* valer bg2 zinc k*
  - • **band**; sensation of a: anac bg2 aur b2.de* chin b2.de* *Con* b2.de* graph b2.de* kreos b2.de* lyc b2.de* merc b2.de* nat-m b2.de* **Nit-ac** b2.de* petr b2.de* phos b2.de* **Puls** b2.de* sabad b2.de* sil b2.de* **Sulph** b2.de*
- **External**: (↗*Pain - externally - constricting*) abrot *Acon* k* *Aesc* aeth aether a1 *Agar* k* *All-c* all-s a1 alum k* alum-sil k2* *Alumn* kr1 am-c k* am-m k* *Aml-ns* k* *Ammc* *Anac* k* ang b2.de* ant-c k* *Ant-t* *Apis* k* aral arg-met k* arg-n k* arn k* *Ars* k* *Ars-i* *Arum-t* asaf k* *Asar* k* atro a1 aur k* *Bar-c* bar-s k2 bell k* berb *Bism* k* borx k* bov k* brom bg2 *Bry* k* *Cact* k* cadm-s bg2 calc k* *Calc-p* cann-i cann-s k* canth k* *Caps* k* carb-ac k* carb-an k* carb-v k* carbn-o a1 *Carbn-s* carc gk6 caust k* cham k* *Chel* k* *Chin* k* **Cimic** k* cina k* coc-c bg2 **Cocc** k* coff k* colch k* *Coloc* k* con k* *Croc* kr1 crot-h bg2 *Cupr* k* dig k* dios *Dros* k* dulc k* euphr k* *Ferr* k* gels k* *Glon* k* **Graph** k* guaj k* haem br1 *Hell* k* hep k* hist mg1.de* hydr-ac k* **Hyos** k* **Ign** b7.de* *Iod* k* *Ip* kali-c k* kali-n k* kreos k* *Lach* k* *Lact-v* br1 laur k* led k* lil-t *Lob* k* *Lyc* k* m-arct b2.de m-aust b2.de mag-c k* mag-m k* *Mag-p* manc bg2 mang k* meny k* **Merc** k* *Merc-c* k* *Merc-i-r* *Mez* k* mosch k* mur-ac k* naja k* nat-c k* nat-m k* **Nit-ac** k* nitro-o a1 nux-m k* **Nux-v** k* oena bg2 olnd k* *Op* k* *Ox-ac* *Par* k* petr k* *Ph-ac* kr1 *Phos* k* phys bg2 pic-ac k2 *Plat* k* **Plb** k* *Puls* k* rad-br ptk1 ran-b k* ran-s k* rat ptk1 rheum k* rhod k* **Rhus-t** k* ric a1 russ a1 ruta k* sabad k* sabin k* sars k* sec k* sel k* *Sep* k* sil k* sin-n a1 spig k* *Spong* k* squil k* **Stann** k* staph k* **Stram** k* *Stront-c* k* *Sul-ac* k* *Sulph* k* *Tab* k* *Tarent* br1 thuj k* *Verat* k* verat-v a1 verb k* viol-o b7a.de* viol-t k* visc sp1 zinc k*
  - • **band**; sensation of a: anac tl1
    - ⁝ **iron**: *Cact* br1 *Coloc* br1*
  - • **belt**: visc sp1
  - • **caged** with wires twisted tighter and tighter; as if: **Cact** k* med bro1
  - • **sensation** of: *Alumn* br1 coll br1
  - • **small** areas, of: hist sp1
- **Glands**; in: calc ptk1 ign ptk1 iod ptk1 plat ptk1 puls ptk1
- **Hollow** organs; of: tab ptk1
- **Internally**: (↗*Pain - externally - constricting*) *Acon* k* *Aesc* agar k* agn k* *Alum* k* alum-sil k2* am-c k* ambr k* aml-ns anac k* ang b2.de* ant-c k* ant-t k* *Apis* br1 arg-met k* *Arn* k* ars k* ars-i asaf k* *Asar* k* aur k* *Bapt* bar-c k* bar-s k2 **Bell** k* benz-ac bism k* borx k* bov k* *Brom* *Bry* k* bufo bg2 **Cact** k* *Calad* k* *Calc* k* calc-sil k2 *Camph* k* cann-i cann-s k* *Canth* k* caps k* carb-an k* carb-v k* carbn-s caust k* *Cham* k* *Chel* k* **Chin** k* *Chlol* cic k* cina k* *Clem* k* *Cocc* k* coff k* colch k* **Coloc** k* *Con* k* croc k* crot-h crot-t cub *Cupr* k* *Dig* k* dios *Dros* k* dulc k* euph k* ferr k* glon graph k* guaj k* haem br1 hell k* hep k* hyos k* **Ign** k* *Iod* k* *Ip* k* kali-c k* kali-n k* kreos k* *Lach* k* lact br1 *Lact-v* br1 *Laur* k* *Led* k* lyc k* m-ambo b2.de* m-arct b2.de m-aust b2.de mag-c k* mag-m k* **Mag-p** mang k* meny k* merc k* merc-c mez k* *Mosch* k* mur-ac k* *Naja* nat-ar nat-c k* **Nat-m** k* **Nit-ac** k* *Nux-m* k* **Nux-v** k* olnd k* op k* ox-ac par k* petr k* *Ph-ac* k* *Phos* k* **Plat** k* **Plb** k* **Puls** k* ran-s k* rheum k* rhod k* rhus-t k* ruta k* sabad k* *Sabin* k* samb k* *Sars* k* sec k* sel k* seneg k* *Sep* k* sil k* *Spig* k* spong k* *Squil* k* stann k* staph k* still **Stram** k* stront-c k* *Sul-ac* k* **Sulph** k* *Sumb* tab bg2 tarax k* *Tarent* br1 teucr k* *Thuj* k* tung-met bdx1• valer k* *Verat* k* *Verat-v* verb k* viol-t k* zinc k*
  - • **band**, sensation of a: acon k* *Alum* alum-p k2 alumn am-br *Ambr* **Anac** k* ant-c k* ant-t k* *Arg-n* k* arn k* ars k* ars-i k2 ars-s-f k2 asaf k* *Asar* k* aur k* aur-ar k2 aur-i k2 aur-s k2 *Bell* benz-ac brom bry **Cact** k* calc k* cann-i **Carb-ac** carb-v k* *Carbn-s* caust k* **Chel** *Chin* k* coc-c *Cocc* k* colch coloc k* **Con** k* croc k* dig dios bg2 gels *Graph* k* hell k* hyos iod k* kreos k* lach bg2 laur k* lyc k* m-ambo b2.de* mag-m *Mag-p* manc k* mang h2 *Merc* k* *Merc-i-r* mosch k* *Nat-m* k* *Nat-n* bg2 **Nit-ac** k*

- **Internally** – **band**, sensation of a: ...
nux-m k* nux-v k* olnd k* op k* petr k* Phos k* pic-ac k2* **Plat** k* **Puls** k* rhus-t bg2 sabad k* sabin k* sang sars k* Sec bg2 sep k* **Sil** k* Spig k* stann k* Stram bg2 sul-ac k* sul-i k2 **Sulph** k* tarent til tril-p ptk1 zinc k* zinc-p k2
  - ⁝ **hot**: gels bg2
  - ⁝ **iron**: Cact br1 Coloc br1
  - ⁝ **tight**; as if bound too: arn b7.de
- • **belt**, sensation of a: Cact sf1.de chin sf1.de phos sf1.de rhus-t sf1.de visc sp1
- • **cough** agg.; during: acon bg2 am-c bg2 ars bg2 dros bg2 mang bg2 squil bg2 sulph bg2
- • **sensation** of: Alumn br1 coll br1
- • **spasm** of sphincter of orifices: Acon alum alum-sil k2* ars ars-i bar-c **Bell** Brom **Cact** calc calc-sil k2 carb-v Chel cic cocc colch con crot-h dig dulc ferr form graph hep Hyos ign iod ip **Lach** Lyc k* **Merc** Merc-c mez Nat-m **Nit-ac** Nux-v k* op phos plat Plb rat rhod **Rhus-t** sabad sars sep **Sil** Staph **Stram** sulph sumb tarax Thuj Verat Verat-v
- ○ • **Organs**; of: plb br1
- - **Joints**; of: acon b2.de* am-m b2.de* **Anac** b2.de* apis sf1.de **Aur** b2.de* calc b2.de* carb-an b2.de* chin b2.de* coloc b2.de* ferr b2.de* **Graph** b2.de* kreos b2.de* lyc b2.de* meny b2.de* **Nat-m** b2.de* **Nit-ac** b2.de* nux-m b2.de* nux-v b2.de* Petr b2.de* ruta b2.de* sil b2.de* spig b2.de* squil b2.de* stann b2.de* Stront-c b2.de* Sulph b2.de* zinc b2.de*
- - **Orifices**; of: alum b2.de* ars b2.de* bar-c b2.de Bell b2.de* calc b2.de* carb-v b2.de* chel b2.de* cocc b2.de* colch b2.de* con b2.de* dig b2.de* dulc b2.de* ferr b2.de* graph b2.de* hep b2.de* hyos b2.de* ign b2.de* iod b2.de* ip b2.de* lyc b2.de* m-ambo b2.de* m-aust b2.de mez b2.de* nat-m b2.de* nux-v b2.de* phos b2.de* plat b2.de* plb b2.de* rhod b2.de* sabad b2.de* sars b2.de* sep b2.de* staph b2.de* stram b2.de* sulph b2.de* tarax b2.de* thuj b2.de* verat b2.de*

CONSUMPTION, PHTHISIS in general: acon b2.de* am-c b2.de* am-m b2.de ambr b2.de* arg-met b2.de* arn b2.de* Ars b2.de* aur b2.de* bar-c b2.de* bell b2.de* borx b2.de* Bry b2.de* calad b2.de* Calc b2.de* carb-an b2.de* carb-v b2.de* caust b2.de* cham b2.de* Chin b2.de* cocc b2.de* con b2.de* cupr b2.de* Dros b2.de* dulc b2.de* Ferr b2.de* graph b2.de* guaj b2.de* hep b2.de* hyos b2.de* ign b2.de* **Iod** b2.de* ip b2.de* **Kali-c** b2.de* kali-n b2.de* kreos b2.de* lach b2.de* laur b2.de* Led b2.de* **Lyc** b2.de* mang b2.de* merc b2.de* nat-m b2.de* nit-ac b2.de* nux-m b2.de* nux-v b2.de* op b2.de* par b2.de* petr b2.de* ph-ac b2.de* **Phos** b2.de* plb b2.de* **Puls** b2.de* ran-b b2.de* rhus-t b2.de* ruta b2.de* sabad b2.de samb b2.de* sec b2.de* sel b2.de* seneg b2.de* Sep b2.de* sil b2.de* spig b2.de* spong b2.de* squil b2.de* **Stann** b2.de* staph b2.de* stram b2.de* Sulph b2.de* teucr b2.de* thuj b2.de* verat b2.de* zinc b2.de*
- **accompanied** by | **weakness**: ars-i ptk1 chinin-ar ptk1
- **fever**; during: bapt ptk1 chinin-ar ptk1 ferr-p ptk1
- **neglected**: kreos ptk1

CONTRACTIONS (= strictures; stenosis): Am-m ptk1 anac ptk1 androc bnm2• calc ptk1 caust ptk1* chim c2 coloc br1* graph ptk1 guaj ptk1 Ign ptk1 lyc ptk1 med c2 nat-c ptk1 nat-m ptk1 Plb br1* plb-xyz c2 prun c2 rhus-t c2 ruta ptk1* sec ptk1 Sep b2.de syph c2 tann-ac br1 ter c2 thiosin c2*
- **inflammation**; after: acon b2.de* Agar k* alum k* Alumn kr1 am-m bg3 ant-c k* arg-met k* Arn b2.de* Ars b2.de* asaf k* Bell k* Bry k* cact k2 calc k* Camph k* canth k* caust k* chel k* Chin k* **Cic** k* Clem k* Cocc k* coloc bg3 con k* dig k* dros k* dulc k* euph k* graph bg3 hyos b2.de* Ign b2.de* lach k* led k* lyc bg3 m-ambo b2.de* m-arct b2.de m-aust b2.de meny b2.de* **Merc** k* Mez k* nat-m k* nit-ac k* **Nux-v** k* op b2.de* petr k* Phos k* plb k* Psor Puls k* ran-b k* **Rhus-t** k* ruta k* sabad k* sec bg3 sep k* Spong k* squil k* staph k* stram k* sulph k* teucr k* thuj k* Verat b2.de* zinc k*
- **pain**; after: abrot ptk1
- **sensation** of: am-m ptk1 asar br1 cact ptk1 coloc br1 guaj ptk1 kali-m ptk1 nux-v ptk1 phos ptk1
- **spasmodic** | **Thorax**: asaf tl1
- ○ - **Aponeurosis**: tub mtf11 tub-r jl2*
- - **Ligaments**: tub mtf11 tub-r jl2
- - **Muscles**: chir-fl bnm4• cimx mtf11 lat-m bnm6• plb tl1 tub mtf11
- ○ • **Flexor** muscles: psor mtf11 syph mtf11
- • **Hollow** organs; muscles of: tab ptk2*

CONTRADICTORY and alternating states: (↗Alternating; Change - symptoms - constant; Many; Metastasis; MIND - Capriciousness; MIND - Mood - changeable) Abrot st1* agar gm1 Aloe st alum gm1 alumn gm1 anac ptk1 apoc k2 arn k2* ars k2* aur gm1 bell jsa* bry jsa* camph gm1 Carc st1* chin gm1 choc srj3• cimic st1* croc crot-t gm1 graph jsa **IGN** k •* kali-bi a kali-c k2* lac-c jsa med gm1 mosch a **Nat-m** k •* op gm1 Plat k* podo k2* psor gm1 **PULS** k •* rhus-t jsa sanic st1 Sep •* Staph st1* Thuj k* tritic-vg fd5.de **Tub** •*

CONVALESCENCE; ailments during: (↗Complaints - acute - recurrent; History; Reaction - lack - convalescence; Weakness - fever - following) ail st Alet hr1* am-c k2* apoc k2* arg-n bg2 Ars lmj aur st Aven bg2* bac st borx bg2 cadm-met jl calad bg2 **Calc** bg2* Calc-p bg2* caps k2* **Carb-v** br1* Carc lmj* Castm bg2* Caust lmj* **Chin** bg2* Chinin-ar bg2* coca sf1.de* cocc st cupr a1* Cur st cypr st Ferr bg2* ferr-act sf1.de guar st iris bg2 Kali-c bg2* kali-chl k13 kali-m k2 kali-p bg2* lac-c bg2 laur k2* lec br1* lob st mang k2* med st meph bg2* Nat-m bg2* nat-p st nux-v bg2 okou jl op bg2* ourl jl2 ph-ac bg2* phos bg2 podo bg2 prot jl3 psor bg2* puls bg2 Scut st Sel bg2* sep bg2 Sil hr1* sul-ac bg2* sul-i mg1.de Sulph bg2* syph k2* **Tub** st* tub-a st zinc bg2*
- **abortion**; after: (↗History - abortion) aur k2 caul cpd• **Cimic** kr1 Helon kr1* Kali-c kr1* Kali-s vh* Lac-c kr1 Lil-t ptk1 Merc kr1 murx ptk1 Plat kr1 Podo kr1 pyrog br1* rheum kr1 ruta ptk1 sabin c1* sec ptk1 Sep cpd* Stram kr1 Sulph kr1* Thlas kr1
  - • **never** well since: sec pfa1*
  - • **repeated** abortions: helon cpd• sep cpd•
- **anesthesia**; from (See Anesthesia [=narcosis] - ailments)
- **antibiotics**; after use of: (↗Medicine - allopathic - abuse) ars cpd• nit-ac cpd• thuj cpd•
- **apoplexy**; after: caust mtf11
- **bones**; fracture of: osteo-mye mtf11
- **burns**; after: agar b4a.de alum b4a.de Ars b4a.de calc b4a.de carb-ac ptk1* Carb-v b4a.de Caust tl1* sulph b4a.de
  - • **never** well since: caust ptk1 suprar mtf11
- **chemotherapy**; after: cadm-s cpd•
- **chest** complaints; after | **never** well since: sulph pfa1*
- **childhood** disease; after: psor cpd• sulph cpd•
- **cortisone**; after use of: (↗Medicine - allopathic - abuse) caust cpd• thuj cpd•
- **croup**; after: arn bg2 bell bg2 Calc k* Carb-v k* dros bg2 Hep bg2 Phos bg2*
- **delivery**; after: arn zzl Graph kr1 sep cpd•
- **diarrhea**: Chin bg2 ferr bg2 kali-c bg2 nat-m bg2 ph-ac bg2 podo bg2 Verat bg2
- **diphtheria**; after: Alet st Cocain st cocc st diph cpd• fl-ac st Helon kr1 Lac-c kr1 pyrog ptk1
  - • **never** well since: lac-c tl1* phyt ptk1 pyrog ptk1
- **dysentery**; after: aloe ptk1 colch ptk1
- **ear**; after discharges from: **Aur** bar-m Cact Calc **Carb-v** Colch k* crot-h k* Hep lach Lyc k* merc k* Nit-ac k* **Psor** **Puls** k* Sulph
- **eczema**; after suppressed: mez tl1 sulph cpd•
- **encephalitis**: coxs mtf11
- **erysipelas**: cupr-act bro1
- **exhausting** diseases; after: aven br1 carb-an br1 carb-v mtf33 lath br1 ph-ac br1 sel br1
- **fever**; after: lyc c1
- **gonorrhea**; after: agn bg2 arg-met bg2 caust bg2 clem b4a.de* colch bg2 cop bg2 guaj bg2 ham bg2 hydr bg2 iod bg2 kali-bi bg2 kali-i bg2 kalm bg2 med bg2* merc bg2 mez bg2 nat-s bg2 nit-ac bg2 nux-v bg2 petr bg2 ph-ac bg2 phyt bg2 podo bg2 rhod bg2 sabad bg2 sabin bg2 sars bg2 sel bg2 sep bg2 spong bg2 staph bg2 sulph bg2 ter bg2 thuj bg2
  - • **never** well since: med pfa1
- **hemorrhages**: stront-c bro1
- **hepatitis**; after: mag-m cpd• nat-s cpd• phos cpd•
  - • **alcoholic** hepatitis: card-m cpd• lyc cpd• sul-ac cpd•
  - • **viral** hepatitis: phos cpd•
- **hormonal** therapy; after: sep cpd•
- **infectious** diseases; after: form-ac sf1.de gels sf1.de psor sf1.de* puls sf1.de pyrog mrr1 sulph sf1.de thuj sf1.de tub sf1.de vario sf1.de
  - • **childhood**; during: carc cpd•
- **influenza**; after: (↗Weakness - influenza - after; HEAD - Pain - influenza - after - neuralgic) abrot st* cadm-met jl carc mlr1• chin csm• chinin-ar cpd• con br1 gels cpd* influ cpd* kali-p csm• lath br1 mand rsj7•

- **influenza**; after: ...
merc-k-i gm1 nat-sal br1* okou jl phyt bg2 psor cpd• scut c1* sul-ac mrr1 sulfonam jl sulph cpd• tub st
  - **never** well since: gels pfa1*
- **injuries**; after: *(↗Injuries) Arn* bro1 carb-v bro1 cic bro1 *Con* bro1 glon bro1 ham bro1 hyper bro1 led bro1 *Nat-s* bro1 *Stront-c* bro1
  - **never** well since (See Injuries - ailments)
- **loss** of fluids; after (See History - loss)
- **lungs**; after inflammation of the: bac cpd• calc st carb-v st* kali-c st lyc st* phos st* sang st sil st* sulph st* tub cpd*
  - **never** well since: *Kali-c* k2* *Lyc* rma2 phos rma2 pneu rma2 sil rma2 sulph rma2 tub rma2
- **malaria**; after: *(↗History - malaria) Chinin-ar* br1
  - **never** well since or recurrent malaria: malar mtf11
- **measles**; after (See Measles - ailments)
- **medicine**; after abuse of allopathic (See Medicine - allopathic - abuse)
- **meningitis**; after: calc st sil st
- **menopause**; after: graph cpd• kreos br1 lach pfa1* puls cpd• sep cpd•
- **milk** leg; after: fl-ac bg2
- **mumps**; after: coxs mtf11 ourl jl2
- **nicotine**; after abuse of: nux-v mtf11
- **ovaries**; after inflammation of: coxs mtf11
- **oxygen** in blood; after decreased | **never** well since: carb-v mtf33
- **pancreatitis**; after: coxs mtf11
- **penicillin**; after use of: penic cpd•
- **perspiration**; after suppressed: calc cpd• merc cpd• sil cpd• sulph cpd• thuj cpd•
- **pocks**; after: merc b4a.de
- **polio**; after: lath cpd•
- **puberty**; after: *(↗Puberty)* puls cpd* sep cpd•
- **puerperal** fever; after | **never** well since: pyrog pfa1
- **radiation** therapy; after: cadm-s cpd•
- **rheumatism** after tonsillitis (See THROAT - Inflammation - tonsils - followed - rheumatism)
- **scarlet** fever; after: am-c b4a.de aur b4a.de *Bar-c* b4a.de *Bell* b4a.de *Hep* b4a.de *Lyc* b4a.de *Merc* b4a.de *Nit-ac* b4a.de *Zinc* b4a.de
- **septic** fever; after: gunp cpd• pyrog br1*
  - **never** well since: pyrog al1*
- **spinal** tap; after: hyper cpd•
- **sprains**; after: am-m bg2 arn bg2 calc bg2 petr bg2 stront-c bg2
- **strain**; after | **never** well since: carb-v pfa1
- **sunstroke**; after: glon tl1 meli mtf11 sang tl1
  - **never** well since: verat cpd•
- **suppuration**; after: chin bg2 phos bg2
- **surgery**; after: hyper cpd• staph cpd•
- **typhoid** fever; after: *(↗History - typhoid)* ars-i bro1 carb-v c1* *Chin* bro1 cocc bro1 hydr bro1 kali-p bro1 nux-v bro1 parathyr jl2 *Psor* bro1 pyrog c1 sulph c1* tarax bro1
  - **never** well since: carb-v pfa1* carc rma2 mang ptk1 *Psor* ptk1* *Pyrog* ptk1* thyr rma2 tub fb* typh rma2
- **urticaria**:
  - **after**: *Apis* b7a.de
  - **suppressed**: apis bro1 urt-u bro1
- **vaccination**; after (See Vaccination)
- **whooping** cough; after: *(↗History - whooping)* carc cpd• *Sang* hr1 tub cpd•

CONVERSATION: | **amel.**: aeth c1

CONVULSIONS: *(↗Neurological)* abrot tl1 absin k* acet-ac k* acetan vh1 *Acon* k* aconin c1* aesc aesc-g a1 aeth k* aether a1* *Agar* k* agar-pa a1 agar-se a1 agre jl3 alco a1 *Alet* hr1* alum k* alum-p k2* alum-sil k2* am-c k* am-caust a1 am-m k* ambr k* ambro bro1 *Aml-ns* kr1* amyg a1 anac androc bnm2• ang b2.de* anis bro1 *Ant-c* k* *Ant-t* k* anth vh *Anthraci* kr1 antip bro1 *Apis* *Aran* k* *Arg-met* *Arg-n* k* arist-cl sp1 *Arn* k* *Ars* k* *Ars-s-f* hr1* **Art-v** k* arum-m hr1* *Asaf* k* asar k1* aster k* **Atro** k* aur k* aur-ar k2 aur-fu j5.de bar-c k* bar-i k2 *Bar-m* k* bar-s k2* bart a1 **Bell** k* ben-n a1* bism j5.de* borx both a1 brom bg2* bruc j5.de *Bry* k* **Bufo** k* bung-fa tsm2 buth-a sp1 cact **Calc** k* calc-ar k2* *Calc-i* k2* *Calc-p* k2 calc-sil k2 *Camph* k* cann-i k* cann-s k* *Canth* k* *Carb-ac* k* carb-an j5.de carb-v carbn c1*

Convulsions: ...
carbn-h a1 carbn-o *Carbn-s* castm c1* **Caust** k* **Cham** k* chen-a k* chin k* *Chinin-s* *Chlf* hr1* chlor c1* **Cic** k* cic-m a1* cimic k* **Cina** k* cit-ac j5.de clem k* coc-c k* coca *Cocc* k* cod a1* coff k* colch k* colchin c1 coloc k* *Con* k* convo-s sp1 cop k* cortico mg1.de* cortiso mg1.de* croc k* *Crot-c* *Crot-h* k* cryp a1 cub k* **Cupr** k* *Cupr-act* a1* *Cupr-ar* k* cupr-s a1 cur k* *Cypr* c1* cyt-l a1* dat-m a1* dat-s a1 *Dig* k* *Dios* bg* diosm br1 diph-pert-t mp4• dor hr1* dulc k* echit a1 euon c1* *Eupi* k* fagu a1 ferr k* ferr-ar ferr-m j5.de* ferr-s c1 form k* frag c1* *Gels* k* *Glon* k* gran a1 *Graph* k* grat k2* guaj guare a1 *Hell* k* helo-s bnm14• hep *Hydr-ac* k* **Hyos** k* hyper bro1* *Ign* k* indg br1* iod k* *Ip* k* iris-fl c1* jasm a1* jatr-c j5.de juni-v a1* kali-ar kali-bi k2 *Kali-br* k* *Kali-c* k* *Kali-chl* k* kali-cy a1 kali-i k* kali-m k2 kali-ox a1* kali-p sf1.de kalm kara c1 keroso a1* kreos lac-e hrn2• lach k* lact j5.de* lat-m sp1* laur k* linu-c a1 linu-u c1* **Lob** k* lol a1 lon-x a1* *Lyc* k* *Lyss* k* m-ambo b2.de* m-arct b2.de* *Mag-c* k* mag-m k* *Mag-p* k* mag-s sp1 manc k* mand sp1 mang med bg* meli meny k* meph k* *Merc* k* *Merc-c* k* merc-d a1 merc-n a1 merc-ns a1 merc-pr-r a1 methyl c1 *Mez* k* morb jl2 morph a1* *Mosch* k* *Mur-ac* k* mygal naja tsm2 nat-c k* nat-f sp1 *Nat-m* k* nat-s k* *Nicot* c1 nit-ac k* nitro-o a1 **Nux-m** k* **Nux-v** k* *Oena* k* ol-an j5.de* ol-j sf1.de olnd k* **Op** k* ox-ac k* oxyurn-sc mcp1• passi c1* pert jl2 petr k* ph-ac k* *Phos* k* phys k* *Phyt* k* pic-ac sf1.de pitu sp1 pitu-p sp1 plat k* **Plb** k* plb-chr c1* *Podo* sf1.de prot jl2* *Psor* *Puls* k* pyre-p c1* ran-b k* ran-s k* *Rat* sf1.de rauw sp1 rheum k* rhod rhus-t k* ric a1 rob k* rumx-act a1* russ a1* ruta k* sabad k* sal-ac sf1.de samb k* *Santin* a1* sars scol c1* *Sec* k* sel seneg sep k* *Sil* k* sin-n k* sium c1* *Sol-crl* c1* *Sol-ni* k* spig k* spirae c1* spong k* squil k* stann k* staph k* staphytox jl2 **Stram** k* stront-c k* **Stry** k* *Stry-s* sf1.de sul-ac k* sul-h c1* sul-i k2* *Sulph* k* syc fmm1• tab k* tanac j5.de* tarax tarent bg2* tax k* *Ter* k* teucr thal jl3 thal-xyz srj8• thea thuj k* thymol sp1* toxo-g jl2 tritic-vg fd5.de *Tub* st1 *Upa* c1* upa-a bro1 valer k* *Vario* hr1* *Verat* k* verat-v k* verb bg* verbe-o br1* vesp k2* vib bg vip k* visc k* zinc k* zinc-cy c1* zinc-m a1* zinc-o bro1 zinc-p k2* *Zinc-s* c1* zinc-val sf1.de* zing k* ziz k* [calc-br stj1 mag-br stj1]

- **one** side: apoc *Art-v* k* bell brom sf1.de *Calc-p* k* caust chinin-s j5.de dulc k* elaps gels graph hell *Ip* k* *Plb* k* sabad b7a.de
  - **accompanied** by | **speech**; wanting: dulc br1*
  - **paralysis** of the other: apis *Art-v* k* bell hell k1 lach sf1.de phos sf1.de *Stram*
  - ○ **Paralyzed** side: *Phos* sec
- **right** side of body: art-v k* *Bell* k* caust chen-a a1* lac-e hrn2• **Lyc** k* *Nux-v* k* sep h2* tarent sf
  - **left** paralyzed: *Art-v* k*
  - ▽ **left**; to: visc
- **left** side of body: bell j5.de *Calc-p* k* chinin-s j5.de colch a1 cupr elaps graph *Ip* k* *Lach* b7a.de nat-m nit-ac j5.de plb sabad j5.de stram j5.de *Sulph* k*
  - **right**; to: *Sulph* h2*
- **daytime**: *Art-v* hr1* *Kali-br* hr1*
- **morning**: arg-n art-v k* *Calc* k* *Caust* k* cocc crot-h k* kalm k* *Lyc* *Mag-p* k* nux-v k* plat k* sec k* sep k* sulph k* tab k* tritic-vg fd5.de
- **forenoon** | 9-10 h: *Nat-m* kr1 plb a1
- **noon**: acon vh1
- **afternoon**: arg-met aster vh stann stram
- **evening**: alum *Alumn* hr1* **Calc** k* *Caust* k* *Croc* gels graph j5.de kali-c j5.de laur k* merc-n k* merc-ns nit-ac j5.de *Op* k* plb-chr a1 stann k* stram k* sulph k*
  - **20** h: ars
  - **21** h: *Lyss*
  - **air** agg.; in open: caust
- **night**: *Arg-n* ars k* *Art-v* k* aur k* bufo k* *Calc* k* calc-ar k* *Caust* k* *Cic* k* *Cina* *Cupr* k* dig k* *Hyos* k* kali-c kalm k* lach j5.de lyc k* *Merc* k* *Nit-ac* k* nux-v k* oena k* **Op** k* *Plb* k* ruta sne *Sec* k* **Sil** k* *Stram* k* sulph k* zinc
  - **midnight**: bufo cina *Cocc* k* santin zinc k*
    - **after**: nit-ac k*
    - **2** h: *Kali-br* hr1
    - **3** h: *Stram* kr1
    - **4** h: *Kali-br* hr1
    - **4-16** h: *Calc*
    - **5** h: plb a1
  - **accompanied** by:
    - **vertigo** | **daytime**: nit-ac ptk1
  - **sleep** agg.: bufo br1*

- **accompanied** by:
  - **asthmatic**; respiration (See RESPIRATION - Asthmatic - accompanied - convulsions)
  - **cholera** (See RECTUM - Cholera - accompanied - convulsions)
  - **chorea** (See Chorea - accompanied - spasms)
  - **gasping**: caust ptk1 laur ptk1
  - **gastrointestinal** complaints: nux-v bro1
  - **saliva** | **bloody**: **Bufo** kr1*
  - **scarlatina**: aeth bro1 ail bro1 am-c bro1 apis bro1 ars bro1 *Bell* bro1 camph bro1 cupr br1* *Cupr-act* bro1 *Hyos* bro1 rhus-t bro1 *Stram* bro1 sulph bro1 zinc bro1
  - O **Abdomen**:
    - **complaints** of (See ABDOMEN - Complaints - accompanied - convulsions)
    - **irritation** of | **dentition**; during: *(↗dentition)* **Colch** bg2
  - **Brain**; complaints of: *(↗brain)* plb bro1
  - **Limb**; flexing and extending: cupr tl1
  - **Ovaries**; complaints of the: vib br1
  - **Spinal** cord; inflammation of (See BACK - Inflammation - spinal cord - accompanied - convulsions)
  - **Teeth**; complaints of: *Bell* b4a.de stann b4a.de
  - **Uterus**; complaints of the: cimic bro1 vib br1
- **Addison's** disease, in: *Calc* k* *Iod* hr1*
- **after** | **agg.**: cic b7.de* *Ferr* b7a.de stram b7a.de
- **air** agg.; draft of: ars cic k2 *Lyss* **Nux-v** phys lp **Stry** k*
- **alcoholic** drinks; after: ran-b c1
- **alternating** with:
  - **complaints**; other: *Ign* b7a.de
  - **diarrhea**: mag-p pd
  - **dyspnea** (See RESPIRATION - Difficult - alternating - convulsions)
  - **excitement** of mind (See MIND - Excitement - alternating - convulsions)
  - **lachrymation**: alum ptk1
  - **laughing** (See MIND - Laughing - alternating - convulsions)
  - **rage** (See MIND - Rage - alternating - convulsions)
  - **relaxation** of muscular system: acet-ac a1
  - **respiration**; difficult (See RESPIRATION - Difficult - alternating - convulsions)
  - **rigidity**: stry a1
  - **stupefaction** (See MIND - Stupefaction - alternating - convulsions)
  - **stupor** (See MIND - Stupor - alternating - convulsions)
  - **tonic** cramps: bell k2* *Cimic* hr1* con sf1.de *Ign* sf1.de *Mosch* sf1.de nux-m sf1.de nux-v sf1.de plat sf1.de sep sf1.de stram k* *Tab* hr1* verat-v sf1.de
  - **trance** (See MIND - Trance - alternating - spasms)
  - **trembling**; external (See Trembling - externally - alternating - convulsions)
  - **unconsciousness** (See MIND - Unconsciousness - alternating - convulsions)
  - **vomiting** (See STOMACH - Vomiting - alternating - convulsions)
- **amenorrhea**, in: art-v kr1
- **anger**; after: *(↗vexation; MIND - Anger)* art-v kr1 *Bufo* **Calc** kr1 **Cham** cina k* **Cupr** kr1 **Kali-br** k* lyss **Nux-v** k* *Op* plat sulph
  - **mother**; in nursling after anger of the (See children - nursing)
  - **nurslings**; in: acon lmj am-c ggd ant-c lmj ars lmj aur lmj carb-v lmj caust lmj **Cham** lmj coff lmj con ggd *Cupr* lmj hell lmj hep lmj *Ign* lmj lach lmj laur ggd *Lyc* lmj *Mosch* lmj nux-m lmj *Nux-v* lmj op lmj ph-ac lmj *Phos* lmj **Puls** lmj sec ggd sep lmj *Staph* lmj *Sulph* lmj verat lmj
- **anxiety**, from: nux-v a1 stram sf1.de
- **apoplectic**: *(↗Apoplexy)* *Bell* k* *Crot-h* k* *Cupr* *Lach* k* nux-v k* plb hr1 stram k* *Verat-v* kr1
- **aroused** from a trance; when forcibly: *Nux-m*
- **aura** (See epileptic - aura)
- **begin** in:
  - O **Abdomen**: aran *Bufo* calc sne
  - **Arm**: arum-t kr1 *Bell* calc ptk1 cic sne *Lach* ptk1 sil ptk1 sulph ptk1
    - **left**: sil st
  - **Back**: ars j5.de sulph
  - **Below**:
    - **extending** to | **Upward**: cupr tl1
  - **Calf**; muscles of: lyc h2
  - **Center**:
    - **extending** to | **Circumference**: cic k2*
  - **Extremities**: verat bg2
  - **Eye**: cic k2
  - **Face**: absin *Bufo* cic k2 cina k* dulc k* *Hyos* *Ign* kali-br bg1 *Lach* santin *Sec* k* stram bg2
    - **left** side: *Lach*
  - **Fingers**: cina bg2 *Cupr* bg2* *Cupr-act* kr1
    - **Toes**, and: (non:cupr br1*) *Cupr-act* kr1*
  - **Hands**: *(↗epileptic - aura - hands)* sec bg2 verat bg2
  - **Head**: cic
    - **extending** to | **Downward**: cic k2
  - **Legs**: *Cupr-act* kr1
  - **Lower** part: *Cupr* tl1
  - **Spine**: acon bro1 *Cic* bro1 cimic bro1 hydr-ac bro1 *Hyper* bro1 ign bro1 nux-v bro1 oena bro1 *Phys* bro1
  - **Throat**: cic k2
  - **Toes**: *Cupr-act* *Hydr-ac* sil sne
- **bending** | **elbow** | **amel.**: nux-v
  - **head**:
    - **backward** | **agg.**: (non:nux-v a1)
- **biting**, with: croc j5.de *Cupr* hr1* lyss k* *Tarent* hr1*
- **bone** in the throat; from: *Cic* k*
- **brain**: *(↗accompanied - brain)*
  - **commotion** of the; from: *(↗injuries - head)* **Arn** kr1 art-v c1 **Cic** kr1 *Hyper* kr1 *Nat-s* kr1
  - **congestion** of:
    - **with**: bell k2
    - **without**: ign bro1
  - **softening** of: *Bufo* kr1 *Caust* k*
- **bright** light, from: *(↗brilliant; light; Shining)* bell *Canth* hr1* lyss k* nux-v op **Stram** k* ter tl1
- **brilliant** objects; from: *(↗bright)* stram dw1*
- **bromides**; suppressed by: *(↗Bromides)* zinc-p bg2
- **changing** | **character**; in: *Bell* k* ign *Puls* k* **Stram** k*
- **children**; in: absin bro1 *Acon* k* *Aeth* k* agar k* agre jl3 am-c lmj *Ambr* *Aml-ns* kr1 ant-c lmj ant-t j5.de* *Apis* arn kr1* ars kr1 **Art-v** k* asaf j5.de aur lmj **Bell** k* borx c1 bry *Calc* k* *Calc-p* bg2* *Camph* *Camph-br* br1* *Camph-mbr* bro1 canth j5.de carb-v lmj caust k* *Cham* k* *Chlol* kr1* *Cic* k* cimic kr1 **Cina** k* cocc k* *Coff* k* colch kr1 con lmj *Crot-c* *Cupr* k* *Cupr-act* kr1 *Cypr* bg2* dol *Gels* glon bro1 *Guare* kr1 **Hell** k* *Hep* *Hydr-ac* k* *Hyos* k* *Ign* k* *Ip* k* *Kali-br* kr1* kali-c kali-p bg2* kreos kr1* lac-e hm2• *Lach* laur k* loxo-lae bnm12• *Lyc* *Mag-p* k* med lmj meli kr1* merc bg* mosch bro1 nat-m lmj nit-ac b4a.de nux-m j5.de* *Nux-v* k* *Oena* bg2* **Op** k* passi c1* ph-ac sf1.de phos bg2* plat prot fmm1• **Puls** lmj *Santin* bro1 scut br1* sec sep lmj *Sil* k* *Stann* b4a.de* *Staph* lmj **Stram** k* *Sulph* k* ter kr1 *Toxo-g* jl2 **Verat** k* *Verat-v* kr1 **Zinc** k* *Zinc-cy* sf1.de zinc-s bro1 *Zinc-val* bg2*
  - **attention** directed to them; when: ant-t fr1*
  - **diarrhea**, with: nux-m ptk1
  - **holding** them amel.; when: nicc ptk1
  - **infants**, in: absin br1* acon bg2* *Aeth* bro1 *Art-v* kr1* *Bell* bg2* bufo kr1 calc bro1 *Camph-mbr* bro1 caust bg2* *Cham* bg2* chlol bro1 *Cic* bro1 *Cina* bg2* cocc bro1 *Coff* bg2 *Cupr* bg2* cypr bro1 glon bro1 **Hell** kr1* *Hydr-ac* kr1* *Hyos* bro1 **Ign** bg2* *Ip* bg2 *Kali-br* bro1 kreos bro1 lach bg2

- **infants**, in: ...
laur bro1 *Mag-p* kr1* *Meli* kr1* *Merc* bg2* mosch bro1 nux-v bg2* *Oena* bro1 *Op* bg2* *Santin* bro1 scut bro1 stann bg2* *Stram* bro1 sulph bg2 *Zinc* bro1 zinc-s bro1
- **newborns**: *Art-v* kr1 bell j5.de* *Cupr* kr1 nux-v j5.de
- **nursing**; while the angered or frightened mother is: bufo ptk1* cham bro1 nux-v bro1 op mtf33
- **playing** or laughing excessively; from: coff ptk1
- **strangers**, from approach of: lyss op k* tarent sf1.de
- **teeth**; during complaints of: *Cham* b7a.de *Cupr* b7a.de *Ign* b7a.de
- **worms**; from: cic c1

- **chill**:
- **after**: *Cina* hr1
- **during**: *Ars* *Camph* b7.de* hyos b7.de *Lach* merc nux-v

- **chorea**-like (See Chorea)
- **clonic**: acon k* **Agar** k* alum k* alum-p k2 am-c k* am-m k* ambr k* ambro vh anac k* ang b2.de* ant-c ant-t k* anth vh *Anthraci* kr1 antip bro1 apis bro1 *Arg-met* k* arg-n bg2 arn k* *Ars* k* *Art-v* (non:asaf k*) asar bg2* aster aur k* aur-ar k2 *Bar-c* k* bar-m bar-s k2 **Bell** k* borx k* bov bg2 brom sf1.de *Bry* k* **Bufo** *Calc* k* calc-i k2 *Calc-p* k* camph k* cann-s k* canth k* carb-ac bro1 carb-v k* carbn-o *Carbn-s* caul bg2 *Caust* k* **Cham** k* chin k* *Chinin-s* *Chlf* kr1 **Cic** k* cimic k* *Cina* k* clem k* cocc k* coff k* coloc k* *Con* k* croc k* **Cupr** k* dig k* dol c1 dulc k* gels bro1 graph k* guaj k* hell k* hep k* **Hyos** k* *Ign* k* indg hr1 iod k* *Ip* k* kali-ar kali-bi bg2 *Kali-c* k* kali-m k2 *Kalm* kreos k* lac-e hm2• lach k* lat-m sp1* lath mrr1 laur k* *Lyc* k* **Lyss** k* m-ambo b2.de m-arct b2.de m-aust b2.de mag-c k* mag-m k* *Mag-p* k* mang k* med c1* meny k* *Merc* k* *Mez* k* mosch k* mur-ac k* mygal k* nat-c k* nat-f sp1 *Nat-m* k* *Nicot* bro1 nit-ac k* *Nux-m* k* nux-v k* *Oena* k* ol-an bg2 olnd b2.de* **Op** k* petr k* ph-ac k* phos k* phys k* *Pic-ac* hr1 *Plat* k* **Plb** k* podo bg2 puls k* ran-b k* ran-s k* rheum k* rhod k* rhus-t k* russ a1 ruta k* sabad k* samb k* sars k* *Sec* k* sel k* seneg k* **Sep** k* *Sil* k* spig k* spong k* squil k* *Stann* k* staph k* **Stram** k* *Stront-c* k* stry bg2 *Stry-s* sf1.de sul-ac k* *Sulph* k* tab bg2 tarax k* tarent k* teucr k* thal-xyz srj8• thuj k* thymol sp1 tub st upa-a bro1 valer bg2 verat k* verat-v k* visc k* *Zinc* k* zinc-p k2 zinc-val bg2*
- **alternating** with tonic: bell bg2* *Cimic* k* con bg2* *Ign* bg2* *Mosch* bg2* nux-m bg2* nux-v sf1.de plat bg2* sep bg2* stram k* *Tab* hr1* verat-v bg2*
- **chill**; during: acon bg2 agar bg2 *Ars* bg2 bell bg2 bry bg2 *Calc* bg2 *Camph* bg2 caust bg2 cham bg2 cic bg2 cina bg2 **Hyos** bg2 ign bg2 lach bg2 lyc bg2 merc bg2 *Op* bg2 sep bg2 stram bg2 sulph bg2
- **fever**; during: **Ars** bg2 **Bell** bg2 bry bg2 calc bg2 **Camph** bg2 **Carb-v** bg2 *Cham* bg2 cic bg2 cocc bg2 cupr bg2 dulc bg2 **Hyos** bg2 ign bg2 ip bg2 kali-c bg2 lyc bg2 merc bg2 nat-m bg2 **Op** bg2 ph-ac bg2 phos bg2 rhus-t bg2 **Sep** bg2 sil bg2 stann bg2 **Stram** bg2 sulph bg2 thuj bg2 **Verat** bg2
- **perspiration**; during: **Bell** bg2 **Cham** bg2 cic bg2 cocc bg2 *Cupr* bg2 *Hyos* bg2 **Op** bg2 *Sep* bg2 stram bg2 thuj bg2 verat bg2

- **closing** a door, on: (*↗noise)* stry
- **coition**:
- **after**: *Agar* k*
- **during**: agar ptk1 *Bufo* k*

- **cold**:
- **air**:
  - **agg.**: agar sne *Ars* bell *Cic* *Indg* kr1 merc *Nux-v*
  - **amel.**: glon k2* op tl1
- **drinks** | **agg.**: caust j5.de cupr lyc j5.de
- **water** | **amel.**: *Caust* cupr tl1 lyc j5.de

- **cold** agg., becoming: art-v mrr bell *Caust* cic *Mosch* k* *Nux-v*
- **exertion** agg.; after: art-v mrr1

- **coldness**; with:
- **side** of body; of one: *Sil* k*
- **Body**; of: anan k1 *Camph* k* caust cic *Hell* k* hydr-ac sf1.de hyos mosch **Oena** k* op stram *Verat* k*
- **Feet**; of: *Cupr* kr1
  - **head** hot; and: bell bro1
- **Hands**; of: *Cupr* kr1

- **colic**, during: bell ptk1 **Cic** hr1* *Cupr* hr1* plb k* sec a1*
- **coma**; with (See MIND - Coma - convulsions)
- **compression** | **Spinal** column; on: *Tarent*
- **congenital**: hell hr1* *Kali-br* hr1* verat hr1*
- **consciousness**:
- **diminished**; with: absin vh1
- **with**: ang b2.de* ars k* aur-ar k2 bar-m k2* bell k* calc k* camph k* *Canth* k* caust k* **Cina** k* *Cupr* vh grat *Hell* k* hyos k* ign bg3* *Ip* k* kali-ar *Kali-c* k* lyc k* m-ambo b2.de *Mag-c* k* merc k* mur-ac k* *Nat-m* k* nit-ac k* *Nux-m* k* *Nux-v* k* *Phos* k* *Plat* k* plb sec *Sep* k* sil k* **Stram** k* stry k* sulph k*
- **without**: *(↗Faintness)* absin acet-ac acon *Aeth* agar hr1* agre jl3 aml-ns kr1 ant-t k* **Arg-n** k* *Ars* k* *Aster* aur k* *Bell* k* **Bufo** k* **Calc** k* *Calc-ar* *Calc-p* hr1* *Calc-s* *Camph* k* **Canth** k* carb-ac *Caust* cham k* chin k* **Cic** k* cina k* *Cocc* k* crot-h *Cupr* k* cupr-act bro1 cupr-ar bro1 cur hr1* dig k* euph hr1 ferr k* gels hr1 glon k* hydr-ac k* **Hyos** k* ign j5.de* *Ip* k* juni-v a1 *Kali-c* lach k* laur k* led k* lyc k* merc k* *Mosch* k* nat-m k* nit-ac k* nux-v k* **Oena** k* op k* phos k* *Plat* **Plb** k* sec k* *Sep* k* *Sil* k* *Stann* j5.de* staph k* *Stram* k* *Sulph* k* tanac *Tarent* verat k* vesp k2* **Visc** k* *Zinc* hr1

- **contortions**; with (See distortions)
- **contradiction**, from: *Aster* k*
- **cough**:
- **after**: cina ptk1 *Cupr* k* ign k2 *Ip* k* just ptk1 nicc c1 *Verat* hr1*
- **during** | **agg.**: bell hr1* *Calc* hr1* cina bro1 *Cupr* bro1 *Cupr-act* bro1 hydr-ac bro1 *Hyos* b7a.de ign hr1* meph hr1* oena bro1 *Sol-crl* bro1 stram a1* *Sulph* hr1*
- **whooping** cough; in: *Brom* hr1* *Calc* hr1* *Cupr* hr1* *Hydr-ac* hr1* *Ip* hr1* **Kali-br** hr1* narc-ps br1

- **croup**; in: *Lach* hr1*
- **cyanosis**, with: *Cupr* hr1* cupr-act bro1 *Hydr-ac* hr1* *Verat* hr1*
- **dead**; appearing to be: cupr tl1
- **delirium** tremens; in: *Hyos* hr1*
- **delivery**: *(↗Paralysis - one - convulsions - after)*
- **after**: *Art-v* sne bell he1 cic al1 cupr st glon hr1 hyos a2 lach hr1 *Mill* hr1* *Plat* kr1 sec a1 stram br1
  - **immediately** after: aml-ns ptk1 ant-t ptk1
- **during**: *Acon* j5.de* aeth bro1 aml-ns bro1 arn bro1 ars bro1 *Bell* j5.de* canth bro1 *Cham* j5.de* *Chin* k2 chinin-s kl chlf kr1 *Chlol* bro1 **Cic** kr1* cimic bro1* cinnm kr1 coff j5.de* *Cupr* kr1* *Cupr-ar* bro1 gels hr1* glon bro1 *Hydr-ac* c1* **Hyos** kr1* **Ign** j5.de* ip j5.de* **Kali-br** kr1* merc-c bro1 merc-d bro1 *Oena* bro1 *Op* bro1 pilo bro1 *Plat* j5.de* *Sec* k2* sol-ni bro1 spira bro1 stram bro1 *Verat-v* bro1 *Zinc* bro1 ziz kr1
- **labor** pains; convulsions from ceasing of: op ptk1

- **dentition**; during: *(↗accompanied - abdomen - irritation - dentition; TEETH - Dentition - difficult)* absin bro1 *Acon* k* *Aeth* k* art-v k* arum-t hr1* *Bell* k* **Calc** k* *Calc-p* hr1* *Camph-mbr* bro1 *Caust* hr1* **Cham** k* chlol bro1 chlor hr1 *Cic* k* *Cina* k* cocc bro1 coff bg2* *Colch* hr1* *Cupr* k* *Cupr-act* kr1 *Cypr* hr1* gels bg2* glon hr1* hell bro1 hydr-ac bro1 hyos k* *Ign* k* *Ip* hr1* **Kali-br** bg2* *Kreos* k* *Lach* hr1* laur bro1 *Mag-p* bg2* *Mand* bg* *Meli* hr1* merc k* mill hr1* mosch bro1 nux-m bg2* nux-v bro1 *Oena* bro1 op bro1* passi sf1.de* *Podo* k* rheum bg2* *Santin* bro1 scut br1* sin-n hr1* sol-ni bro1 *Stann* k* *Stram* k* strept-ent jl2 sulph j5.de* ter c1* thyr jl3 *Verat-v* bg2* *Zinc* bg2* *Zinc-br* bro1 zinc-s bro1
- **newborns**; in: strept-ent jl2

- **diarrhea**:
- **after** | **agg.**: mag-p ptk1 zinc ptk1
- **amel.**: lob
- **children**; in: nux-m ptk
- **during**: nux-m c1*

- **discharges**; from suppressed: *Asaf* cupr k* mill *Stram* k*
- **distortions**; with bizarre: **Cic** mrr1
- **downwards**, spread: *Cic* k* sec
- **drawing**-up of legs, alternately: cyt-l sp1
- **drinking**:
- **after**:
  - **agg.**: ars art-v kr1 bell k* *Hyos* k* *Stram* bg2
  - **water** | **agg.**: calc kl canth kl

- **drugs**; after: acon hr1* **Arn** hr1* **Bell** hr1 cham hr1 coff hr1 *Cupr* hr1 *Hyos* hr1 ign hr1 *Nux-v* hr1 **Op** hr1

- **drunkards**; in: *Absin* sne *Anthraci* kr1 glon *Hyos* hr1* *Nux-v* *Op* sne *Ran-b* k*
- **eating** | **after** | **agg.**: *Arg-n* hr1 aster hr1* *Calc-p* hr1* cina grat k* hyos k* nux-v sf1.de
  - **while** | **agg.**: bufo sne plb
- **emission** of semen, during: art-v k* grat k* *Nat-p* k*
  - **from**: *Lach* kr1
- **epileptic**: *(↗MIND - Unconsciousness - frequent)* abrot tl1 *Absin* k* acet-ac acon b2.de* *Aeth* k* *Agar* k* agarin mtf11 agre jl3 alco a1 alet hr1 all-c a1 *Alum* k* alum-p k2* alum-sil k2* alumn hr1* *Am-br* hr1* am-c k* *Ambr* hr1* ambro c1* *Aml-ns* bg2* amyg c1* *Anac* k* *Anag* hr1* anan vh ang b2.de* anil a1 anis bro1 ant-c b2.de* ant-t b2.de* antip c1* apis bg2 aran-ix mg1.de **Arg-met** k* arg-mur vh **Arg-n** k* arn b2.de* *Ars* k* *Art-v* k* asaf b2.de* *Aster* k* *Atro* hr1* atro-s mtf11 aur b2.de* aur-br c1* aven br1* *Bar-c* **Bar-m** k* bar-s k2* *Bell* k* ben-n c1* bism bg2* borx br1* bry b2.de* **Bufo** k* caj hr1* *Calc* k* **Calc-ar** k* *Calc-p* k* *Calc-s* calc-sil k2* camph k* cann-i k* *Canth* k* *Carb-an* k* carb-v k* carbn-s caste jl3 *Castm* kr1 *Castor-eq* kr1* caul bg2* **Caust** k* *Cedr* k* *Cham* b2.de* chen-a c1* *Chin* k* *Chinin-ar* kr1* chinin-s *Chlol* hr1* chlorpr jl3 *Cic* k* cic-m a1* *Cimic* hr1* *Cina* k* cinnm hr1* *Cocc* k* coleus-a bnj1 coloc b2.de* *Con* k* convo-s sp1* cori-r a1 cot br1 *Crot-c* *Crot-h* k* **Cupr** k* *Cupr-act* a1* *Cupr-ar* k* *Cur* k* *Cypr* hr1* dat-m c1* des-ac jl3 dig k* diph-t-tpt jl2 dros b2.de* dulc b2.de* fago a1 fagu c1* ferr b2.de* *Ferr-cy* bro1 ferr-i hr1 ferr-p hr1* *Form* k* galv c2 *Gels* k* germ-met srj5• *Glon* k* graph k2* *Hell* k* hell-v c1* hep bro1 hydr-ac k* **Hyos** k* *Hyper* hr1* *Ictod* kr1 *Ign* k* *Indg* k* iod k* *Ip* b2.de* irid-met br1* kali-ar k2* kali-bi hr1* *Kali-br* k* kali-c k* *Kali-chl* *Kali-cy* a1* kali-i gm1 kali-m bg2* *Kali-p* hr1* kali-s kres mg1.de* *Lach* k* *Laur* k* led b2.de* levo jl3 lith-br c1* lol bg2* loxo-recl bnm10• luna c2 *Lyc* k* *Lyss* k* m-ambo b2.de *Mag-c* k* *Mag-p* k* mand jl3 *Med* k* meli c1* meli-xyz c2 merc k* merc-i-r hr1 methyl br1* mill c1* mosch k* mur-ac b2.de* naja narc-ps ah1* *Nat-m* k* nat-s k* nicot c1* nit-ac k* nitro-o c1* nux-m k* *Nux-v* k* **Oena** k* oest bro1 onis c1* onon c1* *Op* k* paeon mg1.de parathyr jl2 parth gm1 passi c1* perh jl3 pert jl2 petr b2.de* *Ph-ac* k* *Phos* k* phys c1* *Picro* bro1* *Plat* k* **Plb** k* plb-xyz c2 polyg-pe c1 polyg-xyz c2 prot jl2* *Psor* k* *Puls* k* ran-b k* ran-s b2.de* rauw jl3 rhus-t b2.de* rib-ac jl3 ruta b2.de* *Salam* bro1* santin c1* *Sec* k* sep k* serot-cs mtf11 **Sil** k* sin-n hr1* *Sol-crl* c2* sol-ni j5.de spirae c1* *Stann* k* staph k* *Stram* k* *Stry* k* sulfon c1* **Sulph** k* sumb c1* syc bka1• *Syph* k* tab k* tanac c1 tarax b2.de* *Tarent* k* *Ter* hr1* teucr b2.de* thal-xyz srj8• thea a1 thiop jl3 thuj b2.de* toxo-g jl2 tub br1* valer b2.de* verat k* verat-v bg2* verb bg2* verbe-h c1 *Verbe-o* br1 verbe-u c2 vip k* **Visc** k* *Zinc* b2.de* zinc-cy c1* zinc-o mg1.de zinc-ox mg zinc-p bg2* *Zinc-val* bg2* zing hr1 *Ziz* a1* [nat-sil stj2]
  - **right** side: caust bro1
  - **night**: calc b4a.de* caust bro1 cic bro1 cupr bro1 kali-br bro1 *Kali-c* b4a.de *Sep* b4a.de sil bro1
  - **accompanied** by (See during)
  - **after** epileptic convulsions; complaints:
    - **blind**: sec
    - **headache**: *Calc* kr1 *Caust* cina cupr kali-br kl
    - **hiccough**: *(↗EXTREMITIES - Convulsion - hiccough)* cic bro1
    - **injuries** of tongue: *Art-v* kr1*
    - **nausea**: *Bell* b4a.de* *Cic* b7a.de kali-c gm1
    - **paralysis**: *Caust* bro1 cur ptk1 *Hyos* ptk1 plb bro1 sec bro1
    - **prostration** (See Weakness - convulsions - epileptic)
    - **ravenous** appetite: calc
    - **restlessness** (See MIND - Restlessness - convulsions - after - epileptic)
    - **tumors**: arg-n bro1 cic bro1
    - **unconsciousness** (See MIND - Unconsciousness - convulsions - after - epileptic)
    - **urine**, copious: caust j5.de *Cupr* lach j5.de
    - **vertigo**: calc ptk1* tarent mp1• visc tl1
    - **vomiting**: acon *Ars* bell bro1 *Calc* kr1 colch *Cupr* glon *Lach* b7a.de
    - **Ear** noises: *Ars* k1 *Caust*
  - **anger**; after: *(↗vexation)* art-v kr1 **Calc** kr1
  - **aura** (= before epileptic convulsions): *Cic* bg2 oena bg2 op bg2 stram bg2
    - **absent**: art-v bro1* hydr-ac sf1.de lach sf1.de oena sf1.de zinc sf1.de zinc-val bro1*
    - **auditory** complaints: *Bell* bro1* calc bro1 cic sf1.de hyos sf1.de sulph bro1*
    - **bellowing**: **Cupr** mrr1

- **epileptic – aura**: ...
    - **blindness**: *Cupr*
    - **cold** | **air** over spine and body: agar k*
    - **coldness**; with: sep h2 sil br1
      - **running** down spine: ars
        - **left** side; on: *Sil* k*
      - **Feet**; of: cina sf1.de *Lach* kr1
      - **Scapulae**; between: sep h2
    - **confusion**: *Lach* kr1*
    - **congestion** of blood to head: calc-ar br1* op sf1.de sulph sf1.de
    - **creeping** down spine: *Lach*
    - **descending** agg.: calc bro1
    - **dizziness**, with: indg br1
    - **drawing** pain in left side of chest: nit-ac h2
    - **drawing** pain in limbs: ars k*
    - **eructations**: *Lach* kr1*
    - **expansion** of body, sensation of: *Arg-n*
    - **fear**: aml-ns kr1 arg-n kr1 cupr kr1* nat-m kr1
    - **flatulence**: *Arg-n* bro1 nux-v bro1 psor bro1 sulph bro1
    - **general** nervous feeling: arg-n k* *Nat-m* k*
    - **headache**: *Bell* kr1 calc kr1 *Calc-ar* kr1 cann-i kr1 caust kr1* cina h1* *Lach* kr1* staph kr1 zinc kr1
    - **heart**, from: *Calc-ar* k* lach naja
    - **heat**, flushes of: calc-ar st
    - **jerk** in nape: *Bry* kr1 bufo
    - **malaise**: cic bro1
    - **memory**; confusion of (See MIND - Memory - confused - epileptic)
    - **morose**: zinc sf1.de zinc-val sf1.de
    - **mouse** running; sensation of a: *(↗Formication - mouse)* ars sf1.de aur sf1.de **Bell** k* **Calc** k* ign k* nit-ac k* sep sf1.de *Sil* k* stram sf1.de **Sulph** k*
      - **left** side: nit-ac a1*
      - **Arm**; up: calc ll1* sulph c1
      - **Back** and arms; up: sulph hr1*
      - **Leg**; up: calc gsd1
        - **right** leg: sulph hr1
    - **nausea**: cupr kr1* hydr-ac ptk1 *Sulph* kr1
    - **numbness** of brain: bufo
    - **palpitation**: *(↗CHEST - Palpitation - convulsions - before - epileptic)* absin bg2* ars *Calc* *Calc-ar* cupr k* ferr bg2 *Lach* k* nat-m sf1.de
    - **perspiration** scalp: *Caust* hell-v c1
    - **quivering** of muscles: *Absin* vh1
    - **ravenous** appetite: *Calc* **Hyos**
    - **restlessness**: arg-n k2 bufo kr1 caust sf1.de
    - **sadness**: art-v kr1 zinc sf1.de zinc-val bg2
    - **sexual** organs; starting in: bufo bg2* plat bg2
    - **shocks**: ars *Laur*
    - **shrieking**: **Cic** kr1* *Cupr* kr1* hydr-ac bro1* stram sf1.de
    - **sighing**: cic bg2
    - **sleeplessness**: zinc-val bg2
    - **speech**, unintelligible: bufo sf1.de
    - **trembling**: absin bg2* arg-n st aster bro1
      - **nervous**: absin br1
    - **urging** stool: calc-ar st
    - **vertigo**: *(↗VERTIGO - Convulsions)* ars *Calc-ar* k* *Caust* **Hyos** k* indg bro1* *Lach* k* *Plb* sil sf1.de *Sulph* *Tarent* visc sf1.de
    - **vesicular** eruption: cic bro1
    - **visual** complaints: *Bell* bro1* calc bro1 hyos sf1.de sulph bro1*
    - **voice**, loss of: calc-ar
    - **vomiting**: *(↗STOMACH - Vomiting - convulsions - before)* *Cupr* k* op
    - **warm** air streaming up spine: *Ars*
    - **waving** sensation in brain: cimic k*
    - **without**: art-v br1* zinc-val br1
    - **Abdomen**: bufo k2

- **aura – Abdomen**: ...
  - **Head**; to: ind ptk1 *Indg*
    - **flushes**: indg br1*
  - **Arms**, in: bell sf1.de calc *Calc-ar* k* *Lach* *Sulph*
    - **left** arm, in: *Calc-ar* kr1* cupr kr1* *Sil* kr1* sulph sf1.de*
    - **Forearms**, in: bell st calc st sulph st
  - **Back**, in: ars j5.de sulph j5.de
    - **and** left arm: *Calc-ar* st sulph st
  - **Chest**; in | **pain**: calc-ar mrr1
  - **Ear** noises: hyos hr1*
  - **Epigastrium** to uterus, legs: **Calc** kr1*
  - **Extremities**; in (See limbs)
  - **Eyes**:
    - **dilated** pupils not reacting to light: *Arg-n* ptk1 bufo hr1*
    - **sparks** before the eyes: *Hyos* k*
    - **turned** upwards to left: bufo
  - **Face**:
    - **chewing** motion: *Calc*
    - **formication** in: nux-v sf1.de
    - **twitching**: laur bg2
  - **Fingers** and toes, in: cupr kr1*
  - **Hands**; in: (↗*begin - hands)* cupr mrr1
    - **right**: cupr kr1*
    - **pain**: calc-ar mrr1
    - **extending** to:
      - **Body**: cupr mrr1
      - **Head**: *Sulph* kr1
  - **Head**, from | **trembling** sensation: *Caust*
  - **Heel** to occiput, right: *Stram* k1
  - **Knees**, in: cupr k* cupr-act st
    - **ascending** agg.: cupr br1*
      - **Hypogastrium**; to: cupr br1* cupr-act ptk1
  - **Legs**:
    - **right** leg to abdomen, from: lyc sf1.de
    - **In**: lyc sf1.de plb sf1.de
  - **Limbs**, in: bell st1 calc st1 cupr mrr1* lyc bro1
    - **left**: cupr mtf33
  - **Mouth** wide open: *Bufo*
  - **Pupils** dilated: (↗*EYE - Pupils - dilated - convulsions - before - epileptic)* **Arg-n** k* *Bufo*
  - **Shoulders**; between | **pain**: indg bg2*
  - **Solar** plexus, from: am-br vh art-v bell *Bufo* k1* *Calc* k1* *Caust* **Cic** cupr k* *Indg* **Nux-v** k* *Sil* k* **Sulph**
    - **extending** to:
      - **Both** sides, chest, and throat: am-br vh
      - **Genitals**: bufo ptk1 cic ptk1 *Nux-v* ptk1 *Sulph* ptk1
    - **Head**; to: calc st *Sil* kr1
      - **flush** of heat to head: indg c1
  - **Stomach**, in: (↗*STOMACH - Epileptic)* art-v bell bism bg2* bufo *Calc* *Caust* st1 **Cic** cupr k* **Hyos** k* *Indg* **Nux-v** k* *Sil* **Sulph**
    - **heat**: *Bell* bro1 calc bro1 sulph bro1
    - **Genitals**; or: lyc bro1
    - **Head**; to: **Calc**
  - **Teeth**, grinding of: *Sulph* kr1
  - **Throat**, narrow sensation: lach sf1.de
  - **Tongue** swelling: plb sf1.de
  - **Uterus**, in: bufo cimic tl1
    - **Stomach**; to: bufo
    - **Throat**; to: *Lach*
- **brain**; from complaints of: plb bro1
- **children**; in: aeth bro1 art-v bro1 *Bell* bro1 bufo bro1 calc bro1 cham bro1 cupr bro1 ign bro1 sil bro1 sulph bro1
- **chill**; during: *Ars* b4a.de *Calc* b4a.de
- **chronic**: chlorpr mtf11
  - **aura**; with marked: plb ptk1
- **cold**; after taking a: caust bro1
- **dullness**; with (See MIND - Dullness - epilepsy - with)
- **during** epileptic convulsions; complaints: (↗*MIND - Delirium - epilepsy - during; MIND - Laughing - epileptic - during; MIND - Laughing - spasmodic; MIND - Shrieking - convulsions - epileptic; MIND - Weeping - convulsions - during - epileptic)*
  - **biting** tongue (See tongue - biting)
  - **constipation**: verbe-o br1
  - **enuresis**: hyos hr1*
  - **erections**; painful: oena ptk1
  - **flatulence**: hera br1
  - **froth**, foam from mouth: (↗*MOUTH - Froth - convulsions - during)* aeth j5.de* agar anan vh ars *Art-v* *Aster* kr1 bell *Bufo* camph canth *Caust* *Cham* *Cic* kr1* *Cina* cocc colch *Cupr* gels *Glon* hydr-ac sf1.de *Hyos* ign kr1 *Ind* kr1 *Lach* kr1 laur j5.de* lyc kr1 lyss med kr1 *Oena* *Op* plb kr1 *Sil* j5.de* staph *Stry* sulph tax vip sf1.de
  - **involuntary** discharges: cocc kr1
    - **urination**: anan vh art-v kr1 **Bufo** kr1 *Caust* kr1 cocc kr1 cupr kr1 **Hyos** kr1 lach kr1 nat-m kr1 nux-v kr1 *Oena* kr1 *Plb* kr1 stry kr1 *Zinc* kr1
  - **laughter**; sardonic: stram tl1
  - **lockjaw**: aeth bro1 cic bro1
  - **mouse** running up a limb; sensation of: bell tl1 calc tl1 sil tl1
  - **palpitation**; irregular: calc-ar mrr1
  - **perspiration**: ant-c b7a.de
  - **pupils**:
    - **contracted**: cic kr1 *Op* kr1 phyt kr1
    - **dilated**: (↗*EYE - Staring - convulsions)* aeth j5.de* *Bell* kr1 carb-ac kr1 cic kr1 *Cina* kr1 cocc kr1 oena kr1 plb kr1 verat-v kr1
  - **shrieking** (See MIND - Shrieking - convulsions - epileptic)
  - **throwing**:
    - **backward**: *Camph* kr1
    - **forwards**: *Cupr* kr1
  - **vertigo**: (↗*VERTIGO - Epileptic)* *Apis* arg-n bro1* ars ptk1 art-v bell bro1 bufo calc bro1* *Calc-ar* calc-s *Caust* k* cocc bro1 crot-h cupr bro1 *Cur* hydr-ac bro1 *Hyos* ptk1 ign *Nat-m* nit-ac bro1 *Nux-m* op bro1 plb *Sil* k* stram bro1 tarent ptk1 thuj *Visc* k*
  - **Extremities**; distorted: cic bro1
  - **Eyes**:
    - **downwards**; turned: (↗*EYE - Turned - downward - convulsions)* aeth j5.de*
    - **protruding**: dros ptk1 hyos hr1*
    - **upwards** to right; turned: *Hydr-ac* kr1
    - **winking** of eyes: kali-bi
  - **Face**:
    - **bluish**: absin kr1 agar kr1 atro kr1 *Bell* kr1 *Cic* cina j5.de* **Cupr** *Hyos* ign j5.de *Ip* nux-v kr1 *Oena* **Op** kr1 phys plb kr1 stry *Verat* kr1
    - **expression** | **stupid**, friendly: stram tl1
    - **pale**: am-c kr1 ars j5.de* bell kr1 calc kr1 caust kr1 chin kr1 cic j5.de* cina kr1 *Cupr* kr1 *Ip* kr1 lach j5.de* mosch j5.de nat-m kr1 plb kr1 puls kr1 sil kr1 stann j5.de* sulph kr1 *Verat* kr1 zinc kr1
    - **purple**: hyos hr1*
    - **red**: (↗*FACE - Discoloration - red - convulsions)* aeth j5.de* *Bell* j5.de* bufo camph j5.de* caust kr1 **Cic** j5.de* cina kr1 cit-ac j5.de cocc j5.de *Cupr* kr1 **Glon** ign j5.de* ip j5.de* lyc j5.de* nux-v kr1 *Oena* **Op** stram j5.de*
    - **yellow**: cic j5.de* plb kr1
  - **Fingers** and toes; spasms in: cupr tl1
  - **Heart**; complaints of the: calc-ar mrr1
  - **Larynx**; spasms in: bell tl1
  - **Lids** | **twitching** of: kali-bi ptk1
  - **Pharynx**; spasms in: calc tl1
  - **Stomach**; swelling of: cic bro1*
  - **Teeth**, grinding of: art-v mrr1 *Bufo* **Hyos** k* sulph tarent
  - **Tongue**:
    - **biting** of: absin kr1* anis br1* *Art-v* k* *Bufo* camph k* *Caust* k* cocc *Cupr* ign gk *Oena* *Op* k* plb a1 sec sil vk1 stram k2 tarent k* valer
    - **swelling** of: *Plb* a1*

- **eruptions**; after suppressed: agar bro1 calc bro1 cupr bro1 psor bro1 *Sulph* bro1
- **excitement** agg.: art-v br1
- **fright**; from: arg-n bro1* art-v br1* bufo bro1 calc bro1 caust tl1 cham bro1 hyos bro1 ign bro1* sil bro1 stram bro1* sulph a1*
- **hysterical**: asaf bro1 cocc bro1 cupr bro1 hyos bro1 *Ign* bro1 mosch bro1 oena bro1 *Sol-crl* bro1 sumb bro1 tarent bro1 visc bg2 *Zinc-val* bro1
- **injuries**; after: con bro1 cupr bro1 meli bro1 nat-s bro1
  - **head**; of: meli br1
- **jealousy**; from: lach bro1
- **loss** of vital fluids; from: lach bro1
- **masturbation**; after: art-v br1 lach bro1
- **menses**:
  - **absent**: puls ptk1
  - **after** | **agg.**: cupr b7a.de puls b7a.de
  - **agg.**: arg-n bro1 bufo bro1 caul bro1 caust bro1 cedr bro1 cimic bro1* cupr bro1 kali-br bro1 *Mill* bro1 oena bro1 puls bro1 sol-crl bro1
  - **before** | **agg.**: *Cupr* b7a.de *Nat-m* b4a.de *Phos* b4a.de puls b7a.de
  - **during** | **agg.**: *Calc* b4a.de caust b4a.de cocc b7a.de coff b7a.de *Cupr* b7a.de ign b7a.de merc b4a.de *Puls* b7a.de
- **moon**:
  - **full**: calc bro1*
  - **new**: caust bro1 cupr bro1 kali-br bro1 sil bro1
- **old** people; in: aven br1
- **periodical**: ars bro1 cupr bro1 vip bg2
- **pregnancy** agg.; during: oena bro1
- **psychomotor** seizures: *Hyos* mrr1
- **quinine** poisoning; from: nat-m tl1
- **rapid** succession; attacks in: absin vh1 art-v bro1
- **recent** cases: bell bro1 caust bro1 cupr bro1 *Hydr-ac* bro1 *Ign* bro1 op bro1 plb bro1 stram bro1
- **recurrent**: art-v bro1 cic bro1
- **sadness**; with (See MIND - Sadness - epilepsy - with)
- **sexual** disturbance; from: art-v bro1 *Bufo* bro1 calc bro1 plat bro1 stann bro1 sulph bro1
- **sleep**; during: bufo bro1 cupr bro1 lach bro1 *Op* bro1 *Sil* bro1 viol-t b7a.de
- **starting**; after (See fright)
- **status** epilepticus: *Acon* bro1 aeth bro1 *Bell* bro1 cocc bro1 oena bro1 plb bro1 zinc bro1
- **stool** agg.; during: nux-v ptk1
- **syphilitic**: kali-br bro1
- **touch**; slightest: bell tl1 cic tl1 nux-v tl1 strych-g tl1
- **traumatic**: naphthoq mtf11
- **tubercular**: kali-br bro1
- **valvular** disease; from: calc-ar bro1
- **vexation**; from: (↗*MIND - Irritability - convulsions - before - epileptic)* ign tl1
- **violent**: aesc tl1 hyos tl1
- **wet**; from exposure to: cupr bro1
- **worms**; from: cic bro1 cina bro1 indg bro1 santin bro1 sil bro1 stann bro1 sulph bro1 teucr bro1

- **epileptiform**: (↗*MIND - Unconsciousness - frequent)* *Absin* hr1* acon aeth k* **Agar** alum alum-sil k2* am-c aml-ns kr1* *Anac* ant-c ant-t arg-met k1 **Arg-n** k* arn *Ars* art-v sf1.de asaf k* aur aur-ar k2 **Bell** k* benzol br1 bism sf1.de bry *Bufo* **Calc** k* calc-i k2* calc-p k2* calc-s *Camph* k* canth k* carbn-s caul hr1* **Caust** k* *Cedr* k* *Cham* chin *Chinin-ar* kr1 chlorpr jl3 **Cic** **Cina** cit-v hr1 *Cocc* k* coloc con *Convo-s* sp1* cortico sp1 **Cupr** k* *Cur* k* dig diosm br1 diph-t-tpt jl2 dros dulc epil c1 ferr ferr-ar gal-ac st1 *Gels* k* **Glon** k* graph k2* hell *Hydr-ac* hr1* **Hyos** k* *Hyper* k* hypoth jl3 ign k* iod *Ip* k* kali-br k* *Kali-c* kali-chl sf* kali-i hr1* kali-m k2* kali-s *Lach* laur led lob sf1.de lol sf1.de *Lyc* mag-c *Med* k* merc mosch mur-ac *Nat-m* *Nat-s* hr1 *Nit-ac* *Nux-m* *Nux-v* oena k* op k* passi sf1.de petr ph-ac phos *Phys* hr1* *Picro* vh *Plat* k* **Plb** k* prot jl3 *Psor* *Puls* k* *Ran-b* k* ran-s rauw jl3 rhus-t ruta salam sf1.de *Sec* k* *Sep* *Sil* stann k* staph **Stram** k* streptoc jl2 *Stry* k* sul-i k2* **Sulph** k* tarax *Tarent* k* teucr thuj valer
- **epileptiform**: ...
verat verat-v k* verbe-h sf1.de vip sf1.de **Visc** k* zinc zinc-cy c1 zinc-p k2* *Zinc-val* sf1.de
  - **children**; in: merc mtf33
    - **infants**: toxo-g jl2
- **errors** in diet: *Cic* lac-f wza1•
- **eructations** | **amel.**: *Kali-c* k*
- **eruptions**: acon bro1 *Bell* bro1 glon bro1 thea bro1 verat-v bro1
  - **suppressed** eruptions; after: *Agar* *Ant-c* kr1 ant-t vh apis bro1 ars bro1 *Bry* *Calc* *Camph* kr1 *Caust* k* cic kr1 *Cupr* bro1* *Cupr-act* kr1* *Hyos* kr1 *Ip* kr1 *Kali-m* kr1 op bro1 *Stram* k* *Sulph* *Urt-u* kr1 *Zinc* k* zinc-s bro1
    - **break** out; or when they fail to: *Ant-t* k* apis k2 *Bry* *Camph* **Cupr** k* *Cupr-act* kr1* *Gels* *Hep* kr1 *Ip* *Stram* *Sulph* **Zinc** k*
- **exanthemas** (See eruptions)
- **excitement** agg.: (↗*Nervousness)* acon k* *Agar* art-v sf1.de *Aster* *Bell* k* bufo gk3 cann-i a1 *Cham* k* cic k* cimic k* *Coff* k* *Cupr* k* *Gels* k* **Hyos** k* *Ign* k* *Kali-br* k* *Nux-v* k* **Op** k* plat k* *Puls* k* sec k* sil c1 tarent k* *Zinc* hr1*
  - **religious**: *Verat* hr1*
- **exertion** agg.; after: alum k* alumn kr1 art-v mrr *Calc* cupr sne *Glon* kalm k* *Lach* k* *Lyss* k* nat-m k* petr k* sacch-a fd2.de• sulph
- **extension** of body amel.; forcible: nux-v stry
- **falling**; with: *Agar* k* alum alum-p k2* am-c *Ars* k* *Aster* **Bell** k* bufo k2 *Calc* calc-i k2* *Calc-p* camph j5.de canth *Caust* *Cedr* **Cham** k* *Chinin-ar* kr1 cic cina cocc *Con* **Cupr** k* dig dol c1 dulc hydr-ac bg **Hyos** k* ign *Iod* k* ip lach j5.de laur lyc lyss hr1* mag-c bg merc nit-ac **Oena** k* op petr ph-ac phos plb sec sep sil *Stann* staph *Stram* k* sulph verat zinc
  - **right** side: bell
  - **left** side: bell k* caust k* lach k* sabad k* sulph st
  - **backward**: ang hr1* *Bell* k* camph hr1* canth k* chin k* cic k* cic-m a1 *Ign* k* *Ip* k* kalm hr1* nux-v k* *Oena* **Op** k* rhus-t k* spig k* *Stram* k* [art-v stj]
  - **circle** to the right; first runs in a: *Caust* k*
  - **forward**: arn k* *Aster* calc-p k* canth k* cic k* cupr k* ferr k* rhus-t k* sil k* sulph k* sumb k*
  - **sideways**: bell hr1* *Calc* h2* con hr1* nux-v hr1* sulph hr1*
- **fear**:
  - **from**: acon sf1.de arg-n st1 art-v ptk1 **Calc** kr1* *Caust* sf1.de cupr sf1.de* glon sf1.de hyos ptk1 ign ptk1 ind ptk1 kali-p sf1.de *Op* sf1.de* sil sf1.de
  - **with** (See MIND - Fear - convulsions - with)
- **fever**:
  - **with** (See heat)
  - **without**: ign bro1 *Mag-p* bro1 *Zinc* bro1
- **fingers**, spread: glon tl1 sec st1
- **flexion** and extension: colch mtf11
- **fright** agg.: (↗*Neurological - fright)* *Acon* k* agar apis arg-n art-v bell sf1.de* *Bufo* **Calc** k* *Caust* k* cic cina sf1.de *Cupr* k* *Gels* hr1* glon sf1.de **Hyos** k* **Ign** k* **Indg** k* **Kali-br** k* *Kali-p* hr1* laur hr1* lyss k* nat-m st1 **Op** k* *Plat* k* *Sec* k* sil sf* *Stram* k* sulph tarent verat *Zinc*
  - **mother** (infant); of the: bufo kr1 **Op** k*
- **gastrointestinal** disturbances, preceded by: aeth bro1 anth vh cupr-ar br1*
- **glistening** objects; from (See brilliant)
- **goitre** | **suppressed**; from: iod ptk1
- **grasping** tight | **amel.**: mez ptk1 nux-v k*
- **grief**; from: *Ars* hr1* art-v k* *Hyos* k* ign k* indg st1 nat-m nux-v gl1.fr• *Op* k*
- **headache**; during: bar-m k2 ign bro1
- **heart** disease; from: calc-ar ptk1
- **heart** valve disease; with: calc-ar k2
- **heat**; during●: (↗*FEVER - Intense - convulsions)* acetan bro1 acon bro1 agar zr ant-c bg2 apis tl1 arn bg2* ars bg2* *Bell* bg2* calc bg2 camph tl1* carb-v ptk1 *Caust* bg2* chin bg2 *Cic* k* *Cina* k* cocc bg2 cupr bg2 cur *Ferr-p* hr1* *Hyos* k* ign bg2* lac-e hm2• lach bg2 *Nat-m* hr1* **Nux-v** k* op k* pert jl2 rhus-t bg2 sep bg2* stann bg2 **Stram** k* sulph bg2 tub gk verat bg2* verat-v hr3
  - **children**; in: | **newborns**; in: camph tl1
- **hemoptysis**; ending in: dros ptk1
- **hemorrhage**:
  - **after**: ars bg2* bell bg2* bry ptk1 calc bg2* cina bg2* con bg2* ign bg2* lyc bg2* nux-v bg2* puls bg2* sulph bg2* verat bg2*

- **suppression** of: mill ptk1
- **with**: Chin k* ferr bro1 hyos ip kl phos bro1 Plat k* plb ptk1 Sec k*

- **hiccough**; after: cupr hr1*
- **hydrocephalus**; with: Arg-n hr1* Art-v hr1* bell mtf Calc hr1* hell mtf Kali-i hr1* Merc hr1* Nat-m hr1* Stram hr1* Sulph hr1* Zinc hr1*
- **hydrophobia** with: Bell hr1* Canth hr1* Cur hr1* gels hr1* lyss hr1 Stram hr1*
- **hypochondriasis** with: mosch bro1 stann bro1
- **hysterical**: (↗MIND - Excitement - hysterical - convulsions) absin k* acet-ac hr1* acon j5.de* agar k2 Alum k* alum-p k2* ambr bg2* Apis ars k* **Asaf** k* asar bg2* Aur k* aur-ar k2 aur-s k2* Bell k* Bry k* Calc k* calc-s cann-i hr1* cann-s k* castm bro1 caul hr1* Caust k* Cedr cham k* chlf hr1* Cic k* Cimic k* Cocc k* coff k* Coll **Con** k* croc k* cupr k2* dig b2.de* Gels k* graph k2* hydr-ac hr1* hyos k* **Ign** k* Iod k* Ip k* kali-ar k2* kali-p bg2* lach k* lact j5.de Lil-t bg2* lyc k* m-ambo b2.de Mag-c bg2* Mag-m k* meph bg2* merc k* Mill hr1* **Mosch** k* narc-ps ah1 Nat-m k* nit-ac k* Nux-m k* nux-v k* oena sf1.de op k* petr k* phos k* Plat k* plb k* puls k* ruta b2.de* sec k* Sep k* stann b2.de* staph k* Stram k* sul-i k2* sulph k* sumb k* tarent k* thyr c1 valer k* Verat k* Verat-v k* vib hr1 zinc k* zinc-p k2 Zinc-val bg2*
  - **menses**; before: hyos sf1.de ign sf1.de lach sf1.de
- **idiocy**; with (See MIND - Idiocy - convulsions)
- **indigestion**; from: **Ip** k*
- **indignation**; from: Staph
- **injuries**; after: Ang hr1* arn k* art-v bufo sne Cic k* con ptk1 cupr mg1.de* cupr-act mg1.de hep ptk1 **Hyper** k* Nat-s k* oena k* Op k* puls hr1* Rhus-t k* sil mg1.de sulph k* Valer k*
  - **slight** injuries: valer ptk1
  - **spinal**: zinc ptk1
  - ○ **Head**, of the: (↗brain - commotion; Neurological - injuries - head) **Arn** kr1* art-v kr1* **Cic** kr1* Cupr kr1 Hyper kr1* Led kr1 meli kr1* Nat-s kr1* oena mrr1
- **intermittent**: absin k*
- **interrupted** by painful shocks: stry
- **jealousy**; from: Lach k*
- **knocking** body, from: hyper ptk1
- **labor**; during: acon bro1 bell bro1 cic bro1 cupr bro1 gels hr1 glon bro1 hyos bro1 ign bro1 kali-br bro1 oena bro1 op b7a.de Sec b7a.de stram bro1 verat-v bro1
- **laughing**:
  - **agg.**: chin k2 Coff k* Cupr graph k*
  - **with**: coff k* graph k*
- **leukorrhea**; with: Caust kr1 Lach kr1
- **lids**, while touching: coc-c k*
- **light**; from: (↗bright) art-v mrr1 Bell k* **Lyss** k* nux-v Op k* Psor ptk1 puls ptk1 Pyrog ptk1 rhus-t ptk1 sabad ptk1 Sep ptk1 **Stram** k*
- **limbs**, on attempting to use: cocc ptk1 **Pic-ac** ptk1
- **liquids** agg.: Bell canth hyos **Lyss** k* **Stram**
- **lochia** | **suppressed**; from: mill c1 stram c1 zinc bg2
- **love**; from disappointed: hyos ign k2
- **lying**:
  - **abdomen** with spasmodic jerking of pelvis upward; on: cupr h2*
  - **back**; convulsively turned on the: Cic
  - **side**; on | **agg.**: puls
- **mania**; with (See MIND - Mania - convulsions)
- **masturbation**; from: art-v c1 Bufo k* calad Calc k* dig elaps kali-br Lach k* naja nux-v **Plat** k* plb sep sil stram k* Sulph k*
- **measles**; during: aeth bro1 apis bro1 Bell bro1 camph bro1 coff bro1 Cupr-act bro1 stram bro1 verat-v bro1 viol-o bro1 zinc bro1
- **meningitis**; during cerebrospinal: (↗Neurological - meningitis; FEVER - Cerebrospinal) ail tl1 Ant-t hr1* Apis kr1 Arg-n hr1* cic tl1* Crot-h hr1* cupr mtf33 ferr-p tl1 Glon hr1* Hell hr1* ip tl1 nat-s tl1 Tarent hr1* Verat hr1* verat-v tl1 zinc mrr1
- **menopause**; during: glon sf1.de Lach kr1*
- **menses**:
  - **after** | **agg.**: chin bg2 kali-br st syph k* verat-v ptk1
  - **before** | **agg.**: apis bg2 art-v bro1 bell bg2* brom bg2* Bufo k* calc-s bro1 cann-xyz bg2 carb-v k* caul bro1* Caust k* cimic bg2* Cocc b7.de* coff b7.de* Cupr k* ferr b7a.de gels bro1 Hyos k* Ign bro1 Kali-br k*
- **menses** – **before** – **agg.**: ... Kali-c b4a.de lach bro1 mag-c sf1.de mag-m bro1* merc b4.de* Mosch bg2 oena k* ph-ac b4a.de plat b4a.de* Puls k* sep b4a.de sulph b4a.de* tarent bro1 verat-v bg2*
  - **during**:
    - **agg.**: apis k* Arg-n k* Art-v hr1* Bell k* bufo k2* calc-s bro1 cann-s b7.de* Caul k* caust k* Cedr k* cham b7.de chin bg2 Cimic k* Cocc k* Coff b7a.de Coll k* Cupr k* gels k* glon bg2* Hyos k* Ign k* **Kali-br** k* kali-chl sf kali-m sf1.de Lach k* mag-m bro1 mosch bg2* Nat-m nux-m k* Nux-v k* **Oena** k* phos bg2 phys k* Plat k* plb k* puls k* Sec k* stram k* Sulph k* tarent k* verat bg2 Zinc k*
    - **beginning** of menses | **agg.**: Acon b7.de* Bry b7.de* Cham b7.de* cocc b7.de* Coff b7.de* **Hyos** b7a.de ign b7.de* ip b7a.de Kali-c b4a.de lach bg2 mag-p bg2 Plat b4.de*
  - **instead** of: cic ptk1 oena k* puls ptk1
  - **suppressed** menses; from: Bufo k* Calc-p k* Cocc k* cupr k* Gels k* glon ptk1 Mill hr1* oena mrr1 Puls k*
- **mental** exertion; after: agar sne bell cann-i a1 Glon k* kali-br tl1 op tl1
- **mercurial** vapors, from: stram
- **metastasis**: apis bro1 Cupr k* zinc bro1
- **metrorrhagia**; during: Hyos b7a.de
- **milk** of mother; from suppression of: Agar k* mill c1
- **mirror** (See shining)
- **miscarriage**, after: ruta k*
- **moon**: sil bg2
  - **full** moon: (↗Moon - full - agg.) bell sne **Calc** kr1* caust sf1.de cupr sne Nat-m kr1 sil sne
  - **new** moon: (↗Moon - new - agg.) Bufo kr1* calc sne Caust kr1* Cupr kr1* Kali-br hr1* Sil j5.de*
- **mortification**; from: (↗unjustly) Calc cham k2 Staph kr1
- **motion** agg.: ars k* bell cic bro1 Cocc graph helo-s bnm14• ign bro1 lyss bro1 Nux-v k* stram bro1 Stry k*
- **nervousness**, from: (↗excitement) Arg-n kali-br bro1
- **noise**: (↗closing)
  - **agg.**: ang j5.de ant-c arn Cic k* ign k* Lyss k* Mag-p hr1* nux-v k* stram bro1 stry k*
  - **arrests** the paroxysm: Hell k*
- **nursing** children when mother is angry or frightened (See children - nursing)
- **odors** agg.; strong: bruc j5.de Lyss k* sil stram stry br1 sulph
- **old** people; in: plb mg1.de
- **opisthotonos**; with: aeth tl1 ang b7a.de apis bro1 arg-n tl1 bell tl1 camph tl1 Caust ptk cham b7a.de Cic b7a.de* cina bro1 cupr-act bro1 Hydr-ac bro1 ign b7a.de* ip b7a.de* mag-p bro1 mosch bro1 nicot bro1 nux-m ptk nux-v bro1* Op b7a.de phys bro1 phyt tl1 plat bro1 plb bro1 rhus-t b7a.de sol-crl bro1 sol-ni bro1 stann ptk1 stram b7a.de* Stry bro1 ter tl1 Upa bro1 verat-v bro1*
- **pain**:
  - **abdominal** pain; with: cic k2
  - **after**: chin ptk1 plat ptk1
    - **Uterus**; in region of: coll tl1
  - **during**: ars a1 Bell a1* chir-fl bnm4• coloc a1* ign a1* kali-c a1* lyc a1* nux-v a1* plb-chr a1*
  - **menses** (= dysmenorrhea): caul ptk nat-m ptk
  - **renewed** convulsion at every attack of pain: bell kr1
- **painless**: cann-s b7.de caps b7.de Cic b7.de Mosch b7.de nux-v b7.de op b7.de Stram b7.de
- **palpitations**; after: glon k*
- **paralysis**:
  - **followed** by (See Paralysis - one - convulsions - after)
  - **with**: arg-n k* bell k* **Caust** k* cic k* cocc k* cupr k* Hyos k* lach k* laur k* Nux-m k* Nux-v k* Phos k* plat k* Plb k* Rhus-t k* sec k* Stann k* Tab k* vib k* zinc k*
- **paresis**, followed by: acon bro1 Elaps bro1 lon-x bro1 plb bro1
- **parturition** (See delivery)
- **periodical**: agar ars bar-m bufo kr1* calc Cedr chin kr1 chinin-s cupr ign indg lach kr1 lyc nat-m nux-v kr1 plb kr1 sec stram
  - **day**:
    - **five** or six days; every: Lyc kr1
    - **ten** days; every: Kali-br kr1

- **day**: ...
  - **fifteen** or twenty days; every: *Tarent* kr1
- **hour**; at the same | **children**; in: ign ptk1
- **week**:
  - **every**: *Agar* bufo sne chinin-s *Indg* *Kali-br* kr1 nat-m
  - **two** weeks; every: cupr *Kali-br* kr1 oena
  - **three** weeks; every: camph k2 *Cupr* kr1 *Ferr* kr1 *Op* kr1 stram kr1
- **summer**; every: *Stram* kr1

- **perspiration**:
  - **after** | **agg.**: acon ars *Bry* kr1 cedr cupr sec stry
  - **during**: ars *Bell* **Bufo** camph nux-v op sep
    - **cold** agg.: camph k2 *Cupr* kr1 *Ferr* stram *Verat* kr1
  - **suppressed** perspiration; from: *Sil* sf1.de
    - **foot**-sweat; after: form c2 **Sil** k*
- **pregnancy** agg.; during (= eclampsia): agar hr1 aml-ns bro1 anan a1 apoc dw5 ars b2.de *Bell* b2.de* bry b2.de calc tl1 camph hr1 castm c1* caust b2.de *Cedr* *Cham* k* chin mtf11 *Chlol* c1 *Cic* k* *Cina* j5.de* cocc b2.de* coff b2.de **Con** b2.de *Cupr* k* ferr b2.de *Gels* hr1* glon bro1* hell bg2* *Hyos* k* **Ign** b2.de* *Ip* b2.de* kreos b2.de lach mrr1* lyc k* lyss c1* mag-c sf1.de mag-m b2.de* mill mosch b2.de* nat-m b2.de nux-m b2.de* *Nux-v* b2.de *Oena* kr1* op mrr1 passi ptk1 phos b2.de pitu sp1 plat b2.de* plb a1 puls b2.de *Rhus-t* b2.de* sec b2.de sep b2.de sol-crl bwa3 spirae br1 *Stann* b2.de staph b2.de stram b2.de* *Stry* ptk1 sul-ac b2.de sulph b2.de tanac a2 thyr ptk1 valer b2.de verat bg2* *Verat-v* bg2* zinc b2.de
- **prepuce** being removed; from adherent: raph ptk1
- **pressure**; from:
  - **part**, on a: cic k2
  - **spine**; on: *Tarent* k*
  - **stomach**; on: canth k* cupr cupr-act a1 nux-v
- **priapism**, with: oena ptk1
- **prodrome**, as a: acon bro1 bell bro1 cham bro1 ip bro1 op bro1 verat-v ptk1
- **prolonged** for months: lat-h bnm5• plb bg2
- **puberty**, at: art-v ptk* caul hr1* caust k* cupr k2* hypoth jl3 lach bg2 puls bg2* zinc sf1.de zinc-val bg2*
  - **girls**; in: art-v br1* caul ptk1 caust ptk1
- **puerperal**: *Acon* hr1* ambr k* *Ant-c* hr1* ant-t hr1* apis *Arg-n* k* arn hr1* ars k* art-v k* *Atro* hr1* **Bell** k* benz-ac hr1* canth k* *Carb-v* k* caul hr1* caust k* *Cham* k* *Chinin-s* kr1* chlf hr1* chlol bg2* **Cic** k* cimic k* cinnm hr1* *Cocc* k* *Coff* k* croc bg2 crot-c *Crot-h* hr1* *Cupr* k* cupr-ar bg2 *Cycl* bg2 *Gels* k* *Glon* k* *Hell* k* *Helon* hr1* hep hr1 hydr-ac k* **Hyos** k* *Ign* k* *Ip* k* *Jab* hr1* **Kali-br** hr1* **Kali-c** hr1* kali-p hr1* *Lach* k* *Laur* k* *Lyc* lyss k* mag-p k* *Merc* kr1 *Merc-c* k* *Mill* hr1* mosch k* *Nat-m* hr1* *Nux-m* k* *Nux-v* oena k* *Op* k* passi br1 ph-ac hr1* *Phos* k* *Pilo* c1* *Plat* k* puls k* *Sec* k* sol-ni c1* **Stram** k* stry bg2 tarent hr1 *Ter* k* thyr c1* *Verat* k* verat-v k* zinc k* ziz hr1
  - **accompanied** by:
    - **Tongue** | **brown** discoloration: crot-t vk1 nux-v kr1*
  - **blindness**, with: aur-m cocc cupr
  - **hemorrhage**; with: *Chin* hyos *Plat* *Sec*
  - **perspiration** and fear, with: stram st1
  - **shrieking**, with: *Hyos* *Iod* *Lach* kr1
- **punishment**, after: agar k2* *Cham* k* cina k* *Cupr* st1* **Ign** k*
- **rage**, then: arg-met ptk1
- **religious** excitement, from: verat k*
- **reproaches**; from: agar kr1* ign kr1*
- **riding** in a carriage | **amel.**: *Nit-ac* k*
- **rubbing** | **amel.**: *Phos* k* *Sec* k* stry st
- **running**; after: sulph
- **runs** in a circle before convulsions: caust hr1*
- **scolded**, after being: agar ptk **Cina** mrr1
- **secretions** and excretions; from suppressed (See discharges)
- **sexual**:
  - **excesses**, from: bufo kr1 *Kali-br* hr1* *Phos* hr1*
  - **excitement**: bar-m ptk1 *Bufo* k* calc bg* **Kali-br** hr1* *Lach* *Plat* stann ptk1 visc ptk1
- **shining** objects, from: *(↗bright; Shining)* bell **Lyss** **Stram** k* ter tl1
  - **mirror**; reflected light from water: lyss mg1.de
- **shock**; after: aesc k2* agar k2 cic tl1 *Op*
- **short** attacks: absin vml3•
- **shrieking**, with: acon j5.de *Aml-ns* kr1 ant-t j5.de *Apis* kr1 *Art-v* hr1* bell j5.de calc j5.de* *Camph* hr1* canth j5.de *Caust* j5.de* cedr hr1* *Cic* j5.de* *Cina* j5.de* *Crot-h* j5.de* *Cupr* hr1* **Hyos** j5.de* *Ign* hr1* *Ip* j5.de* *Lach* j5.de* lyc j5.de *Merc* j5.de* nit-ac hr1* *Nux-v* j5.de* oena sf1.de **Op** j5.de* stann hr1* *Stram* hr1* sulph j5.de* verat-v hr1* vip j5.de *Zinc* hr1*
- **shuddering**; with: mosch ptk1
- **sleep**:
  - **between** convulsions; sleeps: agar *Bufo* *Ign* **Oena** **Op** plb
  - **deep** sleep after convulsions: aeth sf1.de bell a1 bufo canth k* *Caust* dat-s a1 *Hell* *Hyos* *Ign* *Lach* **Nux-v** k* *Oena* k* **Op** k* plb sec k* *Sulph* tarent
  - **during**:
    - **agg.**: acon bg2 *Arg-n* bg2* ars ptk1 *Bell* hr1* bufo calc j5.de *Caust* k* cham sf1.de *Cic* k* cina j5.de cocc bg2* *Cupr* k* cupr-ar sf1.de *Gels* hr1* *Hyos* k* *Ign* k* *Kali-c* k* *Lach* k* mag-c j5.de* merc j5.de naja gm1 oena k* *Op* k* puls j5.de* *Rheum* b7a.de* *Rhus-t* j5.de* sec sep ptk1 *Sil* k* *Stram* *Sulph* ptk1 tarent bg2* [art-v stj]
    - **amel.**: agar bg2 hell bg2
  - **going** to sleep; on | **agg.**: aeth c1 arg-met sf1.de sulph sf1.de
  - **loss** of; from: **Cocc** k1*
  - **sleeplessness**; with or after: alum bg2* art-v kr1 bell bg2* bry bg2* calc bg2* carb-an bg2* carb-v bg2 *Cic* kr1 cupr bg2* cypr kr1 hep bg2* hyos j5.de* ign bg2* ip bg2* **Kali-br** kr1 kali-c bg2* merc bg2* mosch bg2* nux-v bg2* passi sf1.de ph-ac bg2* phos bg2* puls bg2* rheum bg2* rhus-t bg2* sel bg2* sep bg2* sil bg2* stront-c bg2* thuj bg2* verbe-h sf1.de zinc sf1.de zinc-val sf1.de
- **smallpox** fail to break out; when: **Ant-t**
- **speak**, on attempting to: *Lyss* k*
- **splinters**: bell k2 cic k2
- **stomach**; from disordered: cic k2
- **stool**:
  - **before**: ars bg2
  - **during** | **agg.**: **Colch** bg2 *Cupr* bg2 hyos bg2 ip b7a.de nux-v ptk1 *Sec* bg2 sulph bg2 tab bg2
- **strange** person, sight of: lyss k* nux-v a1 **Op** kr1* tarent sf1.de
- **strength**; with increased: *Agar* b4a.de
- **stretching** out:
  - **bending**; or | **elbow** amel.: nux-v ptk1
  - **elbow** amel.: nux-v ptk
  - **limbs**; of:
    - **before** convulsions: *Calc* k*
    - **during** convulsions: bell h1
  - **parts** amel.: sec
- **sudden**: ars bg2* art-v bg2 atro bg2 *Bell* k* bufo k2 camph bg2 canth bg2 cham bg2 cic bg2* cupr bg2 cupr-ar bg2 dios bg2 hydr-ac bg2* mez sf1.de nat-s bg2 oena bg2* plb bg2* podo bg2 stry k* tarent bg2 valer bg2 *Verat-v* hr1* zinc bg2
- **sunshine**: acon bg2
- **suppressions**, from: absin ptk1 agar dgt1 caust ptk1 mill ptk1
- **suppuration**, during: *Ars* k* *Bufo* k* canth lach *Tarent* k*
- **swallow**, during attempt to: **Lyss** k* *Mur-ac* k* nux-m k* nux-v a1 *Stram* k*
- **swing** excites convulsions; letting legs: calc
- **syphilitic**: aur hr1* iod hr1* *Kali-br* hr1* **Kali-i** hr1* merc-c hr1* mez hr1* *Nit-ac* k*
- **terminal** stage: op bro1 plb bro1 zinc bro1
- **tetanic** rigidity: abel jl3 absin k* acet-ac a1 *Acon* k* aconin c1* aesc k* agar-ph a1 agre jl alum k* alum-p k2 *Am-c* k* am-m b2.de* ambr k* amyg a1* *Anac* k* ang b2.de* *Ant-t* b2.de* aran-ix jl3 arg-met b2.de* *Arn* k* *Ars* k* art-v hr1 asaf k* *Atro* hr1* *Bell* k* ben-n a1* both a1 bruc j5.de bry b2.de* *Calc* b2.de* calc-f jl3 calc-p bg2* *Calen* c1* camph k* cann-i cann-s k* canth k* carbn c1* carbn-h c1* carbn-o carbn-s c1* *Castm* kr1* caust k* *Cham* k* chin b2.de* *Chinin-s* chlf hr1* *Chlol* k* **Cic** k* cic-m c1* cimic bg2 cina b2.de* *Cocc* k* *Coloc* b2.de* *Con* k* cori-m a1 cortico sp1 crot-h hr1* *Cupr* k* cupr-act mg1.de cupr-ar *Cur* k* dig bg2* diph-t-tpt jl2 dros k* dulc a1 galv c2 *Gels* k* graph bg2* grat j5.de* *Hell* k* hep k* *Hydr-ac* k* *Hyos* k* **Hyper** k* *Ign* k* *Ip* k* jasm a1* juni-v c1* kali-bi a1 *Kali-br* hr1* kali-c b2.de* kali-cy a1 kali-n a1 kreos k* kres mg1.de *Lach* k* lat-h bnm5• lath sf1.de *Laur* k* **Led** k* linu-c a1 *Lob* *Lyc* k* *Lyss* k* m-arct b2.de mag-c bg2* mag-m jl *Mag-p* k* meph jl *Merc* k* methys jl *Mill* hr1* morph a1* *Mosch* k* mur-ac nat-f jl3 nicot c1* nit-ac b2.de* nux-m bg2

- **tetanic** rigidity: ...
Nux-v k* *Oena* k* ol-an bg2 *Olnd* b7a.de **Op** k* ox-ac c1* passi c1* **Petr** k* phos k* *Phys* k* *Phyt* k* **Plat** k* *Plb* k* plb-xyz c2 *Puls* k* pyre-p st rhod k* *Rhus-t* k* santin c1* scor a1* *Sec* k* seneg k* **Sep** k* sil b2.de* sium c1* sol-crl c1* *Sol-ni* k* solin c1* stann bg2* *Stram* k* *Stry* k* stry-p sf1.de *Stry-s* sf stry-xyz c2 sul-ac a1 sul-h c1* sulph k* tab hr1* tanac a1 *Ter* hr1* teucr k* *Ther* k* thuj b2.de* thyr c1* upa c1* valer bg2 verat k* verat-v k* verin c1* vib-p c1* zinc k*
  - **accompanied** by | **opisthotonos**: bell b4a.de clem b4a.de stann b4a.de stry br1
  - **alternating** with | **delirium** (See MIND - Delirium - alternating - convulsions)
  - **cold** applications agg.: thyr ptk1
  - **dashing** cold water on face amel.: ben-n
  - **injured** parts become cold as ice and spasms begin in the wound: **Led**
  - **menses**; from suppressed: *Hell* b7a.de
  - **motion** of limbs possible (passive): acon b7.de* chin b7.de* *Cic* b7.de* puls b7a.de **Stram** b7.de* *Verat* b7a.de
  - **splinters**, from: bell k2 cic k2
  - **traumatic**: acon hr1* *Arn* hr1* *Chlol* hr1* *Cic* hr1* *Cur* hr1* *Hell* hr1* *Hydr-ac* hr1* **Hyper** hr1* *Led* hr1 *Nux-v* hr1* stram st1 tetox st1 teucr c1
  - **trismus**, with: amyg hr1 *Ant-t* hr1* *Bell* hr1* *Cupr-act* kr1 ign gk *Oena* hr1* *Stram* hr1* ther c1 *Verat-v* hr1*
  - **wiping** perspiration from face agg.: nux-v k*
  - **wounds** in the soles, finger or palm; from: *Bell* **Hyper** *Led*
- **throat** irritation, from: cic k2
- **thunderstorm**: agar *Gels*
- **tight** grasp amel. (See grasping - amel.)
- **tightly** binding the body amel.: merc k* mez
- **tobacco** swallowing, from: ip tl1*
- **tonic**: acon k* agar k* alum k* alum-p k2* alum-sil k2* am-c k* am-m k* ambr b7a.de* anac k* **Ang** b2.de* ant-t k* apis arg-met k* arn k* ars b2.de* asaf k* asar k* **Bell** k* borx k* bry k* **Bufo** k* *Calc* k* camph k* cann-s k* canth k* caps k* carbn-o *Caust* k* *Cham* k* chin k* chlf hr1* **Cic** k* cina k* clem k* cocc k* coloc k* con k* croc b7a.de cupr k* cur bg2 cycl k* dig k* dulc k* euph k* *Ferr* k* ferr-ar graph k* guaj k* hell b7a.de hep k* hydr-ac hr1* hyos k* hyper bg2* *Ign* k* *Ip* k* kali-c k* lac-e hrn2• lath sf1.de laur k* led k* *Lyc* k* m-ambo b2.de* m-arct b2.de mag-p k* mang k* med hr1* meny k* *Merc* k* mez k* *Mosch* k* nat-c k* nat-m k* nit-ac k* *Nux-m* b7a.de nux-v k* oena mrr1 olnd k* op k* **Petr** k* ph-ac k* *Phos* k* phys bg2* phyt bg2* pic-ac hr1 **Plat** k* *Plb* k* puls k* rhod k* rhus-t k* sabad k* sars k* *Sec* k* seneg k* **Sep** k* sil k* spig k* spong k* squil b7a.de stann k* **Staph** b7a.de *Stram* k* stry bg2 *Stry-s* sf1.de *Sulph* k* sumb k* tab bg2* thuj k* *Upa* br1 *Verat* k* verat-v hr1* visc sp1 zinc k* zinc-p k2*
  - **accompanied** by | **diarrhea**: ter ptk1
  - **alternating** with clonic (See clonic - alternating)
  - **chill**; during: bell bg2 caust bg2 cic bg2 cocc bg2 coloc bg2 ign bg2 lyc bg2 merc bg2 mosch bg2 petr bg2 phos bg2 sep bg2 sulph bg2 verat bg2
  - **fever**; during: **Bell** bg2 calc bg2 **Camph** bg2 cham bg2 cic bg2 *Cocc* bg2 **Hyos** bg2 ign bg2 ip bg2 kali-c bg2 lyc bg2 merc bg2 mosch bg2 nat-m bg2 *Nux-v* bg2 **Op** bg2 petr bg2 phos bg2 plat bg2 rhus-t bg2 **Sep** bg2 sil bg2 **Stram** bg2 sulph bg2 **Verat** bg2
  - **perspiration**; during: *Bell* bg2 cic bg2 *Cocc* bg2 nux-v bg2 petr bg2 plat bg2 sep bg2 *Verat* bg2

○ · **Single** parts: ign ptk1
- **tooth** extraction, after: bufo st*
- **touch** agg.: acon agar sne ang vh* *Bell* k* bufo sne *Carbn-o* **Cic** k* cina k2* cocc cupr sne ign bro1 *Lyss* k* *Mag-p* hr1* *Nux-v* k* *Stram* k* *Stry* k*
  - **slight** touch: cic tl1 nux-v tl1 *Stry* br1*
- **turned** in bed; from being gently: chen-a a1*
- **turning** the head backwards during convulsions (See HEAD - Drawn - backward - convulsions)
- **unconsciousness**; with (See consciousness - without)
- **uncovering** | **amel.**: op tl1
- **unjustly** accused, after being: (*↗mortification; MIND - Admonition - agg.; MIND - Ailments - reproaches)* *Staph* k1*
- **uremic**: apis ptk1 apoc ars ptk1 bell bro1 *Carb-ac* bro1 chlf kl chlol bro1 cic bro1 crot-h *Cupr* cupr-act bro1 cupr-ar k* *Dig* glon bro1 hell bro1 hydr-ac k* **Kali-br** kr1* *Kali-s* lon-x br1 merc-c k* *Mosch* oena br1* *Op* bro1 pilo c1* *Plb* k* stram st *Ter* urt-u c1* *Verat-v* bro1*

Convulsions: ...
- **urination**:
  - **after** | **agg.**: *Coloc* b4a.de
  - **attempting** to: ter tl1
  - **during** | **agg.**: hyos b7.de*
  - **involuntary**: art-v kr1 **Bufo** kr1 *Caust* kr1 cocc kr1 *Cupr* kr1 **Hyos** kr1 lach kr1 nat-m kr1 nux-v kr1 *Oena* kr1 *Plb* kr1 stry kr1 *Zinc* kr1
  - **painful** | **agg.**: elat hr1
- **vaccination**; after: carc mlr1• caust mr cic mr **Sil** k* thuj bro1 vario mr
- **vermifuges**; from use of: cina tl1
- **vertigo**; after: hyos ptk1* tarent ptk1
- **vexation**; after: *(↗anger; epileptic - anger)* agar sf1.de ars bell *Calc* camph cham sf1.de **Cupr** k* *Ign* k* *Ip* nux-v plat k2 *Staph* k1* sulph verat sf1.de zinc sf1.de
- **violent**: bell tl1 *Bufo* sne *Camph* br1 **Cic** tl1* cocc tl1 *Cupr* sne glon br1 ign k2 kara c1 oena mrr1* plb hr1 stram k2*
  - **accompanied** by | **Brain**; congestion of: glon br1
- **vomiting**:
  - **amel.**: agar k*
  - **during**: aeth bro1* *Ant-c* h2* bar-m k2 cic mrr1 **Cupr** bg2* guar guare k* hyos bg2 *Ip* hr1* merc bg2 oena hr1* op k* upa hr1*
- **waking**; on: bell k* *Ign* hr1* lac-e hrn2• lyss hr1*
- **walking** agg.: lach tl1
- **wander**; with desire to (See MIND - Wandering - desire - convulsions)
- **wandering**: dios bg2
- **warm**:
  - **agg.**: cic mrr1
  - **bathing** | **agg.**: *Apis* glon nat-m op
  - **room** | **agg.**: bufo sne glon op k2
- **water**:
  - **hearing** of: lyss jl2
  - **sight** of; at the: *Bell* canth j5.de **Lyss** k* **Stram** k*
- **waving** of arms: cyt-l sp1
- **weakness**; during: *(↗Weakness - convulsions)* arn bg2 calc-p tl1 hura a1 kali-c a1*
  - **nervous**: sep
- **wet** agg.; getting: calc *Cupr* k* rhus-t
- **worms**; from: *Anth* vh1 ars bg2 art-v bg* asaf j5.de bar-m hr1* *Bell* hr1* *Cham* hr1* *Cic* bg2* **Cina** k* cupr bg2* cupr-o bg2* *Hyos* k* *Ign* k* *Indg* bg2* kali-br bro1* kali-c bg2 *Nux-v* bg2 petr bg2 plat bg2 sabad k* *Santin* bro1 sil k* spig bro1 *Stann* k* stram hr1* sulph bg2 tanac br1* *Ter* k*
- **yawning** agg.: agar sne cic sne graph k* oena sne

○ - **Extensor** muscles: **Cina** k*
- **Internally**: acon k* agar k* alum b2.de* am-c k* ambr k* anac k* ang b2.de* ant-c b2.de* ant-t b2.de* arg-met k* arn k* ars k* *Asaf* k* asar b2.de* bar-c b2.de* *Bell* k* bism k* borx b2.de* bov k* *Bry* k* calad k* *Calc* k* camph k* canth k* caps k* carb-an b2.de* *Carb-v* k* **Caust** k* *Cham* k* chel b2.de* chin b2.de* cina k* **Cocc** k* coff k* colch k* coloc k* con k* *Cupr* k* dig k* dulc b2.de* euph b2.de* *Ferr* k* graph k* hep b2.de* **Hyos** k* **Ign** k* iod k* *Ip* k* *Kali-c* k* kali-chl k13 kali-m k2 kali-n b2.de* kreos k* lach k* laur k* led k* *Lyc* k* m-ambo b2.de* m-arct b2.de mag-c k* *Mag-m* k* merc b2.de* *Mosch* k* mur-ac k* nat-c k* nat-m k* nit-ac k* nux-m k* **Nux-v** k* op k* petr k* ph-ac k* *Phos* k* *Plat* k* plb k* **Puls** k* rhod k* rhus-t b2.de* sabad k* sars b2.de* *Sec* k* seneg k* *Sep* k* sil k* spong k* **Stann** k* *Staph* k* stram k* stront-c k* sul-ac k* sulph k* teucr k* thuj k* valer k* verat k* *Zinc* k* zinc-p k2
- **Isolated** groups of muscles, of: acon bro1 *Cic* bro1 cina bro1 cupr bro1 ign bro1 lat-m bnm6• lyss hr1 nux-v bro1 *Stram* bro1 *Stry* bro1
- **Muscles**; striated: bell bro1
- **Single** parts: *Agar* bg2 laur bg2

CONVULSIVE movements: acon aeth a1 *Agar* alco a1 *Alum* alum-p k2* ant-t apis *Arg-n* arn ars ars-i *Asaf* bar-c bar-i k2* **Bell** k* bry *Bufo* cact *Calc* calc-i k2* *Camph* k* cann-s *Canth* *Caust* **Cham** *Chinin-s* chir-fl bnm4• *Chlor* hr1 **Cic** *Cina* **Cocc** coff *Con* cori-m a1 croc **Cupr** k* cupr-ar dig dulc ferr-m hr1 *Gels* hr1 *Hell* helo-s bnm14• hydr-ac a1 **Hyos** k* **Ign** *Iod* **Ip** kali-ar kali-bi a1 lach laur k* lyc *Mag-p* meny merc morph a1 mosch *Mygal* nat-c nux-m k* *Nux-v* olnd **Op** petr ph-ac phos plat *Plb* ran-s *Rheum* rhus-t *Ruta* sabad samb **Sec** k* spig k* spong *Squil* *Stann* staph **Stram** sulph *Tarent* *Verat* *Verat-v* hr1 *Zinc* k*

COPPER:
- **fumes** agg.: camph k* *Ip* k* lyc k* *Merc* k* nux-v k* op k* *Puls* k*
- **vessels** of copper agg.: hep st

CORPSE REVIVER (See Death)

CORYZA:
- **agg.**: acon b2.de* alum b2.de* *Am-m* b2.de* ambr b2.de* anac b2.de* ant-t b2.de* arn b2.de* **Ars** b2.de* bar-c b2.de* bell b2.de* borx b2.de* bov b2.de* bry b2.de* calad b2.de* *Calc* b2.de* camph b2.de* canth b2.de* caps b2.de* carb-an b2.de* *Carb-v* b2.de* caust b2.de* **Cham** b2.de* chin b2.de* cic b2.de* cina b2.de* cocc b2.de* coff b2.de* cupr b2.de* dig b2.de* dulc b2.de* euph b2.de* euphr b2.de* *Graph* b2.de* hell b2.de* *Hep* b2.de* ign b2.de* ip b2.de* kali-c b2.de* kali-n b2.de* kreos b2.de* *Lach* b2.de* laur b2.de* *Lyc* b2.de* m-arct b2.de m-aust b2.de mag-c b2.de* mag-m b2.de* mang b2.de* **Merc** b2.de mez b2.de mosch b2.de mur-ac b2.de nat-c b2.de* nat-m b2.de* nit-ac b2.de* nux-m b2.de* **Nux-v** b2.de* par b2.de* petr b2.de* ph-ac b2.de* phos b2.de* plat b2.de* **Puls** b2.de* rhod b2.de* rhus-t b2.de* *Sabad* b2.de* samb b2.de* sars b2.de* seneg b2.de* *Sep* b2.de* sil b2.de* *Spig* b2.de* spong b2.de* squil b2.de* stann b2.de* staph b2.de* sul-ac b2.de* sulph b2.de* teucr b2.de thuj b2.de* verat b2.de* zinc b2.de*
- **amel.**: *Thuj* bg2*
- **suppressed** coryza; from: *Acon* kr1 am-c b2.de* *Am-m* b2.de* ambr b2.de* ars b2.de* **Bry** b2.de* calad b2.de* **Calc** b2.de* carb-v b2.de* caust b2.de* cham b2.de* *Chin* b2.de* cina b2.de* con b2.de* *Dulc* b2.de* *Fl-ac* bg2 graph b2.de* hep b2.de* *Ip* b2.de* *Kali-bi* bg2 kali-c b2.de* kreos b2.de* **Lach** b2.de* laur b2.de* lyc b2.de* m-arct b2.de m-aust b2.de mag-c b2.de* mag-m b2.de* mang b2.de* merc b2.de* mill sf1.de nat-c b2.de* nat-m b2.de* *Nit-ac* b2.de* nux-m b2.de* **Nux-v** b2.de* par b2.de* petr b2.de* phos b2.de* *Puls* b2.de* rhod b2.de* sabad b2.de* samb b2.de* sars b2.de* *Sep* b2.de* *Sil* b2.de* spig b2.de* spong b2.de* stann b2.de* stram b2.de* sul-ac b2.de* sulph b2.de* teucr b2.de* thuj b2.de* verat b2.de* zinc b2.de*

COSMETICS; after abuse of: bov ptk1

COTTON; sensation of: onos ptk1

COUGH:
- **after**:
  - **agg.**: ars b2.de* calad b2.de* chin b2.de* *Cina* b2.de* croc b2.de* cupr b2.de* dros b2.de* ferr b2.de* *Hyos* b2.de* ip b2.de* nux-v b2.de* *Phos* b2.de* *Sep* b2.de* squil b2.de* sulph b2.de*
  - **amel.**: apis bro1 *Guaj* b4a.de *Kali-n* b4a.de m-ambo b7.de *Phos* b4a.de *Sep* b4a.de stann b4.de*
- **before** | **agg.**: *Cina* b2.de* croc b2.de* led b2.de*
- **during**:
  - **agg.**: abies-n br1 *Acon* b2.de* adam srj5• alum b2.de* am-c b2.de* am-m b2.de* ambr b2.de* anac b2.de* ang b2.de* ant-c b2.de* *Ant-t* b2.de* arg-met b2.de* *Arn* b2.de* *Ars* b2.de* asaf b2.de* asar b2.de* aur b2.de* bar-c b2.de* **Bell** b2.de* bism b2.de* borx b2.de* *Bry* b2.de* calad b2.de* *Calc* b2.de* camph b2.de* cann-s b2.de* canth b2.de* *Caps* b2.de* carb-an b2.de* carb-v b2.de* caust b2.de* cham b2.de* chel b2.de* *Chin* b2.de* *Cina* b2.de* cocc b2.de* coff b2.de* *Colch* b7.de* coloc b2.de* con b2.de* croc b2.de* cupr b2.de* dig b2.de* **Dros** b2.de* dulc b2.de* euph b2.de* euphr b2.de* ferr b2.de* graph b2.de* guaj b2.de* hell b2.de* *Hep* b2.de* hyos b2.de* ign b2.de* iod b2.de* **Ip** b2.de* kali-c b2.de* kali-n b2.de* kreos b2.de* lach b2.de* laur b2.de* led b2.de* lyc b2.de* m-ambo b2.de* m-arct b2.de* m-aust b2.de* mag-c b4.de mag-m b2.de* mang b2.de* meny b2.de* merc b2.de* mez b2.de* mosch b2.de* mur-ac b2.de* nat-c b2.de* *Nat-m* b2.de* nit-ac b2.de* nux-m b2.de* **Nux-v** b2.de* olnd b2.de* op b2.de* ozone sde2• par b2.de* petr b2.de* ph-ac b2.de* **Phos** b2.de* plb b2.de* **Puls** b2.de* rhod b2.de* **Rhus-t** b2.de* ruta b2.de* sabad b2.de* sabin b2.de* samb b2.de* sars b2.de* sec b2.de* sel b2.de* seneg b2.de* **Sep** b2.de* sil b2.de* spig b2.de* spong b2.de* *Squil* b2.de* stann b2.de* staph b2.de* stront-c b2.de* sul-ac b2.de* *Sulph* b2.de* tell bro1* teucr b2.de* thuj b2.de* valer b2.de* *Verat* b2.de* verb b2.de* zinc b2.de*
    - **short** cough | **agg.**: nux-v b7.de
  - **amel.**: apis ptk1 stann ptk1

COVERING:
- **mouth** | **amel.**: rumx bro1

COVERS:
- **agg.**: *(↗Clothing - intolerance; Warm - wraps)* acon b7a.de* aloe bg2* *Apis* bg2* asar bg2* *Aur-s* wbt2• calc ptk1 *Camph* bg2* *Cham* b7.de* chin b7.de corh br1 ferr bg2* galeoc-c-h gms1• hydrog srj2• ign b7.de* iod bg2* kali-i bg2* kali-s ptk1 *Lach* b7.de* led b7.de* lil-t bg* **Lyc** ptk1 med st1 merc h1 mur-ac bg2* op bg2* phos bg2* puls bg2* rhus-t b7.de* sanic bg* sec bg2* spig b7.de* sulph bg2* tab bg2 tritic-vg fd5.de verat b7.de*
- **amel.** | **desire** for; and: arge-pl rwt5• *Ars* bg2* aur bg2* bell sf1.de choc srj3• clem bg2* colch bg2* hep bg2* nux-v b7.de* psor jl2 *Puls* bg2* rhus-t b7.de* samb bg2* sep brm sil bg2* squil bg2* stront-c bg2* symph fd3.de• tub ptk1
- **aversion** to: acon ptk1 camph ptk1 iod ptk1 lac-cp sk4• puls ptk1 sec ptk1 sulph ptk1
- **kicks** off: **Bry** st1 camph sf1.de *Cham* sf1.de iod sf1.de
  - **coldest** weather; in the (See Uncovering - kicks - coldest)

CRACKING; sensation of:
- ○ - **Internal** parts: bar-c b2.de* calc b2.de* caust b2.de* cham b2.de* cocc b2.de* coff b2.de* graph b2.de* kali-c b2.de* kali-i bg2 meny b2.de* nat-m b2.de* nux-v b2.de* petr b2.de* sabad b2.de* sep b2.de* spig b2.de*
- **Synovial** membranes: nat-p ptk1
- **Tendons**: kali-m ptk1

CRACKLING, creaking, rustling; sensation of: **Acon** b2.de* agar bg2 alum b2.de* ars b2.de* aur b2.de* bar-c b2.de* bry b2.de* **Calc** b2.de* carb-v b2.de* coff b2.de* con b2.de* lach b2.de* m-ambo b2.de* m-arct b2.de* mosch b2.de* nit-ac b2.de* par b2.de* phos b2.de* puls b2.de* **Rheum** b2.de* sabad b2.de* sabin b2.de* sep b2.de* *Spig* b2.de*

CRACKLINGS, like tinsel: acon bg3* calc bg3* cean bg1 coff bg3* hep bg3* rheum bg3* sep bg3*

CRAMPED: | **sensation** of lying in a cramp: ferr-i k2

CRAMPS of muscles (See Pain - muscles - cramping)

CRAWLING (See Formication)

CROSSING A BRIDGE agg.: *(↗EXTREMITIES - Crossing - legs)*
- **narrow** bridge; a: ang ptk1 *Bar-c* b2.de* ferr b2.de* sulph b2.de*
- **running** water; over: ang b2.de* bar-c bg2 brom bg2 *Ferr* b2.de* *Sulph* b2.de*

CROSSING OF LIMBS: *(↗EXTREMITIES - Crossing - legs)*
- **agg.**: agar b2.de* alum b2.de* ang b2.de* arn b2.de* *Asaf* b2.de* aur b2.de* bell b2.de* bry bg2 *Dig* b2.de* kali-n b2.de* laur b2.de* lyc bg2* mur-ac b2.de* nux-v b2.de* phos b2.de* plat b2.de* rad-br bg2 rheum b2.de* rhod bg2 *Rhus-t* b2.de* squil b2.de* valer b2.de* verb b2.de*
- **amel.**: abrot bg2 ant-t ptk1 lil-t ptk1 murx ptk1 rhod bg2* *Sep* bg2* thuj ptk1

CROWDED ROOM (See Room - full)

CRUMBS OF FOOD agg.: nux-v b2.de* staph b2.de*

CRUSHING (See Compression; Pain - crushed)

CRUSTS, scabs (See SKIN - Eruptions - crusty)

CRYPTOCOCCOSIS: cryptc mld2

CURVATURE of bones: am-c bro1 **Asaf** ptk1 **Calc** ptk1 calc-i ptk1 **Calc-p** bro1* hep ptk1 iod bro1 *Lyc* ptk1 *Merc* ptk1 ph-ac ptk1 **Phos** ptk1 puls ptk1 sep ptk1 *Sil* bro1* *Sulph* ptk1

CUSHING's syndrome: cortico sp1* cortiso sp1*

CYANOSIS: *(↗Laboratory - blood - oxygen - decreased; CHEST - Cyanosis; FACE - Discoloration - cyanotic)* absin a1 acetan c1* acon k* agar k* alum k* *Am-c* k* amyg a1 ang b2.de* anil a1 *Ant-ar* bro1* ant-c k* *Ant-t* k* antip br1* apoc c1 *Arg-n* k* arn k* *Ars* k* asaf k* asar k* aur k* bar-c k* *Bell* k* ben-n a1* bism k* both a1 bry k* cact mrr1 calc k* calc-p bg2 **Camph** k* canth bg2 carb-an k* **Carb-v** k* carbn-o a1 caust k* cedr k* cham k* chel k* chin k* chinin-ar chir-fl bnm4• cic k* cina k* cocc k* cod a1 *Con* k* *Crot-h* bro1* **Cupr** k* cupr-ar sf1.de **Dig** k* diph-t-tpt jl2 dros k* ferr k* glon bg2* helo-s bnm14*• hep k* *Hydr-ac* a1* hyos k* ign k* iod bg2 *Ip* k* kali-c bg2 *Kali-chl* kali-n a1 **Lach** k* **Laur** k* led k* *Lob* hr1* lyc k* lycps-v bro1 mang k* merc k* merc-c bg2 merc-cy br1* meth-ae-ae a1 mez bg2 mosch k* mur-ac k* *Naja* nat-m k* nat-n c* nat-ns c1* nit-ac k* nux-m k* nux-v k* **Op** k* ox-ac bg2* oxyurn-sc mcp1• pert jl2 petr a1 ph-ac k* phenac c1* phos k* physala-p bnm7• phyt bg2 pilo bro1 plb k* psor bro1 puls k* ran-b k* *Rhus-t* k* ruta k* sabad k*

Cyaonosis: ...
Samb k* santin a1 sars k* *Sec* k* seneg k* sil k* sin-n hr1 spong k* staph k* stram k* stroph-h c1 stry a1 sul-ac k* sulfon c1* sulph k* tab bro1 thuj k* trinit br1 tub jl2 uva br1 **Verat** k* **Verat-v** bg2* vip a1 xan k* zinc bg2*
- **accompanied** by:
  - **respiration**; complaints of the (See RESPIRATION - Complaints - accompanied - face)
  - ○ **Tongue** | **blue** discoloration: *Dig* kr1* helo-s bnm14• *Podo* kr1*
- **children**; in:
  - **birth**; from: borx ptk1 cact ptk1 dig ptk1 lach ptk1 laur ptk1
  - **infants**: ant-t tl1* arn k* ars k* *Borx* k* *Cact* k* calc j5.de *Camph* *Carb-v* k* chin k* **Dig** k* **Lach** k* **Laur** k* *Naja* k* op k* *Phos* k* psor k* rhus-t k* sec k* sulph k*
- **fever**; during: arund a1 crot-h a1

CYSTS (See Tumors - cystic)

DA COSTA'S SYNDROME (See CHEST - Palpitation - irritable)

DAMP (See Wet)

DANCING: *(↗MIND - Dancing)*
- **after** dancing agg.: spong bg2
- **agg.**: *(↗MIND - Dancing - agg.)* borx b2.de* spong b2.de*
- **amel.**: *(↗MIND - Dancing - amel.)* cann-xyz bg2 caust b2.de* *Ign* b2.de* nat-m b2.de* **Sep** b2.de* sil b2.de* stann b2.de* *Tarent* mrr1

DARK complexion (See Complexion - dark)

DARKNESS:
- **agg.**: *(↗MIND - Darkness - agg.)* acon bg2 alum sf1.de *Am-m* b2.de* anac bg2 ang bg2 *Arg-n* bg2* *Ars* b2.de* bar-c b2.de* **Calc** b2.de* camph b7a.de* cann-xyz bg2 *Carb-an* b2.de* carb-v b2.de* caust bg2* con bg2 galeoc-c-h gms1• *Gels* bg *Lyc* bg2* nat-m bg2 *Phos* bg2* *Plat* bg2* **Plb** bg2* *Puls* bg2* *Rhus-t* bg2 staph b2.de* **Stram** b2.de* stront-c b2.de* sul-ac bg2 valer b2.de* zinc sf1.de [astat stj2 aur stj2 aur-m stj2 aur-s stj2 bar-br stj2 bar-i stj2 bar-met stj2 bism-sn stj2 caes-met stj2 cinnb stj2 hafn-met stj2 irid-met stj2 lanth-met stj2 merc stj2 merc-d stj2 merc-i-f stj2 osm-met stj2 plb-m stj2 plb-p stj2 polon-met stj2 rhen-met stj2 stront-m stj2 stront-met stj2 tant-met stj2 thal-met stj2 tung-met stj2]
- **amel.**: *Acon* b2.de* agar b2.de* agn b2.de* am-c b2.de* *Am-m* b2.de* *Anac* b2.de* anh sp1* *Ant-c* b2.de* arg-n kr1* arn b2.de* *Ars* b2.de* *Asar* b2.de* *Bar-c* b2.de* *Bell* b2.de* *Borx* b2.de* bry b2.de* **Calc** b2.de* camph b2.de* carb-an b2.de* *Caust* b2.de* *Cham* b2.de* *Chin* b2.de* cic b2.de* *Cina* b2.de* *Clem* b2.de* coc-c hr1* coca bro1 cocc b2.de* *Coff* b2.de* *Colch* b2.de* **Con** b2.de* *Croc* b2.de* *Dig* b2.de* *Dros* b2.de* **Euphr** b2.de* **Graph** b2.de* *Hell* b2.de* *Hep* b2.de* *Hyos* b2.de* *Ign* b2.de* kali-c b2.de* kali-n b2.de* lach b2.de* *Laur* b2.de* *Lyc* b2.de* m-arct b2.de mag-c b2.de* *Mag-m* b2.de* *Mang* b2.de* *Merc* b2.de* mez b2.de* mur-ac b2.de* *Nat-c* b2.de* nat-m b2.de* *Nit-ac* b2.de* nux-m b2.de* *Nux-v* b2.de* petr b2.de* *Ph-ac* b2.de* **Phos** b2.de* *Puls* b2.de* rhod b2.de* rhus-t b2.de* ruta b2.de* *Sang* bro1* *Sars* b2.de* sel b2.de* *Seneg* b2.de* *Sep* b2.de* *Sil* b2.de* *Spig* b2.de* staph b2.de* *Stram* b2.de* *Sulph* b2.de* tarax b2.de* tarent hr1* thuj b2.de* tung-met bdx1• valer b2.de* verat b2.de* zinc b2.de*

DEAD; affected parts look as if: ars bg2 carb-v bg2 graph bg2 mez bg2 plb bg2 sel bg2 thuj bg2

DEATH APPARENT: *Acet-ac* k2 acon ptk1 ant-t b2.de* arn k* bell k* *Carb-v* b2.de* chin k* *Coff* b2.de* *Colch* kr1 coloc k* crot-h j5.de hydr-ac j5.de laur k* merc k* nit-ac k* *Op* b2.de* petr ptk1 ph-ac k* phos k* plat ptk1 *Rhus-t* kr1 sin-n kr1 stram k* sul-h c1 tab kr1
- **accompanied** by | **Head**; heat of the: carb-v br1
- **asphyxia** (See RESPIRATION - Asphyxia)
- **carbon** monoxide, poisoning from: *(↗Coal gas; Sewer-gas)* acon j5.de bell j5.de op j5.de
- **children**; in: **Op** b7a.de
- **drowned** persons, of: lach j5.de
- **frozen** persons; of: acon j5.de ars j5.de bry j5.de carb-v j5.de
- **hanged**, strangled persons; of: op j5.de
- **hemorrhage**; after: chin j5.de
- **injuries**; after: arn j5.de
- **lightning**-stroke; after: lach j5.de nux-v j5.de

DEBAUCH: *(↗Reveling; MIND - Ailments - debauchery)*
- **after** a debauch, agg.: *(↗MIND - Ailments - debauchery)* *Agn* ptk1 *Ant-c* sf1.de arg-n c1* ars sf1.de *Bry* sf1.de **Carb-v** c1* *Coff* sf1.de dig c1 ip b7a.de* nat-c sf1.de **Nux-v** b7a.de* *Puls* sf1.de sars k2 sel c1 staph sf1.de sulph sf1.de
- **during**, agg.: acon k* bell k* *Op* k*
- **sensation** as after: *(↗MIND - Delusions - debauch)* caj a1 conin a1 kreos a1 lyc a1 op a1 ox-ac a1

DEBILITY (See Weakness)

DEFENSE MECHANISM: | **poor** (See Cold; taking - tendency; Complaints - acute - recurrent; Reaction - lack)

DEGENERATION OF TISSUES, tendency to: *(↗Fatty)* arn br1 ars br1 med jl2 vanad br1
- **old** people; in: | **men**; old: bar-c br1
- ○ **Blood** vessels; of (See Blood vessels - degeneration)

DEHYDRATION (See Loss - fluids; STOMACH - Thirst - large)

DELICATE CONSTITUTION: *(↗MIND - Elegance; MIND - Sensitive)* ars ptk1 calc ptk1 calc-p ptk1 caust ptk1* cimic ptk1 cocc mrr1 colch ptk1 con ptk1 croc ptk1 cupr ptk1 *Ign* ptk1 kali-p ptk1 *Lyc* ptk1* nat-c ptk1 nux-m ptk1 phos ptk1* pic-ac ptk1 psor ptk1 sep ptk1 *Sil* ptk1* stront-c ptk1 sulph ptk1 tab ptk1 teucr ptk1 verat ptk1 xan br1 zinc ptk1 [calc-sil stj2 ferr-sil stj2 mag-sil stj2 mang-sil stj2 nat-sil stj2 sil-met stj2]
- **children**; in (See Children - delicate)
- **nervous** persons; in: cocc mrr1 *Xan* br1

DELIRIUM (See MIND - Delirium)

DELIVERY (See FEMALE - Delivery)

DELUSIONS (See MIND - Delusions)

DENTITION (See TEETH - Dentition)

DENUDED:
- ○ **Bones**: ars ptk1 asaf ptk1 aur ptk1 calc ptk1 chin ptk1 con ptk1 hep ptk1 lach ptk1 lyc ptk1 merc ptk1 mez ptk1 nit-ac ptk1 ph-ac ptk1 puls ptk1 ruta ptk1 sabin ptk1 sep ptk1 sil ptk1 staph ptk1 sulph ptk1
  - **suppuration**; from: ars bg2 asaf bg2 aur bg2 calc bg2 chin bg2 con bg2 hep bg2 lach bg2 lyc bg2 merc bg2 mez bg2 nit-ac bg2 ph-ac bg2 puls bg2 ruta bg2 sabin bg2 sep bg2 sil bg2 staph bg2 sulph bg2

DERMATOMYOSITIS: *(↗Connective; Sjögren's)* sulph mtf

DESCENDING:
- **agg.**: *(↗MIND - Fear - falling)* acon alum k* am-m k* *Arg-met* k* bar-c k* bell k* berb bg2* **Borx** k* bry k* canth k* coff k* *Con* k* *Ferr* k* gels bg2* *Lyc* k* meny k* nit-ac k* phys bg2* plb k* *Rhod* k* rhus-t k* *Ruta* k* sabin k* sanic bg1 *Stann* k* stram bg2* sulph k* *Verat* k* verb k*
  - **altitude** to the lowlands; from: borx st1
- **amel.**: *Acon* b2.de* *Alum* b2.de* *Alumn* kr1 *Am-c* b2.de* anac b2.de* *Ang* b2.de* ant-c b2.de* arg-met b2.de* arn b2.de* **Ars** b2.de* asar b2.de* *Aur* b2.de* *Bar-c* b2.de* bell b2.de* *Borx* b2.de* **Bry** b2.de* calc b2.de* *Cann-s* b2.de* canth b2.de* carb-v b2.de* caust b2.de* chin b2.de* coff b2.de* *Cupr* b2.de* dig b2.de* dros b2.de* *Euph* b2.de* *Graph* b2.de* *Hell* b2.de* hep b2.de* *Hyos* b2.de* *Ign* b2.de* kali-c b2.de* *Kali-n* b2.de* kreos b2.de *Lach* b2.de* led b2.de* *Lyc* b2.de* m-ambo b2.de m-arct b2.de m-aust b2.de mag-c b2.de* mag-m b2.de* *Meny* b2.de* *Merc* b2.de* mosch b2.de* mur-ac b2.de* *Nat-c* b2.de* nat-m b2.de* *Nit-ac* b2.de* nux-m b2.de* *Nux-v* b2.de* *Par* b2.de* *Petr* b2.de* ph-ac b2.de* phos b2.de* plat b2.de* plb b2.de* ran-b b2.de* *Rhus-t* b2.de* ruta b2.de* sabad b2.de* *Seneg* b2.de* *Sep* b2.de* sil b2.de* *Spig* b2.de* **Spong** b2.de* *Squil* b2.de* *Stann* b2.de* *Staph* b2.de* sul-ac b2.de* *Sulph* b2.de* *Tarax* b2.de* *Thuj* b2.de* verb b2.de* *Zinc* b2.de*
- **stairs**:
  - **agg.**: am-m b7.de *Arg-met* b7.de* bar-c b4.de bell b4.de borx k2 bry b7.de canth b7.de coff b7.de *Con* b4.de* *Ferr* b7.de* lyc b4.de meny b7.de nit-ac b4.de plb b7.de *Rhod* b4a.de rhus-t b7.de *Ruta* b7.de* sabin b7.de stann b4.de sulph b4.de verat b7.de verb b7.de [bor-pur stj2]
    - **high** steps; from: phyt ptk1

DEVELOPMENT: *(↗Children; Dwarfishness; MIND - Development; MIND - Talking - slow)*
- **arrested**: *(↗Children; Dwarfishness; MIND - Development)* *Agar* bg2 aloe sne ant-c vh bac jl2 *Bar-c* bg2* borx k2 bufo k2* *Calc* bg2 **Calc-p** bg2*

- **arrested**: ...
Carc mrr1* cupr a1 des-ac jl3 hypoth mtf11 kreos br1 lyc mrr1 nat-m k2* nep jl3 ol-an mrr1 *Phos* bg2* rad-br c11 rhod kgp5• *Sil* mrr1* sulfa a1* syph jl2 thym-gl mtf11 thyr br1 toxo-g jl2 tub mrr1 vip a1 [bar-m stj1 bar-p stj1 bar-s stj1]
  - **vaccinations**; from: thuj tl1
○ • **Muscles**: lyc mtf11
- **complaints** of: agar bg2 *Bar-c* bg2 **Calc-p** bg2 chin bg2 kali-c bg2 nat-m bg2 ph-ac bg2 *Phos* bg2 sil bg2 sulph bg2
- **rapid**; too: ferr bg2 iod bg2 ph-ac bg2 phos bg2*
- **slow**: bac bro1 bar-c bg2* bufo mtf33 *Calc* bro1 calc-p bro1* caust bro1 cupr mtf33 kreos bro1 lac-d bro1 mag-m bg2 med bro1 nat-m bro1 pin-s bro1 sil bg2* sulph bg2 thyr bro1 toxo-g jl2
○ • **Bones**: *(↗Walking - learning - late - development)* agar bg2* *Calc* bg2* calc-f bg2* *Calc-p* bro1* ferr ptk1 ph-ac ptk1 puls bg2 sil bg2* succ-ac mtf11
  - **Joints**: guaj bg2

DIABETES INSIPIDUS: abrom-a mta2 acet-ac bro1* acon bro1 alf br1* all-c bro1 am-act bro1 ambr mtf11 apoc bro1 arg-met bro1* arg-mur bro1 arg-n gtr1 ars bro1 ars-br mtf *Aur-m* bro1 bell bro1* bry bro1 cain bro1 *Cann-i* bro1 canth hr1 caust bro1 chinin-s bro1 chion bro1* chlorpr jl1 cina bro1 *Cod* bro1 conv bro1 cortico mtf11 crat mtf dulc bro1 *Equis-h* bro1 eup-per hr1 eup-pur hl9* *Ferr-m* bro1 ferr-n bro1 gels bro1* *Glon* bro1 glyc bro1 gnaph bro1 gua bro1 hell bro1* helon br1* ign bro1* indol bro1 jab hr1 kali-c bro1* kali-i bro1 kali-n hr1* kreos bro1* lac-ac bro1 led bro1 lil-t bro1* *Lith-c* bro1 lyc bro1* mag-p bro1 merc-c bro1 mosch bro1* murx bro1* *Nat-m* bro1 nicc-s bro1 *Nit-ac* bro1 nux-v bro1* ol-an bro1* *Oxyt* bro1 ph-ac bro1* phos bro1 phys bro1 pic-ac bro1 plat-m-n bro1 podo hr1* puls bro1 quas bro1 rhus-a bwa3* samb bro1* sang bro1 santin bro1 saroth bro1* sars bro1 sec mtf sel jl1* *Sin-n* bro1 squil bro1 staph bro1 stroph-h bro1* *Sulph* bro1 tarax bro1 ter bro1* thymol bro1 thyr bro1 uran-m hsa1 uran-n bro1* verat-v bro1 verb bro1
- **accompanied** by:
  - **appetite** increased: lyc mta2
  - **emaciation**: rhus-a c1
- **injury** of the head; after: arg-met mtf

DIABETES MELLITUS: *(↗Family - diabetes; Kimmelstiel-wilson; Laboratory - blood - glucose; URINE - Sugar)* abrom-a mta2* acet-ac gtr1 adren mtf aether btw2 alf gtr1 all-s c1* allox sp1 aloe he1 alumn hr1* am-act mtf anthraco c1* apoc vh1* arg-met hr1* arg-n gtr1 arist-m c1 ars hr1* *Ars-br* ah1* asc-c hr1 aspar hr1* aur mtf aur-m-n mtf bar-m bkh1 *Bor-ac* br1 bov hr1* brid-fr jsx1.fr calc cda1 calc-p hr1* calc-sil k2 canth cda1 carb-ac gtr1* carb-v ptk1* carc sp1* card-m br1 *Carl* br1 caust hr1* cean gtr1 cephd-i bnu chel hr1 chim hr1* *Chion* br1* chlol pks1 chlorpr jl1 clem bkh1 coca ksk4 cod a2* coff hr1 coloc hr1* con hr1* cop hr1 cortico mtf11 cortiso mtf11 cub mtf cupr hr1 cupr-ar br1 cur br1* diph-pert-t mp4• eup-pur br1 ferr-i hr1* ferr-m hr1* ferr-p hr1* fl-ac hr1* flor-p jl1 friedr mgb1 gal-ac cda1 galeg mtf11 glyc ah1* *Gymne* mta2* hed sp1 helon a2* hydrang c1 hygroph-s bnj1* indgf-a mtf ins br1 *Inul* br1 iod a2* iris ptk1 kali-act mtf11 kali-br hr1* kali-chl hr1* kali-i mgb1 kali-p hr1* kiss c1* kreos hr1* *Lac-ac* hr1* lac-d al2* lach gvt2* led bkh1 lept mgb1 lith-c gtr1 lyc hr1* lycps-v hr1* mag-act mtf11 mag-o btw2* mag-p mtf mag-s br1 mang-act mtf* med hr1* meny br1 merc mtf* merc-d mtf11 moni jl2 morind-l jsx1.fr morind-m jsx1.fr morph a1* mosch hr1* mur-ac bkh1 murx mta1 nat-ch hsa1 nat-lac mtf nat-m br1* nat-p hr1* **Nat-s** hr1* nauc-l jsx1.fr nep jl1 nit-ac hr1* nux-v hpc2 *Op* hr1* orthos-s lsr4.de• oxyg c1 pancr gtr1* peps vma2 perh jl1 ph-ac hr1* *Phase* br1* phlor c1* phos hr1* pic-ac gtr1 pilo mtf plan c1 plb ptk1* podo hr1* rad-br lp2 rad-met bwa3 ran-b ptk1 rat hr1* *Rhus-a* br1* rhus-r bkh1 rhus-t tl1 sacch-l c1 sal-ac hr1* sanic c1 sarcol-ac mtf11 saroth jl1 sep ptk1 *Ser-ang* mtf sil hr1 spong cvl1 *Squil* ptk1* stict c1 stront-c bwa3 stry-ar pks1 sul-ac hr1* sulfonam mtf11 sulph lp2* syph hr1 **Syzyg** br1* tarent ptk1* **Ter** ptk1 *Terebe* mtf term-a bnj1* thuj ptk1* thyr al2* uran-m hsa1 *Uran-n* hr1* *Urea* br1* vanad br1 vichy-g c1 vinc-r jsx1.fr vince pks1 [cupr-act stj2]
- **accompanied** by:
  - **abscesses**: ars mrr5
  - **acne**: ars-br pks1
  - **albuminuria**: helon mtf11
  - **apoplexy**: con mgb1
  - **appetite**; ravenous: graph mgb1 iod ksk4 kali-p br3 lac-ac bwa3 rat hr1 sec al2 uran-n pfa2

Diabetes mellitus – **accompanied** by: ...
  - **arteriosclerosis**: *(↗Arteriosclerosis)* aur gtr1* chlorpr jl1 plb mta2* syzyg mtf
  - **boils**: *Anthraci* gtr1* *Anthraco* c1 arn a2* ars mtf cephd-i ksk4 chlorpr jl2 graph mgb1 ins mtf* iod ksk4 led mgb1 nat-p br3* ph-ac dw1*
  - **carbuncles**: abrom-a bnj1 ars lsr6* cephd-i ksk4 *Crot-h* mtf* graph mgb1 gymne bnu ins br1* kreos lsr6 *Lach* mtf led mgb1 ph-ac sk2•
  - **constipation**: carl pks1 graph mgb1 kreos mgb1 lac-d al2 nat-s gt2
  - **diarrhea**: ars bro1 gal-ac cda1 kali-act pks1 pancr mta2
  - **dropsy**: acet-ac al1* kali-act pks1
  - **eczema**: ins br1
  - **emaciation**: ars hr1 ars-br ah1 cupr hr1 cur a1* dig mgb1 graph mgb1 helon bro1 kali-br hr1 lac-d mta1 merc c1 nat-s gt2* pancr mta2 ph-ac hr1 rat hr1 tarent mta2 uran-met btw2
  - **gallstones**: but-ac mtf
  - **gangrene**: *(↗Inflammation - gangrenous - diabetics; EXTREMITIES - Gangrene - diabetic)* *Ars* br1 con ptk1 cupr-ar mta1 kreos lsr6 lach ptk1 merc mgb1 *Sec* al2 solid ptk1
  - **gastric** disorder: uran-n bro1
  - **glycosuria**; true: ph-ac tl1
  - **gout**: *Lac-ac* bro1 *Nat-s* bro1 phase mp4• phos dw5
  - **heat**; flushes of: | **menopause**; during: bor-ac pks1
  - **hypertension**: *(↗Hypertension)* sec vml4
  - **hyperthyroidism**: kali-i sk2•
  - **impotency** (See accompanied; MALE GENITALIA/SEX - Erections - wanting - diabetes)
  - **indigestion**: nux-v mgb1 podo mgb1 uran-n cp1*
  - **leukorrhea**: abrom-a zzc1•
  - **paralysis**: cur bro1
  - **psoriasis**: mang-act mtf9
  - **raw** food; constant desire for: tarent tl1
  - **respiration**; asthmatic: *(↗CHEST - Lungs; complaints of the - accompanied - diabetes; CHEST - Phthisis - accompanied - diabetes)* nat-s mrr1
  - **rheumatic** pains: helon mta2 lac-ac mrr1 *Led* mgb1 *Sarcol-ac* mp4• syph hr1
  - **sexual** desire | **decreased**: cupr hr1 kali-c mgb1 mosch btw1 ph-ac hs2
  - **sleeplessness**: carc mp1• chlol pks1 kreos mgb1 ph-ac hr1 uran-n hl9
  - **thirst**: helon bro1
  - **tuberculosis** (See CHEST - Phthisis - accompanied - diabetes)
  - **ulcers**: *(↗SKIN - Ulcers - indolent)* sec mta1 syzyg br1*
  - **urea**; high (See Uremia)
  - **urination**; frequent and copious: vince pks1
  - **urine**; constant urging of: nat-p tl1
  - **weakness** (See Weakness - diabetes)
○ • **Abdomen**:
    - **complaints** of: spig b7.de verat b7.de*
    - **distention** of; tympanitic: uran-n mtf
  - **Ankles**; swelling of the: arg-met ptk2
  - **Feet**; numbness of: *(↗Neurological - accompanied - diabetes)* helon gtr1
  - **Kidneys**; complaints of (See KIDNEYS - Complaints - accompanied - diabetes)
  - **Liver**; complaints of: chion mta2 kali-br c1 kali-c mgb1 mag-c mgb1 nat-p br3* podo mgb1
  - **Nervous** system; complaints of the (See Neurological - accompanied - diabetes)
  - **Parotid** gland; swelling of | **left**: con hr1
  - **Pituitary** gland; complaints of: flor-p jl1

- **accompanied** by: ...
  - **Retina**; inflammation of (See EYE - Inflammation - retina - diabetic)
  - **Skin**; itching of the: con mgb1 graph mgb1 sul-ac hr1
  - **Spleen**; enlarged: chin mgb1 eup-per mgb1
  - **Stomach** | **sinking** sensation in stomach: apoc c1 lac-ac cda1
  - **Tongue**:
    - **cracked**: bor-ac br1
    - **dry**: bor-ac br1
    - **red** discoloration of the tongue: bor-ac br1
      - **bright**: *Nat-s* kr1*
    - **white** discoloration of the tongue: helon kr1* uran-n kr1*
  - **Urinary** tract; inflammation of: canth mgb1 helon hl1 rhus-a gtr1*
  - **Vagina**; coldness of: bor-ac pks1
  - **Vulva**; itching of the: pic-ac k2 sep btw2
- **alcoholism**; with (See MIND - Alcoholism - diabetes)
- **anxiety**; with (See MIND - Anxiety - diabetes)
- **bronze** diabetes: adren mtf
- **children**; in: calc-p mtf33 crat ptk1
- **coma**; with (See MIND - Coma - diabetes)
- **dullness**; with (See MIND - Dullness - diabetes)
- **fright** or shock; after (See Shock - followed - diabetes; MIND - Fear - sudden - followed - diabetes)
- **grief**; with (See MIND - Grief - diabetes)
- **hepatic** form: ars bro1 *Ars-i* bro1 bry bro1 calc bro1 cham bro1 chel bro1 kreos bro1 *Lac-ac* bro1 lept bro1 lyc bro1 nat-p tl1 *Nux-v* bro1 *Uran-n* bro1
- **incipient**: staph mtf11
- **inflammation** of central nervous system; after: lycps-v mtf
- **insulin** dependent: ins mtf nat-p gk7 sulph mtf
- **irritability**; with (See MIND - Irritability - diabetes)
- **memory**; with weakness of (See MIND - Memory - weakness - diabetes)
- **nervous** origin: ars bro1 aur-m bro1 calc bro1 *Ign* bro1 *Ph-ac* bro1 stry-ar bro1
- **pregnancy** agg.; during: allox mtf murx mta2 podo pks1 zinc mtf [zinc-i stj2 zinc-m stj2 zinc-n stj2]
- **rapidly**; developing: cur bro1 morph bro1
- **sadness**; with (See MIND - Sadness - diabetes)
- ○ - **Pancreas**; from complaints of iris bro1 pancr bro1 phos bro1

DIARRHEA:

- **amel.**: abrot k2* *Acon* vh1 aur sne bry st merc-sul c1 nat-s k2* ph-ac k2* podo k2 sulph k13 *Zinc* k*
  - **yellow** amel.: saroth sp1

DIGITALIS: | **abuse** of; after: chin bro1* laur ptk1 nit-ac bro1* thal-xyz srj8•

DINNER:

- **after**:
  - **agg.**: *Agar* bg2 *Aloe* ptk1 alum bg2 ars bg2* *Bry* bg2* grat ptk1 ign bg2 mag-m bg2* merc-i-r ptk1 nat-c bg2 nux-m bg2 *Nux-v* bg2* phos bg2 sul-ac ptk1 zinc bg2*
  - **amel.**: chel bg2* cinnb ptk1 lol bg2 nat-s bg2

DISABLED:

- **children**; in: **Agar** lmj am lmj aur lmj bar-c lmj *Bufo* lmj cact ggd *Calc-p* lmj **Carb-v** lmj carc lmj **Caust** lmj cic lmj hell ggd *Ign* lmj **Med** lmj **Merc** lmj naja ggd op lmj stram lmj zinc lmj
- **congenital**: syph mrr1

DISCHARGES: (↗*Mucous secretions*)

- **amel.**: (↗*Mucous secretions - amel.; Mucous secretions - suppressed*) abrot vh1 achy-a bnj1 acon lsa1.de agar lsa1.de *Anthraci* vh1 arist-cl sp1 ars bg3* asaf vh bell ptk1 borx lsa1.de *Bry* bg3* calad lsa1.de *Calc* bg3* camph ptk1 cham ptk1 chin ptk1 cimic bg2* colch ptk1 con bg cupr sf1.de* dig bg *Dulc* sf1.de* ferr bg graph sf1.de* ham bg hell ptk1 hyper lsa1.de *Ip* bg3* kali-bi lsa1.de kali-chl lsa1.de **Lach** bg2* lyc ptk1 med lsa1.de* merc mrr1 mill bg* mosch bro1* nat-m lsa1.de nux-v sf1.de* *Op* ptk1 petr ptk1 *Ph-ac* bg3* **Phos** bg *Psor* lsa1.de* **Puls** bg3* *Rhus-t* bg3* sec bg senec bg* *Sep* bg3* *Sil* bg3* stann bro1 stict lsa1.de* stram ptk1 **Sulph** bg2* tab lsa1.de thuj sf1.de verat bg3* *Zinc* bg3* [zinc-i stj2 zinc-m stj2 zinc-n stj2 zinc-p stj2]
- **black**: elaps bg3*
- **bland**: euphr ptk1 *Hep* ptk1 kali-m ptk1 *Merc* ptk1 *Puls* ptk1 sil ptk1 sulph ptk1

Discharges: ...

- **bloody**:
  - **frothy**: op ptk1
  - **streaked**: ars ptk1 asaf ptk1 bry ptk1 chin ptk1 crot-h ptk1 *Ferr* ptk1 hep ptk1 ip ptk1 lach ptk1 *Merc* ptk1 nit-ac ptk1 *Phos* ptk1 rhus-t ptk1 sang ptk1 senec ptk1 seneg ptk1 sil ptk1 *Sulph* ptk1 tub ptk1 zinc ptk1
- **burning**: all-c ptk1 ars ptk1 calc ptk1 kali-i ptk1 kreos br1* *Merc* ptk1 merc-c ptk1 puls ptk1 sin-n ptk1 sulph ptk1
- **continuous**: merc ptk1
- **curdled**: borx ptk1 helo-s rwt2• helon ptk1 merc ptk1 til ptk1
- **destroying** hair: bell-p ptk1 lyc ptk1 merc ptk1 nat-m ptk1 nit-ac ptk1* rhus-t ptk1 sil ptk1
- **dirty**: arg-met ptk1 *Ars* ptk1 berb ptk1 calc ptk1 caust ptk1 *Chel* ptk1 cupr ptk1 dig ptk1 diph ptk1 ferr-p ptk1 **Kali-c** ptk1 kali-m ptk1 lach ptk1 *Lyc* ptk1 *Merc* ptk1 merc-cy ptk1 nit-ac mtf33 ox-ac ptk1 ph-ac ptk1 **Phos** ptk1 sil ptk1 sulph ptk1
- **dripping**: agar bg2 all-c bg2 ars bg2 chin bg2 *Phos* bg2 **Rhus-t** bg2 *Sep* bg2
- **excoriating**: all-c ptk1 *Am-c* ptk1 **Ars** ptk1 ars-i ptk1 arum-t ptk1 brom br1* carb-an ptk1 carb-v ptk1 caust ptk1 cham ptk1 cist ptk1 colch ptk1 eucal ptk1 euphr ptk1 fl-ac ptk1 *Graph* ptk1 hep ptk1 hydr ptk1 *Iod* ptk1 iris ptk1 kali-i ptk1 *Kreos* br1* lil-t ptk1 lyc ptk1 *Med* ptk1 **Merc** ptk1 merc-c ptk1 mez ptk1 mur-ac ptk1 nit-ac ptk1* phos ptk1 prun ptk1 ran-s ptk1 *Rhus-t* ptk1 sabin ptk1 sang ptk1 *Sep* ptk1 *Sil* ptk1 sul-ac ptk1 sul-i ptk1 **Sulph** ptk1 tell ptk1 thuj ptk1 tub ptk1
- **fetid** (See offensive)
- **fibrinous**: iod ptk1 kali-chl ptk1 *Kali-m* br1* merc-d ptk1
- **flesh** colored: alum bg2 cocc bg2 kreos bg2 merc bg2 nit-ac bg2 sabin bg2
- **foul** (See offensive)
- **frothy**: apis ptk1 arn ptk1 asc-t ptk1 chel ptk1 cob ptk1 elat ptk1 grat ptk1 *Ip* ptk1 *Kali-bi* ptk1 kali-c ptk1 kali-i ptk1 kreos ptk1 laur ptk1 led ptk1 *Mag-c* ptk1 merc ptk1 nat-s ptk1 oena ptk1 *Podo* ptk1 rheum ptk1 rhus-t ptk1 rumx ptk1 sabad ptk1 sep ptk1 **Verat** ptk1
- **green** | **grass**; turning green like: calc-f ptk1
- **gushing**: ars ptk1 bell ptk1 berb ptk1 bry ptk1 **Crot-t** ptk1 elat ptk1 *Gamb* ptk1 grat ptk1 *Jatr-c* ptk1 kali-bi ptk1 mag-m ptk1 *Nat-c* ptk1 nat-m ptk1 *Nat-s* ptk1 phos ptk1 podo ptk1 sabin ptk1 stann ptk1 *Thuj* ptk1 tril-p ptk1 verat ptk1
- **hardened** (= dried): agar bg2 bry bg2 con bg2 **Kali-bi** bg2 kali-m ptk1 *Mosch* bg2 nat-c bg2 nit-ac ptk1 *Phos* bg2 *Sep* bg2 *Sil* bg2 *Sulph* bg2 *Thuj* bg2
- **hot**: acon ptk1 *Am-c* ptk1 *Bell* ptk1 borx ptk1 cham ptk1 euphr ptk1 iod ptk1 kreos ptk1 op ptk1 *Puls* ptk1 sabin ptk1 sulph ptk1
- **itching**; causing: *Calc* ptk1 fl-ac ptk1 led ptk1 mang ptk1 *Med* ptk1 par ptk1 rhod ptk1 *Rhus-t* ptk1 sulph ptk1 tell ptk1
- **loose**: kali-s bg2 puls bg2
- **lumpy**: aeth ptk1 aloe ptk1 *Ant-c* ptk1 calc-s ptk1 *Cham* ptk1 *Chin* ptk1 coc-c ptk1 croc ptk1 *Graph* ptk1 **Kali-bi** ptk1 kali-m ptk1 kreos ptk1 **Lyc** ptk1 mang ptk1 *Merc* ptk1 *Merc-i-f* ptk1 **Plat** ptk1 rhus-t ptk1 sep ptk1 sil ptk1 stann ptk1
- **meat** water; like: ars ptk1 calc ptk1 ferr-p ptk1 kali-i ptk1 kreos ptk1 mang ptk1 merc-c ptk1 nit-ac ptk1 rhus-t ptk1 stront-c ptk1
  - **acrid**: canth ptk1
- **milky**: calc ptk1 kali-m ptk1 kali-p ptk1 nat-s ptk1 **Ph-ac** ptk1 *Puls* ptk1 sep ptk1
- **molasses**; like: croc ptk1 ip ptk1 mag-c ptk1 phos ptk1
- **musty**: *Borx* ptk1 carb-v ptk1 *Coloc* ptk1 crot-h ptk1 *Merc* ptk1 nux-v ptk1 *Phos* ptk1 *Puls* ptk1 *Rhus-t* ptk1 sanic ptk1 *Stann* ptk1 staph ptk1 teucr ptk1 thuj ptk1 thyr ptk1
- **odor**:
  - **almonds**; bitter: benz-ac ptk1
  - **ammoniacal**: am-c ptk1 asaf ptk1 aur ptk1 benz-ac ptk1 iod ptk1 lac-c ptk1 lach ptk1 mosch ptk1 *Nit-ac* ptk1 phos ptk1 stront-c ptk1
  - **fish**-brine: bell ptk1 calc ptk1 graph ptk1 iod ptk1 med ptk1 ol-an ptk1 sanic ptk1 sel ptk1 **Tell** ptk1 thuj ptk1
  - **urine**; like: benz-ac ptk1 canth ptk1 *Coloc* ptk1 nat-m ptk1 nit-ac ptk1 ol-an ptk1 sec ptk1 urt-u ptk1
- **offensive**, fetid: *Am* br1 cist mtf11 eucal ptk1 *Kreos* ptk1 meph ptk1 *Psor* br1 **Pyrog** br1* rhus-g br1 *Sulph* br1 tell br1
  - **accompanied** by | **Mammae**; cancer of the (See CHEST - Cancer - mammae - accompanied - discharge - offensive)
- **persistent**: iod ptk1
- **profuse**: *All-c* bg2 *Ars* bg2* *Nat-m* bg2 podo ptk1 **Rhus-t** bg2 verat ptk1
- **putrid** (See offensive)
- **rancid**: alum ptk1 carb-v ptk1 *Puls* ptk1 tell ptk1 thuj ptk1 valer ptk1
- **red**: ars-i ptk1 kreos ptk1 merc ptk1 rhus-t ptk1
- **scanty**: acon bg2 bry bg2

- **scanty**: ...
  - **amel.**: apis ptk1 arg-met ptk1 lach ptk1 squil ptk1
- **serous**: anemps br1
- **slimy**: borx ptk1 calc ptk1 chin ptk1 *Kali-bi* ptk1 lyc ptk1 mag-c ptk1 merc-d ptk1 nat-m ptk1 par ptk1 ph-ac ptk1 phos ptk1 *Puls* ptk1
- **staining**: carb-ac ptk1 lach ptk1 *Mag-c* ptk1 mag-p ptk1 med ptk1 merc ptk1 pulx ptk1 sil ptk1 *Thlas* ptk1 thuj ptk1 vib ptk1
  - **yellow**: bell ptk1 carb-an ptk1 graph ptk1 kreos ptk1 lach ptk1 merc ptk1 sel ptk1
- **sticky**: ant-t ptk1 arg-n ptk1 ars-i ptk1 borx bg2 bov ptk1 bry ptk1 caust ptk1 coc-c bg2* croc ptk1 graph bg2* hydr bg2* **Kali-bi** bg2* kali-c ptk1 kali-m ptk1 *Lach* ptk1 lappa ptk1 lyc ptk1 *Merc* bg2* mez ptk1 myric ptk1 nat-m ptk1 osm ptk1 *Phos* ptk1 phyt ptk1 plat ptk1 *Puls* ptk1 rumx ptk1 **Stann** bg2* sul-ac ptk1 thuj ptk1 ust ptk1 verat ptk1 viol-t ptk1
- **suppressed**: camph ptk1 hydr-ac ptk1 stram ptk1 thlas ptk1 verat ptk1
- **tar**; like: lept ptk1 mag-c ptk1 mag-m ptk1 nux-m ptk1 plat ptk1
- **thick**: arg-met ptk1 *Ars* ptk1 ars-i ptk1 borx ptk1 *Calc* ptk1 calc-s ptk1 canth ptk1 carb-v ptk1 con ptk1 croc ptk1 dulc ptk1 graph ptk1 *Hydr* ptk1 *Kali-bi* ptk1 kali-i ptk1 kali-m ptk1 merc ptk1 merc-cy ptk1 nat-m ptk1 psor ptk1 **Puls** ptk1 sil ptk1 sulph ptk1
- **thin**: ars ptk1 *Asaf* ptk1 canth ptk1 *Caust* ptk1 cham ptk1 crot-h ptk1 cupr ptk1 fl-ac ptk1 gamb ptk1 *Graph* ptk1 grat ptk1 iod ptk1 iris ptk1 kali-i ptk1 mag-m ptk1 *Merc* ptk1 mur-ac ptk1 nat-s ptk1 nit-ac mtf33 phos ptk1 *Podo* ptk1 rhus-t ptk1 sabin ptk1 sec ptk1 sil ptk1 *Sulph* ptk1 verat ptk1
- **vicarious**: *Bry* ptk1 con ptk1 dig ptk1 ferr ptk1 ham ptk1 *Lach* ptk1 lycps-v ptk1 mill ptk1 nux-v ptk1 *Phos* ptk1 *Puls* ptk1 sec ptk1 senec ptk1 *Sep* ptk1 sulph ptk1
- **yellow**:
  - **serous**: kali-s br1
  - **sticky**: hydr ptk1 kali-bi ptk1 sumb ptk1
  - **tenacious**: sumb ptk1

DISCOLORATION (See SKIN - Discoloration)

DISORDERED STOMACH: | **complaints** from: *Acon* b2.de* **Ant-c** b2.de* ant-t b2.de* *Arn* bg2 *Ars* b2.de* bar-c b2.de* *Bry* b2.de* calc b2.de* caps b2.de* *Carb-v* b2.de* caust b2.de* cham b2.de* chin b2.de* cocc b2.de* *Coff* b2.de* colch b2.de* con b2.de* cycl b2.de* euph b2.de* ferr b2.de* hep bg2 ign b2.de* **Ip** b2.de* lyc b2.de *Nat-c* b2.de* nat-m b2.de* nux-m b2.de* **Nux-v** b2.de* phos b2.de* **Puls** b2.de* rhus-t b2.de* sep b2.de* sil b2.de* stann b2.de* *Staph* b2.de* sul-ac b2.de* sulph b2.de* verat b2.de*

DISTENSION blood vessels: (↗*Relaxation - blood)* acon k* aesc bg2* agar k* alum k* alum-p k2 alum-sil k2* *Am-c* k* ambr bg2 amyloc-m br1 ant-t bg2 apoc k2 arg-n k2 *Arn* k* ars k* aur bg2* aur-i k2 *Aur-m* k2* aur-s k2 bacls-7 fmm1• *Bar-c* k* *Bar-m* bar-s k2 **Bell** k* bov bg2 bry k* cact k2 calc k* calc-f calc-p c1 calc-sil k2 *Camph* k* carb-an br1 *Carb-v* k* *Carbn-s* caust bg2 celt a1 *Chel* k* **Chin** k* chinin-ar *Chinin-s* cic k* clem bg2 cocc bg2 coloc k* con k* *Croc* k* cycl k* dig **Ferr** k* ferr-ar ferr-i k2 ferr-p fl-ac bg2* *Graph* k* *Ham* k* hep bg2 **Hyos** k* kreos bg2 *Lac-d* st1 lach k* laur bg2 *Led* *Lil-t* bg2 lyc k* m-arct b2.de* m-aust b2.de* mag-c bg2 meny k* merl mosch k* nat-c bg2 nat-m k* nat-s k2 nit-ac k2 *Nux-v* k* olnd k* op k* ph-ac k* *Phos* k* pilo a1 *Plb* *Podo* **Puls** k* rheum bg2 rhod k* rhus-t k* ruta bg2 sabin k2 sars k* sec sel bg2 sep k* sil k* spig k* *Spong* k* staph k* stront-c k* sul-ac bg2 sul-i k2 *Sulph* k* **Thuj** k* thymu br1 vip zinc k*

- **evening**: mill k2 **Puls**
- **atony**, from: mill k2
- **chill**; during: ars bg2 *Bell* bg2 calc bg2 **Chel** b7a.de* **Chin** bg2 ferr bg2 hyos bg2 lyc bg2 meny bg2 nux-v bg2 **Phos** b4a.de* puls b7a.de* sep bg2 sulph bg2 *Thuj* bg2
- **fever**; during: *Agar* am-c bg arn bg *Bell* k* *Camph* **Chin** k* *Chinin-s* *Cocc* bg **Croc** bg **Cycl** bg *Ferr* bg **Hyos** k* **Led** k* mosch bg **Ph-ac** bg **Puls** k* **Ran-s** bg *Rhus-t* bg staph bg thuj bg
- **menses**:
  - **agg.**: ambr ptk1 ferr ptk1
  - **during** | **agg.**: *Hyos* b7a.de
- **motion** agg.: spong h1
- **standing** agg.: sulph k2
- **warm** room from cold air; when entering a: sulph k2

○ - **Arterioles**; of: thyr br1

DISTENSION of abdomen agg.: *Ign* b2.de*

DISTENSION; sensation of: acon b2.de alum b2.de am-m b2.de ambr b2.de anac b2.de ant-c b2.de ant-t b2.de arg-met b2.de arn b2.de ars b2.de asaf b2.de asar b2.de aur b2.de bar-c b2.de *Bell* b2.de *Bism* b2.de bov b2.de *Bry* b2.de calc b2.de canth b2.de *Caps* b2.de carb-v b2.de caust b2.de cham b2.de chin b2.de cina b2.de cocc b2.de colch b2.de con b2.de cycl b2.de dig b2.de dulc b2.de euph b2.de *Glon* ptk1 *Guaj* b2.de hell b2.de hep b2.de hyos b2.de ign b2.de ip b2.de kali-c b2.de kali-n b2.de kreos b2.de lach b2.de *Laur* b2.de led b2.de lyc b2.de m-ambo b2.de m-aust b2.de mag-c b2.de* mang b2.de merc b2.de mez b2.de mosch b2.de nit-ac b2.de nux-m b2.de nux-v b2.de olnd b2.de op b2.de **Par** b2.de petr b2.de ph-ac b2.de phos b2.de plat b2.de plb b2.de **Puls** b2.de ran-b b2.de* ran-s b2.de rhod b2.de **Rhus-t** b2.de ruta ptk1 sabad b2.de sabin b2.de samb b2.de sars b2.de seneg b2.de sep b2.de sil b2.de **Spig** b2.de spong b2.de stann b2.de staph b2.de stram b2.de sul-ac b2.de sulph b2.de tarax b2.de thuj b2.de valer b2.de verat b2.de zinc b2.de

- **pain**; during: puls ptk1

DISTORTION: agar ptk1 bell ptk1 caust ptk1 cic ptk1 guaj ptk1 hyos ptk1 plat ptk1 ruta ptk1 sec ptk1 sil ptk1 stram ptk1 tarent ptk1

○ - **Face**; (active distortion) of muscles of | **agg.**: bry b2.de* olnd b2.de* puls b2.de* spig b2.de*

DIZZINESS (See VERTIGO - Vertigo)

DOUBLING UP of the body: (↗*Bending - double - amel.)* aloe bg2 ant-t b2.de* *Ars* bg2* caust bg2* chin bg2* choc srj3• cimic bg2* *Cocc* b2.de* *Coloc* b2.de* cycl sf1.de dios sf1.de dros bg2 lat-m bnm6• lil-t a1 mag-m bg mag-p bg2* plat bg plb bg2 rhus-t bg2* sabin bg2* sec b2.de* sin-n a1 sulph bg2*

- **chill**; during: merc b4.de

DOWN's syndrome: carc jl2 morg-p mtf11 pert mtf11 toxo-g mtf11

DRAGGING (See Pain - tearing)

DRAWING BACKWARD: (↗*Bending - affected - agg.)*

- **cord**; as by a: crot-t bg2 par bg2 plb bg2

○ - **Limbs** | **agg.**: mosch b2.de*

DRAWING IN:

- **abdomen**:
  - **agg.**: acon b2.de* ambr b2.de* ant-c b2.de* *Ant-t* b2.de* asaf b2.de* *Asar* b2.de* bar-c b2.de* bell b2.de* bov b2.de* calc b2.de* lyc b2.de* *Nux-v* b2.de* phos b2.de* valer b2.de* *Zinc* b2.de*
  - **amel.**: *Ign* b2.de* sabin b2.de*
- **affected** part:
  - **agg.**: asar b7.de
  - **amel.**: sabin b2.de*
- **shoulders** | **agg.**: *Calc* b2.de* cycl b2.de*
- **soft** parts; of: (↗*Retraction - soft)* acon b2.de* agar b2.de* am-c b2.de* arn b2.de* ars b2.de* bar-c b2.de* bell b2.de* *Calad* b2.de* carb-v b2.de* caust b2.de* chel b2.de* chin b2.de* con b2.de* cupr b2.de* *Dros* b2.de* dulc b2.de* euph b2.de* euphr b2.de* hell b2.de* kali-c b2.de* lach b2.de* laur b2.de* *Mosch* b2.de* nat-c b2.de* nux-v b2.de* **Plb** b2.de* rhus-t b2.de* ruta b2.de* sil b2.de* staph b2.de* sulph b2.de* valer b2.de* zinc b2.de*

DRAWING UP the limb, flexing: (↗*Bending - affected - agg.)*

- **agg.**: am bg *Bry* bg carb-v ptk1 *Caust* bg cimic bg kali-bi bg lach bg lyc bg puls ptk1 rhus-t ptk1 sec ptk1 sep bg sulph bg valer bg
- **amel.**: *Alum* k* am-c k* am-m k* anac k* ang k* *Ant-c* k* arg-met k* arn k* aur k* bar-c k* bell k* bov k* *Bry* k* **Calc** k* cann-s cann-xyz bg2 caps k* carb-v k* caust k* cham k* *Chin* k* cina k* clem k* *Coloc* sf1.de con k* croc k* crot-h bg2* dig k* dros k* dulc k* ferr k* graph k* guaj k* *Hep* b4a.de* ign k* kali-c k* lach bg2* laur k* lyc k* *Mang* k* *Meny* k* merc k* merc-c ptk1 mur-ac k* nat-m k* nux-v k* petr k* phos k* plat k* plb k* puls k* ran-b ptk1 rheum k* rhus-t k* *Ruta* k* sabin k* sel k* **Sep** b4a.de* sil bg2* spig k* spong k* stann k* staph k* **Sulph** b4a.de* **Thuj** b4a.de* valer k* verat k*

DRAWN DOWNWARD; sensation as if: camph bg2 cann-s b2.de colch bg2 kali-bi bg2 kreos bg2 merc b2.de* nux-v b2.de* puls bg2

DRAWN TOGETHER; sensation as if: carb-v ptk1 *Chin* ptk1 merc ptk1 naja ptk1 nat-m ptk1 *Nux-v* ptk1 par ptk1 puls ptk1 *Rhus-t* ptk1 *Sel* ptk1 *Sulph* ptk1

DRINKING:

- **after**:
  - **agg.**: acon b2.de* ambr b2.de* anac b2.de* ang b2.de* ant-t b2.de* arn b2.de* **Ars** b2.de* asaf b2.de* asar b2.de* aur b2.de* *Bell* b2.de*

- **after** – **agg.**: ...
  Bry b2.de* cann-s b2.de* Canth b2.de* caps b2.de* Carb-v b2.de* caust b2.de* cham b2.de* Chin b2.de* cic b2.de* cina bg2 Cocc b2.de* colch b2.de* coloc b2.de* con b2.de* Croc b2.de* cupr b2.de* dros b2.de* Ferr b2.de* graph b2.de* hell b2.de* Hep b2.de* hyos b2.de* Ign b2.de* ip b2.de* kali-c b2.de* lach b2.de* laur b2.de* lyc b2.de* Merc b2.de* mez b2.de* mosch b2.de* mur-ac b2.de* Nat-c b2.de* Nat-m b2.de* nit-ac b2.de* Nux-v b2.de* op b2.de* petr b2.de* ph-ac b2.de* phos b2.de* plb b2.de* Puls b2.de* rhod b2.de* Rhus-t b2.de* ruta b2.de* sabad b2.de* sabin b2.de* sec b2.de* sel b2.de* sep b2.de* Sil b2.de* spig b2.de* squil b2.de* staph b2.de* stram b2.de* Sul-ac b2.de* Sulph b2.de* Tarax b2.de* teucr b2.de* thuj b2.de* Verat b2.de*
  - **amel.**: acon bg2* alum bg2 bapt bg2 bar-c bg2 brom bg2* Bry b2.de* carb-an b2.de* Caust bg2* cist bg2* clem sf1.de coc-c sf crot-h bg2 Cupr b7a.de ferr b2.de* graph b2.de* ip b2.de* lac-c bg2 lat-m bnm6• lob bg2* lyc bg2* mosch b2.de* nat-m bg2 nit-ac bg2 nux-v b2.de* olnd b2.de* Phos b2.de* psil jl psor bg2* puls sf1.de rhus-t b2.de* sep sf Sil b2.de* spig b2.de* Spong bg2* sulph bg2 tarax b2.de* verat sf1.de
  - **heated**; when: Bry b7a.de
- **agg.**: acon hr1* Aeth bg2* anac b2.de* apis sf1.de Apoc sf1.de Arg-n bg2* Ars b2.de* aur hr1* Bell b2.de* Bry b2.de* Calc bg2* Canth b2.de* caps bg2* cham b2.de* Chin ptk1 chinin-ar sf1.de Cina b2.de* Cocc j5.de* colch b2.de* coloc bg2* con b2.de* Crot-t bg2* cupr b2.de* dig hr1* Digox c1 Eup-per sf1.de ferr b2.de* gink-b jl3 grat sf1.de hedeo stx1 hell j5.de Hyos b2.de* ign b2.de* Iod b2.de* kali-c bg2* Lach b2.de* laur b2.de* med hr1* Merc b2.de* merc-c ptk1 mez sf1.de nat-ar kr1 nat-m b2.de* nux-v bg2* Phos b2.de* phyt sf1.de* plect stx1 Podo bg2* pop-cand c1 Puls bg* rhus-g stx1 rhus-r bg rhus-t b2.de* sabad b2.de* sabin b2.de* Sel hr1* sep b2.de* sil bg2* squil b2.de* Stann bg2* Stram b2.de* sul-ac ptk1 Trom br1 verat bg2*
  - **rapidly**: Ars b2.de* cina hr1 Hell sf1.de hep sf1.de ip b2.de* nat-m b2.de* Nit-ac b2.de* Nux-v b2.de* Sil b2.de* sulph b2.de* verat sf1.de
- **amel.**: bism ptk1 bry k2* Caust ptk1 cist ptk1 coc-c ptk1 cupr ptk1 lac-h htj1• lavand-a ctl1• lob ptk1 nux-v b7.de* Phos ptk1 sep ptk1 Spong ptk1
- **aversion** to drink in spite of thirst: cann-i sf1.de canth sf1.de stram sf1.de
- **eating** agg.; after: Bry b7a.de
- **lying**; can drink only while: Bell b4a.de
- **sips**; in:
  - **agg.**: merc ptk1
  - **amel.**: bell ptk1 cist ptk1 kali-n ptk1 lob ptk1 squil ptk1

DROPS; sensation of (See Trickling)

DROPSY: Acet-ac bro1 acetan bro1 acon bro1 Adon bro1 aegle-f mtf11 am-be bro1* ampe-tr bro1 Apis bro1* apoc bro1* arg-p bro1 Ars bro1 ars-i bro1 asc-c bro1 atp rly4• benz-ac bro1 Blatta-a bro1 brass bro1 bry bro1 cact bro1 Cain bro1 calc bro1 calc-ar bro1 card-m bro1 Chin bro1 coch bro1 coffin bro1 colch bro1* Conv bro1 cop bro1 cortiso mtf11 Crat bro1 dig bro1* dulc bro1 elat bro1 eup-pur bro1 euph bro1 ferr bro1 Fl-ac bro1 gali bro1 hell bro1* hep bro1 hippoz mtf11 iod bro1 iris bro1 iris-g bro1 jatr-u bro1 Juni-c bro1 kali-act bro1 kali-ar bro1 kali-c bro1 Kali-i bro1 Kali-n bro1 lac-d bro1* Lach bro1 lact-v bro1 Liat bro1 lyc bro1 med mtf11 merc-d bro1 nast bro1 nit-s-d bro1 onis bro1 Oxyd bro1 Phase bro1 phos bro1 Pilo bro1 prun bro1 psor bro1* querc bro1 rhus-t bro1 samb bro1 Samb-c bro1 sol-ni bro1 solid bro1 Squil bro1 Stroph-h bro1 stry-ar bro1 Ter bro1 teucr-s bro1 thlas bro1 toxi bro1 ur-ac bro1 urin bro1 vince bro1

- **acute**: apis mtf11
- **external** dropsy (= anasarca; edema): (➚EXTREMITIES - Swelling - dropsical; EXTREMITIES - Swelling - lower - dropsical; SKIN - Swelling - dropsical) abel jl acet-ac k* acetan bro1 acon b2.de* adam srj5• adon bg2* adren sf1.de aeth kr1* agar alco a1 all-c kr1 am-be c2* am-c bg2 ambr bg2 Ammc kr1 ampe-qu c2 Anac-oc kr1 Anag kr1* ancis-p tsm2 Ant-c k* Ant-t k* anthraci kr1 Apis k* Apoc k* apoc-a c2 Arg-n kr1* arn bro1 Ars k* ars-i k* Ars-s-f kr1 Asaf kr1* Asc-c k* Asc-t kr1 Aspar kr1* aur k* aur-ar k2 aur-i k2 Aur-m k* Aur-m-n kr1 aur-s k2 Bar-m kr1* Bell k* Bism k* blatta-a c2 bor-ac c1* bov bg2* brass-n-o c2 Brom kr1 Bry k* bufo c2 Cact k* cain c1* Caj kr1* calad Calc k* Calc-ar k* calc-p bg2 Calc-s kr1* calc-sil k2 calth br1 camph k* cann-xyz bg2 Canth k* caps hr1* carb-v b4a.de* Carbn-s Card-m k* casc kr1* cedr cham a1* chel k* Chen-a kr1* Chim kr1* Chin k* Chinin-ar chinin-s c2 Chlol kr1* cinnb cinnm kr1 cit-l c2 coc-c br1 coca Coch kr1 coff bg2 Colch k* Coll coloc k* Con k* Conv br1* convo-a j5.de cop k* cortiso jl crat bg2* Crot-h k* Dig k* Dulc k* Elat kr1* equis-h c2 erig kr1 ery-a c2 euonin c2 eup-pur k* euph k* Ferr k* ferr-ar ferr-i ferr-p ferr-s kr1 Fl-ac kr1* Form kr1* frag c1* Gamb kr1 Graph k*

Dropsy – external dropsy: ...
Grat kr1* guaj k* Ham kr1 Hell k* Helon kr1 Hep j5.de* Hippoz kr1* hom-xyz c1* Hydr kr1 hyos k* iber kr1* Ictod k* Iod k* iris kr1 iris-g c2 jal c1 jatr-u c1* junc-e c2 juni-c c2 kali-act c2 kali-ar k* Kali-c b2.de* kali-chl c1* Kali-i bg2* Kali-m kr1* kali-n k* kali-p kali-s Kalm bg2* kreos j5.de* Lac-d k* Lach k* lact kr1 lat-k c1* Laur bg2* Led k* lept kr1 Liat bg1* lith-c bg2* luna c2 Lyc k* lycps-v bg2* mag-m bg2* mang b4a.de Med k* Merc b2.de* Merc-c b4a.de* merc-sul c2 mez k* mur-ac k* myric sne Naja kr1 nat-ar nat-c k* Nat-m bg2* nat-s kr1* nat-sal c1* Nit-ac k* Nux-m k* Olnd k* Op k* oxyd c2* ped c1* phase-xyz c2 phos k* phyt ptk1 pic-ac k* plat k* Plb k* polytr vs prim-vl c2 prot fmm1• Prun bg2* Psor kr1 Puls k* pyrog bg2* ran-b kr1* rauw jl reser jl rhod k* rhus-t k* rumx ptk1 Ruta k* sabad kr1 Sabin k* sacch c2 Sal-ac kr1* Samb k* sanic c2 sars k* sec k* senec c2* Seneg k* Sep k* sil k* solid k* Squil k* staph bg2 stram k* Stront-c j5.de* stroph-h c2* Sulph k* Ter k* Teucr k* thlas c2 Thyr c1* toxi c1* uran-n kr1* urea a1* urin c1* Urt-u bg2* ust ptk1 Verat k* verat-v kr1 Verb k* vesi c2 vesp c1 vesp-xyz c2 vip j5.de* zinc k* Zing kr1* ziz c2

- **morning**: chin Nat-c
- **accompanied** by:
  - **anemia**: acet-ac br1 crat gm1
  - **diarrhea** (See RECTUM - Diarrhea - accompanied - anasarca)
  - **menses** | **suppressed** menses; from: apis bro1 apoc bro1 asc-c c1 Kali-c b4a.de*
  - **renal** failure: oxyd gm1
  - **urine**:
    - **copious**: squil ptk1
    - **pale**: colch tl1
    - **red** sand in urine: lyc tl1
    - **suppressed**: apoc gk aral-h k1 Hell kr1
  - **Heart** disease (See heart)
  - **Skin**:
    - **discoloration**; yellow: merc-d br1
    - **dry**: cain br1
  - **Tongue**:
    - **pale**: Ars kr1*
    - **red** discoloration of the tongue | **bright** red: Ars kr1*
  - **Uterus**; pain in: conv bro1
- **albuminuria**; with: (➚kidney; KIDNEYS - Nephrotic; URINE - Albuminous) apis mrr1 apoc gk Aur-m kr1* Chin kr1 Eup-pur kr1 Helon kr1 Hep kr1
- **body**; over whole (See external)
- **cardiac** (See heart)
- **fever** | **during** | **agg.**: Ferr b7a.de
  - **intermittent** fever; from: Ars b4a.de chim kr1 Dulc kr1 hell bro1
    - **suppressed** intermittent fever; from: Ars kr1 carb-v bro1 chim kr1 chin bro1 dulc kr1 ferr bro1 Ferr-m kr1 hell bro1 lac-d bro1 merc kr1 Sulph kr1
- **heart** disease; from: (➚CHEST - Weakness - heart - accompanied - dropsy) Adon br1* aml-ns kr1 Apis kr1* Apoc kr1* arn bro1 Ars kr1* ars-i bro1 asc-c br1* asc-t bro1 aur bro1 Aur-m kr1* Bry kr1 Cact kr1* Calc-p kr1 chinin-ar kr1 Chlol kr1 Coffin bro1 Colch kr1* Coll kr1* conv br1* cop kr1 Crat bro1* crot-h kr1 Dig kr1* Digin bro1 Fl-ac kr1 Hell kr1 iod bro1* kali-c k2 Kali-m kr1 kalm bro1 Lac-d kr1* Lach kr1* liat br1* Lyc kr1* lycps-v sf1.de merc-d br1* merc-sul kr1 Nat-m kr1 ph-ac kr1 phos kr1 Prun kr1* rauw jl* scop ptk1 Sep kr1 ser-ang br1 spartin bwa3 Squil kr1* Stroph-h c1* ter kr1 vip br1
- **hemorrhage**; after: apoc k2 chin k2*
- **hepatic** (See liver)
- **injuries**; after: bell-p ptk1
- **kidney** disease, from: (➚albuminuria; KIDNEYS - Nephrotic; KIDNEYS - Renal - chronic) acon tl1 ampe-qu br1 ampe-tr bro1 ant-t bro1 Apis kr1* apoc k2* Arg-n sf1.de ars bro1* Asc-c kr1* aspar bro1 aur sf1.de Calc-p kr1 Chim kr1* Colch kr1* coloc kr1 cortiso mtf11 crot-h kr1 Dig bro1 digin bro1 eup-pur kr1* Hell sf1.de helon bro1 juni-c br1 lac-d bro1* lach mtf11 liat c1* Merc sf1.de Merc-c bro1 merc-d br1* nit-ac sf1.de phos sf1.de plb bro1 rauw jl* Sal-ac kr1 senec k2 Solid sf1.de squil mtf11 ter br1* ur-ac bro1 urea br1 vac mtf11

- **external** dropsy: ...
  - **liver** disease, from: *Apoc* bro1 ars bro1 ars-s-f k2 asc-c br1* aur bro1 **Aur-m** kr1* **Calc** kr1 *Card-m* kr1* cean bro1 chel bro1 *Chim* kr1* *Chin* kr1 cop kr1 cupr kr1 *Ferr* kr1 *Fl-ac* kr1* iris kr1 kali-ar k2 *Kali-m* kr1 lac-d k2* **Lach** kr1* lept kr1 liat br1* **Lyc** kr1* merc kr1 merc-sul kr1 mur-ac bro1 *Nat-m* kr1 *Nux-v* kr1 polym bro1 tarax sp1
  - **menstrual** disorder during puberty or menopause: puls bro1
  - **old** people; in: **Kali-c** br1*
  - **painful**: dulc h2
  - **pregnancy** agg.; during: *Apis* kr1 *Apoc* kr1 *Ars* kr1 aur-m kr1 colch kr1 *Dig* kr1 dulc kr1 hell kr1 helon kr1 *Jab* kr1 lyc kr1 merc a1 merc-c kr1 sanic c1* uran-n kr1
  - **renal** (See kidney)
  - **scarlatina**; after: *Acet-ac* kr1 acon bro1 *Ambr* kr1 **Apis** kr1* apoc bro1 **Ars** kr1* *Asc-c* kr1* **Aur-m** kr1* bar-c kr1 *Bar-m* kr1* *Calc* kr1 *Colch* kr1* coloc kr1 cop kr1 *Crot-h* kr1 dig b4a.de* *Dulc* kr1* **Hell** kr1* *Hep* kr1* juni-c bro1 **Lach** kr1* *Merc* b4a.de* *Nat-m* kr1 nat-s kr1 *Phos* kr1* pilo bro1 squil bro1 *Stram* kr1* **Ter** kr1* verat-v kr1 zinc kr1
  - **serum** oozing, with: ars bro1 hep sne lyc bro1 *Rhus-t* bg2*
  - **spleen** disease, from: cean bro1* **Lach** kr1* liat br1* querc c1* querc-r c1* squil c1*
  - **sudden**: *Kali-n* br1*
  - O **Nervous** system: pitu-p sp1
- **general**; in: anag br1 *Apoc* br1* asc-c br1 *Blatta-a* br1 *Cain* br1 calad hr1* calc-ar br1 cortiso mtf11 cyna mtf11 elat br1 gali br1 juni-c br1 kali-act mtf11 kali-c br1* lac-h sze9• mom-b br1 nat-m br1 nit-s-d br1 onis br1 puls mtf33 solid mtf11 spartin-s bwa2* *Uran-n* br1
  - **morning**:
    - **agg.**: apis ptk1 aur ptk1 kali-chl ptk1 phos ptk1 sep ptk1 sil ptk1
    - **amel.**: bry ptk1
  - **accompanied** by:
    - **asthma**; bronchial (See RESPIRATION - Asthmatic - accompanied - edema)
    - **discharge** of serum: ars ptk1 lyc ptk1 rhus-t ptk1
    - **jaundice**: merc-d ptk1
    - **numbness**: fl-ac ptk1
    - **paralysis** (See Paralysis - accompanied - dropsy)
    - **respiration**; difficult: eup-pur ptk1
    - **thirst**: apoc br1
    - **ulcers**: ars bg2* graph bg2* hell bg2* lyc bg2* merc bg2* rhus-t bg2* squil bg2* sulph bg2*
    - **urination** | **profuse**: squil ptk1
    - **urine**; pale: colch tl1
    - **Heart**; complaints of (See external - heart)
    - **Heart**; weakness of (See CHEST - Weakness - heart - accompanied - dropsy)
    - **Kidneys**; complaints of: apoc ptk1 ars ptk1 *Dig* ptk1 helon ptk1 *Merc-c* ptk1 ter ptk1
      - **Heart**; and complaints of: *Merc-d* ptk1
    - **Liver** complaints: *Apoc* ptk1 asc-c br1 card-m ptk1 fl-ac ptk1 lac-d ptk1 lach ptk1 lyc ptk1 mur-ac ptk1
    - **Pelvis**; congestion of (See ABDOMEN - Congestion - pelvis - accompanied - dropsy)
    - **Skin**; red discoloration of: com ptk1
    - **Spleen**; complaints of: lach ptk1
    - **Stomach** | **irritation** of: apoc br1
  - **alcoholism**, from: apoc hr1 ars bro1* fl-ac k2* sulph bro1*
  - **alternating** with:
    - **diarrhea** (See RECTUM - Diarrhea - alternating - dropsy)
    - **discharges**: apoc k2
  - **baglike**: apis ptk1 ars ptk1 kali-c ptk1
  - **children**; in: | **newborns**: apis bro1* carb-v bro1* coffin bro1 dig bro1* lach bro1* sec ptk1
  - **eruptions**:
    - **after**: ars ptk1 hell ptk1 rhus-t ptk1 sulph ptk1
    - **suppressed** eruptions; after: **Apis** kr1* apoc kr1 *Ars* kr1* asc-c kr1 canth bro1 dig kr1 dulc bro1 *Hell* kr1* sulph kr1 zinc bro1

Dropsy – general; in: ...
  - **exanthema** (See eruptions)
  - **glands**; from pressure of: kali-i ptk1
  - **hemorrhage**; after: acet-ac ptk1 apoc ptk1 chin ptk1 ferr ptk1 helon ptk1 senec ptk1
  - **menses**; before: foll mtf11
  - **motion** | **amel**.: nat-c h2
  - **ovulation**; during: foll mtf11
  - **puberty** or menopause; during: puls ptk1
  - **quinine**; from abuse of: apoc bro1*
  - **scarlet** fever; after: asc-c br1 colch tl1
  - **sprains**; from: bov ptk1
  - **sudden**: kali-n ptk1
  - **thirst**:
    - **with**: *Acet-ac* ptk1 *Apoc* k2* ars tl1*
    - **without**: apis bro1* ars tl1 hell bro1* puls mtf33
- **inflammatory**: apis mtf11
- **internal** dropsy: (↗*ABDOMEN - Dropsy; CHEST - Dropsy; EXTREMITIES - Swelling - joints - edematous; FEMALE - Swollen - ovaries - dropsical; FEMALE - Swollen - uterus - dropsical; GENERALS; HEAD - Dropsy; MALE GENITALIA/SEX - Swelling - dropsical; RECTUM - Dryness)* *Acet-ac* c1* *Acon* b2.de* *Adon* c1* agn k* alco a1 am-be c1 am-c k* ambr k* ampe-qu c1 anag c1 ancis-p tsm2 ant-ar sf1.de ant-c k* *Ant-t* anthraco j5.de **Apis** k* apisin sf1.de *Apoc* apoc-a c1 arg-met k* arg-n a1 arn k* **Ars** k* ars-i asc-c c1 aspar c1 aur k* aur-ar k2 aur-i k2 *Aur-m* aur-s k2 *Bar-m* j5.de **Bell** k* benz-ac *Blatta-a* c1 blatta-o sf1.de brass c1 *Bry* k* bufo c1 *Cact* c1 *Cain* c1* caj c1 *Calc* k* *Calc-ar* c1* calc-s c1 calc-sil k2 camph k* cann-s k* canth k* caps k* carb-v k* **Card-m** casc c1 chel j5.de chen-a c1 chim c1 **Chin** k* *Chinin-ar* chinin-s c1 chlol c1 cina k* cit-l c1 coca a1 **Colch** k* coloc k* *Con* k* *Conv* sf1.de *Crat* sf1.de crot-h j5.de **Dig** k* *Dulc* k* elat c1 equis-h c1 ery-a c1 euonin c1 eup-pur c1* euph k* *Ferr* k* ferr-ar ferr-i k2 ferr-p *Fl-ac* c1* form c1 graph c1* grat c1 guaj k* **Hell** k* hep k* hyos k* iber c1 ictod c1 ign b2.de* iod k* *Ip* k* iris-g c1 junc-e c1 *Juni-c* c1* *Kali-act* a1* *Kali-ar* kali-bi sf1.de kali-bit sf1.de *Kali-c* k* *Kali-i* c1* kali-m c1 *Kali-n* j5.de* kali-p kali-s *Kalm* c1* lac-d c1 lach k* lact laur k* *Led* k* *Liat* c1 lith-c sf1.de lyc k* lycps-v sf1.de med k2 *Merc* k* merc-c sf1.de merc-d sf1.de merc-sul c1* mez k* mur-ac k* nat-ar sf1.de nat-m c1* nat-s k2 nit-ac k* *Nit-s-d* sf1.de nux-m a1 nux-v b2.de* olnd j5.de *Op* b2.de* *Oxyd* c1 ph-ac k* *Phase* c1* phos k* *Plb* j5.de* prim-v c1 prun c1* puls k* ran-b c1 *Rhod* j5.de *Rhus-t* k* *Ruta* j5.de sabad k* *Sabin* j5.de sacch a1* samb k* sanic c1 sars k* sec j5.de senec c1 *Seneg* k* *Sep* k* sil k* *Solid* sf1.de spig k* spong k* *Squil* k* stann k* stigm c1 stram k* *Stroph-h* c1* sul-i k2 **Sulph** k* tarent a1 *Ter* bg2* teucr k* thlas c1 thyr c1 urea c1 urea-n sf1.de urt-u sf1.de verat k* vesi c1 vince viol-t k* zinc bg2 zing c1 ziz c1
  - O **Serous** membranes: apis tl1 bry br1* *Chel* br1 colch tl1 med br1 ran-b tl1 sulph tl1
- O **Joints**, of (See EXTREMITIES - Swelling - joints - edematous)

DRUGS:
- **allopathic** drugs (See Medicine)
- **homeopathic** drugs (See Remedies)
- **psychotropic** drugs (See Psychotropic - ailments)

DRUNK; as if: visc sp1

DRY sensation: apis bg2 cortico sp1 cortiso sp1 hist sp1 tritic-vg fd5.de
- O **Body**; whole: aloe bg2 phos bg2
- **External** (See SKIN - Dry)
- **Internal** parts; in: *Acon* b2.de* **Alum** b2.de* *Alumn* br1 am-m b2.de* arg-met b2.de* arn b2.de* ars bg2* *Asaf* b2.de* *Asar* b2.de* bar-c b2.de* *Bell* b2.de* *Bry* b2.de* *Calad* b2.de* camph b2.de* cann-i sf1.de cann-s b2.de* canth b2.de* caps b2.de* carb-v b2.de* caust b2.de* chin b2.de* cic b2.de* cina b2.de* cinnb bg2* cocc b2.de* coff b2.de* con sf1.de croc b2.de* cypra-eg sde6.de• dros b2.de* euph b2.de* ferr b2.de* ign b2.de* ip b2.de* kali-c b2.de* m-ambo b2.de* m-arct b2.de* m-aust b2.de* meny b2.de* merc b2.de* mez b2.de* mosch b2.de* nat-m bg2* **Nux-m** b2.de* nux-v b2.de* olnd b2.de* par b2.de* petr b2.de* *Ph-ac* b4a.de phos b2.de* *Pieri-b* mlk9.de plb b2.de* positr nl2• *Puls* b2.de* rheum b2.de* **Rhus-t** b2.de* ruta b2.de* sabad b2.de* sal-fr sle1• sec bg2* seneg b2.de* sil b2.de* spig b2.de* squil b2.de* stann b2.de* staph b2.de* *Stram* b2.de* sul-ac b2.de* sulph bg2* tarax b2.de* teucr b2.de*

- **Internal** parts; in: ...
thuj b2.de* tritic-vg fd5.de valer b2.de* *Verat* b2.de* viol-o b2.de* viol-t b2.de* *Zinc* bg2*
- **Joints**: *Canth* b2.de* croc b2.de* gnaph ptk1 lil-t ptk1 *Lyc* b2.de* m-arct b2.de* **Nux-v** b2.de* ph-ac b2.de* **Puls** b2.de*
- **Mucous** membranes (See Mucous membranes - dryness)

DRY weather (See Weather - dry)

DRYNESS of usually moist internal parts: (↗*Sicca; Sjögren's)* *Acon* b2.de* adam srj5• aesc ptk1 agar b2.de* agn b2.de* alum b2.de* am-c b2.de* am-m b2.de* ambr b2.de* anac b2.de* ang b2.de* ant-c b2.de* ant-t b2.de* apis bg2* arg-n bg2* arn b2.de* *Ars* b2.de* asaf b2.de* asar b2.de* atro sf1.de aur b2.de* *Bar-c* b2.de* **Bell** b2.de* borx b2.de* bov b2.de* **BRY** b2.de* **Calad** b2.de* **Calc** b2.de* camph b2.de* *Cann-i* sf1.de **Cann-s** b2.de* canth b2.de* caps b2.de* carb-ac bg2 carb-an b2.de carb-v b2.de carbn-o bg2 caust b2.de* *Cham* b2.de* chel b2.de* chin b2.de* cic b2.de* cina b2.de* clem b2.de* cocc b2.de* coff b2.de* colch b2.de* con b2.de* cor-r sf1.de croc b2.de* cupr b2.de* cycl b2.de* dig b2.de* dros b2.de* dulc b2.de* euph b2.de* euphr b2.de* ferr b2.de* gels bg2* *Graph* b2.de* guaj b2.de* hell b2.de* hep b2.de* hist sp1 *Hyos* b2.de* ign b2.de* iod b2.de* ip b2.de* *Kali-bi* bg2* kali-c b2.de kali-i bg2* kali-n b2.de* kreos b2.de* lach b2.de* laur b2.de* led b2.de* *Lyc* b2.de* m-ambo b2.de* m-arct b2.de m-aust b2.de mag-c b2.de mag-m b2.de* *Mang* b2.de* menis br1 meny b2.de* *Merc* b2.de* *Mez* b2.de* mosch b2.de* mur-ac b2.de* nat-c b2.de* **Nat-m** b2.de* neon srj5• *Nit-ac* b2.de* **Nux-m** b2.de* nux-v b2.de* olnd b2.de* onos vml3• op b2.de* *Par* b2.de* *Petr* b2.de* ph-ac b2.de* **Phos** b2.de* plat b2.de* plb b2.de* psil vml3• *Puls* b2.de* ran-b b2.de* ran-s b2.de* rheum b2.de* *Rhod* b2.de* *Rhus-t* b2.de* rumx ptk1 ruta b2.de* sabad b2.de* sabin b2.de* samb b2.de* sang bg2* sars b2.de* sec b2.de* sel b2.de* **Seneg** b2.de* **Sep** b2.de* *Sil* b2.de* spig b2.de* spong b2.de* squil b2.de* stann b2.de* staph b2.de* *Stram* b2.de* *Stront-c* b2.de* sul-ac b2.de* sul-i bg2* **Sulph** b2.de* tarax b2.de* *Thuj* b2.de* vanil fd5.de *Verat* b2.de* verat-v bg2* *Zinc* b2.de*

DUCHENNE-FRIEDRICH SYNDROME (See Complaints - muscles; Dystrophy - muscles)

DUST:
- **agg.**: (↗*Allergic; Stone-cutters; NOSE - Hay - dust; RESPIRATION - Asthmatic - dust)* am-c ptk1 ars bg2* bell ptk1 *Brom* bg2* calc bg2* chel ptk1 chin ptk1 des-ac rbp6 **Dros** ptk1 hep ptk1 ign ptk1 just ptk1 lyc bg2* *Lyss* tl1* nat-ar bg2 ph-ac ptk1 puls ptk1 rumx ptk1 sil bg2* sul-ac mrr1 sulph ptk1 [am-br stj2 bar-br stj2 calc-br stj1 cupr-act stj2 kali-br stj1 mang stj1 mang-act stj2 nat-br stj2]
  - **fine** dust in air: bell ptk1
- **sensation** of dust:
  - ○ **External** parts are coated with dust; sensation as if: plut-n srj7•
  - **Internal** parts; sensation of dust in: *Am-c* b2.de* ars b2.de* *Bell* b2.de* **Calc** b2.de* chel bg2* chin bg* cina b2.de* cocc bg2 crot-c bg2 dros b2.de* hep b2.de* *Ign* b2.de* ip bg2 *Lyc* bg* op bg2 *Ph-ac* b2.de* plat bg2 puls bg* rheum b2.de* rumx bg* sulph b2.de* teucr b2.de* zinc bg2

DWARFISHNESS: (↗*Development; Development - arrested)* ambr ptk1 aster jl3 bac c1 **Bar-c** k* bar-i br1 *Bar-m* k* borx st *Calc* k* **Calc-p** k* *Carbn-s* carc mg1.de* *Con* ptk1 iod lyc k* mag-m sf1.de *Med* k* merc k* merc-pr-a c1* nat-m st1 nep jl3 nux-m sys *Ol-j* k* ph-ac st1 sec *Sil* k* sulfa jl3 **Sulph** k* **Syph** hr1* thyr c1* *Tub* hr1* zinc [bar-p stj1 bar-s stj1]
- **children**; in: carc mlr1• med br1
- **emaciated** babies: ol-j mtf11

DYSENTERY; after: aloe bg2 colch bg2 ham bg2 lyc bg2 nux-v bg2 ph-ac bg2 sul-i bg2 sulph bg2

DYSTONIA; autonomic: adren mtf11 agar mtf med jl2 mucor jl2 rauw jl1 syph jl2 tetrac mtf11

DYSTROPHY: | **Muscles**; of: (↗*Atrophy - muscles; Muscles)* calc mrr1 calc-p sne cur sne dub sne* *Hydroph* mtf *Karw-h* jl2 *Parot* mtf perh mtf phos sne plb sne verat-v sne* [kali-p stj *Mang* stj oryz-s stj plb-m stj *Plb-p* stj]

EASE, cozy, comfortable; feeling at: agar bg2 ars bg2 coca bg2 lach bg2 nat-p bg2 op bg2 pic-ac bg2

EATING:
- **after**:
  - **agg.**: abies-n k* acon k* aesc bro1 **Aeth** bg2* *Agar* k* agn k* all-c **Aloe** k* alum k* alum-p k2* alum-sil k2* am-c k* *Am-m* k* ambr k* **Anac** k* ang b2.de* ant-c k* ant-t k* *Apis* apoc arg-met b2.de* *Arg-n* k* arn k* **Ars** k*

Eating – after – agg.: ...
Ars-s-f k2* arum-t hr1* *Asaf* k* asar k* aur k* aur-ar k2 aur-s k2* bar-act sf1.de *Bar-c* k* bar-i k2* bar-s k2* *Bell* k* *Bism* k* *Borx* k* both-ax tsm2 bov k* *Brucel* sa3• **Bry** k* bufo cain calad k* **Calc** k* calc-i k2* **Calc-p** k* *Calc-sil* k2* camph k* cann-s k* canth k* caps k* *Carb-an* k* *Carb-v* k* *Carbn-s* **Caust** k* *Cham* k* *Chel* k* *Chin* k* *Chinin-s* kr1 chion bro1 chir-fl gya2 chloram jl3 cic k* cina k* cinnb k2* clem k* *Coc-c* *Cocc* k* *Coff* k* colch k* **Coloc** k* **Con** k* croc k* *Crot-t* k* cupr-ar sf1.de *Cycl* k* dig k* dros k* dulc k* echi sf1.de eup-per euph k* euphr k* *Ferr* k* ferr-ar *Ferr-i* ferr-p *Gran* *Graph* k* grat k* guat sp1* hell k* hep k* hydrog srj2• *Hyos* k* ign k* *Indg* k* iod k* ip k* *Jug-r* kali-ar **Kali-bi** k* **Kali-c** k* kali-chl k13 kali-m k2 kali-n k* kali-p k* kali-s kali-sil k2* kreos k* **Lach** k* laur k* led k* **Lyc** k* m-ambo b2.de* m-arct b2.de* m-aust b2.de* mag-c k* mag-m k* manc hr1* mang k* meny b2.de* meph bg2 merc k* *Mez* k* mosch k* mur-ac k* nat-ar *Nat-c* k* **Nat-m** k* nat-s k* nat-sil k2* neon srj5• *Nit-ac* k* *Nuph* hr1* nux-m k* **Nux-v** k* ol-an bro1 olnd k* op k* *Ox-ac* oxyt ptk2 par k* *Petr* k* *Ph-ac* k* **Phos** k* phyt plat k* plb k* *Podo* k* *Psor* k* *Ptel* **Puls** k* *Ran-b* k* ran-s k* raph hr1* rauw jl3 *Rheum* k* rhod k* *Rhus-t* k* **Rumx** k* ruta k* sabad k* sabin k* samb k* sang sanguis-s hrn2• sars k* sec k* *Sel* k* *Seneg* k* **Sep** k* **Sil** k* sphing k* spig k* spong k* squil k* stann k* staph k* stront-c k* stry bro1 sul-ac k* sul-i k2* **Sulph** k* *Tarax* k* ter k* teucr k* thea bro1 *Thuj* k* tril-p k* tritic-vg fd5.de trom k* valer k* verat k* verb k* vesp ptk2 viol-t k* **Zinc** k* zinc-p k2* [tax jsj7]
  - **long** time after; a: aeth ptk1 anac ptk1 carb-v ptk1 ferr ptk1 grat bg2 *Kali-bi* ptk1 kali-i bg2 kreos bg2* murx bg2 nat-m ptk1 *Phos* bg2* **Puls** bg2* sulph ptk1 zinc ptk1
  - **only** after eating: iod tl1 mez tl1
- **amel.**: acon k* adon sf1.de agar hr1* alet sf1.de aloe alum k* alumn k* am-c k* am-m k* ambr k* amor-r jl3 *Anac* k* ang b2.de* arn k* ars k* ars-i *Aster* hr1* bar-c k* bar-i k2* bell-p jl3 *Bov* k* brom *Bry* k* buth-a mg1.de* cadm-met mg1.de* calc k* calc-f mg1.de* calc-i k2* *Calc-s* k* cann-i hr1* *Cann-s* k* carb-an k* carbn-s *Caust* k* cham k* *Chel* k* chin k* cist sf1.de con sf1.de *Cupr* bg2 dicha mg1.de* dios k* euphr falco-pe nl2• *Ferr* k* fl-ac k* gamb k* goss st *Graph* k* guat sp1 hed mg1.de* hell k* *Hep* k* hydrog srj2• *Ign* k* **Iod** k* kali-bi k* kali-br kali-c k* *Kali-s* kalm sf1.de kola stb3• kreos hr1* **Lac-ac** sf1.de* lac-h sze9• lach k* *Laur* k* lith-c lob sf1.de lol sf1.de lyss hr1* m-aust b2.de* mag-c b2.de* mag-m mand mg1.de mang k* med st melal-alt gya4 meny k* merc k* mez k* mosch k* murx mgm• **Nat-c** k* nat-m h2 *Nat-p* nicc k* nux-v k* *Onos* ox-ac bg2 paeon petr k* **Phos** k* plan plat hr1* prot jl2 *Psor* jl2 *Puls* k* rad-br c11 ran-b k* rhod rhus-t k* rob sf1.de ruta fd4.de *Sabad* k* *Sacch* sst• sars k* **Sep** k* sil k* spig k* **Spong** k* squil k* stann k* *Stront-c* k* sul-i k2* sulph k2* tarent k2* tung-met bdx1• valer k2* verat k* zinc sf1.de zinc-p k2* [am-p stj1 am-s stj1 heroin sdj2 *Lith-i* stj2 tax jsj7]
- **agg.**: guat sp1
- **before** | **agg.**: acon k* alum k* am-c k* am-m k* *Ambr* k* anac k* ang b2.de* arn k* ars k* *Ars-i* ars-s-f k2* aur-ar k2 bar-c k* bar-i k2* bell k* *Bov* k* bry k* *Calc* k* calc-i k2* *Cann-s* k* carb-an k* carb-v k* carbn-s caust k* cham k* *Chel* k* *Chin* k* colch k* *Croc* k* dulc k* euphr k* *Ferr* k* **Fl-ac** bg2 *Graph* k* hell k* hep k* *Ign* k* **Iod** k* kali-c k* *Lach* k* **Laur** k* m-aust b2.de mag-c k* mang k* meny k* merc k* mez k* mosch k* **Nat-c** k* *Nat-p* nit-ac k* nux-v k* olnd k* petr k* **Phos** k* *Plb* k* *Puls* k* ran-b k* *Rhus-t* k* *Sabad* k* sabin k* sars k* seneg k* sep k* sil k* spig k* squil k* stann k* staph *Stront-c* k* *Sulph* k* *Tarax* k* valer k* verat k* verb k*
- **fast** agg.: ars k* fic-m gya1 *Ip* k* led k* *Nux-v* k* sil ptk1 sulph k*
- **food** in the stomach | **amel.**: anac k2 fl-ac k2
- **frequently**:
  - **agg.**: aeth ptk1
  - **amel.**: fl-ac ptk1 sulph ptk1
- **lying**; can eat only while: *Bell* b4a.de
- **not** eating; when | **amel.**: *Cocc* b7.de
- **overeating** agg.; after: abies-c vml3• abies-n vml3• acon bg2 aeth ptk1 all-s c1* alum bg2 **Ant-c** b7a.de* ant-t b7a.de* arg-n st *Arn* bg2 ars bg2 asaf bg2 bry bg2* calc ptk1 carb-v bg2* caust bg2* chin bg2 *Coff* bg2* dios c1* hep bg2 ign bg2 **Ip** b7a.de* *Lyc* ptk1 mag-c bg2 nat-c bg2* nat-p ptk1 nux-m bg2* *Nux-v* b7a.de* petr-ra shn4• **Puls** bg2* staph bg2* *Sulph* ptk1 tritic-vg fd5.de tub k2
  - **children**; in: aeth bg2* nat-p bg2*
- **satiety**; after eating to:
  - **agg.**: bar-c k* bar-s k2 *Calc* k* carb-v k* **LYC** k ● nat-c k* nat-m k* nux-v k* **Phos** ● **PULS** k ● sep k* sil k* *Sulph* k* zinc h2
  - **amel.**: ars k* *Iod* k* phos k*

- **small** quantities:
  - **agg.**: alet bg2 am-c bg2 arg-n bg2 bar-c bg2 bell bg2 **Bry** bg2* canth bg2 carb-an bg2* *Carb-v* bg2 *Chin* bg2* *Con* bg2* crot-t bg2 cuc-p stx1 cycl bg2 ferr bg2 hep bg2 *Ign* bg2 kali-bi bg2 *Kali-c* bg2* kali-p fd1.de• kali-s bg2 led bg2 lil-t bg2 **Lyc** bg2* merc bg2 nat-m bg2 nat-p bg2* **Nux-v** bg2* petr ptk1 **Phos** bg2* puls bg2* rhod bg2 rhus-t bg2 sars bg2 *Sep* bg2 sulph bg2* thuj bg2 verat bg2 zinc bg2
  - **amel.**: abel sf1.de alum-sil k2 guat jl* ignis-alc es2• lob ptk1 spong ptk1
- **while**:
  - **agg.**: abies-n bro1 aesc bro1 aeth bro1 agar bro1 aloe k* alum k* **Am-c** k* am-m k* ambr k* anac bg2 ang b2.de* ant-c k* ant-t k* arg-met k* *Arg-n* bro1 arn k* ars k* aur k* aur-ar k2 aur-s k2* *Bar-c* k* bar-s k2* bell k* bism k* *Borx* k* both-ax tsm2 bov k* *Bry* k* *Calc* k* calc-f st1 calc-sil k2* cann-s k* canth k* *Carb-ac* **Carb-an** k* **Carb-v** k* *Carbn-s* k1 *Caust* k* *Cham* k* chin k* chion bro1 *Cic* k* cina bro1 clem k* *Cocc* k* coff k* colch k* *Coloc* bro1 **Con** k* *Crot-t* bro1 cycl k* dig k* dros k* dulc k* euph k* ferr k* *Graph* k* hell k* *Hep* k* hyos bro1 ign k* iod k* *Ip* bro1 kali-bi bg2* **Kali-c** k* kali-n k* kali-p k* kreos bro1 lac-h htj1• lach k* laur k* led k* *Lyc* k* m-ambo b2.de* m-arct b2.de* m-aust b2.de* mag-c k* *Mag-m* k* mang k* merc k* mur-ac bg2 *Nat-c* k* *Nat-m* k* **Nit-ac** k* nux-m k* nux-v k* ol-an bro1 *Olnd* k* petr k* ph-ac k* *Phos* k* plat b2.de* plb k* *Puls* k* ran-b k* ran-s k* rauw jl3 rheum bro1 rhod k* rhus-t k* *Rumx* k* ruta k* sabad sabin k* samb k* sars k* sec k* *Sep* k* sil k* spig k* spong k* squil k* staph k* stram k* stry bro1 sul-ac k* **Sulph** k* tarax teucr k* thea bro1 thuj k* *Trom* br1 ulm-c jsj8• valer k* verat k* verb b2.de* zinc k* [am-p stj1 kali-met stj2]
  - **amel.**: acet-ac bro1 adam srj5• aloe *Alum* k* *Alumn* kr1 am-m k* *Ambr* k* **Anac** k* androc srj1• ap-g vh aq-mar jl3 arn k* aur k* *Auran* kr1 bar-c j5.de bell k* brom bro1* buth-a sp1* cadm-met bro1* cadm-s calc-p cann-i *Caps* k* carb-an k* carb-v k* cham k* *Chel* k* chin k* cimic bro1* cist bro1 *Cit-v* hr1 cocc k* con bro1 *Croc* k* cur hr1* cyn-d jl3 dig k* dros k* ferr k* ferr-act bro1 fl-ac st graph k* guat sp1 haliae-lc srj5• hed sp1 *Hep* bro1 hom-xyz bro1 hydrog srj2• **Ign** k* iod k* *Kali-p* bro1 lac-h htj1• **Lach** k* laur k* led k* *Lith-c* bro1 lyc k* m-arct b2.de* m-aust b2.de mag-c k* mang k* merc k* methys jl *Mez* k* nat-c k* nat-m bro1 nit-ac k* nux-v k* onop jl onos bro1 par k* perh jl *Petr* bro1 ph-ac k* phos k* phyt bg2 pip-n bro1 plat b2.de* prot jl3 psor bro1* puls k* rheum k* rhod k* rhus-t k* sabad k* sabin k* sanic c1 *Sep* k* sil k* *Spig* k* spong k* squil k* stann k* staph k* sul-ac k* sulph k* tarax k* *Thlas* bg1* thymol jl3 v-a-b jl3* **Zinc** k* [am-br stj2 am-caust stj2 am-f stj2 am-s stj1 astat stj2 aur-m stj2 aur-s stj2 bar-br stj2 *Bar-i* stj2 bar-met stj2 bism-sn stj2 caes-met stj2 calc-br stj1 *Calc-lac* stj2 cinnb stj2 *Ferr-lac* stj2 hafn-met stj2 ind stj2 irid-met stj2 kali-br stj1 kali-i stj1 *Lac-ac* stj2 lanth-met stj2 mag-i stj1 merc-d stj2 *Merc-i-f* stj2 nat-br stj2 nat-i stj1 *Nat-lac* stj2 osm-met stj2 plb stj2 plb-m stj2 plb-p stj2 polon-met stj2 rhen-met stj2 stront-m stj2 stront-met stj2 tant-met stj2 thal-met stj2 tung-met stj2 *Zinc-i* stj2]
    - **evening**: hed sp1
    - **only** while eating: *Iod* tl1
  - **beginning** to eat: ang b7.de*
  - **end** of eating: ign b7.de

EBULLITION of blood (See Orgasm)

ECLAMPSIA (See Convulsions - pregnancy)

EDEMA (See Swelling - puffy)

EFFICIENCY: (↗*Vigor)*

- **increased**: agar a1* alco a1 ars sf1.de bell a1 bov a1 bry a1 calc-f sp1 choc srj3• clem a1 cob a1 coca sf1.de coff a1* corn a1 cot a1 elae a1 erech a1 ferr a1 fl-ac a1 gast a1 gels a1 gins a1 helon a1 kola sf1.de* lach sf1.de lil-t a1 meny a1 nat-p sf1.de nept-m lsd2.fr ol-j a1 olib-sac wmh1 op sf1.de ped a1 phos a1 pic-ac sf1.de pieri-b mlk9.de pip-m a1* plat a1 sars a1 stram a1* *Tung-met* bdx1• vanad jl3 wies a1

EFFUSION: calc ptk1 carb-an ptk1 graph ptk1 iod ptk1 kali-i ptk1 kali-m ptk1 rhus-t ptk1 sul-i ptk1 sulph ptk1

- **threatening**: *Apis* bro1 *Bry* bro1 *Chin* bro1 cic bro1 *Hell* bro1 iodof bro1 op bro1 tub bro1 *Zinc* bro1

ELECTRICAL EQUIPMENT; failure of: plut-n nl positr nl2•

ELECTRICITY of the atmosphere; ailments from: (↗*Shock - electric-like - touching)* nat-c dw1* phos k2*

ELECTRICITY; sensation of static: (↗*Shock - electric-like - touching)* bit-ar wht1• cypra-eg sde6.de•

ELECTROSHOCK; ailments from: morph c1 phos c1*

ELEPHANTIASIS: *Anac* c1* ars bro1* calo bro1 card-m bro1 *Elae* bro1 graph bro1* ham bro1 hell hr1* hippoz c1* *Hydrc* hr1* hydrochl-ac ptk1 iod bro1* **Led** mrr1 lyc bro1* *Myris* c* sil hr1* still hr1*

- **arabum**: ars c1* elae c1* *Hydrc* hr1* myris c1* *Sil* hr1*

ELONGATION: | **Tonsils** agg.; of: *Staph* b7a.de

EMACIATION: (↗*Cachexia; Fasting - amel.; Lean people; Malnutrition; FACE - Emaciation)* **Abrot** k* acal br1* *Acet-ac* k* adren st *Agar* alco a1 *Alet* hr1* alf br1 all-s br1* *Alum* k* alum-p k2* alum-sil k2* alumn k* am-c k* am-caust a1* am-m *Ambr* k* ambro c1* anac k* androc srj1• ang c1 ant-c k* ant-t k* anthraci jl2 *Apis* apoc a1* aq-mar jl3 *Arg-met* k* *Arg-n* k* arn k* **Ars** k* **Ars-i** k* ars-met a1* ars-s-f k2* arum-i a1 asc-t k* astra-e jl3 astra-m br1 *Aur* hr1* aur-ar k2 aur-m k* bac jl2 bar-act a1 **Bar-c** k* bar-i k2* *Bar-m* k* bar-s k2* *Bell* hr1* ben-n a1 benz-ac a1* beryl jl3 bism ptk1 borx k* both a1 brach a1* brass-n-o srj5• *Brom* hr1* *Bry* k* *Bufo* buni-o jl3 *Cact* k* **Calc** k* calc-ar sf1.de calc-f mg1.de* calc-hp sf1.de **Calc-i** k* calc-m a1 calc-ox gm1 *Calc-p* k* *Calc-sil* k2* *Camph* k* cann-s a1 *Canth* k* *Caps* hr1* *Carb-an* bg2* *Carb-v* k* carbn-o a1 *Carbn-s* carc mlr1• carl a1 carneg-g rwt1• *Caust* bg2* cench k2* cere-b a1* *Cetr* hr1* *Cham* k* *Chel* k* **Chin** k* chinin-ar chinin-s j5.de* *Chion* chlol a1 *Chlor* k* cic jl3 cimic mg1.de cina k* *Cist* hr1* *Clem* k* cob-n jl3 coca a1* *Cocc* k* coff mrr1 *Colch* *Coloc* k* con k* cor-r cordyc mp4• cory br1 *Crot-c* crot-t k* cub a1* cund hr1* *Cupr* k* dig k* digin a1 diph-pert-t mp4• diphtox jl2 dros k* dulc k* echi a1* echit a1 euphr hr1* eupi a1 **Ferr** k* *Ferr-ar* k* *Ferr-i* k* *Ferr-m* k* ferr-p br1 *Fl-ac* fuc a1 gaert fmm1• *Gamb* hr1* gels a1 germ-met srj5• *Glycyr-g* cte1• gran j5.de* **Graph** k* *Guaj* k* haliae-lc srj5• hed mg1.de **Hell** k* helo bg2* helo-s c1* *Helon* k* *Hep* k* *Hippoz* k* hura a1 *Hydr* k* hydrog srj2• *Ign* k* **Iod** k* *Ip* k* jal mrr1 jug-c a1 kali-ar k* kali-bi k* *Kali-br* a1* *Kali-c* k* *Kali-i* k* *Kali-p* k* kali-s k* *Kali-sil* k2* kali-t a1 *Kreos* k* kres mg1.de* *Lac-ac* hr1* lac-c hr1* *Lac-d* hr1* *Lach* k* lat-k a1 lat-m bnm6• *Laur* hr1* lec br1 led ptk1 lil-t a1 *Lith-c* kr1 luf-op mg1.de* **Lyc** k* *Lycps-v* kr1 lyss hr1* mag-c k* mag-m k* mag-p c1 mang bg2* mang-act br1* med k2* *Merc* k* *Merc-c* a1 merc-k-i gm1 mez k* moly-met jl* morph a1 *Mucor* jl2 *Mur-ac* h2* myos-a sf1.de *Myos-s* hr1* naja a1 *Nat-ar* *Nat-c* k* **Nat-hchls** **Nat-m** k* *Nat-n* sf1.de *Nat-p* k* *Nat-s* k* nat-sil k2* *Nicc* hr1* **Nit-ac** k* nit-s-d sf1.de nuph a1 nux-m k* **Nux-v** k* *Ol-j* k* *Op* k* ox-ac a1 ozone sde2• parathyr jl3* pers jl *Petr* k* *Ph-ac* k* phel hr1* **Phos** k* *Phyt* br1* pic-ac hr1* pilo a1 pin-s sf1.de pip-m a1 *Plan* hr1* **Plb** k* plb-xyz c2 *Podo* hr1* *Psor* k* *Puls* k* pyrog bg2* raph j5.de* *Rheum* kr1 rhus-g a1 *Rhus-t* bg2 rhus-v j5.de* *Rumx* kr1 ruta k* sacch a1* samb k* *Sanic* c1* saroth jl3 *Sars* k* *Sec* k* **Sel** k* *Senec* hr1* sep k* **Sil** k* spig k* spong k* **Stann** k* *Stann-i* sf1.de staph k* still a1 *Stram* k* *Strept-ent* jl2 *Stront-c* k* *Sul-ac* a1* sul-h a1 sul-i k2* sulfa jl3 **Sulph** k* sumb k* symph fd3.de• *Syph* hr1* syzyg br1 tab j5.de* *Tarent* k* *Ter* *Teucr* hr1* thal a1* thal-xyz srj8• ther hr1* *Thuj* b4a.de* thuj-l jl3 thyr br1* tritic-vg fd5.de **Tub** k* tub-a jl2 tub-m vn* tub-r jl3 (non:uran-met k) uran-n k* v-a-b jl2 vanad br1* vanil fd5.de *Verat* k* *Verat-v* hr1* vesp a1 vip j5.de* voes a1 x-ray jl *Zinc* bg2* zinc-m a1* zinc-val c1* [*Spect* dfg1]

- **accompanied** by:
  - **acne**: abrot ptk1
  - **cough**: *Acet-ac* ptk1 ambr ptk1 *Chin* b7.de* ferr b7.de* lyc ptk1 *Nit-ac* ptk1 *Nux-v* b7.de* *Puls* b7.de*
    - **dry**: lyc ptk1
  - **diabetes** (See Diabetes mellitus - accompanied - emaciation)
  - **hands**; heat of the: ol-j br1
  - **perspiration**: led bg2
    - **cold** agg.: ars bro1 *Tub* bro1 *Verat* bro1
  - **phthisis** pulmonalis (See Cachexia - tuberculosis)
  - **plethora**; false: ferr tl1
  - **weakness**: *Acet-ac* br1 ars bro1 iod tl1 kreos tl1 tub bro1* *Verat* bro1
  - ○ **Abdomen**:
    - **distention** of: bufo bg2
    - **enlarged** (See ABDOMEN - Enlarged - children - marasmus)
  - **Glands**; enlargement of: iod tl1*
  - **Head**:
    - **heat** of the: ol-j br1
    - **perspiration** of the: calc tl1

- **acute** diseases; with: verat mtf33
- **anemia**; from (See Anemia - accompanied - emaciation)
- **appetite** with emaciation; ravenous: *Abrot* k* acet-ac bro1* ars ptk1 ars-i br1* bac jl2 bar-c bro1* bar-i k2 brom tl1 **Calc** k* calc-f jl chin hr1* cina ptk1* con bg1* elaps gk gaert fmm1• hydrog srj2• **Iod** k* ip bg1 *Kali-i* vh kola stb3• luf-op jl3 *Lyc* bg2* mag-c ptk1 **Nat-m** k* **Petr** k* *Phos* psor k* sanic bro1* sec bg1* sel bg1 sil sf1.de* sul-i k2* *Sulph* k* thyr br1* *Tub* k* tub-r jl2 (non:uran-met st) uran-n bg2*
  - **children**; in: *Abrot* ars-i bar-c k* *Bar-i* k13* **Calc** *Calc-p Caust Chin* k* **Cina** k* **Iod** k* *Lyc* k* *Mag-c* **Nat-m** k* *Nux-v* petr sanic mtf33 *Sil* sul-i k2 *Sulph* k* tub gk*
    - **infants**; in●: (↗*children - infants)* *Abrot* k* ars-i *Bar-c* k* bar-i **Calc** k* *Calc-p Caust Chin* k* **Cina Iod** *Kali-i* bg1* *Lyc Mag-c* **Nat-m** k* *Nux-v* petr k* sanic tl2* *Sil* sul-i k2 *Sulph*
    - **malarial** regions; born in: nat-m mtf33
    - **newborns**: sanic mtf33
- **beginning** | **Legs**; in (See extending - upward)
- **cancerous** affections; in: (↗*Cancerous - cachectic)* brom tl1 carc mlr1• cory br1
- **cares**; from: caust br1
- **causeless**: x-ray mtf11
- **children**; in: (↗*Children)* *Abrot* k* **Acet-ac** kr1* aeth kr1 alum ant-c *Apis* kr1 *Arg-n* k* arn j5.de **Ars** k* **Ars-i** ars-s-f c1* **Arum-t** kr1 bac bro1 bar-c k* bell j5.de borx k2* brom mtf33 **Calc** k* **Calc-p** k* *Calc-sil* k2* *Carb-v* caust k* cham j5.de chin cina coca c1 con b4a.de* *Ferr* j5.de* hecla st hep b4a.de* *Hydr* **Iod** k* ip mtf33 kali-c kali-i c1 *Kreos* lac-d k2 *Lyc* k* *Mag-c* k* med k2 merc mtf33 moni rfm1• **Nat-m** k* *Nux-m Nux-v Ol-j* k* *Op* petr k* *Phos* k* *Plb Podo* kr1* *Psor* k* *Puls Sanic* bro1* sars k* *Sep* **Sil** k* *Staph* kr1 sul-i k2 *Sulph* k* syph mtf33 tarent mtf33 ther kr1 thyr bro1 tritic-vg fd5.de *Tub* br1*
  - **boys**; pining: (↗*Children - delicate)* **Aur** k* **Lyc** k* *Nat-m* k* *Ph-ac* hr1* **Tub** k*
  - **infants**; in: (↗*appetite - children - infants)* abr bg abrot br1* *Acet-ac* bro1 ant-i bro1 arg-met bro1 *Arg-n* bro1 ars bro1* ars-i bro1* aur bg* bar-c bro1* borx ptk1* *Calc* bg* calc-hp ptk1 calc-i tl1 calc-p ptk1 *Calc-sil* bro1 caps hr1 carb-an bro1 carb-v bro1 caust bro1 cetr bro1 chin bg* clem bro1 ferr bro1 *Ferr-p* bro1 fl-ac bro1 *Gaert* fmm1• glyc br1* helon bro1 *Hep* bro1 *Hydr* bro1 iod bro1* kali-i bro1 kali-p bro1 kreos bro1* led bro1 lyc bg* mag-c ptk1* mang-act bro1 merc br1* *Merc-c* bro1 nat-c bro1 nat-m bro1* nux-m ptk1 *Ol-j* br1* op bro1 *Ph-ac* bro1 phos bro1 phyt bro1 plb hr1* *Plb-act* bro1 plb-i bro1 *Plb-m* bro1 psor bro1 rhus-t bro1 ric bro1 *Samb* bro1 sanic bro1* sars br1* sec bro1 sel bro1 sep mtf33 *Sil* bro1* stann bro1 staph bro1 *Sulph* bg* syph bro1* ter bro1 ther ptk1 *Thuj* bro1 thyr br1 tritic-vg fd5.de tub bg* uran-n bro1 vanad bro1 *Verat* bro1 zinc bro1*
  - **newborns**; in (= marasmus): abrot vh1* borx mtf33
    - **accompanied** by:
      - **Umbilicus**:
        - **discharge** from umbilicus: **Abrot** mrr1*
        - **eruption** on umbilicus: **Abrot** mrr1
    - **birth** trauma; after: (↗*History - birth)* borx mtf33
    - **bottle** fed: nat-p ptk1
- **chronic**: caust br1 parathyr jl2
- **diarrhea**; during: *Borx* hr1 calc k2* chin k2 *Lach* hr1 *Mag-c* hr1 med hr1 *Merc* hr1 *Nat-m* hr1 nat-s mtf33 *Ol-j* hr1 *Petr* hr1* *Ph-ac* hr1 phel br1 plan hr1 podo hr1 prot jl3 *Rheum* hr1 sep hr1* sul-i k2 sulph hr1 teucr hr1 tub br1
- **downwards**; spread (See extending - downward)
- **eating** well; though (See appetite)
- **except** the abdomen; general emaciation (See ABDOMEN - Fat - accompanied - emaciation)
- **excitement** agg.: iod mtf33
- **fright**; from: caust mtf33
- **grief**; after: calc-p vh *Caust* mtf33 petr k* ph-ac k*
- **infantile** marasmus (See children - infants)
- **insanity**; with: arn ars calc chin graph lach lyc nat-m k* nit-ac nux-v phos puls sil k* sulph verat
- **long**-lasting disease; from: caust br1*
- **loss** of animal fluids; from: **Chin** k* **Lyc** k* **Sel** k*
- **menses**; after: phos bg2
- **neuralgia**; after: plb hr1*
- **nutrition**; gradual emaciation from impaired: (↗*Malnutrition)* ars br1

Emaciation: ...

- **old** people; in: *Ambr* k* anac bg2* **Bar-c** k* carb-v bg2* chin ptk1 chinin-s j5.de *Fl-ac* bg2* **Iod** k* **LYC** k ●* nit-ac bg2* op ptk1 rhus-t bg2* *Sec* k* *Sel* k* *Sil* st
- **painful**: caps ptk1 plb ptk1
- **partial** (See single)
- **perspiration**; during: nat-n bg2
- **pining** boys (See children - boys)
- **progressive**: acal br1 arg-n mtf33 ars bro1 carbn-s bro1 hyper bro1 kali-hp bro1 *Phos* bro1 phys bro1 *Plb* bro1 sanic tl1 sec bro1 sil tl1
  - **acute** disease; in: arn ptk1 guaj ptk1 verat ptk1
  - **loss** of appetite; with: bac jl2 calc mtf11
- **rapid**: ars tl1* calc-hp ptk1 chlor ptk1 ferr tl1* iod br1* kreos tl1 nat-sil mtf33 plb br1* samb bro1 tarent hr1* *Thuj* br1* thyr ptk1 tub br1*
- **seaside** | **amel.**: med tl1
- **sensation** of: acon bg2 agar bg2 berb bg2 naja bg2* nat-m bg2 psor bg2
- **suddenly**: bar-c ptk1 graph ptk1 samb ptk1
- **typhoid** fever; after: parathyr jl2
- **upwards**, spreads (See extending - upward)
- **vomiting**; from continued: kali-bi tl1

▽ - **extending** to:
- ○ **Downward**: (↗*Obesity - thighs)* calc k2* cench k2* **Lyc** k ●* **Nat-m** k ●* psor k2* sanic sf1.de* sars k*
- **Upward**: abrot k* arg-n k* pin-s mtf11

○ - **Affected** parts: *Ars* k* bry k* calc bg2* *Carb-v* k* *Caust* bro1 cupr h2 dulc k* **Graph** k* **Led** k* *Lyc Mez* k* nat-m k* *Nit-ac* k* nux-v ph-ac k* *Phos* k* *Plb* k* **Puls** k* **Sec** k* sel k* sep sil k* sulph ptk1
- **Glands**; of: (↗*Atrophy - glands)* con bg* iod bg* kali-p k2
  - **great**: nat-m tl1 petr tl1 ph-ac tl1 phos tl1
- **Painful** parts, of: plb k2
- **Single** parts, of: all-s vh1 bar-c bg2 bry k* calc k* caps carb-v k* *Caust* bg2 con dulc k* graph k* *Iod* k* led k* *Mez* k* nat-m k* nit-ac k* ph-ac k* phos bg *Plb* mtf33 *Sel* k* sil k*
- **Upper** part of body: calc ptk1 lyc gm1 nat-m ptj1• plb ptk1
  - **accompanied** by | **Lower** limbs; well nourished: lyc hr1* nat-m tl1

EMBOLISM: (↗*EYE - Embolism)* kali-m hr1*
- **prophylaxis**: fuma-ac mtf11

EMISSIONS SEMINAL: (↗*Loss - fluids)*
- **agg.**: abrot sf1.de agar *Alum* k* ars aven sf1.de *Bar-c* borx bov bufo sf1.de *Calc* k* cann-i k* cann-s carb-ac sf1.de carb-an carb-v *Caust* k1* *Chin* k* cob k* con sf1.de* dig ferr-br sf1.de glycyr-g cte1• *Iod* kali-br tl1 **Kali-c** k* led *Lyc* k* merc k* mez nat-c **Nat-p** k* **Nux-v** k* petr *Ph-ac* k* *Phos* k* *Pic-ac* plat sf1.de plb *Psor* puls ran-b rhod sabad **Sel Sep** *Sil* stann sf1.de *Staph* k* stram sf1.de *Sulph* k* thuj
- **amel.**: agn kr1 calc-p kr1* *Lach* kr1* *Zinc* kr1*

EMPTINESS, sensation of: (↗*MIND - Delusions - emptiness)* alum b2.de* am-c b2.de* am-m b2.de* ant-c b2.de* ant-t b2.de* arg-met b2.de* arn b2.de* astra-m c1* aur b2.de* bar-c b2.de* bry b2.de* calad b2.de* calc b2.de* caps b2.de* carb-an bg2* carb-v b2.de* caust b2.de* cham b2.de* *Chin* b2.de* cina b2.de* **Cocc** k* coff b2.de* coloc b2.de* croc b2.de* cupr b2.de* dig b2.de* dulc b2.de* euph b2.de* glon bg2* graph b2.de* guaj b2.de hep b2.de* hydr bg2* **Ign** k* ignis-alc es2• iod b2.de* ip b2.de* **Kali-c** b2.de* kali-n b2.de* lach b2.de* laur b2.de* **Lyc** k* mag-c b2.de* mang b2.de* med bg2* meny b2.de* merc b2.de* mez b2.de* *Mur-ac* b2.de* murx bg* myos-a rly4• nat-c b2.de* nat-m b2.de* nux-v b2.de* *Olnd* k* op b2.de* oxyt br1* par b2.de* petr b2.de* **Phos** b2.de* plat b2.de* plb b2.de* podo bg2* **Puls** k* rhus-t b2.de* ruta b2.de* sabad b2.de* **Sars** k* seneg b2.de* **Sep** k* spig b2.de* squil b2.de* **Stann** k* staph bg2* stram b2.de* sul-ac bg2* *Sulph* k* tab k1* tell k1* teucr b2.de* vanil fd5.de verat b2.de* verb b2.de* vib k1* vinc a1* zinc b2.de* *Zing* k*
- **eating**; after: grat ptk1
- **faintness**; with sensation of: **Sep** k1*
- **general**: ail a1 apoc a1 aur a1 cob-n sp1 hydr-ac a1 kali-c a1 merc a1 **Sep** a1 zing a1

○ - **Internally**: aur k1*
- **Organs**; in: tab ptk1
- **Stomach**; of | **agg.**: glycyr-g cte1•
- **Whole** body is hollow; as if: aur bg2* cob-n sp1 galeoc-c-h gms1• kali-c bg2* pall a1*

ENCAGED (See Constriction - external - caged)

END STAGE OF A DISEASE (See Euthanasia)

ENDARTERITIS OBLITERANS (= arteritis obliterans): x-ray sp1

ENDOMETRIOSIS (See FEMALE - Endometriosis)

ENDURANCE: | **increased**: (↗*Strength)* *Kola* stb3• *Lac-lup* hrn2• tritic-vg fd5.de

ENERGY:

- **excess** of energy: (↗*Activity - increased; Activity - physical; Strength)* agar bg2 amp rly4• anthraq rly4• atp rly4• cartl-s rly4• chir-fl gya2 cob ptm1• *Coff* bg2 coli rly4• corian-s knl6• cupr sst3• cystein-l rly4• ephe-si hsj1• ger-i rly4• helo-s rwt2• iod mtf33 *Kola* stb3• lac-h htj1*• lach bg2 loxo-recl knl4• mang-p rly4• med mtf33 medul-os-si rly4• myos-a rly4• nat-ox rly4• nat-p bg2 nat-pyru rly4• nicotam rly4• op bg2* orot-ac rly4• oxal-a rly4• phos mtf33 plac-s rly4• querc-r svu1• ribo rly4• sep mtf33 stram bg2 streptoc rly4• suis-em rly4• suis-hep rly4• suis-pan rly4• suprar rly4• tarent mtf33 thiam rly4• thioc-ac rly4• tritic-vg fd5.de vero-o rly4*• zinc bg2 [*Buteo-j* sej6 tax jsj7]
  - **morning**: ger-i rly4• oxal-a rly4• ribo rly4• tritic-vg fd5.de
  - **forenoon**: ger-i rly4•
  - **afternoon**: nicotam rly4• orot-ac rly4• oxal-a rly4• suis-pan rly4• tritic-vg fd5.de
    - **15** h: suis-pan rly4•
    - **16** h: pyrid rly4•
    - **17** h: cystein-l rly4•
  - **evening**: orot-ac rly4• oxal-a rly4•
    - **18** h; after: lac-h htj1•
  - **alternating** with:
    - **low** energy: [*Buteo-j* sej6]
    - **sadness** (See MIND - Sadness - alternating - energy)
  - **children**; in: (↗*MIND - Restlessness - children)* *Agar* lmj anac mrr1 ant-c mtf33 *Arn* lmj ars-i mrr1 *Aur* lmj *Carc* mlr1• chin mtf33 gaert fmm1• hyos mrr1 iod mtf33 **Lach** lmj* lyc mrr1 *Lyss* lmj **Med** lmj* nux-v lmj* op mtf33 phos mtf33 rhus-t mrr1 sep mtf33 stram mrr1 sulph mrr1 *Tarent* mrr1* *Tub* mrr1 *Verat* mrr1 zinc mrr1
  - **waking**; on: orot-ac rly4• suis-hep rly4•
  - ○ **Muscles**: fl-ac ptk1
- **lack** of energy (See Weakness)
- **moving** upward from the ground through the legs: agath-a nl2•
- **sensation** of: melal-alt gya4 thres-a sze7•

ENERVATION (See Weakness)

ENLARGED (See Hypertrophy; Swelling)

EOSINOPHILIA: abrom-a mtf allox mtf ars mtf aza mtf bamb-a mtf brass-n-o srj5• carc mtf crat mtf loxo-parr mtf loxo-recl mtf lyc mtf musa mtf nat-m mtf nat-s mtf phos mtf rad-br mtf saroth mtf thal mtf thyroiod mtf toxo-g jl2 v-a-b jl2

EPILEPSY (See Convulsions - epileptic)

ERGOT agg.: chin bro1 lach bro1 nux-v bro1 sec bro1 sol-ni bro1

ERUCTATIONS:

- **agg.**: *Agar* b2.de* agn bg2 alum b2.de* am-c b2.de* ant-c b2.de* bar-c b2.de* bell b2.de* bry b2.de* calad b2.de* *Cann-s* b2.de* caps b2.de* **Cham** b2.de* *Cocc* b2.de* cycl b2.de* hep b2.de* kali-c b2.de* *Lach* b2.de* merc-c bg2 nux-v b2.de* par b2.de* *Phos* b2.de* plb b2.de* puls b2.de* rhod b2.de* *Rhus-t* b2.de* sabin b2.de* *Sep* b2.de* sil b2.de* spong b2.de* stann b2.de* staph b2.de* sulph b2.de* *Verb* b2.de* *Zinc* b2.de*
- **amel.**: acet-ac *Acon* aesc agar k* all-c aloe alum k* alum-p k2 alum-sil k2 am-c b2.de am-m k* ambr k* **Ant-t** k* **Arg-n** k* ars b4a.de* *Aur* k* aur-i k2 aur-s k2 *Bar-c* k* bar-i berb borx b2.de* *Bry* k* camph b2.de* cann-s *Canth* k* **Carb-v** k* **Carbn-s** cassia-s cdd7*• cench k2 *Chel* k* cob-n sp1 coc-c cocc k* colch k* coloc k* cop cortico tpw7 *Dig* k* *Dios* k* *Fl-ac* glycyr-g cte1• **Graph** k* *Hydr* iber vml3• **Ign** k* ignis-alc es2• iod k* jug-r vml3• **Kali-bi** **Kali-c** k* *Kali-i* kali-n h2 kali-p fd1.de• *Kali-s* kali-sil k2 *Lac-ac* *Lach* k* laur b2.de* **Lyc** k* mag-c k* mag-m k* marb-w es1• melal-alt gya4 meph a1 mosch k* *Nat-c* k* nat-m nat-ox rly4• *Nit-ac* k* *Nux-v* k* ol-an bro1 olnd b2.de* op par k* petr k* ph-ac phos k* *Pic-ac* *Plat* k* puls ptk1 rhod b2.de* rumx ruta fd4.de sabad b2.de* sabin b2.de* **Sang** k* sars b2.de* *Seneg* st *Sep* k* *Sil* k* stront-c b2.de* sul-ac k* sul-i k2 *Sulph* k* *Tarent* ter thuj bg2 tritic-vg fd5.de zinc k* zinc-p k2

ERUCTATIONS and FLATUS both amel.: arg-n ctj4 carbn-s pfa2 hep hs1

EUTHANASIA; to induce: aml-ns hr1* ant-t bro1* ars bro1* carb-v bro1* lach br1* lachn c1 phos br1 rumx k2 tarent bro1* tarent-c k2* [heroin sdj2]

- **respiratory** complaints; in: *Ant-t* mrr1

EXCORIATION (See Mucous membranes - excoriation; SKIN - Excoriation)

EXERTION; physical: (↗*Activity - physical; MIND - Exertion - physical)*

- **ability** for | **increased**: dendr-pol sk4•
- **agg.**: acon k* *Act-sp* vh1 adam srj5• aesc k2* *Agar* k* agn k2* allox jl **Aloe** sne **Alum** k* *Alum-p* k2 alum-sil k2 *Alumn* am-c k* am-m k* *Ambr* k* ammc j5.de *Anac* ant-c k* *Ant-t* k* apis apoc *Arg-met* *Arg-n* arist-cl sp1 **Arn** k* **Ars** k* **Ars-i** k* ars-s-f k2 asaf k* asar k* atra-r skp7• aur k* aur-ar k2 aur-i k2 aur-m k2 aur-s k2 bacls-7 fmm1• bar-c bar-i k2 *Bar-s* k2 bell-p br1* *Benz-ac* berb sf1.de* beryl jl* blatta-o mrr1 *Bol-la* borx k* both-a rb3 both-ax tsm2 bov k* brom bg2* **Bry** k* buni-o jl buth-a mg1.de* *Cact* **Calc** k* *Calc-ar* k2 calc-f mg1.de* calc-i k2 *Calc-p* k* **Calc-s** k* calc-sil k2 *Cann-s* k* carb-an c1* *Carb-v* k* carc mlr1• *Caust* k* *Chel* *Chin* k* chinin-ar chinin-s j5.de cic k* cimic c1 cina k* cist k2 coca c1* **Cocc** k* coff k* *Colch* k* **Con** k* crat br1 croc k* *Crot-h* cupr c1 cur sf1.de cycl **Dig** k* dulc k2 epiph c1 erig mg1.de euphr k* *Ferr* k* *Ferr-ar* **Ferr-i** *Ferr-p* fl-ac bg2* flor-p jl **Gels** k* glon k2 graph k* *Guaj* *Ham* hell k* *Helon* k* *Hep* k* hydrog srj2*• ign k* **Iod** k* ip k* *Kali-ar* k* *Kali-bi* *Kali-c* k* kali-m k2 kali-n k* *Kali-p* kali-s kali-sil k2* *Kalm* ketogl-ac rly4• *Kreos* k* *Lac-d* k2* lac-h sk4• *Lach* k* lact j5.de **Laur** k* led k* lil-t *Lob* *Lyc* k* *Lycps-v* k* m-arct j5.de mag-c b2.de mag-p k2 malar jl2 mang-p rly4• medul-os-si rly4• meny *Merc* k* *Merc-c* mill c1 *Mur-ac* k* murx naja **Nat-ar** **Nat-c** k* **Nat-m** k* *Nat-p* *Nat-s* ptk1 nat-sil k2 nit-ac k* nux-m k* *Nux-v* k* olnd k* ovi-p c1 *Ox-ac* pall c1* paro-i jl pert jl2 petr j5.de petr-ra shn4• *Ph-ac* k* *Phos* k* **Pic-ac** k* *Pieri-b* mlk9.de plat k* *Plb* k* *Podo* prot jl2 *Psor* *Puls* k* *Rheum* k* rhod k* **Rhus-t** k* *Ruta* k* sabad k* *Sabin* k* sacch-l c1 *Sang* sanic c1 sarcol-ac sp1 sars k* scut c1 sec k* **Sel** k* **Sep** k* *Sil* k* sol-ni **Spig** k* **Spong** k* squil k* **Stann** k* **Staph** k* stront-c bg2 stroph-h ptk1 stroph-s jl suis-em rly4• sul-ac k* sul-i k2 **Sulph** k* symph fd3.de• *Tarent* tax jl tell jl ter c1 ther k2 thuj k* *Tub* k* tub-d zs* tub-m vn* tub-r jl2 v-a-b jl2 *Valer* verat k* *Zinc* k* zinc-p k2 [ant-m stj2 ant-met stj2 bell-p-sp dcm1 beryl-m stj2 ferr-n stj2 kali-met stj2 lith-c stj2 lith-f stj2 *Nat-caust* stj2 oxyg stj2 pop dhh1]
  - **prolonged** exertion: tub-m jl2
  - **slight** exertion: malar jl2 nux-m bg2 sul-i ptk1 thyr ptk1 tub-d jl2
  - **violent** exertion: lappa ptk1 mill ptk1 symph ptk1
- **amel.**: (↗*Idleness - agg.; MIND - Exertion - physical - amel.)* adon ptk1* aesc ptk1* agar bg2* aloe sne alumn bro1 *Apis* mrr1 aur-m-n wbt2• aur-s wbt2• brom bro1 canth k* carc gk6* cartl-s rly4• cupr sst3• *Cycl* bg2* dulc fd4.de ferr sne fl-ac st* galeoc-c-h gms1• haliae-lc srj5• helon sf1.de *Hep* bg2* *Ign* k* ignis-alc es2• *Iod* mrr1 kali-bi gk kali-br ptk1 kali-c jl **Lil-t** bg2* *Mag-m* lp nat-m k* nat-sil fd3.de• olib-sac wmh1 *Orig* mrr1 phys bg2 plb k* rad-br c11 rauw jl* **RHUS-T** k ●* sacch-a fd2.de• sanguis-s hrn2• **SEP** k ●* sil k* spong fd4.de stann k* suis-em rly4• *Tarent* mrr1 thlas ptk1 tril-p tub-r vn* vanil fd5.de [ferr-f stj2 ferr-lac stj2 ferr-sil stj2]
  - **air**; in open: aloe sne galeoc-c-h gms1• nat-sil fd3.de• rad-br sze8• rauw sp1 sacch-a fd2.de• vanil fd5.de
  - **sexual** excitement: galeoc-c-h gms1•
- **aversion** for: calc br1 caps br1 *Chel* br1 lac-del hrn2• lac-loxod-a hrn2• nat-n br1 pall br1
- **desire** for: (↗*MIND - Activity - desires)* bufo br1 lac-del hrn2• limen-b-c hrn2• phos mtf33
- **impossible**: calc-i k2 ham fd3.de• hydrog srj2• kali-p fd1.de• pert-vc vk9
- **sensation** as if: petr-ra shn4•

EXFOLIATION: | **Periosteum**: asaf bg2 merc bg2 ph-ac bg2 sil bg2

EXHAUSTION (See Weakness)

EXOSTOSIS: (↗*EXTREMITIES - Exostosis)* am-c j5.de ang c1 *Arg-met* k* **Aur** k* **Aur-m** k* calc k* *Calc-f* k* *Calc-p* hr1* colch gk crot-c daph c1* *Dulc* k* *Ferr-i* hr1* *Fl-ac* k* graph hr1* hecla k* hep bg *Kali-bi* c1* *Kali-i* k* lap-a bro1* *Maland* bro1* **Merc** a1* *Merc-c* k* *Merc-p* bro1 *Mez* k* *Nit-ac* ph-ac j5.de* **Phos** k* *Plb* j5.de* *Plb-act* bro1 plb-xyz c2 *Puls* rhus-t k* *Ruta* k*

Exostis: ...
Sars hr1* **Sil** k* staph k2* still bro1* sulph k* syph k2* *Zinc* j5.de* zinc-m st1 [*Am-f* stj2 *Bar-f* stj1 *Cupr-f* stj2 *Fl-pur* stj2 *Kali-f* stj1 *Lith-f* stj2 mag-f stj1 *Nat-f* stj1*]
- **eruptions**; after suppressed: sulph ptk1
- **injuries**; after: calc-f ptk1
- **painful**: aur ptk1 daph ptk1 kali-i ptk1 merc ptk1 syph ptk1
- **syphilitic**: fl-ac ptk1 hep ptk1 merc ptk1

EXPANSION; sensation of: *Arg-met* br1 *Arg-n* br1 par br1 sanguis-s hrn2•

EXPECTORATION:
- **after** | **agg.**: *Calad* b2.de* chin b2.de* sep b2.de*
- **agg.**: coc-c ptk1 dig bg2* *Led* bg2* *Nux-v* bg2*
- **amel.**: ant-t b7.de* apis bg2* aral ptk1 arg-met bg2 asaf b7.de coc-c bg2* grin ptk1 hep bro1 hyper ptk1 kali-bi bg2* kali-n ptk1 lach bg2 psor jl2 sep ptk1 stann bg2* sul-i ptk1 zinc bg2*

EXPIRATION:
- **agg.**: agn b2.de* ambr b2.de* anac b2.de* ang b2.de* ant-c b2.de* ant-t b2.de* *Arg-met* b2.de* ars b2.de* asaf b2.de* aur b2.de* bry b2.de* cann-s b2.de* carb-v b2.de* caust b2.de* cham b2.de* chel b2.de* chin b2.de* *Chlor* bg2* cic b2.de* cimic bg2 cina b2.de* clem b2.de* coff b2.de* **Colch** b2.de* *Dig* b2.de* *Dros* b2.de* dulc b2.de* euphr b2.de* *Fl-ac* bg2 *Ign* b2.de* *Iod* b2.de* *Ip* hr1* kreos b2.de* laur b2.de* led b2.de* mang b2.de* med ptk1 meph ptk1 mur-ac b2.de* nat-c b2.de* nux-v b2.de* *Olnd* b2.de* ph-ac b2.de* **Puls** b2.de* rhus-t b2.de* ruta b2.de* sabad b2.de* samb bg2* *Sep* b2.de* **Spig** b2.de* spong b2.de* squil b2.de* stann b2.de* *Staph* b2.de* tarax b2.de* verat b2.de* *Viol-o* b2.de* *Viol-t* b2.de* zinc b2.de*
- **amel.**: **Acon** b2.de* agar b2.de* am-m b2.de* anac b2.de* ang b2.de* arg-met b2.de* arn b2.de* asaf b2.de* asar b2.de* bar-c b2.de* *Borx* b2.de* **Bry** b2.de* calc b2.de* camph b2.de* canth b2.de* caps b2.de* carb-an b2.de* caust b2.de* cham b2.de* chel b2.de* chin b2.de* cina b2.de* clem b2.de* croc b2.de* cycl b2.de* euphr b2.de* guaj b2.de* hell b2.de* hep b2.de* ip b2.de* kali-c b2.de* kali-n b2.de* kreos b2.de* lyc b2.de* m-arct b2.de *Meny* b2.de* merc b2.de* mosch b2.de* nux-m b2.de* olnd b2.de* op b2.de* plat b2.de* plb b2.de* ran-b b2.de* ran-s b2.de* **Rhus-t** b2.de* sabad b2.de* **Sabin** b2.de* sars b2.de* sel b2.de* seneg b2.de* sep b2.de* spig b2.de* spong b2.de* *Squil* b2.de* stann b2.de* sul-ac b2.de* sulph b2.de* tarax b2.de* valer b2.de* verat b2.de*

EXUDATES; to facilitate the absorption of (See Absorption)

FAILURE to thrive (See Children - delicate)

FAINTNESS: (*↗Collapse; Convulsions - consciousness - without; Flabby - internally; MIND - Unconsciousness*)
abies-c k* acet-ac k* acetan c1* **Acon** k* *Aesc* aeth bg2* aether a1 agar k* agar-em a1 alco a1 alet bro1 all-c aloe bg2* *Alum* alum-p k2 alum-sil k2 alumn am-br a1 am-c k* *Am-caust* br1 am-m ambr k* *Aml-ns* kr1* amyg a1* anac ant-c k* ant-m kr1 *Ant-t* k* apis k* *Apoc* bg2* apom a1* *Arg-n* k* *Arn* k* **Ars** k* ars-h *Ars-i* ars-s-f a1* ars-s-r a1* asaf k* asar kr1 atp rly4• atro bacls-7 pte1*• bapt bar-c k* bar-i k2 *Bar-m* bars-s k2 bell k* ben-n a1 benz-ac berb beryl tpw5* bism bg2* bol-la a1 bol-s a1 borx k* *Both* a1* bov k* brom k2 *Brucel* sa3• **Bry** k* bufo k* cact k* calad k* calc k* calc-ar k2 calc-i k2 calc-m a1 calc-p calc-sil k2 calo a1 *Camph* k* cann-i *Cann-s* k* *Canth* k* carb-ac *Carb-v* k* *Carbn-o* *Carbn-s* carl a1 cass a1 castm kr1 castor-eq **Caust** k* cedr cench cere-s a1 **Cham** k* *Chel* chim **Chin** k* *Chinin-ar* chinin-s k* chlol chlor k1 cic k* *Cimic* k* cina k* cinnm kr1 cit-v c1* **Cocc** b2.de* *Coch* kr1 coff bg2* colch k* *Coll* k* *Coloc* k* *Con* k* conin a1 conv bg2* convo-d a1 cot a1 croc k* *Crot-c* **Crot-h** k* crot-t culx k2 cupr k* cupr-act *Cupr-ar* a1* cupr-s cur k* cycl cyclosp sa3• cyt-l a1* **Dig** k* digin a1 digox a1 dios k* dros k* dubo-h a1* dubo-m a1 dulc k* elaps ephe-si hsj1• ery-a a1 eucal a1* eup-per bg2 eup-pur *Euph* a1* euph-c a1 *Ferr* k* *Ferr-ar* *Ferr-i* ferr-p *Form* gala br1 gamb gels gent-c a1 **Glon** k* gran a1 *Graph* k* grin hedeo a1 hell k* hell-f a1 helo-s bnm14• **Hep** k* hippoz hura *Hydr* c1* hydr-ac k* hydrog srj2• *Hyos* k* **Ign** k* **Iod** k* iodof kr1 **Ip** b2.de* iris jab jal k* jasm a1 jug-c kali-ar kali-bi kali-br kali-c k* kali-cy kali-m k2 kali-n k* kali-ox a1 kali-p kali-sil k2 kalm kola stb3• *Kreos* k* lac-ac k* *Lac-d* kr1* **Lach** k* lat-k a1* *Laur* k* lavand-a ctl1• *Led* k* lept *Lil-t* k* *Lina* c1* lob c1* loxo-recl bnm10• luf-act a1 luf-op rsj5• lup a1 *Lyc* k* lycps-v kr1 lyss m-ambo b2.de* m-arct b2.de* m-aust b2.de* mag-c k* *Mag-m* k* magn-gl c1* magn-gr c1* manc mang med hr1* merc k* *Merc-c* merc-cy merc-d merc-ns a1 merc-pr-r a1 mez k* mom-b a1 **Mosch** k* mur-ac *Naja* k* narc-po a1 narc-ps a1* nat-chl br1 *Nat-hchls* *Nat-m* nat-ns c1* nat-p a1 nit-ac k* nitro-o a1 **Nux-m** k* **Nux-v** k* oena ol-an k* olnd k* *Op* k* orot-ac rly4• oscilloc jl2 ox-ac ozone sde2• paeon kr1 pana a1 parth c1* *Petr* k* petr-ra shn4• *Ph-ac* k* phase bro1 *Phos* k*

Faintness: ...
phys *Phyt* a1* picro a1 pip-m a1 plan plat bg2* **Plb** k* plut-n srj7• **Podo** k* *Psor* ptel k* **Puls** k* puls-n a1 ran-a a1 ran-b k* ran-s k* raph a1* rhodi a1 rhus-t k* rob ruta k* sabad k* sacch a1 sal-ac kr1 sal-fr sle1• *Sang* k* sapin a1 *Sars* k* sec k* senec c1* *Seneg* k* senn br1 **Sep** k* sieg mg1.de *Sil* k* sin-n sol-t a1 sol-t-ae *Spig* k* spong c1* stann bg2* staph k* **Stram** k* stroph-h ptk1 stry sul-ac sul-i a1* **Sulph** k* **Sumb** k* suprar rly4• *Tab* k* tanac a1 tarent tax k* *Ter* a1* thea a1 ther k* thuj thyr c1* til *Tril-p* bg2* trinit br1 tub k2 uran-n kr1 ust valer k* **Verat** k* *Verat-v* k* verin a1 vesp k* vesp-xyz c2 *Vib* viol-o k* vip k* wies a1 zinc k* zinc-m zinc-p k2 zing [heroin sdj2 lac-mat sst4]
- **morning**: alumn k* **Ars** k* borx h2* *Carb-v* k* *Cocc* *Con* k* culx k2* dios k* kali-c j5.de* kali-n j5.de *Kreos* k* lach j5.de mag-m h2 med k* nat-m k* nit-ac j5.de **Nux-v** k* petr j5.de pitu-gl skp7• plb k* puls k* *Sang* k* sep j5.de staph j5.de stram k* stry k* **Sulph** k*
  - **7** h: dios
  - **8** h: dios a1 ped a1
    - **8**-9 h: phos
  - **air** agg.; in open: mosch k* nux-v k*
  - **bed** agg.; in: carb-v h2 *Con* hr1*
  - **eating**:
    - **amel.**: nux-v
    - **before** | **agg.**: *Calc* k*
    - **while** | **agg.**: lach
  - **house**, on entering: petr k*
  - **rising**, on: **Bry** k* calc h2 **Carb-v** **Cocc** k* *Iod* k* *Kreos* k* *Lac-d* hr1* *Lach* k* nat-m h2 petr j5.de sep k*
    - **quickly** from stooping or turning head: *Sang*
  - **stepping** on the floor: lac-d k2
  - **stool** agg.; during: phys k*
  - **waking**; on: graph a1
- **forenoon**: kali-n j5.de phos k* sep k* staph stram k*
  - **9** h: ped a1
  - **10** h: ven-m jl*
    - **phthisis**; in: *Kali-c* kr1*
  - **11** h: ind *Lach* *Sulph*
    - **11**-13 h: germ-met srj5•
  - **standing** erect agg.: dios
  - **walking** in open air agg.: lycps-v
- **noon**: bov k* cic h1 dios a1 ign h1* sal-fr sle1• vib hr1
- **afternoon**: anac k* *Asar* k* borx colch rsj2• dios k* phys a1 pitu-gl skp7• seneg j5.de* sulph k* thuj a1
  - **13** h: lycps-v
  - **14** h after chill: gels
  - **16** h after mental exertion: rhodi a1
  - **17**.30 h: nux-m
- **evening**: *Aesc-g* hr1* alet am-c k* asaf k* *Calc* k* coff j5.de glon k* *Hep* k* kali-n h2* *Lac-d* hr1* lach j5.de lyc k* lycps-v mosch *Nat-m* k* nux-v k* ozone sde2• phos k* rhus-t j5.de *Sep* k*
  - **18** h: glon
  - **19** h: lycps-v seneg
  - **20**-21 h: *Nux-v*
  - **21** h: mag-m meli rhus-t
  - **cardiac** depression, from: lycps-v
  - **exertion** agg.: nat-m nat-n a1
  - **stiffness** of fingers and arms, with: petr h2
  - **stool** agg.; during: sars a1
  - **undressing**, on: chel k*
- **night**: am-c k* ars j5.de bar-c k* calc j5.de carb-v j5.de dios a1 graph j5.de *Mosch* k* nit-ac k* nux-m *Nux-v* j5.de* sep b4.de* *Sil* k* suprar rly4• ther k* vip j5.de
  - **midnight**: sep k*
    - **before** | **23** h: propr sa3•
    - **after** | **3** h: dios suprar rly4•
- **abortion**:
  - **after**: rosm a1

- **during**: puls bro1
- **accompanied** by:
  - **coldness**; sensation of: coloc b4a.de
  - **constipation**: verat bro1
  - **mental** symptoms (See MIND - Mental symptoms - accompanied - faintness)
  - **nausea**: ail a1 alum alumn kr1 ang kr1* ant-t tl1 *Arg-n* k* *Ars* a1 bar-c bg2 borx bg2* *Bry* bro1 calad kr1* calc k* carb-an st1 carbn-s caust st1 cham k* chel **Cocc** k* coff bg2 coff-t a1 colch bro1 crot-t bg2 fago *Glon* graph k* hep bro1 **Ip** kr1* kali-bi bg2 *Kali-c* bg2* **Lach** k* lob kr1* luna kg1• lyc bg2 mag-m bg2 nat-m **Nux-v** k* op petr st1 picro a1* plan kr1* plat bro1 *Puls* bro1 pulx br1 sep a1* sul-ac sulph k* *Tab* kr1* ther bg2 valer kr1* verat k* verat-v vesp a1*
    - **rising** agg.: luna kg1•
  - **palpitations** (See palpitations - during)
  - ○ **Heart** failure (See CHEST - Heart failure - accompanied - faintness)
  - **Heart**; complaints of (See heart - disease)
  - **Legs**; weakness of (See EXTREMITIES - Weakness - leg - accompanied - faintness)
  - **Teeth**; pain in (See TEETH - Pain - accompanied - faintness)
- **Addison's** disease, in: *Calc* hr1*
- **after** faintness agg.: acon b2.de* ars b2.de* chin b2.de* *Mosch* b2.de* nux-v b2.de* *Op* b2.de* sep b2.de* stram b2.de*
- **afterpains**; at every attack of: hep *Nux-v* k*
- **air**; in open:
  - **agg.**: *Mosch* j5.de* nit-ac h2 *Nux-v* h1*
  - **amel.**: borx h2* crot-c a1 dios a1 tab hr1 trif-p a1
- **amenorrhea**, in: glon kr1
- **anemia**, in: (*↗Anemia)* acet-ac k2* ferr-i k2 *Mosch* kr1 *Spig* kr1
- **anger**; after: *(↗MIND - Anger)* *Cham* st1 *Gels* mosch k2 *Nux-v* kr1* o p wbt• phos gl1.fr• staph kr1* vesp k2*
- **angina** pectoris, in: *(↗heart - disease; heart - pressure; pain - heart)* *Am* hr1* *Hep* hr1* *Spong* hr1*
  - **precordial** anguish; with: *Aml-ns* kr1* *Merc-i-f* st plb a1 tab kr1*
- **anguish**, after: nux-v kr1 verat kr1
- **anxiety**, after: cench k2
- **aperitif**; after drinking:
  - **evening** | **20** h: brucel sa3•
- **ascending**:
  - **hills** | **agg.**: agar
  - **mountains** | **agg.**: *Coca* st
  - **stairs** | **agg.**: aether a1* *Anac* k* iod lycps-v nept-m lsd2.fr plb k*
- **asthma**, from: *Ars* st1 *Atro* hr1* berb st1 kreos st1 lach st1 morph st1
- **bed** agg.; in: caust k* dios k*
- **bending** | **forward** | **agg.**: pitu-gl skp7•
  - **head**:
    - **backward** | **amel.**: ol-an
- **blood**; after loss of: *(↗Loss - blood)* am-caust vh1 chin sf1.de ferr k2 *Ip* sf1.de op k2* tril-p sf1.de
- **blood**, at sight of: *(↗wounds; MIND - Blood; MIND - Unconsciousness - blood)* aloe vh1 **Alum** st1 nux-m k* *Verat* st1
- **blowing** an instrument, when: kali-n h2
- **breakfast** | **after** | **agg.**: bufo naja
  - **before** | **agg.**: *Calc* hr1* cimic hr1 dios hr1 *Kali-c* hr1
- **breathing** deep | **amel.**: asaf
- **cardiopathy**; in (See heart - disease)
- **chest**; with constriction of: acon ars h2
- **chill**:
  - **before**: *Ars* hr1*
  - **during**: acon b7.de* alumn a1* ars k* asar k* bry bg2 *Calc* hr1* calen j5.de cham bg2 chin bg2 **Coff** b7.de* coloc bg2* kali-c j5.de morph st1 **Nux-v** b7.de* op bg2 phos bg2 **Puls** bg2 sapin a1* **Sep** k* stram bg2* valer b7.de* verat bg2
- **chilliness** with: zing kr1
- **church**, in: *(↗crowded - room; kneeling)* *Ign* k2* merc-i-f a1* ozone sde2•
- **closed** room; in: *Acon* k* *Asaf* k* ip *Lach* *Lil-t* hr1 plb ptk1 **Puls** k* *Tab* trif-p a1 vesp k2*
- **closing** the eyes agg.: ant-t bg1
- **coition**:
  - **after**: **Agar** k* **Asaf** k1* *Dig* k* *Nat-p* k* plat bg2 *Sep* k*
  - **during**: murx bro1 orig bro1 *Plat* bg*
    - **women**; in: murx ptk1 orig ptk1 *Plat* ptk1
- **cold**; after taking a: petr k* *Sil* k*
- **cold water** | **amel.**: glon k* vip j5.de
- **coldness** of skin, with: *Camph* hr1* carb-v hr1* *Chin* hr1* *Laur* hr1* mosch hr1* *Tab* hr1* *Verat* hr1*
- **colic**, during intestinal: asaf kr1 *Castm* kr1 *Coll* st1 *Coloc* kr1 hydr st1 *Manc* kr1 *Nux-m* kr1 stram kr1
- **convulsions**; after: ars-s-f hr1* nux-v a1 *Verat* hr1*
- **cough**:
  - **after**: sil h2
  - **between** spells: *Ant-t* kr1*
  - **during** | **agg.**: *Ars* cadm-s cina coff *Cupr* ip kl *Phos* kr1* sep bro1
- **crowded**; in:
  - **room**●: *(↗church; MIND - Fear - crowd; MIND - Fear - narrow)* *Am-c* ambr ars asaf vh bar-c con elaps gk hippoc-k szs2 *Ign* k1* *Lyc* k* nat-c *Nat-m* *Nux-m* k1* *Nux-v* k1* *Phos* *Plb* **Puls** k* sulph
  - **street**: *(↗MIND - Fear - crowd; MIND - Fear - crowd - street; MIND - Fear - going; MIND - Fear - narrow; MIND - Fear - open)* asaf
- **dark** places, in: *(↗MIND - Darkness - agg.; MIND - Light - desire)* *Stram*
- **descending** stairs agg.: ery-a a1 stann hr1*
- **diarrhea**: *(↗Weakness - diarrhea - from)*
  - **after** | **agg.**: *(↗Collapse - diarrhea; Weakness - diarrhea - from)* aloe bro1* ars k* colch sf1.de con bro1 crot-t bro1 *Merc* bro1 *Nux-m* bro1 **Nux-v** kr1* paeon bro1 **Podo** mrr1 sars bro1 *Ter* bro1 verat bro1
  - **before**: ars gard-j vlr2• sulph sumb
  - **during**: aloe bro1* ars bro1* crot-h bro1 crot-t kr1 *Cupr-act* kr1 *Merc* bro1 *Nux-m* kr1* paeon st podo st* *Puls* kr1 sulph bro1 verat st
- **dinner** | **after**:
  - **agg.**: mag-m ptk1 nux-v ptk1
    - **exertion** in open air agg.: am-m *Kali-c* kr1* *Nux-v* kr1*
  - **during** | **agg.**: asaf k* lyc k* *Mag-m* k* *Nux-v* k*
- **diphtheria**; in: *Brom* hr1* *Canth* hr1* kali-chl st kali-m st1 *Lach* st1 *Sulph* hr1*
- **discouraged**, when: ars k*
- **drowsiness**; with: ars
- **drug**, on thinking of: asaf k*
- **dying**; sensation as if: dig br1 vinc ptk1
- **easy**: ign ptk1 mosch ptk1 olnd bg2
- **eating**:
  - **after** | **agg.**: bar-c k* bufo k* *Caust* k* dios hr1* *Kali-bi* hr1* kali-c hr1* *Mag-m* k* mosch mrr1 *Nux-v* k* *Ph-ac* k* phos b4a.de plan k* sang k* sil h2* sul-ac bg2
  - **agg.**: bufo bg2 nux-v bg2 ph-ac bg2 sil bg2 sul-ac bg2
  - **before** | **agg.**: *(↗hunger)* asaf k* bufo crot-c a1 *Culx* vh ignis-alc es2• ind k* lach a1 phos ran-b k* sulph
  - **must** eat: phos k2*
  - **while** | **agg.**: mosch k2*
- **egg**; on smelling freshly beaten: colch
- **emissions** agg.; after: **Asaf** k* ph-ac k*
- **emotions**; from (See MIND - Excitement - faintness)
- **empty** stomach | **amel.**: pitu-gl skp7•
- **endocarditis**, with: ars k2
- **epistaxis**: *(↗hemorrhages)*
  - **before**: *Carb-v* hr1*
  - **from**: *Acon* hr1* *Cann-s* hr1* croc st1 crot-h hr1* *Ip* hr1* *Lach* hr1*
  - **with**: *Calc* bg2* cann-s bg carb-v k* croc bg2* lach gt1*
- **eructations**:
  - **after**:
    - **agg.**: *Arg-n* kr1* *Nux-v*

- **after**: ...
  - **amel.**: mag-m
- **agg.**: Arg-n Carb-v kr1* nux-v kr1*

- **excitement** agg.: Acon k* am-c Asaf k* aster st camph Caust Cham k* cocc bg2 Coff k* croc bg2 glon k2 Ign k* kali-c bg2 Lach mag-m bg2 mosch bg2* Nat-c Nux-m Op Ph-ac k* puls mrr1 samb bg2 Sumb k* Verat k* vesp k2*
- **exertion** agg.: Arn st1 Ars k* bacls-7 fmm1• calc Calc-ar hr1* Carb-v Caust k* Cocc k* ferr k2* glon k2 hyper k* Iod hr1* Lach hr1* Lob hr1* mosch bg2* nat-m nux-v orot-ac rly4• pitu-gl skp7• plan k* plb k* propr sa3• Rhus-t st1 Senec k* Sep k* sulph Ther k* Verat k*
  - **sudden**: bacls-7 fmm1•
- **face**, with:
  - **blue**: morph st
  - **pale**: acon st berb st Cimic hr1* Ip hr1* Lach hr1* Lob hr1* nat-m st nux-v st puls hr1* Stram hr1* Tab hr1*
  - **red**: acon st Ptel hr1*
- **falling**; with: Ars hr1* Camph hr1* helo-s bnm14• Stram hr1*
  - **backward**: Lac-d hr1*
  - **left** side; to: mez kr1*
- **fasting** amel.: alum-sil k2*
- **fever**:
  - **after**: sal-ac hr1*
  - **before**: ars b4a.de* hep b4a.de sep b4a.de sulph b4a.de
  - **during**:
    - **agg.**: Acon Arn k* ars j5.de bell dendr-pol sk4• Dig bro1 Eup-per bg2* Ign bg2* lil-t bg Nat-m k* Nux-v k* op Petr b4a.de* Phos k* Puls hr1* Sep k* sul-ac bro1 sulph bg2* thuj bg2 verat bro1
      - **intermittent**: Phos hr1*
      - **puerperal**: cimic hr1* Coloc hr1*
- **fire**; near: pitu-gl skp7•
- **flatulence**; from: Carb-v mrr1 lyc k2
- **fluids**; after loss of: (↗weakness) ars st1 bar-c j5.de Carb-v kr1* Chin k* Ip bg2* kreos st1 merc st1 nux-m st1 nux-v st1 Ph-ac k1* Tril-p bg2* Verat kr1*
- **flushes** of heat; with: Crot-t kr1 ignis-alc es2• Sep kl Sulph kr1*
- **frequent**: acet-ac br1 alum-p k2 Ars k* Bapt hr1* Both a1 Camph hr1* carbn-s kr1* Hyos hr1* Merc hr1* Merc-cy hr1* Mosch br1 Murx hr1* Op hr1* Phos k* Sulph k*
- **fright**; after: (↗MIND - Ailments - fright) Acon k* Gels k* Ign k* Lach k* Nux-v gl1.fr• Op k* Phos gl1.fr• Staph gl1.fr• Verat k*
- **fruit** amel.; acid: naja
- **gastric** affections, in: (↗pain - stomach) Alumn a1* Arg-n hr1* bufo kr1 carb-v mrr1 dios hr1* Dor hr1* elaps kr1 Kali-bi hr1* Mag-m hr1* Mez k* Nat-s hr1* ol-an ptk1 sang hr1* sin-n hr1 Sulph hr1*
- **grief**; from: Ign hr1* Staph hr1*
- **headache**; during: ang c1 ars a1 Calc kr1* carb-v kr1* castm kr1 Gels kr1* glon graph st hep k2 hippoz kr1 lil-t k2 lyc h2* mez h2* mosch st nat-m st nux-v bro1 sang k2 Sil kr1* stram Sulph kr1* Ter kr1 verat k* zing
- **heat**:
  - **from**: ant-c hr1* berb st1 nux-v st1 petr hr1* sumb a1
  - **then** coldness: Sep k*
- **heated**; when: ip ptk1 tab j5.de*
- **hematemesis**, from: Ars st
- **hemoptysis**, after: sil h2
- **hemorrhages**; from: (↗epistaxis) chin hr1* ferr bro1 ip k2 phos bro1 Tril-p br1 verat ptk1
  - **delivery**; after: Cann-s kr1* Croc kr1* Ip st Tril-p st
  - ○ **Rectum**: Ign kr1* Nux-v kr1*
  - **Uterine**: Apis kr1* Chin kr1* Coc-c st Kreos kr1* merc kr1* Phys kr1* tril-p c1
- **hemorrhoids**; after: chin k2
- **hunger**; from: (↗eating - before - agg.) calam sa3• cocc hr1* crot-c a1* culx k2* cupr sst3• ignis-alc es2• Lyc hr1 oci-sa sk4• Phos psor al2 Sulph k* ulm-c jsj8•
- **hysterical**: (↗MIND - Hysteria - fainting) Acon bro1 agar vh1 am-c k2* apisin bro1 arn kr1* ars asaf bro1 cench k2 Cham k* cimic Cocc k* cupr bro1 Dig kr1* Ign k* kali-ar k2 lac-d lach bro1 Mosch k* Nat-m Nux-m k* Nux-v puls Sep kr1 stict kr1 sumb tarent mtf33 ter
- **indigestion**; from: Carb-v mrr1

- **injury**:
  - **concussion** of brain, from: Hyos kr1*
  - **shock** in; from: (↗wounds; Shock - injuries) arn j5.de atro kr1 Camph kr1 Cham kr1 dig kr1 Hyper kr1
- **kneeling** in church, while: (↗church) Sep k*
- **labor**:
  - **after**: Cann-s st1 Croc st1
  - **during**: Cimic k* cinnm hr1* coff Nux-v k* Puls k* Sec k* Verat
- **leukorrhea**; with: bar-c kr1 cycl kr1 Lach kr1 Nux-m kr1 sulph kr1
- **lights**, from being in a room with many: nux-v k*
- **listening** to reading, from: agar-em a1
- **looking**:
  - **steadily** at any object directly before eye: sumb k*
  - **upward**: tab ptk1
- **lying**:
  - **after** | **agg.**: calad mag-c
  - **agg.**: berb hr1* calad k* Calc hr1 Carb-v hr1* caust j5.de iod lyc k* merc a1 peti a1 pitu-gl skp7• sulph k* sumb a1
  - **amel.**: alumn k* dios k* hedeo st helo-s bnm14• Merc-i-f k* Nux-v k* verat-v a1
  - **side**; on | **agg.**: lyc sil
- **meningitis**; during: Ant-t hr1* Dig hr1* Glon hr1*
- **menopause**; during: Acon kr1* chin bg2* cimic bg2* cocc kr1* Coff kr1* crot-h bro1 ferr bro1 Glon bg2* hydrc kr1* Kali-c kr1* Lach bg2* Mosch kr1* Nit-ac kr1* nux-m bg2* nux-v bg2* Phys kr1 sep bg2* Sulph bg2* tab bg2* tril-p bro1 valer kr1* Verat kr1* viol-t kr1*
- **menses**:
  - **after** | **agg.**: Chin k* Lach Lyc k*
  - **before**:
    - **agg.**: am-c sf1.de ars bro1 chin bro1 cimic hr1* cocc k* ign bro1 lach k* Lyc k* mosch bro1* Mur-ac Murx Nat-m h2* Nux-m k* nux-v k* Sep k* Thuj k* verat bro1 visc c1
      - **pain**; from: arg-n hr1
  - **during**:
    - **agg.**: Acon bg2* apis Arg-n bg2* ars bro1 berb k* Calc k* cham k* chin j5.de* cimic k* Cocc k* glon bg2* hyos b7a.de Ign k* Ip hr1* kali-c bg2 Lach k* laur kr1* lyc b4.de* mag-c ptk1 mag-m k* med hr1 Mosch k* murx st nat-m k* nux-m k* Nux-v k* plb puls k* raph k* Sars k* Sep k* sulph k* thuj bg2 tril-p ptk1 uran-n bg2* verat k* Vib bg2* wies a1*
      - **pain**; from: Cocc kr1* kali-s k* Lap-a k* lyc ptk1 nux-m ptk1 Nux-v kr1* Sars kr1* Sep kr1*
    - **beginning** of menses | **agg.**: merc ptk1 nux-v bg2 sulph b4a.de
  - **suppressed** menses; from: cocc j5.de kali-c bro1 Nux-m br1* op bro1 Stram b7a.de
- **mental** exertion; from: calad Calc kr1 coff kr1* Nux-v kr1* Par kr1
- **metrorrhagia** with: Chin j5.de
- **motion**:
  - **agg.**: Ars k* Bry hr1* Cocc k* Croc st (non:cupr slp) cupr-act a1* Hyos hr1* kali-c k* Lob hr1* nat-hchls a1 Nit-ac k* nux-v j5.de phys k* propr sa3• spig st Spong k* Verat k*
    - **rapid** motion: samb sumb a1
  - **amel.**: jug-c pitu-gl skp7•
- **music**, on hearing: cann-i sumb k*
- **mydriasis**, with: morph st1
- **nausea**:
  - **after**: Kali-bi k*
  - **before**: dig a1 glon a1 Verat hr1*
  - **during** (See accompanied - nausea)
- **nervous**: abies-c bro1 ant-t bro1 aqui bro1 Arg-n bro1 arn bro1 ars bro1 asar bro1 Caul bro1 Caust bro1 cench k2 cham bg2 Chin bro1 Cimic bro1 cocc bg2* coff bg2 croc bg2 Gels bro1 Hyos bro1 kali-c bg2 lach bro1 lat-m bro1 mag-m bg2 Med bro1 mosch bg2* murx bro1 Nux-v bro1 ph-ac bg2 puls bro1 raph bro1 samb bg2 sep bro1 stry bro1 Sul-ac bro1 sulph bro1 tarent bro1 valer bro1 Zinc bro1
- **noise** agg.: ant-c k2 asaf borx k2 lyc k2 merc nat-m k2
- **numbness**, tingling; with: Acon kr1 borx st nat-m st nux-v st

- **odors**; from (See smell; MIND - Sensitive - odors)
- **operation**:
  - **after**: stront-c mrr1
  - **talking** about an operation: alum st
- **pain**; from: *(↗MIND - Sensitive - pain)* *Acon* bg2* ant-t vh1 apis k* ars bg2* asaf k* bism st1 bol-la a1* **Cham** k ●* *Cocc* k* coff bg2 coloc k* *Gels* hr1* **Hep** bg2* iod bg2 lach lp mosch ptk1 *Nux-m* k* *Nux-v* k* oper br1 phos hr1* phyt ran-s bg2* sacch sst1• sil bg2 stront-c br1* *Valer* k* *Verat* bg2* vib bg2* vip bg2
  - **children**; in: sacch sst1•
  - **prick** of a needle, from: calc h2
  - **stool** agg.; during: *Cocc* kr1*
  - ○ **Abdomen**, in: *Cocc* k* *Coll* st1 hydr bro1 plb stram st1
  - **Anus**, in: sulph h2
  - **Ear**, in: *Cur* *Hep* k* *Merc* k*
  - **Head**, in: mez h2 verat-v hr1
  - **Heart**, in: *(↗angina; heart - disease; heart - pressure)* arn *Cact* kr1* **Lach** *Manc* kr1
  - **Occiput**: gels psa
  - **Sacrum**, in: dios a1 hura a1
  - **Sciatic** nerve: cham bro1 hep bro1 morph bro1
  - **Spermatic** cords, in: calc-ar kr1*
  - **Stomach**, in: *(↗gastric)* *Ars* kr1* **Bism** *Coll* cupr-s kr1 *Dios* kr1 laur c1 *Nux-v* puls ran-b c1 ran-s k* sin-n kr1 *Sulph* kr1
  - **Teeth**, in: chin *Puls* verat
  - **Testes**; in: ham c1 *Laur* kr1* plb a1 ust al2
- **palpitations**: *(↗heart - disease)*
  - **after**: am-c gsy1*
  - **during**: **Acon** kr1* *Am-c* bg2* arg-n bg2* beryl tpw5* cact *Cham* bro1 cimic *Cocc* k* crot-h bg2* *Hydr* bg2* hydr-ac bg2* *Iod* *Kalm* kr1 **Lach** k* laur bg2* lil-t bg2* *Manc* kr1 naja mrr1 nat-m bro1 **Nux-m** k* petr k* puls bg2* sul-i k2 tab bg2* ther bg2 *Verat* k* verat-v bg2
- **paroxysmal**: *Mosch* br1
- **periodical**: cact *Coll* hr1* fl-ac lyc k* nit-ac j5.de staph j5.de
  - **day**; every: *Hydr* kr1*
- **perspiration**:
  - **after** | **agg.**: *Apis* kr1* arn a1* *Chin* st1 sal-ac hr1*
  - **amel.**: *Olnd* hr1*
  - **cold**, with: *Bry* hr1* *Camph* hr1* caps hr1* carb-v hr1* *Chin* hr1* **Dig** hr1* helo-s rwt2• *Hydr* hr1* lach st* *Tab* hr1* ther hr1* *Verat* hr1*
  - **during**: agar k* ant-t hr1* apis arn bg2 *Ars* *Bry* b7.de* *Calc* hr1* carb-v dig ptk1 hydr ptk1 hydr-ac a1 hyos *Ign* k* *Lob* hr1* morph st1 *Nux-v* bg2 *Petr* bg2 *Sel* b7a.de* *Sep* hr1* sulph k* ther k2 *Thuj* b4a.de*
  - **feet**; from suppressed perspiration of: *Sil* kr1*
- **pregnancy** agg.; during●: *Bell* *Kali-c* st1 *Nux-m* *Nux-v* *Puls* sec *Sep* *Verat* kr1
  - **motion** of fetus; from slightest: *Lach* kr1*
- **pressure**; from:
  - **stomach**; in: merc-c bg2
  - **waist**; in: *Lac-c* kr1* *Lac-d* hr1 *Merc* st
- **pressure** of tight clothes agg.: kali-n h2
- **prolonged**: *Hydr-ac* k* *Laur* k*
- **puerperal**: cimic hr1* *Coloc* kr1*
- **pulse**:
  - **imperceptible**; with: *Chin* kr1* *Crot-h* kr1* morph st
  - **irregular**: **Dig** kr1* morph st
  - **slow**: **Dig** kr1*
- **raising**:
  - **arms** above head agg.: *Lac-d* k* lach spong k*
  - **head** | **agg.**: apoc k* *Bry* ip
- **reading**:
  - **after**: asaf cycl k* merc-i-f ptk1 tarax
  - **standing** agg.; while: glon k*
- **restlessness**; after: calc
- **riding**:
  - **after**: berb a1 sep a1
  - **agg.**: *Berb* k* cocc st grat k* *Sep* k* sil
- **rising**:
  - **after** | **agg.**: **Carb-v** hr1* *Iod* hr1* op tl1 phyt tl1
  - **agg.**: *(↗sitting - erect - agg.; sitting up)* acon bg2* ambr k* apoc bg2 *Bapt* hr1 *Bry* k* **Cadm-s** bg2* calad k* *Calc* kr1* carb-v bg2 cere-b a1 chel k* cina bg2 cocc bg2 crot-h cupr k* hydrog srj2• ind *Iod* bg2* *Lach* kr1* *Merc-i-f* bg2* neon srj5• olnd bg2 op bg2 *Phyt* bg2* plb k* ran-a a1 rhus-t bg2 vac kr1* vario kr1* *Verat* bg2 verat-v bg2* vib bg2* vip bg2
  - **bed**; from | **agg.**●: acon apoc k2 berb j5.de **Bry** calad *Calc* kr1 *Carb-v* *Cina* colch kl *Iod* k1* nat-m h2 op **Phyt** rhus-t rob sep trom a1
  - **sitting**; from | **agg.**: carb-v h2 staph sumb trom
  - **stooping**; from | **agg.**: sang a1
- **running** upstairs: sumb k*
- **sauna**; entering a: *(↗Warm - room)* *Apis* mrr1
- **scolding**, from: *Mosch* st1
- **sexual** excesses; after: *Dig* hr1* ol-an sf1.de
- **shivering**; during: puls b7.de
- **shock**; after: *Atro* hr1* [resc rcb1]
- **sitting**:
  - **agg.**: iod kali-n nat-s nux-v j5.de
  - **erect** | **agg.**: *(↗rising - agg.)* acon st calad st chin a2 phyt nh8 sep c1
- **sitting** down agg.: bov j5.de kali-n j5.de
- **sitting up** in bed agg.: *(↗rising - agg.)* **Acon** k* arn **Bry** k* calad st carb-v chin sf1.de *Dig* c4* dios *Ip* *Nux-v* **Phyt** fr3* *Ran-b* hr1* *Sep* kr1* sulph verat-v k* *Vib* k* vip sf1.de
  - **suddenly**: ery-a *Verat-v*
- **sleep**:
  - **after** | **agg.**: **Carb-v** hr1* thuj a1
  - **followed** by sleep; faintness: *Nux-m* kr1*
  - **loss** of sleep; from: cocc gk nux-v gk phos gk pitu-gl skp7• syph kr1*
  - **side**; sleeping on left: asaf dig k2
- **smell**; from: *(↗MIND - Sensitive - odors)* **Colch** ptk1* hippoc-k szs2 ign **Nux-v** k* **Phos** k* sang a1
  - **cooking** food; of: *(↗food)* **Colch** ip
  - **eau** de Cologne amel.: sang a1*
  - **eggs**, of: *Colch* kr1
  - **fish**, of: colch
  - **flowers**; of: **Phos** k1* sang k*
  - **food**; of: *(↗cooking)* colch k2
  - **perfume** or vinegar, of: agar kr1*
  - **stool**; from smell of: dios
- **smoking** | **after** | **agg.**: *Caust* hr1* *Lob* hr1*
  - **agg.**: *Ign* hr1* *Ip* hr1* sil k*
- **snoring**, with: stram st1
- **standing** | **after** | **long** time; for a: bacls-7 fmm1•
  - **agg.**●: acon mrr1 **Alum** k* **Alumn** kr1 am-br vh1 apis berb j5.de *Bry* cur st *Dig* dios a1 glon a1 kali-n j5.de lil-t k* luf-op rsj5• lyc j5.de *Nux-m* k* nux-v phyt pitu-gl skp7• rhus-r sil *Sulph* k* *Zinc*
    - **church** during menses; in: *Lyc* *Nux-m* *Puls*
    - **prolapse** of uterus, from: *Lil-t* st
    - **urination** agg.; during: acon kr1*
- **starting** at something falling to the floor, from: merc a1
- **steam** bath; entering a: *(↗Warm - room)* *Apis* mrr1 kali-bi bg2
- **stomach**; sensation of something rising from: am-br k* ars bro1 **Calc** hr1* chin bro1 hydrog srj2• mosch bro1 nux-m bro1 nux-v bro1 ph-ac bro1
- **stool**:
  - **after**:
    - **agg.**: aloe bg2* apis kr1* *Ars* k* *Ars-s-f* k2* *Bism* b7a.de *Bol-la* kr1* *Calc* k1* carb-v bg2 *Cocc* k* colch k* **Con** k* crot-t hr1* cur dig bg2* dios k* gal-ac br1 hydr hr1* kiss a1 *Lyc* k* morph k* nat-s *Nux-m* k* *Phos* k* phyt k* plan k* **Podo** k* sarr bg* sars bg2 sulph k* *Ter* k* *Verat* k*
    - **amel.**: rhodi a1

- before: *Ars* k* dig k* glon k* puls k* samb sars *Sulph* hr1* sumb verat b7.de*
- **during** | **agg.**: aloe ars bg2 borx kr1* colch bg2* coll k* con ptk1 crot-t st1 dios k* *Dulc* hydr bg2 *Merc* b4a.de* *Nux-m* k* nux-v ptk1 ox-ac k* petr b4.de* plan hr1* podo ptk1 *Puls* k* *Sars* k* spig b7.de* stann bg2* stront-c bg2 *Sulph* k* tab bg2 *Verat* b7a.de* verat-v bg*
- **straining** at | **agg.**: verat-v bg2
- **urging** to | **agg.**: *Cocc* k*

- **stooping** agg.: elaps k* pitu-gl skp7* sumb k*
- **storm**; before: petr h2* *Rhod* mrr1
- **stove**, near a: vesp k2
- **sudden**: acon vh1 ant-c k2* camph st1 cham c1 cimic hr1 cycl a1 hydr-ac sf1.de ip ptk1 kali-cy st1 lac-h sze9• mosch a1* op a1 petr h2* *Phos* k* podo bg2* ran-b bg2* rhus-t k* *Sep* k* syph hr1 thuj a1 valer bg2*
- **summer** heat, from: (*↗sunstroke*) *Ant-c* k* *Ip* k*
- **sun**: pitu-gl skp7•
- **sunstroke**; from: (*↗summer*) carb-v mrr1
- **surprise**; from a: gels k2
- **talking** agg.: *Ars* k*
- **temples** with both hands, on rubbing: merc
- **tendency** to: aether a1* arg-n br1 ars-h hr1 asaf hr1 carbn-o a1* carbn-s a1* colch a1* cupr-s a1* cypra-eg sde6.de• dig a1* elaps a1* euph a1* *Hyos* hr1 iod j5.de kali-ox a1* *Magn-gl* k* mosch hr1 nux-m j5.de* ol-an a1* *Sep* hr1 sol-t-ae a1* sulph a1* *Sumb* st1 tab a1* thea a1* urol-h rwt• verat j5.de
  - **morning**: urol-h rwt•
- **tetanic** spasm:
  - **after**: nux-v a1
  - **before**: sul-h a1
- **thunderstorm**; before: petr k* sil k*
- **toilet**; going to | **night**: ozone sde2•
- **transient**: *Carb-v* h2* lach a1 merc a1 *Mur-ac* hr1* nux-m hr1* nux-v h1* petr h2*
- **trembling**; with: asaf a1* caust bg2* hydrog srj2• ignis-alc es2• *Lach* hr1* nux-v st1 petr st1
- **trifles**; from: *Sep* k* sumb ptk1*
- **turning** head agg.: ery-a a1 ptel sang a1
- **urination**:
  - **after** | **agg.**: **Acon** k* all-c k* med
  - **agg.**: stann bg2
  - **during** | **agg.**: acon bg2 *Med* sf1.de* stann sf1.de
- **uterine** complaints; in: *Cimic* kr1* *Cocc* kr1 *Murx* kr1
- **vertigo**; with: (*↗MIND - Unconsciousness - vertigo; VERTIGO - Unconsciousness*) acon b7a.de* alet br1* alum k* apis b7a.de arg-n bg2* ars bar-c b4.de* berb k* brucel sa3• *Bry* k* camph bro1* canth k* *Carb-v* k* cartl-s rly4• *Cham* k* chin bg2 cina bg2 cocc bg2* coff bg2 colch rsj2• con bg2 *Croc* k* cystein-l rly4• eup-per bg2 eup-pur bg ger-i rly4• glon k* helo-s bnm14• *Hep* k* hipp ign b7.de* kali-br a1 lach k* lat-h bnm5• laur b7.de* luna kg1• mag-c k* mez b4.de* mosch k* nat-c bg2 nat-m bg2 nicotam rly4• nux-m bg2 *Nux-v* k* ol-an bg2 olnd bg2 *Op* bg2 paeon *Phos* k* physala-p bnm7• phyt bg2 plac-s rly4• plat b4.de* positr nl2• rhus-t bg2 ribo rly4• sabad k* sel b7a.de* sep b4a.de* sil b4a.de* suis-pan rly4• sulph k* tab bro1* ther ptk1 thuj b4a.de verat bg2 zinc bg2
- **vomiting**:
  - **after**: **Ars** k* bism sf1.de *Cocc* hr1* dig k* elaps *Gamb* k* kali-c h2 **Nux-v** hr1* *Stict* hr1* verat hr1*
  - **amel.**: colch rsj2•
  - **before**: **Ars** hr1* crot-h hr1* **Ip** hr1*
  - **with**: agar hr1* ant-t a1* apom st1 arg-n bg2 bar-c bg2 borx bg2 *Calc* bg2 cham bg2 cocc ptk1 coff bg2 crot-t bg2* graph bg2 **Ip** hr1* kali-bi bg2 *Kali-c* bg2* lach bg2 lyc bg2 mag-m bg2 nit-ac h2 nux-v bg2* *Phyt* hr1* sulph bg2 **Tab** hr1* ther bg2 **Verat** bg2*
- **waking**; on: **Carb-v** k* dios k* graph k* lach ptel k* ther j5.de
- **walking**:
  - **after** | **agg.**: berb k* *Con* hr1* nux-v j5.de* paeon k*
  - **agg.**: acon vh1 aether a1* arn k* *Ars* k* berb j5.de* bov k* *Con* hr1* cur k* dor k* ferr k* get a1 merc gl1.fr* nat-s k* *Verat-v* k*
  - **air**; in open:
    - **after** | **agg.**: *Nux-v*
    - **agg.**: berb j5.de borx j5.de caust h2 lycps-v mosch j5.de seneg k* sep

Faintness – walking – air; in open: ...
    - **amel.**: am-c j5.de
    - **rapidly**; walking: petr
  - **continued** | **amel.**: *Anac*
  - **upstairs**, from going (See ascending - stairs - agg.)
- **warm** | **bathing** | **agg.**: *Lach* k*
  - **room** | **agg.**: *Acon* ant-c kr1* *Apis* mrr1 calc-i k2 ina-i mlk9.de *Ip* k* kreos *Lach* **Lil-t** k1* lyc *Nat-m* nux-v **Puls** k* **Sep** k* spig tab trif-p a1* vesp k2
- **water** on him amel.; by dashing cold: glon a1
- **weakness**; from: (*↗fluids*) ant-t j5.de *Ars* kr1 bism bg2 *Carb-v* j5.de* caust j5.de chin bg2 *Coca* kr1* *Ferr* k* *Hydr* kr1 hydrog srj2• *Lach* kr1 murx bro1 nux-m bg2* nux-v bg2 ran-b kr1 *Sang* k* sep bro1 *Sulph* bro1 *Verat* bg2* zinc bro1 *Zing* k*
- **weather**; from cold: sep
- **well**, feels especially before the attack: psor vh
- **wet**; after getting: *Sep* k*
- **wine** agg.: sumb a1
- **wounds**, from slight: (*↗blood at; injury - shock*) *Verat* k1*
- **writing**; after: calad k* *Calc* hr1* mosch op

○ - **Heart**:
  - **disease**; in: (*↗pressure; angina; pain - heart; palpitations*) *Arn* st *Ars* kr1* *Cact* kr1* *Chel* kr1* *Dig* kr1* *Kali-p* kr1* lach gm1 *Lina* br1 lycps-v kr1* naja mrr1 *Spig* kr1*
  - **pressure** about; with: (*↗disease; angina; pain - heart*) cimic *Manc* kr1 petr k* plb
  - **weakness** of heart, from: am-c bg2 ars kl conv bg2 crat sys dig kl hydr-ac kl lach bg2* laur bg2* verat kl

FAIR complexion (See Complexion - fair)

FALL; tendency to: (*↗EXTREMITIES - Fall liability; VERTIGO - Fall tendency*) anac b2.de* ang b2.de* ars b4.de* asar b2.de* *Bell* b2.de* *Bism* bg2 bov b2.de* *Brom* bg2* calc b4.de* camph b2.de* caps b2.de* *Caust* b2.de* cic b7.de* cina b2.de* *Cocc* b2.de* colch b2.de* coll ptk1 con ptk1 dros b2.de* *Gels* bg2 hell b2.de* hydr-ac bg2 *Hyos* b2.de* *Ign* b2.de* iod b2.de* ip b2.de* kreos ptk1 laur ptk1 m-ambo b2.de* *Mag-c* b2.de* mang b2.de* merc b2.de* nat-c b2.de* nat-m b2.de* nit-ac b4.de* nux-m b2.de* *Nux-v* b2.de* **Ph-ac** b2.de* *Phos* b2.de* plat b2.de* plb b2.de* puls b2.de* rat ptk1 sabad b2.de* sec b2.de* *Sil* bg2 spig b2.de* spong b2.de* *Stann* b2.de* *Stram* b2.de* sulph b2.de* *Verat* bg2
- **consciousness**; with: *Ang* b7.de* camph b7.de* *Cina* b7.de* hell b7.de* m-ambo b7.de* *Mag-c* b4.de* merc b4.de* *Nux-m* b7a.de nux-v b7.de* *Phos* b4.de* *Plat* b4.de* stram b7.de* stront-c bg2 *Sulph* b4a.de
- **cough** agg.; during: (*↗MIND - Unconsciousness - cough - during*) nux-v ptk1 phos ptk1
- **unconsciousness**; with: *Aur* b4a.de *Bell* b4.de* **Calc** b4.de* *Camph* b7.de* caust b4.de* cic b7.de* *Cina* b7a.de cocc b7.de* cupr b7.de* glon bg2 hydr-ac bg2 *Hyos* b7.de* *Ip* b7.de* lach b7.de* laur b7.de* plb b7.de* sec b7.de*

FALLING APART; sensation as if: agar bg2 arg-n bg2 bapt bg2 calc-p bg2 sulph bg2 *Tril-p* bg2

FALLING; sensation of: bell bg2* crot-t bg2 guaj bg2 mosch bg2 thuj ptk1
- **away**: bar-c bg2
- **forward**:
  - **something** | **Internal** parts: dig b2.de* sulph b2.de* verat b2.de*
- **out**: *Bell* ptk1 cocc ptk1 laur ptk1 *Lil-t* ptk1 nux-v ptk1 podo ptk1 sep ptk1

○ - **Internal** parts; of: agn b2.de* bell b2.de* bov b2.de* bry b2.de* con b2.de* graph b2.de* kali-c b2.de* kreos b2.de* lyc b2.de* m-arct b2.de* merc b2.de* mosch b2.de* nat-c b2.de* nux-v b2.de* *Plat* b2.de* plb b2.de* ran-b b2.de* *Sep* b2.de* spig b2.de* staph b2.de* *Sulph* b2.de* thuj b2.de* zinc b2.de*

FALLS (See Injuries)

FALSE STEP; at a: | **agg.**: anac b4a.de ars b4.de *Bry* b7.de *Caust* b4.de* *Led* b7.de* *Ph-ac* b4a.de phos b4.de *Puls* b7.de *Rhus-t* b7a.de seneg b4.de spig b7.de sulph b4.de valer b7.de

FAMILY HISTORY of: (*↗History*)
- **alcoholism**: (*↗MIND - Ailments - alcoholism; MIND - Alcoholism*) absin gmm1.fr* aethyl rma2 asar bro1* carc mlr1• lach mp1* med sne* nux-v rma2 psor a* ran-b gmm1.fr* sars sne sil rma2 staph mrr1* sul-ac bro1* sulph a* *Syph* a* tub a*

- **alcoholism**: ...
  - • **children**; in: | **infants**; in: absin gmm1.fr* aethyl gmm1.fr* syph mg*
- **allergies**: calc rma2 lyc rma2 sulph rma2
- **anemia**: carc sp1*
- **aortic** complaints: aur zs4.fr* bar-c zs4.fr* merc zs4.fr* syph zs4.fr*
- **apoplexy**: *Acon* bro1 arn bro1 ars bro1 aur zs4.fr* bar-c bro1* *Bell* bro1 calc-f bro1 *Gels* bro1 *Glon* bro1 gua bro1 hyos bro1 *Lach* bro1 laur bro1 merc zs4.fr* *Nux-v* bro1 *Op* bro1 *Phos* bro1 stront-c bro1 syph zs4.fr* verat-v hr1
- **asthma**: bac rma2 carc fb* lyc dmd1.fr* med ghs1* merc rma2 nat-s mta1* psor abm2.fr* sulph rma2 thyr rma2 tub knr1.de*
- **cancer**: brom cda1* calc-ar dgt1 carb-an samkn *Carc* br1* con rmk1• cund gw1* med rma2 sacch rma2 *Scir* rmk1• *Trif-p* br1
- **chest** complaints: bac c1*
- **chicken** pox: carc sk1•
- **diabetes** mellitus: (↗*Diabetes mellitus)* carc fb* sacch sst1* thuj klr1*
- **eczema**: carc rma2 lyc dmd1.fr* psor al1* sulph bl* thuj bl* tub mir1*
  - • **accompanied** by | **urination** at night; involuntary (See BLADDER - Urination - involuntary - night - accompanied - eczema)
- **emotions**: *Plut-n* srj7•
- **goitre**: dros tl1 tub tl1
- **gonorrhea**: *Med* dry1* *Thuj* rma2
- **gout**: calc dmd1.fr* lyc dmd1.fr*
- **heart** disease; early: *Med* mrr1
- **hemiplegia**: verat-v hr1
- **hepatitis**: toxo-g jl2
- **insanity**: carc dy* syph cdh1*
- **lung** complaints: lob samkn
- **malaria**: carc sk1• **Chin** mrr1* *Nat-m* mrr1*
- **measles**: carc sk1•
- **medicine**; abuse of allopathic: bar-c zs4.fr* graph zs4.fr* med zs4.fr* sil zs4.fr* thuj zs4.fr*
- **mumps**: carc sk1•
- **numerous** serious diseases; of: *Carc* mlr1•
- **paraplegia**: verat-v hr1
- **respiratory** complaints: bac bl* tub bl*
- **rheumatism**: sep nh4
- **skin**; complaints of: aur rma2 bac rma2 *Sulph* mg* zinc mg*
- **suicidal** deaths: carc dy* syph cdh1*
- **sycosis**: (↗*Sycosis)* bar-c zs4.fr* graph zs4.fr* *Med* mnc1* sil zs4.fr* *Thuj* zs4.fr*
- **syphilis**: (↗*History - syphilis; Syphilis)* aethi-a c1 aur rma2 bar-c rma2 calc-f rma2 carc skb1* *Fl-ac* zs4.fr* merc zs4.fr* nat-s mta1* nit-ac zs4.fr* phyt mrr1* sulph mp1* *Syph* cda1* thuj awy2*
- **tuberculosis**: acet-ac gsk1* agar br1 ars-i rma2 *Bac* bn* carc sp1* dros tl1* kali-c br1* lob mrr1 mag-c kr* pert jl2 phos mrr1* senec mg* seneg bnk* sep br1 spong br1* stann br1 sulph gsk1* ther br1* thuj rma2 *Tub* bn* *Tub-a* rma2 *Tub-d* rma2 *Tub-k* rma2 *Tub-m* jl2* *Tub-r* rma2 *Tub-ro* wl1* *Tub-sp* rma2
  - • **accompanied** by | **diarrhea** (See RECTUM - Diarrhea - tuberculosis - family)
- **typhoid** fever: carc sk1• parathyr jl2
- **ulcers** of stomach: carc fb*
- **vaccination**; repeated: bar-c zs4.fr* graph zs4.fr* med zs4.fr* sil zs4.fr* thuj zs4.fr*
- **whooping** cough: carc mlr1•

FANNED; being: (↗*Air; draft - sensation)*
- **agg.**: lyss mrr1 mez ptk1
- **amel.**: ant-t ptk1 apis ptk1 *Arg-met* bro1 arg-n ptk1 bapt ptk1 *Carb-v* bro1* *Chin* bro1* chlol ptk1 crot-h ptk1 ferr ptk1 hist jl kali-n ptk1 lac-leo hm2• lach bro1* med bro1* sec ptk1* xanth ptk1
- **desire** to be: ant-t mrr1 apis bg2 ars bg2 bapt bg2 **Carb-v** bg2* caust bg2 chin bg2* chlol c1* chlor bg2 ferr lp glon k2* hist vml3• kali-n bg2* lach bg2* lyc bg2 med bg2* mim-p skp7* nux-m bg2 petr-ra shn4• positr nl2• puls bg2 *Sec* bg2* sulph hr1* tab bg2 zinc bg2
  - • **cough**; during (See COUGH - Accompanied - fanned)
  - • **rapidly**: carb-v br1*
  - • **sleep**; to: pitu-gl skp7•
  - • **slowly**: chin mtf33 lach mtf33

FASTING:
- **agg.**: acon k* aloe alum k* am-c k* *Am-m* b2.de* *Ambr* k* anac b2.de* ars k* *Bar-c* k* bar-i k2 bov k* brass-n-o srj5• bry b2.de* cact bg2 **Calc** k* calc-i k2 cann-s k* canth k* *Carb-ac Carb-an* k* carb-v k* castm bg2 caust k* *Chel* k* chin k* cina k* *Coc-c* **Croc** k* dios c1* ferr k* ferr-p *Fl-ac* ptk1 gran *Graph* k* hell k* *Hep* k* *Ign* k* **Iod** k* *Kali-c* k* *Kola* stb3• kreos k* **Lac-ac** stj*• **Lach** k* laur k* lyc k* mag-c k* mag-m k* merc k* *Mez* k* nat-c k* nat-m brm nat-p k2 nit-ac k* *Nux-v* k* petr k* *Phos* k* **Plat** k* **Plb** k* *Psor* k* puls k* **Ran-b** k* ran-s k* rhod k* rhus-t k* *Rumx Sabad* k* **Sep** k* *Spig* k* **Staph** k* stront-c b2.de* *Sulph* k* **Tab** k* *Tarax* k* teucr k* *Valer* k* verat k* *Verb* k* vero-o rly4• [am-caust stj2 astat stj2 aur stj2 aur-m stj2 aur-s stj2 bar-br stj2 bar-met stj2 bism-sn stj2 caes-met stj2 *Calc-lac* stj2 calc-sil stj2 cinnb stj2 *Ferr-lac* stj2 ferr-sil stj2 hafn-met stj2 irid-met stj2 *Kali-i* stj1 kali-sil stj2 lanth-met stj2 *Lith-i* stj2 *Mag-i* stj1 mag-sil stj2 mang-sil stj2 merc-d stj2 *Merc-i-f* stj2 *Nat-i* stj1 *Nat-lac* stj2 nat-sil stj2 osm-met stj2 plb-m stj2 plb-p stj2 polon-met stj2 rhen-met stj2 sil stj2 sil-met stj2 tant-met stj2 thal-met stj2 tung-met stj2 *Zinc-i* stj2]
- **amel.**: (↗*Emaciation)* agar b2.de* alum b2.de* alum-sil k2* am-m b2.de* ambr b2.de* anac b2.de* ant-c b2.de* arn b2.de* ars b2.de* asaf b2.de* bar-c b2.de* bell b2.de* borx b2.de* *Bry* b2.de* calc b2.de* calc-sil k2* caps b2.de* carb-an b2.de* carb-v b2.de* *Caust* b2.de* **Cham** b2.de* *Chin* b2.de* cocc b2.de* **Con** b2.de* cycl b2.de* *Dig* b2.de* euph b2.de* ferr b2.de* graph b2.de* hell b2.de* hep b2.de* hyos b2.de* ign b2.de* iod b2.de* *Kali-c* b2.de* kali-n b2.de* kali-p k2* kali-s k2* lach b2.de* laur b2.de* lyc b2.de* mag-c b2.de* mang b2.de* nat-c b2.de* **Nat-m** b2.de* nit-ac b2.de* *Nux-m* b2.de* nux-v b2.de* par b2.de* petr b2.de* *Ph-ac* b2.de* phos b2.de* plb b2.de* puls b2.de* rhod b2.de* rhus-t b2.de* ruta fd4.de sabin b2.de* sars b2.de* sel b2.de* sep b2.de* *Sil* b2.de* stann b2.de* stront-c b2.de* sul-ac b2.de* sulph b2.de* thuj b2.de* tritic-vg fd5.de valer b2.de* verat b2.de* *Zinc* b2.de* [*Bar-i* stj2]

FAT PEOPLE (See Obesity)

FATIGUE (See Weariness)

FATTY DEGENERATION: (↗*Degeneration)* *Ars* bro1 aur bro1 *Cupr* bro1 kali-c bro1 *Phos* bro1 vanad bro1
- O - **Blood** vessels; of: phos br1*
- **Glands**: kali-s k2
- **Joints**: pic-ac tl1
- **Organs**: *Ars* ptk1 **Aur** kr1* *Calc-ar* kr1 cupr ptk1 kali-c br1* *Lac-d* kr1 *Lyc* ptk1 mang ptk1 merc ptk1 **Phos** kr1* vanad ptk1
- **Tissues**; of: *Phos* br1

FEASTING (See Reveling)

FEATHER BED agg.: *Asaf* cocc k* *Coloc* k* led k* lyc k* **Mang** k* *Merc* k* *Psor* k* *Sulph* k*

FEATHERS (See Dust)

FEEL every muscle and fibre; as if she could: sep
- **right** side; of her (See MIND - Delusions - body - fibre)

FEVER:
- **after**: ant-c b2.de* ant-t b2.de* arn b2.de* **Ars** b2.de* *Bell* b2.de* bry b2.de* carb-v b2.de* **Chin** b2.de* cina b2.de* dig b2.de* *Hell* b7a.de *Hep* b2.de* kali-c b2.de* nat-m b2.de* *Nux-v* b2.de* phos b2.de* puls b2.de* sep b2.de* sil b2.de* staph b7a.de verat b2.de*
- **before**: acon b2.de* ant-c b2.de* ant-t b2.de* *Arn* b2.de* **Ars** b2.de* bar-c b2.de* bell b2.de* bry b2.de* *Calc* b2.de* caps b2.de* *Carb-v* b2.de* caust b2.de* **Chin** b2.de* *Cina* b2.de* cocc b2.de* ferr b2.de* graph b2.de* hep b2.de* hyos b2.de* ign b2.de* *Ip* b2.de* kali-c b2.de* kali-n b2.de* lach b2.de* lyc b2.de* mag-c b2.de* merc b2.de* nat-c b2.de* nat-m b2.de* nit-ac b2.de* nux-v b2.de* ph-ac b2.de* phos b2.de* **Puls** b2.de* rhod b2.de* *Rhus-t* b2.de* ruta b2.de* sabad b2.de* sabin b2.de* samb b2.de* sep b2.de* sil b2.de* spig b2.de* spong b7.de *Sulph* b2.de* *Verat* b2.de*
- **during**:
  - • **agg.**: acon b2.de* agar b2.de* alum b2.de* am-c b2.de* am-m b2.de* ambr b2.de* anac b2.de* ang b2.de* *Ant-c* b2.de* ant-t b2.de* arn b2.de* **Ars** b2.de* aur b2.de* bar-c b2.de* bell b2.de* borx b2.de* bov b2.de* *Bry* b2.de* calad b2.de* *Calc* b2.de* canth b2.de* caps b2.de* carb-v b2.de* caust b2.de* *Cham* b2.de* **Chin** b2.de* cina b2.de* cocc b2.de* coff b2.de* con b2.de* croc b2.de* dig b2.de* dros b2.de* dulc b2.de* euph b2.de* *Ferr* b2.de* graph b2.de* hell b2.de* hep b2.de* hyos b2.de* ign b2.de* iod b2.de* *Ip* b2.de* *Kali-c* b2.de* kali-n b2.de* kreos b2.de* lach b2.de* laur b2.de* led b2.de* *Lyc* b2.de* mang b2.de* meny b2.de merc b2.de* mez b2.de* mosch b2.de* mur-ac b2.de* nat-c b2.de* *Nat-m* b2.de*

- **during** – **agg.**: ...
  nit-ac b2.de* nux-m b2.de* **Nux-v** b2.de* *Op* b2.de* petr b2.de* ph-ac b2.de* *Phos* b2.de* plat b2.de* *Puls* b2.de* ran-b b2.de* rheum b2.de* rhod b2.de* *Rhus-t* b2.de* ruta b2.de* sabad b2.de* samb b2.de* sars b2.de* sec b2.de* *Sel* mrr1 **Sep** b2.de* sil b2.de* spig b2.de* staph b2.de* stram b2.de* stront-c b2.de* sul-ac b2.de* *Sulph* b2.de* tarax b2.de* teucr b2.de* thuj b2.de* valer b2.de* verat b2.de* zinc b2.de*
  - **amel.**: chinin-s mrr

FIBROSITIS (See Connective; Pain - rheumatic; EXTREMITIES - Pain - rheumatic)

FINAL STAGE OF A DISEASE (See Euthanasia)

FISTULAE: (↗*Abscesses)* alum c1* aur-m c1* bac c1* bar-m c1* berb c1* both a1 bry sf1.de* bufo kr1 cact c1* *Calc* c1* *Calc-f* sf1.de* calc-hp sf1.de *Calc-p* c1* calc-s c1* *Calen* c1* carb-v sf1.de* *Caust* c1* con sf1.de* cop c1* cund c1* eucal c1* *Fl-ac* c1* *Hep* hr1* hydr c1* iris c1* kali-bi gk kali-c ptk1 kreos sf1.de lach sf1.de **Lyc** ptk1 maland c1* mez k2* myris br1 nat-c ptk1 *Nat-s* hr1* *Nit-ac* c1* ol-j c1* petr c1* *Phos* hr1* puls sf1.de* pyrog c1* querc c1 querc-r c2 **Sil** hr1* stram ptk1 stront-c sf1.de *Sulph* k2* syph k2* thuj sf1.de *Tub* c1* tub-k c1 [kali-f stj1 mag-f stj1]
- **abscess**; fistulous: **Calc-s** c1* *Nat-s* hr1*
- **chronic**: stram mtf33
- **operation**; after: *(↗Injuries - operation - ailments)* berb k2 calc k2 calc-p c1* caust k2 graph k2 sil k2 sulph k2 thuj k2
- ○ - **Bones**, of: ang sf1.de* *Asaf* sf1.de* aur sf1.de bufo kr1 calc-f bg2* calc-hp bg2* calc-p mg1.de calc-sil mg1.de fl-ac mg1.de *Hep* bg2* lyc sf1.de merc sf1.de mez *Nat-s* kr1* *Ol-j* kr1 phos bg2* **Sil** bg2* stront-c mtf11 succ-ac mtf11 tub mtf11 tub-m jl2
- **Glands**: cist sf1.de lyc sf1.de merc sf1.de nit-ac sf1.de *Phos* phyt sf1.de *Sil* *Sulph*
- **Joints**: *Calc* hep ol-j k* **Phos** k* **Sil** *Sulph*
- **Skin**; with ulcers of: *Agar* ant-c ars *Asaf* aur bar-c *Bell* **Bry** **Calc** calc-m sf1.de *Calc-p* calc-s carb-ac *Carb-v* carbn-s **Caust** chel *Cinnb* clem *Con* elaps gk *Fl-ac* *Hep* *Hippoz* *Kali-bi* gk kreos *Lach* j5.de led **Lyc** *Merc* mez *Mill* kr1 nat-c *Nat-m* nat-p *Nit-ac* *Petr* ph-ac j5.de **Phos** **Puls** rhus-t ruta sabin sel sep **Sil** stann j5.de *Staph* stram *Sulph* *Thuj*

FLABBY feeling: *(↗Relaxation - physical; Weakness; Weariness)* *Acon* k* agar k* agn k2 am-m k* ambr k* ant-t k* arg-met k* arn k* **Ars** k* asaf k2 asar k* aur-m-n sne *Bar-c* k* bar-s k2 bell k* bov k* bry k* **Calc** k* *Calc-p* k* calc-s calc-sil k2* canth k* **Caps** k* carb-an k* carb-v k* **Caust** k* *Cham* k* *Chel* k* chin k* chinin-ar k2 cic k* cina k* clem coff k* cory br1 **Croc** k* *Cycl* k* *Dig* k* euph k* euphr k* *Ferr* *Fl-ac* graph k* hep k* **Ign** k* iod k* *Ip* k* *Kali-ar* *Kali-c* k* kali-n k* kali-p kali-s laur k* **Lyc** k* m-ambo b2.de m-arct b2.de mag-c k* mag-m k* meny k* merc k* merc-d bg *Mosch* k* mur-ac k* **Nat-c** k* nat-m b2.de nat-p k2 nat-sil fd3.de• nit-ac k* nux-m k* *Nux-v* k* olnd k* ozone sde2• par k* petr k* **Phos** k* *Plat* k* *Psor* puls k* rhod k* rhus-t k* *Sabad* k* sabin k* seneg k* *Sep* sil k* spong k* *Staph* k* stront-c k* **Sulph** k* *Tarax* k* teucr k* *Thuj* k* tril-p c1 tritic-vg fd5.de vanil fd5.de **Verat** k* *Zinc* k*
- ○ - **Hard** parts, in: bar-s k2* caust k* *Merc* k* mez k* *Nit-ac* k* nux-m k*
- **Internally**: *(↗Faintness)* *Calc* k* cypra-eg sde6.de• kreos k* **Sep** k*
- **Muscles**: *Aeth* ptk1 ant-t ptk1 calc ptk1 caps ptk1 carb-ac ptk1 *Chin* ptk1 cocc ptk1 colch ptk1 *Gels* ptk1 *Lyc* ptk1 mur-ac ptk1 ph-ac ptk1 phos ptk1 stram ptk1 sulph ptk1

FLATULENCE agg. (See Flatus - amel.)

FLATUS; PASSING:
- **agg.**: am-br c1* chin gka1* cocc bg2* *Fl-ac* bg2*
- **amel.**: acon k* all-c aloe k* ambr k* anac k* ant-t k* arg-met bg2 *Arg-n* k* arn k* ars bg2 asaf k* asar k* aur k* aur-s k2 bell bg2 bism k* borx k* bov bg2 bry k* but-ac sp1 *Calc* bg2 calc-p k* canth k* caps k* carb-an bg2 **Carb-v** k* *Carbn-s* caust bg2 *Cham* k* chel *Chin* k* cic k* cob-n sp1 *Cocc* k* coff k* *Colch* *Coloc* k* con k* corn bro1 crot-t k* eup-per euphr bg2 *Fl-ac* bg2 gels bg2 glycyr-g cte1• *Graph* k* grat bg2* guaj k* hell bg2 hep k* hom-xyz mgm• hyos k* *Ign* k* iris bro1 jug-r vml3• kali-bi bg2 kali-c k* kali-chl bg2 kali-n bro1 kali-p k2 kali-s kali-sil k2 kola stb3• lach k* laur k* **Lyc** k* m-ambo b2.de* m-arct b2.de* m-aust b2.de mang bg2 marb-w es1• meny k* *Merc-c* bg2 mez k* *Moni* rfm1• nat-m k* nat-n bg2 **Nat-s** k* nept-m lsd2.fr nit-ac k* nux-m k* **Nux-v** k* orot-ac rly4• ox-ac k2 *Ph-ac* k* *Phos* k* plat k* *Plb* k* psor bg2 **Puls** k* rheum k* *Rhod* k* rhus-t k* rumx k2 ruta k* sabin k* **Sang** k* scop ptk1 sel b2.de* sep b2.de* sil b2.de* *Spig* b2.de* spong b2.de* squil b2.de* **Staph** b2.de* stram k* **Sulph** k* teucr k* thuj k* *Verat* k* verb k* viol-t bg2 zinc k* zinc-p k2
- **not** amel.: arg-n tl1* *Camph* h1* **Cham** hr1* **Chin** k* cocc h1* graph h2* mang h1*

FLEXIBILITY:
- **want** of (= stiffness):
  - ○ • **Joints**: am-m b2.de ambr b2.de anac b2.de ang b2.de ars b2.de aur b2.de *Bell* b2.de bov b2.de bry b2.de calc b2.de canth b2.de *Caps* b2.de *Carb-an* b2.de carb-v b2.de *Caust* b2.de cham b2.de chel b2.de chin b2.de cina b2.de *Cocc* b2.de *Coloc* b2.de con b2.de dig b2.de dros b2.de dulc b2.de euph b2.de euphr b2.de *Graph* b2.de hell b2.de hep b2.de hyos b2.de ign b2.de *Kali-c* b2.de kali-n b2.de lach b2.de led b2.de *Lyc* b2.de m-arct b2.de m-aust b2.de merc b2.de mez b2.de nat-c b2.de nat-m b2.de nux-m b2.de nux-v b2.de **Petr** b2.de ph-ac b2.de plb b2.de *Puls* b2.de ran-b b2.de rheum b2.de rhod b2.de *Rhus-t* b2.de ruta b2.de sabin b2.de sars b2.de sec b2.de **Sep** b2.de sil b2.de stann b2.de staph b2.de sul-ac b2.de *Sulph* b2.de thuj b2.de verat b2.de zinc b2.de

FLOATING; as if: abrot bg2 acon bg2* agar bg2 am-c bg2 arg-n ptk1 asar bg2* *Bell* bg2 bism bg2 bov bg2 bufo bg2 calc-ar ptk1 calc-s bg2 cann-xyz bg2* caps bg2 caust bg2 chin bg2 cimic bg2 clem bg2 cocc ptk1 coff ptk1 dig bg2 *Euon* bg2 *Glon* bg2 hura bg2 hyos ptk1 hyper bg2* iod bg2 kali-bi bg2 kali-c bg2 kali-n bg2 *Lac-c* bg2* lach bg2* lact-v bg2 lyc bg2 mag-c bg2 mez bg2 nat-m bg2* nit-ac bg2 **Nux-m** bg2* nux-v bg2 op ptk1 petr bg2 *Ph-ac* ptk1 phos bg2 phys bg2* rheum bg2 sars bg2 sep b4a.de sil bg2 spig bg2* stann bg2 stict bg2* stram bg2* *Sulph* bg2 tell bg2 ter bg2 thuj bg2* valer bg2* verb bg2 visc sp1 xanth bg2 zinc-i ptk1

FLORID complexion (See Complexion - florid)

FLOWING (See Trickling)

FLU (See Influenza)

FLUID RETENTION (See Dropsy - general)

FLUIDS (See Loss - fluids)

FLUSHES (See Heat - flushes)

FLUTTERING (See Vibration)

FLYING in an airplane agg. (See Aviator's)

FOLDING arms: | **agg.**: staph b7.de

FOOD and DRINKS: *(↗Allergic; STOMACH - Disordered; STOMACH - Indigestion)*
- **acids** (See sour drinks)
- **alcoholic** drinks:
  - • **agg.**: absin stx1 acet-ac stx1 acon k* adam srj5• aesc-g stx1 aeth c1 *Agar* k* agav-t jl3* aids nl2• ail vh1 alco stx1 aloe sf1.de* alum k* alum-p stx1 alum-sil stx1 alumn *Am-c* bg2* am-m k* ambr stx1 anac k* ang bt3* anis kr1 *Ant-c* k* ant-t k2* anthraci stx1 apis stx1 apoc c1* apom bt3 aran-ix mg1.de* arg-met stj2* *Arg-n* k* arn k* **Ars** k* arum-i stx1 **Asar** k* astac c1* aur cp1* **AUR-M** mg1.de aur-m-n wbt2• aven br1* bamb-a stx1 **Bar-c** k* *Bell* k* ben-d c1 benz-ac vml3• berb kr1* bism sf1.de* borx k* bov k* brucel sa3• bry c1 bufo stx1 cadm-s k* calad stx1 *Calc* k* *Calc-ar* calc-f mg1.de* calc-s stx1 calc-sil k2* *Cann-i* bt3 caps br1 *Carb-ac* ld1.de* carb-an k* *Carb-v* k* *Carbn-s* k* card-m bt3* caust k* cerev-lg mtf11 *Chel* k* chim-m c1* *Chin* k* chinin-m br1 chir-fl gya2 chlol k* chlor stx1 cic stx1 cimic ptk1 cina stx1 coc-c stx1 *Coca* kr1* cocc k* *Coff* k* *Coloc* stx1 *Con* k* cor-r kkb cortiso sp1 crat c1 *Crot-h* k* cupr stx1 cupr-ar stx1 daph stx1 *Dig* k* dulc fd4.de eup-per hr1 *Ferr* kr1 ferr-i c1* fl-ac bg2* gaul stx1 gels k* gink-b sbd1*• *Glon* kr1* gran c1* grat k2 guar c1* ham fd3.de• hed sp1 *Hell* bg2 hep k* hippoz c1* hyos k* *Ign* k* ignis-alc es2• ina-i mlk9.de kali-bi k* *Kali-br* kr1 kali-m stx1 kali-n stx1 *Lac-e* hrn2• **Lach** k* lat-m wm2 laur k* *Led* k* *Lob* c1* *Luna* kg1*• *Lyc* k* mand mg1.de* *Merc* j5.de* mez stx1 naja k* *Nat-c* k* *Nat-m* k* nat-p stx1 nit-m-ac br1 *Nux-m* k* **Nux-v** k* **Op** k* osm stx1 ozone sde2• paull vml3* *Petr* k* petr-ra shn4• phasco-ci rbp2 phel c1 *Phos* ptk1* phyt bt3* pic-ac stx1 psil stx1 *Puls* k* querc c1 **Ran-b** k* rauw stx1 *Rhod* k* *Rhus-t* k* rumx br1 *Ruta* k* sabad k* sal-al blc1• *Sang* sars k2 *Sec* stx1 **Sel** k* sep k* *Sil* k* *Spig* k* spong fd4.de stann stx1 staph stx1 *Stram* k* stront-c k* stroph-h k* succ-ac vml3• **Sul-ac** k* **Sulph** k* sumb stx1 symph fd3.de• *Syph* kr1* tab ter c1* thea mg1.de thuj trinit br1 tritic-vg fd5.de tung-met bdx1• vanil fd5.de verat k* zinc k* zing kr1* [alumin-s stj2 am-br stj2 am-caust stj2 am-f stj2 am-p stj1 am-s stj1 ant-m stj2 ant-met stj2 arg-p stj2 ars-met stj2 aur-s stj2 cadm-m stj2 chr-s stj2 cinnb stj2 cob stj2 cob-m stj2 cob-p stj2 ferr-sil stj2 gal-s stj2 kali-ar stj2 kali-sil stj2 lith-c stj2 lith-s stj2 mag-sil stj2 mang-p stj2 mang-sil stj2 moly-met stj2 nat-ar stj2 nat-sil stj2 nicc-s stj2 oxyg stj2 sil-met stj2 stront-m stj2 stront-met stj2 titan-s stj2]

- **agg.**: ...
  - **hangover**; excessive: acet-ac c1 aesc-g stx1 *Agar* br1 anis stx1 ant-t br1 apom br1 *Ars* br1 asar br1 astac c1 aur br1 calc-ar br1 carb-v br1 carbn-s br1 card-m br1 coca br1 cocc br1 *Luna* kg1• nux-v br1* olib-sac wmh1 plat-m mtf11 positr nl2• querc br1 *Ran-b* br1 stry br1 sul-ac br1 sulph br1 *Verat* br1 [heroin sdj2]
  - **intoxicated**; easily: *(↗beer - agg. - intoxicated; Intoxication)* adam srj5• aids nl2• alum bg2 bov bg2* chinin-m c1* **Con** bg2* haliae-lc srj5• lac-h htj1• luna kg1• naja a1 nat-sil fd3.de• nux-v sne ozone sde2• positr nl2• ruta fd4.de sal-fr sle1• tritic-vg fd5.de vanil fd5.de *Zinc* kr1*
- **ailments** from: *Agar* bro1 alumn c2 ant-c bro1 apom bro1 **Ars** bg2* asar bro1 aur c2* calc c2 calc-ar bro1 *Carb-v* bg2* *Carbn-s* br1* card-m bro1 coca bro1 cocc bro1 coff bg2 colch bro1 eup-per bro1 ferr-i c2 guar c2 hydr bro1 ip bro1 *Kali-bi* bg2 lach bro1 led bg2* *Lob* bro1 lyc bro1 **Nux-v** bg2* positr nl2• querc bro1 querc-r-g-s br1 *Ran-b* br1* ruta fd4.de sep c2 stry bro1 **Sul-ac** bg2* *Sulph* bg2* tritic-vg fd5.de *Verat* bro1
- **amel.**: *(↗MIND - Timidity - alcohol)* acon ptk1 agar ptk1 androc stx1 arg-n stx1 bufo stx1 canth ptk1* castm stx1 *Con* ptk1 dicha mg1.de **Gels** st* *Granit-m* es1• hell stx1 ign stx1 kali-s fd4.de kreos stx1 lach ptk1 naja stx1 nat-m mrr1 op ptk1 phos stx1 sel ptk1 sep stx1 sul-ac b4.de* thea stx1 [nat-caust stj2]
- **aversion**: ail kr1* alco a1* ang bg* ant-t k* arn stx1 ars ars-met a1* ars-n a bell bry sf1.de* calc ld1.de* calc-ar ld1.de* carb-v bt3 cham sf1.de* chin sf1.de* cocc sf1.de* con tl1 cypra-eg sde6.de• gink-b sbd1*• hipp gsw1 *Hyos* k* ign k* ignis-alc es2• kali-s fd4.de lac-h sze9• lec ld1.de* lyc gk manc mand mg1.de* melal-alt gya4 merc k* nat-sil fd3.de• nux-v k* ph-ac phos ld1.de* phyt st* positr nl2• psor ld1.de* puls stx1 ran-b tl1* *Rhus-t* k* ruta fd4.de sacch-a fd2.de• sil bro1* spig sf1.de* spong sf1.de* stram stroph-h c1* *Sul-ac* ld1.de* sulph sf1.de* symph fd3.de• thiop vml3• tritic-vg fd5.de tung-met bdx1• zinc sf1.de* [am-c stj1 am-m stj1 am-p stj1 ant-c stj2 ant-m stj2 ant-met stj2 mag-sil stj2 mang-s stj2]
- **desire**: *(↗MIND - Alcoholism)* absin kr1 acon k* adam srj5• **Agar** kr1* agav-t jl3* ail sf1.de* alco a1* aloe k* alumn c1 am-c k* am-m br1 anac gl1.fr• anan vh1 *Anis* kr1 ant-c kr1* ant-t k* apis stx1 apom c1 arg-met b7.de* arg-n sf1.de* arge-pl rwt5• arizon-l nl2• arn k* **Ars** k* *Ars-i* *Ars-met* kr1 ars-s-f k2* *Asar* k* astac c1 aster k* *Aur* k* aur-ar k2* aur-i k2* aur-m stj2*• aur-s k2* aven cp1* bac bn* bamb-a stb2.de• bar-c kr1* *Bell* kr1 bism br1 bov k* bry k* bufo k* cadm-s kr1* calc k* *Calc-ar* k* calc-i k2* calc-s cann-i kr1* canth ld1.de* *Caps* k* *Carb-ac* bro1* carb-an *Carb-v* bg2* carbn-s k2* carc mrr1 card-m br1 caust k* chim kr1* chin k* chinin-m c1 cic k* *Cimic* kr1* cisplat vml3• coc-c kr1* *Coca* kr1* cocc bro1* coff kr1 colch br1 con *Crot-h* k* cub cupr k* cupr-ar br1 dig kr1 eup-per k2 falco-pe nl2• ferr-p bro1* fl-ac k* *Gaul* kr1 gels kr1* gink-b sbd1*• gins k* glon sf1.de granit-m es1*• graph sf1.de ham fd3.de• hell *Hep* k* hydr c1* hydrog srj* *Hyos* kr1* iber kr1* ichth br1* ign bg2 *Iod* k* *Kali-bi* bro1* kali-br kr1* kali-i br1 kali-s fd4.de *Kola* stb3• *Kreos* k* lac-ac sf1.de lac-c k* lac-loxod-a hrn2• **Lach** k* lap-la sde8.de• lat-m wm2 lec bro1* *Led* k* levo vml3• *Lob* kr1* lup br1 *Lyc* k* **Mag-f** stj1*• *Med* k* melal-alt gya4 meph stx1 merc k* mez bt2 mosch b7a.de* *Mur-ac* k* myos-a rly4• nad rly4• naja k* nat-c kr1 nat-m b4a.de* nat-p k* nat-s kr1* nux-m bg2 **Nux-v** k* olib-sac wmh1 olnd sf1.de* onos c1 *Op* k* ozone sde2*• passi bt2* *Pegan-ha* tpi1• petr gl1.fr• petr-ra shn4• *Phos* k* pin-con oss2• plat bt2* plb k* positr nl2• pot-e rly4• *Psor* k* *Puls* k* quas sf1.de* querc c1* rad-br sze8• *Ran-b* kr1* raph c1* rhod stx1 rhus-t bg2* ruta fd4.de* sabad stx1 sacch-a fd2.de• *Sel* b7.de* *Sep* k* sil bg2* sol-t-ae k* *Spig* k* spong fd4.de stann ptk1 *Staph* k* stram kr1* stront-c bro1* stroph-h c1 stry-n st suis-pan rly4• *Sul-ac* k* sul-i k2* **Sulph** k* sumb k* symph fd3.de• *Syph* k* tab k* taosc iwa1• tarax stx1 ter ther k* thiop jl tritic-vg fd5.de *Tub* k* tung-met stj2*• vanil fd5.de *Verat* gl1.fr• zing kr1* ziz kr1* [*Alum* stj2 alumin-s stj2 am-caust stj2 *Am-f* stj2 am-s stj1 ant-m stj2 ant-met stj2 arg-p stj2 astat stj2 bar-br stj2 *Bar-f* stj1 bar-i stj2 bar-met stj2 beryl stj2 bism-sn stj2 caes-met stj2 *Calc-f* stj1 chr-s stj2 cinnb stj2 *Cupr-f* stj2 *Ferr-f* stj2 *Fl-pur* stj2 gal-s stj2 hafn-met stj2 heroin sdj2 irid-met stj2 *Kali-f* stj1 kali-n stj1 lanth-met stj2 *Lith-f* stj2 lith-s stj2 mag-s stj1 mang-s stj2 merc-d stj2 merc-i-f stj2 nat-caust stj2 **Nat-f** stj1* nicc stj1 nicc-met stj2 nicc-s stj2 osm-met stj2 oxyg stj2 pall stj2 plb-m stj2 plb-p stj2 polon-met stj2 rhen-met stj2 ruth-met stj2 spect dfg1 tant-met stj2 thal-met stj2 titan-s stj2]
  - **disgust** for; but: thiop jl3
  - **disliked**; which she: med ptk1
  - **menses**; before: **Sel** k*

- **alcoholic** drinks – **desire**: ...
  - **remove** the habit of drinking; to (See MIND - Alcoholism - remove)
- **ale**:
  - **agg.**: *(↗beer - agg.)* *Gamb* kr1* *Spong* kr1 *Sulph* kr1
  - **aversion**: ferr **Nux-v** k* positr nl2•
  - **desire**: ferr-p k* *Med Sulph*
- **almonds** | **desire**: cub k* nat-sil fd3.de•
- **anchovies** | **desire**: *(↗herring - desire; sardines - desire)* atro a2 atro-pur a dulc fd4.de mag-m dgt verat b7.de* [zinc-p stj2]
- **animal** food:
  - **agg.**: helon stx1 phos kr1*
  - **aversion**: graph tl1 ptel tl1 sil ptk1
- **appetizing** food (See delicacies)
- **apples**: alum bg2 ant-t bg2 arg-n bg2 con bg2 merc-c bg2 nat-s bg2 phos bg2 puls bg2 rumx bg2 sep bg2 thuj bg2
  - **agg.**: alum a1* ant-t st* arg-met stj2* arg-n bt3* ars bt3* ars-i ptk1* bell ptk1* bell-p stx1 borx h2* chin bt3* chinin-s a1* fago a1* kali-c dbp lac-lup hrn2• lyc a* mang h2 merc-c vml3• moni rfm1• op oss• ox-ac k2 phos bt3 puls bt3 rumx hr1* sep bt3 spong fd4.de sulph bt3* thuj bt3 vanil fd5.de [arg-p stj2 tung-met stj2]
    - **sour**: merc-c a1*
  - **amel.**: guaj hr1* ham fd3.de• tab c1 ust a1*
    - **sour**: merc-c ptk tab c1
    - **sweet**: merc-c a1
  - **aversion**: ant-t ld1.de guaj ld1.de **Hell** vh* lac-lup hrn2• lyss k*
  - **desire**: aloe k* *Ant-t* k* ap-g br1* arge-pl rwt5• bros-gau mrc1 dulc fd4.de fel a1* *Guaj* k* ham fd3.de• kali-p fd1.de• kali-s fd4.de lyss a malar al2 menth sf1.de ozone sde• polys sk4• spong fd4.de stront-c sk4• sulph k* symph fd3.de• tell k* tritic-vg fd5.de ust a1* vanil fd5.de [*Bor-pur* stj2 calc-s stj1 *Titan* stj2 *Titan-s* stj2]
    - **acid** (See sour)
    - **juice** | **cold**: ozone sde2*•
    - **sour**: carc sst* dulc fd4.de
- **aromatic** drinks | **agg.** | **smell** of: agn vml3• ign bg2* puls bg2*
  - **desire**: anan k*
- **artichokes**:
  - **aversion**: abel vh1 abies-c vh1* acon vh* *Mag-c* vh merc mrr1 sulph vh
  - **desire**: abies-c br1* [card-m stj]
- **artificial** food | **agg.**: alum br1* calc ptk1 gaert ptj1*• mag-c ptk1 nux-v kr1* op br1 podo kr1 sulph ptk1 [alumin stj2 alumin-p stj2 alumin-s stj2]
- **ashes** | **desire**: *(↗indigestible - desire)* tarent k*
- **asparagus** | **desire**: [*Nicc* stj1 *Nicc-met* stj2 *Nicc-s* stj2 *Sel* stj2]
- **aubergines**:
  - **agg.**: suis-pan rly4•
  - **aversion**: *Med* vh*
  - **desire**: med vh*
- **avocado** | **desire**: [moly-met stj2]
- **bacon**:
  - **agg.**: polym bg sanic c1 [arg-n stj2 ferr-n stj2 mag-n stj2 mang-n stj2 nitro stj2 zinc-n stj2]
  - **amel.**: ran-b k* ran-s k*
  - **aversion**: rad-br c1* [arg-n stj2 bar-n stj1 mag-n stj2 mang-n stj2 nat-n stj1 nitro stj2 zinc-n stj2]
  - **desire**: *(↗fat - desire; ham - desire - fat)* *Ars* sf1.de* calc ptk1 *Calc-p* k* carc fb* *Caust* vh* cench k* cystein-l rly4• elaps gk lac-h htj1• limen-b-c hrn2* *Mez* k* musca-d szs1 *Plut-n* srj7• rad-br ptk1* *Sanic* k* sulph ctc* symph fd3.de• tell jl3* *Tub* k* [bar-n stj1 beryl stj2 *Calc-n* stj1 cupr stj2 heroin sdj2 mag-n stj2 nat-n stj1]
    - **enjoy**; yet does not: limen-b-c hrn2•
    - **fatty** bacon: tell rsj10•
    - **fried** bacon: [*Arg-n* stj2 *Ferr-n* stj2 *Mag-n* stj2 *Mang-n* stj2 *Nitro* stj2 *Zinc-n* stj2]
    - **well**-fried: puls gk
- **bananas**:
  - **agg.**: kali-p fd1.de• rumx pd* thiam rly4• [bor-pur stj2]

- **aversion**: bar-c hr1* elaps k* sulph ser
- **desire**: ara-maca sej7• dulc fd4.de haliae-lc srj5• ham fd3.de• ignis-alc es2• nid vml3• nit-ac dgt ozone sde• petr-ra shn4• podo fd3.de• ruta fd4.de sulph dgt ther k* tritic-vg fd5.de tub vh* tung-met bdx1• vanil fd5.de
  - **green**: ozone sde2*•

\- **beans**:

- **agg.**: (↗*flatulent - agg.)* aloe vh1 ars k* **Bry** k* *Calc* k* carb-v k* chin *Coloc* vh cupr erig mg1.de* hell kali-c k* **Lyc** k* nat-m k* *Petr* k* phos bt3 pin-con oss2• puls sep sil k* sulph bt3* vanil fd5.de verat [arg-n stj2 ferr-n stj2 mag-n stj2 mang-n stj2 nitro stj2 zinc-n stj2]
- **amel.**: *Coloc* vh
- **aversion**: anac vh1 ars vh1* bell mrr1 *Kali-act* vh *Lyc* vh* med vh* nat-m vh spong fd4.de [arg-n stj2 ferr-n stj2 mang-n stj2 nitro stj2 zinc-n stj2]
  - **broad** beans: [mang-n stj2]
- **desire**: acon a2 *Acon-l* st *Alum* ld1.de calc vh

\- **beef**:

- **agg.**: kali-n stj1* staph stx1
  - **beefsteak**: kali-n mtf
- **aversion**: crot-c k* graph mtf merc k* polym bg3 ptel k* [kali-n stj1]
  - **beefsteak**: sulph mtf
  - **smell**; to: ptel a1*
- **desire**: elaps a2* lach mtf malar al2*
  - **beefsteak**: mag-c mtf med mtf *Phos* mtf staph mtf tub mtf
  - **raw**; fresh: malar al2
  - **sour** sauce; with: elaps mtf

\- **beer**:

- **agg.**: (↗*ale - agg.)* acon k* act-sp kr1* adlu vml3• aids nl2• alco mtf11 all-c stx1 *Aloe* k* alum bg2* ant-t stx1 ars k* ars-s-f stx1 asaf k* bamb-a stx1 bapt bg2* bell k* *Bry* k* cadm-s k* calc-caust sf1.de* caps vh carbn-s k* carc mlr1• card-m br1* caust stx1 chel *Chim* vml3• chim-m stx1 chin k* chinin-m stx1 chlol k* chlor ld1.de* coc-c k* coloc k* con k2 cor-r stx1 crot-t k* cupr stx1 euph k* *Ferr* k* fl-ac bg2 gamb stx1 ign k* ind stx1 ip stx1 *Kali-bi* k* kali-m kr1 kali-n c1* kali-p fd1.de• lac-h sze9• lach stx1 *Led* k* *Lyc* b2.de* *Merc* stx1 merc-c bg2* mez k* mur-ac k* *Nat-m* stx1 nat-sil fd3.de• nux-m c1* **Nux-v** b2.de* pieri-b mlk9.de *Puls* b2.de* *Rhus-t* k* sal-fr sle1• *Sang* k2 sec bg2* sep k* *Sil* b2.de* stann k* staph k* stram k* *Sulph* b2.de* sumb stx1 teucr k* thea stx1 *Thuj* bg2* trinit br1 tritic-vg fd5.de vanil fd5.de *Verat* b2.de* vinc stx1 zinc sne zinc-p k2 [cadm-met stj2 ferr-f stj2 ferr-lac stj2 ferr-n stj2 ferr-sil stj2]
  - **bad**: nux-m c1
  - **cold**: gink-b sbd1*•
  - **intoxicated**; easily: (↗*alcoholic - agg. - intoxicated)* *Chim* kr1* *Chin* kr1* coloc kr1* ign sf1.de kali-m kr1* tritic-vg fd5.de vanil fd5.de
  - **malt**: kali-bi ptk1
  - **new**: *Chin* b2.de* chinin-m bt3 *Lyc* b2.de* *Puls* b2.de* teucr b2.de
  - **smell**: cham j* phos stx1
- **amel.**: aloe bg2* camph stx1 dulc fd4.de falco-pe nl2• **Lob** vh mur-ac kr1* nat-p c1* pieri-b mlk9.de pull-g vl *Thea* stx1 *Verat* bg2*
- **aversion**: *Alum* k* alum-p k2* asaf k* atro k* bamb-a stb2.de• bell k* bry k* calc k* carbn-s a1* *Cham* k* **Chin** k* *Clem* k* *Cocc* k* crot-t k* *Cycl* k* *Ferr* k* gink-b vml3• *Kali-bi* tl1* kali-s fkr2.de lyc ptk1 med c1 merc k2 mez tl1 mur-ac c1 nat-m k* *Nat-s* **Nux-v** k* pall k* ph-ac *Phos* k* positr nl2• puls bg2* *Rhus-t* k* ruta fd4.de sang bg2* sep k* spig k* spong k* *Stann* k* suis-em rly4• *Sulph* k* [alumin stj2 alumin-p stj2 alumin-s stj2 cadm-m stj2]
  - **morning**: *Nux-v*
  - **evening**: bry nat-m sulph
  - **cold** beer: gink-b sbd1• spong fd4.de
  - **smell** of: *Cham* a1*
- **desire**: **Acon** k* agar k* agath-a nl2• aloe k* am-c k* ant-t a1* arn ars k* asar k* bac wz *Bell* *Bry* k* calad k* calc k* camph k* caps gm1 carbn-s k* carc gk6* card-m br1 *Caust* k* chel chin k* chord-umb rly4• cic jl3* coc-c k* *Cocc* k* cod a1* *Coloc* k* cupr dig digin a1 dulc fd4.de falco-pe nl2• ferr-p a2 galla-q-r nl2• gink-b vml3• *Graph* k* ham fd3.de• hyos j iod a1 *Kali-bi* k* kali-i ld1.de kali-p fd1.de• kali-s fd4.de *Kola* stb3• *Lach* k* m-ambo b2.de* mang k* *Med* st* *Merc* k* mosch k* nat-ar *Nat-c* k* *Nat-m* k* nat-p k* *Nat-s* nat-sil fd3.de• **Nux-v** k* op k* pall sne *Petr* k*

\- **beer – desire**: ...
ph-ac k* *Phel* k* phos k* podo fd3.de• psor k* *Puls* k* *Rhus-t* k* *Sabad* k* sacch-a fd2.de• *Sang* k2 sep sil c1 *Spig* k* spong k* staph stram k* *Stront-c* k* stroph-h bt3* **Sulph** k* sumb a2* symph fd3.de• taosc iwa1• tell k* tritic-vg fd5.de vanil fd5.de verat sne *Zinc* k* zinc-p k2* [am-caust stj2 ant-m stj2 ant-met stj2 beryl stj2 chr-m stj2 *Chr-met* stj1* chr-s stj2 stront-m stj2 stront-met stj2 zinc-i stj2 zinc-m stj2]
  - **morning**: agath-a nl2• musca-d szs1 *Nux-v* a1 phel a1* *Puls* kr1*
  - **forenoon**: agar a1* phos a1*
  - **afternoon**: psor a1* sulph a1*
  - **evening**: coc-c a1* falco-pe nl2• *Kali-bi* a1 mang a1 *Med* st* nux-v a1 sulph a1* *Zinc* k*
  - **bitter**: dulc fd4.de podo fd3.de• vanil fd5.de
  - **chill**, during: ant-c bg2* *Nux-v* bg2* psor bg2 puls bg2
  - **cold** beer: *Cocc* kr1* galla-q-r nl2• gink-b sbd1*•
  - **colic**, after: ph-ac h2*
  - **disliked**; which she: med ptk
  - **eating**; after: sulph b4a.de
  - **fever**:
    - **after**: puls a1*
    - **during**: acon a1* bac wz* nux-v k* puls k*
  - **mastitis**, in: phel a
  - **thirst**: cocc tl1
    - **with**: *Calad* vh
    - **without**: *Calad* kr1*

\- **beetroot** | **desire**: choc srj3*•

\- **berries**:

- **agg.**: ip ptk1
- **aversion**: chin gl3• mag-m stx1 ox-ac gl3• prot jl3* sulph gl3•

\- **biscuits**:

- **agg.**: plan a1 plb a1
- **amel.**: gels a1
- **desire**: calc mtf dulc fd4.de kali-s fd4.de nat-m mtf neon srj5• plb k* positr nl2• tub mtf
  - **chocolate** biscuits: rhus-g tmo3•

\- **bitter** drinks:

- **agg.**: acon aloe ld1.de cod a1* dig *Nat-m* nat-p ptk1 tarax vml3• ter ther ld1.de
- **desire**: acon k* aids nl2• aloe bt3 arist-cl rbp3• cocc sys1 *Cod* a2* dig graph bg *Nat-m* k* nux-v st sep k2* ter vanil fd5.de

\- **bitter** food:

- **agg.**: nat-p c1*
- **desire**: acon k2* arist-cl rbp3• cod kr1* dig k* glycyr-g cte1• graph bg2* ign gk *Nat-m* k* nux-v k2* rhus-g tmo3• sep k2 [niob-met stj2]

\- **bland** food | **desire**: graph mrr1 nat-m mtf pert-vc vk9 ph-ac mtf

\- **blood**; her own | **desire**: plut-n srj7•

\- **boiled** food | **aversion**: calc bro1*

\- **brandy**:

- **agg.**: agar k* *Ars* k* ars-met kr1 arum-i stx1 bell k* calc k* carb-ac ld1.de carb-v c1 chel b2.de* chin k* cocc k* fl-ac bg2 hep k* hyos k* ign k* kali-s fd4.de lach k* laur k* *Led* k* med st **Nux-v** k* **Op** k* puls k* *Ran-b* k* rhod k* *Rhus-t* k* ruta k* spig k* spong fd4.de *Stram* k* sul-ac k* **Sulph** k* verat k* zinc k* [nicc-met stj2 nicc-s stj2]
  - **and** wine amel.: *Sul-ac* kr1*
  - **bad**; from: carb-v c1
- **amel.**: ars c1 crot-h a1 glon br olnd sf1.de* plb stx1 prot jl3 sel sf1.de
- **aversion**: ant-t hr1* *Carb-ac* a1* ign k* lob ld1.de lob-e br1* *Merc* k* ph-ac bg2* rhus-t k* spong fd4.de stram ld1.de* zinc k*
  - **brandy** drinkers; in: *Arn* k*
- **desire**: acon k* *Agar* a ail k* alum sf am-m sf anac sf ant-c sf* arg-met b2.de arg-n k* *Arn* k2 ars k* ars-met asar sf1.de* aster *Bell* k13 borx k13 bov k* bry k* bufo calc k* carb-v ld carbn-s ld caust ld *Chel* ld chin k* cic k* coc-c ld1.de* coca k* *Cocca* *Coff* a con a crot-h a cub k* ferr-p k* glon br ham fd3.de• *Hep* k* hyos st *Ign* st kali-s fd4.de kola stb3• lach k* laur st led k2 lyss al2 *Mag-f* stj1*• *Med* st merc a mosch k* mur-ac k* myos-a rly4*• *Nat-c* a *Nat-m* b4a.de* *Nux-m* a **Nux-v** k* olnd **Op** k* *Petr* *Phos* puls k* *Rhod* a *Rhus-t* a *Ruta* a sabad a *Sel* k* *Sep* k*

- **desire**: ...
  Spig k* spong fd4.de *Staph* k* stram stront-c *Sul-ac* k* *Sulph* k* ther k* [ant-m stj2 ant-met stj2 ant-t stj2 cadm-met stj2 cadm-s stj2 stront-m stj2 stront-met stj2]

- **bread**:
  - **agg.**: acet-ac vml3• acon b7.de aids nl2• *Ant-c* k* arg-n stx1 *Ars* b4a.de asaf b7.de* *Bar-c* k* bell b4a.de bit-ar wht1• **Bry** k* carb-an k* *Caust* k* chin k* chinin-ar stx1 cina bg2* clem k* coff k* *Coloc* b4a.de crot-c sk4• crot-h k* crot-t k* cupr ld1.de euph b4a.de *Ferr* b7.de* *Hydr* kr1* ign b7.de* kali-bi gk kali-c k* *Lach* b7a.de *Lec* sne lith-c ld1.de *Lyc* b4a.de* manc stx1 meny vml3• merc k* *Merc-c* b4a.de mez b4a.de mur-ac b4a.de nat-c sne *Nat-m* k* neon srj5• nept-m lsd2.fr *Nit-ac* k* *Nux-v* k* olnd k* ph-ac k* phos k* pin-con oss2• plat b4.de* **Puls** k* ran-s k* *Rhus-t* k* rob c1 ruta k* *Sars* k* sec k* *Sep* k* sil b4a.de stann b4a.de staph k* stram b7a.de sul-ac k* *Sulph* k* symph fd3.de• teucr k* *Verat* b7.de* *Zinc* k* zinc-p k2* zing k* [ant-m stj2 ant-met stj2 ant-t stj2 ind stj2]
    - **black**, agg.: bry k* ign k* *Kali-c* k* *Lyc* k* nat-m k* nit-ac k* nux-v k* *Ph-ac* k* phos k* *Puls* k* sep bg2 sulph k* symph fd3.de•
    - **butter** agg.; and: *(↗butter - agg.; MIND - Confusion - bread)* acet-ac kr1* carb-an k* caust k* *Chin* k* crot-t k* cycl k* meny k* nat-m k* nat-s bg2 *Nit-ac* k* nux-v k* phos k* **Puls** k* *Sep* k* sulph k*
    - **rye** bread: bry kr1 lyc kr1 merc-c stx1 nat-m kr1 *Nit-ac* h2* nux-v c1 ph-ac kr1 *Phos* kr1 psor bgs
  - **amel.**: *Caust* b2.de* dulc fd4.de lact ld1.de laur b2.de* *Nat-c* b2.de* phos b2.de* ruta fd4.de sabal c1
  - **aversion**: agar k* ant-c stj2* aphis c1* bacls-10 ptj1*• *Calc* vh cassia-s ccrh1*• chen-a gsw1* **Chin** k* *Con* k* corn a1 cortiso gse cur k* *Cycl* k* elaps k* ferr-ar ld1.de gaert ptj1*• hipp gsw1 hydr ld1.de ign k* *Kali-act* vh *Kali-c* k* *Kali-p* k* kali-s kola stb3• *Lach* k* lact k* lavand-a ctl1• lec sne lil-t k* *Lyc* k* *Mag-c* k* manc mang gsw1 meny k* **Nat-m** k* *Nat-p* k* *Nat-s* k* *Nit-ac* k* nux-m a1 *Nux-v* k* ol-an k* *Ph-ac* k* *Phos* k* *Puls* k* *Rhus-t* k* ribo rly4• ruta fd4.de sanic c1* *Sep* k* *Sulph* k* syc ptj1*• symph fd3.de• tarent k* tritic-vg fd5.de [aur-s stj2 cadm-s stj2 chr-s stj2 cinnb stj2 gal-s stj2 lith-s stj2 mang-s stj2 neon stj2 nicc-s stj2 pop dhh1 tax jsj7 titan-s stj2]
    - **black**: *Kali-c* k* *Lyc* k* merc sf1.de *Nat-m* b4a.de* *Nux-v* b2.de* ph-ac b4a.de* puls k* sulph k* tritic-vg fd5.de
    - **brown**: aphis kr1 irid-met srj5• *Kali-c Lyc* nux-v puls sulph
    - **butter**, and: carc fd2.de• *Cycl* k* *Mag-c* k* meny k* nat-p k* sang bg2
    - **pregnancy**, during: ant-t h2 laur vml3• nat-m c1 *Sep* hr1*
    - **rye** bread: kali-c hr2* *Lyc* h2* nat-m h2 *Nux-v* b7.de* *Ph-ac* h2 puls b7.de* *Sulph* gsw1
  - **desire**: abrot k* agath-a nl2• aloe k* am-c k* androc srj1• *Ars* k* *Aur* k* aur-ar k2* aur-m-n wbt2• bar-m vh *Bell* k* bov k* calc sne cann-i a1* carc zzh castm vml3• castor-eq gsw1 *Cham* vh* chen-a c1 *Cina* k* coca-c sk4• *Cocc* stx1 *Coloc* k* con cub k* dulc fd4.de *Ferr* k* ferr-ar ferr-m ld1.de* galeoc-c-h gms1• grat k* hell k* hera vml3• hydr k* ign k* kali-p fd1.de• kali-s fd4.de limest-b es1*• lyc ld1.de *Mag-c* k* mag-f vml3• *Merc* moly-met vml3• nat-ar *Nat-c* k* *Nat-m* k* nat-s zf nept-m lsd2.fr nit-ac vh* ol-an a1* op k* pin-con oss2• plac rzf5• *Plb* k* plut-n srj7• podo fd3.de• propl ub1*• *Puls* k* rhus-g tmo3• ruta fd4.de *Sabad* b7a.de sabal c1 sec k* sep mrr1 sil k* spong fd4.de staph k* streptoc rly4• *Stront-c* k* suis-em rly4• sumb k* symph fd3.de• tell jl3* thiam rly4• tritic-vg fd5.de ulm-c jsj8• vanil fd5.de [am-caust stj2 aur-m stj2 aur-s stj2 bar-br stj2 bar-i stj2 bar-met stj2 bism-sn stj2 bor-pur stj2 caes-met stj2 cinnb stj2 hafn-met stj2 irid-met stj2 lanth-met stj2 merc-d stj2 merc-i-f stj2 nat-caust stj2 osm-met stj2 plat stj2 plb-m stj2 plb-p stj2 rhen-met stj2 stront-m stj2 stront-met stj2 tant-met stj2 tax jsj7 thal-met stj2 tung-met stj2]
    - **evening**: castm a1* dulc fd4.de tell rsj10*
    - **boiled** in milk: abrot k*
    - **butter**, and: agar k* arg-n sne *Bar-m* ld1.de* bell k* carc fd2.de• dulc fd4.de *Ferr* k* grat hell hydr ign k* kali-s fd4.de kola stb3• *Mag-c* k* **Merc** k* *Merc-sul* kr1 nat-m kl phasco-ci rbp2 puls k* sacch sht*• sep kl stront-c bg2* symph fd3.de•
    - **cheese**; and: galeoc-c-h gms1•
    - **dry**: aur bg2 *Bar-m* kali-s fd4.de ruta fd4.de
    - **only**: bov grat ol-an c1 stront-c c1
    - **rye** bread: anis c1 *Ars* carl k* *Ign* k* plb k*
      - **boiled** in milk: abrot vml3•

- **bread – desire**: ...
  - **toasted**: aur mtf aur-m-n mtf calc-p mtf mag-s mtf staph mtf
  - **white**: aur bg2 bar-m bg1 kali-p fd1.de• kali-s fd4.de lac-h sze9• ruta fd4.de spong fd4.de tritic-vg fd5.de vanil fd5.de
- **breakfast** | **aversion**: bacls-10 ptj1*• cench k2 con k* lyc k* mag-s k* pic-ac a2 sel a2* syc pte1*• symph fd3.de• thuj mtf33 *Verat* mtf33
- **broccoli**:
  - **agg.**: [calc-sil stj2 ferr-sil stj2 kali-sil stj2 mag-sil stj2 mang-sil stj2 nat-sil stj2 sil stj2 sil-met stj2]
  - **aversion**: caust sne [calc-sil stj2 ferr-sil stj2 kali-sil stj2 mag-sil stj2 mang-sil stj2 nat-sil stj2 sil stj2 sil-met stj2]
  - **desire**: mag-c mtf mag-m mtf
- **broth**:
  - **agg.**: acon stx1 colch stx1 mag-c k1 mez btw mur-ac k2 rob c1
    - **smell** of; sensitive to the (See NOSE - Smell - acute - broth)
  - **aversion**: *Arn* b2.de* *Ars* b2.de* bell b2.de* *Cham* b2.de* graph b2.de* kali-i a1* rhus-t b2.de* sil h1*
  - **desire**: camph c1 dulc fd4.de mag-c k2 plut-n srj7• tritic-vg fd5.de
- **buckwheat**:
  - **agg.**: fago vh ip k* *Phos* bg2* **Puls** k* *Sep* bg2* verat k*
  - **aversion**: puls c1
- **burned** food | **desire**: nat-m mrr1
- **butter**: *(↗dairy)*
  - **agg.**: *(↗bread - agg. - butter; dairy - agg.)* acet-ac vml3• acon k* ant-c k* ant-t k* *Ars* k* asaf k* bell k* carb-an k* **Carb-v** k* caust k* chin k* colch k* *Cycl* k* dros k* euph k* *Ferr* k* ferr-ar ham fd3.de• hell k* hep k* ip k* mag-m k* meny k* merc-c bg2* nat-ar nat-c k* nat-m k* nat-p nit-ac k* nux-v k* *Phos* k* *Ptel* k* **Puls** k* *Sep* k* spong k* sulph k* *Tarax* k* *Tarent* ld1.de* thuj k* vanil fd5.de [alum stj2 nat-caust stj2 oxyg stj2 plat stj2 sil stj2]
  - **amel.**: arum-m c1
  - **aversion**: ars k* carb-an ld1.de* carb-v k* carc fb* **Chin** k* choc srj3*• *Cycl* k* ferr gk gaert ptj1*• hep bro1* mag-c k* mang gsw1 meny k* *Merc* k* morg-g vml3• nat-m ld1.de nat-p gsw1 petr k* *Phos* k* prot pte1*• *Ptel* k* **Puls** k* sacch sht*• sang k*
  - **desire**: *(↗dairy - desire)* all-s k* arg-n sne *Bung-fa* mtf carc pc* chin gk1* chlam-tr bcx2• dulc fd4.de ferr b7.de* ham fd3.de• ign b7.de* irid-met srj5• kali-p fd1.de• kali-s fd4.de limest-b es1*• mag-c b4.de* mand sp1 merc k* *Morg* jl* morg-p pte1*• nit-ac sf1.de ozone sde2*• plut-n srj7• prot pte1* puls b7.de* querc-r svu1• sacch sht*• sal-fr sle1• spong fd4.de sulph ctc• syc ptj1*• tub gk1* vanil fd5.de
- **buttermilk**:
  - **agg.**: bry h1* calc-p tl1 podo stx1 puls h1* [moly-met stj2]
  - **amel.**: arum-t c1
  - **aversion**: ant-c vld *Cina* ld1.de* [nat-lac stj2]
  - **desire**: *(↗milk - desire - sour)* ant-t bg1* chinin-s ptk1* *Chion* bg1* con dgt elaps bg1* kola stb3• *Lac-ac* stj2*• mag-c dgt mag-m dgt petr-ra shn4• *Puls* zr raph dgt *Sabad* vh sabal bg1* spong dgt stram dgt stront-c sk4• *Thlas* bg1* [calc-sil stj2 mag-lac stj2]
    - **sweetened**: elaps br1
- **cabbage**:
  - **agg.**: *(↗flatulent - agg.)* ars k* **Bry** k* calc k* carb-v k* *Chin* k* colch gk cupr k* erig mg1.de* hell k* kali-c k* **Lyc** k* *Mag-c* k* nat-m k* *Nat-s* **Petr** k* phos bg2* podo k2* *Puls* k* rob ptk1* sacch-a fd2.de• sep k* sil k* sulph bt3* verat k* [*Arg-met* stj1* *Arg-n* stj2 *Arg-p* stj2]
  - **aversion**: bry ld1.de carb-v ld1.de cocc ld1.de kali-c ld1.de lyc ld1.de* petr tl1* ptel gk [*Arg-met* stj1 coch-o stj nicc stj]
  - **desire**: acon a1* *Acon-l* st* alum ld1.de **Cic** b2.de* con bg2 ruta fd4.de tritic-vg fd5.de
- **caffeine** | **desire**: des-ac rbp6
- **cakes** (See pastry)
- **canned** food | **agg.**: podo ptk1
- **carbonated** drinks: *(↗coca; soda pop; soda water)*
  - **aversion**: phos mrr1

- **desire**: choc srj* colch bro1* hydrog srj* *Med* ez medul-os-si rly4• nat-c sne *Ph-ac* kr1* phos kr1* sulph gy tritic-vg fd5.de [arg-n stj2 ferr-n stj2 heroin sdj2 mang-n stj2 nitro stj2 zinc-n stj2]

- **carrots**:
  - **agg.**: calc k* *Lyc* k*
  - **desire**: [heroin sdj2]
- **cauliflower**:
  - **aversion**: [calc-sil stj2 ferr-sil stj2 kali-sil stj2 mang-sil stj2 sil-met stj2]
  - **desire**: mag-c mtf mag-m mtf mag-s mtf tritic-vg fd5.de [mag-lac stj2 mag-met stj2]
    - **béchamel**; with: carl km•
- **caviar**: *(↗fish)*
  - **agg.**: chinin-ar mtf lyc mtf
  - **desire**: phos mtf
- **celery** | **aversion**: nux-v mtf
- **cereals**:
  - **amel.**: nat-c mtf
  - **aversion**: ars phos
  - **desire**: amp rly4• carc mtf thuj mtf
- **chalk**: | **desire**: **Alum** bg2* ant-c ptk1 calc bg2* cic bg2* con bg2 ferr bg2 hep bg2 hyos bg2 ign bg2* *Nat-m* b4a.de nit-ac b4.de* *Nux-v* b7a.de* oci bg2 psor ptk1 *Puls* b7a.de *Sep* b4a.de sil bg2* sulph bg2* tarent bg2*
- **chamomile**:
  - **agg.**: acon bg2 bell stx1 *Cham* k2* *Chin* br1* cocc bg2 coff bg2* ign bg2* nux-v bg2* puls bg2* valer bro1 vip stx1
  - **amel.**: gink-b sbd1•
  - **desire** for: gink-b sbd1•
- **champagne**:
  - **agg.**: *Calc* st digox stx1 vanil fd5.de
  - **desire**: lac-h sze9• ozone sde2• vanil fd5.de
    - **aggravates**; but: carc az1.de•
- **charcoal**:
  - **desire**: *(↗indigestible - desire)* alum k* *Calc* kr1* *Cic* k* con k* ign ld1.de nit-ac k* nux-v k* *Psor* ld1.de*
    - **accompanied** by | **chlorosis**: alum kr1*
- **cheese**: *(↗dairy)*
  - **agg.**: *(↗dairy - agg.)* arg-n stj2*• ars bg2* *Bry* stx1 carb-v stx1 coloc b2.de* crot-c sk4• dios c2 ham fd3.de• kali-c b4a.de musca-d szs1 nit-s-d kr1* nux-v bg2* ph-ac stx1 ptel bg2* *Rhus-t* stx1 sep b4a.de* spong fd4.de staph gl1.fr*• tub hu [alum stj2 bism-sn stj2 ferr-n stj2 mag-n stj2 mang-n stj2 nat-caust stj2 nitro stj2 oxyg stj2 sil stj2 zinc-n stj2]
    - **old** cheese: *Ars* k* *Bry* k* coloc dios c1* nit-s-d c2 ph-ac k* *Ptel* k* *Rhus-t* k*
    - **smell**: olib-sac wmh1
    - **spoiled** cheese: ars sf1.de bry sf1.de ph-ac sf1.de rhus-t sf1.de
  - **aversion**: *Arg-n* st* cac srj *Chel* k* chin bg2 choc srj3• *Cocc* vh coli rly4• coll ld1.de ferr gk hep st* ign zf kola stb3• lyc mtf merc st* nat-m hu nat-ox rly4*• **Nit-ac** st* *Olnd* k* podo fd3.de• ptel tl1* ruta fd4.de *Sil* vh* spong fd4.de *Staph* st* sulph st* suprar rly4• syc ptj1*• tritic-vg fd5.de tub a* vanil fd5.de [bar-n stj1 calc-sil stj2 *Ferr-n* stj2 *Mag-n* stj2 *Mang-n* stj2 moly-met stj2 nat-n stj1 *Nitro* stj2 *Zinc-n* stj2]
    - **gruyère**: *Merc* st* sulph st*
    - **Roquefort**: *Hep* st*
    - **smell** of cheese: lyc mtf
    - **strong**: *Hep* st* *Merc* st* *Nit-ac* st* *Sulph* st*
  - **desire**: acon-ac rly4• adam srj5• aeth vh* aran-ix mtf arg-n k* arizon-l nl2• aster k* bamb-a stb2.de• bung-fa mtf calc vh* *Calc-n* stj1* calc-p mg1.de* carc fd2.de*• caust vh* *Chel* vh* chir-fl gya2 chlam-tr bcx2• *Cist* k* coll ld1.de* dendr-pol sk4• dulc fd4.de fuma-ac rly4• gaert pte1* galeoc-c-h gms1• ham fd3.de• hera vml3• hyos vh ign k* kali-c zf kali-s fd4.de lyc dgt mag-m dgt mand mg1.de* med vh medul-os-si rly4• mosch k* musca-d szs1 nat-m ser* nat-sil fd3.de• nicotam rly4• *Nit-ac* vh* olib-sac wmh1 *Phos* vh* *Plut-n* srj7• podo fd3.de• pot-e rly4• puls k* rhus-g tmo3• rhus-t vh* ribo rly4• ruta fd4.de sep bg2* spong fd4.de stront-c sk4• sulph mtf syc ptj1*• tarent mtf tritic-vg fd5.de tub hu vanil fd5.de [bar-n stj1 bor-pur stj2 cupr stj2 *Ferr-n* stj2 *Mag-n* stj2 *Mang-n* stj2 nat-n stj1 *Nitro* stj2 *Zinc-n* stj2 zirc-met stj2]

- **cheese – desire**: ...
    - **acrid**: ign bg2
    - **butter** cheese: bamb-a stb2.de•
    - **cottage** cheese: bamb-a stb2.de•
    - **feta**: arg-n mtf aster mtf calc-p mtf lyc mtf mag-m mtf med mtf nit-ac mtf nux-v mtf phos mtf sulph mtf
    - **khaloumi**: carb-v mtf caust mtf nat-m mtf nat-p mtf phos mtf
    - **sauce**: calc-p mtf
    - **strong**: arg-n k* aster k* ham fd3.de• ign sf1.de spong fd4.de tritic-vg fd5.de vanil fd5.de
- **cherries**:
  - **agg.**: chin b7.de* mag-m stx1 merc stx1 merc-c ptk1* nat-m ctc• tritic-vg fd5.de [ant-c stj2 ant-m stj2 ant-met stj2 ant-t stj2]
  - **desire**: chin k* choc srj3*• dulc fd4.de podo fd3.de• ruta fd4.de tritic-vg fd5.de
- **chicken**:
  - **agg.**: bac k2* bry k2
  - **aversion**: **Bac** k* **Nat-m** vh* *Sulph* vh* vanil fd5.de
  - **desire**: calc-p mtf dulc fd4.de *Ferr-i* vh* *Graph* vh* ham fd3.de• lap-la rsp1 nat-m gk nat-sil fd3.de• *Phos* vh* pitu-gl skp7• rat mrr1 spong fd4.de sulph mtf tritic-vg fd5.de tub mtf [arg-p stj2 cupr-p stj2 lith-p stj2 mang-p stj2 nat-caust stj2 nat-lac stj2 plb-p stj2]
    - **tandoori**: *(↗smoked - desire)* abies-c mtf aster mtf carc mtf caust mtf kali-p mtf kreos mtf nat-m mtf nat-p mtf nux-v mtf phos mtf puls mtf sacch mtf sulph mtf tub mtf
- **chicory** | **aversion**: [mag-sil stj2]
- **chili** (See red pepper)
- **chocolate**:
  - **agg.**: benz-ac vml3• *Borx* kr1* bry bg2* calad kr1* caust bg2* choc srj3*• coca bg2* dream-p sdj1• dulc fd4.de ham fd3.de• kali-bi bg2* kali-s fd4.de lap-la rsp1 lil-t bg2* *Lith-c* kr1* **Lyc** bg2* nat-m ctc• nat-sil fd3.de• nept-m lsd2.fr ox-ac bg2* positr nl2• prot jl3* ptel gk *Puls* bg2* *Raph* stx1 ruta fd4.de sacch sht*• sang gk spong fd4.de tritic-vg fd5.de vanil fd5.de [*Am-br* stj2 bar-br stj2 beryl-m stj2 **Brom** stj1* calc-br stj1 kali-br stj1 lith-f stj2 lith-i stj2 lith-m stj2 lith-met stj2 lith-p stj2 lith-s stj2 mag-br stj1 mag-sil stj2 *Nat-br* stj2]
    - **bitter**: brom mtf nat-m mtf
  - **amel.**: arge-pl rwt5• calc-s a2 vichy-g stx1
  - **aversion**: calc-sil gg* haliae-lc srj5• kali-s fd4.de lac-e hrn2• myos-a rly4*• osm k* oxal-a rly4• petr-ra shn4• plut-n srj7• positr nl2• prot jl3* ruta fd4.de sacch-a fd2.de• spong fd4.de symph fd3.de• tarent k* tritic-vg fd5.de vanil fd5.de [heroin sdj2]
  - **desire**: *Aegop-p* vml3• agath-a nl2• aids nl2• androc srj1*• anthraci vh1* arg-n st* arge-pl rwt5• arizon-l nl2• *Ars* sne* *Aur-m-n* wbt2• *Aur-s* wbt2• bacls-10 ptj1*• bamb-a stb2.de• bros-gau mrc1 bry gk calc st *Carc* hbh* carneg-g rwt1• caust gk* chin br1 chlam-tr bcx2• choc srj3*• coch-o j5.de* dream-p sdj1• dulc fd4.de elaps gk falco-pe nl2• fum rly1*• galeoc-c-h gms1• ger-i rly4• germ-met srj5• gink-b sbd1*• haliae-lc srj5• ham fd3.de• irid-met srj5• jal vml3• kali-c bl kali-p bl7* kali-s fd4.de kola stb3• lac-del hrn2• lac-h htj1*• lac-loxod-a hrn2• lap-la sde8.de• lepi k* *Lyc* gk* lyss k* mang-p rly4*• med gk medul-os-si rly4• meph vml3• moly-met stj2*• moni rfm1• musca-d szs1 nad rly4• nat-m vh* nat-p sne nat-pyru rly4• nat-sil fd3.de• neon srj5• nept-m lsd2.fr ozone sde2*• pant-ac rly4• petr-ra shn4• phasco-ci rbp2 *Phos* vh* pitu-a a* podo fd3.de• positr nl2• puls gk* pycnop-sa mrz1 pyrog cp1* rad-br sze8• rhus-g tmo3• ruta fd4.de *Sacch* sht*• *Sacch-a* fd2.de• sal-fr sle1• *Sep* st* sinus rly4• spong fd4.de *Staph* mp* *Sulph* vh* taosc iwa1• tarent vh* thuj a* tritic-vg fd5.de tub gk vanil fd5.de [*Am-br* stj2 *Am-c* stj1 *Am-caust* stj2 *Am-f* stj2 *Am-m* stj1 *Am-p* stj1 arg-met stj1* arg-p stj2 *Bar-br* stj2 bar-s stj1 bell-p-sp dcm1 beryl-m stj2 *Brom* stj1* calc-br stj1 calc-m stj1 cupr-p stj2 heroin sdj2 kali-br stj1 kali-sil stj2 lith-p stj2 mag-br stj1 *Nat-br* stj2 nat-caust stj2 nat-lac stj2 plb-p stj2 ruth-met stj2 *Spect* dfg1 tax jsj7 tell stj2 *Zirc-met* stj2]
    - **bitter** chocolate: nat-m gk* phos mtf sep mtf
    - **menses**; before: ephe-si hsj1• sulph mrr1
- **chocolate** milk:
  - **desire**:
    - **cold** chocolate milk: phos mtf
    - **warm** chocolate milk: lyc mtf med mtf puls mtf

- **cider**:
  - **agg.**: ant-c stx1 aster jl3* calc-p stx1 chion stx1 phos bg2 podo br*
  - **amel.**: bell bg2*
  - **desire**: anan vh1 ben benz-ac ld1.de* benzol c1 puls bg2 sulph
- **cinnamon** | **desire**: urol-h rwt•
- **citric** acid | **desire**: (↗lemons - desire) puls b7.de* verat b7.de*
- **citrus** | **agg.** (See lemons - agg.; oranges - agg.)
- **clam** | **aversion**: lac-f vml3•
- **cloves**:
  - **aversion**: [zinc stj2 zinc-i stj2 zinc-m stj2 zinc-n stj2 zinc-p stj2]
  - **desire**: Alum k* Chlor k* stront-n vh
- **coal** | **desire**: (↗indigestible - desire) Alum k* Calc Cic k* ham fd3.de• ign ld1.de psor ld1.de
- **coarse** food:
  - **agg.**: chinin-ar c1*
  - **desire**: abies-c c1* alum ptk1 ant-c ptk1 calc ptk1 calc-p ptk1 ign ptk1 pip-n c1 psor bgs sil ptk1 sulph ptk1 tarent ptk1
- **coca** cola: (↗carbonated)
  - **amel.**: phos fd*
  - **aversion**: des-ac rbp6
  - **desire**: Arg-n mtf Carc mtf chin mtf des-ac rbp6 fl-ac mtf Lyc mtf Med mtf merc mtf nat-m sej3* nat-s mtf ph-ac mtf Phos mtf rad-br sze8• sil mtf stram mtf sulph mtf Tarent mtf tritic-vg fd5.de Tub mtf vanil fd5.de Verat mtf [helium stj2]
    - ⁝ **ice**-cold: phos fd
- **cocoa** | **aversion**: Osm a1* tarent kr1
- **coffee**:
  - **agg.**: abrot vml3• acet-ac stx1 acon sys1 act-sp stx1 Aeth k* agar bg2* aids nl2• alet sf1.de* all-c k* ambr stx1 anac jl3* anan vml3• ang c1* antip c1 arg-n a1* arn stx1 ars k* arum-i stx1 arum-t k* aster k* aur-m kr1* bart a2* bell k* benz-ac vml3• bov k* bry Cact cain stx1 calc k* Calc-p k* calo stx1 camph stx1 cann-i br1* cann-s stx1 **Canth** k* Caps k* carb-v k* carc mlr1• caul kr1* **Caust** k* **Cham** k* chin bg2* chinin-s stx1 chlor stx1 cist clem st* cob stx1 coca stx1 Cocc k* coff k2* colch coloc b2.de* cuc-c vml3• cycl k* cypr vml3• Dig stx1 dulc fd4.de erech stx1 ferr-p c1 Fl-ac bg2* form k* gink-b sbd1*• glon grat k* guar c1* Hep k* hera vml3• hyper stx1 **Ign** k* Ip k* Kali-ar stx1 kali-bi kali-c bro1* kali-n k* kali-p fd1.de• lac-ac c1 lil-t stx1 Lyc k* lyss stx1 m-ambo b2.de* mag-c k* mand mg1.de* mang k* Merc k* merc-sul stx1 mill c1* morph stx1 mosch stx1 nat-m k* Nat-s nit-ac k* **Nux-v** k* ol-an vml3• olnd stx1 osm vml3• ox-ac k* pall stx1 paull c1* petr-ra shn4• Ph-ac Pin-con oss2• plat k* podo fd3.de• psor br1* Puls k* rhus-t k* rumx stx1 ruta fd4.de sal-fr sle1• sep k* spig lsa1.de* spong fd4.de Stann jl3* stram sul-ac k* sulph k* symph fd3.de• tax vml3• Thuj k* tritic-vg fd5.de trom vml3• tub al2 vanil fd5.de verat stx1 vinc k* wies c1 xan stx1 [beryl stj2 bor-pur stj2 chr-s stj2 ferr-n stj2 lith-c stj2 mag-n stj2 mang-n stj2 nicc stj1 nicc-met stj2 nicc-s stj2 nitro stj2 zinc stj2 zinc-i stj2 zinc-m stj2 zinc-n stj2 zinc-p stj2]
    - ⁝ **hot**: caps ld1.de*
    - ⁝ **overuse**: acet-ac c1 antip c1 arg-n stx1 bell stx1 cham br1 chir-fl gya2 Coff k2 cypr vml3• grat c2 guar stx1 guare br1 Ign br1* nux-v c2* ox-ac c2 pall stx1 paull stx1 puls stx1 thuj c2
    - ⁝ **smell** of coffee: (↗NOSE - Smell - acute - coffee) fl-ac bg2* lach bg2* nat-m bg2* osm bg2* sul-ac k* tub bg2*
      - ⁝ **sensitive** to the (See NOSE - Smell - acute - coffee)
    - ⁝ **sweetened** coffee: lol vml3•
  - **amel.**: acon acon-f c1 act-sp vml3* adel stx1 agar alet a* anag vml3* androc srj1*• anth vh1 aran-ix mg1.de* arg-met k* arn c1 Ars k* atra-r bnm3• brom bg2* calo c1 cann-i canth k* carl stx1 **Cham** k* chel bg2* chir-fl gya2 coca stx1 Coloc k* colocin c1 conin-br c1 corn c1 crot-h a1* crot-t stx1 cyt-l c1 dicha mg1.de eucal eug stx1 Euph ld1.de* euphr k* fago ptk1* fil stx1 fl-ac bro1* gink-b sbd1*• glon bg2 hell-o c1 hipp stx1 hydr-ac vml3* hyos k* **Ign** bg2* lach k* lact c1 Lec sne levo jl* mag-c h2 morph c1* mosch bg2* Nux-v bg1* ol-an stx1 op k* phos k* phyt stx1 podo fd3.de• ran-g c1* ruta fd4.de tab c1 thal vml3• til c1 vanil fd5.de verin c1 [arg-n stj2 arg-p stj2]
  - **aversion**: Acon ld1.de* aeth tl1 alum-sil k2* aur-m kr1* bamb-a stb2.de• Bell k* Bry k* **Calc** k* calc-s carb-v k* carc mlr1• cardios-h vml3• Caust ld1.de* Cham k* chel k* Chin k* chinin-s vml3*• cinnb bg1* coc-c k* Coff k* coli rly4• con ld1.de Dulc k* falco-pe nl2• ferr-p tl1 fl-ac k* gink-b sbd1*• hydrog srj* ign tl1 kali-bi kr1* kali-br kali-i ld1.de kali-n k*

- **coffee** – **aversion**: ...
  kali-p fd1.de• lec ld1.de* lil-t k* lol bg2* Lyc k* mag-p mand sp1 Merc k* nat-c k* Nat-m k* **Nux-v** k* olib-sac wmh1 osm k* ox-ac k* ph-ac k* Phos k* phys k* podo fd3.de• puls h1* rheum k* rhus-t k* ribo rly4• sabad k* senec c1* Spig k* spong fd4.de suis-em rly4• Sul-ac k* Sulph ld1.de* vanil fd5.de [chr-s stj2 nicc stj1 nicc-met stj2 nicc-s stj2 osm-met stj2 pop dhh1]
    - ⁝ **morning**: lyc a1 nat-n a2 vanil fd5.de
    - ⁝ **noon**: ox-ac a1*
    - ⁝ **smell**: osm vml3• Puls b7a.de sul-ac h2*
    - ⁝ **sweetened**: aur-m kr1*
    - ⁝ **unsweetened**: rheum b2.de*
  - **desire**: abrom-a ks5* adam srj5• Alum k* alum-p k2* **Ang** k* arg-met k* arg-n k* Ars k* ars-s-f k2* aster k* Aur k* aur-ar k2* aur-i vml3• aur-m vml3• Aur-m-n wbt2• aur-s k2* bamb-a stb2.de• bell bg2* bit-ar wht1• bros-gau mrc1 brucel sa3• Bry k* calc bt3* calc-p k* Canth mgm• Caps k* Carb-v k* carc fb1* cham k* chel Chin k* chinin-s bt3* chir-fl gya2 Coff k2 colch k* coli rly4• Con k* conch fkr1* Cur kr1 cypra-eg sde6.de• des-ac rbp6 dulc fd4.de* Fl-ac bg2* gink-b sbd1*• gran k* grat c1 guar a2* haliae-lc srj5• helo-s rwt2• hera vml3• kali-i ld1.de kali-p fd1.de• kali-s fd4.de ketogl-ac rly4• kola stb3• lach k* lec k* lepi a1* lob merc-c vml3• Mez k* moly-met vml3• mosch k* musca-d szs1 nat-m k* nat-sil fd3.de• Nux-m k* nux-v k* olib-sac wmh1 paull a1* ph-ac k* plac-s rly4• puls bt3* rhus-g tmo3• ruta fd4.de sabin k* sal-al blc1• Sel k* senec ptk2 Sep vh ser-ang vml3• sol-t-ae k* staph sne stroph-h ptk1 sulph k* suprar rly4• symph fd3.de• tarax vml3• tritic-vg fd5.de vanil fd5.de vip fkr4.de Xan bg1* Xanth vh* [alumin stj2 alumin-p stj2 alumin-s stj2 Am-br stj2 Am-c stj1 Am-caust stj2 Am-f stj2 Am-m stj1 Am-p stj1 am-s stj1 arg-p stj2 ars-met stj2 beryl-m stj2 heroin sdj2 kali-ar stj2 lith-c stj2 lith-f stj2 lith-i stj2 lith-m stj2 lith-met stj2 lith-p stj2 lith-s stj2 nat-ar stj2 tung-met stj2]
    - ⁝ **accompanied** by | **dysmenorrhea**: Lach kr1*
    - ⁝ **beans** of: alum sf1.de Chin kr1* nux-v sf1.de sabin sf1.de
    - ⁝ **black**: mez a1* mosch a1* symph fd3.de•
    - ⁝ **burnt**: alum k* chin
    - ⁝ **cold** coffee: petr-ra shn4•
    - ⁝ **grounds** of: Alum sf1.de* con tl1 med mtf33
    - ⁝ **nauseates**; which: Caps k*
    - ⁝ **strong**: Bry kr1* mosch st tritic-vg fd5.de
    - ⁝ **vertigo**; during: nux-m b7a.de
- **cold** drink, cold water:
  - **agg.**: acet-ac br1* Acon stx1 aeth c1 Agar k* agra stx1 All-s kr1* allox sp1* Alum k* alum-p k2* alum-sil k2* Alumn kr1* anac k* Ant-c k* apis Apoc k* aq-mar stx1 aran-sc stx1 arg-n k* Ars k* ars-s-f k2* aur-ar k2* bad stx1 bar-c b4.de Bell k* bell-p st* borx k* bry b7.de* bufo stx1 cadm-s k2* calad bro1* calc k* calc-f k* calc-p calc-s stx1 calc-sil k2* camph bg2* **Canth** k* Caps bg2* carb-an k* Carb-v cham b7.de* Chel k* Chin bg2* chr-ac stx1 cimic stx1 Cina b7.de* clem k* Cocc k* coff-t c1* colch b7.de coloc k* Con b4a.de* Croc k* crot-c stx1 crot-t bro1* Cupr stx1 cycl bro1* Dig k* dros bro1 dulc k* elae stx1 elaps br1* **Eup-per** stx1 **Ferr** k* ferr-ar k* ferr-m ld1.de ferr-p k2 Graph k* grat k* guare c1* gymno c1 haliae-lc srj5• Hep b4a.de* hyos k* Ign k* ip b7.de* jatr-c stx1 kali-ar kali-c k* kali-i k* kali-m k2* kali-p Kali-sil k2 Kreos kr1* lac-c stx1 lach sf1.de* lept bg2* lim stx1 lob bro1 Lyc k* M-ambo b7.de* m-arct b2.de Mag-p manc c1* mang k* Meph vml3* merc k* merc-i-r ptk1 mez b4.de mur-ac k* nat-ar Nat-c k* nat-m b4a.de nat-p nat-sil k2 nit-ac sf1.de Nux-m k* Nux-v k* oci-sa sp1* ol-an vml3* op bg2* Par b7a.de Ph-ac k* phys c1 plb b7a.de psil ft1 puls k* pycnop-sa mrz1 raph stx1 rauw sp1* Rhod k* **Rhus-t** k* sabad bro1* samb ptk1 sarcol-ac vml3• sars k* seneg b4.de **Sep** b4.de* Sil k* sol-t-ae c1 Spig k* spong bg2* squil b7.de* staph b7.de* stram k* Sul-ac k* Sulph k* Syph stx1 Tarent tell rsj10• Teucr k* thea stx1 thuj k* trios hl1* trom stx1 tus-p stx1 verat k* Verat-v vml3* ziz hl1
    - ⁝ **accompanied** by | **pneumonia** (See CHEST - Inflammation - lungs - right - lower - accompanied - thirst)
    - ⁝ **heated**, when: Acon stx1 ars stx1 bell-p c1* Bry k2* Coloc stx1 crot-t stx1 Kali-ar k* Kali-c k* Nat-c Rhus-t k2* samb
    - ⁝ **hot** weather, in: Bry k* carb-v stx1 Kali-c k* Nat-c k* nat-s stx1 Nux-m stx1 verat ptk1
    - ⁝ **ice** water: Acon kr1 **Ars** kr1 carb-v kr1* dig ptk1 elaps stx1 ip stx1 kali-c cp1 kali-i k2 meph stx1 merc kr1 nat-c stx1 puls kr1 rhus-t kr1* Verat-v kr1*

- **agg.**: ...
  - : **perspiring**; when: bell-p mrr1
- **amel.**: acon bg2* acon-f agar stx1 *Agar-em* c1* all-c allox tpw3 aloe k* *Alumn* vml3* *Ambr* k* aml-ns c1 anac k* ang b7.de *Ant-t* k* ap-g c1 apis k* aq-mar stx1 arg-n ptk1* ars k* *Asar* k* aster sf1.de* bamb-a stx1 bar-m c1* *Bell* ptk1 **Bism** k* borx k* brom bg2* **Bry** k* calc k* camph bro1 cann-i bro1 cann-s bt3 cann-xyz ptk1 canth b7.de *Carb-ac* kr1* carc stx1 cassia-s cdd7*• **Caust** k* cham k* chim stx1 *Clem* k* coc-c k* coff coff-t c1 cortico stx1 *Cupr* k* dros stx1 euphr stx1 fago bro1 *Fl-ac* bg2 galla-q-r nl2• hydroph rsj6• hyper stx1 ign ptk1 *Jatr-c* bro1* kali-c k* kali-m ptk1 lac-c br1 **Lach** ptk1 laur k* *Led* bro1 lob-c c1 lob-s c1 mangi vml3• meph jl* merc-i-f ptk1* moly-met jl* *Onos* k* op bg2* petr-ra shn4• **Phos** k* phyt bg2* pic-ac bro1* *Puls* k* rad-br c1* rauw stx1 ruta fd4.de sang ptk1 sanic c1* sel ptk1* **Sep** k* sil sne stann jl3* stel vml3• sumb tab bg2* tep c1 thuj k* trios jl3* tritic-vg fd5.de tung-met bdx1• verat k* xan c1 zinc k* zinc-p k2 [cupr-act stj2 cupr-f stj2 cupr-m stj2 cupr-p stj2]
  - : **ice** water: xan kr1*
- **aversion**: *Acet-ac* vh1 acon bt3 alum-p k2* ant-t ld1.de arg-n sne arn ld1.de* *Ars* ld1.de* bell k* brom k* bry k* *Calad* k* *Calc-ar* ld1.de* canth k* carb-an b4a.de* caust k* chel k* chin k* *Chinin-ar* k* cycl bg2 dig ld1.de elaps ld1.de kali-i ld1.de kali-p fd1.de• **Lyc** mrr1* lyss k* mag-c st *Med* vh musa vml3• nat-m k* *Nat-p* vh nat-s ld1.de neon stj2*• nux-v k* onos ld1.de* *Phel* k* phos ld1.de* phys k* puls ld1.de* pycnop-sa mrz1 rhus-t ld1.de* **Sabad** ld1.de* *Stram* k* sul-ac k2 sulfonam ks2 sulph ld1.de* symph fd3.de• tab k* thyr st1 *Verat* ld1.de*
- **desire**: abel jl3 abrom-a ks5 achy jl **Acon** k* agar k* agar-em bro1 agath-a nl2• ail k* allox tpw4* aloe sne *Alum* ld1.de* *Alumn* k* am-c k* am-m b7.de* anan vh1 anders bnj1 androc srj1*• *Ang* k* ant-c b7a.de* *Ant-t* k* apis b7a.de* apoc k2* *Arg-n* k* arge-pl rwt5• arizon-l nl2• arn k* **Ars** k* arum-t kr1 asaf asim k* aster k* aur k* aur-ar k2* aur-s k2* aza c1 bamb-a stb2.de• bar-ox-suc rly4• *Bell* k* *Bism* k* bit-ar wht1• borx ld1.de* *Bov* k* brass-n-o srj5• **Bry** k* cadm-s k2* *Calc* k* *Calc-ar* calc-f nh *Calc-s* camph kr1* cann-i cann-s bt3 cann-xyz bg2 *Caps* k* carb-ac c1 carb-an h2 carb-v k2 carbn-s k* carc vh* cassia-s ccrh1• *Caust* k* cedr k* *Cench* k* **Cham** k* chel **Chin** k* *Chinin-ar* k* *Chinin-s* kr1 chlam-tr bcx2• choc srj3*• cimic **Cina** k* cinnb k* clem k* coc-c k* *Cocc* k* colch k* *Coloc* b4a.de cop gsw1 corn kr1 *Croc* k* crot-c sk4• *Cuc-c* vml3• *Cupr* k* *Cupr-act* kr1* *Cupr-ar* vml3• cypra-eg sde6.de• dig k* diph ptk1 dream-p sdj1• *Dulc* k* *Echi* k* **Eup-per** k* euph k* ferr-p mrr1 fl-ac k* germ-met srj5• gink-b sbd1*• *Glon* *Graph* k* guaj bc haliae-lc srj5• ham fd3.de• *Hell* hep kr1 hera vml3• hir rsj4• hydrog srj* hydroph rsj6• *Ign* b7.de* ip vh irid-met stj2*• jug-r vml3• kali-bi k* kali-br a1 *Kali-m* bg1* kali-n k* *Kali-p* k* *Kali-s* ketogl-ac rly4• kola stb3• lac-del hrn2• lac-h sk4• lac-leo hrn2• lap-a k* lat-m wm2 *Led* k* *Lepr* vml3• lept ptk1* limen-b-c hrn2* lob-c c1 *Luna* kg1*• *Lyc* *Lycps-v* k* mag-c k* mag-p bg2* malar al2* manc k* mand rsj7• *Med* c1* **Merc** k* **Merc-c** k* mez k* moni rfm1• myos-a rly4*• nat-ar *Nat-c* k* nat-m k* nat-ox rly4*• *Nat-p* k* **Nat-s** k* nat-sil fd3.de• neon srj5• nept-m lsd2.fr nux-v k* oci-sa sp1* oena k* olib-sac wmh1 *Olnd* k* onos k* op br1* orot-ac rly4*• oxal-a rly4• ozone sde2*• paro-i jl3* petr-ra shn4• *Ph-ac* k* **Phos** k* pic-ac pieri-b mlk9.de pin-con oss2• pitu-gl skp7*• plat k* *Plb* k* *Podo* k* polyg-h bg2* positr nl2• propr sa3• psor k* puls k* puls-n c1 pyrog a* rad-br c1 rauw tpw8* *Rhus-t* k* ruta k* *Sabad* k* sabin bg2* *Sacch* sht*• sacch-l bg1* sal-fr sle1• sang hr1 sanic c1 santin c1 sars k* sec k* sel b7.de* *Sep* k* sil kr1* spig k* spong k* squil k* stann jl3* stram kr1 stront-c sk4• succ-ac rly4• suis-em rly4• sulfonam ks2 sulph k* symph fd3.de• *Tama* vml3• tanac hl1 *Tarent* k* tell jl3* *Thuj* k* *Thyr* ptk1* tril-p c1 trios vml3• tritic-vg fd5.de tub a* vanil fd5.de ven-m rsj12* **Verat** k* vip k* vip-a jl3* vip-t gsw1 wye c1* x-ray al2 zinc k* *Zinc-o* c1 zinc-p k2* ziz c1 [alumin-s stj2 am-caust stj2 arg-p stj2 aur-m stj2 bar-br stj2 bar-i stj2 bar-met stj2 bell-p-sp dcm1 *Bism-sn* stj2 caes-met stj2 calc-p stj1 chr-s stj2 cupr-f stj2 cupr-m stj2 *Cupr-p* stj2 gal-s stj2 hafn-met stj2 heroin sdj2 lanth-met stj2 *Lith-p* stj2 lith-s stj2 *Mang-p* stj2 mang-s stj2 merc-d stj2 merc-i-f stj2 moly-met stj2 nicc-s stj2 osm-met stj2 plb-m stj2 *Plb-p* stj2 rhen-met stj2 tant-met stj2 thal-met stj2 titan-s stj2 tung-met stj2 zinc-i stj2 zinc-m stj2]
  - : **afternoon**: bism kr1 bov c1 caust a1* *Croc* a1 nat-m kr1 petr-ra shn4• ruta kr1* sars h2
    - : **15** h: caust a1*
  - : **evening**: bism hr1* bov c1 eug kr1 mag-c c1 oena a1* spong fd4.de
    - : **amel.**: ven-m rsj12•

- **cold** drink, cold water: ...
  - : **night**: *Calc* kr1* dulc fd4.de eup-per a1 mag-c c1 petr-ra shn4• rhus-t k2 ruta fd4.de spong fd4.de sulfonam ks2
    - : **midnight**:
      - . **after** | **2** h: petr-ra shn4•
  - : **accompanied** by | **hoarseness**: bamb-a stb2.de• hir skp7•
  - : **chill**, during: bry k2* carb-v k2 *Eup-per* gk* nat-s k2 sulfonam ks2 tub k2 wye br1
  - : **cough**; during: cassia-s ccrh1•
  - : **everything** else; with an aversion to: acet-ac vh1 sanic c1 tril-p c1
  - : **fever**, during: **Acon** bg2 ang bg2 *Ars* bg2 bell bg2 bism bg2 *Bry* b7a.de calc bg2 caps k2 *Cham* bg2 **Chin** bg2 cupr bg2 *Ign* bg2 **Merc** bg2 *Nat-m* k2 nat-s k2 nux-v bg2 oci-sa sp1 olnd bg2 phos bg2 plb bg2 puls bg2 rhus-t bg2 sabad bg2 squil bg2 sulfonam ks2 thuj bg2 tub k2 verat bg2
  - : **ice** water: acon kr1* *Agar-em* c1* ars kr1* benzol c1 caps k2 lept kr1* nat-s br1 nux-m k2 onos kr1* phos kr1* sil kr1* tril-p c1 *Verat* kr1* wye c1
  - : **ice**-cold water: cupr sst3• lept vml3• mag-p ptk1 nat-m bg2* nat-s mtf33 onos vml3• phos ptk1* ruta ptk1 tril-p vml3• trios rsj1• verat mtf33 wye vml3• [ant-met stj2]
  - : **small** quantities: (↗*STOMACH - Thirst - small)* bung-fa mtf
  - : **thirst**; without: ars bg2 calad ptk1 camph bg2* cocc bg2* coloc bg2* graph bg2 nux-v bg2 phos bg2
- **cold** food:
  - **agg.**: (↗*frozen - agg.)* acet-ac k* acon bg2* agar k* alum k* alum-p k2* alum-sil k2* *Alumn* kr1* *Ant-c* k* *Arg-n* arist-cl wm2 **Ars** k* ars-s-f k2* bar-c k* *Bell* bg2* bell-p sp1* *Bov* k* brom *Bry* k* calad k* calc k* calc-f *Calc-p* calc-sil k2 canth k* *Carb-v* k* *Carbn-s* k* caust k* cham k* chel k* *Cocc* k* coff-t c1 coloc *Con* k* crot-t bg2* cupr bg2 dig dros ptk2 **Dulc** k* elaps kr1* ferr bg2 fl-ac bg2 *Graph* k* hell k* *Hep* k* *Hyos* bg2 ign k* ip bg2 kali-ar **Kali-bi** bg2* *Kali-c* k* kali-i k* kali-m k2 *Kali-n* k* kali-sil k2 *Kreos* k* **Lach** k* lept bg2* limest-b es1*• **Lyc** k* mag-c k* mag-m k* mag-p bg2 *Mang* k* *Merc* k* merc-i-r vml3• mez bg2 mur-ac k* nat-ar nat-c k* nat-m k* nat-p *Nat-s* nat-sil k2 *Nit-ac* k* *Nux-m* k* **Nux-v** k* par k* *Ph-ac* k* plb k* psil vml3• *Puls* k* *Rhod* k* **Rhus-t** k* rumx sabad k* *Sep* k* **Sil** k* *Spig* k* squil bg2* *Staph* bg2* stram bg2* sul-ac b2.de* *Sulph* k* *Syph* st* thuj k* *Verat* k* [mang-act stj2 mang-m stj2 mang-met stj2 mang-n stj2 mang-s stj2]
    - : **overheated**; when: bell-p br1* kali-ar mrr1
  - **amel.**: acon b2.de* adlu kr1* agn b2.de* alum b2.de* alumn kr1* am-c b2.de* *Ambr* b2.de* *Anac* b2.de* ang b2.de* ant-t b2.de* apis bg2* arg-n kr1* ars b2.de* *Asar* b2.de* *Bar-c* b2.de* *Bell* b2.de* bism bg2* borx b2.de* brom bg2* **Bry** b2.de* *Calc* b2.de* cann-s kr1* canth b2.de* *Carb-v* b2.de* *Caust* b2.de* *Cham* b2.de* clem b2.de* coc-c bg2* *Cupr* b2.de* dros b2.de* *Euph* b2.de* *Ferr* b2.de* graph bg2 hell b2.de* *Kali-c* b2.de* *Lach* b2.de* *Laur* b2.de* lyc bro1* m-arct b2.de *M-aust* b2.de mag-c b2.de* mag-m b2.de* *Merc* b2.de* merc-i-f vml3• *Mez* b2.de* *Nat-m* b2.de* *Nux-m* b2.de* nux-v b2.de* op bg2* par b2.de* *Ph-ac* b2.de* **Phos** b2.de* phyt bg2* **Puls** b2.de* pyrog bg2* rhod b2.de* rhus-t b2.de* sars b2.de* *Sep* b2.de* sil b2.de* spig b2.de* squil b2.de* stann bg2* *Sul-ac* b2.de* sulph b2.de* tab bg2* thuj b2.de* verat b2.de* *Zinc* b2.de* [bar-br stj2 calc-br stj1 kali-br stj1 nat-br stj2]
  - **aversion**: acet-ac k* alum-p k2* arg-n sne chel k* cycl k* germ-met srj5• kali-i ld1.de lyc mrr1 *Med* vh phos ld1.de sabad k2 [brom stj1 kali-br stj1]
  - **desire**: abel jl3 acon ptk1 am-c k* ang b7.de* *Ant-t* k* *Apis* k2 arg-n k2* *Ars* b4a.de* asaf kr1* bell b4.de* bism b7.de* *Bov* b4a.de *Bry* b7.de* cadm-s ptk1 calc b4a.de* *Camph* vml3• carc fd2.de• caust b4.de* *Cham* b7.de* chin kr1* cina b7.de* cocc b7.de* croc b7.de* cupr k* cupr-ar k* dendr-pol sk4• diph ptk1 dulc b4a.de* *Elaps* vh *Eup-per* ptk1* euph b4.de* ferr-p bg2 fl-ac st* glycyr-g cte1• *Ign* b7.de* kali-p bg2* *Kali-s* k* lach k2* lept ptk1* *Lyc* manc ptk1 merc b4.de* merc-c k* nat-ar bl nat-m k* nat-p bl *Nat-s* kr1* *Nux-v* k* olnd b7.de* onos ptk1 ph-ac b4a.de **Phos** k* pic-ac ld1.de* pieri-b mlk9.de pip-n bg2* plb b7.de* **Puls** k* rhus-g tmo3• rhus-t b7.de* ruta b7.de* sabad b7.de* sanic vh sars k2* sec bg2* *Sil* k* sulph b4a.de *Thuj* k* tritic-vg fd5.de tub a ven-m rsj12* *Verat* k* zinc k* [cupr-act stj2 cupr-f stj2 cupr-m stj2 cupr-p stj2 mag-sil stj2 nat-sil stj2 stann stj2 zinc-i stj2 zinc-m stj2 zinc-p stj2]
    - : **afternoon**: nat-m a1
    - : **accompanied** by | **menses**: am-c k*

- **desire**: ...
  - **fever**; during: **Acon** bg2 ant-t bg2 ars bg2 bell bg2 bism bg2 borx bg2 *Bry* bg2 calc bg2 cham bg2 **Chin** bg2 croc bg2 cupr bg2 ign bg2 **Merc** bg2 olnd bg2 puls bg2 rhus-t bg2 ruta bg2 sabad bg2 sil bg2 squil bg2 sulph bg2 thuj bg2 verat bg2
  - **milk** (See milk - desire - cold)
  - **pregnancy**, in: *Verat* kr1
  - **thirst**; without: *Camph* vh *Coloc* vh
- **condiments** (See spices)
- **cooked** food:
  - **agg.**: *(↗warm food - agg.)* ars jl* podo k2
    - **smell** of; sensitive to the (See NOSE - Smell - acute - cooking)
  - **aversion**: *(↗warm food - aversion)* am-c b4.de* anac b4.de* ars b4.de* asar jl3* bell k* bov k* calc k* chel k* choc srj3*• cupr k* *Graph* k* guare k* ham fd3.de• ign k* *Kreos* hr1* lach k* *Lyc* k* mag-c k* merc k* nat-sil fd3.de• petr k* phos k* psor sars b4.de* *Sil* k* sulph b4.de* verat k* zinc k* zinc-p k2* [mag-i stj1 mag-lac stj2 *Mag-met* stj2 mag-sil stj2]
    - **overcooked** food: [zirc-met stj2]
  - **desire**: cycl bg2 ferr bg2 lyc bg2 mag-c b4.de* nit-ac h2
- **corn**:
  - **agg.**: calc-ar stx1 chin gl1.fr*• kali-c gl1.fr• puls gl1.fr*• sulph gl1.fr*•
    - **meal**: calc-ar
- **corned** beef and piccalilli | **desire**: falco-pe nl2•
- **crab**:
  - **agg.**: tet stx1
  - **aversion**: [tell stj2]
- **cranberries**:
  - **agg.**: ox-ac k2
  - **aversion**: mag-m jl prot jl3*
  - **desire**: ign h1
- **cream**: *(↗whipped)*
  - **aversion**: adam srj5• puls bl1 syc ptj1*• tritic-vg fd5.de
  - **desire**: carc mlr1• elaps vml lac-h sk4• **Puls** mrr1
    - **sour** cream: [ant-m stj2]
    - **whipped** cream (See whipped)
- **creamy** food | **desire**: lac-lup hrn2• puls zr
- **crispy** food | **desire**: calc mtf calc-p mtf lach mtf nat-m mtf nux-v mtf phos mtf puls mtf sulph mtf
- **crunchy** food | **desire**: sep vh
- **cucumbers**: *(↗gherkins)*
  - **agg.**: *All-c* sf1.de* apis bg2 ars bg2* *Ign* sf1.de* lap-la rsp1 *Nat-m* sf1.de* puls sf1.de* *Rhus-t* sf1.de* sul-ac h1* verat bg2* [*Arg-met* stj1* *Arg-n* stj2 *Arg-p* stj2]
  - **aversion**: *All-c* mrr1 falco-pe nl2• prot jl3* [ant-c stj2 ant-m stj2 ant-met stj2 ant-t stj2 *Arg-met* stj1]
  - **desire**: abies-n k* *Ant-c* k* lac-leo hrn2• lac-loxod-a hrn2• *Phos* vh* *Sulph* vh* symph fd3.de• tritic-vg fd5.de *Verat* k* [*Ant-m* stj2 *Ant-met* stj2 *Ant-t* stj2]
- **curd** | **desire**: cassia-s ccrh1*•
- **curry** | **desire**: [ang stj4]
- **dainties** (See delicacies)
- **dairy** products: *(↗butter; cheese; milk)*
  - **agg.**: *(↗butter - agg.; cheese - agg.; milk - agg.)* agar zr coli vml3• lac-c mtf lac-d mtf levo vml3• vanil fd5.de
  - **aversion**: [heroin sdj2]
  - **desire**: *(↗butter - desire; milk - desire)* cisplat vml3• lac-c mtf lac-d mtf mag-f vml3• tritic-vg fd5.de
- **dates** | **desire**: plut-n srj7•
- **delicacies**:
  - **agg.**: puls ptk1
  - **aversion**: caust k2 petr ld1.de sang ld1.de
  - **desire**: *(↗sweets - desire)* *Acon-l* a1* aeth bg1 anan a2 arg-n k13* *Aur* k* bufo k* calc k* carc a **Chin** k* cub k* cupr k* cupr-ar ld1.de* elaps gk guar vml3• **Ip** k* kali-c kali-s fd4.de lil-t c1* mag-c mag-m b4a.de* melal-alt gya4 nat-c k* paull a2* petr k* plb mtf33 plb-act vh podo fd3.de•

- **delicacies** – **desire**: ...
  psor k* rauw sp1* *Rhus-t* k* *Sabad* k* *Sacch* c1* sacch-l sna* sang k* *Spong* k* symph fd3.de• **Tub** k*
  - **and** salt: **Arg-n** st *Calc* st carb-v st carc st caste st* castm vml3• *Med* st nat-sil fd3.de• *Plb* st
  - **and** sour: *Bry* st *Calc* st *Carb-v* st *Kali-c* st kali-s fd4.de *Med* st *Sabad* st *Sec* st *Sep* st **Sulph** st
  - **sexual** desire; with: chin ptk1
- **diet** | **agg.** | **errors** in diet: *(↗RECTUM - Diarrhea - indiscretion; STOMACH - Slow)* all-c ptk1 all-s kr1* ant-c mrr1* bry stx1 calc-ar kr1* carb-v stx1 cham stx1 chin stx1 *Cic* stx1 coff stx1 dios c1* fl-ac ptk1 graph ptk1 guar stx1 ip stx1 iris stx1 kali-p mrr1 lyc stx1 mag-c c2 nat-c ptk1* nux-m mrr1 nux-v c1* olnd mrr1 paull stx1 puls kr1* sal-ac kr1* sul-ac ptk1 sulph mrr1 xan stx1 xanth stx1
  - **aversion** | **ordinary** diet: ign br1
- **digest**; food he cannot | **desire**: *(↗indigestible - desire)* bry b7.de* *Chin* b7.de* phos bg2 *Puls* b7.de* rheum b7.de*
- **dinner** | **aversion**: carb-an k* coc-c k* malar c1 mygal c1 verat k*
- **dirt**: *(↗indigestible)*
  - **desire**: calc br1 cic mrr1
- **drinks**: *(↗liquids)*
  - **agg.**: absin stx1 art-v stx1 *Bell* stx1 bry stx1 canth c1 *Cimx* stx1 *Cocc* stx1 con stx1 *Hyos* stx1 *Lyss* stx1 plect stx1 podo c1 pop-cand c1 rhus-g stx1 *Stram* stx1 trom br1 *Verat* k2
  - **aversion**: *(↗liquid food - aversion)* acet-ac vh1 agar k* *Agn* k* aloe k* ang k* *Apis* arn k* *Ars* kr1 *Bell* k* berb k* borx bg2* bov bg2* bry bg2* bufo k* calad bg2* calc st* calen c1 camph bg2* *Canth* k* carb-an k* caust b4a.de* cham bg2* chin k* chinin-s bg2* chlor a1* coc-c cocc k* coff k* colch bg2 coloc ld1.de con k* corn cupr k* cupr-act c1 cycl tl1 dros ld1.de **Ferr** k* graph k* ham kr1* hell b7.de* **Hyos** k* ign k* kali-bi bro1* kali-m ckh1 kola stb3• *Lac-c* lach k* lyc bg2* *Lyss* k* m-aust b7.de* merc k* nat-m bg2* *Nit-ac* **Nux-v** k* op b7.de* phys k* plb plb-chr a1* *Puls* rat k* sabin bg2* samb k* sec k* staph ld1.de* *Stram* k* verat bg2* [arg-met stj2 arg-n stj2 arg-p stj2]
    - **accompanied** by:
      - **thirst**: agn b2.de ang k* arizon-l nl2• arn b2.de* ars ptk1 **Bell** b2.de* cann-xyz bg2 canth b2.de* caust b2.de* cocc k* falco-pe nl2• galeoc-c-h gms1• *Hell* ptk1 **Hyos** b2.de* ix bnm8• kola stb3• lac-lup hrn2• lach b2.de* lyc b2.de* merc bg2 merc-c mez nat-m k* *Nux-v* k* rhus-t b2.de* samb b2.de* spong fd4.de **Stram** b2.de* [bell-p-sp dcm1]
      - **Head**; pain in: **Ferr** k* sep tl1
    - **alternating** with | **thirst**: berb k* hell *Lac-c* gsw1 sel gsw1 stram bg3
    - **children**, in: borx bg2 bry bg2
    - **heat**, during: agn bg2 arn bg2 ars bg2 *Bell* bg2 *Canth* bg2 caust bg2 *Cocc* bg2* con k* **Hell** b7.de* *Hyos* bg2 ign bg2 ix bnm8• lach bg2 lyc bg2 merc bg2 naja bg2 nat-m bg2 *Nux-v* bg2 rhus-t bg2 samb bg2 *Stram* bg2 sulph bg2 *Verat* bg2*
    - **vomiting**: ix bnm8•
    - **weather** | **warm**: ix bnm8•
  - **desire**: bell h2* camph a2 cob-n sp1 coloc a2 ferr b7.de* lac-ac stj5• lyc ld1.de plect c1 staph b7a.de wies a2 [*Beryl* stj2 chr-m stj2 chr-met stj2 germ-met stj2 lith-c stj2 lith-f stj2 lith-i stj2 lith-m stj2 lith-met stj2 mag-s stj1 stann stj2]
    - **accompanied** by:
      - **disgust** of drinks: *Bell* b4a.de caust b4a.de lyc b4a.de nat-m b4a.de
      - **swallowing**; difficult: *Bell* b4.de
      - **thirstlessness**: aeth *Ars* k* bell a1* *Calad* k* *Camph* k* *Cimx* cocc k* coloc k* graph k* nux-m k* ph-ac b4.de phos k* wies a1*
        - **fever**; during: *Ars* bg2 calad bg2 camph bg2 cocc bg2 *Coloc* bg2 graph bg2 nux-m bg2 ph-ac bg2 phos bg2
    - **capricious**, but refuses when offered: bell h1*
    - **eating**; while: am-c b4a.de nit-ac b4a.de
- **dry** food:
  - **agg.**: agar k* bov bg2* bry mrr1 calad bt3* **Calc** k* chin k* ip k* *Lyc* k* *Nat-c* k* nit-ac k* nux-v k* ox-ac bt3 petr k* ph-ac k* *Puls* k* raph bt3* sars k* sil k* sulph k*
  - **aversion**: dream-p sdj1• merc b4.de* phos dx1 ruta fd4.de

- **desire**: *Alum* k* lach sne lap-la rsp1 sanguis-s hrn2• [alumin stj2 alumin-p stj2 alumin-s stj2]

- **duck** | **desire**: med mtf phos mtf
- **earth** | **desire**: alum bg2* calc bg2* cic bg2 con bg2 ferr bg2 hep bg2 hyos bg2 ign bg2 *Nat-m* b4a.de *Nit-ac* b4.de* *Nux-v* b7a.de* oci bg2 puls b7a.de *Sep* b4a.de sil bg2 sulph bg2 tarent bg2
- **eaten**; just | **aversion**: nux-v k2
- **eel** | **desire**: *Med* ld1.de
- **eggplants** (See aubergines)
- **eggs**:

- **agg.**: androc stx1 anthraci st* bacls-10 ptj1*• *Calc* bg2* calc-f sf1.de* c a r b - v a1* carc fb* card-m vml3• *Chinin-ar* k* *Cocc* vh colch k* coli vml3• con bg1 *Ferr* k* ferr-m k* ign vh led ptk1 lyc bg2 lyss stx1 merc-c bg2* morg ptj1*• morg-p fmm1• musa vml3• nat-m vh nux-v br1 oscilloc jl2 pitu-a vml2* plb mrr1* prot ptj1*• psor bgs ptel gk **Puls** bg2* *Sulph* bg2* syc a* tub bgs [aur-s stj2 cinnb stj2 ferr-f stj2 ferr-lac stj2 ferr-n stj2 *Ferr-s* stj1 gal-s stj2]
  - **bad** eggs: carb-v c1
  - **smell** of: (↗*NOSE - Smell - acute - eggs*) anthraci st *Colch* k* s u l p h stx1 upa c1
- **amel.**: calc tl1
- **aversion**: agar vh* *Anthraci* vh1* bacls-10 ptj1*• bell bg2* bry sf1.de* c a l c gk calc-f mg1.de* carc c1* colch st* con xyz61 *Ferr* k* ferr-m stj1*• gink-b sbd1*• helo-s rwt2• kali-n mrr kali-s k* morg vml3• morg-g ptj1*• morg-p ptj1*• nat-m vh *Nit-ac* k* ol-an bg3 phos vh* prot pte1* *Puls* st* s a r o t h mg1.de* *Sulph* k* *Syc* ptj1*• tritic-vg fd5.de tub dx1* tung-met bdx1• upa c1* [alumin-s stj2 ant-c stj2 aur-s stj2 beryl-m stj2 c a d m - s stj2 calc-s stj1 chr-s stj2 cinnb stj2 ferr-f stj2 ferr-i stj1 ferr-lac stj2 ferr-n stj2 ferr-p stj1 *Ferr-s* stj1 gal-s stj2 lith-s stj2 mag-s stj1 mang-s stj2 nicc-s stj2 sul-ac stj1 titan-s stj2]
  - **morning**: gink-b sbd1•
  - **boiled**:
    - **aluminium** pans; in: alum tl1
    - **hard** boiled: bry h1* prot pte1*
    - **soft** boiled: sulph mrr1
  - **egg** white: nat-m mrr1
  - **raw** eggs: [*Gal-s* stj2]
  - **smell** of: anthraci vh1* *Colch* k* upa c1
- **desire**: agar a* amp rly4• bac a* bar-c a* *Calc* k* calc-p bg2* carb-an mrr1 *Carc* c1* cartl-s rly4• cassia-s ccrh1*• caust vh* corian-s knl6• cortiso vml3• cystein-l rly4• dream-p sdj1• dulc fd4.de ephe-si hsj1• gaert ptj1*• ham fd3.de• helo-s rwt2• hydr k* kali-s fd4.de lac-h sk4• loxo-recl knl4• *Morg* vml3• morg-g ptj1*• morg-p a* nat-p k* nat-pyru rly4• nat-sil stj2*• ol-an k* olnd ld1.de* pant-ac rly4• phos mrr1 prot pte1* *Puls* vh rhus-g tmo3• ruta fd4.de sanic vh* seneg b4a.de sil vh* spong fd4.de s u i s - p a n rly4• sulph zf tub hu vanil fd5.de [calc-f stj1 *Calc-lac* stj2 *Calc-met* stj2 *Calc-sil* stj2 coch-o stj kali-sil stj2 mag-sil stj2 mang-sil stj2 nat-caust stj2 nat-lac stj2 sil-met stj2 tax jsj7]
  - **boiled**:
    - **hard** boiled: **Calc** carbn-dox knl3• nat-sil fd3.de• puls mrr1 ruta fd4.de spong fd4.de vanil fd5.de [*Beryl* stj2]
    - **soft** boiled: *Calc* k* nat-p ld1.de nit-ac gk ol-an k* olnd ld1.de *Puls* vh* sanic mrr1 [*Beryl* stj2 calc-met stj2]
  - **fried** eggs: calc-p mtf dulc fd4.de haliae-lc srj5• ham fd3.de• kali-s fd4.de nat-p k* ruta fd4.de sil vh* spong fd4.de tub mtf [tax jsj7]

- **everything**:

- **aversion** to: acon-l a1* alum alumn gsw1 am-m k* bov k* caps k* cupr k* grat k* hyos k* ip k* kali-c h2 lyc k* merc k* mez k* mur-ac h2 nit-ac h2 n u x - v k* plat k* plb gsw1 *Puls* k* rheum k* rhod k* rhus-t c1 *Sabad* k2 sars k* senec c1 sep k* sulph k* syph k2 thea k* ther k* thuj k*
  - **daytime**: sep
  - **morning**: lyc plb
  - **forenoon**: sars
  - **afternoon** | **13** h: grat
  - **except** to cold water (See cold drink - desire - everything)
- **desire**: plat ptk1 santin gsw1 sulph ptk1* [ang stj4]

- **farinaceous**: (↗*wheat*)

- **agg.**: *All-c* kr1 alum bg2* *Bry* bg2* *Carb-an* kr1 *Carb-v* bg2* *Caust* k* *Chin* kr1* coloc bg2* *Cop* vml3• euph vml3• *Iris* bg1* kali-bi bg2* kali-c bg2 levo vml3• *Lyc* k* mag-c bg2* moni rfm1• *Nat-c* k* **Nat-m** k* **Nat-s** k* nux-v k* ox-ac k2 *Plb* kr1 psor bg2* **Puls** bg2* rhus-t kr1 rob br1 sulph k* tub bgs verat bg2* [ant-c stj2 ant-m stj2 ant-met stj2 ant-t stj2 lith-m stj2 n a t - a r stj2 nat-br stj2 nat-caust stj2 nat-lac stj2 nat-met stj2 nat-sil stj2]
- **amel.** in children: nat-c ptk1
- **aversion**: (↗*flour - aversion*) abrom-a vml3• ars k* chin ld1.de* *Kali-act* vh lyc ld1.de *Nat-c* ld1.de nat-m bg2* nat-s tl1* nux-m zf ph-ac ld1.de* phos k* plan ld1.de* ptel bg2* puls zf *Sulph* ld1.de* [aur-m stj2 cob-m stj2 cupr-m stj2 nat-ar stj2 nat-br stj2]
- **desire**: (↗*pasta - desire*) adam srj5• aeth vh aloe sne *Alum* k* aq-mar mgm• atri st* aur vh aur-m-n wbt2• *Calc* k* calc-p bro1* carc mlr1* chir-fl gya2 cic cypra-eg sde6.de• *Ferr-act* vh foll asm• *Galeoc-c-h* gms1• germ-met srj5• ignis-alc es2• kali-sil vh lac-h sze9• lach k* lyc hr1 *Nat-m* k* nept-m lsd2.fr nid vml3• nit-ac k* nux-v phos gk2* positr nl2• psor vh puls zf sabad k* sal-fr sle1• sanguis-s hrn2• *Sulph* vh sumb k* tritic-vg fd5.de tub mtf tung-met bdx1• vanil fd5.de [alumin stj2 alumin-p stj2 alumin-s stj2 ant-m stj2 aur-m stj2 bar-i stj2 beryl-m stj2 cadm-m stj2 calc-s stj1 *Chlor* stj2 chr-m stj2 cob-m stj2 cupr-m stj2 *Iod* stj2 kali-m stj1 lith-i stj2 lith-m stj2 m a n g - i stj2 mang-m stj2 merc-d stj2 merc-i-f stj2 mur-ac stj2 nat-ar stj2 nat-br stj2 nat-caust stj2 nat-f stj2 nat-lac stj2 nat-met stj2 nat-sil stj2 plb-m stj2 stront-m stj2 zinc stj2 zinc-i stj2 zinc-m stj2 zinc-p stj2]

- **farsan**:

- **agg.**: lach mtf
- **amel.**: nux-v mtf
- **aversion**: chin mtf
- **desire**: aur mtf aur-s mtf calc mtf calc-p mtf med mtf nat-c mtf nat-m mtf nit-ac mtf nux-v mtf puls mtf sulph mtf

- **fat**:

- **agg.**: (↗*heavy - agg.; meat - agg. - fat; oil - agg.; pork - agg.; rich - agg.*) acon k* adlu vml3• agn bg2* alet sf1.de* ange-s oss1• ant-c k* ant-t k* aran-ix mg1.de* arg-n bg1* *Ars* k* ars-s-f k2* *Asaf* k* bacls-10 ptj1*• bell k* bell-p stx1 bros-gau mrc1 bry k* buni-o jl3* but-ac sp1* calc bg2* calc-f mg1.de* caps fkm1• carb-an k* **Carb-v** k* carbn-s k* *Carc* st1* card-m vml3• *Caust* k* chin k* chinin-ar vml3• cladon vml3• *Colch* k* conv stx1 convo-s jl* cortico vml3• cortiso vml3* cupr ld1.de **Cycl** k* *Dros* k* dulc fd4.de dys fmm1• erig mg1.de* euph k* **Ferr** k* *Ferr-ar* *Ferr-m* k* *Gaert* ptj1*• *Gink-b* vml3• **Graph** bg2 ham bg2 *Hell* k* hep k* hir jl* *Ip* k* jug-r st* kali-ar kali-c k* *Kali-chl* *Kali-m* c1* kali-n k* kali-p fd1.de• kali-s bl kali-sil k2* *Lept* vh* *Lyc* bg2* lyss stx1 mag-c k* *Mag-m* k* mag-s mg1.de* mand mg1.de* meny k* merc k* merc-c k* m e r c - c y ld1.de morg vml3• morg-p ptj1*• myos-a vml3• *Nat-ar* nat-c k* nat-m k* *Nat-p* k* nat-sil k2* *Nit-ac* k* nux-m gk nux-v k* oena vml3• o r o t - a c vml3• phos k* pin-con oss2• pitu-a vml2*• podo k2* psor bg2* *Ptel* k* **Puls** k* rob k* ruta k* sang gk* sanic c1 *Sep* k* sil k* sin-n vml3* *Spig* stx1 *Spong* k* staph k* *Sulph* k* syc ptj1* symph fd3.de• **Tarax** k* **Tarent** ld1.de* *Thuj* k* tritic-vg fd5.de tub bgs *Tub-a* st1 vanil fd5.de verat k* [alum stj2 calc-sil stj2 ferr-f stj2 ferr-lac stj2 ferr-n stj2 ferr-sil stj2 mag-lac stj2 mag-met stj2 mag-n stj2 mag-sil stj2 mang-n stj2 mang-sil stj2 moly-met stj2 nat-caust stj2 nitro stj2 oxyg stj2 sil-met stj2 tung-met stj2 zinc-n stj2]
  - **infants**, in: but-ac sp1* *Gaert* fmm1•
  - **rancid**: ars c1* carb-v c1*
- **amel.**: nux-v ptk1
- **aversion**: (↗*meat - aversion - fat*) acon-l a1* adam srj5• aeth vh1 ambr gk* ang k* aran-ix vml3• arg-n vh* *Ars* k* ars-s-f k2* asar vh* *Aur-m-n* wbt2• bac vml3• bacls-7 ptj1*• bell k* *Bry* k* calc k* *Calc-f* mg1.de* *Carb-an* k* *Carb-v* k* carbn-s k* *Carc* st* **Chin** k* chinin-ar choc srj3*• *Colch* k* convo-s sp1 croc k* *Cycl* k* dros k* dulc fd4.de erig mg1.de* f a l c o - p e nl2• ferr bg2 ferru-g sys1 grat k* guare k* ham fd3.de• hell k* *Hep* k* *Ip* st* ipom-p sp kali-bi bl kali-c gk kali-m ptk1 kali-s gk *Lac-c* al2 lac-f wza1• luf-op vml3• lyc ld1.de lyss mag-m mrr1 mag-s mg1.de* mand mg1.de* *Mang* gsw1 med vh meny k* *Merc* k* morg vml3• morg-g ptj1*• morg-p ptj1*• nat-ar k* nat-c k* *Nat-m* k* nat-n a* nat-p fkr6.de nat-sil fd3.de• nit-ac tl1* nux-v ld1.de* ozone sde2*• **Petr** k* phos k* podo fd3.de• **Ptel** k* **Puls** k* rheum k* rhus-t k* rib-ac jl3* *Rob* vml3• sacch sht*• sang sanic gk sec k* *Sep* k* *Sil* mrr1 sil-mar vh s p o n g fd4.de staph mrr1 *Sulph* k* syc ptj1*• symph fd3.de• syph gk tarent bg2* tax vml3• thyr jl3* tritic-vg fd5.de ulm-c gk [ant-c stj2 ant-m stj2

• **aversion**: ...
ant-met stj2 ant-t stj2 *Arg-met* stj1* *Arg-p* stj2 ars-met stj2 bar-n stj1 beryl-m stj2 erech stj ferr-n stj2 kali-ar stj2 *Mag-n* stj2 *Mang-n* stj2 nat-br stj2 *Nitro* stj2 spect dfg1 tung-met stj2 *Zinc-n* stj2]

⋮ **smell** of: *Colch* b7a.de

• **desire**: *(↗bacon - desire; fried - desire; ham - desire - fat; lard - desire)* arg-n vh* arge-pl rwt5• ars k* aur-m-n wbt2• calc st* *Calc-p* bg2* *Carc* mg1.de* cench a chel a crot-h a cypra-eg sde6.de* dream-p sdj1• dys ptj1* elaps gk hep k* ign zf irid-met srj5• *Kali-n* vh* *Lepr* vml3• lob vh* mag-s mg1.de *Med* vh merc c1 mez bg2* *Morg* vml3• morg-g ptj1*• morg-p ptj1*• nat-c bg1 nat-m bg2 nat-s vh* **Nit-ac** k* *Nux-v* k* phos vh* plb a* plut-n stj2*• positr nl2• prot pte1* puls zf pycnop-sa mrz1 rad-br bg1* ran-b vh rat mrr1* rhus-t vh ruta fd4.de sacch sht*• sal-fr sle1• sanic bg2* *Sil* vh succ-ac rly4• sul-ac vh* *Sulph* k* syc ptj1*• tub bg1* vanil fd5.de [alumin-s stj2 ant-c stj2 ars-met stj2 aur-s stj2 bar-n stj1 cadm-s stj2 chr-s stj2 cinnb stj2 ferr-n stj2 gal-s stj2 kali-ar stj2 lith-s stj2 mag-n stj2 mang-n stj2 mang-s stj2 moly-met stj2 nat-ar stj2 nat-n stj1 nicc-s stj2 *Nitro* stj2 titan-s stj2 zinc-n stj2]

- **figs** | **desire**: plut-n srj7•
- **fish**: *(↗caviar)*

• **agg.**: *(↗oysters - agg.)* androc stx1 arg-n stx1 ars ptk1* astac c1* calad k* carb-an k* carb-v bg1* carbn-s k2* caust stx1 chin bg2* chinin-ar k* conch fkr1* ferr-p vh *Fl-ac* bg1* hom-xyz mgm• kali-c k* kali-n vml3• kali-p fd1.de• *Kali-s* bg2* lach b7a.de* lyc sf1.de mag-m ld1.de *Medus* bg2* moni rfm1• nat-s br1* phenob ld1.de* phos a *Plb* k* pull-g vl* *Puls* bg2* sanic bgs *Sep* bg2* thuj bg2* urt-u bg2* [chr-m stj2 cob-m stj2 nat-br stj2]

⋮ **fresh**-water fish: astac vml3•

⋮ **fried**: kali-c ptk1

⋮ **pickled**: arg-n stx1 calad bg2*

⋮ **poisonous**: *Ars* bg2 **Berb** bg2 *Carb-v* bg2 **Cop** bg2 euph bg2 *Lach* bg2 lyc bg2 *Pyrog* bg2 rhus-t bg2

⋮ **smell** of; sensitive to (See NOSE - Smell - acute - fish)

⋮ **spoiled**: *All-c* hr1* ars k* bell bg2* **Berb** bt3* *Carb-an* hr1* *Carb-v* k* chin k* **Cop** bg2* euph vml3• *Kali-c* kr1 *Lach* sf1.de *Plb* kr1* psor bgs *Puls* k* *Pyrog* sf1.de* rhus-t bg2* ter sf1.de* ther sf1.de

• **amel.**: lac-c ptk1

• **aversion**: acon zf aq-mar mgm• ars-i vh1 asar vh* aur mgg• *Aur-m-n* wbt2• *Aur-s* wbt2• bell vh* calc-s sej carb-v ld1.de* carbn-s k2* caust mtf33 *Colch* k* conch fkr1* cortiso vml3• dulc fd4.de ferr-m vml3• gaert ptj1*• gal-ac vh1 **Graph** k* grat st* guare k* irid-met srj5• kali-i ld1.de kali-s gk limest-b es1*• marb-w es1*• med ser nat-m k* *Phos* k* pin-con oss2• ptel tl1 puls zf stram zf sulph k* vanil fd5.de *Zinc* k* [alumin-p stj2 arg-p stj2 aur-m stj2 calc-p stj1 cob-m stj2 cupr-m stj2 cupr-p stj2 kali-p stj1 lith-p stj2 mag-p stj1 mang-p stj2 nat-ar stj2 nat-br stj2 nat-caust stj2 nat-f stj2 nat-p stj1 ph-ac stj1 plb-m stj2 plb-p stj2 tell stj2 zinc-i stj2 zinc-m stj2 zinc-n stj2 zinc-p stj2]

⋮ **salty**: *Phos* k*

⋮ **soup**: phos mrr1

• **desire**: abrom-a gsb acon vh* adam srj5• aids nl2• ambr tsm1 atro a2 aur-m-n wbt2• bacls-10 ptj1• calc-p mg1.de* carc dgt* caust vh chir-fl gya2 coli rly4• cycl c1 cystein-l rly4• ferr-i stj1* haliae-lc srj5• ham fd3.de• hippoc-k szs2 *Kali-i* vh *Kali-p* fd1.de*• kali-s fkr2.de lac-ac stj5• lac-c dyb lac-loxod-a hrn2• lac-lup hrn2• lach mtf lyc he mag-m dgt mand sp1 *Med* vh* *Meny* vh* *Nat-m* k* nat-p k* nat-s vh* nat-sil stj2*• nit-ac vh ozone sde• pert-vc vk9 phos k* plac-s rly4• podo fd3.de• prot mtf rad-br knl• sep mtf sul-ac bro1* suprar rly4• symph fd3.de• thres-a sze7• tritic-vg fd5.de tub mtf vanil fd5.de *Verat* stx1 [alumin-p stj2 *Arg-p* stj2 aur-m stj2 *Chlor* stj2 chr-m stj2 cob stj2 cob-m stj2 cob-p stj2 coch-o stj cupr stj2 cupr-m stj2 *Cupr-p* stj2 ferr-m stj1 ferr-p stj1 hydrog stj2 *Lith-p* stj2 *Mag-p* stj1 *Mang-p* stj2 mur-ac stj2 nat-ar stj2 nat-br stj2 nat-caust stj2 nat-f stj2 nat-lac stj2 *Nat-met* stj2 ph-ac stj1 sel stj2 tax jsj7 zinc-m stj2 zinc-p stj2]

⋮ **fried**: bacls-10 jl* nat-p kr1*

⋮ **salty**: ferr-i vh* *Nat-m* vh *Nat-s* vh* nit-ac vh* tritic-vg fd5.de [*Plb-p* stj2]

⋮ **smoked**: atro a2 ozone sde2*•

- **flatulent** food | **agg.**: *(↗beans - agg.; cabbage - agg.; peas - agg.; sauerkraut - agg.)* ars k* *Bry* k* calc k* carb-v k* *Chin* k* cupr k* hell k* kali-c k* **Lyc** k* nat-m k* nat-p ld1.de *Nat-s* mtf **Petr** k* psor bgs puls k* rob c1* sep k* sil k* sulph mtf vanil fd5.de verat k*
- **flour**:

• **agg.**: pot-a stx1

- **flour**: ...

• **aversion**: *(↗farinaceous - aversion)* ars k* ph-ac k* *Phos* k*

• **desire**: *Calc* k* lach sabad k* [calc-s stj1 kali-m stj1]

- **food**:

• **agg.**: acon b7.de agar b4.de alet bro1 alum b4.de am-c b4.de *Ambr* b7.de amyg-p bro1 *Ant-c* b7.de arn b7.de ars b4.de asaf b7.de bism b7.de *Bry* b7.de calc b4.de *Canth* b7.de *Caps* b7.de carb-an b4.de carb-v b4.de* caust b4.de *Cham* b7.de *Chel* b7.de* **Chin** b7.de chion c1 cic b7.de *Cocc* b7.de con b4.de *Ferr* b7.de graph b4.de hedeo stx1 hyos b7.de *Ign* b7.de kali-c b4.de lach bro1 lyc b4.de m-arct b7.de m-aust b7.de meny b7.de merc b4.de mosch bro1 nat-c b4.de* nat-m b4.de nit-ac b4.de nux-m b7.de **Nux-v** b7.de petr b4.de ph-ac b4.de *Phos* b4.de plect stx1 podo c1 pop-cand c1 *Puls* b7.de ran-b b7.de rhus-g stx1 *Rhus-t* b7.de *Ruta* b7.de scroph-n c1 sep b4.de sil b4.de staph b7.de sul-ac b4.de sulph b4.de sym-r stx1 *Tarax* b7.de trom br1 valer b7.de *Verat* b7.de verb b7.de wye stx1 zinc b4.de zinc-m stx1 [spect dfg1]

⋮ **sight** of: mosch b7a.de

⋮ **smell** of: *(↗NOSE - Smell - acute - food)* aegop-p vml3• *Ars* k* bell bg2* caust chin stx1 *Cocc* k* **Colch** k* *Dig* k* dros bg2 eup-per gamb gk *Ip* lach bg2 merc-i-f bg2* nat-m bg2 nux-m sf1.de nux-v bg2 osm bg2* par vml3• ph-ac bg2* phos bg2* podo bg2* psor stx1 ptel bg2* sang bg2* sanic stx1 *Sep* k* *Sil* ld1.de* stann k* sul-ac bg2* sulph bg2* syc stx1 sym-r ah* *Thuj* upa stx1 *Vac* jl2 xan bt3 xanth bg2

⋮ **sensitive** to the (See NOSE - Smell - acute - food)

• **amel.** | **rough** food: ign bg2

• **aversion**: absin c1 acet-ac k* *Acon* k* acon-l c1 act-sp a* aesc-g a2 aeth a2 agar k* ail kr1 alco a2 alet kr1* all-c k* *Alum* k* alum-p k2 alum-sil k2 alumn h* amyg-p br1 anac k* androc srj1• *Ang* k* *Ant-c* k* ant-i hl1 ant-s-aur c1 ant-t k* apis arg-met k* *Arg-n* k* *Arn* k* **Ars** k* *Ars-i* ars-s-f k2 *Asaf* k* asar aur k* aur-ar k2 aur-i k2 aur-s k2 bamb-a stb2.de• bapt k* bar-act a2 *Bar-c* k* *Bar-i* k* *Bar-m* bar-s k2 *Bell* k* benz-ac k2 berb kr1 berb-a c1 beryl tpw5 bism k2 borx h2 *Bry* k* bufo k* *Cact* calc k* calc-i k2 calc-sil k2 *Canth* k* caps b7.de* *Carb-an* k* *Carb-v* carbn-s castm c1 castor-eq k* cench stx1 cephd-i bnj1 cham k* chel k* **Chin** k* *Chinin-ar* k* *Chinin-s* k* chion stx1 cimic k* cina bg2 cinnb k* coc-c k* **Cocc** k* coff k* coff-t a2 **Colch** k* *Coloc* con k* conch fkr1• corn c1 crot-c crot-t a cupr k* cupr-act c1 cupre-au c1 *Cycl* k* *Dig* digox c1 dios *Dulc* k* elaps k* erio br1* eup-per k* euph a falco-pe nl2• **Ferr** k* *Ferr-ar* ferr-i ferr-p gamb k* gink-b sbd1• *Glon* graph k* *Grat* k* *Guaj* k* guare k* *Hell* k* hep k* hera c1 hir skp7* *Hydr* hydr-ac kr1 hydrc c1 hydrog srj hyper *Ign* k* *Iod* **Ip** k* ix bnm8• kali-ar kali-bi k* *Kali-c* k* kali-i k* kali-m k2 kali-n stx1 kali-p kali-s kali-sil k2 *Kreos* b7a.de* lac-c al2 lach k* lact gsw1 *Laur* k* lepi **Lil-t** k* lob a2 lyc k* m-aust b7.de* *Mag-c* k* (non:mag-m a) *Mag-s* k* malar al2* manc stx1 mang k* *Merc* k* merc-c k* merc-cy c1 *Merc-i-f* k* merc-meth a2 mez b4.de* mosch mur-ac k* mygal c1* narz a2 nat-ar k2 nat-c k* nat-m k* nat-p k* nat-s k13* nat-sil k2 nicc h nit-ac h **Nux-v** k* ol-an k* olnd k* *Op* k* paull a2 petr petros st ph-ac phos k* phys c1 phyt c1 *Pic-ac* *Plat* k* plb k* *Podo* k* prun k* ptel *Puls* k* raph k* rat k* rham-f c1 rheum k* *Rhus-t* k* *Ruta* k* *Sabad* k* sacch c1 sang k2* sapin c1 sars kr1* sec k* senec c1* *Sep* k* sil k* spong fd4.de *Squil* b7a.de* *Staph* k* stram cda stront-c k* stroph-h c1 sul-ac k* sul-i k2 sulph k* sumb ptj• syc ptj1• sym-r c1* syph k2* *Tarent* k* thea k* thuj til k* trios br1 *Tub* k* upa c1 vac al2* valer a* verat k* vib c1 wies a2* zinc k* zinc-p k2

⋮ **daytime**: mag-s k*

⋮ **morning**: cench k2 con guare a2 lyc mag-s manc a2 phyt c1 syc ptj1•

⋮ **noon**: borx h2 dulc fd4.de lact c1 pic-ac c1 verat

⋮ **evening**: ars mag-c ruta fd4.de sil

⋮ **accompanied** by:

⋮ **diarrhea**; chronic: nux-m ptk

⋮ **hunger**: act-sp *Agar* all-s hr1* *Alum* ang c1* ant-c bg2 *Ars* asar bg2 aur bg2 bar-act a2 *Bar-c* k* bry caps hr1* carb-v *Carbn-s* *Chin* k* chinin-ar ld1.de* *Chinin-s* **Cocc** k* *Dulc* granit-m es1• *Grat* hr1 *Hell* *Hydr* k* hydrog srj *Kali-n* *Lach* **Nat-m** k* nicc **Nux-v** k* olnd op *Phos* plat bg2 psor *Rhus-t* ruta ld1.de sabad sal-fr sle1• sang a2* seneg bg2 *Sil* stann bg2* *Sul-ac* *Sulph* tax *Tub* verb k*

⋮ **Head**; pain in: **Ant-c** kr1 bamb-a stb2.de• cench k2 ferr kr1* sep kr1*

⋮ **Stomach**; feeling of emptiness in: *Bar-c* carb-v carbn-s *Chin* *Cocc* coff dulc *Grat* *Hell* *Hydr* hydrog srj2• mur-ac h2 *Nat-m* *Nux-v* podo k2 *Rhus-t* *Sil* stann *Sulph* verb

⋮ **children**; in: syph mtf33

- **aversion**: ...
  - **convalescence**; during: kreos tl1*
  - **dinner**; during: carb-an coc-c malar c1 mygal c1 ol-an verat
  - **eating**:
    - **attempting** to eat; on: *(↗STOMACH - Appetite - wanting - eating - attempting)* ant-t k2 chion c1 petros st* rheum c1* ruta kr1 *Sil*
    - **honey**; after: *Nat-m* kr1*
    - **little**; after eating a: *(↗STOMACH - Fullness - eating - after - agg. - ever)* am-c c1 *Bar-c* *Bry* bg3* caust bg3* *Cham* bg1* *Cina* bg1* *Cycl* k* hura c1 *Ign* bg1* kali-p fd1.de* *Lyc* bg1* *Nux-v* prun bg1* *Rheum* k* *Rhus-t* bg1 *Ruta* k* sil sul-ac h2 *Sulph*
    - **sudden**; while eating: *Bar-c* k* puls ptk1 *Ruta* k*
    - **while**: am-c tl1 nux-m ptk1
  - **fever**; during: *Am-c* bg2 *Ant-c* b7a.de* ant-t bg2 apis bg2 arn bg2 **Ars** bg2 asar bg2 bell bg2 *Bry* b7a.de* canth bg2 *Cham* b7a.de* chin bg2 cocc bg2 colch bg2 cupr bg2 cycl bg2 dig bg2 euph bg2 guaj bg2 hell bg2 *Ip* b7a.de* **Kali-c** bg2 lach bg2 lyc bg2 merc bg2 mosch bg2 nat-m bg2 nux-v bg2 op bg2 petr bg2 plat bg2 plb bg2 puls bg2 *Rheum* b7a.de* ruta bg2 sars bg2 sec bg2 seneg bg2 sep bg2 sil bg2 sul-ac bg2
  - **green** things: mag-c bg1
  - **perspiration**; during: am-c bg2 *Ant-c* bg2 **Ars** bg2 bry bg2 **Cham** bg2 ip bg2 kali-c bg2 rheum bg2
  - **pregnancy**; during: ant-t kr1* *Laur* kr1* *Nat-m* kr1 *Sep* h2*
  - **seen**; if food is: *(↗sight - aversion)* ail hr1 ant-c bro1 arn hr1 **Ars** hr1* caust tl1 cocc bro1* colch bro1* dig br1* mang h2 merc-i-f hr1 mosch hr1 nux-v bro1* phos ptk1 ptel bg1 sang mha **Sep** bro1* *Sil* k* squil stann bro1 sym-r bro1 tritic-vg fd5.de tub al2 vac al2*
  - **smell** of: *(↗NOSE - Smell - acute - food)* aegop-p vml3• ant-c bro1* *Ars* k* bell ld1.de caust k2* **Cocc** k* **Colch** k* dig br1* gamb gk **Ip** k* lyc ld1.de lycps-v vml3• nux-v bro1* phos kr1* *Podo* k* sang k2 *Sep* k* sil bro1 stann bro1* sym-r bro1* tub al2 vac al2*
  - **supper**; during: am-c h2 lyc gsw1 m-arct al2 sulph k*
  - **tastes** it, then he is ravenous; until he: **Lyc** k*
  - **thinking** of eating; when: ant-t vh arg-met h1* *Ars* hr1* bamb-a stb2.de• carb-v bg* caust tl1 **Chin** hr1* cocc tl1 colch st* dulc fd4.de kola stb3• mag-s malar al2 mosch hr1 nux-m ptk1 nux-v kr1 sang k2 sars h2* *Sep* h2* sym-r ah tanac hl1 upa stx1 *Zinc* hr1* zinc-chr ptk1
    - **pregnancy**; during: ars tl1 caust tl1 cocc tl1 *Sep* h1*
- **desire**: *Maland* al2 ozone sde2• vichy-g c1
  - **he** hates: chir-fl gya2
  - **smell** of: *Lycps-v* bc*
  - **worse**; which makes him: ars st calc stx1 *Carc* mlr• hep st morg-p stx1 nat-c bg2 nit-ac st puls k2* sulph st tub st

- **French** fried potatoes: *(↗fried)*
  - **desire**: *(↗potatoes - desire - fried)* calc-p mtf carc mtf med mtf puls mtf tub mtf
- **fresh** food | **desire**: [am-f stj2 *Arg-met* stj1* *Arg-n* stj2 *Arg-p* stj2 calc-sil stj2 cupr-f stj2 fl-ac stj2 mag-i stj1 mag-lac stj2 mag-met stj2 nat-f stj2]
- **fried** food: *(↗french)*
  - **aversion**: adel a1* mag-s sp1* plb ptk1
  - **desire**: *(↗fat - desire)* agath-a nl2• lac-cp sk4• limen-b-c mlk9.de nicotam rly4• pant-ac rly4• petr-ra shn4• plb k* positr nl2• [alumin-s stj2 ant-c stj2 aur-s stj2 cadm-s stj2 chr-s stj2 cinnb stj2 gal-s stj2 lith-s stj2 mag-lac stj2 mag-met stj2 mag-n stj2 mag-sil stj2 mang-s stj2 nicc-s stj2 sulph stj2 titan-s stj2]
- **frozen**:
  - **agg.**: *(↗cold food - agg.)* arg-n k* *Ars* k* bry *Calc-p* k* *Carb-v* k* coloc bg2 dulc k* elaps gk hep sf1.de *Ip* k1* kali-bi ptk1 oxal-a rly4• psor bg2* **Puls** k* rhus-t sf1.de rob ptk1 rumx
  - **amel.**: phos sf1.de xan ptk1
  - **desire**: arg-met sf1.de eup-per sf1.de nat-s sf1.de phos sf1.de
- **fruit**:
  - **agg.**: acon act-sp k2 *Aloe* alum-sil stx1 *Ant-c* k* ant-t k* arg-met stx1 **Ars** k* ars-s-f k2* aster sf1.de* *Borx* k* **Bry** k* calc *Calc-p* k* *Carb-v* k* carc mlr1• *Caust* bro1* **Chin** k* *Chinin-ar* k* chinin-m kr1 *Cist* k* colch bg2* **Coloc** k* *Crot-t* k* cub k* elaps kr1* *Ferr* k* glon ptk1 ign k* *Ip* k* *Iris* kali-bi bro1 kali-s fd4.de kreos k* lac-ac stj5• lach k* lith-c k* *Lyc* k* mag-c

- **fruit** – **agg.**: ...
  Mag-m k* merc bg2* merc-c bg2* *Mur-ac* k* *Nat-ar* k* *Nat-c* k* nat-p **Nat-s** k* *Olnd* ox-ac bg2* petr-ra shn4• *Ph-ac* phos k* pitu-a vml2* *Podo* k* prun stx1 *Psor* **Puls** k* rheum k* *Rhod* k* *Rumx* bro1* ruta k* samb kr1* *Sel* k* *Sep* k* sul-ac sulph bt3 tarax k* tarent ld1.de* trom k* tub stx1 **Verat** k* zing vml3• [ant-m stj2 ant-met stj2 ars-met stj2 bor-pur stj2 fl-ac stj2 hydrog stj2 iod stj2 kali-ar stj2 lith-f stj2 lith-i stj2 lith-m stj2 lith-met stj2 lith-p stj2 lith-s stj2]
  - **juicy** fruits: ant-c ptk1 calc ptk1 iod ptk1 puls ptk1 sulph ptk1
  - **raw** fruit: *Puls* b7a.de rob vml3• *Verat* b7a.de
  - **sour**: *Ant-c* k* ant-t k2* chinin-m kr1 cist sf1.de* ferr kr1* *Ip* k* kali-m stx1 lac-c stx1 lach ptk1* mag-c sf1.de nat-p bl **Olnd** mrr1 ox-ac k2* *Ph-ac* k* podo sf1.de* *Psor* k* *Sul-ac* kr1* ther kr1*
  - **spoiled**: act-sp k2*
  - **stone** fruits: colch gk kali-bi gk [ant-c stj2 ant-m stj2 ant-met stj2 ant-t stj2]
  - **unripe**: aloe stx1 chinin-ar c1* ip c1* rheum c1* rob c1* sul-ac c1*
  - **watery**: *Ars* c1* kali-n vml3•
- **amel.**: lach k* ptel gk
  - **sour**: lach sf1.de* naja ptk1* **Ptel** gk
- **aversion**: aeth vh* aloe ld1.de *Ant-t* tl1* *Ars* h2* *Bar-c* k* bell vh* bry zf carb-v ld1.de *Carc* c1* *Caust* ld1.de* **Chin** st* chir-fl gya2 ferr-m ld1.de *Hell* vh hyos zf **Ign** k* kali-bi ld1.de kali-br ld1.de kali-s fd4.de *Mag-c* mrr1 nat-m gk oena vml3• **Phos** ld1.de* **Puls** h1* *Rumx* ld1.de* spong fd4.de *Sul-ac* ld1.de* *Sulph* vh* vanil fd5.de [ant-c stj2 ant-m stj2 ant-met stj2 bor-pur stj2 cupr stj2]
  - **citrus** fruit: [moly-met stj2]
  - **green**: ferr vh *Mag-c* h2*
  - **sour**: ferr k2* [spect dfg1]
- **desire**: *Acon-l* a1* adam srj5• adel a2 agath-a nl2• aloe k* *Alum* k* alum-p k2* alumn k* androc vml3• *Ant-t* k* ap-g vh1 aq-mar rbp6 ara-maca sej7• aran ccrh1• ars k* ars-s-f k2* asar jl3* calc a2 calc-s *Carb-v* bg2* carc c1* caust vh chin k* choc srj3• cist k* coli rly4• conch fkr1* cub k* dioxi rbp6 dream-p sdj1• dulc fd4.de ger-i rly4• gran k* guaj bg2* guar a2* ham fd3.de• hep ign k* ina-i mlk9.de irid-met srj5• kali-act vh kali-c zf kali-p fd1.de• kali-s fd4.de ketogl-ac rly4• lach lavand-a ctl1• lepi a1 *Mag-c* k* mag-f vml3• mag-m vh* mag-s mg1.de* med bro1 nat-m nat-sil stj2*• orot-ac rly4*• oxal-a rly4• ozone sde2* paull a1* petr-ra shn4• **Ph-ac** k* phos bro1* pieri-b mlk9.de pitu-a a* podo fd3.de• propl ub1*• propr sa3• ptel sys1 puls k* pycnop-sa mrz1 ruta fd4.de sacch-a fd2.de• sars a2 staph bt3 succ-ac rly4• suis-pan rly4• *Sul-ac* k* symph fd3.de• ther c1* tritic-vg fd5.de tub-a a tung-met bdx1• urol-h rwt• vanil fd5.de **Verat** k* [alumin-s stj2 *Ant-c* stj2 *Ant-m* stj2 ant-met stj2 arg-met stj1* arg-n stj2 arg-p stj2 ars-met stj2 aur-s stj2 beryl-m stj2 cadm-s stj2 calc-sil stj2 chr-s stj2 cinnb stj2 gal-s stj2 heroin sdj2 kali-ar stj2 kali-sil stj2 lith-s stj2 mag-i stj1 mag-lac stj2 *Mag-met* stj2 mag-n stj2 mag-sil stj2 mang-s stj2 mang-sil stj2 nat-ar stj2 nat-f stj2 nicc-s stj2 oxyg stj2 sil stj2 sil-met stj2 sulph stj2 tax jsj7 *Tell* stj2 *Titan* stj2 *Titan-s* stj2 zinc stj2 zinc-i stj2 zinc-m stj2 zinc-p stj2]
  - **dried**: adam srj5• tritic-vg fd5.de
  - **fruit** juice: carc sde• choc srj3*• dioxi rbp6 dulc fd4.de kali-s fd4.de spong fd4.de tarax vml3• [heroin sdj2]
  - **green**: calc a1* calc-s k* lepi a1 lept gsw1 *Med* k*
  - **juicy** fruits: agath-a nl2• aloe sne ant-t ptk1 dream-p sdj1• ger-i rly4• germ-met srj5• hippoc-k szs2 lac-leo hrn2• lac-loxod-a hrn2• nux-m k2 ph-ac ptk1 sars a2* staph ptk1 sul-ac c1* tritic-vg fd5.de vanil fd5.de verat ptk1
    - **afternoon** | **16** h: germ-met srj5•
  - **red**: choc srj3*•
  - **sour**: adel a1* ant-t k2* *Ars* k* ars-s-f vh1 calc k* calc-s k* chin k* *Cist* k* cub k* cypra-eg sde6.de* ferr vh ham fd3.de• ign k* irid-met srj5• lach sf1.de lyc zf mag-c sf1.de *Med* vh* ptel gk1* symph fd3.de• ther hl1* thuj k* **Verat** k*
  - **unripe**: **Med** mrr1
  - **vomiting**; after: gard-j vlr2•
- **garlic**:
  - **agg.**: hydrog stj2* lyc kl nat-m gk nat-sil fd3.de• **Phos** vh podo fd3.de• sabad kr1 tritic-vg fd5.de vanil fd5.de
    - **smell** of garlic; from the: *(↗NOSE - Smell - acute - garlic)* asar bc hydrog stx1 **Phos** kr1 sabad b2.de*
  - **aversion**: asar vh* *Phos* vh* podo fd3.de• prot jl3* *Sabad* k* *Thuj* mrr1

- **aversion**: ...
  - ⁝ **smell** of: sabad b7a.de
- **desire**: agar vh* all-c vh* all-s vh* anan vh1 cand vml3• carc vh* cub a2* kali-s fd4.de kola stb3• nat-m bg2* phos zf sabad vh* sulph vh* *Thuj* mrr1 tritic-vg fd5.de [sel stj2]

- **gherkins**: (*↗cucumbers; pickles)*
  - **aversion**: abies-c vh1 arund vh1 [ant-c stj2 ant-m stj2 ant-met stj2 ant-t stj2]
  - **desire**: abies-c vh1 naja mtf sul-i k2 verat a1* [ant-c stj2 ant-m stj2 ant-met stj2 ant-t stj2 mag-lac stj2 yttr-met stj2 zinc-p stj2]
    - ⁝ **sour**: carc gk6 verat h1
- **ginger**:
  - **agg.**: nux-v stx1
  - **aversion**: [beryl stj2]
  - **desire**: *Lac-h* vml3• phos fd [heroin sdj2]
- **grapefruit**:
  - **aversion**: bar-c gk4 [stront-met stj2]
  - **desire**: lyc gk2 sol-br vml3• [aur stj2 mang-m stj2]
- **grapes**:
  - **agg.**: chin gl1.fr*• chir-fl gya2 ox-ac k2* petr-ra shn4• ruta stx1 verat gl1.fr*•
  - **desire**: ozone sde2*• petr-ra shn4• tritic-vg fd5.de vanil fd5.de [titan stj2 titan-s stj2]
- **gravy** (See broth)
- **green** food:
  - **aversion**: ars b4a.de *Hell* b7.de* mag-c b4.de*
  - **desire**: calc-s ptk1 med ptk1* neon srj5• positr nl2•
- **green** peppers: *(↗pepper; red pepper; sweet peppers)*
  - **agg.**: [*Arg-met* stj1]
  - **desire**: *Lepr* vml3• [niob-met stj2]
- **grilled** food: *(↗smoked)*
  - **agg.**: calc mtf calc-sil mtf puls mtf
  - **desire**: kreos mtf
- **gruel** (See porridge)
- **ham**:
  - **aversion**: puls st* [arg-n stj2 ferr-n stj2 mag-n stj2 mang-n stj2 nitro stj2 zinc-n stj2]
  - **desire**: calc sne *Calc-p* bg2* carc st card-b st dulc fd4.de ham fd3.de• kali-s fd4.de kola stb3• mez bg2* ozone sde2*• plac-s rly4• *Sanic* mrr1 spong fd4.de symph fd3.de• **Tub** mrr1 *Uran-n* kr1* [arg-n stj2 ferr-n stj2 mag-n stj2 mang-n stj2 nitro stj2 plut-n stj2 zinc-n stj2]
    - ⁝ **fat**: *(↗bacon - desire; fat - desire)* calc-p k* *Carc* st* *Card-b* st *Mez* k* *Sanic* k* *Tub* k*
    - ⁝ **raw**: *(↗raw - desire)* ham fd3.de• (non:uran-met c1) *Uran-n* k*
- **hamburger** | **desire**: calc-p mtf phos mrr1* tub mtf
- **hard** things | **agg.**: sin-a stx1 sin-n stx1
- **haricots**; green | **aversion**: prot jl2
- **healthy** food | **desire**: haliae-lc srj5• lac-f wza1• positr nl2•
- **hearty** food | **desire**: kali-s fd4.de olib-sac wmh1 positr nl2• rhus-t a1* spong fd4.de symph fd3.de• tritic-vg fd5.de ust a1* vanil fd5.de
- **heavy** food: *(↗rich)*
  - **agg.**: *(↗fat - agg.; rich - agg.)* ars-s-f k2 bry k* calc k* *Caust* k* cupr k* des-ac rbp6 dioxi rbp6 **Iod** k* lyc k* mag-c h2 nat-c k* ozone sde2• *Puls* k* ruta fd4.de sang stx1 sulph k*
  - **aversion**: ang vh1 ars-s-f k2 chinin-ar k2
- **herbs** | **desire**: bufo bg2
- **herring**:
  - **agg.**: *(↗sardines - agg.)* ferr-p st* fl-ac bg2* lyc bg2* nat-m bg2
  - **aversion**: ferr tl1 gal-ac vh1* phos k*
  - **desire**: *(↗anchovies - desire; sardines - desire)* atro a2 cist med a **Nit-ac** k* *Puls* k* spong fd4.de syph a tub a *Verat* k* [*Bism* stj2]
- **highly** seasoned food (See spices)
- **honey**:
  - **agg.**: apis bgs ars bgs calc-p stx1 caust bgs nat-c k* *Nat-m* kr1* *Nit-ac* b4a.de phos bg2* psor bgs puls bgs *Sil* vh sulph vh*
  - **amel.**: colch c1
- **honey**: ...
  - **aversion**: nat-c st nat-m vh*
  - **desire**: aq-mar rbp6 ham fd3.de• sabad k* suis-em rly4• tritic-vg fd5.de verat bg2*
- **hot** dogs | **desire**: calc-p mrr1 tub vh vanil fd5.de
- **hot** drinks (See warm drinks)
- **hot** food (See warm food - agg. - hot)
- **ice**:
  - **agg.**: agra stx1 arg-n c1* **Ars** bg2* bell bg2* bell-p bg2* *Bry* bg2 calc-p bg2* **Carb-v** bg2* dulc ptk1 hep bg2 ip bg2* kali-bi ptk1 kali-c bg2 kali-i k2 nat-sil fd3.de• *Nux-v* bg2* *Puls* bg2* rhus-t bg2* rob ptk1 [mang stj1]
  - **amel.**: cench stx1 ozone stx1 phos bg2 xan kr1*
    - ⁝ **holding** ice in mouth amel.: coff bro1
  - **desire**: acon ptk ange-s oss1• arg-met bg2* arg-n k2* ars bg2* bry sne *Calc* st* choc srj3*• clem c1 *Elaps* k* eup-per bg2 irid-met srj5• lept bg1* *Med* k* merc-c k* merc-i-f ld1.de* *Nat-s* k* oci-sa sk4• onos ptk paro-i jl3* petr-ra shn4• phos bg2* puls tl1 ruta tl1 sil k2* tritic-vg fd5.de tub sne **Verat** k*
    - ⁝ **pain**; during: med ptk1
- **ice** cream:
  - **agg.**: am-c a arg-n kr1* ars kr1* ars-h stx1 bell-p stx1 calc-p gk* *Carb-v* stx1 carc mlr1• chinin-s stx1 cladon vml3• dig stx1 dulc fd4.de* *Ip* stx1 kali-ar k2* kali-i k2 nat-s k* orot-ac rly4• oxal-a rly4• podo fd3.de• puls kr1* pyrog stx1 rob c1* sep stx1 [ars-met stj2 mang stj1 mang-act stj2 mang-m stj2 mang-met stj2 mang-n stj2 mang-s stj2 nat-ar stj2]
  - **aversion**: aran ccrh1• carc dx1* choc srj3*• kola stb3• puls c1* rad-br c1* ruta fd4.de
  - **desire**: aids nl2• amp rly4• anthraq rly4• arg-n k2* bit-ar wht1• *Bung-fa* mtf *Calc* k* calc-p mrr1 carc fb* carneg-g rwt1• *Cuc-c* vml3• dendr-pol sk4• dream-p sdj1• dulc fd4.de elaps vh *Eup-per* k* germ-met srj5• helodr-cal knl2• *Kola* stb3• lac-del hrn2• loxo-recl knl4• mang-p rly4*• *Med* st nat-m gk nat-p mrr1 nat-s vh nat-sil fd3.de• nept-m lsd2.fr orot-ac vml3• **Phos** k* podo fd3.de• puls k2* rad-br c1* *Sil* k2* spong fd4.de suis-em rly4• *Sulph* mrr1 suprar rly4• tama vml3• tritic-vg fd5.de tub k* vanil fd5.de verat k* [arg-p stj2 cupr-p stj2 lith-p stj2 plb-p stj2 tell stj2]
- **idli** | **desire**: *(↗rice - desire - dry)* calc mtf sil mtf
- **incredible** things | **desire**: cycl tl1
- **indigestible** things: *(↗dirt)*
  - **agg.**: ant-c stx1 ars stx1 bell stx1 bry bg2 calc bg2 *Caust* bg2 cham stx1 cupr bg2 ferr-i c1 **Iod** bg2* ip c1* lyc bg2 nat-c bg2 nux-v stx1 *Puls* bg2 rhus-t stx1 ruta ptk1 sulph bg2*
  - **amel.**: ign ptk1
  - **desire**: *(↗ashes - desire; charcoal - desire; coal - desire; digest - desire; lime [=- desire; lime slate - desire; paper - desire; sand - desire; strange - desire; tea - desire - grounds)* abies-c bg2*] *Alum* k* alumn k* *Aur* st* bell bry k* *Calc* k* *Calc-p* k* cic bg2* con st *Cycl* k* ferr sf1.de* ign br1 lac-c sne **Lach** st* nat-m st *Nit-ac* bg2* nux-v bg2* petr-ra shn4• positr nl2• psor bt3 **Sil** bt3 sulph vh* *Tarent* kr1
- **indistinct** desire (See STOMACH - Appetite - capricious)
- **insects**:
  - **desire** | **black** beetles, slugs, grasshoppers: choc srj3•
- **insipid** food | **aversion**: rheum b7.de*
- **intoxicating** drinks | **desire**: bufo br1*
- **invigorating** food | **desire**: puls b7.de*
- **iron** pots; agg. from food cooked in: sulph b4a.de
- **irritating** food | **agg.**: *Stann* b4.de
- **juicy** things:
  - **aversion**: aloe ld1.de
  - **desire**: *(↗refreshing - desire)* abrom-a ks5* aloe k* *Ant-t* bro1* ars bg2 atis zzc1• bamb-a stb2.de* chin bro1* choc srj3*• gran k* graph bg2* hippoc-k szs2 ketogl-ac rly4• kola stb3• lac-leo hrn2• mag-c bro1 med bro1* nat-ar k* nux-v k2* oci-sa sk4• petr-ra shn4• **Ph-ac** k* phos bg2* pieri-b mlk9.de positr nl2• puls k* sabad bg2* *Sabin* sal-fr sle1• sangin-n c1 sars sol vml3• staph bg2* sul-ac ptk verat k*
- **kiwi**:
  - **agg.**: lyc pcr [ant-c stj2 ant-m stj2 ant-met stj2 ant-t stj2]
  - **desire**: [titan stj2 titan-s stj2]
- **kohlrabi** | **aversion**: [*Arg-met* stj2 *Pall* stj2]

- **lamb** | **desire**: sol vml3•
- **lard** | **desire**: *(↗fat - desire)* ars k* calc-p c1 ruta fd4.de [calc-n stj1 nat-n stj1]
- **lasagna**: *(↗pasta)*
  • **desire**: [calc-sil stj2]
- **leek** | **aversion**: [ang stj4]
- **lemonade**:
  • **agg.**: ant-c stx1 calc st cit-ac stx1 oci-sa sk4• phyt k* *Sel* k* stram stx1
  • **amel.**: *Bell* bg2* cycl bg2* petr-ra shn4• phyt bg2* **Ptel** vh* puls stx1
  • **desire**: *Am-m* bg2* ars gk **Bell** k* calc carc fd2.de• cartl-s rly4• cycl k* eup-per bg2* eup-pur fl-ac bg2* *Jatr-c* k* kali-p fd1.de• kola stb3• lac-e hrn2• lach bg2* malar al2* nat-m gk nat-sil fd3.de• *Nit-ac* k* oci-sa sk4• petr-ra shn4• phasco-ci rbp2 **Ptel** vml3• puls k* sabad a2* *Sabin* k* sec k* suis-pan rly4• sul-ac vh *Sul-i* k* tritic-vg fd5.de vanil fd5.de xan bt3 xanth bg2
    ⁝ **hot**: calc sne *Puls* kr1
- **lemons**:
  • **agg.**: *Olnd* mrr1 puls hu vanil fd5.de
  • **amel.**: bell ptk1 cann-i hs ptel gk* stram ptk1*
  • **aversion**: nux-v vh [nat-caust stj2 nat-lac stj2]
  • **desire**: *(↗citric - desire)* ars k* atis zzc1• *Bell* kr1* ben k* benz-ac k* benzol c1 chel vh cor-r vh ferr mtf33 hep vh* ign gk luf-op vml3• mag-f stj1*• med vh* medus mgm• *Merc* vh nabal c1* nat-m vh* podo fd3.de• ptel gk* puls st* rad-br knl• *Sabad* vh* sabin vh* sacch sht*• sal-fr sle1• sul-ac vh *Sul-i* vml3• tarent vh thea a2* vanil fd5.de verat k* [ars-met stj2 kali-ar stj2 mag-m stj1 nat-ar stj2]
- **lentils**:
  • **agg.**: *Ars* b4a.de *Calc* b4a.de carb-v b4a.de kali-c b4a.de *Lyc* b4a.de *Nat-m* b4a.de pin-con oss2• sil b4a.de
  • **aversion**: *Chel* vh*
  • **desire**: lyc mtf nat-s mtf sulph mtf
- **lettuce**:
  • **agg.**: *Ars* kr1 *Bry* kr1 *Calc* kr1 carb-v kr1 lach kr1 lyc kr1
  • **aversion**: [bor-pur stj2]
  • **desire**: [beryl stj2]
- **licorice** | **desire**: *(↗sweets - desire)* lyc sne sacch sht*• vanad stj1*• [chr-s stj2 nicc-met stj1* nicc-s stj2 tung-met stj2 zinc stj2 zinc-i stj2 zinc-m stj2 zinc-p stj2]
- **light** food:
  • **amel.**: nat-s k2
  • **desire**: *Mag-m* mrr1 rumx k2
- **lime** [=derived from limestone] | **desire**: *(↗indigestible - desire)* **Alum** bg2 calc bg2 cic bg2 con bg2 ferr bg2 hep bg2 hyos bg2 ign bg2 *Nat-m* b4a.de *Nit-ac* b2.de* *Nux-v* b2.de* oci bg2 *Sep* b4a.de sil bg2 sulph bg2 tarent bg2
- **lime**, slate pencils, earth, chalk, clay: | **desire**: *(↗indigestible - desire)* *Alum* k* *Alumn* ld1.de* ant-c sys1 *Calc* k* calc-p sf1.de chel bg1* cic k* ferr ign bro1* lac-f c1 nat-m k* **Nit-ac** k* *Nux-v* k* oci bt3 petr-ra shn4• psor bro1* *Sil* bg1* sulph bt3 tarent bg1* tub a
- **limes** [=citrus fruit]:
  • **desire** | **lime** juice: hydrc mtf*
- **liquid** food:
  • **agg.**: crot-t vml3• gran vml3•
  • **aversion**: *(↗drinks - aversion)* *Bell* ld graph k1 hydrc vml3•
  • **desire**: *(↗soup - desire)* *Ang* k* bell bry k* *Calc-ar* caps cere-b vml3• cob-n sp1* *Ferr* k* kali-i vh *Merc* k* nat-m vh ph-ac *Staph* k* *Sulph* k* verat k*
- **liquids**: *(↗drinks)*
  • **aversion**: bell b4.de* graph k* hyos ptk1 nat-m b4a.de nux-v ptk1 stram ptk1
  • **desire**: cob-n sp1* staph ptk1 sulph ptk1
- **liquor**:
  • **agg.**: *Agar* bro1 ant-c k1* ars k1 bell k1* bov k1 *Cann-i* k2* *Carb-v* k2* cimic k1* coff tl1 guar stx1 *Lach* bro1 led k1* *Nux-v* bro1 paull stx1 *Ran-b* k1* rhod k1* rhus-t k1* sel k1* stram bro1 *Sul-ac* bro1 sulph k1 verat k1* *Zinc* bro1
  • **aversion**: ang bg2*
- **liquor – aversion**: ...
    ⁝ **strong**: cur vml3•
  • **desire**: anan vh1 iod tl1 kola br1 kreos tl1 lach tl1 med kr1* mez tl1 petr-ra shn4• sanic tl1 spong fd4.de symph fd3.de• [lith-f stj2]
- **liver**:
  • **aversion**: sulph dx1* [erech stj]
  • **desire**: kali-c dgt loxo-recl knl4• plut-n srj7•
- **lobster** | **agg.**: kali-n vml3•
- **lukewarm** water | **desire**: aegop-p vml3•
- **mango** | **desire**: chin mtf cina mtf mag-m mtf *Mangi* vml3• puls mtf
- **many** things | **desire**: *(↗STOMACH - Appetite - capricious)* bry bro1 carc mlr1• cham bro1 *Chin* bro1 cic ptk1 **Cina** k* fl-ac bro1 ham fd3.de• kreos phos rheum bro1 *Rhus-g* tmo3• sang bro1 spong fd4.de staph ptk1
- **marinade** | **desire**: ars st aster st* *Cist* st* *Fl-ac* st *Hep* st *Lac-c* st nat-p st ph-ac st* *Sang* st*
- **marrow** | **desire**: aur hu
- **marshmallows** | **desire**: lac-h sze9• tub ser
- **mayonnaise**:
  • **agg.**: *(↗STOMACH - Nausea - mayonnaise)* puls mtf [mag-sil stj2]
  • **aversion**: mag-p rly4• sep gk5* [arg-met stj1 mag-sil stj2]
  • **desire**: bar-c gk1 calc gk1* hep mrr3 lyc mtf phos gk1 sul-ac gk1 [aur stj2]
- **meat**:
  • **agg.**: act-sp stx1 agar stx1 all-s bt3* ant-c stx1 arg-n bt3* ars bro1* astac vml3• bamb-a stx1 bell sf1.de borx bro1* *Bry* bro1* *Calc* bg2* camph stx1 carb-an k* carb-v bro1* carc mlr1• card-m vml3• caust k* *Chin* br1* *Colch* k* cupr dulc fd4.de *Ferr* k* ferr-ar ld1.de ferr-i ld1.de ferr-p ld1.de graph bg2* *Kali-bi* k* *Kali-c* kr1 kali-n stx1 kreos bg2* *Lec* sne lept vml3• lyc gl1.fr• *Lyss* mag-c k* mag-m k* med st merc k* nat-m bro1 nit-m-ac br1 nux-v k2* podo fd3.de• psor stx1 *Ptel* k* *Puls* k* rob vml3* *Rumx* stx1 ruta k* sabal c1 sanic c1 sel bro1 sep bg2* sil k* staph k* sulph k* tarent stx1 ter ther ld1.de* thuj c1 tub stx1 vac stx1 vanil fd5.de verat bro1* zinc stx1 [arg-met stj2 arg-p stj2 chr-s stj2 ferr-f stj2 ferr-lac stj2 ferr-n stj2 ferr-sil stj2]
    ⁝ **bad** meat (See spoiled)
    ⁝ **fat**: *(↗fat - agg.)* *Ptel* mrr1 thuj c1
    ⁝ **fresh**, agg.: ars bg1* *Caust* k* *Chin* bg2* kali-c bg1
    ⁝ **much** meat; too: all-s bro1
    ⁝ **pickled**: act-sp vh* carb-v st
    ⁝ **smell** of meat: ars b2.de* colch b2.de* sep k2 upa c1
      ⁝ **cooking** meat; of: ars k* colch k* psor bgs sanic bgs
      ⁝ **fat** meat: colch bg2
    ⁝ **smoked**, agg.: *Calc* b2.de* *Sil* b2.de*
    ⁝ **spoiled** meat: *(↗sausages - agg. - spoiled)* absin vml3• acet-ac vml3• **Ars** k* bell sf1.de* bry sf1.de* camph bt3 carb-an bt3 *Carb-v* k* chin k* *Crot-h* *Cupr-ar* vml3• *Lach* k* ph-ac sf1.de* *Puls* k* *Pyrog* k* rhus-t sf1.de* urt-u bt3 *Verat* bt3 vip sf1.de*
  • **amel.**: lat-h ld1.de *Verat* b2.de*
  • **aversion**: abies-c k* adel a1 agar k* all-s ld1.de* aloe bg2* *Alum* k* alum-p k2* alum-sil k2* alumn k* am-c k* am-m ld1.de* *Ang* k* anthraci vh1 aphis k* ara-maca sej7• arb-m oss1• *Arg-n* stj2* *Arn* k* *Ars* k* ars-s-f k2* asar k* aster k* atro a1* *Aur* k* aur-ar c1* aur-s k2* bamb-a stb2.de• bell k* borx ld1.de* bros-gau mrc1 *Bry* k* *Cact* **Calc** k* calc-f mg1.de* **Calc-s** k* calc-sil k2* *Cann-s* k* carb-an h2 *Carb-v* k* **Carbn-s** k* carc jl* card-m bro1* cary a1* caust k* cham k* chel k* chen-a kr1* **Chin** k* chin-b kr1* *Chinin-ar* k* *Coc-c* k* colch bro1* coli rly4• conch fkr1* convo-s sp1 cortiso vml3• crot-c k* crot-h bro1* *Cycl* k* der a1 des-ac rbp6 dros stx1 dulc fd4.de *Elaps* k* *Ferr* k* *Ferr-ar* ferr-i k* *Ferr-m* k* ferr-p k* gaert ptj1*• **Graph** k* hell k* helo-s rwt2• hep b4a.de hipp gsw1 hydr k* hydr-ac vml3• *Ign* k* ipom-p sp *Kali-ar* k* *Kali-bi* k* *Kali-c* k* kali-m k2 kali-n stx1 kali-p kali-s kali-sil k2* kola stb3• kreos lachn k* lact k* *Lap-a* k* lec sne lepi *Lyc* k* mag-c k* mag-m ld1.de* mag-s k* manc k* meny ld1.de* *Merc* k* *Mez* k* morg-g ptj1*• morph bro1* **Mur-ac** k* nat-ar k* nat-c k* *Nat-m* k* nat-p nat-s k* nat-sil k2* nicc k* *Nit-ac* k* **Nux-v** k* ol-an k* olnd ld1.de* op k* orot-ac rly4*• ov stx1 **Petr** k* petr-ra shn4• *Phos* k* plan k* *Plat* k* podo fd3.de• pop-cand c1 prot ptj1*• psor stx1 *Ptel* k* **Puls** k* rad-br c1* *Rhus-t* k* ruta k* *Sabad* k* sal-fr sle1• saroth mg1.de* sec k* sel ld1.de* **Sep** k* **Sil** k* stront-c k* **Sulph** k* sumb k* syc ptj1* symph fd3.de• *Syph* k* *Tarent* k* tep ter k* thal vml3• ther ld1.de*

- **aversion**: ...
thuj k* til tip a4 tril-c a1 (non:tril-p a1*) tritic-vg fd5.de *Tub* k* upa k* uran-met sf1.de* uran-n hl1* urol-h rwt• vanil fd5.de verat bt3 x-ray sp1* *Zinc* k* zinc-p k2* [alumin stj2 alumin-p stj2 alumin-s stj2 am-br stj2 am-caust stj2 am-f stj2 am-p stj1 ant-m stj2 *Arg-met* stj1* *Arg-p* stj2 ars-met stj2 aur-m stj2 bar-br stj2 bar-i stj2 bar-m stj1 bar-met stj2 bar-n stj1 beryl-m stj2 bism-sn stj2 bor-pur stj2 cadm-m stj2 chlor stj2 chr-m stj2 cinnb stj2 cob-m stj2 ferr-n stj2 ferr-sil stj2 hafn-met stj2 heroin sdj2 irid-met stj2 kali-met stj2 lanth-met stj2 lith-m stj2 mag-br stj1 mag-lac stj2 mag-met stj2 mag-n stj2 mag-sil stj2 mang-m stj2 mang-n stj2 mang-sil stj2 merc-d stj2 merc-i-f stj2 nicc-met stj2 nicc-s stj2 nitro stj2 osm-met stj2 plb stj2 plb-m stj2 plb-p stj2 rhen-met stj2 sil-met stj2 stront-m stj2 stront-met stj2 tant-met stj2 tell stj2 thal-met stj2 tung-met stj2 zinc-m stj2 zinc-n stj2]
  - **noon**: ol-an olnd ld1.de sulph
  - **evening**: sulph
  - **and** salt: **Graph** mrr1
  - **and** sweets: **Graph** mrr1
  - **boiled**: ars calc sf1.de chel k* nit-ac k*
  - **dinner**, during: nat-c
  - **fat**: *(↗fat - aversion)* anthraci vh1* ars vh1 bamb-a stb2.de• carb-an h2 *Carb-v* k* carc c1* hell k* phos sec hs* tritic-vg fd5.de
  - **fresh**: *Thuj* k* tub vh
  - **men**, in: x-ray sp1
  - **menses**:
    - **before**: amp rly4•
    - **during**: plat
  - **pickled**: carb-v sf1.de* card-m vml3•
  - **raw** meat: [bism-sn stj2]
  - **roasted**: agar mg1.de *Ptel* bg1* tarent tl
  - **salted**: carb-v sf1.de* card-m ptk1*
  - **scrap** meat: mag-c st
  - **smell** of: ars a1* upa c1
  - **smoked**: mag-m dgt
  - **soup**: arn bg2 cham bg2 rhus-t bg2
  - **spicy**: mag-c st
  - **thinking** of it, while: **Graph** k* mur-ac c1* nat-sil fd3.de• nit-ac c1 podo fd3.de• symph fd3.de• upa stx1
- **desire**: abies-c k* acon-ac rly4• agath-a nl2• all-s br1* aloe k* amp rly4• anth a1* anthraq rly4• ara-maca sej7• arum-t vh1 atro a2 aur k* aur-m-n vh* bell-p sp1* bit-ar wht1• borx mtf33 bros-gau mrc1 bry vh* *Calc* st *Calc-p* bg2* canth carc jl* carneg-g rwt1• caust bg2* choc stx1 chord-umb rly4• coca bg2* cocc b7a.de* cori-r a2 cur vml3• cycl dulc fd4.de* elaps a2 erig mg1.de* ferr k* *Ferr-m* k* germ-met srj5• gink-b sbd1*• graph k* hell k* helo-s rwt2• hydr ld1.de iod k* irid-met stj2*• kali-p fd1.de• kali-s fkr2.de kola stb3• *Kreos* k* lac-leo hrn2• lac-lup hrn2• lach zf *Lepr* vml3• *Lil-t* k* limest-b es1*• lyc zf *Mag-c* k* mand mg1.de* *Mang* gsw1 marb-w es1*• med st* medul-os-si rly4• *Meny* k* merc k* morg-g ptj1*• morph a1* myos-a rly4*• nat-m k* nat-sil fd3.de• nicotam rly4• nit-ac sf1.de nux-m zf *Nux-v* st oena zf olib-sac wmh1 ozone sde2*• petr-ra shn4• phos bg* pot-e rly4• puls stx1 rad-br stx1 rhus-g tmo3• sabad k* sacch-a fd2.de• *Sanguis-s* hrn2• sanic sep hs* *Staph* st* *Sulph* k* symph fd3.de• taosc iwa1• thiop jl3* tritic-vg fd5.de tub tub-m jl urol-h rwt• vanil fd5.de verat mtf33 viol-o ptk1* [am-s stj1 astat stj2 aur-m stj2 aur-s stj2 bar-br stj2 bar-i stj2 bar-met stj2 *Beryl* stj2 bism-sn stj2 caes-met stj2 cinnb stj2 cob stj2 cob-m stj2 cob-p stj2 *Cupr* stj2 ferr-f stj2 ferr-i stj1 ferr-lac stj2 ferr-n stj2 ferr-p stj1 ferr-s stj1 ferr-sil stj2 gal-s stj2 hafn-met stj2 heroin sdj2 kali-n stj1 lanth-met stj2 mag-br stj1 mag-f stj1 mag-i stj1 mag-lac stj2 mag-m stj1 *Mag-met* stj2 mag-n stj2 mag-s stj1 mag-sil stj2 merc-i-f stj2 osm-met stj2 pall stj2 plat stj2 plb stj2 plb-m stj2 plb-p stj2 polon-met stj2 rhen-met stj2 ruth-met stj2 *Sel* stj2 tant-met stj2 thal-met stj2 zinc stj2 zinc-i stj2 zinc-m stj2 zinc-p stj2]
  - **barbecued** meat: sol vml3•
  - **boiled**: caust bg2*
  - **children**, in: arum-t vh borx mtf33 calc sne caust mtf33 iod mtf33 mag-c st* sanic c1 staph mtf33 sulph mtf33 tritic-vg fd5.de vanil fd5.de
  - **cold**: *Phos* c1 sil k2
  - **fat**: apis vh1 carc jl2 *Med* mrr1 [arg-n stj2 ferr-n stj2 mag-n stj2 nitro stj2 ruth-met stj2 zinc-n stj2]
  - **hacked**: tub gk
  - **lean**, low in fat: hell b7.de*

- **meat – desire**: ...
  - **mincemeat**: staph mtf sulph mtf
  - **must** have: *Calc* st* nicotam rly4• *Nux-v* st *Staph* st* *Sulph* st* tritic-vg fd5.de
  - **pickled**: abies-c bg2* ant-c bg2* calc-p fr cori-r a1 hyper bg2* *Mag-c* st tub-m jl3
  - **rare** meat: adam srj5•
  - **raw**: *(↗raw - desire)* marb-w es1*• *Phos* vh plut-n stj2*• tub vh
  - **salted** meat: abies-c sf1.de ant-c sf1.de arg-n gsw1 calc-p fr* cor-r gsw1 mag-c tl1 sanic tl1 tub-m jl3
  - **smoked**: atro a2 *Calc-p* k* carc vh* **Caust** k* kreos plut-n srj7• symph fd3.de• tritic-vg fd5.de **Tub** k* tub-m jl3
  - **supper**, at: graph a1
  - **without** being able to eat it: olib-sac wmh1
- **melons**:
  - **agg.**: ars sf1.de* bry stx1 fl-ac bg2* petr stx1 petr-ra shn4• puls sf1.de zing bg2* [ars-met stj2 kali-ar stj2 nat-ar stj2 tell stj2]
  - **aversion**: *Ars* st* *Chin* st* verat st* zing ld1.de* [tell stj2]
  - **desire**: bar-ox-suc rly4• cartl-s rly4• ger-i rly4• hippoc-k szs2 lac-loxod-a hrn2• petr-ra shn4• puls sf1.de* tritic-vg fd5.de vanil fd5.de [*Tell* stj2]
    - **watermelon**: staph mtf
- **milk**: *(↗dairy)*
  - **agg.**: *(↗dairy - agg.; RECTUM - Diarrhea - milk - agg.)*
a-dnitroph a acon b7a.de* acon-l vml3• **Aeth** k* aloe sne *Alum* k* alum-p k2* alum-sil k2* alumn kr1* *Ambr* k* *Ang* b2.de* *Ant-c* k* ant-t k* *Arg-met* arist-cl stx1 *Ars* k* ars-s-f k2* asim mtf11 atro stx1 aur-m-n wbt2• bar-c stx1 bell b4.de* brom k* *Bry* k* bufo gk* but-ac jl1 calad vml3• **Calc** k* **Calc-s** k* calc-sil k2* carb-ac vml3• carb-an k* *Carb-v* k* carbn-s k* carc fb4* card-m a2* *Cham* k* *Chel* k* **Chin** k* *Cic* cocc b7a.de coch stx1 coli jl2* **Con** k* cortico vml3* cortiso vml3* crot-t k* cuc-c vml3• cuph c1 *Cupr* k* cur a1* fago vml3• ferr kr1 hell k* **Hom-xyz** bg2* hyper stx1 ign k* iod stx1 ip hs2 *Iris* k* kali-ar kali-bi bg2 *Kali-c* k* kali-cy stx1 *Kali-i* k* kali-n bg2 kali-p kali-sil k2* lac-c mg1.de* **Lac-d** k* lac-h vml3• lac-v c1* lach k* lact vml3• lact-v bro1 *Lec* sne levo jl* luna c1 *Lyc* k* *Mag-c* k* mag-f mg1.de **Mag-m** k* mag-p stx1 *Mag-s* vml3* med gk merc k2* merc-d stx1 moni rfm1• morph oss* mur-ac stx1 *Nat-ar* k* *Nat-c* k* *Nat-m* k* nat-ox vml3• *Nat-p* k* *Nat-s* nat-sil k2* *Nicc* kr1* **Nit-ac** k* nux-m k* *Nux-v* k* *Ol-j* k* oscilloc jl2 past c1* petr stx1 ph-ac stx1 *Phos* k* phys a2* phyt stx1 pin-con oss2• pitu-a vml2* podo bro1* *Psor* ptel bl6 *Puls* k* raph kr1* rheum bro1* rhus-t k* rob stx1 ruta cka1* sabin k* samb k* sanic stx1 **Sep** k* sil k* spong k* **Staph** st* stram sul-ac k* **Sulph** k* trios vml3• **Tub** hu* *Vac* stx1 valer k* vip a2* *Zinc* k* zinc-p k2 [alumin stj2 alumin-p stj2 alumin-s stj2 *Ant-m* stj2 *Ant-met* stj2 beryl stj2 *Ferr-sil* stj2 lac-ac stj2 *Mag-sil* stj2 *Mang-sil* stj2 moly-met stj2 nat-br stj2 nat-caust stj2 *Nat-lac* stj2 nat-met stj2 pall stj2 *Sil-met* stj2 stann stj2]
    - **boiled**: nux-m hr1* sep c1*
    - **clotted**: chel b7a.de
    - **cold**: calc-sil k2* carc mlr1• kali-i c1* spong ptk1*
    - **curds**: med mtf nat-s mtf thuj mtf tub mtf
    - **hot**: bry ld1.de*
    - **mother's**: acet-ac stx1 *Ant-c* stx1 *Arg-n* k2 calc stx1 chel sne *Cina* bg2* coch stx1 crot-t stx1 ip stx1 jal vml3• nat-c bg2* *Ph-ac* stx1 *Sanic* stx1 **Sil** bg2* *Vac* stx1 *Valer* stx1
    - **warm**: *Ambr* k* *Ang* vml4*
  - **amel.**: acon ptk1* aegop-p vml3• ambr vh1 ant-c bt3 *Apis* k* aran jl3 arist-cl sp1* *Ars* k* arum-m c1 asar vh1 bry samkn* calc-hp ll1 cassia-s vml3• *Chel* bg2* cina bg2* diph bg3* ferr bg2* graph bg2 hydr mrr3 iod k* kali-cy stx1 lact ld1.de merc bg2* merc-cy c1 mez k* *Nux-v* ptk1 op stx1 ph-ac bg2* rhus-t bg2* ruta k* sabal c1* scor sys1 squil bg2* staph bg2* vanil fd5.de verat k*
    - **cold**: ant-c he1 iod ptk1
    - **hot**: ars-h hs1 asar jl1 chel tl1* croc lpc2 crot-c sk4• crot-t hr1*
    - **mother's** milk: ant-c bg2 ars bg2 crot-t bg2 mez bg2
      - **cold**: apis bg2
      - **warm**: chel bg2
    - **sips** of milk: diph ptk1*
    - **warm**: androc srj1*• ars gg *Chel* coloc c1 crot-t vml3* graph k2 lac-h sze9• op stx1 plb-chr c1 scor sys1

- **aversion**: acet-ac br1 acon-l a1* adam srj5• *Aeth* k* alum-p k2* am-c k* ammc a1* *Ant-t* k* *Arn* k* ars b4a.de* arum-t vh1 aur-m-n wbt2• bell k* borx hr1 bov bg2* *Bry* k* *Cact* ld1.de* calad k* *Calc* k* calc-p stx1 *Calc-s* calc-sil k2* *Carb-v* k* carbn-s k* carc c1* chin bg2* cimic gk *Cina* k* con st convo-s sp1 crot-t vml3• elaps ld1.de esp-g kk1.de* ferr k2* ferr-p k* gink-b sbd1*• *Guaj* k* guare k* *Ign* k* iod bg2* ipom-p sp iris tl1 kali-c lsa1.de kali-i ld1.de *Lac-ac* stj5*• **Lac-d** k* lac-f wza1• lac-h vml3• lach bg2 *Lec* k* *Lepr* vml3• lyc gk m-arct b2.de* m-aust b2.de* mag-c k* *Mag-m* ld1.de* merc bg2* *Mez* vh **Nat-c** k* *Nat-m* bg2* nat-p *Nat-s* k* nicc br1* nicot ld1.de nit-ac bg2* nux-m bg2 nux-v k* ol-j a1* par kr1 past bro1* pers jl3* ph-ac br1 *Phos* k* pin-con oss2• podo ld1.de* *Puls* k* rheum k* rhus-t bg2* ribo rly4• ros-d wla1 sabal br1 sacch sht• *Sep* k* *Sil* k* stann k* **Staph** st* suis-hep rly4• sul-ac bg2* *Sulph* k* syc ptj1*• tub c1* vanil fd5.de [am-br stj2 am-caust stj2 ang stj4 brom stj1* calc-br stj1 calc-lac stj2 cob stj2 cob-m stj2 cob-p stj2 ferr-lac stj2 *Ferr-sil* stj2 heroin sdj2 kali-br stj1 *Kali-sil* stj2 mag-br stj1 mag-lac stj2 *Mag-sil* stj2 *Mang-sil* stj2 moly-met stj2 nat-f stj2 nat-lac stj2 *Nat-sil* stj2 nicc-met stj2 nicc-s stj2 niob-met stj2 pall stj2 sel stj2 *Sil-met* stj2 titan stj2 titan-s stj2 tung-met stj2 zinc stj2 zinc-i stj2 zinc-m stj2 zinc-n stj2 zinc-p stj2]
  - **morning**: m-aust al2 puls
  - **boiled**: *Phos* k*
  - **cold**: ph-ac bg2 tub bg2
  - **curds**: lyc mtf phos mtf
  - **desire** appears when drinking a little; but: bry h1*
  - **mother's** milk: acet-ac br1* aeth tl1 ant-c k* ant-t kr1* *Borx* lmj bry st calc-p mtf33 *Cina* k* jal vml3• lac-ac stj5• lach k* mag-c st merc k* nat-c bg2* nat-m hr1 *Ph-ac* br1 rheum b7.de* sabal br1* **Sil** k* stann k* stram k* sulph br1 verat kr1 [*Calc-sil* stj2 *Ferr-sil* stj2 *Kali-sil* stj2 *Mag-sil* stj2 *Mang-sil* stj2 *Nat-sil* stj2 *Sil-met* stj2]
    - **child** refuses: *Acet-ac* br1 ant-c lmj ant-t kr1* apis lmj *Borx* k* bry lmj *Calc* k* **Calc-p** k* cina k* kali-c lmj lach k* lyc lmj *Mag-c* st* *Merc* k* nat-c lmj nat-m lmj *Ph-ac* br1 rheum c1* sabal br1 sec lmj **Sil** k ●* stann st* stram lmj sulph br1 verat kr1
      - **night**: apis ptk
  - **smell** of: bell k* par kr1
  - **warm**: chel ptk1 crot-t ptk1 graph ptk1 sacch sht*•
- **desire**: *(↗dairy - desire)* abrot k* adlu jl3 aids nl2• aloe sne amp rly4• anac k* androc srj1*• *Apis* k* aran jl3* *Ars* k* ars-i vh1* asar vh* *Aur* k* aur-ar k2* aur-m-n wbt2• aur-s k2* bac wz* bapt k* borx k* bov k* *Bry* k* bufo a1 *Cact* ld* *Calc* k* calc-p k2 calc-sil k2* *Carc* c1* *Chel* k* chelin bg3 cisplat vml3• cist ptk1 cur a1* dys ptj1*• *Elaps* k* gaert ptj1*• graph ham fd3.de• hyper kali-i k* **Lac-ac** stj2*• *Lac-c* k* lac-f wza1• lac-h sk4*• lac-leo hrn2• lach bg2 lact ld1.de* lap-la rsp1 limest-b es1*• loxo-recl knl4• *Lycps-v* ld1.de* m-ambo b2.de* mag-c k* mang k* *Merc* k* mercs-n a1 mez tl1 moly-met stj2*• moni rfm nat-c mrr1 *Nat-m* k* nat-s *Nux-v* k* ozone sde• petr-ra shn4• *Ph-ac* k* phel k* *Phos* mrr1 raph c1 **Rhus-t** k* ribo rly4• ruta fd4.de *Sabad* k* sabal bg2* sabin k* *Sacch* sht*• sanic bg1* sep gk *Sil* k* spong fd4.de *Staph* k* *Stront-c* k* suis-hep rly4• sulph k* suprar rly4• syc ptj1*• symph fd3.de• taosc iwa1• thiam rly4• tritic-vg fd5.de *Tub* st* vanil fd5.de *Verat* ld1.de* *Vip* bg2* [ars-met stj2 beryl-m stj2 calc-lac stj2 calc-met stj2 ferr-lac stj2 kali-ar stj2 kali-sil stj2 mag-lac stj2 mag-sil stj2 mang-sil stj2 nat-ar stj2 nat-caust stj2 nat-lac stj2 nat-sil stj2 sil-met stj2 stront-m stj2 stront-met stj2 tax jsj7]
  - **boiled**: abrot k* nat-s k* raph c1*
  - **cold**: adlu jl3* *Apis* bg2* bar-ox-suc rly4* carc dx1* kola stb3• lac-cp sk4• med ser moni rfm1• ozone sde2*• ph-ac k* phel k* *Phos* k* *Rhus-t* k* ruta fd4.de sabad k* sacch sht*• sanic bg3* spong fd4.de staph k* streptoc rly4• *Tub* k* vanil fd5.de
    - **ice**: acon-ac rly4• sanic hsa*
  - **curds**: bac mtf bry mtf calc mtf elaps mtf mag-c mtf mag-m mtf mag-s mtf morg-p mtf nat-c mtf nat-s mtf nux-v mtf ph-ac mtf sep mtf sil mtf
  - **hot**: calc chel graph k* hyper kola stb3•
  - **milk**-shake: conch fkr1•
  - **sour**: *(↗buttermilk - desire)* ant-t bg1* mand sp1 mang k* nat-s a*
  - **warm**: androc srj1• ars sys1* *Bry* k* calc ptk1 chel ptk1 ign sne lac-h sze9• lyss al2 sacch sht*• suprar rly4• tritic-vg fd5.de vanil fd5.de

- **milkshake** | **desire**: med mtf phos mtf tub mtf
- **mixtures** | **agg.**: ant-c bg2* coff bg2 ip bg2* *Puls* bg2*
- **mother's** milk (See milk - agg. - mother's; milk - aversion - mother's)
- **mushrooms**:
  - **agg.** | **poisonous**: camph bro1
  - **aversion**: bamb-a stb2.de• calc-p mtf nat-s dx1 [zinc stj2 zinc-i stj2 zinc-m stj2 zinc-n stj2 zinc-p stj2]
  - **desire**: lyc mtf mag-m mtf
- **mussels**:
  - **agg.**: *(↗oysters - agg.)* **Lyc** b2.de* staph gk
    - **poisoning**: camph cp1*
  - **aversion**: [cupr stj2]
- **mustard**:
  - **agg.**: sin-n vml3•
  - **desire**: alco vml3• ars k* bac vh* cic jl3 *Cocc* k* colch haliae-lc srj5• halo vml3• hep kali-s fd4.de *Lac-c* kr1* mez mill k* nat-sil fd4.de* nicc k* rhus-t ser ruta fd4.de sacch sht*• sacch-a fd2.de• tritic-vg fd5.de [ars-met stj2 kali-ar stj2 nat-ar stj2]
- **mutton**:
  - **agg.**: arg-n ptk1 *Ars* ptk1 borx h1* carb-v ptk1 caust ptk1 chin ptk1 *Colch* ptk1 *Ferr* ptk1 kali-bi ptk1 lept ptk1 lyss ptk1 merc ptk1 ov ptel ptk1 *Puls* ptk1
  - **amel.**: verat ptk1
  - **aversion**: calc b4a.de* mag-c vh ov k*
  - **desire**: nit-ac dgt pitu-gl skp7• plb dgt
- **new** food (= never eaten before):
  - **agg.**: chin bg2 lyc bg2 puls bg2 teucr bg2
- **noodles** (See pasta)
- **nursery** foods | **desire**: arizon-l nl2•
- **nuts**:
  - **agg.**: bamb-a stx1
  - **aversion**: [ferr stj2 ferr-f stj2 ferr-lac stj2 ferr-n stj2 ferr-sil stj2]
  - **desire**: ara-maca sej7• asar vh* calc mrr1* cub k* dulc fd4.de kali-p fd1.de• kali-s fd4.de ozone sde2*• plut-n srj7• ruta fd4.de sep gk* spong fd4.de symph fd3.de• tritic-vg fd5.de vanil fd5.de
    - **salted**: ozone sde2*•
- **oatmeal**: *(↗porridge)*
  - **agg.**: tanac hl1
  - **desire**: ap-g c1* gaert ptj1•
- **oil**:
  - **agg.**: *(↗fat - agg.)* ant-c ptk1 ars ptk1 bry b2.de* calc ptk1 *Canth* b2.de* **Carb-v** ptk1 *Chin* ptk1 **Cycl** ptk1 *Ferr* ptk1 *Graph* ptk1 kali-m ptk1 lyc ptk1 *Meny* vml3• nat-p ptk1 podo fd3.de• **Puls** b2.de* rob ptk1 sep ptk1 sulph vh tarax ptk1
    - **olive**: *Nat-m* vh puls k2 *Sulph* vh
  - **aversion**: ars vh germ-met srj5• *Meny* vh *Nat-m* vh* nat-sil fd3.de• *Puls* vh*
    - **olive**: **Ars** vh *Meny* vh* *Nat-m* vh *Puls* vh
  - **desire**: ars mtf33 jal vml3•
    - **olive**: **Ars** vh dulc fd4.de tritic-vg fd5.de
- **okra**:
  - **agg.**: nat-m mtf
  - **amel.**: nat-s mtf
  - **aversion**: calc mtf caust mrr2 cob mrr2 med hu2 nat-m mtf puls mtf zinc mtf
  - **desire**: lyc mtf nat-s mtf staph mtf sulph mtf tub mtf
- **olive**:
  - **aversion**: **Sulph** vh* tritic-vg fd5.de
  - **desire**: ars mtf33 calc vh* dulc fd4.de kali-p fd1.de• **Lyc** vh* sulph vh symph fd3.de• tritic-vg fd5.de
- **onions**:
  - **agg.**: acon-l c1* alum bg2* alumn vml3• asar bc brom bro1* *Bry* b7a.de carb-v vh carc mlr1* *Ign* vh **Lyc** k* murx bg2* nat-m vh nux-v k* orni bg1* phos vh polym bg *Puls* k* ruta fd4.de sep bg* *Sulph* vh* syc ptj1* thuj b2.de*
  - **amel.**: all-c ptk1*

- **aversion**: alum tl1 asar vh* brom ld1.de* lyc tl1* med hu nit-ac gl1.fr• op vh *Phos* ld1.de* prot jl3* *Sabad* k* sep ld1.de *Thuj* h1* [am-br stj2 ang stj4 calc-br stj1 kali-br stj1 mag-br stj1]
  - **smell** of: aegop-p vml3•
- **desire**: all-c tl1* bell-p ptk1* carc mrr1 cop bg2 cub bg2* form-ac ccrh1• ham fd3.de• lac-del hrn2• loxo-recl knl4• pitu-gl skp7• ruta fd4.de sabad mrr1 symph fd3.de• *Thuj* mrr1 tritic-vg fd5.de
  - **raw**: *(↗raw - desire)* *All-c* all-s ld1.de* bell-p mg1.de* carc vh* cop vml3• cub k* kali-s fd4.de kola stb3• med st *Rhus-g* tmo3• ruta fd4.de *Sabad* vh staph mtf* *Thuj* bg1*

- **oranges**:
  - **agg.**: androc srj arg-n dgt irid-met srj5• med hu* **Olnd** vh* ph-ac ptk1 scor sys1 spong fd4.de syc bka1* [titan stj2 titan-s stj2 tung-met stj2]
    - **juice**: androc srj1*• med hu scor sys1 thal-xyz srj8•
  - **aversion**: elaps ld1.de irid-met srj5•
  - **desire**: amp rly4• androc vml3• ap-g c1* choc srj3*• cub k* dendr-pol sk4• elaps k* galeoc-c-h gms1• ham fd3.de• kali-s fd4.de ketogl-ac rly4• med k* neon stj2*• olnd vh petr-ra shn4• podo fd3.de• positr nl2• sal-fr sle1• sol-t-ae k* spong fd4.de symph fd3.de• ther k* vanil fd5.de [tax jsj7 titan stj2 titan-s stj2]
    - **blood** orange: choc srj3•
    - **orange** juice: germ-met srj lavand-a ctl1• tritic-vg fd5.de vanil fd5.de
- **ordinary** food (See simplest)
- **oysters**:
  - **agg.**: *(↗fish - agg.; mussels - agg.; shellfish - agg.)* *Aloe* k* bell stx1 *Brom* k* bry k* calc st carb-v bg2* *Coloc* bg2 cop stx1 ip stx1 kali-n vml3• **Lyc** b2.de* *Podo* k* *Puls* bg2* sapin stx1 *Sul-ac* k*
  - **amel.**: lach bg2*
  - **aversion**: acon vh calc st lyc br1* med vh *Nat-m* br1 *Phos* k* sep dx1 [alumin-p stj2 arg-p stj2 cupr-p stj2 gal-s stj2 lith-p stj2 mang-p stj2 plb-p stj2 zinc-p stj2]
  - **desire**: apis k* brom *Bry* k* *Calc* **Lach** k* *Lyc* k* **Lycps-v** ld1.de* *Nat-m* k* phos vh *Rhus-t* k* sil dgt sulph vh
- **pancakes** | **agg.**: *Bry* k* ip k* *Kali-c* k* mag-s stx1 **Puls** k* verat k* [beryl stj2]
- **papadam**:
  - **agg.**: *Nux-v* mtf
  - **aversion**: lyc mtf
  - **desire**: ars mtf chin mtf mag-p mtf med mtf merc mtf nux-v mtf
    - **fried**: nux-v mtf
    - **roasted**: ars mtf
- **paper** | **desire**: *(↗indigestible - desire)* lac-c sne lac-f bg1*
- **pasta**: *(↗lasagna)*
  - **desire**: *(↗farinaceous - desire)* calc-p mtf dulc fd4.de kali-s fd4.de lach vh nat-m vh plac rzf5• tritic-vg fd5.de tub mtf vanil fd5.de [alumin-s stj2]
- **pastry**:
  - **agg.**: *(↗sweets - agg.)* **Ant-c** bg2* arg-n k* ars k* bamb-a stx1 *Bry* bg2* *Calc* kr1* cann-i a1* carb-v k* cean c1 cycl sf1.de dios hr1* ferr-p kr1* ip k* *Kali-c* kr1* *Kali-chl* k* kali-m bg2* lob hr1 *Lyc* k* nat-s bg2* *Phos* k* psor bgs ptel bg2* **Puls** k* rob vml3• sanic bgs sarr a1 sulph st* sumb a1* symph fd3.de• *Verat* kr1*
    - **fat**: *Puls* b7a.de
    - **warm**: ant-c bg2 cycl bg2 ip bg2 kali-c b2.de* lyc bg2 nat-s bg2 puls b2.de* verat bg2
  - **aversion**: *Ars* kr1 ferr-p tl1 lyc ld1.de morph c1 *Phos* kr1 *Ptel* kr1* *Puls* sf1.de* sumb a1*
  - **desire**: ap-g c1 aur gk* aur-m-n wbt2• bamb-a stb2.de• bufo k* *Calc* k* carc sys1* chin corn hr1* corn-f hr1* dulc fd4.de kali-p fd1.de• kali-s fd4.de kola stb3• mag-m jl merc-i-f st* naja mtf nat-sil fd3.de• pitu-a ft* plb k* podo fd3.de• positr nl2• puls k2* ruta fd4.de sabad bg1* sacch sht*• suis-em rly4• sulph st* symph fd3.de• thiam rly4• tritic-vg fd5.de vanil fd5.de x-ray al2 [heroin sdj2]
- **peaches**:
  - **agg.**: all-c bro1* *Fl-ac* bg2* glon bg2* psor k* verat gl1.fr*•
    - **smell** of; to the: *(↗NOSE - Smell - acute - peaches)* all-c k*
  - **desire**: aids nl2• tritic-vg fd5.de vanil fd5.de
- **peanut** butter | **desire**: bit-ar wht1• medul-os-si rly4• *Puls* vh* staphycoc rly4• streptoc rly4• tub hu
- **peanuts** | **agg.**: [moly-met stj2]
- **pears**:
  - **agg.**: borx k* bry k* merc-c bg2* naja pd nat-c bg2 psor bgs puls bgs puls-n c1* tub bgs *Verat* k* [bor-pur stj2]
  - **desire**: [bor-pur stj2 titan stj2 titan-s stj2]
- **peas**:
  - **agg.**: *(↗flatulent - agg.)* ars k* **Bry** k* *Calc* k* carb-v k* chin k* *Coloc* vh cupr k* erig mg1.de hell k* kali-c k* **Lyc** k* nat-m k* *Petr* k* phos bg2 puls k* sep k* sil k* sulph gl1.fr• verat k* [zinc-n stj2]
  - **amel.**: *Coloc* vh
  - **aversion**: ars mrr1 *Kali-act* vh *Lyc* vh* med mrr1 nat-m vh
  - **desire**: acon a2 *Acon-l* st *Alum* ld1.de
- **pepper**: *(↗green peppers; red pepper; sweet peppers)*
  - **agg.**: alum k2* ars k* caps vh* *Chin* bg2* *Cina* k* nat-c k* *Nux-v* bg2* sep k* sil k* [aur-s stj2 cinnb stj2 *Gal-s* stj2 sulph stj2]
  - **aversion**: alum tl1 [nicc-s stj2]
  - **desire**: alco vml3• caps k2* carc mlr1• choc srj *Lac-c* ptk1* merc-c nat-m mtf33 nux-v mtf33 vanil fd5.de [*Niob-met* stj2]
    - **black**; for: caps vh kali-s fd4.de *Lac-c* *Nat-m* vh nux-v c1*
- **peppermint**:
  - **aversion**: [tung-met stj2]
  - **desire**: carc sde• galeoc-c-h gms1•
- **pickles**: *(↗gherkins)*
  - **agg.**: ant-c vh carb-v bg2 nat-m ld1.de
  - **aversion**: abies-c k* arund ld1.de*
  - **desire**: abies-c k* alum ld1.de* am-m ld1.de* *Ant-c* k* arn ld1.de* ars ld1.de* bac bn* calc-f nh* cand vml3• carb-an ld1.de* carc zzh cassia-s ccrh1*• chel ld1.de* cod ld1.de* corn kr1 cortiso vml3• falco-pe nl2• ham hep k* hyper k* ign ld1.de kali-bi ld1.de *Lach* k* lact ld1.de* mag-c ld1.de *Myric* ld1.de* nat-ar k* orot-ac rly4*• rib-ac jl3* ruta fd4.de sec ld1.de* *Sep* ld1.de* staph gsw1 *Sul-i* k* *Sulph* k* symph fd3.de• tritic-vg fd5.de verat k* [ant-m stj2 ant-met stj2 ant-t stj2]
    - **spicy** Indian pickles: abies-c mtf *Ars* mtf carc mtf chin mtf cist mtf fl-ac mtf *Hep* mtf lac-c mtf nat-m mtf nat-p mtf *Nux-v* mtf sep mtf stry-p mtf sulph mtf *Tub* mtf *Verat* mtf
- **pineapple**:
  - **aversion**: tub dx1*
  - **desire**: graph dgt **Hydrog** srj*
    - **juice**: oci-sa sk4•
- **pizza**:
  - **agg.**: bamb-a stx1
  - **desire**: calc-p mtf ferr mtf gaert mtf med mtf *Nat-m* mtf nat-pyru rly4• nit-ac mtf phos mtf puls mtf staph mtf stront-c mtf* sulph mtf *Tub* mtf [calc-sil stj2]
- **plain** food | **desire**: rhus-g tmo3•
- **plants** growing near water | **agg.**: nat-s bro1
- **plums**:
  - **agg.**: agar stx1 *Ars* b4a.de ham stx1 mag-c h2* *Merc-c* bg2 puls gl1.fr*• rheum b7.de*
    - **sour** plums: calad vml3•
  - **aversion**: bar-c k* elaps kr1 sul-ac ld1.de
  - **desire**: arg-n kr1 podo fd3.de• ruta fd4.de sul-ac k* tritic-vg fd5.de [titan stj]
    - **sauce**: arg-n
- **poppy** seeds | **desire**: nux-v mtf
- **pork**:
  - **agg.**: *(↗fat - agg.)* acon k* acon-l c1* *Ant-c* k* ant-t k* ars k* asaf k* bamb-a stx1 bell k* **Carb-v** k* caust k* clem bg2* *Colch* k* **Cycl** k* dros bg2* **Graph** bg2* ham k* *Ip* k* *Nat-ar* *Nat-c* k* *Nat-m* k* nux-m stx1 psor bgs **Puls** k* rhus-v stx1 **Sep** k* tarax k* tarent ld1.de* thuj k* tub bgs [alum stj2 nat-caust stj2 oxyg stj2 sil stj2]
    - **smell** of pork agg.: *Colch* b2.de*
  - **amel.**: mag-c kr1* nat-m sf1.de ran-b sf1.de ran-s sf1.de*
    - **smell** of pork: ran-b bg2 ran-s bg2
  - **aversion**: *Ang* b7a.de* arg-n vh1* calc-caust zf carb-v gm1 *Colch* k* cycl br1* *Dros* k* prot pte1* *Psor* k* *Puls* k* sep b4.de*
    - **roasted**: ptel bg1

- **desire**: ant-c mtf33 *Calc-p* bg2* caust vh *Crot-h* k* elaps fkr8.de *Mez* bg2 nit-ac bg2* nux-v bg2* rad-br bg3* rad-met st *Tub* k* [plut-n stj2]
- **porridge**: *(↗oatmeal)*
  - **agg.**: bell gl1.fr*• chin gl1.fr*• kali-c gl1.fr• puls gl1.fr*• sulph gl1.fr*•
  - **amel.**: crot-t stx1
  - **aversion**: ars k* *Calc* k*
  - **desire**: ap-g vml3• bell gl3• chin gl3• gaert fmm1*• lac-ac stj2*• sulph gl3• [mag-lac stj2]
- **potato** chips | **desire**: calc-p mtf med mtf nat-m mtf stram mtf *Tub* mtf
- **potatoes**:
  - **agg.**: *Alum* k* alum-p k2* *Alumn* kr1* am-c bg2* am-m k* amp rly4• *Bry* kr1* calc *Coloc* k* gran bg2* kali-bi vh mag-c st* mag-s k1* merc ld1.de merc-c k* merc-cy ld1.de *Nat-s* k* psor bgs *Puls* bg2* *Sep* k* *Sil* bt3* *Sulph* bg2* tub bgs *Verat* k* [*Alumin* stj2 alumin-p stj2 alumin-s stj2 am-br stj2 am-caust stj2 am-f stj2 am-p stj1 am-s stj1]
    - **watery**: kali-n vml3•
  - **amel.**: acet-ac ptk1* ruta fd4.de
  - **aversion**: alum k* alum-p k2* camph k* carc zzh cupr sht*• lec sne nat-s tl1 *Phos* vh sep ld1.de* syc ptj1*• thuj k* [calc-s stj1]
    - **boiled**: cupr sst3*• [cupr-act stj2 cupr-f stj2 cupr-m stj2 cupr-p stj2]
    - **fried**: cob-n vml3•
  - **desire**: adam srj5• alum vh* calc kr1* calc-p bg2* carc dx1* cardios-h vml3• cic k2 cob-n sp1* des-ac rbp6 dulc fd4.de ham fd3.de• hep ld1.de kali-p fd1.de• lac-leo hrn2• limest-b es1*• malar al2* med st* nat-c k* nat-m mtf nicotam rly4• ol-an k* olnd bg2* pant-ac rly4• pitu-a ft plac-s rly4• plut-n srj7• positr nl2• puls vh ruta fd4.de sacch sht• staph mtf sulph gy tub vh* vanil fd5.de [alumin-s stj2 bor-pur stj2]
    - **boiled**: germ-met srj5• ruta fd4.de
    - **fried**: *(↗french - desire)* alum gk cob-n sp1* kali-p fd1.de• pitu-a ft* sacch sht• [tax jsj7]
    - **mashed**: lac-h sze9• [cupr stj2]
    - **raw**: *Calc* k* carc pc* cic k2* med mtf33
- **poultry**:
  - **agg.**: carb-v c1*
  - **desire**: bac st
- **puddings**:
  - **agg.**: *(↗sweets - agg.)* ptel kr1* sabal c1
  - **aversion**: ars k* calc dx1 *Phos* k* *Ptel* k* syc bka1*•
  - **desire**: gaert pte1*• lac-h htj1• rad-br sze8• sabad k* spong fd4.de tritic-vg fd5.de x-ray al2
- **pungent** things:
  - **agg.**: acon kr1 *Ant-c* kr1 apis stx1 ars kr1 *Carb-v* kr1 dros stx1 *Ferr* kr1 *Hep* kr1 kreos stx1 *Lach* kr1 *Nat-m* kr1 *Nux-v* kr1 *Ph-ac* kr1 *Phos* kr1 *Sil* kr1 *Sul-ac* kr1 *Sulph* kr1 verat stx1
  - **amel.**: arg-n kr1 ign kr1
  - **aversion**: *(↗spices - aversion)* *Fl-ac* ld1.de *Hep* vh sang ld1.de *Sulph* vh
  - **desire**: *(↗salsa - desire; spices - desire)* abies-c gk* acon c1* alum sys1 am-c gk* ang kr1 ant-c sys1 arg-n sys1 ars aster k* aur mtf33 bac stx1 *Bry* kr1 calc-f sys1 calc-p sys1 caps bg1* carc cd caust k2* chel sys1 chin b7a.de* chir-fl gya2 cic sys1 *Cist* cocc stx1 cory-b vml3• crot-h gk *Fl-ac* glycyr-g cte1• *Hep* k* kali-p fd1.de• kali-s fd4.de *Lac-c* lac-leo sk4• lach mrr1 mag-s vml3• med mtf nat-m gk nat-p nat-sil fd3.de• nit-ac k2 nux-v k2* ozone vml3• petr-ra shn4• ph-ac phos vh* puls b7a.de* ruta fd4.de sacch stx1 sacch-a fd2.de• *Sang* sep k2* ser-ang vml3• staph sys1 stront-c sk4• stry-p sf1.de succ-ac vml3• sulph kr1* symph fd3.de• tritic-vg fd5.de tub vh* vanil fd5.de verat gk* *Zing* vml3•
- **quark** | **desire** (See cheese - desire - cottage)
- **rabbit** | **desire**: asar dgt kali-ar dgt
- **radishes**:
  - **agg.**: mand sp1
  - **aversion**: abel vh1 abies-c vh1 [*Osm-met* stj2]
  - **desire**: abies-c br1* lac-loxod-a hrn2• sabad vh sep vh [niob-met stj2]
- **rags**, clean | **desire**: alum k* alumn ld1.de*
- **raisins** | **agg.**: ip br1*
- **raw** food:
  - **agg.**●: ars k* bry k* cham stx1 chin k* chinin-ar stx1 hypoth vml3• lyc k* psor bgs *Puls* k* rhus-v c1* **Ruta** k* *Verat* k*
  - **aversion**: prot fb*
  - **desire**: *(↗ham - desire - raw; meat - desire - raw; onions - desire - raw)* *Abies-c* bg2* ail k* all-c bg1 alum bg2* androc srj ant-c bt3 calc bg2 calc-p pd carb-an gk cub vml3• haliae-lc srj5• ign bg2* lept vml3• *Lycps-v* ld1.de* *Mag-s* vml3• podo fd3.de• prot vml3• psor bgs sil k* **Sulph** k* symph fd3.de• tarent k* tritic-vg fd5.de [heroin sdj2 mag-met stj2 mag-n stj2 mag-sil stj2 nicc-met stj2 nicc-s stj2 ruth-met stj2]
- **red** cabbage | **agg.**: lyc b4a.de petr b4a.de
- **red** food | **desire**: choc srj3*•
- **red** pepper: *(↗green peppers; pepper; sweet peppers)*
  - **agg.**: lac-lup hrn2• phos ptk1
  - **amel.** | **cayenne** pepper: coff-t c1*
  - **desire**: merc-c bg2
    - **cayenne** pepper: choc srj3*• merc-c k*
- **refreshing** things:
  - **agg.**: sang ld1.de
  - **amel.**: petr-ra shn4•
  - **aversion**: *Fl-ac* ld1.de phos ld1.de rheum ld1.de sang ld1.de
  - **desire**: *(↗juicy - desire)* adam srj5• allox jl3* aloe k* ant-t bg2* *Ars* k* *Calc* k* calc-f mg1.de* *Calc-p* ld1.de* calc-s carb-an k* *Caust* k* *Chin* choc srj3*• *Cist* *Cocc* k* ferr-p vh *Fl-ac* k* germ-met srj5• hep bg2 iod bg2* irid-met srj5• m-ambo b2.de* mag-f stj1*• mag-s jl* med ptk1 nat-ar k* nept-m lsd2.fr petr-ra shn4• **Ph-ac** k* *Phos* k* *Puls* k* rheum k* *Sabin* k* sacch-a fd2.de• sang k* sars sec cda sel bg2* sol vml3• sul-ac br1 symph fd3.de• thal vml3• thuj til k* *Tub* valer k* **Verat** k* wies c1 [arg-met stj1 ars-met stj2 bar-f stj1 fl-pur stj2 kali-ar stj2 kali-f stj1 mag-i stj1 mag-n stj2 mag-sil stj2 nat-f stj1 stann stj2]
    - **chill**; during: *Cocc* b7.de* ph-ac bg2 phos bg2 puls bg2
- **rhubarb** | **agg.**: cham stx1 coloc stx1 merc stx1 nux-v stx1 ox-ac k2* puls stx1
- **rice**:
  - **agg.**: bry gl1.fr• *Ign* vh* kali-n vh* puls gl1.fr*• sulph gl1.fr*• tell c1*
  - **desire**: mand sp1 *Musa* vml3• myos-a rly4*• *Phos* mrr1* plac rzf5• ruta fd4.de *Staph* mtf33 ter gsw1 vanil fd5.de [alum stj2 alumin stj2 alumin-p stj2 alumin-s stj2]
    - **dry**: *(↗idli - desire)* *Alum* k* mand sp1 *Phos* vh *Staph* vh ter ther ld1.de
- **rice** puddings | **aversion**: ptel tl1
- **rich** food: *(↗heavy)*
  - **agg.**: *(↗fat - agg.; heavy - agg.)* aeth stx1 alum-sil vh1 ant-c arg-n ars ptk1* asaf stx1 bacls-10 ptj1• *Bry* k* buni-o jl3* calc st* carb-an **Carb-v** k* carc mlr1* caust ld1.de* cupr ld1.de cycl dros k* ferr ferr-m stx1 gaert ptj1• iod ld1.de *Ip* k* kali-chl kali-m c1* morg-p ptj1• myos-a rly4• nat-c ld1.de nat-m *Nat-s* k* *Nit-ac* k* orot-ac rly4• ozone stx1 ph-ac k2 phos pitu-a vml2* *Ptel* mrr1* **Puls** k* samb stx1 *Sep* k* spong stx1 staph sulph ld1.de* tarax thuj tub ptj1• tung-met bdx1•
  - **aversion**: ars mtf33 *Carb-v* mtf33 carc mlr1* choc srj3• falco-pe nl2• merc mtf33 *Nat-m* mrr1 ozone sde2• ptel c1 tritic-vg fd5.de
    - **eating**; while: kali-m ptk1
  - **desire**: act-sp bg arizon-l nl2• carc mlr1• cypra-eg sde6.de• lac-h sk4• nux-v br1 pin-con oss2• plac-s rly4• succ-ac rly4• *Sulph* b4a.de syc ptj1•
- **roast** beef | **aversion**: *Ptel* vml3•
- **rolls**:
  - **desire**: aur b2.de* spong fd4.de vanil fd5.de
    - **stale** rolls; for: *Aur* h2
    - **sweet**: aur bg2
- **root** vegetables | **agg.**: *Calc* b4a.de **Lyc** b4a.de
- **salad**:
  - **agg.**: ars k* bry k* *Calc* k* caps bg2 carb-v k* carbn-s stx1 ip bg2* lach k* lyc k* nux-v bt3* psor bgs *Puls* bg2* sanic bgs spong fd4.de sulph bt3* thal vml3• til stx1

- **aversion**: ham fd3.de• kali-s fd4.de *Mag-c* st podo fd3.de• prot jl3*
- **desire**: ail vml3• androc srj1• apis vh1 chir-fl gya2 cub vml3• *Elaps* k* h a m fd3.de• lavand-a ctl1• lepi a1 lept gsw1* lycps-v ld1.de* mag-m mrr1 mag-s mg1.de* med vh orot-ac rly4*• ozone vml3• petr-ra shn4• sacch-a fd2.de• spong fd4.de suis-hep rly4• symph fd3.de• tritic-vg fd5.de vanil fd5.de verat vh

- **salami** | **desire**: calc-p zr* kali-s fd4.de nux-v sej3 ruta fd4.de spong fd4.de stry sej4 tub vh* vanil fd5.de verat-v sej3 [gali stj2]
- **salmon**:
  - **agg.**: fl-ac ptk1
  - **aversion**: lac-loxod-a hrn2•
  - **desire**: adam srj5• phos mtf
- **salsa** | **desire**: *(↗pungent - desire)* med mtf nux-v mtf tub mtf
- **salt**:
  - **agg.**: *Alum* k* *Alumn* vml3• *Aq-mar* vml3• ars k* aur-m-n wbt2• bell bg1* calc k* caps vh *Carb-v* k* carc mlr1• *Coca* kr1* coch c1* *Dros* k* halo jl3 ignis-alc es2• lyc k* *Mag-m* k* med ser **Nat-m** bg2* nit-ac stx1 nit-s-d kr1* *Nux-v* k* **Phos** k* puls bg2* sabad b7a.de *Sel* k* sep vh sil bg2* vanil fd5.de [bor-pur stj2 chr-m stj2 moly-met stj2 nat-br stj2]
  - **amel.**: *Aq-mar* vml3• halo jl* mag-c b2.de* nat-m bg2*
  - **aversion**: acet-ac k* allox tpw3* alum tl1 arund bg* bufo bg2* *Carb-v* k* *Carc* c1* card-m k* chin bg2* cimic gk *Con* ld1.de **Cor-r** k* cortico tpw7* e l a p s bg *Fl-ac* bg **Graph** k* haliae-lc srj5• ignis-alc es2• irid-met srj5• kali-s fd4.de lyc h2* lyss st merc mrr1 *Nat-m* k* nit-ac ld1.de nux-v st phos b4a.de* puls bg2* *Sel* k* *Sep* k* sil k* syc ptj1*• vanil fd5.de [alumin-p stj2 arg-p stj2 aur-m stj2 calc-p stj1 calc-sil stj2 cob-m stj2 cupr-m stj2 cupr-p stj2 ferr-sil stj2 kali-p stj1 kali-sil stj2 lith-p stj2 mag-m stj1 mag-p stj1 mag-sil stj2 mang-p stj2 mang-sil stj2 nat-ar stj2 nat-br stj2 nat-caust stj2 nat-lac stj2 nat-met stj2 nat-p stj1 nat-sil stj2 ph-ac stj1 plb-m stj2 plb-p stj2 sil-met stj2 zinc-p stj2]
    - **meat**; and: **Graph** mrr1
    - **sweets**; and: **Graph** mrr1
  - **desire**: abrom-a ks5* acet-ac ld1.de* aegop-p vml3• aeth vh* agar vh1* *Aloe* k* *Ambr* tsm1* anac vh anthraq rly4• *Aq-mar* sf1.de* **Arg-n** k* atp rly4• atro k* aur-m-n vh* bac vh* bit-ar wht1• bros-gau mrc1 *Calc* k* calc-f mg1.de* *Calc-p* k* calc-s *Cand* vml3• **Carb-v** k* *Carc* c1* cassia-s cdd7*• caste jl3* *Caust* k* *Chin* vh* chinin-m hs chord-umb rly4• cocc coch c1 *Con* k* *Cor-r* k* dulc fd4.de dys a* fuma-ac rly4• galeoc-c-h gms1• galin jl germ-met srj5• gink-b sbd1*• *Glycyr-g* cte1• halo jl* ham fd3.de• jal vml3• kali-p fd1.de*• kali-s fd4.de lac-ac stj5• **Lac-c** k* lac-h htj1*• lac-leo hrn2• *Lycps-v* ld1.de* *Lyss* k* *Manc* *Med* k* medus vml3• meph k* merc ld1.de* merc-i-f k* merc-i-r k* *Moni* rfm1• morg vml3• morg-g a* morg-p ptj1• nat-ar a* nat-c a* **NAT-M** k* nat-p mrr1* nat-pyru rly4• nat-s a nat-sil stj2*• *Nit-ac* k* nit-s-d c1 orot-ac vml3• oxal-a rly4• ozone sde2*• pers jl3* petr-ra shn4• **PHOS** k* pin-con oss2• *Plb* k* plut-n srj7• podo fd3.de• prot pte1* rat mrr1* rhus-g tmo3• ruta fd4.de sabin mrr1 sacch sht*• sal-ac vml3• *Sanic* k* scarl vh sel k* sep hbh* ser-ang vml3• sil vh* sol vml3• spong fd4.de staph kr1 suis-em rly4• sul-ac vh sulfonam ks2 sulph k* suprar rly4• syc ptj1*• *Tarent* k* tell rsj10* teucr *Thuj* k* tritic-vg fd5.de *Tub* k* tung-met bdx1• uva vh vanil fd5.de **VERAT** k* [alumin-p stj2 am-caust stj2 ant-m stj2 arg-met stj2 arg-p stj2 a u r - m stj2 bar-m stj1 *Beryl* stj2 beryl-m stj2 cadm-m stj2 calc-sil stj2 *Chlor* stj2 chr-m stj2 cob-m stj2 cupr-m stj2 cupr-p stj2 ferr-n stj2 hydrog stj2 kali-sil stj2 lith-m stj2 lith-p stj2 mag-n stj2 mag-p stj1 mag-sil stj2 mang-m stj2 mang-n stj2 mang-p stj2 mang-sil stj2 merc-d stj2 mur-ac stj2 nat-br stj2 *Nat-caust* stj2 nat-f stj2 nat-lac stj2 *Nat-met* stj2 nitro stj2 ph-ac stj1 plb-m stj2 sil-met stj2 stront-m stj2 tax jsj7 zinc stj1 zinc-n stj2]
    - **and**:
      - **dainties** (See delicacies - desire - and salt)
      - **sweets**: **Arg-n** gsd1* aur-m-n stx1 calc st* calc-f stx1 calc-p vh calc-s vh *Carb-v* mtf33 carc stx1 caste st* **Chin** stx1 meph stx1 merc stx1 moni stx1 morg-g stx1 morg-p stx1 nat-m vh **Nit-ac** stx1 *Phos* vh *Plb* st* staph stx1 sulph vh tarent stx1 tritic-vg fd5.de tub vh
    - **pregnancy**; during: *Nat-m* kr1 *Verat* kr1
- **sand** | **desire**: *(↗indigestible - desire)* sil bg1* **Tarent** k*
- **sardines**:
  - **agg.**: *(↗herring - agg.)* eupi stx1 fl-ac st *Lyc* st
  - **desire**: *(↗anchovies - desire; herring - desire)* *Cycl* k* *Ferr-i* mrr1* spong fd4.de *Verat* k*
- **sauces** with food | **desire**: arg-n ld1.de* nicotam rly4• nux-v a1* [*Arg-met* stj2 *Arg-p* stj2]
- **sauerkraut**:
  - **agg.**: *(↗flatulent - agg.)* arist-cl sp1* ars k* **Bry** k* *Calc* k* carb-v k* *Chin* k* cupr k* hell k* *Lyc* k* nat-m k* **Petr** k* *Phos* k* *Puls* k* sep k* verat k* [chr-s stj2]
  - **aversion**: hell k* sulph sf1.de [cupr stj2 cupr-act stj2 cupr-f stj2 cupr-m stj2 cupr-p stj2 mur-ac stj2]
  - **desire**: carb-an k* cham k* choc srj3*• hep vh *Lycps-v* ld1.de* mang-p rly4• *Nat-m* vh ruta fd4.de
- **sausages**:
  - **agg.**: acet-ac bro1* adlu vml3• *Ars* c1* bell c1* bry ptk1 psor bgs puls bro1* sanic bgs
    - **sight** of: squil vml3•
    - **spoiled**: *(↗meat - agg. - spoiled)* acet-ac c1 **Ars** k* **Bell** k* *Bry* k* ph-ac k* rhus-t k* verat bg2
  - **aversion**: *Ars* st* kali-s fd4.de mag-s jl3 puls st spong fd4.de tritic-vg fd5.de
  - **desire**: abrot sbd acet-ac ld1.de* calc-p sf1.de* choc srj dulc fd4.de f u m a - a c rly4• kali-p fd1.de• kali-s fd4.de olib-sac wmh1 puls k2 sil vh suprar rly4• symph fd3.de• tritic-vg fd5.de tub vh* vanil fd5.de [tax jsj7]
- **seafood**:
  - **agg.**: pitu-a vml3•
  - **desire**: ambr tsm1
- **seasoned** food (See spices)
- **seeds** | **desire**: calc mtf33
- **shellfish**:
  - **agg.**: *(↗oysters - agg.; SKIN - Eruptions - urticaria - shellfish)* apis stx1 astac c1* bell j5.de* carb-v k* *Coloc* bg2 cop j5.de* euph bg2* ferr-s stx1 ind a1* levo jl* *Lyc* k* phenob jl3* rhus-t bg2* staph gk ter bg2* tet stx1 *Urt-u* k*
  - **desire**: calc-p mtf lac-h htj1* lach vh mag-p mtf nat-m mtf nat-p mtf phos mtf sep mtf
- **shrimps**:
  - **agg.**: [calc-f stj1]
  - **desire**: [ruth-met stj2]
- **sight** of food:
  - **agg.**: aegop-p vml3• aeth br1* alum-sil k2 ant-c he ant-t **Colch** k* crot-c stx1 *Kali-bi* kali-c *Lyc* merc-i-f mosch k* ph-ac sabad sil bg1* spig squil bg1* **Sulph** k* sym-r br1 thiam rly4• *Vac* jl2 xan [stann stj2]
  - **aversion**: *(↗food - aversion - seen)* ail kr1* *Arn* kr1* **Ars** bell a2 c a u s t k2* chin k2 cocc bwa *Colch* k1* dig ld1.de lyc ld1.de mang h2 *Merc-i-f* kr1* *Mosch* kr1 nux-v ld1.de* ptel bt3 *Sil* squil k* stann ld1.de* *Tub* al2 vac al2
- **simplest** food | **agg.**: *Carb-v* bg2
- **slimy** food | **aversion**: *Calc* vh* med vh* *Nat-m* vh* puls gk [zirc-met stj2]
- **smell** of food:
  - **agg.** (See food - agg. - smell)
  - **aversion** (See food - aversion - smell)
- **smoked** food: *(↗grilled)*
  - **agg.**: *Calc* k* psor bgs *Sil* k* tub bgs
  - **desire**: *(↗chicken - desire - tandoori)* adam srj5• atro a2* calc-p k* carc gk6* **Caust** k* gal-ac vh1* ham fd3.de• kali-p fd1.de• *Kreos* k* meph c1 oxal-a rly4• ozone sde2• puls bg2* symph fd3.de• tritic-vg fd5.de *Tub* ptk1* tub-m sne
- **snails** | **agg.**: [sel stj2]
- **snow** | **desire**: crot-c k*
- **soap** | **desire**: calc bl1*
- **soda** pop drinks: *(↗carbonated; soda water)*
  - **desire**: arizon-l nl2• lac-ac stj5• nux-v mtf phos kr1*
- **soda** water: *(↗carbonated; soda pop)*
  - **desire**: choc srj3• colch ptk* nux-v mtf plut-n srj7• sacch-a fd2.de• spong fd4.de vanil fd5.de [heroin sdj2]
- **soft** food:
  - **agg.**: nit-ac stx1 tanac hl1
  - **desire**: *Alum* b4a.de* alumn a1* pyrus a1* sacch c1* sulph h2*

- **solid** food:
  - **agg.**: alco vml3• bapt stx1 bar-m stx1 morph stx1 olnd stx1 _Ph-ac_ stx1 podo stx1 staph stx1
  - **aversion**: aether a1* ang k* bell bg2 bry b7a.de* choc srj3*• coca kr1* cocain br1 coff c1 _Ferr_ k* lyc k* merc k* _Puls_ b7a.de sacch c1* _Staph_ k* _Sulph_ b4a.de*
  - **desire**: pitu-a a*
- **soup**:
  - **agg.**: acon stx1 alum b4a.de* alumn kr1* ambr stx1 anac b4a.de* _Aran_ stx1 carb-v b4a.de* castm stx1 chin ld1.de* indg vml3* kali-c b4a.de* kali-n vml3• laur b7.de _Mag-c_ stx1 nat-s stx1 ol-an vml3* phos b4a.de prun stx1 puls stx1 sars b4a.de* sep stx1 _Stann_ stx1 staph ld1.de* _Stram_ stx1 zinc stx1
  - **amel.**: acon a2* castm vml3* gent-c c1 _Kali-bi_ hs kali-c stx1 mag-c h2* nat-c stx1 ox-ac stx1 ph-ac stx1
  - **aversion**: _Arn_ k* ars k* bell k* carb-v bt3* carc sht* cham k* chin bt3* _Graph_ k* kali-c ld1.de* kali-chl ld1.de kali-i lac-h htj1• lyc ptk1 merc-cy bg2* nat-m gl1.fr• ol-an a1* puls bt3* _Rhus-t_ k* staph bt3*
  - **desire**: (_↗liquid food - desire; warm drinks - desire; warm food - desire)_ acon-ac rly4• adam srj5• ang vh* bry gsw1 _Calc-ar_ k* carc a* dulc fd4.de **Ferr** gsw1* hep sne kali-chl ld1.de kali-p fd1.de• mag-m dgt nat-m bl1* ol-an a1* phel a2* ruta fd4.de sacch-a fd2.de• spong fd4.de staph kr1* streptoc rly4• tritic-vg fd5.de vanil fd5.de
    - **warm**: (_↗warm drinks - desire)_ bry _Calc-ar_ ferr nat-m phel ruta fd4.de vanil fd5.de
    - **watery** soup: bell b4.de*
- **sour** drinks:
  - **agg.**: _Ant-c_ ptk1 ant-t ptk1 arg-n ptk1 ars ptk1 carb-v ptk1 dros ptk1 fl-ac ptk1 lach stx1 merc-c ptk1 nat-m ptk1 nat-p ptk1 ph-ac ptk1 podo ptk1 _Puls_ ptk1 sep ptk1 sulph ptk1
  - **amel.**: arg-n ptk1 ign ptk1 lach ptk1 ptel ptk1 puls ptk1 sang ptk1
  - **aversion**: arund vh1
  - **desire**: _Acon_ ptk1 aloe sne am-m a2* anan vh1 ant-c gsw1 ant-t ptk1 arn bg2* ars bg2* arund vh1 bell ptk1 borx h2* _Bry_ b7a.de* calc a2* cham kr1* con ptk1 cor-r ptk1 corn kr1* corn-f kr1* cypra-eg sde6.de• dig b4a.de* eup-per kr1 _Hep_ kr1* _Hipp_ jl2 _Kali-bi_ bg2* _Mag-c_ bg2* malar jl2 mang bg2 med ptk1* merc-i-f kr1* mez kr1 myric ptk1 phel bg2* plb gsw1 podo ptk1 _Puls_ kr1* rad-br ptk1 sec lp* sep bg2* squil gsw1* _Stram_ kr1* _Sulph_ ptk1 ther kr1* vanil fd5.de **Verat** kr1*
- **sour** food, acids:
  - **agg.**: **Acon** bg2* aloe kr1* **Ant-c** k* ant-t k* apis kr1* _Arg-n_ k* _Ars_ k* ars-s-f k2* asaf stx1 aster sf1.de* _Bell_ k* borx k* brom k* calad k* calc bg2 **Carb-v** bg2* castm stx1 caust k* chin cimic bg2 cist stx1 cub k* cyn-d vml3• dros k* dulc stx1 _Ferr_ k* ferr-ar ferr-m ld1.de ferr-p fl-ac st* guare c1* **Hep** bg2 ip ld1.de _Kali-bi_ kr1 kali-m stx1 kreos k* lac-ac stj5• lach k* _Lepr_ vml3• mand mg1.de merc-c k* merc-cy ld1.de _Merc-d_ bg1* morph stx1 mur-ac stj2* nat-c k* nat-m k* _Nat-p_ k* nux-v k* **Olnd** vh ph-ac k* phos k* podo ptk1 _Psor_ ld1.de* _Puls_ bg2* ran-b k* _Rhus-t_ bg2* sabad b7a.de sanic c1* sel k* _Sep_ k* staph b2.de* stram stx1 sul-ac bg2* _Sulph_ k* tarax vml3• thuj c1* [_Ant-m_ stj2 _Ant-met_ stj2 ars-met stj2 bor-pur stj2 ferr-f stj2 ferr-lac stj2 ferr-n stj2 ferr-sil stj2 hydrog stj2 kali-ar stj2 moly-met stj2 nat-ar stj2]
    - **smell** of; sensitive to (See NOSE - Smell - acute - sour)
  - **amel.**: arg-met bg2* arg-n bg2* ign ptk1 lach bg2* _Merc_ sf1.de* **Ptel** c1* puls ptk1 sang br1* stram stx1
  - **aversion**: abies-c k* arg-n dx1* arund ld1.de* aur-s stj2*• _Bell_ k* chin ld1.de* clem bg2* _Cocc_ k* _Con_ ld1.de dros bro1* elaps ld1.de _Ferr_ k* ferr-m k* _Fl-ac_ ld1.de* ger-i rly4• glycyr-g cte1• ign k* kali-bi bg2 kreos tl1 lac-ac stj2*• _Lac-h_ vml3• lyc ld1.de mand mg1.de nat-m ld1.de nat-p bg1 nux-v k* petr-ra shn4• ph-ac k* _Sabad_ k* _Sulph_ k* tritic-vg fd5.de tub vh [alumin-s stj2 ant-c stj2 ant-m stj2 ant-met stj2 ant-t stj2 arg-met stj2 arg-p stj2 cadm-s stj2 chr-s stj2 cinnb stj2 _Cob_ stj2 _Cob-m_ stj2 _Cob-p_ stj2 gal-s stj2 hydrog stj2 lith-f stj2 lith-s stj2 mag-lac stj2 mang-s stj2 moly-met stj2 mur-ac stj2 nat-caust stj2 _Nat-f_ stj2 nicc-s stj2 plb stj2 sul-ac stj1 titan stj2 titan-s stj2]
  - **desire**: _Abies-c_ bro1* abrom-a gsb* **Acon** bg2* adel gsw1 aegop-p vml3• alum k* alum-p k2* alumn k* am-c k* am-m k* _Ant-c_ k* _Ant-t_ k* _Apis_ arg-n k* _Arn_ k* _Ars_ k* ars-s-f k2* arund k* aur-m-n vh* bamb-a stb2.de• bell k* bism bg2* bol-la k* _Borx_ k* _Brom_ k* _Bry_ k* _Calc_ k* calc-f nh* calc-s calc-sil k2* carb-an k* _Carb-v_ k* carbn a1* carbn-s k* caust vh cean c1*

- **sour** foods, acids – **desire**: ...
  Cham k* chel k* chin k* chinin-ar k* chinin-m hs _Cist_ k* _Cocc_ b7a.de cod bro1* _Con_ k* conv k* **Cor-r** k* corn k* cortiso vml3• cory-b vml3• cory-c mg1.de crot-h vml3• cub k* cupr cupr-act a1* cur c1* cypra-eg sde6.de• der a1 dig k* dor a1* elaps k* erig mg1.de* eup-per kr1 _Ferr_ k* ferr-ar _Ferr-m_ k* ferr-p _Fl-ac_ k* gaert vml3• glycyr-g cte1• gran k* granit-m vml3• guaj bc **Hep** k* hipp k* _Ign_ k* irid-met srj5• joan bro1 _Kali-ar_ k* kali-bi k* _Kali-c_ k* kali-chl c1 kali-i vh kali-p k* kali-s ketogl-ac rly4• kreos k* _Lac-ac_ stj2*• _Lach_ k* lact ld1.de* lact-v bro1 _Lepr_ vml3• lil-t ptk* lyc ld1.de* lyss al2 _Mag-c_ k* mag-f stj1*• malar al2 mang k* mangi vml3• _Med_ k* merc-i-f k* musca-d szs1 _Myric_ a1* nabal a1 _Nat-m_ k* nat-s c1* petr-ra shn4• _Ph-ac_ bro1* phel k* _Phos_ k* plb k* _Podo_ k* psor k* ptel k* _Puls_ k* rad-br c1* rauw sp1* rhus-g tmo3• rhus-t ribo rly4• _Sabad_ k* _Sabin_ k* sacch gsw1* sacch-a fd2.de• sacch-l gsw samb xxb1 _Sec_ k* _Sep_ k* spira c1 spirae a1 _Squil_ k* stann kr1* staph kr1* _Stram_ k* stront-c sk4• stry-p sf1.de succ-ac vml3• suis-pan rly4• sul-ac vh* _Sul-i_ k* _Sulph_ k* symph fd3.de• thea k* ther k* thuj k* tritic-vg fd5.de tub vh ust k* uva vh vanil fd5.de **Verat** k* ziz k* [alumin-s stj2 am-br stj2 am-caust stj2 am-f stj2 am-p stj1 _Ant-m_ stj2 _Ant-met_ stj2 arg-met stj1* arg-p stj2 ars-met stj2 aur-s stj2 bar-f stj1 _Beryl_ stj2 beryl-m stj2 cadm-s stj2 chr-s stj2 cinnb stj2 cupr-f stj2 fl-pur stj2 gal-s stj2 _Hydrog_ stj2 kali-f stj1 lith-s stj2 mag-lac stj2 mang-s stj2 mur-ac stj2 nat-ar stj2 nat-f stj1* titan-s stj2]
  - **morning**: phel a2* ptel a2
  - **accompanied** by:
    - **allergy**: _Cor-r_ mrr1
    - **coryza**: _Cor-r_ mrr1
  - **coryza**; during: _Cor-r_ mrr1
  - **fever**; during: _Ars_ b4a.de*
  - **headache**, after: nat-s kr1*
  - **pregnancy**; during: _Verat_ kr1
  - **salt**; and: _Arg-n_ st* _Calc_ st _Calc-s_ st **Carb-v** st _Con_ st **Cor-r** st* _Med_ st _Merc-c_ vml3• _Merc-i-f_ st **Nat-m** st* **Phos** st* _Plb_ st* sanic vh _Sulph_ st* _Thuj_ st **Verat** st*
  - **sweets**; and: _Bry_ st _Calc_ st _Carb-v_ st _Kali-c_ st* kali-p bl* kali-s k2* _Med_ st* _Sabad_ st sacch-a fd2.de• _Sec_ st _Sep_ st suis-pan rly4• **Sulph** st*
  - **sweets**; with agg. from: acon bg2 cham bg2 ferr bg2 ign bg2 sulph bg2
- **spices** (= condiments, highly seasoned food):
  - **agg.**: aloe hr alum stx1 ars stx1 bism bg2* chin stx1 cina stx1 cyn-d vml3• guat stx1 ign bg2 kali-m bg2* lac-h htj1• mangi vml3• naja bg2 nat-c stx1 nat-pyru rly4• **Nux-v** bg2* petr-ra shn4• phos k* rob stx1 sel bg2* sep ld1.de sil stx1 trios vml3• vanil fd5.de zinc bg2* [beryl-m stj2 moly-met stj2 ruth-met stj2]
  - **amel.**: hep bg2* nux-m bg2*
  - **aversion**: (_↗pungent - aversion)_ chord-umb rly4• _Fl-ac_ ld1.de haliae-lc srj5• _Hydrog_ srj* _Lac-ac_ stj5• lac-loxod-a hrn2• luf-op rsj5*• mag-s c1* petr-ra shn4• phos ld1.de puls bg2* _Sang_ ld1.de suis-em rly4• suprar rly4• tarent ld1.de [ang stj4 nat-caust stj2 nat-lac stj2 ruth-met stj2 spect dfg1]
  - **desire**: (_↗pungent - desire)_ abies-c bg1* acon k2 acon-ac rly4• alum bro1* am-c gk1* ant-c bg2* aq-mar mgm• arg-n bg2* arge-pl rwt5• arizon-l nl2• ars bg2* aster a1* aur gk* _Aur-m-n_ wbt2• aur-s stj2*• bamb-a stb2.de• bar-ox-suc rly4• bit-ar wht1• brucel sa3• calc-f ld1.de* calc-p bg2* caps ptk1* _Carc_ vh* caust b4a.de* _Chel_ bg2* chelin bg **Chin** k* choc stx1 chord-umb rly4• cic jl3* cist ptk1 cortiso vml3• crot-c sk4• crot-h gk1 _Cuc-c_ vml3• dendr-pol sk4• dulc fd4.de _Fl-ac_ k* germ-met srj5• _Hep_ k* hyper bg2* kali-s fd4.de kola stb3• _Lac-c_ k* lac-cp sk4• lac-lup hrn2• lavand-a ctl1• **Lepr** vml3• lyc lt **Mag-f** stj1*• mag-s sp1* mand mg1.de* med hbh meph kr1* merc-c stx1 nat-m bg2* nat-p gsw1* nit-ac k2 nux-m br1* _Nux-v_ k* oci-sa sk4• oena vml3• ozone sde2• petr-ra shn4• ph-ac b4a.de* **Phos** k* pin-con oss2• podo fd3.de• positr nl2• _Puls_ k* rhus-g tmo3• ruta fd4.de sacch-a fd2.de• _Sang_ k* sep spong fd4.de staph bg2* staphycoc rly4• stront-c sk4• stry-p sf1.de _Sul-ac_ br sulfonam ks2 **Sulph** k* symph fd3.de• tama vml3• _Tarent_ k* tritic-vg fd5.de tub al2* vanil fd5.de verat gk1* _Zing_ st* [alumin-p stj2 alumin-s stj2 _Am-f_ stj2 ang stj4 arg-p stj2 ars-met stj2 _Bar-f_ stj1 bar-m stj1 beryl-m stj2 cadm-s stj2 chr-s stj2 cinnb stj2 cob stj2 cob-m stj2 cob-p stj2 cupr stj2 _Cupr-f_ stj2 cupr-p stj2 _Ferr-f_ stj2 ferr-p stj1 ferr-s stj1 _Fl-pur_ stj2 gal-s stj2 heroin sdj2 kali-ar stj2 _Kali-f_ stj1 kali-p stj1 _Lith-f_ stj2 lith-p stj2 lith-s stj2 mag-p stj1 mang-p stj2 mang-s stj2 nat-ar stj2 **Nat-f** stj1* nicc-met stj2 nicc-s stj2 niob-met stj2 plb-p stj2 sel stj2 tax jsj7 titan-s stj2 zirc-met stj2]

- **spinach**:
  - **aversion**: *Chel* vh* hep dgt
  - **desire**: calc-p dgt2 lac-leo hrn2• stram dgt2 symph fd3.de•
    - ⁝ **raw**: haliae-lc srj5•
- **sprouts**:
  - **agg.**: mag-c mtf phos mtf [arg-met stj1* arg-n stj2 arg-p stj2]
  - **aversion**: [arg-met stj1 coch-o stj cupr stj2 *Zinc* stj2 *Zinc-i* stj2 *Zinc-m* stj2 *Zinc-n* stj2 *Zinc-p* stj2]
  - **desire**: [nat-f stj2]
- **squash** | **aversion**: sulph mrr1
- **stale** rolls (See rolls - desire - stale)
- **starchy** (See farinaceous)
- **sticky** things | **desire**: nat-m bg2
- **stimulants**:
  - **agg.**: *(↗tonics - agg.)* agar k2 ant-c c2* ars-s-f k2* cadm-s bro1* *Caps* vh chion bro1* chlol br1* cocc kr1 coloc c1 con c1 fl-ac bro1 *Glon* bro1 ign bro1 lach bro1 led bro1 naja bro1* nat-sil k2 *Nux-v* br1* op bro1 osm stx1 petr-ra shn4• positr nl2• *Spig* stx1 thuj k2* vanil fd5.de *Zinc* bro1*
  - **amel.**: arg-n stx1 ars c1 cyt-l c1 **Gels** k1* glon bro1
  - **aversion**: bapt c1 petr-ra shn4•
  - **desire**: alco a1* aloe a1* androc srj1• ant-t a1 ars-i k2* ars-s-f k2* aster a1* aur a1 aur-m-n wbt2• aur-s k2* calc-i a2* caps k2* carb-ac br1* caust bg2* chin sf1.de* crot-h tl1* ferr-p br1 *Fl-ac* sf1.de gins a1* hep bg2 iber a1 iod a1* kali-i a1 med bg3* mosch br1 mur-ac k2 naja a1 nat-p a1 nux-v k2* pin-con oss2• *Puls* a1 sel ptk1 sep vh sol-t-ae a1* staph bg2* *Sul-ac* br1 sul-i k2* sulph k2* sumb a1* tab a1 *Valer* c1 vanil fd5.de ziz a1* [tax jsj7]
- **stodgy** food (See indigestible)
- **stout** | **desire**: sumb a2*
- **strange** things:
  - **aversion**: [graph stj2 lith-c stj2]
  - **desire**: *(↗indigestible - desire)* alum br1 atri br1 *Bry* k* *Calc* k* *Calc-p* k* carb-v br1 *Chel* k* cic br1* *Cycl* *Hep* k* *Lyss* ld1.de mag-c *Manc* sep br1 ter kr1
    - ⁝ **pregnancy**, during: *Alum* br1* calc br1* carb-v br1* *Chel* k* **Lyss** k* *Mag-c* k* sep br1*
- **strawberries**:
  - **agg.**: ant-c k* ars c1* bry kr1 cardios-h vml3• ferr kr1 frag c1 ox-ac k* sep k* sulph gk thlas bg1* [ant-m stj2 ant-met stj2 ant-t stj2 ars-met stj2 kali-ar stj2 nat-ar stj2]
  - **amel.**: frag stx1
  - **aversion**: chin h1* ox-ac st* *Sulph* st*
  - **desire**: ox-ac ld1.de
- **sugar**:
  - **agg.**: *Arg-n* c1* bell sf1.de *Calc* kr1* crot-t stx1 gamb stx1 ign stx1 lyc hu med sne *Merc* br1* nat-p c1* ox-ac kr1* psor stx1 sacch c1 sang sf1.de* *Sel* kr1* **Sulph** kr1* tarent-c stx1 thuj sf1.de* trom stx1 tub hu* zinc kr1* [gal-s stj2]
  - **amel.**: bell bg2 colch c1 op stx1 sacch c1 sulph stx1
  - **aversion**: ars sf1.de caust sf1.de chloram jl3 graph sf1.de merc sf1.de nit-ac mtf33 phos sf1.de rauw tpw8* sin-n sf1.de syc ptj1*• symph fd3.de• *Zinc* h2*
  - **desire**: am-c k* am-m ld1.de* **Arg-n** k* *Calc* carb-v b4a.de* carc pc* caust gk chin b7a.de chir-fl gya2 coc-c mgm• coca bg corian-s knl6• crot-h br1 dulc fd4.de dys ptj1* falco-pe nl2• fic-m gya1 foll asm• gaert ptj1*• gink-b sbd1• ip b7a.de* *Kali-c* k* *Lyc* b4.de* nat-m b4a.de nit-ac b4a.de nux-v b7a.de op a1* *Phos* vh prot jl3* rhus-t b7a.de sabad b7.de* *Sacch* c1 *Sec* staph vh* sulph b4a.de* tub jl2
    - ⁝ **evening**: *Arg-n* k*
    - ⁝ **digest** it; but does not: arg-n tl1*
    - ⁝ **digest** only if he eats large amounts of sugar; can: nux-v vh* **Staph** vh*
    - ⁝ **water**; sugared: bufo a1* sulph a1*
- **sunflower** seeds | **desire**: ara-maca sej7•
- **sushi** | **desire**: phos mtf tub mtf
- **sweet** drinks | **desire**: arg-n kr1 bufo c1* cur vml3• sulph a2
- **sweet** peppers: *(↗green peppers; pepper; red pepper)*
  - **agg.**: [*Arg-met* stj2 *Arg-n* stj2 *Arg-p* stj2]
  - **aversion**: hep fbv
  - **desire**: galeoc-c-h gms1• hep fbv tritic-vg fd5.de
- **sweets**:
  - **agg.**: *(↗pastry - agg.; puddings - agg.)* acon k* am-c k* *Ant-c* k* **Arg-n** k* ars bg1* aster sf1.de* bad bg1* bamb-a stx1 bell bg2* benz-ac vml3• caj vml3• calc k* calc-f mg1.de* calc-s stx1 carb-v k2* carc mlr1• *Cham* k* choc srj3*• cina ptk1* cycl sf1.de dys fmm1• ferr bg2 fil stx1 fl-ac gaert fmm1* gamb vml3• *Graph* k* guat vml3* hep gl1.fr• hera vml3• hypoth vml3• **Ign** k* ip kr1* iris c1 kali-p fd1.de• lac-ac stj2*• lach bg1 limest-b es1• *Lyc* bro1* mand mg1.de* mangi vml3• med bro1* *Merc* k* merc-i-f vml3* *Moni* rfm1• mur-ac stx1 nat-c k* *Nat-p* bg2* nat-sil fd3.de• nux-v bt3* ox-ac k* ozone stx1 phos pin-con oss2• podo fd3.de• *Puls* sf1.de* raph vml3* ruta fd4.de sacch sht*• sacch-a fd2.de• sang bg2* sanguis-s hrn2• *Sel* k* spig k* spong c1* *Sulph* k* symph fd3.de• tanac hl1 tarent-c stx1 thuj k* tritic-vg fd5.de trom vml3* vanil fd5.de zinc k* zinc-p k2* [aur-s stj2 cinnb stj2 gal-s stj2 mag-lac stj2 mag-met stj2 mag-n stj2 mag-sil stj2 rhodi stj2 zinc-i stj2 zinc-m stj2 zinc-n stj2]
    - ⁝ **smell** of; sensitive to the (See NOSE - Smell - acute - sweets)
    - ⁝ **sour** things; with desire for (See sour food - desire - sweets; and)
  - **amel.**: am-c jl3 *Arg-n* vh bell ptk1 dulc fd4.de **Lac-ac** stj2*• *Lyc* vh psil stx1 sacch c1* seneg stx1 spong stx1 sulph stx1 [calc-lac stj2 ferr-lac stj2]
  - **aversion**: abrot c1* acon-ac rly4• anthraq rly4• *Arg-n* ld1.de* *Ars* k* bar-c k* beryl tpw5* cadm-s vh* calc c1* calc-p vh calc-sil vml3• carc bg* card-m vh* *Caust* k* chloram jl3* choc srj3*• crot-c sk4• cuc-c vml3• cypra-eg sde6.de• erig jl* galeoc-c-h gms1• glycyr-g cte1• **Graph** k* haliae-lc srj5• ham fd3.de• helo-s rwt2• hipp k* hippoz bg1* hyos zf ign tl1 iod c1 *Kali-c* ld1.de kali-s fd4.de kola stb3• lac-ac stj2*• lac-c k* lac-h htj1• *Lepr* vml3• lol sf1.de* *Lyc* ld1.de mag-m mg* med al2* *Merc* k* nat-m c1 nat-sil fd3.de• nit-ac k* nux-v h1* oena vml3• olib-sac wmh1 oxal-a rly4• ozone sde2*• petr ld1.de petr-ra shn4• ph-ac vh *Phos* k* podo fd3.de• positr nl2• puls st* rad-br bg3* rad-met ld1.de* rauw sp1* rheum ld1.de* ruta fd4.de sacch sht*• sacch-a fd2.de• sanguis-s hrn2• senec bg1* sil vh *Sin-n* k* spong fd4.de *Sul-ac* ld1.de* *Sulph* k* syc vml3• symph fd3.de• tritic-vg fd5.de tub c1 vanil fd5.de verat-v tl1 *Zinc* k* zinc-p k2* [cadm-met stj2 heroin sdj2 nat-lac stj2 spect dfg1]
    - ⁝ **meat**; and: **Graph** mrr1
    - ⁝ **salt**; and (See salt - aversion - sweets)
    - ⁝ **sour**; or: bell bg2
  - **desire**: *(↗delicacies - desire; licorice - desire)* abrom-a ks5* acon-l a2 aegop-p vml3• aeth tl1 agar vh* agath-a nl2• aids nl2• *Alf* bro1* *Am-c* k* amp rly4• anac vh anan a2 anthraci vh1* anthraq rly4• aq-mar rbp6 aran ccrh1• aran-ix sf1.de* **Arg-met** k* **Arg-n** k* arge-pl rwt5• arizon-l nl2• ars k* ars-s-f k2* atp rly4• aur mrr1* *Aur-m-n* vh **Aur-s** stj2*• aza c1 bacls-10 ptj1*• bamb-a stb2.de• bar-c k* bar-ox-suc rly4• bar-s k2* bell vh* bit-ar wht1• *Bry* bufo k* cael jl caj vml3• *Calc* k* *Calc-f* mg1.de* calc-p vh* *Calc-s* k* **Cann-i** vh *Carb-v* k* carc c1* cassia-s ccrh1*• caste jl3* caust vh cere-b a1* **Chin** k* chinin-ar k* **Chinin-s** vh* choc srj3*• chord-umb rly4• *Cina* bro1* coca bro1* coca-c sk4• *Cocain* bro1* coli rly4• conch fkr1* corian-s knl6• crot-h bro1* cub a2 cypra-eg sde6.de• des-ac rbp6 dream-p sdj1• dulc fd4.de dys a* *Elaps* ephe-si hsj1• *Euphr* vh falco-pe nl2• ferr bg2* fic-m gya1 *Foll* vml3• fum rly1*• fuma-ac rly4• gaert ptj1*• galeoc-c-h gms1• germ-met srj5• gink-b sbd1*• glycyr-g cte1• granit-m es1• *Graph* mrr1* *Hep* kr1 *Hera* vml3• hydrog srj* iber vml3• ign zf ignis-alc es2• *Ip* k* irid-met stj2*• joan bro1 kali-ar k* *Kali-bi* mrr1 *Kali-c* k* kali-p k* *Kali-s* k* kola stb3• lac-ac stj2*• lac-c sne lac-cp sk4• lac-h htj1*• lac-loxod-a hrn2• lach zf lepr vml3• lil-t bg2* limest-b vml3• lob vh* loxo-recl knl4• **Lyc** k* *Mag-m* k* mand mg1.de* mang-p rly4*• mangi vml3• *Med* k* melal-alt gya4 *Meny* vh* meph jl* *Merc* k* merc-d bg1* merc-i-f c1* *Moni* rfm1• *Morg* vml3• morg-g a* morg-p a* naja mtf nat-ar k* *Nat-c* k* nat-m k* nat-p fkr6.de nat-s zf nat-sil fd3.de• *Nit-ac* vh nux-m zf nux-v k* oena zf onop jl* op ozone sde2• pant-ac rly4• paull a2 penic vml3• petr k* petr-ra shn4• *Phos* tl1* pieri-b mlk9.de pitu-a a* plac rzf5• plat dx1* *Plb* k* podo fd3.de• positr nl2• propl ub1• prot a* psor al pull-g vl1.nl* *Puls* rb2* pycnop-sa mrz1 rad-br c1* rat mrr1* *Rheum* k* *Rhus-g* tmo3• *Rhus-t* k* rib-ac jl3* ruta fd4.de *Sabad* k* *Sacch* sht*• sacch-a fd2.de* *Sacch-l* sna* sal-al blc1• sang kr1 sanguis-s hrn2•

• **desire**: ...
sanic vh* *Sec* *Sep* k* ser-ang vml3• sil kr1* spong hr1* *Staph* gk* staphycoc rly4• *Stram* mrr1 suis-em rly4• suis-pan rly4• *Sul-ac* vh* **Sulph** k* suprar rly4• syc ptj1*• symph fd3.de• tarax vml3• tarent ccrh1• tetox pin2• thiam rly4• thuj mrr1 thyr br1* tritic-vg fd5.de *Tub* k* tung-met stj2*• ulm-c jsj8• urol-h rwt• vanad dx* vanil fd5.de vero-o rly4*• vip fkr4.de x-ray jl* [*Alumin-s* stj2 am-br stj2 am-caust stj2 am-f stj2 am-m stj1 am-p stj1 *Ant-c* stj2 *Arg-p* stj2 aur-m stj2 bar-br stj2 bar-i stj2 bar-m stj1 bar-met stj2 bar-p stj1 beryl-m stj2 bism-sn stj2 bor-pur stj2 *Cadm-s* stj2 caes-met stj2 *Calc-lac* stj2 calc-m stj1 *Calc-met* stj2 *Calc-n* stj1 *Calc-sil* stj2 chr-m stj2 chr-met stj1* *Chr-s* stj2 *Cinnb* stj2 cob stj2 cob-m stj2 cob-p stj2 cupr-p stj2 ferr-lac stj2 *Gal-s* stj2 hafn-met stj2 heroin sdj2 ind stj2 kali-i stj1 kali-met stj2 kali-n stj1 kali-sil stj2 lac-mat sst4 lanth-met stj2 lith-c stj2 lith-p stj2 *Lith-s* stj2 mag-lac stj2 mag-met stj2 mag-n stj2 mag-s stj1 mag-sil stj2 *Mang-s* stj2 moly-met stj2 *Nat-caust* stj2 *Nat-lac* stj2 nicc stj1 nicc-met stj2 nicc-s stj2 osm-met stj2 plb-m stj2 plb-p stj2 pop dhh1 rhen-met stj2 ruth-met stj2 tant-met stj2 tax jsj7 thal-met stj2 *Titan* stj2 *Titan-s* stj2 zinc stj1* zinc-i stj2 zinc-m stj2 zinc-p stj2 zirc-met stj2]

⁝ **morning** | **waking**; on: *Propl* vml3•

⁝ **evening**: *Arg-met* a2 sacch sht*•

⁝ **accompanied** by | **weakness** (See Weakness - accompanied - sweets)

⁝ **aggravates**; but: *Am-c* st1 **Arg-n** st1* *Calc* st1 carc mlr• lyc mg1.de mag-c mg1.de *Nat-c* st1 spong fd4.de **Sulph** st

⁝ **dinner**; after: sacch sht*• tritic-vg fd5.de [tax jsj7]

⁝ **eating**; after: *Arg-n* vh *Med* vh nux-v vh* sulph vh*

⁝ **headache**; during: **Calc** kr1*

⁝ **menses**; before: *Arg-n* vh1 dream-p sdj1• pitu-a a sacch sht*• **Sulph** kr1*

⁝ **only** sweets: kali-p ptk1

- **syrup**:

• **aversion** | **smell** of: sang a1*

- **tamarind**:

• **agg.**: nux-v mtf sep mtf sulph mtf

⁝ **water**: sel ptk1

• **desire**: *Tama* vml3•

- **tea**:

• **agg.**: abies-c bg2* *Abies-n* c1* *Aesc* agar bg2* ambr stx1 arg-n stx1 ars bg2* aur-m kr1* brach stx1 calad ptk1* carb-ac vml3• cham bg2* *Chin* k* choc srj3*• chr-ac stx1 cocc bg2* coff k* cypr vml3• dios k* dulc fd4.de *Ferr* k* ferr-p c1 fl-ac k2 guar vml3* hep bg2 hydrog stj2* hyper stx1 kali-bi bg2 kali-hp bro1 kali-i stx1 lac-h sk4• lach k* lob c1* luna c1 *Nat-m* stx1 *Nux-v* c1* ox-ac stx1 par stx1 paull vml3* ph-ac bg2* puls bg2* *Rhus-t* kr1* rumx k* ruta fd4.de **Sel** k* **Sep** bg2* sphing c1 *Spig* bg2* stroph-h c1* symph fd3.de• *Thea* stx1 *Thuj* k* verat k* [ferr-f stj2 ferr-lac stj2 ferr-n stj2 ind stj2]

⁝ **overuse**: abies-n br1* camph-br stx1 *Chin* br1* cypr vml3• *Dios* br1* ferr br1* guar stx1 lob c1 nux-v c1* paull stx1 puls br1* *Sel* br1* thea stx1 thuj br1*

• **amel.**: aloe ptk1 carb-ac k* cimic stx1 cot vml3* dig k* ferr k* ferr-p stx1 glon ptk1 iris-t stx1 kali-bi bg2* lina c1 pyrus ld1.de spong fd4.de

• **aversion**: adam srj5• bacls-10 ptj1*• carb-ac k* carb-an ld1.de chin ld1.de* choc srj3*• des-ac rbp6 dios ld1.de ferr-m ld1.de* hydrog srj* kali-hp ld1.de lac-loxod-a hrn2• lil-t vml3• nux-v gl3• *Phos* k* *Sel* ld1.de* spong fd4.de syc ptj1*• symph fd3.de• thea k* thuj ld1.de trinit br1 [heroin sdj2]

• **desire**: abrom-a ks5* alum bro1* aster k* bung-fa mtf calc-s k* *Casc* kr1 chen-a c1 *Chin* st* coca-c sk4• des-ac rbp6 galeoc-c-h gms1• ham fd3.de• hep k* hydr k* kali-p fd1.de• kali-s fd4.de kola stb3• lac-h sk4• lavand-a ctl1• lepi a1 luna kg1• lyss al2 musa vml3• nat-m sne nat-sil fd3.de• nux-v st* olib-sac wmh1 petr-ra shn4• plac-s rly4• podo fd3.de• positr nl2• *Puls* st* pyrus k* rhus-g tmo3• ruta fd4.de *Sacch* sht*• sel bg2* sep kr1* spong fd4.de staph sne suis-em rly4• thuj st* uran-n kr1* vanil fd5.de vip fkr4.de

⁝ **cold**: lac-cp sk4•

⁝ **cookies**; and: galeoc-c-h gms1•

⁝ **grounds**: (↗*indigestible - desire*) *Alum* k* con tl1

⁝ **hot**: galeoc-c-h gms1• pyrus c1

- **thought** of food | **agg.**: alum-sil k2 ant-c k2* *Ant-t* k2 arg-n bg2* borx bg2* cann-s bt3 cann-xyz bg2 carb-v bg2* colch tl1 dros bg2 dulc fd4.de graph bg2* lach bg2 lat-m bnm6• lil-t bg2 merc-cy c1 nat-m bg2* *Puls* bg2* sang k2 sars bg2* *Sep* bg2* thuj bg2* tritic-vg fd5.de
- **tobacco** (See Tobacco)
- **tomatoes**:

• **agg.**: ferr gk* lith-c bg2* lycpr c1 *Olnd* mrr1 op oss• ox-ac k2 phos bg2* sep sne [ferr-f stj2 ferr-lac stj2 ferr-n stj2 ferr-sil stj2 mang-act stj2 mang-m stj2 mang-met stj2 mang-n stj2 mang-p stj2 mang-s stj2 mang-sil stj2]

• **aversion**: bacls-10 ptj1*• falco-pe nl2• ferr gk* hyos vh lyc gm1 *Phos* vh* *Psor* vh* syc ptj1*• [ferr-f stj2 ferr-i stj1 ferr-lac stj2 ferr-m stj1 ferr-n stj2 ferr-sil stj2 mang-act stj2 mang-i stj2 mang-m stj2 *Mang-met* stj2 mang-n stj2 mang-p stj2 mang-s stj2 mang-sil stj2 nicc stj1]

• **desire**: bell mtf33 dulc fd4.de *Ferr* k* ign st* med gk nat-sil fd3.de• phos gk psor vh sulph dgt tritic-vg fd5.de vanil fd5.de [ferr-f stj2 ferr-i stj1 ferr-lac stj2 ferr-m stj1 ferr-n stj2 ferr-p stj1 ferr-s stj1 ferr-sil stj2 mang-act stj2 mang-i stj2 mang-m stj2 *Mang-met* stj2 mang-n stj2 mang-p stj2 mang-s stj2 mang-sil stj2 nicc stj1 nicc-met stj2 nicc-s stj2]

⁝ **ketchup**; tomato: carc mtf nux-v mtf stram mtf sulph mtf tub mtf

⁝ **raw**: dulc fd4.de ferr k* ign vh tritic-vg fd5.de

- **tonics**:

• **agg.**: (↗*stimulants - agg.*) carb-ac ld1.de

• **aversion**: sul-ac ld1.de*

• **desire**: aloe caps k2* carb-ac carb-an caust *Cocc* gels c1 med k2* nux-v *Ph-ac* phos k2* *Puls* k* rheum *Rhus-t* sul-ac *Valer*

- **tube** shaped food | **desire**: choc srj3*•
- **tuna** fish | **desire**: gink-b sbd1*• phos mtf
- **turnips**:

• **agg.**: *Bry* k* calc-ar k* *Lyc* k* *Puls* k* rob c1* sulph gl1.fr*•

• **aversion**: bry h1* puls ld1.de sulph h1*

• **desire**: abies-c br1*

- **variety** of tastes (See many)
- **veal**:

• **agg.**: ars k* *Calc* k* *Caust* k* chin k* **Ip** k* **Kali-n** k* lyc bg2 nux-v k* *Sep* k* sulph k* verat k* *Zinc* k*

• **aversion**: phel k* *Zinc* k* [kali-n stj1]

⁝ **roast** veal: *Calc* b4a.de merc bg2 zinc b4.de*

- **vegetables**:

• **agg.**: *Acet-ac* vh1* *Alum* k* ambr stx1 anan stx1 ars k* asc-t vml3• *Bry* k* calc st* caps ptk1 *Carb-v* kr1* cist stx1 cund stx1 cupr k* cypr stx1 *Hell* k* hydr kr1* *Kali-c* kr1 lept ptk1* lyc k* *Mag-c* kr1* mag-m mtf mag-s mtf nat-ar k2 *Nat-c* k* nat-m stx1 **Nat-s** k* petr bg2* phos stx1 pitu-a vml2* psor bgs *Puls* stx1 sabal c1 sep stx1 sil stx1 *Sulph* stx1 verat k* zing vml3•

⁝ **decayed**: *Carb-an* kr1* **Carb-v**

⁝ **green**: *Ars* kr1* *Bry* b7.de* *Calc* kr1 carb-v kr1* *Cupr* b7.de* *Hell* kr1 *Kali-c* kr1 lach stx1 lyc kr1 mag-c kr1 *Nat-c* kr1 psor bgs *Verat* b7.de*

⁝ **watery**: nat-s br1

• **aversion**: agath-a nl2• anac stx1 arb-m oss1• ars b4a.de* asar stx1 bell k* calc sne carc zzh caust vh* chel stx1 conch fkr1• cur vml3• **Hell** k* hydr k* *Ign* b7a.de kali-act stx1 kali-s fd4.de lyc stx1 lyss ld1.de *Mag-c* k* *Mag-m* hr1* med stx1 *Nat-m* vh nicc stx1 parth vml3• *Phos* vh pot-e rly4• prot stx1 psor stx1 ruta k* sabad stx1 sacch sht*• sulph gk* syc ptj1*• thuj stx1 tub ser* [bor-pur stj2 mag-i stj1 mag-lac stj2 mag-met stj2 mag-n stj2 mag-sil stj2 plb stj2]

⁝ **cooked**: sacch sst1*• [nicc-met stj2 nicc-s stj2]

⁝ **raw**: lap-la rsp1 nat-n dgt sep dgt [ant-c stj2 ant-m stj2 ant-met stj2 ant-t stj2]

• **desire**: abies-c bro1* abies-n stx1 adam srj5• adel a1* *Alum* k* alumn k* androc stx1 ant-c stx1 ars asar jl3* bell vh* calc-s carb-an k* cham k* elaps stx1 ham fd3.de• *Kali-i* vh lac-leo hrn2• lac-loxod-a hrn2• lepi stx1 *Lycps-v* ld1.de* *Mag-c* k* mag-f vml3• *Mag-m* k* mag-s stx1 med stx1 onos ld1.de orot-ac rly4*• ozone sde2*• phos stx1 podo fd3.de• positr nl2• ruta fd4.de sabad stx1 succ-ac rly4• *Sulph* vh symph fd3.de• tritic-vg fd5.de urol-h rwt• vanil fd5.de verat stx1 [beryl-m stj2 calc-sil stj2 cupr stj2 mag-lac stj2 mag-met stj2 mag-n stj2 mag-sil stj2 nicc-s stj2 tell stj2]

⁝ **fresh**: lac-leo hrn2•

- **desire**: ...
  - **green**: abies-n stx1 androc stx1 ant-c stx1 apis vh1* calc-s kr1 elaps stx1 lac-leo hrn2• lepi stx1 lycps-v stx1 mag-s stx1 phos stx1 sulph stx1 verat stx1
  - **juicy**: *Ph-ac* b4a.de
  - **raw**: adam srj5• lac-leo hrn2• *Sacch* sst1*• [*Ant-c* stj2 *Ant-m* stj2 ant-met stj2 ant-t stj2 mag-c stj mag-m stj mag-p stj mag-s stj]

- **vinegar**:
  - **agg.**: *Acon* bg2* aloe alum k2* **Ant-c** k* ant-t k2 *Ars* k* *Bell* k* borx k* calad k* *Carb-v* bg2* caust k* dros k* *Ferr* k* ferr-ar *Graph* bg2 guat vml3• hep bg2 kreos k* lac-ac stj5• lach k* merc-c b4a.de* morph c1* nat-ar nat-c k* nat-m k* *Nat-p* nux-v k* ph-ac k* phos k* *Puls* bg2* ran-b k* *Sep* k* staph k* sul-ac bg2* *Sulph* b2.de* teucr stx1 [hydrog stj2]
    - **smell** of; sensitive to the (See NOSE - Smell - acute - vinegar)
  - **amel.**: agar-em c1 *Asar* k* bry carb-an c1 euon-a hl1 hell ptk1 ign k* lacer c1 meny k* op *Puls* k* sang ld1.de stram k* tab sf1.de tong br* vesp c1*
  - **aversion**: alum tl1 ant-t tl1 syc ptj1*• vanil fd5.de
  - **desire**: ant-c mrr1* apis k* aq-mar mgm• arn k* ars k* asar jl3* bac vh* bell-p mg1.de* carc fb* chel k* *Cor-r* kkb **Hep** k* jal vml3• *Kali-m* vh kali-p k* lepi mang-p rly4• musca-d szs1 *Nat-m* vh oena vml3• puls st rib-ac jl3* sacch-a fd2.de* *Sep* k* stram tl1 sulph symph fd3.de• vanil fd5.de [ars-met stj2 kali-ar stj2 nat-ar stj2]
    - **dilute**: luf-op vml3•

- **vitamin** C | **desire** for: germ-met srj5•
- **wafers** | **desire**: calc-p mtf med mtf nat-m mtf stram mtf tub mtf
- **waffles** | **desire**: calc-p mtf nat-m mtf puls mtf
- **warm** drinks:
  - **agg.**: agn b7.de* allox stx1 ambr b7a.de* ant-c vh apis k2* arum-t stx1 atro stx1 bell stx1 beryl stx1 *Bism* stx1 brom h bry b7a.de* **Carbn-s** ld1.de* carc stx1 *Cham* b7.de* chel ld1.de* chin c1* chion vml3• chlol vml3• choc srj3*• *Dros* b7.de* dulc fd4.de elaps stx1 euph vml3• fl-ac k2* gels a1* graph bro1* hell b7a.de ign sf1.de iod stx1 *Lach* b7a.de* m-arct b7.de *M-aust* b7.de* merc b4.de* *Merc-i-f* vml3* *Mez* b4a.de nat-ar stx1 nux-m b7.de *Nux-v* b7.de oena vml3• ol-an vml3• *Par* b7a.de *Phos* bro1* phyt ptk1 *Puls* b7a.de* pyrog bro1* rhus-r ld1.de **Rhus-t** b7.de* rhus-v stx1 sal-al blc1• sars k2* sec c1 sep br1* sil b4.de* squil b7.de stann br1* *Sulph* ld1.de* verat ld1.de* voes stx1 zinc-p k2 ziz hl1 [alum stj2 alumin stj2 alumin-p stj2 alumin-s stj2 am-caust stj2 cupr stj2 cupr-act stj2 cupr-f stj2 cupr-m stj2 cupr-p stj2]
    - **hot**: am-c kr1 ambr kr1* anac kr1* anis sf ant-t kr1* apis kr1* asar kr1 *Bar-c* kr1 *Bell* kr1* **Bry** kr1* calc kr1* *Carb-v* kr1* caust kr1 *Cham* kr1* chion br1* chlol br1 cupr kr1 euph kr1 ferr kr1 graph sf1.de hell kr1 ign sf1.de kali-c kr1 kali-m kr1 *Lach* kr1* laur kr1 *Merc-i-f* kr1 *Mez* kr1* oena a1* ol-an c1 *Ph-ac* kr1* **Phos** kr1* *Phyt* c1* **Puls** kr1* pyrog sf1.de sanic c1* sep kr1* sil k2* stann br1* sul-ac kr1 ter stx1
  - **amel.**: ail ptk1* allox stx1 *Alum* k* alum-p stx1 am-br c1 androc srj1*• apoc k2* arg-n k* **Ars** k* bac stx1 beryl stx1 *Bry* calc-f c1* canth b7.de *Carbn-s* k* carc mlr1* casc c1* castm stx1 *Cedr* k* cench stx1 *Chel* k* chinin-ar k2* coc-c stx1 coloc stx1 cortiso stx1 crot-t sf1.de cuc-c vml3• cupr sf1.de des-ac rbp6 eupi stx1 glycyr-g cte1• *Graph* guare k* hep stx1 hydrog stx1 kali-p fd1.de• lac-c vh* lach k2 *Lyc* k* *Mang* k* mim-p vml3• *Nux-m* k* **Nux-v** k* pyrog slp* (non:pyrus slp) **Rhus-t** k* sabad k2* sec stx1 spong k* sul-ac ptk1 *Sulph* k* verat k* visc stx1
    - **hot**: ail ptk1 antip c1 ars k* carc mlr1• chel sf1.de* lyc kr1* mag-p kr1* mang kr1 morph stx1 nux-m kr1 nux-v k* pyrog kr1* *Rhus-t* kr1 sul-ac k* *Verat* kr1
  - **aversion**: *Apis* k2 bell mtf33 bry ld1.de* caust ld1.de* *Cham* k* *Cupr* b7.de* graph ld1.de hydrog srj* kali-s bro1* lac-ac stj5• lach k2 med gk medul-os-si rly4• merc-cy c1 nat-m sne oena vml3• **Phos** ptel vml3• **Puls** k* pyrog ld1.de* rib-ac jl3* sanic gk sil kr1 *Verat* b7.de* zinc-p k2* [cob stj2 cob-m stj2 cob-p stj2 zinc stj2 zinc-i stj2 zinc-m stj2 zinc-n stj2]
    - **hot**: caust k2* cham sf1.de* chin k2* ferr k* graph ld1.de hydrog srj *Kali-s* k* *Lyc* ld1.de mang h2 merc-cy c1 nat-sil fd3.de• oena a1* ptel bt3 *Puls* sf1.de* sil kr1*
      - **cold**; hot drinks seem: (↗*THROAT - Coldness - warm*) camph ptk1

- **warm** drinks: ...
  - **desire**: (↗*soup - desire; soup - desire - warm*) abrom-a ks5 adam srj5• alum c1 androc srj1*• ang k* apoc vml3• **Ars** k* ars-s-f k2* bac vml3• bamb-a stb2.de• bell bit-ar wht1• **Bry** k* *Calad* k* calc sne carb-v carc mlr1• casc k* cassia-s ccrh1*• castm bg2* castn-v k* castor-eq gsw1 cedr k* *Chel* k* chinin-ar k2* choc srj3*• cocc bg2* cupr k* dream-p sdj1• eup-per k* eup-pur ferr b7.de* ferr-p st* graph hep k2 *Hyper* k* irid-met srj5• kali-ar kali-c jl* kali-i bg2* kali-p fd1.de• kola stb3• kreos **Lac-c** k* lac-h htj1• limen-b-c hrn2• *Lyc* k* med kr1* merc-c k* neon srj5• ozone sde2*• phos gk phyt vh plut-n srj7• pyrus ribo rly4• *Sabad* k* spig bg1* *Sulph* symph fd3.de• tub al* vanil fd5.de [heroin sdj2 kali-sil stj2 pop dhh1 tax jsj7]
    - **accompanied** by:
      - **angina** pectoris: spig kr1*
      - **Lungs**; inflammation of: chel mrr1
    - **chill**, during: **Ars** *Cedr* *Eup-per* *Kali-ar* k2
    - **fever**, during: *Casc* cedr chel cda *Eup-per* *Lyc* sabad cda
    - **hot**: alum c1 ang kr1 bell kr1 **Bry** kr1* calad kr1* casc kr1 *Castn-v* kr1* cedr kr1* chel kr1* cupr kr1 eup-per kr1 eup-pur kr1 ham fd3.de• hyper kr1 kali-i sf1.de kreos kr1 **Lac-c** kr1 *Lyc* kr1 med kr1* **Phos** kr1* *Puls* kr1 sabad kr1 spig ld1.de* vanil fd5.de [heroin sdj2]
    - **menses**; before: bamb-a stb2.de•
    - **small** quantities: ars mtf11
      - **short** intervals: abrom-a ks5

- **warm** food:
  - **agg.**: (↗*cooked - agg.*) acon k* acon-f c1 agn k* all-c alum k* *Alum-p* k2* alum-sil k2* am-c k* *Ambr* k* *Anac* k* ang b2.de* ant-t k* apis k2 ars b2.de* arum-t stx1 asar k* *Bar-c* k* *Bell* k* bism k* borx k* brom stx1 **Bry** k* calc k* canth k* *Carb-v* k* carbn-s k* caust k* *Cham* k* clem k* *Coc-c* k* *Cupr* k* dros k* dulc fd4.de *Euph* k* ferr k* gels a1* gran k* guat jl hell k* *Kali-c* k* kali-s fd4.de **Lach** k* laur k* *Lob* stx1 m-arct b2.de* m-aust b2.de* *Mag-c* k* mag-m k* merc k* *Mez* k* nat-ar stx1 nat-m k* *Nit-ac* nux-m k* nux-v k* par k* *Ph-ac* k* **Phos** k* phyt ptk1 **Puls** k* rhod k* *Rhus-t* k* sanic stx1 sars k* *Sel* b7a.de sep k* sil k* spig k* squil k* stann k* sul-ac k* sul-i k2* sulph k* thiop jl3* thuj k* verat k* voes stx1 zinc k*
    - **hot**: acon kr1* alum-sil k2* alumn kr1* *Am-c* kr1* *Ambr* kr1* *Anac* kr1* ang kr1* *Ant-t* kr1* apis kr1* ars kr1* arum-t *Asar* kr1 *Bar-c* kr1* *Bell* kr1 borx kr1* *Bry* k* *Calc* kr1* canth kr1* caps carb-v k* *Caust* kr1* *Cham* kr1* chin ld1.de* chlol ptk1* clem kr1* coff *Cupr* kr1 *Euph* kr1* ferr k* graph guat vml3• *Hell* kr1 kali-c kr1* *Lach* kr1 *Laur* kr1* mag-c kr1* mag-m kr1 *Merc* kr1 *Mez* kr1 mill stx1 nat-m kr1 *Nat-s* k* nux-m kr1 nux-v kr1* par kr1* *Ph-ac* kr1* **Phos** kr1* phyt *Puls* k* rhod kr1* rhus-t kr1* sars kr1* *Sep* k* sil kr1 squil kr1* *Sul-ac* kr1* sulph kr1* thuj kr1* trios vml3• tub bt3 verat kr1* zinc kr1*
  - **amel.**: *Ars* ptk1 asar ld1.de chel k2* chinin-ar k2* kreos k2* *Laur* ld1.de* lyc bro1* *Nux-v* ptk1 pull-g vl rhus-t ptk1 sabad k2* *Spong* c1 [plb stj2]
    - **hot**: agar b2.de* ail vml3• alum b2.de* alumn kr1* ant-c b2.de* **Ars** b2.de* bar-c b2.de* bell bg2* bov b2.de* bry b2.de* calc b2.de* canth b2.de* carb-v b2.de* caust b2.de* cham b2.de* chel bg2* *Con* b2.de* *Graph* b2.de* hell b2.de* *Ign* b2.de* kali-c b2.de* *Kali-n* b2.de* *Kreos* b2.de* **Lyc** b2.de* mag-c b2.de* mag-m b2.de* *Mang* b2.de* merc b4a.de *Mez* b2.de* *Mur-ac* b2.de* nat-c b2.de *Nat-m* b2.de* nit-ac b2.de* *Nux-m* b2.de* **Nux-v** b2.de* par b2.de* ph-ac b2.de* *Plb* b2.de* puls b2.de* **Rhus-t** b2.de* sep b2.de* *Sil* b2.de* *Spig* b2.de* sul-ac b2.de* *Sulph* b2.de* thuj b2.de* *Verat* b2.de*
  - **aversion**: (↗*cooked - aversion*) *Alum-p* k2* *Apis* k2 bamb-a stb2.de• *Bell* k* bov vh* bung-fa mtf *Calc* k* cham vh* chel vh* *Chin* k* cupr k* cupr-ar vml3• ferr vh* **Graph** k* guare k* ham fd3.de• hydrog srj* *Ign* k* kali-s k2* lac-ac stj5• *Lach* k* *Lyc* k* mag-c k* mag-s k* merc k* *Merc-c* k* merc-cy ld1.de nat-m sne nat-sil fd3.de• *Nux-v* b7.de* petr k* **Phos** k* psor **Puls** k* sacch sht*• *Sil* k* *Verat* k* zinc k* [cob stj2 cob-m stj2 cob-p stj2 cupr-act stj2 cupr-f stj2 cupr-m stj2 cupr-p stj2 zinc-i stj2 zinc-m stj2 zinc-n stj2 zinc-p stj2]
    - **hot**: calc st **Chin** k* ferr k* hydrog srj* kali-s *Merc-c* k* petr pyrog ld1.de rib-ac vml3• sil k2* verat c1*
  - **desire**: (↗*soup - desire*) amp rly4• ang k* **Ars** k* ars-s-f k2* *Bry* bg2* calc vh caps k2 cassia-s ccrh1*• castm bg2* cedr bg2* *Chel* k* chinin-ar k2* *Cocc* k* cupr k* cycl k* elaps gk *Ferr* k* *Glycyr-g* cte1• kali-i bg2 *Lac-h* vml3• limen-b-c hrn2• *Lyc* k* med st morg-g ptj*• myos-a rly4• *Ph-ac* k* plut-n srj7• ruta fd4.de *Sabad* k* sil k* streptoc rly4• tub vh

- **desire**: ...
[ars-met stj2 calc-sil stj2 kali-ar stj2 kali-sil stj2 mang-sil stj2 nat-ar stj2 oxyg stj2 sil-met stj2 tax jsj7]
  - **hot**: ang kr1* ars kr1 chel kr1 cupr kr1* cycl kr1 *Ferr* kr1 **Lyc** kr1 morg-g ptj*• myos-a vml3• ph-ac kr1 phos k* rhus-g tmo3• *Sabad* kr1*

- **water**:
- **agg.**: *Acon* b7a.de alum b4.de* anac b4a.de apoc k2 arg-n sf1.de* ars b4a.de* ars-h kr1* borx b4a.de bry ld1.de* calc ld1.de canth b7.de* *Carb-v* kr1 carl stx1 cean c1 cench stx1 chinin-ar bro1* *Cocc* b7a.de* *Croc* b7a.de *Crot-t* ld1.de* dros ld1.de ferr-m ld1.de* hyos b7.de lach ld1.de *Lec* sne lob ld1.de lyc ld1.de m-arct b7.de nat-c b4a.de nux-m b7.de* *Oena* c1 phel c1 puls b7a.de* raph kr1 *Rhod* b4a.de sabad ld1.de* sep ld1.de* sin-a stx1 spig b7a.de spong ld1.de* stann ld1.de stram b7.de sul-ac b4a.de sulph b4a.de* teucr b7.de* **Verat** b7a.de
  - **bad**: all-s kr1* alst stx1 alst-b stx1 anthraci kr1* *Ars* stx1 camph stx1 carb-v stx1 chin c1* crot-h c1* merc-c stx1 podo stx1 zing kr1*
  - **too** much: grat ptk1
- **amel.**: *Agar-em* c1* anac b4.de ars ld1.de **Bry** ld1.de caust b4a.de *Cupr* b7.de* lacer c1 op stx1 paeon stx1 *Phos* b4.de* *Puls* b7a.de sal-al blc1• verat b7.de
  - **sips**: kali-n bro1
- **aversion**: aloe sne am-c c1* *Apis* ars k2* bac vh* *Bell* k* berb a1* brom k* *Bry* k* *Calad* k* cann-i *Canth* k* carl k* caust k* cedr k* chel ld1.de* *Chin* b2.de* chinin-ar ld1.de* coc-c k* coloc crot-c c1 elaps k* ham k* hell k* **Hyos** k* *Kali-bi* k* lac-c al2* lach k2* lyc k* *Lyss* k* maland al2 manc merc ld1.de merc-c k* merc-cy ld1.de musca-d szs1 *Nat-m* k* *Nux-m* kr1* **Nux-v** k* onos ox-ac k* phel k* *Phys* k* *Puls* k* **Staph** st* **Stram** k* sul-ac st* *Tab* bg2* thea k* wies c1 zinc zing ld1.de*
  - **accompanied** by | **thirst**: hell ptk1
  - **cold** (See cold drink)
  - **liquor** or brandy is added; unless: *Sul-ac* mrr1
  - **pregnancy**; during: phos ptk1
  - **thinking** of it; when: ham a1*
- **desire**: acet-ac vh1 ant-t kr1 bapt c1 caesal-b zzc1• caps k2 castm c1 cean c1 cench br1 hell c1 kola stb3• lac-c kr1 lac-d k2 lina c1 mag-c c1 *Nux-v* br1 ptel c1 ruta kr1* sacch sst1• *Sanic* c1 sars h2 tritic-vg fd5.de tub al2 vanil fd5.de [cadm-met stj2 cadm-s stj2 heroin sdj2 *Spect* dfg1]
  - **aerated** water (See soda water - desire)
  - **chalybeate** waters of health springs: ferr tl1
  - **children**; in: sanic tl1
  - **cold** water (See cold drink)
  - **lukewarm** (See lukewarm - desire)
  - **only** water: apoc k2 vanil fd5.de
  - **vomiting**; after: gard-j vlr2•
  - **warm** water (See warm drinks)

- **wet** food | **desire**: rhus-g tmo3•
- **wheat**: (↗*farinaceous)*
- **agg.**: calc mtf [chr-m stj2 chr-met stj2 chr-s stj2]
- **whipped** cream: (↗*cream)*
- **desire**: elaps vml puls mrr1* ulm-c jsj8•
- **whiskey**:
- **agg.**: alum stx1 caps vh led tl1 merc stx1 puls stx1 sars k2 trinit br1
- **amel.**: phyt stx1 prot jl2 sel bg2
- **aversion**: ant-t kr1 arn vh1 *Carb-ac* vml3• *Ign* kr1 merc kr1
- **desire**: acon k* *Agar* a ail vh1* alum sf am-m sf anac sf ant-c sf *Arn* k* *Ars* k* cadm-s vml3• calc k* caps k2 carb-ac k* *Carb-an* k* carb-v ld carbn-s ld* chin k* cocc a *Coff* a cub k* fl-ac k* hep k* **Lac-c** k* *Lach* k* led k2 merc k* nux-v k* op *Phos* puls k* *Ran-b* k2 *Sel* k* *Spig* k* staph k* **Sulph** k* ther k* visc vml3• [arg-met stj2 arg-n stj2 arg-p stj2]
- **wine**:
- **agg.**: acon k* acon-l c1* aeth h2* agar k* ail stx1 all-c stx1 *Alum* k* am-m k* ambr stx1 amyg-p c1 anan vml3• *Ant-c* k* ant-t k2* aran-ix mg* *Arn* k* **Ars** k* arum-i stx1 aur aur-m k* bell k* benz-ac bg2* *Borx* k* bov k* bry cact k* *Calc* k* calc-ar stx1 calc-caust stx1 calc-sil k2* camph vml3* caps stx1 carb-an k* carb-v k* carbn-s carc mlr1• **Chin** k2* chlol k* chlor ld1.de* cob-n mg1.de* coc-c k* cocc stx1 **Coff** k* coloc k* *Con* k* conch fkr1* cor-r cur vml3• des-ac jl* eup-per k2 ferr stx1 ferr-i stx1 ferr-m stx1 ferr-p stx1 ferr-s stx1 *Fl-ac* k* flav jl2 *Gels* gins stx1 *Glon* k*

Food – wine – **agg.**: ...
hyos j5.de iber c1* ign k* iod stj2* kali-chl kali-m stx1 kali-n c1* lac-h sze9• *Lach* k* *Led* k* **Lyc** k* mag-m jl meph k2 *Merc* j5.de* mez stx1 mill c1* *Naja* *Nat-ar* *Nat-c* k* *Nat-m* k* nat-s stx1 nat-sil k2 *Nit-ac* b4a.de *Nux-m* k* **Nux-v** k* **Op** k* ox-ac k* ozone stx1 perh stx1 petr k* **Ph-ac** b4a.de phos h1* plb stx1 prot jl3* ptel gk puls k* **Ran-b** k* *Rhod* k* rhus-t k* ruta k* *Sabad* k* sal-fr sle1• sars k2 *Sel* k* sep kr1 **Sil** k* spong fd4.de stann b4.de* staph bg2* stront-c k* *Sulph* j5.de* sumb stx1 tax vml3• thea stx1 thuj k* vanil fd5.de verat k* **Zinc** k* *Zinc-p* k2* zinc-val stx1 [ant-m stj2 ant-met stj2 bar-i stj2 bor-pur stj2 cob stj2 cob-m stj2 cob-p stj2 lith-i stj2 merc-i-f stj2 oxyg stj2]
  - **bad**: carb-v c1*
  - **lead**; containing: alum b2.de* ars b2.de* *Bell* b2.de* chin b2.de* nux-v b2.de* *Op* b2.de* plat b2.de* sul-ac b2.de* *Sulph* b2.de*
  - **overuse**: nux-v k2*
  - **red**: fl-ac bg2* kali-p fd1.de• ozone stx1 vanil fd5.de [zinc stj1* zinc-i stj2 zinc-m stj2 zinc-n stj2 zinc-p stj2]
  - **smell** of; sensitive to the (See NOSE - Smell - acute - wine)
  - **sour**: **Ant-c** k* ant-t k* *Ars* k* chin c1 ferr k* nat-m k2 sep k* sulph k*
  - **sulfurated**: *Ars* b2.de* chin b2.de* *Merc* b2.de* **Puls** b2.de* *Sep* b2.de*
- **amel.**: *Acon* k* acon-l c1* agar k* apis stx1 arg-n stx1 ars bell k* brom bry *Canth* k* *Carb-ac* k* chel chen-v kr1* coc-c stx1 coca br1* cocc *Con* k* dios stx1 ferr hr1* gels k* glon graph k* kalm stx1 lach k* mez nat-m bg2 nit-ac stx1 nux-v k* onos bg2* *Op* k* osm k* phos k* ran-b ld1.de* sel sul-ac k* sulph k* tab c1 thea k* *Thuj* stx1 visc vml3* zea-i br* [osm-met stj2]
  - **sour**: (non:ferr hr1)
  - **sour**; if not: ferr hr1
- **aversion**: **Acon** ld1.de* agar k* alum ld1.de* ars-met carb-v ld1.de* carbn-s ld1.de* carc mlr1• cina kr1 coff ld1.de* crot-c c1 fl-ac k* glon ld1.de hipp gsw1 hyper ld1.de *Ign* k* jatr-c k* jug-r k* lach k* lact ld1.de* m-aust b2.de* manc k* mand sp1 mang-p rly4• *Merc* k* nat-m k* nux-v ld1.de* ph-ac k* puls ld1.de* *Rhus-t* k* ruta fd4.de **Sabad** k* sil ld1.de* spong fd4.de stram kr1 *Sulph* k* tub st* *Zinc* k* zinc-p k2* [pop dhh1]
  - **white**: adam srj5• *M-aust* al2
- **desire**: *Acon* k* adam srj5• *Aeth* k* ant-c mrr1 arg-met k* arg-mur a1 arge-pl rwt5• *Ars* asaf bov k* *Bry* k* *Calc* k* calc-ar calc-s **Canth** ld1.de* carc mlr1• chel k* chin k* chinin-ar k* chlor bg2* chord-umb rly4• *Cic* k* colch crot-h vml3• cub k* cur vml3• dulc fd4.de eup-per k2 *Ferr* gsw1 fl-ac k* galeoc-c-h gms1• germ-met srj5• ham fd3.de* *Hep* k* hyper k* iod bg2* kali-bi k* kali-br k* kali-i k* kali-s fd4.de *Kola* stb3• lac-loxod-a hrn2• lac-lup hrn2• *Lach* k* *Lec* k* **Lycps-v** ld1.de* merc k* *Mez* k* nat-m k* nux-v c1* op ld1.de* ozone sde2*• **Phos** k* plac-s rly4• puls k* ruta fd4.de sal-ac vml3• sec k* sel k* *Sep* k* *Spig* k* spong fd4.de staph k* suis-em rly4• sul-i bg2* **Sulph** k* *Sumb* k* ther k* thiop jl3* tritic-vg fd5.de vanil fd5.de verat vh vichy-g a1* visc a2 [arg-n stj2 arg-p stj2 heroin sdj2]
  - **accompanied** by | **appetite**; ravenous: asar gm1 kali-s fd4.de
  - **claret**: calc-s k* dulc fd4.de ham fd3.de• kali-p fd1.de• kali-s fd4.de pieri-b mlk9.de podo fd3.de• ruta fd4.de sacch-a fd2.de• staph *Sulph* ther tritic-vg fd5.de vanil fd5.de
  - **fever**; during: *Cic* b7a.de*
- **wine** grapes (See grapes)
- **wood** | **desire**: nat-m b4a.de *Nux-v* b7a.de *Puls* b7a.de sep b4a.de
- **yoghurt**:
- **agg.**: nat-p stx1 *Podo* kr1* rhus-t vh
- **aversion**: cypra-eg sde6.de• fuma-ac rly4• *Nat-s* vh* pot-e rly4• suprar rly4• vanil fd5.de
- **desire**: ant-t a2 carc fd2.de• (non:caust k) cypra-eg sde6.de• daph sys elaps mrr1 fuma-ac rly4• ham fd3.de• lac-leo hrn2• lac-loxod-a hrn2• nat-c dgt nat-m gk nat-s mrr1* nat-sil fd3.de• petr-ra shn4• pot-e rly4• rhus-t samkn ribo rly4• suprar rly4• symph fd3.de• tritic-vg fd5.de vanil fd5.de [ant-m stj2]

FOOD POISONING: (↗*Wounds - dissecting; FEVER - Typhoid; RECTUM - Cholera - morbus)* absin bro1 acet-ac bro1 all-c bro1 *Ars* br1* camph bro1 carb-an bro1 carb-v bro1* crot-h bro1* *Cupr-ar* bro1* gamb mrr1 gunp bro1 kreos bro1* lach ptk1 lat-m bnm6• puls ptk1 pyrog c1* urt-u bro1 *Verat* bro1*

FOOT-BATHS:
- **agg.**: all-c bg2 *Bar-c* bg2 bry bg2 calc bg2 *Camph* bg2 caps bg2 cham bg2 *Colch* bg2 cupr bg2 *Dulc* bg2 fl-ac bg2 graph bg2 guaj bg2 *Lach* bg2 lem-m bg2 *Lyc* bg2 merc b4a.de* *Nat-c* b4.de* nit-ac bg2 nux-m bg2 **Nux-v** bg2 phos bg2 **Puls** bg2 rhus-t bg2 *Sep* bg2 **Sil** b4.de* stram bg2 tub bg2

- **amel.**: calad bg2 led bg2 puls bg2

FORCED through a narrow opening, as if: bar-c bg2* bell bg* bufo bg2* carb-ac ptk1 carb-an bg2 card-m bg2 coc-c bg* cocc bg* dig bg2* glon bg* Lach bg* op bg2* plb bg2* puls bg* sul-ac bg2 sulph bg2* tab bg2* thuj bg* Tub bg valer bg*

FOREIGN BODIES: (↗Ball)
- **expulsion** of foreign bodies; excessive (See Abscesses - foreign)
- **sensation** of foreign bodies: acon ptk1 anac ptk1 calc-f ptk1 hep ptk1 lob ptk1 sil ptk1
  - ○ · **Skin**; under the (See SKIN - Foreign)

FORESTS: | **pine** forests amel.; in: Tub mrr1

FORMICATION: (↗Cobweb) Acon b7.de* ail ptk1 am-m b7.de ambr b7.de ant-c b7.de aran ptk1 arg-met b7.de Arn b7.de cann-s b7.de caps b7.de carb-v b4.de caust b4.de cham b7.de chin b7.de cic b7a.de cina b7.de cist ptk1 cocc b7.de Colch b7.de* Croc b7.de dig ptk1 Euphr b7a.de hyos b7.de Ign b7.de Ip b7.de kali-c b4.de lach b7.de laur b7.de m-ambo b7.de m-arct b7.de m-aust b7.de mag-m b4a.de* med ptk1 merc b4.de* mez b4.de nat-c b4a.de nux-v b7.de op b7.de par b7.de Ph-ac b4.de* Phos b4.de* Plat b4a.de Plb b7.de* puls b7.de* Ran-s b7.de* Rhod b4.de* Rhus-t b7.de* sabad b7.de* samb b7.de Sec b7.de* Sep b4a.de Spig b7.de* staph b7.de* Stram b7.de* sulph b4.de* teucr b7.de* Verat b7.de verb b7.de zinc-p ptk1
- **accompanied** by:
  - · **atrophy** (See Atrophy - accompanied - formication)
  - · **numbness** (See Numbness - accompanied - crawling)
  - · **paralysis** (See Paralysis - accompanied - formication)
- **chill**; during: acon bg2 Am-c bg2 arn bg2 caust bg2 coloc bg2 merc bg2 nux-v bg2 puls bg2 Rhus-t bg2 sabad bg2 Samb bg2 sec bg2 sep bg2 spig bg2 sulph bg2
- **delivery**; during: sec bro1
- **emissions** agg.; after: mez h2
- **mouse** creeping or running in muscles; sensation of a: (↗Convulsions - epileptic - aura - mouse) bell a3* Calc ptk1 cimic ptk1 lyc ptk1 nit-ac ptk1 phos ptk1 rhod ptk1 sep ptk1 Sil ptk1 staph ptk1 Sulph ptk1
- **pain**; from: calc-p tl1 hyper ptk1
- **painful** sensation of crawling through whole body if he knocks against any part: spig k*
- **small** spots, in: hist vml3•
- **suffering** parts, of: con h2
- ○ - **Affected** parts: Arn b7a.de coloc ptk1 con h rhus-t b7a.de
- **Bones**: acon k* arn k* cham k* colch k* ign bg2* kali-bi bg2 merc k* mez bg2 nat-c k* nat-m k* nux-v k* ph-ac k* plat k* Plb k* puls k* rhod k* Rhus-t k* sabad k* sec k* Sep k* spig k* sulph k* zinc k*
- **External** parts: abrot bg2 Acon k* acon-c a1 acon-f a1 aconin a1 aesc k* aether a1 agar k* agarin mtf11 agn k2* alco a1 all-s k* aloe bg2* Alum k* alum-p k2* alum-sil k2* Alumn kr1 am-c k* am-m k* ambr k* anac k* ang b2.de* ant-c k* ant-t k* apis bg2 Aran hr1* arg-met k* Arg-n bg2* Arn k* ars k* ars-i ars-s-f k2* arum-t st1 arund k* asaf k* asar k* aur k* aur-ar k2 aur-s k2* Bamb-a stb2.de• Bar-c k* bar-i k2* bar-m bar-s k2* bell k* borx k* bov k* bruc a1 bry k* bufo bg2 cadm-met tpw6 cadm-s k2 calad calc k* calc-p k* camph k* cann-i k* cann-s k* canth j5.de* caps k* carb-an k* carb-v k* carbn-s k2 card-b a1 Carl a1 Castm bg2* Caust k* cedr a1* cham k* Chel k* chin k* cic k* cina k* cist k* clem k* coc-c mtf11 Cocc k* Colch k* coloc k* con k* conin a1 Croc k* cupr-ar a1 cupr-s hr1* cur st1 cypra-eg sde6.de• dros k* dulc k* euon j5.de* euphr k* fago a1 ferr k* ferr-ma j5.de fl-ac a1 gamb a1* gels hr1 gent-c a1 Gran graph k* guaj k* guare a1 halo jl3 ham a1 hep k* hist mg1.de hydr-ac hr1* hyos k* Hyper bg2* ign k* iod ip k* kali-ar Kali-br bg2* Kali-c k* kali-chl k13 kali-m k2 kali-n k* kali-sil k2 Kalm bg2* kreos k* kres srb2.fr lach k* lath sf1.de laur k* led k* Lyc k* m-ambo b2.de M-arct b2.de* m-aust b2.de* mag-c k* Mag-m k* mang k* Med k2* Merc k* merc-c k* merc-i-r a1 Mez k* morph a1 mosch k* mur-ac k* nat-ar Nat-c k* Nat-m k* nat-p nat-sil k2* nit-ac k* nit-s-d a1 nux-m k* Nux-v k* oena ptk1 ol-an bg2 ol-j a1 olnd k* onos op k* osm ptk1 pall k* par k* petr bg2* Ph-ac k* Phos k* phys sf1.de Pic-ac k* pieri-b mlk9.de Plat k* plb k* Puls k* Ran-b k* ran-s k* rheum k* Rhod k* Rhus-t k* rumx bg2* Sabad k* sabin k* samb k* sang ptk1 sars k* Sec k* sel k* seneg k* Sep k* sil k* Spig k* spong k* Squil j5.de stann k* staph k* stram k* stront-c k* sul-ac k* sul-i k2* Sulph k* tab bg2* taosc iwa1• tarax k* Tarent k* tell ptk1 teucr k* thuj k* tub k2* urt-u valer k* vario ptk1 verat k* verb k* viol-t k* Visc bg2* Zinc k* zinc-p k2*

Formication – External parts: ...
  - · **one** side: prim-v mtf11
  - · **accompanied** by:
    - ⁝ **cold** feeling: agar mtf11
    - ⁝ **neuralgia**; complaints of: acon mtf11
- **Glands**: acon k* Arn k* bell k* calc k* cann-s k* canth k* chin b7.de Con k* ign laur k* m-aust b2.de* merc k* nat-c k* ph-ac k* Plat k* puls k* rhod k* Rhus-t k* sabin k* Sep k* Spong k* sulph k* zinc k*
- **Internally**: Acon k* acon-f k* agar agn k* aloe bg2 alum k* alum-sil k2* am-c k* am-m k* ambr k* ant-t k* apis bg2 arg-met k* Arn k* ars k* asaf k* bar-c k* bar-s k2 bell k* borx bg2 bov bg2 brom bg2 Bry k* cadm-s k2 calc k* Calc-p br1 Canth k* caps bg2 carb-an bg2 carb-v k* caust k* Cham bg2 chel k* Chin k* cic k* cina bg2 cocc k* Colch k* coloc k* con bg2 cupr k* dig bg2 dros k* dulc k* euphr k* ferr bg2 graph k* guaj k* hep k* hyos k* ign k* iod k* Ip bg2 kali-ar k2 kali-c bg2 kali-m k2 kali-n bg2 kres srb2.fr Lach bg2 laur k* led k* M-aust b2.de mag-c bg2 mag-m bg2 med ptk1 meny k* merc k* mez k* mur-ac bg2 nat-ar nat-c k* Nat-m bg2 nat-p nat-sil k2 nux-m k* nux-v k* olnd bg2 ph-ac k* phos k* Plat k* plb k* prun bg2 Puls k* rheum k* rhod k* Rhus-t k* Rumx bg ruta fd4.de Sabad k* sabin k* Sang Sec sel k* seneg k* sep k* sil k* spig k* spong k* stann k* staph k* sul-i k2 Sulph k* tarax k* teucr bg2 thuj k* Verat bg2 viol-o k* Zinc k* zinc-p k2
  - · **ants** running through the body; as if: cist a1*
    - ⁝ **air**; fresh | **amel.**: cist tl1
    - ⁝ **lying** down agg.: cist tl1
- **Nerves**; along course of: alum-sil k4

FRACTURES: | **Bones**; fractures of (See Injuries - bones)

FRAGILE people (See Delicate)

FRAIL; as if body were (See MIND - Delusions - body - brittle)

FROSTBITE, ailments from: Abrot bg2* Agar b2.de* Ars b2.de* bell b2.de* Borx b2.de* bry b2.de* camph b2.de* Canth sne Carb-v b2.de* Colch b2.de* Ferr-p c2 hep b2.de* kali-c bg2 m-aust b2.de* mur-ac b2.de* nit-ac b2.de* nux-m c2 nux-v b2.de* Petr b2.de* ph-ac b2.de* Phos b2.de* Puls b2.de* Rhus-t bg2* sul-ac b2.de* sulph b2.de* zinc c1

FROSTY air (See Weather - frosty)

FULLNESS; feeling of:
- **painful** | **right** side of body: lim br1
- ○ - **Externally**: Aesc aloe k2 ars k* aur aur-m bar-i k2 caust k* kali-n k* laur k* nux-m k* par k* phos k* sul-i k2 verat k*
- **Internally**: Acon k* Aesc k* agar k* aloe bg2* alum k* alum-sil k2 am-c k* am-m k* ambr b2.de aml-ns anac k* ant-c k* Ant-t k* Apis arg-n bg2* Arn k* ars k* Asaf k* Asar k* aur k* aur-m k2 aur-s k2 Bar-c k* bar-i k2 bar-m bar-s k2 Bell k* borx k* bov k* Bry k* cact calc k* calc-i calc-s k2 calc-sil k2 camph k* cann-i cann-s k* Canth k* Caps k* Carb-an k* Carb-v k* Carbn-s caust k* cench k2 Cham k* chel k* Chin k* cic k* Cimic k* clem a1 coc-c a1 cocc k* coff k* Colch k* coloc k* com Con k* conv bg2* croc k* Crot-t Cycl k* Dig k* dirc a1 Ferr k* ferr-ar k2 galeoc-c-h gms1• gels bg2* Glon k* Graph k* guaj k* halo jl Ham k* Hell k* hyos k* ign k* iod k* Iris Kali-c k* kali-m k2 Kali-n k* kreos k* lach k* laur k* led k* Lil-t bg2* lol bg2 Lyc k* m-ambo b2.de m-arct b2.de m-aust b2.de mag-c k* mag-m k* mang k* Meli k* meny k* merc k* mez k* Mosch k* mur-ac k* naja bg2* Nat-ar nat-c k* nat-m k* nat-s k2 nept-m lsd2.fr Nit-ac k* Nux-m k* Nux-v k* olnd k* op k* par k* petr k* ph-ac k* Phos k* phys a1 Phyt plat k* plb k* Psor Puls k* Ran-s k* rheum k* rhod k* Rhus-t k* ruta k* sabad k* Sabin k* sars k* Sep k* sil k* spig k* spong k* stann k* staph k* stict stront-c k* sul-ac k* sul-i k2 Sulph k* thuj k* ust bg2* Valer k* verat k* verat-v verb k* vip sf1.de zinc k*
  - · **right** side of body: galeoc-c-h gms1•
  - · **playing** piano, after: anac k1

FUMES (See Smoke)

FUNGOID diseases: kali-i br1

FUNGOID GROWTH (See SKIN - Excrescences - fungus)

FUR in inner parts; sensation as if covered with: Alum ptk1 ars bg2 caust k* chin ptk1 Cina vh cocc k* colch ptk1 Dig ptk1* dros k* Hep vh Iris ptk1 kali-c ptk1 merc k* nux-m k* nux-v b2.de Ph-ac ptk1* Phos k* Pip-n bg Puls k* rhod ptk1 Sulph vh verat ptk1

GAIT REELING, staggering, tottering and wavering (See EXTREMITIES - Tottering)

GALLSTONES (See ABDOMEN - Gallstones)

GARGLING: | **agg.**: carb-v b2.de*

GASSES (= vapors):

- **agg.**: ars bg2 bell bg2 caust bg2 *Gels* bg2 op bg2 sul-ac bg2
- **sensation** of | **Internally**: *(↗Smoke - sensation)* apis bg2 ars bg2 brom bg2 bry bg2 camph bg2 carb-v bg2 chin bg2 ferr bg2 ign bg2 ip bg2 lyc bg2 merc bg2 mosch bg2 nux-v bg2 par bg2 puls bg2 rhus-t bg2 sabad bg2 thuj bg2 verat-v bg2 zinc bg2

GATHERED TOGETHER (See Constriction)

GLAIRY (See Mucous secretions - albuminoid)

GLANDERS: acon bro1 *Ars* k* calc k* chinin-s bro1 *Crot-h* bro1 hep bro1 hippoz c1* *Kali-bi* c1* kreos b7a.de *Lach* c1* *Merc* bro1 ph-ac k* phos bro1 sep bro1 sil bro1 sulph k* thuj bro1

GLASS; sensation as if made of: | **Bones**: thuj tl1

GLYCOGEN STORAGE DISEASES: *(↗Pompe's)* calc mtf

GONORRHEA, suppressed: *(↗URETHRA - Discharge - gonorrheal)* *Acon* bg2 agn k* ant-t bro1 arg-n bg3 aur aur-m k2 benz-ac k* brom *Calc* *Cann-s* bg3 **Canth** b7.de* *Chel* kr1 *Clem* k* *Coca* kr1 con b4a.de crot-h daph gels hr1 graph bro1 kali-i bro1 kalm **Med** k* merc k* mez *Nat-m* ptk1 *Nat-s* kr1* *Nit-ac* k* psor al2* *Puls* k* *Sars* k* *Sel* b7a.de sep k2 sil k2 *Staph* **Sulph** bg2* **Thuj** k* verat viol-t kr1* x-ray bro1 zinc

- **asthma**; in patients with: med awy2* nat-s awy2* puls awy2* sil awy2* thuj awy2*

GOOD HEALTH before paroxysms (See Well - unusually)

GRAND MAL (See Convulsions - epileptic)

GRASPING OBJECTS:

- **agg.**: acon b2.de* *Am-c* b2.de* am-m b2.de* arg-met b2.de* arn b2.de* bell b2.de* bov b2.de* bry b2.de* *Calc* b2.de* *Cann-s* b2.de* *Carb-v* b2.de* **Caust** b2.de* **Cham** b2.de* chin b2.de* dros b2.de* ferr-p bg2 graph bg2 kali-c b2.de* kali-n b2.de* laur b2.de* led b2.de* *Lyc* b2.de* merc b4.de* nat-c b2.de* nat-m b2.de* nat-s bg2 nux-m b2.de* nux-v b2.de* op b2.de* phos b4a.de* plat b2.de* *Puls* b2.de* rhus-t b2.de* sabad b2.de* sec b2.de* *Sil* b2.de* spig b2.de* verat b2.de*
- **amel.**: anac ptk1 cimic bg2* lith-c ptk1 med bg2 spig b7.de* stann bg2 sulph bg2

GRAVES' DISEASE (See EXTERNAL - Goitre - exophthalmic)

GRAYISH, dirty, etc.: arg-met bg *Ars* bg berb bg calc bg *Caust* bg *Chel* bg cupr bg dig bg **Kali-c** bg kali-m bg lach bg *Lyc* bg *Merc* bg **Phos** bg sil bg sulph bg

GREASY, oily, fatty: *Bry* bg **Caust** bg *Iod* bg iris bg **Mag-c** bg maland bg *Merc* bg *Nat-m* bg phos bg plut-n srj7• psor bg puls bg sel bg *Thuj* bg*

- **application** | **amel.**: euph ptk1 euph-l bro1

GREENISH: acon bg **Ars** bg *Carb-v* bg cham bg con bg ip bg kali-i bg lyc bg mag-c bg **Merc** bg *Nat-s* bg phos bg **Puls** bg *Sep* bg stann bg *Sulph* bg *Verat* bg

GRIEF agg.: aur b4a.de caust b4a.de *Cocc* b7a.de *Cupr* b7a.de *Ign* b7a.de *Ph-ac* b4a.de *Staph* b7a.de

GRINDING (See Pain - boring)

GRIPPE (See Influenza)

GROWLING in body (= roaring, humming, buzzing): agn b2.de ambr b2.de ars b2.de aur b2.de bar-c b2.de bell b2.de calc b2.de cann-s b2.de carb-v b2.de *Caust* b2.de cic b2.de cocc b2.de coff b2.de con b2.de croc b2.de ferr b2.de graph b2.de hyos b2.de *Kreos* b2.de lach b2.de m-ambo b2.de **M-arct** b2.de meny b2.de mosch b2.de mur-ac b2.de **Nux-m** b2.de *Nux-v* b2.de **Olnd** b2.de op b2.de ph-ac b2.de phos b2.de plat b2.de **Puls** b2.de *Rhus-t* b2.de sabad b2.de sars b2.de *Sep* b2.de **Spig** b2.de squil b2.de stann b2.de staph b2.de **Sulph** b2.de teucr b2.de thuj b2.de verat b2.de viol-t b2.de zinc b2.de

GROWTH: *(↗Children; Pain - growing; Tall; Weakness - growing)*

- **complaints** of growth process: bar-c ptk1 calc ptk1 calc-p ptk1 ph-ac ptk1 phos ptk1 sil ptk1 *Thyr* ptk1

Growth: ...

- **length** too fast; in: *(↗Children; Pain - growing; Tall; Weakness - growing)* bar-c bg cadm-met gm1 *Calc* bro1* *Calc-p* bg* ferr-act bro1* guaj ptk1 hipp hr1* (non:hippoz br1) iod sf1.de* irid-met c1* jug-r vml3• kreos c1* nat-m kl **Ph-ac** j5.de* **Phos** kr1* sil bg sulph kl
  - **girls**; in: jug-r vml3•
  - **young** people, in (See Growth)

GUILLAIN-BARRÉ SYNDROME: *(↗Paralysis - extending - upward)* aconin c1* alum dgt1 aran-ix jl1 calc gk1 cimic jl1 con c1* lyss c1* mand jl1 meph jl1 plb tl1 psil jl1

HAIR: *(↗SKIN - Hair)*

- **brushing** back agg.: carbn-s bg2* puls b2.de* rhus-t b2.de*
- **cutting** | **agg.**: *(↗HEAD - Hair - cutting)* acon bro1 **Bell** b2.de* *Glon* bg2* kali-i bg2* lappa bg2 led b2.de* lyc brm *Phos* bg2* psor k2* puls b2.de* *Sep* b2.de* tub ser
- **distribution** in women; masculine (= hirsutism): *(↗FACE - Hair - growth - women; FEMALE - Virilism; MIND - Mannish - women)* bar-c rti2 cimic kkv1 cortico sp1 ign dgt1* lyc dgt1 puls mrr1 *Sep* dgt1* thuj dgt1*
- **falling**: alum k2 ph-ac mrr1 prot jl2 *Sel* mrr1 syph jl2 thuj mtf33
  - **rapidly**: thal ptk1
- **pulled**; sensation as if hair were: *Acon* bg2 alum bg2 arg-n bg2 arn bg2 ars bg2 bar-c bg2 bry bg2 canth bg2 caust bg2 chin b7.de* coloc bg2 *Kali-c* bg2 kali-n bg2 kreos bg2 *Laur* bg2 lyc bg2 mag-c bg2 mag-m bg2 mur-ac bg2 ph-ac bg2 *Phos* bg2 *Rhus-t* bg2 sel bg2 sulph bg2
- **sensation** of a: all-c bg2 arg-met bg2 *Arg-n* k* *Ars* k* bell bg2 bry bg2 caps bg2 carbn-s caust bg2 coc-c k* croc bg2 *Ign* bg2 *Kali-bi* k* lac-c bg2 lach bg2 laur bg2* lyc k* m-aust b2.de mosch bg2 nat-m k* nat-p k* nux-v bg2 par bg2 pieri-b mlk9.de *Plat* bg2 ptel bg2 *Puls* k* ran-b k* rhus-t bg2 *Sabad* bg2 **Sil** k* *Sulph* k* tab st1 ther bg2 thuj *Valer* bg2
- **thick**: ant-c ptk1 graph ptk1 lyc ptk1 ust ptk1 viol-t ptk1
- **touch** agg.: ambr b2.de* **Apis** bg2* **Ars** b2.de* *Bell* b2.de* *Carb-v* bg2* chin b2.de* *Ferr* b2.de* *Ferr-p* hr1* hep bg2 ign b2.de* lach bg* mez bg2 nit-ac sf1.de *Nux-v* b2.de* ph-ac b2.de* phos b2.de* *Puls* b2.de* rhus-t b2.de* **Sel** b2.de* sep ptk1 stann b2.de* trios rsj11• tub ser verat ptk1 *Zinc* hr1*

HAMMERING sensation: acon tl1 am-c b2.de* am-m b2.de* calc b2.de* chin b2.de* cic b2.de* clem b2.de* coff b2.de* dros b2.de* ferr b2.de* hep b2.de* lach b2.de* m-ambo b2.de* mez b2.de* nat-m b2.de* *Phos* b2.de* sil b2.de* sulph b2.de* thuj b2.de* verb b2.de*

HAND on the part; laying one's: *(↗Magnetism)*

- **agg.**: kali-n h2
- **amel.**: *(↗Magnetism)* *Bell* k* calc k* canth k* carb-an bg2* *Croc* k* *Cupr* ptk1 dros k* *Mang* b2.de* meny k* mur-ac k* nat-c k* olnd k* par k* **Phos** k• **Rhus-t** k • sabad k* **Sep** k • sil h2 spig k* sulph k* thuj k*
  - **hand** near part amel.: sul-ac h2

HANDICAPPED physically (See Disabled)

HANG DOWN; letting limbs:

- **agg.**: *Alum* k* *Am-c* k* ang b2.de* bar-c ptk1* **Bell** ptk1 berb **Calc** k* *Carb-v* k* *Caust* k* cina k* con ptk1 dig k* hep k* ign k* lyc k* m-aust b2.de* nat-m k* nux-v k* ox-ac par k* ph-ac k* phos k* phyt plat k* plb k* *Puls* k* ran-s k* ruta k* *Sabin* k* sil bg2 stann k* stront-c b2.de* sul-ac k* sulph k* thuj k* valer k* *Vip* k* vip-a jl
- **amel.**: acon k* am-m k* anac k* ant-c k* arg-met k* arg-n *Arn* k* asar k* *Bar-c* k* *Bell* k* berb ptk1 borx k* *Bry* k* calc b2.de* camph k* caps k* caust k* chin k* cic k* cina k* *Cocc* k* coff k* colch k* coloc k* **Con** k* cupr k* dros k* euph k* ferr k* graph k* hep k* ign k* *Iris* *Kali-c* k* kreos k* *Lach* k* *Led* k* lyc k* m-aust b2.de *Mag-c* k* *Mag-m* k* mang ptk1 merc k* *Mez* k* nat-c k* nat-m k* nit-ac k* nux-v k* olnd k* *Petr* k* phos k* plb k* puls k* ran-b k* rat ptk1 *Rhus-t* k* ruta k* *Sil* k* stann k* sul-ac k* sulph k* teucr k* thuj k* verat k* verb k*
- **sensation** of hanging down: *(↗Relaxation - physical)* ulm-c jsj8•

HANGOVER:

- **alcohol**; from excessive use of (See Food and - alcoholic - agg. - hangover)
- **amel.**: mand sp1
- **sensation** as if from a hangover (= without use of alcohol): luna kg1• olib-sac wmh1 [spect dfg1]

HARD BED, sensation of: acon k* agar alum bg2 **Arn** k* *Ars* bamb-a stb2.de• **Bapt** bg2* bar-c *Bell* b4a.de bry k* (non:canth gk) caust k* cham sf1.de con k* dros k* eup-per sf1.de euphr bg2* fago a1 *Ferr* *Ferr-p* gels bg3* get a1 graph k* hep j5.de ip irid-met srj5• kali-c k* kali-p fd1.de• kola stb3• lach bg2 lyc k* m-ambo b2.de* m-aust b2.de* mag-c k* mag-m k* manc merc *Morph* bro1 *Nat-s* bg2* nux-m k* nux-v k* *Op* k* petr h2* phos k* plat k* podo bg2* *Psor* bg2* puls k* **Pyrog** k* *Rhus-t* k* **Ruta** k1* sabad k* sanic c1 **Sil** k* spong stann k* sulph k* tarax k* thuj k* til a1* verat k*

- **everything** on which he lies seems too hard: am br1* bapt mrr1 lyc a petr a *Pyrog* mrr1 rhus-t mrr1

HARDNESS, induration: (↗*Indurations)* alum k* ant-c bg3* *Ars* k* bad ptk1 bar-c k* **Bell** k* brom ptk1 *Bry* k* *Calc* k* *Calc-f* k* *Carb-ac* bg3 **Carb-an** ptk1 carb-v ptk1 chin ptk1 cist bg3* **Clem** k* **Con** k* fl-ac ptk1 *Graph* k* *Iod* k* *Kali-m* bg3* lach ptk1 *Lyc* k* mag-m ptk1 merc bg3* merc-i-r ptk1 **Phos** k* *Phyt* bg3* *Plb* k* **Rhus-t** k* sel ptk1 **Sep** k* **Sil** k* spong ptk1 staph ptk1 *Sulph* k* tarent bg3 tarent-c ptk1

HAT; from pressure of a: agar bg2 alum bg2 ang bg2 arg-met bg2 carb-an bg2 *Carb-v* bg2* hep bg2 kali-n bg2 lach bg2 laur b7.de* led bg2 lyc bg2 *Nit-ac* bg2* *Sil* bg2* stront-c bg2 sulph bg2 *Valer* b7.de*

HAWKING UP mucus agg.: *Ambr* b7.de* coff b7.de hyos b7.de nux-v b7.de puls b7.de rhus-t b7.de sabin b7.de *Spig* b7.de* *Teucr* b7.de*

HEAT:

- **accompanied** by:
  - **nausea** (See STOMACH - Nausea - accompanied - heat)
  - **respiration**; complaints of (See RESPIRATION - Complaints - accompanied - heat)
  - ○ **Head**; complaints of (See HEAD - Complaints - accompanied - heat)
  - **Lower** limbs | **coldness**: mag-c bg2
  - **Teeth**; pain in (See TEETH - Pain - accompanied - heat)
- **air**; in open | **amel.**: brucel sa3•
- **amel.** (See Warm - amel.)
- **flushes** of: (↗*Circulation; Congestion - blood; Orgasm; Weakness - heat; MIND - Anxiety - flushes - during)* acet-ac k* *Acon* k* adam srj5• aesc k* aeth a1 agar bg2* agath-a nl2• agn k* ail k* *All-c* a1 *Aloe* bg2* alum k* alum-p k2 alum-sil k2* *Alumn* am-c k* am-m k* ambr k* **Aml-ns** bg2* anders zzc1• androc srj1• ang k* ange-s oss1• ant-c mrr1* ant-t k* apis k* apoc a1 aran-ix mg1.de* *Arg-n* sf1.de* arge-pl rwt5• arist-cl mg1.de *Arn* k* ars k* *Ars-i* ars-s-f k2 arum-t asaf b2.de* asar k* atp rly4• aur k* bamb-a stb2.de• bapt k* bar-act a1 bar-c k* bar-s k2 *Bell* k* berb bism k* bol-la a1 bor-ac c1 borx k* bov k* brom k* bruc j5.de bry k* bufo k* buth-a sp1 *Cact* **Calc** k* calc-f mrr1 calc-i k2 *Calc-s* calc-sil k2* camph k2* cann-s b2.de* canth b2.de* carb-an k* *Carb-v* k* carbn-dox knl3• *Carbn-s* carc fd2.de• *Carl* a1* **Caust** k* cedr a1 cench k2* *Cham* k* chel chim a1 *Chin* k* chinin-s chir-fl gya2 chlam-tr bcx2• chord-umb rly4• cic sf1.de *Cimic* a1* cimx *Cina* kr1* cit-ac rly4• clem bg2* **Cocc** k* coff k* *Colch* k* coll ptk1 coloc k* con a1 corn k* croc k* *Crot-h* k* *Crot-t* k1* cupr k* cupr-am-s a1 cyt-l mg1.de dig k* dros b2.de* dulc j5.de *Elaps* erech br1 ery-a a1* eucal st1 eup-per euphr bg2* fago a1 *Ferr* k* ferr-ar ferr-i ferr-p fl-ac sf1.de* flav jl3 flor-p mg1.de* foll oss• frax a1* galeoc-c-h gms1• galin jl3 galla-q-r nl2• *Gamb* k* **Gels** hr1 ger-i rly4• **Glon** k* *Graph* k* guaj sf1.de hell-o a1* helon k* hep k* hura hydr-ac st1 hydrog srj2• hyos k* **Ign** k* ignis-alc es2• *Iod* k* ip k* *Jab* c1* jug-r a1 kali-ar k* *Kali-bi* k* kali-br sf1.de **Kali-c** k* *Kali-i* k* kali-n j5.de* *Kali-p* k* *Kali-s* kali-sil k2 ketogl-ac rly4• kiss a1 kola stb3• *Kreos* k* kres srb2.fr lac-ac k* lac-h htj1• **Lach** k* lachn a1 lat-m jl3 laur b2.de* lil-s a1 lipp a1 lob k* luna kg1• **Lyc** k* lyss m-arct b2.de* m-aust b2.de* mag-c b2.de* mag-m k* **Mang** k* mang-p rly4• marb-w es1• med hr1* medul-os-si rly4• melal-alt gya4 meny k* meph sf1.de *Merc* k* merc-i-r a1 methys jl3 mit a1 morg-p fmm1• morph a1 mosch a1 nat-ar nat-c k* nat-m k* nat-ox rly4• nat-p **Nat-s** k* nep jl3* nid jl3 **Nit-ac** k* nit-s-d a1* *Nux-v* k* ol-an a1* ol-j a1 olnd k* op k* orot-ac rly4• *Ov* c2* *Ox-ac* k* oxal-a rly4• *Petr* k* ph-ac k* phasco-ci rbp2 **Phos** k* pip-m a1 **Plat** k* plb b2.de* podo positr nl2• psil ft1 **Psor** k* ptel hr1* **Puls** b2.de* ran-b b2.de* raph k* rauw jl3 *Rhus-t* k* ribo rly4• ros-d wla1 rumx ruta k* sabad k* sabin k* sal-ac hr1* sal-fr sle1• samb b2.de* *Sang* k* saroth jl3 sec sf1.de sel sf1.de* seneg k* **Sep** k* *Sil* k* sinus rly4• sol-a k* spig k* *Spong* k* squil sf1.de stann k* staph b2.de* staphycoc rly4• *Stram* k* streptoc rly4• *Stront-c* bg2* **Sul-ac** k* **Sul-i** k2* **Sulph** k* **Sumb** k* suprar rly4• tab a1* tanac a1 *Ter* st1 teucr k* thala jl3 thiam rly4• thioc-ac rly4• thres-a sze7• **Thuj** k* thyr ptk1* til a1 tritic-vg fd5.de trom hr1* **Tub** k* tung-met bdx1• uran-n sf1.de urol-h rwt• *Ust* sf1.de valer k* vesp-xyz c2 vinc sf1.de viol-t b2.de* vip a1 visc jl3 voes a1 *Xan* yohim c1 zinc k* zinc-p k2 zinc-val sf1.de [alumin-s stj2 aur-s stj2 bell-p-sp dcm1

Heat – flushes of: ...
cadm-s stj2 chr-s stj2 ferr-f stj2 ferr-lac stj2 *Ferr-n* stj2 gal-s stj2 heroin sdj2 lith-s stj2 *Mag-n* stj2 *Mang-act* stj2 *Mang-n* stj2 mang-s stj2 mang-sil stj2 moly-met stj2 *Nat-n* stj1 *Nitro* stj2 spect dfg1 stront-m stj2 stront-met stj2 tax jsj7 titan-s stj2 *Zinc-n* stj2]

- **daytime**: *Bar-c* hr1* bism a1 borx a1 bry a1 kali-s fd4.de *Lach* hr1* nit-ac a1 *Petr* hr1* ribo rly4• *Senec* hr1*
- **morning**: bism k* borx carb-v k2 carc fd2.de• ox-ac hr1* ruta fd4.de
  - **eating**; after: thuj
- **forenoon**: sabad a1
  - **11** h | **hunger**; with: **Sulph** kr1
- **afternoon**: ambr bell k* borx kr1 cit-ac rly4• colch k* con k* fago a1 kola stb3• laur meny *Nat-p* k* plb k* pyrid rly4• samb k* **Sep**
  - **14** h: ptel a1
  - **16** h: cupr sst3• trios rsj11•
  - **16**-21 h: arum-t a1*
- **evening**: acon k* all-c arum-t k* borx carb-an k* carb-v k* *Elaps* k1* kali-p fd1.de• kali-s fd4.de ketogl-ac rly4• *Lyc* k* merc-c k* nat-p k* *Nat-s* k* nit-ac k* phos k* *Psor* k* ruta fd4.de **Sep** k* spong fd4.de *Stann* kr1* *Sulph* k* [heroin sdj2]
  - **19** h: gins a1
  - **20** h | **nausea**; with: ferr
  - **20**.30 h: arum-t cimic a1 cina sep
  - **bed** agg.; in: ruta fd4.de
    - **sleep**; preventing: gink-b sbd1•
  - **eating**; after: carb-v k* choc srj3• upa a1
  - **falling** asleep, before: carb-v
- **night**: (↗*Orgasm - night; SLEEP - Sleeplessness - menopause)* ange-s oss1• arum-t hr1* bar-c k* flav jl3* haliae-lc srj5• *Kali-i* hr1* kali-p fd1.de• petr h2 psil ft1* *Rhod* hr1* sal-fr sle1• *Sep* hr1* spig k* spong fd4.de *Sulph* hr1* thioc-ac rly4•
  - **midnight**:
    - **after** | **3** h: bapt a1* cupr sst3• fago a1
  - **sensation** as if perspiration would break out: bapt
- **accompanied** by:
  - **metrorrhagia** (See FEMALE - Metrorrhagia - accompanied - heat)
  - **numbness** (See Numbness - accompanied - heat)
  - **palpitations** (See palpitations)
  - **vertigo** (See VERTIGO - Accompanied - heat)
  - **Hands**; trembling of (See EXTREMITIES - Trembling - hand - accompanied - heat)
- **air**; in open | **amel.**: malar jl2 mosch a1
- **alternating** with:
  - **anxiety** (See MIND - Anxiety - alternating - heat)
  - **chills**: acon k* ang a1 ars k* asar *Calc* k* calc-f mrr1 *Chinin-s* k1* corn k* galla-q-r nl2• gels vh* iod jug-c a1 *Kali-bi* k* kalm a1 med k* morph a1 musca-d szs1 pin-s a1 plut-n srj7• sal-fr sle1• *Sep* spig tub c1
  - **coldness**; arctic: helo c1 helo-s c1*
  - **Chest**; pain in: lachn a1
  - **Head**; pain in (See HEAD - Pain - alternating - heat)
- **anger**; after: (↗*MIND - Anger)* irid-met srj5• *Petr* kr1 *Phos* [tax jsj7]
- **back** or stomach, from: phos k2*
- **bed** agg.; in: (non:eupi a1) ruta fd4.de
- **chill**:
  - **after**: ail hr1* cimx hr1*
  - **before**: **Caust** k* kali-i kr1 sang spig kr1
- **chilliness**:
  - **after**: corn a1 gast a1 gels a1 nat-p a1* nit-ac a1 *Puls* hr1* rhus-t a1 ruta fd4.de sang a1
  - **with**: agar am-br a1 apis *Ars* k* aur k2 *Carb-v* k* *Colch* k* corn k* erech br1 eup-per kali-bi lach lob malar jl2 mang k2 *Merc* k* *Petr* hr1* plat k* puls sang hr1* sep spong fd4.de sulph ter thuj k*
- **coition**; after: *Dig* hr1*
- **dinner** | **after** | **agg.**: par a1 sumb a1

- **dinner**: ...
  - **during** | **agg.**: calc-s nux-v spong fd4.de
- **eating**:
  - **after**:
    - **agg.**: alum arg-n carb-v card-b a1 cinnb hr1* ignis-alc es2• *Lach* hr1* par k* sumb k* tub c1* upa a1
    - **amel.**: chin h1
  - **agg.**: bov kr1 *Calc-s* nux-v psor k*
- **emotions** agg.: *Calc* lach *Phos* k*
  - **Upper** part: *Aml-ns* vh1
- **excitement** agg.: dys fmm1• nept-m lsd2.fr
- **exertion**, from least: alum ferr mrr1 *Merc* hr1* *Olnd* hr1* ox-ac k2 ruta fd4.de *Sep* k* spong fd4.de sul-i k2 *Sumb* [lac-mat sst4]
- **faintness**; with: *Crot-t* hr1* sep lp* **Sulph** hr1*
- **headache**; during: agar h2 sang ptk1 [tax jsj7]
- **intolerance** of: (non:arg-n br1)
- **leukorrhea**; with: *Lach* kr1 lyc kr1 *Sulph* kr1
- **lying** down:
  - **agg.**: gard-j vlr2•
  - **amel.**: nux-v a1* thuj a1
- **menopause**; during: (↗*Congestion - blood - menopause*) acon bro1* *Aml-ns* kr1* *Arg-n* kr1 aur k2* *Bell* kr1* bor-ac c1* calc bro1* calc-p bro1 carc pd* cham mrr1 *Cimic* bro1 con kr1 *Croc* sf1.de *Crot-h* kr1* *Dig* kr1* dros gk *Eucal* kr1 ferr bro1* foll oss• *Glon* kr1* hydr-ac kr1 *Ign* bro1 ignis-alc es2• jab kr1* *Kali-bi* kr1* *Kali-br* kr1* kali-c bro1* **Lach** kr1* lyc kr1 **Mang** kr1* *Mang-act* bro1 meli vml3• morg fmm1• nat-m ser nicc-s bro1 nux-v bro1* ol-an sf1.de ov bro1* ph-ac bro1* phos mrr1 pilo bro1 *Plat* kr1 psor gk puls gg* *Sang* kr1* sed-ac bro1 *Sep* kr1* staph gk stront-c bro1* **Sul-ac** b4a.de* **Sulph** kr1* sumb kr1* *Ter* kr1 tub bro1* *Ust* kr1* valer kr1* verat-v bro1 vesp bro1 vinc bro1* xan kr1 zinc-val bro1* [lac-mat sst4]
- **menses**:
  - **after** | **agg.**: med jl2
  - **before** | **agg.**: alum ferr bro1 glon bro1 iod k* kali-c hr1* *Lach* bro1* mang-p rly4• ph-ac b4a.de *Sang* bro1 sulph bro1
  - **during** | **agg.**: ferr bro1 glon bro1 *Lach* bro1 nat-m ptk1 nat-p ph-ac hr1* *Sang* bro1 sulph bro1
- **mental** exertion agg.: *Lach* kr1 olnd k* [lac-mat sst4]
- **motion** agg.: *Helon* k* nux-v a1 *Sep* hr1* spong fd4.de streptoc rly4•
- **nausea**; with: hydrog srj2• *Merc* hr1* *Nux-v* hr1* sang hr1*
- **palpitations**; with: aml-ns bg2 ant-c bro1 arg-n a *Calc* hr1* calc-ar a calc-f mrr1 coloc a glon a iod hr1* **Kali-c** k* lach gt1* mosch bg2 petr bro1 puls bg2 sep gt1* sul-ac bg2 sul-i k2 valer bg2
- **perspiration**:
  - **anxiety**; and: ang kali-bi
  - **with**: acet-ac am-m k* ant-c aran-ix mg1.de* aur bell camph k2* *Carb-v* caust sne *Chin* st cimic hr1 cob hr1* **CON** ●* *Fl-ac* vh *Hep* hipp st hydrog srj2• *Ign* hr1* ignis-alc es2• ipom-p kr1 jab sf1.de kali-bi k* *Kali-i* hr1* kres jl **Lach** k ● lyss hr1* nat-m ser nux-v sf1.de op *Ox-ac* hr1* petr h2* plut-n srj7• psil ft1 **PSOR** ●* ros-d wla1 **Sep** k ●* spig hr1 spong fd4.de **Sul-ac** k1* **Sulph** k ● *Ter* hr1* **TUB** k ●* valer sf1.de *Xan* [heroin sdj2 tax jsj7]
    - **night**: sep mrr1
      - **0-1 h**: *Fl-ac* vh
    - **Face** and hands: calc h2
  - **without**: **Lach** st [tax jsj7]
- **pregnancy** agg.; during: glon sf1.de *Sulph* hr1* *Verat* hr1*
- **rest** agg.: ferr mrr1
- **restlessness**; with (See MIND - Restlessness - heat - during - flushes)
- **room** agg.: helon a1 [heroin sdj2]
- **running** agg.: sul-i k2
- **sadness**; with (See MIND - Sadness - heat - flushes - during)
- **sexual** excesses; after: *Dig* hr1*
- **sitting** agg.: sep h2
- **sleep**:
  - **before**: *Carb-v* hr1*
- **sleep**: ...
  - **during** | **agg.**: alum-sil k2 carb-an k2 cham kali-p k2 nat-m *Phos* k* ran-b a1 sil zinc
  - **preventing** sleep: *Psor* kr1* *Puls* kr1* spong fd4.de
- **stool**; after | **amel.**: agar a1
- **tired**; when: helo-s rwt2• helon ptk1
- **trembling**; with: sep ptk1 sul-ac br1*
- **vomiting**; after: tab a1
- **walking**:
  - **air**; in open | **after** | **agg.**: petr hr1
    - **agg.**: caust hydrog srj2• tarax a1
  - **amel.**: fago a1
- **warm** | **air**:
  - **as** from warm air: acon bg2 *Alum* bg2 aster bg2 bry bg2 calc bg2 ol-an bg2 puls bg2 verat bg2
    - **hot** air blowing on parts: hyos bg2 ol-an bg2
  - **room** agg.: trios rsj11•
- **warm** water; as if:
  - **dashed** over one: (↗*Water - dashing*) **Ars** b4a.de* bry bg2 calc cann-s k* nat-m k* ph-ac bg2 phos k* *Puls* k* *Rhus-t* k* sep k*
    - **idea** occurs vividly; when: *Phos*
  - **poured** over one; were: **Ars** k* bry ph-ac phos **Psor** k* *Puls* k* *Rhus-t* k* **Sep** k*
- **weakness**; with: *Phos* kr1 sep br1 symph fd3.de•
  - **after** flushes of heat: dig c1 **Sep** kr1* **Sulph** kr1 *Xan* st
- **wine** agg.: carb-v k2 flav jl2 [tax jsj7]
- ▽ **extending** to:
  - **Downward**: (↗*HEAD - Heat - flushes - extending - stomach*) aesc kr1* chir-fl gya2 glon hydrog srj2• sang xan kr1
    - **Down back**: *Nat-c* kr1* *Sumb* kr1*
    - **Face** to body: cench k2
  - **Upward**: alum alum-sil k2 alumn ars ars-h kr1 asaf bamb-a stb2.de• *Calc* calc-sil k2 carb-an carb-v chin cinnb *Ferr* ferr-ar fic-m gya1 **Glon** k* *Graph* hydrog srj2• indg iris kali-bi *Kali-c* lac-h htj1• lach k2* laur *Lyc* mag-m mang naja k2 nat-s nit-ac ox-ac k2 *Phos* plb *Psor* **Sep** k* *Spong* *Sulph* *Sumb* tarent *Valer*
    - **Back**; from: *Sumb* kr1*
    - **Hips**; from the: alumn

- **intolerance** of heat (See Warm - agg.)
- **lack** of vital heat: (↗*Cold - feeling; Coldness; CHILL - Chilliness*) acetan br1 *Acon* bg2* adam srj5• *Aesc* *Aeth* bro1 *Agar* k* agn bg2 aids nl2• allox jl* *Alum* k* *Alum-p* k2 **Alumn** k1 am-br sf1.de *Am-c* k* am-m bg2* am-n a1 ambr br1 anac bg2* *Androc* srj1• ang j5.de* anh mg1.de* *Ant-c* k* ant-t bg2* *Anth* br1* *Apis* mrr1 apoc mrr1 aral bg2 **Aran** k* aran-ix mg1.de* *Arg-met* *Arg-n* arist-cl mg1.de* **Arn** ptk1 *Ars* k* ars-h kr1* *Ars-i* ars-s-f k2 *Asar* k* atha bro1 *Aur* k* *Aur-m-n* wbt2* aur-s k2* *Bamb-a* stb2.de* **Bar-c** k* *Bar-m* k* bar-s k2 bell ptk1 *Bit-ar* wht1• *Bor-ac* br1* borx bov bg2 *Brom* *Bry* b7a.de* bufo bg2* buth-a mg1.de* cact cadm-s k* calad bg2 **Calc** k* **Calc-ar** k* *Calc-f* **Calc-p** k* *Calc-s* calc-sil k2* calen st **Camph** k* camph-mbr bro1 cann-xyz bg2 *Caps* k* **Carb-an** k* *Carb-v* k* carbn-dox knl3* carbn-o br1 *Carbn-s* k* cartl-s rly4• *Caul* k* **Caust** k* cham bg2 *Chel* k* *Chin* k* chlor kr1 chloram jl chlorpr jl choc srj3* *Chol* bro1 chord-umb rly4• cic bg2* *Cimic* *Cinnb* **Cist** k* cob-n mg1.de coc-c k2 *Cocc* k* *Colch* br1* coli rly4• *Con* k* cory br1 croc bg2 **Crot-c** cupr bro1 cupr-act kr1 cycl k* cystein-l rly4• cyt-l mg1.de* dicha mg1.de* *Dig* k* *Dros* b7a.de **Dulc** k* *Elaps* k* erech br1 esp-g mg1.de* eucal kr1 eucol br1 *Eup-per* ptk1 euph h2* euphr bg2* **Ferr** k* *Ferr-ar* k* ferr-p k2 fum rly4• galla-q-r nl2• gamb mrr1 *Gels* ptk1 ger-i rly4• germ-met srj5• gink-b sbd1• glycyr-g cte1• **Graph** k* *Guaj* haliae-lc srj5• hed jl hell mrr1 **Helo** k* helo-s c2* **Hep** k* hippoc-k szs2 hir jl hydr-ac j5.de* *Hydrog* srj2• *Hyos* mtf33 hyper bg2 ign bg2* ina-i mlk9.de *Ip* k* *Jatr-c* bro1 **Kali-ar** k* **Kali-bi** k* kali-br kr1* **Kali-c** k* kali-chl br1 kali-cy br1 kali-m br1 kali-n bg2* **Kali-p** k* kali-perm br1 kali-sil br1 *Kalm* k* *Kreos* k* lac-ac *Lac-c* mrr1 *Lac-d* lac-h htj1• *Lach* k* lachn bro1 lat-m jl* *Laur* b7a.de* lavand-a ctl1• **Led** k* limest-b es1• lina br1 luf-op bro1 luna kg1• *Lyc* k* lycps-v kr1 *Mag-c* mag-m k* **Mag-p** k* mag-s k1* malar jl2 *Mang* marb-w es1• *Med* meli br1 meny bg2 *Merc* k* *Merc-c* bg2 merc-cy br1 *Mez* k* *Moni* rfm1• *Mosch* k* mur-ac bg2 musca-d szs1 *Naja* k* *Nat-ar* k* nat-c k* *Nat-m* k* *Nat-p* **Nat-s** bg2 *Nat-sil* k2 neon srj5• nep mg1.de **Nit-ac** k* *Nux-m* k* **Nux-v** k* *Ol-j* olib-sac wmh1 **Olnd** bg2 op bg2* orot-ac rly4• ox-ac k2 par bg2 penic jl* perh jl *Petr* k* **Ph-ac** k* phasco-ci rbp2 **Phos** k* pieri-b mlk9.de

- **lack** of vital heat: ...
plac-s rly4• *Plat* bg2 *Plb* k* positr nl2• **Psor** k* *Puls* bg2* **Pyrog** k* *Ran-b* k* *Rhod* k* **Rhus-t** k* ribo rly4• *Rumx* *Sabad* k* **Sabin** bg2 sal-fr sle1• sanic mrr1* sapin c2 sarcol-ac jl saroth mg1.de* sars sec br1* *Senec* *Sep* k* **Sil** k* sinus rly4• *Spig* k* spong fd4.de **Squil** bg2 *Stann* *Staph* stram bg2 *Stront-c* k* suis-em rly4• suis-pan rly4• *Sul-ac* k* *Sulph* k* *Sumb* symph ptk1 *Tab* br1* **Tarax** bg2 *Tarent* k* **Teucr** b7a.de* thal jl *Ther* *Thuj* k* thyr br1 *Tub* tub-sp zs ulm-c jsj8• urol-h rwt• v-a-b jl* vac br1 valer bg2 ven-m rsj12• verat c1* *Viol-t* bg2 vip-a jl x-ray sp1 zinc k* zinc-p k2 [*Buteo-j* sej6 heroin sdj2 spect dfg1 vip bcj1]
  - **morning** | **early**: mur-ac ptk1
  - **afternoon**: aids nl2•
    - **siesta**; after: con h2 mucs-nas rly4•
  - **night**: meny ptk1 phos ptk1
  - **accompanied** by:
    - **air**; desire for open (See Air; open - desire - accompanied - coldness)
    - **diarrhea** (See RECTUM - Diarrhea - accompanied - heat)
    - **hemorrhage** (See Hemorrhage - accompanied - coldness)
    - **illness**; recurrent acute (See Complaints - acute - recurrent - accompanied - heat)
    - **numbness** (See Numbness - accompanied - coldness)
    - **paralysis** (See Paralysis - accompanied - body)
    - **phthisis** pulmonalis (See CHEST - Phthisis - accompanied - coldness)
    - **respiration** | **complaints** of: *Ars* bg2
    - **sciatica**: agar bro1 ars bro1 *Meny* bro1 mez bro1 nat-m bro1 nux-v bro1 plat bro1 puls bro1 *Rhus-t* bro1 sep bro1 spig bro1 verat bro1
    - **Face** and heat of head; with redness of (See HEAD - Heat - accompanied - face - redness - coldness)
    - **Skin**; hot: verat-v ptk1
  - **alternating** with:
    - **heat**; sensation of (See sensation - alternating)
    - **Face**; heat of (See FACE - Heat - alternating - chilliness)
  - **bed**; lying in: lavand-a ctl1•
  - **cough** agg.; during: lyc ptk1
  - **covered**; but aversion of being: **Camph** br1* **Carb-v** mrr1 cor-r br1 sanic mtf33 *Sec* mrr1
    - **Abdomen** uncovered; wants: *Tab* br1
  - **covers** | **agg.**: *Apis* ptk1 calc-s ptk1 cann-xyz ptk1 *Ip* ptk1 led ptk1 *Puls* ptk1 sec ptk1 sep ptk1
  - **exertion** agg.: plb k* *Sil* k* zinc-val ptk1
  - **fanned**; wants to be: *Carb-v* ptk1
  - **frozen**; as if (See Cold - feeling - frozen)
  - **menopause**; during: *Chin* st
  - **menses**:
    - **during**:
      - **agg.**: *Cham* b7a.de *Coff* b7a.de led ptk1 sil ptk1
      - **beginning** of menses | **agg.**: jab ptk1
    - **suppressed** menses; from: puls b7a.de
  - **nausea**; with: arist-cl sp1
  - **old** people; in: alum br1 ambr br1
  - **operation**; from: stront-c br1
  - **pain**; during: agar ptk1 alum-sil br1* ars ptk1 caust ptk1 dulc ptk1 led ptk1 mosch ptk1 sil ptk1
  - **rising** from stooping agg.: merc-c ptk1
  - **sleep**; during: ambr b7a.de
  - **terminal** patients; in: ant-t mrr1
  - **walking** agg.; after: gins
  - **warm** covering does not amel.: *Asar* bit-ar wht1• haliae-lc srj5• laur k2* luna kg1•
  - **warmth** agg.; and: (↗*Warm - agg.)* *Agar* st **Alum** st ant-c st **Apis** st* *Arg-n* st *Ars-i* st aur st *Bar-c* st* borx st **Bry** st *Calc-sil* br1 **Camph** st **Carb-an** st carb-v st* **Carbn-s** st caust bg2* cimic bg2 cocc st dig st *Dros* st *Dulc* st ferr mrr1 **Graph** st guaj st *Ip* st *Kali-s* st lach st laur st **LED** st* **Lyc** st

- **lack** of vital heat – **warmth** agg.; and: ...
Merc st **Mez** st moni rfm1• nat-c st *Nat-m* st *Nat-s* st *Ph-ac* st *Phos* st **PULS** br1* sabad st spig st staph st *Sulph* st* *Thuj* st zinc st
    - **terminal** patients; in: ant-t mrr1
- **menses**; before: tub-sp jl2
- **sensation** of: (↗*affected)* acet-ac k2* achy jl3 **Acon** bg adam srj5• agar k* agn k* aids nl2• allox sp1 aloe k2* *Alum* k* *Alumn* hr1* am-c k* am-m bg ambr h1 anac bg androc srj1• ang bg* anh mg1.de* *Ant-c* mrr1 ant-t k* **Apis** k* ara-maca sej7• aran-ix mg1.de *Arg-n* k* arge-pl rwt5• arn bg ars k* ars-i k* ars-s-f k2 asaf k* *Asar* b2.de* *Aur* *Aur-i* *Aur-m* *Bar-c* bell br1* bell-p sp1 bism bg borra-o oss1• bov k* brass-n-o srj5• *Brom* bg bry k* **Calad** bg *Calc* k* *Calc-f* mrr1 *Calc-i* **Calc-s** *Camph* k* **Cann-s** k* canth k* caps k* carb-v bg carc dgt* cartl-s rly4• caust k* *Cham* bg* chel k* chin k* chlam-tr bcx2• choc srj3• cic h1* cina k* cit-ac rly4• clem bg* cob ptm1• cob-n sp1 **Coc-c** cocc k* **Coff** k* colch k* coloc bg com **Con** bg conch fkr1* *Croc* k* *Cupr* bg cycl k* cyt-l jl3 dig bg *Dros* dulc h1* ephe-si hsj1• euph k* *Ferr-i* mrr1 **Fl-ac** k* flor-p mg1.de* franc br1 galeoc-c-h gms1• galla-q-r nl2• ger-i rly4• gink-b sbd1• graph k* guaj bg haliae-lc srj5• hed mg1.de hell k* helo-s rwt2• hep bg hip-ac sp1 hist mg1.de* *Hydrog* srj2*• *Hyos* bg* hypoth jl3 ign k* ina-i mlk9.de **Iod** k* *Ip* k* jab br1 kali-ar dgt kali-c k* *Kali-i* k* kali-n k* kali-p fd1.de* **Kali-s** k* kreos k* lac-ac stj2*• lac-h htj1*• lac-leo hrn2• *Lach* k* lap-la sde8.de• *Laur* k* *Led* bg **Lil-t** limen-b-c hrn2* loxo-recl knl4• luna kg1• **Lyc** k* lyss mg1.de m-arct b2.de m-aust b2.de mag-c k* *Mag-m* k* manc mrr1 mand sp1 *Mang* k* meli br1 *Meny* bg meph bg2* *Merc* k* merc-c bg *Mez* bg *Mosch* bg mur-ac h2* nat-c k* **Nat-m** k* nat-ox rly4• **Nat-s** k* neon srj5• *Nit-ac* h2 *Nux-m* k* *Nux-v* k* oci-sa sp1* *Olib-sac* wmh1 olnd bg *Op* mrr1 oxal-a rly4• ozone sde2• pant-ac rly4• par bg petr h2* petr-ra shn4• ph-ac k* *Phos* k* *Plat* k* *Plb* bg *Plut-n* srj7• podo mrr1 positr nl2• psil ft1 *Psor* *Ptel* **Puls** k* rad-br mrr1 ran-b k* ran-s bg rauw sp1 rheum k* rhod k* rhus-t k* ribo rly4• ruta fd4.de *Sabad* k* *Sabin* k* samb k* sars k* **Sec** k* *Seneg* k* **Sil** bg3 sinus rly4• spig bg *Spong* squil bg **Stann** bg staph k* stram bg suis-em rly4• **Sul-ac** k* **Sul-i** **Sulph** k* suprar rly4• tab bg2* tarax bg teucr k* thioc-ac rly4• thuj k* *Tub* k* urol-h rwt• valer k* vanil fd5.de *Verat* k* vero-o rly4*• viol-t bg vip fkr4.de *Zinc* k* [bell-p-sp dcm1 beryl stj2 buteo-j sej6 *Fl-pur* stj2 heroin sdj2 spect dfg1]
  - **one** side warm, the other cold (See Cold - feeling - one)
  - **right** side: aids nl2•
    - **left** side cool: aids nl2•
  - **left** side: galla-q-r nl2•
  - **daytime**: bamb-a stb2.de• petr-ra shn4•
  - **evening** | **bed** agg.; in: *Bry* fl-ac k2*
  - **night**: acon-ac rly4• aq-mar rbp6 bamb-a stb2.de• bar-c h2 bros-gau mrc1 cench k2 cham choc srj3• colch rsj2• con h2 dulc fd4.de fl-ac k2* kali-p fd1.de• mag-c cp nat-m nat-sil fd3.de• neon srj5• olib-sac wmh1 phasco-ci rbp2 *Phos* plut-n srj7• podo fd3.de• puls h1* rhus-t h1 ruta fd4.de samb bat1• sil spong fd4.de **Sulph** sne thioc-ac rly4• zinc
    - **midnight**:
      - **before**:
        - **waking** | **amel.**: calad hr1
    - **coryza**; during: lyc b4.de*
    - **first** sleep; on: adam srj5•
    - **waking**; on: hydrog srj2•
      - **amel.**: calad hr1
  - **accompanied** by:
    - **coryza**: acon bg2 ars bg2 hep bg2 lach b7a.de* **Merc** bg2 nat-c bg2 *Nux-v* bg2 sabad bg2 *Spig* b7.de*
    - **stool**; complaints of: cupr bg2 valer bg2
    - **Abdomen**:
      - **complaints** of (See ABDOMEN - Complaints - accompanied - heat)
      - **pain** in (See ABDOMEN - Pain - accompanied - heat)
  - **alternating** with sensation of coldness: arizon-l nl2• hist jl3 olib-sac wmh1 ozone sde2• solid br1 [heroin sdj2]
  - **anxious** | **pollutions**; after: petr b4.de*
  - **ascending** agg.: cob-n sp1 fic-m gya1
  - **atmosphere** seems hot: aster bg2 bry bg2 puls bg2 verat bg2
  - **beer**; after: bell st
  - **cough** agg.; during: bry tl1 irid-met srj5• sep h2 squil h1

- **currents**; sensation of hot: arg-n bg2 dulc bg2 m-ambo b2.de* *Sumb* bg2
- **eating** | **after** | **agg.**: calc b4a.de con b4a.de cycl k2* mag-c b4a.de nit-ac b4a.de par b7a.de petr b4a.de phos b4a.de sep b4a.de spig b7a.de viol-t b7a.de
  - **while** | **agg.**: spig b7a.de valer b7a.de
- **exertion** agg.: alum choc srj3• squil vanil fd5.de
- **external**: agath-a nl2•
- **fever**:
  - **sensation** as from: limen-b-c hrn2•
  - **without**: cham ptk1 graph ptk1 ign ptk1 lach ptk1
- **hand** has lain, where: hyos h1
- **layer** around body: bit-ar wht1•
- **menses** | **before** | **agg.**: am-c b4.de bamb-a stb2.de•
  - **during** | **agg.**: hyos b7a.de lyc b4.de mag-m b4.de nux-v b7.de sep b4a.de
- **motion**, at least: squil h1
- **nausea**; with: chel st1 fl-ac hr1 kali-s fd4.de
- **perspiration**; during: *Cham* b7.de mag-c cp **Op** b7.de *Stram* b7.de
- **rest** agg.: achy jl3
- **restlessness**; with (See MIND - Restlessness - heat - sensation - during)
- **stool**:
  - **during** | **agg.**: puls b7a.de
- **talking** agg.: squil h1
- **urination**; during | **night**: visc c1
- **waking**; on: bamb-a stb2.de• **Bar-c** carc fd2.de• choc srj3• fl-ac *Graph* hydrog srj2• ina-i mlk9.de limen-b-c hrn2* nat-m *Sil* zinc [bell-p-sp dcm1]
- **walking** agg.: samb h1
- **warm** | **drinks** | **agg.**: mag-c k2
  - **food** | **after**: *Carb-v Ferr Kali-c* lach *Mag-c* **Phos** podo fd3.de• **Puls** sep *Sul-ac*
- **weather**; even in cold: lavand-a ctl1• luna kg1•

○ - **Blood** vessels: agar am-m k2 **Ars** *Aur* aur-ar k2 benz-ac st *Bry Calc Hyos* med k* nat-m nit-ac op **Rhus-t** sec ptk1 *Sulph* syph k2* *Verat*
  - **Veins**: xan c1
- **Glands**: cocc b7.de
- **Internally**: limen-b-c hrn2•
  - **accompanied** by | **External** coldness: galla-q-r nl2•
- **Nerves**, along: acon k2
- **Single** parts, in: pime a1 spirae br1
- **Upper** part of body: *Syzyg* br1
  - **accompanied** by | **coldness** of lower half of body: arn mrr1

- **waves**; in: agath-a nl2•

○ - **Affected** parts: (↗*sensation)* colch br1
- **right** side: op a1
- **left** side: bell a1 lac-ac a1 rhus-t a1 ulm-c jsj8•
- **intense** heat as if scalding examiner's hand: **Bell** mrr1

HEAT STROKE (See HEAD - Sunstroke)

HEATED, BECOMING: acon k* am-c k* **Ant-c** k* ant-t vh *Arg-n* arge-pl rwt5• *Arn* atp rly4• *Bell* k* *Brom* k* **Bry** k* calc bg2* calc-s calc-sil k2 *Camph* k* caps k* carb-an b4a.de* *Carb-v* k* cham bg2 coff k* *Cycl Dig* k* dros dulc k2 *Ferr* fic-m gya1 fl-ac bg2 gels k2 *Glon* k* *Graph* mg1.de* hep k* ign k* **Iod** *Ip* k* kali-ar k2 **Kali-c** k* *Kali-n* bg2 **Kali-s** lac-lup hrn2• lach bg2 lyc bg2* merc mez k* *Nat-m* k* *Nit-ac* b4.de* nux-m k* nux-v k* olnd k* *Op* k* *Phos* k* **Puls** *Ran-b Sep* k* **Sil** k* staph k* *Thuj* k* trios rsj11• tung-met bdx1• *Zinc* k*

- **old** drunkards: *Bar-c*

HEAVINESS: (↗*Weakness; Weariness; MIND - Dullness)* aesc ptk1 alet ptk1 aloe ptk1 alum ptk1 apis ptk1 arg-n ptk1 ars-i ptk1 bell ptk1 bism ptk1 bit-ar wht1• *Bry* ptk1 *Calc* ptk1 cartl-s rly4• chel ptk1 chlam-tr bcx2• chord-umb rly4• cob-n sp1 *Con* ptk1 cortico tpw7 ephe-si hsj1• fum rly1*• galeoc-c-h gms1• **Gels** ptk1 ger-i rly4• haliae-lc srj5• helon ptk1 hippoc-k szs2 ip ptk1 ketogl-ac rly4• lac-leo sk4• lac-lup hrn2• lach ptk1 lap-la rsp1 lappa ptk1 lil-t ptk1 lith-c ptk1 lyc ptk1 meny ptk1 *Nat-m* ptk1 **Nux-v** ptk1 par ptk1 petr ptk1

Heaviness: ...
ph-ac ptk1 **Phos** ptk1 pic-ac ptk1 pieri-b mlk9.de *Positr* nl2• **Puls** ptk1 pyrid rly4• ran-b ptk1 rhus-g tmo3• *Rhus-t* ptk1 ruta fd4.de scop ptk1 **Sep** ptk1 sil ptk1 spig ptk1 *Spong* ptk1 *Stann* ptk1 stict ptk1 **Sulph** ptk1 thuj mlk1 tritic-vg fd5.de vanil fd5.de [heroin sdj2]

- **morning**: lac-h sze9•
  - **waking**; on: hydroph rsj6• plut-n srj7• [tax jsj7]
- **afternoon**: [heroin sdj2]
- **night**: hell-o a1
- **exertion** agg.; after | **slight** exertion: *Spong* br1
- **menses** | **after** | **agg.**: bufo bg2 graph bg2
  - **during** | **agg.**: graph bg2
- **rising** agg.: spig ptk1
- **sleepiness**; with: bit-ar wht1•
- **stool** agg.; after: agar bg2

○ - **Blood** vessels: merc bg2
- **Bones**, of: ham fd3.de• sulph ptk1
- **Externally**: (↗*MIND - Dullness; MIND - Prostration)* acon k* adam srj5• **Aesc** agar k* *Agath-a* nl2• agn k* aloe *Alum* k* alum-p k2* alum-sil k2* am-c k* ambr k* ammc j5.de anac k* androc srj1• ang b2.de* ant-c k* ant-t k* apis bg3 arg-n bg2* arn k* *Ars* k* *Ars-i* asaf k* asar k* aur k* aur-ar k2 *Bar-c* k* bar-m bar-s k2 **Bell** k* berb j5.de borx k* bov k* **Bry** k* cact calc k* camph k* cann-i cann-s k* canth k* caps k* carb-ac carb-an j5.de *Carb-v* k* *Carbn-s* caust k* cham k* chel k* *Chin* k* cic k* cimic bg2 cina j5.de clem k* cocc k* coff k* colch k* coloc k* **Con** k* croc k* crot-h crot-t cupr k* cur dig k* dulc k* euph k* euphr k* *Ferr* k* ferr-ar k2 **Gels** k* ger-i rly4• germ-met srj5• graph k* grat j5.de haliae-lc srj5• hell k* hep k* hippoc-k szs2 ign k* iod k* *Ip* k* irid-met srj5• kali-c k* kali-m k2 kali-n k* kali-s *Kreos* k* lac-loxod-a hrn2• lach j5.de lap-la sde8.de• laur k* *Led* k* lyc k* m-ambo b2.de m-arct b2.de* m-aust b2.de* mag-c k* mag-m k* marb-w es1• *Meli* meny k* *Merc* k* *Mez* k* *Mosch* k* mur-ac k* musca-d szs1 *Nat-c* k* *Nat-m* k* nat-sil k2 neon srj5• nit-ac k* nux-m k* **Nux-v** k* ol-an j5.de olib-sac wmh1 *Onos* op k* par k* *Petr* k* ph-ac k* **Phos** k* pic-ac k* plat k* plb k* positr nl2• *Psor* k* **Puls** k* ran-b k* rheum k* *Rhod* k* **Rhus-t** k* *Ruta* k* *Sabad* k* sabin k* samb k* sanguis-s hrn2• sars k* sec k* **Sep** k* *Sil* k* **Spig** k* *Spong* k* squil k* **Stann** k* *Staph* k* stram k* stront-c k* sul-ac k* sul-i k2 **Sulph** k* teucr b2.de* ther j5.de *Thuj* k* valer k* *Verat* k* verb k* viol-o k* *Zinc* k* *Zinc-p* k2
  - **thinking** of it | **amel.**: marb-w es1•
- **Glands**: *Bell* b2.de* chin b2.de* cupr b2.de* lyc bg2 m-arct b2.de merc b2.de* nux-v b2.de* *Phos* b2.de* puls b2.de* rhus-t b2.de* sil b2.de* stann b2.de* staph b2.de* sulph b2.de*
- **Internally**: **Acon** k* adam srj5• *Agar* k* *Agath-a* nl2• agn k* ail a1 *Alet* vh1 **Aloe** k* alum k* alum-p k2 alum-sil k2 *Am-c* k* *Am-m* k* ambr k* anac k* androc srj1• ang b2.de* ant-t k* apoc-a a1 aran vh1 arg-n k* arn k* ars k* ars-s-f k2 arund a1 asaf k* asar k* aster sze10• atro a1 aur k* aur-ar k2 bamb-a stb2.de• *Bar-c* k* bar-m k* bar-s k2 *Bell* k* **Bism** k* *Borx* k* *Bov* k* brach a1* *Bry* k* calad k* **Calc** k* calc-sil k2* camph k* *Cann-i* cann-s k* canth k* carb-ac k* *Carb-an* k* *Carb-v* k* carbn-s caust k* cham k* **Chel** k* chen-v hr1 *Chin* k* choc srj3• chr-ac a1 cic k* cich a1 cinnb a1 cinnm a1 clem k* coc-c a1 *Cocc* k* cod a1 coff k* colch k* *Coloc Con* k* *Croc* k* *Cupr* k* cycl a1 cypra-eg sde6.de• *Dig* k* dor a1* dros k* dulc k* euph a1 euphr k* ferr k* ferr-ar k2 ferr-ma a1 **Gels** gins a1 glon a1 *Graph* k* *Hell* k* helo-s rwt2• helon hr1 hep k* hydrc a1 hydrog srj2• hyos k* hyosin a1 hyper a1 ign k* iod k* ip k* *Iris* kali-bi bg2* *Kali-c* k* kali-chl k13 kali-m k2 kali-n k* kreos k* lac-loxod-a hrn2• *Lach* k* lap-la sde8.de• *Laur* k* *Led* k* lepi a1 *Lob Lyc* k* m-arct b2.de m-aust b2.de *Mag-c* k* *Mag-m* k* manc a1 mang k* melal-alt gya4 *Meny* k* *Merc* k* *Merc-i-f* hr1 mez k* morph a1 mosch k* *Mur-ac* k* musca-d szs1 nabal a1 nat-c k* **Nat-m** k* nat-p hr1* nat-sal a1 nat-sil k2 nauf-helv-li elm2• nit-ac k* *Nux-m* k* **Nux-v** k* ol-an a1 *Olnd* k* *Onos Op* k* ozone sde2• par k* **Petr** k* ph-ac k* **Phos** k* pic-ac br1 plat k* *Plb* k* *Plut-n* srj7• positr nl2• *Prun* psor bg2* **Puls** k* ran-b k* ran-s k* raph a1 rheum k* rhod k* **Rhus-t** k* ruta k* *Sabad* k* *Sabin* k* salin a1 samb k* *Sang* k* sars k* sec k* sel k* *Senec Seneg* k* **Sep** k* **Sil** k* *Spig* k* spirae a1 spong k* squil k* **Stann** k* *Staph* k* stram k* stront-c k* sul-ac k* sul-i k2 **Sulph** k* tarax k* ter hr1 thuj k* til a1 trif-p a1 tung-met bdx1• valer k* verat k* verb k* viol-o k* viol-t k* zinc k* *Zinc-p* k2 zinc-s a1 [spect dfg1]
  - **morning**: agar bg kali-c h2 lyc h2 nat-c h2 nat-sil fd3.de• zinc h2
  - **night**: mag-c h2
  - **accompanied** by | **bruised** feeling (See Pain - sore - accompanied - heaviness)
  - **alternating** with | **lightness**: musca-d szs1 nux-v ptk1

- **Internally**: ...
  - **load**; like a: ozone sde2•
  - **menses**; during: kali-c h2
  - **sleep** agg.; after: rheum h
  - **storm**, before and during: sil h2
  - **waking**; on: galeoc-c-h gms1• ozone sde2•
  - **walking** in open air agg.: dulc fd4.de nit-ac h2
- **Muscles**, of: bapt ptk1 mand mg1.de*
- **Single** parts; in: *Aran* br1 cur ptk1 nit-ac ptk1 rhod ptk1 ruta ptk1

HEMATOMA: *(↗SKIN - Ecchymoses)* calc-f ptk1 merc ptk1 sil ptk1 x-ray mtf11

HEMIPLEGIA (See Paralysis - one - apoplexy)

HEMOPHILIA (See Hemorrhage - blood - non-coagulable)

HEMORRHAGE: *(↗Thrombocytopenia)* abies-n c1* acal bro1 acet-ac k* *Acon* k* *Adren* br1* *Agar* b2.de* alet k2 aln c1* aloe *Alum* k* alumn c1* am-c k* am-caust br1* am-m k* ambr k* *Ammc* hr1* anac b2.de* ancis-p tsm2 *Ant-c* k* ant-t b2.de* anthraci br1* *Apis* apoc k2* *Aran* k* arg-met b2.de* *Arg-n* **Arn** k* *Ars* k* ars-h bro1 ars-i arum-t sf1.de asaf b7a.de* asar b2.de* aur c1* aur-m c1* bapt sf1.de *Bar-c* k* bar-i k2* bar-m **Bell** k* bell-p sf1.de* bism b2.de* bit-ar wht1• blum-o mtf11 borx b2.de* **Both** k* both-a rb3 both-ax tsm2 *Bov* k* brom sf1.de *Bry* k* bufo kr1 *Cact* k* **Calc** k* calc-f sf1.de calc-i k2 *Calc-ln* c1 **Calc-s** k* calc-sil k2* cann-s b2.de* **Canth** k* *Caps* k* carb-an k* **Carb-v** k* *Carbn-s* carc gk6* card-m hr1* casc hr1* caust b2.de* cench tsm2 *Cham* k* **Chin** k* chinin-ar chinin-s j5.de* cina b2.de* cinnb *Cinnm* k* cit-l c1* clem b2.de* cloth tsm2 cob c1* coc-c c1* cocc b2.de* *Coff* k* coff-t st1 colch b2.de* coll hr1* *Coloc* k* con b2.de* cop hr1 *Croc* k* crot-c st1* **Crot-h** k* *Cupr* k* des-ac jl3 dig k* dor sf1.de* *Dros* k* *Dulc* k* *Elaps* k* emetin mp4• equis-h mg1.de erech c1* ergot c1* **Erig** k* erod c1* eucal br1 euphr b2.de* eupi c1* **Ferr** k* *Ferr-ar* *Ferr-i* *Ferr-m* hr1* *Ferr-p* k* ferr-s c1* fic-r c1* fic-v br1 gal-ac c1* gelin bro1 gels hr1 *Ger* c1* glon mg1.de *Graph* k* **Ham** k* **Hell** hr1* hep b2.de* hir c1* hydr bg* *Hydrin-s* bro1 *Hyos* k* ign b2.de* *Iod* k* **Ip** k* jug-c sf1.de juni-c c1* kali-c k* *Kali-chl* k* kali-i k* kali-m k2 kali-n k* *Kali-p* k* *Kreos* k* *Lac-c* hr1 **Lach** k* lachn hr1* lat-m mtf *Led* k* leon c1* lept bg* *Lyc* k* *Lycps-v* bg2* m-ambo b2.de* m-arct b2.de* m-aust b2.de* mag-c b2.de* mag-m b2.de* mang ptk1 **Meli** k* **Merc** k* **Merc-c** k* merc-cy c1* *Mez* k* **Mill** k* mit hr1 mosch k* mur-ac k* **Murx** hr1* nat-c k* **Nat-m** k* *Nat-n* sf1.de* *Nat-s* sf1.de* nat-sal br1 nat-sil bro1 **Nit-ac** k* nux-m k* **Nux-v** k* op b2.de* par b2.de* petr b2.de* *Ph-ac* k* **Phos** k* *Plat* k* plb b2.de* *Psor* k* **Puls** k* pyrog k2* rat j5.de* rhod k* rhus-a c1* rhus-g c1* *Rhus-t* k* ruta b2.de* sabad b2.de* **Sabin** k* sal-ac sf1.de sang k* *Sanguiso* bro1* sars k* scir c1* **Sec** k* sel b2.de* *Senec* k* **Sep** k* *Sil* k* solid bg* squil k* stann k* staph b2.de* stict hr1* *Stram* k* stront-c c1* **Sul-ac** k* sul-i k2 sulfa jl3 **Sulph** k* syph st1 tann-ac br1 tarax b2.de* *Ter* k* thlas c1* thuj k* til br1* tril-p k* urt-u hr1* ust br1* valer b2.de* vanil fd5.de verat b2.de* vib ptk1 vinc j5.de* vip j5.de* vip-a jl3 wies c1* x-ray jl* xan bro1 zinc b2.de* [am-p stj1 bar-p stj1]

- **morning**: *Acal* br1
- **accompanied** by:
  - **coldness**: *Chin* bro1 ferr bro1 phos bro1
  - **congestion**: erech br1
  - **coryza**: crot-h bg2 lach bg2
  - **cough** | **whooping** cough (See COUGH - Whooping - accompanied - hemorrhage)
  - **faintness** (See Faintness - hemorrhages)
  - **gasping**: ip ptk1
  - **myoma**; uterine (See FEMALE - Metrorrhagia - fibroids)
  - **nausea**: **Ip** c*
  - **ringing** in ears: chin tl1
  - **sight**; loss of: chin tl1
  - **twitches** (See Twitching - accompanied - hemorrhage)
  - **urination**:
    - **copious**: calc ptk1 gels ptk1 ign ptk1 lach ptk1 mosch ptk1 sars ptk1 stram ptk1 sulph ptk1 vib ptk1
    - **frequent**: vib ptk1
  - **vertigo**: *Tril-p* br1
  - **vomiting**: ip mrr1
  - **weakness**; severe: crot-h tl1 kreos mtf11
  - O **Ear**; noises in: *Chin* bro1 ferr bro1 phos bro1

Hemorrhage – **accompanied** by: ...

  - **Head**; complaints of (See HEAD - Hemorrhage - after)
  - **Heart**; complaints of the (See CHEST - Heart; complaints - accompanied - hemorrhage)
  - **Liver**; complaints of (See ABDOMEN - Liver - accompanied - hemorrhage)
  - **Skin**; yellow: crot-h tl1 phos br1
  - **Tongue** | **cancer** (See MOUTH - Cancer - tongue - accompanied - hemorrhage)
- **acute**: *Acon* ptk1 *Bell* ptk1 croc ptk1 ferr ptk1 hyos ptk1 mill ptk1 puls ptk1
- **agg.**: *Chin* ptk1 ferr ptk1 ip ptk1 nat-m ptk1 ph-ac ptk1 stict ptk1 sul-ac ptk1
- **amel.**: ars bg2* bov k* brom bg2 bufo bg2* calad ptk1 card-m bg2* coloc bg2 ferr ptk1 ferr-p bg2* *Ham* bg2* kali-n bg2 *Lach* bg2* mag-c bg2 meli bg2* pyrog k2 sars k* sel k* tarent bg2 thiop jl
- **atonic** (See passive)
- **beginning**; at the: ferr-p tl1
- **blood**: *(↗Blood)*
  - **acrid**: am-c j5.de ars j5.de bar-c j5.de bov j5.de canth j5.de carb-v j5.de graph j5.de hep j5.de *Kali-c* j5.de* *Kali-n* j5.de* rhus-t j5.de sars j5.de *Sil* j5.de* sul-ac j5.de* sulph j5.de* zinc j5.de
  - **black**: am-c j5.de* anthraci jl2 arn j5.de ars hr1* asar j5.de bapt k2* ben-n a1 both a1* canth j5.de carb-v j5.de* carc fd2.de• *Chin* j5.de *Croc* j5.de* crot-h bg2* elaps bg2* *Ferr* j5.de* fl-ac bg2 ham k2 kali-bi tl1 *Kali-chl* hr1 kali-n j5.de *Kali-p* hr1 kreos j5.de lach k2* led k2* *Mag-c* j5.de mag-m j5.de mag-s j5.de nat-c j5.de *Nat-m* j5.de* nat-s j5.de nit-ac j5.de ol-an j5.de op a1 *Puls* j5.de *Rhus-t* hr1 sec j5.de* stram j5.de **Sul-ac** hr1 sulph j5.de ust mtf11
  - **bright** red: abrot bg2* **Acon** bg2* am-c j5.de ant-t j5.de* *Arn* j5.de* *Ars* j5.de* bar-c j5.de *Bell* j5.de* borx j5.de bov j5.de bry j5.de calc j5.de* canth j5.de carb-an j5.de carb-v j5.de* chin j5.de cinnm sf1.de *Crot-h* sf1.de dig j5.de dros j5.de* *Dulc* j5.de* erech bro1* *Erig* bg2* *Ferr* j5.de* *Ferr-p* hr1* *Graph* j5.de* *Ham* hr1* *Hyos* j5.de* **Ip** j5.de* kali-n j5.de* *Kali-p* hr1* kreos j5.de laur j5.de led j5.de* *M-aust* j5.de mag-m j5.de meli bg2* **Mill** bg2* nat-c j5.de *Nat-m* hr1* nit-ac j5.de* nux-m j5.de ph-ac bro1* *Phos* j5.de* plb ptk1 *Puls* j5.de *Rhus-t* j5.de* sabad j5.de *Sabin* j5.de* *Sec* j5.de* *Sep* j5.de sil j5.de stram j5.de stront-c j5.de *Sulph* j5.de* *Tril-p* bg2* ust bro1* vanil fd5.de zinc j5.de [calc-p stj1 mag-p stj1 nat-p stj1]
    - **dark** clots; with: ferr ptk1 sabin ptk1 sang ptk1 ust ptk1
    - **frothy**: led ptk1
    - **gelatinous** clots; with: laur ptk1
  - **brownish**: ben-n a1 bry j5.de* calc j5.de *Carb-v* j5.de* *Con* j5.de* ferr k2* puls j5.de rhus-t j5.de sul-h a1
  - **charred** straw; like: lach mtf33
  - **clots**: am-m j5.de arn j5.de* ars k2* *Bell* j5.de* bry j5.de *Cact* br1 calc bg2 canth j5.de* carb-an j5.de caust j5.de cean br1 **Cham** j5.de* *Chin* j5.de* con j5.de *Croc* j5.de* *Ferr* j5.de* ferr-p hr1* *Hyos* j5.de* *Ign* j5.de* *Ip* j5.de* *Kali-chl* sf* *Kali-m* k2* kali-n j5.de *Kali-p* hr1* lac-c tl1 lach bg2* mag-m j5.de *Merc* j5.de* *Nat-m* a1* nat-s j5.de nit-ac j5.de* nux-v j5.de* ph-ac j5.de phos k2* **Plat** j5.de* *Puls* j5.de* **Rhus-t** j5.de* rhus-v j5.de *Sabin* j5.de* sec j5.de* sep j5.de *Stram* j5.de* stront-c j5.de sul-ac sf1.de sulph a1* *Thlas* kr1* zinc j5.de
    - **dark**: alum bro1 androc srj1• anthraci bro1 chin bro1 **Croc** hr1* crot-h bro1 *Elaps* bro1 kali-m k2 merc bro1 merc-cy bro1 mur-ac bro1 plat bro1 *Puls* hr1* *Sec* hr1* *Sul-ac* bro1 ter bro1 *Thlas* bro1 tril-p bro1
    - **fluid**; partly: ferr bg2 plat bg2
    - **liver**; looking like: sabin bg2
  - **clotting**:
    - **quickly**: cham bg2 chin bg2 croc bg2 ip ptk1 kali-m bg2 merc bg2 nit-ac bg2 puls bg2 rhus-t bg2 sul-ac bg2
    - **slowly**: calc bg2 carb-v bg2 crot-h bg2 elaps bg2 ham bg2 lach bg2 nat-m bg2 phos bg2 sec bg2 vip bg2
  - **dark**: acon j5.de* agar bg2* *Am-c* j5.de* *Ant-c* j5.de* anthraci st1 arn j5.de *Asar* j5.de* atra-r bnm3• bell j5.de* *Bism* j5.de both fne1* bov bg2* bry j5.de canth j5.de* *Carb-v* j5.de* carbn-h a1 carbn-o a1 card-m bg2* caust bg2* *Cham* j5.de* *Chin* j5.de* cocc j5.de con j5.de croc j5.de* crot-c mrr1 *Crot-h* bg2* cupr j5.de cycl bg2 dig j5.de dros j5.de *Elaps* ptk1* *Ferr* j5.de* graph j5.de *Ham* bg2* helon ptk1 ign hr1 kali-chl k13 kali-m k2 kali-n j5.de *Kreos* j5.de* *Lach* j5.de* led j5.de lyc j5.de* mag-c j5.de mang-i bro1 merc bg2* merc-cy br1 *Nat-m* hr1 nit-ac j5.de* *Nux-m* j5.de* **Nux-v** j5.de*

- **blood – dark**: ...
Ph-ac j5.de* phos j5.de plat j5.de Puls j5.de* Sec j5.de* sel j5.de Sep j5.de* Stram j5.de* sul-ac bg2* sulph j5.de* ter br1 Thlas kr1* ust bg2* verat bg2
    - ⁝ **thin**; and: am-c ptk1 carb-v bg2 crot-h bg2 ham bg2 lach bg2 nit-ac bg2 sec bg2 sul-ac bg2* ust ptk1
  - **decomposed**: acet-ac bro1 am-c bro1 anthraci bro1* cic j5.de Crot-h j5.de* Lach j5.de* puls bg sec bg ter bro1 Vip j5.de
  - **frothy**: led ptk1
  - **hot**: acon bg2* anac a1 Bell bg2* dulc bg2 sabin bg2*
  - **non**-coagulable (= hemophilia): Adren bro1* ail bro1 am-c ancis-p tsm2 anthraci Apis aran kr1 Arn bg2* ars k* **Both** k1* both-ax tsm2 bov bro1* calc br1* calc-lac bro1* calc-p sf1.de carb-an sf1.de* Carb-v carc mlr1• cench tsm2 chin k* chlol chloram jl cloth tsm2 cortico sp1 croc sf1.de **Crot-c** Crot-h k* dig dor Elaps Erig k1 **Ferr** kr1* ferr-m sf1.de gal-ac br1 Ham bg2* **Hir** st* ip sf1.de* Kali-p kreos bro1* lac-c tl1 **Lach** k* **Lat-m** k1* led sf1.de merc bro1* mill bro1* nat-m nat-n sf1.de Nat-s bg2* Nat-sil bro1* **Nit-ac** op a1 ph-ac sf1.de* **Phos** k* puls sf1.de rad-br st Sec k* sil sf1.de* staphytox jl2 stront-c k2* Sul-ac sulph a1* ter kr1* vip a1 visc ptk1 x-ray st
  - **offensive**: ars j5.de* bapt k2* Bell j5.de Bry j5.de Carb-an j5.de carb-v j5.de caust j5.de Cham j5.de chin j5.de Croc j5.de ign j5.de kali-c j5.de Kali-p k2* merc j5.de mur-ac bg2 phos j5.de plat j5.de rheum j5.de sabin j5.de sec j5.de* sil j5.de sulph j5.de ter br1
  - **pale**: apis a1 carb-ac bg2 carb-an bg2 carb-v bg2 ferr bg2* graph bg2* kreos bg2 Phos bg2* sabad bg2 sulph bg2 tarent a1 til br1*
  - **ropy**, tenacious: anthraci kr1 apis kr1 **Croc** j5.de* crot-h bg Cupr j5.de* kali-chl j5.de Kali-m kr1 kreos bg2 lach bg2 mag-c j5.de* Merc bg2* naja bg2* sec j5.de* ust ptk1 verat bg2
  - **sticky**: crot-h bg2 lach bg2
  - **stringy** (See ropy)
  - **thick**: agar bg2* anthraci jl2 bov bg2* carb-v j5.de cham bg2 chin bg2 Croc bg2* cupr ptk1 Ferr-m a1 kali-n j5.de kreos j5.de lach j5.de laur j5.de mag-c j5.de mag-s j5.de Nux-m j5.de* plat j5.de* Puls j5.de rhus-t bg2 sep bg2 sulph j5.de
  - **thin**: agar hr1 ant-t a1 ben-n a1 both a1 carb-v bg2* chin hr1 crot-h bg2* elaps bro1 ferr k2* graph ptk1 lach bg2* laur ptk1 loxo-lae bnm12• merc-cy br1 Mill hr1 nit-ac ptk1 phos a1 rhus-t ptk1 sabin ptk1 Sec bg2* sul-ac bg2* tab a1 til br1 ust bg2
  - **watery**: alum j5.de am-c j5.de ant-t j5.de Berb j5.de borx j5.de bov j5.de carb-v j5.de crot-h j5.de dulc j5.de* Ferr j5.de* Graph j5.de hir c1* kali-c j5.de kreos j5.de lat-m c1 laur j5.de mang k2* nat-m hr1* nat-s j5.de* nit-ac j5.de phos j5.de prun j5.de Puls j5.de rhus-t j5.de sabin j5.de sec j5.de* stram j5.de sulph j5.de
    - ⁝ **mixed** with clots: arn ptk1 bell ptk1 caust ptk1 Erig bro1 ferr bro1 plat bro1 puls bro1* rat bro1 sabin br1* ust bro1
- **cancer**; in: mill gm1 **Phos** gm1* **Sang** rmk1• strych-g br1
- **cough** agg.; during: vanad br1
- **easy**: dys mtf11 kali-chl ptk1 phos tl1
  - **accompanied** by | **death**; fear of: *(↗MIND - Fear - death - hemorrhage)* acon tl1 ars tl1
- **exertion** agg.; after: bell-p mg1.de Mill k* **Nit-ac** hr1* petr hr1
- **exudation**, hemorrhagic: anthraci kr1
- **fever**; during paroxysmal: cact br1
- **gushing**: acon ptk1 bell bg2* cham ptk1 erig bg2* ham ptk1 ip bg2* lac-c tl1* ox-ac ptk1 puls ptk1 sabin bg2* sec ptk1 tril-p bg2*
  - **intermittently**: psor ptk1 sulph ptk1
- **hepatic** disorders; from: card-m mtf11
- **hysteria**; with (See MIND - Hysteria - hemorrhage - with)
- **injuries**; from: aran bro1 Arn bro1 bov bro1 euph-pi bro1 ham bro1 Mill bro1 tril-p bro1
- **lifting** agg.: petr ptk1
- **local** application: mati mtf11
- **mechanical** damage; from: arn tl1
- **menopause**; in: calc gg ham gg lach gg Phos st puls gg zinc gg
- **menses** | **during** | **agg.**: ham mrr1
  - **suppressed**; from: ham mrr1
- **motion**; from slightest: **Erig** mrr1
- **offensive**: bapt k2 bell ptk1 bry ptk1 carb-v ptk1 helon ptk1 sabin ptk1

Hemorrhage: ...
- **oozing** (See passive)
- **orifices** of the body, from: acet-ac br1 Adren br1 am-caust vh1 anthraci br1* aran **Both** k* carb-v br1 carc gk6* Chin k* **Crot-h** k* elaps erech br1 erig a1 ferr tl1 ferr-p br1* ham lp* Ip bg2* Lach merc-cy br1 mill a1 **Phos** k* sil hr1 Sul-ac k* ter tl1 vip mtf11 zinc bg2
- **painful**: xan br1
- **painless**: mill bro1
- **pale** anemic people: ferr-p tl1
- **passive**, oozing: adren br1 ars-h a1 bov ptk1 bufo ptk1* carb-v k2* Chin bg2* Crot-c mrr1 crot-h ptk1 ferr-p ptk1 gal-ac br1 ham br1* kreos ptk1 lycps-v br1 Mangi br1 menis mtf11 ph-ac tl1* sec bg2* stront-c br1 tarent a1 ter br1* til mtf11 ust ptk1*
  - **accompanied** by:
    - ⁝ **pulse**; weak: gal-ac br1
    - ⁝ **Skin**; cold: gal-ac br1
- **pathological**: acal mtf11
- **pregnancy** agg.; during: thlas mrr1
- **profuse**: Ger br1 Ip br1 mur-ac ptk1
- **prolonged** hemorrhage | **agg.**: plat ptk1
- **putrid**: kali-p k2
- **riding** in a carriage agg.: petr ptk1
- **scratching** agg.: psor ptk1
- **sensation** of hemorrhage:
  - ○ **Blood** vessels | **evening**: adam skp7•
- **septic**: crot-h bg2 kali-p k2 Lach bg2
- **slight** hemorrhage: sep k2
  - **agg.**: bufo bg2* Carb-an bg2* Chin ptk1 ham bg2* **Hydr** bg2* sec ptk1
- **suppression** of hemorrhage agg.: thlas ptk1
- **tendency** to: ail br1 arn br1* both br1 chin mtf33 cinnm mtf11 Crot-h mrr1 ferr mtf11 ham mtf11 ip tl1 kali-i br1 Lach br1 merc-cy br1 mill mtf11 nat-n mtf11 Phos tl1* senec mtf11
- **vicarious**: abrot sf1.de acet-ac bro1 bry k2* ham k2* ip sf1.de kali-c sf1.de Lach hr1 phos hr1* Sec k2*
- **wounds** bleed much (See Wounds - bleeding)
- ○ **Arterial**: acon bg2 aml-ns bg2 bell bg2 coff bg2 ferr bg2 ferr-p bg2 gels bg2 glon bg2 lach bg2 ol-an bg2 sec bg2 seneg bg2
  - **accompanied** by | **phthisis**; incipient (See CHEST - Phthisis - incipient - accompanied - arteries)
- **Internally**: acon gt1* alumn kr1 Arn hr1 Bell bg2* bry bg2 Calc hr1 cham bg2 Chin bg2* cic bg2 con bg2 dulc bg2 eucal br1 euph bg2 ferr bg2 ferr-p gt1* ham br1* hep bg2 hyper bg2 iod bg2 lach bg2 laur bg2 mill gt1* nux-v bg2* par bg2 petr bg2 phos bg2* plb bg2 puls bg2 rhus-t bg2 ruta bg2 sabin gt1* sec bg2 sul-i k* sulph bg2 thlas bg2
- **Mucous** membranes, from: ail bg2* aloe bg2 alum bg2 am-c bg2 am-caust vh1 arg-n bg2 arn bg2 ars bg2* ars-i k2 ars-s-f k2 brom bg2 bry bg2 calc-sil k2 carb-v bg2 ferr-p bg2 ham bg2* kreos bg2 lach br1 merc bg2 mur-ac bg2 nat-n br1 nit-ac bg2 nux-v bg2 phos bg2* puls bg2 sal-ac tl1 sul-ac bg2 Ter br1 thuj bg2
- **Venous**: aloe bg2 arn bg2 carb-v bg2 ham bg2 **Puls** bg2 sep bg2 Sulph bg2

HEMORRHOIDS agg.: coll ptk1

HEPATITIS (See ABDOMEN - Inflammation - liver)

HICCOUGH agg.: acon b2.de* **Am-m** b2.de* bell b2.de* borx b2.de* Bry b2.de* cic b2.de* cocc b2.de* cupr b2.de* Cycl b2.de* Hyos b2.de* Ign b2.de* lyc b2.de* mag-m b2.de* merc b2.de* nat-c b2.de* nux-m b2.de* Nux-v b2.de* par b2.de* puls b2.de* ran-b b2.de* ruta b2.de* sars b2.de* spong b2.de* staph b2.de* stram b2.de* stront-c b2.de* sulph b2.de* Teucr b2.de* verat b2.de* verb b2.de* zinc-val ptk1

HIDRADENITIS (See Inflammation - perspiratory)

HILL (See Mountain)

HIRSUTISM (See Hair - distribution)

HISTORY; personal: *(↗Convalescence; Family)*
- **abortion**; of: *(↗Convalescence - abortion)* alet mp1* Caul mp1* pyrog rma2 Sabin mp1* sec ptk2* sep mp1* Syph bnu*
  - **never** well since (See Convalescence - abortion - never)

- **abscesses**; of recurrent: *(↗boils; Wounds - reopening)* anthraci ptk1* arn mtf ars mtf berb mtf calc mtf calc-f k2 calc-m mtf calc-p mtf calc-s ptk1* crot-h mtf echi mtf hep mtf med gk nat-sil mtf33 psor mtf33 *Pyrog* k* sil mtf33 sulph lp* *Syph* k* tub mtf33
  - ○ **Fingers**; on: hydrog srj2•
  - **Teeth**; of roots of: sulph mrr1
  - **Tonsils**; on: apis bg2 bar-c bg2 guaj bg2 lach bg2 sil bg2
- **abuse**; of: lac-f wza1•
- **antibiotics**; of use of: *(↗medicine; Weakness - antibiotics; SKIN - Eruptions - antibiotics)* carb-v gm1 lach rma2 mag-p gm1 myris rma2 *Nux-v* rma2 op gm1 puls rma2 *Sulph* rma2 thuj rma2
- **birth** trauma; of: *(↗Emaciation - children - newborns - birth; MIND - Eating - refuses - children - birth)* *Arn* rma2 borx mtf33 carc rma2 cic rma2 hell rma2 hyper rma2 nat-m br* nat-s rma2 [bell-p-sp dcm1]
- **bite** of animal: *Lyss* mrr1
  - **immunized** animal: lyss mrr1
- **boils**; of recurrent: *(↗abscesses)* anthraci ptk1 arn bg2* ars bg2* berb bro1 calc bro1* *Calc-m* bro1 calc-p bro1 *Calc-pic* bro1 cephd-i zzc1• echi bro1 hep bg2* hydr bg2 kali-i mrr1 kreos bg2 lyc bg2 nat-m bg2 nat-s bg2 penic mtf11 rhus-t bg2 sec bg2 sul-i bg2 sulph bg2* syph mtf11 tub bro1*
- **bronchitis**; of recurrent: carc mrr1 diph mtf11 dys mtf11 *Phos* mrr1 *Tub* mrr1 tub-d jl2 v-a-b jl2*
- **cancer**; of: carc br1 *Con* mrr1 med jl2 morb tl1 *Trif-p* br1
  - **mammae**; of: **Con** mrr1
- **chest** complaints; of: bac c1*
  - **never** well since (See Convalescence - chest - never)
- **childhood** diseases; of:
  - **absent**: carc gk*
  - **appearing** late in life: carc mtf33
  - **severe**: carc mtf33
- **colds**; of frequently recurrent (See Cold; taking - tendency)
- **complaints**; of recurrent: *(↗Paroxysmal)* bar-c bg2 bar-m bg2 carb-v bg2 coloc bg2 hep bg2 kali-bi bg2 kali-i bg2 lyc bg2 merc bg2 merc-d bg2 mez bg2 plb bg2 psor bg2 puls bg2 rhus-t bg2 seneg bg2 sep bg2 sil bg2 staph bg2 sul-i bg2 sulph bg2* tub bg2
- **cornea**; of recurrent inflammation of the: graph ptk1 syph jl2*
- **coryza**; of recurrent: *(↗Cold; taking - tendency)* abrot bg2 calc bg2 cinnb bg2 coloc bg2 dulc bg2 graph bg2 kali-bi bg2 lach bg2 nat-c bg2 nux-v bg2 puls bg2 **Sil** bg2 *Sulph* bg2 syph mtf33
- **croup**; of recurrent: *Calc* k* **Calc-s** **HEP** k ● *Lyc* bg2 **Phos** bg2*
- **cystitis**; of recurrent: aq-mar mgm• gonotox jl2 hep mrr1 lyc h2 med mrr1 moni rfm1• puls h1 sep h2 tub mrr1
  - **children**; in: apis lmj asaf ggd borx lmj canth lmj caps lmj lach lmj lyc lmj **Med** lmj nux-v lmj sars lmj *Sep* lmj **Staph** lmj tub lmj
- **diarrhea**; of recurrent: *(↗RECTUM - Diarrhea - periodical)* tub mrr1
- **diphtheria**; of: anthraci vh1 diph ptk1 lac-c gsd1 lach br1*
- **discharges**; of | **suppressed**: *(↗EAR - Discharges - suppressed; NOSE - Discharge - suppressed)* alum vh3 lach rma2 psor jl2 puls rma2 sulph rma2 zinc kr2*
- **dislocations** (= luxations): tub jl2
- **domination** by others; of | **children**; in (See MIND - Ailments - domination - children)
- **ear**:
  - **discharges** from: viol-o ptk1
  - **inflammation** | **Internal**; of recurrent: *Merc* vh*
- **eczema**: com ptk1 streptoc jl2
- **epididymis**; recurrent inflammation: coli jl2
- **epistaxis**; of recurrent: aids nl2• ars bro1 carb-v k* carc mlr1• chin bg1* croc bg1 ferr-p bro1 ip c1 kali-c meli ptk1 mill bro1 **Phos** hr1* puls k*
  - **young** people; in: card-m ptk1
- **eruptions**; of: mez tl1
  - **suppressed**: *(↗SKIN - Eruptions - suppressed)* kali-c ptk1 lach rma2 psor mtf33 puls rma2 sulph rma2 zinc kr2*
- **erysipelas**; of recurrent: *Apis* k* calen vml3• *Crot-h* ferr-p bro1* graph hr1* hydr ptk1 lappa mtf11 nat-m bro1* *Rhus-t* bro1* strept-ent jl2 *Sulph* bro1*
- **external** throat; of recurrent fibroids on: *Sil*
- **eyes**:
  - **recurrent** inflammation of the; of: ars bry **Calc** lyc brm *Sulph*
  - **recurrent** styes on the; of: alum anthraci mtf11 apis ptk1 calc-f st1 carbn-s carc mlr1• *Con* k* ferr-py mtf11 *Graph* k* kola stb3• med gk *Psor* k* puls k2* *Sil* k* staph tl1 **Sulph** k* tub jl2*
- **fevers**: carc mlr1•
- **gastrointestinal** complaints; of: *Bac* wda* calc wda* calc-p wda* *Chel* wda* kali-s wda* nat-s wda* *Nux-v* wda* *Phos* wda*
- **gonorrhea**; of: agn br1 med k2* *Nat-s* mrr1* phyt rma2 *Thuj* gsk1*
  - **never** well since (See Convalescence - gonorrhea - never)
  - **suppressed** gonorrhea in patients with asthma; of (See Gonorrhea - asthma)
- **gravel** in urine; of: berb mta1* epig mta1* sars mta1*
- **head** injury; of (See HEAD - Injuries)
- **hydrocephalic** children; of delivering: calc-p c1
- **inflammations**; of frequent: carc sp*
- **influenza**; of: | **never** well since (See Convalescence - influenza - never)
- **laryngitis**; of recurrent: *Brom* *Calc* diphtox jl2
- **lids**; of recurrent tarsal tumors on the: **Calc-f** st *Puls* *Staph*
- **liver**; inflammation of: chin mtf33
- **loss** of fluids; of: *(↗Loss - fluids)* carc rma2 *Chin* wt1* *Ferr* cpd* ph-ac cpd*
- **lungs**:
  - **complaints** of the: lob samkn
  - **inflammation** of the: *Bac* rma2 carc sp* **Kali-i** mrr1 lob mrr1 morg skb1* *Phos* mrr1 *Tub* mrr1
    - **never** well since (See Convalescence - lungs - never)
- **malaria**; of: *(↗Convalescence - malaria)* chinin-s mrr1 nat-m mrr1
  - **suppressed**: chinin-s br1 elat br1
- **mammae**; of recurrent inflammation of the: phyt bl6
- **measles**; of: | **never** well since (See Measles - ailments - never)
- **medicine**; of abuse of allopathic: *(↗antibiotics)* *Lach* wt1* *Nux-v* wt1* *Puls* rma2 *Sulph* wt1* *Thuj* rma2 *Zinc* rma2
- **mononucleosis**; of: ail vml3• bar-c vh1 bar-m vh1 **Carc** mrr1 hep mrr3 lyc hu2 mag-m mrr4• nat-s hu
- **nose**; of recurrent pimples on wings of: bamb-a stb2.de•
- **penis**; of recurrent ulcers on: *Sep*
- **pharynx**; inflammation of: alumn bro1 *Bar-c* bro1 graph bro1 lach bro1 *Sil* mrr1 sulph bro1
- **pleuritis** (= pleurisy): lob mrr1
- **pneumonia**; of (See lungs - inflammation)
- **puerperal** fever; of | **never** well since (See Convalescence - puerperal - never)
- **septic** fever; of: | **never** well since (See Convalescence - septic - never)
- **sexual** abuse; of (See MIND - Ailments - abused - sexually)
- **sinusitis**; of recurrent: carc mrr1* *Kali-i* mrr1 sil mrr1
- **stomach**; of pain in | **cramping** pain: graph bro1 iris mrr1
- **strain** or injury; of: nat-c bro1 nat-m bro1 psor bro1 *Sil* bro1
  - **never** well since (See Convalescence - strain - never)
- **syphilis**; of: *(↗Family - syphilis; Syphilis)* *Kali-bi* br1
- **throat**; recurrent inflammation of: diphtox jl2 psor jl2* *Sil* mrr1
- **tonsillitis**; of recurrent: *Alumn* aur-m-n wbt2• **Bar-c** k* *Bar-m* calc-p st carc fb* dys pte1*• guaj st* *Hep* ign mtf33 lach lyc morg-g pte1*• morg-p pte1*• nat-m mtf33 nit-ac mtf33 penic mtf11 phyt ptk1 *Psor* k* *Sang* sep *Sil* k* sulph syc fmm1• syph xxb thuj mtf33 thymul ttm **Tub** st*
  - **autumn** agg.: merc hr1
- **tuberculosis**; of: agar br1 aur-i klr1* aur-m rma2 bac bn* bov tl1 calc k2 dros tl1* kali-c br1 kali-n rma2 med rma2 nat-m dmd1.fr* nit-ac bl* phos mrr1* phyt bci1* sep br1 sil k2 *Spong* br1 stann br1* ther br1 tub bn* tub-m jl2 v-a-b jl2
- **typhoid** fever; of: *(↗Convalescence - typhoid)* carb-v rma2 carc rma2 parathyr jl2 *Psor* rma2 *Pyrog* ptk2* thyr rma2 tub fb* typh rma2
  - **never** well since (See Convalescence - typhoid - never)
- **urethra**; of discharge from: thuj mrr1
- **urticaria**; of recurrent: hep ptk1 stroph-h ptk1
- **vaccination** or repeated vaccination; of: *(↗Vaccination)* ant-t rma2 carc kr1* lepr rma2 maland dwm1* sil rma2 sulph rma2 *Thuj* br*

- **vaccination** or repeated vaccination; of: ...
  - **never** well since (See Vaccination - never)
- **vertigo**: helo-s bnm14•
- **vomiting**; of: iris mrr1
- **whooping** cough; of: *(↗Convalescence - whooping)* carc sp* coc-c rma2 *Dros* rma2 kali-c rma2 pert rma2

HOARFROST (See Weather - frosty)

HODGKIN'S disease: *(↗Cancerous; Cancerous - lymphoma; Leukemia)* *Acon* c1* acon-l c1* *Ars* c1* ars-br vh ars-i bro1* bar-c mrr1 bar-i bro1* bufo dgt1 buni-o jl3 calc sne *Calc-f* c1* carc mlr1• *Cean* mrr1 cist tl1* con sne ferr-pic bro1 iod bro1* kali-bi jsa *Kali-chl* c *Kali-m* c1* lap-a sne *Nat-m* c1* phos bro1* saroth jl3 scroph-n br1* syph hr1* tub mrr1

HOLDING parts close together: | **agg.**: bry bg2 *Ign* b2.de* staph b2.de*

HOLDING something tight:
- **agg.**: coff b2.de* *Rhus-t* b2.de* spig b2.de*
- **amel.**: anac bro1

HOLLOW (See Emptiness)

HOUSE (See Air - indoor)

HUNGER: | **agg.**: *(↗Sick - hunger)* *Alum* *Anac* bg2* ars-i k2* *Aur* k* bar-c sne brass-n-o srj bung-fa mtf *Cact* calc-f mg1.de* canth k* *Caust* k* chel bg2* cina bg2* **Crot-h** k* *Crot-t* ferr **Graph** k* hell k* **Iod** k* **Kali-c** k* lac-leo sk4• lyc bg2* nat-m sne olnd k* ph-ac sne *Phos* k* plat k* *Psor* *Rhus-t* k* sang sne **Sil** k* *Spig* k* stann staph bg2* **Sulph** k* valer verat k* *Zinc*

HYDROCHLORIC ACID; complaints after: *Bry* b4a.de *Mez* b4a.de

HYPERLIPIDEMIA: *(↗KIDNEYS - Nephrotic)* all-s vml3• aur mtf calc mtf calc-f mtf *Chel* mtf chin mtf *Chion* mtf11 chr-ac vml3• colch jl1 cortiso jl1 ferr-i vwe *Hydr* mtf *Lec* vml3• med vwe nux-v mtf perh-mal jl1* *Tarax* vml3• thuj mtf *Thyreotr* jl1 *Vanad* vml3• zing vml3•
- **dialysis**; from: calc-f mtf lyc mtf mag-m mtf nux-v mtf stront-c mtf sulph mtf

HYPERTENSION: *(↗Diabetes mellitus - accompanied - hypertension)* acon sf1.de* adon sf1.de* *Adren* br1* agar sf1.de* aids nl2• ail vh1 all-s br1 *Am-m* vh1 *Ambr* vh1 aml-ns sf1.de* androc bnm2• anh st* ant-ar k* aran st* aran-ix st* arg-n k* arn mg1.de* ars k* asar sf1.de* aster st* atra-r bnm3• *Aur* br1* aur-br k* aur-i sf1.de* aur-m k* aur-m-n k* *Bar-c* sf1.de* bar-m br1* bell mrr1* benz-ac dgt1 boerh-d zzc1• borra-o oss1• cactin-m hs1 cal-ren k* calc k* calc-f sf1.de* calc-p k* caust k* chinin-s st chir-fl bnm4• chlor a1* chloram st* chlorpr st* choc srj3• coff a1* **Con** ptk1* convo-s st* cortico st* cortiso st* crat br1* crot-c mrr1 cupr k* cupr-act st cupr-ar k* cyna st* cyt-l st* dig k* diph mtf11 diph-t-tpt jl2 dulc mrr1 ergot st* esp-g st* ferr-i mrr1* fl-ac sf1.de* gels a1* glon sf1.de* glycyr-g cte1• *Grat* k* grin br1 ign k* iod sf1.de* iris sf1.de* kali-c k* kali-chl st kali-m k* kali-p k* kali-sal k* kres st* lac-c mrr1 lach mg1.de* lat-h bnm5• lat-m st* loxo-lae bnm12• lyc k* lycps-v ptk1 mag-c k* mand st* med mrr1 meli mrr1 methys st* morg-p mtf11 naja st* nat-m mrr1 nit-ac k* nux-v sf1.de* onop st* ph-ac k* phos k* phys br1 pic-ac k* pitu st* pitu-gl br1 pitu-p sp1 *Plb* br1* plb-i sf1.de* psor k* pulm-a st* puls k* rad-br k* *Rauw* st* reser st* rhus-t gt1* sang k* scop ptk1 *Sec* br1* sep k* *Ser-ang* br1 sil k* spartin bwa3 spartin-s br1 squil sf1.de* *Stront-c* br1* *Stront-i* sf1.de* sulph k* *Sumb* k* syph mtf11 tab k* thal st* thlas k* thuj k* tub mtf11 tub-d jl2 tub-m jl2* uran-n br1* valer sf1.de* vanad k* vanil fd5.de **Verat** k* verat-v ptk1* *Visc* sf1.de* [ferr-m stj1 ferr-p stj1 ferr-s stj1 nat-met stj2]
- **accompanied** by:
  - **apoplexy** (See Apoplexy - accompanied - hypertension)
  - **diabetes** (See Diabetes mellitus - accompanied - hypertension)
  - **nephrosis** (See KIDNEYS - Nephrosis - accompanied - hypertension)
  - **urine**; albuminous: visc br1
  - ○ **Face**; red discoloration of: acon mtf *Arn* mtf *Astac* mtf *Bell* mtf *Bry* mtf chin mtf coff mtf *Ferr* mtf *Glon* mtf hyos mtf *Lach* mtf lyc mtf *Meli* mtf nux-v mtf *Op* mtf phos mtf stram mtf stront-c br1 *Sulph* mtf verat-v mtf
  - **Head**; pain in: loxo-lae bnm12•
    - **morning**: fuma-ac mtf11

Hypertension – **accompanied** by: ...
  - **Heart** | **hypertrophy** (See CHEST - Hypertrophy - heart - accompanied - hypertension)
  - **Kidney**; complaints (See KIDNEYS - Complaints - accompanied - hypertension)
- **dialysis**; from: acon-f mtf adren mtf ser-ang mtf
- **excessive**: toxo-g mtf11
- **lung** complaints; after: nat-ox-act mtf11
- **nervous** mechanism; due to disturbed: aur-m-n br1
- **pulmonary**: brass-n-o srj5•
- **sudden**: adren mtf11 coff ptk1 lat-m bnm6•

HYPERTHYROIDISM: *(↗EXTERNAL - Thyroid)* bell br1 coli jl2 con mrr1 dys mtf11 ferr-i mrr1 *Iod* mrr1 kali-i mrr1 lach mrr1 lycps-v mrr1 nat-m br1* penic mtf11 spig mrr1 spong mrr1 thyr mtf11 thyreotr mtf11 v-a-b mtf11
- **accompanied** by:
  - **diabetes** (See Diabetes mellitus - accompanied - hyperthyroidism)
  - ○ **Heart**:
    - **complaints** of (See CHEST - Heart; complaints - accompanied - hyperthyroidism)
    - **failure** (See CHEST - Heart failure - accompanied - hyperthyroidism)

HYPERTROPHY: *Ant-c* ptk1 ars ptk1 calc ptk1 *Clem* ptk1 *Dulc* ptk1 *Graph* ptk1 ran-b ptk1 rhus-t ptk1 sep ptk1 *Sil* ptk1 sulph ptk1
- **one** sided | **menopause**; during: lyc ptk1*
- ○ **Connective** tissue: hydrc br1
- **Mucous** membranes: ars-i bg2 bar-c bg2 calc bg2 calc-i bg2 calc-p bg2 cist bg2 hydr bg2 iod bg2 kali-bi bg2 kali-i bg2 kali-n bg2 phos bg2 psor bg2 sang bg2 sul-i bg2 sulph bg2 tab bg2 teucr bg2 thuj bg2

HYPNOTICS; from: am-c gm1 carb-v gm1 lach gm1 op gm1

HYPOGAMMAGLOBULINEMIA: calc mtf carc mtf thuj mtf tub mtf

HYPOGLYCEMIA (See Laboratory - blood - glucose)

HYPOTENSION: acetan br1* acon mg1.de adlu jl3 adren mtf11 agar mg1.de ancis-p tsm2 aran mg1.de bacls-7 mtf11 bit-ar wht1• both tsm2 both-ax tsm2 bung-fa tsm2 *Cac* a1 cact br1* cench tsm2 chir-fl bnm4• chlorpr jl3 cloth tsm2 coli jl2* coll br1 cortico jl3* crat br1 crot-c tsm2 crot-h tsm2 cur st1 dendr-pol tsm2 *Diph-t-tpt* jl2 diphtox jl2 elaps tsm2 enteroc jl2 gels ptk1 guips br1 halo jl3 helo-s bnm14• hist sp1 influ jl2* lac-ac stj5• lach mg1.de lat-m sp1* levo jl3 loxo-lae bnm12• lyc k2* lycps-v br1 meph jl3 naja mg1.de* nat-f sp1 oscilloc mtf11 psor jl2 rad-br br1* rauw sp1* reser jl3 rib-ac jl3* ser-a-c jl2* spartin-s br1 staph mg1.de sulfa jl3 ther ptk1 thiop jl3 thymol sp1 thyr br1 toxo-g mtf11 tub-d jl2 v-a-b jl3* vario jl2* verat mg1.de verat-v br1 vip tsm2 visc br1 voac-af jsx1.fr [ferr-[illegible] stj1 ferr-m stj1 ferr-p stj1 ferr-s stj1]
- **accompanied** by:
  - **slow** pulse (See Pulse - slow - accompanied - hypotension)
  - ○ **Heart** failure (See CHEST - Heart failure - accompanied - hypotension)
  - **Kidney** complaints (See KIDNEYS - Complaints - accompanied - hypotension)
- **chronic**: v-a-b jl2
- **dialysis**; from: cac mtf carb-v mtf guips mtf naja mtf verat mtf visc mtf
- **sudden**: *Diph-t-tpt* jl2 helo-s bnm14•

HYPOTHERMIA: acetan vh1 ant-t vh *Antip* vh1 arg-n hr1* *Ars* hr1* ars-h hr1* cact kr1* chlor hr1* cupr-act kr1 eucal hr1* influ mp4• kali-bi kr1 kali-br hr1* kali-p ptk2 loxo-lae bnm12• lycps-v kr1 *Pyrog* jl2
- **persistent** subnormal temperature: cact br1

HYPOTHYREOSIS (See Hypothyroidism)

HYPOTHYROIDISM: *(↗Myxedema; EXTERNAL - Goitre; EXTERNAL - Swelling - thyroid cartilage; EXTERNAL - Swelling - thyroid gland; EXTERNAL - Thyroid)* alum mrr5 ange-s jl1 arg-n mrr5 bacls-7 mtf11 calc mrr1* calc-i mtf carc mp4• con mrr5 cortico jl1 cortiso mtf11 gels mrr5 graph mrr5 hist mtf11

Hypothyroidism: ...
hypoth mtf11 *Iod* mtf kali-c br1* kali-i mrr1 levo jl1 luf-op mp4• lyc mrr5 merc mtf *Nat-m* mrr5* nux-v mrr5 penic mtf11 psor jl2 rib-ac mtf11 sep mrr5 thala mtf11 thiop jl1 *Thyr* mtf11 [am-br stj2 calc-met stj2 *Calc-sil* stj2 *Lith-met* stj2 lith-p stj2 lith-s stj2]
- **acute** diseases; after: thyr br1

HYPOTONY: (↗*Relaxation - physical)* *Psor* jl2 ser-a-c jl2

IDLENESS: | **agg.**: (↗*Exertion - amel.)* alum b2.de* bar-c b2.de* *Con* b2.de* croc b2.de* ferr b2.de* *Ign* b2.de* lyc b2.de* mag-m b2.de* *Nat-c* b2.de* nat-m b2.de* nux-v b2.de* petr b2.de* plb b2.de* **Sep** b2.de* sil b2.de* tarax b2.de* verat b2.de*

ILL FEELING (See Sick)

ILLNESSES (See Complaints)

IMMATURITY; endocrine: pitu-gl mtf11

IMPRESSIONS; deep (See SKIN - Impressions - deep)

INDOLENCE and luxury, ailments from: (↗*Sedentary)*
all-s br1 carb-v st1 clem h1* dig ptk1 helon br1* nux-v st1

INDURATIONS: (↗*Hardness)* *Agn* k* alum k* alum-sil k2* *Alumn* k* ambr k* *Anthraci* k* *Apis* bg2* *Arg-met* *Arg-n* arn k* *Ars* k* ars-i ars-s-f k2* asaf k* *Aur* k* aur-ar k2 aur-i k2* *Aur-m* k* **Aur-m-n** hr1* aur-s k2* **Bad** k* *Bar-c* k* bar-i k2* bar-m j5.de **Bell** k* bov j5.de *Bry* k* *Calc* k* **Calc-f** k* calc-i k2* camph k* cann-i hr1* cann-s k* caps k* **Carb-an** k* **Carb-v** k* carbn-s caust k* cham k* chel k* **Chin** k* cina k* cist sf1.de **Clem** k* cocc j5.de coloc k* **Con** k* cupr k* cycl k* dulc k* ferr k* ferr-ar fl-ac bg2* *Graph* k* *Hep* k* *Hydrc* hr1* hyos k* ign k* *Iod* k* kali-c k* *Kali-chl* *Kali-i* k* *Kali-m* k2 **Lach** k* lap-a sf1.de led k* *Lyc* k* mag-c k* **Mag-m** k* mang bg2* *Merc* k* merc-i-r bg2 mez k* nat-c k* nux-v k* op k* *Petr* j5.de **Phos** k* *Phyt* bg *Plb* k* *Psor* *Puls* k* ran-b bg2* ran-s k* rhod k* **Rhus-t** k* ruta k2 sec k* **Sel** k* **Sep** k* **Sil** k* spig k* spong k* squil j5.de **Staph** k* stram k* sul-i bg2 *Sulph* k* syph st1 thuj k* valer k* verat k*
- **cancerous**: aur-ar k2
- **inflammation**; after: alum b4a.de bry b7a.de *Carb-an* b4a.de *Carb-v* b4a.de *Con* b4a.de dulc b4a.de *Iod* b4a.de *Kali-c* b4a.de lyc b4a.de nux-v b7a.de ph-ac b4a.de ran-b b7a.de *Rhod* b4a.de rhus-t b7a.de sep b4a.de sil b4a.de spong b7a.de *Sulph* b4a.de
- **painful**: bell h1
- **pressure** agg.: cic k2 sep ptk1 *Sulph* k*
- **sensation** of: vesp br1*

○ - **Cartilages**: arg-met k2 aur k2
- **Cellular** tissue: anthraci bro1* carb-an bro1 graph bro1 kali-i bro1* kreos bro1 merc bro1 merc-i-r ptk1 plb-i bro1 rhus-t bro1* sil bro1
- **Connective** tissue (See Connective - induration)
- **Fibrous** tissue: kali-i br1
- **Glands**: (↗*Glands; Swelling - glands - hard)* acon c1 aethi-a sf1.de agar agn k* *Alum* k* alumn k2* am-c k* *Am-m* bg2* ambr k* ant-c k* *Anthraci* kr1* *Apis* kr1 *Arg-n* kr1 arn k* ars k* ars-br br1* ars-i *Asaf* k* astac kr1 *Aster* bro1 *Aur* k* aur-ar k2 aur-i k2 *Aur-m* k* *Aur-m-n* kr1 aur-s k2 **Bad** k* *Bar-c* k* *Bar-i* k2* **Bar-m** k* bar-s k* **Bell** k* berb-a bro1 bov k* **Brom** k* *Bry* k* bufo bg2 **Calc** k* calc-chln bro1 **Calc-f** k* *Calc-i* sf1.de *Calc-s* kr1* calc-sil k2 camph k* cann-s k* canth k* caps k* **Carb-an** k* *Carb-v* k* carbn-s caust k* cham k* *Chin* k* chir-fl gya2 *Cinnb* kr1 cist k* **Clem** k* *Cocc* k* *Coloc* k* **Con** k* cupr k* cycl k* *Dig* k* *Dulc* k* ferr k* *Ferr-i* *Graph* k* *Hecla* kr1* hep k* hydr k2 hyos k* ign k* **Iod** k* kali-c k* *Kali-chl* *Kali-i* k* *Kali-m* k2 kali-n kr1 kali-sil k2 *Lap-a* bro1* *Lyc* k* *Mag-m* k* mang k* *Merc* k* *Merc-aur* sf1.de *Merc-c* kr1 merc-d bg2* *Merc-i-f* kr1* merc-i-r bg2* merc-sul kr1 nat-ar *Nat-c* k* nat-m bg2* nat-sil k2 nit-ac k* nux-v k* oper bro1 petr k* phos k* **Phyt** k* plb k* *Psor* *Puls* k* raph j5.de rhod k* *Rhus-t* k* *Sars* sel ptk1 sep k* *Sil* k* spig k* **Spong** k* squil k* staph k* **Sul-i** bg2* **Sulph** k* syph st1 thuj k* thyr bro1 toxo-g jl2 trif-r bro1 tub bg2* v-a-b jl2 verat k* viol-t kr1
  - **accompanied** by | **itching** in gland: con mrr1
  - **children**; in: med jl2
  - **chronic**: calc-f bg2
  - **cords**; like knotted (See knotty)
  - **foreign** bodies; sensation of small: cocain
  - **hot**: asaf bg2
  - **indolent**: calc-f bg2
  - **injuries**; after: **Con**

Induratons – Glands: ...
  - **knotty** like ropes: (↗*Swelling - glands - knotted)* **Bar-m** *Calc* *Cist* con *Dulc* hep k* *Iod* k* lyc rhus-t *Sil* sul-i k2 *Tub*
  - **malignant**: carb-an bg2
  - **nodes** under the skin, like: bry *Calc* caust mag-c nit-ac *Still* vh
  - **painless**: iod bg2
  - **stony**: alum bg2 calc-f bg2 carb-v bg2
  - **suppurating**; but seldom: brom br1*
- **Joints**: acet-ac br1
- **Muscles**, of: (↗*Complaints - muscles)* alum k* *Anthraci* *Bad* bar-c k* *Bry* k* **Calc-f** k* calo br1 carb-an k* carb-v k* *Caust* k* con k* dulc k* hep k* hyos k* iod k* kali-c k* kali-chl kali-m k2 kali-sil k2 lach k* *Lyc* k* nat-c k* nux-v k* ph-ac k* puls k* ran-b k* rhod k* rhus-t k* sars k* sep k* sil k* spig spong k* sul-i k2 sulph k* thuj k*
  - **neuralgia**; after: bry ptk1
- **Periosteum**: aur tl1 ruta k2*
- **Veins**: ham ptk1 nux-v ptk1
  - **whipcord**; like a: calc-hp ptk1

INFECTIOUS disease: acon mtf11 bell mtf11 cortiso mtf11 echi mtf11 leptos-ih jl2 morb jl2 nat-ox-act mtf11 pyrog jl2 ser-ang br1
- **accompanied** by | **development**; difficult: mal-ac mtf11
- **acute** | **anaerobic**: pyrog mtf11
- **chronic**: med mtf11
- **streptococcus**: (↗*Laboratory - bacteria - streptococcus)* ail br1* arn ptk1 chir-fl bnm4• sul-ac ptk1

INFILTRATION (See Effusion)

INFIRMITY (See Weakness)

INFLAMMATION: abrot bro1* *Acon* b7.de* *Agrosti-a* bro1 ant-c b7.de* apis bro1* *Arn* b7a.de* *Ars* bro1* aur tl1 **Bell** bro1* bell-p sp1 bry b7.de* calc ptk1 cann-xyz ptk1 *Canth* bro1* cham ptk1 chel bro1 chin bro1 cortiso sp1 echi ptk1* ferr-p bro1* **Gels** ptk1 hep bro1* **Hyos** ptk1 *Iod* bro1* ip b7.de kali-bi bro1 kali-c bro1* kali-i bro1 kali-m bro1 kali-s bro1 *Lach* ptk1 merc tl1* *Nat-n* bro1 nux-v b7.de* *Phos* ptk1 plb ptk1 *Puls* b7.de* **Rhus-t** ptk1 sec ptk1 sep ptk1 **Sil** ptk1 spig b7.de *Spira* bro1 *Staph* ptk1 sulph bro1* ter ptk1 *Verat-v* bro1* vib-od bro1
- **acute**: merc-cy br1
  - **chronic** inflammation; acute manifestation of: *Iod* br1
- **cellulitis**: apis bro1* arn bro1* ars bro1* bapt bro1 bry ptk1 canth tl1 crot-h bro1 lach bro1* led mrr1 loxo-recl bnm1• mang-act br1* merc ptk1 *Merc-i-r* bro1 myris br1 pyrog mrr1 *Rhus-t* k2* *Sil* c1* sulph mrr1 tarent-c ptk1 vesp bro1*
  - **delivery**; after: hep bro1 *Rhus-t* bro1 verat-v bro1
  - **patches**: streptoc jl2
  - **phlegmonous**: vac jl2
  - **subacute**: mang ptk1 sil ptk1
- **chronic**: kali-p mtf11 sil tl1
- **cold** applications | **amel.**: loxo-recl bnm10•
- **destructive**: merc br1
- **fever**; at the beginning of: ferr-p tl1
- **first** stage before exudation: *Ferr-p* br1
- **followed** by:
  - **convulsions**: cupr tl1
  - **delirium**: cupr tl1
- **gangrenous**: (↗*SKIN - Gangrene)* abrot tl1 agar c2 all-c c2 anthraci c2* apis c2 **Ars** k* bapt k2 *Bell* bism c2 both c2* brass-n-o c2 bufo gk camph tl1 **Canth** carb-ac c2 *Carb-an* k* *Carb-v* k* *Chin* chr-o c2 *Colch* *Crot-h* k* *Echi* c2* ergot c2 euph h2* hep *Iod* kali-n h2 *Kali-p* k* kreos k2* **Lach** k* merc nat-pyru mtf11 *Phos* *Plb* ran-a c2 *Rhus-t* ric c2 sacch mtf11 **Sec** k* **Sil** sul-ac c2
  - **accompanied** by:
    - **blood** circulation; complaints of: aesc mtf11 nat-pyru mtf11
    - **sepsis**: crot-h mtf11
  - **diabetics**; in: (↗*Diabetes mellitus - accompanied - gangrene)* ars bro1 nat-pyru mtf11 sec mtf11
  - **dry**: lepr mtf11 psor mtf11
  - **moist**: vip-t mtf11
  - **old** people; in: adren mtf11 ergot mtf11 sec mtf11 vip-t mtf11
  - **painful**: ars mtf11 stram mtf11
  - **Raynaud's** gangrene: sec mtf11

- **tendency** to: am-c tl1 canth tl1
- **warm** application:
  - ⁝ **agg.**: ars tl1 sec tl1
  - ⁝ **amel.**: ars tl1
- **wet**: anthraci mtf11

- **ice** | **amel.**: loxo-recl bnm10•
- **intense**: ars tl1 bell tl1 canth tl1 merc-c tl1 *Tarent-c* br1
- **later** stages: kali-s br1
- **operation**; after: acon bro1 *Anthraci* bro1 arn bro1 ars bro1 ars-i bro1 *Bell* bro1 bell-p bro1 calc-s bro1 calen bro1 echi bro1 gunp bro1 *Hep* bro1 hyper bro1 iod bro1 merc-c bro1 merc-i-r bro1 myris bro1 *Pyrog* bro1 rhus-t bro1 *Sil* bro1
- **passive**: *Dig* bro1 *Gels* bro1 puls bro1 sulph bro1
- **subacute**: *Kali-m* br1
- **sudden**: bell h1*
- **suppurative**: hep tl1
- **tendency** to: camph h1 ferr-p br1
  - **hemorrhagic**: canth mtf11
- **wounds**, of: (↗*Wounds - suppurating)* *Acon* j5.de *Apis* b7a.de arist-cl sp1 arn j5.de bell b7a.de calc-f kr1 calen a1* canch br1 *Cham* j5.de* *Con* kr1 eucal br1 formal br1 graph mtf33 hyper k2 kali-bi a1 lach j5.de led k2* med ser mez h2* *Myris* br1 myrt-c br1 nat-m j5.de nit-ac gk plb j5.de plut-n srj7• positr nl2• *Puls* b7.de* *Rhus-t* j5.de* ruta fd4.de sacch br1 sil mrr1 staph mrr1 *Sul-ac* j5.de *Sulph* j5.de tarent gk vip a1

O - **Aponeurosis**: bry k2

- **Blood** vessels: acon k* *Ant-t* k* apis bg2 **Arn** k* **Ars** k* ars-i aur k2 **Bar-c** **Bell** bg2 bufo k2 calc canth bg2 carb-v bg2 cham k* chin bg2 *Cupr* *Ham* k* hell bg2 *Kali-c* k* kreos k* lach k* lyc k* nux-v bg2 *Puls* k* rhus-t bg2 sep bg2 sil k* spig k* **Sulph** k* thuj k* **Verat** bg2 *Verat-v* bg2 **Vip** bg2 zinc k*
  - **injuries**; after: rhus-t sf1.de
  - **thrombophlebitis**: hir mtf11

O • **Arteries**: (↗*Blood vessels - complaints - arteries)* ars bro1 *Calc* kr1 carb-v bro1 eberth jl2 echi bro1 hist jl *Kali-i* bro1 lach bro1 *Nat-i* bro1 sec bro1 sulfa jl

- **Veins**: (↗*Thrombosis; Varicose; EXTREMITIES - Milk)* acon bro1* agar bro1 *All-c* ant-c *Ant-t* hr1* apis kr1* arist-cl mg1.de* *Arn* k* *Ars* k* *Bapt* hr1 *Bell* k1* both st **Bry** *Bufo* **Calc** k* calc-ar sf1.de *Calc-f* sf1.de carb-v sf1.de* carbn-s *Cham* j5.de* *Chin* k1* chlorpr jl3 *Crot-h* hr1* eberth jl2 *Ferr-p* hr1* graph *Ham* k* hecla jl hep *Hippoz* hr1 hir jl *Iod* *Kali-c* k1* kali-chl sf kali-m sf1.de kreos k* **Lach** hr1* *Led* *Lyc* k* *Lycps-v* mag-c mg1.de mag-f jl merc k1* merc-cy c1* merc-i-r mg1.de morg-p pte1*• *Mur-ac* hr1 *Nat-s* nux-v b2.de* parathyr jl2 phos hr1* prot pte1* *Puls* k* rhod **Rhus-t** hr1* *Sep* k1 *Sil* k* spig k* streptoc jl2 stront-br c1* stront-c c1* sulfa jl *Sulph* k* thiop jl thuj b2.de* verat **Vip** c1* vip-a jl zinc k*
  - ⁝ **accompanied** by | **swelling**: *Vip* br1
  - ⁝ **chronic**: arn bro1 merc bro1 *Puls* bro1 ruta bro1
  - ⁝ **delivery**; after forceps: all-c bro1*
  - ⁝ **thrombophlebitis**: ham mrr1

- **Bones**; of (= osteitis): *Acon* k* *Ang* b2.de* ars k* ars-i *Asaf* k* aur k* aur-ar k2 aur-i k2* *Aur-m* aur-s k2 *Bell* k* bry k* *Calc* k* calc-f bg2* calc-sil k2 chin k* clem k* coloc k* con k* conch a1* cupr k* dig k* dys fmm1• euph k* **Fl-ac** guaj hecla kr1* hep k* iod k* *Kali-i* a1* kreos k* *Lac-ac* lach k* *Lyc* k* mag-m k* *Mang* k* mang-act br1 **Merc** k* merc-c bg2 merc-k-i gm1 merc-sul st **Mez** k* nat-c k* nat-sil k2 *Nit-ac* k* **Ph-ac** k* *Phos* k* *Phyt* kr1 plb k* *Psor* **Puls** k* rhus-t k* sep k* **Sil** k* spig k* **Staph** k* staphycoc jl2 still bro1* stront-c bro1* *Sulph* k* *Symph* kr1 thuj k* tub jl2 tub-m jl2 verat k*
  - **children**; in: syph jl2
  - **tubercular**: tub-m jl2

O • **Bone** marrow; of (= osteomyelitis): achy jl acon bro1* arg-met jl arn ptk1 bell bg2* calc ptk1 carc mlr1• cham mrr1 chinin-s bro1* conch a1 des-ac jl* eberth jl2 fl-ac mrr1 gunp bro1* kali-i mrr1 lat-m bnm6• merc mtf11 ph-ac c1* phos br1* puls bg2 *Sil* bg2* staphycoc jl2* syph mrr1 tub mrr1

- **Periosteum** (= periostitis): *Acon* bg2* agar tl1 ant-c k* *Apis* k* aran bro1 *Ars* k* *Asaf* k* aur k* aur-ar k2 *Aur-m* k* *Bell* b2.de* calc k2* calc-f ptk1 calc-p bg2* calc-sil mg1.de chin k* clem bro1 colch bro1 con bro1* conch a1 dros tl1 *Ferr-i* kr1* *Ferr-p* kr1* **Fl-ac** graph bro1 *Guaj* bro1 *Hecla* kr1* hep ptk1 *Iod* bro1* *Kali-bi* bg2* *Kali-i* k* lach tl1* led k* *Mang* k* mang-act bro1 mang-s mtf11 *Merc* k* *Merc-c* k* **Mez** k* myris br1 nat-sal c1* *Nit-ac* k* **Ph-ac** k* phos c2* *Phyt* kr1* plat-m bro1 *Psor* puls k* rhod bro1 rhus-t k* **Ruta** c2* **Sabin** bg2 sars bro1 sep ptk1 *Sil* k* *Staph* k* *Still* c1* sulph ptk1 *Symph* kr1* tell ptk1

- **Bones – Periosteum**: ...
  - ⁝ **accompanied** by | **sensitivity** to touch: mez mtf11
  - ⁝ **rheumatic**: asaf tl1 dros tl1 lach tl1 mez tl1 phyt tl1 ruta tl1
- **Bursae**; of (= bursitis): (↗*EXTREMITIES - Bursae; EXTREMITIES - Inflammation - fingers - joints - bursitis; EXTREMITIES - Inflammation - knee - bursae)* ant-c kr1 apis kr1 ars kr1 bell kr1 *Bell-p* st bry mrr1 chel mrr1 ferr mrr1 ferr-p mrr1 graph kr1 hep kr1 iod kr1 kalm mrr1 *Lycpr* st **Phyt** mrr1 puls kr1 rhod mrr1 *Rhus-t* mrr1 *Ruta* c1* *Sang* mrr1 **Sil** kr1 *Stict* kr1 succ-ac mtf11 *Sulph* kr1* syc bka1•
- **Cartilages**; of: (↗*Cartilages)* **Arg-met** k* asaf k2 *Bell* c1* cham c1* *Cimic* c1* lob-s c1 *Nat-m* olnd c1* *Plb* c1* *Ruta* c1* sil k2 stram k2
  - **children**; in: syph jl2
- **Connective** tissue: anthraci br1 *Apis* bg2 ars bg2 bell bg2 graph bg2 *Hep* bg2 *Med* jl2 myric bg2 rhus-t bg2* sil bg2 sul-i bg2 sulph bg2
- **Externally**: *Acon* k* agar k* agn j5.de alum st1 alumn k2* am-c k* ambr k* ant-c k* *Apis* bg2* arn k* **Ars** k* ars-i asaf k* asar k* aur k* aur-ar k2 bar-c k* **Bell** k* borx b2.de* bov k* *Bry* k* *Cact* *Calc* k* calc-i k2* calc-sil k2* camph k* cann-s k* canth k* caps k* carb-an k* carb-v k* caust k* *Cham* k* chel k* chin k* chinin-s j5.de cina j5.de clem k* cocc k* coff k* colch j5.de coloc k* *Con* k* cortiso sp1 croc j5.de crot-h crot-t j5.de cupr k* cupr-act j5.de dig k* dulc k* **Echi** euph k* *Euphr* k* *Ferr* k* ferr-ar k2 **Ferr-p** hr1* *Fl-ac* *Gels* hr1* gran j5.de graph k* *Gunp* st1 hell k* *Hep* k* hyos k* **Ign** k* iod k* ip k* *Kali-ar* kali-c k* kali-m k2 kali-n k* kreos k* **Lach** k* lact j5.de led k* *Lyc* k* m-ambo b2.de *M-arct* b2.de* m-aust b2.de mag-c k* mag-m k* mang k* *Merc* k* *Merc-d* j5.de mez k* mur-ac k* nat-ar nat-c k* nat-m k* *Nat-n* br1 nat-sil k2* *Nit-ac* k* nux-v k* op k* *Petr* k* ph-ac k* *Phos* k* plb k* **Puls** k* ran-b k* *Rhus-t* k* sabad k* sabin k* samb k* sars k* sep k* **Sil** k* *Spig* k* spira br1 spong k* squil hr1* stann k* **Staph** k* stram k* sul-ac k* *Sulph* b2.de* tarax k* teucr k* *Thuj* k* *Valer* k* verat k* **Verat-v** hr1* zinc k*
- **Fibrous** tissue: bacls-7 fmm1• calc mtf33 dys fmm1• morg-p fmm1• prot fmm1• syc fmm1•
  - **dampness** | **agg.**: *Syc* fmm1•
  - **rest** after a period of agg.: syc fmm1•
- **Glands**; of: (↗*Glands)* abrot mrr1 *Acon* k* ail bro1 *Alumn* k* *Anan* k* *Apis* bg2* arn k* ars k* ars-i k* ars-s-f k2 *Aur* k* aur-ar k2 aur-i k2 *Aur-m* aur-s k2 *Bad* *Bar-c* k* bar-i k2* **Bar-m** bar-s k2 **Bell** k* berb j5.de *Brom* *Bry* k* bufo k* **Calc** k* calc-f mg1.de calc-hp mg1.de calc-i mg1.de *Calc-sil* k2* *Camph* k* canth k* caps bg2 *Carb-an* k* carb-v k* *Carc* mlr1• *Cham* k* *Cist* k* clem k* *Con* k* cor-r c1* crot-h bg2* dros st dulc k* echi bg2* ferr-ar fl-ac mg1.de *Graph* j5.de* helo-s bnm14• *Hep* k* hippoz kr1* iod bro1* *Iodof* bro1 jug-r vml3• kali-ar *Kali-c* k* *Kali-i* k* *Kali-m* kr1 kali-p lach k* laur k* loxo-lae bnm12• *Lyc* k* m-aust b2.de* mag-m j5.de **Merc** k* merc-c a1 *Merc-i-r* bro1* nat-s bg2 *Nit-ac* k* *Nux-v* k* oper bro1 petr k* ph-ac k* **Phos** k* *Phyt* k* plb k* *Psor* *Puls* k* pyrog bg2 raph j5.de rhus-t k* samb k* sanic mg1.de sars k* scroph-n mg1.de sieg mg1.de *Sil* k* *Sil-mar* c1* spig k* spong k2* squil k* staph k* still mg1.de sul-ac k* sul-i k2* **Sulph** k* tarent-c bg2 thuj k* toxo-g jl2 tub mg1.de* v-a-b jl2 verat k* zinc k*
  - **accompanied** by | **measles**: kali-bi bro1 merc-i-r bro1
  - **acute**: carc mlr1•
  - **children**; in: med jl2
  - **chronic**: *Carc* mlr1•
  - **dentition**; during: *Mucor* jl2
  - **gonorrheal**: acon bro1 apis bro1 *Bell* bro1 hep bro1 *Merc* bro1
  - **scarlet** fever; after: brom bro1 hep bro1 lach bro1 *Merc-i-r* bro1 phyt bro1
  - **slow**: *Fil* br1
  - **smallpox**; after: *Merc-i-r* bro1 rhus-t bro1
  - **tubercular**: carc mlr1• merc-k-i gm1 tub jl2
- **Internally**: **Acon** k* agar k* aloe bg2 alum k* ang b2.de* ant-c k* ant-t k* *Apis* arg-met k* *Arg-n* bg2 arn k* **Ars** k* ars-i ars-s-f k2* *Arum-t* asaf k* *Aur* k* aur-ar k2 aur-i k2* aur-s k2* bar-c k* bar-i k2* **Bell** k* bell-p sp1 *Berb* bism k* **Bry** k* *Cact* calad k* calc k* calc-i k2 calc-sil k2* camph k* *Cann-s* k* **Canth** k* caps k* carb-ac carb-v k* *Cham* k* chin k* cic k* cina k* clem k* coc-c cocc k* coff k* colch k* coloc k* *Con* k* cortiso sp1 crot-h *Cub* cupr k* dig k* dros k* dulc k* **Echi** equis-h euph k* *Ferr* k* ferr-ar k2* **Ferr-p** hr1* **Gels** k* graph k* guaj k* ham hell k* hep k* hydr-ac sf1.de *Hyos* k* ign k* **Iod** k* ip k* *Kali-ar* *Kali-c* k* *Kali-chl* *Kali-i* kali-m k2 *Kali-n* k* **Lach** k* laur k* lil-t *Lyc* k* mag-m k* mang k* **Merc** k* **Merc-c** bg2 mez k* nat-ar nat-c k* nat-m k* *Nat-n* br1 nat-s sf1.de nit-ac k* nux-m hr1* **Nux-v** k* op k* par k* pareir petr k* ph-ac k* **Phos** k* phyt **Plb** k* podo sf1.de **Puls** k* ran-b k* ran-s k* rheum k* rhus-t k* ruta k* sabad k* sabin k* samb k* sang sangin-n **Sec** k* senec seneg k* sep k*

- **Internally**: ...
sil spig k* spira br1 spong k* *Squil* k* stann k* stram k* stront-c k* sul-ac k* sul-i k2* *Sulph* k* tab sf1.de tarent sf1.de **Ter Teucr** b2.de thuj k* uva *Verat* k* *Verat-v* sf1.de vip sf1.de
  - **gangrenous**: (↗*Blackness*) **Ars** *Bell* **Canth** *Carb-an Carb-v Chin Colch Crot-h* hep *Iod Kali-p* **Lach** merc *Phos Plb Rhus-t* **Sec Sil** k*
- **Joints**; of: (↗*EXTREMITIES - Inflammation - joints; EXTREMITIES - Pain - joints; EXTREMITIES - Pain - joints - rheumatic; EXTREMITIES - Pain - rheumatic)* abrot sf1.de **Acon** k* *Agn* b7a.de am-be sf1.de am-c sf1.de am-caust sf1.de am-m sf1.de am-p sf1.de ambr b7.de* *Ang* ant-c b7.de* *Ant-t* b7.de* **Apis** k* aran mg1.de* aran-ix mg1.de arb a1* arg-met mrr1 arist-cl sp1 *Arn* k* ars sf1.de asar sf1.de *Aur* aur-m-n wbt2• bar-c sf1.de **Bell** k* *Benz-ac* bg2* berb sf1.de* borra-o oss1• botul jl2 brass-n-o srj5• **Bry** k* *Calc* k* calc-hp sf1.de calc-p sf1.de* carb-ac br1 carc mlr1• caul sf1.de* *Caust* k* cham c1* chin b7.de* chinin-s sf1.de* cimic mrr1 clem sf1.de cocc b7.de* *Colch* sf1.de* coloc sf1.de conch a1 cortico sp1 cortiso sp1 crot-h sf1.de cycl sf1.de *Dulc* bg2* eos br1 eup-per sf1.de euphr mg1.de ferr sf1.de *Ferr-p* k* fl-ac bg2 form bg2* *Form-ac* sf1.de* gamb mrr1 *Gaul* sf1.de germ-met srj5• gins sf1.de graph mrr1 *Guaj* k* hed mg1.de hep sf1.de hyper ichth c1* ign mrr1 *Iod* junc-e br1 kali-ar k2 *Kali-c Kali-i* k* kali-m sf1.de kali-p mrr1 kali-s mrr1 *Kalm* k* *Kreos Lac-ac* lac-c mrr1 lach **Led** k* *Lith-be* sf1.de lith-c k* lith-sal sf1.de *Lyc* k* lyss mrr1 mand mg1.de* *Mang* mang-act br1 meny *Merc* k* mez sf1.de moni jl2 morg fmm1• *Nat-m Nat-s* k* nit-ac br1 nux-v mrr1 ph-ac sf1.de phos sf1.de* *Phyt* k* podo mrr1 *Psor Puls* k* pyrog sf1.de rad-br c11* ran-b sf1.de* *Rhod* k* *Rhus-t* k* *Ruta* k* sabad sf1.de sabin k* sal-ac sf1.de sang sf1.de* *Sars Sep* **Sil** k* spong sf1.de *Stel* sf1.de stict sf1.de* streptoc jl2 stront-c sf1.de sul-i mg1.de *Sulph* k* syph k2 tarax sf1.de thuj sf1.de* toxo-g jl2 tub br1* tub-r jl2 uncar-tom mp4• urt-u sf1.de valer mrr1 ven-m jl verat sf1.de verat-v visc mg1.de [brach stj]
  - **night**: cimic tl1
  - **accompanied** by:
    - **sensitivity**; excessive: colch tl1
    - **Skin**; complaints of: (↗*EXTREMITIES - Pain - joints - accompanied - rash; EXTREMITIES - Pain - joints - gouty - accompanied - eczema; EXTREMITIES - Pain - rheumatic - accompanied - eczema)* rad-br mrr1
  - **chronic**: *Caust* br1 mang-act br1 rad-br br1 scarl jl2
  - **deformans**; arthritis: abrot sf1.de *Am-p* sf1.de ant-c sf1.de apat mtf11 aran mg1.de aran-ix mg1.de arb bro1 *Arn* bro1* *Ars* bro1* aur bro1* bacls-7 mtf11 *Benz-ac* bro1* *Brom* b4a.de *Calc* bro1* calc-caust sf1.de calc-f mg1.de* calc-p bro1* caps bro1 caul bro1* *Caust* c2* *Cimic* bro1* clem sf1.de *Colch* bro1* colchin bro1 cupr ptk1* *Dulc* bro1 euphr mg1.de ferr-i bro1 ferr-pic bro1 fl-ac mg1.de form-ac sf1.de* graph sf1.de *Guaj* bro1* hecla bro1 hed mg1.de* hep sf1.de* ichth sf1.de *Iod* br1* kali-c bro1* *Kali-i* bro1* kalm mg1.de lac-ac bro1 *Led* bro1* lith-be sf1.de lith-c sf1.de lith-sal sf1.de lyc bro1* mand mg1.de mang sf1.de mang-act bro1 **Med** lz merc ptk1* *Merc-c* bro1 methyl bro1 nat-p bro1 nat-s sf1.de nit-ac bro1* onop jl *Pip-m* br1* *Puls* bro1* rad-br sf1.de* rhod bro1* *Ruta* dgt1 *Sabin* bro1* sal-ac bro1 sars sf1.de sep bro1* *Sil* sf1.de* staph sf1.de sul-i mg1.de sul-ter bro1 *Sulph* bro1* syc mtf11 symph mg1.de *Thuj* sf1.de thym-gl bro1 thyr bro1 tub-d dp* urt-u sf1.de visc mg1.de
  - **fails**; when all else: morg-p mtf11
  - **gonorrheal**: clem bg2 kali-i bg2 med bg2 nat-s bg2 puls bg2 rhus-t bg2 sulph bg2 thuj bg2
  - **infectious**: coli jl2 influ jl2 osteo-a jl2 syph jl2
  - **injuries**; after: arn mrr1
  - **osteoarthritis**: bacls-7 fmm1• cassia-s zzc1• dys fmm1• prot fmm1•
  - **rheumatic**: gaul br1 lil-t br1 rad-br br1 *Rham-cal* br1 thyr br1
    - **acute**: *Chinin-s* br1 guaj br1
      - **Large** joints: asc-c br1
    - **infective**: influ jl2
    - **monoarticular**: acon bro1 apis bro1 *Bry* bro1 caust bro1 chin bro1 cop bro1 *Merc* bro1
    - **polyarticular**: arn bro1 *Bry* bro1 guaj bro1 *Puls* bro1
  - **subacute**: dulc bro1 *Led* bro1 merc bro1 *Puls* bro1 rhus-t bro1
  - **wet** damp weather: nat-s tl1
  - ○ **Bones**; long: caust tl1
  - **Large** joints: *Arb* br1

- **Joints**; of: ...
  - **Periosteum**: bell bro1 cham bro1 colch bro1* cycl bro1 guaj bro1 *Kali-bi* bro1 kali-i bro1 merc bro1 *Mez* bro1 phos bro1 phyt bro1 sars bro1 sil bro1
  - **Small** joints: act-sp bg2 aloe bg2 benz-ac bg2 carb-an bg2 **Caul** bg2 colch bg2 kali-bi bg2 led bg2 lith-c bg2 nat-c bg2 rhod bg2 streptoc jl2
- **Liver**; of (See ABDOMEN - Inflammation - liver)
- **Lymphatic** vessels (= lymphangitis): aethi-a sf1.de all-c sf1.de *Anthraci* bro1* *Apis* bro1* arn sf1.de *Ars* sf1.de* ars-i bro1* *Bell* bro1* both bro1* **Bufo** br1* *Buth-a* sp1 carb-v sf1.de *Chinin-ar* sf1.de crot-h bro1* cupr st *Echi* bro1* euph sf1.de graph sf1.de *Gunp* sne hep sf1.de hippoz bro1 **Hyper** sne iod st *Lach* bro1* lat-h bnm5• lat-k bro1 lat-m bnm6• led mrr1 *Merc* bro1* merc-i-r bro1 mygal bro1* *Myris* sf1.de nat-s sf1.de *Pyrog* bro1* *Rhus-t* bro1* sil sf1.de sulph sf1.de* *Tarent-c* sf1.de toxo-g jl2 tub jl2
  - **gonorrheal**: acon bro1 apis bro1 *Bell* bro1 hep bro1 *Merc* bro1
  - **septic**: bufo br1
  - ○ **Nodes**: lat-m bnm6• streptoc jl2 toxo-g jl2
    - **chronic**: streptoc jl2
- **Mucous** membranes: **Acon** b2.de* *Agar* b2.de* agn b2.de* **All-c** hr1 alum b2.de* am-c b2.de* am-m b2.de* ambr b2.de* anac b2.de* ant-c b2.de* **Ant-t** b2.de* apis br1 arg-met b2.de* *Arg-n* bg2* arn b2.de* **Ars** b2.de* arum-d br1 arum-i br1 arum-m hr1* arum-t br1 asaf b2.de* asar b2.de* aur b2.de* aur-ar k2 bar-c b2.de* **Bell** b2.de* bism b2.de* *Borx* b2.de* bov b2.de* *Bry* b2.de* calad b2.de* *Calc* b2.de* *Calc-act* br1 camph b2.de* cann-s b2.de* *Canth* b2.de* caps b2.de* carb-an b2.de* carb-v b2.de* caust b2.de* *Cham* b2.de* chin b2.de* cic b2.de* cina b2.de* clem b2.de* cocc b2.de* coff b2.de* colch b2.de* coloc b2.de* con b2.de* crot-t br1 cupr b2.de* cycl b2.de* dig b2.de* *Dros* b2.de* *Dulc* b2.de* euph b2.de* euphr b2.de* **Ferr-p** hr1 graph b2.de* guaj b2.de* hell b2.de* hep b2.de* hyos b2.de* *Ign* b2.de* *Iod* b2.de* ip b2.de* kali-c b2.de* kali-n b2.de* kreos b2.de* lach b2.de* laur b2.de* lyc b2.de* m-ambo b2.de m-arct b2.de m-aust b2.de mag-c b2.de* mag-m b2.de* mang b2.de* meny b2.de* **Merc** b2.de* mez b2.de* mosch b2.de* mur-ac b2.de* nat-c b2.de* *Nat-m* b2.de* *Nit-ac* b2.de* nux-m b2.de* *Nux-v* b2.de* op b2.de* *Par* b2.de* petr b2.de* ph-ac b2.de* *Phos* b2.de* plat b2.de* plb b2.de* *Puls* b2.de* ran-b b2.de* ran-s b2.de* rhod b2.de* rhus-t b2.de* ruta b2.de* sabad b2.de* samb b2.de* sars b2.de* sec b2.de* sel b2.de* seneg b2.de* *Sep* b2.de* *Sil* b2.de* spig b2.de* spong b2.de* *Squil* b2.de* stann b2.de* staph b2.de* stront-c b2.de* sul-ac b2.de* **Sulph** b2.de* teucr b2.de thuj b2.de* verat b2.de* zinc b2.de*
  - **discharging**: *Calc-act* br1
  - **slow** and intense: kali-bi tl1
- **Muscles**; of: (↗*Complaints - muscles; Myopathia)* *Arn* bro1 bell bro1 *Bry* bro1 cimic sne ham k2 hep bro1 kali-i bro1 lat-m bnm6• merc bro1 *Mez* bro1 *Rhus-t* bro1 streptoc jl2 thuj tl1 toxo-g jl2
  - **fibromyalgia**, fibromyositis: *Calen* oss•
  - ○ **Back**; in: syc pte1•
- **Nerves** (= neuritis): **Acon** k* adren br1 aesc bro1 *All-c* bro1 *Alum-sil* anan bro1 *Ant-c* aran-ix mtf11 arg-n bro1 *Arn* bro1 *Ars* k* atro vh **Bell** k* bell-p bro1* ben-d c2* berb bro1 bry b7a.de* bufo k2 buni-o mtf11 *Cact Carbn-s* bro1 caust k* *Cedr* c1* *Cic* cimic bro1 *Coca Coff* mrr1 con bro1 diph jl2 diphtox jl2 ferr-p bro1 form mtf11 *Gels* k* *Hep Hyper* k* iod *Ip* kali-i *Kalm* lac-c *Lec Led* malar jl2 *Merc* k* *Nat-m* nit-ac k2 *Nux-v* k* pareir bro1 pert jl2 ph-ac bro1 **Phos** k* plb br1* plb-p bro1 *Puls Rhus-t* k* sang bro1 *Sil Stann* bro1 stram *Stront-c* br1* stry bro1 sulph syc fmm1• *Thal* c1* thal-met br1 thal-xyz srj8• thiop mtf11 tub-m jl2 *Urt-u* br1* vip br1 zinc zinc-p bro1
  - **accompanied** by | **sleeplessness**: con bro1*
  - **alcohol**; from: nux-v bro1 stry bro1
  - **chronic** | **injuries**; after: all-c br1* hyper ptk1 stram ptk1
  - **cold** agg.: stront-c br1
  - **diphtheritic**: gels bro1
  - **injuries**; from: *All-c* bro1 arn bro1 calen bro1 *Hyper* bro1
  - **multiple**: ars ptk1 bov bro1* con bro1* morph bro1* stront-c ptk1 thal bro1* vip ptk1
  - **touch** | **amel.**: sang ptk1
  - ○ **Peripheral**: carbn-s br1 lat-m bnm6• lepr mtf11 rhus-t mtf11
- **Organs**: ars-s-f k2
- **Ovaries**; of (See FEMALE - Inflammation - ovaries)
- **Parenchymatous** tissues: *Apis* br1
- **Perspiratory** gland (= hidradenitis): **Calc-s** mrr1

- **Prostate** gland; of (See PROSTATE - Inflammation)
- **Serous** membranes, of: abrot bg *Acon* k* am-c ant-t bg **Apis** k* *Apoc* k* arg-met **Ars** ars-i asaf *Asc-t* vh *Aur* aur-ar k2 aur-i k2 *Aur-m* aur-s k2 bell **Bry** **Calc** calc-p canth bg *Carb-v* colch ferr fl-ac **Hell** indg *Iod* *Kali-c* lac-ac bg lach *Led* **Lyc** mag-m *Merc* *Nat-m* *Ph-ac* *Phos* k* plat *Psor* *Puls* rhus-t bg samb seneg **Sil** *Squil* *Stram* sul-i bg *Sulph* *Ter* zinc
  - **effusion**; with: apis br1
- **Sinuses**; of (= sinusitis): *(↗EAR - Catarrh - eustachian; FACE - Pain - inflammatory; NOSE - Catarrh - followed - frontal; NOSE - Coryza - followed - frontal; NOSE - Sinuses)* aids nl2• am-c mrr1* ant-c mg1.de arg-n ser ars a1 ars-i sf1.de* aur mrr1 aur-m mrr1 aur-m-n wbt2• bell mrr1 berb dgt1 *Calc* kr1* calc-f mg1.de* calc-s st* carb-ac mrr1 carc gk6* caust mrr1 cinnb sf1.de* cor-r mgm• cupre-l mtf11 distemp-vc mtf11 dulc mrr1 elaps mrr1 euph mtf11 fl-ac mg1.de flav jl2 hecla jl *Hep* sf1.de* *Hydr* sf1.de* ign ser influ jl2* *Kali-bi* sf1.de* kali-c mg1.de* kali-i hr1* kali-n mrr1 kali-s st* lac-c mrr1 lob mrr1 luf-op rsj5* lyc sf1.de* mag-c mg1.de mag-f mg1.de mag-m mg1.de med mg1.de* *Merc* sf1.de* morg-g fmm1• morg-p pte1*• mucoc mtf11 mucot mtf11 nat-m sf1.de nat-ox-act mtf11 nat-s mrr1 nit-ac sf1.de* nux-v mtf11 oscilloc jl2* ozone sde2• penic jl *Phos* sf1.de pneu jl2 prun-v mtf11 puls sf1.de* pyrog st sal-fr sle1• scut mrr1 sep mrr1 **Sil** kr1* spig mrr1 stann mg1.de* *Stict* mg1.de* streptoc jl2 *Sulph* sf1.de* syc fmm1• teucr sf1.de thuj mrr1 *Trios* rsj11• tub-a jl2 [am-m stj1 am-p stj1 am-s stj1 calc-br stj1 calc-m stj1 *Chr-met* stj1 heroin sdj2 kali-m stj1 mag-br stj1 nicc stj1]
  - **right**: trios rsj11•
  - **left**: [am-m stj1]
  - **accompanied** by:
    - **vertigo** (See VERTIGO - Accompanied - sinuses)
    - **Head**; pain in: luf-op rsj5• streptoc jl2 syc bka1•
  - **acute**: penic mtf11
  - **children**; in: calc mtf33 carc mtf33
    - **infants**; in: med mrr1
  - **chill**; after: dulc mrr1
  - **chronic**: calc mtf33 carc fb* *Cist* mrr1 hed mtf11 *Kali-bi* mrr1 kali-n mrr1 *Med* mrr1 merc-k-i gm1 mucor jl2 oscilloc mtf11 ozone sde2• penic mtf11 psor mrr1 *Sil* mrr1 strept-ent jl2 thuj mrr1
  - **discharges**; after suppressed: thuj mtf11
  - **infection**; from: morg-g fmm1• morg-p fmm1• syc fmm1•
  - **menses**; during: am-c mrr1 *Mucor* jl2
  - **painful**: trios rsj11•
  - **purulent**: hep br1 luf-op mtf11
  - **recurrent** (See History - sinusitis)
  - **suppressed**: scut mrr1
  - **weather**:
    - **change** of weather: kali-i mrr1
    - **cold**:
      - **wet** | **agg.**: dulc mrr1
  - ○ **Polysinusitis**: sil mtf11
    - **chronic**: influ mtf11
- **Synovial** membranes; of (See EXTREMITIES - Inflammation - joints - synovitis)
- **Tendons**; of (= tendinitis): *(↗EXTREMITIES - Inflammation - tendons)* anac st ant-c c2* bry mrr1 caust mrr1* **Phyt** mrr1 *Rhod* st *Rhus-t* st* **Ruta** mrr1 sil mtf33
- **Tonsils**; of (See THROAT - Inflammation - tonsils)

INFLATED, blown up, filled by air; sensation of being: par b2.de* ran-b b2.de*

○ - **Glands**: spong bg2

INFLUENZA: *Acon* b7a.de* aesc bro1 all-c c2* ant-ar bro1 ant-i bro1 ant-t bro1* apis mrr1 arn b7a.de* ars b4.de* ars-i br1* ars-s-r c2* arum-d c2 asc-c c2 asc-t c2* aven c2 bamb-a stb2.de• bapt bg2* *Bell* bg2* *Brom* bro1 bry b7a.de* calc bro1* camph b7a.de* camph-br c2 canch c2* capp-crc br1 carb-ac c2* carb-v c2 card-m c2* caust b4.de* cent c2 cham c2 chel bg2* chin b7a.de* *Chinin-s* bro1 cimic bg2 *Cinnb* bro1 cupr bg cupr-ar bro1 cycl bro1 des-ac rbp6 dioxi rbp6 diph-pert-t mp4• diphtox jl2 dros bro1 dulc c2* erio c2 ery-a c2* *Eucal* br1* eug c2 *Eup-per* bg2* euph c2* euphr c2* ferr-p bg* *Gels* bg2* germ-met srj5• glon bro1 glyc bro1 *Graph* c2 gymno bro1 haff jl2 influ c1* iod bro1 ip bg2* kali-bi bro1 kali-c bro1 kali-i c2* kali-s bro1 *Kreos* b7a.de

Influenza: ...
lach bro1* lob-c bro1 lob-p c2* lob-s c2 lyc c2* *Lycpr* br1 menth c2 **Merc** bg2* merc-c mtf11 merc-k-i c2 *Nat-n* br1 nat-s c2* *Nat-sal* bro1 *Nux-v* b7a.de* oci-sa sp1 oscilloc jl2 oxyg c2 ozone sde2• phel c2 phos bg2* phyt bg2* podo bro1 *Psor* c2* puls bg2* pyrog c2* rad-br mrr1* rhus-r bro1 *Rhus-t* b7a.de* ribo rly4• rumx bro1 sabad b7a.de* sal-ac bro1 salin c2 salol c1* *Sang* bg2* sangin-n c2* sanic c2 sarcol-ac bro1* sarr c2 seneg c2* *Sil* bg2* silphu bro1 spig bg2* spong bro1 squil bg2 stict bg2* still c2 stram mtf11 stry-xyz c2 sul-i c2 sulo-ac c2 *Sulph* c2* *Thymul* ttm trios c2* *Tub* c2* tub-a c2* vario jl2 *Verat* c2* verat-v bg2* wye c2 yers jl2 ziz c2 [bell-p-sp dcm1 **Spect** dfg1]

- **accompanied** by:
  - **ailments**; at the beginning of other: gels tl1
  - **chill**: leptos-ih jl2
  - **pain**:
    - **bruised**: *Bapt* mrr1
    - **radiating**: leptos-ih jl2
  - **palpitations** (See CHEST - Palpitation - accompanied - influenza)
  - **retching** (See STOMACH - Retching - accompanied - influenza)
  - **typhoid** conditions: bapt tl1
  - **vomiting** | **violent** (See STOMACH - Vomiting - violent - accompanied - influenza)
  - ○ **Bones**; pain in: **Eup-per** c1*
  - **Head**; pain in: leptos-ih jl2
  - **Liver**; complaints of (See ABDOMEN - Liver - accompanied - influenza)
  - **Lungs**:
    - **inflammation** of | **catarrhal** (See CHEST - Inflammation - lungs - catarrhal - accompanied - influenza)
  - **Occiput**; pain in (See HEAD - Pain - occiput - influenza)
  - **Pleura**; pain in (See CHEST - Pain - pleura - accompanied - influenza)
  - **Tongue**:
    - **brown** discoloration: chel kr1*
    - **cracked**: chel kr1*
    - **white** discoloration of the tongue: *Merc-i-r* kr1*
- **beginning**:
  - **rapidly**: bapt tl1 camph tl1
  - **slowly**: gels tl1
- **catarrhal**: silphu br1
- **children**; in: calc tl1 ph-ac tl1
- **complaints** after (See Convalescence - influenza)
- **epidemic**: *Sarcol-ac* br1
- **prophylactic**: eucal ptk1 *Gels* tl1
- **sensation** as if: cadm-met sp1 leptos-ih jl2 luna kg1• olib-sac wmh1 rad-br sze8•
  - **beginning** stage: vult-gr sze5•

INHERITANCE (See Family)

INJURIES: *(↗Convalescence - injuries; Injuries - contusion; Shock; EXTREMITIES - Injuries; EXTREMITIES - Paralysis - lower - injuries)* absin kr1 acet-ac bro1* *Acon* j5.de* *Agn* kr1 all-c c1* aloe ptk1 alst-b jsx1.fr alum j5.de* *Am-c* j5.de* anemps br1 ang bg2* ant-c kr1 apis c1* *Arg-met* kr1* arg-n bg2 **Arn** k* *Aur-m* kr1 *Bad* bell b7a.de* *Bell-p* bg2* bid-b jsx1.fr bid-p jsx1.fr borx b2.de* both-ax tsm2 bril-p jsx1.fr bry k* bufo bg2* calc k* calc-p bg2 calc-s c1 **Calen** bg2* **Camph** st1 **Cann-i** st1 **Cann-xyz** ptk1 canth k* *Carb-v* k* *Caust* j5.de* cham k* chin k* chinin-s j5.de *Cic* k* **Con** k* crats-ce jsx1.fr croc k* crot-t bro1* cupr ptk1 dig ptk1 *Dros* kr1 *Dulc* k* echi bg2* erig c1 eug j5.de euph bg2 euph-pi c1* euphr k* ferr-p c1* *Form* kr1* gamb c1 *Glon* bg2* guare-ce jsx1.fr *Ham* bg2* hein-cr jsx1.fr hell c1* **Hep** k* hib-su jsx1.fr hydrc jsx1.fr hyos k* **Hyper** k* *Iod* k* ip c1 kal jsx1.fr kali-c k* kali-i ptk1 kali-m c1 kali-p c1 kali-s c1 kreos k* lac-c c1 lac-d c1 lac-h sze9• *Lach* k* laur k* *Led* k* *Lith-c* kr1* lyc k* m-ambo b2.de* mag-c c1* merc k* mez k* *Mill* bg2* mir-j jsx1.fr mosch kr1 musa-p jsx1.fr *Naja* ptk1 nat-c k* nat-m k* *Nat-s* k* *Nit-ac* k* nux-m bg2 nux-v k* oena c1 *Olnd* kr1 paeon c1 par k* pareir kr1 *Petr* j5.de* ph-ac k* *Phos* k* phys bg2* pin-con oss2• *Plan* kr1* plat k*

Injuries: ...
plb k* polyg-h kr1 psor c1* **Puls** k* ran-b c1 *Rhod* kr1 **Rhus-t** k* *Ruta* k* sacch-a fd2.de• sal-ac tl1 samb k* sec k* seneg k* *Sep* j5.de* *Sil* k* spig ptk1 spong fd4.de *Staph* k* stict c1 stront-c bro1* **Sul-ac** k* sul-i k2 *Sulph* k* **Symph** k* synad-g jsx1.fr tab ptk1 tarent c1* tell c1 ter c1 teucr kr1* tritic-vg fd5.de urt-u c1 valer c1 vanil fd5.de vario c1 verat k* *Verb* kr1* verbe-o br1 zinc k* [bell-p-sp dcm1 spect dfg1]

- **ailments** from; chronic: acon mrr1 **Arn** br1* carb-v pfa1* cic st1 *Con* st1 glon st1 ham st1 hyper st1 led st1 *Nat-s* st1 ruta bg2 stram mrr1 *Stront-c* st1* [bell-p-sp dcm1]
- **blunt** instruments; from: arn tl1 *Symph* tl1
- **cold** applications | **amel.**: *(↗ice - amel.; warmth - heat)* loxo-recl bnm10•
- **concussion**: acon b2.de* *Anac* b2.de* **Arn** b2.de* *Aur* b2.de* **Bad** hr1* *Bell* b2.de* berb kr1* bry j5.de *Calc* b2.de* calen hr1* camph b2.de* cann-s b2.de* caust b2.de* chin b2.de* *Cic* b2.de* cina b2.de* *Cocc* b2.de* con j5.de* cupr b2.de* euphr hr1* *Glon* bg2* *Hell* hr1* *Hyos* b2.de* **Hyper** hr1* *Iod* hr1* *Kali-p* kr1 kreos b2.de* *Lach* hr1* laur b2.de* *Led* b2.de* lil-t kr1* lyc b2.de* m-ambo b2.de* m-arct b2.de* mag-m b2.de* *Mang* b2.de* mez b2.de* *Nat-m* b2.de* **Nat-s** hr1* nux-m b2.de* *Nux-v* b2.de* onos hr1* ph-ac b2.de* *Puls* b2.de* *Rhus-t* b2.de* seneg b2.de* *Sep* b2.de* *Sil* b2.de* *Spig* b2.de* staph b2.de* stry sf1.de sul-ac j5.de* valer b2.de* vanil fd5.de *Verat* b2.de* viol-t b2.de*
    - • **agg.**: arn-c sf1.de **Arn** sf1.de cic bro1 *Hyper* sf1.de petr sf1.de valer sf1.de
    - • **brain**; ailments from commotion of the: *(↗Shock - electric-like - concussion)* sul-ac c1 teucr c1
- **contusion**: *(↗Injuries)* acet-ac bro1 acon b2.de* ant-c b2.de* *Arg-met* b2.de* arn b2.de* *Bell-p* bro1* calen bg2 canth b7.de carb-an b4.de* carb-v b4.de* caust b2.de* cham b7.de *Cic* b2.de* *Con* b2.de* *Dros* b2.de* echi bro1 euphr b2.de* ham bro1* hep b2.de* hyper bg2* iod b2.de* kali-c b2.de* lach b2.de* led b2.de* nux-m b2.de* *Olnd* b2.de* par b2.de* petr b2.de* phos b2.de* plat b2.de* puls b2.de* rhod b2.de* rhus-t b2.de* **Ruta** b2.de* sep b2.de* staph ptk1 stict ptk1 *Sul-ac* b2.de* sulph b2.de* symph bro1* tell ptk1 teucr b2.de* verat b2.de* verb b2.de*
    - • **agg.**: *Arn* b7.de* *Bell* b7a.de canth b7.de cham b7.de *Con* b4a.de *Dulc* b4a.de *Euphr* b7a.de hep b4a.de iod b4a.de kali-c b4a.de *Lach* b7.de* phos b4a.de plat b4a.de *Puls* b7.de *Rhus-t* b7.de* *Ruta* b7.de *Samb* b7a.de *Sul-ac* b4a.de sulph b4a.de
    - • **bruises**; and: con mtf11
    - • **exertion**; with: *Rhus-t* b7a.de
    - ○ • **Glands**: cic bg2 con bg2 hep bg2 iod bg2 kali-c bg2 merc bg2 *Petr* bg2 *Phos* bg2 puls bg2 sil bg2 sulph bg2
- **deadness** in the bruised part; sensation of: arn k1
- **dislocation** (= luxation): *(↗EXTREMITIES - Dislocation)* **Agn** b2.de* *Am-c* b2.de* *Ambr* b2.de* ang b2.de* **Arn** b2.de* bar-c b2.de* *Bell* bg2* bov b2.de* *Bry* b2.de* **Calc** b2.de* calc-p bg2 cann-s b2.de* caps j5.de* *Carb-an* b2.de* *Carb-v* b2.de* *Carl* a1 *Caust* b2.de* *Coloc* bg2 con b2.de* *Croc* b7.de* *Ferr-s* kr1 *Form* kr1* *Graph* b2.de* hep b2.de* **Ign** b2.de* *Kali-n* b2.de* kreos b2.de* lach j5.de led bg2 **Lyc** b2.de* m-ambo b2.de* m-arct j5.de m-aust b2.de* mag-c j5.de* *Merc* b2.de* mez b2.de* mosch b2.de* **Nat-c** b2.de* **Nat-m** b2.de* *Nit-ac* b2.de* *Nux-v* b2.de* par j5.de **Petr** b2.de* **Phos** b2.de* psor c1 **Puls** b2.de* rheum c1 *Rhod* b2.de* **Rhus-t** b2.de* *Ruta* b2.de* sabin b2.de* sep b2.de* sil bg2 *Spig* b2.de* stann b2.de* staph b2.de* *Sulph* b2.de* tub jl2 zinc b2.de*
- **distortion** of joints (See sprains)
- **extravasations**, with: *Acet-ac* kr1 agar kr1* arist-m c2 **Arn** k* *Bad* bell-p st1* both st1 bry k* calen kr1* cham k* chin k* cic *Con* k* crot-h j5.de* dulc k* euphr k* ferr k* *Ham* kr1* *Hep* k* hyper st1 iod *Lach* k* laur k* *Led* bg2* mill kr1 nux-v k* par k* plb k* *Puls* k* rhus-t k* *Ruta* k* sec k* staph st1 stront-c mrr1 **Sul-ac** k* sul-i k* *Sulph* k* symph st1 tritic-vg fd5.de vanil fd5.de [bell-p-sp dcm1]
- **heal** | **slowly**: mim-p skp7•
- **ice** | **amel.**: *(↗cold - amel.; warmth - heat)* loxo-recl bnm10•
- **mechanical** lesions: aesc tl1
- **operation**:
    - • **ailments** from: *(↗Fistulae - operation; Pain - operation; Weakness - operation)* acet-ac bro1 *Acon* kr1* all-c c1* apis c1* *Arn* c1* *Bell-p* br1* berb bro1* calc-f br1* calc-p c1 *Calen* k2* camph br1* carb-v k2* chin sf1.de croc c1* echi ptk1 ferr-p bro1 ham br1* *Hyper* c1* kali-s bro1 led k2 merc c1 mill bro1 naja bro1 nit-ac bro1 nux-v sf1.de op sf1.de ph-ac c1* pop sf1.de raph bro1* rhus-t br1* ruta k2 **Staph** c1* *Stront-c* c1* stroph-h br1 sul-ac c1* verat bro1 zinc c1*

- **operation – ailments** from: ...
    - ⁝ **deeper** tissues and after major surgical work; to: *(↗ABDOMEN - Injury - deep)* *Bell-p* br1*
    - ⁝ **fistulae**; for (See Fistulae - operation)
    - ⁝ **Bladder**; on stones in (See BLADDER - Stones - operation)
    - ⁝ **Ovaries**; excision of the: ars bro1 *Bell* bro1 *Bry* bro1 chin bro1 coff bro1 *Coloc* bro1 hyper bro1 ip bro1 lyc bro1 naja bro1 nux-v bro1 orch bro1 ov br1* *Staph* bro1
    - • **prophylaxis** | **rectal** operations: coll br1*
    - • **stretching**; with: staph k2
- **overexertion**, strain, from: *Agn* br1* *Arn* hr1* *Ars* hr1* **Bell-p** ptk1* **Calc** hr1* calc-f c1* carb-an hr1* carb-v c1 cocc c1 *Con* hr1* graph ptk1 *Ham* hr1* helon br1 kali-m ptk1 lach ptk1 lyc c1* *Mill* hr1* nat-c c1 nux-v tl1 onos ptk1 ovi-p c1 petr ptk1 *Rhus-t* hr1* *Ruta* ptk1* sanic c1 sil c1* ter c1
    - ○ • **Flexor** muscles; of: *Ruta* br1
- **prone** to (See MIND - Accident-prone)
- **rupture**:
    - ○ • **Blood** vessel; of: bar-c br1 mill kr1
    - • **Muscles**, of: calen kr1
    - • **Tendons**, of: rhus-t st
- **sharp** instruments: dulc fd4.de ham fd3.de• staph k2 tritic-vg fd5.de
- **sprains**: *(↗Lifting straining; Lifting straining of muscles and tendons - from; EXTREMITIES - Sprains)* acet-ac bro1 acon b2.de* **Agn** j5.de* all-s c1* *Am-c* j5.de* am-m c1* am-p bg2 amyg-p c1* anemps br1 ang b2.de* arist-cl sp1 **Arn** b2.de* ars b2.de* *Asaf* b2.de* asar sf1.de bell b2.de* *Bell-p* br1* benz-ac bg2 *Bit-ar* wht1• bov sf1.de *Bry* b2.de* **Calc** j5.de* calc-f c1* calc-p sf1.de calc-sil k2 calen bro1 camph b2.de canth b2.de* *Carb-an* j5.de* carb-v j5.de* carl c1* caust j5.de* *Cham* b2.de chin b2.de* *Cic* b2.de* cocc b2.de con ptk1 cupr b2.de* dulc fd4.de ferr-p kr1* *Ferr-s* kr1 form bro1 graph b2.de* guaj bg2 hell b2.de hyos b2.de* *Hyper* bro1 *Ign* j5.de* kali-i bg2 kali-m c1* kreos c1 lach c1* laur b2.de *Led* bg2* lith-c bg2 **Lyc** j5.de* *M-aust* j5.de mag-c sf1.de maland al2 med al2 merc b2.de mez sf1.de **Mill** kr1* **Nat-c** j5.de* **Nat-m** j5.de* *Nit-ac* j5.de* *Nux-v* b2.de* onos ptk1 *Op* b2.de **Petr** b2.de* **Phos** j5.de* phyt mrr1 **Plat** b2.de plb b2.de polyg-h kr1* polyg-pe c1 *Prun* c1* psor c1* *Puls* b2.de* rad-br bg2 ran-b b2.de rheum b2.de rhod c1* **Rhus-t** c1* rhus-v c1 **Ruta** b2.de* *Sec* b2.de seneg c1 sep j5.de* sil bg2* sol-ni j5.de spig b2.de* stann b2.de staph sf1.de **Stram** b2.de stront-c kr1* sul-ac c1* *Sulph* b2.de* sumb a1 *Symph* kr1* tarent a1 thuj bg2 tritic-vg fd5.de verat b2.de [bell-p-sp dcm1]
    - • **chronic**: am-m ptk1 nat-m ptk1 stront-c br1*
    - • **easy**: carb-an ptk1 phos ptk1 rhus-t ptk1
    - • **swelling** of the joints; with a soft: samb hr4
    - ○ • **Muscles** | **riding** agg.: arist-cl sp1
    - • **Parts** lain on: mosch ptk1
- **strains** (See overexertion)
- **stretching** of tissues: staph k2
- **stump** neuralgia (See Pain - amputation)
- **tennis** elbow (= epicondylitis): *(↗EXTREMITIES - Injuries - elbow - tennis)* agar st ambr st* *Rhus-t* st spirae mtf11
- **tetanus**; prophylaxis of (See Tetanus - prophylaxis)
- **traumatic** fever: *Acon* kr1* *Apis* st **Arn** kr1* *Ars* c1* cact c1 *Calen* kr1* *Chin* c1* *Coff* kr1* *Iod* st1 *Lach* c1* *Lyss* st1 merc st1 *Sulph* k2
- **warmth** agg. | **heat** agg.: *(↗cold - amel.; ice - amel.)* loxo-recl bnm10•
- **wrenching** of joints (See sprains)
- ○ - **Bones**; fractures of *(↗Brittle; Shock - injuries; EXTREMITIES - Fractures)* acon bro1* ang bg2* *Arn* b2.de* asaf kr1 asar b7.de* bell-p mg1.de* bry mrr1 calc k* *Calc-f* bg2* calc-p k* *Calen* j5.de* **Carb-ac** kr1 con b2.de* cortico sp1 cortiso sp1 croc bg2 dulc fd4.de *Eup-per* c1* ferr bg2* hecla c1 hep b2.de* **Hyper** sne iod b2.de* kali-i bg2* led sne lyc kr1 nit-ac kr1 *Petr* bg2* *Ph-ac* b2.de* phos b2.de* *Puls* b2.de* ran-b sne rhus-t b2.de* rob sne **Ruta** k* *Sil* b2.de* **Spig** sne staph b2.de* stront-c st *Sul-ac* sulph bg2* *Symph* k* valer bg2 vanil fd5.de [bell-p-sp dcm1]
    - • **compound** fracture: **Arn** kr1* *Calen* bg2* crot-h kr1 hyper c1* *Lach* kr1
    - • **slow** repair of broken bones: *(↗HEAD - Fractures - skull - slow)* anthraci sne asaf k* **Calc** k* calc-ar mtf11 calc-f bg2* calc-i mtf11 **Calc-p** k* calen bro1* des-ac jl* *Ferr* k* fl-ac k2* iod bro1* lyc k* mang st mang-act bro1 merc k* *Mez* k* nit-ac k* *Ph-ac* k* phos k* puls k* **Ruta** b2.de* sep k* *Sil* k* staph k* succ-ac mtf11 sulph k* **Symph** k* *Thyr* c1*
        - ⁝ **children**; in: *Calc* st* *Calc-f* st *Calc-p* st* sil st

- **Connective** tissue; to (See Connective)
- **Glands**: _Arn_ k* aster bro1 bell-p ptk1* cic k* **Con** k* _Dulc_ k* hep k* _Iod_ k* kali-c b4a.de kalm hr1* merc k* _Petr_ b4a.de* _Phos_ k* puls k* rhus-t k* _Sil_ k* _Sul-ac_ k* _Sulph_ b2.de*
- **Joints**: calen bro1
- **Muscles**, of: (↗_Complaints - muscles)_ arn b2.de* calc k2* calen bro1 nat-c b2.de* nat-m b2.de* phos b2.de* **Rhus-t** b2.de*
- **Nerves**: (↗_EXTREMITIES - Injuries - nerves)_ all-c br1* arn mrr1 bell-p br1* helon c2 hyper bg2* led mrr1 meny c1 ph-ac bro1* phos ptk1 xan c1*
  - **cold** bathing agg.: bell-p br1
  - **pain**; with great: bell-p br1* _Cur_ kr1 glon sf1.de **Hyper** k* led k2 mag-p kr1 meny c1 _Phos_ tarent kr1 ther kr1 [bell-p-sp dcm1]
- **Periosteum**, of: calc k2* _Ruta_ k* spong fd4.de symph c1*
- **Soft** parts, of: **Arn** k* bell-p st1 cham k* **Con** k* dulc k* euphr k* ham st1 hyper tl1* lach k* _Nat-c_ j5.de nat-m j5.de phos j5.de _Puls_ k* _Rhus-t_ j5.de* samb k* _Sul-ac_ k* sulph k* _Symph_ st1
- **Tendons**, of (= tendinitis): acon bg2 am-c bg2 _Anac_ k* apis bg2 arn bg2 ars bg2 ars-i bg2 bell bg2 benz-ac bg2 bry bg2 calc-p bg2 calen bro1* canth bg2 ferr bg2 guaj bg2 hep bg2 iod bg2 kali-i bg2 osteo-a jl2 rhod mrr1 rhus-t bg2* ruta bg2* sil bg2 sulph bg2 symph br1 taosc iwa1• thuj bg2 vac jl2

INSENSIBILITY (See Anesthesia [=insensibility])

INSPIRATION:

- **agg.**: **Acon** b2.de* _Agar_ b2.de* agn b2.de* alum b2.de* am-c b2.de* am-m b2.de* _Anac_ b2.de* ang b2.de* _Arg-met_ b2.de* arg-n st _Arn_ b2.de* ars b2.de* asaf b2.de* _Asar_ b2.de* aur b2.de* bar-c b2.de* _Borx_ b2.de* both-a rb3 bov b2.de* brom sf1.de **Bry** b2.de* _Calc_ b2.de* camph b2.de* cann-s b2.de* canth b2.de* _Caps_ b2.de* carb-an b2.de* carb-v b2.de* caust b2.de* _Cham_ b2.de* _Chel_ b2.de* chin b2.de* cic b2.de* cina b2.de* clem b2.de* cocc b2.de* colch b2.de* coloc b2.de* con b2.de* croc b2.de* _Crot-h_ bg2* cupr b2.de* cycl b2.de* dulc b2.de* euphr b2.de* _Guaj_ b2.de* hell b2.de* hist mg1.de hyos b2.de* ign b2.de* iod b2.de* _Ip_ b2.de* _Kali-c_ b2.de* _Kali-n_ b2.de* _Kreos_ b2.de* laur b2.de* led b2.de* lob ptk1 _Lyc_ b2.de* m-arct b2.de* mag-c b2.de* mag-m b2.de* _Meny_ b2.de* _Merc_ b2.de* _Mez_ b2.de* mosch b2.de* mur-ac b2.de* nat-c b2.de* nat-m b2.de* nit-ac b2.de* nux-m b2.de* nux-v b2.de* olnd b2.de* op b2.de* par b2.de* ph-ac b2.de* phos b2.de* plat b2.de* plb b2.de* puls b2.de* _Ran-b_ b2.de* ran-s b2.de* rhod b2.de* **Rhus-t** b2.de* rumx sf1.de ruta b2.de* _Sabad_ b2.de* **Sabin** b2.de* sars b2.de* _Sel_ b2.de* _Seneg_ b2.de* sep b2.de* sil b2.de* spig b2.de* _Spong_ b2.de* **Squil** b2.de* stann b2.de* stront-c b2.de* sul-ac b2.de* sulph b2.de* sumb ptk1 tarax b2.de* teucr b2.de* _Valer_ b2.de* verat b2.de* verb b2.de* viol-t b2.de* zinc b2.de*
- **amel.**: ant-t b2.de* asaf b2.de* bar-c b2.de* bry b2.de* cann-s b2.de* caust b2.de* _Chin_ b2.de* chir-fl gya2 cina b2.de* **Colch** b2.de* _Cupr_ b2.de* _Dig_ b2.de* dros b2.de* dulc b2.de* **Ign** b2.de* iod b2.de* _Lach_ b2.de* mang b2.de* meny b2.de* nux-v b2.de* _Olnd_ b2.de* ph-ac b2.de* _Puls_ b2.de* ruta b2.de* sabad b2.de* sep b2.de* **Spig** b2.de* squil b2.de* _Stann_ b2.de* staph b2.de* tarax b2.de* verat b2.de* verb bg2* viol-o b2.de* viol-t b2.de*
- **hot** air; ailments from inspiration of: carb-v c1

INSTABILITY OF BODY: (↗_Relaxation - physical)_

acon b2.de agar b2.de agn b2.de alum b2.de ant-t b2.de _Arn_ b2.de ars b2.de _Asar_ b2.de aur b2.de _Bell_ b2.de bism b2.de bry b2.de camph b2.de caust b2.de cham b2.de chel b2.de chin b2.de _Cic_ b2.de cina b2.de **Cocc** b2.de coff b2.de colch b2.de cupr b2.de cycl b2.de dig b2.de dulc b2.de euph b2.de ferr b2.de hep b2.de hyos b2.de ign b2.de ip b2.de _Kali-c_ b2.de kali-n b2.de lach b2.de lyc b2.de m-arct b2.de m-aust b2.de meny b2.de merc b2.de nat-c b2.de _Nat-m_ b2.de nit-ac b2.de nux-m b2.de _Nux-v_ b2.de olnd b2.de op b2.de par b2.de petr b2.de ph-ac b2.de phos b2.de plat b2.de plb b2.de ran-s b2.de rhod b2.de rhus-t b2.de ruta b2.de sabad b2.de sabin b2.de sel b2.de sep b2.de _Sil_ b2.de spig b2.de spong b2.de stann b2.de _Staph_ b2.de stram b2.de sulph b2.de _Tarax_ b2.de **Verat** b2.de viol-o b2.de viol-t b2.de zinc b2.de

INSULIN SECRETION: | decreasing: cortiso sp1*

INTOXICATION, after: (↗_Food and - alcoholic - agg. - intoxicated; MIND - Alcoholism; MIND - Drunkenness; MIND - Libertinism)_

abies-c a1 absin a1 acet-ac a1 acon k* aether a1 agar k* agn a1 aids nl2• _Am-m_ k* aml-ns a1 amyg a1 ang b2.de* _Ant-c_ bg2 arg-met k* ars a1 asar ptk1 atro a1 bart a1 bell k* bov _Bry_ k* calc bg2 camph a1 cann-s a1 _Caps_ a1* carb-an a1 _Carb-v_ k* carbn-s mrr1 chel a1 chin k* chinin-s a1 cic a1 cinch a1 coca a1 _Cocc_ k* _Coff_ k* con a1 conin a1 cori-r a1 dat-m a1 dulc bg2 eucal a1 fagu a1 ferr a1 _Gels_ a1 grat a1 hyos a1 ign a1 ip k* kali-bi a1 kali-c k* kali-i a1 kali-n k* kiss a1 kreos k* lact a1 _Laur_ k* led a1* lol a1 merc a1 mez a1 mill a1 morph a1 nabal a1 naja a1 nat-c bg2 nat-m k* nit-ac bg2 nux-m k* **Nux-v** k* **Op** k* ph-ac k* phel a1 phos bg2 pip-m a1 positr nl2• _Puls_ k* rheum k* rhod a1 rhus-t bg2 sabad a1 sal-fr sle1• samb k* sec a1 _Spong_ k* squil k* staphytox jl2 _Stram_ k* sul-ac ptk1 sulph bg2 tab a1 tax a1 ter a1 teucr k* thea a1 til a1 tus-fr a1 valer k* verat a1 vip a1 zinc a1 [heroin sdj2]

- **as** from (See HEAD - Intoxication)

IODINE, after abuse of:

ant-c sf1.de ant-t hr1* _Ars_ j5.de* bell hr1* camph hr1* chin hr1* chinin-s kr1 coff hr1* _Conv_ bg2* _Hep_ bg2* hydr bro1* lycps-v sf1.de merc hr1* _Op_ bg2* phos j5.de* _Sec_ bg2* spong hr1* sulph j5.de*

IODINE deficiency symptoms:

calc-i mtf11 fuc mtf11 sil mtf11 spong mtf11 thyr mtf11

IRON, after abuse of: (↗_Allergic - chemical)_

ars k* calc-p sf1.de _Chin_ bg2* chinin-ar sf1.de cupr bg2* _Hep_ bg2* iod hr1* ip hr1* merc hr1* nat-m sf1.de _Puls_ k* _Sulph_ k* _Zinc_ k*

- **children**; in: chin mtf33

IRRITABILITY, physical:

- **excessive**: (↗_MIND - Irritability)_ absin k* acon k* agar k* alum c1 _Ambr_ k* anac k* ant-c k* ant-t b2.de* **Apis** k* **Arn** k* _Ars_ k* _Asaf_ k* **Asar** k* **Aur** k* aur-ar k2 _Aur-m_ kr1 bar-c k* bar-m kr1 **Bell** k* _Berb_ c1 borx k* bov k* bry k* _Calad_ c1 calc b2.de* camph k* cann-i k* **Canth** k* carb-ac c1 _Carb-v_ b2.de* carbn-s cartl-s rly4• caust k* _Cham_ k* **Chin** k* _Chinin-s_ k* _Chlol_ kr1 cina b2.de* _Coc-c_ c1 _Coca_ kr1 _Cocc_ k* **Coff** k* _Coll_ c1 con b2.de* croc k* cupr k* dig b2.de* _Dulc_ c1 ery-a kr1 _Ferr_ k* ferr-ar k2 ferr-i a1 fuma-ac rly4• _Gels_ k* ger-i rly4• graph k* hell k* hep k* hyos k* _Ign_ k* indg kr1 kali-c b2.de* kreos k* _Lach_ k* lat-m bnm6• laur k* _Lil-t_ k* _Lyc_ b2.de* _M-arct_ b2.de* m-aust b2.de mag-c k* mag-m k* mang k* **Med** k* meny b2.de* **Merc** k* mez k* _Morph_ c1 _Mosch_ k* mucs-nas rly4• nat-ar k* nat-c k* _Nat-m_ k* nat-ox rly4• nat-p k* nat-sil k2 **Nit-ac** k* nux-m b2.de* **Nux-v** k* orot-ac rly4• par k* ped c1 petr k* _Ph-ac_ k* _Phos_ k* plat k* podo kr1 _Puls_ k* pyrid rly4• rhus-t k* _Rhus-v_ c1 _Rumx_ c1 sabin k* sars b2.de* sec k* sel k* sep k* **Sil** k* spig k* spong b2.de* squil k* **Staph** k* staphycoc rly4• stram k* suis-pan rly4• sulph k* **Tarent** k* **Teucr** k* thiam rly4• tub br1 tub-d zs _Valer_ k* _Verat_ k* _Vib_ kr1 ziz kr1 [spect dfg1]
- **false**: merc ptk1 mur-ac ptk1 phos ptk1
- **lack** of: (↗_Analgesia; Anesthesia [=insensibility]; Painlessness; Reaction - lack; MIND - Irritability - weakness - with)_ acon b2.de* agn k* aloe sne _Alum_ k* alum-p k2 _Am-c_ k* am-m b2.de* _Ambr_ k* _Anac_ k* ang b2.de* ant-c k* ant-t k* arn k* _Ars_ k* asaf k* asar b2.de* bar-c k* bell b2.de* bism k* borx b2.de* brom bry k* **Calc** k* **Calc-i** _Camph_ k* cann-s k* canth b2.de* **Caps** k* _Carb-an_ k* **Carb-v** k* carc gk6* caust k* cham b2.de* chel b2.de* chin b2.de* cic k* clem b2.de* _Cocc_ k* colch k* coloc k* **Con** k* cory br1 croc k* cupr k* dig b2.de* _Dulc_ k* euph k* ferr k* ferr-i k2 **Gels** graph k* _Guaj_ k* **Hell** k* hep b2.de* hyos k* ign b2.de* _Iod_ k* _Ip_ k* _Kali-br_ k1 kali-c k* kali-s k2 lach k* **Laur** k* led k* _Lyc_ k* m-ambo b2.de m-aust b2.de mag-c k* mag-m k* merc b2.de* mez k* _Mosch_ k* mur-ac k* nat-c b2.de* nat-m b2.de* _Nit-ac_ b2.de* nux-m k* nux-v b2.de* **Olnd** k* **Op** k* petr k* **Ph-ac** k* phos k* plb k* **Psor** puls b2.de* _Rhod_ k* rhus-t k* sec k* seneg k* _Sep_ k* sil b2.de* spong k* stann k* staph b2.de* _Stram_ k* stront-c k* _Sulph_ k* **Teucr** st thuj k* valer k* verat j5.de* verb k* _Zinc_ k* [heroin sdj2]
  - **chronic** disease; in: cory br1
- **remedies**; after too much (See Remedies - fail - oversensitive)

IRRITABLE HEART (See CHEST - Palpitation - irritable)

ITCHING:

○ - **Affected** parts: agar ptk1 dig h2 galeoc-c-h gms1•
- **Blood** vessels: ambr bg2 graph bg2
- **Bones**, of: caust ptk1 cocc bg2* _Cycl_ b2.de* kali-m ptk1 kali-n b2.de* phos b2.de* verat b2.de*

○ • **Near** bones: caust bg2
- **Glands**: alum b4a.de am-c k* _Anac_ k* ant-c k* canth k* carb-an k* carb-v k* _Caust_ k* cocc k* **Con** k* _Kali-c_ k* mag-c k* merc k* nit-ac h2 _Phos_ k* plat bg2 ran-s k* rheum k* rhus-t k* sabin k* sep k* _Sil_ k* _Spong_ k* sulph bg2
- **Internally**: acon b2.de* agar b2.de* alum b2.de* am-c b2.de* am-m b2.de* **Ambr** b2.de* amph a1 anac b2.de* ang b2.de* ant-t b2.de* apis bg2 arn b2.de* asar b2.de* bar-c b2.de* bell b2.de* borx b2.de* bov b2.de* brom bg2 bry b2.de* calc b2.de* caps b2.de* carb-v b2.de* caust b2.de* cham b2.de* chin b2.de* chir-fl gya2 cic b2.de* cina b2.de* cocc b2.de* colch b2.de* _Con_ b2.de* croc b2.de* cupr b2.de dig b2.de* euph b2.de* _Ferr_ b2.de* fl-ac bg2 graph b2.de* hep b2.de* hyos bg ign b2.de* **Iod** b2.de* ip b2.de* _Kali-bi_ bg2 kali-c b2.de* lach bg2 _Laur_ b2.de* led b2.de* mag-c b2.de* mag-m b2.de* meny b2.de* merc b2.de* mosch b2.de* nat-c b2.de* nat-m bg nit-ac b2.de* nux-m b2.de* **Nux-v** b2.de* olnd b2.de* petr b2.de* ph-ac b2.de* **Phos** b2.de* plb b2.de* puls b2.de*

- **Internally**: ...
rhod b2.de* rhus-t b2.de* *Rumx* bg ruta b2.de* sabad b2.de* sabin b2.de* sang bg2 seneg b2.de* sep b2.de* sil b2.de* spig b2.de* spong b2.de* squil b2.de* *Stann* b2.de* sulph b2.de* tarax b2.de* teucr b2.de* thuj b2.de* valer b2.de verat b2.de* vero-o rly3• zinc b2.de*
  • **evening** | **amel.**: amph a1
  • **accompanied** by | **burning** pain internally (See Pain - internally - burning - accompanied - itching)
- **Mucous** membranes; of (See Mucous membranes - itching)
- **Skin**; of the (See SKIN - Itching)

JAR, stepping:
- **agg.**: *(↗MIND - Fear - tread)* *Acon* k* aloe bg2* alum k* alum-p k2* alum-sil k2* am-c k* ambr k* *Anac* k* *Ang* b2.de* *Ant-c* k* apis mtf11 arg-met k* *Arg-n* **Arn** k* ars k* *Asar* k* bapt bg2 bar-c k* **Bell** k* berb bg1* borx k* **Bry** k* *Cact* calad k* *Calc* k* calc-p k2* calc-sil k2* camph k* canth k* carb-ac bg2 carbn-s *Caust* k* cham k* chel k* *Chin* k* **Cic** k* cina bg2 *Cocc* k* coff k* **Con** k* crot-h bro1 dros k* dulc k* eup-per sne euphr k* *Ferr* k* ferr-ar ferr-p k2* form bg1 glon k* *Graph* k* *Ham* *Hell* k* *Hep* k* ign k* kali-c k* *Kali-i* k* kali-n k* kali-sil k2* *Lac-c* sf1.de* **Lach** k* lat-m mgm• *Led* k* *Lil-t* *Lyc* k* m-ambo b2.de* mag-c k* *Mag-m* k* mang k2 meny k* merc k* nat-ar *Nat-c* k* *Nat-m* k* nat-p nat-s bg2 nat-sil k2* **Nit-ac** k* nux-m k* *Nux-v* k* *Onos* pall sne par k* petr k* *Ph-ac* k* *Phos* k* plat k* plb k* podo bg2 *Puls* k* rhod k* **Rhus-t** k* ruta k* *Sabad* k* sabin k* sang ptk1 *Sanic* sec k2 seneg k* *Sep* k* **Sil** k* *Spig* k* spong k* stann k* staph k* stry sne *Sulph* k* tab bg2 **Ther** k* *Thuj* k* tor sne valer sf1.de verb k* viol-t k* [ferr-n stj2 mag-n stj2 mang-n stj2 nitro stj2 zinc-n stj2]
- **amel.**: ars ptk1 caps k* gels ptk1 hell bg2 *Nit-ac* ptk1
- **sudden** agg.: vib ptk1

JERKING: *Bell* ptk1 borx ptk1 calc ptk1 caust ptk1 cic ptk1 colch ptk1 hyos ptk1 hyper ptk1 lyc ptk1 meny ptk1 merc ptk1 nux-v ptk1 plat ptk1 *Puls* ptk1 rat ptk1 sep ptk1 spig ptk1 stann ptk1 sul-ac ptk1 sulph ptk1 tab ptk1 tarent ptk1 *Valer* ptk1 *Zinc* ptk1 zinc-i ptk1
- **night**: dig k2 zinc ptk1
- **convulsions**, as in: acon agar *Alum* am-c j5.de am-m j5.de **Ambr** ant-c ant-t j5.de arg-met arn *Ars* asaf j5.de bar-c j5.de bar-m j5.de bell bry bufo k2 *Calc* camph cann-s canth j5.de caps carb-v **Caust** *Cham* chin chinin-s j5.de chlol st1 *Cic* k* cina j5.de cocc j5.de coff j5.de colch j5.de coloc crot-h j5.de *Cupr* cupr-act j5.de cupr-c j5.de dig dros dulc graph j5.de hep *Hyos* *Ign* ip kali-c kali-chl j5.de kreos j5.de lach lact j5.de laur led j5.de *Lil-t* lob j5.de lyc m-arct j5.de mag-c mag-m j5.de mang j5.de *Meny* *Merc* mez mosch j5.de mur-ac *Mygal* vh nat-c **Nat-m** nat-s j5.de nit-ac nux-v op *Petr* ph-ac j5.de phel j5.de *Phos* plat **Plb** puls j5.de *Ran-b* ran-s j5.de rat j5.de rhod rhus-t j5.de sabad *Sec* sep sil sol-ni j5.de squil staph *Stram* stront-c sul-ac *Sulph* tarent k2* teucr j5.de thuj valer j5.de verat viol-t vip j5.de *Zinc* k*
  • **night**: staph h1
- **menses**; during | **beginning** of menses: hyos b7a.de
- **pain**; during: coloc ptk1 ign ptk1 lyc ptk1 meny ptk1 sul-ac bg2
- **painful**: rhod ptk1
- **sensation** of: bamb-a stb2.de•
- **sudden** strong jerks: cic mrr1 stront-c br1

○ - **Bones**: asaf ptk1 chin ptk1 phos b2.de* rhod b2.de* sil ptk1 sulph ptk1
- **Internally**: *(↗Shock - electric-like; Twitching - internally)* *Acon* k* agar k* ambr k* anac k* ang b2.de* aran-ix mg1.de arg-met ptk1 arn k* ars k* asaf bg3 *Bell* k* bov k* bry k* calad k* **Calc** k* **Cann-i** *Cann-s* k* caust k* *Chin* bg3 cic k* clem k* coca cocc ptk1 colch k* *Con* k* *Croc* k* cupr ptk1 dig k* dulc k* **Glon** ign bg3 kali-c bg3 kreos k* *Lyc* k* m-ambo b2.de m-arct b2.de m-aust b2.de mag-c k* mag-m a1 mang k* meny bg3 mez k* mur-ac k* nat-c k* nat-m k* *Nux-m* k* *Nux-v* k* op ptk1 petr k* phos k* **Plat** k* podo ptk1 **Puls** k* ran-b ptk1 ran-s k* rhod k* rhus-t k* ruta k* samb k* sep k* *Sil* k* **Spig** k* *Spong* k* **Stann** k* stront-c k* sul-ac k* tarax bg3 teucr k* thuj k* *Valer* k* *Verat* ptk1 zinc ptk1 zinc-chr ptk1
  • **pain**; from: arg-n ptk1 cina ptk1 lyc ptk1 plat ptk1 podo ptk1 sul-ac ptk1
  • **painful**: zinc-chr ptk1
  • **shivering**; during: m-arct b7.de
  • **sudden**: cic ptk1 ign ptk1
  • **violent**: stront-c ptk1
    ⁝ **pain**; as from: plat ptk1
- **Joints**: alum b2.de* bell b2.de* bry b2.de* bufo bg2 *Coloc* bg2 graph b2.de* m-aust b2.de nat-m b2.de* puls b2.de* sil b2.de* spig b2.de* spong b2.de* *Sul-ac* b2.de* sulph b2.de* *Verat* b2.de* [spect dfg1]

Jerking: ...
- **Muscles**, of: *(↗Complaints - muscles)* acon k* aesc *Agar* k* alum k* alum-p k2 alum-sil k2 am-c ambr b7a.de* *Anac* k* ang b7a.de ant-c k* *Ant-t* k* *Apis* aran-ix mg1.de *Arg-met* *Arg-n* arn k* ars k* *Asaf* k* asar k* *Bar-c* k* bar-s k2 *Bell* k* berb j5.de *Bry* k* bufo k2 cadm-s calc k* calc-f mg1.de* **Calc-p** *Cann-i* caps k* carbn-s card-m k2 caust j5.de* cham k* chin k* *Chion* **Cic** k* *Cimic* cina b7.de clem j5.de cocc k* *Colch* k* coloc j5.de* *Con* *Croc* *Cupr* k* cyt-l mg1.de dulc k* eucal sf1.de euph k* euphr k* *Ferr* k* ferr-ar *Gels* *Glon* *Graph* k* hist mg1.de* **Hyos** k* hyper k2 ign b7.de* ind jl3 iod sf1.de ip k* kali-c k* kali-i kali-n j5.de kali-p k2 kali-s *Lach* laur b7.de *Lil-t* lyc b4a.de* lyss mg1.de *M-ambo* b2.de *M-arct* b2.de* m-aust b2.de* mag-c k* mag-m k2 *Meny* k* *Merc* k* merc-c k* merc-cy br1 **Mez** k* mosch *Nat-c* nat-f mg1.de nat-m k* nit-ac k* *Nux-m* k* *Nux-v* k* olnd k* *Op* k* pert jl2 petr k* ph-ac k* *Phos* k* phyt k2 *Plat* k* *Plb* psor al2 *Puls* k* ran-b b7.de* *Rhus-t* k* ruta k* sabad k* sabin k* sal-ac sf1.de sec j5.de* **Sep** k* sil k* *Spig* k* spong b7.de *Stann* k* staph k* **Stram** k* *Stront-c* k* *Stry* mrr1 **Sul-ac** k* sul-i k2 **Sulph** k* tarax jl3 *Tarent* k* ter teucr j5.de *Valer* k* verat b7a.de viol-t k* *Visc* k* **Zinc** k* **Zinc-p** k2
  • **lying** down; while: tub jl2
  • **sleep**:
    ⁝ **amel.**: agar k2
    ⁝ **during** | **agg.**: *(↗Shock - electric-like - sleep - during - agg.)* aeth a1 agar aloe *Alum* ambr anac ant-t k* arg-met *Ars* *Bell* k* bry calc j5.de castm cham cimic cina k2 cob *Cocc* vh colch k* *Con* cor-r *Cupr* k* cupr-ar sf1.de daph dulc gard-j vlr2• hep ign ip k* *Kali-c* lyc *M-arct* b7a.de merc mez b4a.de nat-c k* *Nat-m* nat-s nit-ac nux-v b7.de* oci-sa sk4• op k* phos puls k* ran-s rheum rhus-t sang a1 sel sep sil stann staph stront-c sul-ac *Sulph* k* thuj tub k2* viol-t zinc k*
    ⁝ **going** to sleep; on | **agg.**: *(↗Shock - electric-like - sleep - going - agg.; Twitching - sleep - going - agg.)* acon *Agar* k* all-s kr1 *Aloe* kr1 *Alum* arg-met **Ars** k* carb-v k2 cob *Colch* k1 cupr br1* hyper *Ign* k* iodof kr1 **Kali-c** k* kali-cy st nux-v k2 phys puls h1 ran-b *Sel* sil *Stront-c* *Stry* *Sul-ac* *Sulph* tub k2* *Zinc*

○ • **Paralyzed** parts: *Arg-n* merc *Nux-v* phos sec k2 stram k2 *Stry*
  • **Side** lain on: *Cimic*
- **Side** lain on: cimic ptk1
- **Side** not lain on: onos ptk1
- **Tendons**: sul-ac ptk1

JET LAG: *(↗Aviator's; Sleep - loss)* arn mtf cocc mtf gels mtf vanad knl•

JUMPING: | **sensation** of | **Internal** parts; in: *Croc* b2.de* mosch b2.de*

○ - **Muscles**: colch ptk1 dios ptk1 hydr ptk1 puls ptk1

KIMMELSTIEL-WILSON syndrome: *(↗Diabetes mellitus; KIDNEYS - Renal - chronic; KIDNEYS - Sclerosis - glomerulosclerosis)* apoc mtf eup-pur mtf jab mtf kiss mtf lyc mtf lycps-v mtf med mtf morph mtf phase mtf phos mtf pic-ac mtf rhus-a mtf sal-ac mtf saroth mtf sulph mtf

KNEELING, on:
- **agg.**: calc bg2 *Cocc* k* mag-c k* puls bg2 sep k* spig bg2 tarent bg2
- **amel.**: aesc ptk1 aloe sne euph bg2*

KNEES; position of (See EXTREMITIES - Knees)

KNITTING:
- **agg.**: kali-c b4.de* mag-c b4.de
- **amel.**: lyc b2.de*

KNOCKING AGAINST something agg.: arn bg2 bar-c b2.de* bell bg2 *Bry* b2.de* carb-v b2.de* *Caust* b2.de* chin bg2 *Colch* bg2 hep b2.de* nux-v bg2 puls b2.de* sep b2.de* sil b2.de* spig b2.de* valer b2.de*

KNOCKING sensation: ant-t bg2

KNOTTED sensation internally: *(↗Ball)* *Abies-n* sf1.de ambr k* ant-t k* arg-n sf1.de arn k* *Ars* k* asaf bg2 bamb-a stb2.de• bell bg2 *Bov* sf1.de bry k* calc sf1.de carb-an k* carb-v sf1.de cham k* cic k* cina bg2 con k* cupr gels graph bg2 hydr bg2 hydr-ac ign bg2 kali-c sf1.de kali-p bg2* kreos k* **Lach** k* lob bg2* mag-m k* mag-p bg2* *Merc-i-r* naja sf1.de nux-v k* petr k* *Phyt* k* puls k* *Rhus-t* k* *Sabad* sec k* sep k* **Spig** k* staph k* stict **Sulph** k* tub mtf11 valer bg2 zinc bg2* [heroin sdj2]

LABORATORY findings:
- **adrenaline** | **decreased**: cur br1
- **agranulocytosis**: sulfa sp1
- **albumin**-globulin ratio inverted: beryl sp1
- **alkalosis**: cortiso sp1
- **bacteria**:
  - **actinomycosis**: sulfa sp1 thymol sp1
  - **coccidioidomycosis**: thymol sp1
  - **colon** bacillus: sulfa sp1
  - **Ducrey's** bacillus: sulfa sp1
  - **dysenteriae**: sulfa sp1
  - **Friedländer's** bacillus: sulfa sp1
  - **gonococci**: guat sp1 sulfa sp1
  - **gram**-negative: sulfa sp1
  - **haemophilus** influenzae: sulfa sp1
  - **meningococcus**: sulfa sp1
  - **pneumococcus**: sulfa sp1
  - **staphylococcus**: sulfa sp1
  - **streptococcus**: *(↗Infectious - streptococcus)* sulfa sp1
- **basal** metabolism rate:
  - **decreased**: pitu-p sp1
  - **increased**: allox sp1
- **blood**:
  - **acidosis**: sulfa sp1
  - **alpha** globulin increased: x-ray sp1
  - **calcium**:
    - **decreased**: nat-f sp1
    - **increased**: beryl sp1
  - **cholesterol** decreased: cortico sp1
  - **glucose**: *(↗Diabetes mellitus)*
    - **decreased**: gluca mtf
    - **increased** | **suddenly**: allox mtf
  - **oxygen**:
    - **decreased**: *(↗Cyanosis)* aspidin br1 carb-v mtf33 graph mtf33 trinit br1
    - **increased**: vanad br1
- **chlorides** decreased: cortiso sp1
- **CO2** combining powder decreased: sulfa sp1
- **corpuscles**; red (See erythrocytes)
- **creatinine** | **increased**: cortiso sp1 lyc mtf morph mtf op mtf phos mtf pic-ac mtf ser-ang mtf
- **electrocardiograph** | **P**-R interval prolonged: stroph-s sp1
- **enzyme**, sulfhydryl, inactivated: x-ray sp1
- **eosinophiles** temporarily increased: cortico sp1
- **erythrocytes**:
  - **decreased**: acetan br1 benzol br1 calc-ar br1 irid-met br1 lec br1 mang-act br1 nat-n br1 plb br1* trinit br1 zinc br1
  - **increased**: *(↗Polycythemia)* cortico mtf11 lat-m bnm6•
- **gastric** secretion increased: hist sp1
- **hemoglobin**:
  - **decreased**: calc-ar br1 ferr-p br1 lec br1 x-ray sp1
  - **increased**: cob-n sp1 loxo-lae bnm12• vanad br1
- **histiocytes**:
  - **increased** | **chronic**: med jl2
- **leukocytes**:
  - **decreased**: ars mtf chin wl1 des-ac jl1* influ jl2 rad-br cp1 rad-met cp1 rib-ac jl1 streptoc jl2* sulfa sp1* x-ray sp1* [cupr stj2]

Laboratory findings – **leukocytes**: ...
  - **increased**: antip br1 *Bar-i* br1 bar-m br1 benzol br1 cortico sp1 ergot br1 hist sp1 lat-m sp1 nat-m br1 tub br1* vanad br1 x-ray sp1
    - **heterophil**: x-ray sp1
    - **neutrophil**: cortico sp1
- **lymphocytes** | **decreased**: cortico mtf11
- **methemoglobinemia**: sulfa sp1
- **nitro** balance negative: cortiso sp1
- **plasma** cells increased: beryl sp1
- **platelets** | **decreased**: *(↗Thrombocytopenia)* bell-p mtf colch mtf crot-h mtf iod mtf kreos mtf lat-m mtf lyc mtf penic jl1* x-ray sp1*
- **potassium** level | **reduced**: cortico sp1* cortiso sp1
- **protein**; total | **increased**: beryl sp1
- **sedimentation** rate:
  - **decreased**: allox sp1
  - **increased**: beryl sp1 cob-n sp1 cortico sp1 v-a-b jl2
- **sperm** count | **low**: aur mtf carb-an mtf *Con* mtf *Iod* mtf med mtf pitu mtf11 staph mtf *Syph* mtf testis mtf tocoph mtf11 x-ray mtf
- **spinal** fluid pressure | **increased**: lat-m sp1 x-ray sp1
- **sulfhemoglobinemia**:
  - **urea**:
    - **decreased**: allox sp1 sulfa sp1
    - **increased**: carc sp1
  - ○ **Vessels** constricted: pitu-p sp1
- **x**-ray:
  - ○ **Bones**:
    - **absorption**: cadm-met sp1 cortico sp1 cortiso sp1
    - **hardening**: nat-f sp1
  - **Trabeculation**: nat-f sp1

LACK of sleep; agg. from (See Sleep - loss)

LACTATION; complaints of: *(↗Ailments - weaning; CHEST - Milk; CHEST - Milk - complaints)* *Acon* c2 bell ptk1 cham ptk1 *Chin* c2 galeg c2 lac-ac stj*• lact-v c2 merc ptk1 nit-ac c2 *Puls* ptk1 ric c2 sep ptk1 *Sil* c2* urt-u c2

LAME feeling: *(↗Pain - bones - paralyzed)* aesc bg2 alum bg2 anac bg2 ang bg2 arg-n bg2 arn bg2* ars bg2 asar bg2 bar-c bg2 bell-p br1 berb bg2 bry bg2 calc bg2 calc-p bg2 cann-s bg cann-xyz bg2 carb-ac bg2 carb-an bg2 carb-v bg2 caust bg2 cham bg2 chin bg2 cimic bg2 coc-c bg2 cocc bg2 con bg2 dios bg2 dros bg2 dulc bg2 echi bg2 ferr bg2 fl-ac bg2 graph bg2 grat bg2 helo bg2 hydr bg2 iod bg2 kali-bi bg2 kali-br bg2 kali-c bg2 kreos bg2 lob bg2 lol bg2 lyc bg2 mang bg2 meph bg2 merc bg2 mez bg2 mur-ac bg2 nat-m bg2 nit-ac bg2 nux-m bg2 nux-v bg2 op bg2 phos bg2 phyt bg2 pic-ac bg2 pyrog bg2 rhus-t bg2 ruta bg2 sars bg2 sel bg2 sep bg2 sil bg2 stann bg2 staph bg2 stram bg2 sulph bg2 tab bg2 thuj br1 tritic-vg fd5.de uran-n bg2 valer bg2 verat bg2 zinc bg2
- **chill**; during: ars bg2 bell bg2 brom bg2 caps bg2 chin bg2 cina bg2 cocc bg2 *Ign* bg2 *Nux-v* bg2 ph-ac bg2 puls bg2 *Rhus-t* bg2 sabad bg2 verat bg2
- **sprains**; after: rheum ptk1 ruta ptk1
- **tremulous**: merc bg2 phos bg2 zinc bg2
- ○ **Nerves**: arg-n bg2 nux-m bg2
- **Single** parts: chel br1

LASSITUDE: *(↗Sluggishness; Weakness; Weariness; MIND - Dullness; MIND - Ennui; MIND - Prostration)* abies-n hr1* absin a1 *Acetan* vh1 **Acon** k* act-sp hr1 adam srj5• *Aesc* aeth *Agar* k* agath-a nl2• ail k* *Alet* kr1 *All-c* hr1 all-s hr1* aloe kr1 **Alum** k* **Alum-p** k2* alum-sil k2* alumn a1* **Am-c** k* *Am-m* kr1 *Ambr* k* *Aml-ns* kr1 ammc hr1* anac hr1* ang h1* anh sp1 ant-c k* *Ant-t* k* anthraq rly4• **Apis** k* apoc k* **Aran** k* aran-ix mg1.de arg-met arg-n kr1 arge-pl rwt5• *Arn* hr1* *Ars* k* ars-h hr1* *Ars-i* k* ars-met kr1 ars-s-f k2* arum-d kr1 arum-m hr1* arum-t hr1* asaf k* asar k* asc-t a1* *Aspar* kr1 astac hr1* aster k* atro kr1 *Aur* k* aur-m-n k* *Bamb-a* stb2.de• *Bapt* k* bar-c k* bar-i k2* bar-m bar-s k2* *Bell* k* bell-p st1 *Benz-ac* k* *Berb* k* berb-a br1 *Bism* k* *Bit-ar* wht1• *Bol-la* kr1 borx *Both* br1 bov k* brach a1* brom hr1 bros-gau mrc1 bry k* cact cadm-met sp1 cain c1* **Calad** **Calc** k* calc-ar hr1* calc-f a1* calc-i k2* **Calc-p** kr1 calc-s hr1* calc-sil k2* calen hr1* *Camph* k* cann-i a1 cann-s k* canth *Caps* k* *Carb-ac* k* *Carb-v* k* **Carbn-s** carc gk6 *Card-m* hr1* cartl-s rly4• *Casc* k* *Caust* k* cedr kr1 cham k* *Chel* k* chen-v hr1* **Chin** k* chinin-ar kr1 *Chinin-s* chir-fl gya2 chlf hr1* chlol hr1* choc srj3• chord-umb rly4• chr-ac hr1* *Cic* k* cimic a1 cina cinnb a1* cist hr1* clem a1 cob-n sp1* coc-c hr1* *Coca* kr1 *Cocc* k* cod a1 coff k* coff-t a1 *Colch* k* coll a1 *Coloc* k* **Con** k*

Lassitude: ...
conv st1 cop corn a1* corn-a br1 croc k* **Crot-c** crot-t kr1 **Cupr** k* _Cupr-ar_ a1* cupr-s a1* _Cycl_ hr1* cyn-d jl3 cystein-l rly4• daph hr1* dicha jl3 _Dig_ k* dios kr1 dirc a1 dor hr1 _Dulc_ h2* ephe-si hsj1• ery-a kr1 eryt-j a1 eucal eup-per hr1 eup-pur hr1* euph hr1* euphr eupi a1 fago a1 **Ferr** k* ferr-ar ferr-p fic-m gya1 _Fl-ac_ a1* _Form_ k* fum rly4• galeoc-c-h gms1• _Gamb_ hr1* gast a1 **Gels** k* germ-met srj5• gins a1 glon a1* goss a1* **Graph** k* grat hr1* guaj _Guar_ kr1 haliae-lc srj5• halo jl3 _Ham_ a1* harp jl3 _Hell_ kr1 _Helon_ hr1 _Hep_ k* hippoc-k szs2 hippoz hr1* _Hydr_ k* hydr-ac a1 _Hydrc_ a1* _Hydrog_ srj2• hyos k* iber a1 _Ign_ k* ina-i mlk9.de ind hr1 iod k* ip k* irid-met srj5• jac-c a1 jug-c a1 kali-ar a1 _Kali-bi_ bg2* _Kali-br_ a1* _Kali-c_ k* _Kali-chl_ hr1* kali-cy a1 _Kali-m_ kr1* kali-n k* _Kali-p_ k* kali-s fd4.de kali-sil k2* kalm a1 ketogl-ac rly4• _Kreos_ hr1 lac-ac hr1* _Lac-c_ hr1* _Lac-d_ hr1* lac-h htj1*• lac-loxod-a hrn2• **Lach** k* _Laur_ k* led _Lept_ kr1 levo jl3 lil-t a1 limest-b es1• _Lob_ lob-s a1 lol a1 luf-op jl3 _Lyc_ k* lyss hr1* m-arct b2.de* mag-c k* mag-m k* manc hr1* _Mang_ _Med_ hr1* medul-os-si rly4• melal-alt gya4 meny k* _Merc_ k* _Merc-c_ hr1 merc-i-f hr1 methys jl3 _Mez_ mit a1 morph a1 mosch k* mur-ac murx a1 musca-d szs1 myos-a rly4• myric a1* naja jl narcot a1 nat-ar _Nat-c_ k* _Nat-m_ k* _Nat-p_ _Nat-s_ hr1* nat-sal br1 _Nat-sil_ k2* neon srj5• nep jl3* nicotam rly4• nit-ac _Nuph_ kr1 _Nux-m_ k* **Nux-v** k* ol-an hr1* ol-j a1* olib-sac wmh1 olnd onop jl3 _Op_ k* osm hr1 _Ox-ac_ k* oxal-a rly4• oxyt ozone sde2• pall hr1* paull a1 petr k* petr-ra shn4• **Ph-ac** k* phel kr1 _Phos_ k* phys a1 phyt k* **Pic-ac** k* plat k* _Plb_ k* plect a1 polyp-p a1 positr nl2• pot-e rly4• _Psor_ k* _Ptel_ a1* puls k* _Pycnop-sa_ mrz1 pyrid rly4• _Ran-b_ k* _Raph_ a1* _Rat_ kr1 rham-cal br1 rhod k* rhus-g a1 _Rhus-t_ k* _Rhus-v_ a1* rib-ac jl3 **Ruta** k* sabad k* sabin k* **Sang** k* sapin a1 sarr a1* sars a1 sec k* sel k* _Senec_ a1* _Seneg_ k* _Sep_ k* **Sil** k* spig k* _Spong_ k* _Stann_ k* staph k* stel br1 _Stram_ k* stront-c stry a1 suis-em rly4• suis-pan rly4• **Sul-ac** k* sul-i k2* sulfa jl3 sulfonam jl3* _Sulph_ k* _Sumb_ k* _Tab_ a1* tanac br1 taosc iwa1• _Tarax_ k* **Tarent** k* tart-ac br1 tell kr1* _Ter_ hr1* tere-la rly4• _Teucr_ k* thal-xyz srj8• ther k* thiop jl3 thuj k* til a1 tritic-vg fd5.de _Tub_ hr1* tung-met bdx1• uran-n kr1 _Ust_ kr1 vac a1* _Valer_ k* vanil fd5.de verat k* verat-v a1 vero-o rly4• vesp hr1 viol-t k* x-ray sp1 **Zinc** k* **Zinc-p** k2* zing hr1* ziz hr1 [bell-p-sp dcm1 _Spect_ dfg1]

- **daytime**: am-m hr1* asc-t hr1* _Calc_ kr1 calc-f hr1* cartl-s rly4• cob-n sp1 _Ferr_ kr1 hydrog srj2• _Kali-bi_ hr1* ketogl-ac rly4• nat-sil fd3.de• _Senec_ hr1* _Sulph_ a1
- **morning**: am-c k* ant-c k* bar-m br1 _Calad_ kr1 calc-sil k2 cham hr1 dulc fd4.de ger-i rly4• germ-met srj5• _Kali-chl_ hr1 _Kali-m_ kr1 lyc _Mag-m_ hr1* nat-c k* nat-p nat-s hr1 nux-v k* ozone sde2• pall hr1 petr c1 petr-ra shn4• sang a1 _Sep_ hr1 spong fd4.de staph kr1 stry a1 suis-pan rly4• _Sulph_ a1* sumb tritic-vg fd5.de vib hr1
  - **and** afternoon: _Bry_ kr1
  - **bed** agg.; in: acon j5.de alum j5.de _Ambr_ j5.de* _Aur_ j5.de _Bell_ j5.de borx j5.de _Bry_ j5.de _Carb-v_ j5.de* _Caust_ j5.de _Cham_ kr1 clem j5.de con j5.de crot-t j5.de dros j5.de dulc fd4.de galeoc-c-h gms1• hell j5.de iod j5.de kali-c j5.de _Lach_ j5.de mag-c j5.de mag-s j5.de mang j5.de nat-m j5.de _Op_ j5.de _Petr_ j5.de* phos j5.de plb j5.de _Puls_ j5.de ran-s j5.de sep j5.de sil j5.de spig j5.de spong fd4.de _Squil_ j5.de thuj j5.de verat j5.de zinc j5.de*
  - **rising**:
    - **agg**.: dig j5.de _Ferr_ kr1 galeoc-c-h gms1• kreos j5.de _Nux-v_ kr1 _Osm_ kr1 petr j5.de ph-ac j5.de plb j5.de _Sep_ kr1 sil j5.de stann j5.de tritic-vg fd5.de vib kr1
    - **amel**.: acon j5.de mag-c j5.de
- **forenoon**: alum k* am-c a1 calad hr1 kali-cy a1 phys a1 ran-b k* ruta fd4.de sabad a1 sars a1 tritic-vg fd5.de
- **noon**: _Cic_ hr1* fago a1 ger-i rly4• haliae-lc srj5• ozone sde2• vanil fd5.de
- **afternoon**: acon-ac rly4• agath-a nl2• aq-pet a1 arg-n arge-pl rwt5• aur a1 _Calc-s_ kr1 _Card-m_ kr1 cartl-s rly4• coloc a1 dulc fd4.de fago a1 ferr a1 galeoc-c-h gms1• gels k* hydr-ac a1 hydrog srj2• hyos h1* ign a1 lac-h htj1• lil-t a1* lyc myos-a rly4• petr h2* petr-ra shn4• phyt a1 ptel a1 sang a1 thuj k* tritic-vg fd5.de zing hr1
  - **13**-17 h: ozone sde2•
  - **16** h: trios jl
  - **16**.30 h: ozone sde2•
  - **17** h: petr-ra shn4•
  - **fever**; with: lil-t bro1
  - **sleep** | **siesta** agg.; after: kali-c h2
- **evening**: am-c k* ars asaf a1 bar-c a1 calc-sil k2* carb-v k* **Caust** coloc a1 dirc a1 dulc fd4.de germ-met srj5• _Graph_ haliae-lc srj5• hep hr1 hydr-ac a1 hydrog srj2• _Ign_ a1* lyc a1 myos-a rly4• _Myrt-c_ hr1* naja nat-m k* nicotam rly4• pall hr1* petr c1 petr-ra shn4• phyt a1 sang st1 senec a1 spig sulfonam jl3 _Sulph_ a1* thuj tritic-vg fd5.de vanil fd5.de

- **evening**: ...
  - **20** h: mang h2
- **night**: calc-sil k2* galeoc-c-h gms1• nat-s hr1 sulph a1
  - **midnight**: galeoc-c-h gms1•
    - **after** | **2** h: trios jl
  - **and** morning: _Nat-s_ kr1
- **accompanied** by | **sadness** (See MIND - Sadness - lassitude)
- **Addison's** disease, in: _Calc_ kr1
- **air** agg.; in open: _Petr_ kr1
- **alternating** with:
  - **activity** (See MIND - Activity - desires - alternating - lassitude)
  - **coldness**, objective or subjective: spig kr1
  - **ideas**; abundant (See MIND - Ideas - abundant - alternating - lassitude)
  - **memory**; active (See MIND - Memory - active - alternating - lassitude)
  - **mental** clarity (See MIND - Ideas - abundant - alternating - lassitude)
- **chemicals** agg.: [spect dfg1]
- **children**; in: _All-s_ vh1
- **chill**; during: merc b4.de
- **chilliness**; with: cimic hr1* corn hr1*
- **coition**; after: _Agar_ j5.de* **Calc** con j5.de graph j5.de led j5.de lyc j5.de nat-m j5.de _Phos_ sf1.de plb j5.de sep j5.de staph j5.de tax j5.de _Ziz_ hr1*
- **conversation**, from: ambr hr1 sil
- **delivery**; after: cupr sst3•
- **driving**: galeoc-c-h gms1•
- **eating**; after: act-sp hr1* ant-c hr1* bar-c h2* bov hr1* _Calc-p_ kr1 _Carb-an_ hr1* _Card-m_ hr1* chin hr1* grat hr1 hydrog srj2• _Lach_ hr1* _Lyc_ lyss hr1* mur-ac _Nat-m_ kr1 _Nux-m_ hr1* ol-an st ozone sde2• **Ph-ac** _Rhus-t_ hr1* sang a1* _Sel_ sep h2 tritic-vg fd5.de
- **emissions** agg.: bar-c j5.de _Ery-a_ hr1* ham hr1* nat-c b4.de* _Nat-m_ hr1 ran-b b7.de* sabad b7.de* _Sep_ b4.de*
- **horse** riding; from too long: cain c1
- **lying**:
  - **must** lie down: cassia-f ckh1 lac-loxod-a hrn2• tritic-vg fd5.de [spect dfg1]
    - **afternoon** | **17** h: lac-loxod-a hrn2•
    - **dinner**; before: _Mez_
    - **eat** frequently; if he does not: _Sulph_ kr1
- **menses**:
  - **after** | **agg**.: berb j5.de* nux-v j5.de* thuj hr1*
  - **before** | **agg**.: alum b4a.de* _Bell_ a1* calc _Chin_ b7a.de kreos b7a.de lyc _Nat-m_ hr1 nux-m b7.de* pot-e rly4•
  - **during**:
    - **agg**.: alum b4a.de* _Am-c_ b4.de* bell a1* borx b4a.de* bov b4.de* calc-p hr1* carb-an b4a.de* castm j5.de _Caust_ j5.de* germ-met srj5• _Graph_ b4.de ign j5.de* iod b4.de* _Kali-c_ b4.de* kali-n j5.de lyc j5.de _Mag-c_ b4.de* mag-m b4.de* _Nit-ac_ b4.de* _Nux-m_ hr1* nux-v b7.de _Petr_ b4.de* phel j5.de phos j5.de sep b4a.de thuj hr1* zinc b4.de
    - **beginning** of menses | **agg**.: iod b4a.de mag-m b4.de
- **mental** exertion: _(↗MIND - Mental exertion - agg. - fatigues)_
  - **agg**.: _(↗MIND - Mental exertion - agg. - fatigues)_ **Aur** hr1* podo hr1* _Puls_ hr1* ruta fd4.de
  - **amel**.: croc br1
- **motion**:
  - **agg**.: cain c1 _Phos_
  - **amel**.: kali-n c1 nat-c h2 tritic-vg fd5.de
- **pregnancy** agg.; during: _Calc-p_ hr1*
- **restlessness**; with: dios hr1* positr nl2• tell hr1*
- **sexual** excesses; after: agn sf1.de
- **sitting** agg.: aur a1 kali-n c1 mang h2 _Merc_ kr1 phos tritic-vg fd5.de
- **sleep** agg.; after: ant-t hr1* _Ars_ hr1 dulc fd4.de kali-c h2 **Puls** hr1* sil
- **spring** agg.: apis kr1 _Bry_ hr1* _Gels_ hr1*
- **stool**:
  - **after** | **agg**.: ip hr1* _Lyc_ hr1* mag-m _Sulph_ hr1

- **before**: *Mez* hr1* *Rhus-t* a1
- **during** | **agg.**: borx kr1 ip hr1*
- **talking**; after: *Alum* dor kr1
- **vomiting**; before: apom br1
- **waking**; on: acon j5.de alum j5.de ambr j5.de *Arg-met* kr1 aur j5.de *Bell* j5.de bit-ar wht1• borx j5.de *Bry* j5.de *Carb-v* j5.de card-m hr1* *Caust* j5.de chin hr1* clem j5.de crot-t j5.de dios hr1* dros j5.de galeoc-c-h gms1• germ-met srj5• hell j5.de hyper hr1* irid-met srj5• *Kali-br* hr1 kreos j5.de lac-ac hr1* *Lach* j5.de mang j5.de *Op* j5.de par hr1 petr j5.de *Ph-ac* j5.de* *Phos* j5.de plb j5.de *Podo* hr1* *Ptel* hr1* puls j5.de ran-s j5.de sep j5.de sil j5.de spig j5.de *Squil* j5.de stann j5.de thuj j5.de verat j5.de xan hr1* zinc j5.de*
- **walking**:
  - **after** | **agg.**: petr h2
  - **air**; in open | **amel.**: agath-a nl2• *Alum* *Am-c* graph h2 tritic-vg fd5.de
  - **amel.**: ambr a1
- **warm** room agg.: iod
- **weather**:
  - **stormy** | **agg.**: psor *Sang* *Tub*
  - **warm** | **agg.**: dulc fd4.de nat-p tritic-vg fd5.de
  - **wet** | **agg.**: **Sang** kr1

LATHE; working the wood: *Sep* b2.de
- **amel.**: *Sep* b4.de*

LAUGHING agg.: *(↗MIND - Laughing - agg.)* *Acon* b2.de* ang b2.de* *Arg-met* b2.de* arg-n bg2 **Ars** b2.de* *Aur* b2.de* **Bell** b2.de* **Borx** b2.de* cann-xyz bg2* **Carb-v** b2.de* carc jl2 **Chin** b2.de* *Coff* ptk1* coloc b2.de* con b2.de* cupr bg2 dros bro1* hyos bg2 *Kali-c* b2.de* laur b2.de* **Mang** b2.de* mang-act bro1 mez b2.de* mur-ac b2.de* nat-m b2.de* nux-v b2.de* pert jl2 **Phos** b2.de* **Plb** b2.de* **Stann** b2.de* sulph bg3* syph ptk1 tell bg2* zinc b2.de*
- **excessive** laughing: coff ptk1
- **loudly**; laughing: calc-f ptk1

LAXATIVES: | **abuse** of: nux-v mtf11

LEAD poisoning; from: *(↗Allergic - chemical; Paralysis - toxic - lead)* *Alum* k* alum-sil c1* *Alumn* k* ant-c kr1 ars k* *Bell* k* carbn-s br1* **Caust** k* chin cocc kr1* *Coloc* c1* crot-t sf1.de cupr sf1.de gels sf1.de hep kr1* iod br1* kali-br bro1 *Kali-i* bro1* kreos kr1 lyc kr1 mang sf1.de merc bro1 *Nat-s* sf1.de nux-v k* *Op* k* petr hr1* pipe c1 *Plat* k* plb mg1.de* sul-ac k* *Sulph* k* zinc kr1

LEAF, valve, skin; sensation of a: alum ptk1 ant-t ptk1 *Bar-c* ptk1 ferr ptk1 iod ptk1 kali-c ptk1 kali-i ptk1 lach ptk1 mang ptk1 *Phos* ptk1 sabad ptk1 *Spong* ptk1 thuj ptk1

LEAN people: *(↗Emaciation; Tall)* acet-ac c1* alum bg2* **Ambr** k* *Arg-met* bg2* *Arg-n* k* ars hr1* ars-i st1 bar-c bg2* beryl sp1* bry k* cadm-met sp1 calc-f sp1 **Calc-p** k* calc-sil stj2* carc fb* caust k* chin hr1* coff hr1* cupr st1 dys fmm1• ferr bg2* fl-ac st1* flor-p jl3 gaert fmm1• graph hr1* *Hep* hr1 ign k* *Iod* k* ip bg2* *Kreos* bg2* lac-ac stj5• lac-c hr1 lach k* *Lyc* k* mag-c bg2* mag-p ptk1* mang bg2* merc hr1* murx mrr1 nat-c sf1.de nat-m hr1* *Nit-ac* k* nux-m bg2* *Nux-v* k* perh jl3 petr bg2* ph-ac st1* *Phos* k* plb hr1* prot jl2* *Psor* ptk1* puls hr1 rat ptk1 sanic ptk1 saroth jl3 sars ptk1 **Sec** k* sep k* *Sil* k* spig hr1 stann c1 staph hr1 **Sulph** k* tub k* *Tub-m* jl2 ust hr1 v-a-b jl3 verat hr1* vib hr1 yohim bwa3* [alumin-p stj2 am-br stj2 am-caust stj2 am-f stj2 am-m stj1 am-p stj1 ant-m stj2 arg-p stj2 ars-met stj2 bar-i stj2 beryl-m stj2 cadm-m stj2 chlor stj2 chr-m stj2 cob-m stj2 cupr-m stj2 cupr-p stj2 ferr-sil stj2 hydrog stj2 lith-f stj2 lith-i stj2 lith-m stj2 lith-p stj2 mag-i stj1 mag-sil stj2 mang-i stj2 mang-m stj2 mang-p stj2 mang-sil stj2 merc-d stj2 merc-i-f stj2 mur-ac stj2 nat-ar stj2 nat-br stj2 nat-caust stj2 nat-f stj1 nat-i stj1 nat-lac stj2 nat-met stj2 nat-p stj1 nat-sil stj2 nicc-met stj2 nicc-s stj2 plb-m stj2 plb-p stj2 sil-met stj2 stront-m stj2 stront-met stj2 thal-met stj2 zinc-i stj2 zinc-m stj2 zinc-p stj2]
- **bony** people: calc bg2 kali-bi bg2 sec bg2
- **children**; in: calc-sil mtf33 phos mtf33 sulph mtf33
- **tuberculinic** state: v-a-b jl2
- **women**: ambr br1

LEANING:
- **against** something:
  - **after**: *Coloc* b2.de*

Leaning – **against** something: ...
  - **agg.**: agar sf1.de arg-met b2.de* arn b2.de* bell b2.de* cann-s b2.de* canth bg2 *Cimic* sf1.de* coloc sf1.de con bg2 cycl b2.de* graph bg2 *Hell* bg2* hep b2.de* mag-m bg2 *Nit-ac* b2.de* phos bg2 plat bg2 samb b2.de* sil bg2 stann bg2 staph b2.de* sulph bg2 *Ther* sf1.de* thuj bg2
  - **amel.**: bell b2.de* *Carb-v* b2.de* dros b2.de* **Ferr** b2.de* gymno ptk1 *Kali-c* b2.de* kali-p ptk1 mang b2.de* merc b2.de* nat-c ptk1 *Nat-m* bg2* nux-v b2.de* ph-ac ptk1 rhod b2.de* rhus-t b2.de* sabad b2.de* sabin b2.de* seneg b2.de* sep sf1.de* spig b2.de* staph b2.de*
- **backward** | **agg.**: atra-r bnm3• nit-ac b2.de* staph b2.de*
- **desire** for leaning: bar-c br1 gymne a1 gymno a1 op a1 tub st1
- **hard**; against something | **amel.**: bell b2.de* *Rhus-t* b2.de*
- **head**:
  - **against** something:
    - **agg.**: hep b4a.de nit-ac b4.de
    - **amel.**: *Bell* b2.de* kali-c b2.de* *Merc* b2.de* rhod b2.de* sabad b2.de* sabin b2.de* seneg b2.de* spig b2.de*
  - **left** side; to | **amel.**: chinin-s bg2
- **sharp** edge; against a:
  - **agg.**: agar b2.de* caust bg2 chinin-s bg2 lyc bg2 ran-b bg2 ruta bg2 *Samb* b2.de* stann bg2 valer bg2
  - **amel.**: nat-c bg2 stann bg2
- **side**; to | **agg.**: meny b2.de*

LEECHES agg.; application of: sec ptk1

LEISHMANIASIS: ars sa lyc brm phos brm
- **children**; in: | **infants**: ars br1

LEPRA:
- **accompanied** by | **clean** tongue: agar kr1*

LEUKEMIA: *(↗Cancerous; Hodgkin's)* acet-ac k* acon hr1* *Aran* hr1* ars k* ars-i bro1* bar-i bro1* bar-m ptk1 ben ptk1 benzo bro1 benzol br1 bry bro1 *Calc* k* calc-ar mtf11 *Calc-p* k* carb-v k* *Carbn-s* *Carc* mlr1• cean bro1* *Chin* k* chinin-s bro1 con bro1 cortiso sp1 crot-h k* *Ferr-pic* bro1 **Hecla** rmk1• hell mrr1 ip k* *Kali-p* k* med mtf11 merc bro1* **Nat-ar** k* *Nat-m* k* *Nat-p* k* **Nat-s** k* *Nit-ac* sne nux-v k* op a1 phos bro1* *Pic-ac* k* rib-ac mtf11 scir rmk1• succ-ac mtf11 sulfa jl3* sulph k* **Symph** rmk1• thuj k* tub st1 *X-ray* br1*
- **children**; in: med mtf33
- **pseudo**-leukemia: ferr-pic br1
- **splenic**: *Cean* bro1* *Nat-s* bro1* querc bro1 succ bro1

LEUKOCYTOSIS: bit-ar wht1• loxo-recl bnm10• tub al* v-a-b jl2

LEUKORRHEA:
- **agg.**: *Alum* b2.de* am-c b2.de* am-m b2.de* ambr b2.de* anac b2.de* ant-c b2.de* ars b2.de* bell b2.de* borx b2.de* bov b2.de* *Calc* b2.de* cann-s b2.de* canth b2.de* carb-an b2.de* carb-v b2.de* caust b2.de* cham b2.de* chin b2.de* cocc b2.de* *Con* b2.de* dros b2.de* ferr b2.de* graph b2.de* hep b2.de* ign b2.de* iod b2.de* *Kali-c* b2.de* kali-n b2.de* kalm ptk1 **Kreos** b2.de* *Lyc* b2.de* mag-c b2.de* mag-m b2.de* **Merc** b2.de* mez b2.de* nat-c b2.de* **Nat-m** b2.de* nit-ac b2.de* ph-ac b2.de* phos b2.de* plat b2.de* psor ptk1 *Puls* b2.de* ran-b b2.de* ruta b2.de* sabad bg2 sabin b2.de sec b2.de* **Sep** b2.de* *Sil* b2.de* sul-ac b2.de* sulph b2.de* thuj b2.de* valer b2.de zinc bg2
- **amel.**: *(↗Mucous secretions - amel.)* arist-cl sp1 carb-v ptk1 cimic bg2 lach bg2 murx ptk1 phyt ptk1 puls bg2
- **before** | **agg.**: am-m b7.de ambr b7.de caust b4.de chin b7.de con b4.de *Ferr* b7.de graph b4.de ign b7.de lyc b4.de mag-c b4.de **Mag-m** b4.de nat-c b4.de nat-m b4.de puls b7.de *Sil* b4.de sulph b4.de zinc b4.de
- **during** | **agg.**: *Alum* b4.de am-m b7.de ambr b7.de bell b4.de *Calc* b4.de chin b7.de *Ferr* b7.de graph b4.de ign b7.de kali-c b4.de *Lyc* b4.de nat-c b4.de puls b7.de sep b4.de *Sil* b4.de

LICKING:
- **amel.**: mang b2.de*
- **lips** | **agg.**: valer b2.de*

LIE DOWN: *(↗Weariness)*
- **desire** to: *(↗MIND - Bed - remain; MIND - Dullness; MIND - Ennui; MIND - Prostration)* abies-c br1* abrot a1 absin a1 **Acon** k* adlu jl aether a1 alet k2 **Alum** k* alum-p k2 alum-sil k2 alumn a1 *Am-c* k* *Ambr* k* amor-r jl *Anac* k* androc srj1• *Ant-c* k* ant-t k* *Apis* k* aq-mar skp7• **Aran** k* *Arg-met* vh1 arn k* **Ars** k* ars-s-f k2 asar k* *Aur* aur-ar k2 aur-s k2 bamb-a stb2.de• *Bapt* k* *Bar-c* k* bar-i k2 bar-m bar-s k2 bell b2.de* bism k*

- **desire** to: ...
borx k* brass-n-o srj5• bry k* buni-o jl caj a1 **Calad** k* *Calc* k* calc-s kr1 calc-sil k2 cann-s j5.de cann-xyz bg2 canth k* *Caps* k* *Carb-an* k* *Carb-v* k* carbn-o a1 **Carbn-s** *Casc* cassia-s cdd7* *Caust* k* cench k2 **Cham** k* *Chel* k* chin k* chinin-ar chir-fl gya2 chlam-tr bcx2• *Chlol* bg2 chlor a1 cic j5.de cina k* clem j5.de *Cocc* k* coff k* colch bg2* coloc a1 *Con* k* croc k* crot-h j5.de crot-t j5.de cupr k* *Cycl* k* daph j5.de dig k* dor a1 dros k* dulc k* euonin j5.de **Ferr** k* ferr-ar k2 ferr-m a1 ferr-p fic-m gya1 form bg2 gels k* gink-b sbd1• gran j5.de *Graph* k* grat j5.de* *Guaj* k* ham a1 hell j5.de* hep h2* hipp a1* hippoc-k szs2 hydr a1 hydrog srj2• hyos h1* iber a1* *Ign* k* ip k* irid-met srj5• **Kali-ar** *Kali-bi* *Kali-br* bg2 **KALI-C** k* kali-m k2 kali-n j5.de* kali-p fd1.de• kali-s *Kali-sil* k2* *Kola* stb3• lac-h sk4*• *Lach* k* laur j5.de lavand-a ctl1• led k* lil-t bg2 *Lyc* k* m-arct j5.de m-aust b2.de mag-c k* mag-m k* manc k* mang h2 merc k* merc-c b4a.de* merc-i-f a1 mez b2.de* mosch kr1 mur-ac k* murx mgm• naja k2 nat-ar nat-c k* *Nat-m* k* nat-p nat-s j5.de* *Nat-sil* k2* neon srj5• nept-m lsd2.fr nicc-met sk4• nicotam rly4• nit-ac b2.de* nux-m j5.de* **Nux-v** k* olnd j5.de* op k* ox-ac j5.de* ozone sde2• par j5.de paull a1 *Petr* k* petr-ra shn4• *Ph-ac* k* *Phos* k* *Phyt* k* *Pic-ac* k* *Plan* bg1* plb j5.de podo fd3.de• polyp-p a1 psor bg2* *Puls* k* ran-b k* raph j5.de *Rhus-t* k* ruta k* sabad k* sabin j5.de sacch-a fd2.de• sal-n a1 sang a1 **Sel** k* senec sf1.de *Seneg* kr1 *Sep* k* **Sil** k* *Spong* k* *Stann* k* staph k* *Stram* k* stront-c k* sulfonam jl* *Sulph* k* *Sumb* k* symph fd3.de• tab a1 taosc iwa1• tarax k* *Tarent* k* teucr k* thea j5.de* ther j5.de thuj k* tub al vanil fd5.de verat k* vip j5.de visc sp1 wildb a1 zinc b2.de* zinc-p k2 *Zing* k* [bell-p-sp dcm1 heroin sdj2]
  - **abdomen** in pregnancy, on: acet-ac bro1 *Podo* bro1*
  - **agg**. thereby; but: alum bg1* murx ptk1
  - **darkness** agg.: tarent st
  - **eating**; after: ant-c h2* caust bg2 chel h1 *Chin* h1* clem h2 ignis-alc es2• *Lach* k* nat-m h2* nit-ac h2 *Sel*
  - **fever**:
    - **before**: ars b4a.de bar-c b4a.de bell b4a.de nat-c b4a.de
    - **during** | **agg**.: *Acon* bg2 **Ars** bg2 *Bry* b7a.de* calad bg2 canth b7.de* cham bg2 *Cocc* bg2 cycl bg2 dros b7a.de* **Nux-v** b7.de* sep bg2
  - **menses**; during: am-c b4a.de
  - **perspiration**; during: *Acon* bg2 apis bg2 **Ars** bg2 *Bry* bg2 calad bg2 canth bg2 *Cham* bg2 cocc bg2 cycl bg2 **Nux-v** bg2 sep bg2
  - **pollution**; after: aq-mar skp7•
  - **stool**; after every: arn br1
  - **uterine** displacement, in: abies-c vml3•
- **must** lie down (See desire)
- **will** not lie down, sits up in bed: (↗*MIND - Sitting - inclination - lie)* kali-br k*

LIFTING, of being lifted; sensation of: **Acon** b2.de* caps bg2 hippoc-k szs2 hyper ptk1 m-ambo b2.de* phos ptk1 stroph-h ptk1

LIFTING, straining of muscles and tendons: (↗*Injuries - sprains)* acet-ac st1 *Acon* st1 *Agn* kr1* alum alumn kr1 *Ambr* arist-cl sp1 **Arn** k* ars bg bar-c bell st1 *Bell-p* st1 *Bov* kr1 *Bry* **Calc** calc-f sp1* calc-p c1 *Calc-s* calen st1 **Carb-an** k* *Carb-v* *Caust* chin *Cocc* coloc **Con** croc cur *Ferr* ferr-p *Form* kr1* get br1 **Graph** *Hyper* st1 *Ign* bg iod *Kali-c* *Kalm* kr1 lach led bg *Lyc* *Mag-c* h2* merc *Mill* mur-ac *Nat-c* nat-m nit-ac olnd *Ph-ac* phos plat podo kr1* prun c1 psor bg* *Puls* bg rhod **Rhus-t** k* ruta bro1 *Sec* **Sil** spig stann staph sul-ac thuj [bell-p-sp dcm1]
- **from**: (↗*Injuries - sprains)* acet-ac st *Acon* st *Agn* a1* alum k* alum-sil k2 alumn kr1 *Ambr* k* arist-cl sp1 **Arn** k* ars bg2 bar-c k* bell st *Bell-p* st *Borx* k* *Bov* kr1 *Bry* k* **Calc** k* calc-f st* calc-p c1* *Calc-s* calc-sil k2 calen st **Carb-an** k* *Carb-v* k* *Carbn-s* *Caust* k* chin k* *Cocc* k* coloc k* **Con** k* croc k* cur *Dulc* b2.de* *Ferr* k* ferr-p *Form* kr1* **Graph** k* *Hyper* k2* *Ign* bg2 iod k* *Kali-c* k* kali-m k2 kali-sil k2 *Kalm* kr1 lach k* led ptk1 *Lyc* k* *Mag-c* j5.de merc k* *Mill* k* mur-ac k* *Nat-c* k* nat-m k* nit-ac k* nux-v k* olnd k* onos ptk1 *Ph-ac* k* phos k* plat k* podo kr1* prun c1* psor c1* puls hr1* rhod k* **Rhus-t** k* **Ruta** b2.de* *Sec* k* sep k* **Sil** k* spig k* stann k* staph k* stront-c st* sul-ac k* sulph k* thuj k* valer k*
  - **amel**.: spig ptk1
  - **arms**, of: rhus-t c1 sul-ac c1
  - **reaching** high: sulph c1*
- **painful**: arn bg2 carb-v bg2 chin bg2 rhod bg2 rhus-t bg2 ruta bg2 sulph bg2
- **tendency** to strain oneself in lifting: arn sf1.de bry sf1.de *Calc* sf1.de carb-v sf1.de con sf1.de graph sf1.de lyc sf1.de *Nat-c* sf1.de* nat-m st nit-ac gk psor st *Rhus-t* sf1.de **Sil** sf1.de* *Symph* st

Lifting, straining of muscles and tendons: ...

○ - **Flexor** muscles: ruta k2

LIGHT; from:
- **agg**.: (↗*MIND - Sensitive - light)* achy jl3 *Acon* b2.de* aesc ptk1 agar b2.de* agn b2.de* alum b2.de* am-c b2.de* am-m b2.de* anac b2.de* anh mg1.de* *Ant-c* b2.de* apis ptk1 arg-n ptk1* arn b2.de* ars b2.de* asar b2.de* *Bar-c* b2.de* **Bell** b2.de* borx b2.de* bry b2.de* buth-a mg1.de **Calc** b2.de* camph b2.de* carb-an b2.de* caust b2.de* cham b2.de* *Chin* b2.de* choc srj3• cic b2.de* cina b2.de* clem b2.de* coca bro1 cocc b2.de* coff b2.de* *Colch* b2.de* **Con** b2.de* *Croc* b2.de* culx k2 cupr b2.de* dig b2.de* *Dros* b2.de* dys fmm1• **Euphr** b2.de* fum rly1• galeoc-c-h gms1• glon c1* **Graph** b2.de* hell b2.de* *Hep* b2.de* hyos b2.de* *Ign* b2.de* kali-c b2.de* kali-n b2.de* lac-d ptk1 lach b2.de* lap-la rsp1 laur b2.de* levo jl3 *Lyc* b2.de* *Lyss* bro1* m-arct b2.de* mag-c b2.de* mag-m b2.de* mag-p ptk1 mang b2.de* *Merc* b2.de* merc-c bg* mez b2.de* mim-p jl3 mur-ac b2.de* *Nat-c* b2.de* nat-m b2.de* *Nat-s* ptk1 nit-ac b2.de* nux-m b2.de* *Nux-v* b2.de* op ptk1* petr b2.de* *Ph-ac* b2.de* **Phos** b2.de* plat b2.de* *Puls* b2.de* rhod b2.de* rhus-t b2.de* ruta b2.de* samb b2.de* sang ptk1 sars b2.de* sec bro1 sel b2.de* seneg b2.de* **Sep** b2.de* *Sil* b2.de* *Spig* b2.de* stann b2.de* staph b2.de* *Stram* b2.de* sul-ac b2.de* *Sulph* b2.de* syc fmm1• tarax b2.de* ther tl1 thuj b2.de* valer b2.de* verat b2.de* zinc b2.de* [fl-ac stj2 hydrog stj2 lith-c stj2 lith-f stj2 lith-i stj2 lith-m stj2 lith-met stj2 lith-p stj2 lith-s stj2]
  - **artificial** light: agn b2.de* am-m b2.de* anac b2.de* *Apis* bg2 *Bar-c* b2.de* *Bell* b2.de* borx b2.de* **Calc** b2.de* carb-an b2.de* caust b2.de* cina b2.de* **Con** b2.de* *Croc* b2.de* **Dros** b2.de* **Glon** bg2* *Graph* b2.de* *Hep* b2.de* *Ign* b2.de* kali-c b2.de* laur b2.de* **Lyc** b2.de* manc bg2 mang b2.de* **Merc** b2.de* mez b2.de* nat-c bg2 nat-m bg2 *Nat-s* bg2 nit-ac b2.de* nux-m b2.de* petr b2.de* *Ph-ac* b2.de* **Phos** b2.de* plat b2.de* **Puls** b2.de* ruta b2.de* sars b2.de* seneg b2.de* *Sep* b2.de* *Sil* b2.de* staph bg2 stram bg2* sulph b2.de* tung-met bdx1•
    - **neon** light: [neon stj2]
  - **blue** light: tab ptk1
  - **bright** light: (↗*Snow ailments)* *Bell* ptk1 bufo ptk1 canth ptk1 chinin-s bg2 galeoc-c-h gms1• glon c1 lyss jl2 stram ptk1 thuj ptk1 [*Titan* stj2 titan-s stj2]
  - **daylight**: acon bg2 am-m b2.de* *Ant-c* b2.de* bell bg2 *Calc* b2.de* **Con** b2.de* *Dros* b2.de* dulc b4a.de **Euphr** b2.de* **Graph** b2.de* hell b2.de* **Hep** b2.de* hyos b2.de* mag-c b2.de* mang b2.de* *Merc* b2.de* nit-ac b2.de* **Nux-v** b2.de* petr b2.de* ph-ac b2.de* **Phos** b2.de* rhod b2.de* samb b2.de* sang bg2 sars b2.de* *Sep* b2.de* **Sil** b2.de* *Stram* b2.de* sulph b2.de* thuj b2.de*
  - **fire**; light of: (↗*Warm - stove - agg.)* *Ant-c* b2.de* bell ptk1 bry b2.de* calc ptk1 caust ptk1 con ptk1 dros ptk1 *Euph* b2.de* *Euphr* ptk1 *Glon* bg2* lyc ptk1 mag-m b2.de* merc b2.de* nat-m ptk1 phos ptk1 puls b2.de* ruta ptk1 sep ptk1 stram ptk1 *Zinc* b2.de*
  - **gas**; light of: caust ptk1 glon bro1* *Merc* ptk1 nat-c bro1* nat-p ptk1
  - **little**; even: galeoc-c-h gms1•
  - **moonlight**: (↗*MIND - Moonlight)* *Ant-c* k* bell k* calc bg2* mucs-nas rly4• ovi-p st1* *Sep* bg2* **Sulph** bg2* thuj k* [ant-m stj2 ant-met stj2 ant-t stj2]
  - **reflected** light: sep ptk1
  - **snow**; light from: acon ptk1 ant-c ptk1 **Ars** ptk1 cic ptk1 *Glon* ptk1
  - **sunlight**: (↗*Sun - exposure)* acon b2.de* adam srj5• agar b2.de* anh mg1.de* *Ant-c* b2.de* ars b2.de* asar b2.de* bar-c b2.de* bell mg1.de* bry b2.de* **Calc** b2.de* camph b2.de* *Chin* b2.de* *Con* b2.de* *Euphr* b2.de* **Glon** bg2* **Graph** b2.de* *Ign* b2.de* kali-bi ptk1 lac-h sze9• lach b2.de* lith-c ptk1 m-arct b2.de* mag-m b2.de* merc-c bg2 *Nat-c* b2.de* nat-m tl1 nux-v b2.de* **Ph-ac** b2.de* phos bg2* plat tl1 prun ptk1 *Puls* b2.de* sang sf1.de sel b2.de* seneg b2.de* sil sf1.de stann b2.de* stram b2.de* *Sulph* b2.de* valer b2.de* vanil fd5.de verat b2.de* zinc b2.de* [cadm-s stj2]
- **amel**.: *Am-m* b2.de* anac b2.de* ars b2.de* bar-c b2.de* **Bell** ptk1 *Calc* b2.de* cann-xyz ptk1 *Carb-an* b2.de* *Carb-v* b2.de* *Caust* kr1 coff bg2 con b2.de galeoc-c-h gms1• *Gels* ptk1 lyc ptk1 *Plat* b2.de* *Staph* b2.de* *Stram* b2.de* **Stront-c** b2.de* *Valer* b2.de* [stront-m stj2 stront-met stj2]
  - **moonlight**: aur ptk1* vanil fd5.de
  - **sunlight**: anac bg2* carbn-dox knl3• choc srj3• con bg2* crot-h ptk1 iod ptk1 kali-m ptk1 *Plat* bg2* positr nl2• rhod ptk1 *Stram* bg2* **Stront-c** bg2* thuj bg2* [spect dfg1]

LIGHTNESS; sensation of (See MIND - Delusions - light [=low)

LIGHTNING, ailments from (See Weather - thunderstorm - lightning)

LIVID (See SKIN - Discoloration - livid)

LOCOMOTOR ATAXIA: *(↗EXTREMITIES - Incoordination; EXTREMITIES - Incoordination - lower; EXTREMITIES - Tottering)* agar bg2*] alumbg2* alumin-m bwa3* *Alumn* c2* am-m bro1 ang bro1 arag br1* *Arg-n* bg2* *Ars* c2* ars-br br1* astra-e vwe2 atro c2* *Aur* c2 *Aur-m* bro1 bar-c bg2 bell bg2* calc hr1 cann-i bro1 carb-v bro1 carbn-s bro1 caust bg2* chlorpr mtf11 chr-s bwa3* cocc bg2* colch he1 con bg2* crot-h hr1 cund c2* cupr bg2 cur c2* der c2 dub c2* dubo-m br1 *Ferr-pic* bro1 *Fl-ac* c2* gels bg2* helo-s c2* hyos bg2* *Ign* c2* iodof c2 kali-br bg2* *Kali-i* c2* kalm c2* lach bg2* lath c2* lol bg2 *Lyc* c2* *Mag-p* c2* merc bg2 merc-c bro1 merc-p bwa3 nat-c ptk1 nat-i bro1 nat-s hr1 nit-ac bro1 nux-m c2* *Nux-v* bg2* onos bg2* ox-ac cp1* oxyt c2 ped bro1 ph-ac c2 *Phos* c2* phos-h c2* phys bg2* *Pic-ac* c2* picro c1* plb br1* *Plb-p* bro1 plb-xyz c2 psor hr1 puls ptk1 rhus-t bg2* ruta bro1 sabad bro1 sec bg2* sil c2* stram c2* *Stry* bro1 stry-xyz c2 sulfon c2 sulph bg2* syph jl2 tab bg2 tarent c2* thal c2* thiosin bro1 verat-v ptk1 zinc ll1* *Zinc-p* bro1 zinc-s bro1

- **accompanied** by:
  - **diphtheria**: ars bro1 bell bro1 lach bro1 mosch bro1 phos bro1
  - **pain** | **lightning**-like (See Pain - lightning-like - accompanied - locomotor)
  - **sexual** excitement: kali-br bro1 phos bro1 pic-ac bro1
  - ○ **Bladder**; complaints of: alum bro1 fl-ac bro1 ign bro1 nux-v bro1 stry bro1 tarent bro1 thiosin bro1
  - **Eyes**; complaints of: bell bro1 con bro1 ferr-pic bro1 phos bro1
  - **Heel**; ulcers on: sil bro1
  - **Muscles**; weakness of: cann-i bro1
  - **Rectum**; complaints of: alum bro1 fl-ac bro1 ign bro1 nux-v bro1 stry bro1 tarent bro1 thiosin bro1
  - **Stomach**; complaints of: *Arg-n* bro1 bell bro1 carb-v bro1 ign bro1 lyc bro1 *Nux-v* bro1 thiosin bro1
- **alcoholism**; from: nux-v vml
- **eating** | **amel**.: nat-c ptk1
- **incipient**: ang bro1 atro bro1 *Bell* bro1 con bro1 ign bro1 nux-v bro1 sec bro1 stry bro1 tarent bro1 zinc bro1 zinc-s bro1
- **painful**: thal-met br1
- **syphilitic**: aur-m-n br1 *Kali-i* bro1 merc-c bro1 nit-ac bro1 sec bro1

LONGER: | **sensation** as if: alum ptk1 hyper ptk1 kali-c ptk1 lac-c ptk1 *Phos* ptk1 stram ptk1 tab ptk1

LOOKING:

- **around** agg.: calc ptk1 *Cic* ptk1 **Con** ptk1 ip ptk1
- **back** | **agg**.: calc b2.de* *Cic* b2.de* **Con** b2.de* ip b2.de kali-c b2.de*
- **bright** objects agg.; at: *Bell* ptk1 canth ptk1 hyos ptk1 *Lyss* ptk1 mur-ac ptk1 stram ptk1
- **concentrated**, focused:
  - **agg**.: agar b2.de* agn b2.de* alum b2.de* am-c b2.de* am-m b2.de* anac b2.de* ang b2.de* arg-met b2.de* **Arg-n** bg2 arn b2.de* *Asaf* b2.de* asar b2.de* *Aur* b2.de* bar-c b2.de* bell b2.de* borx b2.de* bry b2.de* **Calc** b2.de* canth b2.de* carb-an bg2 *Carb-v* b4.de* *Caust* b4.de* cham b7.de* chel b7.de* chin b7a.de* *Cic* b7.de* **Cina** b7.de* cocc b2.de* coff b2.de* *Con* b2.de* **Croc** b2.de* cupr b2.de* dros b2.de* dulc b2.de* ferr b2.de* gels bg2 *Graph* b2.de* hep b2.de ign b2.de **Kali-c** b2.de kreos b2.de laur b2.de* led b2.de* **Lyc** b2.de* m-arct b2.de mag-c b2.de* mag-m b2.de* mang b2.de* meny b2.de* merc b2.de* mez b2.de* mosch b2.de* mur-ac b2.de* *Nat-c* b2.de* **Nat-m** b2.de* nit-ac b2.de* nux-m b2.de* nux-v b2.de* *Olnd* b2.de* **Onos** bg2 par b2.de* petr b2.de* ph-ac b2.de* *Phos* b2.de* plat b2.de* puls b2.de* ran-b b2.de* rheum b2.de* **Rhod** b2.de* rhus-t b2.de* **Ruta** b2.de* sabad b2.de* *Sars* b2.de* sel b2.de* **Seneg** b2.de* *Sep* b2.de* **Sil** b2.de* *Spig* b2.de* *Spong* b2.de* staph b2.de* stram b2.de* stront-c b2.de* sul-ac b2.de* sulph b2.de* thuj b2.de* valer b2.de* verb b2.de* viol-o b2.de* zinc b2.de*
  - **amel**.: agn b2.de* ferr b2.de* *Nat-c* b2.de* petr b2.de* ph-ac b2.de*
- **distance**; into the:
  - **agg**.: dig ptk1 euphr b2.de* *Ruta* b2.de*
  - **amel**.: bell bg2*

Looking: ...

- **distress** agg.; others in: tarent ptk1
- **downward**: [pop dhh1]
  - **agg**.: acon b2.de* alum bg2 arg-n ptk1 borx ptk1 *Calc* b2.de* ferr bg2 kali-c ptk1 kalm bg2* nat-m bg2 *Olnd* b2.de* *Phos* ptk1 phyt bg2 *Spig* b2.de* sulph b2.de*
  - **amel**.: *Sabad* b2.de*
  - **front** of him; in | **agg**.: acon b2.de *Calc* b2.de *Olnd* b2.de *Spig* b2.de sulph b2.de
- **eclipse** agg.; at: hep ptk1
- **glistening** objects; at | **agg**.: acon bg2 ars bg2 **Bell** b2.de* *Canth* b2.de* glon bg2 *Hyos* b2.de* lach b2.de* phos b2.de* *Stram* b2.de* ter bg2
- **light**; at | **bright** light: am-m b2.de* bell b2.de* *Bry* b2.de* *Calc* b2.de* caust b2.de* chel b2.de* colch b2.de* ign b2.de* kali-c b2.de* kreos b2.de* *Mag-m* b2.de* *Merc* b2.de* nux-v b2.de* ph-ac b2.de* *Phos* b2.de* sabad b2.de* sep b2.de* zinc b2.de*
- **long** time; at something for a:
  - **agg**.: acon ptk1 aur ptk1 cic b2.de* kreos b2.de* nat-m ptk1 rheum b2.de* *Ruta* b2.de* sep ptk1 *Spig* b2.de*
  - **amel**.: dig ptk1 *Nat-c* ptk1 sabad ptk1
- **mirror** agg.; into: kali-c ptk1
- **moving** things; at | **agg**.: agar ptk1 **Bell** ptk1 brom ptk1 canth ptk1 *Con* ptk1 *Ferr* ptk1 hyos ptk1 jab ptk1 lyss ptk1 stram ptk1 sulph ptk1
- **one** point agg.; at: agn ptk1
- **plane**; over a large | **agg**.: *Sep* b2.de*
- **red** objects agg.; at: lyc ptk1
- **sideways**:
  - **agg**.: *Bell* b2.de* calc bg2 *Cic* bg2 *Con* bg2* gels bg2 ip bg2 kali-c bg2 merc-c ptk1 olnd b2.de* op bg2 seneg b4a.de spig b2.de* thuj bg2
  - **amel**.: chinin-s ptk1 *Olnd* b2.de* sulph ptk1
- **snow** agg.; at: apis ptk1
- **straight** ahead:
  - **agg**.: *Olnd* b2.de*
  - **amel**.: *Bell* b2.de* olnd b2.de* spig b2.de*
- **turning**; at something | **agg**.: lyc b2.de*
- **upward**:
  - **agg**.: alum b2.de* ars b2.de* benzo bro1 **Calc** b2.de* carb-v b2.de* caust b2.de* chel ptk1 cupr b2.de* graph b2.de* petr b2.de* *Phos* ptk1 plat b2.de* plb b2.de* *Puls* b2.de* *Sabad* b2.de* sabin b2.de* sang ptk1 *Sel* b2.de* sep b2.de* sil b2.de* spig b2.de* sulph bro1 *Thuj* b2.de* zinc b2.de*
    - **high** buildings; at: arg-n ptk1
    - **walking** in open air agg.: arg-n ptk1 sep ptk1
- **water**; on (running):
  - **agg**.: ang b7.de arg-met b2.de* **Bell** b2.de* brom bg2 *Ferr* b2.de* *Hyos* b2.de* stram b2.de* sulph b2.de*
  - **amel**.: bell bg2
- **white**; at something | **agg**.: apis ptk1 ars bg2* cham b2.de* graph b2.de* kali-c b2.de* lyc ptk1 nat-m b2.de* stram b2.de* tab ptk1
- **window**; out the | **agg**.: camph ptk1 carb-v ptk1 **Nat-m** ptk1 ox-ac ptk1

LOOSE: | **skin** hanging loose in affected part; sensation of: iris bg2 lach bg2 phos bg2 *Sabad* bg2 thuj bg2

LOOSE; as if flesh were: apis bg2 bell bg2 *Bry* b7.de* canth b7.de* dros b7.de* *Ign* bg2 kali-c bg2 kreos b7a.de* lach bg2 led b7.de* lyc bg2 *Merc* bg2 mosch bg2 nat-m bg2 nit-ac b4a.de* nux-v b7.de* ol-an bg2 **Rhus-t** b7.de* staph b7.de* *Sulph* b4a.de* *Thuj* b4a.de*

LOSS:

- **blood**; of: *(↗Faintness - blood; after; Nursing; Weakness - epistaxis; Weakness - loss - blood)* abrot sf1.de arn sf1.de calc bro1 *Calc-p* bro1 carb-an sf1.de carb-v b4a.de* caul hr1 *Chin* k2* chinin-ar sf1.de con bro1 *Ferr* k2* ferr-pic c1* ham br1* helon sf1.de hydr sf1.de ip c1 *Kali-c* bro1 *Kali-p* bro1 *Nat-m* sf1.de nux-v bro1 *Ph-ac* b4a.de* phos bro1* puls bro1 *Sel* bro1 senec k2 sep k2* staph k2* stict ptk1 *Stront-c* br1* (non:stront-met) stroph-h br1 *Sulph* b4a.de zinc b4a.de
- **fluids**, of: *(↗Emissions; History - loss; Nursing; Weakness - loss)* abrot bg2 acon ptk1 agar k* alet sf1.de alum k* anac k* ant-c k* ant-t k* arg-met k* arn k* *Ars* k* ars-i *Aven* sf1.de bell k* bism bg2 borx k* bov k* brom bg2 bry k* bufo bg2 *Calad* k* **Calc** k* **Calc-p** k* calen vml3• cann-s k* canth k* caps k* carb-ac bg2 *Carb-an* k* **Carb-v** k* *Carbn-s* caust k* cham k* **Chin** k* *Chinin-ar*

- **fluids**, of: ...
Chinin-s k* cimic ptk1 cina k* coff k* coli jl2 *Con* k* *Crot-h* *Cupr* bg2* dig k* dulc k* elat vml3• *Ferr* k* ferr-ar **Graph** k* ham bg2* helo bg2 helon sf1.de hep k* ign k* *Iod* k* ip k* *Kali-c* k* *Kali-p* k* lach bg2* led k* lyc k* m-ambo b2.de* m-aust b2.de* mag-m k* med jl2 *Merc* k* mez k* mosch k* nat-c k* nat-m k* *Nat-p* nit-ac k* nux-m b2.de* *Nux-v* k* parathyr jl2 petr k* **Ph-ac** k* *Phos* k* plat bg2 plb k* psor al2* **Puls** k* ran-b k* rhod k* rhus-t k* ruta k* sabad k* samb k* sec k* **Sel** k* **Sep** k* *Sil* k* spig k* *Squil* k* stann k* **Staph** k* stram bg2 sul-ac st *Sulph* k* thuj k* valer k* verat k* zinc k* [spect dfg1]
  - **children**; in: psor jl2
    - **nurslings**: psor jl2
  - **exhaustion**; after: phos mtf11

LOW-FEVER STATES: arn br1

LYING: (↗*Bending - affected - amel.*)
- **abdomen**; on:
  - **after** | **amel.**: am-c bg2 ambr bg2
  - **agg.**: ambr bg2 kali-p gk puls gk
  - **amel.**: *Acet-ac* k* adlu jl aloe am-c k* ambr ant-t bro1 ars k* atra-r bnm3• bar-c k* **Bell** k* bell-p bg2 bry calc k* calc-p st* *Chel* k* chion bg2* *Cina* k* *Coloc* k* crot-t k* cupr bg2* *Elaps* k* *Eup-per* bg2* ind bg1* lach k* lept st* mag-c *Med* bg1* *Nit-ac* k* par st* *Phos* k* phyt k* plb k* *Podo* bro1* psil jl *Psor* ptk1 rhus-t k* rib-ac jl sel sep k* *Stann* k* *Tab* bro1 thyr ptk1 [calc-lac stj2 *Calc-met* stj2 calc-sil stj2]
    - **nates** in the air: med jl2
    - **pregnancy** agg.; during: podo kl*
- **across** | **amel.**: con bg2
- **after**:
  - **agg.**: acon k* agar agn alum *Am-c* am-m **Ambr** ant-c ant-t *Arg-met* arn **Ars** ars-s-f k2 *Asaf* asar **Aur** aur-ar k2 bar-c bell bism borx bov bry calad k* calc canth *Caps* k* carb-an carb-v caust *Cham* chel chin *Clem* cocc coff colch coloc *Con* croc cupr *Cycl* dros **Dulc** *Euph* *Euphr* *Ferr* graph guaj hell hep *Hyos* ign ip *Kali-c* kali-chl k13 kali-m k2 kali-n lach laur led **Lyc** *Mag-c* *Mag-m* mang *Meny* merc mez mosch mur-ac nat-ar nat-c nit-ac nux-m nux-v olnd op par petr ph-ac phos **Plat** *Plb* **Puls** ran-b ran-s rhod **Rhus-t** ruta *Sabad* sabin **Samb** sars sel k* seneg *Sep* sil spig stann staph **Stront-c** sul-ac *Sulph* *Tarax* teucr thuj valer verat verb viol-o viol-t zinc
    - **immediately** after lying: cench k2 ferr-i k2
  - **amel.**: acon agar agn am-m ambr anac ant-c ant-t arg-met arn **Ars** asaf aur bar-c *Bell* bov **Bry** caj calad **Calc** calc-f camph cann-s *Canth* caps carb-an *Carb-v* carbn-s caust chel chin cic *Cina* cocc coff colch coloc con *Croc* crot-h cupr dig dios dros dulc euphr *Fl-ac* *Graph* guaj hell *Hep* hyos ign *Iod* ip kali-c kali-n kreos *Lach* laur led lyc mag-c mag-m meli *Merc* nat-c **Nat-m** **Nit-ac** nux-m **Nux-v** *Olnd* pall par petr ph-ac phos **Puls** ran-b rheum rhod rhus-t sabin sacch-a fd2.de• samb sars sec sel *Sep* sil sin-n *Spig* spong **Squil** stann *Staph* *Stram* sul-ac sul-i k2 *Sulph* tarax thuj valer verat verb
- **agg.**: abies-n *Acon* k* adon ptk1* aesc bg2* *Agar* k* agn b2.de* alum k* alum-p k2 *Alumn* hr1* am-c k* *Am-m* k* *Ambr* k* anac k* androc srj1* ang b2.de* ant-c k* *Ant-t* k* **Apis** k* *Apoc* aral k* aran bg2 *Arg-met* k* arn k* **Ars** k* ars-i ars-s-f k2* arum-t bro1 *Asaf* k* asar k* **Aur** k* aur-ar k2 *Aur-i* k2* aur-s k2* *Bapt* bar-c b2.de* *Bell* k* bism k* borx k* bov k* brom tl1 *Bry* k* cact calad k* calc k* calc-p camph k* cann-i cann-s k* canth k* **Caps** k* carb-an k* carb-v k* carbn-s caust k* cench k2* **Cham** k* chel k* chin k* cic k* cina k* clem k* cocc k* coff k* colch k* coloc k* **Con** k* croc k* crot-h bg2 crot-t cupr k* *Cycl* k* dig k* dios k* **Dros** k* *Dulc* k* eup-per bg2 **Euph** k* *Euphr* k* **Ferr** k* ferr-ar ferr-i ferr-p fl-ac k* fum rly1*• gels *Glon* k* gnaph st1 graph k* grin guaj k* *Hell* k* hep k* **Hyos** k* iber bro1 ign k* iod k* ip k* kali-bi *Kali-br* **Kali-c** k* kali-chl k13 kali-i kali-m k2 *Kali-n* k* kali-s k2* *Kalm* bg2* kreos k* *Lach* k* lact laur k* led k* *Lil-t* bg1* **Lyc** k* lycps-v ptk1 *M-ambo* b2.de* m-arct b2.de* m-aust b2.de* mag-c k* *Mag-m* k* mang k* **Meny** k* meph bg2* merc k* mez k* *Mosch* k* *Mur-ac* k* murx naja nat-ar *Nat-c* k* nat-m k* **Nat-s** k* nit-ac k* nux-m k* *Nux-v* k* olnd k* *Op* k* ox-ac bg2 par k* petr k* *Ph-ac* k* phel **Phos** k* **Plat** k* plb k* prot jl3* *Ptel* c1 **Puls** k* *Ran-b* k* raph rheum k* *Rhod* k* **Rhus-t** k* **Rumx** k* *Ruta* k* *Sabad* k* sabin k* sal-ac **Samb** k* **Sang** k* sars k* sec k* sel k* seneg k* *Sep* k* *Sil* b2.de* sphing kk3.fr spig k* spong k* squil k* stann k* staph k* stict stram k* *Stront-c* k* sul-ac k* sul-i k2* *Sulph* k* **Tarax** k* teucr k* thuj k* *Trif-p* bro1 *Valer* k* verat k* *Verb* k* viol-o k* *Viol-t* k* visc sp1 x-ray bro1 zinc k* *Zing* [astat stj2 aur-m stj2 bar-br stj2 bar-i stj2 bar-met stj2 bism-sn stj2 caes-met stj2 cinnb stj2 hafn-met stj2 irid-met stj2 lanth-met stj2 merc-d stj2 merc-i-f stj2 osm-met stj2 plb-m stj2 plb-p stj2 polon-met stj2 rhen-met stj2 tant-met stj2 thal-met stj2 tung-met stj2]
- **amel.**: acon k* adam srj5• agar k* agn k* aids nl2• alum k* alum-sil k2* alumn hr1* am-c k* **Am-m** k* ambr k* anac k* *Androc* srj1• ang b2.de* anh bro1* ant-c k* ant-t k* arg-met k* *Arn* k* ars k* **Asar** k* *Bar-c* k* bar-i k2* **Bell** k* bell-p bro1 borx k* brom bro1 brucel sa3• **Bry** k* calad k* **Calc** k* calc-i k2* *Calc-p* calc-sil k2* camph k* cann-s k* *Canth* k* caps k* carb-ac *Carb-an* k* *Carb-v* k* carbn-s cassia-s cdd7*• *Caust* k* cham b2.de* chel k* chin k* chir-fl gya2 cic k* cimic cina k* clem *Coc-c* kr1 cocc k* coff k* *Colch* k* coloc k* con k* conv croc k* cupr k* cycl bg2* cypra-eg sde6.de• dicha mg1.de dig k* dios dros k* dulc k* equis-h bro1 euph k* **Ferr** k* fic-m gya1 fl-ac bg2* form ptk1 gels bg2* *Glon* granit-m es1• *Graph* k* guaj k* haliae-lc srj5• hell k* hep k* hyos k* *Ign* k* iod k* ip k* kali-c k* kali-n k* kalm k* kreos k* lach k* laur k* *Led* k* lyc k* m-arct b2.de m-aust b2.de mag-c k* mag-m k* mag-s j5.de mand sp1 **Mang** k* *Mang-act* bro1* meny b7.de merc k* merc-c bg2 methys jl mez k* mur-ac k* nat-c k* **Nat-m** k* nat-sil k2* *Nit-ac* k* nux-m k* **Nux-v** k* olnd k* onos bro1 op k* par k* petr k* ph-ac k* phos k* **Pic-ac** k* plat bg2* plb k* *Psor* k* puls bro1* pulx br1* rad-br c11* ran-b k* rheum k* rhus-t k* ruta k* sabad k* sabin k* sang bg2* sars k* sec k* sel k* seneg k* sep k* sieg mg1.de *Sil* b2.de* *Spig* k* *Spong* k* **Squil** k* *Stann* b2.de* *Staph* b2.de* *Stram* b2.de* stroph-s jl3 stry bro1 sul-ac b2.de* sulfonam ks2 *Sulph* k* symph bro1 teucr b2.de* thioc-ac rly4• thuj b2.de* tub-r jl *Verat* b2.de* zinc b2.de* [alumin stj2 alumin-p stj2 alumin-s stj2 am-br stj2 am-caust stj2 am-f stj2 am-s stj1 cadm-met stj2 cadm-s stj2 cob stj2 cob-m stj2 cob-p stj2 *Cupr-act* stj2 hydrog stj2 lith-f stj2 stront-m stj2 stront-met stj2]
- **back**; on:
  - **agg.**: acet-ac k* acon k* agar bg2* aloe alum k* alum-p k2* alum-sil k2* alumn hr1* am-c k* *Am-m* k* ang b2.de* *Arg-met* k* arg-n bg2* arn k* *Ars* k* ars-s-f k2* aur-m bar-c k* bar-i k2* bell k* borx k* bry k* bufo cact ptk1 calc canth k* carb-v h2 *Caust* k* *Cham* k* chin k* cimic bg2* cina k* clem k* *Colch* b2.de* *Coloc* k* *Cupr* k* *Cycl* bg2 dulc k* eup-per euph k* ferr-p k2 hyper **Ign** b2.de* *Iod* k* kali-c k* *Kali-n* b2.de* kreos bg2* lach k* lob bg2 m-ambo b2.de mag-m b2.de* mag-p bg2* merc k* merc-i-f ptk1 nat-c k* nat-m k* *Nat-s* k* **Nux-v** k* *Op* k* par k* **Phos** k* plat k* *Plb* bg2 *Puls* b2.de* ran-b k* *Rhus-t* k* rib-ac jl sang bg2* *Sep* k* *Sil* k* *Spig* k* spong k* stront-c k* sul-i k2* *Sulph* k* thuj k* zinc-chr ptk1 [mag-s stj1]
  - **amel.**: *Acon* k* aeth am-c k* **Am-m** k* *Anac* k* ang b2.de* *Apis* arn k* bar-c k* bell k* borx k* **Bry** k* cact calad k* **Calc** k* calc-sil k2* *Camph* st *Canth* k* *Carb-an* k* caust k* chin k* cimic cina k* clem k* *Colch* k* con k* conv crot-h bg2* cycl bg2* *Dig* bg2* ferr k* grat hell *Ign* k* ip k* *Kali-c* k* *Kalm* k* kreos k* lach k* *Lyc* k* m-ambo b2.de* mag-m b2.de* *Mang* vh merc k* **Merc-c** k* mosch k* nat-c k* *Nat-m* k* *Nat-s* nux-v k* ox-ac par k* *Phos* k* plat k* **Puls** k* ran-b k* **Rhus-t** k* *Ruta* b7a.de* sabad k* sabin bg2* *Sang* k* senec *Seneg* k* sep k* sil k* spig k* *Spong* k* *Stann* k* sulph k* sym-r br1 tell jl3 *Thuj* k* verat k* viol-t k* [ind stj2 mag-s stj1 pop dhh1]
    - **shoulders** elevated; with: acon bro1 ars bro1
  - **turn**; cannot: *Cic* elaps
- **bed**; in:
  - **agg.**: acon k* *Agar* k* agn k* aloe alum k* alum-sil k2 *Am-c* k* am-m k* **Ambr** k* anac k* ang b2.de* ant-c k* *Ant-t* k* *Arg-met* k* arn k* *Ars* k* ars-i asaf k* asar k* *Aur* k* aur-i k2 aur-s k2 bar-c k* bar-i k2 bell k* bism k* *Borx* k* bov k* *Bry* k* bufo bg2 calad k* calc k* calc-i k2 camph k* cann-s k* canth k* caps k* carb-an k* carb-v k* caust k* cham k* chel k* chin k* cic k* cina k* *Clem* k* cocc k* coff k* colch k* *Coloc* k* con k* croc k* cycl k* dig k* dios *Dros* k* dulc k* *Euph* k* euphr k* **Ferr** k* **Ferr-i** ferr-p k2 fl-ac bg2 graph k* guaj k* hell k* hep k* hyos k* ign k* **Iod** k* *Kali-c* k* kali-i kali-m k2 kali-n k* kali-p kali-s *Kalm* kreos k* **Lach** k* laur k* *Led* k* *Lil-t* *Lith-c* **Lyc** k* *M-ambo* b2.de* *M-arct* b2.de* m-aust b2.de* *Mag-c* k* mag-m b2.de* *Mang* k* *Mec* ptk1 meny k* **Merc** k* merc-c bg2 *Merc-i-f* *Mez* k* mosch k* mur-ac k* nat-c k* *Nat-m* k* nit-ac k* nux-m k* *Nux-v* k* olnd k* op k* *Ox-ac* par k* petr k* *Ph-ac* k* phor-t mie3• **Phos** k* phyt *Plat* k* *Plb* k* **Puls** k* ran-b k* rheum k* *Rhod* k* *Rhus-t* k* **Rumx** k* ruta k* sabad k* sabin k* samb k* **Sang** k* *Sars* k* sec k* *Sel* k* seneg k* **Sep** k* **Sil** k* *Spig* k* spong k* squil k* stann k* staph k* stict stram k* *Stront-c* k* sul-ac k* sul-i k2 **Sulph** k* tarax k* *Tell* teucr k* thuj k* valer k* *Verat* k* verb k* viol-o k* viol-t k* x-ray sp1 *Zinc* k* zinc-p k2
  - **amel.**: *Acon* k* agar k* alum hr1 alum-sil k2 am-c hr1 *Am-m* k* ambr k* anac k* ang b2.de* ant-c k* ant-t k* arg-met k* arn k* *Ars* k* ars-s-f k2 asaf hr1 asar k* aur k* aur-ar k2 *Bar-c* k* bell k* bism hr1 bov k* **Bry** k*

- **amel.**: ...
calad k* calc k* calc-sil k2* camph k* cann-s k* *Canth* k* caps k* carb-an k* carb-v k* *Caust* k* cham k* chel k* chin k* **Cic** k* cina k* clem k* *Coc-c* **Cocc** k* coff k* colch k* coloc k* *Con* k* croc k* cupr k* cycl hr1 dig k* diphtox jl2 dros hr1 dulc k* euph hr1 ferr k* **Gels** hr1 graph k* guaj k* hell k* **Hep** k* hipp jl2 hyos k* ign k* iod k* ip k* kali-c k* kali-n k* kreos k* *Lach* k* laur k* led k* *Lyc* k* m-ambo b2.de* m-arct b2.de m-aust b2.de mag-c k* mag-m b2.de* *Mang* vh meny hr1 merc k* mez k* mosch hr1 mur-ac k* nat-c k* *Nat-m* k* *Nit-ac* k* nux-m k* **Nux-v** k* olnd k* op hr1 par k* petr k* ph-ac k* phos k* plat hr1 plb hr1 puls k* pyrog ptk1 ran-b k* rheum k* rhod k* *Rhus-t* k* sabad k* sabin k* samb k* sars k* sec k* sel k* seneg hr1 sep k* *Sil* k* spig k* spong k* **Squil** k* **Stann** k* *Staph* k* *Stram* k* stront-c k* sul-ac k* sulfonam jl3 sulph k* tarax k* teucr hr1 thuj k* valer k* verat k* verb k* viol-t k* zinc hr1
  - **abdomen**; on: bar-c bg2 bell bg2 calc bg2 calc-p bg2 cina bg2 **Coloc** bg2 *Eup-per* bg2 *Med* bg2 pareir bg2 podo bg2 sep bg2
- **desire** to (See Lie - desire)
- **hard** bed, on a | **sensation** as if (See Hard bed)

- **double**; bent:
  - **agg.**: hyos bg2 lyc bg2 spong bg2 teucr bg2 valer bg2
  - **amel.**: bell bg2 cham bg2 cocc bg2 *Colch* b2.de* **Coloc** b2.de* mag-m bg2* mag-p bg2* merc-c bg2 plat bg2 *Puls* b2.de* *Rheum* b2.de* rhus-t b2.de* staph bg2 stram bg2 *Sulph* hr1* verat bg2 [mag-br stj1]
    - **hands** between thighs; with: granit-m es1•
- **down**; desire to lie (See Lie - desire)
- **face**; on the | **amel.**: hyper ptk1 led bg2* *Psor* bg2*
- **ground**; on the | **amel.**: lach bg2
- **hands** and knees; on | **amel.**: con ptk1 eup-per ptk1 euph ptk1 *Lach* ptk1 med ptk1 pareir ptk1 sep ptk1 tarent ptk1
- **half** reclining posture; in a | **amel.**: acon bg2 gels bg2* kalm ptk1 led ptk1 sang bg2* thyr ptk1
- **hard** bed; on a:
  - **agg.**: *Arn* sf1.de bapt sf1.de bar-c sf1.de graph sf1.de kali-c sf1.de lach sf1.de puls sf1.de *Rhus-t* sf1.de sil sf1.de
  - **amel.**: bell sf1.de
- **hard**; on something | **amel.**: acon bg2 bell b2.de* kali-c ptk1 mag-m bg2 nat-m bg2* *Rhus-t* b2.de* sanic ptk1 *Sep* bg2* stann ptk1
- **head** high; with the | **amel.**: *Ant-t* b2.de* apis ptk1 aral ptk1 *Arg-met* ptk1 **Ars** b2.de* bell ptk1 cact ptk1 cann-s b2.de* caps b2.de* *Chin* b2.de* clem b2.de *Colch* b2.de *Con* ptk1 gels ptk1 glon ptk1 *Hep* b2.de* kali-c ptk1 *Kali-n* b2.de* lach b2.de* m-aust b2.de nux-v b2.de petr b2.de* phos b2.de puls b2.de* samb ptk1 sang ptk1 *Spig* b2.de* spong sf1.de* *Squil* b7a.de stront-c b2.de sulph b2.de
- **head** low; with the:
  - **agg.**: *Ant-t* b2.de* apis bg2 aral vh *Arg-met* b2.de* arn b7a.de* **Ars** b2.de* bell bg2 cact bg2 *Cann-s* b2.de* *Caps* b2.de* carb-v bg2 *Chin* b2.de* *Clem* b2.de* *Colch* b2.de* con bg2 gels bg2 glon k2 *Hep* b2.de* **Kali-n** b2.de* *Lach* b2.de* m-aust b2.de* *Nux-v* b2.de* *Petr* b2.de* phos b2.de* **Puls** b2.de* sang bg2 *Spig* b2.de* spong b7a.de* stront-c b2.de* *Sulph* b2.de*
  - **amel.**: apis bg2 *Arn* bg2* bell bg2 calc bg2* caust bg2* lach bg2 nat-m bg2* psor jl2 sang bg2* *Spong* bg2* tab bg2 *Verat* bg2 *Verat-v* st
- **horizontal** position; in a:
  - **agg.**: arn bg2 bell bg2
  - **amel.**: apis bg2* arn b2.de* bell bg2* both-ax tsm2 con ptk1 cycl bg2 laur ptk1 psor ptk1 spong b2.de* tab ptk1 ther ptk1 *Verat-v* ptk1
- **knee** elbow position | **amel.**: carc fd2.de• *Con* bg2* eup-per bg2 euph bg2* kali-c ptk1 *Lyc* bg2* med bg2* pareir bg2 petr bg2 sep bg2
- **knees** and chest; on | **amel.**: choc srj3• sep bg2
- **knees**, body bent backward; on: nux-v ptk1
- **legs** drawn up; with | **amel.**: *Abies-c* vh1 bell sf1.de cocc sf1.de coloc sf1.de *Mag-p* sf1.de stram sf1.de verat sf1.de
- **must** (See Lie - desire)
- **quietly** | **amel.**: bry ptk1 psor ptk1
- **side**; on:
  - **affected** side | **agg.**: *Acon* b7.de* am-m b7.de *Ambr* b7.de* arn b7.de bry b7.de *Chin* b7.de* croc b7.de *Dros* b7.de *Ign* b7.de* *Mosch* b7a.de *Nux-m* b7.de* nux-v b7.de *Rheum* b7.de* *Rhus-t* b7.de *Ruta* b7.de* sabad b7.de spong b7.de staph b7.de tarax b7.de verat b7.de

- **side**; on: ...
  - **agg.**: **Acon** k* am-c k* am-m k* **Anac** k* *Ang* b2.de* *Arg-n* k* arn k* ars h2 aur bar-c k* bell k* borx k* **Bry** k* *Calad* k* **Calc** k* canth k* **Carb-an** k* caust k* chin k* *Cina* k* clem k* colch k* *Con* k* *Ferr* k* *Ign* k* *Ip* k* **Kali-c** k* kali-n h2 *Kreos* k* lach k* *Lil-t* bg1* **Lyc** k* m-ambo b2.de* mag-m b2.de* *Merc* k* *Merc-c* k* mosch k* *Nat-c* b2.de* nat-m k* *Nat-s* k* nux-v k* *Par* k* *Ph-ac* k* *Phos* k* plat k* *Puls* k* ran-b k* **Rhus-t** k* sabad k* *Seneg* k* sep k* *Sil* k* spig k* spong k* **Stann** k* *Sulph* k* *Thuj* k* verat k* viol-t k*
  - **amel.**: acon k* alum k* am-c k* am-m k* anac br1* ang b2.de* arn k* ars k* bar-c k* bell k* borx k* bry k* calc-p canth k* caust k* cham k* chin k* cina k* clem k* **Cocc** k* colch k* *Coloc* b2.de* cupr k* dulc k* euph k* ign k* iod k* kali-c k* *Kali-n* b2.de* lach k* lept ptk1 m-ambo b2.de* mag-m b2.de* merc b2.de* nat-c b2.de* nat-m k* **Nux-v** k* par k* *Phos* k* plat k* puls b2.de* ran-b k* rhus-t k* *Sep* k* *Sil* b2.de* spig k* spong k* stront-c k* sulph k* thuj k*
  - **left**:
    - **agg.**: *Acon* k* ail k* *Am-c* b2.de* anac k* ang b2.de* ant-t apis ptk1 *Arg-n* k* arn k* *Bar-c* k* *Bar-m* sf1.de bell k* brom sf1.de* bry k* *Cact* k* calad br1* calc b2.de* canth k* carb-an k* cean sf1.de chin k* coc-c bro1 *Colch* k* con k* crot-h sf1.de cycl bg2 dig bg2* elaps gk eup-per k* glon bg2* hydroph jl *Iber* bg1* ind bg1* ip k* kali-ar kali-bi gk kali-c k* kalm k* kreos k* **Lach** vh* lil-t ptk1 lyc k* mag-m magn-gr bro1 merc k* mez bg2 *Naja* k* *Nat-c* k* *Nat-m* k* nat-p *Nat-s* k* op *Par* k* petr k* **Phos** k* plat k* *Ptel* bg2* **Puls** k* rhus-t rumx bg2* seneg k* *Sep* k* sil k* *Spig* b2.de* *Stann* b2.de* *Sulph* k* tab k* *Thuj* k* tub ptk1 vib bg2* visc bro1 zinc-i ptk1 [alumin-p stj2 am-br stj2 bar-br stj2 calc-br stj1 cupr-p stj2 kali-br stj1 lith-p stj2 mang-p stj2 nat-ar stj2 nat-br stj2 nat-caust stj2 nat-lac stj2 nat-met stj2 nat-sil stj2 plb-p stj2 zinc-p stj2]
    - **amel.**: acon b2.de* *Am-m* b2.de* anac b2.de* ang c1 arg-n bg2* *Borx* b2.de* bry b2.de* calc b2.de* carb-an b2.de* *Caust* b2.de* cina b2.de* clem b2.de* con b2.de* fum rly1*• ign bro1* ip b2.de* kali-c b2.de* kreos b2.de lach b2.de* lil-t bg3* lyc b2.de* m-ambo b2.de m-arct b7.de *Mag-m* b2.de* *Merc* b2.de* mur-ac bro1* nat-c b2.de* nat-m bro1* *Nux-v* b2.de* phyt ptk1 puls b2.de* ran-b b2.de* sang ptk1 *Sec* b7a.de seneg b2.de* spig b2.de* *Spong* b2.de* stann b2.de* sulph b2.de* thuj b2.de*
  - **pain** goes to side: *(↗Pain - parts lain)*
    - **Lain** on: aral a1* bapt a1
    - **Not** lain on: calc-ar bg2 cur bg2 fl-ac bg2 graph bg2 ign bg2 kali-bi bg2
  - **painful** side:
    - **agg.**: *Acon* k* agar k* am-c k* am-m k* ambr k* anac k* ang b2.de* *Ant-c* k* arg-met k* arn k* *Ars* k* ars-i *Bapt* **Bar-c** k* *Bell* k* bry k* **Calad** k* calc k* calc-f cann-s k* caps k* carb-an k* carb-v k* caust k* *Chin* k* cina k* clem k* croc k* cupr k* **Cycl** h1* dios *Dros* k* *Graph* k* guaj k* **Hep** k* hyos k* ign k* **Iod** k* *Kali-c* k* *Kali-i* k* kali-m kr1* kali-n k* **Lach** b2.de* *Laur* bg2 led k* *Lyc* k* *Mag-c* k* **Mag-m** b2.de* mang k* *Merc* k* mez k* *Mosch* k* mur-ac k* nat-m k* *Nit-ac* k* **Nux-m** k* *Nux-v* k* olnd k* *Par* k* petr k* *Ph-ac* k* *Phos* k* plat k* puls pyrog bg2* ran-b k* ran-s k* *Rheum* k* rhod k* *Rhus-t* k* *Rumx* **Ruta** k* *Sabad* k* sabin k* samb k* sars k* sel k* sep k* **Sil** k* *Spong* k* staph k* stram k* sulph b2.de* tarax k* tell bg2* teucr k* thiop jl thuj k* tub gk valer k* verat k* verb k* vib bro1
    - **amel.**: am-c bro1* ambr k* arn k* bell k* borx bro1 **Bry** k* *Calc* k* cann-s k* carb-an b4.de carb-v k* caust k* *Cham* k* chel bg2 *Coloc* k* cupr-act bro1 esp-g kk1.de fl-ac bg2 ign k* kali-c k* lyc k* m-ambo b2.de m-aust b2.de* mag-p bg2* nux-v k* plb bg2* ptel bro1 *Puls* k* pyrog tl1 rhus-t k* *Sec* b7a.de* *Sep* k* *Stann* b4a.de stram k* sul-ac bro1 sulph viol-o k* viol-t k*
  - **painless** side:
    - **agg.**: *Ambr* k* *Arg-met* arn k* bell k* **Bry** k* *Calc* k* cann-s k* carb-an b4.de carb-v k* *Caust* k* **Cham** k* chel k* chin h1* **Coloc** k* con bg2 cupr **Fl-ac** bg2* hyper *Ign* k* *Kali-c* k* lyc k* *M-ambo* b2.de* *M-aust* b2.de* merc-i-r naja *Nat-c* *Nat-m* bg2 nat-s ptk1 nux-v k* phos k* plan ptel bro1 **Puls** k* *Rhus-t* k* **Sec** bg2* *Sep* k* stann k* sul-ac ter bg2 viol-o k* viol-t k*
    - **amel.**: acon k* agar k* am-c k* am-m k* ambr k* anac k* ang b2.de* ant-c k* arg-met k* arn k* ars k* *Bapt* *Bar-c* k* *Bell* k* bry k* *Calad* k* calc b2.de* calc-f cann-s k* caps k* carb-an k* carb-v k* caust k* chin k* cina k* clem k* croc k* cupr k* dios dros k* graph k* guaj k* *Hep* k* hyos k* ign k* *Iod* k* *Kali-c* k* kali-m k2 kali-n k* lach k* led k* lyc k* m-aust b7.de mag-c k* *Mag-m* b2.de* mang k* merc k* mez k* mosch k*

- **painless** side – **amel**.: ...
  mur-ac k* naja jl nat-m k* nit-ac k* *Nux-m* k* *Nux-v* k* olnd k* par k* petr k* ph-ac k* *Phos* b2.de* plat k* puls ran-b k* ran-s k* rheum k* rhod k* rhus-t k* *Ruta* k* sabad k* sabin k* samb k* sars k* sel k* sep k* *Sil* k* *Spong* k* staph k* stram k* sulph b2.de* tarax k* teucr b2.de* thuj k* valer k* verat k* verb k*
- **part** on which he is lying agg.: aloe bg2 am-c bg2 *Arn* bg2 ars bg2 bar-c bg2 *Bry* bg2 calc bg2 caust bg2 *Chin* bg2 *Graph* bg2 hep bg2 hyper bg2 mag-m bg2 merc bg2 mosch bg2 nat-s bg2 nit-ac bg2 ph-ac bg2 **Puls** bg2 rhus-t bg2 sep bg2 sil bg2 thuj bg2
- **right**:
  - **agg**.: acon k* *Alum* k* *Am-c* k* *Am-m* k* anac k* arg-n ptk1 bad bg2* bell bg2* *Benz-ac* k* *Borx* k* bry k* bufo k* calc b2.de* cann-i br1* carb-an k* caust b2.de* cean vml3• cimic jl cina k* clem k* con k* hydr ptk1 ip k* iris ptk1 *Kali-c* k* kali-i kali-m k2 kalm ptk1 kreos k* lach b2.de* lil-t bg3* lyc k* lycps-v bg2* m-ambo b2.de* mag-c bg1 *Mag-m* k* mag-p ptk1 **Merc** k* mur-ac k* nat-c b2.de* *Nux-v* k* *Phos* k* prun psor puls b2.de* ran-b k* rhus-t bg2* rumx bg2* sang bg1 scroph-n bro1 sec bg2 seneg k* spig b2.de* *Spong* k* *Stann* b2.de* sul-ac sul-i ptk1 sulph k* thuj k*
  - **amel**.: *Acon* b2.de* *Ail* vh1 *Am-c* b2.de* anac b2.de* ang b2.de* ant-t bro1* arn b2.de* *Bar-c* b2.de* bar-m bg2 bell b2.de* brom bg2 *Bry* b2.de* cact bg2 calc b2.de* canth b2.de* *Carb-an* b2.de* cassia-s ccrh1• chin b2.de* colch b2.de* con b2.de* crot-h bg2 ip b2.de* *Kali-c* b2.de* kreos b2.de* *Lyc* b2.de* mang bg2* merc b2.de* naja ptk1 *Nat-c* b2.de* *Nat-m* b2.de* *Par* b2.de* **Phos** b2.de* plat b2.de* ptel bg2* **Puls** b2.de* seneg b2.de* *Sep* b2.de* *Sil* b2.de* spig b2.de* *Stann* b2.de* *Sulph* b2.de* tab bro1* *Thuj* b2.de* tub gk
    - **head** high; with: ars bro1* cact bro1* spig bro1* spong bro1*
- **sliding** down in bed (See Weakness - paralytic - sliding)
- **still**:
  - **long** time; for a | **agg**.: nat-s ptk1
- **stretched** out; lying | **agg**.: cham bg2 colch bg2 coloc bg2 plat bg2 puls bg2 rheum bg2 rhus-t bg2 staph bg2
- **wet** floor agg.; on a: *Ars* bg2* *Calc* bg2* calc-p bg2* caust b4a.de* *Dulc* bg2* *Hep* b4a.de *Nit-ac* b4a.de *Nux-v* ptk1 *Phos* b4a.de rhod ptk1 *Rhus-t* b7a.de* *Sars* b4a.de *Sep* b4a.de *Sil* bg2* *Sulph* b4a.de*
  - **cold** floor; wet and: *Bry* b7a.de
- **wrong** position agg.; from lying in a: staph b2.de* *Tarax* b2.de*

LYING DOWN:
- **after**:
  - **agg**.: acon b2.de* agar b2.de* agn b2.de* alum b2.de* *Am-c* b2.de* am-m b2.de* **Ambr** b2.de* ang b2.de* ant-c b2.de* ant-t b2.de* aran bg2 *Arg-met* b2.de* arn b2.de* **Ars** b2.de* *Asaf* b2.de* asar b2.de* **Aur** b2.de* bar-c b2.de* *Bell* b2.de* bism b2.de* borx b2.de* bov b2.de* *Bry* b2.de* calad b2.de* *Calc* b2.de* camph b7.de cann-s b7.de canth b2.de* *Caps* b2.de* carb-an b2.de* *Carb-v* b2.de* caust b2.de* *Cham* b2.de* chel b2.de* chin b2.de* *Clem* b2.de* cocc b2.de* coff b2.de* colch b2.de* coloc b2.de* con b2.de* croc b2.de* cupr b2.de* *Cycl* b2.de* dros b2.de* **Dulc** b2.de* *Euph* b2.de* *Euphr* b2.de* *Ferr* b2.de* *Fl-ac* bg2 *Graph* b2.de* guaj b2.de* hell b2.de* *Hep* b2.de* *Hyos* b2.de* ign b2.de* ip b2.de* *Kali-c* b2.de* kali-n b2.de* lach b2.de* laur b2.de* led b2.de* **Lyc** b2.de* m-ambo b2.de* *M-arct* b2.de* m-aust b2.de* *Mag-c* b2.de* *Mag-m* b2.de* mang b2.de* *Meny* b2.de* *Merc* b2.de* mez b2.de* mosch b2.de* mur-ac b2.de* nat-c b2.de* nat-m bg2 nit-ac b2.de* nux-m b2.de* nux-v b2.de* olnd b2.de* op b2.de* par b2.de* petr b2.de* ph-ac b2.de* *Phos* b2.de* **Plat** b2.de* *Plb* b2.de* **Puls** b2.de* ran-b b2.de* ran-s b2.de* rheum b7.de rhod b2.de* **Rhus-t** b2.de* ruta b2.de* *Sabad* b2.de* sabin b2.de* **Samb** b2.de* sars b2.de* *Sel* b2.de* seneg b2.de* *Sep* b2.de* sil b2.de* spig b2.de* squil b7.de stann b2.de* staph b2.de* stram b7.de **Stront-c** b2.de* *Sul-ac* b2.de* *Sulph* b2.de* *Tarax* b2.de* teucr b2.de* thuj b2.de* valer b2.de* verat b2.de* verb b2.de* viol-o b2.de* viol-t b2.de* zinc b2.de*
  - **amel**.: acon b2.de* agar b2.de* agn b2.de* am-m b2.de* ambr b2.de* anac b2.de* ang b2.de* ant-c b2.de* ant-t b2.de* arg-met b2.de* arn b2.de* asaf b2.de* aur b2.de* bar-c b2.de* *Bell* b2.de* bov b2.de* **Bry** b2.de* calad b2.de* **Calc** b2.de* camph b2.de* cann-s b2.de* *Canth* b2.de* *Caps* b2.de* carb-an b2.de* *Carb-v* b2.de* caust b2.de* cham b2.de* chel b2.de* chin b2.de* cic b2.de* *Cina* b2.de* cocc b2.de* coff b2.de*

Lying down – **after** – **amel**.: ...
colch b2.de* coloc b2.de* con b2.de* *Croc* b2.de* cupr b2.de* dig b2.de* dros b2.de* dulc b2.de* euphr b2.de* fl-ac bg2 *Graph* b2.de* guaj b2.de* hell b2.de* *Hep* b2.de* hyos b2.de* ign b2.de* *Iod* b2.de* ip b2.de* kali-c b2.de* kali-n b2.de* kreos b2.de* lach b2.de* laur b2.de* led b2.de* lyc b2.de* m-ambo b2.de* m-arct b2.de m-aust b2.de mag-c b2.de* mag-m b2.de* merc b2.de* merc-c bg2 nat-c b2.de* **Nat-m** b2.de* nit-ac b2.de* nux-m b2.de* **Nux-v** b2.de* *Olnd* b2.de* par b2.de* petr b2.de* ph-ac b2.de* phos b2.de* psor bg2 puls b2.de* ran-b b2.de* rheum b2.de* rhod b2.de* rhus-t b2.de* sabin b2.de* samb b2.de* sars b2.de* sec b2.de* sel b2.de* sep b2.de* sil b2.de* *Spig* b2.de* spong b2.de* **Squil** b2.de* stann b2.de* *Staph* b2.de* *Stram* b2.de* sul-ac b2.de* sulph b2.de* tarax b2.de* thuj b2.de* valer b2.de* verat b2.de* verb b2.de*
- **before** | **agg**.: nux-v b7.de ran-b b7.de

LYME DISEASE: chin-su mtf gaul mtf

LYMPHANGITIS (See Inflammation - lymphatic)

LYMPHATIC constitution (See Sluggishness; Weakness)

LYMPHATIC GLANDS (See Abscesses - glands; Indurations - glands; Inflammation - glands; Pain - glands; Swelling - glands)

LYMPHOMA (See Cancerous - lymphoma)

MAGNESIA agg.: nux-v bro1 rheum bro1

MAGNETISM amel.: *(↗Hand on; Hand on - amel.; MIND - Magnetized; MIND - Magnetized - amel.)* acon k* bar-c k* *Bell* k* *Calc* k* calc-p chin k* con k* **Cupr** k* graph k* ign k* iod k* lach ptk1 m-ambo b7.de m-arct b2.de nat-c k* *Nux-v* k* **Phos** k* sabin k* sep k* *Sil* k* sulph k* teucr k* viol-o k* [am-p stj1 calc-sil stj2 cupr-act stj2 cupr-f stj2 cupr-m stj2 cupr-p stj2 ferr-sil stj2 kali-sil stj2 mag-sil stj2 mang-sil stj2 nat-sil stj2 sil-met stj2]

MALAISE (See Sick)

MALARIA: alst-s br1 am-pic br1 anemps br1 aran br1 arn tl1* ars tl1* bapt br1 basil jsx1.fr bid-p jsx1.fr canch br1 caps tl1 cean tl1 cedr br1* chin tl1* chinin-s br1* conyz-sm jsx1.fr cymbop-ci jsx1.fr *Eucal* br1 eup-a c2 *Eup-per* br1* eup-pur mtf11 gard-t jsx1.fr germ-met srj5• guiz-sc jsx1.fr ip tl1 lept br1 malar c2* markh-l jsx1.fr methyl br1 mik-c jsx1.fr mom-ch jsx1.fr nat-m tl1* nat-s tl1 oci-g jsx1.fr oci-sa sp1 parth br1 plan c2 *Pop* br1 pyrog tl1 senec-ma jsx1.fr sulph c2 tarax c2 triclis-g jsx1.fr urt-u mrr1 verbe-h c2 vern-am jsx1.fr
- **accompanied** by:
  - **anemia**: alst-s br1
  - **cachexia** (See Cachexia - malaria)
  - **diarrhea**: alst-s br1
  - **dysentery**: alst-s br1
  - **indigestion**: alst-s br1
  - ○ **Head**; pain in: *Ars* bro1 caps bro1 cedr bro1 chin bro1 chinin-s bro1 cupr-act bro1 *Eup-per* bro1 gels bro1 *Nat-m* bro1
  - **Spleen**; enlargement of: *(↗FEVER - Intermittent - spleen)* cean br1
  - **Tongue** | **green** discoloration of the tongue: *Nat-s* kr1*
- **chronic**: anders mtf11 bol-la btw2 calc-ar lp2* carb-v btw1 corn br1 corn-f br1 gent-q hl9 grin br1 nat-m gm1 pyrog br1 querc-r-g-s br1 stigm c2 ter tl1 tub jl2 verbe-h c2
- **erratic** course of symptoms: sep tl1
- **followed** by | **Hypochondria**; complaints of: ars bg2 cean bg2 cedr bg2 *Chin* bg2 ferr bg2 ign bg2 kali-i bg2 nat-m bg2
- **old**: helia br1*
- **prophylaxis**:
  - **getting** into infected territory:
    - **before**: nat-m c1
    - **on**: ars gm1
- **suppressed** (See History - malaria - suppressed)

MALFORMATION of anatomy (See Disabled)

MALIGNANT disease processes: *(↗Cancerous)* ail br1* am-c ptk1 ars ptk1 *Cadm-s* br1 carb-ac br1 crot-h ptk1 diph br1 echi br1 hell br1 kali-ar br1 lach ptk1 nit-ac ptk1 *Tarent-c* br1*

MALNUTRITION: *(↗Emaciation; Emaciation - nutrition)* abrot ptk1* alf br1 aln br1 bac bro1 **Bar-c** bro1* berb-a br1 borx ptk1* *Calc* br1* *Calc-hp* ptk1 **Calc-p** bro1* caust bro1 crot-h br1 glyc br1 *Graph* ptk1 *Ichth* br1 iod br1 kreos bro1 *Lac-c* ptk1 lac-d br1* lec br1 *Lyc* br1* med bro1 **Nat-m** bro1* ol-j br1 pin-s bro1 sabal br1 sacch br1 sanic ptk1 sil br1* thyr br1*

MANUAL labor: *Am-m* b2.de* *Bov* b2.de* ferr b2.de* kali-c b2.de* *Lach* b2.de* mag-c b2.de* merc b2.de* **Nat-m** b2.de* nit-ac b2.de* phos bg2 *Sil* b2.de* symph fd3.de• *Verat* b2.de* [caes-met stj2]

MANY SYMPTOMS: *(↗Contradictory)* agar ptk1 *Carc* mlr1• kali-i ptk1 merc ptk1 syph ptk1 tub ptk1

MAPPED skin (See SKIN - Discoloration - mottled)

MARASMUS (See Emaciation - children - infants)

MARROW; as if without: | **Bones**: *Lyc* b2.de* sulph bg2 zinc b4a.de

MASTURBATION; ailments from: *(↗MIND - Ailments - masturbation; MIND - Ailments - sexual excesses; MIND - Nymphomania)* abrot bg2* agar k* agn bg2* aloe c1* alum k* *Ambr* anac k* anan a1 ant-c apis c1* *Arg-met* k* arg-n c1* ars k* aur j* aven sf1.de bar-c br1* bell j* bell-p c1* bov k* *Bufo* calad k* **Calc** k* *Calc-p* bg2* calc-s calc-sil k2* cann-i sf1.de cann-xyz bg2 *Carb-v* k* carc st1* *Caust* st1* **Chin** k* cina b2.de* cob c1* **Cocc** k* *Coff* st1* **Con** k* *Dig* k* *Dios* c1* dulc b2.de* ferr k* **Gels** k* graph hr1* grat c1* *Hyos* ign b2.de* *Iod* k* *Kali-br* bg2* kali-c k* *Kali-p* k* *Lach* bg2* *Lyc* k* *Mag-p* k* med c1 *Merc* k* *Merc-c* k* mosch k* nat-c k* *Nat-m* k* **Nat-p** k* nux-m k* *Nux-v* k* op a1* **Orig** k* petr k* **Ph-ac** k* *Phos* k* *Pic-ac* bg2* plat hr1* plb k* *Puls* k* *Sal-n* c1* sars hr1* **Sel** k* **Sep** k* sil k* *Spig* k* squil k* stann bg2* **Staph** k* stict sf1.de still bro1 stram bg2* **Sulph** k* tab c1* *Tarent* hr1* *Thuj* bg2* trib br1* ust hr1* zinc c1* zinc-o bro1

MEASLES:
- **ailments** after: *(↗SKIN - Eruptions - measles)* acon b2.de* am-c bro1 ant-c k* *Ant-t* ptk1 *Apis* b7a.de *Arg-met* kr1 *Ars* b2.de* bar-c k2 *Bell* k* bry k* *Calc* kr1 **Camph** k* **Carb-v** k* *Carbn-s* *Caust* kr1 cham k* chin k* cina bg2 coff b2.de* cupr-act bro1* *Dros* b2.de* *Dulc* j5.de* euphr kr1 ferr-p bg3 *Hell* bg2 *Hyos* k* ign k* iod j5.de *Ip* b2.de* *Kali-bi* bg3 *Kali-c* k2* *Kali-m* kr1* lob st mag-c b2.de merc bro1 merc-c bro1 **Morb** st* mosch k* nux-m kr1 nux-v k* op bro1 oxyd st *Phos* b2.de* **Puls** k* *Rhus-t* k* sang bro1 *Sep* bg2* *Stict* kr1* stram b2.de* *Sulph* k* *Tub* bro1 zinc bro1*
  - **never** well since: carb-v pfa1* carc sk* *Morb* tl1* *Puls* rma2
- **eruption** is suppressed; when the: jatr-c br1 *Phos* j5.de *Puls* j5.de rhus-t j5.de

MEDICINE: *(↗Remedies; Remedies - fail - oversensitive)*
- **allopathic**:
  - **abuse** of: *(↗Analgesics; Convalescence - antibiotics; Convalescence - cortisone; Narcotics; Paralysis - toxic; Purgatives)* agar a1 agn mrr1 *Aloe* br1* ars ptk1 bapt st1 bry vh1 camph sf1.de* carb-v bg2* cham j5.de* chin c1 coff j5.de coloc ptk1 hep ptk1 *Hydr* bro1* kali-i ptk1 lach mrr1 laur bg2 *Lob* st1 mag-s sp1 nat-m ptk1 nit-ac ptk1 **Nux-v** j5.de* op sf1.de* *Ph-ac* mrr1 *Puls* sf1.de* sec ptk1 *Sulph* ptk1 teucr kr1* thuj c1 tub mrr1
    - **antibiotics** (See History - antibiotics)
    - **castor** oil: bry ptk1 *Nux-v* ptk1
    - **cod**-liver oil: *(↗Cod-liver)* hep ptk1
    - **heart** medicine: lycps-v ptk1
    - **morphine**: *(↗Anesthesia [=narcosis] - ailments)* aven br1 ham br1 hyper br1 op gk
    - **opium**: cham ptk1 mur-ac ptk1 nat-m ptk1 *Puls* ptk1 verat ptk1
    - **syphilis**; nonspecific gross medication against: hep br1
    - **vegetable** medicine: camph bro1 *Nux-v* bro1
  - **addiction** to: *(↗Narcotics - desire; MIND - Morphinism)* buth-a sp1 op mrr1 tab c1 [heroin sdj2]
  - **oversensitive** to: acon st arn st carc mlr1• cham st coff st cupr ptk1* lyc st nit-ac k2 **Nux-v** k2* **Puls** st* sep st* sil st* **Sulph** st teucr c1
    - **influenza**; medicine against: am-c gm1 carb-v gm1 lach gm1 op gm1
  - **quick** reaction: *Bell* k2 *Cupr* k2 *Nux-v* k2 *Zinc* k2
  - **schistosomiasis**; injections for (= bilharziasis): ant-t br1*
  - **stimulants**; as if taken: bit-ar wht1•
  - **thinking** of it agg.: asaf ptk1

Medicine: ...
- **homeopathic** (See Remedies)

MEMBRANES, MUCOUS (See Mucous membranes)

MEMORY:
- **exertion** of | **agg.**: m-ambo b2.de

MENOPAUSE: *(↗FEMALE - Menopause; MIND - Menopause)* *Aml-ns* br1 ange-s oss1• aqui br1 arist-cl sp1 bell mrr1 con br1 cyt-l sp1 helon c2 **Lach** br1* mag-c br1 manc mrr1 nicc-s br1 nit-ac c2 nux-m c2 *Ov* br1 phys c2 sal-ac c2 sang c2* sars c2 semp c2 **Sep** mrr1 ther c2 tril-p c2 ust c2* vip br1 x-ray sp1
- **ailments** from: ange-s oss1• aur bg2 calc b4a.de caps bg2 caul bg2 cimic bg2 con bg2 croc bg2 crot-h bg2 ferr-p bg2 glon bg2 graph bg2 kali-bi bg2 **Lach** bg2 lyc bg2 nat-m bg2 nit-ac bg2 nux-v bg2 ol-an bg2 phos bg2 plat bg2 plb bg2 puls bg2 rhus-t bg2 sabin bg2 *Sang* bg2 sep bg2 stront-c bg2 sul-ac b4a.de* *Sulph* bg2 ther bg2 ust bg2 zinc bg2
- **premature**: absin ptk1

MENSES: calc st1 glycyr-g cte1• *Plat* st1 verat st1
- **after**:
  - **agg.**: *All-s* vh1 alum k* alum-p k2* am-c k* arist-cl mg1.de* ars j5.de *Bell* mrr1 berb j5.de **Borx** k* *Bov* k* bry k* *Calc* k* calc-sil k2* canth k* carb-an k* carb-v k* *Carbn-s* chel chin k* *Cocc* sf1.de *Con* k* cupr k* *Ferr* ferr-i **Graph** k* iod k* *Kali-c* k* **Kreos** k* lac-c ptk1 **Lach** k* *Lil-t* k* lith-c ptk1 *Lyc* k* mag-c k* merc k* *Nat-m* k* nat-p *Nit-ac* **Nux-v** k* *Ph-ac* k* *Phos* k* plat k* puls k* rhus-t k* ruta k* sabin sal-fr sle1• **Sep** k* sil k* *Stram* k* sul-ac k* sulph k* tarent sf1.de* verat k* *Zinc* k* *Zinc-p* k2 [ant-m stj2 beryl-m stj2 cadm-m stj2 chlor stj2 chr-m stj2 cob-m stj2 cupr-m stj2 lith-m stj2 mang-m stj2 mur-ac stj2 pall stj2 plb-m stj2 stront-m stj2 zinc-m stj2]
    - **days** after; few: borx bro1 bov bro1
  - **amel.**: aran bg2* arist-cl sp1 calc bg2* cimic bg2* kreos sne lycps-v bg2 pitu-a vml2• thyr jl3 *Zinc-p* k2*
- **before**:
  - **agg.**: abies-c oss4• alum k* alum-p k2* *Am-c* k* am-m k* arg-n k* arist-cl mg1.de* asaf asar k* *Aster* mgm• *Aur-m-n* wbt2• *Bamb-a* stb2.de• *Bar-c* k* bar-i k2* bar-m k* bar-s k2* bell k* berb j5.de *Bit-ar* wht1• borx k* **Bov** k* brom bg2 bry k* **Calc** k* **Calc-p** k* calc-sil k2* canth k* carb-an k* *Carb-v* k* carbn-s carc mrr1* caul bg2* *Caust* k* cham k* chin k* cimic ptk1* cina k* cocc k* coff k* *Coloc* bg2 *Con* k* croc k* **Cupr** k* cypra-eg sde6.de• dig bg2 dream-p sdj1• dulc k* elaps mrr1 ferr k* ferr-i foll jl3* gels k* germ-met srj5• granit-m es1• graph k* hep k* *Hyos* k* ign k* iod k* ip k* *Kali-c* k* kali-chl k13 kali-m k2 kali-n k* *Kreos* k* lac-h htj1• **Lach** k* *Lil-t* mrr1 luna kg1• **Lyc** k* *Mag-c* k* mag-f mg1.de* mag-m k* mag-s mg1.de* *Mang* k* *Merc* k* mez k* mosch k* mur-ac k* nat-c k* **Nat-m** k* *Nat-p* *Nit-ac* b4.de* nux-m k* nux-v k* ol-an j5.de petr k* *Ph-ac* k* *Phos* k* pin-con oss2• *Plat* k* pneu jl2 psor bg2* **Puls** k* rhus-t k* rob st1 ruta k* sabad k* sars k* *Sec* b7.de **Sep** k* sil k* spig k* spong k* stann k* staph k* sul-ac k* **Sulph** k* thuj st1 tub-m vn* tub-sp zs valer k* **Verat** k* *Vib* k* vip-a jl3 **Zinc** k* zinc-p k2* [am-br stj2 ant-c stj2 ant-m stj2 ant-met stj2 ant-t stj2 beryl-m stj2 cadm-m stj2 chlor stj2 chr-m stj2 cob-m stj2 cupr-m stj2 lith-m stj2 mang-m stj2 pall stj2 plb-m stj2 rubd-met stj2 sel stj2 stront-m stj2 vanad stj2 zinc-m stj2]
    - **accompanied** by:
      - **chocolate**; desire for (See Food and - chocolate - desire - menses)
      - **sweets**; desire for (See Food and - sweets - desire - menses)
      - **warm** drinks; desire for (See Food and - warm drinks - desire - menses)
  - **amel.**: lavand-a ctl1• murx ptk1*
- **between** | **amel.**: bell bro1 bov bro1 elaps bro1 ham bro1 magn-gr bro1
- **delayed** menses agg.: fl-ac k2
- **during**:
  - **agg.**: acon k* agar k* aids nl2• aloe alum k* alum-p k2* **Am-c** k* *Am-m* k* ambr k* *Ant-c* **Arg-n** k* ars k* ars-i ars-s-f k2* asar k* aur bg2* *Bamb-a* stb2.de• bar-c k* bar-i k2* bar-m bar-s k2* bell k* berb j5.de borx k* **Bov** k* bry k* *Bufo* but-ac jl3 *Calc* k* calc-p calc-sil k2* cann-s k* canth k* caps k* carb-an k* carb-v k* **Carbn-s** castm j5.de* *Caust* k* **Cham** k* chel k* chin k* chinin-s j5.de *Cimic* k* *Cocc* k* *Coff* k* con k* croc k* crot-h

- **during** – **agg.**: ...
crot-t j5.de cupr k* dream-p sdj1• ferr k* ferr-i ferr-p gels germ-met srj5• gran j5.de granit-m es1• **Graph** k* ham bg2* hep k* **Hyos** k* *Ign* k* iod k* **Kali-c** k* *Kali-chl* k13 kali-i j5.de *Kali-m* k2 kali-n k* *Kreos* k* lac-c ptk1 lach k* laur k* *Luna* kg1• *Lyc* k* **Mag-c** k* *Mag-m* k* *Mag-s* j5.de* merc k* mosch k* *Mur-ac* k* murx mgm• nat-c k* *Nat-m* k* nat-p nat-s j5.de* nicc j5.de nit-ac k* *Nux-m* k* **Nux-v** k* oena ol-an j5.de* olib-sac wmh1 op k* petr k* ph-ac k* phel j5.de *Phos* k* *Plat* k* polys sk4• prun j5.de psor bg2* **Puls** k* rat j5.de rhod k* rhus-t k* sabin k* sars k* sec k* sel k* **Sep** k* *Sil* k* spong k* stann k* staph j5.de* stram k* stront-c k* sul-ac k* **Sulph** k* thea thuj ptk1 thyr jl3 *Tub* bro1 *Verat* k* *Vib* k* vinc j5.de **Zinc** k* **Zinc-p** k2* [ant-m stj2 astat stj2 aur-m stj2 aur-s stj2 bar-br stj2 bar-met stj2 beryl-m stj2 bism-sn stj2 cadm-m stj2 caes-met stj2 chlor stj2 chr-m stj2 cinnb stj2 cob-m stj2 cupr-m stj2 hafn-met stj2 irid-met stj2 kali-ar stj2 kali-met stj2 kali-sil stj2 lanth-met stj2 lith-m stj2 mang-m stj2 merc-d stj2 merc-i-f stj2 osm-met stj2 plb stj2 plb-m stj2 plb-p stj2 polon-met stj2 rhen-met stj2 stront-m stj2 tant-met stj2 thal-met stj2 tung-met stj2 zinc-m stj2]
  - **beginning** of; at: *Acon* k* *Arg-n* bg2 asar k* *Bamb-a* stb2.de• bell k* bry k* *Cact* k* **Calc-p** *Caust* k* *Cham* k* cimic bg2 cocc k* coff k* graph k* **Hyos** k* ign k* iod k* ip k* **Kali-c** lac-c st **Lach** bg2 lyc k* mag-c k* mag-m k* mag-p bg2* merc k* mosch k* nat-m k* nit-ac k* *Phos* k* *Plat* k* plb bg2 *Puls* k* ruta k* sars k* *Sep* k* *Sil* k* staph k* tub br1 zinc bg2 [*Bar-m* stj1]
  - **close** of; at: lach bro1
- **amel.**: all-s bg2* alum k* am-c bro1 apis k* aran k* arg-n bg2 arist-cl mg1.de* bell k* calc k* calc-f k* cimic k* cortiso sp1* cycl k* dicha mg1.de* ferr-p bg2 foll jl3 gels bg2 ign bg2 iod bg2 kali-bi k* *Kali-c* k* kali-p lac-c **Lach** k* lycps-v kr1 mag-p sne mand jl3 *Mosch* k* murx ptk1 phenob k1* phos k* plb sf1.de plut-n srj7• puls k* rhus-t k* senec k* sep k* *Stann* k* sulph k* tub-sp zs ust verat k* vip-a jl *Zinc* k* [zinc-i stj2 zinc-m stj2 zinc-n stj2 zinc-p stj2]
- **beginning** of menses:
  - **agg.**: *Acon* b2.de* *Aq-mar* sf1.de asar b2.de* bell b2.de bry b2.de calc-p ptk1 *Caust* b2.de* *Cham* b2.de cocc b2.de coff b2.de cupr b7.de graph b2.de* **Hyos** b2.de* ign b2.de* iod b2.de* ip b2.de jab ptk1 kali-c ptk1 lac-c ptk1 lach bg2* *Lyc* b2.de* mag-c b2.de* mag-m b2.de mag-p bg2 merc b2.de mosch b2.de nat-m b2.de* nit-ac b2.de* *Phos* b2.de* *Plat* b2.de* plb bg2 *Puls* b2.de ruta b2.de sars b2.de *Sep* b2.de* sil b2.de* staph b2.de* zinc bg2
  - **amel.**: anthraci vh aster bro1* cer-ox bro1 *Cycl* bro1 cypra-eg sde6.de• eupi bro1 glycyr-g cte1• haliae-lc srj5• hydrog srj2• **Lach** bro1* *Mag-p* bro1* plb sf1.de sal-fr sle1• *Senec* bro1 *Zinc* bro1*
- **premenstrual** symptoms in mid-cycle: adam srj5•
- **retarded** (See FEMALE - Menses - late)
- **suppressed**; menses are (See FEMALE - Menses - suppressed)
- **suppressed** menses; from: *Acon* b2.de* agn b2.de alum b2.de *Am-c* b2.de arn b2.de ars b2.de aur b2.de *Bar-c* b2.de bell b2.de borx b2.de bry b2.de* *Calc* b2.de carb-an b2.de carb-v b2.de *Caust* b2.de *Cham* b2.de* chel b2.de chin b2.de *Cocc* b2.de* colch b2.de coloc b2.de **Con** b2.de croc b2.de* *Cupr* b2.de* dig b2.de dros b2.de **Dulc** b2.de euphr b2.de *Ferr* b2.de* **Graph** b2.de guaj b2.de hell b2.de hyos b2.de* ign b2.de iod b2.de **Kali-c** b2.de lach b2.de **Lyc** b2.de m-arct b2.de mag-c b2.de mag-m b2.de mang b2.de merc b2.de *Nat-m* b2.de nit-ac b2.de nux-m b2.de petr b2.de ph-ac b2.de *Phos* b2.de plat b2.de **Puls** b2.de* rhod b2.de rhus-t b2.de ruta b2.de *Sabad* b2.de sabin b2.de sars b2.de sec b2.de *Sep* b2.de *Sil* b2.de *Staph* b2.de* stram b2.de* stront-c b2.de **Sulph** b2.de thuj b2.de *Valer* b2.de* verat b2.de* zinc b2.de

MENTAGRA (See FACE - Eruptions - beard - folliculitis)

MENTAL EXERTION: | **agg.** (See MIND - Mental exertion - agg.)

MENTHOL; from: carb-v gm1

MERCURY: (↗*Paralysis - toxic - mercurial)*
- **abuse** of: (↗*Paralysis - toxic - mercurial)* acon b2.de* agn b2.de* alumn st1 anan st1 ang bg2* *Ant-c* k* ant-t bro1 *Arg-met* k* arn b2.de* ars b2.de* *Asaf* k* **Aur** k* aur-m hr1* aur-s k2* *Bell* k* *Borx* st bry b2.de* calad b2.de* *Calc* k* camph hr1* **Carb-v** k* caust bg2* *Chel* *Chin* k* cic k* cina b2.de* *Clem* k* cocc b2.de* coff b2.de* *Colch* k* con *Cupr* k* dig b2.de* dulc k* *Euph* k* euphr b2.de* ferr b2.de* fl-ac bg2* germ-met srj5• graph k* *Guaj* k* **Hep** k* *Hydr* bg2* *Iod* k* iris sf1.de kali-bi *Kali-chl* bg2* **Kali-i** k* **Lach** k* laur b2.de* *Led* k* *Lyc* b4a.de* merc hr1* merc-i-r c1 *Mez* k* *Mur-ac* k* *Nat-m* b2.de* **Nat-s** k* **Nit-ac** k* nux-v b2.de* op b2.de* *Ph-ac* k* **Phyt** k* plat b2.de* plat-m c1* podo k*

Mercury – **abuse** of: ...
Puls k* rheum k* rhod k* rhus-g bro1 rhus-t b2.de* sabad b2.de* sal-ac bg2 *Sars* k* sel k* sep k* *Sil* k* spong k* **Staph** k* still hr1* stram k* stront-c k* sul-i k2* **Sulph** k* syph k2 thuj k* valer k* verat b2.de* viol-t k* zinc k*
- **fumes** of: carb-v b2.de* *Chin* b2.de* puls b2.de* *Stram* b2.de*

METASTASIS: (↗*Alternating; Change - symptoms - constant; Contradictory)* **Abrot** k* agar k2* aloe ptk1 *Ambr* ptk1 anag vh1 *Ant-c* k2* apis bg2 arn ptk1 *Ars* bg2* asaf sf1.de bell ptk1 benz-ac k2* *Berb* sf1.de* bry sf1.de cact sf1.de *Calc* bg2* *Cann-xyz* ptk1 *Carb-v* k* *Carc* mlr1• *Caul* sf1.de *Cimic* sf1.de* *Cocc* ptk1 colch coll sf1.de conv sf1.de croc ptk1 crot-h sf1.de *Crot-t* sf1.de *Cupr* k* dig sf1.de *Dulc* sf1.de elat sf1.de erig sf1.de ferr-p ptk1 glon ptk1 graph sf1.de grat sf1.de *Ham* sf1.de hep bg2 *Ign* ptk1 ip sf1.de iris ptk1 kali-bi sf1.de kali-c sf1.de *Kalm* sf1.de kreos bg2 lac-c k* *Lach* bg2* lil-t sf1.de lith-c sf1.de lyc bg2* mag-c mg1.de merc bg2 mez sf1.de mut fmm1• *Nat-m* sf1.de nat-p gt1* *Nux-v* sf1.de phos sf1.de* *Plat* sf1.de podo sf1.de psor ptk1* *Puls* k* rham-cal br1 rhus-t sf1.de sabad sf1.de sang k* sec sf1.de *Senec* sf1.de *Sep* bg2* sil bg2* stram ptk1 sul-ac ptk1 sulph k* tril-p sf1.de tub sf1.de* ust sf1.de valer ptk1 verat-v hr1 xan ptk1 zinc sf1.de*

MICTURITION (See Urination; BLADDER - Urination)

MILK:
- **weaning** | **complaints** after (See Ailments - weaning)

MINING; ailments from: (↗*Stone-cutters)* carbn-s ptk1 card-m br1* nat-ar bro1* sulph k2

MOBILITY; excessive (= flexibility etc.): alum b2.de* arn b2.de* *Bell* b2.de* camph b2.de* caust b2.de* cocc b2.de* *Coff* b2.de* con b2.de* croc ptk1 cupr b2.de* hyos b2.de* m-arct b2.de ph-ac b2.de* rhus-t b7.de *Stram* b2.de*

MONONUCLEOSIS: calen mtf11 carc fb* influ jl2* mur-ac mrr1 ph-ac mrr1
- **acute**: carc mlr1•
- **children**; in: carc fb* toxo-g jl2
- **chronic**: (↗*Chronic fatigue)* carc mlr1•

MOON:
- **decreasing** moon (See waning)
- **first** quarter | **agg.**: ars bg3* bry bg3* nat-m bg3*
- **full** moon:
  - **agg.**: (↗*Convulsions - moon - full)* **Alum** b2.de* *Apis* st* aral vk5 arn bg2* **Ars** bg2* ars-i vk5 bar-c st* *Bell* bg2* bov sf1.de* brom bg2* bry st* **Calc** b2.de* calc-p st* canth st* carc mlr1• *Caust* bg2* *Cina* st* *Croc* bg2* cupr st* *Cycl* b2.de* dream-p sdj1• *Fl-ac* bg2* gels st* glycyr-g cte1• *Graph* b2.de* hep st* hyos vk5 ign st* kali-bi sf1.de* kali-n bg2* kali-p fd1.de• *Lach* kr1* led st* **Lyc** bg2* melal-alt gya4 *Merc* st* nat-c b2.de* *Nat-m* k1* nit-ac st* nux-v st* ovi-p vk5 ph-ac k1* **Phos** bg3* *Psor* bg2* **Puls** st* *Rhus-t* st* *Sabad* b2.de* sang st* *Sep* bg2* *Sil* b2.de* sol-mm st* sol-t-ae st* *Spong* b2.de* sul-i st* **Sulph** b2.de* syph vk5 teucr b2.de* thuj st* tub vk5 verat-v st* [ant-c stj2 ant-m stj2 ant-met stj2 ant-t stj2 calc-sil stj2 ferr-sil stj2 hydrog stj2 kali-sil stj2 mag-sil stj2 mang-sil stj2 nat-sil stj2 sil-met stj2]
    - **amel.**; and: clem ptk1 phel ptk1 tarent ptk1
    - **periodical** | **alternate** full moon; every: syph ptk1*
  - **amel.**: carc mlr1• cypra-eg sde6.de• oxal-a rly4•
  - **new** moon agg.; and: alum bg2 croc bg2 kali-bi bg2 sil bg2
- **increasing** and decreasing with the moon; complaints are: clem bg2 emetin mp4• phel bg2
- **increasing** moon (See waxing)
- **last** quarter | **agg.**: lyc bg3* sep bg3*
- **new** moon:
  - **agg.**: (↗*Chorea - moon - new; Convulsions - moon - new)* *Agar* st* *Alum* b2.de* *Am-c* b2.de* **Apis** st* aral vk5 arg-n st* arn bg2* **Ars** bg2* ars-i st* bell st* *Bry* st* bufo bg2* **Calc** b2.de* *Calc-p* st* canth st* carc gk6* **Caust** b2.de* *Chin* st* **Cina** bg2* *Clem* k1* croc bg2* **Cupr** b2.de* daph k1* graph st* hep st* hyos vk5 kali-bi sf1.de* kali-br ptk1* *Lach* st* *Lyc* b2.de* merc st* merc-c st* merc-i-f st* nat-m st* nit-ac vk5 **Nux-v** bg3* **Phos** st* phyt st* **Puls** st* **Rhus-t** bg3* sabad b2.de* **Sep** b2.de* **Sil** b2.de* staph vk5 stram vk5 **Sulph** st* syph vk5 teucr vk5 *Thuj* bg2* tub vk5 zinc vk5
  - **amel.**: carc mlr1• choc srj3•

- **waning** moon:
  - **agg.**: alum kl *Apis* st* *Ars* st* bry st* *Calc* st* clem vk5 *Daph* j5.de* *Dulc* b2.de* gels st* kali-bi st* kali-c st* *Lach* st *Lyc* st* *Merc* st* merc-i-r st* *Nat-m* st* *Nux-v* st* ph-ac st* phel kr1* **Phos** st* phyt st plat st* **Puls** st* **Rhus-t** st* **Sep** st* sil st* sul-i st* **Sulph** bg2* tab st* thuj st* tub st* verat st*
    - **crescent** moon; waning: *Apis* vk5 *Ars* vk5 bry vk5 **Calc** vk5 kali-bi vk5 lach vk5 merc vk5 merc-i-r vk5 nat-n vk5 *Nux-v* vk5 ph-ac vk5 **Phos** vk5 phyt vk5 **Puls** vk5 **Rhus-t** vk5 sil vk5 staph vk5 **Sulph** vk5 syph vk5 thuj vk5 tub vk5 zinc vk5
    - **gibbous** moon; waning: hyos vk5 sil vk5
- **waxing** moon:
  - **agg.**: *Alum* bg2* apis st* arn kr1* **Ars** st* arum-t st* bell st* *Bry* st **Calc** st* calc-p st* caust st* chin kr1* cimic st* *Clem* bg2* *Cupr* b7a.de* graph st* ign st* kali-bi st* kali-c st* *Lach* st* *Lyc* bg2* *Med* st* merc-i-f st* *Nat-m* st* nit-ac st* *Nux-v* st* phel kr1* **Phos** st* **Puls** st* *Rhus-t* st* sang st* **Sep** st* *Sil* st* staph bg2* sul-i st* **Sulph** st* **Thuj** j5.de*
    - **crescent** moon; waxing: bell vk5 **Calc** vk5 cupr vk5 graph vk5 ign vk5 kali-bi vk5 kali-c vk5 *Lyc* vk5 med vk5 nux-v vk5 **Phos** vk5 **Puls** vk5 **Rhus-t** vk5 sang vk5 **Sep** vk5 *Sil* vk5 staph vk5 *Sulph* vk5 thuj vk5 tub vk5
    - **gibbous** moon; waxing: aral vk5 ars-i vk5 hyos vk5 lach vk5 nux-v vk5 sil vk5 staph vk5 syph vk5 tub vk5

MOONLIGHT:

- **agg.** (See Light; from - agg. - moonlight)
- **amel.** (See Light; from - amel. - moonlight)

MORPHINE (See Medicine - allopathic - abuse - morphine)

MOTION:

- **affected** part; of:
  - **agg.**: *Acon* **Aesc** agar am-c k* anac k* ang b2.de* *Ant-t* **Arn** k* *Ars* k* asaf k* asar k* bar-c k* *Bell* k* **Bry** k* bufo bg2 camph k* *Cann-s* k* *Caps* k* caust k* **Cham** k* chel k* *Chin* k* cic k* cimic clem *Cocc* k* coff k* **Colch** *Coloc* *Com* con k* croc k* cupr dig k* ferr-ar form *Gels* *Glon* guaj hep k* ign k* iod k* kali-bi bg2 kali-c k* *Kalm* *Lach* **Led** k* m-ambo b2.de* mag-c k* mang k* meny k* *Merc* k* *Mez* nat-c k* nat-m k* nux-m nux-v k* olnd k* petr k* *Phos* phyt plan c1 (non:plat b2.de*) *Puls* k* *Ran-b* k* *Rheum* *Rhod* **Rhus-t** k* rumx ruta k* sabad k* *Sabin* k* samb k* *Sang* *Sars* k* sel k* sep k* *Sil* **Spig** k* *Stann* staph k* *Sulph* k* thuj k* zinc k*
  - **amel.**: abrot acon k* *Agar* k* agn k* *Am-m* k* ang b2.de* apis bg2 arn k* *Ars* k* ars-i asaf k* asar k* *Aur* k* *Aur-m-n* wbt2* bell bg2 calc k* **Caps** k* cham k* *Chin* k* chir-fl gya2 cina k* *Con* k* croc k* **Dulc** k* *Euph* k* **Ferr** k* hyos bg2 *Kali-bi* kali-c k* lith-c bg2 *Lyc* k* mag-c k* *Mag-m* k* meny k* *Mosch* k* mur-ac k* nat-c k* *Ph-ac* k* **Puls** k* *Rhod* k* **Rhus-t** k* *Sabad* k* *Samb* k* *Sep* k* squil k* stann k* stront-c k* **Sulph** k* *Tarax* k* thuj k* valer k* verb k* viol-t k*
- **after**:
  - **agg.**: **Agar** k* am-c k* anac k* arn k* **Ars** k* aspar calad k* camph k* **Cann-s** k* *Carb-v* k* caust k* cocc k* coff k* *Croc* k* dros k* *Hyos* k* iod k* *Kali-c* k* laur k* m-aust b2.de* merc k* *Nit-ac* k* nux-v k* olnd k* phos k* plb k* **Puls** k* **Rhus-t** k* *Ruta* k* sabin k* sep k* spig k* **Spong** k* **Stann** k* staph k* *Stram* k* sul-ac k* **Valer** k* zinc k*
  - **amel.**: *Agar* b4a.de
- **agg.**: abrot *Achy* jl* *Acon* k* act-sp vh1 adam srj5• adlu jl3 adon sf1.de aesc k2* *Agar* k* agav-t jl3 *Agn* k* *Ail* vh1 aloe k* alum k* alum-p k2* alum-sil k2* alumn kr1 am-c k* am-m k* ambr k* aml-ns bro1 anac k* *Anan* vh1 *Ang* b2.de* ange-s jl3 anh bro1* ant-c k* ant-t k* *Apis* k* apoc aq-mar jl3 arg-met b2.de* arg-n st1 *Arn* k* *Ars* k* ars-h *Ars-i* ars-s-f k2 *Asaf* k* *Asar* k* *Aspar* aster jl3 *Aur* k* aur-ar k2 aur-i k2* aur-m k2 aur-s k2* *Bac* jl2 bapt *Bar-c* k* bar-i k2* bar-m sf1.de bar-s k2* **Bell** k* *Berb* k* beryl jl3 **Bism** k* borx k* both-a rb3 both-ax tsm2 bov k* **Bry** k* bufo k* *But-ac* bro1 *Cact* k* cadm-met mg1.de* cadm-s k* *Calad* k* calc k* calc-ar bro1 *Calc-p* k* *Calc-s* calc-sil k2* *Camph* k* cann-i *Cann-s* k* *Canth* k* *Caps* k* *Carb-an* k* *Carb-v* k* *Carbn-s* card-m cassia-s cdd7*• caust k* cean bro1 cham k* **Chel** k* **Chin** k* chinin-ar *Chion* cic k* *Cimic* k* *Cimx* cina k* *Cinnb* clem k* coc-c k* **Cocc** k* *Coff* k* coff-t st1 **Colch** k* **Coloc** k* *Con* k* cortico sp1 *Croc* k* *Crot-h* crot-t cupr k* cupr-ar cur st1 *Cycl* b2.de* des-ac jl3 *Dig* k* diphtox jl2 dros k* dulc b2.de* equis-h bro1 *Erig* sf1.de *Eup-per* k* euph k* euphr b2.de *Ferr* k* ferr-i ferr-p bg2* *Fl-ac* k* foll jl3 form k* *Gels* k* germ-met srj5• get bro1 *Glon* k* *Graph* k* **Guaj** k* guat jl3 haliae-lc srj5• hed sp1 *Hell* k* helon bro1 *Hep* k* hip-ac sp1* hist mg1.de* hoit jl3 hyos k* *Iber* bro1 ign k* *Iod* k* *Ip* k* *Iris* jac-g jug-c bro1 jug-r st1 *Kali-bi* k* *Kali-c* b2.de* kali-chl k13 kali-i sf1.de kali-m k2* *Kali-n* k* kali-p k* kali-sil k2* *Kalm* k* *Kreos* b2.de* lac-ac sf1.de

Motion – agg.: ...

lac-c k2* *Lac-d* k2* *Lach* k* lap-la rsp1 lat-m jl3 laur k* **Led** k* lil-t sf1.de lina bro1 lob bro1 lyc b2.de* lycpr bro1 lycps-v m-ambo b2.de* m-arct b2.de* *M-aust* b2.de* mag-c k* mag-m k* *Mag-p* k* *Mang* k* med k* *Meli* k* meny k* meph j5.de **Merc** k* merc-c k* mez k* mim-p jl3 mosch k* mur-ac b2.de* myos-a rly4• naja bg2* *Nat-ar* nat-c b2.de* *Nat-m* k* *Nat-p* k* *Nat-s* k* nat-sil k2* nit-ac k* nux-m k* **Nux-v** k* ol-an olnd k* onop jl3 *Onos* k* op k* osm ovi-p st1 *Ox-ac* pall k* par k* paro-i jl3 parot jl penic jl3* *Petr* k* ph-ac k* *Phos* k* *Phyt* k* pic-ac bro1 plan c1 plat k* *Plb* k* psil jl3 *Psor* ptel puls k* puls-n bro1 pulx bro1 pyrog tl1* rad-br c11 **Ran-b** k* ran-s k* *Rheum* k* rhod b2.de* rhus-t b2.de* rumx ruta b2.de* sabad k* **Sabin** k* sal-ac sf1.de sal-fr sle1• samb k* *Sang* k* *Sanic* sarcol-ac sp1* *Sars* b2.de* *Sec* k* *Sel* k* senec seneg k* *Sep* k* sieg mg1.de **Sil** k* sol-t-ae vml3• *Spig* k* spong k* *Squil* k* *Stann* k* *Staph* k* stel br1* still bro1 stram k* stront-c k* stroph-s sp1* stry bro1 stry-p br1 sul-ac k* sul-i k2* **Sulph** k* sumb syph st1 tab bro1* tarax k* *Tarent* bro1* teucr k* thea bro1 *Ther* thuj k* thymol bro1 tril-p trios jl3 tub br1* tub-d zs tub-r jl valer b2.de* vario jl2 *Verat* k* verat-v sf1.de verb k* vesp ptk2 viol-o k* viol-t k* *Visc* k* x-ray jl *Zinc* k* zinc-p k* [alumin-p stj2 arg-p stj2 bar-f stj1 bell-p-sp dcm1 cupr-p stj2 kali-ar stj2 kali-met stj2 *Lith-c* stj2 *Lith-i* stj2 lith-p stj2 *Mang-i* stj2 mang-p stj2 *Merc-i-f* stj2 plb-m stj2 plb-p stj2 stront-m stj2 stront-met stj2 thal-met stj2 *Zinc-i* stj2]

  - **rapid** motion: *Ars* ptk1 *Bry* ptk1 but-ac br1 ferr tl1* sil ptk1 sulph ptk1 symph ptk1
  - **slow** motion: sep bg2
  - **sudden** motion: cocc ptk1 ferr ptk1 kali-c ptk1
  - **violent** motion: acon bg2 arn bg2 ars bg2 bry bg2 calc bg2 camph bg2 lyc bg2 mag-c bg2 nux-v bg2 rhus-t bg2 ruta bg2 sep bg2 sil bg2 sul-ac bg2 sulph bg2 [bar-f stj1]
- **agility**: coff bg stram bg
- **air**; in open:
  - **agg.**: bell bg2 bry bg2 *Calc* bg2 cocc bg2 colch bg2 led bg2 nux-v bg2
  - **amel.**: *Iod* bg2 *Lil-t* bg2 mag-m bg2 **Puls** bg2 sacch-a fd2.de• streptoc jl2 tritic-vg fd5.de vanil fd5.de
- **amel.**: abrot bro1 *Acon* k* aesc bro1 *Agar* k* agn b7.de all-c sf1.de *Aloe* *Alum* k* *Alumn* kr1 *Am-c* k* *Am-m* k* ambr k* *Anac* k* androc srj1• *Ang* b2.de* ant-c b2.de* ant-t k* apis b7a.de* apoc sf1.de aq-mar mgm• aran-ix mg1.de* *Arg-met* k* *Arg-n* k* arge-pl rwt5• arist-cl mg1.de* arn k* *Ars* k* ars-s-f k2* asaf k* asar k* *Atro* **Aur** k* **Aur-m** k* *Aur-m-n* k* bar-c k* bar-m bell b2.de* bell-p bro1* benz-ac *Bism* k* borx k* bov k* *Brom* k* brucel sa3• bry b2.de* cact sf1.de calc k* calc-f k2* calc-p cann-s b7.de canth k* **Caps** k* carb-ac carb-an k* carb-v k* *Caust* k* cham k* chel b7.de chin k* *Chinin-ar* chir-fl gya2 choc srj3• cic k* cimic sf1.de* *Cina* k* coc-c hr1* coca k* *Cocc* k* *Coloc* k* *Com* k* **Con** k* croc b7.de cupr k* **Cycl** k* des-ac rbp6 *Dios* k* *Dros* k* **Dulc** k* erig mg1.de **Euph** k* euphr k* **Ferr** k* ferr-ar ferr-p *Fl-ac* bro1* *Gamb* *Gels* k* guaj k* ham fd3.de• hed mg1.de* *Helon* bro1 hep k* hom-xyz bro1 hydrog srj2• hyos k* ign k* ignis-alc es2• *Indg* k* **Iod** bg1* irid-met stj2*• iris bro1 kali-br sf1.de* *Kali-c* k* *Kali-i* k* *Kali-n* k* *Kali-p* k* **Kali-s** *Kola* stb3• *Kreos* k* lach k* laur k* *Lil-t* lith-c k* lith-lac bro1 lob k* **Lyc** k* *M-ambo* b2.de* m-arct b2.de* m-aust b2.de *Mag-c* k* *Mag-m* k* magn-gr bro1 manc mrr1 mand sp1 mang k* *Med* *Meny* k* meph c1 *Merc* b2.de* *Merc-c* *Merc-i-f* k* mez b2.de* *Mosch* k* *Mur-ac* k* *Nat-c* k* nat-m b2.de* *Nat-s* nat-sil fd3.de• nit-ac k* nux-m k* olib-sac wmh1 olnd k* op k* ozone sde2• par k* parth bro1 petr k* *Ph-ac* k* phel j5.de phos b2.de* pip-m bro1 *Plat* k* plb b2.de* plut-n srj7• pneu jl3 podo fd3.de• **Puls** k* **Pyrog** k* rad-br sze8• rad-met bro1 raja-s jl *Rat* **Rhod** k* **Rhus-t** k* *Ruta* k* **Sabad** k* sabin b2.de* sacch-a fd2.de• **Samb** k* sars b2.de* sel k* seneg k* *Sep* k* sil b2.de* spig k* spong b2.de* *Stann* k* staph b2.de* stel bro1 *Stront-c* k* sul-ac k* **Sulph** k* syph bro1 **Tarax** k* **Tarent** teucr k* thala jl3 thiop jl thuj k* tritic-vg fd5.de *Tub* tub-r vn* vac jl2 **Valer** k* vanil fd5.de ven-m jl3 verat k* *Verb* k* *Vib* *Viol-t* k* visc jl3 xero bro1 *Zinc* k* zinc-p k2* zinc-val sf1.de [am-f stj2 arg-p stj2 astat stj2 aur-s stj2 bar-br stj2 *Bar-i* stj2 bar-met stj2 bism-sn stj2 caes-met stj2 calc-br stj1 cinnb stj2 cupr-f stj2 *Fl-pur* stj2 graph stj2 hafn-met stj2 kali-ar stj2 kali-f stj1 kali-met stj2 kali-sil stj2 lanth-met stj2 lith-f stj2 *Lith-i* stj2 mag-f stj1 *Mag-i* stj1 *Mang-i* stj2 merc-d stj2 nat-br stj2 nat-f stj1* *Nat-i* stj1 osm-met stj2 plb-m stj2 plb-p stj2 polon-met stj2 rhen-met stj2 tant-met stj2 thal-met stj2 tung-met stj2 *Zinc-i* stj2 zinc-m stj2]
  - **rapid** motion: am-m ptk1 ars bg2* aur-m ptk1 brom ptk1 *Ferr* k2 fl-ac bg2* graph ptk1 ign ptk1 nit-ac ptk1 sacch-a fd2.de• scop ptk1 sep bg2* stann ptk1 sul-ac ptk1 tarent ptk1 thlas ptk1 *Tub* ptk1 vanil fd5.de [calc-f stj1 mag-f stj1]
  - **slow** motion: agar bg2* alum ptk1 ambr bg2* *Anac* vh1 androc srj1• asaf k2 *Aur* ptk1 bell bg2 calc kl caust ptk1 cimic lp coloc bg2* **Ferr** bg2* ferr-act bro1 ferr-ar k2 ferr-p k2* glon bg2* kali-bi bg2 kali-p bg2* *Mag-m* bg2* plat bro1 **Puls** bg2* spong fd4.de stann bro1 *Sulph* kl sumb ptk1

- **amel.** – **slow** motion: ...
  symph fd3.de• **Syph** st* tarent ptk1 zinc bro1 [cupr-act stj2 ferr-f stj2 ferr-i stj1 ferr-lac stj2 ferr-m stj1 ferr-n stj2 ferr-s stj1 ferr-sil stj2 kali-br stj1 pop dhh1]
  - **sudden** motion: rhod ptk1 sabad ptk1
  - **violent** motion: aesc bg2* **Ars** bg2 **Brom** bg2* dulc bg2 phys bg2 **Sep** bg2* sil bg2 *Sul-ac* bg2* [am-br stj2 am-f stj2 calc-f stj1 cupr-f stj2 fl-pur stj2 lith-f stj2 mag-f stj1 nat-f stj1*]
- **angular**: agar ptk1
- **arms**; of:
  - **agg.**: *Acon* b2.de* am-m b2.de* *Anac* b2.de* *Ang* b2.de* ant-c b2.de* bar-c b2.de* borx b2.de* bov bg2 camph b2.de* *Dig* b2.de* ferr b2.de* *Led* b2.de* m-arct b2.de* nux-m b2.de* plb b2.de* puls b2.de* *Ran-b* b2.de* *Rhus-t* b2.de* sep b2.de* *Spig* bg2 spong b2.de* sulph b2.de* thuj b2.de* viol-t b2.de*
  - **backward** agg.: sanic bro1
- **automatic**: bell bg lyc bg *Stram* bg
- **aversion** to: abrot st1 **Acon** k* agar a1 alco a1 *Aloe* a1* alum k* alum-p k2* alum-sil k2 am-c k* ambr k* anac k* ant-c k* ant-t k* arn k* **Ars** k* ars-s-f k2* asar k* atro a1 bapt bg2* *Bar-c* k* bar-s **Bell** k* bol-la a1 borx k* **Bry** k* cadm-s k* **Calad** k* **Calc** k* **Calc-s** k* cann-i a1 canth k* *Caps* k* *Carb-an* k* *Carb-v* k* *Carbn-s* caust k* cham k* *Chel* k* *Chin* k* chinin-ar cina k* coc-c a1 *Cocc* k* coff k* colch k2* *Con* k* croc k* cupr k* *Cycl* k* *Dig* k* dios a1 dros k* dulc k* eryt-j a1 ferr k* ferr-i *Gels* k* gins a1 *Graph* k* **Guaj** k* ham a1 hell j5.de hydr-ac a1 hyos k* hyper hr1* *Ign* k* iod j5.de ip k* irid-met srj5• kali-ar *Kali-bi* k* *Kali-c* k* kali-p kali-sil k2* *Kola* stb3• **Lach** k* led k* lob a1 *Lyc* k* *Lyss* sne m-aust b2.de* mag-c k* mag-m k* malar jl2 merc k* *Mez* k* mur-ac k* myric a1 *Nat-ar* nat-c k* *Nat-m* k* nit-ac k* nux-m a1 **Nux-v** k* oena a1 ol-eucal br1 op k* peti a1 petr k* *Ph-ac* k* phos k* phys a1 *Pic-ac* sne pitu-gl skp7• psor ptel a1 puls k* **Ruta** k* *Sang* k* sapin a1 sep k* **Sil** k* stann k* stront-c k* sul-i k2 sulfonam ks2 **Sulph** k* tab a1 tarax k* *Tarent* a1 teucr k* *Thuj* k* tritic-vg fd5.de vanil fd5.de zinc k* zinc-p k2*
  - **evening**: pitu-gl skp7•
  - **chilliness** agg.: pitu-gl skp7•
  - **coldness** agg.: pitu-gl skp7•
  - **downward** motion: borx k2
  - **sitting**; when: kali-p ptk1
- **beginning** of | **agg.**: *(↗Walking - beginning)* *Agar* am-c st ant-t asar k* berb sf1.de bry b2.de* cact k* calc k* calc-f sf1.de **Caps** k* *Carb-v* k* *Caust* k* chin k* cina k* cocc k* **Con** k* cupr k* dig h2 dros k* **Euph** k* **Ferr** k* fl-ac k* graph k* hecla jl hed mg1.de iris sf1.de kali-bi gk *Kali-p* lach k* led k* **Lyc** k* m-ambo b2.de* mag-c k* mand jl med st nit-ac k* osteo-a jl2 petr k* *Ph-ac* *Phos* k* plat k* plb k* *Psor* **Puls** k* rhod k* **Rhus-t** k* ruta k* *Sabad* k* sabin k* *Samb* k* sanic bg1* sars k* sep k2 *Sil* k* stront-c bro1 *Ther* thuj k* tub st tub-r vs valer k* verat *Zinc* zinc-p k2 [ang stj4]
- **continued** motion:
  - **agg.**: rhus-t k2
  - **amel.**: aesc sf1.de agar *Am-m* k* *Ambr* k* anac ptk1 aran-ix mg1.de bac jl2 bell-p mg1.de bry k* *Cact* calc-f sf1.de* **Caps** k* carb-v k* caust k* chin k* cimic hr1 *Cina* k* cob ptk1 com **Con** k* *Cycl* k* *Dros* k* **Euph** k* **Ferr** k* **Fl-ac** bg2 gels graph bg2 hecla jl hed mg1.de ign ptk1 ind k* iod mg1.de iris k* kali-bi gk kali-c k* kali-i mrr1 kalm ptk1 *Lyc* k* m-ambo b2.de mag-c mg1.de mand mg1.de* med k2 osteo-a jl2 phor-t mie3• phos ptk1 plat k* plb k* *Ptel* **Puls** k* pyrog tl1 rad-br c11* rauw jl *Rhod* k* **Rhus-t** k* ruta k* *Sabad* k* sabin k* sacch-a fd2.de• **Samb** k* sep k* *Sil* k* stel mrr1 streptoc jl2 **Syph** st* tarax k* thuj k* *Valer* k* vanil fd5.de *Verat* k* zinc bg2*
- **desire** for: acon b2.de* agar b2.de* alum b2.de* am-c b2.de* *Ambr* b2.de* arg-met bg2 arg-n bg2 *Arn* b2.de* ars b2.de* *Ars-i* k2 asar b2.de* aur bg2 aur-ar k2 *Bell* b2.de* bell-p mg1.de* bism bg2 borx b2.de* bry b2.de* calc b2.de* cann-s b2.de* canth b2.de* cench k2 **Cham** b2.de* **Chin** b2.de* coff b2.de* coloc b2.de* con b2.de* *Cupr* b2.de* dulc fd4.de euphr b2.de* **Ferr** b2.de* ferr-ar k2 ferr-i k2 hydrog srj2• hyos b2.de* ign b2.de* ignis-alc es2• iod b2.de* ip b2.de* kali-i k2 kali-s fd4.de kreos b2.de* lap-la sde8.de• lyc b2.de* m-ambo b2.de *M-arct* b2.de m-aust b2.de macro a1 mag-c b2.de* mag-m b2.de* mang b2.de* merc b2.de* mosch b2.de* mur-ac b2.de* nat-c b2.de* nit-ac bg2 nux-m b2.de* nux-v b2.de* olib-sac wmh1 op b2.de* petr a1 ph-ac b2.de* phos bg2 plac-s rly4• podo fd3.de• puls b2.de* pyrog jl2 ran-b b2.de* rhod b2.de* **Rhus-t** b2.de* ruta b2.de* sacch-a fd2.de• samb b2.de* sec b2.de* sep b2.de* sil b2.de* spong fd4.de squil b2.de* stann b2.de* staph b2.de* stront-c bg2 sul-i k2 sulph b2.de* *Teucr* b2.de* tritic-vg fd5.de tub k2* valer b2.de* vanil fd5.de verat b2.de*

Motion: ...

- **difficult**: acon bg2 agar bg2 alum bg2 am-c bg2 am-m bg2 ambr bg2 anac bg2 *Ang* bg2 ant-c bg2 ant-t bg2 arg-met bg2 arn bg2 *Ars* bg2 asar bg2 aur bg2 bar-c bg2 **Bell** b4.de* borx bg2 bov bg2 *Bry* bg2* *Calc* bg2 camph b7.de* cann-xyz bg2 canth bg2 caps bg2 *Carb-an* bg2 carb-v b4.de* **Caust** bg2* *Cham* bg2 chel b7.de* chin bg2 *Cic* b7.de* cina bg2 *Cocc* bg2 coff bg2 colch bg2 *Coloc* bg2 con bg2 croc bg2 cupr bg2 cycl b7.de* dig bg2 dros bg2 dulc b4a.de* euph bg2 euphr bg2 ferr bg2 *Gels* bg2 *Graph* bg2 guaj bg2 hell bg2 hep bg2 hyos bg2 *Ign* bg2 ip bg2 *Kali-c* bg2 kali-n bg2 kreos bg2 lach bg2 laur b7.de* led bg2 **Lyc** bg2* m-ambo b7.de mag-c bg2 mag-m bg2 mang bg2 meny bg2 *Merc* bg2 mez bg2 mosch bg2 mur-ac b4.de* nat-c bg2 *Nat-m* bg2 nit-ac bg2 nux-m bg2 *Nux-v* b7.de* olnd bg2 op bg2 par bg2 **Petr** bg2* ph-ac bg2 phos bg2 plat bg2 plb bg2 *Puls* bg2 ran-b bg2 rheum bg2 rhod bg2 **Rhus-t** bg2* ruta bg2 sabad b7.de* sars b4a.de* sec bg2 sel bg2 seneg bg2 **Sep** b4.de* *Sil* b4.de* *Spig* bg2 spong bg2 squil bg2 stann bg2 *Staph* bg2 stram b7.de* stront-c b4.de* sul-ac bg2 *Sulph* bg2 tarax b7.de* *Thuj* bg2 valer bg2 *Verat* b7.de* zinc bg2
- **downward** motion agg.: **Borx** bg2* carb-v bg2 **Gels** bg2* sanic bro1* sep bg2 sulph bg2 *[Bor-pur* stj2*]*
- **eyelids**; of | **agg.**: coloc b2.de* mosch b2.de*
- **eyes**; of | **agg.**: acon b2.de* agn b2.de* alum b2.de* arn b2.de* ars b2.de* *Bell* b2.de* **Bry** b2.de* camph b2.de* *Caps* b2.de* carb-v b2.de* *Cham* b2.de* chin b2.de* clem b2.de* cocc k2 coloc b2.de* con b2.de* cupr b2.de* dig b2.de* dros b2.de* *Hep* b2.de* ign b2.de* kalm bg2 *M-arct* b2.de* m-aust b2.de* mang b2.de* merc b2.de* mosch b2.de* mur-ac b2.de* nat-m b2.de* *Nux-v* b2.de* olnd b2.de* *Op* b2.de* pic-ac tl1 plb b2.de* puls b2.de* ran-s b2.de* rhus-t b2.de* sabad b2.de* sabin b2.de* seneg b2.de* sep b2.de* *Sil* b2.de* *Spig* b2.de* spong b2.de* stann b2.de* stront-c b2.de* *Sulph* b2.de* *Valer* b2.de* zinc b2.de*
- **false** move; from a: ars b2.de* *Bry* b2.de* lyc b2.de*
- **foot**; of | **agg.** | **forward**; setting foot: hyos b7.de *Kreos* b7a.de
  - **amel.**: ars bg2* rhus-t bg2* *Zinc* bg2*
- **head**; of | **agg.**: acon b2.de* am-c b2.de* *Arn* b2.de* bar-c b2.de* *Bell* b2.de* *Bry* b2.de* *Calc* b2.de* cann-s b2.de* canth b7.de *Caps* b2.de* carb-v b2.de* chin b2.de* cocc b2.de* coloc b2.de* *Cupr* b2.de* euph b2.de* fl-ac bg2 graph b2.de* ip b2.de* kali-c b2.de* *Lyc* b2.de* mang b2.de* mez b2.de* *Mosch* b2.de* nat-c b2.de* nat-m b2.de* ph-ac b2.de* plat b2.de* puls b2.de* rhod b2.de* samb b2.de* *Sep* b2.de* sil b2.de* *Spig* b2.de* stann b2.de* staph b2.de* sul-ac b2.de* sulph b2.de* tub ptk1 verat b2.de* viol-o b2.de*
- **involuntary**: acon b2.de* agar tl1 alum b2.de* aur b2.de* bell b2.de* calc bg2 camph b2.de* canth b2.de* caust b2.de* cham b2.de* chin b2.de* cimic tl1 *Cocc* b2.de* colch b2.de* con b2.de* *Cupr* b2.de* **Hyos** b2.de* *Ign* b2.de* kali-c b2.de* *Lach* b2.de* lyc b2.de* m-ambo b2.de* m-arct b2.de meny b2.de* mosch b2.de* nux-m b2.de* *Op* b2.de* *Phos* bg2 plb b2.de* rhus-t b2.de* samb b2.de* sep b2.de* spig b2.de* staph b2.de* **Stram** b2.de* verat b2.de*
  - **waking**; while: agar tl1
    ⁝ **sleep** amel.; during: agar tl1
- **oscillatory**: agar ptk1 elaps ptk1 stram ptk1
  - **must** have: elaps br1
- **rhythmical**: agar ptk1 cupr bg2 elaps ptk1 lyc ptk1 phos bg2 stram bg2*
- **sensation** of: acon b2.de* alum b2.de* am-c b2.de* anac b2.de* ang b2.de* ant-t b2.de* arn b2.de* ars b2.de* asar b2.de* aur b2.de* **Bell** b2.de* bry b2.de* *Calc* b2.de* cann-s b2.de* cham b2.de* chin b2.de* cocc b2.de* **Croc** b2.de* cycl b2.de* dig b2.de* dulc b2.de* guaj b2.de* hyos b2.de* *Ign* b2.de* iod b2.de* kali-c b2.de* kreos b2.de* lach b2.de* laur b2.de* led b2.de* m-ambo b2.de* mag-m b2.de* **Meny** b2.de* merc b2.de* mosch b2.de* nat-m b2.de* nux-v b2.de* petr b2.de* ph-ac b2.de* phos b2.de* plb b2.de* rheum b2.de* *Rhod* b2.de* *Rhus-t* b2.de* sabad b2.de* sec b2.de* *Sep* b2.de* *Sil* b2.de* spig b2.de* spong b2.de* stront-c b2.de* **Sulph** b2.de* tarax b2.de* thuj b2.de* verat b2.de* viol-t b2.de* zinc b2.de*

O • **Blood** vessels; in: pip-n bg2
- **stumbling**: visc sp1
- **upward** and downward motion; sensation of: calc bg2 ferr bg2 lach b2.de* plb b2.de* *Spong* b2.de*
- **wrong**:
  - **agg.**: bry ptk1 lyc ptk1
  - **amel.**: am-m ptk1

MOTION sickness (See Riding - streetcar; on - agg.)

MOTIONLESS; holding part: | **agg.**: coff b7.de

MOTIONLESSNESS (= immobility): cic b7.de lycps-v ptk1 mang ptk1 stront-c ptk1
- **one** side: stront-c ptk1
- ○ - **Affected** parts: *Acon* b2.de* agar b2.de* alum b2.de* am-c b2.de* am-m b2.de* ambr b2.de* anac b2.de* ang b2.de* ant-c b2.de* arg-met b2.de* arn b2.de* ars b2.de* asar b2.de* aur b2.de* bar-c b2.de* *Bell* b2.de* bov b2.de* bry b2.de* calc b2.de* cann-s b2.de* canth b2.de* caps b2.de* carb-v b2.de* *Caust* b2.de* cham b2.de* chel b2.de* chin b2.de* cic b2.de* **Cocc** b2.de* colch b2.de* coloc b2.de* con b2.de* cupr b2.de* cycl b2.de* dig b2.de* dros b2.de* *Dulc* b2.de* euphr b2.de* ferr b2.de* gels bg2 graph b2.de* guaj b2.de* hell b2.de* hep b2.de* hyos b2.de* ign b2.de* iod b2.de* ip b2.de* kali-c b2.de* lach b2.de* laur b2.de* led b2.de* lyc b2.de* m-ambo b2.de m-aust b2.de meny b2.de* merc b2.de* mez b2.de* mur-ac b2.de* *Nat-m* b2.de* nit-ac b2.de* nux-m b2.de* *Nux-v* b2.de* olnd b2.de* op b2.de* petr b2.de* ph-ac b2.de* phos b2.de* *Plb* b2.de* puls b2.de* rhod b2.de* **Rhus-t** b2.de* ruta b2.de* sabin b2.de* sars b2.de* sec b2.de* sel b2.de* seneg b2.de* sep b2.de* *Sil* b2.de* spig b2.de* stann b2.de* stram b2.de* stront-c b2.de* sul-ac b2.de* *Sulph* b2.de* tarax b2.de* *Verat* b2.de* zinc b2.de*

MOUNTAIN:
- **agg.** in mountains: med jl2
- **amel.** in mountains: falco-pe nl2• irid-met srj5• merc sne prot jl2 *Syph* bro1* tub a*
- **climbing**; ailments from mountain: *Arn* ptk1 ars c1* *Coca* br1* [oxyg stj2]
- **sickness**: (↗*Ascending high - agg.*) *Acon* kr1 *Arn* mp1• *Ars* c1* aur st1 bell st1 **Calc** st1 *Carb-v* st1 caust st1 **Coca** kr1* con st1 conv st1 cordyc mp4• cupr st1 gels st1 guaj st1 kola sf1.de* *Lach* st1 lyc st1 nat-m st1 olnd st1 *Op* mp1• puls st1 **Sil** mp1• spig st1 verat c1 [oxyg stj2]

MUCOUS SECRETIONS: (↗*Discharges*)
- **acrid**: (↗*Acridity*) aesc st *Alum* j5.de *Am-c* j5.de* *Am-m* j5.de anac j5.de ant-c j5.de *Ars* j5.de* arum-t k2* *Borx* j5.de* bov j5.de calc j5.de calen br1 cann-s j5.de canth j5.de carb-an j5.de *Carb-v* j5.de* carc gk6* *Caust* mtf33 *Cham* j5.de chin j5.de *Con* j5.de euph j5.de *Ferr* j5.de* fl-ac k2* hep j5.de *Ign* j5.de* *Iod* j5.de* kali-c j5.de kali-i j5.de* *Kreos* j5.de* *Lach* j5.de* *Lyc* j5.de* m-arct j5.de mag-c j5.de *Mag-m* j5.de mang j5.de *Merc* j5.de* *Mez* j5.de mur-ac j5.de *Nat-m* j5.de* *Nit-ac* j5.de* *Nux-v* j5.de ph-ac j5.de *Phos* j5.de prun j5.de *Puls* j5.de* *Ran-b* j5.de ruta j5.de sang k2* *Sep* j5.de* *Sil* j5.de *Spig* j5.de *Squil* j5.de *Sul-ac* j5.de *Sulph* j5.de* thuj j5.de* zinc mtf33
- **albuminoid**: alum ptk1 am-m j5.de* berb ptk1 borx j5.de* bov j5.de calc-p ptk1 coc-c ptk1 enteroc jl2 graph k2 grat k2 jatr-c j5.de* *Kali-m* kr1 mez j5.de* *Nat-m* ptk1 pall ptk1 petr j5.de* phyt ptk1 plat j5.de* seneg ptk1 sep ptk1 stann ptk1 tarent ptk1
- **altered**: *Ant-t* ptk1 arg-met ptk1 arg-n ptk1 *Ars* ptk1 **Calc** ptk1 calc-s ptk1 caust ptk1 *Cham* ptk1 graph ptk1 hep ptk1 hydr ptk1 **Kali-bi** ptk1 *Lyc* ptk1 *Merc* ptk1 **Nat-m** ptk1 *Nit-ac* ptk1 nux-v ptk1 *Phos* ptk1 **Puls** ptk1 **Sep** ptk1 sil ptk1 *Stann* ptk1 *Sulph* ptk1
- **amel.**: (↗*Discharges - amel.; Leukorrhea - amel.*) arist-cl mg1.de* *Bry* sf1.de cimic sf1.de cupr sf1.de dulc sf1.de graph sf1.de kali-bi sf1.de **Lach** k2* merc mrr1 mosch sf1.de nux-v sf1.de *Puls* sf1.de* senec sf1.de sep sf1.de **Sulph** sf1.de thuj sf1.de *Zinc* sf1.de
- **bland**: alumn k2 arg-n sf1.de cycl sf1.de kali-s sf1.de *Merc* sf1.de **Puls** bg2*
- **bloody**: acon j5.de* ail bg2 aloe bg2 alum j5.de* alum-sil k2 am-c j5.de* am-m j5.de aphis j5.de arg-n bg2* arn bg2* ars j5.de* ars-h br1 *Ars-s-f* k2 *Asar* j5.de *Bar-c* j5.de* bar-m k2* *Bell* j5.de* borx j5.de brom bg2 bry bg2 bufo mtf33 *Calc-s* hr1* calc-sil j5.de* *Canth* j5.de* caps j5.de carb-an sf1.de *Carb-v* j5.de* caust j5.de* *Chin* j5.de* cocc j5.de* cop j5.de *Crot-h* bg2* daph j5.de diphtox jl2 dros bg2 euon j5.de ferr j5.de* form sf1.de graph j5.de* ham kr1* hep j5.de iod j5.de* kali-ar k2 kali-c j5.de* kali-chl j5.de kali-n j5.de kreos bg2* *Lach* j5.de* led j5.de lyc j5.de* mag-c j5.de mag-m j5.de mang sf1.de *Merc* j5.de* mez j5.de mur-ac bg2 murx j5.de nat-m j5.de* *Nit-ac* bg2* nux-m j5.de *Nux-v* j5.de* op j5.de par j5.de petr j5.de *Phos* j5.de* *Puls* j5.de* sabin j5.de* *Sep* j5.de* *Sil* j5.de* sul-ac j5.de* sul-i k2 sulph j5.de* *Ter* hr1* thuj j5.de* verat j5.de vip j5.de zinc j5.de* zinc-p k2
    - • **streaked**: acon bg2 ail bg2 aloe bg2 alum bg2 am-c bg2 arg-n bg2 arn bg2 ars bg2 bar-c bg2 bell bg2 brom bg2 bry bg2 canth bg2 carb-v bg2 *Chin* bg2 cocc bg2 crot-h bg2 dros bg2 ferr bg2 iod bg2 kreos bg2 lach bg2 lyc bg2 merc bg2 mur-ac bg2 nat-m bg2 nit-ac bg2 *Nux-v* bg2 phos bg2* puls bg2 sabin bg2 sep bg2 **Sil** bg2 sul-ac bg2 sulph bg2 thuj bg2 zinc bg2
- **bluish**: ambr j5.de* ars j5.de* cupr bg2 cupr-act j5.de lach sf1.de
- **brownish**: am-m j5.de ambr bg2 ars j5.de* bapt ptk1 *Bell* j5.de* berb ptk1 bism j5.de borx j5.de* *Bry* ptk1 carb-v j5.de* chel ptk1 grat j5.de hyos ptk1 iod ptk1 kreos ptk1 lyc ptk1 lycps-v ptk1 manc ptk1 nit-ac j5.de* op ptk1 petr ptk1 phos ptk1 *Rhus-t* ptk1 sec ptk1 **Sep** ptk1 staph ptk1 sulph j5.de* thuj ptk1 verat ptk1

Mucous secretions: ...
- **burning**: acon sf1.de aesc sf1.de *Ail* bg2* all-c sf1.de alum j5.de alum-p k2 am-c j5.de* am-m j5.de* *Ars* j5.de* ars-i sf1.de* ars-s-f k2 arum-t sf1.de bad sf1.de brom bg2* calad j5.de *Calc* j5.de canth sf1.de caps sf1.de carb-ac sf1.de *Carb-an* j5.de* carb-v sf1.de castm j5.de chin j5.de* chlor sf1.de cina j5.de *Con* j5.de crot-h sf1.de fl-ac k2* *Gels* bg2* graph sf1.de guaj sf1.de hep sf1.de hydr sf1.de iod sf1.de kali-c sf1.de *Kali-i* j5.de* kreos sf1.de lach sf1.de lyc sf1.de mag-s j5.de *Merc* sf1.de merc-c mrr1 mez j5.de mur-ac sf1.de nat-m sf1.de *Nit-ac* sf1.de* petr sf1.de phos sf1.de phyt sf1.de puls j5.de ran-s sf1.de *Sabad* bg2* sang sf1.de sep sf1.de sil sf1.de sul-ac j5.de* *Sulph* j5.de* ter mrr1
- **cold** agg.: verat k2*
- **complaints** from: ars b4.de *Caust* b4.de kali-c b4.de
- **corrosive**: **Alum** bg2 am-c bg2* *Am-m* bg2 ant-c j5.de **Ars** j5.de* ars-i br1* *Ars-s-f* k2* arum-t k2* borx bg2 *Bov* bg2 brom br1 carb-v bg2* **Caust** bg2* *Cham* j5.de* *Con* j5.de ferr j5.de* **Hydr** bg2 ign bg2* *Iod* sf1.de* ip j5.de kali-ar k2 *Kali-bi* bg2 *Kali-i* bg2* *Kreos* bg2* *Lach* j5.de* lyc sf1.de* **Merc** j5.de* merc-c mrr1 mez bg2 nat-m j5.de* **Nit-ac** bg2* *Nux-v* bg2 *Phos* j5.de* *Puls* bg2* rhus-t bg2 ruta bg2 sep bg2* **Sil** j5.de* staph bg2 sul-ac bg2* *Sulph* j5.de* ter mrr1 *Thuj* bg2* zinc mtf33
- **egg** white; like: *Am-m* br1 nat-m mtf33
- **flocculent**: agar bg2 ambr bg2 kali-bi bg2 kali-c bg2 kreos bg2 mag-c bg2 merc bg2 phos bg2 sabad bg2 sep bg2 sil bg2 sulph bg2 thuj bg2
- **frothy**: *Aphis* j5.de ars j5.de ferr j5.de **Nat-m** hr1* op j5.de sec j5.de sul-ac j5.de
- **gelatinous**: *Aloe* kr1* arg-met j5.de* *Arg-n* ptk1 bell bg2 berb j5.de* caust bg2 chinin-s j5.de cocc k2* **Colch** ptk1 coloc ptk1 dig ptk1 *Hell* j5.de* *Kali-bi* k2* laur j5.de* podo ptk1 *Rhus-t* j5.de* sabin bg2* sel j5.de* sep ptk1
- **gray**: *Ambr* j5.de* anac j5.de* *Arg-met* j5.de* ars j5.de* carb-an j5.de* caust j5.de* chin j5.de* cop j5.de kali-chl sf kali-m sf1.de kreos j5.de* lach j5.de* *Lyc* bg2 mag-m j5.de* merc j5.de* sep j5.de* *Sil* j5.de* thuj j5.de*
- **greenish**: *Ars* j5.de* asaf j5.de aur j5.de borx j5.de* *Carb-v* j5.de* caust j5.de colch j5.de *Dros* j5.de* ferr j5.de* hyos j5.de* *Kali-bi* j5.de* kali-c j5.de *Kali-i* hr1* kali-s hr1* kreos j5.de* lach j5.de led j5.de* *Lyc* j5.de* m-aust j5.de *Mag-c* j5.de* mang j5.de med st *Merc* j5.de* murx j5.de nat-c j5.de* nat-m j5.de nat-s k2* nit-ac j5.de nux-v j5.de *Par* j5.de* *Phos* j5.de* **Puls** j5.de* rhus-t j5.de sabad j5.de *Sep* j5.de* sil j5.de *Stann* j5.de* *Sulph* j5.de* thuj j5.de* tung-met bdx1•
- **hard**: stict sf1.de
- **honey**-like: ars-i k2* graph mtf33
- **hot**: *Ars* bg2 *Bell* mtf33 borx mtf33 *Iod* bg2 *Puls* mtf33 *Sulph* bg2
- **increased**: acet-ac acon k* agar k* agn j5.de **All-c** *Alum* k* alum-p k2 alum-sil k2 alumn k2 am-c k* *Am-m* k* ambr k* *Ammc* anemps br1 ang b2.de* *Ant-c* k* ant-t k* aphis j5.de apoc br1 *Arg-met* k* *Arg-n* k* arn k* *Ars* k* ars-i ars-s-f k2 arum-m j5.de asaf j5.de* asar k* aur k* aur-ar k2 aur-m k2 aur-s k2* *Bar-c* k* *Bar-m* *Bell* k* bell-p br1 *Benz-ac* bism k* bond a1 *Borx* k* bov k* brom k2 bry k* **Calc** k* calc-i br1 calc-s k2 calc-sil k2* calen br1 camph k* *Cann-s* k* canth k* *Caps* k* carb-an k* **Carb-v** k* *Carbn-s* *Caust* k* *Cham* k* chel k* *Chin* k* chlor a1 chr-ac a1 cimic bg3 cina k* cinnb a1* cist k2 *Coc-c* cocc k* coff k* colch k* coloc k* *Con* k* *Cop* k* croc k* crot-t br1 cupr k* dig k* dros k* **Dulc** k* *Eup-per* bg3 euph k* *Euphr* k* *Ferr* k* ferr-ar k2 ferr-i gels bg3 *Graph* k* grat j5.de guaj k* hell k* *Hep* k* **Hydr** k* *Hyos* k* ign k* **Iod** k* *Ip* k* *Iris* bg2* jab br1* kali-ar **Kali-bi** k* *Kali-c* k* kali-chl j5.de* *Kali-i* k* kali-m k2 kali-n k* kali-s k2* kali-sil k2* kreos k* lac-d k2 **Lach** k* lact j5.de laur k* **Lyc** k* m-ambo b2.de m-arct b2.de* m-aust b2.de* mag-c k* mag-m k* mang k2 mec a1 med st* **Merc** k* mez k* mur-ac j5.de* myric hr1* myrt-c br1 nat-ar *Nat-c* k* *Nat-m* k* *Nat-s* j5.de* nicc j5.de *Nit-ac* k* *Nux-m* k* **Nux-v** k* olnd b2.de* op ptk1 *Par* k* **Petr** k* ph-ac k* *Phel* j5.de **Phos** k* plat k* plb k* podo **Puls** k* pyrog jl2 ran-b k* raph j5.de rat j5.de rheum k* rhod k* *Rhus-t* k* *Rumx* ruta k* sabad k* sabin k* sacch br1 *Samb* k* sang k2 sars k* sec k* sel k* senec k2 *Seneg* k* *Sep* k* *Sil* k* sin-n hr1* spig k* spong b2.de* *Squil* k* *Stann* k* staph k* sul-ac k* sul-i k2* **Sulph** k* **Tab** k* tann-ac br1 tart-ac [illegible] tax a1 teucr k* thal a1 thuj k* tong j5.de urt-u br1 valer k* verat k* zinc k*
    - • **accompanied** by | **Skin**; dry: dulc br1
    - • **serous**: anemps br1 apoc br1 kali-s br1
    - • **vomiting**; before: apom br1
- **intermittent**: kali-s br1
- **lumpy**: *Calc-s* hr1* *Hep* hr1* kali-c j5.de kreos j5.de phos j5.de sabad j5.de sabin j5.de sin-n hr1* stann j5.de
- **membranes**; formation of: brom k2
- **metallic** taste: calc j5.de cupr j5.de ip j5.de nux-v j5.de rhus-t j5.de
- **milky**: *Calc* j5.de carb-v j5.de con j5.de ferr j5.de *Kali-m* k2 lyc j5.de phos j5.de *Puls* j5.de sabin j5.de sep j5.de *Sil* j5.de sul-ac j5.de
- **musty** smell: borx j5.de *Carb-v* j5.de

- **offensive**, fetid: ail sf1.de alum sf1.de anthraci sf1.de arg-n sf1.de arn bg2* *Ars* j5.de* ars-i br1 *Ars-s-f* k2* *Asaf* k2* *Aur-s* k2 bals-p sf1.de **Bapt** bg2* bell j5.de* *Calc* j5.de* calc-f sf1.de calc-sil k2 caps j5.de carb-ac sf1.de carb-an br1* *Carb-v* bg2* *Chel* j5.de chin sf1.de chlor sf1.de cist k2* con j5.de* cop sf1.de crot-h sf1.de cupr j5.de cur st *Diph* br1 echi sf1.de euph-c sf1.de fago br1 ferr j5.de fl-ac k2* *Graph* j5.de* *Guaj* hr1* helon sf1.de hep j5.de* ign sf1.de kali-ar k2* kali-bi sf1.de* kali-br sf1.de kali-c mtf33 kali-i sf1.de kali-p k2* kali-perm sf1.de kali-s sf1.de **Kreos** j5.de* **Lach** bg2* lyc sf1.de* mag-c j5.de* *Merc* j5.de* mur-ac j5.de* **Nat-c** j5.de* **Nit-ac** j5.de* *Nux-v* j5.de petr sf1.de phos mtf33 pix sf1.de *Psor* bg2* *Puls* j5.de* *Pyrog* bg2* rhus-t sf1.de *Rob* hr1* *Sabin* j5.de sang sf1.de **Sanic** mrr1 sec bg2 *Sep* j5.de* sil j5.de* stann j5.de *Sulph* j5.de* ter sf1.de ther sf1.de thuj mtf33 tril-p kr1 vip sf1.de
  - **cadaverous** like carrion: psor mtf33
  - **cheese**; like rotten: hep mrr1 *Sanic* mrr1*
  - **fishy** odor: calc ptk1 graph ptk1 med ptk1 ol-an ptk1 **Sanic** ptk1* sep ptk1 tell ptk1 thuj ptk1
- **purulent**: *Aur* bg2 blatta-o br1 **Calc** bg2 calc-s br1* carb-v mtf33 **Con** bg2 cop j5.de *Graph* bg2 ign j5.de lyc sf1.de *Merc* j5.de* nat-c sf1.de *Psor* mrr1 *Puls* bg2 sep j5.de* *Sil* bg2 *Sulph* st*
- **ropy**, tenacious: acon j5.de agn j5.de *Alum* j5.de* alum-p k2 am-m j5.de anac j5.de *Ant-c* j5.de ant-s-aur a1 ant-t j5.de arg-met bg2* arg-n bg2 *Ars* j5.de asaf j5.de bar-act sf1.de bar-c j5.de* bar-m sf1.de *Bell* j5.de *Borx* sf1.de *Bov* j5.de* bry j5.de* calc j5.de* cann-s j5.de canth j5.de* carb-an j5.de carb-v j5.de* carbn-s k2 caust j5.de* *Cham* j5.de chin j5.de *Chinin-s* j5.de *Cist* j5.de *Coc-c* k2* cocc j5.de colch j5.de con j5.de culx k2 dulc j5.de* euphr j5.de form sf1.de graph j5.de* hep j5.de *Hydr* k2* iod j5.de **Kali-bi** k2* kali-c j5.de* *Kali-chl* k13 *Kali-m* k2 kali-s k2* lach j5.de* lact j5.de laur j5.de lob j5.de m-arct j5.de m-aust j5.de *Mag-c* j5.de mag-m j5.de *Merc* j5.de* *Mez* j5.de nat-c j5.de nux-v j5.de ol-an j5.de *Par* j5.de *Ph-ac* j5.de *Phos* j5.de phyt sf1.de plat j5.de plb j5.de* puls j5.de* *Ran-b* j5.de raph j5.de rhus-t j5.de sabad j5.de sabin j5.de *Samb* j5.de scroph-n j5.de *Seneg* j5.de sep j5.de* sin-n hr1* spig j5.de spong j5.de squil j5.de **Stann** j5.de staph j5.de *Sulph* j5.de sumb c1 *Tab* j5.de thuj sf1.de tong j5.de verat j5.de zinc j5.de
- **salty** taste: alum j5.de *Ambr* j5.de *Ars* j5.de *Bar-c* j5.de calc j5.de chin j5.de dros j5.de fl-ac st *Graph* j5.de *Iod* sf1.de *Kali-i* sf1.de *Lyc* j5.de* mag-c j5.de mag-m j5.de *Merc* j5.de *Nat-c* j5.de nat-m sf1.de nux-v j5.de *Petr* j5.de *Phos* j5.de puls j5.de samb j5.de *Sep* j5.de *Sil* j5.de stann j5.de staph j5.de sulph j5.de zinc j5.de
- **sour** taste: calc j5.de graph j5.de *Hep* j5.de* kali-c j5.de kali-n j5.de lam j5.de lyc mtf33 mag-c mrr1 mag-m j5.de merc j5.de nat-c j5.de nat-p st nit-ac st nux-v j5.de *Plb* j5.de *Rheum* mrr1 sep j5.de sul-ac mrr1 sulph j5.de* tarax j5.de
- **suppressed**: *(↗Discharges - amel.)* abrot k1* agar a1* *Ant-c* hr1* arist-cl k1* ars k2* asaf k1* **Asar** k1* aur-m k1* *Bar-c* k1* bell k2* *Bry* bg2* bufo k2* calc k2* carb-v k2* chin k1* cinnb k1* coloc k1* cupr k2* *Dulc* bg2* glon k1* *Graph* k2* ip k1* kali-bi k1* *Lach* bg2* led c1* *Lob* k1* med k1* merc k1* mill k1* *Mosch* hr1* *Nux-v* bg2* op k1* plb k1* *Psor* k1* *Puls* bg2* rumx br1 sanic k1* senec k1* sep k1* *Sil* bg2* **Stram** bg2* *Sulph* bg2* thuj k1* verat k1* verat-v sf viol-o c1* zinc k1*
- **sweetish** taste: asar j5.de *Calc* k2 cham a1 lach j5.de* mag-c j5.de merc-c j5.de phos k2 stann k2
- **thick**, slimy: acon j5.de agar j5.de *Alum* j5.de alum-sil k2 am-m j5.de ant-c j5.de arg-met j5.de* *Arg-n* sf1.de *Ars* j5.de ars-i k2 ars-s-f k2 *Aur-s* k2 bals-p sf1.de *Bar-c* j5.de berb j5.de *Borx* j5.de* calc j5.de calc-s k2* carb-an j5.de carb-v j5.de carbn-s k2 carc gk6* castm j5.de caust k2 cist k2* coc-c k2 con j5.de cop j5.de cycl sf1.de *Ery-a* br1 graph j5.de *Hep* sf1.de *Hydr* k2* iod j5.de ip j5.de kali-bi k2* kali-br sf1.de *Kali-i* j5.de* *Kali-m* kr1* *Kali-s* k2* kali-sil k2 kreos j5.de lac-ac sf1.de lam j5.de lith-c sf1.de lyc j5.de m-arct j5.de *Mag-m* j5.de *Mag-s* j5.de mang sf1.de merc k2* mur-ac j5.de murx j5.de *Nat-c* j5.de* *Nat-m* j5.de* nat-s k2 nat-sil k2 nicc j5.de nit-ac j5.de ol-an j5.de op j5.de par j5.de **Puls** j5.de* ruta j5.de sabad j5.de samb j5.de sars j5.de scroph-n j5.de sec j5.de sel j5.de seneg j5.de *Sil* j5.de* staph j5.de *Sulph* j5.de* tong j5.de tub st tung-met bdx1• zinc j5.de zing j5.de
- **thin**: ambr j5.de ant-t j5.de *Ars* k2* *Ars-s-f* k2* *Asaf* sf1.de asar j5.de *Bell* j5.de* borx j5.de bov j5.de *Calc* j5.de canth j5.de caps j5.de *Carb-v* j5.de* caust j5.de colch j5.de *Con* j5.de ferr j5.de *Fl-ac* k2* gels sf1.de *Graph* j5.de iod mtf33 *Kali-i* j5.de* kali-n j5.de *Kali-s* k2* laur j5.de lyc j5.de* *Mag-c* j5.de merc mtf33 mez j5.de mur-ac sf1.de nat-m j5.de* **Nit-ac** hr1* nux-v j5.de ol-an j5.de *Puls* j5.de* rhus-t j5.de seneg j5.de *Sil* sf1.de stann j5.de staph j5.de sul-ac j5.de* sulph mtf33 ter j5.de* thuj sf1.de
- **transparent**: aesc st alum j5.de castm j5.de crot-h j5.de ferr-m j5.de fl-ac st graph j5.de kali-i j5.de mag-s j5.de mang j5.de **Nat-m** j5.de* phos j5.de puls j5.de sabad j5.de *Sep* j5.de *Sil* j5.de *Stann* j5.de sul-ac j5.de

Mucous secretions: ...

- **typhoid** fever; during (See FEVER - Typhoid - accompanied - mucus)
- **watery**: acon sf1.de* aesc st *Agar* j5.de alum j5.de *Am-c* j5.de *Am-m* j5.de* ambr j5.de ant-c j5.de arg-met j5.de *Ars* j5.de* ars-i br1 *Asaf* k2 asar j5.de bell j5.de *Bov* j5.de brom sf1.de calc j5.de cann-s j5.de *Carb-an* j5.de *Carb-v* j5.de* castm j5.de *Cham* j5.de *Chin* j5.de chlor sf1.de clem j5.de coff j5.de con j5.de elat hr1* fl-ac k2* *Gels* hr1* *Graph* j5.de *Guaj* j5.de ign j5.de iod j5.de* kali-i j5.de* kali-n j5.de *Kali-s* k2* kreos j5.de* *Lach* j5.de lyc mtf33 *M-arct* j5.de *Mag-c* j5.de *Mag-m* j5.de meny j5.de *Merc* j5.de* *Mez* j5.de *Mur-ac* j5.de murx j5.de **Nat-m** hr1* nicc j5.de *Nux-v* j5.de par j5.de phos j5.de *Plb* j5.de *Puls* j5.de* ran-b j5.de rhus-t j5.de seneg j5.de *Sep* j5.de *Sil* j5.de *Squil* j5.de stann j5.de staph j5.de sul-ac j5.de *Sulph* j5.de* thuj j5.de verat k2*
- **white**: bell k2 ferr j5.de graph j5.de grat j5.de hell j5.de *Kali-chl* hr1* *Kali-m* kr1* kali-n j5.de kreos j5.de lyc j5.de* m-arct j5.de mag-c j5.de *Merc* j5.de **Nat-m** j5.de* nat-s k2 nux-v j5.de ol-an j5.de *Phos* j5.de prun j5.de *Puls* j5.de raph j5.de rat j5.de sabin j5.de *Sep* j5.de* *Sil* j5.de sul-ac j5.de tab j5.de
- **yellow**: *Acon* j5.de agar hr1* agn j5.de *Alum* j5.de alum-p k2 alum-sil k2 alumn k2 am-c j5.de am-m j5.de ambr j5.de anac j5.de ang j5.de *Ant-c* j5.de arg-met j5.de* *Arg-n* sf1.de* *Ars* j5.de ars-i k2* *Ars-s-f* k2* aur j5.de aur-ar k2 *Aur-i* k2 *Aur-s* k2 bar-c j5.de bar-i k2 bar-s k2 *Bell* j5.de *Berb* j5.de bov j5.de *Bry* j5.de *Calc* j5.de calc-i br1 calc-s k2* calc-sil k2 *Cann-s* j5.de *Canth* j5.de caps j5.de *Carb-an* j5.de *Carb-v* j5.de* castm j5.de caust j5.de cench k2 *Cham* j5.de *Cic* j5.de cist k2* clem j5.de con j5.de cor-r j5.de croc j5.de cycl sf1.de *Daph* j5.de *Dros* j5.de dulc j5.de *Ery-a* br1 *Eug* j5.de form sf1.de gran j5.de *Graph* j5.de *Hep* j5.de *Hydr* k2* *Iod* j5.de kali-ar k2 kali-bi st* *Kali-c* j5.de* *Kali-chl* hr1 *Kali-m* kr1* kali-n j5.de *Kali-s* hr1* kali-sil k2 *Kreos* j5.de lac-ac sf1.de lach j5.de *Lyc* j5.de mag-c j5.de mag-m j5.de mag-s j5.de mang j5.de merc j5.de* mez j5.de mur-ac j5.de nat-ar a1 *Nat-c* j5.de *Nat-m* j5.de *Nat-p* hr1* nat-s hr1* *Nat-sil* k2 *Nit-ac* j5.de *Nux-v* j5.de ph-ac j5.de *Phos* j5.de prun j5.de *Puls* j5.de* rhus-t j5.de ruta j5.de sabad j5.de sabin j5.de sec j5.de *Sel* j5.de seneg j5.de *Sep* j5.de *Sil* j5.de* *Spig* j5.de *Stann* j5.de staph j5.de sul-ac j5.de* *Sul-i* k2 *Sulph* j5.de* sumb c1 *Thuj* j5.de* tung-met bdx1• verat j5.de viol-t j5.de zinc-p k2
- **yellowish** green: ars-i k2* *Calc-sil* k2* kali-bi st mang sf1.de *Merc* k2 nat-s k2 **Nit-ac** hr1* **Puls** hr1* sulph k2*

MUCOVISCIDOSIS: abrom-a mtf bar-m dgt1 calc-p mtf nicc vml3• op gk sel dgt1 tub mtf

MULTIPLE SCLEROSIS: *(↗Neurological)* acet-ac bro1 *Agar* mrr1 alum mrr1 arg-met jl arg-n bro1* ars bro1 asar mrr1 atro bro1* *Aur* bro1* aur-m c1 bar-c bro1* bar-m br1* bell bro1 bufo dgt1 calc bro1* carbn-s c1 caust bro1* chel bro1 chlorpr jl1 cocc mrr1 *Con* mrr1 crot-h bro1* *Cur* mrr1 des-ac jl3* diphtox jl2 form-ac mtf11 gels bro1* germ-met srj5• halo jl3* hyosin c1 *Hyosin-hbr* bro1 kali-p mrr1 *Lath* c1* lyc bro1* mand jl3* nat-c mrr1 nat-m ctc1* nux-v bro1* ox-ac bro1* p-benzq mtf11 *Phos* bro1* *Phys* c1* *Pic-ac* c1 *Plb* kr1* polio mtf11 psil jl3 sel jl1 sep gk sil bro1* staph mrr1 *Stry* bro1 sulph bro1* tarent c1* tetox mtf11 thala jl3 thuj bro1* toxo-g jl2 wildb c1

- **progressive**: coenz-q mtf11

MUMPS (See FACE - Inflammation - parotid - mumps)

MUSCULAR ATROPHY (See Atrophy - muscles; Complaints - muscles)

MUSCULAR DYSTROPHY (See Complaints - muscles; Dystrophy - muscles)

MUSHROOM POISONING: *Absin* br1* agar hr1* ars st1 atro bro1* *Bell* bro1* camph bro1* pyrog bro1*

MUSIC:

- **agg.**: *(↗Pulsation - externally - music - agg.; MIND - Ailments - music; MIND - Music - agg.; MIND - Sensitive - music)* *Acon* b2.de* aloe bg2 ambr b2.de* anac bg2 bry b2.de* bufo ptk1 calc b2.de* carb-an b2.de* *Cham* b2.de* coca-c sk4• *Coff* b2.de* croc bg2* *Dig* bg2* **Graph** bg2* ign b2.de* kali-c b2.de* kreos b2.de* *Lyc* b2.de* med ptk1 nat-c b2.de* nat-m ptk1 nat-s bg2 *Nux-v* b2.de* pall bg2* *Ph-ac* b2.de* phos b2.de* phys bg2 puls b2.de* *Sabin* b2.de* **Sep** b2.de* stann b2.de* staph b2.de* sulph bg2 sumb ptk1 symph fd3.de• tarent bg2* thuj bg2* tub ptk1 *Viol-o* b2.de* zinc b2.de* [ant-c stj2 ant-met stj2 zinc-i stj2 zinc-m stj2 zinc-n stj2 zinc-p stj2]
  - **menses**; during: nat-c ptk1
- **amel.**: aur bg2* bufo k2 cann-xyz bg2 croc bg2 positr nl2• sul-ac bg2 sumb bg2 tarent bg2* *Thuj* bg2 tub bg2
- **loud**, wild music | **amel.**: *Tarent* mrr1
- **organ** music | **agg.**: lyc b2.de*

- **piano** music | **agg.**: anac bg2 sep bg2 zinc bg2

MYALGIA (See Pain - muscles)

MYASTHENIA GRAVIS: *Alum* mtf *Caust* mtf33 con mtf cur mrr1* cytin sne diph mtf dub mtf gels mrr1 nat-m sne *Parathyr* mp1• pic-ac sne sep mtf stann mtf stroph-h mtf sulph sne thuj mtf

MYATROPHY, progressive spinal: *(↗Atrophy - muscles)* carbn-s c1 **Phos** hr1* phys c1 *Plb* hr1*

MYCOSIS FUNGOIDES: carb-an mtf11

MYOGELOSIS: kola stb3•

MYOPATHIA: *(↗Inflammation - muscles; Pain - muscles)* alum mrr1 *Caust* mtf33 germ-met srj5•

MYXEDEMA: *(↗Hypothyroidism; MIND - Cretinism)* *Ars* hr1* cortico jl3 dor c1* penic jl3 prim-o bro1 sulfa jl3 *Thyr* c1*

NARCOSIS (See Anesthesia [=narcosis] - ailments)

NARCOTICS: *(↗Medicine - allopathic - abuse; MIND - Delusions - opiate - influence; MIND - Morphinism)*

- **agg.**: *(↗MIND - Libertinism)* acet-ac c1* acon k* agar k* am-c bg2 apom bro1 ars k* aur k* *Aven* bro1* **Bell** k* bry k* calc k* *Camph* bro1* cann-i bro1 canth k* carb-v k* caust k* **Cham** k* chin k* cic bg2* cimic bro1 **Coff** k* colch k* croc k* cupr k* *Dig* k* dulc k* euph k* *Ferr* k* *Graph* k* hep k* *Hyos* k* ign k* *Ip* k* kali-perm sf1.de **Lach** k* lob st1 *Lyc* k* macro bro1 mag-s sp1 merc k* mosch k* mur-ac bg2* nat-c k* nat-m k* nat-p bg2* nit-ac k* nux-m k* **Nux-v** k* *Op* k* ox-ac st1 oxyg c1 passi sf1.de ph-ac k* phenob jl3 phos k* plat k* plb k* *Puls* k* rhus-t k* seneg k* *Sep* k* staph k* sulph k* thuj bro1 *Valer* k* verat k* zinc k* [caes-met stj2]
- **ailments** from: *(↗Psychotropic - ailments)* am-c ptk1 bell ptk1 carb-v ptk1 cham br1* *Coff* ptk1 ip c1 *Lach* ptk1 merc ptk1 *Nux-v* ptk1 op mrr1 oxyg c1 puls ptk1 verat c1 [heroin sdj2]
- **desire** for: *(↗Medicine - allopathic - addiction; MIND - Morphinism)* buth-a sp1 chlam-tr bcx2• op a1 tab a1* [caes-met stj2 heroin sdj2 oxyg stj2]
- **opium**, as if had taken: *(↗MIND - Delusions - opiate)* tela vh

NECROSIS: *(↗EXTREMITIES - Necrosis)* ancis-p tsm2 bac c2 bit-ar wht1• both tsm2 both-ax tsm2 calc-i ptk1 cench tsm2 chir-fl bnm4• cloth tsm2 crot-h tsm2 loxo-lae bnm12• naja tsm2 phos tl1 rad-br ptk1 sal-ac c2 sil c2 ther c2*

- **cold** applications | **amel.**: loxo-recl bnm10•
- **ice** | **amel.**: *(↗warm applications; warmth - heat)* loxo-recl bnm10•
- **warm** applications agg.: *(↗ice - amel.; warmth - heat)* loxo-recl bnm10•
- **warmth** agg. | **heat** agg.: *(↗ice - amel.; warm applications)* loxo-recl bnm10•

○ - **Bone**: *(↗Bones; Caries - bone; Softening; Softening bones)* *Ang* bro1* aran sf1.de *Arg-met* bro1* **Ars** k* asaf k* *Aur* bg2* aur-i bro1 *Aur-m* hr1* bac c1 bell k* both a1* *Calc* hr1* *Calc-f* hr1* calc-hp bro1* calc-i sf1.de calc-p bro1* calc-sil bro1 caps sf1.de carb-ac k* carb-an sf1.de chin bro1* *Cist* sf1.de con k* euph k* **Fl-ac** hr1* graph bro1* hecla br1* *Hep* k2* *Iod* bg2* kali-bi bro1* kali-c sf1.de kali-i hr1* kreos k* lach bro1* lap-a sf1.de lyc sf1.de mang k2* med bro1* *Merc* k* *Merc-c* mez k2* *Nat-sil-f* bro1 *Nit-ac* bg2* ph-ac k* *Phos* k* plat sf1.de plat-m bro1 plb k* psor sf1.de* puls bg2 *Sabin* k* sal-ac hr1* sec k* sil k* staph bro1 stront-c sf1.de sul-ac c1* sulph k* symph bro1 syph k2* teucr sf1.de thea bro1 ther k* thuj k* *Tub* br1* vitr-an bro1 vitr-cor br1
  - **avascular**: *(↗EXTREMITIES - Necrosis - hip - joint - avascular)* syph mtf

○ • **Femur**: stront-c bro1

- **Cartilages**: arg-met k2
- **Long** bones: ang bro1 asaf bro1 *Fl-ac* bro1 mez bro1 stront-c bro1

NEPHRITIS (See KIDNEYS - Inflammation)

NETTED CAPILLARIES (See SKIN - Nevi)

NEURALGIA (See Pain - neuralgic)

NEUROCIRCULATORY ASTHENIA (See CHEST - Palpitation - irritable)

NEUROLOGICAL complaints: *(↗Amyotrophic; Anesthesia [=insensibility]; Chorea; Convulsions; Multiple; Paralysis; Paralysis agitans; Poliomyelitis; Polyneuropathy)* agar bg2 *Alum-sil* br1 anac bg2 ant-t b7.de* arag br1 aran br1 *Arg-n* bg2* asar b7.de* asc-c br1 aven br1 bell br1 *Bry* b7.de* bufo br1 caj br1 calc mrr1 *Cann-i* br1 caps b7.de* *Caust* mrr1 cham b7.de* *Chin* b7.de* cic br1* cimic bg2 cina b7.de* coca bg2 *Cocc* b7.de* coff b7.de* *Con* mrr1 cupr b7.de* *Cur* mrr1 dubo-m br1 *Gels* br1 germ-met srj5• glon br1 gua br1 *Hyos* b7.de* ign b7.de* indg br1 kali-p br1 lach mrr1 lath mrr1 laur b7.de* lyss br1 *M-arct* b7.de* m-aust b7.de **Mag-p** bg2 med br1 mygal br1 nat-c mrr1 nat-m mrr1 nat-pyru mtf11 *Nux-v* b7.de* olnd br1 op mrr1 orig br1 oxyt br1 phos bg2 *Plb* br1* *Puls* b7.de* rhus-t b7.de* serot-cs mtf11 spartin-s br1 spig b7.de* stann br1 stram b7.de* syph jl2 tarent bg2* *Teucr* b7.de* valer b7.de* vanil br1 *Verat* b7.de* *Verbe-o* br1 *Viol-o* b7a.de xan br1 zinc bg2* [bell-p-sp dcm1]

- **accompanied** by:
  - **diabetes**: *(↗Diabetes mellitus - accompanied - feet)* helon hr1
  - **polyneuropathy**: brass-n-o srj5•
  - **sleepiness**: lath mrr1
  - **worms**; complaints of: art-v sf1.de
  - **yawning** agg.: lath mrr1

○ • **Spine**; complaints of (See BACK - Spine - accompanied - neurological)

  - **Tongue**:
    - **white** discoloration of the tongue | **Sides**: kali-ar kr1*
- **alternating** with | **physical** complaints: sabad ptk1*
- **children**:
  - **accompanied** by | **Teeth**; complaints of: calc-br mtf11
- **cigar**-makers; of: gels br1
- **discharges**; from suppression of: asaf bro1 merc bro1
- **eruptions**; after suppressed: caust mrr1 cic mrr1 **Cupr** mrr1 zinc mrr1
- **fright**; from: *(↗Convulsions - fright)* stram mrr1
- **injuries**; after: | **Head**; of the: *(↗Convulsions - injuries - head)* stram mrr1
- **irritation** of nervous system: verb br1 verbe-o br1
  - **children**; in: scut br1
- **masturbation**; from: *Gels* bro1 kali-p bro1
- **meningitis**; from: *(↗Convulsions - meningitis)* stram mrr1
- **menses**; from suppressed: *Cocc* b7a.de
- **tobacco**; from: gels bro1
  - **sedentary** habits; in persons with: sep bro1
- **vaccination**; after (See Vaccination - never)
- **worms**; from: cina bro1 psor bro1 sabad bro1

○ - **Central** nervous system carb-ac br1 yohim br1

- **Sympathetic** nervous system: kali-p br1

NEUROPATHY (See Neurological)

NEVER WELL SINCE a complaint (See Convalescence)

NICOTINISM (See Tobacco - agg. - nicotinism)

NITRATE OF SILVER: | **agg.**: nat-m bro1

NITRIC ACID; complaints after: *Petr* b4a.de

NODOSITIES:

○ - **Bones**: asaf bro1 *Aur-m* bro1 bufo bg2 *Cinnb* bro1 fl-ac bro1 kali-bi bg2* *Kali-i* bro1 merc bro1 mez bro1 nux-v bro1 phyt bro1 *Sil* bro1 *Still* bro1

- **Glands**; in: dulc bg2 graph bg2 iod bg2 phos bg2 phyt bg2 sil bg2

NOISES:

- **agg.**: **Acon** k* aloe bg2 alum k* am-c k* anac k* *Ang* k* ant-c k* *Arn* k* ars k* asar k* aur k* bar-c k* **Bell** k* borx b2.de* *Bry* k* calad k* *Calc* k* cann-s k* caps k* carb-an k* **Caust** k* *Cham* k* chin k* chinin-ar ptk1 cimic gk cocc k* **Coff** k* *Colch* k* *Con* k* ferr bro1* glon bro1 *Ign* k* iod k* ip k* kali-c k* kali-p k* *Lyc* k* lycpr bro1 m-ambo b2.de* m-arct b2.de* mag-c k* mag-m bro1* mang k* med bro1 merc k* *Nat-c* k* nit-ac k* nux-m bro1 *Nux-v* k* onos bro1 op k* *Ph-ac* k*

- **agg.**: ...
phos k* *Plat* k* puls k* sabad k* sang k* seneg k* *Sep* k* *Sil* k* *Spig* k* stann k* stram k* sulph k* syph k* tarent bro1* *Ther* k* tub ptk1 v-a-b jl2 *Valer* b7a.de zinc b2.de* [ant-met stj2 bar-i stj2 ferr-f stj2 ferr-lac stj2 ferr-n stj2 ferr-sil stj2 lith-i stj2 mang-i stj2 merc-i-f stj2 oxyg stj2 zinc-i stj2 zinc-m stj2 zinc-n stj2 zinc-p stj2]
- **amel.**: *(↗MIND - Sensitive - noise)* apoc k2* aur-ar k2 calad hr1* calc bg2 carb-an bg2 graph bg2* hell bg2 kali-ar k2* kali-c bg2 mag-p k2* med k2* puls bg2 pyrog k2* sec bg2 tarent k2*
- **rustling** of paper agg.: [ferr stj2 ferr-f stj2 ferr-lac stj2 ferr-n stj2 ferr-sil stj2]
- **voices** agg.; sound of: mur-ac bg2

NUMBNESS: **Acon** bg2* agar bro1* alum-sil bro1 *Ambr* bro1 *Anac* ptk1 ant-t b7a.de apis ptk1 *Aran* ptk1 ars bro1* bar-c ptk1 berb ptk1 bov bro1 cadm-s ptk1 *Calc* b4a.de *Calc-p* bro1 carb-v ptk1 caust b4a.de* *Cedr* bro1 cham bro1* *Chel* b7a.de chir-fl bnm4• cic b7a.de* cimic hr1 *Cocain* bro1 **Cocc** ptk1 cod bro1 con b4a.de* crot-h ptk1 diph ptk1 gels ptk1 glon ptk1 **Gnaph** bg2 **Graph** ptk1 helo bro1 helo-s bnm14• hipp jl2 hyos ptk1 ign bro1 irid-met bro1 kali-br bro1 *Kali-c* ptk1 *Kalm* ptk1 lappa ptk1 lyc b4a.de* mag-c ptk1 med ptk1 nat-m ptk1 nux-m ptk1 nux-v b7a.de* *Olnd* bro1* onos bro1 *Op* ptk1 *Ox-ac* bro1 *Ph-ac* ptk1 phos b4a.de* pic-ac ptk1 *Plat* bro1* *Plb* bro1* **Puls** ptk1 rad-br ptk1 raph bro1 **Rhus-t** bro1* *Sec* b7a.de* stann bro1 *Stram* ptk1 sul-i ptk1 tarent ptk1 tell ptk1 thal bro1 *Thuj* b4a.de* xan ptk1 zinc b4a.de*

- **left** side of body: sumb br1
- **morning**: ambr ptk1
- **accompanied** by:
  - **coldness**: plat ptk1 sumb ptk1
  - **crawling**: sec bg2 tab bg2
  - **dropsy** (See Dropsy - general - accompanied - numbness)
  - **heat**; flushes of: agath-a nl2•
- **bad** news; after: calc-p ptk1
- **chill**; during: *Puls* b7a.de
- **cold** agg.; becoming: *Sumb* br1
- **cold**; exposure to: acon k2
- **fever**; during: cedr bro1
- **hysteria**; in: ign mrr1
- **lying** agg.: zinc ptk1
- **menses**; during: graph bg2
- **music** agg.: sabin c1
- **old** people; in: *Ambr* br1
- **pain**:
  - **after**: acon bg2 agar bg2 asaf k2 graph bg2 mez bg2 plat bg2
  - **during**: *(↗during; painful; Pain - neuralgic - accompanied - numbness)* *Acon* bro1 agar br1 asaf ptk1 calc-p tl1 cann-i bro1 cham bro1* *Cimic* bro1 cocc tl1 *Coloc* ptk1 gnaph ptk1 hyper ptk1 kalm bro1* lat-m bnm6• mez ptk1 nat-m ptk1 plat bro1* puls ptk1 rhus-t bro1* stann bro1 staph bro1
- **paroxysmal**: *Kali-br* hr1
- **sedation**; as if under: convo-s sp1
- **sleep** | **after** | **agg.**: asaf
  - **during** | **agg.**: bufo bg2
- **spots**, in: ambr ptk1 bufo br1* cadm-s k2* caust st1 ign gk *Lyc* k* *Plat* k* sul-i bg*
- **stool** agg.; during: *Ars* b4a.de
- **unilateral**: ign gk
- **waves**; in: agath-a nl2•
- ○ **Affected** parts: *Acon* k* *Agar* bg2 alum k* alum-sil k2 ambr k* *Anac* k* ang b2.de* ant-t k* aran bg2 arn *Ars* k* ars-i *Asaf* k* aur k* aur-ar k2 aur-i k2 bell k* borx k* bov k* bry k* calc k* calc-sil k2 cann-s k* carb-an k* carb-v k* caust k* **Cham** k* chel k* chin k* cic k* cina k* *Cocc* k* coff k* colch k* coloc k* **Con** k* croc k* cupr k* cycl k* dig k* dulc k* elaps euphr k* ferr k* ferr-ar ferr-p *Gnaph* k* *Graph* k* hell k* helo-s bnm14• hep k* hyos k* hyper br1 ign k* iod k* kali-c k* *Kali-n* b2.de* **Kalm** bg2 kreos k* led bg* *Lyc* k* m-arct b2.de m-aust b2.de mag-m k* mang bg2 merc k* mez k* mur-ac k* nat-m k* nux-m k* nux-v k* *Olnd* k* petr k* ph-ac k* phos k* **Plat** k* **Plb** k* **Puls** k* rheum k* rhod k* *Rhus-t* k* ruta k* samb k* sec k* sep k* sil k* spong k* stann k* staph k* stram k* stront-c k* sul-ac k* sul-i k2 sulph k* thuj k* tung-met bdx1• verat k* verb k* viol-o k* zinc k* [heroin sdj2]
  - ○ **Bruised** parts: *Arn*
- **Blood** vessels; along: aml-ns bg2
- **Body**; of whole: acet-ac ptk1 asc-t ptk1 bar-m ptk1 cedr ptk1 chel ptk1 cimic hr1 *Kali-br* ptk1 ox-ac ptk1

Numbness – Body; of whole: ...
  - **accompanied** by | **Head**; pain in (See HEAD - Pain - accompanied - numbness - body)
- **Bones**: abrot bg2 chin bg2
- **Externally**: abrot absin acet-ac a1 *Acon* k* acon-f a1* adam srj5• aesc bg2* agar k* agath-a nl2• ail k* aloe bg2* alum k* alum-p k2* alum-sil k2* alumn k2 am-c k* am-m k* *Ambr* k* **Anac** k* ancis-p tsm2 ang b2.de* anh sp1 ant-c k* *Ant-t* k* *Apis* k* aran sf1.de aran-ix sp1 *Arg-met* bg2* *Arg-n* arn k* *Ars* k* ars-i asaf k* asar k* asc-t a1 aur k* *Bapt* k* *Bar-c* k* bar-m *Bell* k* **Berb** bism k* both tsm2* both-ax tsm2 bov k* brom bry k* bufo bung-fa tsm2 cact k* cadm-s k2 caj k* calad hr1 calc k* *Calc-p* hr1* calc-sil k2 camph k* cann-i k* cann-s k* canth k* caps a1 carb-ac k* *Carb-an* k* *Carb-v* k* **Carbn-s** *Caust* k* cedr k* cench tsm2 *Cham* k* *Chel* k* chin k* chlor *Cic* k* cimic k* cinnb cob-n sp1 coca **Cocc** k* cod a1* colch k* coloc k* *Con* k* conin c1* croc k* *Crot-c* k* *Crot-h* k* crot-t j5.de cupr k* cur cycl j5.de dendr-pol tsm2 dig k* dios k* dulc k* elaps euph bg2 euphr k* falco-pe nl2• ferr k* fl-ac k* form sf1.de gast a1 *Gels* k* *Glon* *Gnaph* **Graph** k* *Guaj* j5.de* haliae-lc srj5• *Hell* k* *Helo* c1 helo-s c2* hep b2.de* hydr-ac hydrog srj2• hydroph rsj6• **Hyos** k* *Hyper* k* *Ign* k* iod k* ip k* irid-met c1* iris kali-ar k2 kali-bi bg2 kali-br k* **Kali-c** k* *Kali-fcy* kali-i bg2 *Kali-n* k* kali-p kalm k* keroso a1 kreos bg2* lacer c1 lach k* lath sf1.de laur k* *Led* k* lepi a1 **Lyc** k* *M-ambo* b2.de* m-aust b2.de* mag-c br1 mag-m k* mag-s sp1 mand mg1.de mang bg2* *Merc* k* *Mez* b2.de* *Mosch* k* *Nat-m* j5.de* neon srj5• nit-ac bg2 nitro-o a1 *Nux-m* k* *Nux-v* k* olnd k* onos k* **Op** k* orot-ac rly4• *Ox-ac* k* oxyt par k* petr k* **Ph-ac** k* *Phos* k* phys k* phyt sf1.de *Pic-ac* k* plac-s rly4• *Plat* k* **Plb** k* *Plb-xyz* c2 positr nl2• *Puls* k* raph a1* rheum j5.de* rhod k* *Rhus-t* k* samb sf1.de sang bg2 *Sec* k* *Sep* k* *Sil* k* sphing k* spig k* spong k* *Stann* bg2 staph k* **Stram** k* stront-c bg2* sul-ac bg2 sulph k* tab k* tanac a1 tang a1 tarent a1 teucr j5.de* thea thuj j5.de* thymol sp1 *Urt-u* k* valer k* verat k* verat-v verb k* vesp br1 vip a1 xan mrr1 *Zinc* k* zinc-p k2 zing sf1.de [heroin sdj2]
  - **one** side: ars ptk1 caust b4a.de* chel ptk1 nat-m ptk1 phos ptk1 *Puls* ptk1
  - **right** half of body: ars bg2* caust ptk1 elaps ptk1 lyc h2 naja ptk1
  - **left** half of body: acon vh1 ars ptk1 caust k* *Lach* vh mez h2 sumb ptk1 xan c1*
  - **morning**: ambr br1
  - **night**: sil h2
    - **waking**; on: mez h2
  - **alternating** with hypersensitiveness: plat bg2
  - **bruised** part, in the: arn
  - **convulsions**; before epileptic: bufo k*
  - **feels** neither heat nor cold: berb bg1*
  - **menopause**; during: *Cimic*
  - ○ **Whole** body: acon a1 ambr hr1 androc srj1• apis a1 **Arg-n** k* asc-t a1 bar-m k* bell a1 caj a1 caps h1* cedr k* chel h1* crot-c a1 gels a1 glon a1 gymno a1 kali-bi a1 **Kali-br** k* kreos a1 lyss merc a1 nitro-o a1 nux-v h1 **Olnd** k* *Ox-ac* k* pic-ac a1 tab a1 tarent a1
    - **pain**; during: asc-t vh
- **Fibrous** tissue: cot br1
- **Glands**: anac k* asaf k* bell k* cocc k* con k* lyc k* *Plat* k* puls k* rhus-t k* sep k* sil k* spong k*
- **Internally**: acon k* agath-a nl2• alum br1 alum-sil k2 am-c k* ambr k* *Ars* k* asaf k* aur-i k2 bar-c k* *Bell* k* *Bov* k* calc k* *Calc-p* br1 carb-an k* carbn-s k* caust k* cham k* chin k* cina k* coff k* colch k* con k* crot-t k* cupr k* dig k* ferr k* galla-q-r nl2• **Gels** k* graph k* hydroph rsj6• *Hyos* k* ign k* *Kali-br* k* kali-c k* laur k* lyc k* m-arct b2.de *M-aust* b2.de mag-c k* mag-m k* merc k* mur-ac k* nat-m k* nit-ac k* nux-m k* olnd k* *Op* k* petr k* phos k* **Plat** k* plb k* puls k* ran-b k* rheum k* sars k* sec br1 seneg k* sil k* *Spig* k* stann k* stram k* stront-c k* thuj k* valer k* verat k* vesp br1 xan mrr1
- **Lower** half of body, of: *Spong* b7a.de*
- **Mucous** membranes: acon bg2 agar bg2 arg-met bg2 bar-c bg2 kali-br bg2 nux-m bg2
- **Muscles**: cot br1
- **Nerves**: acon bg2 con bg2 sec b7a.de
- **Painful** parts: *(↗pain - during; Pain - neuralgic - accompanied - numbness)* alum-sil k2 cham br1
- **Parts**, lain on: am-c k* *Ambr* arn bg2* ars *Bar-c* k* bufo bg2 *Calc* k* calc-sil k2 carb-an bg1 *Carb-v* k* *Carbn-s* *Chin* bg2* cimic cop *Graph* ign kali-c *Lach* lyc gk mag-c bg1* *Nat-m* k* pall st *Phos* **PULS** k ●* **Rhus-t** k* sep st sil k* staph gk sumb zinc
- **Side** lain on | **Not** lain on: fl-ac ptk1

- **Single** parts, in: *Acon* k* agar k* alum k* alum-p k2* alum-sil k2* am-c k* am-m k* *Ambr* k* *Anac* k* ang b2.de* anh sp1 ant-c k* *Ant-t* k* aran ptk1* aran-ix sp1 *Arg-met* k* *Arg-n* arn k* ars ars-i asaf k* asar k* aur k* aur-ar k2 aur-i k2* aur-s k2* *Bar-c* k* bar-s k2* bell k* borx k* bov k* bry k* bufo bg2 cadm-s k2* *Calc* k* calc-i k2* *Calc-p* calc-sil k2* camph k* cann-s k* canth k* caps k* **Carb-an** k* *Carb-v* k* **Carbn-s** caust k* *Cham* k* chel k* *Chin* k* cic k* cina k* **Cocc** k* coff b2.de* colch k* *Coloc* k* con k* **Croc** k* cupr b2.de* cycl b2.de* dig k* dros k* dulc k* euph k* euphr k* *Ferr* k* ferr-ar k2* ferr-p **Graph** k* *Guaj* k* ham fd3.de• hep k* hydrog srj2• hyos k* *Ign* k* iod k* ip k* kali-ar **Kali-c** k* kali-chl k13 *Kali-fcy* kali-m k2 *Kali-n* b2.de* kali-p kali-s k2* kreos k* laur k* led k* **Lyc** k* m-ambo b2.de *M-arct* b2.de *M-aust* b2.de mag-c k* *Mag-m* k* mang k* **Merc** k* mez k* mosch k* *Mur-ac* k* naja bg2 nat-c k* *Nat-m* k* nat-p nit-ac k* *Nux-v* k* olnd k* op k* *Par* k* *Petr* k* ph-ac b2.de* *Phos* k* plat k* plb k* **Puls** k* *Rheum* k* *Rhod* k* **Rhus-t** k* sabad k* sabin k* samb k* *Sars* k* *Sec* k* *Sep* k* **Sil** k* spig k* spong k* squil k* stann k* staph k* *Stram* k* sul-ac k* sul-i k2* *Sulph* k* teucr k* thuj k* valer k* *Verat* k* *Zinc* k* **Zinc-p** k2*

○ • **Peripheral**: anh sp1

- **Upper** half of body, of: *Bar-c* k*

NURSING, suckling agg.: (↗*Loss - blood; Loss - fluids; Trembling - externally - nursing; Weakness - nursing women)* abrot sf1.de *Acet-ac* bro1 acon b2.de* agn b2.de* ant-t kk2.de ars b2.de* *Bell* b2.de* *Borx* b2.de* **Bry** b2.de* **Calc** b2.de* *Calc-p* bg2* carb-an b2.de* carb-v b2.de* carc mlr1• castor-eq kk2.de caust kk2.de *Cham* b2.de* chel b2.de* *Chin* b2.de* chinin-ar sf1.de chion c1 cina b2.de* *Cocc* kr1 con k* crot-h kr1 crot-t kk2.de *Dulc* b2.de* ferr b2.de* graph b2.de* ign b2.de* iod b2.de* ip b2.de* kali-bi bg *Kali-c* b2.de* lac-c kk2.de lach b2.de* lyc b2.de* *Merc* b2.de* mill kk2.de nat-c b2.de* nat-m b2.de* *Nit-ac* kk2.de nux-v b2.de* olnd bg2* *Ph-ac* b2.de* phel bg2* phos b2.de* **Phyt** bg2* **Puls** b2.de* rheum b2.de* *Rhus-t* k* samb b2.de* sec b2.de* sel b2.de* **Sep** b2.de* **Sil** k* spig b2.de* squil b2.de* stann b2.de* *Staph* b2.de* stram b2.de* *Sulph* b2.de* zinc b2.de*

NURSLINGS: (↗*Children - newborns)* abrot mtf33 *Acon* kk2.de aeth kk2.de* ant-c kk2.de* ant-t kk2.de *Arn* kk2.de *Ars* kk2.de aur mtf33 bar-c mtf33 *Bell* kk2.de* **Borx** kk2.de* **Bry** kk2.de bufo mtf33 **Calc** kk2.de* *Calc-p* kk2.de* calc-s mtf33 *Camph* kk2.de carb-v kk2.de* carc mtf33 **Cham** kk2.de* chin kk2.de* cina kk2.de* coloc kk2.de crot-t kk2.de dulc kk2.de ferr kk2.de graph kk2.de hep kk2.de ign kk2.de iod mtf33 *Ip* kk2.de kali-c kk2.de* lach kk2.de* *Lyc* kk2.de* *Mag-c* kk2.de* med mtf33 *Merc* kk2.de* nat-c kk2.de nat-m kk2.de **Nat-p** kk2.de nat-s mtf33 nit-ac mtf33 nux-v kk2.de* **Op** kk2.de* ph-ac kk2.de phos kk2.de plb mtf33 podo kk2.de psor kk2.de* **Puls** kk2.de* rheum c2* *Rhus-t* kk2.de samb kk2.de sanic mtf33 sec kk2.de sep mtf33 *Sil* kk2.de* stann kk2.de staph kk2.de stram kk2.de *Sulph* kk2.de* syph mtf33 tarent mtf33 verat kk2.de* zinc kk2.de

NUX VOMICA; abuse of: *Zinc* b4a.de

OBESITY: (↗*ABDOMEN - Obesity)* *Acon* bg2 adam srj5• adon sf1.de agar k* ail c1 alco a1 all-s br1* *Am-br* hr1* *Am-c* h2* *Am-m* k* ambr k* **Anac** gg *Ang* b2.de* *Ant-c* k* ant-t b2.de* apis bg2 aq-mar mgm• aran-ix mg1.de arist-cl mg1.de* arn b2.de* *Ars* hr1* *Asaf* k* *Aur* k* bac c1 bar-c k* *Bell* b2.de* berb br1 blatta-o c1* borx k* brom bg2* bry k* bufo ptk1 calad sf1.de **Calc** k* calc-act sf1.de *Calc-ar* k* calc-caust sf1.de calc-o ttm2.fr *Calc-p* mrr1 calc-s mrr1 *Calo* br1* camph k* canth k* **Caps** k* carb-v bg2* carc zzh *Carl* br1* caust bg2 cham b2.de* chin k* chlorpr c1 cic b2.de* cimic mg1.de* clem b2.de* *Coc-c* hr1* coca c1 cocc k* coloc b2.de* con k* cortiso jl3 *Croc* b2.de* crot-h j5.de* *Cupr* k* cyna jl3 dig b2.de* dulc mrr1 *Elaps* st euph k* euphr hr1* falco-pe nl2• **Ferr** k* ferr-i mrr1 *Fuc* c1* gamb lwz1 gink-b sbd1• glycyr-g cte1• **Graph** k* guaj k* hell b2.de* *Hura* st *Hyos* b2.de* ign mrr1 iod k* ip k* *Kali-bi* k* kali-br hr1* *Kali-c* k* kola stb3• lac-c sne *Lac-d* k* lac-h sze9• lach k* laur k* lith-c c1* lob br1* lob-e c1 *Lyc* k* lycpr c1* mag-c k* mag-p c1 mang-act bro1 med st1 merc k* merc-d sf1.de* mur-ac k* nat-ar a1 nat-c k* **Nat-m** ●* nux-m k* nux-v gl1.fr• olnd k* op k* ozone sde2• pert-vc vk9 *Phos* bg2* **Phyt** bg2* pitu-a vml2• plat k* plb k* positr nl2• *Puls* k* rauw sp1 rheum b2.de* rhus-t bg2 rumx ptk1 ruta fd4.de sabad k* sabal c1* sacch c1* sars k* sel bg2 seneg k* sep k* sil k* spig k* spong k* stram b2.de* stront-c bg2 stroph-h br1 *Sulph* k* thuj k* *Thyr* a1* *Thyroiod* c1* tus-fr a1* valer bg2 vanil fd5.de verat k* viol-o b2.de* [am-caust stj2 am-f stj2 *Arg-n* stj2 aur-m stj2 aur-s stj2 bar-br stj2 bar-i stj2 bar-met stj2 bism-sn stj2 calc-lac stj2 calc-m stj1 calc-met stj2 chr-m stj2 chr-met stj2 chr-s stj2 cinnb stj2 *Ferr-n* stj2 hafn-met stj2 irid-met stj2 kali-met stj2 lanth-met stj2 lith-f stj2 lith-i stj2 lith-met stj2 lith-p stj2 lith-s stj2 *Mag-n* stj2 *Mang-n* stj2 merc-i-f stj2 moly-met stj2 nicc-met stj2 nicc-s stj2 *Nitro* stj2 osm-met stj2 plb-m stj2 plb-p stj2 rhen-met stj2 tant-met stj2 thal-met stj2 tung-met stj2 *Zinc-n* stj2]

Obesity: ...

- **accompanied** by:
  - • **appetite**; diminished: gink-b sbd1•
  - • **goitre** (See EXTERNAL - Goitre - accompanied - obesity)
  - • **indigestion** (See STOMACH - Indigestion - accompanied - obesity)
  - • **respiration**:
    - ⁝ **asthmatic** (See RESPIRATION - Asthmatic - accompanied - obesity)
    - ⁝ **difficult** (See RESPIRATION - Difficult - accompanied - obesity)
    - ⁝ **wheezing** (See RESPIRATION - Wheezing - accompanied - obesity)
  - • **sexual** organs; underdevelopment of: hydroq mtf11
  - • **weakness** (See Weakness - accompanied - obesity)

○ • **Heart**; weak (See CHEST - Weakness - heart - accompanied - obesity)

- **children**; in: (↗*ABDOMEN - Distension - children - potbellied)* *Ant-c* hr1* *Bad* hr1* bar-c bro1* bell ptk1 *Brom* b4a.de **Calc** b4.de* *Caps* k2* cina br1* *Coloc* b4a.de *Ferr* bro1* graph b4a.de* guaj b4a.de *Ip* hr1* *Kali-bi* hr1* kali-c mtf33 puls mtf33 sacch c1* sars b4a.de seneg c1* sulph b4a.de
  - • **nurslings**: acon tl1 lap-a br1
  - • **thyroid** gland; from dysfunction of: influ mtf11
- **endocrine**: cimic mtf11 hypoth mtf11 pitu-gl mtf11
- **flabby**: lac-d mtf11
- **menopause**; during: calc-ar c1 **Graph** sf1.de* sep sf1.de
- **nutrition**; from improper: calc tl1 graph tl1
- **old** people; in: am-c st1 **Aur** st1 bar-c sf1.de* fl-ac st1 **Kali-c** k1* op st1 sec st1
- **overweight**; slightly: [brom stj1]
- **sadness**; during (See MIND - Sadness - obesity)
- **women**; in: am-c br1 calc-ar br1 cer-ox br1
  - • **accompanied** by | **menses**; painful (See FEMALE - Menses - painful - accompanied - obesity)
- **young** people; in: *Ant-c* j5.de* calc j5.de calc-act sf1.de lach sf1.de

○ - **Abdomen**: pip-n a1

- **Legs** thin; body fat but: am-c dw1* *Am-m* k* ant-c mtf33 plb ptk1 [graph stj2 lith-c stj2]
- **Thighs** and buttocks: (↗*Emaciation - extending - downward)* lyc mrr1 nat-m mrr1

OBSTINATE complaints (See Remedies - fail)

OBSTRUCTION:

- **sensation** of: anac ptk1 coc-c ptk1 med ptk1 *Sangin-n* br1 spong ptk1

○ • **Internal** parts: ang b2.de* bism b2.de* bry b2.de* cham b2.de* chel b2.de* chin b2.de* guaj b2.de* m-ambo b2.de* meny b2.de* nat-c b2.de* nux-m b2.de* **Op** b2.de* phos b2.de* puls b2.de* rhus-t b2.de* sep b2.de* spig b2.de* spong b2.de* *Tab* bg2 verb b2.de*

ODOR OF THE BODY: (↗*EXTREMITIES - Odor)*

- **cadaverous**: ars bg2 pyrog bg2
- **cheese**; like old: bry ptk1 calc bg2 *Con* bg2 *Hep* bg2* sanic ptk1 sulph bg2
- **offensive**: (↗*CHEST - Perspiration - axilla - offensive; EXTREMITIES - Odor)* ail ptk1 *Aq-mar* jl arn bg2* *Ars* bg2* asaf ptk1 aster sze10• aur-s wbt2• *Bapt* bg2* bism bg2 brom bg2 bry bg* cadm-s mrr1 carb-ac bg2* carb-an ptk1 **Carb-v** bg* chin bg2 con ptk1 crot-h ptk1 graph bg2* *Guaj* br1* hep bg2* kali-chl ptk1 kali-i bg2* kali-p bg* kreos bg2* lach bg2* med ptk1 *Merc* bg2* mur-ac ptk1 *Nit-ac* bg2* osm ptk1 phos ptk1 podo bg* **Psor** bg2* pyrog bg2* *Rhus-t* bg2* sabin ptk1 sacch-l c2 sec bg* sep bg2* *Sil* bg* sol-t-ae c2 stann ptk1 stram bg2 sul-ac ptk1 sulph bg2* *Syph* ptk1 tell bg* thuj bg2* tril-p ptk1 ust ptk1 wies c2
  - • **cancerous** affections; in: bufo gm1 cinnm br1 strych-g br1
  - • **himself**; to: sulph bg2
  - • **inflamed** parts: *Kreos* mrr1
  - • **menses**; during: psor ptk1 stann ptk1
  - • **suicidal** thoughts; with (See MIND - Suicidal - thoughts - offensive)
- **oily**: petr bg2

- **sour**: *(↗Sourness)* calc bg2* cham bro1 colos bro1 graph bro1 hep bg2* kreos bro1 lac-d bro1 *Mag-c* bg2* *Rheum* bg2* sul-ac bg2* sulph bro1 urt-u bg2
  - **children**; in: med ptk1
  - **dentition**; during: kreos bro1
- **strong**: rhus-t bg2 stram bg2
- **urinous**: ust ptk1
- **voluptuous** | **menses**; during: *Stram* b7.de*

ODORS:
- **acute** smell (See NOSE - Smell - acute)
- **dirty** clothes; of: | **agg.**: carb-an bg2*
- **offensive** | **eggs**; spoiled: arn ptk1 asc-t ptk1 cham ptk1 psor ptk1 staph ptk1 sulph ptk1
- **sensitive** to (See MIND - Sensitive - odors)

OEDEMA (See Dropsy - external; Swelling - puffy)

OFFENSIVENESS, fetor (See Odor of - offensive)

OLD AGE: *(↗Weakness - old)*
- **old** people; in: *Abies-n* vh1 acet-ac c1* *Acon* *Agar* k* *Agn* st *All-s* st *Aloe* k* *Alum* bg2* alumn k* *Am-c* k* am-m st **Ambr** k* *Ammc* k* *Anac* k* *Ant-c* k* ant-t k* apis c1 *Arg-n* st *Arn* bg2* *Ars* k* ars-s-f k2 **Aur** k* bapt c1 **Bar-c** k* *Bar-m* br1* bism b7a.de *Bry* b7.de* calc bg2* *Calc-p* camph k* cann-i st caps br1* *Carb-an* k* *Carb-v* k* carc gk6 *Caust* k* *Cham* c1* chin b7.de* chinin-s j5.de* chlam-tr bcx2• cic k* cit-v bro1 **Coca** cocc b7a.de* coff br1 *Colch* k* *Con* k* crot-h bro1 cupr k2 dig st *Fl-ac* k* gali mtf11 gamb st gins bg2 *Graph* c1* ham fd3.de• *Hydr* kr1* hydrog srj2• hyos bg2 *Iod* k* *Irid-met* c1* *Iris* st juni-c br1 kali-ar st kali-bi st **Kali-c** k* kreos bg2* **Lach** b7a.de* **Lyc** k* mag-f jl merc st* *Mill* kr1* nat-c st *Nat-m* k* nat-s c1 *Nit-ac* k* nux-m c1* nux-v b7.de* **Op** k* orch c1* *Ov* st perh jl ph-ac bg2 *Phos* bg2* puls st rhus-t bg2 ruta bg2* sabad sabal ptk2 sanic ptk1 sarcol-ac jl sars ptk1 **Sec** k* **Sel** k* *Seneg* k* sep st *Sil* st* squil ptk1 stann bg2 sul-ac k* *Sulph* b4a.de* sumb ptk1 syph ptk1 ter c1* **Teucr** k1* thiosin st thuj st tub ptk1 *Verat* bg2* zinc st
  - **bachelors**; old: con br1
  - **beer** drinkers; old: aloe br1
  - **maids**; old: bov ptk1 cocc ptk1 con br1* lil-t ptk1 mag-m ptk1 plat ptk1
  - **men**; old: bar-c br1 sabal ptk1 *Sel* br1
  - **women**; old: | **thin**, scrawny: sec br1
- **premature**: *(↗FACE - Expression - old)* *Agn* hr1* alco a1 alum br1* *Ambr* k* ant-c bg3 anthraci vh arg-met k2* arg-n ptk1* ars bg3 *Aur* bg3 *Bar-c* k* berb k2* bufo carb-ac bg3 carb-v k2 carc svb• chinin-s k1 coca a1 *Con* bg2* cortico jl3 *Cupr* k2 des-ac jl3 esp-g jl3* *Fl-ac* bg2* gins bg3 hydr bg3 hydrog srj2• *Kali-c* k* kres jl3 **Lach** bg3 lyc k* mag-f mg1.de nit-ac bg3 nux-v k2 op a1 phos bg3 prot jl3* psor sf1.de* reser jl3 sars k2 sec bg3 **Sel** k* sep k2 staph sf1.de stram c1* sulph sf1.de sumb ptk1 verat bg3 *Vip* a1*
  - **men**; in: med jl2
  - **sexual** excess; from: agn br1
- **sadness**; with (See MIND - Sadness - old)
- **senile** decay: *Agn* bro1 *Arg-n* bro1 ars bro1 *Bar-c* bro1 cann-i bro1 *Con* bro1 cordyc mp4• fl-ac bro1 ham fd3.de• iod bro1 *Lyc* bro1 med jl2 orch c2 *Ov* bro1 phos bro1 psor mtf11 thiosin bro1

ONANISM (See Masturbation)

OPENING:
- **shutting**; and | **sensation** of: *Cann-xyz* bg2

OPENING THE EYES:
- **agg.**: acon b2.de* arn b2.de* aur b2.de* bell b2.de* borx b2.de* *Bry* b2.de* *Calc* b2.de* canth b2.de* chin b2.de* cic b2.de* *Clem* b2.de* coff b2.de* con b2.de* *Croc* b2.de* euph b2.de* *Ign* b2.de* *Lyc* b2.de* m-ambo b2.de* mag-m b2.de* *Nux-v* b2.de* phos b2.de* plat b2.de* *Spig* b2.de* tab bro1 zinc b2.de*
- **amel.**: agar b2.de* arn b2.de* ars b2.de* *Bell* b2.de* **Bry** b2.de* calad b2.de* calc b2.de* carb-an b2.de* caust b2.de* chel b2.de* *Chin* b2.de* *Clem* b2.de* con b2.de* croc b2.de* dig b2.de* ferr b2.de* *Hell* b2.de* hep b2.de* ign b2.de* kali-c b2.de* lach b2.de* *Led* b2.de* m-aust b2.de *Mag-m* b2.de* mang b2.de* nux-v b2.de* op b2.de* ph-ac b2.de* phos b2.de* *Puls* b2.de* sars b2.de* sep b2.de* spong b2.de* staph b2.de* sulph b2.de* thuj b2.de*

OPENING THE MOUTH:
- **agg.**: am-m b2.de* *Ang* b2.de* arum-t ptk1 bry b2.de* caust b2.de* cham b2.de* cocc b2.de* dros b2.de* hep b2.de* *Lach* ptk1 **Merc** b2.de* merc-c ptk1 nux-v b2.de* petr b2.de* *Phos* b2.de* puls b2.de* rhus-t b2.de* *Sabad* b2.de* sabin b2.de* sil b2.de* spig b2.de* spong b2.de* sul-ac b2.de* thuj b2.de* verat b2.de*

Opening the mouth: ...
- **amel.**: mez ptk1 nat-c b4.de

OPERATION; ailments from (See Injuries - operation - ailments)

ORGASM of BLOOD: *(↗Congestion - blood; Heat - flushes; MIND - Anxiety - flushes)* acet-ac k2 **Acon** k* aloe alum k* alum-p k2* alum-sil k2* alumn *Am-c* k* *Am-m* k* *Ambr* k* *Aml-ns* k* androc srj1• ant-c ant-t k* anthraco kr1 arg-met k* **Arg-n** k* *Arn* k* ars b2.de* *Ars-i* *Asar* k* astac a1 **Aur** k* aur-ar k2 *Aur-i* k2* aur-s k2* bar-c k* bar-s k2* **Bell** k* berb k* borx bg2* *Bov* k* *Bry* k* **Calc** k* *Calc-ar* calc-i k2* calc-s calc-sil k2 cann-i cann-s k* carb-an k* *Carb-v* k* **Carbn-s** *Caust* k* cench k2 *Cham* k* chel hr1 chin k* cina cocc coff k* *Con* k* corn hr1 *Croc* k* *Cupr* dig k* digin a1 dulc k* erig mg1.de **Ferr** k* ferr-ar *Ferr-i* ferr-p fl-ac bg *Gels* k* **Glon** k* *Graph* k* guaj k* *Hep* k* hydrog srj2• hyos ign k* imp a1 *Iod* k* jab bg2 kali-bi bg2 kali-br bg2 *Kali-c* k* kali-p kali-s kali-sil k2* kiss k* **Kreos** k* **Lach** k* laur bg lil-t k* lipp a1 **Lyc** k* m-aust b2.de* mag-c bg2 mag-m k* mang *Meli* k* *Merc* k* merl *Mill* k2* mosch k* nat-c k* *Nat-m* k* nat-p nit-ac k* *Nux-m* k* *Nux-v* k* *Op* k* ox-ac k2* *Petr* k* **Ph-ac** b2.de* **Phos** k* plb *Puls* k* rhod *Rhus-t* k* sabad k* sabin k* *Samb* k* sang k* *Sars* k* *Sel* bg2 *Seneg* k* *Sep* k* *Sil* k* **Spong** k* *Stann* k* staph k* **Stram** *Stront-c* bg2* stroph-h ptk1 *Sul-ac* bg2* sul-i k2* **Sulph** k* tab k* tell ter bg2 *Thuj* k* til a1 ust bg2 valer bg2 verat k* voes a1
- **morning**:
  - **rising** | **amel.**: nux-v
  - **sleep**:
    - **after** restless: calc
    - **during** | **agg.**: ang
  - **waking**; on: calc h2 graph kali-c h2 lyc nux-v
- **evening**: arn k* *Asar* k* *Caust* dig digin a1 kali-c h2 lyc k* *Merc* hr1* petr k* phos k* rhus-t k* sars hr1* thuj k*
  - **lying** down agg.; after: ign samb sars h2 sil
  - **sexual** excitement; during: clem
  - **sitting** | **amel.**: thuj k*
- **night**: *(↗Heat - flushes - night; SLEEP - Sleeplessness - menopause)* *Am-c* k* arg-n k* *Calc* k* *Carb-an* k* *Carb-v* hep k* ign mag-c *Merc* k* mur-ac k* *Nat-c* nat-m k* *Phos* k* *Puls* ran-b raph hr1* senn st1 *Sep* k* *Sil* k* *Sulph* k*
  - **anxiety**; with (See MIND - Anxiety - night - orgasm)
  - **bed**, drives him out of: iod k*
  - **beer**; after: sulph
- **accompanied** by | **vomiting** (See STOMACH - Vomiting - accompanied - blood)
- **anxiety** with: *(↗MIND - Anxiety - flushes - during)* *Acon* hr1* aloe kr1 am-m hr1* *Bar-c* hr1* chel hr1*
- **ascending** stairs agg.: thuj h1
- **burning**:
  - ○ **Hands**; with burning in: **Sulph** kr1
  - **Skin**, of: *Sang* kr1
- **coition**; after: am-c *Sep*
- **cough** agg.; during: arn b7.de* *Calc* bg2 chin b7.de*
- **disagreeable** news, from: *(↗MIND - Ailments - bad)* lach k*
- **eating**:
  - **amel.**: alum chin k*
  - **warm** food agg.: mag-c
- **emotions**; after: *(↗FACE - Discoloration - red - excitement; MIND - Blushing; MIND - Timidity - bashful)* *Acon* apis *Aur* aur-m-n wbt2• *Bell* bry calc **Cham** coff colch *Coloc* *Con* cupr **Hyos** **Ign** kali-c *Kali-p* *Lach* lyc mag-c nat-m *Nat-p* *Nit-ac* *Nux-v* op *Petr* *Ph-ac* *Phos* plat **Puls** *Sep* *Staph* stram teucr thuj verat
- **faintness**; with: petr hr1*
- **fever**; during: *Arn* b7.de ars b4.de* bell b4a.de bov b4a.de chin b7.de cocc b7.de croc b7.de *Ferr* b7.de* *Mosch* b7a.de *Ph-ac* b4a.de phos b4.de* rhus-t b7.de *Sars* b4a.de sep b4.de* staph b7.de* sulph b4.de*
- **lying** on left side agg.: *Bar-c* k*
- **menses** | **before** | **agg.**: *Alum* k* *Cupr* k* merc k*
  - **during** | **agg.**: *Calc* k* ign b7a.de merc b4a.de *Merl*
- **motion** agg.: iod nat-c nat-m h2 thuj h1
- **moving** in body; as if everything were: croc
- **nervousness**, from: ambr *Bell* calc k* ferr kali-n *Merc* *Nit-ac* *Ph-ac* k* *Phos* sep k*

- **palpitations**; with: kali-c h2* petr hr1 phos h2 sabad bg2 sul-i k2
- **restlessness**; with: aloe kr1 ph-ac kr1
- **sensual** impressions, from: *Phos* k*
- **sitting** agg.: *Mag-m*
- **sleep**; during: *Sep* b4a.de
- **sleep**, when falling asleep agg.: petr sep h2
- **smoking** tobacco, on: phos h2
- **talking** agg.: iod nat-c thuj h1
- **vertigo**; during: *Acon* b7a.de nat-c k*
- **vexation**; after: *Acon* **Cham** coloc ign merc *Petr* **Sep** staph
- **vomiting**; after: verat h1
- **walking**:
  - **after** | **agg.**: arg-n k* berb *Petr* kr1 sul-i k2
  - **air**; in open:
    - **after** | **agg.**: ambr br1
  - **amel.**: mag-m
  - **continued**:
    - **after** | **agg.**: *Arg-n* k*
- **wine** agg.: sil h2

OSSIFICATION:
- **slow** (See Development - slow - bones)

○ - **Arteries**; of: (↗*Arteriosclerosis; Blood vessels - complaints - arteries)* aur br1 *Bar-c* br1 lith-c c2 vario ptk1

OSTEOCHONDROSIS: abrot mtf11 cortiso mtf11 fl-ac mtf11 p-benzq mtf11 syph mtf11

OSTEOGENESIS IMPERFECTA TARDA: p-benzq mtf11

OSTEOMALACIA: *Iod* ptk1 merc-c ptk1 ph-ac ptk1

OSTEOMYELITIS (See Inflammation - bones - bone)

OSTEOPOROSIS: (↗*Brittle; EXTREMITIES - Osteoporosis)* arg-met jl3 bacls-7 pte1• calc-f jl3 cortico sp1 cortiso jl3* dys pte1*• fl-ac mtf11 morg-p pte1*• palo jl3
- **old** people; in: germ-met srj5•

OVARITIS (See FEMALE - Inflammation - ovaries)

OVERUSE of organs (See Lifting, straining of muscles and tendons - from)

PAIN: *Abies-n* ↓ abrot ↓ acetan ↓ **Acon** ↓ acon-c ↓ acon-f ↓ aconin ↓ *Act-sp* ↓ adam ↓ adon ↓ adren ↓ *Aesc* ↓ aeth ↓ **Agar** ↓ agav-t ↓ *Agn* ↓ agro ↓ aids ↓ ail ↓ *All-c* ↓ *Aloe* ↓ **Alum** ↓ *Alum-p* ↓ *Alum-sil* ↓ *Alumn* ↓ *Am-be* ↓ *Am-c* ↓ **Am-m** ↓ am-p ↓ am-pic ↓ am-s ↓ am-val ↓ *Ambr* ↓ aml-ns ↓ ammc ↓ ampe-qu ↓ amyg-p ↓ **Anac** ↓ **Anag** ↓ ancis-p tsm2 *Androc* ↓ **Ang** ↓ anh ↓ *Ant-c* ↓ *Ant-met* ↓ *Ant-t* ↓ anthraci ↓ ap-g ↓ aphis ↓ apiol ↓ **Apis** ↓ apoc ↓ apoc-a ↓ aral ↓ aran ↓ aran-ix ↓ **Arg-met** ↓ **Arg-n** ↓ arge-pl ↓ arist-cl ↓ arist-m ↓ **Arn** ↓ ars tl1 ars-i ↓ *Ars-s-f* ↓ ars-s-r ↓ arum-dru ↓ *Arum-t* ↓ arund ↓ **Asaf** ↓ **Asar** ↓ *Asc-t* ↓ astac ↓ aster ↓ atp ↓ atra-r ↓ *Atro* ↓ **Aur** ↓ aur-ar ↓ aur-i ↓ aur-m ↓ aur-m-n ↓ *Aur-s* ↓ *Bad* ↓ bamb-a ↓ *Bapt* ↓ bar-act ↓ *Bar-c* ↓ bar-i ↓ bar-m ↓ bar-s ↓ bart ↓ bell br1 bell-p ↓ bell-p-sp ↓ benz-ac ↓ **Berb** ↓ berb-a ↓ beto br1 **Bism** ↓ bomb-pr ↓ borx ↓ both tsm2 both-ax tsm2 *Bov* ↓ brass-n-o ↓ **Brom** ↓ **Bry** ↓ bufo ↓ bung-fa tsm2 buni-o ↓ *Cact* ↓ cadm-met ↓ caj ↓ *Calad* ↓ **Calc** ↓ calc-caust ↓ calc-f ↓ calc-i ↓ *Calc-p* ↓ calc-s ↓ *Calc-sil* ↓ calen ↓ *Camph* ↓ canch ↓ *Cann-i* ↓ *Cann-s* ↓ cann-xyz ↓ **Canth** ↓ **Caps** ↓ carb-ac ↓ *Carb-an* ↓ **Carb-v** ↓ carbn-o ↓ *Carbn-s* ↓ carc ↓ card-m ↓ carneg-g ↓ cassia-s ↓ *Caul* ↓ **Caust** ↓ cean ↓ *Cedr* ↓ cench tsm2 cent ↓ cere-b ↓ cerv ↓ **Cham** ↓ **Chel** ↓ **Chin** ↓ *Chinin-ar* ↓ chinin-m ↓ *Chinin-s* ↓ chion ↓ chir-fl ↓ chlor ↓ chr-met ↓ **Cic** ↓ *Cimic* br1 **Cina** ↓ cinnb ↓ cist ↓ cit-v ↓ *Clem* ↓ cloth tsm2 cob ↓ cob-n ↓ *Coc-c* ↓ **Cocc** ↓ cocc-s ↓ **Coff** ↓ **Colch** ↓ coll ↓ **Coloc** ↓ colocin ↓ *Com* ↓ **Con** ↓ conch ↓ *Cor-r* ↓ corn ↓ corn-f ↓ cot ↓ *Croc* ↓ crot-c tsm2 crot-chlol ↓ crot-h tsm2 *Crot-t* ↓ culx ↓ cund ↓ cupr sst3• cur ↓ **Cycl** ↓ cypr ↓ cypra-eg ↓ cystein-l ↓ daph ↓ dendr-pol tsm2 der ↓ dig ↓ digin ↓ *Dios* br1 diosm ↓ diph-t-tpt jl2 dirc ↓ *Dol* ↓ *Dor* ↓ **Dros** ↓ **Dulc** ↓ echi ↓ elaps tsm2 elat ↓ eos ↓ ephe-si ↓ epil a1* erig ↓ ery-a ↓ esp-g ↓ eucal ↓ eug ↓ euon ↓ **Eup-per** ↓ eup-pur ↓ *Euph* ↓ *Euphr* ↓ eupi ↓ fago ↓ **Ferr** ↓ *Ferr-act* ↓ ferr-ar ↓ ferr-m ↓ *Ferr-n* ↓ ferr-p ↓ ferul ↓ *Fl-ac* ↓ flor-p ↓ form ↓ form-ac ↓ franc ↓ galeoc-c-h ↓ galla-q-r ↓ *Gamb* ↓ gast ↓ gaul ↓ **Gels** ↓ germ-met ↓ *Get* ↓ *Glon* ↓ *Gnaph* ↓ goss ↓ **Graph** ↓ grat ↓ *Guaj* ↓ guare ↓ haliae-lc ↓ **Ham** ↓ hecla ↓ hed ↓ hedeo ↓ *Hell* ↓ helo ↓ helo-s ↓ helon ↓ **Hep** ↓ heroin ↓ hip-ac ↓ hipp ↓ hippoc-k ↓ hist ↓ hom-xyz br1 *Hydr* ↓ hydr-ac ↓ *Hydrc* ↓ hydrog ↓ hydroph ↓ **Hyos** ↓

Pain: ...
Hyper ↓ iber ↓ ichth ↓ ictod ↓ **Ign** ↓ ina-i ↓ ind ↓ influ mp4• iod ↓ iodof ↓ **Ip** ↓ irid-met ↓ **Iris** ↓ jac-c ↓ juni-v ↓ kali-ar ↓ **Kali-bi** ↓ **Kali-c** ↓ *Kali-chl* ↓ kali-cy ↓ *Kali-fcy* ↓ *Kali-i* ↓ kali-m ↓ *Kali-met* ↓ *Kali-n* ↓ kali-p ↓ **Kali-s** ↓ kali-sil ↓ *Kalm* ↓ kola ↓ *Kreos* ↓ lac-ac ↓ **Lac-c** ↓ lac-cp ↓ lac-loxod-a ↓ **Lach** ↓ lact ↓ lam ↓ lap-la ↓ lappa ↓ lat-h ↓ lat-m bnm6• **Laur** ↓ lavand-a ↓ *Lec* ↓ **Led** ↓ lepi ↓ lept ↓ **Lil-t** ↓ *Lith-c* ↓ *Lob* ↓ loxo-lae bnm12• loxo-recl ↓ lup ↓ **Lyc** ↓ *Lycpr* br1 lycps-v ↓ lyss ↓ **M-ambo** ↓ *M-arct* ↓ *M-aust* ↓ *Mag-c* ↓ *Mag-m* ↓ *Mag-n* ↓ *Mag-p* ↓ *Mag-s* ↓ magn-gr ↓ malar jl2 *Manc* ↓ mand ↓ *Mang* ↓ mang-act ↓ *Mang-n* ↓ *Med* ↓ *Meli* br1 mentho ↓ **Meny** ↓ meph ↓ **Merc** ↓ *Merc-c* ↓ *Merc-i-f* ↓ merc-i-r ↓ methyl ↓ *Mez* br1 mill ↓ mit ↓ morph ↓ **Mosch** ↓ *Mur-ac* ↓ *Myric* ↓ naja tsm2 narcin ↓ *Nat-ar* ↓ *Nat-c* ↓ nat-f ↓ *Nat-m* ↓ nat-n ↓ nat-p ↓ nat-s ↓ *Nat-sil* ↓ neon ↓ nicc ↓ nicc-s ↓ **Nit-ac** ↓ nit-s-d ↓ *Nitro* ↓ *Nux-m* ↓ **Nux-v** ↓ oci-sa ↓ *Ol-an* ↓ olib-sac wmh1 **Olnd** ↓ *Onos* ↓ *Op* ↓ *Osm* ↓ *Ox-ac* ↓ ozone ↓ paeon ↓ pall ↓ **Par** ↓ paraf ↓ passi ↓ paull ↓ pert-vc vk9 petr ↓ petr-ra shn4• **Petros** ↓ **Ph-ac** ↓ **Phel** ↓ **Phos** ↓ phys ↓ physala-p ↓ **Phyt** ↓ pic-ac ↓ *Pieri-b* ↓ pime ↓ pip-m ↓ pip-n ↓ *Plan* ↓ **Plat** ↓ **Plb** ↓ plb-i ↓ plect ↓ *Plut-n* ↓ pneu ↓ podo ↓ polyg-h ↓ polyg-xyz ↓ polys sk4• pop-cand ↓ positr ↓ pot-e ↓ prim-v ↓ prot ↓ **Prun** ↓ psil ↓ *Psor* ↓ ptel ↓ **Puls** ↓ puls-n ↓ pulx ↓ pyrid ↓ **Pyrog** ↓ pyrus ↓ *Rad-br* ↓ ran-a ↓ **Ran-b** ↓ **Ran-s** ↓ raph ↓ rat ↓ rauw ↓ *Rheum* ↓ **Rhod** ↓ rhus-g ↓ **Rhus-t** ↓ rhus-v ↓ rob ↓ ros-d ↓ *Rumx* ↓ **Ruta** ↓ **Sabad** ↓ sabal ↓ **Sabin** ↓ sacch ↓ sacch-a ↓ sacch-l ↓ *Sal-ac* ↓ salin ↓ salol ↓ *Samb* ↓ *Sang* ↓ sanic ↓ *Sars* ↓ scop ↓ scut ↓ *Sec* ↓ sel ↓ senec ↓ *Seneg* ↓ **Sep** ↓ sieg ↓ **Sil** ↓ sin-n ↓ sol-ni ↓ sol-t-ae ↓ *Sphing* ↓ **Spig** ↓ **Spong** ↓ **Squil** ↓ **Stann** ↓ **Staph** ↓ stel ↓ **Stict** ↓ still ↓ stram ↓ *Stront-c* ↓ stroph-h ↓ stroph-s ↓ *Stry* ↓ suis-hep ↓ **Sul-ac** ↓ sul-i ↓ sulfonam ↓ **Sulph** ↓ sumb ↓ symph ↓ syph ↓ *Tab* ↓ *Tarax* ↓ tarent ↓ *Tarent-c* ↓ tart-ac ↓ tax ↓ tell br1 ter ↓ *Teucr* ↓ *Thal-met* ↓ thal-xyz ↓ thea ↓ ther ↓ thlas ↓ **Thuj** ↓ thyr ↓ til ↓ tong ↓ trach-xyz ↓ tril-p ↓ tritic-vg ↓ *Tub* ↓ tub-m ↓ tung-met ↓ ulm-c c2 uran-n ↓ urt-c ↓ urt-u ↓ *Usn* ↓ ust ↓ uva ↓ vac ↓ **Valer** ↓ vanil ↓ vario ↓ ven-m ↓ **Verat** ↓ *Verat-v* ↓ **Verb** ↓ verin ↓ vero-o ↓ vesp ↓ *Vib* ↓ *Viol-o* ↓ *Viol-t* ↓ vip tsm2 vip-a-c tsm2 vip-d tsm2 *Visc* ↓ vitamin-d ↓ voes ↓ wies ↓ wye ↓ x-ray ↓ xan ↓ **Zinc** ↓ zinc-chr ↓ zinc-i ↓ zinc-o ↓ zinc-ox ↓ **Zinc-p** ↓ *Zinc-val* ↓ zing ↓ [*Buteo-j* sej6]

- **one** side: cocc b7.de cupr b7.de stann ↓
  - **stitching** pain | **crawling**: stann h2
- **right**: arist-m a1 ars ↓ bad ↓ brach a1 bry a1 carb-an ↓ carc ↓ cedr a1 chel ↓ con ↓ crot-c sk4• cupr ↓ galla-q-r nl2• hura ↓ hyos ↓ kali-bi ↓ merc-i-f ↓ mosch ↓ oena a1 phos ↓ pic-ac a1 plect ↓ sep ↓ sil ↓ sin-n ↓ sol-t-ae ↓ sulph a1 tarent a1 tritic-vg fd5.de wye a1 yuc a1
  - **benumbing**: ars h2
  - **drawing** pain: sep h2
  - **jerking**: cupr h2
  - **neuralgic**: merc-i-f mrr1
  - **pinching** pain: sep
  - **stitching** pain: bad a1 carb-an a1 carc fd2.de• chel a1 con a1 hura a1 hyos a1 kali-bi a1 mosch a1 phos a1 plect a1 sil a1 sin-n a1 sol-t-ae a1

  ▽ - **extending** to | **left**: sabad b7a.de
- **left**: aesc ↓ all-c ↓ ant-s-aur ↓ asaf vh benz-ac a1 brom a1 chel a1 cinnb a1 coc-c ↓ crot-c a1* crot-h a1 daph a1 **Ign** ↓ ind a1 kalm a1 lac-cp sk4• lach ↓ lepi a1 lil-t a1 lycps-v a1 merc a1 merc-i-f a1 morg-g ↓ nicc ↓ oena a1 ol-j a1 olib-sac wmh1 op a1 ox-ac a1 phys a1 pic-ac a1 plan a1 plut-n srj7• puls-n a1 *Sil* ↓ sphing ↓ **Squil** ↓ stann ↓ *Sulph* ↓ sumb ↓ tax ↓ tritic-vg fd5.de ulm-c ↓ zinc ↓
  - **night**: lyc ↓
    - **midnight** | **after**: asaf vh
    - **drawing** pain: lyc h2
  - **neuralgic**: morg-g fmm1•
  - **stitching** pain: aesc a1 all-c a1 ant-s-aur a1 coc-c a1 crot-h a1 **Ign** a1 lach a1 lepi a1 merc a1 nicc a1 *Sil* a1 sphing a1 **Squil** a1 stann a1 *Sulph* a1 sumb a1 tax a1 ulm-c jsj8• zinc a1
- **daytime**: ham ptk1
- **morning**: aesc ↓ bomb-chr mlk9.de bry ↓ carb-an ↓ chin ↓ cob ↓ dulc fd4.de euphr ↓ form ↓ galeoc-c-h gms1• lyc ↓ lyss ↓ mag-m ↓ nat-c ↓ ox-ac ↓ *Phyt* ↓ polyp-p ↓ positr ↓ sarr ↓ sil h2 tab ↓ thuj ↓ xan c1
  - **bed** agg.; in: anac ↓ grat ↓ nat-m ↓ petr ↓ rhod ↓ sacch-a ↓ stann ↓ viol-o ↓
    - **sore**: anac a1 grat k* nat-m k* petr h2 rhod k* viol-o a1*
    - **stitching** pain: sacch-a fd2.de• stann sf1.de
  - **ceases** toward evening: pert-vc vk9

- **rising**:
  - **after**:
    - **agg.**: am-m ↓ *Graph* ↓ mag-c ↓ phos ↓ sulph ↓
      - **drawing** pain: *Graph*
      - **sore**: am-m k* mag-c h2 phos k* sulph k*
  - **agg.**: nat-ar ↓ sulph ↓
    - **sore**: nat-ar sulph h2
  - **amel.**: anac ↓ crot-h ↓ grat ↓ viol-o ↓
    - **sore**: anac a1 crot-h a1 grat a1 viol-o a1*
- **sleep**; after insufficient: mag-m ↓
  - **sore**: mag-m
- **sore**: aesc bry k* carb-an k* chin h1 cob a1 euphr k* form k* lyc k* lyss hr1* mag-m h2* nat-c h2 ox-ac k* *Phyt* a1 polyp-p a1 positr nl2• sarr a1 tab k* thuj k*
- **sun**; increasing and decreasing with the: acon bg2 glon bg2* kali-bi bg2 kalm bg2* nat-m bro1 nux-v bg2 sang bg2* spig bg2* stann vml2* stram bg2 sulph bg2 tab bro1
- **waking** | **after**:
  - **agg.**: *Bry* ↓ carb-ac ↓ coloc ↓ crot-h ↓ sep ↓ sulph ↓
    - **drawing** pain: coloc
    - **sore**: *Bry* a1 carb-ac k1* crot-h k* sep k1 sulph a1
  - **on**: aesc ↓ bar-c ↓ calc ↓ crot-h ↓ lac-leo ↓ thuj ↓ til ↓ zinc ↓
    - **sore**: aesc k* bar-c k* calc h2 crot-h a1 lac-leo sk4• thuj k* til k* zinc h2

- **forenoon**: mag-m ↓ mag-s ↓ sars ↓
  - **sore**: mag-m h2 mag-s a1 sars h2
- **afternoon**: sang ↓
  - **sleep**:
    - **siesta**: | **after**:
      - **agg.**: bar-c ↓ eug ↓
        - **sore**: bar-c h2 eug
      - **during**: graph ↓
        - **sore**: graph h2*
  - **sore**: sang a1
- **evening**: agar ↓ all-c ↓ am-c ↓ ars caust ↓ coc-c ↓ colch ↓ lyc ↓ par ↓ puls bro1 raph ↓ ruta fd4.de
  - **20** h: rhus-t ↓
    - **drawing** pain: rhus-t
  - **drawing** pain: coc-c k* raph k* ruta fd4.de
  - **lying** down agg.; after: mag-m ↓ mag-s ↓ petr ↓
    - **sore**: mag-m k* mag-s k* petr h2
  - **sitting** agg.: brom ↓
    - **sore**: brom
  - **sore**: agar h2 am-c caust h2 lyc k* par sf1.de
  - **sunset** | **sunrise**; until: syph br1
  - **tearing** pain: colch br1
  - **thread**; like a: all-c st*
- **night**: *Asaf* br1 *Aur* mrr1 carb-an ↓ caust ↓ chir-fl bnm4• coc-c ↓ colch ↓ con h2 cory br1 euphr ↓ ferr-i ↓ kali-c h2 lac-h sk4• lat-m bnm6• mez tl1 phyt tl1 *Sil* ↓
  - **22** h: bry ↓
    - **drawing** pain: bry
  - **midnight** | **before**:
    - **23** h: fago ↓
      - **sore**: fago
    - **after**: caust ↓
      - **sore**: caust k*
  - **drawing** pain: coc-c k*
  - **sleep**; in: alum j5.de aur j5.de bell j5.de kali-n j5.de lach j5.de lyc j5.de *Merc* j5.de mosch j5.de *Nit-ac* j5.de vip j5.de
  - **sore**: carb-an h2 caust h2 ferr-i k* mez tl1 phyt tl1 *Sil* k*
  - **stitching** pain: euphr h2
  - **tearing** pain: colch br1
- **accompanied** by:
  - **appetite**; increased: sep bg2

- **accompanied** by: ...
  - **apyrexia**: led bro1
  - **eructations**; ineffectual: *Carb-an* b4a.de sep b4a.de
  - **salivation**: *Epiph* bg3* *Kali-bi* vk1 phos bg3*
  - **urination**: phos bg2 rhus-t bg2
    - **complaints** of (See BLADDER - Urination - complaints - accompanied - pain)
  - ○ **Ears**; complaints of: *Ars* bg2 lach bg2 spig bg2
  - **Head**; pain in (See HEAD - Pain - accompanied - pains)
  - **Upper** limbs; complaints of: verat bg2
- **aching**: agar ptk1 arn ptk1 *Bapt* ptk1 bell-p ptk1 bry ptk1 cadm-met sp1 carb-v ptk1 *Chin* ptk1 cimic ptk1 cystein-l rly4• dulc ptk1 echi ptk1 erig ptk1 *Eup-per* ptk1 flor-p rsj3• franc br1 *Gels* ptk1 hyos ptk1 ign ptk1 kalm ptk1 lach ptk1 lappa ptk1 lat-m bnm6• lept ptk1 loxo-recl bnm10• mand sp1 mang-act br1 merc-i-f ptk1 nat-f sp1 nux-v ptk1 *Onos* ptk1 physala-p bnm7• phyt br1* pot-e rly4• pyrog ptk1* *Rad-br* br1* rauw sp1 rhus-t ptk1 ruta ptk1 suis-hep rly4• sulfonam ks2 ter ptk1 vario ptk1 verat-v ptk1 [bell-p-sp dcm1 heroin sdj2]
- **after** | **agg.**: bry b7.de
- **agonizing**: chir-fl bnm4• helo-s bnm14• lat-m sp1* x-ray br1
- **ailments** from: *(↗Sensitiveness - pain; MIND - Sensitive - pain)* cham c1 scut c1
- **air** agg.; draft of: calc-p mtf11
- **air**; in open:
  - **amel.**: caust ↓
    - **sore**: caust
- **alternating** with:
  - **cheerfulness** (See MIND - Cheerful - alternating - pain)
  - **itching**: stront-c ptk1
- **amputation**; after: *(↗amputation - neuralgic; EXTREMITIES - Injuries - fingers - amputated; EXTREMITIES - Pain - amputations)* acon k1* *All-c* bg2* am-m bg2* arn bg2* *Asaf* k* asar ↓ bell k1* cupr k1* cupr-ar sne hell k1* *Hyper* bg2* ign k1* kalm bg2* *Ph-ac* bg2* phos k1* rauw k1* spig k1* *Staph* k1* symph bg2* verat k1*
  - **breathing** deep:
    - **amel.**: ph-ac ↓
      - **neuralgic**: ph-ac ptk1
  - **neuralgic**: *(↗amputation)* all-c bg2* am-m bg2* arn bg2* asar ptk1 hyper bg2* kalm bg2 ph-ac bg2* staph ptk1 symph bg2*
- **anemia**; from: *Ars* ↓ chin ↓ *Ferr* ↓ kali-fcy ↓ puls ↓
  - **neuralgic**: *Ars* bro1 chin bro1 *Ferr* bro1 kali-fcy bro1 puls bro1
- **anger**; after: *Cham* mrr1 coloc ↓
  - **neuralgic**: coloc tl1
- **appear** gradually: *(↗Complaints - appearing - gradually)* acon bry calc-sil bro1 carbn-o caust chin bro1 con ign lact lob psil ft1 rad-br bro1 sars sul-ac tell bro1
  - **disappear**; and:
    - **gradually**: acon arg-n bg2* arn ars k* bar-c k* bufo cact bg2 chel bg2 coloc bg2 crot-h epiph bg2 euphr bg2 form bg1 gels bg2* glon k* ign bg1 jab kali-bi sf1.de *Kalm* k* lach bg2* lob sf1.de lol bg2 mez *Nat-m* k* op *Phos* k* pic-ac **Plat** k* psor *Puls* bg2* sabin sang bg2* sars sel bg2 *Sep* bg1* *Spig* **Stann** k* staph stront-c k* *Sul-ac* sulph **Syph** k2* verb xan c1
    - **suddenly**: *Arg-met* k* *Arg-n* kr1 bell bg2 caust k* ign bg2* psil ft1* *Puls* k* rad-br bg2 rhus-t bg2 *Sul-ac* k*
- **appear** suddenly: *(↗Complaints - appearing - suddenly)* *Acon* sf1.de* agar am-c sf1.de anh sp1 apoc vml3• *Arg-met* k* *Ars* sf1.de aster atra-r bnm3• atro sf1.de *Bamb-a* stb2.de• bar-act sf1.de **Bell** k* berb k* both-ax tsm2 camph k* *Canth* bg1* carb-ac sf1.de caust sf1.de chir-fl bnm4• cimic cob-n mg1.de *Coloc* sf1.de croc *Crot-h* sf1.de *Cupr* sf1.de cupr-ar sf1.de daph st dendr-pol sk4• *Dios* sf1.de eup-per bg1 ferr form sf1.de *Glon* sf1.de kali-bi sf1.de lat-m bnm6• loxo-lae bnm12• lyc mag-c sf1.de mag-p sf1.de med st mez k* morph *Nat-s* sf1.de neon srj5• **Nit-ac** *Nux-v* sf1.de ovi-p br1 ox-ac sf1.de petr-ra shn4• phos br1 phys plb sf1.de *Podo* sf1.de prot fmm1• *Puls* k* ran-b sf1.de rhus-t bro1 ruta fd4.de *Sabin* sep sil sf1.de *Spig* bg1* stann sf1.de *Stry* br1 stry-p sf1.de sul-ac sf1.de *Tab* *Tarent* sf1.de thal-xyz srj8• thala jl3 thuj sf1.de tritic-vg fd5.de tung-met bdx1• *Valer* vanil fd5.de *Verb* sf1.de vip sf1.de zinc sf1.de zinc-val sf1.de
  - **neuralgic**: *Med* jl2

- **disappear**; and:
  - **gradually**: asaf bell bg2* buni-o jl calc coloc bg2* fl-ac *Hyper* bg1* ign sf1.de lach bg2* med bg1 *Puls* k* rad-br bg2* ran-s sabin bg2* sep k1 sul-ac bro1
  - **suddenly**: *Arg-n* arum-t vh asaf aster *Bamb-a* stb2.de* **Bell** k* borx bg2 cact bro1 canth k* *Carb-ac* bg2* carbn-s caust bg2 cham st chr-met dx coff k2* colch tl1 crot-h bg1 cupr bg1 dios bg2 eup-per bg2* eup-pur k* fl-ac ictod bro1 ign k* irid-met srj5• **Kali-bi** k* kali-s tl1 kalm loxo-lae bnm12• lyc k* mag-p k* mang-p rly4• merc-c *Mez* sne nat-f mg1.de neon srj5• **Nit-ac** k* nux-m bg2 ovi-p bg1* oxyt br1* pert-vc vk9 petr bro1* *Phyt* puls bg2* *Rhus-t* bg1* ruta fd4.de sabin spig bg2* stry bro1 sul-ac bg2 sulph bg2 thal jl thuj bg2 tritic-vg fd5.de tub nh* valer bg2 vanil fd5.de [tax jsj7]
- **ascending** agg.: spig ↓
  - **stitching** pain: spig h1*
- **bathing** agg.: rhus-t ↓ sulph ↓
  - **burning**: rhus-t ptk1 sulph ptk1
- **beaten**; as if: ang vh anh sp1 arn br1* bell-p sp1 ham fd3.de• ruta fd4.de
- **beaten** off the bones; as if flesh were: *Bry* b2.de canth b2.de dros b2.de *Ign* b2.de kreos b2.de led b2.de mosch b2.de nit-ac b2.de nux-v b2.de **Rhus-t** b2.de staph b2.de *Sulph* b2.de *Thuj* b2.de
- **bee** stings; like: apis tl1* gels ptk1
- **bending** forward | **amel**.: atra-r bnm3•
- **benumbing**: *Acon* k* agar k* agn k* am-c k* anac k* ant-c k* ant-t k* arg-met k* arn k* asaf k* asar k* aur k* bell k* bov k* bry k* *Calc* k* cann-s k* carb-an k* carb-v bg2 **Cham** k* chin k* cic k* *Cina* k* cocc k* con k* croc k* cupr k* cycl k* dros k* dulc k* euph k* euphr k* *Gnaph* st1 *Graph* hell k* hep k* hyos k* ign k* *Iris* kali-n k* laur k* led k* m-ambo b2.de* mag-c k* mag-m k* mang k* meny k* *Mez* k* mosch k* mur-ac k* nat-c k* nat-m k* nux-m k* nux-v bg2 **Olnd** k* op k* par k* ph-ac k* phos k* **Plat** k* *Puls* k* *Rheum* k* rhus-t k* ruta k* **Sabad** k* sabin k* *Samb* k* seneg k* sep k* stann k* staph k* sul-ac k* sulph k* tarax k* valer k* *Verat* k* **Verb** k* zinc k*
  - **numb** aching: cot br1
- **biting** pain: acon k* agar k* agn k* aloe a1 alum k* am-c k* am-m a1 *Ambr* k* ang b2.de* ant-c k* ant-t k* arg-met k* arn k* ars k* arum-t ptk1 asar k* aur k* bar-m j5.de bell k* *Berb* j5.de* *Bov* j5.de bry k* calad k* calc k* camph k* cann-s k* *Canth* k* *Caps* k* carb-an k* **Carb-v** k* caust k* cench k2 cham k* chel j5.de *Chin* k* cist ptk1 *Clem* k* cocc k* colch k* coloc k* con k* croc k* *Dros* k* dulc k* euon a1 *Euph* k* *Euphr* k* fl-ac ptk1 graph k* grat j5.de *Hell* k* hep k* hydr ptk1 hyos k* *Ign* k* iod k* *Ip* k* *Kali-c* k* kali-chl k13 kali-m k2 kali-n k* *Kreos* k* lac-ac stj5• lach k* lact j5.de* lam j5.de laur k* led k* lyc k* m-ambo b2.de m-arct b2.de* m-aust b2.de* mag-c k* mang j5.de meli ptk1 *Merc* k* *Mez* k* mosch k* mur-ac k* nat-c k* nat-m k* nicc j5.de *Nit-ac* k* nux-m k* **Nux-v** k* ol-an j5.de* olnd k* op k* paeon k* par k* petr k* **Petros** k* ph-ac k* phos k* plat j5.de polyg-h ptk1 *Prun* k* puls k* *Ran-b* k* **Ran-s** k* rheum k* rhod k* *Rhus-t* k* *Ruta* k* sabad k* sabin k* sang ptk1 sars k* sel k* seneg k* *Sep* k* sil k* spig k* *Spong* j5.de squil k* stann k* *Staph* k* stram k* stront-c k* sul-ac k* **Sulph** k* *Teucr* k* thuj k* valer k* verat k* viol-t k* voes a1 **Zinc** k* **Zinc-p** k2* [am-p stj1 am-s stj1]
- **bitten**; as if: bufo bg2
- **blow**; pain as from a: *Acon* b7.de* agar bg2 alum bg2 am-c bg2 am-m b7.de* *Anac* bg2 *Ang* b7.de* ant-t bg2 **Arn** b7.de* asaf b7.de* asar bg2 aur bg2 bar-c bg2 bell bg2 bry b7.de* calc bg2 camph bg2 *Cann-s* b7.de* caust bg2 cham bg2 chin bg2 *Cic* b7.de* **Cina** b7.de* clem bg2 cocc b7.de* colch b7.de* con bg2 *Croc* bg2 cupr b7a.de* cycl b7.de* dig bg2 dros b7.de* *Dulc* bg2 euph bg2 ferr bg2 glon bg2 graph bg2 *Hell* b7.de* hep bg2 hyos b7.de* ign b7.de* iod bg2 ip b7.de* kali-c bg2 kali-n bg2 kreos b7a.de* lach bg2 lyc bg2 **M-ambo** b7.de* m-arct b7.de mang bg2 merc bg2 *Mez* bg2 *Mur-ac* bg2 nat-c bg2 nat-m bg2 *Nux-m* b7.de* nux-v bg2 *Olnd* b7.de* par bg2 petr bg2 **Plat** bg2 podo bg2 puls b7.de* rhod bg2 rhus-t b7a.de* **Ruta** b7.de* samb bg2 sars bg2 sil bg2 *Spig* bg2 squil bg2 stann bg2 stram bg2 **Sul-ac** bg2 sulph bg2 tarax b7.de* teucr bg2 thuj bg2 valer bg2 verat b7.de* viol-o bg2 viol-t bg2 zinc bg2
- **boring** pain: acon k* *Agar* k* aloe alum k* alum-p k2* alum-sil k2* am-c k* am-m k* anac k* ang b2.de* ant-c k* ant-t k* apis *Arg-met* k* **Arg-n** k* arn k* ars k* *Asaf* k* **Aur** k* aur-ar k2 aur-m-n vml3• *Aur-s* k2* bar-c k* bar-s k2* **Bell** k* **Bism** k* borx k* bov k* *Calc* k* calc-sil k2* canni-i canth k* caps k* carb-an k* carb-v k* carbn-s *Caust* k* chin k* cimic *Cina* k* clem k* coc-c cocc k* colch k* coloc k* con k* cupr k* cycl k* dig k* dios k* dros k* *Dulc* k* euph k* euphr k* *Hell* k* *Hep* k* ign k* ip k* *Kali-c* k* kali-n k* kreos k* *Lach* k* laur k* led k* lyc k*
- **boring** pain: ... m-ambo b2.de m-arct b2.de* mag-c k* mag-m k* mag-n bg2 mag-p ptk1 mang k* med ptk1 meny k* *Merc* k* merc-i-f a1 *Mez* k* mur-ac k* *Nat-c* k* *Nat-m* k* nat-sil k2* nit-ac k* nux-m k* nux-v k* olnd k* par k* petr k* *Ph-ac* k* phos k* plan bg2 plat k* *Plb* k* psil ft1 **Puls** k* ran-b k* **Ran-s** k* *Rhod* k* rhus-t k* ruta k* sabad k* sabin k* sel k* *Seneg* k* *Sep* k* *Sil* k* **Spig** k* spong k* stann k* staph k* stram k* stront-c k* *Sulph* k* *Tarax* k* *Thuj* k* valer k* xan ptk1 *Zinc* k* zinc-chr ptk1 *Zinc-p* k2* [chr-met stj1]
  - **inward**: alum k* bell k* calc k* cocc k* *Kali-c* k* mang k* zinc k*
  - **outward**: ant-c k* asaf k* bell k* *Bism* k* bov k* calc k* dros k* *Dulc* k* ip k* puls k* sep k* *Spig* spong k* *Staph* k*
- **broken**; as if: *Ang* b2.de* arn b2.de* bell b2.de* borx b2.de* bov b2.de* calc b2.de* calc-p ptk1 carb-an b4a.de caust b2.de* *Cham* b2.de* *Chel* b2.de* cina b2.de* **Cocc** b2.de* cupr b2.de* *Dros* b2.de* **Eup-per** ptk1 graph b2.de* guaj ptk1 hep b2.de* hyos b2.de* **Ign** b2.de* kreos b2.de* lyc b2.de* m-arct b2.de* mag-m b2.de* merc b2.de* mez b2.de* mosch b2.de* nat-m b2.de* nux-v b2.de* par b2.de* ph-ac b2.de* **Phos** b2.de* puls b2.de* ran-b ptk1 rhus-t b2.de* **Ruta** b2.de* samb b2.de* sep b2.de* sil ptk1 staph b2.de sulph ptk1 *Thuj* ptk1 valer ptk1 **Verat** b2.de* zinc b2.de*
- **bruised** (See sore)
- **burning**: *Acon* bro1 *Agar* bro1 agro bro1 *All-c* bro1 anthraci bro1 *Apis* bg2* *Ars* bro1 bell bg2* *Calad* bro1 *Canth* bro1 *Caps* bro1 carb-an bro1 *Caust* bro1 cham bro1 *Dor* bro1 eos bro1 ign bg2 kreos bro1 ol-an bro1 ph-ac bro1 *Phos* bro1 pip-m bro1 pop-cand bro1 rhus-t bro1 *Sang* bro1 sec bro1 *Sulph* bro1 tarent bro1 tritic-vg fd5.de
  - **accompanied** by | **septicemia** (See Septicemia - accompanied - pain)
  - **hot** coals; as from: *Apis* ptk1 ars h2* *Bell* ptk1 carb-an ptk1 carb-v h2 chir-fl bnm4• guaj ptk1 kali-c ptk1 kreos ptk1 mez ptk1 phos ptk1 rad-br ptk1 sabad a1 spig ptk1 *Tarent-c* ptk1 *Tub* ptk1 vesp ptk1
  - **hot** water; as from: *Sang* br1
  - **intense** and intolerable: anthraci mtf11
  - **pepper**; like: coc-c ptk1 lach ptk1 mez ptk1 nat-s ptk1 xan ptk1
  - **steam**; as from: pulx ptk1
  - **stinging**: ant-c ptk1 **Apis** ptk1 *Ars* ptk1 *Berb* ptk1 *Con* ptk1 *Dulc* ptk1 *Glon* ptk1 iris ptk1 lyc ptk1 mez ptk1 nux-v ptk1 ph-ac ptk1 *Phos* ptk1 rhus-t ptk1 sil ptk1 urt-u ptk1 verat-v ptk1
  - ○ **Internally**: canth ↓ *Phos* ↓
    - **sore**: canth bg2 *Phos* bg2
- **burnt**; as if: *Agar* aloe alum k* ambr k* anac bg2 *Apis* ars bg2* *Arum-t* *Bapt* *Bar-c* k* bell k* *Berb* bov bg2 bry k* cann-s k* canth ptk1 carb-ac bg2 *Caust* k* chin k* *Coloc* cycl ptk1 ferr k* ham fd3.de• hist sp1 *Hydr* ptk1 hyos k* *Ign* k* **Iris** k* kali-c k* lach bg2 lat-m sp1 *Lil-t* lyc ptk1 *Mag-m* k* merc k* mez mur-ac nat-c k* **Nux-v** k* op k* osm par k* phos k* *Phyt* k* *Plat* k* *Plut-n* srj7• *Puls* k* ran-b ptk1 *Ran-s* rauw sp1 rhus-t bg2 ruta bg2 *Sabad* k* *Sang* k* *Sec* bg2 *Sep* k* still stram bg2 sul-ac k* tarent thal-xyz srj8• thuj k* verat k* *Verat-v* ptk1 zinc bg2
- **bursting** pain: acon b2.de* act-sp ptk1 am-c b2.de* am-m b2.de* anac b2.de* ant-c b2.de* ant-t b2.de* arg-n bg2 arn bg2 ars b2.de* asaf b2.de* *Asar* b2.de* bar-c b2.de* **Bell** b2.de* bism b2.de* borx b2.de* bov b2.de* **Bry** b2.de* **Calc** b2.de* camph b2.de* cann-s b2.de* *Caps* b2.de* carb-ac ptk1 carb-an b2.de* carb-v b2.de* **Caust** b2.de* cham b2.de* chel b2.de* chin b2.de* cina b2.de* cocc b2.de* coff b2.de* colch b2.de* coloc b2.de* *Con* b2.de* croc b2.de* dig b2.de* dulc b2.de* eup-per bg2* *Euph* b2.de* euphr b2.de* ferr b2.de* *Gels* bg2 *Glon* ptk1 *Graph* b2.de* guaj b2.de ham bg2* hell b2.de* hep b2.de* hyos b2.de* **Ign** b2.de* iod b2.de* ip b2.de* iris bg2 *Kali-c* b2.de* kali-m ptk1 kali-n b2.de* kreos b2.de* lac-c ptk1 lach b2.de* lat-m bnm6• laur b2.de* lept ptk1 lil-t ptk1 *Lyc* b2.de* m-ambo b2.de m-arct b2.de m-aust b2.de mag-c b2.de* mang b2.de* merc b2.de* mez b2.de* mosch b2.de* mur-ac b2.de* nat-c b2.de* *Nat-m* b2.de* nit-ac b2.de* nux-m b2.de* nux-v b2.de* olnd b2.de* op b2.de* *Par* b2.de* petr b2.de* ph-ac b2.de* phos b2.de* plat b2.de* plb b2.de* puls b2.de* **Ran-b** b2.de* ran-s b2.de* rat ptk1 rhod b2.de* rhus-t b2.de* sabad b2.de* *Sabin* b2.de* samb b2.de* sanic ptk1 sars b2.de* seneg b2.de* **Sep** b2.de* *Sil* b2.de* **Spig** b2.de* spong b2.de* squil b2.de* stann b2.de* staph b2.de* stram b2.de* *Stront-c* b2.de* sul-ac b2.de* sulph b2.de* tarax b2.de* thuj b2.de* thyr ptk1 *Usn* bg2 *Valer* b2.de* verat b2.de* verb b2.de* viol-t b2.de* *Vip* br1* zinc b2.de*
- **cancerous** affections, in: acon st1 alco sne anthraci bro1 *Apis* bro1 arn sne *Ars* bro1* aster bro1 bell sne* bism-o gm1 bry bro1 bufo st* cadm-ar sne cadm-o sne *Calc* bro1 *Calc-act* c1* calc-ox bro1 carb-an k2 carc k4* cedr bro1 cham gm1 chel sne cinnm br1* *Cit-ac* kr1* cod-p gm1 coloc kr1 con bro1 crot-h gm1 cund bro1 echi br1* *Euph* br1* euph-he bro1* ferr-p sne germ-met srj5•

- **cancerous** affections, in: ...
Hydr br1* kali-p sne kreos sne lupin mtf11 mag-p bro1 merc k2 morph bro1 naja gm1 nit-ac sne op bro1 ovi-p bro1 ox-ac sne* ph-ac br1* phyt gm1 rham-cal sne ruta sne sil bro1* tarent-c sne
  - **burning**: calc-ar ptk1 euph-he gm1
- **chill**; during: arn ↓ ars h2 bapt ↓ *Bell* ↓ chin ↓ coff bro1 dulc bro1 hom-xyz ↓ lyc ↓ nat-m ↓ nux-v ↓ petr h2 puls bro1 rhod ↓ *Rhus-t* b7a.de sabad b7a.de sil bro1 sulph ↓ tarent ↓ verat ↓
  - **drawing** pain: lyc h2
  - **sore**: arn bg2 bapt bro1 *Bell* bg2 chin bg2 hom-xyz bro1 nat-m bg2 nux-v bg2 rhod bg2 rhus-t bro1 sulph bg2 tarent k* verat bg2
- **choking** pain: acon b2.de* agar b2.de* am-c b2.de* ambr b2.de* asar b2.de* bell b2.de* bry b2.de* cann-s b2.de* canth b2.de* carb-an b2.de* chel b2.de* *Chin* b2.de* cocc b2.de* coff b2.de* cupr b2.de* dros b2.de* graph b2.de* hep b2.de* **Hyos** bg2 *Ign* b2.de* kreos b2.de* m-arct b2.de m-aust b2.de mag-c b2.de* nat-c b2.de* *Nux-v* b2.de* plb b2.de* **Puls** b2.de* ran-s b2.de* ruta bg2 sabin b2.de* *Spong* b2.de* stram b2.de* sul-ac b2.de* sulph b2.de* verat b2.de* zinc b2.de*
- **chronic**: *Arn* ↓ kreos ↓ *Phos* ↓ sulph ↓ thlas ↓ thuj ↓ vib ↓
  - **neuralgic**: *Arn* bro1 kreos br1* *Phos* bro1 sulph bro1 thlas br1 thuj bro1 vib tl1
- **coffee**; from abuse of: grat ↓
  - **neuralgic**: grat ptk1
- **coition**; after: **Sil** ↓
  - **male**; in: cedr ↓
    - **neuralgic**: cedr ptk1
  - **sore**: **Sil** k*
- **coition** agg.: coloc ↓ cupr ↓ graph ↓
  - **cramping**: coloc ptk1 cupr ptk1 graph ptk1
- **cold**:
  - **agg.**: kali-c tl1 mag-p tl1 ruta tl1
  - **air** agg.: bell-p ↓ ran-b ↓
    - **sore**: bell-p sp1 ran-b k2
  - **amel.**: chir-fl lmj led tl1 phos tl1 sal-ac tl1
- **cold** parts, in: sec ↓ verat ↓
  - **burning**: sec tl1* verat ptk1
- **colic** (See cramping)
- **company**; agg. after being in: pall br1
- **compressed**; as if forcefully: agar b2.de* alum b2.de* ambr b2.de* anac b2.de* ang b2.de* **Arn** b2.de* *Ars* b2.de* asar b2.de* **Bell** b2.de* bov b2.de* bry b2.de* *Calc* b2.de* cann-s b2.de* canth b2.de* *Caps* b2.de* carb-an b2.de* carb-v b2.de* caust b2.de* *Cham* b2.de* cina b2.de* clem b2.de* cocc b2.de* *Colch* b2.de* coloc b2.de* con b2.de* croc b2.de* dros b2.de* dulc b2.de* *Euph* b2.de* graph bg2 guaj b2.de* hell b2.de* hep b2.de* ign b2.de* iod b2.de* kali-c b2.de* kali-n b2.de* kreos b2.de* laur b2.de* lyc b2.de* m-arct b2.de m-aust b2.de mag-m b2.de* mang b2.de* meny b2.de* *Merc* b2.de* *Mez* b2.de* mur-ac b2.de* *Nat-c* b2.de* nat-m b2.de* nit-ac b2.de* nux-m b2.de* **Nux-v** b2.de* op b2.de* par b2.de* petr b2.de* *Phos* b2.de* *Plat* b2.de* *Puls* b2.de* ran-b b2.de* ran-s b2.de* *Rheum* b2.de* rhod b2.de* *Rhus-t* b2.de* ruta b2.de* *Sabad* b2.de* sabin b2.de* sars b2.de* seneg b2.de* sep b2.de* sil b2.de* spig b2.de* *Spong* b2.de* stann b2.de* staph b2.de* stront-c b2.de* *Sulph* b2.de* teucr b2.de* thuj b2.de* valer b2.de* verat b2.de* verb b2.de* zinc b2.de*
- **concussion**; as from: *Am-c* b2.de* arn bg2 hell bg2 mang b2.de* merc bg2 petr b2.de*
- **contracting**: ars bg2 par bg2 puls bg2 sep bg2 zinc bg2
- **convulsions**; developing into: plat ↓
  - **cramping**: plat tl1
- **corrosive** (= as if from an acid): calc-p bg2 con b2.de* *Lach* bg2 phos bg2 ruta b2.de* sabad bg2 teucr b2.de*
- **cough** agg.; during: alum ↓ am-m ↓ ambr ↓ arg-met ↓ arn ↓ ars ↓ bar-c ↓ *Bell* ↓ **Bry** ↓ calc ↓ caps ↓ carb-an ↓ **Carb-v** ↓ *Caust* ↓ chin ↓ cina ↓ ferr ↓ hep ↓ kali-c ↓ kreos ↓ lach ↓ *Lyc* ↓ mag-m ↓ mang ↓ meph ↓ merc ↓ nat-c ↓ nat-m ↓ nat-s ↓ nit-ac ↓ nux-m ↓ **Nux-v** ↓ **Phos** ↓ puls ↓ rhus-t ↓ sep ↓ sil ↓ spig ↓ squil ↓ **Stann** ↓ **Sulph** ↓ zinc ↓
  - **bursting** pain: **Bry** bg2 caps bg2 *Lyc* bg2 merc bg2 nat-m bg2 **Nux-v** bg2 phos bg2 sulph bg2 zinc bg2
- **cough** agg.; during: ...
  - **sore**: alum bg2 am-m bg2 ambr bg2 arg-met bg2 arn bg2 ars bg2 bar-c bg2 *Bell* bg2 calc bg2 **Carb-v** bg2 *Caust* bg2 chin bg2 cina bg2 ferr bg2 hep bg2 lach bg2 lyc bg2 mag-m bg2 meph bg2 merc bg2 nat-c bg2 nat-m bg2 nat-s bg2 nit-ac bg2 nux-m bg2 **Nux-v** bg2 **Phos** bg2 sep bg2 sil bg2 spig bg2 **Stann** bg2 **Sulph** bg2 zinc bg2
  - **stitching** pain: caps bg2*
  - **violent**: carb-an bg2 kali-c bg2 kreos bg2 mang bg2 nit-ac bg2 puls bg2 rhus-t bg2 squil bg2 sulph bg2
- **cramp**, after: plat ↓
  - **sore**: plat h2
- **cramping**: agar ptk1 *Bell* ptk1 **Berb** mrr1 *Cact* br1* **Calc** ptk1 carneg-g rwt1• caul tl1 caust ptk1 cench k2 *Cham* ptk1 *Cimic* br1 cocc ptk1 **Coloc** ptk1 **Cupr** br1* *Dios* ptk1 dulc ptk1 *Graph* ptk1 hippoc-k szs2 hyos ptk1 *Ign* ptk1 lac-loxod-a hrn2• lach ptk1 lat-h bnm5• lat-m sp1* *Lyc* ptk1 mag-m ptk1 mag-p tl1* *Nit-ac* ptk1 **Nux-v** ptk1 *Plat* ptk1 plb ptk1 rauw sp1 rheum ptk1 scop ptk1 sec ptk1 sil ptk1 stann ptk1 staph ptk1 **Sulph** ptk1 *Thal-met* br1 tril-p br1 valer mrr1 verat ptk1 verat-v ptk1 *Vib* br1* [bell-p-sp dcm1 *Mag-s* stj1]
  - **followed** by:
    - **paralysis**: tab ptk1
    - **stiffness**: sec ptk1 sel ptk1
  - **nervous**: *Cimic* br1
  - **wandering** pain: caust bg2 dios bg2 graph bg2
- **crushed**; as if: anh sp1 apis a1 asaf vh *Canth* a1 lap-la rsp1 ran-b bg2 verb bg2
- **cutting** pain: acon tl1* ambr b7a.de ang b7a.de arg-met b7a.de bell tl1* brass-n-o srj5• bry ptk1 *Calc* ptk1 calc-p ptk1 calc-s ptk1 *Canth* ptk1 carc gk6 **Coloc** ptk1 *Con* ptk1 dios ptk1 hyos b7a.de* *Ign* b7a.de kali-c tl1* kali-m ptk1 lat-m bnm6• loxo-lae bnm12• lyc ptk1 merc ptk1 *Nat-m* ptk1 nit-ac ptk1 *Nux-v* ptk1 petr ptk1 plan ptk1 polyg-h ptk1 puls ptk1 rat ptk1 sabal ptk1 sil ptk1 *Sulph* ptk1 tell ptk1 verat ptk1 xan mrr1 zinc ptk1
  - **knife**; as with a: paraf br1
- **darting** (See stitching)
- **deep**: bar-c bg2 eup-per bg2 gels bg2 mang ↓
  - **sore**: mang ptk1
- **digging** pain (= burrowing, rooting sensation): *Acon* k* *Agar* k* alum k* alum-p k2 alum-sil k2 am-c k* *Am-m* k* ambr k* anac k* *Androc* srj1• ang b2.de* ant-c k* ant-t k* arg-met k* arg-n *Arn* k* ars k* *Asaf* k* asar k* aur k* bar-c k* bar-m *Bell* k* bism k* borx k* *Bov* k* *Bry* k* *Calc* k* cann-s k* canth k* caps k* carb-an k* carb-v k* *Caust* k* cham k* chel k* chin k* *Cina* k* clem k* cocc k* colch k* *Coloc* k* con k* croc k* dig k* dros k* **Dulc** k* euph k* ferr k* graph k* guare a1 hell k* hep k* ign k* *Kali-bi* *Kali-c* k* kali-n k* kreos k* laur k* led k* lyc k* m-ambo b2.de* m-arct b2.de* m-aust b2.de* mag-c k* mag-m k* mang k* merc k* mez k* mur-ac k* *Nat-c* k* nat-m k* nux-m k* nux-v k* olnd k* petr k* ph-ac k* *Phos* k* *Plat* k* psil ft1 puls k* rheum k* **Rhod** k* *Rhus-t* k* *Ruta* k* sabad k* sabin k* samb k* seneg k* *Sep* k* sil k* **Spig** k* spong k* squil k* *Stann* k* staph k* stront-c k* sul-ac k* sulph k* thuj k* valer k* zinc k*
- **disappear** suddenly: arum-t hr1* **Bell** hr1* carb-ac hr1* cimic hr1* *Dios* sf1.de helo-s bnm14• mag-p sf1.de stry-p sf1.de thuj sf1.de tung-met bdx1•
- **dragging** (= hard pulling, tugging): acon b2.de* cann-s b2.de* canth b2.de* caust b2.de* coloc b2.de* lil-t ptk1 m-ambo b2.de* merc b2.de* mez b2.de* nux-v b2.de* petr b2.de* podo bg2 puls b2.de* sep b2.de* staph b2.de* verat b2.de*
  - **load**; as from a: aloe ptk1
- **drawing** pain: acon k* adon sf1.de agar j5.de aloe alum j5.de am-c k* ambr j5.de anac k* ang j5.de ant-t j5.de aphis j5.de apoc-a br1 aran-ix mg1.de arg-met arn j5.de* ars j5.de asar j5.de aur-m k2* bar-act a1 bar-c k* bell j5.de* berb sf1.de borx j5.de* *Bry* k* calc j5.de* calc-p k2* calen j5.de *Camph* k* cann-s j5.de canth j5.de caps j5.de carb-ac sf1.de carb-an j5.de **Carb-v** k* card-m k2* *Caul* caust k* *Cham* j5.de* **Chel** k* chin j5.de* chinin-ar chinin-s j5.de cic j5.de cimic k2* cist j5.de clem k* coc-c k* cocc j5.de colch k* **Coloc** k* *Crot-t* cycl j5.de* dig digin a1 *Dulc* j5.de* esp-g kk1.de euon k* eupi k* ferr-ar *Gamb* k* goss k* **Graph** k* guaj k2* guare k* hell hep j5.de hist mg1.de hydrc k* hyos j5.de ip j5.de kali-bi k* kali-c k* kreos k* lach k* lact k* lam j5.de led j5.de* lil-t ptk1 lup j5.de lyc k* m-arct j5.de mag-c mg1.de mag-m j5.de* *Mang* k* med k2* merc k* merc-c j5.de mez k* *Mosch* j5.de mur-ac j5.de nat-c j5.de **Nit-ac** k* nux-m j5.de *Nux-v* k* *Ol-an* k* olnd j5.de petr j5.de ph-ac j5.de* phos k* phyt k2* plat k* **Plb** j5.de* *Puls* k* ran-s j5.de raph k* rhod k* **Rhus-t** j5.de* sabad j5.de sabin j5.de samb j5.de sars h2* sec k* sep k* *Sil* h2* stann k* staph k* stram j5.de sul-ac j5.de sulph k* tab k* ter j5.de thuj k* tritic-vg fd5.de tub k2 **Valer** k* verat j5.de viol-o j5.de *Zinc* k2* zinc-o j5.de zinc-ox j5.de

- **alternating** with | **Heart** symptoms (See CHEST - Heart; complaints - alternating - drawing)
- **backward** as by a cord: crot-t mrr1 par mrr1 plb mrr1
- **cold**; as from taking a: plat h2
- **cramping**: am-c b4a.de *Calc* b4a.de **Coloc** b4a.de con b4a.de *Graph* b4a.de kali-c b4a.de kali-n b4.de *Lyc* b4a.de nit-ac b4a.de petr b4.de phos b4a.de plat b4a.de* *Sil* b4.de* sul-ac b4a.de zinc b4a.de
- **downward**: agn b7a.de ant-t b7a.de bism b7a.de *Bry* b7a.de camph b7a.de caps b7a.de chel b7a.de chin b7a.de cina b7a.de croc b7a.de *Ferr* b7a.de laur b7a.de *M-aust* b7a.de sabin b7a.de squil b7a.de verat b7a.de verb b7a.de
- **paralyzed**; as if: coc-c k* staph h1
- **string**; as if with a (See backward)
- **upward**: *Arn* b7a.de cann-s b7a.de colch b7a.de *M-arct* b7a.de nux-v b7a.de *Ol-an* puls b7a.de sacch-a fd2.de• spong b7a.de

- **dull** pain: **Agar** b2.de* agn b2.de* alum b2.de* anac b2.de* *Ant-c* b2.de* ant-t b2.de* asar b2.de* bism b2.de* borx b2.de* bov b2.de* bry b2.de* calc b2.de* camph b2.de* canth b2.de* carb-v b2.de* caust b2.de* chel b2.de* *Chin* b2.de* cic b2.de* cina b2.de* clem b2.de* cocc b2.de* coff b2.de* coloc b2.de* con b2.de* cycl b2.de* dros b2.de* *Dulc* b2.de* euph b2.de* ferr b2.de* *Hell* b2.de* hep b2.de* **Hyos** b2.de* *Ign* b2.de* *Kreos* b2.de* lat-m bnm6• *Laur* b2.de* led b2.de* *Lyc* b2.de* m-aust b2.de mang b2.de* meny b2.de* merc b2.de* mez b2.de* mosch b2.de* nat-c b2.de* nat-m b2.de* nit-ac b2.de* nux-v b2.de* olnd b2.de* ph-ac b2.de* phos b2.de* plat b2.de* plb b2.de* puls b2.de* ran-s b2.de* rheum b2.de* rhod b2.de* rhus-t b2.de* sabad b2.de* samb b2.de* sars b2.de* sec b2.de* seneg b2.de* sep b2.de* sil b2.de* spig b2.de* spong b2.de* squil b2.de* stront-c b2.de* sul-ac b2.de* teucr b2.de* thuj b2.de* verat b2.de* verb b2.de* viol-o b2.de* viol-t b2.de* zinc b2.de*
- **during** | **agg.**: *Acon* b7a.de *Ant-t* b7.de* *Ars* b4.de* bov b4.de* *Bry* b7.de *Carb-v* b4a.de caust b4.de *Cham* b7.de* cimic ptk1 *Coff* b7a.de coloc b4a.de* dulc b4a.de euph b4a.de graph b4.de* *Hep* b4a.de ign ptk1 *Ip* b7a.de *Kali-n* b4a.de lyc ptk1 *Mag-c* b4a.de mang b4a.de mez b4.de* *Nat-c* b4.de* *Nat-m* b4a.de nux-v b7.de onos ptk1 plat b4a.de *Puls* b7.de* *Ran-s* b7a.de rhus-t ptk1 ruta b7.de sabad b7.de *Sars* b4a.de* sep b4.de* sil b4.de* sulph b4.de thuj ptk1 *Verat* b7.de*
- **eating** | **after**:
  - **agg.**: camph ↓ lach ↓
    - **drawing** pain: camph h1
    - **sore**: lach b7a.de
  - **while** | **agg.**: phos b4a.de
- **electric** shock; as from an: cimic br1 cina ptk1 hippoc-k szs2 phyt tl1 thal-xyz srj8• zinc-chr ptk1
- **eructations** | **amel.**: jal st
- **eruptions**:
  - **herpetic**; after: caust ↓ dol ↓ kali-chl ↓ kalm ↓ mez ↓ plan ↓ prun ↓ ran-b ↓ vario ↓ zinc ↓
    - **neuralgic**: *(↗SKIN - Eruptions - herpetic - neuralgia)* caust ptk1 dol ptk1 kali-chl ptk1 kalm ptk1 mez ptk1 plan ptk1* prun ptk1 ran-b ptk1* vario ptk1 zinc ptk1
    - **touch**:
      - **agg.**: petr ↓
        - **neuralgic**: petr ptk1
      - **amel.**: zinc ↓
        - **neuralgic**: zinc ptk1
  - **suppressed** eruptions; after: mez ↓
    - **neuralgic**: mez mrr1
- **everywhere**: hydr-ac ↓ olnd ↓
  - **cramping**: hydr-ac ptk1 olnd ptk1
- **excitement**: canth tl1 coff tl1
  - **agg.**: alum-sil k2*
- **exertion** agg.: *Berb* ↓
  - **radiating**: *Berb* br1
- **exertion**; on prolonged: mag-p ↓
  - **cramping**: mag-p ptk1
- **fall**; as from a: **Arn** b7.de *Ruta* b7.de
- **fever**; during: anders ↓ androc ↓ *Arn* ↓ *Ars* ↓ bapt ↓ *Cham* b7a.de *Coff* ↓ franc ↓ mosch ↓ nux-v ↓ phyt ↓ *Rhus-t* ↓ spig ↓
  - **intolerable**: *Ars* b4a.de *Cham* b7.de* *Coff* b7.de nux-v b7.de
- **fever**; during: ...
  - **sore**: anders zzc1• androc srj1• *Arn* bro1 bapt tl1 franc bro1 mosch b7.de phyt bro1 *Rhus-t* bro1 spig b7.de
- **flu**-like pain (See sore)
- **followed** by:
  - **soreness**: sang a1
  - **thirst** | **burning**; and (See STOMACH - Thirst - pain - after)
- **gnawing** pain: agn sf1.de* alum bg2 alum-sil k2* am-m b7.de* arg-met bg2 arg-n bg2 *Ars* k* bar-c bg2 bar-s k2* *Bell* bg2 berb ptk1 bry ptk1 calad bg2 *Calc* bg2 cann-xyz bg2 canth b7.de* carb-an bg2 carb-v bg2 caust k* cham ptk1 chel bg2 cocc bg2 coloc br1* *Con* bg2 *Cupr* bg2 dros b7.de* dulc bg2 glon bg2 graph ptk1 guaj bg* hep bg2 ign ptk1 iod bg2 kali-bi bg2 kali-c bg2 kali-i bg2 kali-s ptk1 *Kreos* bg2* lach b7a.de* laur b7.de *Lyc* bg2* mag-m ptk1 meny b7.de **Merc** k* mez bg2* nat-m bg2* nat-s bg* nit-ac bg* nux-v bg2 olnd bg2* ox-ac bg* par b7.de ph-ac bg2 phos bg2* *Plat* bg2* psor bg2 puls bg2* ran-b bg2 *Ran-s* b7.de* rhod bg2 rhus-t ptk1 **Ruta** bg2* sec bg* seneg bg2 sep ptk1 sil k* spong ptk1 stann bg2 staph k* sul-ac bg* sulph k* tarax b7.de thuj ptk1 verat bg2* zinc-chr ptk1
  - **itching** pain: *Agn* br1
- **gouty**: acon b7a.de* agar bg2 **Agn** b7.de* alum bg2 am-c bg2 am-m bg2 ambr b7.de* anac bg2 ang bg2 ant-c b7.de* ant-t b7a.de* **Arg-met** bg2 *Arn* b7.de* ars bg2 *Asaf* bg2 asar bg2 aur bg2 *Bar-c* bg2 **Bell** bg2 bism bg2 borx bg2 bov bg2 **Bry** b7.de* *Calc* bg2 camph bg2 cann-xyz bg2 canth b7a.de* caps bg2 carb-an bg2 carb-v bg2 *Caust* bg2 cham b7.de* chel b7a.de* *Chin* b7.de* cic b7a.de* cina bg2 clem bg2 *Cocc* b7.de* **Colch** b7.de* coloc bg2 con bg2 croc b7a.de cupr bg2 cycl bg2 dig bg2 dros bg2 dulc bg2 euph bg2 euphr bg2 *Ferr* b7.de* *Graph* bg2 guaj bg2 hell bg2 hep bg2 *Hyos* bg2 *Ign* b7a.de* iod bg2 **Kali-c** bg2 kali-n bg2 kreos bg2 laur bg2 **Led** b7.de* lyc bg2 m-ambo b7.de* mag-c bg2 mag-m bg2 *Meny* b7a.de* **Merc** bg2 *Mez* bg2 mosch bg2 mur-ac bg2 *Nat-c* bg2 *Nat-m* bg2 nit-ac bg2 nux-m b7.de* nux-v b7.de* olnd bg2 par bg2 petr bg2 ph-ac bg2 *Phos* bg2 plat bg2 plb bg2 *Puls* b7.de* ran-b b7a.de* ran-s b7a.de* rheum bg2 rhod bg2 **Rhus-t** b7.de* ruta bg2 sabad bg2 **Sabin** b7.de* samb bg2 *Sars* bg2 sec bg2 *Sep* bg2 sil bg2 spig b7a.de* **Spong** b7a.de* squil b7.de* *Stann* bg2 **Staph** b7a.de* stram bg2 *Stront-c* bg2 sul-ac bg2 *Sulph* bg2 tarax bg2 teucr bg2 *Thuj* bg2 valer bg2 verat b7.de* verb bg2 viol-o bg2 viol-t bg2 *Zinc* bg2
  - **wandering**: *Arn* b7a.de *Puls* b7a.de
  - ○ **Joints**: acon b2.de agar b2.de **Agn** b2.de alum b2.de am-c b2.de am-m b2.de ambr b2.de anac b2.de ang b2.de ant-c b2.de ant-t b2.de **Arg-met** b2.de arn b2.de* ars b2.de *Asaf* b2.de asar b2.de* aur b2.de bar-c b2.de* bell b2.de* bism b2.de borx b2.de bov b2.de bry b2.de* *Calc* b2.de camph b2.de cann-s b2.de canth b2.de caps b2.de carb-an b2.de carb-v b2.de *Caust* b2.de cham b2.de chel b2.de *Chin* b2.de* cic b2.de cina b2.de clem b2.de *Cocc* b2.de *Coff* bg2 **Colch** b2.de coloc b2.de con b2.de cupr b2.de* cycl b2.de dig b2.de* dros b2.de dulc b2.de euph b2.de euphr b2.de *Ferr* b2.de *Graph* b2.de guaj b2.de hell b2.de hep b2.de hyos b2.de* ign b2.de* iod b2.de ip bg2 **Kali-c** b2.de kali-n b2.de kreos b2.de laur b2.de* **Led** b2.de lyc b2.de m-ambo b2.de m-arct b2.de *M-aust* b2.de mag-c b2.de mag-m b2.de mang b2.de *Meny* b2.de merc b2.de* *Mez* b2.de mosch b2.de mur-ac b2.de *Nat-c* b2.de *Nat-m* b2.de nit-ac b2.de nux-m b2.de nux-v b2.de* olnd b2.de par b2.de petr b2.de ph-ac b2.de phos b2.de* plat b2.de plb b2.de puls b2.de* ran-b b2.de ran-s b2.de rheum b2.de rhod b2.de rhus-t b2.de* ruta b2.de sabad b2.de **Sabin** b2.de samb b2.de *Sars* b2.de sec b2.de *Sep* b2.de sil b2.de* spig b2.de **Spong** b2.de squil b2.de *Stann* b2.de **Staph** b2.de stram b2.de* *Stront-c* b2.de sul-ac b2.de *Sulph* b2.de tarax b2.de teucr b2.de *Thuj* b2.de valer b2.de verat b2.de verb b2.de viol-o b2.de* viol-t b2.de *Zinc* b2.de
  - **Nerves**: *Colch* bro1 coloc bro1 sulph bro1
- **gradually** increasing (See appear gradually)
- **grasping**, griping, clutching pain: acon b2.de* alum b2.de* *Am-c* b2.de* arn b2.de* bar-c b2.de* *Bell* b2.de* borx b2.de* cact bg2* **Calc** b2.de* *Carb-an* b2.de* carb-v b2.de* caust b2.de* cham b2.de* chin b2.de* cocc b2.de* *Coloc* b2.de* con b2.de* dros b2.de* *Euph* b2.de* gels bg2 graph b2.de* hep b2.de* hyos b2.de* *Ign* b2.de* ip b2.de* kali-c b2.de* kali-i bg2 kali-n b2.de* kreos b2.de* *Led* b2.de* lil-t ptk1 *Lyc* b2.de* m-arct b2.de m-aust b2.de mag-c b2.de* mag-m b2.de* meny b2.de* *Merc* b2.de* mosch b2.de* nat-c b2.de* nat-m b2.de* *Nux-v* b2.de* petr b2.de* phos b2.de* *Puls* b2.de* samb b2.de* sep b2.de* **Sil** b2.de* **Stann** b2.de* *Stront-c* b2.de* sul-ac b2.de* sulph b2.de* thyr ptk1 verat b2.de* zinc b2.de*
- **growing** pains: *(↗Growth; Growth - length; EXTREMITIES - Pain - leg - growing)* acon a1 agar bg2* ap-g br1* apiol ggd1 asaf ggd1 aur ggd1 bell bg2 calc ptk1 calc-f ggd1 calc-p k2* cimic hr1* conch mtf11 eup-per ggd1 *Ferr-act* bg2* *Guaj* b2.de* hipp bro1 m-aust b2.de* mang ptk1* mang-act br1*

- **growing** pains: ...
nat-m brm ol-an bg2 **Ph-ac** b2.de* phos bg2* plan ggd1 sil st1 syph mrr1 vitamin-d mtf11 [kali-p stj1 mag-p stj1 nat-p stj1]
- **hacking** pain (= as with a hatchet): am-c bg2* ars bg2* aur b2.de* calc bg2 clem ptk1 kali-n ptk1 lyc bg2* ph-ac b2.de* ruta bg2* staph b2.de* thuj b2.de*
- **headache**; during: seneg↓
  - **sore**: seneg k*
- **heat**; during: agar↓ androc↓ mang↓
  - **sore**: agar h2 androc srj1• mang h2
- **heated** walk and rapid cooling, after: *Bry*↓ **Rhus-t**↓ **Tub**↓
  - **sore**: *Bry* k* **Rhus-t Tub** gk
- **herpes**; before: staph ptk1
- **herpes** zoster; after: ars↓ caust↓ cimic↓ dol↓ hep↓ kalm↓ merc↓ mez↓ morg-p↓ morph↓ petr↓ plan↓ prun↓ ran-b↓ sil↓ stict↓ still↓ sul-ac↓ syph↓ thal↓ thuj↓ vac↓ vario↓ zinc↓
  - **neuralgic**: ars br* caust ptk cimic sne dol br* hep sne kalm br* merc br mez br* morg-p br morph br* petr ptk plan c2 prun br* ran-b br* sil br stict c2 still br sul-ac sne syph a1 thal dx* thuj tl1 vac jl2 vario br* zinc br*
- **idiopathic**: acon↓ ars↓
  - **neuralgic**: acon bro1 ars bro1
- **increase** (See appear gradually; appear suddenly)
- **increasing** and decreasing suddenly: *Med*↓ nit-ac↓
  - **drawing** pain: nit-ac h2
  - **neuralgic**: *Med* jl2
- **influenza**:
  - **after**: *Lycpr* br1 lycps-v ptk1
  - **agg.**: ars↓
    - **neuralgic**: ars bro1
  - **during**: bapt↓
    - **sore**: bapt tl1
- **injuries**; after:
  - ○ **Nerves**: all-c↓
    - **neuralgic**: all-c br1
- **intermittent**: *Asaf* b7a.de chir-fl bnm4• *Cupr* br1 lat-m sp1 *Stry* br1 *Valer* b7a.de
- **intolerable**: (↗*Sensitiveness - pain - unendurable; MIND - Sensitive - pain)* acon b7a.de* ars h2* *Cham* b7a.de* chir-fl bnm4• cimic hr1 **Coff** b7a.de* colch hr1 lat-m bnm6• med br1 nux-v h1* sars hr1 syph hr1
  - **burning**: sabin ptk1
- **intractable**: chir-fl bnm4•
- **jabbing**: rauw sp1
- **jerking** pain | **lightening**; sudden: daph br1
- **labor** like pain:
  - **accompanied** by | **leukorrhea**: *Bell* bg2 dros ptk1 ign bg2 kali-c bg2*
- **lancinating**: **Asaf** bg2 aster br1 lat-m bnm6•
- **lightning**-like: **Acon** bg2 agar bg2 *Alum* bg2 am-m bg2 anac bg2 apis bg2 *Arg-met* bg2 arg-n bg2 arn bg2 ars bg2 *Bell* bg2 carbn-s mrr1 *Cimic* bg2 **Coloc** bg2 *Dios* bg2 fl-ac bg2 gels bg2 *Graph* bg2 hydr-ac bg2 *Kalm* bg2 kreos bg2 lyc bg2 nat-m bg2 nux-m bg2 *Plb* bg2 sulph bg2 *Valer* bg2 zinc bg2
  - **accompanied** by | **locomotor** ataxia: *Acetan* bro1 *Aesc* bro1 agar bro1 alum bro1 *Am-m* bro1 ang bro1 arg-n bro1 *Ars* bro1 ars-i bro1 *Atro* bro1 bar-m bro1 *Bell* bro1 berb bro1 dig bro1 *Fl-ac* bro1 guaj bro1 hyos bro1 ign bro1 *Kalm* br1* lyc bro1 merc-c bro1 nit-ac bro1 nux-m bro1 *Nux-v* bro1 ol-sant bro1 *Phos* bro1 *Phys* bro1 pilo bro1 plb bro1 plb-i bro1 sabad bro1 santa bro1 *Sec* bro1 sil bro1 *Stront-c* bro1 stry bro1 thal bro1 thiosin bro1 zinc bro1 *Zinc-p* bro1 zinc-s bro1
- **line**; in a: all-c a1* bell ptk1 bufo ptk1* caps ll1* caust ptk1 fago ptk1 ox-ac c1* pyrog ptk1 syph hr1* tell a1*
- **lying**:
  - **abdomen**; on | **amel.**: atra-r bnm3•
  - **agg.**: ruta tl1
  - **back**; on | **amel.**: pert-vc vk9
  - **side**; on:
    - **affected** side:
      - **agg.**: kali-c tl1
      - **amel.**: bry tl1
- **malarial**: aran↓ *Ars*↓ *Cedr*↓ chin↓ chinin-ar↓ *Chinin-s*↓ meny↓ nat-m↓ nicc-s↓ stann↓ sulph↓
  - **neuralgic**: aran bro1 *Ars* bro1 *Cedr* br1* chin bro1 chinin-ar br1 *Chinin-s* bro1 meny bro1 nat-m bro1 nicc-s br1* stann bro1 sulph bro1
- **menopause**; during: lach↓
  - **neuralgic**: lach bro1
- **menses**:
  - **after**:
    - **agg.**: berb↓ *Bry* bro1 chin↓ cimic↓ cupr↓ ham bro1 iod bro1 kreos bro1 puls↓ *Sep* bro1
      - **cramping**: chin ptk1 cupr bg2* puls ptk1
      - **inflammatory**: cimic bro1
      - **neuralgic**: cimic bro1
      - **tearing** pain: berb bg2
  - **before**:
    - **agg.**: alum b4a.de caust↓ coff↓ con↓ cupr↓ iod b4a.de lach↓ mag-c↓ merc↓ nit-ac↓ phos↓
      - **cramping**: caust bg2 coff bg2 cupr bg2 mag-c bg2 merc bg2 phos bg2
      - **sore**: con bg2 lach bg2 nit-ac bg2
  - **during**:
    - **agg.**: alum b4a.de* am-c bg2 ambr↓ aml-ns↓ aran↓ ars b4a.de bar-c bg2 *Bell* bg2 berb bg2 bry bg2 cact bg2 canth b7a.de carb-v bg2 caul bg2 *Cham*↓ chel b7.de cimic bg2 *Cocc* b7a.de *Coff*↓ con↓ croc b7a.de cupr↓ gels bg2 graph b4a.de* *Hyos*↓ *Ign*↓ iod b4.de kalm↓ **Lach**↓ mag-c b4a.de* mag-m↓ nat-c b4.de* nit-ac bg2 nux-m bg2 nux-v bg2 petr bg2 phos↓ *Puls* bg2 sabin bg2 *Sel*↓ sep b4a.de spong↓ stram bg2 tarent bg2 verat bg2 zinc bg2
      - **cramping**: *Cham* b7.de* *Cocc* b7.de* *Coff* b7a.de *Croc* b7a.de cupr b7.de* *Hyos* b7.de *Ign* b7a.de **Lach** b7a.de mag-m ptk1 *Puls* b7.de *Sel* b7a.de
      - **drawing** pain: phos k*
      - **neuralgic**: aml-ns bg2* aran ptk1 berb bg2 gels bg2 kalm bg2 verat bg2
      - **sore**: ambr bg2 carb-v bg2 cimic a1* con bg2 nat-c k* nit-ac bg2 petr h2* sep b4a.de* spong bg2 stram bg2
      - **stitching** pain: nat-c b4.de
  - **suppressed**; from: kalm↓
    - **neuralgic**: kalm ptk1
- **motion**:
  - **agg.**: acon↓ act-sp br1 *Aesc*↓ alum-sil k2 *Arn*↓ bapt↓ bov↓ *Bry*↓ calc↓ cassia-s cdd7*• chel↓ colch↓ cupr br1 cycl↓ *Hep*↓ lach↓ lat-h bnm5• loxo-lae bnm12• merc-c↓ ox-ac br1 phyt↓ plb↓ sil tl1 *Spig*↓ staph↓ ther k2 zinc-chr↓
    - **drawing** pain: calc k* cycl k*
    - **sore**: acon tl1 *Aesc* a1* *Arn* kr1 bapt bov a1 *Bry* k* chel colch tl1 *Hep* kr1 lach merc-c a1 phyt k* plb staph h1
    - **stabbing** pain: *Bry* tl1 *Spig* tl1
    - **stitching** pain: *Bry* br1* *Spig* tl1 zinc-chr ptk1
    - **tearing** pain: *Bry* br1
  - **amel.**: androc↓ ars-h↓ brucel↓ caust↓ galeoc-c-h gms1• kali-c br1 lat-m bnm6• *Pyrog*↓ rad-br↓ *Rhus-t*↓ *Tub*↓
    - **aching**: rad-br br1
    - **sore**: androc srj1• ars-h kr1 caust *Pyrog Rhus-t Tub*
    - **wandering** pain: brucel sa3•
  - **bed** agg.; in: sol-t-ae↓
    - **sore**: sol-t-ae
  - **must** move: mag-c↓
    - **shooting** pain: mag-c bg
- **nail**; as from a: hist sp1
- **neuralgic**: acetan bro1 *Acon* c2* acon-c c2 acon-f c2 aconin c2* adren br1 agar c2* all-c br1* am-pic c2* am-val bro1 aml-ns bro1 anag c2 apoc c2* aran c2* arg-met mrr1 arg-n c2* *Arn* bro1 *Ars* b4a.de* ars-s-r c2 asaf c2 astac c2 aster br1 atro c2* *Bell* b4a.de* berb mrr1 *Bry* bg* cact c2* caj bro1 calc c2 calc-caust c2 *Cann-i* bro1 canth c2 caps c2 carb-ac c2* card-m c2 caust bg* *Cedr* c2* cere-b c2 *Cham* bg* *Chel* c2* *Chin* bg* *Chinin-ar* bro1 chinin-m c2 *Chinin-s* c2* cimic c2* cina c2 cit-v c2 *Clem* br1 cocc-s br1 coff c2* *Coloc* c2* colocin c2* com c2* con bro1 corn-f bro1 crot-c sk4• crot-chlol c2 crot-t c2 cupr c2 cur c2 cypr c2 dendr-pol sk4• dios bg* dirc c2 dol c2 dulc c2* elat c2* eupi c2 ferr c2 ferr-m c2

- **neuralgic**: ...
ferr-p c2 form-ac mtf11 gaul c2* gels c2* *Glon* c2* *Gnaph* bro1 grat c2 guaj c2* hecla c2 helo mtf11 helo-s c2 hyos c2 hyper bg* ichth c2 **Ign** bg* ip bro1 irid-met c2 iris c2* kali-ar c2* *Kali-bi* bg* kali-chl c2 kali-cy c2 kali-fcy bro1 *Kali-i* c2* *Kalm* c2* kreos c2* lac-c c2 lach bg* lat-h bnm5• lob mrr1 loxo-lae bnm12• *Lyc* bg* lyss c2 mag-c c2* mag-m mrr1 *Mag-p* bg* mag-s c2 malar c2 *Med* br1* mentho br1 meny bro1 merc bg* methyl c2* *Mez* c2* morph c2* nat-m bg* nicc-s bro1 *Nux-v* bg* onos br1* ox-ac c2* par c2* passi br1 paull c2 *Phos* bg* *Phyt* c2* pime c2 pip-m c2 pip-n c2 *Plan* c2* *Plat* c2* plb br1* plect c2 polyg-xyz c2 prim-v c2 prot jl2 prun c2* *Psor* bg* *Puls* bg* ran-a c2 *Ran-b* c2* ran-s c2 *Rhod* c2* rhus-t c2* rob c2* rumx ptk1 ruta mrr1 sabad c2 sabal c2 sacch-l c2 sal-ac mtf11 salol c2 sang c2* sanic c2 sec c2 sep c2 sil b4a.de* *Spig* bg* *Stann* c2* *Staph* c2* stict c2 sul-ac c2* *Sulph* bg* sumb c2* syph c2* tarax c2 ter c2 *Thal-met* br1 thea c2* ther bro1* thuj c2* til c2 tong br1 trach-xyz c2 tub bro1* vac br1 *Valer* c2* vario c2 *Verat* bg* *Verb* bg* verin c2 visc br1 xan c2* zinc c2* *Zinc-p* c2* *Zinc-val* br1*
  - **accompanied** by:
    - **colic**: alumn bro1 ant-t bro1 ars bro1 *Atro* bro1 *Bell* bro1 cham bro1 *Cocc* bro1 coloc bro1* cupr bro1 cupr-ar bro1 *Dios* bro1 euph bro1 hydr-ac bro1 hyos bro1 kali-c bro1 mag-p bro1* *Nux-v* bro1 op bro1 *Plb* bro1 plb-act bro1 santin bro1 tab bro1 verat bro1 zinc bro1
    - **constipation**: alum gm1 alum-sil gm1 alumn gm1 plb gm1
    - **coryza**: verb bg2
    - **formication**: acon mtf11
    - **numbness**: (↗*Numbness - pain - during; Numbness - painful*) *Kalm* br1
    - **tearing** pains; severe: coloc tl1 ruta tl1
    - **Brain**; congestion of (See HEAD - Congestion - brain - accompanied - pain)
  - **agonizing**: kali-cy br1
  - **excruciating**: helo-s bnm14• mag-p tl1
  - **followed** by | **mania** (See MIND - Mania - neuralgia)
  - **gouty**: cimic bro1 *Colch* bro1 coloc bro1 kalm bro1 phyt bro1 ran-b bro1 *Rhod* bro1 rhus-t bro1 sulph bro1
  - **hot** needles touched the parts; as if: agar tl1 ars tl1
  - **ice** touched the part; as if: agar tl1
- **noise** agg. the pains: ars gm1 canth tl1 coff k2* *Ther* br1
- **nursing** agg.: cham ↓
  - **cramping**: cham ptk1
- **operation**; after: (↗*Injuries - operation - ailments*) cupr ↓ hyper br1*
  - **neuralgic**: cupr ptk1
- **oppressive** (= causing a sensation of oppression): agar b2.de* ant-c b2.de* ars b2.de* *Bell* b2.de* bov b2.de* bry b2.de* calc b2.de* cann-s b2.de* caust b2.de* cham b2.de* chin b2.de* cic b2.de* cina b2.de* cocc b2.de* coff b2.de* colch b2.de* *Con* b2.de* euphr b2.de* hyos b2.de* ign b2.de* kreos b2.de* *Mag-c* b2.de* mag-m b2.de* **Mosch** b2.de* nat-m b2.de* nux-v b2.de* plat b2.de* plb b2.de* puls b2.de* rhus-t b2.de* ruta b2.de* sabad b2.de* sec b2.de* seneg b2.de* sep b2.de* spig b2.de* staph b2.de* teucr b2.de* viol-t b2.de*
- **paralyzed**; as if: acon k* agar k* agn k* alum k* alum-sil k2* am-c k* am-m k* ambr k* ang b2.de* ant-c k* arg-met k* arg-n bg2 *Arn* b7a.de ars k* ars-i asaf k* asar k* *Aur* k* bar-c k* **Bell** k* *Bism* k* bov k* *Bry* calc k* cann-s k* canth k* caps j5.de carb-v k* caust k* *Cham* k* chel k* *Chin* k* **Cina** k* **Cocc** k* coff k* **Colch** k* coloc k* con k* croc k* crot-h **Cycl** k* dig k* dros k* *Dulc* k* eug j5.de euph k* euphr k* *Ferr* k* ferr-ar ferr-m j5.de gels bg2 graph k* grat bg2 hell k* hep k* hyos k* ign k* iod k* kali-c k* kali-n k* kali-p kreos k* lach j5.de *Laur* led k* lyc k* m-arct j5.de m-aust b2.de mag-c k* mag-m k* mang k* meny k* meph j5.de merc k* *Mez* k* mosch k* mur-ac k* nat-c k* *Nat-m* k* **Nux-v** k* olnd k* par k* petr k* ph-ac k* phos k* plat k* plb k* puls k* ran-s k* raph a1 rheum j5.de rhod k* *Rhus-t* k* ruta k* sabad k* **Sabin** k* sars k* sel k* seneg k* sep k* *Sil* k* spig k* stann k* *Staph* k* stram k* stront-c k* sul-ac k* sulph k* teucr k* thuj k* valer k* *Verat* k* verb k* zinc k*
- **paroxysmal**: lat-m bnm6• rauw sp1
- **periodical**: cact ↓ nicc-s ↓ parth ↓ toxi ↓
  - **daily** at the same hour: kali-bi ↓ sulph ↓
    - **neuralgic**: kali-bi tl1 sulph tl1
  - **neuralgic**: cact ptk1 nicc-s c2* parth c2 toxi c2
- **perspiration**:
  - **amel.**: clem ↓
    - **neuralgic**: clem br1
- **pierced**; as if: apis ptk1 lat-m bnm6• mill ptk1 nat-s ptk1
- **pierced**; as if: ...
  - **hot** iron; by a: *Alum* b2.de*
- **pinching** pain: acon bg2 adam srj5• agar k* alum k* alum-sil k2* *Am-c* hr1* **Am-m** b7.de* ambr anac k* ang bg2 ant-c b7.de* arg-met b7.de* **Arn** k* *Ars* ars-i asar aur bg2 bar-c a1 **Bell** k* berb bg2 bov k* bry k* *Calc* k* calc-i k2* cann-s k* canth k* *Caps* k* carb-an k* carb-v k* caust k* *Cham* *Chel* bg2* *Chin* b7.de* cina k* clem cocc k* *Colch* coloc con k* croc k* daph a1 dig bg2 dros k* dulc k* *Euph* k* euphr b7.de* *Gamb* a1 *Graph* hr1* guaj hell k* hep *Hyos* b7.de* ign k* iod k* *Ip* b7.de* kali-c k* kali-chl k13 kali-i a1 kali-m k2 kali-n kreos k* lat-m bnm6• *Laur* k* led b7.de* lyc k* m-arct b2.de m-aust b7.de mag-c bg2 mag-m k* mang k* meny k* *Merc* k* *Mez* **Mosch** b7.de* mur-ac k* *Nat-c* k* nat-m k* nit-ac nux-m k* **Nux-v** k* olnd b7.de* op par k* petr k* ph-ac bg2* *Phos* k* *Plat* k* **Plb** bg2 *Puls* k* ran-b ran-s *Rheum* rhod k* *Rhus-t* k* ruta k* *Sabad* k* sabin k* samb bg2 sars k* seneg k* sep k* sil k* spig k* *Spong* k* stann k* staph k* stront-c k* sul-ac bg2 *Sulph* k* teucr thuj k* tub k2* valer k* verat k* verb k* viol-t bg2 zinc k*
  - **sensation** of sudden pinch: arg-n br1
- **pneumogastric** complaints; arising from: arn ↓
  - **neuralgic**: arn br1
- **pressing** pain: hist sp1 vanil fd5.de [bell-p-sp dcm1]
  - **blunt** instrument; as from a: *Anac* bg2 carb-v b2.de* cina b2.de* hyos b2.de* lith-c ptk1 mur-ac b2.de* nat-m b2.de* rheum b2.de* valer bg2
  - **inward**: acon k* agar k* alum k* **Anac** k* ant-c k* ant-t k* asaf k* asar k* aur k* bar-c k* bell k* bism k* borx k* bry k* *Calc* k* cann-s k* carb-an k* caust k* *Chel* k* chin k* *Cocc* k* coff k* croc k* cycl k* *Dulc* k* *Hell* k* hep k* ign k* kali-c k* *Kreos* k* laur k* m-ambo b2.de* m-arct b2.de mez k* mosch k* *Nit-ac* k* nux-m k* nux-v k* *Olnd* k* ph-ac k* **Plat** k* prun st1 ran-s k* rheum k* rhod k* rhus-t k* ruta k* sabad k* sabin k* sars k* sep k* sil k* *Spig* k* **Stann** k* *Staph* k* sul-ac k* *Sulph* k* tarax k* teucr k* thuj k* valer k* verb k* viol-t k* *Zinc* k*
    - **deep** inward as if with instruments: *Bov* k* ign ptk1 verat k*
  - **load**; as from a: *Abies-n* **Acon** k* *Aesc* agar k* aloe k* alum k* am-c k* *Am-m* k* *Ambr* k* *Ant-t* k* aral bg2 aran arg-met k* *Arg-n* arn k* *Ars* k* asaf k* asar k* aur *Bar-c* k* **Bell** k* bism k* borx k* bov k* **Brom** **Bry** k* *Cact* k* calad k* calc k* camph k* cann-s k* carb-an k* carb-v k* caust k* cham k* *Chel* chin k* cina k* cinnb cocc k* colch k* coloc k* *Com* *Con* k* corn croc k* crot-t *Cupr* k* dig k* ferr k* gels glon bg2 graph k* hell k* hep k* hyos k* ign k* iod k* **Ip** kali-c k* kali-chl kali-n k* *Kreos* k* laur k* led k* **Lil-t** lyc k* m-ambo b2.de* *M-arct* b2.de mag-c k* mag-m k* mang k* *Meli* **Meny** k* merc k* mosch k* *Nat-c* k* nat-m k* nit-ac k* nux-m k* **Nux-v** k* olnd k* *Op* k* **Par** k* petr k* *Ph-ac* k* phel bg2 **Phos** k* plat k* plb k* *Psor* *Puls* k* **Ran-b** rheum b2.de* rhod k* **Rhus-t** k* sabad k* sabin k* *Samb* k* sars k* *Sec* k* seneg k* **Sep** k* *Sil* k* *Spig* k* spong k* squil k* stann k* staph k* **Stict** stront-c k* sul-ac k* **Sulph** k* thuj k* valer k* *Verb* k* viol-o k* zinc k* zing
  - **outward**: asaf ptk1 bry ptk1 cimic ptk1 puls ptk1 sulph ptk1
  - **plug**; as from a: anac c1
  - **together**: acon k* aeth bg2 agar k* **Alum** k* am-m k* ambr k* *Anac* k* ang b2.de* ant-c k* ant-t k* arg-met k* arg-n bg2 *Arn* k* *Ars* k* asaf k* **Asar** k* aur k* bar-c k* *Bell* k* *Bov* k* bry k* cact bg2 calc k* camph k* *Cann-s* k* *Canth* k* caps k* carb-an k* carb-v k* caust k* cham k* chel k* chin k* cic k* cimic bg2 cina k* **Cocc** k* coff k* coloc k* con k* cupr k* dig k* *Dros* k* dulc k* euph k* ferr k* graph k* guaj k* *Hell* k* helo bg2 hydr-ac bg2 hyos k* ign k* iod k* *Ip* k* kali-c k* kali-i bg2 kali-n k* laur k* led k* lil-t bg2 lyc k* m-arct b2.de mag-c k* mag-m k* meny k* merc k* mez k* *Mosch* k* *Nat-m* k* nat-sil fd3.de• nit-ac k* nux-m k* **Nux-v** k* olnd k* op k* petr k* ph-ac k* phos k* **Plat** k* plb k* puls k* ran-s k* rhod k* rhus-t k* ruta k* sabad k* sabin k* *Sars* k* seneg k* sep k* sil k* spig k* *Spong* k* squil k* *Stann* k* staph k* stram k* stront-c k* *Sul-ac* k* **Sulph** k* symph fd3.de• tarax k* teucr k* thuj k* valer k* verat k* verb k* viol-o k* viol-t zinc k*
  - **upward**: calc-p bg2
  - **within** outward, from: *Acon* k* *Aloe* k* alum k* am-c k* am-m k* anac k* ang b2.de* ant-c k* arg-met k* arn k* **Asaf** k* asar k* *Aur* k* bar-c k* *Bell* k* berb k* bism k* borx k* **Bry** k* calc k* camph k* cann-s k* canth k* caps k* carb-v k* caust k* chel k* chin k* **Cimic** k* cina k* clem k* cocc k* coff b2.de* colch k* coloc k* con k* *Cor-r* k* croc k* cupr k* dig k* *Dros* k* dulc k* euph k* *Ferr* k* graph k* guaj k* hell k* hep k* *Ign* k* ip k* kali-c k* *Kali-i* k* kali-n k* kreos k* lach k* laur k* led k* *Lil-t* *Lith-c* lyc k* *M-arct* b2.de m-aust b2.de mag-m k* mang k* meli k* meny k* *Merc* k* *Merc-c* k* *Mez* k* *Mur-ac* k* nat-c k* *Nat-m* k* nit-ac k* nux-m k* *Nux-v* k* *Olnd* k* op k* *Par* k* petr k* ph-ac k* *Phos* k* plat k* *Prun* k* psil ft1 **Puls** k* ran-b k* ran-s k*

- **within** outward, from: ...
rheum k* rhod k* *Rhus-t* k* ruta k* sabad k* *Sabin* k* samb k* seneg k* *Sep* k* *Sil* k* *Spig* k* *Spong* k* *Squil* k* *Stann* k* staph k* stront-c k* sul-ac k* **Sulph** k* tarax k* *Teucr* k* *Thuj* k* **Valer** b2.de* *Verb* k* viol-t k* zinc k*

- **pressure**:
  - **agg.**: alum-sil ↓ bry ↓ kali-c ↓ **Plat** ↓ plb ↓ sulph ↓ ven-m ↓
    - **cramping**: plat tl1
    - **sore**: alum-sil k2* bry h1 kali-c tl1 **Plat** k* plb k* sulph k2 ven-m rsj12•
    - **stitching** pain: bry br1
  - **amel.**: atra-r bnm3• bry ↓ cassia-s cdd7*• *Coloc* ↓ galeoc-c-h gms1• mag-p ↓
    - **neuralgic**: *Coloc* br1 mag-p tl1
    - **sore**: bry tl1 mag-p tl1
- **pulsating** (See Pulsation - externally; Pulsation - internally)
- **radiating**: *Agar* bg2* androc srj1• apis sf1.de *Arg-n* k* ars bg2* bamb-a stb2.de* bapt bg2 *Berb* k* caust bg2 chir-fl bnm4• cimic bg2 coloc bg2 cupr bg2* *Dios* k* helo-s bnm14• hyper bg2 influ jl2 kali-bi tl1 kali-c sf1.de kali-n bg kalm bg2 lat-h bnm5• lat-m bnm6• lil-t sf1.de mag-m bg2 *Mag-p* k* merc bg2 mez bg2 plb bg2 sil bg2 spig bg2* *Tell* xan c1
- **raw**; as if: am-c ptk1 arum-t ptk1 berb ptk1 *Canth* br1* caps ptk1 carb-v ptk1 *Caust* br1 erig ptk1 *Get* br1 hydr ptk1 lyc ptk1 manc ptk1 meli ptk1 nux-v ptk1 ran-s ptk1 sin-n ptk1 sul-i ptk1 sulph ptk1
- **red** hard nodules: petr ↓
  - **sore**: petr
- **rest**:
  - **agg.**: kali-c ↓ kreos ↓ magn-gr ↓ thuj ↓ tub ↓
    - **drawing** pain: tub k2*
    - **neuralgic**: kreos br1
    - **sore**: kali-c tl1 magn-gr br1
    - **tearing** pain: thuj br1 tub k2*
  - **amel.**: *Bry* ↓ cassia-s cdd7*•
    - **sore**: bry tl1
    - **tearing** pain: *Bry* br1
- **restlessness**; with | **aching** (See MIND - Restlessness - pain, from)
- **rheumatic**: (↗*EXTREMITIES - Pain - rheumatic)* abrot tl1 acon b7.de* act-sp br1 adren br1 aesc tl1 agar tl1 alf br1 am-c ↓ *Ambr* b7.de* ang b7.de* *Ant-c* b7.de* *Ant-t* b7.de* anthraco br1 apoc-a br1 arb c1* arn b7.de* asaf b7.de* aspar br1 asper ktp2 aur tl1 aza br1 bell tl1 bell-p br1* *Berb* bg2* bry b7.de* *Bufo* br1 calc-f sp1 camph b7a.de cann-s b7.de* carb-v ↓ carc br1 caust tl1* cham b7.de* chel ↓ chin b7.de* cimic bg2* clem br1 *Cocc* b7.de* coff b7.de* colch b7.de* croc b7a.de cupr b7.de* cycl b7.de* *Dulc* bg2* elaps br1 euphr b7.de* ferr bg2 ferr-p tl1 form bg2 franc br1 gels bg2 get br1 *Gins* br1 gnaph br1 *Guaj* br1 hipp jl2 hyos b7.de* *Ign* b7.de* irid-met br1 jac-c br1 kali-s tl1 kalm br1 lac-ac br1 lac-c br1 lat-m bnm6• *Led* b7.de* lyc bg2 *Lycpr* br1 m-ambo b7.de* mag-s sp1 magn-gr br1 *Med* jl2 nat-m br1 nat-p tl1 **Nux-v** b7.de* nvct br1 ol-j br1 phor-t mie3• phyt bg2 pin-s br1 plb b7.de* prim-v br1 psor jl2 puls b7.de* rad-br c11* ran-b b7a.de* *Rham-cal* br1 *Rhod* br1 *Rhus-t* b7.de* sabad b7.de* sabin b7.de* sal-ac br1* sang bg2 sec bg2 sil bg2 *Spig* c1* spira br1 squil b7.de* *Stel* br1 *Stict* br1 stront-c br1 sul-ac ↓ syph br1 teucr b7.de* tub tl1 tub-m jl2 *Valer* b7.de* verat b7.de* verat-v tl1 visc br1* xan br1
  - **alternating** sides: lac-c bro1
  - **left** side: *Ox-ac* br1
  - **accompanied** by:
    - **dysentery** (See RECTUM - Dysentery - accompanied - rheumatic)
    - **dyspepsia**: nat-c ptk1
    - **eczema** (See EXTREMITIES - Pain - rheumatic - accompanied - eczema)
    - **hemorrhoids**: *Berb* br1
    - **menses**; painful (See FEMALE - Menses - painful - accompanied - rheumatic)
    - **paraplegia** (See Paralysis - paraplegia - accompanied - rheumatism)
    - **perspiration**: asc-t ptk1
    - **pollutions**: gins bro1
    - **stiffness** | **chronic**: ol-j ptk1

- **rheumatic – accompanied** by: ...
    - **urticaria**: pin-s br1 *Urt-u* br1*
    - **Bronchial** tubes; complaints of the (See CHEST - Complaints - bronchial tubes - accompanied - rheumatic)
    - **Extremities**; heaviness of: *Cimic* br1
    - **Heart**:
      - **complaints** of the (See CHEST - Heart; complaints - accompanied - rheumatic)
      - **inflammation** | **Pericardium** (See CHEST - Inflammation - heart - pericardium - accompanied - rheumatism)
    - **Kidneys**; inflammation of (See KIDNEYS - Inflammation - accompanied - rheumatism)
    - **Ovaries**; irritation of: *Cimic* br1
    - **Uterus**; cramping pain in: *Cimic* br1
  - **air**; in open | **amel.**: kali-m bro1 puls bro1
  - **alternating** with:
    - **chorea** (See Chorea - alternating)
    - **respiration**; asthmatic (See RESPIRATION - Asthmatic - alternating - pain)
    - **Urinary** organs; complaints of (See URINARY - Complaints - alternating - rheumatic)
  - **chill**; during: bapt bro1 hom-xyz bro1 rhus-t bro1
  - **chronic**: anthraco br1 bell tl1 carbn-s br1 *Caust* br1 coli jl2 euon-a br1 get br1 ichth br1 led tl1 lith-c br1 *Med* br1* petr tl1 phyt br1 rhod tl1 *Stel* br1 syph br1 tax br1 tub-d jl2 vanad br1
  - **colchicum**; in abuse of: led bro1
  - **cold** agg.: led bro1 *Merc* bro1
  - **degenerative**: coli jl2
  - **diarrhea**; from suppressed: abrot mrr1
  - **discharges**; from suppressed: abrot bro1
  - **drawing** pain: am-c h2 carb-v k* chel k* sul-ac k*
  - **fever**; during: ars b4a.de led b7.de* lyc b4a.de
  - **gonorrheal**: franc br1 methyl br1 thuj ptk1
  - **loquacity**; with (See MIND - Loquacity - rheumatic)
  - **measles**; during: puls bro1
  - **menses** | **before** | **agg.**: mag-c bg2
    - **during**:
      - **beginning** of menses | **agg.**: senec bg2
  - **motion**:
    - **agg.**: abrot ptk1 act-sp bro1 apis bro1 *Arn* bro1 *Bry* bro1 *Calc* bro1 *Chin* bro1 cimic bro1 clem bro1 colch bro1 form br1* get bro1 guaj bro1 iod bro1 *Kali-m* bro1 kalm bro1 lac-c bro1 led bro1 *Merc* bro1 nux-v bro1 phyt bro1 ran-b bro1 sal-ac bro1 *Stel* bro1
    - **amel.**: cham bro1 chin bro1 dulc br1* ferr bro1 lyc bro1 *Med* jl2 *Puls* bro1 rhod bro1 *Rhus-t* bro1 verat bro1
    - **slight** motion | **agg.**: ferr-p tl1 *Med* jl2
  - **nervous** persons; in (See MIND - Excitement - nervous - rheumatic)
  - **periodical** | **day**; every other: chin bro1
  - **pregnancy** agg.; during: acon bro1 alet bro1 *Cimic* bro1 op bro1 rhus-t bro1
  - **pressure** | **amel.**: bry bro1 form br1*
  - **recurrent**: nat-s ptk1 senec ptk1
  - **rest**:
    - **agg.**: euph-l br1 rhus-t tl1
    - **amel.**: bry bro1 get bro1 visc sp1
  - **seasons**:
    - **spring** | **amel.**: calc-p tl1
  - **snow** agg.; melting: calc-p bro1
  - **swelling** begins; before: abrot al1*
  - **touch** agg.: acon bro1 act-sp bro1 apis bro1 *Arn* bro1 *Bry* bro1 *Chin* bro1 *Colch* bro1 iod bro1 lac-c bro1 ran-b bro1 rhus-t bro1 sal-ac bro1
  - **touching** cold things agg.: sal-ac tl1

- **tubercular**: tub-r jl2
- **warm | applications | amel.**: *Ars* bro1 bry bro1 caust bro1 kali-bi bro1 nux-m bro1 rhus-t bro1 *Sil* bro1
  - **bed | agg.**: led tl1 merc tl1
- **weather**:
  - **cold**:
    - **agg.**: *Camph* br1 influ jl2 rhus-t br1
    - **dry | agg.**: *Acon* bro1 bry bro1 caust bro1 nux-m bro1 *Rhod* bro1
    - **wet | agg.**: dulc br1
  - **warm**:
    - **agg.**: **Colch** ptk1 kali-bi ptk1 kali-s ptk1 rhod br1*
    - **wet | amel.**: *Caust* tl1
  - **wet**:
    - **agg.**: influ jl2 rhod tl1
    - **amel.**: caust bro1
  - **windy** and stormy: *Rhod* br1
    - **before**: puls bro1 *Rhod* bro1 rhus-t bro1

○ • **Fibrous** tissue: arn bro1 bacls-7 fmm1• form-ac bro1 get bro1 morg-g fmm1• phyt bro1 rhod bro1 *Rhus-t* bro1 syph jl2

- **Joints**: *(↗EXTREMITIES - Pain - joints - rheumatic; EXTREMITIES - Pain - rheumatic)* am-p mtf11 bell-p sp1 form br1 gonotox jl2 mag-s sp1 med jl2 merc br1 streptoc jl2 *Tub* ↓
  - **acute**: *Tub* br1*
  - **Small** joints: *Act-sp* br1
- **Muscles**: *Acon* bro1 am-p mtf11 ang mtf11 ant-t bro1 apis bro1 arn br1* bell-p sp1 *Bry* bro1 calc bro1 calc-f sp1 *Casc* bro1 caust bro1 chin bro1 chinin-s bro1 *Cimic* bro1* colch bro1 cygn-ol sze3• dulc bro1 *Ferr* bro1 form mtf11 gels bro1 glyc bro1 gnaph bro1 ham bro1 hyper bro1 jac-c c1* leptos-ih jl2 lyc bro1 *Macro* bro1 med jl2 merc bro1 nux-m mtf11 osteo-a jl2 phos bro1 phyt bro1 ran-b bro1* rhod bro1 rhus-t bro1 sacch-a fd2.de• sang bro1 sil bro1 streptoc jl2 sulph bro1 syph bro1 verat-v bro1
- **Nerves**: bell-p sp1
- **Periosteum | chronic**: still br1
- **Tendons**: arn br1 sacch-a fd2.de•
- **Upper** part of body | **right**: viol-o br1

- **rising**:
  - **after**:
    - **agg.**: coloc ↓
      - **drawing** pain: coloc k*
  - **agg.**: mim-p ↓ pic-ac ↓ ptel ↓
    - **aching**: mim-p rsj8•
    - **sore**: pic-ac k* ptel k*
  - **amel.**: grat ↓ mag-c ↓
    - **sore**: grat mag-c
- **sawing** pain: aesc bg2* brom ptk1 hyper bg2* phos bg2* spig bg2* spong ptk1 sulph bg2* syph bg2* tarent bg2*
- **scarlet** fever; after: elat ↓
  - **neuralgic**: elat vml3•
- **scraped**; as if: *Acon* aesc alum alumn *Arg-n* arn k* asaf k* *Asar* hr1* *Bell* **Brom** k* bry carb-v carbn-s cham k* *Chin* k* *Coc-c* coloc k* *Con* crot-t dig **Dros** k* hydrog srj2• *Kali-bi Kali-chl Lach* led k* lepi a1 *Lyc* k* *Mez* **Nux-v** k* *Osm Par* k* ph-ac k* *Phos* phyt **Puls** k* *Rhus-t* k* *Rumx Sabad* k* sel seneg spig k* *Stann* **Sulph** k* tell **Verat** k* [chr-met stj1]
- **screaming**; from: chir-fl bnm4• lat-m sp1
- **screwed** together; as if: aeth ptk1 alum b2.de* ambr b2.de* bov b2.de* *Coloc* ptk1 elaps ptk1 naja ptk1 nux-m b2.de* *Onos* ptk1 ox-ac ptk1 sars bg2* *Stront-c* b2.de* zinc b2.de*
- **sharp** (See cutting)
- **shattered**; as if: aeth ptk1 ars ptk1 *Bell* ptk1 bry ptk1 carb-an ptk1 *Coff* ptk1 dig ptk1 glon ptk1 *Mur-ac* ptk1 *Nit-ac* ptk1 *Nux-v* ptk1 **Puls** ptk1 **Rhus-t** ptk1 sil ptk1 *Stann* ptk1 staph ptk1 sulph ptk1 verat ptk1
- **shifts** to part lain on: arn bg1 bry bg1 *Graph* bg1* kali-c bg1 merc bg1 mosch bg1 *Ph-ac* bg1* sil bg1
- **shooting** pain: acon bg2* agar bg2* alum bg2* apis bg2 arg-n bg2* ars bg2* bell bg2* berb bg2* cham bg2 chir-fl bnm4• cimic bg2* coff bg2 coloc bg2* cupr ptk1 dendr-pol sk4• dios bg2* ferr ptk1 hell bg2 helo-s bnm14• hippoc-k szs2 hydr-ac ptk1 hyos ptk1 hyper ptk1 iris bg2 kali-bi bg2* kali-c ptk1 kali-i bg2
- **shooting** pain: ...
  kali-m ptk1 kalm bg2* lat-h bnm5• mag-c bg2* mag-m ptk1 mag-p bg2* mez bg2* nit-ac ptk1 nux-v bg2* ox-ac bg2* paeon ptk1 phos br1 plb bg2* prun ptk1 puls bg2 rad-br ptk1 ran-b bg2* rauw sp1 rhus-t bg2* rumx ptk1 sabin ptk1 sang bg2 sep bg2* sil bg2 spig bg2* **Sulph** ptk1 tab bg2 tell ptk1 *Thal-met* br1 xan ptk1* zinc ptk1
- **simultaneous** with headache (See HEAD - Pain - accompanied - pains)
- **sitting**:
  - **agg.**: agar ↓ am-m ↓ caust ↓ samb ↓ spig ↓ **Valer** ↓
    - **drawing** pain: samb k* **Valer**
    - **sore**: agar a1 am-m a1 caust h2* spig st1
  - **chair**; in a | **agg.**: pert-vc vk9
- **sleep**:
  - **after | agg.**: phyt ptk1
  - **during**:
    - **agg.**: *Ars* bg2* aur ptk1 bell bg2* carb-an bg2* carb-v bg2 cham ptk1 con bg2 graph bg2* lyc bg2* merc bg2* *Nit-ac* bg2* nux-m ptk1 plat bg2 rhus-t ptk1 sul-ac bg2* sulph ptk1 til ptk1
      - **waking | amel.**: sul-ac ptk1
  - **half** sleep, during: nit-ac h2
- **somnambulism**, after: sulph ↓
  - **sore**: sulph h2
- **sore** (= bruised): abrot bro1 *Acon* k* adam srj5• adon sf1.de *Aesc* k* agar k* agn k* aloe *Alum* k* *Alum-p* k2* alum-sil k2* alumn k* *Am-c* k* am-m b2.de* ammc k* ampe-qu bro1 anac b2.de* *Ang* b2.de* ant-c k* ant-t k* apis k* **Arg-met** k* arg-n sf1.de arge-pl rwt5• **Arn** k* *Ars* k* ars-i k2* arum-t asaf b2.de* *Asar* k* atra-r bnm3• *Aur* b2.de* aur-ar k2 *Bad* k* *Bapt* k* bar-act a1 bar-c k* bar-i k2* bar-m bell b2.de* bell-p bg2* berb k* borx k* bov k* *Brom* hr1* *Bry* k* calc k* calc-sil k2* calen *Camph* b2.de* canch br1 cann-s b2.de* *Canth* k* caps bg2* (non:carb-ac k*) carb-an k* carb-v k* carbn-o a1 *Carbn-s* cassia-s ccrh1• *Caust* k* cedr k* cent a1 cerv a1 cham k* chel k* **Chin** b2.de* chion bg* chir-fl gya2 chlor k* **Cic** k* **Cimic** k* **Cina** k* cinnb k2* clem k* cob k* cob-n sp1 **Cocc** b2.de* coff b7.de colch b2.de* coloc k* con k* cot a1 *Croc* b2.de* crot-h k* crot-t k* culx k2* cund a1 cupr k* cycl k* dig k* **Dros** k* dulc k* echi k* elaps ephe-si hsj1• eucal bg2* **Eup-per** bg2* euph k* eupi k* fago k* **Ferr** b2.de* ferr-ar ferr-p form a1 gamb k* **Gels** bg2* germ-met srj5• goss k* graph b2.de* grat k* guare a1 haliae-lc srj5• **Ham** k* hedeo a1 *Hell* b2.de* helo bg2 helon sf1.de hep k* hip-ac sp1 hipp k* hist sp1 *Hydrc* hr1* hydrog srj2• hyos k* *Hyper* hr1* iber a1* ictod sf1.de ign k* ina-i mlk9.de ind a1 iod k* ip k* juni-v a1 kali-bi k2 kali-c k* kali-chl k13 kali-i bg2* kali-m k2 kali-n k* kalm k* kola stb3• kreos b2.de* lach k* lappa ptk1 laur b2.de lavand-a ctl1• *Lec Led* k* lil-t k* *Lith-c* k* loxo-recl bnm10• lyc k* lycpr bro1 lyss a1* **M-ambo** b2.de *M-arct* b2.de* *M-aust* b2.de *Mag-c* b2.de* mag-m k* mag-p k2* mag-s k* magn-gr br1 *Mang* k* mang-act br1* *Med* k* meli br1 merc k* *Merc-i-f* hr1* merc-i-r k* mez b2.de* mill bg* mit a1 morph a1* mosch k* *Mur-ac* b2.de *Myric* hr1* narcin a1 *Nat-ar* nat-c k* nat-m k* nat-n bg2 nat-p a1* nat-s k2* nat-sil k2* neon srj5• nicc hr1* nit-ac k* *Nux-m* k* nux-v k* oci-sa sp1 ol-an ptk1 *Olnd* k* onos ptk1 ox-ac k2* ozone sde2• pall bg2* par k* paull a1 petr k* *Ph-ac* b2.de* *Phos* k* phys a1 *Phyt* k* pic-ac hr1* pieri-b mlk9.de plan ptk1 **Plat** k* plb k* plect a1 positr nl2• prun bg2* psil ft1 psor bro1 ptel bg2* *Puls* k* puls-n a1 **Pyrog** k* *Rad-br* bro1 *Ran-b* k* raph k* rat j5.de* *Rhod* k* **Rhus-t** k* rhus-v a1 ros-d wla1 rumx sf1.de **Ruta** k* sabad k* sabin k* sacch-a fd2.de• samb b2.de sars b2.de* sec a1 seneg k* sep k* **Sil** k* sin-n a1 sol-ni sol-t-ae a1 spig k* spong k* squil b2.de *Stann* b2.de* staph b2.de* stel br1 stict bg2 still a1* stry a1 *Sul-ac* k* sul-i k2* sulph k* tarax b2.de* tarent k* tart-ac a1 tell k* ter ptk1 teucr k* thuj k* til ptk1 *Tub* uva kr1 *Valer* b2.de* ven-m rsj12• verat k* verb k* viol-o k* viol-t b2.de wies k* wye bro1 x-ray sp1 zinc k* zinc-p k2*
  - **accompanied** by:
    - **coryza**: hep bg2
    - **heaviness**: chir-fl gya2
    - **metrorrhagia** (See FEMALE - Metrorrhagia - accompanied - pain - sore)
  - **exertion**, as after great: bell-p sp1 chel ptk1 clem k*
  - **march**, as after a long: chel k*
  - **pain**; after: gels bg2 glon bg2
- **splinters**; as from: *(↗stitching)* *Aesc* k* **Agar** k* *Alum* k* **Anag** st1 **Arg-n** k* asaf bg2 *Bar-c Carb-v* k* carc fd2.de• cic k* colch k* coll *Dol* k* *Fl-ac* k* **Hep** k* kali-c bg2 kali-s fd4.de **Nit-ac** k* petr k* plat k* ran-b k* *Sil* k* stann bg2 sulph k* [*Ferr-n* stj2 *Mag-n* stj2 *Mang-n* stj2 *Nitro* stj2]

- **sprained**; as if: arn ptk1 asaf ptk1 bell-p br1 calc ptk1 cham ptk1 *Chel* ptk1 graph ptk1 *Ign* ptk1 nat-m ptk1 petr ptk1 *Phos* ptk1 *Puls* ptk1 *Rhus-t* ptk1 *Sulph* ptk1 thuj ptk1
- **squeezed**; as if: acon b7.de* alum bg2* ambr bg2 *Anac* bg2* **Ang** b7.de* ant-c b7.de *Ant-t* ptk1 arg-met b7.de* arn b7.de* asar b7.de* bar-c bg2 *Bell* bg2 bell-p ptk1 berb ptk1 bry bg2* *Cact* ptk1 calad bg2 *Calc* bg2* camph bg2 cann-xyz bg2 *Carb-v* bg2* caust b4.de* cham bg2 chel bg2 cic b7a.de* cimic ptk1 *Cina* b7.de* cocc bg2* colch bg2 coloc bg2* croc bg2 *Cupr* b7a.de cycl b7.de* dig bg2 dros b7.de* dulc bg2 euphr bg2 graph bg2* hyos bg2 ign b7.de* iod bg2 ip b7.de kali-c bg2 kali-i ptk1 *Kali-n* bg2 kalm ptk1 kreos bg2 lap-la rsp1 led b7.de* lyc bg2 m-ambo b7.de mang bg2 meny bg2* merc bg2* mez bg2 mosch bg2 nat-c b4.de* nat-m bg2* nat-s ptk1 nit-ac bg2* nux-m b7.de nux-v bg2 olnd b7.de* par b7.de petr bg2 ph-ac bg2 phos bg2 **Plat** b4a.de* puls bg2 ran-b bg2 rhod bg2 rhus-t b7.de* ruta b7.de* sabad bg2 sep bg2 sil bg2 spig bg2 squil bg2 staph ptk1 stront-c bg2 sulph bg2 teucr bg2 thuj bg2* valer bg2* verat b7.de* verb b7.de* viol-t bg2 zinc bg2*
  - **tongs**; by a pair of: verb bg2
- **stabbing** pain: apis bg2 *Bry* tl1 cob-n sp1 helo-s bnm14• *Kali-c* tl1 rauw sp1 *Spig* br1*
- **standing** agg.: *Berb* ↓
  - **radiating**: *Berb* br1
- **stinging**: acon ptk1 **Apis** bg2* arn ptk1 *Ars* ptk1 berb ptk1 bry ptk1 chir-fl bnm4• cina ptk1 kali-c ptk1 lat-m bnm6• loxo-lae bnm12• lyc ptk1 merc ptk1 nit-ac ptk1 *Phos* ptk1 plat ptk1 puls ptk1 ruta ptk1 sabal ptk1 *Sep* ptk1 **Sil** ptk1 sul-ac ptk1 *Sulph* ptk1 tarent bg2 ther ptk1 thuj ptk1 zinc ptk1
- **stitching** pain: (↗*splinters)* **Acon** hr1* aconin a1 adam srj5• aesc ptk2 aids nl2• ail a1 alum-p k2 *Alum-sil* k2* *Alumn* k* *Am-m* hr1* amyg-p a1 anac a1 apis a1* arg-n sf1.de* arist-cl sp1 arist-m br1 *Arn* hr1* ars a1* *Ars-s-f* k2* arum-dru c2 **Asaf** a1* *Asc-t* bro1 astac a1 aur-ar k2 aur-i k2* aur-m k2* aur-s k2* bapt hr1 bar-c a1 bar-i k2* bar-s k2* bart a1 **Bell** hr1* benz-ac sf1.de berb bg* bomb-pr mlk9.de borx ptk1 *Bov* hr1* **Bry** a1* bufo sf1.de buni-o jl3 **Calc** a1* calc-f sf1.de calc-i k2* *Calc-sil* k2* cann-i a1* **Canth** j5.de* *Caust* a1* cean vml3• cham a1 *Chel* a1* **Chin** hr1* *Cimic* mrr1 cina sf1.de *Cocc* hr1* coff k2* *Colch* hr1* *Coloc* sf1.de **Con** a1* culx k2* cupr a1 cypra-eg sde6.de• dig a1 *Dros* hr1* dulc fd4.de esp-g kk1.de eucal a1 ferr-ar k2* ferul a1 galla-q-r nl2• *Gamb* a1 gast a1 germ-met srj5• *Graph* a1* haliae-lc srj5• *Hell* hr1* *Hep* tl1* hippoc-k szs2 hist mg1.de* hydr sf1.de hydroph jl3 hyos a1 hyper k2* **Ign** hr1* irid-met srj5• jac-c a1 kali-ar k2* **Kali-c** a1* kali-chl k13 kali-i sf1.de kali-m k2* kali-n a1 kali-s ptk1* kali-sil k2* *Kreos* hr1* lac-ac a1 lac-c a1 lach a1 *Laur* hr1* led a1* lyc a1 *Mag-c* a1* *Mag-m* hr1* mag-p bro1 *Manc* a1 *Meny* hr1* **Merc** hr1* merc-c k2* merc-i-f a1 mez a1 mosch a1 *Mur-ac* a1* naja a1 *Nat-c* hr1* *Nat-m* a1* nat-s bro1 *Nat-sil* k2* neon srj5• **Nit-ac** a1* nux-v sf1.de* *Op* gl1.fr• pall c1 *Par* hr1* *Ph-ac* a1* **Phos** a1* *Pieri-b* mlk9.de plat a1 *Plb* hr1* plb-i sf1.de pneu jl3 **Puls** hr1* ran-b bro1* *Ran-s* hr1* rauw sp1 **Rhus-t** a1* rumx bro1 ruta fd4.de *Sabad* hr1* *Sabin* hr1* sang sf1.de *Sars* a1* scut a1 **Sep** hr1* *Sil* a1* **Spig** hr1* *Spong* a1* squil bro1* *Stann* hr1* **Staph** hr1* stel br1 stict sf1.de stroph-h bg* stroph-s sp1 sul-ac sf1.de sul-i k2* **Sulph** hr1* symph ptk1 *Tarax* hr1* tarent a1 **Thuj** a1* tub k2* tung-met bdx1• ulm-c jsj8• urt-c a1 vanil fd5.de verat a1 **Verb** hr1* verin a1 vesp fkr7.de *Viol-t* hr1 vip a1* visc c1 *Zinc* hr1* zinc-chr ptk1 **Zinc-p** k2* [*Ant-met* stj2 *Kali-met* stj2]
  - **burning**: am-m j5.de bell j5.de *Berb* a1 dig j5.de gamb a1 ign j5.de m-aust j5.de nat-s j5.de rat j5.de rhod j5.de
  - **crawling**: am-m b2.de* anac b2.de* arg-met b2.de* **Arn** b2.de* bar-c b2.de* caust b2.de* chin b2.de* kali-c b2.de* lyc h2 m-arct b2.de meny b2.de* mez b2.de* plat b2.de* *Sabad* b2.de* *Sep* b2.de* sil b2.de* spig b2.de staph b2.de* thuj b2.de* zinc b2.de*
  - **downward**: ant-c k* arn k* *Asc-t* bell k* borx k* canth k* caps k* **Carb-v** k* *Caust* k* chel cimic cina k* coloc k* dios dros k* **Ferr** k* gels graph h2 hydrog srj2• kalm k2 kreos k* lyc k* m-arct b2.de mang k* mez nat-ar k2 nit-ac k* nux-v k* pall petr k* ph-ac k* *Phyt* *Puls* k* *Ran-s* **Rhus-t** sabin k* sars k* sep k* squil k* still *Sulph* k* tarax k* ust *Valer* k* zinc k*
  - **drawing** pain: mang h2
  - **dull** pain: mang h2
  - **inward**: acon k* alum k* am-m k* ang b2.de arg-met k* **Arn** k* *Asaf* bar-c k* bell k* bov k* *Bry* k* *Calc* k* cann-s k* **Canth** k* caps k* carb-v k* caust k* cina k* clem k* cocc k* coloc k* croc k* dros k* guaj k* hyos k* *Ign* k* ip *Laur* k* m-arct b2.de mang k* meny k* mez k* nux-v k* olnd k* par k* petr k* ph-ac k* phos k* *Phyt* *Plb* k* **Ran-b** rhus-t k* *Sabin* k* samb k* sel sil b2.de squil k* staph k* sul-ac k* tarax k* thuj k* verb k*
  - **itching**: carb-v h2 euphr h2 stann h2
- **stitching** pain: ...
  - **jerking** pain: ang b2.de* arn k* *Bry* *Calc* k* carbn-s caust k* **Cina** k* cocc k* coff k* *Coloc* euph k* guaj k* *Lyc* k* mang k* *Meny* k* mez k* mur-ac k* **Nux-v** k* ph-ac k* plb k* sep k* sil k* spong k* **Squil** stann k* zinc k*
  - **needles**; as from: agar ptk1 all-c ptk1 alum ptk1 am-c bg2 anac bg2 apis ptk1 **Arg-n** ptk1 *Ars* ptk1 asaf bg2 bar-c bg2 bell bg2 bry ptk1 calc bg2 camph bg2 caps ptk1 chin bg2 cimic bg2 coloc bg2 **Hep** ptk1 kali-bi ptk1 *Kali-c* bg2* lyc bg2 manc bg2 mang bg2 nat-m bg2* **Nit-ac** ptk1 paeon ptk1 phos bg2 rhus-t ptk1 sabad ptk1 **Sil** ptk1 sulph ptk1 syph ptk1 tarent ptk1 valer ptk1 verat ptk1
    - **cold** needles: *Agar* ptk1 ars ptk1
    - **hot** needles: acon bg2 ars bg2
  - **outward**: *Alum* k* am-m k* ant-c k* **Arg-met** k* arn k* **Asaf** k* asar k* *Bell* k* *Bry* k* *Calc* k* cann-s k* canth k* carb-v k* *Caust* k* cham k* **Chel** **Chin** k* clem k* cocc k* coff k* colch k* **Con** k* dros k* *Dulc* k* hell k* hyos k* kali-c k* kali-chl k13 kali-m k2 *Lach* *Laur* k* *Lith-c* *Lob* *Lyc* k* m-arct b2.de mang k* meny k* **Merc** *Mez* k* mur-ac k* *Nat-c* k* nat-m k* nit-ac k* *Ol-an* olnd k* ph-ac k* **Phel** phos k* phyt **Prun** puls k* rhod k* *Rhus-t* k* *Sabad* k* *Sabin* k* sars h2 *Sil* k* **Spig** k* **Spong** k* **Stann** k* *Staph* k* stront-c k* **Sulph** k* *Tarax* k* ther thuj k* **Valer** k* verat k* verb k* *Viol-o* k* viol-t k*
  - **paralyzed**; as if: sep h2
  - **tearing** pain | **wandering** pain: euphr h2
  - **tensive**: *Asaf* b2.de* *Calc* b2.de* cina b2.de* cocc b2.de* dig b2.de* kali-c b2.de* mang b2.de* nat-m b2.de* olnd b2.de* ph-ac b2.de* ruta b2.de* **Spig** b2.de* *Staph* b2.de* sulph b2.de* tarax b2.de* viol-t b2.de*
  - **transversely**: acon k* ambr k* anac k* arg-met k* *Asc-t* *Atro* **Bell** k* bov k* bry k* calc k* canth k* caust k* cham k* *Chin* k* cimic cocc k* cupr dig *Kali-bi* kali-c k* kali-chl k13 kali-m k2 laur k* lyc k* merc k* mur-ac k* phos k* *Plb* *Ran-b* rhod rhus-t k* seneg k* *Sep* k* *Spig* k* *Stict* stront-c k* sul-ac k* *Sulph* k* tarax k*
  - **upward**: acon k* alum k* arn k* ars k* bar-c k* **Bell** k* bry calc k* canth k* carb-v k* *Caust* k* *Cham* k* chin k* cimic cina k* coloc k* dios *Dros* euphr k* gels *Glon* *Guaj* hyper k2 kali-c k* *Lach* *Lith-c* m-arct b2.de mang k* *Meny* merc nat-ar k2 nat-s petr k* **Phyt** *Plb* puls k* rhus-t k* rumx ruta k* **Sep** k* *Spong* k* *Stann* k* *Sulph* k* *Tarax* k* *Thuj* k*
  - **wandering** pain: *Cina* a1 cypra-eg sde6.de• sul-ac bg2 zinc bg2
- **stool**:
  - **after**:
    - **agg.**: *Calc* ↓ grat ↓ nat-m bg2 nit-ac ↓ phos ↓
      - **beaten**; as if: *Calc* bg2
      - **sore**: calc b4.de* grat nit-ac b4a.de phos b4a.de
    - **long**-lasting: calc bg2 graph bg2 ign bg2 nit-ac bg2 rat bg2
  - **during**:
    - **agg.**: aesc ↓ nit-ac mtf11
      - **sore**: aesc tl1 nit-ac tl1
- **stooping** agg.; after: berb ↓
  - **sore**: berb k*
- **subcutaneous** injections; from: anh ↓
  - **intractable**: anh sp1
- **sudden** (See appear suddenly)
- **syphilis**; from: *Kali-i* ↓ mez ↓ phyt ↓
  - **neuralgic**: *Kali-i* bro1 mez bro1 phyt bro1
- **talking** agg.: all-c ptk1
- **tearing** pain: bell tl1 *Bry* br1 calc-f sp1 cham tl1 colch br1 rauw sp1 *Visc* br1
  - **asunder**: agar k* alum k* am-m k* anac k* arn k* ars k* asar k* calc k* carb-an k* carb-v k* caust k* **Coff** k* colch con k* dig k* ferr k* graph k* ign k* m-ambo b2.de* m-aust b2.de *Mez* k* mur-ac k* nat-m k* **Nit-ac** **Nux-v** k* op k* puls k* raph rhus-t k* sabin k* sep k* spig k* *Staph* k* sul-ac k* sulph k* *Teucr* k* thuj k* zinc k*
  - **away**: act-sp ars bg2 bell bg2 berb bg2 bry bg2 calc bg2 coloc k* dig dros bg2 hep k* ign bg2 **Kali-bi** k* kreos bg1 led m-ambo b2.de* mosch k* nat-m bg2 nux-v k* ol-an bg2 paeon petr k* phos k* *Plb* k* psor bg2 puls bg2 **Rhus-t** k* *Ruta* bg2 sep k* sil bg2 stann bg2 sulph k* thlas bg1 thuj k* uran-n bg1 urt-u bg1

- **downward**: *Acon* k* *Agar* k* *Agn* k* alum k* anac k* ant-c k* ant-t k* arg-n k2* ars k* ars-s-f k2* asaf k* aur k* aur-s k2* *Bar-c* k* bar-i k2* bar-m bar-s k2* **Bell** k* bism k* *Bry* k* calc k* canth k* **Caps** k* *Carb-v* k* *Carbn-s* caust k* chel k* *Chin* k* cina k* colch k* *Coloc* con k* croc k* dulc k* euphr k* *Ferr* k* ferr-p *Graph* k* ign k* *Kali-c* k* kali-chl k13 kali-m k2 kali-n k* kali-p *Kali-s* kalm k2 laur k* **Lyc** k* *M-aust* b2.de mag-c k* *Meny* k* *Merc* k* mez k* mur-ac k* nat-ar *Nat-c* k* nat-m k* nit-ac k* *Nux-v* k* ph-ac k* phos k* *Puls* k* rhod k* **Rhus-t** k* sabin k* sars k* seneg k* *Sep* k* sil k* *Spig* k* squil k* stann k* staph k* **Sulph** k* thuj k* valer k* *Verat* k* verb k* zinc k*
- **outward**: all-c am-c bell bov *Bry* *Calc* cann-s caust *Cocc* cycl elaps euph ip mang mez mur-ac nat-c par ph-ac **Prun** puls *Rhus-t* *Sil* *Spig* spong stram
- **upward**: acon k* alum k* *Anac* k* ant-c k* arn k* *Ars* k* asaf k* asar aur k* **Bell** k* bism k* borx k* bov b4a.de calc k* carb-v k* caust k* chin k* clem k* colch k* *Con* k* *Dulc* k* euphr k* m-arct b2.de mag-c k* meny k* merc k* *Nat-ar* *Nat-c* k* nat-m k* *Nit-ac* k* *Nux-v* k* ph-ac k* phos k* puls k* rhod k* rhus-t k* samb k* sars k* **Sep** k* **Sil** **Spig** k* spong k* *Stront-c* k* sulph k* thuj k* valer k*

- **thinking** of the pain agg.: *Ox-ac* br1
- **thread**; like a: (↗*bones - drawing - thread*) *All-c* br1*
- **thrusting** pain: ars-s-f k2
- **tingling** pain: *Act-sp* br1 arum-dru c2 atp rly4• con k2 galeoc-c-h gms1• hed sp1 lat-m bnm6• pyrid rly4• vero-o rly3•
- **touch**:
  - **agg.**: acon ↓ act-sp br1 alum-sil ↓ ars-s-f ↓ bov ↓ brach ↓ *Bry* ↓ calc-p ↓ calc-sil ↓ *Caust* ↓ clem ↓ *Colch* ↓ cupr br1 graph ↓ helo-s ↓ kali-c tl1 loxo-lae bnm12• mang ↓ mang-act ↓ nat-m ↓ nicc ↓ nux-v ↓ **Plb** ↓ *Rhus-t* ↓ *Ruta* ↓ sacch-a ↓ sil ↓ spig ↓ staph tl1 stram ↓ stry ↓ thuj ↓
    - **sore**: acon a1 alum-sil k2* ars-s-f k2* bov a1 brach a1 *Bry* a1 calc-p a1 calc-sil k2* *Caust* h2* clem a1 *Colch* a1 helo-s bnm14• mang h2* mang-act br1 nat-m a1 nicc a1 nux-v a1 **Plb** c1 *Rhus-t* a1 *Ruta* a1 sacch-a fd2.de• sil a1 spig a1 stram a1 stry a1 thuj a1
    - **tearing** pain: colch br1
    - **wandering** pain | **suddenly**: graph h2
- **twinging**: acon sf1.de *Agar* sf1.de aloe alum k* **Am-m** k* ant-c k* apis arg-n sf1.de *Ars* sf1.de **Asaf** bg aur k* bell k* berb *Bov* k* canth k* carb-an k* caust k* *Cham* sf1.de *Chel* k* *Cimic* sf1.de cocc k* coff sf1.de coloc *Crot-t* *Dios* dros k* *Ferr* iod k* iris sf1.de *Kali-bi* sf1.de kali-c k* *Kali-i* sf1.de kali-m k2 *Kalm* sf1.de lact a1 **Laur** k* lyc k* m-aust b2.de *Mag-c* k* mag-m k* *Mag-p* sf1.de merc k* *Mez* sf1.de **Mosch** k* mur-ac k* nat-p nux-v sf1.de ph-ac k* phos k* phys a1 plan **Plb** k* plb-i sf1.de *Prun* puls sf1.de *Rhus-t* k* sabin k* sang sf1.de sars k* seneg k* *Sep* sf1.de sieg a1* sil k* *Spig* sf1.de staph k* stel sf1.de stront-c k* sul-ac k* *Tab* sf1.de *Valer* k*
- **twisting** pain: *Agar* k* alum k* am-m k* anac k* ant-c k* ant-t k* *Arg-n* arn bg2 ars k* asaf k* bar-c k* *Bell* k* berb borx k* *Bry* k* calad k* calc k* canth *Caps* k* cham k* *Cina* k* clem bg2 *Coloc* bg2* con k* dig k* *Dios* k* dros k* dulc k* elaps ptk1 *Ign* k* ip k* kali-c k* kali-n k* led k* *Merc* k* mez k* nat-c k* nat-m k* nux-m k* *Nux-v* k* olnd k* ox-ac ph-ac k* phos k* *Plat* k* plb k* podo puls ptk1 ran-b k* ran-s k* *Rhus-t* k* ruta k* *Sabad* k* sabin k* sars k* seneg k* sep k* **Sil** k* staph k* sul-ac k* sulph k* thlas bg1 thuj k* valer k* **Verat** k*
- **twitching**: agar ptk1 asaf b7a.de asar b7a.de bell bg2 calc bg2 chin b7a.de* cina b7a.de cocc b7a.de colch b7a.de ign bg2 kali-c bg2 kreos b7a.de meny ptk1 mosch b7a.de puls b7a.de* sep bg2 sil bg2 sulph bg2 thuj bg2 valer b7a.de*
- **ulcerative** pain (= as from subcutaneous ulceration): agn b2.de* *Alum-sil* k2* am-c b2.de* **Am-m** hr1* anac b2.de* arn b2.de* ars b2.de* asaf b2.de* aur b2.de* bar-c b2.de* *Bry* b2.de* bufo ptk1 calc b2.de* *Cann-s* hr1* carb-v b2.de* *Caust* hr1* chin b2.de* *Cic* hr1* colch b2.de* con b2.de* *Cycl* b2.de* dros b2.de* euph b2.de* *Graph* b2.de* *Hep* b2.de* hyos b2.de* *Ign* hr1* iod b2.de* iodof hr1* *Kali-c* b2.de* kali-chl k13 kali-m k2 **Kali-s** k2* kreos b2.de* **Lach** hr1* led b2.de* *Mang* hr1* *Merc* hr1* *Mur-ac* hr1* *Nat-m* b2.de* nit-ac b2.de* *Nux-v* b2.de* par b2.de* petr b2.de* **Phos** b2.de* **Puls** b2.de* **Ran-b** b2.de* rhod b2.de* **Rhus-t** b2.de* ruta b2.de* sars b2.de* sec b2.de* sil b2.de* stann b2.de* staph b2.de* sulph b2.de* tarax b2.de* valer b2.de* verat b2.de* zinc b2.de*
- **undulating** (See waves)
- **unrelenting**: rhus-g tmo3•
- **urination**:
  - **after** | **agg.**: canth bg2 caust bg2
  - **amel.**: gels ↓
    - **neuralgic**: gels mrr1
- **urination**: ...
  - **during**:
    - **agg.**: canth ↓ psor ↓ sep ↓
      - **cutting** pain: canth ptk1 psor bg2 sep ptk1
- **vaccination**; after: thuj ↓
  - **neuralgic**: thuj br1
- **violent**: aeth tl1 carb-ac br1 *Cupr* br1 helo-s bnm14• lat-m bnm6• mag-p tl1 mez tl1 *Ox-ac* br1 syph jl2 *Tarent-c* br1 verat tl1
  - **tearing** pain: acon ptk1 anac ptk1 *Arn* ptk1 ars ptk1 bell ptk1 bry ptk1 *Calc* ptk1 caps ptk1 *Carb-v* ptk1 *Caust* ptk1 cham ptk1 *Chin* ptk1 colch ptk1 con ptk1 kali-c ptk1 *Lyc* ptk1 *Merc* ptk1 nat-c ptk1 *Nit-ac* ptk1 *Nux-v* ptk1 *Plat* ptk1 *Puls* ptk1 *Rhod* ptk1 **Rhus-t** ptk1 sep ptk1 sil ptk1 staph ptk1 stront-c ptk1 sulph ptk1 vip ptk1 xan ptk1 zinc ptk1
- **waking** | **after**:
  - **agg.**: grat ↓ mag-s ↓ sep ↓ sulph ↓
    - **sore**: grat a1 mag-s k* sep sulph a1*
  - **on**: *Aesc* ↓ chir-fl ↓ cystein-l ↓ hydr ↓ hydrc ↓ pot-e ↓ ptel ↓ spong ↓ sulph ↓ thuj ↓
    - **aching**: cystein-l rly4• pot-e rly4•
    - **sore**: *Aesc* hr1* (non:carb-ac k*) chir-fl gya2 hydr hydrc k* ptel hr1* spong k* sulph thuj k*
- **walking**:
  - **agg.**: calc ↓ cassia-s cdd7• coca ↓ *Staph* ↓
    - **drawing** pain: calc k* coca
    - **sore**: *Staph* k*
  - **amel.**: coloc ↓ rhus-t ↓ tub ↓
    - **drawing** pain: rhus-t h1* tub k2*
    - **sore**: coloc
- **wandering** pain: (↗*Alternating; EXTREMITIES - Pain - wandering*) acon k* adam srj5• adon sf1.de aesc k* agar sf1.de agav-t jl3 alum-sil k2* *Am-be* sf1.de am-c *Am-m* k* ambr sf1.de aml-ns a1 ant-t bg2 *Apis* bg2* apoc k* apoc-a a1* arg-met *Arn* k* ars k* ars-s-f hr1* arund a1 asaf k* *Aur* k* aur-ar k2 bapt a1 bar-c *Bell* k* benz-ac k* *Berb* bg2* berb-a sf1.de bry k* buni-o jl3 calc bg2* calc-caust sf1.de *Calc-p* k* camph caps k* *Carb-v* k* *Carbn-s* *Caul* k* *Caust* cedr k* *Cham* hr1 chel k* *Chin* k* *Cimic* bg2* clem k* *Colch* k* coloc a1 com sf1.de con j5.de* croc k* *Cupr* bg2* daph j5.de* der a1 dig sf1.de *Dios* k* diosm br1 elat a1 ery-a hr1* eup-per sf1.de eup-pur fago a1 ferr ptk1 ferr-p k2* fl-ac a1 form sf1.de gels k* goss k* graph h2* haliae-lc srj5• ham fd3.de• *Hydr* bg2* *Hyper* sf1.de ictod kr1 ign k* iod k* *Iris* k* **Kali-bi** k* kali-c k* *Kali-fcy* kali-n ptk1 **Kali-s** k* *Kalm* k* **Lac-c** k* lac-cp vml2• *Lach* k* lact j5.de **Led** k* lil-t k* lyc sf1.de lycps-v mag-c h2 mag-m bg2 *Mag-p* k* magn-gr br1 *Manc* k* *Mang* k* meny bg1 meph a1 merc bg2* merc-i-r sf1.de* mez a1 myric a1 naja a1 nat-m k* nat-s nit-s-d a1* *Nux-m* k* nux-v sf1.de ox-ac sf1.de pall bg2* phos a1 *Phyt* k* plan a1* plat *Plb* k* polyg-h prun sf1.de* psil ft1 **Puls** k* puls-n c1 pyrog sf1.de pyrus a1 *Rad-br* bg2* *Ran-b* rhod k* *Rhus-t* bg1* rhus-v a1 *Rumx* bg2* sabad sf1.de *Sabin* k* sacch a1 *Sal-ac* k* salin a1 sang k* sars k* sec j5.de* senec sf1.de sep k* sil bg2* *Sphing* k* *Spig* k* spong sf1.de stel bg1* (non:still k1) *Sulph* k* symph fd3.de• syph k2* tab bg2 tarent k* tax j5.de tell a1 thuj bg1* *Tub* tub-m vn* valer k* *Verat* hr1* verat-v hr1* zinc k* zinc-chr ptk1 [chr-met stj1]
  - **sharp** points moving all around body: adam srj5•
  - **suddenly**: ambr ptk1 arn ptk1 benz-ac br1* colch ptk1 form vh irid-met srj5• kalm br1 rad-br ptk1 rhod ptk1
- **warm**:
  - **applications**:
    - **amel.**: ars ↓ kali-c ↓ *Mag-p* ↓
      - **burning**: ars br1* kali-c tl1
      - **neuralgic**: *Mag-p* br1*
  - **food**:
    - **agg.**: mag-c ↓
      - **neuralgic**: mag-c mrr1
  - **room** | **agg.**: puls bro1
- **warmth**:
  - **agg.**: bry tl1
  - **amel.**: alum-sil k2 *Coloc* mrr1 galeoc-c-h gms1• mag-p tl1
- **washing**; as from: m-aust bg2

- **waves**; in: acon k* anac k* ant-t k* arn k* asaf k* bamb-a stb2.de• bell bg2 chin k* chir-fl bnm4• cocc k* coff bg2 coloc ptk1 dulc k* fl-ac bg2 glon bg2 hyos bg2 lach k2 lat-m bnm6• mez k* nux-v bg2 olnd k* par bg2 plat k* rhod k* senec bg2 sep k* spig k* stict bg2 sul-ac h2 teucr k* viol-t k* zinc-i ptk1
- **weather**:
  - **bad** weather agg.: rhod ↓
    - **neuralgic**: rhod tl1
    - **drawing** pain: rhod
  - **dry**:
    - **amel.**: thuj ↓
      - **tearing** pain: thuj br1
  - **stormy**:
    - **agg.**: cham ↓
      - **sore**: cham
    - **before**: *Med* ↓
      - **neuralgic**: *Med* jl2
  - **wet**:
    - **agg.**: *Med* ↓ thuj ↓
      - **neuralgic**: *Med* jl2
      - **tearing** pain: thuj br1
- **wedge**; as from a: ant-c b2.de* bov b2.de* caust b2.de* dros b2.de* par b2.de* spong b2.de* stram bg2
- **working** amel.: caust ↓
  - **sore**: caust k*
- **writhing**: lat-m sp1
- **wrong** position, from: staph ↓
  - **drawing** pain: staph h1
- **young** people; in: *Acon* ↓ *Bell* ↓ coloc ↓ *Gels* ↓ kalm ↓ spig ↓
  - **neuralgic**: *Acon* bro1 *Bell* bro1 coloc bro1 *Gels* bro1 kalm bro1 spig bro1

▽ - **extending** to:
  - **radiating** (See radiating)

○ - **Crosswise**, across, etc.: acon bg2 agar b4a.de* alum bg2 ambr bg2 anac bg2 apis bg2 arg-met bg2 asc-t bg2 *Bell* bg2 berb bg2 borx bg2 bov bg2 bry bg2 calc b4a.de* canth bg2 caust bg2 cham bg2 chel bg2 chin bg2 cocc bg2 ferr bg2 hell bg2 kali-bi bg2 kali-c bg2 kalm bg2 *Lac-c* bg2* lach bg2 laur bg2 lyc bg2 mang b4a.de* merc bg2 mur-ac bg2 murx bg2 nat-c bg2 nit-ac bg2 nux-v bg2 phos bg2 *Rhus-t* bg2 seneg bg2 *Sep* bg2 sil bg2 spig bg2 stict bg2 stront-c bg2 sul-ac bg2 sulph bg2 tarax bg2 valer bg2 verat bg2
  - **Downward**: *(↗Complaints - extending - downward)* acon bg2 agar bg2 agn bg2 alum bg2 alumn kr1 ant-t bg2 apis st arn bg2 asaf sf1.de aur bg2 bar-c bg2 bell bg2 benz-ac bg2* berb bg2 bry bg2 canth bg2 *Caps* bg2 *Carb-v* bg2 caust bg2 chel bg2 chin bg2 cina bg2 coff bg2 **Ferr** bg2 goss a1 graph bg2 hydrog srj2• hyper bg2 kali-c bg2 **Kalm** bg2* lach bg2 lat-m bnm6• led st **Lyc** bg2 merc bg2 mez k2 nat-ar k2 nat-c bg2 nat-m bg2 nux-v bg2 ph-ac bg2 *Puls* bg2 rheum kr1* rhus-t bg2 sars bg2 sel bg2* seneg bg2 sep bg2 sil bg2 sulph bg2 *Valer* b7a.de verat bg2 verb bg2 zinc bg2
  - **Ears**: *Mang* ↓
    - **drawing** pain: *Mang* b4a.de
  - **Eyes**: staph ptk1
  - **Fingers**: apis ↓
    - **drawing** pain: apis
  - **Fingers**; tips of: *Lob* ↓
    - **stitching** pain | **outward**: *Lob*
  - **Head**: bell bg2 carb-v bg2 plb bg2
  - **Heart**: benz-ac bg2 **Kalm** bg2
  - **Inward**: alum bg2 arg-n bg2 **Arn** bg2* bell bg2 bov bg2 *Calc* bg2 cann-xyz bg2 **Canth** b7a.de* carb-v bg2 caust bg2 chin bg2 cina bg2 con bg2 hyos bg2 *Ign* bg2 *Laur* bg2 meny bg2 merc bg2 mez bg2 *Olnd* b7a.de petr bg2 phel bg2 phyt sf1.de *Plb* bg2* ran-b bg2* rhus-t bg2 *Sabin* bg2* sep bg2 spig bg2 spong bg2 squil bg2 stann bg2 staph bg2 sul-ac bg2 sulph bg2 valer bg2 verb bg2
  - **Lower** limbs: lat-m bnm6•
  - **Outward**: alum bg2* am-m bg2 anh jl* *Arg-met* bg2 arg-n bg2* arn bg2 **Asaf** b7a.de* bell bg2 berb bg2 bry bg2 calc bg2 canth bg2 carb-v bg2 chel bg2* *Chin* bg2* cimic bg2* cocc bg2 **Con** bg2* dros bg2 dulc bg2

- **extending** to – **Outward**: ...
  hyos bg2 kali-c bg2* kali-m bg2 led k2 lith-c bg2 lyc bg2* mang bg2 merc bg2* mez bg2 mur-ac bg2 nat-c bg2 nit-ac bg2 phel sf1.de phos bg2 phyt bg2* plat bg2 plb bg2 prun bg2* ran-b bg2* rhod bg2 rhus-t bg2 sabad bg2 sabin bg2 *Sep* bg2* sil bg2* spig bg2* spong bg2* stann bg2* stann-i sf1.de staph bg2 **Sulph** bg2* tarax bg2 *Valer* bg2* viol-t bg2 zinc bg2
  - **Thighs**: cham ptk1 *Staph* ptk1 xan ptk1
  - **Toes**: apis ↓
    - **drawing** pain: apis
  - **Upward**: *(↗Complaints - extending - upward)* acon bg2 aloe bg2 alum-sil k2 anac bg2 arn bg2 ars bg2 *Asaf* bg2* aur bg2 **Bell** bg2 calc bg2 canth bg2 caust bg2 cham bg2 chin bg2 colch bg2 con bg2 cupr bg2* dulc bg2 eup-per bg2 eup-pur br1* euphr bg2 gels bg2 *Glon* bg2 helo-s rwt2• hyper sf1.de **Ign** bg2 kali-p fd1.de• kalm k2 **Lach** bg2* *Led* bg2* mag-c bg2 mang bg2 meny bg2 mez br1 naja bg2 nat-ar k2 nat-c bg2 nat-m bg2 nept-m lsd2.fr nit-ac bg2 nux-v bg2 **Phos** bg2 puls bg2 rhus-t bg2 sabad bg2 samb bg2 **Sang** bg2 **Sep** bg2* **Sil** bg2 spong bg2 stront-c bg2 sulph bg2 valer bg2 zinc bg2

○ - **Affected** parts: arn ↓ *Bry* ↓ camph ↓ *Canth* ↓ carb-v ↓ cham ↓ chin ↓ cocc ↓ coloc ↓ con h2 dig h2 *Ham* ↓ hyper ↓ m-arct ↓ merc ↓ **Nit-ac** ↓ nux-v ↓ par ↓ **Puls** ↓ ran-b ↓ rhus-t ↓ sabin ↓ spong ↓ squil ↓ staph ↓ zinc ↓
  - **burning**: *Canth* mrr1 carb-v br1 hyper br1
  - **cough** agg.; during: alum ↓ *Am-c* ↓ am-m ↓ ambr ↓ anac ↓ *Ars* ↓ aur ↓ **Bell** ↓ *Borx* ↓ **Bry** ↓ calc ↓ caps ↓ carb-v ↓ caust ↓ chin ↓ con ↓ crot-h ↓ dig ↓ dros ↓ ferr ↓ grat ↓ hep ↓ iod ↓ kali-c ↓ kali-m ↓ kreos ↓ lach ↓ lyc ↓ nit-ac ↓ nux-v ↓ *Petr* ↓ phos ↓ puls ↓ rhus-t ↓ *Sabad* ↓ sep ↓ sil ↓ spong ↓ squil ↓ stront-c ↓ **Sulph** ↓ *Verat* ↓ zinc ↓
    - **pressing** pain: ambr bg2 anac bg2 bell bg2 *Borx* bg2 bry bg2 caps bg2 chin bg2 dig bg2 grat bg2 iod bg2 phos bg2 sil bg2 spong bg2 squil bg2 stront-c bg2 **Sulph** bg2
    - **stitching** pain: alum bg2 *Am-c* bg2 am-m bg2 anac bg2 *Ars* bg2 aur bg2 **Bell** bg2 borx bg2 **Bry** bg2 calc bg2 caps bg2 carb-v bg2 caust bg2 chin bg2 con bg2 crot-h bg2 dros bg2 ferr bg2 hep bg2 iod bg2 kali-c bg2 kali-m bg2 kreos bg2 lach bg2 lyc bg2 nit-ac bg2 nux-v bg2 *Petr* bg2 phos bg2 puls bg2 rhus-t bg2 *Sabad* bg2 sep bg2 squil bg2 **Sulph** bg2 *Verat* bg2 zinc bg2
  - **drawing** pain: *Bry* b7a.de staph b7.de*
  - **eating**; after: graph b4a.de
  - **menses**; after: chin bg2 kreos bg2
  - **pressing** pain | **stitching** pain: camph b7.de chin b7.de par b7.de
  - **raw**; as if: merc br1
  - **sore**: *Ham* br1 merc br1
  - **stitching** pain | **tearing**: arn b7.de* *Bry* b7.de* camph b7.de* cham b7.de* chin b7.de* cocc b7.de* coloc bg2 m-arct b7.de merc bg2 **Nit-ac** bg2 nux-v b7.de* **Puls** b7.de* ran-b b7.de* rhus-t b7.de* sabin b7.de* spong b7.de* squil b7.de* staph b7.de* zinc bg2
  - **stool**; when straining at: nux-v bg2
  - **tearing** pain | **stitching** pain: bry b7.de canth b7.de cocc b7.de nux-v b7.de staph b7.de
- **Blood** vessels: agar ↓ **Ars** ↓ *Aur* ↓ brom ↓ *Bry* ↓ calc bg2 carb-v ↓ chel ↓ chin ↓ com ↓ fago bg2 *Ham* bg2* *Hyos* ↓ kali-bi ↓ lil-t ↓ med ↓ merc ↓ nat-m ↓ nit-ac ↓ *Op* ↓ phos ↓ plb ↓ *Puls* ptk1 **Rhus-t** ↓ sec ↓ sep ↓ *Sulph* ↓ syph ↓ thuj ptk1 verat ↓ *Vip* ↓ xanth ↓ zinc sf1.de*
  - **night**: **Ars** ↓
    - **burning**: **Ars** h2
  - **burning**: agar k* **Ars** k* *Aur* k* brom bg2 *Bry* k* *Calc* k* carb-v bg2* chin bg2 com bg2 *Hyos* k* med k* nat-m k* nit-ac *Op* k* phos bg2 plb bg2 **Rhus-t** k* sec bg2 *Sulph* syph bg2 verat k* xanth bg2
    - **fire**; like: op b7.de rhus-t b7.de
  - **bursting** pain: chel bg2 *Ham* bg2 kali-bi bg2 lil-t bg2 phos bg2 sep bg2 *Vip* bg2
  - **cutting** pain: calc bg2
  - **drawing** pain: aur bg2
  - **fever**; during: *Ars* ↓ bry ↓ hyos ↓ op ↓ rhus-t ↓ verat ↓
    - **burning**: *Ars* b4a.de* bry b7.de* hyos b7.de op b7.de rhus-t b7.de verat b7.de
  - **perspiration**; during: *Ars* ↓ bry ↓ hyos ↓ rhus-t ↓
    - **burning**: *Ars* bg2 bry bg2 hyos bg2 rhus-t bg2
  - **sleep**; during: *Ars* ↓

- **sleep**; during: ...
  - **burning**: *Ars* b4a.de
- **sore**: ham bg2* puls ptk1
- **stitching** pain: *Ham* bg2 merc b2.de*

- **Body**; all over: acon b7.de ambr b7.de anac b4a.de ant-t b7a.de arn b7.de *Bry* b7.de* cann-s b7a.de canth b7.de cina b7.de* cocc b7.de* coff b7.de* colch b7.de* ephe-si↓ fic-m↓ gamb↓ germ-met↓ hell b7.de kali-c b4a.de lat-m bnm6• led b7.de loxo-lae bnm12• mag-c b4a.de med↓ pyrid↓ sep b4a.de spig b7.de* *Staph* b7.de* *Tarax* b7a.de usn↓
  - **sore**: ephe-si hsj1• fic-m gya1 gamb ptk1 germ-met srj5• med c1 pyrid rly4• usn a2
  - **touch** agg.: mang↓
    - **sore**: mang ptk1

- **Bones**: (↗*Sensitiveness - bones)* abies-n abrot↓ acon k* aesc↓ aeth↓ *Agar* k* agn k* all-c a1 alum j5.de am-c k* am-m k* *Ambr* j5.de anac k* androc↓ ang b2.de* anis↓ ant-c b7.de* ant-t↓ *Apis*↓ aran kr1 *Arg-met* k* *Arg-n* hr1 arn k* ars k* ars-i **Asaf** k* asc-t a1 atha↓ *Aur* k* aur-ar k2 aur-i k2 aur-m k2* aur-s k2 bar-c k* bar-i k2 bar-s k2 bell k* bell-p-sp↓ *Berb* k* bism k* borx↓ bov↓ brom↓ bry k* bufo↓ *Calc* k* calc-f sp1 *Calc-p* k* calc-s k* calc-sil↓ camph j5.de cann-i↓ cann-s k* canth k* *Caps* k* carb-ac↓ carb-an k* carb-v k* carbn-s cartl-s rly4• castor-eq bro1 caust k* cedr↓ celt a1 *Cham* k* chel k* *Chin* k* chinin-m kr1* chinin-s chir-fl↓ cic k* *Cina*↓ *Cinnb* cinnm kr1* clem k* cob br1* cob-n jl3 coc-c↓ *Cocc* k* colch k* coloc k* *Con* k* conch a1 *Cor-r*↓ crot-c a1* *Crot-h* j5.de* crot-t↓ *Cupr* k* cycl k* *Daph* j5.de dig k* dios dros k* dulc k* **Eup-per** k* euph k* euphr↓ ferr k* ferr-ar k* *Fl-ac* k* form↓ gamb↓ *Gels* bg2 glon graph k* guaj k* halo jl3 hell k* *Hep* k* hom-xyz c1* hyper↓ ictod j5.de ign k* indg↓ iod k* **Ip** k* jab↓ kali-bi k* kali-c k* *Kali-i* a1* kali-m↓ *Kali-n*↓ kali-p↓ kali-s *Kalm*↓ kreos k* lac-d k2 lach k* lact↓ lat-m bnm6• laur↓ led k* *Lith-c*↓ *Lyc* k* *Lyss* k* m-arct b2.de* m-aust↓ mag-c k* mag-m k* malar↓ mang k* mang-act bro1 mang-m c1* mang-o↓ meny↓ meph↓ **Merc** k* merc-c bro1 merc-i-f merc-i-r mtf11 merc-k-i gm1 *Mez* k* *Mur-ac* b4a.de* nat-c k* nat-m k* *Nat-s* kr1 nat-sil k2 nicc↓ **Nit-ac** k* nit-s-d↓ nux-m j5.de* nux-v j5.de oci-sa sp1* ol-an bg2 olnd k* op k* osm↓ pant-ac rly4• *Par*↓ petr k* **Ph-ac** k* phel↓ *Phos* k* *Phyt* bg2* plat↓ plb k* plut-n srj7• pot-e rly4• prun↓ **Puls** k* pyrog k2* ran-s k* raph a1 *Rhod* k* *Rhus-t* k* **Ruta** k* sabad k* *Sabin* k* sacch a1 samb k* sarr a1* *Sars* k* sec k* *Sel* seneg↓ *Sep* k* *Sil* k* sol-t-ae a1 *Spect*↓ spig k* spong k* stann↓ *Staph* k* still stront-c k* sul-ac↓ sul-i k2 *Sulph* k* *Symph* bro1* syph lp* *Tab*↓ tarax↓ *Tarent*↓ tax↓ ter↓ teucr k* ther k* thuj k* toxo-g jl2 tub k2* *Vac*↓ valer k* vanil fd5.de verat k* verat-v hr1 **Verb**↓ viol-t k* *Vip*↓ vitr-an bro1 wildb c1* zinc k* zinc-o↓
  - **daytime**: **Staph** b7a.de
  - **morning**: sil h2
  - **night**: *Asaf* k* **Aur** k* aur-m k2 calc-s k2 caust *Cham* cinnb *Fl-ac* k* guare a1 hep bro1 iod bro1 kali-bi k2 **Kali-i** k* kalm lach bro1 *Lyc* ptk1 *Mang* mang-act bro1 **Merc** k* *Merc-i-f* merc-k-i gm1 *Mez* k* **Nit-ac** k* *Ph-ac* k* phos↓ *Phyt* k* rhod bro1 *Sars* k* sil k2* staph k2 still bro1 syph bro1* thuj verat
    - **burning**: *Mez* kr1 ph-ac phos a1
    - **digging** pain: mang h2 mang-act br1
    - **lancinating**: syph jl2
    - **scraped**; as if: ph-ac ptk1
    - **tearing** pain: caust br1
  - **accompanied** by:
    - **influenza** (See Influenza - accompanied - bones)
    - **psoriasis**: phyt mrr1
    - **vertigo** (See VERTIGO - Accompanied - bones)
    - **weakness**: calc tl1
  - **aching**: [*Spect* dfg1]
  - **beaten**; as if: *Tub* jl2
  - **boring** pain: agar k* anac j5.de ang b2.de* aran *Asaf* k* **Aur** k* *Bar-c* k* *Bell* k* brom *Calc* k* carb-an clem k* dulc k* hell k* hep k* kali-c j5.de kali-i bg2 lach k* led a1 *Lyc* k* mang k* **Merc** k* *Mez* k* nat-c k* nat-m k* nit-s-d a1 ph-ac k* phos k* plb bg2 *Puls* k* ran-s j5.de rhod k* rhus-t k* sabad k* sabin k* *Sep* k* *Sil* k* *Spig* k* staph k* sulph k* *Thuj* k*
  - **broken**; as if: agar k2 am-c bg2* *Ang* kr1 arg-met a1 *Arn* k2 ars k2* *Aur* *Bry* caust bg2 *Cham* kr1 *Chel* kr1 coc-c kr1 **Cocc** kr1* cupr k* *Dros* kr1 *Eup-per* bg2* hep k* **Ign** kr1 lyss kr1 mag-m kr1 *Merc* kr1* *Nat-m* nit-ac ptk1 nux-v k2 **Phos** kr1 puls k* *Pyrog* bg2* rhus-t k2 *Ruta* k* *Samb* kr1 sep k*

- **Bones – broken**; as if: ...
  Sil a1 *Symph* kr1 *Tarent* a1 ther k* *Thuj* kr1* *Vac* jl2 valer bg1* *Verat* k* *Vip* [bell-p-sp dcm1]
  - **burning**: ang bg2 ant-t j5.de arn j5.de ars k* *Asaf* k* *Aur* k* bell a1 bry k* *Carb-v* k* caust k* chel bg2 coloc bg2 con dros bg2 *Euph* k* fl-ac bro1 form *Hep* ign kali-i bg2* *Lach* k* lyc k* mang merc k* **Mez** k* nat-c k* nit-ac k* par k* *Ph-ac* k* phos k* puls k* *Rhus-t* k* *Ruta* k* sabin k* *Sep* k* sil k* staph k* *Sulph* k* symph fd3.de• tarent kr1 thuj k* **Zinc** k*
  - **burrowing**: asaf b2.de* calc b2.de* *Carb-an* b2.de* *Cocc* b2.de* dulc b2.de* *Mang* b2.de* rhod b2.de* ruta b2.de* sep b2.de* spig b2.de* thuj b2.de*
  - **caries**: calc-f↓
    - **night**: asaf mtf11
    - **boring** pain: calc-f br1
  - **chill**; during: ars b4.de bar-c↓ bell↓ borx b4a.de caust↓ chin↓ kali-c↓ lyc↓ merc↓ nat-m b4.de* nux-m c1 phos↓ rhod↓ staph↓ verat↓
    - **tearing** pain: bar-c bg2 bell bg2 caust bg2 chin bg2 kali-c bg2 lyc bg2 merc bg2 phos bg2 rhod bg2 staph bg2 verat bg2
  - **cold** agg.: kali-bi↓
    - **sore**: kali-bi bro1
  - **constricting**: alum *Apis* bro1 carb-ac bro1 hep bro1 nit-ac bro1 sulph bro1
  - **cutting** pain: anac ptk1 aur ptk1 aur-m bg2 dig ptk1 kali-bi bg2 kali-m bg2* lach ptk1 osm ptk1 sabad b7a.de*
  - **deep** in: plut-n srj7•
  - **digging** pain: aran arg-met a1 asaf bufo bg2 calc *Carb-an* *Cocc* dulc *Mang* rhod ruta sep spig thuj
  - **drawing** pain: acon j5.de agar j5.de* agn b7.de* anac j5.de ang j5.de ant-t b7.de* *Arg-met* b7a.de *Arn* b7a.de asaf j5.de* atha j5.de aur j5.de* *Bar-c* j5.de bry b7.de* calc-f bg2 cann-s b7.de* canth b7.de* *Carb-v* j5.de caust j5.de cham b7.de* *Chin* b7.de* *Cocc* b7.de* colch b7.de* crot-h j5.de cupr j5.de cycl b7.de* gels bg2* graph h2 hell bg2 ign j5.de indg j5.de ip b7.de* kali-bi bg2 kali-c b4.de* kreos j5.de led b7.de* *Lyc* j5.de m-arct b7.de* m-aust b7.de malar jl2 mang j5.de meny j5.de merc b4.de* nat-m bg2 nit-ac bro1 nux-m b7.de* olnd b7.de* par b7.de* petr h2 ph-ac j5.de plb j5.de puls b7.de* rhod b4.de* rhus-t b7a.de ruta b7a.de sabad b7.de* **Sabin** b7.de* samb b7.de* seneg b4.de* sil bg2 spig b7.de* stann j5.de *Staph* b7.de* sulph bg2 ter j5.de teucr b7.de* thuj b4.de* valer b7.de* verat b7.de* zinc b4a.de* zinc-o j5.de
    - **tearing** pain: *Hep* b4a.de *Merc-c* b4a.de nit-ac b4a.de ph-ac b4a.de phos b4a.de *Rhod* b4a.de *Zinc* b4a.de
    - **thread**; as from a: (↗*thread; Threads)* bry
  - **drinking** agg.; after: hell b7a.de
  - **eating**; after: hell b7a.de
  - **fever**:
    - **before**: *Arn* b7a.de calc b4a.de *Carb-v* b4a.de chin b7a.de ip b7a.de puls b7a.de rhod b4a.de rhus-t b7a.de sabad b7a.de sabin b7a.de verat-v hr1
    - **during**:
      - **agg.**: arg-met↓ *Arn* b7.de* *Bell*↓ calc↓ caust↓ chin bg2 con↓ cycl↓ **Eup-per** al4* *Hell*↓ ign b7.de* kali-c↓ merc↓ nat-m b4a.de* *Puls* b7.de* rhod↓ sabin↓ sars↓ sep↓ staph↓
        - **stitching** pain: *Bell* bg2 calc bg2 caust bg2 con bg2 *Hell* bg2 merc bg2 *Puls* bg2 sars bg2 sep bg2
        - **tearing** pain: arg-met bg2 *Chin* bg2 cycl bg2 kali-c bg2 merc bg2 rhod bg2 sabin bg2 staph bg2
  - **flesh** is thin over bones; where: cycl a1* merc k2* sang ptk1
  - **fracture**; point of: mag-m bg2 symph br1
  - **gnawing** pain: am-m k* arg-met k* *Aur* bro1 **Bell** k* brom canth k* carb-ac bro1 colch bg2 *Con* bg2* *Dros* k* graph k* kali-bi bg2 kali-i k* lyc k* *Mang* k* mang-act bro1 merc bro1 nat-s bg2* *Ph-ac* k* phos k* plb a1 puls k* rhod bg2 *Ruta* k* samb k* *Staph* k* stront-c k* sulph bg2* symph bro1
  - **increasing** and decreasing gradually: syph jl2
  - **injuries**; from: ign↓
    - **tearing** pain | **loose**; as if flesh were: ign ptk1
  - **jerking**: anac j5.de **Asaf** k* aur k* bell k* *Calc* k* caust k* *Chin* k* clem k* colch k* lyc k* mang bg2 merc k* *Nat-m* k* nux-v k* ol-an bg2 petr k* phos k* *Puls* k* rhod k* rhus-t k* sep k* sil k* sul-ac j5.de **Sulph** k* *Symph* kr1 *Valer* k*

- **lancinating**: *Syph* jl2
- **menses**; during: carb-v b4a.de
  - **burning**: *Carb-v*
  - **sore**: carb-v h2
- **paralyzed**; as if: *(↗Lame)* **Aur** k* bell k* chin k* *Cocc* k* *Crot-h* j5.de cycl k* dig *Lach* j5.de led k* mez k* nat-m k* nux-v k* petr k* phos bg2 puls k* rhus-t k* sabin k* *Sil* k* staph k* verat k* zinc k*
- **perspiration**; during: arg-met ↓ *Arn* bg2 *Bell* ↓ *Calc* ↓ caust ↓ chin bg2 con ↓ cycl ↓ *Hell* ↓ ign bg2 kali-c ↓ merc ↓ nat-m bg2 *Puls* bg2 rhod ↓ sabin ↓ sars ↓ sep ↓ staph ↓
  - **stitching** pain: *Bell* bg2 *Calc* bg2 caust bg2 con bg2 *Hell* bg2 merc bg2 *Puls* bg2 sars bg2 sep bg2
  - **tearing** pain: arg-met bg2 *Chin* bg2 cycl bg2 kali-c bg2 merc bg2 rhod bg2 sabin bg2 staph bg2
- **pinching** pain: bell calc cina ign mez nux-m a1 osm petr *Ph-ac* k* plat **Verb** k*
- **pressing** pain: *Alum* k* am-m j5.de anac k* ang b2.de* anis j5.de *Arg-met* k* arn j5.de ars k* asaf k* aur k* *Bell* k* *Bism* k* bry k* cann-i cann-s j5.de canth k* carb-v j5.de carbn-s cham k* chel j5.de cocc k* colch k* *Coloc* k* con k* *Cupr* k* *Cycl* k* *Daph* j5.de dros k* graph k* *Guaj* k* hell k* hep k* ign k* kali-bi bg2 *Kali-c* k* kali-n k* *Led* j5.de m-arct b2.de* m-aust b2.de* mang-o a1 merc k* mez k* nux-m k* nux-v j5.de *Olnd* k* petr h2 phos k* plat k* puls k* rhod k* *Rhus-t* k* *Ruta Sabin* k* sil k* spong k* stann k* *Staph* k* teucr j5.de *Thuj* k* valer k* verat k* viol-t k* zinc k*
  - **sticking** pain: anac b2.de* mez k* ruta b2.de* staph k*
  - **tearing** pain: arg-met k* bell k* cham k* coloc k* thuj k*
- **pressure** agg.: kali-bi k2
- **sawing** pain: aesc bg2 hyper bg2 phos bg2* spig bg2 sulph bg2* syph bg2* tarent bg2*
- **scraped**; as if: *Asaf* b2.de* berb kr1 **Chin** b2.de* coloc b2.de *Ip* bro1 par b2.de* **Ph-ac** b2.de* puls b2.de* **Rhus-t** b2.de* *Sabad* b2.de* spig b2.de* thuj ptk1
- **shattered**; as if: graph bg2
- **sleep** agg.; on going to: graph ↓
  - **pressing** pain: graph h2
- **sore**: acon *Agar* k* am-m k* androc srj1• ang b2.de* **Arg-met** *Asaf* k* aur k* bar-c k* bov k* *Bry* j5.de* bufo bg2 *Calc* k* calc-sil k2 cann-s k* canth j5.de carb-v h2* chin k* chir-fl gya2 **Cocc** k* *Con* conch bro1 *Cor-r* *Crot-h* kr1 *Cupr* dros j5.de* **Eup-per** bg2* graph k* **Hep** k* *Ign* k* **Ip** k* jab kr1 *Kali-bi* kali-p fd1.de• kreos kr1 lac-d k2* *Led* k* *Lith-c* lyss kr1* m-aust b2.de* mag-c k* *Mang* meph j5.de merc b2.de* *Mez* k* nat-m k* nit-ac kr1 nux-m a1 nux-v k* *Par* k* petr k* ph-ac b2.de* *Phos* k* phyt bro1 *Puls* k* *Rhus-t* j5.de* **Ruta** k* sabad k* sabin j5.de sarr kr1 sep k* *Sil Spig* staph j5.de sulph kr1 syph k2 teucr bg2 ther kr1* thuj kr1 tub k2* valer k* *Verat* k* zinc k*
  - **wandering** pain: kali-bi bro1
- **squeezed**; as if: alum bg2* ang b2.de* bell b2.de* calc b2.de* ign b2.de* mez b2.de* olnd bg2 petr b2.de* *Ph-ac* b2.de* plat b2.de*
- **stitching** pain: abrot bg2 acon k* aeth j5.de agar k* agn k* am-c k* anac k* ant-c k* arg-met k* arn bro1* ars k* *Asaf* k* aur k* **Bell** k* berb j5.de **Bry** k* **Calc** k* canth k* carb-v k* **Caust** k* cedr chel k* *Chin* k* cocc k* colch k* **Con** k* daph j5.de *Dros* k* dulc k* euph k* euphr b7.de* graph k* **Hell** k* iod k* *Kali-bi* kr1 kali-c k* kali-n j5.de *Kalm Lach* k* laur j5.de lyc k* m-arct b2.de mag-c k* mag-m j5.de mang k* **Merc** k* mez k* mur-ac j5.de nat-c j5.de nat-s j5.de nit-ac k* nit-s-d a1 nux-v k* ol-an j5.de par k* petr k* ph-ac k* phel j5.de phos k* *Phyt* sf1.de prun j5.de **Puls** k* *Ran-s* k* raph j5.de *Ruta* k* sabin k* samb k* **Sars** k* **Sep** k* sil k* spig k* staph k* stront-c k* **Sulph** k* *Symph* bro1* tarax j5.de tax j5.de *Thuj* k* valer k* verb k* viol-t k* zinc k*
  - **burning**: arg-met b2.de* euph b2.de* zinc b2.de*
  - **ice**-cold needles; as from: aran mtf11
  - **pressing** pain: anac b4.de* ruta b7.de*
  - **sudden**: phos bg2
  - **tearing**: acon b2.de* *Ars* b2.de* calc a1 camph a1 chel b2.de* merc b2.de* phos b2.de* sabin a1 thuj b2.de*
- **syphilitic**: nit-ac tl1 phyt br1

- **Bones**: ...
  - **tearing** pain: acon k* *Agar* k* alum k* *Am-m* k* anac k* ang b2.de* *Arg-met* k* arn k* ars k* asaf k* **Aur** k* *Aur-m* aur-s k2 *Bar-c* k* *Bell* k* *Berb* bism k* borx k* bov k* bry k* calc-p cann-s k* canth k* *Caps* *Carb-v* k* *Caust* k* cham k* chel k* **Chin** k* *Cina* k* *Cocc* k* colch bro1 coloc k* con k* crot-t *Cupr* k* *Cycl* k* dig k* *Dros* k* dulc k* *Ferr* fl-ac bro1 gamb a1 graph k* hell k* hep k* ign k* iod k* kali-bi bg2* **Kali-c** k* *Kali-n* k* *Kalm* kr1 **Lach** k* lact j5.de laur k* *Lyc* k* lyss kr1 *Mag-c* k* mag-m k* mang k* meph j5.de **Merc** k* *Merc-c* *Mez* mur-ac j5.de* nat-c k* nat-m k* nicc j5.de *Nit-ac* k* nit-s-d a1 nux-v k* *Ph-ac* k* *Phos* k* plb k* puls k* **Rhod** k* rhus-t k* *Ruta* k* sabad j5.de *Sabin* k* samb k* sars k* sep k* **Spig** k* spong k* stann k* *Staph* k* *Stront-c* k* sul-ac k* sulph k* *Tab* *Teucr* b2.de* *Thuj* k* valer k* verat k* verb k* *Zinc* k*
    - **burning**: sabin k*
    - **cramping**: aur k* olnd k* *Valer*
    - **jerking** pain: agn b2.de* ang *Bry* **Chin** k* cupr k* mang k*
    - **loose**; as if flesh were: apis ptk1 bell bg2 bry bg2* dios bg2 dros ptk1 ign bg2 lach ptk1 nat-c ptk1 nat-m bg2 ol-an bg2* ph-ac ptk1 rhus-t bg2* *Ruta* bg2* sulph bg2 thuj bg2
    - **paralyzed**; as if: bell k* *Bism* chel k* chin k* *Cocc* k* dig k* nat-m bg2 ol-an bg2
    - **pressing** pain: **Arg-met** k* arn k* asaf k* bism k* bry k* coloc k* **Cycl** k* staph k* teucr k*
    - **sticking** pain: bell k* cina mur-ac k* sabin k*
  - **touch** agg.: kali-bi k2 mez tl1
  - **ulcerative** pain: am-c k* am-m k* *Bry* k* bufo bg2 caust k* cic k* graph k* ign k* mang k* nat-m k* *Puls* k* rhus-t k*
  - **wandering** pain: kali-bi tl1 plut-n srj7•
  - **weather**:
    - **change** of weather: rhod bro1
    - **stormy**:
      - **before**: tub ↓
        - **beaten**; as if: tub jl2
    - **wet | agg.**: merc bro1 mez bro1 nit-ac bro1 phyt bro1 rhus-t bro1 still bro1* syph bro1
  - ○ **Condyles**: verat-v bg2
  - **Epiphyses**: arg-met ↓ calc-p ↓
    - **tearing** pain: arg-met h1 calc-p bg
  - **Long** bones: anac ↓ asaf tl1 bry ↓ calc ↓ cinnb bro1 dig ↓ dros tl1 eup-per bro1 lach tl1 mez tl1 osm ↓ ph-ac ↓ plut-n srj7• *Sabad* ↓ staph bro1 stront-c bro1 syph bro1*
    - **night**: syph jl2
    - **cutting** pain: anac j5.de* calc dig j5.de* osm sabad k*
    - **scraped**; as if: bry ph-ac k2 *Sabad* k*
  - **Marrow**: am-c bg2 bar-c bg2 chin ptk1 crot-h bg2 mag-m bg2 naja bg2 ol-an bg2 op bg2
  - **Parts** lain on: mosch ↓
    - **broken**; as if: mosch a1
  - **Skin** is thin over bones; where (See flesh)
  - **Sutures**; along: calc-p ↓
    - **stitching** pain: calc-p bg2
- **Cartilages**: *(↗Sensitiveness - cartilages)* arg-met c1* lob-s c1* *Rhod* ↓ *Rhus-t* ↓ ruta c1* stram k2
  - **sore**: **Arg-met** *Rhod Rhus-t* ruta k2
- **Distant** parts: ars ↓ ign ↓
  - **cramping**: ars bg2 ign bg2
- **Distant** parts; to: dios ↓
  - **wandering** pain: dios bg2
- **External** parts: acon ↓ agar ↓ agn ↓ alum ↓ am-c ↓ am-m ↓ *Ambr* ↓ anac ↓ ang ↓ ant-c ↓ ant-t ↓ **Arn** ↓ ars ↓ *Asar* ↓ aur ↓ bar-c ↓ bell ↓ bell-p ↓ bov ↓ *Bry* ↓ bufo ↓ calad ↓ **Calc** ↓ calc-p ↓ camph ↓ canth ↓ caps ↓ carb-an ↓ *Carb-v* ↓ *Caust* ↓ cham ↓ chel ↓ chin ↓ cina ↓ cocc ↓ coloc ↓ con ↓ croc ↓ cupr ↓ cycl ↓ dig ↓ dros ↓ dulc ↓ euph ↓ graph ↓ hell ↓ hep ↓ *Ign* ↓ ip ↓ kali-c ↓ kali-n ↓ kreos ↓ *Led* ↓ lyc ↓ *M-ambo* ↓ m-arct ↓ m-aust ↓ mag-c ↓ mag-m ↓ meny ↓ merc ↓ *Mez* ↓ mosch ↓ mur-ac ↓ nat-c ↓ **Nat-m** ↓ nit-ac ↓ nux-m ↓ nux-v ↓ olnd ↓ par ↓ **Petr** ↓ ph-ac ↓ *Phos* ↓ plat ↓ plb ↓ *Puls* ↓ ran-b ↓ *Rhod* ↓ **Rhus-t** ↓ *Ruta* ↓ sabin ↓ sars ↓ seneg ↓ *Sep* ↓ sil ↓ *Spig* ↓ spong ↓ *Stann* ↓ staph ↓ stront-c ↓ **Sulph** ↓ thuj ↓ valer ↓ verat ↓ verb ↓ zinc ↓

• **dislocated**; as if: acon b2.de* agar b2.de* agn b2.de* alum b2.de* am-c b2.de* am-m b2.de* *Ambr* b2.de* anac b2.de* ang b2.de* ant-c b2.de* ant-t b2.de* **Arn** b2.de* ars b2.de* *Asar* b2.de* aur b2.de* bar-c b2.de* bell b2.de* bell-p bg2 bov b2.de* *Bry* b2.de* bufo bg2 calad b2.de* **Calc** b2.de* calc-p bg2 camph b2.de* canth b2.de* caps b2.de* carb-an b2.de* *Carb-v* b2.de* *Caust* b2.de* cham b2.de* chel b2.de* chin b2.de* cina b2.de* cocc b2.de* coloc b2.de* con b2.de* croc b2.de* cupr b2.de* cycl b2.de* dig b2.de* dros b2.de* dulc b2.de* euph b2.de* graph b2.de* hell b2.de* hep b2.de* *Ign* b2.de* ip b2.de* kali-c b2.de* kali-n b2.de* kreos b2.de* *Led* b2.de* lyc b2.de* *M-ambo* b2.de* m-arct b2.de m-aust b2.de* mag-c b2.de* mag-m b2.de* meny b2.de* merc b2.de* *Mez* b2.de* mosch b2.de* mur-ac b2.de* nat-c b2.de* **Nat-m** b2.de* nit-ac b2.de* nux-m b2.de* nux-v b2.de* olnd b2.de* par b7.de **Petr** b2.de* ph-ac b2.de* *Phos* b2.de* plat b2.de* plb b2.de* *Puls* b2.de* ran-b b2.de* *Rhod* b2.de* **Rhus-t** b2.de* *Ruta* b2.de* sabin b2.de* sars b2.de* seneg b2.de* *Sep* b2.de* sil b2.de* *Spig* b2.de* spong b2.de* *Stann* b2.de* staph b2.de* stront-c bg2 **Sulph** b2.de* thuj b2.de* valer b2.de* verat b2.de* verb b2.de* zinc b2.de*

- **Externally**: abrot ↓ acet-ac ↓ achy ↓ **Acon** ↓ acon-c ↓ acon-f ↓ *Act-sp* ↓ adam ↓ adon ↓ *Aesc* ↓ **Agar** ↓ **Agn** ↓ all-c ↓ *Aloe* ↓ *Alum* ↓ *Alum-p* ↓ **Alum-sil** ↓ alumin-s ↓ *Alumn* ↓ *Am-c* ↓ **Am-m** ↓ am-p ↓ am-s ↓ *Ambr* ↓ *Ammc* ↓ *Anac* ↓ *Androc* ↓ **Ang** ↓ *Ant-c* ↓ *Ant-t* ↓ *Antho* ↓ *Anthraci* ↓ aphis ↓ **Apis** ↓ **Apoc** ↓ **Arg-met** ↓ *Arg-n* ↓ **Arn** ↓ **Ars** ↓ ars-i ↓ *Ars-met* ↓ **Ars-s-f** ↓ **Arum-t** ↓ **Asaf** ↓ *Asar* ↓ *Aspar* ↓ atha ↓ atro ↓ *Aur* ↓ aur-ar ↓ aur-i ↓ *Aur-m* ↓ *Aur-s* ↓ *Bad* ↓ bamb-a ↓ **Bapt** ↓ bar-act ↓ *Bar-c* ↓ bar-i ↓ *Bar-m* ↓ bar-s ↓ **Bell** ↓ benz-ac ↓ **Berb** ↓ *Bism* ↓ *Borx* ↓ bov ↓ brom ↓ bruc ↓ **Bry** ↓ *Bufo* ↓ buni-o ↓ cact ↓ *Cadm-s* ↓ *Calad* ↓ **Calc** ↓ calc-act ↓ calc-ar ↓ calc-caust ↓ calc-f ↓ calc-i ↓ *Calc-p* ↓ **Calc-sil** ↓ calen ↓ *Camph* ↓ **Cann-i** ↓ *Cann-s* ↓ *Canth* ↓ *Caps* ↓ *Carb-ac* ↓ carb-an ↓ **Carb-v** ↓ carbn-o ↓ **Carbn-s** ↓ castm ↓ **Caust** ↓ *Cedr* ↓ *Cham* ↓ *Chel* ↓ chelo ↓ **Chin** ↓ chinin-ar ↓ **Chinin-s** ↓ *Chr-s* ↓ **Cic** ↓ *Cimic* ↓ *Cina* ↓ cinnb ↓ cist ↓ *Clem* ↓ cob ↓ coc-c ↓ **Cocc** ↓ coff ↓ **Colch** ↓ *Coloc* ↓ com ↓ **Con** ↓ conv ↓ convo-d ↓ cop ↓ *Corn* ↓ *Croc* ↓ crot-c ↓ crot-h ↓ *Crot-t* ↓ culx ↓ cupr ↓ *Cycl* ↓ cyt-l ↓ *Daph* ↓ *Dig* ↓ *Dios* ↓ dor ↓ **Dros** ↓ *Dulc* ↓ elaps ↓ *Eucal* ↓ euon ↓ euonin ↓ **Eup-per** ↓ euph ↓ euph-l ↓ **Euphr** ↓ fago ↓ **Ferr** ↓ *Ferr-ar* ↓ ferr-m ↓ ferr-ma ↓ ferr-p ↓ fl-ac ↓ form ↓ *Gal-s* ↓ *Gamb* ↓ *Gels* ↓ germ-met ↓ *Glon* ↓ *Gran* ↓ *Graph* ↓ *Grat* ↓ *Guaj* ↓ guare ↓ haliae-lc ↓ **Ham** ↓ *Hell* ↓ helo-s ↓ helon ↓ **Hep** ↓ hera ↓ hist ↓ hydr ↓ *Hydrog* ↓ *Hyos* ↓ **Hyper** ↓ **Ign** ↓ *Indg* ↓ iod ↓ *Ip* ↓ **Iris** ↓ juni-v ↓ kali-ar ↓ **Kali-bi** ↓ kali-br ↓ **Kali-c** ↓ *Kali-chl* ↓ *Kali-i* ↓ *Kali-m* ↓ *Kali-n* ↓ **Kali-p** ↓ **Kali-s** ↓ kali-sil ↓ kali-sula ↓ *Kalm* ↓ *Kreos* ↓ lac-ac ↓ *Lach* ↓ lachn ↓ lact ↓ lam ↓ lap-a ↓ lat-m ↓ *Laur* ↓ **Led** ↓ *Lil-t* ↓ *Lith-c* ↓ *Lith-s* ↓ *Lob* ↓ **Lyc** ↓ lyss ↓ m-ambo ↓ m-arct ↓ *M-aust* ↓ *Mag-c* ↓ mag-m ↓ *Mag-p* ↓ mag-s ↓ *Manc* ↓ mand ↓ *Mang* ↓ *Mang-s* ↓ *Med* ↓ **Meny** ↓ **Merc** ↓ *Merc-c* ↓ merc-i-r ↓ merc-sul ↓ merl ↓ *Mez* ↓ **Mosch** ↓ *Mur-ac* ↓ naja ↓ *Nat-ar* ↓ **Nat-c** ↓ *Nat-hchls* ↓ **Nat-m** ↓ *Nat-p* ↓ **Nat-s** ↓ *Nat-sil* ↓ neon ↓ *Nicc* ↓ *Nicc-s* ↓ nig-s ↓ **Nit-ac** ↓ *Nux-m* ↓ **Nux-v** ↓ *Ol-an* ↓ *Olnd* ↓ *Op* ↓ *Osm* ↓ *Ox-ac* ↓ oxyt ↓ paeon ↓ *Par* ↓ pareir ↓ **Petr** ↓ petr-ra ↓ *Petros* ↓ **Ph-ac** ↓ phel ↓ **Phos** ↓ *Phyt* ↓ pic-ac ↓ pip-n ↓ plan ↓ **Plat** ↓ *Plb* ↓ plb-i ↓ *Plut-n* ↓ pneu ↓ **Podo** ↓ *Prun* ↓ psil ↓ *Psor* ↓ **Puls** ↓ pycnop-sa ↓ **Pyrog** ↓ **Ran-b** ↓ **Ran-s** ↓ raph ↓ **Rat** ↓ rauw ↓ *Rheum* ↓ **Rhod** ↓ **Rhus-t** ↓ rhus-v ↓ *Rumx* ↓ **Ruta** ↓ **Sabad** ↓ **Sabin** ↓ sal-ac ↓ *Samb* ↓ *Sang* ↓ *Sars* ↓ **Sec** ↓ *Sel* ↓ *Seneg* ↓ **Sep** ↓ **Sil** ↓ sol-ni ↓ **Spig** ↓ **Spong** ↓ *Squil* ↓ **Stann** ↓ **Staph** ↓ stel ↓ *Stict* ↓ still ↓ stram ↓ *Stront-c* ↓ *Sul-ac* ↓ *Sul-i* ↓ **Sulph** ↓ sumb ↓ tab ↓ **Tarax** ↓ *Tarent* ↓ tarent-c ↓ *Ter* ↓ teucr ↓ **Thuj** ↓ til ↓ *Titan-s* ↓ tong ↓ trib ↓ *Tub* ↓ urt-g ↓ ust ↓ **Valer** ↓ **Verat** ↓ **Verb** ↓ vib ↓ vinc ↓ *Viol-o* ↓ *Viol-t* ↓ vip ↓ vip-a ↓ wies ↓ **Zinc** ↓ zinc-o ↓ zinc-ox ↓ **Zinc-p** ↓

• **left** upper part of body: kreos ↓

⁝ **burning**: kreos

• **burning**: acet-ac a1 achy jl3 *Acon* k* acon-f c1 *Agar* k* all-c sf1.de aloe alum k* *Alum-p* k2* *Alum-sil* k2* am-c k* *Am-m* k* ambr k* anac k* ang b2.de* ant-c k* ant-t k* *Antho* bg2 *Anthraci* **Apis** k* arg-met k* *Arn* k* **Ars** k* ars-i **Ars-s-f** k2* **Arum-t** k* *Asaf* k* asar k* atha a1 atro a1 aur j5.de aur-ar k2 *Aur-m* k2* *Bapt* *Bar-c* k* bar-m bars-s k2* bell k* *Berb* bism k* *Borx* k* bov k* brom a1 **Bry** k* *Bufo* k* buni-o jl3 calad k* calc k* calc-ar k2* calc-i k2* *Calc-p* camph k* cann-s k* *Canth* k* *Caps* k* carb-ac a1 carb-an k* **Carb-v** k* carbn-o a1 **Carbn-s** **Caust** k* cham k* *Chel* k* chin k* chinin-s j5.de* cic k* *Cimic* k* cina k* *Clem* coc-c cocc k* coff k* colch k* *Coloc* k* com sf1.de *Con* k* convo-d a1 cop a1 *Corn* croc k* crot-c a1 crot-h crot-t k* culx k2* cupr k* *Cycl* k* dig k* dor br1 *Dros* k* *Dulc* k* *Eucal* st1 euon j5.de euph k* euph-l a1 **Euphr** k* fago a1 *Ferr* k* fl-ac bg2* *Gels* a1* germ-met srj5• *Graph* k* *Grat* guaj k* hell k* helo-s bnm14• helon hep k* hist mg1.de* *Hydrog* srj2• *Hyos* j5.de *Ign* k* iod k* ip k* **Iris** k* juni-v a1 kali-ar *Kali-bi* k* kali-br a1 *Kali-c* k* kali-chl k13 kali-m k2 kali-n k* kali-s

- **Externally – burning**: ...
kali-sula a1 *Kreos* k* lac-ac sf1.de* *Lach* k* lachn a1 lap-a sf1.de lat-m sp1 laur k* led k* lil-t a1 lob *Lyc* k* m-ambo b2.de* m-arct b2.de* m-aust b2.de* mag-c k* mag-m k* mag-s j5.de *Manc* k* mand mg1.de mang k* *Med* ptk1 meny k* **Merc** k* *Merc-c* k* merc-sul hr1* merl a1 mez k* mosch k* *Mur-ac* k* *Nat-ar* k* *Nat-c* k* **Nat-m** k* *Nat-s* j5.de nat-sil k2* neon srj5• nicc j5.de *Nit-ac* k* nux-m k* **Nux-v** k* ol-an j5.de* *Olnd* k* *Op* k* ox-ac k2* paeon par k* petr k* petr-ra shn4• **Ph-ac** k* phel j5.de **Phos** k* phyt pic-ac sf1.de* pip-n br1 plan a1 plat k* plb k* plut-n srj7• *Prun* k* psil ft1 *Psor* *Puls* k* pycnop-sa mrz1 *Ran-b* j5.de* ran-s k* raph j5.de* **Rat** k* rauw sp1 *Rheum* k* rhod k* **Rhus-t** k* rhus-v a1 *Rumx* *Ruta* k* *Sabad* k* sabin k* sal-ac samb k* sang j5.de* sars k* **Sec** k* sel k* seneg k* **Sep** k* **Sil** k* sol-ni a1 spig k* spong k* squil k* **Stann** k* *Staph* k* stram k* stront-c k* sul-ac k* sul-i k2* **Sulph** k* tab j5.de *Tarax* k* *Tarent* a1* tarent-c sf1.de *Ter* ptk1 teucr k* *Thuj* k* til a1 trib a1 valer k* verat k* *Viol-o* b7a.de* viol-t k* vip bg2* wies a1 *Zinc* k* zinc-p k2* [alumin-s stj2 am-p stj1 am-s stj1 *Ars-met* stj2 *Cadm-s* stj2 *Chr-s* stj2 *Gal-s* stj2 *Lith-s* stj2 *Mang-s* stj2 *Nicc-s* stj2 *Titan-s* stj2]

• **constricting**: (↗*Constriction - external; Constriction - internally*) acon k* acon-c a1 agar alum k* alum-sil k2* *Am-c* ambr k* *Anac* k* **Ang** b2.de arg-met k* *Arg-n* arn k* bar-c k* *Bell* k* bry k* cact k2* calad k* *Calc* k* camph k* cann-s k* *Canth* j5.de caps fkm1• *Carb-v* k* caust k* cham k* chel k* cic k* *Cina* k* cocc k* colch k* coloc k* **Con** j5.de croc k* cycl k* *Dig* k* dros k* dulc k* euphr k* *Gamb* a1 graph k* hist mg1.de* hyos k* **Ign** j5.de iod k* kali-c k* *Kali-n* k* kreos k* led k* lyc k* m-arct b2.de mag-m j5.de mang k* meny k* merc k* mez k* mosch k* nat-c k* *Nat-m* j5.de *Nit-ac* k* *Nux-v* k* olnd k* petr k* ph-ac k* *Phos* k* **Plat** k* pneu jl3 **Puls** k* ran-b k* rhod k* rhus-t k* ruta k* sabad k* samb sep k* sil k* spig k* squil k* stront-c k* sulph k* sumb teucr k* thuj k* valer k* verat k* verb k* viol-t k* zinc k*

• **cutting** pain: acon k* *Alum* k* alum-p k2* alum-sil k2* *Alumn* hr1* ambr k* anac k* *Androc* srj1• ang b2.de* ant-c k* arg-met k* arn k* ars-s-f k2* asaf k* asar k* aur k* aur-ar k2 aur-s k2* **Bell** k* berb bg2 bism k* borx k* brom bry k* *Calad* hr1* **Calc** k* calc-i k2* **Calc-sil** k2* camph k* cann-s k* canth k* carbn-s castm bg2 caust k* chin k* chinin-s j5.de cimic cina b2.de* clem k* colch k* *Coloc* k* **Con** k* conv dig k* **Dros** k* dulc k* euph k* *Graph* k* hell k* hep k* *Hydrog* srj2• hyos k* *Ign* k* kali-c k* *Kali-chl* k13 *Kali-m* k2 kali-s kalm k2 led k* *Lyc* k* m-ambo b2.de m-arct b2.de mag-c k2* mag-m k* mang k* meny k* *Merc* k* mez k* mosch k* *Mur-ac* k* **Nat-c** k* nat-m k* *Nat-sil* k2* neon srj5• nit-ac k* *Nux-v* k* olnd k* osm ox-ac k2* oxyt par k* **Petr** k* *Ph-ac* k* phos k* plat k* puls k* ran-b k* *Rheum* kr1 rhod k* *Rhus-t* k* ruta k* sabad *Samb* k* sang k2* sars k* seneg k* *Sep* k* *Sil* k* spig k* stann k* staph k* stel br1 stram k* *Stront-c* kr1 *Sul-ac* k* sul-i k2* *Sulph* k* teucr k* thuj k* verat k* *Viol-t* k* *Zinc* k* **Zinc-p** k2*

• **gnawing** pain: acon agar k* **Agn** k* alum k* *Alumn* kr1 am-c k* ambr k* arg-met k* arn k* aur k* *Bar-c* k* bar-m bell k* bry k* calad k* calc k* calc-p a1 *Canth* k* caps k* *Cham* k* *Crot-t* cycl k* dig k* *Dros* k* dulc k* euph k* ferr gamb a1 *Glon* k* graph k* hell k* hyos k* ign k* *Kali-c* k* kreos k* laur k* led k* lyc k* m-ambo b2.de m-aust b2.de mag-c k* mag-m k* mang k* *Meny* k* merc k* merc-i-r a1 mez k* mur-ac k* nat-c k* nux-v k* olnd k* op k* *Par* k* *Ph-ac* k* *Phos* k* **Plat** k* plb k* *Puls* k* **Ran-s** k* rheum k* rhod k* rhus-t k* *Ruta* k* samb k* sep k* sil k* spig k* **Spong** k* stann k* **Staph** k* stront-c k* sulph k* *Tarax* k* thuj k* urt-g a1 verat k* zinc k*

• **here** and there: **Bar-c** ↓ sul-ac ↓ zinc ↓

⁝ **stitching** pain: **Bar-c** st1 sul-ac sf1.de zinc sf1.de

• **jerking**: acon k* agar k* agn k* *Alum* k* alum-p k2* alum-sil k2* *Alumn* hr1* ambr k* anac k* ang b2.de* ant-c k* ant-t k* arg-met k* *Arn* k* ars k* **Asaf** k* asar k* *Aur* k* bar-c k* *Bar-m* bar-s k2* *Bell* k* bism k* borx k* bov k* *Bry* k* **Calc** k* calc-act sf1.de calc-i k2* calc-sil k2* camph k* *Cann-s* hr1* canth k* caps k* carb-v k* *Carbn-s* k* **Caust** k* cham k* *Chin* k* cic k* cimic k2* *Cina* k* *Clem* k* cocc k* coff k* colch k* coloc k* con b2.de* croc b2.de* cupr h2* cycl b2.de* dig b2.de* dros b2.de* dulc b2.de* *Graph* b2.de* hell b2.de* hep b2.de* hyos b2.de* **Ign** b2.de* iod k* kali-bi bg2 kali-c k* kali-chl k13 kali-m k2 kali-s kreos k* lach k* laur k* led k* *Lyc* k* m-ambo b2.de m-arct b2.de *M-aust* b2.de mag-c k* *Mag-p* mang k* **Meny** k* *Merc* k* mez k* mosch k* mur-ac k* *Nat-c* k* **Nat-m** k* *Nit-ac* k* *Nux-m* hr1* **Nux-v** k* olnd k* op k* par k* *Petr* k* *Petros* hr1* ph-ac k* phos k* phyt plat k* plb k* **Puls** k* *Ran-b* k* ran-s k* rheum k* rhod k* **Rhus-t** k* ruta k* sabad k* sabin k* sec k* *Sep* k* *Sil* k* spig k* spong k*

- **Jerking**: ...
Squil k* *Stann* k* staph k* stront-c k* sul-ac k* sul-i k2* sulph k* **Tarax** k* teucr k* thuj k* **Valer** k* verat k* verb k* viol-t k* zinc k*
- **perspiration**; during: cann-s ↓
⁝ **stitching** pain: cann-s st1
- **pinching** pain: acon k* anac k* ang b2.de ant-c k* arg-met k* arn k* bell k* bry k* *Calc* k* cann-s k* caps k* carb-v k* caust k* chel k* chin k* cina k* *Clem* cocc k* con k* croc k* dig k* dros k* dulc k* euph k* euphr k* *Hyos* k* *Ip* k* kali-c k* kreos k* led k* m-aust b2.de mang k* **Meny** k* *Mur-ac* k* nat-c k* nit-ac k* nux-v k* olnd k* *Osm* par k* ph-ac k* phos k* **Rhod** k* *Rhus-t* k* ruta k* **Sabad** k* sabin k* samb k* sars k* sil k* *Spig* **Spong** k* **Stann** k* staph k* sul-ac k* *Sulph* k* thuj k* verat k* **Verb** k* viol-t k* zinc k*
- **pressing** pain: abrot *Acon* k* adam srj5• *Aesc* **Agar** k* agn k* aloe alum k* *Alum-p* k2 *Alum-sil* k2* *Am-m* k* ambr k* *Ammc* *Anac* k* ang b2.de* ant-c k* *Ant-t* k* **Apoc** arg-met k* arn k* ars k* ars-i **Ars-s-f** k2* *Asaf* k* asar k* *Aspar* *Aur* k* aur-i k2* aur-m k2* *Aur-s* k2* *Bapt* bar-c k* bar-i k2* bar-m bar-s k1* *Bell* k* berb j5.de bism k* borx k* bov k* *Bry* k* *Calad* *Calc* k* calc-i k2* *Calc-p* calc-sil k2* calen j5.de *Camph* k* **Cann-i** *Cann-s* k* canth k* caps k* *Carb-ac* carb-an k* *Carb-v* b2.de* carbn-s **Caust** k* cedr *Cham* k* *Chel* k* *Chin* k* **Chinin-s** cic k* *Cimic* cina k* cinnb clem k* cob coc-c *Cocc* k* coff k* *Colch* k* *Coloc* k* *Con* k* crot-t cupr k* *Cycl* k* daph j5.de dig k* dios **Dros** k* *Dulc* k* elaps **Eup-per** euph k* euphr k* **Ferr** k* ferr-ar *Gels* germ-met srj5• *Glon* *Graph* k* *Guaj* k* haliae-lc srj5• *Hell* k* hep k* *Hyos* k* *Ign* k* iod k* *Ip* **Kali-bi** kali-c k* kali-chl k13 kali-m k2 kali-n k* kali-p *Kalm* *Kreos* k* lach k* *Laur* k* *Led* k* *Lil-t* k* *Lyc* k* m-ambo b2.de* m-arct b2.de m-aust b2.de mag-c k* mag-m k* mang k* meny k* merc k* *Mez* k* **Mosch** k* mur-ac k* nat-ar nat-c k* *Nat-m* k* nat-sil k2* **Nit-ac** k* nux-m k* **Nux-v** k* *Olnd* k* *Ox-ac* par k* pareir *Petr* k* *Ph-ac* k* **Phos** k* phyt k* pip-n br1 plat k* plb k* plut-n srj7• **Podo** prun psil ft1 *Psor* **Puls** k* ran-b k* ran-s k* rheum k* **Rhod** k* **Rhus-t** k* **Ruta** k* *Sabad* k* sabin k* *Samb* k* *Sang* *Sars* k* *Sec* *Seneg* k* **Sep** k* **Sil** k* **Spig** k* spong k* *Squil* **Stann** k* **Staph** k* *Stict* stront-c k* sul-ac k* *Sul-i* k2* **Sulph** k* tab *Tarax* k* teucr k* thuj k* ust valer k* *Verat* k* verb k* vib viol-o k* viol-t k* *Zinc* k* zinc-p k2*
- **rest** agg.: tub ↓ valer ↓
⁝ **stitching** pain: tub k2* valer k2*
- **rising** from bed agg.: mag-c ↓
⁝ **jerking**: mag-c h2
- **sore**: *Acon* k* *Aesc* *Agar* k* agn b7.de aloe *Alum* k* am-c k* am-m k* ambr b2.de* anac k* *Ang* b2.de* *Ant-c* b2.de* ant-t k* *Apis* k* **Arg-met** k* **Arn** k* ars k* asaf k* *Asar* k* *Aur* k* *Bad* **Bapt** k* bar-c k* **Bell** k* *Berb* bism b2.de* borx b2.de* bov k* *Bry* k* calad k* *Calc* k* calc-p bg2 camph k* cann-s k* canth k* caps k* carb-an k* carb-v k* carbn-s *Caust* k* cedr *Cham* k* chel **Chin** k* cic k* *Cimic* bg2* *Cina* k* *Clem* k* **Cocc** k* coff k* *Colch* k* *Coloc* k* con k* *Croc* k* cupr k* cycl k* *Daph* j5.de dig k* dros k* *Dulc* k* **Eup-per** euph k* euphr b2.de* *Ferr* k* fl-ac form *Gran* graph k* guaj k* **Ham** hell k* **Hep** k* hyos k* *Ign* k* iod b2.de* ip k* kali-bi bg2 kali-c k* *Kalm* *Kreos* k* lach k* laur k* *Led* k* *Lith-c* *Lyc* k* m-ambo b2.de* m-arct b2.de* *M-aust* b2.de* *Mag-c* k* mag-m k* *Mang* k* med meny k* *Merc* b2.de* mez k* mosch b2.de* mur-ac k* *Nat-c* k* **Nat-m** k* nig-s bg nit-ac b2.de* *Nux-m* k* **Nux-v** k* olnd b2.de* *Ox-ac* par k* petr k* *Ph-ac* k* *Phos* k* *Phyt* k* plat k* plb k* podo bg2 psil ft1 *Puls* k* **Pyrog** **Ran-b** k* ran-s k* rheum k* *Rhod* k* **Rhus-t** k* rhus-v j5.de **Ruta** k* *Sabad* k* **Sabin** k* samb sars k* sec b2.de* sel j5.de seneg k* *Sep* k* **Sil** k* *Spig* k* **Spong** k* squil k* *Stann* k* staph k* stict bg2 stram k* stront-c k* sul-ac k* **Sulph** k* tab j5.de* tarax k* teucr b2.de* thuj k* *Valer* k* **Verat** k* viol-t k* *Zinc* k*
⁝ **skin** were off; as if: chelo br1
- **stitching** pain: abrot *Acon* k* aesc k2 *Agar* k* agn k* *Aloe* *Alum* k* alum-p k2 am-c k* *Am-m* k* ambr k* anac k* ang b2.de* ant-c k* ant-t k* apis arg-met k* arg-n sf1.de *Arn* k* ars k* ars-i **Asaf** k* asar k* aur k* *Bar-c* k* bar-m **Bell** k* benz-ac sf1.de *Berb* bism k* borx k* bov k* **Bry** k* bufo sf1.de calad k* **Calc** k* calc-f sf1.de *Calc-p* camph k* *Cann-i* cann-s k* canth k* *Caps* k* carb-ac carb-an k* carb-v k* **Carbn-s** *Caust* k* cedr cham k* *Chel* k* *Chin* k* chinin-ar chinin-s j5.de **Cic** k* *Cimic* cina k* cinnb cist k2 *Clem* k* *Cocc* k* coff b2.de* colch k* *Coloc* k* **Con** k* croc k* crot-h crot-t cupr k* cycl k* *Daph* j5.de dig k* *Dios* *Dros* k* dulc k* euon j5.de euonin j5.de euph k* euphr k* *Ferr* k* ferr-ar ferr-ma j5.de ferr-p fl-ac bg2 form *Gels* *Graph* k* *Guaj* k* *Hell* k* hep k* hydr *Hydrog* srj2• hyos k* *Ign* k* *Indg* iod k* ip k* kali-ar *Kali-bi* **Kali-c** k* kali-i sf1.de *Kali-n* k* **Kali-p** **Kali-s** kreos k* lach k* lact j5.de laur k* **Led** k* *Lith-c* *Lob* **Lyc** k* m-ambo b2.de* m-arct b2.de* m-aust b2.de* mag-c k* mag-m k* mag-p k2 *Manc* k* mang k* *Med* *Meny* k* **Merc** k* merc-c j5.de* *Mez* k* mosch k* *Mur-ac* k* naja nat-ar *Nat-c* k* *Nat-hchls* *Nat-m* k* *Nat-p* *Nat-s* nicc j5.de **Nit-ac** k* nux-m k* *Nux-v* k* *Ol-an* olnd k* op j5.de *Ox-ac* *Par* k* petr k* *Ph-ac* k* phel j5.de *Phos* k* *Phyt* plat k* *Plb* k* plb-i sf1.de prun j5.de psil ft1 psor **Puls** k* **Ran-b** k* *Ran-s* k* *Rat* rheum k* rhod k* **Rhus-t** k* ruta k* *Sabad* k* *Sabin* k* samb k* sang sars k* sel k* seneg k* *Sep* k* *Sil* k* **Spig** k* *Spong* k* squil k* *Stann* k* **Staph** k* stict sf1.de still stram k* stront-c k* sul-ac k* **Sulph** k* tab j5.de **Tarax** k* teucr k* **Thuj** k* tub k2 *Valer* k* verat k* verb k* viol-o k* *Viol-t* k* vip j5.de* vip-a j5.de **Zinc** k*
⁝ **burning**: *Acon* j5.de alum j5.de *Anac* j5.de arg-met j5.de arn j5.de ars j5.de *Asaf* j5.de aur j5.de *Bar-c* j5.de bell j5.de berb j5.de *Bry* j5.de cann-s j5.de caps j5.de caust j5.de cina j5.de *Cocc* j5.de con j5.de *Dig* j5.de *Hep* j5.de *Hyos* j5.de ign j5.de *Lach* j5.de *Lyc* j5.de m-arct j5.de m-aust j5.de mag-c j5.de meny j5.de *Merc* j5.de *Mez* j5.de mur-ac j5.de nat-s j5.de nicc j5.de *Nux-v* j5.de *Ph-ac* j5.de phel j5.de phos j5.de plat j5.de *Puls* j5.de *Ran-b* j5.de *Ran-s* j5.de *Rhus-t* j5.de sabad j5.de sel j5.de *Sep* j5.de *Sil* j5.de spig j5.de *Spong* j5.de squil j5.de *Stann* j5.de *Staph* j5.de *Sul-ac* j5.de *Sulph* j5.de *Thuj* j5.de *Viol-t* j5.de
⁝ **needles**; as from: *Plut-n* srj7•
- **tearing** pain: **Acon** k* *Act-sp* a1* adon sf1.de aesc *Agar* k* agn k* *Alum* k* alum-p k2* **Alum-sil** k2* *Alumn* kr1 *Am-c* k* *Am-m* k* *Ambr* k* *Anac* k* ang b2.de* ant-c k* ant-t k* aphis j5.de apis bg2 arg-met k* **Arn** k* *Ars* k* ars-s-f k2* *Asaf* k* asar k* aur k* aur-ar k2 aur-i k2* aur-m a1* aur-s k2* bamb-a stb2.de• bar-act sf1.de bar-c k* bar-i k2* bar-m bar-s k2* **Bell** k* **Berb** k* *Bism* k* borx k* bov k* brom bruc j5.de **Bry** k* cact calad k* *Calc* k* calc-caust sf1.de calc-i k2* calc-p k* *Calc-sil* k2* camph k* cann-s k* canth k* *Caps* k* carb-an k* *Carb-v* k* **Carbn-s** *Caust* k* *Cedr* *Cham* k* *Chel* k* **Chin** k* chinin-ar chinin-s j5.de cic k* *Cimic* sf1.de cina k* cist j5.de* clem k* coc-c j5.de* cocc k* coff k* **Colch** k* *Coloc* k* con k* croc k* *Crot-t* k* cupr k* cycl k* cyt-l mg1.de dig k* dros k* *Dulc* k* eucal a1 euph k* euphr k* *Ferr* k* *Ferr-ar* ferr-m j5.de ferr-p *Gamb* k* *Gels* graph k* *Guaj* k* guare a1 hell k* hep k* hera j5.de* hist mg1.de hyos k* **Hyper** ign k* *Indg* k* iod k* ip k* kali-ar *Kali-bi* k* **Kali-c** k* *Kali-i* k* *Kali-n* k* **Kali-p** **Kali-s** kali-sil k2* *Kalm* sf1.de *Kreos* k* lach k* lact j5.de* lam j5.de laur k* **Led** k* **Lyc** k* lyss m-ambo b2.de* m-arct b2.de m-aust b2.de *Mag-c* k* mag-m k* mag-p k2 mang k* med k2* meny k* *Merc* k* merc-c k2* *Mez* k* mosch k* mur-ac k* nat-ar k* *Nat-c* k* **Nat-m** k* nat-p **Nat-s** *Nat-sil* k2* *Nicc* k* **Nit-ac** k* nux-m k* *Nux-v* k* olnd k* op k* ox-ac k2* par k* petr k* ph-ac k* *Phos* b2.de* phyt plan hr1* plat k* plb k* **Puls** k* *Ran-b* k* ran-s k* *Rat* rheum k* *Rhod* k* *Rhus-t* k* ruta k* sabad k* sabin k* samb k* sang k2* sars k* sec k* *Sel* k* seneg k* **Sep** k* **Sil** k* *Spig* k* spong k* squil k* stann k* *Staph* k* stram k* *Stront-c* k* sul-ac k* sul-i k2* **Sulph** k* tarax k* teucr k* thuj k* til a1 tong j5.de *Tub* k2* *Valer* k* verat k* verb k* vinc j5.de viol-o k* viol-t k* wies a1 **Zinc** k* zinc-o j5.de zinc-ox j5.de
- **ulcerative** pain: acon k* agar k* alum k* am-c k* **Am-m** k* ambr k* anac k* ang b2.de* ant-c k* arg-met k* arn k* ars k* aur k* bar-c k* bell k* bov k* **Bry** k* calc j5.de camph k* cann-s k* *Canth* k* caps k* carb-an k* carb-v k* *Caust* k* cedr cham k* chin k* *Cic* k* cocc k* colch k* cycl k* dros k* dulc k* ferr k* *Graph* k* hep k* *Ign* k* *Kali-c* k* kali-n k* **Kali-s** kreos k* lach k* laur k* m-arct b2.de mag-c k* mag-m k* *Mang* k* merc k* *Mur-ac* k* nat-c k* *Nat-m* k* nit-ac k* *Nux-v* k* petr k* ph-ac k* phos k* plat k* **Puls** k* **Rhus-t** k* ruta k* sars k* *Sep* k* **Sil** k* spig k* spong k* staph k* sul-ac k* sulph k* teucr k* thuj k* verat k* *Zinc* k*
- **vexation**; after: rhus-t ↓
⁝ **stitching** pain: rhus-t
- **warmth**:
⁝ **amel.**:
⁝ **heat** amel.: alum ↓ **Ars** ↓ *Ars-met* ↓ *Caps* ↓ carb-v ↓ lyc ↓ *Nat-ar* ↓
. **burning**: alum st **Ars** st* *Caps* st carb-v st lyc st [*Ars-met* stj2 *Nat-ar* stj2]

○ • **Affected** parts: arn ↓ *Merc* ↓
⁝ **jerking**: arn h1 *Merc* k*

- **Fibrous** tissue: *Caust* ↓ cot ↓
  - **benumbing** | **numb** aching: cot br1
  - **drawing** pain: *Caust* br1
  - **tearing** pain: *Caust* br1

- **Glands**: (↗*Sensitiveness - glands)* acon k* agn ↓ all-s a1 *Alum* k* *Am-c* k* *Am-m* ↓ ambr k* anac ↓ *Ang* ↓ ant-c k* ant-t k* apis bg2 arg-met ↓ **Arn** k* ars k* *Ars-i* arund a1* asaf bg2 asar ↓ *Aur* k* aur-ar k2 aur-i k2 aur-s k2 *Bar-c* k* bar-i k2 bar-m bar-s k2 **Bell** k* berb j5.de borx j5.de bov ↓ brom ↓ *Bry* k* bung-fa tsm2 calc k* calen j5.de *Cann-s* k* canth k* *Caps* ↓ *Carb-an* k* *Carb-v* k* *Carbn-s* *Caust* k* cham k* chin k* cic k* cina ↓ clem ↓ *Cocc* ↓ *Coloc* k* con k* cor-r j5.de cupr ↓ cycl ↓ dendr-pol tsm2 dulc k* elaps tsm2 euph ↓ euphr ↓ ferr ↓ graph k* grat ↓ guaj ↓ ham bg2* hell k* helo-s bnm14• hep k* hyos ↓ ign k* *Iod* k* kali-c k* kali-m ↓ kali-s kreos ↓ lach bg2* lat-m bnm6• laur ↓ **Lyc** k* m-ambo b2.de* m-arct j5.de m-aust ↓ mag-c k* mag-m j5.de *Mang* ↓ meny ↓ **Merc** k* *Mez* ↓ mur-ac ↓ murx j5.de naja tsm2 *Nat-c* ↓ *Nat-m* k* nicc ↓ *Nit-ac* k* nux-v k* ol-an ↓ osm ↓ par ↓ petr k* *Ph-ac* k* phel ↓ **Phos** k* phyt ↓ *Plat* ↓ *Plb* ↓ prun ↓ *Psor* ↓ *Puls* k* *Ran-s* ↓ raph ↓ rheum k* *Rhod* ↓ rhus-t k* *Ruta* ↓ sabad ↓ sabin ↓ sang ↓ sel k* *Seneg* ↓ sep k* sil k* *Spig* k* spong k* squil k* stann k* staph k* stram k* *Sul-ac* k* sul-i k2 *Sulph* k* ter ↓ teucr ↓ **Thuj** k* verat k* *Zinc* ↓
  - **night**: *Aur* b4a.de *Mez* b4a.de
  - **boring** pain: *Bell* k* lyc j5.de* puls k* sabad k* sabin j5.de
  - **burning**: alum ant-c arn **Ars** k* *Bell* k* brom bry calc *Cann-s* k* carb-v k* caust cic clem cocc k* *Con* graph *Hep* k* *Ign* kali-c laur k* merc k* mez nat-m nux-v *Phos* k* phyt plat **Puls** k* rheum b2.de* rhus-t *Sep* *Sil* k* staph sul-ac sulph ter j5.de teucr *Zinc*
  - **burrowing**: acon b2.de* am-m b2.de* arn b2.de* asaf b2.de* bell b2.de* bov b2.de* bry b2.de* calc b2.de* *Dulc* b2.de* kali-c b2.de* nat-c b2.de* phos b2.de* plat b2.de* *Rhod* b2.de* rhus-t b2.de* ruta b2.de* sep b2.de* spig b2.de* stann b2.de*
  - **compressed**; as if forcefully: ign b7.de*
  - **constricting**: *Acon* b2.de* alum b2.de* am-c anac arn b2.de* bell k* *Borx* b2.de* *Calc* carb-v caust chin k* cocc b2.de* con b2.de* ign k* iod k* kali-c lyc k* *Mang* b2.de* nat-c *Nit-ac* b2.de* nux-v k* ph-ac phos b2.de* *Plat* *Plb* b2.de* *Puls* k* *Rhus-t* b2.de* sabad sep k* sil spong k* sul-ac b2.de* *Sulph* b2.de*
  - **cutting** pain: arg-met k* *Bell* k* calc k* con k* graph k* ign k* *Lyc* k* nat-c k* ph-ac k* *Sep* k* sil k* staph k* sulph k*
  - **digging** pain: acon am-m arn asaf bell bov bry calc *Dulc* kali-c nat-c phos plat *Rhod* rhus-t ruta sep spig stann
  - **drawing** pain: agn b7.de* alum j5.de *Bell* b4.de* bov b4.de* calc b4.de* cann-s b7.de* cham b7.de* *Chin* b7.de* cycl b7.de* dulc b4a.de guaj a1 *Ign* b7.de* *Merc* j5.de mez b4.de* nit-ac b4.de* phos h2* *Puls* b7.de* *Seneg* b4.de* *Sil* b4.de* sulph b4.de* thuj b4.de*
  - **gnawing** pain: bar-c k* cham k* mez k* nat-m bg2 ph-ac k* *Plat* k* ran-s k* *Spong* k* staph k*
  - **jerking**: arn k* asaf k* aur k* bell k* bry k* *Calc* k* caps k* caust k* chin k* *Clem* k* graph k* lyc k* meny k* merc k* nat-c k* *Nat-m* k* nit-ac k* nux-v k* petr k* *Puls* k* rhus-t k* sep k* sil k* sulph k*
  - **menses**; before: *Con* b4a.de
  - **motion** agg.: bry ↓
    - **stitching** pain: bry tl1
  - **pinching** pain: bry k* *Calc* k* m-arct b7.de* meny k* mur-ac k* prun j5.de *Rhod* k* rhus-t k* sabad k* stann k* sulph k* verat k*
  - **pressing** pain: alum j5.de arg-met k* ars k* asar aur k* *Bell* k* *Calc* k* carb-v k* caust k* chin k* cina k* cocc k* con j5.de cycl k* hyos ign k* kali-c k* *Lyc* k* m-arct b2.de* mag-m j5.de mang k* meny k* **Merc** k* mur-ac nat-m j5.de nit-ac j5.de osm par k* ph-ac k* puls k* rheum k* rhus-t k* sabin k* *Spong* k* stann k* *Staph* k* stram k* *Sulph* k* teucr b2.de* verat k* zinc k*
    - **blunt** instrument; as from a: asar b2.de* carb-v b2.de* hyos b2.de* mur-ac b2.de*
    - **inward**: aur k* *Calc* k* cocc k* cycl k* rheum k* *Staph* k* zinc k*
    - **outward**: arg-met k* cina k* ign k* lyc k* m-arct b2.de mang k* meny k* *Merc* k* par k* puls k* rhus-t k* *Spong* k* sulph k* teucr b2.de*
  - **sore**: alum k* ant-c k* arg-met k* *Arn* k* ars k* bry k* calc k* *Carb-an* k* caust k* *Cic* k* clem b2.de* **Con** k* cupr k* graph b2.de* *Hep* k* *Ign* b2.de* iod k* kali-c k* m-arct b2.de merc k* mez k* nat-m k* nicc a1 nux-v b2.de* *Petr* bg2 phos k* plat k* *Psor* puls k* rhod k* rhus-t k* *Ruta* k* *Sep* k* staph k* sul-ac k* sulph k* teucr k* zinc k*
  - **squeezed**; as if: anac b2.de* *Ang* b2.de* ars b4a.de bell b2.de* *Calc* b2.de* carb-v b2.de* caust b2.de* chin b2.de* iod b2.de* kali-c b2.de* lyc b2.de* m-arct b7.de m-aust b2.de nat-c b2.de* ph-ac b2.de* phos b4a.de *Plat* b2.de* sabad b2.de* sep b2.de* sil b2.de* staph b7.de

- **Glands**: ...
  - **stitching** pain: acon k* agn k* alum k* *Am-m* k* ang b2.de* apis bg2 arg-met k* arn k* *Asaf* k* bar-c k* bar-m **Bell** k* berb j5.de borx k* *Bry* k* *Calc* k* carb-an k* carb-v bg2 caust k* chin k* *Cocc* k* *Con* k* cupr k* cycl k* euph k* euphr j5.de graph k* grat j5.de hell k* hep k* *Ign* k* *Iod* k* kali-c k* kali-m k2 kreos k* lach k* laur b7.de lyc k* m-ambo b2.de* m-arct b2.de* **Merc** k* *Mez* k* mur-ac k* murx j5.de *Nat-c* k* *Nat-m* k* **Nit-ac** k* nux-v b2.de* ol-an j5.de ph-ac k* *Phos* k* plb k* **Puls** k* *Ran-s* k* raph j5.de rheum k* *Rhus-t* k* sabad k* sang j5.de *Sep* k* sil k* spig k* *Spong* k* stann k* staph k* sul-ac k* *Sulph* k* thuj k* verat k* zinc k*
  - **tearing** pain: agn k* am-c k* *Ambr* k* *Arn* k* bar-c k* bar-s k2 *Bell* k* bov k* *Bry* k* *Calc* k* cann-s k* *Caps* k* *Carb-an* k* *Carb-v* k* caust k* *Cham* k* **Chin** k* cocc k* con k* cycl k* *Dulc* k* ferr k* graph k* grat j5.de ign k* *Kali-c* k* kali-s kreos k* *Lyc* k* **Merc** k* mez k* nat-c k* nit-ac k* nux-v k* ol-an j5.de phel j5.de phos k* **Puls** k* *Rhod* k* *Rhus-t* k* sel k* seneg k* sep k* *Sil* k* staph k2 *Sulph* k* thuj k* *Zinc* k*
  - **ulcerative** pain: am-c k* *Am-m* k* aur k* bell k* bry k* calc k* canth k* caust k* cham k* chin k* cic k* cocc k* graph k* hep k* ign k* kali-c k* merc k* mur-ac k* nat-c k* nat-m k* nit-ac k* petr k* **Phos** k* *Puls* k* *Rhus-t* k* ruta k* **Sil** k* staph k* sul-ac k* teucr k* *Zinc* k*
- ○ • **Around**: con ↓
    - **cutting** pain: con h2
    - **stitching** pain: con h2
- **Internal** parts: agar ↓ alum ↓ am-m ↓ ambr ↓ **Ang** ↓ ant-t ↓ apis ↓ arg-n ↓ brom ↓ calad ↓ calc ↓ carb-v ↓ caust ↓ cina ↓ croc ↓ dulc ↓ euph ↓ ign ↓ kali-bi ↓ kali-c ↓ *Lyc* ↓ mur-ac ↓ nux-m ↓ *Nux-v* ↓ *Petr* ↓ ph-ac ↓ phos ↓ **Plat** ↓ podo ↓ puls ↓ ran-b ↓ ran-s ↓ rhod ↓ samb ↓ sang ↓ spig ↓ staph ↓ sulph ↓ tarax ↓ thuj ↓ valer ↓ verat ↓ verb ↓ zinc ↓
  - **cramping**: **Ang** b2.de* ant-t b2.de* calad b2.de* calc b2.de* cina b2.de* croc b2.de* ign b2.de* kali-bi bg2 kali-c b2.de* mur-ac b2.de* *Petr* b2.de* ph-ac b2.de* **Plat** b2.de* podo bg2 puls b2.de* ran-b b2.de* ran-s b2.de* samb b2.de* staph b2.de* thuj b2.de* valer b2.de* verat b2.de* verb b2.de* zinc b2.de*
  - **dislocated**; as if: agar b2.de* alum b2.de* am-m b2.de* ambr b2.de* apis bg2 caust b2.de* dulc b2.de* euph b2.de* kali-c b2.de* *Lyc* b2.de* nux-v b2.de* petr b2.de* plat b2.de* puls bg2 rhod b2.de* spig b2.de* staph b2.de* sulph b2.de* tarax b2.de* thuj b2.de*
  - **raw**; as if: arg-n bg2 brom ptk1 carb-v ptk1 nux-m ptk1 *Nux-v* ptk1 phos ptk1 sang ptk1
- **Internally**: abies-c ↓ abies-n ↓ abrot ↓ acet-ac ↓ achy ↓ **Acon** ↓ acon-f ↓ aconin ↓ *Act-sp* ↓ adam ↓ *Aesc* ↓ aeth ↓ **Agar** ↓ agn ↓ *Ail* ↓ all-c ↓ *Aloe* ↓ *Alum* ↓ *Alum-sil* ↓ alumin-s ↓ alumn ↓ *Am-br* ↓ *Am-c* ↓ *Am-m* ↓ **Ambr** ↓ ammc ↓ amor-r ↓ *Anac* ↓ *Ang* ↓ ant-c ↓ *Ant-t* ↓ *Apis* ↓ *Arg-met* ↓ **Arg-n** ↓ **Arn** ↓ **Ars** ↓ *Ars-i* ↓ *Ars-met* ↓ **Ars-s-f** ↓ **Arum-t** ↓ **Asaf** ↓ *Asar* ↓ *Aspar* ↓ atra-r ↓ *Aur* ↓ aur-ar ↓ aur-i ↓ aur-m ↓ aur-s ↓ *Bamb-a* ↓ **Bapt** ↓ *Bar-c* ↓ bar-i ↓ bar-m ↓ bar-s ↓ **Bell** ↓ bell-p ↓ **Berb** ↓ *Bism* ↓ **Borx** ↓ *Bov* ↓ **Brom** ↓ **Bry** ↓ *Bufo* ↓ *Cact* ↓ cadm-s ↓ *Calad* ↓ **Calc** ↓ calc-ar ↓ calc-i ↓ *Calc-p* ↓ calc-sil ↓ **Camph** ↓ **Cann-i** ↓ *Cann-s* ↓ cann-xyz ↓ **Canth** ↓ *Caps* ↓ carb-ac ↓ *Carb-an* ↓ **Carb-v** ↓ **Carbn-s** ↓ carc ↓ card-m ↓ *Carl* ↓ **Caust** ↓ *Cedr* ↓ *Cham* ↓ **Chel** ↓ chen-a ↓ **Chin** ↓ chinin-ar ↓ choc ↓ *Chr-s* ↓ *Cic* ↓ **Cimic** ↓ *Cina* ↓ cist ↓ *Clem* ↓ *Coc-c* ↓ **Cocc** ↓ *Cod* ↓ coff ↓ *Colch* ↓ *Coll* ↓ **Coloc** ↓ *Com* ↓ **Con** ↓ conv ↓ cor-r ↓ *Croc* ↓ crot-h ↓ crot-t ↓ cub ↓ cund ↓ **Cupr** ↓ cycl ↓ delphin ↓ *Dig* ↓ **Dios** ↓ *Dol* ↓ dor ↓ *Dros* ↓ *Dulc* ↓ elaps ↓ *Elat* ↓ *Equis-h* ↓ eucal ↓ eug ↓ *Eup-per* ↓ eup-pur ↓ *Euph* ↓ euphr ↓ *Ferr* ↓ *Fl-ac* ↓ form ↓ *Gal-s* ↓ *Gamb* ↓ **Gels** ↓ germ-met ↓ *Glon* ↓ goss ↓ *Gran* ↓ **Graph** ↓ *Guaj* ↓ **Ham** ↓ *Hell* ↓ helo-s ↓ hep ↓ hist ↓ hydr ↓ *Hydr-ac* ↓ *Hydrog* ↓ hydroph ↓ **Hyos** ↓ hyper ↓ **Ign** ↓ iod ↓ *Ip* ↓ *Iris* ↓ kali-ar ↓ **Kali-bi** ↓ **Kali-c** ↓ kali-chl ↓ *Kali-i* ↓ kali-m ↓ *Kali-n* ↓ **Kali-s** ↓ kali-sil ↓ *Kalm* ↓ *Kreos* ↓ lac-ac ↓ **Lach** ↓ lat-h ↓ *Laur* ↓ **Led** ↓ lepi ↓ *Lept* ↓ **Lil-t** ↓ *Lith-c* ↓ *Lith-s* ↓ *Lob* ↓ loxo-lae ↓ loxo-recl ↓ **Lyc** ↓ m-ambo ↓ m-arct ↓ *M-aust* ↓ *Mag-c* ↓ *Mag-m* ↓ manc ↓ *Mang* ↓ *Mang-s* ↓ *Med* ↓ **Meny** ↓ **Merc** ↓ **Merc-c** ↓ *Merc-i-f* ↓ merc-i-r ↓ merc-n ↓ merc-ns ↓ **Mez** ↓ mosch ↓ *Mur-ac* ↓ murx ↓ *Naja* ↓ narc-ps ↓ *Nat-ar* ↓ *Nat-c* ↓ **Nat-m** ↓ *Nat-s* ↓ *Nicc-s* ↓ **Nit-ac** ↓ nux-m ↓ **Nux-v** ↓ oena ↓ *Ol-an* ↓ ol-j ↓ olnd ↓ onos ↓ **Op** ↓ *Osm* ↓ *Ox-ac* ↓ *Par* ↓ **Petr** ↓ **Ph-ac** ↓ phel ↓ **Phos** ↓ *Phys* ↓ *Phyt* ↓ *Pic-ac* ↓ pip-n ↓ plan ↓ **Plat** ↓ **Plb** ↓ *Podo* ↓ **Prun** ↓ psil ↓ *Psor* ↓ **Puls** ↓ **Pyrog** ↓ **Ran-b** ↓ *Ran-s* ↓ rat ↓ *Rheum* ↓ *Rhod* ↓ **Rhus-t** ↓ rhus-v ↓ rob ↓ *Rumx* ↓ **Ruta** ↓ **Sabad** ↓ *Sabin* ↓ samb ↓ **Sang** ↓ **Sangin-n** ↓ *Sars* ↓ **Sec** ↓ sel ↓ **Seneg** ↓ **Sep** ↓ **Sil** ↓ sin-n ↓ **Spig** ↓ **Spong** ↓ **Squil** ↓ **Stann** ↓ *Staph* ↓ stel ↓ stict ↓ stram ↓ *Stront-c* ↓ stry ↓ sul-ac ↓ sul-i ↓ **Sulph** ↓ tab ↓ *Tarax* ↓ tarent ↓ *Tell* ↓ *Ter* ↓ *Teucr* ↓ *Thal* ↓ *Ther* ↓ **Thuj** ↓ *Titan-s* ↓ uran-n ↓ ust ↓ uva ↓ **Valer** ↓ **Verat** ↓

- **Internally**: ...
Verat-v↓ **Verb**↓ vesp↓ *Vib*↓ viol-o↓ *Viol-t*↓ vip↓ wye↓ xan↓ **Zinc**↓ **Zinc-p**↓ zing↓ *Ziz*↓

- **left**: *Ran-b*↓
  - **sore**: *Ran-b* bg2
- **night**: euphr↓
  - **stitching** pain: euphr h2
- **burning**: abies-c k* acet-ac k* achy jl3 **Acon** k* acon-f k* aconin a1 aesc bg2* *Agar* k* aloe sf1.de *Alum* k* alum-sil k2 alumn k* *Am-br* am-c k* *Am-m* k* ambr k* amor-r jl3 anac a1 ang b2.de* ant-c k* ant-t k* *Apis* k* arg-met k* *Arg-n* *Arn* k* **Ars** k* ars-i k* **Ars-s-f** k2* **Arum-t** k* *Asaf* k* asar k* atra-r bnm3• *Aur* k* aur-ar k2 aur-i k2* aur-m k2 bamb-a stb2.de• *Bapt* k* *Bar-c* k* bar-m k* bar-s k2 **Bell** k* **Berb** *Bism* k* borx k* bov k* brom bg2* **Bry** k* *Bufo* k* cadm-s mrr1* calad k* *Calc* k* calc-ar k2 calc-i k2 *Calc-p* k* calc-sil k2* camph k* **Cann-i** cann-s k* **Canth** k* caps k* carb-ac carb-an k* *Carb-v* k* **Carbn-s** carc k4* *Carl* a1 *Caust* k* cedr cham k* *Chel* k* *Chin* k* choc srj3• *Cic* k* cina k* *Clem* k* cocc k* coff k* *Colch* k* *Coloc* k* *Com* k* *Con* k* crot-t k* cund *Cupr* k* delphin a1 dig k* *Dios* dol dor br1 *Dros* k* *Dulc* k* equis-h eucal sf1.de eup-pur *Euph* k* euphr k* *Fl-ac* k* form sf1.de *Gamb* k* goss a1 **Graph** k* hell k* helo-s bnm14• hep k* hist jl3 hydr *Hydrog* srj2• hydroph rsj6• hyos k* ign k* iod k* ip k* *Iris* k* kali-ar **Kali-bi** k* kali-c k* *Kali-i* kali-m k2 kali-n k* kali-s kalm a1* *Kreos* k* lac-ac a1* *Lach* k* lat-h bnm5• *Laur* k* led k* *Lil-t* k* *Lith-c* *Lob* loxo-lae bnm12• loxo-recl bnm10• *Lyc* k* m-ambo b2.de* m-arct b2.de* m-aust b2.de* mag-c k* mag-m k* manc a1 mang k* *Med* ptk1 **Merc** k* **Merc-c** k* *Merc-i-f* k* **Mez** k* mosch k* mur-ac k* narc-ps c1* *Nat-ar* k* *Nat-c* k* *Nat-m* k* **Nit-ac** k* nux-m k* **Nux-v** k* oena sf1.de ol-an br1 ol-j sf1.de *Op* *Osm* *Ox-ac* k* par k* *Petr* k* *Ph-ac* k* **Phos** k* phyt k* pic-ac ptk1 pip-n br1 plat k* plb k* **Prun** k* *Psor* **Puls** k* pyrog sf1.de *Ran-b* k* ran-s k* rat k* *Rhod* k* **Rhus-t** k* rhus-v a1 rob *Rumx* ruta k* **Sabad** k* *Sabin* k* **Sang** k* sangin-n *Sars* k* **Sec** k* *Seneg* k* **Sep** k* *Sil* k* sin-n **Spig** k* **Spong** k* *Stann* k* staph k* stram k* stront-c k* stry a1 sul-ac k* sul-i k2 **Sulph** k* tab bg2 tarax k* tarent a1* *Tell* *Ter* k* *Thuj* (non:uran-met k) uran-n ust uva *Verat* k* verat-v viol-o k* viol-t k* wye **Zinc** k* **Zinc-p** k2 [alumin-s stj2 *Ars-met* stj2 *Chr-s* stj2 *Gal-s* stj2 *Lith-s* stj2 *Mang-s* stj2 *Nicc-s* stj2 *Titan-s* stj2]
  - **accompanied** by:
    - **itching**: *(↗SKIN - Itching - accompanied - heat)* mez ptk1
    - **shivering**: acon ptk1 ars ptk1 *Bry* ptk1 chin ptk1 ip ptk1 samb ptk1 verat-v ptk1
- **chill**; during: *Mez*↓ nat-c↓
  - **burning**: *Mez* b4a.de nat-c b4a.de
- **constricting**: *Acon* k* agn k* alum-sil k2 am-m k* **Ambr** k* anac k* *Ang* b2.de* ant-t k* arg-met k* arn k* ars k* asaf k* asar k* aur k* bar-c k* bell k* bism k* borx k* bry k* cact k2* *Calc* k* camph k* canth k* caps k* carb-an k* *Carb-v* k* cham k* chel k* chin k* cina k* *Cocc* k* *Colch* k* *Coloc* k* con k* croc k* cycl k* dig k* dros k* dulc k* ferr k* germ-met srj5• graph k* hyos k* **Ign** k* iod k* *Kali-c* k* lach k* led k* lyc k* mag-c k* meny k* merc k* *Mez* k* mur-ac k* nat-m k* *Nux-v* k* olnd k* petr k* **Ph-ac** k* phos k* **Plat** k* puls k* ran-s k* rheum k* rhod k* rhus-t k* sabin k* sars k* sel k* seneg k* sep k* sil k* spong k* squil k* stann k* *Staph* k* stram k* stront-c k* sul-ac k* *Sulph* k* *Teucr* k* thuj k* valer k* verat k* *Zinc* k*
- **cough** agg.; during: arg-met↓ **Calc**↓ hep↓ *Kali-bi*↓ kali-c↓ *Kali-n*↓ lach↓ mag-m↓ nat-m↓ phos↓ **Sil**↓ staph↓ *Sulph*↓ verat↓
  - **cutting** pain: arg-met bg2 *Kali-n* bg2 nat-m bg2 verat bg2
  - **ulcerative** pain: **Calc** bg2 hep bg2 *Kali-bi* bg2 kali-c bg2 lach bg2 mag-m bg2 phos bg2 **Sil** bg2 staph bg2 *Sulph* bg2
- **cutting** pain: abies-n k* acon k* aesc k* aeth k* agar k* agn k* all-c k* alum k* alum-sil k2 am-c k* am-m k* ambr k* anac k* *Ang* b2.de* ant-c k* ant-t k* arg-met k* arg-n k* *Arn* k* ars k* ars-i a1 ars-s-f k2 asaf k* asar k* aur k* aur-ar k2 aur-s k2 bar-c k* bar-m **Bell** k* *Berb* k* bism k* borx k* bov k* bry k* *Calad* k* **Calc** k* calc-i k2 calc-p calc-sil k2 camph k* cann-i cann-s k* **Canth** k* caps k* carb-an k* carb-v k* caust k* cham k* *Chel* k* *Chin* k* cic k* cina k* clem k* coc-c cocc k* coff k* colch k* *Coll* k* **Coloc** k* **Con** k* conv croc k* crot-h crot-t cub cupr k* cycl k* dig k* **Dios** k* dros k* *Dulc* k* *Elat* *Equis-h* ferr k* *Gamb* k* gels graph k* guaj k* hell k* hep k* hydr *Hydrog* srj2• **Hyos** k* ign k* iod k* *Ip* k* iris **Kali-c** k* kali-chl k* kali-m k2 *Kali-n* k* *Kali-s* kalm k2 lach k* laur k* led k* lepi br1 **Lyc** k* m-ambo b2.de* m-arct b2.de* m-aust b2.de* mag-c k* mag-m k* mang k* meny k* **Merc** k* merc-c mez k* mosch k* *Mur-ac* k* nat-c k* **Nat-m** k* nit-ac k* nux-m k* **Nux-v** k* *Op* k* ox-ac k2 *Par* k* *Petr* k* ph-ac k* *Phos* k* plat k* plb k* **Puls** k* ran-b k* ran-s k* *Rheum* k* rhod k* rhus-t k* ruta k* sabad k* sabin k* samb k* sars k* sec k2 sel k* seneg k* *Sep* k* **Sil** k* *Spig* k* spong k* squil k* *Stann* k* *Staph* k* stel br1 *Stront-c* k* sul-ac k* sul-i k2 **Sulph** k* teucr k* thuj k* valer k* **Verat** k* verb k* *Vib* viol-t k* **Zinc** k* zinc-p k2 zing k*
- **external** coldness; with: carb-v↓
  - **burning**: carb-v mtf33
- **gnawing** pain: agar alum k* am-m k* arg-met k* *Ars* k* bar-c k* *Bell* k* calad k* *Calc* k* cann-s k* canth k* *Carb-v* k* **Caust** k* chel k* cocc k* *Coloc* *Con* k* *Cupr* k* dig dros k* dulc k* *Gamb* hep k* iod k* kali-bi kali-c k* kali-i sf1.de *Kreos* k* lach k* *Lyc* k* merc k* mez k* nat-m sf1.de nux-v k* olnd k* ph-ac k* phos k* *Plat* k* **Puls** k* ran-b sf1.de *Ran-s* k* rhod k* **Ruta** k* seneg k* **Sep** sil k* stann k* staph sf1.de stront-c sf1.de sulph k* teucr k* verat k*
- **jerking**: acon k* agar k* aloe am-m k* ambr k* anac k* ang b2.de* arn k* ars k* **Bell** borx k* bry k* *Calc* k* cann-s k* carb-v k* caust k* cham k* **Chin** k* *Cina* br1 clem cocc k* colch k* con k* croc k* cupr h2 graph k* **Ign** k* **Kali-c** k* lyc k* *M-aust* b2.de mang k* meny k* *Merc* mez k* nat-m k* **Nit-ac** k* nux-v k* petr k* ph-ac k* plat k* plb k* podo c1 **Puls** k* ran-b k* ran-s k* rhus-t k* *Sep* k* **Sil** k* *Spig* k* *Stann* stront-c k* sul-ac k* **Sulph** k* teucr k* **Thuj** *Valer* k*
- **pinching** pain: acon k* *Agar* k* agn k* alum k* *Am-c* k* am-m k* anac k* ang b2.de* ant-c k* ant-t k* arg-met k* arn k* ars k* ars-i asaf k* asar k* aur k* bar-c k* *Bell* k* *Bism* k* borx k* bov k* *Bry* k* **Calc** k* camph k* *Cann-s* k* *Canth* k* caps k* carb-an k* *Carb-v* k* caust k* cham k* **Chel** k* *Chin* k* cic k* *Cina* k* coc-c **Cocc** k* coff k* *Colch* k* **Coloc** k* com con k* croc k* cupr k* cycl k* dig k* dros k* *Dulc* k* eug a1 euph k* euphr k* *Gamb* k* **Graph** k* guaj k* *Hell* k* hep k* hyos k* **Ign** k* iod k* *Ip* k* *Kali-c* k* kreos k* **Lyc** k* m-ambo b2.de* m-arct b2.de m-aust b2.de mag-c k* mag-m k* mang k* *Meny* k* *Merc* k* mez k* mosch k* *Mur-ac* k* *Nat-c* k* *Nat-m* k* nit-ac k* nux-m k* nux-v k* olnd k* *Par* k* *Petr* k* ph-ac k* *Phos* k* plat k* *Plb* k* *Puls* k* *Ran-b* k* ran-s k* rheum k* *Rhod* k* *Rhus-t* k* *Ruta* k* *Sabad* k* sabin k* samb k* sars k* seneg k* *Sep* k* sil k* *Spig* k* *Spong* k* squil k* *Stann* k* *Staph* k* stront-c k* sul-ac k* *Sulph* k* tarax k* teucr k* *Thuj* k* valer k* verat k* **Verb** k* viol-t k* *Zinc* k*
- **pressing** pain: *Acon* k* adam srj5• aesc agar k* agn k* *Ail* *Aloe* *Alum* k* alum-sil k2 am-c k* am-m k* *Ambr* k* *Anac* k* ang b2.de* ant-c k* ant-t k* arg-met k* **Arg-n** **Arn** k* **Ars** k* *Ars-i* ars-s-f k2 *Arum-t* **Asaf** k* asar k* *Aur* k* aur-ar k2 aur-i k2* aur-m k2 aur-s k2 bamb-a stb2.de• bar-c k* bar-i k2 bar-s k2 **Bell** k* berb *Bism* k* *Borx* k* bov k* **Brom** *Bry* k* cact calad k* **Calc** k* calc-i k2 calc-sil k2 *Camph* k* *Cann-i* cann-s k* **Canth** k* caps k* *Carb-an* k* **Carb-v** k* carbn-s *Caust* k* *Cedr* cham k* chel k* chen-a k* **Chin** k* cic k* **Cimic** cina k* clem k* *Coc-c* *Cocc* k* *Cod* coff k* *Colch* k* **Coloc** k* *Con* k* cor-r croc k* crot-t *Cupr* k* cycl k* *Dig* k* dios dros k* dulc k* elaps euph k* euphr k* *Ferr* k* *Gamb* *Gels* k* *Glon* k* goss *Graph* k* guaj k* **Ham** *Hell* k* hep k* hydr *Hydr-ac* hyos k* hyper *Ign* k* iod k* ip k* iris kali-bi *Kali-c* k* *Kali-i* kali-m k2 kali-n k* *Kalm* kreos k* **Lach** k* *Laur* k* led k* *Lept* **Lil-t** *Lith-c* **Lyc** k* m-ambo b2.de* m-arct b2.de m-aust b2.de mag-c k* mag-m b2.de* mang k* **Meny** k* *Merc* k* *Merc-c* merc-i-f *Mez* k* mosch k* mur-ac k* murx naja nat-ar nat-c k* **Nat-m** k* *Nit-ac* k* nux-m k* **Nux-v** k* olnd k* onos **Op** k* osm *Ox-ac* par k* **Petr** k* *Ph-ac* k* **Phos** k* *Phys* *Phyt* *Pic-ac* pip-n br1 *Plat* k* *Plb* k* *Podo* *Prun* psor **Puls** k* **Ran-b** k* ran-s k* *Rheum* k* *Rhod* k* **Rhus-t** k* *Rumx* **Ruta** k* sabad k* *Sabin* k* samb k* **Sang** **Sangin-n** sars k* **Sec** k* **Seneg** k* **Sep** k* **Sil** k* **Spig** k* **Spong** k* *Squil* k* **Stann** k* staph k* stict stram k* stront-c k* sul-ac k* sul-i k2 **Sulph** k* tab *Tarax* k* tarent *Ter* teucr k* thuj k* ust **Valer** k* **Verat** k* *Verat-v* verb k* vesp vib viol-o k* viol-t k* vip xan **Zinc** k* **Zinc-p** k2*
- **sore**: acon k* *Aesc* agar k* alum k* am-c b2.de* am-m k* ambr k* anac k* ang b2.de* ant-c b2.de* ant-t b2.de* *Apis* k* *Arg-met* b2.de* arn k* *Ars* k* ars-i asaf k* asar b2.de* *Aur* k* aur-i k2* **Bapt** bar-c k* bar-m bell b2.de* bell-p ptk1 bism b2.de* borx b2.de* bov k* bry k* *Calc* b2.de* calc-sil k2* **Camph** k* cann-i cann-s k* cann-xyz ptk1 canth b2.de caps b2.de* carb-ac k* carb-an k* carb-v k* carbn-s caust k* cham k* **Chin** k* cic b2.de* cina k* clem k* *Cocc* k* coff k* colch b2.de* *Coloc* k* con k* croc b2.de* *Cupr* k* dig b2.de* *Dros* *Eup-per* bg2 euph k* euphr k* ferr k* **Gels** glon graph k* *Hell* k* hep k* ign k* iod k* *Ip* k* kali-c k* kali-n b2.de* kreos k*

- **sore**: ...
lach k* *Laur* k* led k* lyc k* m-ambo b2.de* m-arct b2.de* m-aust b2.de* mag-c k* mag-m k* *Mang* k* meny k* merc k* **Merc-c** *Mez* b2.de* mosch k* mur-ac k* nat-c k* *Nat-m* b2.de* nit-ac k* nux-m b2.de* *Nux-v* k* olnd b2.de* *Op* k* petr b2.de* ph-ac k* phos k* phyt k* plat b2.de* plb b2.de* **Puls** k* **Pyrog** **Ran-b** k* ran-s k* rhod k* rhus-t k* rumx ruta k* sabad b2.de* sabin k* samb k* *Sang* bg2 sars k* seneg b2.de* sep k* *Sil* k* spig k* spong k* **Stann** k* staph k* stram k* stront-c k* sul-ac k* sul-i k2 *Sulph* k* tab bg2 teucr b2.de* thuj k* valer k* *Verat* k* viol-o b2.de* viol-t k* *Zinc* k*
- **stitching** pain: abrot *Acon* k* *Aesc* *Agar* k* agn k* all-c aloe *Alum* k* alum-sil k2 am-c k* am-m k* ambr k* ammc anac k* ang b2.de* ant-c k* ant-t k* apis k* arg-met k* arg-n k* arn k* *Ars* k* ars-i ars-s-f k2 **Asaf** k* *Asar* k* *Aspar* *Aur* k* aur-ar k2 aur-i k2 aur-m k2 aur-s k2 *Bamb-a* stb2.de• bar-c k* bar-i k2 bar-m bar-s k2 *Bell* k* **Berb** bism k* **Borx** k* *Bov* k* **Bry** k* *Cact* calad k* *Calc* k* calc-i k2 calc-p calc-sil k2 camph k* **Cann-i** **Canth** k* caps k* carb-an k* carb-v k* **Carbn-s** card-m *Caust* k* cham k* **Chel** k* **Chin** k* chinin-ar cic k* cimic *Cina* k* cist k2 clem k* *Coc-c* cocc k* coff k* *Colch* k* coll *Coloc* k* *Con* k* *Croc* k* crot-t cupr k* cycl k* dig k* dios *Dol* k* dros k* *Dulc* k* euph k* euphr k* *Ferr* k* *Gamb* gels *Glon* graph k* *Guaj* k* hell k* hep k* hydr *Hydrog* srj2• hyos k* hyper k2 **Ign** k* iod k* ip k* kali-ar *Kali-bi* k* **Kali-c** k* *Kali-i* kali-m k2 *Kali-n* k* **Kali-s** kali-sil k2 *Kalm* *Kreos* k* **Lach** k* *Laur* k* **Led** k* *Lyc* k* m-ambo b2.de* m-arct b2.de m-aust b2.de *Mag-c* k* *Mag-m* k* mang k* meny k* **Merc** k* **Merc-c** merc-i-r merc-n merc-ns mez k* mosch k* mur-ac k* *Naja* nat-ar *Nat-c* k* *Nat-m* k* *Nat-s* **Nit-ac** k* nux-m k* *Nux-v* k* *Ol-an* olnd k* *Op* k* ox-ac *Par* k* petr k* *Ph-ac* k* phel **Phos** k* phyt plan plat k* **Plb** k* prun psil ft1 psor **Puls** k* **Ran-b** k* *Ran-s* k* rheum k* rhod k* *Rhus-t* k* *Rumx* ruta k* *Sabad* k* sabin k* samb k* sang *Sars* k* sec k* sel k* *Seneg* k* **Sep** k* **Sil** k* **Spig** k* spong k* **Squil** k* stann k* *Staph* k* stram k* stront-c k* sul-ac k* sul-i k2 *Sulph* k* tab *Tarax* k* tarent k2 teucr k* *Thal* *Ther* *Thuj* k* valer k* verat k* verb k* *Viol-t* k* *Zinc* k* zinc-p k2 *Ziz*
  - **burning**: **Ars** aur *Mez* *Ol-an* spig
  - **needles**; as from:
    - **cold** needles: **Agar** k* ars ptk1
    - **hot** needles: acon tl1 agar a1* ars tl1* lith-c ptk1 ol-an ptk1 vesp ptk1
- **tearing** pain: acon k* *Act-sp* br1 aesc *Agar* k* agn k* aloe alum k* *Alum-sil* k4 am-c k* am-m k* *Ambr* k* anac k* ang b2.de* ant-c k* *Ant-t* k* apis *Arg-met* k* arn k* ars k* ars-i ars-s-f k2 asaf k* asar k* *Aur* k* aur-ar k2 aur-i k2 aur-m k2 aur-s k2 bar-c k* bar-i k2 bar-s k2 **Bell** k* **Berb** bism k* borx k* bov k* **Bry** k* cact k2 calad k* calc k* calc-i k2 calc-p bg2 calc-sil k2 camph k* cann-s k* canth k* *Caps* k* carb-an k* **Carb-v** k* *Carbn-s* carc k4* caust k* *Cham* k* *Chel* k* chin k* chinin-ar cic k* cimic bg2 cina k* cist k2 clem k* cocc k* coff k* colch k* *Coloc* k* **Con** k* croc k* crot-h cupr k* cycl k* dig k* dios dros k* dulc k* euph k* euphr k* ferr k* *Gran* graph k* guaj k* hell k* hep k* hyos k* *Ign* k* iod k* ip k* kali-ar kali-bi bg2 kali-c k* *Kali-n* k* **Kali-s** kali-sil k2 *Kalm* kreos k* *Lach* k* laur k* **Led** k* **Lyc** k* m-ambo b2.de* m-arct b2.de m-aust b2.de *Mag-c* k* mag-m k* mang k* *Meny* k* **Merc** k* mez k* mosch k* mur-ac k* nat-ar nat-c k* *Nat-m* k* nit-ac k* nux-m k* **Nux-v** k* olnd k* op k* ox-ac k2 par k* petr k* ph-ac k* *Phos* k* plat k* plb k* **Puls** k* ran-b k* ran-s k* *Rhod* k* rhus-t k* ruta k* sabad k* sabin k* samb k* sang sars k* sec k* sel k* seneg k* **Sep** k* **Sil** k* **Spig** k* spong k* squil k* *Stann* k* staph k* stram k* stront-c k* sul-ac k* sul-i k2 **Sulph** k* *Tarax* k* teucr b2.de* thuj k* uva valer k* verat k* *Verat-v* verb k* viol-o k* viol-t k* *Zinc* k*
- **ulcerative** pain: acon k* alum-sil k2 *Am-c* k* *Arg-n* ars k* bell k* borx k* bov k* *Bry* k* *Cann-s* k* canth k* *Caps* k* carb-an k* carb-v k* carbn-s *Caust* k* cham k* chel k* cocc k* *Coloc* cupr k* dig k* *Gamb* hell k* hep k* kali-c k* kali-m k2 kreos k* **Lach** k* laur k* mag-c k* mag-m k* mang k* *Merc* k* mur-ac k* nit-ac k* *Nux-v* k* ph-ac k* phos k* *Psor* **Puls** k* **Ran-b** k* *Rhus-t* k* ruta k* sabad k* sep k* **Sil** k* spig k* stann k* staph k* stront-c k* *Sulph* k* valer k* verat k*
- **warmth**:
  - **amel.**:
    - **heat** amel.: *Ars*↓ *Ars-met*↓ *Nat-ar*↓
      - **burning**: [*Ars* stj2 *Ars-met* stj2 *Nat-ar* stj2]

▽ • **extending** to | **Skin**: anh sp1

\- **Joints**: (↗*EXTREMITIES - Pain - joints*) abrot↓ acon k* *Acon-c* a1 *Act-sp*↓ aesc k* agar k* agar-ph a1 *Agn*↓ all-c k* aloe↓ *Alum* k* alumn↓ am-c↓ am-m↓ *Ambr*↓ *Anac*↓ **Ang**↓ anh sp1 *Ant-c*↓ ant-s-aur↓ *Ant-t*↓ anthraq rly4• *Apis* k1 *Apoc* k* *Apoc-a* a1 aran k* arb↓ **Arg-met** k1* arg-n↓ arist-cl↓ **Arn** k* *Ars* k* *Ars-i* k* asaf k* *Asar*↓ asc-t k* aster k* aur k* aur-m↓

\- **Joints**: ...
bacls-7 fmm1• bar-c k* *Bell* k* bell-p↓ benz-ac↓ berb↓ bism↓ *Bol-la* k* *Bov*↓ brass-n-o srj5• **Bry** k* bufo↓ cact↓ cadm-s↓ caj k* calad↓ *Calc* k* *Calc-f*↓ **Calc-p** k* calc-s k* camph↓ cann-i k* cann-s↓ cann-xyz↓ canth↓ *Caps* k* carb-ac k* carb-an k* **Carb-v**↓ *Carbn-s* k1 *Carl*↓ cartl-s rly4• casc kr1 caul mrr1 *Caust* k* cedr k* *Cham* k* chel↓ *Chin* k* chinin-ar k1 chlf↓ cic↓ cimic↓ *Cimx* k* cina↓ *Cinnb* k* cist k* *Cit-v* kr1 clem↓ *Cocc* k* coff br1 *Colch* k* *Coloc* k* com br1 con k* cop k* croc k* *Crot-h*↓ crot-t k* cupr b7.de cycl k* daph k* dig k* dios k* diph jl2 diph-t-tpt jl2 *Dros*↓ *Dulc* k* **Euph**↓ euphr↓ *Ferr* k* *Ferr-ar* k* ferr-i k* *Ferr-p* k* fic-m gya1 flav jl2 *Form*↓ galla-q-r↓ gast↓ gels k* *Graph*↓ grat↓ *Guaj* k* guare↓ *Ham*↓ harp jl3 hell k* *Hep*↓ hera↓ hip-ac↓ hist sp1 hydr k* hydrc k* hyos↓ *Hyper*↓ ign k* indg↓ *Iod* k* ip k* iris k1 jac-c k* jatr-c k1 *Kali-bi* k* *Kali-c* k* kali-i↓ kali-n k* kali-p k* *Kalm* k* *Kreos*↓ *Lac-ac* k* *Lac-c* k* lach↓ lat-m bnm6• laur↓ **Led** k* *Leptos-ih* jl2 *Lith-c*↓ loxo-recl bnm10• *Lyc* k* lyss k* m-ambo b7.de m-arct↓ *M-aust*↓ mag-c↓ mag-f jl3 *Mag-m*↓ mand sp1* *Mang* k* meli↓ *Meny*↓ *Merc* k* merc-c↓ mez k* morph k* mosch↓ *Mur-ac*↓ *Nat-ar* k* nat-c↓ nat-f jl3 nat-m k* *Nat-p*↓ *Nat-s* k* nit-ac k* nit-s-d↓ nux-m b7.de **Nux-v** k* ol-an k* **Olnd**↓ op↓ par k* penic mtf11 *Petr*↓ *Ph-ac* k* phor-t↓ *Phos* k* phys↓ *Phyt* k* **Plat**↓ **Plb** k* plect↓ podo mrr1 *Prun*↓ **Puls** k* pyrus↓ rad-br sze8• ran-a↓ ran-b↓ ran-s k* raph k* rham-cal br1 *Rheum* b7.de* *Rhod* k* **Rhus-t** k* *Ruta* k1 sabad k* *Sabin* k* samb↓ *Sang* k* sarcol-ac↓ *Sars*↓ scarl jl2 *Sec*↓ sel k* senec k* *Seneg*↓ *Sep*↓ *Sil* k* sol-ni k1 sol-t-ae k* **Spig**↓ *Spong*↓ squil↓ *Stann*↓ *Staph* k* stict↓ *Stram*↓ strept-ent jl2 streptoc jl2 **Stront-c**↓ stroph-s jl3 sul-ac k* *Sulph* k* symph ptk1* syph al* tab↓ **Tarax**↓ ter k* *Teucr*↓ thala jl3 thuj k* toxo-g jl2 tub jl2 tub-m jl2 tub-r jl3* v-a-b jl2 **Valer**↓ vanil fd5.de *Verat*↓ verat-v k* *Verb*↓ vesp↓ viol-o↓ viol-t↓ vip↓ **Zinc**↓ [heroin sdj2 spect dfg1]

- **morning** | **7 h**: mand sp1
- **afternoon**: kali-i↓ mang-act↓ *Merc*↓
  - **digging** pain: kali-i bro1 mang-act bro1 *Merc* bro1
- **night**: caust↓ mang-act↓
  - **digging** pain: mang-act br1
  - **tearing** pain: caust br1
- **accompanied** by:
  - **menses**:
    - **absent** (See FEMALE - Menses - absent - accompanied - joint)
    - **painful** (See FEMALE - Menses - painful - accompanied - joint)
- **alternating** places: bell tl1 colch tl1 kali-bi tl1
- **broken**; as if: bov b2.de* calc b2.de* carb-an bg2* caust b2.de* dros b2.de* hep b2.de* merc b2.de* mez b2.de* par b2.de* sep b2.de*
- **burning**: abrot bg2* anac jl3 ant-t bg2* arg-n bg2 berb bg2 carb-v bg2 caust bg2 cimic bg2 guare a1 hist jl3 ign j5.de kali-n bg2 lyc bg2 nit-ac j5.de* plat bg2 rhus-t bg2 sabin k2 sulph bg2 thuj bg2* zinc bg2
- **catarrh**; from: ran-b tl1
- **chill**; during: bell↓ bry↓ calc↓ caust↓ chin↓ *Hell*↓ kali-c↓ led↓ lyc↓ mang↓ merc↓ nux-v↓ ph-ac↓ **Rhus-t**↓ sep↓ sil↓ stront-c↓ sulph↓ zinc↓
  - **stitching** pain: calc bg2 *Hell* b7.de* mang bg2 merc bg2 rhus-t bg2 sil bg2
  - **tearing** pain: bell bg2 bry bg2 calc bg2 caust bg2 chin bg2 kali-c bg2 led bg2 lyc bg2 merc bg2 nux-v bg2 ph-ac bg2 **Rhus-t** bg2 sep bg2 stront-c bg2 sulph bg2 zinc bg2
- **cold** applications | **amel.**: **Guaj** mrr1 lac-c mrr1 **Led** mrr1 puls mrr1 rad-br mrr1 sulph mrr1
- **constricting**: ang bg ph-ac bg *Plat* bg pyrus a1
- **cramping**: acon b2.de* am-m b2.de* *Anac* b2.de* **Ang** b2.de* arn b2.de* ars bg2 aur b2.de* bar-c b2.de* *Bell* b2.de* bov b2.de* *Bry* b2.de* **Calc** b2.de* camph b2.de* cann-s b2.de* canth b2.de* carb-an bg2 caust b2.de* cham b2.de* chel b2.de* chin b2.de* cic b2.de* cocc b2.de* colch b2.de* coloc bg2 con b2.de* cupr b2.de* dulc b2.de* euph b2.de* hep b2.de* hist jl hyos b2.de* ign b2.de* kali-c b2.de* kali-n b2.de* kreos b2.de* lach b2.de* laur b2.de* led b2.de* lyc b2.de* m-arct b2.de* meny b2.de merc b2.de mez b2.de* nux-v b2.de* olnd b2.de* op b2.de* par b2.de* petr b2.de* ph-ac kr1 phos b2.de* **Plat** b2.de* plb b2.de* rhus-t b2.de* sarcol-ac jl *Sec* b2.de* sel b2.de* spig b2.de* spong b2.de* staph b2.de* stram b2.de* *Sulph* b2.de* tab bg2 verat b2.de* verb b2.de*
- **cutting** pain: cadm-s j5.de* guare j5.de* hyos j5.de* *Sabad* j5.de* vesp a1

- **deep** in: rad-br c11
- **digging** pain: bell a1 colch a1 *Mang* b4a.de rhod b4a.de
- **dislocated**; as if: acon b2.de* agar b2.de* agn b2.de* alum b2.de* am-c b2.de* am-m b2.de* *Ambr* b2.de* anac b2.de* ang b2.de* ant-c b2.de* ant-t b2.de* **Arn** b2.de* ars b2.de* asar b2.de* aur b2.de* bar-c b2.de* bell b2.de* bov b2.de* *Bry* b2.de* calad b2.de* *Calc* b2.de* *Calc-f* bg2 camph b2.de* caps b2.de* carb-an b2.de* carb-v b2.de* *Caust* b2.de* cham b2.de* chel b2.de* chin b2.de* cina b2.de* cocc b2.de* con b2.de* croc b2.de* cycl b2.de* dig b2.de* dros b2.de* dulc b2.de* euph b2.de* *Graph* b2.de* hell b2.de* hep b2.de* **Ign** b2.de* ip b2.de* kali-c b2.de* *Kali-n* b2.de* kreos b2.de* led b2.de* lyc b2.de* *M-ambo* b2.de* m-arct b2.de m-aust b2.de mag-c b2.de* mag-m b2.de* mang b2.de* meny b2.de* merc b2.de* mez b2.de mosch b2.de* mur-ac b2.de* nat-c b2.de* *Nat-m* b2.de* nit-ac b2.de* nux-m b2.de* nux-v b2.de* olnd b2.de* *Petr* b2.de* ph-ac b2.de* **Phos** b2.de* plat b2.de* plb b2.de* *Prun* bg2 **Puls** b2.de* ran-b b2.de* *Rhod* b2.de* **Rhus-t** b2.de* *Ruta* b2.de* sabin b2.de* sars b2.de* seneg b2.de* sep b2.de* sil b2.de* *Spig* b2.de* spong b2.de* stann b2.de* staph b2.de* *Stront-c* bg2 **Sulph** b2.de* thuj b2.de* valer b2.de* verat b2.de* verb b2.de* zinc b2.de*
- **drawing** pain: acon b7.de* agn b7.de* am-c b4a.de* ang b7.de* *Ant-c* b7.de* ant-s-aur a1 *Ant-t* b7.de* *Arg-met* b7.de* asaf b7.de* asar b7.de* bar-c b4.de* bell b4.de* *Bry* a1 calc j5.de cann-s b7.de* canth b7.de* caps b7.de* *Carl* a1 *Caul* bg2 cham b7.de* chel b7.de* chin b7.de* cina b7.de* cist j5.de* clem a1 cocc b7.de* colch b7.de* cupr b7.de* cycl b7.de* graph b4a.de* hep j5.de hyos b7.de* ign b7.de* kali-c j5.de kreos b7a.de led b7.de* lyc j5.de* m-ambo b7.de* m-arct b7.de *M-aust* b7.de* meny b7.de* merc b4.de* mez b4.de* nat-c b4.de* nat-m a1 nat-s a1 nit-ac j5.de* nit-s-d a1 *Nux-m* kr1 nux-v b7.de* olnd b7.de* par b7.de* petr b4a.de phor-t mie3• phos a1 plat b4.de* plb b7.de* puls b7.de* rheum b7.de* *Rhod* b4.de* rhus-t b7.de* sabad b7.de* sabin b7.de* *Sars* b4a.de sec b7.de* seneg b4.de* sep b4a.de* spig b7.de* spong b7.de* **Staph** b7.de* *Stram* b7a.de *Sulph* b4a.de tarax b7.de* teucr b7.de* tub jl2 valer b7.de* verat b7.de* viol-o b7.de*
- **exertion** agg.: [bell-p-sp dcm1]
- **fever**:
  - **before**: calc ↓ caust ↓ kali-c ↓ kali-n ↓ nat-m ↓ sep ↓ sulph ↓
    - **tearing** pain: calc b4a.de caust b4a.de kali-c b4a.de kali-n b4a.de nat-m b4a.de sep b4a.de sulph b4a.de
  - **during**:
    - **agg.**: agn ↓ bar-c ↓ *Calc* ↓ *Caust* ↓ hell b7a.de kali-c ↓ *Lyc* ↓ merc ↓ nux-v ↓ ph-ac ↓ phos ↓ **Rhus-t** ↓ sil ↓ spig ↓ stront-c ↓ *Sulph* ↓ tarax ↓ thuj ↓ zinc ↓
      - **stitching** pain: bar-c bg2 *Calc* bg2 **Hell** bg2 kali-c bg2 merc bg2 **Rhus-t** bg2 sil bg2 spig bg2 tarax bg2 thuj bg2
      - **tearing** pain: agn bg2 *Calc* b4.de* *Caust* bg2 **Hell** bg2 kali-c bg2 *Lyc* bg2 merc bg2 nux-v bg2 ph-ac bg2 phos bg2 **Rhus-t** bg2 stront-c bg2 *Sulph* bg2 thuj bg2 zinc bg2
- **gnawing** pain: am-c k* aur-m k2 canth k* colch k* *Dros* b2.de* dulc k* graph k* mag-c k* mang k* phos k* **Ran-s** k* stront-c k* zinc k*
- **hysterical**: *Arg-n* bro1 cham bro1 cot bro1 hyper bro1 *Ign* bro1 zinc bro1
- **menses** | **before** | **agg.**: caul bro1 sabin bro1
  - **during** | **agg.**: caul bro1 sabin bro1*
- **neuralgic**: arg-met bro1 *Cedr* bro1 coloc bro1 plb bro1 zinc bro1
- **paralyzed**; as if: acon b2.de* agn b2.de* am-c b2.de* ambr b2.de* anac b2.de* arg-met b2.de* *Arn* b2.de* ars b2.de* *Asar* b2.de* **Aur** b2.de* bell b2.de* bism b2.de* *Bov* b2.de* calc bg2 **Caps** b2.de* *Carb-v* b2.de* caust b2.de* cham b2.de* *Chin* b2.de* cina b2.de* cocc b2.de* colch b2.de* coloc b2.de* con b2.de* *Croc* b2.de* dig b2.de* *Dros* b2.de* **Euph** b2.de* ferr b2.de* graph b2.de* hell b2.de* ign b2.de* kali-c b2.de* kali-n bg2 laur j5.de *Led* b2.de* lyc b2.de* m-ambo b2.de* m-aust b2.de mag-m b2.de* meny b2.de* merc b2.de* *Mez* b2.de* nat-c b2.de* nat-m b2.de* nit-ac b2.de nux-v b2.de* *Par* b2.de* petr b2.de* ph-ac b2.de* phos b2.de* *Plb* b2.de* *Puls* b2.de* rhus-t b2.de* ruta b2.de* sabad b2.de* *Sabin* b2.de* samb b2.de* sars b2.de* *Seneg* b2.de* sep b2.de* stann b2.de* **Staph** b2.de* stram b2.de* stront-c b2.de* sulph b2.de* **Valer** b2.de* verat b2.de* verb b2.de* zinc b2.de*
- **perspiration**; during: agn ↓ bar-c ↓ *Calc* ↓ *Caust* ↓ **Hell** ↓ kali-c ↓ lyc ↓ merc ↓ nux-v ↓ ph-ac ↓ phos ↓ **Rhus-t** ↓ sil ↓ spig ↓ stront-c ↓ *Sulph* ↓ tarax ↓ thuj ↓ zinc ↓
  - **stitching** pain: bar-c bg2 *Calc* bg2 **Hell** bg2 kali-c bg2 merc bg2 **Rhus-t** bg2 sil bg2 spig bg2 tarax bg2 thuj bg2
- **perspiration**; during: ...
  - **tearing** pain: agn bg2 *Calc* bg2 *Caust* bg2 **Hell** bg2 kali-c bg2 lyc bg2 merc bg2 nux-v bg2 ph-ac bg2 phos bg2 **Rhus-t** bg2 stront-c bg2 *Sulph* bg2 thuj bg2 zinc bg2
- **pinching** pain: kreos b7a.de
- **pressing** pain: *Agn* b2.de* *Alum* b2.de* anac b2.de* arg-met b2.de* asaf b2.de* asar b2.de* bar-c b2.de* bell b2.de* calc b2.de* camph b2.de* carb-an b2.de* caust b2.de* cham b2.de* chel b2.de* chin b2.de* clem b2.de* colch b2.de* coloc a1 dulc b2.de* graph b2.de* hep b2.de* hyos b2.de* ign b2.de* iod b2.de* *Kali-c* b2.de* *Led* b2.de* lyc j5.de meny b2.de* merc b2.de* mez b2.de* mosch b2.de* nat-s a1 nit-ac b2.de* nit-s-d a1 nux-v b2.de* petr b2.de* rhus-t b2.de* sabad b2.de* sabin b2.de* sep b2.de* sil b2.de* spong b2.de* stann b2.de* staph b2.de* stront-c b2.de* sulph b2.de* tarax b2.de* thuj b2.de* viol-o b2.de* viol-t b2.de* zinc b2.de*
  - **sticking** pain: ph-ac b2.de* sars b2.de* staph b2.de* zinc b2.de*
  - **tearing** pain: anac k* ang b2.de* arn k* asaf k* bell k* bism k* carb-v k* caust k* cham k* hyos k* led k* lyc k* ruta k* spong k* stann k*
- **pressure** agg.: phor-t ↓
  - **sore**: phor-t mie3•
- **rising** after a long rest agg.: tub-r jl2
- **sore**: abrot a1 acon b2.de* agar b2.de* alumn kr1 am-m bro1 anac b2.de* ang bg2 ant-c b2.de* apis bro1 apoc a1 **Arg-met** b2.de* **Arn** b7a.de* ars b2.de* **Aur** b2.de* bell b2.de* bell-p bro1 berb k2 *Bov* b2.de* bry b2.de* calad kr1 calc b2.de* camph b2.de* carb-an b2.de* carb-v b2.de* *Caust* b2.de* *Cham* b2.de* **Chin** b2.de* chlf a1 cic b2.de* clem a1 coff b2.de* *Colch* bro1 coloc b2.de* *Con* b2.de* croc b2.de* *Crot-h* kr1 *Cupr* b7a.de cycl b2.de* *Dig* b2.de* *Dros* b2.de* dulc b2.de* *Ferr* b2.de* graph b2.de* guaj k2* *Ham* bro1 hep b2.de* hip-ac sp1 hyos b2.de* *Hyper* a1* ign b2.de* kali-c b2.de* kali-i a1 kalm bro1 led b2.de* *Lith-c* kr1* *M-ambo* b2.de* m-aust b2.de* mag-c b2.de* mang j5.de meli bro1 merc-c b4a.de *Mez* b2.de* *Mur-ac* b2.de* nat-c b2.de* *Nat-m* b2.de* *Nat-p* a1* *Nit-ac* b2.de* *Nux-v* b2.de* par b2.de* petr k2 ph-ac b2.de* phor-t mie3• phos b2.de* phys a1 phyt k2* plat b2.de* prun bg2 **Puls** b2.de* ran-a j5.de* **Rhus-t** b2.de* *Ruta* b2.de* sabad b2.de* sabin bro1 *Sep* b2.de* *Spig* b2.de* stann b2.de* staph b2.de* stict bro1 sul-ac b2.de* sulph b2.de* thuj b2.de* tub k2 valer b2.de* *Verat* b2.de* *Verb* bro1 viol-o b2.de* zinc b2.de*
- **standing** agg.: *Tub* jl2
- **stitching** pain: acon b2.de* agar b2.de* *Agn* b2.de* aloe a1 alum b2.de* am-c b2.de* am-m b2.de* anac b2.de* ang b2.de* ant-c b2.de* ant-t b2.de* apis bg2 arg-met b2.de* arg-n bg2 arist-cl sp1 *Arn* b2.de* ars b2.de* *Asaf* b2.de* asar b2.de* *Bar-c* b2.de* *Bell* b2.de* benz-ac bg2 berb bg2 *Bov* b2.de* **Bry** b2.de* bufo bg2 **Calc** b2.de* calc-f bg2 camph b2.de* cann-xyz bg2 canth b2.de* caps b2.de* carb-an b2.de* carb-v b2.de* carl a1 *Caust* b2.de* cham a1 chel b2.de* chin b2.de* cic b7.de cina b2.de* clem b2.de* *Cocc* b2.de* *Colch* b7.de* coloc b2.de* *Con* b2.de* crot-t bg2 *Dros* b2.de* dulc b2.de* euph b2.de* euphr b2.de* ferr b2.de* gast a1 *Graph* b2.de* guaj b2.de* **Hell** b2.de* *Hep* b2.de* hydr bg2 hyos b2.de* *Ign* b2.de* indg a1 iod b2.de* **Kali-c** b2.de* kali-i bg2 *Kali-n* b2.de* *Kreos* b2.de* lac-ac a1 laur b2.de* led b2.de* lyc b2.de* m-aust b2.de* mag-c b2.de* *Mag-m* b2.de* **Mang** b2.de* *Meny* b2.de* **Merc** b2.de* merc-c bg2 mez b2.de* mosch b2.de* mur-ac b2.de* nat-c b2.de* *Nat-m* b2.de* nat-p bg2 nit-ac b2.de* nit-s-d a1 nux-m b2.de* nux-v b2.de* olnd b2.de* par b2.de* petr b2.de* ph-ac b2.de* phor-t mie3• *Phos* b2.de* plat b2.de* plb b2.de* plect a1 *Puls* b2.de* ran-b b2.de* ran-s b7.de rheum b2.de* *Rhod* b2.de* **Rhus-t** b2.de* ruta b2.de* sabad b2.de* *Sabin* b2.de* samb b2.de* sang bg2 *Sars* b2.de* *Sep* b2.de* **Sil** b2.de* **Spig** b2.de* *Spong* b2.de* squil b2.de* *Stann* b2.de* *Staph* b2.de* stict bg2 *Stront-c* b2.de* stroph-s sp1 *Sul-ac* b2.de* *Sulph* b2.de* **Tarax** b2.de* **Thuj** b2.de* valer b2.de* verat b2.de* verb b2.de* viol-t b2.de* vip bg2 *Zinc* b2.de*
  - **burning**: ign a1 mez b2.de* plat b2.de* plb b2.de* sul-ac b2.de* thuj b2.de*
  - **tearing**: ang b2.de* ars b2.de* asaf b2.de* *Asar* b2.de* calc a1 camph a1 carb-v b2.de* caust b2.de* clem b2.de* dulc b2.de* ferr b2.de* merc b2.de* mur-ac b2.de* *Puls* b2.de* *Sabin* b2.de* stann b2.de* **Staph** b2.de* sul-ac b2.de* sulph b2.de* tarax b2.de* *Thuj* b2.de* verb b2.de* zinc b2.de*
- **tearing** pain: acon b2.de* *Act-sp* br1 agar b2.de* *Agn* b2.de* alum b2.de* am-c b2.de* am-m b2.de* *Ambr* b2.de* anac b2.de* ang b2.de* ant-s-aur a1 ant-t b2.de* **Arg-met** b2.de* arist-cl sp1 arn b2.de* ars b2.de* ars-i k2 asaf b2.de* asar b2.de* *Aur* b2.de* bar-c b2.de* bell b2.de* bism b2.de*

• **tearing** pain: ...
Bov b2.de* *Bry* b2.de* cact a1 *Calc* b2.de* camph b2.de* canth b2.de* carb-an b2.de* carb-v b2.de* *Carl* a1 **Caust** b2.de* cham b2.de* chel b2.de* *Chin* b2.de* cic b2.de* cina b2.de* cist j5.de* clem b2.de* cocc b2.de* *Colch* b2.de* con b2.de* cupr b2.de* cycl b2.de* dig b2.de* dros b2.de* dulc b2.de* euphr b2.de* ferr b2.de* graph b2.de* grat a1 guaj b2.de* hell b2.de* hep b2.de* hera j5.de hyos b2.de* ign b2.de* iod b2.de* **Kali-c** b2.de* *Kali-n* b2.de* kreos b2.de* lach j5.de laur b2.de* *Led* b2.de* **Lyc** b2.de* m-ambo b2.de* m-aust b2.de* mag-c b2.de* mag-m b2.de* mang b2.de* meny b2.de* **Merc** b2.de* mez b2.de* mosch b2.de* mur-ac b2.de* nat-c b2.de* nat-m b2.de* nat-s a1 nit-ac b2.de* nit-s-d a1 nux-m b2.de* *Nux-v* b2.de* olnd b2.de* par b2.de* petr b2.de* *Ph-ac* b2.de* *Phos* b2.de* plb b2.de* puls b2.de* ran-b b2.de* rheum b2.de* rhod b2.de* **Rhus-t** b2.de* ruta b2.de* sabad b2.de* sabin b2.de* samb b2.de* *Sars* b2.de* sec b2.de* *Sep* b2.de* sil b2.de* spig b2.de* spong b2.de* stann b2.de* staph b2.de* **Stront-c** b2.de* **Sulph** b2.de* tarax b2.de* *Teucr* b2.de* thuj b2.de* valer b2.de* verat b2.de* verb b2.de* viol-o b2.de* **Zinc** b2.de*

⁝ **burning** pain: *Carb-v* b2.de* caust bg2 nat-c b2.de* nit-ac b2.de*

⁝ **cramping**: anac b2.de* ars b2.de* aur b2.de* bov b2.de* kali-c b2.de* **Olnd** b2.de* phos b2.de* *Plat* b2.de*

⁝ **jerking** pain: acon b2.de* caust b2.de* **Chin** b2.de* cupr b2.de* laur b2.de* mang b2.de* olnd b2.de* *Rhus-t* b2.de* *Sulph* b2.de*

⁝ **paralyzed**; as if: bell b2.de* carb-v b2.de* chel b2.de* chin b2.de* cocc b2.de* con b2.de* dig b2.de* kali-c b2.de* meny b2.de* nat-m b2.de* nit-ac b2.de* phos b2.de* sars b2.de* stann b2.de* **Staph** b2.de*

⁝ **pressing** pain: agn b2.de* anac b2.de* ang b2.de* arg-met b2.de* bism b2.de* **Carb-v** b2.de* chin b2.de* coloc b2.de* graph b2.de* guaj b2.de* kali-c b2.de* lyc b2.de* m-aust b2.de* mez b2.de* ph-ac b2.de* ruta b2.de* sabad b2.de* sars b2.de* sep b2.de* stann b2.de* staph b2.de* zinc b2.de*

⁝ **sticking** pain: agn b2.de* bar-c b2.de* chin b2.de* colch b2.de* dulc b2.de* graph b2.de* hyos b2.de* **Led** b2.de* mag-c b2.de* merc b2.de* mur-ac b2.de* nat-c b2.de* nat-m b2.de* puls b2.de* sabin b2.de* sep b2.de* staph b2.de* *Zinc* b2.de*

• **touch** agg.: fic-m gya1

• **wandering** pain: ang kr1 *Ant-t* kr1 arb br1 colch tl1 *Form* mrr1 galla-q-r nl2• *Hyper* kr1 kali-bi k2 led bg puls tl1 rhod tl1 symph fd3.de• tub k2

○ • **Spots**; in: *Mang* ↓

⁝ **burning**: *Mang* kr1

- **Legs**; in | **growing** pains (See EXTREMITIES - Pain - leg - growing)

- **Ligaments**: get br1

• **rest** | **amel.**: get br1

- **Mucous** membranes: am-m ↓ ambr ↓ bar-m ↓ benz-ac ↓ camph ↓ canth ↓ caps ↓ caust ↓ hep ↓ nux-v ↓ sul-ac ↓ sul-i ↓

• **burning**: canth mtf11 caps mrr1

• **scraped**; as if: am-m bg2 ambr bg2 bar-m bg2 benz-ac bg2 camph bg2 caust bg2 hep bg2 nux-v bg2 sul-ac bg2 sul-i bg2

- **Muscles**: (↗*Complaints - muscles; Myopathia*) abrot ↓ achy jl3 *Acon* c1* adon ↓ aesc ↓ agar ↓ agav-t jl3 agn ↓ alet c1* *Alum* ↓ am-c ↓ am-caust a1 *Am-m* ↓ *Ambr* ↓ **Anac** ↓ **Ang** ↓ **Ant-c** ↓ *Ant-t* c1* anthraq rly4• apis ↓ *Arg-met* ↓ arge br1 *Arn* bro1* ars bro1 *Ars-i* ↓ ars-s-f ↓ **Asaf** ↓ *Asar* ↓ aster jl3 *Aur* ↓ aur-s ↓ bad ↓ *Bapt* ↓ bar-c ↓ bar-i ↓ bar-m ↓ bell bro1 bell-p c1* benz-ac mtf11 berb ↓ *Bism* ↓ *Borx* ↓ botul jl2 bov ↓ brach a1 brass-n-o srj5• bros-gau mrc1 bruc ↓ *Bry* c1* bufo ↓ calad ↓ **Calc** ↓ *Camph* ↓ *Cann-s* ↓ *Canth* ↓ caps br1 carb-ac ↓ *Carb-an* ↓ **Carb-v** ↓ carbn-s bro1 cartl-s rly4• *Castm* ↓ caul mrr1 *Caust* c1* **Cham** ↓ *Chel* ↓ chin mrr1 chlorpr pin1• cho ↓ cic ↓ *Cimic* c1* **Cina** ↓ *Clem* ↓ **Cocc** ↓ coff br1 *Colch* c1* **Coloc** ↓ *Con* ↓ conin ↓ cot ↓ croc ↓ **Cupr** ↓ *Cupr-act* ↓ *Cupr-f* ↓ *Cupr-m* ↓ *Cupr-p* ↓ **Cycl** ↓ cyt-l ↓ *Dig* ↓ *Dios* ↓ dioxi rbp6 dros ↓ *Dulc* c1* ephe-si ↓ eryt-j a1 *Euph* ↓ *Euphr* ↓ ferr ↓ ferr-p sf1.de ferr-s mtf11 form a1 galla-q-r nl2• *Gels* c1* *Glon* ↓ *Graph* ↓ **Guaj** ↓ haliae-lc ↓ ham ↓ harp jl3 *Hell* ↓ *Helon* ↓ *Hep* ↓ hip-ac ↓ hist sp1 hydr ↓ hyos ↓ ign sf1.de iod ↓ ip ↓ *Iris* ↓ jab ↓ jac-c ↓ kali-bi ↓ *Kali-br* ↓ **Kali-c** ↓ *Kali-m* ↓ *Kali-n* ↓ kali-s ↓ kalm ↓ kreos ↓ lac-h ↓ lach ↓ lat-m sp1* *Laur* ↓ led bro1 *Leptos-ih* jl2 loxo-recl bnm10• *Luf-op* rsj5• lup ↓ lyc a1 **M-ambo** ↓ *M-arct* ↓ *M-aust* ↓ *Macro* c1* *Mag-c* ↓ *Mag-m* ↓ *Mag-p* ↓ mag-s sp1* *Magn-gr* ↓ malar ↓ mand sp1* **Mang** ↓ med jl2 *Meny* ↓ merc bro1 merc-c a1 merc-i-r ↓ **Mez** ↓ morph bro1 *Mosch* ↓ *Mur-ac* ↓ myric ↓ **Nat-c** ↓ nat-f sp1* nat-m a1* **Nit-ac** ↓ nitro-o ↓ **Nux-m** ↓ nux-v bro1 oci-sa ↓ ol-an ↓ *Olnd* ↓ op a1 osteo-a ↓ ozone ↓ *Par* ↓ penic mtf11 *Petr* ↓ *Ph-ac* ↓ *Phos* ↓ *Phyt* sf1.de

- **Muscles**: ...
plan ↓ **Plat** ↓ plb a1 plb-act ↓ prot ↓ prun ↓ puls sf1.de pyrog ↓ rad-br sze8• *Ran-b* bro1 *Ran-s* ↓ raph ↓ rauw sp1 rham-cal c1* rheum ↓ **Rhod** ↓ *Rhus-t* br1* *Ruta* bro1 *Sabad* ↓ *Sabin* ↓ sal-ac bro1 sal-al ↓ samb ↓ sang ↓ sarcol-ac ↓ *Sars* ↓ *Sec* ↓ sel ↓ seneg ↓ **Sep** ↓ ser-a-c jl2 sil sf1.de **Spig** ↓ *Spong* ↓ *Squil* ↓ **Stann** ↓ staph sf1.de stram bro1 *Strept-ent* jl2 streptoc jl2 **Stront-c** ↓ stroph-s jl3 *Stry* a1* **Sul-ac** ↓ sulfa jl3 **Sulph** ↓ symph fd3.de• syph al tab a1 tarax jl3 tetox ↓ *Teucr* ↓ thal sf1.de* thuj a1 toxo-g jl2 trinit ↓ tub jl2 tub-a jl2 tub-m ↓ valer bro1 vanil ↓ *Verat* a1* *Verat-v* c1* **Verb** ↓ vib ↓ viol-o ↓ viol-t ↓ zinc a1 **Zinc-p** ↓

• **morning**: mag-s ↓

⁝ **cramping**: mag-s sp1

• **night** on waking: sulph ↓

⁝ **cramping**: sulph h2*

• **aching**: bapt ptk1 caps br1 mand sp1 nat-f sp1 rauw sp1

• **air**; in open:

⁝ **amel.**: mag-s ↓

⁝ **cramping**: mag-s sp1

• **bed**; on going in a cold: calc ↓

⁝ **cramping**: calc tl1

• **benumbing** | **numb** aching: cot br1

• **burning**: mez br1

• **chill**; during: **Ars** ↓ **Bell** ↓ borx ↓ calc ↓ carb-v ↓ caust ↓ chin ↓ ip ↓ kali-c ↓ *Kali-n* ↓ lach ↓ *Led* ↓ **Lyc** ↓ merc ↓ mosch ↓ nit-ac ↓ *Nux-v* ↓ ph-ac ↓ phos ↓ puls ↓ rhod ↓ **Rhus-t** ↓ sep ↓ sil ↓ stann ↓ staph ↓ stront-c ↓ sulph ↓ verat ↓ zinc ↓

⁝ **tearing** pain: **Ars** bg2 **Bell** bg2 borx bg2 calc bg2 carb-v bg2 caust bg2 chin bg2 ip bg2 kali-c bg2 *Kali-n* bg2 lach bg2 *Led* bg2 **Lyc** bg2 merc bg2 mosch bg2 nit-ac bg2 *Nux-v* bg2 ph-ac bg2 phos bg2 puls bg2 rhod bg2 **Rhus-t** bg2 sep bg2 sil bg2 stann bg2 staph bg2 stront-c bg2 sulph bg2 verat bg2 zinc bg2

• **coition**; during: bufo ↓ *Cupr* ↓

⁝ **cramping**: bufo br1 *Cupr* mrr1

• **cramping**: abrot tl1 acon k* agar k* alum k* am-c k* am-m k* *Ambr* k* **Anac** k* **Ang** b2.de* *Ant-t* b2.de* arg-met b2.de* *Arn* k* *Ars* k* *Asaf* b2.de* asar k* aur k* bar-c k* **Bell** k* bism k* bov b2.de* brass-n-o srj5• bry k* bufo bg2 **Calc** k* camph k* *Cann-s* k* canth b2.de* caps k* carb-an k* carb-v k* carbn-s a1 *Castm* kr1 *Caust* k* cham b2.de* *Chel* b7a.de chin k* cho bro1 cic k* cimic bg2* **Cina** b2.de* clem k* *Cocc* k* coff b2.de* colch k* **Coloc** b2.de* *Con* k* conin a1 croc k* **Cupr** b2.de* *Cupr-act* kr1* cyt-l jl3 dig k* *Dios* kr1 dros k* *Dulc* k* euph b2.de* *Euphr* k* ferr k* gels k* *Glon* *Graph* k* haliae-lc srj5• hell k* hep k* hist jl3 hyos k* *Ign* k* iod k* ip k* *Iris* kr1 jab *Kali-br* kr1 *Kali-c* k* kali-n k* kreos k* lac-h sze9• lach k* lat-m sp1* laur b2.de **Lyc** k* m-ambo b2.de *M-arct* b2.de mag-c k* *Mag-m* b2.de* *Mag-p* bg2* mang k* meny k* **Merc** k* mez k* morph a1 mosch k* *Mur-ac* k* nat-c k* nat-f jl3 nat-m k* *Nit-ac* k* nux-m k* **Nux-v** b2.de* olnd k* *Op* b2.de* osteo-a jl2 par k* *Petr* k* ph-ac k* phos k* phyt bg2* **Plat** b2.de* *Plb* k* plb-act bro1 prot fmm1• puls b2.de* ran-b k* ran-s b2.de rhod k* *Rhus-t* k* ruta b2.de* sabad k* samb k* sang bg2 sarcol-ac jl3 *Sec* k* **Sep** k* **Sil** k* *Spig* k* *Spong* k* squil k* *Stann* k* staph k* stram k* stront-c b2.de* **Sul-ac** b2.de* **Sulph** k* syph bro1 *Tab* bg2* tetox mtf11 *Thuj* k* trinit br1 tub-m jl2 *Valer* k* vanil fd5.de verat b2.de* *Verb* k* vib viol-o k* viol-t k* zinc k* [*Cupr-f* stj2 *Cupr-m* stj2 *Cupr-p* stj2]

⁝ **violent**: cupr tl1

• **dialysis**; from: cho ↓ eupi ↓

⁝ **cramping**: cho mtf eupi mtf

• **drawing** pain: *Acon* b7.de* agn b7.de* alum b4.de* ambr b7.de* anac b4.de* ang b7.de* **Ant-c** b7.de* **Ant-t** b7.de* apis bg2 arg-met b7.de* arn b7.de* asaf b7.de* asar b7.de* aur b4.de* bar-c b4.de* **Bell** b4.de* berb bg2 bism b7.de* bov bg2 bry b7.de* calc b4.de* *Camph* b7.de* cann-s b7.de* canth b7.de* *Caps* b7.de* carb-ac bg2 *Carb-v* b4.de* *Caust* b4.de* **Cham** b7.de* *Chel* b7.de* *Chin* b7.de* cic b7.de* *Cina* b7.de* *Clem* b4.de* **Cocc** b7.de* coff b7.de* *Colch* b7.de* croc b7.de* cupr b7.de* **Cycl** b7.de* dig b4.de* dros b7.de* dulc b4a.de* euph b4.de* euphr b7.de ferr b7.de* *Graph* b4.de* hell b7.de* hep b4.de* hydr a1 hyos b7.de* *Ign* b7.de* iod b4a.de ip b7.de* kali-bi bg2 kali-c b4.de* kali-n b4.de* kreos b7a.de led b7.de* lup br1 *Lyc* b4.de* **M-ambo** b7.de* *M-arct* b7.de *M-aust* b7.de* mag-m b4a.de malar jl2 *Mang* b4a.de *Meny* b7.de* merc b4.de* mez b4.de* morph a1 *Mosch* b7.de* *Mur-ac* b4a.de nat-m b4.de* nit-ac b4.de* *Nux-m* b7.de* nux-v b7.de* olnd b7.de* par b7.de* petr b4.de* ph-ac b4.de*

- **drawing** pain: ...
phos b4.de* **Plat** b4.de* *Plb* b7.de* **Puls** b7.de* ran-b b7.de* ran-s b7.de* raph a1 **Rhod** b4.de* *Rhus-t* b7.de* ruta b7.de* sabad b7.de* sabin b7.de* samb b7.de* sec b7.de* sep b4.de* sil b4a.de* spig b7.de spong b7.de* *Squil* b7.de* staph b7.de* stram b7.de* *Stront-c* b4a.de sul-ac b4.de* *Sulph* b4.de* tarax b7.de* *Teucr* b7.de* *Thuj* b4.de* tub jl2 **Valer** b7.de* *Verat* b7.de* verb b7.de* viol-o b7.de* viol-t b7.de* *Zinc* b4.de*
- **exertion** agg.; after: cimic ↓
  - **sore**: cimic ptk1
- **fever**; during: *Acon* ↓ ant-c ↓ **Arn** ↓ **Ars** ↓ *Bell* ↓ **Bry** ↓ **Calc** ↓ caps ↓ **Carb-v** ↓ caust ↓ cham ↓ chel ↓ **Chin** ↓ *Cocc* ↓ colch ↓ dulc ↓ eup-per br1 ferr ↓ hep ↓ ign ↓ kali-c ↓ kali-n ↓ led ↓ **Lyc** ↓ *Merc* ↓ nit-ac ↓ *Nux-v* ↓ phos ↓ *Puls* ↓ *Rhod* ↓ **Rhus-t** ↓ **Sep** ↓ *Sil* ↓ spig ↓ staph ↓ stront-c ↓ *Sulph* ↓ tarax ↓ thuj ↓ tub-a jl2 *Verat* ↓ zinc ↓
  - **cramping**: *Cocc* b7.de* *Verat* b7a.de
  - **stitching** pain: *Bell* bg2 **Bry** bg2 calc bg2 merc bg2 *Puls* bg2 **Rhus-t** bg2 spig bg2 staph bg2 sulph bg2 tarax bg2 thuj bg2
  - **tearing** pain: *Acon* bg2 ant-c bg2 **Arn** bg2 **Ars** bg2 bell bg2 *Bry* bg2 **Calc** bg2 caps bg2 **Carb-v** bg2 caust bg2 cham bg2 chel bg2 **Chin** bg2 colch bg2 dulc bg2 ferr bg2 hep bg2 ign bg2 kali-c bg2 kali-n bg2 led bg2 **Lyc** bg2 *Merc* bg2 nit-ac bg2 *Nux-v* bg2 phos bg2 puls bg2 *Rhod* bg2 rhus-t bg2 **Sep** bg2 *Sil* bg2 staph bg2 stront-c bg2 *Sulph* bg2 tarax bg2 verat bg2 zinc bg2
- **friction** of clothes; from: bad ↓
  - **sore**: bad br1
- **hysterical**: ign bro1 nux-v bro1 plb bro1 puls bro1
- **influenza** agg.: cimic mtf11 eup-per br1
- **motion**:
  - **agg.**: bad ↓ bell-p sp1 *Sil* a1
    - **sore**: bad br1
  - **amel.**: galeoc-c-h gms1• mag-s ↓
    - **cramping**: mag-s sp1
- **nervous**: *Cimic* br1
- **overexertion**; after: **Arn** mrr1 helon br1 [bell-p-sp dcm1]
  - **burning**: helon br1
- **perspiration**; during: acon ↓ ant-c ↓ *Arn* ↓ *Ars* ↓ *Bell* ↓ **Bry** ↓ **Calc** ↓ caps ↓ *Carb-v* ↓ caust ↓ *Cham* ↓ chel ↓ *Chin* ↓ colch ↓ dulc ↓ ferr ↓ hep ↓ ign ↓ kali-c ↓ kali-n ↓ led ↓ *Lyc* ↓ *Merc* ↓ merc-c ↓ nit-ac ↓ **Nux-v** ↓ phos ↓ puls ↓ rhod ↓ *Rhus-t* ↓ **Sep** ↓ sil ↓ spig ↓ staph ↓ stront-c ↓ *Sulph* ↓ tarax ↓ thuj ↓ verat ↓ zinc ↓
  - **stitching** pain: *Bell* bg2 **Bry** bg2 calc bg2 merc bg2 puls bg2 *Rhus-t* bg2 spig bg2 staph bg2 sulph bg2 tarax bg2 thuj bg2
  - **tearing** pain: acon bg2 ant-c bg2 *Arn* bg2 *Ars* bg2 bell bg2 *Bry* bg2 **Calc** bg2 caps bg2 *Carb-v* bg2 caust bg2 *Cham* bg2 chel bg2 *Chin* bg2 colch bg2 dulc bg2 ferr bg2 hep bg2 ign bg2 kali-c bg2 kali-n bg2 led bg2 *Lyc* bg2 *Merc* bg2 merc-c bg2 nit-ac bg2 **Nux-v** bg2 phos bg2 puls bg2 rhod bg2 *Rhus-t* bg2 **Sep** bg2 sil bg2 staph bg2 stront-c bg2 *Sulph* bg2 tarax bg2 verat bg2 zinc bg2
- **pinching** pain: bruc j5.de cann-s j5.de lyc j5.de m-aust j5.de sulph j5.de*
- **pollution**; after: aq-mar skp7•
- **pressing** pain: agar k* agn k* am-m k* *Anac* k* ang b2.de* arg-met k* arn k* *Asaf* k* *Asar* k* aur k* bell k* bism k* bry k* calc k* camph k* cann-s k* *Caps* k* *Carb-an* k* caust k* chel k* chin k* cina k* clem k* cocc k* con k* *Cupr* k* **Cycl** k* dig k* dros k* euph k* euphr k* graph k* hell k* hep k* *Ign* k* kali-n k* *Led* k* lyc k* m-ambo b2.de* m-arct b2.de* m-aust b2.de* mag-c k* mag-m k* mang k* meny k* merc k* mez k* *Mosch* k* mur-ac k* nat-c k* nat-m k* nitro-o a1 **Nux-m** k* nux-v k* *Olnd* k* petr k* *Ph-ac* k* *Phos* k* *Plat* k* plb k* puls k* ran-b k* ran-s k* rheum k* rhod b2.de* rhus-t k* **Ruta** k* *Sabad* k* sabin k* samb k* sil k* spig k* spong k* *Stann* k* *Staph* k* stront-c k* *Sul-ac* k* sulph k* *Tarax* k* *Teucr* k* thuj k* *Valer* k* *Verat* k* **Verb** k* viol-t k* zinc k*
  - **sticking** pain: am-m b2.de* anac k* arg-met b2.de* arn b2.de* asaf k* bar-c b2.de* bell k* calc k* chin b2.de* colch b2.de* coloc k* cycl k* dros k* euph k* *Ign* k* kali-c b2.de* mez b2.de* *Mur-ac* k* olnd k* phos b2.de* plat k* rhus-t b2.de* ruta b2.de* sabad b2.de* sars k* sep k* spong b2.de* stann b2.de* staph b2.de* sul-ac k* tarax b2.de* thuj k* verb b2.de* viol-t b2.de* *Zinc* b2.de*
- **pressing** pain: ...
  - **tearing** pain: agar k* anac k* *Ang* b2.de* arg-met k* arn k* asaf k* asar k* aur k* *Bell* k* bism k* calc k* *Camph* k* cann-s k* carb-v k* chin k* colch k* cupr k* cycl k* hyos k* led k* meny k* petr k* ph-ac k* ruta k* sars k* sep k* spig k* spong k* stann k* sulph k* zinc k*
  - **twitching**: petr h2
- **pressure** agg.: aq-mar skp7•
- **sleep** agg.: *Cupr* ↓
  - **cramping**: *Cupr* mrr1
- **sore**: acon tl1 ang bro1 arn bro1* bad br1* *Bapt* br1* bell bro1 bell-p c1* bry bro1* caust bro1 cic bro1 *Cimic* bro1 cupr-act bro1 dioxi rbp6 ephe-si hsj1• *Gels* bro1 guaj bro1 ham bro1 *Helon* bro1 hip-ac br1* jac-c bro1 kali-c h2 *Magn-gr* bro1 merc bro1 myric bro1 oci-sa sp1 ozone sde2• *Phyt* bro1 pyrog bro1 ran-b tl1 *Rhus-t* bro1 ruta bro1* sal-al blc1• sang bro1 verat h1
  - **accompanied** by:
    - **typhoid** fever: arn bro1 bapt bro1 bry bro1 gels bro1 *Rhus-t* bro1
    - **Head**; pain in: gels bro1 rhus-t bro1
- **splinters**; as from: *Nit-ac* b4a.de
- **stitching** pain: *Acon* k* agar k* agn k* *Alum* k* am-c k* *Am-m* k* ambr k* anac k* ang b2.de* ant-c k* ant-t k* arg-met k* *Arn* k* ars k* *Ars-i* **Asaf** k* asar k* aur k* bar-c k* bar-m **Bell** k* bism k* borx k* bov k* **Bry** k* calad k* **Calc** k* camph k* cann-s k* canth k* caps k* carb-an k* carb-v k* *Caust* k* cham k* chel k* *Chin* k* cic k* cina k* clem k* *Cocc* k* colch k* coloc k* *Con* k* croc k* cupr k* cycl k* dig k* dros k* dulc k* euph k* euphr k* ferr k* *Graph* k* *Guaj* k* *Hell* k* hep k* hyos k* *Ign* k* iod k* ip b7.de **Kali-c** k* *Kali-m* k2 kali-n k* kreos k* lach k* *Laur* k* led k* lyc k* m-ambo b2.de* *M-arct* b2.de* m-aust b2.de* mag-c k* mag-m k* mang k* *Meny* k* **Merc** k* merc-c b4a.de* merc-i-r a1 mez k* mosch k* *Mur-ac* k* *Nat-c* k* *Nat-m* k* *Nit-ac* k* nux-m k* nux-v k* olnd k* *Par* k* petr k* ph-ac k* *Phos* k* plan a1 plat k* plb k* prun a1 **Puls** k* ran-b k* *Ran-s* k* rheum k* rhod k* **Rhus-t** k* ruta k* *Sabad* k* *Sabin* k* samb k* sang bg2 *Sars* k* seneg b4.de *Sep* k* *Sil* k* **Spig** k* *Spong* k* squil k* *Stann* k* **Staph** k* stront-c k* stry a1 sul-ac k* **Sulph** k* **Tarax** k* teucr b2.de* **Thuj** k* valer k* verat k* verb k* viol-o b7.de viol-t k* *Zinc* k*
  - **burning**: *Acon* *Alum* k* am-m k* anac k* apis k* *Arg-met* k* arn k* **Asaf** k* aur k* bar-c k* bry k* bufo bg2 calc k* caust k* cic k* cina k* **Cocc** k* colch b2.de* *Dig* k* euph glon ptk1 ign k* laur k* lyc k* *M-ambo* b2.de* m-arct b2.de m-aust b2.de mag-c k* mang k* merc k* **Mez** k* mur-ac k* **Nux-v** k* *Olnd* k* par phyt plat k* plb k* rhod k* **Rhus-t** k* *Sabad* k* sabin k* samb k* sep k* spig k* stann k* **Staph** k* **Sul-ac** k* tarax k* **Thuj** k* viol-t k* zinc
    - **needles**; as from | **hot** needles: **Ars** *Kali-c* st ol-an
  - **tearing**: acon k* agn k* alum k* am-c k* am-m k* ambr k* **Anac** k* ang b2.de* arg-met k* *Ars* k* asaf k* asar k* aur k* bell k* bism k* borx k* **Calc** k* *Camph* k* cann-s k* canth k* caps k* caust k* chel *Chin* k* cina k* clem k* coloc k* con k* cycl k* dig k* dros k* **Guaj** k* hell k* kali-c k* kreos k* led k* m-arct b2.de* **Mang** k* merc k* mez k* mur-ac k* nat-m k* nux-v k* olnd k* ph-ac k* phos k* **Puls** k* rheum k* *Rhus-t* k* ruta k* sabin k* samb k* *Sars* k* sep k* sil k* spig k* spong k* squil k* staph k* sul-ac k* tarax k* **Thuj** k* verb k* zinc k*
- **stretching** agg.: mag-s sp1
- **surgery**, from: calen oss•
- **tearing** pain: acon k* adon bg2 aesc bg2 agar k* agn k* alum k* am-c k* *Am-m* k* *Ambr* k* anac k* ang b2.de* ant-c k* ant-t k* *Arg-met* k* arn k* *Ars* k* ars-i ars-s-f k2 *Asaf* k* asar k* *Aur* k* aur-s k2 bar-c k* bar-i k2 bar-m *Bell* k* *Bism* k* *Borx* k* bov k* *Bry* k* **Calc** k* camph k* *Cann-s* b7.de* *Canth* k* caps k* *Carb-an* k* **Carb-v** k* **Carbn-s Caust** k* cham k* *Chel* k* *Chin* k* cic k* cimic bg2 *Cina* k* clem k* cocc k* coff b7.de *Colch* k* coloc k* con k* croc k* cupr k* cycl k* dig k* dros k* *Dulc* b2.de* euph k* ferr k* *Graph* k* guaj k* hell k* *Hep* k* hyos k* ign k* iod k* ip k* **Kali-c** k* kali-m k2 *Kali-n* k* kali-s kalm bg kreos k* lach k* laur k* led k* **Lyc** k* m-ambo b7.de m-aust b2.de* *Mag-c* k* *Mag-m* k* *Mang* k* meny k* **Merc** k* mez k* mosch k* *Mur-ac* k* *Nat-c* k* *Nat-m* k* **Nit-ac** k* nux-v k* olnd k* par k* petr k* ph-ac k* *Phos* k* plat k* plb k* *Puls* k* ran-b k* rheum k* **Rhod** k* rhus-t k* *Ruta* k* sabad k* *Sabin* k* samb k* sang k2 sars k* sec k* sel k* seneg k* **Sep** k* **Sil** k* spig k* spong k* squil k* *Stann* k* **Staph** k* **Stront-c** k* sul-ac k* **Sulph** k* tarax k* *Teucr* k* thuj k* valer k* verat k* verb k* viol-o k* viol-t k* **Zinc** k* **Zinc-p** k2

- **tearing** pain: ...
  - **burning**: bell k* *Carb-v* k* caust k* kali-c k* led k* lyc k* m-ambo b2.de* *Nit-ac* k* ruta k* sabin k* tarax k* zinc k*
  - **cramping**: **Anac** k* ang b2.de* ant-c k* arg-met k* asaf k* aur k* bism k* *Calc* k* caust k* chel k* *Chin* k* dulc k* euph k* graph k* iod k* kali-c k* m-aust b2.de mang k* *Meny* k* mosch k* *Mur-ac* k* **Nat-c** k* nat-m k* nux-v k* *Petr* k* ph-ac k* phos k* **Plat** k* ran-b k* ruta k* samb k* sil k* stann k* stront-c k* thuj k* valer k*
  - **downward**: kalm bg2
  - **jerking** pain: acon k* agar k* agn k* alum k* bell k* calc k* camph k* **Chin** k* cina k* *Cupr* k* dig k* dulc k* guaj k* lyc k* mang k* merc k* nat-c k* ph-ac k* phos k* plat k* **Puls** k* rhus-t k* spig k* *Staph* k* stront-c k* sul-ac k* sulph k*
  - **paralyzed**; as if: agn k* ant-c k* asaf k* carb-v k* *Cham* k* *Chin* k* cic k* *Cina* k* cocc k* con k* dig k* graph k* *Hell* k* **Kali-c** k* mez k* mosch k* nat-m k* nit-ac k* phos k* *Sabin* k* *Sars* k* seneg k* sil k* stann k* verb k*
  - **pressing** pain: acon k* ambr k* anac k* ang b2.de* ant-c k* arg-met k* arn k* asar k* bism k* camph k* cann-s k* **Carb-v** k* caust k* chin k* colch k* cupr k* cycl k* dig k* euph k* guaj k* *Kali-c* k* kali-n k* laur k* led k* lyc k* m-arct b2.de* m-aust b2.de nat-c b4.de ph-ac k* ran-b k* ruta k* sabin k* sars k* sep k* spig k* **Stann** k* *Staph* k* stront-c k* sulph k* teucr k* viol-t k* zinc k*
  - **sticking** pain: acon k* agn k* ambr k* ang b2.de* ant-t k* arg-met k* arn k* bar-c k* bell k* bry k* camph k* cann-s k* canth k* caps k* chin k* cic k* *Colch* k* coloc k* con k* dros k* dulc k* *Euph* k* guaj k* hyos k* ign k* iod k* kali-c k* *Lyc* k* mag-c k* mang k* merc k* mur-ac k* nat-m k* ph-ac k* phos k* rheum k* sars k* spong k* staph k* sulph k* teucr k* thuj k* **Zinc** k*
- **touch** agg.: acon ↓ arn ↓ bry ↓ ran-b ↓ ruta ↓
  - **sore**: acon tl1 arn tl1 bry tl1 ran-b tl1 ruta tl1
- **warm** | **bathing**:
  - **amel.**: lat-m ↓
    - **cramping**: lat-m bnm6•
    - **hot** bath: galeoc-c-h gms1• lat-m sp1
  - **bed**:
    - **agg.**: carb-v ↓
      - **stitching** pain: carb-v k*
- **weather** agg.; cold wet: phyt tl1

○ • **Attachment** of muscles: rhus-t br1
- **Flexor** muscles: scroph-n br1
- **Parts** lain on: kali-c ↓
  - **pressing** pain: kali-c h2

- **Nerves**: acon ↓ calc-f ↓ coloc tl1 gels ↓ hyper ↓ kali-c k2 mag-p tl1 nat-m ↓ ph-ac k2 spig tl1 syph k2 ter ptk1 visc sp1 zinc-p ↓
  - **burning**: acon k2
  - **cutting** pain: spig mtf11
  - **influenza** agg.: cimic mtf11
  - **stitching** pain: hyper k2
  - **tearing** pain: calc-f sp1 gels k2 hyper k2 zinc-p k2
  - **tight**; as if pulled: nat-m bg2
  - **violent**: mag-p tl1

▽ • **extending** to:
  - **Body** | **injuries**; after: hyper k2
- **Neuralgic** nerve; tracks of: gels ↓
  - **shooting** pain: gels hr1*
- **Paralyzed** parts: *(↗Paralysis - painful)* agar k* arn *Ars* k* bell cact ptk1 cadm-s k2 calc *Caust* k* cina k1 *Cocc* k* crot-t *Helo-s* rwt2• *Kali-n* k* lat-m k* nux-v phos *Plb* k* rhus-t sil sulph
- **Parts**:
  - **affected** with cramping pain: **Plat** ↓
    - **sore**: **Plat**
  - **changing** parts: kali-bi tl1
  - **grasped** with the hand: bry ↓ **Caust** ↓
    - **burning**: bry **Caust** k*
  - **injured** long ago: des-ac rbp6 glon st
  - **uncovered**, of: bell h1 kali-c tl1

- **Parts**: ...
  - **various** parts of body: acon ↓ *Agar* ↓ apis ↓ *Ars* ↓ *Canth* ↓ caps ↓ *Carb-an* ↓ ph-ac ↓ *Phos* ↓ sulph ↓
    - **burning**: acon bro1 *Agar* bro1 apis bro1 *Ars* bro1 *Canth* bro1 caps bro1 *Carb-an* bro1 ph-ac bro1 *Phos* bro1 sulph bro1
  - **various** parts of body; in: arist-m ↓
    - **stitching** pain: arist-m br1

○ • **Distant** parts | **spine**; from pressure on: sil ptk1 tarent ptk1
- **Parts** lain on: *(↗side lain; Lying - side - pain goes)* **Arn** ↓ *Bapt* ↓ bry ↓ carb-v ↓ caust h2 cimic bg graph bg hep h2 kali-c h2 *Mosch* ↓ nat-m bg nit-ac sne *Nux-m* ↓ phos h2 phys bg polys sk4• **Pyrus** ↓ **Ruta** ↓ sep h2 sil h2 syph al thuj ↓
  - **night**; at: *Sulph* ↓
    - **burning**: *Sulph* a1*
  - **perspiration**; during: nux-v b7a.de
  - **recently** lain on: ph-ac k2 **Puls**
  - **sore**: **Arn** k* *Bapt* bry h1 caust h2 graph h2 *Hep* *Mosch* *Nux-m* k* (non:pyrog k1*) **Pyrus** k1 **Ruta** k* *Sep* sil h2 thuj
  - **sprained**; as if: mosch ptk1*
  - **stitching** pain: carb-v h2
- **Periosteum**: *(↗Sensitiveness - periosteum)* *Acon* bg2 **Am-c** st ang mrr1 ant-c k* **Arn** st **Asaf** k* aur k* **Aur-m** st bell k* bry k* *Camph* k* cann-s st *Cham* *Chin* k* *Colch* b2.de* coloc k* cycl k* dys fmm1• fl-ac ptk1 graph guare st hell k* ign k* kali-c st **Kali-i** st* kali-n ptk1 *Kalm* led k* m-ambo b2.de* *M-arct* b2.de* m-aust b2.de *Mang* k* med k2 *Merc* k* *Merc-c* b4a.de* *Mez* k* mur-ac h2* nat-m ↓ *Nit-ac* st **Ph-ac** k* phos ptk1 *Phyt* k* *Puls* b2.de* *Rhod* k* rhus-t k* **Ruta** b2.de* sabad k* sabin k* sars br1 *Sil* k* spig k* *Staph* b2.de* sul-ac k2 sulph ptk1 symph c1* syph k2* thuj ↓ tub k2
  - **drawing** pain: bry b7.de *Cann-s* b7a.de m-arct b7.de*
  - **scraped**; as if: *Asaf* k* bry bg2 **Chin** k* coloc k* nat-m bg2 **Ph-ac** k* puls k* **Rhus-t** k* *Sabad* k* spig k* thuj bg2
  - **sore**: mang k2* symph br1 tub k2
  - **stitching** pain: *Symph* br1
  - **tearing** pain: *Acon* bg2 bry k* **M-arct** b2.de* *Mez* ph-ac k* *Rhod* k*
  - **weather** agg.; wet: mez tl1

○ • **Lain** on; parts recently: ph-ac k2
- **Side** lain on: *(↗parts lain)* ars ptk1 *Bry* ptk1 *Calc* ptk1 hep br1 *Kali-c* ptk1 merc ptk1 *Nux-v* ptk1 *Ph-ac* ptk1 **Puls** ptk1 sep ptk1 sil ptk1
- **Sides**: abrot ↓ acon ↓ bry ↓ puls ↓ ran-b ↓ sang ↓ sulph ↓
  - **stitching** pain: abrot ptk1 acon ptk1 bry ptk1 puls ptk1 ran-b ptk1 sang ptk1 sulph ptk1
- **Single** parts: chel ↓ dros ↓ form ↓ ox-ac ↓
  - **cramping**: dros bg2 form bg2 ox-ac bg2
  - **drawing** pain | **paralyzed**; as if: chel br1
- **Skin**; below the: asaf ↓ *Bry* ↓ led ↓ par ↓ *Puls* ↓ valer ↓
  - **ulcerative** pain: asaf b7.de *Bry* b7.de* led b7.de par b7.de *Puls* b7.de valer b7.de
- **Small** spots; in (See spots; in small)
- **Spots**; in: agar ↓ aloe ↓ ambr ↓ apis ↓ **Arn** ↓ atha ↓ bar-act ↓ calc-p ↓ carb-ac ↓ carb-v ↓ caust ↓ chin ↓ colch ↓ coloc ↓ daph ↓ galeoc-c-h ↓ glon ↓ ign ↓ **Kali-bi** ↓ lim ↓ lith-c ↓ lyc ↓ mand ↓ merc ↓ nat-s ↓ *Nux-v* ↓ *Ox-ac* ↓ petr ↓ phos ↓ plat ↓ *Ran-b* ↓ raph ↓ **Sabad** ↓ sang ↓ sel ↓ sul-ac ↓ **Sulph** ↓ verat-v ↓ viol-o ↓
  - **burning**: agar a1* ambr a1 apis a1 atha a1 carb-v a1 chin a1 coloc a1 galeoc-c-h gms1• glon ptk1 ign a1 lim a1 lyc a1 mand jl3 nat-s a1 plat a1 ran-b ptk1 raph a1 sabad mrr1 sang ptk1 sel ptk1 **Sulph** a1* verat-v ptk1 viol-o a1
  - **pinching** pain: caust a1 daph a1 lyc a1
  - **pressing** pain: bar-act a1 sul-ac a1
  - **sedentary** living; from: ran-b ↓
    - **burning**: ran-b ptk1
  - **sore**: aloe **Arn** k* calc-p carb-ac k2* colch k2* glon bg* **Kali-bi** k* lith-c ptk1 merc bg* *Nux-v* *Ox-ac* petr phos bg* plat k* *Ran-b* ptk1 **Sabad** k* sulph bg*

- **Spots**; in small: adam srj5• bamb-a stb2.de• *Calc-p* st *Colch* sf1.de dios sf1.de fl-ac galeoc-c-h gms1• hist sp1 ign k* irid-met srj5• **Kali-bi** k* kali-p fd1.de• kola stb3• lil-t k* lith-c mag-p neon srj5• nux-m ol-an sf1.de *Onos* ox-ac k* ozone sde2• pert-vc vk9 psor ran-b k* *Rhod* a1* rhus-v a1 spig h1* symph fd3.de• *Thuj* ulm-c jsj8•
  - **left** side: kali-c br1
  - **boring** pain: fl-ac a1
- **Tendons**: am-m bg2 arn bg2 benz-ac bg2 berb bg2 *Bry* kr1 caust bg2 colch bg2 coloc bg2 harp jl3 iod bg2 kali-bi bg2 kalm bg2 mag-f jl3 nat-m ↓ pot-e rly4• prun bg2 **Rhus-t** bg2* *Ruta* bg2* sabin bg2* syph jl2 thuj bg2 zinc bg2
  - **drawing** pain: am-m k2 kali-bi bg2 nat-m bg2 rhus-t bg2 thuj bg2
- **Thorax**: tub-m ↓
  - **neuralgic**: tub-m jl2
- **Transverse**: ant-c bg2 mag-m bg2 ruta bg2 zinc bg2
- **Upper** part of body: *Arn* ↓
  - **burning**: *Arn* b7a.de
- **Veins**: syph ↓
  - **burning** | **hot** water; as from: syph ptk1
- **Wounds**; in: | **stinging** (See Wounds - painful - stinging)

PAINLESSNESS of complaints usually painful: *(↗Analgesia; Irritability - lack; MIND - Insanity - insensibility)* agath-a nl2• aloe sne am-c ptk1 ant-c br1* ant-t ptk1 calc sne **Cann-s** b7a.de cic sne con b4.de* *Hell* k* *Hyos* b7a.de *Kreos* bg *Laur* b7.de* *Lyc* b4a.de mosch b7.de* *Olnd* b7a.de **Op** k* ph-ac b4a.de* positr nl2• psil ft1* sacch sst• sec b7.de* **Stram** k* **Sulph** b4a.de *Syph* st1 tung-met bdx1• [heroin sdj2]

PARADOXICAL (See Contradictory; MIND - Contradictory)

PARALYSIS: *(↗Neurological; Poliomyelitis)* absin bro1 *Acon* c2* aesc-g c2 agar c2* agro c2 alum c2* *Alumn* c2 ambro c2 anac c2 anac-oc c2 ang br1* *Ant-t* ptk1 arag br1* arg-i c2* *Arg-n* c2* *Arn* c2* *Ars* ptk1 ars-i bro1 asaf bro1 *Aur* c2* *Bar-act* bro1 *Bar-c* c2* bar-m c2* *Bell* c2* both-a rb3 brucin c2 caj c2 calc c2 calc-caust c2* calc-hp c2 calen bro1 *Cann-i* c2* caps c2 carb-ac br1 carb-v ptk1 carbn-o c2* carbn-s bro1 castm c2 caust c2* chen-a c2 chin ptk1 chinin-s bro1 cic c2* *Cocc* c2* colch bro1* *Con* c2* crot-c mrr1 *Cupr* c2* cupr-act c2 cur c2* diph-t-tpt jl2 dub c2 dulc c2* elec c2 equis-h c2 form c2 galv c2 gast c2 *Gels* c2* glon c2 *Graph* c2* grin bro1 gua c2* hell br1* helo bro1* helo-s c2* *Hydr-ac* br1* hydroph rsj6• *Hyos* c2* *Hyper* c2* *Ign* c2* iodof c2 iris-fl bro1 kali-br c2* *Kali-c* bro1 *Kali-i* c2* kali-p c2* kara c2 lach c2* lat-h bro1 lat-m sp1* lath mrr1 lol c2* lyc c2* lyss c2* mang ptk1 mang-act br1 meny c2 *Merc-c* c2* naja br1 nat-m bro1 nux-v c2* olnd c2* onos c2 *Op* c2* *Ox-ac* c2* oxyt c2* par c2 pert jl2 peti c2 *Phos* c2* phys c2* physal-al bro1 *Pic-ac* c2* *Plat* br1* *Plb* bro1* *Plb-act* bro1 plb-i c2* *Plb-xyz* c2 plect bro1 *Rhus-t* c2* rumx-act c2 ruta c2 sang ptk1 *Sec* c2* sil ptk1 sol c2 spartin bwa3 stann c2* staph bro1* stram br1 stry-af-cit bro1 stry-p br1 strych-g c2* sulph bro1* tab bro1 tang c2 tarent c2 tep c2 *Thal* bro1 thal-xyz srj8• thala mtf11 thea c2 thuj c2 thyr c2* tub c2 verat c2* verb ptk1 verin c2 vib c2 xan br1* zinc bro1 zinc-p c2* zinc-phic ptk1 [*Alumin* stj2 *Alumin-p* stj2 *Alumin-s* stj2 *Plb-m* stj2 *Plb-p* stj2]

- **one** side: *(↗Brown-séguard; EXTREMITIES - Paralysis - hemiplegia)* acon k* acon-c a1 adren st agar k* *Alum* k* *Alum-p* k2 alumn kr1 am-m k* ambr bro1 *Anac* k* *Apis* arg-met k* arg-n arn k* *Ars* k1* ars-s-f k2 asar k* *Aur-m* bro1 bapt k* bar-c k* bar-m *Bar-s* k2 *Bell* k* *Both* k1* bov k* bufo gk cadm-s caj kr1* calc k* carb-v k* carbn-o a1 carbn-s k* **Caust** k* chel k* chen-a c1* chin k* chinin-s j5.de cob-n jl *Coc-c* *Cocc* k* colch k* *Con* sne conin c1 cop cur bro1 cycl k* dig k* diph-t-tpt jl2 dulc k* *Elaps* k* *Graph* k* guaj k* hell k* hep k* *Hydr-ac* kr1* hyos k* ign k* irid-met bro1 *Kali-c* k* *Kali-i* kali-m k2 kali-p *Lach* k* laur k* led k* lyc k* merc k* mez k* *Mur-ac* k* nat-c k* nat-m k* nit-ac k* nux-v k* olnd k* *Op* k* ox-ac perh jl petr *Ph-ac* k* *Phos* k* phys bro1 pic-ac c1* plb k* podo rhod k* *Rhus-t* k* sabin k* *Sars* k* *Sec* bro1 sep spig k* stann k* staph k* *Stram* stront-c k* stry c1* *Sul-ac* k* syph tab k1 tarax k* thuj verat-v bro1 vip j5.de* xan c1* zinc k* zinc-p k2
  - **accompanied** by:
    - **constipation**: alum gm1 alum-sil gm1 alumn gm1 plb gm1
    - **epistaxis**: ham ptk1
  - **anger**; after: staph kr1*
  - **aphasia**, with: *(↗MIND - Aphasia)* both fne1* canth mp1• cench st chen-a mp1•
  - **apoplexy**; after: *(↗Apoplexy; HEAD - Cerebral hemorrhage)* acon b7.de* *Alum* k1 anac apis k1 arn k* ars bro1* *Aur-m* ptk1 *Bar-c* k* bell k* both bro1* bufo c1* cadm-s k1 caj st calc-f sf1.de calen st *Caust* k1*

Paralysis – one side – **apoplexy**; after: ...
chen-a br1* *Cocc* b7.de* con *Crot-c* k1 *Crot-h* k1 crot-t sf1.de *Cupr* b7.de* cur bro1 elaps ptk1 form sf1.de *Gels* k1 glon sf1.de *Hyos* b7.de* kali-br sf1.de kali-cy c1 lach k* laur merc sf1.de nat-ox-act mtf11 nux-v k* olnd br1* **Op** k1* **Phos** k* *Plb* k1* puls b7.de* rhus-t bro1* sec k1 sep j5.de* stann k* stram *Stront-c* sf1.de sulph sf1.de toxo-g jl2 verat-v sf1.de *Vip* bro1* *Xan* br1* *Zinc* k*
  - **coldness** of the paralyzed part, with: *Ars* *Caust* k* *Cocc* k* *Dulc* k* graph led k2 *Nux-v* plb **Rhus-t** *Zinc*
  - **convulsions**:
    - **after**: *(↗Convulsions - delivery)* *Ars* hr1* *Bell* hr1* **Caust** k* **Cic** hr1* *Cocc* hr1* con st **Cupr** hr1* *Hyos* k* *Ip* hr1* laur hr1* *Nux-v* hr1* *Plb* j5.de* *Sec* hr1* *Sil* hr1* *Stann* hr1* stram hr1* sulph hr1* *Vib* hr1*
    - **Well** side; of the: apis k1 *Art-v* k1 bell k1 hell k1* *Stram* k1*
  - **diphtheria**; after: nux-v ptk1
  - **eruptions**; after suppressed: *Caust* *Dulc* k1 hep *Lach* bg3 *Psor* k1 *Sulph* k1
  - **excitement**; after: stann
    - **shock**; after: apis k*
  - **headache**; after: ars h2
  - **heat** in the paralyzed part, with: *Alum* k1* phos k*
  - **here** and there, now: bell mp1•
  - **hyperesthesia** of the well side: plb k*
  - **involuntary** motion of the paralyzed limb: *(↗EXTREMITIES - Paralysis - lower - accompanied - ankle)* arg-n h1 merc h1 phos h2
  - **menses**, with vicarious: **Dig** kr1
  - **now** here, now there: bell h1
  - **numbness**:
    - **Paralyzed** side; with numbness of the: *Apis* kr1 cann-i st *Caust* kr1 *Coc-c* kr1 *Rhus-t* kr1 staph st
    - **Well** side; with numbness of the: cocc k1* plb ptk1
  - **pain**; from: nat-m
  - **spasms**; after: cocc bg cupr bg elaps bg *Sec* bg stann k*
    - **other** side; of the: bell kl lach kl phos kl stram kl
  - **twitching**:
    - **Paralyzed** side; of the: apis *Arg-n* merc nux-v phos *Sec* stram k* stry
    - **Well** side; of the: *Apis* k1* art-v k1 *Bell* k1 *Stram* k1
  - ○ **Joints**: aur bg caps bg euph bg puls bg staph bg valer bg
    - **paralyzed** side, of: *Phos* k1 sec k1
- **right**: acon a1 apis *Arn* *Bell* k* both a1* bufo gk *Calc* *Canth* carbn-s a1 **Caust** k* *Chel* ptk1 chen-a c1* colch **Crot-c** k1 crot-h cur bro1 diph-t-tpt jl2 *Elaps* k* *Graph* irid-met c1* iris-fl c1 iris-foe a1 kali-i merc-i-r ptk1 *Nat-c* nat-m ptk1 *Op* *Phos* bg1* *Plb* k1* *Rhus-t* sang k1 sil stront-c sulph k1 *Thuj* bg1* vip j5.de
  - **aphasia**; with (See MIND - Aphasia - paralysis - right)
  - **persistent**: androc bnm2•
- **left**: acon k1 *All-c* kr1 ambr bro1 *Anac* *Apis* k* arg-n *Arn* k* ars art-v kr1 *Bapt* k* *Bar-m* bell k* brom caust k1 cocc k* cupr-ar c1* elaps gels k* hydr-ac karw-h jl lacer a1* **Lach** k* lyc k1* *Nit-ac* k* **Nux-v** k* op ptk1 ox-ac petr phys a1* *Plb* a1* podo **Rhus-t** k* santin c1 stann *Stram* stront-c ptk1 stroph-h ptk sulph thal-xyz srj8• verat-v bro1 vip ptk1 xan bro1
- **accompanied** by:
  - **congestion**: | **Nerve** centres; of: carbn-s br1
  - **constriction**: alum ptk1
  - **dropsy**: hell br1
  - **formication**: cadm-s ptk1 phos ptk1 sec ptk1
  - **hemorrhage**: plb ptk1
  - **pain**:
    - **drawing**: cham tl1
    - **tearing**: cham tl1
  - **urine**; sugar in: cur br1
  - **vertigo**: graph bg2
  - ○ **Body**; icy coldness of: *Bar-m* br1*
  - **Skin** | **sensitiveness** of: *(↗Brown-séguard)* plb mrr1
- **agitans** (See Paralysis agitans)
- **air** | **draft** of air or wind; after: caust kl

- **alcohol**, after abuse of: ant-t hr1* *Ars* hr1* calc hr1* *Lach* hr1* nat-s hr1* *Nux-v* hr1* **Op** hr1* ran-b hr1* sep hr1* *Sulph* hr1*
- **aluminium** poisoning; from: alum tl1
- **anger**; after: nat-m k* *Nux-v* staph
  - **one**-sided (See one - anger)
- **apoplexy**; after: acon bg2 arn bg2* ars bg2 bar-c bg2 bell bg2* calc-f bg2 calen br1 caust bg2 cocc bg2* crot-t bg2 cupr bg2 form bg2 gels bg2 glon bg2 kali-br bg2 lach bg2* merc bg2* nux-v ptk1 op bg2 phos bg2* plb bg2 sep bg2 stann ptk1 stram bg2 stront-c bg2 sulph bg2 verat-v bg2 vip bg2 zinc bg2*
- **appearing** gradually: *(↗EXTREMITIES - Paralysis - appearing)* alum-sil vh1 **Caust** k* con mp1• syph ptk1*
- **ascending** (See extending - upward)
- **atrophy**, with: *(↗Atrophy)* ars mtf33 cupr hr1* **Graph** hr1* *Kali-p* hr1* phys cda *Plb* hr1* *Sec* hr1* *Sep* hr1*
  - **sensation** of: cur bro1 *Phos* bro1 thyr bro1
- **bathing** | **river** bath in summer; from: *(↗EXTREMITIES - Paralysis - river)* bell-p mp1• *Caust* rhus-t mp1•
- **children**; in: plb br1
  - **infants**: *Bell* bg2 bung-fa ptk1 calc bg2* caust ptk1 coloc bg2 gels ptk1 kali-p ptk1 lath ptk1 **Merc** bg2 plb ptk1 rhus-t bg2 vip ptk1
  - **nurslings**: lath br1
- **coition**; after: phos k*
- **cold**:
  - **agg.**: caust tl1 rhus-t tl1 sulph tl1
  - **bathing** | **amel.**: caust ptk1 con ptk1
- **cold**; after taking a: dulc k1 rhod k1
- **consciousness**; with (See MIND - Consciousness - paralysis)
- **convulsions**; after: cocc ptk1 cupr ptk1 cur ptk1 elaps ptk1 hyos ptk1 *Sec* ptk1 stann ptk1 vib ptk1
- **cramps**; after: tab ptk1
- **delivery**; after: **Phos** hr1* **Rhus-t** hr1*
- **dentition**; during: kali-p ptk1
- **diphtheria**; after: ant-t k* apis k1* arg-met k1 *Arg-n* bg2* arn k* *Ars* aven br1 *Bar-c* kr1 botul br1* camph k* carb-ac k* *Caust* k* **Cocc** k* *Con Crot-h Diph* bg2* diphtox jl2 *Gels* k* helon kr1 *Hyos* kali-br k1 kali-p k* *Lac-c* k* *Lach* k* lyc tl1 *Nat-m* k* nux-v *Phos* k* *Phys* bg2* phyt *Plb* k* rhod c1 *Rhus-t* bg2* sec k* sil sulph kr1 thuj kr1 zinc kr1
- **eruptions**; after suppressed: *Caust* k* *Dulc* k1 hep *Lach* bg3 *Psor* k1 *Sulph* k1
- **excitement**: caust tl1
  - **emotional** excitement; from: gels k2* ign ptk1 lach ptk1 nat-m tl1* stann ptk1 stram ptk1
- **exertion** agg.; after: ars k1 *Caust* k1 *Gels* k1 nux-v k1 *Rhus-t* k1*
- **fever** | **after** | **intermittent**: arn hr1* *Ars* hr1* gels *Lach* hr1* **Nat-m** k* *Nux-v* hr1* vinc-ma fr1
  - **during** | **agg.**: **Ars** b4a.de*
- **flaccid** paralysis: diphtox jl2 plb ptk1
- **fright**; as from: nat-m h2
- **hysterical**: acon bro1 arg-n bro1* asaf bg2* atro vh aur sne caust bg2 cham bg2* cimic bg2 cocc bro1* con bg2 ign bg2* mag-m bg2 mosch bg2 nux-m bg2* nux-v bg2 phos bg2* plb ptk1 sabin bg2 *Tarent* bro1* valer bg2*
- **injuries**; after: *(↗Brown-séguard; BACK - Injuries; EXTREMITIES - Paralysis - Lower - injuries)* arn mrr1
- **Landry's** ascending paralysis (See Guillain-barré)
- **lying** on a moist ground; from: rhus-t kl
- **masturbation**; from: *Chin* kr1 stann k*
- **menses**; during: plb bg2
- **mental** emotion, after: *Apis* k* caust kl **Ign** k1 nat-m k1 nux-v k1 stann k1
- **nervous** (See excitement)
- **nettle** rash; after disappearance of: cop
- **neuralgia**, with: abrot k1
- **nicotinism**, from: nux-v mg1.de
- **numbness**; with: *(↗sensation; impaired)* con k2 helo-s br1 sec ptk1
- **old** people; in: *Bar-c* k* *Con* k* *Kali-c* k* **Op** kr1*
- **pain**; preceded by: plb br1
- **painful**: *(↗Pain - paralyzed parts)* *Agar* k* alum-sil k2* arn k* *Ars* k* bell k* cadm-s k2* calc k* *Caust* k* cina k1 *Cocc* k* crot-t k* helo-s rwt2• *Kali-n* k* *Lat-m* k* nux-a ptk *Phos* k* *Plb* k* sil k* sulph k* thal dx
- **painless**: abies-c k* absin acon aeth alum k* alum-p k2* ambr k* *Anac* k* ang b2.de* *Arg-n* arn k* *Ars* k* ars-s-f k2 *Aur* k* aur-ar k2 aur-s k2 *Bapt Bar-c* k* bar-s k2* bell k* bov k* bry k* *Bufo* cadm-s calc k* camph k* **Cann-i** cann-xyz bg2* carb-v k* *Carbn-s Caust* k* cham k* chel k* chin k* chinin-s chlor cic k* **Cocc** k* colch k* coloc k* **Con** k* crot-h *Cupr* cur ferr k* **Gels** k* graph k* hell k* hydr-ac *Hyos* k* ign k* ip k* kali-c k* kalm karw-h jl3 lath br1 laur k* led k* **Lyc** k* m-ambo b2.de m-arct j5.de *Merc* k* nat-m k* nux-m k* nux-v k* **Olnd** k* *Op* k* ph-ac k* phos k* **Plb** k* *Puls* k* rhod k* **Rhus-t** k* *Sec* k* sil k* staph k* stram k* stront-c k* sulph k* *Verat* k* zinc k* zinc-p k2*
- **paraplegia**: *(↗lower; EXTREMITIES - Paralysis - lower)* acon bro1 agar ptk1 alum bro1 anh c1* *Arg-n* bro1* arn bro1 ars bg2* bapt bg* *Bell* bro1 botul mtf11 caul hr1* *Caust* bro1 *Cocc* hr1* *Con* bro1 *Cupr* bro1 cur bro1 diph mtf11 dulc bro1 form hr1* gels c1* *Hyper* bro1 kali-i bro1 kali-t c1* kalm c1* lach bro1 lat-h bro1 lath c1* laur hr1 lepr mtf11 mang c1* mang-act br1* merc-c bro1 nat-m bg* **Nux-v** bro1* *Ox-ac* bro1 peti c2 *Phos* bro1 phys c1* pic-ac c1* pip-m c1* plb hr1* *Plb-act* bro1 rhus-t bro1* rhus-v c1* ruta ptk1 sec hr1* stry c1* stry-xyz c2 sulph bg* ter hr1 thal c1* thal-met br1 thyr c1* toxo-g jl2* vip br1* wildb c1*
  - **accompanied** by:
    - **atrophy**: ars ptk1
    - **rheumatism**: *Caust* bro1 dulc bro1 lath bro1 phos bro1 *Rhus-t* bro1 sulph bro1
    - **urine**; retention of: apoc ptk1
  - **appetite**; with increased: cina ptk1
  - **delivery**; after: caul ptk1 caust ptk1 plb ptk1 *Rhus-t* ptk1
  - **diphtheria**; after: *Arg-n* bro1 ars ptk1 aur-m bro1 aven bro1 botul bro1 *Caust* bro1 *Cocc* bro1 con bro1 *Diph* bro1 *Gels* bro1 kali-i bro1 *Lach* bro1 nat-m bro1 nux-v bro1 phos bro1 phyt bro1 plb bro1 plb-act bro1 rhod bro1 rhus-t bro1 sec bro1
  - **exertion** agg.; after: nux-v ptk1 rhus-t ptk1
  - **fever**; after: rhus-t ptk1
  - **hysterical**: cocc bro1* con bro1 cupr bro1 ign bro1* nux-v bro1 plb bro1 tarent bro1*
  - **progressive**: mang ptk1 mang-act br1
  - **sensation** of: aesc ptk1 aur ptk1
  - **sexual** excesses; after: rhus-t ptk1
  - **spastic**: gels bro1* hyper bro1* *Lath* bro1* nux-v bro1* plect bro1 sec bro1*
  - **spinal**: alum bro1 bell bro1 cann-i bro1 *Con* bro1 irid-met bro1 *Lath* bro1 *Phos* bro1 phys bro1 *Pic-ac* bro1 plb bro1 xan bro1
  - **vaccination**; after: ars ptk1
- **partial** (See Paralysis)
- **perspiration**, from suppressed: *(↗Perspiration - suppression)* *Colch* k1 *Gels* k1* *Lach* k1* *Rhus-t* k1
- **poliomyelitis** (See Poliomyelitis)
- **pollutions**; after: nat-m bg2 sil bg2
- **postdiphtheric** (See diphtheria)
- **progressive**: alum mrr1 arg-n he1 ars btw2 *Caust* br1* cocc mrr1 *Cur* bg2* gels btw2* kali-p br1 karw-h jl1 lach k2 merc-c a1 nat-m nh8 op gsd1 perh-mal jl1 phos btw2 pic-ac k2* *Plb* bg2* sulfon c1 tab a2
- **rheumatic**: *(↗EXTREMITIES - Paralysis - rheumatic)* acon bg2 ang bg2 arn bg2 bar-c ptk1 caust bg2 cham bg2 chin ptk1 colch bg2* dulc bg2 ferr bg2* kalm bg2 puls bg2 rhod bg2 rhus-t bg2 ruta bg2* sulph bg2
- **sensation**; impaired: *(↗numbness)*
  - **without** impaired sensation: cur br1
- **sensation** of: bung-fa mtf musca-d szs1 phos h2 *Prim-o* br1 sang hr1
  - **right**: arn bg2
  - **left**: bapt bg2
  - ○ **Externally**: am-c bg2 anac bg2 caust bg2 croc bg2 lach bg2 nat-m bg2 phos bg2 rhus-t bg2 sep bg2 sil bg2 stront-c bg2
- **senses**; of (See Paralysis of)
- **sexual** excesses, from: *(↗EXTREMITIES - Paralysis - sexual)* *Kali-br* hr1 *Nat-m* k* *Nux-v* k* **Phos** kr1* *Rhus-t* k* sil k1
- **spastic** paralysis: ben-d c1 cocc tl1 gels c2 hyper c1 lath br1 *Nux-v* c1* phos k2 plect c1 sec c1*
- **spastic** spinal: *(↗spinal)* alum bro1 bar-act bro1 ben-d c1 *Con* bro1 gels c1* hyper c1 kres mg1.de lachn c1 lath c1* led bro1 *Nux-v* c1 *Ox-ac* bro1 phos k2* phys c1* pic-ac c2* plb tl1 plect hsa1* sec c1* wildb c2
- **threatening**: glon bg2 hydr-ac bg2 verat bg2
- **toxic**: *(↗Medicine - allopathic - abuse)* *Apis Ars* bapt crot-h kr1 gels lac-c *Lach* mur-ac rhus-t

- **arsenic**: *(↗Arsenical)* *Chin* kr1 ferr kr1 graph kr1 *Hep* kr1 *Nux-v* kr1
- **lead**: *(↗Lead)* *Alumn* bro1 *Ars* kr1 caust bro1 cupr kr1* kali-i bro1 nux-v bro1 *Op* kr1* pipe c1* *Plat* kr1 plb bro1 *Sul-ac* c1*
- **mercurial**: *(↗Mercury; Mercury - abuse)* **Hep** st1 *Nit-ac* st1 staph st1 stram st1 *Sulph* st1

- **typhoid** fever; in: *Agar* k1* caust k1* *Lach* k1* *Rhus-t* k1*
- **vasomotor**: carb-v tl1 gels tl1 puls k2
- **weather**:
  - **change** of weather | **warm** to cold wet; from: *Caust* st *Dulc* st *Rhus-t* st
- **wet**; after getting: **Caust** k1 **Rhus-t** hr1*

▽ - **extending** to:

○ - **Downward**: *Bar-c* k* merc k* zinc ptk1
- **Upward**: *(↗Guillain-barré)* agar k* *Ars* k* bar-act br1 bar-c a1* *Con* k* hydr-ac *Kali-c* k* karw-h jl3 lyss c1* mang k* ox-ac ptk1 phos st* pic-ac ptk1 plb bg2* sarcol-ac mtf11 sulfon c1* thal-xyz srj8• vip br1*

○ - **Affected** parts: colch b7a.de *Plb* b7a.de *Rhus-t* b7a.de
- **Glands**: calc-sil k2
- **Internally**: absin hr1 *Acon* k* ant-c k* arg-n bg2 *Ars* k* bar-c k* bar-s k2 **Bell** k* calc k* cann-s k* canth k* caps k* caust k* chin k* cic k* *Cocc* k* coloc k* *Con* k* cycl k* dig k* **Dulc** k* euphr k* *Gels* k* graph k* helo bg2 helo-s rwt2• **Hyos** k* ip k* kali-c k* lach k* *Laur* k* lyc k* m-aust b2.de meny k* merc k* mur-ac k* nat-m k* *Nux-m* k* *Nux-v* k* *Op* k* petr k* phos k* plb k* *Puls* k* ran-b bg2 rheum k* *Rhus-t* k* sec k* sel bg2 seneg k* sep k* sil k* spig k* **Stram** k* sulph bg2 tab bg2 tarent zinc bg2
  - **mucoviscidosis**: op gk
  - **sensation** of: alum bg2 caust b2.de* cina b2.de* cocc b2.de* ip b2.de* *Lyc* b2.de* meny b2.de* nux-m bg2 puls b2.de* seneg b2.de* sil b2.de* sulph b2.de*
- **Lower** half of body, of: *(↗paraplegia; EXTREMITIES - Paralysis - lower)* alum-p k2 alum-sil k2* arg-n br1 ars a1 graph k2
- **Muscles**: *(↗Complaints - muscles)* both tsm2 both-ax tsm2 bung-fa tsm2 cocc tl1 crot-c tsm2 crot-h tsm2 cupr mtf33 cur br1 dendr-pol tsm2 elaps tsm2 ix bnm8• lat-h bnm5• naja tsm2 visc c1*

○ - **Extensor** muscles: alum k1* ars k1* calc k1 *Cocc* k1* *Crot-h* k1* cur k1* **Plb** k1*
  - **Flexor** muscles: caust k1* mez ptk1 *Nat-m* k1*
- **Organs**, of: absin *Acon* k* agar k* agn k* alum k* alum-p k2* am-c k* am-m k* ambr k* *Anac* k* ang b2.de* ant-c k* ant-t k* arn k* ars k* asaf k* asar k* aur k* aur-s k2* *Bar-c* k* bar-s k2* **Bell** k* bism k* borx k* bov k* *Bry* k* *Calc* k* calc-sil k2 camph k* cann-s k* canth k* *Caps* k* carb-ac carb-an k* carb-v k* carbn-s *Caust* k* cham k* chel k* chin k* cic k* *Cocc* k* colch k* coloc k* con k* croc k* cupr k* cycl k* dig k* dros k* **Dulc** k* euphr k* gels graph k* hell hep k* hydr-ac **Hyos** k* ign k* iod k* ip k* kali-br kali-c k* kali-chl k13 kali-m k2 kreos k* lach k* laur k* led k* *Lyc* k* m-ambo b2.de m-arct b2.de m-aust b2.de mag-c k* mag-m k* mang k* meny k* merc k* mez k* mur-ac k* nat-c k* nat-m k* *Nit-ac* k* nux-m k* nux-v k* *Olnd* k* *Op* k* par k* petr k* ph-ac k* *Phos* k* *Plb* k* **Puls** k* rheum k* rhod k* *Rhus-t* k* *Ruta* k* sabad k* sabin k* sars k* **Sec** k* seneg k* *Sep* k* **Sil** k* spig k* spong k* squil k* stann k* staph k* *Stram* k* stront-c k* *Sul-ac* k* *Sulph* k* thuj k* *Verat* k* verb k* zinc k* zinc-p k2*
- **Single** parts; of: anac k1 *Ant-t* ptk1 *Ars* k1 bar-c ptk1 bell ptk1 **Caust** k* diph-t-tpt jl2 *Dulc* k* gels ptk1 hyos ptk1 nux-v k2* *Op* ptk1 phos ptk1 *Phys* c2 plb k2 puls ptk1 sec ptk1 sil ptk1 sulph ptk1
- **Sphincters**; of: ars bro1 *Caust* bro1 gels bro1 naja br1* nux-v bro1 phos bro1 phys bro1
- **Spinal**: *(↗spastic spinal)* carb-an b4a.de carb-v b4a.de graph b4a.de ign b7a.de irid-met c1* *Kali-c* b4a.de lyc b4a.de nat-c b4a.de nat-m b4a.de nux-v b7a.de petr b4a.de phos b4a.de puls b7a.de *Rhus-t* b7a.de sep b4a.de sil b4a.de sulph b4a.de
  - **children**; in: | **infants**: rhus-t c1*
- **Veins**: alumn k2

PARALYSIS AGITANS: *(↗Neurological)* *Agar* bg2* alum mrr1 ant-t bg* aran mg1.de* aran-ix mg1.de* arg-met sf1.de* *Arg-n* bg2* arn bg3 *Ars* bro1* aur sf1.de *Aur-s* c1* aven br1* bar-c k* bar-m mtf11 bell bg3 bufo k* buth-a mg *Camph-br* br1* *Camph-mbr* bro1 cann-i bro1 *Carb-v* bg3 **Caust** k* chin bg3 chin-b kr1 chinin-s hs chlorpr jl3 cimic jl3 cocain bro1 *Cocc* bg2* colch bg3 *Con* bg2* cortico mtf11 dub bro1* dulc bg3 *Gels* k* halo jl3* hell bg3 helo k* helo-h bwa3 helo-s c1* *Hyos* k* *Hyosin* c1* *Hyosin-hbr* c1* ign he *Kali-br* k* kres mg1.de *Lach* bg3 lath c1* levo jl lil-t ptk1 *Lol* bg2* lyc c1* lyss mtf11 *Mag-p* k* mang h2* mang-act br1* **Merc** k* nicot bro1* nux-v ptk1 *Op* bg3 perh jl3

Paralysis agitans: ...
Phos k* *Phys* bg2* *Plb* k* plb-xyz c2 psil jl3 *Puls* vh rauw sp1* reser jl3* **Rhus-t** k* scopin-hbr br1 scut bro1 sec bg3 sil bg3 staph bg3 stram br1* sulph bg3 tab k* *Tarent* k* thiop jl3* yers jl2 **Zinc** k* zinc-cy c1* *Zinc-pic* c1*

- **accompanied** by | **trembling**: lac-c mtf11
- **alcohol**; after abuse of: *Hyosin-hbr* c1
- **old** people; in: aven br1

PARALYSIS OF SENSES: *Cocain* bro1 cocc tl1 cyt-l bro1 kali-n h2 phys br1 plat bro1

PARESIS (See Weakness - paralytic)

PARKINSON'S DISEASE (See Paralysis agitans)

PAROXYSMAL or recurrent complaints: *(↗History - complaints)* acon bg2* *Agar* ptk1 ars bg2* bar-c ptk1 bar-m ptk1 bell bg2* *Calc* ptk1 *Caust* ptk1 **Cham** ptk1 chin bg2* **Cocc** ptk1 coff bg2 **Coloc** ptk1 cupr bg2* dios bg2* ferr bg2 gels ptk1 hep ptk1 ign ptk1 kali-i ptk1 lach ptk1 lyc ptk1 mag-p bg2* mez ptk1 nat-m bg2* **Nux-v** ptk1 phos ptk1 plat ptk1 plb bg2* *Psor* ptk1 puls ptk1 **Sep** ptk1 stann ptk1 sulph ptk1 tab ptk1 tub ptk1 valer bg2* verb bg2* zinc bg2

- **right**: thuj bg2
- **left**: caust bg2

PARTURITION; ailments from (See FEMALE - Delivery - after)

PECKING (= picking sensation): ambr b2.de* aur b2.de* carb-an b2.de* **Chin** b2.de* cocc b2.de* dros b2.de* m-ambo b2.de m-arct b2.de mez b2.de* nux-v b2.de* rhus-t b2.de* ruta b2.de* verb b2.de*

PELLAGRA: ars ptk1 bov ptk1 gels br1* *Hep* br1* sec ptk1

PERIARTERITIS NODOSA: eberth jl2

PERIODICITY: acon k* adam srj5• *Agar* k* aloe st **Alum** k* alum-sil k2* **Alumn** kr1 am-br am-c sf1.de am-m sf1.de ambr b2.de* ammc sf1.de *Anac* k* ancis-p tsm2 *Ant-c* k* ant-t k* aran k* **Arg-met** k* *Arg-n* hr1* *Arn* k* **Ars** k* ars-h hr1 ars-met br1* ars-s-f k2* asaf sf1.de *Asar* atro sf1.de *Bar-c* k* bell k* benz-ac sf1.de both-ax tsm2 bov k* *Brucel* sa3• bry k* bufo k* *Cact* k* *Calc* k* calc-sil k2* cann-s k* *Canth* k* *Caps* k* *Carb-v* k* **Carbn-s** kr1* carc mrr1 carl br1* **Cedr** k* cent a1* chap br1 chel sf1.de **Chin** k* **Chinin-ar** k* **Chinin-s** k* chr-ac br1* chr-met dx cina k* cist sf1.de clem k* cocc k* colch k* coloc sf1.de croc k* crot-h cupr k* dros k* dulc fd4.de *Eucal* st1 *Eup-per* br1* eup-pur sf1.de ferr k* ferr-ar *Gels* k* graph k* ham fd3.de• hep ptk1 hydrog srj2• *Ign* k* **Ip** k* iris sf1.de *Kali-ar* kali-bi k* kali-c ptk1 kali-n k* lac-d k2* *Lach* k* lact j5.de lept sf1.de lil-t sf1.de *Lyc* k* *Mag-c* mag-p sf1.de* mag-s mg1.de meny k* merc k* mez sf1.de naja sf1.de nat-ar k* nat-c sf1.de **Nat-m** k* nat-n sf1.de *Nat-s* nat-sil fd3.de• nicc hr1* nicc-s st1 **Nit-ac** k* *Nux-v* k* *Ox-ac* br1 par sf1.de petr k* *Phos* *Plb* k* positr nl2• prim-o br1* psor al2 *Puls* k* ran-s j5.de* *Rhod* k* *Rhus-t* k* rhus-v a1* ruta fd4.de *Sabad* k* samb k* *Sang* sec k* sel sf1.de senec sf1.de **Sep** k* **Sil** k* *Spig* k* spong fd4.de *Stann* *Staph* k* *Stry* br1* sul-ac st1 *Sulph* k* symph fd3.de• tarent a1* *Tela* bro1 teucr sf1.de thal jl3 ther sf1.de thuj bro1* tritic-vg fd5.de *Tub* k* tub-r vn* urol-h rwt• urt-u bro1* v-a-b jl2 valer k* vanil fd5.de *Verat* k* verb sf1.de vip j5.de* visc c1 x-ray sp1 zinc k* [*Buteo-j* sej6 mag-lac stj2 mag-met stj2 mag-n stj2 mag-sil stj2 tell stj2 thal-met stj2]

- **day**:
  - **alternate** day: *Alum* b4a.de* anac b4a.de* ars b4a.de* calc b4a.de* canth ptk1 carb-v b4a.de cham sf1.de *Chin* h1* chinin-s j5.de clem ptk1 crot-h j5.de* dros gk fl-ac bro1 *Ip* sf1.de* kali-n b4a.de lyc b4a.de* lycps-v st nat-c b4a.de* nat-m h2* nit-ac b4a.de* nux-v h1* oxyt bro1 psor al2* puls h1* *Rhod* b4a.de rhus-t ptk1 sep b4a.de [buteo-j sej6]
    - **morning**: *Alumn* kr1
    - **evening**: *Puls* j5.de*
  - **eighth**; every: iris tl1
  - **fourth**; every: ars j5.de* aur sf1.de eup-per sf1.de ign sne kali-br st lyc k* polys sk4• puls k* sabad k*
  - **tenth**; every: kali-p sf1.de lach sf1.de* phos ptk1
  - **every**: ars mrr1 caps fkm1• chinin-s mrr1 lac-h htj1• thal mg [thal-met stj2]
  - **third**; every: anac sf1.de aur sf1.de chinin-s j5.de eup-pur sf1.de hydr sf1.de kali-ar k2 kali-br st
    - **pregnancy**; in: *Lyc* st *Mag-c* kr1
  - **Saturdays**: med jl2

- **day**: ...
  - **Sundays**: med jl2
  - **twice** a day: verb ptk1
- **afternoon** | **every**: **Alum** bg2
- **night** | **every**: lil-t bg2
- **hour**:
  - **12** hourly: lac-h htj1•
  - **half**: melal-alt gya4
  - **half** an hour; lasting:
    - **four** hours; up to: **Cupr** b4a.de
    - **one** and a half hours; up to: **Cupr** b7a.de
  - **same** hour; complaints return at the: ant-c k* *Aran* k* ars ptk1 bov ptk1 *Cact* k* **Cedr** bg2* cench st chin k2 *Chinin-s* j5.de* cina ptk1 cocc j5.de ign k* ip sf1.de* kali-bi k2* kali-br st lyc ptk1 nat-m ptk1 sabad k* sel k1 (non:sil k1) tarent st* tub st verb ptk1
    - **15** h: chinin-s mrr1
    - **neuralgia** every day: cedr vh chinin-s c1 **Kali-bi** k* sabad cda sulph k2
- **week**:
  - **every**: am-m ars k2* ars-h kr1* aur-m sf1.de bit-ar wht1• calc-act sf1.de canth k* cedr sf1.de *Chin* k* croc sf1.de eup-per sf1.de gels ptk1 iris bg2* kali-ar k2 lac-d sf1.de* lyc k* nat-sil fd3.de• nux-m sf1.de phos sf1.de* plan polys sk4• positr nl2• rhus-t sabad sf1.de sang bg1* sil sf1.de* **Sulph** k1* tell a1* tritic-vg fd5.de tub
  - **two** weeks; every: am-m **Ars** k* ars-met kr1* brucel sa3• bufo vh *Calc* k* canth st chel sf1.de *Chin* k* chinin-s *Con* k* *Ign* sf1.de iris tl1 kali-br st **Lach** k* nat-sil fd3.de• nicc bro1* phyt sf1.de plan psor *Puls* k* sang ptk1 sulph sf1.de* tritic-vg fd5.de [kali-ar stj2]
    - **amel.**: mag-m ptk1
    - **two** to four weeks: carl br1* ox-ac br1* sulph br1*
    - **two** to three weeks: ars-met bro1
  - **three** weeks; every: ant-c ars bro1* ars-met br1* *Aur* k* brucel sa3• *Chinin-s* k* *Mag-c* k2* psor sulph symph fd3.de• *Tarent* k* *Tub* k* [kali-ar stj2]
  - **four** weeks; every: brucel sa3• germ-met srj5• mag-c j5.de nat-sil fd3.de• nux-m k1* **Nux-v** k* puls k* **Sep** k* tub k*
  - **six** weeks; every: ant-c ptk1 mag-m ptk1
- **month**:
  - **six** months; every: adam srj5• germ-met srj5• lach ptk1 sep ptk1 tritic-vg fd5.de
  - **three** months; every: chin c1*
  - **December**: [ambro stj]
  - **November**: [mill stj]
  - **October**: [helia stj]
  - **September**: [ruth-met stj]
- **year** | **every**: am-c sf1.de* ammc sf1.de ancis-p tsm2 aran mgm• **Ars** bg2* buth-a jl* carb-v bg2* carc mg1.de* cench cina sf1.de crot-h j5.de* dulc fd4.de echi ptk1 elaps ptk1 gels bg1 hydrog srj2*• ign sf1.de kali-bi bg2 *Lach* j5.de* lat-m mgm• lyc ptk1 mez sf1.de naja ptk1 nat-m bg2 nicc bg2* petr sf1.de positr nl2• psor bg2* rhus-r bro1 rhus-t bg2* rhus-v a1* staph sne sulph bg2* tarent k* ther mgm• thuj k* toxi mtf2• urt-u bg2* vip bg2*
- **regular** intervals; complaints return at: **Carbn-s** st ham fd3.de•
- **absent**: *Acon* br1
- **exact**: aran ptk1 ars ptk1 cedr ptk1 chinin-s ptk1 nat-m ptk1 tarent ptk1

PERSONAL HISTORY (See History)

PERSPIRATION:

- **after**:
  - **agg.**: *Acon* ant-t hr1* arn hr1* ars k* ars-i sf1.de ars-s-f k2* bell k* bry *Calc* k* canth sf1.de carb-an h2 carb-v k* castm sf1.de cham **Chin** k* chinin-s bro1 cinnb k2* *Con* k* ferr hr1* *Hep* bro1* ign k* iod k* *Ip* kr1* kali-c k* kali-i sf1.de lyc k* *Merc* k* merc-c bro1 mur-ac hr1* nat-c k* nat-m k* nit-ac bg2* nux-v k* op bro1 petr k* **Ph-ac** k* *Phos* k* *Psor* sf1.de *Puls* k* samb sf1.de sel k* **Sep** k* sil k* spig k* *Spong* hr1* squil k* *Stann* sf1.de *Staph* k* stram bro1 sul-i *Sulph* k* tub sf1.de verat bro1

Perspiration -- **after**: ...

  - **amel.**: *Acon* k* aesc am-m k* ambr k* ant-t k* apis kr1 *Ars* k* aur bg2* bapt bg2 bar-c k* bell k* bov k* *Bry* k* *Calad* k* *Calc* bg2* *Camph* bg2* *Canth* k* **Cham** k* chel k* *Cimx* kr1 clem k* cocc k* coloc k* *Cupr* bg2* elat kr1 eup-per bro1 ferr-p bg2* *Fl-ac* hr1* franc bro1 **Gels** k* glon bg2 *Graph* k* hell k* *Hep* k* hyos k* *Iod* bg2* ip k* kali-i bg2* kali-n k* *Lach* hr1* lat-m bnm6• led k* lyc k* lyss hr1* m-arct b2.de mag-m k* *Nat-c* b4.de **Nat-m** k* nat-sil fd3.de• nit-ac k* nux-v k* *Olnd* k* op k* **Psor** k* puls k* ran-b bg2* rhod k* **Rhus-t** k* sabad k* sabin k* samb k* sel k* seneg bro1 sep b4a.de spong k* stram k* *Stront-c* k* sul-ac k* *Sulph* k* tab bg2 tarax k* *Thuj* k* urt-u bg2* valer k* *Verat* k* vip bg2* vip-a jl visc bg2*
    - **cold** perspiration: nux-v k*
- **during**:
  - **agg.**: *Acon* k* ambr b2.de anac b2.de ant-c b2.de ant-t k* arn k* **Ars** k* bar-c b2.de bell b2.de* benz-ac ptk1 bol-la bro1 **Bry** b2.de* calc k* camph b2.de cann-s b2.de carb-v b2.de **Caust** k* **Cham** k* chel b2.de* *Chin* k* chinin-ar chinin-s bro1 cimx cina b2.de cocc b2.de coff b2.de coloc b2.de con b2.de croc k* dig b2.de* dros b2.de dulc b2.de eup-per *Ferr* k* ferr-ar **Form** k* graph b2.de hep bro1* hyos b2.de ign k* *Ip* k* kali-n b2.de kreos b2.de led b2.de lyc k* m-arct b2.de m-aust b2.de *Mang* b2.de **Merc** k* merc-c bro1 mez b2.de mosch b2.de mur-ac b2.de nat-ar nat-c k* nat-m b2.de *Nit-ac* b2.de* *Nux-v* k* **Op** k* par b2.de ph-ac b2.de* phos k* plb b2.de *Psor* puls k* *Pyrog* bro1* ran-b b2.de rhod b2.de **Rhus-t** k* *Sabad* b2.de sabin b2.de samb b2.de* sel b2.de **Sep** k* spong k* stann b2.de staph b2.de **Stram** k* stront-c b2.de **Sulph** k* tarax b2.de tarent-c ptk1 thuj b2.de til ptk1 tub ptk1 valer b2.de **Verat** k*
  - **amel.**: *(↗PERSPIRATION - Symptoms - amel.)* *Acon* k* aesc aeth k* anac b4a.de apis *Ars* k* bapt k* bell *Bov* k* **Bry** k* *Calad* k* calc k* camph canth k* *Cham* k* *Chinin-s* cic hr1 cimx **Cupr** k* elat k* eup-per k* fl-ac b4a.de* franc br1* **Gels** k* *Graph* *Hep* iod ptk1 kali-i ptk1 lacer a1* *Lach* lyc k* lyss c1 nat-c k* **Nat-m** k* psor k* *Puls* b7a.de **Rhus-t** k* samb sec *Sep* b4a.de *Stront-c* tarent ptk1 tere-ch jl *Thuj* k* *Verat* k* [stront-m stj2 stront-met stj2 zinc stj2 zinc-i stj2 zinc-m stj2 zinc-p stj2]
  - **no** relief; gives: *Acon* anac androc srj1• *Ant-c* *Ant-t* k* apis k2 arn **Ars** ars-s-f k2 bar-c bell k* benz-ac bol-la br1* *Calc* camph cann-s carb-v **Caust** **Cham** chel *Chin* k* chinin-ar sf1.de chinin-s bro1 cimx cina cinnb *Cocc* coff *Colch* k1 coloc k* con croc *Dig* dros dulc eup-per *Ferr* k* ferr-ar **Form** k* graph *Hep* k* hyos *Ign* *Ip* *Kali-c* kali-n kreos lach bg2* led lyc *Mang* **Merc** k* mez mosch mur-ac nat-ar *Nat-c* nat-m *Nit-ac* **Nux-v** **Op** k* par ph-ac k* *Phos* plb psor *Puls* pyrog bro1 ran-b rhod **Rhus-t** k* *Sabad* sabin *Sal-ac* sf1.de samb sel **Sep** k* spong stann staph **Stram** k* stront-c sul-ac bg2 **Sulph** tarax thuj *Til* k* valer **Verat** *Verat-v*
    - **hot**: til st
- **suppression** of perspiration; complaints from: *(↗Paralysis - perspiration)* *Acon* k* **Act-sp** hr1* am-c k* anthraci apis k* apoc mrr1 arn k* *Ars* k* ars-s-f k2 *Asc-c* hr1 *Aspar* hr1* atro a1 *Aur-m-n* kr1 bar-c hu **Bell** k* bell-p bro1 **Bry** k* *Cact* hr1 cadm-s *Caj* kr1* **Calc** k* **Calc-s** calc-sil k2 camph mrr1 cann-s k* *Carb-v* k* *Carbn-s* cary a1 **Cham** k* **Chin** k* *Clem* coff k* **Colch** k* coloc k* cupr k* dubo-m br1 **Dulc** k* *Eup-per* *Ferr* ferr-p c1 *Gels* hr1 *Graph* k* *Hep* k* hyos k* *Ign* hr1 iod k* ip k* kali-ar k* **Kali-c** b2.de* kali-sil k2 **Lach** ptk1 led k* *Lyc* k* mag-c k* *Merc* k* mill sf1.de nat-c k* *Nat-m* k* *Nat-s* nit-ac k* **Nux-m** b2.de* *Nux-v* k* olnd k* op k* ph-ac k* *Phos* k* plat k* *Plb* **Psor** k* puls k* **Rhus-t** k* sabad k* sec k* sel senec sf1.de seneg k* **Sep** k* **Sil** k* spong k* squil k* staph k* **Stram** k* **Sulph** k* ter hr1 teucr k* valer hr1 verb k* viol-o k*
    - ○ **Foot**; of: *(↗EXTREMITIES - Perspiration - foot - suppressed)* am-c apis ars bad **Bar-c** *Bar-m* bar-s k2 cham coch colch *Cupr* *Form* graph haem *Kali-c* lyc merc nat-c *Nat-m* nit-ac ol-an c1 ph-ac phos plb *Puls* *Rhus-t* k* sal-ac c1 sel **Sep** **Sil** k* sulph *Thuj* **Zinc** zinc-p k2

PEST (= the plague): arn b7a.de ars b4a.de* *Bell* b4a.de bry b7a.de colch b7a.de crot-h br1* *Ign* b7a.de* *Iod* br1 lach ptk1 *Nux-v* b7a.de phos b4a.de* pyrog ptk1 *Rhus-t* b7a.de sec b7a.de sil b4a.de sul-ac b4a.de tarent-c ptk1

- **bubonic** plague: ant-t bro1 anthraci bro1 *Ars* bro1 bapt bro1 bell bro1 carb-v bro1 chin bro1 *Crot-h* bro1 hippoz mtf11 *Ign* b7a.de* iod bro1 *Lach* bro1 naja bro1 oper br1* *Phos* bro1 *Pyrog* bro1 raja-s mtf11 rhus-t bro1 tarent-c br1* yers bro1
  - **prophylaxis**: tarent-c br1
- **prophylaxis**: ign ptk1

PETIT MAL (See MIND - Unconsciousness - frequent)

PHANTOM pain (See Pain - amputation)

PHEOCHROMOCYTOMA: aran-ix mtf11 hist sp1

PHOSPHORUS agg.: cupr-s bg2 kali-perm bg2 lach bro1 nux-v bro1 ter bg2

PHYSICAL SYMPTOMS:
- **alternating** with:
  - **cheerfulness** (See MIND - Cheerful - alternating - physical)
  - **diarrhea** (See RECTUM - Diarrhea - alternating - physical)
  - **insanity** (See MIND - Insanity - alternating - physical)
  - **mental** symptoms (See MIND - Mental symptoms - alternating - physical)
  - O **Head**; pain in (See HEAD - Pain - alternating - physical)
- **predominate** | **mental** symptoms: mur-ac tl1 ph-ac tl1

PICKING TEETH (with a tooth-pick): | **agg.**: kali-c b2.de* *Puls* b2.de*

PINCHING:
- **amel.**: *(↗Pressure - hard - amel.)* apis bg2* ars bg2* pip-n bg2
- **sensation** of; sudden (See Pain - pinching - sensation)
- **together**; sensation of pinching: *Cocc* b2.de* ran-s b2.de*

PINING PEOPLE (See Delicate)

PLAYING PIANO agg.: *(↗Weariness - playing)* anac k* calc k* cham st1 kali-c k* *Nat-c* k* phos k2* *Sep* k* zinc k*

PLETHORA: *(↗Congestion - blood; ABDOMEN - Congestion)* *Acon* k* adon bro1 *Aesc* k2* *Aloe* bg2* alum k* *Am-c* k* ambr k* arg-n sne *Arn* k* *Ars* k* asaf kr1* **Aur** k* aur-ar k2 aur-i k2 aur-s k2* *Bar-c* k* bar-i k2* **Bell** k* bell-p bro1 bov k* brom bg* **Bry** k* **Calc** k* calc-hp bro1 camph bro1 canth k* caps k2* *Carb-an* k* *Carb-v* k* *Carbn-s* caust k* cham k* chel k* *Chin* k* chinin-s bro1 clem k* cocc k* *Coll* bro1 coloc k* con k* conv bro1 *Croc* k* cupr k* dig k* digin a1 dulc k* *Ferr* k* ferr-ar ferr-i a1* ferr-p fl-ac bro1 glon c1* *Graph* k* guaj k* *Ham* bro1 hep k* **Hyos** k* ign k* iod k* ip k* **Kali-bi** k* kali-br bro1 *Kali-c* k* kali-n k* *Lach* k* led k* lept bro1 lil-t k2 **Lyc** k* m-aust b2.de mag-m k* *Merc* k* mosch k* nat-c k* **Nat-m** k* nit-ac k* *Nux-v* k* *Op* k* perh jl3 petr k* *Ph-ac* k* **Phos** k* plb bro1 *Podo* bro1 *Puls* k* rauw jl3 rhod k* *Rhus-t* k* sabin k* sacch a1 sars k* sec k* sel k* seneg k* **Sep** k* **Sil** k* spig k* spong k* stann k* staph k* stel bro1 *Stram* k* *Stront-c* k* sul-i k2* **Sulph** k* *Thuj* k* tus-fr c1* valer k* verat k* verat-v hr1 verb bro1 zinc k*
- **constitution**; plethoric: *(↗FEMALE - Menses - absent - plethoric; FEMALE - Menses - copious - plethoric; FEMALE - Menses - scanty - plethoric; FEMALE - Menses - suppressed - plethoric; FEMALE - Metrorrhagia - women - plethoric; MIND - Hysteria - plethoric; NOSE - Epistaxis - plethoric)* **Acon** kr1 arn kr1* *Aur* kr1 **Bell** kr1 bry k2 *Cact* kr1* *Calc* kr1 *Ferr* ser ferr-pic br1 *Glon* kr1 led kr morg-p fmm1• *Nux-v* kr1 *Op* kr1 puls mrr1 ruta kr1 seneg kr1 sulph gk* *Verat-v* kr1*
  - **children**; in: | **nurslings**: acon tl1
- **false**: ferr br1* ferr-p br1
  - **accompanied** by | **emaciation** (See Emaciation - accompanied - plethora)
  - **children**; in: ferr mtf33
- **portal** stasis (See ABDOMEN - Congestion - liver)
- **pregnancy** agg.; during: acon bro1
- **pyelostasis** (See KIDNEYS - Congestion)
- **young** people; of: chim br1

PLUG, sensation of: *(↗Ball)* agar ptk1 *Anac* ptk1 arn ptk1 asaf ptk1 *Coff* ptk1 hep ptk1 *Ign* ptk1 lith-c ptk1 mosch ptk1 *Plat* ptk1 *Ran-s* ptk1 rat ptk1 *Ruta* ptk1 spong ptk1 *Sul-ac* ptk1 sulph ptk1 **Thuj** ptk1 valer ptk1
- **blunt**: ruta ptk1 sul-ac ptk1
- **rough**: ruta ptk1
- O **Externally**: agar k* *Anac* bg3* ang bg2 arn k* asaf bg3 bufo bg2 *Coff* bg3 coloc bg2 *Crot-t* hell k* hep bg3 hyper bg2 **Ign** bg3 *Kali-bi* lach k* plat k* prun bg2 *Ran-s* bg3 ruta k* spong bg3 *Sul-ac* bg3 sulph bg3 **Thuj** bg3
- **Internally**: acon k* *Agar* k* **Aloe** k* am-br am-c k* ambr k* *Anac* k* *Ant-c* k* ant-s-aur sf1.de apoc bg2* arg-met k* arg-n bg1 *Arn* k* *Asaf* k* aur k* *Bar-c* k* bell k* bov k* bufo bg1 calc k* caust k* cham k* chel k* cimic bg2* coc-c k* cocc k* coff k* con k* croc k* dros k* ferr k* graph k* hell k* *Hep* k* **Ign** k* iod *Kali-bi* bg2* kali-c k* kreos k* lach led k* lyc k* *M-ambo* b2.de* merc k* mez k* mosch bg1 mur-ac k* nat-m k* *Nux-v* k* olnd k* par k* plat k* plb k* ran-s k* rhod k* *Ruta* k* sabad k* sabin k* sang sep k* spig k* *Spong* k* staph k* sul-ac b4a.de* *Sulph* k* **Thuj** k*

POISON IVY poisoning (See SKIN - Eruptions - rhus)

POISONINGS: mag-s sp1
- **barbiturate**: mag-s sp1
- **barium**: mag-s sp1
- **charcoal**: am-c tl1
- **cyanide**: cob-n sp1 hip-ac sp1

POISONOUS plants; intoxication by: *Bell* b7a.de

POLIOMYELITIS: *(↗Neurological; Paralysis; Reflexes - diminished)* *Acon* hr1* aeth bro1 alum st1 arg-n st1 arn hr1* ars st1 bell hr1* bung-cd br1 *Calc* bro1 carb-ac st1 *Caust* hr1* chinin-ar st chr-s bro1 cur st1 dulc st1 ferr-i st1 ferr-p st1 **Gels** hr1* hydr-ac st1 hydroph jl3* hyos hr1* kali-i st1 kali-p hr1* karw-h jl3 kres mg1.de lach st1 lath bro1* merc hr1* nux-v hr1* phos bro1* phys br1* *Plb* bro1* plb-i st1 rhus-t hr1* sec bro1* stry-p st1 sulph hr1* verat st1 verat-v st1 vip br1
- **bulbar** form: ant-t gm1 op gm1
- **paralysis** of diaphragm, with: cupr op sil
- **prophylaxis**: cocc gm1 cur gm1 gels gm1 **Lath** gm1

POLLUTIONS: | **agg.**: agar b2.de* agn b7.de *Alum* b2.de* ars b2.de* borx b2.de* bov b2.de* *Calad* b7.de *Calc* b2.de* cann-s b2.de* *Canth* b7.de carb-an b2.de* carb-v b2.de* caust b2.de* chin b2.de* con bg2 *Iod* b2.de* **Kali-c** b2.de* led b2.de* lyc b2.de* m-aust b2.de* merc b2.de* mez b2.de* nat-c b2.de* nit-ac b4.de **Nux-v** b2.de* petr b2.de* ph-ac b2.de* phos b2.de* plb b2.de* puls b2.de* ran-b b2.de* rhod b2.de* sabad b2.de* *Sel* b7.de *Sep* b2.de* sil b2.de* spig bg2 *Staph* b2.de* thuj b2.de* viol-o b7.de

POLYARTHRITIS (See EXTREMITIES - Pain - joints)

POLYCYTHEMIA: *(↗Laboratory - erythrocytes - increased)* cean mrr1 cob-n sp1 cortico sp1 lach mrr1 phos br1* x-ray sp1
- **accompanied** by | **Spleen**; enlarged and tender: **Cean** mrr1

POLYNEUROPATHY: *(↗Neurological)* brass-n-o srj5•

POLYPUS: all-c bro1* alum bg2* alumn c1* ambr k* ant-c k* *Aur* k* bell k* berb c1* cadm-s bg2* **Calc** k* calc-i bg2* **Calc-p** k* *Calc-s* k* *Carb-an* k* carc mlr1• *Caust* k* coc-c ptk1 **Con** k* *Form* bg2* graph k* *Hep* k* iod mtf33 *Kali-bi* bg2* kali-i bg2* kali-m sf1.de kali-n c1* kali-s hr1* lem-m c1* lyc k* *Med* bg1* *Merc* k* merc-i-r sf1.de *Mez* k* nat-m k* nat-s bg2 nit-ac k* petr k* ph-ac k* **Phos** k* *Psor* bg2* puls k* sang k* *Sangin-n* c1* sep k* *Sil* k* **Staph** k* sul-ac k* sulph k* **Teucr** k* *Thuj* k*
- **accompanied** by | **metrorrhagia** (See FEMALE - Metrorrhagia - accompanied - polyps)
- **bleeding**: sang bg2
- O **Mucous** membrane bell-p mtf11 calc mtf11

POMPE'S DISEASE: *(↗Glycogen)* ars mtf ars-i mtf glyco mtf

POSITION:
- **chair**; feet on | **amel.**: con bro1
- **erect**; half | **amel.**: ant-t bro1 apis bro1 bell bro1
- **hands and feet** | **amel.**: eup-per bro1

POUNDING (See Pulsation)

PREGNANCY (See FEMALE - Pregnancy)

PRESSURE:
- **agg.**: acon k* **Agar** k* alum k* alum-sil k2* alumn kr1 am-br k* am-c k* am-m k* ambr k* anac k* *Ang* b2.de* ant-c k* **Apis** k* aq-mar jl3 *Arg-met* k* *Arg-n* sf1.de* arn k* *Ars* k* *Ars-i* asaf k* *Bapt* **Bar-c** k* bar-i k2* bar-m bar-s k2* bell k* bism k* borx k* bov k* *Bry* k* cact *Calad* k* calc k* calc-p camph k* *Cann-s* k* *Canth* *Caps* k* carb-an k* *Carb-v* k* carbn-s card-m caust k* cench bro1 *Chel* k* chin k* cimic jl3 **Cina** k* coc-c coca-c sk4• cocc coloc k* cortiso jl3 crot-t culx k2 cupr k* daph ptk2 dig k* dros k* dulc k* equis-h bro1 fl-ac bg2 *Guaj* k* hecla jl hell k* **Hep** k* hyos k* ign k* **Iod** k* ip k* *Kali-bi* *Kali-c* k* *Kali-i* k* kali-n k* kali-p kali-sil k2* **Lach** k* laur k* led k* **Lil-t** k* *Lob* sf1.de **Lyc** k* *Mag-c* k* mag-m k* mang k* meny k* *Merc* k* **Merc-c** k* mez k* *Mosch* k* mur-ac k* nat-ar k* nat-c k* *Nat-m* k* *Nat-s* k* *Nit-ac* k* nux-m k* *Nux-v* k* *Olnd* k* onos bro1 *Op* ovi-p bro1 ox-ac ph-ac k* phos k* phyt bg2* *Plat* k* psor bg* puls k* *Ran-b* k* *Ran-s* k* rhus-t k* *Ruta* k* sabad k* *Sabin* k* samb k* sars k* *Sel* k* seneg k* sep k* **Sil** k* sol-t-ae vml3• spig k* *Spong* k* *Stann* k* *Staph* k* stram k* stront-c k* sul-ac k* sul-i k2* sulph k* tarent ptk1 tell ptk1* *Teucr* k* thal jl3 thal-xyz srj8• ther c1* thuj k* *Valer* k* verat k* *Verb* k* vib ptk1 vip-a jl3 zinc k* zinc-chr ptk1 [cob stj2 cob-m stj2 cob-p stj2 ferr-n stj2 lith-i stj2 mag-i stj1 mag-n stj2

- **agg.**: ...
mang-i stj2 mang-n stj2 merc-i-f stj2 nat-i stj1 nitro stj2 ruth-met stj2 spect dfg1 thal-met stj2 zinc-i stj2]
  - **dorsal** vertebrae; on: arn a1
    - **last** dorsal vertebra; on: *Arn* a1
  - **painless** side agg.; on: *Ambr* k* arn k* bell k* **Bry** k* *Calc* k* cann-s k* carb-an k* carb-v k* *Caust* k* *Cham* k* *Coloc* k* *Fl-ac* bg2 **Ign** k* *Kali-c* k* lyc k* *M-ambo* b2.de* *M-aust* b2.de nux-v k* **Puls** k* *Rhus-t* k* *Sep* k* *Stann* k* viol-o k* *Viol-t* k*
- **amel.**: abies-c abrom-a ks5 acon k* adon sf1.de agar *Agn* k* alum k* alum-p k2* alum-sil k2* *Alumn* kr1 *Am-c* k* *Am-m* k* ambr k* anac k* ant-c k* *Apis* arg-met k* *Arg-n* k* arn k* ars k* *Asaf* k* atra-r jl3* *Aur* k* bar-m k2* bell k* bell-p st* bism k* *Borx* k* bov k* **Bry** k* cact cadm-met jl3 calc k* calc-f camph k* *Canth* k* caps bro1* carb-ac carb-an sf1.de *Carbn-s* cassia-s ccrh1• *Castm* sf1.de* caust k* cham ptk1 *Chel* k* **Chin** k* cimic sf1.de* cina k* cinnb k* *Clem* k* *Cocc* b2.de* **Coloc** k* **Con** k* *Croc* k* crot-t cupr sf1.de cupr-act bro1 cupr-ar ptk1 dig k* dios k* **Dros** k* *Dulc* k* esp-g kk1.de euon bro1 ferr sf1.de form k* galeoc-c-h gms1• gels sf1.de *Glon* *Graph* k* guaj k* hell k* hip-ac jl3 hist mg1.de* ign k* indg j5.de* ip k* *Kali-bi* kali-c k* *Kali-i* kali-p kreos k* *Lac-d* k2* *Lach* laur k* led k* **Lil-t** k* mag-c k* **Mag-m** k* **Mag-p** k* *Mang* k* med st **Meny** k* merc k* mez k* mosch k* *Mur-ac* k* murx mgm• **Nat-c** k* nat-f mg1.de* *Nat-m* k* nat-p *Nat-s* k* nat-sil k2* *Nit-ac* *Nux-m* k* nux-v k* olnd k* pall sne *Par* k* *Ph-ac* k* phos k* pic-ac bro1 **Plb** k* **Puls** k* pyrog sf1.de* rad-br c11 rad-met bro1 *Rhus-t* k* ruta k* sabad k* sabin k* sang *Sep* k* **Sil** k* *Spig* k* stann k* staph sf1.de stict sf1.de sul-ac k* sulfonam jl3 sulph k* thuj k* *Tril-p* verat k* verb k* vib ptk1 vip-a jl zinc k* [astat stj2 aur-m stj2 aur-s stj2 bar-br stj2 bar-i stj2 bar-met stj2 bism-sn stj2 caes-met stj2 hafn-met stj2 irid-met stj2 lanth-met stj2 mag-br stj1 mag-f stj1 mag-lac stj2 *Mag-met* stj2 mag-n stj2 mag-sil stj2 merc-d stj2 merc-i-f stj2 osm-met stj2 plat stj2 plb-m stj2 plb-p stj2 polon-met stj2 rhen-met stj2 tant-met stj2 thal-met stj2 tung-met stj2]
- **hard**:
  - **agg.**: pip-n bg2 spig bg2 tell bg2
  - **amel.**: *(↗Pinching - amel.)* achy jl arn bg2 ars sne atra-r bnm3• *Chin* mrr1 coloc bg2* culx k2 ign k2 lach mag-m jl malar jl2 plb bg2 rauw jl sep k2 stann jl [tax jsj7]
- **hard** edge; against a:
  - **agg.**: ruta ptk1
  - **amel.**: bell ptk1 *Chin* ptk1 **Coloc** ptk1 con ptk1 ign ptk1 *Lach* ptk1 mag-m ptk1 *Meny* ptk1 nux-v ptk1 pall sne psor ptk1 samb ptk1 sang ptk1 sep sne stann ptk1 zinc ptk1
- **opposite** side; on | **agg.**: viol-t ptk1
- **shoes** agg.; of: borx ptk1 paeon ptk1
- **slight**:
  - **agg.** | **hard** pressure amel.; but: *(↗Rubbing - Amel.)* aloe bg2 bell bg2* *Castm* ptk1 caust bg2 **Chin** bg2* culx k2 ign bg2* kali-c bg2 lac-c k2 *Lach* bg2* *Mag-m* mrr1 *Mag-p* bg2 nux-v bg2* plb bg2* psor ptk1 sulph bg2
- **spine** agg.; on: agar ptk1 arn ptk1 bell ptk1 *Chin* ptk1 kali-c ptk1 *Phys* ptk1 sep ptk1 **Sil** ptk1 ther ptk1
- **steady** pressure | **amel.**: nit-ac ptk1 spig ptk1

PRICKLING:

○ - **Externally**: abrot bg2 acon k* agar k* agath-a nl2• *Ail* alum k* ant-c k* ant-t k* *Apis* bg2* arg-n mrr1 arn hr1* ars bg2* arum-t k2* bar-c bg2 bell k* borx bg2 brom a1 *Brucel* sa3• bry ptk1 calc k* calc-p a1 cann-i cann-s k* caps k* carbn-s carl a1 caust k* chin a1 chlor a1 chr-ac a1 cimic k* clem a1 coloc k* con croc k* *Crot-c* delphin a1 *Dros* k* elaps a1 ferr-m a1 ferr-ma j5.de glon grat j5.de ham bg2* helo-s bnm14• hep k* hydr-ac a1 hyos a1 ign bg2 ip hr1* kali-bi bg2 kali-br kali-p ptk1 laur k* linu-c a1 *Lob* k* lyc k* m-ambo b2.de* m-arct b2.de* med *Mez* k* mosch k* nat-m ptk1 nat-p ptk1 nit-ac bg2 *Nux-m* k* nux-v bg2 onos *Phos* hr1* **Plat** k* **Ran-s** k* rhod bg2 rhus-t bg2* ruta k* sabad k* *Sec* k* sep k* sil bg2 spira a1 staph k* stram a1 sul-ac k* sulph k* symph ptk1 tarent hr1* tep a1 thuj j5.de urt-u ptk1 verat bg2* *Verat-v* ptk1 xan hr1* zinc k*

- **Internally**: abrot acon k* agath-a nl2• *Ail* arum-t k2* aur k* bar-s k2 *Brucel* sa3• cann-s k* carc fd2.de* dios dioxi rbp6 lach malar jl2 **Nit-ac** *Osm* ph-ac k* *Phos* k* plat k* *Ran-b* *Sabad* k* *Sang* sec k* seneg k* verb k* viol-o k*
  - **sides** of body were separated; as if: bamb-a stb2.de•

PROGRESSIVE MUSCULAR ATROPHY (See Atrophy - muscles; Complaints - muscles)

PROLAPSUS: aloe ptk1 arg-met ptk1 arg-n ptk1 aur ptk1 *Bell* ptk1 borx ptk1 *Calc* ptk1 gels ptk1 helon ptk1 *Ign* ptk1 kali-cy ptk1 lach ptk1 lil-t ptk1 *Merc* ptk1 *Mur-ac* ptk1 nat-m ptk1 nux-v ptk1 pall ptk1 phos ptk1 plat ptk1 podo ptk1 *Puls* ptk1 *Rhus-t* ptk1 sep ptk1 stann ptk1 *Sulph* ptk1

PROPHYLAXIS (See Poliomyelitis - prophylaxis; Tetanus - prophylaxis; COUGH - Whooping - prophylaxis; FEVER - Scarlet - prophylaxis; MIND - Hydrophobia - prophylaxis)

PROSTRATION:

- **body**; prostration of the (See Weakness)
- **mental** prostration (See MIND - Prostration)

PROTRUDING:

- **tongue** | **agg.**: cist bg2 cocc b2.de* *Kali-bi* bg2

PROTRUSION:

- **sensation** of: *Acon* ptk1 aur ptk1 *Bell* ptk1 *Cocc* ptk1 ferr ptk1 *Glon* ptk1 hyos ptk1 iod ptk1 **Lach** ptk1 *Lyc* ptk1 lycps-v ptk1 **Nux-v** ptk1 op ptk1 spig ptk1 stram ptk1 sul-ac ptk1

○ • **Bones**: rad-br bg2

PSORA: acon st adlu jl3 aesc st *Agar* h2* alco a1 aln c1* alum h2* alumn k2 am-c h2* am-m h2* ambr st1 amyg st1 anac h2* ang st anh jl3 *Ant-c* h2* ant-t st1 apis st aran jl3 arg-met st* arg-n sf1.de* arn st1 ars h2* ars-br br1* *Ars-i* kr1* ars-s-f k2 asaf sf1.de* asar st1 astra-e jl3 aur h2* aur-m st1 bac c1* *Bar-c* h2* bell h1* berb st berb-a jl3 beryl jl3 bism st borx h2* bov sf1.de* bry st1 bufo st buni-o jl3 *Calc* h2* calc-act st calc-f jl3 *Calc-p* sf1.de* calc-s st1 camph st1 cann-s st1 canth st1 caps st1 *Carb-an* h2* *Carb-v* c1* carc jl2 caust h2* cham st1 chel st1 chin st1 cic h1* cina st cinnb st1 cist br1 clem h2* coc-c st1 coca st cocc st1 coff st colch jl3* coloc h2* con h2* cortiso jl3 croc st1 *Cupr* h2* cycl st1 cyna jl3 daph st des-ac jl3 dig sf1.de* diphtox jl2 dros st dulc h2* euph h2* euph-cy st euph-l st euphr st ferr st1 ferr-ar k2 ferr-ma st ferr-p st fl-ac st flav jl3 galph jl3 graph h2* guaj h2* guat jl3 halo jl3 ham st harp jl3 hell st helon st *Hep* h2* hip-ac jl3 hir jl3 hist jl3 hydr st hydr-ac st hyos st hypoth jl3 iber jl3 ign st iod h* ip st kali-ar k2 kali-bi a1* *Kali-c* h2* kali-i st kali-n h2* kali-p st kreos kr1 kres jl3 lac-c st lac-d st lach st laur st led st levo jl3 lil-t st lob st *Lyc* h2* m-arct st m-aust st *Mag-c* h2* *Mag-m* h2* *Mag-p* br1 mag-s jl3 mand jl3 mang h2* *Merc* st* merc-c st mez h2* mill st mim-p jl3 moni jl2 morph st mosch st mur-ac h2* murx st *Nat-c* h2* *Nat-m* h2* nicc st1 *Nit-ac* h2* nux-v st oci-sa jl okou jl3 *Ol-j* a1* olnd sf1.de* onop jl3 op st orig st palo jl3 par st paraph jl3 ped c1 perh jl3 pers jl3 *Petr* h2* ph-ac h2* phenob jl3 phos h2* plat h2* plb st1 plb-act st pneu jl3* podo st prot jl3 **Psor** kr1* puls st ran-b st rauw jl3 reser jl3 rheum st rhod st1 rhus-t st1 rib-ac jl3 rumx st ruta st sabad st1 sabin st samb st saroth jl3 sarr st sars st sec st sel st1 seneg st1 *Sil* h2* skook br1 spig st1 spong st1 squil st stann sf1.de* staph st stram st stront-c st sul-ac h2* **Sulph** h2* tarax st tell jl3 teucr st thala jl3 thiop jl3 thuj st thyr jl3 trif-p st trios jl3 tub st* tub-r jl3 ven-m jl3 verat st visc jl3 zinc st

PSYCHOTROPIC drugs:

- **ailments** from: *(↗Narcotics - ailments)* arb-m oss1• chin tl1 sep mrr1
- **desire** (See MIND - Drugs - desire - psychotropic)

PTOMAINE POISONING, ailments from (See Food poisoning)

PUBERTY: *(↗Convalescence - puberty)*

- **ailments** in: *Acon* hr1* agar bg2 *Ant-c* bg2* apoc c1 aur hr1* bell hr1* *Calc* hr1* *Calc-p* bg2* caust sf1.de* cimic bg2* croc sf1.de* cupr sf1.de ferr sf1.de* *Ferr-p* sf1.de* **Gels** hr1* *Graph* bg2* guaj ptk1 hell ptk1 helon sf1.de hep sne ign c1 iod sf1.de jug-c bg2 *Jug-r* sf1.de kali-br ptk1 *Kali-c* bg2* kali-p ptk1 *Lach* ptk1 mag-p c1 manc mrr1 mill c1 *Nat-m* bg2* *Ph-ac* bg2* **Phos** bg2* plat k* **Puls** j5.de* *Senec* bg2* sep c1 sil sf1.de stram c1 ther j5.de verat c1 viol-o ptk1
  - **girls**; in: *Aur* kr1* *Bar-c* kr1* *Bell* kr1 *Calc-p* kr1* *Ferr* kr1 fil kr1 hypoth jl **Lach** kr1 *Phos* kr1* *Puls* kr1*
- **complaints** develop at: carc mrr1 puls br1*
- **delayed** puberty: bar-c mtf33 rhod kgp5•
  - **girls**; in: calc-p ptk1

PULSATION: acon ptk1 anh sp1 ara-maca sej7• arg-n bg2 aster ptk1 **Bell** ptk1 *Bell-p* ptk1 bry ptk1 *Calc* ptk1 chin ptk1 chir-fl bnm4• coc-c ptk1 ferr ptk1 glon bg2* jab ptk1 kali-bi bg2 kali-c bg2* kreos ptk1 lach ptk1 lil-t ptk1 meli ptk1 nat-m bg2* *Phos* ptk1 polyg-h ptk1 **Puls** ptk1 *Sep* ptk1 sil ptk1 stroph-h ptk1 sulph ptk1

- **accompanied** by | **Teeth**; pain in (See TEETH - Pain - accompanied - pulsation)
- **eating**; after: lyc bg2
- **general**; in: acon ptk1 alum ptk1 ambr ptk1 *Ant-t* ptk1 *Bell* ptk1 calc ptk1 calc-hp ptk1 *Carb-v* ptk1 ferr ptk1 **Glon** ptk1 *Graph* ptk1 *Kali-c* ptk1 *Kreos* ptk1 lach ptk1 lil-t ptk1 lyc ptk1 nat-m ptk1 **Phos** ptk1 **Puls** ptk1 sang ptk1 sel ptk1 *Sep* ptk1 *Sil* ptk1 sulph ptk1 verat-v ptk1 zinc ptk1
- **reverberating** in head: bell bg2
- **violent**: *Sabin* br1
- **walking**:
  - **air**; in open:
    - **after** | **agg.**: ambr br1
- **warm** agg.: *Com* br1

O - **Affected** parts: led b7.de
- **Blood** vessels | **Arteries**: bell ptk1 chin ptk1 glon ptk1
- **Blood** vessels; in:
  - **eating**; after: sel b7a.de
  - **fever**; during: bell b4a.de
  - **perspiration**; during: *Acon* bg2 *Ars* bg2 **Bell** bg2 calc bg2 chin bg2 graph bg2 hep bg2 merc bg2 *Nux-v* bg2 op bg2 phos bg2 puls bg2 *Rhus-t* bg2 sabad bg2 *Sel* bg2 **Sep** bg2 sulph bg2 thuj bg2 zinc bg2
- **Bones**: *Asaf* k* *Calc* k* carb-v k* lyc k* *Merc* k* nit-ac k* phos k* rhod k* ruta k* sabad k* sep k* sil k* *Sulph* k* thuj k*
  - **night**: *Asaf* a2
- **Externally**: acet-ac k2* *Acon* k* acon-s a1 *Aesc* agar k* alum k* alumn k* am-c k* am-m k* *Ambr* k* ammc k* anac k* ang b2.de* *Ant-t* k* *Arg-met* k* *Arg-n* k* arn k* *Ars* k* *Ars-i* ars-s-f k2* *Asaf* k* asar *Aur* b4a.de *Bar-c* k* bar-i k2* bar-m bar-s k2* bell k* benz-ac berb k* bov k* brom bry k* bufo bg2 *Cact* calad **Calc** k* calc-i k2* *Calc-p* *Calc-s* calc-sil k2* cann-s k* canth k* caps k* carb-an *Carb-v* k* *Carbn-s* cassia-s ccrh1• *Caust* k* cham k* chel k* chin k* chinin-ar chlol chlor a1 cina k* clem k* coc-c cocc k* coff k* *Coloc* k* *Con* k* cop k* croc k* cupr dig k* dros k* dulc k* euph bg2 euphr k* **Ferr** ferr-ar **Ferr-i** ferr-p *Fl-ac* gamb k* gast a1 gels **Glon** k* **Graph** k* guaj k* hell k* helo helo-s rwt2• hep k* hydrog srj2• hyos k* *Ign* k* *Iod* k* kali-ar *Kali-bi* **Kali-c** k* kali-chl k13 kali-m k2 kali-n k* kali-p **Kali-s** kali-sil k2* kiss k* **Kreos** k* **Lach** laur k* led hr1* *Lil-t* k* *Lyc* k* *Lyss* *M-ambo* b2.de* *M-arct* b2.de* *M-aust* b2.de* macro a1 mag-c k* mag-m k* manc k* mang k* med **Meli** meny b7.de *Merc* k* mez k* mosch k* mur-ac k* nat-ar *Nat-c* k* **Nat-m** k* *Nat-p* *Nat-s* nat-sil k2* *Nit-ac* k* nitro-o a1 nux-m k* *Nux-v* k* **Olnd** k* op k* par k* petr k* ph-ac k* *Phos* k* phys k* phyt k* *Plat* k* plb k* positr nl2• **Puls** k* ran-b k* rheum k* *Rhod* k* rhus-t k* *Rumx* *Ruta* k* **Sabad** k* sabin k* samb k* sang k* sarr br1 sars k* sec k* *Sel* seneg k* *Sep* k* *Sil* k* spig k* spong k* squil k* stann k* staph k* *Still* *Stram* k* *Stront-c* k* *Sul-ac* k* sul-i k2* **Sulph** k* *Tarax* k* teucr k* *Thuj* k* til *Urt-u* verat k* *Zinc* k* zinc-p k2* [bell-p-sp dcm1]
  - **morning** | **waking**; on: *Bell* k*
  - **afternoon** | **14**.30 h: pall
  - **evening**: arn *Carb-an* caust nat-m rumx a1 sep
    - **rest** agg.: nat-m
    - **sleep**; before going to: sil h2
  - **night**: am-m k* *Bry* cact k* nat-m k* *Sil* sulph k*
    - **midnight**: phys k*
      - **after**: iris trios a1
    - **cough** agg.; during: *Calc* k*
    - **half** awake, while: sulph k*
  - **air**; in open | **amel.**: *Aur*
  - **bed** agg.; in: arn carb-an caust nat-m sep upa k*
  - **breath**; when holding his: cact k2*
  - **coition**; after: nat-c j5.de
  - **cough** agg.; during: *Calc* k*
  - **dreams**; after: nit-ac j5.de
  - **eating**; after: arg-n k* camph *Clem* lyc k* **Sel** k*
  - **excitement** agg.: ferr kreos
  - **exertion** | **after** | **agg.**: anac h2
    - **agg.**: ferr iod
  - **fever**; during: *Bell* bro1 *Lil-t* bro1 puls bro1 thuj bro1 zinc h2*
  - **headache**; during: lach pall c1
  - **hemorrhage** from anus, after: kali-c h2

- **Externally**: ...
  - **lying**:
    - **agg.**: calad clem h2 coloc h2 *Glon* k* sel ptk1
    - **side**; on:
      - **right** | **agg.**: arg-n k2 clem h2
  - **menses**; before: cupr thuj
  - **motion**:
    - **agg.**: ant-t *Graph* k* *Iod* sil ptk1
    - **amel.**: *Kreos* k* *Nat-m* k*
  - **music**:
    - **agg.**: (↗*Music - agg.*) kreos
    - **plaintive**: kreos
  - **painful**: acon ptk1 am-m ptk1 *Bell* ptk1 bry h1* *Ferr* ptk1 *Ign* ptk1 polyg-h ptk1 psil ft1 sep ptk1
  - **pregnancy** agg.; during: *Kali-c*
  - **rest**, in: kreos a1
  - **sitting** agg.: anac h2 eupi k* phys k* *Sil* k*
  - **sleep** agg.; during: aesc k2* nat-m sulph
  - **speaking** in company, while: carb-v k*
  - **standing** agg.: alum
  - **starting**, on: *Camph* a1
  - **touches** anything; when body: bell k2 glon
  - **tremulous**: nat-c k*
  - **waking**; on: *Bell* hr1* ferr-i glon k2 *Nat-m* j5.de* nit-ac j5.de sulph j5.de
  - **walking**:
    - **agg.**: *Cact* a1 dig k* ferr
    - **air**; in open:
      - **after** | **agg.**: ambr
- **Glands**: *Am-m* k* arn k* asaf k* bell k* bov k* bry k* *Calc* k* caust k* cham k* clem k* con ptk1 *Kali-c* k* lach j5.de lyc k* m-ambo b2.de* **Merc** k* nat-c k* nit-ac k* *Phos* k* rhod k* *Sabad* k* sep k* *Sil* k* *Sulph* k* thuj k*
- **Internally**: acet-ac k2 **Acon** k* act-sp br1 adren vh1 *Aesc* sf1.de aeth agar k* aloe **Alum** k* alum-p k2* alum-sil k2* am-c k* *Am-m* k* ambr k* *Aml-ns* anac k* ang b2.de* ant-c k* **Ant-t** k* antip vh1 apis bg2 arg-met *Arg-n* k* arn k* *Ars* k* *Ars-i* k* *Asaf* k* asar k* *Atro* sf1.de *Aur* k* aur-ar k2 aur-i k2* aur-s k2* bamb-a stb2.de• bar-c k* bar-i k2* bar-m k2* bar-s k2 *Bell* k* berb j5.de *Borx* k* bov k* **Bry** k* *Cact* calad k* **Calc** k* calc-i k2 calc-p calc-s k2 calc-sil k2* *Camph* k* **Cann-i** *Cann-s* k* canth k* *Caps* k* carb-an k* carb-v k* carbn-s carc tpw2* cassia-s ccrh1• caust k* cedr cench k2* *Cham* k* chel k* chin k* chinin-ar chinin-s j5.de *Cic* k* clem h2* **Cocc** k* coff k* colch *Coloc* k* *Con* croc k* crot-h crot-t cycl k* cypra-eg sde6.de• dendr-pol sk4• *Dig* k* dros k* dulc k* **Ferr** k* ferr-ar k2 **Ferr-i** ferr-s sf1.de galla-q-r nl2• gels k* **Glon** k* *Graph* k* *Ham* sf1.de hell k* helo-s bnm14• hep k* hydrog srj2• hyos k* *Ign* k* *Iod* k* ip k* kali-ar k2 kali-bi bg2* kali-c k* kali-i bg2* kali-m k2 kali-n k* *Kola* stb3• *Kreos* k* lach k* *Laur* k* led k* *Lil-t* sf1.de lyc k* m-aust b2.de mag-c k* mag-m k* mang k* **Meli** *Merc* k* *Merc-c* mez k* mosch k* murx nat-c k* *Nat-m* k* nat-p *Nat-s* nat-sil k2 nit-ac k* nux-m k* *Nux-v* k* ol-an j5.de* *Olnd* k* op k* par k* petr k* ph-ac k* **Phos** k* phys phyt bg2 pic-ac plac-s rly4• *Plan* *Plat* k* *Plb* k* plut-n srj7• positr nl2• *Psor* **Puls** k* pyrog sf1.de ran-b k* rheum k* rhod k* *Rhus-t* k* ruta k* *Sabad* k* sabin k* *Sang* sarr br1 sars k* sec k* **Sel** k* seneg k* **Sep** k* **Sil** k* *Spig* k* *Spong* k* stann k* *Stram* *Stront-c* sf1.de sul-ac k* sul-i k2 *Sulph* k* tab sf1.de *Thuj* k* verat k* verat-v verb k* *Zinc* k* zinc-p k2* [tax jsj7]
  - **chill**; during: *Zinc* b4a.de
  - **eating**; after: lyc b4a.de
  - **fever**; during: *Ars* b4a.de zinc b4a.de
  - **sleep**; preventing: sel c1

O · **Blood** vessels: **Acon** b2.de* **Anac** b2.de* **Ant-t** b2.de* apis bg2 arg-n bg2 **Arn** bg2 ars b2.de* asaf bg2 asar b2.de* aur b4a.de* **Bell** b2.de* bov b2.de* bry b2.de* calad b2.de* **Calc** b2.de* *Canth* b2.de* caps b2.de* *Carb-an* b2.de* carb-v b2.de* chin bg2 *Clem* b2.de* *Coloc* b2.de* *Con* b2.de* croc bg2 cupr b2.de* ferr bg2 *Glon* bg2 graph b2.de* hell b2.de* **Hep** b2.de* **Ign** b2.de* **Iod** b2.de* **Kali-c** b2.de* kali-n b2.de* **Kreos** b2.de* **Merc** b2.de* nat-c b2.de* *Nat-m* b2.de* nit-ac b2.de* *Nux-v* b2.de* ph-ac b2.de* *Phos* b2.de* plat bg2 plb b2.de* positr nl2• **Puls** b2.de* *Rhus-t* b2.de* **Sabad** b2.de* sabin b2.de* sars b2.de* *Sel* b2.de* **Sep** b2.de* *Sil* b2.de* staph b2.de* **Stront-c** b2.de* sulph b2.de* **Thuj** b2.de* *Zinc* b2.de* [tax jsj7]
    - **air**; in open | **amel.**: sabin hr1

- **Blood** vessels: ...
  - **ascending** stairs agg.: petr bg2
  - **cough** agg.; during: *Calc* b4.de
  - **excitement**: stront-c bg2
  - **fever**; during: **Acon** bg2 **Ars** bg2 bell bg2 *Calad* b7.de* chin b7.de* kreos bg2 op b7.de* zinc bg2
  - **motion** agg.: thuj bg2
  - **sleep**; during: nat-m b4.de* phos b4a.de sulph b4.de* zinc b4a.de
  - **ticking** like a clock: ambr bg2
  - **Body**; all over: aesc bg2 alum bg2 ambr bg2 aml-ns bg2 cact bg2 gels bg2 ham bg2 kali-bi bg2 kali-i bg2 lach bg2 lil-t bg2 mag-p bg2 nat-m bg2 ol-an bg2 petr bg2 phos bg2 pyrog bg2 sang bg2 staph bg2 tab bg2 verat-v bg2
- **Joints**: am-m b2.de* arg-met b2.de* dros b2.de* led a1 m-ambo b2.de* *Merc* b2.de* mez b2.de* olnd b2.de* ph-ac b2.de* rhod b2.de* rhus-t b2.de* *Ruta* b2.de* sabad b2.de* spig b2.de* thuj b2.de*
- **Veins**: asaf k1* glon ptk1 ham bg2

- **Upper** part of body: hydrog srj2• nit-ac h2

PULSE:

- **abnormal**: **Acon** k* adon br1 adon-ae hl1 agar k* agn k* am-c k* am-m k* ambr k* ang b2.de* ant-c k* *Ant-t* k* arg-met k* *Arg-n* *Arn* k* **Ars** k* **Ars-i** asaf k* asar k* aur k* bar-c k* **Bell** k* bism k* borx k* bov k* *Bry* k* **Cact** bg2 calad k* calc k* *Camph* k* cann-s k* canth k* caps k* carb-an k* *Carb-v* k* *Carbn-s* caust k* cham k* chel k* *Chin* k* chinin-s bg2 cic k* cina k* cocc k* colch k* coloc k* *Con* k* croc k* **Cupr** k* **Dig** k* dulc k* ferr k* *Gels* *Glon* k* graph k* guaj k* hell k* *Hep* k* **Hyos** k* ign k* **Iod** k* ip k* *Kali-c* k* kali-n k* kalm bg2 **Kreos** k* **Lach** k* *Laur* k* led k* lyc k* m-ambo b2.de* m-arct b2.de m-aust b2.de mang k* *Meli* bg2 meny k* *Merc* k* mez k* mosch k* mur-ac k* nat-m k* nit-ac k* nux-m k* nux-v k* olnd k* **Op** k* par k* petr k* **Ph-ac** k* **Phos** k* plat k* plb k* puls k* pyrog bg2 ran-b k* ran-s k* rheum k* rhod k* **Rhus-t** k* sabad k* sabin k* samb k* sang bg2 *Sec* k* senec seneg k* *Sep* k* **Sil** k* spig k* spong k* squil k* stann k* staph k* **Stram** k* stront-c k* sul-ac k* *Sulph* k* thuj k* valer k* **Verat** k* viol-o k* viol-t k* zinc k*
- **atrial** fibrillation: lyc ser toxo-g jl2
- **audible**: ant-t k* *Camph* bg2 con bg2 *Dig* bg2 hell bg2 iod bg2 kali-c bg2 kreos bg2 merc bg2 neon srj5• op bg2 phos bg2 plb bg2 pyrog c sep bg2 **Spig** bg2 sulph bg2 *Thuj* bg2
- **bounding**: *Acon* hr1* aether a1 alco a1 ars k* atro a1 *Bell* hr1* benz-ac k* calad b7.de* camph k* cann-i k* canth k* chinin-s chlol a1 chlor a1 colch hr1* corn-f a1 dulc hr1* eup-per k* *Eup-pur* hr1* fago a1 gels a1 glon k* iod k* jatr-c a1 kali-chl k* lil-t k* naja paro-i jl3 plan k* raph k* trif-p a1 tub-a jl2 verat-v hr1 visc a1*
  - **ascending** stairs agg.: petr h2
  - **walking** agg.: petr h2
- **contracted**: (↗*hard; spasmodic; thready; wiry*) acet-ac k* acon k* agar k* ant-t k* arn k* ars k* *Asaf* k* aster k* bell k* bism k* borx h2* calc k* calth a1 cann-i k* canth k* chin bg2 cina colch k* crot-t k* cupr bg2 cupr-act a1 hyos k* iod k* *Kali-bi* k* *Kali-br* hr1* kali-s a1 kali-sula a1* kiss a1 lach b7a.de* lact hr1 laur k* merc-cy k* morph a1 nit-ac k* op k* ox-ac k* paeon a1 petr k* phos k* plb k* russ a1 *Sec* k* spira a1 squil a1 stann stram a1 stry a1 sul-ac k* *Tarent* hr1* vip a1 zinc zinc-m a1
- **discordant** with temperature: eberth jl2 *Echi* sne kalm sne lil-t bro1* pic-ac tl1 **Pyrog** c* thyr ptk1 verat-v sne
- **double**, dicrotism: acon bg2* agar k* aml-ns bg2* anan kr1 apis bg2* apoc bg2* *Arg-n* hr1 bell k* cycl k* eberth jl2 ferr bg2* *Gels* bg2* glon iber bg2* *Kali-c* ptk1* *Phos* pilo a1 plb k* rhod bg2 *Stram* k* zinc bg2* zinc-s a1
  - **sitting** agg.: dig br1
- **empty**: alco a1 camph chin ferr bg2 *Lach* hr1* petr k* *Sec* kr1 *Verat* hr1*
- **excited**: ant-t k* anth a1 bar-m hr1 cac a1 caru a1 caust hr1 cyt-l a1 dig bg2 iod k* *Lach* hr1 *Nux-v* k* petr k* plumbg a1 *Ran-b* hr1 sol-t-ae a1 *Verat-v* hr1
  - **evening**: caust tl1
  - **night**: all-c a1 *Nat-c* hr1
- **extrasystoles**: bell-p sp1
- **febrile**: *Acon* k* alum alumn a1 anthraco a1* *Ars* k* *Bell* k* bov k* croc hr1* gins a1 lac-ac k* merc-c k* mez k* morph a1 plb k* sars k* sec k* *Stram* k* *Sulph* hr1* thuj k* vip a1
- **fluttering**: acetan bro1 acon k2* *Adon* bro1 adren bro1 aeth bro1 *Agarin* bro1 ail bro1 am-m bro1 ant-ar bro1 ant-t bro1 apis k* *Arn* k* *Ars* k* *Ars-i* bro1 aspar bro1 *Aur* bro1 bar-m bro1 *Cact* bro1 *Camph* bro1 cann-i k2* carb-ac a1* carb-v bro1 cench k2 cimic k2* coff k2* *Coffin* bro1 colch k* coll bro1 *Conv* bro1 crat bro1 *Crot-h* k* dig k2* diph bro1 *Ferr* bro1 ferr-p tl1 gels k* gins a1 *Hydr-ac* bro1 hyosin-hbr bro1 iod bro1 juni-v a1 *Kali-bi* k* *Kali-c* bro1 kali-chl bro1 kali-n k* kalm bro1 *Lach* bro1 *Lat-m* bro1 *Laur* bro1 lycps-v bro1 merc-c bro1 *Merc-cy* bro1 morph a1* *Mur-ac* bro1 naja bro1 **Nux-v** k* op k* ox-ac bro1 ph-ac k* *Phase* bro1 *Phos* k* phys bro1 plb bro1 ptel a1 pyrog k* rhus-t bro1 sang bro1 *Sapo* bro1 *Saroth* bro1 sec k* ser-ang bro1 *Spig* bro1 stann k* stram k* sul-h a1 sulph bro1 tab bro1 ter bro1 thea a1 *Thyr* bro1 *Verat* hr1* *Verat-v* bro1 visc bro1 (non:zinc k*) zinc-m a1*
  - **fever**; during: eberth mtf11
  - ○ **Body**; all over: dig k2
- **frequent** (= accelerated, elevated, exalted, fast, innumerable, rapid): *Abies-n* bro1 abrot a1 acal st **Acon** k* act-sp vh1 adon bro1* adren bro1* aesc *Aeth* k* aether a1 *Agar* k* agar-pa a1 agar-se a1 *Agn* bro1 *Ail* k* alco a1 all-c k* aloe alum k* alum-p k2 alum-sil k2 alumn kr1 am-be kr1 am-br a1 am-c k* am-m k* am-val bro1 ambr k* *Aml-ns* a1* ammc kr1 amyg a1* anac k* anan kr1 *Ang* b2.de* ant-ar a1* ant-c k* ant-m kr1 *Ant-t* k* anthraco a1* antip bro1 aphis a1* **Apis** k* apoc bro1 apom a1 aq-pet a1 ara-maca sej7• aran-ix jl arg-met k* *Arg-n* **Arn** k* **Ars** k* *Ars-h* kr1 **Ars-i** k* ars-s-f kr1* arum-d a1* arum-i a1 arum-t kr1 *Arund* kr1 *Asaf* k* asar k* asc-c kr1 asc-t a1 asim a1* aster atra-r bnm3• *Atro* a1* **Aur** k* aur-ar k2 aur-i k2 *Aur-m* **Aur-s** k2 aza jl *Bapt* k* bar-act a1 bar-c k* bar-i k2 bar-m k* **Bell** k* ben-n a1 *Benz-ac* **Berb** beryl sp1 bism k* bit-ar wht1• borx k* both a1 bov k* brom k* **Bry** k* bux a1 cac a1 *Cact* bro1 cain a1 caj a1 calad calc k* calc-ar k2* *Camph* k* cann-i cann-xyz bg2 *Canth* k* *Carb-ac* a1* **Carb-an** bg2* carb-v k* carbn-h a1 carbn-o a1 carbn-s k2 cary a1 catal a1 caust k* cedr celt a1 *Cham* k* chel k* *Chim* kr1 chin k* chin-b kr1 chinin-ar *Chinin-s* k* chir-fl gya2 chlf br1 *Chlol* kr1 chlor kr1 chloram jl chlorpr jl chr-ac kr1 cic a1* cimic a1* *Cina* k* cinnb a1 clem k* coc-c coca a1* cocc k* *Coch* kr1 cod a1 coff k* coff-t a1 *Colch* k* **Coll** k* coloc k* **Con** k* *Conv* k* convo-s sp1 cop kr1 corian-s knl6• corn a1* *Crat* bro1* **Croc** b2.de* **Crot-c** k* *Crot-h* k1 crot-t cub a1* cund a1 **Cupr** k* cupr-act a1 cupr-ar kr1 cupr-n a1 cupr-s kr1 cur st cycl cymin br1 cyna jl cyt-l jl* daph kr1 dat-m a1 **Dig** k* digin a1 diph bro1 dor a1* dros tl1 dubo-h hs1 dubo-m a1 dulc a1 dys fmm1• *Echi* emetin mp4• equis-h a1 erech a1 erio a1 ery-a a1 eucal a1* euph fago a1 fagu a1 *Ferr* k* ferr-i ferr-m a1 **Ferr-p** k* fl-ac k* foll jl *Form* kr1 gad a1 gala br1 gamb a1 gast a1 **Gels** k* ger-i rly4• gins a1 **Glon** k* gran a1 grat k* guaj k* guat sp1 gymno a1 hall a1 halo jl ham hed jl *Hell* hell-o a1* helo-s bnm14• hep k* hipp hippoz kr1 hist sp1 hoit jl hydr-ac a1 hydrc a1 *Hyos* k* *Hyper* *Iber* a1* *Ign* k* ignis-alc es2• **Iod** k* ip k* iris a1 ix bnm8• jab a1 jatr-c a1 jug-r a1 kali-ar a1 kali-bi k* kali-br kr1 kali-c k* kali-chl a1* kali-i *Kali-m* kr1 kali-n k* kali-ox a1 *Kali-p* kr1 kali-sula a1* kalm bro1 keroso a1 ketogl-ac rly4• *Kola* stb3• kreos k* *Lac-c* kr1 lac-h htj1*• lacer a1* *Lach* k* lapa a1 lat-m br1* *Laur* k* **Led** b2.de* levo jl lil-s a1 *Lil-t* bro1 linu-c a1 lipp a1 lob loxo-lae bnm12• loxo-recl bnm10*• lyc k* *Lycps-v* k* lyss kr1 m-arct b2.de* m-aust b2.de* *Mag-c* b4a.de* *Mag-m* bg2 *Manc* mang k* med kr1 *Meny* b2.de* **Merc** k* merc-c k* merc-cy merc-d a1 merc-i-f a1 merc-pr-a a1 merc-sul kr1 merl kr1 meth-ae-ae a1 methys jl *Mez* k* mill mom-b a1 *Morph* a1* *Mosch* k* *Mur-ac* k* muscin a1 mygal a1* myric a1 *Naja* k* narc-ps a1* narcot a1 nat-ar *Nat-c* k* nat-f jl* **Nat-m** k* *Nat-s* neon srj5• nicc *Nit-ac* k* nit-s-d a1 nitro-o a1 *Nux-m* k* **Nux-v** k* oena a1 *Ol-j* a1* olib-sac wmh1 olnd k* onos **Op** k* osm ox-ac oxal-a rly4• par k* penic jl* petr k* **Ph-ac** k* phase bro1 phase-vg a1 phel **Phos** k* *Phys* *Phyt* k* pic-ac pieri-b mlk9.de pilo a1* plac-s rly4• *Plat* plat-m a1 *Plb* k* plect a1 podo prun st *Psor* kr1* *Ptel* a1* *Puls* k* pycnop-sa mrz1 pyre-p a1 **Pyrog** k* ran-b k* *Ran-s* k* raph a1 rham-f a1 rheum k* (non:rhod bro1*) rhodi a1 rhodi-o-n slp **Rhus-t** k* *Rhus-v* ric a1 *Rumx* kr1 rumx-act a1 *Ruta* bg2 sabad sabin b2.de* samb k* *Sang* santin a1 sapin a1 saroth jl* sarr a1* sars k* scroph-n a1 scut st **Sec** k* *Sel* b7a.de* seneg k* *Sep* k* ser-ang bro1 **Sil** k* sin-n a1 sol-ni a1 sol-t-ae a1 solin a1 spartin bwa3 **Spig** k* spig-m a1 *Spong* k* **Stann** k* staph k* still kr1 **Stram** k* streptoc rly4• *Stront-c* bg2 stroph-h bro1 stry a1 stry-p br1* suis-em rly4• sul-ac k* sul-h a1 sulfa sp1 sulo-ac jl **Sulph** k* sumb a1 suprar rly4• *Tab* k* tanac a1 tarax a1 **Tarent** a1* tax a1 *Tell* k* tep a1 ter k* *Teucr* bg2 thal jl thal-xyz srj8• thea a1* ther a1 thioc-ac rly4• thiop jl thlas kr1 thuj k* thymol jl* *Thyr* bro1* til a1 tox-th a1 trom a1 tub jl2 tub-a jl2 tung-met bdx1• urt-u a1 vac a1* *Valer* k* vanil fd5.de vario kr1 *Verat* k* **Verat-v** k* vesp viol-o kr1 **Viol-t** b2.de* vip a1 vip-a jl visc a1* wies a1 xan a1 yohim mp4• **Zinc** k* zinc-m a1 **Zinc-p** k2 zinc-s a1 [heroin sdj2]
  - **daytime**: nat-ar nat-m k*
  - **morning**: agar k* ail k* *Ars* k* *Ars-met* kr1 asaf k* atro a1 *Canth* k* cedr k* cench k2 chin chinin-s k1 fago a1 *Graph* k* ign *Kali-c* k* merc-c k* *Mez* hr1* mit a1 myric a1 oena a1 onop jl3 ox-ac k* phos k* phys k* podo k* sang k* suis-em rly4• sulph k* sumb a1 ther a1 thuj k* upa a1 vanil fd5.de
    - **slow** during the day and in the evening; but: **Agar** b4a.de* alum bg2 **Ars** b4a.de* calc bg2 canth bg2 chin bg2 graph bg2 *Ign* bg2* **Kali-c** b4a.de* lyc bg2 mez b4a.de* nux-v bg2 phos bg2 sulph mtf33
    - **waking**; on: alumn a1

- **forenoon**: aphis a1 calc k* chin k* com a1 kola stb3• lyc a1 merc-sul a1 mez k* nat-p a1 oena a1 op k* plan k* ptel a1 trom kr1
- **noon**: ars-h hr1 mit a1 oena a1 ox-ac a1
- **afternoon**: agar hr1* bapt hr1* chel a1 chinin-s a1 chr-ac hr1* ferr-i a1 gels a1 gins a1 kali-chl a1 kali-n h2 lyc merc-sul a1 nat-m a1 oena a1 phos a1 phys a1 phyt a1 podo a1 ptel a1 sumb a1 vanil fd5.de
  - **14 h**: bapt hr1
  - **slow** in the morning, but: **Kali-n** b4a.de* thuj b4a.de* zinc b4a.de*
- **evening**: acon k* alum-sil k2* am-caust a1 anth a1 anthraco kr1 aphis kr1 *Arg-met Arg-n* ars a1 arum-i a1 aster a1 atha a1 bry k* calam sa3• *Caps* hr1 *Carb-an* k* **Caust** k* cench k2 chinin-s a1 *Cinnb* k* *Crot-h* k* *Dulc* euph euphr k* *Ferr* k* gent-l a1 graph k2 ham a1 hell k* hyper a1 *Iod* hr1 jug-r a1 *Lach* k* *Lyc* k* mez k* mill a1 *Mur-ac* murx k* *Nat-c* nat-sil k2* *Nux-v* oena a1 olnd k* ox-ac a1 *Ph-ac Phos* k* plan k* *Puls* k* ran-b k* rheum kr1 sars k* sep *Sil Sulph* sumb a1 teucr a1* *Thuj Tub* upa a1 vanil fd5.de *Zinc* k*
  - **bed** agg.; in: sul-ac h2
  - **slow** in the morning, but: arg-met bg2 arn bg2 asar bg2 carb-an bg2 caust bg2 chin bg2 *Kali-c* bg2 **Kali-n** bg2 *Lyc* bg2 mez bg2 **Olnd** b7a.de* petr bg2 phos bg2 puls bg2 **Ran-b** b7a.de* *Sars* bg2 sep bg2 **Spig** b7a.de* teucr bg2 **Thuj** bg2 **Zinc** bg2
- **night**: alum-sil k2* anthraco a1 *Arn* hr1 arum-i a1 aster a1 cinnb k2* con a1 dulc hr1 *Nat-c* hr1 nat-sil k2* nux-v a1 plect a1 ptel a1
  - **midnight** | **after**: *Benz-ac* hyper a1
  - **slow** by day, but: am-c bg2 borx bg2 *Bry* bg2* calc bg2 carb-an bg2 dulc bg2 hep bg2 kali-n bg2 mag-c bg2* *Merc* bg2* mur-ac bg2 nat-c bg2 nat-m bg2 phos bg2 ran-s bg2 sabin bg2 **Sep** b4a.de* *Sil* bg2 sulph bg2
- **accompanied** by:
  - **heat** of body; increasing: hell-o a1 malar jl2 *Pyrog* jl2
  - **Lungs**; inflammation of the (See CHEST - Inflammation - lungs - accompanied - pulse)
- **alternating** with | **slow** pulse (See slow - alternating)
- **and** intermittent: acon *Adren* vh1 agar k* aloe alum am-m amyg a1 ars *Aur* bell k* benz-ac bism cann-i k* canth carb-ac a1 chin chinin-s colch cupr k* *Dig* gels glon k* grat k* hyos ign kali-chl lob merc-c merc-cy mez mur-ac nat-ar nit-ac nux-m *Nux-v* olnd op ox-ac phos phys plb quinid br1 sep stram k* *Sulph* tab verat-v zinc
- **and** small: acet-ac hr1 **Acon** aeth *Agar* hr1 ail k2 alum amyg a1 apis arn **Ars** k* ars-h a1 ars-i k* asaf *Aur Aur-m* bar-c hr1 bell benz-ac bism bry cain kr1 *Camph* canth k* chin cocc colch coloc *Con* crot-t k* cupr a1 *Dig* k* dulc a1 ferr-m hr1* fl-ac k* gels k* glon grat *Hell* k* hyos ign *Iod* kali-bi kali-br hr1 kali-chl kali-n h2 *Lach* k1 **Laur** led lob k* lyc *Lycps-v* merc-c k* merc-cy *Mur-ac* nat-m nit-ac *Nux-m* **Nux-v** olnd op ox-ac petr phos phyt pic-ac puls ran-s raph rhod rhus-t samb **Sil** sol-t-ae a1 staph **Stram** sul-ac tab k* valer k2 **Verat** visc c1 zinc
  - **and** irregular: *Fl-ac* hr1 visc st
- **and** strong and small: acon apis arn ars bell chin crot-t gels hyos merc-c merc-cy op raph stram
- **breath**; when holding his: cact k2
- **chill**; during: chinin-s a1 coloc a1 crot-t a1 gels a1 zinc a1
- **convulsions**; during: aeth bro1* lac-del hrn2• oena a1 op a1* stram hr1 stry a1 verat-v hr1
- **drinking** agg.; after: nat-m k*
- **eating**; after: *Arg-n* ars-h a1 graph k2 *Iod* **Lyc** k* mez h2* nat-m b4a.de* *Nux-v Phos Puls* rhus-t *Sulph*
- **excitement** agg.: anthraco kr1 bar-m kr1 bell k2 cain kr1 con a1 digox a1 kreos tl1 merc a1
- **exertion** agg.; after: arn tl1
- **faster** than the heartbeat: acon k* arn k* *Rhus-t* k* *Spig* k*
- **fever**; with: malar jl2 pyrog bro1
- **fever**; without: camph tl1
- **headache**; during: bamb-a stb2.de• naja k2
- **motion** agg.: alum-sil k2 ant-t k* apoc bro1 *Arn* bell *Bry* chir-fl gya2 *Dig* k* digin a1 ferr-i gk fl-ac *Gels* glon a1 *Graph Iod Lac-e* hrn2• *Lycps-v* **Nat-m** *Nux-v* ozone sde2• petr k* *Phos* sep k* staph stram
- **noticing** it, when: *Arg-n* k*

- **frequent**: ...
  - **pneumonia**; during (See CHEST - Inflammation - lungs - accompanied - pulse)
  - **rest** agg.: *Mag-m*
  - **restlessness**; with internal: *Kola* stb3•
  - **rising** agg.: *Bry Dig*
  - **sitting** agg.: aspar a1* gins a1 indg a1 *Mag-m* nat-m h2* oena a1
  - **standing** agg.: nat-m h2
  - **stool** agg.; after: *Agar* **Con** glon a1
  - **supper** agg.; after: cupr h2
  - **thinking** of past troubles; when: sep
  - **urine**, with copious: dig h2
  - **vexation**; after: acon arg-n **Cham** coloc ign *Nat-m Nux-v Petr* **Sep** *Staph*
  - **warm** applications, from: sulph
  - **weak**; and: ars b4.de *Guaj* b4a.de iod b4.de *Kali-c* b4a.de mang b4a.de merc b4a.de nat-m b4.de *Phos* b4.de*
- **full**: acet-ac k* **Acon** k* aesc k* aeth c1 aether a1 agar hr1* agar-pa a1 alco a1 *All-c* k* aloe **Alum** bg2* alumn kr1 am-m bro1 *Aml-ns* kr1* *Amyg* a1* anan hr1* ancis-p tsm2 **Ant-t** k* anth a1 antip bro1 apis k* apoc k* aq-pet a1 *Arn* k* ars k* ars-h a1* ars-i ars-met a1* arum-d a1* arum-t hr1* asaf k* asar k* asc-c hr1* asim a1 atro a1* *Aur* bg2* bapt k* bar-c k* bar-i k2* bar-m k* **Bell** k* benz-ac k* **Berb** k* bism k* brom k* **Bry** k* cac a1 *Cact* bro1 cain a1* caj a1 calad a1 **Calc** bg2* camph k* cann-i a1 *Canth* k* carb-ac a1 carbn-o a1 cedr k* celt a1 cent a1 cham k* **Chel** k* *Chin* k* chinin-ar kr1* chinin-s chlf a1 chr-ac a1* cic a1 cimic k* clem a1 coff k* coff-t a1 coffin a1 colch k* coloc k* con k* cor-r k* cori-m a1 cori-r a1 crot-c a1 crot-h k* crot-t k* cub a1* *Cupr* k* cupr-act a1 cupr-s a1* cycl k* cyt-l a1 daph dat-f a1 **Dig** k* digin a1 dirc a1 dor a1 *Dulc* k* (non:eup-per slp) *Eup-pur* a1* fago a1* ferr k* ferr-p k* gast a1 **Gels** k* gins k* *Glon* k* **Graph** b4a.de* ham k* hell k* *Hep* k* hydr-ac a1 **Hyos** k* iber a1* ictod bro1 *Ign* k* iod k* jab a1 jug-r a1 juni-v a1 kali-bi k* *Kali-c* k* kali-chl k* kali-i k* kali-m kr1* **Kali-n** k* kali-ox a1 kreos bg2* lac-ac a1 *Lach* k* laur k* *Led* k* *Lil-t* bro1 linu-c a1 lipp a1 lyc k* lycps-v bro1 m-arct b2.de menth a1 *Merc* k* merc-c k* merc-cy k* merc-pr-a a1 merl hr1* *Mez* k* mill k* morph a1 *Mosch* k* mur-ac k* myric a1 *Naja* nat-m k* *Nat-n* sf1.de nat-p bg2 nit-ac k* nitro-o a1 *Nux-v* k* ol-an a1 olnd k* onos bro1 *Op* k* ox-ac k* par k* *Petr* k* *Ph-ac* k* phel k* *Phos* k* *Phys* a1* phyt k* pilo a1* plan k* plb k* plect a1 ptel c1 puls bg2* ran-b k* ran-s k* raph a1 rat a1 rhus-t k* sabad k* *Sabin* k* samb k* sang k* sarr k* sars scroph-n a1 sec bg2 *Sel* seneg k* *Sep* k* *Sil* k* sin-a a1* sin-n a1* sium a1 sol-ni a1 *Spig* k* spira a1 spirae a1 spong k* **Stram** k* stront-c k* sul-ac k* *Sulph* k* sumb a1 *Tab* k* tanac a1 tarax a1 tarent k* tell k* tep a1 thea a1 thuj k* til a1 toxi a1 trif-p a1 trom a1 valer k* vanil fd5.de *Verat* k* *Verat-v* k* vinc a1 viol-o k* vip a1 visc a1* yuc a1 zinc zing a1
  - **right**: kali-chl ptk1
  - **morning**: *Canth* hr1* cedr a1 jac-c a1 phos k* phyt k* sep zinc
  - **forenoon**: nat-ar a1 trom kr1 zing a1
  - **afternoon**: iod k* nat-ar a1 phyt a1 zinc zing a1
  - **evening**: acon k* anth a1 anthraco kr1 hell k* myric a1 olnd k* ran-b k* scut a1 seneg sulph k* thuj k* zinc zing a1*
  - **night**: com a1 *Merc* sep a1* vanil fd5.de
  - **hard**; and: *Acon* b7.de* bar-c b4a.de bell b4.de* *Bry* ptk1 canth b7.de chel b7.de cupr b7.de *Kali-n* b4a.de **Phos** b4.de* stram b7.de
  - **weak**; and: *Ferr-p* ptk1 gels ptk1 verat ptk1
- **hard**: (↗*contracted*) **Acon** k* aesc k* aeth hr1* aether a1 agar-cps a1 agar-pa a1 agro a1 alco a1 *All-c* k* all-s hr1* alum hr1 am-c k* am-caust a1 am-m k* *Aml-ns* kr1 ammc hr1* *Amyg* a1* anan hr1* anil a1 ant-c k* ant-m kr1 *Ant-t* k* apis b7a.de* *Arn* k* ars k* ars-h a1* ars-i k* ars-s-f a1* arum-d a1* asaf k* asar k* aster k* atro a1 *Bar-c* k* bar-i k2* bar-m **Bell** k* *Benz-ac* k* **Berb** k* bism k* brom k* **Bry** k* *Cact* k* calad k* *Calc* hr1 calth a1 camph k* *Canth* k* carb-ac a1 carbn-s a1 cent a1 cham k* **Chel** k* *Chin* k* chlol a1 chlor a1 cimic k* *Cina* k* clem bg2 cocc k* coff k* coffin a1 colch k* coloc k* con k* cor-r k* corn a1* crot-h a1 cub a1 *Cupr* k* *Cupr-act* a1 cupr-s a1* cycl k* cyna jl3 daph *Dig* k* digin a1 dulc k* *Ferr* k* gast a1 gels k* glon k* gran a1 **Graph** b4a.de* ham k* hell k* *Hep* k* **Hyos** k* hyper a1* iber a1 *Ign* k* indg a1 iod k* jatr-c a1 kali-bi k* *Kali-c* k* kali-chl k13 kali-i k* kali-m k2 *Kali-n* k* *Kreos* k* *Lach* k* laur bg2 *Led* k* lyc k* *Lycps-v* kr1 m-ambo b2.de m-arct b2.de *Merc* k* merc-c k* merc-cy k* merc-d a1 *Merc-pr-r* a1 mez k* morph a1 *Mosch* k* mur-ac k* nat-c h2* nat-m k* nat-sil fd3.de• *Nit-ac* k* nit-s-d a1 nitro-o a1 *Nux-v* k* olnd k* op k* ox-ac k* par k*

- **hard**: ...
petr k* ph-ac k* phel k* *Phos* k* phyt k* plb k* plect a1 plumbg a1 ptel c1 puls bg2* pyrog tl1 ran-b k* ran-s k* rauw sp1 rhus-t hr1 sabin k* samb k* sang hr1* sec k* seneg k* *Sep* k* serp a1 *Sil* k* sin-a a1 sol-mm a1 sol-t-ae a1 spig k* spira a1 spong k* squil k* **Stram** k* **Stront-c** bg2* stroph-s sp1 *Stry* a1 sul-h a1 *Sulph* k* tab k* tanac a1 tarent k* tep a1 *Ter* k* thuj a1 til a1 uva a1 valer k* verat k* verat-v k* vinc a1* viol-o k* vip a1 wies a1 zinc k* zinc-m a1
  - **morning**: petr k* phyt k* zinc
  - **forenoon** | **11** h: zing a1
  - **noon**: ox-ac k*
  - **evening**: all-c k* aster hr1 *Bapt* k* dulc k* plb plumbg k* ran-b hr1* zing a1*
  - **climbing**, after: rauw sp1
  - **convulsions**; during: aeth bro1*
  - **excitement**; with: stroph-s sp1
  - **exertion**, after sudden: rauw sp1
  - **old** people; in: **Ant-t** hr1*
  - **slow**, and: stroph-s sp1
- **heavy**: abies-n br1 crot-c a1 phos k* stram k* *Verat-v* hr1* yuc a1
  - **night**: com a1
- **imperceptible**: *(↗soft; weak)* **Acon** k* aeth hr1* agar a1 agn k* am-c hr1* amyg a1* anil a1 ant-t k* *Apis* b7a.de* *Arg-n* hr1* arn bg2 *Ars* k* ars-h hr1* ars-s-f a1* atra-r bnm3• bell k* benz-ac *Cact* k* cadm-br a1 **Camph** b7a.de* cann-i cann-s k* *Canth* k* *Carb-ac* k* **Carb-v** k* carbn a1 carbn-h a1 chel k* chin k* chlol a1* chlor a1 cic k* cic-m a1 cit-l a1* *Cocc* k* **Colch** k* coloc con h2* crot-h k* cub a1 **Cupr** k* cupr-ar a1 cyt-l a1* dig bg2 digin a1 dulc k* ferr k* gels a1* gins a1 guaj k* hell k* **Hydr-ac** bg2* hyos k* iod b2.de* *Ip* k* kali-cy a1 kalm k* kreos k* lach k* laur k* *Led* bg2 m-aust b2.de* mand sp1 med k2 *Merc* k* merc-c k* morph a1 *Mosch* bg2* *Naja* nit-s-d bg nux-v k* oena a1 *Op* k* ox-ac k* petr a1 ph-ac k* phase-vg a1 phos k* *Phyt* hr1* plat k* plb k* *Podo* hr1* puls k* rhus-t k* *Sec* k* **Sil** k* stann k* stram k* stry a1 sul-ac k* sul-h a1 sulph k* tab k* tanac a1 tax a1 thuj bg2 **Verat** k* zinc k*
  - **almost**: acetan bro1 **Acon** k* *Adon* bro1 adren bro1 aeth gt1* agar h2 *Agarin* bro1 agn a1 ail bro1 am-c am-m bro1 aml-ns a1 ant-ar bro1 ant-t k* *Apis* k* apoc k2 arn bro1 *Ars* k* *Ars-i* bro1 aspar bro1 *Aur* bro1 bar-m bro1 bell *Cact* bro1 **Camph** k* carb-ac bro1 carb-v bro1 carbn-o a1 chin chlor a1 cic-m a1 cimic bro1 coff-t a1 *Coffin* bro1 colch bro1 coll bro1 *Conv* bro1 crat br1* crot-h k* cub c1 cyt-l sp1 dig k* digin a1 diph bro1 ferr k* **Gels** k* glon ham hell *Hydr-ac* a1* hydrc a1 hyosin-hbr bro1 iod bro1 *Ip* kali-bi *Kali-c* bro1 kali-chl bro1 kali-n bro1 kalm bro1 *Lach* k* *Lat-m* bro1 *Laur* k* lycps-v bro1 mand sp1 mang *Merc* merc-c a1* *Merc-cy* bro1 morph a1* *Mur-ac* bro1 *Naja* k* nit-s-d bg olnd op k* ox-ac k* ph-ac k* *Phase* bro1 phos k* phys bro1 plb k* *Podo Puls Rhus-t* k* *Ric* a1 sang bro1 *Sapo* bro1 *Saroth* bro1 sec bro1 seneg ser-ang bro1 sol-ni a1 sol-t a1 *Spig* bro1 *Spong Stram* sulph bro1 *Tab* k* ter bro1 tere-ch jl3 thea a1 ther *Thyr* bro1 *Verat* k* *Verat-v* bro1 vip a1 visc bro1 zinc k*
    - **convulsions**; during: nux-v olnd
    - **stupor**; during: hep
  - **chill**; during: ars b4a.de
- **intermittent**: acet-ac k* *Acon* k* acon-c a1 adon ptk1 *Aeth* k* *Agar* k* agar-pa a1 aloe alum k* alumn a1* am-c k* am-m k* amyg hr1* ang k* ant-t bg2* apis k* *Apoc* bg2* *Arg-n* k* arn bg2* *Ars* k* ars-h hr1* ars-i k2* ars-s-f k2* asaf k* *Atro* a1* *Aur* k* bapt bg2* bell k* ben-n a1 benz-ac k* bism k* brom *Bry* k* *Cact* bg2* calc-ar k2 calth a1 *Camph* k* cann-i a1 *Canth* k* *Caps* k* carb-ac k* carb-an a1 *Carb-v* k* *Cedr* k* cere-b a1 **Chin** k* chinin-s *Chlol* a1* chlor a1 cic-m a1 cimic a1 *Cimx* k* cinnb a1 cocc-s hr1 coff k* coff-t a1 coffin a1 *Colch* k* *Con* k* conv k* *Crat* bro1* *Croc* hr1 *Crot-h* k* cub a1* cupr k* cupr-act a1 daph dat-m a1 **Dig** k* digin a1 digox a1 *Dios* hr1 dulc a1 fago a1 ferr k* ferr-m bro1 frag a1 gast a1 *Gels* k* glon k* grat k* *Hep* k* hura a1 hydr-ac a1* hyos k* *Iber* bro1* ign k* *Iod* k* jatr-c a1 juni-v a1 kali-bi *Kali-c* k* kali-chl k* *Kali-i* k* kali-m k2 kali-p k* *Kalm* k* keroso a1 *Kola* stb3• *Kreos* hr1* *Lach* k* lapa a1 *Laur* k* *Lil-t* k* lipp a1 lob k* *Lyc* hr1 *Lycps-v* k* lyss hr1* mag-p bg2 meny bg2 **Merc** k* *Merc-c* k* merc-cy a1* merc-sul a1 meth-ae-ae a1 mez k* morph a1 mur-ac k* murx bg2 naja nat-ar **Nat-m** k* *Nit-ac* k* nit-s-d hr1* nitro-o a1 nux-m k* nux-v k* olnd k* *Op* k* *Ox-ac* k* **Ph-ac** k* phos k* phys a1 phyt k* pip-n bro1 plan a1 *Plb* k* prun-v st1 *Ptel* a1* *Ran-s* hr1* *Rhus-t* k* sabin k* *Samb* k* scut a1 **Sec** k* *Sep* k* *Spig* k* staph bg2 *Stram* k* *Stroph-h* bro1* stry a1 sul-ac k* *Sulph* k* *Tab* k* *Tarent* hr1* ter bg2* thea k* thuj k* trif-p a1 trom a1* vario hr1 verat k* **Verat-v** k* vip a1 xan c1 *Zinc* k* *Zinc-p* k2*
- **intermittent**: ...
  - **dinner**; after: nat-m h2*
  - **eating**; after: nat-m b4a.de
  - **every** second beat: *Spig* kr1
  - **fifth** beat: ars-h kr1 *Chel* kr1 *Coca* kr1* crot-h sf1.de nit-ac sf1.de *Nux-v* kr1
  - **fortieth** to sixtieth beat: agar kr1 ars-h kr1
  - **fourth** beat: *Apis* kr1 *Calc-ar* kr1* cimic bg2* dig bg2 iber kr1 *Mur-ac* kr1 **Nit-ac** b4a.de* *Nux-v* kr1 *Sulph* kr1 tab bg2
    - **fifth** beat; or: colch b7a.de nux-v b7a.de*
    - **skips** every: nit-ac k2
  - **menses**; before: *Kali-c* k13*
  - **old** people; in: bapt br1 tab k*
  - **one** to two beats: nat-m bg2 ph-ac b4a.de*
  - **seventeenth** beat: *Cina* hr1
  - **sixth** beat: acon bg2 ars-h kr1 *Chel* kr1
  - **tenth** beat after exertion or vexation: gels sf1.de
  - **tenth** to thirtieth beat: agar b4a.de* *Cina* kr1 kali-m kr1 lach bg2
  - **third** beat: *Apis* bg2* ars-h kr1 arum-t bg2 cimic bg2* dig bg2 iber kr1 kali-c sf1.de *Mur-ac* b4a.de* nat-m bg2* nit-ac sf1.de* phase kl *Sulph* kr1 vib kr1
    - **fifth** beat; or: crot-h sf1.de *Nit-ac* kr1*
    - **fourth** beat; or: apis kl *Cimic* sf1.de*
    - **seventh** beat; to: dig bro1* mur-ac bro1*
- **irregular**: *(↗CHEST - Palpitation - irregular)* abies-n bg2 acetan bro1 *Acon* k* acon-c a1 acon-s a1 *Adon* bg2* *Adren* bro1* aeth hr1* *Agar* k* agar-pa a1 *Agarin* bro1 aloe alum k* alum-p k2* am-c bg2 am-caust a1 aml-ns anac jl3 ang k* anh jl3 anil a1 **Ant-c** k* ant-t k* antip bro1 apis apoc k* arg-met *Arg-n* k* arn k* **Ars** k* ars-h hr1* *Ars-i* k* ars-s-f k2* arum-d a1* asaf k* asar jl *Aspar* k* *Atro* a1* *Aur* k* aur-ar k2 *Aur-s* k2* bapt bar-act a1 bar-c hr1* bar-m a1 bell k* bell-p sp1* ben-n a1 benz-ac k* bism k* bol-lu a1 *Bry* k* bufo bg2 *Cact* k* cael jl3 calc k* calen a1* *Camph* k* cann-i k* cann-xyz bg2* *Canth* k* *Caps* k* carb-ac k* carb-an *Carb-v* k* carbn a1 carbn-o a1 cary a1 caust bg2 *Cedr* hr1 cere-b a1 cham k* chel k* **Chin** k* chinin-s k* chlam-tr bcx2• chlf a1 *Chlol* a1* chlor a1 chlorpr jl3 chr-ac a1* *Cimic* k* *Cimx* cinch a1 clem a1 coff coffin a1* *Colch* k* *Con* k* *Conv* br1* convo-s sp1* cor-r k* cortico jl3 *Crat* br1* *Crot-h* k* cub a1* cupr k* cupr-act a1 cyt-l a1* **Dig** k* *Digin* a1 digox a1 dirc a1* dulc a1 euph a1 fago a1 ferr k2* ferr-p bg2 form a1 gala br1 *Gels* k* gins a1 glon k* glycyr-g cte1• guare a1 ham k* hed jl3 hell k* *Hep* k* hir jl3 hist jl3 home a1 *Hydr-ac* a1* *Hyos* k* *Iber* a1* ign k* iod k* jab a1* jatr-c a1 juni-v a1 *Kali-bi* k* *Kali-c* k* kali-chl kali-cy a1 *Kali-i* k* kali-m k2 kali-n a1 kali-p k* kali-s a1 kali-sula a1* *Kalm* k* ketogl-ac rly4• *Kola* stb3• kou br1 **Lach** k* lachn hr1* lat-m bnm6• laur k* *Lil-t* hr1* lob k* lol a1 *Lycps-v* k* lyss hr1 m-ambo b2.de* mag-p bg2 mag-s sp1* manc bg2* mang k* meny meph jl3 *Merc* k* *Merc-c* k* merc-cy k* merc-i-f a1* merc-sul a1* mez k* morph a1 *Mosch* hr1 *Mur-ac* b2.de* myric hr1* *Naja* k* nat-ar nat-f sp1* **Nat-m** k* nat-n sf1.de nat-s a1 nicc a1 nit-ac k* nit-s-d a1 nux-m bg2* nux-v k* oena a1 *Olnd* k* onop jl3 *Op* k* ox-ac k* ozone sde2• parathyr jl2 penic jl3 **Ph-ac** k* *Phase* bro1 *Phos* k* phys k* *Phyt* k* pic-ac a1 pilo bro1 pip-n bg2 *Plan* k* *Plb* k* prun-v st1 psor k2* ptel a1 puls bg2* pyrog rauw sp1 *Rhus-t* k* sabad k* sabin k* sacch a1 *Samb* k* *Sang* k* sangin-t c1 santin a1 *Saroth* bro1* **Sec** k* seneg k* *Sep* k* ser-ang bro1 *Sil* k* sol-ni a1 sol-t-ae a1 *Spig* k* *Squil* bg2* stann bg2 *Still* k* **Stram** k* stroph-h bg* stroph-s sp1 stry a1 stry-ar bro1 stry-p br1* sul-ac k* sul-h a1 sulfa jl3 sulo-ac a1 *Sulph* k* *Sumb* bg2* symph fd3.de• *Tab* k* tanac a1 tarent a1* tax a1 ter a1* thea k* thiop jl3 thuj k* trach a1 trif-p a1 tritic-vg fd5.de *Tub* jl2* uva a1* valer k* vanil fd5.de *Verat* k* **Verat-v** k* vib hr1* vip bg2* vip-a jl3 visc c1* wies a1 xan a1* yuc a1 zinc k* *Zinc-p* k2*
  - **morning**: atro a1 caust h2* fago a1 myric a1 phos a1 still a1 sumb a1
  - **and** slow: acon arn ars asaf bell camph cann-i chel chin cimic colch **Dig** dulc ham hell hyos iod *Kali-br* hr1 **Kalm** laur lob merc-c merc-cy mez *Naja* k* nit-ac nux-v olnd op ox-ac ph-ac phys phyt plb rhus-t seneg sul-ac tab verat **Verat-v** zinc
    - **and** violent: dig k2
  - **coma**; with (See MIND - Coma - pulse - irregular)
  - **exertion**, on slight: *Arg-n* dig k2 meny *Nat-m*
  - **lying** | **back**; on | **agg.**: arg-n tell rsj10•
    - **side**; on | **left** | **agg.**: *Nat-m* kr1
      - **right** | **agg.**: tell rsj10•
  - **lying** down agg.: lycps-v a1 still a1 vanil fd5.de

- **irregular**: ...
  - **sitting** agg.: dig br1
  - **stool** agg.; after: *Agar*
- **irritable**: agar hr1 ant-t hr1 arg-met ars k* ars-i br1 bar-m hr1 camph a1* chlol hr1 colch k* cop hr1 cupr hr1 cupr-ar a1* dig k* hydr-ac a1 iod k* kali-bi k* kali-br k* meny k* nux-v hr1 ox-ac k* psor hr1 puls hr1 raph a1 serp a1 stram k* sulph hr1 tab k* tarent hr1 vario hr1
  - **accompanied** by | **apoplexy** (See Apoplexy - accompanied - pulse - irritable)
- **jerking**: acon k* agar bg2 aml-ns bg2* *Arn* bg2 ars bg2* arum-d bg2* aur bar-c k* calad bg2* canth bg2 con bg2 dig bg2* digin a1 dulc k* fago bg2* gins bg2* glon bg2* **Iber** a1* jatr-c bg2* nat-m bg2 nat-p bg2* nux-v bg2 plb k* thuj bg2
- **labored**: *Apoc* vh1 crot-h hr1* cupr cupr-act a1 dig k2 hydr a1 iris kreos k* merc merc-c a1 merc-i-f a1* mit a1 morph a1 op k* stram k*
  - **motion**; from slightest: dig k2
- **large**: acon ptk1 **Apis** kr1 atro a1 *Aur-m* hr1 **Bell** a1* *Bry* a1 camph a1 cench a1 *Chel* a1 chinin-s a1 colch hr1* **Con** a1* cupr-act a1 ferr a1 *Ferr-p* ptk1 gels hr1 gins a1 **Iod** a1* ip hr1* jatr-c a1 kali-cy a1 lycps-v ptk1 manc ptk1 op a1 phos ptk1 plb a1 spira a1 stry a1 sul-ac a1 syph ptk1 *Tab* hr1* *Verat-v* ptk1
- **rapid** (See frequent)
- **shaking** the body: arg-n bg2 nat-m bg2
- **slow** (= bradycardia): *Abies-n* bro1 acet-ac k* *Acetan* vh1 achy jl3 *Acon* k* acon-c a1 acon-f k* acon-l a1 adon br1* adren bro1 aesc bg2* aeth k* aether a1 *Agar* k* agar-cps a1 agar-pa a1 agn k* *All-c* hr1* alumn hr1 am-caust a1 am-n a1 aml-ns a1* *Amyg* k* *Anac-oc* hr1 anan hr1* anh sp1* anil a1 ant-c k* *Ant-t* k* apis bg2 apoc k* arn k* ars k* ars-met kr1 ars-s-f a1* asaf k* asc-c c1 asc-t hr1* *Aspar* k* atra-r bnm3• atro a1 bacls-7 fmm1• bapt k* bar-act a1 bar-i k2 *Bell* k* ben-n a1 benz-ac k* benzol br1 **Berb** k* bit-ar wht1• both a1 brom k* cact bro1 cain a1 *Camph* k* **Cann-i** k* *Cann-s* k* cann-xyz ptk1 *Canth* k* *Caps* k* carb-ac a1* carbn-o a1 carbn-s k2 catal a1 caust k* cench a1 cent a1 *Chel* k* chin k* *Chinin-s* chir-fl bnm4• chlf a1 chlol a1 chlor a1* chr-ac a1 cic k* cimic k* cinch a1 coca a1 cocc tl1 coff-t a1 colch k* coli jl2 coloc k* *Con* k* croc a1 *Crot-h* k* cryp a1 cub a1* cund a1 *Cupr* k* cupr-am-s a1 cupr-cy hsa1 cur st1 cyt-l a1 daph hr1* dat-f a1 delphin a1 **Dig** k* digin a1 digox a1 dios hr1 dirc a1 dub a1 dubo-m a1 dulc k* enteroc jl2 eryt-j a1 esin bro1 euph hr1 euph-c a1 eupi a1* fago a1 ferr k* ferr-ma a1 gast a1 **Gels** k* gins a1 glon k* glycyr-g cte1• grat a1* ham k* *Hell* k* hell-o c1 helo bro1 helo-s rwt2• hep k* hippoz hr1* home a1 hydr bg2* hydr-ac k* hyos k* ign k* iod k* iris jab a1 jac-c a1 jatr-c a1 juni-v a1 kali-bi k* *Kali-br* hr1* kali-c k* kali-chl k* kali-cy a1 kali-m k2 kali-n k* kali-s a1 kali-sula a1* **Kalm** k* kou br1 kreos k* kres jl3 lach k* lachn k* lact a1* lat-k a1 lat-m a1* *Laur* k* lept hr1 *Lob* k* lon-x a1 *Lup* a1* lycpr bro1 *Lycps-v* mag-c bg2 *Mag-m* hr1 mag-s j5.de* *Manc* k* *Mang* b4a.de* mec a1 meny k* meph jl3 merc k* merc-c k* merc-cy k* merc-sul hr1* meth-ae-ae a1 mez k* *Morph* a1* mosch k* mur-ac k* myric k* *Naja* k* naphthoq mtf11 narc-ps br1 narcot a1 nat-ar kr1 nat-c h2* *Nat-m* b4a.de* nat-n bg* nit-ac k* nit-s-d a1* nitro-o a1 *Nux-m* k* nux-v k* oena a1 ol-an bg* olnd k* **Op** k* ox-ac k* par k* parathyr jl2 pen a1 petr k* ph-ac k* phel a1 phos k* phys k* phyt k* pic-ac k* pip-n bg2* pitu sp1 pitu-p sp1 plb k* *Podo* k* prop a1 prun a1 prun-p a1* puls k* ran-b bg2 raph a1 rauw sp1 rhod k* rhus-t k* ruta samars a4 samb k* *Sang* k* sars k* *Sec* k* **Sep** k* sil k* sol-ni a1 solin a1 spartin-s br1 spig k* spong k* squil k* **Stram** k* stroph-s sp1 stry a1 sulo-ac a1 sumb a1 *Tab* k* tanac a1 *Tarent* hr1* tax a1 *Tela* vh ter hr1 thal-xyz srj8• thea a1 ther hr1* thiop jl3 thuj k* thymol sp1* trif-p a1 trios rsj11* upa a1 uva a1 valer k* **Verat** k* **Verat-v** k* verb a1 vip a1 visc a1* wies a1 wye a1 zinc k* zing hr1*
  - **daytime**: dulc kr1 graph k2* *Mur-ac* k* sep k*
  - **morning**: arg-met chinin-s grat k* jac-c a1 lycps-v a1 myric a1 olnd k* petr k* ran-b hr1 sars hr1 sep h2 thuj hr1 zinc hr1
  - **forenoon**: cinnb k* myric a1
  - **afternoon**: chinin-s gins a1 myric a1 ox-ac k*
  - **evening**: ars k* cund a1 *Graph* k* mez hr1 myric a1 nat-ar phyt k* ran-b k2
  - **night**: phys a1
  - **accompanied** by:
    - **apoplexy** (See Apoplexy - accompanied - pulse - slow)
    - **hypotension**: nat-pyru mtf11
    - **nausea**: kalm br1
  - **alternating** with frequent pulse: bell bg2 chin bro1* cic jl cimic jl dig bro1* *Gels* bro1* iod bro1* lat-m bnm6• *Morph* bro1* rhus-t bg2* stroph-h ptk1 stroph-s sp1
  - **bounding**, full and: visc st1

- **slow**: ...
  - **chill**; during: brach hr1 cann-i a1 gins a1 glon a1 hipp a1 *Hydr* hr1 meny hr1 mur-ac h2* sep a1
  - **coma**; with (See MIND - Coma - pulse - slow)
  - **dullness**; with (See MIND - Dullness - pulse)
  - **fever**; with: chinin-s bro1 karw-h jl3 nat-m sne op bro1
  - **headache**; during: gels psa
  - **lying** agg.: dig h2*
  - **masturbation**; after: dig ptk2
  - **old** people; in: gels br1
  - **pregnancy**: gels c1
  - **puberty**; in: dig ptk1*
  - **rest** agg.: arn tl1 dig bg2
    - **faster**; and | **exertion** agg.; after: arn tl1
  - **sexual** abuse; after: dig ptk2*
  - **sexual** excess; after: dig ptk2*
  - **slower** than the beat of heart: agar k* cann-s k* *Dig* k* dulc k* hell k* **Kali-i** bg2 *Kali-n* k* kola stb3• kres srb2.fr laur k* lyc bg2 *Nat-m* bg2 sec k* verat k*
  - **vertigo**; with (See VERTIGO - Pulse - slow)
  - **very**: cub c1
  - **vomiting**, on: squil h1
- **small**: abrot hr1 acal hr1 **Acon** k* acon-c a1 acon-f a1 acon-s a1 *Aeth* a1* aether a1 *Agar* k* agar-pa a1 agn c1 agro a1 ail a1 alco a1 ald a1 alum k* am-c b2.de* am-caust a1 ammc hr1* amyg a1 ant-c k* ant-m a1* *Ant-t* k* apis k* apoc hr1* *Arg-n* hr1 arn k* **Ars** k* ars-h a1* *Ars-i* ars-s-f a1* arum-d a1* asaf k* asc-t a1* aspar a1 aster hr1* atro a1* *Aur* k* aur-ar k2 *Aur-m* k* *Aur-s* k2* *Bapt* hr1 bar-c k* bar-i k2* bar-m *Bell* k* ben-n a1 benz-ac bism k* bol-lu a1 *Brom* hr1 bry k* *Cact* hr1 caj a1 calad k* calc k* calth a1 **Camph** k* cann-i k* cann-s k* canth k* carb-ac k* carb-an bg2 **Carb-v** k* carbn-h a1 cary a1 catal a1 caust a1 *Cham* k* **Chel** bg2* *Chin* k* *Chinin-ar* kr1 chinin-s kr1 chlf a1 *Chlor* a1* cic k* *Cina* b2.de* cinch a1 clem bg2* coca kr1 *Cocc* k* *Coch* hr1 cod a1 coff hr1* coff-t hr1 *Colch* k* coll tl1 *Coloc* b4a.de* *Con* k* conin a1 cop a1 croc bg2* *Crot-h* hr1* crot-t a1 cub a1* cund k* **Cupr** k* cupr-ar a1* cupr-n a1 cupr-s hr1* cyt-l a1 delphin a1 **Dig** k* digin a1 *Dulc* k* euph-l a1 ferr k* ferr-m a1* fl-ac a1* frag a1 gels k* glon a1* graph bg2 grat k* **Guaj** k* gymno a1 haem a1 *Hell* k* helo a1 helo-s rwt2• helon a1 *Hep* hr1 hippoz hr1* hydr-ac a1 *Hyos* k* iber a1 ign k* *Iod* k* ip k* juni-v a1 kali-ar a1* kali-bi k* *Kali-br* hr1* *Kali-c* k* kali-chl k* kali-cy a1 kali-fcy a1 kali-i k* kali-m kr1* kali-n k* *Kali-p* hr1* kali-s a1 kali-sula a1* *Kalm* hr1 keroso a1 *Kreos* k* lac-ac k* lac-c hr1 *Lach* k* **Laur** k* led k* lil-t a1 *Lob* k* lyc k* *Lycps-v* kr1 lyss hr1 m-ambo b2.de* m-aust b2.de* *Mag-m* hr1 mang k* meny k* *Merc* k* merc-br a1 merc-c k* merc-cy k* merc-d a1 merc-n a1 merc-ns a1 *Merc-pr-r* a1 merc-sul hr1* meth-ae-ae a1 *Mez* hr1* morph a1 mosch bg2 *Mur-ac* k* naja bg2 narcot a1 nat-br a1 nat-m k* nat-n a1 nat-s a1 nit-ac k* nit-s-d a1 *Nux-m* k* nux-v k* oena a1 *Ol-j* hr1* olnd a1 *Op* k* ox-ac k* past a1 peti a1 petr k* *Ph-ac* k* *Phos* k* phys k* phyt k* pic-ac k* *Plat* k* plb k* plumbg a1 podo k* prun a1 prun-p a1* ptel a1 puls k* pyrog bro1* ran-a a1 ran-b k* ran-s k* *Raph* k* rhod k* rhus-t k* ric a1 rumx-act a1 russ a1 ruta a1 sabad k* sal-ac hr1* *Samb* k* *Sang* hr1* sarr a1* **Sec** k* seneg k* serp a1 **Sil** k* sol-ni a1 sol-t a1 sol-t-ae a1 solin a1 spartin-s bwa2 spig k* spirae a1 spong bg2* squil k* *Stann* k* staph k* **Stram** k* stroph-h ptk1 stry a1 *Sul-ac* k* *Sulph* k* sumb a1 tab bg2* tanac a1 *Tarent* hr1* tax a1 *Ter* k* thea a1 ther ptk1 thuj k* til a1 upa a1 uva a1* valer k* **Verat** k* *Verat-v* ptk1 vesp a1* viol-o k* vip a1 visc a1* wies a1 zinc k* *Zinc-m* a1 *Zinc-p* k2* zinc-s a1
  - **left** side: kali-chl ptk1
  - **accompanied** by | **apoplexy** (See Apoplexy - accompanied - pulse - small)
  - **convulsions**; during: aeth bro1*
  - **frequent**; and: ars b4.de* aur b4.de* bry b7a.de *Calc* b4a.de carb-v b4a.de *Chel* b7a.de ign b7.de iod b4.de lach b7.de meny b7.de *Merc-c* b4a.de nux-v b7a.de phos b4.de* **Samb** b7a.de sil b4.de* *Stann* b4.de *Stram* b7.de* zinc b4.de
  - **regular**; and: cupr-n a1
- **soft**: (↗*imperceptible; weak*) acal bro1 acet-ac k* *Acon* k* aesc k* aeth k* aether a1 agar k* agn k* ancis-p tsm2 ant-c k* ant-s-aur a1 **Ant-t** k* anth a1 apis apoc arn k* *Ars* k* ars-h hr1* arum-d a1 aspar a1 aster k* atra-r bnm3• atro a1 *Aur* k* bapt k* bar-c k* bar-m k* bell k* bism k* brom hr1

- **soft**: ...
bry k* cact hr1 calc-ar st1 calc-i a1 camph k* cann-i cann-s k* canth k* *Carb-ac* **Carb-v** k* carbn-o a1 carbn-s a1 cham k* chel a1 chin k* chlf a1 *Chlor* a1* cic k* cinch a1 cit-l a1 clem a1 cocc k* *Coffin* bro1 *Colch* k* con k* conv k* crot-h k* cub hr1* **Cupr** k* cupr-s hr1* cyt-l a1 **Dig** k* digin a1 digox a1 dulc k* ery-a a1 euph k* ferr k* ferr-m k* *Ferr-p* bg2* *Gels* k* glon a1 *Guaj* k* ham k* hell k* helo-s bnm14• hep k* hydr-ac k* hyos k* hyper hr1 iber a1* iod k* ip k* ix bnm8• jab a1 jal jatr-c a1 juni-v a1 kali-bi k* kali-br kali-c k* kali-chl kali-cy a1 *Kali-m* kr1* kali-n k* *Kalm* kreos k* lac-ac k* **Lach** k* lat-m jl3 laur k* *Lob* k* loxo-lae bnm12• lyc *Lycps-v* kr1 m-arct b2.de *Manc* hr1* mang k* *Merc* k* merc-cy k* mez k* morph a1 **Mur-ac** k* myric a1 *Naja* narcot a1 nat-ar nat-m k* nat-n a1 nitro-o a1 nux-v k* oena a1 *Ol-j* hr1* olnd k* **Op** k* *Ox-ac* k* ph-ac k* *Phos* k* phys k* phyt k* *Plat* k* plb k* polyp-p a1 puls k* ran-b hr1 ran-s k* rhod b2.de* rhus-t k* sabin hr1 *Sang* k* santin a1 sec k* seneg k* sep hr1 sil k* sin-n a1 sol-ni a1 solin a1 *Spig* k* spirae a1 **Stram** k* stry a1 sul-ac k* *Sulph* hr1* *Sumb* a1* syph ptk1 *Tab* k* tarax a1 **Ter** k* thuj k* toxi a1 trios jl3 uva a1 valer k* **Verat** k* *Verat-v* k* vip a1 zinc k* zinc-m a1
  - **accompanied** by | **heart** failure (See CHEST - Heart failure - accompanied - pulse)
- **spasmodic**: (↗*contracted*) *Ang* b7.de* arn b7.de* ars k* bism k* carbn-s kr1* chin bg2 **Cocc** b7.de* colch a1 cupr k* cupr-act a1 *Dig* bg2* indg a1 iod bg2 kali-bi bg2 merc *Merc-c* b7a.de* nux-m nux-v a1 plb bg2 sabad k* *Sec* b7.de* sep k* *Stram* hr1* verat hr1 zinc k* zinc-s a1
- **strong**: achy jl3 acon k* aether a1 agar bg2* agar-pa a1 alco a1 aloe k* am-c k* aml-ns bg2* amyg a1* ant-t k* apis k* arg-n bg2 arn k* ars b4.de* ars-h hr1* ars-i a1* asaf bg2 asar k* aster jl3 aur b4.de* aza jl3 bar-c b4a.de* *Bell* k* bism b7.de* bov bg2 bry bg2 cact hr1 caj a1 calc b4.de* camph bg2 cann-i cann-xyz bg2 canth b7.de* *Caps* hr1 catal a1 chel b7.de* chin k* chinin-ar kr1 chlf a1 cic bg2 cimic br1 cinnb a1 clem a1 coca a1 coff bg2 con k* crot-h a1 crot-t k* *Cupr* b7a.de* cycl bg2 *Dig* b4.de* dulc b4.de* fago a1 ferr-p k2* gast a1 gels k* germ-met srj5• gins a1 glon bg2 grat bg2 hell b7.de* hoit jl3 hydrc a1 hyos k* iber a1 iod b4.de* jatr-c a1 kali-bi bg2 *Kali-chl* hr1 *Kali-m* kr1 kali-n bg2 kali-sula a1* kreos bg2 *Lac-c* hr1 lach b7a.de* lappa a1 laur bg2 *Led* hr1 lyc bg2 lycps-v a1 m-arct b7.de *Merc* bg2* merc-c k* merc-cy k* merc-i-r a1 mill k* morph a1 mur-ac b4a.de* nat-c bg2 nat-s a1 nat-sil fd3.de• neon srj5• *Nux-v* bg2 op k* par a1 paro-i jl3 petr b4.de* **Ph-ac** k* phos b4.de* phys k* plac-s rly4• plb bg2 *Puls* hr1* ran-b b7.de* raph k* rhod bg2 rumx bg2 sabad k* **Sabin** b7.de* sang k* sarr a1* sec bg2 seneg k* sep bg2 serp a1 sium a1 sol-t-ae a1 **Spig** b7.de* spong bg2 stram k* stront-c b4a.de* stry a1 *Sulph* b4a.de tanac a1 tarent tl1 ter hr1* *Thuj* b4a.de uva a1 valer bg2 *Verat* b7.de* verat-v hr1 **Viol-o** b7.de* zinc bg2
  - **and** slow: dig k2
- **suppressed**:
  - **one** side: led bg2 op bg2
  - **almost** suppressed: kali-sula a1*
- **temperature**; discordant with (See discordant)
- **tense**: (↗*wiry*) acon bg2 adren st1 agro a1 all-c all-s a1 am-c k* *Am-m* k* ammc hr1* *Ant-t* k* aphis a1 ars k* ars-h hr1 atro a1 bar-m br1 bell k* ben-n a1 bism k* **Bry** b7.de* *Cact* hr1 camph k* cann-i k* canth k* cham k* chel bg2 chin k* clem k* coca a1 *Cocc* hr1 coff-t a1 colch k* con k* corn-f a1 *Cupr* bg2* dig bg2 **Dulc** b4a.de* ferr k* hyos k* kali-i k* m-ambo b7.de merc-c b4a.de* *Mez* k* morph a1 nat-c k* nit-ac k* op hr1 ox-ac k* petr k* plb k* rhus-t hr1 sabad k* **Sabin** b7.de* sang k* sec k* sep hr1 sol-t-ae a1 spira a1 spirae a1 squil bg2* stram bg2 til a1 *Valer* b7.de* verat a1 verat-v zinc bg2*
- **thin**: ferr bg2
- **thready**: (↗*contracted; wiry*) acon k* agar-pa a1 *Ail* bg2* alum k* alumn hr1 aml-ns bg2* amyg a1* *Ant-t* hr1* *Apis* b7a.de* arn k* *Ars* k* ars-s-f hr1* ars-s-r hr1* *Bapt* hr1 bell k* *Cact* hr1 *Calc* ptk1 camph k* canth k* carb-v k* carbn-h a1 *Chin* hr1 chinin-s br1 chlf a1 chlol a1 colch k* cop a1 crat a1* *Crot-h* a1* cupr k* dig k* digin a1 hell k* helo-s bnm14• *Hydr-ac* bg2* hyos k* iod k* jatr-c a1 kali-bi k* kali-n a1 lach bg2* **Lat-m** sp1* loxo-lae bnm12• merc-c b4a.de* *Merc-cy* hr1 merc-n a1 merc-ns a1 morph a1 naja k* nat-f sp1* olnd k* op k* ox-ac k* petr k* phos k* phys a1 phyt k* *Plat* hr1* plb k* ptel a1 *Pyrog* bg2* raja-s jl3 rhus-t k* sal-ac sf1.de santin a1 sec hr1* sol-t-ae k* solin a1 *Spig* bg2* stram b7a.de* sul-ac a1 sulph tab bg2* tax a1 *Ter* a1* **Verat** b7.de* verat-v bg2* *Verb* kr1 vip a1 *Zinc* hr1* zinc-m a1
  - **coma**; with (See MIND - Coma - pulse)
- **ticking** of a clock; sensation like the: ambr b7.de* verb b7.de*
- **tremulous**: acon k* agar bg2 ambr k* ang b2.de* **Ant-t** k* apis kr1 arg-n bg2 *Arn* b7a.de *Ars* k* asaf bg2 aur b2.de* *Bell* k* bov bg2 bufo bg2 **Calc** k* camph k* cann-i canth k* carb-ac *Cic* k* cimic ptk1 cina k* cinnb a1 coc-c k* cocc k* colch bg2* con bg2 crot-h k* *Cupr* bg2 cycl bg2 dig k* fago a1 fl-ac bg2 gels k* gins a1 *Hell* k* hyos bg2 *Iber* a1* iod k* kali-bi bg2 kali-c k* kalm ptk1 *Kreos* k* lach k* lil-t bg2 lith-c bg2 lyc bg2 merc k* merc-c k* merc-sul a1* mez bg2 naja ptk1 nat-m k* nit-ac bg2 nux-m k* *Olnd* bg2 op k* ox-ac k* phos k* plat b4a.de* plb k* *Rhus-t* k* ruta k* *Sabin* k* *Sep* k* sil bg2 **Spig** k* *Staph* k* stram k* sul-ac k* tab bg2 valer k* verat bg2 zinc bg2
  - **night**: *Calc* narc-po a1
  - **eating**; after: *Calc*
- **unaltered**, unchanged: agar b2.de* agn b2.de* *Alum* b2.de* am-c b2.de* am-m b2.de* *Anac* b2.de* *Ang* b2.de* *Ant-c* b2.de* arg-met b2.de* *Asaf* b2.de* asar b2.de* bism b2.de* *Borx* b2.de* calad b2.de* camph b2.de* cann-s b2.de* canth b2.de* *Caps* b2.de* caust b2.de* chel b2.de* cic b2.de* *Cina* b2.de* *Clem* b2.de* cocc b2.de* *Coff* b2.de* colch b2.de* coloc b2.de* **Cycl** b2.de* **Dros** b2.de* dulc b2.de* *Euph* b2.de* **Euphr** b2.de* fl-ac bg2 graph b2.de* hell b2.de* ip b2.de* kali-n b2.de* lach b2.de* laur b2.de* led b2.de* lyc b2.de* *M-ambo* b2.de* *M-arct* b2.de m-aust b2.de **Mag-c** b2.de* mag-m b2.de* mang b2.de* meny b2.de* mez b2.de* mur-ac b2.de* **Nat-c** b2.de* nit-ac b2.de* nux-m b2.de* *Olnd* b2.de* *Par* b2.de* plat b2.de* ran-b b2.de* *Ran-s* b2.de* *Rheum* b2.de* rhod b2.de* *Ruta* b2.de* *Sec* b2.de* sel b2.de* sep b2.de* spig b2.de* spong b2.de* squil b2.de* stront-c b2.de* sul-ac b2.de* *Tarax* b2.de* *Teucr* b2.de* valer b2.de* *Verb* b2.de* viol-o b2.de* viol-t b2.de* zinc b2.de*
- **undulating**: agar h2* amyg a1 *Ars* k* camph k* carb-ac a1 carbn-o a1 chlf a1 crot-h k* dig k* digin a1 gins a1 iber a1 *Lach* hr1 op k* plb k* *Zinc* hr1
- **vibrating**: sang bg2
- **violent**: acon ptk1 aml-ns ptk1 bar-c bg2 dig bg2 glon bg2 lach bg2 lycps-v ptk1 merc-c bg2 nat-m bg2 sabin bg2 sep bg2 spig bg2 stront-c bg2
  - **accompanied** by | **perspiration**: coca ptk1
- **weak**: (↗*imperceptible; soft*) *Abrot* hr1 acet-ac k* acetan bro1 acon k* acon-c a1 acon-f a1 *Adon* br1* adren bro1 aesc k* aeth k* aether a1 agar b4.de* agar-cps a1 agar-em a1 *Agarin* bro1 **Agn** b7a.de* *Ail* hr1* ald a1 aloe alum-p k2* am-caust a1 am-m k* ampe-qu a1 amyg a1* ancis-p tsm2 *Ant-ar* bro1* ant-c b7a.de* ant-m kr1 **Ant-t** k* anth a1 anthraci jl2 apis k* apoc hr1* apom a1 *Arg-n* hr1 *Arn* k* **Ars** k* ars-h a1* *Ars-i* hr1* ars-s-f k2* ars-s-r hr1 arum-d a1 asaf k* asc-c a1* *Aspar* k* aster hr1* atra-r bnm3• *Atro* a1* **Aur** k* aur-ar k2 aur-m hr1* *Aur-s* k2* aza jl3 bapt k* **Bar-c** b4.de* bar-m bro1 bar-s k2* bell k* benz-ac hr1* **Berb** k* bism b7.de* both tsm2 both-ax tsm2 *Brom* hr1 bry k* bung-fa tsm2 buth-a sp1 cact hr1* caj a1 calad a1 **Camph** k* cann-i k* **Cann-s** b7.de* *Canth* k* carb-ac a1* carb-an **Carb-v** k* carbn-chl a1 carbn-o a1 cary a1 cass a1 catal a1 cedr k* cench a1* *Cham* b7.de* chel b7a.de* chen-a a1* *Chin* k* (non:chinin-ar slp) chinin-s a1 chion hr1 chir-fl bnm4• chlf a1* chlol a1* chlor a1 **Cic** b7.de* cimic k* *Cimx* k* cinch a1 cinnb a1 coca a1* *Cocc* hr1* cod a1 coff bg2* coff-t a1 *Coffin* bro1 colch k* coll bro1 *Coloc* b4a.de* con b4.de* conin a1 *Conv* bro1 *Crat* br1* crot-c tsm2 **Crot-h** k* crot-t k* cub hr1* *Cupr* k* *Cupr-act* a1* cupr-ar a1* cycl k* cyt-l a1 dendr-pol tsm2 *Dig* k* digin a1 digox a1 dios hr1* diph bro1 dirc a1* dor a1* elaps tsm2 erio a1 ery-a a1 eryt-j a1 eup-per hr1 *Eup-pur* hr1 euph hr1 fago a1 fagu a1 ferr a1* ferr-m k* gal-ac br1 gast a1 **Gels** k* *Glon* k* guaj b4a.de* ham k* hell k* helo-s bnm14• hydr-ac a1* hydrc a1 hyos k* hyosin-hbr bro1 iber a1* *Ign* k* *Iod* k* *Ip* k* iris ix bnm8• jal hr1 jasm a1 jatr-c a1 juni-v a1 kali-ar a1* *Kali-bi* k* *Kali-br* k* *Kali-c* b4a.de* kali-chl bro1 kali-n a1* kali-ox a1 kali-t a1 *Kalm* k* keroso a1 kreos k* lac-ac k* *Lac-c* hr1* **Lach** k* lact a1 lat-k a1 **Lat-m** br1* **Laur** k* lil-t k* lob k* lyc bg2* *Lycps-v* k* *Lyss* a1* *Mag-m* hr1 manc mang k* *Merc* k* *Merc-c* k* merc-cy k* merc-i-f a1* merc-n a1 merc-ns a1 merc-pr-r a1 merc-sul a1* meth-ae-ae a1 mez k* mom-b a1 morph a1* *Mosch* bg2* *Mur-ac* k* **Naja** k* narcot a1 nat-f sp1* nat-m k* *Nat-s* hr1 nit-ac a1 nit-s-d a1 *Nux-m* bg2* nux-v k* oena a1* olnd k* op k* ox-ac k* past a1 peti a1 **Ph-ac** k* *Phase* bro1 *Phos* k* phys k* phyt k* plan hr1 **Plat** b4.de* plb k* plumbg a1 podo k* polyp-p a1 prop a1 psor hr1* ptel a1 *Puls* k* pyre-p a1 raja-s jl3 ran-b hr1 rhod k* *Rhus-t* k* rhus-v k* ric a1 rumx-act a1 sabin a1 sacch a1 sal-ac hr1* sal-p a1 samb hr1* *Sang* k* santin a1 sapin a1 *Sapo* bro1 *Saroth* bro1 *Sec* k* seneg k* sep k* ser-ang bro1 sil bg2* sol-t-ae a1 solin a1 spartin-s bwa2 *Spig* k* spira a1 spirae a1 spong hr1* stann hr1 *Staph* k* *Still* a1* *Stram* k* stront-c bg2 stry a1* stry-p br1 sul-ac k* sul-h a1 sulo-ac a1 *Sulph* hr1* sumb a1 *Tab* k* tanac a1 *Tarent* hr1* tart-ac a1 tax a1 ter a1* tere-ch jl3 thea a1 *Thuj* b4.de* thymol sp1 thyr br1* trif-p a1 trim a4 tub jl2 upa a1 *Ust* hr1* uva a1 *Valer* b7.de* *Vario* hr1* verat k* *Verat-v* k* verb a1 vesp a1* vip bg2* vip-a jl3 visc bro1 xan a1 zinc k* *Zinc-m* a1 zinc-p k2* zinc-s a1 zing a1
  - **morning**: cimic a1* olnd hr1 sep h2 thuj hr1

- **accompanied** by:
  - **apoplexy** (See Apoplexy - accompanied - pulse - weak)
  - **hemorrhage**; passive (See Hemorrhage - passive - accompanied - pulse)
  - **weakness** in general (See Weakness - accompanied - pulse)
  - **Stomach**; uneasiness in: ant-t tl1
- **headache**; during: lach k2
- **motion** agg.: apoc bro1 bar-s k2

- **wiry**: *(↗contracted; tense; thready)* acon bg ammc hr1 amyg a1* ars k* ben-n a1 bol-la a1 cupr cupr-act a1 dig k* gels k* *Glon* hr1* ham k* iber a1 *Kali-br* hr1 kreos k* *Lac-c* hr1* *Lach* hr1 *Lycps-v* kr1 oena a1 ox-ac k* phos k* p h y s k* *Plb* hr1 pyrog bro1 sec k* seneg hr1 tax a1 ter hr1* verat-v hr1 zinc k*

PULSE and temperature dissociated (See Pulse - discordant)

PUNISHMENT agg.: ambr bg2 con bg2 dig bg2 lach bg2 stann bg2 s t a p h bg2

PURGATIVES, abuse of: *(↗Medicine - allopathic - abuse)* hydr bg2* lyc ptk1 *Nux-v* bg2* op bg2* sulph bg2*

PURGING: | **amel.**: abrot ptk1 nat-s ptk1 zinc ptk1

PURPURA IDIOPATHIC THROMBOCYTOPENIC: raja-s mtf11

PUS (See Abscesses - pus)

PUTRID PHENOMENA (See Discharges - offensive)

PYEMIA: *(↗Septicemia)* ars-i ptk1 chin ptk1 lach ptk1 methyl br1 phos tl1* pyrog ptk1

- **prophylaxis** for pus infections: arn br1

QUININE, abuse of: am-c k* am-m bro1 *Ant-t* k* *Apis* apoc lp aran bro1 **Arn** k* *Ars* k* ars-i bro1 ars-s-f k2 asaf k* aza c1 *Bell* k* bry k* **Calc** k* calc-ar bro1* caps k* carb-an c1 **Carb-v** k* cean bro1 cham k* chelo c1* chin mrr1 *Chinin-ar* bro1 *Cina* k* coloc bro1 corn-f br1 cupr k* cycl k* dig k* eucal c1* eup-per bg2* **Ferr** k* ferr-ar gels (non:hell k*) *Hep* kr1 *Hydr* bro1 ign tl1 **Ip** k* kali-ar k2 lac-d k2 *Lach* k* maland bro1 malar bro1 mang b4a.de* meny bg2* merc k* **Nat-m** k* nat-p st1 nat-s k2 nux-v k* parth br1* *Ph-ac* k* phos k* plb k* *Polym* bro1 **Puls** k* ran-s bg2 samb k* sel bg2* *Sep* k* stann k* sul-ac k* *Sulph* k* *Verat* k*

- **cachexia**; with quinine (See Weakness - quinine)
- **cachexia**; without quinine: ant-t sf1.de aran kr1 arn kr1* *Ars* j5.de* bell j5.de* calc j5.de* carb-v j5.de* cham kr1 coff kr1 corn-f br1 eup-per kr1 *Ferr* kr1* *Hell* kr1 **Hep** kr1 iod kr1* *Ip* j5.de* lach j5.de* led k* meny j5.de* merc j5.de* nat-c kr1 *Nat-m* kr1* nux-v kr1* ph-ac sf1.de *Puls* kr1* rhus-t kr1 *Sel* k* sep kr1* sulph kr1* verat j5.de*
- **epilepsy**; causing (See Convulsions - epileptic - quinine)
- **quinine** sulfate: chinin-s mrr1

QUIVERING: *(↗Shaking)* *Agar* b2.de* agn b2.de* aids nl2• alum b2.de* *Am-c* k* am-m b2.de* ambr b2.de* *Ang* b2.de* ant-c b2.de* ars b2.de* **Asaf** b2.de* bapt k2* bar-c b2.de* **Bell** k* berb bism bov b2.de* bry b2.de* *Calc* k* calc-p a1 camph b2.de* canth b2.de* caps k* carb-v b2.de* caust k* chel b2.de* chin b2.de* cic b2.de* *Clem* cocc k2* colch b2.de* coloc b2.de* com **Con** k* croc b2.de* cupr b2.de* dig dros b2.de* gels c1 graph b2.de* guaj b2.de* hell b2.de* hep hyos k* ign k* iod ip b2.de* kali-c k* kali-n kali-s k2* kreos b2.de* lyc k* m-ambo b2.de* *M-arct* b2.de* mag-c mag-m b2.de* med hr1* meny b2.de* merc b2.de* **Mez** b2.de* mosch mur-ac b2.de* **Nat-c** b2.de* nat-m b2.de* *Nit-ac* nux-v k* par b2.de* petr k* phos b2.de* plat b2.de* plb b2.de* puls b2.de* pyrog k2 rhod b2.de* rhus-t b2.de* ruta b2.de* sabin b2.de* sars sel b2.de* seneg b2.de* *Sep* k* sil k* *Spig* b2.de* stann k* stram b2.de* stront-c k* sul-ac k2* **Sulph** k* tarax b2.de* tarent ptk1 thuj b2.de* thyr ptk1 tub ptk1 valer b2.de* verb viol-t b2.de* *Zinc* b2.de*

- **accompanied** by:
  - **weakness**: granit-m es1•
  - ○ **Abdomen**; pain in (See ABDOMEN - Pain - shivering)
  - **Stomach**; pain in (See STOMACH - Pain - accompanied - shivering)
  - **Teeth**; pain in (See TEETH - Pain - shivering)
- **delivery**; during first stage of: cimic tl1
- **heat**; during: ferr k2
- **lying** agg.: *Clem* k* melal-alt gya4
- **motion** agg.: nux-v tl1

Quivering: ...

- **rest** agg.: dros tl1
- ○ **All** over: lyss ptk1
  - **followed** by vertigo: *Calc* k*
- **Glands**; of: *Ang* b2.de* bell k* calc k* kali-c k* mez k* nat-c k* sil k*
- **Internal** parts; in: bov b2.de* *Cann-s* b2.de* seneg b2.de*
- **Nerves**: med br1

RABIES (See MIND - Hydrophobia)

RACHITIS (See Rickets)

RADIANT HEAT (See Warm - stove)

RADIATION THERAPY; from: ars-br rmk1• cadm-i gm1 fl-ac gm1 germ-met srj5• phos gm1 rad-br mrr1* stront-c gm1 x-ray gm1 [calc-sil stj2 ferr-sil stj2 kali-sil stj2 lith-f stj2 lith-m stj2 lith-met stj2 lith-p stj2 lith-s stj2 mag-sil stj2 mang-sil stj2 nat-sil stj2 plut-n stj2 sil stj2 sil-met stj2]

- **x-rays**: caust mtf11

RADIUM TREATMENTS; from: cadm-met gm1 caust mtf11 rad-br mrr1

RAIN (See Weather - rain)

RAISING:

- **affected** limbs:
  - **agg.**: acon b2.de* am-m b2.de* anac b2.de* ant-c b2.de* arg-met b2.de* *Arn* b2.de* asar b2.de* *Bar-c* b2.de* *Bell* b2.de* borx b2.de* both-ax tsm2 bry b2.de* calc b2.de* camph b2.de* caps b2.de* caust b2.de* chin b2.de* cic b2.de* cina b2.de* cocc b2.de* coff b2.de* colch b2.de* coloc b2.de* **Con** b2.de* cupr b2.de* dros b2.de* euph b2.de* *Ferr* b2.de* graph b2.de* h e p b2.de* ign b2.de* *Kali-c* b2.de* kreos b2.de* lach b2.de* *Led* b2.de* lyc b2.de* m-aust b2.de* mag-c b2.de* mag-m b2.de* merc b2.de* mez b2.de* nat-c b2.de* nat-m b2.de* nit-ac b2.de* nux-v b2.de* olnd b2.de* petr b2.de* phos b2.de* plb b2.de* puls b2.de* ran-b b2.de* *Rhus-t* b2.de* ruta b2.de* *Sil* b2.de* stann b2.de* sul-ac b2.de* sulph b2.de* teucr b2.de* thuj b2.de* verat b2.de* verb b2.de*
  - **amel.**: *Alum* b2.de* *Am-c* b2.de* ang b2.de* **Calc** b2.de* caust b2.de* cina b2.de* dig b2.de* hep b2.de* ign b2.de* lyc b2.de* m-aust b2.de nat-m b2.de* nux-v b2.de* par b2.de* ph-ac b2.de* phos b2.de* plat b2.de* p l b b2.de* puls b2.de* ruta b2.de* *Sabin* b2.de* stann b2.de* stront-c b2.de* sul-ac b2.de* sulph b2.de* thuj b2.de* valer b2.de*
- **arms** | **agg.**: *Acon* b2.de* ambr bg2 anac b2.de* ant-c b2.de* apis bg2 arg-met b7.de *Bar-c* b2.de* borx b2.de* bry b2.de* caps b2.de* chin b2.de* **Con** b2.de* cupr b2.de* dig bg2 ferr b2.de* graph b2.de* guaj bg2 ip bg2 k a l i - b i bg2 kali-c bg2 lach b2.de* *Led* b2.de* lyc bg2 plb b2.de* puls bg2 r a n - b b2.de* **Sang** bg2 sil bg2 sulph b2.de* thuj b2.de* zinc bg2
- **eyes** | **agg.**: ars b2.de* bell b2.de* *Bry* b2.de* caps b2.de* *Chin* b2.de* m-arct b2.de* puls b2.de* sabin b2.de*
- **head**:
  - **agg.**: caps b7.de tarax b7.de
  - **amel.**: ars bro1 gels bro1

RAPIDLY GROWING children (See Growth)

REABSORBENT action (See Absorption)

REACHING up with the hands agg.: lach b7a.de

REACTION: aloe sne

- **lack** of: *(↗Irritability - lack; Sluggishness; Weakness - reaction; FEVER - Reaction)* abrot mtf33 aeth ptk1* agar aloe sne *Alum* **Am-c** k* **Ambr** k* *Anac* ant-c ant-t k* apis st arn *Ars* k* **Ars-i** k* ars-s-f k2* *Asaf* *Bar-c* bar-s k2* bell st1 bism *Brom* *Bry* k* **Calc** k* calc-f bg2* *Calc-i* *Calc-s* *C a m p h* k* **Caps** k* *Carb-an* k* **Carb-v** k* carbn-s bro1 carc gk6* *Castm* k* c a u s t k* cham *Chin* k* cic k* *Cocc* k* coch br1 coff **Con** k* cory br1 *Cupr* k* c y p r st1 dig ptk1 *Dulc* k* euph *Ferr* k* ferr-i *Fl-ac* *Gaert* st1* **Gels** k* *Graph* *Guaj* **Hell** k* hep bg2* **Hydr-ac** k* hyos *Iod* k* *Ip* kali-bi bg2* *Kali-br* *Kali-c* k* kali-chl k13 kali-m k2 *Kali-s* kola stb3• lac-c br1 *Lach* k* **Laur** k* luf-op jl3 *Lyc* k* mag-c mag-f mg1.de mag-m k* **Med** k* *Merc* k* mez *Mosch* k* *Mur-ac* nat-ar bro1* nat-c nat-m nat-p nat-s bro1 nit-ac bg2* **Nit-s-d** h *Nux-m* **Olnd** k* **OP** b7a.de* ped st1 petr **Ph-ac** k* *Phos* *Plb* prot st1 **Psor** k* puls bg2* rad-br bro1 *Rhod* scut st1 *Sec* seneg *Sep* k* spong *Stann* **Staph** sne *Stram* k* stront-c sul-i k2* **Sulph** k* *Syph* k* **Tarent** k* thal jl3 ther ptk1 *Thuj* k* **Tub** bg2* **Valer** k* vario sf1.de *Verat* k* verb k* vinc bg2 x-ray br1* **Zinc** k* *Zinc-p* k2* [heroin sdj2]

- **lack** of: ...
  - **accompanied** by:
    - **alternating** states (See Alternating - accompanied - reaction)
    - **syphilis**: calc-f bg2 hep bg2 kali-bi bg2 nit-ac bg2 syph bg2
    - **Brain**; complaints of the: zinc bg2
    - **Chest**; complaints of the: *Laur* br1
    - **Heart**; complaints of the: *Laur* br1
  - **acute** danger (See MIND - Danger - lack)
  - **chill**; after: *Camph* bg2 dulc bg2
  - **chronic** diseases; in: cory br1
  - **convalescence**, in: *(↗Convalescence)* castm bg2 ph-ac bg2
  - **eruptive** diseases, in (See SKIN - Eruptions - break - fails)
  - **fluids**; after loss of: *Chin* bg2
  - **menopause**; during: con bg2
  - **nervous** patients, in: ambr bg2 laur bg2 op bg2 **Valer** bg2* zinc bg2
  - **old** people; in: con bg2
  - **pain**; to: alum mrr1 cocc tl1
  - **remedies**, to (See Remedies - fail)
  - **suppression**, after: lach bg2
    - **eruptions**, of: *(↗SKIN - Eruptions - suppressed)* ars-s-f k2*
  - **suppuration**, in: *(↗Abscesses)* calc-f bg2 hep bg2 merc mtf33
  - **women**; in: | **obese**: am-c br1
- **slow** reaction to pain (See lack - pain)
- **violent**: bell ptk1 *Cupr* ptk1 *Nux-v* ptk1 zinc ptk1
  - **allopathic** medicine (See Medicine - allopathic - oversensitive)
  - **homeopathic** remedies, to (See Remedies - violent)

READING:
- **agg.**: agar b2.de* *Agn* b2.de* alum b2.de* am-c b2.de* ang b2.de* apis bg2 arg-met b2.de* arg-n ptk1 arn b2.de* ars b2.de* *Asaf* b2.de* asar b2.de* aur b2.de* bar-c b2.de* *Bell* b2.de* borx b2.de* bry b2.de* **Calc** b2.de* canth b2.de* carb-ac ptk1 carb-v b2.de* caust b2.de* *Chin* b2.de* *Cina* b2.de* *Cocc* b2.de* coff b2.de* *Con* b2.de* croc b2.de* cupr b2.de* dros b2.de* *Dulc* b2.de* *Graph* b2.de* *Hep* b2.de* ign b2.de* *Kali-c* b2.de* lil-t bg2* lith-c bg2 lyc b2.de* m-arct b2.de* mag-m b2.de* mang b2.de* meny b2.de* merc b2.de* mez b2.de* mosch b2.de* naja ptk1 nat-c b2.de* **Nat-m** b2.de* nit-ac b2.de* nux-m b2.de* *Nux-v* b2.de* *Olnd* b2.de* onos ptk1 par bg2 petr b2.de* ph-ac b2.de* **Phos** b2.de* phys bg2* plat b2.de* puls b2.de* rad-br ptk1 *Rhod* b2.de* rhus-t ptk1 *Ruta* b2.de* sabad b2.de* sars b2.de* sel b2.de* seneg b2.de* sep b2.de* **Sil** b2.de* staph b2.de* stram b2.de* *Sul-ac* b2.de* *Sulph* b2.de* tarax b2.de* thuj b2.de* valer b2.de* *Verb* b2.de* viol-o b2.de* zinc b2.de*
- **aloud**:
  - **agg.**: ambr ptk1 **Carb-v** b2.de* cocc b2.de* *Mang* b2.de* nit-ac b2.de* *Par* b2.de* ph-ac bg2 **Phos** b2.de* sel b2.de* seneg bg2 *Verb* b2.de*
  - **amel.**: nat-c ptk1
- **amel.**: ferr b2.de* *Nat-c* b2.de*

REBELS against poultice (See MIND - Rebels)

RECOVERING slowly (See Convalescence)

RED complexion (See Complexion - red)

REDNESS: **Acon** bg* *Apis* bg* *Arg-n* bg* ars bg **Bell** bg* *Bry* bg* *Cham* bg* chin bg* equis-h a1 *Ferr* bg germ-met srj5• jab ptk1 lach bg* meli bg* *Merc* bg* neon srj5• *Nux-v* bg* op bg* phos bg* *Rhus-t* bg* sabin ptk1 *Sang* bg* sep bg* **Sulph** bg*
- **spots**; in: merc ptk1 pic-ac ptk1 rhus-t ptk1 stict ptk1 sulph ptk1

○ - **Affected** parts: bell mtf33 colch br1
- **Glands**: *Apis* bg2 *Bell* b4a.de *Carb-an* b4a.de *Merc* b4a.de *Phos* b4a.de sil b4a.de sulph b4a.de
  - **bluish** red: *Carb-an* b4a.de hep b4a.de lach b4a.de

REFLEXES: *(↗EXTREMITIES - Reflexes)*
- **absent** (See lost)
- **diminished**: *(↗Poliomyelitis)* alum bg2* arg-n bg2* cur bg2* germ-met srj5• kali-br bg2* oena k* op a1 phys bg2* plb dgt1*

Reflexes – diminished: ...
  - **delirium**; after: agar br1
- **increased**: *(↗EXTREMITIES - Paralysis - lower - accompanied - ankle)* bar-c a1 cann-i br1 cic bg2* cocc bg2* lat-m bnm6• lath bg2* *Mang-act* br1 morph a1 nux-v bg2* op a3 plb hs1* sil br1 stry br1* vip br1
- **lost**: brass-n-o srj5• cur mta1 morph a1 nat-br a1 op a3 oxyt br1 sulfon c1*

REITER'S SYNDROME: *Med* gg*

RELAXATION:
- **physical**: *(↗Flabby; Hang down - sensation; Hypotony; Instability; Weakness; Weariness)* acon k* *Aeth* ptk1 agar k* agn k* agra br1 aids nl2• alet ptk1 aloe ptk1 alum k* ant-c mrr1 ant-t bg2* aran mtf11 arn k* ars k* asar k* aster br1 aur k* bar-c ptk1 bell k* bism k* borx mtf33 bov ptk1 bry k* calc ptk1* camph k* *Caps* br1* caust k* cham k* chel bg2* chin bg2* cic k* cina k* cocc k* coff k* colch k* coli rly4• cory br1 cupr k* cycl k* cystein-l rly4• dig k* dulc k* euph k* ferr k* fuma-ac rly4• gels br1* graph ptk1 hell ptk1 hep bg2 hydr-ac a1 hydrog srj2• hyos k* ign bg2* ip k* kali-c k* kali-n k* ketogl-ac rly4• *Lac-h* htj1• lach bg2* lil-t ptk1 linu-c a1 lob br1* lyc k* *Mag-c* ptk1 mangi br1 med ptk1 meny k* merc k* merc-cy ptk1 micr br1 morph a1 **Mur-ac** ptk1 nat-c k* *Nat-chl* br1 nat-m k* nit-ac k* nux-m k* nux-v k* olnd k* op k* oxal-a rly4• par k* *Passi* br1* petr k* ph-ac k* phos k* plat k* plb k* ran-s k* rhod k* rhus-t k* ribo rly4• ruta k* sabad k* sabin k* sel k* seneg ptk1 sep k* sil k* spig k* spong k* stann k* staph k* stram k* streptoc rly4• suis-pan rly4• sulph k* tarax k* tritic-vg fd5.de tub br1 ulm-c jsj8• valer ptk1 vanil fd5.de verat k* viol-o k* viol-t k* zinc k*
  - **accompanied** by:
    - **Face** | **discoloration**; red: *Aster* br1
  - **children**; in: borx mtf33 calc-i br1 *Calc-p* br1
  - **chronic** disease; during: cory br1
  - **coition**; after: *Agar* hr1* sep a1
  - **fever**:
    - **before**: caps b7a.de ip b7a.de puls b7a.de sabad b7a.de verat b7a.de
    - **during** | **agg.**: apis bg2 *Chin* bg2 **Lyc** bg2 **Petr** bg2 *Ph-ac* bg2 rhod bg2 spong bg2 teucr bg2 valer bg2
  - **perspiration**; during: apis bg2 carb-v bg2 caust bg2 **Chin** bg2 *Lyc* bg2 merc bg2 *Petr* bg2 *Ph-ac* bg2 phos bg2 samb bg2 *Sel* bg2 spong bg2 stann bg2 valer bg2
- **sensation** as if | **Blood** vessels; of: bell bg2

○ - **Blood** vessels; of: *(↗Distension blood)* arn br1 bar-c br1 fl-ac br1 ham br1
- **Connective** tissue; of: *(↗Complexion - fair - lax)* *Aeth* bg aids nl2• aloe bg *Ant-t* bg ars bg calc k2* calc-br c1 caps c1 **Caust** bg chin bg cocc bg *Colch* bg ferr-i c1 **Gels** bg hell bg hep c1 *Hyos* bg kali-c c1 ketogl-ac rly4• **Lyc** bg mag-c c1 merc-c c1 merc-i-r c1 **Mur-ac** bg nat-c bg nat-m bg nit-ac c1 op bg **Ph-ac** bg sec bg sep mrr1 spong c1 verat bg
- **Mucous** membranes: *Hydr* br1
- **Muscles**; of: *(↗Complaints - muscles)* acet-ac br1* *Agar* k* alum bg2 ambr k* amyg kr1 ang b2.de* anh mg1.de *Ant-c* b7a.de ant-t k* arg-met k2 arn k* *Ars* asaf k* atra-r bnm3• atro a1 bar-c mtf bar-m a1 bar-s k2 bell kr1 borx k* bry k* **Calc** k* calc-sil k2 camph k* canth k* **Caps** k* carb-an a1 carbn-o a1 carbn-s a1 caust bg2* *Cham* k* chin k* chinin-ar chlam-tr bcx2• chlf br1 chlor a1 cic k* *Clem* k* coca bg2 **Cocc** k* colch k2 coll br1 *Con* k* *Croc* k* *Crot-c* cupr k* cur bg2 cycl b7.de* dig k* *Dios* dros bg2 *Dulc* b4a.de euph k* *Ferr* k* ferr-ar ferr-i c1 fl-ac bg2 **Gels** k* ger-i rly4• glor-si jsx1.fr glor-su jsx1.fr *Graph* k* guare a1 *Hell* k* helo bg2 helo-s rwt2• hep c1 hydr k* hydr-ac a1 hydrog srj2• *Hyos* k* *Iod* k* *Ip* k* jug-r a1 kali-ar a1 **Kali-c** k* kali-m k2 kali-n bg2 kali-p bg2 kali-s k2 ketogl-ac rly4• lach k* laur k* lob br1 *Lyc* k* *Mag-c* k* mang k2 mangi br1 meli br1 merc k* morph a1 mur-ac k* murx k2 naja mg1.de nat-c k* *Nat-m* b4a.de nat-p k2* nit-ac c1 nux-m k* nux-v b7a.de* olnd bg2 op k* oscilloc jl2 oxal-a rly4• oxyt **Phos** k* phys a1 pic-ac mtf plat k* plb k* psor b4a.de puls k* rheum k* ribo rly4• sabad k* *Sec* k* *Seneg* k* *Sep* sil k* sol-ni spig k* *Spong* k* stram b7.de sul-ac k* sul-h a1 *Sulph* k* tab bg2* ter a1 thal-xyz srj8• thuj k* tril-p zr *Verat* b2.de* (non:verat-v slp) viol-o k* zinc bg2
  - **alternating** with | **convulsions** (See Convulsions - alternating - relaxation)
- **Sphincters**; of: apoc br1 oxyt br1 podo ptk1 sulfon br1

REMEDIES: *(↗Medicine)*
- **acting**:
  - **deep**: alum-sil br1 ars br1 calc-sil br1 carbn-s br1 cench br1 cist br1 glyc br1 kali-sil br1 med br1 sil br1

- **acting**: ...
  - **long**: calc-sil br1 glyc br1
  - **quick**: spartin-s br1
  - **short**: acon br1
  - **slow**: sil br1 squil br1
- **allopathic** medicine (See Medicine)
- **aversion** to homeopathic remedies (See MIND - Remedies - aversion)
- **fail** to act; well selected remedies: *(↗EAR - Noises - remedies)* alum gl1.fr• camph b7a.de carb-v gl1.fr• *Carc* mrr1 laur b7.de* *Mosch* b7.de* op b7.de* psor c1* stram b7.de* sulph c1* teucr kr1* ther br1 tub k2* valer br1
  - **acute** diseases; in: **Sulph** br1
  - **coryza**; during: *Am-c* bg2 *Calc* bg2 caust bg2 *Gels* bg2 hep bg2 **Lach** bg2 nat-m bg2 **Nux-v** bg2 *Sulph* bg2
  - **oversensitive** state; when too much medicine has produced an: *(↗Medicine)* cupr ptk1 ph-ac k* **Teucr** k*
- **violent** reaction to homeopathic remedies: acon gl1.fr• ant-c b7a.de arn gl1.fr• asar b7.de* carc mlr1• cham b7.de* *Chin* b7.de* coff gl1.fr• *Ign* b7.de* lyc gl1.fr• *M-arct* b7.de nit-ac gg nux-v b7.de* *Puls* b7.de* sep gl1.fr• sil gl1.fr• *Sulph* gl1.fr• teucr b7.de* *Valer* b7.de*
  - **high** potencies, to: ars-i k2* lyc mtf33 **Nit-ac** j5.de* nux-v k2

REST:

- **agg.**: acon b2.de* *Adon* vh1 *Aesc* bg2* *Agar* b2.de* alum b2.de* *Alumn* kr1 am-c b2.de* *Am-m* b2.de* *Ambr* b2.de* anac b2.de* ang b2.de* ant-c b2.de* *Ant-t* b2.de* aran-ix jl3 *Arg-met* b2.de* *Arn* b2.de* *Ars* b2.de* *Asaf* b2.de* asar b2.de* **Aur** b2.de* aur-m k2* aur-m-n vml3• bar-c b2.de* bell b2.de* bell-p jl3 benz-ac bg2* *Bism* b2.de* *Borx* b2.de* *Bov* b2.de* **Brom** b4a.de bry b2.de* calc b2.de* calc-f bro1 **Caps** b2.de* carb-ac jl3 carb-v b2.de* carc fd2.de• caust b2.de* *Cham* b2.de* chel b7.de chin b2.de* cic b2.de* cimic jl3 *Cina* b2.de* cocc b2.de* coli jl2 *Coloc* b2.de* com bro1 **Con** b2.de* cortiso jl3 cupr b2.de* **Cycl** b2.de* *Dros* b2.de* **Dulc** b2.de* **Euph** b2.de* *Euphr* b2.de* **Ferr** b2.de* ferr-ar k2* ferr-p k2* fl-ac bg2* foll jl3 gels bg2 glon bg2 **Graph** b4.de* guaj b2.de* hecla jl hep b2.de* hyos b2.de* ign b2.de* indg bro1 *Iod* bg2* iris bro1 kali-c b2.de* kali-i bg2* *Kali-n* b2.de* kali-s k2* *Kreos* b2.de* *Lach* b2.de* laur b2.de* lith-lac bro1 **Lyc** b2.de* *M-ambo* b2.de* m-arct b2.de* m-aust b2.de* *Mag-c* b2.de* **Mag-m** b2.de* mang b2.de* *Meny* b2.de* *Merc* b2.de* *Merc-c* bg2 merc-i-f k2* mez b2.de* *Mosch* b2.de* *Mur-ac* b2.de* *Nat-c* b2.de* nat-f mg1.de* *Nat-m* b2.de* nat-s bg2* nit-ac b2.de* *Nux-m* b2.de* olnd b2.de* *Op* b2.de* par b2.de* pert jl2 petr b2.de* *Ph-ac* b2.de* phenob jl* phor-t mie3• phos b2.de* *Plat* b2.de* plb b2.de* pneu jl3* **Puls** b2.de* pyrog bg2 ran-b b7.de *Rhod* b2.de* **Rhus-t** b2.de* *Ruta* b2.de* **Sabad** b2.de* sabin b2.de* sacch-a fd2.de• **Samb** b2.de* sars b2.de* sel b2.de* seneg b2.de* **Sep** b2.de* sil b2.de* spig b2.de* spong b2.de* stann b2.de* staph b2.de* *Stront-c* b2.de* sul-ac b2.de* sulph b2.de* **Tarax** b2.de* tarent bro1 tell jl3* teucr b2.de* *Thuj* b2.de* tub k2* tub-r jl3* **Valer** b2.de* vanil fd5.de *Verat* b2.de* *Verb* b2.de* *Viol-t* b2.de* *Zinc* b2.de* zinc-val sf1.de [*Arg-n* stj2 *Arg-p* stj2 astat stj2 aur-s stj2 bar-br stj2 *Bar-i* stj2 bar-met stj2 bism-sn stj2 caes-met stj2 cinnb stj2 hafn-met stj2 irid-met stj2 lanth-met stj2 lith-c stj2 *Lith-i* stj2 *Mag-i* stj1 *Mang-i* stj2 merc-d stj2 *Nat-i* stj1 osm-met stj2 plb-m stj2 plb-p stj2 polon-met stj2 rhen-met stj2 tant-met stj2 thal-met stj2 tung-met stj2 *Zinc-i* stj2]
  - **night**: pneu jl2
  - **exertion**; after previous: agar bg2 anac bg2 ars bg2 cann-xyz bg2 hydr bg2 kali-c bg2 puls bg2 rhus-t bg2 ruta bg2 sep bg2 spong bg2 stann bg2 stram bg2 valer bg2 zinc bg2
  - **long** rest: tub-r jl2
  - **motion** agg.; rest as well as: am-c bg2 bov bg2 calc bg2 carb-an bg2 carb-v bg2 caust bg2 get br1 mez bg2 ph-ac bg2 phos bg2 sulph bg2
- **amel.**: abrom-a ks5 achy jl3 acon b2.de* adlu jl aesc bro1 agar b2.de* *Agn* b2.de* alum b2.de* alum-sil k2* alumn kr1 *Am-c* b2.de* am-m b2.de* ambr b2.de* *Anac* b2.de* *Ang* b2.de* anh jl3 ant-c b2.de* *Ant-t* b2.de* aq-mar jl3 arg-met b2.de* *Arn* b2.de* ars b2.de* asaf b2.de* *Asar* b2.de* aur b2.de* bar-c b2.de* bar-m bg2* **Bell** b2.de* bism b2.de* *Borx* b2.de* both-ax tsm2 bov b2.de* **Bry** b2.de* buth-a mg1.de* cadm-s bro1* *Calad* b2.de* *Calc* b2.de* calc-f k2* calc-p bg2* *Camph* b2.de* cann-i k2* *Cann-s* b2.de* *Canth* b2.de* caps b2.de* *Carb-an* b2.de* *Carb-v* b2.de* carc mlr1• caust b2.de* cham b2.de* *Chel* b2.de* chin b2.de* *Cic* b2.de* cina b2.de* clem b4.de coc-c bg2* *Cocc* b2.de* *Coff* b2.de* **Colch** b2.de* *Coloc* b2.de* con b2.de* crat bro1 *Croc* b2.de* *Cupr* b2.de* cycl b2.de* des-ac jl dicha jl3 *Dig* b2.de* dros b2.de* dulc b2.de* *Echi* bg2* euph b2.de* ferr b2.de*

Rest – amel.: ...

fl-ac bg2 **Gels** hr1* get bro1 gink-b jl3 *Graph* b2.de* *Guaj* b2.de* guat jl3 gymno bro1 *Hell* b2.de* *Hep* b2.de* hydr k2* hydrog srj2• hyos b2.de* ign b2.de* *Iod* b2.de* *Ip* b2.de* kali-bi k2* kali-c b2.de* kali-i k2* kali-n b2.de* kali-p bro1 kalm k2* kreos b2.de* lac-d k2* lach b2.de* laur b2.de* **Led** b2.de* lyc b2.de* m-ambo b2.de* m-arct b2.de* *M-aust* b2.de* mag-c b2.de* mag-m b2.de* mag-p k2* malar jl2 mand jl3 *Mang* b2.de* meny b2.de* *Merc* b2.de* merc-c bg2* *Mez* b2.de* mosch b2.de* mur-ac b2.de* nat-c b2.de* *Nat-m* b2.de* *Nit-ac* b2.de* *Nux-m* b2.de* **Nux-v** b2.de* olnd b2.de* onop jl op b2.de* oscilloc jl2 *Par* b2.de* penic srb2.fr *Petr* b2.de* ph-ac b2.de* phenob jl3* *Phos* b2.de* phyt bro1 pic-ac mrr1 plat b2.de* *Plb* b2.de* prot jl3 psor jl2 pulx bro1 *Ran-b* b2.de* *Rheum* b2.de* rhod b2.de* rhus-t b2.de* ruta b2.de* sabad b2.de* sabin b2.de* samb b2.de* sang bg2 *Sars* b2.de* *Sec* b2.de* *Sel* b2.de* seneg b2.de* sep b2.de* ser-a-c jl2 sieg mg1.de sil b2.de* *Spig* b2.de* *Spong* b2.de* *Squil* b2.de* stann b2.de* *Staph* b2.de* *Stram* b2.de* stront-c b2.de* stroph-s jl3 stry-p br1* *Sul-ac* b2.de* sulph b2.de* symph fd3.de• teucr b2.de* ther k2* thuj b2.de* trios jl tub-d jl2 tub-m jl2 vanil fd5.de verat b2.de* verb b7.de vib bro1 viol-t b2.de* zinc b2.de* [ant-m stj2 ant-met stj2 *Bar-i* stj2 bell-p-sp dcm1 *Lith-i* stj2 *Mang-i* stj2 *Merc-i-f* stj2 *Nat-caust* stj2 *Zinc-i* stj2]
- **desire** for: gymno br1
- **interrupted** rest agg.: both-a rb3
- **must** rest: aesc bg2* alum bg2* alum-sil k2 anac bg2* arn bg2* brom bg2* bry bg2* hydrog srj2• lach bg2* lyc bg2* nux-v bg2* op bg2* ph-ac bg2* sabad bg2* stann bg2*

RESTING hand or elbow on knee: | **amel.**: euph b2.de*

RESTING head on table:

- **agg.**: verb b7.de
- **amel.**: con bg2 ferr b2.de* nux-v bg2 *Sabad* b2.de* sulph bg2

RESTING limbs:

- **agg.**: am-m b2.de* ang b2.de* arg-met b2.de* *Arn* b2.de* asar b2.de* *Bell* b2.de* camph b2.de* caust b2.de* *Cimic* bg2 cina b2.de* *Con* b2.de* croc b2.de* graph b2.de* *Kali-c* b2.de* mag-m b2.de* nux-m b2.de* phos b2.de* *Rhus-t* b2.de* ruta b2.de* sabin b2.de* samb b2.de* *Sil* b2.de* spong b2.de* squil b2.de* stann b2.de* sulph b2.de* teucr b2.de* *Ther* bg2 thuj b2.de* valer b2.de* verb b2.de*
- **amel.**: alum b2.de* *Am-c* b2.de* *Calc* b2.de* caust b2.de* dros b2.de* hep b2.de* ign b2.de* *Kali-c* bg2 **Nat-m** bg2 nux-v b2.de* phos b2.de* *Puls* b2.de* ruta b2.de* sabin b2.de* *Staph* b2.de* sulph b2.de* thuj b2.de*

RESTLESSNESS: *(↗MIND - Restlessness)* abrot bg2 absin bro1 **Acon** b2.de* adon bg2 agar b2.de* *Aids* nl2• alum b2.de* am-c b2.de* am-m bg2 ambr b2.de* **Anac** b2.de* androc srj1• ant-t b2.de* *Apis* bg2* arag bro1 arg-met bg2 arg-n bg2* arn b2.de* **Ars** b2.de* asaf b2.de* asar b2.de* aur bro1 bamb-a stb2.de• *Bapt* bg2* bar-c b2.de* **Bell** b2.de* bism bg2* borx b4a.de* bov bg2 *Bry* b2.de* bufo bg2 *Calc* b2.de* calc-p ptk1 camph b2.de* cann-i bro1 *Cann-s* b2.de* canth b2.de* carb-an b2.de* *Carb-v* b2.de* caul bg2 caust b2.de* cench br1* *Cham* b2.de* *Chin* b2.de* cimic bg2* cina b2.de* cocc b2.de* cod c2 *Coff* b2.de* colch bg2 coloc b2.de* con b2.de* *Croc* b2.de* crot-c sk4• cupr b2.de* dulc b2.de* eup-a br1 eup-per bg2 euph b2.de* euphr b2.de* *Ferr* b2.de* fic-m gya1 galla-q-r nl2• gels bg2 glon bg2 graph b2.de* hell b2.de* **Hyos** b2.de* *Ign* b2.de* iod b2.de* ip b2.de* kali-bi bg2 kali-br bg2* kali-c b2.de* kali-i bg2 *Kola* stb3• *Kreos* b7a.de lac-c bro1 lach bro1 laur bro1 led b2.de* lil-t bro1 lol bg2* luna kg1• *Lyc* b2.de* *M-ambo* b2.de m-arct b2.de* m-aust b2.de* mag-c b2.de* mag-m b2.de* mag-p ptk1 mang b2.de* med bro1 melal-alt gya4 meny b2.de* meph bg2 **Merc** b2.de* **Merc-c** b4a.de mez b2.de* *Morph* bro1 mosch b2.de* mur-ac b2.de* mygal bg2* nat-c b2.de* nat-m b2.de* nit-ac b2.de* nux-m b2.de* *Nux-v* b2.de* ol-an bg2 olnd b2.de* *Op* b2.de* par b2.de* pert-vc vk9 petr b2.de* ph-ac b2.de* phos b2.de* phyt bg2* *Plat* b2.de* plb b2.de* psor bg2* puls b2.de* pyrid rly4• pyrog bg2* rad-br c11* ran-b b2.de* rhod b4a.de **Rhus-t** b2.de* ruta b2.de* sabad b2.de* sabin b2.de* *Samb* b2.de* scor a1* sec b7a.de* **Sep** b2.de* sil b2.de* *Spig* b2.de* spong b2.de* squil b2.de* stann b2.de* **Staph** b2.de* stict bg2 **Stram** b2.de* stront-c bg2 *Sulph* b2.de* tab bg2 tarax bg2 **Tarent** bg2* teucr b2.de* ther bg2 thuj b2.de* tritic-vg fd5.de tub mrr1 tub-a jl2 tung-met bdx1• uran-n bg2 urt-u bro1 *Valer* b2.de* vanil fd5.de verat b2.de* verat-v bro1 vero-o rly4*• vib bg2* viol-t b2.de* vip bg2 *Zinc* b2.de* zinc-val bro1 [spect dfg1 tax jsj7 temp elm1]
- **daytime**: lavand-a ctl1•
- **night**: caust br1 ol-j br1 vanil fd5.de
  - **midnight**:
    - **after**:
      - **2** h: ambr a1
      - **3** h: agar a1
  - **amel.**: galla-q-r nl2•

- **chill**; during: acon$_{bg2}$ alum$_{bg2}$ am-c$_{bg2}$ **Ars**$_{bg2}$ asaf$_{bg2}$ **Bell**$_{bg2}$ bov$_{bg2}$ bry$_{bg2}$ calc$_{bg2}$ caps$_{bg2}$ carb-v$_{bg2}$ cham$_{bg2}$ chin$_{bg2}$ coff$_{bg2}$ ferr$_{bg2}$ hyos$_{bg2}$ ign$_{bg2}$ *Kreos*$_{bg2}$ **Lyc**$_{bg2}$ *M-ambo*$_{b7a.de}$ *Merc*$_{bg2}$ nux-v$_{bg2}$ op$_{bg2}$ ph-ac$_{bg2}$ **Rhus-t**$_{bg2}$ *Sabad*$_{bg2}$ sep$_{bg2}$ sil$_{bg2}$ spig$_{bg2}$ staph$_{bg2}$ stram$_{bg2}$
- **convulsive**: sol-ni$_{br1}$
- **fever**:
  - **during** | **agg.**: **Acon**$_{bg2}$ am-c$_{bg2}$ anac$_{bg2}$ ant-t$_{bg2}$ *Arn*$_{bg2}$ *Ars*$_{bg2}$ **Bar-c**$_{bg2}$ *Bell*$_{bg2}$ **Bov**$_{bg2}$ *Bry*$_{bg2}$ *Calc*$_{bg2}$ cann-xyz$_{bg2}$ carb-v$_{bg2}$ cham$_{bg2}$ chin$_{bg2}$ coff$_{bg2}$ ferr$_{bg2}$ *Hyos*$_{bg2}$ ign$_{bg2}$ ip$_{bg2}$ *Lyc*$_{bg2}$ **Mag-c**$_{bg2}$ mag-m$_{bg2}$ *Merc*$_{bg2}$ merc-c$_{bg2}$ **Mosch**$_{bg2}$ **Mur-ac**$_{bg2}$ nit-ac$_{bg2}$ nux-v$_{bg2}$ op$_{bg2}$ ph-ac$_{bg2}$ phos$_{bg2}$ plat$_{bg2}$ puls$_{bg2}$ rheum$_{bg2}$ **Rhus-t**$_{bg2}$ **Ruta**$_{bg2}$ **Sabin**$_{bg2}$ samb$_{bg2}$ sep$_{bg2}$ sil$_{bg2}$ spong$_{bg2}$ staph$_{bg2}$ stram$_{bg2}$ thuj$_{bg2}$ valer$_{bg2}$ verat$_{bg2}$
- **influenza**; during: pyrog$_{tl1}$
- **motion** | **amel.**: galeoc-c-h$_{gms1•}$
- **sleep**; during: hyos$_{b7.de*}$
- **sun**; after exposure to: pert-vc$_{vk9}$
- **violent**: sol-ni$_{br1}$

○ - **Affected** parts: **Arn**$_{b7a.de}$ bry$_{b7.de*}$ chin$_{b7.de*}$ ferr$_{b7.de*}$ *Rhus-t*$_{b7.de*}$
- **Joints**: ign$_{bro1}$

RETCHING: | **agg.**: *Asar*$_{b2.de*}$ olnd$_{b2.de*}$

RETRACTION: aster$_{ptk1}$ cic$_{ptk1}$ clem$_{ptk1}$ crot-t$_{ptk1}$ *Cupr*$_{ptk1}$ hydr$_{ptk1}$ lach$_{ptk1}$ *Merc*$_{ptk1}$ nat-m$_{ptk1}$ nux-v$_{ptk1}$ op$_{ptk1}$ par$_{ptk1}$ *Phyt*$_{ptk1}$ **Plb**$_{ptk1}$ sars$_{ptk1}$ sil$_{ptk1}$ thuj$_{ptk1}$ *Zinc*$_{ptk1}$
- **sensation** of: dig$_{b2.de*}$ hep$_{b2.de*}$ mur-ac$_{b2.de*}$ nux-v$_{b2.de*}$ plb$_{b2.de*}$ rhus-t$_{b2.de*}$ sulph$_{b2.de*}$ verb$_{b2.de*}$

○ - **Soft** parts; of: *(↗Drawing in - soft)* acon$_{b2.de*}$ **Ang**$_{b2.de*}$ ant-c$_{b2.de*}$ arn$_{b2.de*}$ ars$_{b2.de*}$ *Bell*$_{b2.de*}$ bov$_{b2.de*}$ calad$_{b2.de*}$ camph$_{b2.de*}$ caps$_{b2.de*}$ carb-v$_{b2.de*}$ chin$_{b2.de*}$ cocc$_{b2.de*}$ coloc$_{b2.de*}$ dulc$_{b2.de*}$ euph$_{b2.de*}$ graph$_{b2.de*}$ hep$_{b2.de*}$ hyos$_{b2.de*}$ ign$_{b2.de*}$ laur$_{b2.de*}$ m-ambo$_{b2.de*}$ **Merc**$_{b2.de*}$ nat-c$_{b2.de*}$ nat-m$_{b2.de*}$ *Nux-v*$_{b2.de*}$ op$_{b2.de*}$ ph-ac$_{b2.de*}$ phos$_{b2.de*}$ rhus-t$_{b2.de*}$ sep$_{b2.de*}$ squil$_{b2.de*}$ staph$_{b2.de*}$ stram$_{b2.de*}$ sulph$_{b2.de*}$

REVELING; complaints from night: *(↗Debauch; MIND - Libertinism; MIND - Reveling)* agar$_{bg2}$ ambr$_{k*}$ ant-c$_{k*}$ *Ars*$_{k*}$ bry$_{k*}$ *Carb-v*$_{k*}$ coff$_{k*}$ colch$_{k*}$ ip$_{k*}$ lac-d$_{c1}$ *Laur*$_{k*}$ led$_{k*}$ nat-c$_{bg2}$ **Nux-v**$_{k*}$ *Puls*$_{k*}$ rhus-t$_{k*}$ sabin$_{b2.de*}$ staph$_{bg2}$ sulph$_{k*}$

RICKETS: *(↗Bones; Softening; Softening bones)* am-c$_{c1*}$ arg-met$_{jl}$ *Ars*$_{c1*}$ ars-i$_{bro1}$ **Asaf**$_{b4a.de*}$ *Bell*$_{b4a.de*}$ **Calc**$_{b4a.de*}$ calc-act$_{bro1}$ calc-hp$_{bro1}$ *Calc-p*$_{kr1*}$ calc-sil$_{bro1}$ con$_{kr1}$ *Ferr*$_{kr1}$ *Ferr-i*$_{kr1}$ ferr-m$_{kr1*}$ ferr-p$_{kr1*}$ fl-ac$_{bro1}$ *Guaj*$_{kr1}$ hecla$_{kr1*}$ hed$_{c1*}$ *Hep*$_{b4a.de*}$ iod$_{kr1*}$ *Ip*$_{kr1}$ *Kali-i*$_{c1*}$ lac-c$_{kr1}$ *Lyc*$_{b4a.de*}$ mag-c$_{mtf33}$ mag-m$_{bro1*}$ med$_{bro1}$ **Merc**$_{b4a.de*}$ mez$_{b4a.de*}$ *Nit-ac*$_{b4a.de*}$ nux-m$_{kr1}$ *Ol-j*$_{kr1}$ op$_{a1}$ petr$_{b4a.de}$ *Ph-ac*$_{br1*}$ **Phos**$_{b4a.de*}$ pin-s$_{br1*}$ *Psor*$_{kr1}$ *Puls*$_{kr1}$ rhod$_{b4a.de}$ *Rhus-t*$_{kr1}$ ruta$_{kr1}$ sacch$_{c1*}$ sanic$_{c1*}$ *Sep*$_{b4a.de*}$ **Sil**$_{b4a.de*}$ *Staph*$_{kr1}$ *Sulph*$_{b4a.de*}$ suprar$_{bro1}$ tarent$_{a1}$ ther$_{kr1*}$ thuj$_{kr1*}$ thyr$_{br1*}$ tub$_{br*}$

RIDING:
- **air**; in open | **amel.**: naja$_{ptk1}$
- **boat**; in a | **agg.**: ang$_{b2.de*}$ ars$_{b2.de*}$ bell$_{b2.de*}$ brom$_{bg2}$ *Cocc*$_{b2.de*}$ *Colch*$_{b2.de*}$ croc$_{b2.de*}$ euph$_{b2.de*}$ *Ferr*$_{b2.de*}$ *Hyos*$_{bg2}$ kreos$_{bg2}$ m-arct$_{b2.de*}$ nat-m$_{bg2}$ nux-m$_{b2.de*}$ op$_{bg2}$ petr$_{b2.de*}$ sec$_{b2.de*}$ sil$_{bg2}$ staph$_{bg2}$ *Tab*$_{bg2}$ ther$_{bg2*}$ verat$_{bg2}$
- **cold** wind; in: sangin-n$_{c1}$
  - **amel.**: *Arg-n* *Tub*$_{k2*}$
- **horse**; a:
  - **agg.**: arg-n$_{st}$ arist-cl$_{sp1}$ ars$_{k*}$ *Bell*$_{k*}$ borx$_{bg2*}$ bry$_{k*}$ *Graph*$_{k*}$ *Lil-t*$_{k*}$ mag-m$_{k*}$ meph *Nat-c*$_{k*}$ nat-m$_{h2*}$ psor$_{bg2}$ *Ruta*$_{kr1*}$ **Sep**$_{k*}$ sil$_{k*}$ spig$_{k*}$ *Sul-ac*$_{k*}$ ther$_{c1}$ valer$_{k*}$
  - **amel.**: brom$_{k*}$ calc$_{k*}$ kali-c$_{bg2*}$ lyc$_{k*}$ tarent$_{bg1*}$
- **streetcar**; downhill on a | **agg.**: *(↗MIND - Fear - falling)* **Borx**$_{k*}$ *Psor*$_{k*}$
- **streetcar**; on a:
  - **after**: graph$_{k*}$ kali-n$_{k*}$ nat-c$_{k*}$ nat-m$_{k*}$ *Nit-ac*$_{k*}$ plat$_{k*}$ **Sil**
  - **agg.**: *(↗Travelling - ailments; MIND - Riding - carriage - aversion; STOMACH - Nausea - Riding - carriage)* acon$_{sf1.de}$ alum-sil$_{k2}$ aq-mar$_{mgm•}$ *Arg-met*$_{k*}$ *Arg-n* *Arn*$_{k*}$ ars$_{k*}$ asaf$_{bg2*}$ *Aur*$_{k*}$ bell$_{bg2}$ *Berb*$_{bg2*}$ *Borx*$_{k*}$ bry$_{k*}$ calc$_{k*}$ calc-p$_{bg2}$ caps$_{brm}$ carb-v$_{k*}$ caust$_{bro1*}$ coc-c$_{bg2}$ **Cocc**$_{k*}$ colch$_{k*}$ *Con* croc$_{k*}$ cycl$_{kr1*}$ dig$_{bg2}$ ferr$_{k*}$ fl-ac$_{bg2*}$ *Form*$_{mgm•}$ galeoc-c-h$_{gms1•}$

Riding – streetcar; on a – **agg.**: ... graph$_{b2.de*}$ grat$_{bg2}$ **Helon**$_{kr1*}$ *Hep*$_{k*}$ hydrog$_{srj2•}$ hyos$_{k*}$ ign$_{k*}$ ina-i$_{mlk9.de}$ iod$_{k*}$ iodof$_{kr1}$ kali-c$_{k*}$ lac-d$_{st}$ lac-h$_{htj1•}$ *Lach*$_{k*}$ lyc$_{k*}$ *Lyss*$_{k*}$ mag-c$_{k*}$ mag-s$_{mg1.de*}$ meph nat-m$_{k*}$ *Nux-m*$_{k*}$ nux-v$_{c2}$ op$_{k*}$ **Petr**$_{k*}$ phos$_{k*}$ plat$_{k*}$ *Psor*$_{k*}$ puls rhus-t$_{k*}$ *Rumx* *Sanic*$_{bro1*}$ *Sel*$_{k*}$ **Sep**$_{k*}$ *Sil*$_{k*}$ spig$_{k2}$ staph$_{k*}$ sul-ac$_{bg2}$ *Sulph*$_{k*}$ **Tab**$_{b7a.de*}$ *Ther*$_{k*}$ thuj tril-p$_{bg2}$ valer$_{k*}$ [zinc-n$_{stj2}$]
  - **accompanied** by | **eczema** (See SKIN - Eruptions - eczema - accompanied - motion)
  - **closed** car: mag-s$_{sp1}$
- **amel.**: androc$_{srj1•}$ arg-n$_{sf1.de*}$ *Ars*$_{k*}$ bar-m$_{bg1}$ brom bry$_{bg2}$ cupr$_{sst3•}$ des-ac$_{jl}$ galeoc-c-h$_{gms1•}$ *Gels*$_{bg2*}$ glon$_{bg1}$ *Graph*$_{b2.de*}$ kali-n$_{k*}$ lyc$_{bg2}$ merc$_{bg2}$ merc-c$_{bg2}$ *Naja*$_{st*}$ nat-m$_{h2*}$ **NIT-AC**$_{k●*}$ nux-m$_{sf1.de}$ phos$_{k*}$ puls$_{sf1.de}$ tarent$_{ptk1}$ thiop$_{jl}$ [ferr-n$_{stj2}$ mag-n$_{stj2}$ mang-n$_{stj2}$ nitro$_{stj2}$]
- **aversion** to: *(↗MIND - Riding - carriage - aversion)* psor$_{st}$
- **train**; in a: | **agg.**: kali-i$_{ptk1}$

RINSING MOUTH agg.: coc-c$_{ptk1}$

RIPPLING; sensation of: cann-xyz$_{bg2}$ form-ac$_{bg2}$

RISING:
- **agg.**: **Acon**$_{k*}$ alum$_{k*}$ alum-sil$_{k2}$ am-c$_{b2.de}$ *Am-m*$_{k*}$ anac$_{k*}$ ang$_{b2.de*}$ ant-c$_{b2.de}$ *Ant-t*$_{k*}$ arg-met$_{k*}$ arg-n$_{sf1.de*}$ *Arn*$_{k*}$ *Ars*$_{k*}$ asar$_{k*}$ aur$_{b2.de}$ bar-c$_{k*}$ bar-m bar-s$_{k2}$ **Bell**$_{k*}$ berb$_{j5.de}$ borx$_{b2.de}$ both-a$_{rb3}$ bov$_{k*}$ brucel$_{sa3•}$ **Bry**$_{k*}$ cact cadm-s$_{ptk1}$ calad$_{k*}$ *Calc*$_{b2.de}$ camph$_{b2.de}$ *Cann-i* *Cann-s*$_{k*}$ canth$_{b2.de}$ caps$_{k*}$ carb-an$_{k*}$ **Carb-v**$_{b2.de*}$ caust$_{k*}$ *Cham*$_{k*}$ *Chel*$_{k*}$ chin$_{k*}$ *Cic*$_{k*}$ *Cina*$_{b2.de}$ clem$_{b2.de}$ **Cocc**$_{k*}$ colch$_{k*}$ coloc$_{k*}$ *Con*$_{k*}$ croc$_{k*}$ **Dig**$_{k*}$ dros$_{k*}$ dulc$_{b2.de}$ euph$_{b2.de}$ *Ferr*$_{k*}$ fl-ac$_{bg2}$ *Graph*$_{b2.de}$ *Guaj*$_{b2.de}$ hell$_{k*}$ hep$_{k*}$ hydrog$_{srj2•}$ hyos$_{b2.de}$ *Ign*$_{k*}$ ip$_{b2.de}$ kali-c$_{k*}$ kali-m$_{k2}$ kali-n$_{b2.de}$ kreos$_{b2.de}$ lac-ac$_{stj2*•}$ lach$_{k*}$ laur$_{k*}$ led$_{b2.de}$ **Lyc**$_{k*}$ *M-ambo*$_{b2.de}$ m-arct$_{b2.de}$ m-aust$_{b2.de*}$ mag-c$_{b2.de}$ mag-m$_{k*}$ mang$_{k*}$ meny$_{k*}$ merc$_{k*}$ *Merc-i-f*$_{ptk1}$ mez$_{b2.de}$ mosch$_{b2.de}$ *Mur-ac*$_{k*}$ *Nat-c*$_{k*}$ *Nat-m*$_{k*}$ *Nit-ac*$_{k*}$ nux-m$_{b2.de}$ **Nux-v**$_{k*}$ *Olnd*$_{b2.de}$ **Op**$_{k*}$ *Osm* par$_{b2.de}$ petr$_{b2.de}$ ph-ac$_{k*}$ *Phos*$_{k*}$ *Phyt*$_{bg2*}$ plat$_{k*}$ plb$_{k*}$ psor$_{k2}$ *Puls*$_{k*}$ rad-br$_{c11*}$ ran-b$_{k*}$ *Rhod*$_{b2.de}$ **Rhus-t**$_{k*}$ rumx ruta$_{b2.de}$ sabad$_{k*}$ *Sabin*$_{b2.de}$ *Samb*$_{b2.de}$ *Sang* sars$_{k*}$ *Sel*$_{b2.de}$ seneg$_{k*}$ sep$_{k*}$ **Sil**$_{k*}$ *Spig*$_{b2.de}$ spong$_{k*}$ *Squil*$_{k*}$ stann$_{k*}$ staph$_{k*}$ stram$_{k*}$ sul-ac$_{k*}$ **Sulph**$_{k*}$ tarax$_{k*}$ *Thuj*$_{b2.de}$ valer$_{b2.de}$ verat$_{k*}$ verat-v$_{k*}$ verb$_{b2.de}$ vib$_{ptk1}$ *Viol-t*$_{k*}$ zinc$_{k*}$ [bell-p-sp$_{dcm1}$ mag-lac$_{stj2}$]
  - **forenoon**: cob-n$_{sp1}$
- **amel.**: acon$_{k*}$ alum$_{k*}$ **Am-c**$_{k*}$ am-m$_{k*}$ ambr$_{bro1}$ ang$_{b7.de*}$ *Ant-t*$_{k*}$ aral$_{ptk1}$ **Ars**$_{k*}$ asaf$_{k*}$ aur$_{k*}$ bar-c$_{k*}$ bell$_{k*}$ *Borx*$_{k*}$ bov$_{k*}$ bry$_{k*}$ **Calc**$_{k*}$ cann-s$_{k*}$ canth$_{k*}$ **Caps**$_{sf1.de}$ carb-v$_{k*}$ caust$_{k*}$ *Cham*$_{k*}$ chel$_{k*}$ chin$_{k*}$ cic$_{k*}$ *Cimic*$_{bg2}$ colch$_{sf1.de}$ coloc$_{k*}$ con$_{k*}$ *Cupr* *Dig*$_{k*}$ ferr$_{k*}$ glon$_{ptk1}$ hell$_{k*}$ hep$_{k*}$ *Hyos*$_{k*}$ *Ign*$_{k*}$ *Kali-c*$_{k*}$ kali-n$_{sf1.de}$ laur$_{k*}$ *Led*$_{sf1.de}$ lith-c$_{bro1}$ *Lyc*$_{k*}$ mag-c$_{k*}$ mang$_{k*}$ merc$_{k*}$ mosch$_{k*}$ naja nat-c$_{k*}$ nat-m$_{k*}$ nux-m$_{k*}$ nux-v$_{k*}$ olnd$_{k*}$ parth$_{bro1}$ petr$_{k*}$ *Ph-ac*$_{j5.de*}$ phos$_{k*}$ **Plat**$_{h2}$ puls$_{k*}$ rhus-t$_{k*}$ sabin$_{k*}$ **Samb**$_{k*}$ **Sep**$_{k*}$ *Sil*$_{k*}$ spig$_{k*}$ squil$_{k*}$ stann$_{k*}$ sul-ac$_{k*}$ sulph$_{k*}$ teucr$_{k*}$ *Valer*$_{b7a.de}$ [tax$_{jsj7}$]
  - **one** hour after: prot$_{jl2}$
- **bed**; from:
  - **after**:
    - **agg.**: acon$_{b7.de*}$ am-c$_{b4.de*}$ **Am-m**$_{b7.de*}$ anac$_{b4.de*}$ ang$_{b7.de*}$ ant-c$_{b7.de*}$ ant-t$_{b7.de*}$ arg-met$_{b7.de*}$ ars$_{b4.de*}$ bar-c$_{b4.de*}$ bell$_{b4.de*}$ borx$_{b4a.de*}$ bov$_{b4.de*}$ bry$_{b7.de*}$ *Calc*$_{b4.de*}$ camph$_{b7.de*}$ cann-xyz$_{bg2}$ canth$_{b7.de*}$ caps$_{b7.de*}$ carb-an$_{b4.de*}$ *Carb-v*$_{b4a.de*}$ caust$_{b4.de*}$ *Cham*$_{bg2}$ cina$_{b7.de*}$ coloc$_{b4.de*}$ con$_{b4.de*}$ croc$_{b7.de*}$ dulc$_{b4.de*}$ euph$_{b4.de*}$ fl-ac$_{bg2}$ *Graph*$_{b4.de*}$ *Guaj*$_{b4a.de*}$ *Hell*$_{b7.de*}$ hep$_{b4.de*}$ hyos$_{b7.de*}$ *Ign*$_{b7.de*}$ ip$_{b7.de*}$ kali-c$_{b4.de*}$ kali-n$_{bg2}$ **Lach**$_{b7a.de*}$ laur$_{b7.de*}$ led$_{b7.de*}$ lyc$_{b4.de*}$ m-ambo$_{b7.de*}$ m-arct$_{b7.de}$ mag-c$_{b4.de*}$ mag-m$_{b4.de*}$ mang$_{b4.de*}$ meny$_{b7.de*}$ merc-c$_{bg2}$ mez$_{b4.de*}$ mur-ac$_{b4.de*}$ nat-c$_{b4.de*}$ *Nat-m*$_{b4.de*}$ nit-ac$_{b4.de*}$ nux-m$_{b7.de*}$ *Nux-v*$_{b7.de*}$ *Olnd*$_{b7.de*}$ par$_{b7.de*}$ ph-ac$_{b4.de*}$ *Phos*$_{b4.de*}$ plat$_{b4.de*}$ *Puls*$_{b7.de*}$ *Ran-b*$_{b7.de*}$ rhod$_{b4.de*}$ **Rhus-t**$_{b7.de*}$ ruta$_{b7.de*}$ sabad$_{b7.de*}$ sars$_{bg2}$ sep$_{b4.de*}$ sil$_{b4.de*}$ *Spig*$_{b7.de*}$ spong$_{bg2}$ squil$_{b7.de*}$ *Staph*$_{b7.de*}$ stram$_{b7.de*}$ sul-ac$_{b4.de*}$ *Sulph*$_{bg2}$ thuj$_{b4.de*}$ valer$_{b7.de*}$ *Verat*$_{b7.de*}$ verb$_{b7.de*}$
    - **amel.**: acon$_{b2.de*}$ agar$_{b2.de}$ agn$_{b2.de}$ alum$_{b2.de*}$ *Am-c*$_{b2.de}$ am-m$_{b2.de}$ **Ambr**$_{b2.de*}$ anac$_{b2.de}$ ang$_{b2.de*}$ ant-c$_{b2.de}$ *Ant-t*$_{b2.de*}$ *Arg-met*$_{b2.de*}$ arn$_{b2.de*}$ *Ars*$_{b2.de*}$ asaf$_{b2.de}$ asar$_{b2.de}$ *Aur*$_{b2.de*}$ bar-c$_{b2.de*}$ *Bell*$_{b2.de*}$ bism$_{b2.de}$ *Borx*$_{b2.de}$ bov$_{b2.de*}$ bry$_{b2.de*}$ calad$_{b2.de}$ calc$_{b2.de*}$ camph$_{b2.de}$ cann-s$_{b2.de}$ canth$_{b2.de*}$

- **bed**; from – **after** – **amel**.: ...
caps b2.de *Carb-an* b2.de* carb-v b2.de* caust b2.de* cham b2.de* chel b2.de chin b2.de* cic b2.de cina b2.de clem b2.de cocc b2.de* coff b2.de* colch b2.de *Coloc* b2.de con b2.de croc b2.de cycl b2.de dig b2.de *Dros* b2.de* dulc b2.de* *Euph* b2.de euphr b2.de *Ferr* b2.de* graph b2.de* guaj b2.de hell b2.de hep b2.de* hyos b2.de *Ign* b2.de* **Iod** b2.de *Kali-c* b2.de* kali-n b2.de* kreos b2.de lach b2.de laur b2.de* *Led* b2.de *Lyc* b2.de* *M-ambo* b2.de* *M-arct* b2.de* m-aust b2.de* *Mag-c* b2.de* mag-m b2.de *Mang* b2.de meny b2.de *Merc* b2.de mez b2.de mosch b2.de mur-ac b2.de nat-c b2.de nat-m b2.de nit-ac b2.de* nux-m b2.de* *Nux-v* b2.de* olnd b2.de* op b2.de par b2.de petr b2.de ph-ac b2.de* *Phos* b2.de* *Plat* b2.de plb b2.de* **Puls** b2.de* ran-b b2.de* rheum b2.de *Rhod* b2.de* *Rhus-t* b2.de* ruta b2.de sabad b2.de* sabin b2.de* samb b2.de sars b2.de* sec b2.de *Sel* b2.de seneg b2.de **Sep** b2.de* sil b2.de *Spig* b2.de* spong b2.de squil b2.de stann b2.de* staph b2.de* stram b2.de *Stront-c* b2.de* sul-ac b2.de* *Sulph* b2.de* tarax b2.de teucr b2.de thuj b2.de valer b2.de *Verat* b2.de* verb b2.de viol-o b2.de* viol-t b2.de zinc b2.de
  - **agg**.: *Acon* b7a.de* am-m b7.de* ang b7.de* ant-c b7.de* ant-t b7.de* *Apis* bg2 ars bg2 asar b7.de* aur b4.de* *Bell* b4.de* bov b4.de* **Bry** b7.de* calad b7.de* *Calc* b4.de* *Caps* b7.de* carb-an b4.de* **Carb-v** b4.de* caust b4.de* *Cham* b7.de* chin b7.de* cic b7.de* cimic ptk1 *Cina* b7.de* clem b4.de* **Cocc** bg2* **Con** b4.de* croc b7a.de* dig b4.de* dulc b4.de* ferr b7.de* *Graph* b4.de* guaj b4.de* hell b7.de* *Hep* b4.de* hyos b7.de* *Ign* b7.de* kali-bi bg2 kali-c b4.de* kreos bg2 **Lach** bg2* led b7.de* lept bg2 *Lyc* b4.de* *M-ambo* b7.de* m-arct b7.de m-aust b7.de mag-c b4.de* mag-m bg2 meny b7.de* merc b4.de* merc-c b4a.de mosch b7a.de* *Nat-m* b4.de* nit-ac b4.de* *Nux-v* b7.de* *Olnd* b7.de* op bg2 par b7.de* petr b4.de* *Ph-ac* b4.de* *Phos* b4.de* plat b4.de* plb b7.de* puls b7.de* ran-b b7.de* *Rhod* b4.de* *Rhus-t* b7.de* ruta b7.de* *Sabin* b7.de* samb b7.de* *Sel* b7a.de* sep b4.de* *Sil* b4.de* *Spig* bg2 squil b7.de* stann b4.de* *Staph* b7.de* stram b7.de* *Sul-ac* b4a.de* *Sulph* bg2* *Thuj* b4.de* valer b7.de* verat b7.de*
  - **amel**.: am-m b2.de* ang b2.de* arg-met b2.de* *Ars* b2.de* **Aur** b2.de* *Caps* b2.de* carb-an b2.de* caust b2.de* chin b2.de* cic b2.de* con b2.de* dig b2.de* **Dulc** b2.de* *Ferr* b2.de* hell b2.de* hyos b2.de* **Ign** b2.de* *Iod* bg2 kali-n b2.de* kreos b2.de* laur b2.de* *Led* b2.de* *Lyc* b2.de* *Mag-c* b2.de* merc b2.de* mosch b2.de* nat-c b2.de* par b2.de* ph-ac bg2* *Plat* b2.de* plb b2.de* **Puls** b2.de* *Rhus-t* b2.de* sabin b2.de* *Samb* b2.de* **Sep** b2.de* stann b2.de* sul-ac b2.de* sulph b2.de* tarax b2.de* teucr b2.de* *Verat* b2.de* zinc b2.de*
- **difficult**: aesc ptk1 agar ptk1 petr ptk1 ruta ptk1 sulph ptk1
- **must** rise | **pain**; from: mez br1
- **sitting**; from:
  - **after**:
    - **agg**.: aesc ptk1 agar ptk1 alum b2.de* ant-t ptk1 berb ptk1 bry b2.de* calc ptk1 *Caps* ptk1 carb-v b2.de* *Caust* ptk1 *Con* ptk1 kali-bi ptk1 laur b2.de* led ptk1 *Lyc* ptk1 m-ambo b2.de* m-aust b2.de* *Nat-s* ptk1 olnd b2.de* petr ptk1 **Phos** ptk1 puls b2.de* rhus-t b2.de* ruta ptk1 sep ptk1 *Spig* ptk1 staph ptk1 **Sulph** ptk1 verat b2.de*
    - **amel**.: acon b2.de* *Agar* b2.de* agn b2.de* alum b2.de* am-c b2.de* am-m b2.de* *Ambr* b2.de* anac b2.de* *Ang* b2.de* ant-c b2.de* ant-t b2.de* *Arg-met* b2.de* ars b2.de* *Asaf* b2.de* asar b2.de* aur b2.de* *Bar-c* b2.de* bell b2.de* bism b2.de* borx b2.de* bov b2.de* calc b2.de* cann-s b2.de* canth b2.de* **Caps** b2.de* carb-v b2.de* caust b2.de* cham b2.de* chel b2.de* chin b2.de* cic b2.de* *Cina* b2.de* cob ptk1 cocc b2.de* **Con** b2.de* cupr b2.de* **Cycl** b2.de* dig b2.de* *Dros* b2.de* **Dulc** b2.de* *Euph* b2.de* euphr b2.de* *Ferr* b2.de* graph b2.de* guaj b2.de* hell b2.de* hep b2.de* hyos b2.de* ign b2.de* iod b2.de* kali-c b2.de* kali-n b2.de* kreos b2.de* *Lach* b2.de* laur b2.de* led b2.de* **Lyc** b2.de* *M-ambo* b2.de* m-arct b2.de m-aust b2.de mag-c b2.de* *Mag-m* b2.de* mang b2.de* *Meny* b2.de* *Merc* b2.de* mez b2.de* *Mosch* b2.de* *Mur-ac* b2.de* *Nat-c* b2.de* nat-m b2.de* nit-ac b2.de* olnd b2.de* op b2.de* par b2.de* petr b2.de* *Ph-ac* b2.de* phos b2.de* **Plat** b2.de* plb b2.de* **Puls** b2.de* *Rhod* b2.de* **Rhus-t** b2.de* *Ruta* b2.de* *Sabad* b2.de* sabin b2.de* samb b2.de* sars b2.de* sel b2.de* *Seneg* b2.de* **Sep** b2.de* sil b2.de* spig b2.de* spong b2.de* stann b2.de* staph b2.de* stront-c b2.de* sul-ac b2.de* sulph b2.de* *Tarax* b2.de* teucr b2.de* thuj b2.de* *Valer* b2.de* verat b2.de* **Verb** b2.de* viol-o b2.de* **Viol-t** b2.de* zinc b2.de*

Rising – **sitting**; from: ...
  - **agg**.: *Acon* b2.de* ambr b2.de* anac b2.de* ang b2.de* ant-c b2.de* *Ant-t* b2.de* *Apis* bg2 arn b2.de* ars b2.de* asar b2.de* aur b2.de* *Bar-c* b2.de* *Bell* b2.de* both-ax tsm2 bov b2.de* *Bry* b2.de* calc b2.de* cann-s b2.de* canth b2.de* **Caps** b2.de* carb-an b2.de* *Carb-v* b2.de* *Caust* b2.de* cham b2.de* *Chin* b2.de* cic b2.de* cocc b2.de* **Con** b2.de* croc b2.de* dig b2.de* dros b2.de* *Euph* b2.de* *Ferr* b2.de* *Fl-ac* bg2 graph b2.de* kali-bi bg2 kali-c b2.de* kali-n b2.de* lach b2.de* *Laur* b2.de* *Led* b2.de* **Lyc** b2.de* m-ambo b2.de* m-arct b2.de* m-aust b2.de* mang b2.de* merc b2.de* merc-i-f bg2 mur-ac b2.de* nat-c b2.de* *Nat-m* b2.de* *Nat-s* bg2 *Nit-ac* b2.de* *Nux-v* b2.de* *Olnd* b2.de* *Petr* b2.de* *Ph-ac* b2.de* **Phos** b2.de* plat b2.de* **Puls** b2.de* ran-b b2.de* rhod b2.de* **Rhus-t** b2.de* *Ruta* b2.de* sabad b2.de* *Sep* b2.de* sil b2.de* **Spig** b2.de* *Staph* b2.de* stram b2.de* stront-c b2.de* *Sulph* b2.de* *Thuj* b2.de* *Verat* b2.de*
  - **amel**.: am-m b2.de* arg-met b2.de* *Aur* b2.de* bar-c b2.de* caust b2.de* chin b2.de* cycl b2.de* *Dulc* b2.de* *Ign* b2.de* kali-c b2.de* lyc b2.de* *Mag-c* b2.de* mang b2.de* merc b2.de* nat-c b2.de* phos b2.de* plat b2.de* *Puls* b2.de* rhus-t b2.de* samb b2.de* *Sep* b2.de* spig b2.de* spong b2.de* teucr b2.de* valer b2.de* *Verat* b2.de* viol-t b2.de*
- **stooping**; from:
  - **agg**.: **Acon** b2.de alum b2.de *Am-m* b2.de anac b2.de ang b2.de arg-met b2.de *Arn* b2.de *Ars* b2.de asar b2.de bar-c b2.de **Bell** b2.de bov b2.de **Bry** b2.de calad b2.de *Cann-s* b2.de caps b2.de carb-an b2.de caust b2.de *Cham* b2.de chel b2.de chin b2.de *Cic* b2.de *Cocc* b2.de colch b2.de coloc b2.de *Con* b2.de croc b2.de dig b2.de dros b2.de *Ferr* b2.de hell b2.de hep b2.de *Ign* b2.de kali-c b2.de laur b2.de *Lyc* b2.de* m-aust b2.de mag-m b2.de mang b2.de meny b2.de merc b2.de *Mur-ac* b2.de *Nat-m* b2.de *Nit-ac* b2.de **Nux-v** b2.de **Op** b2.de ph-ac b2.de *Phos* b2.de* plat b2.de plb b2.de *Puls* b2.de* ran-b b2.de **Rhus-t** b2.de sars b2.de seneg b2.de sep b2.de spong b2.de *Squil* b2.de *Stann* b2.de staph b2.de stram b2.de sul-ac b2.de **Sulph** b2.de tarax b2.de verat b2.de *Viol-t* b2.de zinc b2.de
  - **amel**.: acon b2.de alum b2.de **Am-c** b2.de am-m b2.de ang b2.de *Ant-t* b2.de **Ars** b2.de asaf b2.de aur b2.de bar-c b2.de bell b2.de *Borx* b2.de bov b2.de bry b2.de **Calc** b2.de cann-s b2.de canth b2.de carb-v b2.de caust b2.de *Cham* b2.de chel b2.de chin b2.de cic b2.de coloc b2.de con b2.de *Dig* b2.de ferr b2.de hell b2.de hep b2.de *Hyos* b2.de *Ign* b2.de *Kali-c* b2.de laur b2.de *Lyc* b2.de mag-c b2.de mang b2.de merc b2.de mosch b2.de nat-c b2.de nat-m b2.de nux-m b2.de nux-v b2.de olnd b2.de petr b2.de phos b2.de puls b2.de rhus-t b2.de *Sabin* b2.de **Samb** b2.de **Sep** b2.de *Sil* b2.de spig b2.de squil b2.de stann b2.de sul-ac b2.de sulph b2.de teucr b2.de

RISING; sensation of something: am-m b2.de* **Arg-n** bg2 *Asaf* b2.de* asar b2.de* borx b2.de* bufo bg2 cedr bg2 **Con** bg2 fl-ac bg2 hep b2.de* *Lach* bg2 laur b2.de* **Led** bg2 lyc b2.de* *Merc* b2.de* mur-ac bg2 nat-c b2.de* nux-v b2.de* *Phos* b2.de* *Plat* b2.de* ran-b b2.de* *Spig* b2.de* sul-ac b2.de* thuj bg2 valer b2.de* *Verat* b2.de* zinc bg2

RIVET or bullet; sensation of a: lil-t ptk1 sulph ptk1

ROBUST people (See Vigor)

ROCKING (= swinging to and fro):
- **agg**.: ars bg2 borx b2.de* carb-v b2.de* *Cocc* bg2* thuj ptk1
  - **forward**; rocking: borx bg2
- **amel**.: carb-an ptk1 cham ptk1 cina ptk1 kali-c ptk1 *Merc-c* ptk1 puls ptk1 pyrog ptk1 rhus-t ptk1 sec ptk1
  - **forward**; rocking: calc bg2 carb-an bg2 cham bg2 cina bg2 kali-c bg2 plb bg2 pyrog bg2 sec bg2
- **to** and fro | **amel**.: bell ptk1 hyos ptk1

ROLLING; sensation of: acon b2.de* agn bg2 aloe bg2 am-c ptk1 am-m bg2 anac bg2 ang bg2 ars ptk1 aur bg2 bell b2.de* *Cact* bg2* crot-h ptk1 cupr ptk1 gels ptk1 graph b2.de* ign b2.de* kali-c bg2* kali-n bg2 *Lach* bg2* lil-t bg2 lyc bg2* m-aust b2.de nat-c bg2 nux-v bg2 ol-an bg2 phos ptk1 plat b2.de* plb b2.de* podo bg2 puls bg2* *Rhus-t* b2.de* ruta bg2 sabad bg2* *Sep* b2.de* tab bg2 tarax b2.de* tarent ptk1

ROMBERG'S sign (See VERTIGO - Standing - eyes)

ROOM:
- **agg**.: *Acon* b2.de* aeth bg2 agar b4.de *Agn* b2.de* all-c bg2 **Alum** b2.de* am-c b2.de* am-m b2.de* ambr b2.de* *Anac* b2.de* ang b2.de* *Ant-c* b2.de* ant-t bg2 apis bg2 *Arg-met* b2.de* **Arg-n** bg2 arn b2.de* ars b2.de* *Asaf* b2.de* *Asar* b2.de* aur b2.de* bar-c b2.de* bell b2.de* borx b2.de* bov b2.de* brom bg2

- **agg.**: ...
  Bry b2.de* calc b2.de* camph b2.de* cann-s b2.de* canth b2.de* caps b2.de* carb-an b2.de* carb-v b2.de* caust b2.de* cham b7.de chel b2.de* chin b7.de cic b2.de* cina b2.de* coff b2.de* colch b2.de* con b2.de* *Croc* b2.de* dig b2.de* dros b7.de dulc b2.de* **Fl-ac** bg2 *Graph* b2.de* *Hell* b2.de* hep b2.de* hyos b2.de* ign b2.de* iod b2.de* *Ip* b2.de* kali-c b2.de* kali-i bg2 kali-n b2.de* kali-s bg2 laur b2.de* led b7.de lil-t bg2 *Lyc* b2.de* m-arct b2.de* m-aust b2.de* **Mag-c** b2.de* *Mag-m* b2.de* mang b2.de* meny b2.de* merc b2.de* *Mez* b2.de* mosch b2.de* mur-ac b2.de* nat-c b2.de* nat-m b2.de* nit-ac b2.de* nux-v b2.de* op b2.de* petr b4.de ph-ac b2.de* *Phos* b2.de* pic-ac bg2 pip-n bg2 *Plat* b2.de* plb b2.de* *Puls* b2.de* ran-b b2.de* *Ran-s* b2.de* rhod b2.de* *Rhus-t* b2.de* ruta b2.de* **Sabin** b2.de* sars b2.de* sel b2.de seneg b2.de* sep b2.de* sil b4.de spig b2.de* *Spong* b2.de* stann b2.de* staph b2.de* stram b7.de stront-c b2.de* sul-ac b2.de* **Sulph** b2.de* tab bg2 tarax b2.de* thuj b2.de* *Valer* bg2 verat b2.de* verb b2.de* viol-t b2.de* zinc b2.de*
  - **air**; as well as open: ars bg2 aur bg2 iod bg2 mez bg2
- **amel.**: *Agar* b2.de* agn b2.de* alum b2.de* am-c b2.de* am-m b2.de* ambr b2.de* anac b2.de* ang b2.de* ant-c b7.de arn b2.de* ars b2.de* aur b2.de* bar-c b2.de* bell b2.de* borx b2.de* bov b2.de* bry b2.de* calad b2.de* calc b2.de* *Camph* b2.de* cann-s b2.de* canth b2.de* caps b2.de* *Carb-an* b2.de* *Carb-v* b2.de* caust b2.de* *Cham* b2.de* *Chel* b2.de* *Chin* b2.de* cic b2.de* cina b2.de* **Cocc** b2.de* *Coff* b2.de* coloc b2.de* *Con* b2.de* dig b2.de* dros b2.de* dulc b2.de* euph b2.de* *Ferr* b2.de* graph b2.de* **Guaj** b2.de* hell b2.de* hep b2.de* hyos b2.de* ign b2.de* iod b2.de* ip b2.de* kali-c b2.de* kali-n b2.de* *Kreos* b2.de* *Lach* b2.de* laur b2.de* led b2.de* lyc b2.de* m-ambo b2.de* m-arct b2.de* m-aust b2.de* mag-c b2.de* mag-m b2.de* mang b2.de* meny b2.de* merc b2.de* mez b2.de* mosch b2.de* mur-ac b2.de* nat-c b2.de* nat-m b2.de* nit-ac b2.de* **Nux-m** b2.de* **Nux-v** b2.de* olnd b2.de* op b2.de* *Petr* b2.de* ph-ac b2.de* phos b2.de* plat b2.de* plb b2.de* puls b2.de ran-b b2.de* rheum b2.de* rhod b2.de* rhus-t b2.de* rumx bg2 ruta b2.de* sabad b2.de* sabin b2.de* sars b2.de* *Sel* b2.de* seneg b2.de* sep b2.de* **Sil** b2.de* *Spig* b2.de* stann b2.de* staph b2.de* *Stram* b2.de* stront-c b2.de* sul-ac b2.de* sulph b2.de* tarax b2.de* tarent ptk1 *Teucr* b2.de* thuj b2.de* *Valer* b2.de* verat b2.de* verb b2.de* viol-t b2.de* zinc b2.de*
- **close** room: (↗*MIND - Fear - narrow)*
  - **agg.**: (↗*MIND - Fear - narrow)* abrom-a ks5 alum k2 aml-ns ptk1 arg-n ptk1 arist-cl jl ars-i k2 bar-s k2 just ptk1 kali-i mrr1 lac-d ptk1 lil-t ptk1 malar jl2* med ptk1 melal-alt gya4 nux-v gl1.fr• podo fd3.de• positr nl2• puls gl1.fr• rauw jl staph gl1.fr• sulph gl1.fr• tub st* vib ptk1
  - **amel.**: euph-l bro1
- **entering** a room; when | **agg.**: *Puls* b7.de *Ran-b* b7.de ran-s b7.de *Rhus-t* b7.de* *Sel* b7a.de spong b7.de *Verat* b7a.de *Verb* b7.de
- **full**:
  - **objects** agg.; of: phys ptk1
  - **people** agg.; of: (↗*MIND - Fear - crowd; MIND - Fear - narrow)* *Ambr* k* ant-c vld *Ant-t* apis bg1* *Arg-n* k* ars k* ars-i sne bar-c k* carb-an k* con k* cypra-eg sde6.de• gard-j vlr2• *Hell* k* hippoc-k szs2 iod bg1* kali-i bg1* lil-t bg1* *Lyc* k* *Mag-c* k* nat-c k* nat-m k* nux-m gk petr k* *Phos* k* *Plb* k* *Puls* k* sabin *Sep* k* stann k* stram k* *Sulph* k* [mang-met stj2]

ROUGH sensation: aesc ptk1 *Alum* ptk1 am-m ptk1 ambr ptk1 arg-n ptk1 *Berb* ptk1 kali-bi ptk1 mang ptk1 naja ptk1 nat-m ptk1 *Nux-v* ptk1 par ptk1 phos ptk1 *Phyt* ptk1 ruta ptk1 *Sulph* ptk1

○ - **Internal** parts: acon b2.de* agar b2.de* *Alum* b2.de* am-c b2.de* am-m b2.de* ambr b2.de* anac b2.de* ang b2.de* ant-c b2.de* arg-met b2.de* ars b2.de* bar-c b2.de* bell b2.de* benz-ac bg2 berb bg2 borx b2.de* bov b2.de* bry b2.de* *Calc* b2.de* cann-s b2.de* canth b2.de* caps b2.de* carb-an b2.de* **Carb-v** b2.de* *Caust* b2.de* cham b2.de* chel b2.de* chin b2.de* cina b2.de* *Cocc* b2.de* coff b2.de* colch b2.de* coloc b2.de* croc b2.de* cycl b2.de* *Dig* b2.de* *Dros* b2.de* dulc b2.de* euph b2.de* ferr b2.de* graph b2.de* hell b2.de* hep b2.de* hyos b2.de* ign b2.de* iod b2.de* ip b2.de* kali-bi bg2 kali-c b2.de* kali-n b2.de* kreos b2.de* lach b2.de* *Laur* b2.de* led b2.de* lyc b2.de* *Mag-c* b2.de* mag-m b2.de* mang b2.de* meny b2.de* merc b2.de* mez b2.de* mur-ac b2.de* nat-c b2.de* nat-m b2.de* nit-ac b2.de* nux-m b2.de* **Nux-v** b2.de* olnd b2.de* *Par* b2.de* *Ph-ac* b2.de* **Phos** b2.de* plat b2.de* plb b2.de* *Puls* b2.de* ran-b b2.de* rhod b2.de* *Rhus-t* b2.de* sabad b2.de* *Sars* b2.de* *Seneg* b2.de* sep b2.de* sil b2.de* spig b2.de* spong b2.de* squil b2.de* *Stann* b2.de* staph b2.de* stram b2.de* *Stront-c* b2.de* *Sul-ac* b2.de* **Sulph** b2.de* thuj b2.de* verat b2.de* verb b2.de* *Zinc* b2.de*

RUBBING:
- **abdomen** | **amel.**: nat-s ptk1 pall ptk1 podo ptk1

Rubbing: ...
- **agg.**: aloe sne *Am-m* k* **Anac** k* arn k* ars k* aur h2 *Bism* k* borx k* *Calad* k* calc k* cann-s k* canth k* *Caps* k* carb-an k* *Caust* k* cham k* chel k* cina ptk1 *Coff* k* **Con** k* cupr k* dros k* guaj k* kreos k* *Led* k* m-ambo b2.de* mag-c k* mag-p ptk1 mang k* merc k* *Mez* k* mosch ptk1 mur-ac k* nat-c k* ol-an ptk1 *Olnd* ptk1 pall ptk1 par k* ph-ac k* phos b2.de* **Plb** ptk1 podo ptk1 **Puls** k* rhus-t ptk1 ruta ptk1 seneg k* **Sep** k* *Sil* k* spig k* spong k* squil k* stann k* staph k* stram k* **Stront-c** k* **Sulph** k* tarent ptk1 tell ptk1* thuj bg2* valer ptk1 zinc ptk1 zinc-val ptk1
- **amel.**: (↗*Pressure - slight - agg. - hard)* acon aeth sne agar k* agn k* *Alum* k* *Alumn* kr1 am-c k* *Am-m* k* ambr k* anac k* ang b2.de* ant-c k* ant-t k* *Arn* k* *Ars* *Asaf* k* bell k* bell-p mg1.de benz-ac hr1* borx k* bov k* bry k* **Calc** k* calc-f st camph k* cann-s k* **Canth** k* caps k* **Carb-ac** k* carb-an k* castm bg2* caust k* cedr chel k* chin k* chir-fl gya2 cic k* cina k* cod sf1.de colch coloc sne croc bg2* *Cycl* k* dios k* *Dros* k* form bro1 *Guaj* k* ham hed mg1.de* hep k* *Ign* k* indg j5.de* iod mg1.de kali-c k* kali-chl k13 kali-m k2 kali-n k* kreos k* laur k* lil-t m-arct b2.de m-aust b2.de mag-c k* mag-m k* *Mag-p* bro1* mang k* melal-alt gya4 meny k* *Merc* k* mim-p jl3 mosch k* *Mur-ac* k* **Nat-c** k* nat-m sne nit-ac k* *Nux-v* k* **Ol-an** k* olnd k* osm pall k* ph-ac k* **Phos** k* plat k* **Plb** k* *Podo* bg2* puls bg2* ran-b k* rhus-t k* *Ruta* k* sabad k* sabin k* samb k* sars k* sec k* sel k* seneg k* sep bg2 spig k* spong k* stann k* staph k* sul-ac k* *Sulph* k* tarax k* *Tarent* bg2* *Thuj* k* valer k* verat-v bg2* viol-t k* *Zinc* k* zinc-p k2* [alumin-p stj2 am-p stj1 arg-p stj2 astat stj2 aur stj2 aur-m stj2 aur-s stj2 bar-br stj2 bar-i stj2 bar-met stj2 bism-sn stj2 caes-met stj2 calc-p stj1 cinnb stj2 *Cupr* stj2 cupr-act stj2 cupr-f stj2 cupr-m stj2 cupr-p stj2 hafn-met stj2 irid-met stj2 kali-p stj1 lanth-met stj2 lith-p stj2 mag-br stj1 mang-p stj2 merc-d stj2 merc-i-f stj2 nat-p stj1 nicc stj1 nicc-met stj2 nicc-s stj2 osm-met stj2 plb-m stj2 plb-p stj2 polon-met stj2 rhen-met stj2 spect dfg1 tant-met stj2 tax jsj7 thal-met stj2 tung-met stj2]
  - **hard** rubbing: med ptk1 rad-br ptk1
- **clothes**; of:
  - **agg.**: olnd ptk1
  - **amel.**: bufo bg2
- **gently**:
  - **agg.**: teucr k*
    ⁝ **hard** rubbing amel.; but: rhus-t bg2
  - **amel.**: arn kr1 *Asaf* kr1 **Calc** kr1 *Caps* kr1 *Cina* kr1 *Croc* kr1 crot-t ptk1 **Cycl** kr1 dios ptk1 *Dros* kr1 form ptk1 guaj kr1 ign kr1 lil-t ptk1 lyss ptk1 mang kr1 med ptk1 meny kr1 *Merc* kr1 *Mur-ac* kr1 **Nat-c** kr1 *Phos* kr1 *Plb* kr1 *Puls* kr1 *Ruta* kr1 sulph kr1 *Thuj* kr1 tritic-vg fd5.de zinc kr1
- **soles** of feet | **amel.**: chel ptk1
- **together**:
  - **sensation** of: cocc bg2* kali-bi bg2* sulph bg2*
    ⁝ **Joints**; in: con bg2*
- **warm** hand; with a | **amel.**: lil-t ptk1

RUNNING:
- **agg.**: (↗*Walking - rapidly - agg.)* alum k* alumn kr1 *Ang* b2.de* arg-met k* *Arn* k* **Ars** k* ars-i ars-s-f k2* aur k* aur-ar k2 aur-i k2* aur-s k2* *Bell* k* borx k* **Bry** k* calc k* *Cann-s* k* *Caust* k* chel k* chin k* cina k* *Cocc* k* coff k* *Con* croc k* *Cupr* k* dros k* *Ferr* ferr-ar k2* hep k* hyos k* *Ign* k* iod k* ip k* *Kali-c* k* laur k* *Led* k* *Lyc* k* *Merc* k* mez k* nat-c k* *Nat-m* k* nit-ac k* nux-m k* *Nux-v* k* *Olnd* k* phos k* plb **Puls** rheum k* *Rhod* k* *Rhus-t* k* ruta k* sabin k* *Seneg* k* sep k* *Sil* k* *Spig* k* spong k* squil k* staph k* sul-ac k* **Sulph** k* verat k* zinc k*
- **amel.**: caust k* *Ign* k* kali-s fd4.de nat-m k* nat-sil fd3.de• *Orig* mrr1 sacch-a fd2.de• **Sep** k* sil k* stann k* vanil fd5.de

RUNNING; as if something were: | **Glands**; in: bell b2.de calc b2.de laur b2.de sep b2.de *Spong* b2.de sulph b2.de

SALMONELLOSIS (See FEVER - Typhoid)

SALT abuse (See Food and - salt - desire)

SAND; sensation of: apis ptk1 ars bg2* berb ptk1 bov ptk1 cist ptk1 coll ptk1 coloc bg2 con ptk1 thuj bg2*

SARCOMA (See Cancerous - sarcoma)

SAUNA amel.: [ant-t stj2]

SCARLET fever: bell tl1 canth tl1 crot-h tl1

- **ailments** after: Am-c b2.de* Am-m aur k* bar-c k* Bell k* Bry k* Calc Carb-ac Carb-an Carb-v Cham k* Con bg2 dulc k* euph k* Hep k* hyos k* Lach k* lyc k* Merc k* nit-ac k* petros c1 phos rhus-t k* Sulph k* verat-v hr1
- **eruptions**; with suppressed: phos j5.de

O - **Glands**; with swollen (See Swelling - glands - scarlet - during)

SCHEUERMANN's disease (See Osteochondrosis)

SCLERODERMA: alum bro1 Ant-c bro1 arg-n bro1 ars bro1 berb-a bro1 brass-n-o srj5• Bry bro1 caust bro1 Crot-t bro1 echi bro1 Elae bro1 Hydr bro1 kali-c mrr1 lyc bro1* petr bro1 Phos bro1 rad-br ptk1 ran-b bro1 rhus-r bro1 sarcol-ac mtf11 sars bro1 sep mrr1 sil bro1 still bro1 sulph bro1 syc mtf11 thiosin br1* thyr bro1* x-ray mtf11

SCLEROSIS; multiple (See Multiple)

SCRATCHING with hands:

- **agg.**: am-m b2.de Anac b2.de* am b2.de ars b2.de* asar ptk1 Bism b2.de bov b2.de Calad b2.de calc b2.de* cann-s b2.de canth b2.de Caps b2.de* carb-an b2.de Caust b2.de cham b2.de chel b2.de coff b2.de Con b2.de cupr b2.de Dol bro1 dros b2.de graph ptk1 guaj b2.de kali-c ptk1 kreos b2.de lach ptk1 Led b2.de m-ambo b2.de mag-c b2.de mang b2.de merc b2.de* Mez b2.de* mur-ac b2.de nat-c b2.de olnd ptk1 par b2.de ph-ac b2.de phos b2.de Puls b2.de* Rhus-t bro1* seneg b2.de sep b2.de Sil b2.de* spig b2.de spong b2.de squil b2.de stann b2.de staph b2.de* stram b2.de Stront-c b2.de sulph b2.de*
- **amel.**: agar b2.de agn b2.de alum b2.de am-c b2.de am-m b2.de ambr b2.de anac b2.de ang b2.de ant-c b2.de ant-t b2.de Arn b2.de* Asaf b2.de* bar-c b2.de bell b2.de borx b2.de bov b2.de Bry b2.de Calc b2.de* camph b2.de cann-s b2.de Canth b2.de caps b2.de carb-an b2.de caust b2.de chel b2.de chin b2.de cic b2.de cina b2.de clem b2.de coloc b2.de com bro1 Cycl b2.de* dig b2.de Dros b2.de Guaj b2.de hep b2.de Ign b2.de Jug-c bro1 kali-c b2.de kali-n b2.de kreos b2.de laur b2.de led b2.de m-arct b2.de m-aust b2.de mag-c b2.de mag-m b2.de Mang b2.de melal-alt gya4 meny b2.de merc b2.de mez b2.de mosch b2.de Mur-ac b2.de* Nat-c b2.de* nit-ac b2.de nux-v b2.de olnd b2.de ph-ac b2.de Phos b2.de* plat b2.de Plb b2.de ran-b b2.de rhus-t b2.de Ruta b2.de* sabad b2.de sabin b2.de samb b2.de sars b2.de sec b2.de sel b2.de seneg b2.de spig b2.de spong b2.de squil b2.de stann b2.de staph b2.de sul-ac b2.de Sulph b2.de* tarax b2.de Thuj b2.de valer b2.de viol-t b2.de Zinc b2.de
- **linen** agg.: asar b2.de*

SCROFULOUS disposition: *(↗Tuberculosis - glandular - lymphatic)*

- **accompanied** by:
  - **syphilis** (See Syphilis - scrofulous)
  - **worms** (See RECTUM - Worms - complaints - accompanied - scrofula)

SCURVY, scorbutus: acet-ac bro1 agav-a c1* agn k* all-s k* aln bro1 alum k* alumn c1* Am-c k* am-m c1* ambr k* ant-c k* aran hr1* arg-met k* Ars k* ars-i arum-m hr1* aur k* bell k* borx k* bov k* brass c1 brass-n-o c2 bry k* Calc k* canth k* caps k* Carb-an k* Carb-v k* cary c1* caust k* cetr hr1* chin k* chinin-s bro1 cic k* Cist k* cit-ac a1 cit-l c1* cit-v coca c1* coch hr1* con k* Dulc k* elat c1* Ferr-p bro1 gali bro1 graph k* Ham c1* Hep k* Iod k* jug-r c1* Kali-c k* kali-chl c1* Kali-m kr1* kali-n k* kali-p hr1* kreos k* lach c1* lyc k* mag-m k* Merc k* Mur-ac k* nat-hchls c1* Nat-m k* Nit-ac k* nit-m-ac c2* nux-m k* Nux-v k* petr k* ph-ac k* phos k* plb a1 psor c1* rat c1* rhus-t k* ruta k* sabin k* sacch a1* sanic c1 sep k* Sil k* sin-n hr1* sol-t-ae c1* stann k* Staph k* sul-ac k* Sulph k* tart-ac br1 tep c1* Urin c1* zinc k*

- **accompanied** by | **fever**: staph b7.de*

SEA:

- **bathing** in the sea (See Bathing - sea)

SEASICKNESS (See STOMACH - Nausea - seasickness)

SEASIDE; at the:

- **agg.**: *(↗MIND - Sadness - seaside)* ambr tsm1 aml-ns bro1 Apom bro1 aq-mar c1* arn bro1 Ars k* aur-m zr* aur-m-n wbt2• brom bg2* brucel sa3• bry a Carc mg1.de* cer-ox bro1 chlol bro1 Cocc bro1 coli jl2 cuc-p bro1 glon bro1 iod mg1.de* kali-br bro1 kali-i k* kali-p bro1 Mag-m k* mag-s mg1.de med bg2* morph bro1 mur-ac mrr1* Nat-m ●* nat-s k* nicot bro1 Nux-v bro1 Petr bro1 Rhus-t ptk1 Sep k ●* sil fb Staph bro1 syph bro1* Tab bro1 thea bro1 Ther bro1 Tub st* [ant-m stj2 bar-i stj2 Beryl-m stj2 cadm-m stj2 calc-m stj1 Chlor stj2 chr-m stj2 cob-m stj2 cupr-m stj2 kali-m stj1 lith-i stj2 lith-m stj2 mag-i stj1 mang-i stj2 mang-m stj2 merc-d stj2 merc-i-f stj2 nat-ar stj2 nat-caust stj2 nat-i stj1 nat-lac stj2 nat-met stj2 plb-m stj2 zinc-i stj2 zinc-m stj2]

Seaside; at the – **agg.**: ...

- • **beginning**; in the: mucor jl2

- **amel.**: *(↗MIND - Seaside - amel.)* acon kr1 ambr tsm1 aq-mar vh1* arb-m oss1• ars-i sne aur-m zr* aur-m-n wbt2• Borx vh brom bg2* bros-gau mrc1 bry a Carc c1* chir-fl gya2 eucal mtf fic-m gya1 Iris vh lac-leo hm2• lyc bg2 mag-s a marb-w es1• Med k1* melal-alt gya4 Nat-m st* puls vh* sal-fr sle1• sep fb* sil a Sul-ac vh Tub st verat a [Am-br stj2 Bar-br stj2 bar-i stj2 beryl stj2 Beryl-m stj2 Calc-br stj1 calc-m stj1 calc-n stj1 Chlor stj2 chr-m stj2 cob-m stj2 cupr-m stj2 Kali-br stj1 lith-m stj2 Mag-br stj1 mag-m stj1 mang-m stj2 merc-d stj2 nat-ar stj2 Nat-br stj2 nat-caust stj2 nat-lac stj2 plb-m stj2]
  - • **prolonged** stay: mucor jl2
- **desire** to be near the sea: *(↗MIND - Seaside - loves)* ambr tsm1 arb-m oss1• taosc iwa1•

SEASONS:

- **autumn**: *(↗MIND - Seasons - autumn)*
  - • **agg.**: all-c c1 Ant-t Aur b2.de* aur-m-n wbt2• bapt bar-m brom k2 bry k* Calc k* calc-p bg2* Chin k* cic Colch b2.de* Coloc bg2* Dulc bg2* Graph k1* hed mg1.de hep ign bg2* iris bg2* Kali-bi bg2* Lach k* lat-m bnm6• Merc b2.de* merc-c bg2* mucor jl2 nat-m bg2* nux-v k* rhod c1* Rhus-t k* Stram k* Verat k*
    - ⁝ **November**: [zirc-met stj2]
    - ⁝ **October**: [zirc-met stj2]
  - • **ailments** since autumn: kali-bi c1
  - • **amel.**: flav jl2
- **spring**:
  - • **agg.**: acon k* all-c bg2* Ambr k* Ant-t k* Apis k* ars-br bro1 Aur k* bar-m Bell k* brom k2* brucel sa3• Bry k* Calc k* Calc-p bg2* Carb-v k* Cench Chel cina h1 Colch k* con c1* crot-h j5.de* dulc k* elaps mgm• Gels bg2* ham bg2 hed mg1.de hep Iris k* Kali-bi k* Lach k* Lyc k* merc-i-f c1 mucor jl2 naja mgm• nat-c bg2* Nat-m k* Nat-s k* nit-s-d bro1* nux-v k* Puls k* Rhod c1* Rhus-t k* Sars k* sec sel bg2 Sep k* Sil k* Sulph k* tub gk urt-u bg2 Verat k* vip mgm•
  - • **ailments** since spring: con c1 kali-bi c1 merc-i-f c1
  - • **amel.**: flav jl2 sacch-a fd2.de•
  - • **early** spring agg.: gels
- **summer**:
  - • **agg.**: Acon k2 Aeth k* aloe bg2* Alum alum-sil k2 Ant-c b2.de* apis bg2* arg-n k* Ars hr1 ars-i bapt kr1* bar-c k* Bell b2.de* borx bov bg2* brom k2* brucel sa3• Bry b7a.de* calc bg2 Camph kr1* Carb-v b2.de* Carbn-s cham k* Chion cina bg2* cinnb coff k2 colch k2 crot-h bg2* crot-t br1* cupr bg2* dulc ptk1 Fl-ac k* Gamb kr1* Gels bg2* ger br1 Glon bg2* graph k* grat ptk1 Guaj Iod k* ip mtf33 iris bg2* Kali-bi k* kali-br st* kali-c sf1.de* kali-i bg2* Lach bg2* lat-m bnm6• Lyc b2.de* mur-ac bg2* Nat-c b2.de* Nat-m k* nux-m bg2* nux-v k* Ph-ac bg2* Phos bg2* Podo bg2* Psor Puls b2.de* rad-br c11 rheum st* rhod bg2* Sel k* sep bg2* sin-n c1 sul-i k2 syph k2* thuj k* Verat kr1* verat-v st1 [am-br stj2 bar-br stj2 bar-i stj2 calc-br stj1 ferr-n stj2 lith-i stj2 mag-br stj1 mag-i stj1 mag-n stj2 mang-i stj2 merc-i-f stj2 nat-br stj2 nat-i stj1 nitro stj2 zinc-i stj2 zinc-n stj2]
    - ⁝ **children**; in: aeth br1 Ip st* typh br1
    - ⁝ **cool** days; after: Bry kr1*
    - ⁝ **September**: [rubd-met stj2 ruth-met stj2]
    - ⁝ **solstice**; at: apis st Bell st brom st Bry st Carb-v st Gels st iris st Kali-bi st Lach st Lyc st nat-c st Nat-m st nux-v st Puls st rhod st sep st Verat st
  - • **ailments** since summer: podo c1 sin-n c1
  - • **amel.**: aesc sf1.de* alum bro1* aran vh1 ars-i sf1.de aur bro1* aur-ar k2* aur-m ptk1 calc-p bro1* calc-sil k2* caust sf1.de* ferr bro1* kali-sil sf1.de Petr sf1.de* phel vml3• psor sf1.de* sil bro1* stront-c sf1.de
- **winter**:
  - • **agg.**: Acon b2.de* Aesc Agar k* Alum k* Am-c b2.de* ammc k* aral vh1 Arg-met k* Arn sne Ars b2.de* ars-i k2 Aur k* aur-ar k2 aur-s k2* Bar-c b2.de* Bell k* borx st bov k* Brucel sa3• Bry b2.de* Calc k* Calc-p calc-sil k2* Camph b2.de* Caps b2.de* carb-an k* Carb-v b2.de* carbn-s k2 Caust k* Cham b2.de* cic k* cina k* cist bg2* Coc-c cocc b2.de* colch k* Con b2.de* Dulc b2.de* Ferr k* ferr-ar Fl-ac k* graph bg2* Hell b2.de* Hep b2.de* Hyos b2.de* Ign b2.de* Ip b2.de* Kali-bi k* Kali-c b2.de* Kali-p kali-sil k2* Kalm ptk1* Lyc b2.de* mag-c k* Mang b2.de* Merc k* Mez k* Mosch b2.de* nat-ar nat-c k* nat-m k* Nux-m b2.de* Nux-v k* Petr b2.de*

- **winter – agg.**: ...
ph-ac k* phel vml3• *Phos* k* prot jl3* **Psor** bg2* **Puls** b2.de* *Rhod* b2.de* **Rhus-t** k* ruta k* *Sabad* k* sangin-n c1* sars k* sec bg2 *Sep* k* *Sil* k* spig k* spong k* stann bg2* **Stront-c** b2.de* *Sulph* b2.de* syph k2* **Verat** b2.de* viol-t [alumin stj2 alumin-p stj2 alumin-s stj2 aur-m stj2 ferr-sil stj2 mag-sil stj2 mang-n stj2 mang-sil stj2 nat-caust stj2 nat-sil stj2 nicc-met stj2 sil-met stj2 stront-m stj2 stront-met stj2]
⋮ **December**: [calc-sil stj2 ferr-sil stj2 kali-sil stj2 mag-sil stj2 nat-sil stj2 sil stj2 sil-met stj2]
⋮ **mid** winter: gels
⋮ **solstice**; at: *Aur* st bry st *Calc* st calc-p st cic st colch st *Dulc* st graph st hep st ign st *Kali-bi* st merc st nat-m st nux-v st *Rhod* st **Rhus-t** st *Verat* st
• **ailments** since winter: sangin-n c1
• **amel.**: glon k2 ilx-a c1* ilx-c kr1* sul-i k2*

SEDENTARY habits: (↗*Indolence*) acon k* aloe c1* alum c1* am-c c1* anac c1* arg-n bro1 ars h2 asar c1* bell b4a.de *Bry* b7a.de* *Calc* b4a.de* *Caps* b7a.de cocc c1 colch b7a.de con k* guar vml3• hydrog srj2• *Lyc* gl1.fr• nat-m c1 **Nux-v** b7.de* petr c1 *Puls* b7a.de rhus-t gl1.fr• sep k* sil c1 staph gl1.fr• sulph c1* ter c1
- **women**; in: coloc br1
• **obese**: am-c br1

SEMI-CONSCIOUS; when: | **agg.**: camph b2.de*

SENILE COMPLAINTS (See Old - old)

SENSIBILITY (See Sensitiveness)

SENSITIVENESS: (↗*MIND - Sensitive*)
- **one** side: cocc bg2 cupr bg2
- **diffused** | **Affected** parts; around: kali-i ptk1
- **everything**; to: merc mtf33 nat-m br1 sul-i ptk1
- **medicines**, to (See Medicine - allopathic - oversensitive)
- **pain**, to: (↗*Pain - ailments; MIND - Sensitive - pain*) *Acon* k* *Agar* k* all-c hr1 *Alum* *Am-c* k* *Ambr* k* anac k* ang b2.de* *Ant-c* k* ant-t k* apis mgm• arg-n bg2 *Arn* k* *Ars* k* ars-h hr1 *Ars-i* ars-s-f k2 asaf k2 *Asar* k* **Aur** k* aur-ar k2 aur-m bro1 aur-s k2 *Bar-c* k* bar-i k2 bar-s k2 *Bell* k* bit-ar wht1• bov hr1 *Bry* k* *Cact* k* calad k* calc k* calc-p calc-sil k2 *Camph* k* cann-s k* *Canth* k* caps k* carb-an k* carb-v k* *Carbn-s* k2* caust hr1 **Cham** k* *Chin* k* chinin-ar cimic bg2* cina k* *Cocc* k* **Coff** k* *Colch* k* coloc hr1 *Con* k* crot-h hr1 *Cupr* k* dig k* *Ferr* ferr-ar k2 ferr-p graph k* hell k* **Hep** k* *Hyos* k* hyper bro1 **Ign** k* iod k* ip k* kali-ar *Kali-c* k* kali-m k2 kali-p k* lac-c bg2 **Lach** k* lact mg1.de lat-m bro1 laur k* led k* **Lyc** k* m-ambo b2.de* m-arct b2.de* m-aust b2.de* *Mag-c* k* mag-m k* mag-p bg2* mang hr1 **Med** k* meli bro1 merc k* mez hr1* *Morph* kr1* mosch bro1 mur-ac k* *Nat-c* k* nat-p *Nat-s* k2* **Nit-ac** k* nux-m k* **Nux-v** k* olnd k* *Petr* k* ph-ac k* **Phos** k* *Phyt* *Plat* bg2 plb k* **Psor** **Puls** k* ran-s bro1 *Rhus-t* k* sabad k* sabin k* sars k* sel k* seneg k* **Sep** k* **Sil** k* *Spig* k* squil k* stann k2 **Staph** k* stram bg2* sulph k* thuj k* *Tub* valer k* verat k* vesp viol-o k* *Zinc* k* zinc-p k2 zinc-val bro1
• **unendurable**: (↗*Pain - intolerable*) cocc k2 coff k2 colch k2*
- **remedies**, to (See Remedies - violent)

○ - **Affected** parts: *Asaf* br1 plb br1
- **Body** oversensitive; whole: acon b7.de* ambr b7.de* ant-c b7a.de *Ant-t* b7.de* *Apis* b7a.de arn b7.de* asaf bg2 asar b7.de* *Aur* bg2 *Bell* bg2 *Bry* b7.de camph b7.de* *Canth* b7a.de caps bg2 castm bg2 *Cham* b7.de* chin b7.de* cina b7.de* *Cocc* b7a.de **Coff** b7.de* cupr b7a.de* hell b7.de hydr-ac bg2 *Ign* bg2 kali-p bg2 lach bg2 m-arct b7.de nit-ac bg2 *Nux-m* b7a.de **Nux-v** b7.de* op bg2 par b7.de phos bg2 plb bg2 pyrog bg2 rhus-t b7.de sang bg2 sel b7.de sil bg2 *Spig* b7.de* spong b7.de squil b7.de staph b7.de sulph bg2 valer bg2 verat bg2
• **fever**; during: mang b4a.de
- **Bones**, of: (↗*Pain - bones*) asaf k* *Aur* k* bell k* bry bufo kr1 calc k* carb-an k* chel chin k* *Chinin-s* cupr **Eup-per** guaj hyper lach k* lyc k* mang ptk1 merc *Merc-c* mez nat-c k* nat-sil k2 nit-ac ptk1 **Phos** puls k* rhus-t k* *Sil* k* *Stram* sulph k* **Tell** zinc
- **Cartilages**: (↗*Pain - cartilages*) **Arg-met**
- **Externally**: *Acon* k* *Aesc* agar k* ail c1 aloe *Alum* k* alum-p k2 alum-sil k2* am-c k* am-m k* ambr k* ang b2.de* ant-c k* ant-t **Apis** k* arg-met k* arg-n ptk1 **Arn** k* ars k* asaf k* *Aur* k* aur-ar k2 *Bapt* *Bar-c* k* bar-s k2* **Bell** k* *Borx* k* bov k* bry k* calc k* calc-p calc-sil k2* camph k* cann-s k* *Canth* k* caps k* carb-an k* carb-v k* carbn-s br1 caust k* *Cham* ptk1 chel k2* **Chin** k* **Chinin-s** k* cic ptk1 cimic cina k* *Clem* coc-c k* *Coff* k* *Colch* k* coloc k* con k* croc ptk1 *Crot-c* cupr k* dig k* euph-pi c1 *Ferr* k* ferr-p *Gels* k* glon c1 graph k2* ham k2* hell k* *Hep* k* hist mg1.de *Hyos* k* ign k* ip k* *Kali-bi* k* *Kali-c* k* kali-i a1* kali-n k*

Sensitiveness – Externally: ...
kali-p kali-s kreos k* lac-c k2 lac-h sk4• **Lach** k* led k* lyc k* lyss ptk1 m-ambo b2.de *M-arct* b2.de mag-c k* mag-m k* mag-p k2 mang ptk1 med ptk1 menth meny bg2 *Merc* k* merc-c bg2* *Mez* k* mosch k* mur-ac bg2 nat-ar *Nat-c* k* *Nat-m* k* **Nat-p** nat-s a1* nat-sil k2* nit-ac k* nux-m k* **Nux-v** k* olnd k* *Op* k* paeon ptk1 par k* petr k* ph-ac k* **Phos** k* *Plat* ptk1 plb k* psor k* **Puls** k* **Ran-b** k* *Ran-s* k* *Rhus-t* k* sabad k* *Sabin* sal-ac sars k* sec k* *Sel* k* *Seneg* k* *Sep* k* **Sil** k* **Spig** k* spong k* squil k* *Stann* k* **Staph** k* stront-c k* sul-ac k* sul-i ptk1 *Sulph* k* tarent ptk1 tell ptk1 ter ptk1 teucr k* thal-xyz srj8• *Ther* ptk1 *Thuj* k* *Tub* br1* valer k2* verat k* vip ptk1 zinc k* zinc-p k2
- **Glands**: (↗*Pain - glands*) arn k* *Aur* k* aur-s k2 **Bar-c** k* bar-i k2 bell k* *Cham* k* chin k* cimic k2 clem cocc k* **Con** k* crot-h cupr k* graph k* hep k* ign k* kali-c k* *Kali-i* br1 laur k* loxo-lae bnm12• *Lyc* k* mag-c k* nat-c k* nat-sil k2 nit-ac k* nux-v k* petr k* ph-ac k* **Phos** k* puls k* *Sep* k* *Sil* k* spig k* squil k* sul-ac k* zinc k*
- **Internally**: (↗*MIND - Senses - acute*) acon k* agar k* *Alum* k* alum-p k2 alum-sil k2* *Am-c* k* ant-c k* ant-t k* apis k* arn k* *Ars* k* ars-i asaf k* *Asar* aur k* aur-ar k2 *Bapt* bar-c k* *Bell* k* bism k* *Borx* k* bov k* *Bry* k* calad k* *Calc* k* calc-sil k2* cann-s k* **Canth** k* *Carb-an* k* carb-v k* carbn-s k* caust k* *Cham* k* chin k* cic k* cimic k2* clem coc-c *Cocc* k* coff k* colch k* *Coloc* k* con k* croc k* crot-h cub cupr k* cycl k* dulc k* *Equis-h* ferr k* *Graph* k* hell k* helon **Hep** k* hyos k* *Iod* k* ip k* *Kali-bi* *Kali-i* kali-p **Lach** k* laur k* led k* *Lil-t* m-arct b2.de mag-c k* *Mag-m* k* mang k* meny k* merc k* *Merc-c* k* *Mez* mosch k* nat-ar *Nat-c* k* **Nat-m** k* *Nit-ac* k* *Nux-v* k* olnd k* *Osm* par k* **Phos** k* puls k* ran-b k* rhus-t k* *Ruta* sars k* *Sec* k* sel k* seneg k* sep k* **Sil** k* spong k* *Squil* k* stann k* *Stram* k* stront-c k* sul-ac k* sulph k* tarax k* tarent teucr thuj k* *Tub* br1 valer k* verat k* zinc k*
- **Periosteum**: (↗*Pain - periosteum*) *Acon* bg2 ant-c k* aur k* bell k* *Bry* *Chin* k* chinin-s bg2 eup-per bg2 guaj k2 ign k* **Led** k* m-ambo b2.de m-arct b2.de m-aust b2.de* mang bg2 merc k* merc-c bg2 *Mez* nit-ac bg2 *Ph-ac* k* phos bg2 *Puls* k* rhus-t k* ruta k* sil k* spig k* staph k* symph c1* tell bg2

SENSORY ILLUSIONS: acon b2.de* *Alum* b2.de* *Anac* b2.de* ant-t bg2 arn b2.de* ars b2.de* *Asaf* b2.de* asar b2.de* bar-c b2.de* *Bell* b2.de* bism b2.de* borx b2.de* bov b2.de* *Brom* b4a.de bry b2.de* *Calc* b2.de* cann-s b2.de* canth b2.de* caps b2.de* caust b2.de* chel b2.de* cocc b2.de* coloc b2.de* con b2.de* *Croc* b2.de* dros b2.de* dulc b2.de* graph b2.de* guaj b2.de* hell b2.de* hep b2.de* hyos b2.de* *Ign* b2.de* iod b2.de* kali-c b2.de* kali-n b2.de* kreos b2.de* *Lach* b2.de* laur b2.de* lyc b2.de* *M-ambo* b2.de* m-arct b2.de* m-aust b2.de mag-c b2.de* mag-m b2.de* meny b2.de* merc b2.de* mosch b2.de* nat-c b2.de* nat-m b2.de* nux-m b2.de* nux-v b2.de* olnd b2.de* op b2.de* *Par* b2.de* petr bg2 ph-ac b2.de* phos b2.de* plat b2.de* *Plb* b2.de* *Puls* b2.de* ran-b b2.de* ran-s b2.de* rheum b2.de* rhod b2.de* **Rhus-t** b2.de* ruta b2.de* sabad b2.de* samb b2.de* *Sec* b7.de* seneg b2.de* sep b2.de* sil b2.de* *Spig* b2.de* spong b2.de* squil b2.de* stann b4.de staph b2.de* **Stram** b2.de* sul-ac b2.de* *Sulph* b2.de* tarax b2.de* thuj b2.de* valer b2.de* verat b2.de* verb b2.de* zinc b4.de*
- **sleep**; during: canth b7.de* cham b7a.de

SEPARATING:
- **extremities**:
• **agg.**: *Ign* b7a.de sulph bg2
• **amel.**: nux-v bg2 psor bg2
- **sensation** of | **Bones**: kali-bi bg2

SEPSIS (See Septicemia)

SEPTICEMIA, blood poisoning: (↗*Pyemia; Wounds - septic*) *Achy* jl3 *Acon* bro1 agar c1 *Ail* k2* am-c k2* ant-t mrr1 anthraci k* *Apis* apisin bro1 arg-met jl arg-n *Arn* k* **Ars** k* ars-i bro1* arum-t sf1.de atro bro1 *Bapt* k* bell bro1* bor-ac c1 both br1* *Bry* k* bufo br1* calc hr1* calc-ar sf1.de* calen bro1* camph mrr1 *Carb-ac* bro1* **Carb-v** k* *Cench* chin mg1.de *Chinin-ar* bro1* *Chinin-s* c1* chlorpr jl3 colch sf1.de conch c1* **Crot-h** k* dor sf1.de eberth jl2 **Echi** c1* elaps sf1.de eucal br1 *Ferr* ferr-p sf1.de gels sf1.de gunp bro1 hell sf1.de hep mtf11 *Hippoz* k* hydroph jl3* hyos bro1* indol mtf11 *Ip* sf1.de* irid-met br1* kali-bi kr1* kali-br hr1 kali-c sf1.de kali-chl br1 *Kali-p* k* kali-perm br1 kreos sf1.de **Lach** k* lat-h bro1 lob-p c1 *Lyc* mag-c mg1.de *Merc* c1* merc-cy bro1* methyl bro1 mur-ac br1* naja sf1.de* nat-s-c bro1 *Nit-ac* sf1.de op sf1.de* paro-i jl3 penic mtf11 ph-ac sf1.de* *Phos* k* phyt sf1.de *Puls* **Pyrog** k* rad-br st raja-s jl3 *Rhus-t* k* *Sal-ac* hr1* *Sec* bro1* sieg mg1.de sil bro1 skat mtf11 staphycoc jl2 stram k2* streptoc bro1 sul-ac sf1.de sulfonam jl3 *Sulph* tarax sf1.de tarent k* tarent-c br1* ter sf1.de toxo-g jl2 trach c1 vac mtf11 vario mtf11 *Verat* hr1* *Verat-v* sf1.de* vince mtf11 *Vip* sf1.de yers jl2 zinc sf1.de

- **accompanied** by:
  - **heart** failure (See CHEST - Heart failure - accompanied - septicemia)
  - **nausea**: ail bg2 bapt bg2 crot-h bg2 elaps bg2 **Lach** bg2 ter bg2 *Vip* bg2
  - **pain**; burning: carb-v br1
  - **typhus** fever (See FEVER - Typhus - accompanied - septicemia)
  - **weakness**: elaps ptk1 pyrog ptk1
- **ailments** from: agar c1 gunp c1 lob-p c1 pyrog c1 tarent c1
- **appearing** suddenly: **Bapt** mrr1
- **children**; in: bapt br
  - **infants**: toxo-g jl2*
- **chill**; during: *Pyrog* bro1 tarent-c bro1
- **coma**; with (See MIND - Coma - septicemia)
- **gram**-negative: streptom mtf11
- **pregnancy** agg.; during: kali-chl bro1
- **prophylaxis** for pus infections: arn br1*
- **restlessness**; with (See MIND - Restlessness - septicemia)
- **smallpox** vaccination; after: maland gm1 sarr gm1

SEQUELAE after an illness (See Convalescence)

SEWER-GAS poisoning: *(↗Coal gas; Death - carbon)* anthraci bro1 *Bapt* c1* phyt c1* pyrog c1* *Tub* st1

SEWING; while: lach b2.de* *Nat-m* b2.de* sul-ac b2.de*
- **amel.**: lach ptk1 *Nat-m* ptk1

SEXUAL DESIRE: *(↗Sexual desire - Suppression - agg.)*
- **suppression** of sexual desire:
  - **agg.**: *(↗Sexual desire; FEMALE - Sexual desire - suppressed - agg.; MALE GENITALIA/SEX - Sexual desire - suppressed - agg.; MIND - Ailments - celibacy)* agn bg2* **Apis** k* bell bg2 berb k* calc k* **Camph** carb-v bg2 *Carbn-o* **Con** k* fl-ac ptk1 graph bg2* *Hell* hyos bg2 kali-n h2* kali-p c1 *Lach* mrr1 *Lil-t* lyc st* **Lyss** m-ambo b2.de* orig st *Ph-ac* **Phos** bg2* pic-ac plat k* **Puls** staph bg2* stram bg2
    - **menopause**; during: *Con* st
  - **amel.**: calad k*

SEXUAL DEVELOPMENT (See Sexual development; FEMALE - Development)

SEXUAL EXCESSES; ailments after: *(↗MIND - Ailments - sexual excesses; MIND - Nymphomania)* acon k* **Agar** k* agn k* alum k* *Alum-p* k2 ambr sf1.de anac k* ant-c k* arg-n c1* arn k* *Ars* k* asaf k* aur k* aur-ar k2 aven c1* bar-c k* bell k* borx k* *Bov* k* bry k* *Calad* b2.de* **Calc** k* calc-p c1 *Calc-s* calc-sil k2 cann-s k* canth k* caps k* carb-an k* **Carb-v** b2.de* caust k* cham k* *Chin* k* *Chinin-ar* cina k* cob sf1.de cocc k* coff k* **Con** k* diaz sa3• *Dig* k* digin bro1 dulc k* ferr k* ferr-pic c1 *Gels* k* gins sf1.de graph k* ign k* *Iod* k* ip b2.de* *Kali-br* k* *Kali-c* k* kali-n **Kali-p** k* led k* *Lil-t* **Lyc** k* lyss br1* m-ambo b2.de* m-aust b2.de mag-m k* *Merc* k* mez k* *Mosch* k* *Nat-c* k* **Nat-m** k* **Nat-p** *Nit-ac* k* **Nux-v** k* ol-an sf1.de onos c1 op k* petr k* **Ph-ac** k* **Phos** k* plat k* plb k* *Puls* k* ran-b k* rhod k* rhus-t k* ruta k* sabad k* samb k* sec **Sel** k* **Sep** k* **Sil** k* *Spig* k* squil k* stann k* **Staph** k* **Sulph** k* symph c1* thuj k* trib bro1 upa c1* valer k* zinc k* zinc-p k2

SEXUAL EXCITEMENT agg.: agar k2 ant-c ptk1 arg-n c1 arn c1 *Bufo* k* calc kr1 chinin-s c1 gins c1 kali-p c1 **Lil-t** k* plat ptk1 sars k* senec ptk1 sep k2 staph c1 tarent ptk1 yohim lp2
- **drunkenness**; during: canth gl1.fr• *Caust* gl1.fr• chin gl1.fr• nux-v gl1.fr• phos gl1.fr•

SHAKING: *(↗Quivering)*

○ - **Head**:
  - **agg.**: acon b2.de* agn b2.de* am-c b2.de* anac b2.de* ang b2.de* ant-c b2.de* ant-t b2.de* *Arn* b2.de* asar b2.de* bar-c b2.de* **Bell** b2.de* borx b2.de* *Bry* b2.de* calad b2.de* calc b2.de* camph b2.de* cann-s b2.de* canth b2.de* carb-an b2.de* carb-v b2.de* caust b2.de* cham b2.de* chel b2.de* chin b2.de* cic b2.de* cocc b2.de* coff b2.de* *Colch* b2.de* croc b2.de* cupr b2.de* dig b2.de* *Glon* bg2 graph b2.de* guaj b2.de* hell b2.de* *Hep* b2.de* iod b2.de* ip b2.de* kreos b2.de* *Led* b2.de* m-aust b2.de* mang b2.de* merc b2.de* mez b2.de* nat-m b2.de*

Shaking – head – agg.: ...
nit-ac b2.de* *Nux-m* b2.de* **Nux-v** b2.de* par b2.de* petr b2.de* phos b2.de* plb b2.de* puls b2.de* ran-b b2.de* rheum b2.de* rhus-t b2.de* ruta b2.de* samb b2.de* sars b2.de* sec b2.de* sel b2.de* sep b2.de* sil b2.de* *Spig* b2.de* spong b2.de* squil b2.de* staph b2.de* stram b2.de* sul-ac b2.de* sulph b2.de* thuj b2.de* verat b2.de*
  - **amel.**: chin b2.de* cina b2.de* *Lach* b2.de*

SHAKING PALSY (See Paralysis agitans)

SHAVING:
- **agg.**: ant-c bg2 aur bg2 caps bg2* *Carb-an* b2.de* cic ptk1 hep bg2 kalm bg2 lyc brm mang bg2 ox-ac bg2* ph-ac bg2* phos bg2* plb bro1* **Puls** bg2* rad-br c11* stroph-s bg*
- **amel.**: brom bg2*

SHINING objects; ailments from: *(↗Convulsions - shining; MIND - Shining - agg.)* bell bro1* canth bro1* cocc-s bro1 glon sf1.de hyos sf1.de* *Lyss* bro1* mur-ac ptk1 stram bro1*

SHIVERING:
- **accompanied** by | **burning** pain internally (See Pain - internally - burning - accompanied - shivering)

SHOCK: *(↗Injuries)* *Acon* c1 ancis-p tsm2 ant-t mrr1 arn tl1 both tsm2 both-ax tsm2 bung-fa tsm2 camph br1 carb-ac mrr1 cench tsm2 cloth tsm2 coff hr1* crot-c tsm2 crot-h tsm2 dendr-pol tsm2 elaps tsm2 hyper c1 mag-c c1* naja tsm2 nux-m mrr1 ph-ac c1 sil a1 stram c1 vip tsm2 [*Cupr-act* stj2 ferr-n stj2]
- **accompanied** by | **heart** failure (See CHEST - Heart failure - accompanied - shock)
- **anesthesia**; during: *Adren* br1
- **electric**-like: *(↗Jerking - internally; MIND - Starting - electric - as; MIND - Starting - electric - shocks - awake)* *Acon* *Agar* k* ail k* alum alum-p k2 am-m bg *Ambr* anac ang apis aran c1* aran-ix mg1.de **Arg-met** k* *Arg-n* k* arn **Ars** k* ars-s-f k2 *Art-v* bar-c *Bar-m* bar-s k2 bell bufo k* calad calc *Calc-p* *Camph* cann-s carb-ac carb-v caust chir-fl bnm4• *Cic* k* cimic k* *Cina* *Clem* *Cocc* k* colch **Coloc** bg con croc cupr *Dig* *Dios* bg dulc *Fl-ac* gels bg graph hell helo-s rwt2• hep *Hydr-ac* bg* kali-c kreos *Laur* *Lyc* mag-m k* manc mang meph a1 mez mur-ac nat-ar nat-c *Nat-m* nat-p k* *Nit-ac* *Nux-m* *Nux-v* ol-an olnd ox-ac sf1.de *Phos* plat plb a1* psil ft1 puls rad-br ptk1 *Ran-b* k* *Ruta* sang sf1.de sep spig squil stram *Stry* sul-ac sulph sumb *Tab* *Thal* ulm-c jsj8• *Valer* k2* **Verat** k* verat-v sf1.de* vesp hr1 xan zinc zinc-p k2
  - **one** side of body: colch br1
  - **right** side of body: agar
  - **morning**: mang h2
  - **evening** | **bed** agg.; in: sulph h2
  - **agg.**: phos ptk1
  - **concussion** of brain, from: *(↗Injuries - concussion - brain)* cic
  - **convulsions**:
    - **before**: *Bar-m* cic hr1 *Laur*
      - **epileptic**: *Ars* k1
    - **interrupted** by painful shocks: stry
  - **lying** agg.: *Clem*
  - **motion**:
    - **agg.**: colch st1 graph
    - **beginning** of | **agg.**: *Arg-n*
  - **rest** agg.: graph
  - **return** of senses, on: cic
  - **sleep** | **during** | **agg.**: *(↗Jerking - muscles - sleep - during - agg.)* ant-t ptk1 *Arg-met* k* arg-n ptk1 *Ars* k* cupr ptk1 iod a1 kreos lyc mag-m ptk1 mez h2 *Nat-m* k* nat-p ptk1 *Nux-m* k* nux-v ptk1 rad-br ptk1 zinc k2
    - **going** to sleep; on | **agg.**: *(↗Jerking - muscles - sleep - going - agg.)* agar k* alum ant-t bro1 **Arg-met** k* **Ars** k* *Bell* calc h2 *Cupr* bro1 ign bro1 *Ip* k* kali-c h2 nat-ar *Nat-m* k* *Nit-ac* k* *Phos* *Stry* thuj h1
  - **slow** pulse, with: *Dig*
  - **touch** agg.: colch st1

- **electric**-like: ...
  - **touching** anything: (*↗Electricity of; Electricity; sensation)* alum k*
  - **waking**, while: alum-p k2 lyc *Mag-m* manc
  - **wide** awake, while: mag-m k* nat-p k*
- **followed** by | **diabetes** mellitus: op hr
- **injuries**; after: (*↗Faintness - injury - shock; Injuries - bones)* *Acet-ac* kr1 **Acon** k* all-c bg2 *Am-c* am-m bg2 **Arn** k* *Ars* kr1* bell both-ax tsm2 *Calc* kr1 calen st1 **Camph** k* *Caps Carb-v Cham Chin* kr1 *Chlf* kr1 *Cic* cocc *Coff Cupr* cupr-ar sf1.de **Dig** kr1 *Gels* hell kr1 hep kr1 *Hydr-ac* kr1 hyos sf1.de **Hyper** k* *Ip* kalm bg2 **Lach** k* *Laur* kr1 lyc kr1 merc *Nat-m* kr1 nat-s bg2 nit-ac kr1 *Nux-m* kr1 nux-v kr1 **Op** k* petr bg2 ph-ac bg2 *Phos* kr1 psor puls bg2 *Ran-b* sec sep kr1 *Staph* stront-c stry-p sf1.de sulph symph bg2 *Tab* kr1 valer bg2 vanil fd5.de **Verat** k*
  - **fractures**; from: acon st1 arn st1
- **nervous**: acet-ac bg2 *Acon* bg2* am-c bg2 ambr ptk1 arn bg2* camph bg2* carb-v ptk1 cham bg2 cic bg2 coff bg2* gels bg2* hep bg2 hyos bg2* hyper bg2* *Ign* ptk1 iod ptk1 merc bg2 nat-m bg2 op bg2* puls bg2 sec bg2 stront-c bg2 sulph bg2 verat bg2*
- **operation**; after: acon ptk1 camph ptk1 carb-v ptk1 *Stront-c* br1* verat br1*

SHOCK; anaphylactic: (*↗Allergic)* ant-t mrr1 apis mrr1 **Carb-ac** mrr1 tetox mtf11 tor br1
- **bee** stings; from: **Carb-ac** mrr1

SHORTENED muscles and tendons: (*↗Complaints - muscles; EXTREMITIES - Contraction; EXTREMITIES - Shortened)* abrot bg2* agar bg alum bg am-c *Am-caust* sf1.de **Am-m** k* ambr k* anac ars aur *Bar-c* calc carb-an k* carb-v **Caust** k* cic *Cimic* coff sf1.de **Coloc** k* con cupr dig dios bg* dros ferr sf1.de form bg2* **Graph** k* *Guaj* k* hell hep hyos iod bg2* kali-c kali-i kreos lach led *Lyc* mag-c *Merc* mez k* mosch *Nat-c* **Nat-m** k* nit-ac *Nux-v* ol-j ptk1 *Olnd* sf1.de ox-ac petr ph-ac phos plb puls k* ran-b rheum *Rhus-t* k* *Ruta* k* samb sec sf1.de *Sep* sil stann sul-ac sulph k* syph bg tell bg2*

SHORTENING of:
- **sensation** of shortening (See Tension - general)

○ - **Muscles**: am-c b2.de* **Am-m** b2.de* ambr b2.de* anac b2.de* ang b2.de* arn b2.de* ars b2.de* aur b2.de* *Bar-c* b2.de* borx bg2 bov b2.de bry b2.de* calc b2.de* carb-an b2.de* carb-v b2.de* **Caust** b2.de* cic b2.de* cimic bg2 coff bg2 *Coloc* b2.de* con b2.de* croc b2.de* cupr bg2 dig b2.de* dros b2.de* euph b2.de* euphr b2.de* ferr bg2 **Graph** b2.de* guaj b2.de* hell b2.de* hep b2.de* hyos b2.de* ign b2.de* kali-c b2.de* kali-i bg2 kreos b2.de* lach b2.de* led b2.de* lyc b2.de* m-ambo b2.de mag-c b2.de* merc b2.de* merc-c b4a.de mez b2.de* mosch b2.de* nat-c b2.de* **Nat-m** b2.de* nit-ac b2.de* *Nux-v* b2.de* olnd bg2 petr b2.de* ph-ac bg2 phos b2.de* plb b2.de* puls b2.de* ran-b b2.de* rheum b2.de* *Rhus-t* b2.de* sabin b2.de* samb b2.de* sec bg2 *Sep* b2.de* sil b2.de* spig b2.de* stann b2.de* sul-ac b2.de* sulph b2.de* tab bg2 verat b2.de*

SHOT rolling through the arteries; sensation of: (*↗Ball)* nat-p k*

SHRINKAGE: (*↗Atrophy)*

○ - **Lymphatic** tissue: (*↗Atrophy)* cortico sp1

SHRIVELLING: *Abrot* sf1.de alum sf1.de am-c j5.de am-m k* ambr j5.de ant-c j5.de* *Arg-n* arn k* *Bar-c* sf1.de bism k* borx sf1.de bry j5.de *Calc* j5.de* camph j5.de cham j5.de chin k* cupr k* fl-ac sf1.de graph j5.de* hell j5.de kali-br sf1.de *Lyc* j5.de* merc k* mur-ac j5.de nux-v j5.de op sf1.de ph-ac j5.de plb j5.de psor k2* rheum j5.de* rhod k* rhus-t j5.de sabad j5.de *Sars* j5.de* *Sec* j5.de* *Sep* j5.de* sil gl1.fr• spig j5.de stram j5.de* *Sulph* j5.de* verat k* viol-o j5.de* vip j5.de zinc k*

○ - **Joints**: caust tl1
- **Mucous** membranes: borx ptk1

SHUDDERING, nervous: (*↗MIND - Anxiety - shuddering; MIND - Restlessness)* absin a1 acon k* acon-l a1 aether a1 agar a1 aloe a1 *Am-m* k* anac antip vh1 **Arn** k* ars ptk1 asar h1* aur *Bell* k* benz-ac blatta-a a1 bond a1 borx a1 both-ax tsm2 *Brom* a1 bry a1 caj a1 calc camph cann-s caps a1 caust cham a1* chin chir-fl bnm4• cic *Cimic* hr1* cina k* clem a1 *Cocc* k* cupr cupr-s a1 cycl a1 dig a1 digin a1 dios bg* dros a1 dulc a1 elae a1 elaps a1 eup-per a1 euph a1 gast a1 *Gels* k* gins a1 glon bg1* graph a1 haem a1 hell a1* hura a1 hydr-ac a1 hydrog srj2• hyos *Hyper* ptk1 ign a1* ip a1* iris-fl a1 junc-e a1 kali-c a1 kali-chl a1 kali-n a1 kali-p k2 kalm a1 kiss a1 kreos *Lach* a1 laur *Led* k* limen-b-c mlk9.de linu-c a1 lyc mag-m mag-s a1 mang merc a1 merc-i-r a1 merc-sul a1 *Mez* k* morph a1 mosch a1* *Nat-m* k* nit-ac a1 nux-m

Shuddering, nervous: ...
Nux-v k* op a1 osm a1 ped a1 ph-ac phos phys ptk1 phyt a1 plat a1 plb a1 podo a1 polyp-p a1 *Puls* k* ran-b ptk1 raph a1 rheum a1* *Rhus-t* k* ruta a1 samb a1 scroph-n a1 seneg sep k* *Sil* k* sin-n a1 *Spig* k* stann a1 staph stram a1 tab a1 tarent a1 thuj a1* til a1 upa a1 valer verat viol-t vip a1 zinc bg* zinc-s a1
- **morning**: mang a1
  - **rising** from bed agg.: coloc h2 rhus-t h1
- **air** agg.; draft of: phys ptk1
- **alternating** with heat: bol-la a1 mang a1 merc a1 puls a1 raph a1 stry a1 tab a1
- **asleep**, when falling: am-c a1 **Bell** a1 calc a1 ign a1 merc-c a1 mez a1 rhus-t a1
- **cold** air agg.: *Cham* h1 mosch ptk1
- **contradiction**; from: elaps ptk1
- **convulsions**; before epileptic: cupr kl
- **dinner**; before: ars a1 cann-i a1 grat a1 sulph a1
- **drawing** pain in abdomen, with: nit-ac h2
- **drinking** | **after** | **agg.**: caps a1* chin a1 elaps a1 lyc a1 nux-v a1 verat a1
  - **agg.**: ars a1 calen a1 caps ptk1 carb-ac bg1
- **eating** | **after** | **agg.**: digin a1 ign a1 lyc h2 rhus-t h1 sulph h2 tab a1
  - **while** | **agg.**: cham a1 lyc h2* staph a1
- **emotions**:
  - **agg.**: asar ptk1
  - **from**; as if: limen-b-c hrn2•
- **emptiness** in stomach, after: phos h2
- **eructations**; with: dulc ptk1 ip h1
- **headache**; from: borx h2 sars h2
- **lying** down agg.: cit-v a1
- **menses** | **before** | **agg.**: *Sep* k*
  - **during** | **agg.**: nux-v a1 sapin a1
- **motion**:
  - **agg.**: caps a1 caust a1 con a1 merc a1 nux-v a1
  - **amel.**: dros a1
- **nausea**; with: mag-c h2 stann h2
- **noise** agg.: asar vh
- **odor** of flowers; from: lac-c ptk1
- **pain**:
  - **after**: glon ptk1
  - **during**: sep a1 sil h2 *Spig* br1
    - **umbilicus**; in: chin h1 ip h1
  - **from**: ars ptk1 bar-c ptk1 caps ptk1 dios ptk1 ign ptk1 mez ptk1 ran-b ptk1 sep ptk1
- **part** touched: *Spig* k*
- **rest** agg.: dros a1
- **rising** | **after** | **agg.**: lyc a1
  - **amel.**: nat-c a1
- **seeing** deformed persons: benz-ac ptk1
- **sitting** agg.: hyper a1 nat-m a1
- **sleep**; on falling in: tub ptk1
- **starting**, with: sulph h1*
- **stool**:
  - **after** | **agg.**: acon-l a1 canth ptk1 grat a1 mag-m a1 mez h2 plat a1 ptel a1 rheum ptk1
  - **before**: merc a1
  - **during** | **agg.**: aesc a1 alum bell k1 calad calc-s a1 castm con ind kali-c mag-m mez a1 nat-c nit-ac h2 plat rheum a1 spig stann verat
- **supper**; during: bov a1
- **thinking** of disagreeable things: benz-ac k* phos k*
- **touch**, slight: kali-c k2
- **twitching** of legs: con h2
- **urination**:
  - **after** | **agg.**: eug a1 iod a1 plat a1
  - **during** | **agg.**: stram ptk1
  - **urging** for urination is not attended; when: sep ptk1
  - **urging** to urinate | **with**: hyper ptk1

- **vomiting**; with: dulc ptk1 sulph h2
- **waking**; on: carc tpw2* ign bg2*
- **walking** | **after** | **agg.**: meny a1
  - **agg.**: arn a1
- **water** brash, with: sil h2
- **wine** agg.: cina k2
- **yawning** agg.: castm a1 *Cina* k* hydr j5.de ip h1 laur c1 mag-m h2 nux-v h1 olnd k* sars h2

○ - **Affected** parts: ars ptk1
- **Bones**: ph-ac b4a.de

SICCA syndrome: *(↗Dryness; Sjögren's; EYE - Xerophthalmia)* brass-n-o srj5•

SICK FEELING; vague: **Acon** b2.de* acon-s a1 agar b2.de* agn b7.de *Alum* b2.de* am-c b4.de ambr b2.de* ang b2.de* ant-c b2.de* *Ant-t* b2.de* apis bg2 arg-met b2.de* arn bg2 *Ars* b2.de* asaf b2.de* asar b2.de* *Bapt* bg2* bar-c b4.de* bell bg2 beryl tpw5 *Bism* b7.de borx b2.de* bov b2.de* bry b2.de* bufo bg2 calc b2.de* calc-f bg2 camph b2.de* cann-s b7.de canth b2.de* carb-an bg2 carb-v bg2 carc mlr1• caust b2.de* cham b2.de* *Chel* b2.de* chin b2.de* cic b2.de* cimic ptk1 cina b7.de *Cocc* b7.de coff b2.de* *Colch* bg2 *Con* b2.de* croc b2.de* cupr b7.de cystein-l rly4• euphr b2.de* ferr b2.de* fl-ac bg2 gels bg2 graph b2.de* guaj b2.de* hell bg2 hep b2.de* ign b2.de* influ jl2* iod b4.de ip b2.de* kali-bi bg2 kali-n b2.de* kali-s fd4.de kreos bg2 lach b7.de* lat-m bnm6• led b2.de* lob ptk1 loxo-lae bnm12• *Lyc* b2.de* m-aust b2.de mag-c b4.de mag-m b2.de* mand rsj7• mang b2.de* merc b2.de* *Mez* b2.de* *Mosch* b2.de* mur-ac b2.de* narc-ps a1* nat-c b4a.de* nat-m bg2 nit-ac b2.de* nux-m b7.de* **Nux-v** b2.de* olnd b2.de* op b2.de* petr b2.de* ph-ac b4.de* phos b4.de* plat b2.de* plb b2.de* *Podo* ptk1 psor bg2* **Puls** b2.de* ran-b b7.de *Rhod* b4.de* rhus-t b2.de* ruta b2.de* sabad b2.de* sabin b2.de* sang ptk1 sec b2.de* sel bg2 seneg b2.de* sep bg2 sil bg2 spig b2.de* *Spong* b2.de* stann b2.de* *Staph* b2.de* stict br1 stront-c b2.de* *Sulph* b2.de* tab ptk1 tarax b2.de* thuj b2.de* tritic-vg fd5.de valer b7.de verat b2.de* zinc b2.de*

- **night**: orni br1
- **causeless**: brom tl1*
- **chill**; during: cann-s b7a.de kali-c b4.de*
- **coryza**; during: phos b4.de*
- **eating**; after: bar-c b4a.de borx b4a.de chin b7a.de lyc bg2 nux-m b7a.de* nux-v b7a.de ph-ac b4a.de rhod b4a.de
- **fever**:
  - **before**: ip b7a.de nux-v b7a.de puls b7a.de
  - **during** | **agg.**: kali-c b4.de
- **hunger**; from: *(↗Hunger - agg.)* lac-loxod-a hrn2• **Phos** bg2
- **menses** | **before** | **agg.**: apis bg2 brom ptk1* calc b4.de* con b4.de kali-c bg2 *Lyc* b4.de*
  - **during** | **agg.**: *Cupr* b7.de
- **pain**; from: ip bg2 stront-c br1*
- **paroxysmal**: *Acon* b2.de* agar b2.de* alum b2.de* *Ambr* b2.de* ang b2.de* ant-c b2.de* ant-t b2.de* arg-met b2.de* *Ars* b2.de* asaf b2.de* asar b2.de bar-c b2.de* *Bell* b2.de* borx b2.de* bov b2.de* bry b2.de* calad b2.de* **Calc** b2.de* camph b2.de* carb-v b2.de* *Caust* b2.de* cham b2.de* chel b2.de* chin b2.de* *Cic* b2.de* cina b2.de* coff b2.de* **Con** b2.de* croc b2.de* **Cupr** b2.de* euphr b2.de* ferr b2.de* graph b2.de* *Hep* b2.de* hyos b2.de* *Ign* b2.de* ip b2.de* *Kali-c* b2.de* led b2.de* *Lyc* b2.de* m-aust b2.de mag-c b2.de* mag-m b2.de* *Mang* b2.de* *Merc* b2.de* mez b2.de* mosch b2.de* mur-ac b2.de* nat-c b2.de* *Nat-m* b2.de* nit-ac b2.de* *Nux-v* b2.de* olnd b2.de* op b2.de* petr b2.de* phos b2.de* plat b2.de* plb b2.de* puls b2.de* rhus-t b2.de* sabad b2.de* sabin b2.de* sel b2.de* seneg b2.de* *Sep* b2.de* **Sil** b2.de* spig b2.de* *Spong* b2.de* stann b2.de* staph b2.de* **Stram** b2.de* stront-c b2.de* *Sulph* b2.de* thuj b2.de* valer b2.de* verat b2.de* zinc b2.de*
- **recovery** from a disease; sensation as if after: *Hell* b7.de*
- **shivering**; during: cann-s b7.de
- **sudden**: carc mlr1• con ptk1
- **waking**; on: cadm-met tpw6

SILICA; from overuse of: camph hr1* **Fl-ac** k* hep hr1* merc hr1* sulph hr1*

SILICOSIS (See Stone-cutters)

SINGING:

- **after** | **agg.**: agar b2.de* *Hep* b2.de* sil bg2

Singing: ...

- **agg.**: agar b2.de* *Am-c* b2.de* carb-an b2.de* **Carb-v** b2.de* cocc b2.de* *Dros* b2.de* mang b2.de* nit-ac b2.de* par b2.de* **Phos** b2.de* sars b2.de* sel b2.de* spong b2.de* *Stann* b2.de* *Sulph* b2.de* verb b2.de*
- **amel.**: sep b4.de

SINKING sensation: alum ptk1 arg-n bg2 ars bg2 bapt bg2 bell bg2 benz-ac bg2 *Bry* bg2* camph bg2 chin bg2 chinin-s ptk1 crot-t bg2 cupr ptk1 dulc bg2* glon bg2* hell ptk1 hydr-ac ptk1 iod bg2 kali-c bg2* *Lach* bg2* laur ptk1 lyc bg2* merc bg2 merc-c bg2 nat-m ptk1 nux-m bg2 ph-ac bg2 phos bg2* rhus-t bg2* sec bg2 tab bg2* verat ptk1 verb bg2 xan ptk1 xanth bg2

SINUSITIS (See Inflammation - sinuses)

SITTING:

- **after**: acon b7.de agar b4.de ambr b7a.de *Ang* b7a.de *Ars* b4a.de asar b7.de bell b4a.de bism b7.de caps b7.de *Carb-v* b4a.de *Caust* b4a.de cham b7.de *Chin* b7.de cocc b7.de con b4a.de croc b7.de dig b4a.de euph b4.de lach b7.de *Led* b7.de lyc b4.de m-arct b7.de *Mag-c* b4a.de *Nit-ac* b4.de nux-v b7.de olnd b7.de ph-ac b4.de *Phos* b4a.de *Puls* b7.de* ran-b b7.de *Rhod* b4a.de rhus-t b7.de* ruta b7.de *Sep* b4a.de *Sil* b4.de* *Sulph* b4a.de zinc b4a.de
- **agg.**: *(↗MIND - Sitting - inclination)* acon k* **Agar** k* agn k* *Aloe* alum k* *Alumn* kr1 am-c k* **Am-m** k* *Ambr* k* anac k* *Ang* b2.de* ant-c k* ant-t k* *Apis* bg2* *Arg-met* k* arn k* **Ars** k* ars-s-f k2 *Asaf* k* asar k* *Aur* k* aur-i k2 *Aur-m* k* *Aur-m-n* aur-s k* *Bar-c* k* bar-m bar-s k2 bell k* bism k* borx k* bov k* *Bry* k* cact calad k* calc k* camph k* cann-s k* canth k* **Caps** k* carb-an k* carb-v k* carc fd2.de• caust k* cham k* chel k* *Chin* k* cic k* cimic jl3 *Cina* k* clem k* cob k* *Cocc* k* coff k* colch k* *Coloc* k* **Con** k* croc k* cupr k* **Cycl** k* dicha mg1.de dig b2.de* dios bro1 *Dros* k* **Dulc** k* equis-h bro1 **Euph** k* *Euphr* k* *Ferr* k* ferr-act sf1.de ferr-ar k2 fl-ac k* *Gamb* graph k* grat j5.de guaj k* hecla jl *Hell* k* hep k* hydrc bro1 hydrog srj2• hyos k* ign k* indg br1* iod k* ip k* *Kali-bi* kali-c k* kali-m k2 kali-n k* kali-p kali-s kreos k* *Lach* k* laur k* *Led* k* **Lyc** k* *M-ambo* b2.de* m-arct b2.de* m-aust b2.de* mag-c k* *Mag-m* k* mang k* *Meny* k* meph jl3 *Merc* k* mez k* *Mosch* k* *Mur-ac* k* *Nat-c* k* nat-m k* nat-p nit-ac k* nux-m k* nux-v k* olnd k* op k* par k* *Petr* k* *Ph-ac* k* phel j5.de phor-t mie3• **Phos** k* phyt bro1 pic-ac k2 **Plat** k* plb k* pneu jl3* *Prun* psor k2* **Puls** k* pyrog k2 ran-b k* ran-s k* rheum k* *Rhod* b2.de* **Rhus-t** k* *Ruta* k* *Sabad* k* sabin k* sacch-a fd2.de• samb k* sars k* sec k* sel k* *Seneg* k* **Sep** k* sil k* *Spig* k* spong k* squil k* stann k* staph k* stram k* stront-c k* sul-ac k* sul-i k2 **Sulph** k* *Tarax* k* teucr k* *Thuj* k* tong j5.de tril-p c1 tritic-vg fd5.de tub k2 **Valer** k* verat k* **Verb** k* viol-o k* **Viol-t** k* vip-a jl3 **Zinc** k* **Zinc-p** k2 [arg-n stj2 arg-p stj2 astat stj2 bar-br stj2 bar-i stj2 bar-met stj2 bism-sn stj2 caes-met stj2 calc-n stj1 cinnb stj2 cob-m stj2 cob-p stj2 hafn-met stj2 irid-met stj2 lanth-met stj2 merc-d stj2 merc-i-f stj2 osm-met stj2 plb-m stj2 plb-p stj2 polon-met stj2 rhen-met stj2 tant-met stj2 thal-met stj2 tung-met stj2]
- **amel.**: *(↗MIND - Sitting - inclination)* *Acon* k* agar k* agn k* alum k* *Alumn* kr1 am-c k* am-m k* *Anac* k* androc srj1• ang b2.de* *Ant-t* k* *Apis* b7a.de aral bg2* arg-met kr1 arn k* ars k* asaf k* asar b2.de* aur k* bar-c k* bell k* borx k* **Bry** k* cadm-s *Calad* k* calc k* camph k* cann-s k* canth k* caps k* carb-an k* carb-v k* caust k* cham k* chel k* chin k* chion choc srj3• cic k* cina k* clem k* cocc k* *Coff* k* **Colch** k* *Coloc* k* con k* croc k* cupr k* cycl k* **Dig** b2.de* *Dulc* kr1 ferr k* ferr-ar k2 gels *Glon* k* *Gnaph* bg2 *Graph* b2.de* guaj k* hell k* hep k* hydrog srj2• hyos k* ign k* iod k* ip k* kali-c k* kali-n k* kreos k* laur k* led k* loxo-recl knl4• m-arct b2.de* m-aust b2.de mag-c k* mag-m k* mang k* meny k* meph c1 *Merc* k* mez k* mosch k* nat-ar nat-c b2.de* nat-m k* nit-ac k* *Nux-m* k* **Nux-v** k* op k* par k* petr k* ph-ac k* phos k* plb k* *Puls* k* pulx br1 ran-b k* ran-s k* *Rheum* k* *Rhod* kr1 *Rhus-t* b2.de* sabad b2.de* sabin k* sacch-a fd2.de• samb k* sars k* sec k* sel k* *Sep* k* *Sil* k* spig k* spong k* *Squil* k* stann k* staph k* stram k* sul-ac k* sulph k* sumb tarax k* thuj k* valer k* verat k* verb kr1 zinc k*
- **aversion** to (See MIND - Sitting - aversion)
- **bent** backward | **amel.**: [zinc stj1]
- **bent** forward:
  - **agg.**: *Acon* b2.de* *Agn* b2.de* alum b2.de* *Alumn* kr1 *Am-m* b2.de* ang b2.de* **Ant-t** b2.de* arg-met b2.de* *Ars* b2.de* asaf b2.de* bar-c b2.de* borx b2.de* bov b2.de* *Bry* b2.de* caps b2.de* carb-v b2.de* caust b2.de* cham b2.de* chel b2.de* *Chin* b2.de* *Cic* b2.de* **Dig** b2.de* *Dulc* b2.de* ferr b2.de* *Hyos* b2.de* ign bg2 meny b2.de* nat-m bg2 *Nux-v* b2.de* *Phos* b2.de* plb b2.de* *Puls* b2.de* ran-b ptk1 *Rhod* b2.de* *Rhus-t* b2.de* *Sabin* b2.de* *Samb* b2.de* *Sep* b2.de* spig b2.de* spong b2.de* *Squil* b2.de* stann b2.de* *Sulph* b2.de* *Verb* b2.de* viol-t b2.de*

- **bent** forward: ...
  - **amel.**: anac b2.de* *Ang* b2.de* ars b2.de* bar-c b2.de* *Bell* b2.de* borx b2.de* bry b2.de* calad b2.de* *Carb-v* b2.de* caust b2.de* *Cham* b2.de* *Chel* b2.de* chin b2.de* cina b2.de* *Colch* b2.de* *Coloc* b2.de* *Con* b2.de* dig b2.de* *Ign* b2.de* **Kali-c** b2.de* kreos b2.de lach ptk1 *Lyc* b2.de* m-aust b2.de mang b2.de* *Merc* b2.de* *Mez* b2.de* mosch b2.de* nux-m b2.de* nux-v b2.de* op b2.de* puls b2.de* *Rheum* b2.de* rhus-t b2.de* *Sabad* b2.de* sars b2.de* *Spig* b2.de* *Spong* b2.de* *Stann* kr1 *Staph* b2.de* sulph b2.de* tarax b2.de* verat b2.de* verb b2.de* viol-t b2.de [kali-ar stj2 kali-met stj2 kali-sil stj2]
- **cold** surface agg.; on a: chim bg2* dulc bg2 *Nux-v* bg2* rhod bg2
- **erect**:
  - **agg.**: acon b7.de anac b2.de* *Ang* b2.de* ars b2.de* aur-s k2* bar-c b2.de* bar-s k2* *Bell* b2.de* borx b2.de* bry b2.de* calad b2.de* *Carb-v* b2.de* caust b2.de* *Cham* b2.de* *Chel* b2.de* chin b2.de* cina b2.de* *Colch* b2.de* **Coloc** b2.de* *Con* b2.de* dig b2.de* *Ign* b2.de* **Kali-c** b2.de* kreos b2.de* *Lyc* b2.de* m-aust b2.de* mang b2.de* *Merc* b2.de* *Mez* b2.de* mosch b2.de* nat-m ptk1 nux-m b2.de* nux-v b2.de* op b2.de* puls b2.de* rheum b2.de* rhus-t b2.de* *Sabad* b2.de* sars b2.de* *Spig* b2.de* *Spong* b2.de* *Staph* b2.de* sulph b2.de* tarax b2.de* verat b2.de* verb b2.de* viol-t b2.de*
  - **amel.**: *Acon* b2.de* *Agn* b2.de alum b2.de* *Alumn* kr1 *Am-m* b2.de* ang b2.de* *Ant-t* b2.de* apis bro1* aral ptk1 arg-met b2.de* *Ars* b2.de* asaf b2.de* bar-c b2.de* bell bro1* borx b2.de* bov b2.de* *Bry* b2.de* caps b2.de* carb-v b2.de* caust b2.de* cham b2.de* chel b2.de* *Chin* b2.de* *Cic* b2.de* con ptk1 **Dig** b2.de* *Dulc* b2.de* ferr b2.de* gels ptk1 *Hyos* b2.de* kali-bi sf1.de* kali-n ptk1 lyc b4a.de meny b2.de* nat-m ptk1 **Nat-s** ptk1 *Nux-v* b2.de* olib-sac wmh1 *Phos* b2.de* plb b2.de* *Puls* b2.de* *Rhod* b2.de* *Rhus-t* b2.de* *Sabin* b2.de* *Samb* b2.de* *Sep* b2.de* spig b2.de* spong b2.de* squil b2.de* stann b2.de* *Sulph* b2.de* verb b2.de* viol-t b2.de
  - **difficult** | **sitting** bent forward in bed; when: lath ptk1
  - **hands** folded on chest: ox-ac ptk1
  - **impossible**: lyc a1 stram a1
- **hard**; on something | **amel.**: bell b4a.de
- **impulse** to sit: *(↗MIND - Sitting - inclination)* acon k* *Agar* k* alum k* am-c k* *Am-m* k* ambr sf1.de anac b2.de* ant-c k* ant-t k* arg-met b2.de* arg-n arn b2.de* *Ars* k* *Ars-i* asar k* *Aur* bar-act sf1.de bar-c k* bar-m *Bell* k* borx b2.de* brom bry k* calc k* camph k* *Cann-s* k* canth k* *Carb-v* k* caust k* cham j5.de* *Chel* k* **Chin** k* *Cocc* k* cod a1 colch k* **Con** k* croc k* cupr k* cycl k* dulc k* *Euphr* k* *Ferr* **Graph** k* *Guaj* b2.de* hell k* hep b2.de* **Hipp** hyos b2.de* ign k* *Iod* k* ip k* jac-c a1 kali-ar kali-c k* kali-p lac-c lach k* lact j5.de laur k* led sf1.de lyc k* m-arct b2.de m-aust b2.de* mag-c k* mag-m k* merc k* mez k* mur-ac k* nat-ar a1 nat-c k* *Nat-m* k* nat-p nat-s bg2* nit-ac b2.de* **Nux-v** k* olnd k* op k* petr k* *Ph-ac* k* **Phos** k* pic-ac a1 plat plb k* puls b2.de* ran-b k* *Ran-s* b2.de* rheum b2.de* rhod k* rhus-t k* ruta b2.de* sabin j5.de *Sec* k* *Sep* k* sil k* *Spong* k* **Squil** k* *Stann* k* staph j5.de stront-c b2.de* sulph b2.de* *Tarax* k* teucr b2.de* verat j5.de* verb k* viol-t k* *Zinc* k*
- **leaning** against something; while | **amel.**: spig b7.de
- **long** time agg.; for a: pneu jl2
  - **after**: ars b4a.de carb-v b4a.de sulph b4a.de
- **low** chair agg.; sitting in a: syph ptk1
- **must** sit up in bed with knees drawn up, rests her head and arms upon knees: **Ars** k* glon a1
- **wet** ground; on (See Wet - ground)

SITTING DOWN:

- **agg.**: *Agn* k* alum k* am-c b4.de **Am-m** k* *Ant-t* k* apis sf1.de arg-met k* aur k* bar-c k* bov k* bry k* caust k* *Chel* k* chin k* cob sf1.de *Coff* k* croc k* cycl k* graph k* *Hell* k* *Ip* k* iris kali-c k* lyc k* *Mag-c* k* mag-m sf1.de mang k* merc k* murx nat-s sf1.de nit-ac k* nux-v sf1.de ph-ac k* phos k* puls k* rhus-t b2.de* ruta k* sabin k* *Samb* k* sars k* sep sf1.de **Spig** k* *Spong* k* squil k* sulph sf1.de thuj k* *Valer* k* verat k* viol-t k* zinc sf1.de
- **amel.**: acon k* ambr k* anac k* ang b2.de* ant-c k* ant-t k* arn k* ars k* asar k* aur k* *Bar-c* k* *Bell* k* bov k* bry k* calc k* cann-s k* canth k* **Caps** k* carb-an k* *Carb-v* k* caust k* cham k* chin k* cic k* cocc k* **Con** k* croc k* cycl b7.de dig k* dros k* *Euph* k* *Ferr* k* graph k* kali-c k* kali-n k* lach k* *Laur* k* *Led* k* lyc k* m-ambo b2.de* m-arct b2.de m-aust b2.de mang k* merc k* mur-ac k* nat-c k* nat-m k* nit-ac k* *Nux-v* k* *Olnd* k* *Petr* k* ph-ac k* *Phos* k* plat k* puls k* ran-b k* rhod k* *Rhus-t* k* ruta k* sabad k* *Sep* k* sil k* *Spig* k* *Staph* k* stram k* stront-c k* *Sulph* k* thuj k* *Verat* k*

SITTING UP in bed: | agg. | hands supporting body; with:

berb ptk1 sulph ptk1

- **amel.**: acon b7a.de am-m b7a.de *Ant-t* b7.de* asaf b7.de cham b7.de ferr b7.de hyos b7a.de *Kali-c* bro1* nux-v b7.de puls b7.de* rhus-t b7.de *Samb* b7.de* *Squil* b7a.de

SJÖGREN'S SYNDROME: *(↗Connective; Dermatomyositis; Dryness; Sicca)* nux-m mrr1 tub vk1 tub-m mtf11

SLEEP:

- **after** sleep:
  - **morning**: *(↗Morning - waking; Waking; Waking - on)*
    - **waking**; on: *Aids* nl2• **Am-m** st **Ambr** st *Arn* st **Ars** st bell-p mg1.de bufo br1* cadm-met mg1.de* **Calc** st *Carb-v* st **Caust** st *Chel* st chin st cob-n mg1.de *Cocc* st *Con* st *Dig* st *Euphr* b7a.de ferr-ar k2 flav jl *Graph* st **Hep** st *Hydrog* srj2• *Hyos* st *Ign* st *Kali-ar* st *Kali-c* st **Lach** st* *Lyc* st mag-c mg1.de neon srj5• **Nux-v** b7a.de* **Phos** st *Phyt* st prot jl **Puls** st **Rhus-t** st sal-fr sle1• samb st **Sep** st *Staph* st **Sulph** st ulm-c jsj8•
  - **afternoon**:
    - **agg.●**: *(↗SLEEP - Unrefreshing - sleep - siesta)* anac k* bar-c h2 bell st *Bry* k* calc-s zf caust bg2 chin k* con h2 *Graph* bg2 *Lach* k* mag-c mg1.de mag-f mg1.de* *Nat-m* h2 phos k* *Puls* k* *Sel* bg2* spong **STAPH** k* *Sulph* k*
    - **amel.**: fl-ac jl granit-m es1• kali-bi jl kola stb3• meph jl nux-m jl nux-v jl ph-ac jl pneu jl rhus-g tmo3• senec jl vanil fd5.de
  - **agg.**: *Acon* k* aesc k* aids nl2• ail kr1 alum-p k2 am-c bg2* am-m k* *Ambr* b2.de* anac k* *Apis* k* apoc vh1* arg-met bg2* *Arn* k* *Ars* k* ars-s-f k2 asaf k* aur-ar k2 bar-m bg2 bell k* borx k* both-ax tsm2 bov k* bry k* bufo kr1* cadm-s k* calad b2.de* calc k* calc-f mg1.de *Camph* k* *Carb-v* k* *Carbn-s* *Caust* k* cham k* *Chel* k* chin k* cina k* cob-n mg1.de coc-c bg2* *Cocc* k* coff k* *Con* k* crat bro1 **Crot-c** *Crot-h* bg2* *Crot-t* k1 dig k* *Dios* kr1 epiph bro1 *Euphr* k* *Ferr* k* ferr-ar graph k* helo-s rwt2• *Hep* k* hom-xyz bro1 *Hydrog* srj2• hyos k* ign k* kali-ar kali-bi bg1* kali-c k* kali-i bg2 kali-n sf1.de kali-p kreos k* lac-c **Lach** k* lob bg2 *Lyc* k* *M-ambo* b2.de* m-arct b2.de* mag-c k* mag-f mg1.de* merc-c bro1 morph bro1 mur-ac murx mgm• myric kr1 naja nat-ar nat-sil k2 nux-m k* nux-v k* olnd k* *Op* k* paeon parth bro1 *Ph-ac* k* *Phos* k* *Phyt* pic-ac bro1 ptel c1 *Puls* k* *Rheum* k* rhus-t k* *Sabad* k* samb k* **Sel** k* *Sep* k* sil bg2 spig k* **Spong** k* squil b2.de* stann k* *Staph* k* **Stram** k* **Sulph** k* syph bro1 thuj k* tub br1* uran-n bg2* valer kr1* *Verat* k* vesp ptk2 ziz bro1
  - **amel.**: acon agar am-m ambr apis *Ars* bry *Calad* k* calc cham chin cocc colch k* con crot-t sf1.de ferr galeoc-c-h gms1• glon k2 hell hydrog srj2• ign ip iris sf1.de kali-s fd4.de kreos lach lob *Med* sf1.de meph sf1.de *Merc* k* mygal bro1 nat-c nid jl *Nux-v* k* onos vml3• oxyt ozone sde2• pall c1 **Ph-ac** k* **Phos** k* pic-ac mrr1 puls ran-b sf1.de rhus-g tmo3• ruta sabal c1 sabin samb sang k* sel *Sep* k* spig thuj tritic-vg fd5.de vanil fd5.de yohim lp2 [cupr-act stj2]
    - **broken** sleep; even after: granit-m es1•
    - **short** sleep; even after a (See short)
- **before** | **agg.**: acon k* agar k* *Agn* k* alum k* am-c k* am-m k* ambr k* anac k* ant-c k* arn k* **Ars** k* ars-s-f k2 asar k* aur k* aur-ar k2 bar-c k* *Bell* k* bism k* borx k* **Bry** k* *Calad* k* **Calc** k* camph k* canth k* caps k* *Carb-an* k* **Carb-v** k* *Caust* k* cham k* chel k* *Chin* k* clem k* cocc k* coff k* coloc k* con k* cycl k* dig k* dulc k* euph k* euphr k* *Graph* k* guaj k* *Hep* k* *Ign* k* ip k* *Kali-c* k* kali-n k* *Kreos* k* lach k* laur k* led k* *Lyc* k* m-ambo b2.de* m-arct b2.de m-aust b2.de mag-c k* mag-m k* mang k* **Merc** k* mez k* mosch k* mur-ac k* nat-ar nat-c k* nat-m k* nit-ac k* nux-m k* nux-v k* par k* petr k* *Ph-ac* k* **Phos** k* plat k* plb k* **Puls** k* ran-b k* rheum k* rhod k* **Rhus-t** k* sabad k* sabin k* samb k* *Sars* k* sel k* seneg k* **Sep** k* *Sil* k* spig k* spong k* stann k* staph k* stront-c k* sul-ac k* **Sulph** k* tarax k* teucr b2.de* thuj k* verat k* verb k* viol-t k* zinc k*
- **beginning** of sleep; at | **agg.**: agar agn k* am-c bg2 am-m k* anac b4a.de ant-c b7.de* aral k* *Arg-met* *Arg-n* arn k* **Ars** k* ars-s-f k2 arum-t bg2 aur k* aur-ar bapt bar-c k* **Bell** k* borx k* **Bry** k* calad k* *Calc* k* camph b7.de *Caps* k* *Carb-an* k* *Carb-v* k* caust k* cench k1 *Cham* b7.de* chin k* cocc k* coff con k* **Crot-h** k* dulc k* *Graph* k* *Grin* k* guaj k* hep k* ign k* ip k* *Kali-ar* **Kali-c** k* kreos k* *Lac-c* **Lach** k* laur k* *Led* b2.de *Lyc* k* m-arct b7.de mag-c k* mag-m k* *Merc* k* mur-ac k* nat-c k* nat-m k* nit-ac b4.de nux-m b7.de nux-v k* *Op* k* ph-ac k* *Phos* k* **Puls** k* ran-b k* *Rhus-t* k* sabin k* samb sf1.de* sars k* sel k* **Sep** k* sil k* *Spong* k* stann bg2 staph k* stront-c k* *Sulph* k* tarax k* teucr k* thuj k* *Valer* verat k*

- **during** sleep:
  - **agg.**: *Acon* k* *Aesc* k2 agn k* alum k* alumn k2 am-c k* am-m k* ambr k* anac k* ang b2.de* ant-c k* *Ant-t* k* *Apis* *Arg-n* **Arn** k* **Ars** k* ars-s-f k2 aur k* aur-ar k2 *Bar-c* k* bar-m **Bell** k* bism k* **Borx** k* both-ax tsm2 brom **Bry** k* *Calad* k* calc k* camph k* *Cann-i* cann-s k* canth k* caps k* carb-ac carb-an k* carb-v k* carbn-s caust k* **Cham** k* *Chel* k* *Chin* k* chinin-ar cic k* cina k* clem k* cocc k* coff k* colch k* coloc k* *Con* k* croc k* crot-h mrr1 cupr k* cycl k* dig k* dros k* dulc k* euph k* *Euphr* b7a.de ferr k* ferr-ar *Graph* k* guaj k* hell k* **Hep** k* **Hyos** k* *Ign* k* ip k* *Kali-ar* kali-br *Kali-c* k* kali-n k* kali-p kreos k* *Lach* k* laur k* led k* *Lyc* k* *M-ambo* b2.de* m-arct b2.de* m-aust b2.de* mag-c k* mag-m k* mang k* meny k* **Merc** k* merc-c bg2 mez k* mosch k* *Mur-ac* k* nat-ar nat-c k* *Nat-m* k* *Nit-ac* k* *Nux-m* nux-v k* **Op** k* par k* petr k* *Ph-ac* k* *Phos* k* plat k* plb k* **Puls** k* ran-b k* ran-s k* *Rheum* k* rhod k* rhus-t k* ruta k* sabin k* *Samb* k* sars k* sel k* seneg k* *Sep* k* **Sil** k* spig k* spong k* squil k* stann k* staph k* **Stram** k* stront-c k* sul-ac k* **Sulph** k* syph st teucr b2.de* thuj k* valer k* verat k* verb k* viol-t k* **Zinc** k* zinc-p k2
  - **amel.**: am-m k* calad k* hell k* *Merc* bg2 phos k* samb k*
- **falling** asleep:
  - **agg.**: puls b7a.de tarax b7a.de verat b7a.de
  - **amel.**: *Merc* k*
- **going** to sleep; on | **amel.**: *Merc* b4a.de
- **half** asleep; when:
  - **agg.**: camph ptk1 nit-ac ptk1 sabad ptk1 valer ptk1
  - **amel.**: *Sel* k*
- **long**; sensation as if slept too: bapt a1
- **long** sleep agg.: ambr k* anac k* arn k* ars asaf k* bell k* borx k* bry k* *Calc* k* camph carb-v k* *Caust* k* cham cimic gk cocc k* *Con* k* dig k* *Euphr* k* ferr *Graph* k* *Hep* k* hyos k* ign k* kali-c k* kreos k* **Lach** lyc k* *M-ambo* b2.de* m-arct b2.de mag-c k* nat-m gk *Nux-v* k* ph-ac k* phos gk puls k* rhus-t k* spig k* *Stram* k* **Sulph** k* verat k*
- **loss** of sleep; from: (*↗Jet; Waking - on - night)* agn vh ambr k* ars sf1.de* bell-p bro1 bry k* calad ph* caps bro1 carb-v kr1* carbn-o bg2 *Caust* k* chin k* *Cimic* k* *Coc-c* ptk1 **Cocc** k* *Coff* kr1* *Colch* k* cortico tpw7 crot-h tl1 *Cupr* k* dip bro1 *Gels* bro1 ign gt* ip k* kali-p ph* kreos bg2 *Lac-d* k1* lach tl1 laur k* med ph* merc ptk1 mygal ph* nat-m *Nit-ac* k* **Nux-v** k* ol-j kr1 olnd op pall ptk1 ph-ac k* **Phos** ptk1 pic-ac k2 puls k* ruta k* sabin k* sang ptk1 *Sel* k* sep k* *Sulph* zinc k* zinc-act c1* zinc-o st [cupr-act stj2 cupr-f stj2 cupr-m stj2 cupr-p stj2 tell stj2 zinc-i stj2 zinc-m stj2 zinc-n stj2 zinc-p stj2]
- **roused** from sleep agg.; being: *Cocc* b7a.de spong ptk1
- **short** sleep:
  - **agg.**: aral ptk1
  - **amel.**: (*↗SLEEP - Need - little)* bamb-a stb2.de• bros-gau mrc1 calad ph* camph tl1 carc tpw* cob a1 cob-n mg1.de* coca-c sk4• conch fkr1• dendr-pol sk4• *Fl-ac* bg2* form a1 galeoc-c-h gms1• granit-m es1• kali-bi bg2* kola stb3• *Lac-loxod-a* hrn2• med bg2* meph bg2* mez a1 nicc-met sk4• nux-m bg2 *Nux-v* bg2* petr-ra shn4• ph-ac bg2* phos tl1* pieri-b mlk9.de psil ft1 ran-r c1* rheum ptk1* senec bg2 sep tl1 vero-o rly4• [alumin-p stj2 arg-p stj2 cupr-p stj2 lith-p stj2 mang-p stj2 plb-p stj2 tax jsj7 zinc-p stj2]
    - **afternoon**: lac-loxod-a hrn2• [tax jsj7]
    - **eating**; after: pneu jl2

SLIDING DOWN in bed (See Weakness - paralytic - sliding)

SLOW manifestation: bros-gau mrc1 bry mrr1 calc-sil br1 *Con* mrr1 diaz sa3• gels br1 gink-b sbd1• *Lyc* br1 rad-br br1 squil br1 tell br1

SLOW repair of broken bones (See Injuries - bones - slow)

SLUGGISH disease process (See Slow manifestation)

SLUGGISHNESS of the body: (*↗Lassitude; Reaction - lack; Weakness; MIND - Dullness; MIND - Ennui; MIND - Prostration; MIND - Slowness)* acon j5.de aesc br1* agar j5.de* *Agath-a* nl2• aids nl2• aloe br1 alum j5.de* *Alumn* k2* *Am-m* k* ammc j5.de anac k* *Ant-t* j5.de* arge-pl rwt5• arn k* ars k* **Asar** a1 aster br1 bar-c b4.de* bell b4.de* bit-ar wht1• borx b4a.de* *Both* br1 bruc j5.de bry j5.de* cact k2* calad j5.de calc k* calc-p j5.de camph cann-s j5.de canth a1 *Caps* k* carb-an k* carb-v k* *Carl* a1 casc j5.de caust b4.de *Chel* chin j5.de chir-fl gya2 cinnb cit-ac rly4• cocc colum-p sze2• *Con* k* croc j5.de cur cycl c1 dig b4.de* dirc a1 dulc k* eup-per br1* ferr-m a1 fic-m gya1 *Gels* graph b4.de* grat j5.de guaj k*

Sluggishness of the body: ...
hell j5.de hep j5.de* hera j5.de hyos a1 ign j5.de indg j5.de iod ip kali-c k* kali-chl k13 kali-m k2 kali-p kali-s k2* lac-leo sk4• lach j5.de* lap-la sde8.de• laur k* lavand-a ctl1• lil-t a1 lob br1 lyc k* m-aust j5.de mag-c b4.de* mag-m k* merc k* mez k* mur-ac k* nat-c k* nat-m k* nat-sil fd3.de• nit-ac k* nux-v k* ol-an j5.de olnd *Op* k* petr k* ph-ac k* phel j5.de phos k* phys a1 *Plb* positr nl2• puls pyrid rly4• rheum j5.de rhod ruta j5.de sabin j5.de sacch-a fd2.de• sanguis-s hrn2• sars j5.de* *Sec* sel j5.de *Sep* k* sil j5.de* spong fd4.de stann k* stel br1 stram stront-c b4.de* sul-i k2* *Sulph* k* symph fd3.de• thal-xyz srj8• thea a1 thuj b4.de* tritic-vg fd5.de tub tl1 vanil fd5.de verb zinc b4.de* zinc-p k2* [heroin sdj2 spect dfg1]

- **morning**: agar k2* carb-an chel nat-c nat-m sacch-a fd2.de• vanil fd5.de verb
  - **sitting** agg.: chel
- **forenoon**: sars a1
- **rising** agg.: ammc a1 sacch-a fd2.de•

SLUMBER: | **amel.**: *Hell* b2.de*

SMALLER; sensation of being: (*↗MIND - Delusions - diminished; MIND - Delusions - small)* acon k* agar k* cact ptk1 *Calc* k* carb-v ptk1 croc k* euphr *Glon* k* kreos k* sabad k* tab ptk1 tarent k*

SMALLPOX: | **ailments** after: cann-xyz bg2

SMOG agg.: arund vh sul-ac st sulo-ac vh

SMOKE:
- **inspiration** of:
  - **agg.**: (*↗Allergic; Allergic - chemical; Allergic - petrochemical)* ars bg2* brom bg2 calc k* caust k* chin bg2* cocc tl1 *Euphr* k* ferr-i mrr1 ign mrr1* kali-bi bg2* lyc bg2* naja bg2 **Nat-ar** mrr1* nat-m k* nux-v k* olnd k* phos ptk1 podo fd3.de• puls bg2 *Sep* k* **Spig** k* **Sul-ac** mrr1 sulph k* suprar rly4• [alum stj2 lac-ac stj2 nat-caust stj2 oxyg stj2 sil stj2]
  - **lamp** agg; smoke of a: aur bg2 nux-v bg2
- **sensation** of: (*↗Gasses - sensation - internally)* apis ptk1 ars bg2* bar-c bg2* berb ptk1 brom ptk1 *Chin* ptk1 croc bg2 euph bg2 ign ptk1 lyc ptk1 nat-ar bg2 nit-ac bg2 petr bg2 *Puls* ptk1 ran-b bg2 sul-ac bg2 thuj bg2 valer bg2 *Verat* ptk1

SMOKING: | **amel.**: aran bro1 tarent-c bro1

SMOOTH; sensation of being: alum ptk1 phos ptk1 ter ptk1

SNEEZING:
- **agg.**: acon b2.de* am-c b2.de* *Am-m* b2.de* ant-t b2.de* arn b2.de* *Ars* b2.de* bar-c b2.de* *Bell* b2.de* *Borx* b2.de* *Bry* b2.de* calc b2.de* canth b2.de* *Carb-v* b2.de* caust b2.de* *Cham* b2.de* chin b2.de* cina b2.de* con b2.de* *Dros* b2.de* euph b2.de* graph b2.de* hell b2.de* hep b2.de* kali-c b2.de* lach b2.de* led b2.de* lol bg *Lyc* b2.de* mag-c b2.de* mag-m b2.de* *Merc* b2.de* mez b2.de* nat-c b2.de* nat-m b2.de* nit-ac b2.de* *Nux-v* b2.de* phos b2.de* *Puls* b2.de* *Rhus-t* b2.de* sabad b2.de* sec b2.de* seneg b2.de* *Sep* b2.de* sil b2.de* *Spig* b2.de* squil b2.de* staph b2.de* sulph b2.de* verb bro1* [tell stj2]
- **amel.**: am-c bg2 am-m bg2 chlol bg2* coca-c sk4• lach bg2* mag-m b2.de* naja bg2* thuj bg2*

SNOW, ailments from bright: (*↗Light; from - agg. - bright; HEAD - Pain - snow - reflection)* ant-c ptk **Ars** ptk glon c1*

SNOWY WEATHER: (*↗Weather - snow)*
- **agg.**: (*↗Weather - snow)* abrom-a-r bnj1 agar ptk1 asar jl3 bry bg2 *Calc* k* *Calc-p* k* caust k* cic **Con** k* fl-ac bg2 *Form* bg2* lach bg2 *Lyc* k* mag-m k* merc k* nat-c k* nux-v b2.de* *Ph-ac* k* *Phos* k* *Puls* k* rhod *Rhus-t* k* **Sep** k* *Sil* k* *Sulph* k* syph ptk urt-u k* vib bg2*
- **ailments** from: con c1 sep c1
- **amel.**: alum vh

SOFT:
- **sensation** of softness of hard parts: caust b2.de* *Merc* b2.de* mez b2.de* *Nit-ac* b2.de* nux-m b2.de*

○ - **Body** had changed into a big, soft bag; sensation as if lac-loxod-a hrn2•
  - **accompanied** by | **heartbeat**; consciousness of (See CHEST - Conscious - accompanied - body)

SOFTENING: (*↗Brittle; Caries - bone; Necrosis - bone; Rickets)*

○ - **Internal** parts: *Calc* b2.de* kreos b2.de*

- **Internal** parts: ...
  - **sensation** of: anac b2.de* ant-t b2.de* arn b2.de* ars b2.de* *Asar* b2.de* aur b2.de* **Bell** b2.de* *Bism* b2.de* bov b2.de* bry b2.de* calad b2.de* *Caps* b2.de* carb-v b2.de* cina b2.de* cocc b2.de* con b2.de* euph b2.de* guaj b2.de* hyos b2.de* **Ign** bg2 kali-c b2.de* laur b2.de* m-ambo b2.de merc b2.de* nux-m b2.de* olnd b2.de* op b2.de* *Par* b2.de* petr b2.de* plat b2.de* plb b2.de ran-b b2.de* ran-s b2.de* rhod b2.de* sars b2.de* *Sep* b2.de* *Spig* b2.de* *Stann* b2.de* tarax b2.de* *Verat* b2.de* zinc b2.de*

SOFTENING bones: *(↗Bones; Brittle; Caries - bone; Necrosis - bone; Rickets)* am-c k* **Asaf** k* aur bg2 bar-c bg2 *Bell* k* bufo bg2 **Calc** k* calc-f *Calc-i* bro1 calc-p k* caust bg2 cic k* con hr1* ferr k* *Ferr-i* hr1* ferr-m hr1* *Ferr-p* hr1* guaj b4a.de* hecla kr1 *Hep* k* iod k* ip k* *Kali-i* hr1* *Lac-c* hr1* *Lyc* k* **Merc** k* mez k* *Nit-ac* k* nux-m hr1* *Ol-j* hr1* parathyr jl petr k* ph-ac k* *Phos* k* plb k* *Psor* hr1* *Puls* k* rhod k* ruta k* *Sep* k* **Sil** k* staph k* *Sulph* k* syph k2* ther k* thuj bg2* [mag-f stj1 mag-p stj1]

- **x-ray**; from: cadm-met sp1 cortico sp1 cortiso sp1

SOLDIER'S HEART (See CHEST - Palpitation - irritable)

SOURNESS: *(↗Acidosis; Odor of - sour)* **Calc** bg* chin bg* cob ptk1 cuph br1 *Graph* ptk1 hep bg2* iris bg2* kali-c ptk1 lappa ptk1 lith-c ptk1 *Lyc* bg* *Mag-c* bg2* merc bg* nat-c bg* nat-m bg* nat-p bg* nat-s ptk1 nux-v bg2* ox-ac ptk1 ph-ac ptk1 phos bg* puls bg* rheum bg2* rob ptk1 *Sacch* br1 sep bg* sil bg2* sul-ac bg2* **Sulph** bg* tarax ptk1

- **bitter**: iris ptk1 nux-v ptk1
- **children**; in: cina ptk1 *Rob* br1

SPARKS; sensation of: agar ptk1 arg-met ptk1 calc ptk1 *Calc-p* ptk1 lyc ptk1 nat-m ptk1 ol-an bg2 **Sec** ptk1 sel ptk1

SPASMS (See Convulsions)

SPECTACLES; wearing: | **agg.**: borx b2.de*

SPINAL SCLEROSIS (See Paralysis - spastic spinal; BACK - Sclerosis - spinal)

SPITTING: | **agg.**: dig b2.de* led b2.de* *Nux-v* b2.de*

SPLASHING (See Swashing)

SPLINTER (See Pain - splinters)

SPONGY:

○ - **Bones**: *(↗Caries - bone)* guaj ptk1

- **Mucous** membranes: caps ptk1 phyt ptk1

SPOTS:

- **symptom** occurring in: agar bg2* alum bg2* am-c bg2 am-m bg2 ambr bg2 apis bg2 arg-met ptk1 *Arg-n* bg2 arge-pl rwt5• arn bg2 *Ars* bg2* asaf bg2 bell bg2 *Berb* ptk1 bry bg2 bufo ptk1 calc bg2 *Calc-p* ptk1 cann-xyz bg2 canth bg2 carb-v bg2 caust bg2* cham bg2 chel bg2 *Cist* ptk1 coff bro1 colch bg2* *Con* ptk1 croc bg2 cupr bg2 dios bg2 ferr bg2 fl-ac bg2* galeoc-c-h gms1• glon ptk1 graph bg2 hep bg2* **Ign** bg2* iod bg2 **Kali-bi** bg2* **Lac-c** ptk1 lach bg2 led bg2 *Lil-t* bg2* lyc bg2 mag-c bg2 mag-m bg2 mag-p bg2 meny bg2 merc bg2 mosch bg2 nat-m bg2* nit-ac bg2 nux-m bg2* ol-an bg2* ol-j ptk1 onos bg2 ox-ac bg2* petr bg2 ph-ac bg2 phos bg2* plat bg2 psor bg2 puls bg2 ran-b bg2 ran-s bg2 rhod bg2 rhus-t bg2* sabin bg2 samb bg2 sars ptk1 sel ptk1 *Sep* ptk1 sil bg2* squil bg2 sul-ac bg2 **Sulph** ptk1 thuj bg2* verat bg2 zinc bg2* [pop dhh1]
- **upward**: morb jl2

▽ · **extending** to | **Downward**: morb jl2

SPRAINS (See Injuries - sprains)

SQUATTING: | **agg.**: calc b2.de* coloc b2.de* graph b2.de* syph ptk1

SQUEEZING (See Constriction)

STAGNATED, sensation as if blood: *(↗CHEST - Stagnation; CHEST - Stagnation - blood; HEAD - Stagnation)* acon k* ambr bg2 bar-c k* bell k* bry k* carb-an bg2 *Carb-v* k* caust k* croc k* crot-t cypra-eg sde6.de• dig k* gels k* glon bg2 graph k2 hep k* ign k* lach bg2 *Lyc* k* m-aust b2.de* nat-m j5.de* nit-ac h2 nux-m bg2 nux-v k* olnd k* *Pic-ac* puls k* rhod k* *Sabad* k* seneg k* sep k* sulph k* sumb zinc k*

STAMINA (See Strength)

STANDING:

- **agg.**: *(↗Weakness - standing)* acon k* aesc bro1 *Agar* k* agn k* aloe k* *Alum* k* alum-p k2* alum-sil k2* *Alumn* kr1 am-c k* *Am-m* k* ambr k* arg-met k* arn k* ars k* ars-s-f k2* asaf k* asar k* atra-r jl3* *Aur* k* aur-s k2* bar-c k* bar-m bar-s k2* *Bell* k* *Berb* k* bism k* borx both-a rb3 both-ax tsm2 *Bov* b2.de* *Bry* k* cact *Calc* k* calc-s calc-sil k2* camph k* cann-s k* *Canth* k* *Caps* k* carb-an k* carb-v k* *Carbn-s* *Caust* k* cham k* chel k* *Chin* k* chinin-ar choc srj3• cic k* cina k* **Cocc** k* coff k* *Coloc* b2.de* **Con** k* cortico jl3 croc k* cupr k* **Cycl** k* dicha mg1.de* *Dig* k* dros k* dulc k* *Euph* k* *Euphr* k* *Ferr* k* ferr-ar ferr-p *Fl-ac* k* graph k* guaj k* hell k* hep k* ign k* *Kali-bi* kali-c k* kali-n k* kali-p lach k* laur k* led k* **Lil-t** k* *Lyc* b2.de* m-ambo b2.de* m-arct b2.de* m-aust b2.de mag-c k* mag-m k* mand mg1.de mang k* meny k* merc k* mez k* mosch k* mur-ac k* *Murx* nat-c k* nat-m k* nat-s ptk1 *Nit-ac* k* nux-m k* nux-v k* olnd k* op k* par k* petr k* *Ph-ac* k* phel j5.de phos k* *Plat* k* plb k* psor jl2 **Puls** k* *Ran-b* k* *Rheum* k* rhod k* *Rhus-t* k* *Ruta* k* *Sabad* k* *Sabin* k* *Samb* k* sarcol-ac jl3 sars b2.de* sec bg2 **Sep** k* sieg mg1.de *Sil* k* spig k* spong k* stann k* staph k* stram k* stront-c k* stroph-s jl3 sul-ac k* **Sulph** k* *Tarax* k* teucr k* thlas bg1 thuj k* *Tub* k* **Valer** k* *Verat* k* *Verb* k* viol-t k* *Zinc* k* *Zinc-p* k2* [lith-c stj2]
- **amel.**: agar k* agn k* am-c k* anac k* *Ang* b2.de* ant-t k* arn k* **Ars** k* *Asar* k* bar-c k* **Bell** k* borx k* *Bov* hr1* bry k* *Calad* k* calc k* camph k* *Cann-s* k* canth k* carb-an k* carb-v k* chel k* chin k* cic k* cina k* cocc k* coff k* *Colch* k* coloc b2.de* croc k* cupr k* dig k* dios dulc hr1 euph k* graph k* guaj k* hell k* hep k* ign k* *Iod* k* ip k* kreos k* *Led* k* m-aust b2.de mang k* meny k* merc k* merc-c bg2 mez k* mur-ac k* naja nat-m k* nit-ac b2.de* nux-m k* *Nux-v* k* par k* petr k* *Phos* k* plb k* *Ran-b* k* rheum k* rhus-t b2.de* ruta k* sars k* sec k* *Sel* k* *Spig* k* spong k* *Squil* k* stann k* staph k* stram k* sul-ac k* sul-i k2* tarax k* tarent thuj k* vip-a jl [cob stj2 cob-m stj2 cob-p stj2]
- **bent** | **amel.**: spong b7.de
- **desire** to stand | **night**: merc mtf33
- **erect** | **amel.**: ars bro1* bell bro1* *Cann-s* b7a.de cedr ptk1 *Dios* bro1* kali-p bro1*
- **eyes** closed agg.; with: arg-n ptk1 calad ptk1 iod ptk1 lath ptk1
- **impossible**: acon a1 acon-f a1 aeth ptk1 ant-t a1 calc-p a1* canth a1 chinin-s ptk1 cocc j5.de* con j5.de* cupr j5.de* cupr-s j5.de dulc a1 hep j5.de* hydrc a1* hyos a1 iod a1 *Kali-br* a1* lach j5.de* lat-m bnm6* loxo-lae bnm12• merc a1 merc-n a1 merc-ns a1 nat-m j5.de* nit-ac j5.de* nux-v j5.de* op a1 phys a1 plb a1 sabad j5.de sec j5.de* stann sf1.de staph j5.de* stram j5.de* sul-ac j5.de tarent a1
  - **till** afternoon: bell a1
  - **fall**; after: arg-n ptk1
- **late** learning to stand: calc-p mtf33
- **toes** agg.; on: cocc ptk1

○ - **Joints** (See EXTREMITIES - Pain - joints - standing)

STARVING: *(↗MIND - Avarice)* Ign k*

STASIS of the venous system: *(↗Circulation)* aesc br1* arist-cl mtf11 arn br1 ars bg2 bell-p c2* *Berb* br1 both-a rb3 calc-f sp1 *Camph* bg2 canth bg2 carb-v br1* card-m mrr1 conv br1 cupr bg2 ham ptk1* puls ptk1 sep br1* stel br1 sulph ptk1 *Verat* bg2 [bell-p-sp dcm1]

- **accompanied** by | **weakness**: sep tl1
- **mechanical** causes; from: bell-p br1
- **portal** congestion; from: *(↗ABDOMEN - Portal)* card-m mrr1 sep br1

STEAM:

- **agg.**: kali-bi ptk1* lyss ptk1
- **amel.**: ars-s-f ptk1* lyss ptk1*

STEIN-LEVENTHAL syndrome: cortico mtf11

STEPPING: | **agg.** (See Jar)

STIFFENING OUT of body: anh sp1 camph ptk1 cham ptk1* *Cina* h1* *Cupr* bg2* ferr-p bg2 *Ign* ptk1 *Ip* ptk1 just bg* phos h2* stram ptk1

- **anger**; with (See MIND - Anger - stiffening)
- **cough**; before: cina kl led bg2*
- **touch** in children; from: apis kl

STIFFNESS: acon vh1 aesc ptk1 aeth tl1 aids nl2• ang br1* apis bg* apoc-a br1 ars-s-f k2 atra-r bnm3• bar-m br1 bell bg* *Bit-ar* wht1• bry bg* *Caust* bg* chel bg* *Cic* ptk1 cimic ptk1 coca-c sk4• cur c2 diph-pert-t mp4• dros ptk1 dulc bg* galeoc-c-h gms1• germ-met srj5• *Guaj* ptk1 hydroph rsj6• ign ptk1 influ jl2* kalm bg* lach bg* *Lec* sne led bg* loxo-recl bnm10• lyc bg*

Magn-gr br1 *Med* ptk1 moni rfm1• nux-v bg* olnd ptk1 onos ptk1 phys ptk1 rad-br c11* rat ptk1 **Rhus-t** bg* *Ruta* mrr1 sec ptk1 *Sep* bg* sil bg* sol-ni br1 stict ptk1 stry-p br1 sul-ac ptk1 *Sulph* bg* syc pte1• ter ptk1 [heroin sdj2]
- **morning**: bit-ar wht1• get br1
- **accompanied** by:
  - **cough**: cina bg2 ip bg2
  - O **Head** bent back: diph-pert-t mp4•
    - **Eyes** open; and: diph-pert-t mp4•
- **chill**; during: acon b7.de *Hyos* b7.de *Op* b7a.de
- **cough** agg.; during: *Cina* b7.de* **Cupr** b7a.de ip b7.de* led b7a.de
- **cramp**-like: cic j
- **cramps**; from: sel ptk1 verat ptk1
- **menses**; during: calc-p bg2 coff bg2 hyos bg2 rhus-t bg2
- **motion**:
  - **agg.**: *Get* br1
  - **impossible**: spong ptk1
- **overexertion**; as from: bar-m br1
- **pain** agg.: nit-ac ptk1 onos ptk1
- **painful**: phyt bg2
- **painless**: olnd ptk1
- **rising** agg.: nat-p tl1
- **waking**; on: sel rsj9•
- O **Joints**: ang br1 anh sp1 bar-m br1 form br1 mez br1 rhus-t br1 stel br1 tub-r jl2
  - **chill**; during: *Acon* bg2 bell bg2 brom bg2 bry bg2 calc bg2 caps bg2 **Caust** bg2 cic bg2 cocc bg2 *Coff* bg2 **Coloc** bg2 graph bg2 **Hell** bg2 hyos bg2 led bg2 lyc bg2 nux-v bg2 **Op** bg2 petr bg2 plat bg2 **Rhus-t** bg2 *Sep* bg2 staph bg2 sulph bg2 thuj bg2
  - **menses**:
    - **during**:
      - **agg.**: *Hyos* b7.de
      - **beginning** of menses | **agg.**: hyos b7a.de ip b7a.de
  - **rising** after a long rest agg.: tub-r jl2
- **Ligaments**: *Get* br1
- **Muscles**: *(↗Complaints - muscles)* ang br1* anh sp1 *Arn* bro1 bad bro1 *Bapt* bro1 bar-m br1 bell bro1 *Bell-p* bro1 *Bry* bro1 caps bg2 caust bro1 cic bro1 *Cimic* bro1 cupr-act bro1 form bg2 *Gels* bro1 guaj bro1 ham bg2* *Helon* bro1 jac-c bro1 lac-lup hrn2• *Magn-gr* bro1 merc bro1 myric bro1 phys br1* phyt bg2* pyrog bro1 rhus-t bg2* *Ruta* bro1 sang bro1 spig bg2 ter ptk1
  - **accompanied** by | **Meninges**; irritation of (See HEAD - Irritation - meninges - accompanied - muscles)
  - **chronic**: franc br1
- **Tendons**; of: rhus-t br1

STONE-CUTTERS; for: *(↗Dust - agg.; Mining)* agar-st jl ars hr1* bell hr1 **Calc** k* chin hr1 *Hep* hr1 ictod sf1.de ip k* *Lyc* k* mag-m jl mucot mtf11 nat-c k* nit-ac k* nux-v hr1 penic jl ph-ac k* phos hr1 *Puls* k* **Sil** k* sulph k*

STONES in organs; formation of: *Bell* ptk1 benz-ac ptk1 *Berb* ptk1 *Bry* ptk1 *Calc* ptk1 *Chin* ptk1 coc-c ptk1 *Coloc* ptk1 dios ptk1 dulc ptk1 hydr ptk1 lach ptk1 **Lyc** ptk1 merc ptk1 *Nux-v* ptk1 oci ptk1 pareir ptk1 podo ptk1 puls ptk1 *Sars* ptk1 sep ptk1
- **deposits**: vario ptk1

STOOL:
- **after**:
  - **agg.**: acon b2.de* *Aesc* bro1 aeth bg2 agar b2.de* agn b2.de aloe bg2 **Alum** b2.de* am-c b2.de* am-m b2.de* ambr b2.de* anac b2.de* ang b2.de* ant-t b2.de apoc bg2 arg-met b2.de* arn b2.de ars b2.de* asar b2.de bar-c b2.de* bell b2.de* borx b2.de* bov b2.de* bry b2.de calc b2.de* calc-p bg2 camph b2.de canth b2.de* caps b2.de* carb-an b2.de* carb-v b2.de* **Caust** b2.de* cham b2.de chin b2.de* cocc b2.de* coloc b2.de* con b2.de* cupr b2.de dig b2.de* dros b2.de* dulc b2.de* euph b2.de* ferr b2.de fl-ac bg2 **Gamb** bg2 graph b2.de* hell b2.de* hep b2.de* hir jl hydr bg2 hyos b2.de **Ign** b2.de* iod b2.de* ip b2.de **Iris** bg2 kali-bi bg2 kali-c b2.de* kali-n b2.de* lach b2.de* laur b2.de* lept bg2 lyc b2.de* m-ambo b2.de* m-arct b2.de mag-c b2.de* mag-m b2.de* merc b2.de* **Merc-c** bg2* mez b2.de* mur-ac b2.de* nat-c b2.de* nat-m b2.de* nit-ac b2.de* nux-m b2.de* **Nux-v** b2.de* olnd b2.de op b2.de* petr b2.de* ph-ac b2.de* **Phos** b2.de* plat b2.de* plb b2.de* podo bg2* puls b2.de* rat bg2 rheum b2.de* rhod b2.de* rhus-t b2.de* ruta b2.de* sabad b2.de* sabin b2.de

Stool – after – agg.: ...
sars b2.de* sec b2.de **Sel** b2.de* seneg b2.de* sep b2.de* sil b2.de* spig b2.de* spong b2.de stann b2.de* staph b2.de* stront-c b2.de* sul-ac b2.de* sulph b2.de* tarax b2.de tell bg2 teucr b2.de* thuj b2.de valer b2.de verat b2.de* zinc b2.de*
  - **amel.**: acon b2.de* agar bg2 aids nl2• aloe bg2 alum bg2 *Am-m* b2.de* ant-c b2.de* ant-t b2.de* ars-i bg2* asaf b2.de* aur b2.de* bar-c b2.de* bism b2.de* *Borx* b2.de* bov b2.de* bros-gau mrc1 **Bry** b2.de* calc-p bg2 canth b2.de* caps b2.de* caust bg2 cham b2.de* cina b2.de* coff b2.de* **Colch** b2.de* coloc b2.de* *Con* b2.de* croc b2.de* cycl b2.de* cyt-l mg1.de* dig bg2 dulc b2.de* ferr b2.de* *Fl-ac* bg2 **Gamb** bg2* glon bg2 guaj b2.de* hell bg2 hep b2.de* ip b2.de* jug-r vml3• kali-bi bg2* kreos b2.de mag-c bg2 mand st mang b2.de* meny b2.de* *Merc* st mur-ac bg2 nat-c b2.de* *Nat-m* b2.de* **Nat-s** ptk1* **Nux-v** bg2* op b2.de* ox-ac bg2* oxyt ptk2 pall ptk1 par b2.de* ph-ac bg2* plb bg2 psor bg2 *Puls* b2.de* rauw jl rheum b2.de* **Rhus-t** b2.de* sabad b2.de* *Sang* bg2 seneg b2.de* sep b2.de* **Spig** b2.de* squil b2.de* *Sulph* b2.de* thuj b2.de* verat b2.de* [bor-pur stj2]
- **before**: acon b2.de agar b2.de agn b2.de alum b2.de am-c b2.de am-m b2.de ambr b2.de anac b2.de ang b2.de *Ant-t* b2.de arn b2.de ars b2.de asaf b2.de asar b2.de *Bar-c* b2.de bell b2.de borx b2.de* bov b2.de *Bry* b2.de calad b2.de calc b2.de camph b2.de cann-s b2.de canth b2.de *Caps* b2.de carb-an b2.de carb-v b2.de *Caust* b2.de *Cham* b2.de chel b2.de chin b2.de cina b2.de cocc b2.de colch b2.de con b2.de croc b2.de cupr b2.de cycl b2.de dig b2.de dros b2.de *Dulc* b2.de euph b2.de ferr b2.de glycyr-g cte1• graph b2.de guaj b2.de hell b2.de hep b2.de ign b2.de *Kali-c* b2.de kali-n b2.de lach b2.de laur b2.de lyc b2.de m-arct b2.de m-aust b2.de mag-c b2.de mang b2.de meny b2.de **Merc** b2.de *Mez* b2.de mosch b2.de nat-c b2.de nat-m b2.de nit-ac b2.de nux-v b2.de olnd b2.de *Op* b2.de petr b2.de ph-ac b2.de *Phos* b2.de plat b2.de *Puls* b2.de rheum b2.de rhod b2.de *Rhus-t* b2.de ruta b2.de *Sabad* b2.de sars b2.de sec b2.de sel b2.de seneg b2.de sep b2.de sil b2.de *Spig* b2.de spong b2.de stann b2.de staph b2.de stram b2.de stront-c b2.de sul-ac b2.de sulph b2.de thuj b2.de valer b2.de **Verat** b2.de viol-o b2.de viol-t b2.de zinc b2.de
  - **agg.**: acon b7.de* agar b4.de **Aloe** bg2* alum b4.de am-c b4.de* am-m b7.de* anac b4.de ang b7.de ant-t b7.de* **Arg-n** bg2 arn b7.de ars b4.de* asar b7.de* aur b4.de bar-c b4.de* bell b4.de borx b4a.de* bov b4.de bry b7.de* calad bg2 calc b4.de* camph b7.de cann-s b7.de canth b7.de* caps b7.de* carb-an b4.de* carb-v b4.de* caust b4.de* cham bg2 chel b7.de chin b7.de* cina b7.de cocc bg2 colch b7.de* coloc b4.de con b4.de croc b7.de cupr b7.de cycl b7.de dig b4.de* **Dios** bg2 dros b7.de dulc b4.de* euph b4.de ferr b7.de* **Gamb** bg2 graph b4.de guaj b4.de hell b7.de hep b4.de *Ign* b7.de kali-c b4.de* kali-n b4.de lach b7.de* laur b7.de lyc b4.de m-aust b7.de **Mag-c** b4.de* mang b4.de* meny b7.de **Merc** b4.de* merc-c bg2 mez b4.de* nat-c b4.de* nat-m b4.de nat-s bg2 nit-ac b4.de nux-v b7.de* op b7.de* petr b4.de* ph-ac b4.de phos b4.de* plat b4.de psor bg2 puls b7.de* **Rheum** b7.de* rhod bg2 rhus-t b7.de* ruta b7.de sabad b7.de* sars b4.de seneg b4.de sep b4.de* sil b4.de spig b7.de* stann b4.de staph b7.de* stram b7.de stront-c b4.de* sulph b4.de* **Thuj** bg2 valer b7.de **Verat** b7.de* viol-t b7.de zinc b4.de
- **during** | **agg.**: acon b2.de* agar b2.de* agn b2.de* alum b2.de* am-c b2.de* am-m b2.de* ambr b2.de* anac b2.de* ang b2.de* ant-c b2.de* ant-t b2.de* apis bg2 arg-met b2.de* arn b2.de* **Ars** b2.de* asaf b2.de* asar b2.de* aur b2.de* bar-c b2.de* bell b2.de* borx b2.de* bov b2.de* bry b2.de* calad b2.de* calc b2.de* camph b2.de* cann-s b2.de canth b2.de* caps b2.de* carb-an b2.de* carb-v b2.de* caust b2.de* **Cham** b2.de* chel b2.de chin b2.de* cocc b2.de colch b2.de coloc b2.de* con b2.de* cupr b2.de* cycl b2.de* dig b2.de* dios ptk1 dros b2.de* dulc b2.de* euph b2.de* ferr b2.de* glycyr-g cte1• graph b2.de* guaj b2.de hell b2.de* hep b2.de* hyos b2.de ign b2.de* iod b2.de ip b2.de* **Iris** bg2 **Kali-bi** bg2 kali-c b2.de* kali-n b2.de* kreos b2.de lach b2.de* laur b2.de* lyc b2.de* m-ambo b2.de m-aust b2.de mag-c b2.de mag-m b2.de* meny b2.de* **Merc** b2.de* merc-c bg2* mez b2.de* mosch b2.de mur-ac b2.de* nat-c b2.de* nat-m b2.de* nit-ac b2.de* nux-m b2.de* nux-v b2.de* olnd b2.de* op b2.de paeon ptk1 par b2.de* petr b2.de* ph-ac b2.de* phos b2.de* plat b2.de* plb b2.de* **Puls** b2.de* ran-b b2.de* rheum b2.de* rhod b2.de* rhus-t b2.de* ruta b2.de sabin b2.de* sars b2.de* sel b2.de* seneg b2.de sep b2.de* sil b2.de* spig b2.de* spong b2.de* squil b2.de stann b2.de* staph b2.de* stram b2.de stront-c b2.de* sul-ac b2.de* **Sulph** b2.de* tarax b2.de thuj b2.de verat b2.de* verb b2.de viol-t b2.de yohim lp2 zinc b2.de*
- **ineffectual** urging to; after | **agg.**: ambr b7.de nux-v b7.de
- **soft** stool:
  - **after** | **amel.**: abrot ptk1 ant-c bg2 **Ars** bg2 **Bry** bg2 guaj bg2 kali-bi bg2 **Lach** bg2 lob bg2 mag-p bg2 mosch bg2 nat-s ptk1 stann bg2 *Zinc* bg2*

- **urging** to | **agg.**: agar ptk1 bell ptk1 carb-an ptk1 ign ptk1 nux-v ptk1 puls ptk1 rat ptk1 rhus-t ptk1 sep ptk1 tell ptk1

STOOP shouldered: agar gk arg-n mtf33 aur gk *Bry* b7a.de *Calc* st1* calc-p bg2 *Carb-v* mtf33 *Cocc* b7a.de coff c1* coloc b4a.de hydrc br1 kali-p bl lac-loxod-a hrn2• *Lyc* st1* med k2* mez b4a.de nat-c k2* nux-v b7a.de* op st1 **Phos** bg2* pieri-b mlk9.de plut-n srj7• psor hr1 puls b7a.de *Sil* st1* spong fd4.de **Sulph** k* *Ter* bg2* thuj mtf33 *Tub* k* ulm-c jsj8• vanil fd5.de
- **children**; in: sulph mtf33 thuj mtf33

STOOPING:
- **after**:
  - **agg.**: alum b2.de *Asar* b2.de* *Bov* b2.de cann-s b2.de* *Caust* b2.de *Hep* b2.de hyos b2.de* meny b2.de* nat-m b2.de *Plat* b2.de viol-t b2.de*
    - **long** time; stooping for a: alum b4.de* *Asar* bg2* *Bov* b4a.de* cann-xyz bg2 *Caust* b4a.de* *Hep* b4a.de* hyos bg2 meny bg2 merc-c bg2 nat-m b4.de* *Plat* b4a.de* viol-t bg2
- **agg.**: *Acon* b2.de* aesc bro1* agar b2.de* *Alum* b2.de* **Am-c** b2.de* am-m b2.de* anac b2.de* ang b2.de* ant-c b2.de* ant-t b2.de* *Arg-met* b2.de* *Arn* b2.de* ars b2.de* asaf b2.de* asar b2.de* aur b2.de* *Bar-c* b2.de* bell b2.de* *Borx* b2.de* bov b2.de* **Bry** b2.de* **Calc** b2.de* camph b2.de* cann-s b2.de* canth b2.de* *Caps* b2.de* carb-an b2.de* carb-v b2.de* caust b2.de* *Cham* b2.de* chel b2.de* chin b2.de* *Cic* b2.de* cina b2.de* *Clem* b2.de* *Cocc* b2.de* coff b2.de* *Coloc* b2.de* con b2.de* *Croc* b2.de* cupr b2.de* cycl b2.de* dig b2.de* *Dros* b2.de* dulc b2.de* ferr b2.de* fl-ac bg2 glon bro1 *Graph* b2.de* haliae-lc srj5• hell b2.de* *Hep* b2.de* ign b2.de* *Ip* b2.de* *Kali-c* b2.de* kali-n b2.de* kreos b2.de* *Lach* b2.de* laur b2.de* *Led* b2.de* lyc b2.de* lyss bro1* m-ambo b2.de* m-arct b2.de* m-aust b2.de* *Mag-m* b2.de* **Mang** b2.de* *Meny* b2.de* *Merc* b2.de* merc-c bg2 mosch b2.de* mur-ac b2.de* nat-c b2.de* nat-m b2.de* nit-ac b2.de* nux-m b2.de* nux-v b2.de* *Olnd* b2.de* op b2.de* par b2.de* *Petr* b2.de* ph-ac b2.de* phos b2.de* plat b2.de* *Plb* b2.de* puls b2.de* ran-b b2.de* rheum b2.de* *Rhod* b2.de* rhus-t b2.de* *Ruta* b2.de* sabin b2.de* samb b2.de* sars b2.de* *Seneg* b2.de* **Sep** b2.de* *Sil* b2.de* **Spig** b2.de* spong b2.de* stann b2.de* staph b2.de* *Stront-c* b2.de* sul-ac b2.de* sulph b2.de* tarax b2.de* tell ptk1 *Teucr* b2.de* ther ptk1 *Thuj* b2.de* **Valer** b2.de* *Verat* b2.de* verb b2.de* viol-t b2.de* zinc b2.de* [lith-c stj2 pop dhh1]
- **amel.**: anac b2.de* ang b2.de* *Ant-t* b2.de* arn b2.de* ars b2.de* bar-c b2.de* bell b2.de* *Bry* bg2 *Cann-s* b2.de* carb-an b2.de* caust b2.de* chin b2.de* cina b2.de* **Colch** b2.de* **Coloc** bg2 *Con* b2.de* dig b2.de* hell b2.de* **Hyos** b2.de* ign b2.de* *Iris* ptk1 lach b2.de* laur b2.de* lyc b2.de* m-aust b2.de* mang b2.de* meny br mez b2.de* mosch b2.de* mur-ac b2.de* nat-m b2.de* nit-ac b2.de* nux-v b2.de* ph-ac b2.de* phos b2.de* puls b2.de* *Ran-b* b2.de* rhus-t b2.de* sabin b2.de* sars b2.de* spong b2.de* staph b2.de* sulph b2.de* tarax b2.de* valer b2.de* verat b2.de* verb b2.de* *Viol-t* b2.de*
- **impossible**: borx ptk1
  - **fall** on coccyx; from: hyper ptk1

STORM (See Weather - thunderstorm; Weather - windy)

STOUT people (See Obesity)

STRAMONIUM agg.: acet-ac bro1 nux-v bro1 tab bro1

STRANGE FEELING through the body: glon bg2 nux-m bg2

STREAMING OF BLOOD; sensation of: alumn *Ox-ac* k*

STRENGTH, sensation of: (↗*Endurance - increased; Energy - excess; Vigor)* adam srj5• *Agar* k* alco a1 anh br1* ars sf1.de bell a1 bit-ar wht1• bov a1 bry a1 *Bufo* bung-fa mtf calc b4.de* calc-f sp1 cann-xyz bg2 carbn-o a1 chinin-s a1 choc srj3• clem a1 cob a1 *Coca* a1* *Coff* k* coli rly4• corn a1 cot a1 dendr-pol sk4• elae a1 erech a1 ferr a1 fic-m gya1 *Fl-ac* gast a1 gels a1 germ-met srj5• gins a1 haliae-lc srj5• ham fd3.de• helon a1 hippoc-k szs2 ignis-alc es2• irid-met srj5• kola sf1.de* lac-cp sk4• lach sf1.de lil-t a1 m-arct b2.de* maias-l hrn2• meny a1 *Nat-p* sf1.de nep mg1.de* nept-m lsd2.fr ol-j a1 *Olib-sac* wmh1 **Op** k* ped a1 petr-ra shn4• phos bg* pic-ac sf1.de pip-m a1* plat a1 plb bg2 plut-n srj7• psil ft1* psor bg pycnop-sa mrz1 sars a1 sinus rly4• stram k* stront-c sk4• symph fd3.de• valer bg2 vanad jl3 wies a1 zinc sf1.de [spect dfg1 temp elm1]
- **alternating** with:
  - **sadness** (See MIND - Sadness - alternating - energy)
  - **weakness** (See Weakness - alternating - strength)
- **anger**; after: carbn-s a1
- **coition**; after: merc-c b4a.de*
- **decreased**: ozone sde2• petr-ra shn4•

Strenght, sensation of: ...
- **perspiration**; during: op a1 pilo a1 stach a1
- **walking** agg.: bapt a1 chin a1 plut-n srj7•

○ - **Muscular**: agar bg2* alco a1 anh sf1.de ars bg2* camph a1 coca a1 cod a1 coli rly4• *Fl-ac* bg2* gels a1 keroso a1 kola sf1.de* *Nat-p* bg2* nat-sil fd3.de• nitro-o a1 phos a1 tab a1 thea a1 zinc bg2*

STRETCHING: (↗*EXTREMITIES - Stretching; MIND - Restlessness - stretching)*
- **agg.**: (↗*Bending - backward - agg.)* *Am-c* b2.de* bry sf1.de *Calc* sf1.de **Cham** bg colch sf1.de iod sf1.de med bro1* meph sf1.de* merc sf1.de merc-c sf1.de **Plat** sf1.de podo sf1.de **Puls** sf1.de rad-br c11* **Ran-b** b2.de* **Rheum** sf1.de *Rhus-t* b2.de* *Sep* sf1.de staph bg2* *Sulph* sf1.de *Thuj* sf1.de [am-br stj2 am-caust stj2 am-f stj2 am-m stj1 am-p stj1 am-s stj1]
- **amel.**: (↗*Bending - backward - amel.)* aml-ns bro1 **Ant-t** sf1.de bell sf1.de berb sf1.de calc st carb-v h2 des-ac rbp6 dios sf1.de dulc bg2 graph bg2 *Guaj* b2.de* halo jl helo-s rwt2• hep sf1.de mand mg1.de nat-f jl3 perh jl phos sf1.de plat h2* plb hr1* podo bg2* psor jl2 **Puls** ●* pyrog bg2* rhus-t bro1 ruta fd4.de sabad bg2* sabin b2.de* sec bro1* sep sne teucr bro1 tub-r jl3* v-a-b jl3* vac jl2 vanil fd5.de [cupr stj2 cupr-act stj2 cupr-f stj2 cupr-m stj2 cupr-p stj2]
- **impossible**: acon phos
  - **pain**; from: bell h1

STRETCHING OUT: (↗*EXTREMITIES - Stretching; MIND - Restlessness - Stretching)* acon k* *Aesc* k* agar k* *Alum* b2.de* alumn kr1 *Am-c* k* ambr k* aml-ns bro1* ang k* ant-t apis arn k* **Ars** k* art-v hr1* arum-t bar-act a1 bar-c *Bell* k* bit-ar wht1• *Bol-la* a1 borx h2 bov k* brach k* *Brom* k* *Bry* b2.de* bufo bg2 caj k* calad k* *Calc* k* calc-p k* calc-s hr1* camph k* cann-s k* canth k* caps *Carb-ac* hr1* carb-an k* *Carb-v* k* **Caust** k* **Cham** k* chel k* chin k* chinin-s j5.de chlf k* choc srj3• cic bg2 cimic k* cimx k* cina k* cit-v hr1* clem b2.de* cocc b2.de* colch k* coloc ptk1 croc b2.de* cur hr1* cycl daph k* dig k* dios dros k* dulc j5.de elat hr1* eup-per hr1 ferr ferr-p bg2 form k* gins k* glon bg2 gran k* *Graph* k* guaj k* haem k* hell b2.de* helo c1 helo-s c1* hep k* hydrc a1 hyos k* ign b2.de* ind k* ip b2.de* kali-bi k* kalm k* kola stb3• kreos k* lach k* lact j5.de laur k* led k* lil-t k* lim a1 lob k* lyc ptk1 lyss hr1 m-ambo b2.de* mag-c k* mang j5.de* med c1 *Menis* a1 meph k* *Merc* k* *Merc-c* k* merc-i-r k* *Mez* k* mur-ac b2.de* nat-c k* *Nat-m* k* nat-s k* neon srj5• nit-ac b2.de* **Nux-v** k* *Olnd* b2.de* onis j5.de* op k* ox-ac k* petr k* ph-ac k* phel k* *Phos* k* plan k* *Plat* k* plb k* podo hr1* polyp-p a1 prun k* **Puls** k* quas bro1 ran-b k* raph k* rhod j5.de **Rhus-t** k* *Rhus-v* k* *Ruta* b2.de* *Sabad* k* *Sabin* bg1* *Sec* b2.de* sel k* senec bg2* seneg b2.de* *Sep* k* sil k* spong k* squil k* stann staph k* stram b2.de* sul-ac b2.de* sulph k* tab j5.de tarent k* tart-ac j5.de* *Teucr* k* tong j5.de* tub-r srb2.fr valer k* verat b2.de* verb k* vinc hr1* viol-o k* wildb zinc k*
- **alternating** sides: androc srj1•
- **daytime**: mang k*
- **morning**: ars *Calc* k* *Carb-v* k* cedr a1 ferr k* graph j5.de hell j5.de* lyc k* nux-v phos puls j5.de rhod j5.de* sep j5.de* sulph h2* tab tarent k* verat k*
  - **6** h: sep
  - **7** h: cedr
  - **8**-11 h: *Nat-m* kr1
  - **amel.**: sec st
  - **arms**; of: petr h2
  - **bed** agg.; in: graph j5.de hell k* meph j5.de merc j5.de petr phos h2* puls j5.de rhod k* sep k* sulph j5.de
  - **benumbed**; as if: meph
  - **desire** to: aml-ns st plb st1 sec st1
  - **waking**; on: dulc k* sep k*
- **forenoon**: aloe ant-t k* bov k* mag-c k* mez k* mill k* mur-ac k* nat-m
  - **11** h: mit
- **noon**: am-c menis a1
- **afternoon**: aml-ns st arum-t k* bell h1 cina a1 form a1 jug-r k* nux-v k* plat k* plb st rhus-t k* sec st
  - **13** h: form
  - **16** h: cina plan
  - **17**-21 h: bell h1
  - **sleep** agg.; after: verat k*
- **evening**: bell j5.de cann-s chin j5.de *Graph* nat-c rhus-t sumb k* tab k* verat k*
  - **chill**; during: tab k*
- **night**: **Caust** k* cocc a1 des-ac rbp6 nat-c sulph k*

- **night**: ...
  - **bed** agg.; in: *Cocc* k*
  - **sleep** agg.; during: nat-m k*
  - **waking**; on: merc
- **air**; in open | **amel.**: ol-an
- **always**: puls j5.de rhod j5.de sabad j5.de staph j5.de tab j5.de
- **anguish**; during: androc srj1•
  - **impending** menses; with: carl
- **anxiety**, from: nat-c
- **arms**; the: spong j5.de squil j5.de stann j5.de tab j5.de
- **backward**: choc srj3• glon k* hydr k*
  - **amel.**: borx h2
- **breakfast** agg.; after: lach k*
- **chill**:
  - **before**: aesc ant-t aran hr1* arn *Ars* bry k* *Eup-per* ign k* ip *Nat-m* nux-v plan rhus-t
  - **during**: alum k* alumn kr1 ars k* bell bg2 bol-la bro1 borx b4a.de* **Brom** b4a.de* bry k* **Calc** bg2 caps k* carb-v bg2 *Caust* b4a.de* cham bg2 coff daph k* elat *Eup-per* k* ferr-p ptk1 hell bg2 hep bg2 ip k* *Kreos* laur led bg2 mur-ac k* *Nat-s* k* nit-ac nux-v k* petr puls bg2 rhus-t k* ruta sep bg2 sulph bg2 tab teucr
- **coldness**, during internal: bol-la kr1 nat-s k*
- **colic**, during: haem k* plb hr1
- **continually** (See always)
- **convulsive**, paroxysmal: ang j5.de bell camph j5.de carbn-h *Chin* cic j5.de* cimic sf1.de cina hydr-ac ip j5.de lach j5.de lyc merc j5.de nux-v h1* op sf1.de sabad j5.de sec j5.de* sil j5.de stram j5.de* sulph j5.de thuj j5.de verat j5.de
- **cough**; after: merc h1* sang k*
- **difficult** | **stooping** easy; but: nat-m ptk1
- **dinner**; after: mag-c k*
- **eating**; after: ip k*
- **fever**:
  - **before**: ars b4a.de bry b7a.de calc b4a.de carb-v b4a.de graph b4a.de hep b4a.de ip b7a.de puls b7a.de rhus-t b7a.de
  - **during**:
    - **agg.**: alum bg2 androc srj1• *Ars* hr1* bell bg2 *Borx* b4a.de* bry bg2 **Calc** b4.de* *Calc-p* hr1* caust b4.de* cham bg2 cina bg2 eup-per hr1* nat-m b4a.de* *Nux-v* b7.de* **Rhus-t** b7.de* **Sabad** b7.de* sep bg2 spong bg2 sulph bg2 thuj
    - **intermittent** fever: cimx br1
- **forcible** | **amel.**: sec ptk1
- **high** up to reach things: rhus-t h1
- **hours**; for: aml-ns ptk1 plb ptk1
- **house**, in the: ruta
- **lying** down agg.; after: **Cocc** hr1*
- **menses**:
  - **after** | **agg.**: carb-an sf1.de
  - **before** | **agg.**: am-c bro1 **Puls** k*
  - **during** | **agg.**: am-c bro1 *Carb-an* k* puls bro1
- **painful**: sec k*
- **perspiration**; during: alum bg2 bell bg2 **Borx** bg2 bry bg2 **Calc** bg2 caust bg2 cham bg2 **Nat-m** bg2 *Nux-v* bg2 **Rhus-t** bg2 *Sabad* bg2 *Sep* bg2 spong bg2 sulph bg2
- **shivering**; during: *Ars* b4a.de rhus-t b7.de
- **shuddering**; while: ars *Puls*
- **sitting** agg.: alum h2
  - **and** reading: euphr
- **sleep** agg.; during: aml-ns bro1 nat-m a1 plb bro1
- **sleepiness** with: ant-t j5.de bell j5.de chin j5.de lach j5.de meph j5.de podo ptk1 sabad j5.de
- **sleeplessness**:
  - **after**: sulph
  - **during**: dulc j5.de
- **slept** enough, as if he had not: am-c mill
- **supper** agg.; after: nit-ac k*
- **tossing** about, with: rhod j5.de
- **unsatisfactory**: aml-ns vh1 *Graph* k*
- **urination** agg.; before: **Puls** k*

Stretching out: ...

- **waking**; on: bell h1 dulc j5.de* hell j5.de *Ign* hr1* meph j5.de merc j5.de* nit-ac h2 phos j5.de sulph j5.de
- **walking** in open air | **amel.**: ox-ac k* plan k*
- **yawning**; with: acon j5.de* aesc hr1* agar j5.de* all-c sf1.de *Alum* bg *Alumn* sf1.de *Am-c* sf1.de ambr sf1.de aml-ns bro1 ang j5.de* ant-t j5.de* arn sf1.de **Ars** j5.de* asar sf1.de bar-c j5.de* *Bell* j5.de* borx sf1.de bov sf1.de *Bry* j5.de* calc sf1.de cann-s sf1.de canth k* caps k* *Carb-v* k* castm sf1.de *Caust* j5.de* **Cham** sf1.de *Chin* j5.de* chinin-s j5.de* cocc j5.de* cur hr1* dig j5.de* dros j5.de* elat sf1.de ferr j5.de* *Form* k* gran j5.de* graph sf1.de *Guaj* j5.de* hell j5.de* hep sf1.de *Ign* sf1.de *Ip* sf1.de kreos j5.de* *Lach* j5.de* lact j5.de* laur j5.de* led sf1.de mag-c j5.de* mang j5.de* meph j5.de* merc sf1.de merc-c sf1.de mez j5.de* mur-ac sf1.de nat-m j5.de* nit-ac sf1.de **Nux-v** j5.de* *Olnd* k* onis j5.de* petr j5.de* ph-ac j5.de* phos j5.de* plat sf1.de plb j5.de* *Puls* j5.de* ran-b sf1.de rhod j5.de* **Rhus-t** sf1.de ruta sf1.de *Sabad* j5.de* sec j5.de* senec k* seneg sf1.de *Sep* j5.de* sil sf1.de *Spong* j5.de* *Squil* k* stann j5.de* *Staph* j5.de* *Sulph* j5.de* tab j5.de* tart-ac j5.de* tong j5.de* vac jl2 valer j5.de* verat j5.de* verb sf1.de viol-o kr1* zinc j5.de*
  - **forenoon**: ant-t j5.de
  - **amel.**: carb-v ptk1 guaj ptk1
  - **chill**; during: ars bro1 elat bro1 lyc bro1 nux-v bro1
  - **menses**:
    - **after** | **agg.**: carb-an b4a.de
  - **sleepiness**; without: vac jl2 viol-o kr1

○ - **Affected** parts | **amel.**: adam srj5•
- **Limbs**:
  - **agg.**: *Alum* b2.de* am-c b2.de* am-m b2.de* anac b2.de* ang b2.de* *Ant-c* b2.de* arg-met b2.de* arn b2.de* aur b2.de* bar-c b2.de* bell b2.de* bov b2.de* *Bry* b2.de* **Calc** b2.de* cann-s b2.de* caps b2.de* carb-v b2.de* caust b2.de* *Cham* b2.de* *Chin* b2.de* cina b2.de* clem b2.de* *Colch* bg2 *Coloc* bg2 con b2.de* croc b2.de* dig b2.de* dros b2.de* dulc b2.de* ferr b2.de* fl-ac bg2 graph b2.de* guaj b2.de* *Hep* b2.de* ign b2.de* **Iod** bg2 kali-c b2.de* laur b2.de* lyc b2.de* m-aust b2.de* mag-m bg2 *Mang* b2.de* meny b2.de* merc b2.de* *Merc-c* bg2 mur-ac b2.de* nat-m b2.de* nux-v b2.de* petr b2.de* phos b2.de* *Plat* b2.de* plb b2.de* psor bg2 *Puls* b2.de* *Rheum* b2.de* *Rhus-t* b2.de* *Ruta* b2.de* sabin b2.de* sel b2.de* **Sep** b2.de* spig b2.de* spong b2.de* stann b2.de* *Staph* b2.de* **Sulph** b2.de* **Thuj** b2.de* valer b2.de* verat b2.de*
  - **amel.**: agar b2.de* alum b2.de* am-m b2.de* anac b2.de* *Ant-t* b2.de* asar b2.de* bell b2.de* berb bg2 borx b2.de* carb-an b2.de* carb-v b2.de* cham b2.de* chel b2.de* chin b2.de* coff b2.de* cupr bg2 dig b2.de* dios bg2 dros b2.de* dulc b2.de* ferr b2.de* guaj b2.de* hep b2.de* ign b2.de* kali-c b2.de* mag-c b2.de* mez b2.de* mur-ac b2.de* nat-m b2.de* nat-s bg2 nux-m b2.de* nux-v b2.de* olnd b2.de* ox-ac bg2 par b2.de* petr b2.de* phos bg2 plat b2.de* puls b2.de* rheum b2.de* rhod b2.de* **Rhus-t** b2.de* sabad b2.de* sabin b2.de* **Sec** b2.de* sel b7a.de *Spig* b7a.de *Spong* b7a.de stann b2.de* staph b2.de* thuj b2.de* verb b2.de* zinc b2.de*
- **Sphincters**; of | **agg.**: staph br1

STROKING with hands (with or without touching): | **agg.**: teucr b2.de*

STRYCHNINE agg.: cur bro1 *Eucal* bro1 kali-br bro1 phys bro1

STUPOR: nat-f sp1

SUBSTANCE: | **abuse** of controlled (See Medicine - allopathic - abuse)

SUCKING (= with the tongue):

- **amel.**: mang b2.de*

○ - **Gums** | **agg.**: bov b2.de* carb-v b2.de* kali-c b2.de* *Nux-m* b2.de* nux-v b2.de* *Sil* b2.de* zinc b2.de*

SUDDEN manifestation: (↗*Complaints - acute; Complaints - appearing - suddenly*) **Acon** bg2* aeth br1* am-c bg2 androc srj1• apis ptk1 *Arg-met* mrr1 ars ptk1 bar-act bg2 **Bell** bg2* **Borx** bg2 camph bg2 canth bg2 carb-ac bg2 choc srj3• *Coloc* bg2* con ptk1 croc bg2 crot-h bg2 *Cupr* bg2* form bg2 glon bg2 hippoc-k szs2 hydr-ac ptk1 hydrog srj2• ign br1 kali-bi bg2 lyc ptk1 mag-c bg2* mag-p bg2* mez bg2* nat-s bg2* ox-ac bg2 *Phos* br1* plb bg2 podo bg2 rad-br ptk1* ran-b bg2 rhus-g tmo3• stann bg2 *Stry* br1 sul-ac bg2 symph fd3.de* tab bg2* tarent bg2* tarent-c ptk1 thal-xyz srj8• thuj bg2 tritic-vg fd5.de tub jl2 tub-d jl2 tung-met bdx1• valer bg2* verat ptk1 vip bg2

Sudden manifestation: ...
[*Ant-c* stj2 *Ant-m* stj2 *Ant-t* stj2 arg-n stj2 bor-pur stj2 cupr-act stj2 cupr-f stj2 cupr-m stj2 cupr-p stj2 ferr-n stj2 mag-n stj2 tax jsj7 thal-met stj2]

SULPHUR, abuse of: acon hr1* ars *Calc* k* camph hr1* cham hr1* chin k* iod hr1* *Merc* k* nit-ac hr1* phos gk **Puls** k* rhus-t hr1* sel bro1 sep k* thuj c1
- **fumes** of sulphur: *Puls* b7a.de

SUN:
- **exertion** in: **Ant-c**
- **exposure** to the sun: (↗*Light; from - agg. - sunlight*) abies-c oss4• abrom-a ks5 *Acon* b7a.de* adlu jl aeth bg2* *Agar* k* agath-a nl2• aloe bg2 aml-ns bg2* anh sp1 **Ant-c** k* *Arg-met* arn bg2 *Ars* kr1* aur-m-n wbt2• *Bar-c* k* **Bell** b2.de* brom *Bry* k* cact c1* cadm-s k* calc k* calc-f mg1.de* *Camph* k* *Carb-v* carc dtp cina bg2* clem k* cob ptk1 cocc c1* crot-h c1 dulc fd4.de elaps gk *Euphr* k* fago bro1 *Gels* bg2* **Glon** k* glycyr-g cte1• graph k* hipp jl2 hyos gk ign k* iod k* ip k* kali-bi gk *Kalm* k* ketogl-ac rly4• **Lach** b2.de* lappa bg1 *Lyss* k* mag-c gk mag-m k* med c1* merc sf1.de merc-c bg2 mur-ac c1* murx ptk1* **Nat-c** k* **Nat-m** k* nat-n bg2* *Nux-v* k* *Op* k* plb gk podo fd3.de• prot jl2 prun c1 psil ft1 *Psor* k* **Puls** k* rhus-t c ros-d wla1 ruta fd4.de sang gk *Sel* k* spig gk stann k* stram bg2* sul-i k2 sulph k* syph c1 tax-br oss1• ther bg2* thuj st tritic-vg fd5.de *Uva* vh *Valer* k* vanil fd5.de verat-v c1 *Zinc* k* [bar-n stj1 beryl-m stj2 cadm-met stj2 hydrog stj2 nat-br stj2 nat-caust stj2 nat-f stj2 nat-lac stj2 nat-met stj2 nat-p stj1 nat-sil stj2]
  - **amel.**: anac b2.de* aur sne brucel sa3• chir-fl gya2 cinnb bg2* con b2.de* crot-h ptk1 ham fd3.de• iod bg2* kali-c st kali-m ptk1 kali-s fd4.de nat-sil fd3.de• *Phos* sne pic-ac bg2* *Plat* b2.de* positr nl2• rhod st* rhus-t b7a.de* ruta fd4.de sacch-a fd2.de• sep sne* *Stram* b2.de* **Stront-c** b2.de* tarent bg2* *Thuj* sf1.de tritic-vg fd5.de [beryl stj2 beryl-m stj2 kali-sil stj2 nat-ar stj2 nat-caust stj2]
  - **chronic**: nat-c c1
- **solstice** | **agg.**: **Calc** vk5
- **sunburn**: acon b2.de* *Agar* bg2 *Ant-c* bg2 **Bell** b2.de* bov ptk1 bry bg2 bufo bro1 *Camph* b2.de* canth bro1* choc srj3• clem b2.de* cortiso jl cyt-l jl euphr bg2 hist mg *Hyos* b2.de* ignis-alc es2• kali-c bro1* lach bg2 *Lyc* bg2 *Mur-ac* hr1* *Nat-c* bg2 *Nat-m* sys op bg2 **Puls** bg2 rob bro1 sel bg2 sol c1* *Sulph* bg2 *Valer* bg2 vanil fd5.de verat bro1* [am-m stj1]
  - **left** side: hydrog srj2•
- **sunlight**:
  - **agg.** (See Light; from - agg. - sunlight)
  - **amel.** (See Light; from - amel. - sunlight)
- **sunstroke** (See HEAD - Sunstroke)

SUNKEN deep in bed when lying down; as if: xan c1

SUNSET (See Evening - sunset)

SUNSTROKE (See HEAD - Sunstroke)

SUPPORT amel.: ferr ptk1 kali-c ptk1 lil-t ptk1 nat-c ptk1 nat-m ptk1 ph-ac ptk1 sep ptk1

SUPPRESSED COMPLAINTS; ailments from: abrot bg2* acon bg2 apis bg2 ars bg2 asaf bg2 bry bg2 cact bg2 calc bg2 camph bg2 caust bg2 cimic bg2 clem bg2 cocc bg2 con bg2 crot-h bg2 crot-t bg2 cupr bg2 dig bg2 dulc bg2 graph bg2 grat bg2 ham bg2 hydr-ac bg2 ign bg2 ip bg2 kali-bi bg2 kali-c bg2 kali-m bg2 kalm bg2 lach bg2 lil-t bg2 lith-c bg2 mez bg2* nat-m bg2 nux-v bg2 phos bg2 plat bg2 podo bg2 psor bg2 puls bg2 rhus-t bg2 sabad bg2 sars bg2 sec bg2 senec bg2 sep bg2* sil bg2 stram bg2 sulph bg2 thuj bg2* tril-p bg2 tub bg2 ust bg2 verat bg2* verat-v bg2 zinc bg2
- **condylomata** (See SKIN - Excrescences - condylomata - suppressed)
- **diarrhea** (See RECTUM - Diarrhea - suppressed)
- **eruptions** (See SKIN - Eruptions - suppressed)
- **exanthemas** (See SKIN - Eruptions - suppressed)
- **gonorrhea** (See Gonorrhea)
- **gout** (See EXTREMITIES - Pain - joints - gouty - suppressed)
- **hemorrhoids** (See RECTUM - Hemorrhoids - suppressed)
- **menses** (See FEMALE - Menses - suppressed)
- **mother's** milk (See CHEST - Milk - suppressed)
- **sinusitis** (See Inflammation - sinuses - suppressed)
- **warts** (See SKIN - Warts - suppressed)

SUPPURATION (See Abscesses)

SURGERY; post effect of: bell-p sp1 [bell-p-sp dcm1]

SURGING through body; sensation of something (= kind of ebullition): acon b2.de* alum b2.de* ars b2.de* bell bg2 calc bg2 carb-v b2.de* caust b2.de* cina b2.de* cocc b2.de* dig b2.de* dulc b2.de* ferr b2.de* fl-ac bg2 *Graph* b2.de* hyos b2.de* laur b2.de* mag-m b2.de* mang b2.de* merc b2.de* *Nux-v* b2.de* plb b2.de* *Rheum* b7.de rhod b2.de* sars b2.de* seneg b2.de* *Sep* b2.de* spong b2.de* *Squil* b7.de* thuj b2.de*

SWALLOWING:
- **after** | **agg.**: cadm-s ptk1 vinc ptk1
- **agg.**: acon b2.de* alum b2.de* am-c b2.de* am-m b2.de* ambr b2.de* anac b2.de* ang b2.de* ant-t b2.de* apis bro1* arg-met b2.de* arn b7.de* ars b2.de* asaf b2.de* aur b2.de* bapt bg2 *Bar-c* b2.de* bell b2.de* borx b2.de* bov b2.de* *Brom* b4a.de* **Bry** b2.de* calc b2.de* camph b2.de* canth b2.de* caps b2.de* carb-an b2.de* carb-v b2.de* caust b2.de* cham b2.de* chel b7.de chin b2.de* cic b2.de* cina ptk1 *Cocc* b2.de* coff b2.de* colch b2.de* con b2.de* *Croc* b2.de* cupr b2.de* dig b2.de* dros b2.de* euph b2.de* ferr b2.de* *Gels* ptk1 graph b2.de* hell b2.de* **Hep** b2.de* hydr-ac ptk1 hyos b2.de* ign b2.de* iod b2.de* ip b2.de* kali-c b2.de* kali-n b2.de* kreos b2.de* lac-c ptk1 lach b2.de* laur b2.de* led b2.de* lyc b2.de* lyss ptk1 m-aust b2.de* mag-c b2.de* mag-m b2.de* mang b2.de* meny b2.de* meph ptk1 *Merc* b2.de* merc-c bg2* merc-i-f bro1* merc-i-r bro1 mez b2.de* mur-ac bg2 nat-c b2.de* nat-m b2.de* *Nit-ac* b2.de* nux-m ptk1 *Nux-v* b2.de* op b2.de* par b2.de* *Petr* b2.de* ph-ac b2.de* *Phos* b2.de* phyt bg2* plat b2.de* plb b2.de* *Puls* b2.de* ran-b b2.de* rhod b2.de* *Rhus-t* b2.de* ruta b2.de* sabad b2.de* sabin b2.de* sars b2.de* seneg b2.de* *Sep* b2.de* sil b2.de* spig b2.de* spong b2.de* stann b2.de* staph b2.de* stram b2.de* stront-c b2.de* sul-ac b2.de* sul-i ptk1 sulph b2.de* tarax b2.de* *Thuj* b2.de* verat b2.de* zinc b2.de*
- **amel.**: alum b2.de* am-m b2.de* *Ambr* b2.de* arg-n bg2 *Arn* b2.de* bell b2.de* *Caps* b2.de* carb-v b2.de* chel b2.de* chin b2.de* cocc b2.de* coloc b4.de* dig b2.de* dros b2.de* graph b2.de* **Ign** b2.de* iod b2.de* ip b2.de* kali-bi bg2 *Lach* b2.de* laur b2.de* *Led* b2.de* m-aust b2.de mag-c b2.de* mang b2.de* merc b2.de* mez b2.de* nat-c b2.de* nit-ac b2.de* nux-v b2.de* olnd b2.de* par b2.de* ph-ac b2.de* phos b2.de* plat b2.de* puls b2.de* rheum b2.de* rhus-t b2.de* ruta b2.de* sabad b2.de* sabin b2.de* spig b2.de* *Spong* b2.de* squil b2.de* stann b2.de* staph b2.de* sul-ac b2.de* sulph b2.de* tarax b2.de* zinc b2.de*
- **cold** drinks | **agg.**: kali-c ptk1
- **continued** swallowing | **amel.**: *Ign* bg2*
- **drinks**:
  - **agg.**: arg-n ptk1 ars ptk1 **Bell** b2.de* brom bg2* *Canth* b2.de* chin ptk1 cina b2.de* *Crot-t* ptk1 cupr b2.de* hyos b2.de* ign b2.de* *Iod* b2.de* kali-br bg2 lach b2.de* lyss ptk1 *Merc* b2.de* merc-c bg2* nat-m b2.de* nux-v ptk1 **Phos** b2.de* phyt bg2 podo bg2 stram b2.de* verat ptk1
  - **amel.**: alum ptk1 nit-ac ptk1 nux-v ptk1
- **empty**:
  - **agg.**: acon bg2 ambr b7.de arg-met b2.de* bar-c b2.de* bell b2.de* borx b2.de* bov b2.de *Bry* b2.de* bufo bg2 calc-p bg2 caps b2.de* chel bg2 **Cocc** b2.de* colch b2.de* croc b2.de* ferr bg2 ferr-p bg2 graph b2.de* *Hep* b2.de* hydr bg2 ign bg2 kali-bi bg2 *Kali-c* ptk1 **Lach** b2.de* mang b2.de* *Merc* b2.de* *Merc-c* bg2* merc-i-r bg2* mez b2.de* nux-v b2.de* ol-an bg2 plat b2.de* *Puls* b2.de* *Rhus-t* b2.de* ruta b2.de* sabad b2.de* sabin b2.de* spig b2.de* sulph b2.de* tell bg2* thuj b2.de* zinc b2.de*
    - **eating** and drinking | **amel.**: ol-an ptk1 tell ptk1
  - **amel.**: alum ptk1 ip b7.de* nux-v b7.de olnd b7.de
- **fast** agg.: ars ptk1 *Nit-ac* ptk1 nux-v ptk1 *Sil* ptk1
- **food**:
  - **after** | **agg.**: *Ambr* b2.de* ars b2.de* bar-c b2.de* *Bry* b2.de* carb-v b2.de* cham b2.de* chin b2.de* colch b2.de* euph b2.de* fl-ac bg2 hep b2.de* ign b2.de* iod b2.de* merc-c bg2 nit-ac b2.de* **Nux-v** b2.de* petr b2.de* *Phos* b2.de* *Puls* b2.de* ran-b b2.de* *Rhus-t* b2.de* sep b2.de* *Sulph* b2.de* **Zinc** b2.de*
  - **agg.**: alum b2.de* am-m bg2 ambr b2.de* ant-t ptk1 apis bg2* ars b2.de* *Bapt* ptk1 *Bar-c* b2.de* bell bg2 brom bg2 **Bry** b2.de* carb-v b2.de* cham b2.de* chin b2.de* cocc bg2 coff bg2 colch b2.de* crot-h ptk1 euph b2.de* **Hep** b2.de* ign b2.de* *Iod* b2.de* kali-c ptk1 lac-c ptk1 lach bg2 merc bg2 merc-i-r ptk1 *Nit-ac* b2.de* *Nux-v* b2.de* *Petr* b2.de* ph-ac b2.de* *Phos* b2.de* plb ptk1 puls b7.de* ran-b b2.de* *Rhus-t* b2.de* *Sep* b2.de* sil ptk1 **Sulph** b2.de* zinc b2.de*

- **food**: ...
  - **amel.**: brom ptk1 ferr ptk1 *Hyos* ptk1 *Ign* b7.de* kali-bi ptk1 kali-br bg2 *Lach* b7a.de* merc-cy bg2* nux-v b7.de* rhus-t b7.de* sanic ptk1
    - **large** amounts: arn bg2
- **not** swallowing; when:
  - **agg.**: alum b2.de* am-m b2.de* *Ambr* b2.de* *Arn* b2.de* bell b2.de* *Caps* b2.de* carb-v b2.de* chel b2.de* chin b2.de* cocc b2.de dig b2.de* dros b2.de* ferr b7.de graph b2.de* **Ign** b2.de* iod b2.de* ip b2.de *Lach* b2.de laur b2.de* *Led* b2.de* m-aust b2.de* mag-c b2.de* mang b2.de* merc b2.de mez b2.de* nat-c b2.de* nit-ac b2.de* nux-v b2.de* olnd b2.de par b2.de* ph-ac b2.de* phos b2.de* plat b2.de* puls b2.de* rheum b2.de rhus-t b2.de* ruta b2.de* sabad b2.de* sabin b2.de* spig b2.de *Spong* b2.de squil b2.de stann b2.de* staph b2.de* sul-ac b2.de* sulph b2.de* tarax b2.de* zinc b2.de*
  - **amel.**: alum bg2 ambr bg2 caps bg2 graph bg2 **Ign** bg2 iod bg2 lach bg2 laur bg2 led bg2 mang bg2 merc bg2 mez bg2 *Nux-v* bg2 plat bg2 puls bg2 sabad bg2 spong bg2 stann bg2 staph bg2 sulph bg2 zinc bg2
- **warm** drinks | **agg.** | **hot** drinks: phyt bg2*
  - **amel.**: alum bg2* kali-c ptk1 nux-v bg2*
- **warm** food:
  - **agg.**: gels ptk1
  - **amel.**: hyos ptk1

SWASHING, splashing, etc. as of water: ars bg* bell b2.de* carb-ac bg* carb-an ptk1 *Chin* bg* cina b2.de* crot-t bg2* dig b2.de* ferr b2.de* glon bg* hell b2.de* *Hep* bg* *Hyos* bg* jatr-c bg2 kali-c bg* laur b2.de* nat-m ptk1 ph-ac b2.de* rhus-t bg2* *Spig* bg*

- **warm**: chin ptk1 hep ptk1 sumb ptk1

SWELLING:

- **absent** | **Affected** parts: ars ptk1 camph ptk1 carb-v ptk1 con ptk1 laur ptk1 op ptk1 ph-ac ptk1 sulph ptk1
- **general**; in: *Acon* k* adam srj5• aeth tl1 agar k* agn k* all-s a1 aloe bg2* alum k* am-c k* am-m k* ambr k* anac k* ancis-p tsm2 ant-c k* anthraco j5.de **Apis** k* arg-met k* arg-n bg2* *Arn* k* **Ars** k* ars-i ars-s-f k2 asaf k* asar k* aur k* aur-m j5.de aur-s k2 *Bar-c* k* *Bar-m* j5.de **Bell** k* bell-p c1* bism k* bit-ar br1* borx k* both tsm2* both-ax tsm2 bov k* **Bry** k* bufo k* buth-a sp1 calad k* *Calc* k* calc-i bg2 calc-sil k2 camph k* cann-s k* *Canth* k* caps k* carb-an k* carb-v k* *Carbn-s* cameg-g rwt1• caust k* celt a1 cench k2 *Cham* k* chel k* *Chin* k* chinin-s j5.de cic k* cina j5.de clem k* cocc k* coff k* colch k* coloc k* com con k* conch a1 cop cortiso sp1 croc k* crot-c tsm2 crot-h crot-t j5.de cupr k* cycl k* *Daph* j5.de dig k* dor a1* dros k* *Dulc* k* eucal a1* euph k* euphr k* *Ferr* k* frag a1* graph k* guaj k* hell k* *Hep* k* hip-ac sp1 hydr bg2 hyos k* ign k* iod k* *Kali-ar* **Kali-bi** k* *Kali-c* k* kali-i j5.de kali-n k* kreos k* lacer c1 lach k* laur k* led k* *Lyc* k* m-ambo b2.de* *M-arct* b2.de* m-aust b2.de mag-c k* mag-m k* mang k* **Merc** k* *Merc-c* j5.de mez k* mosch k* mur-ac k* naja narcin a1 *Nat-c* k* nat-m k* *Nit-ac* k* nux-m k* **Nux-v** k* olnd k* op k* par k* ped a1 petr k* *Ph-ac* k* *Phos* k* phyt bg2 plat j5.de *Plb* k* **Puls** k* ran-b k* ran-s j5.de raph a1 rauw sp1 rhod k* **Rhus-t** k* rhus-v a1 ruta k* sabad k* sabin k* samb k* saroth sp1 sars k* sec k* seneg k* *Sep* k* *Sil* k* *Spig* k* spong k* squil k* stann k* staph k* *Stram* k* stront-c k* sul-ac k* *Sulph* k* tarent a1 ter j5.de teucr b2.de* thal jl3 *Thuj* k* urea a1 urt-u a1 valer k* verat k* *Vip* vip-a-c tsm2 vip-d tsm2 zinc k* ziz a1
  - **right** side: ars h2 sang bg2
  - **baglike**: apis ptk1 ars ptk1 kali-c ptk1 rhus-t ptk1
  - **children**; in: sacch br1
  - **chronic**: *Cist* br1*
  - **cold** swelling: asaf ptk1 *Cocc* ptk1 con ptk1 *Dulc* ptk1 *Merc* ptk1 *Sulph* ptk1
  - **hard**: ars ptk1 bell ptk1 chin ptk1 con ptk1 hep ptk1 iod ptk1 lach ptk1 merc ptk1 puls ptk1 rhus-t ptk1 sil ptk1 spong ptk1 *Tarent-c* ptk1
    - **Various** parts; in: phos ptk1
  - **pale**: **Apis** bg2 bar-c ptk1 *Bry* ptk1 lach ptk1 lyc ptk1 rhus-t ptk1 *Sulph* ptk1
  - **red**: **Bell** bg2
    - **dark**: asaf ptk1
    - **shiny**: sabin ptk1
- **inflammatory**: **Acon** k* agn k* alum k* am-c k* ant-c k* ant-t bg2 *Apis* arn k* **Ars** k* ars-i ars-s-f k2 asaf k* *Aur* j5.de bar-c k* **Bell** k* *Borx* j5.de *Bry* k* **Calc** k* calc-sil k2 cann-s k* **Canth** k* carb-an k* carb-v k* *Caust* k* chin k* cocc k* colch k* *Con* k* crot-h j5.de* cupr k* euph k* gamb hr1 gran j5.de graph k* guaj k* guare hr1 hep k* hyos j5.de *Iod* k* *Kali-ar* **Kali-bi** **Kali-c** k* *Kali-chl* hr1 *Kali-i* k*

Swelling – inflammatory: ...
kali-n j5.de led k* *Lyc* k* m-arct b2.de mag-c k* *Mang* j5.de **Merc** k* mez j5.de mur-ac j5.de nat-c k* *Nat-m* k* *Nit-ac* k* nux-v k* petr k* ph-ac j5.de *Phos* k* *Phyt* k* plb k* *Puls* k* *Rhus-t* k* sabin k* samb k* sars k* sec k* seneg j5.de **Sep** k* *Sil* k* spong k* stann k* stram j5.de **Sulph** k* thuj k* zinc k*

- **bites** and stings; after: **Led** mrr1
- **painful**: anan br1 bit-ar wht1• dig h2
- **puffy**, edematous: *Acet-ac* ptk1 *Acon* k* *Agar* k* am-c k* *Am-m* k* ancis-p tsm2 **Ant-c** k* antip vh1 **Apis** k* *Apoc* k* arn k* **Ars** k* ars-i k2 ars-s-f k2 *Asaf* k* aur k* *Aur-m* bar-c k* *Bell* k* both tsm2* both-ax tsm2 bov mrr1 *Bry* k* cain br1 **Calc** k* calc-sil k2 canth ptk1 **Caps** k* *Carbn-s* card-m ptk1 cedr cench tsm2 cham k* chin k* cina k* cloth tsm2 cocc k* colch k* coloc k* *Com* ptk1 con k* crat br1 crot-c tsm2 crot-h tsm2 culx vml3• **Cupr** k* **Dig** k* diph jl2 dros k* *Dulc* k* **Ferr** k* ferr-ar k2 **Graph** k* guaj k* **Hell** k* helo-s bnm14• hyos k* *Iod* k* ip k* kali-br hr1 kali-c k* kali-i ptk1 kreos k* lach k* laur k* led k* *Lith-c* kr1 *Lyc* k* mag-c k* med ptk1 merc k* mez k* mosch k* naja br1* nat-c k* *Nat-m* kr1* nat-pyru rly4• *Nit-ac* k* nux-m k* nux-v b2.de* **Olnd** k* op k* phos k* *Phyt* plb k* puls k* rheum k* *Rhus-t* k* sabin k2 samb k* sars k* senec-sp bta1• *Seneg* k* *Sep* k* sil k* *Spig* k* spong k* **Squil** k* staph k* stram k* stront-c ptk1 *Sulph* k* ter ptk1* *Teucr* k* thyr br1 til ptk1 verat *Verb* vip tsm2 vip-a-c tsm2 vip-d tsm2 zinc k* ziz kr1
  - **accompanied** by | **Kidneys**; inflammation of (See KIDNEYS - Inflammation - accompanied - edema)
  - ○ **Mucous** membranes: apis bg2* kali-bi bg2 kali-i bg2
- **receding**: ars ptk1 calc ptk1 hep ptk1 kreos ptk1 lach ptk1 lyc ptk1 merc ptk1 sep ptk1 sil ptk1
- **rheumatic**: bry br1
- **sensation** of: acon bg2 *Aloe* bg2 alum b4a.de* am-m bg2 ambr bg2 *Aml-ns* bg2 anac bg2 ant-c bg2 ant-t bg2 apis bg2 apoc-a br1 aran bg2 arg-met bg2 **Arg-n** bg2 arn bg2 ars bg2 asaf bg2 asar bg2 aur bg2 bapt bg2 bar-c bg2 *Bell* bg2 berb bg2 *Bism* bg2 bov b4a.de* *Bry* bg2 *Caj* br1 calc bg2 cann-xyz bg2 canth bg2 *Caps* bg2 carb-v bg2 caust bg2 cham bg2 chin bg2 cic bg2 cina bg2 cocc bg2 colch bg2 con bg2 cycl bg2 dig bg2 dulc bg2 euph bg2* gels bg2 *Glon* bg2 *Guaj* bg2 hell bg2 hep bg2 hyos bg2 ign bg2 ip bg2 kali-c bg2 kali-n b4a.de* kreos bg2 lach bg2 *Laur* bg2 led bg2 lyc bg2 mag-c bg2 *Mang* bg2 merc b4a.de* mez bg2 mosch bg2 nit-ac bg2 nux-m bg2 nux-v bg2 olnd bg2 op bg2 **Par** bg2 petr bg2 ph-ac bg2 phos bg2 *Plat* bg2 plb bg2 **Puls** bg2 ran-b bg2 ran-s bg2 rhod bg2 **Rhus-t** bg2 sabad bg2 sabin bg2 samb bg2 sars bg2 seneg bg2 sep bg2 sil bg2 **Spig** bg2 spong bg2 stann bg2 staph bg2 stram bg2 sul-ac bg2 sulph bg2 tarax bg2 thuj bg2 valer bg2 verat bg2 zinc bg2
  - ○ **Body**; whole: bufo ptk1
  - **Internal** organs; of all: jug-c br1
    - **left** side: jug-c br1
  - **Single** parts; of: *Aran* br1 ars-met br1
- **wounds** (See Wounds - swelling)
- ○ **Affected** parts, of: **Acon** k* **Act-sp** agn k* alum k* alum-sil k2* ant-c k* ant-s-aur *Apis* k* arn k* *Ars* k* *Ars-i* asaf k* aur k* aur-s k2 bar-c k* bar-i k2* **Bell** k* bit-ar wht1• bov k* **Bry** k* calc k* calc-i k2* calc-sil k2* cann-s k* *Canth* k* carb-an k* carb-v k* *Caust* k* cedr cham k* chin k* cic k* clem k* cocc k* colch k* coll con k* **Crot-h** k* crot-t cub cupr k* dig k* dulc k* euph k* **Euphr** *Ferr* k* ferr-ar k2* ferr-p *Fl-ac* **Gels** graph k* guaj k* *Guare* hr1* hell k* *Hep* k* hippoz hr1* hydr ign k* *Iod* k* *Kali-bi* **Kali-c** b2.de* kali-chl hr1* *Kali-i* kali-m k2 ketogl-ac rly4• *Lach* k* *Led* k* *Lyc* k* mag-c k* mang k* **Merc** k* **Merc-c** k* *Mur-ac* k* *Nat-c* k* *Nat-m* k* *Nit-ac* k* *Nux-v* k* ox-ac *Petr* k* ph-ac k* *Phos* k* *Phyt* plb k* *Psor* **Puls** k* ran-b k* **Rhod** k* **Rhus-t** k* ruta k* sabin k* *Samb* k* sang sars k* sec k* **Sep** k* **Sil** k* spig k* **Spong** k* *Stann* k* staph bg2 *Stram* k* **Sulph** k* thuj k* *Valer* zinc k*
  - **Blood** vessels; of: apis ptk1 celt a1 lyc ptk1 paeon ptk1 *Puls* ptk1 visc br1
    - **fever**; during: am-c bg2 arn bg2 bell bg2 **Camph** b7.de* **Chin** b7.de* *Cocc* b7.de* **Croc** b7a.de* **Cycl** b7.de* *Ferr* b7a.de* hyos bg2 m-arct b7a.de mosch bg2 **Ph-ac** bg2 *Puls* b7.de* **Ran-s** bg2 *Rhus-t* b7.de* staph bg2 thuj bg2
    - **perspiration**; during: am-c bg2 arn bg2 *Bell* bg2 *Camph* bg2 **Chin** bg2 cocc bg2 *Croc* bg2 cycl bg2 **Ferr** bg2 hyos bg2 lyc bg2 *Ph-ac* bg2 phos bg2 puls bg2 *Rhus-t* bg2 *Sep* bg2 staph bg2 sulph bg2 *Thuj* bg2
  - **Bones**; of: am-c k* ambr j5.de ang bg2 ant-c j5.de *Arg-met* bg2 **Asaf** k* *Aur* k* bell k* bry k* bufo bg2 **Calc** k* calc-f bg2* *Calc-p* carb-an k* clem k* coloc k* con k* conch a1 daph j5.de* dig k* dulc k* euph k* ferr k* fl-ac k* guaj k* hep k* iod k* *Kali-i* k* kreos k* lac-ac c2* lach k* led j5.de *Lyc* k* mang k* *Merc* k* *Mez* k* nat-c k* nat-m k* *Nit-ac* k* petr k* **Ph-ac** k* **Phos** k* *Phyt* kr1 pitu-gl bro1 plb k*

- **Bones**; of: ...
Puls k* rhod k* rhus-t k* *Ruta* k* sabin k* sep k* **Sil** k* spig k* **Staph** k* stront-c bg2 **Sulph** k* thuj k* thyr bro1 tub bg2 verat k*
  - **sensation** of swelling (See Swollen - bones)
○ · **Condyles** | **Epiphyses**; and: conch bro1 rhus-t bro1
- **Cartilages**; of: *(↗Cartilages; Tumors - enchondroma)* **Arg-met** *Calc* kr1 *Sil* kr1
- **Connective** tissue: kali-i br1
- **Fibrous** tissue: kali-i br1
- **Glands**; of: *(↗Glands)* abrot mrr1 acon k* acon-l c1 *Aesc* aeth br1 agn k* *Ail* bg2* *Aln* c1* alum k* alum-sil k2 *Alumn* kr1 am-c k* *Am-m* k* ambr k* ancis-p tsm2 ant-c k* ant-t k* *Anthraci* k* *Apis* bg2* aq-mar sf1.de arg-met k* arn k* *Ars* b2.de* **Ars-i** k* ars-s-f bg2* *Arum-t* k* asaf k* astac kr1* aur k* aur-ar k2 aur-i k2 *Aur-m* kr1 aur-s k2 *Bad* bg2* *Bapt* k* **Bar-c** k* **Bar-i** **Bar-m** k* bar-s k2 **Bell** k* *Berb* k1 bit-ar wht1• borx k* both tsm2 both-ax tsm2 bov k* **Brom** k* *Bry* k* *Bufo* k* calad k* *Calc* k* calc-ar sf1.de* *Calc-f* bg2* calc-hp sf1.de **Calc-i** k* calc-m c1* calc-p k* **Calc-s** k* *Calc-sil* k2 *Calen* c1* camph k* cann-s k* *Canth* k* caps k* **Carb-an** k* **Carb-v** k* *Carbn-s* k* carc mlr1• caust k* cench tsm2 *Cham* k* chim c1 chin k* cic k* cinnb j5.de **Cist** k* **Clem** k* cloth tsm2 coc-c a1 cocc k* coloc k* **Con** k* cor-r j5.de* cory sf1.de croc k* crot-c tsm2 crot-h k* cupr k* cycl k* dig k* dros st* **Dulc** k* *Eucal* a1* euph k* euphr c1* eupi c1* **Ferr** b2.de* ferr-ar ferr-i k* fl-ac bg2* fuc sf1.de* **Graph** k* hall c1 ham bg2* *Hecla* kr1 hed mg1.de hell k* **Hep** k* hippoz kr1* hydrc sf1.de hyos k* ign k* **Iod** k* *Iris* bg2* jug-r vml3• *Kali-ar* *Kali-bi* kr1 kali-br kr1 *Kali-c* k* *Kali-chl* *Kali-i* k* kali-m bg2* kreos j5.de lac-c k2 lach k* *Lap-a* c1* lat-m bnm6• led k* *Lith-c* kr1* **Lyc** k* mag-c k* mag-m k* mang k* med **Merc** k* **Merc-c** k* merc-d *Merc-i-f* *Merc-i-r* merc-k-i gm1 mez k* mur-ac k* *Nat-c* k* nat-m k* *Nat-p* kr1* nat-s bg2* **Nit-ac** k* *Nux-v* k* ol-j sf1.de ozone sde2• petr k* *Ph-ac* k* **Phos** k* *Phyt* k* plb k* psor k* *Puls* k* pyrog mtf11 ran-b k* ran-s k* raph j5.de rhod k* **Rhus-t** k* *Rumx* br1 ruta k* sabad k* sabin k* samb k* sars k* scir c1 scol a1 scroph-n c1* sec kr1* *Sep* k* **Sil** k* sil-mar c1 sol-a c1* sol-o c1* spig k* **Spong** k* squil k* *Stann* k* staph k* stict c1* stram k* streptoc mtf11 stront-c k* *Sul-ac* k* *Sul-i* bg2* **Sulph** k* symph c1 *Syph* kr1* tab c1 tarent tl1 ter j5.de teucr k* ther k2 thiosin c1* **Thuj** k* toxo-g jl2* *Tub* bg2* tub-a vs tub-m vn* uran-n kr1 urea br1 v-a-b jl2 *Verat* k* viol-o k* viol-t b7.de* vip tsm2 *Zinc* k* [*Bar-f* stj1 bar-p stj1 kali-f stj1 mag-f stj1]
  - **accompanied** by:
    - **herpes** (See SKIN - Eruptions - herpetic - accompanied - glands)
    - **Tongue** | **white** discoloration of the tongue: *Bar-m* kr1*
  - **bead**-like (See knotted)
  - **bluish**: arn k* ars k* aur k* *Carb-an* k* carb-v k* con k* ferr-i hep k* *Lach* k* mang k* merc k* merc-i-f puls k* sil k* sul-ac k*
  - **children**; in: *Brom* br1 med jl2
  - **chronic**: acon-l bro1 *Ail* bro1 *Aln* bro1 apis bro1 ars bro1 ars-br bro1 *Ars-i* bro1 arum-t bro1 astac bro1 aur-m bro1 *Bad* bro1 *Bar-c* bro1 *Bar-i* bro1 bar-m bro1 *Brom* bro1 *Calc* bro1 *Calc-f* bro1 *Calc-i* bro1 calc-p bro1 calen bro1 *Carb-an* bro1 *Cist* bro1 *Clem* bro1 *Con* bro1 cory bro1 crot-h bro1 dulc bro1 ferr-i bro1 fil bro1 graph bro1 hep bro1 *Iod* bro1 *Kali-i* bro1 lach bro1 *Lap-a* bro1 lyc bro1 med bro1 merc bro1 merc-cy bro1 merc-i-f bro1 *Merc-i-r* bro1 nit-ac bro1 *Phyt* bro1 psor bro1 rhus-t bro1 *Rumx* bro1 sal-mar bro1 scir bro1 *Scroph-n* bro1 *Sil* bro1 sil-mar bro1 *Spong* bro1 *Sulph* bro1 tax bro1 thiosin bro1 thuj bro1 tub bro1
  - **cold** agg.: *Ars* k* asaf k* bell k* *Cocc* k* **Con** k* cycl k* dulc k* lach k* rhod k* spig k* thuj kr1
  - **contusions**, after: bell-p k* phos k2
  - **emaciation**; with: *Ars* kr1 *Ars-i* kr1 *Bar-c* kr1 *Calc* kr1 *Calc-i* kr1 *Calc-p* kr1 carb-v kr1 caust kr1 *Cist* kr1 *Con* kr1 *Graph* kr1 iod tl1* *Mag-c* kr1 *Mag-m* kr1 nat-m kr1 nit-ac kr1 *Ol-j* kr1 petr kr1 ph-ac kr1 phos kr1 psor kr1 *Sil* kr1 staph kr1 sul-ac kr1 sulph kr1 ther tl1*
  - **eruptions**; with: dulc h2
  - **fever**; during: *Bell* bg2* *Calc* bg2 *Kali-c* bg2* lyc bg2 merc bg2 nit-ac bg2 phos bg2 *Phyt* bg2 rhus-t bg2 *Sep* b4.de* **Sil** b4a.de* sulph bg2
  - **hard**: *(↗Indurations - glands)* agn k* ail tl1 alumn k2 am-c tl1 ant-c k* arn k* ars k* ars-i k2 asaf k* *Bad* kr1 bar-c k2 *Brom* k2* *Bry* k* calc tl1 calc-f st calc-sil k2 *Carb-an* caust k* chin k* **Con** k* dig k* graph k* hep k2 **Iod** k* *Kali-i* lach k* led k* loxo-lae bnm12• merc k* mez k* nux-v k* *Phos* k* *Phyt* bg2* *Puls* k* **Rhus-t** k* sabin k* samb k* *Sil* mrr1 *Spong* k* staph k1 stront-c k* sul-i k2 *Sulph* k* [calc-br stj1 mag-br stj1]

Swelling – Glands; of: ...
  - **hot**: *Acon* k* am-c k* ant-c k* ant-t bg2 arn k* asaf k* *Bar-c* b4a.de **Bell** k* **Brom** b4a.de **Bry** k* *Calc* k* canth k* *Carb-an* k* carb-v k* *Cham* kr1 chin k* clem k* cocc k* euph k* *Hep* k* kali-c k* led k* **Merc** k* nux-v k* petr k* **Phos** k* *Phyt* k* puls k* rhus-t k* sars k* sil k* *Sulph* k*
  - **hypertrophy**: iod tl1
  - **inflammatory**: *Acon* k* agn k* am-c k* ant-c k* *Arn* k* ars k* asaf k* *Bad* *Bar-c* bar-m k2 **Bell** k* borx k* *Bry* k* calc k* *Carb-an* k* *Carb-v* k* caust k* *Cham* kr1 cinnb *Clem* cocc k* **Con** k* dros st *Hep* k* hyos k* kali-ar *Kali-i* *Lyc* k* mang k* **Merc** k* mez k* mur-ac k* nat-c k* petr k* *Phos* k* *Phyt* k* puls k* *Rhus-t* k* sars k* **Sil** k* spong mrr1 sulph k* *Thuj* k*
  - **injuring**; after: con tl1
  - **knotted** cords, like: *(↗Indurations - glands - knotty)* aeth ptk1 aur ptk1 bar-i ptk1 **Bar-m** k* berb ptk1 *Calc* k* calc-i ptk1 *Cist* k* con *Dulc* k* hep k* *Iod* k* lyc k* nit-ac ptk1 rhus-t k* *Sil* sul-i k2* tub k*
  - **menses**; during: kali-c k* lac-c k*
  - **moon**; full: glycyr-g cte1•
  - **nodes**, like: bry k* iod k2 nit-ac k*
  - **painful**: acon k* am-c kr1 anan kr1 ant-c k* *Anthraco* kr1 *Arn* k* ars kr1 aur k* aur-i k2 *Bar-c* b4a.de* **Bar-m** **Bell** k* bit-ar wht1• calc k* *Calc-p* kr1 canth k* *Caps* kr1 *Carb-an* k* carb-v kr1 carc gk caust kr1 *Cham* kr1 *Chin* k* clem k* cocc tl1 **Con** kr1* cop kr1 cor-r crot-t kr1 cupr kr1 graph bg2 *Hep* ign kr1 *Iod* k* kali-c kr1* *Kali-i* kola stb3• lyc bg2 *Merc* kr1 merc-i-r ptk1 mosch bg2 nat-m kr1 *Nit-ac* k* nux-v k* phos bg2 phyt psor kr1 *Puls* k* rhus-t k* *Sil* k* spig k* stann k* *Staph* k* sulph kr1 [brom stj1 calc-br stj1 mag-br stj1]
  - **painless**: ars asaf **Calc** k* cocc k1 *Con* k* cycl dulc k* *Ign* k* lach merc bg2 *Nit-ac* k* *Ph-ac* k* plb k* *Sep* k* sil k* staph k* sulph k* thuj *Tub* st* [brom stj1 calc-br stj1 mag-br stj1]
  - **perspiration**; during: *Bell* bg2 lyc bg2 merc bg2 nit-ac bg2 phos bg2 rhus-t bg2 *Sep* bg2 *Sil* bg2 sulph bg2
  - **pregnancy** agg.; during: calc-f dgt1
  - **scarlet** fever:
    - **after**: am-c kl **Bar-c** *Lac-c* kr1
    - **during**: am-c br1*
  - **scrofulous**: aur br1 bar-i mtf11 calc-chln mtf11 calc-s tl1 cham mtf11 ferr-i mtf11
- **Joints**; of: *Abrot* acon **Act-sp** agn anag *Ant-t* *Apis* apoc *Arn* *Ars* asc-t aur *Aur-m* bacls-7 fmm1• **Bell** berb k* bov sf1.de **Bry** bufo *Calc* calc-f canth sf1.de caust k2 cedr sf1.de chin chinin-s sf1.de *Cimic* clem *Cocc* **Colch** con dulc k2 *Ferr-p* k* *Guaj* *Ham* **Hep** hip-ac sp1 *Iod* sf1.de kali-ar k2 kali-bi k2 *Kali-chl* kali-i kali-m sf1.de *Kalm* *Lac-ac* lac-c k2 *Lach* **Led** *Lyc* mang med *Merc* *Nat-m* *Nux-v* phor-t mie3• *Ran-b* sf1.de rham-cal br1 *Rhod* *Rhus-t* sabin *Sal-ac* samb sf1.de sil sol-t-ae spong ptk1 stict **Sulph** tarent *Ter* thuj *Verat-v*
  - **fever**; during: calc bg2
  - **fractures**; after: bov ptk1
  - **red**; but little: ferr-p tl1
- **Mucous** membranes; of: aesc br1 *Am-caust* br1 arg-n k* ars-i k* hydr k*
- **Muscles**: lyc b4a.de rad-br sze8• sulph b4a.de
  - **progressive**: carbn-s mtf11 plb-i mtf11
- **Periosteum**: *Acon* bg2 ant-c k* **Asaf** k* *Aur* k* bell k* bry k* chin k* *Kali-i* *Led* b7a.de mang k* *Merc* k* mez k* *Nit-ac* **Ph-ac** k* *Puls* k* rhod k* rhus-t k* ruta k* sabin k* *Sil* k* staph k* sulph bg2
- **Tendons**: | **hard**: calc-f ptk1
- **Uncovered** parts: *Rhus-t* b7a.de
- **Veins**; of: aesc mrr1 aml-ns tl1 brom tl1 *Calc-f* br1 carb-v tl1 chel tl1 dig mtf11 glon tl1 lach tl1 ruta c2
  - **evening**: carb-v h2
  - **fever**; during: *Puls* bro1 thuj bro1
  - **knotty**: sabin k2*
  - **painful** | **chill**; during: chin bro1 chinin-s bro1

SWIMMING:
- **desires** (See MIND - Swimming - desires)
- **while** | **agg.**: cocc ptk1

SWOLLEN sensation: (↗*MIND - Delusions - swollen*) *Acon* k* aesc sf1.de agar aloe alum k* am-c j5.de am-m ambr anac ant-c ant-t apis *Aran* k* arg-met *Arg-n* k* arn ars asaf asar aur *Bamb-a* stb2.de• bapt k* bar-c *Bell* k* berb bg1 *Bism* bov k* bry caj calad calc *Calc-p* cann-i canth *Caps* carb-ac carb-an j5.de carb-v carbn-s caust *Cedr* cench st1 cham chin cimic cina *Coc-c* *Cocc* k* colch coll ptk1 *Coloc* *Com* con *Cor-r* crot-c sk4• crot-h crot-t *Cupr* cycl dig dulc euph *Euphr* gels ptk1 gink-b sbd1• *Glon* k* graph j5.de **Guaj** k* ham sf1.de hell hep hyos ign k* ip kali-br hr1 kali-c kali-n kreos **Lach** k* *Laur* led lyc mag-c mang **Merc** k* **Merc-i-f** k* mez mosch nit-ac nux-m nux-v k* olnd *Op* k* **Paeon** k* **Par** k* petr ph-ac phos plat plb **Puls** k* *Ran-b* k* ran-s rhod **Rhus-t** k* sabad sabin samb *Sang* sanic ptk1 sars *Seneg* sep sil **Spig** k* spong stann staph stram sul-ac *Sulph* tarax thuj valer verat zinc

- **chill**; during: acon bg2
- ○ - **Bones**; of: aloe bg2 ant-c k* ars h2* bell k* chel guaj k* mez tl1* *Puls* k* rhus-t k* spig k*
- **Glands**; of: ant-c k* aur k* aur-i k2 *Bell* k* bry k* carb-v k* chin k* clem con k* dulc k* hep k* ign k* kali-n k* lach k* m-ambo b2.de* m-arct j5.de m-aust b2.de merc k* nat-m j5.de nit-ac k* nux-m k* nux-v k* **Puls** k* *Rhus-t* k* sabin k* spig k* *Spong* k* staph k* sulph j5.de zinc k*
- **Part** of the body: *Brucel* sa3•

SYCOSIS: (↗*Family - sycosis; URETHRA - Discharge - gonorrheal*) acet-ac br1 adlu jl3 aesc st1 *Agar* agn sf1.de alum alumn am-c st1 am-m st1 anac *Anan* hr1* ang st1 ant-c ant-t k* *Anthraco* a1* *Apis* k* aran k* **Arg-met** k* **Arg-n** k* arn hr1* *Ars* bg2* asaf hr1* asar jl3* asim st1 aspar st1 *Aster* k* aur k* *Aur-m* k* aur-m-n c1* *Bar-c* *Benz-ac* c1* berb hr1* berb-a jl3 borx st bov st1 bry bufo st calad st1 *Calc* k* cann-i st1 cann-s st1 canth st1 caps sf1.de* carb-ac k* carb-an k* carb-v k* carbn-s carc mlr1• castm c1* caul st1 *Caust* k* cedr st1 cham k* chim st1 chin st1 chlam-tr bcx2• cic jl3* cimic st1 cinnb k* clem k2* cob-n jl3 coc-c st1 coch st1 colch sf1.de* coloc st1 con k* cop st1 croc st1 crot-h st1 crot-t st1 cub st1 cupr-act st cycl st1 cyna jl3 dig st1 diph-t-tpt jl2 dor st1 *Dulc* k* epig st1 erech st1 erig st1 ery-a sf1.de* eup-pur st1 euph st euph-pi st1 euphr k* fago st1 *Ferr* *Fl-ac* k* flav jl3* gamb st1 gels st1 gnaph st1 *Graph* k* guaj sf1.de guat jl3 helon st1 hep k* hydr sf1.de* influ jl2* *Iod* kali-bi hr1* kali-c kali-chl c* kali-i sf1.de* kali-m c1* kali-n st1 **Kali-s** k* kalm k2* kreos hr1* kres jl3 lac-c st1 *Lach* k* lil-t st1 lith-c st1 *Lyc* k* mag-c hr1* *Mang* **Med** k* merc k* *Merc-c* hr1* merc-d st1 *Merc-sul* hr1* *Mez* mill c1 moni jl2 mosch st1 murx st1 nat-c hr1* *Nat-m* hr1* *Nat-p* hr1* **Nat-s** k* **Nit-ac** k* nux-v st1 ol-j st1 orig st1 (non:orig-v st1) pall st1 parathyr jl2 pareir st1 penic jl3* petr k* petros sf1.de* ph-ac hr1* phos st1 *Phyt* pic-ac c1* pip-n st1 plat st1 plb st1 pneu jl3* prun st1 psor sf1.de* puls k* rat st1 rauw jl3 rhus-t st1 sabad sf1.de* sabin k* sacch-l st1 sanic st1 sarr st1 *Sars* k* *Sec* *Sel* k* senec st1 seneg st1 **Sep** k* *Sil* k* spig st1 **Staph** k* still st1 stram st1 *Sulph* k* tab st1 tell jl3 ter st1 **THUJ** b4.de* thyr jl3 tor br1 uran-n st1 vac br1 ven-m jl3 vib st1 zing sf1.de

- **chronic**: gonotox jl2 med jl2 thuj bg2 vac jl2
- **suppressed**: merc ptk1 nit-ac ptk1 staph ptk1 thuj ptk1

SYNALGIA: apis ptk1 tarent bg3*

SYNCHRONICITY:

- **pulse**; of:
  - **Ear**; with crackling noises in (See EAR - Noises - crackling - synchronous)
  - **Ear**; with hissing noises in (See EAR - Noises - hissing - synchronous)
  - **Ear**; with humming noises in (See EAR - Noises - humming - synchronous)
  - **Ear**; with noises in (See EAR - Noises - synchronous)
  - **Ear**; with rushing noises in (See EAR - Noises - rushing - synchronous)
  - **Ear**; with snapping noises in (See EAR - Noises - snapping - synchronous)
  - **Fingers**; with twitching in (See EXTREMITIES - Twitching - fingers - synchronous)
  - **Head**; with pain in (See HEAD - Pain - synchronous)
  - **Head**; with pulsating in (See HEAD - Pulsating)
  - **Head**; with shocks in (See HEAD - Shocks - synchronous)
  - **Heart**; with palpitation of (See CHEST - Palpitation - synchronous)

Synchronicity – puke; of: ...

- **Teeth**; with pulsating pain in (See TEETH - Pain - pulsating - synchronous)
- **Thigh**; with twitching in (See EXTREMITIES - Twitching - thigh - synchronous)
- **Upper** limbs; with pulsation in (See EXTREMITIES - Pulsation - upper limbs - synchronous)

SYNCOPE (See Faintness)

SYPHILIS: (↗*Chancre; Family - syphilis; History - syphilis*) aethi-a c1* *Aethi-m* bro1 agn sf1.de ail c1* allox jl3 aln c1* am-c bg2 anac br1* anag hr1* *Anan* hr1* *Ang* hr1* ant-c bro1* *Ant-t* hr1* *Apis* kr1* arg-i c1* arg-met *Arg-n* hr1* arn hr1* *Ars* k* ars-br br1* **Ars-i** k* ars-met c1* *Ars-s-f* k* *Asaf* k* asar jl3 *Asc-t* hr1* astra-e jl3 **Aur** k* aur-ar c1* aur-i c1* **Aur-m** k* **Aur-m-n** k* aur-s k2 bad k* bapt bro1 bell st1 benz-ac k* berb hr1* berb-a c1* buni-o jl3 cadm-met sf* *Calc-f* c1* *Calc-i* *Calc-s* k* calo c1* *Carb-an* k* carb-v k* *Caust* hr1* *Cean* hr1* *Chim* hr1* chinin-ar c1* chr-o c1* *Cinnb* k* clem k* cob-n jl3 *Colch* sf1.de* *Con* k* convo-s jl3 cop sf1.de cor-r k* cory c1* crot-h k* cund hr1* cupr sf1.de cupr-s c1* *Daph* hr1 diphtox jl2 echi c1* ery-a sf1.de eryth c1* eucal c1* euph hr1* ferr c1* ferr-i hr1* *Fl-ac* k* flav jl2 franc c1* gels bro1 *Graph* c1* *Gua* br1* guaj k* ham sf1.de hecla kr1* *Hep* k* hip-ac jl3 *Hippoz* hr1* hir jl3 hydr c1* hydrc c1* hypoth jl3 iber jl3 *Iod* k* *Iris* kr1 jac-c hr1* *Jac-g* kr1* jug-r c1* *Kali-ar* k* *Kali-bi* k* kali-br c1* kali-c st1 *Kali-chl* k* **Kali-i** k* *Kali-m* kr1* **Kali-s** k* *Kalm* hr1* *Kreos* hr1* *Lac-c* hr1* lac-d st1 *Lach* k* **Laur** hr1* *Led* lith-c c1* lon-x br1* *Lyc* hr1* maland c1 mang-act br1 **MERC** b4.de* merc-aur bro1* merc-br bro1 **Merc-c** k* *Merc-d* hr1* **Merc-i-f** k* **Merc-i-r** k* merc-k-i gm1 *Merc-n* bro1 *Merc-pr-r* bro1 merc-tn bro1 *Mez* k* mill st1 morb tl1 nat-s k2 nep jl3 **Nit-ac** k* nux-v sf1.de ol-sant sf1.de oscilloc jl2 osm c1* penic jl3 perh jl3 petr k* petros sf1.de *Ph-ac* k* *Phos* k* **Phyt** k* pilo c1 pitu jl3 plat bro1* *Plat-m* bro1 psor c1* ran-p bta1• reser jl3 rhod sf1.de rhus-g bro1 *Sabad* sf1.de *Sang* hr1* *Sars* k* sec st1 sel c1* *Sep* hr1* **Sil** k* sol-mlg bta1• spong sf1.de *Staph* k* stict c1* **Still** k* strych-g c1* *Sul-i* *Sulph* k* **Syph** k* tarent-c mrr1 ter sf1.de thala jl3 thiop jl3 *Thuj* k* thymol jl3 *Thyr* c1* toxo-g jl2 ulm-c c1* vac c1 *Viol-t* hr1* with-s bta1• xan sf1.de

- **accompanied** by:
  - **emaciation**: *Ars* bro1 *Aur* bro1 calo bro1 carb-an bro1 carb-v bro1 ferr-i bro1 ferr-lac bro1 *Iod* bro1 merc bro1 sars bro1
  - **exostosis**: *Calc-f* bro1 fl-ac bro1 *Hecla* bro1 merc-p bro1 phos bro1
  - **fever**: *Bapt* bro1 chin bro1 *Chinin-s* bro1 gels bro1 *Merc* bro1 phyt bro1
  - **pain** | **night**: asaf bro1 *Aur* bro1 calc-f bro1 cinnb bro1 *Cory* bro1 *Eup-per* bro1 fl-ac bro1 hep bro1 *Kali-bi* bro1 *Kali-i* bro1 lach bro1 lyc bro1 *Merc* bro1 *Mez* bro1 phos bro1 *Phyt* bro1 sars bro1 still bro1
  - **salivation**: *Clem* kr1* iod kr1* **Merc** kr1* **Nit-ac** kr1*
  - ○ **Glands**; complaints of: *Bad* bro1 carb-an bro1 graph bro1 *Hep* bro1 iod bro1 merc bro1 *Merc-i-f* bro1 *Merc-i-r* bro1 phyt bro1
  - **Hair** falling out: *Ars* bro1 aur bro1 carb-v bro1 cinnb bro1 *Fl-ac* bro1 graph bro1 *Hep* bro1 kali-i bro1 *Lyc* bro1 merc bro1 merc-i-f bro1 *Nit-ac* bro1 *Phos* bro1 sulph bro1
  - **Nails**; felon at root of: *Aethi-m* bro1 *Ant-c* bro1 ars bro1 graph bro1 kali-i bro1 *Merc* bro1 *Merc-act* bro1 *Merc-aur* bro1 *Merc-br* bro1 *Merc-c* bro1 *Merc-cy* bro1 *Merc-d* bro1 *Merc-i-f* bro1 *Merc-i-r* bro1 *Merc-ns* bro1 *Merc-p* bro1 *Merc-pr-r* bro1 *Merc-tn* bro1
  - **Tongue**:
    - **swelling**: crot-h kr1*
    - **white** discoloration of the: phyt kr1*
- **congenital**: *Aethi-m* br1* ars-i bro1 ars-met bro1 *Aur* bro1 aur-ar vh calc-f br1* *Calc-i* bro1 carc hbh cor-r bro1 kali-i bro1 kreos c1* *Merc* bro1 *Merc-d* bro1 *Nit-ac* bro1 pilo c1 psor br1* syph c1*
  - **accompanied** by | **keratitis**; interstitial: lob-e c1
- **first** stage (See Chancre)
- **infants**; in: bad ptk1
- **mercury**; from abuse of: ang bro1 *Aur* bro1 calo bro1 carb-an bro1 fl-ac bro1 *Hep* bro1 kali-i bro1 *Nit-ac* bro1 rhus-g bro1 sulph bro1
- **scrofulous** patients; in: aur br1 merc-i-r br1
- **second** stage: *Aur* bro1 berb-a br1* calo br1* *Cinnb* bro1 fl-ac bro1 *Graph* bro1 guaj br1* iod bro1 *Kali-bi* bro1 kali-i br1* lyc bro1 *Merc* br1* merc-br bro1 merc-c bro1 *Merc-i-f* bro1 *Merc-i-r* bro1 *Nit-ac* bro1 osm bro1 phos bro1 phyt bro1 rhus-g bro1 sars bro1 *Still* bro1 thuj bro1
- **serology**; with irreducible: astra-e jl

- **third** stage: *Aethi-m* bro1 ars-i bro1 *Aur* bro1 aur-m bro1 cal-ren bro1 calc bro1 calc-act bro1 calc-ar bro1 calc-br bro1 calc-caust bro1 calc-cn bro1 calc-f bro1 calc-hp bro1 calc-i bro1 calc-lac bro1 calc-lp bro1 calc-m bro1 calc-ox bro1 calc-p bro1 calc-pic bro1 calc-s bro1 calc-sil bro1 calc-st-s bro1 carb-v bro1 cinnb bro1 *Fl-ac* bro1 graph bro1 guaj bro1 iod bro1 *Kali-bi* bro1 kali-i br1* lap-a bro1 lyc bro1 *Merc* bro1 *Merc-act* bro1 *Merc-aur* bro1 *Merc-br* bro1 *Merc-c* bro1 *Merc-cy* bro1 *Merc-d* bro1 *Merc-i-f* bro1 *Merc-i-r* bro1 merc-k-i gm1 *Merc-ns* bro1 *Merc-p* bro1 *Merc-pr-r* bro1 *Merc-tn* bro1 *Mez* bro1 *Nit-ac* bro1 ph-ac bro1 phos br1* *Phyt* bro1 psor br1* staph bro1 strych-g br1* sulph bro1 thuj bro1

TAKING OFF something:

- **boots** | **agg.**: apis bg2 calc b2.de* graph b2.de*

TALKING:

- **agg.**: (↗*Weakness - talking; MIND - Conversation - agg.; MIND - Talking - agg.)* acon b2.de* agar b4a.de* alum b2.de* am-c b2.de* am-m b2.de* ambr b2.de* **Anac** b2.de* arg-met b2.de* arg-n bg2* *Arn* b2.de* ars b2.de* arum-t bg2* aur b2.de* bar-c b2.de* *Bell* b2.de* borx b2.de* both-a rb3 *Bry* b2.de* **Calc** b2.de* **Cann-s** b2.de* cann-xyz ptk1 canth b2.de* caps b2.de* *Carb-v* b2.de* carc jl2 caust b2.de* *Cham* b2.de* **Chin** b2.de* chinin-s bro1 cic b2.de* **Cocc** b2.de* coff b2.de* colch bg2 con b2.de* croc b2.de* dig b2.de* *Dros* b2.de* *Dulc* b2.de* euphr b2.de* ferr b2.de* ferr-p bg2 fl-ac bg2 *Graph* b2.de* hell b2.de* *Hep* b2.de* hyos b2.de* ign b2.de* *Iod* b2.de* ip b2.de* kali-c b2.de* led b2.de* lyc b2.de* mag-c b2.de* *Mag-m* b2.de* **Mang** b2.de* *Mang-act* bro1 merc b2.de* merc-c bg2 merc-cy bg2 mez b2.de* mur-ac b2.de* **Nat-c** b2.de* **Nat-m** b2.de* nux-m b2.de* nux-v b2.de* par b2.de* petr b2.de* **Ph-ac** b2.de* *Phos* b2.de* phyt bg2 plat b2.de* plb b2.de* puls b2.de* raja-s jl ran-b b2.de* **Rhus-t** b2.de* *Sars* b2.de* **Sel** b2.de* *Sep* b2.de* sil b2.de* *Spig* b2.de* spong bg2* squil b2.de* **Stann** b2.de* staph b2.de* stram b2.de* stront-c b2.de* sul-ac b2.de* **Sulph** b2.de* teucr b2.de* *Verat* b2.de* verb bro1
  - **long** time agg.; for a: nat-m ptk1
- **amel.**: ferr b2.de* rhus-t bg2 sel bg2 tritic-vg fd5.de
  - **conversation**: aeth c1

TALL people: (↗*Growth; Growth - length; Lean people)* calc-p ptk1 *Coff* br1 goss br1 mag-p ptk1 phos br1* tub mtf33 [alumin-p stj2 arg-p stj2 cupr-p stj2 ferr-sil stj2 lith-p stj2 mag-sil stj2 mang-p stj2 mang-sil stj2 nat-sil stj2 ph-ac stj1 plb-p stj2 sil stj2 sil-met stj2 zinc-p stj2]

- **children**; in: phos mtf33
- **obese**; and | **children**; in: cina br1*
- **thin**; and | **children**; in: calc-p ptk1

TEARING OUT of something; sensation of: alum ptk1 ang bg2 ars bg2 bell b2.de* bov b2.de* bry b2.de* calc b2.de* cann-s b2.de* caust b2.de* cocc b2.de* cycl b2.de* elaps ptk1 euph b2.de* ip b2.de* kreos bg2 m-arct b2.de mang b2.de* mez b2.de* mur-ac b2.de* nat-c b2.de* nat-m bg2 osm bg2 par b2.de* ph-ac b2.de* phos bg2 plat bg2 *Prun* ptk1 rhus-t b2.de* sep bg2 sil b2.de* spig b2.de* spong b2.de* stram b2.de*

TEETH:

- **biting** teeth together (See Biting - teeth)
- **brushing** teeth (See Brushing)
- **dentition** (See TEETH - Dentition)

TEMPERATURE:

- **change** of: acon k* act-sp kr1* aesc k2 all-s vh alum k* alumn kr1 *Ant-t* kr1* **Ars** k* bamb-a stb2.de• bar-c bg2* *Bell* vh* brom k2 brucel sa3• bufo bg2 calc sf1.de *Calc-p* bg2* *Carb-v* k* caust k* colch rsj2• dulc bg2* fic-m gya1 **Fl-ac** kr1* graph k* haliae-lc srj5• **Hep** vh* ip bg2* kali-i bg2* *Lach* bg2* lob vh* lyc k* *Mag-c* k* merc-c bg2* nat-c c1 nat-m bl nit-ac sf1.de *Nux-v* b2.de* *Pert* jl2 *Phos* b2.de* phys a1 *Puls* k* **Ran-b** k* ran-s k* rhod bg2* *Rhus-t* b2.de* rumx bg2* sabad bg2* *Sabin* k* sacch sst1• sang bg2* sep bg2 sil bg2* *Spong* b2.de* stict br1 sulph k* verat k* **Verb** k* [mang stj1 mang-act stj2 mang-m stj2 mang-met stj2 mang-n stj2 mang-s stj2 mang-sil stj2]
  - **cold** to warm: brom k2 ferr bg2 puls b7a.de ran-b b7a.de* rhus-t b7a.de sulph bg2
- **extreme** | **agg.**: ant-c ptk1 carb-v ptk1 caust ptk1 ip ptk1 lach ptk1 sul-ac ptk1 syph ptk1
- **moderate** | **amel.**: prot jl2

TEMPERATURE and pulse dissociated (See Pulse - discordant)

TENDERNESS (See Pain - sore)

TENSION: **Acon** bg2 am-c b4a.de *Am-m* b7a.de bar-c b4a.de cact bg2 carb-an b4a.de chin bg2 kali-c bg2 mang b4a.de *Mez* b4a.de nat-c bg2 olnd bg2 petr bg2 phos b4a.de puls b7a.de* rhus-t b7a.de sep b4a.de sulph b4a.de*

- **general**; in: agar bg2 alum ptk1 am-c bg2 am-m bg2* ambr bg2 apis bg2 ars ptk1 asaf ptk1 bar-c bg2* bell ptk1 *Bry* ptk1 cact ptk1 carb-an bg2 caust bg2* *Coloc* ptk1 con ptk1 dig ptk1 dios ptk1 graph bg2* guaj ptk1 kali-m ptk1 lach bg2* lyc ptk1 mag-p ptk1 merc ptk1 mez ptk1 *Nat-m* ptk1 *Nux-v* ptk1 par ptk1 **Phos** ptk1 plat ptk1 **Puls** ptk1 ran-b ptk1 rhus-t bg2* senec ptk1 *Sep* ptk1 stront-c ptk1 sulph bg2* syph ptk1 verb ptk1 viol-o ptk1 visc ptk1
  - **fever**; during: op bro1
- ○ - **Arteries**; of: (↗*Blood vessels - complaints - arteries)* acon br1 chlor a1 *Coff* a1* gels a1
  - **accompanied** by | **Head**; pain in: acon bro1 *Bell* bro1 *Glon* bro1 glyc bro1 ictod bro1 meli bro1 usn bro1 *Verat-v* bro1
  - **decreased**: coli jl2
- **Bones**; of: agar j5.de arg-met a1 *Asaf* k1 bar-c kr1 **Bell** k* bry *Chin* a1* cimic cocc *Con* crot-h dig dulc kali-bi mang j5.de merc nit-ac rhod *Ruta* k* *Sulph* *Valer* zinc k*
- **Externally**: acon k* agar k* agn k* aloe *Alum* k* alum-p k2* alum-sil k2* *Alumn* kr1 am-c k* *Am-m* k* ambr k* anac k* ang b2.de* ant-c k* ant-t k* apis bg2* ara-maca sej7• arg-met k* *Arg-n* *Arn* k* ars k* *Asaf* k* asar k* *Aur* k* *Aur-m-n* wbt2• aur-s k2* **Bar-c** k* bar-i k2* bar-m bar-s k2 *Bell* k* berb bism k* borx k* bov k* **Bry** k* calc k* camph k* cann-s k* canth k* caps k* *Carb-an* k* carb-v k* **Caust** k* cham k* *Chel* k* chin k* chinin-s j5.de cic k* clem k* cocc k* colch k* **Coloc** k* **Con** k* croc k* crot-h crot-t br1 *Cupr* k* dig k* dros k* dulc k* euph k* euphr k* *Ferr* k* germ-met srj5• glon graph k* guaj k* hell k* hep k* hyos k* ign k* iod k* ip k* kali-ar *Kali-c* k* kali-n k* kreos k* lach k* laur k* *Led* k* lyc k* m-ambo b2.de* *M-arct* b2.de* m-aust b2.de mag-c k* mag-m k* mang k* med hr1* meny k* *Merc* k* *Mez* k* *Mosch* k* mur-ac k* *Nat-c* k* nat-m k* nat-p nit-ac k* nux-m k* *Nux-v* k* *Olnd* k* op k* orot-ac rly4• par k* *Petr* k* ph-ac k* **Phos** k* pieri-b mlk9.de **Plat** k* plb k* **Puls** k* ran-b k* *Rheum* k* rhod k* **Rhus-t** k* ruta k* sabad k* *Sabin* k* sal-fr sle1• samb k* sars k* *Sec* seneg k* *Sep* k* sil k* *Spig* k* *Spong* k* squil k* stann k* *Staph* k* stram k* **Stront-c** k* sul-ac k* sul-i k2* **Sulph** k* tarax k* teucr k* *Thuj* k* valer k* verat k* **Verb** k* *Viol-o* k* viol-t k* x-ray sp1 *Zinc* k*
  - **prevents** motion: apis st
  - **tremulous**: petr h2
- **Glands**; of: alum k* am-c j5.de ambr k* ang b2.de* arg-met k* arn k* aur k* *Bar-c* k* bell k* bov k* *Bry* k* calc k* carb-an k* *Caust* k* clem k* coloc k* *Con* k* dulc k* graph k* kali-c k* lyc k* m-ambo b2.de* m-arct b2.de* merc k* mur-ac k* nux-v k* **Phos** k* *Puls* k* *Rhus-t* k* sabad k* sabin k* sep k* sil k* *Spong* k* staph k* stront-c k* *Sulph* k* thuj k*
- **Internally**: acon k* aesc agar k* agn k* aids nl2• alum k* alum-sil k2 am-m k* ambr k* anac k* ang b2.de* ant-c k* *Ant-t* k* apis bg2 arg-met k* arn k* *Ars* k* **Asaf** k* asar k* *Aur* k* bar-c k* bar-i k2 bar-s k2 **Bell** k* *Berb* bov k* bry k* *Calc* k* camph k* cann-s k* *Caps* k* *Carb-ac* carb-an k* carb-v k* *Caust* k* cham k* chel k* chin k* *Cic* k* *Clem* k* coc-c cocc k* coff k* colch k* *Coloc* k* com con k* croc k* crot-t k* cupr k* cycl k* dig k* dros k* *Dulc* k* euph k* euphr k* ferr k* gels *Glon* *Graph* k* guaj h2 hell k* hep k* hydr-ac hyos k* *Hyper* ign k* iod k* ip k* kali-c k* *Kali-n* k* kola stb3• kreos k* lac-lup hm2• lach k* lact bg1 laur k* led k* lob **Lyc** k* m-ambo b2.de* m-arct b2.de m-aust b2.de mag-c k* mag-m k* mang k* med br1 meny k* *Merc* k* mez k* moni rfm1• *Mosch* k* mur-ac k* naja nat-c k* nat-m k* *Nit-ac* k* nux-m k* **Nux-v** k* olnd k* *Op* k* osm ozone sde2• **Par** k* petr k* ph-ac k* **Phos** k* pieri-b mlk9.de plat k* plb k* positr nl2• **Puls** k* **Ran-b** ran-s k* rauw sp1 *Rheum* k* rhod k* *Rhus-t* k* ruta k* sabad k* sabin k* sal-fr sle1• samb k* sec k* seneg k* **Sep** k* sil k* *Spig* k* spong k* squil k* *Stann* k* *Staph* k* *Stram* k* **Stront-c** k* sul-ac k* sul-i k2 **Sulph** k* tab tarax k* teucr k* thuj k* tritic-vg fd5.de valer k* *Verat* k* verb k* *Zinc* k* [spect dfg1]
  - **electric**-like: ozone sde2•
- **Joints**; of: am-c j5.de *Am-m* b7a.de anac b2.de* ant-t b2.de* **Arg-met** b2.de* arn b2.de* ars b2.de* asaf b2.de* bell b2.de* *Bov* b2.de* **Bry** b2.de* calc b2.de* caltha a1 caps b2.de* carb-an b2.de* carb-v b2.de* *Carl* a1 **Caust** b2.de* cham b2.de* clem a1 colch b2.de* coloc b2.de* con b2.de* *Croc* b2.de* dig b2.de* dros b2.de* euph b2.de* euphr b2.de* graph b2.de* hell b2.de* hep b2.de* iod b2.de* *Kali-c* b2.de* kali-n b2.de* kreos b2.de* lach b2.de* laur b2.de* **Led** b2.de* **Lyc** b2.de* *Mag-c* b2.de* manc a1 *Mang* b2.de* merc b2.de* *Mez* b2.de*

- **Joints**; of: ...
mur-ac b2.de* **Nat-m** b2.de* *Nit-ac* b2.de* nux-v b2.de* par b2.de* petr b2.de* phos b2.de* plat b2.de* **Puls** b2.de* rheum b2.de* *Rhod* b2.de* rhus-t b2.de* ruta b2.de* samb b2.de* *Seneg* b2.de* **Sep** b2.de* sil b2.de* spig b2.de* spong b2.de* *Stann* b2.de* sul-ac b2.de* **Sulph** b2.de* *Teucr* b2.de* verat b2.de* verb b2.de* zinc b2.de*
- **Ligaments**; of: guaj bg2 sep bg2
- **Muscles**; of: *(↗Complaints - muscles)* **Acon** k* acon-ac rly4• agar mrr1 am-c j5.de am-m k* anac k* ang h1* ant-c k* arn k* ars k* bell k* berb bg2 bufo bg2 cann-i cann-s k* canth caps bg2 carb-v k* caust k* chin k* cupr sst3* dulc k* graph k* *Guaj* k* haliae-lc srj5• kali-ar k2 kali-c k* kali-m k2 lac-e hrn2• lach k* led k* *Mosch* k* *Nat-c* k* *Nat-m* k* nat-p k2 **Nit-ac** k* **Nux-v** k* olnd k* ph-ac k* **Phos** b2.de* **Phys** phyt *Plat* k* plb k* prot fmm1• *Puls* k* *Rhus-t* k* sal-fr sle1• **Sep** k* *Sil* stann k* staph k* sulph k* verb k* wies a1 zinc k* zinc-p k2
  - **menses**; from suppressed: *Phos* b4a.de
- **Nerves**; in | **sensation** as if a nerve were drawn tight, then suddenly let go: nat-m bg2

TETANUS: *Acon* bro1 aconin bro1 aml-ns bro1 anac tl1 ang bro1* arn bro1 bell bro1* calen bro1 camph bro1 carbn-s bro1 chlol bro1 cic br1* cocc br1* con bro1 cortico sp1 cupr bro1* *Cur* bro1 diph-t-tpt jl2 *Gels* bro1 hydr-ac bro1* hyos bro1* hyper br1* ign bro1* ip bro1* kali-br bro1 lach bro1 lat-m br1* laur bro1 led br1* lyss bro1 mag-p bro1 morph bro1 mosch bro1 nicot bro1 nux-v bro1* oena bro1 op bro1* ox-ac bro1 *Passi* br1* petr ptk1 *Phys* br1* phyt br1* plat bro1 scor a1* stram bro1* strept-ent jl2 *Stry* br1* tab bro1* ter bro1 thebin bro1 *Upa* br1* verat bro1 verat-v ptk1 zinc bro1
- **accompanied** by:
  - **narcolepsy**: hydr-ac br1
  - ○ **Muscles**; twitching of muscles near wound: led br1
- **convulsions** (See Convulsions - tetanic)
- **lasting** for days: lat-m ptk1
- **prophylaxis**: **Arn** st1 hell k2 **Hyper** k2* lat-m br1* **Led** k2* phys bro1 scor a1* tetox st1 thuj st1
- **tobacco**; from swallowing: ip ptk1

THALASSEMIA: cadm-met mtf11

THIN people (See Lean people)

THIRST (See STOMACH - Thirst)

THIRSTLESS (See STOMACH - Thirstless)

THREADS, sensation of: *(↗Pain - bones - drawing - thread)* all-c bg2 arg-met bg2 *Ars* bg2 bell bg2 bry k* caps bg2 caust bg2 choc srj3• coc-c k* croc bg2 ign k* *Kali-bi* bg2 lac-c bg2 lach k* laur bg2 lyc bg2 mosch bg2 *Nat-m* bg2 nat-p bg2 nux-v bg2* *Osm* k* par k* *Plat* k* ptel bg2 puls bg2 ran-b bg2 rhus-t bg2 *Sabad* bg2* *Sil* bg2 *Sulph* bg2 ther bg2 **Valer** k*

THROBBING (See Pulsation)

THROMBOANGITIS obliterans: kres mtf11

THROMBOCYTOPENIA; idiopathic: *(↗Hemorrhage; Laboratory - platelets - decreased; SKIN - Purpura; SKIN - Purpura - idiopathica)* both mtf cortico sp1 cortiso sp1 phos mtf sec mtf
- **chronic**: chlorpr mtf11

THROMBOEMBOLISM: cortico sp1

THROMBOSIS: *(↗Inflammation - blood - veins)* acetan c1* am-caust br1 *Apis* kr1* arn br1* *Ars* k* bit-ar wht1• *Both* br1* calc-ar hr1* carb-v h2* cortico sp1 ham ptk1* *Kali-chl* hr1* *Kali-m* bg2* kres srb2.fr lach br1* *Nat-s* hr1* quinhydr mtf11 sec c1* *Vip* bg2*
- **albuminuria**, in: calc-ar hr1*
- **hard**: card-m ptk1 fl-ac ptk1
- **pneumonia**; in: am-c hr1*
- **wet** agg.: *Nat-s* st1

THUNDERSTORM (See Weather - thunderstorm)

TICKLING: sep bg2
- **amel.**: sep ptk1
- ○ **Glands**: *Kali-c* b2.de plat b2.de

TICKLING internal (See Itching - internally)

TICKLISH (See MIND - Touched - aversion - ticklishness)

TICS (See MIND - Gestures - tics)

TIME table; generalized:
- **1** h: [abel stj1 abrot stj1 agar stj1 agav-t stj1 agre stj1 all-c stj1 aran stj1 aran-ix stj1 aran-sc stj1 ars stj1 ars-br stj1 ars-h stj1 ars-i stj1 ars-met stj1 ars-n stj1 ars-s-f stj1 ars-s-r stj1 aster stj1 buni-o stj1 but-ac stj1 cadm-ar stj1 calc-ar stj1 camph stj1 canth stj1 carb-v stj1 caul stj1 cent stj1 chin stj1 chinin-ar stj1 chlorpr stj1 cic stj1 cocc stj1 com stj1 crot-c stj1 crot-h stj1 cur stj1 dirc stj1 dol stj1 ferr-ar stj1 foll stj1 gal-ac stj1 haem stj1 inul stj1 iodof stj1 jac-c stj1 kali-ar stj1 lachn stj1 lept stj1 mez stj1 nat-ar stj1 pall stj1 pers stj1 plb stj1 psor stj1 quas stj1 rob stj1 sarcol-ac stj1 sarr stj1 spig stj1 spig-m stj1 spirae stj1 sulo-ac stj1 syph stj1 tab stj1 tax stj1 ter stj1 thal stj1 trios stj1]
- **3** h: aral vh ars-s-f vh [adlu stj1 aeth stj1 am-ar stj1 am-be stj1 am-br stj1 am-c stj1 am-caust stj1 am-i stj1 am-m stj1 am-n stj1 am-p stj1 am-pic stj1 am-s stj1 am-t stj1 am-val stj1 am-van stj1 ant-t stj1 anth stj1 ap-g stj1 arist-cl stj1 arn stj1 arum-m stj1 arum-t stj1 asc-t stj1 aur stj1 bac stj1 benz-ac stj1 berb stj1 bufo stj1 cain stj1 carb-v stj1 chin stj1 chinin-ar stj1 chloram stj1 cimic stj1 cist stj1 coc-c stj1 coch stj1 coff stj1 coff-t stj1 com stj1 con stj1 corn stj1 crot-h stj1 cub stj1 cupr stj1 der stj1 dig stj1 digin stj1 digox stj1 dros stj1 ferr stj1 ferr-act stj1 ferr-ar stj1 ferr-br stj1 ferr-c stj1 ferr-cit stj1 ferr-cy stj1 ferr-i stj1 ferr-lac stj1 ferr-m stj1 ferr-ma stj1 ferr-o-r stj1 ferr-p stj1 ferr-p-h stj1 ferr-pern stj1 ferr-pic stj1 ferr-prox stj1 ferr-py stj1 ferr-r stj1 ferr-s stj1 ferr-t stj1 gent-c stj1 gent-l stj1 gent-q stj1 gink-b stj1 gins stj1 gnaph stj1 grin stj1 hed stj1 helio stj1 hydroph stj1 hyper stj1 ign stj1 ind stj1 inul stj1 iris stj1 iris-fa stj1 iris-ps stj1 iris-t stj1 jac-c stj1 jal stj1 jug-c stj1 kali-act stj1 kali-ar stj1 kali-bi stj1 kali-biox stj1 kali-bit stj1 kali-br stj1 kali-c stj1 kali-caust stj1 kali-chl stj1 kali-chls stj1 kali-chr stj1 kali-cit stj1 kali-cy stj1 kali-f stj1 kali-fcy stj1 kali-hp stj1 kali-m stj1 kali-n stj1 kali-ox stj1 kali-perm stj1 kali-pic stj1 kali-s stj1 kali-s-chr stj1 kali-sal stj1 kali-sil stj1 kali-sula stj1 kali-sulo stj1 kali-t stj1 kali-x stj1 kalm stj1 led stj1 lil-t stj1 lyss stj1 med stj1 menis stj1 merl stj1 phyt stj1 raph stj1 raphani stj1 rat stj1 rumx stj1 samb stj1 samb-c stj1 samb-e stj1 sarr stj1 sars stj1 sec stj1 sel stj1 spig stj1 stict stj1 stront-br stj1 stront-c stj1 stront-i stj1 stront-met stj1 stront-n stj1 tanac stj1 tell stj1 ter stj1 thea stj1 thuj stj1 thuj-l stj1 uran-n stj1 wildb stj1 xanth stj1 zinc stj1]
- **5** h: [abies-c stj1 abies-n stj1 abrot stj1 absin stj1 allox stj1 aloe stj1 alum-sil stj1 am-s stj1 aml-ns stj1 ang stj1 ant-c stj1 ant-s-r stj1 ars-s-f stj1 ars-s-r stj1 aspar stj1 aur-s stj1 bol-la stj1 bol-lu stj1 bol-s stj1 bov stj1 cadm-ar stj1 cadm-br stj1 cadm-f stj1 cadm-i stj1 cadm-m stj1 cadm-met stj1 cadm-o stj1 cadm-s stj1 caj stj1 calc-s stj1 carb-ac stj1 cedr stj1 chin stj1 chinin-s stj1 chlor stj1 chr-ac stj1 chr-met stj1 chr-o stj1 chr-s stj1 cob stj1 con stj1 cupr-s stj1 dig stj1 dios stj1 dulc stj1 euph stj1 euphr stj1 ferr-p stj1 ferr-s stj1 fl-ac stj1 gamb stj1 hep stj1 iod stj1 kali-i stj1 kali-s stj1 kali-s-chr stj1 mag-s stj1 meph stj1 merc-s-cy stj1 merc-sul stj1 nat-s stj1 nat-s-c stj1 nuph stj1 nux-v stj1 ox-ac stj1 par stj1 penic stj1 phyt stj1 pyre-o stj1 pyre-p stj1 pyre-r stj1 raph stj1 rat stj1 rheum stj1 rumx stj1 ruta stj1 sabal stj1 sacch stj1 sel stj1 seneg stj1 sul-ac stj1 sul-i stj1 sul-ter stj1 sulfon stj1 sulfonam stj1 sulo-ac stj1 sulph stj1 sumb stj1 tanac stj1 tarax stj1 tell stj1 ther stj1 tril-p stj1 trom stj1 uva stj1 verat stj1 verat-n stj1 verat-v stj1 vesp stj1 xanth stj1]
- **7** h: arg-met vh [acal stj1 ail stj1 apoc stj1 arn stj1 benzo stj1 chion stj1 cop stj1 crot-h stj1 crot-t stj1 eup-per stj1 eup-pur stj1 gnaph stj1 haem stj1 halo stj1 harp stj1 iris-t stj1 lac-ac stj1 lach stj1 lachn stj1 mag-act stj1 mag-bcit stj1 mag-c stj1 mag-f stj1 mag-i stj1 mag-m stj1 mag-p stj1 mag-s stj1 mag-u stj1 myric stj1 paull stj1 petr stj1 podo stj1 spig stj1 spig-m stj1 trif-p stj1 trif-r stj1 tril-p stj1 ust stj1 uva stj1 verat-v stj1 vesp stj1 xanth stj1]
- **9** h: [aesc stj1 all-c stj1 alst stj1 alum stj1 alum-p stj1 alum-sil stj1 alumin stj1 alumin-act stj1 alumn stj1 aqui stj1 asaf stj1 astra-e stj1 bol-la stj1 cann-i stj1 cann-s stj1 caps stj1 carb-ac stj1 carbn-s stj1 cham stj1 cimx stj1 cina stj1 cocc stj1 conv stj1 cop stj1 cub stj1 cycl stj1 dirc stj1 dros stj1 elaps stj1 fago stj1 form stj1 hir stj1 hura stj1 hydr stj1 ign stj1 ille stj1 iod stj1 ip stj1 lac-ac stj1 lac-c stj1 lachn stj1 leon stj1 meli stj1 meny stj1 mez stj1 nat-n stj1 peti stj1 ptel stj1 sep stj1 sil stj1 sumb stj1 tell stj1 valer stj1 verb stj1 verb-n stj1 vesp stj1 wye stj1]
- **11** h: [abrot stj1 absin stj1 ambr stj1 arg-met stj1 arum-t stj1 asaf stj1 asar stj1 bapt stj1 berb stj1 borx stj1 caps stj1 carb-v stj1 castm stj1 chin stj1 chinid stj1 chinin-ar stj1 chinin-br stj1 chinin-brh stj1 chinin-m stj1 chinin-s stj1 chinin-sal stj1 chinin-val stj1 chlor stj1 cimic stj1 coll stj1 corn stj1 daph stj1 equis-a stj1 equis-h stj1 euphr stj1 gels stj1 guaj stj1 hydr stj1 ign stj1 ind stj1 iod stj1 ip stj1 jac-c stj1 kalm stj1 lob stj1 mag-p stj1 nat-act stj1 nat-ar stj1 nat-be stj1 nat-bic stj1 nat-br stj1 nat-c stj1 nat-cac stj1 nat-ch stj1 nat-f stj1 nat-hchls stj1 nat-hsulo stj1 nat-i stj1 nat-lac stj1 nat-m stj1 nat-n stj1 nat-ns stj1 nat-p stj1 nat-s stj1 nat-s-c stj1 nat-sal stj1 nat-sel stj1 nat-sil stj1 nat-sil-f stj1 nat-suc stj1 nat-sula stj1 nat-sulo stj1 nat-taur stj1 nat-tel stj1 ox-ac stj1 pall stj1 phyt stj1 plan stj1 plb stj1 psor stj1 raph stj1 sec stj1

- **11 h**: ...
sel stj1 spig stj1 squil stj1 stann stj1 stann-i stj1 stann-m stj1 stann-pchl stj1 sulph stj1 til stj1 vanad stj1 viol-o stj1 viol-t stj1 zinc stj1 zing stj1]
- **13 h**: [ail stj1 anh stj1 arg-col stj1 arg-met stj1 arg-mur stj1 arg-n stj1 arg-o stj1 arg-p stj1 arge stj1 aster stj1 bad stj1 cic stj1 cina stj1 cist stj1 clem stj1 coca stj1 cocain stj1 coff stj1 coff-t stj1 coffin stj1 coll stj1 com stj1 dirc stj1 elat stj1 euphr stj1 gent-l stj1 graph stj1 grat stj1 ham stj1 hura stj1 ind stj1 iodof stj1 kalm stj1 lac-ac stj1 laur stj1 lycps-v stj1 lyss stj1 nicc stj1 nicc-s stj1 nux-m stj1 ol-an stj1 paeon stj1 pall stj1 phel stj1 phos stj1 plan stj1 plat stj1 polyg-h stj1 polyp-p stj1 ptel stj1 sabad stj1 sanic stj1 sars stj1 sel stj1 senec stj1 sil stj1 sol-t-ae stj1 spig stj1 squil stj1 stann stj1 stann-i stj1 stann-m stj1 stann-pchl stj1 still stj1 teucr stj1 teucr-s stj1 ust stj1 valer stj1 vanad stj1 verat-v stj1]
- **15 h**: anth vh aster vh caul a caust a cean a cedr a [agar stj1 ang stj1 ant-ar stj1 ant-c stj1 ant-i stj1 ant-o stj1 ant-s-aur stj1 ant-t stj1 apis stj1 apisin stj1 apoc stj1 arn stj1 asaf stj1 asar stj1 asc-t stj1 aza stj1 bad stj1 bell stj1 bol-la stj1 bol-lu stj1 bol-s stj1 borx stj1 brom stj1 buth-a stj1 calc stj1 calc-act stj1 calc-ar stj1 calc-br stj1 calc-caust stj1 calc-chln stj1 calc-f stj1 calc-hp stj1 calc-i stj1 calc-lac stj1 calc-ln stj1 calc-lp stj1 calc-m stj1 calc-o-t stj1 calc-ox stj1 calc-p stj1 calc-pic stj1 calc-s stj1 calc-sil stj1 calc-st-s stj1 cench stj1 chinin-s stj1 chr-ac stj1 cinnm stj1 clem stj1 clem-vir stj1 clem-vit stj1 coca stj1 cocc stj1 coff stj1 com stj1 con stj1 cur stj1 erio stj1 fago stj1 ferr stj1 ferr-i stj1 fl-ac stj1 gent-l stj1 gnaph stj1 guaj stj1 helon stj1 hura stj1 hura-c stj1 iber stj1 iris-t stj1 jac-c stj1 kalm stj1 kreos stj1 lat-m stj1 laur stj1 led stj1 lycps-v stj1 meny stj1 naja stj1 ol-an stj1 par stj1 phel stj1 pip-m stj1 plan stj1 plb stj1 reser stj1 sal-ac stj1 sal-n stj1 sal-p stj1 sang stj1 sangin-n stj1 sarr stj1 sars stj1 senec stj1 sol-t-ae stj1 staph stj1 still stj1 tab stj1 tax stj1 tell stj1 tell-ac stj1 thea stj1 thuj stj1 vesp stj1 wye stj1]
- **17 h**: anth vh [anac stj1 ange-s stj1 arg-n stj1 arum-t stj1 berb stj1 berb-a stj1 berbin stj1 bov stj1 bufo stj1 buth-a stj1 buth-af stj1 buth-oc stj1 caps stj1 carb-an stj1 carbn-s stj1 carc stj1 card-m stj1 castm stj1 cench stj1 chel stj1 colch stj1 coloc stj1 con stj1 cupr stj1 cupr-act stj1 cupr-ar stj1 cupr-c stj1 cupr-cy stj1 cupr-m stj1 cupr-n stj1 cupr-o stj1 cupr-s stj1 cyno stj1 cyt-l stj1 dig stj1 dios stj1 dol stj1 elaps stj1 equis-a stj1 eys stj1 fago stj1 ferr-p stj1 gamb stj1 gent-l stj1 ham stj1 hell stj1 hip-ac stj1 hyper stj1 ign stj1 indg stj1 jab stj1 kali-br stj1 kali-perm stj1 lac-c stj1 lac-d stj1 lil-t stj1 lyc stj1 mang stj1 mang-coll stj1 mang-m stj1 mang-o stj1 mang-s stj1 methys stj1 mill stj1 myric stj1 nep stj1 nux-m stj1 ox-ac stj1 paeon stj1 petr stj1 phel stj1 phys stj1 pic-ac stj1 ptel stj1 puls stj1 puls-n stj1 sabad stj1 sabin stj1 sacch-l stj1 sarr stj1 sars stj1 sep stj1 sin-a stj1 sin-n stj1 sol-t-ae stj1 stram stj1 tarent stj1 thuj stj1 til stj1 trios stj1 trom stj1 tub stj1 v-a-b stj1 valer stj1 x-ray stj1 zing stj1]
- **19 h**: [aesc stj1 agn stj1 ambr stj1 arum-i stj1 bad stj1 bals-p stj1 bar-c stj1 bov stj1 brom stj1 cain stj1 caj stj1 calc stj1 canth stj1 carb-an stj1 carbn-s stj1 castm stj1 caust stj1 cedr stj1 cic stj1 cimic stj1 cocc stj1 cocc-s stj1 com stj1 culx stj1 cycl stj1 cyno stj1 dirc stj1 elaps stj1 elat stj1 euph stj1 fago stj1 ferr stj1 fl-ac stj1 form stj1 gamb stj1 gins stj1 grat stj1 guaj stj1 gymno stj1 ham stj1 hep stj1 hyper stj1 ip stj1 iris-fa stj1 jab stj1 kreos stj1 lachn stj1 lil-t stj1 lob stj1 lycps-v stj1 mag-c stj1 ol-j stj1 osm stj1 palo stj1 ph-ac stj1 phos stj1 phys stj1 pyrog stj1 raph stj1 rauw stj1 rhod stj1 rhodi stj1 rhus-a stj1 rhus-c stj1 rhus-d stj1 rhus-t stj1 rhus-v stj1 sabad stj1 seneg stj1 sin-n stj1 spira stj1 stict stj1 stry stj1 stry-ar stj1 stry-n stj1 stry-p stj1 stry-s stj1 stry-val stj1 sulfa stj1 sulfon stj1 sumb stj1 tarax stj1 tarent stj1 tarent-c stj1 ter stj1 trom stj1 tub stj1 zing stj1]
- **21 h**: ant-c vh asc-t vh [all-c stj1 all-s stj1 arum-i stj1 arum-t stj1 bar-m stj1 brom stj1 bry stj1 calc-p stj1 carbn-s stj1 castm stj1 cham stj1 cinnb stj1 cist stj1 coca stj1 croc stj1 cycl stj1 elaps stj1 erig stj1 eupi stj1 ferr-i stj1 ferr-ma stj1 fl-ac stj1 form stj1 gels stj1 gnaph stj1 ham stj1 hecla stj1 helon stj1 hypoth stj1 indg stj1 jug-c stj1 jug-r stj1 kali-n stj1 kreos stj1 laur stj1 led stj1 lyss stj1 mag-c stj1 mag-p stj1 meli stj1 merc stj1 merc-act stj1 merc-aur stj1 merc-br stj1 merc-c stj1 merc-cy stj1 merc-d stj1 merc-i-f stj1 merc-i-r stj1 merc-k-i stj1 merc-meth stj1 merc-n stj1 merc-p stj1 merc-pr-a stj1 merc-pr-f stj1 merc-pr-r stj1 merc-sul stj1 merc-tn stj1 merl stj1 mur-ac stj1 myric stj1 nit-ac stj1 nit-m-ac stj1 osm stj1 palo stj1 ph-ac stj1 phel stj1 phos stj1 phys stj1 pic-ac stj1 polyg-a stj1 ptel stj1 saroth stj1 sarr stj1 sep stj1 sil stj1 stroph-h stj1 sul-ac stj1 sym-r stj1 tarax stj1 tax stj1 trom stj1 urt-u stj1 valer stj1]
- **23 h**: ant-c vh [acon stj1 acon-a stj1 acon-c stj1 acon-f stj1 acon-l stj1 acon-s stj1 aconin stj1 am-m stj1 ant-t stj1 aral stj1 aral-h stj1 bell stj1 berb stj1 berb-a stj1 berbin stj1 bism stj1 cact stj1 calad stj1 caps stj1 carb-an stj1 castm stj1 cere-b stj1 cina stj1 cist stj1 coc-c stj1 coff stj1 coff-t stj1 con stj1 cop stj1 corn stj1 croc stj1 dulc stj1 elaps stj1 euph stj1 euphr stj1 fago stj1 fel stj1 form stj1 form-ac stj1 grat stj1 indg stj1 iod stj1 iris stj1 iris-fa stj1 iris-ps stj1 iris-t stj1 kalm stj1 laur stj1 lec stj1 lyss stj1 meph stj1 merc stj1 merc-i-f stj1 merc-i-r stj1 mill stj1 myric stj1 naja stj1 op stj1 podo stj1 prun stj1 ran-a stj1 ran-b stj1 ran-fi stj1 ran-fl stj1 ran-g stj1 ran-r stj1 ran-s stj1 raph stj1 rumx stj1 spong stj1 squil stj1 stram stj1 sumb stj1 valer stj1 vib stj1]

TINEA CAPITIS (See HEAD - Eruptions - ringworm)

TINEA VERSICOLOR (See SKIN - Eruptions - pityriasis versicolor)

TINGLING: *Acon* br1* agath-a nl2• ail tl1 bov br1 croc br1 hyper br1 kalm ptk1 sec ptk1 thyr br1
- **pain**:
  - **after**: sec ptk1
  - **during**: agar br1

○ - **Nerves**: med br1

TIRED (See Weakness)

TOBACCO:
- **agg.**: (↗*MIND - Smoking*) *Abies-n* bg2* acon k* act-sp hr1* agar k* *Alum* k* *Alumn* k* ambr k* amp rly4• anac b4.de* ang b2.de* *Ant-c* k* aral vh arg-met k* arg-n k* arn bg2 **Ars** k* ars-i ptk1 asc-t c1* aur-m-n sf1.de* bell k* borx bro1 brom k2* *Bry* k* cact bg2* caj vml3• *Calad* k* calc k* calc-caust sf1.de calc-p bro1 camph k* cann-i br1* carb-an k* carbn-s caust hr1 cham bg2* chel chin k* chinin-ar c1* chinin-m c1* cic k* *Clem* k* coc-c k* coca k* *Cocc* k* *Coff* bg2* coloc k* con conv bg2* cupr bg2 *Cycl* k* dig k* dor hr1* *Dros* b7a.de *Euphr* k* ferr k* ferr-i mrr1 *Gels* k* granit-m es1*• ham a1 *Hell* k* hep k* hydr iber vml3• ictod vml3• **Ign** k* ina-i mlk9.de iod k* *Ip* k* kali-bi bg2* kali-br bg2* kalm bg2* lac-ac k* *Lach* k* lob c1* *Lyc* k* *M-ambo* b2.de* m-arct b2.de* *Mag-c* k* mag-m jl3 mand mg1.de *Meny* k* merc b4.de* mur-ac bro1 naja bg2* **Nat-ar** sne nat-c bg2 *Nat-m* k* nep vml3• nicot c1* **Nux-v** k* okou jl3 osm k* *Par* k* paraf vml3• petr k* phasco-ci rbp2 *Phos* k* **Plan** k* plb bro1 psil jl3* **Puls** k* rad-br ptk1 ran-b k* rhus-t k* *Ruta* k* sabad k* sabin k* sars k* scut c1* sec bro1 *Sel* k* seneg b4.de sep k* sil k* sol-mm c1* **Spig** k* **Spong** k* stann b4.de* **Staph** k* stel bro1* strept-ent jl2 stront-c bg2 stroph-h c1* succ-ac vml3• sul-ac k* sulph k* tab bg2* *Tama* vml3• *Tarax* k* *Thuj* k* verat k* zinc b4.de [alumin stj2 alumin-p stj2 alumin-s stj2 am-br stj2 arg-p stj2 bar-br stj2 cadm-m stj2 cadm-met stj2 cadm-s stj2 calc-br stj1 mag-br stj1 nat-br stj2 osm-met stj2 tung-met stj2]
  - **boys**; in: arg-n bro1 ars bro1 verat bro1
  - **nicotinism**: ign mg1.de nux-v mg1.de okou jl tab mg1.de
    - **accompanied** by | **Tongue**; cracked: nux-v kr1*
  - **smell** of: *Asc-t* vml3• gink-b vml3• osm vml3•
  - **smoke** of tobacco; by: acon bro1* alum tl1 aran vh1 brom ptk1 cic br1* cocc bro1* ferr-i mrr1 ign bro1* staph bro1
  - **smoking**, when breaking of: calad k* led tl1
- **amel.**: aran k* aran-ix mg1.de* arn sf1.de borx k* carb-ac k* coloc k* *Hep* k* levo jl3* lycpr vml3• melal-alt gya4 merc k* naja bg2* nat-c k* *Nat-s* hr1 plat ptk1 *Sep* k* spig k* stront-c ptk1 tarent bg2*
  - **smell** of: lycps-v vml3•
- **aversion** to: abrom-a ks5* acon acon-l a1 alum b4.de* alum-p vml3• androc srj1• ant-t k* arg-met vh arg-n st arn k* ars b4a.de asar b7.de* asc-t vml3• bell b4.de* borx k* bov gsw1 brom k* bry k* **Calc** k* *Camph* k* *Canth* k* *Carb-an* k* chen-a vml3• chin b7.de* chlol gsw1 chlor k* cimic k* clem a1 coc-c k* cocc b7.de* coff b7.de* con k* crot-h vml3• dream-p sdj1• ger-i rly4• gink-b vml3• grat bg2* hera vml3• hydrc c1* hydrog vml3• *Ign* k* ip b7.de* jug-r a1* kali-bi bg2 *Lach* k* led b7.de* *Lob* j5.de* *Lyc* k* m-ambo b7.de* mag-s k* mand sp1 meph k* mez b4.de* nat-ar a1 *Nat-c* b4a.de *Nat-m* k* nep vml3• nux-m b7.de* **Nux-v** k* olnd b7.de* *Op* oxal-a rly4• par b7.de* paraf vml3• *Phos* k* phys vml3• phyt c1* plan br1* plat b4.de* positr nl2• psor *Puls* k* rhus-t b7.de* sars b4.de* sep b4.de* sil b4a.de spig k* stann b4.de* staph bg2* stry st suis-em rly4• *Sulph* k* symph fd3.de• tarax k* thal vml3• thuj k* til k* v-a-b jl valer zing k* [tell stj2]
  - **morning**: meph positr nl2•
  - **cigarettes**: v-a-b jl2
  - **smell** of tobacco; sensitive to: agar a1 ars-h kr1 *Asc-t* kr1 *Bell* *Casc* kr1* chin elaps hr1 gink-b sbd1• *Ign* k* *Lac-ac* vml3• *Lob* kr1* *Lyc* kr1 lyss *Nux-v* phos *Puls* sol-ni a1* spig hr1 symph fd3.de• tab a1 [heroin sdj2]
  - **smoking** his accustomed cigar: alum alum-p k2 alumn gsw1 ant-t kr1 arg-met *Arn* asar k* borx *Brom* k* bry k* *Calc* calc-p k* *Camph* carb-an k* *Casc* kr1 chen-a c1 clem k* coc-c coff k* con h2 euphr k* ferr k2* ferr-i a1 gink-b sbd1• grat k* haliae-lc srj5• **Ign** k* jug-r a1 kali-bi k* kali-n k* lach k* led h1 lil-t tl1 *Lyc* k* mag-s k* nat-ar nat-m nat-s k* nat-sil fd3.de• nicc k* *Nux-v* kr1* olnd k* op k* ox-ac k* phos k* plat h2 positr nl2• psor k* *Puls* k* sars h2 sep k* spig k* *Sulph* symph fd3.de• tarax k* tell k* v-a-b jl vip fkr4.de
    - **morning**: ox-ac
    - **forenoon**: kali-bi

- **aversion** to – **smoking** his accustomed cigar: ...
  - ⁝ **afternoon**: ign k*
  - ⁝ **evening**: *Arg-n* kr1
  - ⁝ **breakfast**; after: psor a1
  - ⁝ **in** spite of his distaste for tobacco; smokes much: thiop jl3
- • **snuff**: spig b7a.de*
- **chewing** tobacco; from: **Ars** k* carb-v ign bro1 lyc k* *Nux-v* *Plan* k* sel bro1 tab kr1* verat k*
- **desire** for tobacco: acon-l vml3• aran-ix mg1.de* *Ars* c1 asar bro1* bell brucel sa3• calad k2* *Calc-p* bg2* *Camph* c1* carb-ac k* carb-v bro1* card-m vml3• castor-eq vml3• *Chin* c1 chir-fl gya2 chlor a1* *Coca* kr1* coff bg1 con a1* daph k* dulc fd4.de eug k* falco-pe nl2• galla-q-r nl2• glon bg2* granit-m es1*• ham a1 hydrog stj2*• ictod vml3• kali-s fd4.de kreos k* lyss mrr1 m-ambo vml3• manc k* med k2* melal-alt gya4 narz a1 nat-c k* nicot st nux-v k* *Olib-sac* wmh1 ox-ac k* pall sne *Phos* c1 pin-con oss2• plan c1* plat k* plb k* positr nl2• rhus-t bg1 sal-fr sle1• *Spig* c1 spong fd4.de *Staph* k* **Tab** k* *Tama* vml3• ther k* thiop vml3• thuj k* tritic-vg fd5.de vanil fd5.de [am-br stj2 am-c stj1 am-caust stj2 am-f stj2 am-m stj1 am-p stj1 kali-n stj1 lith-c stj2 lith-f stj2 lith-i stj2 lith-m stj2 lith-met stj2 lith-p stj2 lith-s stj2 nat-caust stj2 nicc stj1 nicc-met stj2 nicc-s stj2]
  - • **evening**: ox-ac a1
  - • **accompanied** by | **impotence** (See accompanied; MALE GENITALIA/SEX - Erections - wanting - accompanied - tobacco)
  - • **dinner**; after: nat-c a1 tritic-vg fd5.de
  - • **smoking**; desire for: androc mtf bamb-a stb2.de• calad k* calc-p ptk1 carb-ac ptk1 carb-an k* card-m castor-eq kr1 coff b7.de* daph bg2 des-ac rbp6 eug k* *Glon* k* ham k* kali-p fd1.de• *Kola* stb3• lach b7a.de* led k* lyc k* m-ambo b7.de med bg1* nat-c b4.de* nux-v b7.de* olib-sac wmh1 pegan-ha tpi1• phasco-ci rbp2 *Positr* nl2• pycnop-sa mrz1 sep b4a.de staph b7a.de* taosc iwa1• ther k* til ban1• tritic-vg fd5.de tub mtf vanil fd5.de [kali-n stj1 ruth-met stj2]
  - • **snuff**: *Bell* k* sil bg2
- **disgust** for tobacco; remedies to increase: arg-n st ars st calad br1* calc st* camph gl1.fr• **Carb-an** h2* *Caust* st* con gl1.fr• *Daph* mgg• ign st* lach st* nep jl* nicot st nux-v st* pall sne petr st* plan st* **Staph** st* stry st sulph st* tab st v-a-b srb2.fr

TOBACCO POISONING (See Tobacco - agg. - nicotinism)

TONSILLITIS (See THROAT - Inflammation - tonsils)

TORPOR: acon b2.de* am-c b2.de* am-m b2.de* ang b2.de* ant-t b2.de* arg-n bg2 ars b2.de* asaf b2.de* bell b2.de* bry b2.de* camph b2.de* cann-s b2.de* cic b2.de* cina b2.de* cupr bg2 dros b2.de* hell b2.de* hyos b2.de* ign b2.de* ip bg2 kali-c b2.de* kali-s ptk1 kreos b2.de* led b2.de* lyc b2.de* *M-arct* b2.de* mosch b2.de* nat-m ptk1 nux-m b7.de* olnd b2.de* op ptk1 petr b2.de* phos b4a.de plat b2.de* plb b2.de* puls b2.de* sec b2.de* sep b2.de* sil ptk1 stram b2.de* sulph b2.de* verat b2.de* zinc b2.de*

- **left** side of the body; of: acon k*
- **sensation** of: alum b2.de* ang b2.de* *Arg-met* b2.de* **Asaf** b2.de* caust b2.de* cham b2.de* chin b2.de* cina b2.de* *Cocc* b2.de* mang b2.de* meny b2.de* merc b4.de merc-c b4a.de mosch b2.de* nit-ac b2.de* petr b2.de* phos b2.de* *Plat* b2.de* rhod b2.de* sabad b2.de* sec b2.de* sil b4.de vip bg2
  - • **vertigo**; during: nux-m b7a.de

TOUCH: (↗*MIND - Touched)*

- **agg.**: (↗*MIND - Senses - acute; MIND - Touched - aversion)* *Acon* k* *Aesc* **Agar** k* *Agn* k* aloe k* am-c k* am-m k* ambr k* anac k* **Ang** b2.de* ange-s jl3 *Ant-c* k* *Ant-t* k* **Apis** k* **Arg-met** k* arg-n st1* *Arn* k* *Ars* k* ars-s-f k2 **Asaf** k* asar k* aur k* aur-ar k2 *Aur-s* k2* bar-c k* bar-i k2* **Bell** k* borx k* bov k* **Bry** k* bufo k2 *Cact* calad k* calc k* calc-f mg1.de* calc-p calc-sil k2* camph k* *Cann-s* k* *Canth* k* *Caps* k* carb-an k* *Carb-v* k* *Castm* sf1.de caust k* **Cham** k* *Chel* k* **Chin** k* *Chinin-ar* **Chinin-s** cic k* cimic hr1* *Cina* k* *Cinnb* k* clem k* coca-c sk4• **Cocc** k* **Coff** k* **Colch** k* *Coloc* k* com bro1 con k* croc k* **Crot-c** crot-h **Cupr** k* cupr-act bro1 cycl k* daph ptk2 der vml3• dig k* dros k* dulc k* elaps hr1 equis-h bro1 eup-per sf1.de *Euph* k* euph-l bro1 euphr k* ferr k* ferr-i ferr-p bg2* fl-ac bg2* foll jl3 galeoc-c-h gms1• graph k* **Guaj** k* **Ham** k* hell k* helon bro1 **Hep** k* **Hyos** k* hyper sf1.de ign k* *Iod* k* ip k* **Kali-ar** k* *Kali-bi* k* **Kali-c** k* kali-chl k13 *Kali-i* k* kali-m k2 *Kali-n* k* *Kali-p* kali-s kali-sil k2* kalm sf1.de *Kreos* k* lac-d k2* lacer c1

Touch – agg.: ...

Lach k* lat-m bnm6• laur k* *Led* k* *Lil-t* bro1 lob bro1 **Lyc** k* lyss hr1 m-ambo b2.de* m-arct b2.de* m-aust b2.de* *Mag-c* k* *Mag-m* k* **Mag-p** k* mand jl3 **Mang** k* *Med* k* meny k* meph j5.de* *Merc* k* *Merc-c* k* *Mez* k* mosch k* mur-ac k* *Murx* bg2* nat-c k* *Nat-m* k* nat-s bg2* nat-sil k2* **Nit-ac** k* nux-m k* **Nux-v** k* olnd k* *Op* k* osm *Ox-ac* bro1* *Par* k* petr k* *Ph-ac* k* *Phos* k* plat k* plb k* *Puls* k* pyrog jl2 **Ran-b** k* ran-s k* **Rhod** k* **Rhus-t** k* ruta k* sabad k* **Sabin** k* sal-ac *Sang* k* sanic ptk1 sars k* *Sec* k* sel c1 *Seneg* k* **Sep** k* sieg mg1.de **Sil** k* sol-t-ae vml3• **Spig** k* *Spong* k* squil k* stann k* **Staph** k* stel mrr1 *Stram* k* *Stront-c* k* *Stry* bro1 suis-em rly4• sul-ac k* sul-i k2* **Sulph** k* syph k2* *Tarax* k* *Tarent* k* *Tell* k* *Teucr* b2.de* thal jl3 thal-xyz srj8• ther c1* *Thuj* k* urt-u bro1 ust sf1.de valer k* *Verat* k* verb k* viol-o k* viol-t k* vip-a jl3 yuc sf1.de *Zinc* k* zing c1 ziz sf1.de [am-br stj2 *Ant-m* stj2 *Ant-met* stj2 arg-p stj2 astat stj2 aur-m stj2 bar-br stj2 bar-met stj2 bell-p-sp dcm1 bism-sn stj2 brom stj1* caes-met stj2 calc-br stj1 hafn-met stj2 hydrog stj2 irid-met stj2 kali-br stj1 kali-met stj2 lanth-met stj2 lith-f stj2 lith-i stj2 mag-i stj1 mag-lac stj2 mag-met stj2 mag-n stj2 mag-sil stj2 mang-act stj2 mang-i stj2 mang-m stj2 mang-met stj2 mang-n stj2 mang-p stj2 mang-s stj2 mang-sil stj2 merc-d stj2 merc-i-f stj2 moly-met stj2 nat-br stj2 nat-i stj1 osm-met stj2 plb-m stj2 plb-p stj2 polon-met stj2 rhen-met stj2 tant-met stj2 thal-met stj2 tung-met stj2 zinc-i stj2 zinc-m stj2 zinc-n stj2 zinc-p stj2]

  - • **children**; in: *Ant-c* mrr1 ant-t j5.de apis kr1 *Cina* j5.de* nat-s mtf33
  - • **limbs** touch each other at night; cannot bear: *Galeoc-c-h* gms1• lac-c ptk1* *Psor* st* sanic ptk1
- **amel.**: agar k* alum k* *Alumn* kr1 am-c k* am-m k* anac k* ant-c k* arn k* *Ars* k* **Asaf** b2.de* bell k* bell-p st *Bism* k* *Bry* k* **Calc** k* *Calc-act* sf1.de canth *Castm* bg2* caust k* chel k* chin k* *Coloc* k* con k* **Cycl** k* dros k* euph k* euphr k* graph ptk1 *Grat* j5.de* hep b2.de* kali-c b2.de* lyc k* m-arct b2.de* *Mang* k* *Meny* k* merc-c bg2 **Mur-ac** k* nat-c k* nat-m k* olnd k* pall ptk1* petr k* ph-ac k* *Phos* k* plb k* sang bg1* sep k* spig b2.de spong k* staph ptk1 sulph k* tarax k* **Thuj** k* viol-t k* zinc k* [arg-p stj2 stront-m stj2]
  - • **vanishes** on touch and appears elsewhere; pain: ant-t kr1 asaf k* sang k* staph bg1*
- **arms** touching body | **agg.**: psor bg2 spig bg2 sulph bg2
- **bones** agg.; of: aur bg2 bell bg2 calc bg2 carb-an bg2 chin bg2 guaj bg2 kali-bi bg2 lach bg2 lyc bg2 nat-c bg2 *Puls* bg2 rhus-t bg2 *Sil* bg2 sulph bg2 symph bg2
- **clothes** agg.; of: *Galeoc-c-h* gms1•
- **feet** agg.; of: galeoc-c-h gms1• **Kali-c** bg2* nux-v bg2
- **illusions** of: acon *Alum* anac ant-t arn ars *Asaf* asar bar-c *Bell* bism borx bov bry *Calc* cann-s canth caps caust chel coc-c cocc coloc con *Croc* dros dulc glon graph guaj hell hep hyos *Ign* indg iod kali-c kali-n kreos *Lach* laur lyc mag-c mag-m meny merc mosch nat-c nat-m nux-v olnd op *Par* ph-ac phos plat *Plb* *Puls* ran-b ran-s rheum rhod **Rhus-t** ruta sabad samb seneg sep sil *Spig* spong squil staph *Stram* sul-ac *Sulph* k1 tarax thuj valer verat verb
  - • **color**; seen as: anh sp1
  - • **rough**, objects seem: par cda*
- **slight** touch agg.: **Acon** bg2* ang vh **Apis** bg2* ars k* *Asaf* nh **Bell** k* *Caps* nh **Chin** k* coff *Colch* elaps hr1 galeoc-c-h gms1• *Ign* k* kali-c k2 *Lac-c* sne lac-h sk4• **Lach** k* lyss kr1 mag-m k* **Merc** k* merc-c bg2 *Mez* *Nit-ac* ptk1 **Nux-v** k* ph-ac k* *Phos* k* plb nh* *Spig* br1 *Stann* k* staph tl1 thal-xyz srj8•
- **throat** agg.; touching: bell b2.de* **Lach** b2.de*

TOUCHING:

- **anything**:
  - • **agg.**: acon k* am-c k* am-m k* arg-met k* arn k* bell k* borx bov b2.de *Bry* k* *Calc* k* *Cann-s* k* *Carb-v* k* *Caust* k* **Cham** k* chin k* dros k* kali-c k* kali-n k* led k* lyc k* merc k* nat-c k* phos k* plat k* *Puls* k* sec k* *Sil* k* spig k* verat k*
  - • **amel.**: spig bg2*
- **cold** things agg.; touching: anth vh calc cench **Hep** k* *Lac-d* mang ptk1 *Merc* k* *Nat-m* k* phos bg2 *Pyrog* **Rhus-t** k* **Sil** k* thuj k* zinc k*
- **warm** things agg.; touching: *Sulph* k*

TRANSPLANT rejection (See Abscesses - foreign)

TRAVELLING:

- **agg.**: [bell-p-sp dcm1]
- **ailments** from: (↗*Riding - streetcar; on - agg.)* arizon-l nl2• ars ptk1 borx ptk1 cain c2 cann-i mrr1 coca bro1 **Cocc** ●* coff c* colch ptk1 colocin c2 con c1* flor-p rsj3• glon ptk1 kreos ptk1 lyss ptk1 mand mtf11 petr ptk1* plat bro1 sanic ptk1 sel ptk1 *Sep* ptk1 ther ptk1 *Tub* ptk1 [bell-p-sp dcm1]

- **ailments** from: ...
  - **nausea**; without: kali-p ptk1
- **amel.**: *Ign* mrr1

TREMBLING:

○ - **Externally** (= whole body) abel jl3 abrot k* absin k* acet-ac k* *Acon* k* acon-f k* adren st *Agar* k* agar-cps a1 agarin bro1 agn k* alco a1 alum k* alum-p k2* alum-sil k2* alumn k* am-c k* am-caust j5.de* am-m k* **Ambr** k* aml-ns *Anac* k* androc srj1• ang b2.de* ant-c k* **Ant-t** k* *Apis* k* *Apoc* a1 apoc-a br1 aq-mar a1 aran k* aran-ix mg *Arg-met* k* **Arg-n** k* arge-pl rwt5• arizon-l nl2• *Arn* k* **Ars** k* ars-h hr1 ars-i ars-s-f hr1* ars-s-r hr1* asaf k* astac hr1 atro a1 *Aur* k* aur-ar k2 aur-i k2* aur-s k2* *Bapt* bg2* *Bar-c* k* bar-i k2* bar-m k* bar-s k2* *Bell* k* ben-n a1 benz-ac a1 berb j5.de bism k* borx k* both st1 bov k* brom k* bruc j5.de *Bry* k* bufo buth-a mg1.de* **Cact** cadm-met mg1.de cadm-s caj a1 *Calad* *Calc* k* *Calc-caust* j5.de* calc-f mg1.de* *Calc-i* k2* calc-m a1 *Calc-p* k* *Calc-s* calc-sil k2* calth a1 *Camph* k* canch a1 cann-i k* cann-s k* *Canth* k* caps k* carb-ac k* carb-an j5.de carb-v k* carbn-h a1 carbn-o a1 *Carbn-s* k* castm kr1 *Caust* k* *Cedr* cham k* *Chel* k* *Chin* k* *Chinin-ar* *Chinin-s* k* chlor chlorpr jl3 choc srj3• **Cic** k* cic-m a1 **Cimic** k* *Cina* k* cinch a1 cinnm hr1* *Cit-v* a1* *Clem* *Coca* kr1 *Cocc* k* *Cod* k* *Coff* k* coff-t a1* coffin a1 colch k* coloc k* *Con* k* cop hr1* cortico mg1.de* cortiso mg1.de croc k* **Crot-c** k* *Crot-h* k* crot-t k* *Cupr* k* cupr-act j5.de cupr-ar sf1.de cupr-s hr1* cur cycl b7.de dendr-pol sk4• dig k* digin a1 dios k* dioxi rbp6 dros k* dubo-h a1* *Dulc* k* echit a1 esp-g kk1.de euph bg2 euphr k* fagu a1 *Ferr* k* ferr-ar k* ferr-ma j5.de* ferr-p k* fl-ac k2* **Gels** k* gins a1* glon k* gran j5.de* *Graph* k* guaj *Hell* helo helo-s rwt2• hep k* hydr-ac j5.de* *Hydrog* srj2• **Hyos** k* *Hyosin-hbr* bro1 *Hyper* hr1* iber a1* **Ign** k* ignis-alc es2* inul a1* *Iod* k* ip *Iris* kr1 jab bg* kali-act a1 *Kali-ar* k* kali-bi a1 *Kali-br* k* **Kali-c** k* kali-cy a1 *Kali-fcy* kali-i a1 kali-n h2* kali-p k* kali-s kali-sil k2* *Kalm* k* kiss a1 kola stb3• kreos k* lac-ac k* *Lach* k* lam a1 lat-m bro1* lath bg2* laur k* *Lec* *Led* k* lil-t bg* lith-chl bro1 lob j5.de* *Lol* bg2* lon-x a1* *Lyc* k* lycps-v kr1* *Lyss* m-ambo b2.de m-arct b2.de* m-aust b2.de* mag-c k* mag-m k* mag-p k* mag-s k* manc bg2* mang k* *Med* k* meny k* meph **Merc** k* *Merc-c* k* merc-d a1 merc-i-f a1 merc-n a1 merc-ns a1 merc-pr-r a1 methyl br1 **Mez** k* morph a1* *Mosch* k* *Mur-ac* mygal k* naja k2* *Nat-ar* **Nat-c** k* nat-hchls a1 *Nat-m* k* *Nat-p* *Nat-s* k* nat-sal br1 nat-sil k2* nicc j5.de* nicot a1 *Nit-ac* k* nux-m k* *Nux-v* k* oena a1 ol-an j5.de* olib-sac wmh1 olnd k* onos **Op** k* ox-ac k* oxyt br1* oxyum-sc mcp1• pall k* *Par* k* ped a1 petr k* *Ph-ac* k* phel j5.de* *Phos* k* phys bg2* *Phyt* k* *Pic-ac* k* pip-n bg2 plan k* plat k* *Plb* k* plut-n srj7• polyg-h positr nl2• prun j5.de* pseuts-m oss1• psil jl3 psor k* **Puls** k* ran-a a1 ran-b k* ran-s k* rauw sp1* reser jl3 rheum k* rhod k* **Rhus-t** k* russ a1 ruta k* *Sabad* k* sabin k* sal-ac sf1.de samb k* sang k* sarcol-ac bro1 sars k* scut a1* *Sec* k* sel senec a1 seneg k* *Sep* k* sieg mg1.de *Sil* k* sol-ni a1 spartin bwa3 *Spig* k* spig-m a1 spong k* squil bg2* *Stann* k* staph k* **Stram** k* stront-c k* *Stry* k* *Sul-ac* k* sul-h a1 sul-i k2* **Sulph** k* sumb k* *Tab* k* tanac k* tarax *Tarent* k* tax a1 teucr k* thal a1* thal-met br1 thal-xyz srj8• ther bg2* *Thuj* k* thyreotr jl3 til a1 tub bg* valer k* vanad br1* vanil fd5.de *Verat* k* verat-v bg* verb k* verin a1 vesp a1* viol-o k* viol-t k* vip j5.de* *Visc* k* wies a1 x-ray sp1 **Zinc** k* zinc-cy a1 zinc-o j5.de zinc-ox j5.de *Zinc-p* k2* zinc-s a1 [heroin sdj2 *Yttr-met* stj2]

- **right** side, of: merc a1
- **morning**: alumn k* *Arg-met* *Arg-n* k* ars k* bar-c k* calc k* carb-v hr1* cimic k* *Con* *Dulc* k* gran a1 graph k* lyc k* mag-c k* nat-m k* nicc sf1.de *Nit-ac* hr1* *Nux-v* k* petr k* phos k* sil sulph k*
  - **amel.**: mag-c h2
  - **rising** agg.: *Bar-c* h2* *Dulc* a1 petr h2*
  - **waking**; on: *Arg-met* bar-c j5.de calc h2* carb-v j5.de carc gk6 caust k* *Dulc* euphr j5.de gard-j vlr2• hyper k* mag-c k* nit-ac k* phos k* tarent k*
- **forenoon**: ars k* carb-v a1 carbn-o lyc k* nat-m ol-an j5.de* *Plat* k* sars k* sulph j5.de
  - **9.30** h: phys a1
  - **10** h: *Borx*
  - **exertion** agg.: gels k*
- **noon**: sulph j5.de
  - **sleep** agg.; after: nat-m
- **afternoon**: ant-t j5.de asaf vh carb-v k* *Gels* k* lyc k* lyss k* pic-ac k*
  - **13** h: verat-v a1
  - **15** h: asaf kr1 *Nux-v* kr1
  - **17** h: ped a1
- **evening**: bruc sf1.de caust sf1.de chel k* iber a1 *Kali-br* hr1 lach sf1.de lyc k* mez mygal k* nat-m k* nit-ac h2* nux-v sf1.de olib-sac wmh1 pic-ac k* plb ran-b k2 sil a1* stront-c sulph k*
  - **19** h: phys a1

Trembling – Externally – evening: ...

  - **bed** agg.; in: anag a1 eupi k* lyc k* nux-v k* samb k*
  - **sleep** agg.; after: carb-v k*
  - **walking** agg.; after: *Sil* k*
- **night**: *Bell* k* hyos k* lyc k* merc k2* *Op* hr1* phos k* rat j5.de
  - **midnight**:
    - **after** | **3** h: *Rhus-t*
  - **dreaming**, after: calc a1 nicc a1 petr-ra shn4• phos k* sil
  - **half** awake, while: sulph h2
  - **sleep** agg.; after: *Sil*
- **accident**; after an: adam srj5•
- **accompanied** by:
  - **atrophy** (See Atrophy - accompanied - trembling)
  - **leukorrhea** (See FEMALE - Leukorrhea - accompanied - trembling)
  - **shrieking** (See MIND - Shrieking - trembling)
  - **Abdomen**; complaints in (See ABDOMEN - Complaints - accompanied - trembling)
  - **Head**; complaints of (See HEAD - Complaints - accompanied - trembling)
- **air**; in open:
  - **agg.**: all-c k2 calc kali-c laur *Plat*
  - **amel.**: clem k*
- **alcoholism**; from: ant-t kr1* *Ars* bg2* cocain bro1 cocc bro1 *Crot-h* kr1 *Lach* kr1 *Mag-p* kr1 *Nux-v* bg2* sul-ac bg2* sulph bg2*
- **alone**; when | **amel.**: ambr a1
- **alternating** with:
  - **convulsions**: merc a1
  - **convulsive** movements of limbs: arn a1
  - **weakness**: ferr a1
- **anger** | **from**: acon k* alum st ambr arg-n *Aur* k* aur-m-n wbt2• cham bg2* chel cop crot-c sk4• daph ferr-p k* gels dx1 lyc m-aust j5.de merc *Nit-ac* k* nux-v bg2* pall pert-vc vk9 petr h2* phos *Plat* kr1 ran-b k* sep *Staph* k* yohim dg *Zinc* k*
- **anticipation** | **from**: **Gels** mrr1
- **anxiety**:
  - **from**: *(↗MIND - Anxiety)* abrot sf1.de acon sf1.de aeth kr1 ambr ant-c sf1.de **Ars** k* aur aur-m-n wbt2• bell borx *Calc* canth carb-v caust *Cham* k* chel *Cina* sf1.de *Coff* *Con* croc cupr dioxi rbp6 euph h2 ferr a1 graph hydrog srj2• iber vml3• ignis-alc es2• *Lach* lyc mag-c k* mez mosch nat-c nit-ac nux-m phos *Plat* psor *Puls* k* *Rhus-t* samb sars sep *Ther* sf1.de valer verat sf1.de
  - **with**: *Abrot* sf1.de acon sf1.de agar h2 ant-c sf1.de aur sf1.de bell sf1.de *Cina* sf1.de *Croc* sf1.de hydrog srj2• petr h2 puls sf1.de samb ptk1 *Ther* sf1.de verat sf1.de
- **ascending** agg.: merc
- **attacks**, before: absin bg1 arg-n bg2 crot-h bg2 ferr bg2 lyc bg2
- **bed** agg.; in: merc a1 merc-n a1 merc-ns a1
- **breakfast**:
  - **after**:
    - **agg.**: arg-n
    - **amel.**: *Calc* *Con* nat-m nux-v staph
  - **before** | **agg.**: *Calc* k* *Con* nat-m nux-v staph
- **burns**; after: calc ptk1
- **caressing**, while: caps k*
- **chills**; with (See CHILL - Trembling)
- **closing** the eyes agg.: merc a1
- **coffee**, from smell of: sul-ac a1*
- **coition**; after: calc sf1.de* kali-c k2*
- **cold** drinks | **amel.**: phos k*
- **coldness**:
  - **during**: borx
  - **with**: bufo kr1 hyos sf1.de *Merc* hr1* *Mosch* hr1* *Nux-m* hr1* *Op* hr1* plat sf1.de sep brm vanil fd5.de [heroin sdj2]
- **company** agg.: *Ambr* lyc

- **conversation**, from: *Ambr* k* borx
- **convulsions**; before: absin ptk1 verat-v ptk1
- **convulsive**: (↗*spasmodic)* am-c a1 ars a1 atro a1 bar-m kr1 canth a1 ign bro1 kali-cy a1 lol a1 merc a1 tab a1
- **cough** agg.; during: am-c b4.de* ambr k2 ant-t bg1 bell *Cupr* k* just ptk1 *Phos* k* seneg k2
- **diarrhea**, suppressed: abrot k2
- **dinner**; during: *Mag-m* k*
- **dreams**:
  - **after**: ferr-ma j5.de nicc j5.de
  - **during**: calc j5.de m-arct j5.de
- **drinking**, after excessive: plb
- **eating** | **after** | **agg.**: alum ant-c caust j5.de lyc h2* mag-m j5.de olnd bg1 phel j5.de tab j5.de zinc j5.de
  - **amel.**: *Kola* stb3• [heroin sdj2]
- **excitement**: | **emotional** excitement; after: arg-n carc mlr1• **Cocc** k* coff sf1.de cycl st dulc fd4.de ferr gels k2 hep ign k2 merc nat-c nat-m nat-sil fd3.de• petr kr1 ph-ac k2 phys kr1 *Plb* k* *Psor* k* **Staph** k* stram teucr ptk1 thyreotr jl *Zinc*
- **exertion** agg.: alco a1 am-caust a1* anac bg2* ant-t bg2* *Arn* bg2* ars bg2* chinin-s bg2* **Cocc** bg2* dulc fd4.de **Gels** mrr1 iod bg2* merc a1 nat-c bg2* *Nat-m* bg2* plan a1 polyg-h a1 polyg-pe vml2• *Rhus-t* bg2* sec bg2* *Sil* bg2* vanil fd5.de
  - **slight** exertion: borx *Cocc* ferr gels c1 *Merc* k* onos vml3• phos *Plat Plb* polyg-h *Rhus-t* sec *Stann Zinc*
- **faintness**, during: asaf a1 *Lach* hr1* nux-v hr1* petr st
- **fatigue**, after: dulc fd4.de plb k*
- **fear**, from (See MIND - Fear - tremulous)
- **fever**; during: acon bg2* *Apis* bg2 arn bg2 ars k* bar-c b4a.de bell bg2 *Borx* b4a.de* bry bg2 calc k* camph k* cann-i sf1.de caps sf1.de *Chin* bg2 cic bg2 cist k* cocc bg2 con b4.de* dulc k2 eup-per k* helo-s bnm14• *Hyos* bg2 **Ign** b7a.de* kali-c lach lyc b4a.de* mag-c k* merc bg2 mygal **Nat-m** b4.de* *Op* bg2 plat b4.de* **Puls** b7.de* *Rhus-t* bg2 ruta b7.de* *Sabad* bg2 *Samb* bg2 sep k* **Stram** bg2 *Sulph* bg2 thuj bg2 valer bg2 *Verat* bg2 **Zinc** b4a.de*
- **fingertips**; felt to: sep k2
- **followed** by | **paralysis**: plb mtf33
- **fright** agg.: (↗*MIND - Ailments - fright)* abrot bg2 *Acon* bg2* ambr bg2 ant-c bg2 arg-n ars bg2 *Aur* k* bell bg2 calc bg2* carb-v bg2 caust bg2 *Cham* bg2 cina bg2 *Coff* k* croc bg2 cupr bg2 dulc fd4.de **Gels** mrr1 glon graph bg2 hura ign lach bg2 mag-c k* merc k* mosch bg2 *Nat-c* bg2 nicc *Op* k* petr-ra shn4• phos bg2 *Plat* hr1* psor al2 puls k* ran-b hr1* rat rhus-t k* sars bg2 sep k* *Stram* hr1* *Tarent* kr1 ther bg2 verat bg2 zinc bg2*
- **hands**, from using the: phos k2
- **headache**; during: arg-n bg1* borx a1* *Gels* bro1
  - **chill**; with: carb-v h2
- **hungry**, when: (↗*STOMACH - Appetite - ravenous - accompanied - trembling)* *Alum* k* *Crot-h* k* ignis-alc es2• *Kola* stb3• olnd ribo rly4• stann *Sulph* k* *Zinc* k*
- **intention** tremor (See something)
- **joy** agg.: acon aur k* cimic hr1* coff cycl hr1* merc tarent dgt valer
- **looking** downward agg.: kali-c k*
- **lying**:
  - **agg.**: clem
  - **side**; on:
    - **left**:
      - **agg.** | **lying** on back amel.: kalm kr1
- **meeting** friends: tarent k*
- **menopause**; during: *Kali-br* kr1* sul-ac k2 ther sf1.de
- **menses**:
  - **after** | **agg.**: *Chin* k*
  - **before** | **agg.**: alum k* hyos bg2* kali-c b4a.de* lyc bg2* *Nat-m* bg2* sep bg2 stann bg2*
  - **during** | **agg.**: agar bg2 arg-n calc-p caul bg2 caust bg2 chin b7a.de* cina kr1 *Graph* k* *Hyos* k* kali-c bg2 *Lec* mag-c j5.de merl nat-m bg2* nicc sf1.de *Nit-ac* k* plat bg2* puls sf1.de *Stram* hr1* wies a1*
- **mental** exertion agg.: aur borx h2* **Calc** hr1* *Plb* k* vinc k*
- **motion**:
  - **agg.**: anac arg-n canth j5.de iod kali-ar k2 phyt puls j5.de sulph h2 zinc
    - **slow** motion agg.: stann ptk1
    - **sudden** motion: kali-ar k2
  - **amel.**: merc plat puls tl1
  - **hands** and feet; of | **agg.**: cann-i a1
- **music** agg.: *Aloe* kr1* **Ambr** k* nat-c kr1 thuj kr1*
- **nausea**; with: ant-t bg2 *Ars* bg2* borx hr1 *Calc* hr1* carb-v a1 chel hr1* cimic a1 eup-per hr1* hydrog srj2• nit-ac bg2 nux-v bg2 plan hr1 plat hr1* sulph bg2 tab a1 vesp a1*
- **nervous**: abies-c bro1 acon bg2 adox a1* agar bg2 ambr bg2 ant-t bro1 aqui br1* arg-n bg2* arn bro1 ars bg2* asar bro1 aur bg2 both br1* *Caul* bro1 *Caust* bro1 *Chin* bro1 cimic bg2* cina bg2 cocc bg2* coff bg2* con bg2 gels bg2* helo bg2 hyos bg2* kali-br bg2 lach bro1 lat-m bro1 lath bg2 lil-t ptk1 lol bg2 mag-p bg2* mang bg2 *Med* bro1 merc bg2 *Mosch* br1* murx bro1 nux-m bg2 *Nux-v* bro1 phos bg2* phys bg2 plb bg2 puls bro1 raph bro1 sep bro1 *Staph* ptk1 stram ptk1 stry bro1 *Sul-ac* bro1 sulph bro1 tab bg2 tarent bg2* teucr bg2 valer bro1 zinc bg2*
  - **old** people; in: aven br1
- **noise** agg.: *Aloe* kr1* bar-c caust *Cocc* k* hura *Kali-ar* k* mosch tab k*
- **nursing** infant, after: (↗*Nursing)* *Olnd* k*
- **old** people; in: alum st ambr st aur st aven br1* bar-c bg2* calc bg2* cann-i bro1 cocain bro1 con bg2* kali-c st merc st op st phos bro1* plb bg2* plb-act sf1.de* sil bg2* stront-c bg2* sulph bg2* zinc st
- **pain**:
  - **after**: bry a1
  - **with**: bism st *Cocc* k* **Nat-c** k* nit-ac bg1 *Plat* k* puls k* sul-ac bg2 zinc ptk1
- **palpitations**; with: acon hr1* asaf bro1 benz-ac hr1* calc-ar hr1* lach bro1 rhus-t bro1 *Sul-ac* bro1 [bell-p-sp dcm1]
- **paroxysmal**: anthraci kr1 crot-h sf1.de ferr sf1.de lyc h2* *Merc* k*
- **periodical**: **Arg-n** k*
- **perspiration**:
  - **after** | **agg.**: *Apis* kr1
  - **cold** | **with**: merc bg2 mosch bg2 *Puls* hr1*
  - **with**: arn bg2 ars b4a.de* bell bg2 borx bg2 both-ax tsm2 bry bg2 *Calc* bg2 camph bg2 cic bg2 cocc bg2 con bg2 hydrog srj2• *Ign* bg2 ignis-alc es2• jab ptk1 lyc bg2 *Mag-c* bg2 merc bg2* mosch b7a.de* **Nat-c** b4a.de* *Nat-m* bg2 op bg2 plat bg2 *Puls* bg2 rhus-t b7a.de* *Ruta* bg2 **Sep** bg2 stram bg2 **Sulph** b4a.de* *Thuj* bg2 valer bg2 verat bg2 *Zinc* bg2
- **playing** the piano, while: nat-c k*
- **rest**:
  - **agg.**: eupi a1
  - **amel.**: merc a1 nep mg1.de
- **rising** agg.: ambr st hydrog srj2• nat-m bg2
  - **sitting**; trembling in affected parts when rising from: **Caust**
- **sensation** of: seneg ptk1
- **sexual**:
  - **excess**; trembling after sexual: *Phos* kr1
  - **excitement**; trembling during sexual: graph
- **shivering**; during: borx b4a.de caps b7.de *Cina* b7.de* nat-m b4.de olnd b7.de
- **sleep**:
  - **before**: carb-an j5.de nat-m k* petr j5.de sep h2*
  - **during** | **agg.**: *Acon* bg2 agn bg2 alum bg2 am-c bg2 anac bg2 ang bg2 ant-t b7.de* apis bg2* arn bg2 *Ars* bg2 bar-c bg2 **Bell** bg2 borx bg2 *Bry* bg2 calad bg2 *Calc* bg2 camph bg2 caps bg2 carb-an bg2 *Carb-v* bg2 caust bg2 *Cham* bg2 chel bg2 *Chin* bg2 *Chlf* hr1* *Cina* bg2 *Cocc* bg2 colch bg2 con k* croc bg2 *Dig* bg2 dros bg2 *Gels* bg2 *Graph* bg2 *Grin* bg2 hep bg2 hyos bg2 ign bg2 *Ip* bg2 kali-bi bg2 kali-c h2* kreos bg2 lach bg2 laur bg2 lyc bg2 mag-c bg2 mag-m bg2 merc bg2 merc-c bg2 nat-c bg2 nat-m bg2 nit-ac bg2 nux-v bg2 *Op* bg2 petr bg2 ph-ac bg2 *Phos* bg2 plat bg2 plb bg2 **Puls** bg2 rheum b7.de* rhus-t bg2 ruta bg2 samb b7.de* sars bg2 seneg bg2 **Sep** bg2 *Sil* bg2 spong bg2 stann bg2 staph bg2 *Stram* bg2 stront-c bg2 sul-ac bg2 **Sulph** bg2 teucr bg2 thuj bg2 verat bg2 zinc bg2

- **sleep**: ...
  - **starting** from: petr h2* sil bg2
- **smoking** agg.: *Hep* k* kali-c bro1* nat-m k* nit-ac bro1* *Nux-v* hr1* sep bro1* sil k* sulph k*
- **sneezing** agg.: **Borx** st
- **something** is to be done, when (= intention tremor): anac bg2 arg-n bg2* bell bg2 cic bg2 *Cocc* bg2* gels bg2 iod bg2 **Kali-br** k* merc bg2 phos bg2 phyt bg2 rhus-t bg2* samb bg2 *Sec* bg2* zinc bg2*
- **spasmodic**: *(↗convulsive)* ang bg2* bar-m bg2* bism bg2* ign bg2* nux-v bg2* op bg2* plb bg2* sabad bg2*
- **standing** agg.: merc k*
- **stitching** in ear, from: thuj h1
- **stool**:
  - **after** | **agg.**: *Ars* k* bov b4a.de bry b7a.de carb-v k* caust **Con** k* lil-t k* *Merc* kr1
  - **before**: hydr k* merc k* sumb k*
  - **during** | **agg.**: carbn-s con bg2 lac-c bg2 merc b4a.de*
- **supper** agg.; after: alum k* caust k*
- **surprise** agg.: merc a1
- **thunderstorm**; during a: agar *Morph* nat-p k* *Phos*
- **touch**, unexpected: *Cocc* k* kali-ar ptk1
- **urination**:
  - **after** | **agg.**: ars h2*
  - **during** | **agg.**: canth bg2 gels a1* stram lmj
  - **profuse**: gels kr1*
- **vertigo** with: am-c ars bell *Camph* carb-v crot-h *Dig Dulc Glon* nat-m puls spong fd4.de
- **vexation** agg.: acon *Aur* cham sf1.de coff k2* lyc nit-ac nux-v sf1.de petr sf1.de ran-b
- **voluptuous**: calc k*
- **vomiting**:
  - **after**: ars a1
  - **while**: ant-t bg2 ars bg2 colch a1 eup-per hr1* gran a1 nit-ac bg2 nux-v bg2 sulph bg2
- **waking**; on: abrot k* bar-c j5.de cadm-met tpw6 calc k* carb-v j5.de* carc sst• caust j5.de *Cina Dulc* hr1* euphr j5.de ferr-ma j5.de *Ign* hr1* lach m-arct j5.de *Merc* k* nicc j5.de nit-ac orig a1 *Petr* j5.de phos j5.de* plac-s rly4• rat samb b7a.de* sil j5.de stront-c j5.de sulph j5.de tarent k* verat bg1*
- **walking**:
  - **after** | **agg.**: cupr h2 ust k*
  - **agg.**: *(↗EXTREMITIES - Trembling - walking)* am-c k* cupr-ar sf1.de lac-ac k* merc k* nux-v stann ptk1 stry a1
  - **beginning** to walk: cupr-ar ptk1
- **weakness**; from: *(↗Weakness - tremulous)* agar bg2* *Anac* bg2* ant-t bg2* apoc-a vh1 *Bapt* bg2* bell bg2* berb bg2 bry bg2* caust bg2* *Chin* bg2* cocc sf1.de con bg2* hydrog srj2• kali-c bg2* mang bg2* *Nat-m* bg2* nit-ac bg2 phos k2 *Stann* bg2* ther bg2* vanil fd5.de verat bg2* vip bg2 zinc sf1.de
- **widows**, in: con k2
- **wine** agg.: *Con*
- **worm** complaints; in: sabad
- **writing** agg.: lyss mg1.de *Phos* k* *Sil* k*
- ○ **Affected** parts: *Arg-n* br1 caust bg1
- **Feet**, on washing: merc a1
- **Muscles**; of: naja k2
  - **chill**; during: olnd b7a.de
- **Side** lain on: cimic ptk1 clem k*

- **Internally**: *Abrot* bg2* acon vh1 aids nl2• ambr k* ang b2.de* *Ant-t* k* apis b7a.de aran-ix mg1.de* arg-met k2 *Arg-n* k* asaf k* astac ptk1 bell k* bell-p sp1 bit-ar wht1• both-a rb3 both-ax tsm2 *Brach* bry k* calad **Calc** k* calc-sil k2 *Camph* k* caps k* carb-v k* carbn-s carneg-g rwt1• *Caul* k* *Caust* k* chim hr1 chinin-s a1 cina k* *Clem* cocc k* colch k* *Con* k* *Crot-h* k* cycl k* cypra-eg sde6.de• dicha jl3 diph ptk1 esp-g kk1.de *Eup-per* k* gard-j vlr2• gels st1 **Graph** k* hep h2* hura a1 *Hydrog* srj2• *Ign* b7a.de **Iod** k* *Kali-c* k* *Kali-n* k* kali-p fd1.de• kali-sil k2 kreos k* lach bg2* lam a1 lap-la sde8.de• *Lec* lil-t *Lyc* k*

Trembling – Internally: ...
m-arct b2.de* mang-p rly4• med hr1* meph merc k* mosch k* nat-ar *Nat-c* *Nat-m* k* nat-s k* nat-sil fd3.de• nep mg1.de* nit-ac k* nux-m k* *Nux-v* k* par petr k* *Phos* k* *Plat* k* positr nl2• *Puls* k* **Rhus-t** k* ruta k* *Sabad* k* sabin k* sacch-a fd2.de• samb k* *Seneg* k* *Sep* k* sil k* spartin bwa3 *Spig* k* *Spong* hr1 **Stann** k* **Staph** k* *Stront-c* k* **Sul-ac** k* sul-i k2* *Sulph* k* *Teucr* k* ther bg2* tritic-vg fd5.de tung-met bdx1• valer k* x-ray sp1 zinc k* [*Buteo-j* sej6 tax jsj7 *Yttr-met* stj2]

- **night**: nat-m h2 nat-sil fd3.de• plat h2
- **abortion**; during: caul bro1
- **anger**; after: positr nl2•
- **chill**; during: *Calc* bg2 iod bg2 lyc bg2 **Plat** b4a.de* rhus-t bg2 staph bg2
- **eating**; after: lyc b4a.de
- **excitement** agg.: teucr ptk1
- **menopause**; during: caul st sul-ac st
- **rage**; after: gard-j vlr2•
- **sun**; after exposure to: pert-vc vk9
- **weakness**; with: caul c1
- ○ **Affected** parts: *Arg-n* br1
- **Blood** vessels: phel vml3•
- **Muscles**: lat-m sp1

TRICKLING sensation, like drops: acon bg2 agar bg2 agath-a nl2• alum bg2 ambr k* arg-n bg2* arn k* ars bg2 bell k* berb bg2 bufo ptk1 camph bg2 **Cann-s** k* *Cann-xyz* ptk1 caust bg2* cedr bg2 chin bg2 cod bg cot bg2 croc bg2 dulc bg2 *Glon* bg2* graph bg2* irid-met srj5• kali-bi ptk1 lach bg2 lap-a ptk1 lyc bg2 mag-m bg2 merc bg2 nat-m bg2* nux-m bg2 petros ptk1 phos bg2* pip-n bg2 rhus-t ptk1 sang bg2 sep k* sil bg2 spig k* stann ptk1 sumb ptk1 tarent ptk1 thuj k* vario ptk1 verat k*

- **falling** from and upon different spots: canch br1
- **hot** drops: hep ptk1 sep ptk1 stann bg2* sulph bg2* sumb ptk1
- ○ **Affected** parts; on: arg-n ptk1
- **Joints**: nat-m tl1

TRIFLES agg.: ambr ptk1 aml-ns ptk1 carb-an ptk1 cocc ptk1 kali-p ptk1 mag-c ptk1 nit-ac ptk1 nux-m ptk1 phos ptk1

TUBERCULOSIS: *(↗CHEST - Phthisis)* agar ptk1 arist-cl sp1 ars ptk1 aven c2 *Bac* c2* *Bell* c2 beta br1 brom c2 *Calc* c2* calc-f br1 **Calc-p** ptk1 calo br1 carc jl2 chinin-ar c2 coli jl2 cordyc mp4• diphtox jl2 dros br1* elaps hr1 ferr-i c2 form br1 formal mtf11 hed sp1 *Hep* ptk1 hippoz c2* *Ichth* br1 iod ptk1* iodof c2 **Kali-c** ptk1 kali-s ptk1 kreos ptk1 lach ptk1 *Lachn* br1 lap-a c2 lec br1 led c2 **Lyc** ptk1 med tl1 myrt-c c2* nat-ar c2 nat-m mtf11 nit-ac ptk1 ol-j ptk1 *Oscilloc* jl2 ox-ac br1 phel ptk1 phos c2* pneu jl2 psor ptk1* **Puls** ptk1 pyrog c2 sang ptk1 senec ptk1 *Sep* ptk1 *Sil* ptk1 spong c2* *Stann* ptk1* *Sulph* ptk1 teucr-s c2 *Ther* ptk1 titan br1 toxo-g jl2 tub c2* tub-sp jl2 urea c2* v-a-b jl2 vac jl2 vanad br1 x-ray sp1 zinc ptk1

- **accompanied** by | **thirst**: nit-ac ptk1
- **cachexia** (See Cachexia - tuberculosis)
- **cavitation**: pyrog jl2*
- ○ **Visceral**: tub-sp mtf11
- **incipient**: ferr mtf11 *Iod* ptk1 malar jl2 mang-act br1 ol-j br1 pert jl2* toxo-g jl2 *Tub* br1* tub-m jl2* tub-sp jl2* vanad br1
  - **accompanied** by | **Tongue**; aphthae on (See CHEST - Phthisis - incipient - accompanied - tongue)
- **lupus** vulgar: abr c1 agar alum alum-sil k2 alumn ant-c arg-n **Ars** *Ars-i* ars-s-f k2 *Aur-ar* c1 aur-m *Bar-c* bell k2* calc calc-ar kr1 calc-p kr1 calc-sil k2 calo c1 *Carb-ac Carb-v Carbn-s* caust chr-o c1 cic k2* *Cist* cund kr1 ferr-pic c1 graph guare c1 hep hippoz c1 *Hydr* kr1* *Hydrc* kali-ar *Kali-bi* kali-c *Kali-chl* kali-m kr1 kali-s *Kreos* lach **Lyc** m-arcl k2* merc-i-r k2* *Nit-ac* ol-j k2* *Phyt Psor* ran-b k2 rhus-t k2* sabin k2* sep *Sil* spong staph sulph thiosin c1 **Thuj** *Tub-k* c1 vario jl2
  - **rings**, in: *Sep*
- **prophylaxis** of: bac st1* sulph st1 tub st1*
- ○ **Bones**: ang bg2 asaf bg2 calc bg2 calc-hp bg2 dros ptk1* hep bg2 *Phos* bg2* *Puls* bg2* *Stann* bg2* tub jl2
- **Fibrous**: tub-r mtf11
- **Ganglion**: tub jl2 v-a-b jl2
- **Glandular**: dros br1* syc mtf11

- **Glandular**: ...

○ • **Lymphatic** glands: *(↗Scrofulous)* abrot mtf11 aethi-a c1 *Aethi-m* br1* aln br1* alum bro1 ampe-qu br1 ars b4a.de* *Ars-i* bro1 aur br1* *Aur-ar* bro1 *Aur-br* bro1 *Aur-i* bro1 *Aur-m* bro1 *Aur-m-k* bro1 *Aur-m-n* bro1 *Aur-s* bro1 bac bro1* bad bro1 *Bar-act* bro1 bar-c bro1* *Bar-i* bro1 *Bar-m* bro1 *Bar-s* bro1 bell b4a.de* brom bro1 *Cal-ren* bro1 calc b4a.de* *Calc-act* bro1 *Calc-ar* bro1 *Calc-br* bro1 *Calc-caust* bro1 *Calc-cn* bro1 *Calc-f* bro1 *Calc-hp* bro1 calc-i br1* *Calc-lac* bro1 *Calc-lp* bro1 *Calc-m* bro1 *Calc-ox* bro1 calc-p br1* *Calc-pic* bro1 *Calc-s* bro1 *Calc-sil* bro1 *Calc-st-s* bro1 camph br1 caps hr1* *Carb-an* br1* *Caust* bro1 chin b7a.de cina b7a.de* cinnb bro1 cist bg2* clem br1* con br1* diph br1* diphtox jl2 *Dulc* bro1 ferr b7a.de* *Ferr-act* bro1 *Ferr-ar* bro1 *Ferr-br* bro1 *Ferr-cit* bro1 *Ferr-cy* bro1 ferr-i br1* *Ferr-m* bro1 *Ferr-ma* bro1 *Ferr-p* bro1 *Ferr-pern* bro1 *Ferr-pic* bro1 *Ferr-prox* bro1 *Ferr-py* bro1 *Ferr-s* bro1 *Ferr-t* bro1 fl-ac bro1 *Graph* bro1 hell bro1 *Hep* bg2* hippoz br1* hydr bro1 ign b7a.de iod br1* iodof bro1 kali-bi bro1 kali-c mtf11 kali-i bro1* kreos bro1 *Lap-a* br1* lyc bro1* mag-c b4a.de mag-m bro1 *Merc* bro1* *Merc-act* bro1 *Merc-aur* bro1 *Merc-br* bro1 *Merc-c* bro1 *Merc-cy* bro1 *Merc-d* bro1 *Merc-i-f* bro1 *Merc-i-r* bro1 *Merc-ns* bro1 *Merc-p* bro1 *Merc-pr-r* bro1 *Merc-tn* bro1 mez bro1 nit-ac bro1 nux-v b7a.de ol-j br1* petr br1* ph-ac bro1 phos bro1 pin-s br1* plb-i bro1 psor br1* puls b7a.de rheum b7a.de ruta bro1 samb bro1 *Scroph-n* br1 sed-ac bro1 sep b4a.de sil bg2* sil-mar bro1 *Spig* br1 still br1* sulph b4a.de* ther br1* tub bro1* viol-t bro1

  ⁝ **children**; in: cina mtf33

- **Joints**: apis ptk1 ars-i bg2 calc ptk1 calc-p bg2* cist bg2 dros mtf33 form bg2 hed sp1 kali-c bg2* kali-i ptk1 merc bg2 ph-ac bg2* phos bg2 puls bg2* sil bg2* sulph bg2 tub mtf11

TUGGING, PLUCKING sensation: chin b2.de cic b2.de

TUMORS: *(↗Cancerous)* anan c2* *Ant-c* ptk1 apis c2 arn c2 ars ptk1 astac c2 aur c2 aur-m-n c2* *Bar-c* c2* bar-i c2* bar-m c2* bell ptk1 bell-p c2* berb c2 bov c2 brom mrr1 *Calc* c2* *Calc-ar* c2* calc-f bro1* calc-s c2 carb-an ptk1 carb-v ptk1 caust ptk1 chel c2 chol br1 *Cist* bro1 clem ptk1 coloc c2* con c2* croc c2 cund br1 cupre-l c2 dulc c2 eucal c2* eupi c2 ferr-i br1* ferr-pic bro1 form-ac bro1 formal br1 gali bro1 goss c2 graph c2* hecla c2* hydr bro1 *Kali-br* bro1 kali-i c2* kreos bro1 lach c2* lap-a c2* laur c2 lec br1 *Lob-e* bro1 *Lyc* bro1* mag-c c2 maland bro1 manc bro1 mand sp1 med bro1* merc-i-r bro1 merl bro1 nat-cac bro1 nat-sil bro1 nat-sil-f c2 *Nit-ac* ptk1 phos c2* phyt c2* *Plb-i* bro1 psor bro1 ran-b ptk1 sang c2 *Semp* br1* sil c2* sol-t c2 staph c2* sulph ptk1 tarent c2 thiosin c2* thuj c2* *Thyr* bro1 *Ur-ac* bro1 urea bro1 vac c2

- **angioma**: *(↗hemangioma; lymphangioma; HEAD - Tumors - angiosarcoma; SKIN - Excrescences - fungus haematodes; SKIN - Spider)* abrot ptk1* ant-t anthraci mtf arg-n mtf **Ars** bar-c mtf bell bell-p mtf benz-ac mtf brom mtf cact mtf *Calc* calc-f mtf **Carb-an** *Carb-v* caust mtf clem con mtf fl-ac mtf kali-br mtf kali-i mtf *Kreos* **Lach** *Lyc* k* m-arct mtf *Merc* mez mtf *Nat-m* *Nit-ac* nux-v k1 **Phos** phyt mtf *Puls* *Rhus-t* k1 sabal gm1 sep **Sil** staph *Sulph* k* **Thuj** vanad mtf
  - **angiocholitis**: guat sp1 ser-a-c jl2
- **atheroma**, steatoma: *Agar* j5.de* ant-c j5.de anthraci kr1 arg-n k2 *Bar-c* k* *Bell* hr1* benz-ac c1* brom sf1.de *Calc* k* caps hr1 caust hr1* clem hr1* *Con* hr1* crat br1 **Graph** k* *Guare* a1* *Hep* k* kali-br hr1* *Kali-c* k* kali-i c1* lac-ac hr1* lach c1* *Lob* k* lyc m-arct j5.de mez sf1.de nat-c *Nit-ac* j5.de* *Ph-ac* hr1* *Phyt* hr1* plb k2 rhus-t hr1* *Sabin* j5.de* *Sil* j5.de* spong j5.de staph c1* *Sulph* j5.de* thuj kr1 vanad c1*
  - **reappearing** every four weeks: *Calc*
  - **suppurating**: *Calc* *Carb-v* *Sulph* j5.de
- **benign** (See Polypus)
- **cheloid** (See SKIN - Keloid)
- **colloid**: *(↗Cancerous - colloid)* (non:carb-ac hr1) carb-an hr1 hydr kr1 phos kr1
- **congestive**: bell-p sp1
- **cystic**: agar k* ant-c b2.de* *Apis* bg2* apoc hr1* ars hr1* *Aur* bg2* aur-m-n vml3• **Bar-c** k* *Bell-p* vh benz-ac sf1.de bov c1* *Brom* k* **Calc** k* calc-f sf1.de calc-p bro1 *Calc-s* k* carc mlr1• *Caust* bg2 *Con* bg2* cory br1 form-ac sf1.de **Graph** k* *Hep* b2.de* hydr bg2 *Iod* bg2* *Kali-br* bro1* kali-c b2.de* lyc sf1.de* m-arct b2.de* *Med* st1 merc-d sf1.de nit-ac k* **Phos** ptk1* platan bro1 *Sabin* b2.de* sil k* spong b2.de* staph c1* sulph k* *Thuj* b4a.de*

○ • **Bones**, of: mez syph jl2*

- **encephaloma**: *(↗HEAD - Cancer - brain; HEAD - Tumors - brain)* acet-ac k* arn hr1* *Ars* k* *Ars-i* k* art-v hr1* aur-i sne bell hr1* *Calc* carb-ac k* *Carb-an* k* caust k* *Croc* hr1* hippoz gm1 hydr hr1* kali-i k* *Kreos* k* *Lach* k* nit-ac k* nux-v hr1* **Phos** k* plb c1 *Sil* k* sulfa sp1 sulph k* *Thuj* k*

Tumors: ...

- **enchondroma**: *(↗Cartilages; Swelling - cartilages)* aran mtf brom mtf *Calc* hr1* calc-f bro1 carb-v mtf conch c1* fl-ac mtf lap-a bro1 *Sil* hr1* thuj mtf
- **erectile**: *Lyc* k* *Nit-ac* k* *Phos* k* staph
- **fatty**: *(↗lipoma)* agar c2 calc k2 thuj c2 ur-ac c2*
- **fibroid** (See FEMALE - Tumors - uterus - myoma)
- **fibrosarcoma**: *(↗Cancerous - sarcoma)* aur mtf cadm-m mtf calc-f mtf sil mtf
- **ganglion**: *(↗EXTREMITIES - Ganglion; SKIN - Ganglia)* acon bg2 am-c k* ant-c bg2 apis bg2 arn k* ars-i bg2 aur-m k* bell bg2 *Benz-ac* bg2* bov bg2* *Calc* hr1 calc-f sf1.de calc-p bg2 *Carb-v* k* carc mlr1• ferr-ma c1 hep bg2 iod bg2* kali-m bg2* mag-p bg2 ph-ac k* *Phos* k* plb k* rhus-t k* *Ruta* k* seneg bg2 sil k* stict bg2 sul-i bg2 sulph k* thuj c1* tub-a jl2 zinc k*
- **gummata**: asaf bro1 *Aur* bro1 berb-a bro1 *Calc-f* bro1 carb-an bro1* cory br1* cund bro1 *Fl-ac* bro1 iod bg2* *Kali-bi* bro1 kali-i bg2* merc bro1 mez bro1 nit-ac bro1 *Phyt* bro1 sil bro1 staph bro1 *Still* bro1 sulph bro1 thuj bro1
- **hard**: calc-f bro1* *Con* mk1• *Hecla* bro1 lap-a bro1 maland bro1 ruta bro1 *Scir* mk1• sil bro1* verb c1
- **hemangioma**: *(↗angioma)* abrot mtf agar mtf ant-c mtf crot-h mtf fl-ac mtf lach mtf vanad mtf vip mtf
- **keloid** (See SKIN - Keloid)
- **lipoma**: *(↗fatty)* agar hr1* *Am-m* hr1* aur ptk1* bacls-10 mtf11 **Bar-c** b4a.de* **Bell** hr1* *Calc* hr1* calc-ar bro1 carc mlr1• croc hr1* graph hr1* *Kali-br* st *Lap-a* hr1* med mtf11 merc b4a.de phos hr1* *Phyt* hr1* sil vh *Spong* b7a.de *Sulph* b4a.de *Thuj* c1* ur-ac c1*
- **lymphangioma**: *(↗angioma)* bar-c mtf rad-br mtf sec mtf vip mtf
- **myeloma**: *Hecla* mk1•
- **neurofibroma**: *(↗neuroma; schwannoma)* astra-e mtf calc mtf calc-f mtf lepr vk
- **neuroma**: *(↗neurofibroma; schwannoma)* *All-c* bro1* *Calc* calen hr1* ruta mrr1 staph
- **nevi** (See SKIN - Nevi)
- **noma** (See MOUTH - Stomatitis - gangrenous)
- **osteoma**: calc-f mtf fl-ac mtf kali-i mrr1 *Mez* h2*
- **papillomata**: *(↗Cancerous - epithelioma)* ant-c bro1 arg-n mrr1 beryl mtf11 *Calc* hr1* nit-ac bro1 staph bro1 *Thuj* bro1
- **rhabdomyosarcoma**: *(↗Cancerous - sarcoma)* con mtf med mtf syph mtf thuj mtf
- **sarcoma** (See Cancerous - sarcoma)
- **schwannoma**: *(↗neurofibroma; neuroma)* calc mtf
- **scrofulous**: mand sp1
- **spongy**: thuj br1
- **steatoma** (See atheroma)

TURNING:

- **affected** part:
  - **agg.**: ang b7.de ant-t b7.de arn b7.de bry b7.de camph b7.de cham b7.de chin b7.de *Cic* b7.de cocc b7.de cycl b7.de dros b7.de ign b7.de ip b7.de laur b7.de nux-v b7.de puls b7.de ran-b b7.de* sabad b7.de samb b7.de *Spong* b7.de* verat b7.de
  - **amel.**: bell ptk1
- **arms** agg.: spig b7.de
- **around** agg.; turning: agar k* aloe anac b4a.de ars b4a.de *Borx* b4a.de bry ptk1 calc k* cham k* cocc ptk1 coloc ptk1 con b4.de* *Hep* b4a.de *Ip* k* kali-c k* merc k* nat-m k* par k* *Phos* k* rhod b4a.de sil k*
- **bed**; in:
  - **agg.**: *Acon* k* agar k* am-m k* anac k* ars k* asar k* bell ptk1 *Borx* k* *Brom* bg2 *Bry* k* cact ptk1 calad ptk1 calc k* *Cann-s* k* *Caps* k* *Carb-v* k* caust k* chin k* cina k* cocc k* *Con* k* cupr k* dros k* *Euph* k* *Ferr* k* graph k* *Hep* k* kali-c k* kreos k* lac-c ptk1 lach k* led k* *Lyc* k* m-ambo b2.de* mag-c k* merc k* *Nat-m* k* nit-ac k* **Nux-v** k* petr k* phos k* plat k* plb k* **Puls** k* ran-b k* rhod k* rhus-t k* ruta k* sabad k* sabin k* samb k* sang ptk1 sars k* *Sil* k* *Staph* k* *Sulph* k* thuj k* valer k* zinc ptk1
  - **amel.**: *Cham* b7a.de nat-m ptk1 *Puls* b7a.de
- **eyes** | **agg.**: bry b2.de* caps b2.de* cupr b2.de* lyc b2.de* nux-v b2.de* puls b2.de* rhus-t b2.de* sep b2.de* *Sil* b2.de* *Spig* b2.de*
- **head**: *(↗HEAD - Turned; HEAD - Turning - head - agg.)*
  - **agg.**: *(↗HEAD - Turned; HEAD - Turning - Head - agg.)* am-m k* anac k* ang b2.de* ant-c k* *Arn* k* asar k* bar-c k* *Bell* k* bov k* *Bry* k* **Calc** k* calc-hp bg2 camph k* cann-s k* canth k* carb-an k* carb-v k*

- **head** – **agg**.: ...
  caust k* cham k* chin k* **Cic** k* cocc k* coff k* coloc k* cupr k* dros k* dulc k* glon **Hep** k* hyos k* *Ign* k* ip k* kali-c k* lach k* *Lyc* k* mag-c k* mez k* *Nat-c* k* *Nat-m* k* nit-ac k* *Nux-v* k* par k* petr k* ph-ac k* *Phos* k* plat k* *Puls* k* *Rhus-t* k* sabad k* sabin k* samb k* *Sang* sars k* *Sel* k* *Sep* k* spig k* **Spong** k* stann k* staph k* sulph k* thuj k* verat k* viol-t k* zinc k*
- **left**; from right to:
  - **agg**.: scop ptk1 sulph ptk1
  - **amel**.: lach bg1 phos bg1
- **rapidly**; as if: mosch ptk1
- **right**; from left to:
  - **agg**.: sulph bg1
  - **amel**.: lach ptk1 phos ptk1 thuj bg2
- **right**; to: carb-v ptk1 spig ptk1
  - **rising**:
    - **agg**.: kali-c ptk1
    - **before**: kali-c ptk1
- **twisting** involuntarily; turning and: lyc h2

TURPENTINE agg.: nux-m bro1

TWILIGHT; in the:
- **agg**.: (↗*Evening - twilight - agg.)* **Ars** bg1* berb ptk1 **Calc** bg1* caust ptk1 mang bg2 nat-s ptk1 **Phos** bg2* plat ptk1 **Puls** bg1* **Rhus-t** bg1* [mang-p stj2]
- **amel**.: (↗*Evening - twilight - amel.)* bry b2.de* meny ptk1* *Phos* b2.de* plat ptk1 seneg ptk1 tab ptk1

TWITCHING: (↗*MIND - Gestures - tics)* abies-c a1 acon k* acon-c a1 **Agar** k* agath-a nl2• agn alum k* alum-p k2* alum-sil k2* alumn a1* am-c am-m k* *Ambr* k* amyg hr1 **Anac** b4a.de androc bnm2• *Ang* b7.de* ant-c k* *Ant-t* k* apis k* aran hr1* *Arg-met* k* *Arg-n* k* arn b2.de* *Ars* k* *Ars-i* ars-s-f a1* ars-s-r a1 arund a1* **Asaf** k* asc-t hr1* aster k* atro k* *Bar-c* k* bar-i k2* bar-m k* *Bell* k* bism bg2 borx brom bruc a1 *Bry* k* bufo **Cact** cadm-s a1* *Calc* k* *Calc-i* k2* calc-p a1 *Calc-s* k* calc-sil k2* *Camph* k* cann-i k* cann-s b2.de* *Canth* k* caps k* carb-ac k* carb-v k* *Carbn-s* carc mg1.de* *Caust* k* *Cedr* hr1* cerv a1 cham k* *Chel* k* *Chin* k* *Chinin-s* chlf hr1* chlor k* *Cic* k* cic-m a1 *Cimic* k* *Cina* k* *Clem* k* *Cocc* k* *Cod* k* *Coff* b7.de* coff-t a1 colch k* coloc k* *Con* k* croc k* crot-h k* *Cupr* k* cupr-s a1* cycl b7.de cypr hr1* cyt-l a1 dig k* dioxi rbp6 dol a1* dor hr1* dros k* dulc b2.de* echit a1 ferr k2* ferr-r bro1 form bg2 *Gels* hr1* *Glon* bg1* *Graph* k* guaj hedeo a1 *Hell* k* hep b2.de* hydr-ac bg2* **Hyos** k* **Ign** k* **Iod** k* ip k* juni-v a1 *Kali-ar* kali-br k* **Kali-c** k* kali-chl hr1* *Kali-i* hr1* kali-m k2 kali-n h2* kali-p k* kali-s kali-sil k2* kreos k* *Lach* k* lact a1 lat-m bnm6• laur k* led b7.de lipp a1 lon-x a1 lup bro1 *Lyc* k* *Lyss* k* m-ambo b2.de* m-arct b7.de *M-aust* b7.de* mag-c b2.de* mag-m k* mag-p k* *Mang* b4a.de meny k* *Merc* k* *Merc-c* k* merc-cy br1 **Mez** k* *Mill* hr1 morph a1* *Mosch* b7.de* *Mur-ac* k* mygal k* *Nat-ar* **Nat-c** k* nat-f sp1 *Nat-m* k* *Nat-p* nat-s k2* nat-sil k2* *Nit-ac* k* nitro-o a1 *Nux-m* a1* *Nux-v* k* oena a1* ol-an bg2 olnd *Op* k* ox-ac k* *Par* k* petr k* *Ph-ac* k* *Phos* k* phys bg2* phyt k2* pic-ac a1 *Pieri-b* mlk9.de plat k* *Plb* k* plb-act bro1 *Podo* sf1.de psor k* puls k* *Ran-b* b2.de* *Ran-s* b7a.de rat bg2* *Rheum* b7.de* rhod k* *Rhus-t* k* *Rhus-v* a1* ruta sabad b2.de* sabin salin a1 *Santin* bro1 sarcol-ac sp1 scut a1 *Sec* k* sel senec-j a1* seneg *Sep* k* *Sil* k* sol-ni a1 *Spig* k* spong k* squil b2.de* *Stann* staph b2.de* **Stram** k* stront-c k* stroph-h ptk1 *Stry* k* stry-p br1 sul-ac k* sul-i k2* *Sulph* k* syph hr1 tab bg2* tanac tarax tarent hr1* ter hr1* teucr b7.de thal-xyz srj8• thuj k* valer k* vanil fd5.de *Verat* b2.de* *Verat-v* bg2* viol-t k* vip bg2* *Visc* k* x-ray sp1 **Zinc** k* zinc-m a1 *Zinc-p* k2* ziz bro1
- **one-sided**: apis kl stront-c sk4•
- **right**: caust chen-a c1 tarent bg2
- **left**: stront-c sk4•
- **daytime**: *Bar-c* hr1* lyss hr1*
- **morning**: rheum a1
  - **waking**; on: chel kr1 menth-pu a1
- **noon**: petr a1 **Zinc** a1
- **evening**: aether a1 vanil fd5.de
  - **bed** agg.; in: ped a1 petr a1 ran-b a1 sil a1
- **night**: ambr a1* cupr-act a1 op a1 staph a1* tab a1
  - **sleep** agg.; during: graph a1 nat-c a1 petr a1 sel a1 **Zinc** a1
- **accompanied by** | **hemorrhage**: *Chin* kr1 croc mrr1
- **alcoholism**, in: *Crot-h* hr1* *Phos* hr1*
- **children**; in: zinc mtf33

Twitching: ...
- **chill**; during: ambr ptk1 ars bg2 caust bg2 coloc bg2 hyos bg2 ign bg2 lach b7a.de* *Merc* bg2 nat-m bg2 *Op* bg2 phos bg2 staph bg2 *Stram* b7.de* sulph bg2
- **convulsions**:
  - **before**: aster ptk1
  - **during**: cic bro1 hyos bro1 verat-v ptk1
- **cough** agg.; during: *Cina* b7a.de cupr b7a.de
- **delirium**; with (See MIND - Delirium - twitching)
- **delivery**; during: cinnm kr1
  - **labor** ceases; twitching begins when: *Sec* kr1
- **dentition**; during: *Cham* hr1* ter hr1* *Zinc* a1*
- **electricity**, as from: acon a1 arn a1 clem a1 cypra-eg sde6.de• *Daph* a1 dulc a1 plb a1 sec a1
  - **motion**; from: colch tl1
- **fever**; during: ars bg2 *Bell* bg2* **Bry** b7a.de* cham bg2 coloc bg2 cupr bg2 dulc fd4.de hyos bg2 ign bg2 meny bg2 merc bg2 *Nat-m* bg2 nit-s-d kr1 **Op** b7.de* *Puls* b7.de* rhus-t b7.de* *Sec* bg2 *Spong* kr1 stram bg2 sulph bg2 thuj bg2 verat bg2 *Viol-t* bg2
- **fright**; after: *Ign* hr1 *Op* *Stram*
- **grief**; after: ign mrr1
- **hemorrhage** with (See accompanied - hemorrhage)
- **here** and there: agar k* alum h2 ant-c bg2 chel bg2* *Cocc* colch k* hyos gk *Kali-c* k* kali-n k* lyc k* mag-c lp mez k* nat-c h2 nat-m k* ph-ac k* phos k* rhod k* sep k* *Stry* sulph k* **Zinc** k*
- **joy**, from excessive: coff k2
- **menses** | **after** | **agg**.: chin bg2* cupr bg2* kreos bg2 *Nat-m* bg2* puls bg2*
  - **during** | **agg**.: acon bg* bell bg2 bry bg* calc bg* calc-s hr1* caust bg* cham bg* chin b7a.de* cocc bg2* coff b7a.de* cupr bg* form bg* hyos b7.de* ign bg* ip bg* kali-c bg2 lyc bg* mag-m bg* merc bg* nat-m bg* nux-v bg* plat bg2 puls bg* sec bg2 sulph bg2*
- **perspiration**; during: ars bg2 bell bg2 *Bry* bg2 caust bg2 *Cham* bg2 coloc bg2 cupr bg2 hyos bg2 ign bg2 meny bg2 merc bg2 nat-m bg2 nux-v bg2 **Op** bg2 puls bg2 *Rhus-t* bg2 sec bg2 stram bg2 sulph bg2 thuj bg2 verat bg2 viol-t bg2
- **rest** agg.: sacch-a fd2.de• valer k2*
- **sensation** of: chin bg2 cic bg2
- **sleep**:
  - **amel**.: agar k2*
  - **during** | **agg**.: *Acon* bro1 *Aeth* bro1 *Agar* bro1 *Alum* k* ambr b7.de* anac k* ant-c bro1 *Ant-t* b7a.de* *Apis* bro1 *Ars* k* *Bar-c* hr1* bell k* borx bro1 brom a1* bry b7.de* calc bro1 camph b7a.de carb-v bro1* castm bro1 caust k* *Cham* b7a.de* chin bro1 *Chlf* hr1* cina bg2* cinnb *Colch* hr1* con k* *Cupr* k* *Cupr-act* bro1 daph bro1 dig ptk1 dulc k* graph b4a.de* *Hell* hr1* *Hep* b4a.de **Hyos** b7.de* hyper hr1* ign b7.de* *Kali-c* k* kiss a1 kreos bg2 lach b7a.de *Lyc* b4a.de* m-ambo b7a.de mag-c k* merc b4a.de* mez k* morph bro1 nat-c k* nat-m k* nat-s bg2* nat-sil mtf33 nit-ac bro1 nux-v bro1 op b7a.de* passi bro1 petr h2 ph-ac k* phos k* pieri-b mlk9.de puls b7.de* rheum b7a.de* rhus-t b7.de* samb bro1 sel b7a.de seneg k* *Sep* b4a.de* sil k* stann k* staph b7.de* *Stram* b7.de* *Stront-c* k* sul-ac k* *Sulph* k* tarent bro1 tep a1 thuj k* valer bro1 viol-t b7.de* **Zinc** k* ziz bro1
  - **going** to sleep; on:
    - **agg**.: (↗*Jerking - muscles - sleep - going - agg.)* acon k* *Agar* all-s kr1 *Aloe* kr1 *Alum* arg-met arg-n ptk1 **Ars** k* **Bell** bg2* borx ptk1 bry ptk1 calc bg2* carb-v k2 cham bg2* cina ptk1 cob ham fd3.de• hyper *Ign* k* iodof kr1 **Kali-c** k* lyc ptk1 mag-m h2* nit-ac ptk1 op ptk1 ozone sde2• phys puls bg2* sacch-a fd2.de• *Sel* k* *Sep* bg2* sil ptk1 stram ptk1 *Stront-c* *Stry* *Sul-ac* *Sulph* vanil fd5.de *Zinc* k*
    - **air**; as from lack of: calc-s ptk1
- **subsultus** tendinum: acon a1 acon-c a1 *Agar* k* *Alco* a1 am-c ambr k* anac b4a.de ant-c b7.de* ant-t b7.de* *Arg-met* bg2 arn b7.de* *Ars* k* *Asaf* k* asar bg2 bar-c b4a.de* bell k* bism bg2 bol-lu a1 borx bg2 bov bg2 bry b7a.de* *Calc* k* *Camph* k* cann-s bg2 *Canth* carb-v bg2 caust bg2 cham bg2 *Chel* chin b7.de* *Chlor* k* cic bg2 cimic bg2 *Clem* b4a.de* *Cocc* b7.de* *Coloc* bg2 con b4a.de* croc bg2 cupr b7a.de* cupr-s a1 dig bg2 *Graph* bg2 hell b7.de* **Hyos** k* ign b7a.de* indg a1 **Iod** k* ip bg2 kali-c b4.de* *Kali-i* k* lach b7a.de* laur b7.de* *Lyc* k* mang bg2 *Meny* b7.de* merc bg2 merc-n a1 *Mez* k* mosch bg2 *Mur-ac* k* *Nat-c* b4a.de* nat-m b4a.de* nit-ac bg2 nux-v bg2 olnd bg2 op a1 *Ph-ac* k* *Phos* k* *Plat* bg2 plb b7.de* puls b7a.de* ran-s b7.de* rheum bg2 rhus-t k* *Sec* k*

- **subsultus** tendinum: ...
sep b4a.de* sil bg2 spig bg2 *Spong* b7.de* squil sf1.de stann bg2 stram bg2* *Stry* k* sul-ac b4a.de* sulph b4a.de* tarax bg2 *Ter* a1 teucr b7a.de* valer bg2 verat a1 viol-t b7.de* vip a1 **Zinc** k*
  - **fever**; during: iod b4.de*
- **sudden**: mez bg2
- **touch** agg.: morph a1 phos a1 *Stry* k*
- **typhoid** fever; during: **Calc** kr1 cham kr1 *Colch* kr1 crot-h kr1 *Cypr* kr1 *Gels* kr1 **Hyos** kr1 *Lyc* kr1 *Ter* kr1 *Zinc* kr1
- **urination** agg.; after: *Coloc* b4a.de
- **waking**; on: *Ars* j5.de *Bell* j5.de *Camph* hr1* carc mg1.de* cham sf1.de chel a1* *Cod* hr1* *Hyos* sf1.de* *Laur* hr1* lyc j5.de mag-m j5.de op a1 sang a1 stront-c j5.de
- **weather** | **thunderstorm**; before: agar mtf33
- **worm** complaints; in: *Cina* sabad kr1* santin br1

○ - **Glands**: caps b7.de* clem b4.de* sulph b4.de*
- **Internally**: (↗*Jerking - internally*) atro bov *Cann-s* cic a1 seneg vanil fd5.de
- **Muscles**: agar bg2 ambr b2.de* ant-c b2.de* ant-t b2.de* *Arg-met* b2.de* arn b2.de* ars b2.de* *Asaf* b2.de* asar b2.de* bar-c b2.de* *Bell* b2.de* bism b2.de* borx b2.de* both tsm2 both-ax tsm2 bov bg2 bry b2.de* bung-fa tsm2 calc b2.de* cann-s b2.de* carb-v b2.de* caust b2.de* cham b2.de* chin b2.de* cic b2.de* cimic bg2 clem b2.de* *Cocc* b2.de* coloc b2.de* con b2.de* croc b2.de* crot-c tsm2 crot-h tsm2 *Cupr* b2.de* dendr-pol tsm2 dig b2.de* elaps tsm2 *Graph* b2.de* hell b2.de* hyos b2.de* ign b2.de* **Iod** b2.de* ip b2.de* kali-c b2.de* lach b2.de* laur b2.de* lup br1 mang b2.de* *Meny* b2.de* merc b2.de* **Mez** b2.de* mosch bg2 naja tsm2 *Nat-c* b2.de* nat-m b2.de* nit-ac b2.de* nux-v bg2 olnd b2.de* ph-ac bg2 phos b2.de* *Plat* b2.de* plb b2.de* puls b2.de* ran-s b2.de* rheum b2.de* rhus-t b2.de* *Scut* br1 *Sec* b2.de* sep b2.de* sil b2.de* spig b2.de* *Spong* b2.de* stann b2.de* stram bg2 sul-ac b2.de* sulph b2.de* tarax b2.de* teucr b2.de* valer bg2 viol-t b2.de* vip tsm2 zinc bg2 zinc-val ll1*
  - **accompanied** by | **Face**; paralysis of (See FACE - Paralysis - accompanied - muscles)
  - **chill**; during: bell bg2 iod bg2 kali-c bg2 mez bg2
  - **fever**; during: *Bell* bg2 coloc bg2 cupr bg2 *Iod* bg2 **Kali-c** bg2 *Mez* bg2 nat-c bg2 plat bg2 *Sec* bg2 spong bg2 viol-t bg2
  - **perspiration**; during: *Bell* bg2 coloc bg2 cupr bg2 iod bg2 *Kali-c* bg2 mez bg2 nat-c bg2 *Op* bg2 *Plat* bg2 **Rhus-t** bg2 sec bg2 spong bg2 viol-t bg2
- **Paralyzed** part, of: apis kr1 *Arg-n* bg1* *Merc* bg1* nux-v kr1 phos bg1* *Sec* bg1* stram bg1* stry kr1
- **Single** parts, of: agar bg2 alum bg2 chin bg2 *Cocc* bg2 nux-v bg2 puls bg2 zinc bg2
- **Upper** part of body:
  - **convulsions**; during: stram bro1
  - **delivery**; after: cic bro1
  - **lying** down agg.: nat-m h2

TYMPANITES (See ABDOMEN - Distension - tympanitic)

TYMPANITIS (See EAR - Inflammation - media)

TYPHUS ABDOMINALIS (See FEVER - Typhoid)

ULCERS:

○ - **Bones**: asaf ptk1 *Merc* b4a.de ph-ac b4a.de phos b4a.de sep b4a.de sil b4a.de sulph b4a.de syph jl2*
- **Cartilages**: arg-met k2 merc bro1 merc-c bro1
- **Glands**: *Ambr* k* ant-c k* arn k* **Ars** k* asaf k* aur k* aur-ar k2 bar-c b4a.de *Bell* k* calc k* *Canth* k* carb-an k* carb-v k* caust k* clem k* coloc k* *Con* k* cupr k* dulc k* *Hep* k* hyos k* ign k* kali-bi bg3 kali-c k* kali-p kreos k* *Lach* k* lyc k* merc k* nit-ac k* *Ol-j* kr1 ph-ac k* **Phos** k* *Phyt* **Puls** bg3 rhus-t k* *Rhus-v* kr1 sars k* sep k* **Sil** k* spong k* squil k* sul-ac k* *Sulph* k* thuj k* zinc k*
  - **cancerous**: **Ars** b4a.de aur b4a.de *Bell* b4a.de **Brom** b4a.de calc b4a.de carb-an b4a.de carb-v b4a.de caust b4a.de clem b4a.de **Con** b4a.de dulc b4a.de *Hep* b4a.de kali-c b4a.de lyc b4a.de merc b4a.de nit-ac b4a.de ph-ac b4a.de phos b4a.de *Sep* b4a.de *Sil* b4a.de **Sulph** b4a.de zinc b4a.de
  - **spongy**: **Carb-an** b2.de* clem b2.de* kreos b2.de* *Lach* b2.de* *Merc* b2.de* nit-ac b2.de* rhus-t b2.de* sep b2.de* **Sil** b2.de* *Sulph* b2.de* *Thuj* b2.de*
- **Joints**: coloc ptk1 hep ptk1 ph-ac ptk1 *Sep* ptk1 sil ptk1

○ • **About**: **Coloc** bg2 **Ph-ac** bg2 **Sep** bg2
  - **Above**: borx bg2 sep bg2
  - **On** joints: nux-v bg2

Ulcers: ...
- **Skin** (See SKIN - Ulcers)

UNCLEANLINESS agg.: (↗*MIND - Cleanness - mania; MIND - Dirty; MIND - Washing - desire - hands*) **Caps** k* *Chin* k* kali-s fd4.de lac-h htj1• *Psor* puls k* *Sulph* k*

UNCOVERING:
- **agg.**: (↗*Cold; becoming - after - agg.; Undressing; SKIN - Itching - undressing*) *Acon* k* acon-f *Agar* k* *Am-c* ant-c k* apoc c1* arg-met k* *Arg-n* arn k* **Ars** k* asar k* astac vh *Atro* *Aur* k* aur-ar k2 *Bell* k* *Benz-ac* k* borx k* *Bry* k* calc-sil k2* camph k* cann-xyz bg2 canth k* *Caps* k* *Carb-an* k* caust bg2* *Cham* k* *Chin* k* *Cic* k* *Clem* k* *Cocc* k* *Coff* k* *Colch* k* *Con* k* dios dros bro1 *Dulc* *Graph* k* hell k* **Hep** k* hyos k* *Ign* k* **Kali-ar** *Kali-bi* k* **Kali-c** k* kali-i *Kali-sil* k2* kalm c1 kreos k* *Lach* k* led b2.de* **Lyc** k* *Lycps-v* m-aust b2.de *Mag-c* k* *Mag-m* k* **Mag-p** k* mang h2 meny k* *Merc* k* mur-ac k* *Nat-c* k* *Nat-m* k* **Nux-m** k* **Nux-v** k* *Ph-ac* k* *Phos* k* psor bg2* puls k* rheum k* **Rhod** k* **Rhus-t** k* *Rumx* k* sabad k* **Samb** k* sangin-n c1 sep k* **Sil** k* **Squil** k* staph k* stram k* **Stront-c** k* sulph bg2 thuj k* **Zinc** zinc-p k2*
  - **least**: hep ptk1 nux-v ptk1 rhus-t ptk1 *Sil* ptk1
- **ailments** from: kalm sangin-n
- **amel.**: *Acon* b2.de* alum bg2 apis k2* ars b2.de* asar b2.de* aur b2.de* *Borx* b2.de* bry b2.de* *Calc* b2.de* calc-s k2 camph bro1 cann-s b7.de* carb-v b2.de* cham b2.de* chin b2.de* coff b2.de* *Ferr* b2.de* hydrog srj2• ign b2.de* **Iod** b2.de* kali-i bg2 lach b2.de* led b2.de* **Lyc** b2.de* *M-ambo* b2.de* *M-arct* b2.de merc b2.de* mosch b2.de* mur-ac b2.de* nit-ac b2.de* nux-v b2.de* onos bro1 op b2.de* phos b2.de* plat b2.de* podo fd3.de• **Puls** b2.de* rhus-t b2.de* sal-fr sle1• *Sec* b2.de* seneg b2.de* sep b2.de* *Spig* b2.de* staph b2.de* sulph b2.de* *Tab* bro1 thuj b2.de* *Verat* b2.de*
- **aversion** to: arg-n st1 *Ars* bg2* aur hr1* *Bell* bg2* calc-s k2* *Camph* hr1 carb-an hr1 clem sf1.de coff hr1 colch sf1.de cor-r hr1 *Hell* hr1* hep sf1.de* mag-c sf1.de *Merc* hr1 nat-m sf1.de* nux-m sf1.de *Nux-v* bg2* ph-ac sf1.de **Puls** hr1 samb sf1.de sil sf1.de *Squil* bg2* *Stront-c* bg2*
  - **heat**; during sensation of: mag-c cp
- **chest** | **amel.**: sars ptk1
- **desire** for: *Acon* bg2* *Aloe* k2* *Apis* sf1.de *Ars* hr1 ars-i k2* asar sf1.de borra-o oss1• *Bry* hr1 calc hr1* calc-s k2* *Camph* bg2* ferr sf1.de hydrog srj2• hyos tl1 *Ign* hr1 *Iod* bg2* iodof hr1 kali-i k2* led k2* *Lyc* hr1* manc a1 med jl2 merc k2* mosch hr1* mur-ac hr1* *Nit-ac* hr1 op k2* podo fd3.de• *Puls* bg2* *Sec* bg2* spig sf1.de *Staph* hr1 stram sf1.de *Sulph* bg2* tab sf1.de verat sf1.de
  - **morning**: fl-ac a1
  - **sleep**:
    - **during**: alum bg2 plat ptk1*
    - **on** going to: *Op* a1
  - **waking**, on: lyc mtf33 *Plat* a1
- **hands**; of | **agg.**: rhus-t b7a.de
- **head**:
  - **agg.**: acon b2.de* agar b2.de* ant-c b2.de* arg-met b2.de* arn b2.de* ars b2.de* *Aur* b2.de* *Bell* b2.de* benz-ac bg2 borx bg2 brom bg2 *Calc-p* bg2 camph b2.de* canth b2.de* cham b2.de* chin b2.de* cic b2.de* clem b2.de* cocc b2.de* coff b2.de* *Colch* b2.de* *Con* b2.de* graph b2.de* **Hep** b2.de* *Hyos* b2.de* ign b2.de* *Kali-bi* bg2 kali-c bg2 kreos b2.de* *Lach* b2.de* led b2.de* m-aust b2.de mag-c b2.de* mag-m b2.de* merc b2.de* naja bg2 nat-c b2.de* nat-m b2.de* *Nux-m* b2.de* **Nux-v** b2.de* ph-ac b2.de* phos bg2 puls b2.de* rhod b2.de* **Rhus-t** b2.de* sabad b2.de* *Samb* b2.de* sep b2.de* **Sil** b2.de* *Squil* b2.de* staph b2.de* stram b2.de* *Stront-c* b2.de* thuj bg2
  - **amel.**: *Acon* b2.de* asar b2.de* aur b2.de* *Borx* b2.de* bry b2.de* *Calc* b2.de* *Carb-v* b2.de* cham b2.de* chin b2.de* *Ferr* b2.de* ign b2.de* **Iod** b2.de* lach b2.de* laur b7.de led b2.de* **Lyc** b2.de* *M-ambo* b2.de* *M-arct* b2.de merc b2.de* mur-ac b2.de* nit-ac b2.de* op b2.de* phos b2.de* plat b2.de* *Puls* b2.de* sec b2.de* seneg b2.de* sep b2.de* *Spig* b2.de* staph b2.de* stront-c b4.de *Sulph* b2.de* thuj b2.de* valer b7.de* *Verat* b2.de*
- **kicks** the covers of: aq-mar rbp6 **Bry** st camph st *Cham* st iod st puls mtf33
  - **coldest** weather; in: calc-s tl1 camph tl1 hep st sanic st sec tl1 sulph st*
- **neck** | **amel.**: sars ptk1
- **feet**, of: *Calc* bro1 con bro1 cupr bro1 nux-m bro1 *Sil* b4a.de*
- **single** part agg.: (↗*Cold; becoming - after - agg.; Cold; becoming - agg. - part; EXTREMITIES - Uncovering; EXTREMITIES - Uncovering - Agg.*) *Bry* **Hep** k* *Ip* hr1* *Nat-m* **Rhus-t** k* **Sil** k* squil k* stront-c k* *Thuj* k*

UNDRESSING agg.; after: (*↗Uncovering - agg.; SKIN - Itching - undressing)* am-m k* **Ars** k* calc carc mg1.de* *Cocc* k* crot-t bg2 **Dros** k* *Dulc* bg2 hep k* mag-c k* marb-w es1• merc bg2 mez k* mur-ac nat-s k* **Nux-v** k* *Olnd* k* plat *Puls* k* **Rhus-t** k* rumx bg2* sep k* *Sil* k* *Spong* k* stann k* sul-ac bg2 tub bg2 [calc-sil stj2 ferr-sil stj2 kali-sil stj2 mag-sil stj2 mang-sil stj2 nat-sil stj2 sil-met stj2 stront-m stj2 stront-met stj2]
- **air**, in open: phos k*

UNMARRIED persons; complaints of: (*↗Women - unmarried)* *Con* b4a.de

UNWELL; attacks of feeling (See Sick - paroxysmal)

UREMIA: (*↗KIDNEYS - Renal - chronic)* am-c bg2* *Apis* bro1* apoc bro1* ars bg2* arum-t ptk1 asc-c c2* aur sne *Bapt* ptk1 *Bell* bro1* benz-ac k2 cann-i c2* *Canth* bro1* *Carb-ac* c2* cic bg2* *Cupr-act* c2* cupr-ar bg2* diph-t-tpt jl2 glon bg2* *Hell* bro1* **Hydr-ac** bg2* hyos bro1* kali-br br1* lesp-c mg1.de lesp-s lsr4.de* *Morph* bro1* *Op* bg2* phenac c2 phos bro1* *Pic-ac* br1* pilo bro1* plb bg2* queb bro1 senec ptk1 ser-ang br1* *Stram* bro1* sulfa sp1* ter c2* urea c2* urt-u c2* verat-v bro1*
- **accompanied** by:
  - **apoplexy** (See Apoplexy - accompanied - uremia)
  - **respiration**:
    - **asthmatic**: solid ptk1
    - **difficult**: aspidin br1 solid ptk1
  - **vomiting**: apoc ptk1 ars bro1* iod bro1 kreos bro1 nux-v bro1 samb ptk1 scop ptk1 senec ptk1
  - ○ **Heart**; complaints of the (See CHEST - Heart; complaints - accompanied - uremia)
- **chronic**: botul jl2*
- **coma**; with (See MIND - Coma - uremia)

URGING, PUSHING (= as if forced): alum b2.de* am-c b2.de* am-m b2.de* ambr b2.de* anac b2.de* ang b2.de* ant-c b2.de* arn b2.de* *Asaf* b2.de* aur b2.de* bell b2.de* bism b2.de* borx b2.de* calc b2.de* cann-s b2.de* *Canth* b2.de* caps b2.de* carb-an b2.de* carb-v b2.de* caust b2.de* cham b2.de* chel b2.de* chin b2.de* cina b2.de* clem b2.de* **Cocc** b2.de* colch b2.de* coloc b2.de* con b2.de* croc b2.de* dig b2.de* dulc b2.de* graph b2.de* hell b2.de* hyos b2.de* ign b2.de* iod b2.de* ip b2.de* kali-c b2.de* kali-n b2.de* laur b2.de* led b2.de* lil-t ptk1 lyc b2.de* m-ambo b2.de* m-arct b2.de m-aust b2.de mag-c b2.de* mag-m b2.de* merc b2.de* *Merc-c* ptk1 **Mosch** b2.de* nat-c b2.de* nat-m b2.de nit-ac b2.de* **Nux-v** b2.de* phos b2.de* plat b2.de* **Puls** b2.de* ran-b b2.de* rhod b2.de* *Rhus-t* b2.de* *Sabin* b2.de* samb b2.de* sars b2.de* seneg b2.de* sep b2.de* spig b2.de* spong b2.de* stann b2.de* stram b2.de* sul-ac b2.de* sulph b2.de* teucr b2.de* thuj b2.de*
- **outward** | **Glands**: spong bg2

URIC ACID:
- **diathesis**, lithemia: am-be mtf11 am-p br1 benz-ac br1* berb ptk1 cal-ren-u mld2 coc-c c2* coff br1 colch bg2 coloc bg2 *Epig* br1 fab br1 franc br1 frax-e mtf gins bg2 *Ichth* br1 junc-e br1 led bg2 lith-be mtf11 lith-m mtf11 *Lyc* bg2* lysd c1* nat-n br1 nat-s ptk1 oci br1 physal-al br1 sang bg2 sars bg2* sep bg2* skook c2* sulph bg2 ter bg2 thlas c2* thuj ptk1 urt-u br1*
- **reduced** excretion: chin mtf11

URINATION:
- **after**:
  - **agg.**: agn b2.de alum b2.de ambr b2.de* *Anac* b2.de* ang b2.de* ant-t b2.de* *Arn* b2.de* ars b2.de* asaf b2.de* asar b2.de* bar-c b2.de *Bell* b2.de* borx b2.de* bov b2.de bry b2.de *Calc* b2.de* camph b2.de cann-i h1 **Cann-s** b2.de* cann-xyz ptk1 **Canth** b2.de* *Caps* b2.de* carb-v b2.de chel b2.de* *Chin* b2.de* clem b2.de* colch b2.de **Coloc** b2.de* *Con* b2.de* *Dig* b2.de* equis-h ptk1 graph b2.de* guaj b2.de* **Hep** b2.de* ign b2.de* kali-c b2.de* kreos b2.de lach b2.de* laur b2.de* led b2.de lyc b2.de* lys bg2 m-ambo b2.de m-arct b2.de* mag-c b2.de* med ptk1 **Merc** b2.de* merc-c bg2* mur-ac b2.de* *Nat-c* b2.de* **Nat-m** b2.de* nit-ac b2.de* *Nux-v* b2.de* *Par* b2.de* petros ptk1 ph-ac b2.de phos b2.de* plat b2.de plb b2.de *Puls* b2.de* rhod b2.de* rhus-t b2.de *Ruta* b2.de* sabad b2.de sars b2.de* sel b2.de* seneg b2.de* sep b2.de* sil b2.de spig b2.de squil b2.de stann b2.de* *Staph* b2.de* sul-ac b2.de *Sulph* b2.de* teucr b2.de **Thuj** b2.de* verat b2.de viol-t b2.de *Zinc* b2.de*
  - **amel.**: aids nl2• ant-t vh benz-ac k2* borx bg2 bry st chinin-s ptk1 cyt-l sp1 *Eug* st* **Gels** bg2* *Ign* bg2* lith-c ptk1 *Lyc* bg2* meli ptk1 *Ph-ac* bg2* sang ptk1 sil bro1* solid ptk1 *Tab* st ter bg2 verat ptk1 zinc a1 [bor-pur stj2]

Urination: ...
- **before**: alum b2.de ang b2.de *Ant-t* b2.de *Arn* b2.de asaf b2.de aur b2.de bell b2.de **Borx** b2.de *Bry* b2.de calc b2.de cann-s b2.de canth b2.de caust b2.de cham b2.de chel b2.de chin b2.de cic b2.de cocc b2.de coff b2.de colch b2.de **Coloc** b2.de con b2.de croc b2.de *Dig* b2.de dulc b2.de graph b2.de hep b2.de hyos b2.de kreos b2.de merc b2.de mosch b2.de nat-c b2.de **Nux-v** b2.de op b2.de *Ph-ac* b2.de plb b2.de **Puls** b2.de rhod b2.de *Rhus-t* b2.de sabad b2.de sul-ac b2.de *Sulph* b2.de tarax b2.de thuj b2.de zinc b2.de
  - **agg.**: acon ptk1 alum b2.de* ang b2.de* *Ant-t* b2.de* *Arn* b2.de* asaf b2.de* aur b2.de* bell b2.de* **Borx** b2.de* *Bry* b2.de* calc b2.de* cann-s b2.de* canth b2.de* caust b2.de* cham b2.de* chel b2.de* chin b2.de* cic b2.de* cocc b2.de* coff b2.de* colch b2.de* **Coloc** b2.de* con b2.de* croc b2.de* *Dig* b2.de* dulc b2.de* graph b2.de* hep b2.de* hyos b2.de* kreos b2.de* *Lyc* br1* merc b2.de* merc-c bg2 mosch b2.de* nat-c b2.de* **Nux-v** b2.de* op b2.de* *Ph-ac* b2.de* plb b2.de* **Puls** b2.de* rhod b2.de* *Rhus-t* b2.de* sabad b2.de* sanic ptk1 sars ptk1 sul-ac b2.de* *Sulph* b2.de* tarax b2.de* thuj b2.de* zinc b2.de*
- **copious** | **amel.**: merc-c b4a.de
- **during**:
  - **agg.**: *Acon* b2.de* aesc ptk1* aloe ptk1* alum b2.de* am-c b2.de ambr b2.de* anac b2.de* ang b2.de* ant-c b2.de* ant-t b2.de **Apis** bg2* arn b2.de ars b2.de* asaf b2.de asar b2.de bar-c b2.de* bell b2.de* berb ptk1* borx b2.de bov b2.de bry b2.de* calad b2.de calc b2.de* camph b2.de **Cann-i** a1* **Cann-s** b2.de* *Cann-xyz* ptk1 **Canth** b2.de* caps b2.de* carb-an b2.de carb-v b2.de* caust b2.de* cham b2.de* chel b2.de chin b2.de* *Clem* b2.de* coff b7.de *Colch* b2.de* coloc b2.de *Con* b2.de* cupr b2.de* cycl b2.de dig b2.de dulc b2.de* euph b2.de ferr b2.de graph b2.de* guaj b2.de hell b2.de **Hep** b2.de* hyos b2.de* ign b2.de* *Ip* b2.de* kali-c b2.de* kali-n b2.de kreos b2.de lach b2.de laur b2.de* lil-t ptk1* **Lyc** b2.de* m-aust b2.de mag-c b2.de mag-m b2.de **Merc** b2.de* merc-c bg2* mez b2.de* mur-ac b2.de* nat-c b2.de* nat-m b2.de* *Nit-ac* b2.de* nux-m b2.de* *Nux-v* b2.de* op b2.de par b2.de petr b2.de* **Ph-ac** b2.de* *Phos* b2.de* plat b2.de plb b2.de **Puls** b2.de* rheum b2.de* rhod b2.de rhus-t b2.de* ruta b2.de sabad b2.de sabin b2.de *Sars* b2.de* sec b2.de seneg b2.de* sep b2.de* sil b2.de spig b2.de* squil b2.de* stann b2.de staph b2.de* stram b2.de stront-c b2.de sul-ac b2.de sulph b2.de* **Ter** bg2* teucr b2.de **Thuj** b2.de* *Verat* b2.de* viol-t b2.de zinc b2.de*
  - **beginning** of | **agg.**: *Acon* ptk1 canth b2.de* caust b2.de* clem b2.de* *Merc* b2.de*
  - **end** of: bry b2.de *Canth* b2.de* equis-h bg3* merc-c ptk1 mez ptk1 nat-m ptk1 petr b2.de phos b2.de sars ptk1 sulph b2.de
    - **agg.**: bry b2.de* *Canth* b2.de* petr b2.de* phos b2.de* **Sars** bg2 sulph b2.de*
- **scanty** | **agg.**: benz-ac ptk1 oci ptk1 solid ptk1
- **sediment** is increased; general amel. when (See URINE - Sediment - amel.)

VACCINATION; ailments after: (*↗History - vaccination)* *Acon* c1* *Ant-t* bg2* *Apis* bg2* arn tl1 *Ars* k* *Bar-c* hu *Bell* c1* bufo st calc gk carc pc* cean tl1 crot-h kr1* cupr hu echi k* graph c1* hep k* kali-chl *Kali-m* bg2* lac-v c1 **Maland** k* *Merc* bg2* **Mez** c1* *Ped* st1 phos c1 *Psor* st1 rhus-t bg2 sabin kr1* **Sars** bro1* sep bro1 **SIL** bg2* skook c1 stram mrr1 **SULPH** bg2* **THUJ** bg2* tub hr* **Vac** c1* *Vario* bg2* **Zinc** mrr1* [calc-sil stj2 ferr-sil stj2 kali-sil stj2 mag-sil stj2 mang-sil stj2 nat-sil stj2 sil-met stj2 *Zinc-i* stj2 *Zinc-m* stj2 *Zinc-n* stj2 *Zinc-p* stj2]
- **allergies**; for: thuj cpd•
- **BCG** vaccination: v-a-b jl2
- **children**; in: carc ot*
- **diphtheria**; for: diph gm1 merc-cy gm1
- **DTP**; for: diph-pert-t cpd• sil cpd•
- **meningitis**; for: apis gm1
- **neurological** complaints: stram mrr1
- **never** well since: carc cpd• pyrog cpd• sil cpd• thuj cpd*
- **prophylaxis**: sulph bg2* thuj bg2* vario bg2
- **rabies**; for: **Lyss** mrr1
- **reaction**; severe: carc mlr1•
- **respond** to vaccination; failure to: thuj mrr1
- **smallpox**; for: maland jl2* thuj mrr1* vac jl2 vario cpd*
- **tetanus**; for: mag-p ptk1
- **tuberculosis**; for: *Abrot* vh1 v-a-b jl2
- **typhoid** fever; for: bapt bro1*
- **variola**; for: vac jl2

- **yellow** fever; for: ars gm1 crot-c cpd•

VARICOSE veins: (↗*Circulation; Inflammation - blood - veins; EXTREMITIES - Varices)* acet-ac c1* *Acon* j5.de aesc bg2* agar bg2 alco a1 aloe bg2* alum j5.de* alum-sil k2 *Alumn* k* *Am-c* j5.de* *Ambr* k* ang j5.de *Ant-t* k* apis bg2* *Arg-n* arist-cl mg1.de **Arn** k* *Ars* k* ars-s-f k2* asaf k* aur bg2 *Bar-c* j5.de *Bell* k* bell-p bg2* *Berb* k* bov bg2 brom hr1* *Bry* j5.de bufo bg2 **Calc** k* calc-f k* *Calc-i* bro1 calc-p calc-s k2* calen c1* camph j5.de caps k2 *Carb-an* k* **Carb-v** k* carbn-s k2 carc gk6* card-b c1* card-m bg2* *Caust* k* chel j5.de* *Chin* j5.de* chinin-s c1* cic j5.de clem cocc bg2 coll bro1* coloc k* con j5.de *Croc* j5.de *Crot-h* k* cycl j5.de falco-ch sze4• *Ferr* k* ferr-ar *Ferr-p* bg2* **Fl-ac** k* form-ac bg2* gels bg2 *Graph* k* **Ham** k* hecla jl *Hep* k* hyos j5.de influ mp4• kali-ar hr1* kali-bi gk kali-n j5.de* *Kreos* k* lac-c c1* lach k* *Lyc* k* **Lycps-v** k* m-aust b2.de* mag-c k* mag-f mg1.de magn-gr bro1 mand mg1.de mangi br1 meli mg1.de meny j5.de merc bg2* merc-cy c1* mez hr1* mill k* morg fmm1• morg-p fmm1• mosch j5.de *Mur-ac* j5.de* nat-c bg2 *Nat-m* k* *Nux-v* k* olnd j5.de op j5.de *Paeon* k* petr c1* ph-ac j5.de* *Phos* j5.de* plat ptk1 *Plb* k* plb-xyz c2 *Polyg-h* br1* psor k2 **Puls** k* pyrog bg2* *Ran-s* hr1* rhod j5.de *Rhus-t* j5.de* ruta bg2* sabin sang ptk1 sars j5.de* scir c1* sec bg2* *Sep* k* sil k* sol-ni c1* *Spig* k* spong j5.de* staph j5.de* stront-br c1* stront-c j5.de* sul-ac k* sul-i bg2 *Sulph* k* thuj k* tritic-vg fd5.de tub-r jl2 *Vip* k* *Zinc* k* [am-s stj1 bar-s stj1 kali-f stj1]

- **accompanied** by | **epistaxis**: **Ham** mrr1
- **alcoholism**, from: crot-h hr1*
- **black**: lach mrr1
- **bleeding**: alumn k2 **Ham** mrr1
  - • **easily**: **Ham** mrr1
- **blue**: am-c bg2 carb-an bg2 *Carb-v* k* fl-ac bg2 *Ham* hr1 *Lycps-v* *Mur-ac* j5.de **Puls** hr1*
- **break** easily: card-m ptk1 mill k2
- **burning**: *Apis* **Ars** k* *Calc* k* carb-v tl1 sec mrr1
  - • **night**: **Ars** k*
- **bursting**, as if: vip st1
- **cold** | **amel.**: puls mrr1 sec mrr1
- **congested**: aesc tl1 agar mrr1 lac-h sze9• mill k2
- **constricting** sensation: ang hr1*
- **eczema**: allox mtf11 arist-cl mtf11 morg-p fmm1• tub jl2
- **inflamed** (See Inflammation - blood - veins)
- **insanity**; with (See MIND - Insanity - varicose - with)
- **itching**: ant-t b7.de* ars b4a.de barb j berb j5.de bruc j5.de *Caps* j5.de carb-v b4a.de* caust j5.de *Graph* k* lach k* m-aust j5.de nux-v j5.de petr hr1 plb j5.de puls j5.de *Sep* j5.de sil j5.de sul-ac j5.de *Sulph* j5.de *Zinc* b4a.de
- **jar** agg.: ham k2
- **large**: **Ham** mrr1
- **menses**; during: ambr b7a.de
- **network** in skin: berb *Calc* *Carb-v* k* *Caust* k* clem *Crot-h* *Lach* lyc k* nat-m ox-ac plat k* sabad thuj k*
- **painful**: ant-t c1 *Brom* k* *Calc* hr1 *Caust* k* coloc a1 *Ham* k* *Lyc* k* *Mill* k* petr hr1* **Puls** k* sang k* vip st1
  - • **ulcerative**: ant-t b7.de *Lach* b7a.de
- **pimples**, covered with: *Graph*
- **pink**: lach mrr1
- **portal** congestion; from: aesc bro1 *Aloe* bro1 card-m mrr1 *Coll* bro1 lept bro1 lyc bro1 *Nux-v* bro1 *Sulph* bro1
- **pregnancy** agg.; during: (↗*EXTREMITIES - Varices - lower - pregnancy)* acon hr1 *Arn* hr1* ars hr1 bell-p c1* calc bro1 *Carb-v* hr1* *Caust* hr1 **Ferr** k* **Fl-ac** hr1 *Graph* hr1 **Ham** hr1* *Lach* hr1 *Lyc* k* *Lycps-v* *Mill* k* *Nux-v* hr1* **Puls** k* sulph hr1* tril-p ptk1 *Zinc* k*
- **pressure**, agg.: ham k2
- **purple**: aesc br1
- **ruptured**: vip bg2
- **soreness**: am-c j5.de ang j5.de bar-c j5.de *Caust* j5.de ferr a1 graph grat j5.de **Ham** k* hep j5.de ign j5.de *Kali-c* j5.de kali-n j5.de m-arct j5.de merc j5.de merc-cy ptk1 mur-ac j5.de nat-m j5.de *Nux-v* j5.de *Phos* j5.de puls k* rhus-t j5.de sil j5.de sul-ac j5.de *Sulph* j5.de vip st1
- **standing** agg.: sulph k2
- **stinging**: *Apis* graph *Ham* k* **Puls** k*
- **stitching**: alum j5.de *Ant-t* b7.de* *Ars* j5.de bar-c j5.de *Caust* j5.de graph b4a.de grat j5.de kali-c *Kali-n* j5.de lyc merc j5.de nat-m j5.de nux-v j5.de phos j5.de *Sil* j5.de sul-ac j5.de sulph j5.de
- **swollen**: *Apis* *Berb* k* graph h2* *Ham* hr1* paeon bg *Puls* k* stront-c mrr1

Varicose veins: ...

- **ulceration**: (↗*EXTREMITIES - Varices - leg - ulceration; SKIN - Ulcers - varicose)* aesc k13* anac ant-t k* arist-cl k2* arn jl3 *Ars* k* *Calc* calc-f jl3 *Carb-v* *Card-m* k* **Caust** k* cecr jl3 *Cham* j5.de cinnb clem ptk1 crot-h crot-t k* des-ac jl3 eucal c2 fl-ac hr1* gast c2 *Graph* grin *Ham* k* hydr hydr-ac influ jl2* ins br1 kali-s kreos k* **Lach** k* **Lyc** k* merc mez k* morg-p pte1*• *Nat-m* parat jl parathyr jl3 **Puls** k* pyrog k* raja-s k* *Rhus-t* rib-ac jl3 sars sec k* *Sil* k* sul-ac *Sulph* k* syph thuj vip ptk1 *Zinc* [am-s stj1]
  - • **cicatrize**; late to: pyrog jl2
  - • **fetid**: pyrog jl2
  - • **old** people; in: | **men**; old: pyrog jl2
  - • **persisting**: pyrog jl2
- **warmth** agg.: sec mrr1
- **young** people; in: ferr-p hr1*

VAULTS, cellars agg.: (↗*Wet - getting - rooms; MIND - Fear - narrow)* ant-t bg2 aran bg2* **Ars** k* atro hr1 *Bry* k* calc k* *Carb-an* k* carc pd* card-m bg2* caust k* dulc br1* form hr1 *Kali-c* bg2 lyc k* merc-i-f bg2 **Nat-s** bg2* **Puls** k* **Rhus-t** b7a.de *Sel* hr1 *Sep* k* *Stram* k* ter c1

VEINS swollen (See Swelling - veins)

VENESECTION, ailments from: *Chin* b7a.de* senec hr1* squil b7a.de* verat-v hr1

VENOUS PULSATIONS (See Pulsation - internally - veins)

VENOUS STASIS (See Stasis)

VERATRUM agg.: camph bro1 coff bro1

VERTIGO; during: **Acon** b2.de* agar b2.de* alum b2.de* am-c b2.de* am-m b2.de* ambr b2.de* anac b2.de* ant-c b2.de* ant-t b2.de* *Arg-met* b2.de* arn b2.de* *Ars* b2.de* asaf b2.de* aur b2.de* bar-c b2.de* *Bell* b2.de* bov b2.de* bry b2.de* calad b2.de* **Calc** b2.de* camph b2.de* canth b2.de* carb-an b2.de* carb-v b2.de* caust b2.de* *Cham* b2.de* chel b2.de* chin b2.de* cic b2.de* cina b2.de* cocc b2.de* coff b2.de* coloc b2.de* con b2.de* croc b2.de* cupr b2.de* cycl ptk1 dig b2.de* dulc b2.de* ferr b2.de* **Gels** bg2* graph b2.de* hell b2.de* hep b2.de* hyos b2.de* ign b2.de* iod b2.de* ip b2.de* kali-c b2.de* kali-n b2.de* *Lach* b2.de* *Laur* b2.de* led b2.de* lyc b2.de* mag-c b2.de* mag-m b2.de* *Merc* b2.de* mez b2.de* *Mosch* b2.de* nat-c b2.de* nat-m b2.de* nit-ac b2.de* nux-m b2.de* **Nux-v** b2.de* olnd b2.de* op b2.de* par b2.de* petr b2.de* ph-ac b2.de* **Phos** b2.de* plat b2.de* plb b2.de* **Puls** b2.de* ran-s b2.de* rhod b2.de* rhus-t b2.de* ruta b2.de* sabad b2.de* sabin b2.de* sars b2.de* sec b2.de* sel b2.de* seneg b2.de* sep b2.de* sil b2.de* spig b2.de* spong b2.de* squil b2.de* stann b2.de* staph b2.de* **Stram** b2.de* stront-c b2.de* sulph b2.de* *Verat* b2.de* verb b2.de* zinc b2.de*

VIBRATION, fluttering, etc.: agn b7.de* *Am-c* b2.de* ambr bg2 ars bg2 aur bg2 bar-c bg2 **Bell** b2.de* bism b2.de* bit-ar wht1• *Brach* br1 brom ptk1 calad br1 calc bg2 cann-xyz bg2 caps b2.de* carb-an bg2 carb-v bg2* *Caust* b2.de* cic b7.de* cimic bg* clem b2.de* cocc bg2 coff bg2 con b2.de* croc b7.de* cypra-eg sde6.de• dig b2.de* ferr bg2 *Glon* bg2* graph bg2 hep b2.de* hyos b2.de* ign b2.de* iod b2.de* kali-c b2.de* kali-n b2.de* *Kreos* bg2 lach bg2 lyc b2.de* m-ambo bg2 **M-arct** b7.de* mag-c b2.de* melal-alt gya4 meli bg* meny bg2 meph ptk1 mosch b2.de* mur-ac bg2 nat-m bg2 *Nit-ac* b2.de* **Nux-m** b7.de* *Nux-v* b2.de* **Olnd** b7.de* op b7a.de* petr b2.de* ph-ac bg2 phos bg2 plat bg2 **Puls** b7.de* *Rhus-t* b7.de* sabad b7.de* *Sang* bg2* sars b2.de* *Sep* b2.de* sil b2.de* **Spig** b7.de* spong fd4.de squil bg2 stann bg2 staph bg2 stront-c b2.de* **Sulph** b2.de* teucr bg2 thuj bg2 tung-met bdx1• vanil fd5.de verat bg2 verb b2.de* viol-t bg2 zinc bg2 [*Buteo-j* sej6]

- **agg.**: colch ptk1
- **lying** down agg.: clem ptk1
- **sensation** as if: melal-alt gya4
- **stepping**; when: am ptk1

○ - **Blood** vessels; sensation of vibration in phel ptk1

VIGOR: (↗*Efficiency; Strength; Vitality)* acon ptk1 asaf ptk1 bell ptk1 *Bry* br1 caps ptk1 coff ptk1 colch tl1 nat-p ptk1 op ptk1 phos ptk1 psor ptk1 [kali-ar stj2 kali-i stj1 *Kali-met* stj2 kali-p stj1 merc stj2]

- **convulsions**; during: agar ptk1
- **decreased**: ars-i k2* carb-an k2* carb-v sf1.de cocc sf1.de ferr-p k2* laur sf1.de mag-m sf1.de op sf1.de ph-ac st phos k2* psor bg sulph sf1.de tub k2* vinc sf1.de
- **lacking** vigor (See Sluggishness)

VINEGAR application: | **amel.**: meli ptk1

VIOLENT COMPLAINTS: **Acon** br1* aeth br1* alum bg* anac bg* *Ars* bg* *Bell* br1* bry bg* canth bg* carb-v bg* **Cham** bg* cic br1* coloc lmj crot-t lmj cupr bg* glon bg* *Hep* ptk1* *Hyos* bg* ign bg* iod bg* **Lach** ptk1* *Lyss* ptk1 merc bg* merc-c ptk1 mez ptk1 nux-v ptk1* ox-ac ptk1 spig ptk1 **Staph** lmj stram tl1* sulph bg* *Tarent* bg* *Verat* bg*

- **children**; in: **Acon** lmj *Agar* lmj **Apis** lmj *Bell* lmj bry lmj cic lmj coloc lmj crot-t lmj hecla lmj *Hep* lmj *Hyos* lmj **Lach** lmj nux-v lmj **Staph** lmj stram lmj sulph lmj *Verat* lmj

VITALITY: (↗*Vigor*)

- **lacking** vitality (See Reaction - lack; Sluggishness)

VOICE; using: | **agg.**: arg-met bro1 arg-n bro1 arum-t bro1 *Carb-v* bro1 *Dros* bro1 mang-act bro1 nux-v bro1 *Phos* bro1 sel bro1 *Stann* bro1 wye bro1

VOLKMANN's syndrome: prot jl2 tub-r jl2*

VOMITING:

- **after** | **agg.**: *Ant-t* b7.de* *Asar* b7.de* cham b7.de cocc b7.de *Colch* b7.de* ferr b7.de mosch b7a.de nux-v b7.de op b7a.de *Puls* b7.de* *Ruta* b7.de* *Verat* b7.de
- **agg.**: acon k* **Aeth** bg2* *Ant-t* k* arn k* **Ars** k* *Asar* k* bell k* *Bry* k* *Calc* k* caps k* cham k* chin k* cina k* cocc k* *Colch* k* coloc k* con k* **Cupr** k* dig k* *Dros* k* ferr k* graph k* *Hyos* k* iod k* **Ip** k* kali-c b4.de lach k* *Lyc* k* merc-sul hr1 mez k* mosch k* nat-m k* *Nux-v* k* op k* *Phos* k* *Plb* k* **Puls** k* ran-s k* ruta k* sabin k* *Sars* k* sec k* *Sep* k* sil k* stann k* **Sulph** k* *Verat* k*
- **amel.**: acon k* agar *Ail* vh1 anac kl ant-t bro1* ars asar b7.de* calc gk carbn-s *Coc-c* colch k* *Dig* k* *Eup-per* bg2 ferr hr1 helia br1* hell bg2 hyos k* ix bnm8• kali-bi bg2* kola stb3• lat-m sp1 nux-v k* op plb bg1 puls k* *Sang* k* *Sec* k* *Tab* bg2
- **before** | **agg.**: colch b7.de cupr b7.de puls b7.de ran-s b7.de
- **bilious** | **amel.**: card-m ptk1 eup-per ptk1 sang ptk1

WAKING: (↗*Sleep - after - morning*)

- **after** | **agg.**: am-m ptk1 ambr ptk1 *Apis* ptk1 *Ars* ptk1 *Bell* ptk1 calc ptk1 caust ptk1 *Chin* ptk1 hep ptk1 hyos ptk1 kali-bi ptk1 **Lach** ptk1 *Lyc* ptk1 lycps-v ptk1 nat-m ptk1 nit-ac ptk1 *Nux-v* ptk1 onos ptk1 *Op* ptk1 *Phos* ptk1 *Puls* ptk1 sel ptk1 sep ptk1 *Spong* ptk1 stram ptk1 *Sulph* ptk1 tarent ptk1 tub ptk1 valer ptk1
- **amel.**: acon bg2 am-c bg2 am-m k* ambr k* *Ars* k* bry k* *Calad* k* calc k* caps bg2 cham k* chin k* cocc k* *Colch* k* crot-t bg2 *Cupr* bg2 epiph bg2 *Fl-ac* bg2 galeoc-c-h gms1• germ-met srj5• hell k* hydrog srj2• ign k* ip k* iris bg2 kali-bi bg2 kali-p bg2 kreos k* lach k* lob bg2 m-arct b2.de meph j5.de* merc bg2 nat-c k* *Nux-v* k* *Onos* ph-ac k* **Phos** k* psor jl2 puls k* rad-br ptk1 ran-b bg2 ruta k* sabal ptk1 sabin k* samb k* sang bg2 sel k* **Sep** k* spig k* thuj k* valer ptk1 vip j5.de
- **on**: (↗*Sleep - after - morning*) acon k* adam srj5• aesc k2 agar k* agn k* *Aids* nl2• alum k* alum-sil k2* *Alumn* kr1 *Am-c* k* **Am-m** k* **Ambr** k* anac k* *Ant-c* k* ant-t k* arg-met b7.de arg-n st1 *Arn* k* **Ars** k* asaf b7.de aur k* bapt sf1.de bar-c k* bell k* *Benz-ac* bism k* borx k* bov k* bry k* bufo k* cact cadm-s calad k* **Calc** k* calc-p calc-s cann-s k* canth k* *Caps* k* *Carb-an* k* *Carb-v* k* carneg-g rwt1• **Caust** k* *Cench* cham k* *Chel* k* *Chin* k* cic k* cina k* clem k* coc-c *Cocc* k* coff k* colch k* *Con* k* corn croc k* *Crot-h* k* crot-t cupr cycl k* *Dig* k* dros k* dulc k* euph k* euphr b2.de* ferr k* ferr-ar k2* fl-ac bg2 form galeoc-c-h gms1• gels tl1 germ-met srj5• *Graph* k* guaj k* haliae-lc srj5• hell b7.de **Hep** k* *Hydr* *Hydrog* srj2• **Hyos** k* *Ign* k* iod b4.de *Ip* k* *Kali-ar* **Kali-bi** k* *Kali-c* k* kali-i kali-n k* *Kali-s* kreos k* **Lach** k* laur k* led k* *Lyc* k* *M-ambo* b7.de* *M-arct* b2.de* m-aust b2.de* mag-c k* mag-m k* mang k* meny k* *Merc* k* merc-c bg2 *Merc-i-f* k* mez k* mosch k* mur-ac k* naja nat-c k* *Nat-m* k* **Nit-ac** k* nux-m k* **Nux-v** k* **Onos** op k* palo jl3 par b7.de* petr k* ph-ac k* **Phos** k* *Phyt* plat k* plb b7.de plut-n srj7• positr nl2• prot jl2 psor **Puls** k* *Ran-b* k* ran-s k* rauw jl3 rheum k* rhod k* rhus-g tmo3• *Rhus-t* k* ruta k* sabad k* sabin k* sal-fr sle1• *Samb* k* *Sang* sars k* sel k* seneg k* **Sep** k* *Sil* k* spig k* spong k* squil k* stann b4.de* *Staph* k* stram k* stront-c k* sul-ac k* **Sulph** k* tarax k* teucr b2.de* thuj k* trios jl3 *Tung-met* bdx1• **Valer** k* ven-m jl3 verat k* verat-v a1 verb b7.de viol-o k* viol-t k* *Zinc* k*
  - **night**: (↗*Sleep - loss*) ambr bg2 bry j5.de* carb-v bg2 chin bg2 **Cocc** bg2 *Colch* bg2 hydrog srj2• ip bg2 lach j5.de nat-c bg2 nat-m bg2 **Nux-v** bg2 ph-ac bg2 *Puls* bg2 ruta bg2 sabin bg2 *Sel* bg2 sep bg2
  - **siesta**; from: caust bg2

WALKING (= general influence of walking): (↗*EXTREMITIES - Walking*)

- **after** | **agg.**: *Agar* ptk1 alum b4a.de am-m b7a.de ambr b7a.de anac b4.de **Ars** ptk1 calad b7.de camph b7.de *Cann-s* b7a.de *Cann-xyz* ptk1 carb-an b4a.de *Carb-v* b4.de* caust b4.de cocc b7.de coff b7.de croc b7.de cycl b7a.de kali-bi bg2 *Kali-c* bg2 *Kali-n* b4a.de laur b7.de* lyc bg2 m-aust b7.de* mang b4.de mosch b7a.de *Nat-c* b4.de* nit-ac b4.de nux-v b7.de olnd b7.de ph-ac b4a.de plat b4.de *Puls* b7.de* rhod b4a.de *Rhus-t* b7.de* ruta b7.de* sabin b7.de sacch-a fd2.de• **Sep** ptk1 spig b7.de* spong b7.de* stann bg2* stram bg2 *Sul-ac* b4a.de* sulph bg2 valer b7.de* verat b7a.de
- **agg.**: *Acon* k* **Aesc** k* *Agar* k* *Agn* k* ail vh1 aloe *Alum* k* alum-p k2* alum-sil k2 am-c k* am-m k* *Ambr* k* anac k* ang b2.de* ant-c k* *Ant-t* k* apis arg-met k* arg-n bg2 *Arn* k* *Ars* k* ars-i asaf k* *Asar* k* atra-r jl3* *Atro* aur k* aur-ar k2 aur-m k2* *Bapt* bar-c k* bar-i k2* bar-s k2* **Bell** k* *Berb* k* bism ptk1 borx b2.de* both-a rb3 both-ax tsm2 *Bov* k* **Bry** k* *Cact* cadm-met jl3 cadm-s *Calad* k* **Calc** k* **Calc-s** k* calc-sil k2 *Camph* k* *Cann-s* k* canth k* caps k* *Carb-ac* *Carb-an* k* carb-v k* *Carbn-s* cassia-s cdd7• **Caust** k* cham k* *Chel* k* **Chin** k* *Chion* cic k* cina k* clem k* **Cocc** k* *Coff* k* **Colch** k* *Coloc* k* **Con** k* conv cortico jl3 *Croc* k* cupr k* cycl k* dicha jl3 *Dig* k* dros k* dulc k* euph k* euphr k* *Ferr* k* ferr-ar k2 ferr-i ferr-p k2* **Fl-ac** bg2 form gels k* *Glon* *Gran* *Graph* k* guaj k* *Hell* k* *Hep* k* hyos k* ign k* *Iod* k* *Ip* k* *Kali-c* k* kali-n k* kali-p k* kali-sil k2* kalm ptk1 kreos k* *Lach* k* laur k* **Led** k* *Lil-t* lyc k* m-ambo b2.de* m-arct b2.de* *M-aust* b2.de* mag-c k* mag-m k* *Mag-p* k* mang k* meny k* *Merc* k* *Merc-c* bg2 methys jl3 *Mez* k* mosch k* mur-ac k* *Murx* nat-c k* *Nat-m* k* *Nat-p* k* *Nat-s* k* nat-sil k2* **Nit-ac** k* nux-m k* **Nux-v** k* olnd k* op k* paeon par k* *Petr* k* *Ph-ac* k* **Phos** k* *Phyt* k* pic-ac ptk1 plat k* plb k* podo ptk1 *Psor* k* ptel c1 puls k* pyrog ptk1 rad-br ptk1 *Ran-b* k* ran-s k* *Rheum* k* rhod k* **Rhus-t** k* *Ruta* k* sabad k* *Sabin* k* samb k* *Sars* k* sec k* *Sel* k* seneg k* **Sep** k* *Sil* k* **Spig** k* *Spong* k* *Squil* k* **Stann** k* *Staph* k* stram k* stront-c k* sul-ac k* sul-i k2* **Sulph** k* sumb ptk1 tab bg2* *Tarax* k* *Tarent* k* teucr k* thiop jl3 thuj k* tril-p ptk1 tub k* tub-m jl2 valer k* verat k* *Verat-v* verb k* vib ptk1 viol-o k* viol-t k* *Zinc* k* zinc-chr ptk1 zinc-p k2* zinc-val ptk1 [alumin-p stj2 calc-p stj1 cupr-p stj2 lith-p stj2 mang-p stj2 *Stront-m* stj2 *Stront-met* stj2]
- **ailments** from walking: sel c1
- **air**; in open:
  - **after** | **agg.**: *Alum* b4.de* *Am-c* b4.de* am-m b7.de *Ambr* b7a.de anac b4.de* ang b7.de arg-met b7.de arn b7.de ars b4.de bell b4.de borx b4a.de bov b4.de bry b7a.de calc b4.de* carb-v b4.de caust b4.de chel b7.de *Chin* b7.de clem b4.de cocc b7.de coff b7.de **Con** b4a.de *Croc* b7.de dros b7.de *Ferr* b7.de graph b4.de* hep b4.de ip b7.de *Kali-c* b4.de* lach b7.de* laur b7a.de *Led* b7.de **Lyc** b4.de* m-aust b7.de mag-c b4.de merc b4.de mez b4.de nat-c b4.de nat-m b4.de nit-ac b4.de *Nux-v* b7.de op b7.de **Petr** b4.de* ph-ac b4.de *Phos* b4.de* plat b4.de *Puls* b7.de *Ran-s* b7.de* *Rhod* b4.de* *Rhus-t* b7.de *Ruta* b7.de* sabad b7.de sabin b7.de sep b4.de sil h2 *Spig* b7.de* spong b7.de stann b4.de* sulph b4.de valer b7a.de verat b7.de verb b7.de zinc b4.de
  - **agg.**: acon k* *Agar* k* agn k* alum k* alum-p k2 *Am-c* k* am-m k* ambr k* anac k* ang b2.de* ant-c k* arg-met k* arn k* **Ars** k* ars-s-f k2 asar k* aur k* aur-ar k2 aur-s k2 bar-c k* *Bell* k* borx k* bov k* *Bry* k* calad k* *Calc* k* calc-sil k2 *Camph* k* cann-s k* canth k* caps k* *Carb-ac* *Carb-an* k* *Carb-v* k* carbn-s k2 **Caust** k* cham k* *Chel* k* chin k* chinin-ar cic k* *Cina* k* clem k* **Cocc** k* *Coff* k* *Colch* k* coloc k* *Con* k* croc k* dig k* dros k* dulc k* euph k* *Euphr* k* ferr k* ferr-ar k2 **Fl-ac** bg2 graph k* *Guaj* k* hell k* *Hep* k* hyos k* ign k* iod k* ip k* *Kali-c* k* kali-n k* *Kali-p* kali-s mrr1 kreos k* lach k* laur k* *Led* k* lina br1 lyc k* m-ambo b2.de* m-arct b2.de* m-aust b2.de* mag-c k* mag-m k* **Mag-p** k* mag-s j5.de mang k* meny k* *Merc* k* merc-c k* mez k* mosch k* mur-ac k* nat-ar nat-c k* nat-m k* nit-ac k* *Nux-m* k* **Nux-v** k* olnd k* op k* par k* petr k* ph-ac k* *Phos* k* *Plan* plat k* plb k* *Psor* *Puls* k* ran-b k* *Ran-s* k* rheum k* rhod k* *Rhus-t* k* ruta k* sabad k* sabin k* sars k* **Sel** k* *Seneg* k* *Sep* k* *Sil* k* **Spig** k* *Spong* k* *Stann* k* staph k* *Stram* k* stront-c k* sul-ac k* **Sulph** k* tarax k* teucr k* thuj k* valer k* verat k* *Verb* k* viol-t b2.de* zinc k*
  - **amel.**: abrom-a ks5 acon k* adon vh1 aesc sf1.de aeth c1 agar aloe **Alum** k* am-c b2.de* am-m k* ambr k* anac k* ang b2.de* ant-c k* ant-t j5.de apis sf1.de aran sf1.de* arg-met k* **Arg-n** k* arn k* ars b2.de* asaf k* *Asar* k* *Aur* k* aur-m-n wbt2• bapt bar-c k* bar-s k2 bell k* bism k* borx k* bov k* *Brom* *Bry* k* calc k* calc-s caps k* carb-ac carb-v k* carbn-s caust k* chel b7.de choc srj3• cic k* cimic jl cina k* coloc b4a.de *Con* k* croc b7.de*

- **air**; in open – **amel.**: ...
dios sf1.de* *Dulc* k* *Euph* b4.de* **Fl-ac** k* gamb *Graph* k* ham fd3.de• hed mg1.de hep b2.de* hyos k* ign k* ignis-alc es2• *Iod* sf1.de* ip j5.de irid-met srj5• kali-c k* **Kali-i** k* kali-n k* kali-p fd1.de• **Kali-s** k* lach sf1.de laur k* *Lil-t* k* **Lyc** k* m-arct b2.de* m-aust b2.de* *Mag-c* k* mag-f mg1.de* *Mag-m* k* mag-s j5.de* mand mg1.de mang k* meny k* merc k* *Merc-i-r* mez k* mosch k* mur-ac k* *Naja* nat-ar nat-c k* nat-m k* nat-s k2* nicc j5.de nit-ac k* nux-v b7.de* op k* ox-ac par k* petr k* *Ph-ac* k* phel j5.de phos k* pic-ac sf1.de pip-n bg2 plat k* plb k* **Puls** k* rauw jl rhod k* **Rhus-t** k* ruta b2.de* *Sabin* k* sal-fr sle1• *Sang* sars k* sel k* *Seneg* k* *Sep* k* sphing kk3.fr spig k* spong b2.de* *Stann* k* staph k* stront-c k* sul-ac k* *Sulph* k* *Tarax* k* tarent k2* *Teucr* k* *Thuj* k* verat k* verb k* vinc j5.de viol-t k* zinc k*
  - **desire** for (See desire - air)
- **amel.**: *Acon* k* agar k* agn k* alum k* alumn am-c k* *Am-m* k* ambr k* anac k* androc srj1• ang b2.de* ant-c k* ant-t k* apis k* apoc aran-ix jl3 arg-met k* arg-n bg2* arn k* *Ars* k* ars-s-f k2* asaf k* asar k* **Aur** k* aur-m bg1* aur-s k2* bar-c k* bell k* bism k* bov k* *Brom* *Bry* k* buni-o jl3 calc b2.de* calen j5.de canth k* *Caps* k* carb-v k* cartl-s rly4• caust k* cham k* chin k* cic k* cina k* cocc k* coloc k* **Con** b2.de* cortiso jl3 crot-h cupr k* **Cycl** k* *Dig* b4.de* *Dios* *Dros* k* **Dulc** k* **Euph** k* euphr k* **Ferr** k* ferr-ar *Fl-ac* k* gels ptk1 glon graph k* guaj k* halo jl helon ptk1 hep k* hyos k* ign k* indg iod k* kali-bi k* kali-c k* **Kali-i** k* kali-n k* kali-p *Kali-s* k* kreos k* lach k* laur k* led b7.de lil-t ptk1 *Lyc* k* lycps-v bg2 *M-ambo* b2.de* m-arct b2.de* m-aust b2.de* *Mag-c* k* *Mag-m* k* mag-p bg2 mang k* *Meli* *Meny* k* meph jl *Merc* k* merc-c ptk1 mez k* *Mosch* k* mur-ac k* nat-c k* *Nat-m* k* nat-s k2* nid jl nit-ac k* nux-m k* olnd k* op k* palo jl3 par k* petr k* *Ph-ac* k* phos b2.de* *Plat* k* plb k* **Puls** k* pyrog k* *Ran-b* k* raph rat sf1.de *Rhod* k* **Rhus-t** k* *Ruta* k* **Sabad** k* sabin k* **Samb** k* sars k* sel k* seneg k* *Sep* k* sil k* spig k* spong b2.de* stann k* staph k* stront-c k* sul-ac k* **Sulph** k* symph fd3.de• **Tarax** k* tarent ptk1 tere-ch jl3 teucr k* thal jl3 thuj k* tub k2* **Valer** k* vanil fd5.de *Verat* k* *Verb* k* *Viol-t* k* vip-a jl *Zinc* k* zinc-p k2 [astat stj2 bar-br stj2 bar-i stj2 bar-met stj2 bism-sn stj2 caes-met stj2 cinnb stj2 cob stj2 cob-m stj2 cob-p stj2 hafn-met stj2 irid-met stj2 lanth-met stj2 mag-f stj1 merc-d stj2 merc-i-f stj2 osm-met stj2 plb-m stj2 plb-p stj2 polon-met stj2 rhen-met stj2 tant-met stj2 thal-met stj2 tung-met stj2]
- **aversion** to: agar a1 aza jl3 cham a1 clem a1 fago a1 kali-bi a1 nit-ac a1
- **backward** agg.: mang ptk1
- **beginning** to walk: *(↗Motion - beginning - agg.)* acon k* *Agar* am-c k* ambr k* anac k* ang b2.de* ant-c k* ant-t k* arn k* ars k* asar k* aur k* bar-c k* bell k* bov k* *Bry* k* *Cact* *Calc* k* cann-s k* canth k* **Caps** k* carb-an k* *Carb-v* k* *Caust* k* cham k* chin k* cic k* cina k* cocc k* **Con** k* croc k* cupr k* cycl k* dig k* dros k* **Euph** k* **Ferr** k* graph k* kali-c k* kali-n k* lach k* laur k* led k* **Lyc** k* m-ambo b2.de* m-arct b2.de m-aust b2.de mag-c k* mang k* merc k* mur-ac k* nat-c k* nat-m k* nit-ac k* nux-v k* olnd k* petr k* ph-ac k* *Phos* k* phyt sf1.de plat k* plb k* **Puls** k* ran-b k* rhod k* **Rhus-t** k* *Ruta* k* *Sabad* k* sabin k* *Samb* k* sars k* sep k* *Sil* k* spig k* staph k* stram k* stront-c k* sulph k* *Thuj* k* valer k* verat k* *Zinc*
- **bent**:
  - **agg.**: *Bry* b2.de*
  - **amel.**: am-m ptk1 arn bg2 cimic sne **Con** b2.de* *Hyos* b2.de* *Lyc* b2.de* nux-v b2.de* phos ptk1 rhus-t b2.de* sabin b2.de* sulph b2.de* *Viol-t* b2.de*
- **circle**, in a: *(↗MIND - Walking - circle)* bell h1 thuj ptk1
- **continued** | **amel.**: bry b7.de dros b7.de *Ferr* b7.de m-ambo b7.de plb b7.de *Puls* b7.de ruta b7.de sabin b7.de
- **dark** agg.; in the: zinc ptk1
- **desire** for: agath-a nl2• ail bg2 arg-met bg2* arg-n sf1.de *Ars* a1* *Aur* sf1.de* bism bg2* caj a1 calc h2* chlor a1 choc srj3• cod a1 dig bg* *Dios* bg* ferr-p bg2 fl-ac bg2 gins a1 guar vml3• *Iod* sf1.de* kali-cy a1 kali-s fd4.de lepi a1 lyc bg2 merc sf1.de mosch sf1.de murx bg* naja a1 nit-ac bg2 nux-v bg2 *Op* sf1.de* paeon ptk1 paull a1 ruta ptk1 sep bg2* spira a1 spirae a1 spong fd4.de *Stront-c* sf1.de* tarent ptk1 thlas bg2 tritic-vg fd5.de vanil fd5.de zinc-act a1 [lith-i stj2]
  - **night**: *Iod* sf1.de merc a1* *Op* sf1.de tritic-vg fd5.de
  - **air**, in open: *(↗MIND - Walking - desire - air)* asaf a1 clem j5.de crot-t j5.de fl-ac st1 ham fd3.de• hydrog srj2• ignis-alc es2• kali-s fd4.de lach j5.de lact j5.de lyc j5.de mez a1 phos j5.de* puls j5.de ruta fd4.de spong fd4.de teucr j5.de tritic-vg fd5.de vanil fd5.de
- **easily**: thuj h1 zinc sf1.de
- **eyes** closed; with:
  - **agg.**: alum ptk1 arg-n ptk1 calad ptk1 iodof ptk1 zinc ptk1
  - **amel.**: con ptk1

Walking: ...
- **learning** to walk | **accompanied** by | **lower** limbs; weakness of: chin bg2 par bg2 stront-c bg2
  - **late**: acon bg3 *Agar* k* all-s k13 arg-n bg3 *Ars* bg3 ars-s-f hr1* aur-m-n wbt2• *Bar-c* k* bell k* **Calc** k* calc-f lmj **Calc-p** k* *Carb-v* lmj **Caust** k* cupr sst3• ferr bg3 fl-ac bg3 kali-i bg3 lil-t bg3 lyc b4a.de* mag-c b4a.de* med mtf33 merc bg2* **Nat-m** k* *Nit-ac* b4a.de nux-v k* *Ph-ac* bg2* *Phos* bg2* pin-s c2* *Sanic* k* sep bg3* *Sil* k* sulph k* thlas bg thuj bg
    - **development** of bones; tardy: *(↗Development - slow - bones)* *Calc* k2
- **level** ground; on | **agg.**: ran-b b2.de* verat bg2*
- **must** walk | **Bones**; during complaints of: ruta ptk1
- **rapidly**:
  - **agg.**: *(↗Running - agg.)* *Alum* k* alum-sil k2* *Ang* b2.de* *Apis* arg-met k* *Arn* k* **Ars** k* ars-i ars-s-f k2* *Aur* k* aur-ar k2 aur-i k2* *Aur-m* aur-s k2* **Bell** k* *Borx* b2.de* **Bry** k* but-ac br1 *Cact* *Calc* k* *Calc-s* calc-sil k2* *Cann-s* k* *Caust* k* chel k* chin k* cina k* cocc k* coff k* **Con** croc k* *Cupr* k* dros k* *Ferr* ferr-ar hep k* hyos k* *Ign* k* *Iod* k* ip k* *Kali-ar* *Kali-c* k* kali-p kali-sil k2* laur k* *Led* k* *Lyc* k* *Merc* k* mez k* nat-ar nat-c k* *Nat-m* k* nit-ac k* nux-m k* *Nux-v* k* *Olnd* k* **Phos** k* *Plb* **Puls** rheum k* *Rhod* k* *Rhus-t* k* ruta k* sabin k* *Seneg* k* sep k* **Sil** k* *Spig* k* spong k* squil k* staph k* sul-ac k* **Sulph** k* verat k* zinc k*
  - **amel.**: *(↗MIND - Anxiety - pursued - walking; MIND - Hurry - Walking; MIND - Restlessness - Anxious - walking - rapidly; MIND - Walking - More)* *Ant-t* bg2 *Arg-n* ars k2* aur-m bg2 brom k2* canth k* carb-ac *Ign* k* *Mag-c* bg2 *Mag-m* bg2 nat-m k* petr *Rhus-t* bg2* *Sabin* bg2 **Sep** k* sil k* *Stann* k* *Sul-ac* **Tub**
    - **mental** symptoms: hist sp1
- **sideways** agg.: *Caust* b2.de* kali-c ptk1
- **slowly** | **amel.**: agar **Aur** aur-i k2* **Aur-m** cact calc-s **Ferr** k* ferr-ar iris *Kali-p* lyc st **Puls** sep syph jl2* *Tarent*
- **stone** pavement agg.; on a: aloe bg2 ant-c b2.de* ars bg2 *Con* b2.de* hep b2.de* nux-v bg2 sep bg2
- **stopping** motionless; when | **agg.**: ign b7.de
- **striding** out, like a man's walk: chlam-tr bcx2•
- **uneven** ground agg.; on: clem bg2* hyos ptk1 lil-t bg2* phos bg2 podo bg2
- **upright** and gracefully: [neon stj2]
- **wind**; in the | **agg.**: acon k* *Agar* *Ars* k* *Asar* k* aur k* aur-ar k2 **Bell** k* *Calc* k* carb-v k* *Cham* k* chin k* con k* euphr k* *Graph* k* lach k* *Lyc* k* mur-ac k* nat-c k* nux-m k* **Nux-v** k* *Phos* k* plat k* *Puls* k* rhus-t k* **Sep** spig k* *Stann* thuj k*

WARM:
- **agg.**: *(↗Heat - lack - warmth)* acon k* adlu jl3 *Aesc* k2* aeth br1* *Agar* k* agn k* *All-c* k* *Aloe* k2* **Alum** k* alum-sil k2 alumn kr1 am-c b4.de* ambr k* *Anac* b2.de* anan vh *Ant-c* k* *Ant-t* k* **Apis** k* aq-mar jl3 **Arg-n** k* arn k* **Ars-i** *Asaf* bro1* *Asar* b2.de* aster jl3 aur k* *Aur-i* k2* *Aur-m* aur-s stj2*• bapt sf1.de bar-c k* bar-i k2* bell k* beryl jl3 *Bism* borra-o oss1• *Borx* k* brom k2* *Bry* k* *Calad* k* *Calc* b2.de* calc-f vh1* *Calc-i* k2* *Calc-s* k2* *Camph* k* cann-s k* canth carb-v k* *Carbn-s* carc hbh* cassia-s cdd7• caust k* cench k2* cham k* chin b2.de* choc srj3• cimic jl3 cina k* clem bro1 *Coc-c* k* cocc k* coff k2* colch k* coloc k* *Com* bro1 conv bro1 cortico sp1 cortiso sp1* *Croc* k* *Crot-h* bg2* *Cupr* bg2* cycl ptk1 dendr-pol sk4• dig *Dros* k* *Dulc* k* euph k* euphr k* ferr b2.de* ferr-i k* ferr-p sf1.de **Fl-ac** bg2* flav jl3* foll jl3 gels k* *Glon* k* *Graph* k* *Grat* st1 *Guaj* k* *Ham* st1 hed mg1.de helia br1* hell k* hep b2.de* hip-ac jl3 hist jl3 hydroph jl3 *Hyos* bg2* iber bro1* ign k* *Ind* k* **Iod** k* *Ip* k* jug-c bro1 just bro1 kali-ar sf1.de kali-bi sf1.de* kali-br kali-c b2.de* **Kali-i** bg2* kali-m bro1* kali-n mrr1 **Kali-s** k* kalm sf1.de lac-ac stj5• *Lac-c* lac-cp sk4• lac-leo sk4• *Lach* k* laur k* **Led** k* *Lil-t* sf1.de* *Lyc* k* m-ambo b2.de* m-arct b2.de* mag-c b4.de* manc mrr1 med bro1* meli sf1.de *Merc* k* *Mez* k* mur-ac k* nat-c k* **Nat-m** k* **Nat-s** k* nit-ac b2.de* nux-m b2.de* nux-v b2.de* *Op* k* ph-ac k* phenob jl3* *Phos* k* phyt k2* pic-ac k2* *Pieri-b* mlk9.de pitu jl3 **Plat** k* podo sf1.de prot jl3* **Puls** k* rat ptk1 rauw sp1* rhus-g tmo3• rhus-t b2.de* ruta fd4.de sabad k* *Sabin* k* sal-fr sle1• *Sang* ptk1 sars b4.de **Sec** k* sel k* *Seneg* k* sep b2.de* sil b2.de* spig k* *Spong* k* staph k* stel bro1 stront-c b4.de sul-ac bro1* *Sul-i* k2* **Sulph** k* tab k* teucr k* *Thuj* k* thyr vh trios jl3 *Tub* st1 *Uva* vh vanil fd5.de *Verat* k* *Vesp* st1 visc jl3 *Zinc* k* [am-f stj2 am-s stj1 arg-met stj1 bar-f stj1 cadm-s stj2 calc-lac stj2 chr-s stj2 ferr-f stj2 ferr-lac stj2 ferr-n stj2 fl-pur stj2 gal-s stj2 lith-f stj2 lith-i stj2 lith-s stj2 mag-br stj1 mag-i stj1 mag-s stj1 mang-n stj2 mang-s stj2 mang-sil stj2 nat-caust stj2 nat-f stj1* nat-i stj1 nicc-s stj2 nitro stj2 oxyg stj2 *Tell* stj2 titan stj2 titan-s stj2 zinc-i stj2 zinc-n stj2]

- **air**:
  - **agg.**: agn k* *Aloe* alum-sil k2 ambr k* aml-ns vh1 anac b2.de* *Ant-c* k* *Ant-t* k* *Arg-n* k* ars-i *Asar* b2.de* aur k* aur-i k2* *Aur-m* *Bry* k* calad k* calc k* calc-i k2 *Calc-s* k* cann-s k* *Carb-v* k* cham k* cina k* *Coc-c* kr1 *Cocc* k* colch k* croc k* dros k* *Euph* k* *Fl-ac* k* **Glon** ign k* *Ind* **Iod** k* *Ip* k* kali-bi **Kali-s** k* lac-ac stj5• **Lach** k* led k* *Lyc* k* m-arct b2.de **Merc** k* merc-c b4a.de *Mez* *Nat-m* k* *Nat-s* *Nit-ac* b2.de* nux-m nux-v k* *Op* k* *Ph-ac* bg2 phenob jl3* *Phos* k* *Pic-ac* plat k* podo **Puls** k* rhus-t b2.de* sabin k* sacch sst1• sars *Sec* k* sel k* *Seneg* k* *Sep* b2.de* spig b7a.de *Sul-i* k2* *Sulph* k* teucr k* thuj k* xan [alum stj2 am-br stj2 am-f stj2 am-s stj1 ant-m stj2 arg-p stj2 aur-s stj2 bar-f stj1 bar-i stj2 bar-n stj1 bar-s stj1 brom stj1* cadm-m stj2 calc-br stj1 calc-f stj1 chr-s stj2 cinnb stj2 cob-m stj2 cupr-f stj2 ferr-f stj2 ferr-i stj1 ferr-lac stj2 ferr-n stj2 ferr-s stj1 gal-s stj2 lith-f stj2 lith-s stj2 mag-f stj1 mag-m stj1 mang-i stj2 mang-s stj2 merc-i-f stj2 nat-br stj2 nat-caust stj2 nat-f stj1* nat-lac stj2 nat-met stj2 nat-n stj1 nicc-s stj2 *Nitro* stj2 oxyg stj2 plb-m stj2 sul-ac stj1 *Tell* stj2 titan-s stj2 zinc-m stj2 zinc-n stj2]
    - ⋮ **slightly** warm: [chlor stj2 chr-m stj2]
  - **amel.**: *Acon* b2.de* aesc bg2 *Agar* b2.de* alum b2.de* alumn kr1 *Am-c* b2.de* anac b2.de* ant-c b2.de* arn b2.de* **Ars** b2.de* ars-i bg2 asar b2.de* **Aur** b2.de* *Bar-c* b2.de* *Bell* b2.de* borx b2.de* *Bov* b2.de* *Bry* b2.de* *Calc* b2.de* **Camph** b2.de* canth b2.de* *Caps* b2.de* *Carb-an* b2.de* *Carb-v* b2.de* **Caust** b2.de* *Cham* b2.de* chin b2.de* *Cic* b2.de* *Cina* b2.de* *Coc-c* hr1* *Cocc* b2.de coff b2.de* *Colch* b2.de* *Coloc* b2.de* *Con* b2.de* dig b2.de* **Dulc** b2.de* *Ferr* b2.de* graph b2.de* **Hell** b2.de* **Hep** b2.de* *Hyos* b2.de* *Ign* b2.de* ip b2.de* **Kali-c** b2.de* kreos b2.de* lach b2.de* laur b2.de* led bro1 *Lyc* b2.de* m-ambo b2.de m-arct b2.de m-aust b2.de mag-c b2.de* mag-m b2.de* mag-p sf1.de *Mang* b2.de* meny b2.de* *Merc* b2.de* *Mez* b2.de* **Mosch** b2.de* mur-ac b2.de* nat-ar k2 *Nat-c* b2.de* *Nat-m* b2.de* nat-s sf1.de *Nit-ac* b2.de* **Nux-m** b2.de* **Nux-v** b2.de* par b2.de* *Petr* b2.de* *Ph-ac* b2.de* phor-t mie3• *Phos* b2.de* psor bg2* pyrog jl2 ran-b b2.de* *Rhod* b2.de* **Rhus-t** b2.de* *Ruta* b2.de* **Sabad** b2.de* samb b2.de* *Sars* b2.de* *Sel* hr1* seneg b2.de* *Sep* b2.de* *Sil* b2.de* *Spig* b2.de* *Spong* b2.de* squil b2.de* staph b2.de* stram b2.de* **Stront-c** b2.de* sul-ac b2.de* *Sulph* b2.de* symph fd3.de• thuj b2.de* tub mrr1 *Verat* b2.de* verb b2.de* viol-t b2.de* zinc b2.de*
  - **sensation** of: aster ptk1 bry ptk1 kali-c ptk1 puls ptk1 sulph ptk1 verat ptk1
- **amel.**: *Acon* b2.de* *Agar* b2.de* alum b2.de* alum-sil k2* alumn kr1 am-br kr1* *Am-c* b2.de* anac b2.de* ant-c b2.de* aral kr1* *Arg-met* b2.de* arist-cl mg1.de* *Arn* b2.de* **Ars** b2.de* asar b2.de* atra-r bnm3• *Aur* b2.de* aur-m bro1 bad bro1 *Bar-c* b2.de* *Bell* b2.de* bell-p mg1.de* *Borx* b2.de* *Bov* b2.de* brucel sa3• *Bry* b2.de* calc b2.de* calc-f k2* calc-p k2* calc-s k2* **Camph** b2.de* *Canth* b2.de* *Caps* b2.de* *Carb-an* b2.de* *Carb-v* b2.de* carc hbh* cassia-s ccrh1• castm sf1.de **Caust** b2.de* cench k2 cham b2.de* chel k2* *Chin* b2.de* *Cic* b2.de* cimic bro1* cist tl1 *Clem* b2.de* *Cocc* b2.de* *Coff* b2.de* *Colch* b2.de* coli jl2 *Coll* bro1 *Coloc* b2.de* *Con* b2.de* cor-r bro1 cupr-act bro1 cycl bro1* cyn-d jl3 *Dig* b2.de* diphtox jl2 dros ptk1 **Dulc** b2.de* *Ferr* b2.de* flor-p jl3 form bro1 germ-met srj5• gink-b jl3 *Graph* b2.de* gymno kr1* *Hell* b2.de* **Hep** b2.de* *Hyos* b2.de* *Ign* b2.de* ip b2.de* kali-ar k2* kali-bi k2* **Kali-c** b2.de* kali-p bro1 *Kreos* b2.de* lac-d k2* lac-h sze9• *Lach* b2.de* lat-m bnm6• laur b2.de* led b2.de* levo jl3 lob bro1 lyc b2.de* lycpr bro1 m-ambo b2.de m-aust b2.de *Mag-c* b2.de* *Mag-m* b2.de* *Mag-p* k2* mand mg1.de* *Mang* b2.de* med k2* *Meny* b2.de* *Merc* b2.de* *Mez* b2.de* mim-p vml3• moly-met jl **Mosch** b2.de* *Mur-ac* b2.de* *Nat-c* b2.de* nat-m b2.de* nid jl nit-ac b2.de* *Nux-m* b2.de* **Nux-v** b2.de* oci-sa sp1 olib-sac wmh1 onop jl oscilloc jl2 *Petr* b2.de* ph-ac b2.de* *Phos* b2.de* phyt bro1 psor bro1* puls b2.de* pyrog k2* *Ran-b* b2.de* *Rheum* b2.de* *Rhod* b2.de* **Rhus-t** b2.de* *Rumx* bro1* *Ruta* b2.de* **Sabad** b2.de* sacch-a gmj3 *Samb* b2.de* sanic mrr1 *Sars* b2.de* seneg b2.de* *Sep* b2.de* ser-a-c jl2 *Sil* b2.de* *Spig* b2.de* *Spong* b2.de* *Squil* b2.de* *Staph* b2.de* *Stram* b2.de* **Stront-c** b2.de* *Sul-ac* b2.de* *Sulph* b2.de* symph fd3.de• syph k2* thea bro1 ther k2* thuj b2.de* tritic-vg fd5.de tub k2* verat b2.de* verb b2.de* viol-t b2.de* xero bro1 zinc b2.de* [*Ars-met* stj2 calc-sil stj2 ferr-sil stj2 heroin sdj2 kali-sil stj2 lith-c stj2 mag-i stj1 *Mag-lac* stj2 *Mag-met* stj2 mag-sil stj2 *Nat-ar* stj2 nat-sil stj2 plb stj2 sil-met stj2 tax jsj7]
- **applications**:
  - **agg.**: apis bg2* **Bell** ptk1 bry bg2 calc ptk1 *Carb-v* ptk1 crot-h ptk1 cupr ptk1 fl-ac bg2* guaj br1 **Iod** ptk1 kali-i ptk1 kali-s ptk1 lach bg2* led bg2* lil-t ptk1 lyc ptk1 *Merc* ptk1 *Nat-m* ptk1 puls bg2* sabin ptk1 sanic ptk1 sec bg2* spig ptk1 *Sulph* ptk1
    - ⋮ **night**: bros-gau mrc1
- **applications**: ...
  - **amel.**: *Alum* b4a.de am-c b4a.de anac ptk1 ars b4a.de* aur b4a.de bar-c b4a.de bry b7a.de* calc-f bro1* canth b7.de *Caust* b4a.de *Cham* b7.de* *Chin* b7a.de cic b7.de coloc b4a.de* fic-m gya1 hell b7.de hep bg2* **Ign** b7.de* kali-c ptk1 lach b7.de* laur b7.de *Mag-c* ptk1 mag-m b4a.de mag-p bro1* mang b4a.de meny b7.de **Nux-m** b7.de* *Nux-v* b7.de* puls ptk1 rad-br bro1* **Rhus-t** b7.de* ruta bg2 *Sabad* b7.de *Samb* ptk1 *Sep* b4a.de* ser-a-c jl2 sil b4a.de* squil ptk1 *Staph* b7.de stront-c b4a.de* sulph b4a.de syph ptk1 thuj bg2
- **artificial** heat | **amel.**: cor-r br1
- **bathing**:
  - **agg.**: acon gl1.fr• aesc k2 ant-c k2 *Apis* bg2* ars-i sf1.de bell gl1.fr• caust k2 iod sf1.de *Lach* bg2* *Op* bg2* pall sne phos bg2* sulph bg2
    - ⋮ **hot** bath: **Apis** bg2* *Arg-n* bg2 bamb-a stb2.de• *Bell* bg2 bell-p ptk1 *Bry* bg2 *Carb-v* bg2 **Gels** bg2 ham fd3.de• **Iod** bg2 **Kali-i** vh **Lach** bg2 **Nat-m** bg2 op bg2* podo fd3.de• *Puls* bg2 *Sec* bg2 spong fd4.de *Sulph* bg2 tung-met bdx1•
  - **amel.**: am-m vh ant-c k2* bamb-a stb2.de• bit-ar wht1• bufo bro1 dulc fd4.de flav jl2 ham fd3.de• kola stb3• lac-h sze9• lat-m jl* mim-p jl nat-sil fd3.de• neon srj5• ozone sde2• positr nl2• rad-br bro1 *Rhus-t* mrr1 sacch-a fd2.de• sec sf1.de spong fd4.de *Stront-c* bro1 symph fd3.de• thea bro1 vanil fd5.de
    - ⋮ **hot** bath: am-m vh anac bg2* **Ars** bg2 chel ptk1 cypra-eg sde6.de• *Hep* bg2 kali-p fd1.de• lat-m bnm6• lyss ptk1* mag-p ptk1 mez ptk1 nat-sil fd3.de• nit-ac sne positr nl2• pyrog ptk1 rad-br c11* rat ptk1 *Rhus-t* bg2 *Sil* bg2 spig bro1 stront-c ptk1 symph fd3.de• *Thuj* bg2 tritic-vg fd5.de tung-met bdx1• [heroin sdj2]
- **bed**:
  - **agg.**: aeth agn k* *Alum* k* alumn kr1 ambr k* anac b2.de* *Ant-c* k* *Ant-t* k* **Apis** k* arg-n arn k* ars-i *Asaf* asar b2.de* aur k* aur-i k2* *Aur-m* aur-s k2 bar-c k* bell-p bro1 bov k* **Brom** b4a.de *Bry* k* calad k* calc k* calc-f mg1.de calc-i k2* *Calc-s* *Camph* cann-s k* *Carb-v* k* carbn-s k2* *Caust* b2.de* cedr **Cham** k* chin k* cina k* cinnb k2* *Clem* k* *Coc-c* *Cocc* k* colch k* coloc bg2 croc k* daph **Dros** k* dulc *Euph* k* *Fl-ac* k* gard-j vlr2• *Glon* goss *Graph* k* hell k* hyos ign k* *Iod* k* *Ip* k* kali-br sf1.de *Kali-c* b2.de* *Kali-chl* kali-m k2 *Kali-s* kreos sf1.de *Lac-c* *Lach* k* **Led** k* lil-t sf1.de *Lyc* k* m-ambo b2.de* m-arct b2.de* *Mag-c* k* med st **Merc** k* *Mez* k* mur-ac k* nat-c k* *Nat-m* k* nit-ac k* *Nux-m* b2.de* *Nux-v* b2.de* **Op** k* petr sf1.de *Ph-ac* k* phenob jl3* phos k* phyt *Plat* k* psor k* **Puls** k* rad-br mrr1 *Rhod* j5.de* *Rhus-t* b2.de* sabad k* **Sabin** k* sang sf1.de sars k* **Sec** k* sel k* *Seneg* k* sep b2.de* *Sil* bg2* spig k* *Spong* k* staph k* stram stront-c bg2 *Sul-i* k2* **Sulph** k* teucr k* *Thuj* k* *Verat* k* visc bro1 x-ray sp1 [bell-p-sp dcm1]
    - ⋮ **cold** extremities, with: **Camph** **Led** *Mag-c* *Med* **Sec**
  - **amel.**: agar k* *Am-c* k* arn k* **Ars** k* ars-s-f k2* *Aur* k* bapt bg2 bar-c k* bell k* **Bry** k* calc-f dp• *Calc-p* camph k* canth k* *Caust* k* choc srj3• cic k* cocc k* *Coloc* k* con k* *Dulc* k* *Graph* k* **Hep** k* hyos k* *Kali-bi* **Kali-c** k* *Kali-i* kali-p lach k* **Lyc** k* *Mag-p* mosch k* nit-ac k* **Nux-m** k* **Nux-v** k* olib-sac wmh1 petr ph-ac k* *Phos* k* **Rhus-t** k* *Rumx* *Sabad* k* *Sep* k* **Sil** k* spong k* squil k* *Stann* staph k* stram k* stront-c k* sul-ac bg2* sulph k* symph fd3.de• *Tarent* thuj sf1.de **Tub** verat b2.de*
  - **desire** for: choc srj3• sacch-a fd2.de• spig a1 symph fd3.de•
  - **yearning** for: olib-sac wmh1
- **cannot** get warm (See Heat - lack - warm covering; CHILL - Warm - desire)
- **clothing**:
  - **agg.**: lac-leo hrn2•
  - **desire**: *(↗MIND - Fur; wraps)* alum k2 ars k2* *Bar-c* sf1.de bell k2 calc k2 caul k2 coca-c sk4• graph k2 hep k2 kali-c k2 nat-c k2 nat-s k2 plb k2 *Psor* br1* *Sabad* sf1.de sacch-a fd2.de• sil k2* spong fd4.de symph fd3.de•
    - ⋮ **afternoon**: nux-v a1
    - ⋮ **in** spite of sensation of heat: achy jl
    - ⋮ **summer** agg.: hep ptk1 *Psor* br1
- **desire** for warmth: *(↗Clothing - intolerance)* abrom-a-r bnj1 alum bg2* am-br sf1.de arg-met bg2* *Ars* bg2* bamb-a stb2.de• bar-c bg2 calc k2 caps bg2* *Caust* bg2* *Colch* bg2* con bg2* dulc fd4.de falco-pe nl2* gymno br1 ham fd3.de• *Hep* bg2* *Kali-c* bg2* moly-met jl ph-ac bg2* psor bg2* *Sabad* bg2* sacch-a fd2.de• *Sil* bg2* spong fd4.de symph fd3.de• tere-la rly4• thuj bg2 tritic-vg fd5.de tub bg2* [tax jsj7]

- **fire**; open:
  - **agg.**: *Ant-c* b2.de bry b2.de* *Euph* b2.de glon br1 mag-m b2.de merc b2.de puls b2.de *Zinc* b2.de
    - **children**; in: glon br1
- **hands** warm; keeping | **amel.**: hell b7.de
- **room**: *(↗Faintness - sauna; Faintness - steam)*
  - **agg.**: acon k* aeth sf1.de *Agn* k* *All-c* k2* aloe k2 *Alum* k* alum-p k2 alum-sil k2* *Alumn* kr1 am-c bg2* am-m b7a.de ambr k* aml-ns vh1 *Anac* b2.de* androc srj1• *Ant-c* k* ant-t k* **Apis** k* aran-ix mg1.de aran-sc bro1 *Arg-n* arn k* ars-i *Asaf* *Asar* b2.de* aur k* aur-i k2* *Aur-m* aur-s k2* bamb-a stb2.de• bapt bg2* bar-c k* bar-i k2* bell k* borx k* *Brom* k* brucel sa3• *Bry* k* bufo k* calad calc k* calc-i k2* calc-p **Calc-s** cann-s k* *Caps* b7a.de *Carb-ac* *Carb-v* k* **Carbn-s** carc tpw2* caust k* cina k* *Coc-c* cocc colch k* conch fkr1* conv br1 crat bro1 **Croc** k* culx k2* *Dros* dulc k* dys fmm1• euphr bro1 *Fl-ac* gard-j vlr2• gink-b sbd1• *Glon* k* **Graph** k* grat k2 hell k* hep b2.de* hip-ac sp1* hyos hyper bro1 iber vml3• ign k* ina-i mlk9.de *Ind* **Iod** k* *Ip* k* kali-c k* **Kali-i** k* **Kali-s** k* lach k2* laur k* *Led* *Lil-t* k* luf-op jl3 **Lyc** k* m-arct b2.de* *Mag-m* k* med st *Merc* k* *Merc-i-f* mez k* mosch mur-ac k* nat-ar *Nat-c* k* nat-m k* *Nat-s* nit-ac k* nux-v b2.de* *Op* k* oxyt ph-ac k* phos k* *Pic-ac* *Pieri-b* mlk9.de plat k* pneu jl3* podo fd3.de• *Ptel* **Puls** k* ran-b k* rhus-g tmo3• rhus-t b2.de* **Sabin** k* *Sanic* **Sec** sel k* **Seneg** k* sep b2.de* sil mrr1 spig k* *Spong* k* squil b7a.de staph k* *Sul-i* k2* **Sulph** k* *Tab* *Thuj* k* *Til* *Tub* vanil fd5.de *Verat* k* *Verb* b7.de vib bro1 viol-t b7a.de
  - **amel.**: aur-ar k2 both-a rb3 carb-v sf1.de *Caust* sf1.de cham sf1.de chel sf1.de chin sf1.de chinin-ar k2 cocc sf1.de cycl k2* guaj sf1.de *Hep* k2* mag-p k2* mang sf1.de merc sf1.de nux-m sf1.de nux-v sf1.de plat sf1.de rhus-t k2* *Rumx* sf1.de *Sil* sf1.de
- **stove**:
  - **agg.**: *(↗Light; from - agg. - fire)* *Ant-c* k* *Apis* *Arg-n* k* arn b7.de* ars bg2 *Bry* k* bufo k* *Cimic* bg2 cina b7a.de *Cocc* *Con* cupr bg2 *Euph* k* **Glon** k* hydrog srj2• *Iod* *Kali-i* k* *Laur* mag-m k* *Merc* k* nat-m k* nat-s bg2 nux-v bg2 op phos bg2 psor bg2 *Puls* k* ruta b7a.de **Sec** spig b7a.de thiop jl *Zinc* bg2*
  - **amel.**: acon k* agar k* am-c k* **Ars** k* aur k* bar-c k* bell k* borx k* bov ptk1 calc-f dp• camph k* canth k* caps k* caust k* choc srj3• cic k* cocc k* con k* conv cor-r br1 *Dulc* k* graph bg2 hell k* **Hep** k* hydrog srj2• hyos k* **Ign** k* kali-c k* lach ptk1 mag-c k* **Mag-p** mang k* meny b2.de* mosch k* *Nux-m* k* **Nux-v** k* petr k* ran-b k* rhod k* **Rhus-t** k* rumx ptk1 sabad k* **Sil** k* *Stront-c* k* sulph k* tub k2*
  - **cold** and stiff on approaching; he is: *Laur*
  - **desire**: bar-c sf1.de cic a1 med brm ptel a1 sacch-a fd2.de• *Sil* sf1.de tub k2 [heroin sdj2]
- **wraps**: *(↗Covers - agg.)*
  - **agg.**: *Acon* k* ant-c k2* ant-t k2* **Apis** *Arg-met* *Arg-n* arn bg2 *Ars-i* *Asar* b2.de* aur k* aur-i k2* *Aur-m* k* aur-s k2* *Borx* k* brom k2* *Bry* k* *Calc* k* calc-i k2* calc-s *Camph* carb-v k* carbn-s *Cham* k* chin k* *Coc-c* coff k* *Ferr* k* ferr-i *Fl-ac* k* glon hydrog srj2• ign k* **Iod** k* kali-bi bg2 **Kali-s** k* *Lac-c* lach k* **Led** k* **Lyc** k* *M-ambo* b2.de* *M-aust* b2.de **Mag-p** bg2 merc k* mosch k* mur-ac k* *Nit-ac* k* nux-v k* op k* phos k* plat k* **Puls** k* rhus-t k* sabin k2* **Sec** k* *Seneg* k* sep k* *Spig* k* staph k* *Sul-i* k2* **Sulph** k* tab thuj k* tritic-vg fd5.de *Verat* k*
  - **amel.**: alum-sil vh1 aral vh1 *Arg-met* b7a.de arge-pl rwt5• *Arn* b7a.de ars b4.de* **Aur** b4.de* calc-f kr1* *Cham* b7a.de choc srj3• colch k2 culx vml3• graph b4.de hell b7.de **Hep** b4a.de* hydrog srj2• ign b7.de lach b7.de *Mag-m* b4.de* merc b4a.de *Mur-ac* b4a.de nat-c b4.de *Nat-m* b4a.de *Nux-m* b7.de* **Nux-v** b7.de* olib-sac wmh1 phos b4.de psor bg2* rhod k2 rhus-t b7.de* sabad bg2 *Sep* b4a.de **Sil** b4.de* *Squil* b7a.de staph b7.de stront-c b4a.de* symph fd3.de• [stront-m stj2 stront-met stj2]
  - **head**; around | **amel.**: bell bro1 graph bro1 *Hep* bro1 *Psor* bro1 rhod bro1 sanic bro1 *Sil* bro1
  - **sensation** as if: bar-c ptk1 cact ptk1 graph ptk1 med ptk1 nux-v ptk1 sulph ptk1

WARM; BECOMING:

- **agg.**: *Acon* hr1* am-c hr1* **Ant-c** hr1* ant-t vh bar-i k2* *Bell* hr1* borx ptk1 brom st **Bry** b7.de* *Calc-sil* br1 *Caps* hr1* *Carb-v* hr1* coff hr1* *Dig* hr1* *Gels* hr1* *Glon* hr1* *Hep* hr1* *Ign* hr1* iod ptk1 *Ip* hr1* **Kali-c** hr1* kali-s ptk1* lach k2* lyss ptk1 merc ptk1 mez hr1* *Nat-c* ptk1 *Nat-m* hr1* *Nux-m* hr1* *Nux-v* hr1* olnd hr1* *Op* hr1* podo fd3.de• *Puls* b7.de* sabad b7.de samb ptk1 *Sel* ptk1* *Sep* hr1* *Sil* hr1* spig b7a.de staph b7.de* ther ptk1 *Thuj* hr1* verat b7.de verat-v ptk1 *Zinc* hr1*

Warm; becoming – **agg.**: ...

- **air** agg.; in open: acon k* agn k* alum k* alumn kr1 ambr k* anac b2.de* *Ant-c* k* asar b2.de* aur k* aur-i k2 *Aur-m* bar-c k* bar-i k2 *Bell* k* borx bov k* **Bry** k* calad k* calc k* cann-s k* *Carb-v* k* caust k* cham k* chin k* cina k* cocc k* coff k* colch k* coloc k* croc k* dros k* *Dulc* k* euph k* **Gels** kr1 *Glon* graph k* ign k* **Iod** k* ip k* kali-c k* lach k* led k* **Lyc** k* m-ambo b2.de* m-arct b2.de mang k* *Merc* k* mez k* nat-c k* nat-m k* *Nat-s* nit-ac k* nux-m b2.de* nux-v b2.de* olnd k* *Op* k* petr k* ph-ac k* *Phos* k* plat k* **Puls** k* rhus-t b2.de* *Sabad* k* sabin k* *Sec* k* sel k* *Seneg* k* sep k* *Sil* k* *Spig* k* spong k* staph k* *Sulph* k* teucr k* thuj k* *Verat* k*
- **amel.**: *Acon* b2.de* *Agar* b2.de* am-c b2.de* ant-c b2.de* *Arn* b2.de* **Ars** b2.de* asar b2.de* *Aur* b2.de* *Bar-c* b2.de* *Bell* b2.de* *Borx* b2.de* bov b2.de* *Bry* b2.de* *Calc* b2.de* *Camph* b2.de* canth b2.de* *Caps* b2.de* carb-an b2.de* carb-v b2.de* *Caust* b2.de* *Cham* b2.de* *Chin* b2.de* *Cic* b2.de* clem b2.de* *Coc-c* hr1* *Cocc* b2.de colch k2* coli rly4• *Con* b2.de* dig b2.de* *Dulc* b2.de* ferr b2.de* **Graph** b2.de* *Hell* b2.de* *Hep* b2.de* *Hyos* b2.de* *Ign* b2.de* **Kali-c** b2.de* *Kreos* b2.de* lach b2.de* *Lyc* b2.de* m-ambo b2.de m-aust b2.de *Mag-c* b2.de* mag-m b2.de* *Mang* b2.de* meny b2.de* *Merc* b2.de* mez b2.de* **Mosch** b2.de* mur-ac b2.de* *Nat-c* b2.de* nat-m b2.de* *Nit-ac* b2.de* *Nux-m* b2.de* **Nux-v** b2.de* *Petr* b2.de* *Ph-ac* b2.de* *Phos* b2.de* ran-b b2.de* rhod b2.de* **Rhus-t** b2.de* ruta b2.de* **Sabad** b2.de* samb b2.de* *Sars* b2.de* sel b2.de* *Sep* b2.de* *Sil* b2.de* spig b2.de* *Spong* b2.de* staph b2.de* stram b2.de* *Stront-c* b2.de* sul-ac b2.de* *Sulph* b2.de* symph fd3.de• *Thuj* b2.de* *Verat* b2.de* *Verb* b2.de* viol-t b2.de* zinc b2.de*

WARMBLOODED persons (See Heat - sensation)

WARMTH; sensation of (See Heat - sensation)

WASHING clothes, laundry, ailments from: am-c bg ant-c bg *Calc* bg clem bg nit-ac bg phos c1* rhus-t bg sep c1* spig bg *Sulph* bg ther c1*

WATER: *(↗MIND - Fear - water)*

- **agg.** (See Bathing - agg.)
- **aversion** to: *Am-c* br1 *Sulph* br1
- **dashing** against inner parts, sensation of: *(↗Heat - flushes - warm water - dashed)* bell cina **Crot-t** dig ferr hell irid-met srj5• kali-m k2 laur ph-ac *Rhod* *Spig*
- **desire** to be near the water: arb-m oss1• hippoc-k szs2
- **hot** water poured on part; sensation as if: verat-v ptk1
- **living** near water agg.: *Aran* br1 *Nat-s* br1 *Thuj* br1
- **pouring** out of water agg.: lyss mg1.de
- **seeing** or hearing of running water agg.: *(↗MIND - Hydrophobia)* ang bg2 apis bg2 arg-met bg2 bell bg2* brom bg2* canth bg2* **Lys** bg2 **Lyss** bro1* nit-ac bg2 *Stram* bg2* sulph bg2* ter bg2
  - **pregnancy** agg.; during: phos ptk1
- **touching** water | **aversion** to: *Am-c* br1*
- **wading** in, ailments from: ars k* dulc k* mag-p k*
- **working** in water:
  - **agg.**: alum ptk1 *Am-c* ptk1 *Ant-c* ptk1 ant-t ptk1 *Aran* ptk1 *Ars* ptk1 atra-r bnm3• bry ptk1 cact ptk1 *Calc* bg2* calc-p bg2* card-m ptk1 caust ptk1 cham ptk1 cimic ptk1 *Clem* ptk1 colch ptk1 **Dulc** ptk1 gels ptk1 kalm ptk1 lyc ptk1 mag-c bg2* mag-p bro1* med ptk1 merc ptk1 *Nat-s* ptk1 nit-ac ptk1 nux-m ptk1 phos ptk1 phyt ptk1 *Puls* ptk1 pyrog ptk1 *Rhod* ptk1 **Rhus-t** ptk1 sabal ptk1 sabin ptk1 senec ptk1 *Sep* ptk1 *Sil* ptk1 sulph ptk1 ter ptk1 tritic-vg fd5.de tub ptk1
  - **hands** in cold water:
    - **agg.**: lac-d bg2 mag-p bg2 phos bg2
    - **amel.**: jatr-c bg2

WAVELIKE sensations: acon bg2* agath-a nl2• aids nl2• am-c aml-ns bg1 anac a1* ant-t hr1 apis bg2 ara-maca sej7• arn hr1 asaf hr1* *Asar* bg2 **Bell** k* *Bism* calc bg2 camph bg2 cann-xyz bg2 caps caust chin hr1 cic a1 clem cocc hr1 coff b2.de* con dig dulc hr1 falco-pe nl2• ferr-p bg1 gard-j vlr2• glon bg1 graph ptk1 helo-s bnm14• hippoc-k szs2 hydrog srj2• hyos b2.de* iod kali-c kali-n lach bg1 lyc mag-c manc bg2 mang a1 mez hr1 mosch bg2 *Nit-ac* nux-v k* olnd hr1 op bg2 par b2.de* petr plat hr1 rhod hr1* sars *Sep* k* sil spig hr1 stann stict bg2* stram bg2 stront-c stroph-h ptk1 **Sulph** teucr hr1 *Valer* bg2 verat bg2 verb viol-t hr1 zinc-i ptk1 [*Buteo-j* sej6 cadm-met stj2 cadm-s stj2 spect dfg1]

- **pins** and needles; like: agath-a nl2•
- **tidal** waves: [spect dfg1]

WEAKNESS: (*↗Chronic fatigue; Collapse; Flabby; Heaviness; Lassitude; Relaxation - physical; Sluggishness; Weariness; MIND - Dullness; MIND - Prostration; PERSPIRATION - Debilitating)*
abies-c k* abies-n abrom-a ks5 abrot k* absin *Acet-ac* k* *Acetan* vh1 achy jl3 *Acon* k* acon-c a1 acon-f a1 adam srj5• adlu jl3 *Adon* vh1 adox a1 adren c1* aesc aesc-g a1* *Aeth* k* aether a1 agar k* agar-cpn a1 agar-em a1 agar-pa a1 *Agar-ph* a1 agar-pr a1 agar-st a1 agath-a nl2• agav-t jl3 *Agn* k* aids nl2• ail k* alco a1 *Alet* kr1* alf br1* all-c all-s allox tpw4 aln vva1• *Aloe* k* alst c1* alst-s a1 *Alum* k* alum-p k2 alum-sil k2* alumn am-br vh1 **Am-c** k* am-caust a1 am-m k* *Ambr* k* *Aml-ns* a1* ammc j5.de* amor-r jl3 amph a1 amyg a1 **Anac** k* *Anag* kr1 anan kr1 ancis-p tsm2 androc bnm2• *Ang* b2.de* anil a1 *Ant-ar* a1* *Ant-c* k* ant-m a1* ant-o a1 **Ant-t** k* anth a1 anthraci k* anthraco a1* anthraq rly4• *Antip* bro1 aphis j5.de* **Apis** k* apoc k* apoc-a a1* apom a1 aq-mar jl3* aq-pet a1 ara-maca sej7• aral a1 *Aran* k* aran-sc a1* arg-cy a1 **Arg-met** k* *Arg-n* k* arist-cl mg1.de* **Arn** k* **Ars** k* ars-h k* ars-i k* *Ars-met* k* ars-s-f ars-s-r kr1 arum-d a1* arum-i a1 arum-m arum-t asaf k* asar k* asc-t asim a1 aspar kr1* astac a1 aster atha j5.de* atra-r jl3* atro a1 *Aur* k* aur-ar k2 aur-fu j5.de* *Aur-m* a1* aur-m-n a1 aur-s k2 *Aven* c1* bac jl2 bacls-7 jl2* *Bals-p* br1* **Bapt** k* bar-act a1* **Bar-c** k* bar-i k2* *Bar-m* k* bar-ox-suc rly4• bart a1 bell k* bell-p bro1* ben ben-n a1 *Benz-ac* k* berb k* berbin a1 beryl mg1.de *Bism* k* bism-o a1 *Bit-ar* wht1• *Bol-la* bol-s a1 borx k* *Both* a1* bov k* brach brass-n-o srj5• **Brom** k* bruc j5.de brucel sa3• brucin a1 *Bry* k* bufo k* bung-fa tsm2 buni-o k* buth-a mg1.de* *Cact* k* cadm-met mg1.de* cadm-s k2* cain caj a1 calad k* **Calc** k* calc-ar k2 calc-caust a1* calc-hp bro1 **Calc-i** k2* calc-m a1 calc-p k* calc-s calc-sil k2* *Camph* k* cann-i cann-s k* *Canth* k* canthin hs1 caps k* car c2 **Carb-ac** k* *Carb-an* k* carb-v k* carbn-chl a1 carbn-h carbn-o a1 *Carbn-s* carc cpd*• card-m k* *Carl* a1* cartl-s rly4• casc j5.de cass a1 cassia-s ccrh1• castm a1* castn-v *Caul* k* *Caust* k* cedr cench a1* cent a1 cere-b a1 cerv a1 *Cham* k* chap br1 **Chel** k* chelo c1* *Chim* **Chin** k* chinin-ar k* *Chinin-fcit* bro1 **Chinin-s** k* chion k* chir-fl gya2 chlam-tr bcx2• chlf chlol chloram jl3 chlorpr jl3 choc srj3• chord-umb rly4• chr-ac a1* *Cic* k* cich a1 cimic cimx *Cina* k* cinnb cinnm kr1* cist c1 cit-l a1* cit-v a1 *Clem* k* *Cloth* tsm2 cob cob-n mg1.de* coc-c k* **Coca** a1* *Cocc* k* coch kr1* cod a1 *Coff* k* **Colch** k* colchin a1* *Coli* jl2 coll a1 coloc k* colocin a1* colum-p sze2• com **Con** k* conin a1 conin-br c1 conv st1 cop cor-r sf1.de cordyc mp4• corian-s knl6• corn a1* corn-a br1 cortico sp1 cortiso tpw7 cot a1 crat br1* croc k* *Crot-c* k* *Crot-h* k* *Crot-t* cub culx k2 *Cupr* k* cupr-act j5.de* *Cupr-ar* cupr-s cur k* *Cycl* k* cyn-d jl3 cypr c2 cypra-eg sde6.de• cystein-l rly4• cyt-l a1* *Daph* j5.de* dendr-pol tsm2* der a1 dicha mg1.de* **Dig** k* *Digin* a1 digox a1 dios dip bro1 diph br1* diphtox jl2 dirc a1* dor k* *Dros* k* dubo-m a1 *Dulc* k* *Echi* bg2* elaps tsm2 elat ephe-si hsj1• equis-h a1 erig a1 ery-a a1 ery-m c1* eryt-j a1 esch br1 eucal a1* eug eup-per eup-pur euph k* euph-a c1* euph-c a1 euph-hy a1 euph-ip a1 euphr k* eupi a1 fab br1 fago fagu a1 ferr k* ferr-ar k* **Ferr-i** k* **Ferr-m** k* ferr-ma j5.de* *Ferr-p* k* ferr-pic bro1 fic-m gya1 fic-r mg1.de fil c1 *Fl-ac* k* flor-p rsj3* *Form* k* frag a1 franz a1* *Fum* rly1• fuma-ac rly4• gad a1 gal-ac a1* galeg c1* galin jl3 galla-q-r nl2• *Gamb* kr1 gard-j vlr2• gast a1* **Gels** k* gent-l k* gent-q c1 germ-met srj5• get a1 gink-b jl3 gins j5.de* glon k* glyc br1 *Glycyr-g* cte1• goss gran *Granit-m* es1• **Graph** k* grat k* guaj k* guan a1 guar kr1 guare haem sf1.de haliae-lc srj5• hall a1 *Ham* hed jl3 hedeo a1 *Hell* k* hell-o a1 helo bg2 helo-s bnm14• helodr-cal knl2• helon k* **Hep** k* hera a1* hip-ac jl3 *Hipp* hippoc-k szs2 hir rsj4* hist sp1* home a1 hura *Hydr* k* *Hydr-ac* k* *Hydrc* a1 *Hydrog* srj2• hydroph rsj6• **Hyos** k* hyosin a1 *Hyper* iber a1* *Ign* k* ind indg **Iod** k* *Ip* k* *Irid-met* c1* iris k* jab jal a1 jasm a1 jatr-c jug-c a1 jug-r juni-v a1 **Kali-ar** k* *Kali-bi* k* *Kali-br* k* **Kali-c** k* kali-chl k* kali-cy a1* **Kali-fcy** k* *Kali-i* k* kali-m k2* kali-n k* kali-ox a1 **Kali-p** k* kali-perm a1* kali-s k* kali-sil k2* kali-sula a1* kali-t a1 **Kalm** k* ketogl-ac rly4• kino a1 kiss a1 kola br1* kou a1* kreos k* kres mg1.de* lac-ac k* *Lac-c* k* *Lac-d* kr1* lac-del hrn2• lac-h sk4• *Lac-leo* sk4• **Lach** k* lachn lact j5.de* lam j5.de lap-la sde8.de• lapa a1 lat-h bnm5• lat-k a1 lat-m sp1* **Laur** k* **Lec** k* led k* lepi lept lev c2 lil-s a1 lil-t k* lim a1* limest-b es1• lina a1 linu-c a1 lipp a1 lith-c bro1 lith-chl bro1 lob k* lob-c a1* lob-p br1* lob-s lobin a1 *Lol* a1* loxo-lae bnm12• loxo-recl bnm10*• luf-op mg1.de* **Luna** kg1• *Lyc* k* lycps-v lyss m-ambo b2.de* m-arct b2.de* m-aust b2.de* macro a1 mag-c k* mag-f mg1.de* mag-m k* *Mag-p* kr1* mag-s k* magn-gr br1 maland jl2 malar jl2 manc mand a1* mang b2.de* mang-o a1 mang-p rly4• **Med** k* mela a1 melal-alt gya4 meli k* menis a1 meny k* meph **Merc** k* merc-br a1 **Merc-c** k* **Merc-cy** k* merc-d a1 merc-i-f merc-i-r k* merc-k-i gm1 merc-meth a1 merc-ns a1 merc-sul a1* merl a1* methys jl3 mez k* mill mim-p rsj8• mit a1 moly-met jl3 *Mom-b* a1 *Moni* rfm1• morph mosch k* **Mur-ac** k* murx k* musca-d szs1 mygal k* *Myric* a1* nabal a1 naja napht a1 narcin a1 narz a1 nat-ar k* *Nat-c* k* *Nat-chl* br1 nat-f sp1 **Nat-hchls** nat-lac a1 **Nat-m** k* nat-n k* **Nat-p** k* **Nat-s** k* *Nat-sal* c1* nat-sil k2 nat-sula a1 nauf-helv-li elm2• nep mg1.de* nept-m lsd2.fr nicc nicc-met br1

Weakness: ...
nicc-s br1 nicot a1 nid jl3 nig-s mp4• **Nit-ac** k* nit-m-ac a1 nit-s-d j5.de* nitro-o a1 nuph *Nux-m* k* *Nux-v* k* oci-sa sk4• oena okou jl3 ol-an *Ol-j* *Olib-sac* wmh1 **Olnd** k* onos c1* op k* opun-v a1 orch c1* orig a1 orni a1* orot-ac rly4• osm ost a1 osteo-a jl2 *Ox-ac* k* oxal-a rly4• oxyg a1 ozone sde2• paeon pall k* palo jl3 pana a1 par k* parathyr jl3 parth c1* paull a1 ped penic jl3* perh jl3 pert jl2 *Petr* k* petr-ra shn4• **Ph-ac** k* phal a1 phel **Phos** k* *Phys* k* physal-al br1 *Phyt* k* **Pic-ac** k* pilo a1 pimp a1 pin-con oss2• pip-m a1 pitu sp1 pitu-gl skp7• pitu-p sp1 pix a1 plac-s rly4• plan *Plat* k* **Plb** k* plb-chr a1 plect a1 plumbg a1 plut-n srj7• pneu jl2 podo polyg-h polyp-p a1 polys sk4• *Positr* nl2• *Prim-o* br1 *Propr* sa3• prun-p a1 psil ft1 **Psor** k* ptel *Puls* k* puls-n a1 pulx br1 *Pycnop-sa* mrz1 pyrid rly4• pyrog sf1.de* pyrus a1 querc-r svu1• rad-br c11* ran-a j5.de **Ran-b** k* ran-s k* *Raph* rat rham-f a1 rheum k* rhod k* rhodi br1 rhus-g a1* **Rhus-t** k* *Rhus-v* a1* ribo rly4• ric a1* *Rob* a1* *Rosm* lgb1 *Rumx* rumx-act a1 ruta k* *Sabad* k* sabal br1 sabin k* sacch br1* sacch-a fd2.de• sal-fr sle1• salin a1 samb k* samb-c a1 *Sang* k* sanguis-s hrn2• *Sanic* k* santin a1 sapin a1 *Sarcol-ac* bro1* saroth jl3 sarr *Sars* k* scarl jl2 *Scor* a1* scroph-n a1 scut a1* **Sec** k* **Sel** k* senec k* *Seneg* k* senn a1* **Sep** k* sieg mg1.de **Sil** k* silphu c1 sin-n sinus rly4• sium a1 sol-mm a1 sol-ni sol-t a1 sol-t-ae solid bg* solin a1 sphing a1* spig k* spira a1 spirae a1 *Spong* k* **Squil** k* **Stann** k* **Staph** k* staphycoc jl2 *Stict* still *Stram* k* stront-c k* stroph-h bro1 stry k* stry-p st1 suis-pan rly4• **Sul-ac** k* sul-h a1 sul-i k* sulfa sp1* *Sulfon* br1* sulfonam jl3* **Sulph** k* sumb suprar rly4• symph fd3.de• syph syzyg br1 **Tab** k* tanac a1* tang a1 tann-ac a1 taosc iwa1• tarax k* **Tarent** k* tarent-c br1* tart-ac a1 tax j5.de* *Tell* k* **Ter** k* tere-ch jl3 teucr k* thal a1* thal-xyz srj8• thea a1* *Ther* k* thiop jl3 thres-a sze7• *Thuj* k* thymol br1* thyr br1* til tox-th a1 toxo-g jl2 trach a1 tril-p tritic-vg fd5.de trom **Tub** k* tub-d jl2 tub-r jl3* tub-sp zs tus-p a1 uncar-tom mp4• upa a1 uran-met sf1.de uran-n a1* urea mg1.de ust uva kr1 v-a-b jl3* vac a1* valer k* vanil fd5.de ven-m rsj12* **Verat** k* verat-v k* verb k* verin a1 vesp vib bg2* vichy-g a1 vinc viol-o kr1 viol-t k* vip k* vip-a jl3 vip-a-c tsm2 vip-d tsm2 visc sp1 voes a1 wies a1 wildb a1 wye a1* x-ray jl xan *Zinc* k* *Zinc-ar* bro1 zinc-m a1 zinc-o j5.de* zinc-p k2* *Zinc-pic* c1* zinc-s a1 zing ziz a1 [bell-p-sp dcm1 calc-lac stj2 calc-met stj2 heroin sdj2 pop dhh1 **Spect** dfg1 techn stj2]

- **right** side; of the: *Chlf* br1
- **left** side; of the: *Arg-n* kr1 *Lach* kr1 [tax jsj7]
- **daytime**: adam srj5• agar k* *Am-c* k* cench k2 cob-n sp1 corn k* ephe-si hsj1• granit-m es1• graph k* hippoc-k szs2 hydrog srj2• indg k* iod k* lac-lup hrn2• *Lavand-a* ctl1• lyc k* lyss hr1* mag-c k* mosch k* nat-ar nat-c k* *Nat-m* k* nat-sil fd3.de• nit-ac k* oci-sa sk4• op k* ph-ac k* phos k* phys k* pip-m k* plan k* *Stann* k* *Sulph* tarent k* ter k* uran-n kr1
  - **heat** of day, during: (*↗heat*) nat-sil fd3.de• sel k*
  - **walking** | **amel.**: (*↗walking - amel.*) ph-ac k*
- **morning**: *Acal* bro1 acon-l a1 agar k* alum j5.de alum-p k2 am-c k* am-m k* *Ambr* k* amph a1 ant-c k* ant-s-aur apoc k* arag br1 aran sf1.de *Arg-met* arn j5.de **Ars** k* *Ars-i* ars-s-f k2* asc-t k* atra-r jl3 atro k* aur k* aur-ar k2 aur-i k2* bar-m bro1 bell k* bism sf1.de borx bruc j5.de *Bry* k* bufo caj a1 *Calc* k* calc-i k2* *Calc-s* calc-sil k2 canth j5.de* caps k* carb-an k* *Carb-v* k* carbn-s celt a1 cham k* chel k* chinin-s cimic k* cinnb k* clem k* coc-c k* colch k* *Con* k* com a1* *Croc* k* crot-h k* cycl k* cystein-l rly4• dig k* digin a1 dios dros k* dulc fd4.de *Elat* hr1 erig k* euphr k* eupi k* fago flor-p jl3 form k* *Gels* k* gnaph k* granit-m es1• *Graph* ham hippoc-k szs2 hom-xyz st hyper k* *Iod* k* jal k* kali-bi k* kali-c k* kali-chl k13 kali-m k2 kali-n k* kali-p kali-sil k2 lac-ac k* lac-c k* lac-h sze9• **Lach** k* lact j5.de levo jl3 limest-b es1• **Lyc** k* *Mag-c* k* *Mag-m* k* medul-os-si rly4• meli k* *Merc* k* merc-c k* merl a1 morph k* mur-ac k* naja *Nat-ar* *Nat-c* k* *Nat-m* k* *Nat-p* k* *Nat-s* k* nat-sil k2* nicc-met sk4• *Nit-ac* k* *Nux-v* k* op k* osm k* ox-ac k* ped k* perh jl3 *Petr* k* **Ph-ac** k* *Phos* k* pic-ac k* plac rzf5• plat k* *Plb* hr1 podo fd3.de• positr nl2• prun k* psor bro1 *Puls* k* rad-br sze8• ran-b rhus-g tmo3• *Rhus-v* k* rob k* ruta sabad k* sang k* **Sep** k* *Sil* k* *Spig* k* stach a1 *Stann* k* *Staph* k* *Stront-c* stry a1 suis-pan rly4• sul-ac h2 sul-i k2* *Sulph* k* sumb k* syph k* tab k* ther k* thuj k* til k* tub bro1 valer k* vanil fd5.de ven-m rsj12• *Verat* k* viol-t k* zinc k* *Zinc-p* k2* [bell-p-sp dcm1]
  - **6** h: pic-ac
  - **6.30** h: ham
  - **7** h: cham elat graph
  - **8** h: dios phys psil ft1
  - **8.30** h: fago
  - **10** h, until: cench k2 nit-ac
  - **day** amel.; during: acal br1*
  - **amel.**: atra-r skp7*•

- **bed** agg.; in: *Ambr* arn *Carb-v* caust chin chinin-s a1 cich a1 *Con* k* ham c1 hell hep hom-xyz st lach mag-c *Nat-m* k* petr c1 phos polys sk4• **Puls** *Sil* *Staph* stront-c vanil fd5.de
  - **sitting** up; while: nat-m
- **fasting** agg.: con k*
- **ideas** at night; after copious flow of: tab
- **lying** agg.: *(↗lying)* **Puls** k*
- **rising**:
  - **after** | **agg.**: alumn k* *Arg-met* *Arg-n* k* bry k* carb-an k* hep k* kali-n k* *Lach* k* *Nit-ac* k* *Nux-v* k* peti a1 **Ph-ac** k* rhod k* til k*
  - **agg.**: *(↗rising - agg.)* alum k* asc-t k* atra-r skp7• aur-m-n k* bov k* **Bry** calc-caust a1 carbn a1 caust k* chin k* cina colch k* corn k* crot-t k* diaz sa3• dig k* dios k* *Dulc* k* eupi k* *Ferr* k* ham k* hep k* ign k* iris lac-ac k* **Lach** k* *Lyc* k* mez k* nat-m j5.de nux-v k* op k* petr k* **Ph-ac** k* phos k* plb k* puls j5.de puls-n rhus-v k* scut a1 *Sep* k* *Sil* k* *Stann* k* sulph k* thuj k* ust k* [tax jsj7]
  - **amel.**: acon k* carb-v k* caust k* con k* kali-c k* kali-p fd1.de• mag-c k* nat-c k* nat-m k* phos k* *Puls*
- **waking**; on: acon k* agar k* alum k* alum-p k2* am-c sf1.de ambr ant-c *Arg-met* k* arn j5.de aur bell j5.de berb k* *Bry* k* *Calc* k* calc-sil k2* cann-s k* carb-an k* carb-v k* castm castn-v a1 celt a1 cham k* chel chin k* clem k* coca colch k* coloc k* con k* corn k* crot-t k* cycl k* dros k* *Dulc* k* euph j5.de fago k* gels k* gnaph k* granit-m es1• graph k* grat k* hep k* hyper k* ign k* ignis-alc es2• iod j5.de jab k* kali-c k* kali-sil k2* *Lach* *Lyc* mag-c k* mag-s j5.de mang h2 nat-m k* *Nux-m* k1 *Nux-v* k* *Phos* k* pic-ac k* plb j5.de podo k* positr nl2• rhus-g tmo3• rhus-t k* ruta fd4.de sabad k* *Sang* k* *Sep* k* *Sil* k* *Spig* k* *Staph* k* stram k* *Syph* k2* tab k* ter k* thuj j5.de vanil fd5.de verat k* xan k* zinc k*
  - **dream**; from a: *Calc-s* k1 celt a1 op teucr
- **forenoon**: abrot a1 acon k* agn alum k* am-c k* ambr k* ang k* ant-t k* bart a1 bruc j5.de **Bry** k* calc h2 carb-an k* carb-v k* corn k* fago k* fl-ac k* flor-p rsj3• gels a1 graph k* grat k* hell k* hippoc-k szs2 indg k* kali-cy k* kali-n k* lach k* *Lyc* k* mag-m k* mang k* nat-m k* nux-m ox-ac k* petr-ra shn4• *Ph-ac* phel k* phys k* *Plat* k* ptel k* ran-b sabad k* sars k* scroph-n a1 sep k* tab k* tarent k* ulm-c jsj8• vanil fd5.de verat h1
  - **9** h: chinin-s cocc merl nat-s ox-ac ped perh jl peti phys ptel sep
    - **9**-11 h: tarent
    - **amel.**: tarent
  - **10** h: aq-mar jl borx sf1.de castm cench k2 equis-h gels lycps-v merc-d ozone sde2• phys
    - **10**-12 h: calc-s
    - **amel.**: *Gels*
  - **11** h: arg-met *Lach* kr1 nat-c sf1.de phos bg1* ptel sep ptk1 *Sulph* k* thuj zinc k*
    - **menses**; during: adam srj5•
- **noon**: bov carb-v k* caust k* cic hr1 clem k* con conch fkr1* cycl dulc fd4.de fago k* haliae-lc srj5• helon k* hyper k* nat-m nept-m lsd2.fr nit-ac k* ox-ac a1 ph-ac j5.de phos k* phys a1 phyt k* ptel k* sacch-a fd2.de• sil k* spong fd4.de sulph k* symph fd3.de• teucr thuj k* tritic-vg fd5.de zinc j5.de
  - **12**.30 h: gels sol-t-ae
  - **12**.30-15.30 h: dendr-pol sk4•
  - **15** h, until: hyos
  - **18** h, until: phyt a1 ptel
  - **amel.**: hyper k*
  - **sleep** agg.; after: *(↗afternoon - sleep)* borx a1 con a1 cycl a1 nat-m a1
- **afternoon**: acon k* aeth k* *Alet* am-c k* amyg k* anac k* apis aq-pet a1 arg-n k* aur k* bar-c h2 bell k* borx h2 brom k* *Bry* k* carb-an h2 carbn a1 castm chinin-s chord-umb rly4• cinch k* coc-c k* coca colch jl3 coloc k* corn k* con h2 digin a1 dulc fd4.de erig k* fago k* ferr k* gard-j vlr2• *Gels* k* glon k* granit-m es1• ham k* helon hydr-ac k* hydrog srj2• hyos k* ign k* iod h iris *Kali-c* j5.de* kali-n h2* kali-s fkr2.de lac-del hrn2• lach sze9• limen-b-c hrn2* lyc k* lycps-v mag-c k* mang-p rly4• merl k* mez k* mur-ac k* nat-c j5.de nat-m k* nat-p k* nat-s k* nept-m lsd2.fr nit-ac k* nux-v k* oci-sa sk4• ol-an j5.de olib-sac wmh1 osteo-a jl2 oxal-a rly4• petr-ra shn4• phys k* phyt plb j5.de psil ft1 ptel k* ran-b j5.de* rhus-g tmo3• rhus-t k* ruta sang k* sep h2 *Sil* k* spirae a1 spong fd4.de staph k* stram k* stry k* **Sulph** k* thuj k* tritic-vg fd5.de vanil fd5.de zinc k* zing k*
  - **13** h: astac a1 ferr-p phys pic-ac verat-v
- **afternoon**: ...
  - 13.30 h: lyc
  - **14** h: chel gels nux-v sulph
    - **14**-15 h: guan a1 plb-chr a1 sanguis-s hrn2• sulph
    - **14**-16 h: ephe-si hsj1• ign
  - **14**.30 h: nept-m lsd2.fr
  - **15** h: chord-umb rly4• *Ham* lyss kr1 mag-c nat-s nep jl* petr-ra shn4•
    - **15**-16 h: cartl-s rly4• lac-del hrn2• reser jl
  - **16** h: caust gad a1 hydr iris lyc mang merc-i-f phys psil ft1 trios rsj11•
  - **17** h: bamb-a stb2.de• coff colch *Lac-d* kr1 lyc merc h1 psil ft1
    - **17**-19 h: sal-al blc1•
    - **17**-23 h: perh jl
    - **until**: tarent
  - **17**.30 h: stram
  - **sleep** agg.; after: *(↗noon - sleep)* borx h2 chinin-s ferr k* gels k* kali-c h2 nat-m h2
  - **walking**:
    - **after** | **agg.**: ery-a euph hyper tritic-vg fd5.de
    - **agg.**: *(↗walking - agg.)* caust h2 lyc mag-c pic-ac ran-b
    - **amel.**: nat-s a1
- **evening**: acon k* aloe alum j5.de *Am-c* k* am-m h2 aphis j5.de* apis apoc ars k* ars-h hr1 asaf k* asar b7a.de* bapt k* bell h1* berb k* borx bov k* brom k* bruc j5.de bry k* calc k* calc-p k* *Calc-s* k* carb-v k* carl k* *Caust* k* chin j5.de clem k* cob k* coc-c k* coca coloc k* colocin a1 con k* *Croc* k* cycl k* dendr-pol sk4• dios k* dirc k* erig k* ery-m a1 euphr k* eupi k* fago k* ferr ferr-ar k2* form k* granit-m es1• *Graph* k* grat k* haem k* haliae-lc srj5• helon hep k* hydr hydr-ac k* *Ign* k* indg k* iris itu a1 jac-c k* jac-g *Kali-bi* k* kali-c k* kali-chl k13 kali-m k2 kali-n h2 kali-sil k2* kalm k* lac-h sk4• *Lach* k* laur j5.de lim a1 limen-b-c mlk9.de lob k* lyc k* lycps-v mag-c k* merc k* merl k* mez k* mur-ac k* murx k* naja **Nat-m** k* nat-n k* nept-m lsd2.fr nicc hr1* nit-ac k* nux-v k* ox-ac k* pall k* *Petr* k* petr-ra shn4• phos k* pitu-gl skp7• plat k* plb k* psor k* puls-n rat j5.de rhus-g rhus-t k* rumx ruta senec k* *Sep* k* sil k* spig j5.de spong fd4.de stach a1 stront-c k* sulfonam jl3 *Sulph* k* sumb k* symph fd3.de• tab k* tarent k2 *Tart-ac* a1 thuj k* tritic-vg fd5.de tub k2* upa valer k* zinc k* zinc-p k2*
  - **18** h: germ-met srj5• helon lyc merc h1 positr nl2•
    - **until**: merc
  - **19** h: gins mag-c nat-m phys pic-ac sep verat-v
  - **20** h: astac a1 bar-c mang pana a1 phys sep
  - **20**.30 h: limen-b-c hrn2• pip-m [tax jsj7]
  - **21** h: dirc mag-s op phys pic-ac podo fd3.de• [tax jsj7]
    - **amel.**: phos
  - **21**.30 h: lyc sep
  - **air**; in open:
    - **agg.**: chel a1 **Con** a1 grat a1 naja a1 nat-m a1 pic-ac a1 sabad a1
    - **amel.**: *(↗air; in open - amel.)* asc-t k* calc-s k* colch k* germ-met srj5• nat-sil fd3.de• nit-ac k*
  - **bed** agg.; in: lyc k* tritic-vg fd5.de
  - **eating**; after: *(↗supper)* bov a1 *Croc* k*
- **night**: acon-l a1* am-c j5.de ambr k* ant-c k* anthraci anthraco a1 atra-r skp7*• calc k* canth k* carb-an k* carb-v k* chel k* coca crot-t j5.de ferr-i k* gnaph k* hell k* hyper k* kreos mur-ac h2* naja nat-m k* nux-v k* *Rhus-g* tmo3• rhus-t k* sep h2 *Sil* k* sulph k* tab k* thuj k* tritic-vg fd5.de
  - **midnight**:
    - **before**:
      - **22** h: elat fago phys
      - **23** h: nat-m ozone sde2•
    - **at**: ambr k* op k* *Rhus-t* k*
    - **after**: nat-m rhus-t k* suprar rly4•
      - **2** h: dendr-pol sk4• sep h2
      - **3** h: am-c k2 nat-m *Sec* kr1 suprar rly4• zing a1
      - **4** h: sulph
      - **5** h: napht a1
  - **amel.**: adam srj5•
- **abortion**:
  - **after**: *Kali-c* hr1 ruta a1

- **weakness**; from: *Sep* sf1.de sil sf1.de

- **accompanied** by:
  - **asthma**: ars vh bry vh carb-v vh *Chinin-ar* br1 *Psor* mrr1 *Stann* vh*
  - **emaciation**: cub mtf11
  - **enuresis** (See BLADDER - Urination - involuntary - accompanied - weakness)
  - **hemorrhagic** tendency: kreos tl1
  - **hemorrhoids** (See RECTUM - Hemorrhoids - accompanied - weakness)
  - **intellect**; keen (See MIND - Intelligent - weakness)
  - **menses**; painful: **Verat** mrr1
  - **mental** symptoms (See MIND - Mental symptoms - accompanied - weakness)
  - **nausea**: ars bro1 bamb-a stb2.de• chir-fl gya2 elat c1* hir rsj4• hydrog srj2• *Kola* stb3• loxo-recl knl4• nept-m lsd2.fr spong fd4.de [heroin sdj2]
  - **obesity**: berb br1 ip br1
  - **phthisis** (See Consumption - accompanied - weakness)
  - **pulse**; weak: *Ant-t* mrr1
  - **quivering** (See Quivering - accompanied - weakness)
  - **respiration**:
    - **complaints**: *Ant-t* mrr1
    - **impeded**: ars bg2
  - **retching** (See STOMACH - Retching - accompanied - weakness)
  - **sensitiveness**: ars bro1 chin bro1 cocc tl1 plb tl1 sil bro1 ter ptk1
  - **sepsis** (See Septicemia - accompanied - weakness)
  - **sexual** desire; diminished | **ovulation**; during: granit-m es1•
  - **stasis**; venous (See Stasis - accompanied - weakness)
  - **stool**; complaints of (See STOOL - Complaints - accompanied - weakness)
  - **sweets**; desire for: thyr ptk1
  - **ulcers**: bapt bro1
    - **Hand**; on back of | **painful** (See EXTREMITIES - Ulcers - hand - back - painful - accompanied - weakness)
  - **vomiting**: *Aeth* mtf33 **Ant-t** tl1 atis zzc1• bism hr1 cadm-s br1
  - ○ **Abdomen**:
    - **complaints** (See ABDOMEN - Complaints - accompanied - weakness)
    - **sinking** in (See ABDOMEN - Sinking - accompanied - weakness)
  - **Bronchial** tubes; inflammation of (See CHEST - Inflammation - bronchial - accompanied - weakness)
  - **Gastrointestinal** inflammation (See ABDOMEN - Inflammation - gastroenteritis - accompanied - weakness)
  - **Head**:
    - **complaints** of: alum bg2 arn bg2 bov bg2 chin bg2 *Chinin-s* bg2 grat bg2 kali-c bg2 kali-n bg2 kreos bg2 lach bg2 mag-m bg2 nux-v bg2 sil bg2
    - **enlarged** (See HEAD - Hydrocephalus - accompanied - weakness)
  - **Heart**:
    - **chronic** disease (See CHEST - Heart; complaints - chronic - accompanied - weakness)
    - **complaints** of the (See CHEST - Heart; complaints - accompanied - weakness)
    - **failure** of (See CHEST - Heart failure - accompanied - weakness)
  - **Intestines** | **inflammation** of (See ABDOMEN - Inflammation - small intestine - accompanied - weakness)
  - **Kidneys**; inflammation of (See KIDNEYS - Inflammation - accompanied - weakness)
  - **Lumbar** region; coldness in: stroph-s sp1

- **accompanied** by: ...
  - **Lungs**; inflammation of (See CHEST - Inflammation - lungs - accompanied - weakness)
  - **Spinal** cord; inflammation of (See BACK - Inflammation - spinal cord - accompanied - weakness)
  - **Stomach**:
    - **emptiness** (See STOMACH - Emptiness - accompanied - weakness)
    - **inflammation** of (See STOMACH - Inflammation - accompanied - weakness)
    - **pain**: calc-p bg2 nat-m bg2 sabad bg2
  - **Teeth**; pain in (See TEETH - Pain - accompanied - weakness)
  - **Uterus**; complaints of the (See FEMALE - Complaints - uterus - accompanied - weakness; FEMALE - Prolapsus - uterus - accompanied - weakness)
- **acute** diseases: *(↗sudden)*
  - **after**: alet bro1 *Chin* ptk1 *Helon* bro1 meph ptk1 psor ptk1 sel ptk1 verat ptk1
  - **during**: *(↗sudden)* abrot bro1 aeth st* ail st* alet bro1 *Alst* bro1 *Anac* bro1 ant-t st* apis st* ars st* aven bro1 calc-p bro1* carb-an bro1 *Carb-v* bro1 carc mlr1• *Chin* bro1 *Chinin-ar* bro1 coca bro1 *Cocc* bro1 colch bro1 cupr bro1 cur bro1 dig bro1 fl-ac bro1 gels bro1* guar st *Helon* bro1 irid-met bro1* kali-fcy bro1 kali-m k2* *Kali-p* bro1 lath bro1 lob-p bro1 macroz bro1 merc-cy st* mur-ac st* nat-sal bro1 nux-v bro1 *Ph-ac* br1* *Phos* bro1 pic-ac bro1 psor br1* sel br1* sil bro1 staph bro1 stroph-h br1* stry-p bro1 sul-ac bro1 *Tarent-c* ptk1 thyr br1 verat br1* zinc-ar bro1
    - **proportion**; but out of: ars ptk1 sul-ac ptk1
- **Addison's** disease, in: *Calc* hr1* *Iod* hr1*
- **air** agg.; want of: meli
- **air**; in open:
  - **agg.**: am-c am-m ambr *Atro* a1 bry k* calc k* chin clem coff coloc con ferr grat hep b4a.de kali-c lavand-a ctl1• mag-c merc merc-c a1 mur-ac nux-v k* *Plat* k* psor tl1 sang *Spig* k* sulph b4a.de verat
  - **amel.**: *(↗evening - air - amel.)* calc k* carb-v bg chel colch **Con** croc fl-ac ptk1 gels grat hed mg1.de* hippoc-k szs2 ignis-alc es2• kali-i k2* lach bg limest-b es1• lyc bg naja nat-m petr-ra shn4• pic-ac sabad sacch-a fd2.de• sep bg staph bg sulph ptk1 tritic-vg fd5.de
- **albuminuria**, in: *Ars* hr1* *Calc-ar* hr1* *Dig* hr1* *Iod* hr1* *Merc-c* kr1 *Nat-c* hr1* *Ter* hr1*
  - **children**; in: syc fmm1•
- **alcoholic** drinks amel.: *Canth* k* nit-s-d a1 thea a1
- **alcoholism**, in (See drunkards)
- **alternating** with:
  - **activity** (See MIND - Activity - desires - alternating - weakness)
  - **activity**; mental (See MIND - Mental exertion - desire - alternating - weakness)
  - **cheerfulness** (See MIND - Cheerful - alternating - weakness)
  - **excitement** (See MIND - Excitement - alternating - weakness)
  - **hopefulness** (See MIND - Hopeful - alternating - weakness)
  - **restlessness** (See MIND - Restlessness - alternating - weakness)
  - **strength**; sensation of: ars j5.de chin j5.de colch jl
  - **trembling**: ferr k* plb st1
- **anemia**, in: *(↗Anemia)* acet-ac br1 *Chin* kr1* **Ferr** bg2* ferr-p tl1 **Kali-c** kr1* *Nat-c* kr1 *Nat-m* kr1* **Phos** kr1 zinc br1
- **anger**; after: arg-n k2 calc-s k2* ferr-p k2 mur-ac sf1.de zinc k*
- **antibiotics**; from: *(↗History - antibiotics)* carb-v gm1
- **anxiety**:
  - **after**: cocc k2
  - **with**: am-c h2 aur h2 calc h2 caust h2 mur-ac a1 rhus-t h1
- **apoplexy**, from: *(↗Apoplexy)* *Anac* b4a.de *Bar-c* b4a.de* nux-v mrr1
- **appetite**; with increased: ail vml3• sec ptk1 sulph br1
- **apyrexia**; during: nat-m bro1

- **ascending** stairs, from: *(↗menses - during - agg. - going)* alum-sil k2 am-c mrr1 *Anac* k* ars ars-i ars-s-f k2* asar a1 bar-m k2* blatta-a a1 **Calc** k* *Calc-p* k* calc-sil k2* carbn-s k2 coff k* colch croc st1 fago k* **Iod** k* kali-ar k2* *Lyc* k* m-arct j5.de mag-c h2 nat-m nat-n a1 nux-v j5.de ox-ac k* ph-ac k* phys k* pic-ac k* puls sarcol-ac bro1 sep a1* spig k* *Stann* k* sul-i k2 sulph k* symph fd3.de• vanil fd5.de zinc-act a1
- **ascites**, from: **Lyc** kl
- **bed** | **going** to bed | **when**: arn k* cinnb k* lycps-v mur-ac rumx ter k*
  - **in** bed: ambr b7a.de carb-v b4a.de con b4a.de nat-m b4a.de phos b4a.de
- **beer**; after: coc-c vanil fd5.de
  - **amel.**: thea
- **breakfast**:
  - **about** the time of: sep
  - **after**:
    - **agg.**: arg-n k* brom k* carb-v k* cham h1 con h2 dig k* lach k* nux-v *Ph-ac* psil ft1 sil still a1 thea verat k*
    - **amel.**: *Calc Con* nat-m nux-v *Staph*
- **businessmen**; in worn-out: *(↗MIND - Businessmen - worn-out)* **Calc** mrr1 carc mlr1• clem a1 lyc a1 toxo-g jl2
- **cancer**; in: cadm-i mtf carb-an mtf carb-v mtf11 nat-c mtf
- **catarrh**, after: kali-m k2 tritic-vg fd5.de
- **causeless**: psor bro1*
- **chemotherapy**; after: *(↗Chemotherapy; STOMACH - Nausea - medicine - allopathic - chemotherapy)* kali-p mrr1 sep mrr1
- **children**; in: aeth vh1 bar-c k* bell brom mtf33 calc k* *Camph* br1 carb-v c1 carc mlr1• cham j5.de cina j5.de ferr mtf33 kali-c j5.de lach *Lyc* k* nux-v phos mrr1 sil staph mtf33 *Sulph* k* zinc k2
  - **causeless**: carc mlr1• sul-ac ptk1
  - **newborns**; in: *Aeth* mrr1
- **chill**:
  - **after**: apis kr1 chin tl1 *Sulph* h2
  - **before**: *Ars Chin* nat-m thuj k*
  - **during**: agar hr1* alum bg2 ambr b7a.de* anac bg2 ant-c bg2 *Ant-t* bg2 apis b7a.de* aran k* arn k* ars k* asar b7.de* astac hr1* bell bg2 borx b4a.de* bry bg2 *Calc* b4.de* caps b7.de* *Carb-v* b4.de* *Caust* b4.de* cham bg2 *Chin* k* choc srj3• coc-c k* coloc bg2 ferr bg2 gels bg2 hell b7.de* hep k* hyos bg2 ign bg2 ip k* kali-c bg2 kreos bg2 lach led bg2 *Lyc* b4.de* meny b7.de* *Nat-m* k* nux-m bg2 *Nux-v* b7.de* op bg2 petr b4.de* ph-ac bg2 *Phos* k* psil ft1 psor puls bg2 rheum bg2 rhod bg2 rhus-t bg2 ruta fd4.de sabad bg2 seneg bg2 *Sep* b4a.de* sil bg2 spong b7.de* stann bg2 stram b7.de* sulph bg2 *Verat* b7.de*
- **chilliness**; with: kola stb3• sep h2
- **coffee**:
  - **amel.**: *(↗stimulants)* eug a1
  - **odor** of; from: sul-ac
- **coition**; after: acet-ac k2 *Agar* k* ambr sf1.de berb **Calc** k* *Carb-an* j5.de chin k* clem *Con* k* cypra-eg sde6.de• *Dig* k* *Graph* k* *Kali-c* k* *Kali-p* k* *Kali-sil* vh* lil-t lyc k* mosch nat-c bro1 *Nat-m* nit-ac k* *Nuph* hr1* olib-sac wmh1 petr k* *Ph-ac* k* *Phos* k* plat sf1.de **Sel** k* *Sep* k* *Sil* staph tarent k* tax a1 vichy-g a1 *Ziz* hr1*
  - **men**; in: *Calc* ptk1 kali-p ptk1 *Sel* ptk1 sil ptk1
  - **shuddering**; with: kali-c ptk1
  - **women**; in: berb ptk1 sep ptk1
- **cold**; after exposure to: ars a1
- **coldness**:
  - **during**: aeth apis atha a1 con k* guare k* kola stb3• nat-m k* spong fd4.de thuj k*
  - **from**: *Ars* hr1* **Carb-v** hr1* **Verat** hr1*
- **company**:
  - **after**: pall c1*
  - **agg.**: granit-m es1• sep h2
- **complaints**; during other: ars b4a.de ip b7a.de sec b7a.de verat b7a.de
- **confinement**, after (See delivery - after)
- **convalescence**; during: ferr bg2 gels bg2 helo-s bnm14• meph bg2 phos bg2
- **conversation**, from: sil h2
- **convulsions**; after: *(↗Convulsions - weakness)* acon k* aeth kr1* agar h2 *Aml-ns* kr1 ars k* art-v hr1* carbn a1 *Cupr* hr1* elaps br1 *Ip* hr1* merc-c k* *Oena* hr1* sec k* stram h1 stry k* sulph h2 tab k*
  - **epileptic**: aeth bro1 *Aster* hr1* camph k* *Chinin-ar* kr1* *Cic* bro1 hydr-ac bro1 *Plb* hr1* sec bro1 sil bro1 *Stry* bro1 *Sulph* hr1*
  - **hysterical**: ars k*
- **coryza**; during: ars b4a.de* ars-i bro1 bapt bro1 calc h2 gels bro1 graph h2 petr-ra shn4• quill bro1 tritic-vg fd5.de
- **cough**:
  - **after**: coff lp cor-r br1* dig bg iod bg spong bg verat ptk1
  - **from**: am-c bro1 *Ant-t* bro1 ars b4a.de* chin b7.de* cor-r bro1 *Cupr* bro1 cur bro1 ferr b7.de* hep bro1 iod bro1 *Ip* bro1 meph bro1 nit-ac bro1 petr hr1 ph-ac bro1 prot jl2 psor bg2 rumx bro1 squil bro1 *Stict* bro1 *Verat* b7.de*
- **dampness**, from exposure to: ars k*
- **death**, as of approaching: *Ars* k* carc mlr1• con j5.de dig j5.de mag-m j5.de nat-c j5.de* olnd k* op j5.de ph-ac k2 sec j5.de spig j5.de *Vinc* j5.de*
- **delivery**:
  - **after**: calc bg2* carb-v k2 *Chin* b7a.de* coff b7a.de **Kali-c** b4a.de* nux-v bg2 ph-ac bg2 samb st *Sulph* bg2 verat b7a.de* viol-o b7a.de
  - **during**: *Caul* kr1* *Con* kr1 *Gels* mrr1 **Kali-c** h2
- **dementia**; with (See MIND - Dementia - weakness)
- **dentition**; during: *(↗TEETH - Dentition - difficult)* ars bro1 *Calc* hr1* calc-p hr1* *Ip* hr1*
- **descending** stairs agg.: stann k*
- **diabetes** mellitus, in: acet-ac bro1 *Arg-met* kr1 *Ars* kr1* carb-v mgb1 carc mlr1• con mgb1 graph mgb1 kali-c mgb1 *Lac-ac* kr1* op bro1 phos mtf33
- **diarrhea**:
  - **from**: *(↗Collapse - diarrhea; Faintness - diarrhea; Faintness - diarrhea - after - agg.)* acet-ac bro1* aeth bro1 agar bro1 *Ail* bro1 aloe bro1 *Alum* alum-p k2 *Alumn* kr1 ambr ango bro1 ant-c kr1 ant-t kr1* *Apis Arg-n* bro1 arn bro1 **Ars** k* bamb-a stb2.de• bapt k2 bar-m kr1 bism bro1 *Borx* both bry calc-i k2 *Camph* bro1 carb-v **Chin** k* chinin-ar k2 colch bro1* coli jl2 coloc con k* *Corn* kr1 coto bro1 crot-t kr1* cupr bro1 *Cupr-ar* bro1 dios bro1 *Dulc* elaps br1* elat bro1 euph-a kr1 *Ferr* k* gamb gk gast a1 gnaph *Graph* hura hydr hyos h1 influ jl2* *Iod Ip* iris k* jatr-c bro1 kali-c kali-chl *Kali-m* kr1 *Kali-p* kr1* kola stb3• lil-t mag-c k* merc merc-cy moni rfm1• **Nat-s Nit-ac** k* *Nuph* kr1 **Nux-m** kr1 *Nux-v* **Olnd** op ox-ac petr ph-ac k2* phel bro1 **Phos** k* phyt **Pic-ac Podo** k* *Rhus-t* k2* *Ric* a1 *Sec* k* senec sep k* serp bro1 **Sil** *Sul-ac* k* sul-i k2 *Tab* k* *Tarent Tart-ac* kr1* *Ter* bro1 tritic-vg fd5.de trom bro1 tub br1* upa bro1 vanil fd5.de **Verat** k* *Zinc*
  - **suppressed** diarrhea; from: ph-ac k2
  - **weaken**; does not (See RECTUM - Diarrhea - weakness)
- **dinner**: *(↗tremulous - dinner)*
  - **after** | **agg.**: alum h2 am-c k* am-m k* ant-c k* ars k* ars-h hr1* asar k* bapt k* bov k* cain calc k* cann-s c1 carb-v k* castm chel k* *Chin* k* chlam-tr bcx2• cob k* cycl k* dig k* euph-a a1 graph k* grat k* ign k* indg k* iod k* *Lach* kr1 lyc k* mag-c k* mur-ac h2 nat-m k* nat-p k* nit-ac h2 ol-an k* ox-ac perh jl3 *Ph-ac* phel k* phos k* plat k* plect k* sars k* sep h2 *Sil* squil k* *Sulph* k* *Thuj* k* tritic-vg fd5.de zinc k*
  - **amel.**: ambr k* sars h2 [tax jsj7]
  - **before**: *(↗walking - dinner)* nat-m k* sabin a1 sapin a1 sil h2 thuj k*
    - **delayed**, if: sulph k2
  - **during** | **agg.**: am-c h2 bov k* nat-ar a1 nat-s teucr k*
- **diphtheria**; in: *(↗paralytic - diphtheria)* *Ail* k* *Alum-sil* k* *Apis* k* *Ars* bro1 bapt bro1 *Brom* k* *Canth* k* *Carb-ac* bro1 *Chinin-ar* k* *Crot-h* k* diph br1* diphtox jl2 *Ign* k* *Kali-bi* k* *Kali-perm* k* lac-c k* **Lach** k* **Merc-cy** k* *Merc-i-f* k* *Mur-ac* k* *Nat-ar* k* *Nux-v* k* **Phyt** k* *Sal-ac* k* *Sec* k* *Sulph* k*
- **drawing** and jerking in limbs, after: sulph k*
- **dream**, after a: *(↗waking - on)* *Calc-s* k* op k* teucr
- **drinking** agg.; after: nat-m h2
- **dropsy**, in: **Apis** kr1 *Ars* hr1* *Eup-pur* hr1* *Hell* hr1* seneg hr1*
- **drugs** | **psychotropic** drugs; from: sep mrr1
- **drunkards**; in: *Ars* k* caps br1 *Carbn-s* k2* eup-per br1* *Kali-br* k* *Nat-s* hr1* *Ph-ac* mrr1 *Phos* k* *Ran-b* st *Sel* k* sep mrr1
- **dyscratic**: abrot bro1 eup-per bro1 hydr bro1 iod bro1 nat-m bro1 nit-ac bro1 *Psor* bro1 sul-ac bro1 *Sulph* bro1 tub bro1 *Zinc* bro1

- **easily** tired (See exertion - agg. - slight)
- **eating**:
  - **after** | **agg.**: (↗*walking - eating*) act-sp k* adam srj5• alum b4a.de* *Anac* k* ant-c bg2 **Ars** k* ars-s-f k2* asar b7a.de* bar-act a1 **Bar-c** k* bar-s k2* brom calc b4a.de* calc-p k* cann-s k* carb-an k* carb-v b4a.de *Chin* k* chir-fl gya2 cina bg1 clem k* *Con* k* *Croc* crot-c k* cycl k* dig k* ferr sf1.de ferr-ma k* graph b4a.de hep k* hippoc-k szs2 hyper k* ignis-alc es2• kali-c k* kali-sil k2* lach b7a.de* lyc k* mag-c k* mag-m bg1 meph k* merc-c k* mur-ac k* *Nat-c* bg2* nat-m k* **Nit-ac** b4a.de* nux-m bg1 nux-v k* ox-ac a1* **Ph-ac** k* phos k* psil ft1 rhod k* rhus-t k* ruta sang k* sars hr1* sel k* sep b4a.de* *Sil* k* *Staph* k* sul-ac k* sulph k* tell k* teucr k* thea thuj k* tritic-vg fd5.de uran-n bg1 vanil fd5.de zinc ptk1
  - **amel.**: aster k* dulc fd4.de *Hep* hr1* hydrog srj2• **Iod** hr1* nat-c h2 petr k* sacch sst1• sapin a1 sil k* vanil fd5.de
  - **before** | **agg.**: cinnb k* vero-o rly3•
  - **while** | **agg.**: am-c hr1* bar-c ptk1 bufo carb-an b4a.de mag-c k* ptel k* stann ptk1 sulph j5.de
- **emaciation**; from (See Emaciation - accompanied - weakness)
- **emissions** agg.; after: acet-ac k* agar k* anac c1 aq-mar skp7• aur k* *Bar-c* k* *Calad* hr1* *Calc* k* calc-p bro1 canth carb-an k* carl k* *Chin* k* chin-b hr1* *Cob* bg2* *Coff* hr1* *Con* k* cupr k* *Cypr* hr1* dam bro1 dig k* *Dios* bg2* ery-a hr1* ferr bg2 form bro1 *Gels* k* glycyr-g cte1• ham hr1* *Hydr* k* iod k* **Kali-br** hr1* *Kali-c* k* kali-p ptk1 lach j5.de led b7.de* **Lyc** k* med hr1* naja *Nat-m* k* nat-p k* *Nuph* hr1* **Nux-v** k* *Op* hr1* **Ph-ac** k* **Phos** k* *Pic-ac* k* plb k* puls k* *Sabad* b7.de* *Sars* k* *Sel* k* *Sep* k* **Sil** k* *Stann* k* **Staph** k* sul-ac bg2 *Sulph* hr1* ust k* zinc bro1
- **epistaxis**; from: (↗*Loss - blood*) carb-v bg2* chin bg2* cina bg2 diph bro1 ferr bg2* ham hr1 sec bg2* verat bg1
- **erections** agg.: (non:aur k*) aur-m a1* carbn-s
- **eruptions**; after suppressed: ars-s-f k2
- **excess**, after any: agar bro1 *Anac* bro1 *Ars* hr1 *Calc-p* bro1 *Carb-v* bro1 caust bro1 *Chin* bro1 chinin-s bro1 corn-f bro1 cur bro1 gins bro1 kali-c bro1 nat-m hr1* *Ph-ac* bro1 *Phos* hr1* plb k* sel bro1 stroph-h bro1
- **excessive**: ant-t b7a.de ars b4a.de* bapt bg2 carc mlr1• chin b7a.de* ephe-si hsj1• ferr bg2 *Ferr-pic* st1 *Gels* bg2 hydrog srj2• hyos b7a.de influ jl2 iod b4a.de laur b7a.de nat-m b4a.de nit-ac b4a.de olnd b7a.de osteo-a jl2 ph-ac b4a.de* phos b4a.de plb b7a.de ruta fd4.de tab bg2 tritic-vg fd5.de tub jl2 tub-r jl2 *Urin* c1 verat b7a.de [bell-p-sp dcm1]
  - **pain**; from: ars tl1
- **excitement**; after: *Con* k* gels psa phos hr1* spong fd4.de stry k* thea
- **exertion**:
  - **agg.**: acon st *Alum-p* k2 ambr st *Arn* st *Ars* bro1 ars-s-f k2 aur-ar k2 aur-m k2 *Bit-ar* wht1• bry bro1* calc bro1* calc-sil k2* caust bro1 chin st cocc b7a.de* coff st cycl bro1 cystein-l rly4• dulc fd4.de ferr bro1 ferr-ar k2 ferr-i k2 helon br1 kali-ar k2 kali-s fd4.de kalm a1 lac-d bro1 lac-del hrn2• macro a1 mag-c st merc bro1* nat-c bro1 nit-m-ac a1 nit-s-d a1 nux-m b7a.de* petr-ra shn4• ph-ac bro1 pic-ac bro1* rhod k2 rhus-d bro1 rhus-t k2* ruta mrr1* sarcol-ac bro1 sel mtf11 sep bro1* sil st spong fd4.de *Stann* bro1 sul-i k2 symph fd3.de• thea bro1 tung-met bdx1• verat bro1* [tax jsj7]
    - ⁝ **slight** exertion: (↗*motion - slightest; Chronic fatigue; MIND - Prostration*) acon *Agar* ail alum alum-p k2 *Am-c* anac k* apis **Ars** k* *Ars-i* ars-s-f k2 aur-ar k2 aur-m k2 bapt berb bit-ar wht1• **Bry** **Calc** k* calc-sil k2 *Carb-v* carbn-s k2 cham clem *Cocc* *Colch* **Con** k* **Crot-h** dig c1* dor equis-h a1 *Ferr* ferr-ar k2 ferr-i *Gels* k* ham st helo-s bnm14• ign jatr-c kali-c kali-n kali-p fd1.de* kalm lac-d k2 lac-lup hrn2• **Lach** *Lyc* mag-c b4a.de *Mag-m* *Merc* *Merc-c* *Nat-ar* **Nat-c** *Nat-m* k* *Nat-p* nux-m nux-v k2 petr petr-ra shn4• **Ph-ac** k* **Phos** k* **Pic-ac** plb *Psor* ptel **Rhus-t** ruta mrr1 **Sel** *Sep* k* sil mtf33 sol-ni *Spig* **Spong** k* *Stann* k* *Staph* stram sul-i k2 *Sulph* sumb ther thuj thyr br1 tritic-vg fd5.de **Tub** k2* vanil fd5.de verat ziz
    - ⁝ **women**; in: helon ptk1
  - **amel.**: ferr k* ham fd3.de• kali-n
  - **as** from excessive exertion: apis ptk1
- **exhilaration**, as after: cinnb
- **faint**-like: ant-t j5.de *Ars* hr1* bar-c j5.de berb j5.de* *Camph* b7a.de *Carb-v* j5.de* **Caust** j5.de* cham b7.de* *Coca* kr1 *Cocc* b7.de* croc b7.de* *Crot-t* hr1 cupr-c j5.de *Dig* hr1* digin a1 dulc j5.de **Eup-per** hr1* ferr j5.de *Goss* hr1* graph a1 hydrog srj2• ign j5.de kali-c j5.de kali-i a1 lyc a1* mez a1 mosch j5.de **Nux-v** b7.de* olnd b7a.de* *Petr* j5.de* petr-ra shn4• psil ft1 sep j5.de* sil j5.de spong b7.de* sulfon br1 sulph j5.de* taosc iwa1• tritic-vg fd5.de upa a1 vanil fd5.de *Verat* b7.de* zinc a1 zing a1*
- **fasting**; as after: brom a1 euphr a1 iod a1 [am-br stj2]
  - **afternoon**: iod h1*
- **febrile** (See fever - during - agg.)
- **feet**, while washing the: merc k*
- **fever**:
  - **after**: *Alst-s* br1 *Apis* a1 *Aran* caesal-b zzc1• carc mlr1* *Chin* b7a.de gent-l a1 morph a1 sal-ac hr1* *Sel* mrr1 stry-p br1 sulph a1 syph hr1*
  - **before**: **Ars** b4a.de calc b4a.de carb-v b4a.de chin b7a.de hep b4a.de *Ip* b7a.de lach b7a.de *Nat-m* b4a.de nit-ac b4a.de *Nux-v* b7a.de ph-ac b4a.de phos b4a.de rhus-t b7a.de sulph b4a.de
  - **during**:
    - ⁝ **agg.**: acon k* ail br1* alum h2* am-m a1 anac b4.de* ang a1 ant-t k* *Anthraci* kr1 *Apis* b7a.de* aran k* arg-met b7.de* *Arn* hr1* **Ars** k* *Bapt* k* bar-c sys bell b4.de* borx b4a.de* *Bry* k* cadm-s br1 calc b4.de* camph bg2* canth bg2 carb-v k* cassia-s ccrh1• caust b4.de* cham a1 *Chin* b7.de* chinin-ar bg2* cocc bro1 coli jl2 crot-h a1* **Cupr** bg2 dig b4.de* dros bg2 elaps bg2* eup-a br1* *Eup-per* hr1* eup-pur ferr k* *Ferr-p* bg2* *Gels* bg2 helon ptk1 *Ign* k* iod bg2 ip b7.de* kali-c bg2 kali-i bg2 kali-n a1 kreos b7a.de* lach bro1 laur b7.de* lyc k* *Meny* b7.de* merc b4.de* morph a1 *Mur-ac* k* nat-c k* *Nat-m* k* nicc a1 nit-ac k* nit-s-d br1* nux-m bg2 **Nux-v** b7.de* petr b4.de* *Ph-ac* k* **Phos** k* phyt bro1 plb b7.de* *Puls* k* pyrog bro1* rheum b7.de* rhod b4.de* *Rhus-t* k* *Rob* sabad b7a.de* sarr *Sel* ptk1 sep b4.de* sil bg2 spig b7.de* spong ptk1 *Stann* bg2 sul-ac a1* sulph k* ter bro1 thuj bg2* tritic-vg fd5.de **Tub** gk tub-m jl2 *Urt-u* bro1 vanil fd5.de **Verat** b7.de* verat-v hr3* zinc-i ptk1
    - ⁝ **accompanied** by | **anemia** and dizziness (See Anemia - accompanied - fever)
  - **following** prolonged fever: (↗*Convalescence*) ambr hr1 *Colch* st mur-ac mrr1 *Psor* st **Sel**
  - **without**: ars bro1 bapt bro1 carb-v bro1 chin bro1
- **flushes** of heat; from: cocc dig c1* hydrog srj2• ignis-alc es2• nat-c h2 samb bat1• **Sep** kr1* **Sulph** kr1 *Xan* st
- **food**, from sour: aloe
- **fright** agg.: coff merc op
- **gout**; after: cypr br1
- **grief**; from: *Carc* mlr1• *Caust* *Ign* k* nat-sil fd3.de• *Ph-ac* k* *Pic-ac* hr1*
- **growing** fast, after: (↗*Growth; Growth - length*) hipp br1* ph-ac st phos mrr1
- **headache**:
  - **after**: arg-n hr1 [bell-p-sp dcm1]
  - **during**: **Ant-c** hr1* aran hr1* ars-h a1 bism hr1* bufo a1 calc-ar hr1* carb-v hr1* chin hr1* chinin-s kr1 cob a1 cycl a1 dulc fd4.de fago a1 glon a1 lil-s a1 naja a1 nept-m lsd2.fr *Sil* hr1* spong fd4.de symph fd3.de• syph hr1 *Thuj* hr1* thymol sp1 tritic-vg fd5.de *Verat* hr1* [tax jsj7]
  - **from**: androc srj1• ars k2 ars-h k* bufo calc h2 cist k2 cob k* fago k* gels k2 glon k* kali-c h2 lac-d st1 lil-s a1 naja pic-ac k2 psil ft1 sil h2 symph fd3.de• vanil fd5.de [tax jsj7]
- **heartburn**, from: lyc h2
- **heat**: (↗*daytime - heat; Heat - flushes*)
  - **bed**, of: aster k*
  - **from**: aster k* *Carbn-s* coc-c k* ketogl-ac rly4• lac-del hrn2• *Lach* *Nat-c* nat-p k* pic-ac mrr1 *Puls* *Puls-n* a1 rhod k* samb bat1• **Sel** k* *Sulph* k* tab k* vesp k*
  - **room**, in hot: (↗*warm - room*) cinnb *Puls*
    - ⁝ **entering**, from bed: aloe
  - **summer**, of: alum *Ant-t* bro1 *Ars* hr1* *Carbn-s* k2* *Corn* **Gels** hr1* **Iod** *Lach* k* **Nat-c** k* nat-m **Sel** k*
  - **sun**; of the | **agg.**: (↗*sun agg.*) *Ars* kr1 **Gels** kr1* lac-del hrn2• **Nat-c** petr-ra shn4• **Sel** tritic-vg fd5.de

- • **walking** (See sun agg.)
- **hemorrhage**; during: alum ptk1 bry ptk1 carb-an ptk1* *Carb-v* kr1 **Chin** kr1* *Chinin-s* kr1 *Ferr* kr1* ham ptk1 hydr ptk1 *Hyper* kr1 *Ign* kr1 ph-ac k2 *Rat* kr1 sec bro1 stront-c ptk1 stroph-h br1
  - • **little** hemorrhage; from a: erig zr
- **high** altitudes; at: coca mrr1
- **humiliation**; after: carc mlr1•
- **humors**; from loss of (See loss)
- **hunger**; from●: *Alum* *Crot-h* hr1* **Iod** *Kola* stb3• nat-c h2 ozone sde2• *Phos* spig k* sul-i k2* **Sulph** k* ter hr1* vanil fd5.de vero-o rly3• *Zinc*
- **hysteric**: cham b7a.de ign b7a.de* mosch b7a.de nat-m b4a.de* nux-m b7a.de phos h2
- **increasing** gradually | **decreasing** gradually: gard-j vlr2• granit-m es1•
- **indifference**; with (See Weariness)
- **indigestion**; from: colch tl1
  - • **sleep**; from loss of: colch tl1
- **influenza**:
  - • **after**: *(↗paralytic - influenza; Convalescence - influenza)* abrot br1* carc mlr1• chin tl1 con br1* cypr c1* irid-met vml3• kali-p br1* lath br1 **Nat-sal** br1* sal-ac br1
  - • **during**: abrot bro1 adon bro1 *Ars-i* bro1 *Aven* bro1 carb-ac bro1 caust tl1 *Chin* bro1 *Chinin-ar* bro1 chinin-s bro1 con bro1 eup-per bro1 gels bro1* *Iber* bro1 lac-c bro1 lath bro1 phos bro1 psor bro1 sal-ac bro1 *Sarcol-ac* br1*
- **injuries**: | **from**: *Acet-ac* hr1* *Arn* bro1* calen bro1 *Camph* hr1* carb-an bro1 dig hr1* hyper bro1 *Sul-ac* bro1* verat bro1
- **intermittent** (See periodical - intermittent)
- **intoxicated**; as if: *(↗MIND - Stupefaction)* olib-sac wmh1 psil ft1
- **irritability**; with (See MIND - Irritability - weakness - with)
- **jaundice**; from: ferr-pic bro1 pic-ac bro1 tarax bro1
- **leaning** | **left**; to:
  - ⁝ **amel.** | **menses**; during: phel k*
  - • **must** lean: bar-c br1
- **leukorrhea**:
  - • **from**: con h2
  - • **with**: *Aesc* kr1 *Alet* kr1* alum bg2* *Arg-n* kr1 bar-c j5.de* berb kr1* **Calc** kr1* calc-p kr1 *Calen* kr1 carb-an bro1 *Caul* kr1* *Caust* kr1* **Chin** bro1* *Cocc* bro1* coll sf1.de con kr1* *Frax* sf1.de* **Graph** kr1 gua bro1 *Ham* kr1 helin bro1 *Helon* kr1* hydr kr1* *Iod* kr1 kali-bi bg2 *Kali-c* sf1.de **Kreos** b7a.de* *Lyc* kr1 lyss kr1 nabal k1 **Nat-m** kr1 nicc sf1.de onos bro1 *Petr* kr1 *Ph-ac* kr1 phos bro1 *Phys* kr1 *Psor* bro1 puls bro1 rob kr1 *Senec* sf1.de* sep bro1 **Stann** b4a.de* sul-ac kr1 tarent a1* tril-p kr1 *Vinc* sf1.de visc ptk1 zinc kr1
- **lifting** agg.: **Carb-an** kali-sil k2* nat-c h2
- **lifting** one's head from the pillow | **impossible**: colch tl1
- **listlessness**; with (See Weariness)
- **looking** downward agg.: kali-c k*
- **loss** of fluids; from: *(↗Loss - fluids)* agar bro1 *Anac* bro1 *Calc* kr1 *Calc-p* bro1 calen vml3• carb-an mrr1 carb-v bro1* caust bro1 **Chin** b7a.de* chinin-s bro1* corn-f kr1* *Cur* kr1* ferr k2 ferr-ar k2 ferr-i br gins bro1 ham st hydr st kali-c bro1 lachn kr1 *Nat-m* kr1* *Nuph* kr1 **Ph-ac** b4a.de* *Phos* kr1* *Psor* kr1 sec kr1 *Sel* bro1* *Sep* b4a.de* stroph-h bro1 sulph b4a.de
  - • **blood**: *(↗Loss - blood)* ham br1
- **love**, from unfortunate: *(↗MIND - Ailments - love)* *Ph-ac* k*
- **lying**: *(↗morning - lying)*
  - • **agg.**: *(↗rest - agg.)* agar k* alum k* bar-c k* bry k* carb-v carl k* coca cycl gels nat-c nat-m nit-ac nux-v petr k* phys k* pip-m k* *Puls* rhus-g a1 sabad bg2 spig k* tritic-vg fd5.de zinc-m k*
    - ⁝ **shower**, before: gels k*
  - • **amel.**: acon-f k* ars bry j5.de hedeo st helo-s bnm14• kali-c tl1 lach k* mag-c k* nat-m j5.de nit-ac j5.de ph-ac h2 psil ft1 *Psor* sabad j5.de *Sep* k* **Stann** mrr1 taosc iwa1• vanil fd5.de
  - • **back**; on | **amel.**: (non:castm a1) castn-v a1
  - • **must** lie down: bar-c br1 taosc iwa1•
- **masturbation**; from: arg-met vh1 aven sf1.de bell-p c1* *Nat-m* hr1* *Phos* hr1* ust hr1
- **medicine**; from abuse of allopathic: carb-v bro1 helon bro1 nux-v bro1
- **meeting** amel.; in an interesting: pip-m
- **menopause**; during: **Chin** bg2* chinin-ar sf1.de *Cocc* st *Con* sf1.de* *Crot-h* kr1* dig bro1 helo bg2 helon kr1* *Kali-p* kr1* *Lach* bg2* magn-gl st phos bg2* sabin k2 *Sep* bg2* sul-ac k2* tab bg2*
- **menses**:
  - • **after** | **agg.**: agar bg2* *Alum* k* *Alumn* kr1 am-c bro1* am-m bro1 apoc k2 aran bg2 *Ars* bg2* bell bg2* benz-ac k* berb k* cact bg2 calc bg2* calc-p carb-ac bg2 *Carb-an* k* carb-v bro1* castm bg2 *Chin* k* *Chinin-s* kr1 *Cimic* k* *Cocc* bg2* cub hr1 ferr bg2* ferr-pic sf1.de glyc bro1* graph bg2* helo bg2 *Helon* hr1* iod k* **Ip** k* kali-c bg2* kali-p bg2* lac-e hrn2• mag-c bro1 nat-m k* nit-ac bg2 nux-v bg2 *Phos* k* pic-ac sf1.de plat k* sapin a1 sec sep bg2 stann bg2 sulph thlas bro1 thuj k* *Tril-p* bro1 *Verat* bro1 vinc bro1
  - • **appearance** of menses amel.: cycl mag-m
  - • **before** | **agg.**: *Alum* h2* *Am-c* bro1 aur-s k* *Bell* k* brom k* calc b4a.de* carb-ac k* carb-an bro1* carb-v bg2 *Chin* bro1 cimic k* cinnb bg2* *Cocc* k* ferr k* gels bg2* germ-met srj5• glyc bro1 graph bro1 *Haem* bro1 *Helon* bro1 ign bg2* iod k* kali-p bg2 *Mag-c* k* merc bg1 *Nat-m* k* nicc bro1 nux-m k* phel k* phos bg2* puls bro1 sec bg2* sulph b4a.de *Verat* bro1 zinc
  - • **disproportionate** to loss of blood: alum pfa ham kr1 *Ip*
  - • **during**:
    - ⁝ **agg.**: *Agar* k* aids nl2• *Aloe* k* *Alum* k* alum-p k2* *Am-c* k* am-m apoc k2 arg-n mrr1 *Ars* k* ars-i ars-s-f k2* bar-c bar-i k2* bar-s k2* bell k* berb k* borx k* bov k* brom st1 bufo k* cact k* calc k* calc-i k2* calc-p k* *Calc-s* cann-xyz bg2 **Carb-an** k* *Carb-v* k* *Carbn-s* caul k* *Caust* k* *Chin* bro1 cimic k* *Cinnb* k* *Cocc* k* eupi k* ferr k* ferr-i glyc bro1 *Graph* k* *Haem* bro1 haliae-lc srj5• helo bg2 *Helon* k* ign k* *Iod* k* ip k* *Kali-c* k* kali-n h2 *Kali-s* *Lach* k* *Lil-t* k* lyc k* *Mag-c* k* *Mag-m* k* mag-s sp1 mosch k* *Murx* k* nat-ar nat-c k* nat-m k* *Nicc* k* *Nit-ac* k* nux-m k* *Nux-v* k* ol-an bg2 *Petr* k* petr-ra shn4• phel *Phos* k* pic-ac ptk1 puls bro1 *Sabin* k* *Sec* k* senec k* **Sep** k* stann k* sul-i k2 *Sulph* k* *Tab* hr1 tarent k* thuj k* tril-p *Tub* k* (non:uran-met k) *Uran-n* *Verat* k* vinc k* wies a1 zinc bg2 zinc-p k2* [beryl stj2 beryl-m stj2]
      - : **breathe**, must lie down; can scarcely: *Nit-ac*
      - : **going** up stairs, when: *(↗ascending)* *Iod*
      - : **lie** down; with desire to: apoc k2 bell ip *Nit-ac*
      - : **painful** menses: bell bufo *Verat* hr1
      - : **scanty**: ip ptk1
      - : **stand**; can scarcely: cocc br1
      - : **stool** agg.; after: *(↗stool - after - agg.)* nux-v
      - : **talk**, can scarcely: *Carb-an* k* *Cocc* hr1* *Nit-ac* h2* *Stann*
    - ⁝ **amel.**: cycl a1 *Sep* k1*
    - ⁝ **beginning** of menses | **agg.**: brom bg2 cocc bg2 ferr bg2 mag-m bg2 phel
  - • **end** of: bov iod
  - • **suppressed** menses; from: *Cocc* b7a.de
- **mental** exertion:
  - • **agg.**: abrot bro1 alet bro1 *Aloe* *Alst* bro1 *Anac* bro1 anag kr1 apis arn ars aur aur-ar k2 aven bro1 bar-act sf1.de *Bell* **Calc** *Calc-p* bro1 calc-sil k2 carb-an bro1 carb-v k2* cham *Chin* kr1* *Chinin-ar* bro1 cist k2 coca bro1 cocc k* colch bro1 **Cupr** k* cur bro1 dig bro1 dulc fd4.de **Ferr-pic** fl-ac bro1 gels bro1 graph ptk1 *Helon* bro1 ign irid-met bro1* *Kali-c* kali-fcy bro1 kali-n kali-p k2* kali-s fd4.de **Lach** lath bro1 **Lec** k* lil-s a1 lob-p bro1 *Lyc* macroz bro1 mag-c st **Nat-c** nat-m nat-sal bro1 *Nux-v* bro1* okou jl *Par* kr1 *Ph-ac* k* phos bro1* *Pic-ac* kr1* **Psor** k* **Puls** ruta fd4.de sabad scut tl1 **Sel** k* sep sil k* spong staph bro1 stry-p bro1 sul-ac bro1 sulfonam jl *Sulph* symph fd3.de* thuj zinc-ar bro1
  - • **amel.**: *Croc* hydrog srj2•
- **mental** symptoms; during acute (See MIND - Mental symptoms - acute - weakness)
- **milk**:
  - • **agg.**: agar zr sul-ac h2
  - • **loss** of milk in nursing women: *(↗nursing women)* chin tl1
- **mononucleosis**; from: *Carc* mlr1•
- **mortification**; from: ign
- **motion**:
  - • **agg.**: agar k* am-c k2 ammc k* apoc k* *Arg-met* **Ars** k* asaf k* bry k* cann-s k* cocc k* hydr-ac k* kali-bi k* kali-n k* kali-s fd4.de lach k*

- **agg.**: ...
mang-o a1 merc k* merl k* mur-ac j5.de narcin a1 nat-m j5.de nit-ac h2 nux-v k* phel *Phos* k* plb k* sep j5.de* spig h1* **Spong** k* stann h2 staph sulph k* tab k* tub br1 vanil fd5.de
  - **horizontal** position; when moved from: rob
- **amel.**: cham h1 colch k* coloc k* con a1 cycl k* gels kali-i k2 kreos k* limest-b es1• *Lyc* k* mosch *Nat-m* hr1 pip-m k* *Plat* plb podo fd3.de• psil ft1 *Rhod* **Rhus-t** hr1 stann j5.de vanil fd5.de
- **arms**; of | **agg.**: nat-m
- **gentle** motion | **amel.**: kali-n
- **slightest** motion agg.: *(↗exertion - agg. - slight)* anac b4a.de* cocc b7a.de dulc fd4.de lyc bg1 nux-m bg1 plb b7a.de spig b7a.de* stann b4a.de staph b7a.de verat b7a.de*

- **music** agg.: lyc st1
- **nausea**; with: aeth a1 *Agar* hr1* aids nl2• alumn hr1* ang hr1* **Ant-t** bg2* **Ars** bg2 *Calc* a1* *Camph* hr1* cimic a1 cob a1 *Colch* hr1 con bg2 crot-t a1 gran a1 hell a1 hydrog srj2• hyos bg2 **Ip** bg2 kali-c bg2 lavand-a ctl1• nept-m lsd2.fr phos bg2 plat bg2* *Podo* bg2 *Psil* ft1 ruta fd4.de sabad a1 sang a1 sep a1 spong fd4.de stront-c a1 sulph bg2 tritic-vg fd5.de *Verat* bg2* *Verat-v* bg2
- **nervous**: acon k* aesc hr1* *Agar* hr1* *Agn* a1* *Alet* hr1* *Alum* k* alum-p k2* alumn hr1* am-c k* am-m hr1* ambr k* *Anac* hr1* *Aran* hr1* *Arg-n* bg2* arn k* ars k* asaf bg2* *Asar* k* aur aven bg2* *Bar-c* k* bar-i k2* *Bell* k* bry *Calc* k* calc-p k* calc-sil k2* calen a1 camph carb-an k* carb-v carbn-s castm bg2* caust bg2* cham **Chin** k* chinin-ar sf1.de chinin-s kr1 cic k* *Cimic* hr1* clem k2 **Coca** kr1* **Cocc** k* *Coff* k* colch *Con* k* croc *Cupr* k* cur k* cycl hr1* cypr c1 dam br1 dig k* dios hr1* *Fl-ac* bg2* **Gels** hr1* graph k* grat k2 *Guaj* hedeo a1 hell *Helon* hr1* hep k* hydr-ac j5.de* *Hydrc* hr1* hyos k* *Ign* k* *Iod* k* **Kali-br** hr1* kali-n **Kali-p** k* kola br1 lac-c hr1* lach k* lact k* lath br1 laur k* **Lec** k* led lob-p br1 lyc k* *M-arct* b7.de* m-aust b7.de mag-c br1 meph sf1.de *Merc* k* methyl br1 mez bg2 *Moni* rfm1• mosch mur-ac **Nat-c** k* nat-m k* **Nat-p** nat-s hr1* **Nat-sil** k2* **Nit-ac** nuph br1 nux-m k* **Nux-v** k* op ox-ac br1 petr k* **Ph-ac** k* **Phos** k* phys hr1* **Pic-ac** k* pip-m sf1.de *Plat* *Plb* k* **Puls** k* rhus-t k* sabin k* sacch br1 sarcol-ac sp1 sars scroph-n a1 scut br1 sec **Sel** k* **Sep** k* **Sil** k* spig spong squil k* **Stann** k* **Staph** k* stram stry-n mg1.de stry-p sf1.de sul-ac *Sulph* k* sumb hr1* tab sf1.de tarent a1* *Teucr* k* *Ther* hr1* tub br1 *Valer* k* verat verbe-o br1 *Viol-o* k* xan br1 zinc k* zinc-m k* **Zinc-p** k2* zinc-pic sf1.de*
  - **afternoon**: cimic k*
  - **accompanied** by | **Stomach**; complaints of: *Anac* bro1 gent-l bro1 nux-v bro1 stry-p bro1
  - **influenza**; after: *Lob-p* br1 scut br1
  - **menses**; during: *Ign* b7a.de
  - **spinal**: sarcol-ac br1
  - **syphilitic**: *Anac* bro1 asaf bro1 *Aur* bro1 iod bro1 *Kali-i* bro1 lyc bro1 merc-n bro1 *Merc-p* bro1 mez bro1 phos br1*
  - **walking** agg.; after: petr
  - **women**; in: alet bro1 aloe bro1 ambr bro1 ars bro1 aur bro1 bell-p bro1 calc bro1 chin bro1 *Cocc* bro1 *Epiph* bro1 ferr bro1 *Helon* bro1 hyos bro1 *Ign* bro1 iod bro1 kali-p bro1 *Lach* bro1 lyc bro1 *Mag-c* bro1 mag-p bro1 ph-ac bro1 *Pic-ac* bro1 puls bro1 *Sep* bro1 sil bro1 sulph bro1 zinc-val bro1
- **numbness**; with: con k2
- **nursing** and staying up with sick person: *(↗MIND - Ailments - cares; MIND - Prostration - cares)* carb-v st *Carc* mlr1• *Cimic* k* **Cocc** k* *Nit-ac* k* *Nux-v* st olnd puls st zinc *Zinc-act* st
- **nursing** women, in: *(↗milk - loss; Nursing)* *Calc* hr1* *Calc-p* hr1* *Carb-an* k* **Carb-v** hr1* **Chin** k* chinin-s bro1 kali-c bro1 lyc hr1* olnd **Ph-ac** k* *Phos* hr1* *Phyt* hr1* sep mp1• *Sil* hr1* *Sulph* hr1*
- **nutrition**; from defective: alet bro1 *Helon* bro1
- **old** people; in: *(↗Old)* alum br1 *Ambr* k* ant-t k2 aur k* **Bar-c** k* carb-v bro1 carc mlr1• caust br1 *Con* k* *Cur* k* eup-per bro1 glyc bro1 hydr br1 nit-ac c1* *Nux-m* k* op k* *Phos* k* sec *Sel* k* *Sul-ac*
- **operation**, from: *(↗Injuries - operation - ailments)* acet-ac bro1* carb-v k2 hyper bro1* *Stront-c* br1* stroph-h br1
  - **cancer** surgery: kali-p mrr1
- **overwork**; from: ambr br1 arn tl1 *Calc* br1 chin tl1 helon br1 kali-p br1 *Nux-v* mrr1
- **pain**; from: androc srj1• *Arg-met* k* **Ars** k* both-ax tsm2 carb-v cham h1* coloc k2 hep k2 hura kali-p k* kalm k2* pic-ac ptk1 plb podo c1 *Rhus-t* k* ruta ptk1* spig k2 spong fd4.de tarent-c br1 tritic-vg fd5.de verat ptk1
  - **sacrum**; in: *Sep*

- **pain**; from: ...
  - **stomach**; in: *Nux-v* kr1 *Podo*
    - **and** back: sep
- **palpitations**:
  - **after**: *Aml-ns* vh1 kali-c ptk1
  - **with**: am-c bg2 aur h2 caust h2 hydr ptk1 sang a1* sul-i k2 vanil fd5.de
- **paralytic**: agar k2* *Alum* k* alum-p k2* *Alumn* k2* am-m k* ambr k2* anac k2* anan a1 ang b2.de* *Arg-met* **Ars** k* *Art-v* hr1* bad br1 bapt k2* *Bar-c* *Bar-m* bell k* *Bism* bry k* *Calc* k* calc-ar k2* camph k* cann-i k2* canth k* caps j5.de carb-v k* *Caust* k* *Cham* k* chel k* *Chin* k* cimic k2* cina k* **Cocc** k* *Colch* k* con k* crot-h cupr st1 cur a1 dig diph-t-tpt jl2 dros k* euph k* *Ferr* k* ferr-ar ferr-ma j5.de* **Gels** k* gins br1 *Gran* a1 **Hell** k* helo-s bnm14• hyos ign k2* ind k* kali-bi br1 kali-c ptk1 kali-n k* kali-p ptk1 kalm br1* lach laur k* lup a1 m-arct b2.de* mang a1 *Merc* k* mez k* mosch k* **Mur-ac** k* nat-c k* nat-m j5.de nat-p k* *Nit-ac* nux-m k2* nux-v k* *Olnd* k* pert jl2 **Ph-ac** k* **Phos** k* plat k2* plb k* psor k2* *Puls* k* *Rhod* k* *Rhus-t* k* sabad k* sarcol-ac jl3 sars k2 sil k* spong fd4.de *Stann* k* stront-c k* *Sulph* ptk1 thuj b4a.de* valer k* vanil fd5.de **Verat** k* vip br1 zinc j5.de*
  - **morning** | **rising** agg.; after: phos h2
  - **accompanied** by:
    - **chorea** (See Chorea - accompanied - weakness)
    - **stiffness**: lith-c ptk1
  - **diphtheria**; after: *(↗diphtheria)* bar-m br1
  - **exertion** agg.: arg-met k2
  - **heat**; with: ferr c1
  - **influenza**; after: *(↗influenza - after)* bar-m br1
  - **motion** agg.: aeth k* arg-met
  - **old** people; in: kali-c br1
  - **pain**; with: *Arg-met* *Verat*
  - **painful** parts, in: cham k* *Verat*
  - **sensation** of: stront-c ptk1
  - **single** parts: rhus-t k2
  - **sliding** down in bed from a half sitting position●: *Ant-t* hr1* *Apis* k* arn sf1.de *Ars* k* arum-t *Bapt* hr1* *Bell* hr1* carb-v *Chin* hr1* colch bg2* crot-h k2 dendr-pol sk4• *Hell* k* hyos k2* *Lach* k* *Lyc* hr1* mosch **Mur-ac** k* nat-m bg2 *Nit-ac* nux-m op bg2 **Ph-ac** **Phos** *Rhus-t* tab ptk1 zinc h2*
    - **chill**; during: ars bg2 *Mur-ac* bg2
    - **fever**; during: ars bg2 *Mur-ac* bg2
    - **perspiration**; during: ars bg2 *Mur-ac* bg2
- **parturition** (See delivery)
- **periodical**: **Arg-n** k* *Hep* hr1* ruta gk symph fd3.de• taosc iwa1•
  - **morning**; every other: nit-ac
  - **intermittent**: *Apis* corn-f br1 nat-ar k* (non:nat-s k1)
- **perspiration**:
  - **awake**, and dry burning heat while sleeping; perspiration while: **Samb**
  - **foot** sweat; from suppressed: *Sil* kr1
  - **from**: *(↗PERSPIRATION - Debilitating; PERSPIRATION - Exhausting; PERSPIRATION - Profuse - debilitating)* acon k* agar am-c k* ambr k* aml-ns anac b2.de* ant-c k* ant-o a1 ant-t bg2 anthraci apis k* arg-met bg2 arn b2.de* *Ars* k* ars-i k2* ars-s-f k2 bar-c k* bell bg2 ben benz-ac k2 berb bg2 borx b2.de* bov **Bry** k* bufo bg2 caj a1 *Calad* k* *Calc* k* **Camph** k* canth b2.de* **Carb-an** k* carb-v k* carl a1 castm bg2* caust b2.de* **Chin** k* *Chinin-ar* **Chinin-s** coca a1 cocc k* croc k* *Cupr* bg2 dig k* dros bg2 **Ferr** k* *Ferr-ar* k* *Ferr-i* ferr-p gels a1* graph k* hep bg2* hist sp1 hura a1 hyos k* ign k* **Iod** k* *Ip* b2.de* jatr-c a1 kali-ar k2 kali-bi kali-c bg2 kali-i bg2 kali-n k* kali-p fd1.de• kreos b2.de* lac-c laur bg2 lyc k* m-arct b2.de* mag-c st meny bg2 **Merc** k* morph a1 nat-c bg2* *Nat-m* b2.de* *Nit-ac* k* nux-m bg2 **Nux-v** b2.de* op *Ph-ac* k* **Phos** k* plb bg2 **Psor** k* puls k* *Pyrog* ran-s a1 rheum b2.de* rhod k* *Rhus-t* bg2 *Sabad* b2.de* **Samb** k* *Sec* senec sf1.de **Sep** k* *Sil* k* spig bg2 *Stann* k* sul-ac bg2 sul-i k2 *Sulph* k* *Tarax* k* tarent a1 thuj bg2 **Tub** k* *Verat* k* *Verat-v*
    - **morning**: carb-v k2
    - **night**: ars bar-c bry *Carb-an* carb-v k2 *Chin* corn-f br1 eupi ferr hall a1 *Merc* nat-c a1 ph-ac a1 *Phos* kr1 *Samb* stann tarax **Tub** k*
    - **delivery**; after: *Samb* st

- **with** perspiration; weakness: **Aloe** kr1 *Calc* kr1 *Chin* kr1* *Chinin-m* kr1 dig kr1 ferr-ar k2 hydrog srj2• *Jab* kr1 *Lyc* kr1 *Ph-ac* kr1 *Rhus-g* br1 ruta fd4.de sal-ac kr1 sul-ac kr1 *Tarent* kr1
  - **perspiration**; cold: *Camph* kr1 *Carb-v* kr1 cupr kr1 *Merc* kr1 *Ph-ac* kr1 *Ter* kr1 **Verat** kr1
- **playing** piano, from: anac a1* nat-c h2
- **pleasant**: cann-s a1 morph a1
- **pleasure**, from: crot-c k* kalm k2
- **pollution**; nocturnal: med jl2
  - **after**: viol-o b7a.de
- **pregnancy** agg.; during: alet k2* alum kr1 alumn hr1* calc-p hr1* *Helon* hr1* murx hr1* *Sulph* kr1 *Verat* hr1*
- **progressive**: acon hr1* *Adren* vh1 ars bg2 caust bg2* cupr-ar hr1* cur mrr1 *Dig* hr1* kreos bg2 *Merc* hr1 *Ol-j* hr1* *Phos* hr1* *Plb* hr1* verat bg2*
- **quinine**; from abuse of: ars-s-f k2 chelo c2 eucal c2 nat-m c2
- **rapid**: *(↗sudden; Collapse - sudden)* **Ars** k* aur bapt bg3* diphtox jl2 ephe-si hsj1• kou br1 *Lach* hr1 laur k* lyc ptk1 merc-cy br1 *Sep* k* *Thuj* br1 tub ptk1 **Verat** k*
- **reaction**, with lack of: *(↗Reaction - lack)* *Am-c* hr1* carc mlr1• *Laur* hr1* **Op** hr1* *Sulph* hr1* *Valer* hr1* [heroin sdj2]
  - **fat** people, in: **Caps** kr1
- **reading**:
  - **agg.**: anac *Aur* k* kali-p fd1.de• ph-ac k* **Pic-ac** mrr1 plb k* podo fd3.de• *Sumb* k*
  - **aloud** | **agg.**: arg-met vh stann
  - **light**; by: sulfonam ks2
- **recurrent** | **ten** to thirty minutes; lasting: marb-w es1•
- **rest**:
  - **agg.**: *(↗lying - agg.; sitting - agg.)* coloc a1 con a1 kreos a1 lyc h2* rhod k2
  - **amel.**: bry a1 helo-s bnm14• hydrog srj2•
- **resting** head on something and closing eyes amel.: anac k*
- **restlessness**; with: *(↗MIND - Restlessness - weakness; MIND - Restlessness - weakness - during)* **Ars** hr1* *Bapt* hr1 *Bism* hr1* *Colch* hr1* gels sys lycps-v kr1 lyss hr1* musca-d szs1 *Ph-ac* hr1* **Rhus-t** hr1* spong fd4.de zinc ptk1
- **riding**:
  - **agg.**: *(↗walking - riding)* card-m ptk1 cere-b a1 cocc k* petr k* *Psor* k1 sep k* sulph k* (non:ter kl) tet k*
  - **air**; in open | **amel.**: cinnb
- **rising**:
  - **after** | **agg.**: am-c k* coc-c k* hydr k* mag-c k*
  - **agg.**: *(↗morning - rising - agg.)* acon-c k* ammc k* arn k* **Ars** atro k* **Bry** k* clem k* coca dulc fd4.de ephe-si hsj1• fago k* ham k* hydr k* hydrog srj2• hyper k* jab k* lach tl1 lyc k* mag-c k* nat-ar *Nat-m* k* olnd k* osm k* phyt k* pic-ac k* pip-m a1 ptel k* rhus-g a1 *Rhus-t* k* sol-t-ae k* teucr k* thuj k* (non:uran-met k) uran-n
  - **sitting**; from | **agg.**: bry h1 *Chin* k* dulc fd4.de vanil fd5.de
- **room**:
  - **agg.**: asar jl3
  - **closed** agg.; from: asar jl
- **sadness**; with (See MIND - Sadness - weakness)
- **sea**-bath, after: *(↗Bathing - sea - agg.)* *Mag-m* k*
- **sedentary** habits agg.: nux-v st1 sulph st1
  - **women**; in: helon ptk1
- **sensation** | **Bones**: bufo bg2 indg bg2
- **sensitiveness**; without: ph-ac bro1
- **sexual**:
  - **desire** increased; with (See sexual; MALE GENITALIA/SEX - Sexual desire - increased - weakness)
  - **excesses**, after: agn mrr1 *Ars* kr1 aven sf1.de calad k2* chin sf1.de coca kr1 con sf1.de* *Dig* kr1 gins sf1.de graph ptk1 kali-c sf1.de lil-t ptk1 *Lyc* ptk1 *Nat-m* kr1* nat-p ptk1 nux-v ptk1 onos ptk1 *Ph-ac* sf1.de* *Phos* kr1* sec ptk1 staph ptk1 sulph ptk1 symph ptk1 *Ust* hr1*
  - **excitement** agg.: pic-ac k2
- **shivering**; during: chin b7.de verat b7.de
- **sit** down; desire to: alum j5.de ambr sf1.de anac j5.de ars sf1.de bar-c br1 bry j5.de* calc sf1.de caps ckh1 caust sf1.de cham j5.de chin sf1.de *Cocc* j5.de* colch sf1.de croc j5.de dulc sf1.de hydrog srj2• kali-n sf1 de led sf1.de *Lil-t* sf1.de* m-aust j5.de *Merc* sf1.de mur-ac j5.de nat-m sf1.de nat-s sf1.de nux-v j5.de* ol-an j5.de olnd sf1.de ph-ac sf1.de rhus-t j5.de sabin j5.de *Stann* bg2* staph j5.de stront-c sf1.de sulph j5.de tarax j5.de tritic-vg fd5.de verat sf1.de
- **sitting**:
  - **agg.**: *(↗rest - agg.; sudden - sitting)* agar k* anac arg-met j5.de *Ars* aur bry k* carl k* caust j5.de chel k* chin k* cocc k* colch k* fago graph k* kali-n k* led j5.de limest-b es1• *Lyc* k* m-aust j5.de *Mag-c* mang k* merc j5.de* merc-i-f k* mur-ac j5.de *Nat-m* k* nit-ac k* nux-v j5.de olib-sac wmh1 phos j5.de *Plat* k* plb k* psil ft1 ptel ran-b j5.de* **Rhus-t** k* ruta k* sabad staph stront-c j5.de *Sulph* thuj j5.de tritic-vg fd5.de
  - **amel.**: bry k* euph-a a1 glon k* hydrog srj2• nux-v sapin a1 trios rsj11•
  - **impossible**: pic-ac k2
  - **walking**; after: **Ruta**
- **sleep**:
  - **after**:
    - **agg.**: agar k* ambr hr1* bor-ac borx camph k* carl k* chel k* chinin-s coca colch k* con cycl k* dor k* ferr gels gent-l k* *Kali-n* bg2* *Lach* lyc k* mez k* nat-n petr-ra shn4• psil ft1 sec k* sep k* sil k* sin-n hr1* vanil fd5.de zinc k*
    - **not** amel.: lavand-a ctl1•
  - **amel.**: alum sf1.de hippoc-k szs2 mez k* *Ph-ac* *Phos* k* tritic-vg fd5.de
  - **during** | **agg.**: bufo
  - **loss** of; from: *Carc* mlr1• chin tl1 **Cocc** k* colch bro1* cupr k* glon kr1 *Hydr* kr1 *Ip* kr1 *Nat-m* a1* nux-v bro1* osm a1 petr-ra shn4• pic-ac k2 *Puls* a1
    - **as** from loss of sleep: plat h2
- **sleepiness**:
  - **agg.**: *Chlol* kr1* *Coff* *Colch* kr1 gran hep a1 melal-alt gya4 nit-ac petr-ra shn4• psil ft1 rhus-t a1 ruta fd4.de spong fd4.de tritic-vg fd5.de vanil fd5.de
    - **morning**: psil ft1 ruta fd4.de verat
    - **afternoon**:
      - **walking** | **amel.**: ruta
  - **as** from sleepiness: *Aeth* kr1 chen-v kr1 cimic dig hydrog srj2• kali-n merc-sul kr1 nept-m lsd2.fr peti a1 petr phel plat *Rhus-t* thuj
- **sleeplessness** agg.: *Carc* mlr1• chlol hr1 *Cypr* a1* *Kreos* hr1*
- **sliding** down in bed (See paralytic - sliding)
- **smoking** agg.: *(↗tobacco; walking - agg. - smoking)* asc-t k* clem j5.de* *Hep* k* vanil fd5.de
- **sneezing** agg.: petr ptk1 sabad bg2
- **somnambulism**, after: sulph k*
- **spinal** origin; of: *(↗BACK - Inflammation - spinal cord - accompanied - weakness)* cocc tl1
- **sporting**: arn st1 ars st1 coca st fl-ac st1 rhus-t st1 spong fd4.de
- **spring** agg.: apis **Bry** hr1*
- **standing** agg.: *(↗Standing - agg.)* *Acon* kr1 acon-c a1 aeth mtf33 agn *Apis* kr1 asaf aster kr1 berb calc-sil k2 *Cic* cocc j5.de crot-h cupr j5.de cur cystein-l rly4• ham a1 hep j5.de *Kali-c* kr1 kali-n j5.de lach j5.de led j5.de merc **Merc-cy** a1* mur-ac nat-m nit-ac j5.de nux-v j5.de ol-an j5.de ped a1 petr-ra shn4• plat j5.de ran-b ribo rly4• spig staph j5.de sul-ac j5.de* *Sulph* ther j5.de zinc h2 zing
- **stimulants** amel.: *(↗coffee - amel.; tea - amel.)* phos k*
- **stomach**; as from in: anan vh1 hydrog srj2• mag-c h2 mag-m h2*
- **stool**:
  - **after**:
    - **agg.**: *(↗menses - during - agg. - stool; tremulous - stool)* aeth k* *Aloe* k* ambr b7.de* ant-t k* apis k* apoc k* arg-n bg2 arn k* **Ars** k* **Ars-met** ars-s-f k2* bapt bg2* bism k* *Borx* b4a.de bov k* bry b7.de* *Calc* k* carb-an b4.de* *Carb-v* k* *Carbn-s* castn-v a1 caust k* chin k* *Chinin-s* clem k* cocc ptk1 coch bg* colch k* coloc k* com k* **Con** k* cop k* crot-h k* crot-t k* cupr b7.de* dios *Dulc* k* eupi k* ferr b7.de* ferr-ma k* gamb mrr1 glycyr-g cte1• *Graph* k* *Hydr* hr1 hyos b7.de* ign k* *Iod* ip k* *Jatr-c* kr1 kali-bi bg2 kali-n bg2 kali-p bg2* *Lach* k* lil-t k* lipp a1 *Lyc* k* mag-c k* mag-m h2 *Med* k* **Merc** k* mez k* nat-m k* nat-p hr1 **Nat-s** k* **Nit-ac** k* *Nux-m* b7.de* *Nux-v* k* olnd b7.de* *Petr* k* ph-ac bg2 *Phos* k* phys k* **Pic-ac** k* plan k* **Podo** k* psil ft1 puls b7.de* pyre-p a1 rham-f a1 rheum b7a.de* sabad k* sacch **Sec** k*

- **after – agg.**: ... *Sep* k* *Sil* b4a.de* *Sulph* k* *Ter* k* thuj k* trios k1* trom k* tub bg* **Verat** k* vinc k* zinc [tax jsj7]
  - : **mucous** stool: borx ptk1
- **before**: hydr k* mez k* nat-hchls *Rhus-t* k* *Verat* k*
- **during** | **agg.**: aesc ant-t bg2 apis k* arg-n bg2 *Ars* b4a.de* atro k* bell k* *Borx* k* carbn-s chin b7a.de* cic bg2 cob k* colch crot-h crot-t hr1* cupr bg2 *Cupr-act* kr1 dulc b4.de* hep b4a.de* hyos bg2 ip b7.de* kali-c b4a.de* kali-i k* lact k* *Nit-ac* hr1* *Nux-v* b7a.de petr b4.de* pic-ac k* plan **Plat** k* podo bg2 *Rheum* b7a.de sec k* sulph bg **Tab** bg2 verat k*

- **stooping** agg.: graph k*
- **storm**:
  - **before** and during a: sil k*
  - **thunderstorm**; during: acon b7a.de caust nat-c nat-p nit-ac petr rhod sil k*
- **sudden**: *(↗acute; acute - during; rapid; Collapse - sudden)* *Acon* k* act-sp k* *Aeth* sf1.de ail bg2 *Am-c* bg2* am-m j5.de* ambr j5.de* *Ant-ar* sf1.de ant-c k2* *Ant-t* bg2* anthraci vh1 *Apis* k* apoc sf1.de *Arg-met* arg-n bg2 arn bg2* **Ars** k* ars-h k* *Ars-i* sf1.de *Bapt* bg2* bell h1* bry bg2* calc calo a1 camph k* cann-s j5.de carb-ac sf1.de *Carb-v* k* *Caust* h2* cham k* chir-fl gya2 chlam-tr bcx2• colch k* con k* **Crot-h** k* *Cupr* bg2 cupr-ar k* dig h2* dulc j5.de* fl-ac bg2 *Gels* bg2* glon bg2 **Graph** k* *Hell* bg2* *Hep* k* hippoc-k szs2 *Hydr-ac* bg2* ign k2 *Ip* k* jatr-c sf1.de kali-br hr1* kali-c h2 kali-cy a1* kalm bg2 ketogl-ac rly4• lac-h sze9• lach k* laur k* lith-c bg2* lyc k* mag-c bg2 marb-w es1* *Merc* ptk1 merc-c bg2 merc-cy bg1* merc-i-f bg2 naja bg1 nit-ac bg2 *Nux-v* k* petr h2* *Phos* k* pycnop-sa mrz1 ran-b k* rhus-t bg2* sabad bg2* sacch sst1• sacch-a fd2.de• sec *Sel* k* **Sep** k* sil bg2 spong k* stann k* stram k* sul-h a1 *Sulph* bg2* *Tab* bg2* tarent k* tax k* thuj bg1 tub-d jl2 vanil fd5.de *Verat* k* *Verat-v* bg2* vip j5.de zinc h2*
  - **afternoon**: lyc k* ran-b k* sacch-a fd2.de• vanil fd5.de
    - : **13.30 h**: iodof
    - : **walking** agg.; after: graph k*
  - **evening**: fl-ac k*
  - **chilliness**; during: sep k*
  - **daily**: *Hep* k*
  - **diarrhea**, with: crot-t kr1
  - **dinner**; after: thuj bg1
  - **dressing** after rising, while: *Stann*
  - **eruption** comes out, after the: ars
    - : **old** people; in: kali-cy st
  - **robust** looking people; in: graph mrr1
  - **sitting** agg.: *(↗sitting - agg.)* cham k* lyc k* ran-b k*
  - **vanish**, as if senses would: ran-b k*
  - **walking** agg.: *(↗walking - agg.)* carb-v h2 con h2* sabad k* wildb
- **sun** agg.; walking in the: *(↗heat - sun - agg.)* dulc fd4.de *Lach* *Nat-c*
- **sunstroke**, from: *Bell* hr1 **Carb-v** mrr1 *Glon* hr1* *Verat-v* hr1*
- **supper** agg.; after: *(↗evening - eating)* alum k* bov chin k* lach k* mag-c k* sil
- **surprise**; from a: gels k2
  - **pleasant**: *Coff* mrr1
- **sweets** | **after**: sacch sst1•
- **symptoms**; with very few: carc mlr1• syph ptk1
- **syphilis**; during: *Kali-i* hr1* *Lyc* hr1* *Staph* hr1*
- **talk** of others agg.: *(↗MIND - Talking - others)* alum am-c ars verat
- **talking** agg.: *(↗Talking - agg.)* act-sp k* **Alum** k* am-c am-caust a1* ambr arn st *Calc* k* *Cocc* k* dor k* elaps gk *Ferr* k* granit-m es1• hydrc a1 *Hyos* k* iod k* jac-c a1 kali-p fd1.de• kali-s fd4.de *Nat-m* k* *Ph-ac* k* *Psor* k* sep k* sil k* **Stann** k* **Sulph** k* *Ust* hr1* wies a1 zinc-p k2
  - **menses**; during: **Alum** al carb-an al cocc al
- **tea** | **amel.**: *(↗stimulants)* dig a1
- **tendency** to: coli jl2
- **thirst**; with: bufo bg2
- **thoughts**:
  - **doing** anything; of: bacls-7 fmm1•
  - **work**; of | **agg.**: bacls-7 fmm1•
- **tobacco**; from: *(↗smoking; walking - agg. - smoking)* calad k2* clem j5.de granit-m es1• hep b4a.de* nux-v b7a.de
- **toothache**:
  - **after**: nat-c h2 ruta fd4.de
  - **with**: clem bg mang h2 verat bg
- **transfusion**; after blood: p-benzq mtf11
- **tremulous**: *(↗Trembling - externally - weakness)* *Agar* aids nl2• *Alum* k* *Anac* k* anag hr1* androc srj1• ant-t sf1.de *Apis* apoc-a br1 **Arg-n** k* arn a1 *Ars* k* *Bapt* bell sf1.de berb hr1* borx j5.de bry sf1.de calc-ar k2* calc-s k2 canth caps j5.de carb-v k* caul caust h2* *Chin* j5.de* chinin-s j5.de clem k* *Cocc* k* **Con** k* *Crot-h* k* cupr h2 dulc fd4.de *Gels* k* granit-m es1• graph j5.de hep k* hydrog srj2• hyos j5.de kali-c h2* kali-n k* *Kalm* **Lach** hr1* lyc k* lycps-v kr1 mang bg2* med k2* merc br1 *Nat-m* h2* *Nit-ac* k* ol-an j5.de* olnd j5.de* ox-ac petr h2* *Phos* k* *Plat* plb j5.de *Puls* k* rhus-t h1 sal-fr sle1• *Sep* spig j5.de spong fd4.de **Stann** k* *Sul-ac* br1* ther thuj bg2 til a1 vanil fd5.de verat sf1.de zinc sf1.de
  - **night** | **waking**; on: brom k*
  - **dinner**; after: *(↗dinner)* ant-c k*
  - **smoking**; after: hep ptk1
  - **stool** agg.; after: *(↗stool - after - agg.)* **Ars** k* carb-v k* caust k* **Con** k*
- **trifles**; from: am-c br1* ars ptk1
- **tuberculosis**; after: acal bro1 ars bro1 *Ars-i* bro1 *Chinin-ar* bro1 elaps br phos bro1 sil bro1 *Stann* mrr1 tub gk tub-a bro1
- **typhoid** fever; during: agar bro1 *Agarin* bro1 apis bro1 *Ars* bro1 bapt bro1 *Bell* bro1 bry bro1 cocc bro1 colch bro1 gels bro1 hell bro1 *Hyos* bro1 *Hyosin-hbr* bro1 *Ign* bro1 lach bro1 lyc bro1 *Mur-ac* bro1 *Ph-ac* bro1 *Phos* bro1 rhus-t bro1 *Stram* bro1 sumb bro1 valer bro1 zinc bro1
- **urination** | **after**:
  - : **agg.**: ars bg2* berb bg2* bufo bg2 calc-p bg2 caust bg2* cimic k* dig bg2 eup-per bg2 ferr bg2* gels bg2* lys bg2 *Lyss* k* med bg2* nux-v bg2* *Phos* k* *Pic-ac* bg2*
    - : **copious**: calc-p bg2* caust gels med
  - **before**: nux-v bg2
- **vertigo**; with: *Acet-ac* kr1 aeth ptk1 ambr bro1 apis b7a.de *Arg-n* bro1 *Bapt* a1* chin bro1 colch ptk1 con bro1 crot-h ptk1 crot-t a1 cupr b7.de* cupr-s kr1 dulc bg2* echi bro1* *Gels* bg2* graph a1 hell a1 helo-s bnm14• hydrog srj2• iod b4.de* kali-bi bg2 kali-n b4.de* laur b7.de* nat-c bg2 olnd bg2 petr-ra shn4• phos bg2 ruta fd4.de sabin b7.de* sel ptk1 *Sil* kr1 spong fd4.de stront-c b4.de* strych-g br1 tab bg2* tritic-vg fd5.de uran-n kr1 vanil fd5.de verat bro1 zinc bg2
- **vexation**; after: *Ars* *Calc-p* calc-s k2 cocc k2 lyc *Nat-m* nux-v petr sep h2 verat
- **vomiting**:
  - **after**: aeth h2 aloe a1 ant-c hr1* ant-t a1 apom a1 ars h2* bar-c a1* cadm-s a1* cinnm hr1 *Colch* hr1* cycl a1 der a1 dulc fd4.de gran a1 kali-bi tl1 mag-c h2* nat-s a1 op a1 phyt a1* sel a1 *Verat* h1* zinc h2
  - **with**: aeth bg2* **Ant-t** b7a.de* ars b4a.de* bol-s a1 cadm-s ptk1 *Calc* hr1* con bg2 crot-t a1 gran a1 guaj k2 hyos bg2 **Ip** b7a.de* kali-c h2* phos h2* plat bg2 *Podo* bg2* **Sang** a1* sulph h2* tab a1 **Verat** b7a.de* *Verat-v* bg2*
- **waking**:
  - **morning** (See morning - waking)
  - **after** | **agg.**: arg-met calc-s k* cedr k* cycl k* iod k* wildb
  - **on**: *(↗dream)* aeth k* alco k* aloe ambr k* aq-pet a1 arg-met ars-h k* aur a1 bell k* bism k* bry k* bufo bg2 cadm-met tpw6 carbn-s card-m k* cham k* chel k* chin k* clem k* colch rsj2• *Cycl* k* dig k* dios k* *Dulc* hr1* *Echi* bg2* ephe-si hsj1• equis-h erig erio a1 euphr j5.de fago a1 ferr k* ferr-p k* form k* haliae-lc srj5• hipp k* hura hyper a1 ign sf1.de lac-ac a1* (non:lac-c k1) luna kg1• lyc k* mang k* myric k* nabal a1 nat-ar nat-m k* nat-p k* nux-m k* nux-v sf1.de* op k* ph-ac pip-n bg2 podo psil ft1 ptel k* **Puls** k* puls-n a1 rhod k* rhus-t k* sang k* sec sf1.de sel sf1.de *Sep* k* staph b7.de sulph k* sumb k* syph hr1* tab k* teucr k* thuj k* upa k* xan k*
- **walking**:
  - **after** | **short** walk; after a: *Nat-c* hr1* ruta kr1 *Sulph* hr1* *Ter* hr1* tub k2*
  - **agg.**: *(↗afternoon - walking - agg.; sudden - walking)* acon acon-f a1 adam srj5• aesc agar **Alum** **Alum-p** k2 alum-sil k2 am-c j5.de* ambr j5.de *Anac* ang a1 arg-met j5.de* arn **Ars** *Ars-i* asc-t a aur-ar k2 aur-m k2 aur-s k2 bar-c bar-i k2 bar-m bar-s k2 *Berb* bov brom **Bry** **Calc** **Cann-i** *Carb-ac* c1 *Carb-an* *Carb-v* *Carbn-s* caust h2 cench k2 cham chel *Chin* chinin-ar clem h2 coca cocc *Coloc* **Con** cupr *Cupr-ar* digin a1 dulc fd4.de ery-a a1 ery-m a1 euph euph-a a1 fago a1 **Ferr** k* ferr-ar ferr-i

- **agg.**: ...
ferr-ma *Fl-ac* franz a1 gins graph j5.de ham helon hep hyper ind indg *Iod* kali-ar k2 *Kali-c* kali-m k2 kali-p kali-s fd4.de kali-sil k2 *Lac-d* **Lach** led j5.de *Lyc* lyss a1 mag-c mag-m mag-s j5.de *Med* meny merc merl mez morph a1 **Mur-ac** narcin a1 *Nat-ar* *Nat-c* nat-hchls *Nat-m* nat-n a1* *Nat-s* nat-sil k2 nicot a1 **Nit-ac** nux-m nux-v j5.de pall petr **Ph-ac** **Phos** phys phyt **Pic-ac** *Plb* polyg-h **Psor** *Puls* puls-n ran-b j5.de* rheum rhod **Rhus-t** ruta sabin **Sep** *Sil* *Spig* k1 **Squil** stann *Staph* stram stront-c j5.de sul-i k2 **Sulph** sumb tarent tell thea j5.de thuj til tril-p tub k2 *Verat* wies a1 wildb a1 *Zinc* zinc-p k2
  - **menses**; during: *Murx* hr1* phel k*
  - **short** walk; a: bar-c a1 *Calc* hr1* cann-i hr1* *Con* hr1* sil a1
  - **smoking** agg.; after: (↗*smoking; tobacco*) sulph k*
  - **storm**, before and during a: sil k*
- **air**; in open:
  - **after** | **agg.**: alum ptk1 cocc ptk1 graph h2 ham fd3.de• rhus-t ptk1 sil h2 spong ptk1 symph fd3.de• tritic-vg fd5.de
  - **agg.**: act-sp agar **Alum** alumn kr1 *Am-c* ambr ang h1 arg-met ars-s-f k2 berb j5.de bry *Calc* calc-sil k2 carb-v caust chel chin j5.de *Cocc* k1 coff *Coll* coloc h2* *Con* euph h2* ferr graph grat j5.de ham fd3.de• hep hyos kali-bi kali-c kali-s fd4.de lact lyc h2* m-arct j5.de m-aust j5.de mag-c mag-m j5.de merc nat-m *Nux-v* ph-ac j5.de puls rhod **Rhus-t** sang sep *Sil* *Spig* sulph symph fd3.de• *Zinc*
  - **amel.**: agar am-c asar jl caust chinin-s j5.de croc j5.de *Fl-ac* gink-b sbd1• grat j5.de ignis-alc es2• *Kali-i* ox-ac sapin a1 *Sulph* tritic-vg fd5.de
- **amel.**: (↗*daytime - walking - amel.*) ambr h1 anac k* bry h1 calc h2* coloc k* ignis-alc es2• kali-i k2 merc k* nat-m k* **Rhus-t** k* *Ruta* k* **Sulph** k*
- **beginning** to walk: *Carb-v*
- **breakfast**; after | **amel.**: coca
- **cough** and expectoration, from: nux-v k*
- **dinner**, before: (↗*dinner - before*) hyper a1
- **eating** agg.; after: (↗*eating - after - agg.*) hep a1
- **house**, in the: agar k* ferr-ma k* sapin a1 sec k* sumb k*
- **rapidly**:
  - **agg.**: agar k* coc-c k* olnd k*
  - **amel.**: *Stann* k*
- **riding** agg.; after: (↗*riding - agg.*) petr k*
- **slowly** | **amel.**: *Ferr* k*

- **warm**:
  - **bathing**; after: aesc k2 lac-e hrn2• puls k2
  - **room** agg.: (↗*heat - room*) aloe ambr croc *Iod* kali-i k2 merl **Puls**
- **warm** from walking and rapidly becoming cold agg.; becoming: bry a1 *Rhus-t*
- **waves**; comes in (See increasing - decreasing)
- **weather**:
  - **cloudy**, damp; in: sang
  - **cold** agg.: apis lach
  - **warm** | **agg.**: aesc k2 **Ant-c** camph bg2 *Iod* lac-e hrn2• lach bg2 *Nat-ar* nat-c bg2 nat-m k* nat-p podo bg2 *Sel* k* **Sulph** k1 vip a1
- **whooping** cough: verat ptk1
- **widows**, in: con k2
- **wine**:
  - **agg.**: ars k1 lyc k1 phos k1 *Thuj* k1
  - **amel.**: ars a1 *Thuj* a1 visc jl
- **women**; in: alet ptk1 helon br1 mag-c br1
  - **exertion**; from: helon bro1
  - **obese**: am-c br1
- **worms**; with: carc mlr1• *Cic* hr1* *Cina* kr1 *Merc* hr1*
- **writing** agg.: cann-s ran-b k* sil
- **yawning**; after: eug k* *Nux-v* k*
- **young** people; in: ferr br1

○ - **Affected** parts: am b7a.de cham b7a.de chin b7a.de
- **Joints**: *Acon* k* aesc agar b2.de* agn b2.de* *Aloe* alum b2.de* am-c b2.de* anac b2.de* ang b2.de* *Ant-t* b2.de* *Arg-met* **Arn** k* ars asar b2.de* aur k* bar-c b2.de* bell b2.de* borx k* bov k* *Bry* k* **Calc** k* calc-p bg2* cann-s b2.de* canth b2.de* *Carb-an* k* carb-v k* carbn-s *Caust* k* cham chel *Chin* k* chinin-ar

Weakness – Joints: ...
cimic clem k* cocc b2.de* colch b2.de* coloc **Con** k* cupr b2.de* cycl b2.de* dig b2.de* dros b2.de* dulc b2.de* euph k* euph-l br1 *Ferr* k* ferr-ar ferr-p get br1 graph hep b2.de* hyos b2.de* ign b2.de* **Kali-c** k* kali-n b2.de* *Kali-s* kreos b2.de* *Lach* k* *Led* k* **Lyc** k* mang k* med ptk1 **Merc** k* merc-c k* mez k* morph mosch b2.de* murx *Nat-c* bg2 *Nat-m* k* *Nit-ac* k* nux-m b2.de* *Nux-v* k* olnd k* par b2.de* *Petr* k* *Ph-ac* b2.de* phor-t mie3• *Phos* k* plat b2.de* plb k* podo **Psor** k* *Puls* k* ran-b b2.de* raph rheum b2.de* rhod k* **Rhus-t** k* *Ruta* b2.de* sabad b2.de* sars b2.de* **Sep** k* *Sil* k* spong b2.de* stann b2.de* *Staph* k* *Stront-c* b2.de* sul-ac b2.de* **Sulph** k* symph fd3.de• tab bg tarax b2.de* thuj k* valer b2.de* *Verat* k* viol-o bg2 viol-t b2.de zinc b2.de* zing
  - **children**; in: abrot mtf11
  - **exertion** agg.: phos ptk1
  - **paralytic**: euph br1 euph-l br1
  - **spasms**; after: rheum ptk1
- **Muscular**: (↗*Complaints - muscles*) acet-ac bro1 acon b7.de* agar b4.de* *Agath-a* nl2• *Alet* bro1 alum b4.de* alumn k2* am-c b4.de* am-caust bro1 am-m b7.de* anac b4.de* anh br1* ant-c b7.de* *Ant-t* b7a.de* *Apis* b7a.de apoc vh1 arg-n bro1 arn bg2* ars b4.de* asaf b7.de* aur b4.de* **Bar-c** b4.de* bar-m hr1* bell b4.de* berb bg2 borx b4a.de both tsm2 both-ax tsm2 *Bov* b4a.de bry b7.de* bung-fa tsm2 *Calc* b4.de* *Camph* b7.de* cann-xyz bg2 canth b7.de* *Carb-ac* bg2 *Carb-v* b4.de* caust b4.de* cham b7.de* *Chin* b7.de* *Chlol* hr1* cimic ptk1 clem b4a.de cocc b7.de* colch b7.de* coll bro1 *Con* b4.de* cortico sp1 *Croc* b7.de* crot-c tsm2 crot-h tsm2 *Cupr* b7a.de dendr-pol tsm2 *Dig* b4.de* dioxi rbp6 dros b7.de* *Dulc* b4.de* elaps tsm2 euphr b7.de* *Ferr* b7.de* ferr-m hr1* ferr-p bg2 **Gels** bg2* germ-met srj5• graph b4.de* guaj b4a.de *Hell* br1* helon br1* hep br1* hydr br1* hyos b7.de* ign bro1 iod b4.de* ix bnm8• kali-bi bg2 kali-br hr1 kali-c b4.de* kali-hp bro1 kali-n b4.de* kali-p bg2* kalm bro1 kola stb3• laur b7.de* *Led* b7a.de lob bro1 *Luf-op* rsj5• *Lyc* b4.de* m-arct b7.de macro a1* mag-c b4.de* mag-m b4.de* mag-p bg2* mang bg2 meny b7.de* merc b4.de* **Merc-c** b4a.de mez b4.de* mur-ac b4a.de* naja tsm2 *Nat-c* b4.de* **Nat-m** b4.de* **Nit-ac** b4.de* *Nux-m* b7a.de nux-v b7.de* olnd b7.de* onos br1* *Op* hr1* pall br1* petr b4.de* ph-ac b4.de* phos b4.de* phys c1* physal-al br1* **Pic-ac** hr1* pip-m br1 *Plat* b4.de* *Plb* b7.de* plb-act bro1 puls b7.de* rad-br ptk1 rheum b7.de* *Rhod* b4.de* **Rhus-t** b7a.de* *Ruta* b7a.de sabad b7.de* sarcol-ac br1* sec b7.de* *Seneg* b4a.de senn br1 *Sep* b4.de* *Sil* b4.de* sin-n hr1* spartin-s bwa2 spig b7.de* stann b4.de* stram b7.de* stront-c b4.de* *Stry* bro1 stry-p br1 sul-ac b4a.de* *Sulph* b4.de* symph fd3.de• tab br1* ter hr1* thuj b4.de* thyr br1 *Verat* b7.de* verat-v bro1* zinc b4.de*
  - **accompanied** by:
    - **Eyes**; complaints of the (See EYE - Complaints - accompanied - weakness)
    - **Head**; complaints of the (See HEAD - Complaints - accompanied - weakness - muscles)
  - **children**; in: | **infants**: bell bg2 **Calc** bg2 caust bg2 *Sil* bg2 *Sulph* bg2
  - **fatigue**; from: am tl1 ferr-p tl1
  - **fever**; during: gels tl1
  - **growing** pains; from: ferr-p tl1
  - **paralytic**: *Alum* br1 *Alumn* k2*
  - **progressive**: caust br1
  - **prolonged** for months: lat-h bnm5•
- **Organs**; of: carl br1
  - **exertion** agg.; after: ferr-pic br1
- **Single** parts; in: valer ptk1

WEANING (See Ailments - weaning)

WEARINESS: (↗*Chronic fatigue; Flabby; Heaviness; Lassitude; Lie; Relaxation - physical; Weakness; MIND - Dullness; MIND - Ennui; MIND - Prostration*) *Acetan* vh1 acon k* adam srj5• adlu jl3 aesc agar k* *Agath-a* nl2• alet c1* aloe br1 **Alum** k* *Alum-p* k2 *Am-c* k* ambr k* *Anac* k* *Androc* srj1• ang b2.de* *Anh* mg1.de* *Ant-c* k* *Ant-t* k* aphis j5.de aran j5.de aran-ix mg1.de arg-met k* *Arg-n* arist-cl mg1.de* arizon-l nl2• *Arn* k* ars k* *Ars-i* asaf k* asar k* aur k* aur-ar k2 aur-m aur-s k2 *Bacls-7* fmm1• *Bamb-a* stb2.de• *Bapt* bar-c k* bar-m bar-ox-suc rly4• bell k* bell-p c2* **Benz-ac** berb beryl sp1 *Bism* k* *Bit-ar* wht1• *Blatta-a* br1 borx h2* bov k* brass-n-o srj5• *Brom* b4a.de bros-gau mrc1 bruc j5.de *Bry* k* cadm-met mg1.de* cain c2 calad j5.de calam sa3• *Calc* b2.de* calc-f sp1 **Calc-p** *Calc-sil* k2 camph k* **Cann-s** k* cann-xyz ptk1 canth k* caps k* *Carb-ac* carb-an k* *Carb-v* k* **Carbn-s** carc mg1.de* cartl-s rly4• *Castm* br1 *Caust* k*

Weariness: ...
cecr jl3 cench k2 cham k* **Chel** k* chin k* *Chinin-ar* br1 chir-fl gya2 choc srj3• chord-umb rly4• cic k* cimic cimx cina k* cist j5.de clem k* cob br1 cob-n mg1.de* *Coc-c* coca-c sk4• cocc k* coff k* colch k* coli jl2 coloc k* *Con* k* conch fkr1• cordyc mp4• corian-s knl6• cortico sp1 cortiso sp1 **Croc** k* *Crot-c* *Cupr* cycl k* cystein-l rly4• dam c2 dicha mg1.de dig k* dioxi rbp6 diphtox jl2 dros k* dulc k* dys fmm1• enteroc jl2 ephe-si hsj1• erig mg1.de esp-g mg1.de* euph k* euphr k* **Ferr** k* ferr-ma j5.de ferr-p **Ferr-pic** c2 fic-m gya1 flor-p rsj3• gaba sa3• gard-j vlr2• **Gels** k* ger-i rly4• germ-met srj5• gink-b sbd1• gran j5.de **Graph** k* grat j5.de guaj j5.de guat sp1 *Ham* harp jl3 hecla jl hed mg1.de* hell k* helon k* *Hep* k* hist mg1.de* *Hydrog* srj2• *Hyos* k* ign k* ina-i mlk9.de influ jl2* interf sa3• iod j5.de *Ip* k* kali-bi bg2* kali-c k* kali-chl j5.de *Kali-m* k2 kali-n k* **Kali-p** kali-s kali-sil k2 kalm k2 ketogl-ac rly4• kola stb3• *Kreos* k* lac-ac *Lac-e* hrn2• lac-h sk4• lac-loxod-a hrn2• **Lach** k* lact j5.de lap-la sde8.de• *Laur* k* lavand-a ctl1• **Lec** k* led k* luf-op mg1.de* **Lyc** k* m-ambo b2.de* m-arct b2.de* m-aust j5.de *Mag-c* k* mag-f mg1.de mag-m k* malar jl2 mand mg1.de* mang k* med jl2* melal-alt gya4 meny k* meph j5.de* **Merc** k* mez k* *Moni* rfm1• mosch k* *Mur-ac* k* murx j5.de naja jl *Nat-c* k* **Nat-m** k* *Nat-s* nat-sil k2 neon srj5• nep mg1.de nicotam rly4• nit-ac k* *Nux-m* k* **Nux-v** k* oci-sa sk4• ol-an j5.de *Olib-sac* wmh1 olnd k* onos br1 op k* oxal-a rly4• ozone sde2• pant-ac rly4• *Par* k* *Parathyr* jl2 *Petr* k* petr-ra shn4• **Ph-ac** k* phenob srb2.fr **Phos** k* phys c1 phyt bg2 **Pic-ac** *Pieri-b* mlk9.de plac rzf5• plac-s rly4• *Plat* k* plb k* plut-n srj7• polys sk4• positr nl2• pot-e rly4• propl ub1• propr sa3• prot fmm1• prun j5.de *Psil* jl* *Psor* k* **Puls** k* *Pycnop-sa* mrz1 pyrog jl2 ran-b k* rauw sp1 *Rheum* k* *Rhod* k* *Rhus-t* k* rib-ac jl3 ribo rly4• *Ros-d* wla1 **Ruta** k* sabad k* sabin k* samb k* sang a1 saroth sp1 sars k* sec k* senec seneg k* **Sep** k* sieg mg1.de **Sil** k* sinus rly4• spig k* spong k* squil k* *Stann* k* **Staph** k* *Stram* k* stront-c k* suis-em rly4• *Sul-ac* k* sulfa sp1 **Sulph** k* sumb suprar rly4• syc fmm1• *Tab* teucr k* ther j5.de thioc-ac rly4• thiop jl3 thuj k* trinit br1 tritic-vg fd5.de **Tub** tub-r jl2 tub-sp jl2 uncar-tom mp4• *Urol-h* rwt• v-a-b jl2* valer k* vanil fd5.de vario jl2 *Verat* k* verb k* vero-o rly3• viol-o k* *Viol-t* b7a.de visc sp1 x-ray sp1 **Zinc** k* zinc-p k2 [bell-p-sp dcm1 heroin sdj2 spect dfg1 tax jsj7]

- **daytime**: olib-sac wmh1
- **morning**: alum j5.de am-c ambr ant-c j5.de *Ars* aur j5.de bamb-a stb2.de• bar-c j5.de bell j5.de bov j5.de brucel sa3• *Bry* k* calad caps h1* carb-an j5.de *Carb-v* k* carbn-s carc fb carneg-g rwt1• castm sf1.de caust j5.de *Cham* k* chel j5.de* chin j5.de clem a1 cob-n mg1.de* con j5.de cortiso sp1 croc j5.de cycl a1 cystein-l rly4• dig a1 digin a1 *Dioxi* rbp6 dros h1* dulc fd4.de erig mg1.de euphr a1 ferr j5.de hep h2* hydrog srj2• ina-i mlk9.de kali-c j5.de *Kali-chl* kali-p fd1.de• kali-s fd4.de kola stb3• lac-ac **Lach** lact j5.de lap-la sde8.de• lyc h2* m-aust j5.de *Mag-c* k* mag-m malar jl2 meph jl3 merc-c a1 merl a1 mur-ac h2* *Nat-m* k* nat-sil fd3.de• **Nux-v** k* olib-sac wmh1 ox-ac a1 peti a1 petr k* petr-ra shn4• phos h2* propl ub1• propr sa3• prun j5.de* puls j5.de rat a1 rhus-t j5.de sabad j5.de **Sep** k* sil h2* spig j5.de* spong fd4.de stann j5.de staph k* stront-c j5.de stry a1 sul-i k2* *Sulph* k* teucr j5.de* ther j5.de thuj h1* tritic-vg fd5.de tub al *Urol-h* rwt• valer j5.de vanil fd5.de zinc
  - **8** h: carc fb
  - **9**-10 h: coca-c sk4•
  - **bed** agg.; in: petr h2
  - **rising** agg.: atra-r bnm3• bov j5.de *Brucel* sa3• carbn a1 caust h2* colch a1 dig a1 dulc fd4.de ferr j5.de gran a1 hep h2* kali-s fd4.de *Lyc* h2* mez a1 nat-sil fd3.de• nux-v h1* puls j5.de rat a1 spong fd4.de stann j5.de teucr j5.de* thuj h1* tritic-vg fd5.de
  - **sleep**; from poor: cob-n sp1
  - **waking**; on: alum j5.de am-c j5.de ambr j5.de ant-c j5.de aur j5.de bar-c j5.de bell j5.de bism j5.de *Bry* j5.de *Calc* j5.de cann-s j5.de *Carb-an* j5.de *Caust* j5.de chel j5.de chin j5.de cob-n sp1 coca-c sk4• *Con* j5.de cycl j5.de cyclosp sa3• cystein-l rly4• dros j5.de dulc j5.de gink-b sbd1• hep j5.de hydrog srj2• kali-c j5.de kali-p fd1.de• lact j5.de *Lyc* j5.de m-aust j5.de *Mag-m* j5.de med al *Nat-m* j5.de *Nux-v* j5.de petr-ra shn4• phos j5.de positr nl2• prun j5.de rhus-t j5.de sabad j5.de sep j5.de spig j5.de staph j5.de stront-c j5.de teucr j5.de ther j5.de *Thuj* j5.de tritic-vg fd5.de valer j5.de vanil fd5.de *Zinc* j5.de
- **forenoon**: am-c j5.de bamb-a stb2.de• dulc fd4.de erig mg1.de esp-g jl3* graph h2* hell j5.de* hydrog srj2• indg a1 kali-s fd4.de lact a1 mag-m j5.de* moni rfm1• nat-s j5.de olib-sac wmh1 phel j5.de* propl ub1• ruta fd4.de sars a1 seneg j5.de spong fd4.de vanil fd5.de
- **noon**: calc a1 caust h2* conch fkr1* digin a1 dulc fd4.de esp-g jl3* ham fd3.de• kali-s fd4.de nat-sil fd3.de• olib-sac wmh1 ox-ac a1 podo fd3.de• ruta fd4.de sacch-a fd2.de• spong fd4.de tritic-vg fd5.de vanil fd5.de
- **afternoon**: adlu jl3 *Agath-a* nl2• am-c j5.de amp rly4• arizon-l nl2• bamb-a stb2.de• *Bry* a1 carc fd2.de• carneg-g rwt1• chel a1 coc-c a1 conch fkr1* digin a1 dioxi rbp6 dulc fd4.de fago a1 gard-j vlr2• gink-b sbd1• hydrog srj2• iod j5.de kali-c h2* kali-s fd4.de* kola stb3• lac-loxod-a hrn2• lac-lup hrn2• lyc a1 mag-c j5.de mag-m j5.de* merl a1 mez a1 nat-c j5.de nat-s a1 nat-sil fd3.de• nux-v h1* ol-an j5.de olib-sac wmh1 ozone sde2• phos j5.de plect a1 ptel a1 rat a1 ros-d wla1 ruta fd4.de sang a1 spong fd4.de staph j5.de* stry a1 thuj j5.de* tritic-vg fd5.de urol-h rwt• vanil fd5.de vip fkr4.de [heroin sdj2]
  - **14**-16 h: bamb-a stb2.de• fic-m gya1 ozone sde2•
  - **14**-21 h: coca-c sk4•
  - **16** h: *Dioxi* rbp6 mang a1
  - **16**.30-19.30 h: androc srj1•
  - **16**-20 h: carneg-g rwt1• ozone sde2•
  - **17** h: rosm lgb1
  - **amel.**: ham fd3.de• kali-c jl ketogl-ac rly4• propr sa3•
- **evening**: androc srj1• bamb-a stb2.de• berb bov a1 carb-v k* caust h2* choc srj3• coc-c a1 cor-r a1 *Croc* a1 cycl a1 dioxi rbp6 dulc fd4.de euphr a1 gink-b sbd1• graph h2* hydr-ac a1 hydrog srj2• ign jac-c a1 kali-bi a1 kali-c a1 kali-n a1 kali-s fd4.de kalm a1 lach a1 lap-la rsp1 laur a1 lyc a1 mang-p rly4• meph jl3 *Merc* h1* merc-c a1 merl a1 methys jl3 mez a1 *Mur-ac* murx a1 nat-sil fd3.de• nit-ac h2* olib-sac wmh1 ox-ac a1 ozone sde2• pall petr h2* psil ft1 ruta fd4.de sabad a1 sacch-a fd2.de• spong fd4.de *Sulph* k* sumb a1 thuj a1 tritic-vg fd5.de tub mtf33 vanil fd5.de visc c1
  - **18** h: androc srj1• carc fd2.de• sacch-a fd2.de•
  - **20** h: mang a1
  - **20**-21 h: lac-loxod-a hrn2•
  - **21** h: trios rsj11•
  - **air** agg.; in open: *Carb-v*
  - **amel.**: conch fkr1• hydrog srj2• propr sa3• spong fd4.de
- **night**: bit-ar wht1• dulc j5.de kreos j5.de merc j5.de olib-sac wmh1 sabad j5.de sabin j5.de
- **agg.**: act-sp ptk1 aml-ns bg2 apis bg2 arg-met bg2 arg-n bg2 arn b7a.de* ars b4.de* berb ptk1 bry bg2 cann-s b7a.de* chin b7a.de* cocc bg2 *Coff* b7a.de* cupr bg2 epiph bg2* *Ferr* bg2 ham bg2 helon ptk1 nat-m bg2 nux-v b7.de* ph-ac ptk1 **Rhus-t** b7a.de* sul-ac bg2 thuj bg2 verat b7a.de*
- **air**; in open | **amel.**: androc srj1• galeoc-c-h gms1• hed mg1.de*
- **alcoholic** drinks; from: olib-sac wmh1
- **ascending** stairs, from: blatta-a br1 calc-p c1 sul-i k2 symph fd3.de• vanil fd5.de
- **bed**; when going to: bapt a1
- **born** tired; as if: kola stb3• onos br1
- **chill**; during: choc srj3• propr sa3•
- **chronic**: lyc tl1 v-a-b jl2
- **coition**; after: *Agar* b4.de* calc b4.de* *Con* b4a.de kali-c b4.de* lyc b4.de* mez b4a.de nit-ac b4.de* petr b4a.de sel b7.de*
- **conversation**, from: ambr
- **coryza**; during: *Ars* b4a.de calc b4a.de **Gels** bg2 graph b4.de* sep b4.de*
- **diarrhea** agg.; after: sul-i k2
- **eating**:
  - **after**:
    - **agg.**: androc srj1• ant-c *Ars* bamb-a stb2.de• *Bar-c* *Calc-p* hr1 cann-s a1* *Carb-an* card-m chin k* *Croc* a1 cycl a1 haliae-lc srj5• hydrog srj2• hyos a1 indg a1 kali-c k* kali-p fd1.de• kali-s fd4.de *Lach* lap-la sde8.de• laur a1 **Lyc** hr1 mur-ac *Nat-m* k* nat-sil fd3.de• *Nux-m* ox-ac a1 ozone sde2• podo fd3.de• positr nl2• pycnop-sa mrz1 *Rhus-t* ruta sacch-a fd2.de• sang staph a1 symph fd3.de• tritic-vg fd5.de vanil fd5.de
    - **amel.**: androc srj1•
  - **while** | **agg.**: *Kali-c* k*
- **exertion**:
  - **agg.**: bar-c ptk1
  - **amel.**: bit-ar wht1• brass-n-o srj5• ham fd3.de• hed sp1 podo fd3.de• tung-met bdx1•
- **leukorrhea**:
  - **after**: con j5.de
  - **with**: prun j5.de
- **menopause**; during: bell-p bro1 calc bro1

- **menses**:
  - **after** | **agg.**: alumn hr1* bell hr1* carb-an hr1* cub hr1* nat-m hr1* nux-v sf1.de phos sf1.de plat hr1* thuj
  - **before** | **agg.**: alum amp rly4• *Bell* carb-an a1 gink-b sbd1• *Nat-m*
  - **during**:
    - **agg.**: *Am-c* androc srj1• bit-ar wht1• borx calc-p carb-an a1 *Caust* k* ign iod kali-c mag-c *Nit-ac Nux-m Petr* petr-ra shn4• sars a1 sul-i k2* thuj vanil fd5.de
    - **amel.**: hed sp1
- **mental** exertion agg.: (↗*MIND - Mental exertion - agg. - fatigues)* alum androc srj1• *Aur* dulc fd4.de kali-p fd1.de• *Lach* **Lec** k* petr-ra shn4• **Pic-ac** k* *Puls* ruta fd4.de *Thuj*
- **music** agg.: lyc c1*
- **old** people; in: bar-c br1
- **periodical** | **winter** at spring; about end of: *Brucel* sa3•
- **playing** piano; from: (↗*Playing)* anac k*
- **reading** agg.: *Aur* ham fd3.de• kali-p fd1.de• kali-s fd4.de podo fd3.de•
- **rest** agg.: dulc fd4.de psil ft1
- **sexual** excitement, from: sars sf1.de
- **sit** down, desire to: dulc j5.de kali-p fd1.de• stann j5.de sulph j5.de
- **sitting** agg.: bry j5.de chin j5.de dulc fd4.de hydrog srj2• led j5.de mag-c j5.de *Merc* ol-an j5.de plat j5.de plb j5.de rhus-t j5.de symph fd3.de• tritic-vg fd5.de vanil fd5.de
- **sleep** agg.; during: bufo bg2
- **standing**:
  - **agg.**: androc srj1• led j5.de *Mur-ac* nat-m j5.de plat j5.de
  - **amel.**: androc srj1•
- **stool**:
  - **after** | **agg.**: ambr a1 *Calc* b4.de* carb-v b4a.de caust bg2 mag-m bg2 merc b4.de* *Nit-ac* b4a.de phos b4a.de
- **sudden**: olib-sac wmh1 trios rsj11•
- **talking**; after: **Alum** *Calc-p* dulc fd4.de kali-p fd1.de• lap-la rsp1 med pc *Sulph*
  - **much** talking: calc h2
- **uncontrollable**: kola stb3•
- **waking**; on: alum j5.de am-c j5.de ambr j5.de ange-s jl3 ant-c j5.de aur j5.de bar-c j5.de bell j5.de bism j5.de bov j5.de bros-gau mrc1 *Bry* h1* *Calc* j5.de cann-s j5.de *Carb-an* j5.de cameg-g rwt1• *Caust* j5.de chel j5.de* chir-fl gya2 *Con* j5.de *Cycl* j5.de* dros j5.de dulc j5.de ferr j5.de hydrog srj2• hyper a1 lact j5.de *Lyc* j5.de m-aust j5.de *Mag-m* j5.de *Nat-m* j5.de prun j5.de rib-ac jl3 sacch-a fd2.de• sep j5.de sol-t-ae a1 spig j5.de sumb a1 tep a1 teucr j5.de *Thuj* j5.de tritic-vg fd5.de valer j5.de vanil fd5.de *Zinc* j5.de
  - **amel.**: thiop jl
- **walking**:
  - **after**:
    - **agg.**: agar j5.de alum j5.de anac jl3 calc-s a1 carb-an j5.de caust j5.de* clem j5.de coff j5.de con j5.de cupr a1 graph j5.de ham fd3.de• iod j5.de kiss a1 *Lac-d* k2* malar jl2 *Mur-ac* nux-v j5.de ph-ac j5.de plat j5.de psil ft1 sabad j5.de sabin j5.de sol-t-ae a1 stann a1 sul-i k2* valer j5.de vanil fd5.de
      - **pregnancy**; in: *Calen* st
  - **agg.**: am-c mrr1 bry j5.de chin j5.de con j5.de ferr j5.de lach j5.de led j5.de mag-c j5.de mag-m j5.de plb j5.de sacch-a fd2.de• stram j5.de
  - **air**; in open:
    - **agg.**: alum j5.de coff j5.de ferr j5.de ham fd3.de• m-arct j5.de mag-c j5.de nat-m j5.de rhod j5.de sacch-a fd2.de• sep j5.de sulph j5.de
    - **amel.**: caust j5.de croc j5.de gink-b sbd1• ham fd3.de• rhus-t a1 ruta j5.de sul-ac j5.de
  - **amel.**: ambr h1
- **weather**:
  - **change** of weather: bamb-a stb2.de•
  - **stormy** weather; during: bamb-a stb2.de•
  - **wet** | **agg.**: bamb-a stb2.de• dulc fd4.de
- **women**; in: | **obese**: am-c br1

WEATHER:

- **bright** (See clear)
- **change** of weather:
  - **agg.**: abrot achy jl acon k2 agar ptk1 alum bg2* alumn *Am-c* b2.de* anh jl ant-c *Ant-t* apis aran bg2* ars k* asar jl bar-c bg2* *Bell* benz-ac k* borx k*

Weather – change of weather – **agg.**: ...
brom *Brucel* sa3• **Bry** b2.de* *Calc* k* calc-f k2* *Calc-p* k* calc-sil k2 carb-v c1* carbn-s *Caust Cham* a1* *Chel* k* chin bro1* cimic hr1 cinnb k2 colch k* con gk crot-c st crot-h bg2* cupr bg2* cur st *Dig* k* **DULC** b2.de* euph k* galph jl *Gels* k* *Graph* b2.de* harp jl *Hep* bg2* hyper k* *Ip* k2* kali-ar jsa kali-bi *Kali-c* k* kali-i bg2* kali-s mrr1 *Kalm* kr1* lach k* lept c1 mag-c bg2* mand jl *Mang* k* mang-act bro1 med jl2 meli *Merc* b2.de* merc-i-f c1 merc-i-r c1 *Mez* k* mosch st *Nat-c* k* nat-m k2* nat-p k2 nat-s a nat-sil k2 nit-ac k* **Nux-m** k* nux-v k* olnd mrr1 oscilloc jl2 *Petr* k* *Ph-ac* **Phos** k* phys bg2* phyt st **Psor** k* *Puls* k* **Ran-b** k* *Rheum* b2.de* **Rhod** k* **RHUS-T** b2.de* *Rumx* k* ruta bro1* sabin ptk1 sang bg2* sep k* **Sil** k* spig bg2* stann k2* stict bro1* stront-c k* sul-i ptk1 *Sulph* k* tarent bro1* *Teucr* bg2 thuj bg2* **Tub** k* *Verat* b2.de* verb ptk1 *Vip* bg2*
- **amel.**; and: mang ptk1
- **Bones**: am-c ptk1

  - **amel.**: bac jl2 onop jl
  - **cold** to warm agg.: ant-c bg2* brom k2 **Bry** k* carb-v *Chel* crot-h bg2* *Ferr* gels k* **Kali-s** *Lach Lyc* nat-c bg2* *Nat-m Nat-s* nux-v bg2* **Psor** *Puls* sep bg2* **Sulph Tub**
  - **desires** change of weather, which amel.: mang ptk1 sep ptk1 tub ptk1
  - **dry** to wet: *Nat-s* br1
  - **rapid** change agg.: sep ptk1
  - **spring** agg.: all-c bro1 ant-t bro1 gels bro1 kali-s bro1 nat-s bro1
  - **warm**:
    - **cold** agg.; to: acon bg2 *Ars* bg2* calc k2 calc-p k2 calc-sil k2 carb-v bg2* *Caust* bg2* **Dulc** bg2* hep k2 **Merc** kl nat-sil k2 nit-ac k2 *Nux-v* bg2* puls bg2* *Ran-b* bg2* *Rhus-t* kl sabad bg2* *Sil* bg2* stront-c bg2* tub k2 **Verat** kl
    - **wet** agg.; to: gels c1
- **clear** weather agg.: acon aloe st asar *Bry* k* *Caust Hep Nux-v* plb k* sabad spong
- **cloudy** weather:
  - **agg.**: aloe bg1* am-c k* ammc bg1 ant-t k2 aran bg2 arn ptk1 ars bg2 ars-i ptk1 aur ptk1* bar-c bg2* *Ben-n* bg1* bry calc calen bg2* *Cham* k* *Chin* k* dulc gels bg2 hydrog srj2*• hyper bg2* lac-ac stj5• lach k2* *Mang* k* merc k* naja bg2 *Nat-c* bg1* nat-m bg2 nat-s bg2* nitrob vh *Nux-m* k* *Physal-al* bg1* plb k* *Puls* k* rhod **Rhus-t** k* sabal ptk1 sabin ptk1 sang bg1 *Sep* k* stram ptk1 sulph k* tub ser verat viol-o ptk1 [astat stj2 aur-s stj2 bism-sn stj2 cinnb stj2 irid-met stj2 merc-d stj2 plat stj2 plb-m stj2 plb-p stj2 polon-met stj2 spect dfg1 thal-met stj2 tung-met stj2]
  - **amel.**: *Bry* b7a.de* caust bg2* kalm ptk1 lappa ptk1
  - **sun** peeks through the clouds; when the | **agg.**: sulph mrr1
- **cold** weather:
  - **agg.** (See Cold - air - agg.)
  - **amel.** (See Cold - air - amel.)
  - **dry**:
    - **agg.**: **Acon** k* agar bro1 alum b2.de* alumn kr1 am-c j5.de apis tl1 apoc bro1 *Ars* k* ars-i ptk1 **Asar** k* aur bro1 bell k* borx k* *Bry* k* calc j5.de* calc-i k2 calc-p k2* *Camph* j5.de caps j5.de carb-an k* carb-v k* **Caust** k* cham k* coc-c k2 cocc j5.de coff k2 *Crot-h* daph j5.de dulc j5.de* ferr-ar k2 fl-ac bg2 **Hep** k* hydrog srj2• *Ip* k* kali-ar ptk1 **Kali-c** k* *Kali-sil* k2 kreos bro1 lach j5.de lappa bg2 laur k* lyc j5.de mag-c k* med ptk1* mez k* mur-ac k* nat-s bg2 nit-ac j5.de* nit-s-d bro1 nux-m j5.de* **Nux-v** k* *Petr* bro1 ph-ac j5.de phos j5.de* phys bg2 physal-al bg2 phyt k2 plat bg2 plb bg2 *Psor* k2 *Puls* bg2 rhod k* rhus-t j5.de* ruta fd4.de *Sabad* k* samb ptk1 sep k* *Sil* k* spig k* *Spong* k* staph k* sulph k* *Verat* kr1 visc bro1 zinc k*
    - **amel.**: carc fb* led bg2* *Puls* mrr1 sil k2
  - **wet**:
    - **agg.**: abies-c oss4• abrot k2* *Acon* tl1 aesc k2 *Agar* k* all-c bg2* all-s k* aloe sne **Am-c** k* *Ant-c* k* *Ant-t* bg2* *Apis Aran* k* *Arg-met* k* *Arg-n* arn bro1 **Ars** k* ars-i ars-s-f k2 asc-t k* *Aster* k* aur k* aur-ar k2 *Aur-m-n* **Bad** *Bar-c* k* bar-i k2 bar-s k2 bell k* bell-p tl1* blatta-o sf1.de borx b2.de* bov k* bry k* **Calc** k* calc-i k2 **Calc-p** k* calc-s calc-sil k2 *Calen* st (non:canth b2.de*) *Caps* bg2* carb-an k* *Carb-v* k* *Carbn-s* cean vml3• cham k* chin k* choc srj3• *Cimic* bg2* clem k* **Colch** k* coloc bg2 con k* cupr k* **Dulc** k* elaps bg2* erig sf1.de eucal bg2* *Ferr* k* *Fl-ac* k* *Form* k* *Gels* k* glon bg2 *Graph Guaj* bro1 hep k* *Hyper* k* *Iod* k* ip k* *Kali-bi* k*

- **wet – agg.**: ...
  kali-c k* kali-i k* kali-m k2 kali-n k* kali-p kali-sil k2 *Lach* k* *Lath* k* laur k* lept bg2* *Lyc* k* mag-c k* mag-p k2 *Mang* k* mang-act bro1* **Med** k* *Merc* k* merc-c bg2 merc-i-f k* *Mez* k* mur-ac k* naja jl *Nat-ar* *Nat-c* k* nat-m bg2* **Nat-s** k* *Nit-ac* k* **Nux-m** k* nux-v k* onop jl paeon penic jl* *Petr* k* phos k* physal-al bro1 *Phyt* k* polyg-h st psil ft1* psor k2 *Puls* k* **Pyrog** k* *Ran-b* k* **Rhod** k* **Rhus-t** k* rumx bg2* *Ruta* k* sang k2 sars k* seneg k* sep k* ser-a-c jl2 **Sil** k* *Spig* k* stann k* staph k* *Still* bg2* *Stront-c* k* *Sul-ac* k* *Sulph* k* *Tarent* teucr bg2 *Thuj* k* **Tub** k* ulm-c jsj8• urt-u bro1 *Verat* k* zinc k* zinc-p k2 *Zing* sf1.de [mang-m stj2 mang-met stj2 uva stj]
  - **old** people; in: ammc c1
  - **amel.**: aur-m k2 kali-s fd4.de
- **dry**:
  - **agg.**: *Acon* b2.de* alum k* alumn kr1 ars k* **Asar** k* aur-m gm1* *Bell* b2.de* borx b2.de* *Bry* k* carb-an k* carb-v k* **Caust** k* *Cham* b2.de* coc-c k2 coff k2 *Fl-ac* vh **Hep** k* *Ip* b2.de* *Kali-c* kali-sil k2 *Laur* b2.de* mag-c b2.de* *Mang* vh *Med* br1* *Merc* vh* mez b2.de* *Mur-ac* b2.de* *Nit-ac* vh nux-m k2 **Nux-v** k* phor-t mie3• phos *Plat* vh* *Rhod* b2.de* sabad k* *Sep* k* sil k* *Spig* b2.de* spong k* staph k* sulph k* zinc k* [alumin stj2 alumin-p stj2 alumin-s stj2 astat stj2 aur stj2 aur-s stj2 bar-br stj2 bar-i stj2 bar-met stj2 bism-sn stj2 caes-met stj2 cinnb stj2 hafn-met stj2 irid-met stj2 lanth-met stj2 merc-d stj2 merc-i-f stj2 osm-met stj2 plb stj2 plb-m stj2 plb-p stj2 polon-met stj2 rhen-met stj2 tant-met stj2 thal-met stj2 tung-met stj2]
  - **amel.**: agar b2.de* *Am-c* b2.de* *Ant-c* b2.de* *Aur* b2.de* bar-c b2.de* bell b2.de* *Borx* b2.de* bov b2.de* bry b2.de* **Calc** b2.de* canth b2.de* *Carb-an* b2.de* *Carb-v* b2.de* card-m vml3• cham b2.de* *Chin* b2.de* choc srj3• *Clem* b2.de* con b2.de* *Cupr* b2.de* **Dulc** b2.de* *Ferr* b2.de* hep b2.de* ip b2.de* kali-c b2.de* *Kali-n* b2.de* *Lach* b2.de* *Laur* b2.de* *Lyc* b2.de* *Mag-c* b2.de* magn-gr bro1 *Mang* b2.de* *Merc* b2.de* merc-c kr1 mez b2.de* moly-met jl *Mur-ac* b2.de* *Nat-c* b2.de* *Nit-ac* b2.de* **Nux-m** b2.de* nux-v b2.de* petr b2.de* phos b2.de* *Puls* b2.de* *Rhod* b2.de* **Rhus-t** b2.de* *Ruta* b2.de* *Sars* b2.de* *Seneg* b2.de* sep b2.de* sil b2.de* *Spig* b2.de* stann b2.de* *Staph* b2.de* still bro1 *Stront-c* b2.de* *Sul-ac* b2.de* *Sulph* b2.de* tub mrr1 *Verat* b2.de* *Zinc* b2.de*
- **dull**, not clear weather | **amel.**: *Bry* b2.de plb b2.de
- **foggy** weather | **agg.**: abrot sf1.de aloe bg2 *Aran* bg2* ars bg2 bapt bro1 bar-c sf1.de bry k* calc b2.de* calen bg2 cham k* chin k* dulc b2.de* *Gels* bg2* **Hyper** k* mang k* merc b2.de* mosch naja bg2 nat-m bg2 *Nat-s* bg2* nux-m k* plb k* *Rhod* k* **Rhus-t** k* sep k* *Sil* k* *Staph* vh sulph k* *Thuj* bg2* verat k* [ant-t stj2 germ-met stj2 mang-act stj2 mang-m stj2 mang-met stj2]
- **frosty** weather (= hoarfrost):
  - **agg.**: *Agar* bg2* *Calc* bg1* carb-v bg2 caust bg1* *Con* bg1* hydrog srj2*• kali-c bg2 *Lac-ac* stj5• lyc bg1* mag-m bg1* merc bg1* nat-c bg1* nux-m bg2 nux-v bg1* ph-ac bg1* phos bg2* *Puls* bg1* rhus-t bg1* *Sep* bg2* sil bg1* spong bg2 sulph bg1* syph bg2* [neon stj2]
- **hot**:
  - **agg.**: *Acon* k2* aeth k2* aloe bro1* *Ant-c* bg2* ant-t sf1.de *Apis* sf1.de aq-mar vml3• bapt sf1.de *Bell* bro1 borx bro1 both-ax tsm2 brom k2 *Bry* bg2* *Carb-v* bg2 cocc bg2 croc bro1 *Crot-h* bro1* crot-t bro1 *Cupr* sf1.de dulc fd4.de *Gels* bro1 *Glon* bro1 kali-bi c1* lach bg2* *Nat-c* bro1 *Nat-m* bro1 nat-s k2 nat-sil fd3.de• nit-ac bro1 *Op* sf1.de phos bg2* pic-ac bro1 *Podo* bro1 *Puls* bg2* sabin bro1 sel bg2* syph bro1 thuj sne [lith-s stj2 neon stj2]
    - **cold** night; and: acon ptk1 dulc ptk1 merc ptk1 rumx ptk1
- **humid** (See wet)
- **rainy**:
  - **agg.**: aran bg2* ars mtf bros-gau mrc1 dulc mtf elaps bg2 erig bg2 glon bg2 ham bg2 lac-c bg2 lach k2* lem-m br1 mag-c bg2 mang bg2 merc br1 nat-s k2* oci-sa jl phyt bg2 plat ptk1 ran-b bg2* *Rhus-t* kl sabin bg2 senn bg2 sil mtf *Sulph* vh tub k2*
    - **heavy** rains; especially: dulc fd4.de lem-m c1*
  - **amel.**: **Caust** mrr1 ign mrr1 [heroin sdj2]
  - **before**: phos zf
- **snow** agg.; melting: *(↗Snowy; Snowy - agg.)* **Calc-p** a1* kali-bi gsd1
- **storm** (See thunderstorm; windy)
- **stormy** weather (See thunderstorm; windy)
- **sultry** | **agg.**: aloe bg2 carb-v bg2 gels bg2 ham bg2 mang bg2 nat-m bg2 *Rhus-t* b7a.de sabad bg2 sep bg2
- **thunderstorm** (= storm):
  - **after**: asar jl calc-p bg1* carc st1* crot-h c1 gels c1 morph c1 nat-c c1 nat-p c1* nit-s-d c1 phos c1 psor c1 puls c1 rhod c1 rhus-r sf1.de rhus-t bg2* sep bg2* syph c1 tub k2
  - **agg.**: agar k* aran bg1 arg-met sf1.de aur *Brucel* sa3• *Bry* k* calc st carb-v caust k* chinin-ar k2 conv bg1 elaps bg1* erig bg1 *Gels* k* glon bg1 ham bg1 hydr-ac ptk1 *Lach* k* mag-c bg1 mand jl mang bg1 *Med* k* meli bro1 mez k2 morph kr1* **Nat-c** k* nat-m k* nat-p k* nat-s hr nat-sil fd3.de• nit-ac k* nit-s-d c1 petr k* *Phos* k* phyt bg1* prot jl psor k* puls kr1* ran-b bg1* *Rhod* k* rhus-t sf1.de* sabin bg1 *Sep* k* *Sil* k* spig sf1.de syph k* thuj tub k2* [alumin-p stj2 arg-p stj2 bor-pur stj2 calc-p stj1 cupr-p stj2 kali-p stj1 lith-p stj2 mag-p stj1 mang-p stj2 ph-ac stj1 plb-p stj2 zinc-p stj2]
  - **amel.**: *(↗MIND - Cheerful - thunders)* carc jl2* psor vh rhus-t ptk1 *Sep* bg2* [beryl stj2]
  - **approach** of a: *Agar* k* arg-met bg2 aur *Bell-p* bro1 berb bg1 bry k* calc k2 calc-f bg1 carc gk6 caust k* *Cedr* k* con gk dulc bg2* falco-pe nl2• *Gels* k* hep bg2* hyper k* *Kali-bi* *Lach* k* *Lyc* mag-p bg2 mand mg1.de mang bg2* med k* meli k* *Nat-c* k* nat-m k* nat-p *Nat-s* bro1 nat-sil fd3.de• nit-ac petr k* *Phos* k* phyt bro1 **Psor** k* puls *Ran-b* **Rhod** k* *Rhus-t* k* *Sep* k* sil k* sul-ac bg1 sulph k* syph thuj *Tub* k* zinc bg2*
    - **amel.**: carc mlr1•
  - **enjoying** (See MIND - Weather - thunderstorm - loves)
  - **lightning**; ailments from: crot-h c1* falco-pe nl2• morph c1 phos c1 rad-br c11
    - **amel.**: [beryl stj2]
- **warm** weather:
  - **agg.** (See Warm - air - agg.)
  - **amel.** (See Warm - air - amel.)
  - **dry**:
    - **agg.**: ant-c c1* carb-v sf1.de cocc sf1.de kali-bi c1 lach c1* tritic-vg fd5.de vanil fd5.de
    - **amel.**: alum bro1 *Calc-p* bro1 choc srj3• *Nat-s* br1* nux-m bg2* penic jl* rhus-t bg2* *Sulph* bg2* tub mrr1
  - **wet**:
    - **agg.●**: *Aloe* bg2* aran-ix mg1.de aur sne bapt bro1 bell sf1.de *Brom* k2* bry bg2 calc-f mg1.de **Carb-v** k* *Carbn-s* k2* card-m vml3• caust k2 *Cedr* br1 erig mg1.de *Gels* k* ham bro1* hep tl1 *Iod* k* *Ip* bg2* *Kali-bi* k* **Lach** k* lath c1 lyc bg2 mand k1* mang sf1.de merc-i-f c1 moni rfm1• nad rly4• nat-m sf1.de* **Nat-s** k* nat-sil fd3.de• nit-m-ac br1 onos vs phos bro1 **Sep** bro1* *Sil* k* sulph sne symph fd3.de• **Syph** c1* tub k2* vip-a jl [calc-n stj1]
    - **amel.**: *Aloe* sf1.de ant-c bg2 ars-i bg2 bell sf1.de brom sf1.de *Carb-v* sf1.de cham bro1 gamb mrr1 *Gels* sf1.de ham sf1.de hep bg2* *Ip* sf1.de kali-bi bg2 kali-c bro1 mag-p bg2 nat-m sf1.de pyrog bg2 sep sf1.de sil bro1 spong fd4.de thuj bg2
- **wet** weather:
  - **agg.**: abies-c oss4• abrot k2 achy jl aesc k2 agar k* aloe ptk1* alum-sil k2 **Am-c** k* amph bro1 anac st ant-c k* *Ant-t* k* **Aran** k1* arg-met k* *Arg-n* k* **Ars** k* *Ars-i* k* ars-s-f k2 aster bro1 aur k* aur-ar k2 **Bad** bapt ptk1 bar-c k* bar-i k2 bar-m bar-s k2 bell k* blatta-o c1 borx k* bov k* brom k* *Brucel* sa3• bry k* **Calc** k* calc-f k2* calc-i k2 *Calc-p* *Calc-s* calc-sil k2 calen bro1* canth k* carb-an b2.de* *Carb-v* k* carbn-s ptk1 caust k2 *Cedr* br1 cham k* chim bro1 chin k* chinin-s bro1 *Cimic* k2 *Cist* clem k* *Colch* k* con k* crot-h bro1 cupr k* cur bro1* **Dulc** k* elaps elat c1* erig bg1 euphr bro1 *Ferr* k* form bro1 *Gels* kr1* *Glon* kr1 *Graph* bg1* *Ham* *Hep* k* hydrog srj2• hyper *Iod* k* ip k* kali-bi k2* kali-c k* *Kali-i* k* kali-m k2 kali-n k* kali-sil k2 *Lac-ac* kr1* lac-d k2 *Lach* k* lath c1* laur k* *Lem-m* k* *Lyc* k* lyss kr1* mag-c k* *Mag-p* k2 magn-gr bro1 *Mang* k* med jl2* meli k* **Merc** k* mez k* mur-ac k* *Naja* *Nat-act* *Nat-c* k* **Nat-hchls** nat-m ptk1 **Nat-s** k* *Nit-ac* k* **Nux-m** k* nux-v k* oci-sa sp1 olnd ptk1 onop jl op ptk1 oscilloc jl2 paeon petr k* phos k* *Phyt* k* pic-ac k2* pneu jl2 psor k2 **Puls** k* rad-br bro1 *Ran-b* rauw sp1 **Rhod** k* **Rhus-t** k* *Ruta* k* sang k2 sars k* senec vml3• seneg k* *Sep* k* *Sil* k* sin-n c1 spig k* stann k* staph k* stict c1 still bro1 strept-ent jl2 streptoc jl2 *Stront-c* k* sul-ac k* sul-i k2 *Sulph* k* sumb syc fmm1• syph c1 teucr *Thuj* k* *Tub* k* tung-met bdx1• vac jl2 *Verat* k* *Zinc* k* zinc-p k2 zing kr1 [*Ant-m* stj2 *Ant-met* stj2 arg-p stj2 bor-pur stj2 *Cadm-met* stj2 calc-lac stj2 *Calc-met* stj2 cob stj2 cob-m stj2 cob-p stj2 ferr-n stj2 kali-f stj1 kali-met stj2 mang-n stj2 *Moly-met* stj2 niob-met stj2 nitro stj2 *Pall* stj2 *Rhodi* stj2 *Rubd-met* stj2 *Ruth-met* stj2 *Sil-met* stj2 spect dfg1 *Stront-m* stj2 *Stront-met* stj2 *Techn* stj2 *Yttr-met* stj2 zinc-n stj2]

- **amel.**: *Acon* b2.de* alum b2.de* alumn kr1 arge-pl rwt5• ars b2.de* **Asar** b2.de* aur-m k* bell b2.de* borx b2.de* bov kr1* **Bry** b2.de* carb-an b2.de* carb-v b2.de* **Caust** b2.de* *Cham* b2.de* falco-pe nl2• **Fl-ac** kr1* **Hep** b2.de* *Ip* b2.de* kali-s fd4.de lach tl1 laur b2.de* mag-c b2.de mang kr1* *Med* bro1* mez b2.de* mur-ac b2.de* *Nit-ac* kr1* **Nux-v** b2.de* oci-sa jl* phor-t mie3• *Plat* kr1* positr nl2• *Rhod* b2.de* *Sabad* b2.de* sang tl1 sep b2.de* sil b2.de* *Spig* b2.de* *Spong* b2.de* staph b2.de* sulph b2.de* tung-met bdx1• *Zinc* b2.de* [alumin stj2 alumin-p stj2 alumin-s stj2]
- **rains**; especially heavy (See rainy - agg. - heavy)

- **wind** (See windy; Wind)
- **windy** and stormy weather: *Acon* k* *All-c* hr1* *Am-c* hr1* androc srj1• arg-met k2 ars k* asar k* aur k* aur-ar k2 **Bad** k* bell k* bry k* carb-v k* carc gk6 caust bg2 *Cham* k* chel bg2 *Chin* k* chinin-ar con k* erig mg1.de euphr k* gels bg2 graph k* *Hep* k* hyper hr1* ip hr1* **Kalm** hr1* *Lach* k* lyc k* mag-c *Mag-p* mez k2* *Mur-ac* k* musca-d szs1 nat-c k* nat-m bg2 nit-s-d c1 **Nux-m** k* *Nux-v* k* petr *Phos* k* plat k* prot jl2 *Psor* k* *Puls* k* ran-b k2* **Rhod** k* rhus-t k* ruta k* *Sep* k* spig k* spong fd4.de sul-ac sulph k* syph jl2 tab bg2 thuj k* tub jl2 [calc-p stj1 mang stj1 mang-act stj2 mang-m stj2 mang-met stj2 mang-n stj2 mang-p stj2 mang-s stj2 tung-met stj2]
  - **after** | **amel.**: rhod bro1
  - **amel.**: carc jl2 [beryl stj2]
  - **before**: *Elaps* ptk1 med ptk1 rhod ptk1 rhus-t ptk1 sul-i ptk1

WEGENER'S GRANULOMATOSIS: aur mtf

WEIGHT; as of a heavy: acon bg* ars bg* bar-c bg* bell bg* **Bry** bg* *Cact* bg* carb-v br1 coll br1 dios bg* dros bg elaps ptk1 lach bg* nux-m bg* **Nux-v** bg* petr bg* ph-ac ptk1 **Phos** bg* positr nl2• *Puls* bg* sep bg* zinc bg*
- **cold** agg.: agar ptk1

WEIGHT; children who fail to gain (See Emaciation - children)

WEIGHT; increasing (See Obesity)

WEIGHT; puts on easily (See Obesity)

WELL:
- **never** well since (See Convalescence)
- **not** well; one feels (See Sick - causeless)
- **says** he is well (See MIND - Well - says)
- **unusually** well:
  - **accompanied** by constipation (See RECTUM - Constipation - accompanied - well)
  - **strong**; feels so (See Strength)
  - **then** agg.: bry bg* carc st1* helon st nux-v bg* phos ptk1 **Psor** bg* sep ptk1

WELLING UP; sensation of: *(↗Bubbling)* *Berb* bg2 caps bg2 coloc bg2 laur bg2 nux-v bg2 puls bg2 rheum b2.de* squil b2.de*

WET:
- **applications**: **Am-c** k* am-m k* **Ant-c** k* bar-c k* *Bell* k* borx k* bov k* *Brucel* sa3• bry k* **Calc** k* canth k* carb-v k* **Cham** k* **Clem** k* con k* crot-h bro1 dulc k* *Kali-c* k* *Kali-n* k* *Lach* sf1.de laur k* *Lyc* k* mag-c k* *Merc* k* mez k* mur-ac k* nat-c k* nit-ac k* nux-m k* nux-v k* phos k* pneu jl2 puls k* **Rhus-t** k* sars k* *Sep* k* sil k* *Spig* k* stann k* staph k* strept-ent jl2 *Stront-c* k* sul-ac k* **Sulph** k* zinc k*
  - **agg.**: am-c bg2 ant-c bg2 bell bg2 calc bg2 canth bg2 cham bg2 clem bg2 kali-n bg2 lach bg2 lyc bg2 merc bg2 rhus-t bg2 sep bg2 sil bg2 stront-c bg2 sulph bg2
  - **amel.**: *Alum* b2.de* *Alumn* *Am-m* k* ant-t k* *Ars* k* **Asar** b2.de* borx k* bry k* caust b2.de* cham k* *Chel* b2.de* *Euphr* b2.de* laur k* *Mag-c* k* mez k* mur-ac k* *Nux-v* k* **Puls** b2.de* *Rhod* k* *Sabad* k* sep k* *Spig* b2.de* staph k* zinc k*
  - **cold** wet applications:
    - **agg.**: **Am-c** kr1 am-m kr1 **Ant-c** kr1 apoc k2 *Ars* sf1.de bar-c kr1 *Bell* kr1 *Borx* kr1 bov kr1 *Bry* kr1 cadm-met jl **Calc** kr1 *Canth* kr1 *Carb-v* kr1 *Cham* kr1 **Clem** kr1 coli jl2 *Con* kr1 dulc kr1 graph sf1.de *Hep* sf1.de *Kali-c* kr1 *Kali-n* kr1 lach sf1.de *Laur* kr1 *Lyc* kr1 mag-c kr1 *Merc* kr1 *Mez* kr1 mur-ac kr1 nat-c kr1 *Nit-ac* kr1* *Nux-m* kr1 nux-v kr1 *Petr* kr1* ph-ac sf1.de *Phos* kr1* puls kr1* **Rhus-t** kr1 ruta sf1.de *Sars* kr1 *Sep* kr1 *Sil* kr1* *Spig* kr1 stann kr1 *Staph* kr1 *Stront-c* kr1 *Sul-ac* kr1 **Sulph** kr1 syph k2 *Zinc* kr1

Wet – applications – cold wet applications: ...
    - **amel.**: aloe sf1.de* aml-ns st anac jl *Apis* sf1.de* arg-n sf1.de* arn st aur st bry k2* fl-ac st glon st iod sf1.de* kali-p st *Led* k2* nat-hchls jl nux-v sf1.de* pic-ac st pieri-b mlk9.de *Puls* sf1.de *Sec* k2* sep sf1.de* spig sf1.de
  - **warm** wet applications:
    - **agg.**: *Apis* sf1.de bry sf1.de *Fl-ac* sf1.de lach k2* *Led* sf1.de phyt k2 *Puls* sf1.de *Sec* sf1.de
    - **amel.**: alum-sil k2 ant-c sf1.de *Ars* k2* calc-f k2* coloc sf1.de fl-ac st *Hep* sf1.de kali-bi sf1.de *Mag-p* st paraph jl ph-ac sf1.de phos k2 ruta sf1.de *Sil* sf1.de* sulfa jl thiop jl thuj sf1.de x-ray jl
- **getting**: *(↗CHILL - Exposure - wet)* *Acon* b7a.de* all-c bro1 **Alum** bg2 am-c k* ant-c k* ant-t b2.de* *Apis* k* aran bro1* *Arn* bg2* ars k* *Bell* k* bell-p ptk1 borx k* *Bry* k* **Calc** k* calc-p k* *Calc-s* camph k* carb-v k* **Caust** k* cham sf1.de *Chin* cocc ptk1 *Colch* k* *Dulc* k* *Elaps* bro1 euph k* fl-ac bg2 *Hep* k* *Hyos* b7a.de* *Ip* k* kali-bi bg2 *Kali-c* b4a.de* kola stb3• lach k* *Lyc* k* malar c1 meli bro1 *Merc* bro1 merc-i-r c1 narc-ps bro1 nat-m bg2 **Nat-s** bg2* nit-ac k* *Nux-m* k* nux-v bg2 phos k* phyt bg2* pic-ac bro1 **Puls** k* ran-b bro1* rhod c1* **Rhus-t** k* ruta bro1 *Sars* k* sec k* **Sep** k* *Sil* bg2 strept-ent jl2 sulph k* ter sf1.de thuj sf1.de tub c1* urt-u bg2 verat k* verat-v hr1 visc c1 xan c1 zinc k*
  - **feet**: agn *All-c* k* *Bar-c* bg2 bry bg2 *Calc* h2* *Camph* bg2 caps bg2 cham k* *Colch* bg2 cupr bg2 *Dulc* k* fl-ac bg2 graph bg2* guaj bg2 *Lach* bg2 lem-m bg2 lob c1 *Lyc* bg2 merc k* nat-c k* nat-m nit-ac bg2 *Nux-m* k* **Nux-v** bg2 *Phos* k* phyt sne **Puls** k* *Rhus-t* k* *Sep* k* **Sil** k* stram bg2 *Sulph* sf1.de tub bg2 xan
    - **amel.**: calad bg2 led bg2 puls bg2
  - **head**: bar-c k* **Bell** k* bry gk hep bg2 hyos bg2 led k* phos bg2 *Puls* k* rhus-t c1 *Sep* bg2 [stront-m stj2 stront-met stj2]
  - **heated**; when: bell-p c1* rhus-t c1
  - **perspiration**; during: *Acon* k* ant-c bg2 ars bg2 *Bell-p* bg2* *Bry* bg2 calc k* *Clem* bg2 *Colch* k* con bg2 *Dulc* k* nat-c bg2 nat-s bg2 *Nux-m* **Rhus-t** k* *Sep* k* *Verat-v* hr1*
  - **rooms**, in wet: *(↗Vaults)* *Aloe* kr1 ant-t bro1 *Aran* bg2* **Ars** b4a.de* atro hr1* *Bry* hr1* *Calc* b4a.de* calc-p sf1.de *Carb-an* b4a.de* carb-v bg2 carc mlr1• caust b4a.de* **Dulc** bg2* form hr1* *Kali-c* b4a.de lyc b4a.de* nat-n sf1.de **Nat-s** bg2* nit-ac sf1.de **Puls** bg2* rhod bg2 *Rhus-t* bg2* *Sel* hr1* *Sep* b4a.de* sil bg2 *Stram* hr1* ter c1* *Thuj* bg2* verat bg2
  - **sheets**, ailments from wet: rhus-t c1
- **ground**; ailments from sitting on wet: *Ars* bg2* calc bg caust bg2* *Dulc* bg2* nat-s gk *Nux-v* bg2* rhod bg *Rhus-t* bg2* sil bg
- **sensation** of being wet:
  - **rain**; as if exposed to soaking: kalm a
  - **sheets** are wet; as if: lac-d ptk1
- **weather** (See Weather - wet)

WETTING a part: | **amel.**: asar b7.de spig b7.de

WHIRLING sensation: ant-t b2.de* arg-met b2.de* croc b2.de* nux-v b2.de* petr b2.de* ran-b b2.de* sabad b2.de* sep b2.de* sil b2.de* sulph b2.de* tarax b2.de*

WHITENESS: ant-t ptk1 ars ptk1 **Calc** ptk1 carb-v ptk1 chel ptk1 *Chin* ptk1 cina ptk1 dig ptk1 *Ferr* ptk1 *Graph* ptk1 *Kali-m* ptk1 **Lac-c** ptk1 **Merc** ptk1 *Nat-m* ptk1 ph-ac ptk1 *Phos* ptk1 *Puls* ptk1 sep ptk1 sulph ptk1 *Verat* ptk1
- **chalk**; like: ant-c ptk1 mez ptk1
- **milky**: *Kali-m* ptk1

○ - **Parts** usually red; of ambr b2.de* anac b2.de* ang b2.de* ant-t bg *Ars* b2.de* **Borx** b2.de* *Calc* b2.de* canth b2.de* carb-v bg caust b2.de* chel bg *Chin* bg cina bg coloc b2.de* dig bg *Ferr* b2.de* *Graph* bg **Hell** b2.de* *Kali-c* b2.de* *Kali-m* bg **Lac-c** bg lac-d bg2 lyc b2.de* **Merc** b2.de* *Merc-c* k13 nat-c b2.de* *Nat-m* bg *Nit-ac* b2.de* *Nux-v* b2.de* *Olnd* b2.de* op b2.de* petr b2.de* ph-ac bg *Phos* b2.de* *Plb* b2.de* puls b2.de* sabin b2.de* *Sec* b2.de* sep b2.de* *Staph* b2.de* *Sul-ac* k* sulph b2.de* valer b2.de* *Verat* b2.de* viol-t b2.de* *Zinc* b2.de*
  - **accompanied** by | **numbness**: sul-i ptk1

WHOOPING COUGH; ailments after: carc fb* **Sang** ●*

WIND: *(↗MIND - Sensitive - wind)* *Acon* k* anac j5.de androc srj1• *Ars* k* ars-i asar k* *Aur* b2.de* aur-ar k2 *Bell* k* bry k* bufo k* calc k* *Calc-p* k* canth b7a.de* caps ptk1 carb-v k* caust **Cham** k* *Chin* k* chinin-ar k2 coca-c sk4• *Coff* k2* colch ptk1 coloc ptk1 con k* cupr elaps *Euphr* k* graph k* helodr-cal knl2• *Hep* ptk1 hyos b7a.de* ip st kali-c ptk1 kalm c1 *Lach* k* **Lyc** k* lyss mrr1 mag-c ptk1 mag-p k2* med ptk1 mur-ac k* nat-c k* nit-ac h2*

Wind: ...
Nux-m b2.de* **Nux-v** k* ph-ac ptk1 **Phos** k* plat k* *Psor* **Puls** k* rheum ptk1 **Rhod** k* *Rhus-t* bg2* samb ptk1 sel ptk1 sep j5.de* **Sil** ptk1 spig k* **Spong** squil ptk1 stram b7a.de* stront-c ptk1 sul-ac sulph k* tab bg2 thuj k* tub bg1 verb ptk1 zinc k* *Zinc-p* k2 [arg-met stj1* arg-p stj2 erech stj mang stj1 *Mang-act* stj2 *Mang-i* stj2 *Mang-m* stj2 *Mang-met* stj2 *Mang-n* stj2 *Mang-p* stj2 *Mang-s* stj2 *Mang-sil* stj2]

- **amel.**: arg-n bg2* hydrog srj2*• lac-ac stj5• nux-m bg2* tub jl2 [niob-met stj2]
- **cold**:
  - **agg.**: *Acon* k* agra br1 *All-c* kr1 apis bg2* arn bg2 *Ars* k* ars-i *Asar* k* **Bell** k* bell-p br1* *Bry* k* cadm-s c1* calc k2 calc-p carb-an k* carb-v k* *Caust* k* cham k* chinin-ar k2 *Coff* vh cupr k* ferr-ar **Hep** k* ina-i mlk9.de ip k* *Kali-bi* kalm k2 lach bg2* mag-c br1 mag-p bg2* nit-ac h2* **Nux-v** k* psor *Rhod* bg2* **Rhus-t** bg2* rumx bg2 sabad k* *Sep* k* *Sil* k* **Spong** k* thlas bg2 tub st1 vanil fd5.de verat hr1* [calc-sil stj2 mag-sil stj2 nat-sil stj2]
    - ⁝ **shelter** amel.: agra c
  - **dry** | **agg.**: *Acon* b2.de* ars b2.de arum-t bro1 asaf tl1 *Asar* b2.de bell b2.de bry b2.de* carb-an b2.de *Carb-v* b2.de* caust b2.de* cham b2.de* cupr bro1 *Hep* b2.de* ip b2.de kali-c tl1 lyc bro1 mag-c bro1 *Nux-v* b2.de* *Phos* b4a.de* puls bro1 *Rhod* bro1 sabad b2.de sep b2.de* sil b2.de* spong b2.de*
  - **wet**: all-c c1* calc c1 kali-bi k2
- **desire** to be in the wind: androc srj1• aq-mar mgm• hydrog srj2• ruta fd4.de *Tub* st* [heroin sdj2]
- **dry** | **agg.**: acon bg2 ars bg2 asar bg2 bell bg2 bry bg2 calc-p bg2 carb-an bg2 *Carb-v* bg2 *Caust* bg2 cham bg2 **Hep** bg2 ip bg2 **Nux-v** bg2 *Puls* bg2 sabad bg2 sep bg2 sil bg2 **Spong** bg2
- **north** wind agg.: ars ptk1 asar ptk1 carb-v ptk1 caust ptk1 hep ptk1 nux-v ptk1 sep ptk1 spong ptk1 zinc ptk1
- **sensation** of: *(↗Air; draft - sensation)* agar k2* calc bg2 canth k* caust bg2 *Chel* k* *Cist* bg2* coloc bg2 cor-r graph k* lach sf1.de *Laur* bg2 **Lyss** m-ambo b2.de m-arct b2.de *M-aust* b2.de *Mez* bg2* *Mosch* *Nux-v* k* olnd k* phos bg2 puls k* rhus-t k* sabin k* samb bg spig k* squil k* stram k* *Thuj* bg2* valer bg2
  - **blowing**:
    - ⁝ **Covered** parts; on: camph
    - ⁝ **Single** parts; on: *Hep* br1
  - **cold** agg.: camph croc *Lac-d* *Laur* **Lyss** *Mosch* rhus-t samb
- **warm**:
  - **south** wind: *Ars-i* asar jl bry bg2* carb-v bg2* euphr bg2* *Gels* kr1* *Ip* lach k2 nat-c bg2 rhod bg2* sil bg2*
  - **wet** wind: *Acon* kr1 **Hep** kr1
- **weather** (See Weather - windy)
- **wet** | **agg.**: all-c bro1 dulc bro1 *Euphr* bro1 ip bro1 *Nux-m* bro1 rhod bro1

WINDOW; close to a: | **agg.**: chin b7.de

WINE (See Food and - wine)

WIPING with the hands: aloe ptk1 *Graph* ptk1 lach ptk1 mur-ac ptk1
- **agg.**: aloe bg2 *Graph* bg2 lach bg2
- **amel.**: alum b2.de* arn b2.de* *Asaf* b2.de* bism b2.de* **Calc** b2.de* canth b2.de* *Caps* b2.de* carb-an b2.de* *Cina* b2.de* croc b2.de* **Cycl** b2.de* *Dros* b2.de* euphr ptk1 guaj b2.de* hep bg2 ign b2.de* mang b2.de* meny b2.de* merc b2.de* mur-ac b2.de* **Nat-c** b2.de* nit-ac bg2 *Phos* b2.de* *Plb* b2.de* puls b2.de* ruta b2.de* sulph b2.de* thuj b2.de* zinc b2.de*

WOMEN; complaints of: acon bg2* agar b2.de* am-m b2.de* ambr b2.de* ang b2.de* ant-t b2.de* apis ptk1 arn b2.de* asaf b2.de* **Bell** b2.de* borx b2.de* *Bry* b2.de* **Calc** b2.de* camph b2.de* canth b2.de* **Caps** b2.de* *Caust* b2.de* **Cham** b2.de* *Chin* b2.de* cic b2.de* cimic ptk1 clem b2.de* **Cocc** b2.de* *Con* b2.de* **Croc** b2.de* cupr b2.de* dig b2.de* euph b2.de* ferr b2.de* fl-ac bg2 graph b2.de* hell b2.de* helon ptk1 *Hyos* b2.de* *Ign* b2.de* iod b2.de* ip b2.de* kali-c b2.de* lach b2.de* laur b2.de* led b2.de* mag-c b2.de* mag-m ptk1 mang b2.de* merc b2.de* merc-c b4a.de* *Mosch* b2.de* mur-ac b2.de* nat-c b2.de* *Nat-m* bg2 *Nux-m* b2.de* nux-v bg2 op b2.de* **Plat** b2.de* plb b2.de* **Puls** b2.de* rheum b2.de* *Rhus-t* b2.de* sabad b2.de* sabal ptk1 **Sabin** b2.de* *Sec* b2.de* *Sel* b2.de* seneg b2.de* **Sep** b2.de* sil b2.de* spig b2.de* spong b2.de* stram bg2 sul-ac b2.de* sulph b2.de* thuj b2.de* *Valer* b2.de* verat b2.de* vib ptk1 viol-o b2.de*
- **unmarried**: *(↗Unmarried)* cocc ptk1 sil ptk1

WOODEN sensation: kali-n ptk1 petr ptk1 rhus-t ptk1 thuj ptk1

WOOL:
- **amel.** (See Clothing - woolen - amel.)
- **intolerance** (See Clothing - intolerance - woolen; SKIN - Itching - wool)

WOOZY (See MIND - Stupefaction)

WORMS:
- **complaints** of (See RECTUM - Worms - complaints)
- O - **Skin**; sensation as if worms under (See SKIN - Worms - under)

WOUNDS: alum bg2 *Am-c* bg2 anag c1* ang bg2 *Apis* k* arg-n bg2 arist-cl mg1.de* *Arn* k* ars c1* *Bell* b7a.de bell-p bg2* bor-ac c1* borx k* bov c1* bry bg2* bufo bg2* calc bg2 calc-p bg2* *Calen* bg2* canth bg2 carb-ac st1 carb-v k* caust bg2 cham bg2* chin bg2 cic k* cist sf1.de con k* croc k* *Dulc* bg2 echi bg2* erig c1* ery-a c1* eup-per c1* euph bg2 euphr b2.de* ferr-p c1 glon bg2 ham bg2* helia c1* hell c1* hep k* hydrog srj2• hyos bg2 *Hyper* bg2* iod k* kali-c bg2 kali-p c1 kreos k* *Lach* k* lappa mg1.de laur bg2 **Led** k* lyc bg2 m-ambo b2.de* mang-act br1 merc k* mez k* mill bg2* nat-c k* nat-m k* nat-s bg2 nit-ac k* nux-m bg2 nux-v bg2 par bg2 petr bg2 ph-ac k* *Phos* k* phys bg2* plan c1* plat bg2 plb k* priva-l bta1• *Puls* k* rhus-t k* ruta k* samb b7a.de* sec bg2* senec c1* seneg k* sil k* spong fd4.de *Staph* k* stront-c sf1.de *Sul-ac* k* sulph k* symph bg2* tritic-vg fd5.de vanil fd5.de verat bg2 with-s bta1• zinc k* zinc-m c1* [bell-p-sp dcm1 gynu-ce dbx1.fr phyll-c dbx1.fr sida-rh dbx1.fr tetrad-f dbx1.fr vang-e dbx1.fr]
- **ailments** from wounds (See constitutional)
- **bites**: *(↗SKIN - Stings)* acet-ac hr1* aids nl2• all-s hr1* am-c bro1 am-caust bro1 anthraci bro1 *Apis* bro1 *Arn* b7a.de* *Ars* bro1 bell bro1 calad bro1 camph bro1 *Cedr* bro1 cist br1 crot-h bro1 dulc fd4.de echi br1* euph-po bro1 gaul bro1 grin c1* gua bro1 gymne bro1 *Hep* brm hydr-ac bro1 *Hyper* hr1* kali-perm bro1 *Lach* bro1* lat-h thj1 *Led* hr1* lob-p st1 merc brm mosch bro1 *Plan* hr1* pyrog bro1 rhus-t brm sela bro1 *Seneg* st1 sil brm sisy bro1 spirae bro1 *Strych-g* bro1 *Sul-ac* b4a.de* vespul-vg k4
  - **cats**; of: *Led* mrr1
  - **discoloration** | **red**: lat-m sp1
  - **dogs**, of: hyper k2* *Lach* hr1* led c1 **Lyss** hr1* *Ter* hr1*
    - ⁝ **rabid**: arist-cl sp1 ars st1 bell st1 canth st1 *Chr-ac* hr1* echi c1 hyos st1 *Lyss* st* spirae br1 [sol-no dbx1.fr]
  - **gnat**: arn tl1 *Canth* tl1
  - **inflamed** (See Inflammation - wounds)
  - **itching**: aids nl2• lat-m sp1 mez sys
  - **pain**:
    - ⁝ **extending** to | **Other** parts: lat-m sp1
  - **poisonous** animals, of: acet-ac k2 *Am-c* j5.de* anthraci ptk1 *Apis* k* arn k* *Ars* k* aur bell k* calad *Caust* j5.de* *Cedr* k* cist br1* *Echi* k* **Gent-l** sne gua sne helo-s rwt2• hep k2 hyper k* kali-perm br1 *Lach* k* *Lat-m* sne **Led** k* *Lob-p* st1 *Lyss* hr1* mosch ptk1 nat-m j5.de* puls j5.de* pyrog ptk1 *Seneg* k* stram sul-ac k* *Tarent-c* sne thuj k2 vip
  - **rabid** animals; of: echi c2 *Lyss* mrr1
  - **rattlesnakes**; of: iod br1
  - **reptiles**; of: lycps-v c2
  - **scorpions**; of: euph-po br1 gua br1
  - **snakes**; of: am-c k2 am-caust br1 anag hr1* *Apis* st arist-cl sp1 arn st1 *Ars* hr1* aur st1 *Bell* hr1* bid-p jsx1.fr calad st1 *Camph* hr1* cassia-o bta1• *Cedr* hr1* cench sne chen-o jsx1.fr cissu-d jsx1.fr clerod-g bta1• *Echi* c1* euph-po br3* euph-pr br3 gua br1* guaj st1 gymne c1* hyper st1 indg br1 ipom-f bta1• kali-perm br1 **Lach** st1 **Led** st1 leont-l bta1• leont-o bta1• lob-p c1* lycps-v c1* mik-c jsx1.fr plan c1* secu-l jsx1.fr *Sela* br1 seneg hr1* sima c1 sol-cp bta1• stram st1 strych-g br1 strych-s bta1• sul-ac st1 thalic-r jsx1.fr *Thuj* k2* viol-o br1 *Vip* st1
    - ⁝ **chronic** complaints after: merc kr1 ph-ac kr1
    - ⁝ **prophylaxis** to snake bites: euph-po br1
  - **spider**; of: cedr br1 euph-po br1 indg br1 kali-perm br1 lach sne lat-m sne sela br1 *Tarent-c* sne
    - ⁝ **swelling**: lat-m sp1
  - **swelling**; with (See swelling)
  - **tarantula**, of: lycps-v c1*
  - **ticks**; of | **abundant** bites: calc-p brm
- **black**: *Chin* hr1* *Lach* hr1* trach a1 vip a1

- **bleeding** freely: *Acon* j5.de* am-c bg1* ancis-p tsm2 ant-t j5.de aran k* *Arn* k* ars j5.de asaf j5.de *Bell* b7a.de bell-p mg1.de bit-ar wht1• borx j5.de both a1 both-ax tsm2 calen mrr1 *Carb-v* k* caust j5.de cench k* *Chin* j5.de* clem j5.de cloth tsm2 con j5.de *Cop* j5.de* croc k* crot-c tsm2 crot-h k* cyn-d zzc1• *Dor* st1 eug j5.de *Euphr* j5.de ferr ferr-p bg2 ham bg2* helo-s bnm14• hep k* **Hir** st1 *Hydr* hr1* *Kreos* k* **Lach** k* **Lat-m** st1 led k2* *M-ambo* b2.de* merc k* mez j5.de mill k* *Nat-c* j5.de nat-m k* **Nit-ac** j5.de* *Nux-m* j5.de *Nux-v* j5.de *Ph-ac* k* **Phos** k* plb j5.de puls k* rhus-t k* ruta j5.de sec bg1* sep j5.de sil j5.de spong fd4.de *Staph* j5.de sul-ac k* *Sulph* k* thlas bg2 tritic-vg fd5.de vanil fd5.de vip j5.de vip-a-c tsm2 vip-d tsm2 *Zinc* k*
  - **black** blood: vip a1
  - **clots**; favors the formation of: cact br1
  - **fall**; after a: *Arn* bro1 ham bro1 mill bro1
  - **small** wounds: am-c k1* carb-v k1* hydr k2* kreos k2* lach k2* ph-ac k1* phos h2* sul-ac k1* tritic-vg fd5.de ulm-c jsj8• *Zinc* k1*
- **bluish**: *Apis* kr1 helo-s bnm14• *Lach* hr1* lyss hr1* *Vip* a1 [echi stj]
- **burns** (See Burns)
- **cold** agg.; becoming: **Led** k ●* *Scor* a1*
- **constitutional** effects of: arn k* bry c1 calen c1 carb-v k* con k* ferr-p c1 glon ptk1 hep hyper c1 *Iod* k* kali-p c1 *Lach* k* **Led** k* nat-m *Nat-s* ptk1 *Nit-ac* k* *Phos* k* plan c1 puls rhus-t senec c1 *Staph* k* *Stront-c* ptk1 *Sul-ac* zinc
- **corrosive**; gnawing: mez h2
- **crushing**: arist-cl sp1 arn ptk1 con ptk1 echi br1 hyper ptk1 ruta ptk1 staph ptk1
- **cuts**: anemps br1 *Arn* k* *Calen* hr1* *Carb-v* hr1* *Cic* hr1* con hr1* dig hr1* dream-p sdj1• dulc fd4.de *Ham* hr1* hep hr1* hyper bro1* kali-chl hr1* kali-m c1 *Lach* hr1* *Led* k* merc k* nat-c k* nat-sil fd3.de• *Nit-ac* hr1* ph-ac k* *Phos* ptk1 plan hr1* plb j5.de* puls ptk1 ruta fd4.de sil k* spong fd4.de **Staph** k* *Sul-ac* k* sulph k* symph fd3.de* tritic-vg fd5.de vanil fd5.de
  - **burnt** appearance; with: plut-n srj7•
  - **green** and odorous: brom tl1
- **decubitus** (See SKIN - Decubitus)
- **discharging** | **viscid** blood-like fluid: naja br1
- **dissecting**: *(↗Food poisoning)* *Anthraci* k* *Apis* k* *Ars* k* crot-h hr1* *Echi* bro1* ham hr1* *Lach* k* led *Pyrog* k* sil sne *Ter* hr1*
- **foreign** bodies, from: *(↗splinters)* arn st1 *Calen* hr1 *Hep* hr1* *Lob* c1* **Sil** hr1*
  - **eye**, in the (See EYE - Injuries - foreign)
- **gangrene** of: acon j5.de* am-c j5.de* *Anthraci* kr1 **Ars** j5.de* *Bell* j5.de* *Brom* kr1 calen kr1* *Carb-v* j5.de* *Chin* j5.de* *Eucal* kr1 euph j5.de* **Lach** j5.de* sal-ac bro1* sec kr1 *Sil* j5.de* sul-ac bro1* trach a1 vip a1 vip-a jl
- **granulations**, proud flesh: *(↗SKIN - Cicatrices; SKIN - Keloid)* *Alumn* hr1* *Anac* kr1 *Anac-oc* hr1 *Ant-t* hr1* **Ars** hr1* *Calc* hr1* *Calen* hr1* chir-fl bnm4• cund hr1* hydr k2* *Kali-chl* hr1 *Kali-m* kr1 *Lach* hr1* *Merc* k2* nit-ac bro1 *Sabin* bro1* **Sil** bro1* **Sulph** ●* thuj bro1
- **greenish**: senec st1
- **gunshot**: am-caust hr1 apis ptk1 **Arn** j5.de* calen bro1* *Euphr* j5.de* *Hyper* hr1* *Lach* hr1* *Led* ptk1 *Nit-ac* bg2* plan ptk1 *Plb* j5.de* puls j5.de* ruta j5.de* *Sul-ac* j5.de* sulph j5.de* symph c1* urt-u sne
- **heal**; tendency to:
  - **quickly**: lyss kr1* manc ptk1
    - **suddenly** disappearing: ars bg2 calc bg2 hep bg2 kreos bg2 lach bg2 lyc bg2 merc bg2 sep bg2 sil bg2
  - **slowly**: *All-c* kr1* alum alum-p k2 alum-sil k2 am-c arist-cl sp1 *Arn* ptk1 ars k2* *Bar-c* bar-s k2 bell-p sp1 *Borx* k* both a1 *Calc* k* calc-s k2* *Calen* br1* *Carb-v* k* carbn-s k2 carc mlr1• caust *Cham* k* chel chir-fl bnm4• clem j5.de con k* cortiso jl* crats-ce jsx1.fr croc j5.de crot-h dulc fd4.de *Graph* k* ham fd3.de• hein-cr jsx1.fr hell j5.de helo-s bnm14• **Hep** k* hib-su jsx1.fr hydrog srj2• hyper k2* kali-bi ptk1 kali-c kali-sil k2 kola stb3• kreos ptk1 **Lach** k* loxo-recl bnm10• lyc k* lyss mg1.de mag-c maland jl2 mang *Merc* k* *Merc-c* mill k2 mir-j jsx1.fr mur-ac musa-p jsx1.fr nat-c j5.de **Nit-ac** k* nux-v j5.de **Petr** k* ph-ac phos plb positr nl2• puls rad-br sze8• *Rhus-t* ruta k2 sacch br1 sars k2 sep **Sil** k* spong fd4.de squil j5.de *Staph* **SULPH** k ●* synad-g jsx1.fr tritic-vg fd5.de *Tub* st vanil fd5.de visc ptk1
    - **cancer**; in: coenz-q mtf11
    - **suppuration**; with: coenz-q mtf11
- **infected** (See Inflammation - wounds)
- **inflamed** (See Inflammation - wounds)
- **injection**, from painful: *Crot-h* st1 *Led* st1
- **itching**: [bell-p-sp dcm1]
- **lacerations**: arist-cl mg1.de* arn bro1* bell-p mrr1 **Calen** bg2* **Carb-ac** bro1* *Ham* hr1* *Hyper* hr1* led bro1* spong fd4.de staph b7a.de* sul-ac bro1* symph bro1* vanil fd5.de

○ - **Sphincters**; of: staph br1
- **large**: hyper ptk1
- **lead** colored: *Lach* hr1* vip a1
- **mottled**: led tl1
- **nail**; stepping on a (See penetrating)
- **numbness** of wounds: plut-n srj7•
- **odors** | **foul**: cist bg2
- **oozing**: mill k2
- **painful**: *(↗pulsating)* *All-c* st1 am-c j5.de *Apis* arist-cl sp1 *Arn* mrr1 bell j5.de calc hr1* calc-f hr1* calen hr1* cham hr1* chir-fl bnm4• con j5.de croc j5.de crot-h a1 eug j5.de* *Ham* br1 helo c1 helo-s c1* *Hep* j5.de **Hyper** k* led nat-c hr1* nat-m k* *Nit-ac* nux-v *Ph-ac* j5.de* ruta fd4.de **Staph** sulph
  - **burning**: *Acon* j5.de arn j5.de *Ars* j5.de bry j5.de *Carb-v* j5.de caust j5.de hyper k2 merc j5.de mez j5.de naja br1 *Nat-c* b4a.de* nat-m j5.de nit-ac b4a.de rhus-t j5.de *Sul-ac* j5.de *Sulph* j5.de zinc st
  - **corrosive**, gnawing: mez h2
  - **old** wounds: all-c ptk1 glon ptk1 kali-i ptk1 nat-m ptk1 *Nat-s* ptk1 *Nit-ac* ptk1 nux-v ptk1 phasco-ci rbp2 sil ptk1 symph ptk1 ulm-c jsj8•
  - **stinging** in wounds: acon k* *Apis* arn bar-c bell j5.de bry caust chin j5.de clem j5.de *Led* merc mez j5.de nat-c k* *Nit-ac* k* sep j5.de sil j5.de *Staph* sulph
    - **small** wounds; in: ulm-c jsj8•

▽ - **extending** to | **Nerve**: hyper tl1
- **pale**: led tl1
- **paralyzed**: led tl1
- **penetrating**, punctured: *(↗splinters; stab)* **Apis** k* aran c1* *Carb-v* k* cic k* con bg2 hep k* *Hyper* k* lach bg2* **Led** k* **Nit-ac** k* phase c1* phase-xyz c2 plan bg* plb k* sil k* sulph k*
  - **bleeding**: aran gm1
  - **painful**: led tl1

○ - **Nerves**; parts rich in (See Injuries - nerves)
  - **Palms** and soles, of: **Hyper** k* **LED** k1* **Plan** sne
- **poisoned**: cist ptk1
- **poisonous** plants, from: echi st
- **pulsating**: *(↗painful)* *Bell* j5.de *Cham* j5.de clem j5.de *Hep* j5.de *Merc* j5.de mez h2 *Puls* j5.de *Sulph* j5.de
- **punctured** (See penetrating)
- **purple** | **dark** purple: naja br1
- **reaction**; without (= deficient reaction): ars bg2 camph bg2 carb-v bg2 con bg2 laur bg2 op bg2 ph-ac bg2 sulph bg2 [heroin sdj2]
- **reopening** of old: *(↗History - abscesses)* asaf k2* *Carb-v* b2.de* *Caust* j5.de* con b2.de* *Croc* b2.de* *Crot-h* j5.de* eug j5.de fl-ac bg* *Glon* j5.de* *Lach* b2.de* m-ambo b2.de nat-c b2.de* *Nat-m* b2.de* *Nit-ac* j5.de *Nux-v* j5.de *Op* ptk1 **Phos** b2.de* *Sil* b2.de* *Sulph* b2.de* *Vip* bg2*
  - **cicatrices** (See SKIN - Cicatrices - break)
- **scurfiness**, with: *Calen* hr1* *Carb-ac* hr1* dulc fd4.de *Hyper* hr1* spong fd4.de
- **septic**: *(↗Septicemia)* ars bg2* hydrog srj2•
- **soft** tissues; with torn: arn st1 calen st1 **Carb-ac** st1 ham st1 *Hyper* st1 led st1 staph st1 sul-ac st1 symph st1
  - **accompanied** by:
    - **gangrene**; tendency to: calad st1 sul-ac st1
    - **pain**: *Hyper* lz
    - **Nail**; tearing of: *Led* st1
- **splinters**, from: *(↗foreign; penetrating)* abrot tl1 acon *Anag* kr1 *Apis* *Arn* k* *Carb-v* k* **Cic** k* colch k* dulc fd4.de *Hep* k* **Hyper** k* lach k* *Led* k* lob c1 nat-sil fd3.de• *Nit-ac* k* petr k* plat k* ran-b k* *Sil* k* *Staph* sulph k* tritic-vg fd5.de
- **stab** wounds: *(↗penetrating)* acet-ac st *All-c* hr1* *Apis* k* arn carb-v k* cic k* con j5.de dulc fd4.de eug j5.de hep b2.de* **Hyper** sf1.de lach **Led** k2* nat-m j5.de nit-ac k* phase sne plb b2.de* *Rhus-t* hr1* sep j5.de* sil k* spong fd4.de *Staph* k* sulph b2.de* vanil fd5.de
- **stinging** (See painful - stinging)
- **stings** of mosquitoes (See SKIN - Stings - mosquitoes)
- **suppurating**: *(↗Abscesses; Inflammation - wounds)* *Anthraci* ptk1 *Apis* ptk1 arist-cl sp1* arn st1 *Ars* ptk1 asaf j5.de* *Bell* j5.de borx a1* *Bufo* kr1 *Calc* kr1 calc-f kr1 calc-s kr1 *Calen* kr1* caust j5.de *Cham* kr1* *Chin* j5.de *Croc* j5.de* echi ptk1* graph tl1* *Hep* kr1* hydrog srj2• lach j5.de led ptk1* liat br1

- **suppurating**: ...
  Merc b4a.de* *Nat-m* kr1 petr tl1* phos ptk1 plb j5.de* plut-n srj7• *Puls* j5.de* pyrog ptk1 *Sil* b4a.de* *Sulph* j5.de* vip-a jl3
  - **prophylactic** of pus infection (See Septicemia - prophylaxis)
- **swelling** of: acon hr1* *Arn* j5.de* *Bell* j5.de* *Bry* j5.de* kali-chl hr1 kali-m kr1 *Led* mrr1 nux-v j5.de* *Puls* j5.de* *Rhus-t* j5.de* ruta fd4.de *Scor* c1 sul-ac j5.de* *Sulph* j5.de* tritic-vg fd5.de vip a1
- **warm** applications | **amel.**: ars tl1

○ - **Nerves**: hyper k2 led k2

WRAPS (See Warm - wraps)

WRITHING: | **Blood** vessels: bell ptk1 hydr-ac ptk1

WRITING:

- **agg.**: acon b2.de* agar b2.de* alum b2.de* am-c b2.de* am-m b2.de* anac b2.de* ant-c b2.de* arn b2.de* *Asaf* b2.de* asar b2.de* aur b2.de* bar-c b2.de* borx b2.de* bry b2.de* calad b2.de* **Calc** b2.de* cann-s b2.de* canth b2.de* carb-v b2.de* caust b2.de* cham b2.de* chel b2.de* chin b2.de* cic b2.de* cimic bg2 *Cina* b2.de* *Cocc* b2.de* coloc b2.de* croc b2.de* dros b2.de* euph b2.de* euphr bg2 ferr b2.de* *Fl-ac* bg2 graph b2.de* hep b2.de* ign b2.de* **Kali-c** b2.de* lach bg2 laur b2.de* led b2.de* *Lyc* b2.de* meny b2.de* mez b2.de* mur-ac b2.de* nat-c b2.de* *Nat-m* b2.de* nit-ac b2.de* nux-m b2.de* *Nux-v* b2.de* *Olnd* b2.de* par b2.de* petr b2.de* ph-ac b2.de* phos b2.de* plat b2.de* puls b2.de* ran-b b2.de* rheum b2.de* *Rhod* b2.de* rhus-t b2.de* *Ruta* b2.de* sabad b2.de* sabin b2.de* samb b2.de* sars b2.de* seneg b2.de* *Sep* b2.de* **Sil** b2.de* spig b2.de* spong b2.de* stann b2.de* staph b2.de* stront-c b2.de* sul-ac b2.de* sulph b2.de* thuj b2.de* valer b2.de* zinc b2.de*
- **amel.**: ferr b2.de* nat-c b2.de*

X-RAY burn or treatments; after: cadm-met gm1 calc-f ptk1 fl-ac gm1 phos ptk1 rad-br ptk1

YAWNING:

- **after** | **agg.**: am-m b2.de* croc b2.de* *Nux-v* b2.de*
- **agg.**: acon b2.de* agar b2.de* aloe ptk1 am-c b2.de* am-m b2.de* anac b2.de* ang b2.de* ant-t b2.de* arg-met b2.de* *Arn* b2.de* ars b2.de* aur b2.de* bar-c b2.de* bell b2.de* borx b2.de* bry b2.de* calad b2.de* calc b2.de* canth b2.de* caps b2.de* carb-an b2.de* *Caust* b2.de* *Chel* b2.de* chin b2.de* **Cina** b2.de* cocc b2.de* croc b2.de* cycl b2.de* dig b2.de* ferr b2.de* *Graph* b2.de* hep b2.de* **Ign** b2.de* ip b2.de* kali-c b2.de* **Kreos** b2.de* *Laur* b2.de* lyc b2.de* *M-arct* b2.de* m-aust b2.de mag-c b2.de* mag-m b2.de* mang b2.de* *Meny* b2.de* mez b2.de* *Mur-ac* b2.de* nat-c b2.de* nat-m b2.de* **Nux-v** b2.de* *Olnd* b2.de* op b2.de* par b2.de* petr b2.de* ph-ac b2.de* *Phos* b2.de* plat b2.de* puls b2.de* **Rhus-t** b2.de* ruta b2.de* *Sabad* b2.de* **Sars** b2.de* sep b2.de* sil b2.de* stann b2.de* *Staph* b2.de* *Sul-ac* b2.de* *Sulph* b2.de* teucr b2.de* thuj b2.de* verat b2.de* viol-o b2.de* zinc b2.de*
- **amel.**: berb ptk1 chinin-s bg2* croc b2.de* guaj ptk1 m-ambo b2.de* plat j5.de *Staph* b2.de*
- **frequent** (See SLEEP - Yawning)

YELLOW: acon bg* *Ars* bg* *Ars-i* ptk1 bry bg* calc bg* carb-an ptk1 cham bg* **Chel** bg* *Chin* bg* con bg* crot-h bg* eup-per bg* ferr bg* hep ptk1 *Hydr* bg* iris bg* kali-bi bg* kali-c bg* kali-s ptk1 *Lach* bg* **Lyc** bg* **Merc** bg* merc-i-f ptk1 nat-s ptk1 nit-ac bg* nux-v bg* *Phos* bg* *Plb* bg* podo bg* **Puls** bg* **Sep** bg* *Sulph* bg*

- **golden**, bright or orange: aeth bg* aloe bg* alum bg* card-m bg* **Chel** bg* cina bg* colch bg* kali-c bg* *Kali-p* bg* *Merc* bg* **Nux-m** bg* phos bg* sang bg* **Sul-ac** bg*
- **green**: ars-i ptk1 mang ptk1 *Merc* ptk1 *Puls* ptk1
  - **turning** green: con ptk1

ZIGZAG sensation or appearance: calc ptk1 rhod ptk1 sars ptk1 sul-i ptk1

ADRENAL GLANDS; complaints of: thal-met br1

- **adrenocortical** damage: cortiso mtf11
- **failure**; adrenal: p-benzq mtf1
- **function**; deficient: naphthoq mtf11

BLOOD: (↗*Hemorrhage - blood)*

- **complaints** of the: ail br1 arn br1 ars-h br1 aur br1 crot-h br1 echi br1 lach br1 merc br1 plb br1 thuj br1 [bell-p-sp dcm1]
- **degradation**: lach mtf11 ser-ang br1
- **disorganization**: ail bro1 am-c bro1 *Anthraci* bro1 arn bro1 *Ars* bro1 ars-h bro1 *Bapt* bro1 carb-ac bro1 *Crot-h* bro1 *Echi* bro1 kreos bro1 *Lach* bro1 *Mur-ac* bro1 phos br1* psor bro1 *Pyrog* bro1 *Rhus-t* bro1 tarent-c bro1

Blood: ...

- **quick** circulation of blood; sensation of too: ars h2
- **thin**, sensation as if: hell a1* loxo-lae bnm12•
- **turmoil**; bloods seems to be in a constant: am-m br1*

BONES; complaints of: (↗*Brittle; Caries - bone; Necrosis - bone; Rickets; Softening bones)* *Arg-met* br1* **Asaf** ptk1 aur br1* *Calc* br1* *Calc-f* ptk1 *Calc-p* br1* castor-eq br1 chin ptk1 chlam-tr bcx2• cocc ptk1 cupr ptk1 daph br1 eup-per ptk1 fl-ac ptk1* hep ptk1 kali-bi br1 kali-i ptk1 lyc ptk1 merc br1* merc-pr-r mtf11 mez br1* *Nit-ac* ptk1 **Ph-ac** ptk1 *Phos* ptk1 *Phyt* br1* **Puls** ptk1 pyrog ptk1 rhod ptk1 rhus-t ptk1 *Ruta* ptk1 sel br1 sil br1* staph ptk1 *Sulph* ptk1 syph ptk1 [bell-p-sp dcm1]

- **night**: merc tl1 mez tl1
- **accompanied** by | **Kidney** complaints (See KIDNEYS - Complaints - accompanied - bone)
- **porous**: phos bg2
- **syphilitic**: arg-met bro1 *Asaf* bro1 *Aur* bro1 aur-m bro1 calc-f bro1 carb-v bro1 *Fl-ac* bro1 hep bro1 *Kali-bi* bro1 *Kali-i* bro1 lach bro1 *Merc* bro1 *Mez* bro1 *Nit-ac* bro1 ph-ac bro1 *Phos* bro1 phyt bro1 sars bro1 *Sil* bro1 staph bro1 still bro1 sulph bro1

○ - **Bone** marrow: bit-ga mtf carb-v mtf carc mtf crot-h mtf *Ferr* mtf ferr-act mtf ferr-cit mtf ferr-i mtf *Ferr-p* mtf kali-m mtf *Merc* mtf nit-ac mtf pip-m mtf pip-n mtf *Plb* mtf syph mtf tub mtf
  - **decreased** activity: carc mtf syph mtf x-ray mtf

- **Condyles**: arg-met ptk1 cycl ptk1 rhus-t ptk1 sang ptk1 verat-v ptk1
- **Epiphyses**: calc-p bg2
- **Hollow** bones: aran bg2 fl-ac bg2 merc bg2 mez bg2 rhus-t bg2 still bg2
- **Long** bones | **Deep** in: ruta ptk1
- **Marrow**: am-c ptk1 chel ptk1 chin ptk1 kali-c ptk1 *Lyc* ptk1 mag-m ptk1 naja ptk1 ol-an ptk1 op ptk1 stront-c ptk1 sulph ptk1
- **Periosteum**: *Colch* br1 ruta br1
  - **chronic**: colch br1
- **Protuberances** of bones: bell bg2 crot-t bg2 mez bg2 sil bg2
- **Symphyses** and sutures: calc bro1 *Calc-p* br1* des-ac rbp6

CIRCULATION; complaints of the blood: (↗*Apoplexy; Arteriosclerosis; Blood vessels - complaints; Congestion - blood; Heat - flushes; Stasis; Varicose; SKIN - Gangrene)* *Acon* bg2 *Bell* br1 *Benzol* br1 bov br1 *Cham* bg2 germ-met srj5• *Glon* bg2 ham mrr1 *Iod* br1 kola br1 lachn br1 lact-v br1 *Phos* bg2 *Plb* mrr1 *Sang* br1 sec mrr1 stry-p br1 vanil br1 *Vip* bg2

- **morning**: agar bg2 alum bg2 *Ars* bg2 calc bg2 canth bg2 chin bg2 ferr bg2 graph bg2 ign b7.de* kali-c bg2 *Lyc* bg2 mez bg2 nat-c bg2 *Nux-v* b7.de* phos b4.de* rhus-t bg2 *Sep* b4.de* *Spig* bg2 thuj bg2
- **forenoon**: aloe bg2 arg-met bg2 cann-xyz bg2 guaj bg2 kali-c bg2 *Nat-c* bg2 nat-m bg2 sabad bg2 *Sep* bg2 sul-ac bg2
- **afternoon**: alum bg2 *Calc* b4a.de* ferr bg2 gels bg2 *Kali-n* bg2 *Phos* b4.de* plb bg2 staph bg2 thuj bg2 zinc bg2
  - **sleep**; during | **agg.**: anac bg2 bry bg2 calc bg2 graph bg2 ign bg2 nux-v bg2 phos bg2 *Puls* bg2 sel bg2 **Staph** bg2 sulph bg2
- **evening**: ang bg2 **Arg-met** b7.de* **Arn** bg2 asar bg2 *Bell* b4.de* bov bg2 *Calc* b4.de* canth bg2 **Carb-an** b4.de* carb-v b4.de* **Caust** b4.de* *Chel* bg2 chin bg2 ferr bg2 graph bg2 ign bg2 *Kali-c* b4.de* *Kali-n* bg2 lach bg2 **Lyc** b4.de* mag-c bg2 mang bg2 merc bg2 **Mez** b4.de* nat-c bg2 nat-m b4.de* *Nit-ac* b4.de* olnd bg2 petr b4.de* phos bg2 **Puls** b7.de* ran-b bg2 rhus-t bg2 sabin bg2 samb bg2 *Sars* b4a.de* sep b4.de* *Spig* bg2 sulph b4.de* *Teucr* bg2 **Thuj** b4.de* *Zinc* b4.de*
- **night**: am-c b4a.de* ant-t bg2 arn bg2 *Ars* b4.de* borx bg2 *Bry* bg2 calc b4.de* carb-an bg2 **Dulc** b4.de* graph bg2 *Hep* bg2 ign bg2 kali-n bg2 lyc bg2 *Mag-c* b4a.de* *Merc* b4.de* mez bg2 mur-ac bg2 **Nat-c** b4.de* nat-m bg2 *Nit-ac* bg2 *Phos* b4.de* *Ran-s* bg2 sabin bg2 **Sep** b4.de* **Sil** b4a.de* squil bg2 sulph bg2 thuj bg2
  - **midnight**: calc bg2
    - **after** | **2**-3 h: benz-ac bg2
- **accompanied** by | **gangrenous** inflammation (See Inflammation - gangrenous - accompanied - blood)
- **air** agg.; in open: nat-m bg2
- **anger**: *Acon* bg2 *Bry* bg2 **Cham** bg2 coloc b4a.de* ign bg2 nat-m bg2 *Petr* b4a.de* **Sep** b4a.de* staph bg2
- **ascending** stairs agg.: acon bg2 *Ars* bg2 *Bar-c* bg2 bell bg2 bry bg2 calc bg2 ferr bg2 graph bg2 kali-n bg2 merc bg2 nat-c bg2 nat-m bg2 **Nit-ac** bg2 nux-v bg2 **Petr** b4.de* rhus-t bg2 ruta bg2 seneg bg2 sep bg2 spig bg2 *Spong* bg2 stann bg2 staph bg2 sulph bg2 **Thuj** bg2 zinc bg2

- **beer** agg.: acon bg2 ars bg2 bell bg2 coloc bg2 *Ferr* bg2 lyc bg2 nux-v bg2 puls bg2 *Rhus-t* bg2 sec bg2 *Sep* bg2 stram bg2 **Sulph** b4a.de* *Thuj* bg2 verat bg2
- **coffee** agg.: canth bg2 caust bg2 **Cham** bg2 chin bg2 cocc bg2 *Ign* bg2 ip bg2 merc bg2 *Nux-v* bg2 ph-ac bg2 puls bg2 rhus-t bg2 sulph bg2 thuj bg2
- **coition** | **agg**.: visc bg2
- **cold** agg.; taking a: dulc bg2
- **collapse**: mal-ac mtf11
- **company** agg.: carb-v bg2
- **cough** agg.: *Acon* bg2 apis bg2 *Arn* bg2 **Ars** bg2 **Bell** bg2 bry bg2 **Calc** bg2 carb-v bg2 chin bg2 *Ip* bg2 nat-m bg2 nit-ac bg2 *Nux-v* bg2 **Phos** bg2 puls bg2 rhus-t bg2 sabad bg2 sec bg2 **Sep** bg2 spong bg2 squil bg2 sulph bg2
- **diminished**: aeth br1 carb-an br1 esch br1 mangi br1
- **disturbed**; peripheral: crat mtf11 hist sp1
- **drinking** agg.; after: acon bg2 anac bg2 ant-t bg2 *Arn* bg2 **Ars** bg2 brom bg2 bry bg2 **Calc** bg2 *Chin* bg2 cocc bg2 coloc bg2 **Con** b4.de* croc bg2 cupr bg2 ferr bg2 hep bg2 *Nat-m* bg2 nit-ac bg2 *Nux-v* bg2 puls bg2 *Rhus-t* bg2 *Sil* bg2 sulph bg2 teucr bg2 *Thuj* bg2 **Verat** bg2
- **eating**:
  - **after**:
    - **agg**.: acon bg2 alum bg2 ang bg2 asaf bg2 *Bry* bg2 cact bg2 *Calc* b4a.de* camph bg2 **Carb-an** b4.de* *Carb-v* bg2 caust bg2 cham bg2 chin bg2 con bg2 hep bg2 ign bg2 kali-c bg2 **Lyc** b4.de* mez b4.de* *Nat-c* bg2 nat-m bg2 *Nit-ac* b4.de* *Nux-v* bg2 par bg2 petr bg2 ph-ac bg2 **Phos** b4.de* *Puls* bg2 ran-b bg2 **Sel** bg2 sep bg2 sil bg2 sul-ac bg2 sulph bg2 thuj bg2 viol-t bg2 zinc b4.de*
    - **amel**.: chin b7.de
  - **before** | **agg**.: calc bg2 **Chin** bg2 con bg2 iod bg2 *Kali-c* bg2 *Nat-c* bg2 phos bg2 sep bg2
  - **while** | **agg**.: am-c bg2 carb-an bg2 carb-v bg2 ign bg2 *Kali-c* bg2 nit-ac bg2 sep bg2 *Spig* bg2
- **emotions**; from: *Acon* bg2 **Aml-ns** bg2 apis bg2 asaf bg2 *Aur* bg2 *Bell* bg2 bry bg2 calc bg2 **Cham** bg2 coff bg2 colch bg2 *Coloc* bg2 *Con* bg2 cupr bg2 **Hyos** bg2 **Ign** bg2 kali-c bg2 *Lach* bg2 lyc bg2 mag-c bg2 nat-m bg2 *Nit-ac* bg2 *Nux-v* bg2 op bg2 *Petr* bg2 *Ph-ac* bg2 *Phos* b4.de* plat bg2 **Puls** bg2 *Sep* bg2 *Staph* bg2 stram bg2 teucr bg2 thuj bg2 verat bg2
- **exertion** agg.; after: acon bg2 *Am-c* b4.de* arn bg2 ars bg2 bry bg2 dig bg2 **Iod** b4a.de* lach bg2 lyc bg2 meph bg2 **Merc** b4.de* nat-m b4a.de* rhus-t bg2 sil bg2 spong bg2 sulph bg2 thuj bg2
- **hanging** down of parts agg.: ph-ac bg2
- **hungry**; when: kali-c b4.de
- **inspiration**:
  - **agg**.: bell bg2 sep bg2
  - **deep** | **amel**.: carb-v bg2
- **irregular** circulation: acon bg2 am-m br1 *Bell* bg2 *Chin* bg2 *Ferr* bg2 *Glon* bg2 *Lach* bg2 nux-v bg2 *Puls* bg2 sep bg2 **Sulph** bg2
  - **blood** seems to be in a constant turmoil (See Blood - turmoil)
- **lying**:
  - **back**; on | **agg**.: alum bg2 am-c bg2 am-m bg2 **Ars** b4.de* caust bg2 cham bg2 chin bg2 coloc bg2 cupr bg2 ign bg2 iod bg2 *Kali-n* bg2 *Nux-v* bg2 *Phos* bg2 plb bg2 *Puls* bg2 rhus-t bg2 *Sep* bg2 *Sil* bg2 spig bg2
  - **bed**; in | **agg**.: acon bg2 agn bg2 alum bg2 ambr bg2 ang bg2 ant-c bg2 ant-t bg2 *Arg-met* b7.de* arn bg2 asaf bg2 asar bg2 aur bg2 borx bg2 bry bg2 **Calc** b4.de* cham bg2 chel bg2 coloc bg2 ferr bg2 graph bg2 *Hell* bg2 ign bg2 iod bg2 *Kali-c* bg2 kali-n bg2 led bg2 **Lyc** bg2 mag-m bg2 mang bg2 meny bg2 merc bg2 mosch bg2 *Nat-m* b4.de* **Nit-ac** b4.de* nux-v bg2 ox-ac bg2 phos bg2 pip-n bg2 *Puls* bg2 *Rhus-t* bg2 **Samb** bg2 *Sel* bg2 seneg bg2 *Sep* bg2 spig bg2 stront-c bg2 *Sulph* bg2 valer bg2 verat bg2 *Viol-t* bg2
  - **side**; on | **left** | **agg**.: acon bg2 am-c bg2 anac bg2 ang bg2 *Bar-c* bg2 *Bry* bg2 calc bg2 canth bg2 carb-an bg2 carb-v bg2 chin bg2 dig bg2 glon bg2 *Graph* bg2 ip bg2 *Kali-c* bg2 lil-t bg2 *Lyc* bg2 merc bg2 mez bg2 **Nat-c** b4.de* **Nat-m** b4.de* **Phos** b4.de* pip-n bg2 **Puls** bg2 *Sep* bg2 sil bg2 *Stann* bg2 sulph bg2 thuj bg2
    - **right** | **agg**.: acon bg2 am-m bg2 anac bg2 **Arg-n** bg2 borx bg2 carb-an bg2 ip bg2 kali-n bg2 lyc bg2 mag-m bg2 *Merc* bg2 **Nux-v** bg2 puls bg2 seneg bg2 spig bg2 spong bg2 *Stann* bg2 tab bg2 viol-t bg2
- **lying** down agg.; after: agn bg2 am-c bg2 *Ambr* bg2 **Arg-met** bg2 *Ars* bg2 asaf bg2 *Aur* bg2 bry bg2 **Calc** bg2 caps bg2 carb-v bg2 cham bg2 chel bg2 clem bg2 cycl bg2 dulc bg2 ferr bg2 glon bg2 graph bg2 hell bg2 **Hep** bg2 hyos bg2 *Kali-c* bg2 *Lyc* bg2 mag-c bg2 mag-m bg2 merc bg2 nux-v bg2 op bg2 *Phos* bg2 *Plat* bg2 plb bg2 *Puls* bg2 *Rhus-t* bg2 sabad bg2 **Samb** b7.de* sel bg2 seneg bg2 *Sep* bg2 spig bg2 spong bg2 squil bg2 stront-c bg2 sul-ac bg2 sulph bg2
- **menses** | **before** | **agg**.: alum bg2 am-c bg2 bar-c bg2 *Calc* bg2 cocc bg2 coloc bg2 con bg2 **Cupr** bg2 iod bg2 **Kali-c** bg2 *Lyc* bg2 merc bg2 nat-m bg2 ph-ac bg2 **Puls** bg2 sec bg2 sep bg2 *Spong* bg2 stann bg2 sulph bg2 verat bg2
  - **during** | **agg**.: ars bg2 calc bg2 chin bg2 **Ign** bg2 iod bg2 phos bg2 **Sep** bg2 *Sulph* bg2
- **motion**:
  - **agg**.: acon bg2 am-m bg2 ant-c bg2 **Ant-t** bg2 arn bg2 bar-c bg2 *Bell* bg2 *Bry* bg2 *Cann-xyz* bg2 chin bg2 colch bg2 **Dig** b4a.de* ferr bg2 *Fl-ac* bg2 *Graph* b4.de* **Iod** b4.de* kali-n bg2 lach bg2 led bg2 mez bg2 nat-c bg2 **Nat-m** b4a.de* *Nit-ac* b4.de* nux-v bg2 olnd bg2 par bg2 **Petr** b4.de* *Phos* bg2 samb bg2 seneg bg2 **Sep** bg2 sil bg2 spig bg2 squil bg2 *Staph* bg2 stram bg2 sulph bg2 *Thuj* b4.de* valer bg2
  - **amel**.: arg-n bg2
  - **arm**; of | **left** arm agg.; of: phos bg2
- **music** agg.: acon bg2 calc bg2 dig bg2 *Lyc* bg2 **Nat-c** bg2 nux-v bg2 *Ph-ac* bg2 **Sep** bg2 *Staph* bg2 **Thuj** bg2 viol-o bg2
- **pain**:
  - **after**: canth b7.de
  - **during**: acon bg2 bov bg2 bufo bg2 cimic bg2 glon bg2 hep bg2 ign bg2 kali-bi bg2 lach bg2 nux-v bg2 spig bg2
- **pressure** agg.: kali-bi bg2
- **relaxation** of mind agg.: acon bg2 asar bg2 *Bell* bg2 bism bg2 *Chin* bg2 cic bg2 dig bg2 mag-c bg2 nat-m bg2 *Petr* bg2 phos bg2 spong bg2 stann bg2 stram bg2
- **rest** agg.: apis bg2 arg-met bg2 arn bg2 aur bg2 bell bg2 *Calc* bg2 caps bg2 cham bg2 chin bg2 coloc bg2 con bg2 cycl bg2 **Dig** bg2 *Dulc* bg2 *Euph* bg2 ferr bg2 *Kali-c* bg2 kali-n bg2 **Kreos** b7a.de* lyc bg2 **Mag-m** bg2 meny bg2 mosch bg2 nat-c bg2 *Nat-m* bg2 par bg2 ph-ac bg2 *Phos* bg2 puls bg2 **Rhus-t** bg2 ruta bg2 sabad bg2 samb bg2 *Seneg* bg2 *Sep* bg2 *Spig* bg2 stann bg2 sulph bg2 tarax bg2 valer bg2
- **rising**:
  - **stooping**; from:
    - **agg**.: *Acon* bg2 ars bg2 bell bg2 *Bry* bg2 nat-m bg2 nux-v bg2 op bg2 phos bg2 rhus-t bg2 squil bg2 sulph bg2 *Verat* bg2
    - **amel**.: aloe bg2
- **singing** in church: | **agg**.: carb-an bg2
- **sitting**:
  - **agg**.: agar bg2 alum bg2 *Anac* b4.de* **Ang** bg2 ant-t bg2 *Asaf* bg2 asar bg2 bar-c bg2 calc b4.de* caps bg2 carb-an bg2 **Carb-v** b4.de* chin bg2 cycl bg2 *Dig* bg2 dulc bg2 ferr bg2 gels bg2 graph bg2 lyc bg2 **Mag-m** b4.de* mang bg2 meny bg2 mosch bg2 mur-ac bg2 **Nat-c** b4.de* ph-ac bg2 **Phos** b4.de* plat bg2 puls bg2 rhod bg2 *Rhus-t* bg2 sabad bg2 seneg bg2 *Sep* bg2 *Sil* b4.de* **Spig** bg2 sulph bg2 *Valer* bg2 verb bg2 viol-t bg2
  - **amel**.: thuj b4a.de
  - **bent** forward | **agg**.: alum bg2 ang bg2 arg-met bg2 bry bg2 cann-xyz bg2 *Chin* bg2 *Dig* bg2 meny bg2 merc bg2 olnd bg2 ph-ac bg2 ran-b bg2 rhod bg2 *Rhus-t* bg2 seneg bg2 *Sil* bg2 *Spig* bg2 spong bg2 stann bg2 staph bg2
- **sleep** | **during** | **agg**.: acon bg2 *Ars* bg2 bell bg2 bufo bg2 *Calc* bg2 camph bg2 cham bg2 chin bg2 hep bg2 hyos bg2 ign bg2 led bg2 merc bg2 *Nat-m* bg2 *Op* bg2 *Ph-ac* bg2 *Phos* bg2 puls bg2 *Rheum* bg2 *Sabin* bg2 *Samb* bg2 sep bg2 sil bg2 stram bg2 *Sulph* bg2 viol-t bg2 *Zinc* bg2
  - **falling** asleep:
    - **agg**.: calc bg2 nat-m bg2 sil bg2
    - **before** | **agg**.: agar bg2 am-c bg2 *Arn* bg2 ars bg2 **Asar** bg2 bar-c bg2 bell bg2 bry bg2 **Calc** bg2 carb-an bg2 carb-v bg2 dulc bg2 graph bg2 ign bg2 lach bg2 *Lyc* bg2 *Mag-c* bg2 mag-m bg2 merc bg2 mur-ac bg2 nat-c bg2 *Nat-m* bg2 nux-v bg2 phos bg2 **Puls** bg2 *Rhus-t* bg2 *Sabad* bg2 sabin bg2 samb bg2 sars bg2 *Sep* bg2 *Sil* bg2 sulph bg2 thuj bg2

- **sleeplessness** agg.: am-c bg2 am-m bg2 arn bg2 *Ars* bg2 asar bg2 borx bg2 *Bry* bg2 **Calc** bg2 camph bg2 *Con* bg2 dulc bg2 hep bg2 kali-c bg2 laur bg2 *Lyc* bg2 mag-c bg2 merc bg2 nat-m bg2 nit-ac bg2 **Phos** bg2 *Plat* bg2 **Puls** bg2 ran-b bg2 **Rhus-t** bg2 **Sabin** bg2 samb bg2 *Sep* bg2 **Sil** bg2 sulph bg2
- **sluggish**, congested: aesc mtf11 aeth bro1 ambr mtf11 anac mtf11 arn mtf11 aster mtf11 bar-c mtf11 both-a rb3 calc bro1 *Calc-p* bro1 carb-an bro1 *Carb-v* bro1 cic mtf11 cimic bro1 cinnm bro1 coxs mtf11 ferr-p bro1 gels br1* hyper mtf11 led bro1 morg fmm1• morg-p fmm1• nat-m bro1 quinhydr mtf11 *Rhus-t* bro1 sec mtf11 *Sil* bro1 sol-ni mtf11 suis-chord-umb mtf11 tab mtf11 uncar-tom mp4•
- **smoking** agg.: acon bg2 ant-c bg2 ars bg2 cic bg2 cycl bg2 *Ign* bg2 nux-v bg2 **Phos** b4.de* *Puls* bg2 sel bg2 seneg bg2 sep bg2 spong bg2 *Staph* bg2
- **standing** agg.: **Agar** bg2 aur bg2 *Con* bg2 cycl bg2 ferr bg2 nat-m b4.de* **Plat** bg2 puls bg2 rhus-t bg2 *Valer* bg2
- **stool** agg.; after: ant-t bg2 *Ars* bg2 caust bg2 nit-ac bg2 *Op* bg2 rhus-t bg2
- **stooping** agg.: acon bg2 agar bg2 alum bg2 am-c bg2 ang bg2 arg-met bg2 *Bry* bg2 cann-xyz bg2 chin bg2 *Dig* bg2 *Graph* bg2 mang bg2 *Merc* bg2 merc-c bg2 nat-c bg2 olnd bg2 ph-ac bg2 ran-b bg2 seneg bg2 *Sep* bg2 sil bg2 **Spig** bg2 squil bg2 **Sul-ac** b4.de* valer bg2 verat bg2
- **stretching** agg.: phos bg2
- **talking** agg.: alum bg2 am-c bg2 *Ambr* bg2 anac bg2 *Arn* bg2 bell bg2 borx bg2 *Bry* bg2 *Calc* bg2 cann-xyz bg2 canth bg2 *Carb-v* bg2 cham bg2 chin bg2 cocc bg2 dulc bg2 graph bg2 *Hep* bg2 ign bg2 iod bg2 *Kali-c* bg2 *Led* bg2 mang bg2 merc bg2 merc-c bg2 mez bg2 mur-ac bg2 nat-c bg2 nat-m bg2 *Ph-ac* bg2 *Phos* bg2 *Plat* bg2 **Puls** bg2 ran-b bg2 *Rhus-t* bg2 *Sel* bg2 sep bg2 spig bg2 squil bg2 *Stann* bg2 stram bg2 sul-ac bg2 *Sulph* bg2 verat bg2
- **tea** agg.: ars bg2 chin bg2 *Ferr* bg2 hep bg2 ph-ac bg2 **Sel** bg2 thuj bg2 verat bg2
- **thinking** of it agg.: arg-n bg2 bar-c bg2
- **turning** in bed agg.: *Acon* bg2 am-m bg2 **Ars** bg2 bry bg2 *Cann-xyz* bg2 caps bg2 carb-v bg2 con bg2 ferr bg2 *Hep* bg2 kreos bg2 *Lyc* bg2 nat-m bg2 nux-v bg2 **Puls** bg2 rhus-t bg2 sil bg2 staph bg2 *Sulph* bg2 thuj bg2
- **urination** agg.; before | **agg.**: lil-t bg2
- **vertigo**:
  - **during** | **agg.**: bell bg2 nat-c bg2 phos bg2
- **vomiting** | **agg.**: ars bg2 cupr bg2 ip bg2 mosch bg2 puls bg2 sulph bg2 *Verat* b7.de*
- **waking**; on: agar bg2 alum bg2 am-c bg2 ambr bg2 arn bg2 *Ars* bg2 bar-c bg2 bell bg2 borx bg2 **Calc** bg2 camph bg2 carb-an bg2 carb-v bg2 chin bg2 cina bg2 cocc bg2 ferr bg2 *Graph* bg2 ign b7.de* ip bg2 kali-bi bg2 *Kali-c* bg2 *Lyc* bg2 mag-c bg2 mez bg2 mosch bg2 *Nat-c* bg2 *Nat-m* bg2 nit-ac bg2 *Nux-v* bg2 petr bg2 ph-ac bg2 *Phos* b4.de* puls bg2 ran-s bg2 *Rhus-t* bg2 sabin bg2 **Sep** bg2 *Sil* bg2 spig bg2 *Staph* bg2 sul-ac bg2 *Sulph* bg2 thuj bg2 verat bg2 *Zinc* bg2
- **walking**:
  - **after** | **agg.**: agar bg2 *Ambr* bg2 anac bg2 ars bg2 cann-xyz bg2 carb-v bg2 ferr bg2 hyos bg2 led bg2 *Lyc* bg2 meny bg2 nux-v bg2 *Petr* bg2 *Puls* bg2 *Rhus-t* bg2 sabad bg2 sabin bg2 *Sep* bg2 stann bg2 valer bg2
  - **agg.**: arg-n bg2 arn bg2 aur bg2 bell bg2 *Bry* bg2 colch bg2 dig bg2 graph bg2 led bg2 lyc bg2 merc bg2 merc-c bg2 nat-m bg2 *Nit-ac* b4.de* *Nux-v* bg2 *Petr* b4.de* phos bg2 samb bg2 sel bg2 spig bg2 squil bg2 *Staph* bg2
  - **air**; in open | **after** | **agg.**: *Petr* b4a.de sep b4.de
    - **agg.**: **Am-c** b4.de* am-m bg2 *Ambr* b7.de* anac bg2 ant-c bg2 arg-met bg2 *Bell* bg2 borx bg2 camph bg2 chin bg2 *Cocc* bg2 con bg2 guaj bg2 *Hep* bg2 lyc bg2 **Nux-v** bg2 petr bg2 ph-ac bg2 rhus-t bg2 *Sel* bg2 **Sep** b4.de* *Spig* bg2 staph bg2 sulph bg2 tarax bg2
  - **amel.**: glon bg2
  - **rapidly** | **agg.**: plb bg2
- **warm** room agg.: agn bg2 am-c bg2 am-m bg2 ambr bg2 anac bg2 ang bg2 ant-c bg2 *Apis* bg2 ars bg2 asar bg2 bell bg2 bry bg2 calc bg2 *Croc* bg2 graph bg2 **Iod** bg2 *Ip* bg2 laur bg2 *Lyc* bg2 nat-m bg2 phos bg2 plat bg2 *Puls* bg2 rhod bg2 rhus-t bg2 *Sabin* bg2 sel bg2 seneg bg2 spig bg2 sul-ac bg2 sulph bg2 thuj bg2 verb bg2
- **weak**: carb-v tl1 cinnm br1 fl-ac mtf11 lyc br1
  - **accompanied** by | **perspiration**; profuse: salv br1
- **weather** | **stormy** | **before**: psor bg2
  - **warm** weather | **agg.**: ant-c bg2 asar bg2 *Bry* bg2 carb-v bg2 cocc bg2 colch bg2 *Graph* bg2 **Iod** bg2 lach bg2 lyc bg2 **Nit-ac** b4.de* op bg2 ph-ac bg2 phos bg2 *Puls* bg2 sec bg2 sel bg2 sep bg2 *Sulph* bg2
- **whiskey** | **agg.**: **Arn** bg2 *Ars* bg2 calc bg2 chin bg2 cocc bg2 **Fl-ac** bg2 hep bg2 ign bg2 *Lach* bg2 led bg2 *Nux-v* bg2 *Op* bg2 rhus-t bg2 stram bg2 sul-ac bg2 sulph bg2

Circulation; complaints of the blood: ...

- **wine** agg.: ant-c bg2 arn bg2 **Ars** bg2 borx bg2 calc bg2 *Carb-v* bg2 coff bg2 fl-ac bg2 *Lach* bg2 **Lyc** bg2 nat-c bg2 **Nat-m** b4.de* nux-m bg2 *Nux-v* bg2 op bg2 *Ran-b* bg2 sabad bg2 sel bg2 **Sil** b4a.de* **Thuj** bg2 *Zinc* bg2

○ - **Veins**: carb-v ptk1 puls ptk1 sulph ptk1

EXTERNAL PARTS; complaints of: acon b2.de* *Agar* b2.de* *Agn* b2.de* alum b2.de* am-m b2.de* anac b2.de* ang b2.de* ant-c b2.de* *Arg-met* b2.de* *Arn* b2.de* ars b2.de* asaf b2.de* asar b2.de aur b2.de* bar-c b2.de* bell b2.de* bism b2.de* bry b2.de* calc b2.de* cann-s b2.de* caps b2.de* carb-an b2.de* carb-v b2.de* *Caust* b2.de* cham b2.de* chin b2.de* cic b2.de* cina b2.de* clem b2.de* cocc b2.de* colch b2.de* coloc b2.de* con b2.de* croc b2.de* cycl b2.de* dig b2.de* dros b2.de* dulc b2.de* euph b2.de* *Euphr* b2.de* ferr b2.de* graph b2.de* hell b2.de* hep b2.de* hyos b2.de* ign b2.de* ip b2.de* *Kali-c* b2.de* kali-n bg2 kreos b2.de* lach b2.de* led b2.de* m-ambo b2.de *M-arct* b2.de m-aust b2.de mag-c b2.de* mag-m b2.de* mang b2.de* *Meny* b2.de* merc b2.de* mez b2.de* mosch b2.de* mur-ac b2.de* *Nat-c* b2.de* nat-m b2.de* nit-ac b2.de* nux-m b2.de* nux-v b2.de* *Olnd* b2.de* op b2.de* par b2.de* petr b2.de* ph-ac b2.de* phos b2.de* **Plat** b2.de* puls b2.de* ran-b b2.de* ran-s b2.de* rhod b2.de* **Rhus-t** b2.de* ruta b2.de* sabad b2.de* sabin b2.de* samb b2.de* sars b2.de* sec b2.de* sel b2.de* seneg b2.de* sep b2.de* sil b2.de* *Spig* b2.de* spong b2.de* squil b2.de* stann b2.de* staph b2.de* stram b2.de* stront-c b2.de* sul-ac b2.de* sulph b2.de* *Tarax* b2.de* teucr b2.de thuj b2.de* valer b2.de* verat b2.de* verb b2.de* viol-o b2.de* viol-t b2.de* zinc b2.de*

GLANDS; complaints of the: *(↗Abscesses - glands; Indurations - glands; Inflammation - glands; Swelling - glands)* apis ptk1 ars ptk1 arum-t ptk1 aur br1* bar-c bg2* *Bell* bg2* berb-a br1 brom ptk1 *Bry* ptk1 *Calc* br1* carb-an ptk1 chim br1 chin ptk1 *Cist* br1* *Clem* br1* con bg2* *Dulc* br1 fuli br1 hep ptk1 *Iod* bg2* kali-m ptk1 *Lach* ptk1 lap-a br1 lyc bg2* med jl2 *Merc* bg2* nit-ac ptk1 phos bg2* *Phyt* br1* **Puls** ptk1 rhod ptk1 rhus-t bg2* sil bg2* spong bg2* staph ptk1 sulph bg2* tab ptk1 tub ptk1

- **activity** increased: *Jab* br1
- **cold**; after taking a: con tl1
- **eruptions**; after suppressed: psor mtf33
- **paroxysmal**: cact bro1 dig bro1 glon bro1 samb bro1

INTERNAL PARTS; complaints of: *Acon* b2.de* aloe bg2 alum b2.de* *Am-c* b2.de* ambr b2.de* ang b2.de* ant-c b2.de* *Ant-t* b2.de* arg-n bg2 ars b2.de* asaf b2.de* asar b2.de* aur b2.de* bell b2.de* bism b2.de* borx b2.de* bov b2.de* *Bry* b2.de* bufo bg2 calad b2.de* **Calc** b2.de* camph b2.de* cann-s b2.de* **Canth** b2.de* caps b2.de* carb-an b2.de* carb-v b2.de* caust b2.de* cham b2.de* chel b2.de* *Chin* b2.de* cic b2.de* cocc b2.de* colch b2.de* coloc b2.de* con b2.de* croc b2.de* cupr b2.de* dig b2.de* dulc b2.de* euph b2.de* ferr b2.de* gels bg2 glon bg2 graph b2.de* *Hell* b2.de* hep b2.de* hyos b2.de* ign b2.de* iod b2.de* ip b2.de* kali-c b2.de* kali-n b2.de* kreos b2.de* lach b2.de* *Laur* b2.de* lyc b2.de* m-ambo b2.de m-arct b2.de m-aust b2.de mag-c b2.de* mag-m b2.de* mang b2.de* meny b2.de* merc b2.de* merc-c bg2 mez b2.de* mosch b2.de* mur-ac b2.de* nat-c b2.de* nat-m b2.de* nit-ac b2.de* nux-m b2.de* **Nux-v** b2.de* olnd b2.de* par b2.de* petr b2.de* ph-ac b2.de* **Phos** b2.de* plat b2.de* plb b2.de* podo bg2 puls b2.de* ran-b b2.de* ran-s b2.de* rheum b2.de* rhod b2.de* rhus-t b2.de* ruta b2.de* sabad b2.de* sabin b2.de* sars b2.de* sec b2.de* *Seneg* b2.de* sep b2.de* sil b2.de* spig b2.de* spong b2.de* squil b2.de* stann b2.de* staph b2.de* stram b2.de* stront-c b2.de* sul-ac b2.de* sulph b2.de* tarax b2.de* teucr b2.de* thuj b2.de* valer b2.de* verat b2.de* verb b2.de* viol-o b2.de* zinc b2.de*

JOINTS; complaints of the: *Arg-met* br1 *Arn* ptk1 bell ptk1 *Benz-ac* ptk1 *Bry* ptk1 *Calc* ptk1 caust ptk1 *Cham* ptk1 cimic ptk1 **Colch** ptk1 dros ptk1 dulc ptk1 graph ptk1 guaj ptk1 kali-bi ptk1 kalm ptk1 led ptk1 lith-c ptk1 lyc ptk1 *Mang* ptk1 **Merc** ptk1 morg fmm1• nat-m ptk1 nux-v ptk1 phyt ptk1 *Puls* ptk1 rad-br ptk1 *Rhus-t* br1* ruta ptk1 *Sabin* ptk1 sep ptk1 *Sil* ptk1 staph ptk1 stront-c ptk1 **Sulph** ptk1 symph br1

- **alternating** with | **eruptions**: staph ptk1
- **cold** agg.; taking a: calc-p ptk1 rumx ptk1
- **lying** down agg.: led tl1
- **subacute**: guaj bro1 *Led* bro1 puls bro1
- **suppressed**: *Caj* bro1 nat-m bro1 ox-ac bro1 rhus-t bro1

○ - **Deep** in: cimic ptk1 rad-br ptk1

- **Small** joints: act-sp ptk1 benz-ac ptk1 *Caul* br1* colch tl1* kali-bi ptk1 led tl1* lith-c ptk1 nat-p ptk1 ran-s ptk1 rhod ptk1 sabin ptk1 sal-ac ptk1 stel mtf stict ptk1 thuj ptk1 [bell-p-sp dcm1]

- **Small** joints: ...
  - **exertion** agg.: [bell-p-sp dcm1]
- **Surfaces** of joints: hip-ac br1
- **Synovial** membranes: *Colch* br1
  - **chronic**: colch br1

MUCOUS MEMBRANES; complaints of: abies-c br1 acon bg* all-c bg* anemps br1 *Ang* br1 ant-t bg* apis bg* arg-n bg* ars b4a.de* bell b4a.de* borx bg* bry bg* canth mrr1 caps bg* *Cham* bg* *Cop* br1 *Crot-t* br1 cub br1 *Dulc* b4a.de* eucal ptk1 *Euph* b4a.de* euphr bg fuli br1 hep b4a.de* hip-ac br1 hydr bg* ichth br1 inul br1 ip bg* kali-bi bg2* kali-c bg* kali-i bg2 kreos tl1 *Merc* b4a.de* *Mez* b4a.de myric br1 nit-ac b4a.de* *Nux-v* bg* pen br1 phos bg* phyt bg2 pix br1 *Puls* bg* *Rhus-t* br1 rumx ptk1 sabad ptk1 sal-ac tl1 *Sang* br1* senec ptk1 seneg b4a.de* skook br1 squil ptk1 *Stann* b4a.de* *Sulph* b4a.de* syph ptk1 ter ptk1 thuj ptk1 tub-sp jl2 xan br1 [bell-p-sp dcm1]
- **bleeding** (See Hemorrhage - mucous)
- **cancer** of: eucal gm1
- **chronic** complaints | **irritability**; with (See MIND - Irritability - mucous)
- **degeneration**: mez tl1 phos br1
- **discoloration** of:
  - **dark**: aesc ptk1 bapt ptk1 carb-v ptk1 ham ptk1 lach ptk1 merc-i-r ptk1 mez ptk1 phos ptk1
  - **pale**: abrot bg2 acet-ac bg2 alum bg2 arn bg2 ars bg2* calc-p bg2 carb-an bg2 carb-v bg2 chin bg2* cupr bg2 ferr bg2* graph bg2 kali-c bg2* mang bg2* nat-m bg2 phos bg2* puls bg2 senec bg2 sulph bg2
  - **red**: acon ptk1 *Ars-i* br1 bell ptk1 canth ptk1
    - **bright** red: acon bg2 arg-n bg2 arum-t bg2 bell bg2 canth bg2 caps bg2 colch bg2 ign bg2 sabad bg2
    - **dark** red: aesc bg2 arg-n bg2 bapt bg2 carb-v bg2 ham bg2 lach bg2 merc bg2 phyt bg2 puls bg2
- **dryness**: acet-ac bg2 acon bg2 aesc bg2* ail bg2 aloe bg2 alum bg2* bar-c bg2 bell bg2* borx bg2 *Bry* bg2* caps bg2 caust bg2* cist bg2 con bg2 cygn-ol sze3• euph bg2 falco-ch sze4• form bg2 gels bg2 guaj bg2 hist sp1 kali-c bg2* lith-c bg2 mag-c bg2 merc bg2 mez bg2 *Nat-m* bg2* *Nux-m* bg2* nux-v bg2 petr bg2 phos bg2 phyt bg2 plb bg2 sabad bg2 sang bg2* seneg bg2 stict ptk1 sul-i bg2 ter bg2 uran-n br1 *Verat* bg2* zinc bg2
- **excoriation**: *Kreos* mrr1
- **glistening**: apis bg2 bell bg2 cist bg2 hyos bg2 phos bg2 stram bg2
- **inflammation** (See Inflammation - mucous)
- **irritation**: alum tl1 arg-n br1 *Ars-i* br1 carb-ac br1 crot-t br1 euph br1 phos br1
- **itching**: ars-i br1
- **pain** | **burning**: ars-i br1 caps tl1 kreos tl1 ter mrr1
- **pale** (See discoloration - pale)
- **raw**: am-c bg2 arum-t bg2* borx bg2 brom bg2 caps bg2 carb-v bg2 kreos bg2* merc bg2 mur-ac bg2 nit-ac bg2 *Nux-v* bg2* phos bg2 sul-ac bg2 thuj bg2
- **relaxation** of (See Relaxation - mucous)
- **serous**: abrot bg2 acon bg2* ant-t bg2 apis bg2* ars ptk1 *Bry* bg2* canth bg2* colch ptk1 *Dulc* mrr1 hell bg* kali-c bg2* lac-ac bg2 lyc ptk1 merc bg2 ran-b bg* rhus-t bg2 sabin br1 seneg ptk1 sil ptk1 squil bg2* sul-i bg2 sulph bg2*
  - **irritation**: phos br1
- **slimy**: merc tl1
- **sticky**: apis bg2 arg-n bg2 arn bg2 ars bg2 canth bg2 carb-v bg2 con bg2 hep bg2 kali-c bg2 lach bg2 nit-ac bg2 nux-v bg2 phyt bg2 puls bg2 sulph bg2 thuj bg2
- **sulci** of: kali-bi bg
- **swelling** of (See Swelling - mucous)
- **ulceration** of: ail bg2* aloe bg2 alum bg2 *Am-caust* br1 apis bg2 arg-met bg2 arg-n bg2* ars bg2* ars-i bg2 arum-t bg2 asaf bg2 aur bg2 calc bg2 caps bg2 carb-ac bg2 carb-an bg2 cupr bg2 hydr bg2* iod bg2 kali-bi bg2 kali-chl bg2 kali-i bg2* kreos bg2* lach br1 merc mtf33 merc-c bg2* mur-ac tl1 nit-ac bg2* phos bg2 phyt bg2* sil bg2* sul-ac bg2* syph mrr1

MUSCLES; complaints of: *(↗Atrophy - muscles; Dystrophy - muscles)* agar ptk1 anac ptk1 arn ptk1 ars ptk1 **Bell** ptk1 **Bry** ptk1 *Calc* ptk1 **Caust** ptk1 *Cimic* bg2* cocc ptk1 con ptk1 *Eup-per* ptk1 gels ptk1 hell ptk1 hyos ptk1 kali-c ptk1 **Lyc** bg2 *Mur-ac* ptk1 *Nat-m* bg2 nux-v ptk1 *Plat* bg2 **Rhus-t** ptk1 sec ptk1 *Sep* bg2 til ptk1 valer ptk1 *Verat* ptk1 zinc ptk1
- **exertion** agg.: [bell-p-sp dcm1]

NERVES; complaints of (See Neurological)

SPHINCTERS; complaints of: laur ptk1 sil ptk1 staph ptk1

LIST OF REMEDY ABBREVIATIONS

10 (Paterson) = bacls-10.	
7 (Paterson) = bacls-7.	
abel.	abelmoschus
abies-a.	abies alba
abies balsamea = abies-c.	
abies-c.	abies canadensis
abies-n.	abies nigra
abr.	abrus precatorius
abrin.	abrusinum
abrom-a.	abroma augusta
abrom-a-fol.	abroma augusta folia
abrom-a-r.	abroma augusta radix
abrot.	abrotanum
absin.	absinthium
absintls.	absintalsem
acac-ar.	acacia arabica
acac-f.	acacia farnesiana
Acacia senegal = acac-ar.	
acal.	acalypha indica
acanthia lectularia = cimx.	
acanthus mollis = bran.	
acanth-v.	acanthus virilis
accip-ge.	accipiter gentilis
acenoc.	acenocoumarol
acer-c.	acer campestre
acer-circ.	acer circinatum
acet-ac.	aceticum acidum
acer negundo = neg.	
acetald.	acetaldehyde
acetan.	acetanilidum
acetars.	acetarsolum
acetaz.	acetazolamide
aceton.	acetonum
acetontl.	acetonitrilum
acetoph.	acetophenonum
acetylar.	acetylarsan
acetylch.	acetylcholine
acetylch-m.	acetylcholinum muriaticum
acetyls-ac.	acetylsalicylicum acidum
achillea millefolium = mill.	
achil-m.	achillea moschata
achil-n.	achillea nana
achil-p.	achillea ptarmica
achras	achras sapota
achy.	achyranthes calea
achy-a.	achyranthes aspera
acicl.	aciclovir
acidum aceticum glaciale = acet-ac.	
acidum ascorbicum = ascor-ac.	
acidum asparticum = aspart-ac.	
acidum benzoicum = benz-ac.	
acidum boricum = bor-ac.	
acidum butyricum = but-ac.	
acidum cis aconiticum = acon-ac.	
acidum folicum = fol-ac.	
acidum glutamicum = gluta-ac.	
acidum hydriodicum = iod-h.	
acidum hydrochloricum = mur-ac.	
acidum hydroiodicum = iod-h.	
acidum lacticum = lac-ac.	
acidum maleicum = mal-ac.	
acidum nicotinicum = nicot-ac.	
acidum oleicum = ol-ac.	
acidum pantothenicum = pant-ac.	
acidum phosphoricum = ph-ac.	
acidum picronitricum = pic-ac.	
acidum salicylicum = sal-ac.	
acidum silicicum = sil.	
acidum tartaricum = tart-ac.	
acioa-d.	acioa dewevrei
acip-st-ov.	acipenser sturio ex ovis
aclad.	acladium castellanii
acok-op.	acokanthera oppositifolia
acon.	aconitum napellus
acon-a.	aconitum anthora
acokanthera schimperi = car.	
acokanthera venenata = acok-op.	
acon-ac.	aconiticum acidum
acon-c.	aconitum cammarum
acon-co.	aconitum columbianum
acon-f.	aconitum ferox
aconin.	aconitinum
acon-l.	aconitum lycoctonum
acon-s.	aconitum septentrionale
acorus calamus = calam.	
acrol.	acroleinum
actin-a.	actinomyces albus
actin-c.	actinomyces citreus
actin-g.	actinomyces griseus
actinidia deliciosa var. deliciosa = actinid-d.	
actinid-ctx.	actinidiae cortex
actea racemosa = cimic.	
actea spicata = act-sp.	
ACTH = cortico.	
actinidia chinensis var. deliciosa = actinid-d.	
actinid-d.	actinidia deliciosa
actin-l.	actinomyces luteus
actaea racemosa = cimic.	
act-sp.	actaea spicata
adam.	adamas
adans-d.	adansonia digitata

adax. adaxukah
adel. Adelheid aqua
Adelheid quelle = adel.
adelpha bredowii = limen-b-c.
adenin. adeninum
adenyl-ac. adenylicum acidum
adeps suillus = adeps-s.
adeps suillus depuratus = adeps-s.
adeps-s. adeps suis
adhatoda = just.
adhatoda vasika = just.
adiant. adiantum capillus veneris
adlu. adlumia fungosa
a-dnitroph. alpha-dinitrophenolum
adon. adonis vernalis
adon-ae. adonis aestivalis
adn = des-ac.
adonin. adonidinum
adox. adoxa moschatellina
adp. adenosinum diphosphoricum acidum
adr-ctx. adrenalis cortex
adp = adp.
adrenal cortex = adr-ctx.
adren. adrenalinum
adren-bt. adrenalinum bitartaricum
adrenocorticotropinum = cortico.
aegle-f. aegle folia
aegle-m. aegle marmelos
aegop-p. aegopodium podagraria
aer-mar-a. aer maritim artificialis
aer-med. aer medicalis
aesc. aesculus hippocastanum
aesc-c. aesculus carnea
aesc-ctx. aesculus hippocastanum e cortice
aesc-g. aesculus glabra
aescin. aesculinum
aeth. aethusa cynapium
aethanolum = alco.
aether aether
aether aethylicus = aether
aether sulphuricus = aether
aethi-a. aethiops antimonialis
aethi-m. aethiops mineralis
aethylicum = aethyl.
aethyl. aethylium
aethyl-act. aethylium aceticum
aethyl-br. aethylium bromidum
aethyl alcohol = alco.
aethylce. aethylcellulose
aethyl-m. aethylium muriaticum
aethyl-n. aethylium nitricum
aethylium nitrosum = nit-s-d.
aethyl-s. aethylium sulfuricum
aethyl-s-d. aethylium sulfuricum dichloratum
ag-ag. agar agar
aethylum aceticum = aethyl-act.
aethylum nitricum = aethyl-n.
aethylum oxidum = aether
agam-g. agamemnon graphium
agap. agapanthus
agaricus laricis = bol-la.
agar. agaricus muscarius
agar-ac. agaricicum acidum
agar-cit. agaricus citrinus
agaricus bulbosus = agar-ph.
agar-cpn. agaricus campanulatus
agar-cps. agaricus campestris
agar-em. agaricus emeticus
agarin. agaricinum
agar-pa. agaricus pantherinus
agar-ph. agaricus phalloides
agar-pr. agaricus procerus
agar-r. agaricus rubescens
agar-se. agaricus semiglobatus
agar-st. agaricus stercorarius
agar-v. agaricus vernus
agath-a. agathis Australis
agav-a. agave Americana
agave rigida = agav-t.
agav-t. agave tequilana
ager-c. ageratum conyzoides
agkistrodon contortrix = cench.
agkistrodon piscivorus = ancis-p.
agn. agnus castus
agra. agraphis nutans
agre. agremone ochroleuca
agri. agrimonia eupatoria
agri-fl. agrimonia eupatoria flos
agrim. agrimony (Bach fl.)
agri-od. agrimonia odorata
agropyron repens = tritic.
agropyrum repens = tritic.
agro. agrostema githago
agrostemma githago = agro.
agrosti-a. agrostis alba
agrosti-ca. agrostis capillaris
agrosti-vg. agrostis vulgaris
aids. aids nosode
ailanthus altissima = ail.
ail. ailanthus glandulosa
aira-fl. aira flexuosa
aju-c. ajuga chamaepitys
aju-r. ajuga reptans
aka joanesia asoca = joan.
alab. alabaster
alam. alamanitra
alan-d. alaninum D
alan-l. alaninum L
album. albuminum
alarconia helenoides = wye.

albz-f.	albizzia fastigiata
alchem-a.	alchemillia alpina
alchem-ar.	alchemilla arvensis
alchem-vg.	alchemilla vulgaris
alchor-c.	alchornea cordifolia
alcohol fortis = alco-de.	
alco.	alcoholus
alco-de.	alcohol dehydratatum
alco-s.	= carbn-s. = alcoholus sulphuris
ald.	aldehydum
aldos.	aldosteron
alet.	aletris farinosa
aleurisma canis = aleur-l.	
aleurisma castellanii = aclad.	
aleur-l.	aleurisma lugdunense
alexandra senna = senn.	
alf.	alfalfa
alh.	alhanodium
alhenna = henna	
alis-p.	alisma plantago
all-a.	allium ascalonicum
alkana tinctoria = anch-t.	
alkekengi = physal-al.	
allant.	allantoinum
all-c.	allium cepa
all-f.	allium fallax
alliar-o.	alliaria officinalis
allox.	alloxanum
all-p.	allium porrum
all-s.	allium sativum
all-u.	allium ursinum
all-v.	allium victorialis
aln.	alnus rubra
allylsulfocarbamida = thiosin.	
aln-g.	alnus glutinosa
aloe	aloe socotrina
alnus serrulata = aln.	
aloe-fe.	aloe ferox
aloe-pe.	aloe perryi
aloe vera = aloe	
alop-p.	alopecurus pratensis
alst.	alstonia constricta
alpha-tocopherolum = tocoph.	
alpina officinarum = galan.	
alpinia officinarum = galan.	
alsidium helminthocorton = helm.	
alsine media = stel.	
alst-b.	alstonia boonei
alst-s.	alstonia scholaris
alth.	althaea officinalis
alth-r.	althaea rosea
alting-e.	altingia excellsa
alum.	alumina
alum-ar-sel.	alumina arsenicum selenium
alumin.	aluminium metallicum
aluminii chloridum hexahydricum = alumin-m.	
aluminii oxidum hydricum = alumin-o.	
aluminii sulfas = alumin-s.	
alumin-act.	aluminium aceticum
alumin-br.	aluminium bromatum
aluminium chloridum = alumin-m.	
alumin-gl.	aluminium gluconicum
aluminium kalium sulphuricum = alumn.	
alumin-l.	aluminium lacticum
alumin-m.	aluminium muriaticum
aluminium oxide = alum.	
alumin-o.	aluminium oxydatum
alumin-p.	aluminium phosphoricum
aluminium silico-sulpho-calcite = slag	
alumin-s.	aluminium sulfuricum
alumin-sil.	aluminium silicicum
alum-in-to.	alumina insulae Tory
alumn.	alumen
alumen chronicum = kali-s-chr.	
alumen crudum = alumn.	
alumn-ust.	alumen ustum
alum-p.	alumina phosphorica
alum-sil.	alumina silicata
ammonii chloridum = am-m.	
am-act.	ammonium aceticum
aluminum chloridum = alumin-m.	
amalg-st.	amalgam standalloy
amanita bulbosa = agar-ph.	
aman-c.	amanita citrina
amanita muscaria = agar.	
amanita phalloides = agar-ph.	
aman-r.	amanita rubescens
am-ar.	ammonium arsenicicum
amanita verna = agar-v.	
amara = ign.	
amaranthus = amar-h.	
amar-h.	amaranthus hypochondriacus
amar-s.	amaranthus spinosus
amar-t.	amaranthus tristis
amary-e.	amaryllis equestris
ammonium auricum = aur-fu.	
am-be.	ammonium benzoicum
am-bi.	ammonium bichromicum
ambr.	ambra grisea
am-br.	ammonium bromatum
ambro.	ambrosia artemisiaefolia
ambro-r.	ambrosia chamissonis
ambra succinum = succ.	
ambr-xyz.	ambra unknown preparation
ammonium bromhydricum = am-hbr.	
am-c.	ammonium carbonicum
am-caust.	ammonium causticum
ammonium chloratum = am-m.	
ammonium chloridum = am-m.	

am-cit. ammonium citricum
amer. americium
amer-n. americium nitricum
am-f. ammonium fluoratum
amfep-m. amfepramonum muriaticum
ammonium hydratum = am-caust.
am-hbr. ammonium hydrobromicum
am-hox. ammonium hydroxynum
am-i. ammonium iodatum
aminoaceticum acidum = glyco.
aminobenzene = anil.
amibe-ac. aminobenzoicum acidum
aminobenzolum = anil.
amicap-ac. aminocaproicum acidum
amidop. amidopyrinum
ami-ncap-ac. amino-n-caproicum acidum
amisuc-ac. aminosuccinicum acidum
aml-act. amylium aceticum
aml-ns. amylenum nitrosum
am-m. ammonium muriaticum
ammoniacum = ammc.
ammc. ammoniacum gummi
amm-fml. ammonium formaldehydum
ammi-m. ammi majus
ammi-v. ammi visnaga
am-mlb. ammonium molybdicum
ammoph-a. ammophilia arenaria
am-n. ammonium nitricum
amn-l. amnii liquor
amoeb-h. amoeba hystolytica
amoracia = coch.
amor-r. amorphophallus riviere
am-ox. ammonium oxalicum
amp. adenosinum monophosphoricum acidum
am-p. ammonium phosphoricum
amp = amp.
ampe-qu. ampelopsis quinquefolia
ampe-tr. ampelopsis trifoliata
ampe-w. ampelopsis weitchii
amph. amphisbaena vermicularis
amph-a. amphisbaena alba
amphet-s. amphetaminum sulfuricum
am-pic. ammonium picricum
am-s. ammonium sulfuricum
am-sal. ammonium salycilicum
amsal-ac. aminosalicylicum acidum
am-sel. ammonium selenicosum
am-spir-a. ammoniae spiritus aromaticus
am-t. ammonium tartaricum
am-val. ammonium valerianicum
am-van. ammonium vanadinicum
am-xyz. am-c. + am-m.
amygdala amara = amyg.
amygdala communis dulcis = amyg-d.
amygdalae = tonsi.
amygdalae amarae aqua = amyg.
amyg. amygdalus communis
amygdalus communis amara = amyg.
amyg-d. amygdalus dulcis
amyg-p. amygdalus persica
amylam. amylaminum hydrochloricum
amylium nitricum = aml-ns.
amylium nitrosum = aml-ns.
amyloc-m. amylocainum muriaticum
amyls. amylase
amylu-t. amylum tritici
anac. anacardium orientale
anac-oc. anacardium occidentale
anac-xyz. anacardium unknow part
anacy-p. anacyclus pyrethrum
anag. anagallis arvensis
anagy. anagyris foetida
anan. anantherum muricatum
anagyroides = cyt-l.
anamirta cocculus = cocc.
anans-c. ananassa comosus
anans-s. ananassa sativa
anas barbariae hepatinii et cardiae extractum = oscilloc.
anas-eu. anas europaea
anas-i. anas indica
anchi-s. anchieta salutaris
anchusa italica = anch-o.
anch-o. anchusa officinalis
anch-t. anchusa tinctora
ancistrodon contortrix = cench.
ancistrodon mokeson = cench.
ancis-p. ancistrodon piscivorus
andalusite rock = alum-sil.
anders. andersonia
andropogon squarrosus = anan.
andr. androsace lactea
andira araroba = chrysar.
andira inermis = geo.
androc. androctonus amoreuxii hebraeus
androctonus amurreuxi hebraeus = androc.
androctonus Australis = buth-a.
androg-p. andrographis paniculata
andromeda arborea = oxyd.
androm-ma. andromeda mariana
androm-ni. andromeda nitida
androm-po. andromeda polifolia
andropogon muraticus = anan.
andropogon muricatus = anan.
andropogon nardus = cymbop-n.
androp-sn. andropogon schoenantus
androst. androsteron
anemps. anemopsis californica
anemone hepatica = hepat.
anemone ludoviciana = puls-n.

anemone montana = puls-m.
ane-n. anemone nemorosa
anemone nuttaliana = puls-n.
anemone pratensis = puls.
anemone pulsatilla = puls-vg.
anemone pulsatilla = puls.
ane-r. anemone ranunculoides
anethum foeniculum = foen-an.
anet-g. anethum graveolens
anethum vulgare = foen-an.
aneur. aneurinum
angustura falsa = bruc.
angustura spuria = bruc.
angustura spuria falsa = bruc.
ang. angustura vera
ange. angelica atropurpurea
ange-ar. angelica archangelica
ange-b. angelicae brasiliensis
ange-s. angelicae sinensis
angelicae sinensis radix = ange-s.
ango. angophora lanceolata
anguillae serum = ser-ang.
anguis-fr. anguis fragilis
anh. anhalonium lewinii
anil. anilinum
anil-s. anilinum sulphuricum
anisum pimpinella = pimp-a.
anis. anisum stellatum
anisatum = anis.
anis-ol. anisi aetheroleum
ankistrodon contortrix = cench.
ankistrodon contortrix mokeson = cench.
annona muriatica = anona
anona anona muricata
antiaris toxicaria = upa-a.
antifebrinum = acetan.
ant-ac. antimonium acidum
antimonium arsenicicum = ant-ar.
ant-ar. antimonium arsenicosum
antimonium chloridum = ant-m.
ant-c. antimonium crudum
ant-f. antimonium fluoratum
anth. anthemis nobilis
anona triloba = asim.
antennaria dioica = gnaph.
anth-a. anthemis arvensis
anth-cot. anthemis cotula
anthemis pyrethrum = pyre-p.
antho. anthoxanthum odoratum
anthraci. anthracinum
anthraci-vc. vaccinum anthracis vivum
anthraco. anthracokali
anthrakokali = anthraco.
anthraq. anthraquinone
anthriscus cerefolium = ceref-s.
anthrokokali = anthraco.
anthyl. anthyllis vulneraria
ant-i. antimonium iodatum
antip. antipyrinum
antip-sal. antipyrinum salicylicum
antirrhinum linaria = lina.
antirr. antirrhinum majus
ant-m. antimonium muriaticum
ant-met. antimonium metallicum
ant-n. antimonium nitricum
ant-n-l. antimonium natrum lacticum
ant-o. antimonium oxydatum
ant-s-aur. antimonium sulphuratum auratum
antimonium sulphuratum aureum = ant-s-aur.
antimonium sulphuratum nigrum = ant-c.
ant-s-r. antimonium sulphuratum rubrum
ant-t. antimonium tartaricum
aorta aorta
apat. apatit
ap-d. apium dulce
apeir-s. apeira syringaria
ap-g. apium graveolens
aphis aphis chenopodii glauci
aphlo-t. aphloia theaeformis
aphthos. aphthosinum
apiol. apiolum
apis apis mellifica
apisin. apisinum
apis-xyz. apis unknown part
apium petroselinum = petros.
apium virus = apisin.
aplop-l. aplopappus laricifolius
apoc. apocynum cannabinum
apoc-a. apocynum androsaemifolium
apocin. apocyaninum
apomorphia = apom.
apomorphini hydrochloridum = apom-m.
apom. apomorphinum hydrochloricum
apom-m. apomorphinum muriaticum
append-xyz. appendictitis nosode unknown species
apus-a. apus apus
aq-calc. aqua calcarea
aqua calcis = aq-calc.
aq-chl. aqua chlorata
aqua glandium quercus robur = querc-r-g-aq.
aq-mar. aqua marina
aq-pet. aqua petra
aq-pur. aqua pura
aqua regia = nit-m-ac.
aqua sanicula = sanic.
aq-sil. aqua silicata
aqui. aquilegia vulgaris
aqueous calendula = calen.
aquil-ch. aquila chrysaetos

aq-vg. aqua vulgaris
arab. arabinosum
arag. aragallus lamberti
aralia quinquefolia = gins.
aral. aralia racemosa
aral-c. aralia californica
aralia ginseng = gins.
aral-h. aralia hispida
aral-nu. aralia nudicaulis
aral-sp. aralia spinosa
ara-maca. ara macao
aranea avicularia = mygal.
aran. aranea diadema
araneae tela = tela
aranearum tela = tela
araneus ixobolus Thorell = aran-ix.
aranin. araninum
aran-ix. aranea ixobola
aran-sc. aranea scinencia
arb. arbutus andrachne
araroba = chrysar.
arbor tristis = nyct.
arbin. arbutinum
arb-m. arbutus menziesii
arb-u. arbutus unedo
arbutus uva ursi = uva
archa-e. archaeopsylla erinacei
arctium lappa = lappa
arctium majus = lappa
arctostaphylos manzanita = manz.
arctostaphylos uva ursi = uva
arctostaphylos uva-ursi = uva
ard-l. ardesius lapis
arec. areca catechu
arecolinum bromhydricum = areco-hbr.
areco-hbr. arecolinum hydrobromicum
aren. arenaria glabra
aren-r. arenaria rubra
aren-s. arenaria serpyllifolia
arg-act. argentum aceticum
arg-ars. argentum arsenicicum
arg-br. argentum bromatum
arg-c. argentum carbonicum
argentum chloratum = arg-mur.
arg-col. argentum colloidale
arg-cy. argentum cyanatum
arge. argemone mexicana
argenti nitras = arg-n.
argent. argentite
arge-pl. argemone pleicantha
arg-f. argentum fluoratum
argentum foliatum = arg-met.
arg-i. argentum iodatum
argilla = alum.
argin. argininum
arg-met. argentum metallicum
arg-mur. argentum muriaticum
arg-n. argentum nitricum
arg-o. argentum oxydatum
argon argon
arg-p. argentum phosphoricum
arg-pr. argentum proteinatum
arg-s. argentum sulfuricum
arg-vi. argentum vitellinicum
arion arion empiricorum
arist-cl. aristolochia clematitis
arist-co. aristolochia colombiana
aristl. aristol
aristolochia cymbifera = arist-m.
aristolochia infesta = arist-cl.
arist-m. aristolochia milhomens
arist-r. aristolochia rotunda
arisaema atrorubens = arum-t.
arisaema triphyllum = arum-t.
aris-vg. arisarum vulgare
aristolochia serpentaria = serp.
arizon-l. Arizona lava
arlo. arlome
armo-r. = coch. = armoracia rusticana (old abbr.)
armoracia lapathifolia = coch.
armoracia rusticana = coch.
armoracia sativa = coch.
arn. arnica montana
arn-xyz. arnica unknown part
arrhenal = nat-meth-ar.
arrh-e. arrhenaterum elatius
ars. arsenicum album
ars-ac. arsenicum acidum
ars-be. arsenobenzolum
ars-br. arsenicum bromatum
arsenicum citrinum = ars-s-f.
ars-h. arsenicum hydrogenisatum
ars-i. arsenicum iodatum
ars-met. arsenicum metallicum
ars-n. arsenicum nitricum
arsenicum tri-iodatum = ars-i.
arsenicum tri-oxidum = ars.
ars-pyr. arseno pyrite
arsenicum rubrum = ars-s-r.
arsenicum stibiatum = ant-ar.
ars-s-f. arsenicum sulphuratum flavum
ars-s-r. arsenicum sulphuratum rubrum
arsynal = nat-meth-ar.
artanthe elongata = mati.
artemisia abrotanum = abrot.
artemisia absinthium = absin.
artemisia cina = cina
artemisia contra = cina
art-d. artemisia dracunculus
arthr-u. uratic arthritis nosode

artemisia judaica = cina
artemisia maritima = cina
art-m. artemisia mutellina
art-tri. artemisis tridentata
artemisia selengensis = art-v.
art-v. artemisia vulgaris
arum arisarum = aris-vg.
arum-d. arum dracontium
arum-dru. arum dracunculus
arum-i. arum italicum
arum-m. arum maculatum
arum seguinum = calad.
arum-t. arum triphyllum
arund. arundo mauritanica
arundo communis = arund-p.
arund-d. arundo donax
arund-p. arundo phragmites
asaf. asa foetida
asar. asarum Europaeum
asagraea officinalis = sabad.
asar-c. asarum canadense
asar-o. asarum officinale
asarum rotundifolium = asar.
ascar-l. ascaris lumbricoides
asc-c. asclepias cornuti
ascaris vermicularis = enterob-v.
asc-cf. asclepias cordifolia
asc-cu. asclepias currassavica
asclepias decumbens = asc-t.
asclepias gigantea = calo.
asc-i. asclepias incarnata
asclepias vincetoxicum = vince.
ascophyllum nodosum = fuc-n.
ascor-ac. ascorbicum acidum
asclepias syriaca = asc-c.
asc-t. asclepias tuberosa
ashoka = joan.
asim. asimina triloba
ask. askalabotes laevigatus
asparticum acidum = aspart-ac.
asp. aspen (Bach fl.)
aspar. asparagus officinalis
asparin. asparaginum
aspart-ac. L-asparticum acidum
asper. asperula odorata
asperg-br. aspergillus bronchialis
asperg-fl. aspergillus flavus
asperg-fu. aspergillus fumigatus
asperg-n. aspergillus niger
aspho. asphodelus albus
asphodelus ramosus = aspho.
aspidium = fil.
aspidium filix mas = fil.
aspidium panna = pann.
aspidosperma quebracho = queb.
aspidospermina = aspidin.
aspidin. aspidospermium
aspirinum = acetyls-ac.
aspl-a. asplenium adiantum nigrum
ast-a. aster asper
assaku = hura
astac. astacus fluviatilis
astat. astatinum
asteriacanthion rubens = aster.
aster. asterias rubens
asthm-r. asthma nosode Reckeweg
astra-ca. astragalus campestris
astra-ci. astragalus cicer
astra-e. astragalus excapus
astra-gl. astragalus glycyphyllos
astra-gu. astragalus gummifer
astra-h. astragalus Hornii
astra-l. astragalus legum
astra-m. astragalus menziesii
astra-mo. = astra-m. = astragalus mollissimus
astragalus mollissimus = astra-m.
atha. athamanta oreoselinum
atis. atista indica
atis-r. atista radix
atox. atoxyl
atp. adenosinum triphosphoricum acidum
atp = atp.
atra-r. atrax robustus
atri. atriplex hortensis
atro. atropinum-pur. + -s. (old abbr.)
atropa belladona = bell.
atropa bella-donna = bell.
atropa mandragora = mand.
atropini sulfas = atro-s.
atro-pur. atropinum purum
atro-s. atropinum sulphuricum
auc-j. aucuba japonica
aug. augopora
aur. aurum metallicum
aurantiacum = ant-s-aur.
aurantii amari floris aetheroleum = cymbop-n-ol.
auran. aurantii cortex
aurantii cortex = cit-v.
aureum = ant-s-aur.
auri solutio colloidalis = aur-col.
aurum arsenicicum = aur-ar.
aur-ar. aurum arsenicum
aur-br. aurum bromatum
aur-col. aurum colloidale
aur-cy. aurum cyanatum
aurantium = cit-v.
aurel-a. aurelia aurita
aureobasidium = clados-m.
aureom. aureomycinum
aur-f. aurum fluoratum

aurum foliatum = aur.
aur-fu. aurum fulminans
aur-i. aurum iodatum
aur-kcy. aurum kalicyanatum
aur-m. aurum muriaticum
aur-m-k. aurum muriaticum kalinatum
aur-m-n. aurum muriaticum natronatum
aur-n. aurum nitricum
aurum natrium chloratum = aur-m-n.
aur-n-f. aurum natrum fluoricum
aur-p. aurum phosphoricum
aur-s. aurum sulphuratum
aur-ts-n. aurum thiosulfuricum natronatum
aven. avena sativa
aven-g. avena germinata
aviaire = tub-a.
avic. avicularia
avocado = pers.
ayahuasca = banis-c.
ayhuasca = banis-c.
aza. azadirachta indica
bac. bacillinum Burnett
baccae juniperi = juni-c.
bacch-c. baccharis crispa
bacls-10. bacillus 10 (Paterson)
bacls-7. bacillus 7 (Paterson)
bac-t. bacillinum testium
bacillus acidophilus = lactob.
bacillus Calmette-Guérin = v-a-b.
bacillus clostridium botulinum = botul.
bacillus Friedländer = mucot.
bacillus leprae = lepr.
bacillus prodigiosus = serrat-ma.
bacillus seven (Paterson) = bacls-7.
bacillus ten (Paterson) = bacls-10.
bacillus Welchii = clostr-we.
bacterium coli = coli.
bacterium coli commune = coli.
bacterium lactis aerogenes = mucot.
bad. badiaga
baj. = bry-la. = baja
bahia-pulver = chrysar.
ball-f. ballota foetida
ball-l. ballota lanata
ballota nigra = ball-f.
balsamodendron myrrha = myrrha
balsamodendron roxburgii = myrrha
balsamum copaivae = cop.
balsamum copaivae siccum = cop.
bals-p. balsamum peruvianum
balsamum toluiferum = bals-t.
bals-t. balsamum tolutanum
bamb-a. bambusa arundinacea
bamb-xyz. bambusa unknown species
bambusa vulgaris = bamb-a.
banana = musa
bananae flos = musa
banis-c. banisteria caapi
baptisia confusa acetica = bapt-c.
bapt. baptisia tinctoria
banisteria quitensis = banis-c.
banisteriopsis caapi = banis-c.
bapt-c. baptisia confusa
baryosma tongo = tong.
bar-act. baryta acetica
bar-ar. baryta arsenicosa
barb. barbae cyprini ova
barbiflora = orthos-s.
barbit. barbital
bar-br. baryta bromata
barbr-vg. barbarea vulgaris
barbu-s. barbula squarrosa
bar-c. baryta carbonica
bar-cn. baryta calcinata
baryta fluorata = bar-f.
bar-f. baryta fluorica
bar-gl. baryta gluconica
bar-i. baryta iodata
bar-m. baryta muriatica
bar-met. baryta metallicum
bar-n. baryta nitrica
bar-o. baryta oxydata
barosma crenata = baros.
baros. barosma crenulatum
barii sulphas = bar-s.
barium aceticum = bar-act.
barium arsenicosum = bar-ar.
barium bromatum = bar-br.
barium calcinatum = bar-cn.
barium carbonicum = bar-c.
barium chloratum = bar-m.
barium fluoricum = bar-f.
barium gluconicum = bar-gl.
barium iodatum = bar-i.
barium nitricum = bar-n.
barium oxalsuccinicum = bar-ox-suc.
barium oxydatum = bar-o.
barium phosphoricum = bar-p.
barium sulfuricum = bar-s.
baros-be. barosma betulina
baros-se. barosma serratifolia
bar-ox-suc. baryta oxalsuccinata
bar-p. baryta phosphorica
bar-s. baryta sulphurica
bart. Bartfelder aqua
basal. = arizon-l. = Basaltic lava (old abbr.)
basaka = just.
basil. basilicum

basil-fol. ocimum basilicum ex foliis
basil-her. ocimum basilicum ex herba
basil-xyz. ocimum basilicum unknown species
bassar-a. bassariscus astutus
bathus tamulus = mesobuth-t.
bcg = v-a-b.
beech beech (Bach fl.)
begon-s. begonia semperflorens
begonia tuberosa = begon-s.
bell. belladonna
bell-fol. atropa belladonna folium
bell-p. bellis perennis
bell-p-sp. bellis perennis spagyricus
benzenum = benzol.
ben. benzinum
b-end. beta endorphine
ben-d. benzinum dinitricum
ben-n. benzinum nitricum
benz-ac. benzoicum acidum
benzc. benzocainum
benzl-be. benzyl benzoicum
benzl-br. benzyl bromatum
benzl-c. benzyl cinnamicum
benzn. benzonaphtolum
benzo. benzoin oderiferum
benzol. benzolum
benzq. benzoquinonum
berb. berberis vulgaris
berb-a. berberis aquifolium
berbin. berberinum
berbin-s. berberinum sulphuricum
berk. berkelium
berlin-w. Berlin wall
bers-l. bersama lucens
beryl. beryllium metallicum
berylla carbonica = beryl-c.
beryl-c. beryllium carbonica
beryllium chloride = beryl-m.
beryl-f. beryllium fluoridum
beryl-m. beryllium muriaticum
beryl-o. beryllium oxydatum
beta rapa = beta
beta beta vulgaris
beta-al. beta vulgaris altissima
beta-co. beta vulgaris conditiva
beta-m. beta maritima
betin. betainum muriaticum
beto. betonica aquatica
betonica officinalis = stach.
betonica stachys = stach.
betu. betula alba
betu-fol. betula alba e foliis
betula pendula = betu.
betu-p. betula pubescens
betu-pi. pix betulina
betula verrucosa = betu.
bid-b. bidens bipinnata
bid-p. bidens pilosa
bigelovia arborescens = aplop-l.
bigelovia veneta = aplop-l.
bignonia caroba = jac-c.
bignonia catalpa = catal.
bignonia copaia = jac-c.
bilinum = fel
bilir. bilirubinum
biot. biotinum
bism. bismuthum-sn. (+ -o.) (old abbr.)
bismithi subsalicylas = bism-sal.
bism-c. bismuthum carbonicum
bism-gl. bismuthum gluconicum
bism-i. bismuthum iodatum
bism-k-i. bismuthum kalium iodatum
bism-m. bismuthum muriaticum
bism-met. bismuthum metallicum
bism-n. bismuthum nitricum
bism-o. bismuthum oxydatum
bism-sal. bismuthum salicylicum
bism-sc. bismuthum subcarbonicum
bism-sg. bismuthum subgallicum
bism-sn. bismuthum subnitricum
bism-sula. bismuthum sulphuratum
bism-val. bismuthum valerianicum
bitis arietans = bit-ar.
bit-ar. bitis arietans arietans
bit-ga. bitis gabonica
bix. bixa orellana
blatta-a. blatta Americana
blatta-o. blatta orientalis
blum-o. blumea odorata
boa-co. boa constrictor
boerh-d. boerhavia diffusa
boerhavia erecta = boerh-h.
boerh-h. boerhavia hirsuta
boerhavia repens = boerh-d.
bofareira = ric.
bold. boldo fragrans
bol-ed. boletus edulis
boletus esculentus = bol-ed.
bol-la. boletus laricis
bol-lu. boletus luridus
boletus pinicola = polyp-p.
bol-s. boletus satanas
bol-su. boletus suaveolens
bomb-chr. bombyx chrysorrhea
bombyx mori = bomb-chr.
bomb-pr. bombyx processionea
bolus alba = alumin-sil.
bombus silvestris = bombu-s.
bombu-s. bombus sylvestris
bomh. bomhenia

bond.	Bondonneau aqua
bop-sc.	bopusia scabra
bor-ac.	boricum acidum
bor-met.	= bor-pur. = borium metallicum (old abbr.)
bor-pur.	borium purum
borra-o.	borrago officinalis
boracicum acidum = bor-ac.	
borago officinalis = borra-o.	
borx.	borax veneta
bos bovis = bos-taur.	
bos primigenius taurus = bos-taur.	
bos-taur.	bos taurus
bos taurus bilis = fel	
bosw-c.	boswellia carterii birdw.
bosw-sac.	boswellia sacra flueck
bosw-soc.	boswellia socotrina
bothrops jacara = both.	
both.	bothrops lanceolatus
both-a.	bothrops alternatus
both-ax.	bothrops atrox
bothrio-l.	bothriocephalus latus
bothrops urutu = both.	
botul.	botulinum
bougainvillea = bougv.	
bougv.	bougenville
bougmanica = dat-a.	
bounafa = ferul.	
bovista gigantea = bov.	
bov.	bovista lycoperdon
bowd-m.	bowdichea major
brach.	brachyglottis repens
brad-tact.	bradykinine triacetate
brahea serrulata = sabal	
brahmi	brahmi
bran.	branca ursina
brass.	brassica napus oleifera (old abbr.)
brassica alba = sin-a.	
brass-c.	brassica campestris
brass-e.	brassica eruca
brass-n-o.	brassica napus oleifera
brassica nigra = sin-n.	
brass-o.	brassica oleracea
brass-o-r.	brassica oleracea rubra
brassica rapa = brass-c.	
brass-r.	brassica rapa rapa
brauneria pallida = echi-pa.	
brayera anthelmintica = kou.	
brid-at.	bridelia atroviridis
brid-fr.	bridelia ferruginea
bril-p.	brillantaisia patula
briz-m.	briza media
brod-e.	brodiaea elegans
brom.	bromium
bro-m.	bromus mollis
brom-ac.	bromium acidum
bromaz.	bromazepam
brom-hac.	bromhydricum acidum
brom-i.	bromium iodatum
bromof.	bromoformium
bromus racemosus = bro-r.	
bro-r.	bromus ramosus
bros-gau.	brosimum gaudichaudi
bruc.	brucea antidysenterica
brucel.	brucella melitensis
brucin.	brucinum
brucin-n.	brucinum nitricum
brugmansia candida = dat-a.	
brun-vg.	brunella vulgaris
bry.	bryonia alba
bry-cr.	bryonia cretica
bry-d.	bryonia dioica
bry-la.	bryonia laciniosa
bryonopsis laciniosa = bry-la.	
bryophyllum calycinum = kal.	
bryophyllum pinnatum = kal.	
bryo-p.	bryophyllum proliferum
brunfelsia hopeana = franc.	
brunfelsia uniflora = franc.	
bry-xyz.	bry. + bry-d.
Buckminster fullerenes = carbo-f.	
bufo cinereus = bufo	
bufo	bufo rana
bufo-s.	bufo sahytiensis
bung-cd.	bungarus candidus
bufo sahytiensis Mure = bufo-s.	
bufo vulgaris = bufo	
bufonis saliva = bufo	
bung-cl.	bungarus caeruleus
bungarus facia = bung-fa.	
bung-fa.	bungarus fasciatus
buni-e.	bunias erucago
buni-o.	bunias orientalis
bunium carvi = caru.	
bupiv.	bupivacaine
bupl-f.	buplevrum falcatum
buthus tamulus = mesobuth-t.	
butyl chloralhydratum = crot-chlol.	
but-ac.	butyricum acidum
bursa pastoris = thlas.	
buteo-b.	buteo buteo
buteo-j.	buteo jamaicensis
buth-a.	buthus Australis
buthotus tamulus = mesobuth-t.	
buthuolus tumulus = mesobuth-t.	
buth-af.	buthus afer
buthus lamblus = mesobuth-t.	
buth-oc.	buthus occitanus
bux.	buxus sempervirens
cac.	cacao

cactus bonplandii = cere-b.
cact. cactus grandiflorus
cachou = catechu
cactin-m. cactinum mexicanum
cactus opuntia = opun-v.
cactus selenicereus grandiflorus = cact.
cactus serpentinus = cere-s.
cact-xyz. cactus unknown part
cadm-act. cadmium aceticum
cadm-ar. cadmium arsenicosum
cadm-bi. cadmium bichromatum
cadm-br. cadmium bromatum
cadm-c. cadmium carbonicum
cadm-calc-f. cadmium calcarea fluoricum
cadm-chl. cadmium chloratum
cadm-chr. cadmium chromatum
cadm-f. cadmium fluoratum
cadm-f-i. cadmium ferrum iodatum
cadm-gl. cadmium gluconicum
cadm-i. cadmium iodatum
cadm-m. cadmium muriaticum
cadm-met. cadmium metallicum
cadm-n. cadmium nitricum
cadm-o. cadmium oxydatum
cadm-p. cadmium phosphoricum
cadm-s. cadmium sulphuratum
cadm-sel. cadmium selenicosum
cael. caela zacatechichi
caer. caerulum
caesal-b. caesalpinia bonducella
caesalpinia pulcherrima = poinc-p.
caes-br. caesium bromatum
caes-hox. caesium hydroxydum
caes-m. caesium chloratum
caes-met. caesium metallicum
caesum muriaticum = caes-m.
caffeinum = coffin.
cahinca = cain.
cahinca racemosa = cain.
cain. cainca
cajanus flavus = cajan.
cajanus indicus = cajan.
caj. cajuputum
cajan. cajanus cajan
cak-m. cakile maritima
calabar = phys.
calad. caladium seguinum
calag. calaguala
calam. calamus aromaticus
calami-a. calamintha acinos
calami-ch. calamintha chenopodii
calami-cl. calamintha clinopodium
calami-g. calamintha grandiflora
calami-o. calamintha officinalis
calcii arsenias = calc-ar.
calcii bromidum = calc-br.
calcii carbonas = calc.
calcii chloridum = calc-caust.
calcii gluconas = calc-gl.
calcii glycerophosphas = calc-glp.
calcii lactas = calc-lac.
calcii panthothenas = calc-pt.
calcium aceticum = calc-act.
calcium arsenicosum = calc-ar.
calcium bromatum = calc-br.
calcium carbonicum = calc.
calcium causticum = calc-caust.
calcium chloratum = calc-m.
calcium chlorinatum = calc-chln.
calcium citricum = calc-cit.
calcium fluoricum = calc-f.
calcium formicum = calc-form.
calcium glutamicum = calc-glt.
calcium hypophosphoricum = calc-hp.
calcium iodatum = calc-i.
calcium lacticum = calc-lac.
calcium metallicum = calc-met.
calcium ovi testae = calc-o-t.
calcium oxalicum = calc-ox.
calcium oxydatum = calc-o.
calcium phosphoricum = calc-p.
calcium picricum = calc-pic.
calcium silicatum = calc-sil.
calcium stibiato-sulphuratum = calc-st-s.
calcium sulphuricum = calc-s.
cal-bil. calculus biliari
calc. calcarea carbonica
calc-act. calcarea acetica
calc-ar. calcarea arsenicosa
calcarea biliaris = cal-bil.
calc-br. calcarea bromata
calc-caust. calcarea caustica
calc-chem. calcarea carbonica chemicalis
calcarea caustica segini = calc-caust.
calc-chln. calcarea chlorinata
calc-cit. calcarea citrica
calc-cn. calcarea calcinata
calcarea fluorata = calc-f.
calc-f. calcarea fluorica
calc-form. calcarea formicum
calc-f-sil. calcarea fluosilicata
calc-gl. calcarea gluconica
calc-glp. calcarea glycerophosphorica
calc-glt. calcarea glutamica
calc-hi. calcarea hydriodica
calc-hox. calcarea hydroxidum
calcarea hypochlorata = calc-chln.
calc-hp. calcarea hypophosphorosa
calc-hs. calcarea hyposulfurosa

calc-i. calcarea iodata
calc-lac. calcarea lactica
calc-ln. calcarea lactica natronata
calcarea lactica phosphorica = calc-lp.
calc-lp. calcarea lactophosphorica
calc-m. calcarea muriatica
calc-met. calcarea metallicum
calc-n. calcarea nitrica
calc-o. calcarea oyxdata
calcarea carbonica Hahnemanni = calc-ost.
calc-ost. calcarea carbonica ostrearum
calc-o-t. calcarea ovi testae
calc-ox. calcarea oxalica
calc-p. calcarea phosphorica
calc-perm. calcarea permanganica
calc-pic. calcarea picrica
calc-pt. calcarea pantothenica
calc-py. calcarea pyrophosphorica
calcarea sulphurata hahnemanni = hep.
calcarea sulphurata stibiata = calc-st-s.
calc-s. calcarea sulphurica
calcarea renalis = cal-ren.
calcarea renalis praeparata = cal-ren.
calc-sil. calcarea silicata
calcarea silicica = calc-sil.
calcarea silico-fluorica = calc-f-sil.
calc-st-s. calcarea stibiato-sulphurata
calc-v. calcarea versaillis
calendula cerate = calen.
calen. calendula officinalis
calculus urinae = cal-ren.
calen-a. calendula arvensis
calic. calici virus
calif. californium
calla aethiopica = zant.
calli-al. calliandra alternans
calli-h. calliandra houstoni
callilaris = pin-c.
callil-l. callilepis laureola
calomel = merc-d.
calo. calotropis gigantea
calluna vulgaris = eric-vg.
calocd-d. calocedrus decurrens
caloct-a. calochortus albus
calo-l. calotropis lactum
calo-p. calotropis procera
cal-ren. calculus renalis
cal-ren-p. calculus renalis phosphorus
cal-ren-u. calculus renalis uricus
cal-sal. calculus salivarii
calth. caltha palustris
calx vivas mineralis = calc-hox.
calyc-o. calycanthus occidentalis
calyp-u. calyptridium umbellatum
calys-s. calystegia sepium
camel-j. camelia japonica
camellia sinensis = thea
campan-ra. campanula rapunculus
campan-ro. campanula rotundifolia
campan-t. campanula trachelium
camphora monobromata = camph-br.
camph. camphora officinalis
camphora racemica = camph.
camph-ac. camphoricum acidum
camph-br. camphora bromata
camph-mbr. = camph-br. = camphora monobromata
campho-m. camphorosma monspeliaca
cancer astacus = astac.
cancer fluviatilis = astac.
cancerinum = carc.
canch. canchalagua
candida albicans = moni.
cand. candida parapsilosis
canis-exc. excrementum caninum
candida pseudotropicalis = kluyv-ma.
canna canna angustifolia
cann-i. cannabis indica
cann-s. cannabis sativa
cann-xyz. cannabis unknown species
canth. cantharis vesicatoria
cantha-c. cantharellus cibarius
canthin. cantharidinum
cany-d. canyon dudleya
capp-crc. capparis coriaccea
capp-crm. capparis corymbifera
capp-g. capparis gueinzii
capre. capreolus capreolus
capsella bursa pastoris = thlas.
capsella bursa-pastoris = thlas.
caps. capsicum annuum
caps-f. capsicum frutescens
car. carissa schimperi
cara-p. carapa procera
carb-ac. carbolicum acidum
carbam. carbamazepine
carbamidum = urea-n.
carb-an. carbo animalis
carbmc. carboxymethylcellulosum
carbo ligni = carb-v.
carb-mi. carbo mineralis
carbn. carboneum
carbn-chl. carboneum chloratum
carbn-dox. carboneum dioxydum
carbn-h. carboneum hydrogenisatum
carbn-o. carboneum oxygenisatum
carbn-s. carboneum sulphuratum
carboneum tetrachloridum = carbn-tm.
carbn-tm. carboneum tetramuriaticum
carbo-f. carbo fullerenum
carb-um. carbo umbra

carb-v. carbo vegetabilis
carc. carcinosinum
carc-bl-adp. carcinosinum bladder adeno papillar
carc-col. carcinoma coli
carcinosinum burnett = carc.
carc-col-ad. carcinosinum colon adeno
carc-col-adp. carcinosinum colon adeno papillar
carc-hepat. carcinoma hepatis
carcinosinum foubister = carc.
carc-in. carcinosinum intestines co.
carc-lar. carcinoma laryngis
carc-lu. carcinoma bronchium
carc-lu-ads. carcinosinum lung adeno squamous
carc-mamm. carcinoma mammae
carc-mel-met. carconisum melanoma metastitic
carcinosinum mammae scirrhus = scir.
carc-rec-ad. carcinosinum rectum adeno
carc-st. carcinosinum stomach
carc-st-ad. carcinosinum stomach adeno
carc-st-sc. carcinosinum stomach scirrhus
carc-ut. carcinoma uteri
carc-ut-ad. carcinosinum uterus adeno
carc-ut-p. carcinosinum uterus papillar
cardam. cardamine pratensis
cardam-a. cardamine amara
cardamo. cardamomum
card-b. carduus benedictus
cardiaz. cardiazol
cardios-h. cardiospermum halicacabum
card-m. carduus marianus
carex-a. carex arenaria
cari-p. carica papaya
carl. Carlsbad aqua
carli-a. carlina acaulis
carli-vg. carlina vulgaris
carneg-g. carnegia gigantea
carnin. carnitinum
carnin-m. carnitinum muriaticum
caroba = jac-c.
caroten. carotenum
carp-b. carpinus betulus
carthamnus ceriferus = myric.
cartl-s. cartilago suis
carum aureum = ziz.
caru. carum carvi
cary. carya alba
caryo. caryophyllus aromaticus
casc. cascarilla
casein. caseinum
cass. cassada
cascabela thevetia = thev.
cascara = cas-s.
cas-s. cascara sagrada
cassia acutifolia = senn.
cassia-a. cassia alata
cassia angustifolia = senn.
cassia-f. cassia fistula
cassia-l. cassia laevigata
cassia-m. cassia medica
cassia obtusa = cassia-ob.
cassia obtusata = cassia-ob.
cassia-o. cassia occidentalis
cassia-ob. cassia obovata
cassia senna = senn.
cassia-s. cassia sophera
castanea vulgaris = castn-v.
caste. castella texana
caste-to. castella totuosa
castm. castoreum canadense
cassia sophora = cassia-s.
castalia pudica = nymph.
castalia speciosa = nymph-a.
castanea sativa = castn-v.
castn-v. castanea vesca
castor-eq. castor equi
castr-ol. castor oil
castoreum muscovitum = castm.
castoreum sibericum = castm.
castoreum sibinicum = castm.
castoreum sibiricum = castm.
catal. catalpa bignonoides
catar. cataria nepeta
catechu catechu
catharanthus roseus = vinc-r.
cath-a. cathartes aura
Caterpillar fungus = cordyc.
catha-ed. catha edulis
catuab. catuaba
cauc-l. caucalis latifolia
caul. caulophyllum thalictroides
caust. causticum
causticum hahnemanni = caust.
Cayenne pepper = caps.
cayratia debilis = cissu-d.
cean. ceanothus Americanus
cean-tr. ceanothus thrysiflorus
ceanothus virginiana = cean.
cecr. cecropia mexicana
cecr-o. cecropia obtusa
cecr-p. cecropia palmata
cedar incense = calocd-d.
cedr. cedron
cedrus-d. cedrus deodara
cedrus-l. cedrus libani
cefur. cefuroxim
celastrus edulis = catha-ed.
celas-s. celastrus scandens
celo-t. celosia trigyna
celt. celtis occidentalis
cem. cement

cench. cenchris contortrix
cent. centaurea tagana
centaurium = canch.
centaurium erythraea = canch.
centau. centaury (Bach fl.)
cenchris piscivorus = ancis-p.
cent-ca. centaurea calcitrada
cent-cy. centaurea cyanus
cent-j. centaurea jacea
cent-n. centaurea nigra
centella asiatica = hydrc.
centr-r. centranthus ruber
cent-u. centaurea umbellata
ceph. cephalanthus occidentalis
cepa = all-c.
cepa vulgaris = all-c.
cephaelis ipecacuanha = ip.
cephd-i. cephalandra indica
ceras-ce. cerastes cerastes
cerast-a. cerastium aquaticum
cerasus padus = prun-p.
cerasus virginia = prun-v.
cerasus vulgaris = prun-cs.
cerat. corato (Bach fl.)
cerevisiae fermentum = tor.
cer-br. cerium bromatum
cer-c. cerium carbonicum
cerbera thevetia = thev.
cerc-o. cercis occidentalis
cerc-s. cercis siliquastrum
cere-b. cereus bonplandii
ceref-s. cerefolium sativum
cereus grandiflorus = cact.
cere-s. cereus serpentinus
cerev-lg. cerevisia lager
cer-f. cerium fluoratum
cer-i. cerium iodatum
cer-lac. cerium lacticum
cer-m. cerium muriaticum
cer-met. cerium metallicum
cer-n. cerium nitricum
cer-o. cerium oxydatum
cer-ox. cerium oxalicum
cer-p. cerium phosphoricum
cer-s. cerium sulfuricum
cer-sil. cerium silicatum
ceratostigma willmottiana = cerstig-w.
cerstig-w. ceratostigma willmottigma
certhec-t. ceratotheca triloba
cerv. cervus brasilicus
cervus brasilicus campestris = cerv.
cerv-elaph. cervus elaphus
ces-m. = caes-m. = cesium muriaticum
cesium bromatum = caes-br.
cesium hydroxydum = caes-hox.
cesium metallicum = caes-met.
cesium muriaticum = caes-m.
ceter-o. ceterach officinarum
ceto. cetonia aurata
cetr. cetraria islandica
chaerophyllum sativum = ceref-s.
chaero-t. chaerophyllum temolum
chalco. chalcosine
chamaelirium = helon.
chamaelirium carolinianum = helon.
chamaelirium luteum = helon.
chamaemelum nobile = anth.
chamaerops serrulata = sabal
cham. chamomilla
chamaecyparis lawsonia = cupre-l.
chamae. chamaedrys
chamomilla foetida = anth-cot.
chamomilla recutita = cham.
chamomilla romana = anth.
chamomilla vulgaris = cham.
chap. chaparro amargoso
chasm-p. chasmanthera palmata
chaul. chaulmoogra
ch-bud chestnud bud (Bach fl.)
cheir. cheiranthus cheiri
chel. chelidonium majus
chel-g. chelidonium glaucum
chelin. chelidoninum
chelo. chelone glabra
chenopodium ambrosioides = chen-a.
chen-a. chenopodium anthelminticum
chenopodii glauci aphis = aphis
chen-al. chenopodium album
chen-bh. chenopodium bonus henricus
chen-bt. chenopodium botrys
chen-g. chenopodium glaucum
chen-hy. chenopodium hybridum
chenopodium olidum = chen-v.
chen-o. chenopodium opulifolium
chenod-ac. chenodesoxycholicum acidum
chen-v. chenopodium vulvaria
chenopodium ugandae = chen-o.
chen-vg. chenopodium vulgare
chicorium intybus = cich.
chic. chicory (Bach fl.)
chim. chimaphila umbellata
chim-m. chimaphila maculata
chim-rot. chimaphila rotundifolia
chin. china officinalis
chin-b. china boliviana
chin-ca. china calisays
chinchonae cortex = chin.
chinid. chinidinum hydrochloricum
chinini hydrochloridum = chinin-m.
chinini sulfas = chinin-s.

chinin-ar. chininum arsenicosum
chinin-br. chininum bromaticum
chinin-brh. chininum bromhydricum
chinin-fcit. chininum ferri citricum
chinin-hcy. chininum hydrocyanicum
chinin-m. chininum muriaticum
chinin-p. chininum phosphoricum
chinin-pur. chininum purum
chinin-s. chininum sulphuricum
chinin-sal. chininum salicylicum
chinin-val. chininum valerianicum
cinchona boliviana = chin-b.
cinchona calisaya = chin-b.
cinchona flava = chin-ca.
cinchona officinalis = chin.
cinchona pubescens = chin-su.
cinchona regia = chin.
chin-su. cinchona succirubra
chiococca densifolia = cain.
chiococca racemosa = cain.
chiogenes hispidula = gaul-h.
chionanthus Americana = chion.
chionanthus latifolia = chion.
chion. chionanthus virginica
chir-fl. chironex fleckeri
chirop. chiroptera
chivx. chivonex
chlam. chlamydinum
chlam-tr. chlamydia trachomatis
chlf. chloroformium
chloroformum = chlf.
chlg-p. chlorogalum pumeriadianum
chlol. chloralum hydratum
chlor. chlorum
chlora perfoliata = gent-pe.
chlorals. chloralosum
chloram. chloramphenicolum
chloramb. chlorambucil
chlorami. chloraminum
chlordia. chlordiazepoxide
chlorinum = chlor.
chlorns-ac. chlornitrosum acidum
chlornitrosum acidum = nit-m-ac.
chloroc-w. chlorocodon whiteii
chlorox. chloroxylenum
chlorpr. chlorpromazinum
chlort. chlortetracycline
chloromycetinum = chloram.
chlp. chlorophyllum
chlquin-p. chloroquinum phosphoricum
cho. cholas terrapina
choc. chocolate
chol. cholesterinum
cholcalc. cholecalciferolum
cholesterolum = chol.
cholin. cholinum
chondodendron tomentosa = pareir.
chondodendron tormentosum = pareir.
chondr-c. chondrus crispus
chopn. chopheenee
chord-umb. chorda umbilicalis
ch-plum cherry plum (Bach fl.)
chr-ac. chromicum acidum
chr-act. chromicum aceticum
chr-ah. chromicum anhydridum
chr-gl. chromium gluconicum
chr-hox. chromium hydroxydum
chr-m. chromium muriaticum
chromium kali sulphuratum = kali-s-chr.
chromium kaliumsulfuricum = kali-s-chr.
chr-met. chromium metallicum
chr-o. chromium oxydatum
chr-p. chromium phosphoricum
chr-s. chromium sulphuricum
chrys-ac. chrysophanicum acidum
chrysan. chrysanthemum leucanthemum
chrysanthellum indicum = chrystl.
chrysanthemum = chrysan-m.
chrysan-b. chrysanthemum balsamita
chrysan-ci. chrysanthemum cinerariaefolium
chrysan-co. chrysanthemum coronarium
chrysan-m. chrysanthemum morifolium
chrysanthemum vulgare = tanac.
chrysanthenum parthenium = pyre-p.
chrysar. chrysarobinum
chrysi. chrysis
chrysol. chrysolite
chrystl. chrysanthellum Americanum
chrysophyllum glyciphloeum = luc-g.
chrysosporium pannorum = aleur-l.
cibot-b. cibotium balantium
cic. cicuta virosa
cice. cicer arietinum
cich. cichorium intybus
cic-m. cicuta maculata
cimic. cimicifuga racemosa
cimx. cimex lectularius
cina cina maritima
cinch. cinchoninum sulphuricum
cinchop. cinchophenum
cine. cineraria maritima
cinis-l. cinis ligni
cinn-ac. cinnamicum acidum
cinnb. cinnabaris
cinnamomi cortex = cinnm.
cinnamomum camphora = camph.
cinnamomum ceylancium = cinnm.
cinnm. cinnamomum zeylanicum
cinnmd-c. cinnamodendron corticosum
cinnamonum verum = cinnm.

circ-l. circaea lutetiana
cirr-hepat. cirrhosis hepatis nosode
cirs-ac. cirsium acaule
cirs-ar. cirsium arvense
cirs-l. cirsium lanceolatum
cisplat. cisplatina
cissa-t. cissampelos torulosa
cissu-c. cissus cuneifolia
cissu-d. cissus debilis
cist. cistus canadensis
cistus vulgaris = cist.
cit-ac. citricum acidum
citrus aurantium = cit-v.
cit-b. citrus bergamia
citrus canadensis = cist.
cit-d. citrus decumana
cit-l. citrus limonum
citrullus colocynthis = coloc.
citrullus lanatus = cuc-c.
citl-vg. citrullus vulgaris
cit-m. citrus medica
cit-p. citrus paradisi
cit-s. citrus sinensis
cit-v. citrus vulgaris
cit-xyz. citrus species unknown
cladon. cladonia pyxidata
cladon-ra. cladonia rangiferina
cladop. cladophora rupestris
clados-l. cladosporium lugdunense
clados-m. cladosporium metanigrum
claus-an. clausena anisata
claus-in. clausena inaequalis
clem. clematis erecta
claviceps purpurea = sec.
clemat. clematis (Bach fl.)
clematis recta = clem.
clem-sax clematis saxicola
clem-vir. clematis virginiana
clem-vit. clematis vitalba
cleom-g. cleome gynandra
clerod-g. clerodendron glabrum
clerod-i. clerodendron infortunatum
clobaz. clobazam
clomip clomipramine
clostridium botulinum = botul.
clostr-we. clostridium Welchii
cloth. = bit-ar. = clotho arietans (old abbr.)
clotho arietans = bit-ar.
cnic-ar. cnicus arvensis
cnicus benedictus = card-b.
coalt. coaltarum
cob. cobaltum metallicum
cob-act. cobaltum aceticum
cobaltum chloratum = cob-m.
cobaltum chloridum = cob-m.
cob-col. cobaltum colloidale
cob-f. cobaltum fluoratum
cob-gl. cobaltum gluconicum
cob-i. cobaltum iodatum
cob-m. cobaltum muriaticum
cob-n. cobaltum nitricum
cob-o. cobaltum oxydatum
cob-p. cobaltum phosphoricum
cob-s. cobaltum sulfuricum
cob-sil. cobaltum silicatum
cob-sula. cobaltum sulphuratum
cobra corallinus = elaps
cobra nigricolis = naja-n.
coca coca
coca-c. coca cola
cocaini hydrochloricum = cocain.
cocain. cocainum hydrochloricum
cocainum muriaticum = cocain.
cocarb. cocarboxylase
cocc. cocculus indicus
cocculus platyphylla = pareir.
coc-c. coccus cacti
coccal bacillus Coccal co. (Paterson)
cocci-i. coccinia indica
coccal co. (paterson) = coccal
coccal compound (paterson) = coccal
cocc-s. coccinella septempunctata
cochenille cactus = opun-c.
cochlearia armoracea = coch.
coch. cochlearia armoracia
coch-o. cochlearia officinalis
cochlearia pyrenaica = coch-o.
cochlearia rusticana = coch.
cocos-n. cocos nucifera
cocos-n-aq. cocos nucifera aqua
cocos-xyz-aq. cocos unknown species aqua
cod. codeinum
codeth. codethylinum
cod-p. codeinum phosphoricum
cod-s. codeinum sulfuricum
coenz-a. coenzyme A
coenz-q. coenzyme Q
coffea arabica = coff.
coff. coffea cruda
coffin. coffeinum
coff-t. coffea tosta
colch. colchicum autumnale
cola acuminata = kola
cola nitida = kola
cola vera = kola
colchin. colchicinum
coleus-a. coleus aromaticus
coli. colibacillinum
coll. collinsonia canadensis
collarg. collargolum

collod.	collodion
col-met.	= niob-met. = columbium metallicum
coloc.	colocynthis
colocin.	colocynthinum
colocynthis citrullus = coloc.	
colombo = chasm-p.	
colos.	colostrum
colubrina = nux-v.	
colum-p.	columba palumbus
columbine = aqui.	
columbium niobium = niob-met.	
columbo = chasm-p.	
colut-a.	colutea arborescens
com.	comocladia dentata
comar-p.	comarum palustre
combr-r.	combretum raimbaultii
coninum = conin.	
con.	conium maculatum
conchae praeparatae = calc.	
conch.	conchiolinum
condurango = cund.	
cones.	conessinum
conessinum bromhydricum = cones-hbr.	
cones-hbr.	conessinum hydrobromicum
congo-r.	congo red
conin.	coniinum
conin-br.	coniinum bromatum
conr-m.	cornus mas
consol-r.	consolida regalis
conv.	convallaria majalis
convlm.	convallamarinum
convo-a.	convolvulus arvensis
convo-d.	convolvulus duartinus
convo-s.	convolvulus stans
convolvulus purga = jal.	
convolvulus purpureus = ipom-p.	
convolvulus scammonia = scam.	
convo-se.	convolvulus sepium
convolvulus turpenthum = oper.	
conyza canadensis = erig.	
conyz-sm.	conyza sumatrensis
conyz-vg.	conyza vulgaris
copahu = cop.	
copaiba = cop.	
copaifera langdorfii = cop.	
copaifera officinalis = cop.	
cop.	copaiva officinalis
coprah	coprah
cordelistris syphilitica = jac-c.	
cord-c.	cordia coffeoide
cordyc.	cordyceps militaris
corh.	corallorhiza odontorhiza
corian-s.	coriandrum sativum
cori-m.	coriaria myrtifolia
cori-r.	coriaria ruscifolia
coqueluchinum = pert.	
corla-o.	corallina officinalis
corn.	cornus circinata
cor-n.	corallium nigrum
corn-a.	cornus alternifolia
corn-f.	cornus florida
corn-s.	cornus sericea
corn-sa.	cornus sanguinea
coron-v.	coronilla varia
cor-r.	corallium rubrum
corpus luteum = lutin.	
cortex gland. adrenalis = adr-ctx.	
cortico.	corticotropinum
cortisoni acetas = cortiso.	
cortiso.	cortisonum
corv-cor.	corvus corax
cory.	corydalis formosa
cory-b.	corydalis bulbosa
corydalis canadensis = cory.	
cory-c.	corydalis cava
coryl-a.	corylus avellana
corynanthe yohimbe = yohim.	
cosmo.	cosmolin
cost-p.	costus pisonis
cost-s.	costus spicatus
cot.	cotyledon umbilicus
cotinus coggygria = rhus-c.	
coto	coto
cotrim.	cotrimoxazol
coumarinum = cumin.	
coxs.	coxsackie virus nosode
cr-apple	crab apple (Bach fl.)
crasp-v.	craspidospermum verticellatum
crass-o.	crassula obliqua
crass-r.	crassula rubicunda
crataegus laevigata = crat.	
crataegus monogyna = crat.	
crat.	crataegus oxyacantha
crat-fr.	crataegi oxyacanthae fructus
crats-ce.	craterispermum cerinanthum
creat.	creatinum
creat-p.	creatinum phosphoricum
cresolum = kres.	
cresylolum = kres.	
crith-m.	crithmum maritimum
croc.	crocus sativus
crocus stigmates = croc.	
crot-ad.	crotalus adamanteus
crot-c.	crotalus cascavella
crot-cam.	croton campestris
croton cascarilla = casc.	
croton chloralhydratum = crot-chlol.	
crot-chlol.	croton chloralum
croton eluteria = casc.	
crot-f.	croton fulvum

crot-h.	crotalus horridus
crot-le.	croton lecheri
crot-t.	croton tiglium
cryp.	cryptopinum
cryptc.	cryptococcinum
ctenoc-c.	ctenocephalides canis
ctenoc-f.	ctenocephalides felis
cub.	cubeba officinalis
cuc-c.	cucurbita citrullus
cuc-m.	cucurbita maxima
cuc-p.	cucurbita pepo
cucumis colocynthis = coloc.	
cucum-h.	cucumis hirsutus
cucum-m.	cucumis melo
culx.	culex musca
culx-p.	culex pipiens
cumin.	cumarinum
cumn-c.	cuminum cyminum
cund.	cundurango
cunila pulegioides = hedeo.	
cuphea petiolata = cuph.	
cuph.	cuphea viscosissima
cupr.	cuprum metallicum
cupri sulfas anhydricus = cupr-s.	
cupr-act.	cuprum aceticum
cupr-alum.	cuprum aluminatum
cupr-am-s.	cuprum ammoniae sulphuricum
cupr-ar.	cuprum arsenicosum
cupr-be.	cuprum benzoicum
cupr-br.	cuprum bromatum
cupr-c.	cuprum carbonicum
cupr-cy.	cuprum cyanatum
cupre-au.	cupressus Australis
cupre-l.	cupressus lawsoniana
cupre-n.	cupressus niger
cupre-s.	cupressus sempervirens
cupr-f.	cuprum fluoratum
cupr-form.	cuprum formicum
cupr-gl.	cuprum gluconicum
cupr-hdr.	cuprum hydrargyrum
cupr-hox.	cuprum hydroxydum
cupr-i.	cuprum iodatum
cupr-m.	cuprum muriaticum
cupr-n.	cuprum nitricum
cupr-o.	cuprum oxydatum nigrum
cupr-ox.	cuprum oxalicum
cupr-p.	cuprum phosphoricum
cupr-pi.	cuprum protoidatum
cupr-s.	cuprum sulphuricum
cupr-sil.	cuprum silicatum
cupr-sula.	cuprum sulphuratum
cur.	curare
curc.	curcuma javanensis
curcuma longa = curc-x.	
curc-x.	curcuma xanthorrhiza
curc-z.	curcuma zedoaria
curi.	curium
cuscus = anan.	
cusc-a.	cuscuta Americana
cusc-ep.	cuscuta epithymum
cusc-eu.	cuscuta Europaea
cuscuta minor = cusc-ep.	
cusparia febrifuga = ang.	
cyanhydricum acidum = hydr-ac.	
cyanoc.	cyanocobalaminum
cyath.	cyathula
cycl.	cyclamen Europaeum
cycl-n.	cyclamen napolitanum
cyclamen purpurascens = cycl.	
cyclop.	cyclophosphamide
cyclos.	cycloserinum
cyclosp.	cyclosporinum
cyd.	cydonia vulgaris
cygn-be.	cygnus bewickii
cygnus columbianus = cygn-be.	
cygn-cy.	cygnus cygnus
cygn-ol.	cygnus olor
cymbop-ci.	cymbopogon citratus
cymbop-n.	cymbopogon nardus
cymbop-n-ol.	cymbopogon nardus oleum
cymin.	cymarinum
cyna.	cynara scolymus
cynanchum = vince.	
cyna-c.	cynara cardunculus
cyn-d.	cynodon dactylon
cyno.	cynoglossum officinale
cynor.	cynorrhodon
cynos.	cynosbati
cyper-l.	cyperus longus
cyper-o.	cyperus olivaris
cypr.	cypripedium pubescens
cyperus rotundus = cyper-o.	
cypra-eg.	cypraea eglantina
cyrtop-p.	cyrtopodium punctatum
cystein.	cysteinum
cystein-l.	L-cysteinum
cystein-m.	cysteinum muriaticum
cysti.	cystisinum
cysto-f.	cystoseira fibrosa
cystisus laburnum = cyt-l.	
cysto-nephr.	cystopyelonephritis nosode
cytid.	cytidinum
cytin.	cytisinum
cyt-l.	cytisus laburnum
cytisus scoparius = saroth.	
daboia = vip-d.	
daboia russellii = vip-d.	
dact-g.	dactylis glomerata
dactylopius coccus = coc-c.	
dam.	damiana

damiana aphrodisiaca = dam.
danaz. danazol
daph. daphne indica
daph-l. daphne laureola
dat-a. datura arborea
dat-f. datura ferox
datura stramonium = stram.
datin. daturinum
daphne mezereum = mez.
daphne odora = daph.
daphne odorata = daph.
datis. datisca cannabina
dat-m. datura metel
dat-s. datura sanguinea
dauc-c. daucus carota
dchlo-de-s. dichlorodiethyl sulfide
delphinium staphysagria = staph.
delphinum consolida = consol-r.
del. delphinus amazonicus
delphin. delphininum staphysagria
delphin-n. delphinium nudicaule
dema. dematium petraeum
dendr-pol. dendroaspis polylepsis
derris elliptica = der.
der. derris pinnata
deoxyribonucleicum acidum = des-ac.
derm-f. dermatophagoides farinae
derm-p. dermatophagoides pteronyssinus
des-ac. desoxyribonucleicum acidum
desch-f. deschampsia flexuosa
descu-s. descurainia sophia
desm-g. desmodium gangeticum
desmon-r. desmoncus rudentum
dictamus fraxinella = dict.
dieffenbachia seguinum = calad.
de-s-oestr. diethylstilboestrolum
deut-o. deuterium oxydatum
deut-t-o. deuterium tritium oxydatum
dexam. dexamethason
dextr. dextrinum
dedleya cymposa = cany-d.
dhchol-ac. dehydrocholicum acidum
deltacortisone = predn.
dhcort. deltahydrocortisone
dhretin. dehydroretinol
dh-strept. dihydrostreptomycine sulfate
dextrum lacticum acidum = sarcol-ac.
diabolus metallorum = stann.
diadema aranea = aran.
dial-f. dialium ferrum
di-ammonii phospas = am-p.
di-ammonii sulfas = am-s.
dianthe-p. dianthera pectoralis
dianthu-c. dianthus caryophyllus
dianthu-f. dianthus fimbriatus
dianthus superbus = dianthu-f.
diastase = amyls.
diaz. diazepam
dicentra canadensis = cory.
dicen-c. dicentra cucullaria
dicentra formosa = cory.
dicha. dichapetalum
diclof. diclofenac
dicoum. dicoumarolum
dictamnus = orig-d.
dict. dictamnus albus
dig. digitalis purpurea
digin. digitalinum
dig-la. digitalis lanata
dig-lu. digitalis lutea
digitalis purpureae folium = dig.
digox. digitoxinum
dikalii carbonas = kali-c.
dikalii phosphas = kali-p.
dikalii sulphas = kali-s.
dinatrii phosphas dodecahydricus = nat-p.
dinatrii tartras = nat-tar.
dion-mus. dionaea muscipula
dios. dioscorea villosa
diosgin. diosgeninum
diosin. dioscoreinum
diosma crenata = baros.
diosm. diosma lincaris
dioscorea paniculata = dios.
dios-p. dioscorea petrea
diosp-k-c. diospyros kaki Creveld
diox. dioxan
dioxi. dioxinum
dip. dipodium punctatum
diphtheriae bacillus = diph-b.
diphthericum = diph.
diphthericum-tetanicum-typho-parathyphoidicum = diph-t-tpt.
diph. diphtherinum
diph-b. bacillus diphtheriae
diph-pert-t. diphtheria, pertussis, tetanus
diph-te-pol-vc. diphthero-tetano-polio vaccinus
diph-te-vc. diphthero-tetano vaccinus
diphtox. diphtherotoxinum
diph-t-tpt. diphthero-tetano-typho-paratyphoidicum
diph-vc. diphthero vaccinus
diplo-t. diplotaxis tenuifolia
dips-s. dipsacus silvestris
dipterix odorata = tong.
dipt-tu. dipterocarpus turbinatus
dirc. dirca palustris
diss-i. dissotis incana
dissotis rotundifolia = hetrt-r.
distemp. distemperinum nosode
distemp-vc. distemperinum vaccinum
dithyr. di-iodo-thyroxinum

ditin. ditainum
divertic. diverticulose nosode
denys = tub-d.
docort-act. deoxycorticosteroni acetas
dna = des-ac.
dodec-h. dodecatheon hendersonii
dol. dolichos pruriens
dolichovespula maculata = vespul-m.
dopa dopa
dopam-chl. dopamine chlorhydrate
dor. doryphora decemlineata
dorema ammoniacum = ammc.
doron-p. doronicum pardalianches
doryphora leptinotarsa = dor.
dovy-r. dovyalis rhamnoides
doxoc. doxycycline
doxor. doxorubicine
drab-vn. draba verna
draconitum foetidum = ictod.
dracunculus vulgaris = arum-dru.
dream-p. dreaming potency
drim-g. drimys granatensis
dros. drosera rotundifolia
dros-l. drosera longifolia
drym-cor. drymaria cordata
drymis winteri = cinnmd-c.
dryopteris filix mas = fil.
dryopteris filix-mas = fil.
dryop-i. dryopteris inaequalis
dryop-p. dryopteris pentheri
dtp-vc. diphthero-tetano-pertussis vaccinus
dub. duboisinum + dubo-m. (old abbr.)
DTTAB = diph-t-tpt.
dt-tab. = diph-t-tpt.
dubo-h. duboisia hopwoodi
duboin. duboisinum
dubo-m. duboisia myoporoides
duboisinum sulphatum = duboin.
dudl-c. dudleya cymposa
dulc. dulcamara
dupuyt. dupuytren nosode
durb. durbital
dys. bacillus dysenteriae (Bach)
dys. co. (bach) = dys.
dysenteriae (bach) = dys.
dysenteriae compound (bach) = dys.
dyspr-br. dysprosium bromatum
dyspr-c. dysprosium carbonicum
dyspr-f. dysprosium fluoratum
dyspr-i. dysprosium iodatum
dyspr-lac. dysprosium lacticum
dyspr-m. dysprosium muriaticum
dyspr-met. dysprosium metallicum
dyspr-n. dysprosium nitricum
dyspr-o. dysprosium oxydatum
dyspr-ox. dysprosium oxalicum
dyspr-p. dysprosium phosphoricum
dyspr-s. dysprosium sulphuricum
dyspr-sil. dysprosium silicatum
dystr-m-pr. dystrophia musculorum progressiva nosode
eaux Eaux Bonnes aqua
eberth. eberthinum
ecballium elaterium = elat.
echiichthys vipera = trach-v.
echi. echinacea angustifolia
echinc. echinococcinum
echinp. echinops spinosus
echi-p. echinacea purpurea
echi-pa. echinacea pallida
echis carinatus = vip-a-c.
echitaminum = ditin.
echit. echites suberecta
echium echium vulgare
eel serum = ser-ang.
eich-c. eichhornia crassipes
einstein. einsteinium
either = aether
eke-me. ekebergia meyeri
elae. elaeis guineensis
elaeo-v. elaeodendron velutinum
elaps elaps corallinus
elat. elaterium
elaterium officinarum = elat.
elea-gr-r. eleaocarpus granitus roxb
elec. electricitas
electricitas frictionale = elec.
electro-magnetismus = m-ambo.
elem. elemuy gauteria
eleph-b. elephantorhiza burchelli
elettaria cardamomum = cardamo.
eleut. eleutherococcus
elm elm (Bach fl.)
elmen Elmen aqua
elymus repens = tritic.
elytrigia repens = tritic.
emb-k. embelia kraussii
emblc. embelica officinalis
emb-r. embelia ribes
emb-sc. embelia schimperi
emeticus = ant-t.
emetin. emetinum
emetin-m. emetinum muriaticum
ems Ems aqua
end-s. endiva sativa
endymion nutans = agra.
entamoeba dysenterica = amoeb-h.
entamoeba hystolytica = amoeb-h.
enterob-v. enterobius vermicularis
enteroc. enterococcinum

enterotoxinum = enteroc.
eos. eosinum
eos-n. eosinum natrum
ephe. ephedra vulgaris
ephe-si. ephedra sinica
ephedrini hydrochloridum = ephin-m.
ephin-m. ephedrinum muriatium
epigaea repens = epig.
epig. epigea repens
epih. epihysterinum
epil. epilobium palustre
epil-a. epilobium angustifolium
epil-h. epilobium hirsutum
epil-s. epilobium spicatum
epil-t. epilobium tetragonum
epinephrinum = adren.
epiphegus Americanus = epiph.
epiph. epiphegus virginiana
epiphysis cerebri = pineal.
epit. epithalia syphilitica
eppa-an. eppalage anemonaefolia
equis-a. equisetum arvense
equis-h. equisetum hyemale
equis-p. equisetum palustre
equis-v. equisetum variegatum
eran. eranthis hymnalis
erb-br. erbium bromatum
erb-c. erbium carbonicum
erb-f. erbium fluoratum
erb-i. erbium iodatum
erb-lac. erbium lacticum
erb-m. erbium muriaticum
erb-met. erbium metallicum
erb-n. erbium nitricum
erb-o. erbium oxydatum
erb-ox. erbium oxalicum
erb-p. erbium phosphoricum
erb-s. erbium sulphuricum
erb-sil. erbium silicatum
erech. erechthites hieracifolia
ergocalc. ergocalciferolum
ergot. ergotinum
ergotam. ergotaminum
ergotam-t. ergotamini tartras
eric-ca. erica carnea
eric-ci. erica cinerea
eric-vg. erica vulgaris
erig. erigeron canadense
erig-a. erigeron acris
erinus lobelia = lob-e.
erio. eriodictyon californicum
eriodyction californicum = erio.
eriodyction glutinosum = erio.
eriog-u. eriogonum umbellatum
erios-co. eriosema cordatum
erlan-c. erlangea cordifolia
erod. erodium cicutarium
erophila vulgaris = drab-vn.
eruca alba = sin-a.
eruca sativa = brass-e.
erv-e. ervum ervilia
erv-l. ervum lens
ery-a. eryngium aquaticum
ery-c. eryngium campestre
ery-f. eryngium foetidum
eryhtrom. erythromycinum
ery-m. eryngium maritimum
erys-a. erysimum alliaria
erysimum barbarea = barbr-vg.
erys-c. erysimum capitatum
erys-o. erysimum officinale
erythrina corallodendron = pisc.
eryth. erythrinus
erythraea centaurium = canch.
erythraea chilensis = canch.
erythr-ca. erythrina caffra
erythron-p. erythronium purpurascens
eryt-j. erythrophlaeum judiciale
erythroxylon coca = coca
escherichia coli = coli.
esch. eschscholtzia californica
escoba amargo = parth.
esin. eserinum
esin-sal. eserinum salicylicum
esp-g. espeletia grandiflora
esponjilla = luf-op.
estrone = foll.
ethanal = acetald.
etherum = aether
ethyl cellulose = aethylce.
ethylene-ethenyl-diamine = lysd.
ethylicum = aethyl.
ethylicum aceticum = aethyl-act.
ethylicum muriaticum = aethyl-m.
ethylicum nitricum = aethyl-n.
ethylicum sulfuricum = aethyl-s.
ethylicum sulfuricum dichloratum = aethyl-s-d.
etna Etna lava
eucal. eucalyptus globulus
eucal-r. eucalyptus rostrata
eucal-t. eucalyptus tereticorti
eucl-l. euclea lanceolata
eucl-n. euclea natalensis
eucalypti aetheroleum = ol-eucal.
eucalypti folium = eucal.
eucol. eucalyptolum
eugenia carophyllata = caryo.
eugenia cheken = myrt-ch.
eugenia jambolana = syzyg.

eug. eugenia jambos
euonymus Europaea = euon.
euon. Euonymus europaeus
euon-a. euonymus atropurpurea
eugenia vulgaris = eug.
euginia chequen = myrt-ch.
euonin. euonyminum
euonymus vulgaris = euon.
eup-a. eupatorium aromaticum
eupatorium aya-pana = eup-a.
eup-c. eupatorium cannabinum
eup-d. eupatorium dendroides
euphorbia sylvatica = euph-a.
euph. euphorbium officinarum
eupatorium satureiaefolium = gua.
eupatorium triplinerve = eup-a.
eupatorium verticullatum = eup-pur.
euph-a. euphorbia amygdaloides
euph-c. euphorbia corollata
euph-cy. euphorbia cyparissias
euph-e. euphorbia esula
euph-he. euphorbia heterodoxa
euph-hero. euphorbia herophylla
euph-hi. euphorbia hirta
euph-hl. euphorbia helioscopa
euph-hy. euphorbia hypericifolia
euph-ip. euphorbia ipecacuanhae
euph-l. euphorbia lathyris
euph-m. euphorbia marginata
euphorbia milii var. splendens = euph-sp.
euph-pa. euphorbia palustris
euph-pe. euphorbia peplus
euph-pi. euphorbia pilulifera
euph-pis. euphorbia pilosa
euph-po. euphorbia polycarpa
euph-pr. euphorbia prostata
euph-pu. euphorbia pulcherrima
euphr. euphrasia officinalis
euph-re. euphorbia resinifera
euph-sp. euphorbia splendida
euphrasia rostkoviana = euphr.
eupi. eupionum
eup-per. eupatorium perfoliatum
eup-pur. eupatorium purpureum
eur-br. europium bromatum
eur-c. europium carbonicum
eur-f. europium fluoratum
eur-i. europium iodatum
eur-lac. europium lacticum
eur-m. europium muriaticum
eur-n. europium nitricum
eur-o. europium oxydatum
eur-ox. europium oxalicum
eur-p. europium phosphoricum
eur-s. europium sulphuricum
eur-sil. europium silicatum
euryangium sumbul = sumb.
euscorpius italicus = scor.
euspongia officinalis = spong.
eut-o. euterpe oleracea
evonymus atropurpureus = euon-a.
evonymus Europeus = euon.
evonymus vulgaris = euon.
exalginum = metald.
exogonium purga = jal.
eys. eysenhardtia polystachia
fab. fabiana imbricata
faba-vg. faba vulgaris
faec. bacillus Faecalis (Bach)
faecalis (bach) = faec.
fago. fagopyrum esculentum
fagu. fagus sylvatica
fagu-p. pix fagus sylvatica
falco-bi. falcon biarmicus
falco-ch. falcon cherrug
falco-co. falcon columbarius
falco-el. falcon eleonorae
falco-me. falcon mexicanus
falco-pe. falcon peregrinus disciplinatus
falco-ru. falcon rusticolus
falco-sp. falcon sparverius
falco-su. falcon subbuteo
falco-ti. falcon tinnunculus
fall-au. fallopia aubertii
farfara = tus-fa.
fasci-h. fasciola hepatica
fax-cae-al. fax caelestis allende
febr-wolhy. febris wolhynia nosode Merck
febr-xyz. febris species unknown
fel fel tauri
fel-s. fel sui
felix domestica lac = lac-f.
fenot-hbr. fenoterolum hydrobromatum
ferm. fermium
ferr. ferrum metallicum
ferr-act. ferrum aceticum
ferr-am-s. ferrum ammonium sulfuricum
ferrum arsenicicum = ferr-ar.
ferr-ar. ferrum arsenicosum
ferr-br. ferrum bromatum
ferrum bromhydricum = ferr-hbr.
ferr-c. ferrum carbonicum
ferrum chloratum = ferr-m.
ferr-cit. ferrum citricum
ferr-coll. ferrum colloidal
ferr-cy. ferrum cyanatum
ferr-f. ferrum fluoratum
ferr-form. ferrum formicum
ferr-fuma. ferrum fumaricum
ferr-gl. ferrum gluconicum

ferr-gp.	ferrum glycero phosphoricum
ferr-hbr.	ferrum hydrobromicum
ferr-hcy	ferrum hydrocyanicum
ferr-i.	ferrum iodatum
ferr-lac.	ferrum lacticum
ferr-m.	ferrum muriaticum
ferr-ma.	ferrum magneticum
ferr-n.	ferrum nitricum
ferr-o-r.	ferrum oxydatum rubrum
ferr-ox.	ferrum oxalicum
ferr-p.	ferrum phosphoricum
ferr-pern.	ferrum pernitricum
ferr-p-h.	ferrum phosphoricum hydricum
ferr-pic.	ferrum picricum
ferr-pm.	ferrum pomatum
ferr-prox.	ferrum protoxalatum
ferr-py.	ferrum pyrophosphoricum
ferr-r.	ferrum reductum
ferrum sulfas = ferr-s.	
ferr-s.	ferrum sulphuricum
ferr-schl.	ferrum sequichloratum
ferr-si.	ferrum sidereum
ferr-sil.	ferrum silicicum
ferr-t.	ferrum tartaricum
ferrosi gluconas = ferr-gl.	
ferru-g.	ferrula galbanum
ferr-val.	ferrum valerianicum
ferula asa foetida = asaf.	
ferula communis = ferul.	
ferul.	ferula glauca
ferula moschata = sumb.	
ferula narthex = asaf.	
ferula rubicaulis = ferru-g.	
ferula scorodosma = asaf.	
ferula sumbul = sumb.	
fest-e.	festuca elatior
fest-r.	festuca rubra
fibr.	fibrinum
ficaria ranunculoides = ran-fi.	
ficaria verna = ran-fi.	
fic-c.	ficus carica
ficus indica = opun-f.	
fic-m.	ficus macrophylla
ficus opuntia = opun-f.	
fic-r.	ficus religiosa
fic-v.	ficus venosa
filipendula ulmaria = spirae.	
fil.	filix mas
fiel di piedra = flor-p.	
fila-l.	filaria loa
fisc-l.	fiscum laxum
fl-ac.	fluoricum acidum
flamm.	flammeus
flaveinum = lutin.	
flav.	flavus
fleum-p.	fleum pratense
flf.	fluoroformium
flor-p.	flor de piedra
flos-sol.	= helia. = flos solis
fl-pur.	fluor purum
fl-sil-ac.	fluosilicum acidum
flos solis = helia.	
flunit.	flunitrazepam
fluor-xyz.	fluor albus nosode species unknown
foen.	foeniculum sativum
foen-an.	foeniculum anethum
foeniculum aquaticum = phel.	
foen-d.	foeniculum dulce
foenm-g.	= trig-f-g. = foenum graecum
foeniculum vulgare = foen-an.	
foenum graecum = trig-f-g.	
fol-ac.	folicum acidum
foll.	folliculinum
form.	formica rufa
form-ac.	formicicum acidum
formaldehydi solutio = formal.	
formal.	formalinum
form-n.	formica nigra
fragaria elatior = frag.	
frag.	fragaria vesca
fram.	framboesinum
franciscaea uniflora = franc.	
franc.	franciscea uniflora
francm.	francium
frangula = rham-f.	
frangulae cortex = rham-f.	
franz.	Franzensbad aqua
frase-crl.	frasera carolinensis
frax.	fraxinus Americana
frax-e.	fraxinus excelsior
frax-o.	fraxinus ornus
friedr.	Friedrichshaller aqua
fruc-m-s.	fructi mixtus sucus
fruct-f.	fructus fructicosus
fuc.	fucus vesiculosus
fuc-c.	fucus crispus
fructus phytolaccae = phyt-b.	
fuchsin = fuch.	
fuch.	fuchsinum
fuc-n.	fucus nodosus
fuc-p.	fucus platycarpus
fuc-s.	fucus serratus
fuli.	fuligo ligni
fum.	fumaria officinalis
fuma-ac.	fumaricum acidum
funiculus umbilicalis = chord-umb.	
funiculus umbilicalis suis = suis-chord-umb.	
furf-i.	furfur iritici
fus.	fusarium oxysporum
gab.	gabbro

gaba	gamma-aminobutyricum acidum
gad.	gadus morrhua
gabro = gab.	
gado-br.	gadolinium bromatum
gado-c.	gadolinium carbonicum
gado-f.	gadolinium fluoratum
gado-i.	gadolinium iodatum
gado-lac.	gadolinium lacticum
gado-m.	gadolinium muriaticum
gado-n.	gadolinium nitricum
gado-o.	gadolinium oxydatum
gado-ox.	gadolinium oxalicum
gado-p.	gadolinium phosphoricum
gado-s.	gadolinium sulphuricum
gado-sil.	gadolinium silicatum
gaert.	bacillus Gaertner (Bach)
gala.	galanthus nivalis
gal-ac.	gallicum acidum
gaertner (bach) = gaert.	
galact.	galactosum
galan.	galanga
galbanum = ferru-g.	
galeg.	galega officinalis
galen.	galena
galeo.	galeopsis ochroleuca
galeob-lu.	galeobdolon luteum
galeoc-c-h.	galeocerdo cuvier hepar
galeopsis dubia = galeo.	
galeopsis grandiflora = galeo.	
galeo-la.	galeopsis ladanum
galeo-n.	galeopsis nodosa
galeo-s.	galeopsis segetum
gallinae stomachi tunica interior = ing.	
gal-f.	gallium fluoratum
gali.	galium aparine
galipea cusparia = ang.	
galipea officinalis = ang.	
gali-al.	galium album
gali-c.	galium cruciata
gali-e.	galium erectum
gali-l.	galium luteum
galeopsis tetrahit = galeo-n.	
galin.	galinsoga parviflora
galium mollugo = gali-al.	
galium odoratum = asper.	
gali-pa.	galium palustre
gali-po.	galium porrigens
galium verum = gali-l.	
galla-q.	galla quercina
galla-q-r.	galla quercina ruber
galla-t.	gallae turcicae
galla-ti.	galla tinctora
galla-tu.	galla turcica
gallus gallus = gallus-d.	
gallus-d.	gallus gallus domesticus
gallus-em.	embryo gallinae
gal-m.	gallium muriaticum
gal-met.	gallium metallicum
gal-o.	gallium oxydatum
gal-p.	gallium phosphoricum
galph.	galphimia glauca
gal-s.	gallium sulphuricum
galv.	galvanismus
gamb.	gambogia
garcinia hanburyi = gamb.	
garcinia morella = gamb.	
garcinia sp. = gamb.	
gardenalum = phenob.	
gard-j.	gardenia jasminoide
gard-t.	gardenia ternifolia
garlic = all-s.	
gast.	Gastein aqua
gaultheria humilis = gaul.	
gaul.	gaultheria procumbens
gaulteriae aetherolum = gaul.	
gaul-h.	gaultheria hispidula
gaultheria repens = gaul.	
geb-k.	gebera kraussii
gelin.	gelatinum
gelsemium nitidum = gels.	
gels.	gelsemium sempervirens
gemi-ve.	gemiasma verdans
genat.	genatosan
genista scoparia = saroth.	
genist.	genista tinctoria
gent.	gentian (Bach fl.)
gent-ac.	gentiana acaulis
gent-am.	gentiana amarella
gent-c.	gentiana cruciata
gent-ch.	gentiana chirata
gent-l.	gentiana lutea
gent-pe.	gentiana perfoliata
gent-pn.	gentiana pneumonanthe
gent-pu.	gentiana purpurea
gentiana quinqueflora = gent-q.	
gent-q.	gentiana quinquefolia
geoffroya inermis = geo.	
geo.	geoffroya vermifuga
geom.	geomycine
ger.	geranium maculatum
ger-i.	= ger-ro. = geranium inodorum (old abbr.)
gerin.	geraninum
gerium robertianum = ger-i.	
germ-met.	germanium metallicum
ger-o.	= pelarg-o. = geranium odoratissimum (old abbr.)
ger-r.	geranium rotundifolium
geranium odoratissimum = pelarg-o.	
geranium pusillum = ger.	

ger-ro. geranium robertianum
geranium robertianum = ger-i.
ger-s. geranium sanguineum
get. Gettysburg aqua
geum geum rivale
geum-m. geum montanum
geum-u. geum urbanum
gilia-c. gilia capitata
gink-b. ginkgo biloba
gins. ginseng quinquefolium
glad-c. gladiolus communis
glam-ch. glucosamine chlorhydrate
glanderinum = hippoz.
glandula adrenalis cortex = adr-ctx.
glandula parathyroidea = parathyr.
glandula parotis = parot.
glandula pinealis = pineal.
glandula suprarenalis = suprar.
glandula thymus = thym-gl.
glandula thyreoidea = thyr.
glech. glechoma hederacea
glinicum = med.
glob-a. globularia alypum
glon. glonoinum
glor-si. gloriosa simplex
glor-su. gloriosa superba
gluca. glucagon
gluco. glucosum
glucagonum = gluca.
glucinium metallicum = beryl.
glucinium muriaticum = beryl-m.
glucinium oxydatum = beryl-o.
glucrl. glucochloral
glucosum anhydricum = gluco.
gluta-ac. glutamicum acidum
glutam. glutaminum
glutat. glutathion
gluten gluten
glyc. glycerinum
glycinum = glyco.
glyco. glycocollum
glycog. glycogenum
glycosmis pentaphylla = atis.
glycyr-g. glycyrrhiza glabra
glycyrrhiza glabra linn. = glycyr-g.
glynicum = med.
glyox. glyoxal
gnaph. gnaphalium polycephalum
gnaph-ar. gnaphalium arenarium
gnaphalium dioicum = gnaph.
gnaph-l. gnaphalium leontopodium
gnaph-o. gnaphalium obtusifolium
gnaph-ul. gnaphalium uliginosum
golondrina = euph-po.
gomph-f. gomphocarpus fructicosus

gonococcinum = med.
gonolubus cundurango = cund.
gonotox. gonotoxinum
gorse gorse (Bach fl.)
goss. gossypium herbaceum
goss-a. gossypium arboreum
goss-h. gossypium hirsutum
gou-l. gouania longispicata
gran. granatum
granite murvey = granit-m.
granit-m. granitum murvey
graph. graphites
graphites naturalis = graph.
graphium agamemnon = agam-g.
grat. gratiola officinalis
grew-oc. grewia occidentalis
grin. grindelia robusta
grin-sa. grindelia subalpina
grin-sq. grindelia squarrosa
grin-xyz. grindelia unknown species
gryl-c. gryllus campestris
gua. guaco
guaj. guajacum officinale
guaiacum officinale = guaj.
guajol. guajacolum
guan. guano Australis
guani. guaninum
guako = gua.
guanin-m. guanidinum muriaticum
guanin-n. guanidinum nitricum
guao = com.
guar. guarana
guarea guidonia = guare.
guare. guarea trichiloides
guaraninum = coffin.
guare-ce. guarea cedrata
guat. guatteria gaumeri
guat-l. guatteria longifolia
guilandina dioica = gymno.
guips. guipsinum
guiz-sc. guizotia scabra
gummi guttae = gamb.
gummi gutti = gamb.
gum-l. gummi laccae
gum-t. gummi tragacanthae
gunn-p. gunnera perpensa
gunp. gunpowder
gutenbergia cordifolia = erlan-c.
gymne. gymnema sylvestre
gymno. gymnocladus canadensis
gymnocladus dioicus = gymno.
gymnocladus distica = gymno.
gynandropsis gynandra = cleom-g.
gynocardia odorata = chaul.
gynu-ce. gynura cernua

haem.	haematoxylon campechianum
gyrotheca tinctoria = lachn.	
haemat.	haematite
haem-i-b-vc.	haemophilus influenzae B vaccinus
haff.	haffkine
hafn-met.	hafnium metallicum
hagenia abyssinica = kou.	
haliae-lc.	haliaeetus leucocephalus
haliaethus leukocapitus = haliae-lc.	
hall	Hall aqua
halo.	haloperidolum
ham.	hamamelis virginiana
hamamelis virginica = ham.	
haplopappus bailahuen = haplo-b.	
haplo-b.	haplopappus baylahuen
haro-ma.	= haru-ma. = haronga madagascariensis (old abbr.)
harpagophyti radix = harp.	
harp.	harpagophytum procumbens
haru-ma.	harungana madagascariensis
haru-pa.	harungana paniculata
hcg.	choriongonadotropinum
heath.	heather (Bach fl.)
hecla	Hecla lava
hed.	hedera helix
hedeo.	hedeoma pulegioides
hedysarum capitatum = onob-s.	
hedy.	hedysarum ildefonsianum
hedyos-a.	hedyosmum arborescens
hein-cr.	heinsia crinita
helia.	helianthus annuus
helia-t.	helianthus tuberosus
helianthus vulgare = helia.	
helichrysum arenarium = gnaph-ar.	
helich-s.	helichrysum staechas
helic-p.	helicobacter pylori
helonias viridis = verat-v.	
helin.	heloninum
hekla lava = hecla	
helianthemum canadense = cist.	
heli-n.	helianthemum nummularium
helio.	heliotropium peruvianum
helios = sol	
helio-eu.	heliotropium Europaeum
helio-i.	heliotropium indicum
helium	helium
hell.	helleborus niger
hell-f.	helleborus foetidus
hell-o.	helleborus orientalis
hell-t.	helleborus trifolius
hell-v.	helleborus viridis
helm.	helminthochortos
helmi-e.	helminthia echioides
heln-ov.	helinus ovata
helo.	heloderma-h. + -s. (old abbr.)
helodr-cal.	helodrilus caliginosus
helo-h.	heloderma horridum
helon.	helonias dioica
helo-s.	heloderma suspectum
helx.	helix tosta
helx-p.	helix pomatia
hemidsm.	hemidesmus indica
henna	henna
hep.	hepar sulphur
hepar sulphuris = hep.	
hepar sulphuris calcareum = hep.	
hepar sulphuris kalinum = kali-sula.	
heparin.	heparinum
hepatica nobilis = hepat.	
hepat.	hepatica triloba
hepati-a-vc.	hepatitis A vaccinus
hepati-b-vc.	hepatitis B vaccinus
hepati-xyz.	hepatitis nosode species unknown
heracleum branca = hera.	
hera.	heracleum sphondylium
herna-p.	hernandia pellata
hern-g.	herniaria glabra
heroin.	heroinum
herp-s.	herpes simplex nosode
herp-z.	herpes zoster nosode
hesp-m.	hesperis matronalis
hetrt-r.	heterotis rotundifolia
heuch.	heuchera Americana
hev-b.	hevea brasiliensis
hexachl.	hexachlorophenum
hydrofluoricum acidum = fl-ac.	
hf-sil-ac.	hydrofluo-silicicum acidum
hib-a.	hibiscus arboreus
hib-sa.	hibiscus sabdariffa
hib-su.	hibiscus surattensis
hier-p.	hieracium pilosella
hier-u.	hieracium umbellatum
hip-ac.	hippuricum acidum
hippomane mancinella = manc.	
hipp.	hippomanes
hippea-e.	hippeastrum equestre
hippoc-k.	hippocampus kuda
hippop-r.	hippophae rhamnoides
hippoz.	hippozaeninum
hir.	hirudo medicinalis
hirudo officinalis = hir.	
histamini dihydrochloridum = hist-m.	
hist.	histaminum
histid.	histidinum
histid-m.	histidinum muriaticum
histaminum hydrochloricum = hist-m.	
hist-m.	histaminum muriaticum
hochst.	aqua Hochstein
histrix prehensilis = sphing.	
histrix subspinosum = sphing.	

hoang-nan = strych-g.
hoit. hoitzia coccinea
holarrhena antidysenterica = kurch.
holc-l. holcus lanatus
holly holly (Bach fl.)
holm-br. holmium bromatum
holm-c. holmium carbonicum
holm-f. holmium fluoratum
holm-i. holmium iodatum
holm-lac. holmium lacticum
holm-m. holmium muriaticum
holm-met. holmium metallicum
holm-n. holmium nitricum
holm-o. holmium oxydatum
holm-ox. holmium oxalicum
holm-p. holmium phosphoricum
holm-s. holmium sulphuricum
holm-sil. holmium silicatum
holothuria physalis = physala-p.
hom-am. homarus Americanus
hom-cap. homarus capensis
homarus vulgaris = hom-g.
home. homeria collina
hom-g. homarus gammarus
hom-xyz. homarus unknown species
honeys. honeysuckle (Bach fl.)
hordeum-g. hordeum semen germinatum
hordeum-m. hordeum murinum
hordeum-vg. hordeum vulgare
hoorali = cur.
hordin-s. hordeninum sulfuricum
hormoflaveinum = progest.
hornb. hornbeam (Bach fl.)
hott-p. hottonia palustris
hoya-c. hoya carnosa
hphos-ac. hypophosphorum acidum
hubertia ambavilla = senec-abv.
hume. humea elegans
humulus lupulus = lup.
hura hura brasiliensis
hura-c. hura crepitans
hyalur. hyaluronidase
hydn-r. hydnum repandum
hydr. hydrastis canadensis
hydr-ac. hydrocyanicum acidum
hydrang. hydrangea arborescens
hydratum = am-caust.
hydraz-m. hydrazinum muriaticum
hydrc. hydrocotyle asiatica
hydrc-vg. hydrocotyle vulgaris
hydrangea frutescens = hydrang.
hydrargyri bichloridum = merc-c.
hydrargyri bijodidum = merc-i-r.
hydrargyri cyanidum = merc-cy.
hydrargyri lactas = merc-lac.
hydrargyri oxycyanidum = merc-o-cy.
hydrargyri oxydum flavum = merc-o-f.
hydrargyri oxydum rubrum = merc-pr-r.
hydrargyri oxydum subsulphuricum = merc-sul.
hydrargyri subchloridum mite = merc-d.
hydrargyrum bichloratum = merc-c.
hydrargyrum bicyanatum = merc-cy.
hydrargyrum bijodatum rubrum = merc-i-r.
hydrargyrum depuratum = merc.
hydrargyrum lacticum = merc-lac.
hydrargyrum metallicum = merc.
hydrargyrum oxydulatum nitricum crystallisatum = merc-n.
hydrargyrum stibiatosulfuratum = aethi-a.
hydrargyrum stibiato-sulfuratum = aethi-a.
hydrargyrum sulfuratum = aethi-m.
hydrargyrum sulphuratum nigrum = aethi-m.
hydrinin-m. hydrastininum muriaticum
hydrinin-s. hydrastininum sulphuricum
hydrin-m. hydrastinum muriaticum
hydrin-pur. hydrastinum purum
hydrin-s. hydrastinum sulphuricum
hydrobr-ac. hydrobromicum acidum
hydrochloricum = amylam.
hydrochl-ac. hydrochloridum acidum
hydrocort. hydrocortisone
hydrog. hydrogenium
hydroph. hydrophis cyanocinctus
hydroq. hydroquinone
hydrophobinum = lyss.
hydrophyllum virginianum = hydro-v.
hydro-v. hydrophyllum virginicum
hydroxp. hydroxyproline
hydroxq. hydroxyquinoleine
hygrophila spinosa = hygroph-s.
hygroph-aur. hygrophilia auriculata
hygroph-s. hygrophilia sphinosa
hymen-ac. hymenocardia acida
hymos. hymosa
hyosciamus niger = hyos.
hyoscinum bromatum = scopin.
hyoscinum bromhydricum = scopin-hbr.
hyoscinum hydriodicum = scopin-i.
hyoscyami folium = hyos.
hyoscyaminum hydrobromatum = hyosin-hbr.
hyoscyaminum sulphatum = hyosin-s.
hyos. hyoscyamus niger
hyosin. hyosciaminum-s. + -hbr. (old abbr.)
hyosin-hbr. hyosciaminum hydrobromatum
hyosin-s. hyosciaminum sulphatum
hyper. hypericum perforatum
hyper-ac. hypericum acutum
hyper-aet. hypericum aethiopicum
hyper-m. hypericum maculatum
hyper-pu. hypericum pulchrum

hyper-q.	hypericum quadrangulum
hypo.	hypophyllum sanguineum
hypericum tetrapterum = hyper-ac.	
hypoes-t.	hypoestes triflora
hypophysinum = pituin.	
hypophysis anterior = pitu-a.	
hypophysis cerebri = pitu-gl.	
hypophysis glandula = pitu-gl.	
hypophysis posterior = pitu-p.	
hypop-m.	hypopitis multiflora
hypoth.	hypothalamus
hypothalamus of the ox = hypoth.	
hypt-p.	hyptis pectinata
hypt-s.	hyptis suaveolens
hyss-o.	hyssopus officinalis
iaspis = jas.	
iber.	iberis amara
ibo.	iboga
iboza riparia = tetrad-r.	
ibupr.	ibuprofen
ichthyolammonium = ichth.	
ichth.	ichthyolum
ichthyotoxinum = ser-ang.	
ictod.	ictodes foetida
illicium anisatum = anis.	
illicium stellatum = anis.	
illicium verum = anis.	
ig-a.	immunoglobulin A
Iecoris aselli oleum = ol-j.	
ign.	ignatia amara
ignis-alc.	ignis alcoholis
ihydr-ac.	iodhydricum acidum
ille.	illecebrum verticillatum
ikshugandha = trib.	
ilx-a.	ilex aquifolium
ilx-c.	ilex casseine
ilex cassine = ilx-c.	
Ilex opaca = ilx-a.	
ilex paraguaiensis = mate	
ilex paraguariensis = mate	
ilx-v.	ilex vomitoria
imp.	imperatoria ostruthium
impa-b.	impatiens balsamina
impa-ca.	impatiens capensis
impa-g.	impatiens glandulifera
impa-n.	impatiens noli tangere
immunoserum diphthericum = diphtox.	
impat.	impatiens (Bach fl.)
impatiens pendulifera = impa-n.	
impatiens roylei = impa-g.	
impa-w-a	impatiens walleriana alba
imperatoria peucedanum = imp.	
ina-i.	inachis io
inca.	incajea
indigofera tinctoria = indg.	
ind.	indium metallicum
indg.	indigo tinctoria
indgf-a.	indigofera atriceps
indol.	indolum
indom.	indometacine
influ.	influenzinum
influ-eq-vc.	influenza equine vaccinus
influenzinum vaccinus = influ.	
ing.	ingluvin
inos.	inositol
ins.	insulinum
insig-m.	Insight meditation
interf.	interferon alpha leucocytaire
inul.	inula helenium
inula conyza = conyz-vg.	
inul-d.	inula dysenterica
inul-g.	inula graveolens
inulin.	inulinum
inul-p.	inula pulicaria
inula squarrosa = conyz-vg.	
inul-v.	inula viscosa
iod.	iodium
iod-act.	iodium aceticum
iod-br.	iodium bromatum
iod-h.	iodium hydrogenisatum
iod-m.	iodium muriaticum
iodium purum = iod.	
iodof.	iodoformium
ipeca = ip.	
ip.	ipecacuanha
iodoformum = iodof.	
iodothyrinum = thyroiod.	
ipat.	ipatropium
ipomea purga = jal.	
ipomea turpenthum = oper.	
ipom-ba.	ipomoea batatas
ipomoea bona-nox = convo-d.	
ipom-f.	ipomoea ficifolia
ipomoea hirsutula = ipom-p.	
ipom-nil.	ipomoea nil
ipom-p.	ipomoea purpurea
ipomoea rubrocaerulea = ipom-vi.	
ipomoea stans = convo-s.	
ipomoea tricolor = ipom-vi.	
ipom-vi.	ipomoea violacea
ip-rd.	ipecacuanhae radix
irid-m.	iridium muriaticum
iridinum = irisin.	
iridium chloride = irid-m.	
irid-met.	iridium metallicum
iris	iris versicolor
iris-fa.	iris factissima
iris-fl.	iris florentina
iris-foe.	iris foetidissima

iris-g. iris germanica
iris-h. iris harwegii
irisin. irisinum
iris minor = iris-t.
iris-ps. iris pseudacorus
iris-pu. iris pumila
iris-t. iris tenax
isoleuc. isoleucinum
ison. isoniazide
isop. isoprenaline
itu itu
ix. ixodes ricinus
ix-vc. ixodes ricinus vaccine
jab. jaborandi
jacaranda braziliensis = jac-c.
jac-c. jacaranda caroba
jac-g. jacaranda gualandai
jac-m. jacaranda mimosifolia
jacaranda ovalifolia = jac-m.
jacaranda procera = jac-c.
jacea = viol-t.
jade jade
jal. jalapa
jas. jaspis
jambos eugenia = eug.
jambosa vulgaris = eug.
janosia = joan.
jararaca = both.
jararacussu = both.
jasm. jasminum officinale
jasper jasper
jateorhiza palmata = chasm-p.
jateorrhiza palmata = chasm-p.
jatr-c. jatropha curcas
jatr-g. jatropha gossypifolia
jatropha manihot = cass.
jatr-u. jatropha urens
jatrorrhiza palmata = chasm-p.
jatz. Jatzfeld aqua
jeff-di. jeffersonia diphylla
jenosia ashoka = joan.
jequiritolum = abrin.
jequirity = abr.
joan. joanesia asoca
juglans cathartica = jug-c.
jug-c. juglans cinerea
jodium = iod.
jonosia asoka = joan.
jugin. juglandinum
jug-r. juglans regia
juncus communis = junc-e.
junc-e. juncus effusus
junc-ja. juncus jaquinii
junc-p. juncus pilosus
juni-br. juniperus brasiliensis
juni-c. juniperus communis
juni-o. juniperus oxycedrus
juni-o-p. juniperus oxycedrus pix
juni-p. juniperus phoenicea
juniperus sabina = sabin.
juni-v. juniperus virginiana
juniperus virginianus = juni-v.
just. justicia adhatoda
justicia cydoniifolia = just.
justicia paniculata = androg-p.
just-r. justicia rubrum
kal. kalanchoe pinnatum
kalag. kalagua
kalam. kalamegh
kali hydriodicum = kali-i.
kali hydriodium = kali-i.
kali hydroiodicum = kali-i.
kali silicatum = kali-sil.
kalii acetas = kali-act.
kalii antimoniotartras = ant-t.
kalii bichromas = kali-bi.
kalii bromidum = kali-br.
kalii chloridum = kali-m.
kalii chromas = kali-chr.
kalii citras = kali-cit.
kalii dihyrogenphosphas = kali-p.
kalii iodidum = kali-i.
kalii nitras = kali-n.
kalii permangas = kali-perm.
kali-act. kalium aceticum
kali-ar. kalium arsenicosum
kali-asp. kalium asparticum
kali-aur-cy. kalium auro-cyanatum
kali-bi. kalium bichromicum
kali-biox. kalium bioxalicum
kali-bit. kalium bitartaricum
kali-br. kalium bromatum
kali-b-t. kalium borotartaricum
kalium bromhydricum = kali-hbr.
kali-c. kalium carbonicum
kali-caust. kalium causticum
kali-chl. kalium chloricum
kali-chls. kalium chlorosum
kali-chr. kalium chromicum
kalium chromicum sulphuricum = kali-s-chr.
kali-cit. kalium citricum
kali-cy. kalium cyanatum
kali-f. kalium fluoratum
kali-fcy. kalium ferrocyanatum
kali-form. kalium formicum
kali-gl. kalium gluconicum
kali-hbr. kalium hydrobromicum
kali-hox. kalium hydroxydum
kalium hypermanganicum = kali-perm.

kali-hp.	kalium hypophosphoricum
kali-i.	kalium iodatum
kalium iodicum = kali-i.	
kali-l.	kalium lacticum
kali-m.	kalium muriaticum
kalium manganicum = kali-perm.	
kali-met.	kalium metallicum
kali-n.	kalium nitricum
kali-nat-t.	kalium natrum tartaricum
kali-o.	kalium oxydatum
kali-ox.	kalium oxalicum
kali-p.	kalium phosphoricum
kali-perchl.	kalium perchloricum
kali-perm.	kalium permanganatum
kali-pic.	kalium picricum
kali-picn.	kalium picronitricum
kali-s.	kalium sulphuricum
kali-sal.	kalium salicylicum
kali-s-chr.	kalium sulphuricum chromicum
kalium stibyltartaricum = ant-t.	
kali-s-cy.	kalium sulfocyanicum
kali-sil.	kalium silicicum
kali-sula.	kalium sulphuratum
kali-sulo.	kalium sulphurosum
kali-t.	kalium tartaricum
kali-tcy.	kalium thiocyanatum
kali-tel.	kalium telluricum
kalium-ns.	kalium nitrosum
kali-x.	kalium xanthogenicum
kalm.	kalmia latifolia
kam.	kamala
kaolinit = kaol.	
kaol.	kaolinum
kaolinum ponderosum = alumin-sil.	
kaolinum ponderosum = kaol.	
kara	karaka
karlsbad aqua = carl.	
karw-h.	karwinskia humboldtiana
kauri	= agath-a. = kauri Australis
katipo = lat-k.	
kauri agathis Australis = agath-a.	
kava-kava = pip-m.	
kell = khell.	
kerose.	kerosenum
keroso.	kerosolenum
ketogl-ac.	ketoglutaricum acidum
khaya-s.	khaya senegalensis
khell.	khellin
kino	kino pterocarpi
khilte = khell.	
kinkeliba = combr-r.	
kino australiense = ango.	
kino-m.	kino malabar
kiss.	Kissingen aqua
Klebsiella pneumoniae = mucot.	
kluyveromyces cicerisporus = kluyv-ma.	
kluyveromyces fragilis = kluyv-ma.	
kluyv-ma.	kluyveromyces marxianus
knau-ar.	knautia arvensis
kobra = naja	
kola	kola
kosen	Kosen aqua
koso = kou.	
kou.	kousso
krameria triandra = rat.	
krent-l.	krentophyllum lanatum
kreos.	kreosotum
kres.	kresolum
kronth.	Kronthal aqua
krypt.	krypton
kurch.	kurchi
lac-ac.	lacticum acidum
laburnum anagyroides = cyt-l.	
lac-as.	lac asinum
lac-c.	lac caninum
lac-cp.	lac caprinum
lac-cp-m.	lac caprinum masculinum
lac-d.	lac vaccinum defloratum
lac defloratum = lac-d.	
lac-del.	lac delphinum
lac delphinum = lac-del.	
lac equie = lac-e.	
lac-e.	lac equinum
lac-eleph-m.	lac elephas maxiumus
lacerta (zootoca) vivipara = lacer-viv.	
lacer.	lacerta agilis
lacer-viv.	lacerta vivipara
lac equinuus assinus = lac-as.	
lac-f.	lac felinum
lachesis alternatus = both-a.	
lachesis lanceolatus = both.	
lach.	lachesis mutus
lac-h.	lac humanum
lachn.	lachnanthes tinctoria
lac-leo.	lac leoninum
lac leonis = lac-leo.	
lac-loxod-a.	lac loxodonta Africana
lac-lup.	lac lupinum
lac-mac-m.	lac macaca mulatta
lac-mat.	lac maternum
lac-o.	lac ovis
lac-pan-tr.	lac pan troglodytes
lac-pr.	lac primatum
lac-sui.	lac suinum
lact.	lactuca virosa (old abbr.)
lacta-d.	lactarius deliciosus
lact-e.	lactuca elongata
lacticum acidum dextrum = sarcol-ac.	
lactis acidum = lac-ac.	
lactis vaccini flos = lac-v-f.	

lactob.	lactobacillus
lactof.	lactoflavinum
lactrm.	lactucarium thridace
lact-sa.	lactuca sativa
lact-sc.	lactuca scariola
lactuca silvestris = lact-v.	
lact-v.	lactuca virosa
lac-urs.	lac ursinum
lac vaccini flos = lac-v-f.	
lac-v.	lac vaccinum
lac-v-b.	lac vaccinum butyricum
lac-v-c.	lac vaccinum coagulatum
lac-v-f.	lac vaccinum flos
lac-v-fe.	lac vaccinum fermentatum
laminaria flexicaulis = lamin-d.	
lam.	lamium album
lam-am.	lamium amplexicaule
Lager beer = cerev-lg.	
lamin-d.	laminaria digitata
lamium galeobdolon = galeob-lu.	
lam-m.	lamium maculatum
lam-p.	lamium purpureum
lampo-cy.	lampona cylindrata
lampr-m.	lampranthus multiradiatus
lampro-sp.	lamprohiza splendidula
lamps-c.	lampsana communis
land.	Landeck aqua
lang.	langebrucken aqua
lanol.	lanolinum
lant-c.	lantana camara
lanth-met.	lanthanum metallicum
lanth-n.	lanthanum nitricum
lanth-o.	lanthanum oxydatum
lanth-s.	lanthanum sulfuricum
lantana spinosa = lant-c.	
lant-t.	lantana trifolia
lapa.	lapathum acutum
lapathum sylvestre = lapa.	
lap-a.	lapis albus
lapis calcareus Burren = limest-b.	
lapis divinus = cupr-alum.	
lapis granites murvey = granit-m.	
lap-la.	lapis lazuli
lapis marmoreus Connemara = marb-w.	
lapis renalis = cal-ren.	
lappa	lappa arctium
lappa major = lappa	
lappa minor = lappa	
lappa officinalis = lappa	
lappa tomentosa = lappa	
laps.	lapsana communis
larch	larch (Bach fl.)
laricifomes officinalis = bol-la.	
lar-d.	larix decidua
lar-e.	larix Europaea
lars-arg.	larus argentatus
lasidora cubana = mygal.	
latex-v.	latex vulcani
lathyrus odoratus = lath.	
lath.	lathyrus sativus
latrodectus curassavicus = ther.	
lat-h.	latrodectus haseltii
lathyrus cicera = lath.	
lath-l.	lathyrus latifolius
lath-sy.	lathyrus sylvestris
lat-k.	latrodectus katipo
lat-m.	latrodectus mactans
latrodectus mactans hasselti = lat-h.	
laur.	laurocerasus
laurus benzoin = benzo.	
laurus camphora = camph.	
lauru-n.	laurus nobilis
lauru-p.	laurus persea
laurus sassafras = sass.	
laurustinus = vib-t.	
lava heclae = hecla	
lava scoriae = hecla	
lavand-a.	lavandula angustifolia
lavand-l.	lavandula latifolia
lavand-o.	= lavand-a. = lavandula officinalis (old abbr.)
lavandula officinalis = lavand-a.	
lavandula spica = lavand-l.	
lavandula vera = lavand-a.	
lavandulae aetheroleum = ol-lav.	
lawr.	lawrencium
lawsonia inermis = henna	
l-dopa = dopa	
lec.	lecithinum
led.	ledum palustre
lem-g.	lemna gibba
lem-m.	lemna minor
leontice thalictroides = caul.	
leontopodium alpinum = gnaph-l.	
leon.	leonurus cardiaca
lens esculenta = erv-l.	
leont-l.	leonotis leonurus
leont-o.	leonotis ovata
lepd-s.	lepidoptera saturniidae
lepi.	lepidium bonariense
lepi-i.	lepidium iberis
lepi-s.	lepidium sativum
lepr.	leprominium
lept.	leptandra virginica
leptilon canadense = erig.	
leptol-e.	leptolobium elegans
leptos-ih.	leptospira ictero-hemorrhagica
lesp-c.	lespedeza capitata
lesp-s.	lespedeza sieboldii
lespedeza thunbergii = lesp-s.	

leuca-g. leucaena glauca
leucanthemum parthenium = pyre-p.
leucanthemum vulgare = chrysan.
leucas-a. leucas aspera
leucantha = bid-b.
leuc-d. leucanthemum discoidum
leucop. leucophyllus
lev. Levico aqua
levist. levisticum officinale
levist-rd. levistici officinalis radix
levoarterenol = noradr.
levo. levomepromazinum
liat. liatris spicata
lichen islandicus = cetr.
lich-i. lichtensteinia interrupta
lignum nephriticum = eys.
lignum vitae = guaj.
lig-vg. ligustrum vulgare
lilium Africanum = agap.
lil-a. lilium album
lilium candidum = lil-a.
lilium lancifolium = lil-t.
lil-l. lilium longiflorum
lil-m. lilium martagon
lil-s. lilium superbum
lil-t. lilium tigrinum
lim. limulus cyclops
lima-ag. limax agrestis
limax ater = arion
limen-b-c. limenitis bredowii californica
limest-ar. limestone Arans
limest-b. limestone Burren
limx. limex ater
lim-xyz. limulus unknown part
lina. linaria vulgaris
lina-e. linaria elatine
lina-sp. linaria spuria
lina-st. linaria striata
lincom. lincomycine
linda. lindane
lindera benzoin = benzo.
lingusticum levisticum = levist.
lini semen = linu-u.
linol-ac. linoleicum acidum
linum cartharticum = linu-c.
linu-c. linum catharticum
linu-u. linum usitatissimum
lip. lippia mexicana
lip-as. lippia asperifolia
lip-c. lippia citriodora
lipp. Lippspringe aqua
liquor ammoni caustici = am-caust.
lir-o. liriosma ovata
lister. listeriosis nosode
lithan-p. pix lithantracis
lithii benzoas = lith-be.
lithii carbonas = lith-c.
lithii citras = lith-cit.
lith-be. lithium benzoicum
lith-br. lithium bromatum
lithium bromhydricum = lith-hbr.
lith-c. lithium carbonicum
lith-chl. lithium chloricum
lith-cit. lithium citricum
lith-f. lithium fluoratum
lith-gl. lithium gluconicum
lith-hbr. lithium hydrobromicum
lith-i. lithium iodatum
lith-lac. lithium lacticum
lith-m. lithium muriaticum
lith-met. lithium metallicum
lith-o. lithium oxydatum
lithosp-a. lithospermum arvense
lith-p. lithium phosphoricum
lith-s. lithium sulfuricum
lith-sal. lithium salicylicum
lithospermum officinale = mil-s.
lithospermum virginicum = onos.
loa-loa = fila-l.
loa. loasa tricolor
lobelia glandulosa = lob-s.
lob. lobelia inflata
lobaria pulmonaria = stict.
lob-a. lobelia acetum
lob-c. lobelia cardinalis
lobelia coerulea = lob-s.
lob-d. lobelia dortmanna
lob-e. lobelia erinus
lobin. lobelinum
lobin-m. lobelinum muriaticum
lobin-s. lobelinum sulfuricum
lobl-m. lobularia maritima
lob-p. lobelia purpurascens
lobelia siphilitica = lob-s.
lob-s. lobelia syphilitica
lob-u. lobelia urens
loleum temulentum = lol.
lol. lolium temulentum
lon-c. lonicera caprifolium
lon-e. lonicera etrusca
lon-n. lonicera nigra
lonicera ochroleuca = lon-x.
lon-p. lonicera periclymenum
lon-x. lonicera xylosteum
lophophora williamsii = anh.
lophophytum leandri = flor-p.
lophophytum mirabile = flor-p.
lophophytum spectabile = flor-p.
loran-sc. loranthus scurrula
loraz. lorazepam

lormet.	lormetazepam
lot-c.	lotus corniculatus
loxoc.	loxosceles (old abbr.)
loxo-ga.	loxosceles gaucho
loxo-lae.	loxosceles laeta
loxosceles nigella = loxo-lae.	
loxo-parr.	loxosceles parrami
loxo-recl.	loxosceles reclusa
loxosceles reclusus = loxo-recl.	
loxo-refr.	loxosceles refescens
lycosa fasciiventris = tarent.	
lycosa tarentula = tarent.	
lsd.	lysergic acid diethylamide
luc-g.	lucuma glycyphloeum
luesinum = syph.	
lueticum = syph.	
luf-act.	luffa actangula
luf-am.	luffa amara
luffa bendaul = luf-ech.	
luffa bendaul = luf-ech.	
luf-b.	luffa bindal
luffa bondel = luf-ech.	
luffa bondel = luf-ech.	
luf-ech.	luffa echinata
luffa longistyla = luf-ech.	
luffa longistyla = luf-ech.	
luf-op.	luffa operculata
luf-s.	luffa sphaerica
lumbr-t.	lumbricus terrestris
lum-uv.	lumen UV
luminal = phenob.	
luna	luna
lup.	lupulus humulus
lupin.	lupulinum
lups-a.	lupinus albus
lute-br.	lutetium bromatum
lute-c.	lutetium carbonicum
lute-f.	lutetium fluoratum
lute-i.	lutetium iodatum
lute-lac.	lutetium lacticum
lute-m.	lutetium muriaticum
lute-n.	lutetium nitricum
lute-o.	lutetium oxydatum
lute-ox.	lutetium oxalicum
lute-p.	lutetium phosphoricum
lute-s.	lutetium sulphuricum
lute-sil.	lutetium silicatum
luteum	luteum
lutin.	luteinum
lyc.	lycopodium clavatum
luzula pilosa = junc-p.	
luzula vernalis = junc-p.	
lychnis githago = agro.	
lyci-b.	lycium barbarum
lycoperdon bovista = bov.	
lycpr.	lycopersicon esculentum
lycopus aqauticus = lycps-eu.	
lycps-eu.	lycopus Europaeus
lycps-v.	lycopus virginicus
lycs-ar.	lycopsis arvensis
lys.	lysinum
lysd.	lysidinum
lysd-dnp.	lysidinum dinitrophenatum
lysi.	lysimachia nummularia
lysi-r.	lysimachia ruhmeriana
lysi-vg.	lysimachia vulgaris
lys-m.	lysinum muriaticum
lyss.	lyssinum
lyss-vc.	vaccinum rabiei ex cellulis
lythrum petiolatum = cuph.	
lythrum salicaria = salic-p.	
lytta vesicatoria = canth.	
macro.	macrotinum
macrotys racemosa = cimic.	
macroz.	macroziama spiralis
madar = calo.	
madura album = calo.	
maesa-l.	maesa lanceolata
maesa-t.	maesa trichophlebia
maeso-f.	maesobotrya floribunda
magnesii chloridum hexahydricum = mag-m.	
magnesii citras = mag-cit.	
magnesii hydroxidum = mag-hox.	
magnesii oxydum = mag-o.	
magnesii subcarbonas levis = mag-c.	
magnesii sulfas = mag-s.	
mag-act.	magnesium aceticum
mag-ar.	magnesium arsenicicum
mag-art.	magnesium artificialis
mag-asp.	magnesium asparticum
mag-bcit.	magnesium borocitricum
mag-br.	magnesium bromatum
magnesium calcinatum = mag-o.	
mag-c.	magnesium carbonicum
mag-chl.	magnesium chloricum
mag-cit.	magnesium citricum
mag-f.	magnesium fluoratum
magnesium fluorosilicatum = mag-sil-f.	
mag-form.	magnesium formicum
mag-gl.	magnesium gluconicum
mag-gp.	magnesium glycerophosphoricum
mag-hox.	magnesium hydroxydum
mag-hp.	magnesium hypophosphorosum
mag-hs.	magnesium hyposulfurosum
mag-i.	magnesium iodatum
mag-lac.	magnesium lacticum
mag-m.	magnesium muriaticum
mag-mang-p.	magnesium manganum phosphoricum
mag-met.	magnesium metallicum
mag-n.	magnesium nitricum

magnetismus animalis = mesmer.
magn-gl. magnolia glauca
magn-gr. magnolia grandiflora
mag-o. magnesium oxydatum
mag-orot. magnesium oroticum
mag-p. magnesium phosphoricum
mag-pox. magnesium peroxydatum
mag-s. magnesium sulphuricum
mag-sal. magnesium salicylicum
mag-sil. magnesium silicatum
mag-sil-f. magnesium silicofluoratum
mag-t. magnesium tartaricum
magenta = fuch.
magistery of bismuth = bism-sn.
magnes artificialis = m-ambo.
magnesia = mag-o.
mag-u. magnesia usta
mahonia aquifolium = berb-a.
mah-p. mahonia palustris
maias-l. maiasaura lapidea
majalis = meloe-m.
majeptilum = thiop.
makar. makaradhwaja
mal-ac. malicum acidum
malachite = cupr-c.
malachium aquaticum = cerast-a.
maland. malandrinum
malar. malaria nosode
malath. malathion
malatox. malariatoxinum
malleinum = hippoz.
mallotus philippinensis = kam.
malosma laurina = rhus-l.
malt-ext. maltum extractum
malus-c. malus communis
malus-d. malus domestica
malus-f. malus fusca
malus-p. malus pumila
malus sylvestris = malus-c.
malva-a. malva alcea
malva-m. malva moschata
malva-ne. malva neglecta
malva-p. malva parviflora
malva-s. malva sylvestris
malvav-a. malvaviscus arboreus
m-ambo. magnetis poli ambo
mamm. glandula mammalis
mamma glandula = mamm.
manaca = franc.
manc. mancinella
mand. mandragora officinarum
mande-ac. mandelicum acidum
mand-r. mandragora e radice siccato
mang. manganum-act. + -c. (old abbr.)
mangana sulfas = mang-s.
mang-act. manganum aceticum
mang-be. manganum benzoicum
mang-c. manganum carbonicum
mang-coll. manganum colloidale
manganum dioxydum = mang-o.
mang-f. manganum fluoratum
mang-gl. manganum gluconicum
mang-gp. manganum glycero phosphoricum
mangi. mangifera indica
mang-i. manganum iodatum
mang-lact. manganum lacticum
mang-m. manganum muriaticum
mang-met. manganum metallicum
mang-n. manganum nitricum
mang-o. manganum oxydatum
manganum oxydatum nativum = mang-o.
manganum peroxydum = mang-o.
mang-p. manganum phosphoricum
mang-s. manganum sulphuricum
manganum silicatum = mang-sil.
mang-sil. manganum silicicum
mang-sil-f. manganum silicofluoratum
manihot utilissima = cass.
manioc = cass.
manni. mannitol
mannitolum = manni.
mannohep. mannoheptulose
mant-r. mantis religiosa
manz. manzanita
mapato = rat.
mapr. maprotiline
marant-a. maranta arundinacea
marb-w. white marble
m-arct. magnetis polus arcticus
marble, white = marb-w.
marien. Marienbader aqua
marigoldin = calen.
markh-l. markhamia lutea
marr. = marr-vg. = marrubium album (old abbr.)
marrubium album = marr-vg.
marr-vg. marrubium vulgare
marsdenia cundurango = cund.
marum verum = teucr.
maruta cotula = anth-cot.
mastoid. mastoiditis nosode
mate ilex mate
mater perlarum = conch.
mati. matico
matricaria chamomilla = cham.
matr-d. matricaria discoidea
matr-i. matricaria inodora
matricaria recutita = cham.
matricaria suaveolens = matr-d.
matth. matthiola graeca
m-aust. magnetis polus Australis

methylacetanilidum = metald.
methylene blue = methyl.

MDMA	methylenedioxy-n methylamphetamine

mauritanica = arund-d.

mec.	meconinum

medicago sativa = alf.

med.	medorrhinum
medic-l.	medicago lupulina
medul-o.	medulla oblongata
medul-os.	medulla ossis
medul-os-si.	medulla ossis suis
medul-ren.	medulla renalis
medul-spi.	medulla spinalis
medul-spi-ce.	medulla spinalis cervicalis
medul-spi-do.	medulla spinalis dorsalis
medul-spi-lu.	medulla spinalis lumbalis
medul-spi-s.	medulla spinalis suis
medul-spi-sa.	medulla spinalis sacralis
medul-supr.	medulla suprarenalis
medus.	medusa
medus-xyz.	medus. + physal-p.
mein-p.	Meinberg Pyrmont aqua
mel	mel
mela.	melastoma Ackermanni
melal-alt.	melaleuca alternifolia
melal-alt-ol.	melaleuca alternifolia oleum
melal-hy.	melaleuca hypericifolia

melaleuca leucodendron = caj.

melam-a.	melampyrum arvense
melan.	melaninum
mel-c-s.	mel cum sale
meli.	melilotus officinalis

melia azadirachta = aza.
melia azadirachta indica = aza.
melia grandiflora = guare.

meli-a.	melilotus alba
meli-alt.	melilotus altissima
melin.	melitine
melis.	melissa officinalis
melit.	melitagrinum
meli-xyz.	melilotus off. + -a.

meloe vesicatoris = canth.

melo.	melolontha vulgaris

melittis melissophyllum = meltis-g.

meloe-m.	meloe majalis

melitococcinum = brucel.
melitotoxinum = brucel.

meltis-g.	melittis grandiflora
menad.	menadion
mendel.	mendelevium
meningoc.	meningococcinum
meningoc-vc.	vaccinum meningococcale
menis.	menispermum canadense

menispermum cocculus = cocc.

menis-r.	menispermum rakta
menth.	mentha piperita
menth-aq.	mentha aquatica
menth-ar.	mentha arvensis
mentho.	mentholum
menth-pu.	mentha pulegium
menth-r.	mentha rotundifolia
menth-s.	mentha sylvestris
menth-v.	mentha viridis
meny.	menyanthes trifoliata
mepacr-chl.	mepacrine chlorhydrate

mephitis americana = meph.
mephitis mephitica = meph.

meph.	mephitis putorius
meprob.	meprobamate
merc.	mercurius solubilis
merc-act.	mercurius aceticus
merc-ar.	mercurius arsenicicus
merc-aur.	mercurius auratus
merc-br.	mercurius bromatus
merc-bs.	mercurius bi-sulfuricus
merc-c.	mercurius corrosivus
merc-chli.	mercurius chloroiodatus
merc-chr.	mercurius chromium oxydulatus

mercurius cum kali = aethi-m.

merc-cy.	mercurius cyanatus
merc-d.	mercurius dulcis

mercurius et kali iodatus = merc-k-i.
mercurius flavus = merc-o-f.

merc-f.	mercurius fluoratum
merc-i-f.	mercurius iodatus flavus
merc-i-r.	mercurius iodatus ruber

mercurius bi-iodatus = merc-i-r.
mercurius biniodatus = merc-i-r.

merc-k-i.	mercurius biniodatus cum kali iodatum
merc-lac.	mercurius lacticus
merc-meth.	mercurius methylenus
merc-n.	mercurius nitricus

mercurius nitricus oxydulatus = merc-ns.

merc-ns.	mercurius nitrosus
merc-o-cy.	mercurius oxy-cyanatus

mercurius oxydatulus niger = merc.
mercurius oxydatus = merc-pr-r.

merc-o-f.	mercurius oxydatus flavus
merc-p.	mercurius phosphoricus

mercurius protoiodatus = merc-i-f.
mercurius proto-iodatus = merc-i-f.

merc-pn.	mercurius proto-nitricus
merc-pr-a.	mercurius praecipitatus albus
merc-pr-f.	mercurius praecipitatus flavus
merc-pr-r.	mercurius praecipitatus ruber
merc-ps.	mercurius proto sulphatum
merc-r.	mercurius rhodanatus
merc-sal.	mercurius salicylicus

mercurius solubilis hahnemanni = merc.
mercurius sublimatus = merc-c.

mercurius sublimatus corrosivus = merc-c.
merc-s-cy. mercurius sulphocyanatus
mercenaria mercenaria = ven-m.
mercs-n. mercuresceinum natricum
merc-sul. mercurius sulphuricus
mercurius sulphuratus niger = aethi-m.
mercurius sulphuratus ruber = cinnb.
merc-s-xyz. mercurius sulphuricum unknown preparation
merc-tn. mercurius tannicus
merl. mercurialis perennis
merl-a. mercurialis annua
mercurius vivax = merc.
mercurius vivus = merc.
mescal. mescalinum
mesembrianthemum cristallinum = mese-c.
mese-c. mesembryanthemum cristallinum
mesmer. mesmerismus
mesobuth-t. mesobuthus tamulus
mesp. mespillus germanica
metacetaldehydum = metald.
metald. metaldehydum
meth-ae-ae. methylium aethyloaethereum
metallum album = ars.
metallum iodatum = ars-i.
metastatic melanoma = carc-mel-met.
methan. methanol
meth-bchl. methylenum bichloratum
methion. methioninum
meth-sal. methylium salicylicum
methyl. methylenum coeruleum
methylenum trichloratum = chlf.
methylenum trichloride = chlf.
methylglycoxalidine = lysd.
methyl-glyox. methylglyoxal
methyl-guanin. methylguanidin
methys. methysergidum
metrosideros costatus = ango.
meum-a. meum athamanticum
mez. mezereum
mica mica
micr. micromeria douglasii
microc. micrococcinum
micrococcus catarrhalis = mucot.
micrococcus melitensis = brucel.
micrococcus tetragenius = mucot.
microg-p. microglossa pyrifolia
microphyllus pennatifolius = jab.
micrurus corallinus = elaps
micrurus fulvius = elaps
mik-c. mikania cordata
mikania guaco = gua.
mik-s. mikania setigera
mikania setigera = mik-s.
mill. millefolium
mil-s. milium solis
mimosa quadrivalvis var. angustata = mim-mi.
mimosa quadrivalvis var. nuttallii = mim-nu.
mim. mimulus (Bach fl.)
millipedes = onis.
mim-h. mimosa humilis
miml-g. mimulus guttatus
miml-lu. mimulus luteus
mim-mi. mimosa microphylla
mim-nu. mimosa nuttallii
mim-p. mimosa pudica
mir-j. mirabilis jalapa
mispickel = ars-pyr.
miss. Mississquoi aqua
mit. mitchella repens
mitom. mitomycine
mitot. mitotane
mitra-st. mitragyna stipulosa
mnng. n-methyl-n'-nitro-n-nitrosoguanidin
mob-ray mobile phone radiation
molin-c. molinia coerulea
molu. molusca
molybdaenum metallicum = moly-met.
moly-ac. molybdenicum acidum
moly-m. molybdenium muriaticum
moly-met. molybdenium metallicum
mom-b. momordica balsamica
momordica balsamina = mom-b.
mom-ch. momordica charantia
momordica elaterium = elat.
mom-f. momordica foetida
mom-in. momordica involucrata
monar-di. monarda didyma
monar-fi. monarda fistulosa
monar-pu. monarda punctata
moni. monilia albicans
moni-c. monilia coerula
mono. monotropa uniflora
mono-h. monotropa hypopitis
mons. monsonia ovata
monst-p. monstera pertusa
morb. morbillinum
morb-vc. vaccinum morbillorum vivum
morg. bacillus Morgan (Bach)
morg-g. bacillus Morgan-Gaertner (Paterson)
morg-p. bacillus Morgan pure (Paterson)
morgan (bach) = morg.
morgan pure (paterson) = morg-p.
morgan-gaertner (paterson) = morg-g.
morind-l. morinda lucida
morind-m. morinda morindoides
moring-p. moringa pterygosperma
morph. morphinum and salts (old abbr.)
morphini hydrochloridum = morph-m.

morphini sulfas = morph-s.
morph-act. morphinum aceticum
morph-m. morphinum muriaticum
morph-pur. morphinum purum
morph-s. morphinum sulphuricum
morus-n. morus nigra
mosch. moschus
moscho-r. moschosma riparia
mudar = calo.
ms. multiple sclerosis nosode
moschus moschiferus = mosch.
mucocatarrhalis = mucot.
mucoc. mucococcinum
mucor mucor mucedo
mucor-a-p. mucor cum aspergillus cum penicillinum
mucot. mucotoxinum
mucs-nas. mucosa nasalis
mucuna pruriens = dol.
muc-u. mucuna urens
mukul balsamodendron mukul
mum-l. mumulus lewisii
mur-ac. muriaticum acidum
muru. murure leite
murx. murex purpurea
musa musa sapientum
musan-c. musanga cecropioides
mus musculus hortulanus = mus-m.
mus rattus rattus = ratt-r.
musa-p. musa paradisiaca
musca-d. musca domestica
muscin. muscarinum
mus-m. mus musculus
must. mustard (Bach fl.)
mut. bacillus Mutabile (Bach)
mustela foetida = meph.
mutabile (Bach) = mut.
myc-ung. mycosis unguis nosode
mygale avicularia = mygal.
mygal. mygale lasiodora
myos-a. myosotis arvensis
myos-s. myosotis symphytifolia
myosotis avicularia = myos-a.
myosotis intermedia = myos-a.
myos-sv. myosotis sylvatica
myric. myrica cerifera
myric-g. myrica gale
myricin. myricinum
myristica fragrans = nux-m.
myristica officinalis = nux-m.
myris. myristica sebifera
myroc-p. = bals-p. = myrocylon peruvianum
myrmexin = form.
myrobalanum chebula = term-c.
myrocylon peruvianum = bals-p.
myrospermum pereirae = bals-p.
myroxylon pereira = bals-p.
myroxylon peruvianum = bals-p.
myrox-t. myroxylon toluiferum
myrrha myrrha
myrrhis-o. myrrhis odorata
myrt-c. myrtus communis
myrtillus = vacc-m.
myrt-ch. myrtus cheken
myrtillocactus = cact.
myrtlc-g. myrtillocactus geometrizans
myrtus jambos = eug.
myrt-p. myrtus pimenta
myrtus pimenta = pime.
mytil. mytilus edulis
nabal. nabalus serpentarius
nabulus albus = nabal.
nack. nackelia
nickterina = mir-j.
nicotiana tabacum = tab.
nad. nicotinamide adenine dinucleotide
naja naja tripudians
nadidum = nad.
naja nigricolis = naja-n.
naja-n. naja nigricollis
nalox. naloxon
nandr-php. norandrostenolon phenylpropion
napellus = acon.
napht. naphtha
naphtaz-m. naphthazolinum muriaticum
naphtaz-n. naphthazolinum nitricum
naphthoq. naphthoquinone
naphtin. naphthalinum
naloxone = nalox.
napin. napellinum
narcin. narceinum
narcot. narcotinum
narcot-act. narcotinum aceticum
narcot-m. narcotinum muriaticum
narc-po. narcissus poeticus
narc-ps. narcissus pseudonarcissus
narz. Narzan aqua
nast. = nast-o. = nasturtium aquaticum (old abbr.)
nasturtium aquaticum = nast-o.
nast-o. nasturtium officinale
natrii acetas = nat-act.
natrii benzoas = nat-be.
natrii bromidum = nat-br.
natrii carbonas monohydricus = nat-c.
natrii chloridum = nat-m.
natrii citras = nat-cit.
natrii fluoridum = nat-f.
natrii hydroxidum = nat-hox.
natrii hydroxydum = nat-caust.

natrii hypophosphis = nat-hp.
natrii iodidum = nat-i.
natrii lactatis solutio = nat-lac.
natrii nitras = nat-n.
natrii nitris = nat-ns.
natrii oxalas = nat-ox.
natrii phosphas = nat-p.
natrii salicylas = nat-sal.
natrii sulfas anhydricus = nat-s.

nat-act.	natrium aceticum
nat-ae-s.	natrium aethylosulphuricum

natrium arsenicicum = nat-ar.

nat-ar.	natrium arsenicosum
nat-be.	natrium benzoicum
nat-bi.	natrium bichromicum

natrium biboracicum = borx.
natrium biboratum = borx.

nat-bic.	natrium bicarbonicum
nat-bis.	natrium bisulfurosum
nat-bor.	natrium boricum
nat-br.	natrium bromatum

natrium cacodylicum = nat-c.

nat-c.	natrium carbonicum
nat-cac.	= nat-c. = natrium cacodylicum
nat-caust.	natrium causticum
nat-ch.	natrium choleinicum

natrium chloratum = nat-m.

nat-chl.	natrium chloricum
nat-chr.	natrium chromicum
nat-cit.	natrium citricum
nat-cy.	natrium cyanatum
nat-f.	natrium fluoratum
nat-form.	natrium formicum
nat-gchol.	natrium glycocholicum
nat-gent.	natrium gentisatum
nat-gl.	natrium gluconicum
nat-glt.	natrium glutamicum
nat-gp.	natrium glycerophosphoricum
nat-hchls.	natrium hypochlorosum
nat-hmp.	natrium hexa-meta-phosphoricum
nat-hox.	natrium hydroxydum
nat-hp.	natrium hypophosphorum
nat-hsulo.	natrium hyposulphurosum
nat-i.	natrium iodatum
nat-lac.	natrium lacticum
nat-m.	natrium muriaticum
nat-mar.	natrium marinum
nat-met.	natrium metallicum
nat-meth.	natrium methylate
nat-meth-ar.	natrium methylarsinicum
nat-mlb.	natrium molybdicum
nat-mvan.	natrium metavanadicum
nat-n.	natrium nitricum
nat-nic.	natrium nicotinicum
nat-ns.	natrium nitrosum
nat-o.	natrium oxydatum
nat-ol.	natrium oleicum
nat-ox.	natrium oxalicum
nat-ox-act.	natrium oxalaceticum
nat-p.	natrium phosphoricum
nat-perm.	natrium permanganicum
nat-prop.	natrium propionicum
nat-pyru.	natrium pyruvicum
natr-n.	natrix natrix
nat-s.	natrium sulphuricum
nat-sal.	natrium salicylicum
nat-s-c.	natrium sulphocarbolicum
nat-sel.	natrium selenicum

natrium silicatum = nat-sil.

nat-sil.	natrium silicicum
nat-sil-f.	natrium silicofluoricum
nat-stann.	natrium stannicum
nat-suc.	natrium succinicum

natrium sulphorinicum = nat-ae-s.

nat-sula.	natrium sulphuratum
nat-sulo.	natrium sulphurosum
nat-tar.	natrium tartaricum
nat-taur.	natrium taurocholicum
nat-tel.	natrium telluricum

natrium tetraboracicum = borx.
natrium tetrachloroauratum = aur-m-n.

nat-tmcy.	natrium thiosinaminum cyanatum
nat-uric.	natrium uricum
nat-val.	natrium valerianicum
nat-van.	natrium vanadicum
nauc-l.	nauclea latifolia
nauf-helv-li.	lignum naufragium helvetiae
nect.	nectandra amara

nectandra cymbarum = nect.

nect-p.	nectandra pichury major
nectrin.	nectrianinum
neg.	negundium Americanum
nego-a.	= neg. = negundo aceroides

negundo aceroides = neg.
negundo Americanum = neg.

nego-f.	negundo fraxinifolium

neisseria flava = flav.

neis-meng-vc.	neisseria meningitidis vaccinus
nelum-lu.	nelumbium luteum
nelum-n.	nelumbo nucifera
nemo-m.	nemophila menziesii
neod-br.	neodymium bromatum
neod-c.	neodymium carbonicum
neod-f.	neodymium fluoratum
neod-i.	neodymium iodatum
neod-lac.	neodymium lacticum
neod-m.	neodymium muriaticum
neod-met.	neodymium metallicum
neod-n.	neodymium nitricum
neod-o.	neodymium oxydatum

neod-ox. neodymium oxalicum
neod-p. neodymium phosphoricum
neod-s. neodymium sulfuricum
neod-sil. neodymium silicatum
neom. neomycine
neon neon
neor-m. neorautanenia mitis
neos-ms. neostigmine methyl sulfate
neot-n-a. neottia nidus avis
nep. nepenthes distillatoria
nepet. = catar. = nepeta cataria
neph-l. nephelium litchi
nept-m. neptunium muriaticum
nept-ox. neptunium oxalicum
ner-od. = olnd. = nerium odorum
nerium odorum = olnd.
nerium oleander = olnd.
neur. neurinum
nicc. niccolum-met. + -c. (old abbr.)
neurohypophysis = pitu-p.
niacinamidum = nicotam.
niacinum = nicot-ac.
nicc-act. niccolum aceticum
nicc-be. niccolum benzoicum
niccolum bromatum = nicc-br.
nicc-br. niccolum bromidum
nicc-c. niccolum carbonicum
nicc-f. niccolum fluoratum
nicc-gl. niccolum gluconicum
nicc-m. niccolum muriaticum
nicc-met. niccolum metallicum
nicc-o. niccolum oxydatum
nicc-s. niccolum sulphuricum
nicc-sil. niccolum silicatum
nicc-xyz. niccolum unknown species
nicotinicum amidum = nicotam.
nicot. nicotinum
nicot-ac. nicotinic acidum
nicotam. nicotinamidum
nid. nidus edulis
nig-d. nigella damascena
nigr-a. nigritella angustifolia
nig-s. nigella sativa
ninhy. ninhydrine
niob-m. niobium muriaticum
niob-met. niobium metallicum
niob-s. niobium sulphuricum
nit-ac. nitricum acidum
nitrogenum oxygenatum = nitro-o.
nitroglycerinum = glon.
nit-m-ac. nitromuriaticum acidum
nitraz. nitrazepam
nitrogenii oxidum = nitro-o.
nitro. nitrogenium
nitrobenzenum = nitrob.
nitrob. nitrobenzolum
nitro-o. nitrogenium oxygenatum
nitroph. nitrophenolum
nitro-pox. nitrogenium peroxydatum
nitroso-muriaticum acidum = nit-m-ac.
nitros-ac. nitrosum acidum
nitri acidum = nit-ac.
nit-s-d. nitri spiritus dulcis
mytilus trossulus = mytil.
myxoedema parotitis = ourl.
nn-diphel. n nitrosodiphenylamin
nitrum = kali-n.
nobel. nobelium
noc-a. nocardia asteroides
nocardia lutea = actin-l.
nopalea coccinellifera = opun-c.
noradrenalini hydrochloridum = noradr.
noradr. noradrenalinum
norepi. = noradr. = norepinephrine (old abbr.)
norepinephrine = noradr.
norleuc. norleucine
nosc. noscapinum
note-st. notechis scutatus
novoc. novocainum
nucl-ac. nucleinicum acidum
nuph. nuphar luteum
nuph-p. nuphar pumilum
nux-a. nux absurda
nux colae = kola
nux juglans = jug-r.
nux-m. nux moschata
nux-v. nux vomica
nyckterinia capensis = zant.
nyct. nyctanthes arbor tristis
nymphaea lutea = nuph.
nymph. nymphaea odorata
nycterinia capensis = zant.
nymph-a. nymphaea alba
nymphea alba = nymph-a.
nymphea odorata = nymph.
nyst. nystatine
oak oak (Bach fl.)
ochn-a. ochna atropurpurea
ocimum basilicum = basil.
oci. ocimum canum
oci-car. ocimum caryophyllatum
oci-g. ocimum gratissimum
oci-m. ocimum micranthum
oci-sa. ocimum sanctum
oci-su. ocimum suave
oct-mac. octopus maculosa
oenanthe aquaticum = phel.
oena. oenanthe crocata
oena-f. oenanthe fistulosa
oenanthe phellandrium = phel.

oeno.	oenothera biennis
oestronum = foll.	
oest.	oestrus cameli
oestrd.	oestradiol
oestrd-be.	oestradiol benzoas
officinalis polyporus = bol-la.	
oidium albicans = moni.	
okou.	okoubaka aubrevillei
ol-ac.	oleicum acidum
oleum animae aetherum dippeli = ol-an.	
ol-an.	oleum animale aethereum
oleum anisum = anis-ol.	
oleum cajuputi = caj.	
oleum carvi = caru.	
ol-car.	oleum caryophyllatum
olden-d.	oldenlandia decubens
olden-h.	oldenlandia herbacea
oleum chaulmoogra = chaul.	
oleum cornu cervi = ol-an.	
oleum dippeli = ol-an.	
oleum elaeis = elae.	
ol-eucal.	oleum eucalyptus
ol-eur.	olea Europea
olea Europea = ol-eur.	
ol-eur-ol.	oleae Europeae oleum
ol-ha.	oleum haarlem
ol-hc.	oleum hydnocarpi
ol-hi.	oleum hippoglossi
oleum sussini non rectificatum = ol-suc.	
oleum terebinthinae = ter.	
oleum verbasci = verb-ol.	
oleum wittnebianum = caj.	
olib-c.	olibanum carteri
olib-sac.	olibanum sacrum
olib-soc.	olibanum socotrinum
olive	olive (Bach fl.)
ol-j.	oleum jecoris aselli
oleum jecoris morrhuae = ol-j.	
ol-lav.	oleum lavandulae
ol-mo.	oleum morrhuae
oleum morrhuae = ol-j.	
oleum mulleini = verb-ol.	
ol-myr.	oleum myristicae
olnd.	oleander
ol-pat.	oleum patchouli
oleum patchouly = ol-pat.	
oleum petrae = petr.	
oleum pogostemon patchouli = ol-pat.	
oleum ricini = ric.	
oleum ricinus = ric.	
ol-sant.	oleum santali
ol-suc.	oleum succinum
onchoryncus tschawytscha = oncor-t.	
oncor-t.	oncorynchus tsawytscha
onis.	oniscus asellus
onob-s.	onobrychis sativa
onon.	ononis spinosa
ononis arvensis = onon.	
onon-n.	ononis natrix
onon-r.	ononis repens
onop.	onopordon acanthium
onos.	onosmodium virginianum
operculina turpethum = oper.	
ophelia chirata = gent-ch.	
opianyl = mec.	
op.	opium
onosmodium virginicum = onos.	
oophorinum = ov.	
oorari = cur.	
oper.	operculina turpenthum
opium crudum = op.	
opl.	oplia farinosa
opop.	opopanax chironium
opun-a.	opuntia aciculata
opun-c.	opuntia coccinellifera
opun-f.	opuntia ficus indica
opun-s.	opuntia spina alba
opun-v.	opuntia vulgaris
opun-xyz.	opun-s. + opun-v.
orch.	orchitinum
orcin.	orcinolum
oreo.	oreodaphne californica
orex-tann.	orexinum tannaticum
origanum hortensis = orig.	
orig.	origanum majorana
origanum majorana = orig.	
orig-cr.	origanum creticum
orig-d.	origanum dictamnus
orig-v.	origanum vulgare
orni.	ornithogalum umbellatum
ornithogalum nutans = agra.	
orni-p.	ornithogalum pyrenaicum
ornith-chl.	ornithine chlorhydrate
orob-m.	orobanche major
orobanche virginiana = epiph.	
orot-ac.	oroticum acidum
orteaga = eys.	
ortho acidum = amibe-ac.	
orthambe-ac.	orthoaminobenzoicum acidum
orthos-s.	orthosiphon stamineus
orthosiphonis folium = orthos-s.	
oryz-s.	oryza sativa
oscilloc.	oscillococcinum
osm.	osmium met. + -ac. (old abbr.)
osm-ac.	osmicum acidum
os-max.	ostitis maxilar nosode
osm-met.	osmium metallicum
osm-o.	osmium oxydatum
osmium tetroxidum = osm-o.	

osmu-r. osmunda regalis
ostrea edulis = calc.
ost. ostrya virginica
osteo-a. osteo-arthriticum
osteo-mye. osteomyelitis nosode
osteo-mye-scl. osteomyelosclerosis nosode
osteos-n. osteospermum nervatum
osyr-a. osysris alba
othon-n. othonna natalensis
otit-m-xyz. otitis media nosode unknown species
ouabin. ouabainum
ourl. ourlianum
ov. ovininum
ova tosta = ovi-p.
oval buchu = baros.
ovar. ovaries
ovi-p. ovi gallinae pellicula
ovi gallinae testa = calc-o-t.
ovi testa = calc-o-t.
ovi-v. ovi vitellus
ox-ac. oxalicum acidum
oxal-a. oxalis acetosella
oxal-c. oxalis corniculata
oxal-s. oxalis semiloba
oxat. oxatomide
oxaz. oxazepam
oxeod. oxeodaphne
oxpren. oxprenololum
oxyd. oxydendron arboreum
oxyg. oxygenium
oxyq-m. oxyquinoleinum muriaticum
oxyt. oxytropis lamberti
oxytrophis = oxyt.
oxyt-c. oxytropis campestris
oxyte-chl. oxytetracycline chlorhydrate
oxytoc. oxytocinum
oxyurn-sc. oxyuranus scuttellatus
oxy-v. = enterob-v. = oxyuris vermicularis (old abbr.)
oxyuris vermicularis = enterob-v.
ozaen. ozaena nosode
ozone ozonum
padus avium = prun-p.
paeon. paeonia officinalis
paico = chen-a.
pakur = fic-r.
pali-a. paliurus aculeatus
pall. palladium metallicum
paliurus Australis = pali-a.
paliurus spina christi = pali-a.
pall-f. palladium fluoratum
pall-m. palladium muriaticum
pall-o. palladium oxydatum
palm-ac. palmiticum acidum
palo. paloondo
papaya vulgaris = asim.
p-ambe-ac. para-aminobenzoicum acidum
p-ambes-ac. para-aminobenzoicumsulfamidum acid
pambt. pambotano
pambotano = calli-h.
p-amsal-ac. para-aminosalicylicum acidum
pana. panacea arvensis
panax ginseng = gins.
panax quinquefolia = gins.
pancr. pancreatinum
pancreatis pulvis = pancr.
pann. panna
pant-ac. pantothenicum acidum
papain. papainum
pap-d. papaver dubium
papaver somniferum = op.
papaver vulgaris = pap-r.
papaverini hydrochloridum = papin-m.
papin. papaverinum
papin-m. papaverinum muriaticum
pap-r. papaver rhoeas
par. paris quadrifolia
paraf. paraffinum
paraffinum liquidum = paraf.
paraph. paraphenylendiaminum
parat. paratyphoidinum
paratyphoidinum a = parat.
parat-b. paratyphoidinum B
parathormonum = parathyr.
parathyreoid glands = parathyr.
parathyr. parathyreoidinum
paravespula germanica = vespul-germ.
paravespula maculifrons = vespul-mf.
paravespula squamosa = vespul-sq.
pareir. pareira brava
pariet. parietaria officinalis
parit-t. paritium tiliaceum
parn-p. parnassia palustris
paro-i. paronychia illecebrum
parot. parotidinum
parotitis nosode = parot.
parot-vc. parotitis vaccinus
parth. parthenium hysterophorus
passi. passiflora incarnata
parthenium hysterophorus lynn = parth.
parthenocissus = ampe-qu.
passi-c. passiflora coerulea
past. pastinaca sativa
past-u. pastinaca urens
paull. paullinia pinnata
p-benzq. parabenzoquinonum
para-benzoquinonum = p-benzq.
p-dchlbe. paradichlorobenzolum
paullinia sorbilis = guar.
pausinystalia yohimba = yohim.

pect.	pecten jacobaeus
pectin.	pectinum
ped.	pediculus capitis
pedclr.	pedicularis canadensis
pediculus inguinalis = ped-p.	
ped-p.	pediculus pubis
pegan-ha.	peganum harmala
pelarg.	pelargonium reniforme
pelarg-o.	pelargonium odoratissimum
pelias berus = vip.	
pellin.	pelletierinum
pen.	penthorum sedoides
penghawar djambi = cibot-b.	
penic.	penicillinum
penic-calc.	penicillinum calcium
penic-cm.	penicillium camemberti
penicillium candidum = penic-cm.	
penicillium caseicolum = penic-cm.	
penicillium cyclopium = penic-cy.	
penic-cy.	penicillium cyclopodium
penic-e.	penicillium expansum
penicillium giordanoi = penic-e.	
penicillium glaucum = penic-e.	
penic-g.	penicillium griseum
penic-n.	penicillium notatum
penic-p.	penicillium piceum
pentac-m.	pentaclethra macrophylla
pentad-b.	pentadiplandra brazzeana
pentaz.	pentazocine
pepsini pulvis = peps.	
peps.	pepsinum
perchlet.	perchlorethylene
perh.	perhexilinum
perh-mal.	perhexilinum maleatum
perhydr.	perhydrol
peri.	periploca graeca
perid-b.	perideridia bolanderi
perill-f.	= perill-o. = perilla frutescens (old abbr.)
perilla frutescens = perill-o.	
perill-o.	perilla ocymoides
periproc.	periproctitic abscess nosode
perkin.	perkinismus
perlarum mater = conch.	
pern-c.	pernus canaliculus
perob.	perobinha
pers.	persea Americana
persea gratissima = pers.	
persica amygdalus = amyg-p.	
persica vulgaris = amyg-p.	
persicaria acris = polyg-h.	
persicaria urens = polyg-pe.	
pert.	pertussinum
pert-vc.	pertussis vaccinus
pest.	pestinum
petan-v.	petanisia variabilis
peti.	petiveria tetandra
petasites fragrans = tus-fr.	
petasites hybridus = tus-p.	
petasites officinalis = tus-p.	
petasites vulgaris = tus-p.	
peti-a.	petiveria alliacea
petr.	petroleum
petr-cr.	petroleum crudum
petr-di.	petroleum diesel
petrola.	petrolatum
petroselinum crispum = petros.	
petroselinum hortense = petros.	
petros.	petroselinum sativum
petros-c.	= petros. = petroselinum crispum (old abbr.)
petr-ra.	petroleum raffinatum
petr-xyz.	petroleum unknow preparation
peucedanum graveolens = anet-g.	
peuc-o.	peucedanum officinale
pg-a1ta1.	prostaglandinum a1 tromboxane a1
pg-a2ta2.	prostaglandinum a2 tromboxane a2
pg-all.	prostaglandinum all types
pg-e1.	prostaglandinum e1
pg-e2.	prostaglandinum e2
pg-f2a.	prostaglandinum f2 alpha
ph-ac.	phosphoricum acidum
peucedanum oreoselo = atha.	
peucedanum ostruthium = imp.	
peumus boldo = bold.	
pexid = perh-mal.	
peyotl = anh.	
phal.	phallus impudicus
pharbitis purpurea = ipom-p.	
phasco-ci.	phascolarctos cinereus
phase.	phaseolus nanus
phase-l.	phaseolus lunatus
phase-vg.	phaseolus vulgaris
phase-xyz.	phase.+ phase-vg.
phel.	phellandrium aquaticum
phell-n.	phellinus nigricans
phenac.	phenacetinum
phenan.	phenanthrenum
phenerg.	phenergan
phenob.	phenobarbitalum
phenol = carb-ac.	
phenolpht.	phenolphtaleinum
phenolum = carb-ac.	
phenoth.	phenothiazinum
phenylaethylimalonylureum = phenob.	
phenylal.	phenylalanine
phenylalaninum = phenylal.	
phenylbe.	phenylbenzene
phenylbu.	phenylbutazone
phenylglycolicum acidum = mande-ac.	
phenylhy.	phenylhydrazinum

phila. philadelphus coronarius
phill-a. phillyrea angustifolia
phill-l. phillyrea latifolia
philo-p. philodendron pertusum
phle. phleum pratense
phlor. phlorizinum
phoen-d. phoenix dactylifera
phorad-fl. phoradendron flavescens
phoradendron serotinum = phorad-fl.
phor-t. phormium tenax
phos. phosphorus
phos-h. phosphorus hydrogenatus
phos-m. phosphorus muriaticus
phosphorus muriaticus = phos-pchl.
phos-pbr. phosphurus pentabromatus
phos-pchl. = phos-m. = phosphorus pentachloratus
phosphorus pentachloratus = phos-m.
phos-ps. phosphorus pentasulfuratus
phosphorus pentichloride = phos-m.
phos-tbr. phosphorus tribromatus
phos-ti. phosphorus triiodatus
phyllitis scolopendrium = scolo-v.
phyld-b. phyllodoce breweri
phragmites communis = arund-p.
phthirus pubis = ped-p.
phyll-c. phyllanthus casticum
phyll-n. phyllanthus niruri
phys. physostigma venenosum
physalia physalis = physala-p.
physalia utriculus = physala-p.
physal-al. physalis alkekengi
physal-an. physalis angulata
phylloquinone = hydroq.
physalia arethusa = physala-p.
physalia caravella = physala-p.
physala-p. physalia pelagica
physal-p. physalis peruviana
physostigminum = esin.
physin-sal. physostigminum salicylicum
phyt. phytolacca decandra
phyt-b. phytolacca berry
pic-ac. picricum acidum
phytolacca tetandra = peti.
picea-e. picea excelsa
picea mariana = abies-n.
picea nigra = abies-n.
picea-p. picea pungens
pichi-pichi = fab.
picraena excelsa = picra-e.
picra-e. picrasma excelsa
picrasma excelsa = picra-e.
picro. picrotoxinum
picro-ac. picrotoxinum acidum
picronitricum acidum = pic-ac.
picror. picrorhiza

pieri-b. pieris briassicae
pilocarpus jaborandi = jab.
pilocarpus microphyllus = jab.
pilocarpus pennatifolius = jab.
pilosella = hier-p.
pil-eq. pilus equinus
pilios-t. piliostigma thonningii
pili-pili = caps.
pilocarpini hydrochloridum = pilo-m.
pilo. pilocarpinum + salts (old abbr.)
pilo-m. pilocarpinum muriaticum
pilo-n. pilocarpinum nitricum
pilo-pur. pilocarpinum purum
pime. pimenta officinalis
pimpinella major = pimp.
pimp. pimpinella saxifraga
pimpinella alba = pimp.
pimp-a. pimpinella anisum
pin-c. pinus cupressus
pinus canadensis = abies-c.
pin-con. pinus contorta
pine pine (Bach fl.)
pineal. pinealis
ping-vg. pinguicula vulgaris
pin-l. pinus lambertiana
pinus maritima = pin-pi.
pin-mo. pinus montana
pinus murrayana = pin-s.
pin-pa. pinus palustris
pin-pi. pinus pinaster
pin-s. pinus silvestris
pinus sylvestris = pin-s.
pin-teo. pinus teocote
pipe. piperazinum
pinus uncinata = pin-mo.
piper angustifolium = mati.
piper angustifolium elongatum = mati.
piper cubeba = cub.
piper elongatum = mati.
pip-g. piper guineense
pip-m. piper methysticum
pip-n. piper nigrum
pir-c. pirus communis
pirox. piroxicam
pisc. piscidia erythrina
pis-s. pisum sativum
pist-l. pistacia lentiscus
pist-v. pistacia vera
pitto-v. pittosporus viridiflorum
pitu. pituitaria posterior (old abbr.)
pitu-a. pituitaria anterior
pituitaria cerebri = pitu-gl.
pitu-gl. pituitaria glandula
pituin. = pitu-gl. = pituitrinum
pitu-p. pituitaria posterior

pituitarium anteriorum = pitu-a.	
pituitarium posteriorum = pitu-p.	
piturinum = dubo-h.	
pityr-o.	pityrosporum orbiculare
pix	pix liquida
plac.	placenta humana
plac-s.	placenta suis
plac-s-f.	placenta fetalis suis
plac-s-m.	placenta materna suis
plan.	plantago major
planifolia = vanil.	
plantago aquatica = alis-p.	
plan-c.	plantago coronopus
plantago ispaghula = plan-p.	
plan-l.	plantago lanceolata
plan-mi.	plantago minor
plantago ovata = plan-p.	
plan-p.	plantago psyllium
plast.	plastic
plat.	platinum metallicum
platan. old = platan-oc. + -or. = platan.	
platan.	platan. species (old abbr.)
platanus acerifolia = platan-or.	
platan-oc.	platanus occidentalis
platan-or.	platanus orientalis
platina = plat.	
platinum chloratum = plat-m.	
plat-col.	platinum colloidale
plat-f.	platinum fluoratum
plat-i.	platinum iodatum
plat-m.	platinum muriaticum
plat-m-n.	platinum muriaticum natronatum
plb.	plumbum metallicum
plumbii acetas = plb-act.	
plb-act.	plumbum aceticum
plb-ar.	plumbum arsenicicum
plb-bchl.	plumbum bichloridum
plb-br.	plumbum bromatum
plb-c.	plumbum carbonicum
plb-chr.	plumbum chromicum
plb-f.	plumbum fluoratum
plb-gl.	plumbum gluconicum
plb-i.	plumbum iodatum
plb-m.	plumbum muriaticum
plb-n.	plumbum nitricum
plb-o.	plumbum oxydatum
plb-o-f.	plumbum oxydatum flavum
plb-o-r.	plumbum oxydatum rubrum
plb-p.	plumbum phosphoricum
plb-s.	plumbum sulfuratum
plb-sact.	plumbum subaceticum
plb-tae.	plumbum tetra-aethylicum
plb-xyz.	plumbum met. + -act. + -c.
plect.	plectranthus fruticosus
plect-b.	plectranthus barbatus
plect-v.	plectronia ventosa
plumbg.	plumbago littoralis
plumbg-eu.	plumbago Europaea
plume.	plumeria celinus
plume-a.	plumeria alba
plut-c.	plutonium carbonicum
plut-f.	plutonium fluoratum
plut-lac.	plutonium lacticum
plut-m.	plutonium muriaticum
plut-met.	plutonium metallicum
plut-n.	plutonium nitricum
plut-o.	plutonium oxydatum
plut-ox.	plutonium oxalicum
plut-p.	plutonium phosphoricum
plut-s.	plutonium sulphuricum
plut-sil.	plutonium silicatum
pluv.	pluvia
pm-br.	promethium bromatum
pm-c.	promethium carbonicum
pm-f.	promethium fluoratum
pm-i.	promethium iodatum
pm-lac.	promethium lacticum
pm-m.	promethium muriaticum
pm-n.	promethium nitricum
pm-o.	promethium oxydatum
pm-ox.	promethium oxalicum
pm-p.	promethium phosphoricum
pm-s.	promethium sulphuricum
pm-sil.	promethium silicatum
pneu.	pneumococcinum
pneu-vc.	vaccinum pneumococcale
pneumococcus = pneu.	
poa-p.	poa pratensis
podo.	podophyllum peltatum
podoin.	podophyllinum
poinc-p.	poinciana pulcherrima
polar.	polaris
pole.	polemonium coeruleum
polio	polio
polio-vc.	vaccinum poliomyelitidis inactivatum
polio-vc-sk.	polio vaccinus salk
polio-vc-sn.	polio vaccinus sabinus
poll.	pollantinum
pollen = poll.	
polon-met.	polonium metallicum
poly bowel compound (bach) = poly-bow.	
polya-po.	polyandra poligama
polyart.	polyarthritis nosode
poly-bow.	poly bowel co. (Bach)
polyg-a.	polygonum aviculare
polygonum acre = polyg-h.	
polyg-am.	polygonum amphibium
polyg-bta.	polygonum bistorta
polyg-btd.	polygonum bistortoides
polygonum hydropiper = polyg-pe.	

polyg-h.	polygonum hydropiperoides
polygl-a.	polygala amara
polygl-o.	polygala oppostifolia
polygala senega = seneg.	
polygl-vg.	polygala vulgaris
polyg-m.	polygonum maritimum
polygn-vg.	polygonatum vulgare
polyg-pe.	polygonum persicaria
polygonum punctatum = polyg-h.	
polyg-s.	polygonum sagittatum
polygonum fagopyrum = fago.	
polyg-xyz.	polygonum h. + -pe. + ?
polym.	polymnia uvedalia
polymix.	polymyxin b
polypodium calaguala = calag.	
polypodium leucotomos = calag.	
polypd-vg.	polypodium vulgare
polyporus nigricans = phell-n.	
polyporus officinalis = bol-la.	
polyp-p.	polyporus pinicola
polys.	polystyrenum
polytr.	polytrichum juniperinum
polytr-c.	polytrichum commune
polyv.	polyvinyle chlorure
populus tremula = pop.	
pop.	populus tremuloides
pop-cana.	populus canadensis
pop-cand.	populus candicans
populus alba = pop-cand.	
populus balsamifera = pop-cand.	
pop-c-t.	populus balsamifera trichocarpa
pop-n.	populus nigra
porc-m.	porcelanum mesniense
portal-p.	portulacca pilosa
portu-o.	portulacca oleracea
positr.	positronium
potamobius astacus = astac.	
pota.	potamogeton natans
potassium xantate = kali-x.	
pot-a.	potentilla anserina
pot-arg.	potentilla argentea
pot-au.	potentilla aurea
pot-e.	potentilla erecta
potentilla tormentilla = pot-e.	
poter-s.	poterium sanguisorba
poter-sp.	poterium spinosum
pot-gl.	potentilla glandulosa
potentilla recta = pot-e.	
pot-r.	potentilla reptans
pot-t.	= pot-e. = potentilla tormentilla (old abbr.)
pothos foetidus = ictod.	
pras-br.	praseodymium bromatum
pras-c.	praseodymium carbonicum
pras-f.	praseodymium fluoratum
pras-i.	praseodymium iodatum

pras-lac.	praseodymium lacticum
pras-m.	praseodymium muriaticum
pras-met.	praseodymium metallicum
pras-n.	praseodymium nitricum
pras-o.	praseodymium oxydatum
pras-ox.	praseodymium oxalicum
pras-p.	praseodymium phosphoricum
pras-s.	praseodymium sulfuricum
pras-sil.	praseodymium silicatum
predn.	prednison
prednisolon = prednl.	
prednl.	prednisolone acetate
pregnan.	pregnandiolum
pren-a.	prenanthes alba
prenanthes serpentaria = nabal.	
prim-a.	primula auricula
prim-f.	primula farinosa
primula obconca = prim-o.	
prim-o.	primula obconica
primula officinalis = prim-v.	
prim-v.	primula veris
prim-vl.	primula vulgaris
primulae veris radix = prim-v.	
prin.	prinos verticillatus
prionurus Australis = buth-a.	
priva-l.	priva leptostachya
procaini hydrochloridum = proc-m.	
proc-m.	procainum muriaticum
progest.	progesteron
prolac.	prolactine
proli.	proline
prolinum = proli.	
prom.	promethazine
prom-chl.	promethazine chlorhydrate
prontos.	protonsil rubrum
prop.	propylaminum
propl.	propolis
propr.	propranololum
propr-chl.	propranololum chlorhydratum
propyl.	propylene glycol
proq.	proquantil
prost.	prostate gland
prostin.	prostatinum
prot.	bacillus Proteus (Bach)
proteus vulgaris = prot.	
protac.	protoactinium
protg.	protargol
protin.	proteinum
protonu.	protonuclein
proteus (bach) = prot.	
proteus mirabilis = prot.	
prot-r.	proteus rettgeri
prots-m.	= prot. = proteus mirabilis
prots-v.	= prot. = proteus vulgaris
prun.	prunus spinosa

prun-am. prunus amygdalus
prun-ar. prunus armeniaca
prun-av. prunus avium
prun-cf. prunus cerasifera
prun-cs. prunus cerasus
prun-d. prunus domestica
prune. prunella vulgaris
prunus dulcis var. amara = amyg.
prunus laurocerasus = laur.
prun-m. prunus mahaleb
prun-p. prunus padus
prun-pe. prunus persica
prun-v. prunus virginiana
psalliota bispora = agar-cps.
psalliota hortensis = agar-cps.
pseudognaphalium obtusifolium = gnaph.
pseud. pseudomonas aeruginosa
pseuts-m. pseudotsuga menziesii
psid. psidium guayava
psil. psilocybe caerulescens
psil-s. psilocybe semilanceata
psoricum = psor.
psor. psorinum
psoral. psoralea bituminosa
psoral-c. psoralea corylifolia
psoral-p. psoralea pinnata
psorias. psoriasis nosode
psychotria ipecacuanha = ip.
psychotria viridis = banis-c.
psyllium = plan-p.
ptel. ptelea trifoliata
pterocarpus erinaceus = kino
pterocarpus marsupium = kino
ptergl-ac. pteroylglutamicum acidum
pteraema excelsa = picra-e.
pteri-a. pteris aquilina
ptraz. pentetrazolum
ptetrocarpus santalinus = santal.
ptycho-ol. ptychopetalum olacoides
ptycho-unc. ptychopetalum uncinatum
ptycho-xyz. ptychopetalum species unknown
pulic-d. pulicaria dysenterica
pull-g. pullus gallinaceus
pulm-a. pulmo anaphylacticus
pulmon. pulmonaria vulgaris
pulmo vulpis = pulm-v.
pulmon-a. pulmonaria angustifolia
pulmon-o. pulmonaria officinalis
pulmon-t. pulmonaria tuberosa
pulm-s. pulmo suis
pulm-v. vulpes pulmo
puls. pulsatilla pratensis
puls-m. pulsatilla montana
pulsatilla nigricans = puls.
puls-n. pulsatilla nuttaliana
puls-vg. pulsatilla vulgaris
pulx. pulex irritans
pulx-c. pulex canis
punica granatum = gran.
putrin. putrescinum
putrin-m. putrescinum muriaticum
pycno-e. pycnostachys eminii
pycnop-sa. pycnoporus sanguineus
pyocy. pyocyaninum
pyocyin. pyocyanotoxinum
pyoderm-xyz. pyodermie nosode species unknown
pyrar. pyrarara
pyren-sc. pyrenacantha scandens
pyre-o. pyrethrum officinarum
pyre-p. pyrethrum parthenium
pyre-r. pyrethrum roseum e floribus
pyridoxini hydrochloridum = pyrid.
pyrid. pyridoxinum hydrochloricum
pyrim. pyrimethamine
pyrola umbellata = chim.
pyro-ac. pyrolignosum acidum
pyrocarb. pyrocarbon
pyrog. pyrogenium
pyrogal-ac. pyrogallicum acidum
pyrogall. pyrogallol
pyrol. pyrola rotundifolia
pyrol-m. pyrola minor
pyrus malus = malus-c.
pyru-ac. pyruvicum acidum
pyrus pyrus Americana
pyrus-c. pyrus communis
quas. quassia amara
quasin. quassinum
queb. quebracho
querc. quercus
quercus fructus = querc.
querc-g. quercus glandium
querc-l. quercus lobata
quercus pedunculata = querc-r.
querc-pu. quercus pubescens
querc-r. quercus robur
querc-r-fl. quercus robur flos
querc-r-g-aq. quercus robur aqua glandium
quercus robur galla = galla-q-r.
querc-r-g-s. quercus robur glandium spiritus
quercus sessilifera = querc-r.
quill. quillaya saponaria
quillaya smegmaderma = quill.
quin-chl. quinacrine chlorhydrate
quinhydr. quinhydrone
quinid. quinidinum
quinid-m. quinidinum muriaticum
quinid-s. quinidinum sulfuricum
quinol. quinoleinum
Rademacher's solution = zinc-act.

rad-br.	radium bromatum
rad-chl.	radium chloratum
rad-met.	radium metallicum
radix angelicae sinensis = ange-s.	
rado.	radon
raja-s.	rajania subsamarata
rana bufo = bufo	
ran-a.	ranunculus acris
ran-b.	ranunculus bulbosus
ran-fi.	ranunculus ficaria
ran-fl.	ranunculus flammula
ran-g.	ranunculus glacialis
ran-p.	ranunculus pinnatus
ran-r.	ranunculus repens
ran-s.	ranunculus sceleratus
raph.	raphanus sativus
raphani.	raphanistrum arvense
raphis-g.	raphispermum gerardioides
rapp.	rappenau aqua
rat.	ratanhia peruviana
ratanhiae peruvianae radix = rat.	
ratt-norv.	rattus norvegus
ratt-r.	rattus rattus
rauvolfia serpentina = rauw.	
rauw.	rauwolfia serpentina
realgar = ars-s-r.	
red-ch.	red chestnut (Bach fl.)
rein.	Reinerz aqua
ren.	kidneys
resina cimifugae = macro.	
resina itu = itu	
resina laricis = tere-la.	
resina piceae = abies-n.	
res.	resorcinum
resc.	rescue (Bach fl.)
reser.	reserpinum
retin.	retinol
retin-ac.	retinoicum acidum
rhamni purshianae cortex = cas-s.	
rham-cal.	rhamnus californica
rham-cath.	rhamnus cathartica
rham-f.	rhamnus frangula
rham-f-cor.	frangulae corticis extractum siccum
rhamnus purshiana = cas-s.	
rham-f-xyz.	rhamnus unknown part
rham-pr.	rhamnus prinoides
rhen-met.	rhenium metallicum
rhen-o.	rhenium oxydatum
rheum officinale = rheum	
rheum	rheum palmatum
rheum-r.	rheum rhaponticum
rhiz.	rhizopus niger
rhod.	rhododendron chrysanthum
rhod-f.	rhododendron ferrugineum
rhizopus nigricans = rhiz.	
rhodallinum = thiosin.	
rhodi.	rhodium metallicum
rhodi-o-n.	rhodium oxydatum nitricum
rhodon.	rhodonitum
rhus-a.	rhus aromatica
rhus canadensis = rhus-a.	
rhus-c.	rhus cotinus
rhus-d.	rhus diversiloba
rhus-g.	rhus glabra
rhus-l.	rhus laurina
rhus-r.	rhus radicans
rhus radicans = rhus-t.	
rhus-s.	rhus succedanea
rhus-t.	rhus toxicodendron
rhus-ty.	rhus typhina
rhus-v.	rhus venenata
rhus-ver.	= rhus-v. = rhus vernix (old abbr.)
rhus vernix = rhus-v.	
rhus-xyz.	rhus-r. + rhus-t.
rib-ac.	ribonucleicum acidum
ribes grossularia = ribes-u-c.	
ribes-n.	ribes nigrum
ribes-r.	ribes rubrum
ribes-u-c.	ribes uva crispa
ribo.	riboflavinum
ric.	ricinus communis
richardia aethiopica = zant.	
ricino-h.	ricinodendron heudelotii
rizoph.	rizophora mangle
rna = rib-ac.	
rob.	robinia pseudacacia
rosa-xyz.	rosa unknown species
rorippa nasturtium aquaticum = nast-o.	
ros-b-a.	rosa bracteata alba
ros-ca.	rosa canina
ros-ca-fl.	rosa canina flos
ros-ce.	rosa centifolia
ros-d.	rosa damascena
ros-g.	rosa gallica
rosm.	rosmarinus officinalis
ros-r.	rosa rubra
rovam.	rovamycine
royal-j.	royal jelly
roye-l.	royena lucida
roye-v.	royena villosa
r-rose	rock rose (Bach fl.)
ruap-l.	ruapehu lava
rub-c.	rubia cordifolia
rubd-br.	rubidium bromatum
rubd-c.	rubidium carbonicum
rubd-m.	rubidium muriaticum
rubd-met.	rubidium metallicum
rubella	rubella nosode
rubella-vc.	rubella vaccinus
rubeol.	rubeolae nosode

rub-par-rub-vc. rubeola-parotitis-rubella vaccinus
rubrum rubrum
rubia tinctoria = rub-t.
rub-t. rubia tinctorum
rubu. rubus villosus
rubus chamaemorus = rubu-c.
rubu-c. rubus chamaerosus
rubu-ca. rubus caesius
rubu-fr. rubus fruticosus
rubu-i. rubus idaeus
rubu-r. rubus rigidus
ruby ruby
rudbeckia angustifolia = echi.
rudb-h. rudbeckia hirta
rumx. rumex crispus
rudbeckia pallida = echi-pa.
rudbeckia purpurea = echi-p.
ruizia fragrans = bold.
rumx-ab. rumex abyssinicus
rumx-acl. rumex acetosella
rumx-act. rumex acetosa
rumx-al. rumex alpinus
rumx-aq. rumex aquaticus
rumex obtusifolius = lapa.
rumx-p. rumex patientia
rusc-a. ruscus aculeatus
russula emetica = agar-em.
russ. russula foetens
ruta ruta graveolens
ruta-a. ruta angustifolia
ruth-met. ruthenium metallicum
rutin. rutinum
r-wat. rock water (Bach fl.)
sabad. sabadilla
sabal sabal serrulata
sabb. sabbatia angularis
sabdariffa = hib-sa.
sabin. sabina
sacch. saccharum officinale
saccharomyces cerevisiae = tor.
saccharomyces ceru = tor.
sacch-a. saccharum album
sacchin. saccharinum
sacch-l. saccharum lactis
saccharum raffinatum = sacch-a.
sacch-xyz. saccharum unknown type
sacmy-a. saccharomyces apiculata
sag-s. sagittaria sagittaefolia
salicylate of soda = nat-sal.
sal-ac. salicylicum acidum
salisburia adiantifolia = gink-b.
sal-al. salix alba
salam. salamandra maculata
sal-am. salix Americana
salam-l. salamandra lacerta
salamandra maculosa = salam.
salbut. salbutamol
sal-fr. salix fragilis
salic-p. salicaria purpurea
salin. salicinum
sal-l. salix lasiolepis
sal-ma. salix madagascariensis
sal amarum = mag-s.
sal glauberi = nat-s.
sal-mar. sal marinum
sal-mo. salix mollissima
salmon-e. salmonella enteridis
salix vitellina = sal-l.
salmo-sal. salmo salar
salmo-trut. salmo trutta
sal-n. salix nigra
salmonella parathyphoidea = parat.
salmonella schotmullieri = parat-b.
salmonella typhi = eberth.
salol. salolum
salix nigricans = sal-p.
sal-p. salix purpurea
salv. salvia officinalis
salv-p. salvia pratensis
salv-sc. salvia sclarea
salv-so. salvia sonomensis
salv-vb. salvia verbenaca
salv-vt. salvia verticillata
samars. samarskite
sambucus humilis = samb-e.
samb. sambucus nigra
sambuci nigrae flos = samb.
samb-c. sambucus canadensis
samb-e. sambucus ebulus
salviae officinalis folium = salv.
sam-br. samarium bromatum
samb-r. sambucus racemosa
sam-c. samarium carbonicum
sam-f. samarium fluoratum
sam-i. samarium iodatum
sam-lac. samarium lacticum
sam-m. samarium muriaticum
sam-n. samarium nitricum
sam-o. samarium oxydatum
sam-ox. samarium oxalicum
sam-p. samarium phosphoricum
sam-s. samarium sulphuricum
sam-sil. samarium silicatum
sang. sanguinaria canadensis
sanguinarinum = sangin-pur.
sangin-act. sanguinarinum aceticum
sangin-n. sanguinarinum nitricum
sangin-pur. sanguinarinum purum
sangin-t. sanguinarinum tartaricum
sanguiso. sanguisorba officinalis

sanguiso-m.	sanguisorba minor
sanguis corvi = corv-cor.	
sanguis-s.	sanguis soricis
sanguisuga officinalis = hir.	
sanic.	sanicula aqua
sanic-eu.	sanicula Europaea
sanochr.	sanochrysine
santalum = ol-sant.	
santa.	santalum album
santal.	santalinus
santin.	santoninum
santol.	santolina chamaecyparissus
sapin.	saponinum
sapo.	saponaria officinalis
sap-o.	sapindus oblongifolius
sapium sylvaticum = still.	
sapo-ca.	sapo castile
sapo-so.	sapo soda
sapot-a.	sapota achras
sap-s.	sapindus saponaria
saraca indica = joan.	
sarcol-ac.	sarcolacticum acidum
saroth.	sarothamnus scoparius
sarr.	sarracenia purpurea
sars.	sarsaparilla officinalis
sass.	sassafras officinalis
sat-h.	satureia hortensis
sat-m.	satureia montanta
saur.	saururus cernuus
saxi.	saxifraga granulata
saxitox.	saxitoxinum
saxon.	saxonitum
scabiosa arvensis = knau-ar.	
scab-c.	scabiosa columbaria
scab-s.	scabiosa succisa
scam.	scammonium
scand-met.	scandium metallicum
scand-o.	scandium oxydatum
scarabaeus melolontha = melo.	
scarlatininum = scarl.	
scarl.	scarlatinum
scat.	scatolum
schin.	schinus molle
schoenocaulon officinale = sabad.	
schot-b.	schotia brachypetala
scir.	scirrhinum
schrankia nuttallii = mim-nu.	
schrankia uncinata = mim-mi.	
scilla bifolia = squil-b.	
scilla maritima = squil.	
scilla-non-scripta = agra.	
scirp-p.	scirpus paludicola
scler.	scleranthus annuus
sclera.	scleranthus (Bach fl.)
sclero-c.	sclerocarya caffra
scol.	scolopendra morsitans
scolopendrium officinale = scolo-v.	
scolo-v.	scolopendrium vulgare
scop.	scopolia carniolica
scopar.	scoparius genista
scopin.	scopolaminum bromatum
scopin-hbr.	scopolaminum bromhydricum
scopolaminum hydriodicum = scopin-i.	
scopolaminum hydrobromidum = scopin-hbr.	
scopin-i.	scopolaminum iodatum
scopla.	scopola
scorodosma foetida = asaf.	
scorpio Australis = buth-a.	
scor.	scorpio Europaeus
scroph-aq.	scrophularia aquatica
scroph-m.	scrophularia marylandica
scroph-n.	scrophularia nodosa
scorpionida = scor.	
scroph-xyz.	scroph-m. + scroph-n.
scutellaria lateriflora = scut.	
scut.	scutellaria laterifolia
scut-g.	scutellaria galericulata
sec.	secale cornutum
sec-ce.	secale cereale
secret.	secretinum
secu-l.	securidaca longipedonculata
sed-ac.	sedum acre
sed-al.	sedum album
sedum alpestre = sed-r.	
sed-c.	sedum cepaea
sedi.	sedinha
sed-r.	sedum repens
sedum purpureum = sed-t.	
sed-rf.	sedum reflexum
sed-ru.	sedum rubens
sed-t.	sedum telephium
sel.	selenium metallicum
selaginella = sela.	
sela.	selaginella apus
selenicereus grandiflorus = cact.	
selenicereus spinulosus = cact.	
sel-col.	selenium colloidale
seli.	selinum carvifolium
sel-o.	selenium oxydatum
semp.	sempervivum tectorum
semp-a.	sempervivum arachnoideum
semecarpus anacardium = anac.	
semen contra = cina	
sem-t.	semen tiglii
seneb-c.	senebiera coronopus
senec.	senecio aureus
senec-abv.	senecio ambavilla
senec-ad.	senecio adonidifolius
senec-atc.	senecio aurantiacus
senecio cineraria = cine.	

senec-c. senecio cordatus
senecio cordifolius = senec-c.
senec-d. senecio doronicum
senec-fa. senecio faniasioides
senec-fu. senecio fuschii
senecio gragglis = senec.
senec-i. senecio incanus
senebiera pinnatifida = lepi.
senecin. senecinum
senec-j. senecio jacobaea
senec-ma. senecio mannii
senec-sa. senecio sarracenicus
senec-sp. senecio speciosus
senec-sy. senecio sylvaticus
senec-vg. senecio vulgaris
senec-xyz. senecio unknown species
seneg. senega
senn. senna
senna obovata = cassia-ob.
senna occidentalis = cassia-o.
sennae folium = senn.
senticosus eleutherococcus = eleut.
sep. sepia officinalis
sep-os. sepia os
sepia succus = sep.
sepsinum = pyrog.
septi. septicaeminum
seq-de. sequoia dendron
seq-g. sequoia gigantea
seq-s. sequoia sempervirens
ser-a-c. serum anti colibacillum
serratula tinctoria = liat.
ser-ang. serum anguillae
ser-eq. serum equi
ser-febr-s. serum febris suis
serenoa repens = sabal
serenoa serrulata = sabal
serin-ca. serinus canaria
serot. serotoninum
serot-cs. serotoninum creatininum sulfuricum
serp. serpentaria aristolochia
ser-pestis-s. serum pestis suis
serrat-ma. serratia marcesens
seven (Paterson) = bacls-7.
shigella dysenteriae = dys.
shig-f. shigella flexneri
sicar-a. sicarius albospinosus
sicar-h-k. sicarius hahnii Karsh
sicar-o. sicarius oweni
sicar-s. sicarius spatulatus
sicar-t. sicarius testaceus
sida-rh. sida rhombifolia
sider. siderite
sieg. siegesbeckia orientalis
sil. silicea terra
sil-col. silica colloidalis
sierra iris = iris-h.
sigillum salomonis = polygn-vg.
sile-i. silene inflata
sil-mar. silica marina
sil-met. silicium metallicum
silpho. silphion cyrenaicum
silphu. silphium lacinatum
silphium laciniatum = silphu.
silybum marianum = card-m.
simaba cedron = cedr.
sima. simaruba amara
simaruba cedron = cedr.
simaruba ferroginea = cedr.
sima-g. simaruba glauca
simaruba officinalis = cedr.
sima-v. simaruba versicolor
simmon-ch. simmondsia chinensis
simul. simulium makara
sin-a. sinapis alba
sin-ar. sinapis arvensis
sin-n. sinapis nigra
sinapsis arvensis = sin-ar.
sinus. sinusitisinum
sin-xyz. sinapis alba + nigra
sison podagraria = aegop-p.
sist-m-b. sistrurus miliarius barbouri
sisy. sisyrinchium galaxoides
sisymbrium alliaria = alliar-o.
sisymbrium officinale = erys-o.
sisym-s. sisymbrium sophia
sium sium latifolium
sium-a. sium angustifolium
sium podagraria = aegop-p.
skat. skatolum
skook. Skookum Chuck aqua
slag slag silica
slate-nwls. Slate of North Wales
smaragd smaragd
smil-a. smilax aspera
smil-c. smilax china
smilcin. smilacinum
smilax offinialis = sars.
smilax sarsaparilla = sars.
smyrnium aureum = ziz.
soja-h. soja hispida
sol sol
sol-a. solanum arrebenta
sol-br. sol britannicus
sol-cp. solanum capense
sol-crl. solanum carolinense
soldan-a. soldanella alpina
sol-ecl. solar eclips
solanum dulcamara = dulc.
sol-er. solanum erythracantum

solidago virga avrea = solid.
solid. solidago virgaurea
solid-n. solidago nemoralis
solin. solaninum pur. + -act. (old abbr.)
sol-in. solanum integri
solalinum = solin.
solania = solin.
solin-act. solaninum aceticum
solin-pur. solaninum purum
sol-mlg. solanum melongena
sol-mm. solanum mammosum
solanum lycopersicum = lycpr.
sol-mx. solanum malacoxylon
sol-ni. solanum nigrum
sol-no. solanum nodiflorum
solanum oleaceum = sol-o.
sol-o. solanum oleraceum
sol-ps. solanum pseudocapsicum
sol-so. solanum sodomoeum
sol-t. solanum tuberosum
sol-t-ae. solanum tuberosum aegrotans
solanum vesicarium = physal-al.
sol-v. solanum villosum
sol-x. solanum xanthocarpum
somatot. somatotrophine
soph. sophora japonica
sor-ac. sorbicum acidum
sorbus Americana = pyrus
sorb-a. sorbus aucuparia
sorb-d. sorbus domestica
sorbit. sorbitolum
sorg-vg. sorghum vulgare
sparg-r. sparganium ramosum
spartin. sparteinum
spartin-s. sparteinum sulfuricum
spartini sulfas = spartin-s.
spart-j. spartium junceum
spartium scoparium = saroth.
spect. spectrum
sper-a. spergula arvensis
sperl-r. spergularia rubra
spermc-n. spermacoce natalensis
sperminum = orch.
sphaerococcus helminthochortos = helm.
sphang-s. sphagnum squarosum
sphing. sphingurus martini
spig. spigelia anthelmia
spigelia anthelmintica = spig.
spig-m. spigelia marylandica
spiggurus martini = sphing.
spil. spilanthes oleracea
spin-o. spinacia oleracea
spira. spiranthes autumnalis
spira-ca. spiranthes casei
spira-ce. spiranthes cernua
spirae. spiraea ulmaria
spirae-f. spiraea filipendula
spir-aeth-c. spiritus aetheris compositus
spira-la. spiranthes lacera
spira-lu. spiranthes lucida
spiram. spiramycine
spira-ro. spiranthes romanzoffiana
spir-n-d. = nit-s-d. = spiritus nitri dulcis (old abbr.)
spiron. spironolacton
spiros-af. spirostachys Africanus sond
spir-q-g. = querc-r-g-s. = spiritus quercus glandium
spiritus aetheris nitrosi = nit-s-d.
spiritus dulcis nitri = nit-s-d.
spiritus glandium quercus robur = querc-r-g-s.
spiritus nitrico-aethereus = nit-s-d.
spir-sula. spiritus sulphuratus
spirul. spirulina
splen. splenum
spongia fluvialitis = bad.
spongia officinalis = spong.
spong. spongia tosta
spongilla fluvialitis = bad.
sporg. sporgon
sporob-r. sporobolomyces roseus
sporob-s. sporobolomyces salmonicolor
sporot. sporothrix schenckii
squil. squilla maritima
sporotricum beurmanni = sporot.
spyrostachys Africanus = spiros-af.
squil-b. squilla bifolia
stach. stachys betonica
stach-a. stachys arvensis
stachys officinalis = stach.
stach-p. stachys palustris
stach-s. stachys sylvatica
stann. stannum metallicum
stann-i. stannum iodatum
stann-m. stannum muriaticum
stann-o. stannum oxydatum
stann-pchl. stannum perchloratum
stann-pox. stannum peroxydatum
stann-s. stannum sulfuratum
staph. staphisagria
staphylocinum = staphycoc.
staphycoc. staphylococcinum
staphytox. staphylotoxinum
stapl-g. stapelia gigantea
staphysagria = staph.
star-bet. star of bethlehem (Bach fl.)
steal steal
stear-ac. stearicum acidum
stellaria aquatica = cerast-a.
stel. stellaria media
ster-c. sterigmatocystis candidum

sterculia acuminata = kola
stereocaulon corallinum = stereo-co.
stereo-co. stereocaulon coralloides
sth = somatot.
stibio-kali tartaricum = ant-t.
stibium acidum = ant-ac.
stibium arsenicosum = ant-ar.
stibium chloridum = ant-m.
stibium crudum = ant-c.
stibium iodatum = ant-i.
stibium metallicum = ant-met.
stibium muriaticum = ant-m.
stibium oxydatum = ant-o.
stibium sulfuratum aurantiacum = ant-s-aur.
stibium sulfuratum nigrum = ant-c.
stibium sulfuratum rubrum = ant-s-r.
stibium sulphuratum auratum = ant-s-aur.
stibium tartaricum = ant-t.
stict. sticta pulmonaria
stigm. stigmata maydis
stigm-p. stigmata maydis putamen
stilboest. stilboestrolum
still. stillingia silvatica
stizolobium pruriens = dol.
stovaine = amyloc-m.
stovarsol = acetars.
stram. stramonium
strepta-g. streptanthus glandulosus
strept-ent. bacillus strepto-enterococcus
streptoc. streptococcinum
streptococcus haemolyticus = streptoc.
streptococcus pyogenes = streptoc.
streptococcus scarlatinae = streptoc.
streptococcus viridans = streptoc.
streptomyces albus = actin-a.
streptomyces citreus = actin-c.
streptomyces griseus = actin-g.
streptom. streptomycinum
streptom-s. streptomycinum sulphatum
stront-ar. strontium arsenicicum
stront-br. strontium bromatum
stront-c. strontium carbonicum
stront-gl. strontium gluconicum
stront-i. strontium iodatum
stront-lac. strontium lacticum
stront-m. strontium muriaticum
stront-met. strontium metallicum
stront-n. strontium nitricum
stront-o. strontium oxydatum
stront-s. strontium sulfuricum
stroph-gr. strophantus gratus
stroph-h. strophanthus hispidus
strophin. strophanthinum
stroph-s. strophanthus sarmentosus
stroph-xyz. strophanthus species unknown
stry. strychninum purum
stry-af-cit. strychninum citricum cum ammonioferri-citricum
strychnini et ferri citras = stry-af-cit.
stry-ar. strychninum arsenicosum
strych-g. strychnos gaultheriana
strych-h. strychnos henningsii
strychnos ignatiae = ign.
strychnos nux vomica = nux-v.
strychnos nux-vomica = nux-v.
strych-s. strychnos spinosa
stry-n. strychninum nitricum
stry-p. strychninum phosphoricum
strychnos tieut = upa.
stryph. stryphnodendron barbatimam
stry-s. strychninum sulphuricum
stry-val. strychninum valerianicum
stry-xyz. strychinum unknown type
subt. bacillus subtilis
succ. succinum
succ-ac. succinicum acidum
succ-xyz. succ. + succ-ac. + ol-suc.
sucr. sucrose
suis-chord-umb. suis (chorda umbilicalis)
suis-cu. cutis suis
suis-em. embryo suis
suis-hep. hepar suis
suis-pan. pancreas suis
suis-s. sanguis suis
sul-ac. sulphuricum acidum
sul-ac-ar. sulphuricum acidum aromaticum
sulfamidochrysoidine = prontos.
sulfa. sulfanilamidum
sulfag. sulfaguanidinum
sulfamrz. sulfamerazine
sulfamtz. sulfamethizol
sulfap. sulfapyridinum
sulfatz. sulfathiazolum
sulfon. sulfonalum
sulfonam. sulfonamidum
sul-h. sulphur hydrogenisatum
sul-i. sulphur iodatum
sulphuricum aromaticum acidum = sul-ac-ar.
sulo-ac. sulphurosum acidum
sulfur = sulph.
sulphamidochrysoidine = prontos.
sulph. sulphur
sulph-tinct. sulphur tinctura
sulph-trit. sulphur trituratum
sulpi. sulpiride
sulphur lotum = sulph.
sulphur sublimatum = sulph.
sul-s-l. sulphur sublimatum lavum
sul-ter. sulphur terebinthinatum

sumbul ferula = sumb.
sumb. sumbulus moschatus
sunoma sage = salv-so.
suprar. suprarenalis
suprarenalis cortex = adr-ctx.
suprarenalis glandula = suprar.
surukuku = lach.
sus-scr. sus scrofa
sutox. sutoxol
sweet-ch. sweet chestnut (Bach fl.)
syc. bacillus Sycoccus (Paterson)
symphoricarpus rivularis = sym-r.
symph. symphytum officinale
swertia carolinensis = frase-crl.
swertia chirata = gent-ch.
sycoccus (paterson) = syc.
sycoccus bacillus (paterson) = syc.
sycotic co. (paterson) = syc.
sycotic compound (paterson) = syc.
symphoricarpos albus = sym-r.
sym-r. symphoricarpus racemosus
symplocarpus foetidum = ictod.
synad-g. synadenium grantii
syph. syphilinum
syriaca = asc-c.
syr. syringa vulgaris
syzygium aromaticum = caryo.
syzygium cumini = syzyg.
syzyg. syzygium jambolanum
syzygium jambos = eug.
tab. tabacum
taber-i. tabernanthe iboga
tabern-s. tabernaemontana stapfiana
tal-m. talauma mexicana
talp-eu-p. talpae Europeus pel
tam. tamus communis
tamarix gallica = tama-c.
tama. tamarix germanica
tama-c. tamarix cinariensis
tamox. tamoxifen
tamrnd. tamarindus indica
tanac. tanacetum vulgare
tanac-b. tanacetum balsamita
tanac-er. tanacetum erectum
tang. tanghinia venenifera
tann-ac. tannicum acidum
tanninum = tann-ac.
tant-f. tantalum fluoratum
tant-met. tantalum metallicum
taosc. Taosca aqua
taper. taperiba
taraktogenos = chaul.
taraktogenos kurzii = chaul.
tarant-xyz. tarantula alive or dead
tarantula cubensis = tarent-c.
tarantula hispanica = tarent.
taraxacum dens leonis = tarax.
tarax. taraxacum officinale
tarent. tarentula hispanica
tarent-c. tarentula cubensis
tart-ac. tartaricum acidum
tartarus depuratus = kali-bit.
tartarus emeticus = ant-t.
tartarus stibiatus = ant-t.
tartr. tartrazine
tax. taxus baccata
tax-br. taxus brevifolia
techn. technetium
tec-p. tecoma pentaphylla
tecoma radicans = tec-p.
tegen-ag. tegenaria agrestis
tegen-at. tegenaria atrica
tegen-do. tegenaria domestica
tegen-gi. tegenaria gigantea
tegenaria magnacava = tegen-ag.
tegen-pa. tegenaria pagana
tein. Teinach aqua
tela tela araneae
tell. tellurium metallicum
tela aranearum = tela
teleamethylthioninum chloridum = methyl.
tell-ac. telluricum acidum
temp. tempestas
tep. Teplitz aqua
ten (Paterson) = bacls-10.
teph-k. tephrosia kraussiana
teph-v. tephrosia vogelii
ter. terebinthinae oleum
teramycin = oxyte-chl.
terb-br. terbium bromatum
terb-c. terbium carbonicum
terb-f. terbium fluoratum
terb-i. terbium iodatum
terb-lac. terbium lacticum
terb-m. terbium muriaticum
terb-n. terbium nitricum
terb-o. terbium oxydatum
terb-ox. terbium oxalicum
terb-p. terbium phosphoricum
terb-s. terbium sulphuricum
terb-sil. terbium silicatum
terebe. terebenum
tere-ch. terebinthina chios
tere-la. terebinthina laricina
term-a. terminalia arjuna
term-c. terminalia chebula
terp-h. terpini hydras
terra terra
ter-xyz. terebinthina unknown preparation

test. testosterone base
test-act. testosterone acetate
terra silicea = sil.
testa praeparata = calc-o-t.
testis testicles
test-pr. testosterone propionate
tet. tetradymitum
tetan. tetanosinum
tetan-vc. tetanus vaccinus
tetox. tetanotoxinum
tetrac. tetracyclinum
tetrabromfluoresceinum = eos.
tetrachl. tetrachloroethylene
tetrac-m. tetracyclinum muriaticum
tetrad-f. tetradenia fructicosa
tetrad-r. tetradenia riparia
teucrium chamaedrys = chamae.
teucr. teucrium marum verum
tetramethylaminum = prop.
teucr-b. teucrium botrys
teucr-s. teucrium scorodonia
teucr-sdm. teucrium scordium
thal. thallium met. + -act. (old abbr.)
thala. thalamus
thal-act. thallium aceticum
thal-ar. thallium arsenicosum
thal-c. thallium carbonicum
thal-f. thallium fluoratum
thalic-r. thalictrum rhynchocarpum
thal-m. thallium muriaticum
thal-met. thallium metallicum
thal-n. thallium nitricum
thal-o. thallium oxydatum
thal-s. thallium sulphuricum
thal-xyz. thallium unknown species
thap-g. thapsia garganica
thaspium aureum = ziz.
thaum-p. thaumetopoea processionnea
thea thea chinensis
thea sinensis = thea
thebaicum = op.
thebin. thebainum
thein. theinum
theobroma cacao = cac.
theob. theobrominum
theoph. theophyllinum
ther. theridion curassavicum
thev. thevetia nerifolia
thiam. thiaminum hydrochloridum
thioc-ac. thiocticum acidum
thiop. thioproperazinum
thiosin. thiosinaminum
thlas. thlaspi bursa pastoris
thom-h. thomandersia hensii
thor-act. thorium aceticum
thor-c. thorium carbonicum
thor-f. thorium fluoratum
thor-lac. thorium lacticum
thor-m. thorium muriaticum
thor-met. thorium metallicum
thor-n. thorium nitricum
thor-o. thorium oxydatum
thor-ox. thorium oxalicum
thor-p. thorium phosphoricum
thor-s. thorium sulphuricum
thor-sil. thorium silicatum
thor-x-ray thorium x-ray
thres-a. threskiornis aethiopica
thuj. thuja occidentalis
thrombidium = trom.
thryallis glauca = galph.
thuj-g. thuja gigantea
thuj-l. thuja lobii
thul-br. thulium bromatum
thul-c. thulium carbonicum
thul-f. thulium fluoratum
thul-i. thulium iodatum
thul-lac. thulium lacticum
thul-m. thulium muriaticum
thul-n. thulium nitricum
thul-o. thulium oxydatum
thul-ox. thulium oxalicum
thul-p. thulium phosphoricum
thul-s. thulium sulphuricum
thul-sil. thulium silicatum
thyam. thyamine
thycho-d. thychosanthes dioica
thym-gl. thymi glandulae extractum
thymine = thyam.
thymi-ac. thyminicum acidum
thymoidinum = thym-gl.
thymol. thymolum
thymus = thym-gl.
thymu. thymus serpyllum
thymonucleicum acidum = des-ac.
thymul. thymuline
thymum. thymum
thymu-vg. thymus vulgaris
thyr. thyreoidinum
thyreostimulinum = thyreotr.
thyreotr. thyreotropinum
thyroid = thyr.
thyroidinum = thyr.
thyroiodinum = thyroiod.
thyroiod. thyro-iodinum
thyrox. thyroxin
tilia cordata = til.
til. tilia Europaea
thyroxinum biiodatum = dithyr.
til-al. tilia alburnum

til-ar. tilia argentea
til-p. tilia platyphyllos
tilia silvestris = til.
til-t. tilia tomentosa
timol. timolol
tinas. tinospora cordifolia
tinctura sine kali = caust.
tinea-xyz. tinea unknown species
tip. tipida aqua
titan. titanium metallicum
titan-ac. titanicum acidum
titanii dioxidum = titan-o.
titan-cy. titanium cyanatum
titan-m. titanium muriaticum
titan-n. titanium nitridum
titan-o. titanium oxydatum
titan-s. titanium sulfuricum
titan-xyz. titan-g. + titan-n.
tocoph. tocopherolum
tod-a. toddalia aculeata
toen-s. toenia saginata
tol. toluidinum
toluen. toluene
toluiferum = bals-t.
tonca = tong.
tong. tongo odorata
tonsi. tonsilinum
tonsils = tonsi.
tormentilla erecta = pot-e.
tor. torula cerevisiae
torm. = pot-e. = tormentilla erecta (old abbr.)
toxi. = ancis-p. = toxicophis pugnax (old abbr.)
toxicodendron diversilobum = rhus-d.
toxicodendron quercifolium vernix = rhus-t.
toxicodendron radicans = rhus-t.
toxicodendron vernixa = rhus-v.
toxicophloea thunbergi = tox-th.
toxo-g. toxoplasma gondii
tox-th. = acok-op. = toxicophlaea thunbergii (old abbr.)
trach. trachinus draco
trachsp-j. trachelospermum jasminoides
trach-v. trachinus vipera
toxoplasmosis nosode = toxo-g.
toxoplasms gondi = toxo-g.
trach-xyz. trach. + trach-v.
trad. tradescantia diuretica
trag-p. tragopogon pratensis
trametes suaveolens = bol-su.
trem-g. trema grisea
trema guineensis = trem-or.
trem-or. trema orientalis
triaetam. triaethanolamine
triamc. triamcinolon
triatema = triat.
triat. triatoma
trib. tribulus terrestris
trich. trichosanthes amara
trich-an. trichosanthes anguina
trichil-e. trichilia emetica
trichin. trichinoyl
trichlact-ac. trichloroaceticum acidum
trichlae. trichloraethylene
trichom. trichomonas vaginalis
trichoph-d. trichophyton depressum
trichoph-p. trichophyton persearum
trichophyton persicolor = trichoph-p.
trichoph-r. trichophyton rubrum
trichoph-ung. trichophytosis unguis nosode
trichosanthes dioica = trich.
trichr. trichuris trichurius
triclis-g. triclisia gilletii
trifolium album = trif-r.
trif-al. trifolium alpinum
trif-ar. trifolium arvense
trif-d. trifolium dubium
trif-e. trifolium elegans
trifolium fibrinum = meny.
trif-p. trifolium pratense
trif-r. trifolium repens
trig-f-g. trigonella foenum graecum
trigonella foenum-graecum = trig-f-g.
trigonocephalus contortrix = cench.
trigonocephalus lachesis = lach.
trigonocephalus piscivorus = ancis-p.
tril-c. trillium cernuum
trillium erectum = tril-p.
tril-p. trillium pendulum
trim. trimeresurus wagleri
trimer-a. trimeria alnifolia
trimeth. trimethadione
trimethylaminum = prop.
trimethylxanthin = coffin.
trinatrii citras = nat-cit.
trinitrophenolum = pic-ac.
trinit. trinitrotoluenum
trion. trional
trios. triosteum perfoliatum
tritic. triticum repens
triticum aestivum = tritic-vg.
tritic-g. triticum germinatum
tritic-s. triticum spelta
tritic-vg. triticum vulgare
trito trito
trium-r. triumfetta rhomboidea
troll-as. trollius asiaticus
troll-eu. trollius Europaeus
troll-la. trollius laxus
trom. trombidium muscae domesticae

trop.	tropaeolum majus
trychs.	trychosanthes
trych-t.	trychophyton tonsurans
tryps.	trypsinum
trypt.	tryptophanum
tub.	tuberculinum bovinum Kent
tsuga canadensis = abies-c.	
tuberculini aviarii derivatum = tub-a.	
tuberculini bovini derivatum = tub.	
tuberculinum aviaire = tub-a.	
tub-a.	tuberculinum avis
tub-d.	tuberculinum Denys
tub-k.	tuberculinum Koch
tub-m.	tuberculinum Marmoreck
tuberculinum pristinum = tub-k.	
tub-r.	tuberculinum residuum Koch
tub-ro.	tuberculinum Rosenbach
tub-sp.	tuberculinum Spengler
tubiporus edulis = bol-ed.	
tul.	tulipa
tung-met.	tungstenium metallicum
turnera aphrodisiaca = dam.	
turnera diffusa = dam.	
turpethum minerale = merc-sul.	
tur-f.	turraea floribunda
tur-o.	turraea obtusifolia
tus-fa.	tussilago farfara
tus-fr.	tussilago fragrans
tus-p.	tussilago petasites
tyl-i.	tylophora indica
typh.	typha latifolia
typhobacillinum = eberth.	
typho-vc.	typhoid vaccinus
tyram.	tyramine
tyran-rex.	tyrannosaurus rex
tyros.	L-tyrosinum
tyrosinum = tyros.	
tyrothr.	tyrothricinum
tyrotox.	tyrotoxicon
ulc-cr.	ulcus cruris nosode
ulc-du.	ulcus duodeni nosode
ulc-ve.	ulcus venticuli nosode
ulm-c.	ulmus campestris
ulmus fulva = ulm-r.	
ulm-m.	ulmus montana
ulm-pra.	ulmus procera
ulmus pyramidalis = ulm-m.	
ulm-r.	ulmus rubra
ulm-xyz.	ulmus unknown species
ulx-eu.	ulex Europaeus
umbellularia californica = oreo.	
umbilicus pendulinus = cot.	
umck.	umckaloabo
uncar-tom.	uncaria tomentosa
undec-ac.	undecylenicum acidum
une-e.	unedo edulis
upa.	upas tieuté
upa-a.	upas antiaris
urginea maritima = squil.	
ur-ac.	uricum acidum
uran-act.	uranium aceticum
uran-ar.	uranium arsenicicum
uran-c.	uranium carbonicum
uran-f.	uranium fluoratum
uragoga ipecacuanha = ip.	
uraninit.	uraninitum
uran-lac.	uranium lacticum
uran-m.	uranium muriaticum
uran-met.	uranium metallicum
uran-n.	uranium nitricum
uran-o.	uranium oxydatum
uranoth.	uranothorium
uran-ox.	uranium oxalicum
uran-p.	uranium phosphoricum
uran-s.	uranium sulphuricum
uran-sil.	uranium silicatum
urea	urea pura
urea-n.	urea nitrica
ureth.	urethane
urg-ind.	urginea indica
urine = urin.	
urin.	urinum
urin-d.	urinum diabeticum
urin-eq.	urina equina
urin-gr.	urinum gravidarum
urol-h.	urolophus halleri
urotrop.	urotropinum
ursin-t.	ursinia tenuiloba
urt-c.	urtica crenulata
urt-d.	urtica dioica
urt-g.	urtica gigas
urt-u.	urtica urens
urt-xyz.	urtica species unknown
usn.	usnea barbata
ust.	ustilago maydis
uva	uva ursi
uvar.	uvaria triloba
uza.	uzara
v-a-b.	vaccin atténué bilié
Vaccin of Haffkine = pest.	
vac.	vaccininum
vacc-m.	vaccinium myrtillus
vacc-v.	vaccinium vitis idaea
vaccinotoxinum = vac.	
vaccinum hepatitidis A inactivatum = hepati-a-vc.	
vaccinum hepatitidis B (ADNr) = hepati-b-vc.	
vaccinum influenzae inactivatum = influ.	
vaccinum parotitidis vivum = parot-vc.	
vaccinum rubellae vivum = rubella-vc.	
vaccinum tetani adsorbatum = tetan-vc.	

vacuum	vacuum
valer.	valeriana officinalis
valer-ac.	valerianicum acidum
valerianae radix = valer.	
valerl-o.	valerianella olitoria
valin.	valinum
vanad.	vanadium metallicum
vanad-m.	vanadium muriaticum
vanad-o.	vanadium oxydatum
vanad-s.	vanadium sulphuricum
vanes-u.	vanessa urtica
vang-e.	vangueria emirnensis
vang-l.	vangueria lasiantha
vanil.	vanilla aromatica
vanilla planifolia = vanil.	
vanilin.	vanillinum
varech = fuc.	
varic.	varicellinum
vario.	variolinum
vasel.	vaselin
vasop.	vasopressine
vauc-s.	vaucheria sessilis
ven-m.	venus mercenaria
venus planetes = ven-s-e.	
ven-s-e.	venus stella errans
velome de mato = crot-f.	
ventus	ventus
ver-ac.	vernix caseosa
verat.	veratrum album
veratrum luteum = helon.	
verat-n.	veratrum nigrum
verat-v.	veratrum viride
verbascum thapsiforme = verb-de.	
verb.	verbascum thapsus
verb-de.	verbascum densiflorum
verbe-h.	verbena hastata
verbe-o.	verbena officinalis
verbe-u.	verbena urticaefolia
verb-f.	verbascum floccosum
verb-n.	verbascum nigrum
verb-ol.	verbasci oleum
verin.	veratrinum
vermic.	vermiculite
vern-a.	vernonia anthelmintica
vern-am.	vernonia amygdalina
vern-co.	vernonia corymbosa
vern-w.	vernonia wooddii
veronal = barbit.	
veronastricum virginicum = lept.	
vero-ab.	veronica abyssinica
vero-b.	veronica beccabunga
vero-c.	veronica chamaedrys
vero-o.	veronica officinalis
vero-p.	veronica persica
vero-t.	veronica teucrium
veronica virginica = lept.	
verr.	verrucinum
verrug-a-c-f.	verrugosa acrochordon chocoe fel
verv.	vervain (Bach fl.)
vesi.	vesicaria communis
vesp.	vespa crabro
vespul-germ.	vespula germanica
vespul-m.	vespula maculata
vespul-mf.	vespula maculifrons
vespul-sq.	vespula squamosa
vespul-vg.	vespula vulgaris
vesp-xyz.	vespa crabro + vespul-m. +vespul-vg.
viburnum oderiferum = vib-od.	
vib.	viburnum opulus
vetiver = anan.	
vetiveria zizanioides = anan.	
vibh.	vibhuti
vib-l.	viburnum lantana
vib-od.	viburnum oderatissinum
vib-p.	viburnum prunifolium
vib-t.	viburnum tinus
vichy-g.	Vichy aqua Grande Grille
vichy-h.	Vichy aqua Hôpital
vinc.	vinca minor
vince.	vincetoxicum officinale
vicia ervilia = erv-e.	
vicia faba = faba-vg.	
vinc-ma.	vinca major
vinc-r.	vinca rosea
vine	vine (Bach fl.)
vineg.	vinegar
vinum	vinum
viola	viola
viol-c.	viola canina
viol-o.	viola odorata
viol-s.	viola sudetica
viol-t.	viola tricolor
vip.	vipera berus
vip-a.	vipera aspis
vip-a-c.	vipera acontica carinata
vipera communis = vip.	
vip-d.	vipera daboia
vip-l-f.	vipera lachesis fel
vip-r.	= vip-a. = vipera redi (old abbr.)
vip-ser.	immunoserum contra venena viperarum
vipera redi = vip-a.	
vipera russelli = vip-d.	
vip-t.	vipera torva
virid.	viridum
virl.	virillium
visc.	viscum album
virola sebifera = myric.	
virus poliomyelitis = polio	
visc-ab.	viscum abietis
visc-ar.	viscum armeniacae

visc-cr.	viscum crataegi
visc-l.	viscum laxum
visc-m.	viscum mali
viscum pini = visc-l.	
visc-pi.	viscum piri
visc-po.	viscum populi
visc-pr.	viscum pruni
visc-q.	viscum quercinum
visc-r.	viscum robiniae
visc-s.	viscum salicis
visc-t.	viscum tiliae
vitamin b12 = cyanoc.	
vitamin b2 = ribo.	
vitamin b3 = nicotam.	
vitamin b4 = adenin.	
vitamin b5 = pant-ac.	
vitamin b6 = pyrid.	
vitamin b7 = inos.	
vitamin b8 = adenyl-ac.	
vitamin c = ascor-ac.	
vitamin d2 = ergocalc.	
vitamin d3 = cholcalc.	
vitamin e = tocoph.	
vitamin f = linol-ac.	
vitamin g = lactof.	
vitamin h2 = amibe-ac.	
vitamin k = menad.	
vitamin pp = nicot-ac.	
vitamine h1 = biot.	
vitex agnus castus = agn.	
vitex agnus-castus = agn.	
vit.	vitex trifolia
vitamin-d	vit d2 and/or vit d3
vitamin b1 = thiam.	
vit-b-x.	vitamin b1+b2+b6+b12
vitis alba = bry.	
vitis quinquefolia = ampe-qu.	
vitis rubra = ampe-qu.	
vitis-v.	vitis vinifera
vitr-an.	vitrum antimonii
vitr-cor.	vitrum coroni
viverra civetta = bassar-a.	
voac-af.	voacanga Africana
voes.	Voeslau aqua
voslau	Voslau aqua
vulpes-s.	vulpes (sanguis)
vult-gr.	vultur gryphus
waln.	walnut (Bach fl.)
wede-n.	wedelia natalensis
weilb.	Weilbach aqua
white-ch.	white chestnut (Bach fl.)
wies.	Wiesbaden aqua
wildb.	Wildbad aqua
wildu.	Wildungen aqua
will.	willow (Bach fl.)
wist-fl.	wisteria floribunda
wist-s.	wisteria sinensis
wither.	witherite
with-s.	withania somnifera
wigardia californica = erio.	
w-oat	wild oat (Bach fl.)
w-rose	wild rose (Bach fl.)
w-viol.	water violet (Bach fl.)
wood alcohol = methan.	
woorali = cur.	
woorara = cur.	
wrightia antidysenterica = kurch.	
wrightia tincto = kurch.	
wyethia = wye.	
wye.	wyethia helenoides
xanthoxylum Americanum = xan.	
xan.	xanthoxylum fraxineum
xan-al.	xanthoxylum alatum
xanrhi.	xanthorrhiza apifolia
xanrhoe.	xanthorrhoea arborea
xanth.	xanthium spinosum
xanthin.	xanthinum
xanth-mc.	xanthium macrocarpum
xanth-st.	xanthium strumarium
xen.	xenon
xero.	xerophyllum asphodeloides
xime-c.	ximenia caffra
xiphosura = lim.	
xiph.	xiphosura Americana
x-ray	x-ray
xyloc.	xylocaine
xylop-a.	xylopia aethiopica
xyma-m.	xymalos monospora
yampah = perid-b.	
yatr.	yatren
yaupon = ilx-v.	
yell-vc.	yellow fever vaccinum
yers.	serum yersiniae
yerba buena = micr.	
yerba mansa = anemps.	
yerba santa = erio.	
Yersin = yers.	
yohimbehe = yohim.	
yohim.	yohimbinum
yohim-m.	yohimbinum muriaticum
yttrb-br.	ytterbium bromatum
yttrb-c.	ytterbium carbonicum
yttrb-f.	ytterbium fluoratum
yttrb-i.	ytterbium iodatum
yttrb-lac.	ytterbium lacticum
yttrb-m.	ytterbium muriaticum
yttrb-n.	ytterbium nitricum
yttrb-o.	ytterbium oxydatum
yttrb-ox.	ytterbium oxalicum

yttrb-p. ytterbium phosphoricum
yttrb-s. ytterbium sulphuricum
yttrb-sil. ytterbium silicatum
yttr-met. yttrium metallicum
yttr-o. yttrium oxydatum
yttr-ox. yttrium oxalicum
yuc. yucca filamentosa
zaluzianskya capensis = zant.
zant. zantedeschia aethiopica
zanthoxylum alatum = xan-al.
zanthox-c. zanthoxylum capense
zanthoxylum fraxineum = xan.
zea-i. zea italica
zincum isovalerianicum = zinc-val.
zinc. zincum metallicum
zinc-act. zincum aceticum
zinc-ar. zincum arsenicosum
zinc-be. zincum benzoicum
zinc-br. zincum bromatum
zinc-c. zincum carbonicum
zinc-chl. zincum chloricum
zincum chromatum = zinc-chr.
zinc-chr. zincum chromicum
zinc-col. zincum colloidale
zinc-cy. zincum cyanatum
zinc-f. zincum fluoratum
zinc-fcy. zincum ferrocyanatum
zinc-form. zincum formicum
zinc-gl. zincum gluconicum
zinc-i. zincum iodatum
zinc-m. zincum muriaticum
zinc-n. zincum nitricum
zinc-o. zincum oxydatum
zinc-ox. zincum oxalicum
zinc-p. zincum phosphoricum (old abbr.)
zinc-phat. zincum phosphoratum
zinc-phic. zincum phosphoricum
zinc-pic. zincum picricum
zinc-pox. zincum peroxydatum
zea mais = stigm.
zea putrefatto = zea-i.
zieria minutiflora = xan-al.
zinci oxidum = zinc-o.
zinci sulphas = zinc-s.
zinc-p-xyz. zinc-phat. + zinc-phic.
zinc-s. zincum sulphuricum
zinc-val. zincum valerianicum
zingiber = zing.
zing. zingiber officinale
zirc-m. zirconium muriaticum
zirc-met. zirconium metallicum
zirc-n. zirconium nitricum
zirc-o. zirconium oxydatum
zisyphus paliurus = pali-a.
ziz. zizia aurea
zootoca vivipara = lacer-viv.
ziz-int. zizia integerima
zizyp-j. zizyphus jujuba
zizyp-m. zizyphus mucronata

LIST OF AUTHOR ABBREVIATIONS

a ALLEN Timothy Field: (1837-1902)

a1 ALLEN Timothy F.: [Encyclopedia of Pure Materia Medica (Vol. 1-10)], New-York / Philadelphia: Boericke & Tafel (1879)

a1.fr ALLEN Timothy F.: Encyclopédie de la Matière Médicale pures : Séléction de remèdes

a2 ALLEN Timothy F.: [Handbook of Materia Medica and Homeopathic Therapeutics], Philadelphia: Boericke & Tafel (1889)

a3 ALLEN Timothy F.: [Primer of Materia Medica], New Delhi: Jain Publishers (1892)

a4 ALLEN Timothy F.: [A general symptom register of homoeopathic materia medica - index to the Encyclopaedia of Pure Materia Medica.], Philadelphia: Boericke and Tafel (1880)

aa anonymous author

aa1 anonymous author: [Indian Pharmacopea]

aa2 anonymous author: [Discussions - Materia Medica by Contempory Homeopaths]

aa3 anonymous author: [Natural History Information - animals]

aa4 anonymous author: [Provings - Contemporary Provings]

aa5 Anonymous author: [The Poultry Doctor] (1990)

abj AMBROS Julio J.

abj1.es AMBROS Julio J.: Semiología Homeopática Infanto Juvenil [2nd Ed.], Argentina: Ambros J. - Yabes E. (1993)

abm AUBIN M.: (1927-1985)

abm1.fr AUBIN M., JOLY P., PICARD P., DEMARQUE D. et JOUANNY J.: Pratique Homéopathique en Gastro-enterologie, Paris: Centre d'Etudes et de Documentation Homéopathique (1982)

abm2.fr AUBIN M., DEMARQUE D., JOLY P., JOUANNY J. et SAINT-JEAN Y.: Concordances homéopathiques, Paris: Centre d'Etudes et de Documentation Homéopathique (1989)

abs ALBIN Steve: Contemporary homeopath [Portland, USA]

abs1 ALBIN Steve: [Poison Oak Miseries], N Eng. J H, Vol 2 nr 1: pg 8-9 (1993)

acl ACKERLY Sarah: Contemporary homeopath [Portland, USA]

acl1 ACKERLY Sarah: [A case of Intractable Constipation], N Eng. J H, Vol 3 nr 2: pg 17-18 (1994)

ada ANDREASSEN Alf: (1953-)

ado AUDASSO Sergio

ado1 = psm1 = AUDASSO Sergio (old abb.): [Corso di primi soccorso omeopatico [Edited by Audasso]]

adp ANDERSCH-HARTNER Peter

ads ADAMS Suzanne C.: Contemporary homeopath [Washington, USA]

ads1 ADAMS Suzanne C.: [Cases: Dermoid Cysts], N Eng. J H, Vol 3 nr 1: pg 19-20 (1994)

aem ACHE M.: (1952-)

aem1 ACHE M. and MATTITSCH G.: [Proving of Aegopodium podagria], Documenta Homoeopathica, 12 (1989)

ag AEGIDI: French homeopathic physician. One of the founders of homeopathy in France.

agh ANGELL Henry C.

agh1 ANGELL Henry C.: [Treatise on diseases of the eye.], Boston (1870)

ah ANSHUTZ Edward Pollock: (1846-1918)

ah1 ANSHUTZ Edward Pollock: [New, old and forgotten remedies [2nd Ed.]], Philadelphia: Boericke & Tafel (1917)

ah2 ANSHUTZ Edward Pollock: [Sexual ills & diseases [2nd Ed.]], Philadelphia: Boericke & Tafel (1910)

ah2.es ANSHUTZ Edward Pollock: Tratamiento Homeopático de las enfermedades sexuales.

ah3 ANSHUTZ Edward Pollock: [Therapeutic by-ways [1st indian Ed.]], New Delhi: World homeopathic links

ah4 ANSHUTZ Edward Pollock: [A guide to the twelve tissue remedies of biochemistry] (1927)

ak ASKENSTEDT F. C.

al ALLEN Henry C.: American homeopathic physician (1836-1909)

al1 ALLEN Henry C.: [Keynotes and Characteristics with Comparisons], Wellingborough: Thorsons Publ. (1898)

al1.de ALLEN Henry C.: Grundzüge und Characteristika der Materia Medica mit Nosoden

al1.fr ALLEN Henry C.: Symptômes clés et caractéristiques des principaux remèdes.

al10 ALLEN Henry C.: [Tuberculinum], Med Adv, Vol 39/1: pg 1 (1901)

al11.es ALLEN Henry C.: Comparaciones de Algunos Medicamentos de la Materia Médica Homeopática

al1a.es ALLEN Henry C.: Keynotes Reordenados y clasificados con Medicamentos sobresalientes de la MM y Nosodes intestinales (9th Ed.), New Delhi: Jain Publishers (2000)

al2 ALLEN Henry C.: [The Materia Medica of some important nosodes], Philadelphia: Boericke & Tafel (1910)

al3 ALLEN Henry C.: [The therapy of fevers], Philadelphia: Boericke & Tafel (1884)

al3.fr ALLEN Henry C.: Matière Médicale de la fièvre, Paris: Similia (1990)

al4 ALLEN Henry C.: [The therapy of intermittent fever], New Delhi: Jain Publishers (1884)

al5	ALLEN Henry C.: [The therapy of tuberculous affections], New Delhi: World Homeopathic links. Reprint in 1983
al6	ALLEN Henry C.: [Gregg consumption], Calcutta: Sett Dey & Co (1889)
al7	ALLEN Henry C.: [Salicylic Acid], International Hahnemannian Association Proceedings (1895)
al8	ALLEN Henry C.: [Silica], Med Adv, Vol 39/1: pg 8 (1901)
al9	ALLEN Henry C.: [Malaria officinalis], Med Adv, Vol 39/4: pg 180 (1901)
alj	ALLEN John H.: American homeopathic physician (1854-1925)
alj1	ALLEN John H.: [The Chronic Miasms, Psora & Pseudopsora], Bombay: Roy and Co (1910)
alj1.es	ALLEN John H.: Los Miasmas Crónicos. Psora y Pseudopsora, Buenos Aires: Editorial Albatros (1985)
alj2	ALLEN John H.: [Diseases and Therapeutics of the Skin], Philadelphia: Boericke and Tafel (1902)
alj3	ALLEN John H.: [Medorrhinum], Med Adv, Vol 32/2: pg 59 (1894)
alj4	ALLEN James H.: [Chronic Miasms: Sycosis], Vol II (1900)
alm	ALEEM Mohammed: Contemporary homeopath [Madras, India] (1954-)
alm1	ALEEM Mohammed: [The Rhythm of Volcano], Links, Vol 1: pg 39-40 (1994)
alw	ALLEN William A.: (1842-)
alw1	ALLEN William A.: [Repertory to Symptoms of Intermittent Fever] (1882)
am	ALTMANN Micha: Contemporary homeopath [Israel] (1950-)
ama	ATMADJIAN Anaïs: Contemporary homeopathic physician [Paris, France], Psycho-analyst, psychiatrist and neurobiologist.
ama1.fr	ATMADJIAN Anaïs: Traité d'Homéopathie appliquée à la Maternité, Paris:Maison Neuve (1992)
amd	AHMAD Shafiq
amd1	AHMAD Shafiq: [A short Repertory on Indian drugs]
ans	ANAND Sunil: Contemporary homeopath [Bombay, India]
ans1	ANAND Sunil: [Prescribing for Children], Links, Vol 2: pg 9-10 (1993)
ar	ARAUJO Claudio: Contemporary homeopathic physician [Rio de Janeiro, Brasil] (1952-)
arg	ARENA Gaetano
arg1	ARENA Gaetano: [Preliminary Investigation into an experimental Homeopathic Application of ETNA LAVA] (2001)
arg1.it	ARENA Gaetano: Ricera Omeopatica Sperimentale su ETNA LAVA (2001)
arg2	ARENA Gaetano: [Experimental Homeopathic Research on OPUNTIA FICUS INDICA] (2002)
arg2.it	ARENA Gaetano: Ricera Omeopatica sperimentale su OPUNTIA FICUS INDICA (2002)
ase	ANSELMI Eugenio E.
ase1.es	ANSELMI Eugenio E.: Lor Remedios Homeopáticos, New Delhi: Jain Publishers
asm	ASSILEM M.: (1942-)
asm1	ASSILEM M.: [Folliculinum: mist or miasm], Nottingham: Society of Homeopaths (1990)
asm2	ASSILEM M.: [The Mad Hatter's Tea Party] (1994)
asm3	ASSILEM M.: [Luna and Sol]
asw	ARMSTRONG W. P.: (1860-1940)
asw1	ARMSTRONG W. P.: [A handbook of the Diseases of the Heart], Chicago (1882)
at	AUSTIN Alonzo E.: (1868-1948)
ath	ARNDT H.R.: (1845-)
ath1	ARNDT H.R.: [First Lessons in the Symptomatology of Remedies]
atj	ATTOMYR Joseph
atj1	ATTOMYR Joseph: [Proving of Ira], Neues Archiv für Homöopatische Heilkunst, Vol 2 (1844)
atj2	ATTOMYR Joseph: [Proving of Anemone nemorosa], Neues Archiv für Homöopathische Heilkunst, Vol 1: pg 180
atj3.de	ATTOMYR Joseph: Brief über Homöopathie, Leipzig: Köhler (1833)
atn	ANTONIOU K.: Contemporary homeopath [Greece]
atn1	ANTONIOU K.: [Unexpected Remedy in a Case of Depression], E J Cl. H, Vol 1 nr 1: pg 19-21 (1995)
atr	ALTHER: Swiss homeopathic physician from the time of Hahnemann (1800-1860)
aw	AGRAWAL M. L.
aw1	AGRAWAL M. L.: [Materia medica of the human mind] (1989)
aw2	AGRAWAL M. L.: [Homeopathy in accidents and injuries]
aw3	AGRAWAL M. L.: [A comparative study of chronic diseases]
aw4	AGRAWAL M. L.: [Diseases of hair and nails]
aw5	AGRAWAL M. L.: [Homeopathy in asthma]
aw6	AGRAWAL M. L.: [Insomnia and sleep]
aw7	AGRAWAL M. L.: [Measles and small-pox]
aw8	AGRAWAL M. L.: [A Repertory of desires and aversions]
aw9	AGRAWAL M. L.: [Dreams and nightmares]
awy	AGRAWAL Y. R.: (1941-)
awy1	AGRAWAL Y. R.: [Treatise on Bowel Nosode] (1981)
awy2	AGRAWAL Y. R.: [Homeopathy in asthma], New Delhi: Vijay Publication (1985)
awy3	AGRAWAL Y. R.: [Homoeopathy in Accidents and Injuries.], Delhi: Vija Publications (India) (1983)
az	ACHTZEHN Hans-Jürgen: Contemporary homeopath [Germany] (1951-)
az1.de	ACHTZEHN Hans-Jürgen: Carcinosinum, H Einblicke, Vol 1: pg 6 (1990)

b	BOENNINGHAUSEN Clemens von: German homeopath (1785-1864). One of the main students of Hahnemann. Received right to practice as a physician from King Wilhelm IV (1843).
b1	BOENNINGHAUSEN Clemens von: [Characteristics of Materia Medica], Münster: Coppenrath (1833)
b1.de	BOENNINGHAUSEN Clemens von: Versuch über die Verwandschaffen der hom. Arzneien., Munster (Germany): Verlag der Coppenrathschen Buch-und Kunsthandlung (1836)
b10.de	BOENNINGHAUSEN Clemens von: Die homöopathische Behandlung des Keuchhustens in seinen verschiedenen Formen, Munster (Germany): Verlag der Coppenrathschen Buch-und Kunsthandlung (1860)
b12.de	BOENNINGHAUSEN Clemens von: Übersicht der Haupt-Wirkungs-Sphäre der Antipsorischen Arzneien, so wie der antisyphilitischen und antisykotschen und ihre charakteristischen Eigenthümlichkeiten, als Anhang zum Repertorium derselben., Münster, Druck und Verlag der Coppenratschen Buch- und Kunsthandlung (1833)
b13.de	BOENNINGHAUSEN Clemens von: Die Homöopathie: ein Lesebuch für das gebildete, nicht-ärztliche Publikum., Münster: Coppenrath (1834)
b14.de	BOENNINGHAUSEN Clemens von: Kleine medizinische Schriften. Rewrited by Klaus-Hennig Gypser., Heidelberg: Arkana Verlag (1853)
b15.de	BOENNINGHAUSEN Clemens von: Der Homöopathische Hausartzt: in kurzen therapeutischen Diagnosen., Münster: Regensberg (1853)
b2	BOENNINGHAUSEN Clemens von: [Therapeutic Pocket Book]
b2.de	BOENNINGHAUSEN Clemens von: Therapeutisches Taschenbuch, Münster: Coppenrath (1846)
b2.es	BOENNINGHAUSEN Clemens von: Manual de Terapéutica Homeopática y Repertorio, México: Nueva Editorial Médico (1993)
b2.fr	BOENNINGHAUSEN Clemens von: Manuel de Thérapeutique Homéopathique
b2a.de	BOENNINGHAUSEN: Additions to b2 collected by the son of Clemens von BOENNINGHAUSEN
b3	BOENNINGHAUSEN Clemens von: [Aphorisms of Hippocrates], Leipzig: Purfürst (1863)
b3.de	BOENNINGHAUSEN Clemens von: Die Aphorismen des Hippokrates: nebst den Glossen eines Homöopathen., Leipzig: Purfürst (1863)
b4.de	BOENNINGHAUSEN Clemens von: Systematisch-Alphabetisches Repertorium der Homoöpathischen Arzneien - Enthaltend die antipsorischen, antisyphilitischen und antisykotischen Arzneien., Münster: Coppenrath (1833)
b4a.de	BOENNINGHAUSEN Clemens von: Additions to b4 collected by the son of Clemens von BOENNINGHAUSEN
b5.de	BOENNINGHAUSEN Clemens von: Übersicht der Haupt-Wirkungs-Sphäre der Antipsorischen Arzneien und ihre charakteristischen Eigenthümlichkeiten, als Anhang zum Repertorium derselben., Munster (Germany): Verlag der Coppenrathschen Buch-und Kunsthandlung (1833)
b6.de	BOENNINGHAUSEN Clemens von: Die Körperseiten und Verwantschaften, Münster (1853)
b7.de	BOENNINGHAUSEN Clemens von: Systematisch-Alphabetisches Repertorium der Homoöpathischen Arzneien - Enthaltend die nicht-antipsorischen Arzneien., Münster: Coppenrath (1833)
b7a.de	BOENNINGHAUSEN Clemens von: Additions to b7 collected by the son of Clemens von BOENNINGHAUSEN
b8	BOENNINGHAUSEN Clemens von: [The Lesser Writings] (1908)
b9	BOENNINGHAUSEN Clemens von: [Whooping Cough]
ban	BANNAN Robert: (1961-)
ban1	BANNAN Robert: [A proving of Tilia cordata], Links, Vol 9: pg 104-106 (1996)
ban2	BANNAN Robert: [Urtica urens]
bat	BERNARD Teresa M.: (1946-)
bat1	BERNARD Teresa M.: [Proving of Sambucus nigra - Linking trees project], Links, Vol 12: pg 174-175 (1999)
bb	BARBANCEY J.
bb1.fr	BARBANCEY J.: Pratique homéopathique en psycho-pathologie
bbj	BARBENCY Jacqueline
bbm	BARBERA Maria Luisa
bbm1.it	BARBERA Maria Luisa: Oltre il dissimile. Le basi storico-filosofiche dell'Omeopatia hahnemanniana, Como: h.m.s. homeopathic medicine software s.r.l. (2001)
bbp	BARBIER Pierrer: (1916-2002)
bbp1.fr	BARBIER Peter: Homéopathie, petits remèdes retrouvés, Maloine, 1994. Zit.: Cah. Hahn., 32 (3), 1995, 116 (1994)
bc	BLACKIE Margery G.: English homeopathic physician. British Queen's physician. (1898-1981)
bc1	BLACKIE Margery G.: [The Challenge of Homoeopathy (The patient Not the Cure)], London: Macdonald and Jane (1976)
bc2	BLACKIE Margery G.: [Classical Homeopathy], Beaconsfield (England): Beaconsfield Publ. (1986)
bc3	BLACKIE Margery G.: [A comparison of Arsenicum, Nitricum. Acidum, Hepar Sulphur and Nux vomica] (1961)
bc4.es	BLACKIE Margery G., CLOSE S., ROBERTS H. y WRIGHT E.: Clinica Homeopática. Translated by

	Raul Ibarra Ovando, Buenos Aires: Editorial Albatros (1993)
bca	BENCE L.
bca1.fr	BENCE L. et Meraux M.: La musique pour guérir
bch	BEUCHELT H.
bch1.de	BEUCHELT Hellmuth: Konstitutions- und Reaktionstypen in der Medizin u.s.w., Heidelberg: Haug [5th Ed.] (1977)
bch2	BEUCHELT H.: [Datisca cannabina.], A H Z. 216 ;156 (1971)
bci	BIANCHI Ivo: Contemporary homeopathic physician [Italia] (1948-)
bci1	BIANCHI Ivo: [Principles of homotoxicology], Baden-Baden: Aurelia - Verlag (1989)
bcj	BECKER Jürgen: Contemporary homeopath [Germany] (1945-)
bcj1	BECKER Jürgen: [Vipera], Links, Vol 4: nr. 2 pg 8 (1991)
bcj10	BECKER Jürgen: [Anacardium orientale]
bcj11	BECKER Jürgen: [Antimonium crudum]
bcj12	BECKER Jürgen: [Argentum metallicum]
bcj13	BECKER Jürgen: [Argentum nitricum]
bcj14	BECKER Jürgen: [Asarum europaeum]
bcj15	BECKER Jürgen: [Baryta carbonica]
bcj16	BECKER Jürgen: [Berberis vulgaris]
bcj17	BECKER Jürgen: [Calcarea fluorica]
bcj18	BECKER Jürgen: [Calcarea phosphorica]
bcj19	BECKER Jürgen: [Cannabis indica]
bcj2	BECKER Jürgen: [Ferrum phosphoricum. A Group Dream proving of Ferrum-phosphoricum.], Links, Vol 5: pg 17-19 (1992)
bcj20	BECKER Jürgen: [Carbo vegetabilis]
bcj21	BECKER Jürgen: [Carcinosin]
bcj22	BECKER Jürgen: [China officinalis]
bcj23	BECKER Jürgen: [Cuprum metallicum]
bcj24	BECKER Jürgen: [Drosera]
bcj25	BECKER Jürgen: [Dulcamara]
bcj26	BECKER Jürgen: [Ferrum metallicum]
bcj27	BECKER Jürgen: [Fluoricum acidum]
bcj28	BECKER Jürgen: [Formica Rufa]
bcj29	BECKER Jürgen: [Graphites]
bcj3	BECKER Jürgen: [Platinum metallicum.], Proc 35th LMHI Congr., Sussex UK pg 49-90 (1982)
bcj30	BECKER Jürgen: [Helleborus niger]
bcj31	BECKER Jürgen: [Hepar Sulphur]
bcj32	BECKER Jürgen: [Hypericum perforatum]
bcj33	BECKER Jürgen: [Kali phosphoricum]
bcj34	BECKER Jürgen: [Lac caninum]
bcj35	BECKER Jürgen: [Lilium tigrinum]
bcj36	BECKER Jürgen: [Magnesium carbonicum]
bcj37	BECKER Jürgen: [Magnesium muriaticum]
bcj38	BECKER Jürgen: [Mandragora officinarum]
bcj39	BECKER Jürgen: [Medorrhinum]
bcj4	BECKER Jürgen: [Aloe socotrina]
bcj40	BECKER Jürgen: [Muriaticum acidum]
bcj41	BECKER Jürgen: [Natrium carbonicum]
bcj42	BECKER Jürgen: [Niccolum]
bcj43	BECKER Jürgen: [Nitricum acidum]
bcj44	BECKER Jürgen: [Opium]
bcj45	BECKER Jürgen: [Petroleum]
bcj46	BECKER Jürgen: [Phytolacca]
bcj47	BECKER Jürgen: [Plumbum]
bcj48	BECKER Jürgen: [Stannum]
bcj49	BECKER Jürgen: [Succinum]
bcj5	BECKER Jürgen: [Astacus fluviatilis]
bcj50	BECKER Jürgen: [Tuberculinum Koch]
bcj51	BECKER Jürgen: [Veratrum album]
bcj52	BECKER Jürgen: [Zincum metallicum]
bcj53	BECKER Jürgen and SANKARAN Rajan: [Naja tripudians]
bcj54.de	BECKER Jürgen und SCHMELZER Wolfgand: Der raffinierte Zucker. Eine Homöopatische Arzneimittelprüfung, Kirchzarten (Germany): SunriseVerlag (1998)
bcj6	BECKER Jürgen: [Allium cepa]
bcj7	BECKER Jürgen: [Alumina]
bcj8	BECKER Jürgen: [Ambra Grisea]
bcj9	BECKER Jürgen: [Ammonium carbonicum]
bcn	BUCKEN Dany: Contemporary homeopathic physician [Bruxelles, Belgium] (1933-)
bcr	BIANCHINI Roberto: Contemporary homeopath [London, Great Britain] (1958-)
bcr1	BIANCHINI Roberto: [A case of Menopausal symptoms], Links, Vol 3: pg 26 (1994)
bcx	BOOCOCK Richard
bcx1	BOOCOCK Richard and SOUTH DOWN SCHOOL: [Proving of Mobile Phone Radiation] (1999)
bcx2	BOOCOCK Richard and SOUTH DOWN SCHOOL: [Proving of Chlamydia Trachomatis] (2000)
bd	BOYD Wm. Ernest: (1891-1955)
bda	BANDELIN Karin: Contemporary homeopathic physician [Germany]
bdc	BARDON Michel: Contemporary homeopathic physician [France]
bdg	BEDAYN Greg: (1952-)
bdg1	BEDAYN Greg: [Corvus Corax] (1998)
bdh	BODDE H. G.: Contemporary homeopathic physician [Netherlands]
bdj	BARNARD Julian
bdj1.es	BARNARD Julian: Obras Completas del doctor Bach....el hombre que descubrió los Remedios Florales., Barcelona (Spain): Editorial Océano Ibis, S.A. reprint: September 1998 (1998)
bdm	BANDOEL Maria Clara
bdm1.es	BANDOEL Maria Clara: Homeopatia Los Sintomas Mentales De Las Experimentaciones Puras Y Su Desarrollo Dinamico Vital - Tomo 1, Buenos Aires: Editorial Albatros (1991)

bdm2.es	BANDOEL Maria Clara: Homeopatia Los Sintomas Mentales De Las Experimentaciones Puras Y Su Desarrollo Dinamico Vital - Tomo 2
bdm3.es	BANDOEL Maria Clara: Homeopatia Los Sintomas Mentales De Las Experimentaciones Puras Y Su Desarrollo Dinamico Vital - Tomo 3
bdm4.es	BANDOEL Maria Clara: Fundamentos Filosoficos De La Clinica Homeopatica, Buenos Aires: Editorial Albatros (1990)
bdt	BALDOTA Sudhir: Contemporary homeopath [Bombay, India] (1955-)
bdt1	BALDOTA Sudhir: [The case of Princess Daisy], Links, Vol 1: pg 36 (1995)
bdt2	BALDOTA Sudhir: [Elegance - A case of eagle], Links, Vol 2: pg 83-86 (1999)
bdx	BOND Annette: Contemporary homeopath [England] (1956-)
bdx1	BOND Annette: [The homeopathic proving of Tungsten], Manchester: North West College of Homeopathy (1997)
bdy	BOYD H.
bdy1	BOYD H.: [Introduction to Homeopathic Medicine], England: Beaconsfield (1982)
be	BOYLE C. C.
be1	BOYLE C. C.: [Therapeutics of the Ear]
bea	BOLTE Angelika
bea1	BOLTE Angelika and Jörg Wichmann: [The Natural Relationship of Remedies] (1997)
bfj	BUFFUM J. H.
bfj1	BUFFUM J. H.: [Essentials of Diseases of Eye and Ear], New Delhi: Jain Publishers (1989)
bft	BRADFORD Thomas Lindsley: (1847-1918)
bft1	BRADFORD Thomas Lindsley: [Homoeopathic Bibliography of the United States], Philadelphia: Boericke & Tafel (Pennsylvania) (1892)
bft2	BRADFORD Thomas Lindsley: [The Life and Letters of Hahnemann], New Delhi: Jain Publishers
bft3	BRADFORD Thomas Lindsley: [Index of Homeopathic Provings], New Delhi: Jain Publishers
bfw	BREYFOGLE William LaMartine: (1845-1915)
bfw1	BREYFOGLE William LaMartine: [Epitome of Homeopathic Medicines] (1879)
bg	BOGER Cyrus Maxwell: (1861-1935)
bg1	BOGER Cyrus Maxwell: [Additions to Kent's Repertory], New Delhi: Jain Publishers (1932)
bg10	BOGER Cyrus Maxwell: [The Study of Materia Medica and Taking the case] (1961)
bg11	BOGER Cyrus Maxwell: [General Analysis (Card repertory)] (1926)
bg12.fr	BOGER Cyrus Maxwell: La Science et l'Art de Guérir et autres articles (1987)
bg2	BOGER Cyrus Maxwell: [Boenninghausens's Characteristics and Repertory], Bombay: Roy & Co. (1936)
bg2a	BOGER Cyrus Maxwell: Boenninghausens's Characteristics and Repertory (Original edition), Parkersburg: W.VA (1905)
bg3	BOGER Cyrus Maxwell: [Synoptic Key of the Materia Medica], New Delhi: Swaran [6th Ed.] (1931)
bg3a	BOGER Cyrus Maxwell: Synoptic Key of the Materia Medica. Repertory part (1928)
bg4	BOGER Cyrus Maxwell: [Times of the remedies and moon phases], New Delhi: Jain Publishers (1988)
bg5	BOGER Cyrus Maxwell: [Studies in the Philosophy of Healing], New Delhi: Jain Publishers [reprint: 2nd Ed.] (1915)
bg6	BOGER Cyrus Maxwell: [Bursa pastoris, Thlaspi], Hom Rec (1924)
bg7	BOGER Cyrus Maxwell: [Xanthoxylum], Med Adv, Vol XXXVIII nr. 5: pg 311 (1890)
bg8	BOGER Cyrus Maxwell: [Calcarea hypophosphorica, Odds and Ends], International Hahnemannian Association, Session 40-45: pg 7
bg9	BOGER Cyrus Maxwell: [Collected writings], London: Robert Bannan (1994)
bgc	BERGERET C.
bgc1	BERGERET C.: [Eschscholtzia californica.], Hom. Monatsbl. 97 ; 84 (1972)
bgg	BOGAERDS G. A.: Contemporary homeopath [Netherlands]
bgk	BERGK-LUCKA
bgk1	BERGK-LUCKA: [Proving of Marienbader kurbrunner], A H Zt, Vol 56: pg 117
bgr	BONGAARTS R.: Contemporary homeopath [Netherlands]
bgs	BURGESS-WEBSTER M.: (1890-)
bgs1	BURGESS-WEBSTER M.: [Medorrhinum], Hom Rec, Vol 47/15 (1932)
bgs2	BURGESS-WEBSTER M.: [Syphilinum], Hom Rec (1935)
bgs3	BURGESS-WEBSTER M.: [Psorinum], Hom Rec, Vol 51/4: pg 147 (1936)
bgt	BOURGARIT: (1916-)
bgt1.fr	BOURGARIT: Thérapeutique homéopathique du nouveau-né et du nourrison, Paris: Maloine (1987)
bgt2.fr	BOURGARIT: Thérapeutique homéopathique de l'enfant
bh	BACH Edward: English Homeopathic physician. Originator of the Bowel Nosodes and Bach Flowers. (1886-1936)
bha	BEHAM A.
bha1	BEHAM A.: [Harpagophytum procumbens.], A H Z. 216; 204 (1971)
bhb	BAEHR Bernhard: (1828-1884)
bhb1	BAEHR Bernhard: [The Science of Therapeutics, According to The Principles of Homoeopathy Vol. I], New York: Boericke & Tafel (1870)

bhb2	BAEHR Bernhard: [The Science of Therapeutics, According to The Principles of Homoeopathy Vol. II], New York: Boericke & Tafel (1870)
bhf	BONSCH Franz: Contemporary homeopathic physician [Germany] (1949-)
bhg	BRIGHAM G. N.
bhg1	BRIGHAM G. N.: [Catarrhal Diseases of the nasal and respiratory Organs], Calcutta: Haren and Brother (3th Ed.)
bhk	BIRCH K.: (1954-)
bhk1	BIRCH K. and ROCKWELL J.: [A Homeopahtic Proving of Sequoia sempervirens] (1994)
bhm	BOMHARDT Martin: (1960-)
bhm1	BOMHARDT Martin: [Materia Medica] (1995)
bhm1.de	BOMHARDT Martin: Symbolische Materia Medica, Germany: Verlag Homöopathie (1995)
bhm2	BOMHARDT Martin: [Opium] (1994)
bhm2.de	BOMHARDT Martin: Opium: Dokumentation der Arzneimittelprüfung in Berlin. (1994)
bj	BHANJA K. C.: (1894-)
bj1	BHANJA K. C.: [Constitutional drug pictures]
bj2	BHANJA K. C.: [Masterkey to Homoeopathic Materia Medica], Darjeeling (1947)
bjj	BERJEAU Jean Philibert H.: (1809-1891)
bjj1	BERJEAU J. P. H. and FROST J. H. P.: [The Homeopathic Treatment of Syphilis, Gonorrhea, etc.], New Dehli: Jain (1870)
bk	BLACK G.
bk1	BLACK G.: [Viscum Album, the common Mistletoe]
bka	BICKLEY Antony: Contemporary homeopath [United Kingdom] (1947-)
bka1	BICKLEY Antony: [The bowel nosodes.], American Homoeopath (2002)
bke	BOEKE E. W.
bkh	BUCK H.: (1825-)
bkh1	BUCK H.: [The Outline of Materia Medica and clinical Dictionary], New delhi: Jain Publishers (1987)
bkl	BOUKO-LEVY: (1947-)
bkl1	BOUKO-LEVY: [Homeopathic and Drainage Repertory] (1992)
bkl2.fr	BOUKO-LEVY: Guide d' Homéopathie (1990)
bl	BORLAND Douglas M.: (1885-1960)
bl1	BORLAND Douglas M.: [Children Types], London: British Homeopathic Association (1948)
bl1.fr	BORLAND Douglas M.: Les Types d'Enfants
bl2	BORLAND Douglas M.: [The Treatment of certain Heart Conditions by Homeopathy], Br Hom J, Vol 38/3 (1948)
bl3	BORLAND Douglas M.: [Influenzas]
bl4	BORLAND Douglas M.: [Pneumonias], New Delhi: Jain Publishers (1987)
bl5	BORLAND Douglas M.: [Homeopathy for mother and infant], London, British Homoeopathic Association (1950)
bl6	BORLAND Douglas M.: [Digestive Drugs] (1940)
bl7	BORLAND Douglas M.: [Homeopathy in Practice], Beaconsfield (England): Beaconsfield Publ. (1982)
bl8	BORLAND Douglas M.: [Some Emergencies of General Practice], Bombay: The homeopathic Medical Publishers [1st Ed.] (1970)
bl9	BORLAND Douglas M: [Blood poisoning]
bla	BELL James Bachelder: (1818-1914)
bla1	BELL James B.: [The homeopathic therapeutics of diarrhea [3rd Ed.]], Philadelphia: Boericke & Tafel (1888)
blc	BALLANCE Sue: Contemporary homeopath [New Zealand] (1948-)
blc1	BALLANCE Sue: [Proving of Salix alba. Linking trees project.], Links, Vol 12: pg 172-173 (1999)
blf	BRADLEY F. J.
blf1	BRADLEY F. J.: [Cancer Latency Prevention and Cure through Miasmatics], New Delhi: Jain Publishers (1988)
blm	BAÑUELOS MARINO Rodrigo
blm1.es	BAÑUELOS MARINO Rodrigo: Cuestionario Del Kent, New Delhi: Jain Publishers (1994)
blp	BAILEY Philip M.: Contemporary homeopathic physician [Australia]
blp1	BAILEY Philip M.: [Homeopathic Psychology], Berkeley: North Atlantic Books (1995)
blp2	BAILEY Philip M.: [Personality Profiles of the Major]
blp3	BAILEY Philip M.: [Constitutional Remedies]
blr	BANDLISH Renu: Contemporary homeopath (India, Student of P. Rastogi.]
blr1	BANDLISH Renu: [Students Guido to Materia Medica], New Delhi: Jain Publishers (1996)
bls	BELLOWS Howard Perry: (1852-)
bly	BLACKLEY J. C.
bmf	BODMAN Frank
bmf1	BODMAN Frank: [Insights into Homeopathy], England: Beaconsfield Publishers (1990)
bmf2	BODMAN Frank: [Grass Therapy.], Homeopathy, Vol 25: pg 8 (1975)
bmh1	= bhm1 = BOMHARDT Martin: [Materia Medica]
bmz	BRONFMAN Zalman J.
bmz1.es	BRONFMAN Zalman J.: El dinero en la materia médica homeopática, Buenos Aires: Editorial Club de Estudio (1999)
bmz2.es	BRONFMAN Zalman J.: El Malhumor de los Homeopatas., Buenos Aires: Editorial Albatros (1992)
bmz3.es	BRONFMAN Zalman J.: Diálogos con un Homeópata, Buenos Aires: Editorial Club de Estudio (1998)
bmz4.es	BRONFMAN Zalman J.: Ilusiones, Sueños y Delirios en homeopatia, Buenos Aires: Editorial Club de Estudio (1999)
bmz5.es	BRONFMAN Zalman J.: La Identidad y el Doble en la Materia Médica Homeopática, Buenos Aires: Editorial Club de Estudio (1995)
bn	BURNETT James Compton: (1840-1901)

bn1	BURNETT James C.: [Enlarged tonsils cured by medicine], New Delhi: Jain Publishers (1972)
bn10	BURNETT James C.: [Natrum muriaticum], London: Gould (1880)
bn11	BURNETT James C.: [Tumours of the breast], London: Epps (1888)
bn12	BURNETT James C.: [Gout and its cure], London: Epps (1895)
bn13	BURNETT James C.: [On neuralgia [2nd Ed.]], London: Epps (1894)
bn14	BURNETT James C.: [Fifty Reasons for being a homeopath]
bn14.fr	BURNETT James C.: Les cinquante Raisons d'être Homéopathe, Maisonneuve (Ste Ruffine) (1969)
bn15	BURNETT James C.: [Organ Diseases of Women] (1896)
bn16	BURNETT James C.: [Vaccinosis] (1960)
bn17	BURNETT James C.: [Fevers and Blood Poisonings], Calcutta: Srih. Dey of A.P. Homeopathic Library [2nd Ed.] (1968)
bn18	BURNETT James C.: [The New Cure of Consumption by its Own Virus [reprint 4th Ed.]], New Delhi: Jain Publishers (1898)
bn19	BURNETT James C.: [Best of Burnett.], New Delhi: H.L. Chitkara Ed. (1992)
bn2	BURNETT James C.: [Diseases of the spleen], London: Epps (1887)
bn20	BURNETT James C.: [Gold as a remedy in Disease notable in some Forms of Organic Heart Disease, Angina Pectoris, Melancholy... and as an Antidote to the Effects of Mercury]
bn21	BURNETT James C.: [On Fistula and its Radical Cure by Medicines]
bn22	BURNETT James C.: [The change of Life in Women and the Ills and Ailings Incident Thereto] (1953)
bn23	BURNETT James C.: [Valvular Disease of the Heart from a New Standpoint]
bn3	BURNETT James C.: [Delicate, backward, puny and stunty children], London: Hom. Publ. (1895)
bn4	BURNETT James C.: [The diseases of the liver [2nd Ed.]], Philadelphia: Boericke & Tafel (1895)
bn5	BURNETT James C.: [Diseases of the skin [3th Ed.]], New Delhi: Jain Publishers (1997)
bn6	BURNETT James C.: [Curability of tumours by medicines], London: Hom. Publ. (1893)
bn7	BURNETT James C.: [Curability of cataract], London: Hom. Publ. (1880)
bn8	BURNETT James C.: [Ringworm], London: Hom. Publ. (1892)
bn9	BURNETT James C.: [Diseases of the veins], London: Epps (1894)
bna	BRAUN Artur
bna1.de	BRAUN Artur: Methodik der Homootherapie, Regensburg: Johannes Sonntag (1975)
bnc	BERNASOCCHI Michele: Homeopathic doctor
bnd	BROWN Donald: (1952-)
bnd1	BROWN Donald and LANGE Andrew: [Candida Parapsilosis] (1992)
bne	BRAUN Eva Maria: Contemporary homeopath [Germany]
bnf	BRIONES Flavio Silva: Veterinary [Chili] (1950-)
bnf1.es	BRIONES Flavio Silva: Manual de medicina veterinaria homeopática [1st Ed.], Santiago de Chile: Editorial Universitaria. (1990)
bnf1a.es	BRIONES Flavio Silva: Manual de medicina veterinaria homeopática (2nd E.), México: Propulsora de Homeopatía (1997)
bnf2.es	BRIONES Flavio Silva: Nomenclatura y sinonimia Homeopática
bnf3.es	BRIONES Flavio Silva: Sintomas Claves de los Principales Medicamentos de la Materia Medica Homeopática
bng	BEHNISCH Gotthard: Contemporary homeopathic physician [Detmold, Germany]. Translator of "Medizin der Zukunft" of George Vithoulkas (1951-)
bnh	BERNARD Henri: (1895-1980)
bnh1	BERNHARD Henri: [The Homeopathic Treatment of Constipation], New Delhi: Jain Publishers (1989)
bni	BRUNINI
bni1	BRUNINI: [Materia Medica Homeopatica] (1992)
bni1.pt	BRUNINI: Materia Medica Homeopathica [2nd. Ed.], São Paulo: Mythos engenharia de mercado ltda (1992)
bni2.pt	BRUNINI: A criança de... 61 remédios Homeopaticos, São Paulo: Mythos engenharia de mercado ltda (1993)
bni3.pt	BRUNINI: Homeopatia Principos doutrina Framacia ia Ibehe
bnj	BANERJEE Prosad: (1945-)
bnj1	BANERJEE Prosad: [Materia medica of Indian drugs], West Bengal (1992)
bnj2	BANERJEE Prosad: [Dysentery]
bnj3	BANERJEE Prosad: [Sexual disease and its treatment]
bnj4	BANERJEE Prosad: [Coronary thrombosis]
bnj5	BANERJEE Prosad: [Chronic disease: its causes and cure], New Dehli: Jain (1985)
bnk	BANERJEE N. K.: (1900-)
bnk1	BANERJEE N. K.: [Realistic Materia Medica with therapeutics repertory], Calcutta: Salzer
bnk2	BANERJEE N. K.: [Blood Pressure its etiology and treatment], New Dehli: Jain (1960)
bnk2.es	BANERJEE N. K.: Tensión arterial.
bnl	BAGNULO
bnl1.it	BAGNULO: Note di Dinamica Miasmatica e Keynotes dei principali Rimedi Omeopatici
bnm	BONNET M. S.: Contemporary homeopath [England] (1944-)
bnm1	BONNET M. S.: [The Loxosceles spider], B H J: Vol 85: pg 205-213 (1996)
bnm10	BONNET M. S.: [The toxicology of Loxosceles reclusa [The brown recluse spider]], N Eng J H, Vol 7 nr 1: pg 26-43 (1998)

bnm11	BONNET M. S.: [The toxicology of Trachinus vipera: The lesser weeverfish], B H J: Vol 89: pg 84-88
bnm12	BONNET M. S.: [The toxicology of loxosceles laeta: the South American Brown Spider.], Boletín Mexicano de Homeopatía Vol 32: pg 9-14 (1999)
bnm13	BONNET M. S.: [The toxicology of the Buthotus tamulus - the Indian red scorpion. 2000], Links, Vol 13 pg 112-118 (2000)
bnm14	BONNET M. S.: [The toxicology of Heloderma suspectum: the Gila Monster], Br Hom J, Vol 89: pg 198-204 (2000)
bnm15	BONNET M. S. and BASSON P.W.: [The toxicology of Amanita phalloides], Homeopathy, Vol 91 pg 249-254 (2002)
bnm16	BONNET M. S.: [The toxicology of Solenopsis invicta : the imported red fire ant.], Boletín Mexicano de Homeopatía Vol 33: pg 17-24, (2000)
bnm2	BONNET M. S.: [The Toxicology of Androctonus scorpion], B H J: to be published (1997)
bnm3	BONNET M. S.: [The Toxicology of the Atrax Robustus spider], B H J: to be published (1997)
bnm4	BONNET M. S.: [The toxicology of the Chironex fleckeri jelly fish: the Australian sea wasp.], Br H J, Vol 88: pg 62-68 (1999)
bnm5	BONNET M. S.: [The toxicology of the Latrodectus hasselti spider. The Australian red back spider.], Br H J, Vol 88: pg 2-6 (1999)
bnm6	BONNET M. S.: [The toxicology of Latrodectus mactans. The black widow spider.], Links, Vol 11: nr 3 pg 161-168 (1998)
bnm7	BONNET M. S.: [The toxicology of Physalia physalis: the Portuguese Man-Of-war.], J Am Inst H, Vol 92 nr 1: pg 23-32 (1999)
bnm8	BONNET M. S.: [Toxicology of Ixodes ricinus, the European tick.], Br H J, Vol 87: pg 22-27 (1998)
bnm9	BONNET M. S.: [Octopus maculosa], Br Hom J, Vol 88: pg166-171 (1999)
bnn	BLINN J. F.
bnr	BUCHNER Joseph Benedict
bns	BARNI Stefano: Contemporary homeopathic physician [Italy]
bnt	BINET: (1911-1985)
bnt1.fr	BINET: Thérapeutique Homéopathique
bnt2.fr	BINET: L'homéopathie pratique
bnu	BANERJEA Subrata Kumar: Contemporary homeopath [Calcutta, India] (1957-)
bnu1	BANERJEA Subrata Kumar: [Thyroidinum], Links, Vol 2: pg 15-17 (1993)
bnu10	BANERJEA Subrata Kumar: [Clinical and Comparative Materia Medica. Schematic Comparison of Remedies.]
bnu11	BANERJEA Subrata Kumar: [Synoptic Memorizer of Materia Medica], New Delhi: Jain Publishers (1980)
bnu2	BANERJEA Subrata Kumar: [Materia Medica made easy] (1993)
bnu3	BANERJEA Subrata Kumar: [Materia Medica of a few Rare Nosodes] (1994)
bnu4	BANERJEA Subrata Kumar: [Fifty homeopathic Indian Drugs]
bnu5	BANERJEA Subrata Kumar: [Essential Guide to Pharmacy]
bnu6	BANERJEA Subrata Kumar: [Essential Guide to Materia Medica]
bnu7	BANERJEA Subrata Kumar: [Miasmatic Diagnosis]
bnu8	BANERJEA Subrata Kumar: [Brain Tumor in Homeopathy]
bnu9	BANERJEA Subrata Kumar: [Homeopathy Around the World]
bnx	BONNEROT
bnx1	BONNEROT and FORTIER-BERNOVILLE: [Ulcer of the Stomach and Duodenum. Translated by Rajkumar Mukerji from the Original French], New Delhi: Jain Publishers (1988)
bnx1.es	BONNEROT y FORTIER-BERNOVILLE: Ulcera del Estómago y del Duodeno. Translated by Gilberto Quintero Ramírez, New Delhi: Jain Publishers
br	BOERICKE William: American homeopathic physician. Highly reputated clinician. (1849-1929)
br1	BOERICKE William: [Pocket Manual of Homeopathic Materia Medica], New Dehli: Jain (1927)
br1.de	BOERICKE William: Handbuch der Homöopathischen Materia Medica, Heidelberg (Germany): Karl F. Haug Verlag GmbH & C° (1996)
br1.es	BOERICKE William: Manuel de bolsillo de Materia Médica Homeopática Comprende. Translated by Javier Vicite Medrano, New Delhi: Jain Publishers
br1.fr	BOERICKE William: Matière Médicale Homéopathique
br1.it	BOERICKE William: Materia Medica
br1.nl	BOERICKE William: Materia Medica
br1.pt	BOERICKE William: Materia Medica
br1a.de	BOERICKE William: Materia Medica und Repertorium. Homöopatische Mittel un ihre Wirkungen., Leer: Verlag Grundlagen un Praxis (1986)
br2	BOERICKE William: [A Compend of the Principles of Homoeopathy], Lahore: Homoeopathic Stores and Hospital (1874)
br3	BOERICKE William and DEWEY Willis A.: [The Twelve Tissue Remedies of Schuessler], Philadelphia: Boericke & Tafel [6th Ed.] (1914)
br4	BOERICKE William: [Materia Medica - Relationships of remedies]
br5.nl	BOERICKE William en PHATAK S.R.: De complete Materia Medica
br6	BOERICKE William: [The Development of Homoeopathy. Presented by Julian Winston.] (1880)
bra	BERRIDGE Edward W.: (1878-1929)

bra1	BERRIDGE Edward W.: [Complete Repertory to the Homeopathic Materia Medica on diseases of the Eyes.[2nd Ed.]], London: Heath (1873)
bra2	BERRIDGE Edward W.: [Repertory Corrections], International Hahnemannian Association (1919)
bra3	BERRIDGE Edward W.: [= bra1 = Complete Repertory on the diseases of Eyes (old abbr.)] (1994)
bra4	BERRIDGE Edward W.: [A proving of Medorrhinum. Presented by Julian Winston.]
brb	BURRETT C. A.: (1890-)
brc	BOERICKE Charles: American homeopathic physician, son of William Boericke, brother of Garth Boericke, he taught at Hahnemann hospital
brd	BARANDIARAN Anselmo: Contemporary homeopathic physician [Spain]
brg	BOERICKE Garth Wilkinson: Homeopathic physician in Philadelphia [son of William Boericke], studied at Hahnemann Hospital (1893-1968)
brj	BAUR Jacques: Contemporary homeopathic physician [France] (1920-2003)
brj1.fr	BAUR Jacques: Avatars et aventures du remède
brj2.fr	BAUR Jacques: La matière médicale homéopathique
brl	BRUK Larry: Veterinary
brm	BÄR Marc: [Switzerland] (1955-)
bro	BOERICKE Oscar Eugene: American homeopathic physician. (1873)
bro1	BOERICKE Oscar Eugene: ["Repertory" in "Pocket Manual of Homeopathic Materia Medica" [by Boericke William]], New-York: Boericke & Runyon (1927)
brr	BENRUBI Raphael: Contemporary homeopathic physician [France]
brw	BREWSTER O'REILLY Wenda
brw1	BREWSTER O'REILLY Wenda: [= h3a = Organon of the Medical Art by Dr. Samuel Hahnemann. Annotated by Wenda Breweter O'Reilly], Edited by Wenda Breweter O'Reilly
brx	BARROS - ST-PASTEUR José
brx1.es	BARROS - ST-PASTEUR José: Homeopatía Medicina del terreno., Caracas: Universidad Central de Venezuela, Ediciones de la Biblioteca (1977)
br-xyz	BR1 or BRO1
bs	BAAS Cees: Contemporary homeopath [Netherlands] (1956-)
bsa	BRIGGS Derek: Contemporary homeopath [New Zealand] (1931-)
bsa1	BRIGGS Derek: [Gelsemium, The Heroic Coward], Links, Vol 1: pg 13-14 (1994)
bsa2	BRIGGS Derek: [Coriaria Ruscifolia = tutu]
bsa3	BRIGGS Derek: [Ruapehu lava]
bsb	BLOESY Bernhard
bse	BROUSSALIAN Edouard: (1962-)
bsi	BAKSHI Jatinder P.S.
bsi1	BAKSHI Jatinder P.S.: [Phoenix repertory]
bsj	BLASIG-JÄGER Thomas
bsj1.de	BLASIG-JÄGER Thomas: Arzneimittelbeziehungen, Greifenberg (Germany): Hahnemann Institut - Privatinstitut für homöopatische Dokumntation Gmbh (1996)
bsk	BAKSHI Kirpal S.
bsk1	BAKSHI Kirpal S.: [Homeopathic remedies in verse], New Dehli: Jain (1991)
bsm	BRUNSON Marc: (1950-)
bsn	BOSE N.C.
bsn1	BOSE N.C.: [SKIN], Hom Herald, Vol III nr 8 (1940)
bsn2	BOSE N.C.: [Index Indicators SKIN], Hom Herald, Vol IV nr 4 (1941)
bsn3	BOSE N.C.: [Index Indicators], Hom Herald, Vol IV nr 5 (1941)
bsn4	BOSE N.C.: [Index Indicators], Hom Herald, Vol V nr 7 (1942)
bsn5	BOSE N.C.: [Malaria in India], Hom Herald, Vol VIII nr 2 (1947)
bsr	BENSON A. REUEL
bsr1	BENSON A. REUEL: [Homeopathic Nursery Manual] (1993)
bss	BOSE Sachindra K.
bss1	BOSE Sachindra K.: [Synopsis of Homeopathic Materia Medica], Calcutta: Sachindra Kumar Bose (1921)
bt	BARTHEL Horst: Contemporary homeopathic physician [Germany]. Creator of the "Synthetic Repertory" [with Dr. Klunker] (1934-)
bt1.de	BARTHEL Horst: Charakteristika Homöopathischer Azneimittel, Berg a. Starnberger See: O Verl. (1984)
bt2	BARTHEL Horst: [Synthetic Repertory: Psychic symptoms. Vol 1], New Delhi: Jain Publishers (1991)
bt3	BARTHEL Horst: [Synthetic Repertory: General symptoms. Vol 2], New Delhi: Jain Publishers (1991)
bta	BRYANT A. T.
bta1	BRYANT A. T.: [Zulu medicine and Medicine-men], Cape Town: C. Struik (1966)
btb	BOTTI Maurizio: Contemporary homeopathic physician [Italy]
btd	BLET Dominique: Contemporary homeopathic physician [France]
bth	BHATTACHARYYA H. CH.
bth1	BHATTACHARYYA H. CH.: [The Homeopathic Family Practice], Calcutta: Bhattacharyya (13th Ed.)
btj	BRYANT J.: (1926-)
btj1	BRYANT J.: [A pocket manual or Repertory of Homeopathy]
btm	BHATTACHARYYA M.
btm1	BHATTACHARYYA M. et al.: [Manual of Materia Medica [with Allen's Clinicals] 2 Vols.], Calcutta: Bhattacharyya
btr	BÖTTCHER - HAASE C.

btr1 BÖTTCHER - HAASE C.: [Croton tiglium]

btr2 BÖTTCHER - HAASE C. and LIDO H. and STUBLER M.: [Luffa operculata], Br H J (1988)

bts BHATT Smruti: Contemporary homeopath [Bombay, India]

bts1 BHATT Smruti: [A case of Eczema], Links, Vol 3: pg 29 (1993)

btv BHATIA V.R.

btv1 BHATIA V.R.: [Influenza and Its Homoeopathic Treatment] (1994)

btw BURT William H.: (1836-1897)

btw1 BURT William H.: [Characteristic Materia Medica], New York/Philadelphia [2nd Ed.] (1873)

btw2 BURT William H.: [Physiological Materia Medica], Chicago [3th Ed.] (1883)

btx BARTHEL Michael

btx1.de BARTHEL Michael: Des kleine Buch der Arzneimittel-Beziehungen (1985)

btx2 BARTHEL Michael, GEISSLER J. and QUAK T.: [T. Cymbopogon citratus]

bty BHATTACHARYA Benoytosh

bty1 BHATTACHARYA Benoytosh: [Tridosha and Homeopathy]

bv BOVINA Giuseppina: Contemporary homeopathic physician [Italy]

bvl BARVALIA Praful M.: Contemporary homeopath [Bombay, India]

bvl1 BARVALIA Praful M.: [A case of depression Travail of "The Outcast"], Links, Vol 2: pg 30-31 (1993)

bw BECKWITH E. C.

bwa BLACKWOOD Alexander L.: (1862-1924)

bwa1 BLACKWOOD Alexander L.: [Diseases of the kidneys and nerves] (1913)

bwa2 BLACKWOOD Alexander L.: [Diseases of the heart] (1901)

bwa3 BLACKWOOD Alexander L.: [Manual of Materia Medica, therapeutics and Pharmacology with Clinical Index] (1906)

bwa4 BLACKWOOD Alexander L.: [The food tract: its ailments and disease of the peritoneum.], Philadelphia: Boericke & Tafel (1909)

bwa5 BLACKWOOD Alexander L.: [Diseases of the Liver, Pancreas and Ductless Glands] (1907)

bwg BIDWELL Glen I.

bwg1 BIDWELL Glen I.: [How to Use the Repertory with a Practical Analysis of forty Homoeopathic Remedies], Calcutta: N.K. Banerjee (1915)

bwg1.es BIDWELL Glen I.: Como manejar el repertorio., New Delhi: Jain Publishers

b-xyz. Boenninghausen's remedies between brackets

byg BAYR G.

byg1 BAYR G.: [Adlumia fungosa.], A H Z. 221 (1976) 45-59 / A H Z. 224 (1979)

c CLARKE John Henry: English homeopathic physician. Published many interesting books. (1853-1931)

c1 CLARKE John H.: [Dictionary of Practical Materia Medica (Vol. 1-3)], London: The Homeopathic Publ. (1904)

c1.de CLARKE John H.: "Der Neue Clarke" Ein Enzyklopädie für den homöopathische Praktiker, Bielefeld (Germany): Stefanovic: Verlag für homöopathische Literatur (1990)

c1.es CLARKE John H.: Diccionario de Materia Médica Práctica

c1.fr Clarke John H.: Dictionnaire de Matière Médicale

c1.pt CLARKE John H.: Materia Medica

c10 CLARKE John H.: [Therapeutics of the serpent poisons], London: Hom. Publ. (1893)

c11 CLARKE John H.: [Radium as an internal remedy] (1908)

c12 CLARKE John H.: [The therapeutics of cancer]

c13 CLARKE John H.: [Cholera, Diarrhoea and dysentery] (1893)

c14 CLARKE John H.: [Non Surgical Treatment of Diseases of the Glands and Bones.], New Delhi: Jain Publishers (reprint) (1986)

c15 CLARKE John H.: [Antimonium natrum lacticum], Hom Rec (1929)

c16 CLARKE John H.: [Bird's Eye view - A Lecture on Organon of Medicine], New Delhi: Jain Publishers (1987)

c17 CLARKE John H.: [Constitutional Medicine with especial reference to the three constitutions of Von Grauvogl]

c18 = lej2 = CLARKE John H. (old abb): [Cough and Expectoration]

c19 CLARKE John H.: [A Dictionnary of Domestic Medicine with a Special Section on Diseases of Infants.]

c1a.es CLARKE John H.: Sintomas mentales., Buenos Aires: Editorial Albatros (1991)

c2 CLARKE John H.: [A Clinical Repertory to the Dictionary of Materia Medica], London: Hom. Publ. (1904)

c20 CLARKE John H.: [Gunpowder as a War remedy]

c21 CLARKE John H.: [Haemorrhoids and Habitual Constipation: their Constitutional Cure- with Chapters on fissure and fistula] (1996)

c22 CLARKE John H.: [Homeopathy explained]

c3 CLARKE John H.: [Whooping cough cured with coqueluchin], New Delhi: Jain Publishers (1908)

c4 CLARKE John H.: [Diseases of the heart and arteries], London: Gould (1895)

c5 CLARKE John H.: [Catarrh, colds and influenzas.] (1899)

c6 CLARKE John H.: [The cure of tumours by medicines], London: Epps (1908)

c7 CLARKE John H.: [Grand characteristics of Materia medica] (1931)

c8 CLARKE John H.: [The prescriber [6th Ed.]] (1900)

c8.it CLARKE John H.: Omeopatia facile: Manuele pratico di prescizione

c9 CLARKE John H.: [Indigestion - its causes and cure] (1928)
cb CLERBAUX
cba CAMPBELL A.C.H.
cba1 CAMPBELL A.C.H.: [Moschus], Br H J (1981)
cbc CHAMBREAU Christina: (1950-)
cbd CHHABRA Divya
cbd1 CHHABRA Divya: [Magnesia sulphate]
cbd2 CHHABRA Divya: [Lac felinum]
cbd3 CHHABRA Divya: [Lac defloratum]
cbl CAMBELL D.M.
cbl1 CAMBELL D.M.: [Radium bromatum] (1993)
cbm CUESTA BRIAND Marie-Joëlle
cbp CALLEBAUT Peter
cbx CAMPBELL Alice B.
cbx1 CAMPBELL Alice B.: [Platina], Medical Adance (1902)
ccn CHURCHILL Nick
ccp CROCKER Pamela: Contemporary homeopath [Concord, USA]
ccp1 CROCKER Pamela: [Asthma in a child], N Eng. J H, Vol 1 nr 1: pg 9-10 (1992)
ccrh1 Central Council for research in Homoeopathy, New Delhi: [A proving of Cassia Sophera] (1987)
cd CANDEGABE Eugenio F.: (1934-)
cd1 CANDEGABE Eugenio F.: [Comparative Materia Medica] (1997)
cd1.es CANDEGABE Eugenio F.: Materia Medica Comparada (1983)
cda CHOUDHURI N. M.: (1858-)
cda1 CHOUDHURI N. M.: [A Study on Materia Medica and Repertory], New Delhi: Jain Publishers (1929)
cda2 CHOUDHURI N. M.: [Hepar sulphuris], Hom Rec, Vol X!!! nr. 9: pg 396 (1898)
cda3 CHOUDHURI N. M.: [Homoeopathic cases from India], Hom Rec, Vol XIII nr. 9: pg 396 (1898)
cdd CHAND Diwan Harish: Contemporary homeopathic physician [India]. Vice President for India at the LIGA. (1934-)
cdd1 CHAND Diwan Harish: [Peptic Ulcer [reprint]], New Delhi: National Homoeopathic Pharmacy (1982)
cdd2 CHAND Diwan Harish: [Follow up of the case [reprint]], New Delhi: National Homoeopathic Pharmacy (1983)
cdd3 CHAND Diwan Harish: [A Fantasy in materia medica [reprint]], New Delhi: National Homoeopathic Pharmacy (1981)
cdd4 CHAND Diwan Harish: [Homoeopathy in geriatrics], New Delhi: National Homoeopathic Pharmacy (1991)
cdd5 CHAND Diwan Harish: [Short biography of Dr. D.H. Chand.], New Colony (1962)
cdd6 CHAND Diwan Harish and SCHMIDT P.: [Kent's final General Repertory of the homeopatic Materia Medica], New Delhi: National Homeopathic Pharmacy(2nd Ed.) (1982)
cdd7 CHAND Diwan Harish: [A proving of cassia sophera], 1986, 35th Liga Medica Hom. Int. congress, 1982 (1982)
cdd8 CHAND Diwan Harish: [Microdoses, Megaresults. Clincial Cases], New Delhi: National Homoepathic Pharamcy (1995)
cdh CHOUDHURY Harimohon: (1940-)
cdh1 CHOUDHURY Harimohon: [Indications of Miasms], New Delhi: Jain Publishers (1988)
cdh2 CHOUDHURY Harimohon: [50 Millesimal Potency in Theory and Practice] (1990)
cdl CASTAÑEDA Luis Zepeda
cdl1.es CASTAÑEDA Luis Zepeda: Clinica homeopatica, Guadalajara: Ediciones de Homeopatía de Guadalajara (1986)
cdl2.es CASTAÑEDA Luis Zepeda: Diccionario Médico Homeopatico Ilustrado, México: CASTAÑEDA Luis Zepeda (1996)
cdl3.es CASTAÑEDA Luis Zepeda: La Homeopatia, México: Edamex (1990)
cdl4.es CASTAÑEDA Luis Zepeda: Los Antecedentes de la Homeopatia, México: CASTAÑEDA Luis Zepeda (1992)
cdl5.es CASTAÑEDA Luis Zepeda: Nueva Farmacopea Homeopatica, México: CASTAÑEDA Luis Zepeda (2000)
cdl6.es CASTAÑEDA Luis Zepeda: Samuel Hahneman - El Triunfo Sobre La Adversidad, CASTAÑEDA Luis Zepeda (1992)
cdm CANDEGABE Marcelo E.
cdm1.es CANDEGABE Marcelo E. y CARRARA Hugo C.: Aproximacion al metodo practico y preciso de la Homeopatia Pura - Casos Clinicos., Vicente López (Argentina): Editorial Lalaye (1997)
cdm2.es CANDEGABE Marcelo E.: Dialogos con Tomas Pablo Paschero: Maestro de la Homeopatía Argentina, Vicente López (Argentina): Editorial Lalaye (1997)
cdm3.es CANDEGABE Marcelo E.: Escritos sobre Homeopatía, Buenos aires: Club de Estudio (1996)
cdm4.es CANDEGABE Marcelo E.: Bases de la doctrina Médico Homeopática
cdv CHAND Diwan Vijay: Contemporary homeopathic physician [India]
cdx CHOUDHURY A.W.K.
cdx1 CHOUDHURY A.W.K.: [A Case Treated With Nux Vom., Stopping the Paroxysm With the First Dose], Homoeopathic Recorder, Vol 14, nr 7 (1899)
cdx2 CHOUDHURY A.W.K.: [Natrum muriaticum], Homoeopathic Recorder, Vol 15, nr 2 (1900)
ce CHARGE A.
ce1.fr CHARGE A.: Traitement homéopathique des organes de la respiration, Paris: L.H.F.
cea CASE Erastus Ely: (1847-1918)
cea1 CASE Erastus Ely: [Some Clinical experiences of Erastus E. Case.], Greenville: Van Hoy Publishers (1916)

cea2 CASE Erastus Ely: [Magnetis polus australis], International Hahnemannian Association Proceedings, Session (1917)
cec CHASE and CULLES
cec1 CHASE: [Proving of Myricin], Trans. Mass Hom. Med. Soc. 1861-1866 (1861)
cen CASTRO ENGLER NASCIMENTO Iracema
ces CHASE Sandra M.: Contemporary homeopath [Fairfax, USA]
ces1 CHASE Sandra M.: [Bufo: The Toad - its Materia Medica], Links, Vol 3: pg 20-24 (1993)
ch COUCH A. S.
chr CHAUHAN R.K.
chr1 CHAUHAN R.K.: [Expressive drug pictures of homoeopathic materia medica [Vol. 1]], New Delhi: Jain Publishers (1999)
chr2 CHAUHAN R.K.: [Expressive drug pictures of homoeopathic materia medica [Vol. 2]] (1990)
cji CHATTERJI A.N.
cji1 CHATTERJI A.N.: [Three in One] (1990)
ck CLARK George Hardy: (1860-)
ck1 CLARK George Hardy: [Homeopathic treatment of asthenopia (weak eye sight)], Jain Publishers (1993)
ck2 CLARK George Hardy: [The ABC manual of materia medica and therapeutics] (1901)
cka CLARKE A. Gladstone: (1885-)
cka1 CLARKE A. Gladstone: [Decachords] (1925)
cka1.de CLARKE A. Gladstone: Decacords
cka1.es CLARKE A. Gladstone: Decacordios. Una guía Concisa a la Materia Medica Homeopática.
ckh CHITKARA H. L.: Contemporary homeopathic physician [New Dehli, India] (1937-)
ckh1 CHITKARA H. L.: [Update Addition to Repertory of Mind], New Dehli: Jain (1995)
ckh2 CHITKARA H. L.: [New Comprehensive Materia Medica of Mind] (1990)
ckh3 CHITKARA H. L.: [Quick Reference Guide to Repertory of Mind symptoms]
ckh4 CHITKARA H. L.: [New Updated Materia Medica of Mind]
ckh5 CHITKARA H. L.: [Relationship of Remedies]
ckp CHIPKIN Peggy: Contemporary homeopath [Albany, USA]
ckp1 CHIPKIN Peggy: [Vulvitis in a Four Year Old Girl], N Eng. J H, Vol 4 nr 4: pg 33-35 (1995)
cks CLARKE Savitri: Contemporary homeopath [Cambridge, USA]
cks1 CLARKE Savitri: [Aversion to Nursing in an Infant], N Eng. J H, Vol 1 nr 1: pg 7 (1992)
cky CHAKRAVARTY B.N.: (1937-)
cky1 CHAKRAVARTY B.N.: [A short proving of S.E.Ray [Solar eclipse]], 35th Liga Medica Hom. Int. congress (1982)
clc COULON Claude
cld COLLINS Deborah: Contemporary homeopath (1953-)
cld1 COLLINS Deborah: [Plumbum in practice.], Links, Vol 6: nr. 3 (1993)
cls CLOSE Stuart M.: (1860-1929)
cls1 CLOSE Stuart M.: [The Genius of Homeopathy. Lectures and Essays on Homeopathic Philosophy]
cmc CREMONINI Cesar: Contemporary homeopathic physician [Argentina]
cn CENERELLI Carlo: Contemporary homeopathic physician [Italy]
cna CHIANESE Francesco: Contemporary homeopathic physician [Italy]
cnc CONANT C. M.
cnc1 CONANT C. M.: [An obstetric Mentor], New Delhi: Jain Publishers
cnj O' CONNOR Joseph T.
cnj1 O' CONNOR Joseph T.: [The American Homoeopathic Pharmacopoeia [2nd Ed.]], New York: Boericke & Tafel (1883)
cnm CANNELL Michael: Contemporary homeopathic physician [England].
cns CHETNA N. SHUKLA: (1968-)
cns1.de CHETNA N. SHUKLA: Diabetes mellitus : ein Fal von Lac asinum, H Zt, Nr 1: pg 33-36 (1999)
cns2 CHETNA N. SHUKLA: [The Soul of the spirit in the substances - The hom. Proving of the Butterfly, the Donkey's Milk & the Rose]
cns3.de CHETNA N. SHUKLA und KITTLER Monika: Anas Indica - Indische Ente: Prüfung und Kasuistik, Zweibrücken:Verlag Karl-Josef Müller (2001)
cns4.de CHETNA N. SHUKLA, Nayana C. Khopade, Guddi makhija, RUSTER Gerhard: Oxygenium: Zwei homöopatische Prüfungen und Kasuistik., Zweibrücken:Verlag Karl-Josef Müller (2000)
cns5.de CHETNA N. SHUKLA und MÜLLER Karl-Josef: Lac asinum: Zwei homöopatische Prüfungen und Kasuistik., Zweibrücken:Verlag Karl-Josef Müller (1999)
cp COWPERTHWAITE Allen Corson: (1848-1926)
cp1 COWPERTHWAITE Allen Corson: [Textbook of Materia Medica and Therapeutics], Chicago (1885)
cp2 COWPERTHWAITE Allen Corson: [Disorders of menstruation]
cp3 COWPERTHWAITE Allen Corson: [Textbook of Gynecology], New Dehli: Jain Publ. (1888)
cpa CHAPIN E.
cpb COOPER Robert T.: (1844-1903)
cpb1 COOPER Robert T.: [Cancer and cancer symptoms] (1900)
cpb2 COOPER Robert T.: [Cocaine], Hom Rec, Vol XIV nr. 2: pg 68 (1899)
cpc COOPER R. M.
cpd COOPER Dorothy: (1915-)
cpg CAMPOS Gelse Mazzoni: Contemporary homeopath [Brasil]

cpg1.pt	CAMPOS Gelse Mazzoni e FREITAS Arlete Faria de: Flores da Terra: Um repertorio de Florais de Todas as Partes da terra, Sao Paolo: Edit. Roca (1995)
cpi	CASPARI
cpi1	CASPARI: [Proving of Electricity], Bibliothek für Homöopatische Medizin Vol 2 [2nd Ed.] (1834)
cpl	COOPER Linda: Contemporary homeopath [Ohio, USA]
cpl1	COOPER Linda: [Cases of Bronchopulmonary dysplasea], Links, Vol 2: pg 23 (1995)
cpm	CRESPO DUBERTY Mario
cpm1.es	CRESPO DUBERTY Mario: Los Comentarios de León Simon al Organon de Hahnemann, Buenos Aire: EDA (2000)
cpm2.es	CRESPO DUBERTY Mario: La Homeopatía Unicista, Buenos Aire: EDA (2000)
cpm3.es	CRESPO DUBERTY Mario: La Homeopatía y el arte de curar, Buenos Aire: EDA (2000)
cpr	CAMPORA Carlos N.
cpr1.es	CAMPORA Carlos Nestor: La Patogenesia de Loxosceles Laeta: La Araña de los rincones. Araña marron o araña asesina., Buenos Aires: Editorial Club de Estudio (1999)
cpy	COPPE Yves: Contemporary homeopathic physician [Belgium] (1953-)
cpy1.fr	COPPE Yves: La grossesse, Gent: Homeoden Book Service (1991)
cr	CHARETTE Gilbert: ((1878-1953)
cr1.fr	CHARETTE Gilbert: Précis d'homéopathie: la matière médicale pratique, Paris: Editions Médicales (1928)
cra	CLARY L.
crb	CORRADO Giovanni Bruno: Contemporary homeopathic physician [Brasil]
crf	CERAMI Fiorella Maria: Contemporary homeopathic physician [Italy]
crg	CAREY George W.
crg1	CAREY George W.: [The Biochemic System of Medicine], St. Louis: Luyties Pharmacal Company (20th Ed.) (1921)
crh	CARRARA Hugo: Contemporary homeopathic physician [Italy]
crm	CURRIM Ahmed N.: Contemporary homeopathic physician [Norwalk, USA]. Collected the work of Grimmer and the lost, last Repertory of Kent. (1940-)
crp	CURIE Paul Francis: (1799-1853)
crp1	CURIE Paul Francis: [Practice of Homoeopathy] (1938)
cry	CHAKRABORTY A.
cry1	CHAKRABORTY A.: [Hom. Drug personalities with therapeutic hints]
cs	CUSHING Alvin Mathew
cs1	CUSHING A. M.: [Leucorrhea, Its Concomitant Symptoms]
csa	CASAUS Angel: Contemporary homeopathic physician [Spain]
csj	CASALE Jorge Alberto
csj1.es	CASALE Jorge Alberto: Los Miasmas cronicos - Perturbacion del tono bioenergético [2nd Ed.], Buenos Aires: Editorial Club de Estudio (1995)
csm	CASTRO Miranda: (1949-)
csm1	CASTRO Miranda: [Borax veneta]
csp	CLAUSER Pierluigi: Contemporary homeopathic physician [Italy]
css	CREASY S.
ct	CROWTHER G.
cta	CUSTIS J. B. G.
ctb	CARTIER François: (1864-1928)
ctb1.fr	CARTIER François: Traité complet de thérapeutique homoeopathique. Vol 1, Paris: Baillière (1929)
ctb1a.es	CARTIER François: Terapeutica Homeopática Vol 1 and 2, New Delhi: Jain Publishers
ctb2.fr	CARTIER François: Traité complet de thérapeutique Homoeopathique. Vol 2, Paris: Baillière (1929)
ctb3.fr	CARTIER François: Traité complet de thérapeutique homoeopathique. Vol 3, Paris: Baillière (1929)
ctb4.fr	CARTIER François: Traité complet de thérapeutique homoeopathique. Vol 4, Paris: Baillière (1929)
ctb5.es	CARTIER François: Tradado de Terapeutica. Translated by Everardo Cruz, New Delhi: Jain Publishers
ctb5.fr	CARTIER François: Traité complet de thérapeutique homoeopathique. Vol 5, Paris: Baillière (1930)
ctb5a.es	CARTIER François: Enfermedades de los Ojos, Nariz, Oidos y Laringe: Su Tratamiento Homeopático. Translated by Everardo Cruz, Madrid (Spain): Dilema Editorial (2004)
ctb6	CARTIER François: [Therapeutics of the Respiratory Organs [Translated from French and Edited by Williams, C.A.] - Vol 6], Philadelphia: Boericke & Tafel (1919)
ctb6.es	CARTIER François: Terapeutica de las Vias Respiratorias segun la ley de los semejantes. Translated by: Everardo Cruz., New Delhi: Jain Publishers (1939)
ctb6.fr	CARTIER François: Traité complet de thérapeutique homoeopathique. Vol 6, Paris: Baillière (1930)
ctc	COULTER Catherine: Contemporary homeopath [USA] (1934-)
ctc1	COULTER Catherine: [Portraits of Homeopathic Medecine, Vol 1], Berkeley: North Atlantic Books (1986)
ctc2	COULTER Catherine: [Portraits of Homeopathic Medecine, Vol 2], Berkeley: North Atlantic Books 1986-1988 (1988)

ctc3	COULTER Catherine: [Portrait of indifference.], Berkeley: North Atlantic Books (1989)
ctc4	COULTER Catherine: [Thuja occidentalis]
ctc5	COULTER Catherine: [Syphillinum & carcinosin: psychological analysis.], Indian J Homoeopath Med, 1989, Apr-Jun; 24(2):140-1,
ctd	CROTHERS Dean: Contemporary homeopathic physician [USA] (1948-)
cte	CHATTERJEE Ardhendu Sekhar: (1958-)
cte1	CHATTERJEE Ardhendu Sekhar: [Glycyrrhiza glabra Linn] (1997)
cte2	CHATTERJEE Ardhendu Sekhar: [A Study over Thyroidinum], Homeopathic practioners conference Chandpara (1984)
ctf	CHRISTO Marcus
ctf1	CHRISTO Marcus: [Proving of MDMA by by the Travelling Homeopaths Collective.]
cth	COULTER Harris L.
cth1	COULTER Harris L.: [Homoeopathic Science and Modern Medicine. The Physics of Healing with Microdoses.], Berkely: North Atlantic Books (1980)
cth2	COULTER Harris L.: [Divided legacy: The conflict between homeopathy and the American medical association.], Richmond: North Atlantic Books (1973)
cth3	COULTER Harris L.: [Aids & Syphilis - The Hidden Links [2nd Ed.]]
cti	CASTELLINI Maurizio: Contemporary homeopathic physician [Italy]
ctj	CHATTERJEE T. P.: (1947-)
ctj1	CHATTERJEE T. P.: [My memorable cures] (1987)
ctj2	CHATTERJEE T. P.: [Highlights of homoeo-practice [2nd Ed.]], New Delhi: Jain Publishers (1991)
ctj3	CHATTERJEE T. P.: [A Handbook of useful thoughts on homoeo-practice and disease terminology], New Delhi: Jain Publishers [1st Ed.] (1991)
ctj4	CHATTERJEE T. P.: [My Random Notes on some Homeopathic Remedies Reprint], New Delhi: Jain Publishers (1994)
ctj5	CHATTERJEE T. P.: [Fundamentals of Homeopathy and Valuable hints for Practice]
ctj6	CHATTERJEE T. P.: [Hints on Homeopathic Practice and Children's Diseases] (1994)
ctk	CHIMTHANAWALA Kasim: Contemporary homeopath [Nagpur, India]
ctk1	CHIMTHANAWALA Kasim: [An unusual case of Amenorrhoea], Links, Vol 2: pg 14 (1993)
ctl	COLLYER Clayton: Contemporary homeopath [England] (1963-)
ctl1	COLLYER Clayton and DAVIS Jackie: [The homeopathic proving of Lavender] (1997)
ctm	CORTENS Mark: Contemporary homeopathic physician [Belgium] (1951-)
cts	CHATTERJEE Sujit: Contemporary homeopath [Bombay, India]
cts1	CHATTERJEE Sujit: [A case of Behavioural Problems], Links, Vol 2: pg 27-28 (1993)
cv	CHAVANON Pierre
cv1	CHAVANON Pierre and LEVANNIER R.: [Emergency homeopathic First-Aid [Translated from French by G.A. Dudley]], Northamptonshire, England: Thorsons Publishers limited (1977)
cva	CLOVER Anne M
cva1	CLOVER Anne M. and Jenkins S. and Campbell Anthony C.: [Report on a proving of Pulsatilla], Br H J, Vol 69: pg 134-147 (1980)
cvl	CLEVELAND Charles Luther
cvl1	CLEVELAND C. L.: [Salient Materia Medica and Therapeutics], Philadelphia (1888)
cvm	CREVELD Marijke: Contemporary homeopath [Netherlands] (1949-)
cvm1	CREVELD Marijke: [Diospyros kaki.], Zwolle (Netherlands): private (2004)
cvm1.nl	CREVELD Marijke: Diospyros kaki., Zwolle (Netherlands): private (2003)
cyj	CLAY J.V.F.
cyj1	CLAY J.V.F.: [Diseases of the Nose and throat]
cza	CROUZET Anne-Marie: (1946-)
cza1.fr	CROUZET Anne-Marie: Ginkgo Biloba: L'arbre qui fait Mémoire
cza2.fr	CROUZET Anne-Marie: Lac Leoninum (2002)
czm	CARRANZA Marta Beatriz
czm1.es	CARRANZA Marta Beatriz: El Milagro Floral. De la Energía sanadora de las flores y hacia la autocuración, [1st Ed.], Córdoba (Argentina): Editorial Cooperativa de Trabajo Dr. Manuel Belgrano Ltda. Grupo Nacional de Cultura la Solapa. Octubre 1998 (1998)
dan	DAS N.C.
dan1	DAS N.C.: [Thunderstorm repertory] (1950)
dar	DAS E. Radha
dar1	DAS E. Radha: [Synopsis of Homeopathic Aetiology.], New Delhi: Jain Publishers (2nd Ed.) (1988)
das	DAS Bishamber: (1945-)
das1	DAS Bishamber: [Select your remedy, revised and enlarged.], New Delhi (1988)
db	DIEFFENBACH Wm. Hermann: (1865-)
dba	DEBATS Fernand J. M.: Contemporary homeopathic physician [Netherlands]
dbb	DEARBORN Frederick Myers: (1876-1960)
dbf	DABBAH Flora: Argentinian homeopathic physician
dbm	DEARBORN Frederick M.
dbm1.es	DEARBORN Frederick M.: Enfermedades de la Piel. Translated by Javier Vicite Medrano, New Delhi: Jain Publishers
dbp	DE BAETS Piet: Contemporary homeopathic physician [Eeklo, Belgium]. Founder of H.R.I.C. [Homeopathic Research and Information Centre] (1953-)
dbx	DUBOIS H. M.: French ethnologist (1898-)

dbx1.fr	DUBOIS H. M.: Monographie des betsileo [Madagascar], Paris: Institut d'Ethnologie (1938)
dc	DECKERS Arnold: Contemporary homeopathic physician [Netherlands]
dcb	DE CASTRO Benedict J.
dcb1.es	DE CASTRO Benedict J.: Logica de Repertorios, New Delhi: Jain Publishers
dci	DORCSI Mathias: Contemporary homeopathic physician [Münich, Germany] (1923-2001)
dci1.de	DORCSI Mathias: Arzneimittellehre, Heidelberg: Haug Verlag (1985)
dci2.de	DORCSI Mathias: Homeopathie [6 vols], Heidelberg: Haug Verlag (1977)
dci3.de	DORCSI Mathias: Stufenplan und Ausbildungsprogramm in der Homoopathie - band 1, Heidelberg: Haug Verlag (2nd Ed.)
dcm	DEACON Louise
dcm1	DEACON Louise and RIBOT-SMITH Alan: [Spagyrical Proving of Bellis Perennis] (1996)
dct	DUNCAN Thomas Cation: (1840-1902)
dct1	DUNCAN Thomas C.: [Children, Acid and Alkaline]
dct2	DUNCAN Thomas C.: [Hand Book on the Diseases of the Heart and their Homeopathic Treatment], Chicago: Halsey Bros. Co. (Illinois) (1898)
dd	DIEUDONNE André: Contemporary homeopathic physician [France]
df	DUFF P. S.
dff	DEL FRANCIA Franco: Contemporary homeopathic veterinary physician [Italy]
dff1.it	DEL FRANCIA Franco e ZUCO Willy: Veterinaria Omeopatica e psicopatologia del Cavallo, Sommacampagna:Demetra (1990)
dfg	DRANSFIELD Gill
dfg1	DRANSFIELD Gill: [The homoeopathic proving of spectrum.], St.Martin by Looe (Cornwall, UK): Penvith Publishing (2000)
dfh	DUFILHO Robert
dfh1.fr	DUFILHO Robert: Les Symptômes mentaux en Homéopathie, Pau (France) (1986)
dfh2	DUFILHO Robert: [Géométrie Homéopathique]
dfh3.fr	DUFILHO Robert: Le piano homéopathique, Paris: Similia (1999)
dg	DUDGEON Robert Ellis: Translator into English of Hahnemann's Materia medica pura (1820-1904) (1880)
dg1	DUDGEON Robert Ellis: [Hahnemanns therapeutic hints], Calcutta (1958)
dg2	DUDGEON R. E.: [Lectures on the Theory and Practice of Homeopathy], New delhi: Jain Publishers (1987)
dg3	DUDGEON R. E.: [= h4 = The Lesser Writings of Samuel Hahnemann (old abbr.)], New delhi: Jain Publishers (1987)
dga	DOUGLAS
dgb	DANGELA Gunther: Contemporary homeopathic physician for internal medicine [Villingen, Germany].
dgh	DOUGLAS H. R.
dgh1	DOUGLAS H. R.: [Lectures on Diseases of Chest], New Delhi: Indian Books & Periodicals Syndicate
dgj	DUGAN J.
dgj1	DUGAN J.: [Collinsonia canadensis], Homoeopathic Recorder, Vol 24, nr 10
dgs	DOUGLASS Melford Eugene
dgs1	DOUGLASS Melford Eugene: [Skin diseases] (1899)
dgs2	DOUGLASS Melford Eugene: [Warts]
dgs3	DOUGLASS Melford Eugene: [Materia Medica]
dgs4	DOUGLASS Melford Eugene: [Pearls of Homeopathy] (1903)
dgs5	DOUGLASS Melford Eugene: [Repertory of new remedies]
dgt	DEGROOTE Filip: Contemporary homeopathic physician [Brugge, Belgium] (1952-)
dgt1	DEGROOTE Filip: [Physical Examination and Observation in Homeopathy], Gent:Homeoden Book Service (1992)
dgt2	DEGROOTE Filip: [Notes on Miasms, heredity and remedy interactions] (1994)
dgt3	DEGROOTE Filip: [Carcinosinum Essay, Articles] (1986)
dh	DUNHAM Carroll: American homeopathic physician at the turn of the century (1828-1877)
dh1	DUNHAM Carroll: [Lectures on Materia Medica], New Delhi: Jain Publishers (1879)
dh2	DUNHAM Carroll: [Homeopathic Science of Therapeutics], New York (1877)
dh3	DUNHAM Carroll: [Lectures of Kent]
dh4	DUNHAM Carroll: [Graphites], International Hahnemannian Association
dh5	DUNHAM Carroll: [Symptoms, their Study or "How to Take the Case"]
dh6	DUNHAM Carroll: [The Science of Therapeutics. A collection of papers] (1877)
dhh	DEN HARTOG Hans: (1959-)
dhh1	DEN HARTOG Hans: [Proving of Populus tremuloïdes - Linking trees project.], Links, Vol 12, Autumn: pg 170-171 (1999)
dhj	DEHOND Jean Pierre: Contemporary homeopathic physician [Belgium]
dht	DEINHART
djr	DUJANY Ruggero: Contemporary homeopathic physician [Italy]
djr1.it	DUJANY Ruggero: Materia Medica Omeopatica, Milano:Rafaello Cortina Ed. (1988)
dk	DIRKEN Rainer: Contemporary homeopathic physician [Germany]
dkk	DEGKWITZ Karin
dkk1.de	DEGKWITZ Kari, CHETNA N. Shukla, KITTLER Monika und MULLER Karl-Josef: Rosa: Zwei Prüfungen und Kasuistik, Zweibrücken:Verlag Karl-Josef Müller (2002)
dkl	DACK Laurie: (1953-)

dkl1	DACK Laurie: [Professional Case Conference 1993] (1993)
dko	DRAKE Olin M.
dko1	DRAKE Olin M.: [Repertory of Warts and Condylomata], New Delhi: Jain Publishers
dko2	DRAKE Olin M.: [Repertory of Foot Sweats], Homoeopathic Physian: Vol 14 (1894)
dko3	DRAKE Olin M.: [General remarks upon polypoid growths with repertory], Hahnemannian Advocate (1897)
dkp	DAHLKE Paul
dkp1	DAHLKE Paul: [Repertorium]
dll	DE LELLIS Luis Pedro
dlm	DHAWLE M.L.
dlm1	DHAWLE M.L.: [Principles and Practice of Homeopathy]
dm	DEL MAS R.: American homeopathic physician (1890-)
dm1	DEL MAS R.: [Clinical Cases], Hom Rec, Vol XLV nr. 7 (1930)
dma	DOMINICI Gustavo
dma1	DOMINICI Gustavo, PITARI Giusi and GULIA Pietro: [Etna Lava: Proving symptomatology and clinical results.] (2002)
dmd	DEMARQUE D.: (1915-1999)
dmd1.fr	DEMARQUE D., JOUANNY J., POITEVIN B. et SAINT-JEAN Y.: Pharmacologie et matière médicale homeopatique., Paris: Centre d'étude et documentation homeopatiques (1993)
dmd1.it	DEMARQUE D., JOUANNY J., POITEVIN B. e SAINT-JEAN Y.: Farmacologia e materia medica omeopatica. (1999)
dmg	DEMANGEAT Georges: [1913-1990]
dmh	DE MEDIO Horacio: Contemporary homeopath [Argentina, Buenos Aires]
dmh1	DE MEDIO Horacio: [Introduction to the veterinary homeopathy] (1995)
dmh1.es	DE MEDIO Horacio: Introducción a la homeopatía veterinaria (1995)
dmk	DAM Kees: (1953-)
dmk1	DAM Kees: [Dreams and homoeopathy], Links, Vol 12: pg 10-13 (1999)
dmk2.de	DAM Kees: Die Furcht, überrascht zu werden. Lac caprinum (Ziegenmilch), H Zt, Vol 1: pg 31-39 (1996)
dml	DE MATTOS Léa
dmm	DRAIMAN Mario
dmm1.es	DRAIMAN Mario: Las Personalidades Homeopaticas Vol 1, Buenos Aires: Edición Argentina (1991)
dmm2.es	DRAIMAN Mario: Las Personalidades Homeopaticas Vol 2, Buenos Aires: Edición Argentina (1999)
dmp	DARMON P.
dmp1.fr	DARMON P.: Dictionnaire des Thèmes de la Matière Médicale
dmt	DIMITRIADIS George: Contemporary homeopath, Australia (1959-)
dmt1	DIMITRIADIS George: [Gleaning of Homeopathic Philisophy]
dmt2	DIMITRIADIS George: [Some Essays on Homeopathy]
dmx	DEMEURES
dmx1	DEMEURES: [Mentholum], Journal de la Société Gallicane de Médicine Homoéopathique
dmx2	DEMEURES: [Menyanthes], Journal de la Société Gallicane de Médicine Homoéopathique
dmx3	DEMEURES: [Pinus sylvestris], Journal de la Société Gallicane de Médicine Homoéopathique
dp	DUPRAT Henry: French homeopathic physician (1878-1968)
dp1.fr	DUPRAT Henry: Traité de matière médicale homéopathique Vol. 1, Trévoux: Patissier (1947)
dp2.fr	DUPRAT Henry: Traité de matière médicale homéopathique Vol. 2, Paris: Baillière (1948)
dp3.fr	DUPRAT Henry: L'Homeoepathie vivante., Genève (1926)
dpa	DUPORT Alain
dpa1.es	DUPORT Alain: Casos
dpa1.fr	DUPORT Alain: Cas Cliniques Vétérinaires
dr	= emd = DURR Elmore (old abb): Contemporary homeopath [USA]
dr1	DURR Elmore: [= emd1 = Acute Versus Chronic: An Unusual Otitis Prescription (old abb)], N Eng. J H, Vol 1 nr 1: pg 4-5 (1992)
drp	DORI Peter
drp1	DORI Peter: [Die Systematische Verlaufsanalyse]
dry	DURY William V.: (1837-)
dry1	DURY William V.: [Eruptive Fevers] (1877)
ds	DESAI Bhanu D.
ds1	DESAI Bhanu D.: [How to find the Similimum with Boger-Boenningshausen's Repertory.], New Delhi: Jain Publishers (1992)
dsa	DAWS Jean: (1938-)
dsa1	DAWS Jean and SCRIVEN Daphne: [The making of the Proving of Sol Brittanic], Turnbridge Wells: Helios (1994)
dsb	DOOMS Pierre: Contemporary homeopathic physician [Belgium]
dse	DESCHERE Martin: (1848-1902)
dse1	DESCHERE Martin: [Proving of Sanicula mineral spring Water], North American Journal of Homoeopathy Vol 45: pg 657
dsj	DESAEDELEER: Contemporary homeopathic physician [Belgium]
dsl	DE SCHEPPER Luc
dsl1	DE SCHEPPER Luc: [Hahnemann Revisited - A textbook of Classical Homeopathy - For the Professional. Santa Fe, 1999] (1999)
dsp	DROSSOU P.: (1944-)
dsp1	DROSSOU P. et al.: [The homeopathic treatment of Carpal Tunnel Syndrome], L M H I, Vol 2 nr 6: pg 22-26 (1989)

dsr	DESAI Rupal
dsr1	DESAI Rupal: [Re-exploring our Magnificient Plants [1st Ed.]]
dsr2	DESAI Rupal: [Magnificent Plants 2]
dt	DIENST G. E.: Student of Kent (1867-1932)
dt1	DIENST G. E.: [What to do for the stomach], Philadelphia (1907)
dta	DUTTA A.C.: Contemporary homeopath [India] (1936-)
dta1	DUTTA A.C.: [Homoeopathy: A systematic of Case Records], New Delhi: Jain Publishers
dtd	DAPTARDAR B. G.: Contemporary homeopath [Bombay, India]
dtd1	DAPTARDAR B. G.: [A case of Asthma], Links, Vol 3: pg 21 (1994)
dtn	DETINIS Luis: Contemporary homeopath [Buenos Aires, Argentina] (1954-)
dtn1	DETINIS Luis: [Mental symptoms in homeopathy], Beaconsfield (1994)
dtn1.es	DETINIS Luis: Síntomas mentales en homeopatia 2
dtn2	DETINIS Luis: [Semiologia homeopatica y bases para un repertorio orgánico]
dtn3.es	DETINIS Luis: Veratrum album: Respuestas a las principales preguntas de la clinica homeopatica
dtn4.es	DETINIS Luis: Congreso del Dr. Luis Detinis
dtp	DETAND Patrick: Contemporary homeopathic physician [Brussel, Belgium]. Teacher at the schools of Brussels and Gent. (1955-)
dv	DOEUVRE Erwin: Contemporary homeopathic physician [Oostende, Belgium]. President of VSU, School for homeopathy, Gent (1950-)
dvm	DAVITS Maria: Contemporary homeopathic physician [Netherlands]
dvr	DEVAUX Renée: Veterinary (1940-)
dvs	DAVIDSON Stephen Myles: Contemporary homeopath [Phoenix, USA]
dvv	DIVANJI V. G.
dvv1	DIVANJI V. G.: [Partial proving of Molybdenum metallicum], Hom Rec (1931)
dw	DEWEY Willis Alonzo: American homeopathic physcian. Professor Materia Medica Michigan. (1858-1938)
dw1	DEWEY Willis Alonzo: [Essentials of Homeopathic Materia Medica], Philadelphia: Boericke & Tafel (1899)
dw1.es	DEWEY Willis Alonzo: Esencialidades de Materia Médica Homeopática. Translated by L. Arriaga, New Delhi: Jain Publishers (1899)
dw2	DEWEY Willis Alonzo: [Essentials of Homeopathic therapeutics], Philadelphia: Boericke & Tafel (1895)
dw3	DEWEY Willis Alonzo: [Twelve Tissue Remedies] (1928)
dw4	DEWEY Willis Alonzo: [Ferrum phosphoricum], Hom Rec, Vol XIV nr. 1: pg 37 (1908)
dw5	DEWEY Willis Alonzo: [Practical Homeopathic Therapeutics] (1933)
dwm	DHAWALE M. L.: (1927-1987)
dwm1	DHAWALE M. L.: [Principles and Practice of Homeopathy [part 1, 2]], Bombay: Institute of clinical research (2nd Ed.) (1986)
dx	DOCKX René: Contemporary homeopathic physician [Knokke, Belgium] (1944-)
dx1	DOCKX René and KOKELENBERG Guy: [Kent's Comparative Repertory of the Hom. Materia Medica], Gent: Homeoden (1988)
dx2.nl	DOCKX René: De Nieuwe Materia Medica van de metalen
dy	DEY H. K.: (1935-)
dy1	DEY H. K.: [Complications of menstruation]
dy2	DEY H. K.: [Rheumatism cured by homoeopathy], Calcutta: Haren and Brothers (1975)
dyb	DIGBY B.: (1950-)
dyb1	DIGBY B.: [Homeopathic Lectures]
dyb2	DIGBY B.: [Lac caninum] (1990)
dyc	DAY Christopher: (1947-)
dyc1	DAY Christopher: [The homeopathic treatment of small animals, principles and practice], New Delhi: Jain Publishers (India) (1988)
dyc2	DAY Christopher: [The Homoeopathic Treatment of Beef and Dairy Cattle]
dzs	DIEZ Susanne
ebh	EBERLE Hans: Contemporary homeopathic physician [Rosenheim, Germany] (1950-)
ebh1.de	EBERLE Hans und RITZER Friedrich: Arzneimittelprüfung Uranium metallicum (1996)
ebh2.de	EBERLE Hans und RITZER Friedrich: Arzneimittellehre: Neue homöopatische Arzneien I, München: Verlag Müller & Steinicke (1999)
ebh3.de	EBERLE Hans und RITZER Friedrich: Arzneimittellehre: Neue homöopatische Arzneien II, München: Verlag Müller & Steinicke (1998)
ec	EICHENBERGER A.: Contemporary homeopath [Switzerland]
ech	EICHELBERGER Otto: Contemporary homeopathic physician [Germany]
ech1	EICHELBERGER Otto: [Lehre und Praxis], Heidelberg: Haug (1989)
ech2	EICHELBERGER Otto: [Praxis und Forschung], Heidelberg: Haug (1987)
ecm	ESCOBAR Mario R.
ecm1.es	ESCOBAR Mario R.: Lecciones de Oftalmología, New Delhi: Jain Publishers
ecr	EICHLER O.
ecr1	EICHLER O. and KOCH Chr.: [Harpagophytum procumbens], Arzneim. Forsch 20; 107 (1970)
eg	EGEL
ege	EGEE J. B.
egp	ENGEL Peter B.
egp1	ENGEL Peter B.: [A proving of Nidus edulis], Br H J, Vol 64: pg 225-230 (1975)

egr	EIGENRAAM Karel: Contemporary homeopath [Netherlands]
egt	EGGERT William
egt1	EGGERT W.: [The Homoeopathic Therapeutics of Uterine and Vaginal Discharges], New York: Boericke & Tafel (1878)
egw	ENGELS W.
egw1	ENGELS W.: [Haplopappus bailahuen], Karlsruhe, Naturwiss.Fa.Diss.v. 29.5.1970
el	ENGLISH John: Contemporary homeopathic physician [UK]
elg	ELLINGER Liesbeth: (1960-)
elk	ELIA Kim
elm	ENGLISH Mary
elm1	ENGLISH Mary: [Tempestas - Storm - A Remedy Proving.], Stud Hom, Vol 84 december (1999)
elm2	ENGLISH Mary: [Proving of Naufragium helvetia] (2002)
elt	ELEFTHERIADIS John: Contemporary homeopath [Greece]
elt1	ELEFTHERIADIS John: [Homeopathic treatment of Pneumonia], E J Cl. H, Vol 1 nr 3-4: pg 16-17 (1995)
em	EMERY J. T. G.
ema	EMMERSON G. C.
emd	ELMORE Durr: Contemporary homeopath [USA]
emd1	ELMORE Durr: [Acute Versus Chronic: An Unusual Otitis Prescription], N Eng. J H, Vol 1 nr 1: pg 4-5 (1992)
emp	EDMONDS Phil.
ens	ENNIS Sylvia
ens1	ENNIS Sylvia: [The Natural Choica Sickle Cell] (1994)
epa	ESPANET A.
epa1.es	ESPANET A.: Tratado Metodico y Practico de Materia Medica y de Terapeutica. Translated by Pio Hernandez Y Espeso, New Delhi: Jain Publishers
epb	ESPECHE Bárbara
epb1.es	ESPECHE Bárbara: Las Flores de Bach, Manual Práctico y Clínico, Buenos Aires: Ed. Continente (1990)
es	EISING Nuala: (1947-)
es1	EISING Nuala: [Granite, Marble and Limestone] (1995)
es1a.fr	EISING Nuala: La Première Pathogénésie de Granit
es2	EISING Nuala: [Provings of Ignis alcoholis and Succinum] (1998)
es2a.de	EISING Nuala: Feuer (Ignis alcoholis): Die Prüfung, Zweibrücken:Verlag Karl-Josef Müller (1998)
es2b.de	EISING Nuala: Bernstein (Succinum) - Die Prüfung, Zweibrücken:Verlag Karl-Josef Müller (1999)
es3	EISING Nuala: [Vacuum: The proving] (2000)
es3.de	EISING Nuala: Vakuum Die Prüfung, Zweibrücken:Verlag Karl-Josef Müller (2001)
esj	EPPS John: (1805-1869)
esj1	EPPS John: [Domestic Homoeopathy: or, Rules for the Domestic Treatment of the Maladies of Infants, Children, and Adults, and for the Conduct and the Treatment during Pregnancy, Confinement, and Suckling.[5th Ed.]], Boston: John Wilson & Son (Massachusetts) (1853)
ev	EVANS W. H.
ev1	EVANS W. H.: [Proving of Naphthalinum], North American Journal of Homoeopathy, Vol 33: pg 415
ez	EIZAYAGA Francisco Xavier: Contemporary homeopathic physician [Buenos Aires, Argentina] (1921-)
ez1	EIZAYAGA Francisco Xavier: [Treatise on Homeopathic Medicine, Lectures and Practice.]
ez2.pt	EIZAYAGA Francisco Xavier: El moderno Repertorio de Kent, Buenos Aires (1979)
ez3.es	EIZAYAGA Francisco Xavier: Enfermedades Agudas Febriles, su tratamiento homeopático, Buenos Aires: Ediciones Marecel (1978)
fb	FOUBISTER Donald M.: English homeopathic physician. Introduced carcinosin in the MM. (1902-1988)
fb1	FOUBISTER Donald and Templeton (Studies of Dr Mabilon and Dr Payen): [Indications for certain nosodes.], Hahnemann Glean, Nov, nr 48 (11), pg: 490-500 (1981)
fb1.fr	FOUBISTER Donald et Templeton (Studies of Dr Mabilon and Dr Payen): Recueil d'études sur les nosodes, Ecole Hahnemannienne Dauphiné Savoie (1981)
fb10	FOUBISTER Donald M.,: [The Significance of Past History in Homeopathic Prescribing]
fb2	FOUBISTER Donald M.: [Homeopathy and pediatrics], Bombay: Hom. Med. Publ. (1978)
fb3	FOUBISTER Donald M.: [Tutorials on Homeopathy], Beaconsfield (England): Beaconsfield Publ. (1989)
fb4	FOUBISTER Donald M.: [The carcinosin Drug Picture], New Delhi: Indian Books & Periodicals Syndicate (1958)
fb5	FOUBISTER Donald M.: [Notes on Helleborus Niger]
fb6	FOUBISTER Donald M.: [Constitutional effects of anaesthesia], New Dehli: Indian Books & Periodicals Syndicate
fb7	FOUBISTER Donald M.: [Therapeutic hints for students of homoeopathy], New Delhi: Indian books & Periodicals Syndicate
fb8	FOUBISTER Donald M.: [A Clinical Study of Carcinosin as a Constitutional Remedy], Br H J, Vol 43/2 (1953)
fb9	FOUBISTER Donald M.: [Clinical Impressions of Carcinosin], Br H J, Vol 44/2 (1954)

fbv	FABBROCINI Vincenzo: Contemporary homeopathic physician [Italy] (1945-)
fc	FAFCHAMPS Jean: Contemporary homeopathic physician [Belgium]
fcj	FRANCOIS Jean Marie: Contemporary homeopathic physician [Belgium]
fck	FINCKE Bernhardt: (1821-1906)
fck1	FINCKE B.: [Galvinismus], H Heritage Vol 18: pg 149-150 (1993)
fck2	FINCKE Bernhardt: [The Proving of X-ray], IHA Transactions 1897 pg 47-76
fd	FRIEDRICH Peter: Contemporary homeopath [Germany] (1947-)
fd1.de	FRIEDRICH Peter und Edeltraud: Charaktere Homöopathischer Arzneimittel Teil I, Höhenkirchen-Sgbr.: Traupe-Vertrieb (1992)
fd2.de	FRIEDRICH Peter und Edeltraud: Charaktere Homöopathischer Arzneimittel Teil II, Höhenkirchen-Sgbr.: Traupe-Vertrieb (1992)
fd3.de	FRIEDRICH Peter und Edeltraud: Charaktere Homöopathischer Arzneimittel Teil III, Höhenkirchen-Sgbr.: Traupe-Vertrieb (1999)
fd4.de	FRIEDRICH Peter und Edeltraud: Charaktere Homöopathischer Arzneimittel Teil IV, Höhenkirchen-Sgbr.: Traupe-Vertrieb (2001)
fd5.de	FRIEDRICH Peter und Edeltraud: Charaktere Homöopathischer Arzneimittel Teil V (2004)
fdo	FRENDO Ramon
fdo1.fr	FRENDO Ramon: Granit en Dix Points.
fdo2.fr	FRENDO Ramon: Cuprum Metallicum (2000)
fdo3.fr	FRENDO Ramon: Luna : Etude et Thèmes
fdo4.fr	FRENDO Ramon: Observations et cas Cliniques
fdo5.fr	FRENDO Ramon: Thèmes et Etude de la Matière Médicale
fdr	FLOYD Rosalind: (1952-)
fdr1	FLOYD Rosalind and AZGARD Izzy: [Cladonia] (1992)
fe	FAYETON S. M-L.: Contemporary homeopathic physician [Brives Charensac, France] (1951-)
fe1	FAYETON S. M-L.: [A striking symptom leads to the simillimum], Links, Vol 9: pg 11-12 (1996)
fff	FRANCOIS-FLORES Fernando Darío
fff1.es	FRANCOIS-FLORES Fernando Darío: = h9.es = Algunos Escritos de Samuel Hahnemann (old abbr.) (1998)
fff2.es	FRANCOIS-FLORES Fernando Darío: = h4.es = Escritos Medicos Menores del Dr. Samuel Hahnemann [1st Ed.], New Delhi: Jain Publishers (1996)
fff3.es	FRANCOIS-FLORES Fernando Darío: Materia Medica Mexicana, México (2000)
fff4.es	FRANCOIS-FLORES Fernando Darío: Samuel Hahnemann : Su vida y recuerdo, México: Corporativo Grupo Balo (2002)
fff5.es	FRANCOIS-FLORES Fernando Darío: Historia de la Escuela libre de Homeopatía y Historia de la Medicina Homeopática en Mexico
fh	FAHENSTOCK J. C.
fh1	FAHENSTOCK J. C.: [A manual of Homeopathic Materia Medica]
fha	FURTH E.
fhb	FISCH
fhh	FELDHAUS Heinz-Werner: Contemporary homeopathic dentist [Germany]
fhm	FISCHER Michael: (1949-)
fk	FRISCHKNECHT Pablo: Contemporary homeopathic physician [Switzerland]
fkm	FUCKERT Manfred: (1958-)
fkm1	FUCKERT Manfred: [An involuntary proving of Capsicum], Links, Vol 12: pg 30-32 (1999)
fkr	FLICK Reinhard: Contemporary homeopath [Germany] (1954-)
fkr1	FLICK Reinhard and KLUN Claudia: [Conchiolinum (Mater perlarum)] (1996)
fkr1.de	FLICK Reinhard und KLUN Claudia: Arzneimittelprüfung von Mater perlarum (Conchiolinum), Documenta Homoeopathica, nr 16 (Herausgeber Dr. Franz Swoboda, Maudrich Verlag) (1996)
fkr2.de	FLICK Reinhard und ABRAHAMIAN H.: Kalium Sulphuricum: Arzneimittelselbsterfahrung, Documenta Homoeopathica, nr 19 (Herausgeber Dr. Franz Swoboda, Maudrich Verlag) (1999)
fkr3.de	FLICK Reinhard: Die Ebene der Träume bei Mercurius solubilis, Documenta Homoeopathica, nr 15 (Herausgeber Dr. Franz Swoboda, Maudrich Verlag) (1995)
fkr4.de	FLICK Reinhard und KLUN Claudia: Homoöpathischen Arzneimittelprüfung von Vipera berus (2004)
fkr5.de	FLICK Reinhard und KLUN Claudia: HAMP von Formica rufa (2004)
fkr6.de	FLICK Reinhard und SCHOITSCH S.: HAMP von Natrium phosphoricum, Documenta Homoeopathica, nr 20 (Herausgeber Dr. Franz Swoboda, Maudrich Verlag) (2000)
fkr7.de	FLICK Reinhard und KLUN Claudia: HAMP von Vespa crabro (2004)
fkr8.de	FLICK Reinhard: Persönliche Prüfung von Conium und Elaps (1997)
fkw	FINK Wilfried: (1960-)
fkw1	FINK Wilfried: [A proving of Larus argentatus [Sea-gull]], Links, Vol 10 Summer: pg 106-108 (1997)
fkw2	FINK Wilfried: [Laurocerasus]
fkw3.de	FINK Wilfried: Porcellanum misniense. Dokumentation der Arzneimittelprüfung (1998)
fl	FELLOWS H. B.: (1838-)
fl1	FELLOWS H. B.: [Antero-spinal paralysis], Chicago (1878)
fla	FIELITZ: German homeopathic physician during the time of Hahnemann (1780-1850)
flg	FOLLAS Greig: Contemporary homeopath [Tauranga, New Zealand]

flg1 FOLLAS Greig: [An inadvertent Proving of Granite?], Links, Vol 2: pg 37-38 (1993)

fli FERNANDEZ de LARA Ignacio

fli1.es FERNANDEZ de LARA Ignacio: Indice Terapeutico para el tratamiento homeopático de las enfermedades en general., New Delhi: Jain Publishers

flk FASSLER Kristy: Contemporary homeopath [Portsmouth, Great Britain]

flk1 FASSLER Kristy: [Attention Sensory Deficit], N Eng. J H, Vol 3 nr 3: pg 29-33 (1994)

fmh FRISHMUTH J.

fmh1 FRISHMUTH J.: [Diseases of Childhood with Therapeutic Indications]

fmj FOURMON J.

fmj1 FOURMON J.: [Flor de piedra], A H Z 213, pg: 127 (1968)

fmm FELDMAN Murray: Contemporary homeopath [Canadal] (1945-)

fmm1 FELDMAN Murray: [A repertory of the Bowel Nosodes] (1994)

fmx FROHMAN Monica: Veterinary

fne FORNIAS Eduardo

fne1 FORNIAS Eduardo: [Bothrops lanceolatus], Homeopathic Recorder, Vol.23, No.10, p.436, Oct. (1908)

fns FORNIAS S.

fns1 FORNIAS S.: [Proving of Parthenium hysterophorus], Homoeopathic Recorder, Vol 1

fr FARRINGTON Ernest A.: American homeopathic physician (1847-1885). Professor of MM at the Hahnemann Medical College in Philadelphia from 1874 onwards.

fr1 FARRINGTON Ernest A.: [Clinical Materia Medica], Philadelphia: Hahnemann Medicall College (1908)

fr1.de FARRINGTON Ernest A.: Klinische Arzneimittellehre, Leipzig: Schwabe (1913)

fr1.es FARRINGTON Ernest A.: Materia Médica clinica

fr2 FARRINGTON Ernest A.: [Comparisons in Materia Medica with Therapeutic Hints.], Philadelphia: Office of the Journal of Homeopathics (1901)

fr3 FARRINGTON Ernest A.: [Therapeutics Pointers and Lesser writings with some clinical cases.], Calcutta: Bagchi Publ. (1880)

fr4 FARRINGTON Ernest A.: [Therapeutic pointers to some common remedies], Calcutta: Bagchi Publ. (1880)

fra FARIAS DIAS Aldo: Contemporary homeopathic physician [Rio de Janeiro, Brasil]

frc FERRO Carlos: Veterinary [Argentina] (-1999), Professor Escuela Médico Homeopática Thomas Pablo Paschero.

frc1 FERRO Carlos: [Medicina homeopática veterinaria], Acta Homeopática Argentinensia, agosto 1987.

frh FARRINGTON Harvey: (1872-1957)

frh1 FARRINGTON Harvey: [Homeopathy and homeopathic Prescribing], Philadelphia: American Institute of Homeopathy (1955)

frl FERREOL M.: Veterinary [France] (1955-)

frl1 FERREOL M.: [Manuel d'homéopathie vétérinaire], GenGoux P. editions Delsoer, Liège, Belgium (1976)

frm FLORES Matilde: Contemporary homeopath [Stow, USA]

frm1 FLORES Matilde: [An Anxious Patient], N Eng. J H, Vol 2 nr 1: pg 12-15 (1993)

fru FRIEDRICH U.

fru1.de FRIEDRICH U.: Ein unbekanntes, charakteristisches Sepiasymptom, Zeitschrift fr Klassische Homeopathie, Vol 5 (1997)

frv FLORES Villalva Fernando

frv1 FLORES Villalva Fernando: [Pathogenesy of croton lecheri [Dragon's blood]], Proc 54th LMHI Congr.,Salvador- Bahia, Brasil (1999)

frv1.es FLORES Villalva Fernando: Patogenesia de Croton Lecheri (Sangre de drago) (1999)

fry FLURY Rudolf: Swiss homeopathic physician (1903-1977). Président of the "Association Suisse des Médecins Homoéopathes" [1947-1955 and 1963-1971].

fry1.de FLURY Rudolf: Praktische Repertorium, bern: Lemberg (1979)

fry2 FLURY Rudolf: [Homoeopathy and the principle of reality] (1979)

fry3 FLURY Rudolf: [Proceedings of the Swiss society of homeopaths] (1977)

fs FIELDS R.: American homeopathic physician, publisher of an index-card repertory (1882-)

fs1 FIELDS R.: [The Symptom Register, Part 1], Philadelphia (1922)

fse FRIES E.S.: Suis homeopath (Zürich)

fse1.de FRIES E.S.: Bönninghausen's Therapeutisches Taschenbuch für Homöopatische Ärzte..., Leipzig: A. Marggraf's homöopatische Officin. (1897)

fsj FISEL J.

fsj1 FISEL J. and GÄBLER and SCHWÖBEL H. and TRUNZLER G.: [Haronga madagascariensis], Dtsch. Apoth. Ztg. 106 ; 1053-60 (1966)

fsp FRASER Peter

fsr FISHER Charles E.: (1853-)

fsr1 FISHER Charles E.: [Homeopathy in obstetric emergencies]

fsr2 FISHER Charles E.: [Handbook on the diseases of children], Chicago: Medical Century (1895)

ft FLORES TOLEDO David: Contemporary homeopathic physician [Mexico] (1926-)

ft1 FLORES TOLEDO David: [Psilocybe caerulescens Murray] (1980)

ft2 FLORES TOLEDO David: [Pituitrinum anterior], Similia Similibus Curentur, Vol 19 nr. 3: pg 83

ft3.es FLORES TOLEDO David: Iniciación a la homeopatía

ftb	FORTIER - BERNOVILLE Maurice: (1896-1939)
ftb1	FORTIER - BERNOVILLE: [What we must not do in Homeopathy], New Delhi: Jain Publishers (1974)
ftb2	FORTIER - BERNOVILLE et al.: [Eruptive Fevers and contagious Diseases of Children [Translated by Raj Kumar Mukerji from French]], New Delhi: Jain Publishers
ftb3	FORTIER - BERNOVILLE et al.: [Therapeutics of the Diseases of Liver and Biliary Ducts [Translated by Raj Kumar Mukerji from French]], New Delhi: Jain Publishers
ftb4	FORTIER - BERNOVILLE: [Remedies for Circulatory and Respiratory System [Translated from French by Raj Kumar Mukerji]], New Delhi: Jain Publishers
ftb5	FORTIER - BERNOVILLE: [Therapeutics of Intoxication [Translated from French by Raj Kumar Mukerji]], New Delhi: Jain Publishers
ftb6	FORTIER - BERNOVILLE: [Diabetes Mellitus [Translated from French by Raj Kumar Mukerji]], New Delhi: Jain Publishers
ftb6.es	BERNOVILLE F.: Diabetes Mellitus. Translated by QUINTERO RAMÍREZ Gilberto, New Delhi: Jain Publishers (1991)
ftb7	FORTIER - BERNOVILLE and ROUSSEAU A.: [Chronic Rheumatism], New Delhi: Jain Publishers (1988)
ftb8	FORTIER - BERNOVILLE: [Syphyilis and Sycosis [Translated by Raj Kumar Mukerji]], New Delhi: Jain Publishers (1998)
ftj	FAUST Jurgen: Contemporary homeopathic physician [Germany]. Translator of “Essences” of G. Vithoulkas
ftr	FOSTER J.
ftr1	FOSTER J.: [Toothache and its cure]
ftv	FOTIADIS Vassilis: Contemporary homeopathic physician [Greece]
fwe	FREIWALD E.
fwe1	FREIWALD E.: [Flor de piedra], A H Z. 209, pg 232-236 (1964)
fyz	FAYAZUDDIN M.: (1936-)
fyz1	FAYAZUDDIN M.: [Pregnant Ladies], Kakinada (1983)
fyz2	FAYAZUDDIN M.: [Anomalies of New born Babies], Kakinada (1987)
fyz3	FAYAZUDDIN M.: [Morbid Fears and Anxieties], Kakinada (1988)
fyz4	FAYAZUDDIN M.: [Peculiar and Characteristic Symptoms], Kakinada (1991)
fyz5	FAYAZUDDIN M.: [Surgeon's Friends in Homeopathy. Succus Calendula], Kakinada
fyz6	FAYAZUDDIN M.: [Hypericum - A Study.], Kakinada: 4th edition (1995)
fyz7	FAYAZUDDIN M.: [Surgeon's Friends in Homeopathy. Arnica Montana], Kakinada: 4th edition (1993)
fzj	FITZ- MATTHEWS J.
fzj1	FITZ- MATTHEWS J.: [Proving of Anagallis arvensis], Medical Advance, Vol 26: pg 358 (1891)
fzr	FINZ R.
fzr1	FINZ R.: [Haronga madagascariensis], Der Prakt. Arzt 21; 676 (1967)
gb	GARBERS Uwe: Contemporary homeopath [Germany] (1956-)
gba	GENBRUGGE Kris: Contemporary homeopathic physician [Belgium]
gbc	GILBERT C.B.
gbc1	GILBERT C.B.: [Sciatica], Homoeopathic Physician, June (1893)
gbd	GAMBY François: Contemporary homeopathic physician [France]
gbg	GREENBERG Alan: Contemporary homeopath [New Jersey, USA]
gbg1	GREENBERG Alan: [Poison Ivy Miseries], N Eng. J H, Vol 2 nr 1: pg 6-7 (1993)
gbh	GÄBLER Hartwig: Contemporary homeopathic pharmacist [Karlsruhe, Germany]
gbh1.de	GÄBLER Hartwig: Über einige Neuere Homöopatische Mittel, H Naturheilk, Vol 10: pg 300-307 (1979)
gbh2	GÄBLER Hartwig: [Harpagophytum procumbens], Hom. Monatslol. 97; 123 (1972)
gbh3	GÄBLER Hartwig: [Valeriana officinalis], A H Z (5) : pg 229 (1980)
gbk	GAUBLOMME Kris: Contemporary homeopathic physician [Belgium] (1953)
gbk1	GAUBLOMME Kris: [Concentration problems in a child], Links, Vol 2: pg 33-34 (1990)
gby	GABANYI Dieter
gby1.de	GABANYI Dieter: Homöpathie für Allgemein und Fachpraxen
gcc	GATCHELL CH.
gcc1	GATCHELL CH.: [Key Notes of Medical Practice], Chicago (1895)
gcj	GILCHRIST J. G.: (1879-)
gcj1	GILCHRIST J. G.: [The Homoeopathic Treatment of Surgical Diseases], Chicago (1873)
gcm	GUIMARAES CAMILO Maria de Lourdes
gds	GUILD-LEGGET S.L.
gds1	GUILD-LEGGET S.L.: [Ferrum sulphuricum], Medical Advance, Vol 46 (1908)
ge	GEE W. S.
gehu	Groupe d'Etude d'Homéopathie Unisiste
gehu1.fr	Groupe d'Etude d'Homéopathie Unisiste: Substance des Remèdes
gehu2.fr	Groupe d'Etude d'Homéopathie Unisiste: Symbolisme des Remèdes
gehu3.fr	Groupe d'Etude d'Homéopathie Unisiste: Notes prises en réunions
gemmh	Groupe d'étude de Matière Médicale Homéopathique P. Deroche
gemmh1.fr	Groupe d'étude de Matière Médicale Homéopathique: Essences des Remèdes

	Homéopathiques, selon la méthodologie du Dr. A. Masi Elizalde (2004)
gemmh2.fr	Groupe d'étude de Matière Médicale Homéopathique P. Deroche: Samarskite
gft	GRIFFIN Tricia: Contemporary homeopath [England]. Teacher at the Sheffield School of Homoeopathy.
gft1	GRIFFIN Tricia: [Iridium Proving] (1997)
gfw	GREIFF Walter: Veterinary
gfw1	GREIFF Walter: [Flor de piedra], A H Z 220: pg 168 (1975)
gg	GHEGAS Vassilis: Contemporary homeopath [Greece] (1948-)
gg1	GHEGAS Vassilis: [Classical Homeopathic Lectures Vol. A], Genk (Belgium): Homeo-Study (1993)
gg2	GHEGAS Vassilis: [Classical Homeopathic Lectures Vol. B], Genk (Belgium): Homeo-Study (1993)
gg3	GHEGAS Vassilis: [Classical Homeopathic Lectures Vol. C], Genk (Belgium): Homeo-Study (1993)
gg4	GHEGAS Vassilis: [Classical Homeopathic Lectures Vol. D], Genk (Belgium): Homeo-Study (1993)
gg5	GHEGAS Vassilis: [Classical Homeopathic Lectures Vol. E], Genk (Belgium): Homeo-Study (1993)
gg6	GHEGAS Vassilis: [Classical Homeopathic Lectures Vol. F], Genk (Belgium): Homeo-Study (1993)
gg7	GHEGAS Vassilis: [Classical Homeopathic Lectures Vol. G], Genk (Belgium): Homeo-Study
gg8	GHEGAS Vassilis: [Classical Homeopathic Lectures Vol. H], Genk (Belgium): Homeo-Study (1999)
gg9	GHEGAS Vassilis: [Classical Homeopathic Lectures Vol. I], Genk (Belgium): Homeo-Study
gga	GUTGE-WICKERT Angelika: (1949-)
gga1	GUTGE-WICKERT Angelika: [Elemente zur Berliner homöopathie: Medusa] (1998)
gga2	GUTGE-WICKERT Angelika: [Medusae]
ggb	GNAIGER Jutta
ggd	GRANDGEORGE Didier: Contemporary homeopathic physician, France (1950-)
ggd1	GRANDGEORGE Didier: [The Spirit of Homeopathic Medicines: Essential Insights to 300 Remedies], Berkeley (California): North Atlantic Books) (1998)
ggd1.es	GRANDGEORGE Didier: El Remedio Homeopático
ggd1.fr	GRANDGEORGE Didier: L'esprit du Remède Homéopathique, Villenueve-Loubet: EdiComm (1992)
ggd1.it	GRANDGEORGE Didier: Lo spirito del rimedio
ggj	GREGOIRE Jean-Claude: Contemporary homeopathic physician [Brussel, Belgium]. President of School in Brussels. Editor Rev B Hom (1938-)
ggp	GREGORY Peter: (1950-)
gh	GALHARDO J. E. R.
ghb	GHOSH B.K.
ghb1	GHOSH B.K.: [Food Desires and Aversions with their Effects] (1996)
ghh	GIENSCH H.
ghh1	GIENSCH H.: [Myrrhis odorata], A H Z 220; 196 (1976)
ghs	GHOSH S. K.: (1916-)
ghs1	GHOSH S. K.: [Clinical Experiences with some rare Nosodes], Calcutta: Sm. Sushama. Rani Ghosh (3th Ed.) (1976)
ght	GEBHARDT K.H.: (1924-)
ght1	GEBHARDT K.H.: [Cajuputum], A H Z, Jan-Feb. 234 (1) :3-9 (1989)
gk	GEUKENS Alfons: Contemporary homeopathic physician [Hechtel, Belgium] Founder of Clinical Training Center Hechtel (1944-)
gk1	GEUKENS Alfons: [Homeopathic Practice - Part 1], Hechtel (Belgium): Centrum voor Homeopathie (1988)
gk1.de	GEUKENS Alfons: Homöopathische Praxis - Vol. 1, Hechtel (Belgium): Centrum voor Homeopathie (1988)
gk10.de	GEUKENS Alfons: Homöopathische Praxis - Vol. 9, Hechtel (Belgium): Centrum voor Homeopathie (1999)
gk11.de	GEUKENS Alfons: Homöopathische Praxis - Vol. 10, Hechtel (Belgium): Centrum voor Homeopathie (2001)
gk2	GEUKENS Alfons: [Homeopathic Practice - Part 2], Hechtel (Belgium): Centrum voor Homeopathie (1989)
gk2.de	GEUKENS Alfons: Homöopathische Praxis - Vol. 2, Hechtel (Belgium): Centrum voor Homeopathie (1889)
gk3	GEUKENS Alfons: [Homeopathic Practice - Part 3], Hechtel (Belgium): Centrum voor Homeopathie (1990)
gk3.de	GEUKENS Alfons: Homöopathische Praxis - Vol. 3, Hechtel (Belgium): Centrum voor Homeopathie (1990)
gk4	GEUKENS Alfons: [Homeopathic Practice - Part 4], Hechtel (Belgium): Centrum voor Homeopathie (1992)
gk4.de	GEUKENS Alfons: Homöopathische Praxis - Vol. 4, Hechtel (Belgium): Centrum voor Homeopathie (1990)
gk5	GEUKENS Alfons: [Homeopathic Practice - Part 5], Hechtel (Belgium): Centrum voor Homeopathie (1993)
gk5.de	GEUKENS Alfons: Homöopathische Praxis - Vol. 5, Hechtel (Belgium): Centrum voor Homeopathie (1991)

gk6 GEUKENS Alfons: [Carcinosinum], Hechtel (Belgium): Centrum voor Homeopathie (1989)

gk7 GEUKENS Alfons: [Homeopathic Practice - Part 6], Hechtel (Belgium): Centrum voor Homeopathie (1995)

gk7.de GEUKENS Alfons: Homöopathische Praxis - Vol. 6, Hechtel (Belgium): Centrum voor Homeopathie (1992)

gk8 GEUKENS Alfons: [Homeopathic Practice - Part 7], Hechtel (Belgium): Centrum voor Homeopathie

gk8.de GEUKENS Alfons: Homöopathische Praxis - Vol. 7, Hechtel (Belgium): Centrum voor Homeopathie (1993)

gk9 GEUKENS Alfons: [Homeopathic Practice - Part 8], Hechtel (Belgium): Centrum voor Homeopathie

gk9.de GEUKENS Alfons: Homöopathische Praxis - Vol. 8, Hechtel (Belgium): Centrum voor Homeopathie (1995)

gka GASKIN A.

gka1 GASKIN A.: [Comparative Study on Kent's Materia Medica] (1994)

gkw GLÜCK Walter

gkw1.de GLÜCK Walter: Mantis religiosa: Arzneimittelselbsterfahrung, Deutsches Journal für Homeopathie, Vol 15, nr 4 (1996)

gl GALLAVARDIN Jean-Pierre: French homeopathic psychiatrist (1825-1898)

gl1.fr GALLAVARDIN Jean-Pierre: Psychisme et Homéopathie, Vienne/Isère: Ternet-Martin (1896)

gl2.fr GALLAVARDIN Jean-Pierre: Pathogénésies Psychiques (1898)

gl3 GALLAVARDIN Jean-Pierre: [Repertory of Psychic Medicines with Materia Medica], New Delhi: Jain Publishers (1993)

gl3.fr GALLAVARDIN Jean-Pierre: Répertoire de Médecine Psychique. Matière Médicale inédite de toutes manifestations psychiques et tendances de l'être humain.

gl4 GALLAVARDIN Jean-Pierre: [Plastic Medicine Homeopathic treatment]

gl4.fr GALLAVARDIN Jean-Pierre: Médcine Plastique. Observations et répertoire d'indications de médicaments pour développer, faire maigrir, modifier et modeler certaines parties du corps.

gl5 GALLAVARDIN Jean-Pierre: [The homeopathic treatment of Alcoholism]

gl5.es GALLAVARDIN Jean-Pierre: Alcoholismo y su tratamiento homeopático. Translated by Don Jesús Villaseñor Ayala., New Delhi: Jain Publishers

glh GILLINGHAM H. P.: (1956-)

glm GALANTE Michel: Contemporary homeopath [USA]

gln GOULLON H.

gln1.de GOULLON H.: Silicea heilt Schwerhörigkeit, Allgemeine Homöopathische Zeitung Vol. 81 pg 29 (1870)

gm GRIMMER Arthur H.: American homeopathic physician (1874-1967). Highly reputed for his treatment of cancer.

gm1 GRIMMER Arthur H.: [The Collected Works [edited by Ahmed N. Currim, Ph.D., M.D.]], Greifenberg (Germany): Hahnemann Institut - Privatinstitut für homöopatische Dokumntation Gmbh (1996)

gm2 GRIMMER A. H. and FORTIER-BERNOVILLE: [Homoeopathic treatment of cancer [1st Indian Ed.]], New Delhi: Jain Publishers (1960)

gm3 GRIMMER Arthur H.: [Carbo vegetalis], H Rec, Januari: pg 43 (1936)

gm4 GRIMMER Arthur H.: [Cadmium salts], H Rec, Vol XLV nr. 9: pg 625 (1930)

gm5 GRIMMER Arthur H.: [Applications of Remedies to Cancer Cases], H Rec, Vol XLV nr. 11: pg 789 (1930)

gm6 GRIMMER Arthur H.: [Cancer cures and specifics], H Rec, Vol XLVI nr. 12: pg 357 (1951)

gma GUTMAN William: (1899-)

gma1 GUTMAN William: [Homeopathy: The fundamentals]

gma2 GUTMAN William: [Cadmium Metallicum], New York (1951)

gmc GOMEZ

gmj GAMARRA Salvador Javier: Contemporary homeopathic physician [Brasil]

gmj1 GAMARRA Salvador Javier: [Colibacillinum] (2000)

gmj2 GAMARRA Salvador Javier: [Selenium metallicum] (2000)

gmj3 GAMARRA Salvador Javier: [Saccharum album] (2000)

gmj4 GAMARRA Salvador Javier: [Aqua coco proving]

gmm GUERMONPREZ M.: (1923-)

gmm1.fr GUERMONPREZ M., PINKAS M. et TORCK M.: Matière médicale homéopathique [3th Ed.], Lyon: Editions Boiron (1989)

gmm1.it GUERMONPREZ M., PINKAS M. e TORCK M.: Materia Medica

gms GRIMES Melanie: Contemporary homeopath [USA] (1951-)

gms1 GRIMES Melanie: [Tiger Shark: A Homeopathic Proving of Galeocerdo Cuvier Hepar], Alethea Book Company (2000)

gms2 GRIMES Melanie: [New proving of Meteorite: Fax caelestis allende] (2002)

gmt GRAMM Theodore J.

gmt1 GRAMM Theodore J.: [Repertory of the Urinary Symptoms] (1888)

gmv GETMAN Volkert L.: (1865-1950)

gmz GOMEZ Juan Agustin

gn GREENE Alice: Contemporary homeopathic physician [UK]

gnc GUINEBERT Colette: Contemporary homeopath [Paris, France] (1950-)

gnc1 GUINEBERT Colette: [Chronic Sinusitis], Links, Vol 3: pg 55 (1990)

gnj GREEN Julia Minerva
gnj1 GREEN Julia Minerva: [A method of remedy study: zinc.]
gnj2 GREEN Julia Minerva: [Repertory making, repertory uses.]
gnj3 GREEN Julia Minerva: [Medorrhinum]
gnm GRANIER Michel
gnm1 GRANIER Michel: [Conferences upon Homoeopathy], London: Leath and Ross (1859)
gnt GRINNEY Tony
gnt1 GRINNEY Tony: [A proving of Thiosinamine] (2001)
gpe GIAMPIETRO Ernesto J.
gpe1.es GIAMPIETRO Ernesto J.: Doctrina y clinica avanzada en Homeopatia, Madrid (Spain): Dilema Editorial (2003)
gpi GASPARINI L.
gpi1.it GASPARINI L.: Studio dí Materia Medica Omeopatica (2000)
gs GROSS Gustav Wilhelm: Student of Hahnemann (1794-1847)
gsb GHOSE S.: (1874-)
gsb1 GHOSE S.: [Drugs of Hindustan with their homeopathic use] (1984)
gsb2 GHOSE S.: [Lachesis trigonocephalus], Br H J, VI: pg 301 (1914)
gsc GRIGGS W. B.: American homeopathic pediatrician (-1970)
gsc1 GRIGGS W. B.: [Subjective proving of Glycerine], Hom Rec, pg 518 (1936)
gsd GIBSON Douglas M.: English homeopathic physician (1888-1977)
gsd1 GIBSON Douglas M.: [Studies of Homeopathic Remedies], Beaconsfield (England): Beaconsfield Publishers, Marianne H (1987)
gsd2 GIBSON Douglas M.: [Elements of Homeopathy]
gsd3 GIBSON Douglas M.: [Fear and Homeopathy]
gsd4 GIBSON Douglas M.: [First Aid Homoeopathy in accidents and ailments.], The British Homoeopathic Association, London. (1977)
gsd4.fr GIBSON Douglas M.: Urgence en Homéopathie (Traduction, Dr J. Lafeuillade)
gse GEERTS Brigitte: Contemporary veterinary homeopath [Herentals, Belgium] (1950-)
gsg GUESS George: Contemporary homeopath [Asherville, USA]
gsg1 GUESS George: [Confirmatory questions]
gsg2 GUESS George: [Two cases of Alcoholism], Links, Vol 3: pg 21 (1991)
gsh GROSS Rud. Hermann: (- 1865)
gsh1 GROSS Rud. Hermann: [Comparative materia medica], Leipzig: Marggraf (1892)
gsh1.de GROSS Rud. Hermann: Vergleichende Arzneiwirkungslehre
gsk GYPSER Klaus-Henning: Contemporary homeopathic physician [Germany]. Editor of several homeopathic Journals. (1947-)
gsk1 GYPSER Klaus-Henning: [Kent's minor writings on homoeopathy [Indian reprint]], New Delhi: Jain Publishers (1988)
gsk2.de GYPSER Klaus-Henning: Fehler im Repertorium von Kent, Zt Klass H, Vol 5 (1987)
gsk3.de GYPSER Klaus-Henning: Zur Problematik Synonymer Rubriken im Repertorium von Kent, Zt Klass H, Vol 1 (1987)
gsk4.de GYPSER Klaus-Henning: Zur Frage der Verlässlichkeit des Homöopathischen Instrumentariums, Zt Klass H, Vol 6 (1987)
gsk5.de GYPSER Klaus-Henning: Entstehung, Struktur und Praktische Anwendung von Bogers Bönninghausen's Characteristics and Repertory, Zt Klass H, Vol 35 nr. 3 (1991)
gsk6.de GYPSER Klaus-Henning und WALDECKER A.: Bestätigungen von Symptomen im Kentschen Repertorium und Nachträge aus der Materia Medica, Zt Klass H, Vol 34 (1990)
gsk7.de GYPSER Klaus-Henning und WALDECKER A.: Gesammelte Arzneimittelprüfungen aus Stapfs "Archiv für die Homöopathische Heilkunst", Heidelberg (1991)
gsk8 GYPSER Klaus-Henning: [Argentum Nitricum], Z Class Homöop Arzn Nov-Dec. (1989)
gsl GRIESSELICH L.: (1804-1848)
gsl1 GRIESSELICH L.: [Proving of Franzensbad], Hygea, Band 3-23
gsl10 GRIESSELICH L.: [Proving of Teinach in Wirtemburg], Hygea Vol 9 pt 3: pg 224 (1836)
gsl11 GRIESSELICH L.: [Proving of Weilbach water], Hygea Vol 9: pt 3 (1836)
gsl2 GRIESSELICH L.: [Proving of Elmen Soolbad], Hygea Vol 9: pt 3 (1836)
gsl3 GRIESSELICH L.: [Proving of Ems], Hygea Vol 9 pt 3: pg 224 (1836)
gsl4 GRIESSELICH L.: [Proving of Kosen, Soolbad, Naumburg], Hygea Vol 9 pt 3: pg 244 (1836)
gsl5 GRIESSELICH L.: [Proving of Jatzfeld, Soolbad in Wurtemberg], Hygea Vol 9: pg 244, 256 (1836)
gsl6 GRIESSELICH L.: [Proving of Kronthal], Hygea Vol 9: pt 3 (1836)
gsl7 GRIESSELICH L.: [Proving of Landeck in Scheinen], Hygea Vol 9 pt 3: pg 224 (1836)
gsl8 GRIESSELICH L.: [Proving of Langebrucken], Hygea Vol 9 pt 3: pg 224 (1836)
gsl9 GRIESSELICH L.: [Proving of Meinberg pyrmont], Hygea Vol 9 pt 3: pg 175 (1836)
gsm GLASS Michael: Contemporary homeopath [New York, USA]
gsm1 GLASS Michael: [Two cases of Emotional First Aid], N Eng. J H, Vol 2 nr 1: pg 27 (1993)
gsr = mlg = GIBSON-MILLER R.
gsr1 = mlg3 = GIBSON-MILLER R.: [Relationship of remedies and sides of the body] (1977)
gss GIBSON S.

gss1 GIBSON S. and GIBSON Robin: [Calcarea fluorica], Homeopath, Jun Vol 13 (2): pg 62-64 (1993)
gss2 GIBSON S. and GIBSON Robin: [Fluoricum acidum], Homeopath, Jun Vol 13 (2): pg 62-64 (1993)
gsw GUERNSEY William Jefferson: (1854-1935)
gsw1 GUERNSEY William Jefferson: [Desires and aversions] (1883)
gsw2 GUERNSEY William Jefferson: [The homeopathic therapeutics of haemorrhoids], Calcutta (India), Sett Dey (1944)
gsw3 GUERNSEY William Jefferson: [Malandrinum], Med Adv, Vol 37/1: pg 338 (1899)
gsw4 GUERNSEY William Jefferson: [Repertory of Menstuation] (1879)
gsy GUERNSEY Henry Newell: (1817-1885)
gsy1 GUERNSEY Henry N.: [Keynotes to the Materia Medica], Philadelphia: Boericke (1887)
gsy1.de GUERNSEY Henry N.: Keynotes zur Materia Medica, Heidelberg (Germany): Karl F. Haug Verlag GmbH & C° (1999)
gsy2 GUERNSEY Henry N.: [Application of Principles of Homeopathy to Obstetrics] (1883)
gsz GUERNSEY Egbert: (1823-1903)
gsz1 GUERNSEY Egbert: [Homoeopathic Domestic Practice. [9th Ed.]], New York: Boericke & Tafel (1871)
gt GENTRY William Daniel: (1836-1922)
gt1 GENTRY William D.: [Concordance Repertory], New-York: Chatterton & Co (1890)
gt2 GENTRY William D.: [Rubrical and Regional Text Book of Homoeopathic Materia Medica Urine and Urinary organs], Philadelphia (1890)
gta GORTON W. D.
gtb GIRTEN: Contemporary German homeopath
gtc GUPTA A. C.
gtc1 GUPTA A. C.: [Materia medica of Bowel nosodes]
gtd GUPTA D. C. D.
gtd1 GUPTA D. C. D.: [Characteristic Materia Medica], Calcutta: Published by the author (6th Ed.)
gtk GUPTA A. K.
gtk1 GUPTA A. K.: [The Problem Child and Homeopathy] (1995)
gtn GHATAK N.
gtn1.es GHATAK N.: Enfermedades Cronicas. Translated by Martha Taylor De Zorrilla, New Delhi: Jain Publishers (1998)
gtr GUPTA Ram Lal
gtr1 GUPTA Ram Lal: [Directory of Disease and Cures in Homeopathy (Vol. 1-2)], New Dehli: Jain (1989)
gtx GERSTER Karl
gtz GOETZE O.
gtz1 GOETZE O.: [Berberis vulgaris], Simillia Simillibus Curentur, Vol 1 (1988)
gv GARVICE I.
gvl GRAUVOGL, Eduard von: (1811-1877)
gvl1 GRAUVOGL, Eduard von: [Text Book of Homoeopathy Part 1 & 2], New York: Boericke & Tafel (1870)
gvt GUNAVANTE S. M.: Contemporary homeopath [Bombay, India] (1959-)
gvt1 GUNAVANTE S. M.: [A case Psychological Disturbed Youth], Links, Vol 1: pg 36-37 (1995)
gvt2 GUNAVANTE S. M.: [The "genius" of homeopathic remedies] (1995)
gw GLADWIN Frederika E.: Student of Kent (1856-1931)
gw1 GLADWIN Frederika E.: [The people of the materia medica world], Philadelphia (1921)
gw1.fr GLADWIN Frederika E.: Le Peuple du Monde de la Matière Médicale - Une Matière Médicale comparative
gw2 GLADWIN Frederika E.: [The Repertory Idea], Hom Rec (1925)
gw3 GLADWIN Frederika E.: [A Study and Revision of Kent's Repertory], Hom Rec, Vol XLIII 15/2 (1928)
gw4 GLADWIN Frederika E.: [A Study and Revision of Kent's Repertory], Hom Rec, Vol XLI 12 (1926)
gww GAWLIK Walter
gww1 GAWLIK Walter: [Der kurze Weg zum homöopathischen Arzneimittel]
gy GRAY Bill: Contemporary homeopathic physician [San Francisco, USA]. Founder hom. school of Berkeley. (1942-)
gy2 GRAY Bill: [Seminar [Part 1] - Burgh Haamstede [Netherlands] May 1988], Amsterdam: Ilse Bos, private (1988)
gy3 GRAY Bill and SHORE Jonathan: [Seminar Burgh Haamstede [Netherlands] April 1989], Amsterdam: Ilse Bos, private (1989)
gy4 GRAY Bill: [Clinical cases.]
gya GRAY Alastair
gya1 GRAY Alastair: [A Homoeopathic proving of Ficus Macrophylla] (2001)
gya2 GRAY Alastair: [A Homoeopathic Proving of Chironex Fleckeri - Box Jellyfish] (2001)
gya3 GRAY Alastair: [A Homeopathic Proving of Lampona Cylindrata (White Tailed Spider)], Sydney: private (2003)
gya4 GRAY Alastair and PEDERSEN Carol: [A Homoeopathic Proving of Melaleuca Alternifolia (Tea Tree)] (2003)
gz GONZALES PEIRONA Enrique: Contemporary homeopathic physician,[Spain] Pres. Spanish Federation Hom. Assoc.
gz1 GONZALES PEIRONA Enrique: [Myrobalanum chebula [Terminalia chebula]]
gz1.es GONZALES PEIRONA Enrique: Myrobalanum chebula [Terminalia chebula]
gzp GARZONIS Peter: Contemporary homeopathic physician [Greece] (1947-)

h	HAHNEMANN Samuel: German Homeopathic Physician (1755-1843). Founder of Homeopathy
h1	HAHNEMANN Samuel: [Materia medica pura] (1880)
h1.de	HAHNEMANN Samuel: Reine Arzneimittellehre, 3 Vermehrte Auflage (Vol. 1-6), Dresden & Leipzig (1833)
h1.es	HAHNEMANN Samuel: Materia Médica Pura
h1.fr	HAHNEMANN Samuel: Traité de Matière Médicale
h1.pt	HAHNEMANN Samuel: Materia Medica Pura
h10.de	HAHNEMANN Samuel: Fragmenta de viribus medicamentorum. Die erste Materia medica homoeopathica, Greifenberg (Germany): Hahnemann Institut - Privatinstitut für homöopatische Dokumntation Gmbh (2003)
h2	HAHNEMANN Samuel: [The Chronic diseases, their Peculiar nature and their Homoeopathic cure. Translated by Louis H. Tafel.], London: Pemberton Dudley (1896)
h2.de	HAHNEMANN Samuel: Die Chronischen Krankheiten, 2 Vermehrte Auflage, Dresden & Leipzig (1839)
h2.es	HAHNEMANN Samuel: Tratado De Enfermedades Cronicas
h2.fr	HAHNEMANN Samuel: Les Maladies Chroniques, leur nature spécifique et leur traitement homéopathique. - Partie théorique., Bruxelles - Ed. de l'Ecole Belge d'Homéopathie
h2.pt	HAHNEMANN Samuel: Doenças Crónicas
h2a.es	HAHNEMANN Samuel: Doctrina y tratamiento homeopático de la enfermedades crónicas. Aumentada y comentarios por David Flores Toledo, México: Universidad Nacional Autónoma de México (1989)
h2b.es	HAHNEMANN Samuel: Las enfermedades cronicas, su naturaleza peculiar y su curación homeopática. Trabajo realizado por la Dra. Cristina Viqueira y colaboradores., Buenos Aires: Escuela Médica Homeopatica Argentina "Tomás Pablo Paschero" (1999)
h2c	HAHNEMANN Samuel: The Chronic Diseases: Their Specific Nature and Homoeopathic Treatment. Charles J. Hempel., Editor: Charles J. Hempel.
h3	HAHNEMANN Samuel: [Organon of Medicine], First translation (1922)
h3.de	HAHNEMANN Samuel: Organon der heilkunst, Heidelberg (Germany): Karl F. Haug Verlag GmbH & C° (1996)
h3.es	HAHNEMANN Samuel: El Organon de la medicina
h3.fr	HAHNEMANN Samuel: Organon de l'art de guérir (5th Ed.) Translated and annotated by Jean-Claude Grégoire, Bruxelles: Ecole Belge d'Homéopathie (1984)
h3.it	HAHNEMANN Samuel: Organon
h3a	HAHNEMANN Samuel: Organon of the Medical Art by Dr. Samuel Hahnemann. [2nd Ed.] Annotated by Wenda Breweter O'Reilly, Edited by Wenda Brewster O'Reilly (1997)
h3b.es	HAHNEMANN Samuel: El Organón de la medicina. [1st Ed.] Comentado por David Flores Toledo, Mexico: Instituto Politécnico Nacional (1999)
h3c.es	HAHNEMANN Samuel: Organon de la Medicina. Translation by Jorge C. Torrent., México: Editorial Porrúa (1999)
h4	HAHNEMANN Samuel: [Lesser writings Hahnemann]
h4.de	HAHNEMANN Samuel: La Medicina dell'Esperienza e altri scritti minori di Samuel Hahnemann, Milano: Editorium (1993)
h4.es	HAHNEMANN Samuel: Escritos Menores Hahnemann
h4.it	HAHNEMANN Samuel: La Medicina dell'Esperienza e altri scritti minori di Samuel Hahnemann, Milano: Editorium (1993)
h5	HAHNEMANN Samuel: [Ninety homeopathic remedies]
h5.es	HAHNEMANN Samuel: Noventa Medicamentos Homeopáticos, Miraguano Ediciones (1986)
h6	HAHNEMANN Samuel: [Coffeinum], Med Adv, Vol 43/6: pg 337 (1803)
h7.de	HAHNEMANN Samuel: Krankenjournal D2 [1801-02], Heidelberg: Haug (1801)
h7.pt	HAHNEMANN Samuel: Diário de Pacientes
h8	HAHNEMANN Samuel: [Effects of Coffee]
h9.es	HAHNEMANN Samuel: Algunos Escritos de Samuel Hahnemann, Quito (México): Red-RADAR (1998)
hbe	= wt = HUBBARD Elizabeth W. (old abbr.)
hbe1	HUBBARD Elizabeth W.: [= wt1 = Homeopathy as Art and Science (old abbr.)] (1990)
hbh	HUI BON HOA Jacques: Contemporary homeopathic physician [France] (1935-)
hbh1.fr	HUI BON HOA Jacques: Recueil des publications du Docteur Jacque Hui Bon Hua, Nîmes: Groupe Mercurius (1978)
hbh2.es	HUI BON HOA Jacques: Compendio de Técnica Repertorial & Homeopática
hbh2.fr	HUI BON HOA Jacques: Précis de technique répertoriale homéopathique de Kent, Angoulème (France): Eds. Coquemard (1963)
hbh3	HUI BON HOA Jacques: [Carcinosin.], Br Homoeopath J, nr 52: pg 189 (1963)
hbh3.fr	HUI BON HOA Jacques: Carcinosinum, Etude Pathogénésique et clinique, Annales Homoéopathiques Françaises, Octobre (1962)
hbh4.fr	HUI BON HOA Jacques: Nosodes intestinaux, Angoulême (1966)
hbj	HÜBNER Jutta
hbj1.de	HÜBNER Jutta: In Morpheus Armen liegen (2001)
hc	HUTCHINSON John H.
hca	HOLCOMBE A. W.: (1897-)

hca1	HOLCOMBE A. W.: [Spasms and Convulsions, an Abbridged Repertory], Calcutta, Salzer & C (1937)
hch	HANCHETT H.G.
hch1	HANCHETT H.G.: [Elements of Modern Domestic Medicine]
hch2	HANCHETT H.G.: [Sexual Health with Modern Homeopathic Treatment]
hcw	HUTCHINSON J. W.
hcw1	HUTCHINSON J. W.: [Seven hundred Redline Symptoms] (1994)
hd	HODIAMONT G.
hd1.fr	HODIAMONT G.: Plantes médicinales en homéopathie, Bruxelles: Debrus-Tensi (1983)
hd2.fr	HODIAMONT G.: La matière médicale & les remèdes végétaux., Paris: Baillière (1985)
hd3.fr	HODIAMONT G.: Nouvelles études d'homéopathie, Bruxelles (1960)
hd4.fr	HODIAMONT G.: Homéopathie et physiologie. Leurs relations., Paris: Similia et Baillière (1983)
hd5.fr	HODIAMONT G.: Venins et remèdes du règne animal en homéopathie., Bruxelles (1957)
hda	HINSDALE A. E.
hdg	HOLDEN Jon: (1942-)
hdh	HEUDENS Hennie: Contemporary homeopath [Leuven, Belgium]
hdh1.nl	HEUDENS Hennie: Themadagen Epilepsie & Silicea
hdh2	HEUDENS Hennie: [Hyoscyamus], Homeopath, Vol XI nr.3 (1994)
hdh3	HEUDENS Hennie: [Personal additions for Carcinosinum]
hdj	HARNDALL J.S.
hdj1	HARNDALL J.S.: [Homoeopathy in Veterinary Practice], Calcutta: Bagchi A. (1993)
he	HOYNE Temple S.: (1841-1899)
he1	HOYNE Temple S.: [Clinical Therapeutics (Vol. 1-2)] (1880)
hg	HOLMGREN Marc: Contemporary homeopathic physician [Belgium]
hgc	HUG Christine: Contemporary homeopath [Freiburg, Germany] (1950-)
hgc1	HUG Christine: [A case of Magnesium metallicum], Links, Vol 4: pg 44 (1994)
hh	HEATH G. E.
hha	HERSHOFF A.
hha1	HERSHOFF A.: [Musculoskeletal Healing]
hhl	HAEHL Richard: (1873-1923)
hhl1	HAEHL Richard: [Samuel Hahnemann: His Life and Work. Vol 1], Edited by J.H.Clarke & F.J. Wheeler (1922)
hhl1.de	HAEHL Richard: Samuel Hahnemann: sein Leben und sein Werk
hhl2	HAEHL Richard: [Samuel Hahnemann: His Life and Work. Vol 2], Edited by J.H.Clarke & F.J. Wheeler (1922)
hhr	HOBHOUSE R.W.
hhr1	HOBHOUSE R.W.: [Life of Christian Samuel Hahnemann]
hj	HIND Jai
hj1	HIND Jai et al.: [Chronic Diseases and Theory of Miasms - Team of Experienced Teachers]
hl	HALE Edwin Moses: (1830-1899)
hl1	HALE Edwin Moses: [Materia Medica and Special Therapeutics of the New Remedies [5th Ed.]], Philadelphia: Boericke and Tafel (1886)
hl10	HALE Edwin Moses: [The Characteristics of the New Remedies [3rd Ed.]], Detroit: Lodge's Homoeopathic Pharmacy (Michigan) (1873)
hl11	HALE Edwin Moses: [The Medical, Surgical, and Hygienic Treatment of Disease of Women, especially those causing Sterility. [2nd Ed.]], New York: Boericke & Tafel (1880)
hl12.de	HALE Edwin Moses: Hale's Neue Amerikanische Heilmittel., Euskirchen: Verlag Homöopathisches Wissen (1873)
hl2	HALE Edwin Moses: [Diseases of the Heart]
hl3	HALE Edwin Moses: [Cases: Spasmodic Cough], N Eng J H, Vol 3 nr.1: pg 26 (1994)
hl4	HALE Edwin Moses: [Clinical Observations on Terebinth], American Homeopathic Review, pg 454 (1863)
hl5	HALE Edwin Moses: [Proving of Nelubrium luteum], Chicago (1871)
hl6	HALE Edwin Moses: [Proving of Viburnum prunifolium], Medical Era, Vol 1: pg 5 (1883)
hl7	HALE Edwin Moses: [Proving of Illex casseine], Washington Govt. Pr. (1891)
hl8	HALE Edwin Moses: [Saw Palmetto]
hl9	HALE Edwin Moses: [Special Symptomatology of the New Remedies Vol. 1] (1875)
hla	HERTLI Rudolf: Contemporary homeopath [Switzerland]
hlb	HARTLAUB Carl Georg Christian: (1795-1839)
hlb1	HARTLAUB Carl Georg Christian and TRINKS C. F.: [Unknown Title], Ann Hom Klin, Vol 3: pg 309-313 (1832)
hlb2.de	HARTLAUB Carl G. C. und TRINKS N.: Reine Arzneimittellehre (Vol. 1-2), Leipzig: Brockhaus (1831)
hll	HILL B.L.: (1813-1871)
hll1	HILL B.L. and HUNT Jas. G.: [The Homeopathic Practice of Surgery, Together with Operative Surgery], Cleveland: J.B. Cobb and Company (Ohio) (1855)
hlo	Homéopathie à Livres Ouverts
hlo1.fr	Homéopathie à Livres Ouverts: Mercurius Corrosivus - Etude et Observation. (Coordonné par FRENDO Ramon), hlo
hlo2.fr	Homéopathie à Livres Ouverts: Haliae Leucocephalus - Etude et Thèmes. (Coordonné par FRENDO Ramon & SAUZIERE D.) (2002)

hlo3.fr	Homéopathie à Livres Ouverts: Séminaire de Vénise 2002-2003. (Coordonné par FRENDO Ramon) (2003)
hlo4.fr	Homéopathie à Livres Ouverts: Thèmes et Etude de la Matière Médicale
hlr	HALE R. Douglas
hlr1	HALE R. Douglas: [Acute Diseases of the Chest] (1875)
hm	HERMACE S. G.: (1940-)
hmb	HAMISH W. Boyd
hmd	HAMOND Declan
hmd1	HAMOND Declan: [Ecstasy [MDMA] proving]
hmd2	HAMOND Declan: [Berlin Wall proving]
hme	HAMILTON Edward: (1824-1899)
hme1	HAMILTON Edward: [Flora Homoeopathica or Illustrations and Descriptions of the Medicinal Plants used as Homeopathic Remedies], New Delhi: Jain Publishers (1852)
hmf	HARTMANN Franz: Student of Hahnemann (1796-1853)
hmf1	HARTMANN Franz: [Arsenicum album], Hom Rec, Vol XIII nr. 1: pg 27 (1898)
hmf2	HARTMANN Franz: [Practical Observations on the Chief remedies] (1841)
hmh	HAUPTMAN Horst: Contemporary homeopathic physician [Germany] (1951-)
hmh1	HAUPTMAN Horst: [The significance of signs], Links, Vol 3: pg 27-28 (1992)
hmh2.de	HAUPTMAN Horst: Homöopathie in der Kinderärtzlichen Praxis, Heidelberg: Haug Verlag (1991)
hmn	HAMILTON Donald
hmn1	HAMILTON Donald: [Homeopathic Care for Cats and Dogs]
hms	HOLMES H.P.
hms1	HOLMES H.P.: [Magnesium phosphoricum], H Heritage, Vol 16: pg 427-430 (1991)
hmw	HELMUTH William Tod: (1833-1902)
hmw1	HELMUTH William Tod: [Surgery and its Adaptation to Homoeopathic Practice], Philadelphia: Moss & Brother (Pennsylvania) (1855)
hn	HONAN W. F.
hnb	HORNIG Bernhard
hnc	HEINIGKE Carl: (-1889)
hnc1	HEINIGKE Carl: [Pathogenetic Outlines of homoeopathic drugs], Philadelphia, Boericke & Tafel (1880)
hnz	HEINITZ M.
hnz1	HEINITZ M.: [Haronga madagascariensis], Therap. Gegenw. 103; 1014 (1964)
homp	UNKNOWN: Different articles, Hom Phys (1881)
hp	HEMPEL H.: Student of Hahnemann (1780-1850)
hp1	HEMPEL H.: [The science of therapeutics vol. 1 (1843-)]
hpc	HEMPEL Charles Julius: (1811-1879)
hpc1	HEMPEL Charles Julius: [Materia Medica and Therapeutics] (1865)
hpc2	HEMPEL Charles Julius: [A New and Comprehensive System of Materia Medica Vol 1 & Vol 2], London: Leath and Ross. (1865)
hr	HERING Constantine: American homeopathic physician. Introduced lachesis in MM. (1800-1880)
hr1	HERING Constantine: [Guiding Symptoms of our Materia Medica (Vol. 1-10)], Philadelphia (1879)
hr1.de	HERING Constantine: Leitsymptome unserer Materia Medica (Vol 1-10), Aachen (Germany): Verlag Renée von Schlick (1992)
hr1.fr	HERING Constantine: Les symptômes guides de notre Matière Médicale, Limoges: Editions Roger Jollois
hr2	HERING Constantine: [Condensed Materia Medica - reviewed by E. A. Farrington [3rd ed.]], Philadelphia (1877)
hr2.de	HERING Constantine: Kurzgefasste Arzneimittlellehre, Greifenberg (Germany): Hahnemann Institut - Privatinstitut für homöopatische Dokumntation Gmbh
hr3	HERING Constantine: [Analytical Repertory of the Symptoms of the Mind], New York (1881)
hr4	HERING Constantine: [The homeopathic domestic physician], Philadelphia: Boericke & Tafel (1883)
hr4.de	HERING Constantine und Richard Haehl: Homöopathischer Hausarzt, Euskirchen: Verlag Homöopathisches Wissen (1998)
hr4a.es	HERING Constantine: Medicina Popular Homeopatica. Refundida y completada por Ricardo Haehl., New Delhi: Jain Publishers (1990)
hr5.de	HERING Constantine: Wirkungen des Schlangengiftes, Leipzig, Allentaun: Kummer (1837)
hr6	HERING Constantine: [Proving of Lithium carbonicum], American Homoeopathic Review, May pg 481 (1863)
hr7	HERING Constantine and MARTIN Henry Noah: [The Journal of Homoeopathic Clinics. Vol 1 & 2], Philadelphia: Hahnemann Medicall College (1870)
hr8	HERING Constantine: [Analytical Therapeutics] (1875)
hr9.de	HERING Constantine: Amerikanische Arzneiprüfungen Vorarbeiten zur Arzneilehre als Naturwissenschaft, Euskirchen: Verlag Homöopathisches Wissen (1857)
hrj	HEEREN Joseph: Contemporary homeopathic physician [Belgium]
hrk	HERON Krista: (1955-)
hrk1	HERON Krista: [Longing for a perfect intimacy. Two cases of Psuedotsuga menziessi], Links, Vol 12: pg 181-183. (1999)
hrn	HERRICK Nancy: Contemporary homeopath [Albany, USA] (1947-)
hrn1	HERRICK Nancy: [A case of Natrium Phosphoricum], Links, Vol 3: pg 28-29 (1993)

hrn2 HERRICK Nancy: [Animal Mind, Human voices: Provings of Eight New Animal Remedies] (1998)

hrn3 HERRICK Nancy: [Dolphin's Milk: a proving], Links, Vol 9: pg 100-103 (1996)

hrn4.de HERRICK Nancy: Die Prüfung von Lac leoninum, H Zt, Nr 1: pg 40-46 (1996)

hrn5 HERRICK Nancy: [Anhalonium Proving]

hs HUGHES Richard: (1836-1902)

hs1 HUGHES and DAKE Jabez Philander: [Cyclopaedia of Drug Pathogenesy (Vol. 1-4)], London (1891)

hs2 HUGHES Richard: [Manual of Pharmacodynamics], Calcutta: Ringer & C° (1876)

hs3 HUGHES Richard: [The principles and practice of homoeopathy.], New Delhi: World Homoeopathic Links (1902)

hs4 HUGHES Richard: [The Knowledge of the Physician. A Course of Lectures delivered at the Boston University School of Medicine]

hs5 HUGHES Richard: [A Manuel of Therapeutics: According to the Method of Hahnemann], London: Leath and Ross (2nd Ed.) (1877)

hsa HANSEN Oscar: (1859-)

hsa1 HANSEN Oscar: [A Text-Book of Materia Medica of Rare Homeopathic Remedies: A Supplement to A. G. Cowperthwaite's "Materia medica"], London: Hom. Publ. (1899)

hsb HAYES Royal Elmore Swift: (1871-1952)

hsb1 HAYES R. E. S.: [Adaxukah Effects and Other Provings], Hom Rec (1928)

hsb2 HAYES R. E. S.: [Vipera torva, clinical reports], Hom Rec, Vol 54/11: pg 34 (1939)

hsb3 HAYES R. E. S.: [A study of Ambergris], International Hahnemannian Association, Session 42: pg 121 (1921)

hsh HOLSTEIN Hermann: Contemporary homeopath [Germany]

hsj HANSEL Jürgen: Contemporary homeopath [Germany] (1951-)

hsj1 HANSEL Jürgen: [Ephedra] (2004)

hsj1.de HANSEL Jürgen: Ephedra und die Zauberpflanzen, Greifenberg (Germany): Hahnemann Institut - Privatinstitut für homöopatische Dokumntation Gmbh (1998)

hsl HANSEN Lise

hsn HUSSAIN Abid

hsn1 HUSSAIN Abid: [Relationships of Homeopathic Drugs], Sargodha: Kent Homeopathic Stores and Hospital (1960)

hsw HAWKES W. J.

hsw1 HAWKES W. J.: [Characteristic Indications for Prominent Remedies] (1884)

ht HOUGHTON Henry Clark: American homeopathic physician (1837-1901)

ht1 HOUGHTON Henry Clark: [Lectures on Clinical Otology], Boston: Clapp (1885)

hta HEATH Alfred: (1850-)

htc HART Charles P.

htc1 HART Charles P.: [Therapeutics of nervous Diseases], New Delhi: Harjet & Co (1989)

htc2 HART Charles P.: [Repertory of the new remedies], Philadelphia: Boericke & Tafel (1876)

htj HOUGHTON Jacqueline: (1949-)

htj1 HOUGHTON Jacqueline and HALAHAN Elisabeth: [The homeopathic proving of Lac humanum] (1993)

htk HÖTZER K.

htk1 HÖTZER K.: [Lespedeza capitata], A H Z 218 ; 7 (1973)

htl HOUAT L.T.

htl1.fr HOUAT L.T.: Homoeopathie et Toxologie (1866)

htl2.fr HOUAT L.T.: Nouvelles Donnees de M.M.H. et de Toxicologie

htp HATHERLY Patricia A.

htp1 HATHERLY Patricia A.: [A proving of Cadmium metallicum] (1998)

hu HERSCU Paul: Contemporary homeopath [USA]. Editor of the New England Journal of Homeopathy (1959-)

hu1 HERSCU Paul: [A case of Failure to thrive], Links, Vol 3: pg 24-25 (1992)

hu2 HERSCU Paul: [The Homeopathic Treatment of Children], Berkeley: North Atlantic books (California) (1991)

hu3 HERSCU Paul: [Stramonium - with an introduction to Analysis using Cycles and Segments], Amherst: New England School of Homeopathy (1996)

hu4 HERSCU Paul: [Alcoholus]

hva HORVILLEUR Alain

hva1 HORVILLEUR Alain: [Matière Médicale]

hvb HAVRANEK Bea: Veterinary

hw HOWARD A. G.

hwc HIWAT Corrie: Contemporary homeopath [Groningen, The Netherlands] (1950-)

hwc1 HIWAT Corrie: [Two Cases], Links, Vol 1: pg 14-16 (1994)

hwj HOWARTH J.

hwj1 HOWARTH J.: [Clinical And Pathogenetic Action of Coffea cruda], H Heritage, May ; 17(5) ; 297-298 (1992)

hzf HEINZE F.

hzf1 HEINZE F.: [Galanthus nivalis], Zeitschrift für Naturheilmethoden 1; 125-131 (1979)

hzw HERZ W.

hzw1 HERZ W.: [Galphimia glauca], A H Z 212; 533 (1976)

ib IMBERECHTS Jacques: Contemporary homeopathic physician [Brussel, Belgium]. Pres. Homeopathia Internationalis. Vice-Pres. Liga Belgium. (1937-)

ib1 IMBERECHTS Jacques: [Carcinosinum, cancerinism and tuberculinism, childhood diseases among adults and other viral, immunological and

	degenerative disturbances], Athene, 31me congrès de la Ligue Homoeopathique intern. (1976)
iba	IBERSHOFF A. E.
ih	IMHÄUSER Hedwig: (1948-)
ih1.de	IMHÄUSER Hedwig: Homöopathie in der Kinderheilkunde, Heidelberg: Haug Verlag (1975)
ilm	ITALIANO Maurizio
ilm1	ITALIANO Maurizio: [Cured Cases]
is	IMS Leif: Contemporary homeopathic physician [Norway]
itm	ISSAUTIER Marie Noëlle and CELVET Henry: (1949-)
iwa	IRWIN Anne
iwa1	IRWIN Anne: [Seven Streams of Taosca Proving] (1998)
iwa2	IRWIN Anne: [A proving of Tory island clay. Red Granite Clay] (2003)
j	JAHR Georg Heinrich Gottlieb: German homeopathic physician (1800-1875)
j1.de	JAHR Georg Heinrich Gottlieb: Die Geisteskrankheiten, dritter Band der Therapie nach den Grundsätzen der Homöopathie von Bernhard Bar, Leipzig: Wilmar Schwabe (1866)
j1.es	JAHR Georg Heinrich Gottlieb: Del tratamiento homeopatico de las Affeciones Nerviosas y de las Enfermedades Mentales. Translated by Silverio Rodriguez Lopez, New Delhi: Jain Publishers
j10	JAHR Georg Heinrich Gottlieb: [Family Practice or Simple Directions in Homeopathic Domestic medicine]
j11	JAHR Georg Heinrich Gottlieb: [The Venereal Diseases, their Pathological Nature, Correct Diagnosis and Homeopathic Treatment]
j11.de	JAHR Georg Heinrich Gottlieb: Die venerischen Krankheiten: ihre pathologische Natur, richtige Erkenntniss und Homöopathische Behandlung., Leipzig: Niedergesaess (1867)
j12.es	JAHR Georg Heinrich Gottlieb: Nociones elementales de homeopathia (1989)
j13.fr	JAHR Georg Heinrich Gottlieb: Du Traitement Homéopathique des Maladies de la Peau et des Lésions Extérieures en général, Paris: Libraire de L'Academie Nationale de Medecine (France) (1850)
j14.de	JAHR Georg Heinrich Gottlieb: Die Lehren und Grundsätze der gesammten theoretischen und praktischen Homöopatischen Heilkunst., Stuttgart: Liesching (1857)
j15.de	JAHR Georg Heinrich Gottlieb: Allgemeine und spezielle Therapie der Geisteskrankheiten und Seelenstörungen: nach homöopathischen Grundsätzen, Leipzig: Weigel (1855)
j16.de	JAHR Georg Heinrich Gottlieb: Alphabetisches Repertorium der Hautsymptome aus Symptomen-Kodex., Euskirchen: Verlag Homöopatisches Wissen (1849)
j2	JAHR Georg Heinrich Gottlieb: [Forty years of practice. Translated with Notes and New Remedies, by Charles J. Hempel, M.D.], New York, William Radde (1869)
j2.de	JAHR Georg Heinrich Gottlieb: Therapeutischer Leitfaden für angehende Homöopathen: Zusammenfassung 40 Praxis etc, Leipzig: Literarisches Institut (1869)
j3.de	JAHR Georg Heinrich Gottlieb: Klinische Anweisungen zu Homöopathischer Behandlung der Krankeiten, Leipzig: Bethman (1849)
j4.de	JAHR Georg Heinrich Gottlieb: Gedrängte Totalübersicht aller zur Zeit eingeführten hom. Heilmittel, Leipzig: Hermann Bethmann (1848)
j5.de	JAHR Georg Heinrich Gottlieb: Systematisch-Alphabetisches Repertorium der Homoöpathischen Arzneimittellehre, Leipzig: Herrmann Bethmann (1848)
j6.de	JAHR Georg Heinrich Gottlieb: Handbuch der Haupt-Anzeigen für die richtige Wahl der homöopatischen Heilmittel, Düsseldorf: Schaub (1835)
j7.de	JAHR Georg Heinrich Gottlieb: Ausführlicher Symptomen-Kodex der homöopatischen Arzneimittel, Übersicht der homöopatischen Heilmittel in ihren Erstwirkungen un Heilan. Vol 1 & Vol 2, Leipzig (1848)
j8	JAHR Georg Heinrich Gottlieb: [Homoeopathic Treatment of diseases of Females and Infants at the Breast], New York (1856)
j9	JAHR Georg Heinrich Gottlieb: [Hull's Jahr : A New Manual of Homoeopathic Practice. Edited with Annotations and Additions by F.G.Snelling. [8th American Ed], with an Appendix of the New Remedies by Charles.J. Hempel], New York: William Radde (1860)
j9.es	JAHR Georg Heinrich Gottlieb: Nuevo Manual de Medicina Homeopática. Translated by: Pedro Rino, New Delhi: Jain Publishers
jb	JOBERT J.: Contemporary homeopathic pediatrician [France]
jc	JACOBS Jennifer: Contemporary homeopathic physician [USA]
jl	JULIAN Othon André: Contemporary homeopathic physician [France] (1910-1984)
jl1	JULIAN Othon André: [Materia Medica of new Homeopathic remedies] (1979)
jl1.fr	JULIAN Othon André: Dictionnaire de Matière Médicale de 130 Nouveaux Homéothérapeutiques, Paris: Masson (1981)
jl2	JULIAN Othon André: [Materia Medica of Nosodes with Repertory] (1983)
jl2.fr	JULIAN Othon André: Matière Médicale des Biothérapiques Nosodes. Traité de Micro-immunothérapie Dynamisée, Paris: Librairie Le François (1977)

jl3 JULIAN Othon André: [Materia Medica of New Homoeopathic Remedies] (1979)

jl3.fr JULIAN Othon André: Matière médicale d'Homéothérapie, Paris: Peyronnet (1971)

jl4 JULIAN Othon André: [Treatise on dynamised micro immunotherapy], New Delhi: Jain Publishers (1992)

jl5 JULIAN Othon André: [Intestinal nosodes of Bach-Paterson [1st Indian Ed.]], New Delhi: Jain Publishers (1981)

jl6 JULIAN Othon André: [Pathogenesis of Nepenthes], Br H J, Vol 53: pg 259-266 (1964)

jl7 JULIAN Othon André: [Pathogenesis of Platinum 1980. A vortico-visceral pharmacodynamic proving,], Br H J(1983) Vol 72: pg 31-50 (1980)

jl8 JULIAN Othon André: [bcg], Hahnemannian Gleanings 1981 48 ;48(2) (1981)

jln JOLLYMAN N. W.

jln1 JOLLYMAN N. W.: [My Practice of Homeopathy], Nex Delhi: Jain Publishers (1991)

jln2 JOLLYMAN N. W.: [Asthma - Causes, Types & Homeopathic Treatment] (1990)

jmb JIMENEZ Benjamin

jmb1.es JIMENEZ Benjamin: Farmacopea homeopática [2nd Ed.], New Delhi: Jain Publishers (1939)

jn JONES Samuel Arthur: (1834-1912)

jnb JAIN B.

jnb1 JAIN B.: [Pocket Medical dictionary of the principal words used in medicine and the collateral sciences]

jnc JAYNE Christopher

jne JONES Eli G.: (1850-1933)

jne1 JONES Eli G.: [Cancer: its Causes, Symtoms and Treatment]

jnj JONAS Julian: Contemporary homeopath [Vermont, USA] (1950-)

jnj1 JONAS Julian: [A case of being accident prone], N Eng. J H, Vol 1 nr 1: pg 8 (1992)

jnm JENAER Maurice

jnm1.fr JENAER Maurice: Homeopathie pour mieux guérir, Brussels: Hatier (1986)

jnm2.fr JENAER Maurice et MARICHAL Bernard: Immunothérapie et Homéopathie, Rev Belg Hom: 44 Vol 2: pg 45-60 (1992)

jns JONES Stacy: (1828-1906)

jns1 JONES Stacy: [The Medical genius; a guide to the cure], Philadelphia (USA), Boericke & Tafel (1912)

jns2 JONES Stacy: [The Bee Line Repertory], Philadelphia (USA), Boericke & Tafel (1894)

jnv JENNI Viktor: Contemporary homeopath [Bern, Switzerland] (1950-)

jnv1 JENNI Viktor: [Opium], Links, Vol 4: pg 21-24 (1993)

jny JOUANNY J.

jny1.fr JOUANNY J., JOLY P., AUBIN M., PICARD PH. et DEMARQUE D.: Pratique Homeopatique en Urologie, Paris: Centre d'études et de documentation homeopatiques (1983)

jny2 JOUANNY J., DEMARQUE D., AUBIN M., SAINT-JEAN Y. and YOLY P.: [Pratique Homeopatique en Medicine Infantile], France: Centre d'études et de documentation homeopatique (1988)

jny3.fr JOUANNY J, CRAPANNE J.B., DANCER H., MASSON J-L: Thérapeutique Homéopathique: possibilités pour pathologies aigues Vol 1, Pioltello: Laboratoires Boiron Italia (1999)

jny3.it JOUANNY J, CRAPANNE J.B., DANCER H., e MASSON J-L: Terapia omeopatica Possibilitá in Patologia acuta (1999)

jny4.fr JOUANNY J, CRAPANNE J.B., DANCER H., MASSON J-L.: Thérapeutique Homéopathique: possibilités pour pathologies chroniques Vol 2, Pioltello: Laboratoires Boiron Italia (1999)

jny4.it JOUANNY J, CRAPANNE J.B., DANCER H., e MASSON J-L.: Terapia omeopatica Possibilitá in Patologia cronica (II edizione) (1999)

jpn JAIN P. N.

jpn1.es JAIN P. N.: Guía para el botiquín familiar homeopático de B. Jain, New Delhi: Jain Publishers (2000)

js JOHNSON B. R.

jsa JACQUES Alexandre: Contemporary homeopathic physician [Namur, Belgium] (1950-)

jsb JANS Johan: Contemporary homeopathic physician [Belgium]

jsg JANSSON Gunnar: Contemporary homeopath [Sweden]

jsh JESSEN H. C.

jsh1 JESSEN H. C.: [Therapeutical Materia Medica], New Delhi: Jain Publishers (1991)

jsi JOHNSON I.D.

jsi1.es JOHNSON I.D.: La Homeopatía en Casa. Arreglada para el uso de las familias. Traducida y puesta al día por Eulalio Dario Flores, New Delhi: Jain Publishers

jsj JANSEN Jean Pierre: Contemporary homeopath [Groningen, The Netherlands] (1954-)

jsj1 JANSEN Jean-Pierre: [Two Bromium cases], Links, Vol 3: pg 17-18 (1994)

jsj2 JANSEN Jean-Pierre and Hiwat Corrie: [Scutellaria laterifolia], Centrum voor klass. Hom. Holland

jsj3 JANSEN Jean-Pierre and Hiwat Corrie: [Aristolochia clematitis], Centrum voor klass. Hom. Holland

jsj4 JANSEN Jean-Pierre and Hiwat Corrie: [Calcarea sulphurica], Centrum voor Klassieke homeopathie, Holland

jsj5 JANSEN Jean-Pierre and Hiwat Corrie: [Calcarea silicata], Centrum voor Klassieke homeopathie, Holland

jsj6	JANSEN Jean-Pierre and Hiwat Corrie: [Protocol provings linking trees.], Links, Vol 12: pg 165-166 (1999)
jsj7	JANSEN Jean Pierre: [Taxus Baccata] (1999)
jsj8	JANSEN Jean Pierre: [Hahnemans proving] (1996)
jsl	JOHNSTON Linda: Contemporary homeopathic physician [Los Angeles, USA] (1950-)
jsp	JOUSSET Pierre: (1818-1910)
jsp1.fr	JOUSSET Pierre: Elements de Pathologie et de Therapeutique Generales [2nd Ed.], Paris: Libraire J.-B. Bailliere et Fils (France) (1900)
jsp2.fr	JOUSSET Pierre: Leçons de Clinique Médicale professées à L'Hopital Homéopathique Saint-Jacques 1877-1885, Paris: Libraire J.-B. Bailliere et Fils (France) (1886)
jsw	JAMES Bushrod Washington: (1836-)
jsw1	JAMES Bushrod Washington: [Tumors], Haryana (1985)
jsx	JANSSENS Pieter G.: (1952-)
jsx1.fr	JANSSENS Pieter G., KIVITS M. et VUYLSTEKE J.: Médecine et hygiène en Afrique centrale de 1885 à nos jours vol. 1, Brussels: Fondation Roi Baudoin (1992)
jtm	JOST Marcus
jtm1.de	JOST Marcus: Die Eiche, Quercus robur (1997)
jws	JAWAHAR Shah
jzk	JEZEWSKI Henry: (1961-)
jzk1	JEZEWSKI Henri: [Vibhuti]
k	KENT James Tyler: American homeopathic physician (1849-1916). Probably the most important homeopath at the turn of the century.
k1	KENT James Tyler: [Kent's personal additions to his Repertory] (1916)
k13	KENT James Tyler: [Source unknown or not mentioned] (1916)
k2	KENT James Tyler: [Lectures on Homeopathic Materia Medica [4th Ed.]], New Delhi: Jain Publishers (1904)
k2.es	KENT James Tyler: Lecturas Homeopáticas de la Materia Médica. Vol 1 and 2 Translated by Anselmo Hernández Jordán, New Delhi: Jain Publishers (1929)
k2.fr	KENT James Tyler: Matière Médicale Homéopathique
k3	KENT James Tyler: [Minor Writings on Homeopathy], Heidelberg: Haug (1987)
k3.es	KENT James Tyler: Homeopatía - Escritos Menores, Aforismos y Preceptos
k4	KENT James Tyler: [New Remedies, clinical cases, lesser writings, aphorisms and precepts], Chicago: Erhart and Karl (1926)
k5	KENT James Tyler: [Kent Lectures on homeopathic philosophy] (1919)
k5.es	KENT James Tyler: Filosofía homeopática, New Delhi: Jain Publishers
k5.pt	KENT James Tyler: Lições de Filosofía Homeopática
k6	KENT James Tyler: [Use of the Repertory "How to Study the Repertory"], Jain Publishers
k6.es	KENT James Tyler: El Uso del repertorio.
k7	KENT James Tyler: [What the doctor needs to Know in Order to Make a Succesfull prescription]
k8	KENT James Tyler: [The Dunham Lectures [merged into Kent]] (1899)
kab	KIANI B.
kab1	KIANI B.: [Haronga madagascariensis], Arzneim.-Forsch. 18; 763 (1968)
kbj	KRICHBAUM J.W.
kbj1	KRICHBAUM J.W.: [The Remedy v.s Mechanics in Cases of Difficult Labor], Homoeopathic Recorder (1900)
kbj2	KRICHBAUM J.W.: [The surgical sphere and indications for hypericum], Medical Advance, Vol 41 (1903)
kbj3	KRICHBAUM J.W.: [Sinapis nigra], Medical Advance, Vol 46 (1908)
kbj4	KRICHBAUM J.W.: [Arsenicum iodatum], Medical Advance, Vol 47 (1909)
kda	KORNDOERFER A.
kda1	KORNDOERFER A.: [C. von Boenninghausen's Homoeopathic Therapia of Intermittent and Other fevers] (1873)
kf	KAUF Christian P.: Contemporary homeopathic physician [Germany]
kg	KING Lesley: Contemporary homeopath [England] (1957-)
kg1	KING Lesley and LAWRENCE Bob: [Luna, a proving], Turnbridge Wells: Helios (1993)
kga	KRÜGER Andreas: (1954-)
kga1.de	KRÜGER Andreas: Lac caninum - Der faule Hund wird langsam bissig, H Zt, Nr 1: pg 69-73 (1996)
kgc	KRÜGER Christiane: Contemporary veterinary homeopath [Germany] (1945-)
kgj	KING Jno. C.
kgj1	KING Jno. C.: [Headaches / Repertory Analysis], Chicago (1891)
kgp	KÖNIG Peter: (1955-)
kgp1	KÖNIG Peter and SWOBODA Franz: [Succinicum acidum], Br H J, Vol 76/19: pg 19-29 (1987)
kgp2	KÖNIG Peter and SANTOS Ute: [Dream Proving of rhododendron chrysantum], Links, Vol 8: pg 19-20 (1995)
kgp3	KÖNIG Peter and SANTOS Ute: [Berberis Vulgaris] (1994)
kgp4	KÖNIG Peter and SANTOS Ute: [Convallaria]
kgp5	KÖNIG Peter and SANTOS Ute: [Dream Proving of rhododendron chrysantum] (1993)
kh	KIRSCH Sarah: German homeopathic physician from the time of Hahnemann (1835-)
khn	KRACH N.
khn1	KRACH N.: [Biotypen], Heidelberg: Haug Verlag (1980)
khu	KÖHLER Ulrich
kjm	KRUG Jean-Marie: (1951-)

kjm1.fr	KRUG Jean-Marie: Observations et Cas Cliniques
kk	KLUNKER Will: Contemporary homeoathic physician [Heiden, Switzerland]. Creator of the Synthetic Repertory with Dr. Barthel. (1932-)
kk1.de	KLUNKER Will: Eine Arzneiprüfung von Espeletia Grandiflora, A H Z, Vol 217: pg 5 - 14 (1972)
kk2.de	KLUNKER Will: Zu den Rubriken der Säuglings- und Stillbeschwerden, Zt Klass H, Vol 17/6: pg 269-272 (1973)
kk3.fr	KLUNKER Will: Spigelia ou Spigurrus?, Rev Belg Hom, Vol 3: pg 41-50 (1992)
kk4	KLUNKER Will and MILLER G.: [Beziehungen der arznien unter sich.], Heidelberg: Haug verlag
kk5.fr	KLUNKER Will: Rêves et Delusions de serpents, Rev B H, Vol XXIII Decembre nr. 4 (1990)
kk6	KLUNKER Will: [Synthetic Repertory: Sleep, Dreams, sexuality. Vol 3], New Delhi: Jain Publishers (1991)
kka	KAFKA Jacob: (1809-1893)
kka1.de	KAFKA Jacob: Die Homeopatische Therapie auf Grundlange der Physiologischen Schule, Sondershausen, Gotha: Eupel (1865)
kkb	KOKELENBERG Guy: Contemporary homeopathic physician [St Niklaas, Belgium] (1948-)
kkc	KUHNKE J.
kkc1	KUHNKE J.: [Luffa operculata], A H Z 212; 558 (1976)
kkp	KRISHNA KUMAR P.
kkp1	KRISHNA KUMAR P.: [Talks on poisons, Metals acids & Nosodes used as Homeopathic Medicines] (1995)
kkp2	KRISHNA KUMAR P.: [The women, female problems and their cure], New Delhi: Jain Publishers (1995)
kkp2.es	KRISHNA KUMAR P.: Enfermedades comunes del Hombre y su curación
kkp3	KRISHNA KUMAR P.: [The man, sexual problems and their cure], New Delhi: Jain Publishers (1995)
kkp3.es	KRISHNA KUMAR P.: Enfermedades comunes del Hombre y su curación
kkv	KULKARNI V.
kkv1	KULKARNI V.: [Gynecology and Obstretics] (1994)
kl	KÜNZLI VON FIMMELSBERG Jost: Homeopathic physician [Switzerland] (1915-1992)
kl1	KÜNZLI VON FIMMELSBERG Jost: [Repertorium Generale], Berg a. Starnberger See (Germany): Barthel & Barthel (1987)
kl2	KÜNZLI VON FIMMELSBERG Jost: [Repertorium Generale - black dots], Berg a. Starnberger See (Germany): Barthel & Barthel (1987)
kl3	KÜNZLI VON FIMMELSBERG Jost: [Collected Lectures]
kla	KEIL
kla1	KEIL: [Proving of Friedrichhaller Bitterwasser], Zeitschrift Für Homöopatische Klinik, Vol 4 (1845)
klb	KAPLAN Brian: Contemporary homeopathic physician [UK]
klb1	KAPLAN Brian: [The Homeopathic Conversation: the art of taking the case], London: Natural Medicine Press (2001)
klg	KELLER Georg von: Contemporary homeopathic physician [Germany]
klg1.de	KELLER Georg von: Eine Quellenstudie zum Kentschen Repertorium, Zt Klass H, Vol 33 (1989)
klg2.de	KELLER Georg von: Computer and Homöopathische Einzelsymptome, Zt Klass H, Vol 34 (1990)
klg3	KELLER Georg von: [Clematis erecta], Br H J, Vol 4 (1993)
klg4.de	KELLER Georg von: Berberis: Symptomensammlungen · homöopatischer Arzneimittel. Heft 10, Heidelberg: Karl F. Haug Verlag (1982)
klg5.de	KELLER Georg von: Gesammelte Aufsätze und Vorträge zur Homöopathie., Greifenberg (Germany): Hahnemann Institut - Privatinstitut für homöopatische Dokumntation Gmbh (2002)
klm	KITTLER Monika
klm1	KITTLER Monika: [Thea chinensis] (1999)
klm1.de	KITTLER Monika: Thea Chinensis: Die Prüfung, Zweibrücken:Verlag Karl-Josef Müller (1999)
klr	KOEHLER Gerhard: (1946-)
klr1	KOEHLER Gerhard: [Lehrbuch der Homöopathie [2 Vols]], Stuttgart: Hippokrates Verlag (1988)
klu	KICHLU K. L.
klu1	KICHLU K. L. and BOSE: [Textbook of Descriptive Medicine]
klx	KNELLE: (1938-)
km	KRAMER Anton: Contemporary homeopath [Netherlands] (1956-)
kma	KUMAR A.V.
kma1	KUMAR A. V.: [Principles of Homeopathic Therapeutics], New Delhi: Indian Books and Periodicals Syndicate, Karol Ba
kmg	KAMAT Gautam: Contemporary homeopath [Bombay, India] (1950-)
kmg1	KAMAT Gautam: [Two cases of Skin Allergy], Links, Vol 1: pg 29-31 (1995)
kmp	KAMINSKI P.
kmp1	KAMINSKI P. and Katz R.: [Flower Essence Repertory - Maleisian herbs]
kmy	KRISHNAMOORTY V. K.: (1939-)
kmy1	KRISHNAMOORTY V. K.: [Homeopathy in Accidents and Injuries], New Delhi: Jain Publishers (2nd revised Ed.) (1979)
kmy2	KRISHNAMOORTY V.: [Beginner's guide to Bach Flower remedies]
kmy3	KRISHNAMOORTY V.: [Advanced Practice of Dr. Bach remedies]
kmy4	KRISHNAMOORTY V.: [New Bach remedies]
kn	KENNEDY Charles Oliver
kna	KHAN L. M.: Contemporary homeopath [Calcutta, India] (1950-)

kna1	KHAN L. M.: [An experience with Cyclamen], Links, Vol 1: pg 25 (1994)
knk	KANODA K. D.
knk1	KANODA K.D.: [Advanced Homeopathy], New Delhi: Jain Publishers (1991)
knk2	KANODA K. D.: [Danger Zones in Homeopathy], New Delhi: Jain Publishers
knl	KLEIN Louis: Contemporary homeopath [Canada] (1946-)
knl1	KLEIN Louis: [Scutellaria], IFH Conference (1990)
knl2	KLEIN Louis: [Helodrilus caliginosus - Information and Synopsis of a New Proving], Links, Vol 11: pg 154-156 (1998)
knl3	KLEIN Louis: [Carbon dioxide] (1990)
knl4	KLEIN Louis: [Loxosceles reclusa - The brown Recluse spider] (1998)
knl5	KLEIN Louis: [Lumbricus terrestris]
knl6	KLEIN Louis: [Coriandrum proving] (2000)
knl7	KLEIN Louis and MANTEWSIWICH Emily: [Hahnemanian Proving of Argentum Sulphuricum]
knp	KRISHNAMURTHY P.S: Contemporary homeopath [India] (1928-)
knp1	KRISHNAMURTHY P.S: [Osteoarthritic nosode proving] (1988)
knr	KASTNER Raimund F.: (1955-)
knr1.de	KASTNER Raimund F.: Boenninghausens Physiognomik der Homeopathischen Arzneimittel und die Arzneiverwandtschaften, Heidelber: Haug Verlag (1995)
kny	KENENY T.
kny1	KENENY T.: [Haronga madagascariensis], Arzneim.-Forsch 21; 421-24 (1971)
kny2	KENENY T.: [Eichornia crassipes. Unveröffentlichter Kurzbericht] (1972)
kow	KARO W.
kow1	KARO W.: [Diseases of Respiratory System]
kow2	KARO W.: [Diseases of the Skin]
kow3	KARO W.: [Homeopathy in Women's Diseases]
kow4	KARO W.: [Diseases of the Male Genital Organs]
kow5	KARO W.: [Urinary and Prostatic Troubles]
kp	KOPP F.
kpg	KAMPIK G.
kpg1	KAMPIK G.: [Myrtillocactus geometrizans - Neue Behandlungsmöglichkeiten bei pekanginösen beschwerden.], A H Z. g. 218; 249-52 (1973)
kpp	KUIPER Pieter: Contemporary homeopath [Netherlands]
kpx	KIPPAX J. R.
kpx1	KIPPAX J. R.: [A Handbook of Diseases of Skin and their Homeopathic Treatment], New delhi: Jain Publishers (1989)
kr	KNERR Calvin B.: American homeopath (1847-1940)
kr1	KNERR Calvin B.: [Repertory of Herings Guiding Symptoms of our Materia Medica], Philadelphia: Davis Co (1896)
kr2	KNERR Calvin B.: [Drug Relationship], Calcutta (1936)
kr3	KNERR Calvin B.: [Life of Hering] (1940)
krr	KÖRNER R.
krr1.de	KÖRNER R. und RAUCH H.: Taraxacum
krs	KOHLRAUSCH Stefan: (1959-)
krs1	KOHLRAUSCH Stefan: [Die Milch von misshandelten Schweinen löst Wut und Aggression aus - Lac suinum], H Zt, Nr 1: pg 27-32 (1999)
krw	KHARIWALA Falguni: Contemporary homeopath [India] (1950-)
krw1	KHARIWALA Falguni: [A case of Cyclamen], Links, Vol 3: pg 27 (1993)
ks	KISHORE Jugal: (1918-)
ks1	KISHORE Jugal: [Cynodon dactylon]
ks2	KISHORE Jugal: [M&B 693 = sulfonamidum] (1977)
ks3	KISHORE Jugal: [Saraca indica]
ks4	KISHORE Jugal: [Tylophora indica]
ks5	KISHORE Jugal: [Abromata augusta] (1974)
ks6	KISHORE Jugal: [Evolution of Homeopathic Repertories and Repertorization [1st Ed.]], New Delhi: Kishore Cards Publication (1998)
ksa	KONSTANTARAS John: Contemporary homeopath [Greece]
ksf	KROSCHEWSKI - KÖNIG Friedel
ksf1.de	KROSCHEWSKI - KÖNIG Friedel: Homöopathie 360 - kristallklar
ksf2.de	KROSCHEWSKI - KÖNIG Friedel: Repertorium Nachträge
ksk	KANSAL Kamal
ksk1	KANSAL Kamal: [The Biochemics] (1993)
ksk2	KANSAL Kamal: [Homeopathic Treatment - Constipation] (1995)
ksk3	KANSAL Kamal: [Homeopathic Treatment - Dental Diseases] (1994)
ksk4	KANSAL Kamal: [Homoeopathic Treatment - Diabetes Mellitus] (1992)
ksk5	KANSAL Kamal: [Homeopathic Treatment - Pet Animals] (1998)
ksk6	KANSAL Kamal: [Kansal's Practice of Medicine with Homoepathic Therapeutics]
ksk7.es	KANSAL Kamal: Usted y su Bebe. Una Guía Homeopática Familiar, New Delhil: Jain publishers (1995)
ksn	KASSIN
ksp	KLOSS P.
ksp1	KLOSS P.: [Flor de piedra], Naturwissensch. 54; 472 (1967)
ksp2	KLOSS P.: [Luffa operculata], Cogn. Arch. Pharmaz. 299; 351-355 (1966)
kss	KHALSA Sat Jit Kaur: Contemporary homeopath [Montreal, Canada] (1950-)
kss1	KHALSA Sat Jit Kaur: [Dupuytren's Contracture], N Eng. J H, Vol 2 nr 1: pg 10-11 (1993)

kt	KUNST M.
kt1	KUNST M.: [Okoubaka aubrevillei], A H Z: 217 pg 116- 121 (1972)
ktj	KERSTEN Jacques
ktj1.fr	KERSTEN Jacques: Ma pratique homéopathique au quotidien - 101 cas cliniques commentés, Esneux (Belgium): Kersten Jacques (2002)
ktm	KHUTELA M.P.
ktm1	KHUTELA M. P.: [Renal calculus], Jaipur: Homeopathic Charilable Trust
ktp	KAMTHAN P. S.: (1934-)
ktp1	KAMTHAN P. S.: [CANCER - Curable under Homoeopathic Treatment (reprint)], New Delhi: Jain Publishers (1982)
ktp1.es	KAMTHAN P. S.: Cáncer curación bajo tratamiento homeopático
ktp2	KAMTHAN P. S.: [Homeopathic therapy in Gout, Arthritis and Rheumatism with concomitants] (1974)
ktp3	KAMTHAN P. S.: [How homeopathy cures Mania, Melancholia and madness] (1974)
ktp4	KAMTHAN P. S.: [How to cure: headache, facial neuralgia, glaucoma, tootache] (1979)
ktp5	KAMTHAN P. S.: [Remedies for Pain & Warts] (1977)
ktp6	KAMTHAN P. S.: [Remedies for Skin and Bone Diseases] (1977)
ktp7	KAMTHAN P. S.: [Specific Remedies for Respiratory, Cardiac and Urinary diseases] (1978)
ktp8	KAMTHAN P. S.: [The Female Prescriber] (1990)
ktp9	KAMTHAN P. S.: [The Haemorrhage Controller] (1995)
kts	KAMTHAN S.K.
kts1	KAMTHAN S.K.: [The Homoeopathic First Aid Prescriber], New Delhi: Jain Publishers (1997)
kyd	KAY Dennis: Contemporary homeopath [Colorado, USA] (1950-)
kyd1	KAY Dennis: [Cases Stamper], N Eng. J H, Vol 3 nr 2: pg 15-16 (1994)
kzh	KUNZE H.
kzh1	KUNZE H.: [Carduus marianus], Homoeopathic Physician, May (1891)
lb	LORBACHER Arnold: German homeopathic physician of the 19th century, publisher of the Allgemeinen Homöopathischen Zeitung (1818-1899)
lba	LOMBARDI A.
lba1	LOMBARDI A.: [Leonurus cardiaca], Gazetta Sanitaria Nr. 3 (1947)
lbk	LÖBISCH Klaus
lbk1.de	LÖBISCH Klaus: Hura brasiliensis, eine Arznei die Zust nde van Aussatzigkeit kennt un zu heilen vermag, Homopatische Einblicke, Vol 35 (1998)
lby	LABORDE Yves: Contemporary homeopath [Germany]
lby1.de	LABORDE Yves: Repertorium miasmatischer Symptome, München: Müller & Steincke (1992)
lby2.de	LABORDE Yves: Die Hereditären Chronischen Krankheiten, München: Verlag Müller & Steinicke (1990)
lby3.de	LABORDE Yves: Dreisprachiges, klinisches Repertorium mit miasmatischen Hinweisen
lby4.de	LABORDE Yves: Klinische und miasmatische Materia Medica, München: Verlag Müller & Steinicke (1994)
ld	LODISPOTO A.: (1920-)
ld1.de	LODISPOTO A.: Diät und Homöopathie, Zt Klass H, Vol IV/3: pg 95-141 (1960)
ld2	LODISPOTO A.: [Persönliche Beobachtung] (1984)
ldg	LINDEMANN G.
ldg1	LINDEMANN G.: [Myrrhis odorata], Dtsch. Apoth. Ztg. 98; 132 (1958)
ldh	LEDUC Herman: Contemporary Belgian homeopath
ldh1.fr	LEDUC Herman: Dictionnaire d'homéopathie pédiatrique
ldj	LARA DE LA ROSA, José Luis
ldj1.es	LARA DE LA ROSA: Repertorio de Síntomas y Remedios, New Delhi: Jain Publishers (1990)
ldm	LIDCHI Maggie: Contemporary homeopath [Pondicherry, India] (1950-)
ldm1	LIDCHI Maggie: [The Story of Madhav], Links, Vol 4: pg 33 (1994)
le	LOE
lej	LEE Edmund J.
lej1	LEE Edmund J.: [Repertory of Characteric Symptoms of Homoeopathic Materia Medica], Philadelphia (1889)
lej2	LEE Edmund J. and CLARK George H.: [Cough and Expectoration] (1894)
lfj	LAFEUILLADE Jean
lfj1.fr	LAFEUILLADE Jean: Diagnostic Energétique en Homéopathie (2000)
lg	LANG Bärbel: Contemporary homeopath [Germany]
lga	LANGE Andrew: (1952-)
lgb	LONG Bernard
lgb1	LONG Bernard and CAYREL P.: [Rosmarinus officinalis], Rev B H, Jun ; 25(2) ; 37-44 (1992)
lgb2.fr	LONG Bernard: Répertoire Homéopathique des Maladies Aigues (2000)
lgb3.fr	LONG Bernard: L'Homéopathie en images. Phosphorus, Le Porteur de Lumière, Nice: CY Editions
lgb4.fr	LONG Bernard, SIMON François et le Groupe DYNAMIS: Cortisone et Glucocorticoïdes - Pathogénésie de Cortisone., Montpellier (France): LONG Bernard, SIMOND François et le Groupe DYNAMIS (2003)
lgb5.fr	LONG Bernard: Absinthium : Etude et nouvelle Pathogénésie
lgr	LOGAN Robin: (1954-)

lgr1	LOGAN Robin: [The Homeopathic Treatment of Eczema], Beaconsfield (England): Beaconsfield Publ.
ljy	LA JOYA: Veterinary [Mexico] (1940-)
ljy1	LA JOYA: [Medicamentos Homeopáticos para los animales.], Ediciones La Habana, Mexico (1980)
lk	LEMBKE L. W. E.
lkc	LASCHKOLNIG Christine: Contemporary homeopath [Vienna, Austria] (1950-)
lkc1	LASCHKOLNIG Christine: [Cases: The Way to the beast of Prey], N Eng. J H, Vol 3 nr 1: pg 22-24 (1994)
lke	LACHKAR Edmond-Paul
lke1.es	LACHKAR Edmond-Paul: La homeopatía en la farmacia, Dolisos España (1993)
lkg	LOUKAS George: Contemporary homeopath [Thessaloniki, Greece] (1950-)
lkg1	LOUKAS George: [A Case Report], Links, Vol 1: pg 28-29 (1995)
ll	LILIENTHAL Samuel: American homeopathic physician of the pioneering time (1815-1891)
ll1	LILIENTHAL Samuel: [Homeopathic therapeutics [2nd Ed.]], Philadelphia: Boericke & Tafel (1879)
llj	LALOY J.L.
lm	LEAMAN
lma	LEMUS TRANSITO Antonio
lma1	LEMUS TRANSITO Antonio: [The Centipede], Journal of the American Institute of Homeopathy (1954)
lmj	LAMOTHE Jacques: Contemporary homeopathic pediatrician [France] (1943-)
lmj1.fr	LAMOTHE Jacques: Homéopathie pédiatrique, Paris: Similia (1996)
lmp	LOMMAERT Philippe: Contemporary homeopathic physician [Antwerpen, Belgium] (1952-)
lmx	LANSMANNE Jean
lmx1.fr	LANSMANNE Jean: Un pas vers la compréhension des dynamisations Homéopathiques., Bruxelles: Editions de l'Ecole Belge d'Homéopathie (2003)
ln	LEONARD W. E.
lp	LIPPE Adolph von: (1812-1888)
lp1	LIPPE Adolph von: [Text Book of Materia Medica], Philadelphia (1866)
lp2	LIPPE Adolph von: [Keynotes and red line symptoms of the materia medica.], New Dehli: Jain Publ. (1915)
lp2.fr	LIPPE Adolph von: Symptômes et traits principaux de la Matière Médicale
lp3	LIPPE Adolph von: [Keynotes of the Homeopathic Materia Medica], Philadelphia, Boerick and Tafel (1915)
lp4	LIPPE Adolph von: [Key to the Materia Medica or Comparative Pharmacodynamic.], Philadelphia: Henry Duffield (1854)
lpa	LEUPEN Alex: Contemporary homeopathic physician [Netherlands] (1950-)
lpc	LIPPE Constantin: (1840-1885)
lpc1	LIPPE Constantin: [Repertory to the more characteristic Symptoms of the Materia Medica] (1879)
lpc2	LIPPE Constantin: [Textbook of Materia Medica] (1865)
lpe	LASPRILLA Eduardo Elias
lpe1.es	LASPRILLA Eduardo Elias: Reflexiones criticas sobre medicina clasica y homeopatica, Buenos Aires: Editorial Albatros (1991)
lr	LORENZ Eric: Contemporary homeopathic physician [switzerland]
lra	LARA Isidre: Contemporary homeopathic physician [Spain]
lra1.es	LARA Isidre y QUERALT José Maria: Semiología de la Psora Latente
lrb	LAURAEUS Ritva: Contemporary homeopathic physician [Finland]
lrj	LAURIE Joseph
lrj1	LAURIE Joseph: [The Homoeopathic Practice of Medicine]
lrj2	LAURIE Joseph: [The homoeopathic domestic medicine Vol 1 & Vol 2], Philadelphia: Boericke (10th Ed.) (1872)
lrj2a	LAURIE Joseph: An epitome of the homeopathic domestic medicine. Enlarged and improved by A.Gerard Hull., New York: William Radde (3th Ed.] (1846)
lrn	LIRA Bernardo
lrn1.es	LIRA Bernardo: Cinco sintomas en un libro. [1st Ed.], New Delhi: Jain Publishers (1997)
lrp	LE ROUX Patricia: (1958-)
lrp1	LE ROUX Patricia: [Lac Caninum, remedy of ailments from child sexual abuse.], Proc 54th LMHI Congr., Salvador-Bahia Brasil (1999)
lrp2.fr	LE ROUX Patricia: Les Lacs
lrp3	LE ROUX Patricia: [The Acids]
lrp3.fr	LE ROUX Patricia: Les Acides
ls	LAWSHE J. Z.
lsa	LEERS Hans: (1946-)
lsa1.de	LEERS Hans: Leerskarten (1950)
lsa2	LEERS Hans: [Sammlung seltener Symptome], Heidelberg: Haug (1988)
lsd	LUSTIG Didier
lsd1.fr	LUSTIG Didier: Germanium (2000)
lsd2	LUSTIG Didier and RAY Jacques: [The proving of Neptunium muriaticum] (2002)
lsd2.fr	LUSTIG Didier et RAY Jacques: La Pathogénésie de Neptunium Muriaticum (2002)
lsd3.fr	LUSTIG Didier: Agraphis Nutans (1998)
lsd4.fr	LUSTIG Didier: Androctonus Amoreuxii Hebraeus (1996)
lsd5.fr	LUSTIG Didier: Plutonium Nitricum (1996)
lsd6.fr	LUSTIG Didier: Ustilago Maydis (2000)
lsg	LESIGANG H.

lsg1 LESIGANG H.: [Latrodectus mactans], Documenta homoeopathica 12 (1992)
lsg2 LESIGANG H.: [Oenanthe crocata], Br H J, Jul ; 81(3), pg 127-131 (1992)
lsr LEESER Otto: (1888-1964)
lsr1.de LEESER Otto: Grundlangen der heilkunde - Vol. 1, Stuttgart/Berlin: Hippokrates (1927)
lsr2.de LEESER Otto: Mineralische Arzneistoffe - Vol. 2, Heidelberg: Haug (1988)
lsr3.de LEESER Otto: Pflanzliche Arzneistoffe I - Vol. 3, Heidelberg: Haug (1987)
lsr4.de LEESER Otto: Pflanzliche Arzneistoffe II - Vol. 4, Heidelberg: Haug (1989)
lsr5.de LEESER Otto: Tierstoffe - Vol. 5, Heidelberg: Haug (1987)
lsr6 LEESER Otto: [Homeopathic Materia Medica], Philadelphia (1935)
lsr7 LEESER Otto: [The Contribution of Homeopathy to the Development of Medicine]
lsy LASSAUW Yvonne: Contemporary homeopath [Amsterdam, The Netherlands] (1960-)
lsy1 LASSAUW Yvonne: [The most sweetest little girl], Links, Vol 3: pg 26 (1992)
lsy2 LASSAUW Yvonne: [Aurum sulphuratum], Simillima, Vol 1 (1993)
lsy3 LASSAUW Yvonne: [Hyoscyamus niger], Simillima, Vol 2 (1993)
lt LATHOUD Joseph-Amedée: French homeopathic physician (1882-1944)
lt1.es LATHOUD Joseph-Amedée: Materia Médica Homeopatica, Buenos Aires: Editorial Albatros (1994)
lt1.fr LATHOUD Joseph-Amedée: Etudes de Matière Médicale Homéopathique, Vienna (1932)
lta LOUTAN Guy: Contemporary homeopathic physician [switzerland]
lta1.fr LOUTAN Guy: Répertoire de Thèmes et de la Matière Médicale Dynamique, Genève: Loutan (2000)
ltp LENTHERIC F.
lvd LEVY David: Contemporary homeopath [Double bay, Australia] (1961-)
lvd1 LEVY David: [Evolution of a Remedy idea], Links, Vol 1: pg 19-22 (1994)
lvd2 LEVY David: [Piper Methysticum], Links, Vol 8: pg 17-19 (1995)
lvr LIVINGSTON R.
lvr1 LIVINGSTON R.: [Homeopathy], London: Ainsworth's Homeopathic Pharmacy (1973)
lvs LEAVITT Sheldon
lvs1 LEAVITT Sheldon: [Homeopathic Therapeutics as applied to Obstetrics], New Delhi: Jain Publishers (1989)
lvs2 LEAVITT Sheldon: [Science and Art of Obstetrics]
lvt LEVRAT
lvt1.fr LEVRAT, PIGEOT, SETIEY et TETAU: Guide de prescription homéopathique
lwj LOWE J.N.
lwj1 LOWE J.N.: [Mind and disposition during parturition] (1895)
lwz LOWENSTEIN J.M.: (1931-)
lwz1 LOWENSTEIN J.M.: [Effect of [-]-hydroxycitrate on fatty acid synthesis by rat liver in vivo], J Biol Chem, Vol 246: pg 629-632 (1971)
lz LINCZ: Contemporary homeopathic physician [Brussels, Belgium] (1908-)
lzf LUTZE F. H.
lzf1 LUTZE F. H.: [Duration of Action and Antidotes of the principal Homeopathic Remedies with their complementary and inimical Relations], New Delhi: Indian Books & Periodical Syndicate
lzf2 LUTZE F. H.: [Facial and Sciatic Neuralgias] (1898)
lzf3 LUTZE F. H.: [Diseases of Respiratory Organs] (1916)
lzr LAZARUS
lzr1 LAZARUS: [Proving of Prenanthus serpens], North American Journal of Homoeopathy, Vol 4: pg 352
mc MARCY E. E.
mca MUSCARI TOMAIOLI Gennaro: Contemporary homeopathic physician [Italy]
mcj METCALL J.W.
mcj1 METCALL J.W.: [Homeopathic Provings]
mcp MASCI Paul
mcp1 MASCI Paul and KENDALL Philip: [The Taipan, the world's most dangerous Snake] (1995)
mct MC CLINTOCK L.
mct1 MC CLINTOCK L.: [The proving of Lac Glama (Llama Milk)]
mcx MARCY and PETERS and FILLIGRAPH
mcx1 MARCY and PETERS and FILLIGRAPH: [The elements of a new Materia Medica]
mcx2 MARCY and PETERS and FILLIGRAPH: [New Provings & Clinical Experiences]
md MUNDY David: Contemporary homeopath [UK] (1941-)
md1 MUNDY David: [Carcinosin] (1982)
mdc MEDINA Conrado
mdc1.es MEDINA Conrado: Doctrina Homeopática, New Delhi: Jain Publishers
mde MEINDERS Edith: Contemporary homeopathic physician [Netherlands] (1955-)
mdg MADAUS Gerhard
mdg1.de MADAUS Gerhard: Lehrbuch der Biologischen Heilmittel, Register für die therapeutische Anwendung (1979)
mdj MICHAUD Jacques: (1918-)
mf MACFARLAN Donald
mf1 MACFARLAN Donald: [Concise pictures of dynamised drugs: personally proven], Philadelphia: Private (1936)
mf2 MACFARLAN Donald: [Provings and clinical observations]

mf3 MACFARLAN Donald: [A re-proving of Calcarea carbonica], International Hahnemannian Association Proceedings, Session (1926)
mfh MONTFORT C. Hector
mfh1 MONTFORT C. Hector: [Mitotane]
mfh1.es MONTFORT C. Hector: Nuevo medicamento homeopático en asma bronquial. Reporte de 120 casos tratados., México: La Homeopatía de México: Vol 61: pg 10-12 (1993)
mfj MOFFAT John L.: (1876-)
mfj1 MOFFAT John L.: [Homoeopathic therapeutics in ophthalmology.], Philadelphia (1916)
mfm MACFARLAN Malcolm: (1950-)
mg MEZGER Julius: (1909-)
mg1.de MEZGER Julius: Gesichtete Homöopathische Arzneimittellehre [3rd Ed.], Ulm: Karl F. Haug Verlag (1949)
mg2 MEZGER Julius: [Hedera helix, Homeopathie], Homeopathie Jan-Feb ; 4(1) ; pg 61-63 (1987)
mga MORGAN L.
mgb MORGAN William
mgb1 MORGAN William: [Diabetes mellitus [Its history, chemistry, anatomy, pathology, physiology and treatment]] (1877)
mgb2 MORGAN William: [Diphteria [Its history, causes, symptoms, diagnosis, pathology and treatment]] (1870)
mgb3 MORGAN William: [The Signs and concomitant Derangements of Pregnancy] (1870)
mgb4 MORGAN William: [Homoeopathic Treatment of Indigestion, Constipation, and Haemorrhoids.], Philadelphia: Rademacher & Sheek (Pennsylvania) (1854)
mgc MORGAN A. R.: (1859-)
mgc1 MORGAN A. R.: [Repertory of Urinary Organs and Prostate Gland], Philadelphia (1899)
mgf MORGAN Fred B.
mgf1 MORGAN Fred B.: [Feldspar in Mononucleosis - Infectious Mononucleosis], The Homoeopathic Recorder, Vol LVIII, Nr 10, 11, 12, (April, May, June) (1943)
mgf2 MORGAN Fred B.: [Feldspar in Mononucleosis - Acute Infectious Mononucleosis], The Homoeopathic Recorder, Vol. LXII, nr 11, May, pg: 332-335 (1947)
mgg MEGENS Gerard: (1950-)
mgm MANGIALAVORI Massimo: Contemporary homeopathic physician [Modena, Italy]. Creator of Consulta soft. (1956-)
mgm1 MANGIALAVORI Massimo: [I Think of Death when I'm alone, 2 Cases of crotalus Cascavella], Links, Vol 9: pg 29-31 (1996)
mgm2 MANGIALAVORI Massimo: [Cured Cases]
mgm3 MANGIALAVORI Massimo: [Remedy Themes]
mgm4 MANGIALAVORI Massimo: [Official Repertory Additions] (2000)
mh MARSCH H. R.: (1912-)
mha MERSCH: Belgian homeopathic physician (1872-)
mhb MEYHOFFER: Austrian homeopathic physician of the first generation after Hahnemann
mhc MENHARD Konrad: Contemporary homeopathic physician [Germany]
mhh MALHOTRA H.C.
mhh1 MALHOTRA H.C.: [Care and Treatment - Fistula, Piles] (1990)
mhh2 MALHOTRA H.C.: [Menses and Health [A Lady's Manual of Homeopathic care]] (1991)
mhn MOHANTY Niranjan: (1945-)
mhn1 MOHANTY Niranjan: [Text book of Homeopathic Materia Medica] (1985)
mhx MARSH A.
mhx1 MARSH A.: [Clinical Drug Pictures]
mie McIVOR E. G.: (1940-)
mie1 McIVOR E. G.: [Proving of Pernus canaliculus] (1980)
mie2 McIVOR E. G.: [Ginkgo biloba - a proving.], Br H J, Vol 64: pg 105-106 (1975)
mie3 McIVOR E. G.: [Phormium tenax - a proving], Br H J, Vol 69: pg 27-32 (1980)
mie4 McIVOR E. G.: [Nepenthes distillatoria], J Am Inst Hom, Mar ; 73(1) (1980)
mie5 McIVOR E. G.: [Penicillium], J Am Inst Hom Sep 73(3) (1980)
mir MCINTYER E. R.: (1951-)
mir1 MCINTYER E. R.: [Stepping Stones to Neurology], New Delhi: Jain Publishers (1991)
mjr MAJUMDAR P. C.
mjr1 MAJUMDAR P. C.: [Appendicitis curable by Medicine], New Delhi: Jain Publishers (1989)
mjs MOORE James
mjs1 MOORE James: [Dog Diseases Treated by Homeopathy], New Delhi: Jain Publishers (1994)
mk MCKENZIE P. L.
mka MUKERJEE A. N.
mka1 MUKERJEE A. N.: [Therapetic Hints of Dr. Mahendralal Sircar], Calcutta: Hahnemann Publ. (5th Ed.)
mkb MOEHRKE Brita: Contemporary homeopathic physician [Germany]
mkj MUKERJI R. K.
mkj1 MUKERJI R. K.: [Constitution and temperament [a compilation of articles published in different french journals]], New Delhi: Jain Publishers (1986)
mkr MUKERJI R. J.
mkr1 = ftb8 = MUKERJI R. J. (old abb.)
mks MUKHERJEE Somnath
mks1 MUKHERJEE Somnath: [Efficacy of homeopathy in Cancer treatment (1st. Ind. Ed.)], Calcutta: Dr. Abinash Ch. Das (1981)
mkw MOSKOWITZ Richard
mkw1 MOSKOWITZ Richard: [Homeopathic Medicines for Pregnancy and Childbirth] (1992)
ml MC LAREN K. A.

ml1	MC LAREN K. A.: [Ephedra vulgaris var. helvetica], Hom Rec, Vol XLV nr.3: pg 184 (1930)
mla	MELLON R. R.
mlb	MÜLLER Josef Oswald: Austrian homeopathic physician [Wien] during the time of Hahnemann (1810-1886)
mlc	MÜLLER Clotar
mlc1.de	MÜLLER Clotar: Charakteristiken der wichtigsten homöopathischen Heilmittel, Leipzig: Schwabe (1935)
mlc2.de	MUELLER Clotar: Systematisch-alphabetisches Repertorium der gesammten homöopathischen Arzneimittellehre, Leipzig: Weigel (1848)
mlc3.de	MÜLLER Clotar: Charakteristik von 30 der wichtigsten homöopatischen Heilmittel behufs ihrer Anwendung in de gewöhnlichsten Erkrangkungsfällen. (1873)
mlc3.es	MÜLLER Clotar: El Indicador Caracteristico de los 30 remedios homeopaticos., Madrid: Las mil y una ediciones (1876)
mld	MACLEOD George: (1912-1995)
mld1	MACLEOD George: [The treatment of cattle by homeopathy], Health Science Press, England (1981)
mld2	MACLEOD George: [Cats: Homeopathic remedies] (1993)
mld3	MACLEOD George: [The homeopathic treatment of dogs], Homoeopathic Development Foundation Ltd, England (1985)
mld4	MACLEOD George: [The homeopathic treatment of horses], Clarke Doble & Brendon Ltd, England (1977)
mld5	MACLEOD George: [A veterinary Materia Medica and clinical repertory, with a materia medica of the nosodes.], Daniel Company Ltd, England. (1995)
mle	MÖLLINGER Heribert: Contemporary Homeopath [Swizerland]
mle1.de	MÖLLINGER Heribert: Homöopatische Arzneimittelprüfung von Calendula, Güttingen, Switzerland (1997)
mle2.de	MÖLLINGER Heribert: Homöopatische Arzneimittelprüfung von Oleum Jecoris Aselli., Güttingen, Switzerland (1998)
mlg	MILLER Gibson R.: (1862-1923)
mlg1	MILLER Gibson R.: [A synopsis of homeopathic philosophy], Glasgow (1909)
mlg2	MILLER Gibson R.: [On the comparative value of symptoms in the selection of the remedy], Br H J, Vol 1: pg 73,97 (1911)
mlg3	MILLER Gibson R.: [Relationship of remedies and Sides of the Body], Hom. Publish C° London (1933)
mlh	MÜLLER Hugbald V.
mlh1.de	MÜLLER Hugbald V.: Die Farbe als mittel zur simillimum findung in der Homoöpathie., Heidelberg: Haug Verlag (1990)
mlk	MÜLLER Karl-Josef: (1959-)
mlk1	MÜLLER Karl-Josef: [Thuja Occidentalis: New aspects of the remedy with Clinical information. A collection of Case Studies.], Zweibrücken:Verlag Karl-Josef Müller (1995)
mlk1.de	MÜLLER Karl-Josef: Thuja occidentalis: Neue Aspekte und deren klinische Bestätigungen, Zweibrücken:Verlag Karl-Josef Müller (1994)
mlk10	MÜLLER Karl-Josef: [Tegenaria atrica Cases] (2003)
mlk11	MÜLLER Karl-Josef: [Tyrannosaurus rex Cases]
mlk12	MÜLLER Karl-Josef: [Apium Cases]
mlk13	MÜLLER Karl-Josef: [Phosphoricum acidum - New aspects of the remedy with clinical confirmation - A collection of Case studies.], Zweibrücken:Verlag Karl-Josef Müller (1999)
mlk13.de	MÜLLER Karl-Josef: Acidum phosphoricum: Neue Aspekte und dere klinische Bestätigungen., Zweibrücken:Verlag Karl-Josef Müller (1995)
mlk14	MÜLLER Karl-Josef: [The Female Lycopodium - New Aspects of the Remedy with Clinical Confirmation - A collection of Case studies.], Zweibrücken:Verlag Karl-Josef Müller (2000)
mlk14.de	MÜLLER Karl-Josef: Lycopodium bei Frauen: Neue Aspekte und deren klinische Bestätigungen., Zweibrücken:Verlag Karl-Josef Müller (1995)
mlk15.de	MÜLLER Karl-Josef: Rhus toxicodendron: Das chronische Bild, Zweibrücken:Verlag Karl-Josef Müller (2002)
mlk16	MÜLLER Karl-Josef: [Calcarea arsenicosa - New aspects of the Remedy with Clinical information - A collection of Case Studies.], Zweibrücken:Verlag Karl-Josef Müller (2003)
mlk16.de	MÜLLER Karl-Josef: Calcium arsenicosum: Neue Aspekte und deren klinische Bestätigungen, Zweibrücken:Verlag Karl-Josef Müller (1997)
mlk17.de	MÜLLER Karl-Josef: Cimicifuga: Neue Aspekte und deren klinische Bestätigungen, Zweibrücken:Verlag Karl-Josef Müller (1997)
mlk18.de	MÜLLER Karl-Josef: Germanium metallicum: Die klinische Entdeckung eines homöopatischen Arzneimittels., Zweibrücken:Verlag Karl-Josef Müller (2001)
mlk19.de	MÜLLER Karl-Josef: Lac humanum: Die klinische Entdeckung eines homöopatischen Arzneimittels., Zweibrücken:Verlag Karl-Josef Müller (1996)
mlk2	MÜLLER Karl-Josef: [Moschus - The Clinical Rediscovery of a Homeopathic Remedy - A collection of Case Studies.], Zweibrücken:Verlag Karl-Josef Müller (1997)
mlk2.de	MÜLLER Karl-Josef: Moschus: Die klinische Neuentdeckung eines Arzneimittels, Zweibrücken:Verlag Karl-Josef Müller (1995)
mlk20.de	MÜLLER Karl-Josef: Mandragora officinarum: Neue Aspekte und deren klinische Bestätigungen, Zweibrücken:Verlag Karl-Josef Müller (2000)
mlk21.de	MÜLLER Karl-Josef: Solanum tuberosum: Die klinische Entdeckung eines homöopatischen

	Arzneimittels., Zweibrücken:Verlag Karl-Josef Müller (1999)
mlk22.de	MÜLLER Karl-Josef: Cuprum aceticum: Die klinische Entdeckung eines homöopatischen Arzneimittels., Zweibrücken:Verlag Karl-Josef Müller (1996)
mlk23	MÜLLER Karl-Josef: [Opium: New Aspects of the Remedy with Clinical Confirmation - A collection of Case Studies], Zweibrücken:Verlag Karl-Josef Müller (2003)
mlk23.de	MÜLLER Karl-Josef: Opium: Neue Aspekte und deren klinische Bestätigungen., Zweibrücken:Verlag Karl-Josef Müller (1998)
mlk24.de	MÜLLER Karl-Josef, SONZ Suzanne und STEWART Robert: Musca Domestica: Zwei Prüfungen und sieben Fälle, Zweibrücken:Verlag Karl-Josef Müller (2003)
mlk3	MÜLLER Karl-Josef: [Argentum nitricum - New Aspects of the Remedy with Clinical confirmation - A collection of Case Studies.], Zweibrücken:Verlag Karl-Josef Müller (1996)
mlk3.de	MÜLLER Karl-Josef: Argentum Nitricum: Neue Aspekte und deren klinische Bestätigungen, Zweibrücken:Verlag Karl-Josef Müller (1994)
mlk4.de	MÜLLER Karl-Josef: Lac defloratum - Die Angst überträgt sich, H Zt, Nr 1: pg 85-86 (1996)
mlk5.de	MÜLLER Karl-Josef: Das Geheimnis der offenen Tur - Schnelle Hilfe bei Warzen durch lac delphinum?, H Zt, Nr 1: pg 29-30 (1996)
mlk6	MÜLLER Karl-Josef: [Lac felinum cases] (1997)
mlk6.de	MÜLLER Karl-Josef: Der "Katzenmensch" und seine Freiheit - lac felinum, H Zt, Nr 1: pg 80-84 (1995)
mlk7	MÜLLER Karl-Josef: [Carcinosinum - new and confirmed clinical symptoms - a case collection], Zweibrücken:Verlag Karl-Josef Müller (1994)
mlk8	MÜLLER Karl-Josef: [Lac caninum - New aspects of the remedy with clinical confirmation - A collection of Case studies.], Zweibrücken:Verlag Karl-Josef Müller (1997)
mlk8.de	MÜLLER Karl-Josef: Lac caninum: Neue Aspekte und deren klinische Bestätigungen, Zweibrücken:Verlag Karl-Josef Müller (1994)
mlk9.de	MÜLLER Karl-Josef, CHETNA Shukla, Nancy HERRICK und Stefan KOHLRAUSCH: Sieben Schmetterlinge: die homöopatischen Prüfungen, Zweibrücken:Verlag Karl-Josef Müller (1998)
mln	MOLIN
mln1	MOLIN: [Proving of Bunafa], Bulletin de la Société Homoeopathique de Paris, Vol 30 (1845)
mlr	MICKLEM R. D.: (1951-)
mlr1	MICKLEM R. D.: [Carcinosin, a Compendium of references], Queensbury (1994)
mlx	MELO Lima Carlos
mlx1	MELO Lima Carlos: [Hepar] (2001)
mly	MAILLE Yves
mly1.fr	MAILLE Yves: De la Stratégie des Barrages à la Prescription Homéopathique des Nosodes
mm	MC MICHAEL A. R.
mmj	MILLEMANN Jacques: Veterinary [France] (1935-)
mmj1	MILLEMANN Jacques: [Nervous Gestation and lactation in bitches] (1993)
mmj1.fr	MILLEMANN Jacques: Gestation et lactation nerveuse de la chienne, Revista Dynamis N°1, edition Similia, septembre 1993 (1993)
mmj2	MILLEMANN Jacques: [Matière médicale homéopathique vétérinaire], Editions Similia
mmp	MITTMAN Paul: Contemporary homeopath [Enfield, USA]
mmp1	MITTMAN Paul: [A seizure Disordered child], N Eng. J H, Vol 1 nr 1: pg 5-6 (1992)
mn	MENEAR Vicky: Contemporary homeopathic physician [USA]
mna	MINOTTI Angel O.: (1944-)
mna1.es	MINOTTI Angel O.: Traumatismos, heridas, complicaciones y secuelas., Buenos Aires: Editorial Albatros (1990)
mna2.es	MINOTTI Angel O.: Ensayos filosóficos Médicos: La enseñanza de un camino curativo (2001)
mna3.es	MINOTTI Angel O.: Semiologia y materia medica de los Tumores de Mama, Buenos Aires: Editorial Albatros (1990)
mnc	MENON C. R. K.: (1939-)
mnc1	MENON C. R. K.: [Some Constitutional Remedies], Cochin: Hom. Study Centre (1981)
mnj	MUÑOZ Jorge Santiago: Contemporary homeopathic veterinary [Argentina] (1953-)
mnj1.es	MUÑOZ Jorge Santiago: Repertorio Veterinario (1997)
mnl	MEYNEL
mnl1	MEYNEL: [Proving of Stannum muriaticum], Deutsche Klinik, N° 4: pg 437 (1851)
mnp	MANNA Pradip Kumar: Contemporary homeopath [India]
mnp1	MANNA Pradip Kumar: [H. C. Allen's Therapeutic Notes], Calcutta: Dipanwita Publishers (1993)
mnt	MONNOT F.: (1949-)
mnt1.fr	MONNOT F.: Progrès et homéopathie, Rev B H (1989)
moa	MONROE A.L
moa1	MONROE A.L: [Method of Memorizing the Materia Medica]
mp	MURPHY Robin: Contemporary homeopath [USA]. Creator of the Homeopathic Medical Repertory. (1950-)
mp1	MURPHY Robin: [Homeopathic Medical Repertory], Pasoga Springs (Colorado): Hahn. Acad. North America (1993)
mp2	MURPHY Robin: [Homeopathy and Cancer]
mp3	MURPHY Robin: [Fundamentals of Materia Medica]
mp4	MURPHY Robin: [Homeopathic Remedy Guide] (1995)

mp5	MURPHY Robin: [Reversed repertory]
mr	MOHR Charles: (1844-1907)
mr1	MOHR Charles: [Verification of Unverified Symptoms in Allen's Encyclopedia], Transactions Homoeopathic Medical Society of Pennsylvania (1881)
mra	MEIRA Adailton: Contemporary homeopathic gynecologist [Curitiba, Brasil] (1950-)
mrb	MORROW H. C.: (1901-)
mrc	MARIM Matheus: Contemporary homeopathic physician [Curitiba, Brasil] (1942-)
mrc1	MARIM Matheus: [Simplified Materia Medica of brosimum gaudichaude], Revista de Homeopatia - AMHB, nr 3 (1999)
mrc2	MARIM Matheus: [Simplified Materia Medica of bothrops jararacussu], Revista de Homeopatia - AMHB, nr 3 (1999)
mrd	MOORE J. M.
mre	MURE Benoit: (1809-1858)
mre1.fr	MURE Benoit: Pathogénésies brésiliennes, São Paulo: Editora Roca (1999)
mre2	MURE Benoit: [Animal and Vegetable Poisons of the Brazilian empire]
mrg	MARING G.
mrg1	MARING G.: [Dichapetalum], A H Z 205, 24u. 127 (1960)
mrg2	MARING G.: [Dichapetalum], J Am Inst Hom June ; 72(2) (1979)
mrj	MUREAU Jules: Contemporary homeopathic physician [Leuze, Belgium]
mrl	MIRILLI Jose
mrl1	MIRILLI Jose: [Thematic Materia Medica]
mrp	MOHR Peter
mrp1.de	MOHR Peter und HERRICK Nancy: Leben zwischen den Polaritäten - Lac equinum, H Zt, Nr 1: pg 48-59 (1996)
mrr	MORRISON Roger: Contemporary homeopathic physician [Berkeley, USA] (1954-)
mrr1	MORRISON Roger: [Desktop Guide to KeyNotes & Confirmatory Symptoms], Albany (1993)
mrr2	MORRISON Roger: [Seminar [Part 1] - Burgh Haamstede [Netherlands] Sept 1987], Amsterdam: Ilse Bos, private (1987)
mrr3	MORRISON Roger: [Seminar [Part 2] - Burgh Haamstede [Netherlands] Sept 1988], Amsterdam: Ilse Bos, private (1988)
mrr4	MORRISON Roger and HERRICK Nancy: [Seminar [Part 3] - Leystad [Netherlands] November 1991] (1991)
mrr5	MORRISON Roger: [Desktop Companion to Physical Pathology] (1998)
mrt	MURATA Shuji
mrt1	MURATA Shuji: [Lessons on Homeopathy] (1990)
mrt1.es	MURATA Shuji: Lecciones de Homeopatía, Mieres: Academia de Homeopatia de Asturias (1990)
mrx	MEERA
mrx1	MEERA: [Repertory of the diseases of mother and newborn], New Delhi: Jain Publishers (1996)
mry	MAURY E. A.
mry1	MAURY E. A.: [Drainage in Homoeopathy. [translated from french by Mark Clement]], England, Sussex: Health Sience Press (1965)
mrz	MORRIS Catherine
mrz1	MORRIS Catherine: [A Proving of Pycnoporus Sanguineus (a south African fungus)] (2002)
ms	MASI Alfonso Elizalde: Contemporary homeopathic physician [Buenos Aires, Argentina]. (1933-2003) Founder IIAEH [Instit. Intern. Altos Estudios Hom.]. Editor Actas IIAEH. (1932-2003)
ms1	MASI Alfonso Elizalde: [Cours supérieur de révision de la doctrine de la technique et de la matière médicale homéopathique], Belgium: Gent (1989)
msa	MAAS H.P.J.A.: Contemporary homeopathic physician [Netherlands]
msc	MESSAGIER René: Contemporary homeopathic physician, France
msd	MASIELLO Domenick John: Contemporary homeopathic physician [USA]
msm	MASOOD M.
msm1	MASOOD M.: [How to Succeed if One Remedy Fails - Alternatives], Lahore: Homeopathic Stores & Hospital
msx	MILLSPAUGH Charles F.
msx1	MILLSPAUGH Charles F.: [American Medicinal plants. An illustrated and descriptive guide to plants indegenous to and naturalized in the United States which are used in medicine.], New York: Dover Publications (1974)
mt	MORTELMANS Guido: Contemporary homeopathic physician [Lier, Belgium]
mt1	MORTELMANS Guido: [Sophie's Choice], Links, Vol 3: pg 61 (1990)
mta	MATHUR K. N.: (1932-)
mta1	MATHUR K. N.: [Systematic materia medica of homoeopathic remedies [1st Ed.]], New Delhi: Jain Publishers (1972)
mta2	MATHUR K. N.: [Diabetes Mellitus Its Diagnosis & Treatment] (1975)
mtb	MARTIN BALLESTERO Juan: Contemporary homeopathic physician [Spain]
mtc	MATUK José: Contemporary homeopathic physician [Mexico]
mtd	MATTITSCH G.
mtd1.de	MATTITSCH G. und HASLINGER-PRÜGER J.: Carcinosin
mte	MATEESCU Roxana: Contemporary homeopath [Roumania] (1971-)
mtf	MASTER Farokh Jamshed: Contemporary homeopath [Bombay, India] (1957-)
mtf1	MASTER Farokh Jamshed: [Acute Surgical Cases Treated], Links, Vol 1: pg 7-9 (1994)
mtf10	MASTER Farokh Jamshed: [Hair Loss] (1992)

mtf11	MASTER Farokh Jamshed: [Homoeopathic bedside clinical tips] (1999)
mtf12	MASTER Farokh Jamshed: [Homoeopathic dictionary of dreams] (1999)
mtf13	MASTER Farokh Jamshed: [Homeopathy in Cancer] (1989)
mtf14	MASTER Farokh Jamshed: [Homeopathy in Cervical Spondylosis] (1995)
mtf15	MASTER Farokh Jamshed: [Homoeopathy in lactose intolerance] (1994)
mtf16	MASTER Farokh Jamshed: [Lycopodium] (1995)
mtf17	MASTER Farokh Jamshed: [Medicine in Mnemonics] (1981)
mtf18	MASTER Farokh Jamshed: [Mysterious Thuja] (1993)
mtf19	MASTER Farokh Jamshed: [Naja Naja Naja [1st Ed.]], New Delhi: Jain Publishers (1990)
mtf2	MASTER Farokh Jamshed: [A proving of Maccasin Snake [Toxicophis]] (1999)
mtf20	MASTER Farokh Jamshed: [Perceiving rubrics of the mind] (1991)
mtf21	MASTER Farokh Jamshed: [Sandy Silicea], New Delhi: Jain Publishers (1994)
mtf22	MASTER Farokh Jamshed: [Snakes in Homeopathic Grass]
mtf23	MASTER Farokh Jamshed: [St-Ignatius Bean] (1994)
mtf24	MASTER Farokh Jamshed: [Suppressed Staphysagria] (1998)
mtf25	MASTER Farokh Jamshed: [Sycotic shame] (2000)
mtf26	MASTER Farokh Jamshed: [The Bed Side Organon of Medicine] (1999)
mtf27	MASTER Farokh Jamshed: [The Fascinating Fungi] (1996)
mtf28	MASTER Farokh Jamshed: [The State of Mind that affects Foetus] (1999)
mtf29	MASTER Farokh Jamshed: [Tubercular Miasm Tuberculins [simplified and explained] [2nd Ed.]], New Delhi: Jain Publishers (1999)
mtf3	MASTER Farokh Jamshed: [Ammoniums: The Sour Prunes] (1998)
mtf30	MASTER Farokh Jamshed: [Tumours and homoeopathy] (1995)
mtf31	MASTER Farokh Jamshed and JAWAHAR Shah: [Cross References Mind] (1996)
mtf32	MASTER Farokh Jamshed: [Bach flower remedies]
mtf33	MASTER Farokh Jamshed: [Clinical Observations of Children's Remedies], Bombay: Homeopathic Health Centre (1st Ed.) (1999)
mtf34	MASTER Farokh Jamshed: [Homeopathic Treatment of Acute Cardio-respiratory failure], Mumbai: Homeopathic Health Centre (2002)
mtf35	MASTER Farokh Jamshed: [Lacs in Homeopathy], Eindhoven: Lutra (2002)
mtf36	MASTER Farokh Jamshed: [A Homoeopathic Proving of Bungarus Fasciatus (Banded Krait)], Mumbai (India): Homeopathic Health Center (2003)
mtf37	MASTER Farokh Jamshed: [Bitis Arietans] (2003)
mtf4	MASTER Farokh Jamshed: [The Web Spinners] (1995)
mtf5	MASTER Farokh Jamshed: [A Patient's guide to homoepathy] (1991)
mtf6	MASTER Farokh Jamshed: [Acid-Base disorders: Basic concepts & clinical management] (1997)
mtf7	MASTER Farokh Jamshed: [Agitated Argentums] (1996)
mtf8	MASTER Farokh Jamshed: [Bed-wetting [Enuresis]] (1985)
mtf9	MASTER Farokh Jamshed: [Diseases of the Skin [Including of Exanthemata]] (1993)
mtg	MARTINEZ Fragoso Gabriel
mtg1.es	MARTINEZ Fragoso Gabriel: Perfil Biográfico de Homeópatas Universales
mtj	MARTINEZ Juan Arsenio
mtj1.es	MARTINEZ Juan Arsenio: Pharmacompendium Homeopatico, Buenos Aires: Editorial Albatros (1990)
mtj2.es	MARTINEZ Juan Arsenio: Farmacia Homeopatica, Buenos Aires: Editorial Albatros (1990)
mtn	MINTON Henry: (1831-1895)
mtn1	MINTON Henry: [Uterine Therapeutics [1st Ed.]], Calcutta: Roy Publishing House (1968)
mtn2	MINTON Henry: [Repertory of Head symptoms.], Hom J Obs (1882)
mtr	MATEU RATERA Manuel: Contemporary homeopathic physician [Spain] (1951-)
mtr1.de	MATEU RATERA Manuel: Erste Hilfe durch Homöopathie, Greifenberg (Germany): Hahnemann Institut - Privatinstitut für homöopatische Dokumntation Gmbh (1997)
mtr1.es	MATEU RATERA Manuel: Primeros auxilios con Homeopatia
mtr1.fr	MATEU RATERA Manuel: Premier secours en Homéopathie
mtr2.es	MATEU RATERA Manuel: Los secretos del Remedio. Materia médica homeopática.
mts	MOUNT S. J. L.: (1943-)
mts1	MOUNT S. J. L.: [Migraine], New Delhi: Jain Publishers (1st Ed.) (1991)
mtt	MARTINEZ Tejero Vicente
mtt1.es	MARTINEZ Tejero Vicente: Lumen Apothecariozum II
mtv	MATHUR R. P.
mtv1	MATHUR R.P.: [Miracles of Healing by Homoeopathy], New Delhi: Jain Publishers (1st Ed.) (1989)
mtv2	MATHUR R. P.: [Common Infectious Diseases with Therapeutic & Repertory in Homeopathy] (1991)
mtx	MITRA B. N.
mtx1	MITRA B. N.: [Tissue Remedies], Calcutta: Roy Publishing House (4th Ed.) (1973)

my	MAYER J.
myv	MEYER Veit
myv1.de	MEYER Veit: Der Kreuzbrunnen und seine Heilwirkungen
mza	MIRZA Anwer: Contemporary homeopath [Bombay, India]
mza1	MIRZA Anwer: [A case of Carcinoma of the Nasopharynx], Links, Vol 4: pg 32 (1995)
mzm	MOIZE Micaela
mzm1.es	MOIZE Micaela: Homeopatia: Doctrina y Práctica, Brasil: Javier Salvador Gamarra (1984)
mzr	MUZUMDAR K. P.
mzr1	MUZUMDAR K. P., AUGUSTINE V. T. and THAKOR K.: [Proving of Abroma Augusta Folia], New Delhi: Central Council for Research in Homeopathy (1986)
nb	NEBEL Antoine: (1870-1954)
nbe	NEATBY Edwin Awdas: (1858-1933)
nbe1	NEATBY Edwin A.: [An index of aggravations and ameliorations] (1974)
nbe2	NEATBY Edwin A.: [A Manual of Homeo Therapeutics]
nbe3	NEATBY Edwin A. and NEATBY T. M.: [Homoeopathy in Tropical Diseases], London
nc	NICOLAI Ton: Contemporary homeopathic physician [Netherlands]
ncc	NICHOLS C.F.
ncc1	NICHOLS C.F.: [Acrochordon chocoe: Characteristics], Homoeopathic Physician, Vol 1, nr 9 (1881)
ndr	NAIDU Rajiv: Contemporary homeopath [Bombay, India]
ndr1	NAIDU Rajiv: [A case of Alopecia Totalis], Links, Vol 3: pg 22 (1994)
ng	NEESGAARD Per: Contemporary homeopath [Denmark] (1950-)
ng1	NEESGAARD Per: [Hypothesis Collection - Primary Psora and Miasmatic Dynamic] (2000)
ng1.da	NEESGAARD Per: Hypotesesamling - Primaer Psora og Miasmatisk - dynamik
nh	NASH Eugene Beauharnais: American homeopathic physician (1838-1917)
nh1	NASH Eugene Beauharnais: [Leaders in Homeopathic Therapeutics], Philadelphia: Boericke & Tafel (1898)
nh1.es	NASH Eugene Beauharnais: Fundamentos de terapéutica homeopática
nh2	NASH Eugene Beauharnais: [Leaders in typhoid fever] (1900)
nh3	NASH Eugene Beauharnais: [Regional leaders [2nd Ed.]], Philadelphia: Boericke & Tafel (1908)
nh3.es	NASH Eugene Beauharnais: Características Regionales
nh3.it	NASH Eugene Beauharnais: Principi de terapeutica omeopatica
nh4	NASH Eugene Beauharnais: [The testimony of the clinic], Philadelphia: Boericke & Tafel (1911)
nh5	NASH Eugene Beauharnais: [Leaders for the use of sulphur], Philadelphia: Boericke & Tafel (1907)
nh5.it	NASH Eugene Beauharnais: I sintomi principali di Sulphur con comparazioni
nh6	NASH Eugene Beauharnais: [Leaders in respiratory organs], Philadelphia: Boericke & Tafel (1909)
nh7	NASH Eugene Beauharnais: [Radium]
nh8	NASH Eugene Beauharnais: [Expanded works of Nash], New Dehli: Jain (1995)
nh9	NASH Eugene Beauharnais: [How to Take the Case and Find the Simillimum]
nh9.es	NASH Eugene Beauharnais: Cómo se debe repertoriar un caso para encontrar EL SIMILIMUM. Translated by L. Arriaga, New Delhi: Jain Publishers
nh9.fr	NASH Eugene Beauharnais: Principes de thérapeutique homéopathique, Paris: Doin (1950)
nhc	NEIDHARD Charles: (1809-1895)
nhc1	NEIDHARD C.: [Pathogenetic and Clinical Repertory of the Most Prominent Sysmptoms of the Head with their Concomitants and Conditions], Philadelphia: F.E. Boericke, Hahnemann Publishing House (Pennsylvania) (1888)
nk	NOACK Alphons
nk1.de	NOACK Alphons, TRINKS und MUELLER: Handbuch der Homöopathischen Arzneimittellehre, Leipzig: Schumann - Weigel (1848)
nl	NORLAND Misha: Contemporary homeopath [Uffculme, Great Britain] (1943-)
nl1	NORLAND Misha: [Thuja, The Tree of Life, the Tree of Death], Links, Vol 2: pg 19-23 (1995)
nl2	NORLAND Misha: [Collected provings] (1999)
nl3	NORLAND Misha: [Collected provings 2]
nlj	NIELSEN Jorgen: (1957-)
nn	NENNING C.
nn1	NENNING C.: [Proving of Betula], A H Zt, Vol 20: pg 130
npl	NAGPAUL V.M.
npl1	NAGPAUL V.M. and DHAWAN I.M. and VICHITRA A.K. and RASTOGI D.P: [Tarantula hispanica - a reproving], Br H J, Vol 78: pg 19-26 (1989)
nsj	NISSEN Jes
nsk	NARASIMHAMURTI K.L.
nsk1	NARASIMHAMURTI K.L.: [Handbook of Materia Medica & Therapeutics of homoeopathy [1st Ed.]], New Delhi: Jain Publ. (1994)
nsr	NEUSTAEDTER Randall: (1949-)
nsr1	NEUSTAEDTER Randall: [Clematis Proving], J Am Inst Homoeopath, Vol 77 nr 2: pg 15-23 (1983)
nta	NORTON A. B.: American homeopathic ophthalmologist (1856-1919)
nta1	NORTON A. B.: [The Homeopathic Treatment of Incipient Senile Cataract, with Tabulated results of 100 cases], N Am J H, pg 3-16 (1891)
nta2	NORTON A.B.: [Ophthalmic Diseases and Therapeutics]

nwa	NEISWANDER A.C.: (1914-)
nwa1	NEISWANDER A.C.: [Niccolum sulphuricum], Hahnemann Homoeopath Sand 1992 Sep ; 16(9): pg 147-150 (1992)
ob	OBARY
oba	OBERBAUM Menachem: Contemporary homeopathic physician [Israel]
obj	OBERG J. U.
odp	O'DRISCOLL P.
odp1	O'DRISCOLL P.: [Ayahuasca, a Prover's Experience], Prometheus Unbound, Spring (1996)
oh	OEHME
oh1	OEHME: [Diphtheritis]
ohn	O'HANLON M.
ohn1	O'HANLON M.: [A short proving of Strophantus sarmentosus], Br H J, Vol 42: pg 13-15 (1952)
os	OLDS C. L.
os1	OLDS C. L.: [Aconitum], Med Adv, Vol XXXII: pg 305 (1894)
os2	OLDS C. L.: [Ammonium carbonate], Hom Rec, pg 153 (1925)
oss	OLSEN Steve: Contemporary homeopath [Canada] (1957-)
oss1	OLSEN Steve: [Trees and Plants that Heal], Maple Ridge, Canada: Legacy Publ. (1997)
oss1.de	OLSEN Steve: Bäume und Pflanzen die heilen. Die Prüfung und Anwendung von fünf neuen homöopatischen Mitteln, Zweibrücken:Verlag Karl-Josef Müller (1997)
oss2	OLSEN Steve: [Sleeping giants - pinus contorta - the shore pine] (1998)
oss3	OLSEN Steve: [Betrayal, isolation, resentment. Pseudotsuga menziesii - a homeopathic proving - Bomen project], Links, Vol 12: pg 178-181 (1999)
oss4	OLSEN Steve: [Arbor Medica] (2004)
ot	ORTEGA Proceso SANCHEZ: Contemporary homeopath [Mexico] (1919-)
ot1	ORTEGA Proceso SANCHEZ: [Notes on the Miasms]
ot1.de	ORTEGA Proceso SANCHEZ: Anmerkungen zu den Miasmen oder chronischen Krankheiten im Sinne Hahnemanns., Heidelberg: Karl F. Haug Verlag (1980)
ot1.es	ORTEGA Proceso SANCHEZ: Apuntes sobre los Miasmas o Enfermedades Cronicas de Hahnemann, México: Biblioteca Homeopatica de México (1999)
ot2.es	ORTEGA Proceso SANCHEZ y collaboratores: Carcinosinum Patogenesia completa., La homeopatía en el mundo. Homeopathía de México (Edition especial) (1997)
ot3.es	ORTEGA Proceso SANCHEZ: Traduccion y definicion de los sintomas mentales del repertorio sintetico de Barthel
ot4.es	ORTEGA Proceso SANCHEZ: Aplicación Practica de la clinica integral homepatica considerando lo miasmatico, México: Cuernavaca, Morelos (2000)
ot5.es	ORTEGA Proceso SANCHEZ: Introducción a la medecina homeopática: Teoria y técnica
oth	OSTROM Homer Irvin
oth1	OSTROM Homer Irvin: [Leucorrhoea and other Varieties of Gynaecological Catarrh] (1910)
otr	OTTER René
ozc	OZANAM C.
ozc1.fr	OZANAM C.: Etudes sur le venin des arachnides et son emploi en thérapeuthique. (1856)
ozx	OZANON Christian
ozx1.fr	OZANON Christian: Observations et Cas Cliniques (2004)
pa	PLA Anna: Contemporary homeopathic physician [Spain] (1956-)
paj	PRAT Jacques
paj1.fr	PRAT Jacques: Des Conférences de Kent, cent ans plus tard..., Société Hahnemanniene de Normandie (2000)
pc	PASCHERO Tomas Pablo: Argentinian homeopathic physician. (1904-1986)
pc1.pt	PASCHERO Tomas Pablo: Sintomas mentales, Buenos Aires (1974)
pc2	PASCHERO Tomas Pablo: [Cross references of Rubrics of the Mind, Anotaciones en el Repertorio de Kent], Buenos Aires
pc3	PASCHERO Tomas Pablo: [Tuberculinum bovinum Kent], J Am Inst Hom, Dec (1986)
pc4	PASCHERO Tomas Pablo: [Homoeopathy], Beaconsfield : Beaconsfield Publishers ltd (1st Ed.) U.K. (2000)
pc4.es	PASCHERO Tomas Pablo: Homeopatia
pcf	PICCART Frank: Contemporary homeopath [Genk, Belgium]
pcf1	PICCART Frank: [Cases: The No Fuss Woman], N Eng. J H, Vol 4 nr 4: pg 17-20 (1995)
pcr	PETRUCCI Roberto: Contemporary homeopath (Italy) (1961-) Founder of CENTRO DI OMEOPATIA MILANO.
pct	PONCET Jacques-Edouard
pct1.fr	PONCET Jacques-Edouard: Homéopathie pédiatrique, Thérapeutique en pathologie aiguë, France: Boiron Eds. [2nd Ed.] (1994)
pct2	PONCET Jacques-Edouard: [Homéopathie pédiatrique, psychopathogie.] (1994)
pd	PLADYS Albert: Belgian homeopathic physician (1920-1981). President Royal Belg Soc Hom. [1978-1981]
pda	PURDOM T. E.
pdb	POLDERMAN Guus O.: Contemporary homeopathic physician [Netherlands]
pdr	PFLEIDERER
pdr1	PFLEIDERER: [Proving of Mercurius rhodanatus], Deutsches Zeitschrift für Homeopathie (1931)
pe	PIERCE Willard Ide: (1857-1913)
pe1	PIERCE Willard Ide: [Plain talks on materia medica with comparisons], Calcutta: Haren & Brother (1911)

pe2	PIERCE Willard Ide: [Repertory of Cough, better and worse], New Delhi (1990)
pet	PETERSEN Fred Julius: (1863-)
pet1	PETERSEN Fred Julius: [Materia Medica and Clinical Therapeutics] (1905)
pew	PAIGE W. H.
pew1	PAIGE W. H.: [Diseases of the Lungs, Bronchi and Pleura], New Delhi: Jain Publishers (1988)
pf	PULFORD Dayton: American homeopathic physician (1899-1964)
pfa	PULFORD Alfred: (1863-1948)
pfa1	PULFORD A.: [Key to Homeopathic Materia Medica], Toledo, Ohio (1947)
pfa2	PULFORD A.: [Homoeopathic materia medica of graphic drug pictures and clinical comments.], New Delhi: Jain Publishers (1944)
pfa3	PULFORD A.: [Homeopathic Leaders in Pneumonia] (1928)
pfa4	PULFORD A.: [Repertory of the Symptoms of Rheumatism and Sciatica]
pfa5	PULFORD A.: [A Repertory of Leucorrhoea], Hom Recorder July 1939 (1939)
pfb	PULFORD B. T.
pfg	PFEIFFER Gabriele: (1949-), Germany
pfm	PFLUGFELDER M.
pfm1	PFLUGFELDER M.: [Cardiospermum halicacabum], Naturheilpraxis 25; 516 (1972)
ph	PATCH Frank Wallace: (1862-1923)
pha	PAYRHUBER Dietmar: Contemporary homeopathic physician [Austria]
pha1	PAYRHUBER Dietmar: [A case of Septicaemia], Links, Vol 1: pg 10 (1991)
pin	PAI P.N.: (1919-)
pin1	PAI P.N.: [A proving of Chlorpromazine], Br H J, Vol 54: pg 102-104 (1965)
pin2	PAI P.N.: [A proving of Tetanus toxin], Br H J Vol 56: pg 94-100 (1967)
pkh	PENNEKAMP Heinrich
pkh1	PENNEKAMP Heinrich: [Kinder-Repertorium nebst pädagogischen und therapeutischen Hinweisen - Osten - Isensee] (1999)
pkj	PEKER Jacqueline: (1936-)
pkj1	PEKER Jacqueline: [Homeopathy en médecine vétérinaire, animaux de compagnie.], Editions Maloine, France (1991)
pks	PAVRI KEKI R. Sharukh
pks1	PAVRI KEKI R. Sharukh: [Essentials of Diabetes Mellitus & its Treatment by Homoeopathy] (1992)
pl	PAULUS Michel: Contemporary homeopathic physician [Belgium]
pln	Pelech Natasha: Student of Homeopathy [Canada]. (1974-)
plr	PELLICO Ramón
plr1	PELLICO Ramón: [Manual veterinario homeopático del ganadero], Edited by F. Olmedo, Mexicio (1990)
pls	PAUL S.: (1950-)
pls1	PAUL S.: [Skin Therapeutics] (1991)
plx	PHELAN Richard A.
plx1	PHELAN Richard A.: [Inaugural Dissertation on Therapeutics. Presented by Julian Winston.] (1867)
pm	PRIESTMAN Kathleen: Contemporary homeopathic physician [England] (1900-)
pmc	PUHLMANN C.G.
pmc1	PUHLMANN C.G.: [Handbook of Homeopathic Practice]
pml	PASTORINO María Luisa
pml1.es	PASTORINO María Luisa: La medicina floral de Edward Bach,, Buenos Aires: Editorial Club de Estudio (1987)
pmr	PALOMARES DURÁN Roberto
pmr1.es	PALOMARES DURÁN Roberto: Le Epilepsia y Sutratamiento Homeopático., New Delhi: Jain Publishers (1995)
pms	PALMER S.
pms1	PALMER S.: [The proving of Aqua Tunbridge Wells]
pn	PLISNIER Emile: Contemporary homeopathic physician [Belgium]
pnb	PANDA B. B.
pnb1	PANDA B. B.: [Significance of Dreams in Homoeopathic Prescribing] (1984)
pnm	PANOS M. B.
pnm1	PANOS M. B. and HEIMLICH J.: [Family Homoeopathic Medicine], New Delhi: Vision Books (1983)
pnz	PLANITZ Christa von der: Contemporay homeopathic physician [Germany]
ppb	PAPARGIRIOU Kriton: Contemporary homeopathic physician [Italy]
ppg	PAPAPHILLIPOU George: Contemporary homeopathic physician [Greece]
ppg1	PAPAPHILLIPOU George: [Differential of violent remedies], Links, Vol 3: pg 17-19 (1991)
ppo	PIPER O. et al
ppo1	PIPER O.: [Proving of Aqua tipida], Homoeopathic Times, London Vol 2: pg 184
ppp	POPOWSKI Pierre
ppp1.fr	POPOWSKI Pierre: Collection d'articles et cas cliniques des Cahiers de Biothérapie
ppp2.fr	POPOWSKI Pierre: Homéopathie Pédiatrique - Articles
ppr	POMPOSELLI Raphaella: Contemporary homeopath [Milano, Italy]
ppr1	POMPOSELLI Raphaella: [A case of Viburnum Opulus], E J Cl. H, Vol 1 nr 2: pg 27 (1995)
ppt	POPOVA Tatiana D.
ppt1	POPOVA Tatiana D.: [Lectures]
prf	PARSONS Philip K.: (1935-)
prj	POIRIER Jean

prj1	POIRIER Jean: [Homeopathic Treatment of the Diseases of Heart] (1998)
prl	PEREIRA Lúcia
prs	PORAS
ps	PIERSON J. T.
psa	POSSART A.: (1823-)
psa1.de	POSSART A.: Homoöpathische Arzneimitellehre (Vol. 1-3), Nordhausen: Büchting (1863)
psj	PETERS John Charles: (1819-1893)
psj1	PETERS John C.: [A Complete Treatise on Headaches and Diseases of the Head. .], New York: William Radde (1859)
psj2	PETERS John C.: [A Treatise on the Inflammatory and Organic Diseases of the Brain.], New York: William Radde (1855)
psm	PONTESILLI Marisa
psm1.it	PONTESILLI Marisa: Corso di primi soccorso omeopatico, Edited by Audasso Sergio
pss	PALSULE S.G.
pss1	PALSULE S.G.: [Asthma and Blood Pressure] (1999)
pss2	PALSULE S.G.: [Dentistry and Homeopathy] (1977)
pss2.es	PALSULE S.G.: Odontologia y Homeopática, New Delhi: Jain Publishers (1977)
pss3	PALSULE S.G.: [Homeopathic Treatment for E. N. T. Diseases] (1983)
ptd	PARENTEAU D.
ptd1.fr	PARENTEAU D.: Thérapeutique Homéopathique en Ophtalmologie, Paris: G. Doin & C (France) (1934)
pte	PATERSON Elisabeth: (1920-)
pte1	PATERSON Elisabeth: [A survey on the Nosodes], B H J, Vol 49: pg 161-186 (1960)
ptg	PRATO Gonzalo M.: Contemporary homeopathic physician [Venezuela]
ptj	PATERSON John: (1890-1954)
ptj1	PATERSON John: [The Bowel Nosodes], London (1950)
ptj1.fr	PATERSON John: Les Nosodes Intestinaux
ptj2	PATERSON John: [Clinical Notes, Observations], London (1933)
ptj3	PATERSON John: [Intestinal Nosodes in diseases of Children], London (1937)
ptj4	PATERSON John: [Sycosis and Sycotic Co.], London (1933)
ptk	PHATAK S. R.: Contemporary homeopathic physician [Bombay,India] (-1981)
ptk1	PHATAK S. R.: [Concise Repertory of Homeopathic Medicines], New Dehli: Jain Publ. (1963)
ptk2	PHATAK S. R.: [Materia Medica of Homoeopathic medicines], New Delhli: Indish Book and Periodicals (1977)
ptk2.es	PHATAK S. R.: Materia Médica de Medicina Homeopática
ptm	PELT Marguerite: (1952-)
ptm1	PELT Marguerite and STUUT H.: [Cobalt], Links, Vol 8: pg 19-21 (1995)
ptn	PORTONE Nicola: Contemporary homeopathic physician [Italy]
ptr	PATEL Ramanlal P.
ptr1	PATEL Ramanlal P.: [Luffa operculata in bronchial asthma]
pts	PETERS R. G.: Contemporary homeopath [Sneek, The Netherlands]
pts1	PETERS R. G.: [A case of depression and headache], Links, Vol 3: pg 15 (1995)
ptt	PRATT N.J.
ptt1	PRATT N.J.: [Double blind proving trials by medical students], Br H J, Vol 60: pg 41-43 (1970)
ptx	PITT Richard: Contemporary homeopath [USA] (1950-)
ptx1	PITT Richard: [Taxus brevifolia - Pacific Yew] (2002)
ptz	PETROZ Antoine
pw	POWEL F.
pwa	POWEL W. R.
pwb	POWEL M.
pwe	POWELL E.F.
pwe1	POWELL E.F.: [The Group Remedy Prescriber]
ql	QUILISCH W.
ql1.de	QUILISCH W.: Homoeopathische Praxis, Stuttgart: Hippokrates Verlag (3rd Ed.) (1987)
ql2.de	QUILISCH W.: Homoeopathische Differentialtherapie, Heidelberg: Karl F. Haug Verlag (1980)
qqh	QUIQUANDON Henri: Veterinary [France] (1928-)
qqh1	QUIQUANDON Henri: [Homéopathie vetérinaire et biothérapie.], Editions du Point Vétérinaire, Francia (1983)
qtg	QUINTERO RAMÍREZ Gilberto
qtg1.es	QUINTERO RAMÍREZ Gilberto: Anemia y Homeopática tratamiento y enfoque homeopático de la anemia y afecciones relacionadas., New Delhi: Jain Publishers (1997)
qy	QUAY George H.
qy1	QUAY George H.: [Diseases of the Nose an Throat], Philadelphia (1897)
qy2	QUAY George H.: [A monograph of diseases of the nose and throat.], Philadelphia: Boericke & Tafel (1901)
radkn	Radar Keynotes
rb	ROBERTS Herbert Alfred: American homeopathic physician (1868-1950)
rb1	ROBERTS Herbert Albert: [Materia Medica] (1941)
rb2	ROBERTS Herbert Albert: [Sensations as if], Calcutta: Economic Hom. Pharmacy (1937)
rb2.fr	ROBERTS Herbert Albert: Les sensations comme si
rb3	ROBERTS Herbert Albert: [The study of remedies by comparison] (1941)

rb3.es ROBERTS Herbert Albert: El Estudio de los remedios por comparacion

rb4 ROBERTS Herbert Albert: [The rheumatic remedies] (1939)

rb5 ROBERTS Herbert A. and WILSON Annie C.: [The principles and practicability of Boenningshausen's therapeutic pocket book.], Philadelphia: Boericke & Tafel.

rb6 ROBERTS Herbert Albert: [Proving of Iridium metallicum], Med Adv, Vol 43/6: pg 345 (1905)

rb7 ROBERTS Herbert Albert: [The Spider Poisons], Hom Rec (1931)

rb8 ROBERTS Herbert Albert: [Bothrops atrox], Hom Rec, May (1938)

rb9 ROBERTS Herbert Albert: [The principles and Art of Cure by Homoeopathy - A Modern Textbook]

rba RICHBERG E. O.

rbb RABE Rudolph Frederick: (1872-1952)

rbb1 RABE Rudolph Frederick: [Lathyrus], Med Adv, Vol XLVIII: pg 281 (1910)

rbe ROBERTS Ernest: Contemporary homeopath [UK]

rbe1 ROBERTS Ernest: [Homeopathy: Principles and Practice], Kent: Winter Press (2001)

rbf ROBERTSON F.

rbf1 ROBERTSON F.: [Mandragora]

rbg RIEBERER Gabriela

rbo RIBEIRO Filho: (1953-)

rbp ROBBINS Phillip: (1956-)

rbp1 ROBBINS Phillip: [Vibhuti]

rbp2 ROBBINS Phillip: [Phascolarctos cinereus [Australian Koala secretion]] (1998)

rbp2.de ROBBINS Phillip: Koala (phascolarctos cinereus): Die Prüfung, Zweibrücken:Verlag Karl-Josef Müller (1999)

rbp3 ROBBINS Phillip and JANSEN Jean-Pierre: [Aristolochia clematis] (2000)

rbp3.de ROBBINS Phillip: Aristolochia clematitis: Die Prüfung, Zweibrücken:Verlag Karl-Josef Müller (2001)

rbp4 ROBBINS Phillip: [Aqua marina]

rbp5 ROBBINS Phillip: [Insight meditation]

rbp6 ROBBINS Phillip: [Evolving Homeopathy. Towards a Developmental Approach to Homeopathy.], Philip Robbins (2003)

rbr RIBEIRO FREITA Gilberto: Contemporary homeopathic physician, Brazil (1953-)

rbs ROBERTS R.

rbs1.fr ROBERTS R.: Precis d'Homeopathie Pratique et Matiere Medicale, France: Boiron

rbt ROBERTS T.G.

rbt1 ROBERTS T.G.: [Calcarea fluorica], Medical Advance, Vol 37, nr 12 (1899)

rbw ROBERTS W. H.

rc RÜCKERT Ernst Ferdinand

rc1.de RÜCKERT Ernst Ferdinand: Systematische Darstellung aller bis jetzt gekannten homöopathischen Arzneien Vol 1 & 2, Leipzig: Schumann (1832)

rcb RICHARDSON-BOEDLER Cornelia: (1954-)

rcb1 RICHARDSON-BOEDLER Cornelia: [The Bach Flower Remedies] (1993)

rcb1.de RICHARDSON-BOEDLER Cornelia: Die Anwendung der Bach-Blütentherapie in den Heildisziplinen. Katalysatoren in der homöopathischen Behandlung, Trans. Cornelia Richardson-Boedler. In Encyclopaedia Homeopathica. Assesse, Belgium: Archibel, 2002.

rcb10 RICHARDSON-BOEDLER Cornelia: [Dicentra cucullaria]

rcb2 RICHARDSON-BOEDLER Cornelia: [Crassula obliqua] (1993)

rcb3 RICHARDSON-BOEDLER Cornelia: [Psychic causes of Illness: Applying Homeopathy and Bach flowers therapy to Psychosomatic illness], Cornelia Richardson Boedler: June 12th, 1995. Revised and expanded May 1997 (1997)

rcb4 RICHARDSON-BOEDLER Cornelia: [The psychological / Constitutional essences of the Bach Flower remedies.], New Delhi: Jain Publishers (1997)

rcb4.de RICHARDSON-BOEDLER Cornelia: Die Anwendung der Bach-Blütentherapie in den Heildisziplinen. Tiefendynamische Bach Blüten für Psyche und Konstitution., Trans. Cornelia Richardson-Boedler. In Encyclopaedia Homeopathica. Assesse, Belgium: Archibel, 2002.

rcb5 RICHARDSON-BOEDLER Cornelia: [The ammonia remedies: their homoeopathic use in head injuries and other head conditions.], 1998 Br H J,Vol 87: pg 203-209 / 1999 Br H J,Vol 88: pg 24-27 (1998)

rcb6 RICHARDSON-BOEDLER Cornelia: [Sicarius [Six-Eyed Crab Spider]: A homeopathic treatment for Ebola haemorrhagic fever and disseminated intravascular coagulation?], Br H J, Vol 88 pg 24-27 (1999)

rcb7 RICHARDSON-BOEDLER Cornelia: [A Potential Antidote for the Necrotic and Systemic Effects caused by the brown recluse spider [Loxosceles reclusa].], J Am Inst H, Vol 91nr 3: pg 277-283 (1998)

rcb8 RICHARDSON-BOEDLER Cornelia: [The doctrine of signatures: a historical, philosophical, scientific view I. [and later II]], Br H J, Vol 88. (1999)

rcb9 RICHARDSON-BOEDLER Cornelia: [Spider remedies]

rcj REICHENBERG-ULLMAN Judyth: Contemporary homeopath [Edmonds, USA]

rcj1 REICHENBERG-ULLMAN Judyth: [Insights into a Common remedy], Links, Vol 2: pg 18 (1995)

rde RUDDOCK Edward Harris: (1822-1875)

rde1 RUDDOCK Edward Harris: [Lady's Homoeopathic Manual], London (1865)

rde2	RUDDOCK Edward Harris: [Diseases of Infants and Children], London (1886)
rde3	RUDDOCK Edward Harris: [The Common diseases of children]
rde4	RUDDOCK Edward Harris: [Homeopathic Treatment of Infants and Children]
rde4.es	RUDDOCK Edward Harris: Tratado Teorico Y Practico De Las Enfermedades De Los Ninos, Madrid (Spain): Dilema Editorial (2003)
rde5	RUDDOCK Edward Harris: [The common diseases of Women]
rde6	RUDDOCK Edward Harris: [The Pocket Manual of Homeopathic Veterinary Medicine [1st Ed.]], New Delhi: Jain Publishers (1972)
rde7	RUDDOCK Edward Harris: [The Stepping Stone to Homeopathy and Health]
rdf	REDIN Fernando Gonzáles: Contemporary homeopathic physician [Ecuador]
rdf1.es	REDIN Fernando Gonzáles: ABC de la Nutricion, Quito: REDIN Fernando Gonzáles (1997)
rdr	RODRIGUES RITA Rogerio
rdr1.pt	RODRIGUES RITA Rogerio: Adiçoes da patogenesia moderna de hydrocyanicum acidum ao repertorio., Revista de Homeopatia (R H AMHB) nr 2, outubro: pg 34-42 (1998)
re	RAYE G.
rea	RICE P.
rea1	RICE P.: [Veratrum viride], Br Hom J, Vol XXIV: pg 343
rec	RAUE Charles Godlove: (1820-1896)
rec1	RAUE Charles Godlove: [Special pathology and diagnostics], Philadelphia: Boericke and Tafel (1882)
res	RAUE Charles Sigmund: (1873-)
res1	RAUE Charles Sigmund: [Diseases of children], Philadelphia: Boericke and Tafel (1899)
rfm	RIEFER Marco: (1958-)
rfm1	RIEFER Marco: [Riefer M. Candida albicans: a proving report and a case.], Homoeopath Links, 1998, Summer;11(2):107-10, (1998)
rfm1.de	RIEFER Marco: Das Arzneimittelbild von Candida albicans, Freiburg: Marco Riefer (1996)
rg	ROGERS Ruth: American homeopathic physician (1926-)
rgm	RIGHETTI Marco: Contemporary homeopathic physician [switzerland]. Psychiatrist.
rgp	ROGIERS Patrick: Contemporary homeopath [Belgium] (1959-)
rha	RONHAAR A.: Contemporary homeopath [De Krim, The Netherlands]
rha1	RONHAAR A.: [Protruded tongue in brain affections], Links, Vol 3: pg 14-15 (1995)
rhj	RUSH John
rhj1	RUSH John: [The handbook of Veterinary homoeopathy] (1997)
rjp	RAJAGOPALARAO P.
rjp1	RAJAGOPALARAO P.: [Most Valuable Tips from Masters of Homeopathy] (1998)
rkb	RAKOW Barbara: Veterinary [Austria] (1949-)
rke	RUCKERT E.F.
rke1	RUCKERT E.F.: [Therapeutics and Outlines of Successful Cures]
rkh	RECKEWEG Hans Heinrich: (1905-1985)
rkh1	RECKEWEG Hans Heinrich: [Homeopathia Antihomotoxica: Symptoms and index of modatilites with Materia Medica] (1980)
rkh1.de	RECKEWEG Hans Heinrich: Homeopathia Antihomotoxica - symptomen und Modalitätenverzeichnis mit Arzneimittellehre. Vol 1 & Vol 2
rkm	RAKOW Michael: Veterinary [Austria]
rl	REILLY David: Contemporary homeopathic physician [UK]
rlg	ROLLIN R. Gregg: (1828-1886)
rlg1	ROLLIN R. Gregg: [An Illustrated Repertory of Pains In Chest, Sides and Back: Their Direction and Character, confirmed by Clinical Cases. [2nd Ed.]], Chicago: Duncan Brothers Publishers (Illinois) (1879)
rly	RILEY David: Contemporary homeopath [USA]. Actively undertaking many provings. (1952-)
rly1	RILEY David: [A proving of Fumaria officinalis], Links, Vol 7: pg 18-20 (1994)
rly2	RILEY David: [Proving of Cardiospermum halicacabum], HomInt nr.1: pg 12 (1996)
rly3	RILEY David: [Veronica officinalis], Br. H. J., Vol 84: pg 144-148 (1995)
rly4	RILEY David: [Collected provings] (1994)
rm	RADEMACHER Johann Gottfried: (1772-1850)
rm1.de	RADEMACHER Johann Gottfried: Erfahrungsheillehre, Lorch: Rohm-Verlag (1939)
rma	REHMAN Abdur: Contemporary homeopathic physician [Lahore, Pakistan]
rma1	REHMAN Abdur: [Related Remedies] (1997)
rma2	REHMAN Abdur: [Family History and Personal History with Intercurrent Reaction and Alternative Remedies] (1997)
rma3.de	REHMAN Abdur: Homoopathische Behandlung Symptomenarmer Falle, Stuttgart: Johannes Sonntag (2001)
rmk	RAMAKRISHNAN A
rmk1	RAMAKRISHNAN A.U. and COULTER C.: [The Homepathic Treatment of Cancer], Ninth House publishing (2001)
rms	RUMANSEDER: Practionner (1927-)
rmt	REUMONT Thomas von: Contemporary homeopath [Germany] (1960-)
rmu	RIMMLER Uli: Contemporary psychotherapist [Germany] (1961)
rmu1	RIMMLER Uli: [The Flight of the Condor - The Andean Condor: Vultur gryphus]
rpd	RESPONDEK U.: (1950-)

rpd1 RESPONDEK U.: [Cardiospermum halicacabum] (1990)

rpd2 RESPONDEK U.: [Croton tiglium], H Arz Vol1 (1990)

rpd3 RESPONDEK U.: [Fabiana imbricata], H Arz Vol 3

rpv RAMPOLD Veronika, Millenium author list 2003

rpv1.de RAMPOLD Veronika: MINDMAT, Vollständige Materia medica der ichnahen Symptome (1998)

rq RISQUEZ F.

rq1 RISQUEZ F.: [Psychiatry and Homeopathy] (1995)

rq1.es RISQUEZ F.: Psiquiatría y Homeopatía (1995)

rr ROHRER Anton: Contemporary homeopathic physician [Austria] 1955-)

rr1 ROHRER Anton: [Characteristics of Angustura Vera], Links, Vol 2: pg 13 (1993)

rs ROSS E. V.: English homeopathic physician (1948-)

rsa RUSSEL D. C.

rsd ROSS T.Douglas: (1932-1964)

rse ROSSI Elio

rsi ROSSETTI Luiz Cesar: (1965-)

rsi1 ROSSETTI Luiz Cesar: [Lepidoptera saturniidae]

rsi1.pt ROSSETTI Luiz Cesar: Lepidoptera saturniidae

rsj RAESIDE John R.: (1926-1972)

rsj1 RAESIDE J.R.: [Fifteen Years of Drug Proving in London], B H J, Vol 61 (1972)

rsj10 RAESIDE J.R.: [A proving of Tellurium], Br H J, Vol 57: pg 216-220 (1968)

rsj11 RAESIDE J.R.: [A proving of Triosteum Perfoliatum], Br H J, Vol 49: pg 269-278 (1960)

rsj12 RAESIDE J.R.: [A proving of Venus Mercenaria], Br H J , Vol 51: pg 200-206 (1962)

rsj13 RAESIDE J.R.: [Arzneimittelprüfung von Esponjilla [Luffa operculata]], Zt Klass H, Vol 9, 49 (1965)

rsj14 RAESIDE J.R.: [Atrax robustus], Br H J 59 (1970)

rsj15 RAESIDE J.R.: [Veronica officinalis], Br H J 84 (1995)

rsj2 RAESIDE J.R.: [A proving of Colchicum autumnale], Br H J, Vol 56: pg 86-93 (1967)

rsj3 RAESIDE J.R.: [A proving of Flor de Piedra [Lophophytum leandri]], Br H J , Vol 58: pg 240-246 (1969)

rsj4 RAESIDE J.R.: [A proving of Hirudo medicinalis], Br H J , Vol 53: pg 22-30 (1964)

rsj5 RAESIDE J.R.: [A proving of Esponjilla [Luffa operculata]], Br H J, Vol 54: pg 36-45 (1965)

rsj6 RAESIDE J.R.: [A proving of hydrophis cyanocinctus], Br H J Vol 48: pg 197-214 (1954)

rsj7 RAESIDE J.R.: [A proving of Mandragora officinarum], Br H J, Vol 55: pg 68-75 (1966)

rsj8 RAESIDE J.R.: [A proving of Mimosa pudica JR.], Br H J, Vol 60: pg 97-104 (1971)

rsj9 RAESIDE J.R.: [Report on a proving of Selenium], Br H J, Vol 50: pg 215-225 (1961)

rsl ROUSSEAU L. A.

rsl1 ROUSSEAU L. A. and FORTIER-BERNOVILLE: [Diseases of Respiratory and Digestive Systems of Children], New Delhi: Jain Publishers (1982)

rsl2 ROUSSEAU L. A.: [Suppurations and Neuralgia], Calcutta: Hahnemann Publ. (1936)

rsp ROSEMBAUM Paulo: Contemporary homeopathic physician [Brasil]

rsp1 ROSENBAUM Paulo et al.: [Lapis Lazuli, a Proving. A pathogenesy developed by the team of Escola Paulista de Homeopatia - São Paulo - Brazil.], São Paulo (Brazil): Escola Paulista de Homeopatia (2001)

rss REIS S.: (1961-)

rss1 REIS S.: [Palladium metallicum], Arch H, 2(4): pg 173-186 (1993)

rst ROSENTHAL Chaim: Contemporary homeopathic physician [Tel Aviv, Israel]. Authority on analysing symptoms by families of remedies.

rsx RHEES

rsx1 RHEES: [Proving of Rhus laurina, Lithrea laurina], North American Journal of Homoeopathy Vol 3

rsy RAMSEYER A. A.

rsy1 RAMSEYER A. A.: [Rademacher's Universal & Organ Remedies] (1975)

rt RUTTEN Lex A. B.: Contemporary homeopathic physician [Breda, Netherlands]. Pres. Samuel Hom. Assoc. Creator Samuel Keynotes, Samuel Ponderation Factor.

rta ROTHENBERG Amy: Contemporary homeopath [Enfield, USA]

rta1 ROTHENBERG Amy: [Cases: It is Nice to Wait], N Eng. J H, Vol 4 nr 2: pg 11-13 (1995)

rti RASTOGI D.P.: (1939-)

rti1 RASTOGI D.P.: [Cuprum oxydatum nigrum], Proc 40th LMHI Congr., Lyon France pg 354-357 (1985)

rti2 RASTOGI D.P.: [Homeopathic Gems] (1997)

rti3 RASTOGI D.P.: [Some Case Reports]

rti4 RASTOGI D.P.: [Use of Indigenous and Other Remedies in Homeopathy as Home Remedies] (1993)

rv REVES Joseph: Contemporary homeopathic [Haifa, Israel]. Creator of soft HomeoData.

rwp RAWAT P. S.: (1947-)

rwp1 RAWAT P. S.: [Select your dose and potency] (1989)

rwp2 RAWAT P. S.: [Homeopathy in Acne and Alopecia] (1977)

rwp3 RAWAT P. S.: [Homeopathy in Angina Pectoris] (1977)

rwt ROWE Todd: (1958-)

rwt1 ROWE Todd: [Carnegia gigantea a proving of Saguaro Cactus] (1997)

rwt2 ROWE Todd: [Heloderma Suspectum proving] (1996)

rwt3 ROWE Todd: [Urolophus Halleri: a pronving of Round Stingray] (1998)

rwt4 ROWE Todd: [Cathartes aura: A proving of Turkey Vulture], Edited by Yolande Grill HMA, CCH. (1999)

rwt5 ROWE Todd: [A proving of Argemone pleicantha] (2000)

rwt6 ROWE Todd: [A proving of Alligator mississipensis] (2001)

rwt7 ROWE Todd: [Proving of Turquoise] (2002)

rwt8 ROWE Todd: [Proving of Larrea tridentata (Creosote)] (2003)

ry ROYAL George: (1853-)

ry1 ROYAL George: [Textbook of Homeopathic Materia Medica] (1920)

ry2 ROYAL George: [Textbook of homoeopathic theory and practice of medicine.], New Delhi: Jain Publishers (1923)

ry3 ROYAL George: [The homoeopathic therapy of diseases of the brain and nerves.], Philadelphia: Boericke & Tafel (1928)

ryj REY Jacques

rym ROY M. M

rym1 ROY M. M: [Manual of Homeopathic Pocket Repertory]

rz REZZANI Carlo: Contemporary homeopathic physician [Como, Italy]. Creator of CHIP soft [Clin. Hom. Invest. Program].

rzf RITZER Friedrich: Contemporary homeopath [Passau, Germany] (1961-)

rzf1 RITZER Friedrich and EBERLE Hans: [Plutonium - the suppression of the person's nucleus], Links: Vol 4: pg 13-16 (1995)

rzf1.de RITZER Friedrich und EBERLE Hans: Plutonium: Die Unterdrücking des Weges zum Grund des eigenen Wesens., Eberle Hans (1995)

rzf2.de RITZER Friedrich und EBERLE Hans: Arzneimittelprüfung von Scorpio europeus (1995)

rzf3.de RITZER Friedrich und EBERLE Hans: Aqua Hochstein (1996)

rzf4 RITZER Friedrich and EBERLE Hans: [Excrementum caninum] (1996)

rzf5 RITZER Friedrich and EBERLE Hans: [Placenta proving] (1995)

rzf6.de RITZER Friedrich und EBERLE Hans: = ebh2.de = Arzneimittellehre: Neue homöopatische Arzneien I (old abb), München: Verlag Müller & Steinicke

rzf7.de RITZER Friedrich und EBERLE Hans: = ebh3.de = Arzneimittellehre: Neue homöopatische Arzneien II (old abb), München: Verlag Müller & Steinicke (1998)

sa SOUK-ALOUN Phou: Contemporary Homeopathic physician [France]. Actively undertaking provings.(1940-)

sa1 SOUK-ALOUN Phou: [New provings : Brucella] (1990)

sa1.fr SOUK-ALOUN Phou: Nouvelles pathogénésies: Brucella, Mélitine .., Rev B H (1990)

sa2 SOUK-ALOUN Phou: [Cyclosporinum] (1992)

sa3 SOUK-ALOUN Phou: [Provings of the french "comite d'experimentation homeopathique".] (1990)

sa4 SOUK-ALOUN Phou: [Unintentional Provings]

saa STADLER Angelika

saa1 STADLER Angelika and ZACHMANN Marion: [Zwischen Mütterlichkeit und Passivität - Lac delphinum], H Zt, Nr 1: pg 16-20 (1996)

sad SOARES Antonius A. Dorta

sad1 SOARES Antonius A. Dorta: [Dicionário de Medicamentos Homeopáticos], Santos Livraria editora 1ed. 2000

samkn SAMUEL: Keynotes (1992)

samkn.de SAMUEL: Keynotes (1992)

sb SCHWABE Willmar

sb1 SCHWABE Willmar: [Homeopathisches Arzneibuch], Berlin (1958)

sb10 SCHWABE Willmar: [Liver-protecting and cholerectic picroside II from Picrorrhiza kurroa]

sb11 SCHWABE Willmar: [Pharmacopoea homeopathica polyglotta. Translated by Semuel Steffens.], Leipzig: Willmar Schwabe (1911)

sb11.es SCHWABE Willmar: Pharmacopoea homeopathica polyglotta.(6th Ed.) Translated by Paz Alvarez., Leipzig: Willmar Schwabe (1911)

sb11.fr SCHWABE Willmar: Pharmacopoea homeopathica polyglotta. Translated by Alphonse Noack, Leipzig: Willmar Schwabe (1911)

sb11.it SCHWABE Willmar: Pharmacopoea homeopathica polyglotta. Translated by Jommaso Cigliano, Leipzig: Willmar Schwabe (1911)

sb11.pt SCHWABE Willmar: Pharmacopoea homeopathica polyglotta. Translated by Francisco José da Costa, Leipzig: Willmar Schwabe (1911)

sb2.de SCHWABE Willmar: Übersicht über neuere Arzneipflanzen, die sich in den letzten 20 Jahren in der Homöopathie und der Phytotherapie bewährt haben., A H Z, Vol 5: pg 217-229 (1980)

sb3 SCHWABE Willmar and HERZ W.: [Flor de piedra], A H Z 209: pg 228 (1964)

sb4 SCHWABE Willmar: [Cardiospermum halicacabum], A H Z 217: pg 146-153 (1972)

sb5 SCHWABE Willmar: [Datisca cannabina], A H Z 217: pg 146-153 (1972)

sb6 SCHWABE Willmar: [Espeletia grandiflora], A H Z 217: pg 146-153 (1972)

sb7 SCHWABE Willmar: [Harpagophytum procumbens], A H Z 217: pg 146-153 (1972)

sb8 SCHWABE Willmar: [Okoubaka aubrevillei], A H Z 217: pg 146-153 (1972)

sb9 SCHWABE Willmar: [Luffa operculata], Erfahr.hk.12; 74 (1963)

sba SCHMALLBACH A.

sba1.de SCHMALLBACH A., CORDEL A. und BROOCK H: Mandragora, die Geheimnisvolle (1996)

sbb SILBERT Barbara: Contemporary homeopath [Newburyport, USA]

sbb1 SILBERT Barbara: [Tingly, Woozy and Full of Rushes], N Eng. J H, Vol 4 nr 4: pg 11-13 (1995)
sbd SWOBODA Franz von: (1956-)
sbd1 SWOBODA Franz von and König Peter: [Ginkgo biloba] (1992)
sbd2 = kgp1 = SWOBODA Franz von and KÖNIG Peter: [Succinicum acidum]
sbd3 SWOBODA Franz von: [Abies canadensis], Br Hom J (1986)
sbd4 SWOBODA Franz and KÖNIG Peter: [Magnesium fluoratum.], Proc 42nd LMHI Congr., Virginia USA: pg 158-162 (1987)
sbd5 SWOBODA Franz: [Abrotanum]
sbe STRAUBE Eva-Maria: Contemporary homeopathic physician [Germany]
sbg SERBAN Gabriella: Contemporary homeopath [Göteborg, Sweden]
sbg1 SERBAN Gabriella: [Case of The Ice-Walls], Links, Vol 4: pg 31-32 (1995)
sbh SCHUBY Hugo: (1850-)
sbj SPILBAUER Jean-Pierre
sbj1.es SPILBAUER Jean-Pierre: Caso Belladonna: La Yegüa "Praline"
sbm STÜBLER M.
sbm1 STÜBLER M.: [Espletia grandiflora], A H Z 217, 14 (1972)
sbx SHERBINO G.W.
sbx1 SHERBINO G.W.: [Case of Sanicula aqua.], Medical Advance (1886)
sca SPENCER C. S.
scc SANCHEZ Caballero Edwiges: (1945-)
scc1 SANCHEZ Caballero E., R. Sanchez, M. Riba et al.: [Pure experimentation and reexperimentation in homeopathy of Mexico carcinosinum.], Proc 54th LMHI Congr., Salvador-Bahia, Brasil (1999)
scn SARCINELLI LUZ Hylton: Contemporary homeopathic physician [Rio de Janeiro, Brasil]
scr SANCHEZ Caballero Rosario
scr1.es SANCHEZ Caballero Rosario: Materia Médica Miasmática, Carcinosinum, México: La Homeopatía en el mundo Nr. 3 (1997)
sd SHEDD Percy William: (1870-1911)
sd1 SHEDD Percy William: [The Clinical Repertory], Philadelphia: Boericke and Tafel (1908)
sda SEIDEL Ray E.: American homeopathic physician, practiced from1936-1980, thaught by Knerr and by Garth Boericke (1952-)
sdb SNADER Edwin
sdb1 SNADER Edwin: [Repertory of Heart Symptoms] (1888)
sde SCHADDE Anne: Contemporary homeopath [Munchen, Germany] (1947-)
sde1 SCHADDE Anne: [My experience with Natrum Carbonicum], Links, Vol 2: pg 22-23 (1993)
sde2 SCHADDE Anne: [Proving of Ozone], München (1996)
sde2.de SCHADDE Anne: Ozon (O3zon) : Eine homöopathische Studie, Munchen: Verlag Müller & Steinicke (1995)
sde3 SCHADDE Anne: [Proving of Carcinosinum], München (1994)
sde4 SCHADDE Anne: [The proving of Ginkgo biloba]
sde4.de SCHADDE Anne: Ginkgo biloba: Eine homöopathische Studie, München: Verlag Müller & Steinicke (2000)
sde5 SCHADDE Anne: [The proving of Lithium carbonicum]
sde5.de SCHADDE Anne: Lithium carbonicum: Eine homöopatische Studie, München: Verlag Müller & Steinicke (2000)
sde6 SCHADDE Anne: [Cypraea Eglantina - Cowrie snail]
sde6.de SCHADDE Anne: Cypraea Eglantina, genannt die Kaurischnecke - eine homöopatische Studie (2002)
sde7.de SCHADDE Anne: Lignum aquilaria agallocha, edelstes Räucherholz der Welt - eine homöopatische Studie
sde8 SCHADDE Anne: [The proving of Lapis lazuli]
sde8.de SCHADDE Anne und HANSEL Jürgen: Lapis lazuli - eine homöopatische Studie (2002)
sdj SNOWDON Janet: (1947-)
sdj1 SNOWDON Janet: [Dreaming Potency] (1999)
sdj2 SNOWDON Janet: [The Homeopathic Proving of Heroin] (2000)
sdl SANDOVAL Luis G.
sdl1.es SANDOVAL Luis G.: Farmacopea Homeopatica Mexicana, New Delhi: Jain Publishers
sdr SPALDING Ray W.
sdr1 SPALDING Ray W.: [Ailments from], Hom Recorder, Vol LXI nr 1 (1945)
sds SUDARSHAN S. R.
sds1 SUDARSHAN S. R.: [Homeopathic Treatment of Non-Malarial Fevers] (1994)
sdx SEIDEL Eduard
sdx1.de SEIDEL Eduard: Geschichte der homöopatischen Heilanstalt zu Leipzig und sämtlicher darin behandelten Krankheitsfälle (1840)
sdy SNADER Edward R.
sdy1 SNADER Edward R.: [Repertory of the Heart Symptoms]
sej SHORE Jonathan: Contemporary homeopath [San Fransisco, USA] (1943-)
sej1 SHORE Jonathan: [Strychninum], Homoeopathy International, Vol 5: nr. 3 (1991)
sej10 SHORE Jonathan: [Investigations into the Psyche of the Spider.]
sej2 SHORE Jonathan: [Seminar Glasgow [Scotland] April 1989] (1989)
sej3 SHORE Jonathan: [Seminar Hapert [Netherlands] September 1990] (1990)
sej4 SHORE Jonathan: [Seminar Hapert [Netherlands] April 1991] (1991)

sej5	SHORE Jonathan: [Seminar Glasgow [Scotland] April 1990] (1990)
sej6	SHORE Jonathan: [Proving buteo jamaicensis] (1995)
sej7	SHORE Jonathan: [Proving ara macao] (2000)
sej8	SHORE Jonathan: [Atrax robustus] (1996)
sej9	= sze2 = SHORE Jonathan: [Columbus Palumba (Dove)]
ser	SCHORE Robert: Contemporary homeopathic physician [USA] (1943-)
sf	STAUFFER Karl: (1870-1930)
sf1.de	STAUFFER Karl: Symptomen-Verzeichnis nebst vergleichenden Zusätzen zur Homoöpathischen Arzneimittellehre, Regensburg: Verlagsbuchhandlang Johannes Sonntag (1929)
sf2.de	STAUFFER Karl: Klinische Hom. Arzneimittelehre [2nd Ed.], Regensburg: Verlagsbuchhandlang Johannes Sonntag (1926)
sf3	STAUFFER Karl: [Homoeotherapie], Regensburg: Verlagsbuchhandlang Johannes Sonntag (1986)
sfa	STAPF Johann Ernst: Student of Hahnemann. Herausgeber des Archivs für Hom. Heilkunst (1788-1860)
sfa1	STAPF Johann Ernst: [Additions to the Materia Medica Pura] (1846)
sfh	STIEFELMANN Henrique: Contemporary homeopathic physician [Brasil]
sfm	SCHEFFER Mechthild
sfm1.es	SCHEFFER Mechthild: La terapía Floral de Bach, teoría y Práctica,, Barcelona (Spain) : Ediciones Urano (1992)
sfm2.es	SCHEFFER Mechthild: Terapía Original de las Flores de Bach [1st Ed.], Barcelona (Spain): Ediciones Paidos (1994)
sfr	SCHAFFER Rodney: (1945-)
sfr1	SCHAFFER Rodney: [Professional Case Conference 1995] (1995)
sfu	STUMPF U.
sfu1	STUMPF U.: [Espeletia grandiflora], Naturwiss. Fak. Diss. Heidelberg (1976)
sg	SHINGAL
sga	SCHLEGEL O.
sgb	SPRING Beat: Contemporary homeopathic physician [switzerland]
sgb1	SPRING Beat: [Suicidal Depression], Links, Vol 1: pg 17 (1990)
sgc	STENGEL E.F.
sgc1	STENGEL E.F.: [Paloondo], Ärztl. Praxis Nr. 15,13 (1955)
sge	STIEGELE A.
sge1.de	STIEGELE A.: Homoeopathische Arzneimittlelehre, Hippokrates Verlag
sge2	STIEGELE A.: [Über Grenzerweiterungen in der Homöopathie [Fabiana imbricata]], Dtsch. Hom. Mschr. 7, 604 (1956)
sgh	SELIGER H.
sgh1	SELIGER H.: [Paloondo], Therapiewoche 4 (1953-54) 350
sgj	SINGHAL J.N.
sgj1.es	SINGHAL J.N.: Una guía para el hogar prescriptor rapido de cabecera con notas sobre Relación clinica de Remedios y Homeopatía en Cirurgía. Translated by Martha Taylor de Zorrilla, New Delhi: Jain Publishers (1995)
sgl	SEHGAL M. L.: Contemporary homeopath [New Delhi, India]
sgl1	SEHGAL M. L.: [Rediscovery of Homoeopathy], Links, Vol 1: pg 31-34 (1994)
sgl2	SEHGAL M. L.: [A brief review of the history of revolutionized homoeopathy.] (1999)
sgl2.it	SEHGAL M. L.: Omeopatia Rivoluzionata (1999)
sgp	SEEGER P.G.: (1933-)
sgp1	SEEGER P.G.: [Harpagophytum procumbens], Erfahr.hk. 22; 255 (1973)
sgr	STÄGER
sgr1	STÄGER Robert: [Proving of Knautia arvensis], A H Zt, Vol 140: pg 145 (1900)
sgs	SEGANTINI Sergio
sgs1	SEGANTINI Sergio: [Proving of pillolinum]
sgs2.it	SEGANTINI Sergio e Maria A. Marchitiello: = h4.it = La Medicina dell'Esperienza e altri scritti minori di Samuel Hahnemann (old abbr.)
sgu	SINGH Subhas
sgu1.es	SINGH Subhas: Mente Un estudio simplificado
sgw	SPRINGER Wolfgang: Contemporary homeopathic physician [Germany] (1952-)
sgw1	SPRINGER Wolfgang: [Cobaltum and Cobaltum nitricum], Links, Vol 4: pg 40-41 (1995)
sgx	SCHLEGEL Emil
sgx1.de	SCHLEGEL Emil: Innere Heilkunst [4th Ed.] (1921)
sh	SINHA N.
sha	SMITH W. L.: (1862-)
shb	STONHAM T. G.
shc	SHREEDHARAN C. K.
shc1	SHREEDHARAN C. K.: [A concise Materia Medica & Repertory of Nosodes] (1994)
shd	SMITH D.T.
shd1	SMITH D.T.: [Before and After Surgical Operations]
shh	STORCH H.
shh1	STORCH H.: [Lespedeza capitata], A H Z 205; 42 (1960)
shj	SHAH JAYESH K.: (1958-)
shj1	SHAH JAYESH K.: [Vipera redi]
shj2	SHAH JAYESH K.: [Rattus Proving]
shl	STERNHEIM Ludwig
shl1.es	STERNHEIM Ludwig: Cada uno su propio médico., New Delhli: Jain Publishers (1996)
shn	SHAH Nandita: Contemporary homeopath [Bombay, India]

shn1	SHAH Nandita: [A case of Extreme Weakness], Links, Vol 2: pg 21 (1993)
shn2	SHAH Nandita: [Lac defloratum], H Zt, Nr 1: pg 87 (1996)
shn3	SHAH Nandita: [Lac delphinum], H Zt, Nr 1 (1996)
shn4	SHAH Nandita: [Benzinum Petroleum] (2000)
shr	SHAH Rajesh: Contemporary homeopath [Bombay, India]
shr1	SHAH Rajesh: [Bufo - a wonderful respiratory remedy], Links, Vol 3: pg 18-20 (1993)
shr2	SHAH Rajesh: [My Experiences with Ferrum Metallicum], Bombay: Shree Publ. (1996)
shs	SINGH Sapuran
shs1	SINGH Sapuran: [Hering's model cures] (1977)
sht	SMITH Trevor: (1925-)
sht1	SMITH Trevor: [A proving of kali carbonicum], Br H J, Vol 68: pg 88-92 (1979)
shw	SCHWARZHAUPT W.
shw1	SCHWARZHAUPT W.: [Fabiana imbricata, Mündliche mitteillung]
shx	SHAH Ronak J.: Contemporary homeopath [India]
shx1	SHAH Ronak J.: [Veratrum - An Egoistic Lily [1st Ed.]], New Delhi: Mayur Jain: Indian Books & Periodicals Publishers (2002)
shy	SINHA Yadubir
shy1	SINHA Yadubir: [Miracles of Mother Tinctures] (1981)
shy1.es	SINHA Yadubir: Tratamiento de las enfermedades con tinturas.
shz	SMITH C.C.
shz1	SMITH C.C.: [A brief study of xanthoxylum], Homoeopathic Physician (1886)
shz2	SMITH C.C.: [Sticta pulmonaria], Homoeopathic Physician (1889)
shz3	SMITH C.C.: [Aconitum napellus in its relation to the female sexual system], Homoeopathic Physician (1881)
shz4	SMITH C.C.: [Calendula, it's place in homoeopathic therapeutics] (1881)
sjc	SUJIT C.
sjc1	SUJIT C.: [The proving of Chocolate]
sjc2	SUJIT C.: [The proving of Ficus Indica (Banyan)]
sk	SANKARAN Rajan: Contemporary homeopathic physician [Bombay, India] (1960-)
sk1	SANKARAN Rajan: [The Spirit of Homeopathy], Bombay: Homeopathic Medical Publishers (1992)
sk10	SANKARAN Rajan: [Iodium]
sk11	SANKARAN Rajan: [Homeopathy, The Science of Healing]
sk12	SANKARAN Rajan: [The System of Homeopathy]
sk13	SANKARAN Rajan: [An Insight into Plants]
sk2	SANKARAN Rajan: [The Substance of Homeopathy], Bombay (1993)
sk3	SANKARAN Rajan: [Tarentula hispanica - A study. [1st Ed.]], New Delhi: Jain Publishers (1991)
sk4	SANKARAN Rajan: [Provings:Similia similibus curentur], Mumbai (India): Homoeopathic medical publishers (1998)
sk5.de	SANKARAN Rajan: Lac equinum, H Zt, Nr 1: pg 60 (1996)
sk6.de	SANKARAN Rajan: Lac leoninum, H Zt, Nr 1: pg 47 (1996)
sk7	SANKARAN Rajan: [The Soul of remedies], Homoeopathic Medical Publishers, Bombay, (1st ed.) (1997)
sk8	SANKARAN Rajan: [Bacillinum Burnett]
sk9	SANKARAN Rajan: [Ferrum metallicum]
ska	SARKANY Endré: Belgian homeopathic physician. (-1993)
skb	SARKAR B. K.: Contemporary homeopathic physician [India] (1899-)
skb1	SARKAR B. K.: [Up to date with Nosodes], Calcutta: Roy Publishing House (1971)
skb2	SARKAR B. K.: [Essentials of Homeopathic Philosophy and the Place of Repertory in Homeopathic Practice.], Calcuta: Roy Publishing House (1961)
skg	SCHWENKER G.
skg1	SCHWENKER G. and KLOSS P. and ENGELS W.: [Haplopappus bailahuen]
skn	SUKUMARAN N.
skn1	SUKUMARAN N.: [Heart Problems of Adult and Aged] (1995)
skp	SANKARAN P.: (1922-1979)
skp1	SANKARAN P.: [The Value of the Repertory], Bombay (1965)
skp2	SANKARAN P.: [Random Notes on Some Drugs], Bombay (1965)
skp3	SANKARAN P.: [The clinical relationships of homoeopathic remedies.], Bombay: The Homoeopathic Medical Publishers (1984)
skp4	SANKARAN P.: [Some notes on the nosodes.], Bombay: The Homoeopathic Medical Publishers (1978)
skp5	SANKARAN P.: [Atrax robustus], Br Hom J, Vol LIX: pg 45 (1970)
skp6	SANKARAN P.: [The indications and Use of Bowel Nosodes], Bombay (1973)
skp7	SANKARAN P.: [Some new provings], Bombay: Homeopathic Medical Publishers (1978)
skp8	SANKARAN P.: [Insulinum]
skp9	SANKARAN P.: [The Elements of Homoeopathy]
skr	SIRKER C.
skr1	SIRKER C.: [A Keynote Repertory of Materia Medica]
sl	SEARLE W. S.
sla	SCHÜSSLER Wilhelm Heinrich: German homeopathic physician. Creator of the Schüssler salts. (1821-1898)
sla1	SCHÜSSLER Wilhelm Heinrich: [The Twelve Tissue Remedies and their Use in Trituration of Dr.

	Schuessler, recommended for Investigation by Dr. C. Hering. 2d editon.] (1874)
sla1.de	SCHÜSSLER Wilhelm Heinrich: Specielle Anleitung zur homöopathischen Anwendung der physiologischen Functionsmittel, Oldenburg (1874)
sla2	SCHÜSSLER Wilhelm Heinrich: [The Biochemical Treatment of Diseases], New Delhi: Jain Publishers (1989)
sla3	SCHÜSSLER Wilhelm Heinrich: [Biochemic pocket guide : Physicians Quick Reference of Dr. Schussler], New Delhi: Jain Publishers
sld	SAELENS Daniel: (1965-)
sle	STIRLING Penelope: (1952-)
sle1	STIRLING Penelope: [The Homeopathic Proving of Crack Willow: Salix Fragilis] (1998)
sle2	STIRLING Penelope: [The proving of Cygnus Bewickii] (2002)
slf	SNELLING Frederick Greenwood: (1831-1878)
slf1	SNELLING Frederick Greenwood: [Symptomatology - Manual of the Homeopathic Materia Medica]
slg	SAELENS Geert: Contemporary homeopathic physician [Wenduine, Belgium]
slh	SCHOELER H.
slh1	SCHOELER H.: [Eichornia crassipes], A H Z. 218; 2 (1973)
slh2	SCHOELER H.: [Diosgeninum]
slm	SOLER-MEDINA Alberto
slm1	SOLER-MEDINA Alberto: [Repertory of Pregnancy, Parturition and Puerperium], Heidelberg: Haug Verlag (1989)
sln	STELLING Nicolas: Contemporary homeopathic dentist [switzerland]
slp	SALAÜN Pierre: Remedy occurence confirmed by the research work of Dr. Salaün. (1934-)
slp1	SALAÜN Pierre: [Staphyse], Contemporary homeopathic physician (Carpentras, France)
slv	SULLIVAN Andrea: Contemporary homeopath [Washington DC, USA]
slv1	SULLIVAN Andrea: [A case of Menorrhagia], N Eng. J H, Vol 4 nr 4: pg 14-15 (1995)
sm	STAMM L. E.
sma	SIJMONS Jan: Contemporary homeopathic physician [St. Niklaas, Belgium] (1953-)
sma1	SIJMONS Jan: [Kleine remedies: 50 Klinische gevallen], Gent (Belgium): Homeoden Book Service (1992)
smb	SIMMONS B.
smb1	SIMMONS B.: [Cough repertory], Liverpool (1870)
sme	STEINMETZ E.F.
sme1	STEINMETZ E.F.: [Poterium spinosum], Research IV; 582 (1964)
smj	SIMAR Jean: Contemporary homeopathic pediatrician [Brussel, Belgium]
smk	KIMBALL Samuel A.
smk1	KIMBALL Samuel A.: [A Repertory of Gonorrhoea, with the Concomitant Symptoms of the Genital and Urinary Organs.], Boston: Otis Clapp and Son (1888)
sml	SMALL Alvan Edmond: (1811-1886)
sml1	SMALL A.E.: [Manual of Homoeopathic Practice, for the use of Families and Private Individuals [6th Ed. Enlarged]], Philadelphia: Rademacher & Sheek (Pennsylvania) (1857)
smn	SAMANT Nitin: Contemporary homeopath [Bombay, India]
smn1	SAMANT Nitin: [A case of Arthritis], Links, Vol 1: pg 27 (1995)
smr1	SIGMAR A. H.: [Applied Homeopathic Medicine]
smr1.es	SIGMAR A. H.: Medicación Homeopática aplicada
sms	SALTZMAN Susanne: Contemporary homeopath [New York, USA]
sms1	SALTZMAN Susanne: [Cases: Fear of Vomiting], N Eng. J H, Vol 3 nr 1: pg 17-18 (1994)
sn	SKINNER Thomas: (1825-1906)f
sn1	SKINNER Thomas: [Grand Characterisitics of the Materia Medica]
sn2	SKINNER Thomas: [Homoeopathy in its Relation to the Diseases of females or Gynaecology], London (1886)
sna	SWAN Samuel: (1814-1893)
sna1	SWAN Samuel: [Proving of "Lager Beer" with cases illustrative of its action] (1855)
sna2	SWAN Samuel: [Nosodes and Morbific Products], New York (1888)
sna3	SWAN Samuel: [Lac felinum], The Homoeopathic Physician, May: pg 160 (1883)
sna4	SWAN Samuel: [Proving of syphilinum], The Homoeopathic Physician, July: pg 318 (1888)
sna5	SWAN Samuel: [Materia Medica and Provings]
sna6	SWAN Samuel: [Triticum], H Heritage Nov ; 16 (1991)
sna7	SWAN Samuel: [Proving Of Ovi Gallina Pellicula - Membrane Of The Egg Shell], International Hahnemannian association - Transactions 1881-83 pages 248-254
snb	SPINELLI Silvestro: Contemporary homeopathic physician [Aquaviva, Italy]
snd	SPINEDI Dario: Contemporary homeopath [Orselina, Switzerland]
snd1	SPINEDI Dario: [Objective Signs], Links, Vol 3: pg 20 (1992)
sne	SAINE André: Contemporary homeopath [Canada] (1953-)
sne1	SAINE André: [Psychiatric patients - Seminar Homeopathy - Hahnemann and Psychological Cases. Lectures on Pure Classical Homeopathy], Eindhoven (Netherlands): Lutra Services (2nd Ed.) (1999)
sns	SHANNON Samuel F.
sns1	SHANNON Samuel F.: [Apis], Medical Advance, Vol 40, nr 5 (1902)

sp	STEPHENSON James Hawley: (1919-1985)
sp1	STEPHENSON James Hawley: [Hahnemannian Provings - A Materia Medica and Repertory 1924-1959], Bombay: Roy & Co. (1963)
spa	SCHEPENS Edouard: Belgian homeopathic physician (1910-)
spa1	SCHEPENS Edouard: [Latrodectus mactans], Rev B H, nr. 1: pg 157-162 (1966)
spa2	SCHEPENS Edouard: [Some cases of Medorrhinum], Rev B H, nr. 1: pg 170-186 (1950)
spb	SHAPIRO: (1951-)
spd	SHEPHERD Dorothy: English homeopathic physician (1885-1952)
spd1	SHEPHERD Dorothy: [Magic of the Minimum Dose]
spd2	SHEPHERD Dorothy: [More Magic of the Minimum Dose]
spd3	SHEPHERD Dorothy: [Homeopathy in Epidemic Diseases]
spd4	SHEPHERD Dorothy: [A physician's Posy]
spd5	SHEPHERD Dorothy: [Homoeopathy for the First Aider.], Health Science Press., Essex - England
spk	SHEPPORD K.
spk1	SHEPPORD K.: [The treatment of cats by homeopathy], Health Science Press, England (1987)
spp	SHARP P.H.
spp1	SHARP P.H.: [Constipation and Diarrhea]
sr	STORA
sra	SCHIER J.
srb	SEROR R.: (1928-)
srb1.fr	SEROR R.: Articles
srb2.fr	SEROR R.: Pathogénésies Homéopathiques Françaises, Cahiers de Biothérapie, 79-86 (1966)
sre	SORENSEN Hans Aage: Contemporary homeopath [Denmark]
srg	SCHNURRENBERGER U.: Veterinary [Switzerland] (1955-)
srj	SHERR Jeremy: Contemporary homeopath [UK]. Actively proving new substances. (1955-)
srj1	SHERR Jeremy: [The Homeopathic Proving of Scorpio [2nd Ed.]], Upton-upon-Severn (GB): Severnside Printers (1990)
srj2	SHERR Jeremy: [The Homeopathic Proving of Hydrogen], Northampton (England): private publ. (1992)
srj2.fr	SHERR Jeremy: Hydrogène (Traduction de la Pathogénésie de Jeremy Sherr par P. Deroche)
srj3	SHERR Jeremy: [The Homeopathic proving of Chocolate] (1993)
srj3.fr	SHERR Jeremy: Pathogénésie de Chocolate. (Traduction: Dr Michèle Camelin)
srj4	SHERR Jeremy: [The Dynamics and Methodology of Homoeopathic Provings], West Malvern (1994)
srj5	SHERR Jeremy: [Dynamic Provings - Volume 1], Malvern: Dynamis Books (1997)
srj5.fr	SHERR Jeremy: Germanium
srj5a.fr	SHERR Jeremy: Adamas
srj6	SHERR Jeremy: [Dynamic Provings - Volume 2], Malvern: Dynamis Books (1998)
srj7	SHERR Jeremy: [The homoeopathic proving of Plutonium nitricum, including the toxicology of ionising radiation] (1999)
srj7.fr	SHERR Jeremy: La pathogénésie de Plutonium Nitricum
srj8	SHERR Jeremy: [Dynamic Materia Medica : Syphilis - A Study of the Syphilitic Miasm through Remedies], Malvern: Dynamis Books (2002)
srl	SCHMIDRAMSL H.
srl1	SCHMIDRAMSL H. and OSTERMAYR B. and VON ARNIM J.: [Strophantus Hispidus], A H Z, May-June, 283(3): pg 106-109 (1993)
srn	SCHLUREN E.
srn1	SCHLUREN E.: [Homoopathie in Frauenheilkunde und Geburtshilfe], Heidelberg (Germany): Karl F. Haug Verlag GmbH & C° (4th Ed.)
srx	STARRE Jeffrey: Contemporary Homeopathic Physician [Ohio, USA] (1950-)
ss	STEARNS Guy Beckly: (1870-1947)
ss1	STEARNS Guy Beckly: [Keynotes for Homoeopathic Remedies in Surgery], New York
sst	SMITS Tinus: Contemporary homeopath [Netherlands] (1946-)
sst1	SMITS Tinus: [The magic sugar Saccharum Officinale], Links, Vol 8: pg 28-36 (1995)
sst2	SMITS Tinus: [Cancer, a deeper understanding. Carcinosinum], Links, Vol 11: pg 16-22 (1998)
sst3	SMITS Tinus: [Cuprum metallicum], Links, Vol 5: pg 10-14 (1992)
sst4	SMITS Tinus: [Lac maternum], Links, Vol 12 n°5: pg 255-261 (1999)
sst5	SMITS Tinus: [Inspiring homeopaty]
sst5.fr	SMITS Tinus: Homéopathie inspirante
st	SCHMIDT Pierre: Swiss homeopathic physician. Creator of the LIGA. and the "Groupement Hahn. Lyon". (1894-1987)
st1	SCHMIDT Pierre: [Cahiers Hahnemanniens] (1987)
st1.it	SCHMIDT Pierre: Quaderni di omeopatia, Perugia: Società Omeopatica Edizioni (1992)
st2.fr	SCHMIDT Pierre: Traumatismes Sportifs, Maisonneuve (1969)
st3	SCHMIDT Pierre: [Defective Illnesses], Calcutta: Hahnemann Publ. (1st Ed.) (1980)
st4	SCHMIDT Pierre: [The Hidden Treasures of the last organon]
st5	SCHMIDT Pierre: [The art of Case Taking]
st6	SCHMIDT Pierre: [The art of Interrogation], New Delhi: Jain Publishers
st6.es	SCHMIDT Pierre: El arte de Interrogar.
sta	SAWTELLE B. A.
stan	SCHMIDT Andreas: (1960-)
stb	SCHUSTER Bernd: Contemporary homeopath [Diez, Germany] (1948-)

stb1	SCHUSTER Bernd: [When the Soul is Liberated], Links, Vol 9: pg 12-13 (1996)
stb2	SCHUSTER Bernd: [Bambus - Homeopathic proving.] (2000)
stb2.de	SCHUSTER Bernd: Bambus: Homöopathische Prüfung und Verifizierung. Mit Kasuistiksammlung., Kronberg: Kent Gesellschaft (1996)
stb2.fr	SCHUSTER Bernd: Bambusa arundinacea (Traduit par CAMELIN Michèle, CHENU Gérard et KRUG Jean-Marie)
stb3	SCHUSTER Bernd: [Cola: Homoeopathic Proving of Cola nitida] (1999)
stb3.de	SCHUSTER Bernd: Cola - Homöopathische Arzneimittelprüfung der Colanuss, Weilburg: Verlag für Homöopathie (1997)
stb4.de	SCHUSTER Bernd: Bambus in der Praxis - Homöopatische Arzneimittelprüfung - Praxisanwendung - Kasuistiken., Weilburg: Verlag für Homöopathie (1999)
stc	SCHMIDT Roger: American homeopathic physician, brother of Pierre Schmidt (-1975)
stc1.fr	SCHMIDT Roger: Brucella. Un Nosode rarement employé, Annales Homéopathique Fr, nr. 2: pg 113 (1959)
std	SCHRETER Gustav Adolf: Student of Hahnemann in Lemberg (1803-1864)
ste	SANTEE E. M.: (1850-)
ste1	SANTEE E. M.: [Repertory of convulsions], New York (1890)
stg	SASTREY G. S. R.
stg1	SASTREY G. S. R.: [Aids and Homepathy]
sth	SCHMIDT H. C.
stj	SCHOLTEN Jan: Contemporary homoeopathic physician [Utrecht, Netherlands]. Co-ordinator of a group practice with 3 other homeopaths. Lecturing intensively all over (1951-)
stj1	SCHOLTEN Jan: [Homeopathy and Minerals] (1993)
stj1.de	SCHOLTEN Jan: Homöpathie und Minerale, Utrecht: Stichting Alonnissos (1997)
stj1.es	SCHOLTEN Jan: Homeopatía y Minerales
stj1.fr	SCHOLTEN Jan: Homéopathie et Minéraux
stj1.nl	SCHOLTEN Jan: Homeopathie en Mineralen, Utrecht (Netherlands): private (1993)
stj2	SCHOLTEN Jan: [Homeopathy and the elements] (2003)
stj2.de	SCHOLTEN Jan: Homöopathie und die Elementen, Utrecht: Stichting Alonnissos (2000)
stj2.nl	SCHOLTEN Jan: Homeopathie en de elementen (1996)
stj3.nl	SCHOLTEN Jan: Tungsten, een proving, Similia Similibus Currentur, Vol 23/3 pg: 15 (1993)
stj4	SCHOLTEN Jan and LEUPEN Alex: [Coffee, the black liquid fuel. Materia Medica of Angustura.], Links, Vol 8: pg 26-27 (1995)
stj5	SCHOLTEN Jan and PELT Marguerite: [Lactic acid - A girl is a girl is a girl], Links, Vol 3: pg 12-13 (1995)
stj6	SCHOLTEN Jan: [Vanadium Metallicum], Links, Vol 7: pg 10-12 (1994)
stj7	SCHOLTEN Jan: [Helianthus annuus proving], Report of the homeopathic postgraduade SHO : Stichting Homeopatische opleidingen 31/10-1.11-1997 (1997)
stj8	SCHOLTEN Jan: [Minerals in Plants], Utrecht: Stichting Alonnissos
stj9	SCHOLTEN Jan: [Wad stories: Homeopathic lectures from a sailing trip on the Wad in the Netherlands], Utrecht: Stichting Alonnissos (2001)
stp	SPEIGHT Phyllis
stp1	SPEIGHT Phyllis: [A Comparison of the Chronic Miasms], Plymouth: Clarke, Doble & Brendon Ltd (1961)
stp1.es	SPEIGHT Phyllis: Comparación de los miasmos crónicos (1961)
stp2	SPEIGHT Phyllis: [Overcoming Rheumatism and Arthritis]
str	STUUT Rienk: Contemporary homeopathic physician [Netherlands] (1957-)
sts	SCHMIDT S.
sts1	SCHMIDT S.: [Harpagophytum procumbens], Therapiewoche 22; 1072-74 (1972)
stu	SANTOS Uta: (1954-)
stu1	SANTOS Uta and KÖNIG Peter: [Dream Proving of Berberis], Links, Vol 7: pg 15-17 (1994)
stx	SMET René
stx1	SMET René: [Fundamental FOOD & DRINK symptomatology, with Repertory, and foreword in English, Dutch and French.] (1995)
sty	SAULT David
sty1	SAULT David: [A Modern Guide to the Mental Rubrics of Kent's Repertory], Haarlem (Holland): Merlyn publishers (1992)
suta	SCHÜTTE Achim
sutr	SCHÜTT R.
sutr1	SCHÜTT R.: [Paloondo], A H Z. 215; 241 (1970)
sv	STEVENS G.: (1894-)
sv1	STEVENS G.: [Grindelia robusta], Proceedings of the International Hahnemannian Association (1934)
sva	SYLVESTROWICZ H.
svb	SOLVAY: (1941-)
svc	SHEVIN William: Contemporary homeopathic physician [USA]
svd	SALVIO Almato D.
svd1.es	SALVIO Almato D.: El Indicador característico de cien medicamentos homeopáticos comprendiendo los treinta.(Dr. Müller), New Delhi: Jain Publishers
svg	SRIVASTAVA G. D.
svg1	SRIVASTAVA G. D. and CHANDRA J.: [Alphabetical Repertory of Characteristics of

	Homoeopathic Materia Medica], New Delhi: Jain Publishers (1990)
svk	SRINIVASAN K. S.
svk1	SRINIVASAN K. S.: [Additions to Classical Materia Medica], New Delhi: Jain Publishers (1990)
svm	SIVARAMAN M.S.
svm1	SIVARAMAN M.S.: [Homeopathic Treatment of Asthma] (1979)
svo	SALVATORE MEIRA Adailton: Contemporary homeopath [Brasil]
svp	SERVAIS Philippe: Contemporary homeopathic physician [France] (1947-)
svp1.fr	SERVAIS Philippe: Le Similimum, histoire d'une vie (vol. 1) (2002)
svp2.fr	SERVAIS Philippe: Le Similimum, histoire d'une vie (vol. 2) (2003)
svr	SIVARAMAN P.: Contemporary homeopath [India] (1927-)
svr1	SIVARAMAN P.: [Concise Repertory of aggravation and amelioration] (1980)
svr2	SIVARAMAN P.: [Corrections and Additions to Kent's Repertory], New Delhi (1982)
svr3	SIVARAMAN P.: [Kent's Repertory of the Homoeopathic Materia Medica Expanded], New Delhi (1995)
svr4	SIVARAMAN P.: [Your Tooth Problems Cured with Homoeopathic Medicine], New Delhi: Jain Publishers (1993)
svr5	SIVARAMAN P.: [Ear, Nose and Throat: Troubles cured with Homoepathy], New Delhi: Jain Publishers (1981)
svr6	SIVARAMAN P.: [Dreams and their homeopathic medicines] (1978)
svr7	SIVARAMAN P.: [Asthma Cured with Homeopathic Medicines] (1978)
svr8	SIVARAMAN P.: [Epilepsy cured with Homeopathic Medicines]
svr9	SIVARAMAN P.: [Haemorrhoids cured by Homeopathic Medicines]
svt	SNEEVLIET Anette: Contemporary homeopath [Bakkeveen, The Netherlands]
svt1	SNEEVLIET Anette: [Belladonna-children], Links, Vol 3: pg 21-22 (1992)
svu	SAVULESCU Geo: (1956-)
svu1	SAVULESCU Geo and CRUMP Sue: [Proving Quercus Robur] (1996)
swc	SOWTON C.
swc1	SOWTON C.: [The proving of Tela Aranea (Spiderweb)]
swm	SANTWANI M.T.
swm1	SANTWANI M.T.: [Common ailments of Children and Their Homeopathic Management] (1979)
swm1.es	SANTWANI M.T.: Enfermedades Comunes de los Ninos y su Tratamiento Homeopático. Translated by Martha Taylor De Zorrilla., New delhi: Jain Publishers (1979)
sws	SONAWALA S.
sws1	SONAWALA S.: [Sepia and Lachesis]
sxj	SAXTON John: (1940-)
syk	SWAYANADAN K. R.
syk1	SWAYANADAN K. R.: [Intestinal Worms] (1981)
syp	SATYA Paul
syp1	SATYA Paul: [Analogy of pain], New Delhi: Jain publishers (1990)
sys	SCHROYENS Frederik: Contemporary homeopathic physician [Gent, Belgium]. President VSU, School Hom Gent [1981-1990]. Homeopathic Coordinator RADAR. (1953-)
sys1	SCHROYENS Frederik: [Synthesis (original English version) (9th Ed.)], London: Homeopathic Book Publishers (2003)
sys1.de	SCHROYENS Frederik: Synthesis (Ed. 8.0) (Translation: Peter VINT), Greifenberg (Germany): Hahnemann Institut - Privatinstitut für homöopatische Dokumntation Gmbh (2001)
sys1.es	SCHROYENS Frederik: Synthesis (Ed. 6.01) (Translation: Fernando REDIN), London: Homeopathic Book Publishers (1998)
sys1.fr	SCHROYENS Frederik: Synthesis (Ed. 7.2) (Traduction: Jacqueline OZANON), London: Homeopathic Book Publishers (2000)
sys1.it	SCHROYENS Frederik: Synthesis (Ed. 8.0) (Translation: Mariella DI STEFANO), London: Homeopathic Book Publishers (2002)
sys1.nl	SCHROYENS Frederik: Synthesis (Ed. 5) (Translation: René OTTER), Eindhoven: Lutra Services (1995)
sys1.pt	SCHROYENS Frederik: Synthesis (Ed. 6.70) (Translation: Claudio ARAUJO), Belgium: Archibel (1998)
sys2	1000 Small remedies
syz	HOMOEOPATHIA EUROPEA GROUPS (1985)
sz	SCHWARZ Erik: Contemporary homeopath [Germany] (1952-)
sze	SCHULZ Elisabeth: (1959-), Germany
sze1	SCHULZ Elisabeth: [Buteo jamaicensis - hawk], Homöopathische Einblicke, December, nr 28 (1996)
sze10	SCHULZ Elisabeth: [Remedy Encounter with Asterias rubens], Naturheilpraxis, nr 11 (2001)
sze2	SCHULZ Elisabeth: [Columba palumbus], Homöopathische Einblicke, December, nr 28 (1996)
sze3	SCHULZ Elisabeth: [Cygnus olor], Naturheilpraxis, March, nr 3 (2001)
sze4	SCHULZ Elisabeth: [Falco cherrug], Homöopathische Einblicke, December, nr 28 (1996)
sze5	SCHULZ Elisabeth: [Vultur gryphus - condor] (1999)
sze6	SCHULZ Elisabeth: [Test Flight], Homöopathische Einblicke, December, nr 28 (1996)

sze7	SCHULZ Elisabeth: [The proving of Holy Ibis] (2000)
sze8	SCHULZ Elisabeth and SHORE Jonathan: [The proving of Radium Bromatum] (1996)
sze9	SCHULZ Elisabeth: [Lac Humanum Proving Vol I & 2] (1996)
szg	SCHLÜTZ G.O.
szg1	SCHLÜTZ G.O. and VENULET J.: [Experientia Basel], 20 (1964) 78, Ref.: Chem. Zbl. (1966) 3281
szh	SCHULZ Hugo: (1853-1932)
szh1	SCHULZ Hugo: [Proving of Semen tiglii], Hom Rec, Vol 4: pg 171 (1889)
szs	SONZ Susan: Contemporary Homeopath in the USA
szs1	SONZ Susan and STEWART Robert: [The proving of Musca domestica] (2002)
szs2	SONZ Susan, SONAM Kushner and STEWARD Robert: [Hippocampus Kuda, a proving of sea horse.] (2003)
szu	SCHMUTZER Ulli
szu1.de	SCHMUTZER Ulli: HAMP von Rosa canina
szw	SCHWARTZ W. H.: (1895-)
szw1	SCHWARTZ W. H.: [The homoeopathic treatment of wounds and injuries.], New Delhi: Jain Publishers (1935)
szx	SCHULTZ
szx1	SCHULTZ: [Proving of Quinine hydrochlorate], Hahnemannian Monthly, Vol 23 (1888)
tac	TOOTHAKER C.G.
tac1	TOOTHAKER C.G.: [Incidental provings, Oil Pennyroyal], Philadelphia Journal of Homoeopathy, Vol 2 (1853)
tbr	THEOBALD R.M.
tbr1	THEOBALD R.M.: [Agnus castus], H Heritage, Nov., Vol 17 (11): pg 709 (1992)
tcs	TALCOTT Selden Haines: (1842-1902)
tcs1	TALCOTT Selden Haines: [Mental Diseases and their Modern Treatment]
tf	TRIONFI Maurizio: Contemporary homeopathic physician [Brescia, Italy] (1950-)
tg	TOGEL Reinhold: Contemporary homeopathic physician [Germany]
thj	TWOHIG Julia: [Australia] (1950-)
thj1	TWOHIG Julia: ["Deadly Romance" A homoeopathic proving Latrodectus Hasseltii - Red back Spider] (1998)
tl	TYLER Margaret Lucy: (1857-1943)
tl1	TYLER Margaret Lucy: [Homeopathic Drug Pictures], London: The Homeopathic Publishing Co (1942)
tl1.pt	TYLER Margaret Lucy: Materia Medica
tl10	TYLER Margaret Lucy: [Repertorizing]
tl11.es	TYLER Margaret Lucy: Curso de Homeopatía para graduados, Buenos Aires: Editorial Albatros (1993)
tl2	TYLER Margaret Lucy: [Pointers to the common remedies], New Dehli: Jain publishers (1934)
tl3	TYLER Margaret Lucy: [Acute conditions, injuries], London, British Homoeopathic Association (1936)
tl4	TYLER Margaret Lucy: [Drosera], British Homoeopath Journal - Vol 17, pg 122 (1927)
tl5	TYLER Margaret Lucy: [Some drug pictures.]
tl6	TYLER Margaret Lucy: [A Study of Kent's Repertory], Hom World (1914)
tl7	TYLER Margaret Lucy: [Different ways of Finding the Remedy], New Delhi: Jain Publishers
tl8	TYLER Margaret Lucy: [Hahnemann's conception of Chronic Disease, as caused by Parasitic Micro-Organisms], New Delhi: Jain Publishers
tl9	TYLER Margaret Lucy: [Homeopathy Introductory Lectures]
tle	THIELENS E.: Contemporary homeopath [Hechtel, Belgium]
tle1	THIELENS E.: [A case of Asthma], Links, Vol 4: pg 29-30 (1995)
tll	TAYLOR Lorraine: Contemporary homeopath [Bern, Switzerland]
tll1	TAYLOR Lorraine: [Two Cases of Alcoholism], Links, Vol 3: pg 20 (1991)
tlr	TAYLOR de Zorrila Martha
tlr1.es	TAYLOR de Zorrila Martha: Prescriptor rapido de cabecera
tlv	TALAVERA
tlv1	TALAVERA: [Proving of Polyandria poligama, Yolotxochitl, Magnolia grandiflora], Reforma Medica, Aug. (1885)
tlx	TAYLOR E.A.
tlx1	TAYLOR E.A.: [Proving of Piper nigrum], Medical Advance, Vol 45, nr 4 (1907)
tm	THOMAS C. H.
tma	TIMMERMAN Alize
tma1	TIMMERMAN Alize: [The symbol in a remedy as a key factor. A case of lac felinum. Timmerman Alize], Links, Vol 9: pg 148-150 (1996)
tme	THOMAS Emlyn
tme1	THOMAS Emlyn: [Homeopathy for Sports, Exercise and Dance], Beaconsfield (England): Beaconsfield Publ.
tmh	THOMAS H.
tmh1	THOMAS H.: [External remedies]
tmo	TUMMINELLO Peter: (1954-)
tmo1	TUMMINELLO Peter: [Rhodonite and the horn of plenty], Links, Vol 12: pg 23-25 (1999)
tmo2	TUMMINELLO Peter: [Molybdenum]
tmo3	TUMMINELLO Peter: [Rhus glabra: A Homoeopathic Proving] (1997)
tmp	TUNMANN P.
tmp1	TUNMANN P. et al.: [Harpagophytum procumbens], Dtsch. Apoth. g. 102 (1962) 1274 / Dtsch. Apoth. g. 103 (1963) 395 / Lieb. Ann. Chem. 712 (1968) 138
tms	THOMAS Sue
tn	TURNER M. W.

tna	THURNEYESEN Andre: Contemporary homeopath [Bern, Switzerland]
tna1	THURNEYESEN Andre: [Case], Links, Vol 2: pg 32 (1990)
tp	TEMPLETON D. M.: (1930-)
tpb	TRIPPI Biaggio
tpb1.it	TRIPPI Biaggio: Lessico pratico omeopatico
tpi	TIRASPOLSKI Ilia: (1966-), Russia
tpi1	TIRASPOLSKI Ilia and TIMOFEEVA Tatiana: [A new homeoptahic remedy: Peganum harmala - Results from provings and clinical experience], Links, Spring, Vol 13: pg 54-57 (2000)
tpw	TEMPLETON W. Lees: (1889-)
tpw1	TEMPLETON W. Lees: [The Homoeopathic Treatment of Influenza], New Delhi: Jain Publishers (1990)
tpw2	TEMPLETON W. Lees: [Provings of Carcinosin], Br Hom J, Vol 44 nr 2: pg 108-115 (1954)
tpw3	TEMPLETON W. Lees: [Provings of Alloxan], Br Hom J, Vol 39: pg 246-281 (1949)
tpw4	TEMPLETON W. Lees: [A third proving of Alloxan], Br Hom J, Vol 41: pg 112-119 (1951)
tpw5	TEMPLETON W. Lees: [Report of Beryllium Provings], Br H J, Vol 43: pg 78-84 (1953)
tpw6	TEMPLETON W. Lees: [Cadmium Metallicum], Br H J, Vol 39: pg 60-64 (1949)
tpw7	TEMPLETON W. Lees: [Provings of cortisone and ACTH.], Br H J, Vol 45: pg 89-97 (1956)
tpw8	TEMPLETON W. Lees: [Report on Rauwolfia Serpentina], Br H J, Vol 45: pg 155-169 (1956)
tpw9	TEMPLETON W. Lees: [Proving of Strophanthus sarmentosus], Br H J, Vol 42: pg 4-13 (1952)
trj	TORRE Blázquez José Ramon: (1953-)
ts	TESSIER Jean-Paul: (1811-1862)
tsc	TRINKS Carl Friedrich: (1800-1868)
tsc1	TRINKS Carl Friedrich: [Reine Arzneimittellehre], Leipzig (1831)
tsg	THOMPSON Gregory: Contemporary homeopath [Maine, USA]
tsg1	THOMPSON Gregory: [Cases: Eruption 2], N Eng. J H, Vol 3 nr 3: pg 35-37 (1994)
tsm	THOMPSON Michael: (1942-)
tsm1	THOMPSON Michael: [Ambra grisea - The Road to Homoeopathic Practice Vol.1] (1996)
tsm2	THOMPSON Michael: [Venomous snakes of the world.] (2003)
tsn	THOMPSON Nick
tt	TESTE Alphonse: (1814-1898)
tt1	TESTE Alphonse: [The homeopathic materia medica], Philadelphia (1854)
tt2	TESTE Alphonse: [A homeopathic treatise of the disease]
tt3	TESTE Alphonse: [Homeopathic Drug Pictures]
tt4	TESTE Alphonse: [Diseases of children]
ttm	TETAU Max: Contemporary homeopathic physician [France] (1927-)
ttm1.fr	TETAU Max: Matière médicale clinique Vol. 1 (1979)
ttm2.fr	TETAU Max: Les polychrestes homéopathiques dans leurs rapports avec les troubles neuro-endocrino-sympathique (1980)
ttm3.es	TETAU Max: Signos mayores de los grandes remedios homopáticos
ttm3.fr	TETAU Max: Signes Majeurs des grands remèdes homéopathiques., Maline (Paris) (1979)
ttm4.es	TETAU Max: Homeopatía
ttm5.es	TETAU Max: Nuevos Aspectos Clinicos de la Organoterapia Diluida y Dinamizada
twd	TYSZKIEWICZ D.
twd1	TYSZKIEWICZ D. and ZELAZOWSKI K.: [Atriplex hortensis], PolTyg. lek. 19, 1166-1167 ref.: Münch.med.Wschr. 111 (1969) 19, 1112
tws	TIWARI Shashi Kant
tws1	TIWARI Shashi Kant: [Homoeopathy and Child Care: Principles, Therapeutics, Children's Type, Repertory], New Delhi: Jain Publishers (1998)
ub	URBAN Eberhard: Contemporary homeopathic physician [Germany] (1947-)
ub1	URBAN Eberhard: [Propolis], Zt Klass H, Vol 4: pg 150-154 (1985)
ub2	URBAN Eberhard: [Propolis], Proc 42nd LMHI Congr., Virginia USA: pg 152-157 (1987)
uba	USUBILLAGA A.
uba1	USUBILLAGA A. et al.: [Espeletia grandiflora], Phytochemistry 12; 2999 (1973)
ugs	UNGEN-STERNBERG von
usda	Agricultural Research Service of the USDA
usda1	Agricultural Research Service of the USDA: [Common weeds of the United States.]
uw	UNDERWOOD Benoni F.: (1843-)
uw1	UNDERWOOD Benoni F.: [Diseases of childhood and their homeopathic treatment]
uw2	UNDERWOOD Benoni F.: [Headache and its Materia Medica], Calcutta: Roy publishing house (1972)
uw3	UNDERWOOD Benoni F.: [Materia Medica of Differential Potency] (1884)
vad	VIOLA Dominique: (1955-)
vbf	VANDEN BERGHE Fons: Contemporary homeopath [Genk, Belgium]
vbf1	VANDEN BERGHE Fons: [A case of Nerves], N Engl. J H, Vol 4 nr 4: pg 9-10 (1995)
vbg	VAN DEN BOGAERT Eduard
vbg1.fr	VAN DEN BOGAERT Eduard: Répertoire Thématique d'Homéopathie Mytho-Bio-logique (2001)
vbg2.fr	VAN DEN BOGAERT Eduard: Les Aigles (2000)
vda	VAN DAELE Paul: Contemporary homeopathic physician [Hasselt, Belgium] (1953-)
vdb	VANDEN EYNDE Eric: Contemporary veterinary homeopath [Brussel, Belgium]
vdc	VAN DEHN R.: Contemporary homeopath [Netherlands]

vdr	VAN DER REYDEN R. L.: Contemporary homeopathic physician [Netherlands]
vg	VOEGELI Adolf: (1898-1993)
vg1.de	VOEGELI Adolf: Magen-, Leber- und Galle-erkrankungen
vg2.de	VOEGELI Adolf: Die Kreislauferkrankungen, Heidelberg: Haug Verl. (1970)
vgh	VANDERGUCHT Henri
vgh1	VANDERGUCHT Henri: [Camphora officinalis)], Rev B H Sep; 43(3) (1991)
vh	VITHOULKAS George: Contemporary homeopath [Alonissos, Greece]. Founder Clinical Teaching Center Athens. Creator VES [Vith. Expert System]. (1932-)
vh/dg	VITHOULKAS George: Changes of degrees (1990)
vh_1	vh_1
vh_2	vh_2
vh_3	vh_3
vh_4	vh_4
vh1	VITHOULKAS George: [Materia Medica Viva (Vol. 1 - Vol 7)], San Francisco: Health and Habitat (1992)
vh1.de	VITHOULKAS George: Materia Medica Viva
vh10	VITHOULKAS George: [Homeopathy: Medicine for the new millennium], Alonnisos: The International Academy of Classical Homeopathy (2000)
vh2	VITHOULKAS George: [Talks on Classical Homoeopathy - The Esalen Conferences 1980 - Part 1], Edited by Jain Publishers (1980)
vh3	VITHOULKAS George: [= vh4 = Essences of Materia Medica] (1988)
vh3.fr	VITHOULKAS George: = vh4.fr = Essence des remèdes homéopathiques (1984)
vh4	VITHOULKAS George: [Essences of Materia Medica], New Delhi: Jain Publishers (1st Ed.) (1988)
vh4.es	VITHOULKAS George: Esencia de la Materia Médica Homeopática
vh4.fr	VITHOULKAS George: Essence des remèdes homéopathiques, Paris: Similia (1988)
vh5	VITHOULKAS George: [Talks on Classical Homoeopathy - The Esalen Conferences 1980 - Part 2], New Delhi: Jain Publishers (Edited by B. P. Rao) (1990)
vh6.it	VITHOULKAS George: Essenzi psicopatologiche del rimedio omeopatico
vh7	VITHOULKAS George: [Talks on Classical Homoeopathy - The Esalen Conferences 1980 - Part 3], New Delhi: Jain Publishers (1980)
vh8	VITHOULKAS George: [The sience of homeopathy], New York: Grove Press, Inc.
vh9	VITHOULKAS George and OLSEN Steve: [Winning Strategies of Case Analysis: A Short Course For Radar and the Vithoulkas Expert System]
vh9.de	VITHOULKAS George und OLSEN Steve: Erfolgsstrategien für die Fallanalyse: Eine kurze Einfürhung in Radar und das Vithoulkas Experten System, Greifenberg: GSP GmbH (1999)
vha	VAN HOOGENBEMT Els: Contemporary homeopathic physician [Belgium]
vhh	VAN HOOTEGHEM Henk: Contemporary homeopath [Koerzel, Belgium]
vhh1	VAN HOOTEGHEM Henk: [On focusing a case], Links, Vol 3: pg 22 (1991)
vhv	VERHEIJ-VAN DER WIEL Jannie
vhv1	VERHEIJ-VAN DER WIEL Jannie: [Recurrent bronchitis - A case of Sambucus nigra], Links, Vol 12 nr 3: pg 175 - Linking trees project (1999)
vhx1	vhdg anterior degree 1 (1990)
vhx2	vhdg anterior degree 2 (1990)
vhx3	vhdg anterior degree 3 (1990)
vhx4	vhdg anterior degree 4 (1990)
vjp	VIJAYAKAR Prafull
vjp1	VIJAYAKAR Prafull: [The Theory of Suppression: seven layers of suppression]
vjp2	VIJAYAKAR Prafull: [The Theory of Acutes]
vk	VAKIL Prakash: Contempory homeopathic physician [Bombay, India]. Profesor at the Govt. Homeoapthic Hospital, Irla, Bombay. (1935-1995)
vk1	VAKIL Prakash: [Tongue that does not lie], Bombay: Vakil Hom. Prakashan Publ. (1988)
vk2	VAKIL Prakash: [New, old and forgotten remedies], Bombay: Vakil Hom. Prakashans Publ. (1992)
vk3	VAKIL Prakash: [Dreams] (1993)
vk4	VAKIL Prakash: [Homeopathic Rainbow] (1987)
vk5	VAKIL Prakash: [Moon Phases Chart], Bombay: Vakil Hom. Prakashans Publ. (1987)
vk6	VAKIL Prakash: [A Text Book of Homeopathic Therapeutics: vol 1: Diseases of the Central Nervous System], Bombay: Vakil Homeopathic Prakashans [2nd Ed.] (1988)
vk7	VAKIL Prakash: [Leprominium: a New Nosode], Homeopath, Vol 8/2: pg 77 (1988)
vk8	VAKIL Prakash: [Therapeutics of the Respiratory System]
vk9	VAKIL Prakash: [A proving of Pertussis vaccine], Proc 52nd LMHI Congr., Pg 100-103 (1997)
vka	VAKIL A.E.
vka1	VAKIL A.E. and VAKIL V.E. and NANABHAI A.S.: [A study of serum elctrolyte and thyroid hormone changes in Iodum provers.], Br H J, Vol 77: pg 152-154 (1988)
vka2	VAKIL A.E. and VAKIL V.E. and NANABHAI A.S.: [A study of Iris versicolor], Br H J, Vol 78: pg 15-18 (1989)
vkm	VENKATARAMAN S.
vkm1	VENKATARAMAN S.: [Mercurius corrosivus], Hahnemannian Gleanings June ; 53(6): pg 178-180 (1986)
vko	VOLK O.H.
vko1	VOLK O.H.: [Harpagophytum procumbens], Dtsch. Apoth. Ztg. 104; 573 (1964)

vkw	VINK Wendy: Contemporary Homeopatic veterinarian [United Kingdom] (1970-)
vl	VRIJLANDT Arie: Contemporary homeopathic physician [Netherlands] (1911-)
vl1.nl	VRIJLANDT Arie: Homeopathische prescriptie in de praktijk, Nijmegen (1982)
vl2	VRIJLANDT Arie: [Pullus gallinaceus], Similia Similibus Currentur
vla	VILLERS A.
vld	VAN DER LINDEN Jean: Contemporary homeopathic physician [Leuven, Belgium] (1960-)
vlr	VALE Regina
vlr1	VALE Regina and M. Lúcia Pereira: [Considerations on placebo effects in different pathogenetic studies preliminary valuation.], Proc 54th LMHI Congr., Salvador - Bahia, Brasil (1999)
vlr2	VALE Regina: [Summary of the Pathogenesis of Gardenia Jasminoides] (2000)
vls	VALLESPIR LOPEZ Solange
vma	VARMA P.N.
vma1	VARMA P.N. and Indu Vaid: [Side effects] (1992)
vma2	VARMA P.N. and Indu Vaid: [Encyclopaedia of Homeopathic Pharmacopoeia Vol 1 and Vol 2] (1995)
vme	VILLANEUVA Montiel Erika
vme1.es	VILLANEUVA Montiel Erika: Pulsatilla: Síntomas Mentales y Análisis medicamentosa., New Delhi: Jain Publishers (1995)
vmh	VOLLMER H.
vmh1	VOLLMER H.: [Leonurus cardiaca], Kli. Wo. 22; 38/39, 566 (1943)
vml	VERMEULEN Frans: Contemporary homeopath [Netherlands] (1948-)
vml1.nl	VERMEULEN Frans: Kindertypes (1985)
vml2	VERMEULEN Frans: [Synoptic Materia Medica. Vol 1], Haarlem (1992)
vml2.fr	VERMEULEN Frans: Synoptic Vol. 1
vml3	VERMEULEN Frans: [Synoptic Materia Medica. Vol 2] (1998)
vml3.de	VERMEULEN Frans: Synoptische Materia Medica 2, Haarlem (Holland): Emryss bv Publishers (1998)
vml4	VERMEULEN Frans: [Concordant Materia Medica] (1997)
vml4.de	VERMEULEN Frans: Konkordanz der Materia Medica, Haarlem (Holland): Emryss bv Publishers (2000)
vml5	VERMEULEN Frans: [Prisma - The Arcana of Materia Medica Illuminated - Similars and Parallels between substance and remedy.], Haarlem (Netherlands): Emryss bv Publishers (1st ed.) (2002)
vmr	VERMEIRE Jean-François: Contemporary homeopathic physician [St Niklaas, Belgium]. Pres. Royal Belg Soc Hom.
vn	VANNIER Léon: French homeopathic physician (1880-1963)
vn1.es	VANNIER Léon: Materia Médica Homeopática
vn1.fr	VANNIER Léon: Materia Medica (1935)
vn1.it	VANNIER Léon: Materia Medica
vn10.fr	VANNIER Léon et POIRIR J.: Precis de Matiere Medicale Homeopathique, France: Boiron (1948)
vn2.es	VANNIER Léon: Terapéutica Homeopática
vn2.fr	VANNIER Léon: Thérapeutique Homéopathique
vn2.it	VANNIER Léon: Terapeutica Homeopatica
vn3.es	VANNIER Léon: Homeopatía - Remedios de Estados Agudos
vn3.fr	VANNIER Léon: Les Maladies Aigues
vn4.fr	VANNIER Léon: Les douleurs abdominales
vn5.fr	VANNIER Léon: Précis de thérapeutique homéopathique, Paris: Doin (1978)
vn6.fr	VANNIER Léon: La pratique de l'homéopathie
vn7.fr	VANNIER Léon: Caractéristiques essentièlles
vn8.fr	VANNIER Léon: La typologie et ses applications (1930)
vn9	VANNIER Léon: [Difficult and Backward Children]
vna	VENANZI Marco: Contemporary homeopathic physician [Italy]
vnk	VIJNOVSKY Bernardo: (1938-)
vnk1.es	VIJNOVSKY Bernardo: Tratado de Materia Medica Homeopatica Vol I, Buenos Aires [8th Ed.] (1978)
vnk10.es	VIJNOVSKY Bernardo: Los Antagonistas Similares en biología y medicina., Buenos Eires: Editorial "La Clínica" (1960)
vnk11.es	VIJNOVSKY Bernardo: Tratamiento Homeopatico de las affeciones y enfermedades agudas. [3th Ed.], Buenos Aires: Estilos Gráficos S.A. (1995)
vnk2.es	VIJNOVSKY Bernardo: Tratado de Materia Medica Homeopatica Vol 2, Buenos Aires
vnk3.es	VIJNOVSKY Bernardo: Traducción y comentarios del Organon de Hahnemann., Buenos Aires: Talleres Gráficos Zlotopioro (1983)
vnk4.es	VIJNOVSKY Bernardo: Síntomas clave de la Materia Médica homeopática en el repertorio de Kent, Buenos Aires: Estilos Gráficos S.A. (1992)
vnk5.es	VIJNOVSKY Bernardo: Aclaranda Dudas (El testimonio de la clínica en los casos crónicos tratados con el método de la dosis únicas)., Capital Federal (Argentina): Alan Centro Gráfico (1988)
vnk6.es	VIJNOVSKY Bernardo: Repertorio de Síntomas Mentales Especiales, Buenos Aires: Vijnovsky (1992)
vnk7.es	VIJNOVSKY Bernardo: Pequeños Grandes remedios., Buenos Aires: Estilos Gráficos S.A. (1995)
vnk8.es	VIJNOVSKY Bernardo: Niños y ancianos en la Materia Médica homeopática y en el Repertorio., Buenos Aires: VIJNOVSKY Bernardo (1955)
vnk9.es	VIJNOVSKY Bernardo: Valor real de los síntomas en la historia clínica homeopática., Buenos Aires: VIJNOVSKY Bernardo (1981)
vns	VIJNOVSKY Selma
vns1.es	VIJNOVSKY Selma: Un Paso mas... Hacia el enfoque homeopático de las Flores de Bach, [1st

	Ed.], Argentina: Libro de Edicion Argentina, December 1998 (1998)
vo	VAN OPROY Flor: Contemporary homeopathic pediatrician [Belgium]
vo1	VAN OPROY Flor: [Pediatrics], Gent (Belgium): Homeoden Book Service (1993)
vpn	VULPIAN
vpn1	VULPIAN: [Proving of Trito, Watersalamander], Zeitschrift des Vereins der Homöopathischen Ärtze Oesterrei (1857)
vpn2	VULPIAN: [Proving of Salamandra lacerta], Allgemeine Homöopathische Zeitung, Vol 46/6
vr	VAN 't RIET: Contemporary homeopathic physician [Netherlands]
vs	VOISIN Henri: French homeopathic physician (1880-1963)
vs1.fr	VOISIN Henri: Matière Medicale (1950)
vs2.fr	VOISIN Henri: Répertoire
vs3.fr	VOISIN Henri: Thérapeutique et Répertoire homéopathique du practicien, Paris: Maloine (1978)
vs4	VOISIN Henri: [En attendant le médecin: comment se soigner par l'homéopathie, sans le médecin ou en l'attendant.]
vs5	VOISIN Henri: [Ce qu'est réellement l'homéopathie]
vs6	VOISIN Henri: [Les Groupes et Familles de Remèdes]
vs7	VOISIN Henri: [L'application rationelle et critique de l'homéopathie.]
vs8	VOISIN Henri: [Clinical homeopathy]
vs8.fr	VOISIN Henri: Homéopathie clinique. Répertoire et thérapeutique. Deuxième édition revue, rectifiée et augmentée.
vs9.pt	VOISIN Henri: Manual de Matéria Médica para o clínico homeopata [2nd Ed.], São Paolo, Organização Andrei (1987)
vsp	VASANI Paresh: Contemporary homeopath [Bombay, India]
vsp1	VASANI Paresh: [A Case Study], Links, Vol 1: pg 20 (1995)
vsr	VERSPOOR Rudy
vsr1	VERSPOOR Rudy and SMITH Patty: [Homeopathy Renewed, A Time for Healing]
vss	VERSTEEG Silke: Contemporary homeopath [Germany] (1950-)
vss1	VERSTEEG Silke: [Bach flowers repertory]
vta	VAN TWILLERT C.: Contemporary homeopath [Netherlands] (1954-)
vtl	VAUGHTERS Lucy: Contemporary homeopathic physician [New York, USA]
vtl1	VAUGHTERS Lucy: [A case of Panic Disorder], N Eng. J H, Vol 1 nr 1: pg 11-14 (1992)
vtp	VINT Peter
vv	VIVIAN: (1965-)
vv1	VIVIAN: [Rubus Chamaemorus]
vv2	VIVIAN: [Simuliidae]
vva	VERVARCKE Anne: (1952-)
vva1	VERVARCKE Anne: [Proving of Alnus rubra - Linking trees project], Links, Vol 12: pg 166-167 (1999)
vwe	VAN WOENSEL Erik: Contemporary homeopath [Groesbeek, The Netherlands] (1962-)
vwe1	VAN WOENSEL Erik: [A case of Carcinosinum], E J Cl. H, Vol 1 nr 2: pg 29-30 (1995)
vwe2	VAN WOENSEL Erik: [Radar keynotes version 4 - Characteristics and pecularities. A compiled Materia Medica.] (2000)
vwm	VAN WASSENHOVEN Michel: Contemporary homeopathic physician [Brussels, Belgium]
vwm1.fr	VAN WASSENHOVEN Michel: Prostaglandines, Rev B H (1985)
vzh	VAN DER ZEE Harry: Contemporary homeopath [Haren, The Netherlands] (1953-)
vzh1	VAN DER ZEE Harry: [A case of cyclamen], Links, Vol 3: pg 25 (1995)
vzh2	VAN DER ZEE Harry: [Miasms in labour: A revision of the homoeopathic theory of the miasms. A process towards health], Utrecht (Netherlands): Stichting Alonnissos (2000)
vzv	VAN ZANDVOORT Roger
vzv1	VAN ZANDVOORT Roger: [The Complete Repertory 4.5]
vzv2	VAN ZANDVOORT Roger and RETZEK H.O.: [The Complete Materia Medica]
vzv3	VAN ZANDVOORT Roger: [Complete Repertory Millenium] (2003)
vzv4	VAN ZANDVOORT Roger: [Repertory Universale] (2003)
wb	WOODBURY Benjamin Collins Sr.: (1836-1915)
wbc	WANSBROUGH C.
wbc1	WANSBROUGH C.: [Ayahuasca and the pineal gland], Prometheus unbound, Spring (1995)
wbt	WULFSBERG Terje: Contemporary homeopath [Bergen, Norway] (1954-)
wbt1	WULFSBERG Terje: [Chronic Diarrhoea], Links, Vol 3: pg 55-56 (1990)
wbt2	WULFSBERG Terje: [Three pieces of Gold], Oslo:HomeopatiBokhandelen (1998)
wcs	WORCESTOR S.
wcs1	WORCESTOR S.: [Repertory to the Modalities]
wd	WARD James William: American homeopathic physician. Former President American Inst. Hom. (1861-1939)
wd1	WARD James William: [Unabridged Dictionary of the Sensations as if: Part I: Pathogenetic], New Dehli: Jain Publ. (1939)
wd2	WARD James William: [Unabridged Dictionary of the Sensations as if: Part II: Clinical], New Dehli: Jain Publ. (1939)
wd6	WADIA S. R.: [= wda6 = Homoeopathy in children's diseases], New Delhi: Jain Publishers (1985)

wda	WADIA S. R.: Contemporary homeopathic physician [India] (1932-)
wda1	WADIA S. R.: [Leucoderma, its homeopathic treatment] (1989)
wda2	WADIA S. R.: [Homeopathy in skin diseases]
wda3	WADIA S. R.: [Homeopathic cures asthma] (1977)
wda4	WADIA S. R.: [Tonsillites cured by homeopathy] (1979)
wda5	WADIA S. R.: [Tips by masters of Homeopathy]
wda6	WADIA S. R.: [Homoeopathy in Children's Diseases], New Delhi: Jain Publishers (1985)
wdi	WUNDERLI J.
wdi1	WUNDERLI J.: [Lespedeza capitata], A H Z 212; 295 (1967)
wdj	WOOD James O. Craven: (1858-1948)
wdj1	WOOD James O. Craven: [Clinical gynaecology]
wdj2	WOOD James O. Craven: [Essentials of Homeopathic Prescribing]
wdx	WADE J.L.
wdx1	WADE J.L.: [Anthemis nobilis], The American Homoeopathic Review (1860)
wf	WAFFENSMITH J. W.: (1904-)
wfa	WULFING Theodor: Contemporary homeopath [Germany]
wfd	WINGFIELD B. Digby
wfd1	WINGFIELD B. Digby: [Venus Flytrap]
wg	WIGG G.
wga	WIRGA Zdzislaw: Contemporary homeopathic surgeon [Poznan, Poland]
wgk	WEINGES K.
wgk1	WEINGES K et al.: [Flor de piedra, Phytochemistry 10; 829] (1971)
wgn	WEGENER Andreas: Contemporary homeopathic physician [Germany]
wgn1.de	WEGENER Andreas: Mittelsverwechslungen im Repertorium von Kent: Borax und Bovista, Teil 1, Zt Klass H, Vol 5 (1987)
wgn2.de	WEGENER Andreas: Mittelverwechslungen im Repertorium von Kent: Ambra und Ammonium bromatum, Teil 2, Zt Klass H, Vol 6 (1987)
wgn3.de	WEGENER Andreas: Mittelverwechslungen im Repertorium von Kent: Juglans cineria und Juglans regia, Teil 4, Zt Klass H (1988)
wgn4.de	WEGENER Andreas: Mittelverwechslungen im Repertorium von Kent: Lepidium und Leptandra, Teil 5, Zt Klass H (1988)
wgn5.de	WEGENER Andreas: Mittelverwechslungen im Repertorium von Kent: Comocladia und Conium, Teil 6, Zt Klass H, Vol 6 (1988)
wgn6	WEGENER Andreas: [Phytolacca], Z Class Homöopath 1993 Mar-Apr (1993)
wh	WINTSCH C. H.
wha	WESTERHUIS Atjo: (1949-), Netherlands
whs	WILHELMER S.
whs1.de	WILHELMER S. und FAES W.: Solanum tuberosum
whs2.de	WILHELMER S. und FAES W.: Galphimia glauca
wht	WRIGHT Craig: (1973-)
wht1	WRIGHT Craig: [Bitis arietans arietans and its venom] (1999)
wkc	WILKINSON Chris
wkc1	WILKINSON Chris: [Hekla Lava] (2001)
wkc2	WILKINSON Chris: [The Homeopathic Proving of Venus Stella Errans] (1999)
wkc3	WILKINSON Chris: [The Homeopathic Proving of Alabaster] (2001)
wl	WHEELER Charles Edwin: (1868-1947)
wl1	WHEELER Charles Edwin: [Introduction to the Principles and Practice of medicine.] (1920)
wl1.es	WHEELER Charles Edwin: Introducción a los principos y la prática de la homeoptía
wl2	WHEELER Charles Edwin: [Chronic Diseases]
wla	WOELFEL Arthur: Contemporary German homeopath (1948)
wla1	WOELFEL Arthur and OSTERMAYR Benno: [Rosa damascena] (2003)
wla1.de	WOELFEL Arthur und OSTERMAYR Benno: Rosa damascena. Eine homöopathische Arzneimittelselbsterfahrung, Die Rose - Botanik, Geschichte, Medizin, Orignalia Homeopathica, Greifenberg (Germany): Hahnemann Institut - Privatinstitut für homöopatische Dokumntation Gmbh (1999)
wlg	WEILAND G.
wlg1.de	WEILAND G.: HAMP von Aqua marina
wlh	WALACH H.
wlh1	WALACH H.: [Does a highly diluted homoeopathic drug act as a placebo in healthy volunteers? Experimental study of Belladonna 30C in double-blind crossover design - a pilot study], J Psy Res , Vol 37 nr 8: pg 851-860 (1993)
wlj	WEILAND Jürgen: Contemporary homeopath [Germany]
wlj1	WEILAND Jürgen, KÖNIG Peter and DAUZ Gerda: [Proving of Vitis vinifera] (2003)
wlj1.de	WEILAND Jürgen, KÖNIG Peter und DAUZ Gerda: Vitis vinifera - Zwei homöopathische Arzneimittelstudien in einem Buch (2003)
wlr	WILLIAMS Robin
wls	WILLEMSE Rob
wlw	WILLIAMSON Walter: (1811-1870)
wlw1	WILLIAMSON Walter: [Diseases of Females and Children and their Homoeopathic Treatment.]
wlx	WILLIRD
wlx1	WILLIRD: [Repertory of Cough]
wm	WHITMONT Edward: (1912-1998)
wm1	WHITMONT Edward: [The Practice of Homeopathy] (1970)
wm2	WHITMONT Edward: [Psyche and Substance], Berkeley (1980)
wm3	WHITMONT Edward: [The Symbolic Quest]
wm4	WHITMONT Edward: [The Alchemy of Healing]

wm5	WHITMONT Edward: [Return of the Goddess]
wmh	WACHSMUTH Jörg H.: (1959-)
wmh1	WACHSMUTH Jörg H.: [Olibanum sacrum] (1999)
wmh1.de	WACHSMUTH Jörg H.: Olibanum Sacrum
wmj	WICHMANN Jorg: (1958-)
wmj1	WICHMANN Jorg: [Proving of Fagus sylvatica - Linking trees project], Links, Vol 12: pg 167-169 (1999)
wmw	WOUTMAN Willem: Contemporary homeopathic physician [Netherlands]
wn	WIJNANTS Paul: Contemporary homeopathic physician [Belgium] (1932-)
wpb	WIPP Benno
wpb1	WIPP Benno: [Homoeopathie in Psychiatrie und Neurologie], Heidelberg: Karl F. Haug Verlag (1979)
wr	WEIR John, Sir: English homeopathic physician (1879-1971)
wr1	WEIR John, Sir: [Difficulties in homoeopathic prescribing], Bombay: The Homoeopathic Medical Publishers (1969)
wr2	WEIR John, Sir: [A system of therapeutics], London (1928)
wr3	WEIR John, Sir: [Science and Art of Homoeopathy], London (1928)
wr4	WEIR John, Sir and TYLER M. L.: [Some of the Outstanding Homoeopathic Remedies for Acute Conditions, Injuries, etc. [2 parts]]
wra	WARD Andrew
wse	WILSEY E.H.
wse1	WILSEY E.H.: [A Repertory of Dreams], Parkersburg (West-Virginia) (1898)
wsf	WOODS Fergie Harold: (1883-1961)
wsf1	WOODS Fergie Harold: [Essentials of Homeopathic Prescribing], London: Homeopathic Publishing Co (1950)
wsf2	WOODS Fergie Harold, KENYON J.D. and WHEELER C.E.: [Drug Proving Committee: Penicillin], Br H J, Vol 37: pg 64-66 (1947)
wsf3	WOODS Fergie Harold: [Rapid Repertory]
wsg	WÜNSTEL G.
wsg1	WÜNSTEL G.: [Picrorhiza], Phys. Med. u. Reh. 15; 71 (1974)
wsh	WEBSTER H. T.
wsh1	WEBSTER H. T.: [Proving of Artemisia tridentata], Medical Advance Vol 13: pg 86 (1886)
wsj	WINSTON Julian: (1941-)
wsj1	WINSTON Julian: [A proving of Glonoine], J Am Inst Hom, Mar Dec ; 76(4) : pg 147-150 (1984)
wsm	WIESENAUER Markus
wsm1	WIESENAUER Markus: [Praxis der Homöopathie], Stuttgart: Hippokrates Verlag (1985)
wsm2	WIESENAUER Markus: [Eichornia crassipes, Neue Heilmittel der Homöopathie.], Modernes Leben natürl. Heilen 105, 2, 43 (1980)
wsp	WELLS Phineus Parkhurst: (1808-1891)
wsp1	WELLS Phineus Parkhurst: [Diarrhoea and Dysentery], New Delhi: Indian Books and Periodical Syndication
wsp2	WELLS Phineus Parkhurst and HERING G.: [Symptomatic Indications of Typhoid Fever], Calcutta: Salzer & Co (3rd Ed.)
wsp3	WELLS P. P. and BOENNINGHAUSEN C., von: [Intermittent Fever]
wsr	WEISS R.F.
wsr1	WEISS R.F.: [Leonurus cardiaca], Dtsch. med. Wschr.; 392 (1938)
wss	WESSELMANN Stefan: (1963-)
wsw	WINSLOW W.H.
wsw1	WINSLOW W.H.: [The Human Ear and It's Diseases], New York: Boericke & Tafel (1882)
wt	WRIGHT- HUBBARD Elizabeth: American homeopathic physician (1896-1967)
wt1	WRIGHT- HUBBARD Elizabeth: [Homoeopathy as Art and Science], Beaconsfield (1990)
wt2	WRIGHT Elizabeth: [A Brief Study course in Homeopathy], New Delhi: Jain Publishers
wta	WINTERBURN George William: (1845-1911)
wta1	WINTERBURN George William: [A Repertory of the Most Characteristic symptoms of the Materia Medica] (1886)
wtc	WITTENBURG Christine: Contemporary homeopath [Cantabria, Spain]
wtc1	WITTENBURG Christine: [The Gift], Links, Vol 3: pg 21-22 (1994)
wth	WOLTER H.
wth1	WOLTER H.: [Flor de piedra], A H Z. 213 (1968) 434 / A H Z. 214 (1969) 433 / A H Z. 224 (1979) 90-99 / Der Prakt. Tierarzt 57 (1976) 9
wtj	WATT J.M.
wtj1	WATT J.M. and BREYER-BRANDWIJK M.G.: [Medical and poisonous plants of southern and eastern Africa.], Livingstone - Edingburgh - London (1962)
wtm	WETTEMANN Marion
wwa	WOODWARD A.W
wwa1	WOODWARD A.W: [Constitutional Therapeutics] (1903)
wz	WITZIG Friedrich: Contemporary homeopath [Germany] (1954-)
wz1	WITZIG Friedrich: [Über Bacillinum Burnett], D J H, Vol 1: pg 3 (1994)
wza	WIRTZ Anne: (1943-)
wza1	WIRTZ Anne: [A caring capricious creature - Lac felinum], Links, Vol 9: pg 145-148 (1996)
xx	In research
xxb	HOMOEOPATHIA EUROPEA BRYONIA (1985)
xxb1	HOMOEOPATHIA EUROPEA BELLADONNA (1988)
xxc	HOMOEOPATHIE EUROPEA CALCAREA
xxh	HOMOEOPATHIA EUROPEA HYPERICUM
xxl	HOMOEOPATHIA EUROPEA LYCOPODIUM

xxl1	HOMOEOPATHIA EUROPEA CARBO V.
xxn	HOMOEOPATHIA EUROPEA NAJA
xxp	HOMOEOPATHIA EUROPEA PHOSPHORUS
xxp1	HOMOEOPATHIA EUROPEA PARIS
xxr	HOMOEOPATHIE EUROPEA RHUS TOX (1985)
xxs	HOMOEOPATHIA EUROPEA STAPHYSAGRIA (1985)
xxs1	HOMOEOPATHIA EUROPEA SEPIA
xxx	Wrong remedy: Wrong remedy for this rubric: the other author references explain why this remedy has to be removed, (1800)
xyz	IN RESEARCH
xyz60	Degroote: [test] (2003)
xyz61	problems with dgt: [test] (2003)
xyz62	problems bg1/bg2: [test] (2003)
xyz63	problems k2: [test] (2003)
xyz64	problems with sz: [test]
xyz65	problems with gb: [test]
xyz66	IN RESEARCH (2003)
xyz67	IN RESEARCH: [Different articles], J Am Inst H (2003)
xyz68	UNKNOWN: [Different articles], Cah Gr Hahn (2003)
ygj	YASGUR Jay: Contemporary homeopath [USA]
ygj1	YASGUR Jay: [Homeopathic Dictionary and Holistic Health Reference], Greenville: Van Hoy Publishers (1990)
yhs	YELDHAM Stephen
yhs1	YELDHAM Stephen: [Homeopathy in Veneral Diseases] (1888)
ykm	YAKIR Michal: Contemporary homeopath [Jerusalem, Israel]
ykm1	YAKIR Michal: [A case of migraine], Links, Vol 4: pg 25-26 (1995)
yl	YINGLING William A.: (1851-1933)
yl1	YINGLING William A.: [The Accouchers Emercency Manual], Calcutta: Set, Day & Co (1895)
yl1.fr	YINGLING William A.: Le Manuel des urgences obstétricales, Esneux: Editions Liégoises d'Homéopathie (1995)
yl2	YINGLING William A.: [Torula cerevisia], International Hahnemannian Association, Session 42: pg 171 (1990)
yl3	YINGLING William A.: [Repertory of Appendicitis], Homoepathic Physian: Vol 15 (1895)
ylc	YUILL Cheryl: (1952-)
yy	INSTITUTO INTERNATIONAL [Masi] GROUPS
yya1	INSTITUTO INTERNATIONAL ARGENTINA, grp 1
yya2	INSTITUTO INTERNATIONAL ARGENTINA, grp 2
yyb	INSTITUTO INTERNATIONAL BELGIUM
yyb1	INSTITUTO INTERNATIONAL BRAZIL
yyc	CHIRON Paul
yyc1.es	CHIRON Paul: Elementos de Materia Médica Homeopáthica, México, D.F.: Ediciones Hahnemann (1974)
yyc1.fr	CHIRON Paul: Matière Médicale
yyd	School of Hom. Medicine, Darlington: Iridium metallicum
yye1	INSTITUTO INTERNATIONAL ECUADOR
yyf	INSTITUTO INTERNATIONAL FRANCE
yyg	GUILD OF HOMOEOPATHS
yyg1	GUILD OF HOMOEOPATHS: [Meditation Provings from Promethius]
yyg2	GUILD OF HOMOEOPATHS: [Meditative repertory]
yyh	Sociedade Gaúcha de Homeopatia
yyh1.es	Sociedade Gaúcha de Homeopatia: Hydrocyanicum acidum, Revista de Homeopatia, Vol 1 (1997)
yyi	INSTITUTO INTERNATIONAL INDIA
yyi1	INSTITUTO INTERNATIONAL ITALIA
yyn	INSTITUTO INTERNATIONAL NETHERLANDS
yys	INSTITUTO INTERNATIONAL switzerland
yys1	INSTITUTO INTERNATIONAL SPAIN
yyv	INSTITUTO INTERNATIONAL VENEZUELA
zb	ZOBY Elias Carlos: (1963-)
zb1.pt	ZOBY Elias Carlos: Concordancia Homeopatica [rubricas mentais] (1963)
zb2.pt	ZOBY Elias Carlos: Concordância Homeopática [sonhos] (1963-), New Delhi: B. Jain publishers (1998)
zf	ZAFIRIOU Vangelis: Contemporary homeopath [Greece] (1955-)
zf1	ZAFIRIOU Vangelis: [Mind additions to the repertory], E J Cl. H, Vol 1 nr 2: pg 11 (1995)
zge	ZIEGLER E.
zge1	ZIEGLER E.: [Luffa operculata], Landarzt 40; 78 (1964)
zk	ZWEMKE Hans: Contemporary homeopathic physician [Germany]
zl	ZALA Michel: Contemporary homeopathic physician [France] (1953-)
zl1.fr	ZALA Michel: Observations et Cas Cliniques
zl2.fr	ZALA Michel: Les Araignées
zl3.fr	ZALA Michel: Synthèse et Remèdes
zmw	ZIMMERMANN W.
zmw1.de	ZIMMERMANN W.: Homoeopathische Arzneitherapie, Regensburg: Johannes Sonntag (1980)
zmw2	ZIMMERMANN W.: [Erfahrungen mith Harpagophytum.], Phys. Med. u. Reh. 18; 317-319 (1977)
znb	ZORN B.
znb1	ZORN B.: [Harpagophytum procumbens], Zeitschrift für Rheumaforschung 17; 134-38 (1958)
zr	ZAREN Ananda: Contemporary homeopath [USA] (1949-)
zr1	ZAREN Ananda: [Core Elements of the Materia Medica of the Mind] (1993)
zr2	ZAREN Ananda: [Seminar Lelystad [Netherlands] May 1989], Amsterdam: Ilse Bos, private (1989)

zrz	ZORZI
zrz1	ZORZI: [Riscoperta Dell'Omeopatia Vol 1-7]
zs	ZISSU Roland: (1919-)
zs1.fr	ZISSU Roland et GUILLAUME: Fiches de Matière Médicale (1979)
zs2.fr	ZISSU Roland: Cahiers de médecine homéopathique
zs3.fr	ZISSU Roland et GUILLAUME: Manuel de médecine homéopathie
zs4.fr	ZISSU Roland: Matiere Medicale Homoeopathique Constitutionnelle [2 Vols], France: Boiron (1989)
zt	ZUMTOBEL Gernot: Contemporary homeopathic physician [Austria]
zv	ZERVOS N.
zz	INTERNATIONAL FOUNDATION (Vithoulkas)
zzb	BAD BOLL: Homeopathische Kreis - Bad Boll (1985)
zzc	CENTRAL COUNCIL FOR RESEARCH IN HOMEOPATHY
zzc1	CENTRAL COUNCIL FOR RESEARCH IN HOMEOPATHY: [Provings] (1995)
zzg	INTERNATIONAL FOUNDATION CENTER ATHENS
zzg1	INTERNATIONAL FOUNDATION CENTER DETMOLD
zzg2	INTERNATIONAL FOUNDATION CENTER LONDON
zzg3	INTERNATIONAL FOUNDATION CENTER SALZBURG
zzh	INTERNATIONAL FOUNDATION CENTER HECHTEL (1990)
zzi	INTERNATIONAL FOUNDATION CENTER FIRENZE
zzl	Centre Liègeois d'Homéopathie: Additions verified by Marc Brunson et al. (1995)
zzm	INTERNATIONAL FOUNDATION CENTER NORWAY
zzn2	INTERNATIONAL FOUNDATION CENTER NETHERLANDS
zzs	INTERNATIONAL FOUNDATION CENTER BERN
zzv	INTERNATIONAL FOUNDATION CENTER CALIFORN
zzz	Remedy from subrubric: This remedy is copied from a analogous (similar) subrubric and awaits confirmation in this current rubric. (1800)